The American Midwest
An Interpretive Encyclopedia

The American Midwest

An Interpretive Encyclopedia

GENERAL EDITORS

Richard Sisson
Christian Zacher
Andrew Cayton

INDIANA UNIVERSITY PRESS
Bloomington and Indianapolis

Firm Amaz 9/07 75.00

This book is a publication of

Indiana University Press
601 North Morton Street
Bloomington, Indiana 47404-3797 USA

http://iupress.indiana.edu

Telephone orders   800-842-6796
Fax orders   812-855-7931
Orders by e-mail   iuporder@indiana.edu

Printed in China

Cataloging information is available from the Library of Congress.

ISBN 0-253-34886-2 (cl.)

1 2 3 4 5   11 10 09 08 07 06

Donors

The Ohio State University

The National Endowment for the Humanities

Wolfe Associates of Columbus

The Ohio General Assembly

The Columbus Foundation

Charlotte R. Haller Fund

Ben and Dana Falter Fund

Paul G. Duke Fund

The Limited Foundation

Chemical Abstracts Service

Indiana University Press

Hattie W. & Robert L. Lazarus Fund

William and Beverly Hirzel

Barbara Brandt

In Praise of the Middle Way

1

From Cretaceous to the Cambrian,
the Midwest Sea encompassed stars and moon,
brew of oozy, reedy depths, whorl
of nautiloid, trilobite, thrash
of xiphactinus, colossal squid.

Then utter cold came down. Glacial drift
laid rich till plains we plow and reap today,
stones strewn among teeth and bones.
Fathoms swell beneath our feet, ice
can shift. Expecting the miraculous,

we tread dream tides, dark tribal fires,
sedimentary rock. We do not go
too far, but if we do we long for depths
of home. We cherish every motherland.
What circles and encloses sets us free.

2

Hulett Unloaders groan, bow, stand,
shore birds. Ore boats, barges bend around
curves of rivers named by native bards.
Taconite and coke explode to steel,
while wind bedecks corn and wheat. What

you need we pour, we forge, we reap. We rise
above the prairie, plain. Serpent mound,
sod hut, silo, spire, skyscraper
mark where they came and lay, those steerage kin
with lovely tongues, to see, and seeing, sing.

We are, we chant, Illini, Hoosier, Hawk,
Buckeye, Husker, Cyclone, Packer, Bear
in red, white, black, yellow, brown.
Insular is all, a way to find,
beyond tornadic, lightning change, ourselves.

3

In this grand sandwich we are the meat.
Here between way left, hardest right,
sweat of get and gone, yea and nay,
too high, too low we broker, stake a claim.
Between the hips, thighs, lips, ears

we mediums of sacred hearth are seers.
We temper, we anneal, cross-pollinate
the very thick of things. Who busts
the sod like us? Who lays down tracks, roads?
This country's middle ear is her balance.

In middle earth we burrow, hunker, root,
and here we take our stand. Look for us
in pit and pith. We mean the mean. Our sense
is place, our privacy. Here we thrive.
In rarefied mid-air, we take pride.

David Citino
2005

General Contents

Reader's Guide

The American Midwest: An Interpretive Encyclopedia is organized topically, as indicated in the general table of contents. Each section begins with a table of contents for the section, and further organizational explanation is offered in the Senior Consulting Editors' overview essays that appear at the start of each section. While those explanations and tables of contents provide a sense of the order of each section, readers wishing to find a particular subject quickly should refer to the general index at the end of the volume. Some subjects not listed in the table of contents, such as business and industry, are treated throughout the encyclopedia. Readers should consult the index to locate the various treatments of them.

The general editors encourage readers who are interested in learning more about any topic to consult the list of references following most entries and essays. These references include sources as well as further readings considered easily accessible to readers and dependable over time. Unpublished manuscripts, speeches, interviews, databases, websites, directories, and reference works generally are not cited for further reading—with the exception of reference works and websites that are specific enough in nature to be helpful as a guide for in-depth exploration of a particular topic.

Photos, other illustrations, and sidebars are listed in the credits index at the end of the volume. In a few cases, in response to specific copyright owner stipulations, illustration captions also include permissions information specified by the copyright holder.

Our source for the spelling of Native American tribal names is Frederick E. Hoxie's *Encyclopedia of North American Indians* (1996), although authors of some articles felt it appropriate to use different spellings.

All entries and essays have gone through an extensive fact-checking process to ensure the greatest accuracy possible. Every effort also has been made to provide information that is as current as possible.

Preface and Acknowledgments

Most Americans have an ambiguous sense of regional identity. If asked to explain who they are, few would think first of regionalism—an expression of imagined identity with people who inhabit a perceived common landscape. Ethnicity, race, gender, religion, and state, among other things, would probably matter more. Twenty-first-century Americans, moreover, live in a society in which mass culture, continual migration, and instantaneous communication have for decades been undermining local and regional cultures. In the 1990s, the Chicago Bulls was a midwestern professional basketball team whose major player was from North Carolina and whose fans lived throughout the United States, indeed, the world.

Yet the Midwest and the Heartland are common and frequent referents in political commentary and in the public imagination as a distinct, if unclearly bounded, geographic entity that harbors distinctive ways of life. Inhabitants of the Midwest are widely thought of as hard-working, thrifty, devoted to family values, strong in character, comfortable with normalcy, rather sedate, and cautious about change. The Midwest, in all its variety, is a particular place whose residents live in a unique landscape. It is as real as the Sears Tower or the cornfields of Iowa or the streets of Detroit; it is also the imagined places of Sherwood Anderson's Winesburg, Ohio, Willa Cather's Nebraska prairies, the Chicago of both James Farrell and Richard Wright, and the Dakota reservations of Louise Erdrich.

The Midwest has always been in the middle, and not just geographically. It is, and was, a place of both industry and agriculture, large and small cities and small towns, massive corporations and powerful labor unions, artistic creativity and cultural repression. Politically, it has for two centuries been a place of close elections, iconoclastic leaders, and egalitarian movements. It is a complicated and unpredictable region, and contrary to its popular image, the Midwest has always been distinguished by the diversity of its residents. In ancient times the region was home to paleohunters, to the important Mound Builder civilizations commonly known as Adena and Hopewell, and to the various Mississippian cultures that found their apogee in the great city-state of Cahokia. In the seventeenth and eighteenth centuries, it was home to a wide variety of Native Americans, including Ojibwe, Sioux, Pawnee, Potawatomi, Delaware, Miami, Shawnee, Illinois, and other American Indians whose names and cultures still shape the cognitive and physical landscapes of the region. No less diverse were the European American immigrants who flooded the area in the 1800s, bringing with them countless languages, customs, and beliefs. In our time, African, Arab, Asian, and Hispanic Americans have established a significant presence in the region. No one particular group of people can lay claim to the Midwest.

While we can argue about whether the Midwest has unique characteristics, we cannot deny that many of its daughters and sons think that the region is unique; think in some certain if inchoate fashion that they are midwestern. There is no more interesting expression of this vague regionalism than singer-songwriter Bob Dylan's ambivalence. He left his home state of Minnesota because "It couldn't give me anything." Almost in the same breath, however, Dylan concedes that Minnesota "wouldn't be such a bad place to go back to and die in. There's no place I feel closer to now, or get the feeling that I'm part of, except maybe New York; but I'm not a New Yorker. I'm North Dakota-Minnesota-Midwestern. I'm that color. I speak that way. I'm from someplace called the Iron Range. My brains and feelings have come from there." (quoted in Chester G. Anderson, ed., *Growing up in Minnesota: Ten Writers Remember their Childhood* [1976], 8–9). Like hundreds before and after him who have left the region—from William Dean Howells to Frank Lloyd Wright to Toni Morrison—Dylan, whatever else he may be, is a creature of the Midwest. However far from the region native Midwesterners may move, on some level they always live there. As Morrison put it in a 1983 interview: "I am from the Midwest so I have a special affection for it. My beginnings are always there. No matter what I write, I begin there." (quoted in Danille Taylor-Guthrie, ed., *Conversations with Toni Morrison* [1994], 158).

The American Midwest: An Interpretive Encyclopedia seeks to explore, interpret, and explain both the Midwest and the elusive sense of identity that Dylan described. It endeavors to portray and analyze the ways in which Midwesterners have historically lived and thought. It assesses their origins; the evolution of their landscapes; the construction of their cities, suburbs, towns, and farms; and the ways in which they eat, dress, speak, worship, relax, vote, and socialize. It describes their political cultures, military experiences, labor movements, and class structures, and in various sections it examines the distinctive commercial and industrial engines of the region's economy. And it details the interaction and contributions of diverse groups who have migrated to the region. It engages issues of race, economic development, work, and family, and it investigates and surveys the cultural expressions of Midwesterners in the rich domains of folklore, art, literature, music, film, and theater. In so doing, its editors hope to have limned what Dylan calls midwestern "color." They have endeavored to make the encyclopedia comprehensive, though not exhaustive, and accessible to and informative for a general readership as well as a useful reference for scholars interested in regionalism in America.

The conception, organization, development, and completion of a complex project like an encyclopedia require a considerable investment of intellectual energy and sustained commitment. The project of which the encyclopedia is a product began in the summer of 1998 when John Gallman, then director of Indiana University Press, approached Richard Sisson, formerly provost and interim president of The Ohio State University and then professor and Trustees Chair in Comparative Politics, and Christian Zacher, professor of English and director of Ohio State's Institute for Collaborative Research and Public Humanities, about producing such a work through the Institute. They were both attracted to the proposal, Sisson given his long-term interest in regionalism and culture in Asia, his position of leadership in a Midwest educational institution, and his roots as a native Ohioan, Zacher given his commitment to public education in the humanities and involvement in other collaborative publishing efforts, and both because of their midwestern heritage. They were successful in securing the participation of Patrick Mullen, a professor of English and folklore at Ohio State and formerly publications editor for the American Folklore Society, who served at the outset as an advisory editor in helping to develop the initial formulation for the project. They ultimately agreed to take on the task as a major interdisciplinary, educational initiative under the auspices of the Institute. Sisson and Zacher were subsequently fortunate in recruiting Andrew Cayton, Distinguished Professor of History at Miami University, a published scholar on the history of the American Midwest, to serve as the third general editor, who provided intellectual leadership throughout the project. Cayton collaborated specifically with Sisson and Zacher in developing the overall table of contents as well as identifying and recruiting the senior consulting editors. He took the lead in drafting the nature and significance section of the ultimately successful proposal for funding to the National Endowment for the Humanities, and he wrote the General Overview essay for the encyclopedia.

Critical to the emergence of the overall structure of the project were two planning conferences convened at Ohio State. The first meeting was devoted to establishing linkages with other institutions, presenting the general editors' conception and scope of the work, obtaining advice on the substance and organization of the project, and identifying colleagues who, if they were to agree, would serve as outstanding senior consulting editors. The participants, experts on the Midwest and scholars of regionalism, included Kathleen Nells Conzen, Henry Glassie, Trudier Harris, and Gary C. Ness, all of whom became members of the encyclopedia's National Editorial Advisory Board; Bert Feintuch and James Grossman of *The Encyclopedia of New England* and *The Encyclopedia of Chicago*, respectively; and Charles Camp, John Gallman, Julie R. Newell, and Judith Sealander. Others who attended this first conference included Lawrence A. Brown, Kermit L. Hall, James P. Leary, James Madison, Deborah L. Miller, and Patrick Mullen, all of whom continued to serve as either senior consulting editors or in other instrumental advisory roles. The conference was invaluable to the general editors in helping them sharpen the intellectual design of the encyclopedia.

After further refining the thematic organization of the encyclopedia in the form of sections, the general editors invited experts highly regarded in their respective fields to serve as senior consulting editors, each with responsibility for a particular section. They and the general editors discussed the further organization and substantive compass of the sections in a series of conference calls, and they were provided the assistance of an experienced consultant in developing a substantial outline and precis for their sections. The general editors were continually and intimately engaged in this process throughout.

A second conference drew together the senior consulting editors and other interested parties for a collective report and analysis of the project in progress, a report on the nature of each section and its proposed table of contents and a collective planning for the road ahead. The occasion also provided a forum for discussing both avoidable and allowable overlaps among the various sections. In these as in previous and future discussions the general editors gained insight into the complexities and challenges of producing such a volume from the editors of other completed or in-progress encyclopedias, particularly *The Encyclopedia of Indianapolis*, *The New Encyclopedia of the American West*, and the *Encyclopedia of the Great Plains*. No less important to the success of the project has been the discovery, early on in the project, in conferences, in various general editors' presentations, and through innumerable inquiries since, of the breadth of enthusiasm for such an encyclopedia and the widespread and growing interest in the field of Midwest and regional studies.

Because of other writing projects as well as his teaching responsibilities at Miami University, Professor Cayton resigned as a general editor in the fall of

2001, but remained with the project as a general consulting editor, along with James H. Madison and Deborah L. Miller. During his leave, Sisson and Zacher assumed responsibility for the organization of all sections, for assisting senior consulting editors in continuing to mold their sections and in attracting contributors, and for editing the first waves of submissions. They divided responsibility for the sections between them, Sisson overseeing fourteen and Zacher eight. They also during this time secured the requisite funding that would allow the completion of the encyclopedia in a timely manner.

The departure of Charlotte Dihoff as managing editor in 2001 resulted in the reorganization of the project, with Sisson and Zacher sharing overall management of the effort through its publication. In the fall of 2002, Cayton resumed his role as a general editor at the request and urging of Sisson and Zacher, given the many contributions he had already made to the project. He supervised to completion the sections on Education, Geography, Language, Peoples, Religion, Rural Life, Small-Town Life, Sports and Recreation, and, in consultation with Sisson and Zacher, the Portraits of the Twelve States. Sisson maintained responsibility for Images, Folklore, Labor Movements and Working-Class Culture, Transportation, Urban and Suburban Life, Constitutional and Legal Culture, Politics, and Military Affairs; and Zacher retained responsibility for Arts, Literature, Cultural Institutions, Media and Entertainment, and Science and Technology/Health and Medicine.

We feel a deep sense of gratitude to the many individuals and organizations who contributed their ideas, time, and treasure to make the production of this volume possible. Our thanks go first to John Gallman, who extended important advice and support at the outset. Kermit L. Hall, then dean of Ohio State's College of Humanities and later one of our senior consulting editors, gave critical support to the project at its inception.

Financial support for the encyclopedia came from a variety of sources: the National Endowment for the Humanities, our most generous external funder, which also offered incisive and constructive comments on our plans; Wolfe Associates of Columbus, a major funder; the Columbus Foundation, which granted funding from the Charlotte R. Haller, Ben and Dana Falter, and Paul G. Duke Funds; the Limited Foundation; Chemical Abstracts Service; Indiana University Press; the Hattie W. & Robert L. Lazarus Fund; William and Beverly Hirzel; and Barbara Brandt. At Ohio State—which has been our largest funder—the Institute for Collaborative Research and Public Humanities offered essential material, staff, and financial aid. Major funding also was provided by several other

contributors at Ohio State: the Office of the President; the Office of Research; the Office of Academic Affairs; the College of Humanities, particularly Deans Hall and Michael J. Hogan, and its Departments of Comparative Studies, English, and History; and the Department of Political Science and its then chair, Paul Allen Beck. Throughout the project, continuous important funding was made available from the Board of Trustees Chair in Comparative Politics. At the start of the project, we received invaluable advice and assistance on fund-raising from Anne Swire and Steven Moore of the OSU University Development Office of Corporate and Foundation Giving and from Roger Addleman, Lisa Wente, and Vince McGrail of University Development Communications. Professor Paul Nini and his students in the Department of Industrial, Interior, and Visual Communication Design suggested design possibilities for the book gratis. At Miami University, Charlotte Newman Goldy, chair of the History Department, and John Skillings, Dean of the College of Arts and Science, made it possible for Andrew Cayton to participate in the project. Miami undergraduate Matthew Wolfe provided invaluable research assistance. The many contributing authors who generously waived payment lessened the burden of our costs.

The scholars, artists, and public figures who make up our National Editorial Advisory Board offered foundational advice and guidance throughout the life of the project. At Ohio State, Steven Westman of the University Libraries coached us on the nature of a potential electronic version of the book; Steven McDonald and John Biancamano of the University's Department of Legal Affairs gave us various needed advice; and the staff of Ohio State's Humanities Information Systems developed invaluable online tracking tools and rescued our staff from sometimes mutinous computers.

The encyclopedia's superb editorial team was the group that made this project happen. Charlotte Dihoff, managing editor from 1999 to 2001, assisted the general and consulting editors in organizing the contents and editorial procedures. Associate Editor Anne Burnham established editorial guidelines for the volume and took the lead in developing the article review process; she also read and edited manuscripts and with tact coordinated their passage from the editors to the authors and back. Assistant Editor Rebecca Zell Fullmer worked with the general and consulting editors during the review process, helped recruit and consult with authors, supervised our editorial assistants, and kept things moving efficiently. Sathyan Sundaram, web developer and rights specialist, also provided technological guidance to the editorial staff; created and maintained the project website; and organized the procurement of photos, maps, tables, and graphs for the volume. Deena Adelman served as a traffic manager, reliably overseeing a host of communication and editorial matters. Editorial Assistant Jennifer Hastings provided invaluable aid and took the lead on the fact-checking process. That work was continued by Editorial Assistant Vanessa Perez and brought to completion by the careful oversight of Senior Editorial Assistant Alyssa von Reuter, who also knowledgeably monitored the final preparation of the manuscript through its copy-editing phase. Working along with them over the several years of the project were a number of dependable student assistants managing various tasks—Akilah Atkinson, Christopher Bernhardt, Bruce Bortner, Peter Bratt, Brady Burkett, Devin Burritt, Esther Coley, Melanie Dean, Sam Dobrozsi, Lindsay Donofrio, Luke Eviston, Allison Fisher, Gabrielle Gethers, Jennifer Jones, Roman Nitze, Andrew Nolan, and Christine Platt. Brookes Hammock and Michael Hissam were especially instrumental in preparing the final manuscript. The Institute's administrative assistant, Elizabeth Lantz, watched over our budget and material needs through the life of the project and assisted importantly in the final readying of the manuscript. Cartographers James DeGrand and Margaret Popovich learnedly prepared the maps for the volume. Consultants Gail Meese, Peter Williams, Barbara Lyons, and Barbara Brandt also lent their expertise to the project. We benefited greatly from advice about fact-checking we received from Rich Groening and Carol Sykes of the Ohio State University Libraries.

The twenty-four senior consulting editors of *The American Midwest: An Interpretive Encyclopedia* have been devoted supporters of the project. Their efforts to ensure the quality of every article in the encyclopedia have made the volume what it is. The general editors also thank our three general consulting editors, James Madison, Deborah L. Miller, and Juliet E. K. Walker, for their valuable counsel and a range of contributions to the effort.

All of us mourn the death of Mary Neth, our Senior Consulting Editor for Rural Life, in September 2005. As creative as she was good-humored, Mary was a joy to work with. Lastly, our special thanks to the staff at Indiana University Press, especially to Editorial Director Robert Sloan, Managing Editor Miki Bird, and Production Director Bernadette Zoss for their assistance in bringing this book into the light of day. Rebecca Hominski, Lewis Parker, and Debbie Masi at Westchester Book Services led us through the final stages and prepared the encyclopedia for print. John Bealle created the index.

Richard Sisson, Christian Zacher, and
Andrew Cayton
September 22, 2005

"*Prodesse quam conspici*" ("To produce rather than to be conspicuous"), the motto of Miami University in Oxford, Ohio, is a fitting credo for the American Midwest as a whole. In the popular imagination, Midwesterners are generally considered proudly ordinary people who speak dialect-free American English and go about their business without fanfare or drama. Performers born there tend to leave, though pride in life and place is given a visible presence. Those who remain daily demonstrate the workings of a democratic culture that embodies what many people consider the fulfillment of the American Dream. "Midwesterners," writes Dennis Preston, our "Language" Senior Consulting Editor, "are thought to be strong, brave, polite, hard working, self-effacing, self-sufficient, generous, friendly, Protestant, white, normal, average, and boring."

The familiar midwestern landscape consists of gleaming silos and white houses amid endless green fields of corn linked by meandering streams and asphalt highways to rectangular towns dominated by stores, banks, and professional offices along Main Streets surrounded by frame homes with wide porches decorated with hanging pots of geraniums and suffused with the aroma of fresh-baked bread. Railroads and expressways join these towns to the vertical skylines, cavernous business districts, and sprawling factories and suburban office buildings of St. Louis, Milwaukee, Kansas City, Cincinnati, Cleveland, Omaha, Wichita, Minneapolis-St. Paul, Indianapolis, Columbus, Detroit, and Chicago.

These iconic images seem so natural and right to so many people that they easily obscure the contingent and contested culture of the American Midwest. In accepting what the region has become and the image it projects (or what other people project onto it), we sometimes lose sight of its diversity, its exceptionalism, and the paths its residents have chosen not to follow. The modesty announced in *prodesse quam conspici* has been accompanied not only by confidence in the institutions of family and community and a capacity to overcome adversity but by an acceptance of the status quo, a distrust of idiosyncrasy, an avoidance of confrontation, and a general lack of self-reflection.

The American Midwest: An Interpretive Encyclopedia is a labor of love by hundreds of people, most of them natives of the region, who believe that the question of whether the Midwest constitutes a distinctive place is one worth pondering. Indeed, the guiding principle of this work is a belief that the process of contemplating that question is as important as any answers offered individually or collectively by our authors. In the largest

sense, we hope the encyclopedia contributes to the civic culture of the United States. We mean to inform. We also hope to provoke public discussion about the Midwest as something more than the sum of its parts. If readers frustrated by the borders we have imposed or irritated by the conclusions reached by some of our authors respond publicly with their own ideas about the Midwest, we will have accomplished our overall goal of encouraging more conversation about the region.

Of one thing, however, we have no doubt: Whatever the Midwest lacks in flamboyance or precision, it gains in significance. The conquest, settlement, and development of what we call the Midwest is one of the most important events in the past quarter millennium of human history. In the nineteenth century, millions of people entered this interior region, forcibly displaced thousands of American Indians, and established a society that dominated North America and much of the globe throughout the twentieth century. This breathtaking transformation amounts to one of the most all-encompassing and significant revolutions in the history of the world. No other place besides the American Midwest better reflects the combined impact of the democratic revolutions of the eighteenth century and the transportation, communication, and industrial revolutions of the nineteenth century. No other place on earth brought so many different human beings together in such a short period of time to negotiate and fashion new ways of life. No other place better exemplifies the values of market capitalism as well as ideals of social equality, civic culture, and local democracy.

Perhaps we tend to slight the significance of the Midwest because its history is largely a narrative of the accumulation of ordinary events into large-scale change rather than a story of dramatic turning points. It has been a place that encourages people to do what is necessary to accomplish an assigned task; a place that nurtured hundreds of women who in the early 1870s suddenly refused to tolerate the effects of intoxication and marched into saloons and stores demanding that the proprietors not sell alcoholic beverages; a place that produced generals like Ulysses S. Grant, William Tecumseh Sherman, John J. Pershing, and Dwight D. Eisenhower, men who did what was necessary to win wars without being seduced by the charms of fleeting glory, and leaders like Jane Addams, Robert LaFollette, and John Dewey, for whom change was always straightforward and practical. Pragmatism underscored the far-reaching reforms advocated by

William Jennings Bryan at the turn of the twentieth century, Hubert H. Humphrey's campaign for civil rights at the 1948 Democratic National Convention, and the promotion of workers' rights by Eugene V. Debs and A. Philip Randolph.

A century ago, when the Midwest was coming into its own, its boosters celebrated their contributions to human progress with fairs, histories, monuments, and public buildings. Characteristically, their stress was on the United States rather than the Midwest. Among the most famous events was the World's Columbian Exposition held in Chicago in 1893 to commemorate the four-hundredth anniversary of the first transatlantic voyage of Christopher Columbus. More than twenty-seven million people visited the exposition, making it one of the greatest attractions of its era. Constructed on more than six hundred acres that ran for two miles along Lake Michigan, the exposition introduced the first elevated electric railway, movable sidewalk, and Ferris wheel. Visitors popularized hamburgers, carbonated beverages, Cracker Jack, Cream of Wheat, Shredded Wheat, Juicy Fruit gum, and Aunt Jemima syrup. The centerpiece of the exposition was the White City, a collection of buildings showcasing exhibits from all over the world that gave birth to the Beaux-Arts style and the City Beautiful movement.

In less than a year, twelve thousand workers raised some four hundred edifices in Roman and Greek styles at a total cost of more than eight million dollars in 1893 dollars. Director Daniel Burnham said that they were imposing a neoclassical white harmony on what had only recently been a wilderness. The exposition was both an illustration and a symbol of the nineteenth-century transformations exemplified by the Midwest. Promoting harmony and order, the exposition married material and artistic achievements into a tribute to both civic ideals and consumer fantasies. "Its white facades," writes our "Cultural Institutions" Senior Consulting Editor Erika Doss, "expressed turn-of-the-century assumptions of white, Anglo-Saxon supremacy and deemed ancient Greece and Rome as the pinnacles of world art and culture." "Villages of non-white and non-Western 'natives' [reinforced] notions of social Darwinism and the supposed evolutionary differences between savagery and civilization. Its rituals of nationalism—the 'Pledge of Allegiance' was written expressly for the Chicago fair—instructed visitors about American patriotism."

The White City and the Columbian Exposition were so remarkable that they overwhelmed even the most hardened visitors. Labor organizer Debs wanted working-class Americans to be able to "look upon the beautiful in art as well as nature, a form of worship entirely devoid of cant and hypocrisy, superior to any worship narrowed by creeds and dogmas" (quoted in Alan Trachtenberg, *The Incorporation of America: Culture and Society in the Gilded Age* [1982, 218]). L. Frank Baum remembered the White City when he imagined a place called the Emerald City in the Land of Oz, and no doubt it influenced the productions of Walt Disney, the son of one of the construction workers.

In its tribute to progress, to the potential of an alliance between commerce and art, to the possibilities inherent in human collaboration and public culture, the White City and its promoters obscured as much as they revealed. The boosterism of the Midwest—its ceaseless interest in promoting itself as the emblem of all that is good and decent—was never more vividly displayed. The result was something not unlike the history and culture of the Midwest: the rapid creation of an enormously attractive and popular place whose glittering lights and gleaming surfaces made invisible the conflicts and challenges that lay all around it.

Outside the White City, the Midwest in the 1890s was in the midst of a crisis that constituted one of the worst periods of economic depression in the history of the United States. Chicago, like other cities in the region, had grown so quickly that it sometimes seemed haphazard, even chaotic. Buildings came down almost as soon as they went up. Hundreds of thousands of people arrived from Europe and the Americas, speaking multitudes of languages and worshipping in multitudes of sacred spaces, finding work in dangerous plants and dismal offices and living in overcrowded and inadequate housing. While working-class immigrants organized to survive and farmers rallied against the powerful railroads, middle-class Midwesterners fretted about being overrun by immigrants whose values and manners affronted their sense of respectability, moderation, and stability. Serious issues, including corporate regulation, currency reform, temperance, public education, and labor unions, bitterly polarized Midwesterners. It was in this context that people rushed to the Columbian Exposition to ride the Ferris wheel and sample the treats in the central area of food stands dubbed the Midway. Many were simply seeking amusement. The White City was a consumer fantasy, a place of escape from a troubled and difficult world.

Implicitly, the exposition celebrated the first century of the American Midwest as much as it celebrated the voyages of Columbus. The White City's blend of pretension and pragmatism, of entertainment and education, as well as the degree to which it obscured conflict and diverted attention from problems, reflected the commonly understood history of the Midwest as a whole. In general, popular narratives of regional history recounted a story of development that unfolded with such speed and thoroughness that people could scarcely remember what came before it or what went into its making. The history of the Midwest was a tale of inevitable, uncontested, and natural progress.

In the middle of the eighteenth century, American Indians and some Europeans lived in villages on the banks of lakes and rivers from the Ohio River to the headwaters of the Mississippi River. Ojibwe and Sioux inhabited what we call Wisconsin; Osages lived along the lower Missouri River; Illinois and Potawatomis were south of Lake Michigan; and Shawnee, Delaware, and Miami dominated the Wabash, Maumee, and Ohio River Valleys. In addition to agriculture, these peoples depended on commerce with French and English traders. They traded furs and skins, some from as far away as what is now the Dakotas, for cloth, guns, alcohol, and steel instruments. The future Midwest was a heavily forested area laced with lakes and rivers that facilitated the commercial ties that connected the Sioux, the Osage, and others with Paris and London, inducing ever-increasing dependence on European and European American technology and trade. Beyond economic ties, Indians sought diplomatic and military alliances with Europeans, exploiting their power and position to play the French and the English off against each other and to use Europeans as leverage against the imperial Iroquois.

The destruction of this world commenced in the middle of the eighteenth century. The 1754 arrival near the forks of the Ohio River (modern-day Pittsburgh) of a party of Virginians under the command of a young George Washington precipitated a world war that lasted until 1763 and resulted in the demise of the French empire in North America. The triumphant British were unable to manage their victory, however, and alienated a wide range of Americans, including the Indians of the Great Lakes as well as the artisans of Philadelphia and Boston. In 1776 thirteen Atlantic colonies declared their independence and established a republic. Along the way to forcing British acceptance of this new order, Americans attacked Indians all the way from New York to Georgia. A series of conflicts after the 1783 Treaty of Paris climaxed in the defeat of Indian warriors just before and during the War of 1812 and the mutual acceptance by Great Britain and the United States of a permanent border at the Great Lakes. Despite sporadic violence in the upper Mississippi Valley, in the 1820s and 1830s the American republic held sway from the Atlantic Ocean to the Great Plains. Ironically, the names of all midwestern states, with the exception of Indiana, would be drawn from Indian cultures.

Within a matter of decades, Americans and Europeans completed the revision of the landscape of the future Midwest. They consumed and laid waste to forests; drained swamps; and constructed roads, canals, and railroads. They planted corn and wheat, tended fruit orchards, and raised hogs and cattle, making their region one of the breadbaskets of the world. They built thousands of small towns along transportation routes that became local entrepôts, communities of rectangular blocks covered with solid brick-and-frame homes emanating from that central Main Street commercial core. Strategically located communities became processing centers, transforming grain into portable goods such as beer and flour or butchering hogs into a multitude of products.

A variety of large cities grew up in the region, but Chicago—established in 1833, only half a century before its White City would dazzle the world—became the transportation, commercial, and cultural capital of the North American interior almost overnight. Railroads built Chicago. Timber from Minnesota and Wisconsin, wheat from the Dakotas, and corn from Iowa filled the warehouses along Lake Michigan. Lawyers and entrepreneurs flocked to the city to bet on the future of grain sales and real estate development. Burned to the ground in 1871, Chicago barely paused in its reconstruction and growth. By 1900 it was a grand place, with a distinctive skyline formed by tall buildings, broad streets, and rectangular squares. Chicago was the primary destination of people eager to move beyond rural and small-town lives. Beyond Chicago, from Ohio to Kansas, the Midwest at the turn of the twentieth century was a commercial and agricultural paradise, unlike anywhere else in the world.

The role of government is often as invisible in the history of the Midwest as the presence of Native Americans. The United States Congress created a territorial policy in the Land Ordinance of 1785 and the Northwest Ordinance of 1787 that would provide the template for American expansion throughout the nineteenth century. Land in the Midwest would generally be surveyed and sold in squares, creating the checkerboard right angles that mark most of the region. An orderly process allowed people to form states, starting with Ohio (1803), and moving through Indiana (1816), Illinois (1818), Missouri (1821), Michigan (1837), Iowa (1846), Wisconsin (1848), Minnesota (1858), Kansas (1861), Nebraska (1867), North Dakota (1889), and South Dakota (1889). As important, the Northwest Ordinance ensured that states would have republican governments, that they would encourage public education and religion, and that they would not permit slavery (except in Missouri). While support for education and opposition to slavery were controversial and sometimes more rhetorical than real, they nonetheless came to define the Midwest in the popular imagination.

By the mid-nineteenth century, in fact, many residents attributed their progress to the cultivation of free labor and to cultural institutions such as schools and churches that molded people of middle-class character. The public culture of the Midwest flourished in a host of activities, from popular Chautauquas to thousands of local voluntary societies committed to the moral and material progress of human beings. More than half of the Carnegie libraries built in the United States were in the Midwest. The region boasted a plethora of Christian denominations whose congregations built beautiful churches and supported dozens of private colleges to train ministers, teachers, and good citizens. States, meanwhile, created public school systems and public universities, and over time designed some of the most innovative curricula in the world. This trend climaxed in the third quarter of the nineteenth century with the founding of the great land-grant universities that would become the public face of the Midwest in the twentieth century, symbols of democratic higher education reflected in the motto of The Ohio State University—*Disciplina in civitatem* ("Education for citizenship").

Nineteenth-century Midwesterners took pride in their development, although their sense of region was ambiguous at best. They spoke of their home as the West or the Great West. (The term *Midwest* did not become common until the early twentieth century.) More often, they talked in terms of states rather than the region as a whole. Although they saw the Union victory in the American Civil War as an affirmation of regional values, they organized themselves, as did the army, by states. When the "boy general" Arthur MacArthur planted the American flag on the top of Missionary Ridge outside Chattanooga, Tennessee, in November 1863, he reportedly exclaimed "On Wisconsin!" not "On Midwest!"

The sons and daughters of the Midwest were everywhere between the mid-1800s and the mid-1900s. From 1860 to 1960 Midwesterners occupied the White House more than half the time. Other prominent politicians included John Sherman, William Jennings Bryan, Eugene Debs, George Norris, and Robert La Follette. The region became the crossroads of national transportation systems and the headquarters of the most important U.S. industries. Inventors and entrepreneurs such as Thomas Edison, Cyrus McCormick, the Wright brothers, John Deere, Richard Sears, Garrett Morgan, Charles Kettering, Henry Ford, Ray Kroc, and William Lear all came from the Midwest. Personal health and diet movements began in the Midwest. The area has encouraged a large number of medical and pharmaceutical advances as well as important medical clinics. Major American writers from William Dean Howells and Mark Twain to Langston Hughes and Willa Cather were midwestern. *Poetry*, the famous literary magazine, made its home in the Midwest. Here were some of the greatest creations of architects like Frank Lloyd Wright and Louis Sullivan and city planners like Daniel Burnham and George Kessler. Here jazz flourished and the issue-oriented media talk show evolved.

By the early twentieth century, the transformation of the landscape into what we think of as the Midwest was largely complete. The dynamic age of revolutionary change gave way to an era of stability and stagnation. Once on the cutting edge of global change, the Midwest came to epitomize the American status quo. Midwesterners were supposedly pragmatic, middle-of-the-road people. When late twentieth-century Americans thought of the Midwest, they thought of Harry S Truman and Oprah Winfrey, Jane Addams and Gerald Ford—plain-spoken, respectable citizens. Many imagined the Midwest as homogeneous, predictable, and boring, the kind of place people dreamed of escaping from to someplace that was brighter and more dynamic. One of the great tropes of American autobiography in the twentieth century is the tale of the small-town midwesterner—like Cole Porter—who goes to New York or Hollywood to make it big, reversing the migration pattern of the nineteenth century.

The Midwest by the middle of the twentieth century seemed to be more a state of mind or attitude than a specific place. Midwesterners were distinguished by their lack of distinguishing characteristics. Anything but flamboyant, they supposedly had no discernible accent or clothing or customs. Their culture, like their history and their landscape, was linear and straightforward, without major drama, without peaks or valleys; no oceans, though bordered by great lakes; no great wars, though war defined the region from the mid-1700s until the early 1800s and in the 1860s; no major problems, despite the existence of agrarian discontent, racial tensions, and urban poverty. Midwestern cuisine (supposedly meat and potatoes) was the midwestern culture in miniature: solid, practical, unimaginative. Midwesterners by definition were not introspective, at least not publicly. They were nice people who produced without being conspicuous, living comfortably within the hermetically sealed world of a Garrison Keillor monologue.

Unlike southerners or westerners, who thrive on, even demand, conversation about regional identity rooted in a profound sense of alienation from some vague American mainstream culture and its government, Midwesterners are apparently happy to identify with the United States as a whole. Their local pride is all about exemplifying the best of America. The Midwest is the Heartland, the nation writ small, the great middle, lacking extremes, lacking diversity.

The American Midwest attempts to complicate this

image, to demonstrate that this apparently stable region has always been a crucible of dramatic political protest, social reform, labor unions, and cultural movements; that its extremes in production are as wide as those in climate. History would have persuaded less foolhardy souls against such a dubious enterprise, for efforts to think about the Midwest as a whole have traditionally foundered on the rock of definition. Rarely have scholars gotten beyond debating whether Ohio and Nebraska belong together. While we recognize the value of such arguments, we have in practical midwestern fashion tried to get on with an examination of the region and to let definitions emerge from the process. We may be taken to the woodshed for our choice of boundaries, but it was an unavoidable trip no matter what we chose to do. The encyclopedia embodies our belief that culture is often a matter of perception, that what people believe to be true matters as much or more than what scholars may demonstrate to be empirically verifiable. Our sense is that people drinking coffee in a café off Interstate 70 have a strong sense of what the Midwest is. They may not be able to explain it formally, but in a phrase popularized by midwesterner and Supreme Court justice Potter Stewart, they know it when they see it.

Our Midwest consists of the states created from the original Northwest Territory plus several covered by the Louisiana Purchase of 1803, the states of the upper Mississippi Valley and those parts of Kansas and Nebraska east of the hundredth meridian and of the Dakotas east of the Missouri River. In part, slavery influenced our decision; only Missouri of the twelve was a slave state. In part, geography dictated selection: Our region is land drained northward into the Great Lakes and southward into the Ohio, Missouri, and upper Mississippi Valleys. Given the rainfall line of the hundredth meridian and the preponderance of rivers as well as the largest bodies of fresh water on the planet, it is heavily forested, generally wet and flat land with ore and coal deposits in its most northern and southern reaches.

The American Midwest is organized topically rather than chronologically to encourage readers to reflect on the region as a whole. Each section was entrusted to a distinguished specialist who in collaboration with the general editors compiled a table of contents and recruited authors to write entries and essays. Although the organization of each section varies, sections tend to move from the general to the specific, introducing broad themes in longer introductory essays with details supplied in the shorter entries that follow. Some sections proceed chronologically and create a narrative; some proceed alphabetically; others combine the two approaches. Rather than have specific sections for

women, African Americans, Native Americans, and other groups traditionally excluded or underrepresented in books such as this one, we decided to incorporate all peoples as much as possible throughout the encyclopedia. We have tried to make sure that no one state or group of states is overrepresented. In a nod to the importance of state identity in the region, we open with a section entitled "Portraits of the Twelve States," which consists of consciously idiosyncratic essays about the particular qualities of the various states.

Among the many themes in the book as a whole, two recur: universalism versus exceptionalism, and homogeneity versus diversity.

Is the Midwest simply a microcosm of the United States? Our authors are divided in their response to the question of universalism. Many do not find anything peculiarly midwestern in their subject, thereby reinforcing the common wisdom that the Midwest is the least recognizable (or interesting) of American regions. One of the revelations of this encyclopedia, however, is the number of authors who do believe that there is something distinctive about the Midwest. Readers will find extensive information documenting the extent to which the cultures and peoples of the Midwest diverge from their counterparts in the South, the Northeast, the Great Plains, or the Far West. To be sure, the region has experienced virtually all of the major developments and issues in the history of the United States—conquest and settlement, immigration and migration, agriculture and industrialization, race and ethnicity, reform and resistance, suburbanization and consumerism—but they have not originated or evolved in precisely the same ways.

Is the Midwest a region of unbroken sameness? Regarding the question of homogeneity in the Midwest, our authors are close to unanimous in answering with an emphatic "No!" As we learn in "Images of the Midwest," the reputation of the Midwest as homogeneous is largely an act of imagination that has flourished with particular vigor since World War II. Beyond easy generalizations, however, lies enormous variety.

At the dawn of the twentieth century, the Midwest was one of the most ethnically and culturally diverse places on earth. Its residents were immigrants and the children of immigrants from the eastern coast of North America, most from Europe, and from parts of Latin America and Asia. Thanks to 1920s congressionally imposed restrictions on immigration into the United States and to the growing visibility of race, the multiple cultures of the Midwest have largely faded from the popular imagination. But in the 1890s, a diaspora of Christian denominations shaped the landscape of parts of the region, like rural Iowa and small-town Kansas. Chicago, Cleveland, and St. Louis teemed with communities of Poles, Russians, Italians, Hungarians, Lebanese, and Greeks, among many others. The Midwest supported hundreds of newspapers and magazines in a staggering number of languages. The German triangle (Cincinnati to St. Louis to Milwaukee) dominated midwestern culture, introducing German words, customs, foods, and music. The upper Mississippi Valley attracted hundreds of thousands of Scandinavians who left their imprint from Wisconsin to the Dakotas. In the last decades of the twentieth century, immigrants arrived in large numbers from the Middle East, South and Southeast Asia, and Africa.

The American Midwest introduces readers to the cultural diversity of the Midwest, including a vast array of foods, languages, styles, religions, and customs. We learn about strong midwestern traditions of agrarian resistance, labor organization, and opposition to corporate and middle-class values as well as the deep conflicts engendered by racism and exclusion. We experience the region as a hothouse of ideas and innovations, reforms and revivals, as well as a setting for social and physical extremes. We see how the influx of different peoples into the region in the twentieth century, from Appalachians to African Americans to emigrants from Mexico and Central America, sub-Saharan Africa, Southeast Asia, and the Caribbean, continues to redefine the American Midwest. Today, the region is home to some of the most numerous and varied immigrant communities in the United States: Somalis in Ohio, Hmong in Wisconsin, Hispanics in Iowa, and Muslims in Michigan.

Ironically, as in the past, the very variety of the Midwest encourages a veneer of public culture that tends to downplay diversity while it highlights superficial conformity. Midwesterners sometimes insist so much on the importance of civic culture, nurtured in schools, churches, and families and expressed in great public buildings and ceremonies, because it has seemed to be the only way to bring any semblance of order to their complex world. The Midwest exemplifies James Madison's argument in *The Federalist Papers* that in an extended territory with a large heterogeneous population it is "less probable that a majority . . . will have a common motive to invade the rights of other citizens; or if such a common motive exists . . . [it will be] more difficult for all who feel it to discover their own strength and to act in unison with each other" (Isaac Kramnick, ed., *The Federalist Papers* [1788; reprint, 1987, 127]). Precisely because the Midwest is so diverse, precisely because it does not have a homogeneous population or a common interest, it is a region defined to a large extent by the construction of a public culture designed to allow people to talk and participate in ways that suppress differences behind facades of civility and the common good. If this ten-

dency promotes conformity, it also nurtures creativity and passion among people determined to express themselves.

The Midwest in fact is not the land of the bland, but a collection of disparate communities held together, more or less, by a civic culture that transcends (or at least ignores) differences, fashioned and buoyed by social engagement and characterized by sustained public participation and philanthropic giving. Thus we emphasize generic institutions of commerce, education, manners, and development. Morality is not specific. It is a general focus on hard work, respect, and politeness. Civic culture is something that Midwesterners, especially midwestern rebels, of whom there are quite a few, want to capture and define. Today, the American Midwest is a source of comfort and conformity, a place transformed from a nineteenth-century symbol of progress into a twenty-first-century symbol of stability, from the home of pioneers pointing the United States toward the future into the residence of guardians of the nation's traditions. Its legacy lies in the settlement of Peoria, Arizona, by people from Peoria, Illinois, and Columbus, Nebraska, by people from Columbus, Ohio; in the creation of Main Street at the Disney theme parks by a native of Marceline, Missouri; in films made on the "Midwest Street" lot at Warner Brothers' California studio; in the annual Iowa reunion picnics in southern California; in the dead zones of the Gulf of Mexico caused by the drainage of chemicals from midwestern farm fields; and even in the perfect Illinois town that explorers from Earth find on Mars in Ray Bradbury's *Martian Chronicles*.

The Midwest, in sum, is a remarkable display of human achievement: a rapidly constructed monument to material progress that hides the ways in which it has been constructed, challenged, and contested, and a set of variations on themes that have created a place unlike any other in the world. We hope our readers occasionally shake their heads and mutter, "I didn't know that!" or, as important, "I don't know *about* that!" According to a contemporary journalist, the World's Columbian Exposition of 1893 was "the latest and most complete, and by far the best illustrated, of an Ecumenical Encyclopedia, published in one enormous volume" (Walter Besant, "A First Impression," *Cosmopolitan* 15 [Sept. 1893]). May our readers find their stroll through this, "the latest and most complete" of encyclopedias, as stimulating as people more than a century ago found a stroll along the Midway and through the exhibits of the White City.

Andrew Cayton
Miami University, Oxford, Ohio

Landscapes and People

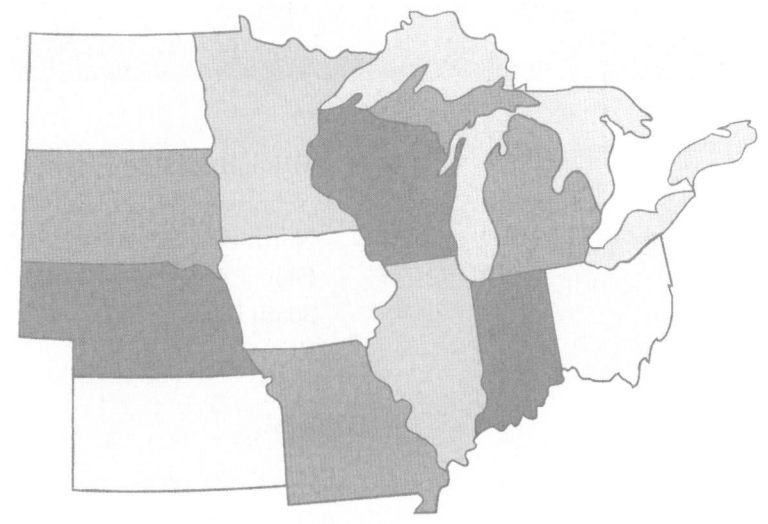

Portraits of the Twelve States

SECTION EDITOR
Deborah L. Miller

Section Contents

Overview

The American Midwest means different things to different people. Its shape and contours shift dramatically, depending on where you are standing. From Ohio, the Missouri River looks like a distant boundary in a different kind of place. From Michigan, Minnesota, and Wisconsin—part farm country and part forested lake terrain, imbued with the ideas and symbols of northern latitudes and defined in part by the Canadian boundary—the Ohio River that marks the southern edge of the Old Northwest looks more like the northern border of the South.

Even the peoples of the Midwest cannot always agree on where the region begins and ends. Citizens of Ohio, Indiana, and Illinois sometimes claim to be the original Midwesterners because their states were the first to emerge from the Northwest Territory in the early 1800s. Residents of the Dakotas, Nebraska, and Kansas, states created in the second half of the nineteenth century, are not sure that Ohio and Indiana are even part of the Midwest. The residents of Wisconsin and Minnesota seek to distinguish themselves within the region by using the term upper Midwest to refer to their area.

Midwestern states are frequently as complicated as the region. The states around the margins have close relationships with other regions. Some actually include parts of other regions, such as the Great Plains, within their boundaries. Even interior states, such as Iowa and Illinois—which may be thought of as the heart of the Heartland, the middle of the Midwest—are divided into sub-regions. Within North and South Dakota, the Missouri River marks an internal rainfall boundary—between tallgrass prairie and shortgrass prairie, between farms and ranches, between East River and West River—which is approximated by the one-hundredth meridian. A similar internal dividing line exists in Nebraska and Kansas, but no river marks it, because the Missouri, heading south, forms the Iowa-Nebraska border before continuing southeast to meet the Mississippi at St. Charles, Missouri.

As is the case everywhere, Midwestern waterways make obvious political boundaries. The Mississippi River divides Missouri from Illinois and Iowa from Wisconsin. The St. Croix River separates Wisconsin and Minnesota. Lake Michigan and Lake Superior form part of the boundary with Canada for Michigan and Wisconsin.

But rivers unite people as well as divide them. Sometimes, political borders artificially separate people who share economic, social, and cultural interests. Fargo-Moorhead in North Dakota and Minnesota and the Quad Cities of Illinois and Iowa demonstrate that phenomenon. Residents of small towns in southern Illinois are more likely Cardinals rather than Cubs fans and may associate more with residents of small towns in Missouri or Kentucky than they do with the denizens of Chicago. Like citizens of border states, the citizens of border cities have formed close relationships with their neighbors.

State boundaries, of course, are arbitrary, no more than invisible lines drawn by politicians in Washington, D.C. But the land they divided was real, and soon the lines took on practical meaning, as surveyors marked them, legislators passed different laws in different capitals, and newspaper editors and guidebook writers relentlessly promoted settlement. Landscape and settlement patterns frequently reinforced the general contours of political boundaries. As James Madison notes in *Heartland: Comparative Histories of the Midwestern States* (1988), "States in the eastern part of the region were settled earliest and have always been the most populous, the most urban, and the most industrial. Later settlement, less rainfall, and harsher climates have left the western edge of the region more sparsely populated." (5)

Over time, despite the importance of natural features, settlement patterns, and economic networks, many Midwesterners have come to think about themselves in terms of their native or adopted state. "Portraits of the States" thus explores the region through a series of essays on the 12 states covered in this encyclopedia. Readers should be aware, however, that this section differs from the others in both tone and content. These essays are more reflective than informative by design. We did not ask our essayists to recount history or summarize data. Rather, we asked them to write about what their state means to them.

We are delighted with the results. Roger Welsch writes about the surprising allure of Nebraska, while Jane Ahlin shares and reveals the passion many North Dakotans feel for their state. Thomas Fox Averill provides both heat and light in his discussion of Kansas, and Herbert Hoover outlines the distinctive history of South Dakota. Susan Allen Toth muses about homegrown place names and infinite horizons growing up in Iowa, and Eric Sandweiss charts his connections from Missouri through the airwaves to the greater Midwest and beyond. South Dakota–born Annette Atkins offers a plainswoman's sideways view of humid, forested Minnesota, and Michael Perry merges personal memory and arguments about state identity in Wisconsin.

American Indians play major roles in Kathleen Stocking's lake-locked Michigan as they do in the essays about states on the Midwest's western edge. Becky Bradway's Illinois story juxtaposes the relationships between Chicago and the central and southern parts of the state, demonstrating that all Illinois is divided into three parts, all contentious. R.W. Apple highlights the people and places of Ohio, and Kurt Vonnegut eloquently explains Indiana's Midwestern qualities.

We invite readers to begin with their own native or adopted state and work out from there to the others. These engaging essays reveal the depth of the complicated emotional connections that Midwesterners feel when they think about home. As important, by revealing the ways in which the experiences of the various states have diverged and converged, they provoke us to consider the extent to which our 12 states constitute something more than the sum of their parts, a place we call the American Midwest.

Deborah L. Miller
Minnesota Historical Society

Illinois

Illinois is three states. Three geographies, three separate spheres representing the three contemporary states of being: urban, rural, and in-between (a suburban or big town identity, depending on the aspirations of those who live there). Illinois is a long, lean state, making it easy to draw the lines that separate Chicago and its suburbs, the central cities/towns, and rural southern Illinois. These divisions generally mark the difference between being a Cardinals or a Cubs/White Sox fan, southern or northern, Republican or Democrat. Only Illinoisans seem to be aware of the split. "I'm from Springfield," you might tell a stranger, and she'll say, "How far is that from Chicago?" Chicago thinks it's Illinois and the rest of the world does, too, and so the Windy City *de facto* defines the state. It dictates the politics (and Illinois is all about politics)—its macho brand of Democratic identity filters down into Republican country, and a tough-guy immigrant industrialism trumps the pastoral agricultural vision. Chicago is, after all, the second city (Los Angeles isn't a city—it's one long strip mall). The rest of the state fights Chicago dominance every step of the way.

Industry was money and power in the nineteenth and twentieth centuries, and Chicago had it. Chicago took off in the early 1800s with the construction of the Illinois and Michigan Canal, which linked the Great Lakes to the Illinois River (and so to the Mississippi). People came to build the canal and to take advantage of the opportunities that would come with expanded trade. Agriculture has always grounded Illinois commerce; food was bought and sold, and the devices to expand crop production were built (like reapers and,

eventually, tractors). Once the canal was wrapped up, the workers turned to railroad construction. By the 1850s, Illinois farmers could use the rails to ship their grain and livestock to Chicago, where the produce was converted to products and shipped around the country. Then the steel mills appeared, and Chicago industry filled the skies with smoke. In the 1860s, the stockyards opened, hanging Chicago with the label "Porkopolis" as New York had a laugh. Along with the pigs came Chicago's reputation as a brutal and smelly place where the only public interest was in making money.

Because of the packinghouses, the railroads, the many immigrants, the steadfast drive to grow at all costs, and the general barroom bluster, Chicago became known for its blue-collar roughness, a "tell it like it is" honesty. Chicago insists that it is relatively classless (at least compared to the East Coast), and while this isn't really true, it remains an optimistic Chi-town belief.

Without the rest of Illinois, there would be no Chicago. While the city dwellers and the downstaters rarely mix, both depend on the other. The farmers' product created the need in the Midwest for the canals and railroads, and the farmers in turn spurred industry by purchasing the agricultural machinery. Still, each of Illinois' north-central-south states protects its own turf. The downstaters resent Chicago for bullying its way into political power, while the Chicagoans think the downstaters are a bunch of rubes. The people in the center believe they're the ones who keep the state in operation, because they do the practical, nuts-and-bolts work (like farming and filing documents). The people in southern Illinois think everyone is corrupt, and look with a fonder eye upon Kentucky than any of their upstate neighbors.

And so what of the farm belt, that section in the middle with all that corn, corn, corn? Central Illinois has flatland with rich dirt, and so, of course, you find farmers. Along with the farmers are those who make their living from the farm industry, the workers for Caterpillar, International Harvester, and John Deere in cities like Peoria, Decatur, and Rock Island-Moline. And don't forget the people who work for the multinational corporations, like Archer Daniels Midland, that turn all that grain into materials. The farm industry kept the downstate cities alive for decades, attracting residents to those middle-sized cities. Farming created that eerie green-and-yellow landscape that seems tedious to many outsiders, but holds a strange beauty. The towns—Riverton, Virden, Petersburg, Pleasant Plains, Maroa, LeRoy, Arcola, Fishhook—proclaim their independence. Each is different from the other. And when people need to get to a city, they go to Springfield, Peoria, Champaign-Urbana, and Bloomington-Normal.

Inside these middle-sized cities, you don't see much corn. You find malls, government buildings, colleges—the usual institutions that serve the usual people, the government workers, insurance execs, factory hands, and schoolteachers. The cities and towns have distinctive characters, based on the backgrounds of their original settlers and the type of work maintained there. Champaign-Urbana is dominated by the University of Illinois; Bloomington-Normal is the site of two major insurance companies and Illinois State University; Springfield is the center of a large and contentious state government; and the industries in Decatur, Peoria, and Rock Island-Moline revolve around agricultural products and machinery.

Central Illinois initially attracted seekers who had been farmers in their old countries or who otherwise were accustomed to a quiet pastoral setting. Other towns were configured around mines, and so they attracted laborers and their families. The isolated nature of the countryside put a town of Irish thirty miles from a town of Italians twenty miles from a town of Germans ten miles from a town of Swedes. Towns and neighborhoods maintained strong ethnic identities (and divisions from their neighbors), which didn't change until the coming of mass media and easy travel.

Moving south, the plain turns into bluffs and hills to the juncture of the Ohio and the Mississippi Rivers; this land was settled mostly by uprooted southerners and Appalachians who liked the free, slow-paced atmosphere and the beauty of the hills. The land is so hilly that it's the only part of Illinois that doesn't have a strong farming connection; what farmland that existed has long since been lost to erosion. Its industry is mining, although now many of the mines have closed. These communities came together like the ones in Chicago: A few people from a country or an ethnic or racial group settled and their families followed in droves, and they all had children, and for decades they stayed, growing descendants and roots. Talk about good names, Southern Illinois has got 'em: Rosiclare, Beaucoup (pronounced BUCK-Up), Cambria, Horseshoe, Boody. The landscape here is astonishingly beautiful and rugged; the wildness of the terrain is exemplified by the Shawnee National Forest, a quarter-million-acre park between the Mississippi and the Ohio Rivers. This land was set aside in the 1930s, when the southern Illinois economy proved to be permanently hard-hit. It is one of Illinois' few ecologically protected areas; although Illinois is the fifth most populated state in the Union, it ranks forty-eighth in the amount of land reserved for public parks. The Shawnee protects five hundred species of wildlife while still allowing humans to ride horses, climb bluffs, and hike. People from all over the country come here to find a sense of isolated freedom that is rarely found in the more popular national parks.

Southern Illinois—once known as "Little Egypt" and the "Illinois Ozarks"—survives independently of the rest of Illinois; its city ties are with St. Louis, not Chicago. The area's biggest college is Southern Illinois University in Carbondale, a former-hippie enclave that holds rowdiness and radicalism in high regard. While southern Illinois is a conservative region, it has pockets of strong liberalism; one of the country's most progressive politicians, Senator Paul Simon, came from a town near Carbondale. More than any other area, the residents of Southern Illinois have retained their populist rural traditions. They insist upon it.

Before the north-middle-south splits, the blues and Studs Terkel and the Daleys and Lincoln's Home, the state had an identity based on hunting, fishing, and planting. Its boundaries were defined by rivers, not politics and ethnic backgrounds. Illinois was long home to the five tribes of the Illini Confederation. These tribes—the Kaskaskia, Cahokia, Peoria, Tamaroa, and Michigamea—occupied lands from Lake Michigan in the north to the Ohio River in the south, to the Wabash in the east, and west across the Mississippi. The five tribes coexisted fairly peacefully (despite skirmishes with outside tribes) until Jacques Marquette and Louis Joliet showed up in 1673. The explorers made a stop at the home of the grand chief of the Illini Confederation near what is now Peoria. Unfortunately for the original Illinoisans, this opened the door to traders and missionaries. The tribes of the Illini Confederacy then made the sad mistake of siding with the French in the French and Indian Wars, which aroused antagonisms among outside tribes and gave the British added impetus to wipe them out. In 1673, the Illinois tribes numbered more than ten thousand people. By 1832, when their land was permanently taken by the government, there remained a single village of less than three hundred. Those who hadn't been killed in the wars were killed by smallpox.

And all of these residents had been preceded by the Cahokian mound builders in southern Illinois, one of the largest pre-Columbian civilizations in North America. In A.D. 900, it was the center of Mississippian culture; one of the mounds, Monk's Mound, covers fourteen acres in four terraces that reach one hundred feet high. The world's largest remaining prehistoric earthen building rested atop it. Long after the demise of this civilization, the Cahokian area was caught in the same vise of English and French settlement. Across the Mississippi, St. Louis grew right alongside the mounds. This sense of the ancient and the new occurs throughout Illinois, in condensed spaces and in juxtaposition. The names of the towns and cities and rivers evoke the tribes. So do the museums, where we try to formally preserve our lost legacies. But the legacy of the original Illinoisans most clearly remains in the isolated parts of the state, along the rivers and in the forests. These dwindling locations continue to contain their spirits. It is easy to forget there that Illinois' identity is really a combative, bloody, and blustering one.

Once the whites settled, the three states of Illinois quickly formed their own obstinate identities. The state's splits play out in the activities for which Illinois has become best known: politics, the creation of music and poetry, architectural innovations, and baseball. The Civil War was the most famous incident to bring out the state's conflicted nature. Though Illinois prides itself on being the "Land of Lincoln," the southern third of the state had Confederate sympathies; the middle was a hodgepodge of Confederates, abolitionists, and those who held out for union while advocating slavery; the north was mostly in favor of ending slavery, with some areas (such as Galesburg) actively abolitionist. The end of the war certainly didn't end Illinois' racial divisions; Chicago was a mecca for freed blacks, and while the downstate cities have strong African American communities, the small towns are generally as European Caucasian as their residents can possibly make them. The farther downstate you go, the fewer blacks you will see until you reach East St. Louis and Cairo. As the poet Vachel Lindsay once noted, the Mason-Dixon line ran right through his backyard in Springfield. These racial and ethnic separations have had an impact upon every facet of Illinois life. The Klan had its strongholds downstate. Race riots took place in Springfield and Chicago. Even now, African Americans are redlined into their own separate communities in Illinois cities.

One striking result of this is the vibrancy of those black communities. African American art and music are an important part of the Illinois identity. Everywhere we go, we hear the echoes of Chicago blues. The riffs run through our national soul and rock consciousness, mutated through guitar solos and rap mixes. Chicago blues are black and evolved southern, mixing the industrial urban and agricultural rural. In Chi-town, Delta Blues met electricity. Chicago was where the jobs were, and it carried the mythology of opportunity; during the Jim Crow era, the black community grew. The strains from the South traveled through Memphis and Kansas City and stopped in the Windy City, where they combined with the rhythms of urban industry to make heart-stopping guitar-based riffing and wailing blues. Chess Records made its base here; among the best-known blues musicians were Muddy Waters, Buddy Guy, Junior Wells, Howlin' Wolf, and B.B. King. Music transcends the state's internal boundaries, truly blending north and south,

urban and rural. Folk, rock, and country music also drift from north to south, south to north; bluegrass and string bands from southern Illinois play upstate; folkies draw their influences from both country and blues; and rockers (the best known being the Smashing Pumpkins) proclaim cynical urban angst while maintaining a baseline midwestern honesty.

Art seems to be the only activity that unifies the state. Sports, for one, exemplifies Illinois' divisions: North of Springfield live the Cubs/Sox fans; below, the Cards fans. When the Cards and the Cubs play each other, tensions are ugly. If Illinoisans are like this on the field of sport, imagine what they must be like in the field of big stakes money: politics.

Illinois makes a glorious industry of politics, raising backstabbing and manipulation into a fine art of control. We residents are fascinated by the state's workings, the moral and immoral and amoral machinations of its structures, and this attitude permeates everything, everywhere, in every field. It's a state of big business, big government, big ideas turned into big practicalities, and buckets of money. Politics is the art of Illinois. Without politics, Illinois might be, well, Indiana or Iowa.

Everyone knows Chicago has been dominated by the Daleys and Madigans and those who work as cogs in the Democratic machine. Downstate is nearly all Republican, except for pockets of Democratic populism. And the center is Lincoln and more Lincoln and his true home, the state capitol. Lanky rail-splitter Abe, whose face is everywhere, defines the land, our license plates, and every American's worthless penny. Lincoln, not a myth, was the quintessential Illinois Politician. He worked the system, walking the middle line until he held power. He didn't begin by holding his open-minded beliefs (at least not publicly), but was forced into his stand through moral necessity. Abe saw himself as a common man—he *was* a common man—a smart man who knew how to play up his populist image. And the image was true: He came from humble beginnings, rose to power, and was unpretentious and intellectual. He struggled with his own melancholy, his wife's depression, and his child's death. He experienced dark contemplations and understandings, and historians puzzle over him, even now. And after equivocation, Lincoln took a stand that was right and acted upon it both oratorically and politically. He had a visionary sense of his place in the context of history, and in this he reflects the strangest of all Illinois characteristics: visionary optimism meshed with bottom-line practicality. In Illinois, visionaries came to set up intellectual enclaves and mystical utopian communes. Gangsters came to feed and feed on the many newcomers as they worked their way into the political system. The populist dream met with populist practicality, leading to high-flown beauty and the basest equation of violence and use. The Chicago that is known for its Louis Sullivan buildings, its community of writers and performers and artists is also famous for the Haymarket Square riot, the Democratic National Convention of 1968, and Al Capone. The Springfield that is famous as the home of Abe Lincoln also had one of the most notorious racial mob attacks in 1908 (as thousands of whites burned down the black section of town and lynched two innocent men). The southern Illinois known for its stunning bluffs and strange beauties is poverty hit hard by the decline of coal mining. In every part of the state, most residents remain stubbornly independent and individualistic. Their ancestors may have stopped moving west, but that was only because they knew they had found a place that they could call their own and make a heap o' money.

Money and home: the American Dream. People in Illinois hope that hard work will get them their just due, as they maintain an optimism hidden by black humor and something between humility and low state-esteem. Illinois was built by outcasts and rebels fleeing the East Coast, forced from the South, and adventuring from Europe; communities were armed pockets based on ethnicity and race, and those in each group came to believe that financial progress was the only true progress. "Get ahead" was their mantra— but in doing so, stay true to self and community. Illinois believes in hard work and gritty competition aided by whatever force is needed to make money and gain power. Along the way, great cities and idyllic towns will be created: This is the belief of the cult of Illinois. The cult's core beliefs are in justice and essential populist opportunity. Optimism is still ingrained in Chicago's attitudes and beliefs about itself (hog butcher to the world and all that) and in those of the rowdy unemployed hill-livers in southern Illinois and the government workers and former hippies and machinists in the central part of the state. The idealistic side of Illinois insists that there is value in the common human.

The ability of people in Illinois to make money allowed for a seeming leveling of opportunity for decades. Some European intellectuals who visited Illinois in the nineteenth century objected to this very sense of possibility, which they feared led to a devaluation of art and a loss of power for the (supposedly more knowing and benevolent) upper classes. The Illinois toughness and bluntness that was celebrated by twentieth-century writers was witnessed with fear and contempt by many from the East Coast and Europe. The democratic experiment that seemed to be playing out in Illinois was seen as a fearful error—the demise of the old world and the rise of the modern.

One of the ways Illinois' democratic tendencies were expressed was through architectural innovation. These new buildings that were to be "for the people" were generally greeted with establishment amusement and, in some cases, dismay. The innovations of the Chicago School of architects, who moved from the ornate styles into a simpler "prairie style" that meshed with the flatness, and who developed ambitious skyscrapers, were initially viewed with scorn. The buildings, so obvious in their strangeness of idea, also drew artists and followers who believed that Chicago would become "the New Athens." Frank Lloyd Wright claimed that "the greatest and most nearly beautiful city of our young nation is probably Chicago. Eventually I think that Chicago will be the most beautiful great city left in the modern world." *Left*, he said, meaning that the world was in decline and that the Windy City held the promise of some shining future. He wasn't the only one who felt that way in those early years of the twentieth century. Chicago had money to spend, and the more progressive thinkers and doers believed that the money (often ill-gotten through industry and worker abuse) should be spent toward the goal of "beauty and goodness." Chicagoans liked their arts to be purposeful, to enclose people and add to the well-being of individuals, who were not patrons, but who existed as a part of and within the art itself. Art should be simple in idea and form, not ostentatious and ornamental—some might even call it naive. It was to be unbound from eastern provincialism and long-entrenched wealthy patrons. It was to be less tired, more vibrant, no longer cynical. A building should not only be looked at, but lived in. Art was to be (according to the dream) a part of everyday life, not only "appreciated" by a single class, but a part of what Wright called "the living city." Other versions of Wright's prairie style are found all over Illinois, existing as a part of their environment.

Illinois is full of artists, and the artists that continue to be identified with the state are the populists. There may well be better ones, but these are the people whose work gets put in the anthologies and called: Chicago, or called: Midwestern Town. Studs Terkel, archetypical old-school Chicago, interviews working guys and gals at the bar, transcribes their stories, is obstinately D(d)emocratic. Who else?: Edgar Lee Masters's *Spoon River Anthology*. "General William Booth Enters into Heaven" ("Are you washed in the blood of the lamb?") –Vachel Lindsay. Richard Wright (*Native Son*). Theodore Dreiser (*Sister Carrie*). Lorraine Hansberry (*A Raisin in the Sun*). Ernest Hemingway (yes, he started in Illinois). Upton Sinclair (slaughterhouse jungles). Edna Ferber (*Showboat; Giant*). Ben Hecht (*The Front Page*). Carl Sandburg ("city of big shoulders"). Harriet Monroe (founder of *Poetry*, the most important literary magazine of the early twentieth century). Langston Hughes ("a raisin in the sun"). And moving near contemporary, Saul Bellow, Ray Bradbury, Gwendolyn Brooks, William Maxwell, John Gardner. Is this enough?—there are plenty of others. For years, Illinois writing was characterized by a merging of social and even journalistic concerns with a populist, talkin'-to-ya, here's-the-straight-stuff approach.

And who is coming next? I can give you that list, but it would be too long, and I would surely leave out people who ought to be there. Contemporary Illinois art, as far as I can tell, has no defining characteristic other than quality. Writers are working in all modes, perspectives, cross-media, and cross-perspectives. Experimentalists and traditionalists coexist, and no type seems to be predominant. The artistic trends and schools of thought tend to be characterized more in terms of universities (and their faculty and students) than around an "Illinois type" or a "Chicago school."

I edited an anthology of contemporary midwestern creative nonfiction (*In the Middle of the Middle West*, 2003) and in this book, place was seen as important by the writers—even obsessively so, and even if its importance was fought against. The geography of Illinois was of fascination to several writers; most remarked upon the beauty of its flatness. Others wrote about Lake Michigan as a mystical body of water; several, about the Chicago "els," the elevated trains; others, about the prejudice that they faced because they were gay or African American (again giving lie to the idea of Illinois as an equality-conscious "Land of Lincoln"). The form of these pieces ranged from the traditional essay to a fragmentary prose that was nearly poetry. So perhaps it would not be a stretch to assert that Illinois writers continue to be strongly aware of place as a context and as a point of impact. Many of the writers seemed at odds with this place, or in a state of mourning or anger; but at every turn, place was acknowledged as important, even life-defining. A regret at the quick changes in place identity came up again and again. And there was a recognition that the sense of opportunity and openness that once existed was coming to an end.

The state is in transition: The work of artists of Illinois now lack firm definition as the state's populist characteristics fade into scattered national trends. All of us are classed less by locale than by movement, given that we are united by transportation and the suburbanization of life. The artistic communities are dominated by universities of expatriates, not original Illinoisans. And the decline of place-identity in the arts may reflect the state of the United States, making the question "What is Illinois?" irrelevant. Chicago still insists that it is a place uniquely of the people, and it still has a tough, muscular quality that makes it

different from the provincialism and pretension of New York, or the laid-back-party of L.A., or the southern strip-mall decorum of Atlanta. Chicago still has Wrigley Field; Chicago still has Cubs fans, loyal though the Cubs never win. People still play the blues, and sometimes the innovators transmute that into punkish rock. There may still be some Studs or Sandburg types out there, along with those who are coming up with another kind of vibrant and insistent music reflecting the next step of the cultural-industrial North-South blend.

Everything is changing. The farms are being sold, one after another. (And we haven't been proud of agriculture here for a while. Unlike Iowa, Illinois has not embraced its farming roots—if anything, it seems embarrassed by them, even while the farms remain an essential part of the Illinois economy). The suburbs are sprawling farther and farther, small towns are linked by highways and malls and blending into the middle-sized cities, industry giving way to smaller parts, people taking jobs behind counters and desks. Neighborhoods and towns struggle to hold on to ethnic identity through advertising and tourist displays, but this is beginning to look like historical nostalgia as the lines blend and the children leave and marry outside state lines. For a state so identified by physical labor—be it in fields or in factories—the changes will be cellular. Big shoulders are no longer necessary.

I am sure, though, that we will always have the blues of the city or the country—everyone has the blues. There will always be unrecorded upstarts in the bars, playing their guitars and chanting their poems. And, for good or evil, we will always have politics, as the quick heartbeat of power goes on. And I like to believe we'll always have in Illinois this idealistic populism, because believers breed believers, and working people will always be here, and the good guys do not always have to win as long as they play good ball and we're hanging out with our friends. This is an understanding that so permeates the state that I can't imagine it disappearing. But then, I'm a native Illinoisan, and we are prone to our illusions.

Becky Bradway
Normal, Illinois

Indiana

"Breathes there not a man, with soul so dead, who never to himself has said, this is my own, my native land." This famous celebration of no-brainer patriotism by the Scotsman Sir Walter Scott (1771–1832), when stripped of jingoistic romance, amounts only to this: Human beings come into the world, for their own good, as instinctively territorial as timber wolves or honeybees. Not long ago, human beings who strayed too far from their birthplace and relatives, like all other animals, would be committing suicide.

This dread of crossing well-understood geographical boundaries still makes sense in many parts of the world—in what used to be Yugoslavia in Europe, for example, or Rwanda in Africa. It is, however, now excess instinctual baggage in most of North America, thank God, thank God. It lives on in this country, as obsolescent survival instincts often do, as feelings and manners which are by-and-large harmless, and which can even be comical.

Thus do I and millions like me tell strangers that we are Middle Westerners, as though we deserved some kind of medal for being that. All I can say in our defense is that natives of Texas and Brooklyn are even more preposterous in their territorial vanity.

Nearly countless movies about Texas and Brooklynites are lessons for such people in how to behave ever more stereotypically. Why have there been no movies about supposedly typical Middle Western heroes, models to which we too might conform?

All I've got now is an aggressively nasal accent.

About that accent: When I was in the Army during World War II, a white southerner said to me, "Do you have to talk that way?"

I might have replied: "Oh yeah? At least my ancestors never owned slaves," but the rifle range at Fort Bragg, N.C. seemed neither the time nor the place to settle his hash.

I might have added that some of the greatest words ever spoken in American history were uttered with such a Jew's-harp twang, including the Gettysburg address by Abraham Lincoln of Illinois and these by Eugene V. Debs of Terre Haute, Ind.: "As long as there is a lower class I am in it, as long as there is a criminal element I am of it, as long as there is a soul in prison I am not free."

I would have kept to myself that the borders of Indiana, when I was a boy, cradled not only the birthplace of Eugene V. Debs, but the national headquarters of the Ku Klux Klan.

Illinois had Carl Sandburg and Al Capone.

Yes, and the thing on top of the house to keep the weather out is the ruff, and the stream in back of the house is the crick.

Every race, sub-race, and blend thereof is native to the Midwest. I myself am a purebred Kraut. Our accents are by no means uniform. My twang is only fairly typical of European-Americans raised some distance north of the former Confederate States of America. It appeared to me when I began this essay that I was on a fool's errand, that we could only be described en masse as what we weren't. We weren't Texans or Brooklynites or Californians or southerners, and so on.

To demonstrate to myself the folly of distinguishing us, one-by-one, from Americans born anywhere else, I imagined a crowd on Fifth Avenue in New York City, where I am living now, and another crowd on State Street, in Chicago, where I went to a university and worked as a reporter half a century ago. I was not mistaken about the sameness of the faces and clothing and apparent moods.

But the more I pondered the people of Chicago, the more aware I became of an enormous presence there. It was almost like music, music unheard in New York or Boston or San Francisco or New Orleans.

It was Lake Michigan, an ocean of pure water, the most precious substance in all this world.

Nowhere else in the Northern Hemisphere are there tremendous bodies of pure water like our Great Lakes, save for Asia, where there is only Lake Baikal. So there is something distinctive about all native Middle Westerners after all. Get this: When we were born, there had to have been incredible quantities of fresh water all around us, in lakes and streams and rivers and raindrops and snowdrift, and no undrinkable salt water anywhere!

Even my taste buds are midwestern on that account. When I swim in the Atlantic or Pacific, the water tastes all wrong to me, even though it is in fact no more nauseating, as long as you don't swallow it, than chicken soup.

There were also millions and millions of acres of topsoil all around us and our mothers when we were born, as flat as pool tables and as rich as chocolate cake.

When I was born in 1922, barely a hundred years after Indiana became the 19th state in the Union, the Midwest already boasted a constellation of cities with symphony orchestras and museums and libraries, and institutions of higher learning, and schools of music and art, reminiscent of the Austro-Hungarian Empire before the First World War. One could almost say that Chicago was our Vienna, Indianapolis our Prague, Cincinnati our Budapest, and Cleveland our Bucharest.

To grow up in such a city, as I did, was to find cultural institutions as ordinary as police stations or fire houses. So it was reasonable for a young person to daydream of becoming some sort of artist or intellectual, if not a policeman or a fireman. So I did. So did many like me.

Such provincial capitals, which is what they would have been called in Europe, were charmingly self-sufficient with respect to the fine arts. We sometimes had the director of the Indianapolis Symphony Orchestra to supper, or writers and painters, and architects like my father, of local renown.

I studied clarinet under the first chair clarinetist of our orchestra. I remember the orchestra's performance of Tchaikovsky's *1812 Overture*, in which the cannons' roars were supplied by a policeman firing blank cartridges into any empty garbage can. I knew the policeman. He sometimes guarded street crossings used by students on their way to or from School 43, my school, the James Whitcomb Riley School.

It is unsurprising, then, that the Midwest has produced so many artists of such different sorts, from world-class to merely competent, as provincial cities and towns in Europe used to do.

I see no reason this satisfactory state of affairs should not go on and on, unless funding for instruction in and celebration of the arts, especially in public school systems, is withdrawn.

Participation in an art is not simply one of many possible ways to make a living as we approach the year 2000. Participation in an art, at bottom, has nothing to do with earning money. Participation in an art, although unrewarded by wealth or fame, and as the Midwest has encouraged so many of its young to discover for themselves, is a way to make one's soul grow.

No artist from anywhere, not even Shakespeare, not even Beethoven, not even James Whitcomb Riley, has changed the course of so many lives all over the planet as have four hayseeds in Ohio—two in Dayton and two in Akron. How I wish Dayton and Akron were in Indiana! Ohio could have Kokomo and Gary.

Orville and Wilbur Wright were in Dayton in 1903 when they invented the airplane.

Dr. Robert Holbrook Smith and William Griffith Wilson were in Akron in 1935 when they devised the 12 steps to sobriety of Alcoholics Anonymous. By comparison with Smith and Wilson, Sigmund Freud was a piker when it came to healing dysfunctional minds and lives.

Beat that! Let the rest of the world put that in their pipes and smoke it, not to mention the works of Ernest Hemingway, Saul Bellow, and Toni Morrison; Cole Porter and Hoagy Carmichael; Frank Lloyd Wright and Louis Sullivan; Twyla Tharp and Bob Fosse; Mike Nichols and Elaine May.

And Larry Bird!

New York and Boston and other ports on the Atlantic have Europe for an influential and importunate neighbor. Midwesterners do not. Many of us of European ancestry are on that account ignorant of our families' past in the Old World and the culture there. Our only heritage is American. When Germans captured me during the Second World War, one asked me, "Why are you making war against your brothers?" I didn't have a clue what he was talking about . . .

Anglo Americans and African Americans, whose ancestors came to the Midwest from the South, com-

monly have a much more compelling awareness of a homeland elsewhere in the past than do I—in Dixie, of course, not the British Isles or Africa.

What geography can give all Middle Westerners, along with the fresh water and topsoil, if they let it, is awe for an Edenic continent stretching forever in all directions.

Makes you religious. Takes your breath away.

Kurt Vonnegut
New York, New York

(Originally written in 1999 for the Indiana Humanities Council under the title, "To Be a Native Middle-Westerner." Published on their website. Reprinted with permission.)

Iowa

When I was young, I thought Iowa went on forever. I had never been to Texas, but I could not imagine any state larger, roomier, more full of sky, than Iowa. Living in Ames, whose surrounding landscape varied from pancake-flat to gently rolling farmland, our little family—widowed mother, my sister, and I—rarely ventured into other terrain. On our summer vacation, when we drove straight north through Iowa to a Minnesota lake, the Iowa cornfields on either side of the bullet-straight highway seemed very much like the cornfields around Ames.

In those years, Iowa's narrow highways had curving concrete curbs on each side. (Were they meant to discourage us from veering off the road and disappearing into one of those endless cornfields?) Since my mother hated those curbs—as well as high speeds, big trucks, and the dangers of passing—we seldom ventured onto those highways just for fun. We did sometimes drive thirty miles south to Des Moines for shopping or a basketball tournament, or north to Osage to an uncle's farm, and once, unusually, on an overnight trip east to the hilly Amana Colonies. But Iowa seemed mostly the same: open land, tidy towns dwarfed by the fields, occasional patches of woods and windbreaks, more open land. On and on and on.

And yet, even as a child, I think I knew that Iowa was not always quite what it seemed. Just fifteen miles west of Ames, the level fields suddenly disappeared at the Ledges State Park, where sandstone bluffs towered almost a hundred feet above a creek that wound past thickly wooded slopes. Nearby, the Des Moines River sometimes rose in flood; a marker in the park showed how alarmingly high this flood could reach. Grownups told us children garbled versions of Indian myths, usually involving lovelorn maidens or braves who had drowned or who had tragically leaped to their deaths from one of the highest bluffs. A picnic at the Ledges was an excursion into another, wilder world, of flowing water, dusky groves, and long-ago romance.

I did wish Iowa had an ocean. Although Ames was quite proud of its campus centerpiece, a human-made pond hopefully christened Lake La Verne, it was muddily murky. I was also dimly aware of two largely ignored, fast-moving streams that snaked through town, but I could sense no mystery in either Squaw Creek or Skunk River. Unlike a watery map of Minnesota, which I studied on our summer car trips, I could only find on the Iowa map a few random, depressingly small blue dots. To my dreamer's eye, the map looked unappealingly monotonous, hundreds of tiny squares divided by blue-and-red lines, accented with endless tiny settlements.

Yet here again Iowa could surprise me. Far from Ames, Iowa did have three lakes, close to the Minnesota border: Spirit Lake, Clear Lake, and Okoboji. (Of the handful on the Iowa map, these were the only three I ever saw.) I never paused long there, just hours on an overnight family reunion, or a dawn-to-dark adventure with high-school friends, or an occasional side excursion as our family headed toward Minnesota. The shores of these shining lakes were lined with vacation cabins, often only yards apart, whose beckoning docks led out into unknown water. I could envision the excitement of staying for days, even a week or more, in one of those cabins, with an unfamiliar, wave-tossed lake at my doorstep, surrounded by fascinating people I'd never met. People who lived right next to the water had to be more glamorous than the other Iowans I knew.

Even now, when I have lived many years in Minneapolis, only minutes from a sizable lake, if I say to myself, "Okoboji," I can still feel a buried tremor of excitement. Okoboji whispers of an imaginative child's fantasies: swimming all afternoon under a blazing blue sky, roasting hot-dogs on the shore at dusk, rowing out on a lake gleaming in the moonlight. Part of Okoboji's charm is its name. For a state that some outsiders, rushing across on the interstate, consider repetitively dull—what Iowan hasn't heard those uninformed comments?—its place names reveal quite a different spirit.

When I first plunged as a teenager into the passionate poems of Stephen Vincent Benét, still widely reprinted in the 1950s, I instantly took to my heart his ballad "American Names." "I have fallen in love with American names, /" he writes, "The sharp names that never get fat, / The snakeskin-titles of mining claims, / The plumed war-bonnet of Medicine Hat, / Tucson and Deadwood and Lost Mule Flat." Benét would have loved Iowa's names. I grew up with those fragments of unintended poetry, taking them for granted, but still absorbing their evocative, often strangely moving voices. Now I can sense how many of those names, counties, cities, towns, and even streets, sing of Iowa's complex heritage. Long after the first Iowans were chased from their ancestral lands, their voices still echo across the state: Pottawattamie, Poweshiek, Winnebago, Winneshiek, Pocahontas, Tama, Maquoketa, Cherokee, Keokuk, Hiawatha, Keosaqua, Osage, Sac City, Sioux City, and, of course, Iowa itself.

In time I also became sensible of the many European ethnic groups who had come to Iowa, settled here, and left their names behind them. After high-school French, I could translate the meaning of "Des Moines," feeling a little embarrassed that I pronounced it, as Iowans do, with a flat nasal twang that firmly eliminates anything French about it. (Iowans do a little better with Dubuque and Fayette.) I knew that Madrid, a settlement west of Ames with a definitively heavy accent on its first syllable, was a relative—a very distant country cousin—of a great city in Spain. I could also faintly hear a certain far-off homesickness in names like Norway, Wales, Guttenberg, Batavia, Schleswig, Westphalia, Macedonia, Montezuma, Panama, and Tripoli.

But the Iowa names I have always liked best are homegrown. Many are plain and no-nonsense: Beaver, Hawkeye, Marsh, Wood, Rock Rapids, Deep River, Red Oak, Clearfield, Eagle Grove. Some are openly patriotic, like Independence and Liberty Center, or a little puzzling, like Diagonal and Gravity, or happily eccentric, like What Cheer. Who can't hear a touch of melancholy in the naming of Lone Tree or Lost Nation? Who wouldn't want to live in a town called Mapleleaf, Morning Sun, Pleasant Valley, Rose Hill, or Strawberry Point? Who could fail to warm to a state boasting two little towns, almost next to each other, called Edna and George?

Perhaps like many others who only learn to appreciate a place after leaving it, I began to recognize my deep-rooted affection for Iowa when I went away for college. Northampton, Massachusetts, was an attractive spot, with spreading old trees arching over its historic streets. But the East seemed crowded. Northampton blended into one outlying town, then another. It was hard to tell where towns stopped and country began. Growing up, I had understood, without thinking much about it, that I lived very close to an infinite horizon. If I wanted to, I could soon find myself alone under a wide sky. I missed knowing that.

During my college years, my mother remarried, and Buell, my new stepfather, loved to drive. When I was home on holidays, Buell and my mother often took me with them on their frequent leisurely tours around the countryside. Years before William Least Heat Moon, my stepfather relished the subtle revelations of blue highways. "Buell wants to drive every single road in Story County," my mother told me once, and several excursions later, I began to grasp how many different back roads one Iowa county could pack into a few dozen square miles.

Buell taught me to see Iowa with a sharper, more focused lens. He often drove without a plan, maybe heading ten miles in one direction and then turning in another. Only twenty minutes out of Ames, we might find ourselves in a wooded dip, not quite a valley, with an abandoned farm sheltered behind trees at the end of a long rutted lane. I wondered why I had never before discovered this secluded gravel road next to a shadowed gurgling creek, a place inconceivably remote from Ames's busy streets.

On these meandering trips, we were alert. We looked for round barns, octagonal barns, and crumbling old barns with massive stone foundations. My mother called out if she saw a barn whose once-bright red had faded to an especially luminous glow. We rolled slowly through small towns, remarking on the clean white lines of old church steeples, ornately decorated banks, grandiose funeral homes, and main-street cafes with homey names like Cozy Nook, Vi's Diner, Sally's Snack Shop, or, succinctly, just Eats. On those unhurried, long afternoons, I learned to pay attention to monumental grain elevators, mellow brick schoolhouses, weathered houses with turrets and rambling porches, leafy avenues hushed by summer heat, and wildly colorful backyard gardens overflowing with hollyhock, zinnias, nasturtiums, petunias, and snapdragons.

I am still exploring Iowa. When my husband James and I drive back to our Minneapolis home from Ames, we sometimes take longer, slower routes just so we can see more. On book promotions, I have been able to investigate parts of the state I hadn't seen before. And Iowa still surprises me. In Davenport, which I'd thought of as a roistering river town linked eastward to the markets of Chicago, I was startled to find hominy and grits on a menu. Then I remembered that Davenport was not far from Missouri, which in turn leads into the Deep South. Recently James and I drove east from Ames to the Mississippi, then north along the river until Iowa ended. So Iowa is flat? Or landlocked? Certainly not here. As we swerved and curved through deep valleys and along panoramic ridges, I realized why Grant Wood's paintings show such seductively undulating hills. Standing high above the great river on Pike's Peak, with its magnificent miles-long vista of water, diverging channels, islands, tributaries, and cliffs, I could easily convince myself I was looking over a foreign country.

Perhaps because I live today in Minneapolis, on my wanderings around Iowa I seldom seek out cities. I have enough of cities. That is not how I felt when I was young. Growing up, I was almost sleepless with pulsing anticipation on the nights before an outing to Des Moines—home of fabled Younkers Department Store, with its moving escalator and classy Tea Room; an Art Center where I am almost sure I was once awed by a world-famous painting of Whistler's mother; a giant indoor arena that sometimes showcased plays guaranteed straight from Broadway. I also knew Iowa had brand-name businesses, though I probably only could have named Quaker Oats in Cedar Rapids, Maytag in Newton, and *Better Homes and Gardens* in Des Moines.

Now twenty-first-century Iowa, far from being a strictly agricultural economy, prospers with varied industries. From Sioux City to Cedar Rapids, Council Bluffs to Waterloo, Davenport to Dubuque, Iowa's cities (not to mention its many college and university towns) offer cultural and historic attractions far richer than those of fifty years ago. (Even then, Iowans revered Iowa City, home of the University of Iowa, as a haven of the arts. After all, that was where creative writers came from all over America to study at the Iowa Writers' Workshop.) Yet what I appreciate most about those cities is that they still do not gobble up all of Iowa's fields and sky.

Many people mourn that our world is increasingly crowded. Fortunately, it is possible to forget that in Iowa. Sometimes James and I stop our car on a deserted back road in Iowa's level center. On a clear day, we try to calculate how many immeasurable miles we can see in all directions. We point out to each other the widely scattered but ubiquitous farms—houses, silos, barns—that look like tiny Monopoly markers on a giant square board. Or we may count the water towers on the horizon, signs of towns once connected only by horseback. They are still too far apart for anyone to walk comfortably from one to another. But the farmhouses and towns are plainly visible. Shelter, houses, churches, stores are never too far away. Iowa's distances are seldom lonely.

Who exactly are the Iowans who live in these farmhouses, small towns, or larger cities? I have never been able to come up with an encompassing answer. When I meet someone from Iowa, and I explain that I'm "from Ames"—a suggestive phrase, as if I were extended on a long invisible cord from the town where I was born—we usually nod, smile knowledgeably at each other, and act as if we somehow shared a secret handshake. "So you're from Belmond? Of course I know where that is," I say confidently. I'm an Iowan, after all. I've heard of Monona, Grundy Center, Harlan, and Charles City. I am conscious that Lamoni is pronounced with a long "i." Mention Oskaloosa, and after I exclaim, "Well, no kidding, I'm from Ames," I might even burst into the old Central Iowa Conference Fight Song: "I don't care 'bout the fame of old Marshalltown, or the feats of Oskie High / And Grinnell is the team that we love to beat / And the same goes for old Boone High, RAH RAH RAH."

The important word about that handshake is "secret." Iowans recognize that nobody outside the state is mindful of them. Because Iowa is so often overlooked—quite literally, as jumbo jets soar overhead, seldom stopping, from New York or Boston to Houston or Los Angeles—it is a state that almost seems like a private enclave. Visitors who pause briefly, perhaps for a sales trip, a convention, or sudden car repair, and who then stay long enough to poke around, usually find themselves unsettled. Things they don't expect happen here. Who could have foreseen, in a state alleged to be boringly flat, Iowa's many unusual caves? Dancehall Cave at Maquoketa Cave Park? Crystal Lake Cave near Dubuque? Or eerie Spook Cave, reachable only by boat through a none-too-large hole in a limestone bluff?

How, puzzled visitors might ask themselves, can a stick-in-the-mud state have produced the Winnebago, a national symbol of America's incurable restlessness? If Iowa is indeed tame, why is one of its parks called Wildcat Den? How can supposedly staid Iowans patronize riverboat gambling? (It floats and flourishes at Council Bluffs, Sioux City, Fort Madison, Dubuque, Marquette, Bettendorf, Osceola, Clinton, and Davenport.) Who could have predicted the emergence of Maharishi University, which has almost taken over the otherwise unremarkable town of Fairfield? Do the maharishi's acolytes really levitate, rising in meditative tranquility from the soil of southern Iowa?

Once anyone looks hard at Iowa, it begins to shimmer with possibilities, rather like the enigmatic cornfields in *Field of Dreams*. Here's an intriguing experiment. Try standing alone, sometime after the middle of July, in front of a long row of sky-high corn. (Find a field large enough to feel as if it might swallow you up.) Stare down this darkening tunnel until all you can see is a disappearing arch of green. If you stare long and hard enough, after a while your vision may blur a little. The row of corn might seem to move, or change, or murmur. You don't even have to wait until dusk. The rustle of leaves, the endless rows, the rippling swells, will all be magic enough. Like Kevin Costner in that quintessentially romantic Iowa movie of 1989, you might then be quite ready to see the fluttering green curtain part and a team of legendary, long-dead baseball players emerge one by one.

Iowans don't usually consider themselves as romantics—which suggests they may not know as much about Iowans as they think. Consider, for example, not only *Field of Dreams*, but also Meredith Willson's joyous *The Music Man*, inspired by Mason City, or Robert James Waller's heartstring-plucker of a novel, then a movie, *The Bridges of Madison County*. The Little Brown Church in the Vale, enshrined in one of America's oldest sentimental ballads—"Come to the church by the wildwood, / Oh, come to the church in the vale"—remains a hallowed site near Nashua.

Instead of seeing themselves as dreamers or visionaries, Iowans like to pretend that they are hardheaded, practical folk. We don't put up with foolishness. We have no time for nonsense. We have a knack, even if we don't always practice it, for keeping things simple. All Iowans like bargains, we joke to each other. We love corn on the cob, chocolate milk, ribs, baked potatoes, lemon meringue pie, fat juicy pork chops. We have faith in high-school basketball tournaments, marching bands, potluck suppers, and Fourth of July parades. Mostly, we would agree, we share what it is like to live somewhere quiet, to enjoy plenty of space, to breathe clean air, to look up at millions of stars at night because artificial lights don't drown them.

But some Iowans aren't like that at all. Since I grew up in a college town, I could see that Iowans came in all sorts. Across our street, Henry Dunnett, a sharp-tongued agricultural economist, was a sober elder in the Presbyterian Church. He was quite different from gentle Aaron Holst, just down the block, a sophisticated nuclear physicist from New York who was also a fine pianist. Those who didn't work at the college were quite different from one another, too. Our unpretentious next-door neighbor, who sold Oldsmobiles, was warm and affable; another neighbor, a prominent dentist, lived in a big house on a hill and kept very much to himself. I couldn't have picked which was the typical Iowan.

Although the classic stereotype of Iowans is probably Grant Wood's satiric painting *American Gothic*, I have never been convinced by that stern, rigid farmer and his humorless wife. My Uncle Bill, who farmed near Osage, was genial, generous, and intensely involved in liberal politics, and his wife, my Aunt Grace, was a dynamo of energy. When I worked as a summer replacement at the Ames newspaper, I often consulted with our county agricultural agent, a ginger-haired man whose frequent jokes and stories livened up our little newsroom. If the rural Iowans I interviewed for the Ames *Daily Tribune*'s Farm Page were sometimes economical with words, they were almost always open, friendly, and helpful. I didn't know Grant Wood's farmers.

So who are typical Iowans? Statistics, which I never entirely trust, could supply endless data about percentages of rural and urban population, ethnic groups, Republicans and Democrats, Catholics and Presbyterians, college degrees, size of families, and much more. But I find it more illuminating to ponder the list compiled by Iowa's largest newspaper, the *Des Moines Register*, of Famous Iowans. The list includes both those born in Iowa, even if they only lived in the state a few years, and those who came to stay long enough to become firmly identified as Iowans. And what a list it is! Try forming a composite of Glenn Miller (born in Clarinda), the Ringling Brothers (who spent twelve years in McGregor), John Wayne (born in Winterset), and legendary labor leader John L. Lewis (an Iowan for six years). Orville and Wilbur Wright lived in Iowa for three years as boys; Herbert Hoover's birthplace was West Branch; opera star Sherrill Milnes attended Drake University in Des Moines.

Add Tennessee Williams, who qualifies because he claimed his time at the University of Iowa changed his name (from Tom to Tennessee) and life. Stir in George Gallup, who grew up in Jefferson and who popularized opinion polls. Think of Ronald Reagan, who entered the entertainment world as a sports broadcaster in Davenport and Des Moines. He probably knew other Hollywood stars of yesteryear from Iowa: Donna Reed, Don Ameche, Neva Patterson, Marilyn Maxwell, Don DeFore.

The once-chic designer Halston, actually Roy Halston Frowick, lived in Des Moines briefly as a child. He makes the list because at age two, he was named "healthiest city boy" at the Iowa State Fair. Think of Halston next to Wyatt Earp, who grew up in Pella, and Bix Beiderbecke, the celebrated cornet player of the 1920s, from Davenport. Amelia Bloomer, a feminist whose name became attached to a new-fangled female garment, lived for years in Council Bluffs, and Amelia Earhart attended high school in Iowa.

But for me, the quintessential Iowans may be the Duesenberg brothers. Frederick and August Duesenberg—whose German background suggests the variety of Iowa's cultures—built their first car in 1904–1905 in Des Moines. The sleek Duesenberg, which became a fabulous success, symbolized luxury and class. According to the *Des Moines Register*, the word turned into American shorthand for anything that was special or extraordinary: hence "Duesie," then "doozie."

That's my Iowa. A doozie of a state, Iowa is deceptively unassuming. Any time someone starts to label it, the reverse pops up. Rural? Not exactly. Conservative? That depends. Flat? Look more closely. Dull? Picture Glenn Miller linking arms with Wyatt Earp, Amelia Bloomer with Ronald Reagan, Herbert Hoover with the Ringling Brothers. Now there's a circus.

Susan Allen Toth
Minneapolis, Minnesota

Kansas

Kansas is in that great middle part of the United States that many people call "flyover country." Flown over, or traversed at night by car, Kansas is rarely seen, except by its own inhabitants, as the place it actually is. Like so many midwestern states, Kansas is an abstraction. Abstractions invite and support stereotypes, as in the humor of an October 3, 1994, *New Yorker* cartoon in which *all* the states between Manhattan and L.A. are labeled Mudville, as though all were nothing but a great expanse of dirt, of agriculture, of cows and chickens and pigs, of mud. Nothing much happens here, except that Casey strikes out.

The places we don't know live only in story, joke, one-liner, phrase; they often come to represent anything but what they really are. Think of the constant misuse of geographic words like *prairie* and *plains*. (Prairie: tall grass, generally east of the hundredth meridian, more than twenty inches of rainfall; Plains: short grass, generally west of the hundredth meridian, less than twenty inches of rainfall.) In any TV map of the United States, or any national news report, Kansas might be part of the "Midwest," the "West," the "Middle West," or the "Western States." In fact, Kansas contains both the geographic center of the United States (before Alaska and Hawaii) and the geodetic center of the United States. Kansas is even at the center of the North American continent, so surely its location shouldn't be so hard to fathom: As the center, it is central.

Though central on the map, Kansas is not central in the popular mind or the popular culture: Kansas is the Timbuktu of the United States, its farthest reach, its unlikely destination, its metaphor for obscurity. Kansas is the place name of choice when Hollywood wants to make a point about flyover country. In *Diamonds Are Forever* (James Bond), evil terrorists steal a weapon of mass destruction, and want to zap the world in order to show their power and capacity for violence. One points out to the group that the orbit of the space weapon will soon put it over Kansas. "If we zap Kansas," a terrorist quips, "the world wouldn't learn about it for a year."

In *Twice Bitten*, an old vampiress needs virgin blood. Her young captives, male and female, have just spoiled her plans by having sex. She laments the scarcity of virgins, and her servant takes her hand to comfort her: "Don't worry, there are others. In places like . . . Kansas."

In these images, the popular culture leaps between two abstractions. The first: Kansas is obscure, desolate, and forgotten. Second: Kansas represents an innocent past when stern and virginal people read their Bibles, and, as L. Frank Baum wrote of Dorothy's Uncle Henry, "did not know what joy was."

Kansas: Obscure, Desolate, Forgotten

> Dorothy lived in the midst of the great Kansas prairies. . . . When Dorothy stood in the doorway and looked around, she could see nothing but the great gray prairie on every side. . . . The sun had baked the plowed land into a gray mass, with little cracks running through it. Even the grass was not green, for the sun had burned the tops of the long blades until they were the same gray color to be seen everywhere. Once the house had been painted, but . . . now [it] was as dull and gray as everything else.
>
> –L. Frank Baum, *The Wonderful Wizard of Oz*

Kansas comes by its image of desolation from many sources. L. Frank Baum, of course. But almost a century before *The Wizard of Oz*, Zebulon Montgomery Pike saw what is now Kansas in his 1806 exploration of the recently acquired Louisiana Purchase. He wrote, "These vast plains of the western hemisphere may become in time as celebrated as the sandy deserts of Africa." Stephen H. Long visited in 1819, "this extensive section of the country . . . [that] is almost wholly unfit for cultivation, and . . . uninhabitable by a people depending upon agriculture for their subsistence." Long's map of the "country drained by the Mississippi" labeled most of the land that is now Kansas with a title that echoes L. Frank Baum: "Great American Desert."

Visitors gather first impressions. People more truly knew Kansas when they settled here. Frank Baker, a Lane County (far western) bachelor, wrote what became a popular folk song about his experiences around 1890, ten years before *The Wizard of Oz*. To know Kansas, unfortunately, was not always to love it. After describing his leaky sod house, his lean diet of "common sop-sorghum, old bacon and grease," his encounters with rattlesnakes, centipedes, bedbugs, and "gay little flea[s]," he sang:

> How happy am I on my government claim,
> For I've nothing to lose nor I've nothing to gain.
> I've nothing to eat and I've nothing to wear,
> And nothing from nothing is honest and fair.

Baker left Lane County around 1891: "I'll no longer remain / And starve like a dog on a Government claim."

He wasn't the last to leave. Earl Thompson left Wichita in the 1940s. His novel *Garden of Sand* (1970) begins:

> Love a place like Kansas, and you can be content in a garden of raked sand. For ground it is the flattest. Big sky, wheat sea, William Inge, bottle clubs, road houses—Falstaff and High Life, chili and big juke road houses—John Brown, Wild Bill Hickok, Carry A. Nation, cockeyed Wyatt Earp, Pretty Boy Floyd, and shades of all those unspoken Indians.

More recently, Frank and Deborah Popper, sociologists from what Kansans call "back East," studied population and land use and encouraged the trend toward Great Plains depopulation. They suggested small population centers for service and industry, surrounded by the presettlement Great Plains, what they labeled "Buffalo Commons."

Given the consensus—from Long's "uninhabitable" Kansas to the Poppers' "de-populated" Plains—nobody should wonder why so many people see Kansas as the flat, boring, Great American Desert of its early nomenclature.

Kansas: Where Have All the People Gone?

Demographers tell us that 70 percent of Americans live within an hour's drive of a coast and that in another ten years 80 percent will. Kansans must drive about sixteen hours to Galveston, Texas, about twenty hours to Washington, D.C., and about thirty hours to San Francisco. Our nearest ocean is the "sea of grass" so often evoked in the poetry and prose of the Midwest.

Poet Kenneth Porter's parents homesteaded near Sterling, in central Kansas. Porter celebrates the Great Plains and those who settled Kansas. They had already given up the familiar East—the rockbound coasts, the forests, the "templed hills." They had learned to love

> rivers "half a mile wide and half an inch deep"—
> or five miles by twenty feet
> at the time of spring rains

They had adjusted to

> the horizon dragging outward at the heart-walls
> the land drought-crucified;
> the hosts of tiny vicious flying dragons;
> the screaming down-rush of the white-hooded three-day blizzard;
> the ocean of grass a stormy sea of flame.

They had put their faith in the agricultural adaptations of dryland farming, winter wheat, windmills, barbed wire, and in their own toughness. Then they suffered the stock market crash of 1929 and the Great Depression. Kansans call that time the "Dirty Thirties," a twice-cussed seven years when the failed economy of the East (center of finance) combined with the drought of the West (center of agriculture) to deliver a double shock. Some admitted defeat—physically, culturally, and psychically.

But the midwestern/rural/agricultural way of life had already become diminished by the 1920s, when urban population overtook rural. Urban images, urban politics, and urban concerns began to dominate the discourse of American life. By the end of the Dust Bowl, Kansas's population had stopped growing through in-migration. Many had left their farms—though Kansas's population was not as diminished as Oklahoma's. Historian C. Robert Haywood points out that the Dust Bowl dispossessed were called "Okies," not "Kansies." But, as Huber Self writes in *Environment and Man in Kansas* (1978): "of the 105 counties in Kansas, seventy-one had reached maximum population forty years or more previous to 1970."

In the first census conducted by the federal government, farmers made up 95 percent of the U.S. population. In the most recent census, farmers were less than 1 percent, so low that in the next census farmers will be part of "OTHER," along with alligator wrestlers, cement sculptors, and blacksmiths.

Culturally, *The Wizard of Oz*, via Hollywood, visited Kansas again after the Dust Bowl. By 1939, Americans could easily believe Kansas to be a flat, gray land of tight-fisted farmers and twisters. By then, the farm implement might best be used as a prop for Judy Garland to lean against while she sang about that place over the rainbow where "happy little bluebirds fly." Dorothy's "over the rainbow" was every young person's desire to leave the farm and head for some city, Emerald or not. Ironic in its perfect timing with the release of *The Wizard of Oz*, Dr. Karl Menninger analyzed Kansas's mental state in an essay, "Bleeding Kansans." He found that Kansans had

> gone off the deep end with desperate seriousness, and in so doing earned for themselves the name of being a humorless, puritanical people, incapable of joy and grudging in their attitude toward those happier than themselves.
> . . .
> I began by saying that we live in a beautiful state, a state settled by brave, intelligent and far-visioned people; then I had to add that our intelligence and our vision do not seem to have prevented us from developing a vast inferiority, not a real inferiority but a feeling of inferiority.

Maybe *The Wizard of Oz* turns on Dorothy's desire to return home. And twentieth-century Americans heard her mantra: "There's no place like home, there's no place like home, there's no place like home." But few, from 1939 on, returned to the agricultural Kansas except as an exercise in nostalgia. After World War II, the comforting war hero Dwight David Eisenhower, from Abilene, Kansas, was elected, twice, to the presidency. At the beginning of his second term, *The Wiz-*

ard of Oz began its interminable run on television. By 1960, John Fitzgerald Kennedy wisely chose "The *New* Frontier" (emphasis mine) to distinguish himself from Ike's America and its nostalgia for an older, agricultural, homogenized, pasteurized nation, as pure and healthy as the milk delivered to American homes during the Eisenhower years.

Since the 1960s, Kansas travel and tourism campaigns have actively evoked stereotypes. One promotion called Kansas "The Land of Ahhh's," which baffled the *Wall Street Journal* because it acknowledged our worst stereotype. On the occasion of the 125th anniversary of statehood, we trumpeted: "125 and Coming Alive," thereby admitting how moribund our state image had become. Since then we have been "America's Central Park," we've claimed that "The Secret's Out" (though who listened?), we asked people to say Kansas "Above a Whisper," and we've been "Simply Wonderful," two words that hardly spark the imagination toward anything but the truth of simplicity and the lie of the wonderful. Such Kansas promotions show our inability to cut through the tangle of stereotypes, assumptions, and images that tie up our imaginations as we think about a place so many of us care deeply about.

Caring About Kansas: Keeper of Firsts. In fact, Kansas has a place in American history that moves well beyond stereotypes of landscape and agriculture. In 1922, William Allen White wrote: "Kansas is the Mother Shipton, the Madame Thebes, the Witch of Endor, and the low barometer of the nation. When anything is going to happen in this country, it happens first in Kansas. Abolition, Prohibition, Populism, . . . the exit of the roller towel . . . —these things came popping out of Kansas like bats out of hell."

Although our popular culture image might make people scoff at White's grandiose claim, our historical reality makes Kansas one of few states—with Massachusetts, Virginia, Texas and California—emblematic of America. As historian Carl Becker wrote in 1910: "The Kansas spirit is the American spirit double distilled. It is a new grafted product of American individualism, American idealism, American intolerance. Kansas is America in microcosm."

Becker and White came to their conclusions because, historically, Kansas has lived on a kind of fault line. For example, the first European explorer to make a significant incursion into North America, Francisco Vásquez de Coronado, ended his journey in Kansas in 1541. A year later, a priest from that expedition returned to what is now Kansas and became the first Catholic martyr in what is now the United States. The first trail to the Southwest, the Santa Fe Trail, was surveyed in 1825, beginning in what is now Kansas City, Missouri, and traversing for over four hundred miles through what is now Kansas. This early trail was soon followed by other routes to faraway places—the Oregon Trail and the Butterfield Overland. After the Civil War, the cattle trails brought beef to a meat-starved nation and America's famous hero, the cowboy, was born. The first cattle towns were all in Kansas—Abilene, Wichita, Dodge City, Hays.

White refers to some of the social and political movements associated with Kansas. Abolition occurred because Free Staters in Kansas territory included the likes of John Brown and James Lane (first to arm blacks in the service of the Union). "Bleeding Kansas" was the Civil War before the Civil War. After the Union victory, Kansas attracted veterans loyal to the Grand Army of the Republic and the Republican Party. Kansas became the first state to adopt Prohibition, and kept it the longest—from 1881 until 1949. In the 1890s, Kansas was the first state to elect officials from America's largest third-party movement—Populism. And in the early part of the twentieth century, Kansas was home to the nation's largest-circulation socialist newspaper, *The Appeal to Reason*, of Girard. Emanuel Haldeman-Julius went from that newspaper to create the first mass-market paperback books, the Little Blue Books, "A University in Print" to educate the working classes.

Free State Kansas became the primary destination of the first mass migration of blacks out of the South when Reconstruction failed. The "Exodusters," who remembered John Brown, knew, too, that Kansas was the first state to ratify the Fifteenth Amendment, black voting rights, in 1867. The first black woman admitted to the practice of law in the United States was Lutie Lytle, of Topeka, in 1897. Ten years later, Kansas elected Charles Curtis as one of the first Native Americans to the Senate (1907) and he later went on to become vice president of the United States in 1929. Wichita's Hattie McDaniel was the first black woman to win an Academy Award in 1939. In the early 1950s, Kansas was targeted by the NAACP in its fight to desegregate schools, and those well-educated Kansas blacks with Exoduster roots struggled all the way to *Brown v. Board of Education, Topeka, Kansas* (1954).

The burgeoning women's movement saw opportunities to influence women's rights in state constitutions being written after the Civil War. Kansas women were granted municipal suffrage. As a result, Dora Salter of Argonia became the first woman mayor in the United States (1887). The first woman dentist began her practice in Lawrence in 1867. The first white woman to explore the Pacific was Osa Johnson in the 1900s. And in 1949, Georgia Neese Clark became the first woman to serve as U.S. treasurer.

After Populism was co-opted by Republican progressivism in the early part of the twentieth century, Kansas led the reform spirit, particularly in the fields of public and mental health. Dr. Samuel J. Crumbine, he of the "roller towel" in the William Allen White quote, took over as secretary of the State Board of Health just as the germ theory became popular medical knowledge, and his campaign against the house fly (the flyswatter is a Kansas invention) in 1906 was followed by equally successful forays against the roller towel (1907) and the common drinking cup (1909). Kansas was the first state to pass food & drug and water & sewage acts. Dr. Karl Menninger's pioneering efforts in mental health reflected his belief in Kansas as a supportive place for his radical ideas. He founded the Menninger Clinic, an open-air sanitarium for the mentally ill, in 1925.

Kansas firsts contain the specifics that allow some generalizations. Kansas, as central, was at a crossroads geographically and politically—from the trails to the coincidence of statehood at the beginning of the Civil War. As a decidedly Republican state, and then a Progressive Republican state, Kansas tended to be in the forefront of those states willing to put the public good before individual rights, hence the racial history, the experiments with social causes like Prohibition, the good record for education, for women's rights and opportunities, and, finally, for the innovations in health. Kansas is no longer seen as a state thinking ahead of the rest of the nation. A fairly recent review of the states called us "The Eclipsed State." But those who know our history have much to be proud of, and we continue to put interesting prototypes onto the national stage—Eisenhower, Gwendolyn Brooks, Langston Hughes, William Inge, William Stafford, Gordon Parks, Robert Dole.

Kansas: Heartland

The people of the camp groaned and stood up.... They were moving West, to escape the past, escape the East. Why didn't they ever look behind them? Did they never wonder why they were so weary and mean? Dorothy knew and despised them. They were all pulling the East with them.

–Geoff Ryman, *Was* (1992)

Kansas, though perhaps "eclipsed," refuses to be left behind. Kansas is dragged behind like some vestigial tail. We remember its wag long after we remember its vitality, or what it meant to the United States. Kansas, along with the rest of the Midwest, has another popular culture role to play: Heartland. This at a time when the heart seems to have gone out of so much of the country. Americans want to believe that somewhere people are innocent, agricultural, close to

God, living out the values of an older America—the "family values" so hypocritically invoked in political rhetoric. Midwestern businesses name themselves "Heartland" in order to establish trust, evoking simpler times, when people kept their word with only a handshake.

"Heartland," though, comes about because, as the population shifted to the urban, Kansas and the Midwest lost the "culture war." Think of the novels of Sinclair Lewis, fueled by a contempt for the Midwest. Lewis took apart the smug, isolated small town in *Main Street* (1920), his first successful novel. That books opens:

> This is America—a town of a few thousand, in a region of wheat and corn and dairies and little groves.
> The town is, in our tale, called "Gopher Prairie, Minnesota." But its Main Street is the continuation of Main Streets everywhere. The story would be the same in Ohio or Montana, in Kansas or Kentucky or Illinois, and not very differently would it be told Up York State or in the Carolina hills.
> Main Street is the climax of civilization. That this Ford car might stand in front of the Bon Ton Store, Hannibal invaded Rome and Erasmus wrote in Oxford cloisters.

Lewis's smugness betrays him, because this "climax of civilization" is the same in New York City, Los Angeles, and Washington, D.C. Every place in the United States has its pious morality, smug comfort, envious consumerism. Kansas certainly does. Joseph Stanley Pennell, in his 1944 novel *The History of Rome Hanks and Kindred Matters*, wrote:

> But what sort of people squatted in Fork City anyway? They all sold each other wheat and bacon and corn and beef and farm machinery and squeaky shoes; they all talked in the same Goddamned flat nasal voice about the same Goddamned trivial things day-in-day-out year-after-year—eating, sleeping and growing more rustic and pompous and proverbial.

In American and Kansan literature of the first half of the twentieth century, a writer could never go wrong criticizing the small town. Or religion, as Sinclair Lewis did in his 1927 *Elmer Gantry*, part of which he both researched and set in Kansas. Or business, as Lewis did in his 1922 *Babbitt*. Nobody can go wrong exposing the hypocrisies in these things, especially if they exist somewhere else, like Kansas.

Nobody can go wrong extolling the virtues of place, either—especially if that place is Kansas, at the metaphoric heart of the nation. When the Clutter family was murdered in Holcomb in 1959—the subject of Truman Capote's *In Cold Blood* (1979)—the country's fascination seemed to be based on the senti-

ment that if such random violence could happen in Kansas, it could happen anywhere! The exclamation was emphasized when Timothy McVeigh bombed the Federal Building in Oklahoma City, having planned the crime and built the bomb in Kansas, with Terry Nichols, who owned a home in Herrington. Terrorism in the Heartland became the story: If it can be planned in Kansas and committed in Oklahoma, is no place safe?

Such a story is based on the Heartland abstraction. Anyone who knows Kansas history will point to "Bleeding Kansas," the period from 1854 to 1861 when Free State radicals traded murders and crimes with proslavery forces. Confederate guerilla William Quantrill burned and looted Lawrence in 1863, killing almost as many people as Timothy McVeigh. Frontier violence, whether committed by Federal troops against Native Americans, or by posses taking justice in their own hands, was common in Kansas and the West. The Great Plains has a richer tradition for fringe groups like the Posse Comitatus than the coastal states. But such history and tradition were not explored deeply during the Murrah Building media blitz. Oklahoma and Kansas are the heart, and the media saw only the tragic poignancy in the innocent deaths of good Heartlanders.

Kansas: Grounded. Kansas as flyover country is rendered insignificant, nowhere special, containing nothing interesting or unique. This echoes the sentiments of another *New Yorker* cartoon, which shows the sign "Heart of America" and, next to it, another sign reading "Bypass," which a car of Easterners has chosen as the best route. On the other hand, Kansas as Heartland, a repository of fundamental American values—religious, agricultural, family—is rendered extremely significant, of great interest to the nation. But neither image is grounded. Both can be maintained only by ignorance—by flying over, or driving through at night.

We in the United States avoid forming deep relationships with particular places. We do so at our own peril. I know how much meaning and richness has come through my own relationship with a particular Kansas. To know one place intimately is to have a *way* of knowing. To learn respect for a single place is to learn to transfer respect to all places close to people's hearts. William Stafford, one of Kansas's very best poets, knew this. In "Allegiances" he wrote:

> It is time for all the heroes to go home
> if they have any, time for all of us common ones
> to locate ourselves by the real things
> we live by.
> . . .

Suppose an insane wind holds all the hills
while strange beliefs whine at the traveler's ears,
we ordinary beings can cling to the earth and love
where we are, sturdy for common things.

Sadly, Americans have had a hard time loving "where we are."

But we need to try, because when the landscape, *all* the landscapes of our lives, comes to be held within ourselves, and is felt and loved, we find the sturdiness in common things that we want of a heartland, a place like Kansas. Only then can we turn our property into our homes. We can turn the anyplace we live into the someplace that matters to us. I am tired of the Kansas that is reduced to "Mudville" or elevated to "Heartland." I prefer to live a life by "real things." My state, central in its history and geography, is just such a real thing, a place that grounds me as American, midwesterner, Kansan.

Thomas Fox Averill
Washburn University, Kansas

Michigan

The state of Michigan is the largest land-locked double peninsula in the world in the midst of the largest freshwater seas in the world. You can see it on the globe in the upper center of the North American continent. The lower peninsula looks like a left-handed mitten with the thumb on the east and a little finger on the other side; the upper peninsula looks like a shark headed west with a big dorsal fin.

The state has a three-thousand-mile coastline around these two peninsulas that are connected by a bridge at the Straits of Mackinac. The gales around the Mackinac Bridge can be fierce, and in the fall of 1989 a woman in a Yugo blew off it. The five-mile bridge was the longest suspension bridge in the world when it was built in 1957. The work was dangerous because of the winds; five men died building it. A Native American workman was luckier and, when the catwalk he was on flew loose, was able to climb two hundred feet to save his own life.

Michigan is surrounded by Lakes Michigan, Superior, Huron, and Erie—with connections to Lake Ontario, the St. Lawrence Seaway, and the Atlantic Ocean; and at the west end of Lake Superior, after a mile or so of portage, with links to the Mississippi River and the Gulf of Mexico. The trading routes provided by the Great Lakes were used by Indians for thousands of years.

The tempests on the Great Lakes, notorious even in Herman Melville's time, were described by him as far more fierce than on any ocean (and the most able and defiant sailor under Ahab had trained on the Great Lakes), storms that have "drowned full many a midnight ship with all its shrieking crew." The "Boreal blasts," as Melville would say, come up suddenly and out of nowhere. Singer Gordon Lightfoot memorialized the wreck of the *Edmund Fitzgerald* in 1975, "when the witch of November" came early and the ship and its twenty-nine-man crew were plunged to the bottom of Lake Superior. I grew up above Lake Michigan's Sleeping Bear Bay. My father logged off South Manitou Island in the 1950s in a wild scheme that nearly broke him. He towed the logs back by ferry to an expensive wharf he'd brashly put in himself (there's a lot more to putting in a pier, it turns out, than what he thought) with huge rented equipment to drill the pilings. My mother used to stand at the picture window in foul weather, looking out. Every November we lost another piece of our dock.

The weather in Michigan can change within minutes and the land itself, in the grand scheme of things, has a history of change. Before the continents found their way to where they are now, Michigan was where Florida is, our pine trees were the ferns of the Jurassic, and a saltwater sea produced the fossilized corals we call Petoskey stones and find along the shore. Michigan was shaped by glaciers, over and over again, the last one receding a mere eleven thousand years ago. My mother's three-hundred-foot hill above Sleeping Bear Bay was once the shore of a different lake. Once my sister and I counted eighteen old shorelines between the base of our hill and the present-day Lake Michigan.

In the spring, we would find trailing arbutus in the woods, tiny, sweet-smelling, pink blossoms hidden under pine needles, reputed to be an aphrodisiac. People pulled it up and made it into garlands. It doesn't grow back, or at least I haven't seen it years. I know my father used to send it to my mother in a box with ice when he was courting her and she treasured it above the most expensive perfume or the flower from the florist.

Michigan is fragile, feminine, changeable. It has soft hills, pink air, millions of songbirds, deep blue-green waters, and winds that can move from the southwest to the northwest in the time it takes you to drive to the beach, usually about thirty minutes from wherever you are. One hot day this summer while I was on the phone with my daughter calling from San Francisco, the temperature dropped fifteen degrees in as many minutes: a front coming in. The wind picked up. I carried the phone off the porch so she could hear the wind chimes just a-going. "It sounds like church," Lilah said. Sudden changes in the Michigan weather make you stop to catch your breath, remind you that nothing is permanent, that the entire expanse of eons can collapse like an accordion back to a time when no life form had lungs to catch a breath, a time when the only life form was a coral.

Deadly lake storms, mosquito swamps, and a short growing season didn't make Michigan the first choice of immigrants who wanted to farm and raise a family. Federal surveyor Edward Tiffin reported after the War of 1812 that only one acre in a thousand would "admit of cultivation." Unbeknownst to Tiffin, there was good farmland in south-central Michigan in the area that would become the farms of Pontiac and the auto industry of Flint, but it was so walled off by impenetrable forests and noxious swamps that no one knew about it for years. And up along Lake Superior, the deep freeze winters protected the rich deposits of iron and copper until the late 1800s.

Yet the land was Paradise to those who'd always lived here and loved it. In his *History of the Ottawa and Chippewa Indians of Michigan* (1887), Andrew Blackbird, an Ottawa who grew up in Harbor Springs in the early 1800s, writes that there was "such an abundance of wild strawberries, raspberries and blackberries that they fairly perfumed the air of the whole coast with fragrant scent of ripe fruit." The passenger pigeons and the whitefish were so plentiful that it took almost no labor to gather them. "Then I never knew my people to want for anything to eat or wear," he writes, "as we always had plenty of wild meat, and plenty of fish, corn, vegetables, and wild fruits. I thought (and yet I may be mistaken), that my people were very happy in those days." I live on the Leelanau Peninsula, where the fresh fruit still perfumes the air and in June the yellow puccoon along Lake Michigan fills the air with a fragrance like that of camellias, but the garish three-million-dollar mansions everywhere you look, muscling each other for a piece of the view, are frightful.

Sometimes in the winter when everyone is gone, when the snow is soft and thick and the silence is infinite, I can imagine Andrew Blackbird's Michigan. One night years ago in the winter, I heard a knock on my door and my neighbor, with a child in a backpack, said, "You have to come out." Above our heads there were magical lights, like acre-sized scarves moving in the sky: blue-green, fuchsia, green, purple, yellow. The northern lights, as I've never seen them since.

Doug McCormick, a man whose parents were the keepers of the Northport lighthouse and grew up in Cross Village in the early 1900s, can recall going to school with mostly Indians and learning to wrestle. "The Indian boys were good at wrestling," McCormick reminisced one soft May morning in 2000 outside the lighthouse. The way many people made a living there was to harvest the passenger pigeons and ship them in barrels to Chicago. Passenger pigeons are flightless when nesting and so settlers would set up smudge fires for five miles in all directions in the pines and go out and gather the delicious game, never imagining that the passenger pigeons would become quickly extinct from all this too-easy harvesting. "No one wanted that to happen," McCormick said. "They didn't know."

The Indians traversed the lakes between Chicago in the winter and Manitoulin Island in the summer. Their coastal campgrounds would become the first frontier settlements and, later on, the first resorts. James Fenimore Cooper, who lived in Michigan for a time, set one of his stories, "The Oak Openings," about the War of 1812, here. He described an outpost on the Kalamazoo River, like the intergalactic bar in *Star Wars* with its random assortment of characters just passing through: a few Indians, a few French traders, a few soldiers of fortune, an outlaw or two, and an Anglo-American eccentric whose specialty was hunting bees. Americans on the move and on the make, with the nearest bookstore 1,500 miles away by canoe. The river itself was visible in the distance, "a beautiful little river that flows westward, emptying its tribute into the vast expanse of Lake Michigan."

Michigan was under the French flag until 1760, then under the British until 1776, and the American presence wasn't real until 1814. The French fur traders were the first Europeans in Michigan, and many married or lived with Indian women so that by the time Cooper visited, there were already grown grandchildren and great-great-grandchildren of these unions. There was a scarcity of European women in early America; the Indian women, on the other hand, were expert in woods lore and accustomed to traveling in the wilderness, and so there were many alliances, marital and otherwise, between non-Indian men and Indian women. Johnny Cash, Elvis Presley, Abraham Lincoln, Aaron Neville, and Cher, to name just a few famous Americans, reportedly had Indian relatives, and what held for the rest of America was also true for Michigan.

The first trickle of immigrants to Michigan came in the 1700s to escape war, poverty, incarceration, and discrimination, and while many were white, there were many blacks, too. Michigan historian Bruce Catton documented the pioneer family of Zachariah and Mary Morgan near Boyne City in *Michigan: A Bicentennial History* (1976). Zachariah was the son of manumitted slaves born in 1840 in North Carolina; his parents were afraid he would be kidnapped and sold south and so moved out of range. Eventually Zachariah and his wife, Mary, the daughter of second-generation fugitive slaves in Canada, would carve out a place for themselves in the Michigan wilderness, establishing a brick factory and, later, a school. So well respected was this family for their hard work and kindness to others that when Mary died in 1951 at the age of 107, the entire town shut down for the funeral.

Michigan wasn't even Michigan until 1837, the twenty-sixth state admitted to the Union, a vast, impenetrable forest. The Michigan wilderness was where slaves who followed the North Star sometimes found safe haven with bands of Indians, a phenomenon documented in the book *Black Indians* (1997) by William Katz. They followed the Big Dipper, or "the drinking gourd," as in the song, a pattern of escape that would eventually be dubbed the Underground Railroad, a metaphor for the four-hundred-year-old secret route to freedom. In my own family on my father's side, a people who headed out for the territory the minute they could see the smoke from a neighbor's chimney, my father alluded to being part Indian and, based on his looks, maybe he was part black, too. Now it's popular to claim this, but a hundred years ago the closest anyone came to admitting ancestry other than English was saying that one might be a little bit French Canadian.

In Michigan, as in other places in America, attitudes toward Indians changed from decade to decade, usually along with government policy. In his *Notes on the State of Virginia (1781–1782)*, Thomas Jefferson advised the Indians to intermarry with European settlers (which they had in any case already done), intermarriage being cheaper than war. In an address to the "Mohiccons [*sic*]" he says, "you will . . . form one people with us . . . you will mix with us by marriage, your blood will run in our veins." But then after the last treaty was negotiated, and Andrew Jackson's soldiers started the Indians west on the Trail of Tears, things changed. Frances Fitzgerald, writing in 1979 in *America Revised*, has a passage delineating the confusing and contradictory way American history textbooks depicted Indians, a treatment that veered wildly from portraying them as blood-thirsty enemies to noble savages, depending on the political situation of the time.

Michigan in the 1800s was like places back east in the 1600s, and there were more Indian alliances and influences in the early days of European immigration than are acknowledged even today in the history books. According to a well-researched essay by Sally Wagner published in 1992 in the *Akwe-kon Journal*, Elizabeth Cady Stanton, Matilda Joslyn Gage, and other early feminists were directly influenced by Iroquois women. The Iroquois were an Algonquin people, like the tribes in Michigan who had come originally from the East by way of the St. Lawrence. According to Wagner, under European law women didn't have property, they *were* property, whereas many Indian tribes, including the Algonquin Michigan tribes, were matrilineal: The women held property in their own right, had custody of children, spoke their mind freely and were respected participants in the selection of leaders and in council. Indian women in Michigan, through marriage and example, brought herbal knowledge and woods lore to pioneer women, a way of raising children without corporal punishment, and the habit of having their own thoughts and expressing them, in private and in public, whenever they felt like it.

Henry Schoolcraft, the government treaty negotiator at Sault Ste. Marie, provides an example of a mixed marriage. Henry met Jane Johnston at a sugaring-off party, the time when maple sap is boiled down in the spring. She was from the influential Johnston family, half Chippewa on her mother's side and half Irish on her father's. Because of the prominence of her family, Jane was described by many important visitors to the Soo. Thomas McKenny, a Washington official, described Jane in a letter to his wife. "Mildness of expression, and softness and delicacy of manner as well as of voice, characterize her," he wrote. "You would never judge, either from her complexion or her language, that her mother was a Chippewa."

Educated in Europe by her father's aristocratic relatives, Jane was fluent in several languages. Henry used Jane to help him translate from Chippewa to English, and also to curry favor with the people he needed to sign treaties. Anna Brownell Jameson, the wife of the Canadian prime minister, went by boat one evening from Mackinac Island to Sault Ste. Marie with Mrs. Schoolcraft and her children. In *Winter Studies and Summer Rambles* (1838), she wrote that they were plagued by mosquitoes. Finally exhausted, Mrs. Jameson fell asleep on the bottom of the boat, "but whenever I woke from uneasy, restless slumber, there was Mrs. Schoolcraft, bending over her sleeping children, waving off the mosquitoes and singing all the time a low, melancholy Indian song; while the northern lights were streaming and dancing in the sky, and the fitful moaning of the wind, the gathered clouds and chilly atmosphere foretold a change in the weather."

A man who can spend his days taking the land away from the relatives of the woman he is making children with by night must be expert in the art of situational ethics. It came as no big surprise when the Schoolcraft marriage collapsed after the last treaty was signed in 1835. Almost immediately, Henry went back East, taking the children away from Jane and putting them in New England boarding schools. Jane died shortly after of a broken heart. Henry, accused by the government he'd served of absconding with funds, changed his name to Colcraft and soon after married a wealthy spinster who had obtained her money by selling her slaves. Together Henry and his second wife wrote a racist tract, *The Black Gauntlet* (1860), in which they give themselves cloying invented names, Ne Na Baim (for him) and Musidora (for her). In this book of thinly disguised fiction Jane is described as "too kind" to her children, a common Indian failing, the authors note, a woman Henry married in a burst of "ethnographic enthusiasm." The coauthors provide a bounty of casuistic arguments to the effect that it was the duty of whites to enslave blacks and civilize Indians in order to bring them closer to God. The work of being a treaty negotiator in the enemy-filled wilderness must have required at least duplicity if not multiple personalities. Henry was an intrepid explorer, a prolific writer, and one of the most dauntless opportunists ever hired by the government. The name Schoolcraft, not Colcraft, has been given in Michigan to a county, a road, and a school.

When Alexis de Tocqueville came up the Detroit River in 1831 to the present-day location of Detroit, there was a fort on one side and an Indian camp on the other. "French appearance of the village. Catholic Church. Cock on the church tower. Scottish soldier in full dress on the bank," Tocqueville wrote in *Democracy in America*, while on the other side were crude huts, naked children. Meanwhile, "two stark naked savages in a canoe, twisting fast as a whirlpool round our boat." Beyond that was the trackless forest, creating a "feeling of isolation, of abandon, greater even than on the ocean." Tocqueville wrote, "The woman dressed like a lady. Strange mixture of prosperity and poverty. The Americans in their log houses have the air of rich folk who have temporarily gone to spend a season in a hunting-lodge."

In 1843, Margaret Fuller, a friend of Ralph Waldo Emerson's and Henry David Thoreau's, came up Lake Michigan on a steamer filled with people who'd accepted government land grants. "It grieved me," she writes in *Summer on the Lakes, in 1843*, "to hear these immigrants who were to be the fathers of a new race, all, from the old man down to the little girl, talking not of what they should do, but of what they should get in the new scene. It was to them a prospect, not of the unfolding nobler energies, but of more ease, and larger accumulation." Fuller could already sense disaster in this rabid materialism, but no one could have predicted that the next century would see the wholesale extinction of species, and such severe industrial pollution of air, soil, and water that the whitefish, so plentiful during Blackbird's time, would be rendered too toxic for pregnant women to eat.

Fuller was not alone in observing the predation of the new race. In *Democracy in America*, Tocqueville describes a budding nation of philistines. "It would be difficult to describe the avidity with which the Ameri-can rushes forward to secure this immense booty that fortune offers," he writes. This is the way it was done, he says: "Three or four thousand soldiers drive before them the wandering races of the aborigines; these are followed by the pioneers who pierce the woods, scare off the beasts of prey, explore the courses of the inland streams, and make ready the triumphal march of civilization." The Manitoulin Ottawas called the ravenous newcomers "the hungry ghosts" and depicted them in a play I saw in 1987 as nine-foot-tall, two-dimensional figures with gaping holes where their stomachs and hearts should have been. Eventually Michigan Indians, along with the tribes from other states, would be force-marched west, many children expiring on the way. Katz and several others give seventy million as the number of Native Americans who died in the first centuries of conquest, based on the theory that the New World contained 15 percent of the world's population at the time of "discovery" by Europe. However, even the most conservative estimates state that over ten million Native Americans would die, more than the number of people killed by Adolf Hitler.

Immigrants from Europe came to Michigan, but Americans who'd been here a long time also arrived, people like my Stocking ancestors who'd come over in 1633 on the *Griffin* initially to find religious freedom, people who after several generations were just restless seekers looking for any kind of freedom. They were a special breed, these early dissidents, adventurers, escapees, and pioneers, black and white; they were people who naturally chafed under the constraints imposed on them by people other than themselves, who had learned to enjoy risk, who'd trained themselves to like living where they had to figure everything out for themselves.

Internal religious communities, too, like those first pilgrims who came to Plymouth Rock, were always attracted to the frontier. In 1847, James Strang heard God tell him to go to Beaver Island in Lake Michigan. Strang and Brigham Young had led a party of Mormons out from New York State, one of my great-great-grandmothers among them, but in Ohio they had a falling out over polygamy, which Young wanted and Strang didn't. As reported by Roger Van Noord in *King of Beaver Island* (1988), Young went on to Utah and Strang went to Beaver Island, where he was promptly elected to the Michigan legislature. A few years passed and Strang had another sacred revelation telling him polygamy was okay after all. This was while his purportedly male secretary was discovered to be pregnant. Strang, who as a teenager had seriously entertained the idea of marrying Queen Victoria, had himself crowned king on Beaver Island. The islanders had a time of it getting Strang's throne puffy enough and so stuffed the arms of the wooden chair with pincushion moss before covering the whole with red velvet.

In Michigan, as in America generally, a person could experiment. Some of these experiments didn't benefit others, but some did. On the eve of the Great Depression, Joseph Maddy decided to build a music camp. This was considered a daft notion by most as it was thought that children would not want to practice the French horn or the violin when they could be fishing. People were wrong and today Interlochen Arts Academy educates children from all over the world. A stroll on campus during a recent visit showed people of every race and nationality enjoying a concert next to Green Lake just as the sun was setting.

Ottawa and Chippewa Indians on the Leelanau Peninsula, struggling with terrible poverty until the 1980s, fought for and won federal recognition. Jackson's Indian Removal Act is snared all of them; a few had escaped during the long march and still more had gone to Canada and hidden out, moving back once the cavalry was gone. Now the tribes run casinos and, although they have not restored themselves to the halcyon days of Blackbird's time, they are surviving. Other Michigan tribes have followed suit.

In a parallel development, Hispanic people, who started coming to Michigan in the summers in the 1940s to pick fruit, now can find winter employment with the tribes and are becoming permanent residents. Hansen's grocery store in Suttons Bay has a sign above the door that reads: Thank you, Gracias, Megwetch (the familiar phrase for "thank you" in the local Ottawa language). Hispanics, or Latinos, a five-hundred-year-old mix of Native American, European, and African with a slightly different process of miscegenation from south of the border, are predicted to be nearly 25 percent of the U.S. population by 2050. Racial lines in Michigan are blurring and Caucasians are fast becoming a minority. The Romans ruled England longer than the English held sway in America; even the Latin language, once forced on students like William Shakespeare, is long dead. The Chinese—successively conquered by Mongols, Tartars, Huns, Anglos, and a host of others—never tried to conquer their conquerors but only to marry them and outlast them, and they succeeded. The only difference between England and China 2,000 years ago and America and Michigan today is that the speed of change has gone from oxcart to fiberoptics. Today we're all on the Internet, great-grandmothers and Indians alike, and we're all just a click away from everything and everybody.

In the Upper Peninsula, where my son-in-law is from, his grandmother Rose tells of growing up in a mining camp outside Negaunee in the 1920s and 1930s with Finnish, Welsh, English, Italian, Polish, and Slav neighbors; another piece of the American melting pot that has long since melted. When miners protested the low wages and unsafe working conditions, soldiers were brought in to send them back to the rat-infested, water-filled mines. Jerry Stanley relates in *Big Annie of Calumet* (1996) that in 1913 at Calumet, "Big Annie" Clemenc wrapped herself in the American flag, stepped in front of the soldiers and said, "Run your bayonets and sabers through this flag and kill me, but I won't move . . . if this flag will not protect me, then I will die with it." Italian Hall that Christmas Eve "under a cold Christmas moon," as Woody Guthrie sings in his song about the Calumet miners' strike, was the scene of one of the most shameful events in mining history. That night, when the children were having their Christmas play upstairs, some unknown person, almost certainly trying to break the strike by beating the spirit of the strikers, shouted "Fire!" and barred the door. Seventy-four people died in the stampede that followed, sixty-three of them children.

My grandparents and great-grandparents homesteaded in Michigan near Coldwater. My grandfather and his father, with whom he came north, were lumbermen in the days when it was work done with an ax: The crosscut saw wasn't even invented until the 1880s. The name Stocking must have come from a long line of woodsmen—*stocking* is an old word that means, variously, a tree-trunk or a measure of standing timber—and so Michigan, described by Tocqueville as "trees, ceaseless trees" was the place for them.

My father had an encyclopedic knowledge of the woods that came from his parents and from being outside all day. He could tell the birds by their songs and imitate them. I recall him pointing out a hermit thrush, that rare American nightingale, deep in the woods, and then his teaching me how to do call and response with a bird. I used to go with him to the woods as a preschooler. He would sit me down on his overshirt with my books, far from the falling trees but near enough to hear "Timber!" and feel the ground shudder each time a tree was felled. When I lived in Manhattan my husband and I used to take our kids to the Metropolitan Museum of Art, the Museum of Natural History, or the Museum of Modern Art, showing them the treasures of the world. I never thought it at the time, but that's what my father did when he took me to the woods. He pointed out things that were beautiful and wonderful: a scarlet tanager, a purple finch, a bluebird, a green-winged luna moth, a baby owl, a newborn fawn, golden jewelweed, pink lady slippers. Now, when people put up a mansion on the shore or on the hill, I wonder if they know they just bulldozed a museum of rare and irreplaceable objects d'art.

My grandparents pushed farther north in the late

1800s, walking on the old Indian trail that went between Newago and Northport. They came by oxcart with several children and all their tools and bedding. The state had been clear-cut from one side to the other, the stumps like yellow plates as far as the eye could see. My grandfather was a big, fair-haired, easygoing guy and my grandmother was a tiny, dark, intense woman who in pictures looks a little like Bruce Lee. My grandmother prepared her sons for the rigors of the backwoods by naming them Rod, Deck, Hale, and Pierce. My father and his twin sister were so small that my grandmother kept them alive in shoe boxes on the back of the woodstove. All her children lived. When the lumber played out, Grandma kept the farm going with butter and eggs. The soil was all sand but she made a go of it.

Henry Schoolcraft, in *Narrative Journal* (1820), recounting his journey up Lake Michigan from Chicago in a canoe, observed a coast of "sand banks, and pines" for mile after mile. When he gets to Sleeping Bear Dunes, where I grew up, he describes, writing in stunned disbelief, "a bank of sand, probably two hundred feet high, and extending eight or nine miles, without any vegetation" with one knoll that resembled a "couchant bear" (hence the name Sleeping Bear Dunes), which in 1970 Congress designated a national lakeshore. I lived in an old farmhouse at the base of the dunes from 1974 to 1976. That house is no longer there because the national park management tore it down, but when the sun would come up over Glen Lake, it would shine through the front windows of the house, ricochet off the golden sand mountain and out the back windows, and fill the entire place with reverberating orange light for the glory hour of sunrise.

Now I live in another, even older, farmhouse twenty-five miles up the Leelanau Peninsula from Sleeping Bear outside the village of Lake Leelanau. My house, or the oldest portion of it, was on the original plat maps when Leelanau County was first surveyed. It was a Schaub homestead. The Schaubs founded the village of Lake Leelanau back in the 1850s. This is the story as my octogenarian friend Theresa Schaub tells it. The Schaubs were Germans from Alsace-Lorraine who left to escape a century of conflict and conscription. Theresa's great-grandmother wanted to have a Catholic church and so took maple sugar back to Buffalo to trade for religious vestments. In a storm on Lake Michigan on the way home, she prayed to the Virgin Mary and promised to name the church after her if she survived. "Mass at St. Mary's was in three languages—French, German, Polish—when they first started," Theresa told me, adding, "and they didn't all get along that well at first—but they learned." These nationalities had just been fighting one another back in Europe but, in a generation or two, intermarriage and learning English ameliorated a lot of the differences. Michigan was settled so recently, relative to other parts of the country, that there are people alive today who can remember the stories of how the community was shaped by immigrants.

I asked Theresa how the families around Lake Leelanau made it through the Depression. She said that they sold off lake lots to resorters and with that had enough to keep going. When the state first opened up to homesteaders, the government was giving away the waterfront property. The land along Lake Michigan, which now sells for $4,000–$9,000 a waterfront foot, was considered worthless in 1850 because it couldn't be farmed. In addition to the Great Lakes, Michigan has over eleven thousand inland lakes and five hundred islands on all the lakes and rivers. Tourists started coming in the early 1890s and haven't stopped yet.

The first summer residents, like Ernest Hemingway's family up near Petoskey, came initially by steamer and then, later, by train. Michigan is still a series of lakeside resort communities, towns that die back to 150 people after Labor Day and come alive again after Memorial Day. But now people fly up or take the thruway and they come from Manhattan and San Francisco, Paris and London, as well as the larger midwestern cities of Detroit, Chicago, Cincinnati, and Indianapolis. And they come for the cherries and the strawberries, the northern lights and the wild flowers, the bonfires and the singing at night on the beach, the sailing and the swimming, and to simply retreat to a more peaceful scene. Andrew Blackbird and his relatives had the right idea all along.

Kathleen Stocking
Lake Leelanau, Michigan

Minnesota

When I grew up in Sioux Falls, South Dakota, it was possible to believe that I occupied a "corner of the world." I lived on a square block—twelve blocks to the mile—lined on all four sides with square houses with straight walls. The block was divided lengthwise by the alley that gave onto squared-off garages that in the 1950s housed even squared-off cars. Our boxy, red Ford station wagon suited our big family, but I do remember longing after the 1958 Thunderbird, nicknamed the "Square Bird."

I could stand at the corner nearest my house at 8th and Summit and see in a straight line in all four directions. So, square it was, and mostly still is. In the 1960s developers in Sioux Falls' south end laid out curved streets, but not in my neighborhood, nor in my times, and too late to change my mind's landscape.

The United States Land Ordinance of 1785 laid out a system for surveying and dividing the country into six-mile squares, counted outward and numbered from a point on the Ohio-Pennsylvania border. Subsequent land-law refinements divided those squares into thirty-six one-mile-square sections, then each of those into four 640-acre quarter sections and so on down to my house's lot on my square block.

This land division system, invented in New England, imposes order and predictability whatever the actual lay of the land. That grid lies awkwardly across many parts of the United States, but just west of Sioux Falls those straight lines actually match the flat contour of the landscape. I always ask for a window seat when flying into and out of Sioux Falls just for the pleasure of seeing that grid.

The first time I visited Scotland, I found that those squares had been etched into my psyche. In the seaside village of Ullapool, I tried—in vain, but repeatedly nonetheless—to go around the block. I hadn't thought "Okay, I'll go around the block," I just found myself peculiarly but deeply puzzled when I couldn't find the square that would take me back to where I'd started.

Living in central Minnesota nearly a half century later teaches me that "corner of the world" is a mixed metaphor. Our house in Collegeville is as square as anything in South Dakota, but here that squareness rebukes the undulating landscape that surrounds it. It's a house at war with its environment. The builder took round, rough, odd-shaped stones and turned them into two-foot thick, straight walls that feel like a barricade against the outside. Built just over a century ago, the house expresses a nineteenth-century farmer's yearning to escape the elements, to find refuge from sun and storm alike in the dark, safe interior.

My husband and I are planning a new addition to the house—all windows and views. Unlike the original farmer-builder, we're indoor people who want protection from mosquitoes, wood ticks, and severe weather, but not from sun and views. We want as much of both as we can get.

This is my Minnesota-born husband's dream house, but not quite mine. The addition will help, but while he loves the views and will love them even better when we have more windows, I will still feel claustrophobic. For me, the landscape itself is the barricade. All those hills and trees get in the way so I can't see anything.

By ten thousand years ago, the last of the most recent glaciers had nearly melted away, but it left behind a landscape organized by and around water—rivers, lakes, and the memory of older, gigantic rivers and lakes. This last glacier had occupied a huge area, most of it north of Minnesota's current outlines, but four of its ice fingers (a metaphor too delicate for the power-

ful force exerted by these ice packs)—Rainy, Superior, Des Moines, and Wadena—left their dramatic mark on the land. They cut, scraped, abraded, sculpted, and plucked their way across the region, and then withdrew, leaving behind debris, rocks, boulders, soils of several types and colors, a lot of water, and two different Minnesotas.

One of those Minnesotas, the north and northeast two-fifths, is hillier, more wooded, and full of lakes. The other Minnesota, the south and southwest two-fifths, is flatter, drier, and more open. The other fifth is a transition zone between the two: lakes, more deciduous than coniferous trees, and flatter with occasional rolling hills. Both of these Minnesotas take their identity from those trees and that water—one side for having them, and one side for not. Politicians, especially, identify the significant state division as metro and outstate. I think this water/trees and no water/no trees division is much more telling and revealing of the state's nature and sense of itself.

The no water/no trees area—we might call it Prairieland, though some Minnesotans certainly consider it the Far Side of Paradise—includes the southwestern corner, a swath of counties along the western border with the Dakotas, and up to Canada. A bit of it in the far southwestern corner never got touched by the glaciers. The rest of it, though, was either flattened by the departing ice or by the lake that formed when part of the glacier got stalled and melted, forming the 116,000-square-mile glacial Lake Agassiz. That lake, long since dried up, left in western Minnesota the Red River of the North and a fertile, flat, and dry lake bed. You can still see the outline of the southern tip of the lake and even its shoreline. This huge lake bed was flat enough, the soil rich enough, the trees few enough that big, rich, commercial, bonanza farms flourished here in the late nineteenth and early twentieth centuries.

Before whites showed up, native people burned the land to keep the stray trees down. These were mostly Dakota people. They had woodland roots, but by the early nineteenth century they had been pushed out onto the prairies by the domino effect of European settlement farther east on more eastern native groups, including the Ojibway.

Later European Americans also burned to clear the prairies for farming and then planted trees in other places for firewood, shade, protection, perhaps even a bit of decoration.

This flat southwestern part of the state probably has more trees now than a century ago. The federal government passed the Timber Culture Act in 1873 to encourage tree planting. Imagined by the same brains who believed that rain followed the plow, the legislation was motivated by the hope that trees would modify the harsh climate and even increase rainfall. These legislators and many of their compatriots also thought trees more civilized, somehow, than open land. Largely unsuccessful at either filling the prairies with trees or at changing the climate (or even at civilizing it, I fear), the legislation was repealed by the early 1890s.

The state of Minnesota went further. From 1873 it paid bounties—up to $25 per year—to farmers who planted at least an acre's worth of trees, not more than twelve feet apart, and kept them alive for six years. Farmers in every county in this western/southwestern region applied for and received tress bounties. E.A. Running, for example, in Chippewa County (two over from the Minnesota–South Dakota border) planted a total of 6¼ acres of trees in 1874, 1875, and 1880 and swore that those trees were in a "thrifty and growing state" one, two, and three years later. Grasshoppers had damaged his trees in the first two years, but he had replanted so he still got credit and his bounty. Among Minnesota's other Johnny Appleseeds I was delighted to find that my maternal great-grandfather, Clark Workman Seely, had planted a total of 16 acres of trees and collected $37.40 in bounties. Minnesotans planted over 25,000 acres of trees in the first decade of bounty distribution.

Then, after the turn of the century, farmers planted trees as shelter belts and windbreaks with a growing recognition of the power and proclivity of the wind to pile up snow in the winter and to whip away the soil the rest of the time. The drought years of 1910–1911 and then the dusty, dirty 1920s and 1930s added a sharp urgency to this need for trees. Planters clustered these trees on the windward side of farmhouses or in a straight line along fence rows. Driving through the southwestern and western counties, you can see these often squared-off "islands of trees" in the "rolling seas of sod," as one state forestry official called them. Even when the farmhouses have been abandoned and fallen in, these trees still interrupt the wind and hold the soil.

With the exception of Lake Agassiz, the glaciers left few so-called orphaned mini glaciers, the kind that resulted in lakes, so many of those counties in the Far Side were left with many fewer lakes than in the other Minnesota. Where Itasca County in the north central part of the state has over a thousand lakes within its boundaries, Roseau and Pennington in the northwest have three and one, respectively; Pipestone in the southwest has one. Its neighbor, Rock County, reports two, but they're both human-made reservoirs, and while the State Conservation Office counted them as lakes—and so, probably, do the people who enjoy them—they're not "official" Minnesota lakes.

But there was surface water, and farmers for much of the twentieth century worked concertedly and de- terminedly to drain it away. Wetlands, according to the State Drainage Commission, "have impeded the progress of development." Drained land, however, could be farmed (at least in drier years) and cultivated into ever more prosperity. In the first three decades of the twentieth century, Minnesotans in the southwest drained between five and six million acres of marsh and wetlands. The net effect of these human efforts only made this flatland more of what it was—drier, with occasional trees.

Our house stands just on the dividing line between these two regions on what geologists call a terminal moraine. That means that the low rises and the distant hills that I see out my windows were made by—and actually are—the debris pushed up and dropped as if by a snowplow at the farthest extent of one particular ice lobe. It also means that the land is good for grow- ing trees and better for pastures (and animals, there- fore) than crop farming because of the land's roll. Out the back window I have another glacial remain—a pond. It's too small to have a name, too shallow to sup- port fish (it freezes solid in the winter), and doesn't qualify as one of Minnesota's 10,000 lakes (or 11,400 according to the Division of Natural Resources, or over 11,800 by the counting of the Minneapolis *Star Tribune*). But there are at least a dozen lakes—with names—within a mile of our house.

The nearest one is Lake Sagatagan, at the heart of the campus that is home to St. John's Abbey and Uni- versity, the St. John's Preparatory School, and the Liturgical Press. The admissions counselors report that if they can just get students to see the campus, the natural surroundings will do the rest of the recruiting.

The sisters of the Order of Saint Benedict—twelve miles away—have held a peculiarly Minnesota kind of grudge for over a century against the monks of the Order of Saint Benedict who, the sisters say, stole the money intended for them by their Bavarian king Lud- wig and bought this property, leaving the sisters to set- tle on the open prairie land nearby. The monks got the choice land: hilly, wooded, and including five lakes. The sisters got stuck on open, flat, dry land of a kind that many Minnesotans—and many Americans, ad- mittedly—consider boring and empty. To my South Dakota eye that land, full of grasses and crops, of mountains of hay in the summer, is a vista worth lin- gering over. But neither the sisters nor the monks would likely agree.

The "Sag," the largest of the lakes (218 acres) that the monks got, is alive with activity all year round. Students, monks, and a few neighbors swim almost as soon as the ice has gone out. People rent canoes there. The crew team practices in the early morning. Walk- ers often hike to the Stella Maris Chapel on the east side. Anglers from the neighborhood put in at the public access on the west side. During the winter, the hockey teams practice indoors but the hardier cross-country skiers and snowshoers and some amateur skaters take to the frozen surface. The really intrepid set up fish houses or an upturned bucket to fish through the ice. Then there's Brother Paul Jasmer, OSB, who doesn't care much for fishing, but receives callers and serves tea in his fish house. These activities—minus the tea service, I imagine—are replicated on the thousands of other lakes in the state.

These lakes have also fostered an ice hockey culture in the state allowing places like Eveleth, Minnesota, to boast that no other place its size "has produced as many quality players or has contributed more to the growth and development of the sport in the United States." Eveleth, too, hosts the United States Hockey Hall of Fame. In this "national shrine," as they call it, you can watch an endlessly repeating film loop highlighting several of its native sons leading the U.S. hockey team to victory over the Soviet Union in the 1980 Winter Olympics.

There are lakes in South Dakota, of course, but pretty muddy and unattractive in my experience. From as early as I can remember until I was ten years old, my mother gave each of us our own cardboard box to pack our stuff, and my whole family spent two luxurious weeks at Big Stone Lake, on the boundary between South Dakota and Minnesota. It was a special treat to go out fishing with my dad in the early morning and for my older sisters to meet boys at Hartford Beach. We all played in the water for hours.

I learned to swim, though, and for years swam nearly every summer day at the Terrace Park city pool. I still prefer pools to lakes. I like seeing the bottom and knowing where the edges are. No fish, either. I feel safer. Minnesotans, though, seem to prefer lakes.

Wherever one lives in Minnesota, going to the lake is a sacred ritual. No one would conclude that there's only one lake; nonetheless, almost all Minnesotans refer only to "the lake." Oddly, they never mean the really big lake, Superior; they call that the "North Shore" even though it's actually the lake's east shore, but never mind. It's all the other lakes that they call "the lake." Maybe they figure that there are so many lakes, and so many with the same name, that it's not worth naming their particular one. I mean, look, if you said you were going to Lake Alice, you could be going to one in Clearwater, Hubbard, Olmstead, Otter Tail, Pope, St. Louis, or Wilkin County. What good would it do, then, to say Lake Alice? It would only require more explanation (which Minnesotans are loathe to give).

And Alice isn't anywhere close to being one of the most common lake names. Nearly one hundred are called some version of Mud and another hundred named Long. Sixty-eight are called Rice (nine in Itasca County alone) and forty-eight are named Bass (ten of those in Itasca County, too). There are twelve Andersons; six Idas, two Mabels and two Ethels, three Josephines, four Johns, three Jacks and one Hungry Jack; five Potatos and two Pomme de Terres. My favorite names are Lost Honeymoon, the ever-hopeful Full-of-Fish, and the despairing Dead (four of them).

A few of those lakes carry Dakota or Menominee names, but more of them carry Ojibwa or Ojibwa-variant names testifying to the association of the Ojibwa with this watered part of the state. They are of the woods and the water, not the prairies.

Mrs. George H. Davis and her daughters, Alice and Kate, made a chronicle of their lake summers, not unlike the records that many Minnesotans have kept or, more often, wish they'd kept at their lakes. Mrs. Davis and her daughters started going to the lake in either 1912 or 1913 (they couldn't remember which) and spent their first few summers renting Spruce Cottage at the Pines, a small resort run by a Mrs. Osborne at Lake Hubert. (There is only one Lake Hubert in the state; it's in Crow Wing County, north of Brainerd, just above the geographic center of the state). In 1915, Mrs. Davis had a cabin of their own built, two lakes away, on Clark Lake (three of that name). On June 10 of that year, she and Kate and Alice arrived for a long, languorous summer at their new cabin, outhouse and all. That was part of the charm. All that summer, the Davises entertained friends and relatives. They swam, took walks, did needlepoint, rowed the boat, made Christmas wreaths, and took pictures of each other. Women weren't the only vacationers, but no Mr. Davis, Sr., ever showed up, nor did Kate and Alice's brother, Fred, a doctor in Faribault. In 1935, a carload of relatives from Tacoma, Washington, made the drive to the cabin and, as Mrs. Davis recounted in her book, next to the photographs of the relatives' departure, "To us their stay seemed all too short."

Despite their best intentions, but typically, I'm afraid, they kept their guest/memory/photo book "Summers at Clark Lake" intermittently. Even one of the Clarks noted that she regretted not having started the guest book in 1915. In 1950, they took to the book with a burst of vigorous energy, and Alice detailed a summer that anyone who's stayed at a lake would recognize:

June 21 baked cake
June 22 to Brainerd for shopping
   thunderstorm
   Mr. and Mrs. Bane called
June 25 to Lake Edward
June 26 Kate fell down stairs
June 30 Drove to dump

July 1 1st row on lake, saw blue heron
July 4 quiet day to ourselves . . .
July 19, 20, 21 blueberrying 8 quarts
Aug. 1 canned blueberries
    and made watermelon pickles

In 1954, a less energetic Kate reported, in the only entry for that year, that the girls were "late getting up this year because of ACD's arthritis." They held on for three more years, but in 1957, the sisters sold the cabin to a woman with the unlikely name of Marthena Drybread. In their final memory-book entry, Kate recalled "Built in 1915 used by KG and AD 42 summers." This isn't a South Dakota story, but it is a familiar one in Minnesota.

Family and state stories, identity, and history in all of Minnesota are steeped in water: the state's name, from "muddy or sky-tinted water"; the state's "Land of 10,000 Lakes" slogan, of course; even the state's shape. Big Stone and Traverse Lakes and the Red River of the North make up the western border. Lake of the Woods, Rainy and Namakan Lakes, Lac La Croix, a string of other lakes, and the Pigeon River form most of the northern boundary. Lake Superior and the St. Croix and Mississippi Rivers mark the eastern border. Those boundaries enclose 92,000 miles of rivers and "more shoreline than California, Florida and Hawaii combined." The two major community events in the Twin Cities are the summer Aquatennial in Minneapolis and the St. Paul Winter Carnival, which had an ice palace as its centerpiece in 2003.

Ojibwa and Dakota people contested control of water (Leech, Cass, and Red Lakes, for example); harvesting wild rice from canoes on northern lakes is still an important Ojibwa cultural activity; white explorers came and went by water; fur traders and trade routes depended on water; water-power milling was the state's first industry, and timber, one of its first products.

Oh, trees. Trees are the other thing. Where the essence and history of South Dakota have most to do with flat, dry, and open, Minnesota's essence and history have most to do with the combination of water and trees.

Of course there are also trees in South Dakota—a few anyway—but in my part of the state they're almost all planned and planted: Dutch elms in front of our house until disease took them all; three big evergreens in the back; a giant catalpa next door that shed petals we could turn into fingernails; and the apple tree across the street. The South Dakota mode, though, is a tree here and a tree there, not this mass of green on the horizon that I see outside the Collegeville house.

It's come as quite a surprise to me to learn that there are so many trees, worth looking at in themselves. My husband can recount the location of the red cedars, the bur oaks, the Norway pines along the route from Minneapolis to Collegeville. I've driven that same route three times a week for over a decade and I've noticed the lilac bushes.

He also knows and pays attention to every tree on the Collegeville property. While I'm scouting around for trees that we might cut down so that I can see something, my husband and the nurseryman have long conversations about which new tree to plant where. Wanting to include me, they ask what I want. For lack of anything else to say, I remember that a friend once oohed over a mountain ash, thereby individuating it from the rest of the green mass, so I say, why not a few mountain ashes. It's the only one I can think of to suggest.

It turns out that thirty-five species of trees are commonly found in Minnesota, and ninety-three are only found there. I'm embarrassed to say that I have had a bit of a hard time remembering what actually is the difference between coniferous and deciduous trees. (Since in reading for this essay I finally made the connection between cones and coniferous, I should be all right from now on.) I don't think that I'm really slow; it's just that my consciousness is neither leafed nor treed. Of the thirty-five, I can now identify my mountain ash and the box elders (especially if there are box-elder bugs around), maples, willows, cottonwoods, birches, and aspen. The other dozen common trees—locust, walnut, hickory, oak, elm, ironwood, hackberry, basswood, balsam, poplar, and cherry—might be identifiable to "real" Minnesotans, but they're beyond me. The evergreens, including the tamarack—which isn't, and the cedars, pines, firs, and spruce—all remain part of the green mass. Beautiful, but somehow without individual personalities.

While Minnesotans in the southwest and the west were madly planting trees in the dirty 1930s, an army of Civilian Conservation Corps workers was deployed across northeastern Minnesota to thin, prune, and clear trees and to fight forest fires. There were six CCC camps in Itasca County alone. The tree thinners were only slightly more successful than the tree planters at changing the natural environment.

Outsiders seem often to think of all of Minnesota—and the rest of the Midwest—as remote. Minnesotans deny it and make a virtue of it. Aleut and Eskimo people don't, apparently, really have a lot of words for snow, but Minnesotans do have various notions of "remote." In the state imagination, the southwestern and western part of Minnesota is remote and desolate. The remote of the north and northeast, however, is heaven.

I went to college in Marshall, Minnesota. I expected to find language classes and history and literature, philosophy and chemistry. I didn't expect to discover nature. I didn't expect to find a different way of looking at the landscape and of feeling about it. My friends came from exotic-sounding places: Silver Lake, Bird Island, Sleepy Eye. They knew birds and wildflowers. They knew about Lake Agassiz and how its melting created a riverbed far too big for the Minnesota River that currently runs through it. They even gave me words for what I hadn't previously seen: Robert Bly's description of trees in a valley as "heavy green smoke close to the ground." Or, Robert Frost's view of spring "Nature's first green is gold, Her hardest hue to hold."

Perhaps this discovery was an accident or the natural result of college life in a rural place. But I've come to believe that it was the work of Minnesota itself, through the instrument of my friends, Minnesotans every one of them. They lived out and taught a particularly Minnesotan relationship to the land, a connection that was intense and immediate and, in that southwestern part of the state, full of longing.

They shared a soulful yearning to be elsewhere. Down there in southwestern Minnesota, many seemed to feel as if they had been exiled to some domestic Siberia. Not because of the cold (we all had that), and it wasn't the hunger for Los Angeles or New York or even Minneapolis that one might expect in such a rural place. They pined, instead, for some more northern place with more water and more trees.

"Up North," including Lake Superior, actually looks quite a bit like the real Siberia, including Lake Baikal: forests, bog lands, lakes and more lakes. But exile? Hardly! The heart of Minnesota and Minnesotans beats most strongly here amid those trees and lakes, on the rivers and in the woods. It's the end of the earth, for sure, but the end where a lot of Minnesotans would prefer to live if they could, if there were enough jobs, if . . . if . . . if. . . . This place nurtures dreams and fires the imagination. Ely, International Falls, Grand Marais, Superior National Forest, Chippewa National Forest, the Boundary Waters Canoe Area. They're all remote, but when you get there you're somewhere, somewhere special and magic.

After college, I left Minnesota for the East Coast and then for graduate school. I'd caught the Minnesota disease, though, so I wrote my dissertation on a Minnesota topic to make sure that I would find my way back. I did, and I've lived here more or less since 1980. I'm almost a native. I'd love to have a lake cabin. I can identify dozens of birds. I've even taken to walking in the woods around our Collegeville house. But I'm still not quite a Minnesotan. When I drive down to see my dad in Sioux Falls, I feel myself start to breathe easier as the landscape flattens out and opens up, as those trees get out of the way and big, flat farm fields take over. My claustrophobia lifts. I relax. I'm reminded that I'm a South Dakotan at heart by how good I feel when I get out of the woods and into the open.

Minnesotans, though, Minnesotans are different. Their relationship to the land is part of who they are, part of how they understand themselves and one another, certainly part of how they make sense out of the world. It's not just that they have an impulse to hike, camp, canoe, fish, boat, ski, hunt—anything that gets them into the woods and onto the water—though they certainly do have that.

It's something more. It's something deeper and more personal, somehow. It's this passion, this visceral connection to trees and water that informs Minnesota history, identity, and life. It's this impulse that makes Minnesotans Minnesotan.

Annette Atkins
St. John's University, Minnesota

Missouri

When you grow up in Missouri, as I did, you look at maps. It's not just that you're scheming (as many midwestern kids do) about how you're ever going to get out of this place, but that you're confronted with the problem of figuring out just where this place *is*. Betweenness is the Missourian's lot in life. Studying the map on the bedroom wall, it didn't take me long to figure out that my state was bordered (some might say hemmed in) by more than any other, or that it was bigger than every state east of it and smaller (with only a couple of exceptions) than any to the west. Or that, if I stretched my hand across those record-setting eight border states and onto the states that *they* connected with—then, like a boy with seventy-league boots, I could stretch from North Carolina clear to Wyoming, from Minnesota to Texas, without taking one finger off of home base. I thought we deserved some sort of prize for such geographic peculiarities, and I still do.

Instead, as I discovered, Missourians pay for their centrality with chronic episodes of geographic delusions of grandeur. Is it any surprise that it was a Missourian—the transcontinental railway advocate Senator Thomas Hart Benton—whom history remembers for pointing west in 1849 and saying, "There is the East"? That another, Logan Uriah Reavis, would thirty years later willingly endure public ridicule by delegating to himself the task of relocating the nation's capital to St. Louis, a place whose central location, he promised, made it "the future great city of America"? Or that the state's best-known literary navigators, Huckleberry Finn and the runaway slave Jim, would manage, disastrously, to drift so far south that they were unable to go east, and thence north, to freedom?

As a late-twentieth-century St. Louisan, my own sense of global orientation was only slightly less ambitious, slightly more dependable. Lying awake at night, fiddling with the tuning knob of a small transistor radio, I listened for precious fragments of a local-news broadcast, a Chinese-restaurant commercial, a hotel-ballroom dance from Chicago, from New York City, even from Miami. Halstead Street, Times Square, Collins Avenue seemed as close to me, in my midcontinental perch, as the corner store. Just past the middle of the dial, the Red Sea of radio static parted to make way for KMOX, the local AM giant whose nightly call-in shows drew insomniacs and night-shift workers from across middle America. Their cacophonous twangs and drawls, shooting through far-flung telephone wires into a small, fluorescent-lit studio located (I imagined) atop an otherwise dark downtown skyscraper, were beamed back out from St. Louis across a flat landscape of rapt porch-sitters that stretched from the North Woods down to the Gulf Coast.

But as a Missourian grows older, he learns that at least some other kids, lulled to sleep by the sounds of a California surf or New Jersey freeway traffic, picture his state not as the nerve center of civilization but as a cultural black hole, populated by Jed Clampetts and Ma and Pa Kettles and threatening to suck into its vortex anyone who makes the mistake of flying too low over the unfortunate dark spot that separates Hollywood from Manhattan Island. (That is, if they picture it at all.) To a person, the acquaintances I would make at my eastern college knew less about my home than I did about theirs. Yet my knowledge of Manhattan theatre listings or Miami coffee shop menus, I found, did little to dim the letters of the neon "rube" sign that somehow attached itself to my head each time I announced where I was from. "Missouri." Even the name, it seems, suggested to them an unfortunate emotional condition.

Still, like many who actually enjoy languishing in the state of Misery, I learned not to be bothered by my fellow citizens' ignorance of their nation's vital center. So what if America's elite didn't know—waiting for their lunch dates at the corner of 59th Street and Fifth Avenue in New York (beside the [Joseph] Pulitzer Fountain and the General William T. Sherman statue), suiting up for their lacrosse games at Berkeley (in the Phoebe Apperson Hearst Gymnasium), meeting for cocktails in the Adolphus (Busch) Hotel in Dallas, posing for pictures atop the Continental Divide at (John C.) Fremont Pass, reading about the latest Robert Altman movie in Clay Felker's trendy *New York* magazine, watching Walter Cronkite while leaning back in their (Charles) Eames chairs—that it was Missourians who shaped their daily experience of the world? Did they really think I cared? That I was *keeping score*? Please. (That's nine, but we're not done yet.)

Besides their shared burden of secretly shaping American culture, it may be argued that Missourians share little in common with one another. Despite their dutiful adherence to the sobriquet "Show-Me State" (a vaguely attributed expression of stubborn pride that seems to me not particularly distinctive; does anyone ever claim to come from the "If You Say So, It Must be True State"? Surely it's time to come up with a new nickname), there truly is little besides sales tax that holds the state's residents together. You may not know it, but every non–St. Louis Missourian who began reading this essay has since turned the page. It's true; they did so at the beginning of paragraph three, when I identified myself as a St. Louisan and they muttered, "Yeah, like he knows something about Missouri."

It is hard for me to blame them. It was after all the people of St. Louis themselves who, in 1875, sought to escape from Missouri's clutches by passing the nation's first home-rule ordinance, and it was St. Louis's deputy mayor who, as recently as 1997, milked local laughs by posing the riddle, "What do you get when you take St. Louis and Kansas City out of Missouri?" (answer: "Arkansas"). For their own part, residents of various parts of Missouri have, at times in the state's history, tied themselves more closely to the culture and economy of Tennessee plantation owners, Mississippi sharecroppers, Kansas ranchers, or Rhineland dairy farmers than they have to their neighbors in the state's largest city. St. Louis itself, for that matter, has never exactly projected a clear civic identity. This is the city that in the mid-nineteenth century was home to a Democratic party newspaper (the *Republican*) and a Republican newspaper (the *Democrat*), that divides its surrounding county into more than ninety suburban municipalities (some with a population of fewer than one hundred souls), and that considers itself the logical home to both a Mardi Gras and a Strassenfest.

The cultural output of the Split Personality State (there, how's that?) bespeaks similarly unresolved divides. Imagine yourself in Mississippi, for the moment, and think about music and literature. The images come readily enough to mind. Southern writers. Delta blues. In Montana, it seems, anyone who applies pen to paper becomes a "Westerner." Minnesotans, proud of their stoic small-town image, might allow for a literary range just wide enough to include Sinclair Lewis and Garrison Keillor. Strong artistic traditions, and an equally strong body of self-affirming critical literature, have taught us what to expect of the writers, artists, and musicians who hail from these and other states. How, then, to account for a place that produces Charlie Parker as well as Porter Waggoner, Chuck Berry as well as Reinhold Niebuhr, Tennessee Williams as well as Lanford Wilson, Langston Hughes as well as Walt Disney? (Seventeen; since you get the point, we'll leave it at that.) To say that these and other talents all came from Missouri says little or nothing about the state's ability to inspire intellectual and artistic creativity; less still about its ability to retain creative individuals (with the exception of Chuck, they all left). Were it New York City, Los Angeles, or Chicago, such cultural overlays might furnish us with evidence of the magnetic powers of a vibrant cultural hearth. In Missouri, they simply attest to the happenstance by which the flotsam of a variety of unassimilated cultural traditions has washed up on the same interior shore.

The landscape of the You Must Be on Your Way Somewhere Else State mirrors its people's disparate cultural identities. It is here that the huddled brick Main Streetscape of the original "national road" (later, U.S. Highway 40) meets the souvenir-stand-and-tourist-court sprawl of its western successor, Route 66. The motorist entering the state from the east encounters a St. Louis streetscape of brick warehouses, begrimed factories, and high-rise housing projects; she departs the state five hours later looking out over the wide streets, frame houses, and front porches of Kansas City, while the sun sets over the dry prairie west of the Missouri River. Somewhere between these east- and west-facing urban andirons, she might have chosen either to diverge north—into a forty-acre checkerboard landscape of soybean and hog farms, small towns, and railroad crossings—or south, among the winding roads of the Ozark and St. Francois Mountains, where town names still reflect the aspirations of the Spanish- and French-colonial founders who dreamed of gold and silver and settled for iron and lead. If there is a middle ground connecting these barely reconcilable landscapes, then perhaps we can credit the state's early legislators for finding it in the city that they named for Thomas Jefferson—the state capital, a place whose chief claim to distinction may be that lawmakers could flee from it with equal speed in any direction.

The legislative dilemmas that occupy the representatives of the Awfully Hard to Govern State, when they do sojourn in sleepy Jefferson City, are not atypical of those facing most states with strong urban/rural divides: mass transit versus highway financing, gun control versus concealed-weapon permits—and their solutions all look quite different according to whether one represents Knox County, with its population density of 8 people per square mile, or the city of St. Louis, where the same area houses more than 5,000. Occasionally, as Benton managed to do in the early nineteenth century, there appears a politician capable of uniting urban and rural interests and taking their support into a position of national leadership: Stuart Symington, a patrician Democrat from St. Louis, gathered up sufficient small-town support to fashion himself a serious Senate power broker in the 1950s and 1960s; Republican John Ashcroft, the Springfield native and one-time governor who appealed to conservative interests both in the farm belt and in the affluent metropolitan suburbs, lost his own senatorial reelection bid in 2000 only to see George W. Bush grant him the opportunity of becoming one of the most activist attorneys general in recent history. Yet even as it offers a proving ground for lawmakers testing their skill in bridging political gaps, Missouri is no Indiana or Ohio, churning out presidential and vice-presidential candidates who "look like America." Only Ulysses S. Grant and Harry S Truman—the latter by the thinnest of margins—have been elected to national office, and in the period between 1964 and the time of this writing, when every U.S. president other than Gerald Ford has come to office from a Sun Belt state, rusty Missouri has shown itself only in George McGovern's abortive choice of Senator Thomas Eagleton to join him aboard the sinking ship of the 1972 Democratic presidential campaign.

What of the future of the Most Frequently Bordered State? No longer "the center of our Western operations," as Jefferson described St. Louis at the time of the Louisiana Purchase, Missouri long ago ceased to function as the entrepôt for a nascent continental empire. By the early twentieth century, when its early status as way station for the entire colonizing enterprise had given way to its current, less dramatic position as transition point between multiple cultural regions—a place between, rather than a place beyond—Missouri had lost some of the capital and creative fuel that stoked the engines of its early growth. Yet the legacy of that earlier time, and of the environmental features that favored the state's early growth, colors the experiences of Missouri's 5.6 million residents today. St. Louis's "initial advantage" (to borrow the geographers' term) as a western urban outpost contributed to a lasting infrastructure of political, cultural, and religious resources there—from a U.S. circuit court of appeals to the nation's second-oldest symphony orchestra to a Catholic basilica—that outweighs anything one expects of the nation's eighteenth-largest metropolitan area. Because the Great Plains will never be extensively urbanized, Kansas City remains the metropole for a vast western hinterland. In few places does the once-dominant French influence on the American interior rise more closely to the surface than it does in the houses of Ste. Genevieve or the clashing street grids of St. Louis. The Missouri River Valley's remnant landscape of German-settled farms and towns rivals Pennsylvania's for its scenery and architecture and, past hamlets that Samuel Clemens knew as a boy, the Mississippi—locked and dammed though it may be—does indeed keep rollin' along, and in dramatic fashion.

While twenty-first-century Missouri will still reflect such indelible influences, it will likely bear, as well, the mark of Bosnians, Vietnamese, Eritreans, Mexicans, and others who have in recent decades found their way there through the cordon of bordering states. With a foreign-born population of under 3 percent, the state is still a long way from being California—or even, for that matter, nineteenth-century Missouri. But its diversifying population, in the wake of post-1966 immigration laws and recent global refugee movements, suggests that international influence on the state will wax again. On the other side of the globalization coin, a Wal-Mart is a Wal-Mart. The outskirts of a Missouri town no longer differ from those of any other American town. Today's restless twelve-year-old need not fiddle desperately with the aerial on his AM radio for a faint glimmer of the Chicago news; he turns on CNN and instantly finds himself facing the same images being conveyed to viewers in Bangkok and Baghdad. Today, the residents of anywhere in the United States, flooded as they are with crosscurrents of global culture and information, are as liable as Huck Finn to lose their bearings, to find themselves adrift in a world at once strange and too familiar. But those who live in more cosmopolitan cities, or along international borders, where such developments have been longer in coming, are likelier to make their way through the fog and to find their course once more, to draw on the good effects of internationalization and resist the bad.

It has been a long time since Missourians knew what it was to live along the uneasy line between British and French empires, between Union and Confederate territory, between urban East and untamed West. Long since curled up in the comfortable lap of the Midwest, Missourians may have to learn all over again of the disorientation—and the creative potential—that come from living amidst the flows of international capital, culture, and people that once more travel across the center of the continent as easily as they do along its more exposed edges. To get along in this new world, the Missourians of the future may need to let down their stubborn guards, swallow their mulish pride, throw up their arms and surrender to the once and, I am now prepared to admit, future state motto, saying—albeit with new meaning—"I'm from Missouri: Show Me."

Eric Sandweiss
Indiana University–Bloomington

Nebraska

The vast grasslands between the Missouri River and the Front Range of the Rocky Mountains are a landscape of square boundaries because there are few obvious natural boundaries. The rolling hills of one state seem to run seamlessly into the rolling hills of the next. But like so much of the geography, culture, politics, economics, biology, and life of this center region of the continent, the boundaries *are* there; they are sometimes subtle, not apparent to the casual eye, and they are made all the less obvious by modern travel, when crossing what were once almost-impossible barriers like the Missouri River is accomplished in a moment, perhaps totally missed if you happen to be tuning the radio in your car or reading a magazine in an airliner. But to those who live in and love eastern Nebraska, the area is distinctive nonetheless.

Eastern Nebraska is defined on its eastern and northern edges by the unequivocal barrier of the Missouri River (and, to a lesser degree in the north, the Niobrara River). Indeed, the Missouri River boundary was seen as so formidable for the frontier, so considerable, that travelers coming from the East knew those hills across the wide, turbulent river as "The Nebraska Coast," as if it were on the other side of an ocean. Soon enough, however, the waters that were once considered a wide moat making expansion almost impossible became the very waterway that carried the frontier to the Nebraska prairies, as steamboats came to use the river as a quick, relatively cheap, and easy passage from St. Louis, Missouri, to Brownville, Nebraska City, and Omaha, Nebraska.

To the south, the loess hills and limestone outcroppings of Nebraska fade with little distinction into the Kansas hills and quarries, but perhaps the most interesting transition of the area is to the west, slowly ascending the slope of the continent across the Plains toward the Rocky Mountains. Within the relatively short distance of a couple hundred miles from the Missouri River to the Nebraska Sandhills, the largest sand-dune area in the Western Hemisphere, a few hours on Interstate 80, minutes in a transcontinental flight, one travels eastward from the woodland prairies of the Missouri-Mississippi basin to the drier, upland short-grass lands of what was once called "the Great American Desert." During the nineteenth century, railroads organized celebratory trips, in fact, from the East to the hundredth meridian, roughly where Cozad, Nebraska, is today, so that adventurers could step off the train, look up the rails ahead, and say with all truth that they had actually seen "The West." Even today, Nebraska communities from Omaha to Scottsbluff boast that they are the Gateway to the West.

That transition from East to West is far more meaningful, however, than the mere length of the native grasses or an invisible line superimposed across rail lines. There are changes in soils, topographical definition, waterways, and rainfall from the East to the West that result in dramatic differences in population density, economic foundations, social understandings, political attitudes, and historical backgrounds. Eastern Nebraska is farm country; the rich loess and river-bottom soils offer heavy earth with gentle surface profiles. In contrast to the even heavier soils in a much wetter Iowa to the east, eastern Nebraska fields, mostly wind-deposited loess and glacial soils in the northeastern parts of the state, are never tiled to run off excessive soil-level moisture, and yet dry-land crops are common.

While the hundredth meridian offered the drama of a grand round number, native Nebraskan author Wright Morris, who spent his youth about one hundred feet west of the ninety-eighth meridian in Central City, Nebraska, was perhaps more accurate when he wrote in the opening paragraph of *Works of Love* (1951), "West of the 98th Meridian—where it sometimes rains and it sometimes doesn't." Lincoln, Nebraska, the state's capital, expects about twenty-five to thirty inches of rain annually. Ogallala, only three hundred miles to the west, gets only fifteen to twenty inches.

It is therefore not so much a cohesive and central nature that defines eastern Nebraska as it is a matter of its role as a dramatic and relatively rapid transition between the larger, more homogeneous regions to the east and west. It is across this relatively narrow band of tallgrass prairies on rolling glacial and wind-formed hills that many eastern and western species of plants, birds, and animals meet, often in narrow biological bridges formed by the river valleys of the Republican, Platte, and Niobrara Rivers in Nebraska.

The same could be said for the region's human occupants: Eastern Nebraska prefers to see itself as urban. Eastern Nebraska looks for its cultural models to the East. While Nebraskans to the west of Kearney or North Platte look to the state's only cities, Omaha and Lincoln, with great suspicion and, sometimes, contempt, eastern Nebraskans want theirs to be seen as cultural equivalents to the shining cities of the East. Lincoln and Omaha are quite different from each other and see themselves as rivals, rather than sister urban enclaves in a sea of corn, the state's principal crop. Omaha started as a rollicking, hard-bitten river town; it is seen by everyone else in the state, including Lincoln, as a crime-ridden, dangerous town with slums, environmental pollution, and all the other vices and failings of any "city." Omaha is a labor town, with a history of slaughterhouses, racial strife, and congestion. Lincoln, on the other hand, prides itself on being a white-collar, intellectual, university town, with clean industries like insurance companies, government administration, and technology. The reality is that Omaha is in many ways the cultural "center" of Nebraska, with a symphony, a major art gallery, world-class zoos, and opera, while Lincoln with its accelerating growth is experiencing a rise also in exactly the

kinds of things it likes to consider its differences from Omaha . . . congestion, crime, and pollution.

The differences between Nebraska's two urban centers are rapidly becoming moot: The distance between Omaha and Lincoln grows less daily as the corridor between them on Interstate 80 fills in with businesses and residential developments. Fifty years ago, the distance between Lincoln and Omaha was considered to be about sixty-five or seventy miles; today that distance is more like forty-five or fifty miles, not much more than a half hour from city limit to city limit, as the cities grow ever closer to each other.

Perhaps the most prominent and generally accepted unifying cultural factor in Nebraska is its perennial University of Nebraska at Lincoln top-ten football team, but even the ferocious devotion that makes Memorial Stadium at the university the third-largest city in the state on football Saturdays causes division: The team mascot, Herbie Husker, is for many Nebraskans a profound embarrassment . . . for the easterners because the bumpkin image detracts from the wish to be seen as cosmopolitan, and for the westerners because the mascot's overalls and bucolic manner are a denial of their cattle-based, westward-looking culture. Small wonder that there are persistent discussions (and occasionally half-serious efforts) on the part of western Nebraskans to "secede" from the state, perhaps joining instead with Wyoming, to establish a new political reality reflecting their very real emotional, cultural, and economic ties with the West.

The bifurcation is not arbitrary. It is based on geographic and economic realities. Nor is it new. Plains Indian populations during the eighteenth and nineteenth centuries reflected the same kind of division: earth-lodge-dwelling farmers—Omaha, Oto, Ponca—in the east; tipi-living nomadic hunters—Lakota, Cheyenne, Arapaho—in the west. The tribes encountered each other perhaps most often on their hunts and travels along the natural route of the Platte River, the single most distinctive and significant geographic feature of the state and, indeed, the very source of its name. "Nebraska" is a distortion of the Omaha word for "broad water," also the foundation for the French name for the river, "Platte."

Curiously, the Platte River, without question the most prominent and influential "boundary" in Nebraska, runs not along an edge of the region but right through its heart. The Platte River is one of the world's most dramatic aggradational rivers, not carving a canyon down into the earth but bringing alluvial soils, sands, and gravels down from the mountains and depositing them ever deeper for millions of years on the plains. The river is hundreds of yards wide between shallow banks and is rarely more than waist deep, sometimes during dry summers completely dry from bank to bank. Despite its shallowness, however, its quicksands and unpredictable holes and channels have historically been a formidable barrier in the state, during settlement years crossable only in the deep winter when it is frozen but with very dangerous holes and hidden channels even then. During the state's formation, the struggle to locate the capital was more than a matter of civic pride: The painful fact was that whoever wound up on the other side of the Platte River from the new capital city would be at a profound disadvantage in business and politics. The name change of the capital city from Lancaster to Lincoln was in fact engineered by Omaha boosters hoping southern sympathies during the Civil War period would be strong enough to keep the capital in *Douglas* County rather than in the city of *Lincoln*. Travel considerations prevailed, however, and Lincoln was nonetheless named capital city of the new state . . . but even then, to thwart Omaha subversions, a contingent of raiding Lincolnites went to the Nebraska Territory capitol, purloined the state seal, and carried it back to Lincoln . . . across the frozen Platte River!

And yet, east and west, the Platte River has historically been the travel route across Nebraska. Tribal people of eastern Nebraska used the broad, flat valley of the Platte for travel to and from the buffalo grounds and the flint quarries of what is now northeastern Wyoming. The Oregon, Mormon, Overland, and Pony Express trails used this same route, with some accommodations to the Platte's singular configurations. Just as the Platte contrarily is depositing alluvial materials rather than gouging out a canyon, it also flows perversely across the landscape. If the river flowed as one might expect—directly across the plains and into the Missouri River, its valley becoming ever wider until it empties into the Missouri—travel across the continent in the early years of settlement would have been much easier. But instead, the Platte makes an inconvenient detour starting near the city of Columbus and the confluence of the Loup River forks with the Platte, going not southeast toward the Missouri but in a huge arc northward, to the current location of Fremont, then plunging twenty-five miles south again to Ashland, finally resuming its eastward course toward the Missouri valley.

Apparently not done with its antic behavior, at Ashland the immense valley of the Platte narrows to less than a half mile, rimmed on each side by steep, heavily eroded limestone cliffs. Thus when travelers on the Oregon, Mormon, or Overland trails were beginning their travels in March, April, or May, the flooding Platte might fill the narrow gorge from valley wall to valley wall. Even if there were no floods, the valley was so narrow there was scarcely room for a road, a reality still true today. So Mormon travelers started their journey near what is now the northern edge of Omaha, following the north side of the Platte and then the Loup Rivers, eventually crossing the Loup and rejoining the Platte near Grand Island. The Oregon and Pony Express trails began on the Missouri River near Kansas City or Nebraska City and crossed open prairie, reaching and traveling along the south bank of the Platte anywhere between Grand Island or Kearney, then westward along the river's south bank.

Despite advancing technologies, the annoying, trickster nature of the Platte remains a reality. Railroad builders loved the broad, flat lands along the Platte to the west . . . but they still had to deal with the curious behavior of the river to the east. The interstate highway avoids the Platte until it reaches Grand Island, where builders could take advantage of the broad, flat, gently rising surface—and abundant construction gravels!—the Platte affords from there west. Conveniently spaced bridges now span the wide, shallow river every couple dozen miles, but it is still a rare winter when some community or other along its banks is not plagued by ice gorges at the bridges and lowland flooding. The Platte has been tamed but not conquered. Its waters are now also diverted at several places for recreation, power generation, and irrigation, so it remains one of the state's most important, if troublesome, resources.

The Platte River has not only determined the topography, history, and economics of Nebraska, it has also profoundly affected perceptions of the state. Perhaps the most common adjective used to describe Nebraska by those who have seen it only from trains, Interstate 80, or Highway 30—the Lincoln Highway—is "flat." Those most commonly traveled routes naturally take advantage of the broad, flat "divide" lands in the east and the river bottoms to the west, and so the traveler sees only flat landscape. A side trip along any other route, however, quickly dispels that misperception. Eastern Nebraska's surface has been determined by wind, glaciers, and water erosion, all three producing a rolling landscape drained by many small, tree-lined waterways.

The Platte River's role in determining the direction of eastern Nebraska is still very active. Nebraska's population is heavily concentrated along the eastern edge of the state. Half the state's population of roughly two million people is concentrated along the first tier of eastern counties, within 50 miles of the Missouri River, leaving the other half scattered across the immense 350 miles of the rest of the state. While that fact is not likely to change for a while, there is another dynamic at work. Most counties of Nebraska are losing population. That is not surprising. Farms are growing larger and larger and becoming ever more mechanized, which means that fewer and fewer people are needed to operate them. So people are leaving the rural countryside, naturally going where there are other economic opportunities: more heavily populated areas. Moreover, the grinding economics of agriculture today mean that in order to farm, a family has to have another source of income. In some cases, a spouse takes a nonagricultural job to support the farming operation, or a farmer may work at another job part of the day and farm in whatever time remains. Jobs mean communities. So population is also shifting, not simply to eastern Nebraska but to the long chain of communities along the transportation routes following the Platte Valley. As the population in outlying counties of Nebraska grows smaller, the populations of communities along the Platte River are growing, thus creating a new, unifying, linear megacommunity. The name *Nebraska*, meaning the Platte River, may become ever more appropriate in the future as the state becomes truly a state centered on the river for which it was named.

Similarly, it was hoped that increased travel opportunities across Nebraska would bring more visitors and build an appreciation and understanding of the state's subtle beauty and interest, but its four hundred miles have gone even more out of focus as travelers speed through on the crowded interstate highway system, seeing and learning little of what the area has to offer. Air travel in the state is almost nonexistent outside of Lincoln and Omaha, making Nebraska truly little more than a "flyover state," with its air travelers seeing only a blanket of clouds or a patchwork of vaguely green or brown squares and blotches far below them.

Politically, Nebraska is an enigma. It is frequently touted as being the most conservative state outside the Deep South and yet it belies any such stereotyping by electing again and again Democrats, from state offices to the U.S. Congress. Omaha, which is a strong labor center and historically the most racially diverse community in the state, is, perversely, Republican; Lincoln, a corporate city, votes Democratic (this moderate liberalism is usually attributed to the university population). Perhaps most accurately, Nebraskans tend to vote in accordance with personal connections, inclinations, and impressions rather than along political lines: Nebraskans vote for people they like, thus accounting for the recent election of a university football coach with virtually no agricultural experience in the overwhelmingly agricultural Third District of Nebraska, representing most of the state other than Lincoln and Omaha. This is reflected, or perhaps even encouraged, by Nebraska's political system, which features the only unicameral, or one-house, nonpartisan legislature in the nation.

A similar internal contradiction persists within the ethnic and cultural makeup of Nebraska. While there is a persistent nostalgia for the immigrant roots of Nebraska communities—largely German, Slavic, and Scandinavian—and almost every town with even a hint of an ethnic past has an annual festival to celebrate it, the prevailing atmosphere is one of dogged and insistent Americanism, a disregard for ethnicity that is too close to its roots, and a preference for artificial cultural re-creation as opposed to anything that is too accurate to conform to a modern American comfort level for foreignness. So a community may celebrate its German roots one day a year but is not likely to make much of a point of that provenance the rest of the time; while one may hear a lament in the morning on Main Street in a community with a Danish heritage that Danish is no longer heard there on a daily basis, before the sun sets there will also be a complaint that newer immigrants to the area are still speaking Spanish two years into their tenancy!

While the Omaha Tribe at Macy, on the Missouri River an hour north of the city of Omaha, and the adjacent Winnebago reservation represent an ancient past—the Omahas are still on land they have occupied for at least four centuries—most Nebraska communities are surprisingly young. Europeans and visitors from the eastern United States are surprised and sometimes amused at the seriousness with which Nebraska towns celebrate centennials, a solemnity that suggests great antiquity when, even in the history of this young nation, a century is little more than a good first step, little more than four generations. At many such celebrations, the town will honor a citizen who is older than the town itself . . . the point seldom being noted that the town has persisted actually no more than the span of one single lifetime!

Nebraskans are the last people to ask what their home region has to offer the visitor or prospective new resident because the state's most valuable assets are subtle, everyday. There are no dramatic scenery or stunning cultural features, no gigantic sources of wealth, no sites of powerful historical impact. The people who live here have come to take their most valuable assets as everyday features of normal life, no more or less than anyone would expect for a decent life.

There is, however, no scarcity of charming small towns and farmsteads with remarkably friendly and honest people; a wealth of beauty in ripening wheat and milo fields and crystal-clear nights with more stars than anyone imagined exist; an incredible variety in weather phenomena from arctic blizzards to withering heat waves quickly forgotten by Nebraska natives interspersed with the occasional placid, idyllic days and nights that the meteorologically amnesiac Nebraskan somehow comes to identify as "typical." Residents still rarely lock their house or car doors. It is considered a common courtesy to wave at anyone you encounter driving toward you on a Nebraska road . . . even strangers. At a small-town café, strangers may find locals joining them at the table and asking how much rain they had over at their place. And the meal will be hot roast beef with plenty of potatoes and gravy, homemade bread, a Jell-O–based salad, and homemade pie with ice cream for dessert, suggesting a presumption that the diner may not be finding another place to eat for the next day or two.

Nebraskans seem to be a little embarrassed by that kind of "Mayberry RFD" image of their homeland and yet they feel an intense affection for their home and a pride when visitors and newcomers recognize the Heartland, homeland character of their state. A distinctive frontier humor survives in the regional affection for the tall tale and the rigor it suggests: "Hot enough for you?" "Cold enough for you?" "Dry enough for you?" The first and central format of any Nebraska conversation is the weather, almost always an expression of how miserable it is. "Too windy to load rocks," "So dry I saw two trees chasing a dog," "So cold folks were going to church just to hear about hell" . . . nowhere in the world does the art of the tall tale prosper as it does in Nebraska. As in pioneer days, laughter is an important method for dealing with adversity—perhaps the only method. Just as the adversity persists, so too does the sense of humor.

Nebraska is something of a backwater, the last place reached by the fashions and fads of the West Coast and the East Coast. That is occasionally a reason for mockery by those who consider the mode of the day, or week, or month important. But for others who find cultural stability and long-term vision more attractive, Nebraska offers a solid rock of tradition and cold-eyed consideration of the newfangled. The single most important factor in my own relocation from the city of Lincoln, insofar as it can be considered a city, to Dannebrog, population 352, was a conversation with a local resident one of the first times I looked down the short, dusty, dead-quiet main street. I looked at the dogs sleeping in the shade of the grocery store and asked, "What do you folks do in this town for excitement?" My new friend said wisely and movingly, "We don't get excited in this town."

Roger Welsch
Dannebrog, Nebraska

North Dakota

To live in North Dakota is to live with the sky pulled open. The view of the world is unobstructed—often startling—winter, summer, spring, and fall, the earth at times meeting the sky in a panorama of brilliant colors and at other times as a subtle demarcation between monochromatic tones. The natural, physical world is open and enormously large, its level topography and the state's low population making boundlessness North Dakota's defining characteristic. That part of the state identifies with the Midwest and part with the West doesn't interfere with the view. Yet in the hopefulness of expansive vistas where everything seems possible, North Dakota hides nothing. With the pulse of progress long attached to outside demand for agricultural and energy-related raw products, the state's ups and downs remain as visible as its dramatic seasons and stunning sunrises and sunsets.

That isn't to say that North Dakota and its people lack complexity. The ongoing struggle for a state identity able to bridge midwestern and western attitudes, deal with urban and rural concerns, meld Native American and middle-American values, and connect it all to economic progress is nothing if not complicated. However, the state's physical openness is a metaphor for the straightforward, what-you-see-is-what-you-get attitude that North Dakotans appreciate. People are not puffed up—just cautious and a bit defensive about being the butt of national jokes, to be sure—yet generally welcoming and caring. Life is good where the air is clean and the ducks fly low, and most residents don't yearn to live elsewhere. Unfortunately, the pace of economic decline in most parts of the state makes the desire to remain moot. Young adults—five or more generations removed from immigrants who staked their future on homesteads—now expect to migrate elsewhere. And unlike many of their parents and grandparents, who left the state to see something of the world comfortable knowing that sooner or later they would return, young people today see North Dakota as a great place to grow up and get an education. Nevertheless, they expect it will be a place they're likely to view through a rearview mirror for the rest of their lives. Particularly those growing up on farms and ranches or in small towns see uncertainty all around them. Their parents and grandparents, struggling to keep farms viable or Main Street businesses alive, teach them by example that loving the land and rural life—even with hard work and perseverance—isn't necessarily enough to make a living. In messages spoken and unspoken, young people learn that their chances for success are greater if they leave the state.

Strong emotional ties tell them something else, however. Ties to family and to a reservoir of spiritual refreshment (which North Dakotans are sheepish to talk about even to one another) pull at and puzzle those who leave. Unfortunately, that magnetism, theoretically capable of repopulating the state with native sons and daughters, is hampered by the iffy nature of economic opportunity awaiting them once they return. North Dakota is more likely to keep accidental migrants, those people whose careers land them in the state only to discover—usually to their surprise—that they have found a wonderful place to live and raise their families. Of course, accidental migrants almost always move into the larger North Dakota cities with lively business, educational, cultural, and social communities. Small towns rarely benefit. And unfortunately, the same pattern holds true for present-day immigrants, the highest number in recent years coming from the former Yugoslavia and sub-Saharan Africa. Brought to North Dakota through programs of Lutheran Social Services, today's immigrants are settled in cities, primarily Fargo and Grand Forks, where there are jobs, social agencies, and others from their homelands to help them adjust. Unlike the Scandinavian and German immigrants who settled the state over a century ago, their hopes and dreams are not bound to the land.

Contrary to what the rest of the country might expect, weather isn't a major factor in the out-migration of young people well aware that their birthplace of extremes is a healthful place to live. Usually known for stoicism, North Dakotans are uncharacteristically immodest in believing that their heartiness and longevity stem from resilience born of cold and heat. (Lots of states get cold in the winter or hot in the summer. But only one registered 60 degrees below zero and 120 degrees above zero in the same calendar year, extremes that occurred in North Dakota in 1936). Oddly enough, winter weather can figure into the visceral desire to return, particularly when former North Dakotans find themselves living in nearby states. Cold and snow make for a common experience throughout the Midwest, but in North Dakota, winter elements come in mythic proportion. Nature cannot be finessed when temperatures plunge to 45 degrees below zero, blizzards roar on unimpeded arctic winds, and staying alive is the order of the day. In those inevitable, life-threatening storms, old survival stories resurface and new ones take root. As birthright, the sagas of man/woman versus nature are woven deeply into the warp and weft of the state's cultural fabric, history, and folklore. And while tornadoes, grasshoppers, fires, and floods all have their place, the most gripping stories are blizzard-based. North Dakotans enjoy grumbling that winter is long and tiresome and spring no more than a few days between winter's cold and summer's heat, but brutal storms and bitter cold hold excitement and challenge and are enemies to outwit and outlast, adversaries not without mystique in the dangers they present. Even in the most heroic tales, there are times the elements win.

Theodore Roosevelt loved the heroic demands of life in the northern part of Dakota Territory, soon to become the state of North Dakota. He first visited in 1883, stayed a good while, got into the cattle business in the Badlands, and became an enthusiast for the frontier. Long before the state knew it would portend the future, the problem of out-migration found embodiment in Roosevelt and his experience. Roosevelt affiliated emotionally with the Badlands and credited the rough and rigorous life he lived on his sojourns to Dakota as having been integral to everything that followed for him, including becoming the twenty-sixth president of the United States. And yet, he lost much of his inherited fortune when his cattle-ranching enterprise suffered terrible losses in the winter of 1886–1887, and he never was able to recoup his investment. Dakota was the place that made him healthy when he embraced the land in 1883, and it was the place he retreated to for healing when grief-stricken after his wife and his mother both died on Valentine's Day in 1884. But it was not a place to stay in for long. Life was good, but making a living was not. And although his passion for the state was sincere, his economic ties to North Dakota were cut before the turn of the century.

Looked at objectively, Roosevelt remained an outsider, an Easterner whose own future never was committed to that of North Dakota. And yet, he was the first truly famous American identified with the state. In turn, North Dakota identified with his "bully" attitude and his great passion for preserving nature's wonders for future generations, so much so that the national park in the North Dakota Badlands bears his name. The state also named its highest award after him. Called the Theodore Roosevelt Rough Rider Award, it was established during the 1961 Dakota Territory Centennial to honor North Dakotans of extraordinary achievement who bring honor to the state, and it has been given to expatriate North Dakotans as different from one another as "Champagne Music Maker" (with his hallmark German brogue) Lawrence Welk and *Ebony* magazine journalist Era Bell Thompson; western author Louis L'Amour and basketball great Phil Jackson. The award also has honored North Dakotans renowned for work within the state, such as Dr. Anne Carlsen, inspirational founder of the Crippled Children's School, now called the Anne Carlsen Center for Children, and entrepreneur Harold Schafer, whose Gold Seal Company fortune transformed the western town of Medora into a popular tourist attraction.

That no American Indians were honored during the first forty years of the award seems odd in a state with a proud and diverse Indian heritage and four large, distinct reservations: the Turtle Mountain Band of Chippewa and the Spirit Lake Sioux (Lakota) on the east side of the hundredth meridian; the Three Affiliated Tribes of Fort Berthold (Arikara, Hidatsa, and Mandan) and the Standing Rock Sioux (Dakota, Lakota, and Yanktonai) on the west side. Of course, there is no public record of the names of people offered the award who turned it down, so it isn't clear whether the lack of Native American recipients speaks to oversight on the part of state leaders or to Indian discomfort with an honor named for Theodore Roosevelt—an unabashed imperialist whose mixed remarks on the worth of Indians are well documented.

Yet, symbolically, the lack of Indian honorees underscores a divided legacy within North Dakota. And although hostility never was a hallmark of interaction between Indians and whites—even during times preceding statehood—today's cooperative relationships between the two groups include the sense of being visitors, rather than participants, in each other's worlds. While historically Indians have spent more time traveling back and forth between cultures, the growth of Indian casinos in recent years has increased interest in the reservations as entertainment spots for Indians and non-Indians, alike. Vestiges of racism exist, and a shared vision for the state's future remains elusive. But understanding for the importance of a shared vision is growing. One changing dynamic that is expected to add to Indian influence and participation across the state is that unlike their white counterparts, young Indians are staying in North Dakota, and, consequently, one of the few places where population is increasing is the reservations.

Dramatic cycles of boom and bust were early ingredients of state character, more prominent for settlers of western ranch ranges than eastern farm fields, but flavor for a stew of contradictions inherent in North Dakota's geographic location. Straddling drift prairie with one foot in the fertile mud of the Red River Valley along the Minnesota border and one foot in the semiarid steppes of the Great Plains spreading west from the Missouri River, North Dakota has struggled with identity, cohesiveness, and economic viability all its days. Although from border to border, citizens revere the land, tying that spiritual connection to practical and progressive policy making often splits perspectives along the Missouri Escarpment where the Central Lowlands give way to the Great Plains. Creating more tension than the east-west split, however, is the separation between rural and urban areas of the state. The emptying out of North Dakota continues to drag at small towns trying to hang on to what they have. For towns that have endured the consolidation of schools, the cutback or total loss of local medical care, and the boarding up of Main Street businesses, policies that help economic development in cities suf-

fering none of those problems are viewed with a degree of bitterness. The urban-rural divide is statewide, although population loss is more dramatic the farther west one goes. Still, the uncomfortable truth for North Dakota—with the exception of towns that have become bedroom communities for the state's largest cities—is that within an hour's drive of North Dakota's eastern border, the dwindling nature of towns begins to be clearly visible.

Dwindling, but not dying, the towns in the eastern half of the state are midwestern, much like "out-state" towns in Minnesota, Iowa, or Indiana. These are towns of the American heartland where midwestern themes, stereotypes, tensions, and contradictions resonate: *Are midwestern folks down home or behind the times, independent or isolated, modest or mediocre, morally superior or sanctimonious?* Settled either mostly by Scandinavians or mostly by Germans from Russia with churches and local café menu items to match their heritage, such towns are places where even a generation ago "intermarriage" was the term used when Catholics and Lutherans married. And although ethnic background has little to do with everyday life anymore, a cook serving *lefse* (a griddle-baked Norwegian potato flatbread) at the same table as *knephla* soup (German potato dumpling soup) still would qualify as a heretic.

The people of these small North Dakota towns are like-minded and resilient. They've seen farm sizes grow, the number of farm families decrease, and businesses, schools, churches, and civic organizations reflect that change with smaller numbers. And yet, in most ways, towns remain vital—amazingly so—with fewer people assuming more and more roles to keep the structure of community life and the amenities it affords in place. But the challenge to maintain vitality in the face of further population loss is immense. And the parade of history marches against them.

In bearing the fault lines Midwest/West and urban/rural typical for the tier of states that share the hundredth meridian, North Dakota's problems resonate regionally. However, North Dakota's special character is bound up in historical themes identified and brought to public attention in 1958 by the late historian and University of North Dakota professor Elwyn B. Robinson. In an address given during the commemoration of the seventy-fifth anniversary of the University of North Dakota, Dr. Robinson named six interrelated themes and, in turn, connected them all to the state's geography: "first, remoteness; second, dependence; third, radicalism; fourth, a position of economic disadvantage; fifth, the Too-Much Mistake; and, sixth, adjustment to the imperatives of a cool, subhumid grassland." A half century later, North Dakota's chances for future prosperity depend upon rethinking those themes and making them work for—not against—economic progress.

Of the six, only radicalism no longer applies. Agricultural subsidies and other federal entitlement and assistance programs, beginning with Franklin Delano Roosevelt's New Deal, softened the effects of outside exploitation by corporations and government that had angered ordinary citizens and sown seeds of radical activism in grassroots groups such as the Farmer's Alliance and Independent Party of the late nineteenth century and the Non-Partisan League (NPL) of the early twentieth century. (Interestingly, despite North Dakota's strong political conservatism today, two state-owned entities that continue to thrive, prosper, and serve the state well—the Bank of North Dakota and the North Dakota State Mill and Elevator—began around 1920 in the heyday of NPL socialistic policies). While populism continues to color the political landscape, primarily through the process of initiative and referendum, bedrock conservatism holds sway in the state legislature. On the up side, North Dakota remains fiscally sound at a time when other state governments swim in red ink; on the down side, conservatism too often translates into aversion to reasonable risk, thus stymieing innovation and new ideas—particularly legislative ideas aimed at young people and young families—and leaving North Dakota stuck in the past, singing tired old verses to the lament of outward migration.

The other five themes identified by Robinson reinforce one another and overlap with like problems in other upper midwestern states, although location intensifies North Dakota's situation. The "Too-Much Mistake"—too many farms, too many counties, too many towns, too many roads, too many schools—has been magnified by "adjustment to the imperatives of a cool, subhumid grassland." In the boom years of settlement, it wasn't far from truth to say that everywhere the train stopped, a town sprang up. What was not recognized was that west of the rich glacial till of the Red River Valley, homesteads of 160 acres were not sufficient for individual farms; in fact, twice that acreage wasn't enough. But settlement occurred as if it were, and towns plotted every few miles could not thrive without large numbers of farmers to support their businesses. State population peaked in 1930 at 680,845 and by 2000 had dropped to 642,200, a number reflecting a steady downward trend in the numbers of farm families and small-town businesses dependent upon their trade. (The population loss is all the more striking when compared to the population of the United States, which more than doubled in the same period, going from 122 million to 281 million.) A double blip of prosperity for energy and agricultural interests in the 1970s—related to the OPEC oil em-

bargo and unexpected Soviet demand for American grain—slowed the trend but did not stop it. And although North Dakota cities gained in population as small towns lost, their economies lacked the kind of diversity that might have offset overall decline. The devastating Red River flood in 1997, which left the city of Grand Forks, along with most of the Red River Valley, under water, also struck a blow to population, causing over eight thousand people, or just under 7 percent of the population, to leave Grand Forks County during the process of rebounding and rebuilding. Located in the most fertile farmland of the state, and home to the University of North Dakota and a nearby Air Force base, Grand Forks is assured of recovery. But the role the city might have played in stemming the tide of outward migration was lost during crucial years.

The other themes, remoteness and dependence, also exacerbate each other and play out on the national stage as economic disadvantage, Robinson's fourth theme. Because agriculture is North Dakota's only major industry, the state's economy is tightly bound to everything that affects production, pricing, and transportation. True long ago and still true today, North Dakota's land-locked, middle-of-North America position makes it unattractive for industry or manufacturing that requires ready access to markets—a fact that underscores the dominance of agricultural dependency. Because agriculture is an industry fraught with variability, relative economic stability for the state depends upon federal programs and subsidies. With the help of strong congressional delegations, North Dakota has a history of not paying into the national coffers nearly what it gets back in subsidies; in fact, the ratio of difference ranks near the top for all states. Of course, two air force bases (Minot and Grand Forks), four Indian reservations, and a strong contingent of senior citizens collecting Social Security also play roles in the amount of federal monies that are returned to the state.

When Robinson identified the historical themes, he understood the state well enough to worry that he had presented "hard disagreeable truths—hurting [North Dakota's] self-esteem." Indeed, there's something paradoxical about North Dakota's combination of boundlessness and dependence, lack of pretense and ongoing search for identity, spiritual surety and operative doubtfulness. North Dakota's openness necessarily exposes flaws and mistakes, but it exposes assets and capabilities, too. For instance, the "Too Much" theme has two sides. On one side are too many secondary schools, colleges, and universities for a small population to support; on the other is top-tier ranking for North Dakota students on standardized testing along with both the second-highest high school graduation rate and the highest percentage of graduates who go on to college in the nation. Not surprisingly, college graduates also stand out and are highly recruited by out-of-state firms for the quality of their educational background and their work ethic. (It is no stretch to imagine the potential for keeping graduates in the state through joint public/private applicable research ventures, an idea already in the works at the universities). In short, North Dakota helps set the curve on raising and educating children well—a selling point for renaissance that cannot be overstated.

In the light of instant communication and information, technological advancements, and Internet potential, Robinson's theme of remoteness also looks different. North Dakota's leadership position in tele-education and tele-health provide good examples. One program, the North Dakota Division of Independent Study, was begun in the 1930s as correspondence education to help the state's rural students get high school diplomas; now it educates students who must depend upon distance learning in all fifty states and more than thirty foreign countries. In the arena of tele-health, Merit Care, the state's largest medical provider, became one of the first hospitals to use minimally invasive robotic technology and the very first in the nation to do a live webcast of robotically assisted heart surgery. In general, a variety of rural challenges is forcing the state to the cutting edge of technological advancement. Rural access to high-speed Internet is key to changing the climate of business opportunity, opening up markets for "boutique" products or consortiums of specialty items, putting entrepreneurs in the rural areas in touch with vendors and consumers, and removing obstacles of "economic disadvantage." (Perhaps this is the arena for "radicalism" able to effect economic transformation in the twenty-first century.)

North Dakota joins other midwestern states in a region nationally dismissed for sameness. In truth, regional sameness is ripe for exploitation—particularly, the theme of dependence might not echo so loudly were there more "interdependence" (regionalism) strengthening the midwestern states. Already seen as promising for the tier of states sharing the hundredth meridian, the idea has taken root in organizations such as the Great Plains Institute for Sustainable Development and the American Indian multistate InterTribal Bison Cooperative.

The environment also holds promise for North Dakota. Wind farms have sprung up to produce energy from a constantly renewable resource. And with the fourth-largest number of wildlife refuges among the fifty states—all of them managed for waterfowl production—North Dakota at present qualifies as a hunter's paradise. The "cool sub-humid grassland" that cannot sustain large numbers of farmers and ranchers has alternate possibilities for ecotourism. For that matter, traditional tourists have become more sophisticated, seeking out places with substance and subtlety, places much like areas along the Lewis and Clark Trail that hardly have changed in two hundred years. Another idea, admittedly romantic, is that North Dakota's beautiful combination of space and simplicity could draw people seeking spiritual renewal. Among many paradoxes revealed in the North Dakota experience is the fact that people fear isolation, even as they covet solitude. Silence, itself, is a rare commodity and a challenge for modern urban sensibilities—a new frontier of sorts.

North Dakota native son and poet the late Thomas McGrath, in his epic poem *Letter to an Imaginary Friend* (1962), plumbed the spiritual depth of the state this way:

> Dakota is everywhere.
>   A condition.
>   And I am only a device of memory
> To call forth into this Present the flowering dead and
>   the living
> To enter the labyrinth and blaze the trail for the en-
>   during journey
> Toward the round dance and commune of light . . .
>   to dive through the night of rock
> (In which the statues of heroes sleep) beyond history
>   to Origin
> To build that Legend where all journeys are one
>   where Identity
> Exists
>   where speech becomes song . . .

North Dakotans with roots pushed deep into the prairie seek that harmony, struggling with the many different dualities of land and people that give the state its character, yet accepting that complexity and commonality don't have to be sorted out to be appreciated. That's why when driving through an overlay of haze on a sultry summer morning, they aren't surprised to see colorful mirages shimmering ahead, as ephemeral and as real as hope. Then the sun has its way, the sky opens up, and the view goes on forever.

Jane Ahlin
Fargo, North Dakota

Ohio

Ohio was admitted to the Union in 1803 as the seventeenth state. It was also the first wholly American state, the original thirteen having begun as British colonies and the next three (Vermont, Kentucky, and Tennessee) having been carved out of them. Today,

Ohio is the most easterly of the midwestern states, but two centuries ago it was the wild west—the first bit of the Northwest Territory, which was created by act of Congress in 1787, to gain statehood.

Ever since, as Michael Barone has remarked, it has seemed the "epitome of American normalcy," a good place to take the temperature of the nation. In 1970, Ben Wattenberg and Richard Scammon chose Dayton to typify what they called "The Real Majority." Seeking in 1996 to understand the grassroots reaction to Bill Clinton, the *New York Times* sent Michael Winerip, a star reporter, to live in Canton for a year. As part of a series exploring unemployment in Ohio's bicentennial year, 2003, the *Washington Post* focused on Newark, which it defined as "the middle of America," in economic if not geographic terms.

Ohio is a squarish state, measuring 220 miles from north to south and the same from east to west. It is part of the Midwest flatlands, with no hill higher than 1,549 feet. The 2000 census confirmed Ohio's standing as the nation's seventh-largest state, with a population of 11,353,140. The state's population was less diverse than that of the nation as a whole, mainly because it had relatively few people of Asian and Hispanic origin; blacks made up 11.5 percent of Ohio's population, compared with 12.3 percent of the country's. The median annual household income, $40,956, closely approximated the national figure, $41,994.

Columbus, the capital and the seat of The Ohio State University, was the largest city, with 711,470 people. But the population of its metropolitan area was much smaller, at 1,612,694, than those of Cleveland (2,148,143) and Cincinnati (2,009,632). In all, Ohio boasted seven of the one hundred largest urban conglomerations, also including Dayton, Akron, Toledo, and Youngstown.

In the years after the Civil War, in which Ohioans like Ulysses S. Grant and William T. Sherman played pivotal roles, Ohio experienced explosive growth. Cleveland was the early headquarters of John D. Rockefeller's Standard Oil Company, and Ohio factories contributed enormously to the nation's growing industrial strength. Cleveland and Youngstown made steel, Toledo made glass and automobiles, Akron made tires, Canton made bearings, Dayton made cash registers, and Cincinnati made soap.

But most of the steel mills have gone dark, and other industries have suffered. Ohio is growing slowly—much less rapidly than states like Texas and California—which has cost it seats in the House of Representatives and the electoral votes that go with them. Its House delegation in 2006 was its smallest since the 1820s. (Cleveland has been shrinking for decades; it was the sixth-largest city in the country as

recently as 1940.) No longer do the major parties turn to Ohioans in assembling presidential tickets.

Between 1840 and 1920, no fewer than eight Ohioans were elected president—William Henry Harrison, Grant, Rutherford B. Hayes, James A. Garfield, Benjamin Harrison, William McKinley, William Howard Taft, and Warren G. Harding. In 1920, in fact, both nominees were Ohio newspaper publishers: Harding from Marion for the Republicans, and James M. Cox from Dayton for the Democrats. Since then, no Buckeye has been nominated for president, though Robert A. Taft was a contender in 1952, and none has been nominated for vice president by a majority party since John W. Bricker in 1944.

William McKinley and Mark Hanna—the first a former governor and former chairman of the House Ways and Means Committee from Canton, the second a coal and iron baron and party boss from Cleveland—put Ohio's imprint on the nation in the state's golden age. It began in 1896 when Hanna, as chairman of the Republican National Committee, engineered McKinley's election as president, inaugurating a thirty-four-year period of GOP dominance, locally and nationally. The two of them stood for hard money, high tariffs, and an aggressive Americanism abroad, verging on imperialism.

The Depression brought sitdown strikes, sometimes marked by violence, and fierce political combat between the unions, especially the new Congress of Industrial Organizations, and the Republican establishment, personified by Robert Taft, a son of the twenty-seventh president. One result was the anti-union Taft-Hartley Act, enacted in Washington in 1947; another was a new equipoise between the parties in Ohio, which made it a major battleground of national politics for the rest of the twentieth century.

But the Republicans reasserted control in 2000 and again in 2004. George W. Bush carried the state, as his father had fatally failed to do in 1992, and the Republicans emerged from the balloting in control of the governorship, all the lesser statewide offices, both senate seats, and both houses of the legislature.

The earliest days of what was to become Ohio belonged, of course, to the Native Americans. Of the prehistoric peoples called the Mound Builders we know little. But their astonishing Serpent Mound, an earthen embankment in the shape of a snake, almost a quarter-mile long, still stands near Peebles, in the countryside east of Cincinnati, as evidence of their sophistication.

When European Americans arrived, they found various tribes, including the Miami, the Shawnee, the Ottawa, and the Iroquois Confederacy. Organized settlement began in 1788, when a group of colonists from New England founded Marietta, on the Ohio River;

the home of General Rufus Putnam, superintendent of the Ohio Company, is preserved there.

Hostile Indians blocked expansion for a time, and in 1791, Indians equipped with British arms inflicted a catastrophic defeat on General Arthur St. Clair, who lost seven hundred of his men in a battle at Fort Recovery on the Indiana border. But three years later, General Anthony Wayne defeated Indians allied with the British at Fallen Timbers, near Toledo, ending British hopes of maintaining control of the Northwest Territory. In 1795, Wayne forced the Indians to cede their lands to the United States. The Indians were pushed farther west, and settlers stormed in. Statehood followed just eight years later.

Ohio's first constitution was a profoundly Jeffersonian document. More democratic than those of the eastern states, it provided for universal male suffrage and imposed strict limitations on executive authority. "They saw their new state as a blank canvass on which they could paint a magnificent future of prosperity and harmony," writes Andrew Cayton in *Ohio: The History of a People* (2002). "The creation of Ohio was one of the great acts of the American Enlightenment."

Traveling through the Ohio Valley in the 1830s, the Frenchman Alexis de Tocqueville was impressed by the young state's progress, in particular its "fine crops" and "elegant dwellings." South of the river, he wrote, slavery made labor degrading, but north of it, where labor was considered honorable, "man appears rich and contented."

Harriet Beecher Stowe, who had lived in Cincinnati for many years, dramatized the differences between Kentucky and Ohio in *Uncle Tom's Cabin* (1852), which tells the story of the young slave Eliza, who risked her life on the ice floes of the Ohio to reach freedom. In real life, fleeing slaves were sheltered in Oberlin and other Ohio "stations" on the Underground Railroad.

On the eve of the Civil War, Ohio was the third-largest state in the country, and Cincinnati was the country's largest inland city.

The pioneers took two main routes, breaching the Appalachian barrier in the north as well as the south. New Englanders and New Yorkers followed the Mohawk Valley and Lake Erie west, replicating in the Western Reserve of northern Ohio the town greens they had left behind, with white-steepled churches. Hudson, chartered in April 1803, by the new General Assembly, still looks like a Connecticut village.

Southern Ohio, on the other hand, was settled largely by Kentuckians and Virginians, many of whom came down the Ohio River. They gave southern Ohio an Appalachian flavor that persists to this day. Cincinnati, the metropolis of the south, has more in common with Louisville, Memphis, and other Southern cities than it does with Cleveland. Ohio is a state of two cultures, with northern accents north of Route 40 and southern accents south of it. In the nineteenth century, they differed in their view of the Civil War, with Butternut and Copperhead sentiment dominant in the south; in the twentieth, voting often divided in the same way.

At the beginning, Ohio was overwhelmingly white and overwhelmingly English-speaking, although there was a significant minority of German speakers. But as coal mines and factories developed, Italians, Poles, Hungarians, Serbs, Slovaks, Slovenes, and Croatians arrived to man them, along with blacks from the South. They gave Cleveland, in particular, a far different character from the rest of the state, culturally and politically. Leaders like Frank Lausche emerged from its "cosmo wards," where the central Europeans lived.

In a speech to the Ohio Society of New York in 1910, Wilbur Wright remarked that if he were to give advice to a young man on how to succeed in life, he would say, "pick out a good father and mother, and begin life in Ohio." An exaggeration, of course, but an exaggeration grounded in reality. In the latter part of the nineteenth century and the early years of the twentieth, a group of practical, down-to-earth, yet visionary Ohioans invented things that revolutionized modern society.

Thomas A. Edison, born in Milan, developed the first workable phonograph and the first workable electric light bulb. Wilbur Wright and his brother, Orville, born in Dayton, achieved the first sustained airplane flight. Charles F. Kettering, born in Loudonville, invented the cash register and the automobile self-starter and, eventually, gave his name to the nation's greatest center for cancer research, in New York.

Rockefeller, a Baptist workaholic, lived in Cleveland for three decades. He became the richest man in the country not through an invention but by perfecting an organization that controlled every aspect of the oil business. He helped to transform Ohio, and not only by turning it from a predominantly agricultural state into a mainly industrial one. Rockefeller money, and that of contemporaries such as Stephen V. Harkness, Jeptha H. Wade, John L. Severance, and Henry Clay Folger, poured into Cleveland's major cultural institutions.

Their philanthropy helps to explain why Cleveland, now in the second rank of American cities in terms of population, has one of the country's two or three best symphony orchestras and one of its half-dozen top art museums. (It also has the popular Rock and Roll Hall of Fame, located there in part because Alan Freed, a local disk jockey, coined the phrase "rock and roll.")

Smaller museums were made possible by other

Ohio fortunes, notably those in Toledo, Youngstown, Columbus, and Oberlin. Cincinnati supports a pair of excellent art museums, though they are less encyclopedic than Cleveland's. And thanks to its big Germanic population (57.4 percent of the total in 1890), the Queen City of the West, as Henry Wadsworth Longfellow called it, has long had a rich musical tradition, beginning in 1873 with the May Festival, now the oldest choral gala in the Western Hemisphere.

Ohio's greatest painter, George Bellows, found his best subjects not in the middle-class Columbus neighborhood where he grew up but in the rawer, more turbulent aspects of big-city life, like trains, factories, slums, and the violent world of boxing.

He was not alone in leaving the state. Ohio-born writers and other intellectuals headed for New York and Chicago in droves, and many of them condemned their native state, especially its small towns, as banal and philistine. William Dean Howells invented a prototype, christened it "Dulldale" and inveighed against "the meanness and hollowness of that wretched little village-life." James Thurber savagely caricatured Columbus in *My Life and Hard Times* (1933).

Sherwood Anderson's portrait *Winesburg, Ohio* (1919) is more subtly drawn. He, too, decried conformity, but he saw it rooted in human nature, not in the Midwest; the problem, Anderson argued, lies in the inability of human beings to connect with each other.

Yet however blinkered it may have seemed, Ohio emphasized higher education in its earliest days, looking to the wider world. Ohio University in Athens was chartered in 1804, the second year of the state's existence; The Ohio State University, the land-grant school, dates from 1870. Although none of the state's 130-odd colleges and universities has quite achieved the academic eminence of midwestern rivals like Wisconsin and Michigan, Ohio State and Case Western Reserve are highly regarded, and liberal-arts colleges such as Oberlin, Denison, Antioch, and Kenyon have all built national reputations.

Ohio State's intellectual achievements are not as well publicized as the achievements of its football teams. In a sports-mad state, the Buckeyes have been a powerhouse for more than half a century. Ohio is known too for producing football coaches, from Woody Hayes, Don Shula, and Ara Parseghian to Paul Brown, who founded both of the state's professional teams, the Cleveland Browns and the Cincinnati Bengals, and helped bring the Pro Football Hall of Fame to Canton, where the pro game started.

The Cincinnati Reds (né Red Stockings), America's first professional baseball team, went 65-0 in 1869, their inaugural season. Since then, the Reds and the Cleveland Indians have fielded future Hall-of-Famers like Tris Speaker, Bob Feller, and Johnny Bench. Sprinter Jesse Owens, from Cleveland, was one of the great Olympic heroes. More recently, golfer Jack Nicklaus, from Columbus, dominated his sport.

As the new millennium began, Ohio faced formidable challenges. Governor Bob Taft, scion of Ohio's greatest political family and great-grandson of the state's next-to-last president, put it bluntly: "We're not moving fast enough to keep pace with our competitors or to replace jobs lost to productivity."

The trouble had been a long time brewing. Musclebound by its dependence on heavy industry at a time when manufacturing jobs were disappearing, it ranked thirty-fourth among the fifty states in the increased value of goods and services produced between 1988 and 1998. Well-paying manufacturing jobs constituted a third of all of the state's jobs in 1969 but less than a fifth by 2000, and most of the service and other jobs that replaced them did not pay as much.

Cleveland had particularly hard going in the quarter-century that began in 1965. The Cuyahoga River became so fouled with industrial wastes that one day in June 1969 it caught fire. At a ceremony designed to demonstrate his solidarity with the city's working men, Mayor Ralph J. Perk set his hair afire. His successor, Dennis Kucinich, mismanaged Cleveland into the first financial default by a major United States city in modern times. People began deriding it as "The Mistake by the Lake."

The postwar years saw a vast African American migration into Ohio's cities. By 1980, Cleveland's population was more than two-fifths black. Cincinnati, Dayton, and Youngstown each were one-third black, and Akron and Columbus were almost one-quarter black. Few of the migrants found the economic security that they had hoped for in their new lives.

In Cleveland's inner-city neighborhoods, largely abandoned in mass flight by the white middle classes, racial discontent mounted. A 1966 uprising in Hough, a black slum, was followed by widespread violence in Glenville in 1968, though a black man, Carl B. Stokes, had been elected Cleveland's mayor in 1967. Cincinnati had its own demonstrations in 1967, and it went through another nasty patch in 2001 following the shooting of a black man by a white policeman.

Unrest of another kind, fueled by opposition to the Vietnam War, led to student demonstrations at Kent State University in 1970. Inexperienced National Guard troops dispatched by Governor James A. Rhodes opened fire, killing four students and wounding nine others. The episode became a metaphor for the chasm that was opening between the war's backers and its foes. "Ohio, once the land of endless beginnings, had become a place of deadly endings," Cayton wrote.

The Rust Belt cities mounted a counterattack, and to some extent it succeeded. Cleveland built itself a Ritz-Carlton, new office towers, a new ballpark and the Rock and Roll Hall of Fame. Cincinnati developed a specialty in avant-garde architecture, hiring Frank Gehry, Michael Graves, Peter Eisenman, and, finally, the British-born Iraqi Zaha Hadid, whose Contemporary Arts Center, her first project in the United States, was widely hailed as a masterpiece.

Both cities, and Columbus as well, emerged as regional banking capitals, and both cities generated new jobs through small-scale manufacturing. As steel mills vanished, machine-tool and other plants multiplied. Akron turned itself into a polymer-technology center, taking up some of the slack caused by the shuttering of tire factories.

Yet Ohio's easy access to coal and to iron ore, together with its dense network of east-west railroads and highways that had powered the state's earlier growth, no longer counted for as much in an era driven by technology. What mattered most in the new age was education, and there Ohio lagged, despite its wealth of degree-granting institutions.

While politicians bragged about low taxes, they spent relatively little on schooling. In 2002, the state ranked forty-first in the percentage of residents twenty-five or older holding bachelor's degrees, thirty-ninth in the percentage holding graduate degrees, and fortieth in per capita spending for higher education. The picture was not much better on the local level. Cleveland's school system was packed with run-down buildings and underachieving students; a superintendent warned that "the future will pass us by" if radical change was not forthcoming.

Even with innovative programs instituted by several governors, Ohio has made slow progress in its effort to share in the knowledge-based economic revolution, as have neighboring or nearby states like Illinois, Pennsylvania, and Michigan. As a whole, the state's economy stands perilously close to stagnation.

R. W. Apple, Jr.
New York, New York

South Dakota

South Dakota entered the Union as the fortieth state on November 2, 1889. It ranks seventeenth among the fifty United States in size, containing 75,885 square miles (49,354,240 acres) of land within boundaries that form a rectangle divided near the center by the Missouri River on a line that approximates the hundredth meridian. South Dakota ranks forty-sixth among the states in population, with 754,844 residents in 2000. Most are descended either from thirteen of fourteen ancestral tribes of Sioux enrolled in nine federally recognized reservation societies or from more than twenty non-Indian ethnic groups that immigrated prior to 1930.

Natural Features. South Dakota derives its continental orientation and regional definition from several natural features. Within its borders are the geographic center of North America, indicated by a marker a few miles north of the capital at Pierre, and the only true continental divide, at the northeast corner. Water flows from Big Stone Lake through the Minnesota and the Mississippi Rivers southward to the Gulf of Mexico and from Lake Traverse through the Red River northward to Hudson's Bay. South Dakota contains the highest elevation above sea level east of the Rocky Mountains, at 7,242 feet, on Harney Peak in the Black Hills. The aquatic artifacts and stunning landscapes of the expansive Badlands east of the Black Hills have inspired Native American legends.

South Dakota is the central state in the massive Missouri River drainage basin. Like the Volga River in Russia, the Missouri is a Northern Hemisphere river that human beings find difficult to manage, especially during floods. One cause is the flow of silt—from which the Missouri gained its nickname "Big Muddy" —mainly washed into the river in western South Dakota. In 1942, federal officials estimated the annual silt flow near Kansas City at 204 million tons. To reduce it, control flooding, maintain barge navigation below Sioux City, facilitate crop irrigation, and serve wildlife preservation and tourism, the congressional Flood Control Act of 1942 authorized the installation of four massive rolled-earth dams and reservoirs along the Missouri's main stem in South Dakota.

The Missouri divides as much as it dominates the state. Eastern South Dakota lies within a glaciated physiographic province called Prairie Plains. The region's black soils and an average annual precipitation as great as twenty-four inches have for more than a century nurtured an agricultural and livestock-feeding economy supported by commercial centers at Sioux Falls, Yankton, Mitchell, Aberdeen, and scores of smaller towns. Native Americans live on four reservations on the periphery of East River with a total acreage of 1,635,000.

Western South Dakota is part of the nonglaciated Great Plains. Porous soils and average annual precipitation as low as fourteen inches have encouraged livestock breeding, feed-grain production, mining and forest industries. Most people live in Rapid City, Hot Springs, Spearfish, Lemmon, Philip, and a few scattered small towns and supply stations. Native Americans retain five reservations close to the Missouri River and its principal tributaries that include more than twelve million acres.

Missouri Valley Culture. In the early nineteenth century, fur traders, the first non-Indian residents of the Dakotas, developed a "Missouri River Valley Culture," or "Steamboat Society," which received legal recognition in the 1858 Yankton tribal treaty. The economy was built around sales of wood for fuel boilers on steamboats; services to tourists and other travelers; and supplies and services to pioneering homesteaders, livestock growers, and Indian agency managers. No less important were gambling, prostitution, and illegal alcoholic beverage sales to Native Americans. The valley culture produced a line of urban centers along the river upstream from North Sioux City, including Jefferson, Elk Point, Burbank, Vermillion, Yankton, Bon Homme, Springfield, Running Water, Tackett Station, White Swan (now Pickstown), Harney City, Wheeler, Oacoma, Chamberlain, Fort Pierre, Pierre (the capital), and Mobridge. The population swelled after the establishment of the Yankton, Whetstone, Fort Thompson, Cheyenne River, and Standing Rock Indian agencies near the river's edge. These commercial centers united people living on both sides of the Missouri as well as those along the river's banks. Even today, however, South Dakotans still often identify themselves as "East River" and "West River."

East River and West River Cultures. Political decisions reinforced the east-west divide created by the landscape. After the Louisiana Purchase of 1803 allowed the United States to claim the Missouri Valley, federal officials at different times attached various parts of the future South Dakota to the Indiana, Louisiana, Missouri, Michigan, Wisconsin, Iowa, Minnesota, and Nebraska Territories. During some periods, there was no governance from any organized federal territory. Yet there existed continuous federal administration for both East River and West River in the jurisdiction of the Upper Missouri Agency upstream from Council Bluffs from 1819 to 1868, and for East River in the jurisdiction of the Mendota Agency in Minnesota from 1820 to 1854. The superintendent of the Upper Missouri Agency held jurisdictional powers similar to those of territorial governors.

The founding of the Dakota Territory in 1861 resolved much of the legal confusion but did little to create a common culture in what would become South Dakota. During the territorial period, which lasted until the Dakotas became states in 1889, settlement patterns intensified the divergence of East River and West River populations. On the east side, mainly

Dakota and Nakota Sioux settled on lands that eventually became four reservations. On the west side, mainly Lakota and some Nakota Sioux settled around agencies that became five reservations in 1889.

At the same time, nearly 350,000 American and western and northern European immigrants settled in the territory, largely east of the Missouri River. Later arrivals, many of whom were from southern and eastern Europe, chose to locate close to the Missouri River or west of it. Thus, ethnic and religious differences within both Native American and European American societies accentuated the internal division of South Dakota.

By 1930, the 692,849 people who lived in the state were a remarkably diverse lot. More than twenty immigrant heritages existed among European Americans. There were French, French Canadian, English, Anglo-Canadian, Scots, Welsh, Norwegian, Swede, Dane, Dutch, Irish, German, Russian, Mennonite, Hutterite, "Plain German," Polish, Austrian, three divisions of Czech, Swiss, Jewish, and extraneous others. Recent additions include Hispanics, Asians, Pacific Islanders, Russians, people from the Balkans, Middle Easterners, Africans, and African Americans. In the early 2000s, the largest non-Indian ethnic groups are Scandinavians and various representations of Germans. The smallest is Jews, with only about 350 reporting the practice of their religion.

By 1936, the population of South Dakota formally included the equally diverse residents of nine reservation societies recognized by the federal government as "domestic dependent nations" whose members had become U.S. citizens under the terms of the National Indian Citizenship Act of 1924. Most Native Americans in South Dakota descend from thirteen of fourteen ancestral tribes of Sioux in three cultural/linguistic divisions. (Only the Assiniboine are missing.) The Dakota includes Mdewakanton and Wahpekute (together called Santee) plus Sisseton and Wahpeton. The Nakota includes Yankton, and Yanktonai. The Lakota includes Oglala, Brule, Minneconjou, Sans Arc, Two Kettle, Blackfoot Sioux, and Hunkpapa.

Immigrant enclaves established religious institutions that sustained ethnic as well as denominational solidarity. In 1890, Roman Catholics were the most numerous. Lutherans ran a close second, and various denominational manifestations of Calvinism and Anabaptism followed. In 2000, Lutherans had become more numerous than Roman Catholics. Other influential groups were Methodist, United Church of Christ, Presbyterian, Episcopal, Baptist, Assemblies of God, Jewish, and Muslim.

For decades, Catholic, Episcopal, Presbyterian, and Congregational missionaries labored to persuade Indians to convert to Christianity as well as to abandon traditional religious practices. Federal officials collaborated with similar acculturation endeavors by hiring missionaries as educators. Although tribal religions were never forbidden by federal law or policy—except, briefly, the Sun Dance and the Ghost Dance—cultural and economic pressures largely drove tribal religions underground.

During the Native American renaissance of the 1970s, tribal religions reemerged in public. Only the Ghost Dance had disappeared. Through the last quarter of the twentieth century, the attendance of tribal members in Christian denominational activities declined steadily while participation in ancestral belief systems grew. The belief system indigenous to the Sioux is defined by the intercessory uses of the sacred pipe, whose introduction is attributed to the appearance of the White Buffalo Calf Woman. It features the dramatic Sun Dance but centers around the Inipi ceremony in the sweat lodge. The other ancestral native religion, which is defined by the use of peyote as a sacrament, entered Sioux Country from the south in about 1902 and gained formal recognition in chapters of the Native American Church of North America. Although Native Americans have not necessarily abandoned a belief in Jesus Christ, many have criticized the behavior of past missionaries.

Educational Institutions. Ethnicity and religion are closely intertwined with education in South Dakota history and contemporary life. A public precollege network of schools evolved in all immigrant rural enclaves through assistance from a federal donation of two sections per township of public land. By 1950, this network included 3,395 independent or common school districts accommodating 86,489 elementary pupils and 283 units educating 28,401 secondary students. High costs, transportation improvements, and changes in state regulations contributed to subsequent consolidation. During the academic year 1999–2000, South Dakota had only 176 school districts. More have disappeared because of state legislation subsidizing consolidation and allowing open enrollment. The policy of open enrollment permits students to transfer to another district, taking with him or her about $2,500 in annual tuition.

Many South Dakotans oppose the consolidation or closure of public schools, arguing for their importance in preserving religious and ethnic traditions as well as the economic health of towns. Some find alternatives to public schools in private educational networks. Religious and private sponsors have opened twenty-four academies to accommodate small groups of students from kindergarten through high school. A lack of resources has forced the closing of eleven but others have been enlarged.

Higher education came to the Dakota territory in the forms of the Congregational Yankton College and the federally commissioned flagship University of South Dakota at Vermillion in October 1882. Since then, state officials have opened ten additional colleges or universities and vocational institutions and closed only one college, at Springfield, which became a medium-security state prison. Religious and private sponsors have founded fifteen additional colleges in the state. Six have subsequently closed, including Yankton College, whose campus became a minimum-security federal prison camp.

As citizens of the United States since 1924, all Native Americans are eligible to attend public, parochial, or private institutions. Children on the nine reservations have had access to federally funded, segregated institutions as well. Dramatic consolidation facilitated by improved transportation and tribal circumstances has drastically reduced the number of precollege schools operated by tribes or the Bureau of Indian Affairs. Twenty remained open in 2000. Since 1969, the U.S. Congress has extended support for the operation of tribally owned colleges and universities. In the academic year 1999–2000, there were accredited colleges on five reservations and learning centers on three others. Incentives for the tribal management of schools include proximity to homes and local control of cultural and historical information.

Health Care Delivery Systems. Four healthcare delivery networks in South Dakota have evolved into a system as complex and expensive as the one to provide education. The first was the network designed to serve federally recognized tribes. It originated in the appointment of a physician at Fort Snelling to try to control epidemics in the jurisdiction of the Mendota Agency. Through the nineteenth century, U.S. government physicians at forts, Indian agencies, and boarding schools were responsible for tribal health care.

In the twentieth century, the U.S. Congress passed several acts to regulate health care for Indians. In 1902, officials opened the controversial Hiawatha Asylum for Insane Indians at Canton, but it was closed by 1934. In 1916, Congress funded the first legitimate reservation hospital at Rosebud, followed by others on most reservations. In 1918, federal officials established a minimum Indian "quarter-blood" standard to determine eligibility for access to all federal services, including health care. In 1921, Congress passed the Snyder Act to establish free health care as a federal trust responsibility for tribal members of quarter-blood Indian heritage or more in all federally recognized tribes. This benchmark act remains in place, although later changes have extended care to persons of less than quarter-blood Indian heritage and allowed tribal influence in Indian Health Service operation and management.

In 1997, the Northern Great Plains Indian Health Service Aberdeen Area Office reported "Service Units" in South Dakota centered at Rapid City as well as on all of the reservations, to which "Health Locations" were attached as clinics in scattered reservation communities. Indian Health Service facilities offered 73,533 people free clinical, hospital, specialist, and referral services, plus long-term care for the disabled and elderly. In 1997, Congress offered free health care on request to 9.7 percent of the resident population of South Dakota. This benefit continues today.

Of the remaining 90.3 percent of the population, only federal employees, active military personnel, and armed forces veterans have access to care free of charge. All others are responsible for paying rising costs that sometimes result in foreclosure and the bankruptcy of patients without medical insurance.

Until the end of the nineteenth century, the non-Indian residents of South Dakota relied on the services of "country doctors" who treated maladies mainly with patent medicines and other intoxicants. No community had access to a legitimate hospital. Public services were restricted to those available at county "poor farms" and were reserved for people who could not care for themselves until the creation of the Social Security system in the 1930s. In the area of mental health, territorial officials opened the Insane Asylum at Yankton in 1879. It is still in operation.

Medical education improved significantly in 1907 with the opening of the School of Medicine at the University of South Dakota. In 1917, the state required formal training for nurses under the governance of a State Board of Nursing. During the 1920s, similar regulatory efforts affected pharmacy and other services while administrative personnel founded the first hospital regulatory association.

Privately, the Catholic religious were the first to provide institutional health care. In 1895 at Yankton, Benedictine Sisters added a health-care apostolate. Two years later, they opened the Sacred Heart Hospital, which remains the central facility in the Benedictines' network of hospitals, clinics, and long-term-care facilities. In 1901 at Aberdeen, Presentation Sisters responded to a cholera epidemic by adding a health-care apostolate and opening St. Luke's Hospital, which remains an important facility in the Presentations' network of hospitals, clinics, and long-term care facilities.

At Rapid City in 1911, Methodist Deaconness Hospital grew out of a private facility operated by a physician to establish the first permanent hospital service in West River, and in 1926, Catholic St. John's

opened nearby. In 1973, the two merged into the Rapid City Regional Hospital. By 1998, its investors and administrators either owned or managed nearly all hospitals, clinics, and long-term-care facilities available to non-Indians across West River.

In 1998, too, the Benedictine Sisters at Yankton and Presentation Sisters at Aberdeen formed partnerships in a managerial network named Avera Health, centered at Sioux Falls, which took control of all purchases, hiring, and management. By the year 2000, Avera Health controlled twenty-three hospitals, fifteen long-term-care facilities, twelve assisted-living complexes, thirteen senior apartment complexes, thirty-five clinics, and thirty-one satellite locations across East River and counties in bordering states.

Also by 2000, most other medical facilities in East River fell under a competing management system of similar size named Sioux Valley and centered at Sioux Falls. Sioux Valley managers claimed to consolidate a "cottage industry" into a network under one administrative umbrella, like the one at Avera Health, including groups of hospitals, clinics, home-health agencies, and insurance services. A few independent competitors remain in East River, but Avera Health and Sioux Valley share a monopoly nearly as complete as the one claimed by Rapid City Regional in West River.

Two other units in mainstream health-care delivery exist at Sioux Falls. An impressive Veterans Administration Hospital opened in 1948 on the campus of the former Columbus College, a Catholic institution. It is a regional center in the network of some 1,300 VA medical facilities scattered across the United States. Much like tribal members at Indian Health Service Units, veterans grumble about changing staff, delays in gaining appointments, and waiting lines. Yet, like the Indians, they receive treatment, hospitalization, and long-term care at little or no expense.

Alternative health-care systems thrive across South Dakota. Along the streets of every city, signs advertise the presence of chiropractors, whose most prominent facility is the Ortman Clinic at Canistota, south of Mitchell. Since 1915, its chiropractors have seen more than three million patients. They have received treatments by Mennonites or Methodists with legitimate credentials in chiropractic medicine who combine scientific strategies with faith healing.

Increasingly since the Native American renaissance of the 1970s, tribal medicine men and women of the Sacred Pipe belief system and roadmen in the Native American Church have combined the use of herbs with faith, treatments in use long before non-Indians arrived in South Dakota. Their services have extended across ethnic boundaries to outsiders, but they work mainly within reservation communities.

Modern Indian Tribes. Tribal influence affects many aspects of life in South Dakota because members of nine reservation societies plus some others comprise more than 10 percent of the state population. The nine tribes still control the use of approximately 6 percent of the land (some 4.7 million acres). Although most of the land is of little use for agriculture or livestock production and exists at locations too remote for industrial development, it accommodates a growing Native American population. The Yankton Reservation's resident Indian population of about 1,200 in 1970 had grown to about half of the 7,148 enrolled members.

Many Indians are returning to the reservations because of renewed interest in cultural origins and traditions. In addition, they enjoy eight advantageous federal "trust responsibilities," known to most tribal members as "treaty benefits," available in perpetuity as a part of the quid pro quo for the cession of all Indian land. These are available to some 2.5 million federally recognized Indians scattered across the United States, but those who occupy federally protected land tend to benefit the most. Federal trust responsibilities include freedom from taxation on land under federal protection, or on business profits derived from protected land, including income from high-stakes casinos authorized by the National Indian Gaming Regulatory Act of 1988; and "Indian preference" as mandatory "affirmative action" in employment, required by Congress in the Indian Reorganization (Wheeler-Howard) Act of 1934.

Trust responsibilities assure the "Buy Indian" advantage, initiated in 1910, which allows tribal members access to reservation business opportunities without competitive bidding, such as housing-construction contracts federally funded on the Pine Ridge Reservation at $9,915,277 for the year 2003. They also provide free health care at Indian Health Service facilities, education at federal expense for reservation residents in grades K–12, and suitable housing for reservation residents at limited cost. Trust responsibilities support tribalism with salaries for elected or appointed officials as well as administrative costs for housing developments and other services. And they assure cultural freedom, initially guaranteed by U.S. Indian Office Circular 2970 in 1934 and reinforced by the American Indian Religious Freedom Act of 1978.

These benefits help explain the fact that since the 1960s the population of the nine federally recognized reservations has been the fastest growing segment of the population in the state as a whole. On every reservation, a general council of voting adults controls a democratic/representative government established by a written constitution and bylaws to define membership standards, jurisdictional powers, and election procedures.

State Governance and Economy. South Dakotans have tended to support different kinds of politicians at different levels of the American federal system. They expect their representatives in Washington, D.C. to derive maximum benefits from congressional allocations. Meanwhile, they send fiscal conservatives to Pierre who respect the constitutional requirement of a balanced budget. South Dakota's economy has thus long depended heavily on spending by the national government even as it is restricted by ceilings on state and local expenditures.

Despite the influx of federal dollars, economic change since World War II has undermined efforts to retain non-Indian population. Historically, federally subsidized farming and ranching have been South Dakota's economic mainstay. Now incomes from tourism are nearly as important. Since Congress passed the Agricultural Adjustment Act of 1948, rural production subsidies have been unreliable due to administrative manipulation of "percentage of parity payments." Federal support of agriculture has plummeted since Congress started to phase out subsidies with the passage of the Federal Agricultural and Reform Act of 1996.

Recent politicians have sought to promote economic development by attracting "clean industries." In 1980, the state altered a historical usury restriction to allow almost unlimited interest charges on loans. This change, along with the absence of state personal or corporate income taxes, lured the credit card division of Citicorp from New York. Other banking and insurance companies followed. In addition, South Dakotans have benefited from the recent operation of Gateway Computers distribution centers and the accommodation of telemarketing facilities.

The federal government, however, remains integral to South Dakota's economy. In West River, U.S. Park Service, Forest Service, and Grasslands installations provide employment and marketing opportunities as does the U.S. Air Force's Ellsworth Air Base. Established in 1942, Ellsworth's future is precarious because it regularly appears on lists of proposed base closings. In East River, the establishment of the U.S. EROS Data Center (for satellite photography) north of Sioux Falls in 1970 added approximately 750 federal jobs.

Cultural Heritage Preservation. People interested in the ethnic and cultural heritage of South Dakota will find ample resources at the South Dakota Cultural Heritage Center in Pierre, which contains a substantial archive; the I.D. Weeks Library at the University of South Dakota in Vermillion, with some 35,000 volumes on Western Americana plus archival and documentary collections connected to an oral history center containing more than 5,000 recorded interviews; and the Augustana College Center for Western Studies in Sioux Falls, with about 25,000 volumes on regional history as well as extraordinary archival and art collections.

Herbert T. Hoover
University of South Dakota

Wisconsin

In the summer of 1998, country music roadies stuffed my boots with cheese. They struck as I slept, right about the time our big bus crossed the Illinois state line into Wisconsin, the state of my birth and residence. The crew furthermore taped my bunk shut and stole my shorts. I know a Hallmark moment when I see it. For two weeks I had been the outsider, hitching a ride while taking notes on the life of an itinerant singer. Now, on this final day of the tour, I was being hazed into the circle. In a world where warm fuzzies are dispensed via spitwads and prodigious wedgies, the pranks were a benevolent send-off. Never mind that the cheese came presliced and processed from a deli tray backstage at the previous night's gig in Chicago, it was a symbolic nod to my home state. The crew made sure I was clear on the relevance. "You're a *cheese-head*," said the sound man. "Cheese-feet for the cheese-head!"

Despite the myriad goodies Wisconsin has laid before the world—Liberace, the typewriter, the Republican Party—our collective identity remains inextricably cheesy. Any near-term hope for an alteration of this perception was pummeled senseless on January 26, 1997, when the Green Bay Packers beat the New England Patriots in Super Bowl XXXI. The stands of the Superdome were studded with exuberant Wisconsinites who—apparently of their own free will—chose to cap their noggins with gigantic wedges of fake cheese. It has been claimed that 800 million citizens of the world were witness to this native display. One suspects the image will endure.

On a recent Tuesday, I pronounced the world's icons to be in a state of accelerated diminution—Barbra Streisand and foam cheese hats included. I made the declaration aloud, in what I intended to be portentous tones. My critics—in this case, a pair of self-regarding squirrels—responded with a flurry of petulant chatter. Squirrels possess a limited worldview. I was alone in the wilderness that Tuesday, having fled to a tiny unfinished shack in the forest after stumbling across a nugget of statistical porn claiming 5,000,000,000,000,000,000 bytes of new information had been committed to storage in the year 2002. The mind fibrillates. As a kindness to those of us whose math abilities are so irremediably blunted that the operation of a bingo card qualifies as an exercise in advanced algebra, it was further illustratively explained that the equivalent information in print form would provide every person on the planet with a stack of books thirty feet high. I took to the woods and enclosed myself within a simple wooden cube.

For millennia, the limited means of recording history emphasized the preservation of only its most remarkable or simplistic elements. Humankind's attention was narrowly focused by default. Even major archival breakthroughs like photography were so rare in the early days as to be pointed mainly toward great events—the War between the States, for instance. But the available information was always increasing, building to our current state of pell-mell. From cave paintings to the digital explosion, the means by which we might record and replicate events and objects have proliferated in ever-contracting cycles. We are rolling up information like a snowball, and the snowball is becoming bigger than the world itself. Today we store our gigabytes in exabytes, but where is next week's shelf space?

For quite a long time, it seems we can corral our memories. Into my early thirties, I had this sense I could review my life at will. Memories arranged themselves in segments and subsets, cross-referenced and divvied by setting and chronology. Childhood. Grade school. High school. College. The cowboy years. Bike racing. Girlfriends. Poets. Jobs. The summer of '89. But then one day you're shifting boxes above the closet and a cassette of REO Speedwagon's *Hi Infidelity* slips out to clip you on the skull and in ten minutes you're still on the floor perusing the j-card, realizing you can't remember if "Out of Season" is supposed to evoke Lisa Ketter under the pine tree or Sandy Neuhiesel in the pickup truck. Life is nothing more than the ceaseless proliferation of time, with every second a potential memory. Experience accumulates, forming a matrix riddled with interconnections, and the interconnections multiply exponentially with each breath we draw. Boundaries blur. The groupings become less discrete. I have made fitful starts at journals, but when I look back through the haphazard notes, I find myself overwhelmed by melancholy and futility. The big fish leaves the little pond and fails to notice the river widening until he is swept into the sea. Immediately, he begins his search for anything familiar. Eventually, he realizes: In the sea, everything is small. And the sea is rising.

We're fresh off a cultural dust-up here in Wisconsin. It recently came our turn to get one of those state-themed commemorative quarters the U.S. Mint has been stamping for a few years now. Three designs were proposed, and citizens were allowed to cast their votes online. The "Scenic Wisconsin" scene—a deer, a lake, a fish—finished a distant third. Things were tighter between the remaining two choices. "Early Exploration," with an image of a Native American greeting a trapper beside a canoe, received 112,907 votes but was edged out by the 137,745 votes cast for "Agriculture," a design featuring your standard cow head beside a cheese wheel garnished with a corn cob. A small barn can be seen on the distant horizon. Citing the fact that the online poll was unscientific and that the agriculture quarter failed to convey the state's ethnic and cultural diversity, the members of the Commemorative Quarter Council voted 12-8 to overrule the vote and adopt the Early Exploration design. Facing a 5:00 P.M. deadline and citing the people's right to be heard, the governor stepped in and overruled the council, reinstating the Agriculture design.

The kinetic state of human affairs requires constant intellectual evolution. Everything will be questioned. And always, in the heart of the tumult, hovers the question of our own identity. The presentation of a collective self depends on our ability to distill something iconographic from the mix. This has never been easy. The process is frequently weighted in favor of the noisy and privileged. Now the proliferation of information brings into question the very possibility of a place or a person achieving character in the recognizable sense. In the *Duino Elegies*, Rainer Maria Rilke asked: "Does the infinite space / we dissolve into, taste of us then?"

My mother used to say she didn't care who she married as long as she didn't marry a farmer. She'd been married to my brainy chemist father just over two years when he bought a farm. The three of us—I was two years old—put the noxious stacks of the Nekoosa-Edwards paper mill in the rearview mirror of our '52 Chevy and headed across state for a new life on eighty tillable acres in the northwestern corner of Chippewa County, Wisconsin.

Ours was a classic Wisconsin homestead: white house, red barn, a few simple outbuildings, all constructed by second-generation Norwegian immigrants in the wake of the lumbering boom. The farm stood at the southern edge of what historians refer to as the "cutover" region. The cutover was once thick with century-old white pines, but by the 1900s they were long gone down the nearest river. As a short-term fix for the suddenly finite lumber supply, the loggers further stripped the land of lower-grade hemlock, cedar, and hardwoods. After the lumberjacks departed, the government encouraged farmers to settle the area, but the denuded sandy soil of the cutover was poorly suited to farming. Although there were many beautiful farm operations scattered throughout northwestern Wisconsin during my childhood, I came of age thinking of farming as a tough gig in which folks scrabbled and hung on—I was surprised in later life when I spent time in the Coulee Region to the southwest and discovered that farm families numbered among the prominent and well-to-do.

A Bohemian neighbor gave us our first milk cow. She was a lumbering Holstein. Dad pulled her home behind our Ford Falcon station wagon. Our next cow was named Angie. She was followed by Belinda. Then Charlotte, who was mostly white. I don't remember how long we stuck with the alphabetical naming system, but in high school I remember departing from the sequence in order that I might name a calf after my girlfriend at the time. We took to honoring many female friends of the family this way. If you were a man, there wasn't much point, since bull calves were sent down the road on the cattle truck shortly after weaning.

Initially, we shipped our milk in steel cans. It was Grade B milk, destined for cheese. The cans were kept cool in a concrete water tank inside a tiny milk house. Later, when we built a new milk house and got a bulk tank, we were qualified to sell Grade A milk, drinking milk. Dad still has the milk cans. He uses them to haul water to his little flock of sheep.

The bulk tank was about as fancy as we got. We never had a pipeline, or a milking parlor. We stuck with what was essentially 1950s technology, dragging DeLaval milkers from cow to cow. When the attached pail was full, it was lugged to the milk house and dumped through a strainer into the bulk tank, where a big stainless steel paddle stirred the milk to even out the temperature and keep the cream from separating. We kids used to go around behind the back of the tank and stick our hands into the water reservoir that housed the cooling coils. They were coated in ice, and in the middle of summer it was delicious to step into the concrete coolness of the milk house, dip into the painfully cold water, and run my fingers over the slippery coils of ice.

Dad went pretty easy on us with the milking. Some of my friends in school had to milk morning and night. Dad only asked that we help with the evening chores, and my brother and I were allowed to switch off every other night. In the summer, the sticky Wisconsin air made milking a sweaty chore, but in the winter the barn was cozy. We usually kept up a running conversation while we waited for each cow to milk out. Dad did a lot of teaching during milking, and we didn't even know it. I remember once he told me to beware the study of philosophy, because I would wind up questioning everything, including my own faith. He was dead right, of course. I can still see him saying that. I was standing by the calf pen, and he was kneeling with his head against the flank of a cow, his arm threaded between her hocks in a sort of half nelson to keep her from kicking the milker. The rolling mercury switch in the vacuum pump spun round and round, the silvery bead splashing from one end of the glass tube to the other, connecting and disconnecting the electrical current that ran the milkers and set up the quiet rhythm behind every milking session: *chit-chhh, chit-chhh, chit-chhh* . . .

In the summers we hayed, trading work with the neighbors, switching back and forth between farms through the first and second crop, and sometimes a third crop. My brothers and I marked our development as men by how high we could stack hay on a wagon. The day I balanced a bale on my forearms and pitched it nine high, I felt my shoulders broaden. From haying I learned to love to sweat. Once we were stacking bales in the peak of the neighbor's steel shed, bale after bale spilling off the elevator, into the palpable air, and the sweat ran from us like water squeezed from a sponge, and the chaff plastered itself to our forearms and the hollow of our necks, and between loads we went to the cool milk-house and drank long drinks of tap water from a steel dipper tasting of brass. In midafternoon, we pulled the thermometer from the milk-house windowsill and took it to the haymow with us, and when we finished the next load, it read 113 degrees. The best sounds of haying are the sounds you hear from a distance—the up-and-down groan of the tractor engine as it lugs against the plunger that drives the hay into the bale chamber, the delicate *clink-a-chunk* of the needles threading through the knotter. We bale the hay so that in the dead of winter we can pop the strings and feed the cows flakes of summer.

It was field work I loved the most. I loved the hours on the tractor, and often worked the dirt late into the night. There is a field in the back forty, a wide square that drops gently to the west, and one night I ran the drag until well past midnight, criss-crossing the field over and over in the small pool of yellow light the headlights made, back and forth, north and south, then in diagonals, the dust rising in the darkness behind me until the soil lay smooth in the night. When the sun had gone down, a coolness came on, and toward the end of the night pockets of cool air gathered in the low spots, and when I passed through them I could feel the heat rising from the crankcase, and I squeezed it between my knees to draw off some of the warmth. When I drove into the yard, the house was dark, but a light was on in the porch. I parked the tractor in the shed, listened to it click and cool as I walked away, and felt the dirt in my teeth, the dirt in my ears, the dust all across my face, and I felt strong and useful and good.

My father's red barn is empty now. The cows are gone, the paint is peeling. But do not brace yourself for an elegy. Every generation has its change. Time has a way of turning even the most revolutionary among us into reactionaries hung up on recollections. I am susceptible, especially when I see yet another vinyl-sided box sprouting in a cornfield. But I am resisting based on the fact that historian Frederick Turner established years ago that the land is a palimpsest, that change and adaptation were constant. Sometimes if the weather is right you can tune in the public radio station that broadcasts from the Lac Courte Oreilles Reservation up north. If you catch the Native American news, you will be reminded that it is never the frontier that is vanquished, it is the people. In *The Wisconsin Frontier* (1998), author Mark Wyman writes that, "Indians were most tested when later waves of newcomers had less need to rely on native inhabitants and often considered them barriers to progress." This line echoes in my head when I see the suburbs devouring the farm fields. An entire culture is being trampled, driven not by Manifest Destiny, but by the fact that people want a house and a garage.

In the year 2000, my Indianhead Regional Telephone Directory arrived with its cover decorated by a stylized illustration of an overalled farmer tilling a field. He rode an old-style green tractor with a narrow front end, just the same as the John Deere B I cut my teeth on. The classic red barn and silo were visible on the horizon beneath a fat yellow sun. It was a sweet scene, evocative of everything that draws me to this place. And it was an utter illusion. These days, if you see a John Deere B, it's owned by a collector, or it's a hobby farm plaything. The farmers who didn't get wiped out in the early eighties got wiped out in the late nineties. The dairy barns are empty or decaying or replaced by monster operations, and as for the silos, several guys I went to high school with make a living tearing them down, stave by stave. Here was this image intended to convey rural Wisconsin, and it amounted to a commemoration of the irretrievable. Even the sun was outdated, drawn as a round earpiece from one of those hefty phone receivers that are becoming as dated as tail fins. The poet Richard Brautigan once said that the "doomed" purpose of one of his books was "to keep the past and the present functioning simultaneously." How far can iconography lag behind reality before it fails to convey identity?

The controversy over the state quarter fueled a nice little run of editorials and chatter. I was driving across the state in the wake of the governor's decision, and heard the issue addressed on Wisconsin Public Radio. Some callers hinted that farmers had conspired to tilt the online vote. Others found the cow-and-cheese image frankly passé. Several pro-cow callers countered that trappers and Indians were hardly unique to Wisconsin. They felt that regardless of the current state of the countryside, dairy products put this state on the map, and so it should remain. Both sides were proud to be from Wisconsin. They weren't so sure they were proud to be from the other guy's Wisconsin. My trip took me through some of the heart of Milwaukee, and as I poked along, I wondered what my Wisconsin life had to do with this urban Wisconsin life. At a truck stop along the interstate, I pondered a rack of picture postcards. There were a lot of red barns and black-and-white cows, with the caption, "America's Dairyland." California has led the nation in milk and butter production for years now.

Somewhere from within the flux and multiplicity, identity emerges. For the moment, in Wisconsin, we are most universally regarded as cheese-heads. On the grounds that a certain amount of reasonable stereotyping is fundamental to both the ascription and appropri-ation of identity, I do not object. If I may register a single reservation, it is that I prefer *cheddar*-head. The specificity of the term imparts an element of sophistication, even as the *thumpy-thump* tempo of the internal rhyme scheme preserves a spirit of novelty. *Cheddar*-head is a smooth blend of self-deprecation and gravitas. *Cheese*-head is a plain goof—a generic dictum along the lines of a United Nations–brokered compromise designed to avoid alienating the Swiss-heads, the Colby-heads, the Gorgonzola-heads, and those little gift-pak Gouda-heads. Unity supersedes, I suppose. Until we are willing to scrub "America's Dairyland" from our license plates, we must bind together in cheese and pretend California never happened.

Michael Perry
New Auburn, Wisconsin

Images of the Midwest

SECTION EDITOR
James R. Shortridge

Section Contents

Overview

Place imagery appears a trivial subject at first glance. The associations of Wisconsin with cheese and Colorado with mountains, to take two popular examples, are known to conceal as much as they reveal. Our educational system rightfully teaches us to be suspicious of such stereotypes. Imagery persists, however. It does so for the practical reason that real places are immensely complicated. People need some kind of geographical shorthand in order to make sense of the world around them, and regional images perform this role. When conceived of in such a way, a consideration of images is critical for understanding the development of the Midwest or any other place. How the residents and others perceive this region has greatly influenced countless decisions, including ones about immigration, business location, and vacation destination.

Any discussion of place imagery is necessarily idiosyncratic. The organization of this section reflects that with longer essays that address generalized images and less lengthy ones that address social and production images, images reflected in literature and popular cul-

American Gothic, by Grant Wood (1930). 1930.934, Oil on beaverboard, 74.3 × 62.4 cm, Friends of American Art Collection. All rights reserved by The Art Institute of Chicago and VAGA, New York, New York.

ture, and images of location and destination. Few definitive studies exist and the subject is almost impossible to quantify. The Midwest is doubly difficult in this regard, for both the term itself and the particular real estate said to be midwestern have varied considerably in their definitions over the last century and a quarter. Even today, I can find maps that depict the region as lying entirely west of the Mississippi River, and others that limit its range to Ohio, Illinois, and the other states of the old Northwest Territory. Sometimes Chicago is the focal city; sometimes it is a peripheral outpost.

Creation of an Image. Most people assume that the regional labels *Midwest* and *West* are associated in some manner. The story most often repeated asserts that after Ohio, Indiana, and Michigan began to develop beyond the frontier stage, people decided that these places no longer were "Western" in the sense of being undeveloped land. They supposedly sought a new name to differentiate themselves from the true frontier territory of the plains and beyond, and so coined the phrase *Middle West* (or *Midwest*). This scenario is logical but wrong. The label actually has a more recent origin. The time is the 1880s, not the 1830s, and the place is Kansas and Nebraska.

A Middle West on the plains was a product of post–Civil War expansion. People from both the North and the South moved westward in large numbers in the late 1860s, and the surge continued throughout the 1870s and 1880s. The process brought a huge swath of country into the public consciousness. Texas was part of this, so was Kansas, and so too the Dakotas. But these three places were hardly alike. Texas, for example, was southern and Spanish in cultural heritage, the land northward from Kansas mostly northern and northern European. Much of Kansas and Texas had been settled for a generation or more by the 1880s, and so exhibited a somewhat rooted character quite unlike the frontier conditions that still existed in the far northern plains. Realizing all this, writers began to compartmentalize the region. They created "Southwest" as a label to describe Texas and Indian Territory, "Northwest" for the Dakotas and Montana, and, of course, "Middle West" for Kansas and Nebraska.

The imagery associated with the plains Middle West in the late nineteenth and early twentieth centuries is interesting for its own sake, but even more so because these same traits were applied as well to the older Northwest Territory. The similarity would soon lead to an expansion of the area said to be midwestern. These traits also are important because most of them have persisted to the present time. Indeed, they are the ones still most fundamental to regional identity.

Three themes predominate: the vastness, fertility, and climatic extremes of the land; the pastoral nature of the society; and the blend there of youthful vigor and mature judgment.

Although settlers had evaluated prairie landscapes somewhat skeptically when they first encountered them in Illinois early in the nineteenth century, the virtues of these big grasslands were fully appreciated by the time of the postwar boom. Technology was then available to drain wet areas, to plow through even the toughest virgin sod, and to import any lumber that might be needed for construction. Beauty, fertility, and a sense of vastness all remained, however. And the descriptions were much the same as this one from a generation before: "Here light predominates instead of shade . . . while the extent of the open scene . . . allows the eye to roam abroad, over an endless diversity of agreeable subjects." Writer after writer perceived a "solitary grandeur" in the immense land. Many compared the waving grass to the swells of an ocean; a few found the vastness reminiscent of the Sahara.

Once the prairie was cultivated, images of oceans gave way to those of fertility. Often this abundance was symbolized by photographs of corn plants fourteen feet tall or stories about grain harvests so big that elevator capacity was exhausted. Plump animals and other exhibits at county and state fairs sent the same message, the kind of fecund symbols later captured in the paintings of Iowan Grant Wood.

Domes of blue sky punctuated by puffs of cumulus clouds have been important components of the image of open space. The sky always has been a varied symbol for the Midwest, however, because it produces thunderheads, blizzards, hailstorms, fierce winds, and searing heat as easily as it generates spectacular sunsets and fair-weather clouds. Changeability and extremes in weather patterns, in fact, are one of the region's defining characteristics. In the early days settlers often saw these events as tests sent by God. More recently they have become badges of pride. Coping with environmental extremes toughens personal resolve, residents feel, and the widespread ravages of a flood or a big snowstorm bring out a cooperative spirit.

Writers about Kansas and Nebraska in the 1890s saw a people who had passed through the difficult years of pioneering. Life in a rewarding but capricious climate had tested their mettle, and they emerged self-reliant and independent, kind and thrifty. According to a typical report, even "the Garden of Eden was not more purely pastoral" than was Nebraska in 1900, and the settlers there were "worthy specimens of a worthy type—plain, sensible, honest men who have never begged any odds in the game of life, and whose strongest wish seems to be to stand square with their fellows."

Descriptions of early Midwesterners sound like idealizations of rural life, but they were meant as fact, not philosophy. The region was portrayed almost universally as a happy middle ground, suspended providently between the untamed wilderness on the one hand and crowded, corrupted cities on the other. Such a pastoral existence was an old dream, of course. It had special meaning for Americans in the late nineteenth century, however, because they needed to reestablish a national identity after the devastation of civil war. Removed from the old scenes of conflict, the plains of the Midwest provided a useful place symbolically and otherwise to start anew with hard work, idealism, and the other traits associated with Thomas Jefferson's view of a nation of yeoman farmers.

The power that the cluster of pastoral traits carried for Americans is demonstrated by a rapid, grassroots expansion of the area said to be midwestern in the first decade of the twentieth century. Without coercion, residents of the northern plains, Iowa, and Missouri, and then, slightly later, those of the old Northwest Territory, began to call themselves Midwesterners. It was an unprecedented event. Part of the explanation for the relabeling must have come from the awkwardness of the existing popular names for most of this territory, the New Northwest and the Old Northwest, respectively. But the biggest reason seems to have been the widespread appeal of the image of independent farmers and wholesome small-town merchants living productively in the fertile interior of the nation. People simply wanted to be a part of it.

A third cluster of images that contributed to the appeal of the Midwest as it expanded into a twelve-state region was a popular comparison made between regions and the human life cycle. In this scheme the West was said to be youthful, and thus energetic and optimistic, but also reckless and radical. The East, in contrast, had passed into old age. Its economy was in decline, its soils exhausted, and its people ridden by conflict. The Midwest avoided both of these extremes. It was analogous to a young adult, a place that still had vigor and idealism, but also good judgment and increasingly sophisticated taste. Many people pointed to the region's mature agriculture and a growing industrial base. Carl Sandburg's Chicago, that half-naked and sweating hog butcher to the nation, epitomized this view.

Modern Images. Pastoral symbols survive in the Midwest today to a remarkable degree. No matter that its people are mostly urban, residents and outsiders alike still associate this regional label with the growing of corn and wheat and the production of milk, beef, and pork. It is a landscape of red barns, silos, John Deere tractors, and two-story, white farmhouses. Small towns punctuate the scene, each full of friendly Main Street merchants, quiet churches, courthouse towers, and grain elevators. Even the land-survey pattern depicts honesty, an almost geometric world where the roads run in cardinal directions and all the fields contain multiples of 160 acres. Midwestern pastoralism also has been symbolized by a host of particular places and the straightforward individuals they have produced. In Kansas it might be the linkage of Abilene with Dwight D. Eisenhower, in Nebraska perhaps that of Norfolk with Johnny Carson. Regionwide the best example may be River City, Meredith Willson's fictionalized version of Mason City, Iowa, where the good citizens once reformed even that rogue traveling salesman known as "The Music Man."

The retention into the twenty-first century of pastoral images as the core of midwestern cultural identity is mysterious. The region still has farms and small towns, of course, but its people are now overwhelmingly urban. They earn their livings in the service sector and in manufacturing plants, and they are increasingly diverse, ethnically and otherwise. Nevertheless, surveys reveal that even residents of Chicago and Detroit associate the region largely with rural symbols. I believe that the explanation for this perception stems from contradictions that exist in the American character. We simultaneously want to see ourselves as the world's industrial leader, as wholesome farmers in touch with the land, and as unfettered and youthful Daniel Boones. Perhaps the only way to hold on to this set of beliefs is to compartmentalize them and assign each one to a specific section of the country.

The image of the Midwest as a young adult has not endured as well as that of pastoralism. In the late 1910s and early 1920s these two traits had combined to make the region the undisputed heart of the nation. Farming was still an admired way of life, and the industrial development that was associated with young adulthood produced the best of all worlds. This pairing, however, proved impossible to maintain symbolically. A combination of several factors—the nation continuing to associate the region with farming, farming beginning to fall from favor as an occupation of choice, and the simple aging of the population—led to two major image shifts. Industry and large cities disappeared as regional symbols, and the farmers and small-town merchants began to be called hicks rather than yeomen. Whereas Midwesterners had once been equated with all manner of progressive ideas—the initiative and the recall in politics, the regulation of railroads and banks, and the prohibition of alcohol—they gradually came to personify an inward-looking conservatism. Fighting Bob La Follette and Sockless Jerry

Simpson yielded to Joseph McCarthy, the earthy goodness of Antonia Cuzak to the narrow and twisted residents of Gopher Prairie, Minnesota, and Winesburg, Ohio. In the process the heartland was transformed into somewhat of a forgotten place. People began to call it flyover country.

The nadir of midwestern imagery occurred about 1970. In more recent years, although some writers continue to portray the region as bypassed America, an opposing view has emerged. The cities of California and the East Coast, which had seemed so alluring in the 1940s and 1950s, lost some of their charm. Crime began to rise in these places; so did congestion and pollution. Realization also grew that something vague but important about belonging to a community was threatened by the new lifestyles. The Midwest came to be perceived by many people thinking in this way as a kind of haven. Its small towns and farmsteads stood for roots, they said, for connectivity to family and environment. Iowa, for example, was a touchstone to a more genuine America, a place where a person might establish a "field of dreams."

Localized Images. If the set of general midwestern images sketched above was matched with those of individual states, the correspondence would be closest for Iowa. Everybody seems to agree on this, and it is easy to find claims that this state represents the core of midwestern values in every decade of the twentieth century. Nowhere else is the land's fertility so uniformly high and the climate so ideal for agriculture. Rural prosperity came easily there. The absence of a large urban center is important to the symbolic dominance as well, because this means no challenges for the pastoral themes. Des Moines, clean and modest, is arguably the capital of the region as much as it is of Iowa. Illinois, the only serious challenger as the midwestern focus, makes its claim at a different scale. Whereas Iowa epitomizes all things midwestern, Illinois, with a far richer mixture of terrains, occupations, and cultures, is more a microcosm of the United States. To the extent that the Midwest also has been viewed as such a microcosm, then Illinois qualifies as a center.

The states of Michigan and Ohio, the eastern outposts of the Midwest and the last two places to adopt this regional name in the 1910s, are now uncomfortably labeled. The cities of Cleveland, Detroit, and Toledo have personified heavy industry throughout most of the twentieth century. Populations are more diverse in these states than elsewhere in the region as well. Work in the automobile and steel plants attracted hundreds of thousands of immigrants from nearly every country in eastern and southern Europe, as well as from Appalachia and the lower South. The original affinity of these states for the Midwest label was based on the same microcosm idea used in Illinois. Ohio especially fit this conception, and people there glorified themselves for having produced eight national presidents between the 1840s and the 1920s. Things are different now. A survey conducted in the 1980s revealed that most young Ohio residents preferred to be called Easterners, not Midwesterners. This is not illogical, given the time zone and the similarity of Ohio's economic structure to that of Pennsylvania.

Midwestern symbolism provides almost as inadequate a generalization for its northern district as it does for the east. A clear line through the midsection of Michigan, Wisconsin, and Minnesota separates a southern, agricultural sector from a land of paper mills, mines, and tourism. This division is partly a product of geology, partly that of climate, but the cultural results are equally striking. The northland was opened up by a lumber boom that extended from the 1840s into the early decades of the twentieth century. Large-scale mining of copper and iron ore were characteristic as well. These activities gave an industrial character to the region, especially to Michigan and Wisconsin, where strong manufacturing traditions were enforced in Detroit and Milwaukee. A more lasting legacy has been a tradition of liberal government produced as a reaction to the conservatism of the lumber and mine bosses. Developed under the leadership of Wisconsin's Robert La Follette and others, it levies high taxes but also promotes social justice with excellent levels of support for public education and health. The idea has been carried to its most extreme in North Dakota. There a large contingent of Norwegian immigrants helped to bring the Non-Partisan League to power in 1916 and produced a system of state-owned banks and grain elevators.

Terrain and settlement history create a third transition away from midwestern imagery in southeastern and southern Ohio, in the southern sections of Indiana and Illinois, and in the southern half of Missouri. All of these places have cultural roots in Virginia. Their people brought with them a taste for the Baptist religion and for timbered, hilly landscapes where they could best practice a mixed, largely subsistence economy. The stereotype of these places has always been more hillbilly than yeoman farmer. This is apparent in the large vernacular regions known as "Little Egypt" in Illinois and "Little Dixie" in Missouri, and by the tone of popular advertising from the resort towns of Brown County, Indiana, and Branson, Missouri. In Missouri the combined effect of the Ozarks, Little Dixie, and the cotton country of the boot-heel region is enough to make midwestern credentials as shaky as those in Ohio.

Finally, midway across Kansas, Nebraska, and the Dakotas, midwestern imagery gives way to that of the West. Most residents of the High Plains still regard themselves as Midwesterners, and both the rural way of life there and the vast expanse of the land certainly conform to core symbols. A Corn Belt economy of 160-acre farms and a dense rural population was not sustainable on the true plains, however. The precipitation totals simply were too low and too variable. As a result, wheat, range cattle, and a boom-and-bust mentality replaced corn, hogs, and predictable prosperity. Many of the farmers transformed themselves into ranchers and learned to live comfortably in this "big sky" country. The cowboy image dominates west of the hundredth meridian.

Sources and Further Reading: Joseph E. Baker, "The Midwestern Origins of America," *American Scholar* 17 (Winter 1947–1948); Andrew R. L. Cayton and Susan E. Gray, eds., *The American Midwest: Essays on Regional History* (2001); James Hall, *Statistics of the West* (1837); Charles M. Harger, "New Era in the Middle West," *Harper's New Monthly Magazine* (July 1918); Rollin L. Hartt, "Middle-Westerners and That Sort of People," *Century Magazine* (Dec. 1916); Graham Hutton, *Midwest at Noon* (1946); John A. Jakle, *Images of the Ohio Valley* (1977); Frank R. Kramer, *Voices in the Valley* (1964); Sinclair Lewis, *Main Street* (1920); William R. Lighton, "The Riches of a Rural State," *World's Work* (1900); Meredith Nicholson, "The Valley of Democracy," *Scribner's Magazine* 63 (June 1918); Richard L. Power, *Planting Corn Belt Culture* (1953); Edward A. Ross, "The Middle West: Being Studies of Its People in Comparison with Those of the East," *Century Magazine* (Feb. 1912); James R. Shortridge, *The Middle West: Its Meaning in American Culture* (1989); Henry Nash Smith, *Virgin Land: The American West as Symbol and Myth* (1950); Booth Tarkington, "The Middle West," *Harper's Monthly Magazine* (Dec. 1902).

James R. Shortridge
University of Kansas

Fertility

Surely the most fundamental and enduring image of the American Midwest is that of agricultural productivity—America's breadbasket. It is not a literal breadbasket, for the midwestern states east of the hundredth meridian have not been leading wheat producers for over a century. But the image of agricultural productivity still dominates Americans' perception of the region.

In the American mind, the Midwest is inseparable from the Corn Belt, the heartland of agriculture that stretches from Ohio to the Great Plains. The agriculture practiced in the public's perception consists of mixed farming—highly diversified farm operations

Harvesting wheat. Photo courtesy John Deere & Company. IMG 41424.

raising crops and livestock, perhaps fruits, vegetables, and poultry, in a predictable, changeless cycle of seasons.

The breadbasket is more than simply a production system; essential to it are the social and settlement systems that support production. Midwestern farms in the American imagination are operated by families who are dedicated to their land and to farming as a way of life. These are decent, self-reliant people who are viewed both by themselves and by others as friendly, honest, forthright, and practical, yet idealistic, egalitarian, traditional, and moral. The Jeffersonian ideal—the yeoman farmer—thrives in this image.

Furthermore, these farmers operate in a specific context—small, vibrant family farms are set in a landscape of picturesque small towns. The Midwest is envisioned as a rural environment, in spite of the historic role of the region's cities and the key role of its major metropolitan regions to this day.

The impressive output of midwestern farms is a product of a concurrence of environmental, demographic, economic, and technological forces. Nature in the Midwest is well suited for agricultural activity. Soils in most of the region are rich and fertile. In particular, the mollisols of the prairie, formed under grassland vegetation, are high in nutrients and are among the world's richest soils. Most of the region has a lengthy growing season, with adequate moisture in summer. Slopes are mostly gentle, and the region contains a very high proportion of arable land.

Into this setting came nineteenth-century migrants from the eastern states and northwestern and central Europe. Although they farmed small acreages in their regions of origin, they were market oriented. Much of their produce was consumed at home, but they were not subsistence farmers. They steadily strove to increase their surplus production in order to increase access to cash and the products it could purchase.

The U.S. economy of the nineteenth century produced the tools farmers needed to till the soil, plant and harvest crops, and transport those crops to market. The growing agricultural economy of the Midwest and the emerging industrial strength of the nation were intricately intertwined. Persistently high labor costs in the American economy spurred farmer demand for labor-saving devices—steel plows and grain-harvesting machinery in the nineteenth century; tractors, planters, and corn pickers in the twentieth. Great distances from midwestern farms to the metropolitan centers of consumption created demand for efficient transportation systems—first canals; soon thereafter, railroads. Rail lines became the link that moved technology from factories to farms and produce from farms to market.

As midwestern farm numbers increased, manufacturing enterprises moved westward to the emerging urban system of the region to produce farm implements and other needs, as well as to process the exploding production of the region's farms. The growth of nearly every city in the region was based on either production of agricultural inputs or processing of farm products. The cities could not have existed without farmers to buy their goods and provide them with raw materials for refinement. Chicago and Moline became headquarters for the manufacturing enterprises of Cyrus McCormick (born in Virginia) and John Deere (born in Vermont). Minneapolis thrived on grain milling. Omaha, Kansas City, St. Paul, and, above all, Chicago converted cattle and hogs into meat for consumers.

It was this interdependence of farm and city, of raw material and fabricator/processor that became the hallmark of the midwestern breadbasket. In truth, the midwestern farm was never the bucolic, self-contained enterprise that has dominated the pastoral image of the Midwest. The very productivity of farmers depended upon the technology supplied by industry, the transportation technology to move massive harvests to markets, and the factories that converted resources into marketable commodities. The farm depended on the city.

So, too, did the exploding midwestern metropolises depend upon farmers. Farm residents were the customers for urban goods and the suppliers of sustenance for cities. Likewise, smaller cities and towns existed in symbiotic relationships with their rural hinterlands. Dependent upon rail connections to Des Moines, Indianapolis, Topeka, and, especially, Chicago, smaller places were the "middlemen" of the region's agriculture. Small towns sold the manufactured goods that farm families purchased. They stored the grain that farmers brought to rail sidings, channeled funds to farming operations, and shipped commodities to processors.

In the twentieth century, they also funneled surplus populations from fertile farm families to the manufacturing-driven labor markets of midwestern cities. For that reason alone most urban residents of Sioux City and St. Joseph, of Peoria and Cedar Rapids, are closely attuned to both the agricultural economy and the rural and farm culture. They are farmers just below the surface—only a generation or two removed from the farm.

Despite the oversimplification of the popular image of the region's agricultural system, the Midwest remains the nation's foremost producer of agricultural commodities. For 150 years the Midwest has been the most productive agricultural region in the country. Approximately 41 percent of the nation's agricultural product sales originate in these twelve states. The top ten states in corn acreage are all midwestern. Only two of the top ten states in number of farms with annual sales over a hundred thousand dollars are *not* found in the Midwest. In 1997, the twelve midwestern states contained half the value of U.S. farm machinery. They accounted for 42 percent of the cattle sold, two-thirds of the hogs sold, and six of every seven bushels of corn harvested. Of the hundred top corn-producing counties in the United States, ninety-four were located in the Midwest east of the hundredth meridian.

Although the farm family of nostalgia, if it ever existed, has disappeared, midwestern farming is still largely family-based. Nowhere else in the country are corporate farms less in evidence than here. Corporate organization of farms has increased, but in only a few counties is more than 10 percent of the farmland operated by corporations. Most of those are family-owned corporations.

Agriculture in the Midwest has been undergoing structural changes that reflect agricultural transformations in the nation as a whole. During the second half of the twentieth century, these changes were associated primarily with the growing size of farms and the rise of industrial agriculture.

At the turn of the twenty-first century, farm ownership patterns have changed dramatically. Family farmers living on their land often do not own much of the land they operate, and they increasingly depend on nonfarm sources of income. Relatively little land is farmed by full owners, except in Missouri, Wisconsin, northern Minnesota, and Michigan's Upper Peninsula. In most of Illinois, less than 20 percent of farmland is operated by full owners. Driven by the need to acquire more farmland so they can maintain an adequate income, farmers have turned to part ownership—some land is owned; quite a bit more is rented. This is the dominant pattern in nearly all of the region. Tenant farmers operate about 12 percent of the farmland, only slightly above the national average. Tenancy has long been particularly important in much of Illinois and is increasingly significant in northern Iowa.

In the Iowa-Illinois core of the region, 30 percent of farmers report more than two hundred days of off-farm work each year. That figure rises to around 40 percent in Indiana, Michigan, and Ohio, where there are greater opportunities for wage labor in urban areas. In just a handful of counties is the figure under 20 percent.

In the post–World War II era, agriculture became increasingly reliant on the standardization and specialization characteristic of manufacturing enterprises. Most important, consumption of energy skyrocketed as farmers substituted fossil fuels for most human and animal inputs—especially labor, fuel, and fertilizer. In effect, farmers learned how to make corn from petroleum.

Not only are most midwestern farms family operated, those operators live on their farms. Typically, over 70 percent of farm operators reside on the farms they operate, unlike agriculture in other major production areas of the United States. Only in the western margins of the region, particularly in western Kansas, with its tradition of *sidewalk* and *suitcase* farmers, is the share of absentee operators especially high.

Purchased energy to operate tractors and raise crop yields increased the capital costs of farming and spurred farm expansion as farmers sought increased income to pay for fixed expenses. The result was growing specialization of agricultural production, both regionally and on individual farms. Farm families reduced their range of production activities and their consumption of home-produced commodities. They sold their chicken flocks and their few milk cows and purchased eggs and milk in grocery stores like urbanites.

Larger farms meant fewer farms, so rural population decline became continuous after about 1935. Fewer farms led directly to declining populations in the small towns that provided services to farmers.

In midwestern counties distant from metropolitan and interstate-highway growth centers, rural population decline has been unabated since the 1930s. Pawnee County in southeastern Nebraska, for example, dropped from nearly 12,000 people in 1900 to only 3,087 in 2000. Not surprisingly, the number of farms has decreased, from an all-time high of 1,409 in 1930 to only 444 in 1997, representing a decrease of 69 percent.

Likewise, the rural landscape has changed with industrialization. The decline in mixed farming has converted the "typical" farm of 1940, with several crops, poultry, cattle, and hogs, to the specialized farm of the present. In the core of the Midwest, this is typically a corn and soybeans operation with no livestock. It needs no fences to keep animals out of fields; old barns, sheds, and corn cribs crumble as industrial metal buildings and grain bins, symbols of industrial mass-production, replace them. Feedlots are found only on specialized factory farms, where manure has become a major waste-disposal problem rather than the resource it represented in 1940.

As industrial farming has grown in importance, it has become less tied to the geographic characteristics that made the Midwest a breadbasket. California now leads the nation in dairy production. North Carolina has become a major center of hog production; Arkansas leads in poultry; and the giant cattle feedlots are in Colorado and western Kansas.

Although industrial elements dominate midwestern agriculture today, the region continues to lead the nation in agricultural output and farming remains primarily a family-based activity. And, in spite of the growing importance of many types of agricultural production outside the Midwest, the region remains the nation's breadbasket both in the nation's consciousness and in reality. The yeoman farmer may have vanished long ago, and the bucolic landscapes of mixed farming may survive only as nostalgia. But the identity of the region as the core of America's food production remains fact.

Sources and Further Reading: Bradley H. Baltensperger, "Larger and Fewer Farms," *Journal of Historical Geography* 19 (June 1993); William Cronon, *Nature's Metropolis* (1991); David B. Danbom, *Born in the Country* (1995); John C. Hudson, *Making the Corn Belt* (1994); Mark Kramer, *Three Farms* (1980); James H. Madison, ed., *Heartland: Comparative Histories of the Midwestern States* (1988); James R. Shortridge, "The Emergence of the 'Middle West' as an American Regional Label," *Annals of the Association of American Geographers* 74 (June 1984); James R. Shortridge, *The Middle West: Its Meaning in American Culture* (1989); John L. Shover, *First Majority, Last Minority* (1976).

Bradley H. Baltensperger
Michigan Technological University

Land of Flatness

Most places in the Midwest are relatively unknown. They are little known because they are extremely rural. Kearny County, Kansas, like others, is *extremely* rural. But unlike others, it is a landscape that is also extremely isolated, part of a quilted pattern of very small counties that, in a precise grid, blanket the High Plains that gradually roll downstream from the Front Range of the Rockies in the west to the Missouri and Mississippi basin in the east. Kearny County was, and still is, farm and ranching country, a mix that characterizes the western border of the Midwest. It is not the homestead landscape like others in the Midwest, where smaller family farms, which slowly exited the agricultural scene in the 1980s, were arranged in tight 160-acre parcels. The Township and Range System— a systematic landscape of one-mile squares—has left its imprint on this land of broken escarpments, sand hills, and high tableland with endless horizons, but the culture of agriculture here never acquired an affinity for diversity like most American farms to the east. In the 1870s settlers from Iowa, Illinois, eastern Kansas, and Missouri came to the High Plains, and later they followed the Atchison, Topeka and Santa Fe Railroad to places such as Lakin, Deerfield, and Garden City. They devoured the open plain; marked their parcels with barbed wire; and blazed trails through short grass, yucca, and sagebrush. Their conventions, and inventions, were not suited for the land, and following a sequence of dry years, most of them left. They left

Flatness of land, North Dakota. Photo by Dawn Charging. Courtesy North Dakota Tourism Department.

behind two important legacies: one, a roughly hewn landscape of abandoned parcels that were quickly nabbed by those who decided to stay—farmers and ranchers with financial backing that allowed them to weather the dust and wind; and, two, a shallow understanding of the land that, for such a short time, they called home.

Only a handful of the first generation of European settlers decided to stay. These families tried to grow gardens—the land speculators who founded Garden City, southwest Kansas's largest town, tried to convince migrants that all kinds of fruits and vegetables could be easily grown there in an attempt to draw settlers. But the small garden plots adjoining the homesteads, the dugouts, and the sod houses made from blocks of earth were the only major attempt at agricultural diversification. The main cash crop was dry-land wheat, which required only a minimal amount of precipitation year in and year out. It was not drought resistant, but suited for the sixteen inches of rain that falls here some years. Farmers also had pigs and sheep, and in the valley of the Arkansas River they had orchards and in the early 1900s began diverting river water for alfalfa and sugar beets.

To the south of the river, which for some time was crossable only by pontoon, a handful of ranchers also grazed cattle. South of the river was a different place. It was the northeastern reach of the desert Southwest, where cactus, sagebrush, and coyotes were indigenous and farmers transplanted from Illinois and Ohio were not. In line with the social climate of America at the time, those who dared to venture into the hills attempted to tame it—first with cattle and barbed wire, later with thousands of trees—aimed at making it an agricultural oasis. During the 1930s, which were

clearly the hardest of times, ranching families marketed surplus eggs, chickens, and cream in nearby communities in order to survive. Wells and springs dried up under the wind and the sun, and the landscape experiment that had become a success in the rest of the Midwest nearly folded.

This was apparently no lesson, and the concerns of an older generation that lived through a decade of dust passed into story and myth. Many present-day residents first witnessed the howl of the wind, dust clouds looming, and survived the moving sand dunes in the early 1970s. Then, children walked, or rode buses, in complete darkness to school. The streetlights on Main Street in Lakin were the only beacons leading them to the school building that, during daylight and dust-free days, was unmistakably the largest such structure in Kearny County. Many would argue they were walking through a vestige of the past, a hallmark of culture in southwest Kansas that recurs every ten or twenty years, when dry weather coupled with wind put the entire place in jeopardy and put most of the small-scale farmers and ranchers out of business. The tenacity of a midwestern cultural trait—a fascination with horizontal space—had manifest itself in the Sand Hills where thousands of acres of rolling desert were effectively wiped clean. This land no longer tells its own story but has been silenced by hundreds of miles of pipelines, irrigation sprinklers, and farm machinery that hum with the sound of progress. Thousands of wells tap limited aquifer water, in some places two hundred feet below the surface, which, in turn, fuels a new agriculture and the contemporary culture of Kearny County.

By the early 1980s, those who could not get big, got out of agriculture in western Kansas. It was at this point that agriculture became agro-industrial. In the decades since, like the rest of southwest Kansas, Kearny County has become highly mechanized. Crop types were diversified—to include corn and alfalfa—but mass production, not diversification, became the goal. Kearny County now plays its own rather small part in an American culture of automobiles, mobility, McDonalds, and Wal-Mart. Most of the smaller family-owned parcels have been gobbled up by larger farms and ranchers and by speculators from places far away. People no longer drive to Lakin to market eggs, chicken, and cream; nor do they come to buy socks, shoes, or invisible tape. The last department store in town closed when the new agriculture in the Sand Hills began, and the fascination with the automobile has led to a fascination with driving twenty-five minutes each way, many times a week, to trade in Garden City. This weekly, if not daily, ritual is mirrored by the daily commute of farmers to and from work, by school buses traveling over and across wide expanses of ranchland to pick up a handful of kids, and by the winds blustering through tassels of corn. In the short tenure of American culture on this landscape, a legacy of linear association—horizontal thinking—has evolved. The linear is manifest in landscape arrangement, where all county roads, town streets, property lines, and the relatively few trees resemble a straight edge, by perfect design.

A few families have been here for over 120 years, and some a bit longer, but this place is still very little known. And it is not only unknown because it is the western range of flyover country, that large, expansive, in-between space that lies somewhere between Denver and Kansas City. But it is *terra incognita*—unknown ground—to most of its occupants. Because of the plight of its inhabitants during the 1930s, this place holds an important place in the American psyche. While "Dusters," as the remaining handful of survivors are called, do not suffer from any John Steinbeck–induced chip on their shoulders, as do the dwellers from the state directly to the south, they do understand how resilience in such a harsh environment takes hindsight and, well, foot-sight. They can look down at their feet and literally and figuratively see their lives rooted in the dust. These connections are represented in nostalgia and museum displays, but little has been said by anyone there about how the Dust Bowl experience has a bearing on the future. This is because conversations, not unlike landscape features, are linear as well, with that which lies directly and inevitably in front. In a timely sense, this is what lies immediately ahead, what can be secured for the rest of the day and, perhaps, tomorrow. But there is little forethought about what might happen in ten years, and this is perhaps because people have easily forgotten what happened ten years gone. No one ever seems to find the time, even in extremely rural Kearny County, to stop and think about what lies beneath them. Conversations never seem to occur perpendicular to the landscape, or in a necessary retrograde fashion that might aid in avoiding another calamity. Convenience stores and grain elevators are full of talk about wind, rain, freezes, and commodity prices—weather and market forecasts that lie ahead—but the land seems to be only a stage where a well-known drama of the 1930s could be reenacted.

While there have been few success stories in agricultural diversification here, cultural diversification appears to be working, for now. The predominant culture of southwestern Kansas is a combination of various forms of southern plains and midwestern cultures—including that of eastern Kansas, which people out here despise—homogenized into a plains culture that does not completely fit any midwestern stereotype or mold. It is an in-between culture, lurking somewhere in the shadows of the agricultural utopia to the north and east and the cultural utopia to the south and west. Its members are divided as a people in the American consciousness as being of the plains, but somewhere between the West of the Rockies, the Southwest of the desert, and the Midwest of the Rust, Corn, and Wheat Belts. There is no use in pretending that the contradictions between these American traits cause confusion for the culture here, because there has been a successful merging of the steadfast Jeffersonian farmer with the Texas oilman and the Colorado rancher.

The lack of a fascination with the distinctiveness of their culture translates, at least in Kearny County, to a detachment from things afar. Very few are overly concerned with events that occur two or three counties away, let alone with what happens in Kansas City, Sacramento, or Beijing. Remarkably, the culture here has accepted, or perhaps required to varying degrees, an ethnically diverse population of migrants from all over Mexico, Central America, and Southeast Asia in order to fuel its agro-industrial machine. This has led to the proliferation of ethnic arts, religion, and food, and a much-needed internationalization of the local schools. But this diversity is in jeopardy, if not because the international cultures do not intersect the dominant one on an even cultural plane, then because it has been the landscape, not places of national or regional origin, that has proven to dictate culture here.

Kearny County lies on the edge of the Midwest, many of its residents have midwestern origins, and they have tried to do some stereotypically midwestern things here, particularly with the land. Only a few (and those who survived the Dust Bowl make up the vast majority) have really come to understand this place as if it were more than a backdrop or setting for the un-folding drama of the creation of American culture, midwestern or not. Nowhere in the Midwest—whether the dells of Wisconsin, the arrowhead of Minnesota, or the South Side of Chicago—has a culture that is as flat as the one here. Kearny County culture is as unique to the Midwest as it is to the rest of the world, but when the remaining few Dusters go with the wind, its most prominent characteristic—a flatness that emulates the level plains—could very well blow away just as so much dust and so many others have the past 120 years.

Sources and Further Reading: Peter McCormick, "Traces in the Sand," *North American Geographer* 1 (Spring 1999); Frank Popper and Deborah Popper, "The Great Plains," *Planning* 53 (1987); Pamela Riney-Kehrberg, *Rooted in Dust* (1994); James Shortridge, *Peopling the Plains* (1995).

Peter J. McCormick
Fort Lewis College, Colorado

Flyover Country

Flyover country is a term of playful condescension toward rural America from an urban perspective. In popular use, it labels the irritatingly wide, relatively empty lands one flies over on the way from one coast of the United States to the other. Symbolically, it refers less to a specific physical place than to any part of the country that Americans have traveled over or through, but have not touched, and would rather not touch. In this sense, it represents more than empty space (forests and deserts may be flown over, but they are, at worst, neutral landscapes); the term assumes settlement and culture, but culture that is dull and irrelevant. Altogether, it implies a land and a people to be avoided. In simple terms, flyover country is rural America, and the Midwest, as the most recognized icon of rural life and culture, is the quintessential flyover country.

The label *flyover country* (sometimes "fly-over country" or "flyover land") first appeared in popular literature in the late 1970s, when urban growth in the United States was just reaching its apex (suburban growth took its place). The term's use has gradually accelerated since then, evolving from a hyphenated form introduced in quotes ("fly-over") in the early 1980s, into a widely recognized synonym for the Midwest by the mid-1990s. The phrase is most consistently defined as the space between the coasts or, more specifically, between New York City and Los Angeles. Though it began as a pejorative applied by those living on the coasts, it is increasingly adopted by Midwesterners as a regional label for home.

This definition has not yet earned a listing in print dictionaries, or until now, even in an encyclopedia, but online slang dictionaries have filled the gap:

> The middle class Midwest that is typically "flown over" by scheduled airlines in their hops between their major hubs. The bounds of flyover country vary from urbanite to urbanite. People from Chicago tend to think it runs from the Mississippi River to the Rockies (and also Indiana). Bay Area, it's the San Joaquin Valley east to Chicago. New York, it's anything that is not within an hour's drive of The City. Pejorative nickname for middle America, most often used by people on the east or west coast. Also: fly-over country.

Flyover country, though a relatively recent label, expresses an attitude much older than powered flight. It seems straightforward and benign at face value, but it veils a deep current in the American psyche about the nature, purpose, and meaning of rural America. It is laden with contemporary urban beliefs about rural places and people as obsolete, backward, superfluous, laughable, and possibly dangerous. Ironically, it also represents the Midwest as the imagined reservoir for the solid, simple virtues upon which Americans still place a high value. Thus, while deriding the Midwest as "flyover country," Americans also cling to the notion that it's a place where people still live simple, wholesome lifestyles, do honest work, and draw health and vitality from proximity to nature.

The label is also significant in its application from an outside perspective. Its wide use and recognition, even by those who live in the region, implicitly verifies the dominance that the American coastal cultures have over the country's humble middle. Denizens of the Midwest have grudgingly accepted the label because, in the face of overwhelming dominance by urban America, they haven't the power to coin an enduring label of their own.

Wherever there's a spot of geographical ignorance in the mind of the American public, fiction rushes to fill the void. This is as true of the rural Midwest as it is of remote corners of Africa or Asia. Fiction has delighted in portraying American rural cultures in a dark or laughable manner at least since the late nineteenth century. Works such as *The Wizard of Oz* (1900) and Sinclair Lewis's novel *Main Street* (1920) are prime examples of a negative take on rural midwestern society. Later works, such as Larry McMurtry's *Last Picture Show* (book: 1966, film: 1971), helped perpetuate the rural myths as the nation settled into its urban identity. Subsequent works of print and film fiction have reinforced these images in the American mind. The colorless landscapes and people of Kansas portrayed in the film version of *The Wizard of Oz* (1939)

Farm patchwork from the air. Photo by Paul Stafford, Minnesota Office of Tourism.

are now a solid part of the canon of American childhood imagery, thanks to the ritual yearly television broadcast. Later films have continued to build on popular assumptions about rural people and places as being laughable, backward, or frightening. Rural culture continues to be depicted as an oppressive force in films like *Footloose* (1984) or as downright evil in films like *Breakdown* (1997).

The Midwest also commonly serves as the butt of jokes by outsiders. Take, for instance, the words of "The Waco Kid" in Mel Brooks's notorious 1974 comedy *Blazing Saddles:* "You gotta remember that these are just simple farmers. These are people of the land, the common clay of the new West. You know: *Morons.*" Kansas seems to bear the brunt of these jokes (perhaps *The Wizard of Oz* set a precedent). A good example is a gratuitous insult to the state made by James Bond's arch nemesis, Blofeld, in the 1971 film *Diamonds Are Forever.* Explaining his plans to attack the Earth with a satellite-mounted death ray, he quips, "As you see, Mr. Bond, the satellite is at present over Kansas. But if we destroy Kansas, the world may not hear about it for years." In a print example, respectable scientists published a tongue-in-cheek article in 2003 titled "Kansas Is Flatter than a Pancake," in which they used legitimate scientific methods to compare the surface of a pancake to the topography of Kansas and concluded that the state's "degree of flatness might be described, mathematically, as 'damn flat.'"

Outsiders also use the Midwest as a convenient metaphor for nothingness, desolation, or predictability. Consider this *New York Times* movie review (1989):

The term "fly-over" is sometimes used dismissively to describe parts of the country between its East and West Coasts, areas that, by implication, hold no surprises and can be fully understood without benefit of a visit. There are fly-over films, too, although a perfect one is rare.

And another *New York Times* movie review by a different author (1999):

The staging ground for Dorothy's adventure [*The Wizard of Oz*], the background against which the foreground can take shape, is Kansas—a state that functions as a peculiar place-holder in the American mind, a kind of psycho-topographical zero.

The appearance of the flyover label seems to coincide with changes in Americans' attitudes toward rural life and culture as reflected in the evolution of television programming over the past few decades. In the 1950s and 1960s, popular television dramas such as *Lassie, Bonanza,* and *Daniel Boone* idealized rural life. Then came the playful ridicule of small-town America in popular 1960s television programs such as *Green Acres, Petticoat Junction,* and *Mayberry RFD.* The trend has since gone from making fun of rural America to dispensing with it altogether. Nearly all rural comedies and dramas disappeared from television by 1973. The void was filled with decidedly urban programs such as *All in the Family, Streets of San Francisco,* and *Barney Miller* in the 1970s, and with the likes of *Dallas, Miami Vice, Hill Street Blues,* and *L.A. Law* in the early 1980s, shows that played on popular stereotypes of the dangers and corruption of urban life. The 1990s brought a slightly different set of popular urban shows, such as *Seinfeld, Friends,* and *Ally McBeal.* These programs show the urban setting's transition from a locus of gritty action and intrigue to a stage for everyman stories of human comedy and drama, perhaps indicating a wider acceptance in the public mind of urban life as the norm.

Rural midwestern residents are acutely aware of the flyover perception, and are not pleased about it. Many of them, especially in the Great Plains states, feel belittled and disenfranchised by the rest of the country to begin with. They resent outsiders' presumptions and find it insulting that urban people, knowing almost nothing about them, feel free to stereotype and criticize them. Many of them complain of feeling left out of most of what happens in America. This makes them quick to become defensive in the face of any bicoastal derision. Their hackles rise when they see outsiders set to interfere materially with their lives or communities. In the Midwest, such interventions evoke a deep suspicion that outside or urban agencies single out hapless rural communities because they lack the political clout of the big coastal cities. For example, people on the Great Plains have passionately fought attempts by outside contractors to dump sewage sludge from New York City on local farmland as an alternative fertilizer. They find especially insulting the notion of accepting sewage from a place considered the epitome of urban degradation (the metaphorical significance of such an arrangement should be obvious). In another case, the attempt by the Department of Transportation to replace the only traffic signal with a stop sign in a small Kansas town infuriated the residents; they saw it as an inept, if not hostile, intervention by ignorant and pretentious bureaucrats and, ultimately, as an attack on the validity of their way of life.

One of the most vivid examples of rural Midwesterners' contempt for outside interference is their reaction to the "Buffalo Commons" proposal. This was the work of two Rutgers University researchers, Frank and Deborah Popper, who had noted a steep decline in population and economic vitality in several rural Great Plains counties. They proposed in a 1987 article that the federal government buy up plains property as people moved out and turn the land back to a natural grazing ground for buffalo. They meant only to stimulate thought on the region's future, but residents took the idea as a challenge by coastal urbanites to their personal worth and way of life. They reacted with self-righteous indignation, and even death threats toward the Poppers. The fact that the Poppers' statistics confirmed an alarming depopulation of the plains only seemed to intensify their reactions.

The interplay of urban attitudes toward flyover country and rural people's reactions to those attitudes reflects a fundamental ambivalence and contradiction in American identity and imagery. Although mainstream Americans have essentially disowned their rural background and rural people, they are to a great extent an urban people with rural ideals. As the Midwest has become America's icon of rural life and culture, urban dwellers have developed nostalgia for this rural world, even as they poke fun at it. Thornton Wilder's *Our Town* (1938), a surprisingly popular play about the mundane lives of people in a small New England village, clearly struck a sentimental chord about small-town life in the American psyche. The popularity of television programs such as *The Waltons* and *Little House on the Prairie,* both of which ran well into the 1980s, shows that a romantic view of America's rural past endures. This nostalgia is probably best exemplified today by the tremendous popularity of Garrison Keillor's often poignant portrayals of the quintessentially rural residents of his fictional Lake Wobegon, Minnesota.

Though urban society may try to laugh off the rural culture of the Midwest, the region plays a vital role in national identity and mythology. Americans' interpretations of democracy, independence, and freedom are deeply rooted in their rural past, as are their beliefs in the sanctity of community, strong family relationships, and a strong work ethic. The Midwest is a repository for these nostalgic rural images and ideals, and is a symbol of quiet spaces and unsullied landscapes. Americans need flyover country as a sort of unchanging secret garden where the essential roots and character of American identity can be safely tucked away. To function as such, it must remain unknown to most of urban America. Thus the Midwest could not play this important symbolic role in the American psyche if it was not, in fact, flown over.

Sources and Further Reading: Thomas Fox Averill, "Flyover Country," *North American Review* 284 (Jan. 1999); Mark Fonstad, William Pugatch, and Brandon Vogt, "Kansas Is Flatter Than a Pancake," *Annals of Improbable Research* 9 (May/June 2003); William Least Heat-Moon, "The Great Kansas Passage," introduction to Daniel D. Dancer, *The Four Seasons of Kansas* (1988); Stuart Klawans, "That Void in Cyberspace Looks a Lot Like Kansas," *New York Times* (June 20, 1999); Janet Maslin, "Expectations Confront Reality," *New York Times* (Oct. 1, 1989); Anne Matthews, *Where the Buffalo Roam* (1992); Frank J. Popper and Deborah E. Popper, "The Great Plains," *Planning* 53 (Dec. 1987); James R. Shortridge, "Cowboy, Yeoman, Pawn, and Hick," *Focus* 35 (Oct. 1985); James R. Shortridge, *The Middle West: Its Meaning in American Culture* (1989).

Cary W. de Wit
University of Alaska–Fairbanks

Genuine America

The Midwest is a land of neat, orderly towns and hospitable, friendly people; a land of rock-solid tradition and unhurried pace. It is uniquely American, and utterly charming. When you wander down Main Street (for midwestern America *always* has a Main Street), you'll pass soda fountains, bakers, barbershops, and family restaurants where old-timers with an aw-shucks rusticity trade tall tales over bottomless cups of coffee. If you venture into the surrounding countryside, you'll pass neatly kept farms and covered bridges, windmills and cornfields. Midwesterners are people connected with the earth, but with a firm, controlling hand placed on her shoulder. Whether you are in town or country, you'll find that the region is permeated by a culture deeply rooted in the tilled soil, and founded on homespun virtues such as family, work, and concern for neighbor that have been lost in the hustle and bustle of modern-day America. It's also seen as the most moderate, the most average, the most normal part of the country, whatever these terms might mean. It's midway between untamed nature and concrete-slab civilization. It's the metaphorical as well as the geographic middle between the extremities of the coasts, those supposed freak shows of crime and degradation and lunacy. It's the sensible, stoic emotional middle ground amid the extreme passions of humanity that explode on the evening news every night. In short, the region represents common sense and decency and normal Americanness incarnate. There's even a phrase, dating from vaudeville days, that encapsulates just how normal Midwesterners are: "Will it play in Peoria?" If so, it's a sure thing. After all, this is a culture of sober, sensible, practical, no-nonsense, plainspoken, honest people. This is the "Heartland," everybody's hometown. This is the genuine America.

You've heard this all before, this image of the land out here between Lake Erie and the hundredth meridian. This particular version is a composite of descriptions found in tourism brochures of the midwestern states, but tourism bureaus certainly didn't invent this vision. It's an image with a history almost as long as that of the region itself, and one held by outsiders and old-time residents alike. It is a vision of what we'd like to think we are as a nation, a symbolic realm where our national heart still beats undisturbed by the onslaught of the here and now.

Of course, as with all images, the "genuine America" so lovingly described here is a highly selective one. Above all else, it's a rural and small-town vision. If you look back at the opening description, you'll see no trace of St. Louis or Milwaukee or Omaha. As geographer Donald Meinig has argued, small-town Main Street is in fact one of the quintessential landscapes symbolizing, in the mind of the public, the true essence of our Americanness. Its image is so wholesome, so squeaky-clean, so symbolically associated with American virtue, that Walt Disney chose it as the centerpiece of Disneyland. People's conceptions of the Midwest simply do not include the urban areas that are home to millions. The lack of an urban component to Virtuous Midwesternness hasn't stopped midwestern city-dwellers from trying to claim a little bit of the aura of wholesomeness for themselves, though. For many decades, starting in the 1920s, the *Chicago Tribune* actively promoted the greater Chicago area as "Chicagoland" (a phrase still used in the state's tourism brochures), presenting it as a super-wholesome antidote to the moral chaos of the East and West Coasts. The fact that such a claim wasn't seen as completely laughable at a time when Al Capone was regularly making Chicago headlines is a measure of just how disconnected midwestern images can be from reality.

Alongside the Midwest's positive image, however, there has long run a parallel counterimage. The quintessential portrait of this is Sinclair Lewis's novel *Main Street*. First published in 1920, *Main Street* explores the fine line that separates "tradition" and "values" from fear of change, closed-mindedness, and xenophobia. Main Street, in *Main Street*, is not an island of virtue in a corrupt world, but a cesspool of small-minded philistinism and knee-jerk conservatism, blind to anything outside its own borders. While the positive elements of Main Street's image persist in the minds of many Americans, this shadow *Main Street* follows ever after right behind.

One part of the midwestern image of virtue is of relatively recent vintage—the nostalgic view of the region as a touchstone for traditional values. Prior to World War II, in the heyday of the small midwestern town, "tradition" was the furthest thing from towns-people's minds—growth and modernity was their goal. Midwesterners saw themselves and their communities as the engines of progress that would drive the prosperity of the whole nation. They believed that their homespun American values of honesty and hard work would create a bright, booming future.

In the middle decades of the twentieth century, however, the national economy bypassed these earnest, hard-working Midwesterners. The numbers of family farms, the bedrock of the small-town economy, declined drastically as agriculture became more mechanized and larger scale. Widespread automobile ownership and the developing spiderweb of interstates and highways crisscrossing the land meant that even long-time residents were no longer economically bound to their hometown. Soon, what had been seen as a hopeful vision of the future was instead viewed as an anachronism. The big city was where opportunity lay, in the factories of Detroit or Chicago, and small towns saw their prestige eroding.

The luster of urban life would fade, however, as race riots, growing unemployment, and crime in the 1960s colored Americans' perceptions of cities. In reaction, an increasingly urbanized America put on its rose-colored glasses, and a growing sense of nostalgia began to enter into people's image of the Midwest. Perhaps, they thought, in our rush to abandon our rural past, we have left something behind. And so, in much the same way as we fence off Yellowstone as the last refuge of the wolf and grizzly, we have mentally fenced off our ideal-ized, romanticized Midwest as the last remaining relict stands of a vanishing America, a land of quiet, modest, honest decency in the midst of a corrupt modern world. As with the national parks, many of us will never even visit this repository of our "true" national selves; it's enough just to know that it is there, preserving the way we were, the way we like to see ourselves.

Curiously, at the same time as the nostalgic image of small-town America has become increasingly com-mon, the reality of the rural Midwest is changing con-siderably. Even Main Street doesn't live up to our image of Main Street much anymore. The hardware stores and malt shops of downtown are rapidly being replaced by homogeneous strips of Wal-Marts and McDonalds out on the edge of town. But that hasn't stopped the *idea* of Main Street from remaining one of the quintessential symbolic American landscapes; if anything, the nostalgic pull is strengthened. As urban areas become increasingly homogenized, we need mom and pop stores to retain a tie to our beloved past.

Many midwestern small towns have tried to capitalize on this nostalgia by catering to outsiders interested in connecting with the nation's rural past. Throughout the region, antiques stores now fill many storefronts where dry-goods stores or florists or lawyer's offices or black-smiths or donut stores once were. Festivals commemo-rating the simple, rural, immigrant life abound—it's a rare small town that doesn't have some sort of Harvest Days or Pioneer Festival. In Lindsborg, Kansas, which promotes its Swedish immigrant heritage and its small-town feel to outsiders, city leaders intent on drawing tourist dollars have banned the use of neon signs (which, fifty years earlier, were a source of immeasurable pride in the town as a visual symbol of its modernity) in order to preserve the feel of a rustic, quaint island of the past. No longer trying to catch up to the big cities, small towns now promote the very lack of urbanity that previ-ously was such an embarrassment. Small towns are no longer beacons lighting the way to the future (as they were to their founders) but, rather, preservers of the past.

But this widespread acceptance of the midwestern small town as the epitome of our "real" national identity also has some disturbing undertones. This vi-sion of "genuine" America, after all, requires us to have a "fake" America, which includes those that are excluded from the image. Nobody refers, for example, to Gary, Indiana, as "the real America," or South Side Chicago, or Postville, Iowa, with its Hassidic Jewish community that runs a kosher slaughterhouse. During the aftermath of the Oklahoma City bombing, the middle-America location of the tragedy was a constant focus of the national news reporters. This attack was so horrifying precisely because of its location in the mythical Heartland. It made us feel personally vulner-able because it felt like an attack on the very soul of our nation. That's all very well, but the unspoken sub-text of that image should give us pause. Would it have been *less* tragic if the blast had occurred somewhere on the East or West Coasts and killed new Chinese immi-grants or beatnik poets or poor black single mothers on welfare? Are these people somehow less genuinely American?

Changing demographics may soon force us to con-front the problematic limitations of our romanticized image. Although urban Americans increasingly view the small-town Midwest through a nostalgic haze, the youth in those towns can't wait to get out. In Iowa, for example, more than 60 percent of college graduates leave the state. Meanwhile, Iowa has the third-highest percentage of elderly residents in the nation. As a re-sult, there are not enough workers to staff many new businesses or to allow existing ones to expand. The crisis became so severe that Governor Tom Vilsack did the previously unthinkable at the outset of the twenty-first century: He actively encouraged highly skilled immigrants to settle in Iowa, currently one of the whitest states in the country. He selected three communities (Mason City, Fort Dodge, and Marshall-town) to promote as immigration zones.

Even before Governor Vilsack's plan, Marshall-town had already undergone notable shifts—this town of twenty-six thousand absorbed more than seven thousand Hispanic newcomers in the last few years of the twentieth century, largely workers attracted by the town's meatpacking plant. The future of such areas will be increasingly nonwhite; a local elementary school in Marshalltown at the turn of the century had a "minority" population of over 60 percent. Grocery stores stock Hispanic food items and Spanish-language magazines, and the local Catholic church now has some Spanish-language masses. After much public and legislative debate, in early 2002 the gover-nor of Iowa signed a bill making English the official language of the state.

Iowa is not alone on this leading edge of the demographic frontier; the face of the entire Midwest is slowly but surely changing, as it always has. While still overwhelmingly white, many midwestern states doubled or even tripled their Hispanic population between 1990 and 2000, the new residents often drawn by job opportunities at meatpacking plants and other agribusiness enterprises. Meanwhile, among the white population, the old are getting older and the young continue to leave.

In many ways, the slowly growing immigrant population of the Midwest is nothing new. Today's new Americans have many of the same forward-looking goals and dreams as the immigrants of 1890. This is a population not timeless and rooted but, rather, one always in motion, always questing in search of the good life. In other words, today's Midwest is about as "genuine America" as it gets, but it's a genuineness of a very different sort than that found in our nostalgia-tinged vision. The question these changes raises is this: Will the nostalgic view of the Midwest as our genuine Heartland, as our touchstone for values, persist in the face of demographic changes? Will the image be able to accommodate the growing diversity of mid-America? Or will it continue in our minds as a Norman Rockwell image of a vanished era, immune to the new reality of the American Heartland?

Sources and Further Reading: Stephen Bloom, *Postville: A Clash of Cultures in Heartland America* (2000); Richard Francaviglia, *Main Street Revisited* (1996); Sinclair Lewis, *Main Street* (1920); D.W. Meinig, "Symbolic Landscapes," in D.W. Meinig, ed., *The Interpretation of Ordinary Landscapes* (1979); James R. Shortridge, *The Middle West: Its Meaning in American Culture* (1989).

Steven M. Schnell
Kutztown University of Pennsylvania

Heartland

The Midwest is often characterized as the Heartland of the United States by insiders and outsiders alike. Indeed, the two labels *Heartland* and *Heartland of America* are nearly synonymous today. But this has not always been the case. In fact, the origin of the term *heartland* emanates from European geopolitical thinking at the turn of the twentieth century. Popular books and magazines indicate that the word's meaning and application shifted during the ensuing decades to eventually include the cultural values already mythologized in the term *Midwest*. The names *The Heartland* and *The Heart of America* literally embody the cultural values long linked to the Midwest. They are also less abstract names, able to carry more emotional weight

because of this embodying quality. Commercial use of Heartland today reveals core and peripheral areas within the region, and intriguing changes in the name's meaning and geographical distribution.

Dictionary entries for *heartland* usually include some or all of the following: the central area of a state, nation, or continent; a large central region of relatively homogeneous political and cultural character; the part of a larger land area deemed essential to the viability of a society; and a central zone where core cultural and economic values are thought to reside. These values typically include economic self-sufficiency, conservative political and religious ideals, and an organic rootedness borne of agrarian life. Heartland is translated into other languages only occasionally, but when it is, the result always includes the idea of centrality: *pays du centre* (French); *zona centrale* (Italian); and *centraal gebied van het land* (Dutch). But the English word relies on the symbolism of the human heart as the center of being. River, railroad, and highway networks represent the veins and arteries through which the economic lifeblood flows. The Heartland is assumed to be rhythmically constant despite periodic changes around it, assuring the existence of a stable truth in the core of the body politic. The population may decline, the economy may dwindle, and strangers may move in, but the persistent beating of older cultural values is thought to remain unchanged. To call a region "the heartland" is, in the end, a humanization and sanctification of place to a degree inadequately attended by other labels.

These images are part of the meaning of the expression today, but they were not present at its creation. "Heart-land" was first used in a 1904 paper presented to the Royal Geographical Society of Great Britain by Sir Halford Mackinder, a British geographer, conservative, and imperialist intellectual concerned with geopolitics and the location of military power in world history. In this paper and in later works, Mackinder used the term to describe the vast north-central part of the Eurasian continent, the region from which several conquerors went forth repeatedly to control the coastal areas of both Europe and Asia. Concerned as he was with Britain's ability to maintain control of the world's seas, Mackinder worried that this heartland remained invulnerable because sea-based military power could be denied access to it. Whoever controlled the heartland, he wrote, could reach out to control the coasts and eventually the seas; the reverse was not possible. Thus he saw those in command of this heartland as a threat to liberty and democratic ideals, values he thought were represented best in Britain.

The term *Heartland* began to undergo an inversion in meaning in the mid-twentieth century, when it started to be used widely in the United States to embody the very political values Mackinder thought to be so distant from it in Europe. But the geopolitical notion of heartlands did not immediately lose favor by any means. It was taught in U.S. military academies and reproduced in Reagan-era U.S. State Department bulletins outlining national security strategies during the cold war.

British writer George Orwell understood the strategic importance of heartlands, but he also saw something more in the idea, something sacrosanct to a society. In *1984*, first published in 1949, he wrote that throughout the twentieth century, the boundaries of the world powers, or "superstates" as he termed them, constantly shifted, but "the territory which forms the heartland of each superstate always remains inviolate." For Orwell, there were at least three heartlands in the world, one of them in North America, and they were of enough cultural significance that an incursion into one was a greater violation than an attack at the edge of the state. In this same year, "Heart of America" was recommended to schoolteachers by the editors of *Senior Scholastic* magazine as a useful description of the Midwest. Such interpretations signaled the shift in meaning. By the 1950s, heartland was no longer just an abstract geopolitical concept discussed in the halls of power. It had gained an additional connotation as something more humanized and meaningful for residents as well as outsiders.

Beginning in the 1950s, one of the major purveyors of the Midwest-as-Heartland idea was the National Geographic Society (NGS). NGS apparently first used the concept in print in 1952, and in the next fifty years published thirty-four articles and maps with heartland in the title, most of these referring to the Midwest. For example, in 1958 a map supplement appeared in *National Geographic* titled "North Central United States," which was described in an accompanying article, "Atlas Map Charts the Nation's Heartland." The Dakotas, Nebraska, Kansas, Missouri, Iowa, Minnesota, Wisconsin, and Illinois were depicted as the "country's meat market, . . . breadbasket, . . . coal cellar" and the location of enduring American traits. Ohio, Michigan, and Indiana were omitted by NGS editors from their Heartland.

A survey of widely read magazines published since 1960, including *Time, Newsweek, Life, U.S. News & World Report*, and *Forbes*, reveals continuous identification of the Midwest as the Heartland or Heart of America, although the boundaries of the region vary and are often vaguely identified. Usage is particularly common in articles discussing national and regional election campaigns and results, a further indication that national publications see in the region the presence of bedrock and bellwether political values.

No less popular has been the academic application of the term. According to the comprehensive on-line database maintained by University Microfilms International in the last four decades of the twentieth century, "heartland" appeared in the title or abstract of nearly 200 doctoral dissertations. After a slow start, more recent use of the term has soared: 7 dissertations in the 1970s; 56 in the 1980s; and 109 in the 1990s. Although some of these scholars used "heartland" to refer to regions outside the United States, in the majority of cases the term was used as a simple substitute for "Midwest."

Although scattered commercial use of heartland exists throughout the United States, it is ubiquitous in the Midwest. The name is found virtually everywhere as part of a business or corporate moniker, although it is less popular among Michigan, Ohio, and Indiana businesses and is common in Wisconsin and North Dakota. The heartland of the "Heartland" is located, unsurprisingly, in Illinois, Iowa, Kansas, Missouri, and Nebraska, but it is not evenly distributed across these states. The basins of the Arkansas, Des Moines, James, Kansas, Missouri, and Platte Rivers are the primary axes. The Mississippi Valley is of secondary importance. Small towns, like Fort Dodge, Iowa; Grand Island, Nebraska; and Kirksville, Missouri, and their surrounding environs have the highest rates. In terms of sheer numbers the Kansas City metropolitan area and Omaha-Council Bluffs top the list in that order.

The range of the heartland has recently started to expand. In Oklahoma, more than a hundred businesses have newly adopted the name in recent years, and when Amtrak reestablished passenger rail service in the state in 1999, "The Heartland Flyer" was selected in a naming contest conducted among the state's schoolchildren. In the Oklahoma City metropolitan area alone, some fifty-seven enterprises now use the name, including a large number of new churches. There were thirty-four such establishments here in 1996; only seven in 1995 and none of them churches. Usage soared immediately after the bombing of a federal building in that city in April 1995, in which 168 people were killed. What we are witnessing is another enlargement of meaning, the use of *heartland* as a repository of grief, a way to embody in place this deepest of sentiments. In such a situation, the event is cast as a strike at the heart of the entire country. On the afternoon of the day of the bombing, CNN broadcasters were already calling the event "Terror in the Heartland," although the term had seldom been applied by anyone to Oklahoma.

"Heartland" has an odd history, throughout which its meaning has expanded. From a geopolitical abstraction, to an embodiment of the longstanding midwestern myth, to a revenue-producing slogan, the interpretations keep multiplying. We can now also expect to see heartland used where the blood of innocents has been shed. Since the 1950s, a kind of comfort has been associated with the term, the kind that comes from imagining home as not irrelevant, but somehow centrally important in a larger context. To this we have now added the comfort that comes for people who hold their suffering very close to the heart.

Sources and Further Reading: Bart Becker, *'Til the Cows Come Home* (1985); Stephen Bloom, *Postville* (2001); Douglas Foley, *The Heartland Chronicles* (1995); Halford J. Mackinder, *Democratic Ideals and Reality* (1919); Halford J. Mackinder, "The Geographical Pivot of History," *Geographical Journal* 23 (Apr. 1904); National Geographic Society, "Atlas Map Charts the Nation's Heartland," *National Geographic* 114 (Nov. 1958); George Orwell, *1984*, rev. ed. (1983); Gearóid Ó Tuathail, "Putting Mackinder in His Place," *Political Geography Quarterly* 11 (Jan. 1992); Senior Scholastic Magazine, "Heart of America," *Senior Scholastic* 50 (May 1949); Ray A. Young Bear, *Black Eagle Child* (1992).

Robert Rundstrom
University of Oklahoma

Movies

Most movies set in the Midwest could happen anywhere. And that is usually precisely the point. The region's reputation as the most generic of American places attracts filmmakers interested in telling American stories.

Midwesterners are often portrayed on film as pragmatic souls who believe that they have realized the American dream. Yet they are also isolated in a provincial world that produces superficiality, hypocrisy, and conformity as easily as corn and cars. Audiences laugh knowingly when the polite Nebraska adulterer played by John Lithgow in *Terms of Endearment* (1983) insults a rude store clerk by asking her if she is from New York. When a small-town couple visits Manhattan in *The Out-of-Towners* (1970, 1999), they are overwhelmed by the complexities and impersonal character of the big city. Southerners or Northeasterners may be loud, flamboyant, even confrontational, but Midwesterners are nice people who suppress personal desires in order to fit into a larger culture of civic responsibility and middle-class rectitude. No wonder movies set in the region often deal with a cultural environment that both nurtures and constricts human beings.

The Wizard of Oz (1939) is a case in point. Dorothy Gale is a sensitive young girl living a black-and-white life on the dusty prairie of Kansas. Bereft of her parents, she has an improvised family consisting of her aunt and uncle, their hired men, and her dog, Toto. Dorothy longs for a place "over the rainbow" where people are happy and contented. Carried by a twister into the colorful Land of Oz, Dorothy and Toto encounter unusual characters, enjoy the pleasures of the Emerald City, and deal with dangerous woods and witches, only to realize that all they really need is in their own backyard: "There is no place like home." Kansas, despite its limitations, is about as good a place as any person has a right to expect.

The popularity of *The Wizard of Oz* rests squarely on the universality of concerns about family, security, and adventure. A young person learning to appreciate what she has through exposure to something else is a clichéd plot in virtually all cultures. Movies about the Midwest, however, not only harp on this theme, they remark on the importance of place as a way of thinking about the relationship between individuals and their larger culture. Journeys of self-discovery are all about whether a person wants to accept life in the Midwest or abandon it altogether.

To be sure, many films celebrate the state of mind that is the Midwest. *The Music Man* (1962), a tougher-than-it-first-appears portrait of small-town Iowans fooled by a charlatan who himself cannot resist the power of simple love, suggests that underneath the petty provincialism of Midwesterners are values of family and community worth sharing. *Meet Me in St. Louis* (1944) creates a community where dreams are limited to the boy next door or the fair at the end of the trolley line, but that no one really wants to leave, even for the glamour of New York City. *Field of Dreams* (1989) transforms an Iowa cornfield into a touchstone of reconciliation and redemption; true happiness lies in developing relationships with members of nuclear families and small towns rather than in pursuing individual dreams.

Midwestern movies rarely deal with the stuff of grand drama: ascents to greatness, tragic failures, or titanic struggles with evil. They confront the mundane dilemma of the extent to which people can make peace with the world around them. Success, if it happens, is portrayed as a triumph of basic American values. What matters is how well people control themselves and become parts of larger social networks. In *Hoosiers* (1986), a small-town high school team and its determined coach win an improbable victory over bigger, richer, and more urban rivals in the state basketball championship. They celebrate with quiet satisfaction in a job well done and resignation to the fact that their moment of glory is fleeting.

Not all films about the Midwest celebrate individual character. More than a few accentuate the variety of its peoples and terrain as well as the impact of weather, distances, economic uncertainty, and prejudice, suggesting that some problems are too complicated and too structural to be resolved by good character. Jan Troell's *The Emigrants* (1970) and *The New Land* (1972) trace a Swedish family's relocation to Minnesota in the middle of the nineteenth century and emphasize the physical and economic challenges to realizing the American dream. *Northern Lights* (1978), *Country* (1984), and *A Thousand Acres* (1997) illustrate political and economic struggles as well as the personal problems behind the regional image of comfortable domesticity.

Films focusing on midwestern economic and social problems have a long ancestry, extending back at least to King Vidor's *Our Daily Bread* (1934) and the short documentary *The Plow That Broke the Plains* (1936). Nor are they all agrarian. Michael Moore's *Roger and Me* (1989) confronts the impact of corporate downsizing on working-class people, especially in Michigan. In these and other movies, the Midwest is hardly a bucolic bastion of traditional values.

Still, the tendency among critics of life in the Midwest is to focus on how its residents are distorted by conformity and repression rather than economic dislocation. In *Boys Don't Cry* (1999), people lead lives of deception and desperation soaked in rage and resentment. Middle-class citizens are also unable to make connections. Any and all attempts at striking out on their own become perverted and are ultimately counterproductive. The criminal ambitions of the businessman in Joel and Ethan Coen's *Fargo* (1996) lead only to failure while the small-town police chief played by Frances McDormand succeeds because she is so resolutely resigned to the ways of her environment. Nebraskan Alexander Payne's *Election* (1999) explores the banality of ambition focused solely on achieving personal validation. In *About Schmidt* (2002), Payne traces the attempts of a retired and widowed insurance agent to connect with his daughter; successful by midwestern standards, Schmidt has no sense of having been present in his own life.

American movies in general make similar points when they touch on the Midwest. The same region whose fields of corn nurtured by decent people mold Clark Kent into the Man of Steel in *Superman* (1978) is the exemplar of American cultural conformity in Woody Allen's visit to Wisconsin in *Annie Hall* (1977). Alfred Hitchcock juxtaposed both images in *North by Northwest* (1959) in the famous scene in which a plane suddenly and anonymously chases the main character through cornfields: An icon of American prosperity becomes a dangerous place where nothing is what it appears to be. More recently, *Traffic* (2000) suggested the pervasiveness of illegal drugs in the United States by focusing on a respectable family in the conservative city of Cincinnati.

Movies set in Chicago, while edgier, diverse, and more cosmopolitan, tend to embody familiar obsessions about the region as a place where manners and morality matter more than long-term structural trends. The Midwest is not about slavery or aridity; it is about relationships. Like an overgrown small town, Chicago is the perfect setting for romantic comedies such as *My Best Friend's Wedding* (1997). Chicagoans may be wealthier, poorer, hipper, or more ethnic—and their city somewhat generic—but they are still nice Midwesterners underneath. Whether the heroine is Julia Roberts or Jennifer Lopez, individual character, middle-class love, and family triumph in the end.

Exciting without being alien, Chicago was the preferred place of escape for suburban white adolescents in films made in the 1980s. Robert Redford's *Ordinary People* (1980) was a devastating portrait of the emotional turmoil (and failed relationships) lurking beneath the surface of suburban life. But in Reagan America, audiences preferred to see suburbs as stultifying rather than dangerous. In *Adventures in Babysitting* (1987), a teenager takes her young charges on a romp through Chicago at night and emerges wiser and more mature. In *Ferris Bueller's Day Off* (1986), clever teenagers outwit naive parents and idiotic authority figures to have more fun and find more enlightenment in one afternoon in Chicago than they do in weeks in their suburban enclave. *The Blues Brothers* (1980) paid tribute to the city's African American heritage by focusing on the antics of a couple of white guys defying suburban respectability by emulating black musicians.

Like Dorothy, however, these characters eventually go home. After running away, they accept who they are and what they will become within the limited palette of midwestern life. The enormously popular *Home Alone* (1990) taught that lesson by reversing the usual plot; the young boy learns to appreciate his family by defending the family home while his parents and siblings are away. *Risky Business*, the 1983 film that made Tom Cruise a major star, was more serious in its depiction of urban possibilities. Yet Cruise's character's success at negotiating that world is ultimately constructed as a rite of passage that ensures his admission to Princeton and the kind of professional, upper-middle-class suburban world of his parents. Even mild acts of rebellion become tests of individual character and lead to conformity.

Films such as *Native Son* (1986) and *Eight Men Out* (1988), John Sayles's account of the 1919 Black Sox scandal, deal with midwestern life realistically. But they are rare. More typical are the excellent documentary *Hoop Dreams* (1994), a kind of inner-city version of *Hoosiers*, and comedies such as *Soul Food* (1997) and *Barbershop* (2002), which are ultimately reassuring and uplifting. Few problems cannot be overcome with the help of family and friends. *The Sting* (1973) was a clever variation on the basic plot: con artists as a fictive family banding together to get rich and happy. The characters in the musical *Chicago* (2002) acknowledge the importance of middle-class values and families by mocking and manipulating cultural assumptions about gender roles and individual success. In the bleak world depicted in *Road to Perdition* (2002), there is redemption in the love between father and son and the healing power of a rural farm family. Diversity itself becomes quaint, a series of variations on familiar themes rather an exploration of serious differences. *My Big Fat Greek Wedding* (2002) is a case in point.

In the end, midwestern movies tend to revolve around characters trying to master the rules of their culture. What do people have to do to enjoy both public approbation and personal happiness? Is it even possible to have both? What does it mean to be middle class or to realize the American dream? Many films address these issues. *Alice Adams* (1935) and *The Magnificent Ambersons* (1942) are classic movies that feature individuals fumbling to achieve or maintain a middle-class status rooted in education, manners, and consumerism as well as income. But none is more evocative than Peter Yates's 1979 version of Steve Tesich's Oscar-winning screenplay *Breaking Away*.

Dave, like Dorothy Gale, lives in a dream world, pretending to be Italian by faking an accent and riding his bicycle. He and his friends are the sons of lower-middle- or working-class families in Bloomington, Indiana, known derisively as "cutters" because previous generations worked in limestone quarries. To these young men, Indiana University represents an upwardly mobile, middle-class world off limits to them because of their lack of money and understanding. The buildings fashioned from local limestone are the territory of wealthy, confident students whose future seems all but assured. Dave's father, now a used car salesman, takes his son to the university library to show him the limestone and to talk about education as the path to material comfort and respectability. At the climax of the film, the cutters defeat their collegiate rivals in the annual Little 500 bicycle race, a victory won because of their determination and self-respect—because of their character—which, the film implies with more hope than evidence, will carry over into the rest of their lives.

Breaking Away is the quintessential midwestern movie because it describes a cultural landscape that is at once safe and restrictive. It ambiguously celebrates the virtues of home and family and criticizes the prejudices and limitations of small-town life. In a setting

that is both generically American and peculiarly midwestern, it confronts issues of class and diversity but ultimately focuses on individual character as the key to success. It promotes ambition as long as it is realistic and pursued within the parameters of the larger culture. And, above all, it imagines Midwesterners as decent people who long for a good life without knowing exactly what that life entails or what they have to do to realize it.

Sources and Further Reading: Richard B. Armstrong, *Encyclopedia of Film Themes, Settings, and Series* (2001); John Belton, *American Cinema, American Culture* (1994); John E. Bodnar, *Blue-Collar Hollywood* (2003); Kenneth MacKinnon, *Hollywood's Small Towns* (1984); Steven Mintz and Randy Roberts, eds., *Hollywood's America* (1999); Leonard Quart, *American Film and Society since 1945*, 3rd ed. (2002); Steven J. Ross, ed., *Movies and American Society* (2002); Robert Sklar, *Movie-Made America*, rev. ed. (1994).

Andrew Cayton
Miami University, Oxford, Ohio

Television

Images of the Midwest on television conform to stereotypes of a bland region somewhere in the middle of the United States where life is neither complicated nor sophisticated. Indeed, the great advantage of the region's reputation for producers of television shows is that it is supposedly the home of people of the middle: earnest, industrious, and loath to commit themselves to any extreme. The Midwest therefore is a kind of blank screen: You can project onto it whatever you choose without being too concerned about offending someone. In the 1990s, the producers of a situation comedy on NBC about aliens living on Earth set *Third Rock from the Sun* in Ohio because they wanted "the best cross-section of America and people that we can find." The state "epitomizes our collective image of what the country should be. . . . There are no trends being set in Ohio."

Substitute any other midwestern state for Ohio and you have a capsule summary of the ways in which television imagines the Midwest as a whole. It is rarely very place-specific in terms of landscape, beyond fleeting visual references to downtown skylines or famous landmarks such as sports stadiums or the arch in St. Louis. Rather than highlight diversity or dissent, the projection of the Midwest on television conjures up a region where what matters is the personal rather than the public, where both the sources of problems and their ultimate solutions lie within the confines of a nuclear family ensconced in the security of their own home.

The role of place in television shows has evolved considerably over the past half century. Early dramas and comedies conveyed a concrete sense of a cultural context, which was usually urban and ethnic. By the late 1950s, however, programs shied away from association with place. The goal was to provide the advertisers who financed productions with wide exposure by appealing to the largest possible audience. Why alienate potential viewers with accents or references to real places? No less important in the growing emphasis on bland backdrops was financial costs. Virtually all television programs were produced on back lots in southern California because it was prohibitively expensive to film on location.

Lacking distinctive visual images, television programs took place in a generic America that could have been anywhere. If people tended to assume they were set in the Midwest, that was fine, given its image as the most American of all regions. Midwestern suggested an absence of local color. Because it was not distinctive, it could not offend. Popular television figures were often from the Midwest: Newscaster Walter Cronkite was a native of Missouri and late-night talk-show host Johnny Carson was from Nebraska. Daytime soap operas were deliberately set in generically midwestern cities. *The Edge of Night* featured the Cincinnati skyline behind its opening credits but made no further use of the setting. Situation comedies took place in bland suburbs, in bland homes among families with no concrete religious, ethnic, or political identification. Even the occupation of fathers was rarely discussed. Programs focused on interpersonal relationships that were at the heart of nuclear family life. Indeed, family was the most significant social institution consistently represented on television. Even when the setting was courts or hospitals, they tended to function as extended fictive families obsessed with personal relationships. In the 1960s, television shows in general rarely confronted the crises in civil rights and foreign policy that dominated the news. The point was to entertain and sell products, not to engage its viewers in civic discussion.

The cultural changes associated with the late 1960s, particularly an amorphous rebellion against the alleged hypocrisy of middle-class suburban respectability, precipitated a change in attitudes toward place. In the early 1970s, an increasing number of television programs were located in a well-defined region. The appeal of the family drama *The Waltons* lay in its creator Earl Hamner's evocation of his Depression childhood in the Blue Ridge Mountains of Virginia, despite the fact that the program was produced in southern California. Similarly, the situation comedy *All in the Family* took place in Queens, New York, and with good reason. Americans could more easily imagine

(and tolerate) the working-class Bunkers confronting one another over issues of race, war, religion, and gender than they would a suburban family in Des Moines or Green Bay. Direct discussions were apparently part of the culture in New York City, where people were simply more opinionated than polite.

The serious problems confronting the Midwest— including the shootings at Kent State University in May 1970, the decline of heavy industry into the Rust Belt, rural economic crises, and serious urban unrest—did not register on fictional television programs. The region served as a backdrop of heartland stability in an era of rapid social change. Mary Richards, the ambitious single, professional woman played by Mary Tyler Moore, lived in Minneapolis with a surrogate family made up of co-workers and neighbors. Bob Newhart played the role of a psychologist, Bob Hartley, on the *Bob Newhart Show*, whose home was Chicago and whose wife worked; the novelty was that they had no children. A divorced woman raised two teenage daughters in *One Day at a Time* in Indianapolis. Later in the decade, the more slapstick *Happy Days* and *Laverne and Shirley* evoked nostalgia for the supposedly simpler days of the Eisenhower era in Milwaukee.

The overall image was of a safe, relatively nurturing place where decent people lived and worked in a relatively timeless world far from the social and cultural upheavals convulsing America. Mary Richards spent much of her life in a newsroom yet the news seemed never to have an impact on her; the stuff of her existence was her relationships with her friends and the tension between career and family. The comedy on *Mary Tyler Moore* flowed from the eccentricities of the characters surrounding the stable star. But their tics were all personal. A major exception was Rhoda Morgenstern, Mary's best friend, and her mother, who were Jews from New York City. Others were simply idiosyncratic, strange for reasons that seemed entirely divorced from any external influence. While these sitcoms sometimes took on serious issues, such as death and divorce, they almost never confronted tough social concerns such as race to the degree that *All in the Family* did. The closest thing to overt social commentary was Norman Lear's *Mary Hartman, Mary Hartman*, which satirized the banality of small-town life in Fernwood, Ohio.

African Americans, at best peripheral characters in television, became leading figures in the late 1970s. One popular sitcom, *Good Times*, was set in the housing projects of Chicago and focused on the lives of a family who were far from affluent. Race mattered on this program, as it did on *The Jeffersons*, which took place in New York City. But these were sitcoms, after all, and the characters verged on stereotypes. It was probably not coincidental that *Good Times* was about a family that, race and poverty aside, faced challenges that could be resolved in under half an hour and mostly within the confines of the household.

In the 1980s and 1990s, television became grittier, more realistic, and more interested in giving people and locations specific characters. Serial dramas such as *Dallas* and *Dynasty* exploited their locales and accentuated the supposed distinctiveness of their cultures, or at least consumer stereotypes. Place as well as family somehow made J.R. Ewing, the central figure on the enormously popular *Dallas*, who he was. Or so viewers were supposed to discern from the facts that he wore ten-gallon hats, worked in the oil industry, and was proud to be from Texas. Similarly, *Seinfeld*, a leading sitcom of the 1990s, was deliberately set in a few blocks on the Upper West Side of New York City and developed its comedy from the place-specific challenges of its proudly ethnic and urban characters. Indeed, a major reason people in the rest of the United States laughed was that they thought the characters were different from them. This willingness to emphasize diversity flowed from the greater openness of American society and the exposure of generations to other places through television itself. As important was the expansion of choices available on cable television.

Programs set in the Midwest, which continued to proliferate, also had more of an edge. *Hill Street Blues*, Steven Bochco's innovative multilayered police drama in the 1980s, was set in Chicago, as was the phenomenally successful hospital drama of the 1990s, *ER*. The sitcom *Family Ties* took place in Columbus, Ohio, and *Home Improvement*, in a Detroit suburb. The prolific television writer and producer David E. Kelley had one of his first successes with *Picket Fences*, a drama about a family and a community of eccentric but lovable people in Wisconsin.

Still, the Midwest on television remained largely a relatively blank canvas on which writers and directors could paint whatever they wanted. If the region was peculiar in some ways, it was more important that it was safe and reliable, far from the upheaval and diversity occurring elsewhere in the United States. The problems people faced in the Midwest, even in *Hill Street Blues* and *ER*, were primarily personal and familial. Race rarely mattered, and religion and ethnicity, even less. To be sure, shows now featured stronger women (the prosecutor in *Hill Street Blues*, the mother in *Picket Fences*) and African Americans, not to mention an occasional Jewish or gay person. But their problems and the ways in which they dealt with them remained traditional.

The nuclear family was the center of the universe, and it taught the core values of honesty, decency, respect for others, hard work, and ambition tempered by realism. There was little that love could not overcome, apparently. In *Family Ties*, the twist was to feature a conservative son with liberal parents, reversing a conventional stereotype of the 1960s and 1970s. Yet the political differences mattered little in the end when family ties triumphed; as always in midwestern television, the private takes precedence over the public, individuals are more important than groups, and family is the alpha and omega of existence. Never mind that this image did not jibe with reality. Its power was undeniable, perhaps because it was a representation of an imagined place.

The Drew Carey Show, a minor hit in the early 2000s though it had its start in 1995, made fleeting attempts to deal with the challenges of working-class life. Much more ambitious and significant was *Roseanne*, a sitcom set in Chicago in the 1990s. Neither beautiful nor ambitious, and far from wealthy, the Conner family had problems that could not be resolved by the affection of a nuclear family. Parents and children do not always get along. No matter how hard this particular family worked and loved, they confronted challenges that simply seemed beyond their control.

Roseanne proved to be exceptional. By and large, the Midwest remained a backdrop for programs obsessed with relationships; the world beyond families scarcely seemed to matter. Even when nationally syndicated talk shows originating in Chicago with hosts such as Jenny Jones and Jerry Springer turned family ties on their heads by featuring people who defied or ignored respectable behavior, they presented their flamboyance as a personal idiosyncrasy or a failure of traditional family structures.

The most popular and most sophisticated of these programs was hosted by Oprah Winfrey. While Oprah hardly shies away from tough issues, as often as not she leads her viewers away from social action to focus on the ways in which they can take control of their lives and improve themselves. We may debate the value of this course, and we certainly may suggest that it reflects larger developments in American society as a whole, but we can hardly miss the extent to which it reflects a consistent image of the Midwest as a place dominated by concerns with family and individual character.

Sources and Further Reading: Eric Barnouw, *Tube of Plenty*, 2nd ed. (1990); S. Robert Lichter, Linda S. Lichter, and Stanley Rothman, *Prime Time: How TV Portrays American Culture* (1994); J. Fred MacDonald, *One Nation under Television* (1994); Alex McNeil, *Total Television*, 4th ed. (1996); Josh Ozersky, *Archie Bunker's America* (2003).

Andrew Cayton
Miami University, Oxford, Ohio

Rust Belt

To understand the phrase *Rust Belt* it is useful to review the early labeling of manufacture regions of the United States. The Northeast became the "Manufacturing Belt" or the "Industrial Belt" initially, but these "belts" ultimately extended from the megalopolitan East Coast to Chicago and St. Louis in the west. Southward, the region came to include northern Virginia, usually West Virginia, and the Ohio River. Louisville, Kentucky, is at the belt's southern edge. To the north, the Manufacturing Belt encompassed western New York State, southern Michigan, and southeastern Wisconsin. Within Canada, southern Ontario was indisputably part of the region. Cities within the Manufacturing Belt were the main industrial ports of the East Coast, steel-making centers, transshipment centers on the Great Lakes, industries along the Ohio River, and urban centers along a few major roads, notably the National Road and the newer highways that parallel it.

The variation "Rust Belt" comes from journalists searching for a popular moniker to apply to the decline of this region of the United States from the 1960s to the 1980s. The term first appeared in Webster's dictionary in the mid-1980s, and an examination of textbooks and print media reveals the nature of the term's usage. Rust Belt is sometimes used interchangeably with terms such as "Snow Belt" or "Frost Belt" to imply the entire industrial core, but just as often means smaller, less diversified, towns suffering the most unemployment and economic decay. Thus typed were cities along the East Coast, the Allegheny Plateau, and the Great Lakes, which had previously seen themselves as the eternal industrial core of America but suffered cost cutting and layoffs resulting from global industrial competition. Baltimore, Buffalo, Pittsburgh, Youngstown, Cleveland, Detroit, Toledo, and Chicago are larger metropolitan areas considered generally Rust Belt, but many of them maintained sufficient economic diversity to outgrow the label. Many smaller industrial communities could not, and toward the turn of the century were the most oft-quoted examples.

The core of the Rust Belt is difficult to define, but much of it is midwestern. The Census Bureau has defined the Rust Belt as the swath of formerly smoke-shrouded midwestern cities identified with big factories, big autos, and big steel—cities like Youngstown and Detroit. Youngstown for decades focused on blast-furnace and open-hearth steel production and suffered severe labor and population losses with job cutbacks and plant closings. For some, Youngstown is the center of the Rust Belt. Detroit—with the decentralization and automation of the automotive industry—has also been labeled the capital of the Rust Belt, but Flint, Michigan, the subject of Michael Moore's ruthless satire aimed at General Motors' continual

Demolition of the Ohio Works, U.S. Steel, Youngstown, Ohio, in the Rust Belt. Ohio Historical Society, SC2419.

layoffs and plant closings in Buickland, seems more representative. Coal and metalworking towns of eastern Pennsylvania like Scranton/Wilkes-Barre and Allentown also are sometimes considered of Rust Belt variety. East Coast decline is typical of the definition, but decay there has not been uniform.

Mentioning any of these cities can prompt Rust Belt talk, but increasingly, the label signifies smaller, less well known, communities stung by industrial decline. Many old industrial river towns north or south of Pittsburgh such as Aliquippa and Brownsville are in areas, in the words of author William Least Heat-Moon, "of almost unrelieved Rust Belt decay." From Pittsburgh westward down the Ohio River are many other small industrial communities, such as Wheeling, Ironton, and Portsmouth, made infirm by Rust Belt deindustrialization. Obviously, the term is closely related to the look of the land where steel mills, factories, and ports lie idle, but Rust Belt is also used to emphasize general industrial contamination of water and soil—and the effects of acid rain.

The term is heard more in common speech than seen in professional writing. For example, authors of human and world geography texts only started using the term with some regularity from about 1995 onward. Most geographers writing on North America do not indulge in Rust Belt language, preferring to discuss the details of the "deindustrialization," "brownfield" land use, and subsequent "diversification" of previously ailing cities. One regional treatise on the Pittsburgh area accompanying conference materials for the ninety-sixth annual meeting of the Association of American Geographers used Rust Belt only once in thirteen articles treating the area's old and new industrial character. Overall, experts generally eschew references to the Rust Belt because of its vagueness, but the label has served a popular need to simplify geography using all-encompassing names. Cultural geographer Wilbur Zelinsky both advocated the study of such vernacular regional terms while railing them as "deplorable." Labels such as "Rust Belt," "Sunbelt,"and "Snow Belt" may lack specificity, but their origins and applications in popular culture are little understood. A search of the Internet book website AddALL found five books with Rust Belt in their title, and the term has made its way into the arts with heavy metal bands, industrial poetry, photographic essays, and museum expositions all prominently using the term.

Comparing popular labels, for example, one finds the opposite "Sunbelt" much more readily used in the vernacular than Rust Belt. People favor regional labels implying optimism, progress, leisure, and retirement rather than those signifying decline, deterioration, and loss. In texts, Sunbelt is repeatedly used with reference to internal migration while Rust Belt is rarely used in similar sections treating industry and manufacturing. By association, the term generally signifies a population trend of out-migration from the industrial Northeast and Midwest. Thus as the Sunbelt rises, the Rust Belt declines.

Few people use Rust Belt to describe Pittsburgh itself now, though they may use it to describe the Pittsburgh of three decades ago. In Joel Garreau's *Nine Nations of North America*, the term is used to mean the decay of the democratic machine of the old labor bosses, so, for some at least, Rust Belt implies sociopolitical change more than the decay of the built environment. Thus one 2002 *Washington Post* article referred to states like Pennsylvania and Ohio, which are highly divided between old industrial pursuits and newer suburban development, as "rust belt swing states." In the political arena, the Great Lakes states are increasingly referred to as the Rust Belt, especially when presidential elections come around. The use of Rust Belt as an all-encompassing regional catchphrase is increasing while its use as an industrial label is lessening.

Though many former industrial areas in the Rust Belt are still hurting, many others such as Pittsburgh, Cleveland, and Indianapolis have seen more economic rebound and diversification than expected. Some textbooks using the name in the early 1990s had abandoned it by 2000, perhaps an indication of this surprising turnaround in much of the Midwest. Richard Preston's book *American Steel* (1991) refers to the "resurrection of the Rust Belt" in its subtitle, though the term is little used in the text. A certain irony is involved, because if the Rust Belt is truly resurrected, is it still the Rust Belt? Detroit has also made remarkable strides in economic redevelopment, even to the point that subsections of the Rust Belt auto economy are now labeled the "Tech Belt" by authors of *Business Week*. Rust Belt, therefore, seems to be increasingly more limited to smaller industrial areas of less industrial diversity, though the Census Bureau reports that many Rust Belt metropolitan areas of less than a hundred thousand people also saw significant growth during the 1990s. Some of this growth may have been due to Internet marketing, largely unheard of before 1990, by traditional Rust Belt companies in heavy industry. One article discussed the Rust Belt at "Net Speed." In other words, "Rust Belt" shows signs of becoming a phrase of optimism and respectability, just as James R. Shortridge has shown to be the case for the "Middle Western" label itself. If the term disappears, however, no industrial rebound will ever again constitute the same number of laborers in heavy manufacturing.

Apart from its use in the Midwest, use of the Rust Belt label has been on the increase in describing foreign industrial areas now rotting, such as England's old mining and manufacturing "Pauperized Belts," Germany's Ruhr Valley, and many old coal and steel towns in northern France. Rust Belt has been aptly applied to the idled industrial regions of the former Soviet Union, but the most popular extra American application has been to older Chinese industry, especially in northeastern China, contrasted with the newer developed zones in southern China. In journalistic reference, Manchuria is becoming the most popular Rust Belt outside the United States. America, or the Midwest, thus has contributed to the origination of internationally applied regional labels.

Sources and Further Reading: Steven P. Dandaneau, *A Town Abandoned* (1996); John P. Hoerr, *And the Wolf Finally Came* (1988); Sherry Lee Linkon and John Russo, *Steeltown U.S.A.* (2002); Michael Moore, *Downsize This!* (1997); Richard Preston, *American Steel: Hot Metal Men and the Resurrection of the Rust Belt* (1991); James R. Shortridge, *The Middle West: Its Meaning in American Culture* (1989); Wilbur Zelinsky, *The Cultural Geography of the United States*, rev. ed. (1992).

Craig S. Campbell
Youngstown State University, Ohio

Seasonality

There are many popular descriptions of midwestern daily weather and climate, ranging from humorous to profane, but inevitably they all center around the concepts of either change or diversity. The middle of the North American continent is a unique physical setting, with several elements that help shape the dynamic midwestern climate. Nowhere else on earth does one find the combination of the following phenomena: (1) a continent that extends from high to low latitudes with significant midlatitudinal area; (2) lack of east-west trending mountain barriers to air movement—allowing ready mixing of cold and dry northern air (central Canadian origin) with warm and moist southern breezes (Gulf of Mexico origin); (3) a large continent with a high western mountain range (the Rockies) to inhibit precipitation "downstream"—encouraging development of dry and hot summer air masses (southwestern U.S. origin) that are also free to join the "mix" above; and, last, (4) the Rocky Mountains' creation of areas of instability in the atmosphere that favor midlatitude cyclone (surface storm) development near the southwestern portions of the Midwest and the establishment of storm tracks that then carry these systems over the entire region. Together these factors forge the characteristic features of midwestern climate that are so familiar to its inhabitants.

First among these features is the distinct nature of the seasons themselves. Winter, spring, summer, and autumn each have special characteristics that set them apart from the other three seasons. This fiercely seasonal aspect of the midwestern climate has obvious implications for native and agricultural vegetation. More precipitation (30 to 48 inches annually) in the east (Michigan, Wisconsin, Indiana, Illinois, and Missouri) is associated with generally deciduous forests in the south grading into mixed coniferous forests in the far north. A rapid westward decline in precipitation (16 to 25 inches annually) in the far west (the Dakotas, Nebraska, and Kansas) results in native grasslands in these areas. Agriculture has replaced native vegetation across large portions of the Midwest because the climate and soils are well suited to grain production, especially corn and wheat. Perhaps less obvious is the effect of the midwestern seasonal cycle on people. The most potent impact is demonstrated by the ways that individuals use weather events to mark the passage of time. Strong public awareness (and even anticipation) of events such as the last spring frost, the first autumn frost (both especially important for farmers and gardeners because of their connections to the growing season), or the first autumn/winter snow is commonplace. Based on my own experience (I grew up in Michigan, moved to Kansas, then to San Francisco, and, finally, to Wisconsin), the "personal climate connection" fostered by living in the Midwest is often not fully realized unless the individual moves to a very different climate, such as California's.

Within each of these four distinct seasons is a wide range of extreme weather events, along with considerable geographic variations in the typical mix of daily conditions. Winter brings several varieties of severe weather, including heavy snow, freezing rain (glaze), and frigid temperatures. In spring (and throughout the nonwinter seasons), severe thunderstorms frequently produce damaging winds, heavy rain, hail, and the midwestern signature natural hazard, the tornado. While tornadoes occur in many places around the world, no area experiences more than the Midwest and (to its immediate south) the states of Oklahoma and Texas. The physical setting of the Midwest and the springtime atmosphere provide ideal conditions for the production of these exceptionally potent phenomena. Summer brings the potential for heat waves, prolonged meteorological droughts, and desiccating winds. Autumn either can be mild and almost summerlike, or can bring the first seasonal snows as early as September.

While the general picture of midwestern weather and climate is complete, more details are necessary in order to appreciate the experience of living in this region. I will now "color in" the specific character and within-region variations of each season using air mass distributions and the range of conditions over a typical thirty-day period.

Tornado over Kansas, by John Steuart Curry (1929). Hackley Picture Fund Purchase, Muskegon Museum of Art, Muskegon, Michigan.

A little more than half of midwestern winter days (sixteen of thirty) are spent under the influence of high-pressure centers originating out of central Canada. These systems bring generally clear skies and cold-dry "continental" conditions. However, low stratus clouds are also common, especially in the vicinity of the Great Lakes (which adds to winter sunshine deprivation for residents). Occasionally within this category, air of a more northern origin (North Pole/Siberia) invades, bringing exceptionally cold temperatures (13 to 31°F), particularly to Minnesota and the Dakotas.

Strong southern-origin winter storms are few in number (two out of thirty days) but of high impact. These low-pressure areas form in the panhandle regions of Oklahoma and Texas and then roar toward the Northeast. Feeding on the contrast of cold-dry northern air and warm-moist southern air, they can spread heavy snows (6 to 18 inches) and freezing rain over any part of the Midwest, depending on their precise tracks. Several of these storms can account for virtually the entire seasonal snowfall (12 to 24 inches) across the southern Midwest.

Snowfall in the northern portions of the Midwest is augmented by low-pressure areas originating in the Canadian Prairie Provinces (e.g., Alberta) and moving generally east along the U.S.-Canada border (three out of thirty days). These systems are associated with moderate Pacific-origin air and generally bring only 2 to 4 inches of snow each. Seasonal snowfall across much of the northern Midwest is pushed to around 24

to 48 inches by these storms and gives travelers there more opportunities to get used to "winter driving conditions" than those in the south. Also, areas around the Great Lakes, especially those to the south and east of Lakes Superior and Michigan (typically "downwind") receive vastly larger annual amounts of snow (48 to 180 inches) due to the "lake effect." The remainder of midwestern winter days (nine of thirty) have shared regional air-mass dominance, with cold-dry continental air common in the east and milder Pacific air prevalent in the west. Variations on this pattern can allow Pacific air to extend across the eastern Midwest as well, bringing the midwinter "thaws" that are also a quasi-regular part of the winter season.

After a cold and harsh winter, no season is more eagerly anticipated in the Midwest than spring. There are several ways to define its start, the most straightforward being the vernal equinox (March 20 or 21), but this fixed astronomical date is generally much too early across most of the region to herald any true improvement in weather conditions. Another is the last "killing" spring frost (generally a date with a minimum temperature at or below 28°F), which is important in defining the start of the agricultural growing season yet occurs too late—generally after weather conditions have improved considerably—to be considered the start of spring. A third definition, and my preference, is measured by plant life-stages, or "phenological" events, such as first leaf and first bloom. While spring plant development is somewhat of a continuum over several months, there are two periods of rapid progress, especially relevant to deciduous forests: (1) first new growth of understory shrubs and the greening of lawns, which typically occurs from around early March in the south to early May in the far north; and (2) first new growth in the dominant forest trees, which starts about April 1 in the south and reaches the Canadian border by June 1.

Once spring gets underway, it exhibits characteristics of the climate system in transition, retaining many winterlike features but flashing promising signs of warmer weather to come. Similar to winter, half of spring days (fifteen of thirty) have cold-dry Canadian-origin high-pressure systems dominating the entire region. Extreme versions of these anticyclones are often responsible for last frost events. Unlike winter, the other half of spring days are under the influence of low-pressure storms and "April showers." Northern-origin systems account for about three of thirty days, bringing mild temperatures and light precipitation. A new "middle-origin" type of low-pressure system accounts for roughly seven of thirty days in spring. These storms have a more southerly track and more moisture (generally with more precipitation) than the northern systems, but they are only slightly stronger. The final group of spring days (five of thirty) contains the most potent set of low-pressure storms. As in winter, these "panhandle" systems draw on abundant Gulf of Mexico moisture and a contrast with cold-dry Canadian-origin air to the north. Add in a little bit of hot-dry air from the southwestern United States, and the stage is set for these low-pressure centers to produce severe thunderstorms with damaging winds, tornadoes, and even heavy snows over any part of the Midwest.

Warm weather brings a partitioning of the Midwest into three subregions dominated by single air masses. Typically on nineteen of thirty days, warm-moist Gulf of Mexico–origin air covers the southeast, cooler Canadian-origin air controls the northeast, and hot-dry southwest U.S.–origin air rules the west. Occasional variations of this pattern allow hot-dry air to overrun the east, bringing extremely high temperatures (from 95 to 105°F) and drought conditions, if it persists. On a second set of days (five of thirty) warm and humid air flows northward over most of the Midwest, bringing high dew-point temperatures (68 to 77°F) and uncomfortably "sticky" weather. Thunderstorms can build as isolated cells across the south, or in the north, with support from weak low-pressure areas traveling along the U.S.-Canadian border on these days. Last, cool-dry air can occasionally (six of thirty days) dominate most of the region in association with Canadian-origin high-pressure areas. Especially strong systems of this type can bring welcome relief from high heat and humidity, even across the extreme southern Midwest.

As in spring, the climate system is in transition during autumn. Summerlike days with high temperatures from 68 to 77°F can occur across the Midwest well into late October or even early November. However, the occasional season with traces of snow in September is also part of the region's expected weather mix. The most numerous set of days (ten of thirty) is dominated by cool Canadian-origin air over the entire region, as was true for the other two nonsummer seasons. Extreme days in this pattern bring the first killing frost and the end of the growing season. Pacific-origin air associated with low-pressure areas traveling along the U.S.-Canada border accounts for another eight of thirty days. These systems generally bring mild temperatures and light precipitation. A three subregion pattern similar to that of summer (cold-dry in the northeast, warm-moist in the southeast, and hot-dry in the west) controls the area for yet another eight of thirty days. However, the west is not as hot as it is in summer, and there is much more mixing of air mass characteristics across the entire Midwest in this pattern.

Finally, the last four of thirty days are under the influence of southern-origin panhandle low-pressure areas. These strong storms can bring severe weather, if summerlike, or early winter snows if they are more winterlike in their makeup, the latter type becoming increasingly common during the later half of November. As autumn winds down, Midwesterners brace for another winter. Yet even as cold weather becomes common, their mood brightens when they remember that spring will inevitably return.

Sources and Further Reading: Reid A. Bryson, "Air Masses, Streamlines, and the Boreal Forest," *Geographical Bulletin* 8 (1966); Jay R. Harman, *Synoptic Climatology of the Westerlies* (1991); Augustus W. Küchler, *Potential Natural Vegetation of the Conterminous United States* (1964); John E. Oliver and John J. Hidore, *Climatology: An Atmospheric Science* (1993); Mark D. Schwartz, "An Integrated Approach to Air Mass Classification in the North Central United States," *Professional Geographer* 43 (Feb. 1991); M.D. Schwartz and Bernhard E. Reiter, "Changes in North American Spring," *International Journal of Climatology* 20 (June 2000); M.D. Schwartz and Brent R. Skeeter, "Linking Air Mass Analysis to Daily and Monthly Mid-tropospheric Flow Patterns," *International Journal of Climatology* 14 (May 1994).

Mark D. Schwartz
University of Wisconsin–Milwaukee

Vastness

There is a pervasive image of the Midwest as vast and flat, a place with little, if any, relief. As used in the description of landscape, the term *relief* means the difference in elevation between the highest and lowest points of a defined area. At a maximum, the relief for most states in the Midwest is around a thousand feet, a far cry from the several thousand feet in many western states. Although the overall relief of the region may be subdued, the region can claim a variety of landscapes. The Ozarks of southern Missouri are as rugged and isolated as parts of the Appalachian Mountains. Hilly southern Indiana stands in marked contrast to the flat northern part of the state. The Flint Hills of eastern Kansas, which support the largest expanse of tallgrass prairie in North America, don't fit the "flatlands" image assigned to the state. The rolling loess bluffs of western Iowa and Illinois and the hills of southeastern Ohio contrast with the vision of physical homogeneity. And the mighty rivers of the region, wandering across broad valleys they carved and continue to modify, have created unique physical landscapes that have left an enduring mark on American art, literature, and music.

Bounded on the east by mountains and on the west by the Great Plains, the Midwest is a region that does not easily evoke description. People readily associate the East with the mountains of northern New England or the shoreline. The West brings to mind a rugged landscape of mountains, broad vistas, and deep canyons. In contrast, the single image that seems to characterize the Midwest is the flatness of the region. It is viewed as lacking the ruggedness of the West and the rolling, forested slopes of the East. "I ain't no Flatlander," claimed a widely circulated T-shirt some years ago. Although other parts of America are as flat as the Midwest (e.g., the Mississippi "delta" area, the

Atlantic Coast plain), the "Flatlander" label was always linked to the vast stretch of the country west of the Appalachians and east of the Rockies.

The image of the region was perhaps best captured years ago by a cover of the *New Yorker* that purported to give the typical New Yorker's view of the world. It showed the skyscrapers of the metropolis, the Hudson River stretching to the north, and then a broad stretch of virtually uninhabited land to the west. The land, of course, was flat and featureless. At the far edge of the cover loomed the Rocky Mountains and the almost mythical landscapes of the West. The message was clear: West of the eastern seaboard is a broad expanse of nothing, a land to be crossed on the way to more interesting landscapes.

In physical size, the Midwest is a large region, stretching approximately a thousand miles from east to west and eight hundred miles from north to south. Crossing the region from east to west, the climate gets progressively drier; from north to south, more humid. Much of the land is cultivated, although large areas still support natural vegetation, such as the broadleaf deciduous forest in the eastern states of the region. The broadleaf forest is also found in the northern states of Wisconsin and Minnesota mixed with larger numbers of evergreen species such as pine. Moving westward into Illinois and Iowa, the summers become progressively drier, partially contributing to a decline in forest cover and an increase in the grass cover of the prairie. But climate alone cannot explain the existence of the prairie. Fire has also played a role in keeping the land clear by burning out young trees. At the western border of the Midwest, the prairie dominates, its tall

Vastness of water, Lake Michigan.
Photo by Sathyan Sundaram.

grasses increasingly mixed with short-grass species. Trees are scarce except along the perennial rivers that cross the area.

To many, the Midwest is not just the physical, but also the cultural, interior of the country. It is viewed as an open land of farms and fields, a land of great distances and few people. Although there are large cities in the Midwest, the image of the region is decidedly rural. With the image of rural comes the impression that Midwesterners are simple, even somewhat naive, in comparison with the "cultured" residents of the eastern and western seaboards. According to this line of reasoning, to the extent that the Midwest has culture, it is regarded as inferior to that available on the coasts.

But it would be misleading to suggest that every image of Midwesterners is negative. There are positive qualities, as well. Its residents are known for their even temperament and hospitality, qualities that may derive from living in a relatively uncongested, low-stress environment. The region is widely held to be a wonderful place to raise a family. Conceivably the size, and sometimes the loneliness, of the region have helped to forge a social network in which people are always ready to lend a hand of support or help. Midwesterners take pride in their work ethic but appear less consumed with career advancement than residents elsewhere in the country. Perhaps the vastness of the midwestern landscape puts human ambitions in a proper perspective. As has been noted, it is the region of the country that is most at peace with itself.

The development of the midwestern landscape has involved a number of processes acting over various lengths of time. Some were active for only short periods, others over great spans of time. Some processes were very localized, or perhaps linear in their impact. Rivers, for instance, have shaped the landscape in a relatively narrow band, although their influence can stretch many hundreds of miles. Other processes impacted a large area. A good example is the role of wind in shaping the land. In the Midwest, it was a major force in shaping the landscape along and downwind of major river valleys, and today wind is a crucial elemental factor at the drier western margin of the region.

Several hundred million years ago, the region that is today the Midwest was covered repeatedly by water. These vast oceans persisted for millions of years, and in them materials accumulated that would eventually become the structure of today's Midwest. The repeated appearance and disappearance of these oceans left behind layer upon layer of materials that were, over time, converted to rock. We call them sedimentary rocks. There are many different types of sedimentary rocks, but all share one characteristic: They were deposited in horizontal layers. Most in the Midwest

have stayed that way, helping to give the region its relatively even surface.

Much later, the great ice sheets of the glacial age moved across the sedimentary rocks. Driven by changes in the global climate that allowed snow to accumulate to great depths around the Hudson Bay area of Canada and eventually convert to ice, the vast ice sheets moved slowly southward beginning about 1.8 million years ago. The exact number of glacial advances and retreats is still debated, but the impact of glaciers on the landscape of the Midwest cannot be missed. The ice carted huge quantities of Canadian soil, sediment, and rock, and spread them across the northern part of the United States. Close to the Canadian border, erosion was the dominant process; farther south, where the ice was thinner, the glaciers dumped their load of rock, soil, and sediment. In some locations, such as across northern Ohio and Indiana, the massive glaciers paused for hundreds of years, depositing materials in linear ridges called moraines. In Minnesota, chunks of ice left behind by the retreating glaciers were buried. When they melted, large circular depressions were left on the landscape. Today many are filled with water to form kettle lakes; they account for many of the more than ten thousand lakes of the state.

But not all of the Midwest was glaciated. The boundary separating the glacial and nonglacial areas runs generally east and west across southern Ohio, Indiana, and Illinois, then turns slightly northward to central Missouri and the northeastern corner of Kansas, before curving northward across eastern Nebraska and into central South Dakota and southwestern North Dakota. North of this line, ice visited at least once between 1.8 million and ten thousand years ago; south of the line, there is no evidence of glaciation, at least not during the last ice age. The exception to this division is the Driftless Area of southwestern Wisconsin, which escaped the ice sheets. As a generalization, nonglaciated areas tend to have more relief than glaciated areas. To the south of the glacial boundary are the rolling hills of southern Ohio, Indiana, and Illinois. More closely aligned with the south than with the north, these relatively isolated parts of the Midwest have a look and feel that is very different from the rest of the region. Only along the Ohio River, the major waterway that forms the region's southern boundary, does the culture become more varied, in cities such as Cincinnati and Louisville.

Related to the ice age but not directly a product of it are the loess deposits and hills. Loess, typically a tan or reddish material, is especially common above the wide valley-bottom lands of the Mississippi and Missouri Rivers. It was spread by strong and persistent westerly winds during the ice age. These winds moved across the sediment-filled valleys of major rivers such as the Mississippi and the Missouri, picking up sediments and spreading them miles downwind. As happens with wind erosion and transport, many of the sediments settled onto the landscape immediately adjacent to the river valley, forming massive bluffs such as those of western Iowa and Illinois. Farther downwind, the loess was deposited in a progressively thinner veneer, forming what one might describe as a ramp that slopes gradually eastward. Some of the most fertile soils of the Midwest, including much of the Corn Belt, subsequently developed in this loess. The soils also support the tallgrass prairie, a landscape that the early settlers found especially difficult to plow because of the dense and deep root systems of the native grasses. Cultivation of the area had to wait for the invention of the steel plow by John Deere in the mid-1800s.

In the end, the image of the midwestern landscape as homogeneous, the same from north to south and east to west, simply crumbles under close examination. Moving westward from its eastern border, the rolling, densely forested hills of eastern Ohio give way to the cultivated fields of Indiana, Illinois, and Iowa. Rich farmland lines the fertile banks of the Ohio, Mississippi, and Missouri Rivers, which themselves flow in broad valleys cut into the surrounding landscape. Along these major waterways local cultural regions have formed, such as the Little Rhine along the Missouri River southwest of St. Louis, an area that supports a thriving tourist business. Continuing westward, the eastern forests slowly give way to the tallgrass prairie of Iowa, and the eastern Dakotas, Nebraska, and Kansas. With the decline in annual precipitation, the cultivated fields are replaced by rangeland. Only where adequate supplies of irrigation water are available, such as along the Platte River in Nebraska or the Kansas River in northeastern Kansas, does cultivation remain the dominant land use. Towns become few and far between. This is the Great Plains at the far western edge of the Midwest. Here, perhaps more than anywhere else in the region, the image of vastness applies. The Great Plains is, indeed, spacious. Sky merges with earth, the horizon stretches as far as the eye can see. But there is variety in the landscape, as well. The Flint Hills and Red Hills of Kansas and the loess hills of southern Nebraska are anything but flat and monotonous. Once again, as is often true throughout the Midwest, reality is at odds with the image.

Sources and Further Reading: Roger C. Anderson, "The Historic Role of Fire in the North American Grassland," in Scott L. Collins and Linda L. Wallace, eds., *Fire in North American Tallgrass Prairies* (1990); Robert Smith Bader, *Hay-*

seeds, Moralizers, and Methodists* (1988); Joel Garreau, *The Nine Nations of North America* (1981); Walter Kirn, "The Heartland of Darkness," *Atlantic Monthly* 289 (Feb. 2002); Antony R. Orme, ed., *The Physical Geography of North America* (2002); James R. Shortridge, *The Middle West: Its Meaning in American Culture* (1989).

Charles W. Martin
Kansas State University

Yeoman Farmer

The yeoman farmer and yeoman farm are midwestern and American ideals or symbols, described and pictured as part of an agrarian past in stock images of rural America regularly appearing on television and in movies, advertisements, and commercials intended to pull at our heartstrings. Such a setting probably never existed, at least full-blown in the idealized Madison Avenue/Hollywood conception; but it is a rich and evocative image used to great effect especially during holidays, times of national tribulation, and political campaigns.

This idealized image, representing self-sufficiency and self-reliance, individualism and independence, and traditional family and community structures, may be descended from the yeoman farms found in the Midwest during the nineteenth century. The term *yeoman farm* comes from England to describe land held freely by an independent farmer standing on the social ladder between the gentry and the landless laborer. Yeoman farms appeared in the American colonies from New England to the Upland and Lowland South and moved west with the settlers. Southern and northern yeoman farmers were overwhelmingly white, lower-middle-class owners of small- to medium-sized tracts. Competition for land resulted in both groups probably holding neither the best nor the worst land. Both groups possessed their own farming equipment and relied on the family for most agricultural labor, although some southern farmers held a few slaves. Both groups strove for economic improvement by achieving at least modest success and prosperity. The stereotype has yeoman farmers producing all they needed on the farm and isolated from the larger economy. In actuality, however, the yeoman farmer was partially self-sufficient and partially engaged in the commercial economy.

In the idealized conception, yeoman farmers were neither poor nor wealthy. Northern or southern, they recognized when conditions required a decision about their future. They faced difficulty expanding their holdings given rising land costs; they sensed flagging soil fertility; they found it hard to compete in the commercial agricultural economy against lower-cost slave labor or larger-scale producers. New, cheaper frontier land in the Midwest lured them, and they had the wherewithal to do something about it. The typical yeoman farmer migrating to the Midwest was not a landless tenant or rural laborer or one of the urban poor. Establishing yeoman farms required funds and farming knowledge. The minimum capital seemingly needed in the 1820s has been estimated at five hundred dollars; by the 1850s the minimum approached a thousand dollars. Considerable costs were faced: transportation, land purchase, shelter, clearing forests or breaking prairie sod, agricultural equipment, and seed grain and food for family and animals prior to the first crop. Travel costs might be reduced for migrants near or already in the Midwest. Sale of the old farm or an inheritance for a younger son might provide capital. Many farmers bought no land or only a small parcel at first, earning money as tenants or laborers to purchase some or more land. Others practiced a craft or skill to generate funds. New land could be bought on time from the government or mortgaged, or the farmer could buy partially improved land. Not all land needed to be readied for crops immediately. Equipment, animals, seeds, and food might be carried from the old home, but more haulage required greater transportation effort and costs. The labor of farmer, family, relatives, or neighbors (with labor returned as needed) overcame shortages in capital.

The yeoman farm supported a self-sufficient and self-reliant family who raised both crops and livestock. In forested regions, small plots initially cleared by girdling or slash-and-burn expanded over time as more land was opened and the remaining trees were removed. In prairie regions, more of the resistant sod was cut or turned year after year. Fences appeared to protect crops, mark boundaries, and signal the application of proper farming techniques. The lean-to, shanty, or log cabin initially housing the family was replaced by a larger frame house and a barn was built to shelter the livestock. Increasing prosperity might result in the construction of a large, two-story brick house. Following the model of agrarian perfection, the yeoman farm eventually evolved into the ordered and well-kept farmstead depicted in the popular county atlases of the late 1800s and early 1900s. The next generation replicated this sequence on the next frontier.

Some key factors may explain why the Midwest supported perhaps the best examples of yeoman farms. Environmentally, it was blessed with a temperate climate (colder to the north) and good soils (better to the west) well suited to supporting the mixed grain and livestock farming imported from eastern regions. During the settlement era, midwestern land was rela-

tively cheap initially and evolving government land policy made it cheaper (and available in larger parcels), especially compared with land costs east of the Appalachians. Beginning in Ohio, most land was surveyed systematically using the Rectangular Public Land Survey, meaning that the boundaries and extent of a particular parcel could be determined fairly accurately. Buying land directly from the government or from a direct purchaser of government lands helped ensure reliable property titles, a critical issue for many yeoman farmers. The lack of clear titles, accurate surveys, and affordable good lands in older settlement areas drove many farmers to look elsewhere for lands offering these characteristics. Thomas Lincoln's travails with unclear titles and surveys in Kentucky, for example, encouraged him to take his family, including young Abraham, across the Ohio River into southern Indiana.

Describing the Midwest as a region uniformly settled by yeoman farmers does not paint a sufficiently diverse portrait because many others purchased land there. Land investment and speculation began as soon as white settlement was permitted in the Trans-Appalachian region: George Washington and other Revolutionary War figures invested in the Ohio Company's holdings in the state's southeastern region. Speculators or investors collected large tracts in the Midwest. If their agents and surveyors were skilled, these included the most promising lands for lumber, minerals, or town building or the best lands for farming. A few purchasers of prairies in the Wabash River Valley of northwestern Indiana and northeastern Illinois hoped to become cattle barons. Corporate entities commonly owned parcels in the mining and lumbering districts and, from Illinois westward, lands granted for railroad construction.

Nonagricultural components of the economy, including mining and lumbering, attracted migrants. Laborers for the lead mines of southwestern Wisconsin and northwestern Illinois arrived quite early, although large-scale extraction of copper and iron from the more remote mineralized areas on the south shore of Lake Superior took longer to develop. Commercial lumbering became dominant in the northern Great Lakes region from Michigan to Minnesota. Mining and lumbering relied on access to markets and demand generated by sparsely wooded areas to the west and developing urban/industrial centers in the Midwest and elsewhere. Iron mining in Michigan's Upper Peninsula expanded greatly after completion of the first locks at Sault Ste. Marie in 1855. Lumbering benefited from the development of narrow-gauge railroads in the pineries and broad-gauge rail line or lake freighter connections to markets in the Midwest and westward.

Even among the yeoman farmers, economic activity was considerably more complex than simple self-sufficient agriculture on family-owned farms. Many did not obtain land directly from the federal government despite this being perhaps conceptually ideal. Some purchased acreage from investors on time, through tenancy arrangements, or using a mortgage; others bought squatters' improvements and then filed legally for the land. During the frontier period, farmers quickly engaged at least partially in the commercial economy. Some let hogs forage for food in the forest mast and herded or hauled them to slaughter at Cincinnati, known for good reason as "Porkopolis." Farmers required market access to sell, trade, or barter their cash crops and surpluses for the manufactured items and other goods they could not or did not produce themselves. Establishing yeoman farms along streams, rivers, and roads, often the most sought-after locations, provided access to the larger world. Crossroads settlements and market towns sprang up as quickly as the farmers' crops. The value of access to commercial markets is apparent from the popular demand for public and private investment in roads and transportation innovations such as canals and railroads.

While their roles as yeoman farmers provided similarities, there was cultural diversity among nineteenth-century Midwesterners and even within their families. Husbands, wives, or children often were born in different states or countries, and children's birthplaces showed a "child ladder" pattern of family movement from place to place. Most settlers came from Pennsylvania, New York, Virginia, and Kentucky. New England, Maryland, and other locations also provided some. Nearly all were descendants of English, Scotch-Irish, German, and Irish ethnic groups. Broadly speaking, settlers focused on certain midwestern areas westward or northwestward of their former homes. Largely following latitudinal lines, Virginians and Kentuckians settled the southern Midwest, the central Midwest was heavily settled by Pennsylvanians, and New Yorkers and New Englanders concentrated farther north but not at the extreme north where farming was least successful. Foreign-born immigrants, often collecting into ethnic communities, added diversity. Some became yeoman farmers; others pursued different occupations such as mining and lumbering. Welsh and English (Cornish) laborers settled in the Wisconsin/Illinois lead-mining district. Many Germans set up homes in rural Wisconsin and east of St. Louis or in cities like Cincinnati and St. Louis. Irish immigrants often labored on canals, roads, and railroads, eventually settling in rural or urban Midwest locations. Large numbers of Dutch arrived in rural southwestern Michigan; Swiss immigrants concentrated in extreme southern Indiana and Wisconsin; Scandinavians settled in Minnesota. African American immigrants from many states, not just the South, were among the yeoman farmers. In some locations, such as southern and eastern Indiana and southwestern Michigan, African Americans closely associated with Quakers from the Carolinas developed strong rural communities. Individual, family, or small groups of American Indians remained, particularly in the northern Midwest.

Beyond the assumed mainline Protestantism of the model yeoman farmer was more religious diversity. There were Roman Catholics and Jews and adherents of minor denominations, such as Quakers in Indiana and Mormons in Illinois. Religious or philosophical associations formed distinctive communities of Shakers in Ohio and Harmonites in southern Indiana. Concentrations of certain ethnic groups were revealed by their religious affiliations, such as Dutch Reformed in southwestern Michigan, Catholicism among the Germans and Irish, and Lutheranism among Germans and Scandinavians. Amish and Mennonite communities developed most notably in Ohio, Indiana, and Iowa. In some way these communities represent the ideal yeoman farm of the past, focused on family farming, an agricultural economy, and a simpler lifestyle, although their religious and cultural structure and, for some, their limited agricultural mechanization distinguish them from the current yeoman farm image.

The concept of a Midwest settled by yeoman farmers represents an American ideal or symbol; the reality was far more complex. But this ideal is supported by realities such as American bounty, prosperity, and economic strength initially built on agriculture. The symbol of the yeoman farmer feeds into many American conceptions and misconceptions: the agrarian myth represented by the Jeffersonian image of citizen-farmers as the ideal Americans, the "goodness" of rural versus the "badness" of urban, the 160-acre family farm, or the "back to the land" movement in the late twentieth century. Although the yeoman farm stereotype presents a simple, bucolic, commercialized image of America, the foundation of America's mythical rural image arguably is the nineteenth-century midwestern yeoman farm, and the yeoman farmer is its symbol.

Sources and Further Reading: Robert E. Ankli, "Farm-Making Costs in the 1850s," *Agricultural History* 48 (Jan. 1974); Jeremy Atack and Fred Bateman, "Yeoman Farming," in Lou Ferleger, ed., *Agriculture and National Development* (1990); Paul W. Gates, *The Farmer's Age* (1968); Henry Glassie, *Pattern in the Material Folk Culture of the Eastern United States* (1968); Richard Hofstadter, "The Myth of the Happy Yeoman," *American Heritage* 7 (Apr. 1956); James T.

Lemon, *The Best Poor Man's Country* (1976); Frank L. Owsley, *Plain Folk of the Old South* (1949); Richard Lyle Power, *Planting Corn Belt Culture* (1953); Malcolm J. Rohrbough, *The Trans-Appalachian Frontier* (1978); James R. Shortridge, *The Middle West: Its Meaning in American Culture* (1989).

Gregory Rose
The Ohio State University–Marion

Midwest as a Young Adult

Traits of young adulthood came to define the Midwest in early twentieth-century scholarship, creative works, and popular thought. This association occurred as part of a broader cultural trend in which three regions of the United States—the East, the Midwest, and the West—were linked respectively to the human life-cycle stages of old age, adulthood, and youth. Following World War I, the Midwest assumed prominence in American regional culture as the country recognized the vigorous leadership found there in both agricultural and industrial production. The East had lost this sort of vitality as it faced the decrepitude of old age, whereas the West still exuded the imprudent optimism and boisterousness of youth. The Midwest's identity as a young adult faced short periods of criticism prior to each of the two world wars but rebounded vigorously in the immediate postwar years. As early as the 1920s, the polarization of rural and urban realities began to challenge the uniform application of youthful maturity to the region. Following World War II, new cores of prosperity in the West began to displace youthfulness in the Midwest, a process that ultimately imbued the region with its current markers of traditionalism and conservatism.

Widespread confusion over the region's symbolic characteristics and physical boundaries prohibited the formation of a coherent label in the nineteenth century. In *The Middle West: Its Meaning in American Culture* (1989), cultural geographer James R. Shortridge wrote that the central plains were identified largely with the untamed West throughout the 1880s. The Old Northwest, by contrast, possessed relatively mature industrial and urban landscapes at the time. It was not until the agricultural depression of the 1890s that the plains subregion began to display more mature attitudes toward resource use and social life.

By the turn of the century, spatial and economic integration brought the plains, prairies, and northern woods together in an overarching geographical arrangement. As historian William Cronon has illustrated in *Nature's Metropolis: Chicago and the Great West*, the region's expanding transportation corridors coordinated goods and services in an impressive network of production, consumption, and exchange. This system linked urban and rural communities in a functional region of agrarian and industrial might. The 1910s witnessed the emergence of a coherent and powerful identity for this newly integrated region. Residents and outsiders alike blended themes of maturity and youthfulness in their descriptions of a confident and growing section of the country. The plains subregion had matured as a result of the 1890s depression, and the entire countryside benefited from technological innovations in agriculture. The urban areas had achieved striking growth in manufacturing, wholesaling, and distribution. Commentators such as Charles Harger began to use symbols of young adulthood to interpret this burgeoning region. Popular literature stressed that the region's plentiful resources and hard-working populace together fostered a vision of self-assurance and vitality.

Chicago was the center of this vast midwestern system. Accordingly, writers found it easy to compare the city's overwhelming strength in the national economy and its supremacy in the popular consciousness with that of a strapping young man. Carl Sandburg's 1916 poem "Chicago" is but the most famous example of this sort of narrative. Sandburg personifies the city as a brawny, overconfident young man who single-handedly directs the nation's most significant heartland industries with an effortlessness that exudes arrogance. Although young adulthood flourished on the grandest scale in cities such as Chicago, the countryside possessed equally remarkable traits of maturity. Chicago no doubt was the "City of the Big Shoulders" and, indeed, "Nature's Metropolis," but the rural areas of the 1910s displayed honest and industrious farmers and loggers who provided much-needed fuel for the machine.

Shortridge has observed that a growing conflict between the urban and the rural realities of the Midwest consistently challenged the uniform application of the young adult label. Throughout the twentieth century, popular thought typically stripped the region of its urban dimension and simplified the place to a pastoral realm. Early on, it was easy to interpret a pastoral Midwest in terms of youthful maturity. By the 1920s, however, a downturn in the agricultural markets generated a brand of rural conservatism and depression that was too visible for writers and other commentators to ignore. Sinclair Lewis's *Main Street* (1920) underscored this sense of provincialism and moral smugness, while the news media emphasized how the depression had undermined the countryside's vivacity. City dwellers began to perceive their small-town counterparts as a source of humiliation and embarrassment. The Great Depression of the 1930s reversed this trend for a time, prompting commentators to em-

❖ "Chicago," Carl Sandburg

Hog Butcher for the World,
Tool Maker, Stacker of Wheat,
Player with Railroads and the Nation's Freight
    Handler;
Stormy, husky, brawling,
City of the Big Shoulders:

They tell me you are wicked and I believe them, for I
    have seen your painted women under the gas lamps
    luring the farm boys.
And they tell me you are crooked and I answer: Yes, it
    is true I have seen the gunman kill and go free to
    kill again.
And they tell me you are brutal and my reply is: On the
    faces of women and children I have seen the marks
    of wanton hunger.
And having answered so I turn once more to those who
    sneer at this my city, and I give them back the sneer
    and say to them:
Come and show me another city with lifted head singing
    so proud to be alive and coarse and strong and
    cunning.
Flinging magnetic curses amid the toil of piling job on
    job, here is a tall bold slugger set vivid against the
    little soft cities;
Fierce as a dog with tongue lapping for action, cunning
    as a savage pitted against the wilderness,
        Bareheaded,
        Shoveling,
        Wrecking,
        Planning,
        Building, breaking, rebuilding,
Under the smoke, dust all over his mouth, laughing with
    white teeth,
Under the terrible burden of destiny laughing as a
young
    man laughs,
Laughing even as an ignorant fighter laughs who has
    never lost a battle,
Bragging and laughing that under his wrist is the pulse,
    and under his ribs the heart of the people,
            Laughing!
Laughing the stormy, husky, brawling laughter of
    Youth, half-naked, sweating, proud to be Hog
    Butcher, Tool Maker, Stacker of Wheat, Player
    with
Railroads and Freight Handler to the Nation.

Source: Carl Sandburg, *Chicago Poems* (1916), 3–4.

During the late 1920s and 1930s, the urban areas remained industrious but they, too, evolved apart from their agrarian complement. This development created yet another point of difficulty in applying the young adult label to the Midwest because Chicago and other cities were increasingly perceived as decadent places that had entered the advanced stages of industrial growth. Sportswriter Roger Kahn summarized this change:

When Carl Sandburg published "Chicago" in 1916, a racket was "a device used to strike a ball or a shuttle-cock." By 1927 . . . *racket* had developed another, darker meaning: "a dishonest business or practice, especially one using fraud or extortion." Chicago still butchered hogs, stacked wheat, and handled freight, but its growth industry now was racketeering. With bootlegging at the center of his underworld trade, Al Capone was said to be earning $100 million a year. Capone had henchmen running sidelines in brothels, heroin, and bookmaking.

The increasing gap between urban and rural areas was not the only source of identity crisis for the Midwest. Prior to each world war, outsiders publicly questioned the region's commitment to national interests because its residents generally were less enthusiastic than others about the prospect of war. Once the United States entered the conflicts, however, the region reaffirmed its youthful maturity by producing millions of dollars worth of equipment, food, and supplies. This agricultural and industrial productivity sparked brief periods of rejuvenation in young adulthood imagery. Taking a slightly different tack in his book *An American Colony: Regionalism and the Roots of Midwestern Culture* (2002), historian Edward Watts argued that industrial and political interests in the East consistently enforced regional perceptions and comparisons that rendered the Midwest inferior, a trend that makes the region's periods of postwar popularity seem more like temporary anomalies than serious cultural resurgences. Another historian, Jon Gjerde, wrote in *The Minds of the West* (1997) that ongoing internal cultural conflicts between natives and immigrants challenge the application of a singular identity to the region at any point in its history.

These differences in interpretation notwithstanding, the Midwest's status as a young adult plummeted dramatically following World War II. It was a fall from which the region would never fully recover. During the second half of the twentieth century, the Pacific Coast and Sunbelt areas of the West emerged as the nation's new cores of economic prosperity and regional popularity. The Central Valley of California became the country's dominant agrarian region, accelerating the economic and social decline of small farm-

phasize the ways that economic hardship had, in fact, fortified agrarian areas through socioeconomic attrition. The regionalist artwork of Grant Wood and Thomas Hart Benton likewise bolstered the image of the midwestern countryside by glorifying the agrarian lifestyle.

ing towns in the central United States. Consequently, themes of traditionalism, conservatism, and blandness came to characterize the rural Midwest. By 1980, a survey of university students revealed that they no longer perceived the region as a vibrant, exciting region conducive to their lifestyles as young adults. Like the early twentieth-century public, most college students considered the Midwest to be a pastoral place and ignored the region's overwhelming urban dimension. However, the survey indicated that this young generation saw the countryside itself as a cultural backwater, not as a vital contributor to national industry. Outsiders expressed this view with particular frequency, a development that accords with the region's contemporary portrayal in popular culture. The success of Garrison Keillor's "News from Lake Wobegon" and the Coen brothers' film *Fargo* rests, in part, on satirizing this overriding perception of midwestern pastoral conservatism.

The fall from young adulthood also was evident in postwar perceptions of urban areas in the region. After the war, Chicago maintained its industrial productivity and a far-reaching agricultural empire, but its image as a healthy and vibrant young adult vanished. Reflecting on childhood excursions from New England to Wisconsin, Cronon described this new version of a sullied midwestern metropolis:

[Chicago] announced itself to our noses before we ever saw it . . . the forest of smokestacks, the great plumes of white and unwhite steam, were unlike any place that . . . I had ever lived. The place remains in my memory as a gray landscape with little vegetation, a clouded sky hovering over dark buildings, and an atmosphere that suddenly made breathing a conscious act. I remember especially one smokestack with dense rusty orange vapor rising like a solid column far into the sky before it dissipated. We always saw it there, every year, and it signaled our entrance into The City.

Cronon's take on Chicago resembles that of Sandburg only in that it highlights industrial activity and urban enormity. The soot, dirt, and waste that Sandburg's Chicago had been able to laugh off finally settled, trapping the city in dark clouds of pollution, corruption, and violence. The riots during the 1968 Democratic National Convention and the appearance of a Cleveland-to-Milwaukee Rust Belt only served to entrench this image. Like their agrarian counterparts, the cities of the Midwest had evolved past their prime.

In twenty-first-century popular thought, the Midwest remains a predominantly pastoral place that has outgrown young adulthood. Yet the region exhibits significant signs of renewed growth and vitality even amid this perceived maturity. Downtown revitalization projects in Chicago, Milwaukee, Kansas City, and Cleveland have garnered nationwide attention and attracted a surge of new residents. Many university towns in the region have become vibrant centers of growth for high-tech industries. Environmentalists and outdoor enthusiasts are imbuing portions of the countryside with new life through preservation and restoration efforts such as the Midewin National Tallgrass Prairie near Joliet, Illinois; the Indiana Dunes National Lakeshore; and the Tallgrass Prairie National Preserve in the Flint Hills of Kansas. These developments underscore the perceptual diversity of the Midwest and, in particular, the localized persistence of young adult imagery.

Sources and Further Reading: William Cronon, *Nature's Metropolis: Chicago and the Great West* (1991); Jon Gjerde, *The Minds of the West* (1997); Roger Kahn, *A Flame of Pure Fire* (1999); James Madison, ed., *Heartland: Comparative Histories of the Midwestern States* (1988); Daniel Nelson, *Farm and Factory: Workers in the Midwest, 1880–1990* (1995); J. Sanford Rikoon, *Threshing in the Midwest, 1820–1940* (1988); James R. Shortridge, *The Middle West: Its Meaning in American Culture* (1989); Edward Watts, *An American Colony: Regionalism and the Roots of Midwestern Culture* (2002).

Soren C. Larsen
University of Missouri–Columbia

Prairie Aesthetics

The prairie's open expanse evokes strong feelings—fear, awe, boredom, excitement. It dominates the Midwest region, giving way to woods to the north and to the east. To some it appears empty, to others pregnant, and to yet others fruitful. It may be liberating or overwhelming. Its beauty, too, is understood in very different ways: as a grassland ecosystem dominated by bluestem or as cropland with bluestem used figuratively for grains. Early European and American travelers recorded their responses to the grassland. William Cullen Bryant's poem "The Prairies," published in 1854, spoke of "unshorn fields, boundless and beautiful." The journals of Lewis and Clark, Francis Parkman, Washington Irving, and others began with the, to them, more comfortable treed landscape, but as they moved deeper into the prairie they were gripped by the height of the grasses and the mix of flowers. They noted the massive herds of bison, the play of prairie chickens, wolves stalking, and bobolinks in flight. Their descriptions show awe, fear, hunger, and thirst. To traveler and writer John C. Van Tramp, the prairie was special; every site varied by season, day,

❖ "The Prairies," William Cullen Bryant

These are the Gardens of the Desert, these
The unshorn fields, boundless and beautiful,
For which the speech of England has no name—
The Prairies. I behold them for the first,
And my heart swells, while the dilated sight
Takes in the encircling vastness. Lo! they stretch
In airy undulations, far away,
As if the ocean, in his gentlest swell,
Stood still, with his rounded billows fixed,
And motionless forever.—Motionless?—
No—they are all unchained again. The clouds
Sweep over with their shadows, and, beneath,
The surface rolls and fluctuates to the eye;
Dark hollows seem to glide along and chase
The sunny ridges. Breezes of the South!
Who toss the golden and the flame-like flowers,
And pass the prairie-hawk that, poised on high,
Flaps his broad wings, yet moves not—ye have played

. . . .

As o'er the verdant waste I guide my steed,
Among the high rank grass that sweeps his sides,
The hollow beating of his footstep seems
A sacrilegious sound. . . . Let the mighty mounds
That overlook the rivers, or that rise
In the dim forest crowded with old oaks,
Answer. A race, that long has passed away,
Built them;—a disciplined and populous race
Heaped, with long toil, the earth, while yet the Greek
Was hewing the Pentelicus to forms
Of symmetry, and rearing on its rock
The glittering Parthenon. These ample fields
Nourished their harvests, here their herds were fed,
When haply by their stalls the bison lowed,
And bowed his maned shoulder to the yoke.

. . . The graceful deer
Bounds to the wood at my approach. The bee,
A more adventurous colonist than man,
With whom he came across the eastern deep,
Fills the savannas with his murmurings,
And hides his sweets, as in the golden age,
Within the hollow oak. I listen long
To his domestic hum, and think I hear
The sound of that advancing multitude
Which soon shall fill these deserts. From the ground
Comes up the laugh of children, the soft voice
Of maidens, and the sweet and solemn hymn
Of Sabbath worshippers. The low of herds
Blends with the rustling of the heavy grain
Over the dark-brown furrows. All at once
A fresher wind sweeps by, and breaks my dream,
And I am in the wilderness alone.

Source: William Cullen Bryant, *Poems* (1848), 218–22.

and hour unlike mountains or deserts. The prairie was a work of art rewarding constant observation. It could appear a wilderness that engulfed those moving through it or a park where the light on the meadow overwhelmed as one emerged from the woods.

As midwestern settlement spread, the prairie aesthetic eased from ecosystem to cropland. Efforts to transform the prairies to cropland dominated the nineteenth century. Promotional brochures were sales pitches that cast a golden glow over the prairies. *A Glimpse of Iowa in 1846; or, Iowa Emigrant's Guide* (1846), for example, calls prairies "the gardens of nature." They were boundless, broad, undulating, fertile, verdant. They held potential. In Willa Cather's *My Ántonia* (1918) they are "not a country at all, but the material out of which countries are made." Walt Whitman's *Specimen Days* (1882) celebrates them as America's characteristic landscape precisely because they appeared so rich in potential; he imagined them filled with farms producing crops to feed the nation.

Travelers' journals gave way to settler accounts, often fictionalized. Hamlin Garland's *A Son of the Middle Border* (1917) captures the altering aesthetic. His description of the Iowa landscape is especially rich in feeling, the two prairies adjoining: the open uncultivated prairie of big bluestem, switchgrass, and Indian grass and the domesticated prairie of cropland. The natural meadows, as he describes them, hint at unknown wilderness, while the cropland prairie required work, cooperation, and responsibility. The wild, waving bluestem became the waving corn or wheat celebrated in "America the Beautiful" (1893). In painting, George Catlin's *Prairie Meadows Burning* (1832) became Sallie Cover's *The Homestead of Ellsworth Bell* (1880s) and, later yet, Grant Wood's *Fall Plowing* (1931). Cropland was the prevailing prairie aesthetic, more productive than pastoral. Prairie soils were praised for their fertility and agricultural production that integrated the Midwest into the nation.

The two aesthetics, ecosystem and cropland, conflict. The ecosystem aesthetic sees in prairie complexity and self-sustainability—that is, independence from people. Adaptability; variety in the mix of grasses and flowers; interdependence of grasses, flowers, and animal life are its central features. The agricultural aesthetic values the landscape for a more singular purpose. The fields are specialized centers of production, each field with one crop. Instead of diversity, its signature is plainness. It is a human construction, measured by its contributions to human needs. The landscape's open flatness underscores the croplands' beauty especially as agriculture becomes increasingly mechanized; it makes the fields easy to work. Crops then fill the fields and the eye. Trees are scarce markers of borders between house and field. The breadth of the prairie matches its increasing production. So many bushels and so many bushels per acre of wheat, corn, soybeans, sugar beets, and sorghum produce neat rows of figures on the page, as neat as the fields themselves.

Frank Lloyd Wright and the Prairie School incorporated the prairie's horizontal lines into their architectural prairie aesthetic. Wright's low-pitched, overhanging roofs blended into the landscape. The buildings' tones and colors were those of mature grains. Pattern books took up the Prairie School designs and purveyed the aesthetic widely. Wright's colleague, landscape architect Jens Jensen, nudged the prairie aesthetic back toward ecosystem. A designer of parks, Jensen strongly advocated using native plantings, "nature's own arrangements." Wildlife biologist and midwesterner Aldo Leopold is perhaps most responsible for firmly reestablishing the aesthetic of the ecosystem. His writings emphasized the incomparable complexity of natural systems. His *Sand County Almanac* (1966) offers exacting testimony to the native prairie's beauty. He decried the farmer's orderly landscape. Health lay in the less manipulated version, in the survival of the delphinium, for example, along railroad right-of-ways or in graveyards.

Leopold inspired many prairie enthusiasts. Ecological restoration—the effort to restore landscapes to their native condition—has been especially active in the Midwest. The impulse feeds both an academic field—University of Wisconsin's Arboretum and Iowa State University's Aldo Leopold Center, for example—and a popular movement. Prairie restorationists form local groups like the Missouri Prairie Foundation or join national land-preservation groups like the Nature Conservancy and the Trust for Public Land and acquire land for prairie restoration, planting, and burning.

Today's prairie aesthetic continues to draw on the experience of openness, the sense of being at the end of the earth and at its center, as writer Michael Martone observes. The Midwest today has little native prairie and much cropland; its inhabitants are mainly urban, but the native prairie inspires. It stimulates the work of writer John Madson and photographers Terry Evans and Frank Oberle. For Madson, the prairie's aesthetic lies in its adaptability and resilience. Forever in motion, it is a place without barriers. It promotes movement, restlessness, interaction, and escape. It has power. Digging in the soil, watching the diversity of plants build, one notes the changing mix of plants from season to season and year to year as variations in rainfall, temperature, fire, and grazers produce an ever-surprising aesthetic. One joins the life of the prairie.

Sources and Further Reading: Terry Evans, *Prairie: Images of Ground and Sky* (1986); Robert E. Grese, *Jens Jensen: Maker of Natural Parks and Gardens* (1998); Joni L. Kinsey, *Plain Pictures* (1996); Dixie Legler, *Prairie Style* (1999); Aldo Leopold, *Sand County Almanac: With Essays on Conservation* (1966); John Madson, *Where the Sky Began* (1982); Michael Martone, *Flatness and Other Landscapes* (2000); Steven Packard and Cornelia F. Mutel, eds., *The Tallgrass Restoration Handbook* (1997); John C. Van Tramp, *Prairie and Rocky Mountain Adventures; or, Life in the West* (1870).

Deborah Popper
College of Staten Island, New York

Barns

Agriculture represents one of the strengths of the American Midwest. The midwestern farmer, depicted in Grant Wood's *American Gothic* painting, is perhaps this country's strongest and most quickly recognized rural icon. In addition, few structures in the rural countryside of the region are as prominent and easily identifiable as the great farm barns. Regardless of type, as one moves through the Midwest, barns tend to be everywhere other than in cities. Many date from the latter third of the nineteenth century or the early twentieth century. Types of structures change generally from east to west and from south to north. To a degree this orientation is the result of changes in farming systems, a partial reflection of different climatic environments. In Ohio and Michigan, barn types are those carried into the region by early settlers from New England, New York, and Pennsylvania.

The smallest barn, usually termed the English or three-bay threshing barn, is typically three bays wide (a central threshing floor separating storage or stabling areas on either side), two bays deep, and has a hayloft above. This early structure often proved inadequate, especially as westward-moving settlers encountered more productive soils. One easy modification was to construct a pent, a triangular projecting roof on one gable to provide protected space for a wagon or other large agricultural equipment. The pent freed up inside space for other uses.

Another modification occurred when the Yankee farmers came into contact with the Pennsylvania Germans. The Pennsylvania bank barn was two and one-half stories high. The ground level was partially excavated into a hillside. Here, cattle and other animals could be housed in comfort in the winter. The second story functioned much as the three-bay barn did, but it was cantilevered to project out over the downslope side of the lower level. Granaries were built into the overhang, allowing feed to be dropped directly into the feeding lot. The projecting overhang is the distinguishing feature of the Pennsylvania German barn.

The westward-migrating Yankees, even before they reached the Midwest, had elevated the three-bay threshing barn by inserting a basement story such as the Pennsylvania barn had. In the new region, however, slopes were more gentle and the basement barn usually was not built into a hillside. A full lower level was constructed of stone, brick, or, later, cement blocks. Access to the upper level was by means of a ramp or barn bridge. Otherwise, the basement barn functioned just as the Pennsylvania barn did. The original single-level three-bay barn gradually disappeared as farming spread westward and the structure proved to be too cramped and unserviceable.

In the Midwest, higher summer temperatures, lower yearly rainfall, and more productive soils changed farming from a system of general crop production mixed with animal husbandry to one more strongly oriented to grains, initially corn and wheat, and, ultimately, soybeans. Barns no longer had to shelter large numbers of livestock. The Pennsylvania and the basement barns were no longer needed even though farms were larger. A smaller, less-expensive structure served the needs of this agriculture.

A subtle shift in the patterns of immigration also affected barn design. More and more, settlers came from northern Germany, where a transverse frame barn, the Saxon barn, was common. This one-and-a-half-story barn had either a central threshing floor or a centered double row of stanchions for a few cows. The side areas of the barn were for storage of grain or equipment. Entrance was on the gable, in contrast to other barns, and the main entry was often supplemented by two smaller doors from which side aisles passed through the length of the structure. In the Midwest, this design is usually termed the transverse frame barn if used primarily for storage and processing, and the feeder barn if used mostly for livestock. Some scholars also have noted a possible connection with transverse crib barns brought into the Midwest from Appalachia and the Southeast.

One important variant of the Saxon barn occurs in the Dutch settlement in southwestern Michigan. There, barns often have a shed attached to one side, which gives the barn an asymmetrical profile when viewed from the end. The shed addition permits cattle to be housed along one side. The main part of the barn houses machinery, grain, and hay.

In the dairy-farming sections of the northern Midwest, a third type of dairy barn joins basement and Pennsylvania barns. This structure, called the Wisconsin barn, was designed at the University of Wisconsin Agricultural Experiment Station in the early part of the twentieth century. A transverse barn (doors on gable), it is characterized by its extended length, large loft for hay storage, and gambrel roof. These features, and the relative ease with which gable extensions could be added, made it suitable for the growing dairy farms of the period.

Each major immigrant group introduced barns into the Midwest that were unique to its area of origin. Although not all of these have yet been given careful study, a few of the better known and studied ones can be cited. The Finns in the upper peninsula of Michigan and northern Wisconsin and Minnesota introduced a number of single-function barns, the most distinctive of which was the *lato*, or hay barn. Its most distinctive feature was loosely fitted, inward-slanting side walls to promote air circulation and to protect

Amish round barn, Kewanee, Illinois. Photo by Dale A. Kooi. Courtesy Lorraine Owens, President, Friends of Johnson Park Foundation, Kewanee, Illinois.

against rain. Scandinavians favored a dual-purpose elongated cow and hay-storage facility. The best remaining concentration of these structures is in the Swedish settled area of Chisago County, Minnesota.

Another multipurpose barn was used by Walloon Belgians in the Door Peninsula of Wisconsin. It is typically elongated and built of logs. Other ethnic communities in the Midwest who introduced distinctive barn types include Welsh in Allen County, Ohio; Czechs in a number of communities in South Dakota; and Germans in the Flint Hills area of Kansas. The latter, as well as some non-Germans in the Flint Hills, built magnificent limestone barns with stone arched doorways, tooled stone lintels (blocks over doors or windows), and corner quoins (stone blocks that form building corners). They are probably the most artistically beautiful barns of the Midwest.

The agricultural landscape of the Midwest also contains a few nonorthogonal barns. Built in the last part of the nineteenth century, these round- and polygonal-plan structures were popularized by the same movement that produced octagonal and hexagonal houses in the United States. Unfortunately, they were more difficult and more expensive to construct and maintain than rectangular-plan barns. Feeding of livestock was inefficient and the popularity of these structures did not last long. Some of them still survive, along with a handful of oval-plan and donut-shaped barns, the latter especially around Stephenson County, Illinois.

One of the most thoughtfully arranged and carefully preserved groups of barns is those collected in the Old World Wisconsin open-air folk museum in Eagle, Wisconsin. Organized as part of small, reconstructed ethnic settlements, the barns effectively communicate the sense of early farming communities.

Sources and Further Reading: Jerry Apps and Allen Strang, *Barns of Wisconsin* (1977); Allan G. Bogue, *From Prairie to Corn Belt* (1968); Robert F. Ensminger, "A Comparative Study of Pennsylvania and Wisconsin Forebay Barns," *Pennsylvania Folklife* 32 (Spring 1983); Lee Hartman, "Michigan Barns," *Michigan Natural Resources* 45 (Spring 1976); Allen G. Noble and Hubert G. H. Wilhelm, eds., *Barns of the Midwest* (1995).

Allen G. Noble
University of Akron, Ohio

Corn Belt Cubes and Other Vernacular Houses

A dwelling of substantial dimensions variously called a Corn Belt cube, a foursquare, or a box provides a fitting symbol for a stereotypically agrarian Midwest.

Constructed between the 1890s and 1920s, cubes are plain-looking houses that express middle-class respectability with restraint. Two stories tall, with four rooms upstairs and down, they are capped by hipped pyramidal roofs sloped steeply enough to accommodate attic dormers. Regardless of generous dimensions, the scarcity of fashionable embellishment on these houses echoes radio-show host Garrison Keillor's portrayal of their inhabitants as deferential and taciturn people. Whether standing on the farm or in town, the foursquare form complements its regional setting. Country cubes conform with checkerboard township-and-range survey fields and straight section-line roads. In cities and towns they reflect rectangular lots and gridiron street patterns.

An apparently good fit notwithstanding, cube dwellings are neither confined to the Midwest nor evenly spread across this region. While found more frequently in the upper Midwest than in its lower reaches, foursquares are also common in Ridge and Valley Appalachia from Pennsylvania southward into Virginia. This coincidence puts their place of origin in question. The former popularity of vernacular cubes stems in part from their frequent promotion in house-plan books distributed among local contractors as well as mail-order marketing to self-builders. Build-your-own house supply firms situated in Bay City and Saginaw, Michigan, circulated catalogs advertising foursquares among a variety of house types. Structural components were shipped to customers for on-site assembly using step-by-step instructions. Additional materials arrived in sequence as construction progressed. Chicago-based Sears Roebuck and Montgomery Ward added diverse house types, including the cube, to a wide array of goods available through local catalog outlets.

Within the Midwest diversity among larger vernacular dwellings began to appear when different folk forms arrived with separate streams of settlers moving inland from the Atlantic seaboard. This divergence is illustrated by a pair of distinctive house types that withstood a transition from laborious time-honored methods of construction to more rapid balloon-frame assembly. Natives of New England and upstate New York brought a two-story upright-and-wing dwelling to the upper Midwest as part of their cultural baggage. This kind of structure was derived by adding a sparingly decorated, two-floor version of a gable-front Greek Revival house to a previously erected Cape Cod cottage. The smaller and older one-and-a-half-story section had been widely built in colonial New England as a modest dwelling. Enlargement occurred when individual circumstances allowed in western New York and places beyond. In effect, the original cottage took on the appearance of an appendage. By positioning fronts of newer and taller uprights farther forward, a more favorable impression was made on passersby and visitors alike. Self-contained floor plans in each unit indicate sequential construction.

Within the lower Midwest, I-houses two stories tall but only one room deep provided a measure of success comparable to upright and wing dwellings built farther north. Over time many of these were enlarged by a rear ell to which the kitchen was usually relegated. This form of dwelling was first identified as a distinctive variety across Indiana, Illinois, and Iowa, though it existed earlier along the Atlantic seaboard and through the Upland South and was later a popular architectural form in places west of the Missouri River.

Beginning around 1900 limited numbers of Corn Belt cubes built in midwestern cities and towns began to display unusual traits at the hands of innovative architects. In suburban Chicago, and farther afield, Frank Lloyd Wright and his Prairie School collaborators converted the boxlike and awkwardly tall foursquare form into one with a decidedly horizontal aspect. This was achieved through lowering the pitch of the roofs and extending their eaves, employing rows of casement windows, and freely applying horizontal banding to outer walls. In a trompe l'oeil manner second-story heights were seemingly compressed by positioning a transition in exterior surface materials at the level of upstairs windowsills. Where skillfully utilized these innovations convey a sense of oneness with low-relief prairie terrain. Extensive areas of glass, open-first-floor plans, and projecting verandas impart an impression of unity between these dwellings and their immediate surroundings.

Whether built with foursquare or more complex footprints, Prairie School–style houses are more closely affiliated with the Midwest than any other kind of dwelling possessing substantial dimensions. Obscuring a confluence between Prairie architecture and this region is the limited number of these houses and their incomplete dispersal. Dwellings displaying elements of Prairie design are encountered most often in cities and towns situated in Illinois, Iowa, Wisconsin, and Minnesota. Municipalities with higher than average numbers include Chicago and several adjacent suburbs as well as Mason City, Madison, La Crosse, and Minneapolis. Prairie-style abodes are found less frequently in Indiana and rarely seen in other midwestern states. Beyond the Midwest, Seattle, Washington, can claim an exceptional collection of period Prairie School dwellings.

Sources and Further Reading: H. Allen Brooks, *The Prairie School* (1972); R. W. Brunskill, *Illustrated Handbook of Vernacular Architecture*, 2nd ed. (1978); Alan Gowans, *The Comfortable House* (1986); John A. Jakle, Robert W. Bastian, and Douglas K. Meyer, *Common Houses in America's Small Towns* (1989); Virginia McAlester and Lee McAlester, *A Field Guide to American Houses* (1984).

Robert W. Bastian
Indiana State University

German America

The Midwest became the most popular destination for German-born immigrants in the nineteenth century, and today the region's farmlands, small towns, and cities are home to more Americans who claim German ancestry than any other. Although German Americans can be found throughout the United States, as a group they are so closely identified with the Midwest that images of the two often conflate: Stolidity, industriousness, unadventurousness, and the close bonds between family and farm are traits frequently said to describe both Germans and Midwesterners more generally. This stereotype—one that is retold to national audiences every Saturday evening during Garrison Keillor's *Prairie Home Companion* radio program as the quiet members of Our Lady of Perpetual Responsibility Catholic Church—nonetheless competes with contrasting images that are products of other eras and media.

During the nineteenth and early twentieth centuries—the era of massive European immigration—German America took root in hundreds of communities across the Midwest. The region's cities developed into the nation's most characteristically German urban environments with German breweries, music halls, restaurants, churches, and beer gardens dominating cityscapes from Cincinnati to St. Louis. By 1890, for example, dozens of German beer gardens provided both badly needed open space in Milwaukee and a total seating capacity of 105,000 for the city's thriving German American community. Likewise, many of the region's small towns took on a distinctly German quality, and hundreds of agricultural counties stretching from Dubois County, Indiana, to Stearns County, Minnesota, became German-language islands in a sea of English.

Such a concentrated immigrant-ethnic presence drew both praise and consternation from non-Germans, who paid especial attention to the sociability and conviviality created by innumerable German social clubs, or *Vereine*. Germans celebrated major events like the founding of the German Empire in 1871 and the German-American Bicentennial of 1883, celebrating the first organized immigration of Germans to Pennsylvania, as well as annual local *Volksfeste*, in a much more public and sensuous way than their

English-speaking neighbors. Even the Fourth of July—with singing, dancing, and beer drinking—became a distinctly German event, and one imbued with *Gemütlichkeit*, or good-natured sociability, throughout German America. Such festive occasions were eventually praised by President John F. Kennedy, who wrote in *A Nation of Immigrants*, "We . . . owe the mellowing of the austere Puritan imprint on our daily lives . . . to the influence of the German immigrants." Not everyone was as pleased with the distinctly German brand of festive culture, however. Prohibitionists and nativists responded angrily to the noisy "damn Dutch" and their Sabbath-desecrating, beer-guzzling picnics. Upon seeing souvenir postcards that cast a negative light on Milwaukee's most numerous group, in 1906 beer baron Frederick Pabst responded defensively in the English-language *Milwaukee Free Press*, "The suggestions . . . are positively indecent and many of them are actually insulting. Milwaukee residents, and especially the Germans, are not drunkards. People who know the Germans understand that the caricatures are of the meanest and most contemptible nature."

Standing alongside such derogatory images were those of Goethe, Beethoven, and Kant—Germany's prestigious icons of European high culture and symbols that German Americans called upon to foster an emerging sense of ethnic awareness. Their middle- and upper-class leaders tapped into a growing self-confidence brought about by increasing political-economic influence in the Midwest as well as pride in Germany's 1871 unification, and they soon began building public and civic structures conspicuously designed to impart a sense of German identity. Sometimes, as in Cincinnati's Music Hall of the 1870s, German associations constructed buildings for their own purposes that could then become important public spaces for all the city's residents. In other cases, such as Milwaukee's Germania Building of 1896, they served specifically German uses like housing America's largest publisher of German books, newspapers, and magazines. Not surprisingly, German America's leaders also embarked on an extensive monument-building campaign designed to glorify German culture. From the end of the Civil War until the beginning of World War I, residents of towns and cities across the Midwest dedicated monuments to cultural heroes like Schiller and Beethoven and to famous German Americans such as Baron Friedrich Wilhelm von Steuben. Perhaps the high point of German pride was constructed on a bluff overlooking New Ulm, Minnesota, where city leaders placed a replica of their homeland's national monument to Arminius, the legendary symbol of German unity.

The two world wars and their aftermath wrought significant changes in German America and its image in American culture. Once a "model" ethnic group, Germans suddenly attained pariah status during the Great War, when everything remotely identified with Germanness became an object of suspicion and derision. The names of towns changed—Berlin, Iowa, for example, became Lincoln—the names of streets changed; the National Guard burned German books in Baraboo, Wisconsin; sauerkraut became "liberty cabbage"; and Theodore Roosevelt advised shooting or hanging any German deemed disloyal—advice carried out by a mob of miners who lynched a German immigrant in southern Illinois. Although such pernicious nativism was not restricted to Germans, their communities were hit especially hard, and trends toward assimilation intensified dramatically. German America went underground, so to speak, where non–public places like churches and homes provided the setting for the quiet maintenance of traditions, especially culinary.

Since the 1960s German culture—like ethnic heritages elsewhere—has experienced a revival of interest that centers, in no small measure, on food. The bratwurst, sauerkraut, strudel, and beer served in German restaurants and during countless festivals across the Midwest have replaced Schiller or the "stupid Hun" as defining symbols. Like the Dutchman bands that play at those festivals and restaurants, such food is recognized and appreciated by Midwesterners as "German," but it often bears only fleeting resemblance to "pure" ethnic or Old World styles. Here and elsewhere German America as a whole has been thoroughly commodified. Developers, architects, and local boosters have selectively refashioned historical images of Milwaukee's German past, for instance, into architectural facades through highly visible historic preservation and architectural projects. Similarly, boosters in places like Frankenmuth, Michigan, devote considerable energy "Bavarianizing" the landscape to make it seem more recognizably "German." While such efforts may attract academic scorn, they are no less "authentic" expressions of German American culture than their nineteenth-century predecessors.

Sources and Further Reading: Kathleen Neils Conzen, "Ethnicity as Festive Culture," in Werner Sollors, ed., *The Invention of Ethnicity* (1989); Steven Hoelscher, Jeffrey Zimmerman, and Timothy Bawden, "Milwaukee's German Renaissance Twice-Told," in Robert Ostergren and Thomas Vale, eds., *Wisconsin Land and Life* (1997); Anne R. Kaplan et al., "The Germans," *The Minnesota Ethnic Cookbook* (1986); John F. Kennedy, *A Nation of Immigrants* (1964); James P. Leary and Richard March, "Dutchman Bands," in Stephen Stern and John Allan Cicala, eds., *Creative Ethnicity* (1991); Frederick C. Luebke, *Germans in the New World* (1990); Frederick Pabst, *Milwaukee Free Press* (Feb. 17, 1906); La Vern J. Rippley, *The German-Americans* (1976); William H.

Tishler, "Midwest Germans," in Dell Upton, ed., *America's Architectural Roots* (1986); Christine M. Totten, "Elusive Affinities," in Frank Trommler and Joseph McVeigh, eds., *America and the Germans*, vol. 2 (1985).

Steven Hoelscher
University of Texas–Austin

Russian-German America

Russian-German America describes areas in the American Midwest settled by approximately 120,000 immigrants who came to the United States from the Volga and Crimea regions of southern Russia from approximately 1870 to the 1920s. The image of a dutiful, pious, German-speaking farmer, newly arrived from Europe, tilling soil on the windswept and treeless plain still resonates in parts of the American Midwest. These midwestern lands were often among the last to be settled by Europeans. The descendants of these immigrants remain in the Midwest and have built large farms, communities, and institutions reflecting lasting traditions of faith and industriousness. Russian-German Americans are not ethnically Russian, however. They are disparate peoples, linked only by German heritage and their common immigration to the United States from Russia.

Beginning in the 1760s Germans streamed into southern Russia at the behest of Catherine the Great, who sought productive settlers to repopulate lands reclaimed from Turkish armies. By the late nineteenth century nearly 1.8 million Germans had resettled throughout the whole of Russia. Although the immigrants came from differing regions within Prussia, they shared a desire for land. Some settlers, especially the (Dutch) Mennonites, who had been living in the Vistula Delta region, and the Hutterites, immigrated because they were promised autonomy by the Russian state, including the continued use of the German language. In time, however, many of these "Russian" Germans became disillusioned when the political, social, and economic climate was radically changed by tsarist edict only a century after the original invitation.

At approximately the same time in the American Midwest, railroad companies, particularly the Burlington and the Santa Fe, were looking for pioneers to populate the prairies. The colonies of Germans in Russia were highly prized because they were thought to be disciplined and productive. Entire Russian-German villages were targets of aggressive marketing campaigns aimed at enticing them to the Midwest, often emphasizing the similarity of landscapes between lands in Russia and those to be settled in the United States. Russian-Germans were lured by the promise of generous agricultural tracts available in Kansas, Nebraska, Minnesota, and the Dakotas. Mennonites, in particular, were coveted because of their legendary agricultural prowess. These immigrants eventually played a substantial role in helping these states become enormous producers of grain and related products. The Russian-Germans are a unique group because of the isolation the settlers experienced in Russia, which fostered distinctive cultural patterns (such as foodways) and forced a measure of self-sufficiency.

While farming was the principal vocation for most of the immigrants, religion is the cornerstone of Russian-German America, particularly the Catholic, Lutheran, and Mennonite faiths. Churches were among the first structures built by the new settlers. Some of these historic sanctuaries remain, such as the Cathedral of the Plains constructed by Catholic Volga Germans in Victoria, Kansas. Because their origins within Europe were varied before emigrating to southern Russia, however, so too are the influences of the Russian-Germans who came to the Midwest. The Russian Mennonite settlers, for example, did not erect cathedrals. Instead, their isolated, autonomous lifestyle led to a series of "mutual aid" activities developed to meet their needs, including food distribution for the needy, credit agencies, and fire insurance. Russian Mennonites in Kansas had a large hand in establishing a college (Bethel College in North Newton), hospitals, newspapers, a mental health care facility, and numerous commercial entities. Another group of Mennonites, the Mennonite-Brethren, developed from the landless class of Mennonites in Russia before their departure to the Midwest. Following the emigration, Mennonite-Brethren adherents throughout the United States looked to Hillsboro, Kansas, as the cultural hearth of their faith. Hutterites, unlike other ethnic groups in the Midwest, continue to live communally on sizable and profitable farms, own few personal items, and remain separated from non-Hutterite culture. Today, over sixty Hutterite colonies thrive throughout the Dakotas and Minnesota.

Aside from the Hutterites' continued isolationist lifestyle, other markers of Russian-German life, such as language, dress, building types, and agricultural practices are fading. Foods remain the most tangible reminder of the past. While no longer a part of daily fare, ethnic food still plays a big part at large festivals and other gatherings. Russian-German cuisine includes borscht (cabbage or beet based), varieties of wurst, and potato dishes. Known by several names, the bierock (sweet dough stuffed with onions, cabbage, and beef) is the best-known Russian-German dish and is the signature entrée of Runza, a Nebraska-based fast-food franchise. Miniature wheat-roll nuggets (coined "peppernuts") spiced with cloves and ginger are holiday favorites. Additionally, Russian-German settlers brought from Europe a strain of blackberries (*Schwartzberren*) still used to make pastries. Among the Russian Mennonites, cottage cheese and dumplings, *verenika*, is a standard dish at food festivals. These Mennonites also transported the seeds of hearty watermelons that thrived in Russia. Melons remain central to the Russian Mennonite "faspa" tradition, a light supper that also features *Zwieback* (hard rolls made from wheat flour), jams, and coffee.

Annual food and culture festivals, thriving century-old churches, and even elderly people chatting in German dialect, all markers of the Russian-German imprint in the Midwest, can still be found in varying degrees in some midwestern communities. Nebraska's capital, Lincoln, has long had a strong Russian-German presence, as does the nearby farming community of Sutton. Among the countless Russian-German communities in North Dakota is Strasburg, home to bandleader Lawrence Welk, the son of Russian-German immigrants. Aberdeen and Eureka are among the many towns in South Dakota that remain linked to this past. Several small towns in west-central Kansas near Hays, including Catherine and Schoenchen, still proudly claim a "Volga" German heritage. Russian Mennonite towns include Goessel, Newton, and North Newton in Kansas; Beatrice and Henderson in Nebraska; Mountain Lake in Minnesota; and Freeman in South Dakota.

By 1940 the number of Russian-German immigrants to the United States swelled to approximately 350,000, the majority of whom settled in the Midwest. Their influence is still evident more than a century after their arrival.

Sources and Further Reading: David M. Emmons, *Garden in the Grasslands* (1971); Donald B. Kraybill and C. Nelson Hostetter, *Anabaptist World USA* (2001); Richard Sallet, *Russian-German Settlements in the United States*, trans. Armand Bauer and La Verne J. Rippley (1974); Norman E. Saul, "Myth and History," *Heritage of the Great Plains* 22 (Summer 1989); William C. Sherman, *Prairie Mosaic* (1983); James Shortridge, *Peopling the Plains* (1995); C. Henry Smith, *The Coming of the Russian Mennonites* (1927); Karl Stumpp, *The German-Russians*, trans. Joseph Height (1967).

Steven Foulke
St. Lawrence University, New York

Nordic America

The Midwest experienced early and substantial Nordic settlement, and it remains the heartland of Nordic America. Swedes and Norwegians, the most numerous, spread heavily throughout the upper Midwest, while Finns localized in northern Michigan and Minnesota. Danes established a swath of settlement from Wisconsin through northern Illinois, southern Minnesota, and parts of Iowa, Nebraska, and South Dakota. Icelandic settlements coalesced at Washington Island, Shawano, and Milwaukee, Wisconsin, early staging areas, as well as places in Minnesota, Nebraska, and North Dakota. Swedish-speaking Finns tended to settle alongside Swedes, and Finns and the Sami, genetically non-Scandinavian, usually came as Norwegians, Swedes, or Finns and settled down in those communities. Chicago was the premier gateway.

While Nordic settlers were intensely interested in land for farming, most settled in urban areas and worked in trades and services. Specialization found expression through Norwegian builders, Danish dairymen, Icelandic fishermen, and Swedish engineers. Norwegians were tobacco farmers in Wisconsin and wheat farmers in Minnesota, and Finns mined copper and iron in the northern ranges. Nordic settlers founded communities based on regional origin, which helped preserve homeland dialects and traditions, in many instances employing place names, such as Denmark and Stockholm, Wisconsin.

Nordic Americans have preserved a strong sense of ethnic identity. They were among the first ethnic groups to chronicle their history, organize ethnic historical societies, and establish museums of ethnic heritage, such as the Norwegian Vesterheim Museum in Decorah, Iowa; the Danish Immigrant Museum in Elk Horn, Iowa; and the Swedish American Museum Center in Chicago. The Naeseth Library in Madison, Wisconsin, is a repository for Norwegian immigrant records, and the Swenson Swedish Immigration Research Center at Rock Island, Illinois, offers the same for Swedish migrants. Hancock, Michigan, the focal point of Finns in the United States, is home to the Finnish American Heritage Center, and the Fiske Collection at Cornell University in New York is a repository for Icelandic Americans.

Nordic immigrants established a rich associational life, from churches and cooperatives to labor unions and temperance orders. Pride in heritage is cultivated in a range of organizations, most of them based in the Midwest, including the Icelandic-American Society, the Swedish American Historical Society, the Swedish Institute, the Sons of Norway, the Vasa Order, the Norwegian American Historical Association, the Danish American Heritage Society, the Finlandia Foundation, and the Swedish Finn Historical Society. Some groups have organized home-area associations, like the Norwegian *bygdelag* and the Sami Siida of North America. Eau Claire, Wisconsin, is home to the Midwest Institute of Scandinavian Culture, and Old

Gunder Hanson's wheat field, Grant County, Minnesota. The Norwegian Emigrant Museum's Photo Archives, neg. no. U-442.

World Wisconsin has a large collection of Scandinavian folk architecture. Furthermore, they have published and maintained ethnic newspapers and journals such as the *Danish Pioneer, Nordisk Tidende*, and the *Finnish American Reporter.*

Religion has played an important role in the maintenance of ethnic traditions. Among the observant most were or are Lutheran, Mission Covenant, Methodist, or Baptist. Nordic Americans, particularly Norwegians, also exhibited religious factionalism, reflecting religious tendencies in their homelands. Religion has also played an important role in the education of Nordic Americans, from folk and parochial schools to colleges. In the case of higher education, for example, Norwegian immigrants founded St. Olaf, Luther, Concordia, Augustana (Sioux Falls, South Dakota), and Augsburg Colleges in the Midwest. Swedes built Augustana College in Rock Island, Illinois, as well as Gustavus Adolphus, Bethany, Lutheran, North Park, and Bethel Colleges, also in the Midwest. Finns established Suomi College (now Finlandia University) at Hancock, Michigan, and the Finnish People's College in Minnesota, and Danes founded Dana and Grand View Colleges in Nebraska and Iowa, respectively. Nordic Americans established health-care facilities such as the Gundersen Clinic in La Crosse, Wisconsin; orphanages; deaconess hospitals; and counseling centers. They created Lutheran Brotherhood, a fraternal insurance company (now Thrivent Financial for Lutherans), today a major sponsor of religious and educational programs.

Ethnic expression is stronger in the Midwest than elsewhere as exemplified in the large number of ethnic symbols, festivals, and traditions. The groups maintain some holiday traditions, especially Christmas, observe independence or constitution days of their respective homelands, and celebrate other special events such as Midsummer. Scandinavian Day is celebrated annually in Chicago, and the Danes observe "Julefest," St. Hans Day, and Denmark's Constitution Day. Finn-Fest is sponsored annually in different locations in the U.S., often combined with the Sami Siida annual meetings. The 17th of May, Norwegian Independence Day, is the most symbolic for Norwegians; Nordic Fest in Decorah, Iowa, and Hostfest in Minot, North Dakota, are also major celebrations. Swedes gather for Swedes Day in Minneapolis as well as Midsummer Day and Santa Lucia in multiple locations.

Even at the outset of the twenty-first century, interest in ethnic foods continues to flourish, and food remains one of the strongest expressions of ethnic identity. Words such as *lutefisk* (cod) and *smorgasbord* are now virtually synonymous with *Scandinavian*. Malt porridge remains an important Finnish Easter food, and *julekake* (Christmas cake), *krumkake* (thin rolled pastry), *pepparkaka* (ginger cookies), herring, and flatbread are common terminology in Scandinavia America. The Nordic Heritage Museum in Seattle is the main repository for Nordic recipes and cookbooks. Similarly, interest in folk art has increased dramatically within Nordic communities in recent decades.

The Nordics in America are descended from literate immigrants who understood the democratic process, practiced the Protestant work ethic, and blended easily as welcome additions to America, yet often differing from host values. Today they are striving to establish modern identities based on changing values and lifestyles in a multicultural world. They are mostly middle class, live in urban areas, and tend to have good education and be civic-minded and politically active. With heightened interest in genealogy and heritage, ethnic communities remain vibrant, with ethnicity an important part of community and personal identity, though identities have been redefined by generations of life in America.

Sources and Further Reading: Frederick Hale, ed., *Danes in North America* (1984); A. William Hoglund, *Finnish Immigrants in America, 1880–1920* (1960); Michael G. Karni, Olavi Koivukangas, and Edward W. Laine, eds., *Finns in North America* (1988); Allan Kastrup, *The Swedish Heritage in America* (1975); Birgit Flemming Larsen and Henning Bender, eds., *Danish Emigration to the U.S.A.* (1992); Odd S. Lovoll, ed., *Nordics in America* (1993); Hans Norman and Harald Runblom, *Transatlantic Connections* (1988); Ingrid Semmingsen, *Norway to America* (1978).

Ann Marie Legreid
Central Missouri State University

Up North

For many Midwesterners going "up north" is synonymous with going on vacation in the northern Midwest. Extending across the northern stretches of Michigan, Wisconsin, and Minnesota is a belt of second-growth forest and tens of thousands of lakes. This region, often called the Northwoods, has attracted summer visitors escaping the Midwest's cities to the south for over a century. The tradition began in the 1870s when the railroads first penetrated the primeval forests. While lumber barons rushed in to exploit the vast sea of timber, the potential for good hunting and fishing was not overlooked. The earliest accommodations were primitive shacks and campsites built for, and often by, sportsmen.

In the 1880s and 1890s more elaborate lodges and resorts began to appear, catering to an elite urban clientele who often stayed for a month or more at a time. The early resorts were operated on what was known as the American plan, which meant that guests were provided with everything from fishing hooks to three square meals a day. They functioned largely as self-contained systems typically consisting of a lodge, cottages, maintenance buildings, cattle and horse barns, an ice house, a small farm, and a boat house. Some even had their own water tower. The lodge was the centerpiece of the resort, for it was there that most social activity took place. Lodges were often constructed of local materials, chiefly logs, with an elaborate fieldstone fireplace serving as the focal point of nighttime activities and conversation.

In the 1920s the relatively expensive American-plan resorts gave way to what were called housekeeping-style resorts. In general, housekeeping-style resorts consisted of several small cottages, typically without an elaborate main lodge. People were expected to bring their own linens and food. In short, they offered a place to stay, not a place to live for several weeks or months. The first housekeeping-style resort appeared in the 1910s, and by the 1920s they outnumbered American-plan resorts. There were several reasons for their popularity: A Northwoods vacation was now affordable for the middle class; better roads and wider use of the automobile allowed people to be more mobile, so it became less attractive to be tied entirely to one place for a long period of time; and many of the wealthier people who had been regular patrons at the American-plan resorts built summer homes of their own.

Since the 1950s there has been a modern evolution and multiplication of accommodation types. The seasonal-home phenomenon accelerated in the 1960s and 1970s with the rise of middle-class disposable income. Chain hotels began to appear in the 1980s. Other types of arrangements like condominiums to own, share, or rent took off during the 1980s and grew with the 1990s' economic boom. This evolution was accompanied by the arrival of fast-food chains, Wal-Mart, and convenience stores. Through it all, however, "up north" for many Midwesterners still evokes strong images of the region's northern resort country, the Northwoods.

Sources and Further Reading: Timothy Bawden, "Reinventing the Frontier: Tourism, Nature, and Environmental Change in Northern Wisconsin, 1880–1930," Ph.D. diss., University of Wisconsin–Madison (2001); John Fraser Hart, "Resort Areas of Wisconsin," *Geographical Review* 74 (Apr. 1984); Patricia Eileen Walsh, "The Last Resort," Ph.D. diss., University of Minnesota (1994).

Timothy Bawden
University of Wisconsin–Eau Claire

Grain Elevators

Since the late nineteenth century, the grain elevator has evolved into one of the most conspicuous and widespread cultural landscape features in western parts of the Midwest. In the early twentieth century, architectural historians romanticized modern grain elevators as works comparable to ancient classical structures. For photographers and painters, grain elevators have served as artistic elements in idyllic, rural settings. For most people, grain elevators have symbolized the bountifulness of the world's richest agricultural region, the excess of which is garnered in

ConAgra grain elevator, Franklin County, Ohio. Photo by Roman Nitze.

towering concrete cylinders anchored firmly in the vastness of the midwestern landscape.

Despite the popular view of grain elevators as agricultural icons, their form is far more powerfully driven by utilitarian aspects of which the public is largely unaware because few people have ever ventured inside them. Grain elevators became components of a collection system through which a region's crops could be funneled to distant markets. As upright, concrete structures they were born of the necessity for fireproof materials and for eliminating the more labor-intensive movement of grain in flat storage units. Internal frictional effects of grain held in large bulk amounts, resulting in relatively little pressure on walls or floors, coupled with evolving elevator technology allowed for storage in tall, upright, concrete bins.

Basic operations occur in both relatively small "country" elevators and the much larger "terminal" elevators, which receive their grain by truck or by rail from country elevators. Operations at terminal elevators are more highly automated and efficient, however. Movement follows the pattern of a rectangular circuit. After leaving the dump pit, grain is lifted by a "leg" to a garner at the top of the "headhouse," the rectilinear structure rising above the circular bins. From the garner, grain flows into the scale hopper and, after weighing, into the distributor, a device that directs the grain either to a bin or to an external loading spout. Grain designated for bins is taken by horizontal conveyor belts housed in the "galleries" extending along the top of the bins; a "tripper," which can be set at any pair of bin-holes the full length of the belt, drops the grain into the bins. Beneath the bins in the "tunnels," bottom slides opened on any number of

bins allow grain to flow in the right "mix" onto another horizontal belt that completes the circuit by conveying grain back to the leg for eventual loading. This basic system of grain movement has evolved to the point where large terminal elevators are capable of loading 120-car "unit trains" within a day.

Continued consolidation in the grain industry and the demise of numerous rail lines suggests that the days of many country elevators are numbered. Trucks still serve elevators abandoned by railroads, however, so they continue to survive even in towns almost completely shorn of other businesses. Even some of the old metal-sheathed, cribbed elevators have endured long past their heyday, their survival based on their use for equipment storage and their limited salvage value. Their continued presence is a reminder of a time when local economies played a much greater role in the agriculture of the Midwest.

Sources and Further Reading: George O. Carney, "Grain Elevators in the United States and Canada," *Material Culture* 27 (Spring 1995); John C. Hudson, *Plains Country Towns* (1985); Le Corbusier, *Towards a New Architecture*, trans. Frederick Etchells (1931); Robert B. Riley, "Grain Elevators," *American Institute of Architects Journal* 66 (Nov. 1977).

Tom Schmiedeler
Washburn University, Kansas

Windmills

The windmill, its vane pointing out the direction of the wind as its metal fan blades whirl, pumping up fresh water for thirsty livestock, was for decades during the late nineteenth and well into the twentieth centuries nearly ubiquitous in the farm lots and pastures of the Midwest.

For centuries wind power had been harnessed worldwide for diverse purposes. The first windmills in North America were modeled after European originals: either the tower model, with a movable wheel mechanism affixed to a stationary tower, or the post model, with all the moving parts mounted on a post and rotating with the wind. A few of these European-style windmills, generally employed to grind grain, are extant, such as the one in Wamego, Kansas.

By the mid-nineteenth century, as settlement in the Midwest and the plains increased, a need arose for a less cumbersome water-pumping windmill. Daniel Halladay, at the instigation of John Burnham, both Vermonters, is credited with inventing the first commercially viable windmill, in 1854. Later that year Halladay, Burnham, and Henry McCray organized the Halladay Wind Mill Company in Connecticut. Soon realizing that the greatest potential market lay in the Midwest, Burnham moved to Chicago in 1856 and started the U.S. Wind Engine and Pump Company. In 1863 his company bought the Halladay firm and moved its operations to Batavia, Illinois, which became a center for windmill manufacturing as other firms set up shop there as well.

In 1866 Leonard Wheeler and his son William perfected a solid-wheel windmill. The following year in Beloit, Wisconsin, their company began its highly successful manufacturing of the Eclipse windmill. Manufacturers found a major market in the railroads, which needed water for steam engines.

Windmills were also used to grind grain (for both flour and livestock feed), saw wood, churn butter, and shell corn. Among the most unusual uses were manufacturing billiard cues and operating a newspaper press. By the turn of the twentieth century windmills were being used to generate electricity. Individual generators supplied electricity to many farm homes in the Midwest before rural electric cooperatives brought power to more remote regions. Early in the twenty-first century large-scale wind factories with hundreds of giant turbines were being installed in many midwestern states.

One of the first all-metal windmills was designed by Thomas O. Perry, who in 1888 teamed with La Verne W. Noyes, an inventor of agricultural machines, to produce the Aeromotor, which became one of the most successful windmills ever, and joined with a number of other manufacturers to establish a dominant presence in the market.

Not all windmills were manufactured, however. Homemade windmills were particularly common in Nebraska and Kansas. These machines, although much less efficient in operation than manufactured ones, could be constructed from scrap materials for only a few dollars.

Today this once indispensable machine of the Midwest has been replaced on many farms and ranches by ponds or by electric or solar-powered pumps.

Sources and Further Reading: T. Lindsay Baker, *A Field Guide to American Windmills* (1985); Erwin Hinckley Barbour, *The Homemade Windmills of Nebraska* (1899); Shaaron Cosner, *American Windmills* (1977).

Jim Hoy
Emporia State University, Kansas

Silos

Silos dot the landscape of the Midwest like agricultural sentinels. Their concentrations are highest in the northern and eastern sections of the region, in the areas of dairying and mixed farming. Midwestern silos are of two types—trench and tower. A device for storing fodder crops in a green state, the North American silo is an idea borrowed from Europe in the latter half of the nineteenth century. Early results were mixed, but the idea showed promise, especially for dairy farmers, who supplied the growing urban demands for fluid milk. Although milk cows "dried up" when green pasturage became unavailable in the winter months, the demand for milk in the cities did not. Feeding the green fodder stored in the silo enabled the cows to produce milk all winter.

Manley Miles, a professor at the University of Illinois, undertook practical experiments in the late 1870s with corn fodder and broomcorn in pits. As a result of his and other successful experiments, farmers began to utilize pits and, later, trench silos, which consist of a partially excavated trench filled with green fodder, with a plastic or similar cover. Experimenting farmers in the dairy farming areas of the northeastern United States hit upon construction of above-ground (tower) silos because the labor of digging pits was prohibitive on any large scale. By 1882 tower silos were being constructed in large numbers throughout the Midwest, especially in Wisconsin.

Tower silos have proven more popular than trench silos. Although the cost of construction is higher, tower silos have much lower rates of spoilage, are less easily waterlogged, and are more convenient to unload. The greatest emphasis on trench silos is in the drier margins of the Midwest. Elsewhere the tower silo predominates.

Prior to 1891 virtually all silos were square or rectangular, a large majority having been constructed inside barns to enable use of existing square framing. Square- or rectangular-plan silos, however, were sometimes unable to withstand the great pressure of the silage, with air consequently being admitted, spoiling the contents. Corner drag caused by the friction between the fodder and the silo walls created air pockets, also leading to spoilage. These serious problems were solved in 1891 by the perfection of the round wooden silo by Professor F.H. King of the Wisconsin Agricultural Experiment Station. These early silos were constructed of either vertical tongue and groove, stacked round hoops, or horizontal wooden staves, secured by steel binding rods tightened by turnbuckles.

After the turn of the twentieth century, farmers began gradually to turn away from wooden silos to more permanent, less permeable materials. Among the most successful of these was poured concrete. The entire silo was constructed as one piece by filling a wooden form. The separate cap was a low dome with an access door or hatch and an enclosed side chute for unloading. Monolithic concrete silos soon gave way to cement stave silos, which remain the most common silos on farms in the Midwest. The form of these silos is the same as that of the wooden stave silo including binding hoops and turnbuckles. A few tile block and brick silos were built, but neither of these materials retained popularity, probably because of the cost of the labor required to erect them.

After World War II a radically new silo design appeared and steadily gained in acceptance. Made of fiberglass bonded to sheets of metal, its construction allowed it to be completely airtight, thus achieving maximum efficiency. These silos, usually known by the trade name of Harvestore, could be unloaded from the bottom, thereby solving one of the major difficulties of earlier silos. The major problem lay in this silo's great cost. A Harvestore silo ultimately came to mark the farm of an efficient, modern, and prosperous dairy farmer.

Sources and Further Reading: N. S. Fish, "The History of the Silo in Wisconsin," *Wisconsin Magazine of History* 8 (Dec. 1924); J. R. McCalmont, *Farm Silos* (1960); Allen G. Noble, "Barns and Square Silos in Northeast Ohio," *Pioneer America* 6 (July 1974); Allen G. Noble, "The Silo in the Eastern Midwest," *Ohio Geographers: Recent Research Themes* 4 (1976).

Allen G. Noble
University of Akron, Ohio

John Deere and Other Tractors

The development of the tractor changed the agricultural landscape of the Midwest more than any other technological innovation. Draft animals, previously used as a power source, were all but eliminated. Tractors replaced field workers and helped to spawn a massive shift in population known as "rural to urban migration." Small rural towns withered and died, one-room schoolhouses disappeared, average farm size in-

John Deere tractor at corn harvest. Photo courtesy John Deere & Company. IMG 21832.

creased dramatically, and eventually less than 2 percent of the nation's population was engaged in farming.

Initially, the transition was slow as mammoth steam-propelled machines weighing between five and ten tons lumbered across the plains, on steel lug wheels, at top speeds of two miles per hour. Then, in 1902, Charles Hart and Charles Parr manufactured and sold the first gasoline traction engine in the United States. The gasoline traction engine was soon shortened to "tractor," and the dawn of a new era was underway. Over the years, more than four hundred companies pursued the development of a viable tractor. Most of these companies failed or merged with other corporations and lost their identity.

Midwestern farm boys from past generations have vivid memories of some of the tractors that impacted their lives. Names like John Deere, Farmall, Ford, Massey-Harris, Allis Chalmers, Case, Oliver, Fordson, McCormick-Deering, and Minneapolis-Moline are quickly recited as old favorites. They remember the days when they walked around the County Fair holding their father's calloused hand as they checked out the tractor displays. They remember racing tractors down flat county roads against the neighbor boys and fistfights at school over whose dad had the best tractor. They remember using new vocabulary words acquired from the hired man the first time they tried to line up a three-point hitch.

Tractors served as status symbols in the community, and the purchase of a new tractor could generate as much pride as an addition to the family. There was strong brand loyalty, and certain models carved a notch in rural history. McCormick's Farmall A, H, C, and M series rocketed the company to a leadership position. The little gray Ford Tractor N series was one of the most beloved tractors of all time. In many collectors' minds, the Massey-Harris 44 was one of the best tractors ever built. However, the manufacturer that outlasted them all was the John Deere Company.

The John Deere Company began as a manufacturer of steel plows in 1837 in Grand Detour, Illinois, and by the early 1960s had become the largest agricultural machinery manufacturer in the world. This phenomenal growth reflects the fierce loyalty of Deere owners who quip, "There are two kinds of farmers, those who drive a John Deere and all of the others."

No single tractor is remembered more fondly than the two-cylinder "Johnny Popper," the all-time favorite of tractor collectors. The familiar *poppa, poppa, poppa* was a lullaby to its owner's ears, although often an irritant to the ears of others. It was simple, dependable, and powerful and it was John Deere green, the most recognizable brand color in the world. It served as the foundation on which the Deere tractor empire was built.

Sources and Further Reading: Wayne G. Broehl, Jr., *John Deere's Company* (1984); T. Herbert Morrell and Jeff Hackett, *Oliver Farm Tractors* (1997); James C. Murphy, "The Development and Diffusion of the Agricultural Tractor, 1880–1954," master's thesis, Southwest Texas State University (2002); Robert N. Pripps, *Ford Tractors* (1990).

Byron D. Augustin
Texas State University–San Marcos

Landscapes of Steel

In 1906 United States Steel chairman Judge Elbert H. Gary broke ground on a windswept tract of Indiana sand dunes and swamps at the head of Lake Michigan for what would become the world's largest integrated steel mill, and an adjacent city of more than a hundred thousand people. Historically, the Gary Works represents the pinnacle of Fordist production techniques; when America was assembling a well-integrated industrial economy tied to mass production, mass consumption, and economies of scale. Relative to today's post-Fordist economy, it has become a bastion of retreat and retrenchment in the face of global competition.

Primary-metals manufacturing evolved and moved west within an expanding North American manufacturing belt, stabilizing along the southern shores of the Great Lakes as a cornerstone of the Midwest's industrial economy. Initially, the component parts of steel production were typically controlled by different firms at different sites, including the coking of bituminous coal; blast-furnace reduction of iron; and steel refining, casting, forging, and milling. The concept of vertically integrating these component parts at single-site locations was advanced first at Carnegie Steel near Pittsburgh in the 1870s, and then diffused through the upper Ohio and Mahoning Valleys to the shores of the Great Lakes.

The steel industry's shift toward the Great Lakes was precipitated by new ore supplies and by the westward expansion of markets for steel rail and wire demanded by western railroads and farms and structural steel for burgeoning midwestern cities. High-quality iron ore from the western rim of Lake Superior was boated down to the cities of the southern shores, where it met metallurgical coal railed north from Appalachian and midwestern coal fields. Limestone needed as a flux to attract impurities during smelting could be found locally or shipped from large quarries in northern Michigan.

Horizontal integration of competing firms into huge conglomerates enabled companies to amass enough capital to build vertically integrated steel mills linked to captive iron and coal mines by fleets of privately owned ore boats and company-controlled railroads. The largest of these concerns was United States Steel, formed in 1901. Through merger, U.S. Steel inherited Chicago's South Works at the mouth of the Calumet River. The corporation's National Tube subsidiary built its largest pipe mill at Lorain, Ohio. This was dwarfed, however, by U.S. Steel's Gary Works, which ultimately came to include eight blast furnaces, fifty-six open hearths, a coke plant, and numerous fabricating mills arranged around its own humanmade harbor and fifteen-thousand-car rail yard.

The Lake Michigan shoreline at Gary was devoted entirely to the mill. Lake freighters docked at the mile-long harbor to unload iron ore and limestone into storage pits paralleling banks of blast furnaces. Fueled by coke, the blast furnaces reduced the iron ore to pig iron, which was converted to steel in adjacent open-hearth furnaces. This arrangement constituted the "hot end" of the plant. The "cold end" was made up of the fabricating mills where steel was converted into the shapes needed by the end users, including National Tube, American Bridge, American Car and Foundry, and American Locomotive, all nearby U.S. Steel subsidiaries. The mill site was surrounded by five large railroads and bounded on the south by the tracks of three major trunk lines, beyond which lay the city of Gary, a speculative grid of streets largely populated by southern and eastern European industrial workers.

Other horizontally and vertically integrated mills gravitated to the lakes, clustering around Chicago, Cleveland, and Detroit. Inland Steel built a massive works at East Chicago, Indiana, in 1901, followed by Youngstown Sheet and Tube in 1916. Up the Calumet River, Republic Steel, a conglomerate assembled to rival U.S. Steel, expanded the old Interstate Iron and Steel mill in 1930. Two integrated steel mills were also built along Cleveland's Cuyahoga River during the 1910s. Republic Steel purchased one in 1935, and Pittsburgh's Jones & Laughlin Steel Corporation bought the other in 1942. Great Lakes Steel built a mill on the Detroit River in Ecorse, Michigan, that was merged with Illinois's Granite City Steel in 1929 to form National Steel Corporation.

The idea of single-site vertical integration was taken one step further at Ford's River Rouge plant in Dearborn, Michigan. During the early twentieth century, rolled sheet steel for automobiles replaced rails as the steel industry's primary product. In 1917 Henry Ford began constructing a gargantuan steel mill and auto assembly plant that would receive raw materials in one end and disgorge finished cars out the other, the epitome of Fordist production. In a similar example of upstream integration, International Harvester produced the steel for its farm equipment at its Wisconsin Steel subsidiary on the Calumet River from 1905 until 1980. Bethlehem Steel built the last integrated mill on the lakes at Burns Harbor, Indiana, in 1964.

When the American steel industry collapsed during the 1980s due to a global glut of steel, peripheral production sites in the West and the Atlantic Tidewater areas susceptible to cheaper imported steel were abandoned. The industry retrenched around a smaller number of modernized midwestern mills using basic oxygen furnaces, continuous casters, and improved electrogalvanizing lines. All three integrated mills along Chicago's Calumet River were closed, as were two more in Youngstown, Ohio, and eight in the Pittsburgh area.

The surviving mills have experienced significant corporate realignment resulting from two decades of mergers and bankruptcies. U.S. Steel centered its Midwest production at Gary and at Lorain Tubular in Ohio and then purchased National Steel in 2003, acquiring National's integrated mills at Granite City, Illinois, and Ecorse, Michigan. Beginning as a Texas construction and engineering firm, LTV Corporation had acquired Jones & Laughlin by 1968, purchased Youngstown Sheet and Tube in 1978, and merged J & L with Republic Steel in 1984. After two bankruptcies, however, LTV's two remaining mills, in Cleveland and East Chicago, were taken over by International Steel Group (ISG) in 2002. A year later ISG absorbed bankrupt Bethlehem's integrated mills at Burns Harbor, Indiana, and Sparrows Point near Baltimore. Ford spun off its River Rouge mill to Rouge Steel in 1989, and Inland Steel's East Chicago mill was acquired by Ispat International.

Although not as large as the Great Lakes production, several steel mills also operate in the Ohio Valley, including AK Steel's integrated plant in Middletown, Ohio, and Wheeling Pittsburgh in Steubenville, located across the Ohio River from Weirton Steel. Despite the rise of scrap-charged, electric-arc-furnace minimills, the demand for raw steel reduced from iron still exists, albeit diminished, and the favored site for making this commodity continues to be the large, integrated mills centered on the Midwest.

Sources and Further Reading: Robert W. Crandall, *The U.S. Steel Industry in Recurrent Crisis* (1981); Anthony P. D'Costa, "State-Sponsored Internationalization," in Helzi Noponen, Julie Graham, and Ann R. Markusen, eds., *Trading Industries, Trading Regions* (1993); Douglas A. Fisher, *Steel Serves the Nation, 1901–1951* (1951); John P. Hoerr, *And the Wolf Finally Came* (1988); John C. Hudson, *Across This Land* (2002); Raymond A. Mohl and Neil Betten, *Steel City: Urban and Ethnic Patterns in Gary, Indiana, 1906–1950* (1986); Powell Moore, *The Calumet Region: Indiana's Last Frontier* (1959).

Kevin J. Patrick
Indiana University of Pennsylvania

Yoopers

"Yoopers," a term that first appeared during the early 1970s, refers to the residents of Michigan's northernmost area, a fifteen-county region called the Upper Peninsula, or U.P. Separated from Michigan's Lower Peninsula by the Straits of Mackinac, the U.P. is bordered by Wisconsin and the Great Lakes of Superior, Michigan, and Huron. The U.P. includes almost 30 percent of Michigan's total area but had only 4 percent of its population in 2000.

The region that now constitutes the U.P. was joined with Michigan only because a small, 468-square-mile section of land along the southern border of the Lower Peninsula—the "Toledo Strip"—had been surveyed incorrectly during the early 1800s. When statehood was achieved in 1837, a political compromise gave the entire Upper Peninsula to Michigan in exchange for the Toledo Strip, which was then attached to Ohio.

After statehood the U.P. began to be exploited for its significant natural resources, including those that had been utilized by American Indians for centuries: forests, fisheries, and mineral deposits. The extraction of ore from the "Copper Country" of the U.P. commenced during the 1840s; one decade later the district had emerged as the nation's commercially viable source of copper ore. Iron-ore mining started on the Marquette, Menominee, and Gogebic Ranges from the 1840s to the 1880s. Most of the copper deposits were exhausted by the late 1960s, and only two iron-ore mines continue to operate on the Marquette Range.

Since the 1840s several unsuccessful efforts have been made to separate the U.P. from Michigan and develop a new state, even after the Mackinac Bridge linked the two peninsulas in 1957. The U.P. Independence Association, formed in 1962 along with representatives from several northern Wisconsin counties, called for the creation of the state of Superior. The organizers' often humorous antics led some Lower Peninsula residents to dub their northern counterparts "Yupes," a term that soon evolved to "Yoopers." The Yoopers countered by terming the southerners "Trolls," because they lived below the Mackinac Bridge.

One of Ernest Hemingway's short stories (1930) is set in the U.P., although attorney and judge John Voekler (pen name Robert Traver) brought national attention to the region through several books, most notably *Anatomy of a Murder* (1958), later transformed into an acclaimed movie (1959). More recently, the music of a local band, Da Yoopers, has stereotyped the contemporary Yooper as someone who endures mosquitoes and black flies in summer, pursues deer hunting in autumn, encounters heavy snowfalls (up to three hundred inches annually) in winter, and deals with high unemployment rates and difficult economic conditions throughout the year. The band's lyrics also reflect the U.P. dialect, sometimes called "Yooper Talk" or "Yoopanese," which is a blending of the region's predominant European immigrant cultures—Finnish, French Canadian, Italian, Swedish, and Cornish. Examples include the substitution of "da" for "the," and the dropping of some prepositions: for example, "Let's go show" rather than "Let's go to the show."

Modern technology and communications have lessened the former geographic isolation of the U.P. Nevertheless, the current image of the Yooper as one of the Midwest's most colorful denizens remains.

Sources and Further Reading: David Binder, "Yes, They're Yoopers, and Proud of It," *New York Times* (Sept. 14, 1995); Ernest Hemingway, "Big Two-Hearted River," in *In Our Time* (1930); Russell M. Magnaghi and Michael T. Marsden, eds., *A Sense of Place: Michigan's Upper Peninsula* (1997); Robert Traver, *Anatomy of a Murder* (1958).

Arnold R. Alanen
University of Wisconsin–Madison

Hedgerows

The word *hedge* is apparently derived from one or more Anglo-Saxon words: *haeg* (hurdle), *hecg* (boundary), and *hega* (border boundary); or, to complicate matters, the Old English word *haga* (enclosure). Contemporary definitions of the term *hedgerows* reduce to a row or "fence" of shrubs or trees serving to enclose or separate parcels of lands. Compositionally, they vary from a single species, for example, Osage orange, to a mix of tree species, shrubs, and forbs. Further, hedgerows can be cultural or natural features on the landscape, the former being typically planted along the boundary of a cultivated field, and the latter emerging from a fence line, usually originating from viable seeds contained within bird droppings.

Hedgerows of the Midwest have long been touted for their many beneficial effects and can serve a number of functions, whether intended or not. Perhaps most apparent is the role of windbreak, which in itself can serve multiple functions: protection and habitat for wildlife and protection for livestock operations, snow management, and enhancement of field microenvironments. Wildlife is afforded not only protection but habitat, including nesting opportunities for a variety of birds and other wildlife such as squirrels, rabbits, and wild turkeys; food sources (e.g., nuts, seeds, and leafy browse) and foraging areas (e.g., insects under bark, nectar sources); a microclimate providing shelter from the elements; and sanctuary in areas of cropland when being pursued or moving among forage areas. Similarly, hedgerows afford considerable protection and shelter for livestock such as cattle, horses, and sheep. Because snow is often wind-driven, the hedgerows' influence on air movement will alter snow accumulation, usually serving to concentrate deposition on the downwind side. Most commonly, the hedgerow is portrayed as a means to modify the environment of otherwise exposed cropland and horticultural plots (e.g., vineyards, orchards): Wind currents and velocity are modified such that soil loss from wind erosion is reduced; decreased wind velocities reduce the evaporative loss of soil moisture; and the rate of surface runoff is reduced, thereby decreasing erosion and encouraging infiltration into the soil zone and perhaps to the water table. A related role of the hedgerow is one of pest control, by providing habitat for insect-eating birds, mammals, and amphibians. Further, hedgerows add aesthetic value to the landscape, which serves to improve quality of life in the rural environment.

Historically, the western fringe states of the Midwest (Kansas, Nebraska, South Dakota, and North Dakota) have been the focus of tree-planting efforts, the grandest of which was the Plains Shelterbelt Project, initiated by President Franklin D. Roosevelt's 1934 Executive Order 6793. Despite intense criticism of this expensive project at the time of its inception, it was implemented and has since been considered a success. Unfortunately, many of the shelterbelts have been allowed to deteriorate or slip into decadence, or have been destroyed through burning and grubbing in order to increase cropland production. In recent years a considerable number of calls have been made for the renovation and establishment of new hedgerows and shelterbelts.

Sources and Further Reading: Wilmon H. Droze, *Trees, Prairies, and People* (1977); Curtis J. Sorenson and Glen A. Marotz, "Changes in Shelterbelt Mileage Statistics over Four Decades in Kansas," *Journal of Soil and Water Conservation* 32 (Nov./Dec. 1977).

William C. Johnson
University of Kansas

Hurley, Hibbing, and Iron-Mining Landscapes

Iron-mining landscapes on opposite sides of Lake Superior contradict conceptions of a monotonously agrarian Midwest. Replacing market towns regularly aligned across checkerboard fields are aberrantly clustered mining communities. These settlements follow contorted outcrops of mineral-bearing rock and are surrounded by second-growth forests. They identify the Marquette, Menominee, Gogebic, Vermilion, Mesabi, and Cuyuna iron ranges of Michigan's Upper Peninsula and northern parts of Wisconsin and Minnesota.

Among iron-mining towns Hurley, Wisconsin, has an enduring reputation as an infamous outpost. For generations local officials turned a blind eye toward establishments providing baser forms of entertainment. Scores of Silver Street saloons prospered until the last Gogebic mines closed during the 1960s. Colorful venues offered dancing girls, gaming tables, and prostitutes. The most substantial structure among the taverns was built by the Hurley National Bank. Since the bank's failure, during the Great Depression, this once exemplary symbol of legitimate commerce has housed the Bank Club Bar and Grill.

In 1914 Minnesota imposed an onerous property tax on unmined iron deposits. Mining companies reacted by relocating the town of Hibbing in order to extract rich beds of underlying ore. Hibbing responded with annexation of nearby unincorporated mineside settlements called locations. This extended tax base paid for diverse and expensive public amenities that gave the community a model-town image. The ultimate gesture was a four million dollar high school built in 1921. Eventually higher-grade ore deposits were depleted and mining properties abandoned on the Mesabi and other iron ranges. Attempting to preserve an industry that also yielded state revenues, Minnesota proposed a statewide referendum on mineral-property tax reduction. In 1964 voters passed a taconite tax amendment giving low-grade iron mines a twenty-five-year exemption from property assessments higher than those paid by other corporations.

Beyond the Mesabi Range mining was done mainly underground. Salient elements of corresponding landscapes included shaft headframes, engine and dry houses, support timber stockpiles, and railroad sidings lined with ore cars. To this day caving grounds mark former subsurface working sites, but few locations with monotonous rows of company-built houses remain. Dominating Mesabi horizons are mesalike dumps of glacial overburden and slate that formerly covered ore deposits. In open pits, now partly flooded with groundwater, power shovels once loaded high-grade hematite directly into railroad cars. Later on, dump trucks and conveyor belts carried ore to the surface. After 1964 depleted mines and modest crushing and washing facilities were phased out. These gave way to sprawling taconite pits and plants that produce one ton of concentrated pellets from three tons of lean iron.

Cornish, Finnish, Greek, Irish, Italian, Jewish, and diverse Slavic immigrants came to iron-range towns in proportions more typical of Cleveland, Detroit, and Chicago than the rural Midwest. Tombstones bearing polyglot surnames are durable monuments to a complex settlement history. Less persistent reminders are ethnic churches, synagogues, and national benefit-society halls, many of which have been vacated, sold, or razed in recent years.

Sources and Further Reading: Robert W. Bastian, "Iron Ore Grades and the Changing Pattern of Lake Superior Mine Shipments," Ph.D. diss., Indiana University (1968); E. W. Davis, *Pioneering with Taconite* (1964); John G. Krier, *Hibbing, the Richest Little Village* (1981); Earle G. Sell, *Ironwood, Michigan, and Surrounding Area* (1990).

Robert W. Bastian
Indiana State University

Duluth Ore Boats

The economic history of Duluth-Superior is the history of its harbor, which is protected from Lake Superior by two narrow sandbars—Minnesota Point, which extends almost six and a half miles from the north shore, and Wisconsin Point, which reaches two and a half miles out from the south shore. Together they form a perfect landlocked basin, and the channel between them, improved with bulkheads, concrete piers, and a breakwater, admits the largest ships on the Great Lakes. Iron ore to feed the huge steel mills of the lower Great Lakes has been one of the chief reasons for the port's existence for over a century. The rich iron mines of Minnesota have long been the impetus for much of the activity at the port and on the lakes in general. Duluth and Superior grew as railroad and harbor towns serving as outlets for the millions of tons of ore brought by train to be loaded onto fleets of ore-carrying vessels, which have become a symbol of the region recognized around the world. From the *Griffon* to the *Edmund Fitzgerald*, ships and shipping contributed greatly to the history and folklore of the Great Lakes. Ore carriers in particular contributed to the popular image.

The steel mills were on Lake Erie, Lake Ontario, and around the southern end of Lake Michigan, near coal and markets but far from the mines. Large quantities of ore had to be moved by water, and had to be moved rapidly. In the mid-1800s, however, the ships that plied the lakes were ill-suited for the iron-ore trade. As a result in 1869, Elihu Peck, a Cleveland shipbuilder, decided to build a steam-powered, propeller-driven ship, the *R. J. Hackett*, specifically de-

signed to haul iron ore. Peck patterned the *Hackett* after small canal barges that carried grain and other bulk cargoes. The *Hackett* had its pilothouse and quarters for the deck crew at the bow end and its machinery and quarters for the galley and engine-room crews at the stern. In between was a continuous, open cargo hold with hatches on twenty-four-foot centers. The *Hackett* carried only enough rigging for emergencies. Peck also built an identical vessel, the *Forest City*, to be the *Hackett*'s consort. Prevented from increasing the size of ships by narrow locks, shallow channels, and the limitations of wooden ship construction, the consort system provided a means for transporting large quantities of ore to the lower lakes. This system depended on a large engine on a tug or propeller to haul the flotilla south. It was not unusual for one powerful tug or wooden propeller to tow up to six sailing ships or specially designed consorts. Because of their heritage and appearance, these types of vessels became known as steambarges.

Sources and Further Reading: William Ashworth, *The Late, Great Lakes* (1986); J. A. Baumhofer, *Where the Boats Are* (1994); Bruce Bowlus, "Changes of Vast Magnitude," Ph.D. diss., Bowling Green State University (1992); Eric Hirsimaki, *The Lakers*, vol. 1 (1987).

Randall Rohe
University of Wisconsin–Waukesha

Garrison Keillor's Lake Wobegon

On July 6, 1974, writer Garrison Keillor introduced radio listeners to a fictional central Minnesota town called Lake Wobegon in the first broadcast of *A Prairie Home Companion*. Modeled after Nashville's *Grand Ole Opry*, Keillor's live performances offer a unique mix of music, storytelling, and satire that made it the flagship program of Minnesota Public Radio and one of the most popular, long-running productions in the United States. In subsequent decades, the hamlet evolved into one of America's most beloved literary landscapes as Keillor continued to spin more elaborate tales about the quirky residents in a series of books launched in 1985 with the best-selling *Lake Wobegon Days*. Based largely upon Keillor's own reminiscences of life in Minnesota, the imaginary town has become a geographic metaphor for the state, a fact that both perplexes and pleases Minnesotans and causes endless debate about the author's sense of place accuracies. Because of the national and international popularity of Keillor's works, Lake Wobegon has also come to symbolize the quintessential culture and landscape of the upper Midwest.

Observers familiar with "outstate" Minnesota (beyond the Twin Cities) will immediately recognize strains of truth in Keillor's satirical portrayals, particularly those involving cultural traits specific to the state's northern European immigrant stock. With his own Anglo-Protestant fundamentalist background as a touchstone, Keillor gently pokes fun at the piety and parochialism of small-town life. Long-standing Lutheran–Roman Catholic rifts are common targets for Keillor's commentary, as are the perceived differences between the two prominent Wobegonian ethnic groups: the Norwegians and the Germans.

Keillor's stories accurately reflect the social divides that exist in small-town Minnesota where civic institutions have historically been segregated by religion and ethnicity. He deftly stereotypes Old World personality traits still perceptible in the rural Midwest—frugality, tidiness, terse speech, reticence to embrace outsiders, and antiurban sentiment. Keillor describes the ubiquitous taverns, cafés, and business establishments, celebrates annual festivals where the residents come together as a community, and endures Christmas lutefisk (lye-soaked cod that resembles fish Jell-O) feeds with the Norwegian Lutherans in church basements.

Wobegonians also exhibit the complex duality of Minnesota's collective state character: a sense of exceptionalism and smugness arising from the belief that they have created a place of clean living, good life, and good government ("where the women are strong, and the men good-looking, and the children all above average") that contrasts starkly with a darker fatalism, self-doubt, pessimism, conservatism, and stoic acceptance of the weather, their limitations, and their unhipness as expressed in the town motto, "*Sumus quod sumus*," or "We are what we are."

Yet for all of the specific Minnesota details associated with the Wobegon phenomenon, Keillor has succeeded in creating a place with universal appeal, a landscape where readers can "stand in praise of common and modest things . . . the pleasure of porches, and small conversation, and fresh vegetables, the pleasure of winter, the pleasure of the familiar, every year, coming around and around."

Sources and Further Reading: Joseph A. Amato and Anthony Amato, "Minnesota, Real and Imagined," in Stephen R. Graubard, ed., *Minnesota, Real and Imagined* (2001); Garrison Keillor, *In Search of Lake Wobegon* (2001); Garrison Keillor, *Lake Wobegon Days* (1985); Mervyn Rothstein, "Keillor Remembers the 'Town That Time Forgot,'" *New York Times* (Aug. 20, 1985).

Cynthia A. Miller
Minnesota State University

Mark Twain's Tom Sawyer and Huckleberry Finn

Samuel Clemens was born in 1835 in the "almost invisible" village of Florida, Missouri. His family moved to the nearby river town of Hannibal four years later. Clemens's fascination with the Mississippi River, which consumed much of his young life, became the centerpiece of much of his fiction. After learning the river while working on steamboats, he adopted a pen name from river-pilot jargon for a depth of twelve feet: Mark Twain.

Although he was from a state often associated with the Midwest, Twain regularly described himself as a southerner. His father was a native Virginian and his mother was from Kentucky. During the Civil War Twain joined the Confederates as a second lieutenant, but resigned after only two weeks service in the field. He later explained that he was "incapacitated by fatigue through constant retreating." Despite his southern identity, Twain had no affection for slavery and distanced Hannibal from the Deep South, writing that "to our whites and blacks alike the Southern plantation was simply hell; no milder word could have described it."

Most people also do not think of Twain as a midwesterner because he spent little time in the region after the age of twenty-six. Moreover, much of Twain's writing occurred well before the evolution of the area into a recognizable region in the American vernacular. Nevertheless, Mark Twain created some of the most enduring literature associated with the heartland. The title character of *The Adventures of Tom Sawyer* (1876) could well be viewed as the embodiment of the emerging Midwest in the nineteenth century. In his youth, energy, and wit, he is an assault on the genteel culture against which many people defined themselves. When Tom Sawyer encounters a stranger who is unusually well dressed for a weekday, Twain remarks: "This was simply astounding. His cap was a dainty thing, his close-buttoned blue cloth roundabout was new and natty, and so were his pantaloons. He had shoes on— and it was only Friday. He even wore a necktie, a bright bit of ribbon. He had a citified air about him that ate into Tom's vitals."

Tom's sidekick, Huckleberry Finn, is even rougher and, ultimately, more pragmatic and compassionate. In *Tom Sawyer*, Huck is first seen shoeless, dressed in rags, and swinging a dead cat. The son of the town drunk, Huck makes his home in doorways and hogsheads, and is "idle, and lawless, and vulgar and bad." He is also the envy of every boy in town. But in *Adventures of Huckleberry Finn* (1884), Twain's most famous hero becomes a complex vehicle for an extended commentary on the themes of abuse, violence, slavery, and freedom. In the end, however, some of the most enduring images from *Huck Finn* are those that create a sense of a distinctive place. "It was kind of solemn, drifting down the big still river, laying on our backs looking up at stars, and we didn't ever feel like talking loud, and it wasn't often that we laughed, only a little kind of low chuckle. We had mighty good weather, as a general thing, and nothing ever happened to us at all."

Sources and Further Reading: Justin Kaplan, *Mr. Clemens and Mark Twain* (1966); Mark Twain, *The Autobiography of Mark Twain* (1959); Mark Twain, *Illustrated Works of Mark Twain* (1979).

G. Scott Campbell
University of Kansas

Dorothy Gale and Oz

Lyman Frank Baum's *The Wonderful Wizard of Oz* (1900) features one of the best-known literary characters in the world, Dorothy. She is not Dorothy Gale, however, until the third Oz book, *Ozma of Oz* (1907). Readers might associate Baum's choice of the surname Gale with the Kansas cyclone of *Wizard*. After all, when Baum edited the *Aberdeen* (Territory) *Saturday Pioneer*, he published frequent accounts of midwestern weather. Or in 1879 he might have read that six Gales, of Irving, Kansas, were killed in a nationally famous double tornado. Or Baum might have been influenced by "Home on the Range" (1876), adapted to many locations in the nineteenth century; its second verse begins, "Oh, give me the gale, of the Solomon vale." In *Ozma of Oz* the gale is a violent sea storm. Dorothy and Uncle Henry are traveling to Australia to visit relatives because Uncle Henry "had been working so hard on his Kansas farm that his health had given way and left him weak and nervous." Dorothy Gale is swept into the sea, and into fairyland. Now surnamed, she is the same midwestern girl. She is the same plucky freedom fighter who destroys evil; the same friend to odd characters; the same democratic uniter of the best forces in fairyland; the same smart, kind, and calm child as in the first book. The only difference: an irritating lisp, which she retains through the rest of Baum's Oz books.

Dorothy also maintains her desire to return to her aunt and uncle. In *Wizard*, she claimed that there was no place like home. By *Ozma of Oz*, when Dorothy checks on Kansas in a magic mirror, her Aunt Em seems fine. Uncle Henry, by himself in Australia, is suffering. Dorothy begs to be transported to him, wanting to comfort him. This echoes her selflessness

Dorothy and friends from the *Wizard of Oz*. Warner Bros. Entertainment Inc. Clip & Still Licensing.

in *Wizard*, when she explains her hurry to get home: Aunt Em will think she's dead, and cannot afford mourning if the crops are no better than the year before. In subsequent Oz books, Baum tired of using natural disasters to transport Dorothy to Oz. In *The Emerald City of Oz* (1910), Dorothy finds a final disaster. Uncle Henry's mortgage is due, and Dorothy says to Ozma, "he 'spected to pay by making money from the farm; but he just couldn't." Because Dorothy Gale is, by then, a princess in Ozma's court, she asks Ozma to rescue them all from the Midwest. Uncle Henry, Aunt Em, and Dorothy Gale leave Kansas to reside in Ozma's court. Henry is relieved, Aunt Em bored for lack of work—they are like a retired farm couple in Florida. Eight Oz books follow *Emerald City*; none refers to Kansas and the Midwest.

L. Frank Baum survived three years (1888–1891) in Dakota Territory and South Dakota, but gave it up for Chicago city life. Dorothy Gale survived a Kansas childhood, but gave it up for the Emerald City. Together, they gave the Midwest one of its admirable citizens, someone with the heart, brains, and courage to thrive in a difficult environment, and to leave when necessary.

Sources and Further Reading: Thomas Fox Averill, "Oz and Kansas Culture," *Kansas History* 12 (Spring 1989); L. Frank Baum, *Dorothy and the Wizard in Oz* (1908); L. Frank Baum, *The Emerald City of Oz* (1910); L. Frank Baum, *The Ozma of Oz* (1907); L. Frank Baum, *The Road to Oz* (1909); David L. Greene and Dick Martin, *The Oz Scrapbook* (1977); S. J. Sackett and William E. Koch, *Kansas Folklore* (1961).

Thomas Fox Averill
Washburn University, Kansas

Sinclair Lewis's *Main Street* and *Babbitt*

A native of Sauk Centre, Minnesota, Sinclair Lewis was the first American to receive the Nobel Prize in Literature. One of the most successful novelists of the early twentieth century, he created considerable controversy with his major famous works, *Main Street* (1920) and *Babbitt* (1922). Despite Lewis's intimations that the novels could have taken place anywhere in America, most people read them, and with good reason, as assaults on the midwestern world in which he was raised.

Main Street relates the story of Carol Milford. Searching for direction after graduating from college, Carol decides to find a small prairie village and "make it beautiful." Opportunity presents itself in the form of marriage to Will Kennicot, a doctor from the small town of Gopher Prairie, Minnesota. Carol is assured by her husband as well as the residents of Gopher Prairie that the town is up-and-coming, the "prettiest place in the Middlewest," and home to the best, "squarest" people on earth.

What Carol finds, though, is a bleak, ugly town, stocked with unimpressive businesses, even less impressive houses, muddy streets, and sickly lawns. Embarking on a campaign to polish this "rough diamond," Carol concludes that the residents of Gopher Prairie are as dull as its landscape. They are a self-righteous, xenophobic people who do not read and do not think. A "blank wall of mediocrity," they view Carol as a heretic, as an affront to the "peace and dignity of the State of Minnesota." Meanwhile, Carol comes to see the ideals of Main Street as "the prohibition of happiness. . . . It is slavery self-sought and self-defended. It is dullness made God. A savorless people, gulping tasteless food, and sitting afterward, coatless and thoughtless, in rocking-chairs prickly with inane decorations, listening to mechanical music, saying mechanical things about the excellence of Ford automobiles, and viewing themselves as the greatest race in the world."

Unlike Carol, George Babbitt avoids reform, except for occasional forays into self-improvement. A real estate dealer in the fictional midwestern city of Zenith, he is in his midforties and married with two children. Through the course of the novel, Babbitt becomes aware of the confinement and desolation inherent in the materialistic culture that he has promoted. Like Carol, Babbitt attempts to rebel, but is pressed back into conformity.

Both novels end with their protagonists taking comfort in their children's future. Babbitt finds consolation in the fact that his son has chosen a life that will allow him to do what he really wants to do. *Main Street* ends with Carol speaking of her sleeping young daughter: "Do you see that object on the pillow? Do you know what it is? It's a bomb to blow up smugness. If you Tories were wise, you wouldn't arrest anarchists; you'd arrest all these children while they're asleep in their cribs. Think what that baby will see and meddle with before she dies in the year 2000!"

Sources and Further Reading: Sinclair Lewis, *Babbitt* (2002); Sinclair Lewis, *Main Street* (1999); Richard Lingeman, *Sinclair Lewis: Rebel from Main Street* (2002).

G. Scott Campbell
University of Kansas

Willa Cather's Alexandra and Ántonia

Born in Virginia in 1873, Willa Cather moved with her family to Red Cloud, Nebraska, at the age of nine. She left the Midwest in 1896, spending much of her life in New York City, where she completed her two best-known novels, *O Pioneers!* (1913) and *My Ántonia* (1918). Both works were inspired by Cather's life on the Nebraska prairie.

The novels tell the stories of two remarkable women—Alexandra Bergson, the daughter of Swedish immigrants, and Ántonia Shimerda, the daughter of Czech immigrants. Both come to Nebraska during its difficult early years, and the settlement landscape that Cather describes is harsh indeed. The prairie is depicted as being "like a horse that no one knows how to break to harness, that runs wild and kicks things to pieces." The land seems as if it "wanted to be left alone, to preserve its own fierce strength, its peculiar, savage kind of beauty, its uninterrupted mournfulness." Despite the unforgiving prairie, and despite blizzards, droughts, and sickness, Alexandra and Ántonia love the land and draw excitement from it. "There was nothing but land," Cather writes, "not a country at all, but the material out of which countries are made. . . . I wanted to walk straight on through the red grass and over the edge of the world, which could not be very far away." It is on the land and with the soil that Alexandra and Ántonia are best able to express and understand themselves.

Alexandra and Ántonia survive the difficult times, and are well-educated by poverty. After years of struggle, the shaggy carpet of prairie grass begins to vanish, replaced by a checkerboard of wheat and corn anchored in mile-long furrows of rich soil. All the human effort of the pioneers comes back in "long, sweeping lines of fertility." Alexandra tells a friend, "The land did it. It had its little joke. It pretended to be poor because nobody knew how to work it right; and then, all at once, it worked itself. It woke up out of its sleep and stretched itself, and it was so big, so rich, that we suddenly found we were rich, just from sitting still."

There is a sense in Cather's writing that the true character of the Midwest comes out of these hard times, and that this spirit is, in fact, challenged by successful times. Some prairie residents become self-righteous, provincial and conceited as they become comfortable, and both Alexandra and Ántonia meet tragedy amid the prosperity.

Still, in the end they both endure. The land, and the noble character of those that care for it, endures. In the closing pages of *O Pioneers!*, Alexandra tells a childhood friend that "the land belongs to the future. . . . We come and go, but the land is always here. And the people who love it and understand it are the people who own it—for a little while."

Sources and Further Reading: Willa Cather, *My Ántonia* (1994); Willa Cather, *O Pioneers!* (1992); Sharon O'Brien, *Willa Cather: The Emerging Voice* (1987).

G. Scott Campbell
University of Kansas

Sherwood Anderson's *Winesburg, Ohio*

Perhaps no other literary work of the twentieth century so compellingly records the societal and emotional consequences of the shift from an agrarian to an industrial economy in rural America as *Winesburg, Ohio.* Published in 1919 as the machine age and the urban experience were increasingly altering the lives of ordinary Americans, Sherwood Anderson's fictional account offers evocative yet contrasting images of the rural Midwest and the American small town. These two powerful symbols had already begun to represent a nostalgic American ideal, although at the time of the book's publication they were both well in decline. In part a novel, in part a collection of short stories, the book's twenty-four sections impart interconnected sketches of various citizens of Winesburg, a fictional settlement modeled after the true-life town of Clyde, Ohio, where Anderson spent his formative childhood years. At once sentimental and critical of an idyllic, pastoral rural America, *Winesburg* has been hailed by many critics as a literary classic. Given that the book has been in print continuously since its initial publication and has been translated into at least twenty-seven languages, public appreciation for Anderson's best-known work appears to mirror such critical praise.

Much of the content of *Winesburg* probably reflects Anderson's own process of coming to terms with his critique of and affection for American small-town life. At the age of thirty-six, following a nervous breakdown, he left Elyria, Ohio, where he was a rather successful businessman, for Chicago to become a serious writer. There he fell in with the group of writers and cultural bohemians who comprised the so-called Chicago Renaissance and quickly distinguished himself as an outspoken critic of American materialism. Early commentators praised *Winesburg* as a splendid example of literary realism, but many subsequent critics have argued that what Anderson achieved is actually the opposite. Anderson was not trying to paint a picture of life in a typical midwestern small town; rather, Winesburg and its odd assortment of inhabitants are meant to represent Anytown, USA, where the ideals and reality of life in an uncertain age and time are in perpetual disconnect.

A central leitmotif running throughout *Winesburg* involves the search for ultimate truths, which are in the end unknowable and unattainable. Each of the twenty-four sections tells the story of characters that pursue a certain "truth" to such an extent that they become "grotesque." In the search for such truths, most of the book's characters become alienated, lonely, and disappointed, cut off from community bonds that are withering away under the influence of materialism and mechanization. In this way *Winesburg* can hardly be seen as an elegiac tribute to the quintessential midwestern small town. Its set of powerful images and themes—alienation, dysfunction, isolation, and loneliness—are in direct conflict with many of the ideals that Americans associate with the Midwest: morality, conservatism, and a strong sense of community. As such, *Winesburg*'s most powerful theme is that of nostalgia—nostalgia for a preindustrial America where the bonds of community instilled in people a common sense of purpose and meaning.

Sources and Further Reading: Malcolm Cowley, introduction to Sherwood Anderson, *Winesburg, Ohio* (1960); John H. Ferres, ed., *Winesburg, Ohio: Text and Criticism* (1996);

William A. Sutton, *The Road to Winesburg* (1972); Ray Lewis White, *Winesburg, Ohio: An Exploration* (1990).

Timothy G. Anderson
Ohio University

Boundary Waters, Minnesota

Straddling the Minnesota-Ontario border, the Boundary Waters offers a striking contrast to the more typical agricultural landscapes of the Midwest. The sounds, the smells, the visual landscape are those of the North. This is the land of moose, wolves, blueberries, clear, dark lakes, and endless forest. Of loon echoes and silence. Of conifer and fish scent. Even the mining and logging history of the place has a northern flavor. For Midwesterners, this is a place apart. A place for escape. A wilderness. One visit can form lifetime memories, so powerful is the impact on those from the more domesticated parts of the Midwest.

The wilderness still exists, thanks to the efforts of leaders, such as Sigurd Olson and the Quetico-Superior Committee, who fought to buy out resorts and prevent further incursion into the area in the 1940s and 1950s, laying the ground for later designation of the over one million–acre Boundary Waters Canoe Area (BWCA) Wilderness. Threats to wild qualities of the region continue, now mainly from second homes and motorized recreation. With North Woods shops now inhabiting midwestern malls, and trinket stores on every corner of Ely, Minnesota, the otherness blurs, but the quiet of the Boundary Waters is still there for those who seek it out. In *Listening Point* (1958), a book that helped define the essence of the Boundary Waters, Sigurd Olson wrote: "I named this place Listening Point because only when one comes to listen, only when one is aware and still, can things be seen and heard."

Sources and Further Reading: Clifford Ahlgren and Isabel Ahlgren, *Lob Trees in the Wilderness* (2001); Sigurd F. Olson, *Listening Point* (1958); Kevin Proescholdt, Rip Rapson, and Miron L. Heinselman, *Troubled Waters: The Fight for the Boundary Waters Canoe Area Wilderness* (1995).

Deborah D. Paulson
University of Wyoming

Brown County, Indiana

Brown County, Indiana, is a central rural woodland county whose border is only about fifteen miles south of the southern suburbs of Indianapolis. With a population of only fifteen thousand, and with less than one thousand in the county seat of Nashville, the county has maintained a backwoods flavor because its soils are too poor for quality agriculture. Given these parameters, the county's rustic popularity is remarkable, perhaps bred by proximity to the state capital nearby. Urban life, however, seems much farther away. Within Brown County are Yellowwood State Forest, Brown County State Park, and the northern reaches of Hoosier National Forest. Brown County has gradually marketed an image of hilly Hoosier paradise that is the envy of many a rural midwestern county.

Its festivals have grown as attractions for thousands of work-weary suburbanites across the central United States. A few typical covered bridges add the necessary spice of folk architecture. Brown County was once known for substantial precious metals in its northern creeks. People still make a hobby of panning for gold, and it is a great achievement to find that minuscule fleck as a memento, even if it is lost in a bottle of sand. A number of artistic folk have claimed Brown County as home, including Kin Hubbard, the writer known for the fictional Brown County character of Abe Martin; the portrait painter T.C. Steele; and photographer Frank Hohenberger. The county is also the home of the Bill Monroe Bluegrass Festival, established by the Father of Bluegrass in 1953 at Bean Blossom.

Sources and Further Reading: Dillon Bustin, *If You Don't Outdie Me* (1982); Lyn Letsinger-Miller, *The Artists of Brown County* (1994); Bill Thomas, *The Brown County Book* (1981).

Craig S. Campbell
Youngstown State University, Ohio

Branson, Missouri

An Ozark resort community located in southwestern Missouri, Branson was incorporated in 1912. Upon publication of Harold Bell Wright's *The Shepherd of the Hills* in 1907, an early-twentieth-century best seller that glorifies the region, thousands of visitors flocked to the area to learn more about local lifestyles. During this period, tourists also arrived to fish, swim, and boat on the White River, recreational opportunities furthered by the construction of Lake Taneycomo in 1913 and Table Rock Lake in 1959. Branson's modern tourism industry emerged in 1959 with the opening of the Baldknobbers Jamboree, a variety show theatre combining country music, Ozark folk songs, and comedy. In 1967 the local Presley family launched the first theatre on what is now the Highway 76 "Strip," a thoroughfare that currently hosts numerous similar venues. In 1960 the Silver Dollar City theme park opened, a site meant to preserve the late-nineteenth-century heritage of the Ozarks that still draws millions of visitors with its combination of crafts displays and thrill rides. In 1983, with the founding of the Roy Clark Celebrity Theater, the town began attracting nationally recognized entertainers. Currently Branson hosts roughly fifty variety show theatres featuring renowned artists such as Andy Williams, Glen Campbell, and the Osmonds. Gaining a reputation throughout the 1980s for wholesome fun replete with patriotic, religious, and rustic subjects, this town of 6,050 residents now welcomes approximately seven million visitors per year. As one of the Midwest's premier vacation destinations, Branson continues to accentuate time-tested pastoral, familial, and pious themes, leading local boosters to label its offerings as "Real American Entertainment."

Sources and Further Reading: Bruce Cook, *The Town That Country Built* (1993); Lynn Morrow and Linda Myers-Phinney, *Shepherd of the Hills Country* (1999); Milton D. Rafferty, *The Ozarks: Land and Life* (1980).

Aaron Ketchell
University of Kansas

Corn Palace, South Dakota

Mitchell, South Dakota, became the location of the self-acclaimed "World's Only Corn Palace" in 1905, although its antecedents date back to 1892, when residents initiated a civic enterprise known as the Corn Belt Exposition. Promoters erected a structure in an attempt to foster the growth and prosperity of the town, situated near the evolving western extension of the Corn Belt. Mitchell's first "palace" had the dual purpose of being a venue for agricultural exhibitions and stage entertainment. By 1904 the Corn Palace presented headliner shows (e.g., John Philip Sousa), with the period of the 1930s, 1940s, and 1950s (often featuring Lawrence Welk) being especially well publicized.

The current structure is the third Corn Palace, dating from 1921. Annual redecoration is a major task because two sides of the building with its multistory murals must be covered again with thousands of corncobs of various colors, sheaths of wheat and native grasses, and other grains during the summer. Mosaics are produced by nailing half ears of split corncobs plus bunches of grain and grasses to the walls. The palace's exterior has become a major attraction for both tourists and birds, and it may well be the world's largest bird feeder, according to some of its visitors. Nationally known acts continue to be booked into the Corn Palace, along with numerous expositions. If the commercial production of corn helps to define the geographical Midwest, it's fitting that a Corn Palace should be located proximal to the western margin as a symbol of this important grain.

Sources and Further Reading: Tom D. Griffith, *South Dakota* (1994); Edward P. Hogan and E. H. Fouberg, *The Geography of South Dakota*, rev. ed. (1998); George M. Smith, *South Dakota: Its History and Its People*, vol. 3 (1915).

Donald J. Berg
South Dakota State University

The Mitchell Corn Palace, South Dakota. Photo courtesy The South Dakota Department of Tourism and State Development.

Door County, Wisconsin

Door County, the "thumb" of northeastern Wisconsin, is a peninsula surrounded by the waters of Green Bay and Lake Michigan. The most distinctive natural feature of Door County is the Niagara Escarpment, a steep limestone cliff that outcrops along the peninsula's western edge. Inland, a veneer of glacial drift masks an underground system of caves and crevices, whereas dunes, ridges, and wetlands characterize the eastern shore.

The *Porte des Morts* passage, located between the northernmost tip of the Door Peninsula and Washington Island, was named by seventeenth-century French explorers for its treacherous currents and rough surface waters. Today a ferry carries tourists to the island, moving steadily over the "door of death" for which Door County is named.

The early economies of fur trading, logging, and stone quarrying have given way to tourism on the peninsula. Both natural scenery and cultural events have attracted tourists to Door County since before the turn of the last century, especially north of Sturgeon Bay. A diverse landscape of water, rock, meadow, forest, and dunes can be observed as one travels along the coasts between small villages with maritime-sounding names like Egg Harbor, Fish Creek, and Jacksonport. Several ethnic groups settled on the peninsula. Washington Island remains the largest Icelandic settlement in the United States today, and the southern part of the county, near Brussels, is part of the largest rural Belgian settlement in the nation.

Sources and Further Reading: Craig Charles, *Exploring Door County* (1999); John Palmquist, ed., *Wisconsin's Door Peninsula* (1989); Kazimierz J. Zaniewski and Carol J. Rosen, *The Atlas of Ethnic Diversity in Wisconsin* (1998).

Carol J. Rosen
University of Wisconsin–Whitewater

Traverse City, Michigan

Traverse City, Michigan, is located on Lake Michigan's Grand Traverse Bay, about three hundred miles by road northeast of Chicago. With a population of 14,523, it is the largest city in the northern half of Michigan's Lower Peninsula and the hub of a rapidly growing area.

Traverse City has not fit much of the stereotypical image of the Midwest despite being closely linked to it. Instead of producing grain and livestock, Traverse City's early decades (1850–1910) centered on the export of lumber and other forest products to Chicago.

When farmers arrived, they emphasized fruit growing, particularly cherries. The dominant activity in the area in recent decades has been tourism and recreation, activities rarely preeminent throughout the Midwest.

Prosperous Midwesterners early on were grateful to escape the oppressive summers for the attractions of boating and fishing in the Grand Traverse area. Today most of the midwestern population lives within a day's drive of Traverse City, and summer crowds come for the outdoor pleasures once enjoyed mainly by the wealthy. Recreation has expanded to other seasons, with people attracted by fall colors, hunting, skiing, and snowmobiling. Large resort complexes have superseded the older lodges and small motels, and increasing numbers of people convene or retire here.

The Traverse City area combines the still energetic older central city with outlying growth. Historic preservation, artists' galleries, and a symphony orchestra thrive. A ring road connects new shopping centers and residential areas, but it is only these last features that may cause visitors to say: "It's just like home."

Source and Further Reading: Lawrence Wakefield, *Queen City of the North: An Illustrated History of Traverse City from Its Beginnings to 1980s* (1988).

Charles Heller
Western Michigan University

Phil Stong's *State Fair*

Grandson of a director for Iowa's first state fair (1854), journalist Phil Stong, from Keosauqua, celebrated the fair and farming in his best-selling 1932 novel *State Fair*, the first published and most successful of his more than forty books. Movies about the Frake family have kept *State Fair* steadily in print and preserved its bucolic picture of midwestern life. Fox released film versions in 1933 (starring Will Rogers), 1945 (a Rodgers and Hammerstein musical), and 1962 (an ineffective relocation to Texas). A stage musical based on the 1945 film premiered in 1995. Mixing sentiment and realism, the book focuses on Margy and Wayne, wholesome Iowa teens who yearn for romantic excitements. At the fair they briefly enjoy worldly partners, who pull them toward a more urban, decadent world. For their parents, Abel and Melissa, whose pig and pickles capture prizes, the fair interrupts farming's relentless, usually unrewarded work. Some 1932 reviewers complained that *State Fair* ignored the Depression and rural discontents, but popular audiences embraced the reassuring story. Despite dramatic changes in midwestern agrarian life since 1932, Stong's images continue to resonate as symbols of core American values

State Fair movie poster. Image courtesy John Shelton Lawrence.

and a western extension of the great Black Swamp of northwestern Ohio. Though born and raised in Wabash County, fifty miles westward, the naturalist and novelist Geneva Stratton-Porter briefly lived in the Limberlost, making it the focus of novels and non-fiction nature writings, a popular genre in the early decades of the 1900s.

A sylvan to pastoral to urban transformation is progressively seen throughout Stratton-Porter's works as the Limberlost swamp was in reality gradually drained for farmland use. Though her writings always focused on the close observation of nature, her point of view gradually changed as the environment that she originally saw as pristine was diluted and done away. Thus, with each novel, "nature" becomes slightly more distant and less an intimate experience. In *Freckles* (1904), though logging takes place in the swamp, the Limberlost is seen as a natural wildlife repository, and this idea peaks with *A Girl of the Limberlost* (1909). Her appreciation does not follow a theme of noninterference—her mode is that of human ecologist, not radical conservationist. In these works nature is a schoolhouse of enlightenment and an escape from the ills of urban life.

As the Limberlost is drained, a separation of people and nature is evident in Stratton-Porter's fiction. *The Harvester* (1911) treats the dilemma of preserving the natural benefits of the marshland over the perceived benefits of farming after drainage. Later she moved to Los Angeles, and this abandonment of rural northern Indiana values is evident in her writings, which still advocated nature study, but saw nature as "inexorable" and somewhat distant. In her book *The Keeper of the Bees* (1925), the effects of World War I on a young soldier's life remove the pristine innocence of the outdoors. Nature becomes tainted both by war and by her urban residence. Killed in a motoring accident in Los Angeles when a streetcar struck her automobile, Stratton-Porter's death was far removed from her Limberlost epiphanies.

Source and Further Reading: Judith Reick Long, *Gene Stratton-Porter: Novelist and Naturalist* (1990).

Craig S. Campbell
Youngstown State University, Ohio

and position rural Iowa as "the heart of the heartland." The big pig barns, dusty roads, pickup trucks, corn, houses with porches, small villages, country stores, fairs, Ma in her apron, the farmer-philosopher, good-hearted teens with city dreams, tantalizing outsiders—whether presented with nostalgia or scorn—still dominate portrayals of the Midwest in popular culture.

Sources and Further Reading: Clarence Andrews, *A Literary History of Iowa* (1972); Chris Rasmussen, "Mr. Stong's Dreamy Iowa," *Iowa Heritage Illustrated* 79 (Winter 1998); Phil Stong, *State Fair* (1996).

John Shelton Lawrence
Marty Knepper
Morningside College, Iowa

Gene Stratton-Porter's Limberlost

The Limberlost was a marshland in southern Adams County, thirty miles south of Fort Wayne, Indiana,

Robert S. Lynd and Helen Merrell Lynd's *Middletown*

Muncie, Indiana, was depicted as Middletown by sociologists Robert S. Lynd and Helen Merrell Lynd because it was seen as typical of the emerging Midwest. Moving from an agricultural base to an industrial society produced stresses in the Muncie community, as it did throughout the region. Middletown is thus a mirror reflecting an emerging, "modern" America. Founded by the Wolf (*Munsee*) clan of the Delaware Indians in a "protected" northern bend of the White River in the late 1700s, Munseytown began as an agricultural center, but the coming of the railroad in 1852 and the discovery of natural gas in 1886 spurred industrial development and population growth. In 1888 Ball Brothers Glass Company was lured from Buffalo, New York, and by 1905 there were twelve hundred workers at Ball, producing sixty million glass jars per year, and Muncie had established its reputation as an industrial "Magic City." Steel-fabrication industries, automobiles, and automobile parts were to follow. When the Lynds published *Middletown* in 1929, Muncie found prominence in this portrait of a twentieth-century city. The Ball Brothers and Ball Corporation placed an indelible stamp on Muncie (Ball Stores, Ball Hospital, Ball State University) as it grew into America's hometown, and even its family life found favor as related by Muncie's own Emily Kimbrough in her book *How Dear to My Heart* (1944). Ball Corporation headquarters left in 1998, and educational and service functions are now dominant in the city's economy.

Sources and Further Reading: Robert S. Lynd and Helen Merrell Lynd, *Middletown: A Study in Contemporary American Culture* (1929); Wiley W. Spurgeon, Jr., *Muncie and Delaware County: An Illustrated Retrospective* (1984).

Tom L. Martinson
Auburn University, Alabama

Harold Bell Wright's *Shepherd of the Hills*

In 1907 Harold Bell Wright published *The Shepherd of the Hills*, a best-seller that would catapult him onto the literary scene and initiate Ozark tourism. Derived from Wright's many years of residence in the region, the book tells the story of Daniel Howitt, a Chicago minister seeking rest and seclusion in this pastoral setting. Befriended by Matt and Molly Matthews and hired as a shepherd, "Dad" Howitt mentors local youths while reckoning with his own troubles. Unbeknownst to the Ozarkers, Howitt's son had traveled to the area years previously, impregnated the Matthewses' daughter, and left his lover to die in childbirth at the urging of his prideful father. At the end of the novel, these indiscretions are revealed as Dad makes peace with locals and is spiritually rejuvenated. By glorifying rural lifestyles and condemning urban vices, Wright's story resonated with early-twentieth-century anxieties concerning the demise of rural existence and wholesome values—themes still emphasized in the contemporary Ozark tourism industry. As early as 1909 travelers ventured to the area to see sites memorialized in the book. In 1926 Lizzie McDaniel purchased the homestead of John and Anna Ross, who functioned as models for the Matthews family, and opened a museum. In 1960 Mark Trimble established an outdoor theater on this site that still conducts nightly renditions of the novel. Currently, visitors encounter many other reminders of the book in the Branson, Missouri area, including Shepherd of the Hills Expressway and Old Matt's Guest House. Thus Wright's idealistic vision of Ozark life continues to influence the region nearly one hundred years after its publication.

Sources and Further Reading: John P. Ferre, *A Social Gospel for Millions* (1988); Lynn Morrow and Linda Myers-Phinney, *Shepherd of the Hills Country* (1999); Lawrence V. Tagg, *Harold Bell Wright: Storyteller to America* (1986).

Aaron Ketchell
University of Kansas

Grant Wood's *American Gothic*

American Gothic by Grant Wood is one of the most recognized paintings in America. It is also one of the most caricatured. The painting of a man and a woman standing in front of a house with a gothic window was first exhibited in Chicago in 1930, where it made Wood famous, and was purchased by the Art Institute of Chicago for three hundred dollars. From the beginning everyone accepted the scene and the couple as quintessentially American, albeit of an earlier time. The precise meaning of the painting, however, remains puzzling to this day. Although Wood denied it, he was accused of satirizing Midwesterners. To some viewers the gloomy faces and stiff poses were an illustration of the dullness and rigidity of midwestern life and the narrowness of its people. Other viewers, however, saw the painting as an expression of the hardships of life in the Midwest and the determination and strength of its inhabitants. The painting, therefore, was a link to America's past of small rural towns, families living in their own house, and a strong work ethic. Caricatures of the painting number in the hundreds, most of them using the painting as a symbol of "middle America" or average Americans. The faces of Jimmy and Rosalynn Carter, as well as those of Ronald and Nancy Reagan, have appeared in place of the two original figures. In advertisements, skis, tennis rackets, and fishing poles have replaced the man's pitchfork. The painting, which measures approximately twenty-five by thirty inches, still hangs at the Art Institute of Chicago. As a national icon its value is incalculable.

Sources and Further Reading: Wanda Corn, *Grant Wood: The Regionalist Vision* (1983); James M. Dennis, *Grant Wood: A Study in American Art and Culture* (1986).

James Kelly
University of Hawaii–Hilo

Johnny Carson (1925–2005)

As host of *The Tonight Show*, Johnny Carson dominated late-night television for thirty years, from 1962 until his retirement in 1992. He received four Emmy awards, the Kennedy Center Lifetime Achievement Award, and the Presidential Medal of Freedom. Key to his popularity was his midwestern demeanor. Viewers were comfortable with him, often perceiving him as a nonthreatening neighbor who joked without malice. Johnny was born in Corning, Iowa, on October 23, 1925, the son of Homer and Ruth (Hook) Carson. The family moved to Norfolk, Nebraska, when he was eight, where Johnny attended public schools. When he was twelve Johnny sent off for a mail-order magic kit, and two years later he was skillful enough to give his first public performance, at the Norfolk Rotary Club. For the next several years he performed at numerous parties, churches, and clubs. After serving in the Navy during World War II, Carson graduated from the University of Nebraska in 1949. That year he was hired by WOW-TV in Omaha to host an afternoon television variety show, *The Squirrels Nest*, where he told jokes, put on skits, and interviewed guests. He went on to host other television shows in Los Angeles and New York, and on October 1, 1962, he began his reign on *The Tonight Show*. After his retirement Johnny Carson lived in Malibu, California, with his fourth wife, Alexis Maas. His previous marriages were to Joanna Holland, Joanne Copeland, and Jody Wolcott, his college sweetheart, with whom he had three boys: Chris, Ricky, and Cory. He died in January 2005.

Sources and Further Reading: Paul Corkery, *Carson: The Unauthorized Biography* (1987); Laurence Leamer, *King of the Night* (1989); Charles Moritz, "Carson, Johnny," *Current Biography* (1982).

James Kelly
University of Hawaii–Hilo

Meredith Willson's *The Music Man*

The musical comedy *The Music Man*, written and composed by Meredith Willson, takes place in 1912 in

"River City, Iowa," a fictitious town based on Willson's home town of Mason City, Iowa. In addition to Willson's delightful music and lyrics, the show takes the audience on a nostalgic trip back to an imaginary turn-of-the-century America, with small-town folk in Iowa who were innocent, honest, and entertaining. The show opened at the Majestic Theatre in New York on December 19, 1957, and ran on Broadway for 1,375 performances. In addition, several road companies toured the country, and the show was made into a movie of the same name. Robert Preston had the starring role in the original Broadway show and in the movie. As one of the most popular Broadway shows, it was acclaimed by both critics and the public, receiving many awards, including a Tony Award for best musical and the New York Drama Circle Award for best musical. The *New York Times* critic Brooks Atkinson described the show as "American as apple pie," illustrating the simplicities of life in Iowa in 1912. The story concerns a fraudulent traveling salesman, Professor Harold Hill, who arrives in River City, Iowa, by train, intending to sell band instruments and uniforms to the unsophisticated townspeople, then skips town with their money. Along the way he falls in love with Marian, the librarian, and miraculously sparks a musical revolution in River City. The musical numbers, all written by Willson, include soft-shoe, ragtime, barbershop quartet, and marches, including the popular "76 Trombones."

Sources and Further Reading: Bernard Beckerman, ed., *On Stage: Selected Theater Reviews from the New York Times, 1920–1970* (1973); Stanley Green, *The World of Musical Comedy*, 3rd ed. (1974); John Skipper, *Meredith Willson* (2000).

James Kelly
University of Hawaii–Hilo

*M*A*S*H*'s "Radar" O'Reilly

"Radar" O'Reilly, one of the key characters in the popular TV show *M*A*S*H* and the original movie by that name, was from a farm near Ottumwa, Iowa, and his personality, as written into the show, reflected the image many people have of Midwesterners. As the *M*A*S*H* unit's company clerk during the Korean War, Corporal O'Reilly was timid, quiet, and unassuming, but also honest and dependable with a strong work ethic. He was shy, particularly around girls. His favorite drink was Grape Nehi, implying he was unfamiliar with the sophisticated alcoholic drinks of cities. Although he was liked by almost everyone, he often complained to the other characters on the show about their lack of respect for him and his occupation. His full name was Walter Eugene O'Reilly. Relatives on the family farm back home included his mother, Edna, and his uncle Ed. He had a dog named Ranger and a cow named Betsy. His tenderness toward livestock and pets reflected his midwestern roots and closeness to nature. His affection for his mother and the family farm were links to a traditional rural society and family life. Although the TV show ostensibly takes place during the Korean War, the attitudes and behaviors of the other characters depicted in the show, such as sympathy for the enemy and ridicule of military leaders, were more typical of the recent Vietnam War era. The character of Radar, in contrast, seemed truly associated with an earlier time, the 1950s and the Korean War era.

Sources and Further Reading: Suzy Kalter, *The Complete Book of M*A*S*H* (1988); George St. John, *M*A*S*H Trivia* (1984).

James Kelly
University of Hawaii–Hilo

Field of Dreams

Physical imagery in *Field of Dreams* (1989) has enthralled millions and supports two flourishing tourist sites at Dyersville, Iowa, the film's shooting location. There visitors see the white, two-story farmhouse with its large front porch; the immaculate baseball diamond surrounded by cornfields; and the beautiful Iowa sky. The repeated exchange "Is this heaven? No, it's Iowa" became a bumper sticker and promotional slogan.

The film is based on *Shoeless Joe* (1982) by W.P. Kinsella, who exploited this Iowa pastoral-magical setting for other stories. This story features a poignant set of fantasies: The disgraced 1919 Chicago White Sox are redeemed; Ray and his father reconcile; the farm evades foreclosure; and the dreams of "Doc" Graham and antiwar writer Terence Mann come true on the field. *Dreamfield*, a 1994 ESPN documentary film on that tourist site, confirms that visitors come to this Midwest locale to enact their dreams, find reconciliation, and celebrate the joys of baseball that existed before it became a corporate enterprise.

Ironically, the film's social imagery plays against this magic of physical place. Stolid, conservative relatives and neighbors see the baseball diamond as a foolish waste of good farmland; scorn Ray and Annie, who "majored in the '60s" at Berkeley, and denounce Mann as a "pervert," "communist," and "advocate of race mongrelization." An identical place/people contrast appears in the film *The Bridges of Madison County* (1995), which also requires an outsider to see the Mid-

west's beauty and to find its potential for pastoral magic.

Sources and Further Reading: W. P. Kinsella, *The Iowa Baseball Confederacy* (1986); W. P. Kinsella, *Magic Time* (1998); Brett H. Mandel, *Is This Heaven?* (2002).

Marty Knepper
John Shelton Lawrence
Morningside College, Iowa

Hamlin Garland's Middle Border Books

Between the 1880s and the 1920s, Hamlin Garland wrote short stories, novels, and autobiographies that interpreted the Midwest, what he called the Middle Border, to the reading public. Garland's writings followed his family's migrations to Wisconsin, Iowa, and the Dakotas and his own migrations to Chicago and then east. Garland's gritty descriptions of the hardships of rural life, best reflected in his most famous work *Main-Travelled Roads* (1891), brought attention to the need for reform and reflected his support for the Populist Party in the 1890s. Garland contrasted the beauty and power of nature with the labor of farmers too hard-pressed to appreciate it. In stories like "Under the Lion's Paw" (1899) he used the communal ethos of farmers and the nobility of their labor to critique the greed and corruption of speculators who used the land only for profit. However, his writing never simply focused on the economic problems of rural life, but also illuminated the social gatherings of rural communities, the beauty of midwestern landscapes, and the diverse ethnicity of the people.

Garland also explored the different cultures of rural and urban Americans. His autobiographical trilogy, one of which (*Daughter of the Middle Border*, 1921) won the Pulitzer Prize, traced not only the difficulties of his own rise to fame from humble roots, but also the development of the "Middle Border." Garland, in both fiction and autobiography, portrayed his own status, crossing classes and cultures, and his own maturation and "rise" as parallel with those of the Midwest, always in between but contributing something vital, new, and central to America's story.

Sources and Further Reading: Jean Holloway, *Hamlin Garland: A Biography* (1960); Mary Neth, "Seeing the Midwest with Peripheral Vision," in Andrew R. L. Cayton and Susan E. Gray, eds., *The American Midwest* (2001); Donald Pizer, *Hamlin Garland's Early Work and Career* (1960).

Mary Neth
University of Missouri–Columbia

Laura Ingalls Wilder's Little House Books

Laura Ingalls Wilder has helped to shape the world's conception of the Midwest since the publication of her first children's book, *Little House in the Big Woods*, in 1932. The nine books that comprise the Little House series, including the most famous title, *Little House on the Prairie* (1935), chronicle Wilder's family's settlement through Wisconsin, Kansas, Minnesota, and Dakota Territory (now South Dakota). In each location, landscape acts as a main character, which, in turn, generates a vision of place. The image is formed largely through vivid descriptions: the sweet smells of grasslands, the wonder of a moonlit winter's night, her mother's fresh cornbread, screams of panthers, and unpredictable weather patterns. In her books, Wilder also talks about the psychological impact of the prairies on the people who lived there. She explains their passions for open spaces, frustrations over failed crops, pleasures in working the land, and fears of being alone in unsettled territory. Ultimately, she suggests that the image of the Midwest is best understood through a people's ongoing interrelationship with the land—where the country's roughness builds or breaks spirit; where hard work, ingenuity, and morality overcome challenges; and where the prairie's wild beauty inspires.

Wilder's impact has been wide ranging both geographically and generationally. Her work has been translated into over forty languages, and the Little House series has sold more than forty million copies to date. Readers continue to identify with the characters, stories, and spirit Wilder created and to believe in the Midwest they find in her books.

Sources and Further Reading: John E. Miller, *Becoming Laura Ingalls Wilder* (1998); Jane M. Subramanian, *Laura Ingalls Wilder: An Annotated Bibliography of Critical, Biographical, and Teaching Studies* (1997).

Katherine Shortridge
Roanoke College, Virginia

O. E. Rølvaag's *Giants in the Earth*

Ole E. Rølvaag's *Giants in the Earth* represents a classic contribution to both American and Norwegian literature. This fictional narrative focuses upon the lives, successes, and misfortunes of several Norwegian immigrant families who settled and attempted farming in the southeastern part of Dakota Territory in the 1870s; it concludes in the following decade.

Giants centers on a vaguely circumscribed area on what would become part of the northwestern margin of the Midwest, with numerous references made to coastal Norway and the characteristics of the ocean, especially those known to fishermen. The immigrants establish themselves at "Spring Creek," located somewhere northwest of Sioux Falls. Rølvaag incorporates many descriptions of and allusions to the nature of the prairie lands at the onset of European settlement. The lack of trees on the extensive glaciated interfluves; the aspect of being upon a broad expanse of an essentially endless ocean of prairie; the feelings of claustrophobia during the long and often bitter winters; and the isolation brought on by the lack of outside contacts, especially for the women in the story, all find exposition in the volume. The author's eye for the details of the physical environment, both within Dakota Territory and compared to and contrasted with the Lofoten Islands of Norway, fashions a rich fabric throughout the novel. Perhaps some of the most fascinating parts of the book focus on the newcomers' struggles to wrest a subsistence livelihood from the new lands and to simply survive the often-brutal winters on the edge of human occupancy.

Ultimately, Rølvaag's pioneers triumph in the process of settling and developing a part of the upper Midwest, but at great cost in terms of human suffering and privation, which generally parallels the experiences of many of the nonfictional peoples and events that constituted the region's geographical, historical milieu.

Sources and Further Reading: Einar Haugen, *Ole Edvart Rølvaag* (1983); Ole E. Rølvaag, *Giants in the Earth* (1927); Harold P. Simonson, *Prairies Within* (1987).

Donald J. Berg
South Dakota State University

Dubuque, Iowa

Called the "Masterpiece on the Mississippi" by its chamber of commerce, Dubuque is the seventh-largest city in the state of Iowa (2000 population, 57,686). Its architectural inventory of Victorian-era mansions, especially those on the bluffs overlooking the mighty river, is impressive. The steep escarpment from the floodplain of the Mississippi to the top of the bluffs makes Dubuque's setting comparable to that of San Francisco. A ride on the funicular to the top of the bluffs is a must for tourists and sometimes a necessity for residents.

Dubuque was founded in 1788 by French Canadian fur trader and lead miner Julien Dubuque, who lived there until his death in 1810. Adding to that French Canadian presence were a considerable number of immigrants from Ireland encouraged by Pierre-Jean-Mathias Loras, the first bishop of the Diocese of Dubuque. This rather large Roman Catholic presence makes Dubuque unique among large cities in Iowa. Manifestations of this Catholic influence include the location of two Catholic colleges in the city—Loras and Clarke—and a Trappist monastery located a few miles outside of the city.

The Midwest in general, and Dubuque in particular, supposedly so lacked urban sophistication that *New Yorker* founding editor Harold Ross suggested in a 1925 prospectus that the magazine would not be for "the little old lady in Dubuque." That comment congealed community solidarity.

Leading industries in Dubuque include meatpacking, especially of pork products, and the manufacture of agricultural machinery. But these traditional industries have been eclipsed by employment in technology-based and service industries.

Sources and Further Reading: Len Kruse, *My Old Dubuque*, ed. Robert Byrne (2000); Randolph Lyon, *Dubuque: The Encyclopedia* (1991); William E. Wilke, *Dubuque on the Mississippi, 1788–1988* (1999).

Thomas L. Bell
University of Tennessee

Uncle John Iowa. With permission of the Jay N. "Ding" Darling Foundation.

Jay N. "Ding" Darling's *Uncle John Iowa* Cartoons

Jay N. "Ding" Darling, the creator of *Uncle John Iowa*, was the political cartoonist for the *Des Moines Register* for forty years and was simultaneously syndicated nationally by the *New York Herald Tribune*, from 1916 until his retirement in 1949. The Michigan native, who won two Pulitzer Prizes for his work, wielded significant national influence in the first half of the twentieth century.

Darling left the *Register* to join the *New York Globe* from November 1911 to February 1913. Following that unhappy experience, he wrote to a friend, "The people of Iowa think more to the square inch than the people of New York think to the square mile."

Darling, who used such familiar characters as Uncle Sam and John Bull in his work, in 1948 wrote that the only character that "has been completely of my own creation is the Iowa Farmer, old Uncle John Iowa." The model for the farmer, who became a symbol for the state, was Samuel H. Cook, a Van Meter, Iowa, farm implement dealer who died in 1932.

Because Darling resided in Des Moines, the capital of a state whose economy was overwhelmingly dependent upon agriculture, his cartoons often addressed state, national, and international farm-policy issues from Uncle John Iowa's perspective. During the early years of the century, Uncle John also personified many of the subscribers to the then-statewide *Register*—family farmers whose extraordinary productivity fed the nation and much of the world while also tending to depress prices for agricultural commodities.

Source and Further Reading: David L. Lendt, *Ding: The Life of Jay Norwood Darling* (2001).

David L. Lendt
Columbia, Missouri

Midwest Living

Midwest Living is to the Midwest what *Southern Living* is to the South, *Sunset* to the West Coast, and *Yankee* to New England. All of these magazines celebrate the local through color photography and articles; all are intent upon boosting their region and encouraging tourism. As part of this effort, *Midwest Living* portrays the high quality of life available to residents of this region, a quality that is already acknowledged by most readers. Golf courses and lake cottages combine with front porches and friendly residents to create an inviting image. Launched in April 1987 by Meredith Corporation of Des Moines, Iowa (also the publisher of *Better Homes and Gardens*), the new publication was intended to respond to a commonality of values among Midwesterners and an increased awareness of regionalism. The circulation of this bimonthly publication is eight hundred thousand, 90 percent by subscription, and the content is focused on middle-class Midwesterners.

Midwest Living is organized into sections on travel and recreation, food and dining, and home and garden. Profiles of resorts, locally favorite restaurants, driving tours, and seasonal crafts are regular features. Topics related to home cooking (including recipes) and to decorating ideas that bring readers into the homes of other families also are popular with a readership that is said to be committed to self-improvement. Abundant advertising includes the products of many regional firms, including Andersen Windows, Ball Home Canning Products, Clabber Girl, and Lands' End.

Source and Further Reading: William Dunn, "*Midwest Living,*" *American Demographics* 9 (Jan. 1987).

Barbara G. Shortridge
University of Kansas

Better Homes and Gardens

Based in Des Moines, Iowa, since its founding in 1922, the highly successful home magazine *Better Homes and Gardens* represents the values and imagery of the Midwest at every turn of the page. Photographs with blue skies, expansive lawns, and outdoor spaces are combined with family-focused features aimed at friendly, unpretentious folk. Edwin T. Meredith originally named his creation *Fruit, Garden and Home*, but changed it to the current title in 1924. Meredith Corporation is now an extended entity with numerous subscription publications, high advertising revenues, and Internet sales, but its flagship publication remains the same. Monthly circulation stands at 7.6 million with 96 percent of sales by subscription. Many more people, of course, read it in their dentist's waiting room.

Better Homes and Gardens is more comprehensive in content than its competition. With sections devoted to gardening, health, home improvement, recipes, crafts, and children's projects, the magazine's appeal crosses divisions of age and gender. Information for prospective advertisers profiles readers who are middle-class America: college educated, home owning, and married. Although it has a national circula-

tion, *Better Homes and Gardens* emphasizes the Midwest in both content and values presented. Its model homes, environmentally sound gardening suggestions, quilt patterns, and comfort foods are most frequently drawn from midwestern examples. The words *friends*, *neighbors*, and *community* are used repeatedly, and the "family values" expressed throughout its pages were there long before the phrase became popular.

Source and Further Reading: Carol Reuss, "Edwin T. Meredith," *Annals of Iowa* 42 (Spring 1975).

Barbara G. Shortridge
University of Kansas

Buckeye

Exactly how and why Ohioan identity came to be associated with a tree species of little commercial or utilitarian importance is shrouded in myth and obscured by folklore. A member of the horse chestnut family and the official state tree since 1953, the Ohio buckeye (*Aesculus glabra*) is indeed native to Ohio, but can be found from northern Texas to the Ohio Valley. Historically, the word certainly stems from the appearance of the nuts of the tree, which resemble the eye of a buck deer; the word is probably a translation of a Native American term for the nuts. In earlier times buckeyes were carried as charms or worn as amulets, suggesting a folk belief in the nut's curative medicinal powers. The use of the term to signify an inhabitant of Ohio dates from the early nineteenth century, when the buckeye began to be used in political oratory as a symbol associated with rugged frontier individualism and independence; William Henry Harrison employed buckeye log cabins and walking sticks as emblems of Ohio in his 1840 presidential campaign. With time a buckeye came to represent someone from Ohio who was stalwart and tenacious, much like the tree itself, which thrives in environments often inhospitable to other species. In this way the symbolism and meaning embodied in the buckeye and its use as a synonym for Ohioans, as well as its use as a mascot for The Ohio State University sports teams, parallels the frontier imagery personified in other midwestern terms such as Jayhawk and Hoosier.

Sources and Further Reading: John Fleischman, "Of Buckeyes and Buckeyes," *Audubon* 91 (Sept. 1989); Ohio Division of Forestry, *Ohio: The Buckeye State* (1998).

Timothy G. Anderson
Ohio University

Hoosier

The word *Hoosier* has been used as a nickname for the people of Indiana since the nineteenth century and has been adopted extensively by Indiana businesses, organizations, and festivals; perhaps the most well-known use is the nickname for the athletic teams at Indiana University in Bloomington. Although Indianans currently embrace the word, its historic meanings are somewhat unflattering. Early-nineteenth-century usage equated "hoosiers" to rough, ill-mannered, thick-headed folk dwelling beyond the margins of civilized society, much as the words *redneck* or *hillbilly* may be used today.

How the term originated invites much speculation and controversy. Common explanations involve frontier residents calling out "Who's here?" or "Who's yer?" to unfamiliar visitors; an apocryphal Louisville contractor named Hoosier, who preferred to hire Indiana men; "hoosa," a rumored but unsubstantiated native term for corn; and "hushers," Indiana scrappers who cowed or "hushed" their opponents. Numerous additional theories, both serious and lighthearted, attract support from various corners as well. The earliest sincere attention came from Indiana historian Jacob Piatt Dunn, who connected the term to an Anglo-Saxon term for hill, "hoo." A "hoosier," therefore, would be a hill-dweller. More recently, William D. Piersen reintroduced the argument that the name derived from an African American Methodist preacher, Harry Hoosier, whose appeal among lower-class whites mostly in the midland and Appalachian regions—primary sources of early white immigrants to Indiana—earned his followers the scorn of the more established segregationist frontier population. According to Piersen, the introduction of the term *Hoosier* for an unintelligent rustic dates to the late eighteenth century, in the latter half of Harry Hoosier's lifetime. Regardless of its original implications, the name today is worn with pride by all classes of Indianans.

Sources and Further Reading: William D. Piersen, "The Origin of the Word 'Hoosier,'" *Indiana Magazine of History* 91 (June 1995); "Sketch of Hoosier History," *Indiana History Bulletin* (Oct. 1965).

David E. Schul
The Ohio State University–Marion

Jayhawk

Today most familiar as the University of Kansas mascot, the mythical, flightless Jayhawk has also been an emotionally charged state and military icon. Jayhawkers gained notoriety in the 1850s as marauding bands of free-state Kansans at war with proslavery Missouri Bushwhackers. The term *Jayhawk* likely derived from a combination of the thieving blue jay and the murderous sparrow hawk (American kestrel). Border ruffians on both sides employed jayhawking, the theft of firearms and livestock, yet the Kansans were increasingly called Jayhawkers. The Jayhawker label shed its stigma as the nickname for the Civil War Seventh Kansas Cavalry, especially with reports of how the unit emancipated, or jayhawked, slaves. In subsequent wars Kansas squadrons have often adopted the Jayhawk nickname and adorned their craft with the name or with a caricature carrying bombs and other paraphernalia.

Through the mid-1900s Kansans were often nicknamed Jayhawkers, but recently the icon's use as a state emblem diminished due to in-state university rivalries and the popular Sunflower State moniker. The University of Kansas Jayhawk connection began in 1886 with the famous "Rock Chalk Jayhawk" chant and achieved pictorial representation and mascot status in 1912. Five iterations have since reflected the nature of the times, including a menacing World War II fighting Jayhawk, but the most enduring design was drawn by Hal Sandy in 1946 as a smiling Jayhawk. Sporting a crimson head, a large yellow beak, and a blue body with KU letters, perhaps the Jayhawk's most surprising attributes are its large yellow shoes, reputably used for kicking opponents.

Sources and Further Reading: Kirke Mechem, "The Mythical Jayhawk," *Kansas Historical Quarterly* 13 (Feb. 1944); Craig Miner, *Kansas: The History of the Sunflower State, 1854–2000* (2002); Richard B. Sheridan, "The Historic Jayhawkers and the Mythical Jayhawk," in Dennis Domer and Barbara Watkins, eds., *Embattled Lawrence: Conflict and Community* (2001).

Kevin S. Blake
Kansas State University

Superman and His Kansas Roots

The formative years for Superman, the prototypical action superhero, were spent in rural Kansas. Mythical Smallville and his adoptive parents, Jonathan and Martha Kent, imbued Superman with his bedrock values—honesty and humility. These virtues reflect midwestern identity and imagery and for decades have fit with the nostalgic American yearning for traditional midwestern pastoral values. Cleveland, Ohio residents Jerry Siegel and Joe Shuster created Superman in the early 1930s, but it was June 1938 before the Man of Steel soared to comic book fame in an Action Comics cover story. Superman was subsequently adapted countless times to comics, radio, film, television, and theatre. The standard plot begins with an orphaned infant from the doomed planet Krypton rocketing to Earth and crash-landing in a Kansas cornfield where he is found by the childless Kents, who name the baby Clark.

A simple farm life amid wide-open expanses fills Clark's boyhood years as his superpowers slowly reveal themselves. As a young adult, Clark leaves Kansas for the big city of Metropolis, where he embarks on a newspaper career and the romantic pursuit of fellow Kansan Lois Lane, all the while surreptitiously switching into superhero mode to combat villains plaguing urban America. A good and true son of the Kansas plains, Superman frequently returns home to Smallville for a respite from the strife of Metropolis. The symbolism of Superman, including patriotism and fulfilling the American dream through "truth, justice, and the American way," continues to dovetail with rural Midwest ideals.

Sources and Further Reading: Scott Beatty, *Superman: The Ultimate Guide to the Man of Steel* (2002); James R. Shortridge, *The Middle West: Its Meaning in American Culture* (1989).

Kevin S. Blake
Kansas State University

Jesse James (1847–1882)

The James family moved from Kentucky in 1842 to Kearney, Missouri, where Jesse was born in 1847. Missouri was the scene of battles between Union troops and pro-South sympathizers. At seventeen Jesse joined William "Bloody Bill" Anderson's guerrilla fighters in 1864 after Union troops reportedly attempted to hang Jesse's stepfather, harassed his pregnant mother, and gave Jesse a severe beating. Later, Jesse James formed an outlaw gang that included his brother Frank and Cole Younger. For years the James Gang carried out stagecoach, bank, and railroad robberies. Due to local support, James was never convicted of any crimes. Hired by the railroads, an agent of the Pinkerton Detective Agency tossed a firebomb into Jesse's parents' home, killing his half brother and blowing his mother's arm off. In 1881 Missouri governor Thomas Crittenden offered a substantial reward for his capture. In 1882 James recruited brothers Bob and Charlie Ford because most of the James Gang had been killed in a bank robbery in 1876. James moved to St. Joseph, Missouri, living under the alias Tom Howard. On April 3, 1882, Bob Ford put a single bullet into the back of James's head and attempted to collect the reward. Instead he was sentenced to hang for murder, but was pardoned by Governor Crittenden. Immortalized in "The Ballad of Jesse James," Bob Ford was killed in a barroom brawl in Creede, Colorado, in 1892. According to legend, James faked his death and disappeared to South America. In 1995, however, DNA testing proved that the body in the box was Jesse James.

Sources and Further Reading: Robert L. Dyer, *Jesse James and the Civil War in Missouri* (1994); William A. Settle, Jr., *Jesse James Was His Name* (1966).

George O. Carney
Oklahoma State University

James Whitcomb Riley's Bucolic Poetry

The poetry of the Hoosier native James Whitcomb Riley made him popular during his lifetime and well beyond. From the late nineteenth through the early twentieth century, Riley wrote on rural life with whimsy and an edge of humor, and his poems often ended with moral directives. Ideals of rustic contentment and simplicity of life were cultivated in his youth in Greenfield, Indiana. Poems oriented to children are full of creatures and critters, with images of "giunts," "griffins," "elves," "gobble-uns," and "great black things." This mode of writing showed his playful verse and reminds the reader of an earlier version of Dr. Seuss.

Though modern poets sometimes dismiss his work, it is clear that Riley was a keen observer of people and land and the rhythms of rural life. An expert mimic of local dialect and poetic style, Riley is most remembered for poems hearkening back to a golden age of bucolic purity. Ambition was Riley's motivation, but this did not change the fact that urban people loved the phrasing and atmosphere of his rural approach. A resident of Indianapolis, Riley almost never mentioned city life or modern technology in his work, and his poems are filled with pasture, wood, barn, and farm. The synopsis of one poem, "The Little Dog Woggy," is a succinct summary of Riley's overall approach to life and land. It preaches that you can travel around the world and see the great cities and sites, but in doing so you may neglect your rural roots of home and family.

Sources and Further Reading: James Whitcomb Riley, *The Complete Poetical Works of James Whitcomb Riley* (1993); Elizabeth J. Van Allen, *James Whitcomb Riley: A Life* (1999).

Craig S. Campbell
Youngstown State University, Ohio

Radio Stations

Radio stations have reflected midwestern culture, and four examples are WHO of Des Moines, WLS of Chicago, WLW of Cincinnati, and KMOX of St. Louis. Each had unique adaptations on the rural to urban alteration of the Midwest. The oldest of the group was WLW, with call letters assigned in 1922. WHO and WLS followed in 1924, and KMOX in 1925.

WHO, founded by Banker's Life Insurance (now the Principal), was oriented toward rural agriculture, music, and sports. "The Voice of the Middle West," its *Barn Dance Frolic* lasted until the late 1950s and its *Country Music USA* program was heard throughout the entire country at night, launching many careers. Chicago's WLS (for World's Largest Store—a Sears venture), with its *National Barn Dance* and later sponsorship by *Prairie Farmer Magazine*, also catered to rural sensitivities. Its popular slogan was "Bringing the World to the Farm," but with the burgeoning influence of suburban Chicago in the 1960s it went to rock and pop. In 1989–1990 it went to all talk.

Once blazing at five hundred thousand watts, WLW was "The Nation's Station." Founded by Cincinnati's wealthy Crosley family, its music programming was mixed, reflecting the Queen City's straddling of the North and the Upland South. Likewise KMOX, "The Voice of St. Louis," began broadcasting music, sports, and news reflective of its varied sponsors. Ozark bluegrass featured prominently. Originally a public Missouri corporation, in 1960 KMOX was the first station in the country to switch to an all-talk format.

Sources and Further Reading: John C. Baker, *Farm Broadcasting* (1981); Dick Perry, *Vas You Ever in Zinzinnati?* (1966); B. Eric Rhoads, *Blast from the Past* (1996).

Craig S. Campbell
Youngstown State University, Ohio

Maids of the Prairie from WHO's *Barn Dance Frolic.* The group appeared on WHO Radio as part of the Iowa "Barn Dance Frolic." With permission by WHO Radio, Des Moines, Iowa. Image courtesy Dave Sichak, Hillbilly-music.com.

Geography

SECTION EDITORS

John Hudson and Lawrence A. Brown

Section Contents

Overview

As defined in this encyclopedia, the Midwest region of the United States encompasses roughly 600,000 square miles, or about one-fifth the area of the Lower 48 states. The region is bounded by Canada and the Great Lakes on the north, by the Great Plains on the west, and by the Upland South and the Northeast along its southern and eastern margins. The U.S. Census Bureau, which does not recognize a separate Great Plains region, defines the midwestern states as the entire states of Ohio, Indiana, Michigan, Illinois, Wisconsin, Minnesota, Iowa, Missouri, North Dakota, South Dakota, Nebraska, and Kansas, an area of roughly 750,000 square miles.

Physical Geography. The Midwest overlaps two major geological divisions of the North American continent, the Canadian Shield and the Central Lowland. The shield has some of the world's oldest known rocks, with ages recorded in the billions of years. Rocks as old as these are exposed at the surface in much of central Canada and along the northern fringes of the Midwest. South of there a cover of more recently formed sedimentary rocks lies above the ancient shield rocks. Known as the Central Lowland, the

sedimentary rock region has a gently sloping or undulating topography, stretching from the base of the Appalachians on the east to the Rocky Mountains on the west. Because the Central Lowland has not been subjected to the forces of mountain building, its rocks remain in roughly horizontal layers. Glaciers covered most of the Canadian Shield and the Central Lowland during the past two million years, which further muted topographic features. In the southern Midwest, where this glacial cover is absent, the topography is noticeably more hilly.

The climate of the Midwest is of the moist, warm-summer variety. Winter temperatures are more variable than summer, ranging from cool along the southern margins to cold in the central portion to very cold in the north. Three types of air masses, originating in distant source areas, produce day-to-day variations in the weather. Cold, dry air from northern Canada produces cold fronts that are associated with precipitation in all seasons. Mild, dry air from the western interior of the United States is responsible for prolonged periods of sunny weather. The third air-mass type, which originates over the Gulf of Mexico and the subtropical Atlantic Ocean, is warm and moist. Tropical air moves northward in all seasons, and it yields significant precipitation wherever it encounters the colder, Canadian air at the surface.

The Midwest's climate has a strong influence on

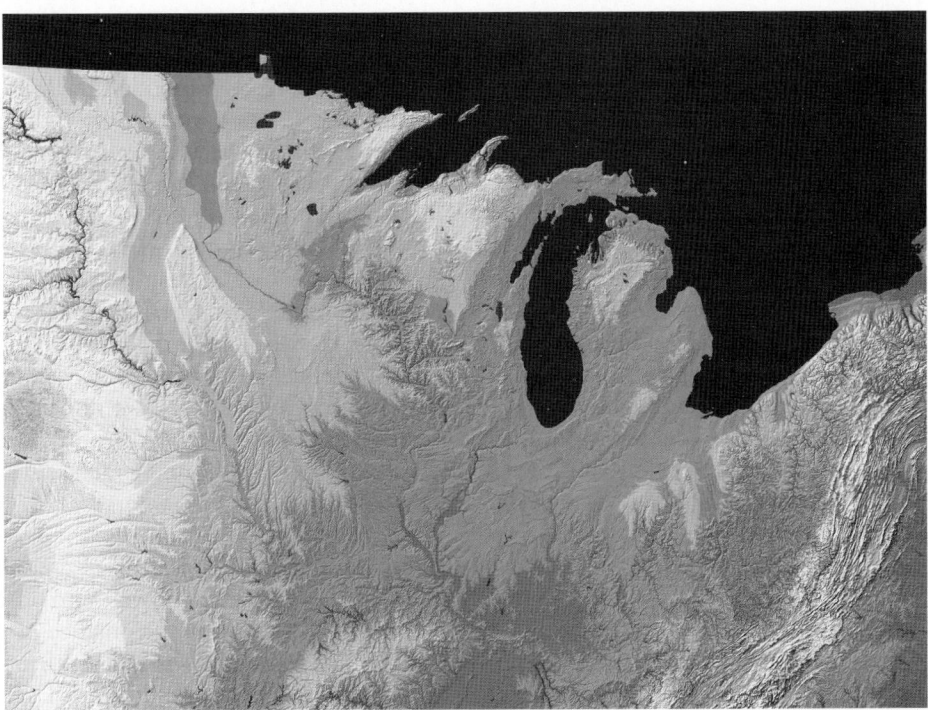

Satellite imagery of the Midwest. Image courtesy United States Geological Survey, United States Department of the Interior.

the pattern of vegetation. Cold winter temperatures in the north favor the growth of boreal forests. Winter-hardy needleleaf and broadleaf deciduous species, including spruce, balsam fir, and aspen, can endure temperatures below –20°F. South of a line through the middle of Wisconsin, extending west and north into Minnesota and eastward into lower Michigan, a variety of broadleaf deciduous species forms the native plant cover. Oak, maple, ash, elm, beech, and hickory are examples of trees found in this belt of temperate, humid climate. Forests composed of these trees once covered most of the Midwest south of the boreal zone, extending south of the Ohio River into the Upland South.

A significant break in the forested pattern appears as a large, wedge-shaped zone that narrows eastward toward the southern end of Lake Michigan. The wedge-shaped zone is the Midwestern Prairies, a zone of mixed grasses and wooded groves that was produced by a combination of droughts and fires within the past ten thousand years. The wedge of prairie (Prairie Peninsula) across the Midwest coincides with an area where summer drought is especially prevalent.

Soils that formed under these conditions of geology and climate are high in natural fertility. Because the glaciers totally altered surface conditions, midwestern soils are relatively youthful, having formed within the past ten to twelve thousand years since the climate warmed and the glaciers disappeared. Soils of the midwestern forest zone are typically black to brown, with abundant humus, and occur as a thick layer above the glacial deposits. Midwestern Prairie soils are similar, although slightly darker in color and even higher in natural fertility. The combination of a temperate climate, adequate precipitation, and relatively recent origin has endowed the Midwest with some of the world's richest agricultural soils.

Regions of the Midwest. Variations in geology, climate, vegetation, and soils combine to produce a mosaic of environmental settings across the Midwest. Although the variations are sometimes difficult to detect and produce only subtle differences from place to place, four distinct geographic subdivisions of the Midwest can be recognized. From south to north they are: the Southern Uplands, the Prairies, the Lower Great Lakes, and the Upper Great Lakes. Each of the four has had a distinctive history of human occupancy dating from prehistoric times.

The Southern Uplands. The several southward advances of glaciers during Pleistocene times (from about two million years ago until ten thousand years ago) reached no farther south than the Ohio River Valley. Southeastern Ohio, southern Indiana, the

southern fringe of Illinois, and the southern half of Missouri were not glaciated; neither was an isolated area in southwestern Wisconsin known as the "Driftless Region" because of the absence of glacial features. As a result, these areas have a more rugged topography that is less suitable for agriculture than much of the rest of the Midwest. In prehistoric times the uplands were used for hunting game because they were unfit for cultivation. Lands such as these held little interest for most white settlers who later moved north of the Ohio River. Hence, the more rugged upland areas have had relatively little human settlement.

Native peoples living in or near the unglaciated Southern Uplands practiced agriculture on the fertile floodplains along rivers, and so did the first white settlers who moved into the region during the early decades of the nineteenth century. The early white settlers came from Virginia, Kentucky, and Tennessee, where they had created a type of agriculture based on raising large crops of corn to fatten cattle and hogs. Although the corn crops they planted owed much to Native American agriculture, the use Upland Southerners made of corn was distinctly different. Native peoples used corn (maize) as their principal bread grain, but pioneering white settlers used it primarily as a feed crop to fatten stock for market. This was the origin of the Corn Belt system of agriculture, which flourished in Kentucky, Tennessee, and southern Ohio by 1840.

Desiring to expand their operations, settlers from the early Ohio River Valley Corn Belt spread northward, especially into good lands of the Miami Valley and the Virginia Military District in Ohio. Soon thereafter, a new migration left the hilly fringes of the Ohio Valley to move into central Indiana and Illinois, where Corn Belt agriculture also was established.

Ohio, Indiana, and Illinois were the first states admitted to the Union out of what had been the Northwest Territory. Although slavery was not totally outlawed in the new states, its practice was severely restricted by the framers of those states' constitutions. Missouri was not part of the Northwest Territory but, rather, became part of the United States through the Louisiana Purchase. No laws discouraged slavery in what became the state of Missouri. Southerners who desired to move west and practice slavery thus had Missouri as their option, whereas those who wished to avoid slavery generally chose to move northward to Ohio, Indiana, or Illinois.

Upland Southerners moved into all of these areas and brought with them the practice of corn-livestock agriculture. Most of Missouri south of the Missouri River is part of the rugged Ozark Highland, an area that offered few amenities to the incoming agricultural settlers because of its topography and inaccessibility. Smoother, more fertile land with a thin cover of older glacial materials lay north of the Missouri River in the state of Missouri. Tobacco and hemp planters from Kentucky and Tennessee brought slaves with them and established a scaled-down form of plantation agriculture in what became known by the 1840s as the "Little Dixie" region of Missouri.

Population growth and economic expansion stagnated in the Southern Uplands after the Civil War. New economic growth was focused on cities, a form of settlement the upland areas lacked. Population slowly declined in many upland areas for the next century. In isolated areas, such as portions of the Missouri Ozarks, this trend was reversed beginning in the 1960s when recreation opportunities were created by reservoir construction.

Urbanization in the southern Midwest took place outside the upland areas. The Ohio and the Mississippi Rivers were the principal arteries of commerce until railroads were built in the Midwest beginning in the 1840s. River commerce was responsible for the early growth of both Cincinnati and St. Louis, and it also contributed to the early importance of Kansas City as a transportation center. Because the Mississippi and its tributaries flow toward the south, river commerce was directed southward until the middle of the nineteenth century.

The Midwestern Prairies. Why is there a large prairie region in the Midwest? Most scientists believe that fire is part of the explanation, although there is disagreement over the cause of the fires. American Indians' practice of deliberate burning to drive game and to improve grassy conditions for grazing animals is the explanation of prairie vegetation favored by many. Other scientists stress the role of lightning-caused fires. Fire eliminates woody vegetation from a landscape. Repeated fires over a long period of time would have been necessary to produce the treeless conditions seen on the Midwestern Prairies when they were first described by European explorers in the eighteenth century. Conditions of drought, common in the central Midwest, are thought to be a necessary precondition for fire. Without fires, the Midwestern Prairies are soon invaded by small trees and shrubs. Grassy vegetation eventually is shaded out by the canopy of forest trees.

Corn-livestock agriculture was developed in the forested domain of the Upland South, but it expanded most rapidly in areas that lacked a heavy forest growth. Lands that had a cover of grasses mixed with open woodlands did not demand hard labor to clear. They became the favored environments for new settlers to colonize in the early decades of the nineteenth century. Beginning with the introduction of livestock feeding in the Virginia Military District of Ohio, corn-livestock agriculture expanded westward from Ohio, across the prairies and plains of Illinois and Iowa, to eastern Nebraska and Kansas in less than two generations. By the 1880s, most of the prairies had been plowed and planted in corn. Growth of American agriculture during the second half of the century was made possible because of the continued expansion of cultivation into new areas. Because the gently sloping, fertile prairies offered the best potential farmland, growth of Corn Belt agriculture was most rapid on prairie lands.

Growth of the prairie–Corn Belt system of agriculture was responsible for much of Chicago's early growth. As agriculture intensified, Chicago's factories grew in size and number, providing employment for thousands of new workers who streamed into the city from all parts of the world. The city's importance in grain marketing led to invention of the practice of futures trading at the Chicago Board of Trade. Chicago was once the world's largest meat packer, and it has long had an important role in food industries using flours, oils, and sweeteners made from wheat, corn, and soybeans. The same industries were responsible for the growth of other cities of the Midwestern Prairies region, including Omaha, St. Joseph, Des Moines, Cedar Rapids, Decatur, and Waterloo. Manufacturing industries devoted to the production of farm implements and food-processing machinery also appeared in these cities.

In contrast to the earlier, river-based system of commerce in the southern Midwest, the push of agricultural settlement across the prairies was based on the growth of railroad transportation. The pattern of urbanization became more dispersed because railroads made new areas accessible to urban growth. Settlement patterns in Indiana, Illinois, Iowa, and eastern Nebraska and Kansas were heavily influenced by railroads. These states are less known for a few large cities than they are for a network of small- to medium-sized cities, each with an economic base that depends on manufacturing industries and trade.

The Midwestern Prairies extend westward across the Missouri River to merge with the Great Plains in the central portion of the Dakotas, Nebraska, and Kansas. Lack of precipitation is the major factor limiting forest growth west of a line running through the center of those states. Wheat was the traditionally favored crop west of this line because precipitation was inadequate for corn. Today, however, large corn crops grow under irrigation throughout much of Nebraska and Kansas. The meat-packing industry has moved westward to the new corn-raising areas as well. Irrigation technology has been largely responsible for the westward extension of Corn Belt agriculture, from the Midwestern Prairies into the Great Plains.

The Lower Great Lakes. Four of the five Great Lakes (Superior, Michigan, Huron, and Erie) lie totally or partially within the Midwest. The Lower Great Lakes region is the southern margins of those four lakes and includes adjacent lands in Canada as well. Compared with the Midwestern Prairies region, the Lower Great Lakes is forested, has a somewhat moister and cooler climate, has a traditional emphasis on wheat raising and dairying rather than corn-livestock production, and supports an economic base that depended on the success of its manufacturing industries, especially heavy industry.

Steel production came to the Lower Great Lakes region in the late nineteenth century. Population had shifted westward and the demand for heavy machinery, electrical equipment, and fabricated metal products was growing. Iron mines in northern Minnesota and the Upper Peninsula of Michigan became the principal source of ores that could be transported cheaply by Great Lakes vessels to steel mills in Chicago, Detroit, Milwaukee, and Cleveland. Coal from the southern Midwest moved north by rail and then traveled by lake boats to the steel mills. Industrial growth was responsible for rapid urbanization. Waves of new immigrants—first from southern and eastern Europe and later from the American South—moved to the Lower Great Lakes' industrial centers.

The growth of individual industries was part of an overall system of regional development in which the typical factory was not only a producer but also a consumer of goods manufactured in nearby factories. Automobile production involves a complex of industries, each of which is a supplier to or customer of many others. Because they need one another's products, it is advantageous for these industries to cluster together. Cities of the Lower Great Lakes region rarely depended on a single industry but, rather, contained factories of many types. Food products, home appliances, motor vehicles, and many other lines of goods were produced in hundreds of factories in the Lower Great Lakes region.

Some of these industries have declined in importance during the past several decades and have moved their operations to other parts of the United States or to foreign countries. Economic problems stemming from industrial decline led to population loss in some cities and to attempts to find replacement economic activities in nearly all cities of the Lower Great Lakes. Most cities of the region now have more diversified economies that focus on the production of services, technology, and information.

Whereas the Southern Uplands and much of the Midwestern Prairies were settled by people familiar with corn-livestock agriculture, the Lower Great Lakes received most of its early American-born population from New York and New England. Wheat farming was an early specialty of farmers from northeastern "Yankee" backgrounds, although by the early decades of the twentieth century their focus shifted to dairying. Thousands of settlers who came to the Lower Great Lakes from Germany, the Scandinavian countries, and other parts of western Europe also became dairy farmers. Dairying remains the most important agricultural industry in many parts of the region today. Fruit, vegetable, and grain crops, along with dairy products, are the basis of a growing food-production sector in the Lower Great Lakes economy.

The Upper Great Lakes. Both the Midwestern Prairies and the Lower Great Lakes held many attractions for white settlers during the nineteenth century. Suitability of the land for agriculture declines in a northward direction, however, and so did the rate of land settlement in the nineteenth century. Roughly coinciding with the transition from temperate broadleaf forests to boreal forests, the northern limit of good agricultural land occurs as a line across the middle portion of lower Michigan, north-central Wisconsin, and northeastern Minnesota. North of that line, the growing season is too short for grain crops to mature, soils are lower in fertility, and the land is poorly drained in many areas due to the comparative recency of its glaciation. This more northern area, known as the Upper Great Lakes, was characterized by slow population growth during most of its history.

Human settlements in the Upper Great Lakes region have been most often associated with resource exploitation. Beginning in the eighteenth century, the fur trade dominated human use of the region, and it involved nearly all of the native and European-derived peoples who lived there. Once the valuable furs were gone, logging for lumber production became the principal economic activity. During the last half of the nineteenth century, logging and sawmilling activities clustered along the region's major rivers, which provided transportation for the logs. Cities such as Grand Rapids, Michigan; Oshkosh and Wisconsin Rapids, Wisconsin; and Brainerd, Minnesota, all began as sawmilling centers, located downstream on rivers that flow out of the great woods to the north.

Logging of the most desirable trees, such as white pine, ended when the last stands of those trees were cut in the early decades of the twentieth century. Forest-products industries in the Upper Great Lakes then turned to paper manufacturing, an industry that makes use of many types and sizes of trees. New manufacturing processes made it possible to convert trees such as aspen, which is unsuitable for lumber, into particle board and other products used in the home-building industry. Forest products are the leading manufacturing sector in the Upper Great Lakes region today.

Other resources of the region, including copper and iron ore, have undergone similar cycles of production, decline, and subsequent revitalization based on the use of less-pure ores. Northern Michigan's and northern Minnesota's iron ranges were depleted of their higher-grade ores by the 1950s, but the invention of taconite pellets made it possible to make use of the large, remaining reserves of low-grade ores. Two iron ranges—the Marquette Range in Michigan's Upper Peninsula and the Mesabi Range north of Duluth, Minnesota—remain in active production today and are important suppliers for Lower Great Lakes steel mills.

While cool temperatures and a landscape dotted with small lakes were not attractive to nineteenth-century pioneer settlers, they became the Upper Great Lakes' most important resource during the twentieth century when the region began serving as a resort vacation destination for the Midwest's city dwellers. Recent decades have seen rapid population growth in the Upper Great Lakes region as more people have chosen to make their year-around homes in a land where lakes and recreation opportunities abound.

Recent Trends. Population growth in the amenity-rich north country, industrial decline in the aging cities, consolidation of farms, increased agricultural production per acre in agriculture, and a newfound interest in environmental protection and restoration are some of the themes that will affect midwestern geography in the decades to come. The possibility of climatic warming suggested by some scientists today would have the effect of shifting the Midwest's climatic regions northward and probably would expand, rather than reduce, the area suitable for raising crops. No decline in demand for the array of food items produced in the Midwest has been forecast nor is one likely.

During the 1970s, some people predicted that the Lower Great Lakes region would become a "Rust Belt" due to industrial decline, but economic restructuring saved many industries from extinction. The rise of a knowledge-oriented and service-based economy will permit further dispersion of the population, which is likely to mean more population growth in amenity areas. That, in turn, will make it more necessary to protect such areas from environmental damage. Overall, the influence of the physical environment will continue to be felt in all areas and on all forms of livelihood.

Sources and Further Reading: Allan G. Bogue, *From Prairie to Corn Belt: Farming on the Illinois and Iowa Prairie in the Nineteenth Century* (1963); John R. Borchert, *America's*

Northern Heartland: An Economic and Historical Geography of the Upper Midwest (1987); William Cronon, *Nature's Metropolis: Chicago and the Great West* (1991); Nevin M. Fenneman, *Physiography of Eastern United States* (1938); Henry H. Glassie, *Pattern in the Material Folk Culture of the Eastern United States* (1968); John Fraser Hart, *The Land That Feeds Us* (1991); John C. Hudson, *Making the Corn Belt* (1994).

John Hudson
Northwestern University, Illinois
Lawrence A. Brown
The Ohio State University–Columbus

Geology

Many people, geologists included, imagine the middle of the North American continent as layer-cake flat, a place where little happens and there is little to see or examine. Yet from the early 1800s to the present, the geology of the Midwest has given rise to ideas and concepts that have found a permanent place in the earth sciences.

Even before scientists began studying the midcontinent, the area's geologic forces made themselves apparent. In December 1811, near the town of New Madrid (pronounced MAD-red) in the boot-heel of Missouri, an earthquake occurred that was among the largest (in terms of the amount of land shaken) in the history of North America. That quake was followed by two others in January and February 1812. The tremors rang church bells on the Atlantic seaboard, created new lakes, changed the course of the Mississippi River, and destroyed large areas of forest.

Damage and loss of life were relatively small because the region was sparsely settled at the time. But the New Madrid quake provided evidence that the stable midcontinent was not really all that stable, and it gave rise to geophysical studies that have been important in earthquake analysis. Should New Madrid produce another earthquake today like the ones almost 200 years ago, the damage would be far greater. Even without moving, these faults raised a ruckus. In the 1980s, a prediction of earthquake activity in the New Madrid fault zone frightened people and sold earthquake insurance. It helped educate the public about earthquakes in places where they are usually forgotten, but it might also have jaded the public when the predicted quake failed to occur.

Glacial features are a more subtle expression of the area's complex geology. Reports in the early 1800s commented on glacial debris in the Ohio River Valley, though its source was attributed to ice rafting—the movement of glacial deposits atop icebergs that then melted and dropped their load of rock to the sea floor.

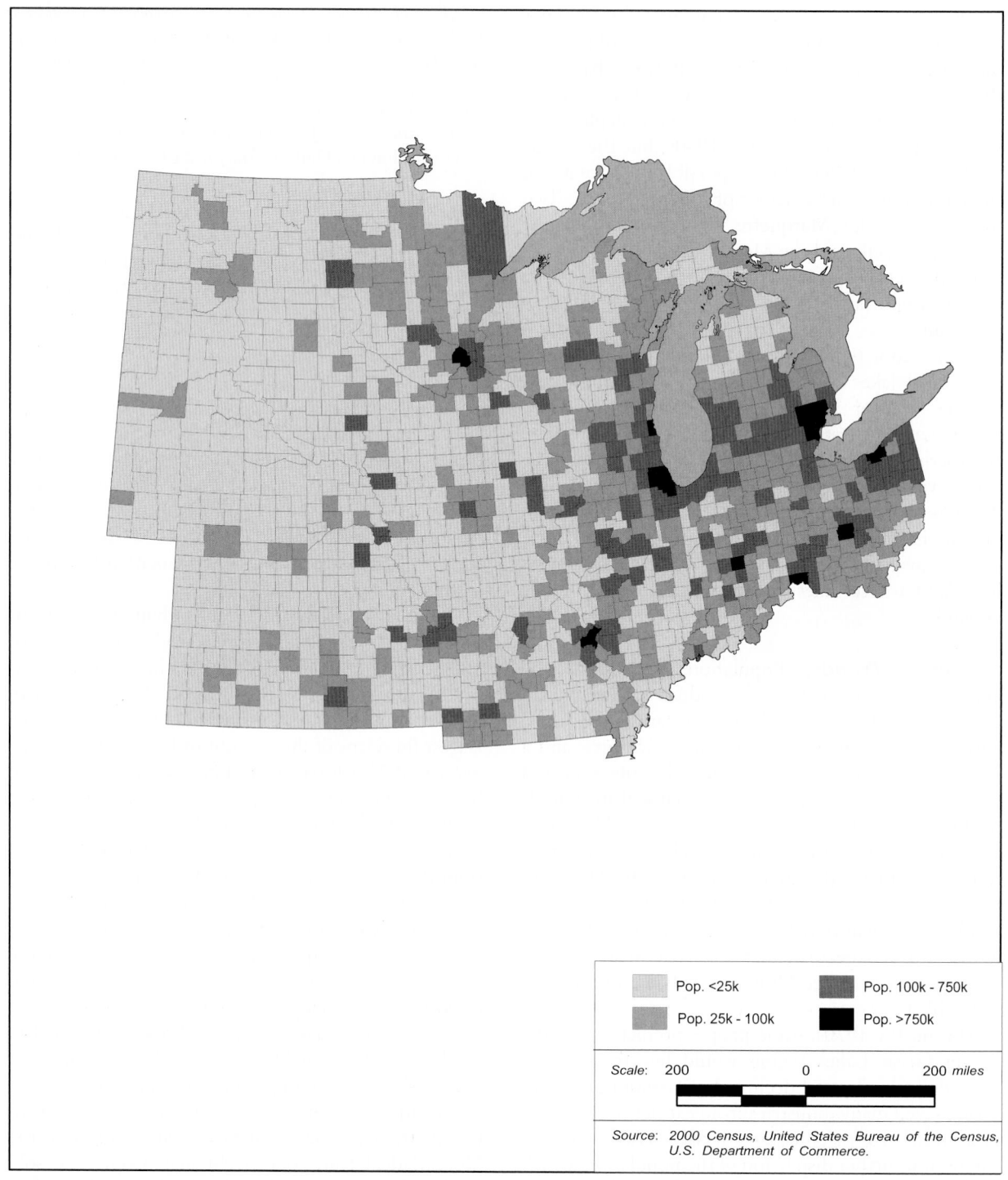

Population density. Prepared by Roman Nitze. *Source:* 2000 Census, United States Bureau of the Census.

By the mid to late 1800s, geologists, working particularly in Ohio and Wisconsin, began to understand the role of glaciation, identifying the movement of lobes of ice onto the landscape and the deposits that were left behind, such as moraines. They also began to understand the role of glaciers in eroding lake basins, scratching glacial striations into bedrock, and causing glacial rebound (the slow uplift of the earth's surface after the weight of the glaciers was removed as they retreated north).

By studying glacial drift (the boulders, gravel, and other debris moved by glaciers), scientists saw that glacial features were not the result of ice rafting or even any single period of glaciation, but represented a series of glaciers. They began teasing apart glacial and interglacial periods. By 1900, they had mapped the extent of the various glacial periods fairly thoroughly, and they had roughly determined glacial and interglacial time periods during the Pleistocene. They also began studying loess (a finely ground, silt-like material that blew out of the streambeds of meltwater from the glaciers). John Newberry, director of the Ohio Geological Survey from 1869 to 1874, and Thomas C. Chamberlin, head of the Wisconsin Geological Survey from 1873 to 1882, were particularly identified with improved understanding of glacial geology in the upper Midwest.

An additional contribution grew out of midwestern geology, one that owed its discovery to that layer-cake geology. In some locations—in stream banks on the plains of Illinois, for example, or in roadcuts along newly constructed highways in Kansas—geologists saw the repetitive nature of the rocks. A layer of limestone was above a layer of shale, which was above another of limestone, and so on. These repeated limestone/shale sequences (with coal beds or sandstone intermixed) gave rise to a concept of cyclic sedimentation, the idea that rocks were deposited in repeated cycles by shallow water as sea levels went up and down. In general terms, shales were deposited in shallow water, limestones in slightly deeper water. The idea that certain packages of rocks (called cyclothems) were deposited in succession originated in Illinois in the early 1900s. The concept then was championed in the 1930s and 1940s in Kansas (where other examples came from the subsurface during explorations for oil and gas).

The cyclothem concept generated arguments over the exact nature of deposition (did dark black shales, for example, represent deep water or very shallow water?) and the mechanism that caused the sea-level changes (were they due to melting and freezing of polar ice caps, or subtle up-and-down movement of the land?). Cyclothems were probably the most home-grown geologic concept to came out of the Midwest.

Finally, geologic resources were crucial in driving exploration and producing geologic information. Almost as early as Europeans arrived, they found important deposits of minerals and fuels. The lead and zinc mines of south-central Missouri were utilized as early as the 1720s. Coal was later mined in Illinois, and concepts of the subsurface were applied in the search for oil in southern Ohio and the plains of Kansas. Hard-rock minerals were mined in the northern Midwest, such as the iron ranges of Minnesota and the lead district of Wisconsin. Mining and drilling generated huge amounts of data, especially subsurface information, that in the 1860s and 1870s helped to drive the creation of organizations, such as state geological surveys, to study the region's geology.

The landscape of the Midwest is both complex and subtle. The region's natural resources on, above, and below the earth's surface, and indeed all the natural features together, have contributed to geologic ideas and understanding around the world.

Sources and Further Reading: Robert H. Dott, Jr., ed., *Eustasy: The Historical Ups and Downs of a Major Geological Concept* (1992); Ellen T. Drake and William M. Jordan, eds., *Geologists and Ideas: A History of North American Geology* (1985); Mott T. Greene, *Geology in the Nineteenth Century: Changing Views of a Changing World* (1982); James L. Penick, *The New Madrid Earthquakes*, rev. ed. (1981); George W. White, *Essays on History of Geology* (1978).

Rex C. Buchanan
University of Kansas

Climate

The climate of the Midwest results from an interplay of several different controls, large-scale features of the environment that determine the kinds and frequency of weather systems and their associated patterns of temperature and precipitation that characterize a region. For the Midwest, these include latitude, continental location, position in the westerlies, and the Great Lakes. A midlatitude location assures that solar radiation varies strongly from winter to summer as day length and sun angle change with the revolution of the Earth about the sun. At the same time, the location of the Midwest within the North American landmass, relatively far from the moderating effects of oceans and within a broad corridor of mountain-free terrain that stretches from the Arctic Ocean to the Gulf of Mexico, allows these strong seasonal radiation changes to produce relatively wide swings of seasonal temperature and permits invasions by contrasting air masses originating from these distant sources. The contrast between these air masses helps account for the range of daily weather changes and also provides energy that occasionally fuels both severe local storms (thunderstorms, hailstorms, and tornadoes) as well as great cyclonic storms during the cold season that generate blizzards and other extreme events.

As a consequence of its mid-latitude position, the Midwest lies within a global belt of winds called the westerlies, which means that weather systems (the familiar "lows" and "highs" on daily weather maps) traveling mainly west to east characterize the midwestern climate, although the surface winds at any one time may be from any direction. Whether over a given period these have northwestern origins, as from the Arctic, or are from the southwest is a result of circulation (jet stream) patterns in the upper atmosphere that determine whether there are episodes of colder or warmer, or drier or wetter, weather than normal because the climatic norms integrate the impacts of a wide range of patterns over the long term. While a great variety of upper-air patterns has been observed over the Midwest, some are more common and thus more characteristic than others, which in combination with seasonally changing radiation receipts assures that the daily weather, though often changeable, falls within certain limits. Abnormal persistence of any one pattern, however, brings repetitive weather that can lead to drought or floods, or sustained heat or cold. Because the upper air winds are stronger in winter than in summer they propel systems in the westerlies at a faster clip during the cold season. Faster travel means more frequent weather changes and fewer sustained periods of one kind of weather or another in the winter.

Finally, the Great Lakes contribute modest amounts of heat and moisture to the atmosphere mostly in fall and winter, when they are warmer than most air masses traversing them, resulting in moderated temperatures and locally augmented snowfall and cloudiness downwind. During other seasons, their influence is limited to cooling shoreline areas or reducing some types of cloud cover.

Fluctuating upper air patterns assure that midwestern weather is variable during all seasons, as different air masses are alternately drawn into the region from different source areas by passing weather systems. In general, however, three kinds of air masses most often dominate the scene. The most common are of continental origin and invade the Midwest from the west or

northwest. If they start out as Pacific air masses, they are warmed and dried in transit over the Rocky Mountains and normally produce temperatures near the seasonal mean. If, however, they originate in northern Canada or the Arctic (or sometimes even Siberia), particularly in winter, they are less modified en route and generally result in the coldest weather of any given season. When this cold air streams over the relatively warm Great Lakes in winter, it is destabilized and yields sometimes heavy lake-effect snowfall on downwind areas within thirty or so miles of the lakes, particularly where higher inland terrain further lifts the air, as in northwest lower Michigan or parts of the Upper Peninsula.

The least common air mass in the Midwest originates over the warm waters of the Gulf of Mexico or the Caribbean Sea and approaches on winds from the south. In summer it accounts for hot, humid weather most common in the southern parts of the region. It becomes less common northward where cold fronts in association with traveling weather systems pass more frequently. In northern Minnesota, Wisconsin, and Michigan, gulf air normally accounts for the weather on only a small fraction of days otherwise dominated by continental air masses. In winter, it is nearly absent in the north and only seldom affects even the southern Midwest, usually in the form of low stratus clouds, fog, and drizzle.

Gulf air's chief importance throughout the Midwest during all seasons is as a source of water vapor for precipitation. It is lifted by passing weather systems and their associated fronts and quite often invades ahead of these systems only at cloud level, unapparent at the surface except for the associated rain or snow-

Devil's Lake, Wisconsin.
Wisconsin Department of Tourism.

fall. Indeed, the majority of water molecules falling on the landscape is traceable back to this air mass. The only important exception is lake-effect precipitation, the water vapor that truly has a local origin, but the overall contribution of this component is small, and its hydrologic significance to the Great Lakes (as spring run-off from the melting snow) is inconsequential because it is water vapor originally acquired from the lakes' surface.

In short, in winter the northern and western parts of the Midwest are the coldest and driest, respectively, owing to the dominance of that region by continental air masses. Southern and eastern parts are wetter and milder because continental air masses are moderated before they reach these areas and tropical air masses (often aloft in association with traveling storm systems) are somewhat more common. In summer, however, slight changes in the upper-air patterns allow tropical air to stream northward from the Gulf of Mexico into central North America more easily. Western parts of the Midwest have hotter, more humid, and somewhat wetter summers than the north or northeastern parts.

Sources and Further Reading: Val Eichenlaub, *Weather and Climate of the Great Lakes Region* (1979); Jay R. Harman, *Synoptic Climatology of the Westerlies* (1991); Kenneth E. Kunkel, Linda D. Mortsch, and Peter Lewis, *The Climate of the Great Lakes–St. Lawrence River Basin* (2001); D. W. Phillips and J.A.W. McCulloch, *The Climate of the Great Lakes Basin* (1972).

Jay Harman
Michigan State University

Landforms

The Midwest is a diverse region. While parts of Illinois, Ohio, Michigan, and the Red River Valley of North Dakota and Minnesota are flat, many midwestern landscapes range from gently rolling to quite hilly. Knowing the origins of these landforms helps explain the appearance of the region's physical landscapes.

It all starts with bedrock. The underlying hard bedrock controls the landforms above because of its general resistance to weathering and erosion. Hard rocks, such as granite, basalt, dolomite, and some sandstones, stand up as ridges and high hills. Softer shales and limestones erode into lowlands and valleys. In southern Indiana, the highly soluble limestones have weathered into a type of landscape called karst, replete with caves, sinkholes, and even disappearing streams. Soft shale and sandstone bedrock is also the underlying explanation for the existence of the Great Lakes—the

areas above the soft rocks were preferentially scoured out by the glaciers of the past two million years.

With the exception of the far north, where the crystalline rocks of the Canadian Shield form the bedrock, the Midwest is a region of gently dipping sedimentary rocks. Sandstones, shales, and limestones/dolomites comprise the bulk of these rocks. After many millennia of erosion by glaciers, wind, and water, most of these rock formations have developed into low, ridgelike landforms called cuestas. Much of southern Wisconsin and Michigan is underlaid by cuestas formed by dolomite, but because they are large-scale landforms, and because they are covered with thick glacial debris, most midwestern cuestas are difficult to discern from the ground. The cuestas of eastern Kansas, best exemplified in the limestone-dominated Flint Hills, are only thinly mantled with glacial deposits and stand out as excellent examples of this type of landform.

Much of the Midwest has long been a gently rolling landscape, largely because the repeated advances of glaciers into the region have eroded the bedrock highs and filled in the lowlands with debris. However, the Driftless Area, a region in southwestern Wisconsin and northeastern Iowa that was never covered by glaciers, remains a very hilly and bedrock-controlled landscape. Dominated by steep slopes, bedrock outcrops, and deep, stream-cut valleys, it is an atypical midwestern region. Similarly, areas south of the glacial limit, such as the Ozark Plateau of Missouri and parts of southeastern Ohio, are much more bedrock-dominated and exhibit more relief than do other, glaciated regions.

Even before glaciers advanced into the region, it had low relief and several large, through-flowing rivers. Glaciers took advantage of these preexisting valleys and the soft rocks below, deepening them into the Great Lakes. Much of the rock and sediment scoured out was then deposited in thick sheets of glacial drift. With each glaciation a new sheet of drift was deposited, eroding or burying any soils that may have formed on the previous materials. The buried soils (called paleosols) preserve within them a fossil environmental record and thus are important stratigraphic marker beds.

Glacial landforms dominate most midwestern landscapes. Ridges of debris formed at the ice margins are called end moraines. Many moraines are quite rolling with many isolated depressions called kettles formed as buried ice blocks melted. The end moraines tend to be low and broad in the southern parts of the Midwest but are more rugged and have higher relief in the north, where the ice sheet was colder and more often frozen to its bed. The looping end-moraine patterns provide important information about the ways in

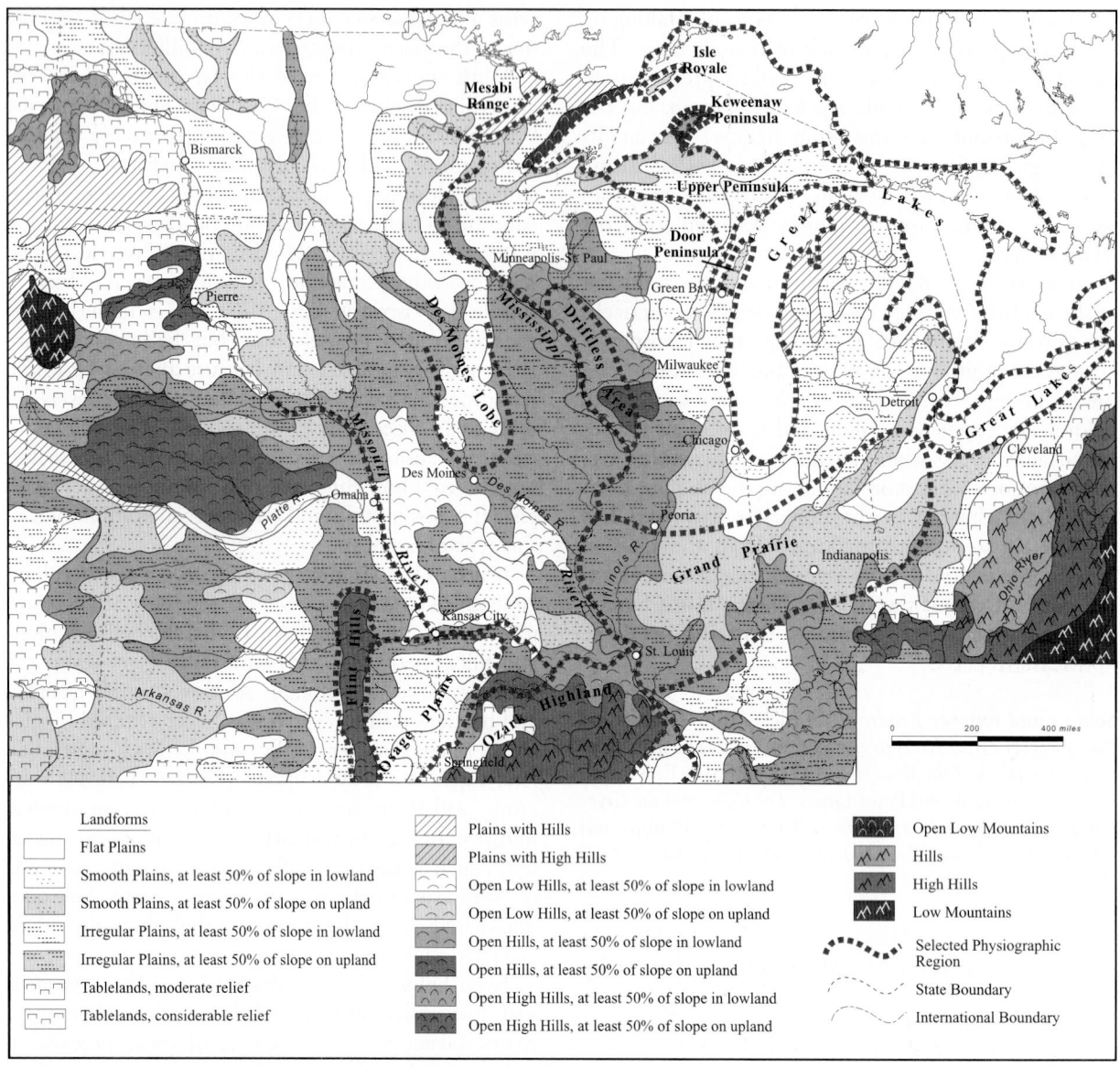

Landforms

☐ Flat Plains

Smooth Plains, at least 50% of slope in lowland

Smooth Plains, at least 50% of slope on upland

Irregular Plains, at least 50% of slope in lowland

Irregular Plains, at least 50% of slope on upland

Tablelands, moderate relief

Tablelands, considerable relief

Plains with Hills

Plains with High Hills

Open Low Hills, at least 50% of slope in lowland

Open Low Hills, at least 50% of slope on upland

Open Hills, at least 50% of slope in lowland

Open Hills, at least 50% of slope on upland

Open High Hills, at least 50% of slope in lowland

Open High Hills, at least 50% of slope on upland

Open Low Mountains

Hills

High Hills

Low Mountains

Selected Physiographic Region

State Boundary

International Boundary

Landforms and key physical geography regions. Prepared by Margaret Popovich. *Source:* "The National Atlas of the United States of America." U.S. Department of the Interior (1970); and E. H. Hammond, "Classes of land surface form in the forty-eight states," *Annals of the Association of American Geographers* 54 (1964), no. 1, Map Supplement Series, no. 4.

which the ice sheets advanced and receded. End moraines that formed where two ice lobes converged are called interlobate moraines. These features are some of the most rolling and lake-strewn of all the glacial landforms; examples include the Kettle Moraine region of Wisconsin and the southeastern Michigan interlobate moraine.

Subglacial landforms were formed beneath the ice sheet. They include drumlins—streamlined, spoon-shaped hills that occur by the hundreds in southeastern Wisconsin, northeastern Minnesota, and northern lower Michigan. Drumlin fields tend to be found where the ice was forced to climb out of a deep lake basin onto a nearby upland. Eskers are long, sinuous

ridges of sand and gravel that formed as tunnels, carved out by subglacial meltwater streams and filled with debris. They are important sources of sand and gravel (aggregate). Equally important as aggregate sources are outwash plains, which formed as meltwater washed out in front of the ice sheet. Outwash plains tend to be flat and sandy; many are irrigated for agriculture.

The flattest but most agriculturally productive landform regions are areas that formerly were beneath glacial lakes. Most of these lakes formed as water ponded between the ice margin and higher topography beyond. Waves and currents beveled the lake bottoms while lake clays filled in the low areas, leaving behind nearly featureless plains. The most expansive of these glaciolacustrine plains are in the Red River Valley of North Dakota (Glacial Lake Agassiz), northern Ohio (Glacial Lake Maumee), and the "thumb" of Michigan (Glacial Lake Saginaw). Were it not for subsurface drains, these areas might still be extensive swamps. Now drained, they form some of the best agricultural lands in the Midwest.

Many landforms, especially those west and south of the Great Lakes, are covered with anywhere from a few inches to a few yards of windblown silt, or loess. The sources for this silt were the Wabash, Mississippi, Illinois, Missouri, and other rivers that carried milky, silt-rich glacial meltwater. During winters, the valleys dried up and the silts were blown onto nearby uplands, where they would eventually develop into extremely fertile soils.

Sand-dune fields have formed on midwestern landscapes where a sufficiently large sand source exists. The largest of these are the Sand Hills of Nebraska. In Michigan and Wisconsin, many dune fields on present-day swamps attest to warmer and drier climates in the past.

Sources and Further Reading: Nevin M. Fenneman, *Physiography of Eastern United States* (1938); Paul F. Karrow and Parker E. Calkin, eds., *Quaternary Evolution of the Great Lakes* (1985); Grahame Larson and Randall J. Schaetzl, "Origin and Evolution of the Great Lakes," *Journal of Great Lakes Research* 27 (2001); Lawrence M. Martin, *The Physical Geography of Wisconsin*, 3rd ed. (1965); David M. Mickelson, Lee Clayton, David S. Fuller, and Harold W. Borns, Jr., "The Late Wisconsin Glacial Record of the Laurentide Ice Sheet in the United States," in *Late-Quaternary Environments of the United States*, vol. 1, Stephen C. Porter, ed., *The Late Pleistocene* (1983); Anthony Orme, ed., *The Physical Geography of North America* (2002); Jean C. Prior, *Landforms of Iowa* (1991); William D. Thornbury, *Regional Geomorphology of the United States* (1965).

Randall Schaetzl
Michigan State University

Flora

The flora of the Midwest is diverse because of complex interactions among climate, soils, natural disturbance, and human activities. The plant cover also is influenced by a decrease in precipitation from east to west, and by a decrease in temperature from south to north. Vegetation types include upland temperate hardwood forest, tallgrass prairie, mixed deciduous forest, and boreal forest.

By eleven thousand years ago the most recent gla-

ciers in the Midwest had melted, and the barren land lacked well-developed soils. New plant assemblages developed as soils formed and individual species migrated northward and westward. In the mid-nineteenth century, when the U.S. government undertook a detailed land survey, surveyors recorded the tree species they encountered, the wetlands they crossed, and the prairies they passed through. From these documents, scholars have reconstructed and mapped the vegetation prior to European settlement. Plant geography has changed significantly since that time, however, largely due to human activities.

The rolling hills of the Ohio River Valley and Missouri Ozarks are clothed with a hardwood forest of broadleaf deciduous trees. The pre-European vegetation of the Ohio River Valley was a mixed forest of maple, buckeye, beech, tulip tree, oak, and linden that graded into oak-hickory forest farther west. Oak-hickory forest gave way to beech-maple forest in Indiana. The current land cover of this region is a mosaic of agricultural fields, pastures, and forest remnants.

Prairie vegetation in the Midwest has a continuous cover of tall grasses and non-woody (herbaceous) plants. Wildflowers such as purple coneflower and black-eyed Susan and nitrogen-fixing legumes such as lupine are common. Moisture demand is close to total precipitation received, so woody species (trees and shrubs) grow only in depressions and stream valleys where there is sufficient soil moisture and where fire is inhibited.

During the past several thousand years, the prairie advanced eastward under drier conditions and retreated westward—encroached upon by deciduous forest—under wetter climate regimes. By the time Europeans arrived, a wedge of tallgrass prairie covered the entire western part of the midwestern region and narrowed to a "Prairie Peninsula" near the Illinois-Indiana border.

Prairie soils are especially fertile because they form in nutrient-rich wind-deposited sediment (loess). There is little excess rain to cause leaching, the deep-rooted plants hold nutrients, and the upper layer of soil is rich in partially decomposed organic matter. The nation's Corn Belt developed in these soils. Most of the land covered by prairie prior to European settlement is now cultivated.

Native Americans had a significant impact on vegetation in some areas. They used fire to manage plant cover and to chase game. Accidental spread from campfires or lightning strikes also ignited prairie fires. Regardless of origin, these fires raged across the grasslands. Every few years a given patch of prairie might be burned. Many grassland species are adapted to fire: The foliage above ground burns, but the roots remain intact. The grasses and wildflowers resprout and the prairie is reborn. Few woody plants can tolerate fire, so an open grassland is maintained. Some trees, like bur oak, can resprout from their burned stumps, and the thick, corky bark of full-grown bur oaks protects them from fire. Oak savanna (also known as oak woodland, oak opening, or prairie parkland) developed where single or multiple fire-tolerant trees punctuated the continuous grass cover.

The mixed deciduous forest, or Big Woods, extended from central Wisconsin through central Minnesota, south of the boreal forest. Prior to European settlement, maple-basswood forest dominated the Big Woods landscape, especially on sites protected from fire. Oak woodlands were on the margins and in fire-prone areas. Sugar maple, basswood, elm, green ash, and ironwood trees compose the canopy today where the forest has not been cleared for agriculture and housing.

Pollen evidence suggests that the Big Woods in Minnesota developed fairly recently. The forest expanded into the prairie about 300 to 400 years ago, when cooler, wetter conditions promoted forest development. Development pressure and invasive species now threaten the limited remaining acreage of this vegetation type.

The southern edge of the boreal forest in northern Michigan, Wisconsin, and Minnesota now is a place for recreation as well as a source of raw materials for the forest-product industry. Large-scale lumbering of the "Pineries" began in the mid-nineteenth century after the timber industry had collapsed in the East. White pine and red pine were the most valuable species; less than 10 percent of the tall pine forest was left uncut in regions such as northeastern Minnesota. Spruce, balsam fir, jack pine, aspen, and birch were spared from the first episode of heavy cutting.

The forest that regenerated following logging in the northern Midwest consists of species native to the area, but in vastly different proportions. For some six thousand to eight thousand years, white pine and red pine had regenerated naturally following disturbance by fire. After logging, however, most of the seed trees were gone, the characteristics of the forest floor and seedbed had changed, and new disease and competition were introduced. Large-scale efforts to replant the forest created such a demand for white pine seedlings that U.S. nurseries could not provide the necessary stock. White pine seedlings imported from Europe were infected with white pine blister rust. Gooseberries and currants—common plants in recently logged areas—served as alternate hosts for the rust, which caused deadly cankers on white pine seedlings and saplings.

Aspen, which is not favored for lumber, regenerated in much of the cutover forest of the Upper Great Lakes region. The species' ability to resprout from its roots gives aspen an advantage over other species following disturbance. As the once-busy lumber mills closed down in the 1920s and 1930s, the paper industry developed and aspen, spruce, balsam fir, jack pine, and birch trees that had been spared during the pine harvest were ground into pulp. Pine trees in plantations are harvested for wood pulp that is processed into printing paper, toilet paper, and boxboard. More recently, aspen chips have been pressed and glued into oriented strand board and wood fiberboard for the construction industry. Pine trees in plantations are harvested for wood pulp that is processed into printing paper, toilet paper, and boxboard.

The future of Midwestern vegetation will depend on how species and individual plants respond to human activities and climate change.

Sources and Further Reading: Clifford Ahlgren and Isabel Ahlgren, *Lob Trees in the Wilderness* (1984); John T. Curtis, *The Vegetation of Wisconsin* (1959); Margaret B. Davis, "Holocene Vegetational History of the Eastern United States," in *Late Quaternary Environments of the United States*, vol. 2, Herbert E. Wright, Jr., ed., *The Holocene* (1983); Eric C. Grimm, "Fire and Other Factors Controlling the Big Woods Vegetation of Minnesota in the Mid-Nineteenth Century," *Ecological Monographs* 54 (Sept. 1984); John C. Hudson, *Across This Land* (2002); James M. Omernik and Alisa L. Gallant, *Ecoregions of the Upper Midwest States* (1988); Robert C. Ostergren and Thomas R. Vale, eds., *Wisconsin Land and Life* (1997); John R. Tester, *Minnesota's Natural Heritage* (1995).

Susy Svatek Ziegler
University of Minnesota–Twin Cities

Fauna

The fauna of the Midwest has changed substantially since the height of the last glacial period eighteen thousand to twenty thousand years ago. The loss of some species and the appearance of others is related in part to the rapidly changing climate. Some shifting patterns of midwestern biogeography, however, are due to human activity.

Large mammals (megafauna) roamed the region following the last glacial retreat. Muskox and mastodon remains have been found throughout the Midwest. Most herbivores with an adult body weight over 270 pounds in North and South America, including mastodons, mammoths, camels, llamas, horses, tapirs, ground sloths, and cave bears, went extinct between twelve thousand and nine thousand years ago. Many large predators—such as saber-toothed tigers, hyenas, and lions—also went extinct at that time.

Some species of large raptors and scavengers, which presumably feasted on the carcasses of the large mammals, died out at about the same time.

What caused these mass extinctions? One theory is that large mammals may have evolved to the point that they could not adapt to the postglacial climate. Temperatures warmed rapidly following the last glacial period, and the food supply for large herbivores may have decreased due to shifting vegetation patterns, triggering a cascade of events that affected all levels of the food web. New competitors that migrated across Beringia (the former land bridge that is now under the Bering Strait) into North America from Asia may have shifted the dynamics of species interactions.

An alternative theory is the overkill hypothesis. Perhaps humans are responsible for the mass extinction of large mammals, and the carnivores and scavengers went extinct as their food sources disappeared. Skilled hunters did colonize North America via Beringia, and they did kill large mammals. Stone points (spear tips) associated with the Clovis people have been found with the remains of mammoths and other large animals. Native mammals in North America had not evolved in the presence of humans (as they had in Africa) so they had no flight instincts. The timing of the arrival of Clovis people and the mass extinctions of megafauna may, however, have been purely coincidental. Scholars continue to debate the details. A complex combination of natural factors and human activities may have caused the extinctions.

Bison (buffalo) are among the large mammals that did not die out by the beginning of the Holocene (ten thousand years ago). Bison grazed abundantly on the western edge of the region, but they, too, came close to extinction by 1890. For centuries, Native Americans had relied on bison for food, shelter, and clothing. European settlers relentlessly hunted the animal in the mid 1800s for buffalo robes and for sport. The bison carcasses were left to rot on the prairie. Later, settlers and Native Americans collected the bleached bones and shipped them by rail to rendering plants in St. Louis and Detroit. By the early 1890s, millions of tons of bones were converted to fertilizer and burned to make carbon black for use as pigments.

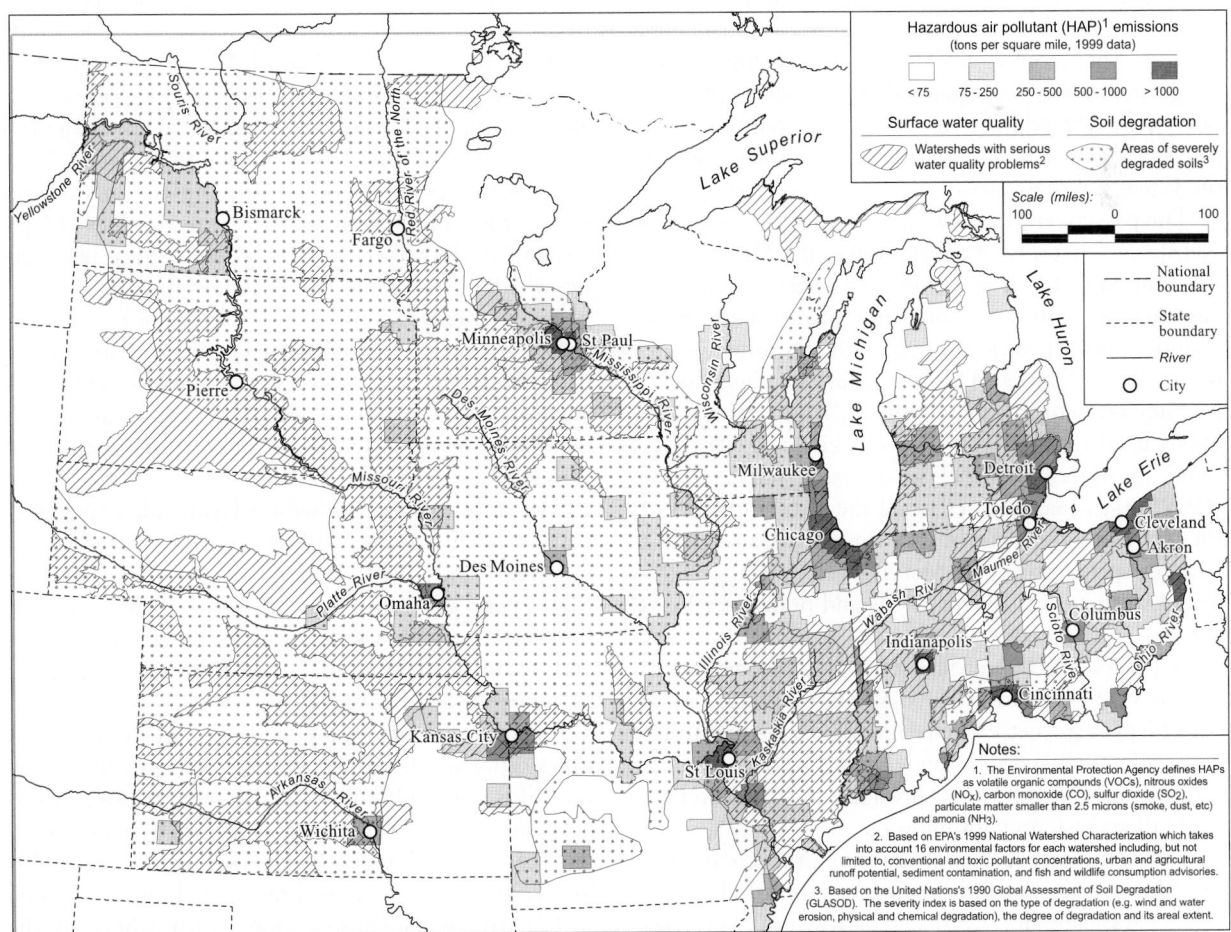

The negative impact of human development on the environment. Prepared by James DeGrand. *Source:* United States Environmental Protection Agency.

Bison are now an important grazer in areas of reconstructed prairie in the western Midwest. Other animals that are characteristic of the region include pronghorn antelope, coyotes, jackrabbits and cottontail rabbits, ground squirrels, prairie dogs, pocket gophers, badgers, migrating waterfowl, and grassland birds.

The fauna of the northern Midwest changed significantly during the Holocene, even before European settlers migrated westward along the timber and agricultural frontiers. Furs were one of the first commodities exported from North America on a large scale. Fur-bearing mammals, adapted to the long, cold winters of the upper Midwest, were trapped for their thick pelts. Beaver, white-tailed deer, muskrat, otter, marten, raccoon, mink, rabbit, fisher, black bear, elk, and bison were among those species that were captured, although beaver pelts formed the basis of the fur-trading economy.

The period of fur trade and exploration lasted for a couple of centuries. The French organized the fur trade in the mid 1600s, the British pursued it next, and Americans took the lead in the 1800s. Native Americans trapped the animals for the European traders. The peak of fur trading in the Great Lakes region occurred in the late eighteenth century, after which beavers were scarce east of the Mississippi River. Larger mammals were trapped and traded in place of beaver. Beaver populations have recovered, and now beaver lodges, dams, and ponds are a familiar sight in the Great Lakes forests.

The passenger pigeon is another example of an animal species that once was common in the Midwest but was hunted ruthlessly—in this case to extinction. The passenger pigeon was at one time probably the most abundant bird species on earth, with an estimated two to five billion birds. The birds flew in huge flocks, feasting on acorns and beechnuts, from at least the 1600s until the last wild bird was killed in Sargents, Ohio, on March 24, 1900. In *A Sand County Almanac* (1949), Aldo Leopold described the awesome sight of the "onrushing phalanx of victorious birds, sweeping a path for spring across the March skies, chasing the defeated winter from all the woods and prairies of Wisconsin." The pigeons were hunted wantonly for their meat (which became a delicacy in East Coast cities) and to stop them from damaging agricultural crops. The birds were netted and killed in large quantities. Ironically, the species' tendency to roost in huge groups to avoid predators through safety in numbers made them easy prey for hunters.

Today, invasive species are causing great concern in the Midwest. Zebra mussels in the Great Lakes and smaller water bodies, European earthworms in forests of northern Minnesota, and gypsy moths in forests of the eastern Midwest region are not native to the area, but are altering aquatic and terrestrial plant and animal communities.

Sources and Further Reading: John R. Borchert, *America's Northern Heartland* (1987); James H. Brown and Mark V. Lomolino, *Biogeography*, 2nd ed. (1998); Jeanne Kay, "Wisconsin Indian Hunting Patterns, 1634–1836," *Annals of the Association of American Geographers* 69 (Sept. 1979); Aldo Leopold, *A Sand County Almanac* (1949); Paul S. Martin and Richard G. Klein, eds., *Quaternary Extinctions* (1984); James M. Omernik and Alisa L. Gallant, *Ecoregions of the Upper Midwest States* (1988); Robert C. Ostergren and Thomas R. Vale, eds., *Wisconsin Land and Life* (1997); David Quammen, *The Song of the Dodo* (1996); Gordon G. Whitney, *From Coastal Wilderness to Fruited Plain* (1994).

Susy Svatek Ziegler
University of Minnesota–Twin Cities

Agriculture

Revolutions in technology and biology that allow fewer farmers to produce more through specialization have been the driving force behind changes in midwestern farming since World War II. A relatively small number of large, full-time, highly capitalized, and technologically oriented farmers have emerged to produce most of the region's crops and livestock. Most farmers, however, have smaller operations and depend on income from jobs in nearby towns or cities. These farmers are less likely to specialize except in beef cattle, which can be cared for during evenings and weekends. An increasing number of farms have been purchased for recreation, hobbies, or investments. This is particularly true near cities, in the Upper Great Lakes and Southern Uplands regions, and in other areas with marginal farmland that may offer the amenities of woods, water, and hills.

Two-thirds of the Midwest is farmland. This is a 17 percent decline since 1950. It occurred because many marginal lands were shifted to other uses such as forestry or recreation, while some farmlands were flooded for reservoirs or were converted to highways and urban developments. The Midwest accounts for 21 percent of the nation's land area, 29 percent of its farmland, and a disproportionate 47 percent of the nation's cropland, but the region produces only 36 percent of the agricultural market value of national products sold because most midwestern farmers grow relatively low value crops. Most Midwest cropland is located in the Midwestern Prairies and most is planted with corn and soybeans, along with wheat in the Dakotas.

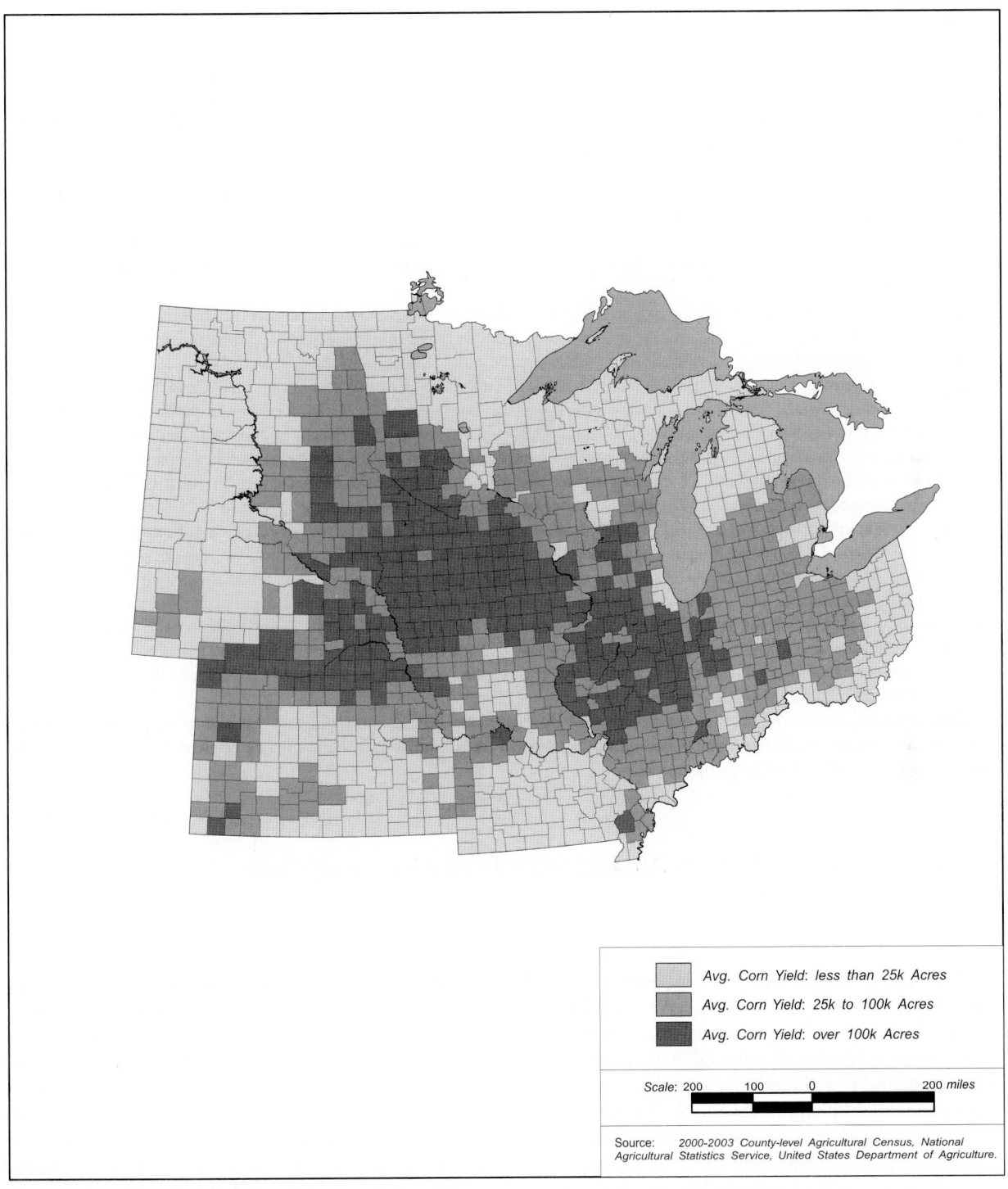

Corn production in the Corn Belt (average corn yield harvested by county, 2000–2003). Prepared by Roman Nitze. *Source:* 2000–2003 County-level Census, United States Department of Agriculture.

❖ Wheat Harvest Time

Christopher arrived when the wheat was ripe and fields waved golden on days when there was a breeze. During his visit, this nephew with ties to Mennonites from Indiana and Iowa accompanied me on a celebration of the wheat harvest in the Hartsburg Bottoms. How fitting, for it was Mennonites who first introduced wheat to the lands of the American Midwest.

In the 1870s, events in distant areas of the world occurred that eventually brought change to vast areas of empty grasslands in Kansas. To speed up change and encourage movement and the sale of lands that it owned after the Civil War, the Santa Fe Railroad broadcast fliers far and wide advertising good land for between two and five dollars per acre. A world away, Mennonite farmers who had emigrated en masse from the Netherlands found their way to Prussia and southern Russia, hoping to find a place to farm and worship in peace. Mennonite teams were also sent to the United States, where they learned of the cheap grasslands, sent teams to survey it, and wrote home of their approval. By 1874, Mennonite groups had begun to settle in Kansas.

They established towns in the region north of Wichita—Newton, Goessel, and Moundridge. In this treeless grassland, they constructed huts and dug wells and brought cherries, potatoes, and mulberry bushes. While local farmers banked on corn, the immigrants planted Turkey Red winter wheat, native to the shores of the Black Sea.

In a single planting season, it was clear that the hardier Turkey Red variety was better than the soft strains of spring wheat then being sown in the Midwest. Quickly the word was out. Letters were sent to other Mennonites in Russia, encouraging them to come to Kansas and bring as much Turkey Red seed as their trunks, pillows, and hatboxes could carry.

Kansas, once a vacant grassland, is today one of the world's largest producers of wheat. Wherever back roads lead you, Mennonites can be found who are still farming wheat—the crop that turned the Midwest into the world's breadbasket. By June, local farmers are busy checking the moisture level of their wheat to determine its ripeness.

"How do you know when it's ready to harvest?" I asked a local farmer. "Bite a kernel or break one and listen to the sound it makes," I was told. "You want it to be hard and brittle so it breaks with a cracking sound. Or you can weigh it, same as you do corn. When moisture is no more than 14 percent of the weight of the kernel, the wheat is ready for harvest."

This week, Christopher and I drove down to the Hartsburg Bottoms. It was hot and dry. Perfect for the huge mechanized combines that thresh the grain from the wheat stalks. We found Orion Beckmeyer and rode in his combine until the lights of the great red machine had to be turned on to guide us back to the grain truck. It was 9:00 P.M. when I finally drove my truck over the freshly cut wheat stubble toward the gravel farm road. There, we passed Orion's wife Barbara on her way to the fields with a basket of sandwiches and sun tea.

How appropriate, I thought, that our friends end their workday during the wheat harvest with a simple meal. A meal built around bread—made from grains brought by European Mennonites who made history by turning empty grasslands into a breadbasket that now feeds the world.

Cathy Salter
Hartsburg, Missouri

Originally published in the *Boon County (Missouri) Journal* and the *Columbia (Missouri) Tribune*

Midwestern farms are favored by both locational and physical advantages. Farmers have favorable access to domestic and international markets because grain can be inexpensively shipped by barge down the Mississippi and its tributaries, across the Great Lakes and to the Atlantic Ocean via the St. Lawrence Seaway, and to all other points by rail and trucking. The region's warm to hot summers are favorable for crops, yet winters are cold enough to slow the decay of organic matter that is critical for fertile soil. Rainfall is normally abundant enough for crop production but not so abundant as to leach soil nutrients. The flat to gently rolling hills of the Midwestern Prairies and the adjacent Lower Great Lakes area impose few barriers to farming. In a broad arc from central Ohio west to Kansas City and north through Omaha and Sioux Falls to Canada, glacial deposits leveled the land and left rich parent material that became some of the world's richest soils. Many of the region's shallow glacial lakes and wetlands were drained and became productive croplands. Today the prairies and the Lower Great Lakes comprise one of the most significant agricultural areas in the world, with less-productive farmlands on the periphery. The Southern Uplands have thin soil and less cropland with more land devoted to pasture and trees, while the cool, boreal forests of the Upper Great Lakes limit farming to the north.

Migrants from the Atlantic Seaboard converged in southwestern Ohio during the early part of the nineteenth century. Their combined farming ideas became the norm for Midwestern Prairie farming until after World War II. This farming was based upon a multiple-year rotation of small grains, corn, and a legume hay crop to restore nitrogen to the soil. The rotation maintained soil fertility and minimized erosion. Most farmers increased the value of their labor by feeding a substantial portion of their harvest to hogs or cattle. The most important crop for these farmers was corn, and the area from central Ohio to central Nebraska became known as the Corn Belt. Today this region should be renamed the Corn-Soybean Belt. Fifty to 70 percent of the land is used for crops, and corn and soybeans account for 60 to 70 percent of the acres harvested.

Other migrants from New England and New York moved west through the Lower Great Lakes along the prairie-forest edge. These farmers raised wheat for the market and dairy cattle. Wheat became a minor crop, but dairy cattle thrived in the cooler northern climate and could be fed silage from chopped corn, which did not have a long enough growing season to reach full maturity. Today, Lower Great Lakes farmers account for one-third of the nation's production of dairy products. Farmers attempted to till the cutover area of the Upper Great Lakes after forestry companies had cut the pines, but the costs of clearing the stumps were enormous and the rewards meager. This area has reforested and agriculture is not significant except where there are pockets of fertile soil or specialty enterprises.

Historically, most farm animals foraged in pastures with supplemental food provided by the farmer. To make the most of their land and time, midwestern farmers have recently enclosed most of their farm animals. Today, virtually all chickens and turkeys, most hogs, and perhaps a majority of dairy cattle are housed in industrial-looking buildings that also enclose the specialized equipment needed to feed and care for each species. This enclosure movement allowed farmers to specialize by concentrating their time and capital on raising the animals, and it has also made the pastures available for other purposes. In the Midwestern Prairies, most of these pastures became cropland, whereas in the Southern Uplands and the Upper Great Lakes, the pastures were often converted to forests or nonfarm uses. The enclosed animal facilities are only cost effective at large scales, so most hogs, chickens, turkeys, and an increasing proportion of dairy cattle are raised by relatively few farmers with large, specialized enterprises. A mere 6 percent of midwestern farmers raise 70 percent of the nation's hogs.

Midwestern farmers also raise one-quarter of the nation's beef cattle. Historically, many farmers purchased additional calves from Great Plains farmers and fed them during the winter before sending them to market. After 1960, Corn Belt farmers specialized in growing cash grain crops; they closed feedlots, abandoned barns, removed fences, plowed pastures, and concentrated their efforts on growing corn and soybeans for market.

Sources and Further Reading: John R. Borchert, *America's Northern Heartland* (1987); John Fraser Hart, "Change in the Corn Belt," *Geographical Review* 76 (Jan. 1986); John Fraser Hart, "Half a Century of Cropland Change," *Geographical Review* 91 (July 2001); John Fraser Hart, *The Land That Feeds Us* (1991); John C. Hudson, *Making the Corn Belt* (1994); John C. Hudson, "The Other America," in Thomas F. McIlwraith and Edward K. Muller, eds., *North America: The Historical Geography of a Changing Continent*, 2nd ed. (2001); Hugh Prince, *Wetlands of the American Midwest* (1997).

Darrell E. Napton
South Dakota State University

Cultural Geography

Culturally, the Midwest is a product of the mixing of ethnic communities moving westward from earlier-settled areas to the east, together with newly arriving communities directly from Europe and, later, the rest of the world. New settlers have tended to concentrate with earlier arrivals, including relatives and those who spoke the same language, followed the same religion, and enjoyed the same food. Not surprisingly, small ethnic settlement islands grew up in the countryside and, similarly, in cohesive neighborhoods in the urban centers. Many of these persist today.

Some settlers came in such numbers that they left a cultural imprint over great expanses of the Midwest. The Germanic peoples, among the earliest and most numerous, came to rival, and even surpass, the Anglo dwellers. Even the great wave of Germanic immigrants was not entirely homogeneous—some were Protestant, some Catholic, some from the north German plain, others from the quite different culture of the Rhineland, and still others from other German-speaking areas. Despite their internal variations, however, they spread a veneer of basic German culture throughout much of the Midwest. In the sea of this Germanness, other immigrant groups established ethnic islands wherever they came in volumes sufficient to ensure some continuity of their culture.

Thus the cultural geography of the Midwest resembles a checkerboard with a majority of the spaces occupied by German-derived settlers and other groups scattered in between them. While the list of other ethnic islands is long, a few places stand out because of their concentration, their relative size, and the success with which those communities have maintained their particular cultural orientation. Among these are the Dutch in southwestern Michigan and around Pella, Iowa; Belgians in the Door Peninsula of Wisconsin; Czechs in Colfax County, Nebraska, and in several communities in southeastern South Dakota; Finns in the cutover pine forest in northern Michigan, Wisconsin, and Minnesota; Norwegians in Vernon County and other areas of western Wisconsin; Swedes in Chisago County, Minnesota, Lindsborg, Kansas, and Clay County, South Dakota; Danes in Lincoln County, Minnesota, and southwestern Iowa; and German Russians in Ellis County and Cheyenne County, Kansas, and several places in North Dakota. Italians and Poles as well as other eastern and southern Europeans emigrated at a time when most available rural land had already been occupied, hence their impact on the midwestern countryside is minimal.

The later arrivals mostly joined their compatriots in urban areas. Some cities came to be dominated by particular groups, for example, Milwaukee by Germans. The groups who arrived in the twentieth century were not as easily absorbed into the central city wards as those of the nineteenth century had been. Settlers in many cities were restricted to small neighborhoods or forced to districts lying on the fringes of the larger cities, where more land under less pressure was available and racial tensions were minimal. Thus, one may trace Polish settlement in Hamtramck, Michigan (outside of Detroit); Puerto Ricans in Lorain, Ohio (outside of Cleveland); and, most recently, Vietnamese between St. Paul and Minneapolis, Minnesota.

Nevertheless, many central-city foreign neighborhoods did develop. A map of Cleveland, Ohio, in the 1960s identified distinct Croatian, Czech, Hungarian, Italian, Russian Jewish, Lithuanian, Polish, Slovak, Slovenian, and Hispanic neighborhoods. Even greater diversity exists in Chicago, where one can encounter a new nationality every two or three blocks along such major avenues as Clark Street. Ethnic neighborhoods are also in smaller cities, as the Italian cluster of North Hill in Akron, the Lebanese in Toledo, and the Finns in sections of Ashtabula, Ohio, attest. In both urban nationality neighborhoods and rural ethnic islands, the successful continuance of a particular culture depends upon many factors, including income, race, religion, and language. First-generation children often wish to assimilate, if they can become prosperous enough to do so.

Among the factors working to maintain ethnic communities in the Midwest, none is stronger than religion. Moving across the countryside today, the careful observer notes the importance of churches and cemeteries, which often mark earlier patterns of ethnicity. The Amish are probably the most easily recognized religious community, with major concentrations in Holmes County, Ohio, northeastern Indiana, and around Arthur, Illinois.

Ultimately, if the community has been able to maintain its viability, third and fourth generations begin to appreciate their unique heritage and develop a sense of ethnicity. The exterior manifestation of this is often the commercialization of celebrations, the preservation of vernacular architecture, and the promotion of restaurants, crafts, and festivals.

Sources and Further Reading: John C. Hudson, "Migration to an American Frontier," *Annals of the Association of American Geographers* 66 (June 1976); John C. Hudson, "North American Origins of Middlewestern Frontier Populations," *Annals of the Association of American Geographers* 78 (Sept. 1988); Terry G. Jordan, "Population Origins in Texas, 1850," *Geographical Review* 59 (Jan. 1969); Frederick C. Luebke, ed., *Ethnicity on the Great Plains* (1980); Allen G. Noble, "The Character and Composition of Rural Ethnic Islands," in Jesse O. McKee, ed., *Ethnicity in Contemporary America*, 2nd ed. (2000); Allen G. Noble, "Identifying Ethnic Regions in Ohio," *Ohio Geographers* 12 (1984); James R. Shortridge, *Peopling the Plains* (1995); Hubert G. H. Wilhelm, *The Original Distribution of Settlement Groups, Ohio, 1850* (1982).

Allen G. Noble
University of Akron, Ohio

Manufacturing

With its vast and highly fertile prairie landscapes drained by broad and slow-moving rivers and steeped in agricultural tradition, the Midwest hardly seems suited to its nickname as the nation's Industrial Heartland. Yet this is the very landscape that spawned the creative geniuses of Henry Ford and Ransom Olds (automobiles), Orville and Wilbur Wright (air flight), John Deere and J.I. Case (agricultural implements), Harvey Firestone (rubber tires), Philip Armour (meatpacking), George Pullman (rail-transport equipment), S.C. Johnson (household chemicals), and Seymour Cray (supercomputers). Economically, the Midwest is as much associated with the Detroit automotive complex; the Chicago–Gary, Indiana, steel works; the petrochemical and rubber industries of Ohio's Cuyahoga River Valley; the former stockyards and packing plants of Chicago and Kansas City; and the defense-related aerospace industry of St. Louis as it is with the prairie landscape.

The development of the Midwest as the nation's industrial heartland owes as much to history and geography as to the entrepreneurship of the likes of Ford and Deere. Cities like Cincinnati, Chicago, St. Louis, and Minneapolis served as staging grounds for settlers embarking west to establish new homesteads throughout the Great Plains and into the Pacific Northwest. As trailheads, these cities were called upon to supply the wagons for overland transportation, nonperishable

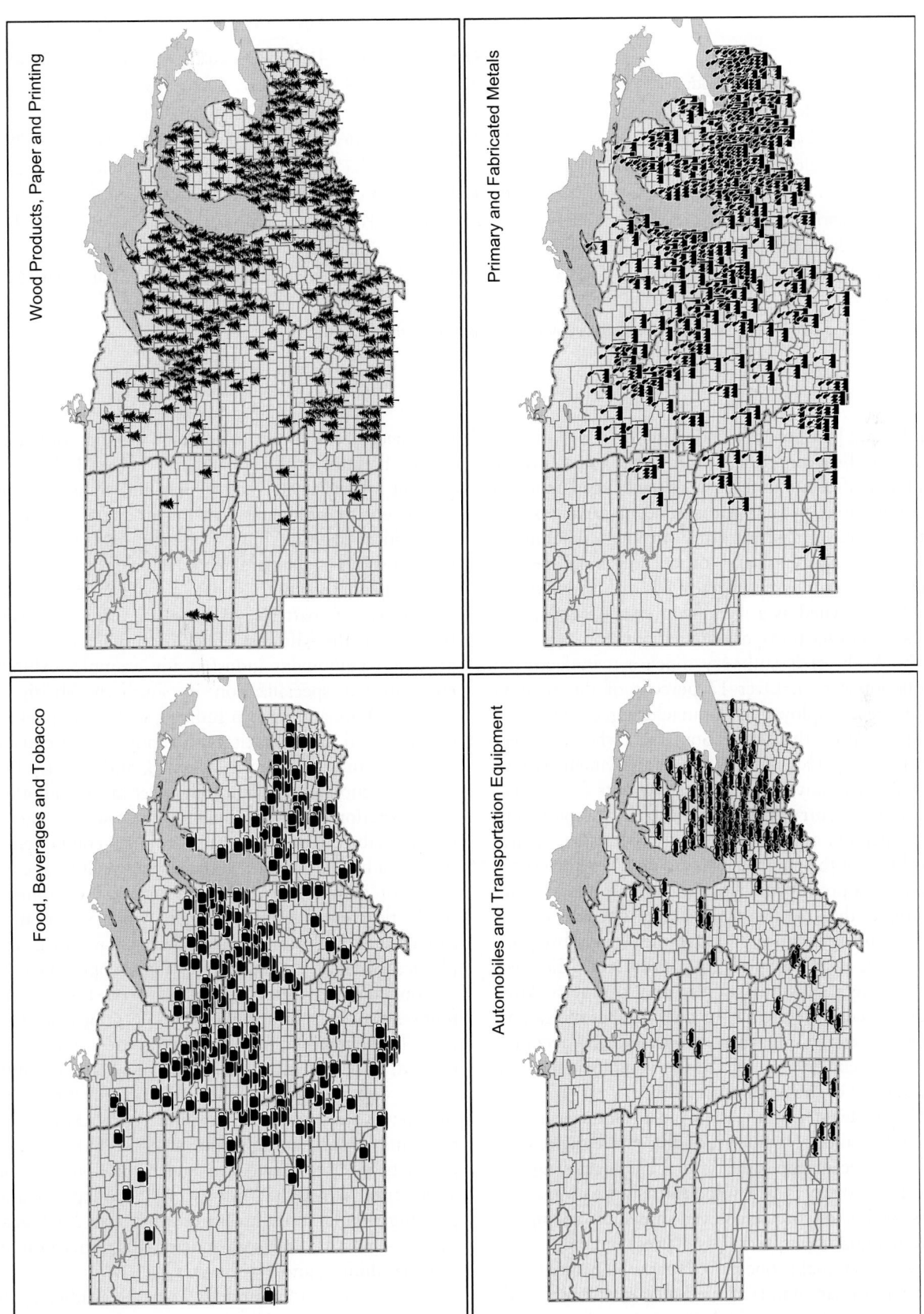

Wood Products, Paper and Printing

Primary and Fabricated Metals

Food, Beverages and Tobacco

Automobiles and Transportation Equipment

Key manufacturing industries by county. Prepared by Andrew Krmenec. *Source:* U.S. Bureau of the Census, *2001 County Business Patterns.*

Table 1. Proportion of Counties Specializing in Manufacturing and Specific Manufacturing Sectors, by State

	IL	IN	IA	KS	MI	MN	MO	NE	ND	OH	SD	WI
Manufacturing	40.2	**71.7**	**51.5**	25.5	**53.0**	41.4	38.3	20.2	8.3	**69.3**	16.7	**65.3**
Food, Beverage & Tobacco Products	11.8	17.4	25.3	8.8	10.8	29.9	9.6	16.7	8.3	22.7	6.7	44.4
Textiles, Apparel & Leather Products	1.0	3.3	1.0	1.0	2.4	1.1	5.2	0.0	0.0	6.8	0.0	5.6
Wood Products, Paper & Printing	19.6	44.6	12.1	12.7	44.6	34.5	33.0	2.4	0.0	38.6	6.7	**79.2**
Petroleum, Chemical Products & Plastics	15.7	41.3	12.1	7.8	32.5	13.8	9.6	4.8	0.0	**56.8**	3.3	26.4
Nonmetal Mineral Products	11.8	19.6	12.1	2.0	13.3	12.6	13.0	2.4	0.0	37.5	1.7	6.9
Primary & Fabricated Metals	26.5	47.8	25.3	12.7	49.4	25.3	16.5	7.1	0.0	**67.0**	6.7	47.2
Automobiles & Transportation Equipment	2.0	31.5	5.1	6.9	37.3	2.3	7.8	0.0	0.0	29.5	0.0	8.3
Machinery, Computer Products & Appliances	25.5	45.7	23.2	22.5	**65.1**	34.5	12.2	10.7	4.2	**50.0**	10.0	**51.4**

Source: 2001 County Business Patterns series produced by the U.S. Bureau of the Census.

food for the long journey, and basic tools for building a home and carving a living out of the tough prairie soil. Later, after homesteads were established, many of the same cities became the source of carriages and farm wagons, furniture, tool-making machinery, ready-made clothing, and other household refinements. By the time of Ford and Olds, the Midwest was already renowned as a manufacturer of wagons, carriages, and other transportation equipment.

The Midwest is still very much a manufacturing production center. Over 17 percent of the region's workforce is employed in manufacturing, compared to 13.8 percent for the United States as a whole. Indeed, with just 24 percent of the total employment base of the U.S. economy, the Midwest accounts for 31 percent of the country's total manufacturing employment and 31 percent of manufacturing output value. Nearly two-thirds of the counties making up the Midwest region have a proportionate labor force in manufacturing greater than the national average. The bulk of that manufacturing is concentrated in the older, more populous parts of the region, from Ohio and Michigan west through Missouri, Iowa, and southern Minnesota. Except for the far western reaches of Kansas, Nebraska, and the Dakotas, manufacturing accounts for 10 percent or more of the total employment base across much of the Midwest.

The Midwest manufactures practically everything. All totaled, about 50 percent of all counties across the Midwest specialize in some form of manufacturing (see table 1). A county is said to specialize if the proportion of its total labor force employed in manufacturing, or some manufacturing sector, is at least one and a half times the national proportion. Nearly 30 percent specialize in primary and fabricated metals; durable goods (equipment, computer products, and appliances); or wood products, paper, and printing. Roughly 20 per-

cent specialize in food and beverage products or petroleum, chemical products, and plastics. And about 10 percent specialize in automobiles and transportation equipment or nonmetal mineral products. The only sector for which the Midwest has no notable specialization is textiles and apparel manufacturing.

The geography of these data reveal a more complex and intricate pattern of manufacturing industry throughout the Midwest. The automobile and transportation equipment industry, for example, exhibits concentrated specialization in southern Michigan, western Ohio, and eastern Indiana, with small pockets of additional specialization occurring in Wisconsin, Illinois, Minnesota, Iowa, Missouri, and Kansas. Because automobiles, agricultural power units, and other transportation equipment incorporate a wide range of plastic, fabricated metal, and rubber components, there is a high degree of similarity between the geography of automobile and transportation equipment production and the geographies of primary and fabricated metals and of petroleum/chemical products and plastics. Similarly, there is an obvious geographic correspondence between these latter two industries and midwestern specialization in durable goods production. These regional industrial complexes, as they are termed, arise as the rational consequence of automotive or durable-goods-producing firms locating near suppliers so as to minimize input costs. For much the same reason, specialization in food and beverage products is concentrated in and around the prime agricultural belt of the Midwest, and wood, paper, and printing amidst the forests of northern Michigan, Wisconsin, and Minnesota and across southern Ohio, Indiana, Illinois, and Missouri.

The key to understanding how the Midwest has maintained its prominence in manufacturing after decades of south- and southwestward population redistribution within the United States and the more recent globalization of world markets lies in the notion of competitive advantage. Other than its rich and highly productive soils, the Midwest boasts only modest endowments of natural resources, many of which were initially developed a century ago and are now largely exhausted. Its rivers are generally too slow for the generation of cheap hydroelectric power, and its labor supply, though ample, is no cheaper than might be found anywhere else in the United States.

The one advantage the Midwest boasts that cannot be exhausted or duplicated is its geographic centrality. Simply put, the Midwest is closer to all other parts of the United States than any other region. The Great Lakes–St. Lawrence Seaway gives access to Canada, the Atlantic Seaboard, and the rest of the world; the Ohio, Mississippi, and Missouri Rivers, to the Caribbean; and the nation's vast network of rail and interstate highways, to all points between the East and West Coasts. No other region within North America can guarantee as much connectivity to continental and global markets through low-cost transportation systems as the Midwest.

Sources and Further Reading: Edgar S. Dunn, Jr., *The Development of the U.S. Urban System*, vol. 1, *Concepts, Structures, Regional Shifts* (1980); John C. Hudson, *Making the Corn Belt* (1994); Philip R. Israilevich, Kenneth N. Kuttner, and Robert H. Schnorbus, "Tracking Midwest Manufacturing and Productivity Growth," *Economic Perspectives* 17 (Sept./Oct. 1993); Thomas H. Klier, "Spatial Concentration in the U.S. Auto Supplier Industry," *Review of Regional Studies* 29 (Winter 1999); D. C. Knudsen, "Manufacturing Employment Change in the American Midwest, 1977–86," *Environment and Planning A* 24 (Sept. 1992); John Rees, Geoffrey Hewings, and Howard Stafford, eds., *Industrial Location and Regional Systems* (1981); James M. Rubenstein, *Making and Selling Cars* (2001).

Andrew Krmenec
Northern Illinois University

Primary Extractive Industries

In many parts of the Midwest, primary extraction industries encouraged European American settlement and played an important role in the overall economic development of the region. The Great Lakes area was economically more important in the American fur trade than any other region. From 1790 to the War of 1812, the center of the fur trade lay east of the Mississippi River and north of the Ohio River. The region contained hundreds of trading posts where Native Americans bartered deerskins and beaver, muskrat, raccoon, and other pelts for alcohol, firearms, tools,

woolen blankets, ornaments, and other manufactured goods. In 1808, John Jacob Astor started the American Fur Company, which established posts in many of the river valleys of Michigan, Wisconsin, Minnesota, and northern Illinois. Besides furs, the company dealt in minerals, "Indian sugar," products of the fisheries, and real estate; it likewise manufactured trade goods and furnished transportation facilities and mail service.

During the mid 1830s, raccoon replaced beaver as the dominant fur in the American trade. Raccoon exports to England more than doubled during the 1830s, and U.S. furriers used substantial numbers of raccoon pelts. The raccoon was trapped in significant numbers only north of the Ohio River.

In 1840, the Midwest produced an estimated $515,000 worth of furs, or roughly 50 percent of the total U.S. fur exports. By the early 1840s, most of the large fur companies had noticeably reduced their operations or curtailed them altogether. Farmers and other permanent settlers who trapped in their spare time replaced them. The value of raccoon exports almost doubled from the 1860s to the 1880s. During the 1860s, the United States exported 32,000 mink pelts to Great Britain annually; by the end of the 1880s, this figure had grown almost ten-fold. This led to the domestication of mink and the establishment of mink ranches in the United States in the mid 1870s. Fur farming became prominent around the turn of the twentieth century. Today, the Great Lakes states produce about half the mink—by far the most important furbearer—raised domestically in the United States.

Following the example of earlier French settlers, Americans began to mine lead ore in the 1820s on the Fever River in northwestern Illinois, which with northeastern Iowa and southwestern Wisconsin formed the upper Mississippi Lead District. The mines of the district remained an important source of lead until 1867 and the discovery of lead in southeastern Missouri (part of the Tri-state Mining District of Missouri, Kansas, and Oklahoma). The rich deposits enabled Missouri to become one of the most productive lead-mining regions in the world. For over seventy years, Missouri led the United States in lead production; total output exceeded seventeen million tons valued at $5 billion.

The existence of copper in the Lake Superior region had been suspected as early as the seventeenth century. The first U.S. mining in the region took place in 1844 on the Keweenaw Peninsula. By 1846, a dozen mining companies had commenced more or less active operations. Michigan led U.S. copper production from 1847 until 1887. From 1844 to 1968, when mining ended, the Keweenaw Peninsula produced over eleven billion pounds of copper, more than any other district in history.

The development of the Keweenaw copper mines encouraged the search for other minerals in the Lake Superior region. In 1845, a group of prospectors from Jackson, Michigan, uncovered an outcropping of iron ore on a wooded hill (the present site of Negaunee) in the Marquette Range. Subsequently, mining began on the Marquette Range (1847), the Menominee Range (1870), and the Gogebic Range (1884). The region's remote location far from coal deposits and eastern markets retarded its development, and real growth awaited improvements in transportation. Annual production peaked in 1918, when Michigan produced over eighteen million tons of iron ore.

Meanwhile, mining of iron ore began in the Lake Superior region of Minnesota on the Vermilion Range (1882), the Mesabi Range (1890), and the Cuyanna Range (1911). The Mesabi Range proved to be the richest, the largest, and the most productive. Its output mounted until it produced nearly 85 percent of the iron ore mined in the United States in 1919. By the end of World War II, mining had exhausted most of the higher-grade deposits, but the iron ranges of Minnesota still contained large deposits of taconite, a hard lower-grade ore with about half the iron of the richer ores. In the mid 1950s, the development of the Davis process made it economically feasible to exploit these lower-grade deposits. In 2002, Minnesota's iron mines produced an estimated thirty-five million tons of iron ore.

The Midwest contains parts of two coalfields. Mining of coal began in Ohio (1804), followed by Indiana (1811), Illinois (1810), Missouri (1817), and Iowa (1839). Illinois has the third-largest total coal resources (and the largest bituminous coal resources) in the United States. The first coal mining in the state apparently occurred in 1810 along the Muddy River in Jackson County. The first production reports are for 1833, when the state produced 6,000 tons of coal. The total grew to almost 17,000 tons in 1840. After 1840, the extension of railroads throughout much of the United States greatly stimulated the mining of coal not only in Illinois but in the rest of the Midwest. In 1850, Illinois produced 300,000 tons of coal. Thirty years later, the figure had grown to over 6.1 million tons. In 1947, the state's coal output reached 68 million tons and Illinois ranked fourth in the United States. Chicago was the world's largest coal market. Currently, Illinois produces about 40 million tons of coal annually.

The lake states contained the only large commercial stands of pine in the upper Midwest and formed a natural lumber region. Lumbering began first in Michigan, which was ideally situated for supplying parts of the eastern market. The spread of lumbering into Wisconsin and Minnesota corresponded with the increasing settlement of the prairie states.

In 1850, Michigan already ranked fifth in the nation in lumber production. By 1856, lake-state lumber had transformed Chicago into the primary wholesale lumber center in the United States. The mass attack on the lake-state forests, however, began after the Civil War. Between 1869 and 1879, lake-state lumber output jumped 75 percent, from 3.6 billion to 6.3 billion board feet. Between 1869 and 1899, the lake states were the primary source of lumber in the nation. By 1899, production in the region had declined to 8.7 billion board feet. Wisconsin, however, led the nation in lumber production between 1899 and 1905. Thereafter, lumber production declined rapidly. In 1926, the three states produced only 2,047 million board feet of lumber while they consumed 3,721 million board feet. Lumbering nevertheless remained important in some parts of the region, and the lake states became major producers of pulpwood.

Sources and Further Reading: Lew A. Chase, "Michigan Copper Mines," *Michigan History* 24 (Oct. 1945); James L. Clayton, "The Growth and Economic Significance of the American Fur Trade, 1790–1890," in *Aspects of the Fur Trade* (1967); Howard N. Eavenson, *The First Century and a Quarter of American Coal Industry* (1942); William B. Gates, *Michigan Copper and Boston Dollars* (1951); Orin G. Libby, "An Economic and Social Study of the Lead Region in Iowa, Illinois, and Wisconsin," *Transactions of the Wisconsin Academy of Sciences, Arts and Letters* 13 (1901); Howard N. Sloane and Lucille L. Sloane, *A Pictorial History of American Mining* (1970); David A. Walker, *Iron Frontier* (1979); Michael Williams, *Americans and Their Forests* (1989).

Randall Rohe
University of Wisconsin–Waukesha

Rectangular Public Land Survey System

An invisible rectangular net—a system of lines and points or corner monuments—covers almost two-thirds of the coterminous United States. The lines and points comprising the net were established by surveyors working under contract with the national government. They played an essential role in the European American settlement of the United States after 1785, when the Continental Congress adopted an ordinance that would privatize the land it already owned and any it would subsequently acquire.

Designed to be quickly and inexpensively prosecuted, the surveys fulfilled two purposes. They provided necessary legal descriptions, defining the boundaries of parcels of land that could be owned as well as their location, and provided all prospective landowners with essential information.

The surveys were merely part of the process

through which the federal government created private landowners: first, by acquiring jurisdiction over an area through armed conflict and treaties with foreign nations; then, by acquiring title to the land surface from American Indian bands; next, by creating parcels of land that could be conveniently owned; and, finally, by conveying title of those parcels to individuals, corporations, and states. The surveys effectively marked the start of European American occupation of the land surface.

Until 1855, when *A Manual of Instructions to Regulate Field Operations of Deputy Surveyors* was published, the surveys were under the control of surveyors general who possessed considerable independence. Under a surveyor general's supervision, deputies ran north-south and east-west lines that intersected at right angles, placing monuments in the ground, usually posts or stones, every half mile and dividing the land surface into a hierarchy of rectangles. The largest rectangle was a township thirty-six square miles in area, defined by four township corners, six miles apart, connected by township lines or exteriors. Section corners, spaced at one-mile intervals and connected by lines one mile apart, subdivided each township into thirty-six sections, each 640 acres in size. The deputies also placed quarter-section monuments halfway between each section corner without running lines between them. As they worked, the surveyors recorded what they did in field notes. They also recorded the character of the land surface, information considered impor-

tant to prospective landowners. Thus, they created a database, a systematic inventory of monuments, lines, plant cover, soil, topographic features, and human activities of the land surface they surveyed.

In the surveyor general's office, draftsmen compiled plats of every township depicting what each deputy did and saw. In addition, they drew lines connecting the quarter-section corners that had been set, creating four quarter-sections, and added lines to create four quarter-quarter sections of forty acres in each quarter-section.

For a variety of reasons, the deputies could not make the net completely rectangular. Water bodies interrupted their lines, requiring them to set "meander corners" where the lines intersected the water and creating parcels called government lots that were often less than forty acres. Similarly, Indian reservation boundaries and the boundaries between states created government lots as the public-land survey lines ended, or closed, where they intersected them.

Even without these "surface irregularities," intersecting north-south and east-west lines could not produce a completely rectangular grid because the Earth's surface is curved. Each east-west line is really a chord of an arc, a problem that was never addressed by the surveying practice described here. All north-south lines converge at the poles, a problem that was addressed in the following manner. East-west lines, called correction lines, were run at specific distances from each other. These lines were run before town-

---

❖ **Mapping the Midwest and the Land Ordinance of 1785**

Passed by Congress, the Land Ordinance of 1785 established a checkerboard of straight lines on the North American landscape west and north of the Ohio River.

An Ordinance for ascertaining the mode of disposing of Lands in the Western Territory.

BE it ordained by the United States in Congress assembled, that the territory ceded by individual States to the United States, which has been purchased of the Indian inhabitants, shall be disposed of in the following manner:

The first line, running due north and south as aforesaid, shall begin on the river Ohio, north from the western termination of a line, which has been run as the southern boundary of the State of Pennsylvania; and the first line, running east and west, shall begin at the same point, and shall extend throughout the whole territory. Provided, that nothing herein shall be construed, as fixing the western boundary of the State of Pennsylvania. The geographer shall designate the townships, or fractional parts of townships, by numbers progressively from south to north; always beginning each range with No. 1; and the ranges shall be distinguished by their progressive numbers to the westward. The first range, extending from the Ohio to the lake Erie, marked No. 1. The Geographer shall personally attend to the running of the first east and west line; and shall take the latitude of the extremes of the first north and south line, and of the mouths of the principal rivers.

. . . The plats of the townships respectively, shall be marked by subdivisions into lots of one mile square, or 640 acres, in the same direction as the external lines, and numbered from 1 to 36; always beginning the succeeding range of the lots with the number next to that with which the preceding one concluded.

Source: J. C. Fitzpatrick, ed., "Land Ordinance of 1785, May 20, 1785," in *Journals of the Continental Congress*, vol. 28 (1904–).

ship exteriors, although they were subsequently used as such. Along these lines, township corners that would govern the township lines to the north were established "correctly" at six-mile intervals. In 1851, correction lines became standard parallels, east-west lines that were run every four or five townships (twenty-four or thirty miles apart). In addition, to ensure greater surveying accuracy, guide meridians (north-south lines spaced four townships, or twenty-four miles, apart) were run and subsequently used as township exteriors.

Each surveyed township was defined with reference to the intersection of two lines that were independently established and later used as township borders. Each was simultaneously part of a row of townships lying either north or south of a baseline—an east-west line—and part of a column of townships (called ranges, following the earliest surveying practice in what is now Ohio) lying either east or west of a principal meridian—a north-south line. "Township 101 North Range 32 West of the Fifth Principal Meridian" is located at 100 township, 600 miles, north of its reference baseline, and thirty-one ranges, 186 miles, west of the fifth principal meridian.

Each subdivision in a township was defined by its location in the hierarchy of rectangles created by the lines and corners; where the section was located in the township, from one to thirty-six; where the quarter-section lay in the section (e.g., the northeast quarter); and, finally, where the quarter quarter-section lay in the quarter-section (e.g., the northeast quarter of the northeast quarter). A complete legal description of a forty-acre parcel was "the south-west quarter of the south-west quarter of Section 1 Township 101 North Range 32 West of the Fifth Principal Meridian." Government lots were defined by a unique number within a section, thus "Lot 1, Section 1."

This reference system allowed townships to be surveyed and subdivided easily, quickly, and relatively precisely in large parts of the United States. As important, the monuments set by the deputies are the corners used today even though they may have been erroneously located in the first place or lost, moved, or stolen since they were set. Thus the survey net continues to function as a dominant organizer of space, providing the essential references for the boundaries that separate not only landowners but units of government.

Sources and Further Reading: Bureau of Land Management, *Manual of Instructions for the Survey of the Public Lands of the United States* (1973); Hildegard Binder Johnson, *Order upon the Land* (1976); Andro Linklater, *Measuring America* (2002); William D. Pattison, *Beginnings of the American Rectangular Land Survey System, 1784–1800* (1964); Lowell O. Stewart, *Public Land Surveys, History, Instructions, Methods* (1935); C. Albert White, *A History of the Rectangular Land Survey* (1983).

Roderick H. Squires
Philip J. Gersmehl
University of Minnesota–Twin Cities

Transportation

Transportation development began in earnest with the post–Revolutionary War settlement of the Ohio Country. As increasing numbers of Americans moved into the region, eastern entrepreneurs realized that the cities that captured the bulk of the Ohio River Valley trade would prosper at the expense of their competitors.

Between 1818 and the early 1850s, three major transport modes (road, canal, and railroad) crossed the Appalachians. The National Road was the first, connecting Baltimore to the Ohio River settlement at Wheeling by 1818. Although the National Road marked an improvement over earlier migration paths and generated passenger travel and regular stagecoach service, the road remained a relatively high-cost route with little commercial viability. It was still cheaper to ship grain downstream on the Ohio and Mississippi Rivers to New Orleans and thence by sailing vessel to Atlantic ports.

The National Road nevertheless gave Baltimore a perceived early advantage over its rivals and stimulated efforts in New York and Philadelphia to develop their own trans-Appalachian penetration lines in the form of canals. The completion of the Erie Canal between the Hudson River and Lake Erie in 1825 was one of the most significant events in U.S. transportation history because it created a low-cost transport linkage between the Great Lakes and New York City. The Erie Canal sparked a canal-building boom in the Midwest between 1830 and 1845. By 1845, a full-fledged canal network had emerged in Ohio. The Ohio and Erie Canal, completed in 1833, connected Cleveland to Portsmouth and was the first major connection between the Great Lakes and the Ohio River. This canal offered farmers a low-cost access to both the Great Lakes–Erie Canal system and the Ohio-Mississippi system. By 1835, the Miami and Erie Canal had been completed from Cincinnati north to Dayton. The ultimate goal of this canal was to reach Lake Erie via the Maumee River and Toledo, which it did in 1843. In Indiana, the Wabash and Erie Canal connected Toledo on Lake Erie to Lafayette on the Wabash River when it was completed in 1843. Farther west, the opening of the Illinois-Michigan Canal in 1848 linked Chicago to LaSalle, Illinois.

During this time, the National Road was extended from Wheeling to Columbus and added Zane's Trace, an extension from Zanesville to the Ohio River port of Maysville, Kentucky. With the goal of reaching the Mississippi, the National Road reached Indianapolis by 1845 and Vandalia, Illinois, by 1850. However, the National Road could not compete for freight with the expanded and lower-cost canal and river networks. By 1850, competition from railroads led, for all practical purposes, to the abandonment of the road.

The change in transport accessibility achieved between the completion of the Erie Canal in 1825 and the additional canal interconnections accomplished by 1850 significantly altered the pattern of commercial trade in the Midwest. In 1835, 78 percent of the grain exported from this region moved down the Ohio River. By 1839, the Great Lakes–Erie Canal system accounted for 51 percent of the grain traffic, and by 1850, more than 66 percent of grain shipments flowed along the Great Lakes-Erie Canal route.

The canal boom came to a screeching halt with the rise of the railroad. Locally promoted lines in Ohio were developed in the early 1850s in the Cincinnati, Cleveland, and Sandusky areas but functioned primarily as adjuncts to the waterways, serving mainly to tap the hinterlands of these river and lake ports. In fact when trans-Appalachian lines entered the Midwest in 1853 there were twenty-two railroads in operation in Ohio, with the longest extending from Sandusky to Cincinnati. Another significant early rail link had been constructed from Detroit to New Buffalo, Michigan, just across the lake from Chicago.

In spite of some impressive beginnings in Ohio, the Midwest had not completed a comprehensive system of transport linkages prior to the coming of the railroad. However, once the railroad arrived, the effect was rapid and general. Almost immediately long-distance travel shifted to the railroads. Road-building projects reverted to a localized role, providing access to railroads and existing waterways.

The overall economic development of the Midwest was spurred on by the improved transport made possible by the railroad. The unmatched speed of the railroad quickly enabled it to replace the canal-road network. Travel times were reduced from weeks to days—even hours in some cases. The shipment of agricultural goods became more profitable, and the U.S. heartland took more definite form. Agricultural expansion was followed by massive industrial development. Once the railroads breached the Appalachians, they spread rapidly across the Midwest; trackage more than tripled from less than ten thousand miles to over thirty thousand miles between 1850 and 1860. By 1860, the process of interconnection was well underway, and by 1890, complete interconnection had cre-

ated a dense network in the regional core of Ohio, Indiana, and Illinois. Chicago became the focus for virtually all railroads (figure 2). Although rail dominance was conspicuous by the end of the nineteenth century, low-cost water transport had not vanished. The Great Lakes shipping lines had steadily increased tonnage as a result of the movement of iron ore, coal, and the heavy industry of the Midwest.

The popularity of automobiles in the early twentieth century led to an emphasis on highways. Once begun, highway transportation developed rapidly and became a serious competitor to the railroads. Federal grants provided funds for states to build roads linking major cities (Chicago-Cleveland-Buffalo-New York; Chicago-Ft.Wayne-Pittsburgh-Philadelphia-New York). Better-connected and higher-quality routes allowed for the expansion of truck transport, and by the end of the 1920s, truck transportation was well-established as a major competitor to the railroads. Following World War II, the railroads lost ground on all fronts. In the 1950s, there were more than a hundred class 1 railroads in the Midwest. (Railroads in North America are classified as class 1, class 2, and class 3 in terms of annual operating revenue. The exact revenues required to be in a particular class have varied through the years as they are adjusted for inflation. Class 1 is the highest.) By the 1990s, only sixteen remained. The airlines had taken over the long-haul passenger business, and the private automobile accounted for the overwhelming majority of short- and medium-haul travel. Trucks had extended their range for general merchandise from short- to medium- and even long-haul delivery. Great Lakes bulk carriers continued to be important, and low-cost barge tows along the waterways also provided strong competition to the railroads for bulk commodities. The public demand, however, was for more and better highways.

Shortly after the end of World War II, several limited-access highway linkages were superimposed on the existing midwestern highway network. State tollway commissions in Indiana and Ohio were formed, and it became possible to travel from New York to Chicago via divided expressways. Plans for building additional toll roads were dropped in 1956 when the massive Interstate Highway System was unveiled by the Eisenhower administration. The system provided a national network of high-priority linkage between major metropolitan areas. Because the Midwest was well established as the dominant core region of the United States and as the location of several major cities, it was well represented by new interstate connections. Ohio alone has six interstate highways.

Winners and losers are to be found in the wake of nearly every transport development. Twentieth-century transportation improvements have reduced the competitive position of the Midwest. Firms today are less tied to the concentration of manufacturing centers that developed around the original transport-dependent heavy industrial bases of the region. The significant changes that have taken place in the speed and flexibility of transportation permit companies to evaluate alternate locations that may provide lower total costs and nicer year-round climates for their productive processes. As a result, the South and the West have become increasingly attractive, as have offshore locations.

The Midwest nonetheless remains a powerful economic region, well positioned to take advantage of the technological changes of the twenty-first century. It retains considerable entrepreneurial talent, a good array of support services, and good regional, national, and international accessibility provided by the combination of water, rail, interstate highway, and commercial airline networks.

Sources and Further Reading: Association of American Railroads, *Railroads of the United States* (1970); William Cronon, *Nature's Metropolis* (1991); John Oliver, *History of American Technology* (1956); Edward Taaffe, Howard Gauthier, and Morton O'Kelly, *Geography of Transportation* (1996); James Vance, Jr., *Capturing the Horizon* (1986).

William V. Ackerman
The Ohio State University–Lima

Urbanization

Urbanization is the process whereby a society is transformed from an essentially rural one to a predominantly urban one. Its most visible expression on the landscape is the growth of cities and an increase in their number, size, and areal extent. The key to the early growth of midwestern cities was the size and richness of the agricultural resource base. Settlement of rich agricultural lands beginning in the 1790s was followed by commercial trade and, shortly thereafter, by the beginnings of industrial production.

Throughout the evolution of the present pattern of Midwest urbanization, two factors—great migrations and major changes in transportation technology—have exercised major influences on the location of metropolitan areas. The concept of "initial advantage" is also helpful in explaining the geographic pattern of urban centers. Once located at an advantageous site, often based on water transport and accessibility to a rich agricultural hinterland, the earliest cities became magnets for new investment.

Urbanization in the Midwest is a recent historical phenomenon. As late as 1830, all of the major metropolitan areas of forty thousand or more inhabitants with the exception of Pittsburgh were east of the Appalachians or in western New York. Although the area of continuous settlement was spreading westward toward the Mississippi River, an effective network of transportation lagged behind this migration. Between 1790 and 1830, Cincinnati and St. Louis emerged as important centers of commerce, each with the initial advantage of proximity to water transportation.

Between 1830 and 1870, major cities began to appear in the Midwest and urban growth in this U.S. subregion accounted for most of the city growth in the nation. Canal development opened the area to increased settlement and advanced commercialization, but it was the coming of the railroad that brought profound changes and rapid urban expansion. A series of regional networks developed, the larger ones converging at critical port locations on the inland waterways that penetrated the vast agricultural land resources of the region.

By 1870, a number of new cities had appeared while existing places continued to expand, including Cleveland, Toledo, Columbus, Springfield, Dayton, and Cincinnati in Ohio; Ft. Wayne, Indianapolis, Lafayette, Terre Haute, and Evansville in Indiana; Detroit, Lansing, Jackson, and Grand Rapids in Michigan; Milwaukee in Wisconsin; and Minneapolis and St. Paul in Minnesota. In addition to Chicago, Illinois had Rock Island, Peoria, Bloomington, and Springfield. The Mississippi River cities of Burlington, Iowa, and Quincy, Illinois, developed, and St. Louis experienced additional growth. Along the Missouri River system, Omaha, Nebraska, St. Joseph, Missouri, and Kansas City, Missouri, had appeared.

These cities laid the metropolitan base for an important part of the market-oriented industrial growth that occurred in that region between 1870 and 1920. Certainly the historical-geographic significance of the Great Lakes, rivers, and canals was very important. Centers that developed along these routes gained an initial advantage that attracted rail connections and served to enhance their early beginnings. The paramount importance of initial rail and terminal-facility advantages to urban-industrial growth is perhaps best exemplified by Chicago. In 1830, Chicago had a population of fewer than 5,000 inhabitants. By 1860, the population had grown to 112,172 and "the city was the nation's most important railroad center, a terminus for eleven trunk roads and twenty branch and feeder lines."

The period from 1870 to 1920 witnessed a rapid expansion of rail transportation that spurred additional urban growth and development in the Midwest. Many of the new urban centers reflected the opening or commercialization of agricultural land resources.

Thus growth occurred in communities along the Missouri River and their accessible hinterlands with notable development at Sioux City, Iowa; Omaha-Lincoln, Nebraska; Leavenworth, Kansas City, Topeka, and Wichita, Kansas; and St. Joseph, Joplin, and Springfield, Missouri. Also, previously settled areas of the Midwest experienced significant additional growth based on a boom in industrialization resulting from the increasing scale of manufacturing, the rise of the steel and auto industries, and the introduction of steel rails that enabled trains to travel faster and to carry heavier loads. Important industrial boom cities of this period included Youngstown, Akron, Canton, Steubenville, Lorain-Elyria, Lima, and Portsmouth in Ohio. Michigan experienced urban growth at Flint, Saginaw-Bay City, Muskegon, Kalamazoo, and Battle Creek. In Minnesota, both Duluth and Superior gained prominence, and in Wisconsin, Green Bay and Madison joined Milwaukee as important centers. Other development resulted from industrial growth based on the forest resources along the frontiers of the agricultural Midwest.

By 1920, the present pattern of settlement was well established in the Midwest, and subsequent metropolitan change had taken place within that pattern. The period from 1920 to 1970 has been aptly named by John R. Borchert as the "auto-air-amenity epoch." A key element was the shift in the main source of energy from steam power to the internal combustion engine. This led to the decline of coal and railroad centers but simultaneously stimulated the automotive industry in southern Michigan.

Following World War II, the increasing shift away from rail to automobile and truck transportation, as well as the development of a dense highway network, combined with the increasing importance of amenities (nicer climate, better access to recreation) to affect many cities negatively. The Midwest core lost some of its competitive locational advantage. Highway and air patterns were and are considerably less concentrated on the Midwest core than was the rail pattern. Lower real costs of transportation have led industries to become more "footloose"; that is, more able to consider alternative locations based on low labor costs, low taxes, cheaper land, and high amenity values. In all of these, the South and the West have advantages over the Midwest, and the metropolitan areas of the Sunbelt are particularly attractive to labor-intensive manufacturing and to the high-growth, high-tech sectors of electronics, aerospace, and petrochemicals. Thus in many midwestern industrial communities the benefits of initial advantage and agglomeration economies have been outweighed by agglomeration diseconomies (higher costs resulting from congestion, pollution, and higher labor costs and land prices), the relatively low

productivity of dated machinery, and lack of amenities. Although the urban pattern has remained unchanged, the overall economic health of the cities has been weakened.

Most cities in the Midwest were dealt an additional economic blow by the deindustrialization of the 1970s and early 1980s. Industries already weakened by a declining economy and rising inflation now faced increasing market penetration from Japanese and European industries and strong competition from a number of newly industrialized countries. Manufacturing, the economic sector most important to the Midwest (which contained the lion's share of U.S. industrial activity), was hardest hit by deindustrialization. This sector, already suffering from the regional decentralization described above, experienced accelerated decline. The postindustrial economy based on information management, computer technologies, global communications, and intercontinental travel favored globally oriented gateway metropolises along the Pacific and Atlantic coasts.

Despite changing economic conditions, the midwestern urban system has demonstrated a surprising degree of resiliency. Although employment in manufacturing (smokestack heavy industry) has declined, the geographic pattern of urban places developed early in the 1900s demonstrates substantial inertia. Midwestern cities are adapting to the requirements of the new global order (information-based, high-tech economic activities). Between 1976 and 1986, ten midwestern cities increased their share of job growth in business and professional services at rates greater than the national average. The Midwest remains a significant part of the economy of the United States, and the existing urban system benefits from a strong entrepreneurial base; good accessibility to regional, national, and global markets; a productive labor force; and a commitment to meet the demands of a postindustrial economy. The challenge, however, remains great. Between 1990 and 2000, of the fifty fastest-growing metropolitan areas in the United States, only two—Lawrence, Kansas (ranked 34th) and Sioux Falls, South Dakota (46th)—were in the Midwest.

Sources and Further Reading: John R. Borchert, "American Metropolitan Evolution," *Geographical Review* 57 (July 1967); John R. Borchert, "America's Changing Metropolitan Regions," *Annals of the Association of American Geographers* 62 (June 1972); Breandán Ó hUallacháin and Neil Reid, "The Location and Growth of Business and Professional Services in American Metropolitan Areas, 1976–1986," *Annals of the Association of American Geographers* 81 (June 1991); Paul Knox, *Urbanization: An Introduction to Urban Geography* (1994); John J. Macionis and Vincent N. Parrillo, *Cities and Urban Life* (1998); Alan Pred, "Industrialization, Initial Advantage, and American Metropolitan Growth," *Geographical*

Review 55 (Apr. 1965); Edward J. Taaffe, Howard Gauthier, and Morton O'Kelly, *Geography of Transportation* (1996); Maurice Yeates and Barry Garner, *The North American City* (1980).

William V. Ackerman
The Ohio State University–Lima

Notable Physical Regions

Des Moines Lobe

The action of glaciers imprinted a distinct character on the midwestern landscape. The Des Moines Lobe region of north-central Iowa displays topography and earth materials from one of the final surges of ice to protrude southward from a massive ice sheet that lay across parts of North America during the Wisconsin episode of geologic time. The Des Moines Lobe region is named for Iowa's capital city, which now stands at the southern limit of this former glacial advance.

Geologic materials underlying the Des Moines Lobe include layers of pebbly clay, erratic boulders not native to Iowa, water-sorted sand and gravel, fibrous black peat, and even occasional bones and teeth of a now-extinct fauna that included mammoths and mastodons. Pieced together, these deposits reveal a dynamic story of glacial ice pushing into Iowa about fifteen thousand years ago, surging southward even as the climate warmed, urged by changing dynamics within the main ice sheet farther north, and with a thin profile of perhaps only two or three hundred feet of ice thickness as it slid along the preferred path of a preexisting lowland, lubricated by abundant meltwater beneath the ice.

The nature of the glacier's advance was to surge and stagnate, readvance and stagnate again. The southernmost Bemis advance reached the present location of Des Moines 14,000 years ago, leaving tell-tale ridges and irregular knobs, especially along its compressed lateral margins. Successive advances did not reach as far south, but they, too, left distinct bands of glacial debris marking the Altamont Moraine 13,500 years ago and the Algona Moraine 12,500 years ago. By 12,000 years ago, glacial forays into Iowa ceased, though enormous volumes of meltwater continued to pour down river valleys, draining the lobe and its parent glacier to the north. Many of the broad spans of today's valleys obtained their width at this time.

Today, relatively level, undissected terrain sets the youthful Des Moines Lobe region apart from the older, more rolling, and better-drained terrain across the rest of Iowa. The region is crossed by prominent crescent-shaped bands of ridges and knobby hills (moraines), which mark the former positions of major ice advances. The landscape includes other features that formed in direct contact with slowly melting, debris-rich stagnant ice, including kames, kettles, eskers, and outwash plains. Clusters of natural lakes, the flats of former lake beds, and wetland bogs and marshes—many linked along former meltwater routes within and beneath the decaying ice—add to the classic appearance of these freshly glaciated landscapes.

Although the expanses of low-relief landscapes are squared off by fences and section-line roads into fields of intensively cultivated agricultural land, the Des Moines Lobe's terrain and earth materials still retain the appearance of direct contact with the Midwest's defining glacial heritage.

Sources and Further Reading: Carrie J. Patterson, "Laurentide Glacial Landscapes," *Geology* 26 (July 1998); Jean C. Prior, *Landforms of Iowa* (1991).

Jean Cutler Prior
Iowa Geological Survey
Iowa Department of Natural Resources

Door Peninsula

The Door Peninsula is located on the eastern side of Wisconsin. Lake Michigan is on its eastern shore and Green Bay is on its western shore. The peninsula is about 80 miles long and 25 miles wide at its base. Its 250 miles of coastline consist of sandy beaches, stony beaches, limestone cliffs, islands, and bays.

Like the majority of the state of Wisconsin, the Door Peninsula was shaped in part by glaciation, and much of its area is covered by glacial till. However, the Niagara Cuesta has had an even greater influence on the physical geography of the Door Peninsula. The Niagara Cuesta was formed during the Silurian period 425 to 413 million years ago. At that time, the area now known as the Door Peninsula was covered by a large inland sea. A layer of dolomite, a resistant type of limestone, was formed from coral reefs. If not for the resistant limestone, the Door Peninsula might have been completely eroded away by glaciers. Over time, the layer of dolomite was uplifted and eroded. The result of this formation is a steep escarpment along the western coast of the peninsula and a gentle eastern slope that continues into Lake Michigan. Local relief of the western limestone cliffs varies from one hundred to two hundred feet. The Niagara Escarpment is higher and steeper north of the city of Sturgeon Bay and lower and farther inland south of Sturgeon Bay. Waves and glacial erosion caused the escarpment to be steeper north of Sturgeon Bay. This geologic formation extends far beyond the Door Peninsula to form cliffs on the eastern shore of Lake Winnebago and the escarpment that Niagara Falls flows over.

Management of water quality is the most significant environmental problem that affects the Door Peninsula. The dolomite of the Niagara Cuesta does not provide for much natural filtration of impurities from water. Dolomite does not absorb much water, and cracks in it allow water to flow through quickly. Thin soils over the northern three-fourths of the peninsula do not allow for much filtration either. As the population of the Door Peninsula has grown, managing water quality has become increasingly difficult.

Some of the main economic activities of the Door Peninsula are tourism, fishing, agriculture, and cheese production. The picturesque landscapes of the Niagara Escarpment attract tourists. Commercial and sport fishing are common in the waters surrounding the Door Peninsula. Most harbors are located on the Green Bay side of the peninsula where the slopes are steeper.

Much of the agricultural production of the peninsula consists of fruit crops. Because of Green Bay and Lake Michigan, temperatures in the summer are not as high as inland areas of Wisconsin and winter frost does not occur as soon. The Door Peninsula is famous for cherries, and a large portion of the state's apple crop is grown on the peninsula. Cheese production is most common south of Sturgeon Bay.

Sources and Further Reading: Craig Charles, *Exploring Door County* (1999); J. M. Moran and E. J. Hopkins, *Wisconsin's Weather and Climate* (2002); Gwen Schultz, *Wisconsin's Foundations* (1986); Wisconsin Cartographers' Guild, *Wisconsin's Past and Present* (1998).

Julie Weinert
The Ohio State University–Columbus

Driftless Area

Drift is a broad term that geographers use to refer to sediments that have been carried and deposited by glacial ice or by the water from a melting glacier. Thus, *driftless* refers to the lack of such sediments and implies that the landscape has not been covered by glacial ice. The Driftless Area of the upper Midwest is one such region. Traditionally defined to include parts of southwestern Wisconsin, southeastern Minnesota, northeastern Iowa, and northwestern Illinois, today the Driftless Area covers southwestern Wisconsin, northeastern Illinois, and the very southeast corner of Minnesota.

The Driftless Area originated nearly 2 million years ago during the Pleistocene epoch's numerous advances and retreats of glacial ice. Although the Driftless Area escaped direct ice contact, and at no time was it ever surrounded completely by ice, significant deposits of sediment related to these episodes of glaciation occur in the Driftless Area. Deposits of outwash, sediment derived from glacial melt water, occur in the major river valleys of the Driftless Area. These include the upper Mississippi River and major tributaries that drained the glaciated landscapes that surrounded the area during the Pleistocene. Upland landscapes in the Driftless Area are also blanketed with deposits of fine wind-blown silt known as loess.

Loess Hills, Iowa. Iowa Division of Tourism.

The Driftless Area has also been referred to as the Paleozoic Plateau, reflecting the geologic period in which its bedrock formations originated. These bedrock formations consist primarily of sandstones, capped at the highest elevations by dolomite. The bedrock formations emerged during a time when an inland sea covered a large area of central North America. Millions of years of stream dissection of the Driftless Area resulted in a region characterized by deep, narrow valleys, often referred to as coulees in southwestern Wisconsin. Relief is greatest along the Mississippi River.

The Driftless Area has a continental humid climate regime with an average annual precipitation of thirty to thirty-four inches. The average January temperature for the region is around 15°F, with an average July temperature of about 75°F.

The native vegetation of the Driftless Area consisted of prairie and oak savanna on ridge tops and dry upper slopes, with deciduous hardwood forest on moister slopes. Wet prairies, marshes, and flood-plain forests were also common on river flood plains. A fascinating feature in some of these valleys is steep, boulder slopes of dolomite rock weathered and mass wasted from bluffs during the Pleistocene. Cold air circulates through these rocky algific (cold-producing) slopes creating a microhabitat for Ice Age relict plant species such as northern monkshood and balsam fir, as well as rare terrestrial snails.

Today, the Driftless Area is a landscape of dairy and corn agriculture with small rural communities and moderate-sized regional urban centers.

Sources and Further Reading: Lawrence Martin, *The Physical Geography of Wisconsin*, 3rd ed. (1965); Richard W. Ojakangas and Charles L. Matsch, *Minnesota's Geology* (1982); Jean C. Prior, *Landforms of Iowa* (1991).

Dean Wilder
University of Wisconsin–La Crosse

Flint Hills

The Flint Hills of Kansas, from Marshall County south into the Osage Hills of Oklahoma, comprise the remaining 2 percent of tallgrass prairie that once stretched from Texas to Indiana. In Kansas, the unplowed five million acres of big bluestem, little bluestem, switchgrass, and Indian grass are renowned as steer country. Their high protein and calcium content have an unsurpassed ability to add weight to cattle efficiently, economically, and naturally.

Texas longhorns from the trail-drive era were fattened in the Flint Hills before being sent to eastern markets. After the overland trails closed, cattle, chiefly aged steers, were shipped by train. After World War II, trucks transported cattle, completely taking over the trade by the mid 1960s. A change to pasturing yearlings instead of aged steers occurred at the same time.

Several distinctive features distinguish Flint Hills ranching from ranching in the West. One is the grazing of cattle raised elsewhere and brought in for a summer grazing season that traditionally ran from mid April through mid October. In recent decades, double-stocking, wherein twice the normal number of cattle are pastured for a half season, has become more common.

Another distinctive element is a three-part arrangement among land owners, cattle owners, and custom graziers (or "pasturemen"). The pasturemen lease grass from landowners and sublease it to cattle owners. Each cattle owner is responsible for transporting cattle and paying exceptional nutritional or medical expenses. The land owner is responsible for taxes and major capital improvements. The pastureman is responsible for repairing fences, receiving and caring for cattle, and shipping. He or she doctors sick cattle, provides salt and water, and accounts for each head of livestock.

Another element is a mix of farming and ranching. In much of the ranching West, crop agriculture is possible only through irrigation, but in the Flint Hills, rich bottom lands and an average annual rainfall of over thirty inches support a variety of crops and hay.

The pastureman is also responsible for the colorful practice of spring burning. Kaw and Osage Indians burned the old grass to attract game to the new growth, a practice that cattlemen adopted during the settlement period. Early opposition from agricultural scientists turned into support following experiments, begun in the 1970s at the Konza Prairie Natural Research Area near Manhattan, that proved that the annual burn-off keeps trees and weeds from invading the prairie, improves the health of grass, and increases weight gains.

In 1997, the National Park Service and the National Park Trust established the National Tallgrass Prairie Preserve on the 11,000-acre Spring Hill/Z-Bar Ranch in Chase County, the heart of the Flint Hills and the subject of William Least Heat-Moon's book *PrairyErth* (1991). Heavyweight boxing champion Jess Willard was a resident of the Flint Hills, as was the legendary Roberts family, which produced world champion rodeo cowboys Ken and Gerald Roberts. In 1931, an airplane crash near Bazaar killed famed Notre Dame football coach Knute Rockne.

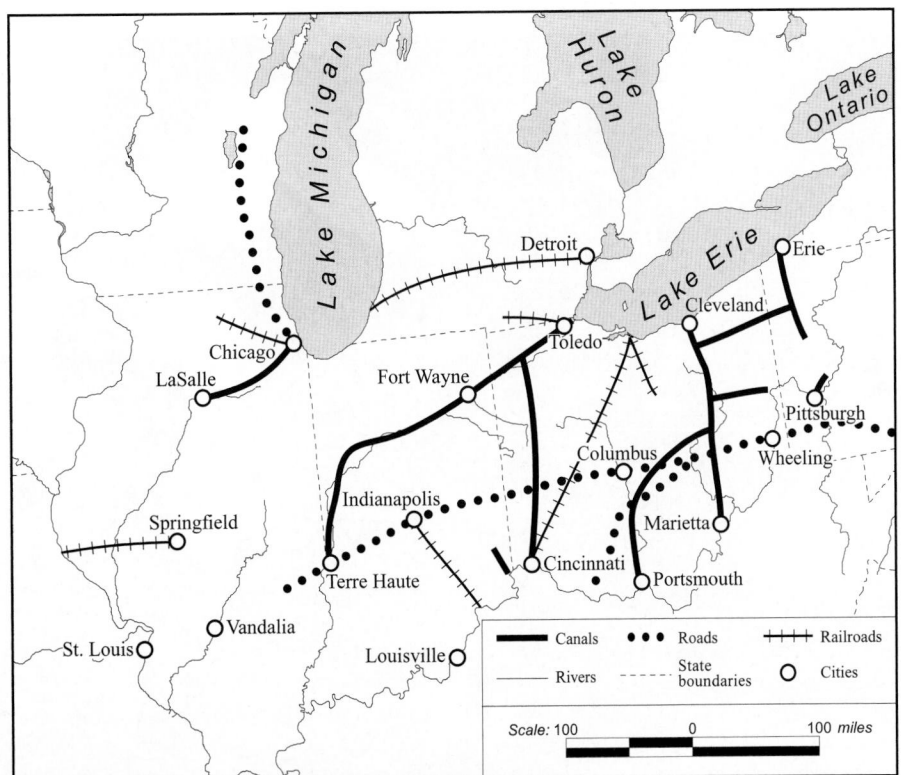

Mid-nineteenth century transportation networks. Prepared by William Ackerman. *Source:* Edward J. Taaffe, Howard L. Gauthier, and Morton E. O'Kelly, *Geography of Transportation* 2nd ed. (1996), 91.

Sources and Further Reading: Thomas D. Isern, "Farmers, Ranchers, and Stockmen of the Flint Hills," *Western Historical Quarterly* 16 (July 1985); Walter M. Kollmorgen and David S. Simonett, "Grazing Operations in the Flint Hills–Bluestem Pastures of Chase County, Kansas," *Annals of the Association of American Geographers* 55 (June 1965); James C. Malin, "An Introduction to the History of the Bluestem-Pasture Region of Kansas," *Kansas Historical Quarterly* 11 (Feb. 1942).

Jim Hoy
Emporia State University, Kansas

Grand Prairie

The Corn Belt of the Midwest replaced an area that was once tallgrass prairie—the Grand Prairie. The region, which also has been called the Prairie Peninsula, is a wedge from Ontario, Canada, and Oklahoma to Indiana, with islands of tallgrass prairie extending into Ohio and Texas. The rich soils that now nurture agriculture developed from windblown and lakebed sediments, glacial outwash, and the accumulated mulch of prairie plants that can reach over ten feet high and penetrate over ten feet into the soil. Across the prairie landscape, poor drainage resulted in scattered fresh-

water marshes and a patchwork of wet and dry prairies. Forests edged rivers, with occasional groves of trees on moraines.

The prairie landscape prior to European settlement is difficult to envision today, but it was vividly described by Eliza R. Steele in 1841:

> A world of grass and flowers stretched around me, rising and falling in gentle undulations, as if an enchanter had struck the ocean swell, and it was at rest forever. . . . Imagine yourself in the centre of an immense circle of velvet herbage, the sky for its boundary . . . whole acres of blossoms all bearing one hue, as purple, perhaps, or masses of yellow or rose; and then again a carpet of every color intermixed, or narrow bands, as if a rainbow had fallen upon the verdant slopes.

The Grand Prairie became established after the last glacial maximum, during a warmer, drier climate about 8,300 years ago, and was maintained by several factors. Winter temperatures and drying winds, and increasing precipitation from west to east, largely define the boundaries. Only 25–35 percent of average annual precipitation occurs in winter, and growing-season rains are often punctuated by severe droughts, conditions that favor grasslands. Rivers and streams provide some

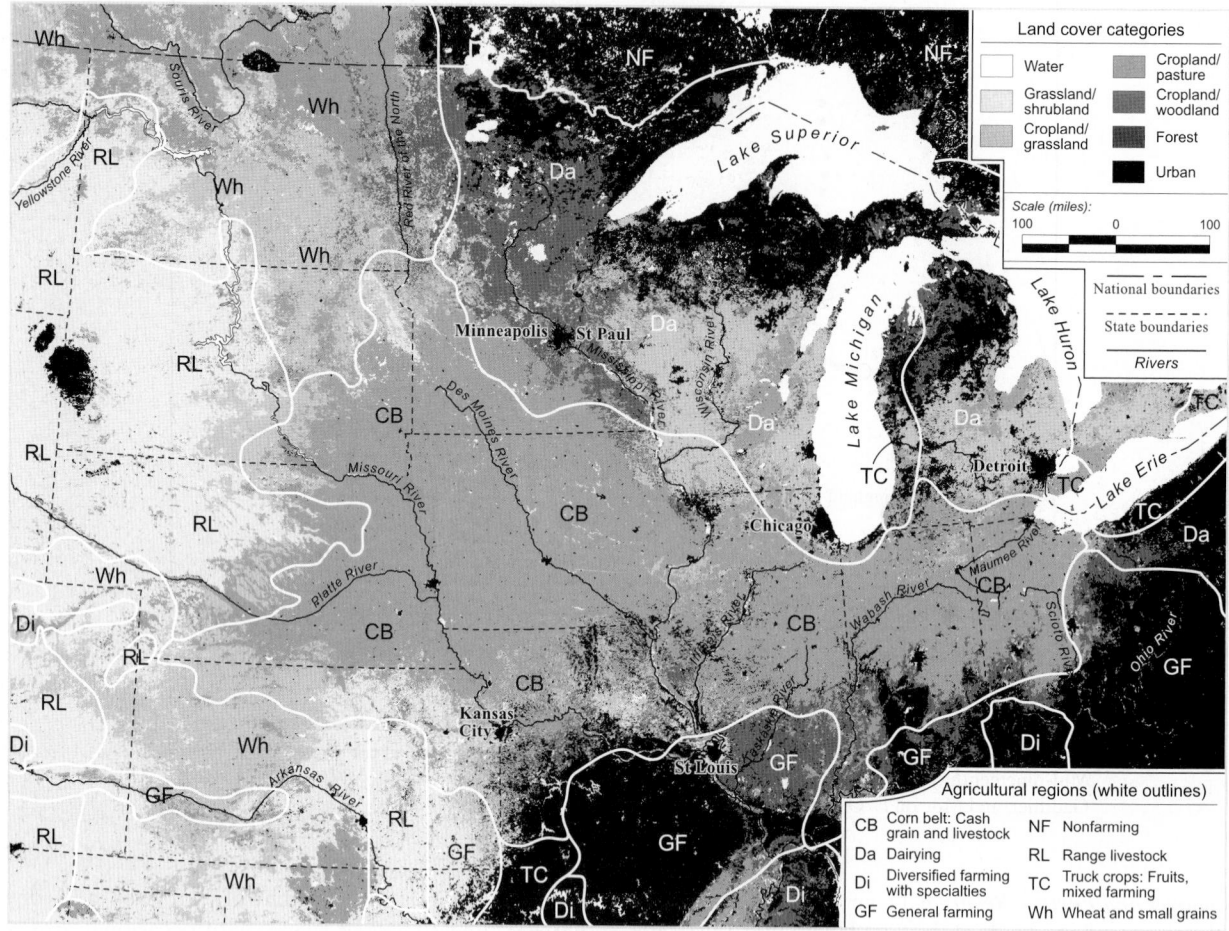

Land cover and use. Prepared by James DeGrand. *Source:* U.S. Geological Survey EROS Data Center, *North American Land Cover Characteristics 2002*, http://www.geo.msu.edu/geo333/agriculture.html.

of the only natural firebreaks in this mostly flat landscape; lightning- and human-induced fires discourage invasion by woody plants. The fire frequencies that were necessary to prevent woody plant encroachment into prairies are not well understood, but are thought to have occurred every one to fifteen years on a given site. Grazing by bison and other ungulates and rodents also maintained the grasslands.

Today, less than 1 percent of tallgrass prairie persists, largely due to three agricultural developments. The most important of them was the "sod-buster," a self-scouring steel-bladed plow invented by John Deere in 1837. Within sixty years, the majority of virgin prairie had been cultivated, returning high crop yields in black soils once thought infertile because no trees grew on them. A second agricultural development was the mass production and installation of clay tiles to improve soil drainage. More recently, economic factors leading to farm consolidation, a decrease in livestock grazing, and the abandonment of

many railroad lines have promoted the cultivation of small, previously unused prairie patches. Nevertheless, a few remnants of the Grand Prairie remain, embedded in a matrix of the most agriculturally productive and valuable land in the world.

Sources and Further Reading: Stanley A. Changnon, Kenneth E. Kunkel, and Derek Winstanley, "Quantification of Climate Conditions Important to the Tall Grass Prairie," *Transactions of the Illinois State Academy of Science* 96 (Mar. 2003); Douglas R. McManis, "The Initial Evaluation and Utilization of the Illinois Prairies, 1815–1840," research paper, University of Chicago, Department of Geography (1964); Kenneth R. Robertson, Roger C. Anderson, and Mark W. Schwartz, "The Tallgrass Prairie Mosaic," in Mark W. Schwartz, ed., *Conservation in Highly Fragmented Landscapes* (1997); Eliza R. Steele, *A Summer Journey in the West* (1841).

Adrienne L. Edwards
Illinois Natural History Survey

Great Lakes

The largest supply of inland fresh water in North America is made up of five major lakes (Erie, Huron, Michigan, Ontario, and Superior) and one minor lake (St. Clair). The Great Lakes were formed twelve thousand years ago during the last period of glaciation (Ice age) when massive glaciers extended across the region and gouged troughs into the landscape. As the glaciers receded, these depressions filled with meltwater. Today, the Great Lakes cover 94,250 square miles and contain 18 percent of the world's freshwater.

The lakes and the St. Lawrence River form an inland waterway connecting the Atlantic Ocean with the interior of North America. Stretching from Duluth, Minnesota, on Lake Superior (average lake surface elevation of 600 feet above sea level) to the Atlantic, the Great Lakes–St. Lawrence Seaway extends 2,342 statute miles through four connecting river systems and nineteen lift locks. As a vital transportation linkage, the Great Lakes facilitate global trade in grain commodities, iron, and coal products. The waterway connects the natural resources and manufacturing cities of Minnesota, Wisconsin, Michigan, Indiana, Illinois, Ohio, Pennsylvania, and New York. Canals have extended this network to connect the Hudson River and Mississippi River inland waterways.

The Great Lakes provide important water resources for cities and offer recreation space for their inhabitants. Three of the United States' major industrial centers and most populous metropolitan areas are located in the region: Chicago on Lake Michigan, Detroit between Lakes Erie and St. Clair, and Cleveland on Lake Erie. Though no major commercial fisheries exist currently, the lakes were a significant supplier of fish for Native Americans and early European settlers. Past industrial and agricultural water pollution and exogenous species such as lampreys and zebra mussels have severely damaged native fish populations and, subsequently, their predators. Since the mid-twentieth century, the Great Lakes have been stocked with a number of oceanic fish species, such as steelhead trout and coho salmon, which flourish and spawn in tributary rivers. Today, recreational fishing and boating draw millions of tourists to the region annually, although some fish species such as walleye are still considered unsafe to eat due to chemical contamination.

The Great Lakes area is an important agricultural region. Sandy soils rich in glacial till, the sedimentary remnants of receding glaciers, line the coastal plains

---

❖ The Greatest Lakes of All

The World Bank predicts that the demand for water will double in the next twenty years. More than fifty countries are expected to experience water shortages by 2025 as the world's population rises to 7.8 billion, a 28 percent increase in just twenty-four years.

Currently, manufacturers, thermoelectric plants, and public drinking-water systems use 55 billion gallons of water daily from the Great Lakes. The U.S.-Canadian International Joint Commission (IJC) is an advisory group sanctioned by both countries to study water issues along their shared borders. Current trade laws permit the two countries to protect their water resources, as long as measures don't purposefully hinder trade and amount to no greater than a 5 percent loss of water in the Great Lakes basin.

In less technical terms, this means that under current trade laws, Great Lakes water may be sold. The Great Lakes contain 20 percent of the world's fresh water, amounting to six quadrillion (six followed by fifteen zeros) gallons of fresh water. The lakes are such huge reservoirs because they are deep, with the bottoms of four of them below sea level.

In 1988, a lengthy wet climatic cycle pushed the Great Lakes' levels to an all-time high, flooding adjacent buildings and land. Some politicians supported efforts to lower lake levels. Simultaneously, the Mississippi Valley was experiencing a serious drought that summer. The flow of the Mississippi River was so low that more than a thousand barges were marooned between Vicksburg, Mississippi, and St. Louis, Missouri.

With Illinois's water-borne transport at a standstill, the governor of Illinois proposed unsuccessfully to divert excess water from Lake Michigan to the Mississippi. Politicians from other jurisdictions around the lakes, however, wisely and successfully opposed the project. Such action would have set a poor precedent for water diversion.

For the present, the issue of whether Great Lakes water can be sold to those in need has been answered. Up until now, there have been few, if any, bulk shipments of water by Great Lakes industries, but that could change. As worldwide demand for water increases, where will the United States and Canada ultimately draw the line on the Great Lakes?

Neal G. Lineback
Appalachian State University, North Carolina

Source: A previous version of this article appeared in *Geography in the News* June 8, 2001. Reprinted by permission of maps.com.

Lake Michigan pier, St. Joseph, Michigan. Photo by Sathyan Sundaram.

along the southern and eastern lakeshores and are well suited for staple crops, mainly corn and soybeans. A variety of specialty crops such as cherries, asparagus, apples, and grapes benefit from the more temperate climate along the lakeshores, where changes in air temperature are less extreme due to the thermal mediation of the large water bodies. Thus the lakes provide an extended frost-free growing season, and the rootstock of perennial plants is less likely to be damaged by soil freezing.

Sources and Further Reading: George Cantor, *The Great Lakes Guidebook* (1978); Kent Fuller, Harvey Shear, and Jennifer Wittig, eds., *The Great Lakes: An Environmental Atlas and Resource Book*, 3rd ed. (1995).

Jon Moore
Utah Valley State College

Isle Royale

Located in the northwest corner of Lake Superior, Isle Royale is at once an example of the beauty of the Midwest and a history lesson in the struggle to tame a wilderness. Consisting of slightly more than two hundred square miles, the island itself is approximately forty-five miles in length and nine miles across at its widest point. Located about fifteen miles off the Ontario shoreline, Isle Royale is actually a part of the state of Michigan some sixty miles to the south. Created from magma released by a midcontinental rift

nearly a billion years ago, the island today features a series of linear ridges trending southwest to northeast. Subsequently ground smooth by countless glacial advances, Isle Royale and its surrounding archipelago of several hundred or so rocky outcrops have supported an array of human cultures.

Human exploration and settlement on the island by indigenous peoples may have begun as long as 4,500 years ago. Native copper was extracted and worked into ornaments and artifacts that were traded throughout the region and as far east as present-day New York. Politically, Isle Royale was claimed by the French in 1671 (hence its name) and was eventually acquired by the United States in 1783, though it appeared on maps within areas marked Chippewa Territory until 1843. Both native and European fur trappers worked the island for pelts, and the waters of Lake Superior were exploited for whitefish and trout until the collapse of commercial fisheries in the twentieth century. Modern copper mining on the island lasted from the mid to the late nineteenth century, and extensive logging was followed by fires that served to rejuvenate vegetation.

Isle Royale became a national park in 1940 and received designation as an international biosphere reserve in 1980. At present, the area of the park is approximately 850 square miles, more than 80 percent underwater and almost all of it classified as federally protected wilderness.

One of the most interesting aspects of Isle Royale has been its use as a natural laboratory in studying predator-prey cycles. Moose and wolves, apparently unknown on the island until they swam and crossed an ice bridge from the mainland around 1900 and 1949, respectively, have been studied in great detail by wildlife biologists. Recently, inadvertent human introduction of diseases harmful to wolves may have upset this delicate balance somewhat, but both groups of animals have so far weathered drought, fire, and inbreeding by the wolf population for over fifty years.

Today, Isle Royale is a sought-after wilderness experience destination. The park annually receives an average of almost twenty thousand visitors during the summer months. Although there are no roads and campsites are primitive, hundreds of miles of trails and canoe portages are available to those willing to brave clouds of insects and a challenging environment. Recreational amenities are few, and the National Park Service continues to debate the level of future development appropriate for the island.

Source and Further Reading: National Park Service, *Isle Royale Official Map and Guide* (2003).

Randy J. Bertolas
Wayne State College, Nebraska

Keweenaw Peninsula

Known locally as Copper Country because of the extensive copper mines that fueled its economy in the late 1800s, the Keweenaw (pronounced KEE-wehnaw) Peninsula is today a forested vacationland with a strong sense of place and a blue-collar history.

Bedrock is close to the surface across much of the peninsula. The physical landscape is controlled by steeply dipping beds of Precambrian basalt that formed as lavas flowed out of large crustal fissures circa 1.1 billion years ago. This series of lava flows, most of them from 6.5 to 16 feet thick with one flow more than 1,300 feet thick, totals more than 12 miles in thickness.

These lava flows have since hardened and tilted as the Earth's crust warped. The more resistant basalt beds stand up today as a series of ridges that parallel the spine of the peninsula and give it its outline. Repeated glaciations during the past two million years did not completely erode these hard rocks, which is why the peninsula juts out into Lake Superior. Rocks beneath the lake are softer and were eroded away by these same glaciers.

The rich copper deposits of the Keweenaw Peninsula were formed as deep-seated, hot, copper-rich fluids circulated through cracks and holes (amygdules) in the rocks, long after they had hardened from lava. These fluids gave rise to the two types of copper mined in the Copper Country: (1) native copper, which is copper colored and metallic, and (2) chalcocite, or copper sulfate. Ojibwe Indians first discovered the native copper about four thousand years ago, but found little use for the soft metal, using it mainly as trinkets and ornaments. Douglass Houghton, Michigan's first state geologist, declared the copper deposits of the peninsula economically valuable in 1841, and by 1844 the first copper mine had opened. The "copper rush" was intense but short, with eleven to fourteen billion pounds of pure copper mined in all. Michigan led the nation in copper production from 1845 to 1887. By the 1960s, most mines had closed.

Most of the miners in the deep, cold, shaft mines were immigrants, especially Finns, Cornish, Germans, and Slovaks, who left a rich imprint on the region. Central to this culture, and still popular, is the pasty (pronounced PAS-tee)—a circle of thick pastry filled with meat, potatoes, and other vegetables that is then folded over to form a filled, semicircular pie. The pasty was brought to the area by Cornish miners. Pasties were prepared the night before and baked in the morning. The filling stayed warm until well into midday, providing the miners with a hot meal in the cold mines.

Today the Keweenaw Peninsula is a land of dense forests, old mining towns, and picturesque lakes. The Lake of the Clouds sits in a structural valley between resistant lava flows. Most of the forest is second- and third-growth hardwoods, having been cut initially in the early twentieth century. Backpacking in the remote, pristine forests is very popular.

Tourism is extremely important to the region. Copper Harbor is a favorite destination, as are the twin cities of Houghton and Hancock—both former mining towns. The Keweenaw National Historical Park in Calumet has preserved the heritage of copper mining, including many of the original structures and landscapes of the copper era.

Sources and Further Reading: David J. Krause, *The Making of a Mining District* (1992); Gene L. LaBerge, *Geology of the Lake Superior Region* (1994); Angus Murdoch, *Boom Copper* (1943); Marc L. Wilson and Stanley J. Dyl II, "Michigan Copper Country," *Mineralogical Record* 23 (Mar.–Apr. 1992).

Randall Schaetzl
Michigan State University

Mesabi Range

The Mesabi (Ojibwa for "sleeping giant") Range is a more or less continuous ridge 120 miles long and 1 to 3 miles wide between Grand Rapids and Babbitt, Minnesota. At its highest point, it rises 500 feet above the plains on either side to an elevation of 1,900 feet. It contains one of the world's greatest concentrations of iron ore—an irregular streak of taconite, limonite, and hematite that extends almost the entire length of the range. The Biwabik Iron Formation, the heart of the Mesabi Range, formed about two billion years ago from water-lain Precambrian sediments. This formation's sedimentary rock type, taconite, usually contains 25–30 percent iron. Approximately 100 million years ago, oxygen-rich alkaline groundwater moving through faults and other fractures in this formation dissolved much of the silica and left concentrations of iron in the form of hematite and limonite, which contain more than 50 percent iron.

After years of searching for iron ore, Leonidas Merritt and his brothers discovered iron ore that contained 65 percent iron and immediately named the spot Mountain Iron in 1890. In 1892, the Duluth, Missabe and Northern Railroad carried the first shipment of Mesabi Range iron ore to Duluth. From Duluth, ships carried it to steel mills around the Great Lakes. By 1893, the Mesabi Range had ten mines in operation. The great steel companies of the East provided the capital needed to develop the mines on an extensive scale, and by 1900 they controlled the Mesabi Range, whose mines were producing more iron than any other region in North America.

The earliest mining on the Mesabi Range consisted of shallow underground mines. However, because most of the iron formations occurred near the surface, covered only by a relatively thin layer of unconsolidated and easily removed glacial sediments, and the high-grade ore proved relatively soft and easy to mine, such operations soon gave way to open-pit mining. The Hull-Rust-Mahoning pit became the most famous of these mines. Here, open-pit mining removed a total of about 1.1 billion tons of material (half of it iron ore) and left a pit with a maximum depth of almost five hundred feet that covers nearly three square miles. (By comparison, the building of the Panama Canal required the removal of only about 40 percent as much rock.)

In the mid-twentieth century, the Mesabi Range consistently produced approximately one-third of the world's iron ore, with the Hull-Rust Mahoning mine alone generating up to 10 percent of the world's iron ore during the 1940s. While only an estimated 132 million tons of high-grade ore remained in 1980, the region had reserves of 39 billion tons of taconite. Crushing, separating, binding with clay, and heating of taconite produces hard, marble-sized pellets that railroads and ore boats carry to steel mills around the Great Lakes region. Today, the Mesabi Range produces about 75 percent of the iron ore mined in the United States.

Sources and Further Reading: Theodore C. Blegen, *Minnesota: A History of the State* (1963); Richard W. Ojakangas and Charles L. Matsch, *Minnesota's Geology* (1982); David A. Walker, *Iron Frontier* (1979).

Randall Rohe
University of Wisconsin–Waukesha

Mississippi River

The Mississippi River formed the original western boundary of the United States from the Treaty of 1783 to the Louisiana Purchase of 1803. Because of its immense size and longitudinal straightness, not deviating more than 3 degrees east or west of longitude 92° W over a length of more than 2,300 miles, the river serves as a convenient dividing line between the eastern and western United States.

The river has three major divisions. Its upper division continues from its source in northern Minnesota downstream to its confluence with the Missouri River near St. Louis. It drains glaciated terrain, and tributaries bring in vast loads of sand that create islands and natural, lakelike stretches in the river. The Wisconsin and Illinois tributaries provide water connections by portage or canal between the Mississippi River and Lake Michigan. The short, middle division lies between the mouths of the Missouri and the Ohio Rivers. Water from the Illinois and the Missouri Rivers practically doubles the size of the Mississippi. In this division, the Mississippi River is a major ecological boundary, separating the biologically diverse Ozarks from the biologically simpler glacial prairies of southern Illinois. The lower division, which lies outside the Midwest, begins at the mouth of the Ohio River and continues to the Gulf of Mexico.

The flow of the Mississippi River can fluctuate greatly, although it is partially regulated by dams, chiefly in the Missouri River basin. The great flood of 1993 set records all along the Mississippi River from Minnesota to the mouth of the Ohio River and ranks as one of the great natural disasters in the history of the United States.

Despite the Mississippi's role as a political boundary, it is perhaps more important as the commercial and cultural artery of the upper Midwest. The historical role of the river as a uniter of diverse peoples is often overlooked because contemporary reliance on personal cars tempts us to interpret the river as a bar-

The banks of the Mississippi River near its junction with the Missouri River. Illinois Department of Commerce and Community Affairs.

rier to movement. Railroads, which first bridged the Mississippi River at Rock Island in the 1850s, greatly lessened dependence on the river, especially above St. Louis. Nevertheless, river transportation continued to grow as barges replaced steamboats in the twentieth century. Twenty-seven low dams with navigational locks between St. Louis and the head of navigation at St. Paul have converted the Mississippi River into a series of stepped pools. St. Louis is the nation's largest inland river port because of its centrality in the inland waterways network and the generally ice-free condition of the Mississippi River below St. Louis.

The Mississippi River in the Midwest figures prominently in American literature and lore. Mark Twain (Samuel Clemens) described life along the river in the mid-nineteenth century, and his and others' depictions remain vivid in the collective memory of Americans. Historical tourism has revived many aging river towns, such as Hannibal and Ste. Genevieve, Missouri; Elsah, Nauvoo, and Galena, Illinois; Dubuque, Iowa; and Prairie du Chien, Wisconsin.

Sources and Further Reading: Frederick J. Dobney, *River Engineers on the Middle Mississippi* (1978); John W. Reps, *Cities of the Mississippi* (1994); Mark Twain, *Life on the Mississippi* (1883).

Walter Schroeder
University of Missouri–Columbia

Missouri River

The Missouri River, formed by the Jefferson, Madison, and Gallatin Rivers in Montana, flows for around 2,300 miles to discharge into the Mississippi River just above St. Louis.

French fur traders of St. Louis explored and mapped the river as far as North Dakota well before the Lewis and Clark expedition of 1804–1806. Long inhabited by American Indians, the Missouri River Valley became a major region in the history of the United States. "To cross the wide Missouri" was to enter the Great Plains and an environment hostile to eastern-style farming. The famous western trails— Santa Fe, Oregon, Mormon, California—began after the Missouri River had been crossed.

Called by Indians the "Smoky River," the Missouri was the premier American "muddy" river because of its heavy load of sediment. Its beds and banks were notoriously unstable, and numerous islands and bars in its shallow channel sustained a diverse aquatic and riparian biology but were the bane of steamboating. Flooding was expected every May and June.

Before railroads, the Missouri River was the commercial artery from St. Louis to Montana. Steamboats entered the Missouri River in 1819, and with exceptional effort the small, shallow-draft boats reached as far as Fort Benton, Montana. Railroads changed the

❖ Where the River Flowed

A river ran through it and became an inland sea. Brown water lived for weeks in the houses and barns that dared to risk sharing the floodplain with such a moody neighbor—the old Missouri River. The buildings are empty now, curiously out of place in the middle of this new sea. Brown. Constantly in motion. A young sea exploring new avenues far beyond the old river channel, beyond the broken levees, beyond Orion Beckmeyer's green Chevy pickup that hangs on stubbornly to the levee wall. Like the spirit of this little town, it has refused to be washed downriver, out to sea. As long as it hangs on, the good folks of Hartsburg will fight this battle against more water than anyone can remember, even Henry Klemme, who has lived all of his ninety-three years in this town.

It was a restless, wild, drunken river. A crummy guest. A reckless dancer. It took over the party. Drove out the people who lived in the houses. Emptied out the American Legion Hall where the town folks come to socialize and dance. And when the river grew tired of its fun, it flowed silently out the door, leaving behind a slippery, dark-brown shadow of its outrageous dance—everywhere.

It will be weeks, months perhaps, before it leaves our sight and a lifetime before it leaves our memory.

It is an eerie thing to enter a house where the river has lived for a month. The seven-foot-high brown watermarks it left on the once-white clapboard walls of Hartsburg's homes and post office show how far it traveled into a town it hadn't entered since 1903. And then it was nothing like this. This time it pushed through doors and opened every cabinet in the kitchens, swam in bathtubs and closets, even moved refrigerators from the foot-high cinder blocks where they had been elevated weeks earlier, setting them back where they had been, upright and filled with mud.

The river still lives all around the neighborhood where I've come to offer help. Five of us have entered an empty house and begun to deal with the river's rampage. We are up to our ankles in mud that feels and looks like thick chocolate pudding gone bad. Smells foul. Clings to everything it touches. Frogs entered the house in the owners' absence and fish swam freely in each room, exiting through the back door when the river pushed it open and caused it to warp. This river, weaving through town like a bad drunk, continues to leave its mark on all that it touches.

We, the fortunate ones, are drawn to the river and the drama being played out in Hartsburg that will come to be known as the Great Flood of '93. In our oldest jeans and highest-topped rubber boots, we attach ourselves to a house and its family for the day. Assembly lines are formed to evacuate the thick, foul mud.

We begin the slow process of reclaiming this house by shoveling and heaving loads of mud. Only not for long. River mud is heavy and leaves the back muscles aching if you carry it too far, or for too long. Squeegees move mud more easily. Four or five pushers in assembly-line fashion direct mud from room to room, until if finally reaches the front door. With a final shove, it flies back into the river, now almost a foot below the door jam. It will take hours of pushing and shoving and hosing down, but finally the floor will reemerge. The once beautiful oak hardwood floorboards were milled in Hartsburg years ago when the town had two operating lumber mills. It will be difficult to rip those up and replace them with new wood. Even now, buckled and splotchy with river residue, they have a nutty richness that seems as old as the town.

Finally, by midday, it begins to look like a small victory over the river has been won—in this one house at least. The mud, here just hours ago, has rejoined the river. Tired, mud-spattered, and hungry, we head to lunch at the fire station cafe—a place to sit among new friends, share stories, and regroup energies for the labors that will continue through the afternoon and over the weeks to come.

Cathy Salter
Hartsburg, Missouri

Originally published in the *Boone County (Missouri) Journal* and the *Columbia (Missouri) Tribune*

economic geography of the Missouri River basin in post–Civil War years by opening up land away from rivers and reorienting traffic away from them. River traffic dwindled and has never fully rebounded with barges as it has on eastern rivers.

In 1944, the Pick-Sloan Plan laid out a comprehensive plan to manage the river essentially for barge navigation and flood prevention. The Army Corps of Engineers, the federal agency in charge of managing the river, built six main-stem dams and many others on tributaries to regulate flow according to a *Master Manual.* The lakes formed by the dams are among the largest human-made lakes in the United States in area

and have spawned a vigorous recreation industry in the Dakotas. The corps also engineered the lower river from its mouth to Sioux City, Iowa, for barge navigation by narrowing and deepening the channel, eliminating islands, and reducing the curvature of bends. Landowners and the corps built levees to protect farmlands and built-up areas.

Severe droughts in the 1980s, sluggish growth in river commerce, rising environmental concerns, and changing uses of river water prompted a revision of the *Master Manual.* The great flood of 1993, which occurred despite efforts to manage high waters (in large part because rains fell downstream from the flood-control dams), complicated attempted revisions. Sharp differences in the interests of upstream and downstream states ensure that management of the river will remain controversial for a long time. Issues include a finite amount of water, Native American water rights, irrigation, public-water supplies, cooling water for power plants, waste-water disposal, commercial navigation, recreation, flood control, and river ecology, especially protection for endangered species. These issues suggest that the water issues of the West are spreading into the more humid Midwest.

Sources and Further Reading: Robert L. Branyan, *Taming the Mighty Missouri* (1974); James M. Denny and James D. Harlan, *Atlas of Lewis and Clark in Missouri* (2003); Henry Cowles Hart, *The Dark Missouri* (1957); Gary E. Moulton, ed., *The Journals of the Lewis and Clark Expedition*, 13 vols. (1983–2001).

Walter Schroeder
University of Missouri–Columbia

Osage Plains

The Osage Plains lies between the Ozarks of Missouri and the Flint Hills of Kansas. It is a cuestaform topography of smooth, shale plains that alternate with north-south-trending belts of low, limestone

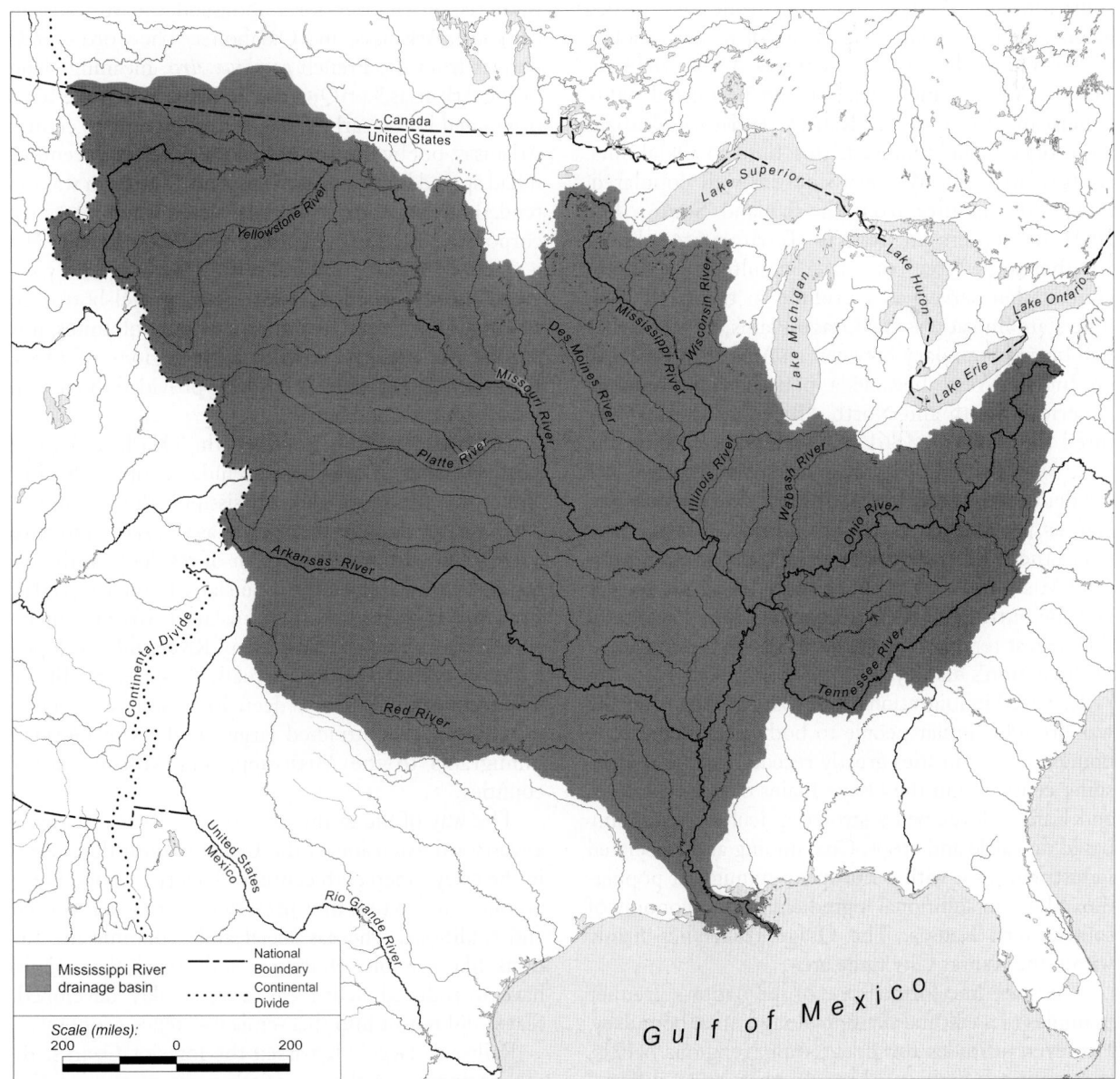

Mississippi River drainage basin. Prepared by James DeGrand. *Source:* www.nationalatlasftp.html#hydroOm.

hills. At the time of European contact, the region was the homeland of the Osage Indians. French fur traders from St. Louis maintained good relations with Osages well into the nineteenth century, although Osages had difficult relations with other Native Americans.

In 1821, the western boundary of the new state of Missouri split the Osage Plains into land open to white settlement and federal territory reserved for Indians. Some thirty Indian tribes being removed from east of the Mississippi were given land in the Osage homeland. Most of the reservations fronted directly on the Missouri state line. For white Americans, the line was an artificial barrier. They could move across Indian space to reach Santa Fe, California, Oregon, and Colorado, but they could not settle in it. The Missouri towns of Westport and Independence crowded against the line as outfitting towns for western trails.

Passage of the Kansas-Nebraska Act in 1854 removed the settlement barrier and permitted white Americans to settle in Kansas Territory. Indians were once again removed, this time to Oklahoma. By this time, the Missouri side was well populated, mostly by families from the Upland South. The right of settlers in Kansas Territory to choose whether to be "free" or "slave" resulted in a violent contest that served as a prelude to the Civil War. The state line across the Osage Plains, which earlier had been a boundary between an American East and an Indian West, became a boundary between an American South and North. "Bleeding Kansas" entered the union in 1861 as a free state. During the Civil War, communities were burned and sacked and residents murdered by Missouri bushwhackers and Kansas jayhawkers. Utter breakdown of civil order led to the U.S. Army's removal of some twenty thousand Missouri residents in counties along the border and the burning of their properties. This was one of the largest territorial expulsions of white Americans in the nation's history.

Renewed immigration to the Osage Plains after the war brought similar people to both sides of the state boundary. Animosities greatly receded during the ensuing century, and the Osage Plains of both Missouri and Kansas developed a strong agricultural economy based on cattle and crops. Coal mining and associated industrialization with a European-immigrant population added an additional ingredient to the economy of southeastern Kansas. The Osage Plains lies firmly within the Kansas City trade area.

The state line formed one of the nation's premier examples of a cultural division along a state boundary. However, attitudes toward taxation, religious beliefs, and political party preferences that once differed along the boundary greatly waned during the twentieth century. Although a region of homogeneous topography, the Osage Plains presents two different historical settlement and cultural regions.

Sources and Further Reading: Michael Fellman, *Inside War* (1989); Willard H. Rollings, *The Osage* (1992); James R. Shortridge, *Peopling the Plains* (1995).

Walter Schroeder
University of Missouri–Columbia

Ozark Highland

The Ozarks is a well-defined physiographic and cultural region of over forty thousand square miles in Missouri, Arkansas, and Oklahoma. The word *Ozarks* derives from the French *pays aux Arcs,* meaning "land of the Arkansas," or Quapaw, Indians. When the term originated in the early 1700s, it applied only to central Arkansas, but by the first half of the nineteenth century it had spread into southern Missouri. The term was extended farther north in popular usage when it was incorporated into the name Lake of the Ozarks in 1931.

Defined physiographically, the Ozarks is a hilly region, mostly wooded, with clear, gravel-bottomed streams. Dominated by limestones and dolomites, it is one of the nation's premier karst regions of caves, sinkholes, and springs. It has long provided the nation with lead, zinc, and barite.

Defined culturally, however, the Ozarks is significantly smaller in area and excludes people who live along the Missouri and Mississippi River borders. They do not think of themselves as Ozarkers and have a way of life different from that of residents of the interior Ozarks. Before the Louisiana Purchase (1803), French Canadians and their enslaved African Americans settled along the Mississippi River and developed a Creole culture that has virtually disappeared. In the mid-nineteenth century, deep loess soils and transportation access attracted large numbers of German immigrants to the Mississippi and Missouri River counties.

The way of life in the interior Ozarks is essentially a westward extension of the Upland South that began in the early nineteenth century. Society was organized around kinship ties, thus preserving vernacular speech and traditions, whereas social and economic institutions like schools, churches, and stores that would have introduced new ideas were weakly developed. Slaves did not fit into this semisubsistence economy.

Railroads largely bypassed the interior Ozarks. By the beginning of the twentieth century, the interior

Ozarks was increasingly isolated and was not participating in national economic development. The standard of living fell behind and *Ozarks* became a term of ridicule.

Transformation of the image of the Ozarks began with the promotion of the region as a "playground" for growing numbers of automobile tourists. Tourism, first promoted in the White River Hills region and at mineral springs, spread to several major lakes by the mid-twentieth century. The Ozark National Scenic Riverways (1964) converted the Current River into a national destination for river recreationists. Large acreages were put into public ownership as national and state forests, conservation areas, and parks. A moderate climate, beautiful scenery, and costs of living well below the national average induced thousands of retirees to move to the Ozarks. The majority of counties experienced population growth in the last two decades of the twentieth century, in contrast to population decline in rural counties elsewhere in the Midwest.

Although vestigial attitudes remain common enough to distinguish the interior Ozarks as a region, they are giving way to more mainstream midwestern attitudes as immigration increases into the Ozarks. At the beginning of the twenty-first century, one can speak of an emerging "Nouveau-zarks."

Sources and Further Reading: Russel L. Gerlach, *Immigrants in the Ozarks: A Study in Ethnic Geography* (1976); Milton D. Rafferty, *The Ozarks: Land and Life*, 2nd ed. (2001); Carl O. Sauer, *The Geography of the Ozark Highland of Missouri* (1920); Walter A. Schroeder, *Opening the Ozarks* (2002).

Walter Schroeder
University of Missouri–Columbia

Notable Cultural Regions

Illinois Military Tract

The Illinois Military Tract consisted of a triangle of well-watered, fertile, and easily accessed land located between the Mississippi and the Illinois Rivers. By the mid-nineteenth century, it was at the center of the transformation of a wide swath of territory from Ohio to Nebraska into the Corn Belt, perhaps the most recognizable landscape associated with the American Midwest.

In 1812, the U.S. Congress set aside public land in Illinois in order to entice men into military service against Great Britain. After the War of 1812, the federal government bribed the Potawatomis living along the Illinois River into ceding their land claims. Congress then authorized the surveying of the military tract, which covered territory that eventually included Adams, Brown, Calhoun, Fulton, Hancock, Henderson, Knox, McDonough, Mercer, Peoria, Pike, Schuyler, Stark, and Warren Counties as well as parts of Bureau, Henry, Marshall, and Putnam Counties. Three and a half million acres reserved for veterans were opened for development in 1817.

Each man was entitled to 160 acres and back pay to help with initial costs. But fears of Indians and concerns about the agricultural potential of tough, treeless prairies made the tract foreboding. Men had to travel to Illinois, choose a parcel, register it at a land office, and received a confirmation from Washington, D.C., before they could sell it. Nevertheless, about three-fifths of the roughly 29,000 veterans who located land did so in the Illinois Military Tract, although many transferred their claims to speculators or lost them because of unpaid taxes.

Land sales boomed in the 1830s as families from the northeastern United States and Europe joined Upland Southerners. In 1836, the federal land office in Quincy sold a record 569,376 acres. [Davis, p. 209] Settlers built their society around the cultivation of corn and other grains used to fatten hogs and cattle that were then driven to local markets for sale and slaughter. The Illinois Military Tract became a model of an emerging characteristic of midwestern culture: the integration of farms and villages. Peoria, the most important urban center, had a plethora of stores, professional offices, banks, and industries specializing in farm equipment, pork packing, and distilling.

The mid-nineteenth century was the most dynamic and innovative era in the region's history. With the rise of industry, cities, and a consumer society, the tract seemed out of step with modern economic and cultural developments, and it has suffered in recent years from serious out-migration as young people leave to seek employment in cities and suburbs. Still, despite the fact that its reputation as the American Heartland reflects its past more than its present, advertisers and politicians continue to ask "Will it play in Peoria?" as a way of judging the mood of the nation as a whole.

Sources and Further Reading: Theodore Carlson, *The Illinois Military Tract* (1951); James E. Davis, *Frontier Illinois* (1998); John C. Hudson, *Making the Corn Belt* (1994); James W. Oberly, *Sixty Million Acres* (1990).

Andrew Cayton
Miami University, Oxford, Ohio

Little Dixie

Little Dixie is a cultural region that extends across central Missouri from Hannibal on the Mississippi River to near Kansas City on the western border. Its distinction is its early settlement by Upland Southerners and enslaved African Americans, producing one of the strongest geographic centers of southernness in the Midwest. The label *Little Dixie* apparently was first applied after the Civil War; it may come from a national Democratic convention when Missouri delegates were referred to as coming from "Little Dixie," described as "more Dixie than Dixie."

After the War of 1812, Kentuckians and Virginians poured into the Boonslick region along the Missouri River, attracted by its rich loessial soils, saline springs, timber, extensive bluestem prairies, and river access to markets. By mid-century, settlement had expanded to the east and west and created a homogeneous region that was the heart of Missouri until the Civil War. Little Dixie provided most of Missouri's governors and state officials. Its leaders were responsible for developing social, political, and economic institutions for the state. Wealth was founded on tobacco and hemp, corn and hogs, mules, high-grade cattle, and supplying westbound emigrants. Residents of Little Dixie constituted the core of support for the Confederacy and supplied most of Missouri's anti-Union soldiers during the Civil War.

The Civil War ended Little Dixie's dominance in Missouri. European immigration, railroads, and the growth of St. Louis and Kansas City created counterbalancing regions. Little Dixie did not turn to manufacturing and commerce and thus stayed primarily

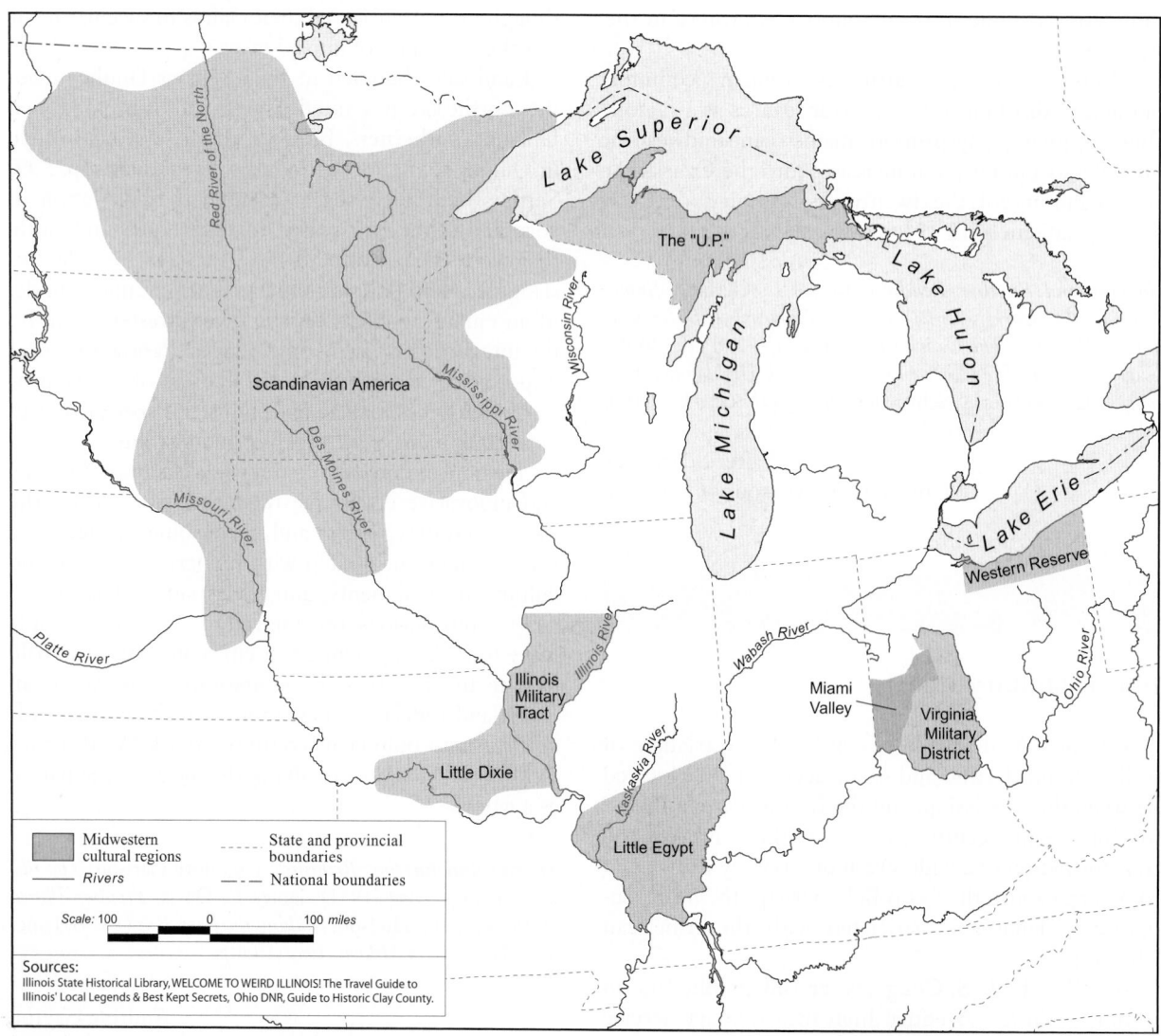

Key cultural geography sites. Prepared by Roman Nitze. *Source:* Illinois State Historical Library, *Welcome to Weird Illinois, Travel Guide to Illinois's Local Legends & Best Kept Secrets*, Ohio Department of Natural Resources; and *Guide to Historical Clay County*.

agricultural and rural, organized around small county-seat towns. Southern traditions continued in tobacco plots, race-horse and mule breeding, fiddle music, grand antebellum mansions, and a conservative Protestant theology. Place names divulge the geographic sources of settlers: Bowling Green and Paris (Kentucky); Danville, Roanoke, and Williamsburg (Virginia). In the twentieth century, Little Dixie's political leadership remained staunchly conservative both fiscally and sociologically. Whereas it once was solidly Democrat, Little Dixie now votes conservative Republican. The rural African American population, formerly the major black element in Missouri, has virtually disappeared. Farm consolidation and lack of nonagricultural opportunities decreased population by as much as half during the twentieth century. Little Dixie is now an "insider's region," keenly felt by its own residents but fading in its perception by outsiders.

Probably the most famous person to come from Little Dixie was Samuel Clemens, or Mark Twain. Born to a slaveholding family in rural Monroe County, Clemens grew up in Hannibal. Twain's best-known novels reflected his formative years in Little Dixie and were notable in their author's efforts at portraying black people as fellow human beings. Twain wrote *Adventures of Huckleberry Finn* (1884), often called the first true American novel because of its bold topic and use of vernacular language, in Little Dixie speech and in a Little Dixie geographic setting.

Sources and Further Reading: Robert Crisler, "Missouri's Little Dixie," *Missouri Historical Review* 42 (January 1948); Howard Wight Marshall, *Folk Architecture in Little Dixie* (1981); Michael J. O'Brien, *Grassland, Forest, and Historical Settlement* (1984); Albert E. Trombley, *Little Dixie* (1955).

Walter Schroeder
University of Missouri–Columbia

Little Egypt

Little Egypt, the southern part of Illinois bounded by the north-south-flowing Mississippi, the east-west-flowing Ohio, and the north-south-flowing Wabash Rivers, is one of the oldest vernacular or locally recognized regions in the Midwest, if not the country. Its northern boundary is not self-evident and has been in flux over time.

The evolution of this vernacular regional term began with a Baptist minister, John Badgley, who, looking over the bluff at what is now Edwardsville, proclaimed the fertile American bottoms the "Land of Goshen," the productive area of Egypt given to the tribes of Israel at the time of Joseph. Other influences were comparisons of the Mississippi River with the Nile River and the apparent resemblance of Native American mounds at Cahokia and Mounds, Illinois, to the pyramids of Egypt. The name was confirmed by two separate phenomena. The first was giving towns Egyptian or Nile place names, such as Cairo, Thebes, Alexandria, Karnak, and Dongola. Second, during a potential famine threatened by the severe winter of 1830–1831 in central and northern Illinois, farmers going to southern Illinois to buy corn for food and seed often said that they were traveling "to Egypt." By the 1840s, the counties south of Mount Vernon became known as Little Egypt. The name persists today in ordinary usage and in a newspaper title.

The persistence of this vernacular term is due to the distinctiveness of southern Illinois culture from that of the rest of the state. The ancestral roots in the region are from the Upland, or Upper, South, particularly Kentucky and Tennessee. Its settlers were not Yankees from New England as in the northern prairies of Illinois. Some were even from the Deep South. Cairo has many African American shotgun houses, a style characterized by being one room wide and several rooms deep and having a small front porch with very thin supports. During the Civil War, southern Illinois had many "Copperheads," the name given to Southern sympathizers in the Union states. The rise of Chicago, with non-Anglo cultures derived from southern and eastern Europe, exacerbated the cultural contrast of southern Illinois with the northern part of the state.

Another important event in shaping the life of Little Egypt was the development of coal mining in the late nineteenth and early twentieth centuries. Coal deposits stretched for almost 150 miles from Carbondale into southwestern Indiana. Many of them were relatively shallow, which resulted in strip-mining in the twentieth century and subsequent massive reclamation projects in the twenty-first.

The decline of coal mining created some of the highest rates of poverty and unemployment in the state. As in other states, communities have sought to obtain prisons as their economic lifeline. The most famous example is the federal penitentiary at Marion. The oldest state prison in the area is at Chester and the newest one is at Tamms.

Sources and Further Reading: John Hudson, "North American Origins of Midwestern Frontier Populations," *Annals of the Association of American Geographers* 78 (Sept. 1988); Jon Musgrave, *Egyptian Tales of Southern Illinois* (2000).

Michael Roark
Southeast Missouri State University

Miami Valley

The Miami Valley, a swath of territory flatter than lands eastward and westward, extends north-northeast into the interior from Ohio's southwesternmost corner. On the valley's west, the Great Miami River meets the Ohio at the Ohio-Indiana border, and on its east, the roughly parallel-flowing Little Miami River joins the Ohio just upstream from Cincinnati. The Miami Valley attracted settlement early, despite being relatively far down the Ohio River. By 1800, it held the farthest inward push of population in Ohio.

Soon thereafter, the greater valley region was Ohio's most densely populated, containing many Middle Atlantic natives, southerners, and African Americans (in urban centers, especially Cincinnati and Dayton, and in rural settlements throughout the valley). It also contained above-average percentages of foreign immigrants, particularly Germans (in Cincinnati, Dayton, and numerous rural communities), English, and Irish. Its people were described in 1815 as "industrious, frugal, temperate, patriotic, religious," intelligent, and enterprising.

The valley comprised one of the first development corridors into Ohio's interior. Its rolling, wooded hills and fertile bottomlands, heavily cultivated by 1825, supported a significant agricultural economy. By 1850, Ohio led the nation in corn production and the Miami Valley, also famous for cattle and, especially, hog raising, led the state. Hinterland agricultural production collected at smaller cities like Lebanon, Xenia, and Troy. Agricultural processing and increasing industrial production supported by the transportation assets of rivers, roads, the Miami and Erie Canal, and, eventually, railroads characterized the incipient industrial cities of Hamilton, Middletown, Springfield, and Dayton. Cincinnati, the Old Northwest's most important city during and after the pioneer period, offered superior accessibility for collecting, concentrating, and shipping agricultural products from the Miami Valley and from Ohio, Indiana, and the Upland South. A concentration of meatpacking, especially pork, gave Cincinnati its "Porkopolis" nickname; slaughterhouse byproducts provided raw materials for soap and candle makers; and distilleries and breweries (particularly associated with Cincinnati) utilized surplus grain. Cincinnati, Dayton, and other valley cities processed agricultural goods and manufactured a wide variety of items. Before long, the valley displayed, arguably for the first time anywhere, what would become quintessential midwestern characteristics—a strong agricultural base supporting, and in places surpassed by, a strong industrial and commercial base.

During the late nineteenth and the first half of the twentieth centuries, the Miami Valley underwent tremendous industrial and commercial development. Building on its initially diverse industrial and commercial economy, Cincinnati came to host industries ranging from consumer products manufacturer Proctor and Gamble, initially making soap from rendering products of the city's famous slaughterhouses, to high-tech jet aircraft engines manufacturing by General Electric. Other cities also experienced rapid manufacturing growth. Dayton already boasted a strong industrial presence based on the National Cash Register Corporation. As a result of the inventiveness of the Wright brothers and Charles Kettering, Dayton became a key center of aircraft manufacturing, research facilities, and related services, and motor vehicle and parts manufacturing. The Miami Valley region's diverse economy and transportation advantages have supported an economic evolution adding high-tech manufacturing to agricultural production, processing, and traditional manufacturing.

Sources and Further Reading: Andrew R. L. Cayton, "The Middle West," in William L. Barney, ed., *A Companion to 19th-Century America* (2001); William T. Utter, *The Frontier State, 1803–1825* (1968); Francis P. Weisenburger, *The Passing of the Frontier, 1825–1850* (1941); Hubert G. H. Wilhelm, *The Origin and Distribution of Settlement Groups: Ohio: 1850* (1982).

Gregory Rose
The Ohio State University–Marion

Scandinavian Regions of the Upper Midwest

Although populations with origins in the Scandinavia region of Europe have a long presence in both the United States and Canada, the Midwest region of the United States and, to a lesser extent, the contiguous "Prairie" region of Canada emerged by the early twentieth century as the heartland of Scandinavian settlement of North America. Deep roots by people of Scandinavian origins have been reflected over the past 150 years in the waxing and waning of specific Scandinavian ethnic neighborhoods in Chicago, Milwaukee, Minneapolis, and in rural and urban communities scattered from Michigan to Kansas and central Iowa to the Dakotas. Each summer and fall, festivals honoring the Midwest region's Scandinavian heritage occur in scattered geographic regions throughout the Midwest, such as Marquette, Michigan's FinnFest USA. In small communities across Iowa, Minnesota, and Wisconsin, Norway's Constitution Day, known as Syttende Mai, is celebrated each May. Each fall, Minot, North Dakota, hosts what is billed as "America's Largest Scandinavian Festival," Norsk Høøstfest.

The association of populations with origins in Scandinavia with certain areas of the Midwest is a pronounced and enduring feature of the region's demographics, traditions, and some of its institutions. Communities with majority populations claiming origins in Norway dot the landscapes of western and southern Wisconsin, the central and northern parts of Iowa, the Red River region of Minnesota, and large parts of North Dakota. Although Finnish communities were traditionally found in many regions of the United States, from northern Massachusetts to Oregon, the association between specific place and Finns is most pronounced in northern Michigan and the Iron Range of northern Minnesota.

In aggregate terms, the ethnic composition of Scandinavian communities in the upper Midwest reflects to a great degree overall migration from northern Europe to the United States, particularly movement in the heyday of this process, roughly 1860 to 1920. However, one distinguishable geographic feature of the upper Midwest region is the representation in significant parts of it of Finns and Norwegians, both in numbers and culturally far beyond their representation in the United States as a whole. In general, the most significant settlements of the upper Midwest were those of Swedes, Norwegians, and Finns. The least significant groups were Danes and Icelanders. In Wisconsin, for example, a permanent, significant Danish presence is usually associated with the area around Racine, while the presence of Norwegians has been widespread throughout the state, being particularly significant in vast areas of western Wisconsin. The presence of Finns and Swedes in Minnesota is etched into the collective consciousness of the state as a whole. In all of the upper Midwest, few communities were ever identified with settlement from Iceland or with an Icelandic identity.

The movement of Scandinavian populations to the Midwest region of the United States represented the third wave of European contact and settlement in the region. By the time Swedes, Norwegians, Danes, and Finns settled the area in significant numbers, they did so against a backdrop of well-established and deeply rooted political and economic institutions that had been established by Anglo Americans, particularly from New York, Pennsylvania, New England, and the South. Anglo-American pioneers to this region were not, however, the first Europeans to make an imprint on the region. Rather, these settlers relied on an intersection with the French, who constituted the first wave of successful European settlement of the region. While in most of the Midwest, including Iowa, Wisconsin, and Minnesota, German-origin peoples and their Scandinavian kin came to vastly outnumber populations claiming Anglo-American roots, Anglo-

American settlement and control laid the political, economic, and social foundations of the Midwest and made possible settlement by millions with origins in northern and central Europe.

Swedes were the largest Scandinavian nationality to come to the United States. Between the end of the Civil War and World War I, more than a million Swedes immigrated to this country. In the Midwest, Swedish populations were particularly high in Illinois and Minnesota. Although Chicago was the hub of the Swedish population in Illinois, with more than 150,000 by World War I, Swedes became one of the dominant ethnic groups in the northwestern region of the state, where the first Swedish-language newspaper, *Hemlandet*, was started in Galesburg in 1855. The substantial Swedish settlement in northern Illinois acted as a springboard to settlement in central and northern Iowa, where government land grants and rich farmland to be had at a cheap price prompted many families to move in the late 1800s.

In Minnesota, the Minneapolis area became the center of Swedish culture. Significant settlement by Swedes in Wisconsin included an identifiable community in Milwaukee and isolated communities in the northern and central regions of the state, such as in Marinette, Lincoln, Vilas, and Price Counties. The most substantial settlements by Swedes took place in northwestern Wisconsin, including in Polk and Burnett Counties and the Superior area, which is located across Lake Superior from Duluth, Minnesota.

Although Norwegians accounted for a smaller number of original immigrants into the United States than did Swedes, no Scandinavian populations—with the possible exception of Finns—have so strongly maintained both an ethnic identity and a connection to their country of origins. While the vast majority of the population with origins in Norway has for a long time been part of the Anglo-American mainstream, a Norwegian presence in Iowa, Wisconsin, Minnesota, and the Dakotas is maintained via churches, private colleges, small towns with high Norwegian-origin populations, and festivals. Many Norwegian American families continue to have relatives in Norway, and informal exchanges by family members and others continue to link local populations with their ancestral country of origin.

Although there is substantial evidence of an ethnic Finnish presence within the original settlement of the Delaware Valley by the Dutch-dominated New Sweden Company in the 1600s, and documented evidence of the presence of Finnish people within the Russian settlement of Alaska in the 1700s, most immigrants from Finland to the United States—like other Scandinavians—came during the years of vast demographic growth that accompanied the geographic and economic expansion of the United States from the late 1860s to the 1920s. During this time, significant communities of Finns were created from northern Massachusetts to the Dakotas. For example, it is estimated that between 1870 and 1920, more than 300,000 Finns immigrated to the United States. Of these, the largest numbers settled in Michigan, followed by Minnesota. In many parts of the country, Finns came to be associated with mining and quarrying, particularly with mining of iron in northern Minnesota and Wisconsin.

Georges G. Cravins
University of Wisconsin–La Crosse

Upper Peninsula, Michigan

Michigan's Upper Peninsula, known as the U.P., is bordered by three of the five Great Lakes. Divided from the Lower Peninsula by the Straits of Mackinac, the Upper Peninsula is known for its unique culture, dialect, and scenic beauty. U.P. residents affectionately refer to themselves as "Yoopers" and humorously refer to individuals from the Lower Peninsula as "Trolls" because they live "Under the Bridge." The Mackinac Bridge, completed in 1957, was built to connect the Upper Peninsula with the rest of the state and, for that matter, the outside world. Prior to construction of the bridge, most individuals traveling to the U.P. opted to go around and through Wisconsin rather than embark on the sometimes perilous ferry crossing between the two peninsulas. Although the bridge and better roads have had a great impact, the peninsula remains famous for its remoteness and separation from the rest of Michigan and the nation.

Along with its isolation, the U.P. is known for its cool, northern summers and long, cold, snowy winters. Lake Superior, which borders the entire northern shore of the peninsula, delivers heavy lake-effect snowfall along the shoreline and in nearby inland areas. Houghton, Marquette, and Sault Ste. Marie are cities well known for extremely heavy lake-effect snowfalls. Lake Superior is also infamously known for severe fall gales. The lake has claimed hundreds of ships over the years due to storms capable of producing thirty-three-foot swells and winds exceeding forty-five knots. One of the most well-known shipwrecks, made famous by the songwriter Gordon Lightfoot, was the wreck of the *Edmund Fitzgerald* off Whitefish Point on November 10, 1975.

The short, cool summers and generally acidic soils do not promote widespread agricultural activity. One exception is dairy farming in the "Banana Belt." This region, in the southern tip of the U.P., is known for lower snowfalls, milder winters, and more fertile soils compared to the rest of the peninsula. The large tracts of forest in the U.P. support widespread commercial logging operations. The timber is primarily sold as pulpwood to the many paper companies scattered across the peninsula and northeast Wisconsin.

The lower Menominee River, which borders Wisconsin, contains the largest number of paper mills and other industries in the Upper Peninsula. With vast tracts of remote forests containing thousands of inland lakes and streams, along with the Great Lakes themselves, tourism makes up a large portion of the economic sector throughout the year. While summer brings in a large number of vacationers, winter tourism, especially in the heavy snow areas along Lake Superior, is just as popular, often generating more revenue than summer tourism. Open-pit iron-mining operations continue as an industrial activity, although this economic sector is in decline.

Sources and Further Reading: Cully Gage, *A Love Affair with the U.P.* (1988); Mary Hunt, *Hunt's Guide to Michigan's Upper Peninsula*, 2nd ed. (2001); Theodore J. Karamanski, *Deep Woods Frontier* (1989); Russell M. Magnaghi, *An Outline History of Michigan's Upper Peninsula* (1979).

Joseph P. Hupy
Michigan State University

Virginia Military District

To maintain its quota of soldiers during the American Revolution, the Commonwealth of Virginia in 1779 began providing warrants redeemable for "good" land across the Appalachians in amounts varying from 200 acres for a private with fewer than three years of service to 15,000 acres for a major general with four years of service. To meet this obligation, Virginia retained two pieces of territory when it ceded its trans-Appalachian land claims to the United States in 1784. Over 1 million Kentucky acres were to be opened first, with 3.9 million acres between the Scioto and Little Miami Rivers (about one-sixth of what would become Ohio) available if needed.

By 1787, Virginia had requested the Ohio lands and some impatient warrant owners already had claims outlined. But Congress did not permit settlement. By the time Ohio lands became available, economic hard times in Virginia and disinterest in migrating made warrant holders susceptible to speculators, who purchased large quantities of warrants at a fraction of their original value. Eventually, seventy-five individuals or partnerships held warrants for approximately one-third of the Ohio District, and twenty-five of them (including Thomas Worthington and Lucas Sullivant) together claimed over 1 million acres.

The district was a midwestern outlier of Virginia's irregular metes-and-bounds survey system in a region otherwise regularly surveyed, primarily through the Congressional Survey System. No comprehensive survey was required prior to land entry, and warrant holders identified their own claims. Surveyors and speculators' agents adeptly outlined the best lands or most promising locations, often before legally permissible and so efficiently that by 1802 some were claiming that no "good" land remained. Unusually shaped parcels looking like gerrymandered political districts encompassed prime parcels: valley bottoms, mill sites, and potential town locations. As typical in metes-and-bounds surveyed areas, lawyers were kept busy sorting out conflicting land claims resulting from unsystematic parcel identification, impermanent survey markers, careless record keeping, and claims to more land than warranted. Speculators' prices and uncertain land identification retarded the district's settlement. A traveler passing through part of the Virginia Military District in 1840 wrote that it contained larger land holdings, more tenancy, and a lower population than other parts of Ohio.

Many Revolutionary War veterans never settled the Ohio lands they earned. Most veterans or their descendants, speculators, and other migrants came from Virginia, Kentucky (heavily settled by Virginians), or North Carolina. Southern cultural characteristics established by the first settlers dominated in the district, visible still in early settlements like Chillicothe. The irregular survey's impact on the land is very clear from the air, on topographic maps, or to a motorist. Midwesterners expecting to travel north-south or east-west country roads along section lines intersecting at square corners will be disconcerted (and potentially lost) by the meandering road system that follows property lines and natural features. Major urban centers have not developed in the Virginia Military District, permitting the area to retain much of its rural character, particularly in the south. Recently, some major industrialization has developed, especially in the north and much of it associated with manufacturing facilities for Honda of America, its suppliers, and the Scotts Company.

Sources and Further Reading: William Thomas Hutchinson, *The Bounty Lands of the American Revolution in Ohio* (1979); Norman J. W. Thrower, *Original Survey and Land Subdivision* (1966); William T. Utter, *The Frontier State, 1803–1825* (1968); Hubert G. H. Wilhelm, *The Origin and Distribution of Settlement Groups: Ohio, 1850* (1982).

Gregory Rose
The Ohio State University–Marion

Western Reserve

Connecticut, one of only two states holding trans-Appalachian territory after the creation of the United States, claimed 3 million acres 120 miles westward from Pennsylvania between 41° and 42°, 2'; N latitude. Initially called New Connecticut and later the Western Reserve, this area formed the northeastern part of Ohio at statehood in 1803. In 1795, Connecticut sold the reserve to the Connecticut Land Company, retaining one-half million acres on the western edge (the "Firelands") to compensate its citizens for Revolutionary War losses. Moses Cleaveland, the company's agent, purchased the land east of the Cuyahoga River from the Native Americans, and a few years later they ceded the area west of the Cuyahoga River.

Some pioneers arrived in 1796 but settlement began slowly, discontinuously moving from east to west. The Western Reserve was relatively isolated and the journey to reach it arduous. The region's attractiveness increased after the War of 1812 when economic difficulties in New England strongly induced emigration, and conditions in the reserve improved as towns and mills were built and churches and schools were established. With the Erie Canal's opening in 1825, migration to the reserve received a major boost.

Yankee population origins and cultural landscapes strongly marked the reserve: In 1850, at least 75 percent of immigrants there were New Englanders. Connecticut, Massachusetts, and Vermont natives concentrated there along with New Yorkers, particularly from Yankee-influenced upstate areas. Pennsylvanians were found in the southern reserve. Yankees transferred New England place names, quickly introduced familiar educational and religious institutions, and dominated social and political leadership. The landscape sprouted town greens overlooked by white clapboard churches and New England house types and supported Yankee farm economies such as dairying. Growing industrial centers such as Cleveland, Akron, and Youngstown attracted a wide range of Southern and European immigrants. But the Yankee influence remained strong in small towns and rural areas.

Industrialization started early and grew most dramatically during the second half of the nineteenth and first half of the twentieth centuries. In Youngstown, iron manufacturing from low-quality local ores began in 1803, with steel production on a massive scale introduced after 1870. Freight cars hauling Lake Superior iron ore from Lake Erie ports to Pittsburgh returned northward with coal to support steel making (using Superior ores) in cities such as Youngstown and Cleveland. Akron's industrial fame was based on tire manufacturing, the demand for which grew explosively along with motor vehicle use in the first half of the twentieth century. Automobile and auto parts manufacturing also developed in the region. Because Cleveland was the largest city, its manufacturing and commercial activities were more diversified, including steel, petroleum products, automobile industries, shipping, retail, banking, and research and educational services. The Western Reserve's heavy-industry base was hard-hit by economic downturns in the 1970s as traditional manufacturing declined. Urban centers, especially those with one dominant industry like Akron (rubber) and Youngstown (steel), became quintessential Rust Belt cities, suffering massive job losses and severe socioeconomic crises that still shadow the region.

Sources and Further Reading: Andrew R. L. Cayton, "The Middle West," in William L. Barney, ed., *A Companion to 19th-Century America*, (2001); Harry F. Lupold and Gladys Haddad, eds., *Ohio's Western Reserve* (1988); Leonard Peacefull, ed., *The Changing Heartland: A Geography of Ohio* (1990); Hubert G. H. Wilhelm, *The Origin and Distribution of Settlement Groups: Ohio, 1850* (1982).

Gregory Rose
The Ohio State University–Marion

Peoples

SECTION EDITOR
Jon Gjerde

Section Contents

Overview

It is not too much to say that the broad outlines of the history of the Midwest are subsumed within the migration to the region and subsequent interaction of its peoples. One could also argue that one of the most distinguishing characteristics of the region is its ethnic and racial heterogeneity. No less an authority than Frederick Jackson Turner, in his influential 1893 essay on the significance of the frontier, wrote about the centrality and distinctiveness of the population of what he called the "Middle region (of the United States)." This area, which was entered by New York harbor, was distinct from regions to the north and south because of its wide mixture of nationalities. It was, Turner argued, "an open door to all Europe." Yet it was also "a region mediating between New England and the South, and the East and the West. It represented that composite nationality which the contemporary United States exhibits," Turner continued, "that juxtaposition of non-English groups, occupying a valley of a little settlement, and presenting reflection of the map of Europe in their variety." This ethnic and racial diversity, Turner contended, extended to the Midwest. When he wrote specifically on the region in the early twentieth century, Turner focused on the diversity of the population in the Midwest with its New England, southern U.S., and European heritages. In outlining the Midwest's transition from an agricultural "frontier" to an industrial colossus, Turner carefully classified the waves of migration and the interactions of peoples—including the Indian, the Yankee, the southerner, and the European—that shaped the region. The organization of this section follows the historical waves of immigration and settlement of peoples in the creation of the American Midwest.

Historians today tend to use Turner as a foil to depict his implicit racism or his unsophisticated endorsement of American exceptionalism. Yet his observations about the peopling of the Midwest, the region of his birth and the region he knew best, are accurate. The history of the Midwest was deeply colored by a series of migrations that peopled and repeopled the region. Migrants from all corners of the globe have arrived, interacted, and often clashed with people already present. They have created communities and thereby contributed to the building of midwestern regional culture. Even after Turner's death, moreover, the story continued as new waves of migrants entered the region to people its cities, towns, and countryside. Although Turner overemphasized the power of the midwestern environment to remake these peoples into assimilated Americans, he was right to argue that a region of ethnic and racial diversity was "typical of the modern United States."

The story of the peoples of the Midwest begins some twelve thousand years ago when the first human inhabitants entered the land that would become the

Michoacán immigrants celebrating Our Lady of Guadalupe feast day, St. Agnes Church, Chicago, 1998. *Chicago Tribune* photo by Kit Welling. All rights reserved. Used with permission.

region. These indigenous peoples adapted to their environments and resource bases and developed a variety of strategies of subsistence from farming to hunting and gathering. They also made changes upon the land varying from effigy mounds found in locales ranging from Iowa to Ohio to the famous Cahokia mounds in Illinois near St. Louis, the largest of which covers fourteen acres at its base and rises one hundred feet high. Yet theirs was not a static world, and tribal groups within the region repeatedly came into contact—and conflict—with one another.

Encounters with Europeans and Africans in the mid-1600s altered the indigenous peoples' world even more dramatically. New diseases against which they had little immunity disrupted the Indians' health, and ultimately they came into conflict with peoples of Europe moving westward and hungry for their land. One historian has suggested that Indians, like Europeans and Africans, faced such radical change in their culture and society that they too lived in a "new world." Indians of course were not powerless. In the era prior to the American Revolution, European imperial authorities of France, England, and Spain were forced to forge alliances between their empires and Indian nations. Native Americans, after all, were skilled hunters who could supply goods—especially furs—coveted by European traders. The negotiated arena of what became the Midwest was what one historian has called the "middle ground" between European and Indian worlds. Skillfully playing European empires against one another, Indian nations augmented their own power and influence.

Shortly after American independence from Britain, however, a huge migration commenced that would dramatically weaken Indian society and repeople the region principally with those of European and African descent. A region of minor importance to the United States in 1800, the Midwest, largely as a result of this migration, became an area of pivotal importance to the nation half a century later. The white population of the Old Northwest (Ohio, Indiana, Illinois, Michigan, and Wisconsin), which was slightly more than a quarter million in 1810, had increased sixtyfold twenty years later to number about 1.5 million people. In the three decades before the Civil War, moreover, the five states of the Old Northwest expanded to nearly seven million inhabitants. As new territories were taken from native peoples, the migration extended farther west. By 1860 Iowa and Minnesota contained nearly one million people. The states of the region, the oldest of which was a mere fifty-seven years old, contained over one-quarter of the American population on the eve of the Civil War.

This migration of American-born peoples, black and white, was composed of distinct migrations from Canada, New England, the middle states, the Upland South, and the Deep South to the Midwest. These migrants' paths tended to follow lines of latitude. French Canadians, for example, moved to the most northerly climes of the region. Yankees, as people from New England were called, and Yorkers, who were born in New York, migrated mainly to the northern Midwest, peopling the Western Reserve near Cleveland and then fanning out into Michigan, Wisconsin, Minnesota, and northern Iowa and Illinois. The midwestern swath of the Upland Southerner settlement was to the south of the Yankee and Yorker migration and was particularly evident in southern Ohio, Indiana, southern Illinois and Iowa, and Missouri.

The migrations from the eastern United States placed a deep cultural imprint on the Midwest. Colleges that continue to thrive, such as Oberlin in Ohio, Carleton in Minnesota, and Ripon in Wisconsin, were established by migrants who strove to transplant their Yankee world of education and religion to the region. In contrast, slavery took root in Missouri, where the 114,931 African American slaves and 3,572 free people of color comprised more than 10 percent of the state's population in 1860. The Missouri legislature passed laws that resembled those of the Deep South. An 1847 ordinance, for example, prohibited the instruction of reading and writing to black or mulatto people at the risk of fines and imprisonment.

As midwestern society was forged, these groups came into contact and often into conflict as episodes of crucial region-shaping cultural clashes pitted Yankees against the southerners. The friction between American groups varied in intensity, but it periodically erupted in brutal violence. Maine-born Elijah Lovejoy was killed by a proslavery mob in 1837 while defending his antislavery newspaper the *Saint Louis Observer* in Alton, Illinois. Some twenty years later, Kansas became a site of guerilla warfare between advocates of slavery and those who wished to make Kansas a free state. Indeed, one could argue that many of the crucial enactments in the years leading up to the Civil War, including the Kansas-Nebraska Bill of 1854, *Dred Scott v. Sandford* (1857), and "bleeding Kansas" in the late 1850s, were cultural battles centered in the Midwest.

As Americans moved westward, they were joined by a stream of migrants from Europe. Immigrants from the German states, Ireland, Scandinavia, the British Isles, and the Low Countries began to move to the vast tracts and growing cities of the region beginning around the 1830s. Because these peoples migrated somewhat later than the American-born, their concentrations of settlement were more to the west. German immigrants created the "German triangle," a huge region of settlement defined by Milwaukee, St. Louis, and Cincinnati, all of which were cities with a particular German stamp. They also dominated regions of Iowa, Minnesota, Missouri, the Dakotas, and Nebraska. Settlements of Norwegians and Swedes dotted Wisconsin, Iowa, and Kansas, but the bulk of the migration was directed to the northern belts of the Midwest in Wisconsin, Minnesota, and the Dakotas. Irish, Dutch, and English communities are also found throughout the midwestern landscape.

Even more than American-born migrants, the Europeans moved in a "chain migration" fashion, where people joined family and friends already settled in the region. These migration patterns created tightly knit settlements in the rural and urban locales that tended to buffer the immigrants from American society and permitted them to create ethnic enclaves where language and religious faith were replanted and maintained. These European immigrants too made a distinctive imprint on the region. Not only did they replant their religious institutions, they introduced new food and drink. Germans transferred the art of brewing to Milwaukee, Cincinnati, and St. Louis, which remain centers of the American beer industry. Place names, from New Prague and New Ulm in Minnesota to Swedesburg and Luxemburg in Iowa to Stockholm and New Holland in South Dakota, attest to the European presence in the small-town Midwest. Perhaps even more remarkable are the agricultural settlements, notably in the upper Midwest, that maintain their European character. Large settlement areas in Wisconsin, Iowa, Nebraska, Kansas, and the Dakotas were peopled almost entirely by Germans (including people of German descent moving from Russia who were often Mennonites and were called Russian-Germans), Norwegians, Swedes, and the Dutch. As late as 1900, regions in the upper Midwest contained among the largest proportion of immigrants of anywhere in the United States.

As the Midwest entered an unprecedented era of industrialization, the origins, motivations, and settlement patterns of the region's migrants shifted in the late nineteenth and early twentieth centuries. These new immigrants—from southern and eastern Europe and Mexico as well as blacks and whites from the American South—moved to rapidly growing cities such as Chicago, Detroit, Milwaukee, Minneapolis, and Cleveland. Others moved to toil in the huge iron-ore mines of Michigan and Minnesota that provided the raw material for the region's huge industrial plants. Still others worked as lumbermen in the vast forests of the upper Midwest. African Americans tended to move permanently to the midwestern cities, fleeing economic decline and enduring racism in the South. The "new" immigrants from Europe, on the other hand, often moved to the United States with the intention of returning home with greater wealth. Most of the im-

migrants were men, often moving singly, without wives and family, to the drudgery of the mills, mines, and factories. Despite dreams of returning home, a significant share of the immigrants remained to build urban communities. Like blacks, they formed urban enclaves, joined labor unions, built churches, and, in so doing, put their own distinctive stamp on the region.

Migrants from the American South and, especially, from southern and eastern Europe dominated the industrial workplace. In the late nineteenth century, it was said that "not every foreigner is a workingman, but . . . it may almost be said that every workingman is a foreigner." European immigrants and their children as a result comprised much of the population of the Midwest's industrializing cities. In 1920, 72 percent of Chicago's population and 69 percent of Cleveland's were immigrants and their children. The black populations of Chicago, Cleveland, and Detroit, in contrast, were between 7 and 8 percent in 1930, but growing rapidly. Detroit's African American population increased twentyfold between 1910 and 1930.

These massive migrations, like those that preceded them, reoriented urban midwestern culture. Migrants and their descendants built religious edifices, ranging from enormous Roman Catholic basilicas to modest storefront churches, which attested to the transplantation and evolution of their religious faiths. They constructed a vast array of ethnic institutions that eased their adaptation to life in the Midwest. Written in English or in their native tongues, newspapers were published to keep their readers informed about life at home and to instruct them about conditions in the United States. An array of ethnic institutions, ranging from banks to burial associations and fraternal organizations, were instituted to temper life in an uncertain industrial workplace. Out of these organizations, an ethnic and racial leadership emerged that tended to play critical roles in the governance of the cities and, ultimately, the states and the nation.

These migrants also profoundly influenced midwestern culture. No better example exists than the new forms that transformed midwestern music. The polka was invented in Europe in the early nineteenth century and was transplanted by Czech, Polish, Slovenian, and German immigrants to the Midwest, where they transformed the musical form into an "old-time" music that became popular among the white working class. More significant was the migration of black music—especially jazz—to the Midwest. By the early 1920s a substantial migration of jazz artists to Chicago, Kansas City, and St. Louis had created particular urban styles in their midwestern homes.

As always, however, these developments were accompanied by ethnic and racial conflict. Immigrants from southeastern Europe were often condemned in the early twentieth century as "new immigrants" who did not possess the superior "racial" qualities of those who preceded them. After the United States entered World War I in 1917, many midwesterners worried about the loyalty of Germans and leftist radicals (a wide variety of people commonly lumped together as "Reds") who might undermine the war effort. One German immigrant, in fact, was lynched in southern Illinois because he was suspected of disloyalty. And the postwar midwestern world was rife with racial tension. When World War I ended, the United States endured an economic downturn and layoffs. Growing unemployment exacerbated racial tension. Race riots exploded in Chicago and East St. Louis in 1917. The effect of this conflict was profound. For one thing, the race riots destroyed whatever hopes remained in the Midwest for peacefully integrated cities. For another, growing concern about the volume and origins of the immigrants resulted in federal laws enacted by Congress in 1921 and 1924 that radically reduced the level of immigration to the United States.

After immigration restriction went into effect in the mid-1920s, the European migration was seriously curtailed as migration within the Western Hemisphere grew. Whites and blacks from the South and Latino/as from Mexico and the Caribbean migrated in increasing numbers in the 1920s and in the decades following the Great Depression and World War II. Between 1940 and 1960 Chicago's black population almost tripled in size from 278,000 to 813,000. During the 1950s the African American population of Detroit increased from 303,000 to 487,000. Unfortunately, many of these more recent migrants were unable to benefit from industrial work because of racism that inhibited their entry into the workforce and deindustrialization that reduced the number of job openings. While urban European ethnic communities persisted well into the twentieth century, they were complemented by rapidly growing Hispanic barrios and African American neighborhoods.

Following a decades-long reduction in international migration, a new immigration from Europe and, especially, Asia, Latin America, and Africa commenced after World War II and swelled after 1965, when immigration law was again altered to permit more foreign immigrants to enter the nation. The backgrounds and motivations of the new immigrants are complex, but we can divide them into three components. First, a changing world economy and an altered immigration law have encouraged a migration of people with marketable skills to the United States. Throughout much of this country, computer engineers, doctors, and academics have moved to locations of high-tech and university settings. The Midwest is no different, as people who are part of a "brain drain"

from nations such as India, Korea, and Taiwan have moved to university cities including Ann Arbor, Columbus, Madison, and Iowa City and to cities with high-tech industry such as Minneapolis-St. Paul and Chicago. Second, as the United States has deindustrialized and labor unions have been weakened, less skilled and more poorly paid service workers and laborers have found new homes in the cities and small towns of the Midwest, working in job sites as diverse as meatpacking plants and sugar-beet fields. Third, waves of political refugees moving to the United States have placed a particular imprint on the Midwest. The Hmong in Wisconsin and Minnesota, Arabs in Detroit, Somalis in Minnesota, and peoples from the former Soviet Union in Chicago exemplify the variety of refugee migrations to the region.

Like the earlier migrations, this new immigration has recast midwestern culture. Mexican restaurants now are common in small midwestern towns; bok choy and lemongrass, in addition to corn and tomatoes, can be purchased at farmers' markets; *matryoshkkas* (Russian nesting dolls) and Hmong tapestries are available in midwestern stores. The demographic influence of the new immigration has been particularly profound in specific locations. Chicago has the third-largest Mexican American population in the United States. One in four adults in Dearborn, Michigan, a city of some 91,000 people, is Arab American, whereas 58 percent of Dearborn's children are Arab American. And it is not only metropolitan areas that have felt the effect of the new immigration. Consider Worthington, Minnesota, where one-fifth of the city's 10,000 people are recent immigrants and their children. Or Wausau, Wisconsin, where Hmong are nearly 12 percent of the city of 38,000 people. Or Postville, Iowa, where over one-tenth of the town with a population of around 1,500 are members of an Orthodox Jewish population. Operating a kosher meat-processing plant, the Jewish population of Postville has perhaps more rabbis per capita than any other city in the United States.

In sum, the peoples of the Midwest have been continually evolving over the past few centuries by migrations that have repeatedly transformed midwestern culture. The interaction that has resulted, to be sure, has not been free of conflict, but the roiling of people, their beliefs, and their cultural practices has created a region dynamic for its cultural change. As Turner argued a century ago, these migrations reflected a particular American modernity and pluralism. The Midwest today is not usually considered a region of immigrants; that honor is reserved for the Sunbelt states where many immigrants *and* midwesterners have relocated in recent decades. Yet it bears emphasizing that the midwestern history is replete with massive waves of immigration and indelibly linked to the movement of its peoples.

Sources and Further Reading: Joseph Amato and John Radzilowski, *Community of Stranger Change, Turnover, Turbulence, and the Transformation of a Midwestern Country Town* (1999); James R. Barrett, *Work and Community in the Jungle* (1987); Juan R. García, *Mexicans in the Midwest, 1900–1932* (1996); Jon Gjerde, *The Minds of the West* (1997); Susan Gray, *The Yankee West* (1996); James R. Grossman, *Land of Hope* (1991); Herbert G. Gutman, *Work, Culture and Society in Industrializing America* (1977); Walter D. Kamphoefner, *The Westphalians* (1987); Jo Ann Koltyk, *New Pioneers in the Heartland* (1997); Nell Irvin Painter, *Exodusters* (1977); Richard Lyle Power, *Planting Corn Belt Culture* (1991); Thomas J. Sugrue, *The Origins of the Urban Crisis* (1996); Frederick Jackson Turner, *The Frontier in American History* (1920); Richard White, *The Middle Ground* (1991); Oliver Zunz, *The Changing Face of Inequality* (1983).

Jon Gjerde
University of California–Berkeley

Eighteenth-Century Native Americans

The rivers and lakes that defined the boundaries of the eighteenth-century area that became the Midwest encompassed a woodlands/prairie region that was remarkably similar in geography, climate, and resources. The geographical core of this region was the Mississippi, and its tributary rivers defined the region's boundaries. The western and southern borders were the Arkansas and Missouri Rivers, while the Ohio River extended the southern boundary eastward to the Appalachian Mountains.

Within this region there was a wealth of natural resources: Woodlands and prairie lands teemed with wildlife, well-watered, rich alluvial soils created an agricultural surplus, and lakes and rivers were well stocked with fish. Lifeways were rarely stressed by the "starving times" that challenged daily life in other regions. During the summer months Indian women grew corn, squash, beans, and melons and they harvested blackberries, raspberries, bearberries, huckleberries, gooseberries, strawberries, and blueberries. The fall brought plentiful nut harvests. In the spring Indians gathered in maple sugar camps to harvest sap for syrup and sugar. Mokucks, or baskets of sugar, were commonly traded along the riverways in exchange for seasonal agricultural produce or other goods. Northern communities had the advantage of plentiful wild-rice harvests. In the north, where the growing season was shorter and where hunting was more important, men rarely hunted far from their villages. Most communities maintained permanent village sites as well as seasonal hunting camps.

The natural landscape of the eighteenth century was a vast patchwork of wetlands and swamplands caused by melting winter snows and seasonal rains, and here fur-bearing animals thrived. European fur traders were a common presence, and many had married Native American women. It was the French who first went west to trade, and they dominated the trade until the 1760s, when the English displaced them following the Seven Years' War. In the eighteenth century the Great Lakes basin was the continent's most profitable fur-trade region. Well-watered lowlands and cold winters produced a rich harvest of pelts, and the vast network of rivers and lakes facilitated the transportation of those furs. While the fur trade changed many Great Lakes Indian communities, involvement in the trade did not result in the demise of Indians.

The European presence, however, had introduced deadly pathogens into this region. Smallpox was problematic in the first half of the eighteenth century and often devastated entire villages. The last smallpox epidemic in the region occurred during the Seven Years' War, and by the last half of the century population levels had begun to recover.

In the eighteenth century the lands of the present-day Midwest were dominated by a variety of Indian cultures and lifeways. Pontiac's Rebellion convinced the British that the colonists should be confined to the lands east of the Appalachian Mountains. King George III issued the Proclamation Line of 1763, which declared the lands west of the Appalachians Indian country. Nor did the last decades of the century equate with American hegemony. Despite winning its independence, the United States did not effectively establish its sovereignty north of the Ohio River. Sovereignty remained contested until Great Britain agreed in the Jay Treaty of 1794 to relinquish control over its forts south of the Great Lakes and was not completely secure until the American victory in the War of 1812.

The waterways of this region facilitated movement both within and across the region and into and out of the region. Plains Cree, Plains Ojibwa, and Cheyenne were initially Minnesota inhabitants. The Cheyenne were first pushed west by Sioux expansion and, like the Cree and the Ojibwa, they continued westward in a pattern of woodland-prairie-plains migration until they moved into their historic homelands and were incorporated into the buffalo-hunting economy. Refugee Neutral, Erie, Huron, Abenaki, and Mohegan were also pushed west and were incorporated into existing communities of the western Great Lakes. This refugee influx further complicated the ethnic diversity of the region. Midwestern Indians were first described by seventeenth-century French explorers, whose writings mentioned the Iliniwek Confederacy (Cahokia, Chipussea, Coircoentanon, Kaskaskia, Michigamea, Moingwena, and Peoria), Arikara, Mandan, Hidatsa,

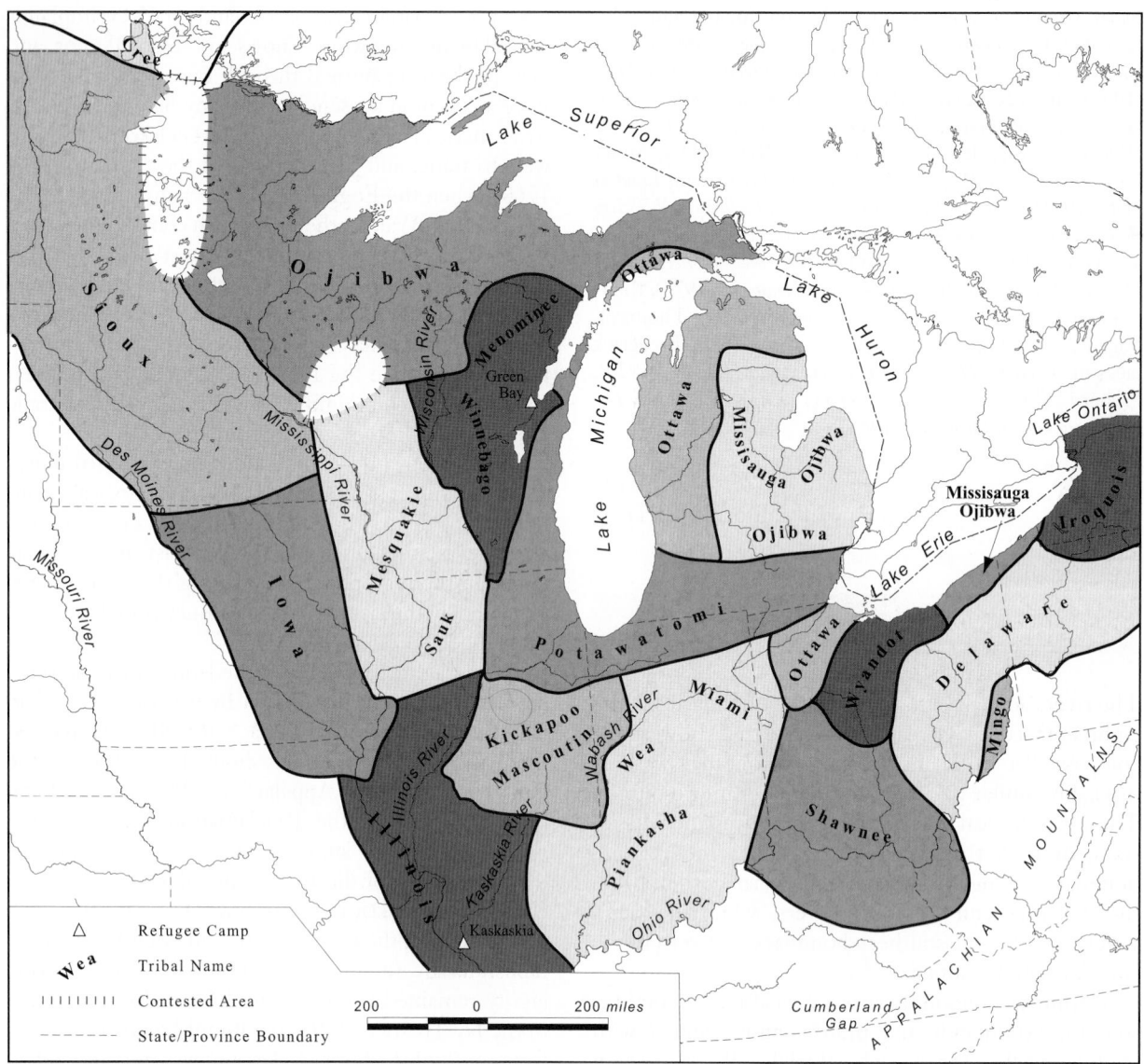

Locations of Native American tribes, 1768. Prepared by Margaret Popovich. *Source:* Helen Hornbeck Tanner, ed., *Atlas of Great Lakes Indian History* (1987).

Pawnee, Iowa, Omaha, Osage, Ponca, Wichita, Fox (Mesquakie), Potawatomi, Sauk, Miami, Odawa (Ottawa), Menominee, Ojibwa, Winnebago, and Sioux. The names that we attribute to these people were often created through the linguistic misunderstandings of French visitors. For instance, the term *Potawatomi* had little meaning in the original Potawatomi language. These people called themselves *Neshnabe*, "man"—or the plural *neshnabek*, "people." The Ojibwa referred to themselves as *Anishinabe*, "original man." Among the Iliniwek the word *ilini* has the same meaning: man. The syllable *wek* represents the plural termination for "man," but the plural was changed to *ois* to conform to

the French ending pattern and thus resulted in the term *Illinois*.

The important demographic shifts that occurred during the seventeenth century were interrupted at the beginning of the eighteenth century when the site of the Fur Trade Wars shifted from the Great Lakes east to the Iroquois homeland. The Iroquois quest for better hunting lands, where beaver were plentiful and where their own dead could be replaced with Great Lakes captives, came to an end in 1801. During the last decades of the previous century the Iroquois had transformed the Midwest into a land of exiles, with large refugee communities located at Kaskaskia and

Green Bay. Both refugee communities reportedly contained close to ten thousand exiles. The Great Kaskaskia Village consisted primarily of Ilini communities, although there were also adjacent Sauk and Fox villages. The Green Bay community was more ethnically diverse and its inhabitants were more removed from their traditional homelands—most had fled from lands east of Lake Michigan. The Green Bay refugees protected themselves by putting Lake Michigan between themselves and their Iroquois aggressors. The Iliniwek Confederacy remained on their homelands and the decision proved disastrous. They became the most frequent target of Iroquois hostility, and by the first decade of the eighteenth century eight tribes had disappeared. Once Iroquois warriors returned to their homelands, the Potawatomi slowly migrated along the western and southern shoreline of Lake Michigan, continuing east until they reached present-day southwestern Michigan. The Potawatomi laid claim to most of the vacant Ilini lands, and they became the most significant nation in the southern Great Lakes during the eighteenth century.

Despite the large number of different communities, the social organization generally consisted of family units, some of which were nuclear while others were extended. Families could be either matrilineal, patrilineal, or bilineal. Regardless of how membership or residence patterns were determined, groups of interrelated families tended to live together in villages and these villages were generally linked by membership in a clan. In the Midwest clans were designated by the name of an animal, a location, an ancestor, or even by the name of a natural phenomenon, such as Thunder. Each clan gathered for ceremonial events, such as the Green Corn Ceremony on the southern prairie lands and the Feast of the Dead among the Ojibwa. Each clan communally possessed names, songs, and rituals. Puberty rites often signaled the acquisition of a clan name. Some clans possessed greater prestige and authority than others, but again the model was that of communally inspired, not individualistically inspired, behaviors. Elders were important members of each community, valued not only for their advice but because they educated children through stories, songs, chants, and dances. Even when a chief existed he had relatively little power. There were generally no more than three or four hundred people loyal to him and all decision-making was consensual, made by tribal councils. Marriage tended to be outside the clan, thus creating kinship links that extended across villages and clans.

The fertile prairie lands of this region gave rise to an agriculturally focused ceremonial calendar that related to the harvesting of those resources. Food production was controlled by women and was sufficient to feed households but was also shared when other families did not have adequate resources to make it through the winter months. The ceremonial calendar coincided with the harvesting of foods and brought people together in festivals of thanksgiving. Both the production of maple sugar and the harvesting of corn were such events. Fall festivals were more frequently devoted to ensuring the success of the hunter, as in the Feast of the Hunter's Moon among the Miami.

Religion did not possess an institutional structure. Instead, Indians believed that spiritual power resided in anthropomorphic beings that included animals, celestial bodies, or other natural features of the landscape. The fulfillment of ceremonial obligations assured that these deities remained favorably disposed toward the communities who respected them. To fail to adhere to ritualistic behaviors jeopardized that community's daily existence. Sacred bundles, retained by village elders or acquired during sacred visions, contained powers bestowed by the supernatural and often determined membership in particular groups, such as war or medicine societies. One of the most prominent societies was the Midewiwin (Grand Medicine Society), whose members acted as spiritual leaders and healers. They were prominent among the Ojibway, Odawa, Potawatomi, Menominee, Winnebago, Sauk, Fox, and Kickapoo. They promoted health through balanced lifestyles, the use of herbs in healing, and the vision quest. Their society remains influential at the beginning of the twenty-first century, although the birch-bark scrolls containing their songs and stories were lost.

From 1745 to 1815 a religiously inspired struggle arose that achieved a type of Pan-Indian unity. From the rebellion led by the Odawa Pontiac (c. 1720–1769) in the 1760s through the work of the Shawnee Prophet Tenskwatawa (1775–1836), brother of Tecumseh (c. 1768–1813), Indian lands of the Midwest were afire with intertribal movements that proclaimed that Indian ceremonies and rituals, which held the key to sacred power, could successfully resist colonial expansion. The emergence of Indian prophets briefly united various peoples into militant factions but these movements were unable to overcome the ethnic diversity of the region. These "nativistic" movements rejected attempts at accommodation to white ways and were, therefore, often opposed by those communities whose lifestyles had been affected through contact with Europeans and involvement in the fur trade.

Fur-trade villages found that access to trade goods enhanced both their social prestige and their political power. Many Potawatomi, Odawa, and Miami villages became increasingly sedentary and were suppliers to the trade, producing sufficient agricultural goods to feed transient Europeans. Once the Seven Years' War ended and Indians no longer supplied warriors on behalf of their French allies, demographic stability returned to the region. Many villages ignored the British call for allies to fight on their behalf against the Americans during the Revolutionary War. In fact, many communities switched their allegiance to the Americans when the French joined the war as colonial allies.

Despite their less than enthusiastic support for the British, the outcome of the American Revolution left Indians in the future Midwest completely unprepared for the destabilizing events of the nineteenth century. There was no longer a government policy that sought to contain the Anglo world on the eastern seaboard. Emigrants and land speculators forced the opening of the West through the Ohio River Valley. The Cumberland Gap, the only natural opening through the mountains, funneled the newcomers directly into the Ohio River Valley. However, the Appalachian Mountains continued to serve as a natural barrier to westward movement, reinforced by Britain's refusal to relinquish control over Forts Detroit and Michilimackinac until the defeat of the Indian coalition at the Battle of Fallen Timbers in August 1794 by a U.S. army under the command of General Anthony Wayne. The geographical heart of the region was broached once the Americans controlled the Mississippi. The region's expansive river network brought a flood of Anglo invaders onto Indian lands. The subsequent defeat of Tecumseh and the Prophet signaled the end of pan-Indian resistance and many, although not all, nineteenth-century communities faced voluntary migration and/or forced removal.

Sources and Further Reading: Emma Helen Blair, *The Indian Tribes of the Upper Mississippi Valley and Regions of the Great Lakes* (1996); James A. Clifton, George L. Cornell, and James M. McClurken, *People of the Three Fires* (1986); Gregory Evans Dowd, *A Spirited Resistance* (1992); R. David Edmunds, *The Potawatomis, Keepers of the Fire* (1978); W. Vernon Kinietz, *The Indians of the Western Great Lakes, 1615–1760* (1991); Michael N. McConnell, *A Country Between: The Upper Ohio Valley and Its Peoples, 1724–1774* (1992); Stewart Rafert, *The Miami Indians of Indiana* (1996); Susan Sleeper-Smith, *Indian Women and French Men* (2001); Helen Hornbeck Tanner, *Atlas of Great Lakes Indian History* (1987); Richard White, *The Middle Ground: Indians, Empires, and Republics in the Great Lakes Region, 1650–1815* (1991).

Susan Sleeper-Smith
Michigan State University

Woodlands

The Woodland peoples have populated the region that became the Midwest for several thousand years. The territory occupied by the Woodland Indians can be roughly defined as the land bordered by the Great Lakes to the north, the Ohio River to the south and east, and the Mississippi River to the west. Some of the earliest Woodland Indians have been generically classified as Mound Builders due to the fact that they built hundreds of earthen mounds. The early Woodland Indians, known as the Adena, constructed impressive conical mounds in the Ohio Valley. A subsequent cultural group know as the Hopewell (200 B.C. to A.D. 500) built a series of mounds, including the monumental Serpent Mound, throughout modern southern Ohio. Its cultural impact spread across the Ohio River, west to the Mississippi River, and north into what is now Michigan. Another major group of Mound Builders was the Mississippian peoples (A.D. 750 to the 1500s). Regardless of the particular group that built them, these mounds contain much of the physical evidence (pottery, jewelry, skeletal remains) of the cultures of these prehistoric peoples. The purpose of the mounds is subject to broad speculation. Some, such as Fort Ancient in southwestern Ohio, appear to have been designed as defensive structures. Others, such as the city-state of Cahokia in Illinois, appear to have been cultural and economic centers as well as possible centers of religious and ceremonial activities.

The pre-Columbian Woodland Indians survived through a combination of hunting and gathering and agriculture. Most Woodland males hunted deer and smaller animals as well as buffalo in the western parts of the future Midwest. Females grew a combination of crops, most notably the "Three Sisters," maize, beans, and squash. Woodland peoples, especially those in the northern Great Lakes region such as the Ojibwa, also relied heavily on fishing to supplement their diets. The Woodland peoples typically lived in semipermanent villages located on or near rivers or lakes. Woodland Indians practiced a wide variety of religions, most based on a creation story involving several gods and demigods.

First contact with Europeans took place along the shores of the Great Lakes in the early to mid-1600s, when French explorers and Jesuit missionaries penetrated the region. A burgeoning fur trade developed between the French and the Woodland Indians, particularly those located in present-day Michigan and Wisconsin. This led to competition among tribes for access to French trade goods, which included metal tools and cooking utensils, cloth and clothing, firearms, and alcohol. By the 1700s many tribes had become dependent on trade goods. Competition for the lucrative Indian trade combined with European affairs led to conflict between the British and the French, culminating in the French and Indian War. The Woodland Indians overwhelmingly sided with the French, reliable trade partners who posed less threat to their lands than the English colonists. The resulting defeat of the French did not quash Native American resistance to the British. In 1763 an Ottawa leader named Pontiac, aided by the religious prophet Neolin, a Delaware, led a multitribal coalition of Woodland peoples against the encroachment of British soldiers and settlers. This war, sometimes called Pontiac's Rebellion, saw the Native American forces nearly defeat the British. However, after toppling many of the western British outposts, Pontiac was unable to capture Fort Detroit and his army disbanded.

For the next thirty years, the Woodland peoples fought irregularly against the Europeans. During the American Revolution, most Woodland people either remained neutral or, like the Shawnee and the Delaware, fought with the British against the American colonists, who threatened to expand unchecked into the Midwest if victorious. Following the colonial victory, Americans began to expand rapidly into Kentucky, and in the late 1780s crossed the Ohio River into present-day Ohio. This sparked wide-scale warfare. In 1790, a coalition of Woodland Indians led by the Shawnee Blue Jacket and Little Turtle of the Miami defeated an American military expedition intent upon burning their winter food supplies. The following year the Indians destroyed an army led by Arthur St. Clair, governor of the Northwest Territory. Then in August 1794, a better organized American army crushed the Indians at the Battle of Fallen Timbers near present-day Toledo, Ohio. The Woodland Indians had no choice but to cede most of present-day Ohio and part of present-day Indiana to the United States.

The first half of the 1800s saw momentous changes in the lives of the Woodland peoples. Through a plethora of treaty agreements, the United States acquired vast amounts of territory in exchange for monetary payments and land set aside for tribes as reservations. Despite efforts to oppose these treaties, most notably the coalition formed by the Shawnee Tecumseh and his brother, Tenskwatawa (the Prophet), from 1805 to 1813, and the brief war conducted by Sauk and Fox chief Black Hawk and his allies in 1832, white expansion into the Woodland homeland proceeded rapidly. Many Native Americans saw little to be gained in resistance and began to acculturate, adopting some white traits such as style of dress, farming techniques, and religion while maintaining a unique cultural identity. In the 1830s President Andrew Jackson's removal policies forced many Woodland tribes such as the Shawnee, the Wyandot, and the Delaware to relocate to the Indian Territory (Oklahoma). Many northern Woodlands peoples such as the Ojibwa and Menominee were restricted to reservations in remote areas of the Midwest.

Following the removal period, Woodland Indians remaining in the Midwest were subject to government efforts designed to eradicate Indian cultures and replace them with European American cultures. Some Woodland peoples were subject to allotment, a process by which the United States abolished the reservation system and replaced it with private land ownership. The Shawnee who had been removed to Kansas in the 1820s and 1830s were compelled to sign an allotment treaty in 1854. This policy escalated from the 1880s onward after passage of the General Allotment Act in 1887.

Native American children were sent to boarding schools scattered throughout the Midwest and other parts of the United States. The Minnesota Ojibwa children who attended the Flandreau boarding school in South Dakota were forced to abandon their language and outward Indian appearance in favor of speaking English and learning trades that included blacksmithing and agriculture. Despite these efforts many students retained their culture privately.

In the latter half of the twentieth century, Woodlands peoples, along with other Native Americans, went through the termination and relocation era. The Menominee tribe of Wisconsin had their reservation status terminated by the United States in 1954 but fought for and regained federal recognition in 1973. Meanwhile, many Woodlands peoples relocated to midwestern cities like Milwaukee, Chicago, and Minneapolis, usually with assurances of government job and housing assistance. These promises often went unmet, but more than half of the Native American population migrated off-reservation and into urban areas.

Since the 1970s many Woodland peoples have successfully regained long violated or ignored treaty rights. One instance involved the Chippewa (Ojibwa) people of Wisconsin, who regained some of their fishing rights through federal court proceedings in the 1980s, though the case caused wide-scale racial tension. Many Woodland peoples also received monetary compensation for lost lands and rights from the Indian Claims Commission. Other groups such as the Miami Nation of Indiana have attempted to establish their status as federally recognized tribal entities, with mixed results. In the early twenty-first century, the Woodland Indians are attempting to bring economic prosperity to their tribal groups by establishing casinos, building fisheries, and selling arts and crafts. They are also supporting educational programs designed to maintain distinctive cultural traits such as language.

Sources and Further Reading: Brenda J. Child, *Boarding School Seasons* (1998); Gregory Evans Dowd, *A Spirited Resistance* (1992); Donald L. Fixico, *Termination and Relocation* (1986); Rita Kohn and W. Lynwood Montell, *Always a People*

(1997); Michael McConnell, *A Country Between* (1992); Helen Hornbeck Tanner, ed., *Atlas of Great Lakes Indian History* (1987); Bruce G. Trigger, ed., *Handbook of North American Indians*, vol. 15 (1978); Richard White, *The Middle Ground* (1991).

Michael L. Cox
Amanda, Ohio

Plains

Scholars studying indigenous peoples in the western portion of what Americans came to call the Midwest frequently refer to the area as the Prairie Plains. The climate of the Prairie Plains, which includes the eastern Dakotas, Iowa, Nebraska, and Kansas, involves more rainfall, less severe winters, and a greater diversity of plants and animals than that of the western Great Plains. Because of the region's environment, Native American populations have continuously utilized a wide array of resources. As early as twelve thousand years ago, small migratory groups hunted the local fauna and gathered plants. By ten thousand years ago, local populations began to focus greater attention on plants and smaller mammals. Local hunters and gatherers more than likely made extensive use of wild seeds, tubers, nuts, roots, and fruits as well as bison, deer, and rabbits.

Because of the region's favorable climate, Native American peoples residing in the Prairie Plains developed agriculture and pottery. They also began to inhabit sedentary villages and, in some cases, construct elaborate burial mounds. By at least 500 B.C., corn, sunflowers, marsh elder, and squash had begun to be domesticated. Soon after the emergence of horticultural practices, dispersed semisedentary villages appeared along the banks of local rivers and their tributaries.

Even though domesticates became an important component of the local diet, the hunting and gathering of a diversity of undomesticated resources continued to be a significant source of food. Presumably, after the planting of crops, village inhabitants left their communities for an extended period of time in order to hunt and gather enough excess resources to ensure an adequate supply of food during the winter months.

At around A.D. 1000, settlements in the eastern Plains began to be fortified with moats and palisades. During this period, the climate became drier and horticulturists from elsewhere began to migrate to the arable lands of the eastern Plains. More than likely, competition for these farmlands led to endemic warfare between the newcomers and the locals.

Linking these early archaeological settlements with present-day indigenous populations in the Prairie Plains has been possible in a number of cases. Linguistically there are two main language families: the Siouan and the Caddoan. Among Siouan groups present in the region, the Hidatsas and the Mandans can be tied to inhabitants residing in the Upper Missouri river region in A.D. 1200. During the early 1700s, a large diaspora of other Siouan-speaking communities migrated into the Prairie Plains. These include the Iowas, Poncas, Omahas, Kansas, Otos, Missouris, Osages, and Quapaws. Apparently these communities originated in the Ohio River Valley and moved westward in response to the expansion of European American settlers and Native American groups.

Two Caddoan-speaking populations can also be linked to archaeological groups residing in the Prairie Plains in A.D. 1200. These include the Arikiras, who lived near the Hidatsas and Mandans in the Upper Missouri River region, and the Pawnees, who inhabited the central and eastern portions of Nebraska and Kansas. Both the Arikiras and the Pawnees migrated into the region from the eastern part of the southern Plains.

Beginning in the 1700s and continuing until the reservation era, disease and warfare decimated indigenous populations in the western portion of what became the Midwest. Smallpox, typhoid, and measles generally killed the elderly, who were the repository of a community's knowledge, as well as the young. Each of the diseases also tended to occur during the planting and harvesting cycle. As a result, populations already weakened by disease often succumbed to starvation rather than the illness itself.

Incursions into the Prairie Plains by nomadic groups and European American settlers during the 1700s and 1800s caused many of the local populations to alter their settlement patterns. A number of the original communities merged into fewer villages in order to provide themselves with greater protection from predatory enemies. The Mandans, the Hidatsas, and the Arikiras as well as the Otos and the Missouris instituted this strategy. In the case of the Pawnees, the entire community chose to relocate to Oklahoma in order to gain relief from the relentless attacks of nomadic Lakotas. Other populations, such as the Omahas and the Poncas, relinquished territory to the more aggressive Lakotas.

During the 1800s, sedentary populations remaining in the Prairie Plains were placed on reservations. The Mandans, the Hidatsas, and the Arikiras share the Fort Berthold reservation in North Dakota. Members of this reservation support a strong educational system that incorporates culturally specific learning. Currently, there are more college graduates living on the Fort Berthold reservation than on any other reservation in North Dakota.

The Omahas currently share a reservation in Nebraska with the Winnebagos. Although the Poncas once had a reservation along the Niobrara River in Nebraska, they were terminated as a tribe during the 1950s. When they finally succeeded in regaining recognition by the federal government in the 1990s, none of their reservation land was given back to them. Nevertheless, the Poncas continue to persevere and are committed to building a strong community. At present both the Omahas and the Poncas are committed to language-retention efforts. In addition, the University of Nebraska at Lincoln offers an advanced four-semester course on the Omaha language.

Unfortunately, the languages of the Kansas, the Otos, the Missouris, the Quapaws, and the Iowas have become extinct. Efforts are being made to reintroduce these languages into the primary schools, but so far federal funds have not been made available for this project. Both the Kansas and the Iowas have reservation lands in Nebraska and Kansas. The Otos and the Missouris, who have merged into one community, have a small reservation in Oklahoma.

The Prairie Plains region has a rich archaeological history and remains a vibrant place for Native American peoples. Powwows, community colleges, and Indian centers often serve as a mainstay for local indigenous groups. Although development of the reservations continues to lag behind the rest of the United States, many local governments are becoming more successful in attracting businesses and tourists.

Sources and Further Reading: Patricia Albers, "Changing Patterns of Ethnicity in the Northeastern Plains, 1780–1870," in Jonathan D. Hill, ed., *History, Power and Identity* (1996); Douglas Bamforth, *Ecology and Human Organization on the Great Plains* (1988); Edward Barry, *The Fort Belknap Indian Reservation* (1974); Eli Paul, *The Nebraska Indian Wars Reader, 1865–1877* (1998); Glendolin Wagner and William Allen, *Blankets and Moccasins* (1987).

Martha McCollough
University of Nebraska–Lincoln

Métis

Métis is a term sometimes used, especially in Canada, to describe people of mixed Native American and European ancestry. The first métis people were the children of fur traders, often French Canadians, and Indian women of the tribes with which they traded.

During the eighteenth and early nineteenth centuries, the traders sought intermarriage in order to create connections between themselves and Native American peoples with whom they hoped to exchange blankets, kettles, guns, and other items for furs. Indians viewed these relationships as methods of incorporating outsiders into kinship networks, with an associated set of obligations for loyalty, honesty, and generosity. Indian wives frequently served as mediators, translators, and cultural interpreters between their own communities and their husbands'. Métis children carried on these traditions of mediation.

Although many métis children grew up in Indian villages, by the late eighteenth century some fur-trade families had founded distinctive towns. Detroit, Green Bay, Peoria, Milwaukee, St. Paul, Chicago, and Vincennes are among over fifty cities founded before 1830 where a high percentage of the residents were métis. Typically the métis spoke French, their mother's Indian language, and often several others. Most were at least nominally Roman Catholic. The métis numbered about ten to fifteen thousand in 1830.

The culture of fur-trade towns reflected a mixture of both Native American and European traditions. Métis women generally dressed in the native style, with loose knee-length dresses and leggings of trade cloth, moccasins, and jewelry of beads and trade silver. Although elite men dressed in European American style, fur trade workers, such as *voyageurs* (boatmen), developed distinctive styles of dress including calico shirts, bright woven belts, and a variety of hats. Métis fiddlers entertained at dances; card parties and sleigh rides enlivened cold winter months. Although métis townspeople did not maintain the seasonal migrations of their Indian cousins, the maple-sugaring season in early spring often lured a large percentage of them to sugar groves, where they camped for weeks at a time. Here they combined traditional Indian sugar-making techniques with Easter celebrations. Crepes were delicious with maple syrup.

The early nineteenth century brought changes to the métis as Anglo Americans and European immigrants came to dominate the old fur-trade towns. Prominent métis included the Brisbois family of Prairie du Chien; the Grignons of Green Bay and Kakauna, Wisconsin; and the LeClaires of Davenport, Iowa. Most métis people, however, did not benefit from the changes. Confronted with new political institutions, court language, economic practices, Protestant churches, and unfamiliar concepts of race and gender hierarchy, some migrated north and westward to Canada. A few joined Indian kin in their villages and reservations. Others lost or sold their land and removed to the countryside or smaller towns. In addition, some métis from the Pembina/Red River region of Minnesota, North Dakota, and Manitoba moved south, as did refugees from Louis Riel's unsuccessful Manitoba rebellion after 1870. Some of the latter joined the Turtle Mountain reservation of North Dakota in 1882.

Sources and Further Reading: Lucy Eldersveld Murphy, *A Gathering of Rivers* (2000); Jacqueline Peterson and Jennifer S.H. Brown, eds., *The New Peoples* (1985); Susan Sleeper-Smith, *Indian Women and French Men* (2001); Tanis Chapman Thorne, *The Many Hands of My Relations* (1996).

Lucy Eldersveld Murphy
The Ohio State University–Newark

Nineteenth-Century Americans

In the early nineteenth century native-born people from New England, the Middle Atlantic region, and the Upland South migrated to the Midwest, where they laid dominant patterns for the region's economic, cultural, and political development. Each group carried distinctive cultural habits, but by midcentury their amalgamation had created a prosperous agrarian capitalism that dominated the region's economy. French Canadians were initially a sizable group in the upper Midwest but eventually assimilated into the larger culture despite a distinct language and religion. In contrast, people of color remained isolated by racial discrimination, confined to urban ghettos or small rural settlements. Nevertheless, all groups laid a foundation for later migrations of more diverse groups of peoples. Furthermore, conflicts between groups of native-born Americans created powerful political parties and forged a strong middle-class ethos that would influence the history of the entire nation.

The timing of the migration of American-born peoples to the Midwest in the nineteenth century can be best explained by availability of government land and an agrarianism that privileged the ideal of the independent farmer. Increasingly liberal government land policies favored the smallholder, so as the pressure of population on land in the East increased, families from eastern regions migrated westward to buy enough land. Wealthy speculators who had purchased large tracts under the terms of the Land Ordinance of 1785 sold their lands rather than pay taxes, increasing the supply of land. The federal grant of military bounties to veterans of the War of 1812 was another way easterners acquired land in the Midwest.

The settlement patterns of native-born Americans in the nineteenth century were dictated by available routes and changing modes of transportation. Early

settlers traveled on the Mississippi and the Ohio Rivers, moving their household goods on flatboats and steamboats. The opening of the Erie Canal in 1825 created a waterway from the Atlantic Ocean to the Great Lakes, bringing settlers from western New York and upper New England. Other settlers traveled in wagons over the National Road and on primitive local roadways. State construction of canals assisted immigration in the 1840s, and after 1850 increasing numbers migrated to the Midwest via railroad, or a combination of boat and rail travel.

Early in the century, most native-born migrants settled in the countryside on freehold farms or in small towns. Regional entrepôts like Cincinnati were "spearheads of settlement," centers of commerce and transportation that served a rural hinterland. Due to their location as rail-transport centers, by 1850 cities like St. Louis and Chicago reached prominence. By the 1870s a pattern of dominant and subordinate cities had been established in the Midwest, anchored by St. Louis, Chicago, Cincinnati, Cleveland, Detroit, Milwaukee, and Indianapolis. Many rural people migrated to the cities, supplying labor for factories and swelling the size of St. Louis to a half million and Chicago to one million people by 1890.

The major American-born groups that settled the Midwest in the nineteenth century originated in three eastern source regions: New England and New York, the Middle Atlantic region, and the Upland South. The prevailing latitudinal migration patterns from east to west resulted in a stronger Yankee/Yorker influence in the northern Midwest and dominance by southerners in the lower parts of the midwestern territories. Those from the Middle Atlantic region tended to be found in the upper and middle Midwest, often mingling with the Yankee/Yorkers. While distinctive cultures and migration patterns can be traced, we must proceed with caution because cultural stereotypes of the period tended to be extreme versions of a more complex reality. Nevertheless, early settlers were well aware of those cultural differences and often found opportunity to ridicule the arrogant Yankee or the lazy southerner.

Yankee/Yorkers migrated westward to what would become the northern tier of midwestern states: Michigan, Ohio, Indiana, Illinois, Wisconsin, and Minnesota. Yankee/Yorkers tended to cluster in small towns where they operated small shops and stores, complemented by raising corn and wheat. They established Protestant churches and set up schools that served as civic centers for a larger rural hinterland. In larger towns, Yankees founded colleges, temperance societies, and fraternal lodges and printed newspapers. While region of origin does not absolutely correlate to the extent of market participation, Yankees were the most eager to embrace the opportunities of the market. The ascendance of Chicago as the region's major metropolis by the century's end resulted in part from the dominance of Yankee/Yorkers who were characterized as highly attuned to the market.

People born in the Middle Atlantic states of Pennsylvania, Delaware, and New Jersey migrated directly westward, some in staged patterns via Ohio and Indiana, before reaching Illinois and Iowa. They were bound by kin ties, but unlike the Yankees were not likely to settle in towns. Experienced in producing for market, they were committed to a diversified agricultural commerce of corn, wheat, and livestock. Many were of Scotch-Irish descent, and they established Presbyterian churches. Because they were neither

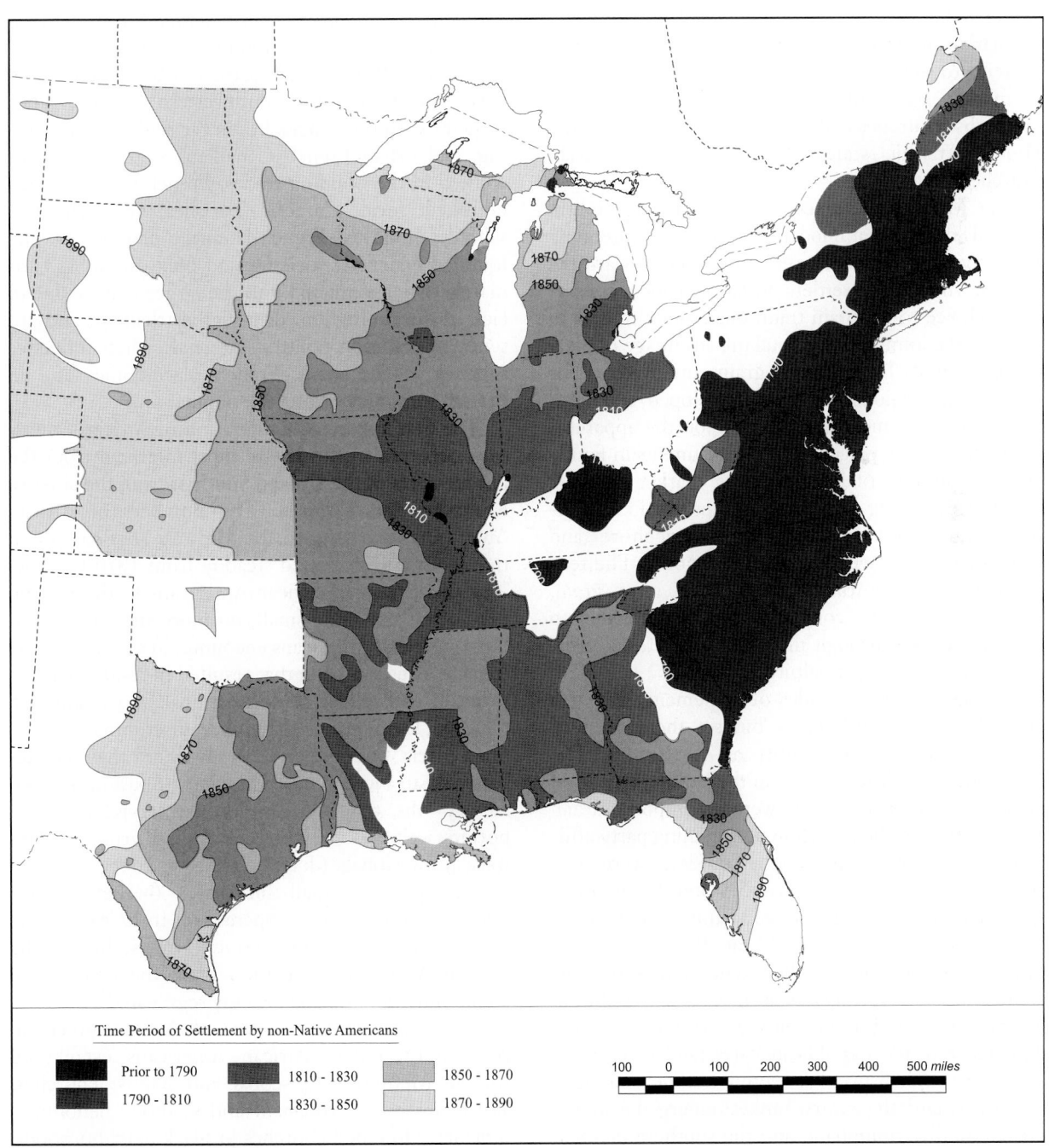

Time Period of Settlement by non-Native Americans

Prior to 1790 | 1810 - 1830 | 1850 - 1870
1790 - 1810 | 1830 - 1850 | 1870 - 1890

The progress of non–Native American settlement, 1787–1850. Prepared by Margaret Popovich. *Source:* Henry Gannett, *Statistical Atlas of the United States, Based Upon Results of the Eleventh Census* (1890).

Yankees nor Southerners, many served as cultural brokers in sectional conflicts.

Upland Southerners entered the Midwest through southern Ohio, Indiana, and Illinois, traveling on the Ohio and Mississippi Rivers and migrating overland on the National Road. They dominated the early settlement of states like Illinois and Indiana, settling on scattered farmsteads in wooded and watered areas where they planted corn and raised hogs on open lands. Kin formed migrant groups, and family ties dominated a gentry style of local politics. While some were thoroughly engaged in producing for market, more commonly the southern-born were content to settle inland and bring their produce to market seasonally. They founded Baptist and Methodist churches and joined with settlers from the Middle Atlantic states to establish Presbyterian churches.

The Midwest's characteristic agrarian capitalism resulted from accommodations to the burgeoning economy by settlers who were ambivalent toward the market. Midwestern settlers on farms made a conservative choice to maintain traditional commitments to family and community while taking advantage of market opportunity by producing grains and livestock for sale. As the regional economy developed and farm families became more dependent upon the apparatus of the market, they made subtle adjustments in family size and division of labor to meet market demand. Differences among settlement groups resulted in diverse approaches to commercial agriculture and strengthened the overall regional economy. The tendency of Middle Atlantic mirgants to grow grain, Southerners to raise corn and hogs, and Yankees to market produce through their stores created a prosperous commercial agriculture.

During the early decades of settlement, migrants noticed sectional differences but set them aside to forge a new regional identity as Westerners. The dominance of political parties in the Jacksonian period meant that sectional loyalties were less important than attitudes toward the market in determining party affiliation. But submerged sectional tensions were provoked at midcentury as Yankees and Southerners sparred over slavery, public education, and temperance movements. The Republican Party evolved in middle-class support for bourgeois values of self-control seen by Democrats as threats to republican liberty. Union victory in the Civil War ensured the dominance of the Republican Party (and its ethos of bourgeois capitalism) that would not be dislodged until the twentieth century. Yankees emerged from the war culturally triumphant, and the southern element of the population was marginalized in the new middle-class midwestern identity.

Smaller groups similarly made their mark on the Midwest. French Canadians from Quebec were originally a significant presence in the northern Midwest, specifically Michigan and Minnesota. At the end of the eighteenth century, French Canadians made up a vast majority of the white population in Michigan, but by the time Michigan became a state in 1837 they were a minority. A second wave of migration peaked in the 1880s, and by 1900 French Canadians made up 3.6 percent of the state's population.

Encouraged by the Catholic hierarchy to cluster to maintain their culture, most settled in rural areas where they engaged in mining or farming. In Minnesota, French Canadians settled in St. Paul, the Red River Valley, and the southwestern prairies. They brought with them skills in the fur trade and lumbering, and urban French Canadians were laborers or worked in the building trades. French Canadians established local Catholic parishes and parochial schools, published French-language newspapers, and founded beneficial societies and political clubs. Ultimately they assimilated into the larger culture due to lack of discrimination, dispersed settlement, and absence of common political interests. Their influence survives in the many French place-names and in French surnames among the population.

The first appreciable migration of African Americans occurred in the 1840s; most migrated from the border states of the Upland South or from the cities of Kentucky and Virginia. The numbers of African Americans migrating to the Midwest rose sharply in the 1860s and increased steadily from 1870 to 1900. The proportion of African Americans to the general population remained small, no more than 3 percent. Urban African Americans encountered systematic patterns of discrimination that resulted in residential segregation and denial of occupational opportunity. In Chicago, Detroit, and Milwaukee, discrimination confined blacks to commercial areas where they had access only to increasingly dilapidated housing. Denied factory jobs, they remained in the service trades as porters, waiters, and domestics. A small group of elites were professionals (doctors, lawyers, educators), and others operated small businesses (barbers, seamstresses, rooming house operators). In its early years the business community served whites, but as the African American population grew the commercial community became increasingly segregated.

Churches were the center of African American community. Urban African Americans established African Methodist Episcopal and Baptist churches, and mainstream Protestant and Catholic denominations later founded churches in black neighborhoods. The churches sponsored schools and women's benevolent societies and hosted political rallies. A vibrant array of other organizations emerged as the size of the urban community grew: fraternal lodges, women's clubs, literary societies, and civil rights organizations. In Chicago, African Americans founded Provident Hospital in 1891 to serve their own community in the face of racial discrimination.

Before the Civil War, Black Laws restricted the civil rights of free African Americans, but after the passage of the Fifteenth Amendment in 1870 they enjoyed a measure of civil equality. Black men could vote, and blacks were no longer legally segregated in schools and other public places (although de facto segregation did exist in the schools). African Americans were loyal to the Republican Party, and it reserved minor political offices for elite blacks. African Americans published their own newspapers to serve community interests and agitate for civil rights.

Before 1860 over three-fourths of the region's African Americans lived in rural areas. They were largely free people of color who had migrated from the Upland South, but some were fugitives from slavery. At least thirty black communities were established, mostly in Ohio and Indiana but also in southern Michigan, Illinois, and Wisconsin. Land ownership was critical to the success of rural blacks in overcoming racial discrimination, and they were freer than urban African Americans to earn a livelihood and pass assets to their children in the form of land. Like urban blacks, they remained segregated in rural enclaves where they founded their own churches, schools, and community organizations.

The Civil War reinforced Yankee dominance, notably a market-oriented culture and a strong federal state that many southern-born residents had resisted. Even the term *Yankee*, which earlier had referred to people from New England, came to symbolize all Americans. The influx of European immigrants in the nineteenth century highlighted the differences between them and native-born Americans, disguising cultural differences among the American-born groups that had settled the Midwest. The result was a homogeneous white identity that would be identified as quintessentially American by the late twentieth century. African Americans remained outsiders in the nineteenth century but would become an integral part of the region's twentieth-century identity.

Sources and Further Reading: Andrew R. L. Cayton and Peter S. Onuf, *The Midwest and the Nation* (1990); John P. DuLong, *French Canadians in Michigan* (2001); Nicole Etcheson, *The Emerging Midwest* (1996); Susan Gray, *The Yankee West* (1996); John C. Hudson, *Making the Corn Belt* (1994); Timothy R. Mahoney, *River Towns in the Great West* (1990); Susan Sessions Rugh, *Our Common Country* (2001); Allan H. Spear, *Black Chicago* (1967); John C. Teaford, *Cities of the*

Heartland (1993); Stephen A. Vincent, *Southern Seed, Northern Soil* (1999).

Susan Sessions Rugh
Brigham Young University, Utah

Yankees/Yorkers

Natives of New England and New York, also called Yankees and Yorkers, formed an important element of the Midwest's frontier population. They accounted for 572,058 immigrants according to the 1850 census (12.3 percent of U.S.-born natives in the Midwest) and 1,072,070 immigrants in 1880 (7.4 percent). Yankees and Yorkers are logically considered together because of the close demographic and cultural connections between them. Many New Englanders migrated roughly westward to upstate New York during its settlement period, perhaps sailing down the coast to New York City and up the Hudson River to Albany or struggling overland to reach the Mohawk River or the Erie Canal once it opened. The majority of Yorker natives in the Midwest came from the upstate regions heavily settled by Yankees, and many Yankees, Yorkers, or their progeny continued migrating westward. Especially throughout the northern Midwest in the nineteenth century, a strong geographical association existed between Yorker and Yankee immigrant settlements.

New England and New York migrants formed an important component of the pioneer population throughout the Midwest. They appeared early among the trans-Appalachian immigrants and founded, for example, the first major settlements in Ohio. In southeastern Ohio surrounding Marietta, the Ohio Company of Associates, an entity largely controlled by residents of Massachusetts, Rhode Island, and Connecticut, promoted 1.5 million acres of land for settlement. Yankees from western Connecticut (primarily), western Massachusetts, and upstate New York populated the Western Reserve area of northeastern Ohio that was originally claimed by Connecticut. In the southern Midwest, Yankees and Yorkers concentrated primarily in northern Ohio, Illinois, and, to a lesser extent, Indiana, but they also were among the migrants to counties near the Ohio River. Preliminary research suggests that the few Yankees and Yorkers in southern Indiana tended to be found in larger proportion in cities, towns, and small settlements than in the surrounding rural districts. Yankees and Yorkers also were a significant presence in the southern Midwest cities of Cincinnati and St. Louis.

Yankee and Yorker settlements are most commonly associated with the northern tier of midwestern states, where immigrants born in New England and

The Hayes family at Spiegel Grove, Fremont, Ohio. The Rutherford B. Hayes Presidential Center, Lucy Webb Hayes Photo Gallery.

New York formed a dominant element of the early-nineteenth-century population. In Michigan and Wisconsin in 1850, 260,303 Yankees and Yorkers accounted for over 48 percent of their U.S.-born population. In Minnesota, just 1,143 of them comprised over 28 percent of the U.S.-born population. By 1880 Yankees and Yorkers in the northern Midwest (including Dakota Territory) averaged just over 17 percent of the U.S.-born population as the number of inhabitants native to midwestern states increased. Still, no other U.S. region provided comparable percentages of immigrants. Yankee and Yorker settlers centered on the southern halves of Michigan, Wisconsin, Minnesota, and the Dakota Territory, where the focus was farming. In the northern portions of Michigan, Wisconsin, and Minnesota dominated by pine forests, the 1850 population was quite low except at key settlement points. By 1880 foreign-born immigrants comprised significant portions of this region's total population.

New York typically provided approximately twice as many immigrants to the Midwest as New England. In 1850 the Midwest's 391,482 New Yorkers heavily outnumbered its 180,576 New Englanders, with Vermont (52,529), Massachusetts (47,569), and Connecti-

cut (44,995) providing the most Yankees. By 1880 there were 770,165 New Yorkers compared to 301,905 Yankees, with 83,972 of them coming from Massachusetts, 81,189 from Vermont, and 51,509 from Maine. According to the 1850 and 1880 censuses, far larger numbers of Yorkers and Yankees lived in the northern Midwest, including Michigan, Wisconsin, Minnesota, and the Dakota Territory as well as northern Illinois, northern Ohio, and, to a lesser extent, northern Indiana, than in the southern Midwest.

Affirming the Yankee-Yorker connection, the more northerly and westerly settlement orientation of New York natives in the Midwest was mirrored by New England natives. The northern tier of midwestern states—Michigan, Wisconsin, and Minnesota—all listed New York plus at least one New England state among the top six domestic sources of settlers in 1850 and 1880. Wisconsin, heavily settled by Vermont and Massachusetts natives, provided the largest number of immigrants (11,685) to the Dakota Territory in 1880. By contrast, New England natives were a less significant portion of the total immigrant population in the southern and western Midwest, although regionally within those states (such as in northeastern Ohio) they were quite important. Among southern Midwest states only Ohio (in which Connecticut ranked sixth for 1850 with 22,855 natives in residence) had any New England state among the leading sources of immigrants in 1850 or 1880.

Genealogical records including the county origins of New Englanders and New Yorkers living in Ohio, Indiana, and Michigan by the middle of the 1800s reveal more information about their birthplaces and/or previous residences than the census. Most New Englanders in the eastern Midwest originated in central and western Massachusetts and western Vermont, although some hailed from the Boston area and others from Connecticut. Only a few migrated from New Hampshire or Maine (usually from the southern parts of those states) or from Rhode Island. Some New York natives came from the eastern Mohawk Valley and southeastern areas along the Hudson River Valley between Albany and New York City. Overwhelmingly, however, the eastern Midwest's pioneer settlers migrated either directly or indirectly from the Genesee Country, the region primarily between Syracuse and Rochester, New York. They had been born or lived in upstate New York, perhaps being married and starting a family there before moving west. Many eastern Midwest settlers born in New England, especially western and central Massachusetts and western Vermont, previously resided in the upstate New York region and perhaps were the Yorkers' parents. It appears that the migration pattern of Yankees or Yorkers to Ohio, Indiana, or Michigan was generational, originating in

New England or upstate New York, pausing in the Genesee Country and then continuing to land south of the Great Lakes.

In the northern Midwest, Yankees and Yorkers quickly established cultural hegemony. Northerners developed social and cultural institutions and soon came to dominate political, educational, and religious life. New England or New York natives such as Lyman Beecher and Rufus Putnam in Ohio, Lewis Cass and William Woodbridge in Michigan, Joshua Atwater and Stephen A. Douglas in Illinois, and Sherman Booth in Wisconsin were key figures. In Illinois and Ohio especially, where Yankees and Yorkers in the northern portions and Upland Southerners in the southern portions faced off across a Pennsylvanian middle zone, cultural and political conflict was perhaps inevitable. The stereotypes have northern and southern natives holding each other in low regard: What northerners considered progressive social, political, and educational reforms and agricultural improvements southerners saw as cultural imperialism and elitism. The geography of midwestern cultural diversity appeared in political struggles over immigration and social opportunities for blacks and each state's response to abolitionism and the Fugitive Slave Act of 1850. Differing economic ties reinforced existing cultural differences: Southern portions of midwestern states were connected to the South via the Ohio and Mississippi Rivers while northern portions linked via the Great Lakes and Erie Canal to the Northeast.

Yankees and Yorkers left significant cultural imprints on the midwestern landscape. Especially where they settled first, their architectural or material culture influences are displayed by older structures in city, town, or country, the plat of a small town with a central village green, or the placement of the barn across the road from the farmhouse. Examples of saltbox houses or Cape Cod cottages, traditional in New England, and the Greek Revival style popular in upstate New York at the turn of the nineteenth century appear throughout the Midwest, especially in northern Ohio, southern Michigan, and Wisconsin.

Place names from New England and New York frequently reappear in the northern Midwest. Directional monikers such as "Center" or "East" or "West" are common transplantations of the old township structure used in New England for small places and crossroads settlements like Liberty Center in northeastern Indiana, Berrien Center in Michigan, Richland Center in Wisconsin, Sioux Center in Iowa, and Brooklyn Center in Minnesota. Many settlements precede the New England or New York place-name with "New": New Boston in Michigan, New Auburn in Wisconsin, New Brighton in Minnesota, New Albany in Kansas. Sometimes repeated Yankee or Yorker names were scattered west by successive waves of settlers: There is a Plymouth (from Massachusetts) in Ohio, Michigan, Indiana, Wisconsin, Iowa, and Minnesota, and a Lansing (from New York) in Ohio, Michigan, Illinois, Iowa, Minnesota, and Kansas. Vermontville, Michigan, shows an even more straightforward connection. Upstate New York place-names derived from classical Greek and Roman sources and popular in the early National Period reappear in the Midwest: Seneca is found in New York, Ohio, Michigan, Wisconsin, South Dakota, Nebraska, and Kansas. Other cultural elements—traditional dialects and word use or common religious denominations like Congregationalism—connect the northern Midwest with Yankee and Yorker cultural hearths. And, mirroring broad similarities in environments, dairying remains a common form of agriculture in New England, New York, and the northern Midwest.

Sources and Further Reading: Henry H. Glassie, *Pattern in the Material Folk Culture of the Eastern United States* (1968); John C. Hudson, "Yankeeland in the Middle West," *Journal of Geography* 85 (Sept.–Oct. 1986); Richard Lyle Power, *Planting Corn Belt Culture* (1953); Malcolm J. Rohrbough, *The Trans-Appalachian Frontier* (1978); Gregory S. Rose, "South Central Michigan Yankees," *Michigan History* 70 (Mar./Apr. 1986); Lois Kimball Mathews Rosenberry, *The Expansion of New England* (1962); Robert P. Swierenga, "The Settlement of the Old Northwest: Ethnic Pluralism in a Featureless Plain," *Journal of the Early Republic* 9 (Spring 1989); Wilbur Zelinsky, "Classical Town Names in the United States: The Historical Geography of an American Idea," *Geographical Review* 57 (Oct. 1967); Wilbur Zelinsky, *The Cultural Geography of the United States* (1973).

Gregory Rose
The Ohio State University–Marion

Middle Atlantic Europeans

Settlers native to the Middle Atlantic states (Pennsylvania, New Jersey, Maryland, and Delaware) accounted for a significant portion of the U.S.-born midwestern population according to the 1850 and 1880 censuses. The four states together provided 443,959 immigrants in 1850 and 684,789 in 1880, or 9.5 percent and 4.7 percent, respectively, of settlers born in the United States. Their presence was proportionally greatest in Ohio, Iowa, and Minnesota in 1850 and, additionally, in Nebraska and Kansas in 1880. Immigrants from the Middle Atlantic states concentrated in a wedge tapering northwestward from Ohio, where they were the largest group in nearly all counties, through northern Indiana and Illinois and into Iowa, Kansas, and Nebraska.

Pennsylvanians were by far the largest group of Middle Atlantic natives in the Midwest, numbering 325,143 in 1850 and 552,256 in 1880. In 1850 three of every four Middle Atlantic natives had a Pennsylvania birthplace; by 1880 it was four of every five. Pennsylvania's leadership as a source of settlers wanes farther west and northwest in the Midwest, but in Ohio it was overwhelmingly the largest provider, domestic or foreign. Early-nineteenth-century Pennsylvanians living in the eastern Midwest mostly came from the southeastern and southwestern regions of the state. Other Middle Atlantic states, smaller both physically and demographically, provided considerably fewer natives to the Midwest. Maryland was the second most important source of Middle Atlantic natives, accounting for 60,944 in 1850 and 63,357 in 1880. Somewhat fewer midwestern migrants were born in New Jersey: 47,554 in 1850 and 60,448 in 1880. Delaware supplied no more than 10,500 settlers in either census year.

The Middle Atlantic impact in the Midwest extended beyond people actually born there. Given the dominance of Pennsylvanians, many next-generation Ohio natives who moved farther west carried their parents' Middle Atlantic culture. Ohio was the largest source of domestic birthplaces in Indiana and Iowa in 1850 and 1880, the second-largest source in 1850 and the largest source in 1880 for Illinois, and the second-largest source for Michigan and Wisconsin in both census years. The large Amish and Mennonite populations in Ohio, Indiana, and Iowa represent another originally Pennsylvanian influence still apparent in the Midwest. The North Carolina–born Quakers concentrated in east central Indiana by 1850 also carried some Middle Atlantic characteristics due to their ancestors' migrations from southeastern Pennsylvania down the Shenandoah Valley to Piedmont North Carolina, which they left for Indiana.

Beyond their demographic impact, Middle Atlantic natives and Pennsylvanians in particular influenced midwestern culture. The majority of traditional midwestern dialects and the predominant religious affiliations in the Midwest originated in the Middle Atlantic states. Elements of midwestern material culture, such as the I-house and the Pennsylvania banked barn, also show Middle Atlantic influence, especially on the southern Midwest landscape. The large-scale mixed farming activity traditionally associated with the Midwest—production of wheat for sale and corn for use as animal feed; production of livestock for meat or dairy purposes—has as its model the agricultural system perfected in southeastern Pennsylvania in the late 1700s. The Pennsylvania Dutch there, like midwesterners a generation or two later, quickly moved production from subsistence agriculture to commercialization.

Sources and Further Reading: Henry H. Glassie, *Pattern in the Material Folk Culture of the Eastern United States* (1968); Gregory S. Rose, "The Southern Midwest as 'Pennsylvania Extended,'" *The East Lakes Geographer* 23 (1988); Robert P. Swierenga, "The Settlement of the Old Northwest: Ethnic Pluralism in a Featureless Plain," *Journal of the Early Republic* 9 (Spring 1989); Wilbur Zelinsky, *The Cultural Geography of the United States* (1973).

Gregory Rose
The Ohio State University–Marion

Upland Southerners

The South provided a considerable portion of the Midwest's nineteenth-century settlers. Many were born in the "older" seaboard states of Virginia and North and South Carolina; few were born in the "newer" seaboard states of Georgia, Alabama, or Mississippi. Kentucky provided the most southern immigrants for much of the Midwest, while Tennessee also sent many settlers. An effective approach to determining the origins of the Midwest's southerners uses the Fall Line to divide the South into lowland and upland areas. The Fall Line, a zone of falls or rapids in the rivers flowing southeastward from the Appalachian Mountains to the Atlantic Ocean, cuts roughly southwest to northeast from Columbia, South Carolina, through Raleigh, North Carolina; Richmond, Virginia; and Washington, D.C. It differentiates the Carolinas and Virginia into eastern, Lowland portions consisting of coastal plains and the Tidewater and western, Upland portions consisting of the Piedmont and the Appalachian Mountains.

Lowland areas are flatter and have better soils. By the early 1800s they had been settled longer; were more developed and prosperous; featured large landholdings supporting commercial, plantation agriculture built on the slave system; and contained large African American populations. Upland areas are topographically more varied, with hills and mountains and poorer, more easily eroded soils. By the early 1800s they were dominated by yeomen, independent farmers holding small acreages, owning few if any slaves, relying on family labor, and engaging primarily in subsistence agriculture. Most of the Upland South had been settled only since the Revolutionary War and contained few African Americans, but some places housed relatively recent German and Scotch-Irish immigrant populations. Many yeoman farmers resented the economic and political power of Lowland Southerners and the labor competition represented by the slave system.

According to nineteenth-century census records, settlers native to states fully or partially in the Upland South comprised a significant portion of the Midwest's

U.S.-born settlers. Most heavily settling the southern Midwest, especially Indiana through Missouri, southerners extended from the Ohio River approximately to the path of the National Road through Columbus, Indianapolis (southern influence bulged farther northward in Indiana), Springfield, and Jefferson City. Middle States, New York, and New England natives dominated northward. In 1850 Virginia, North Carolina, Kentucky, and Tennessee supplied 585,544 immigrants to the Midwest, 12.6 percent of the U.S.-born population. In 1880 their number had increased to 767,422, but their percentage fell to 5.3. Due to an increasing midwestern-born population, the percentage of residents born outside the Midwest decreased between 1850 and 1880, with the Upland South region experiencing the greatest decline.

Kentucky was the leading state of origin for the Midwest's Upland Southerners. Kentucky natives numbered 212,658 (4.6 percent of U.S.-born settlers) in 1850 and 326,883 in 1880 (2.3 percent). Their influence was especially strong in the southern portions of Indiana closest to northern Kentucky, but they also formed a major component of the population northward into central Indiana and across southern Illinois into Missouri. Virginia was the next-largest source of Upland Southerners, proportionally more significant in 1850 (4.4 percent, or 204,090 natives) than in 1880 (1.6 percent, or 228,834 natives, including West Virginians). Ohio contained the most Virginians (85,762 in 1850, 64,459 in 1880), primarily in the south, but Illinois and Indiana also housed between 24,697 and 41,819 each year. North Carolinians were significantly numerous in east-central and southern Indiana in 1850: Its 33,175 North Carolina natives (3.6 percent of U.S.-born settlers) accounted for over 45 percent of North Carolinians in the Midwest; another 17,009 lived in Missouri in 1850.

West of the Mississippi River, upland southern nativity was greatest in Missouri, where 172,450 (33.1 percent of U.S.-born settlers) lived in 1850 and 247,923 in 1880. Kentucky provided 40.4 percent of Missouri's Upland Southerners in 1850 and 41.5 percent in 1880; Tennessee and Virginia provided about 25 percent each in both years. Iowa's 23,718 Upland Southerners in 1850 (13.9 percent of U.S.-born settlers) increased to 40,334 in 1880 but fell to 3 percent of the U.S.-born population. The second-generation influence of Upland Southerners may be more significant west of the Mississippi River. Settling later than more easterly midwestern states, Kansas and Nebraska drew numerous immigrants from them: Illinois provided 106,992 natives to Kansas and 45,583 to Nebraska in 1880 (no state provided more settlers to either); Ohio was the birthplace of 93,396 and 31,800, respectively. Both Illinois and Ohio had strong upland southern population origins. Unless all these natives came from northern Illinois and Ohio, where northern immigrants were dominant, considerable second-generation upland southern cultural influence existed in those western Midwest states by 1880.

The Upland Southerner immigration stream included African Americans. Most were freed slaves who came on their own or with their former owners; some were escaped slaves. The Northwest Ordinance forbade the introduction of slavery north of the Ohio River. State Black Laws, however, curtailed the rights of African Americans. Southern blacks migrated to urban centers like Cincinnati and St. Louis (where slavery was permitted by the Missouri Compromise of 1820), and to rural areas. By 1850 east-central Indiana contained many African Americans born primarily in North Carolina. Southwestern Michigan was another center of African Americans from Virginia and South Carolina.

Most Upland Southerners were whites migrating from a few specific regions. Research on Indiana highlights the Shenandoah Valley from northern Virginia to eastern Tennessee, Piedmont North Carolina (also the Quaker region), and especially north-central Kentucky (roughly, Lexington to Louisville) as the key regions. Scattered other areas, such as upland South Carolina and northwestern Virginia (now West Virginia) also contributed immigrants. Ohio's Upland Southerners primarily migrated from northwestern Virginia near the Ohio River, especially the panhandle region around Wheeling, while some also came from northern Virginia's Shenandoah Valley.

Upland Southerners found the Midwest attractive and accessible, especially in the southern zones where the climate, environment, and topography were relatively familiar. Cheap, fertile lands were easily reached, and parcels were clearly delineated by a regular survey system and guaranteed by government-supplied titles. Accurately surveyed and titled land was important to Upland Southerners because in their old homes many had been plagued by unclear titles for lands surveyed using the irregular, unsystematic metes-and-bounds method and sold by private landholders. The inability to gain clear title to his land in Kentucky helped lure Abraham Lincoln's father, Thomas (born in Virginia's Shenandoah Valley), and his young family to southern Indiana.

Upland Southerners typically were the first settlers in the southern Midwest, initially controlling territorial and state governments and establishing the political and social culture. They influenced the enactment of Black Laws in Ohio, Indiana, Illinois, and Michigan, which were intended to limit immigration by African Americans; require the posting of bonds to ensure economic self-sufficiency; and block them from voting, serving on juries, testifying in court, or having their children educated by public funds. Illinois went further, substituting a fixed period of indentured servitude for slavery outlawed by the Northwest Ordinance. As northern Ohio, Indiana, and Illinois filled with Yankees, Upland Southerners' political and cultural dominance faded. Political conflict underlain by cultural differences emerged over African American immigration and civil rights, state support for internal improvements, public support for education, and other issues. Cultural perceptions or misperceptions added fuel to political conflicts. Many Upland Southerners believed that Yankees regarded them as socially, educationally, and economically inferior. The spread of anti-slavery sentiments reinforced the sense that Yankees were insensitive to Upland Southern settlers' historical, cultural, and economic ties with the slaveholding South.

The culture of the Upland South, much of which originated in southeastern Pennsylvania and spread down the Shenandoah Valley, accompanied its migrating population. Especially strong in the southern Midwest, upland southern culture was characterized by distinctive dialect, expressions, and word selections; unique architectural and material culture styles (folk housing, barns, fencing); and the prominence of Baptists, Methodists, and Quakers. Major figures in the nineteenth-century Midwest also had upland southern connections. Thomas Worthington of Ohio was born in what is now West Virginia. The Methodist circuit rider Peter Cartwright, native to Virginia's Shenandoah Valley, moved from Kentucky to central Illinois. And the Midwest's most famous Upland Southerner was Abraham Lincoln, who was born in north-central Kentucky, grew up in southern Indiana, and built his reputation in central Illinois.

Sources and Further Reading: John D. Barnhart, "Sources of Southern Migration into the Old Northwest," *Mississippi Valley Historical Review* 22 (June 1935); Russel L. Gerlach, *Settlement Patterns in Missouri* (1986); Henry H. Glassie, *Pattern in the Material Folk Culture of the Eastern United States* (1968); John C. Hudson, "North American Origins of Middlewestern Frontier Populations," *Annals of the Association of American Geographers* 78 (Sept. 1988); Milton Newton, "Cultural Preadaptation and the Upland South," *Geoscience and Man* 5 (June 1974); Richard Lyle Power, *Planting Corn Belt Culture* (1953); Gregory S. Rose, "Upland Southerners: The County Origins of Southern Migrants to Indiana by 1850," *Indiana Magazine of History* 82 (Sept. 1986); Wilbur Zelinsky, *The Cultural Geography of the United States* (1973); Wilbur Zelinsky, "The Population Geography of the Free Negro in Ante-bellum America," *Population Studies* 3 (Mar. 1950).

Gregory Rose
The Ohio State University–Marion

French Canadians

Shortly after New France became a royal colony in 1663, the French crown began sponsoring expeditions into the interior of North America. As a result, explorers and missionaries from French Canada were among the first people of European ancestry to establish a presence in the vast territory that became the Midwest. Father Jacques Marquette, Louis Jolliet, Cavalier de la Salle, and Henri de Tonti were soon followed by *coureurs de bois* engaged in the fur trade, some of whom settled in the region. A small number of settlers later established communities at Peoria, Kaskaskia, St. Genevieve, Kankakee, Vincennes, St. Paul, and Detroit.

Most of the region was under the administration of the royal government located in Québec until 1717, when its southern reaches were transferred administratively to the French government of Louisiana. The Treaty of Paris of 1763, which ceded the region east of the Mississippi to Great Britain, temporarily ended most immigration from Canada to the territories east of the Mississippi, as would the Louisiana Purchase of 1803 for those west of the Mississippi. Prior to the Treaty of Paris, France had ceded the latter possessions to Spain, though Spanish governance frequently remained in the hands of French administrators. France would regain the vast Louisiana territory in 1800 before selling it to the United States in 1803. At the time, Missouri had the largest number of residents of French Canadian ancestry in the Midwest.

French Canadians were active in the development of the region. Pierre Ménard, born in Québec, became Illinois's first lieutenant governor when it gained statehood in 1818; Gabriel Richard, the pastor of a French Canadian parish in Detroit, was elected Michigan's delegate to Congress in 1823. French Canadian immigration, especially to Michigan but also to Wisconsin and Minnesota, began anew in the 1850s as the forest and later the mining industries expanded. Well before the Civil War, a new immigration was also noted in Illinois, particularly around Bourbonnais and adjoining Kankakee, where French Canadians found fertile farmland and where their numbers were sufficiently large by 1848 for them to support a resident French Canadian priest. Others were attracted to Chicago, which was growing substantially, particularly after the Civil War. They were a sufficiently large presence in the city for Louis Fréchette, who would become a major French Canadian poet, to found two French newspapers while living there from 1866 to 1871. French Canadians, however, tended to concentrate in certain regions and cities. They never became a substantial percentage of the population of any of the midwestern states as they did in New England. They also worked in a variety of economic sectors, in contrast to French Canadians in the Northeast, most of whom were factory workers.

French Canadians in the United States retained a high level of loyalty to the Catholic Church, and as soon as their numbers were sufficient they founded parishes served by French-speaking clergy. By 1892 there were four such parishes in Chicago and three in Minneapolis-St. Paul. Numerous other cities and towns in the Midwest supported French Canadian churches. (Illinois and Michigan each had more than a dozen communities with such parishes, but these could be found in villages in Wisconsin, Minnesota, North Dakota, and Kansas as well.) In Minnesota, beyond Minneapolis-St. Paul, which had a French-Canadian population of approximately eighteen thousand in 1891, the largest settlements were in Polk County in the Red River Valley. The strong communitarian inclinations of French Canadians also led them to found fraternal and social organizations, such as the Saint-Jean-Baptiste societies, that complemented parish life.

By 1868 the increasing number of French Canadians in the Midwest led to the establishment of Saint Viator College in Bourbonnais, Illinois, by the French Canadian religious order the Clercs de Saint-Viateur, for the purpose of serving the educational needs of francophones living in the Midwest. Saint Viator, which was granted a university charter in 1874 by the state of Illinois, was especially important in training young men who would in turn serve the French-speaking community as priests, doctors, and lawyers. French Canadians founded approximately three dozen French-language newspapers in the Midwest in the nineteenth century, mostly in Michigan, Illinois, and Minnesota. While most were short-lived, a few, such as *Le Courrier de l'Illinois* (Kankakee) and *Le Canadien* (St. Paul) lasted more than two decades. The French Canadian community of the Midwest was considered sufficiently important for Americans of French Canadian descent, most of whom lived in New England, to hold their national convention in Detroit in 1869 and in Chicago in 1872. Their highest concentrations in the Midwest were in Michigan, Illinois, Wisconsin, and Minnesota.

By the early twentieth century, some French Canadian organizations in the Midwest were corresponding with one another in English, and by the mid-1930s, some leaders of French Canadian social organizations were no longer able to hold meetings in French, a clear sign that facility with the language had waned. At Saint Viator College, the only French-speaking college of liberal arts to have been founded in the Midwest, most of the instruction was by then given in English. Immigration ceased after the imposition of strict border-crossing rules with the advent of the Great Depression, and with few new immigrants to maintain the links with the original culture, the assimilation of French-Canadians into the larger American culture accelerated. Saint Viator College, battered by the financial crisis of the thirties, was forced to close its doors in 1939.

While the community has today lost much of its cohesion and identity, its historical role can still be detected in the toponomy of the region: in the ending of the name of the state of Illinois; in the names of cities such as Des Moines, Dubuque, Duluth, Detroit, Eau Claire, Prairie du Chien, and Sault Ste. Marie; in those of rivers such as the Des Plaines and the St. Croix; and even in the motto of the state of Minnesota: *L'Étoile du Nord*.

Sources and Further Reading: D. Aidan, "French Canadian Communities in the Upper Midwest during the Nineteenth Century," in Dean Lowder and Eric Waddell, eds., *French America* (1993); Charles Balesi, *The Time of the French in the Heart of North America, 1673–1818* (1992).

Émile J. Talbot
University of Illinois–Urbana-Champaign

African Americans

The nineteenth-century Midwest was a contested borderland for African Americans who imagined it as a promised land free from slavery and experienced it as a place where they were largely unwelcome. To a significant extent, the national debate over slavery and African American civil rights focused on the Midwest, centering on such famous events as the Missouri Compromise of 1820, the Kansas Nebraska Act of 1854, and the *Dred Scott v. Sandford* decision of 1857.

The Northwest Ordinance of 1787 made slavery illegal north of the Ohio River, and the midwestern states with the exception of Missouri formally abolished the institution when they were admitted to the Union. In Indiana and Illinois, proslavery forces mounted strong campaigns that ultimately failed, largely because white settlers feared that slavery would devalue their labor and create an aristocracy. Because of exceptions and lax enforcement, some African Americans remained enslaved until the mid-1800s. Missouri was the midwestern anomaly due to the Missouri Compromise, which balanced the admission of slave Missouri with free Maine. When Missouri finally abolished slavery in 1865 more than 114,000 slaves were freed.

Many whites feared that the region would prove irresistible to free African Americans and fleeing slaves. The majority of white residents wanted to be free of both slavery and African Americans. Before the Civil

War, all territories and states created "Black Laws" to keep African Americans from entering or settling. Most demanded that African American settlers post a five hundred dollar bond and possess papers of freedom. Some, including Illinois, Indiana, and Iowa, enacted exclusion laws that technically barred any free African Americans from entering their states at all. While most of these laws were repealed after the Civil War, Illinois and Indiana retained legal restrictions to African American immigration as late as the 1880s.

Although small in number, African American settlers were extremely mobile, with a fierce sense of self-determination. They created strong networks of kinship, friendship, and business. The Midwest's free African American population grew rapidly throughout the nineteenth century, from 69,291 in 1860, living primarily in Indiana and Ohio, to 495,751 in 1900, with over half living in Missouri, Kansas, Illinois, and Michigan.

The first significant wave of free African American immigrants occurred between the 1830s and the 1850s. In that twenty-year period around 32,500 free African Americans came to the Midwest, with the majority settling in Ohio and Indiana. Although some of these immigrants were escaping slavery, the majority were free African Americans from North Carolina and Virginia fleeing increasingly oppressive legal and social restrictions in their home states. The nineteenth-century Midwest offered African Americans an opportunity to shape their lives and define their own identities. African Americans mixed freely with Native Americans, complicating notions of racial and ethnic identity.

In general, African Americans lived in rural communities. Some were created by radical abolitionists as places for African Americans to find refuge on their trek north to freedom. Ohio was a favorite destination for abolitionists. Oberlin, Antioch and Wilberforce Colleges, which accepted African American students, were centers of antislavery activity. Brooklyn, Illinois was among the towns founded by African Americans.

Blacks endured despite the often violent opposition of large numbers of whites. Cincinnati was home to both African Americans and white abolitionists and experienced serious racial unrest in the 1820s, 1830s, and 1840s. During the Civil War, racial conflict intensified throughout the region. There were race riots in Detroit in 1863. Nevertheless, many black men defied rising racial tensions and laws prohibiting them from joining state militias in order to fight against the Confederacy. The first black regiments formed on the East Coast actively recruited in the Midwest. By 1863 the demands of African Americans led most state governments to form black regiments, many of which saw active duty.

In the aftermath of the Civil War, some states made progress in extending the rights of citizenship to black men. In 1868 Minnesota and Iowa became the first states in the Midwest to make African American suffrage legal; in 1867 and 1868, respectively, Michigan and Iowa passed legislation that outlawed school segregation. Other states followed, with African Americans winning the right to vote, the right to attend school, and the right to sit on a jury, among others. African Americans were quick to take advantage of these rights. They won political offices from the township to the state level, sent their children to school, and encouraged their friends and families in the South to move north. Perhaps the most famous migration in this period occurred in the late 1870s; "Exodusters" from southern states moved to Kansas, where they created vibrant all–African American communities such as Nicodemus.

Black civil rights in the nineteenth-century Midwest existed more on paper than they did in practice. In the 1870s, African Americans across the United States lost the civil rights they had gained in the immediate aftermath of the Civil War. Still, despite the persistence of racial tensions and inequalities, midwestern African Americans had many advantages that southern African Americans did not, including more landownership, greater political power, and effective social organizations. Segregation was more a matter of custom than of law, and lynchings provoked legislation in Ohio condemning them.

As the century came to a close, midwestern African Americans became increasingly urban, moving from farms and rural communities to seek work in industry and commerce. They created vibrant urban communities that nurtured many important figures, including Scott Joplin, who created ragtime music in St. Louis; Dr. Daniel Williams, who performed the world's first open-heart surgery in Chicago in 1893; Ida B. Wells, who made 1890s Chicago the base of her antilynching activities; and George Washington Carver, who owed his early successes to his education at Iowa colleges. These African Americans, along with many others, proved that they had the courage and ability to succeed despite the many challenges facing them in the Midwest.

Sources and Further Reading: Lillian Anthony-Welch, "Black People: The Nation-Building Vision," in *Broken Hoops and Plains People* (1976); Sundiata Cha-Jua, *America's First Black Town* (2000); Zachary Cooper, *Black Settlers in Rural Wisconsin* (1977); David Gerber, *Black Ohio and the Color Line: 1860–1915* (1976); Kenneth Hamilton, *Black Towns and Profit* (1991); Nell Painter, *Exodusters* (1977); Henry Louis Taylor, Jr., *Race and the City* (1993); Emma Lou Thornbrough, *The Negro in Indiana* (1957).

Anna-Lisa Cox
Newberry Library, Chicago, Illinois

Early and Rural Nineteenth-Century Europeans

During the nineteenth century the Midwest became a homeland for European immigrants who came in search of economic opportunity, both on the countryside and in its developing cities. On the one hand, the opening of successive midwestern settlement frontiers during the middle to latter decades of the century coincided with the timing of early waves of mass emigration from Europe. This coincidence of opportunity and demand drew millions to the region's forests and prairies, where they acquired land through purchase or homesteading, developed farms and communities, and settled in to a life in which the values and practices of their European pasts were gradually adapted to the environmental, social, and political realities of their new homeland. In 1880 25.6 percent of the 1.8 million farmers in the Midwest were foreign born compared to 14.4 percent in the United States as a whole. On the other hand, cities and towns were the destinations of millions of others from Europe who toiled as laborers, craftspeople, and domestics; formed ethnic enclaves; and built vibrant institutional structures. Immigrants comprised 40.7 percent of the population of Chicago, 39.9 percent of Milwaukee, 39.2 percent of Detroit, 37.1 percent of Cleveland, and 36.3 percent of St. Paul. The successful settlement of such large numbers of Europeans on the land, as well as in towns and cities, did much to shape the Midwest's early cultural and social identity and remains today an important part of the region's heritage.

The majority of these agricultural settlers came from northern and western Europe, particularly from the British Isles, Scandinavia, the Low Countries, and the German-speaking regions of central Europe. Often referred to as "old immigrants," they came in a series of waves that began in the 1840s and continued one after another into the 1880s. Many traveled together, coming as families, partial families, or extended kinship groups, and we often think of their emigration as family based, although some came as individuals as well. Many also came with a fairly well developed idea of where they were going and what they might expect to find there, having been recruited by agents representing the individual states or railroad companies, or having received advance information and even tickets from relatives and acquaintances already in America. This flow of information and advice, whether formal or informal, often led to the development of streams of migration that emanated from particular places or districts in Europe and terminated in particular parts of the Midwest. These highly directed streams of movement, often referred to as "chain migrations," played a critical role in bringing immigrants to the region.

The timing of immigration affected settlement patterns in the Midwest. Native-born Americans tended to dominate Ohio, Indiana, Illinois, and southern Michigan, because these states were settled before the onset of mass migration from Europe in the second quarter of the nineteenth century. Midwestern states developed after the 1830s, however, had a far greater proportion of European residents. In 1880 50 percent of the farms in Minnesota, Wisconsin, Michigan, and Dakota Territory were operated by immigrants. Europeans arriving in the late-1860s found that the greatest opportunity lay along a wedge-shaped frontier zone, the leading point of which stood just to the northwest of Minneapolis, and the trailing flanks of which extended eastward across the forest margins of Wisconsin and Michigan and southward across the prairies of southern Minnesota, Iowa, Nebraska, and Kansas.

Exactly where people might settle along within zones of opportunity was often determined by information flow. Once a few people had decided to take land in a particular place or district, the chain-migration process would take over, encouraging others to follow. In this way, large parts of the rural Midwest came to represent a vast patchwork quilt of cluster settlements, often consisting of people with common origins in particular provinces, districts, or even parishes in Europe. Subsequent streams from existing settlements to "daughter" settlements on newly established frontiers added further layers of complexity to the process, creating what might be thought of as scattered "archipelagos" of related settlements.

The character of urban enclaves also stemmed from a combination of the timing of migration streams from Europe and levels of economic opportunity in the United States. Germans immigrating in large numbers in the 1840s soon dominated Milwaukee, Cincinnati, and St. Louis. In 1850, they comprised over a quarter (27 percent) of Cincinnati's population, many of them living in the Over-the-Rhine neighborhood. Later-arriving immigrants, such as Scandinavians, tended to cluster in cities that developed later, like the Twin Cities.

This tendency to cluster among one's own kind was especially apparent in the rural immigrant settlements, which have been referred to as "spatial communities." Their spatiality derives from the facts that they were culturally homogeneous, that relatively discrete boundaries separated one community from another, and that most centered on some kind of institutional focus. The immigrant church often played an essential role as an organizing force in midwestern rural immigrant communities. Most of these churches were founded early in the settlement process by local settlers and developed over time into social as well as religious centers for the entire community. The church was instrumental in bringing people together and helping to instill a common sense of local place identity. Indeed, many rural immigrant settlements were identified by the name of the church on which they were centered. The tall spire of the church tower, often visible from miles around, and the nearby cemetery were reassuring symbols of the community's permanence and vitality. These churches, many of them still in use today, are the most visible reminders of the communities founded by immigrant settlers more than a hundred years ago.

The strong combination of religious and ethnic identity could sometimes bring communities into conflict with neighboring settlements. The immigrant spatial community tended to be self-conscious and inward looking. Neighboring communities were often separated by different languages, different dialects of the same language, and different religious affiliations. These differences led to a certain amount of prejudice and caution. Marriage across community boundaries, for example, might be discouraged or only grudgingly accepted.

The immigrant community also tended to distance itself from the local American-born population, which often preceded the immigrants into an area and set itself up as the dominant commercial and political element in the nearest market town. Part of the adaptation process that all rural immigrants had to grapple with was the fact that they were dependent on the local Yankee population for credit, the purchase of goods and implements, and the sale of what was produced on the land. Only gradually did rural immigrant populations begin to move into such commercial activity themselves and to wrest local political control from the older American-born population.

Conflict also occurred within spatial communities, especially those that were large and recently settled. Even quite culturally homogeneous enclaves were often divided between two or more regional groups. A large Norwegian community, such as the Koshkonong settlement in southern Wisconsin, might have substantial numbers of settlers hailing from a number of valleys or districts in Norway. Rapidly settled communities, too, were often more culturally heterogeneous than communities that were settled over a longer period of time, the main reason being that chain migration was most effective when land remained available for long enough that late arrivals could still find land nearby. If the frontier passed too quickly, this "filling in" function was foreclosed, and emigrants from a specific area in Europe might fail to achieve the numbers

necessary to establish themselves as the dominant element within a spatial community.

Sometimes these internal differences became apparent in religious disputes. The classic example of this is the wave of schisms that rocked immigrant congregations of Norwegian Lutherans during the latter part of the nineteenth century. The schisms were caused by a theological dispute over the question of predestination—whether people were chosen for salvation by the grace of God or by their own good works. So heated was the debate that in numerous Norwegian settlements an element of the population left the established Lutheran congregation to set up a rival Lutheran church, often across the road or a short distance away. Studies have shown that the cleavage that took place within these communities often reflected differences in places of origin and premigration religious experience. The same can be said for the impact of various late-nineteenth-century religious revivals and competition from rival denominations on established immigrant congregations in other ethnic communities.

Immigrants to the city also often moved in a chain-migration fashion that produced tightly knit urban enclaves. The large gathering of people of common nationality and language was instrumental in engendering a vibrant institutional structure of print media, theatre, and ethnic and religious organizations. As in rural locales, different political and cultural beliefs sparked conflict among those in distinct ethnic enclaves. To take one telling example, a law against drinking beer on Sunday in Chicago resulted in hundreds of arrests of Germans and the subsequent beer riots of 1855. Likewise, the presence of large immigrant populations in Milwaukee was a critical factor in the election of the first socialist mayor in the United States in 1910.

The cultural lives of midwestern rural immigrant communities can be measured in generations. The generation that uprooted itself and made the transatlantic journey to a new land was the one that clung most tenaciously to the language, traditions, attitudes, and values of the homeland. The second generation, whether born to the first generation in Europe and brought to America as children or born in America, learned English and generally were more receptive to American values and social practices, although it should be noted that the first generation for all its cultural and social conservatism was anything but bashful about embracing the American market economy for the purpose of improving itself. By the third generation, the relevance of the old language, traditions, attitudes, and values had waned considerably. American participation in World War I, which in many parts of the Midwest coincided with the coming of age of the third or fourth generation, was an important catalyst in leading immigrant communities to redefine themselves as American.

Indeed, the way in which the old European communities of the Midwest have projected their identity to others over time is an interesting topic. The most public displays of ethnic identity come in the form of community celebrations, such as pageants and festivals, and in tourism promotions of various kinds. A close examination of the history of these celebrations shows that the character and emphases of the events have evolved from the post–settlement era to the present. Early celebrations, set in rural communities in the late nineteenth century, tended to celebrate the accomplishments of the first pioneering generation and pay fond tribute to the Old World roots of the community. Celebrations set against the backdrop of World War I and the Depression tended to emphasize the patriotic contribution of the ethnic community to traditional American values and causes, such as the Swiss as a democratic people who resisted oppression. After World War II, as might be expected, many such celebrations became entirely Americanized, with only scarce or slight mention of ethnic identity.

Beginning in the 1970s, however, the ethnic celebration began to enjoy a renaissance driven by the search for "roots" along with a nostalgic, and sometimes overly commercialized, interest in anything ethnic. Now in the twilight of their ethnicity, midwestern communities continue to mark their old European past. Any reading of the listings of current summer celebrations put out by the tourism agencies of the various states reveals an abundance of community events that celebrate ethnic identity, all of which underscores the enduring heritage of old Europeans in the Midwest.

Sources and Further Reading: Michael P. Conzen, ed., *The Making of the American Landscape* (1990); Jon Gjerde, *From Peasants to Farmers* (1985); Steven D. Hoelscher, *Heritage on Stage* (1998); Steven D. Hoelscher and Robert C. Ostergren, "Old European Homelands in the American Middle West," *Journal of Cultural Geography* 13 (Spring/Summer 1993); Walter D. Kamphoefner, *The Westfalians* (1987); Anne Kelly Knowles, *Calvinists Incorporated* (1997); Ann Marie Legreid, "Exodus, Transplanting, and Religious Reorganization of a Group of Norwegian Lutheran Immigrants in Western Wisconsin," Ph.D. diss., University of Wisconsin-Madison (1985); Robert C. Ostergren, *A Community Transplanted* (1988); Mary Beth Schlemper, "The Regional Construction of Identity and Scale in Wisconsin's Holyland," Ph.D. diss., University of Wisconsin–Madison (2003).

Robert C. Ostergren
University of Wisconsin–Madison

English

The English were among the first Europeans in the region that became the Midwest. In the middle of the eighteenth century, English colonists challenged the French in the Ohio River Valley and along the southern shores of Lake Erie. They established trade with Native Americans such as the Miami and Shawnee by offering them lower prices on higher-quality goods. English traders and officials were present in the region during the last half of the eighteenth century, but their influence waned with the victory of an American army over a coalition of Indians at the Battle of Fallen Timbers in August 1794. Evacuating most of their posts south of the Great Lakes, English officials became marginal figures and disappeared entirely after the American victory in the War of 1812.

English people began migrating to the Midwest in large numbers after the end of the Napoleonic Wars in 1815. They quickly became critical citizens. Many English migrants lived in the eastern United States before they moved west. After 1825 the Erie Canal conveniently channeled English immigrants from Liverpool directly to the Midwest.

The English who arrived in the nineteenth century were part of a long tradition of migration from England to America that dates back to the seventeenth and eighteenth centuries. The earlier migrants formed links, or migration networks of information, that allowed English people to write to family members or neighbors who had preceded them, get accurate information, and prearrange their migration, often to the extent of prearranging their employment—even their land purchases. Methodists were overrepresented because of a long tradition of Methodist migration to America that was rooted in discrimination against them in England in the eighteenth and early nineteenth centuries.

During the 1850s Illinois, Michigan, Wisconsin, Ohio, and Iowa were among the top ten destinations of English heading to the United States. In 1850 Wisconsin had a greater percentage of English-born inhabitants (6.2 percent) than any other state in the Midwest. The U.S. census indicated in 1850 that over a quarter (28.5 percent) of all the English-born in the United States were living in the Midwest. That figure grew to a third (32.4 percent) in 1860, and then fell to around a quarter for the rest of the century. Illinois, Wisconsin, and Michigan saw large increases of English residents during the 1850s because of the growing opportunities for farming and mining in the Lake Superior region and the upper Mississippi River.

A number of qualities distinguished the English and made them uniquely important to midwestern development. The English came from a remarkably wide spectrum of economic and occupational backgrounds because Great Britain, the world's first industrial nation, had a labor force with the greatest variety of backgrounds and skills. English immigrants transferred much of the industrial revolution to the Midwest. The mining industry, the iron industry, textiles, pottery, machine making, and many others were to a large extent brought by English immigrants. Perhaps the best example is the role of Cornish and other English lead miners in developing the lead-mining region of the upper Mississippi River Valley.

Particularly before the late nineteenth century, most of the English entering the Midwest became farmers, and a large portion had skills with which to earn capital for land purchases. Many combined farming with their craft. Agriculture was an irresistible draw for the English, who could buy land in the Midwest for the cost of renting it for a few years in England. Most were tenant farmers or farm laborers, but many were experts in advanced farming techniques, especially in drainage and animal breeding. Many others had little or no agricultural experience and yet succeeded on American farms, especially after Britain repealed its protective Corn Laws in 1847 and opened itself up to American agricultural products from the rich wheat lands of the Midwest.

The English were also uniquely "invisible." That is, they found it relatively easy to blend in because they shared a basic language, culture, and political heritage with the majority of the Midwest's white population, most of whom were themselves of British extraction. Generally, they did not form separate communities or enclaves but interacted more immediately with the native-born residents of the Midwest and participated more quickly and fully in local society. They did not have to establish their own separate churches because the Americans and the English already shared many major denominations, especially Methodist, Congregationalist, Baptist, and Episcopalian. Not surprisingly, the available data indicate that among all immigrants the English had the highest rate of marriage with native-born Americans.

By the late nineteenth century English immigrants were showing a preference for Canada, and those entering the United States were looking farther west. In the twentieth century English migration to the United States, and specifically the Midwest, slowed dramatically. Increasingly, migrants were professionals and academics drawn to industries and universities in the Midwest. Like their predecessors, the newer English immigrants blended in quickly, illustrating the fact that England and the United States, despite their differences, still had important cultural similarities.

Sources and Further Reading: Rowland T. Berthoff, *British Immigrants in Industrial America, 1790–1950* (1953); Charlotte J. Erickson, *Invisible Immigrants* (1972); Charlotte J. Erickson, *Leaving England* (1994); David Jeremy, *Transatlantic Industrial Revolution* (1981); Maldwyn A. Jones, "The Background to Emigration from Great Britain in the Nineteenth Century," in *Perspectives in American History*, vol. 7 (1973); William E. Van Vugt, *Britain to America* (1999).

William E. Van Vugt
Calvin College, Michigan

Scots

Scots were among the first Europeans to settle America. Prominent in all of Britain's North American colonies, Scots had crossed the Ohio River by 1779. After 1820 more came directly from Scotland. Economic depression and unemployment in the Lowlands and enclosure in the Highlands, in which small arable fields were consolidated for sheep pasturage and the tenants were evicted, caused many to leave Scotland in the first two decades of the nineteenth century, while the abundance of fresh land and greater social and political equality attracted many to the Midwest. The most famous Scot was Arthur St. Clair, a general in the Continental Army, member of the Continental Congress, and governor of the Northwest Territory from 1787 through 1802.

The early Scots often formed clusters in the Midwest. This was due to their tight ethnic identity and the fact that many migrated in small groups, often led by a clan leader or clergyman, through "chains" of information formed by earlier migrants. There were "Scotch Settlements" in many townships throughout the early Midwest. Scots retained some cultural traditions and organized the St. Andrews Society in order to assist fellow Scottish immigrants who needed help. But with their wide use of the English language the Scots successfully blended in with the larger society and intermarried with non-Scots.

In the 1820s unemployed Scottish handloom weavers formed societies to assist emigration to the United States, which continued until the 1860s. During the "hungry" 1840s, the failure of the potato crop stimulated more emigration, as did economic distress in the Lowlands. Between 1820 and 1851 about ten thousand Scots emigrated to the United States, and roughly half of them settled in the Midwest. In the second half of the century, more Scots took up land in Illinois, Michigan, and Wisconsin. Scots were quite prominent in Illinois and Chicago. By 1850 there were nearly five thousand Scottish-born people in that state. They were also heading farther west. The number of Scots in Iowa rose from about seven hundred in 1850 to three thousand in 1860. Missouri had a Scotland County by 1841, and many other Scottish place-names were established throughout the region. By the late nineteenth century most Scottish Americans lived in the Midwest.

Because Scotland, like the rest of Britain, was far ahead of the United States in industrialization, Scottish immigrants provided invaluable skills to the Midwest's growing industries, especially iron production, mining, quarrying, machine building, engineering, shipbuilding, and, of course, textiles. They were also overrepresented in the professions and clerical work and thus were not as preponderant in agriculture as other immigrant groups, especially in the late nineteenth and the twentieth centuries.

Sources and Further Reading: Gordon Donaldson, "Scots," in Stephen Thernstrom, ed., *Harvard Encyclopedia of American Ethnic Groups* (1980); Gordon Donaldson, *The Scots Overseas* (1966); Malcolm Gray, "Scottish Emigration: The Social Impact of Agrarian Change in the Rural Lowlands, 1775–1875," *Perspectives in American History* 7 (1973).

William E. Van Vugt
Calvin College, Michigan

Welsh

The Welsh are a small but locally important group in midwestern history. As Protestant Europeans long familiar with English culture, nineteenth-century Welsh immigrants fit easily into American society. Yet the fact that most were Welsh speakers, and the dominance of that language in historically separate Welsh religious denominations, insulated them from rapid assimilation wherever their numbers were sufficient to form significant communities. The Welsh experience in the Midwest had more in common with those of Dutch, Luxembourg, and Swiss immigrants than with those of the English or the Scots.

Pennsylvania and New York attracted the largest number of Welsh immigrants throughout the nineteenth century, but Ohio and Wisconsin developed sizeable Welsh communities. By 1860 almost every state in the Midwest had at least a few Welsh settlements. Some bore telltale Welsh place-names, such as Radnor, Ohio, and Bala, Kansas. The region's largest Welsh communities formed where hundreds of immigrant families were able to buy inexpensive farmland in close proximity to one another. Welsh industrial workers were also concentrated in skilled and supervisory positions at iron and steel works from Youngstown to Chicago, as well as at coal mines in Illinois.

Midwestern Welsh ethnic identity took root most strongly in agricultural settlements and small towns, such as Wisconsin's Waukesha and Columbia Counties and the town of Racine, a leading port for Welsh immigrants heading for land in Wisconsin, Minnesota, and Iowa. While the clannishness of industrial Welsh workers made them formidable opponents in labor disputes, group identity among the rural Welsh tended to focus on religious piety and respectability. The roughly three thousand immigrants who settled in Ohio's Jackson and Gallia Counties supported twenty-two Welsh chapels. Although these simple wood-frame structures appeared outwardly American, they were sanctuaries of Welsh culture, preserving the language in religious services well into the twentieth century in Jackson-Gallia as in many rural midwestern settlements. Chapels were also sites of community meetings, musical and literary competitions, and Welsh hymn-singing and preaching festivals. The latter, called the *gymanfa ganu* (guh-MAHN-vah GAH-nee), became increasingly popular in the early twentieth century as an occasion to reunite families and remind Welsh Americans of the close ties between their ancestral language, hymnody, and religion.

Few midwestern cities had significant Welsh populations. Middle-class Welsh neighborhoods in Cincinnati and Columbus were less concentrated than true ethnic enclaves. More typical was Chicago's scattered Welsh population, though its members managed to stage ambitious choral performances at the Columbian Exposition of 1893. One of the last barriers to formal assimilation fell when the Welsh Calvinistic Methodist Church merged with the Presbyterian Church in the 1920s. Interest in Welsh culture revived in the last decades of the twentieth century, spurred by the monthly national newspapers *Y Drych* ("The Mirror") and *Ninnau* (roughly, "We Welsh") and ethnic tourism to Wales. In keeping with the low profile of the Welsh throughout their history, however, sites and celebrations marking Welsh American heritage are little known outside the ethnic community: the roving annual national gymanfa ganu, which draws up to three thousand participants; local Welsh hymn-sings; and the Welsh-American Heritage Museum in Oak Hill, Ohio.

Sources and Further Reading: Alan Conway, ed., *The Welsh in America* (1961); Aled Jones and William Jones, *Welsh Reflections* (2001); Anne Kelly Knowles, *Calvinists Incorporated* (1997); R. D. Thomas, *A History of the Welsh in America*, trans. Phillips G. Davies (1983).

Anne Kelly Knowles
Middlebury College, Vermont

French

French migration to the Midwest reached its peak in the late 1860s. By 1870 four out of ten French people in the United States lived in one of the midwestern states—almost fifty thousand of them mostly in Ohio, Illinois, Indiana, and Missouri. Many settled in the cities of St. Louis, Cincinnati, Chicago, and Detroit, where they had industrial, service, and business jobs. Others lived in midwestern rural counties and became farmers. By the late nineteenth century fewer French migrants to the United States were choosing midwestern destinations. However, about a third of all French-born migrants and their descendants in the United States could be found in the midwestern states in 1900.

Nineteenth-century French migrants partook in the larger migration movements from France to the Americas that drew several hundred thousand French men and women across the Atlantic to North and Latin America between the 1810s and World War I. Many of them came from the peripheries of France. Those who went to the Midwest were no exception, often leaving the eastern French provinces of Alsace and Lorraine in search of better lands, better jobs, and a better life.

They built upon a tradition of French presence in the Midwest that went back to the seventeenth century and remained lively into the nineteenth century in the fur-trading upper Great Lakes areas as well as in Ohio, Indiana, Michigan, and along the Mississippi River. Although St. Louis, Vincennes, Detroit, and Sainte Genevieve had lost much of their French character by the mid-nineteenth century, place-names and rural landscapes throughout the region reminded recent French migrants of early French colonial settlements. Particularly in urban areas, French migrants developed various ethnic institutions, including newspapers, fraternal societies and other networks that fostered French regional or national cultures. Other migrants from Alsace and Lorraine hardly spoke French and decided to join more powerful German ethnic networks. In Michigan and Wisconsin, recent French migrants were often drawn to the ranks, networks, and institutions of the more numerous French Canadians, resulting in a particular brand of French American culture.

In the early twentieth century French migration to the Midwest became insignificant, resulting in the quasi disappearance of French American cultural and social traits in the region. Since the 1970s, however, renewed popular and academic interest has led to the progressive rediscovery of French heritage and memory in the Midwest, a trend that is likely to endure.

Sources and Further Reading: Charles J. Balesi, *The Time of the French in the Heart of North America, 1673–1818* (1992);
Carl J. Ekberg, *French Roots in the Illinois Country* (1998); Judith A. Franke, *French Peoria and the Illinois Country, 1673–1846* (1995); Leroy R. Hafen, ed., *French Fur Traders and Voyageurs in the American West* (1997).

François Weil
L'Ecole des Hautes Études en Sciences Sociales,
Paris, France

Germans

Few groups of immigrants rival the pervasive influence of Germans on the landscape and culture of the Midwest. Germans were in the initial waves of settlement in the early nineteenth century. The first significant numbers floated down the Ohio River from Pennsylvania to places such as Cincinnati. The 1825 opening of the Erie Canal connecting the Hudson River with Lake Erie led directly to German migration into the Great Lakes region, especially the cities of Cleveland, Detroit, Chicago, and Milwaukee. Others arrived via steamboats that brought them up the Mississippi River to St. Louis and, eventually, the upper Midwest. By midcentury, railroads were replacing waterways as the primary means of access for German immigrants.

In the early 1800s Pennsylvania Germans were accompanied into the Midwest by Germans fleeing the economic and political upheaval associated with the Napoleonic Wars. By the 1830s and 1840s Germans interested in building new lives elsewhere were emigrating in huge numbers. The so-called Grays, or liberal idealists, of the 1815–1840s period fled Germany for political freedom and to fulfill their dreams of a democratic "New Germany." Their hopes were raised by figures such as Gottfried Duden, who, after living in Missouri in the mid-1820s, published a glowing report of the state. Thousands took his advice to seek utopia, thereby also conveniently relieving German states of excess population.

Many Germans who moved to the Midwest were members of religious groups. Conservative Lutherans who fled Saxon Germany because they refused to join the Prussian-mandated union of the Reformed Church with the Lutheran Church in 1817 arrived to form the Missouri Synod. So-called Old Lutherans of similar vintage shaped the Wisconsin Lutheran Synod—the more conservative wing of the Lutheran Church in America today. In the decades that followed, Lutheran agencies in Neuendettelsau near Nuremberg fostered emigration, supplying the Midwest with missionaries and settlements, including the Frankenmuth colonies in central Michigan.

Organized on many levels, German Protestants enjoyed centralized support in America with their *Der Deutsche Kirchenverein des Westens* (the German Evangelical Society of the West, founded in St. Louis in 1840) and their leadership centers at Fort Wayne, Indiana; Watertown, Wisconsin; and New Ulm, Minnesota. The missionary activities of the Catholic Church were of even greater significance. Agencies of the Ludwigmissionsverein sponsored by Bavarian king Ludwig in Munich and the Vienna-based Leopoldinenstiftung were behind these efforts. Sustaining forces among German Catholics were such organizations as the lay Central-Verein in St. Louis; the German-born or -speaking bishops in Wisconsin, Illinois, the Dakotas, and Ohio; as well as Catholic publications such as the Ohio *Waisenfreund,* the *Seebote* of Milwaukee, and the *Wanderer* of St. Paul.

Germans were the dominant immigrant group numerically in the nineteenth-century Midwest. Midwestern Germans welcomed refugee leaders from the 1848 revolutions in Germany, who toyed with the idea of creating a separate German-speaking state within the United States. Forty-eighters argued that a German-speaking region in America would model a democratic society in Germany. For at least a decade, they called for abolishing the Senate, countermanding

John M. Lipp married Eva Baumgartner at Blessed Trinity Catholic Church, Krasna, North Dakota, in 1923. Jolenta Fischer Masterson Collection. North Dakota State University.

the office of president, and implementing "pure" democracy. In later years, particularly during World War I, critics argued that these Germans were trying to perpetuate and extend the German political homeland.

The Missouri and Wisconsin Territories were briefly candidates to be an idealized "Germany." But the Civil War shifted attention to perpetuating German culture within the United States rather than through secession. Germans advocated publicly funded schools taught in German, an effort that succeeded in areas where Forty-eighters held sway. German-language instruction ended abruptly with World War I when state laws forbade it. More practical efforts beguiled Germans with dreams of a German presence in farming and manufacturing.

States and railroads with non-German leadership also sought to attract German immigrants because they idealized German homesteaders. The first state legislature to establish a commission to procure German immigrants was Michigan's, in 1849. In its wake, American consul to Germany Charles L. Fleischmann sought to purchase six hundred thousand dollars' worth of Michigan farmland for resale to German immigrants. Even though his scheme failed, thousands of Germans arrived with cash to acquire the state's land.

In 1852 Wisconsin's commissioner of immigration appointed Dutch-born Gysbert Van Steenwyck to recruit German immigrants. Minnesota created its board of immigration in 1867, followed in 1870 by Iowa, whose German-born Mathias J. Rohlfs sent agents to Germany to acquire newcomer "capital" that Iowans thought was bypassing them for Minnesota. Kansas, the Dakotas, and Nebraska posted official state-immigrant offices in Germany and/or New York harbor to direct Germans to their agricultural lands. Wisconsin in 1882 printed 20,000 copies of a brochure in German, while the Minnesota immigration commissioner reported that his office answered 220,000 German letters of inquiry. In 1881 the Wisconsin commissioner estimated that the "total value of the labor . . . conveyed to the United States during the last five years" from Germany was roughly $700,000,000.

Railroad agents also spurred immigration from Germany. Prominent in Wisconsin was Kent K. Kennan, while Friedrich Hedde labored in Nebraska. Working for the Burlington route from Chicago to Denver was George Harris. Energetic for the Northern Pacific from St. Paul to Seattle was the German immigrant Henry Villard (Heinrich Hilgard), who exhibited the line's products in Germany and at the Vienna Exposition of 1873. Bismarck, the capital of North Dakota, got its name when Samuel Wilkinson, secretary of the Northern Pacific, suggested honoring the Prussian chancellor, rather than an engineer named Edwinton, to attract more Germans to North Dakota. Due especially to the Milwaukee Road line to Aberdeen and Eureka, Germans from Russia, accustomed to farming the treeless steppes, poured into the Dakota Territory after Russia's 1874 revocation of their privileges on the Black Sea and the Volga River. Other mechanisms effective in steering Germans to the Midwest were the agencies of Friedrich Missler in Bremen, newspapers such as the *Deutsche Auswander-erzeitung*, and employment offices in New York such as the *Arbeits-Nachweisungs-Bureau*, which directed Germans to Chicago, Detroit, St. Louis, and Davenport, Iowa.

After 1890 most German immigrants concentrated in the industrial centers of the Midwest heartland. While the first immigrants tended to be from the small farms of the German southwest (the Palatinate and Hesse), later German immigrants were often day laborers and servants from German central regions and the northwest, where estate-based commercial agriculture excluded young men once power machinery replaced them. After 1880 immigrant sources shifted eastward to Posen, Silesia, and West and East Prussia. Prime destinations were both pivotal German cities in the Ruhr or Berlin as well as Detroit, Chicago, Indianapolis, St. Louis, St. Paul, and Milwaukee, all of which competed for the immigrants' industrial skills.

In fact, as in the Ruhr, industrial magnates in American cities enticed Polish-speaking—but officially Prussian-born—immigrants to work in their factories. Milwaukee owes the Polish-speaking section on its near-south side to invited Prussian-born Polish speakers. Meanwhile, Detroit and Chicago attracted Germans born beyond the borders of imperial Germany, including those from Bohemia, Russia, and the Austro-Hungarian Empire. Although early German-speaking Swiss settlers chose Wisconsin for its dairy husbandry, others arrived because guidebooks emphasized that the bishops of Milwaukee and Green Bay were German-Swiss immigrants. In Minnesota, publicist-priest Father Franz Pierz from Slovenia and his invitee Father Alexander Berghold from Graz made their St. Cloud and New Ulm regions attractive for extraterritorial German immigrants. By contrast, Davenport and Grand Island, Nebraska, lured northern Germans and German-speaking Danes from impoverished agrarian Schleswig-Holstein and Mecklenburg.

The process of "chain migration" increased the concentrations of German settlement in the Midwest. Wisconsin always had the greatest proportion of Germans measured as a percentage of its population— triple the share warranted by the national population. Close behind, judging from the 1920 census, were Minnesota, Iowa, Nebraska, Missouri, and Illinois.

Historians suggest that Germans in the rural regions of Germany avoided industrialization by leaving their peasant status for American farming regions. After 1900 economic conditions impelled them into the factories, even *from* the American farming regions of the Midwest. Thus Chicago in 1900 had 204,000 German-born, many in the industrial workforce because of the accomplished apprentice system in Germany, which prepared immigrants for skilled jobs like tool-and-die maker in American cities. Practitioners of crafts such as bakers, carpenters, and brewers gave the German element economic advantages in cities. Germans specialized in butchering and crafts like cigar making, cabinetry, and tailoring; few were doctors, lawyers, teachers, or bookkeepers. In the German community, women were noticeably underrepresented in the workforce and tended to toil as nurses, shopkeepers, tailors, and in clerical jobs.

Except in Chicago, Milwaukee, St. Louis, and Cincinnati, Germans were uncommon in the management circles of large firms. However, they made their mark in other fields, such as engineering. German names such as Roebling, on cable bridges at Cincinnati and New York; Studebaker and Chrysler, on wagons and automobiles; Weyerhaeuser in lumber, Villard (Hilgard) in railroading, Brumder in publishing in Milwaukee, and Walther in labor organization suggest the German influence. Few entered politics, although Carl Schurz of Watertown, Wisconsin, served as a U.S. senator and as secretary of the interior.

On the whole, rural Germans were conservative in politics, although less so in cities such as Chicago, Detroit, Columbus, and Milwaukee. Some were active socialists. Whereas they tended to vote for Republican Abraham Lincoln in 1860, Germans in Wisconsin in later decades supported Milwaukee's Victor Berger, who led the Socialists in the U.S. House of Representatives, and Progressive governor and senator Robert La Follette. When Democrat Woodrow Wilson asked for a declaration of war on Germany in April 1917, one of Wisconsin's senators and nine of eleven House members voted against it with the explanation that they voted the consciences of their constituents.

At the beginning of the twenty-first century, people of German ancestry continue to dominate the Midwest. More than a quarter of the Midwest population reports itself as "German." In every midwestern state at least 20 percent of the population has German roots: North Dakota, with Germans comprising almost 44 percent of the population; Wisconsin, with a German population of about 42 percent; and South Dakota, with around 40 percent of its residents claiming German ancestry, have particularly high populations.

Although Germans in America today are largely assimilated, many acknowledge their German heritage in censuses and in festivals that celebrate the German birthright across the Midwest. What is commemorated, however, is a regional sense of place that most German American populations have carved out of their homeland, retaining a romantic image, an "elective Germany," equated with Bavaria rather than Germany as a whole. German music is omnipresent, both in concert halls and ballrooms, with polkas and waltzes. During summers, numerous German marching, oompah, and concert bands tour the Midwest entertaining audiences, usually corresponding to this selective memory of Bavaria.

Place-names of German origin persist, despite efforts to eradicate them during World War I. Huge, fortresslike late-nineteenth-century breweries embody the determination of brewers to resist prohibition. On occasion a monument such as that to Hermann the Cherusker in New Ulm graces a city skyline. But despite the prominent Turner Halls in Indianapolis, Chicago, Davenport, St. Paul, and New Ulm, and regardless of the many statues of Schiller and Goethe in city parks, the German heritage in the American Midwest has now been largely silenced.

Sources and Further Reading: David W. Detjen, *The Germans in Missouri, 1900–1918: Prohibition, Neutrality, and Assimilation* (1985); Melvin G. Holli, "The Great War Sinks Chicago's German Kultur," in Peter d'A. Jones and Melvin G. Holli, eds., *Ethnic Chicago* (1981); June Drenning Holmquist, ed., *They Chose Minnesota: A Survey of the State's Ethnic Groups* (1981); Walter D. Kamphoefner, *The Westfalians: From Germany to Missouri* (1987); Frederick C. Luebke, ed., *Ethnic Voters and the Election of Lincoln* (1971); LaVern J. Rippley, "Official Action by Wisconsin to Recruit German Immigrants, 1850–1890," *Yearbook of German-American Studies* 18 (1983); La Vern J. Rippley, *The Immigrant Experience in Wisconsin* (1985); William C. Sherman and Playford V. Thorson, eds., *Plains Folk: North Dakota's Ethnic History* (1988); Robert M. Taylor, Jr., and Connie A. McBirney, eds., *Peopling Indiana: The Ethnic Experience* (1996); Charles Van Ravenswaay, *The Arts and Architecture of German Settlements in Missouri: A Survey of a Vanishing Culture* (1977); Kazimierz J. Zaniewski and Carol J. Rosen, *The Atlas of Ethnic Diversity in Wisconsin* (1998).

La Vern J. Rippley
St. Olaf College, Minnesota

Irish

The Irish have played a role in the history of the Midwest since the earliest days of European settlement. In sheer numbers, only the Germans, and perhaps the English, have been more important than the Irish. According to the Census 2000, the Irish are the second-largest ancestry group in the region. A total of 11.8 percent of midwesterners report Irish and another 1.3 percent indicate Scotch-Irish as their first or second ancestry.

Irish immigrants to the Midwest came from a troubled land. Irish Catholics, who made up over three-quarters of Ireland's population and accounted for the overwhelming majority of Irish immigrants to the Midwest, detested the centuries-long English domination of their country. At the beginning of the nineteenth century they still lacked equal political rights, supported an established Anglican church, and lived under an onerous land system in which most landlords were Protestants of English heritage.

Perhaps the first Irish in the present-day Midwest were soldiers serving with the French Army in military posts like Detroit and St. Louis. Among the first permanent settlers were thousands of Irish Protestants, who came to the colonies in significant numbers beginning in the early eighteenth century and who in the late eighteenth and early nineteenth centuries migrated across the Appalachian Mountains and helped populate the southern areas of Ohio, Indiana, and Illinois as well as Missouri.

During the 1830s immigration from Ireland increased significantly and shifted from being mainly Protestant to being overwhelmingly Catholic. As a result of the Great Famine, in the late 1840s and early 1850s immigration from Ireland reached tidal-wave proportions. Although never at the level of the famine years, Irish immigration remained significant until 1930. While most Irish settled in the Northeast, in 1880 25 percent of Irish immigrants in the United States lived in the Midwest.

In the decades before the Civil War thousands of Irish immigrants worked on the construction of canals and railroads. Many of them eventually made their way to growing cities such as Chicago, St. Louis, Cleveland, and Cincinnati, where they often lived in slumlike neighborhoods. Irish immigrants were more often than not unskilled workers. Nonetheless, Irish immigrants in the Midwest did somewhat better economically than their counterparts in the East.

Although the majority of the Irish in the Midwest lived in urban areas, a considerable minority settled on farms and in small towns. In 1870, 30 percent of the Irish-born workforce in the Midwest was engaged in agriculture compared to only 9 percent in the Northeast. Similarly, in 1870, 46 percent of the Irish-born in the Midwest lived in rural areas and small towns compared to 24 percent of them nationwide. Few Irish settled in organized colonies such as those in southwestern Minnesota sponsored by the Catholic Colonization Bureau of St. Paul. Instead, the vast majority migrated with family and friends as part of "chain migration." Generally settling in small clusters, the Irish had few large, concentrated settlements. Some left the land, although as late as 1900 26 percent of the Irish (first- and second-generation) workforce in the Midwest was engaged in agriculture.

The most significant impact that Irish Catholics have had on the Midwest was the crucial role they played in the growth and development of Catholicism. English speaking, accustomed to a nonestablished Catholic Church, and the victims of religious discrimination in their own country, the Irish were well suited to the task of building the church in the United States. Along with German Catholics, who made up a larger proportion of the Catholic population in the Midwest than they did in the Northeast, the Irish took what was a skeletal structure and within a few decades transformed it into a flourishing institution with churches, schools, and charitable institutions.

From the beginning, linguistic and cultural differences created problems between the English-speaking Irish and the Germans, who resented Irish domination of the American hierarchy. In urban areas much of the tension was diffused through the creation of separate national parishes for the Germans. In rural areas such a solution was impractical; if two groups found themselves in the same area they simply had to attend the same church. No doubt anti-Catholic organizations such as the Know-Nothings in the 1850s, the American Protective Association in the 1890s, and the Ku Klux Klan in the 1920s strengthened the bonds between Irish and German Catholics. In time, as the German communities became English speaking, the differences between the two groups became less significant, although ethnic tensions would continue as other non-English-speaking Catholic groups like the Poles and the Italians began to settle in several midwestern cities in large numbers at the end of the nineteenth century.

Another area where the Irish had a significant impact was urban politics. As in the East, the Irish in the Midwest were overwhelmingly Democratic. Fluency in English and experience with political campaigning in Ireland gave Irish immigrants an advantage over non-English-speaking immigrants, while dependence on municipal patronage jobs gave them an economic incentive for political involvement. From the late nineteenth century onward, Irish political power became particularly noticeable in city governments. Among the most noteworthy big-city politicians of Irish heritage were Tom Pendergast in Kansas City and Richard J. Daley in Chicago. Outside of urban areas Irish political power has been less visible. Individual Irish Americans such as Populists like Ignatius

Donnelly of Minnesota, twentieth-century Democrats such as Frank Murphy of Michigan, and Republicans like Joseph McCarthy of Wisconsin have left their mark on American politics, but it is hard to make the case that the Irish as a group have stood out from others on the state or the national level as they have on the local.

The Irish in the Midwest, like those in the rest of the country, have supported Irish organizations. The most noteworthy of these were the several nationalist groups, both constitutional and revolutionary (like the Fenians and Clan na Gael), that sent millions of dollars to Ireland in the nineteenth and early twentieth centuries to assist in the struggle for Irish self-government. After the creation of the Irish Free State in 1922, which granted independence to most of the island, nationalist activity greatly declined, though it revived somewhat, at least in some of the larger cities, after the Troubles broke out in Northern Ireland in the late 1960s. Besides nationalist organizations, the Midwest Irish have supported a plethora of cultural and fraternal organizations such as the Ancient Order of Hibernians.

In the twentieth century, as the numbers of first- and second-generation Irish dwindled and as intermarriage with other groups grew, it became difficult to distinguish the Irish from other European Americans. Only 21 percent of those claiming Irish ancestry in the 1980 U.S. census reported Irish ancestry alone. In this respect the Irish in the Midwest have assimilated to a greater degree than those in the Northeast, where 32 percent of people reporting themselves as Irish indicated only Irish ancestry. The difference is at least partly explained by the fact that Irish immigrants never made up as large a percentage of the population of the Midwest as the East.

The midwestern Irish experience has diverged, therefore, in certain respects from that of the Irish in the Northeast, the chief region of Irish settlement, although the Irish experience in both regions has been very similar, particularly with regard to the Catholic Church and urban politics. Besides overall regional differences, there have also been significant variations among Irish communities within the Midwest. An Irish farming community adjacent to a German Catholic settlement no doubt evolved differently than one near a Norwegian Lutheran one. Similarly, the Irish community in Chicago, because of its size and because Chicago attracted significant numbers of Irish immigrants over a longer period than other midwestern cities, was quite distinct from other Irish midwestern urban communities, so much so that Irish Chicago was more like the Irish community in New York than communities in St. Paul or Detroit.

Sources and Further Reading: Michael F. Funchion, "Irish Chicago: Church, Homeland, Politics, and Class—The Shaping of an Ethnic Group, 1870–1900," in Melvin G. Holli and Peter d'A. Jones, eds., *Ethnic Chicago*, 4th ed. (1994); Michael Glazier, ed., *The Encyclopedia of the Irish in America* (1999); Lawrence J. McCaffrey et al., *The Irish in Chicago* (1987); Grace McDonald, *History of the Irish in Wisconsin in the Nineteenth Century* (1976); Timothy J. Meagher, ed., *From Paddy to Studs* (1986); Ann Regan, "The Irish," in June Drenning Holmquist, ed., *They Chose Minnesota* (1981); James P. Shannon, *Catholic Colonization on the Western Frontier* (1957); JoEllen Vinyard, *The Irish on the Urban Frontier* (1976); Mark Wyman, *Immigrants in the Valley* (1984).

Michael F. Funchion
South Dakota State University

Peoples of the Low Countries (Belgium, the Netherlands, Luxembourg)

The Low Countries lie astride the delta of Europe's Rhine River, gateway to the North Sea and the Atlantic world. Various efforts over the past several centuries to unite these lands into one nation have failed, mainly because of profound cultural and religious differences.

Four language groups, Dutch, French, Frisian, and German, overlap the religious and political borders. The northern Netherlands province of Friesland holds to the Frisian language. Dutch is the common language in the remainder of the Netherlands and in the Flemish region of northern Belgium. French is spoken in Belgium's Walloon region south of the language border, except in the Belgian province of Luxembourg and in the Grand Duchy of Luxembourg, where German is also spoken. Religiously, Dutch Reformed dominate the north, Flemish Catholics the center, and Walloon and Luxemburg Catholics the south.

Immigrants brought these distinctive characteristics to North America. Dutch and Belgians colonized New Netherlands (later New York) in the years 1614–1664, and their descendants increased to 100,000 by 1790. Since then official immigration numbers to the United States are: Belgium, 200,000; the Netherlands, 380,000; and Luxembourg, 75,000. These gross estimates are roughly proportional to their relative national populations. The main influx was from the 1840s through the 1890s, and the primary destination for all three nationalities was the Midwest.

Lesser numbers arrived after World War II. They chose the major metropolitan centers, especially in the Far West. According to self-reported ethnic identities in the 2000 federal census, the sample estimate of "single ancestry" and "multiple ancestry" Belgians is 360,000; Netherlanders, 4,500,000; and Luxembourgers, 45,000.

The three groups have formed a variety of settlements in the Midwest. Belgian and Dutch Catholics have congregated in and around Detroit; Green Bay, Wisconsin; Rock Island-Moline, Illinois; and South Bend-Mishawaka, Indiana. Dutch Protestants have lived mainly within fifty miles of Lake Michigan—from Muskegon, Holland, and Grand Rapids, Michigan, to Chicago and Sheboygan, Wisconsin, as well as in Marion (Pella) and Sioux Counties in Iowa. Luxembourgers were centered from Chicago and Milwaukee

The first Dutch settlers of Grand Rapids, Wisconsin. Wisconsin Historical Society, WHi-22829.

to Green Bay, Dubuque, Iowa, and St. Paul, where they settled comfortably among German immigrants. Walloons sought out French Canadian settlements with French-speaking priests.

Most Lowlanders farmed and did so successfully; their axiom was "big barns and small houses." Each nationality also brought particular job skills. Belgians were experienced in the textile, glass, and coal-mining industries. Dutch farmers specialized in draining swamplands for truck gardening, and in dairying for the Chicago milkshed. Urban Dutch were concentrated in the furniture factories and publishing houses of Grand Rapids and the private refuse businesses of Chicago.

The Dutch have shown a penchant for establishing family-owned businesses. Among the most prominent in the late twentieth century were "America's Dutch Twins," Richard De Vos and the late Jay Van Andel of Michigan, the billionaire founders of Amway, one of the largest direct-marketing enterprises in America. The Dutch emphasis on education and religion made Grand Rapids a national locus of Christian book publishing.

Cultural customs and institutions are mainly a product of the nineteenth-century enclave migration built around the church. But the Protestant-Catholic distinction was crucial. The Dutch Reformed worshiped in the mother tongue in hundreds of homogeneous congregations, while Flemish and German Catholics joined mixed-nationality parishes that intoned the universal Latin mass. Each nationality formed its own clubs and societies, newspapers and periodicals, and kept traditional foods and shops. Dutch and Belgian culture flourished more than Luxembourger culture. Luxembourgers were too few, and they melded into German parishes, except in a few Chicago suburbs (Park Ridge, Evanston) and in small towns such as Belgium and St. Nicholas, Wisconsin; Remsen, Iowa; and Rollingstone, Minnesota. Belgians enjoyed their traditional gaming sports of archery, darts, and bicycle and pigeon racing, while the Dutch adopted the American pastimes of softball and bowling. Belgians also became enthused about bowling and American football.

Dutch Reformed church life has been rich but fractious. The two main denominations are the Reformed Church in America, which dates from 1628, and the Christian Reformed Church in North America, an 1857 offshoot. The Christian Reformed Church held more tightly to its Netherlandic roots and won most of the new immigrants after 1880. It established a system of private Christian day schools and maintained Dutch-language worship into the 1920s. Both Dutch Reformed denominations established academies and colleges in the Midwest: Hope College (1866), Calvin

College (1876), Northwestern College (1882), Central College (founded in 1853, it became Dutch Reformed in 1916), Dordt College (1955), and Trinity Christian College (1959). Flemish Catholics founded St. Norbert's College (1898).

Politically, the Dutch Reformed voted Democratic until the Civil War and solidly Republican thereafter (except in Pella, Iowa); Flemish and Luxemburg Catholics, by contrast, remained staunch Democrats. The Lowlanders left public office to others until after 1945, when the third generation gained the skills, education, and money to enter politics. Michigan's Fifth Congressional District has often gone to the Dutch, beginning with Gerrit J. Diekema of Holland in 1907 and his successors Bartel Jonkman, Richard Vander Veen, and, since 1993, Vernon Ehlers. Guy Vander Jagt represented Michigan's Ninth Congressional District for twenty-five years, followed by Peter Hoekstra.

The high point of ethnic pride for the Lowlanders was the period from 1900 to 1930, augmented by a brief surge of immigrants after World War II. Dutch-language newspapers thrived, including *Onze Toekomst* ("Our Future") of Chicago, the *Gazette van Detroit*, and the *Gazette van Moline* (Illinois), as did social clubs, benevolent societies, and sporting clubs. All three Lowlander groups are now largely assimilated, except for Dutch Reformed adherents who still maintain private Christian schools.

Sources and Further Reading: Nicholas Gonner, *Luxembourgers in the New World* (1987); Henry Lucas, *Netherlanders in America: Dutch Immigration to the United States and Canada, 1789–1950* (1955); Philemon D. Sabbe, *Belgians in America* (1960); Robert P. Swierenga, *Faith and Family* (2000); Jacob Van Hinte, in Robert P. Swierenga, ed., *Netherlanders in America: A Study of Emigration and Settlement in the Nineteenth and Twentieth Centuries in the United States of America*, (1985); Henry A. Verslype, *Belgians of Indiana* (1987).

Robert P. Swierenga
Hope College, Michigan

Norwegians

During Norway's century of emigration, 1825–1925, nearly 800,000 Norwegians moved overseas, overwhelmingly to the United States.

The move overseas began with the arrival of the sloop *Restauration* in the port of New York on October 9, 1825, carrying fifty-three voyagers. They were Quakers, Quaker sympathizers, and followers of the lay preacher Hans Nielsen Hauge and thus subject to persecution by the religiously monopolistic Norwegian Lutheran state church. In the mid-1830s, most moved from their initial settlement in western New York to the fertile Fox River Valley southwest of Chicago. Flocks of Norwegian peasants, mainly from the central highland valleys and western coastal districts, responded to the good news about life in North America. By the end of the Civil War, nearly 78,000 Norwegians had crossed the Atlantic.

Migration became massive in the half-century after 1865. About 677,000 Norwegians relocated to the United States. Immigrants and American-born generations moved from older settlements to new homes in a region extending from the southern tip of Lake Michigan to eastern Montana, including Iowa. In 1910 more than 80 percent of the first generation lived within this vast area.

Norwegians succeeded as farmers and showed a dedication to farming as a way of life. As recently as 1940 over half of all midwestern Norwegians made a living in agriculture or plied a variety of trades in small villages and towns. An attachment to the land, passed on through generations, strongly influenced their religious and secular institutions. A conservatism in spirit and mind prevailed and preserved Old World traditions and values.

Norwegians also established colonies in America's metropolitan areas, including Chicago and Minneapolis, which became major cultural centers. Women typically found work as domestics while men labored in construction and carpentry as well as the fishing industry. In addition, Norwegian-trained engineers, architects, and other professionals were attracted by the financial prospects of an expansive American economy. Social mobility through education, entrepreneurship, and public service moved later generations of Norwegian Americans into the middle class.

The Lutheran church, which traced its founding back to the pioneer Wisconsin settlements of the 1840s, became in its various manifestations the main institution erected by Norwegian immigrants, even though it was plagued with disharmony and dissent. Perhaps the divisiveness was evidence of the strength of Norwegian-American Lutheranism and an ethnoreligious identity that for many Norwegian Americans continues in force. In 1917 the different Lutheran directions united in the Norwegian Lutheran Church of America. Converts were made to non-Lutheran denominations, but never in large numbers. Some Norwegians joined the Methodists and the Baptists and formed Norwegian-language congregations within these denominations.

A strident Norwegian denominationalism and competing educational and theological convictions produced institutions of many kinds. Six four-year colleges and one two-year college are a living legacy of the educational mission of Norwegian-American Lutheranism. These colleges are today associated with the Evangelical Lutheran Church in America and there constitute a major educational enterprise within this large and diverse Lutheran church union.

A flourishing Norwegian American press, including *Skandinaven*, *Decorah-Posten*, and *Minneapolis Tidende*, helped nourish a separate ethnic life. There was an explosive growth of voluntary societies and social and cultural activities; the many charitable organizations that came into being were a response to the social

Student body and faculty of St. Olaf School, Northfield, Minnesota, 1875. St. Olaf College Archives.

needs of the immigrants. Some of these institutions have evolved into large medical and other care institutions.

Newspapers promoted assimilation by educating Norwegians about American ways and public affairs. From a modest start in 1847 with the publication of *Nordlyset* in the Muskego settlement in eastern Wisconsin, newspapers sprang up in shifting centers of Norwegian settlement and served individual political ambitions. A strong Republican conviction characterized the press and its subscribers, though in specific regions of the upper Midwest, such as the wheat-producing areas of North Dakota and northwestern Minnesota, newspapers had a pronounced reformist bent. In Minnesota, Norwegian voters sought social democratic reform within the Democratic Farmer-Labor political camp. Others maintained a conservative and traditional Republican affiliation.

In 1990 about 3.9 million Americans identified themselves subjectively as being of Norwegian ancestry, either as their first or second ethnicity. Norwegian Americans in general value a generational transfer of moral and ethical values associated with a specific ethnicity. They seek knowledge of where ancestors came from and even visit modest homesteads where their roots are located. There has also been an increase in observances of Norway's Constitution Day, May 17, and other ethnic festivals. These are frequently community affairs, indicating both open ethnic boundaries and a mainstreaming of ethnic cultures.

Not only those of Norwegian ancestry but people of a great variety of ethnic backgrounds join in the traditional lutefisk suppers still served by many Lutheran churches of Norwegian-immigrant origin, practice peasant arts and crafts of rose painting and woodcarving, and enthusiastically participate in folk-dance groups. Norwegian Americans thus preserve their distinctive cultural traditions within their larger role as citizens of the United States.

Sources and Further Reading: Theodore C. Blegen, *Norwegian Migration to America, 1825–1860* (1931); Einar Haugen, *The Norwegian Language in America*, 2 vols. (1969); Odd S. Lovoll, *A Century of Urban Life* (1988); Odd S. Lovoll, *The Promise Fulfilled* (1998); Odd S. Lovoll, *The Promise of America*, 2nd ed. (1999); E. Clifford Nelson and Eugene L. Fevold, *The Lutheran Church among Norwegian-Americans*, 2 vols. (1960); Orm Øverland, *The Western Home* (1996); Carlton C. Qualey, *Norwegian Settlement in the United States* (1938).

Odd S. Lovoll
St. Olaf College, Minnesota, and
University of Oslo, Norway

Swedes

The Midwest experienced early Swedish settlement, with Illinois serving as the cradle of Swedish America, Minnesota the heartland, and Chicago the center of Swedish organizations. Mass immigration was well-established by the 1860s, with Chicago and Minneapolis serving as gateways. The earliest movement was into Illinois, Minnesota, Iowa, and Kansas, and later into Wisconsin, Michigan, Nebraska, and the Dakotas. Old established settlements, especially those in Illinois, gave birth to new colonies farther west. Most subsequent migration has been internal, with people relocating from farm communities to urban areas such as Minneapolis and Omaha.

Propaganda from states, railroads, and steamship companies, as well as individual efforts of ethnic colonizers, originally enticed Swedes to the United States. Gustaf Unonius established a colony called New Uppsala near Pine Lake, Wisconsin, in 1841, and although the colony failed, Unonius's written accounts of life in the upper Midwest helped to propel mass migration from Sweden. Bishop Hill, an early communal colony established by Erik Jansson in Illinois in the 1840s, became symbolic of Swedish community building. Swedish settlers in rural areas focused on mixed-grain and dairy agriculture, while urban immigrants, the majority, distinguished themselves in business and the trades.

Illinois was the major destination of Swedes through most of the nineteenth century, yet settlement did not extend much beyond the northern portion. In addition to Chicago's Swede Town and suburbs, the best-known centers were Rockford and the Fox River Valley in the northeast and Bishop Hill, Galesburg, Rock Island, and Moline in the northwest. Swedes in Wisconsin concentrated in the northwest, establishing places like Stockholm (1854) in Pepin County. Many Swedes were farmers who supplemented their incomes with seasonal work in the lumber camps. Others were iron miners or found employment in Superior, a port for grain and iron exports. The oldest Swedish colony in Iowa, New Sweden, was established in 1845 by Peter Cassel. Swedes were taken westward by the Chicago, Burlington, and Quincy Railroad. In fact, Burlington, Iowa, received so many Swedes in transit that a section of the city became known as Swede Town.

Swedes settled heavily throughout Minnesota, with the largest contiguous Swedish area in Isanti and Chisago Counties near the Twin Cities. In 1930 Swedes were among the largest foreign-born ethnic groups in Minnesota, constituting more than 50 percent of the populations of Isanti, Chisago, Mille Lacs, Kanabec, Meeker, and Kittson Counties. Today

Minneapolis-St. Paul has more people of Swedish stock than any other place in the state.

Swedish settlers in Michigan were primarily lumbermen, miners, and small-time farmers in the northern cutover. Ishpeming was the central settlement. Swedes took up mining jobs alongside Finns at the Marquette, Menominee, and Penokee-Gogebic iron ranges of Michigan and Wisconsin. Small settlements of Swedes grew from lumber camps, and port cities like Marquette and Escanaba drew large numbers of Swedish workers.

Ohio's few Swedes live mostly in industrial centers like Cleveland, Akron, and Youngstown. The greatest relative numbers are in the port of Ashtabula, whose north end was once known as Swedetown. Swedes were not attracted to Indiana in large numbers, although there were clusters in the northwestern counties of Lake, LaPorte, and Porter. Missouri attracted only a small number of Swedes, the greater share settling in Kansas City, yet the state was important in the transit of Swedish settlers to points west.

People of Swedish ancestry are found throughout Kansas, with most in eastern and central counties. The First Swedish Colonization Company founded the Lindsborg Colony (1869) in Saline and McPherson Counties, today the largest rural concentration of Swedes in Kansas. Swedish Americans are found throughout Nebraska, but primarily in Omaha and Lincoln. Swedes were attracted by the Northern Pacific and Great Northern Railways into the Dakotas and settled in farm and small-town settings among the more numerous Norwegians. Swedes have a notable presence in Fargo, Grand Forks, Minot, Bismarck, and Williston. In South Dakota, Swedes are most numerous in Sioux Falls and Minnehaha County, on the eastern border.

Swedes established many ethnic organizations, newspapers, medical facilities, schools, and universities. Those with a religious affiliation tended to be Augustana Lutheran, Mission Covenant, Free Church, Methodist, or Baptist. Swedish Lutherans established Augustana College in Rock Island, Illinois (1860); Gustavus Adolphus College in St. Peter, Minnesota (1862); Bethany College in Lindsborg, Kansas (1881); and Luther College in Wahoo, Nebraska (1883). Swedish Baptists established Bethel College and Seminary in Arden Hills, Minnesota (1871), and the Swedish Covenant group established North Park College (now University) and Theological Seminary in Chicago (1891). Among the most influential newspapers were *Hemlandet* (1855), *Svenska Tribunen* (1876), and *Svenska Amerikanaren* (1877), all published in Chicago.

The Swedish Council in America (1972), based in Minneapolis, serves as the umbrella organization for over three hundred affiliated groups. The Vasa Order (1896), the largest of the Swedish-American organizations with more than two hundred lodges in North America, is dedicated to the preservation of Swedish culture.

Swedes celebrate their heritage in the Santa Lucia, Midsummer, and other ethnic festivals. Large Midsummer celebrations are held in Chicago; Lindsborg, Kansas; and Scandia, Minnesota, while Swedish Day is celebrated in Minneapolis's Minnehaha Park each June. Among the leading centers for Swedish-American history are the Swedish-American Historical Society in Chicago; the Swenson Swedish Immigration Research Center at Rock Island, Illinois; the Bishop Hill Museum in Illinois; the Swedish Institute in Minneapolis; and the Swedish American Museum Center in Chicago.

Contemporary Swedish immigrants are mostly professionals, live in metropolitan areas, and usually do not build links to established Swedish American communities or join ethnic organizations. The Swedish Women's Educational Association (SWEA), which aids immigrants, is a notable exception.

Most Swedish Americans today are American-born and live in urban areas, and while use of the ethnic language is limited, Swedish America has increased numerically via a heightened interest in ethnic identity. In the U.S. census of 1970 about 800,000 people identified themselves as Swedish; in the 1990 census the number was 4.6 million; and in the 2000 census, about 4 million.

Sources and Further Reading: Philip J. Anderson and Dag Blanck, eds., *Swedish-American Life in Chicago* (1992); Ulf Beijbom, ed., *Swedes in America: New Perspectives* (1993); Allan Kastrup, *The Swedish Heritage in America* (1975); Helge Nelson, *The Swedes and the Swedish Settlements in North America* (1943); Hans Norman and Harald Runblom, *Transatlantic Connections* (1988); George M. Stephenson, *The Religious Aspects of Swedish Immigration* (1932); Swedish Council of America, "Immigration Jubilee," *Sweden and America* (Autumn 1995); Alan Winquist, *Swedish-American Landmarks* (1995).

Ann Marie Legreid
Central Missouri State University

Danes and Icelanders

Although the first Danish immigrant arrived in America before the Revolutionary War, Danish migration grew in the years following the American Civil War and peaked in 1882, when 11,618 Danes migrated. Because the Midwest was then the primary focus of immigration to the United States, Danes tended to move to the region.

Although most Danish migrants had agricultural backgrounds, they settled in both rural and urban areas of the Midwest. Wisconsin had been a destination for some Danes before the Civil War and newcomers joined them after the war, especially near Hartland and Neenah. The largest rural settlement in Wisconsin was in Polk County, in the northwestern part of the state. During the 1870s and 1880s Wisconsin led all other states in the number of Danish residents.

Iowa became the midwestern center of Danish immigration between 1890 and 1920. Although Danes were distributed throughout the state, the major concentration was in Shelby and Audubon Counties, between Des Moines and Council Bluffs. Elk Horn is now the home of the Danish Immigrant Museum. Grand View College in Des Moines, affiliated with the Evangelical Lutheran Church of America, has Danish roots.

In Minnesota, Tyler and Askov were founded by Danish Lutherans who wished to establish a setting for Danes interested in maintaining their Lutheran faith and Danish ways. Both communities sponsored folk schools, boarding schools where young people could get a broad education and learn the Danish heritage.

Other states in the Midwest with rural Danish concentrations include Michigan (Montcalm County), Illinois (Sheffield County), Nebraska (Howard County), Kansas (Lincoln County), and South Dakota (Turner County).

A substantial number of Danes became farmers. Racine, Wisconsin was the home of Danes who worked in the farm-implement factories. Each year at the end of May the city commemorates its Danish heritage with the Kringle (the name of a pastry) Festival.

Chicago attracted the largest number of Danes. By 1900 there were more than ten thousand. The major concentration near North and Kedzie Avenues and Humboldt Park was called Little Denmark. A full range of Danish businesses, churches, clubs, and social societies thrived in Chicago. On Kedzie, just off of North, the Dania Society built a hall that became a social center. *Den Dansk Pioneer* ("The Danish Pioneer"), originally published in Omaha, is now located in the Chicago suburb of Elmwood Park.

Omaha also attracted Danes and became the home of the Danish Brotherhood, a fraternal organization. Insurance was its initial focus, and it founded branch societies all over the United States. It fosters the preservation of Danish heritage. A short distance north of Omaha is the town of Blair, the home of Dana College, a school with a Danish tradition.

Because Iceland remained under Danish rule until 1918 and continued as a kingdom under the Danish monarch until 1944, the U.S. census includes Icelanders in the Danish totals. Yet the Icelanders possess a distinct language and culture. An estimated five thousand migrated to the United States between 1870 and 1930, with the largest concentration in the northeastern North Dakota counties of Pembina and Cavalier.

Sources and Further Reading: Thomas P. Christensen, *A History of the Danes in Iowa* (1952); Enok Mortensen, *The Danish Lutheran Church in America* (1967); George R. Nielsen, *The Danish Americans* (1981); Peter L. Petersen, *The Danes in America* (1987).

George R. Nielsen
Concordia University, Illinois

Swiss

For the past five centuries Swiss have left their multilingual and multiethnic nation for opportunities abroad in agriculture, the trades, industry, commerce, and the professions. Some 290,000 emigrants went to the United States between 1820 and 1930, and about 63,000 between 1930 and 1990.

Swiss in the Midwest were distributed as shown in table 1. Although Swiss dispersed widely, as of 1990 areas of concentration included the Chicago (1,990); Madison, Wisconsin (2,625); Minneapolis-St. Paul (1,582); Milwaukee (1,014); and St. Louis (1,170) areas, as well as in rural areas such as Green County, Wisconsin (3,620); Adams County (3,104) and Elkhart County, Indiana (1,780); and Holmes County, Ohio (1,407).

Swiss also founded several settlements that often lost their national-ethnic character by the third generation. In 1804 winegrowers from Vevey, Switzerland, settled Vevay, Indiana, as the result of a land grant to Jean Jacques Dufour (1767–1827). In 1817 Mennonites from the Swiss Jura Mountains established Sonnenberg, Ohio; in 1825, Chippewa, Ohio; and in 1838, Berne, Indiana. In 1825 several Swiss families left the Red River colony in Canada for Gratiot's Grove northeast of Galena, Illinois. In 1831 Kaspar Koepfli (1774–1854) founded Highland, Illinois. Swiss families located in Sauk City, Wisconsin, in 1841. Four years later Swiss from the Swiss canton Glarus established New Glarus in Greene County, Wisconsin, where many Swiss also settled in towns such as Monroe. In 1848 Bernese Swiss founded Alma on the Mississippi River, and in 1852 Swiss Benedictines established St. Meinrad, Indiana, from which several daughter foundations emerged, among them Blue Cloud Abbey in South Dakota. In 1858 Swiss

Table 1. Swiss-born in American Midwestern States, 1870, 1900, 1930, and People of Declared Single Swiss Ancestry, 1980

State	1870	1900	1930	1980
Ohio	12,727	12,007	7,624	20,425
Illinois	8,980	9,033	7,315	9,897
Missouri	6,597	6,819	3,578	5,298
Wisconsin	6,069	7,666	7,669	15,534
Indiana	4,287	3,472	1,624	11,515
Iowa	3,937	4,342	2,096	4,305
Minnesota	2,162	3,258	2,041	4,626
Michigan	2,116	2,617	2,834	5,613
Kansas	1,328	3,337	1,594	4,305
Nebraska	593	2,340	1,364	2,665
S. Dakota	33*	585	618	1,141
N. Dakota		374	369	530
TOTAL MIDWEST	48,829	55,850	38,726	85,854
TOTAL US**	75,153	115,593	113,010	235,355

Source: J. P. von Grueningen, *The Swiss in the United States* (1940): 68–69, based on US census data; * for both Dakotas; ** see Bureau of the Census, *Historical Statistics of the United States, Colonial Times to 1970* (1975), Part 1, 117; 1980 figures in J. P. Allen and E. J. Turner, *We the People. An Atlas of America's Ethnic Diversity* (1988), Appendix 2: "Ethnic Population Data for States and Counties—1980," pp. 226–304; "Single Ancestry" included those who reported only one national ancestry: see ibid., 2–3 for details.

settled Tell City, Indiana, on the Ohio River, and Swiss from the canton Graubünden settled Badus, South Dakota, northeast of present-day Ramona, in 1877.

Swiss Americans have made an impact on the Midwest in a variety of ways. Beginning in the 1830s Swiss promoted their faith among American Indian peoples. Swiss Reformed missionary Jacob Stucki (1857–1930) labored among the Winnebago, and the Benedictine Martin Marty (1834–1896), the first abbot of St. Meinrad and a missionary among the Lakota, became the first Catholic bishop of South Dakota in 1889. Anselma Felber (1843–1883) founded a Benedictine monastery in Clyde, Missouri, and Getrud Leupi (1825–1904) established one in Yankton, South Dakota. Swiss established dairies in Ohio, Wisconsin, and South Dakota and played a leading role in processing milk for urban markets.

Peter Rindisbacher (1806–1834) and Karl Bodmer (1809–1883) left unique paintings of midwestern landscapes as well as of American Indians. In Chicago, Rudolph Ganz (1877–1972) was a noted pianist, conductor, and composer. During her years at the University of Chicago, psychiatrist Elisabeth Kübler-Ross (1926–2004) revolutionized approaches to death and dying.

Despite the fact that their lack of a common native language leads others to mistake them for Germans, Italians, or French, the Swiss have made many significant contributions to the history of the American Midwest.

Sources and Further Reading: John Paul von Grueningen, ed., *The Swiss in the United States* (1940); Leo Schelbert, "Swiss," in Robert M. Taylor and Connie A. McBirney, eds., *Peopling Indiana* (1996); Leo Schelbert, "Swiss in South Dakota," *Swiss-American Historical Society Review* 37 (Nov. 2001); Urspeter Schelbert, ed., *Swiss Colonists in 19th Century America* (1995).

Leo Schelbert
University of Illinois–Chicago

Late Nineteenth-Century Europeans, Mexicans, and Asians

With the exception of the initial wave of settlement by old-stock Americans, no other single migration wave did more to shape the character of the Midwest than the migration of Europeans (and, later, Mexicans and Asians) that occurred between the end of the Civil War and the 1920s. Virtually every city, large and small, bears the marks of this great influx.

Between 1870 and 1900 the settler immigration that helped fill up the rural areas of the Midwest gradually tapered off. This migration stream was dominated by peoples from northern and western Europe. Germans, Norwegians, and Swedes were among the most prominent, especially in states such as Wisconsin, Michigan, Minnesota, and Iowa. There were also groups of Dutch, Belgians, Danes, Czechs, and Poles. This rural migration never completely ended, and efforts to form rural ethnic colonies continued into the 1920s among such diverse groups as Jews, Danes, and Poles. Nevertheless, the recruits from these colonies were drawn more and more from North American urban ethnic communities than from European countries.

As settlement in rural areas declined, the growth of urban areas and the gradual expansion of extractive industries such as timber and mining drew greater numbers of immigrants to wage labor. Cities such as Detroit, Chicago, St. Louis, Milwaukee, and St. Paul, which had been dominated by German and Irish immigrants, attracted large numbers of people from east-central, southern, and, finally, southeastern Europe. The largest groups were Italians, Poles, Jews, Czechs, and Slovaks, but a plethora of other groups also arrived: Greeks, Ukrainians, Carpatho-Rusyns, Lithuanians, Hungarians, Finns, Romanians, Serbs, Croatians, Slovenes, Bulgarians, Albanians, Lebanese, Latvians, Estonians, and Roma (Gypsies).

In addition, Germans from eastern Europe and Russia joined preexisting German communities or formed distinct communities of their own. This wave of immigration was effectively ended by the outbreak of World War I. Little immigration from central and eastern Europe occurred between the two wars, although some refugees from countries such as Belgium were admitted during the war. Following World War II, a new wave of immigrants, mostly refugees, arrived in the Midwest from war-torn Europe. Jews and Poles were the largest groups, but there were also many Latvians, Lithuanians, Estonians, and Ukrainians. After the 1956 Hungarian revolution, refugees settled in the Midwest.

Mexican immigrants began to arrive in the Midwest just before World War I, with the earliest migrants in villages and cities. Some were itinerant laborers; others gravitated toward skilled or semiskilled jobs that they might have known in Mexico, such as tile making. After immigration from eastern and southern Europe was effectively banned following World War I, Mexicans came north in increasing numbers to work in factories and on farms. Farm laborers often came north to work each year. This connection sometimes persisted over two or three generations until laborers settled permanently in larger cities. Mexicans in Chicago and St. Paul worked mainly as meatpackers, following earlier groups such as Poles, Lithuanians, and other east-central Europeans. In Detroit most worked in the automobile industry, which had a voracious demand for workers and often used African Americans, southern whites, and Mexicans as counterweights in labor disputes with the largely eastern European workforce. In the 1930s, many Mexicans were deported or left under threat of deportation, but the communities themselves survived, providing a nucleus for the next wave of Mexican immigration after 1965.

Asian immigration to the Midwest was small, though more consistent than Mexican. Chinese were the most numerous group. Very small communities sprang up in the larger cities, but by 1900 small Chinese-owned establishments, especially the ubiquitous laundry, were common in smaller towns and cities. Such businesses tended to be rather ephemeral. While Japanese were not numerous enough to form communities, scattered individuals and groups of men worked on railroad repair and construction gangs. Following the American takeover of the Philippines in 1898–1899, some Filipinos arrived in the Midwest.

Most were young, male college students who tended to find jobs as waiters and servants. Chicago had the largest Filipino community by the early 1920s. Because of an acute gender imbalance, intermarriage with Polish or Irish women was common enough to merit a sociological study by the University of Chicago.

As the Midwest industrialized, these "new" immigrants were drawn to unskilled and semiskilled wage labor in industries such as meatpacking (Chicago, Omaha, St. Paul), steel (Chicago, Gary, Cleveland), milling and brewing (Minneapolis, St. Louis, Milwaukee), automobile production (Detroit), and a host of other manufacturing and production fields. Although the big cities drew the largest number of new arrivals, many smaller towns and cities, such as Duluth, Toledo, Green Bay, and Saginaw, also had large, even predominantly foreign-born, populations.

Extractive industries also drew large numbers of immigrants. Logging in Minnesota, Wisconsin, and Michigan; iron mining in Minnesota; and copper mining in Michigan's Upper Peninsula were all powered by immigrant labor. Finnish immigrants were most heavily concentrated in the Upper Peninsula and northern Minnesota, which respectively held the largest and second-largest Finnish populations in the United States. The northern mines also drew large numbers of Serbs, Croatians, and Slovenes, who, like the Cornish they often succeeded, seemed to specialize in certain types of mining.

The peopling of the Midwest also took place through secondary migration. The development of the auto industry and its spin-off manufacturing concerns drew numerous foreign-born central and eastern European workers and their children from places such as Pennsylvania's coal fields. Auto-dependent towns like Hamtramck, Michigan, home to such giant plants as Dodge Main and Chevrolet Gear and Axle, were peopled through secondary migration. These migrants were later joined by migrants from the rural South, both black and white.

The heavy influx of southern, central, and eastern Europeans, and the choices made by both employers and workers, resulted in heavy ethnic concentrations in particular industries. By 1940 half of all workers in heavy industry were Slavic. In Detroit, Poles alone made up half the workforce in auto production. Polish became a kind of lingua franca on the shop floor, spoken not only by eastern and central Europeans but even by many Italians and blacks. These immigrant communities would play a crucial role in the struggle for worker's rights in the 1920s and 1930s. Massively concentrated in heavy industry and possessing a high level of communal solidarity, these immigrants, once they were admitted to the union movement, proved vital to its success. Although by and large quite conservative—radical movements never got more than a small toehold in most communities—the immigrants fiercely defended their rights as workers and as new Americans.

Large ethnic concentrations gave a special flavor to midwestern cities. Ethnic neighborhoods became cities within cities, where business, family life, worship, courtship, and socializing took place in the native dialect (though often peppered with English words such as *pajczek*—"pay check"). Each neighborhood had its own sights, sounds, and smells. Communities developed distinct ethnic cultures that were a cocreation of immigrants and their American-born children. Old-country ideas merged with American forms and methods. Rituals and holidays took on new and sometimes different meanings, while other cultural products were "ethnicized." Polka, a popular working-

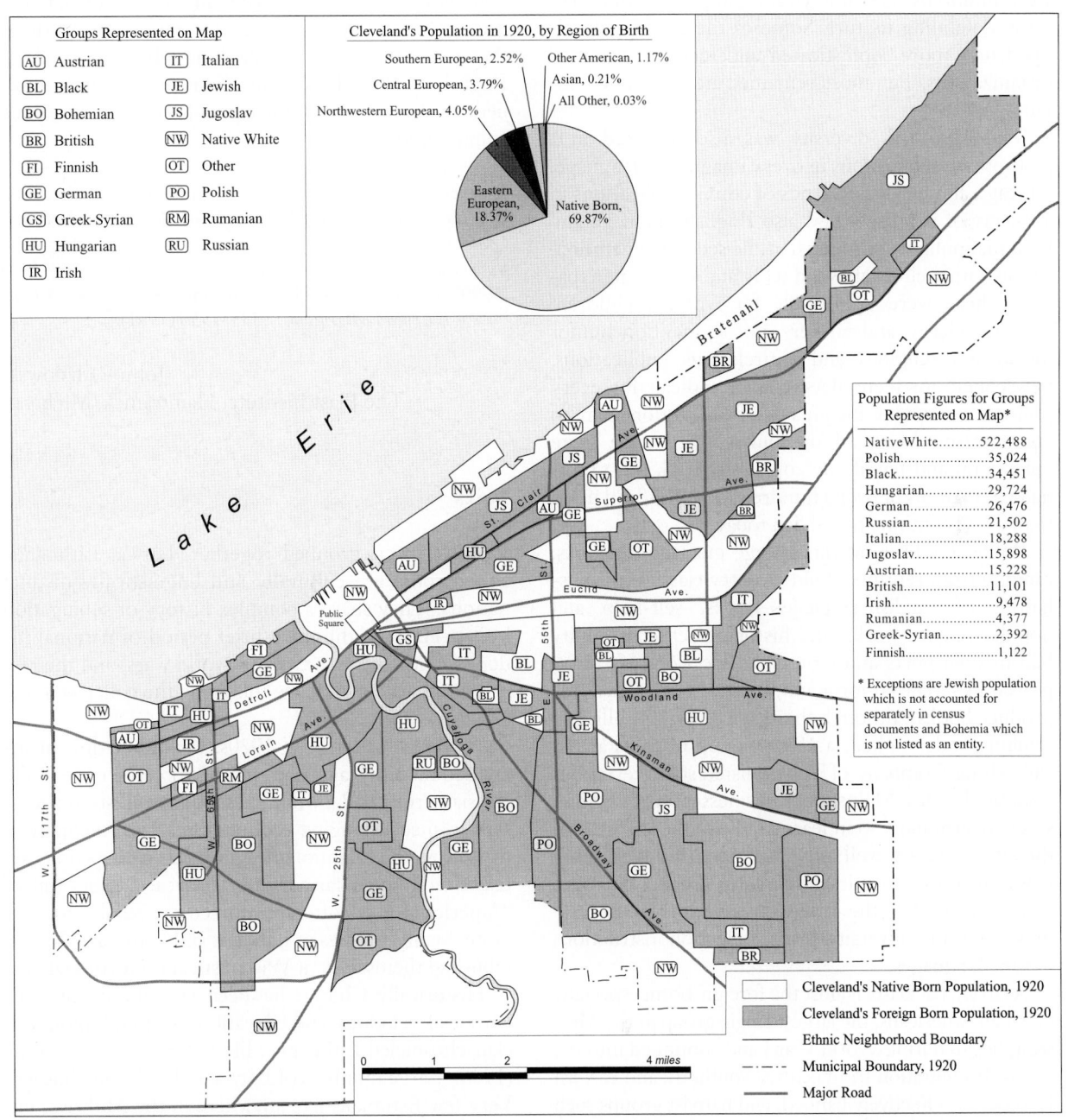

Ethnic enclaves in Cleveland, 1920. Prepared by Margaret Popovich. *Source:* U.S. Bureau of the Census, *Fourteenth Census of the United States Taken in the Year 1920*, Volumes II and III (1922); Helen Hornbeck Tanner, *The Settling of North America* (1995); David D. Van Tassel and John J. Grabowski, *The Encyclopedia of Cleveland History* (1987).

class music created in mid-nineteenth-century Europe, became a "traditional" ethnic music for central, eastern, and southern Europeans, with each group developing its own variants.

Urban ethnic communities were usually tightly focused and based around religious institutions and community organizations. National ethnic associations, often based in fraternal organizations, developed out of these local institutions. In addition to formal institutions, each community had informal groups for socializing and self-protection. In Chicago, there were hundreds of ethnic youth gangs, each one jealously defending its turf. Some of these gangs developed into more sophisticated and lucrative criminal organizations, but most remained neighborhood affairs.

The Midwest's diversity was also reflected in a plethora of publications in every imaginable language. Chicago alone had thousands of ethnic publications in a variety of languages and also English-language and bilingual publications aimed at the second generation. Along with well-established daily and weekly newspapers, there were periodicals for women, children, workers, clergy, and farmers, not to mention humor magazines, religious and antireligious publications, newspapers for teetotalers, and periodicals for every political viewpoint imaginable, from nationalism to communism. Many of the publications were quite ephemeral and few if any copies survived, but others had circulations of over a hundred thousand, and more than a few continue to publish today.

Publishers brought out a huge quantity of books, ranging from reprints of old-country classics to translations of English-language books, self-help and popular-science works, and history. Each community had its own poets and writers, whose work often appeared in serialized form and, later, in cheap, easy-to-produce books. Although the scope of such publishing remains understudied, a 1940 catalog of the Paryski Publishing Company of Toledo listed some ten thousand book titles. Mainstream businesses and local and state governments soon learned to use the medium of the ethnic press as well. Advertisements for everything from cigarettes to miracle cures to Coca-Cola were common. In 1896 the state of Minnesota, in an early bow to cultural diversity, printed election instructions in nine languages.

A strong backlash against the foreign-born, especially German Americans, the largest single group in the Midwest, began during World War I and continued into the 1920s. Immigration from central, southern, and eastern Europe was effectively banned, and nativist groups such as the Ku Klux Klan gained a following in the Midwest by preaching hatred toward "foreign" Catholics and Jews. Such developments, however, revealed the resiliency of ethnic communities. Many actively and creatively redefined themselves in the American context, using new ethnic markers—such as "traditional" folk costumes and dances—and holidays, such as Columbus Day. Rather than foreign sojourners, they were now an integral part of America. Many groups celebrated heroes of the American Revolution, such as Friedrich Wilhelm Augustus von Steuben, Tadeuz Kosciuszko, or Marie Joseph Paul Yves Roch Gilbert de Motier La Fayette. Some found forebears who had "discovered" America, such as Leif Erickson or Saint Brendan. Not only did such groups write themselves into the American story, they recast that story as something other than a tale of English-speaking Protestants. This process has continued in various forms throughout midwestern ethnic communities.

Sources and Further Reading: Ewa Morawska, *For Bread with Butter* (1985); James S. Pula, *Polish Americans: An Ethnic Community* (1995); Julianna Puskás, ed., *Overseas Migration from East-Central and Southeastern Europe, 1880–1940* (1990); Rudolph J. Vecoli and Suzanne Sinke, eds., *A Century of European Migrations, 1830–1930* (1991).

John Radzilowski
The Piast Institute, Hamtramck, Michigan

Balts

Though often grouped together, Latvia, Lithuania, and Estonia are culturally and linguistically distinct nations. They share a complex history of subjugation by powerful neighbors, a brief period of national independence between the two world wars, and the restoration of independence following the collapse of the Soviet Union in 1991.

From 1880 until the 1920s, a combination of increased mobility, agrarian reform, forced service in the Russian army, and a willingness to take all steps necessary to meet changing economic realities (including a trip across the Atlantic) brought Baltic craftspeople, artisans, and small farmers to America. Letters full of "America stories" often reinforced the resolve to emigrate. Small colonies of Latvians and Estonians first established themselves in Wisconsin and North Dakota.

Historically, Chicago has been a significant Lithuanian social, religious, and educational center. Upton Sinclair chronicled Lithuanian life in his novel *The Jungle* (1906). Large numbers of Latvians also live in Chicago. Very few Estonians live anywhere in the Midwest, but members of all three groups live in Cleveland, Detroit, Indianapolis, and Minneapolis.

Following World War II, Balts arrived as political refugees under the Displaced Persons Act of 1948 after spending five years in refugee camps. DPs, as they called themselves, resisted the rapid assimilation of their predecessors. In general, they were more urban, literate, and skilled than their earlier counterparts. Most arrived as extended families. In contrast to the turn-of-the-century Balts who settled into ethnic enclaves, these immigrants were dispersed by resettlement organizations to sponsors who guaranteed work and housing for one year. Thus former bankers, clerks, lawyers, once-affluent housewives (and the occasional farmer) milked cows; tended fields; and worked as gardeners, cooks, and housekeepers. After their stint with sponsors, most gradually migrated to cities. Despite menial jobs, they developed a vital ethnic life, seeking economic integration without cultural assimilation.

Identifying themselves as exiles rather than immigrants, they considered themselves as the only ones at liberty to preserve and perpetuate "true" culture during a period of foreign occupation of the homeland. In interviews, they recall the "packed suitcases under beds" in preparation for a quick return: "Do you know, what I felt when I boarded that ship, 'I am still going home, just the long way' . . . I felt, I felt and hoped that's my detour back home." As decades passed, the desired "When I go back" shifted to the children—"When you go back." Several hundred people from each group, predominately the young, had "returned" by the mid-1990s.

In 2000 more than 770,000 Americans claimed Estonian, Latvian, and Lithuanian descent; more than one-quarter of them lived in the Midwest. The observations of a Latvian sociologist forty years ago remain largely true for Baltic activists in general: They live among Americans geographically, economically, and educationally, but live as Latvians—or Estonians, or Lithuanians—socially, aesthetically, and personally. Partly in jest, partly in sadness, they typically claim the middle of the Atlantic Ocean—the crossroads between here and there—as home.

Sources and Further Reading: Anna Asars, Interview, Immigrant Groups in Indiana Project, Indiana University Center for the Study of History and Memory (1978); Algirdas M. Budreckis, ed. and comp., *The Lithuanians in America* (1976); Inta Gale Carpenter, "Baltic Peoples: Lithuanians, Latvians, and Estonians," in Robert M. Taylor, Jr., and Connie A. McBirney, eds., *Peopling Indiana* (1996); Maruta Karklis, Liga Streips, and Laimonis Streips, eds. and comps., *The Latvians in America, 1640–1973* (1974); Jann Pennar, ed. and comp., *The Estonians in America* (1975).

Inta Gale Carpenter
Indiana University–Bloomington

Greeks

Greeks can be defined as an ethnic and cultural group that traces its heritage to classical Greek civilization, Byzantine/Eastern Christianity, and the new Hellenic civilization after the Greeks gained their independence from the Ottoman Turks in the early nineteenth century. Greeks have been in the United States for more than a century. Along with other southeastern Europeans, they represent the "new immigrants," as opposed to the "old immigrants," who came primarily from northwestern Europe.

Most midwestern Greeks came during the mass immigration early in the 1900s and then again after World War II. Because the second wave was associated with the heroic resistance of Greeks to fascist Germany and Italy, these immigrants brought a new era of "respectability" to American-born Greeks, many of whom had worked in industry. Greeks generally have achieved a comfortable middle- and upper-middle-class standing in American society. Greek communities are found in most cities in the Midwest, with the strongest in the Chicago metropolitan area.

The overwhelming majority of early Greek immigrants were working class. They tended to be poor young men from agricultural backgrounds with limited education and skills. Later immigrants were more educated and moved as families as well as individuals. A substantial number were international students and professionals. It is estimated that between 250,000 and 300,000 Greeks and Greek Americans live in the Midwest, the majority of them American-born.

The most important institutions sustaining Greeks throughout the two major phases of migration were the Greek Orthodox Church and the family. More than a place of worship, the church was the hub around which religious, ethnic, and cultural activities (including Greek-language instruction) revolved. What the family was to the individual, the church was to the community. The same was true of practically every Greek community in the United States. To be a Greek meant to be a Greek Orthodox Christian. The identities were inseparable.

As of 2004 the Greek Orthodox Archdiocese listed about 540 parishes in the United States, with around 800 priests serving them. The Midwest counts 112 parishes and some 116 priests. Most members of these parishes are American-born Greeks and converts to Greek Orthodoxy from mixed marriages.

Greek schools were established at about the same time as the parishes. Most Greek Orthodox parishes operate Greek schools, usually on the weekends or after the public schools let out, for a few hours each week.

Early Greek immigrants worked on the railroads.

During the 1900s 5,000 or more Greeks were itinerant railroad workers in Kansas City. By 1912, the railroad town of Minot, North Dakota, had 250 Greek men, most employed on the Great Northern Railway. In Omaha, about 2,000 early Greeks worked in meatpacking and railroads. But it was as small-business entrepreneurs (especially as restaurateurs) that Greeks made their mark in American society. Both early and late Chicago Greek immigrants were heavily represented in service-oriented occupations.

By the 1920s Greek immigrants were prominent restaurant owners, ice-cream manufacturers, florists, fruit and vegetable operators, and confectionery merchants in Chicago, St. Louis, Detroit, and other cities. The *Chicago Herald and Examiner* reported in 1927 that Chicago Greeks operated more than 10,000 stores—500 of them in the Loop. By 1923 there were 1,035 Greek-owned restaurants. One of the leading enterprises was John Raklios's chain of restaurants. Post–World War II Greek immigrants followed the same path. Greek-owned restaurant establishments increased dramatically with the arrival of the "new" Greek immigrants during the 1960s and 1970s.

Other Greeks went into other kinds of businesses including groceries, dry goods, shoeshine parlors, movie theaters, construction, and real estate. Most of these operations were family owned. In St. Louis, the Skouras brothers started in the movie business. By 1926 they owned thirty-seven theaters in St. Louis, and by the 1930s the chain had grown to more than four hundred nationwide. By 1942 one of the brothers, Spyros, had become president of Twentieth Century Fox.

Greek American professionals are largely a post–World War II phenomenon. The 1994–1995 survey of *Hellenic Who's Who* reported over 900 professionals in the Midwest. In addition, the 2002 *Greek Orthodox Yearbook* lists eighteen Greek radio/TV programs. By far the three most common professions are business, medicine, and law. The 2000 *Directory of the Hellenic American Academic Community* lists more than 450 academics, fifty of whom are in the Midwest. The 2001 Modern Greek Studies Association lists six American universities in the Midwest with programs in Modern Greek studies. There are also five Greek and Greek American newspapers and two Greek American magazines—all located in the Chicago area.

Greeks have formed numerous organizations, Greek towns, and ethnic institutions. Both the 2002 *Yearbook* of the Greek Orthodox Archdiocese and the 1994–1995 *Hellenic Who's Who* list approximately ten national federations/organizations with headquarters in Chicago and two headquartered in Ohio. The American Hellenic Educational Progressive Association (AHEPA) is by far the largest Greek American association, with chapters in most midwestern cities.

There is also a Greek American Nursing and Rehabilitation Center in Wheeling, Illinois, and a Hellenic Museum and Cultural Center in Chicago.

Sources and Further Reading: John Gurda, *New World Odyssey* (1986); Milton Kouroubetis, *The Greeks of Michiana* (1987); George A. Kourvetaris, *Studies on Greek Americans* (1997).

George Andrew Kourvetaris
Northern Illinois University

Hungarians

In the second half of the nineteenth century, the spread of a capitalist market economy brought demographic, economic, and social changes to Hungary. Transition from feudalism to capitalism was drawn out, incomplete, and fraught with contradictions. Industrialization was narrowly based, and the industrial sector could not absorb the surplus agrarian population. Millions of peasants did not have land to provide a living or the means to acquire any. Meanwhile, innovations in transportation and the spread of literacy broadened horizons and created new expectations.

These developments created the first and largest wave of emigrants, from the 1880s to 1924. Their ethnic and linguistic diversity was striking. Most numerous were the Slovaks and the Magyars. Together they constituted more than 50 percent of the ten ethnic groups of migrants from Hungary. Jewish merchants, Slovak miners, and German and Magyar craftspeople were the pioneers, but when the multinational agrarian population joined them in increasing numbers, the large-scale movement became what is now known as a peasant migration.

A few political emigrants from the revolutions of 1848 had found asylum in the United States. Most Hungarians, however, were economic migrants, hoping to return with their savings to the place of their birth. Many achieved that goal. Nevertheless, Hungarians established settlements near the mines, ironworks, and steel mills where many of them worked. In spite of their efforts to live near familiar people, social and cultural differences among the multiethnic Hungarians shaped the evolution of their communities.

One of the cultural characteristics of the Magyars was the fact that they belonged to various religious denominations. Besides the Roman Catholic majority, there were sizable groups of Reformed Protestants, Jews, and Greek Catholics and a smaller number of Lutherans, Baptists, and Unitarians.

Neighborhoods of Magyars emerged in Cleveland, where they represented the largest ethnic group

A Hungarian wedding, East Chicago, Indiana, 1916. Immigration History Research Center, University of Minnesota.

among immigrants from Hungary. From Cleveland they often migrated to the steel mills on the southern side of Lorain, Ohio. Magyar neighborhoods developed in Toledo, Youngstown, and Dayton, Ohio. The Dayton Malleable Iron Works's Hungarian settlement consisted of factory-owned houses on the eastern side of the city. Similarly, in Columbus, Ohio, a small, more closely formed settlement was established. Those who could escape the mines of Pennsylvania looked for work in Cleveland. Others went to Delray, an outer suburb of Detroit, Michigan, mainly to work in the Ford factory. In Illinois, they went to the factory areas in the outskirts of Chicago, where most of the men worked in the enormous mills of the Illinois Steel Company.

Magyars organized social and cultural institutions such as churches and fraternal organizations. Often they cooperated with Slovaks in this work. Still, the diversity of the Hungarian community caused social and political conflicts over the nature of Hungarian nationalism, especially during World War I.

Generational change had a great impact on the course of ethnic identification. When the majority of American-born children of Magyars grew up, they wanted to work out their own identity. It became evident that many of them did not want to belong to their parents' ethnic communities.

During the Great Depression, the new immigrants, including Magyars with their second generation, participated in the strikes, organized drives, and struggled to gain unemployment insurance. Magyars took part in mass activities of workers, mostly in Cleveland, Toledo, Detroit, and Chicago.

In the middle of the twentieth century, the United States received two more waves of Hungarian immigrants. In the spring of 1945, hundreds of thousands of civilians and soldiers crossed the western border of Hungary in the wake of their liberation from Nazi Germany. While the majority returned after the "farewell to the arms," almost seventeen thousand mostly middle- and upper-class immigrants settled in the United States between 1949 and 1953.

On October 23, 1956, an uprising broke out in Budapest against the Communist government of Hungary. When it was mercilessly suppressed, two hundred thousand Hungarians fled the country, and nearly forty thousand of them settled in the United States. They were well-trained young people, 66.4 percent of them under thirty years old and 11.07 percent of them professional, technical, and kindred workers. Members of this second wave of Hungarian refugees were warmly welcomed and celebrated as freedom fighters.

Neither of these post–World War II waves of refugees merged with the "old-timer" Hungarian immigrants. The newcomers generally preferred to form their own associations to satisfy their intellectual and political needs and aspirations. The traditional Hungarian neighborhoods were disintegrating by the 1970s. As mines and iron- and steelworks were closed, descendants of immigrants turned to other occupations and moved to suburban neighborhoods. The local institutions that sustained traditional identities—national parishes, lodges, newspapers—were gravely weakened, and in many cases completely disappeared.

Sources and Further Reading: Thomas E. Barden and John Ahern, eds., *Hungarian American Toledo* (2002); Malvina Hauk-Abonyi and James A. Anderson, *Hungarians of Detroit* (1977); Eugen M. Kulischer, *Europe on the Move* (1948); Michael Pap, "Hungarian Communities in Cleveland," in Michael Pap, ed., *Ethnic Communities of Cleveland* (1973);

Susan Papp, *Hungarian Americans and Their Communities of Cleveland* (1981); Robert Perlman, *Bridging Three Worlds* (1991); Julianna Puskás, ed., *Overseas Migration from East-Central and Southeastern Europe, 1880–1940* (1990); Steven Bela Vardy, *The Hungarian-Americans* (1985); S. Alexander Weinstock, *Acculturation and Occupation* (1969).

Julianna Puskás
Hungarian Academy, Budapest, Hungary

Italians

Of the almost 16 million people who claimed Italian ancestry in the 2000 U.S. census, some 2.5 million resided in the Midwest. The states of Illinois, Ohio, and Michigan collectively reported almost 1.9 million people of Italian ancestry. Indiana, Minnesota, Missouri, and Wisconsin each had more than 100,000 but fewer than 200,000, while the other midwestern states each counted fewer than 100,000. The Midwest clearly has not been the favored region of Italian settlement. Vast stretches of the region recorded less than 2 percent of their residents as being of Italian ancestry. Because Italian immigrants preferred urban areas, the midwestern Italian American population is clustered about the metropolitan areas of Chicago, Cleveland, and Detroit.

From the 1850s Italians were itinerants pursuing traditional migratory trades; political refugees from the failed uprisings of the Risorgimento; as well as artists, musicians, and adventurers. By the 1870s there were small Italian colonies in several midwestern cities. Led by nationalist expatriates, they formed societies, published newspapers, and celebrated Columbus Day. Despite their anticlericalism, several Italian Catholic parishes were established. One of the first was the Church of the Assumption in Chicago in 1881.

A new wave of Italian immigrants commenced in the 1880s, including *contadini* (peasants) from the southern regions of Basilicata, Campania, and Calabria. Sojourners, their goal was to save money and return to Italy. Railroad companies recruited these laborers to work on the railroads of the Midwest and the Far West. Meanwhile, Sicilians recruited for the sugar plantations of Louisiana migrated up the Mississippi River. Cleveland, Milwaukee, St. Louis, Omaha, St. Paul, and, above all, Chicago became labor markets where *padrones* enlisted gangs of Italians to work on the *tracca* (railway tracks).

Until World War I, the Italian population of midwestern cities was largely composed of this floating labor force. Although few Italians were employed in heavy industries, garment manufacturing became a major source of employment for both women and men. As immigrants secured steady work, they established Little Italies in both large cities and rural communities.

Mining was the other occupation that attracted Italians to the Midwest. Italian miners moved first to the coal-mining areas of Indiana, Illinois, Iowa, and Kansas. Others migrated to the iron and copper mines of Michigan's Upper Peninsula. From there, Italian miners subsequently migrated to the iron-ore ranges of northern Wisconsin and Minnesota. In contrast to the railroad workers, who tended to be from the southern regions, central and northern Italians predominated among the miners.

Italian artists and artisans, stone cutters, sculptors, and stucco workers played a special role in the embellishment of public buildings, churches, and mansions

Italian society parade, Cumberland, Wisconsin. Immigration History Research Center, University of Minnesota.

throughout the Midwest. Barbers, musicians, and cooks elevated the quality of life in the region. The Italian influence upon the culinary arts has been perhaps the most enduring. As truck farmers and vendors, they introduced artichokes, broccoli, zucchini, and other vegetables, and as importers of pasta, oranges, olive oil, and wine, they enriched midwestern cuisine. Italian bakeries, delicatessens, restaurants, and saloons in time attracted a cosmopolitan clientele. For many Italians, the purveying of food and drink became the path to fortune in America.

Through a process of "chain migration," relatives and *paesani* (townspeople) were sent for and provided with lodgings and jobs. Wives arrived, families were established, and a second generation was born. The so-called Little Italies were clusters of village groupings according to the spirit of *campanilismo* (in-groupness). Relying on one another for assistance and comfort, paesani formed mutual-aid societies bearing names of patron saints or national heroes. Slow to establish churches, the contadini's folk beliefs and practices sustained them. Celebrations of the feast days of saints, such as that of the Madonna of Pompeii by Sicilians in Milwaukee, were both expressions of piety and affirmations of communal identities.

Emigration and revolutionary movements were contemporary expressions of popular discontent in late-nineteenth-century Italy. Many immigrants had participated in socialist and anarchist activities in mining areas as well as cities. Spring Valley, Illinois, became notorious in the early 1900s as a hotbed of Italian anarchists. Chicago was a stronghold of Italian socialists. These radicals were active in strikes, such as those of Chicago garment workers of 1910 and Minnesota mine workers of 1916. Atheists, they formed free-thought societies, circulated anticlerical literature, and harassed religious processions.

The twentieth century brought great change to Italian American communities in the Midwest. World War I inspired a spirit of nationalism among apolitical immigrants. With the rise of Benito Mussolini to power in Italy in the 1920s, Fascist propaganda was promulgated in the Midwest through Italian newspapers, lodges of the Sons of Italy, and national parishes. Most Italian Americans basked in the glory of a new, powerful Italy. For too long they had been derided as "dagos" and discriminated against in housing, employment, and public life. Particularly offensive was their widespread image as *Mafiosi*, a criminal stereotype reinforced by allegations of "Black Hand" extortion and bootlegging.

The 1920s marked the end of mass migration and hastened the assimilation of Italians. Italian families acquired consumer goods, homes, and automobiles. Hard hit by the Depression of the 1930s, Italian Americans lost homes, businesses, and jobs. Peasant traditions, however, enabled them to cope with long stretches of unemployment. Vegetable gardens and chicken coops provided food for the table, while kinship and paesano bonds led to sharing of scarce resources. Italian Americans for the most part supported the Democratic Party and President Franklin Delano Roosevelt's New Deal. They also played an important role as both leaders and rank and file in the region's massive labor strikes and organizing campaigns led by the CIO (Congress of Industrial Organizations).

Many Italian Americans retained their attachment to Fascist Italy until the outbreak of World War II in 1941. Italy's military conquest of Ethiopia (1935–1936) brought Italian Americans into conflict with African Americans in Cleveland and other midwestern cities. With Italy's declaration of war on the United States on December 11, 1941, the Italian American flirtation with Fascism came to an end. Proclaiming their American patriotism, Italian Americans purchased war bonds and sent their sons and daughters to fight the Axis powers. Mike Colalillo of Duluth was one of the few to be awarded the Congressional Medal of Honor in World War II. Nonnaturalized immigrants were declared "enemy aliens." This stigma was removed on Columbus Day 1942 on the grounds that Italians had proven their loyalty to the United States.

World War II constituted a watershed in the history of Italian Americans. When the second generation left the Little Italies for military service and war jobs, they made friends with and married people from other ethnic backgrounds. After the war, full employment and the benefits available through the Servicemen's Readjustment Act of 1944 (the GI Bill) enabled many to realize their dream of owning a home in the suburbs. Factors that hastened the demise of Little Italies were the massive highway construction and "urban renewal" programs of the 1950s. The suburban exodus was also a response to the influx of large numbers of African Americans into midwestern cities. In becoming "white Americans," many of the descendants of the racially "in-between" Italian immigrants had also become racists.

Prior to World War II, the educational attainment of Italian Americans was one of the lowest among ethnic groups. Considerations of family economy and cultural values discouraged such aspirations among immigrant children. The GI Bill opened the portals of universities and technical colleges to the second generation. Italian Americans increasingly pursued higher education, resulting in accelerated social mobility. While a substantial number continued as blue-collar workers, many of the offspring of the contadini attained middle-class status.

In politics, Italian Americans such as Bruce Vento

of St. Paul and Frank Annunzio of Chicago were elected to the U.S. Congress, but few achieved high office nationally. Although Chicago has the largest Italian American population in the region, no representative of the group has been elected mayor of the city or governor of the state of Illinois. This limited political achievement has been attributed to the alleged ties of Italian American politicians with organized crime. As Italians became affluent and conservative suburbanites, they tended to move into the ranks of the Republican Party.

Sociologist Richard Alba has asserted that Italian Americans have entered the "twilight of ethnicity," that they have largely assimilated into a "white ethnic" population. Surviving traces of ethnic culture are symbolic and without meaning in everyday lives. This view is opposed by the concept of the "invention of ethnicity," which contends that while ethnic culture has changed from generation to generation, ethnicity as a shared identity has persisted. Only this can explain the continuation of certain forms of ethnic expression, such as the celebration of the feast days of saints and Columbus Day; the revitalization of organizations, such as the Order Sons of Italy in America; and the creation of new ones, such as the Joint Civic Committee of Italian Americans in Chicago.

This ethnic revival is part of the larger transformation of our image of America as a melting pot into that of a multicultural society. Proud of their ancestors, many midwestern Italian Americans embrace and celebrate their ethnic identity.

Sources and Further Reading: Richard Alba, *Italian Americans: Into the Twilight of Ethnicity* (1985); James Paul Allen and Eugene James Turner, eds., *We the People* (1988); Graziano Battistella, ed., *Italian Americans in the '80s* (1989); Robert F. Harney and J. Vincenza Scarpaci, eds., *Little Italies in North America* (1981); Salvatore J. LaGumina, Frank J. Cavaioli, Salvatore Primeggia, and Joseph A. Varacalli, eds., *The Italian American Experience* (2000); Tom W. Smith, *A Profile of Italian Americans* (1992); Rudolph J. Vecoli, "The Formation of Chicago's 'Little Italies,'" *Journal of American Ethnic History* 2 (Spring 1983); Rudolph J. Vecoli, "Italian-American Ethnicity: Twilight or Dawn?" in John Potestio and Antonio Pucci, eds., *The Italian Immigrant Experience* (1988); Rudolph J. Vecoli, ed., *Italian Immigrants in Rural and Small Town America* (1987).

Rudolph J. Vecoli
University of Minnesota–Twin Cities

Jews

Jews built a vibrant and varied life for themselves in the Midwest. The first Jews in the region were migrants fleeing political and economic turmoil in Europe's German-speaking lands in the 1820s to the 1850s. By and large, they were drawn into the South and Midwest, where they saw greater economic opportunities in areas that reminded them of rural Germany. In general, Jews became small merchants or artisans. Although they had practiced a traditional form of Judaism in Europe, most of them gave up all but the most basic Jewish religious practices. It took years to establish congregations and burial societies.

Some of our earliest evidence of Jewish settlement comes from Indiana. A land-development company seems to have been responsible for bringing Jews into the territory as early as the 1810s. The first Jewish settler in Vincennes, Samuel Judah, appears in records by 1818.

More typical of the settlement pattern is St. Louis, Missouri. Individual Jews apparently lived in the area as early as the late 1820s or the early 1830s. Records indicating that Jewish New Year services were conducted in 1837 give us our first hard evidence of a critical mass of Jews. Other communities coalesced at a slightly later date. The core of Cleveland's Jewish community arrived from Bavaria in 1839. They, along with Jews already in the region, immediately chartered the first Jewish organization in the city, the so-called Israelite Society. A few years later a second congregation, Anshe Hesed, was established. The same pattern can be seen in Chicago. There are scattered references to Jews there as early as 1832, but the first organized activity was the creation of a congregation in 1845 to celebrate the Jewish New Year. Shortly thereafter a burial society was founded.

Organized Jewish communities appear somewhat later farther west. Jews began arriving in Nebraska in the mid 1850s, before the area was even a territory. The first Jewish congregation in Iowa was organized in Keokuk in 1855, with a synagogue appearing in 1877. Minnesota's first Jewish congregation, Mount Zion Hebrew Congregation, was organized in Saint Paul in 1856, and the Mt. Zion Cemetery Association in Leavenworth, Kansas, appeared in 1857.

Within this overall pattern, Cincinnati, Ohio, was somewhat unusual. The city attracted a large number of German migrants, including a correspondingly larger number of Jews, and became the major center of Jewish life in the Midwest. A small Orthodox congregation was organized in 1824 by a group of Jews from England. The first German Jewish congregation appeared in 1840, a second in 1848, and a third in 1855. It is no surprise that the first rabbinical seminary in North America (Hebrew Union College), founded in 1875, was located in Cincinnati, which had perhaps the largest German Jewish community in the country.

German Jewish migration had largely come to a

halt by the 1860s. First the Civil War made travel impossible, and improving conditions in Europe reduced the incentive to leave. This reduction led to a number of profound changes. Most significantly, the German Jewish community in North America evolved from an immigrant community to a native-born one. The community also became wealthier, more self-assured, and more organized, as the foundation of Hebrew Union College exemplifies. Finally, the German language was abandoned in favor of English. By the 1870s virtually every Jewish congregation in the Midwest had substituted English for German in prayers, sermons, and synagogue records.

This Americanized and comfortably assimilated community of roughly a quarter-million souls soon found itself inundated by a massive wave of Jews from eastern Europe escaping repressive laws enacted by Tsar Alexander III in 1881. Because the eastern European Jewish immigration was part of a much more massive migration of peoples from eastern and southern Europe, it is hard to determine with any exactitude the number of Jews who arrived. It appears, however, that between 1881 and the new immigration laws of 1924, some 2.5 million "Russian" Jews came to North America. The vast bulk of these Jewish immigrants remained where they disembarked, especially in New York City.

Significant numbers, however, found their way across the Appalachians and into the Midwest. These Jews—Yiddish speaking, Orthodox in practice, medieval in dress and mannerisms—discovered that they had very little in common with the existing, highly Americanized, "German" Jewish community and so quickly set about the task of organizing their own synagogues, schools, social centers, and other institutions. In St. Louis, there were three congregations in 1851, only one of which was traditional in its liturgy. In the decades between 1880 and 1930, Russian Jews established four new congregations, all much more Orthodox in character. Other cultural and social institutions were established as well, including a Jewish Hospital in 1902 (no crosses or crucifixes in the rooms, kosher meals, and Sabbath worship), a Young Men's Hebrew Association (modeled on the Young Men's Christian Association), a Jewish Orphan's Home, and an old-age home.

This pattern repeated itself in many other midwestern communities. Columbus, Ohio, had only one small congregation in the 1860s but saw three traditionalist, Russian congregations open between 1883 and 1907. A Jewish community center was established in 1913 and a community newspaper, the *Ohio Jewish Chronicle*, in 1922. Cleveland not only saw the size of its Jewish community almost triple during this time, but witnessed the establishment of the Jewish Relief

Society in 1895, a Jewish settlement house in 1898, Mt. Sinai Jewish Hospital in 1903, and an Orthodox home for the aged in 1906. Cleveland also had for a while a Yiddish newspaper, *Di yidishe Velt*. The most dramatic example of the impact of the eastern European Jewish migration can be seen in Detroit. In 1880 the Detroit Jewish community numbered about one thousand, with one Reform and four Orthodox congregations. Four decades later, the community numbered thirty-five thousand and offered a full range of Jewish religious and social organizations.

These changes were, of course, modest in comparison with what was happening in New York and other East Coast cities. To relieve the pressure on those areas, a number of initiatives were undertaken to encourage Russian Jews to leave the coast and settle in the Midwest and the South. One of the more innovative initiatives called for the establishment of Jewish homesteading opportunities. Baron Maurice de Hirsch, a leading New York Jewish philanthropist, established the Jewish Colonization Association in 1882 to create a Jewish population center on the Missouri River in what was to become North Dakota. Another attempt, the so-called Russian-Jewish Farmer Settlement, commenced in the same region around 1892. Neither, however, had much success.

With the imposition of immigration quotas in 1924, large-scale migration into the Jewish communities of the Midwest virtually stopped. In the decades that followed, two opposing trends emerged. On the one hand, the "Russian" Jewish community underwent the same process of Americanization and assimilation that their German predecessors had undergone two generations earlier. On the other hand, a strong sense of Jewish identity arose because of growing anti-Semitism. One of the centers of this Jew-hatred was Detroit, where Father Charles Coughlin broadcast a weekly radio show in which he preached about the wickedness of the Jews and where Henry Ford had subsidized the publication of the rabidly anti-Jewish pamphlet *The Protocols of the Elders of Zion*.

Anti-Semitism virtually disappeared in America in the wake of the Nazi horrors of the Holocaust. The American Jewish community found unprecedented acceptance in the country, and Jews were able fully and openly to participate in the political, social, and cultural lives of their communities. Because of economic, demographic, social, and economic trends in the United States following World War II, the Jewish community became more homogeneous and the midwestern Jewish community lost its particular character. Like the rest of North American Jewry, the Jews of the Midwest have since the 1970s undergone a process of renewed ethnic and religious identification. This is due to a number of factors, including a delayed reaction to the massacre of Europe's Jews, the creation and success of the state of Israel, and the general growth of ethnic pride in the late 1900s.

In the last few decades, Jews have been leaving rural areas and small towns and migrating to urban areas where they can find employment and Jewish communal support. At the same time, many of the large cities of the Midwest—such as Cleveland, Detroit, and St. Paul—are struggling economically. In combination, these two trends have resulted not only in the disappearance of many small midwestern Jewish communities, but a steady out-migration of Jews to the two coasts.

Sources and Further Reading: Roberta R. Farber and Chaim I. Waxman, eds., *Jews in America* (1999); Lee Levinger, *A History of Jews in the United States* (1970); Tina Levitan, *First Facts in American Jewish History* (1996); Pamela Susan Nadell, ed., *American Jewish Women's History* (2003); Cecil Roth and Geoffrey Wigoder, eds., *Encyclopedia Judaica*, 18 vols. (1972–1991); Howard M. Sachar, *A History of the Jews in America* (1992); Robert M. Seltzer and Norman J. Cohen, eds., *The Americanization of the Jews* (1995); Joseph Telushkin, *The Golden Land: The Story of Jewish Immigration to America* (2002); Gary Phillip Zola, ed., *The Dynamics of American Jewish History* (2004).

Peter J. Haas
Case Western Reserve University, Ohio

Poles

The Midwest contains the largest concentrations of Polish Americans in the United States. Chicago is famously said to have more Poles than any city save Warsaw. In Wisconsin, nearly one in ten residents claims Polish ancestry. Polish communities can be found in every midwestern state. Poles settled in isolated rural colonies and large urban neighborhoods. The earliest communities date from the 1850s, with the largest numbers arriving between 1880 and 1924. Refugees from Nazi Germany and Soviet domination arrived in large numbers after World War II. Immigration resumed in the 1960s and picked up dramatically in the 1980s and 1990s to the point that in the late 1990s Poles were again the largest single immigrant group in the city of Chicago.

Although a few political refugees from partitioned Poland could be found in the Midwest as early as the 1840s, the first Polish settlement dates from the late 1850s. Small numbers arrived in rural or mixed urban-rural settlements prior to the Civil War: Polonia, Wisconsin; Winona, Minnesota; Parisville, Michigan; and Washington, Missouri. A few also followed waves of German immigrants to cities such as Milwaukee, De-

troit, and Chicago. Rural, settler immigration continued to draw Poles from German-ruled western Poland from the 1860s to the 1880s. Settlements sprang up in many areas of Wisconsin, Minnesota, Michigan, central Illinois, and eastern North Dakota. Planned colonization efforts brought families from urban centers such as Chicago to central Nebraska, northern Wisconsin, and western Minnesota.

By the 1870s, the great majority of Polish immigrants were going to the region's industrializing cities. Chicago and Milwaukee attracted the largest number of Poles. Later waves and secondary migration built up Polish communities in cities such as Detroit. By World War II, first- and second-generation Polish Americans numbered about five hundred thousand in Chicago and three hundred thousand in Detroit.

Although the first Polish immigrants came from western Poland, their numbers were soon dwarfed by larger waves from the Austrian- and Russian-controlled regions of southern and northeastern Poland. Milwaukee's Polonia, the name given to the city's Polish neighborhood, remained largely dominated by the early arrivals. In Chicago, the near northwest side was home to all three groups but was dominated politically and socially by the westerners who established businesses and major ethnic fraternal organizations. The South Side was dominated numerically by Poles from Galicia. Detroit presents yet a third pattern. An early settlement of western Poles was dwarfed by a secondary migration of Poles, mainly from the coal mines of Pennsylvania, who came in the first two decades of the twentieth century to take jobs in the growing auto industry.

Leaving aside the 10 percent who settled on farms, and some small mining or logging communities, the majority of Poles in the Midwest worked in heavy industry. Poles were given, and took, the dirtiest, toughest, and most dangerous jobs in the meatpacking, steel, automobile, tire and rubber, and milling industries. In Detroit, half of all workers in heavy industry in the 1920s and 1930s were Poles.

Poles were involved in some of the bitterest labor struggles of the early twentieth century. In 1893 striking Polish canal diggers in Lemont, Illinois, were attacked by armed black strikebreakers led by white foremen, who killed at least eight and wounded some two dozen more. As the movement for workers' rights gained momentum, Poles proved crucial to its success. In Detroit, the United Auto Workers would not have succeeded without strong support from the Polish community. The use of Polish in the city's auto plants was so prevalent that union organizing appeals on Polish-language radio attracted workers from other ethnic groups as well, including Ukrainians, Bulgarians, Italians, and African Americans.

Members of the St. Joseph Society, St. Paul,
Minnesota, 1918. Immigration History
Research Center, University of Minnesota.

The foremost Polish American institutions were Roman Catholic parishes. They formed the symbolic and spiritual glue that bound the new communities together, and also provided practical benefits. Parishes were cultural centers, rallying points in times of crisis, social service agencies, and supported the parochial schools that educated children. St. Stanislaus Kostka (founded in 1867) in Chicago was the largest Catholic parish in the United States in 1900 with forty thousand parishioners, while a few blocks away Holy Trinity (1872) had twenty thousand members. Many churches, such as Sweetest Heart of Mary in Detroit, were spectacular architectural achievements created by people who just a few years before had been living in thatched-roof huts with dirt floors.

The parishes were also centers of political and communal strife. Some Poles, disgruntled by discrimination at the hands of Irish or German bishops, broke with the Catholic Church to form independent parishes. Some of these eventually coalesced into the Polish National Catholic Church, based in Scranton, Pennsylvania, which had adherents in Michigan, Illinois, Wisconsin, Minnesota, and Ohio. Most Polish parishes remained within the mainstream Roman Catholic fold, although internal church conflicts wracked many communities. In 1908 the American church hierarchy finally allowed ordination of the first Polish-American bishop, Reverend Paul P. Rhode of Chicago (later bishop of Green Bay).

After the church, the school was perhaps the most important Polish American institution. Virtually all parish schools were run by nuns from Polish chapters of American orders or largely Polish and Polish Amer-

ican orders, such as the Sisters of St. Felix (Felicians). Joining these orders represented an attractive avenue for education and social mobility for young immigrant women and the mobilization of a large talent pool for the good of their young communities. Polish teaching sisters developed teaching materials that were emphatically Polish and Catholic.

The most important Polish lay organizations were fraternal insurance societies. The largest and oldest were based in Chicago. The Polish Roman Catholic Union of America (1873) emphasized loyalty to the church, Polish Catholic positivism, and self-help. The rival Polish National Alliance (PNA; 1880) was secular and emerged from romantic nationalism, emphasizing the liberation of the Polish homeland. The Polish Women's Alliance of America (1898) focused on women's rights, suffrage, and Polish nationalism. All three national associations maintain Chicago headquarters. In addition, there were several regional fraternal groups and a plethora of single-society death-benefit organizations. Although the organizations often squabbled among themselves, they agreed on aiding the Polish homeland in times of need. In 1944 this agreement was institutionalized in the Polish American Congress, an ethnic umbrella organization headquartered in Chicago and eventually dominated by the largest fraternal organization, PNA.

Polish communities developed a vast range of other institutions. One of the most durable has been the Orchard Lake Schools, founded in Detroit in 1886. In addition, two other colleges were founded in the Midwest: a now-closed two-year school in Chicago and Madonna University, founded by Polish Felicians near

Detroit. There were also colleges, hospitals, orphanages, old-age homes, settlement houses, social welfare organizations (e.g., today's Polish American Association), veterans' groups (e.g., the Polish Legion of American Veterans), amateur and professional theatrical circles, libraries, folk-dance groups, cultural clubs, choir and musical societies, athletic leagues, and scouting and youth organizations. With the arrival of post–World War II émigrés and refugees from Nazi Germany and the Soviet Union, a whole new set of institutions sprang up including branches of Polish armed forces veterans' groups and *harcerstwo* (Polish scouts).

The first regular Polish-language newspaper, *Orzel Polski* ("Polish Eagle") appeared in Washington, Missouri, in 1870. Chicago alone has been home to hundreds of periodicals. Milwaukee and Detroit also supported daily papers into the 1960s and 1970s. Scores of publications were also found in smaller communities, such as Omaha (*Gwiazda Zachodu* ["Western Star"], 1904–1945), St. Paul (*Nowiny Minnesockie* ["Minnesota News"], 1915–1978), and Stevens Point, Wisconsin (*Gwiazda Polarna* ["The North Star"], founded in 1908, and *Rolnik* ["The Farmer"], 1891–1960). The largest newspaper was *Ameryka-Echo*, published by Toledo's Antoni Paryski, which had a weekly circulation of over a hundred thousand in the years after World War I.

Paryski also published books. A partial catalog from his company dating to the late 1930s lists nearly ten thousand titles. Midwestern communities also supported many small publishers who reprinted works of Polish literature; translated English-language books, practical nonfiction, and history; and published literary, religious, and polemical works by immigrant authors. At the turn of the twenty-first century, Chicago supported three Polish-language dailies while weeklies and monthlies continued to thrive in several communities serving Polish-speaking, bilingual, and English-speaking readers.

Poles have remained relatively weak in politics. There has never been a Polish mayor of Chicago and there has been only one Polish mayor of Detroit. Discrimination, poverty, the internal focus of many communities, a distrust of power, ineffective leadership, excessive focus on the affairs of the old country, and failure to build coalitions with other groups are some of the factors cited by scholars and activists for this weakness.

The success of the union struggles, the demographic impact of World War II, and postwar prosperity brought about a gradual suburbanization as Polish Americans made their way into the American middle class. Until the 1970s Poles remained below the national average in terms of education and career attain-

ment but since then have made up ground quickly and moved away from traditional, blue-collar occupations.

Unlike many other so-called white ethnics, however, Poles have retained strong loyalties to home neighborhoods and parishes, often driving many miles each week to attend church services or social events. Some older Polish communities such as Hamtramck, Michigan, escaped the worst ravages of urban blight and have managed to blend gentrification with a degree of ethnic flavor.

This process has been aided by additional waves of Polish immigrants who have arrived since World War II. In the late 1940s and the 1950s, a significant number of political refugees, displaced people, veterans of the Polish armed forces in exile, and survivors of Nazi and Soviet oppression arrived in the Midwest. Settling in major urban centers such as Chicago, Detroit, or Cleveland, these émigrés were highly political and helped refocus the community on the plight of Communist-dominated Poland. A small number of economic immigrants arrived in the late 1960s and the 1970s. In the 1980s martial law in Poland created a new wave of political immigrants, who in the late 1980s and the 1990s were followed by an even larger wave of economic immigrants, some of them illegal. Each of these waves had an often-tempestuous relationship with previously established Polish Americans and Polish immigrants. Nevertheless, the new waves have brought new blood to many older communities and have aided in language retention.

Today midwestern Polish communities present a picture of diversity. The large number of vital Polish ethnic organizations in nearly every midwestern state indicates that this is not a community set to disappear from the American scene anytime soon. Its complex relationship with the now-free homeland remains to be defined, as do relations among its diverse and diffuse subgroups. Still, Polish Americans have defied expert predictions of their imminent demise for over a century by remaking and redefining themselves in a changing America, and there is little doubt they will do so again in the future.

Sources and Further Reading: John Bukowczyk, *And My Children Did Not Know Me* (1987); Waclaw Kruszka, *Historya Polska w Ameryce* (1905); F. Niklewicz, *Polacy w Stanach Zjednoczonych* (1937); James S. Pula, *Polish Americans: An Ethnic Community* (1995); John Radzilowski, *The Eagle and the Cross: A History of the Polish Roman Catholic Union of America* (2003); Thaddeus C. Radzialowski, *Polish Americans in the Detroit Area* (2001); Adam Walaszek, ed., *Polska Diaspora* (2001).

John Radzilowski
The Piast Institute, Hamtramck, Michigan

Romanians

Romanian immigrants and their American-born descendants established numerous communities in the Midwest. Significant Romanian immigration to the region began only after 1870 and through World War I was characterized by a high proportion of men seeking jobs in industry. Return migration rates were as high as two-thirds of all arrivals. Immigration during this early period was also heavily weighted to Romanian communities in Austria-Hungary, as well as in Macedonia and even Albania. From the 1920s to the 1990s, Romanian immigration was small save for about ten thousand refugees admitted after World War II. In the early 1990s about thirty-three thousand Romanians entered the United States, though it is unclear how many of them have settled in the Midwest.

Major Romanian communities developed in Cleveland and Youngstown, Ohio; Detroit and Dearborn, Michigan; and the Gary-Chicago area. Smaller communities appeared in St. Paul, St. Louis, Cincinnati, and industrial towns in northeastern Ohio. Early on, Cleveland emerged as a major Romanian center and home to numerous ethnic organizations and newspapers. Romanian men and their American-born sons found jobs primarily in the steel and metallurgical industries, as well as in the auto factories of Michigan. By 1920 Detroit had the largest single Romanian concentration in the Midwest.

Romanian American cultural and organizational life in the Midwest centered mostly in Cleveland. The first mutual benefit society emerged there in 1902 and the first Romanian-language newspaper, *Tribuna* ("Tribune"), a year later. The first Romanian Orthodox and Catholic parishes were founded in Cleveland in 1904 and 1905, respectively. The largest Romanian periodical in the United States, *America*, an Orthodox publication and the organ of the Union of Romanian Beneficial and Cultural Societies, was published in Cleveland. By World War I it had 10,500 subscribers nationwide.

Because of the lack of Romanian clergy, midwestern communities tended toward local independence and schism. The Romanian Orthodox Church, the largest denomination, established over a dozen parishes in the Midwest. In 1929 Detroit became the home of a separate Romanian episcopate established for the United States. Under the leadership of Bishop Policarp Morusca, it established a cultural center in 1937 at Grass Lake, Michigan, which remains the most significant Romanian cultural institution in the country. In 1950 the Orthodox split over support for the new Communist regime in Romania. Independent Orthodox parishes could be found in St. Paul and Alliance, Ohio. Catholic Romanians of the Orthodox rite also established a number of midwestern parishes and their own fraternal societies but have never been numerous enough to support a separate bishop. A Romanian Baptist association was founded in 1913 in Cincinnati, and a smaller Pentecostal community was active in Dearborn, Michigan.

Since the fall of Communism in Romania, there has been renewed immigration as well as renewed contacts between the diaspora and the home country. The relatively small size of most Romanian communities precludes a significant ethnic infrastructure, but there are active cultural, social, religious, and student groups in many areas, testifying to a continuing ethnic identity.

Sources and Further Reading: Theodore Andrica, *Romanian Americans and Their Communities of Cleveland* (1977); Josef J. Barton, *Peasants and Strangers* (1975); Mary Leuca, "Development in Ethnic Heritage Curriculum: A Case Study of Romanian Americans in Lake County, Indiana," Ph.D. diss., Purdue University (1979); Vladimir Wertsman, *The Romanians in America, 1748–1974* (1975).

John Radzilowski
The Piast Institute, Hamtramck, Michigan

Slovaks

Slovak migration to the Midwest was part of a larger movement to the urban-industrial heartland in the late nineteenth and early twentieth centuries. More than 650,000 Slovaks migrated to the United States between 1870 and 1920 and approximately 500,000 stayed for good. While half settled in Pennsylvania, the 1920 census counted almost 79,000 in Ohio, 44,400 in Illinois, over 10,000 each in Indiana and Michigan, and smaller numbers in Minnesota and Wisconsin.

Initially single or newly married young men migrated in search of work. Their ancient homeland of Hungary was largely agricultural and failed to provide enough work for a growing population that had only been freed from serfdom in 1848. America's rapid industrialization required cheap, unskilled labor. Slovaks flocked to the steel mills of Cleveland, Gary, East St. Louis, and Superior; to Illinois's bituminous coal mines (in the Streator region); to Chicago's meatpacking industry; and to Detroit's automobile factories. Smaller numbers made their way to Milwaukee's meatpacking plants and to the flour mills of distant Minneapolis. A very small number tried their luck at farming in Illinois, Iowa, Wisconsin, and Minnesota.

The earliest arrivals congregated in saloons and boardinghouses near their places of work operated by their linguistic neighbors, the Czechs and the Poles, who had preceded the Slovaks by a generation. Later, enterprising Slovak men opened their own saloons while married Slovak women earned extra income for their families with their own boardinghouses. Anglo-American observers decried the overcrowding and supposed immorality of these boardinghouses, but they were an absolute necessity for men earning only about one dollar and fifty cents a day (two dollars a day was considered a living wage) because the women who opened their four-room shanties to large numbers of boarders were able to double the family income.

Even though most Slovak immigrants to the United States in the late nineteenth and early twentieth centuries were initially sojourners who had come to earn their thousand-dollar "fortunes" and then return home, over three-quarters of them stayed. Like fellow Slavs who had come before them, they established institutions that made their life in America worth living. Responding to the need for fellowship plus cheap accident or illness insurance, Slovak immigrants in the 1880s established fifty local fraternal-benefit societies, which by 1890 began to merge into national bodies. Among them were the First Catholic Slovak Union of the United States, established in Cleveland in 1890, and its female counterpart, the First Catholic Slovak Ladies' Association, also headquartered in Cleveland and established in 1892. More than two hundred thousand Slovaks joined about a dozen national fraternal organizations.

Local fraternal-benefit societies led the way in the creation of the second pillar of the Slovak-American community—the parish church. The majority Roman Catholics and the minority Lutherans, Greek Catholics, and Calvinists established parishes in all their major settlements. Of the 241 Roman Catholic parishes that the Slovaks built by 1930, 53 were in the Midwest. The largest settlements, in greater Cleveland and Chicago, boasted 10 Roman Catholic parishes each. While Greek Catholics built 155 churches by 1930, they were of mixed Rusyn-Slovak ethnicity and it is impossible to estimate the number of such parishes that the Slovaks controlled. Lutheran Slovaks, meanwhile, created 69 parishes, 22 of which were in the Midwest, with Chicago and greater Cleveland having 4 each. Smaller communities, such as in Minneapolis, had 1 Roman Catholic, 1 Lutheran, and 1 Greek Catholic church. Most of the Roman Catholic parishes also built parochial schools for their younger members and until the 1950s taught in both English and Slovak.

Slovak Roman Catholics established religious orders for both men and women. The largest of the men's was the Benedictine Order of St. Andrew Svorad Abbey in Cleveland. It was founded in 1929 by Slovak graduates of the Czech Benedictine Abbey and College of St. Procopius in Lisle, Illinois. The Slovak monks subsequently founded Cleveland's famous Benedictine High School. Meanwhile, Slovak Franciscan Fathers established a second monastery (the first was in Pittsburgh) in Valparaiso, Indiana, in 1929.

The first of the women's orders appeared in the Midwest in 1923: the Slovak Sisters of the Third Order of St. Dominic, in Oxford, Michigan. It was followed by the Vincentian Sisters of Charity, who created their second province (the first was in Pittsburgh) in Bedford, Ohio, in 1928. After World War II the Slovak Daughters of St. Francis of Assisi organized themselves and built a permanent home in Lacon, Illinois. Finally, in 1953 the Slovak Benedictine sisters were canonically established in Tinley Park, Illinois. All these religious orders served their Slovak communities as teachers, nurses, and spiritual leaders.

The third pillar of the Slovak community in America was the press. Immigrants were curious about news from home, as well as job opportunities in America. To satisfy their thirst for news, entrepreneurs and fraternal leaders established over 220 dailies, weeklies, semimonthlies, and monthlies for Slovak-American communities between 1885 and the present. Seventy-one of these newspapers were published in the Midwest, with 30 appearing in Cleveland and 28 in Chicago. One of the longest-lasting Slovak newspapers in America is the *Jednota* ("Union"), published weekly by the First Catholic Slovak Union of Cleveland since 1891.

After World War II a few thousand Slovak political refugees came to America, fleeing either Communism in their homeland in 1948 or the Soviet-led invasion of Czechoslovakia in 1968. (Slovakia became a part of Czechoslovakia in 1918 and achieved independence in 1993.) Many of these refugees, plus their predecessors from before World War I, moved to California in search of new opportunities or to Florida to retire. While the first two generations of American Slovaks worked largely as unskilled, semiskilled, or skilled laborers in American heavy industry, the third and fourth generations, with better education, moved into white-collar and professional employment and are now largely members of the American middle class.

Sources and Further Reading: Ján Body, ed., *History of the Slovak Zion Synod LCA* (1976); Konštantín Culen, *Slovenské Casopisy v Amerike* (1970); George Dolak, *A History of the Slovak Evangelical Lutheran Church in the United States of America, 1902–1927* (1955); First Catholic Slovak Union of America, *Slovak Catholic Parishes and Institutions in the United States and Canada*, comp. Philip A. Hrobak (1955); František Hrušovský, *Slovenské rehole v Amerike* (1955); Joseph C. Krajsa et al., *Slovaks in America: A Bicentennial Study* (1978); M. Mark Stolarik, *Immigration and Urbanization: The Slovak Experience, 1870–1918* (1989); M. Mark Stolarik, "The Slovak-

American Press," in Sally M. Miller, ed., *The Ethnic Press in the United States* (1987); M. Mark Stolarik, *The Slovak Americans* (1988).

M. Mark Stolarik
University of Ottawa, Ontario, Canada

South Slavs

Over 40 percent of Americans of South Slavic ancestry reside in the Midwest. They originated in southeastern Europe and spoke related languages, but resided along the cultural frontier between Habsburg central Europe, Orthodox Byzantium, and the Ottoman Middle East. Their religious differences illustrated cultural disparity. Catholic Slovenes and Croatians employed the Latin alphabet; Orthodox Serbs, Montenegrins, Macedonians, and Bulgarians used the Cyrillic alphabet. Non-Christians included Bosnian Muslims and Sephardic Jews.

Slovenian Catholic missionaries were among the few South Slavs in the Midwest before 1890. Frederic Baraga, now a candidate for sainthood, became bishop in Michigan's Upper Peninsula (1853). Joseph Buh not only evangelized Minnesota Indians, he sponsored *Amerikanski Slovenec*, the first Slovenian-language newspaper in the United States (1891).

South Slavs emigrated primarily from Austro-Hungarian and Turkish territories between 1890 and 1914. To improve their poor economic status or to escape military service, they sought jobs in the metallurgical, mining, and meatpacking industries; railroading; or construction. Their numbers constantly fluctuated, for many were young married men and bachelors who returned to their native villages after accumulating a small fortune, or who crossed the Atlantic several times. If they decided to remain permanently, they sent for their families or for a young woman from their hometown to marry.

One-seventh of Montenegro's males between the ages of nineteen and twenty-four worked in the Midwest in 1914. When a Bosnian Serb assassinated Archduke Franz Ferdinand and provoked a chain of events that led to World War I, young Serbian, Montenegrin, and Bulgarian men heeded government calls to defend their homelands. Many never returned to the Midwest for they were battle casualties or died in prisoner-of-war camps.

Typically, a Slavic immigrant neighborhood contained a significant job source (factory, mill, mine), a church, a clubhouse (the "national home" for meetings, choral, and dramatic performances), a grocery store, a boardinghouse, a corner saloon or coffee-house, and a barber shop. Housing typically was recently constructed or had just been vacated by native-born or earlier Irish and German immigrants.

Oliver Iron Mining Company recruited Slovenes, Croatians, and Montenegrins to work the strip mines of the Mesabi iron range around Eveleth, Hibbing, and Ely in northeastern Minnesota. Croatians labored in the copper fields around Calumet, Michigan after 1881 and played a leading role in the 1913–1914 Michigan copper strike. Armour Packing in Kansas City employed them in slaughterhouse jobs. The Balkan Udruga (home-loan association), founded in St. Louis (1907), financed home mortgages for one thousand families. The conservative Croatian Catholic Union organized in Gary, Indiana, in 1921. Although Croatians resided in Cleveland and St. Louis, Chicago became the major center of Croatian culture, with roughly fifty thousand Croatians living there in the 1990s. Of the thirty-two Croatian Catholic churches in America, over half are located in the Midwest.

The largest Slovenian settlement outside Europe was in Cleveland, where Slovenes located near steel mills along St. Clair Avenue and railroad yards in Collinwood. National Malleable Castings Company recruited Slovenes in their native villages and settled them in Indianapolis's Haughville district. Other Slovenes found work in United States Steel plants on Chicago's South Side and in Joliet, Illinois, and in the factories of Milwaukee. Their two largest fraternal insurance societies were the religious American Slovene Catholic Union (KSKJ; founded in Joliet in 1894) and the secular Slovene National Benefit Society (SNPJ; founded in Chicago in 1904).

Serbs organized a patriotic society in Chicago before 1880. They resided in Steubenville, Youngstown, Akron, and Cincinnati, Ohio; along the Lake Michigan shoreline from Indiana Harbor (East Chicago) north to Milwaukee; and in Duluth, Minnesota. Many were employed in the stockyards and packing plants of South St. Paul. The American seat of the Serbian Orthodox Church was established in Libertyville, Illinois, in 1927.

After an abortive anti-Turkish uprising (1903), Macedonians and Bulgarians arrived in Cleveland, Toledo, Ohio, and Gary. Some ten thousand Macedonians settled around St. Louis to take jobs in rolling mills, foundries, and railroading. The first Bulgarian Orthodox church in North America organized in Granite City, Illinois, in 1909. The Macedonian Political Organization (now called the Macedonian Patriotic Organization), advocating an independent Macedonia, organized in Fort Wayne, Indiana, in 1922 and published *Makedonska Tribuna* in Indianapolis in 1927.

In the 1930s Indianapolis was the administrative seat of the Bulgarian Orthodox Church in America.

After the U.S. Congress passed immigrant quota legislation (1924), the only South Slavs admitted were political refugees and displaced persons from Communist Yugoslavia and Bulgaria after World War II. After 1965 immigrants were urban and educated, in sharp contrast to the illiterate peasantry of earlier decades. Like the English-speaking children of previous immigrants, they entered business and the professions. Their higher economic status permitted them to reside in suburbs and decentralized ethnic communities. Serbs relocated from Cleveland to nearby Parma and other southwest suburbs. Slovenes reside on Indianapolis's far west side and in Indiana's Hendricks County, in Cleveland's Euclid and Milwaukee's West Allis, and in suburban Detroit and Chicago.

Post–World War II refugees revived the neighborhood of the few hundred Bosnian Muslims who had helped construct Chicago's subway. Soon the newcomers obtained white-collar jobs and moved to northern suburbs such as Northbrook (where an Islamic center was constructed in 1976). Refugees fleeing the conflicts following the 1991–1992 breakup of Yugoslavia settled in Detroit's Hamtramck.

South Slavs formed part of the large, unskilled work force in Chicago, Cleveland, Detroit, Indianapolis, Milwaukee, St. Paul, St. Louis, and Kansas City and became a major ethnic contingent in the Midwest. According to Census 2000 data, 62 percent of the nation's Slovenes, 46 percent of Serbs, and 42 percent of Croatians live in the region. An estimated sixteen thousand Macedonians and Bulgarians live in Michigan.

Three-quarters of the country's Bosnian Muslims live in the Milwaukee-Chicago-Gary area. South Slavs are well represented in midwestern politics. Frank J. Lausche (Slovenian) and George Voinovich (Serbian/Slovenian) served as Ohio governors and U.S. senators; Rudolph G. Perpich (Croatian) was a two-term governor of Minnesota. Businessman Ivan Lebamoff (Macedonian) became mayor of Fort Wayne (1972).

New immigrants, family memories, and nostalgia preserve ethnic consciousness and encourage attendance at traditional church services, participation in national home activities and cultural festivals, membership in the old societies and choral groups, and preparation of traditional cuisine. The proclamation of Slovenian, Croatian, and Macedonian independence (early 1990s) also strengthened ethnic pride.

Sources and Further Reading: Nikolay G. Altankov, *The Bulgarian-Americans* (1979); June Drenning Holmquist, ed., *They Chose Minnesota* (1981); George J. Prpic, *South Slavic*

Immigration in America (1978); Robert M. Taylor, Jr., and Connie A. McBirney, eds., *Peopling Indiana* (1996).

James J. Divita
Marian College, Indiana

Czechs

The Czechs are a Slavic-speaking people concentrated in the Czech Republic, which, along with Slovakia, is a successor state to both the former Czechoslovakia (1918–1993) and the Austro-Hungarian Empire (1867–1918). Czech migration to the Midwest began following the 1848 central European revolutions and peaked between 1890 and 1914. The 1939 German annexation of Czech lands, the 1948 Communist takeover of Czechoslovakia, and the 1968 Warsaw Pact invasion also contributed to Czech migration into the region.

Czech immigrants in the 1848–1914 period arrived largely in family groups rather than as individuals. Causes for emigration were primarily economic, though political repression and avoidance of service in the Austro-Hungarian army also played a role. Incentives for immigration to the Midwest included opportunities created by the 1862 Homestead Act, railroad and state-government advertisements encouraging settlement, and industrial job opportunities. A high literacy rate enabled Czech immigrants to move into skilled trades or to become business owners. The 1910 U.S. census lists 539,000 foreign-born people of Bohemian stock, but it is not clear what percentage was actually Czech. The preponderance of pre–World War I Czech immigrants came from village or rural backgrounds. Once in the Midwest they settled in urban and rural communities, with Milwaukee and St. Louis early centers. St. Louis had a Czech Catholic Church and a Czech fraternal society by 1854.

Standard Oil Company attracted Czech workers to Cleveland in the 1860s. Many were coopers who built barrels to contain refined oil. In the 1870s Czechs were skilled workers in Cleveland's steel industry, but their compatriots arriving in the late 1870s and early 1880s entered that industry as unskilled workers, or even as strikebreakers. The garment, baking, and building trades also employed Cleveland's Czechs. Many from the second and third generations moved out of working-class ranks to become self-employed contractors, shopkeepers, city and county employees, or white-collar workers in insurance and banking. The Czech population in Cleveland numbered fifty thousand in 1920.

The largest Midwest Czech urban center is in the Chicago area. In the 1870s there were about 10,000

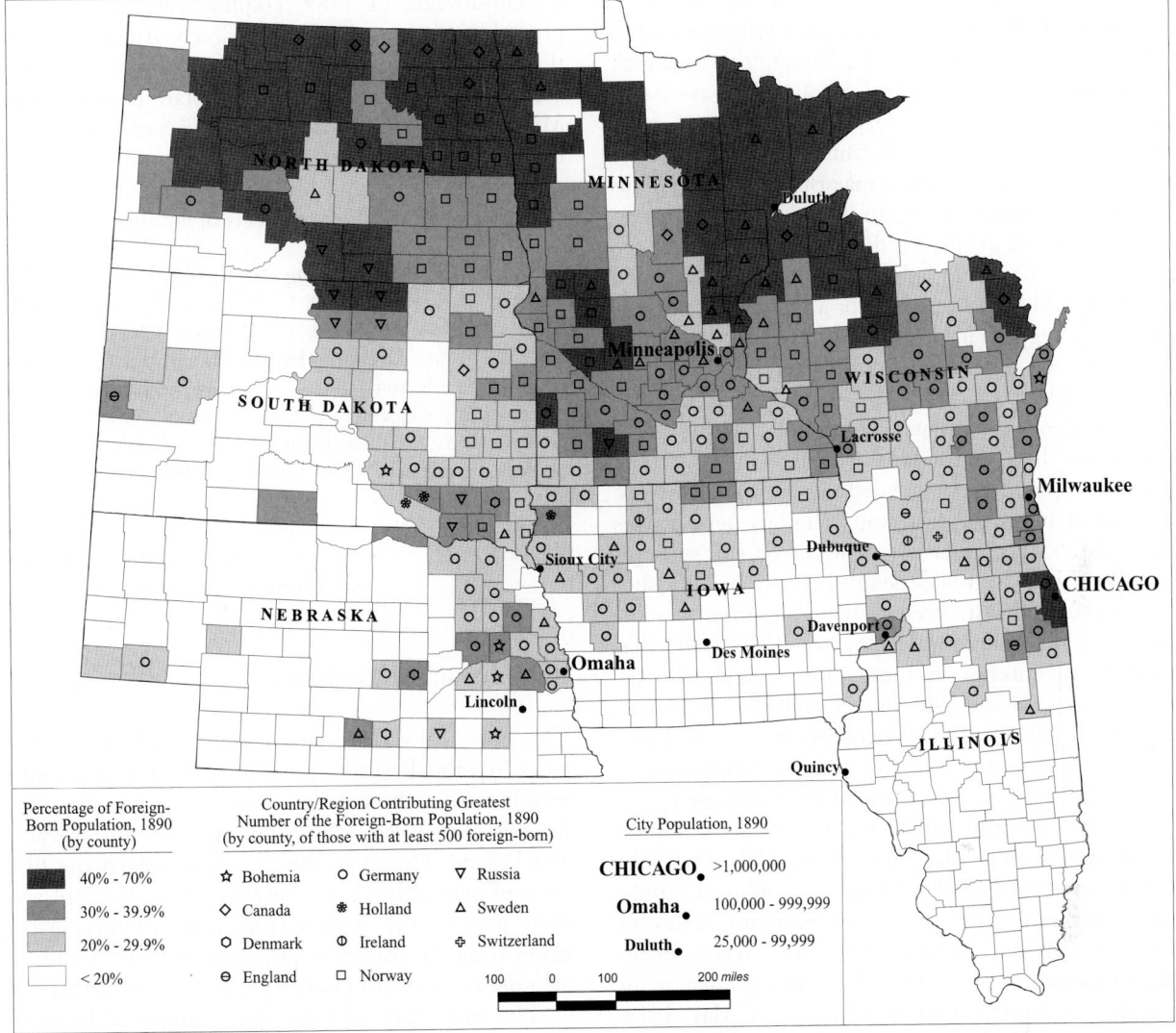

Ethnic origins of the upper Midwest, 1890. Prepared by Margaret Popovich. *Source:* U.S. Bureau of the Census, *Report on Population of the United States at the Eleventh Census: 1890* (1895), Part I, Tables 4, 6, and 33.

Czech-born or Czech-descended inhabitants, and by 1920 that number had grown to 113,000. The Czech community formed in the 1860s southwest of the Loop, and over a sixty-year span, spread west as far as suburban Cicero and Berwyn. Czechs entered vocations ranging from unskilled factory work to skilled artisanship and trades. They also became owners and managers of manufacturing concerns such as breweries and shoe factories. In 1900 Western Electric, located in a Czech neighborhood, employed hundreds of Czechs.

Minnesota's Twin Cities and Omaha also attracted Czech immigrants. By 1930 there were over 12,000 "Czechoslovaks" in Minneapolis, its western suburb of Hopkins, and St. Paul. Many worked for local farm-

implement factories, breweries, or railroads. Czechs in Omaha were involved in a variety of trades and businesses, including banks, wholesale houses, and funeral homes.

In the rural Midwest, homestead and railroad lands drew Czechs to the states west of Illinois. Towns such as New Prague, Prague, Bechyn, Protivin, Brno, Trebon, and Tábor were scattered throughout the region. In 1914 more than 60,000 first- and second-generation Czechs were living in Nebraska, nearly one-eighth of the state's population.

Czech American institutions flourished between the Civil War and World War I. Czechs organized churches along with theatrical, reading, music, gymnastic, fraternal-benefit, and cemetery societies A three-way division among Catholics, Protestants, and religious liberals affected their institutional life. Although most Czech immigrants were nominally Catholic, they associated the Catholic Church with Austrian repression. Consequently, many Czech immigrants broke with it once they were in America, and a majority became religious liberals or minority Protestants. Religious liberals established their own gymnastic, theatrical, and fraternal organizations. Until Catholics and liberals cooperated during World War I to lobby for a Czechoslovak state, they often engaged in vituperative feuds.

The Czech American press reflected these disputes. Religious liberals pioneered Czech American journalism, but the Catholics quickly followed. By the 1870s papers on both sides of the religious divide had sprouted up and were engaged in vigorous polemics. Czechs of many political and religious perspectives formed 326 Czech journals, of which 85 still survived in 1920. Czech Catholics established national parishes across the Midwest. Presbyterians organized a midwestern Czech-language presbytery (1910–1948) that supported churches in these same neighborhoods. Catholics established the only Czech American college, the College of St. Procopius, in 1887 in Lisle, Illinois. An attempt to found a Czech religious-liberal college in Cedar Rapids, Iowa, in 1881 collapsed.

Czech American political activities took several forms. American involvement in World War I brought Czech Americans of all religious and political groupings together to work for an independent Czechoslovakia. Tomáš. G. Masaryk, Czechoslovakia's "President-Liberator," opened his American campaign for Czechoslovak statehood in Chicago in May 1918. Similarly, Czech American organizations lobbied for Czechoslovakia's reconstitution after its liquidation by Nazi Germany in 1939. Among prominent Czech American politicians were Chicago mayor Anton Čermák, Wisconsin lieutenant governor Charles Jonáš, Illinois and Ohio U.S. congressional representatives Adolph Sabath and Charles Vanik, and Nebraska U.S. senator Roman Hruska.

Assimilation into the American mainstream since 1945 has weakened Czech identification, though several factors have served to maintain it. One is continued immigration. Somewhere around 62,000 people emigrated from Czechoslovakia to America between 1945 and 1990, half of whom are presumed to be Czech. Second, gymnastic and fraternal-benefit societies, churches, and cultural institutions have perpetuated Czech ethnicity. Festivals and dinners served in churches or *sokol* meeting halls also maintain Czech visibility. Nearly every Czech community still has music and folk-dance groups.

Since the collapse of the Communist regime in Czechoslovakia in 1989, communications have improved between midwestern Czech Americans and their European cousins. The University of Chicago has a chair in Czech Studies, and the state universities of Michigan, Ohio, Indiana, Illinois, Wisconsin, Iowa, and Nebraska teach the Czech language. Interest in Czech cuisine and genealogy has led to the publication of cookbooks and countless projects of family genealogy.

Sources and Further Reading: Tomáš Čapek, *The Čechs (Bohemians) in America* (1920); C. Winston Chrislock, *Charles Jonas (1840–1896)* (1993); C. Winston Chrislock, "The Czechs," in June Drenning Holmquist, ed., *They Chose Minnesota* (1981); Karen Johnson Freeze, "Czechs," in Stephen Thernstrom, ed., *Harvard Encyclopedia of American Ethnic Groups* (1981); Jan Habenicht, *History of Czechs in America* (1996); Vera Laska, *The Czechs in America, 1633–1977* (1978).

C. Winston Chrislock
St. Thomas University, Minnesota

Russians and East Slavs

The East Slavs—Russians, Ukrainians, Belorussians, and Carpatho-Rusyns—came from an area that is now mostly within the current countries of Ukraine, Belorussia, and Russia and small areas within Slovakia and Poland. However, the area from which the first wave of immigrants came between 1880 and 1914 was then part of the Austro-Hungarian Empire. Most came from the Austrian province of Galicia and an area of northeastern Hungary called Subcarpathia.

The first wave of East Slavs numbered between 300,000 and 400,000 people. Somewhat less than one-fourth settled in the Midwest. Of the 2,652,214 people of Russian descent living in the United States in 2000, 446,933, or about 17 percent, were in the Midwest. Of the 892,922 people of Ukrainian descent, 189,167, or about 21 percent, resided in the Midwest.

Early immigrants generally identified themselves in religious rather than national terms. They were members of a church loyal to the pope in Rome but with an Eastern-Byzantine-Greek ritual. People generally called themselves Rusyns, or some variant of that term. One of the highest priorities for Rusyns was to establish their own church because they did not feel comfortable with the unfamiliar rites of the Polish, Slovak, or Hungarian churches. The early missionaries attempted to establish the Greek Catholic Church, as it was most often called, among the new immigrants but were blocked by the Latin-rite bishops. In spite of these obstacles, Rusyns from both Galicia and Subcarpathia continued to build churches and bring priests over from the old country. When Bishop John Ireland of St. Paul, Minnesota, prevented Father Alexis Toth from serving the new St. Mary's Greek Catholic Church among the Rusyns in Minneapolis in 1889, that parish was accepted into the Russian Orthodox Church. Father Toth then served as a missionary to convert other Rusyn parishes to Russian Orthodoxy. Because of the Latin bishops' opposition to a Byzantine rite in the United States, Toth was reasonably successful in his conversion efforts.

Father Toth cooperated with others in establishing the first union of Rusyn fraternal (mutual aid) societies. In 1892 they organized the *Sojedinenije*, now called the Greek Catholic Union. This organization was open to Rusyns from both Subcarpathia and Galicia. The Greek Catholic Union still publishes its official newspaper, the *Americansky Russky Viestnik*. Very shortly after the Greek Catholic Union was organized, the Rusyn immigrant community split into three separate groups. The Greek Catholic Union was dominated by the Subcarpathian Rusyns, so the Galician Rusyns separated in 1894 and formed their own mutual aid society called the *Rus'kyj Narodnyj Soiuz*, now the Ukrainian National Association. This association has published an official newspaper, *Svoboda*, since 1893. In 1895 the Russian Orthodox Church and Father Toth helped organize the third major society to serve the Russian community, the Russian Orthodox Mutual Aid Society, which publishes *Svit*.

The formation of the three mutual aid societies indicated that the Rusyn immigrants were adopting three incompatible national identities. The Greek Catholic Union increasingly identified itself as Carpatho-Rusyn representing the Rusyns from Subcarpathia, while the Ukrainian National Union represented Rusyns from Galicia influenced by priests who belonged to the "American Circle." These were priest-intellectuals who championed the Ukrainian identity for the Galician Rusyns. The Russian Orthodox Mutual Aid Society represented Rusyns who joined the Russian Orthodox Church and adopted a Russian national identity, obscuring the fact that very few Russians from Russia emigrated to the United States before 1914.

This first wave of East Slavs settled in large numbers in Ohio, Michigan, and Illinois, with Indiana, Wisconsin, Minnesota, and North Dakota also receiving significant numbers. Chicago, Cleveland, and Detroit supported the three largest populations. The settlement pattern in North Dakota differed from that of the other states because most immigrants to North Dakota came by way of Canada and settled on farms.

Religion frequently divided East Slavs. By 1924, when the Ukrainians and the Carpatho-Rusyns were given separate Greek Catholic bishops, there were more than 235,000 members of the Ukrainian diocese (headquartered in Philadelphia) and more than 285,000 members of the Carpatho-Rusyn diocese (headquartered in Pittsburgh). By that time the Russian Orthodox Church (headquartered in New York City) had more than 105,000 members.

The second wave of East Slavic immigrants to the United States occurred during the interwar years 1920 to 1939 and was strongly influenced by the Russian Revolution. For the first time significant numbers of these immigrants were ethnic Russians and eastern Ukrainians from the former Russian Empire. Most of them settled in New York and other eastern cities, but significant numbers made their way to the Midwest, where they changed the cultural, political, and religious nature of the various Russian and Ukrainian communities.

The new immigrants to the Russian American community brought with them a new church hierarchy, a Synod of Bishops that claimed to be the Russian Orthodox Church in Exile. The Russian Orthodox Church in America continued to recognize the Moscow Patriarchate, so the New Synod of Bishops organized a few new churches that were also actively anti-Communist. It was the Synod of Bishops in Exile that canonized the former Tsar Nicholas II. While this church had its greatest presence on both the East and the West Coasts, it also established a few parishes in the Midwest.

In the Ukrainian community, the new immigrants revitalized the Ukrainian identity of the Ukrainian Catholic Church and led a political shift in secular and fraternal circles. Until the 1920s the Ukrainian National Union had been strongly influenced by the socialist ideas of American Circle. By the mid-1930s the Ukrainian National Union and many other newly established Ukrainian organizations had shifted to a right-wing political stance. They were strongly anti-Communist, favoring political and military action to establish an independent Ukraine. Several youth organizations established paramilitary branches in the United States. In the 1920s the new Ukrainian immigrants also founded an American diocese of the Ukrainian Autocephalous Orthodox Church, which had been founded in Ukraine as an alternative to the Russian Orthodox Church.

The Carpatho-Rusyn community was not joined by significant numbers of new immigrants. They were, however influenced by a papal decree, "Cum Data Fuerit," enforcing celibacy among the Eastern-rite priests. Because this was viewed as unwanted Latinization, thirty to forty thousand Carpatho-Rusyns organized several Carpatho-Russian or Rusyn Orthodox churches. These churches were authorized by the Ecumenical Patriarch of Constantinople.

The third wave of Russian and Ukrainian immigration occurred after World War II. About one hundred thousand East Slavs came to this country, most of them Ukrainians, about one-fourth of whom settled in the Midwest. The Russians generally associated with the Russian Orthodox Church in Exile. Their focus on theological purity and anti-Communism created a barrier between them and the previous waves of Russian immigrants and certainly impeded their absorption into mainstream American society.

Third-wave Ukrainians were better educated than their predecessors and came to the United States with organizational structures they had developed in the displaced persons camps in Europe. They also had a passionate commitment to the creation of an independent Ukraine. Because they were better educated, better organized, and had a common experience, they moved quickly to construct their own organizations and churches. About two-thirds were Ukrainian Catholics from western Ukraine and one-third of them were Orthodox from eastern Ukraine. These immigrants were also politically active in their attempts to create an independent Ukraine. As influential members of the Captive Nations organization, they publicized the plight of the eastern European nations under Soviet control and lobbied the U.S. Congress and presidents to work for the freedom of those countries. To the extent that they participated in partisan politics, the overwhelming majority were Republicans.

The fourth wave of Russians and Ukrainians occurred after the fall of the Soviet Union in 1991. About five hundred thousand people migrated from the Soviet Union and its successor states between 1980 and 1997. Most of them were Jews. However, about one hundred thousand Russians and an equal number of Ukrainians have emigrated from the former Soviet Union. Of them, about 15 percent settled in the Midwest.

This fourth wave of immigrants differed markedly from the previous immigration. As a general rule, they were well educated, often from professional occupations, individuals or families, and not strongly integrated into the established Russian and Ukrainian communities. They used established communities to make initial contacts in their new homeland but were eager to make contacts outside their ethnic communities.

Sources and Further Reading: Keith P. Dyrud, "The East Slavs—Rusins, Ukrainians, Russians, and Belorussians," in June Drenning Holmquist, ed., *They Chose Minnesota* (1981); Keith P. Dyrud, *The Quest for the Rusyn Soul* (1992); Oksana Irena Grabowicz, "Persistence and Change in Values, Attitudes, and Beliefs: A Study of the Ukrainian Community in

the U.S.," Ph.D. diss., University of Massachusetts (1988); Thomas Kochman and Miroslav Semchyshyn, eds., *Ukrainians in Illinois* (1976); G. Kulchycky, *The Ukrainian Community in Ohio, 1885–1976* (1977); Myron B. Kuropas, *The Ukrainian Americans* (1991); Paul Robert Magocsi, *Our People* (1994); Dariia Markus, *Ukrainians in Chicago and Illinois* (1989); Theodore B. Pedeliski, "Slavic Peoples," in William C. Sherman, ed., *Plains Folk* (1988); Kazimierz J. Zaniewski and Carol J. Rosen, *The Atlas of Ethnic Diversity in Wisconsin* (1998).

Keith P. Dyrud
St. Paul, Minnesota

Mexicans and Mexican Americans

People of Mexican descent, who have been a significant presence in the Midwest since the early twentieth century, today constitute the fastest-growing minority population in the region.

Although less than nine percent of U.S. Hispanics (of whom 71 percent identified themselves as Mexican) lived in the Midwest in 2000, their numbers had increased by 81 percent during the 1990s. Today, over one million Hispanics (of whom 65 percent are of Mexican descent) reside in Cook County, Illinois. One out of every five Chicagoans is Hispanic, the third largest concentration of Spanish-speaking peoples in the United States.

Mexicans and Mexican Americans live in places other than Chicago, Milwaukee, Detroit and other cities of the Great Lakes. In Nebraska, Kansas, Wisconsin, and Minnesota the population of Mexicans and Mexican Americans grew between 48 and 68 percent during the 1980s and 1990s. Youthfulness (the average age is 25.9), high birthrates, and sustained immigration from Mexico and the southwestern United States mean that these growth rates will likely continue.

Mexicans and Mexican Americans began settling in the Midwest in the early 1900s to work for the railroad, meatpacking, steel, automobile, and sugar-beet industries. The first major wave of immigration from Mexico and the Southwest to the Midwest, however, began during World War I. Mexicans were initially recruited by labor contractors and employers in the railroad and sugar-beet industries. Once here, they pursued opportunities in the steel, meatpacking, and auto industries. One of the earliest Mexican *colonias* in the Midwest was in the twin cities of Kansas City, Kansas, and Kansas City, Missouri. After World War I other major Mexican settlements developed in Chicago, Detroit, Indiana Harbor, and Gary, Indiana.

For the most part, this was a highly mobile population that primarily consisted of young single or unattached males. In many communities the ratio of men to women was quite skewed. In Detroit the ratio of men to women was 300:100, in Gary it was 274:100, and in Chicago it was 210:100. This differed markedly from the Southwest, where male-female ratios were more evenly matched.

Most employers preferred to hire men and discouraged the immigration of family units. This practice was, in part, designed to discourage permanent settlement. Initially the sugar-beet industry followed this pattern, but it changed after World War I when labor grew scarce and recruiting more difficult. Labor contractors and employers realized that it was more cost-effective to recruit families because all family members contributed their labor to harvesting sugar beets. Furthermore, if men brought their families with them they were more likely to remain in the area during the off-season, thus saving the company time and money in recruiting a new labor force. To encourage Mexicans and Mexican Americans to remain, companies offered them low-cost or free housing during the off-season and other incentives. Mexicans engaged in beet work often traveled to other cities and towns during the off-season in search of work.

Although the largest percentage of Mexicans and Mexican Americans were working class, a small but influential group of middle-class Mexicans also found their way to the region. They established small businesses or professional practices to meet the needs of immigrants. They also spearheaded organizational efforts to help expatriates in their communities. The most common form of organization was the mutual-aid society (*mutualista*), which provided social activities for the community at large and assiduously promoted continued loyalty to Mexico.

Mexican consuls also worked to defend the legal and civil rights of Mexican nationals and to promote loyalty to Mexico. Along with *Comites Patrioticas* (Patriotic Committees), they sponsored celebrations to commemorate Mexican Independence Day (September 16), and Cinco de Mayo. Efforts to promote loyalty and discourage naturalization among Mexican nationals proved effective because the majority did not intend on settling permanently in the region. Their goal was to earn enough money to return to Mexico and the Southwest and make a better life for themselves and those they had left behind. Furthermore, the discrimination they encountered in the United States led many to adopt a "*Mexico Lindo*" attitude, which created an idealized view of their homeland. Thus, unlike their southwestern counterparts, midwestern Mexicans were strongly antiassimilationist and less likely to become naturalized. Only 4 percent of midwestern Mexicans were naturalized in the early twentieth century. Nevertheless, they regularly cele-

brated U.S. national holidays such as the Fourth of July and participated in the rapidly growing consumer culture.

Mexicans and Mexican Americans suffered from the effects of prejudice and discrimination. Discrimination manifested itself in substandard housing and in the workplace, where they were relegated to the lowest-paying and most hazardous jobs. Segregation, discrimination, and poor treatment by local police and the courts added to their difficulties. They were accused of increasing crime rates, disease, and violence. Labor unions saw them as scabs and strikebreakers who lowered wages, undermined organizational efforts, and deprived citizens of jobs.

During the early years of the Great Depression, Mexicans were repatriated in large numbers. Initially, local consuls and Mexican organizations helped nationals return to Mexico. But as the Depression deepened, forced repatriation became more common and less discerning in terms of nationals versus Mexicans who were U.S. citizens. The repatriations, whether voluntary or forced, led to the removal of about sixty-four thousand of the approximate two hundred thousand Mexicans and Mexican Americans in the Midwest.

During World War II Mexicans volunteered in large numbers and fought on all fronts for the United States. The war created a renewed demand for laborers. *Mexicanas* entered the workforce in greater numbers out of a sense of patriotic duty, loyalty to their loved ones in the service, and monthly allotments that proved inadequate to support their families. Mexican Americans who did not enter the military or the workforce supported the war in other ways. When the war ended the participation of Mexican American women in the labor force declined noticeably. However, there was one notable change—young married women who needed or wanted to now worked until the birth of their children.

In the late 1940s and early 1950s Mexican Americans from South Texas and the Southwest, migrant workers, and Mexican nationals (including *braceros*—Mexican contract workers) traveled north in increasing numbers to join those who had avoided repatriation. Chicago, which had been home to a sizable Mexican population before the Great Depression, resumed its status as the main destination for many Mexicans and Mexican Americans. The growth of the Mexican-descent population in the Midwest continued during the 1960s when the United States benefited from government spending and the Vietnam War.

Then in the 1970s, high inflation, a shortage of oil caused by events in the Middle East, and growing competition from foreign markets (especially Japan) caused a major economic downturn in the Midwest. Although many European Americans either left the Rust Belt or fled to the suburbs, the Mexican-descent population continued to expand. Between 1970 and 1988 the Hispanic population increased by 40 percent, and it accounted for 56 percent of the region's total population increase of eight hundred thousand during the 1980s.

Mexican Americans had returned from World War II determined to achieve the freedom and equality they had fought to preserve. Unfortunately, their hopes and expectations faced serious challenges from a society that still looked upon them as aliens. To combat discrimination in urban and rural workplaces, Mexican Americans joined unions in increasing numbers. In the process of actively promoting the rights of workers, they gained important political and organizational experience. They also joined two Texas-based organizations: the League of United Latin American Citizens (LULAC; formed in 1929) and the American G.I. Forum (established in 1948). Committed to ensuring the civil rights of Mexican Americans, both organizations promoted the "Americanization" of Mexicans, ballot-box politics, educational advancement, and legal challenges to segregation and discrimination. The LULAC and the forum established chapters throughout the Midwest in the 1950s and 1960s.

Among Mexican Americans the movement for reform was by no means homogeneous or harmonious. Divisions occurred over strategies, leadership, philosophy, and goals. The community was also divided by the Vietnam War, which tended to pit the "G.I. Generation," who had fought in World War II and the Korean War, against the younger generation. Usually the latter group embraced the ideas and strategies of the Chicano Movement, which emerged during the volatile 1960s. More confrontational and nationalistic in asserting their self-identity, those involved in the movement generally eschewed the accommodationist practices of the G.I. Generation.

Although prosperity returned in the 1990s, anti-alien feelings remained strong. These attitudes were especially prevalent in communities where people of Mexican descent were relative newcomers. But even in places where they had a long-established presence, their increasing numbers gave rise to new concerns and the resurgence of negative stereotypes. Because the majority of Mexicans and Mexican Americans remained concentrated in low-paying unskilled or semi-skilled work, they did not benefit from the renewed prosperity. The situation for undocumented Mexican immigrants is often worse. Their "illegal" status makes them highly vulnerable and susceptible to exploitation and mistreatment.

The largely urban Hispanic population in the Midwest became more diverse in the second half of the twentieth century. Starting in the 1950s, a growing number of immigrants arrived from the Caribbean (especially Puerto Rico), Central, and South America. Still, Mexicans and Mexican Americans make up roughly 71 percent of the Hispanic population, according to the 2000 U.S. Census.

Today Hispanics are drawn to the Midwest for different reasons. Many come in search of new opportunities or employment. In places such as Iowa, Nebraska, and Minnesota, Mexican nationals are recruited by the meatpacking and poultry industries. Others, including people from Central America, migrate to the region in order to escape poverty, persecution, or the ravages of war. Compared to their homelands, the United States offers safety, employment, higher rates of pay, and the promise of a better standard of living. Others travel to the region via "chain migration," which has been a long-established process of facilitating migration into the region. For Mexican Americans coming from the Southwest, the appeal is being able to live in smaller communities, which they perceive as safer, friendlier, and better able to provide quality education.

Whether they are citizens of the United States or recent arrivals, people of Mexican descent clearly have played an important and continuing role in the growth and development of the Midwest.

Sources and Further Reading: Robert Aponte and Marcelo Siles, *Latinos in the Heartland* (1994); Juan R. García, *Mexicans in the Midwest, 1900–1932* (1996); Louise Año Nuevo Kerr, "Mexican Chicago: Chicano Assimilation Aborted, 1939–1954," in Melvin G. Holli and Peter d'A. Jones, eds., *The Ethnic Frontier* (1977); James B. Lane and Edward J. Escobar, eds., *Forging a Community* (1987); Félix Padilla, *Latino Ethnic Consciousness* (1985); Richard Santillán, "Midwestern Mexican American Women and the Struggle for Gender Equality: A Historical Overview, 1920s to 1960s," in Juan R. García and Thomas Gelsinon, eds., *Perspectives in Mexican American Studies*, vol. 5 (1995); Michael M. Smith, "Beyond the Borderlands: Mexican Labor in the Central Plains, 1900–1930," *Great Plains Quarterly* 1 (Fall 1981); Paul S. Taylor, *Mexican Labor in the United States: Chicago and the Calumet Region* (1932); Dionicio Nodín Valdés, *Barrios Norteños* (2000); Zaragosa Vargas, *Proletarians of the North* (1993).

Juan R. García
University of Arizona

Finns

In 1864 around twenty Finns from Norway's copper region became the first of their national group to arrive in the Midwest. Recruited by the Mining Emigrant Association to work in the new copper mines around Hancock and Calumet in northern Michigan, they soon were followed by immigrants from Finland, which was then a grand duchy of Russia. By the 1870s copper miners were leaving Michigan for employment in Minnesota, and a decade later Finns settled there to work, particularly in iron mines. Others worked on the ore docks of northern Ohio or farmed in Wisconsin and North and South Dakota.

In 1900 Michigan, with almost 19,000, and Minnesota, with more than 10,000, had nearly 85 percent of all midwestern Finns. Wisconsin and Ohio both had Finnish populations of more than 2,000. South Dakota had more than 1,000 Finns and Illinois had just under 900. All other midwestern states had fewer than 500 Finns—no Finns were present in Kansas, Missouri, and Nebraska. Forty percent of the arrivals from Finland headed for Minnesota and Michigan between 1900 and 1920.

By the 1920s an estimated 300,000 had emigrated from Finland. Most were young migrants from rural areas who were unable to find jobs in cities. Midwestern mining areas in particular became gateways to Finnish American communities. Because of their strong presence in Michigan and Minnesota, Finns gained cultural leadership among their compatriots.

While Apostolic Lutherans were establishing the first centers of organized religion, Finns in Calumet and Hancock also introduced newspaper publishing in 1876 that soon extended from New York Mills in Minnesota to Ashtabula in Ohio. The Apostolic Lutherans, pietist disciples of Lars Laestadius, were critical of the Lutheran state church of Finland. In 1890, however, church supporters organized the Finnish Evangelical Lutheran Church, or Suomi Synod. The Synod Lutherans established Suomi College and allied with the Finnish National Temperance Brotherhood. The Finnish National Evangelical Lutherans formed a rival "people's" church in 1898 and supported the Friends of Temperance. The majority of immigrants remained unattached. In addition, workingmen's societies appeared, though initially they were stronger in the East.

The struggle between secularism and religion intensified as Socialism gained a foothold, recruiting both immigrant new arrivals and members of established organizations. In 1905 the main Socialist newspaper, *Työmies* ("Workingman"), moved from Massachusetts to Hancock, and one year later a convention in Hibbing, Minnesota, established the Finnish Socialist Federation. Labor radicals were prominent supporters of the Minnesota iron strike of 1907 and the Michigan copper strike of 1913–1914. By World War I Finnish industrial unionists were also strong in Minnesota. These formative years coincided with the movement of miners and other workers to farms in the Midwest. Although homestead lands were still available until the 1890s, most Finns arrived too late to obtain them. Instead, they used credit to purchase so-called cutover lands from which trees had been stripped. But the buyers had to devote hard labor to clearing rocky and swampy stump lands. It was said that stumps only understood the Finnish "language."

In 1920 70 percent of Finland-born farm operators in the United States were in the Midwest, mainly Michigan, Minnesota, and Wisconsin. Farm building continued in the 1920s as mining jobs disappeared. In 1930 nearly 36 percent of all midwestern Finns were rural farm residents; 19 percent, rural nonfarm residents; and 44 percent, urban. Only a minority became farmers in the Midwest, however, and 68 percent of Finns elsewhere were urban. Michigan and Minnesota still had about three-fourths of all midwestern Finns.

In spite of limited immigration from Finland and the effects of the Great Depression, midwestern Finns maintained their cultural life between 1920 and 1940. Lutherans appealed to the second-generation Finnish Americans who outnumbered the immigrants. Most temperance societies faded away. The Finnish Workers Federation regrouped Communist sympathizers, and industrial unionists remained strong. Immigrant newspapers appeared in New York Mills, Duluth, Superior, Calumet, and Hancock as well as Ironwood in Michigan. Cooperative stores flourished among consumers and farmers, who often relied on the Socialist-originated Central Cooperative Wholesale of Superior after World War I. Upwards of 175 cooperatives appeared in the first four decades of the twentieth century, notably in Michigan, Wisconsin, and Minnesota.

After decreasing almost 30 percent between 1920 and 1940, Midwest Finns became even fewer after World War II. Their numbers declined 53 percent between 1940 and 1960 and even faster between 1960 and 1980, leaving the Midwest with only 23 percent of all immigrant Finns in the United States. By 1980 Finnish immigrants and their American-born children were a minority among midwesterners with ancestors from Finland. The immigrant generation had decreased more than 87 percent in number since 1940; the third and later generations became the majority of Finnish American descendants. In 2000 there were just over 296,000 people of Finnish ancestry in the Midwest, representing 47 percent of all Finnish descendants in the United States. More than two-thirds of them lived in Michigan and Minnesota.

These demographic changes paralleled a cultural decline. The suspension of the *Päivälehti* ("Daily Journal") of Duluth in 1948 began the end of the newspaper era that closed when the *Työmies-Eteenpäin* ("Workingman-Forward") of Superior ceased publishing in 1998. While labor halls suspended activities, the

Suomi Synod merged with non-Finnish Lutherans, and only seven cooperatives survived in 2001. One-time activists commemorated immigrant culture by erecting monuments and publishing a history of Minnesota's Finns. Although churches and the renamed Suomi College (now Finlandia University) acknowledge their ethnic roots, ties to one-time centers of immigrant culture have been weakened. Only a minority of Finnish Americans are organizing cultural activities such as festivals and arts and crafts fairs to affirm their "Finnishness" or ethnic identity.

Sources and Further Reading: Armas K. E. Holmio, *History of the Finns in Michigan*, trans. Ellen M. Ryynanen (2001); Michael G. Karni, Matti E. Kaups, and Douglas J. Ollila, Jr., eds., *The Finnish Experience in the Western Great Lakes Region: New Perspectives* (1975); Timo Riippa, "The Finns and Swede-Finns," in June Drenning Holmquist, ed., *They Chose Minnesota* (1981); Hans R. Wasastjerna, ed., *History of the Finns in Minnesota*, trans. Toivo Rosvall (1957).

A. William Hoglund
University of Connecticut

Twentieth-Century Southern Migration

During the course of the twentieth century, ten million people—black and white—would leave the South, perhaps the largest migration in recent American history. Race remains an important criterion in understanding southern out-migration. Even though they were outnumbered overall by whites, the proportion of nonwhite southerners who left the South was larger, and perhaps because of race the exodus of southern African Americans has gained more attention by scholars.

Migration scholars often speak of pulls and pushes when attempting to understand the mass movement of people. On the one hand, immigration had long been the fuel of industrialization in the urban Midwest. When World War I stopped this flow of people, mostly from Europe, a labor shortage resulted. Forced to look to domestic supplies of labor, industries sent southward labor agents who made big promises of northern opportunity. And when black newspapers, such as the *Chicago Defender* or the *Indianapolis Recorder*, began trumpeting to southern readers the benefits of leaving the South, another substantial pull existed for southern people of color. On the other hand, the push to leave the South was long felt by African Americans there. Several generations of postbellum black people had come of age under the tightening grip of segregation, and the social and cultural strictures were accompanied by economic problems, including low wages and the debt peonage of the sharecropping system. The advance of the boll weevil, which destroyed cotton crops in the South, served as another push. Together, the pull of northern labor needs and the push of racist southern society accounted for what historians call the "Great Migration," which began after 1915.

Neither black nor white migrants all came directly from fields to midwestern factories. In fact a substantial movement began from southern fields first to southern urban areas, because the South's major cities were swelling with African Americans after World War I. They were, after all, pulled and pushed to these southern cities for the same reasons that would impel people to move to northern urban areas. By the 1960s, moreover, most black migration to the Midwest was interurban—from southern city to northern city.

❖ **Origins of the Great Migration: Mississippians Seek Information about Life in the Midwest**

Vicksburg, Miss. May the 5th, 1917
Sir: Just wants you to give me a few words of enfermation of labor situations in your city or South Dakota grain farms what is their offers and their adress. Will thank you for any enformation given of same.

Marcel, Miss., 10/04/17
Dear Sir: Although I am a stranger to you but I am a man of the so called colored race and can give you the very best or reference as to my character and ability by prominent citizens of my community by both white and colored people that knows me although am native of Ohio whiles I am a Northern desent were reared in this state of Mississippi. Now I am a reader of your paper the Chicago Defender. After reading your writing ever wek I am compell & persuade to say that I know you are a real man of my color you have I know heard of the South land & I need not tell you any thing about it. I am going to ask you a favor and at the same time beg you for your kind and best advice. I wants to come to Chicago to live. I am a man of a family wife and 1 child I can do just any kind of work in the line of common labor & I have for the present sufficient means to support us till I can obtain a position. Now should I come to your town, would you please to assist me in getting a position I am willing to pay whatever you charge I don't want you to loan me not 1 cent but *help* me to find an occupation there in your town now I has a present position that will keep me employed till the first of Dec. 1917. now please give me your best advice on this subject. I enclose stamp for reply.

Source: Emmett J. Scott, "Letters of Negro Migrants of 1916–1918," *Journal of Negro History* 4 (July 1919): 292, 293.

Original location and kinship were two important determinants of destinations of migrants of color. Railroad lines in the first half of the twentieth century (and later, of course, interstate routes) mattered, just as they would for white southerners trying to decide upon a destination. The Illinois Central Railroad, for example, paralleled the Mississippi River from the Delta to Chicago. Not surprisingly, many African American newcomers in Chicago hailed from western Tennessee and Mississippi and Louisiana. The Louisville and Nashville Railroad connected towns in Kentucky and Tennessee with destinations in Indiana and Ohio, primarily Indianapolis and Cincinnati. Kinship also was very important—for white migrants as well as black—since "trail-blazing" migrants would influence destinations of later migrants because the former could offer the latter temporary housing, food, information, and, not unimportantly, an antidote to homesickness.

Clara Brooks, for example, was born and raised in Giles County, Tennessee, and came of age on a tenant farm. After her father died, her mother decided to move the family to Indianapolis in 1936 because Clara's "oldest brother had been living here since 1921," she explained. "After my father died, he wanted the family close to home so he could help raise the rest of the kids until they was of age."

Compared to black migrants, southern white migrants always had more choices. To be sure, when the Cumberland Plateau was settled by the 1890s, there was no other regional economic frontier to move to, so population tended to be stuck there. Massive population growth and the subdivision of family farms led to the beginning of poverty in the region. As timber and coal quickly transformed parts of the region into wage-earning economies, many mountaineers jumped at the chance to abandon agriculture. But when timber and coal reserves began to disappear, a desperate situation existed. Many saw no other solution than leaving the South for the North.

Yet if black migrants opted for larger urban areas, white southerners sometimes found smaller towns in agricultural areas more palatable. A sizable migration emerged in the twentieth century, for example, that brought white southerners to work in Indiana's tomato fields, Ohio's onion fields, and Michigan's orchards. One historian argues that the least prepared chose outlying industrial areas and even farms, while those who were more prepared chose urban areas peppered with jobs in automobile parts and assembly. Although many migrants and their children eventually ended up in factories, the fact that the migration began as an agricultural one tempers the stereotypical view of rural-to-urban, field-to-factory migration.

The Great Depression was a crushing blow to those white southerners who had begun to overcome the difficulty of adjusting to a new northern way of life only to experience the shutdown of a factory. Orbie Berry, for example, caught a bus in 1925 from Tennessee to Flint, Michigan, and liked his job at a Chevrolet plant. Returning to Flint after a visit to the South, Berry was shocked to learn that the plant had shut down. "I said, 'They's other people that need the job worse than I do,'" Berry explained. "I seen them crying on the street during the time them days I wouldn't be a working. They was laying them off you know—pitiful." So Berry joined thousands of other whites who returned to ride out the Great Depression close to the land. Gypsy Chandler, from Lawrence County, Kentucky, remembered how "the highways was crowded with people traveling, those who were away from home and trying to get back close to relatives, where they could have some security." Returnees quickly realized, however, that in some places, particularly the Upland South, the land simply could not support such large numbers of people, a reason for out-migration in the first place.

When recovery associated with World War II emerged, a massive migration of both whites and blacks followed. The places of origin of black migrants would shift from the upper South to the deep South after 1940, especially Mississippi; by 1970 Mississippi-born blacks in the Midwest would constitute over a quarter of the entire southern black out-migration. The black population in Chicago, for example, jumped more than sevenfold in the 1940s, to almost half a million. At one point in the 1950s, 2,200 African Americans were arriving in Chicago each week. For black southerners, agricultural life virtually ceased to exist after the birth of the mechanical cotton picker and the death of the sharecropping system. Among whites, larger numbers would come from the highlands after 1940. In the southern Appalachian region alone, 704,000 people left between 1940 and 1950 compared to a paltry 81,000 between 1935 and 1940. Between 1950 and 1957, another 784,000 fled, and between 1940 and 1970 a total of 3.2 million mountaineers bolted. Out-migration was significant enough to produce losses through interstate migration for each southern state.

Popular lore—particularly in the Midwest—maintains that all southern whites who came to the Midwest were from the mountains, but this is not true. Census data reveal that almost twice as many people left western Tennessee as left eastern Tennessee between 1955 and 1960, most of them bound for Chicago. More western Kentuckians migrated to Indiana than eastern Kentuckians during the same period, although twice as many Tennesseans bound for Indiana left middle and eastern areas than western areas. Despite the stereotype of a hillbilly migration to the Midwest, white out-migration in reality was a southern, and not exclusively an Appalachian, phenomenon—not an exodus from the hills but, rather, from the Upland South.

One of the strongest reasons to suggest that white and black southerners were part of the same Great Migration concerns their reception in the Midwest; southern migrants were generally unwelcome there. Hostility to both groups of newcomers was based on class, of course, but black migrants suffered doubly because of racial scorn. White newcomers found residential patterns divided by class; often the poorest, most densely settled urban areas became the ports of entry for whites, such as Uptown in Chicago or Over the Rhine in Cincinnati. Native midwesterners opposed southern whites because they were said to be dirty, alcoholic, violent, fecund, and generally unaware of "civilized" city ways. Migrants tell stories about signs outside apartments warning "No Hillbillies." Native whites were also hostile because employers were said to prefer southern whites, presumably because southerners knew little about labor unions. One migrant reported that managers preferred southerners because "we did not know anything to begin with, so they didn't have to take it out of us before they told us what they wanted us to know." Historians disagree over the extent of labor-union knowledge and awareness among southern whites; generalizations are difficult to make about a diverse group of people. Nonetheless, as time went on, southern whites earned an average income that differed little from northern-born whites. They found the economic success for which they were looking.

Money and dignity were two things for which African Americans migrated; generally they found more of the former in the North than the latter. Residential patterns were rigidly divided by race. Black newcomers' only choice of residence was in neighborhoods already established by local blacks. In Chicago, housing options were limited to "kitchenettes": crowded one- or two-room flats with an icebox, a hot plate, and a shared bathroom. And migrants quickly learned that stories circulating back home about northern freedoms were simply false. Maxie Connie, for example, who as a child moved to Indianapolis, must have spoken for many when she said simply, "I knew there were certain places I just wasn't allowed to go." Realtors and bankers joined anxious white homeowners (under "improvement associations") and zealous white thugs were prone to firebombing to make sure that midwestern cities remained segregated.

Following World War II, Chicago experimented with integrating public housing, but after a nasty white riot in 1946 the city decided to build segregated black public housing inside segregated black neighborhoods. Bricks, stones, and bombs were a common white response throughout much of the Midwest when black migrants tried to improve their circumstances. In 1943, an especially violent confrontation between blacks and whites took place in Detroit. Riots broke out in many midwestern cities in the late 1960s, most notably in 1966 in Chicago and in 1967 in Detroit. Forty-three people died during the violence in Detroit. Even smaller cities fell prey to the hate and despair of rioting, including Dayton and South Bend.

Black rioting appeared to prove that discrimination had pushed black people to the breaking point. If southern whites found jobs rather easily in numerous midwestern factories, black southerners often were relegated to janitorial positions or the most dangerous jobs, even if employment options widened as time went on. A 1963 Detroit study found that there were only twenty black salespeople in area shopping malls, proving that black retail positions were behind the scenes. Eventually, black migrants achieved parity with midwestern-born blacks, and some began to narrow the gap with whites. Nevertheless, if both white and black southerners received hostile welcomes, stark differences remained between white and black job opportunities. Charles Denby, a black migrant from Alabama who had worked in the Mobile shipyards, was rejected for a Detroit riveting job in favor of a white Tennessean who told Denby he "had just come in from the fields."

Taverns and churches were two of the most common associational outlets for southern whites, yet both institutional forms felt foreign for many a migrant to the North. Before long, however, white southerners were frequenting more comfortable bars that advertised "Live Hillbilly Music." Chicago by the 1950s had many such bars to choose from. Meanwhile, Protestant denominations preferred by white southerners grew rapidly. On November 5, 1951, eight southwestern Michigan Southern Baptist congregations (SBCs) met in Roseville and voted to form the Motor Cities Association of Southern Baptists in Michigan. Chicago in 1950 had nine SBC churches; just nine years later, there were more than seventy. In the 1950s and 1960s the fastest-growing denomination in Ohio was the Southern Baptist.

Black migrants also worshipped in their own churches ranging from African Methodist Episcopal congregations to storefront churches, but they had additional associational opportunities as well. Generally, black migrants were far more active and effective in community organizations than whites. The YMCA and YWCA had black branches in midwestern cities, and local chapters of the NAACP, CORE, the Urban League, and even the Black Panthers were sometimes effective in carrying the message that all black issues were migrant issues because so many black residents in the Midwest had been born in the South. Additionally, black newspapers championed the cause of readers. As for whites, the music that black migrants brought with them spoke to and represented the plight of the millions of people who left the South for a better life.

Sources and Further Reading: J. Trent Alexander, "Great Migrations: Race and Community in the Southern Exodus, 1917–1970," Ph.D. diss., Carnegie Mellon University (2001); Chad Berry, *Southern Migrants, Northern Exiles* (2000); Neil Fligstein, *Going North* (1981); Peter Gottlieb, *Making Their Own Way* (1987); James N. Gregory, "The Southern Diaspora and the Urban Dispossessed: Demonstrating the Census Public Use Microdata Samples," *Journal of American History* 82 (June 1995); James R. Grossman, *Land of Hope: Chicago, Black Southerners, and the Great Migration* (1989); Lewis M. Killian, *White Southerners* (1970); Jack Temple Kirby, "The Southern Exodus, 1910–1960: A Primer for Historians," *Journal of Southern History* 49 (Nov. 1983); Nicholas Lemann, *The Promised Land* (1991); Thomas J. Sugrue, *The Origins of the Urban Crisis* (1998).

Chad Berry
Maryville College, Tennessee

African Americans

In the twentieth century, the Midwest became an important center of African American life. In 1900 just under five hundred thousand African Americans resided in the Midwest. By 2000 that number had multiplied almost fourteen times over.

Early in the 1900s midwestern industries, looking for a new laborers to replace European immigrants, began hiring African Americans. By 1920 the Ford Motor Company of Detroit employed 1,675 African Americans. These economic opportunities, juxtaposed with harsh conditions and limited prospects in the South, helped to give rise to one of the largest movements of people in American history. This "Great Migration" became a social movement in the early twentieth century as African Americans migrated out of the South in search of better educational and job opportunities. By 1920 more than one million African Americans had left the South. Many have compared this migration to the Jews' flight from Egypt.

This migration was not always a positive experience. In many rural communities, especially in Missouri, African Americans became sharecroppers and were forced to revert to a lifestyle similar to the one they had fled. Elsewhere, many whites were very hostile to the influx of African Americans. Town ordinances and/or local custom forbade African Americans to appear in public after sunset. Whites instigated

racial unrest and race riots. Lynchings also occurred. Whereas lynchings in the South were used as a means of social control to keep African Americans "in their place," in the Midwest, lynchings were intended to drive African Americans out of the community. In a race riot in 1908 in Springfield, Illinois, the hometown of Abraham Lincoln, whites assaulted and killed African Americans and destroyed their property.

African Americans mobilized to resist these and other injustices. In 1909 African Americans formed the National Association for the Advancement of Colored People (NAACP). The National Urban League was founded in 1911. With these and other organizations, African Americans began a period of community building and "self-help" in the Midwest. Programs were so successful that by 1930 50 percent of the employed African American workforce in Detroit had received their jobs through contacts at the Detroit Urban League. Trade unions such as the Brotherhood of Sleeping Car Porters sprang up with branches across the Midwest to organize African Americans. The Nation of Islam, founded in Detroit around 1930, soon after moved its headquarters to Chicago. African American newspapers such as the *Chicago Defender* and the *Pittsburgh Courier* disseminated information. Fraternal orders grew in prominence.

Economic expansion during World War I and World War II created prospects in the Midwest for African Americans seeking educational and vocational opportunities. World War I allowed African Americans some involvement with the military and some jobs on the home front. During World War II, the Fair Employment Practices Committee integrated the war industries and opened up many new jobs to African Americans. In 1948, President Harry S Truman issued an executive order to desegregate the military, which affected the Great Lakes Naval Station in Illinois as well as army and air force installations throughout the region. These and other gains, however, were sometimes met with violence by whites opposed to increased opportunities for African Americans. During World War I, whites rioted against blacks in the 1917 East St. Louis race riot and in racial disturbances throughout the "Red Summer" of 1919 in Chicago. Opposition to the integration of World War II industries precipitated a major riot in Detroit in 1943.

Two competing visions of race relations emerged in the Midwest after World War II. One was an integrationist vision of race relations more radical than many Southern African Americans envisioned; another envisioned a separatist nation. Although neither attracted large numbers, their influence would prove great.

Civil rights attorneys chose the Midwest as the locus for a milestone decision in the civil rights move-

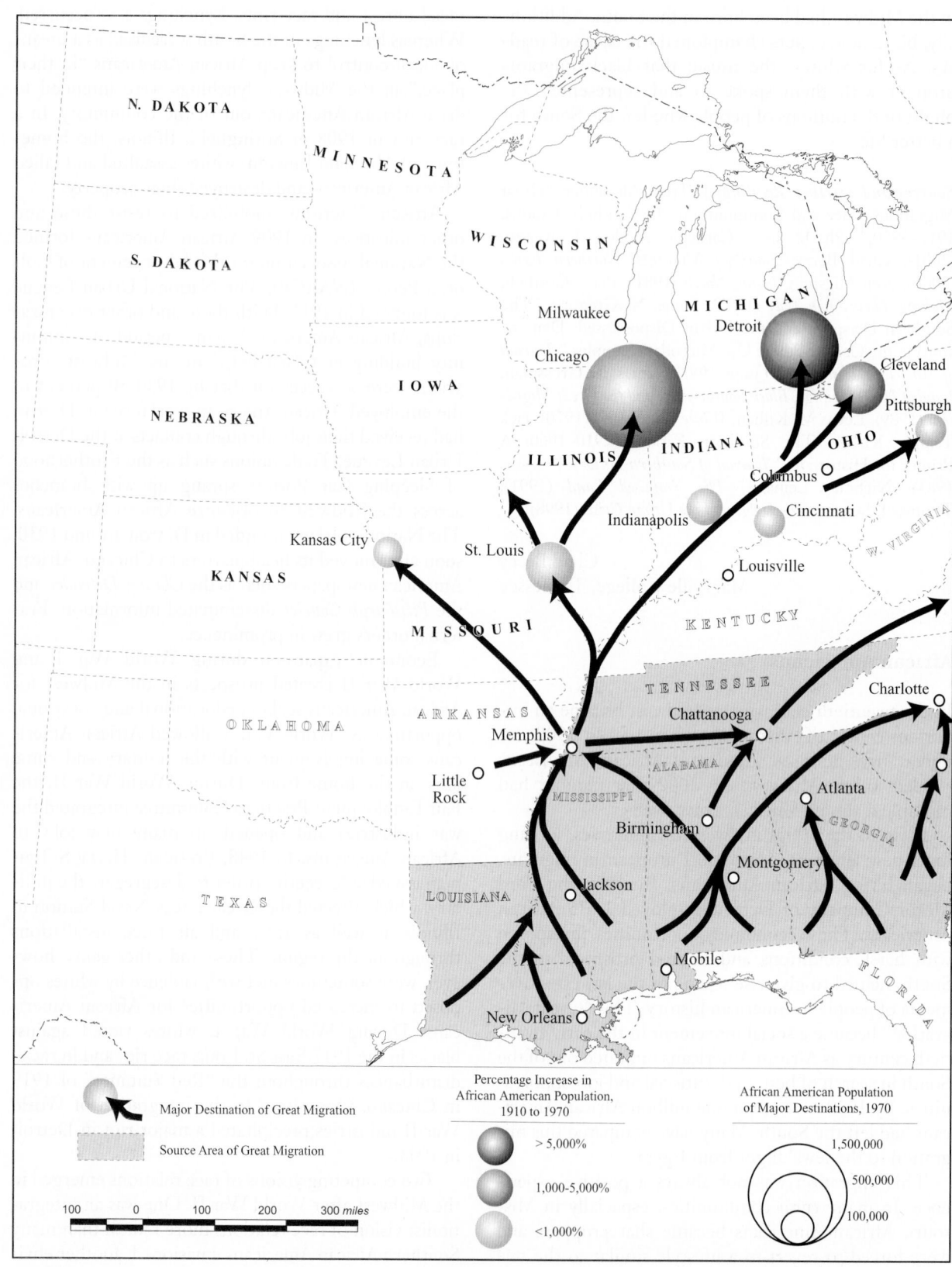

The Great Migration, 1910–1970. Prepared by Margaret Popovich. *Source*: Stephen A. Flanders, *Atlas of American Migration* (1998), 163; Helen Hornbeck Tanner, *The Settling of North America* (1995); U.S. Bureau of the Census, *Thirteenth Census of the United States Taken in the Year 1910* (1913), vol. 1, table 37; U.S. Bureau of the Census, *1970 Census of Population* (1973), vol. 1, table 67.

ment. The Supreme Court in *Brown v. the Board of Education of Topeka, Kansas*, challenged the "separate but equal" doctrine that allowed the segregation of public schools. Linked with four cases from the South, *Brown* was selected as the lead case because Topeka was not a southern community. With momentum from the *Brown* decision, African Americans from the Midwest, as well as across the nation, continued to organize to promote social change.

Yet, almost all African American children were still going to school in all-black schools. School integration in the Midwest was actually losing ground as whites fled to suburbs. Job opportunities were extremely limited. African American men in the Midwest had trouble getting jobs, decent housing, or an adequate education. Midwestern big-city fire and police departments were all white; construction crews were all white. In large urban ghettos of the Midwest, there were more African American dropouts from high school than there were semiskilled or unskilled jobs waiting for them. The gap between the median income of African American families in the United States and the median income of white families was growing larger even as there were more opportunities for college-educated, middle-class African Americans.

Anger at unfair conditions roiled as African Americans reacted to the poverty and hopelessness of ghetto life. Race riots, this time originated by African Americans, erupted in summer of 1966 in Chicago's West Side and in Detroit. In Detroit, forty-three people, most of them African American, died.

Midwestern civil rights leaders such as James Farmer began to devise programs to attack the enduring problem of a culture of poverty, not by achieving immediate integration, or even by using direct action techniques, but by building community institutions and power bases. They reasoned that political power was necessary to secure the economic programs needed to cure the ills of the ghetto. Political power required community organization.

When Dr. Martin Luther King, Jr., decided in 1966 to focus on the Campaign to End Slums, he chose Chicago. This was an important turning point in the civil rights movement because Americans were forced to confront their racism as a national phenomenon, not something limited to the South. Demonstrators protested throughout the city against unfair and discriminatory housing and employment practices. King remarked that in Chicago he had encountered more hostility than from any other group of whites. Other civil rights leaders came to realize that their constituencies in the northern slums were not likely to be moved by the abstract and otherworldly Christian rhetoric of King: To love and forgive one's enemies is not an easy calling. King nonetheless went ahead with a peaceful march in Cicero, the most obdurate and recalcitrant of Chicago's all-white suburbs.

As long as the target of the civil rights movement was the exposed and clearly visible system of segregation in the South, direct-action techniques designed to achieve specific, short-term, usually legislative goals were very appropriate. Direct action focused attention on a tangible goal, and nonviolence dampened the hostility of southern whites while it stimulated sympathy outside the South.

However, as more and more African Americans from the Midwest and the large cities poured into the civil rights movement, the nature of the movement changed. An important indicator of this shift was the chairman of the Student Nonviolent Coordinating Committee Stokely Carmichael's enunciation in 1966 of the slogan "Black Power."

Black Power was a concept that appealed to the young and militant within the movement; to those from the North and, especially, the Midwest; or those who had cosmopolitan outlooks, rather than to movement workers with strong ties to the local community in the South. Young midwestern African Americans, energized by the southern civil rights movement, soon discovered that its goals were not appropriate to the North and that its rhetoric had no resonance in urban ghettos.

Instead, the "bopping gang" worldview prevailed, in which life is a conflict between "us" and "them," and "we" must defend our turf from "them" and impose our will on "them." Malcolm X articulated such feelings in powerful language. Because the news media were fixed on the South in those years, the concept of Black Power did not frequently transcend its local settings in the North until it was enunciated through the southern movement. Many prominent figures of the southern civil rights movement such as Jesse Jackson, Diane Nash, and James Bevel have made the Midwest, especially Chicago, their home.

Even before the civil rights movement, the Midwest was a hotbed of African American political grassroots activism. In 1928 Oscar DePriest of Chicago became the first African American elected to the United States Congress since the end of the nineteenth century, and in 1934 Arthur Mitchell, also of Chicago, became the first African American Democrat elected to the House. Following Carl Stokes's election in Cleveland, Ohio, in 1967 as the first African American mayor of a large city, blacks began to make significant electoral gains, electing mayors all across the Midwest, even in cities such as St. Louis and Kansas City without African American majority populations.

The Midwest has nurtured its share of famous African Americans. In 1992 Carol Mosley-Braun of Chicago became the first African American woman elected to the United States Senate, and in 2004 she ran for nomination as the Democratic candidate for president. Michael Jordan played basketball for the Chicago Bulls; Oprah Winfrey lives and tapes her popular television show in Chicago; Toni Morrison calls Ohio home; Magic Johnson, Diana Ross, and Stevie Wonder all hail from Michigan; and Michael and Janet Jackson come from Gary, Indiana.

Despite these examples of individual success, discrimination in housing and education continue to this day—especially in the large metropolitan centers of the Midwest. Gains have been made but significant problems remain under or unaddressed.

Sources and Further Reading: Sundiata Keita Cha-Jua, *America's First Black Town* (2000); Leonard N. Moore, *Carl B. Stokes and the Rise of Black Political Power* (2002); Kimberley L. Phillips, *Alabama North* (1999); Thomas J. Sugrue, *The Origins of the Urban Crisis* (1996); Jeanne Theoharis and Komozi Woodard, eds., *Freedom North* (2003); Joe William Trotter, *The Great Migration in Historical Perspective* (1991); William M. Tuttle, Jr., *Race Riot* (1996).

Orville Vernon Burton
Matthew Cheney
University of Illinois–Urbana-Champaign

Southern Whites and Appalachians

Southern whites and Appalachians have contributed significant levels of migration to the Midwest during much of the twentieth century. This migration consisted primarily of rural southerners and Appalachians moving to urban areas in the Midwest. Migrants from the mountains of eastern Kentucky, Tennessee, and West Virginia had destinations in Chicago, Detroit, Cincinnati, Columbus, and Youngstown. Areas such as Chicago's Uptown, Cleveland's West Side and Cincinnati's Over-the-Rhine came to be referred to as "hillbilly ghettos" and have lent themselves to stereotypes of Appalachian migrants.

There were two significant waves of migration—the first from the 1920s through the early 1950s and the second during the 1960s. Migrants from the South and Appalachia were drawn by economic opportunities and were pushed from their areas of origin by poverty and unemployment. Despite stereotypes to the contrary, migration to the Midwest from the southern Appalachians was typically selective by age and education—migrants were generally younger adults with better-than-average educations in their area of origin. The common perception that the "hillbillies" came with a large social cost in the form of increased demand on the welfare systems is inaccurate. Although white

southerners began in marginal positions economically, they typically did better or returned home.

Appalachian migrants had much in common with other migrant groups. First, they moved in "chain migration" fashion—from a rural community to an urban area where other members of their community already lived. A chain migration of more than two thousand people linked Columbiana County, Ohio, and the environs of Youngstown, Ohio, with Appalachia. Many people from West Virginia moved to Cleveland and folks from eastern Kentucky ended up in Cincinnati or Chicago. In addition to facilitating the process of migration, this "stem" family system helped the migrants adjust in the new location. Family members already in the city provided a place to stay as well as information on where to find jobs.

Second, white southern Appalachians were drawn primarily by economic opportunities. Young high school graduates from the rural South migrated to cities to seek their fortunes when they did not perceive opportunity in their home communities. Finally, the large amount of migration from the South and the southern Appalachians as well as the perceived differences of many of the migrants encouraged the perpetuation of negative stereotypes of rural Appalachians in particular. Nevertheless, many of these migrants have made significant contributions to the Midwest and continue to add to the diversity of the region.

Sources and Further Reading: Bruce Ergood and Bruce Kuhre, eds., *Appalachia: Social Context Past and Present* (1983); George Hillery, James Brown, and Gordon DeJong, "Migration Systems of the Southern Appalachians: Some Demographic Observations," *Rural Sociology* 30 (Mar. 1965); William W. Philliber, Clyde B. McCoy, and Harry C. Dillingham, eds., *The Invisible Minority: Urban Appalachians* (1981); Harry Schwarzweller, James Brown, and Joseph Mangalam, *Mountain Families in Transition* (1971).

J. Marvin Pippert
North Georgia College and State University

Late-Twentieth-Century Immigration

Immigration to the Midwest in the last half of the twentieth century was a story of multiple immigration streams and of new peoples following well-beaten paths. Unlike the mass immigration of the period 1880–1920, immigration in the last half of the twentieth century was stimulated by multiple factors. Wars, poverty, and unrest in regions such as East Africa, Southeast Asia, Latin America, and eastern and central Europe all played a part in sending people to the

United States and to the Midwest. Also important were structural changes in the economy. A growing service sector and the dispersion of manufacturing and processing, especially in meatpacking and light industry and electronics assembly, created new demands for wage labor and, often, local labor shortages. The increasingly global nature of labor markets also drew white-collar workers and educated people from a variety of backgrounds. Some came to escape oppression or a lack of opportunity for professionals. Others came seeking an education at one of many midwestern universities or colleges and then stayed to work.

Another significant change during this era was the federal Immigration and Nationality Act of 1965, which reopened the opportunities for legal immigration and removed national-origin quotas. This change in the law coincided with a change in the nature of who sought to come to the United States. More and more, immigrants from Latin America, Asia, or Africa sought homes in the Midwest.

Prior to World War I, the Midwest had been a major destination for immigrants. In the last half of the twentieth century, however, other regions of the country surpassed the Midwest as a prime immigrant destination. In 1955 about one-fifth of resident aliens in the United States lived in the Midwest. Between 1961 and 1970, as immigration laws were loosened, 164,000 immigrants were naturalized in the midwestern states, just under one-fifth of the total. Yet all the midwestern states together naturalized fewer immigrants than either New York or California alone. By 2000 only slightly more than 10 percent of admitted legal immigrants listed the Midwest as their intended place of settlement.

Illinois continued to be the most attractive midwestern state, particularly the Chicago area. After New York and Los Angeles, Chicago was the third-most-favored American city for new arrivals until it was displaced by Miami in the 1990s. Among the other midwestern states, Michigan and Ohio held second and third place, respectively, as immigrant destinations.

The new wave of post-1965 immigrants often chose destinations other than the Midwest for two main reasons. First, the decline of the Midwest's traditional manufacturing base left fewer entry-level jobs for immigrants. Second, immigration was dominated by arrivals from Latin America and Asia whose migration patterns traditionally favored the West Coast, the Sunbelt, and, to some extent, New York City and its environs. The Midwest continued to be the paramount destination only for central and eastern Europeans.

The first major waves of newcomers after World War II included refugees and displaced persons. They were Jews, Poles, Ukrainians, Hungarians, Czechs, and other peoples of central and eastern Europe whose lives, families, and homes had been destroyed, disrupted, or severely threatened by the Nazi and Soviet regimes. Most were civilians admitted under special legislation, but other groups were veterans of the Polish armed forces in the west and Hungarian freedom fighters who left their homeland after the 1956 revolution.

These immigrants usually settled in or near communities of their co-ethnics, who had lobbied hard to get them admitted. Chicago and Detroit probably received the largest numbers. Refugees with specialized or skilled occupations often had to go farther from the confines of the old community neighborhoods. Ethnic support networks and relatives played an important role in place of settlement. But the new immigrants were often very different from their American cousins, in terms of culture, education, politics, and life experience. These differences created tension with the more established and Americanized brethren. The newcomers formed their own clubs and associations. Despite cooperation with older ethnic associations and the sharing of certain facilities, they maintained separate social circles.

Growing immigration from Latin America, Asia, Africa, and the Middle East was the most obvious change in the late twentieth century. In the Midwest, Latin American migration has long been dominated by Mexicans and Mexican Americans, although Central Americans, Puerto Ricans, and some Cubans made their presence felt, particularly by the 1990s. Mexicans and Mexican Americans first established communities in midwestern cities such as Chicago, Detroit, and St. Paul in the 1920s. Migrant farm labor, used widely for crops such as sugar beets, drew workers from south Texas and Mexico proper and, save for a hiatus during the Depression, has been almost continuous since then.

A new wave of Mexican immigration to the Midwest was evident by the late 1980s. This movement was larger and more widespread than any previous Mexican migration to the region. Although many Mexicans and Mexican Americans continued to come as farm laborers, the new immigrants were much quicker to look for job opportunities in other sectors. The widespread dispersion of the meatpacking industry drew many of these immigrants, though poor working conditions and high turnover rates resulted in a fairly fluid population. Like an earlier generation of eastern European immigrants, many new Mexican arrivals focused on earning money to support families in Mexico or elsewhere in the United States. Yet growing Hispanic communities in major cities and small towns demonstrate that a portion of this migrant stream has settled permanently in the region. In virtually every midwestern state, Mexicans are one of the fastest-growing ethnic groups.

Prior to 1965, the Asian and Asian American population in the Midwest was small, with Chinese predominating in most places. Subsequent immigration has not always followed this pattern. After the 1975 fall of Saigon, groups of Vietnamese refugees were resettled by social service agencies in many communities. They were widely dispersed to reduce the burden on any single community, with many refugees sent to very small towns. Within several years, most of these refugees had left their initial host communities to join family members elsewhere. Although California was the prime destination, the Minneapolis-St. Paul metropolitan area attracted a significant number of Vietnamese and other Southeast Asians.

Hmong immigrants were the second major Southeast Asian group to arrive in the Midwest in significant numbers. Many followed the Vietnamese to Minnesota and Wisconsin. In the 1990s many Hmong settled in California, but facing discrimination and competition from other new immigrants, they resettled in the Midwest in large numbers. St. Paul and Minneapolis developed the largest Hmong communities. Smaller towns, such as La Crosse, Wisconsin, were also popular.

Immigrants from the Middle East, North Africa, and south Asia settled in many of the larger midwestern cities. Detroit, with one of the nation's largest Arab populations, has become home to a diverse mixture of Palestinians, Lebanese, Iraqi Chaldeans, and others. While newcomers were often Muslim, Christians continued to form a disproportionate percentage of this migrant stream. Asian Indians formed a "quiet migration" that most often consisted of well-educated professionals and academics. Many were attracted to universities, research facilities, and high-technology and engineering firms. Others opened small businesses.

In the last decades of the twentieth century, war, famine, and economic hardship in sub-Saharan Africa spurred an increase in immigration from several countries. Immigrants from Nigeria and other west African nations settled in most of the larger cities. Immigration from East Africa led to the creation of compact communities in several cities. Ethiopian immigrants, particularly Oromo and Eritreans, first arrived in the early to mid-1980s, followed by a large wave of Somalis who came as refugees. Significant Somali communities developed in Milwaukee and Minneapolis, as well as in smaller towns such as Marshall, Minnesota, where immigrants found jobs in small meatpacking and electronics-assembly firms.

One of the most noteworthy patterns of immigration to the Midwest in the 1980s and 1990s was the settlement of many immigrants in small, rural towns, especially in Iowa, Minnesota, and Missouri. Drawn by the regional dispersion of the meatpacking industry in particular, these newcomers represented the largest immigrant influx to the rural upper Midwest since the period of initial settlement a century or more earlier. They met with reactions ranging from mild hostility to open acceptance from local populations undergoing great demographic change.

Attracted by inexpensive housing in farm towns, new Latin American, Asian, or African immigrants allowed many communities to retain schools that otherwise would have closed or consolidated with larger neighbors. More than a few immigrants also cited the less hectic and seemingly less threatening atmosphere of small-town life as the reason for settling in these communities. At the same time, the new immigrants did not always see the towns as a place of long-term residence, and the high turnover rate of the meatpacking industry created a high degree of demographic turbulence that sometimes exceeded that of urban centers.

In the larger cities, new immigrants were often attracted to old ethnic neighborhoods that had survived suburbanization and urban renewal. These neighborhoods offered older, inexpensive but well-maintained housing stock, which allowed immigrants to buy property as a family-investment strategy, mirroring a pattern laid down by immigrants of the previous century. Hamtramck, Michigan, a traditionally Polish enclave of Detroit, attracted not only recent immigrants from Poland but also Albanians, Yemeni Arabs, Bosnians, Bangladeshis, and Macedonians. By 2000 children in the city's schools spoke twenty-seven languages. Similar patterns occurred in Chicago, Minneapolis, St. Paul, and elsewhere.

Although there were many similarities between immigrants at the beginning and the end of the twentieth century, there were also crucial differences. Immigrants in the late 1900s arrived in a region whose patterns of economic, social, political, and cultural life were well established. The legal atmosphere and attitudes toward immigration were also different. Previous waves of immigrants had received little assistance in adjusting to their new homes. But in most states during the twentieth century a significant array of public and private social service agencies had developed that sought to better the lives of immigrants. The greater degree of public appreciation for the "diversity" that immigrants brought to the region was often fairly shallow, however, as controversies over language revealed. While many midwestern states continued to translate some official documents into immigrant languages, particularly Spanish, there was a growing unease in some quarters. A few communities even passed ordinances making English the official town language.

The end of the twentieth century did not signal the

end of this newest wave of immigrant newcomers. Always sensitive to economic conditions and shifting labor market and housing conditions, immigrants continue to find the Midwest a good place to settle, find a job, and raise a family, just as their predecessors had a century before.

Sources and Further Reading: Joseph Amato and John Radzilowski, *Community of Strangers* (1999); Joseph A. Amato, John Meyer, John Radzilowski, Donata DeBruyckere, and Anthony Amato, *To Call It Home* (1996).

John Radzilowski
The Piast Institute, Hamtramck, Michigan

Asian Indians

The history of Asian Indians (or Indian Americans) in America is more than two hundred years old. In earlier years, their numbers were small and their influence insignificant. Between 1820 and 1965, in part because of discriminatory legislation that targeted them, fewer than seventeen thousand Asian Indians came to North America. Settling on both the West and East Coasts, few went inland. Things changed significantly with the passage of the Immigration and Nationality Act of 1965, which both abolished discriminatory quotas based on national origins and privileged those who possessed skills as technicians and professionals. Asian Indian immigration grew to include doctors, engineers, scientists, academics, and other professionals in addition to members of the working class. Many of the jobs they took were in the Midwest.

The 1990s saw a second wave of immigration from India, when the globalization of capital and labor markets accelerated dramatically, bringing about an unprecedented expansion of Western economies. The new, knowledge-based economy of America needed people with training in engineering and computer technology. The highly ranked Indian Institutes of Technology (originally established with assistance from Western nations) provided thousands of workers for high-tech industries in the United States. The highly skilled, elite Asian Indian immigrant was generally followed by his wife and children, his lesser-skilled blood relatives, and, sometimes, aging parents.

Many in this second wave of immigrants from India went to the vibrant economic nodes in Chicago, Detroit, Cleveland, Columbus, Minneapolis–St. Paul, Indianapolis, and St. Louis. The data from Census 2000 show that the Indian American community was the fastest-growing ethnic group in the United States, increasing 106 percent in ten years to reach almost 1.7 million today.

Because the statistics displayed in table 2 need to be complemented with detailed demographic surveys and related social research pertaining to individual states and the region as a whole, they mask the ethnic, linguistic, and religious disparities among Asian Indians living in the Midwest. Padma Rangaswamy's comprehensive sociological study of Asian Indians living in metropolitan Chicago can, however, serve as a surrogate for Asian Indians in the Midwest and, indeed, for all immigrants from India living in the United States. According to this study, languages spoken at home by Chicago-area Asian Indian immigrants expressed in percentages were English (37%), Gujarati (29%), Hindi (17%), Punjabi (9%), Telugu (8%), Malayalam (7%), Tamil (6%), Kannada (5%), Bengali (4%), and Urdu (2%)—indicating ethnic and linguistic diversity as well as the community's acceptance of English. Education and income diversity also exists among Asian Indians, though together in 2000 they had the highest median family income of any racial/ethnic group in the United States and were easily one of the most highly educated groups in the nation, earning the moniker "model minority."

The processes of adaptation by Asian Indian immigrants into the mainstream culture of America have been both general and particular. Asian Indian immi-

Table 2. Indian American Population by State, and State Population as a Percentage of Indian American National Population

State	1990	2000
Illinois	64,200 (7.87%)	124,723 (7.43%)
Michigan	23,845 (2.92%)	54,631 (3.25%)
Ohio	20,848 (2.56%)	38,752 (2.31%)
Minnesota	8,234 (1.01%)	16,887 (1.01%)
Indiana	7,095 (0.87%)	14,685 (0.87%)
Wisconsin	6,914 (0.85%)	12,665 (0.75%)
Missouri	6,111 (0.75%)	12,169 (0.72%)
Kansas	3,956 (0.49%)	8,153 (0.49%)
Iowa	3,021 (0.37%)	5,641 (0.34%)
Nebraska	1,218 (0.15%)	3,273 (0.19%)
North Dakota	482 (0.06%)	822 (0.05%)
South Dakota	287 (0.04%)	611 (0.04%)
Total in Midwest	146,211 (17.93%)	293,012 (17.46%)
Total for US	815,447	1,678,765

Notes: Numbers provided are population by state and that population as a percent of the national Indian American population. Data derived from US Census 2000 by the US-India Lobby. States ordered by Indian American population in 2000.

Source: Ram Narayanan, U.S. India Lobby, May 29, 2001, https://lists.cs.columbia.edu/pipermail/ornet/2001-May/000889.html.

grants all share a common socialization in the ways of the West, through their history of British colonization of India. They often adjust well to life in the United States, having experienced English as the language of instruction in their university-level education and training. Therefore, they are able to join the discourses of economy, politics, and culture in their new land—notwithstanding the initial disadvantages of their native accents.

The Asian Indians of the Midwest do not by any means stand outside the history of Asian Indian immigration elsewhere in America. Nor is their experience much different from the near-universal emigration/immigration experience of the 175 million others in the world today who have left India. Like many other immigrant groups, they were pushed by relative poverty, social exclusion, and political violence, and pulled by promises of freedom, personal security, and new beginnings for themselves and their children in a new place. Like others before them, they have faced discrimination and exclusion. Initially, the realities of dual cultural identities, conflicting pulls of attachments and core identifications, and personal inability to participate in society and politics have been hard to take.

The short period since the watershed year of 1965 does not permit much analysis of the social and cultural history of Asian Indians. Yet the emergence of new, layered identities for second-generation Asian Indians and the dynamics of their incorporation into the new host culture is unmistakable. While electronic-communication technologies have made contacts with home more frequent and films and music easy to acquire, the assimilation process has by no means been thwarted or slowed.

Assimilation is proceeding in many directions: economic (ownership of businesses, from grocery stores and motels to high-tech companies); political (organization of ethnic interest groups; control of print and broadcast media; candidates for political offices at local and state levels); social (including the popularity of Indian cuisine and clothing among non–Asian Indians); and cultural (ways of contemplating, celebrating, and grieving). Birthdays have taken on a new cultural color.

Indian women are seeking to redefine themselves, though within the frame of their Indian culture. Patterns of finding spouses and the wedding ceremonies that follow are a hybrid of East and West. A survey of Indian immigrants who got married in the United States showed that 24.6 percent of men and 8.3 percent of women had married outside the race. Rituals surrounding death and dying have been adapted to the requirements of local laws and the "architecture" of American funerals. This fusion assists the new generation of Asian Indians to develop a "trans-nationalism of the heart" on their way to becoming truly Indian Americans.

Sources and Further Reading: H. S. Bhola, "Asian Indians in Indiana," in Robert M. Taylor, Jr., and Connie A. McBirney, eds., *Peopling Indiana* (1996); Arthur W. Helweg and Usha M. Helweg, *An Immigrant Success Story* (1990); Padma Rangaswamy, *Namaste America* (2000).

Harbans S. Bhola
Indiana University–Bloomington

Chinese

Chinese have been an important presence in the Midwest since at least the middle of the nineteenth century. Their experiences have been similar to Asian Pacific American midwesterners in general. On the one hand, Chinese Americans are a thread in the multiethnic fabric of America's "Heartland"; on the other hand, theirs is a strand that is largely unknown and unappreciated.

Nevertheless, finding signs of today's Chinese Midwest is not hard. In 2000 Chinese midwesterners were in every state of the region. A sample drawn from Illinois, Michigan, Ohio, Missouri, Kansas, Nebraska, and North Dakota reveals that self-identified Chinese residents range from 0.1 percent of a state's population (North Dakota) to 0.6 percent (Illinois), but their absolute numbers are not insignificant. The Chinese populations of Illinois, Michigan, Ohio, and Missouri are 76,725, 33,190, 30,425, and 13,667, respectively.

Both the absolute numbers and the percentages of Chinese in midwestern states have increased recently, contributing to the general growth of the midwestern Asian American population. At the same time, there is diversity in the category *Chinese*. Given the long history of a worldwide Chinese diaspora, it is not surprising to find midwestern Chinese coming from numerous migration flows and immigration experiences. Whether it describes an American-born graduate student from Connecticut attending the University of Wisconsin or a restaurant worker from Beijing in central Michigan; a researcher from Hong Kong in Chicago or a third-generation Chinese American freshman from Los Angeles attending Ohio State, the term *Chinese* covers a multitude of starting points.

If finding the contemporary Chinese midwestern presence is not hard, locating its past is. The history points to a midwestern legacy that first formed when many states in the region emerged from the Civil War as an increasingly self-conscious "middle West." Illinois, the "Land of Lincoln," was an early recipient of internal Chinese American migration. Old-timers in

Chicago's Chinese district recounted how pioneers in the 1870s walked from Rocky Mountain locales to Great Lakes' destinations. Other Chinese communities developed in Milwaukee, Detroit, and Cleveland.

The 1870s to the 1880s were years of crucial growth. Nearly all the midwestern states showed "take offs" that were truly modest, often starting from 0 or 1 "Chinese" recorded for a state. Indiana, Wisconsin, and Minnesota began with "zero" Chinese in 1870. Ten years later, 29 Indianans, 16 Wisconsinites, and 24 Minnesotans were called Chinese. Michigan began with 1 and went to 27. But the real growth spurt occurred in Illinois and Ohio. Illinois had 1 Chinese resident in 1870 and 209 ten years later, while Ohio counted 1 in 1870 and 111 in 1880.

Chinese in the 1870s Midwest were always noticeable. Newspapers would often report the arrival of a "Chinaman." The *Milwaukee Sentinel* noted the coming of a solitary new Chinese denizen in Watertown, Wisconsin, in 1878. The reception, often curious, would at times turn hostile, which attracted comment from newspapers outside the region. The *Atlanta Constitution* reported that Chinese Chicagoans requested help from the Chinese consul because laundrymen were being harassed in the Windy City. In 1889 Milwaukee, Wisconsin, experienced the only citywide midwestern version of contemporary anti-Chinese violence when up to three thousand of that city's non-Chinese residents mobbed, stoned, and attacked Chinese laundries while threatening its Asian laundrymen.

Nevertheless, it was during these post–Civil War years that the Chinese Midwest took hold. In Chicago, Chinese community organizations established themselves near Clark and Van Buren Streets in the 1880s. After 1910, a Chicago Chinese community began to grow at a new location near Wentworth and 22nd Steets. A sizeable Chinatown developed along Chicago's Cermak Road, and city directories in communities as varied as Madison, Wisconsin, and Detroit, Michigan, listed Chinese businesses. This persistence is noteworthy because it occurred in the midst of the Chinese exclusion years, the sixty-one-year era of immigration controls directed specifically against people of Chinese descent that began with passage of the Chinese Exclusion Act of 1882. Despite this drag on population growth, a small but significant American-born second generation emerged within Chinese American midwestern communities in the first decades of the twentieth century. One of these American-born midwesterners wrote a dissertation at the University of Chicago about Chinese laundrymen. His examination of Chicago laundry workers is one of the most detailed and illuminating studies of Chinese American labor during the late exclusion era.

The stubborn fact of Chinese America became an invigorated demographic force with the repeal of the Exclusion Act in 1943, the availability of U.S. naturalization to Chinese immigrants, and the reforms forged by the immigration acts of 1952 and 1965, both of which scaled back the anti-Asian provisions of earlier immigration laws. The late-twentieth-century story of the Chinese American Midwest might have remained a largely undramatic narrative of local population growth were it not for an incident that occurred in the midst of the Midwest's deindustrialization and came to symbolize the racial tensions that accompanied the "Rust-Belting" of the region. In 1982 Vincent Chin, a native Detroiter, was killed by two laid-off autoworkers who saw him as the embodiment of job-threatening competition from Japan's automobile industry. Chin's death and its handling in the courts (where his assailants received three years' probation and $3,780 in fines at the state level; the attempt to prosecute them for federal civil rights violations later failed) led to a nationwide Asian American rights mobilization.

That this galvanization occurred in the 1980s Midwest is telling. The Chinese American presence in the Midwest is, at first glance, modest in numbers, but its configuration, drawing upon and contributing to the racial dynamics of the region, makes it a key component. In that sense, Chinese in the Midwest transcend their small numbers and exemplify the need to rethink and recast our understanding of the Midwest in ways that complicate and enrich our notion of the American Heartland.

Sources and Further Reading: Victor Jew, " 'Chinese Demons': The Violent Articulation of Chinese Otherness and Interracial Sexuality in the U.S. Midwest, 1885–1889," *Journal of Social History* 37 (Winter 2003); Adam McKeown, *Chinese Migrant Networks and Cultural Change* (2001); Paul Siu, *The Chinese Laundryman* (1987).

Victor Jew
University of Wisconsin–Madison

Japanese

The forces that brought a significant Japanese population to the Midwest are unique to this ethnic group and postdate by several decades the arrival of much of the original immigrant population on the West Coast. Japan permitted its population to emigrate beginning in 1884, but large-scale migration to the mainland United States did not begin until 1900. By 1940 nearly 90 percent of the 127,000 Japanese in America lived in the three Pacific-coast states, the great majority in California. Because the Midwest was remote from western ports of entry and offered few work opportunities not found in the West, it attracted few Japanese in the early years of their immigration. No midwestern state had even 500 Japanese in 1940; Chicago, with 390, was the largest urban area of concentration.

Soon after Japanese settlement began on the Pacific coast, anti-Japanese sentiment developed, just as prejudice had against the Chinese earlier. California passed laws to prevent noncitizens, and even their American-born children, from owning or leasing land. Largely because of pressure from western states, the federal government denied Japanese the right of naturalization in 1922, and the Immigration Act of 1924 banned further Japanese immigration, a situation that prevailed until 1952. After the Japanese attack on Pearl Harbor brought the United States into World War II, the government succumbed to racist agitation and fears about the loyalty of its Japanese residents. On February 19, 1942, President Franklin Roosevelt signed Executive Order 9066, authorizing the military to remove anyone from strategic areas at its discretion. By mid-1942, more than 110,000 Japanese, two-thirds of them American-born citizens, had been taken from California and parts of Oregon, Washington, and Arizona to ten barbed-wire-encircled concentration camps, euphemistically called relocation centers, in the remote interior West and in southeastern Arkansas.

The civilian agency in charge of these camps, the War Relocation Authority, began efforts to resettle Japanese from the camps almost immediately. Camp residents could leave for three principal purposes: to serve in the military, to pursue higher education, or to seek employment. Most who sought education or employment chose the Midwest because it was closer to both the western interior and the Arkansas camps than the East. In 1941 more than 90 percent of Japanese college students attended Pacific-coast institutions, but in 1945–1946 nearly half were studying in the Midwest; Chicago and Minneapolis-St. Paul had the largest number of students.

The most important factor in the dramatic growth of the Midwest's Japanese population was jobs. Chicago was the greatest magnet, with its vast industrial and service economy. Estimates in late 1945 placed the Japanese population of Chicago at between twenty and twenty-five thousand. Smaller numbers relocated to other major cities such as Detroit, Cleveland, and Indianapolis.

Minneapolis-St. Paul attracted a surprising number of resettlers because of its pioneering establishment of local committees to aid the Japanese and the large number of educational institutions that welcomed Japanese students. Most important was the location near the Twin Cities of the Military Intelligence Service Language School, whose task was to increase the effectiveness of American-born Japanese soldiers as linguists. This was necessary because Americanization had pro-

ceeded to the point that very few Japanese Americans were proficient in Japanese. By the time the school returned to California in 1946, more than six thousand Japanese soldiers had graduated. Family members often accompanied them, and many of those who attended the school chose to return to Minneapolis-St. Paul after their military service.

The closing of the concentration camps and the reopening of the West Coast to the Japanese in 1945 set off a large out-migration from the Midwest. The Japanese population had fallen by about half by the time of the 1950 census. Nonetheless, the states of Illinois, Ohio, Michigan, and Minnesota each had more than one thousand Japanese, and nearly twelve thousand lived in Chicago. In the larger urban Japanese populations, a variety of ethnic institutions developed, including social-welfare, religious, and recreational organizations. For a time, Chicago had several identifiable Japanese neighborhoods. As the years passed, however, residential clusters dispersed, and the smaller Japanese populations had difficulty maintaining ethnic institutions, which often disappeared or lost their vitality.

In recent decades, Japanese American population growth has been slow compared with that of other Asian Americans. Japanese American fertility is the lowest of all Asian groups, and larger numbers of immigrants from other parts of Asia have arrived in the Midwest, especially since 1960. That year, Japanese ranked first or second in all midwestern states, but by 2000 they ranked fifth or sixth, behind Chinese, Koreans, Filipinos, Asian Indians, and, often, Vietnamese. Japanese Americans remain concentrated in states with large metropolitan areas. In the twelve midwestern states, 63,012 people identified themselves as Japanese in the census; the total rises to 92,369 when those who reported Japanese and one or more other ancestries are included. Metropolitan Chicago is still the Japanese American metropolis. Nearly eighteen thousand Chicagoans reported Japanese as their only race and 6,000 more had Japanese and one or more other backgrounds.

Previous censuses permitted only one racial identification, which makes direct comparison of 2000 with earlier years difficult. The growing number who report Japanese and one or more additional ancestry groups indicates a high rate of intermarriage. A large majority of marriages among third- and fourth-generation Japanese Americans nationally are intermarriages, and the rate tends to be highest in areas where their populations are relatively small, as is the case in the Midwest.

Since World War II, midwestern Japanese Americans have made great advances. They are more than twice as likely to have completed undergraduate and graduate degrees compared to the general population, and they enjoy significantly higher incomes. The Midwest offered a social and economic environment that caused thousands of displaced Pacific-coast residents to choose not to return and, instead, to make new homes and prosper in communities throughout the region.

Sources and Further Reading: Michael D. Albert, "The Japanese," in June Holmquist, ed., *They Chose Minnesota* (1981); Roger Daniels, *The Politics of Prejudice* (1962); Sharon M. Lee, "Asian Americans: Diverse and Growing," *Population Bulletin* 53 (June 1998); Brian Niiya, ed., *Encyclopedia of Japanese American History* (2001); David J. O'Brien and Stephen S. Fugita, *The Japanese American Experience* (1991); Paul R. Spickard, *Japanese Americans: The Formation and Transformation of an Ethnic Group* (1996); Jere Takahashi, *Nisei/Sansei: Shifting Japanese American Identities and Politics* (1997); Michi Weglyn, *Years of Infamy* (1976).

Michael D. Albert
University of Wisconsin–River Falls

Koreans

On January 13, 2003, Korean Americans in the Chicago metropolitan area marked the centennial celebration of Korean immigration to the United States with a pictorial exhibition of their history at the Daley Center. Why January 13? Because on January 13, 1903, around 100 Koreans arrived in Honolulu, Hawaii, aboard the ship *Gaelic* and began the official Korean immigration to America. By the time the Korean government abruptly halted immigration in 1905, another seven thousand Koreans had joined this first group.

Around 1905, several of these immigrants moved to Chicago. About the same time, a well-known expatriate, Yong Man Park, established a military-training camp in Nebraska to train Koreans to fight against Japan in Manchuria, although this camp did not contribute much to establish a Korean community. The Chicago area was the hub of the Korean presence in the Midwest from the beginning. Even though a few Koreans lived in the Midwest in the 1890s, there was no Korean American community in the Midwest to speak of until the mid-1910s. By the late 1910s, Koreans had organized an ethnic church in Chicago. Until the end of World War II, the Korean population increased very little, never exceeding several hundred.

With the onset of the Korean War in 1950, about fifteen thousand Korean women and children immigrated to the United States as wives of American soldiers and adoptees. What proportion of them settled in the Midwest is unknown. A great majority of these post–Korean War immigrants maintained few ties with the Korean American community. They are also the least-studied group among Koreans in America.

The Korean population in the Midwest as well as in the nation grew exponentially with the 1965 revision of U.S. immigration law. According to Census 2000, a little over 12 percent of 1.23 million Koreans reside in the Midwest, with nearly 40 percent of them in Illinois. As in other regions, the great majority of Koreans in the Midwest are the post-1965 immigrants and their descendants. Korean immigration grew until 1987–1988 and has declined steadily ever since. In the 1990s, the annual Korean immigration was less than half the peak number of 35,000. As Korean immigration declined, the Midwest's share of the total Korean population also declined, from close to 20 percent in the 1970s to 18 percent in the 1980s, 14 percent in the 1990s, and a bit over 12 percent in the 2000s. The Midwest's share of new immigrants also declined, only more rapidly.

A greater proportion of the Korean population in the Midwest consists of long-term settlers and their native-born children compared to the proportion in other regions. Midwestern Koreans are mostly suburbanites; in the Chicago area, 75 percent report living in various suburbs. Homeownership among suburbanites is also high, ranging from 60 to 80 percent. City dwellers include two groups: the elderly and young adults, single or married without school-age children. Wherever they live, Koreans generally are quite active in ethnic Protestant churches.

Koreans have traditionally been self-employed. Because many small-business owners are reaching retirement age in the Midwest and a great majority of their children are in professional/managerial occupations, Korean small businesses in minority areas of urban areas are on the decline. This phenomenon, called ethnic succession, is occurring more swiftly among Koreans in the Midwest than in any other region.

Koreans in the Midwest are mainly "Korean Americans" rather than "Koreans living in America." This point applies to not only the children of immigrants, as expected, but also the immigrants themselves. As the immigrants' perspective changes to that of Korean Americans, all other aspects of daily living such as family/kin; community, including church life; and intergenerational relations are affected. One indication is the growing acceptance of non-Korean marriage partners of the immigrants' children. Without an unexpected upsurge in new immigration from South Korea, this integration will continue in the foreseeable future, although the process will not be linear or smooth.

Native-born children of Korean immigrants are reaching the stage of young adulthood in large numbers. A great majority of them hold professional/managerial occupations and are in the early stage of their career. Their out-marriage rate is one of the highest among Asian Americans. Given the tender age of their children (i.e., the grandchildren of immigrants), it is not clear what type of ethnic identity will prevail among Koreans in the Midwest in the future. Yet as long as they maintain Asian phenotypic features, their ethnic identity will likely not dilute to the level of "symbolic ethnicity" of the mainstream whites in America.

Sources and Further Reading: Hyock Chun, Kwang Chung Kim, and Shin Kim, eds., *Koreans in the Windy City: A Collective Reflection on 100 Years of Korean American Life Experience in the Chicago Area* (2004); Elaine Kim and Eui Young Yu, eds., *East to America: Korean American Life Stories* (1996); Kwang Chung Kim, ed., *Koreans in the Hood: Conflict with African Americans* (1999); Shin Kim and Kwang Chung Kim, "Intimacy at a Distance, Korean American Style: Invited Korean Elderly and Their Married Children," in Laura Katz Olson, ed., *Age through Ethnic Lenses: Caring for the Elderly in Multicultural Society* (2001); Ho-Youn Kwon, Kwang Chung Kim, and R. Stephen Warner, eds., *Korean Americans and Their Religions: Pilgrims and Missionaries from a Different Shore* (2001); Ho-Youn Kwon and Shin Kim, eds., *The Emerging Generation of Korean-Americans* (1993); Pyong Gap Min, *Changes and Conflict: Korean Immigrant Families in New York* (1998); In-Jin Yoon, *On My Own: Korean Businesses and Race Relations in America* (1997).

Kwang Chung Kim
Western Illinois University

Filipinos

Filipinos comprise the second-largest Asian group in the United States, with a population of approximately 2.3 million. Although post-1965 immigration accounts for dramatic growth in the Filipino American community, Filipinos have been in the Midwest from the turn of the twentieth century. In fact, the history of Filipinos in the Midwest aptly illustrates two important themes in Filipino American history: the vexed colonial relationship between the United States and the Philippines, and the changing patterns of Filipino migrations to the United States in the twentieth and the twenty-first centuries.

After three centuries of Spanish colonial rule, the Philippines became a U.S. colony after the United States defeated Spain in the 1898 Spanish-American War and, subsequently, a Filipino independence movement in the Philippine-American War (1899–1902). In the late nineteenth and early twentieth centuries, world's fairs exhibited Filipino bodies in ways that popularized the contrast between Filipino sav-

agery and American civilization. The Philippine Reservation at the 1904 World's Fair in St. Louis displayed nearly eleven hundred Filipinos living in villages on a forty-seven-acre site. The exhibits of the scantily clad Filipino "wild tribes"—Bagobos, Negritos, Igorots, and Moros—were the most popular displays of the reservation. Although these exhibits popularized images of Filipino savagery, Americans' inhumane treatment of Filipinos at these fairs resulted in disease and death.

In the early twentieth century, labor and education provided avenues for Filipino migration to the United States. While business associations utilized the colonial status of Filipinos as U.S. nationals in order to recruit thousands of Filipinos to work on Hawaiian plantations, U.S. colonial government–sponsored scholarship programs provided a different way for an elite group of young Filipino men and women to come to the United States. The major objective of these programs was to train Filipino students who would eventually return to the Philippines and assume positions in U.S. colonial institutions there. Starting in 1903, government-sponsored students known as *pensionados* arrived to study in colleges and universities located primarily in the Midwest, such as the University of Illinois and Ohio State University, and on the East Coast. Many of them organized student clubs that defended Filipinos' worthiness of independence through pamphlets and newsletters.

Although the vast majority of the approximately forty-five thousand Filipinos on the mainland United States in 1940 lived in California and the Pacific Northwest, *pensionados* inspired more Filipinos to come to the United States as self-supporting students, some of whom made the Midwest their permanent home. Despite their well-educated backgrounds, most Filipinos in Illinois found work in low-ranking service employment as cooks, waiters, busboys, bellboys, and chauffeurs. Some Filipinos also worked as postal clerks and Pullman Company attendants.

The majority of Filipinos throughout the United States during the first half of the twentieth century were male. Unlike in California, where they were targets of antimiscegenation laws, Filipino men in Illinois were able to marry white women. These interracial marriages produced an interracial Filipino American second generation.

Passage of the Tydings-McDuffie Act in 1934 granted the Philippines gradual independence but severely curtailed further Filipino migration to the United States. However, the eligibility of Filipinos who had served in the U.S. Army during World War II in the First and Second Filipino Infantry Regiments and in non-Filipino units fighting in Europe to become U.S. citizens increased the population. So, too, did the War Brides Act of 1945 and the Fiancées Act of 1946, which enabled the formation of a new second generation of Filipino Americans born to Filipino fathers and mothers.

During World War II, several thousand Filipino midwesterners left the region for more lucrative war-industry work on the West Coast. In the 1950s and 1960s the U.S. Exchange Visitor Program became a new avenue for Filipino migration to the Midwest. Hospitals in Illinois, Michigan, and Ohio actively recruited Filipino nurses (who had trained in Americanized hospital schools of nursing established during the U.S. colonial period in the Philippines) to alleviate critical nursing shortages.

The passage of the Immigration Act of 1965, with preference categories for skilled workers, facilitated Filipino professional immigration. Nursing, in particular, became an international specialty of the Philippines. By the late 1960s, the Philippines was becoming the leading supplier of foreign-trained nurses to the United States. The active recruitment of Filipino nurses and physicians by health-care institutions led to the formation of Filipino American communities in the Midwest with larger percentages of health professionals than those on the West Coast.

Although the aggressive recruitment of Filipino nurses to alleviate shortages in health-care institutions in Missouri, Wisconsin, and Minnesota continues in the twenty-first century, not all contemporary Filipino migration to the Midwest is highly skilled and professional. Filipino contract workers in Rapid City, South Dakota, are employed primarily in entry-level custodial, housekeeping, and light-manufacturing jobs. Recent complaints of these contract workers about unfair working conditions remind us that, despite the legislative and economic gains of Filipinos in the second half of the twentieth century, racial and economic inequality in the Midwest persist.

Filipinos continue to change the cultural landscape of the region. Elizabeth Punsalan, who was raised in Ohio and lives in Michigan, is a five-time U.S. national ice dance champion. Ohio state representative Steve Austria was elected to a four-year term as a state senator. After twenty-five years of planning, the Filipino Association of Greater Kansas City inaugurated its Filipino Cultural Center Building in June 2000. More recently, the Philippine Study Group of Minnesota together with other Filipino American organizations convinced the Minnesota legislature to correct the text of a plaque at the capitol, which commemorated the service of Minnesota volunteers in the Philippines during the Spanish-American War. The new plaque acknowledges that the Spanish-American War "was fought to defeat Spain, not to free the Filipinos" and that Filipinos fought unsuccessfully for full independence against the United States in the Philippine-American War. In the new millennium, the Filipino American community continues to inform the rich diversity of contemporary life in the Midwest.

Sources and Further Reading: Catherine Ceniza Choy, *Empire of Care* (2003); Barbara M. Posadas, *The Filipino Americans* (1999); Benito M. Vergara, Jr., *Displaying Filipinos* (1995).

Catherine Ceniza Choy
University of Minnesota–Twin Cities

Vietnamese

The fall of Saigon and the end of the Vietnam War in 1975 resulted in the exodus of thousands of Vietnamese refugees to the United States. In 1975 125,000 Vietnamese refugees, primarily from South Vietnam, were resettled in the United States. A few thousand Vietnamese were admitted annually from 1976 to 1978. In 1979 the border war between China and Vietnam stimulated the acceptance of more than 44,000 Vietnamese refugees by the United States. In 1980 and 1981 combined, over 180,000 Vietnamese refugees were admitted into the country. The number dropped to 42,000 in 1982 and, with the exception of 1985, continued to exceed 20,000 each year through the mid-1990s. From 1989 through the mid-1990s, Amerasians (the children of Vietnamese mothers and American servicemen fathers) and former South Vietnamese prisoners of war, under the auspices of special refugee resettlement programs, constituted one-third to one-half of the Vietnamese refugees admitted into the United States. Since the mid-1990s, Vietnamese immigrants sponsored by family members in the United States have replaced refugees as the most significant portion of the arriving Vietnamese population.

The 1990 census enumerated 593,213 persons of Vietnamese origin residing in the United States. Ten years later, U.S. census takers counted 1,122,528 Vietnamese—a near doubling of the population. While the refugee flow has largely ended since the mid-1990s, the Vietnamese population has continued to expand due to family-reunion immigration and natural increase. In 2000 Vietnamese families were somewhat larger and younger than the United States population as a whole.

In 2000 Vietnamese in the United States were concentrated in the West Coast states of California (447,032) and Washington (46,149) as well as in Texas (134,961). In the midwestern region, the largest Vietnamese populations were in Illinois (19,101) and Minnesota (18,824). Sizable numbers of Vietnamese also lived in Michigan (13,673), Kansas (11,623), Missouri (10,926), Ohio (9,812), Iowa (7,129), and Nebraska (6,364). More modest numbers of Vietnamese were in Indiana (4,843), Wisconsin (3,891), South Dakota (574), and North Dakota (478).

Among midwestern metropolitan areas, Minneapolis-St. Paul and Chicago possessed the largest Vietnamese communities (15,905 and 15,894, respectively). There were sizable Vietnamese communities in the metropolitan areas of Wichita (7,284); Grand Rapids-Muskegon-Holland, Michigan (5,611); St. Louis (5,537); Detroit-Flint-Ann Arbor (5,237); and Kansas City (5,140). More modest communities were in Lincoln, Nebraska (3,774); Cleveland-Akron (2,625); and Des Moines (2,588).

Probably the most identifiable Vietnamese neighborhood in the Midwest is the Argyle Street area of the Uptown neighborhood on the North Side of Chicago. Over the past quarter century, the Vietnamese experience in Uptown has earned a place in the storied history of immigrant and ethnic neighborhoods in the city of Chicago. Beginning in 1975, resettlement agencies placed many Vietnamese refugees in the vicinity of Argyle Street. Uptown has had a well-known and well-documented history as a "port of entry" for a diverse group of low-income residents, including Appalachian migrants in the 1950s and 1960s, Native Americans in the 1960s and 1970s, and ex-mental hospital patients in the 1970s and 1980s.

In Uptown, Vietnamese refugees were resettled in dilapidated apartment buildings. Recent refugees were often the victims of crime. Despite these difficulties, the Vietnamese population in Uptown continued to grow through the 1980s and 1990s. In the mid-1980s, ethnic Vietnamese and ethnic Chinese from Vietnam began opening restaurants, supermarkets, video stores, and other businesses intended to serve the growing Vietnamese community in the Chicago area. With the expanding number of Vietnamese businesses, the Argyle area had earned the nickname "Little Saigon" by the early 1990s. At that time, the neighborhood also acquired a visible identifying landmark when the Chicago Transit Authority remodeled the Argyle el subway stop with an Asian-style pagoda. The Argyle Street area continues to serve as a weekend shopping destination for Vietnamese from around the Chicago region.

Although socioeconomically mobile Vietnamese residents in the Chicago area have been moving to outlying suburban communities, Uptown is still the home of the Vietnamese Association of Illinois—the primary social-services agency aiding people of Vietnamese origin in the Chicago area. The neighborhood surrounding Argyle Street in Uptown has three Vietnamese Buddhist temples, a Vietnamese Catholic con-gregation, and several ethnic Vietnamese Protestant churches of various denominations. Small but geographically cohesive institutional districts also serve growing Vietnamese communities in St. Paul, Minneapolis, St. Louis, Kansas City, Des Moines, and Wichita.

Homeownership data suggest that Vietnamese living in midwestern states have experienced considerable socioeconomic advancement. In 1990, just over 43 percent of enumerated Vietnamese households across the United States lived in owner-occupied dwellings. By 2000, 69.8 percent of Vietnamese households in Minnesota and 58.1 percent in Illinois lived in owner-occupied units. In Michigan, Kansas, Missouri, Ohio, Iowa, and Nebraska, the homeownership rates of Vietnamese households exceeded 60 percent. As they have throughout the United States, many people of Vietnamese origin in the Midwest have achieved upward mobility over the past decade through advancement into mainstream professions as well as entrepreneurship, with a particularly pronounced concentration in nail-salon ownership.

Sources and Further Reading: J.M. Freeman, *Changing Identities* (1995); J. Hein, *From Vietnam, Laos, and Cambodia* (1995); M.H. Hung and D.W. Haines, "Vietnamese," in D.W. Haines, ed., *Refugees in America in the 1990s* (1996); N.M. Shelley, "Building Community from 'Scratch': Forces at Work among Urban Vietnamese Refugees in Milwaukee," *Sociological Inquiry* 71 (Fall 2001); Min Zhou and Carl Bankston, *Growing Up American* (1998).

Mark E. Pfeifer
Hmong Cultural Center, St. Paul, Minnesota

Hmong and Cambodians

The Hmong people are an ethnic group whose origins go back at least three thousand years in China. In Asia, Hmong live in southwestern China, Thailand, Burma, Laos, and Northern Vietnam. The first Hmong migration of notable size to the United States began with the fall of Saigon and Laos to Communist forces in 1975. Many Hmong had worked with pro-American anti-Communist forces during the conflicts in Vietnam and Laos. As a result, they were subject to violence and retribution in Laos. Many Hmong escaped Laos to Thailand, where they were incarcerated in refugee camps.

From the late 1970s to the mid-1990s, large numbers of Hmong refugees were resettled in the United States. The peak was 1980, when 27,000 Hmong refugees were admitted. From 1981 to 1986, the number of Hmong refugees slowed to a few thousand each year, but admissions picked up again between 1987 and 1994, when about 56,000 Hmong refugees were accepted. After 1994 Hmong refugee admissions slowed to a trickle because most of the Thai camps were by then empty, with the remaining Hmong repatriated to Laos.

The 1990 census enumerated 94,439 Hmong Americans across the United States, with more than half of the population residing in California. During the 1990s, the Hmong population shifted away from California and toward the Midwest. According to the 2000 U.S. census, about half of the Hmong now live in the Midwest, mostly in Minnesota (41,800), Wisconsin (33,791), and Michigan (5,383), compared to 41 percent in 1990.

By 2000 there were 169,428 Hmong enumerated in America, representing a nearly 90 percent increase in the population from 1990. Due to language and cultural barriers in the enumeration of the Hmong population, this figure is probably a significant undercount. Minneapolis-St. Paul claimed 40,707 Hmong residents. Other midwestern metropolitan areas with smaller but sizable Hmong populations included the Wisconsin cities of Milwaukee-Racine (8,078), Appleton-Oshkosh-Neenah (4,741), Wausau (4,453), Green Bay (2,957), Sheboygan (2,706), La Crosse (2,285), Madison (2,235), and Eau Claire (1,920), as well as Michigan's Detroit-Ann Arbor (3,926).

Why did Minneapolis-St. Paul emerge as the new Hmong American capital? The opportunity to make a better life seems to be a key motivating factor for migration to the Twin Cities region. "The cost of living is cheaper here than in California," Lee Pao Xiong, president of the Urban Coalition in St. Paul, told the Associated Press. "The quality of education is better here, and jobs are available here." A 2002 community directory lists thirteen Hmong community organizations and thirty-nine Hmong religious congregations in the Minneapolis-St. Paul area. A sizable Hmong business and institutional district has grown near St. Paul's University Avenue.

As a result of starvation, disease, and executions, an estimated 2 million Cambodians, one-quarter of Cambodia's population, perished between 1975 and 1978 under Pol Pot and the Khmer Rouge. The Vietnamese invasion of Cambodia in December 1978 pushed out the Khmer Rouge regime, and hundreds of thousands of Cambodian refugees fled to Thailand. Only modest numbers of Cambodians were resettled in the United States during the 1975–1978 period. The numbers of Cambodian refugees coming into the United States increased to 6,000 in 1979 and exceeded 10,000 each year from 1980 to 1986 before leveling off significantly in the late 1980s.

In comparison with the Hmong's, the Cambodian presence in the Midwest is relatively small. According to census figures, 171,937 people of Cambodian origin resided in the United States in 2000, compared to 149,047 in 1990. Of them, 70,232 were counted in California, almost 20,000 in Massachusetts, nearly 14,000 in Washington State, and more than 8,000 in Pennsylvania. In the Midwest, the largest numbers of Cambodians were enumerated in Minnesota (5,530), Illinois (2,879), and Ohio (2,725).

In the midwestern states, the most sizable Cambodian enclaves are located in Minneapolis-St. Paul (4,149); Chicago (2,764); and Columbus, Ohio (1,464). Minneapolis-St. Paul and the Chicago area serve as the primary institutional centers for Cambodians living in the midwestern states. The St. Paul–based Cambodian Association of Minnesota provides a range of social services and cultural programs for Cambodian youth, adults, and elderly residing across the Twin Cities metropolitan area. A large Cambodian Buddhist temple is located near Farmington, about thirty miles south of St. Paul.

In Chicago, many Cambodian refugees initially moved to the Uptown neighborhood on the city's North Side in the late 1970s and throughout the 1980s. The Uptown community continues to be home to many Cambodians though the population has dispersed somewhat through the Chicago metropolitan area over time. The Argyle Street area of Uptown is the site of a Cambodian Buddhist temple and the Cambodian Association of Illinois, the primary Cambodian social service organization in the Chicago area.

Sources and Further Reading: Dia Cha and Norma Livo, *Teaching with Folk Stories of the Hmong* (2000); D.C. Everest Area Schools, *The Hmong and Their Stories* (2001); Jeremy Hein, *From Vietnam, Laos, and Cambodia: A Refugee Experience in the United States* (1995); Lourdes Medrano Leslie, "Leave West, Buy a House," *Minneapolis Star-Tribune* (29 Apr. 2002); Fungchatou Lo, *The Promised Land: Socioeconomic Reality of the Hmong in Urban America, 1976–2000* (2001); Darina Siv, *Never Come Back* (2000); Nancy J. Smith-Hefner, *Khmer American* (1999).

Mark E. Pfeifer
Hmong Cultural Center, St. Paul, Minnesota

Lebanese

Lebanese began migrating to the United States in the mid-1870s. At that time they were referred to as Syrians because they came from the Syrian province of the Ottoman Empire. In 1946 part of this province became the independent Republic of Lebanon. Some 90 percent of these early Lebanese immigrants were Christians, either Maronite Catholic or Orthodox; the

Arab American teenagers, Dearborn, Michigan, 1997. Courtesy Steve Gold.

rest were Muslim or Druze. The Lebanese were the largest group of Arab immigrants in the United States at the time and were a significant part of turn-of-the-twentieth-century migration. Like many other immigrants, the Lebanese intended to return to their homeland after saving money from years of hard work.

A large proportion of immigrant Lebanese women and men worked as pack peddlers selling needed household goods—linens, tablecloths, handkerchiefs, and fabrics—to rural housewives and urban families. Pack peddling led Syrian/Lebanese to all parts of the United States, but there was a high concentration of sales networks and settlement within the Midwest. Many specialized in the industrial and coal-mining areas of Illinois, Ohio, Indiana, and Michigan. A network of distribution centers and settlement towns developed in areas such as Detroit, Michigan; Toledo, Ohio; Chicago, Bloomington, and Spring Valley, Illinois; Sioux Falls, South Dakota; and Omaha, Nebraska. Michigan City and Fort Wayne, Indiana, hosted some of the earliest documented Syrian/Lebanese enclaves.

Syrian/Lebanese Christians and Muslims established numerous religious institutions, including a large number of churches. They built the first known Islamic center in the United States in 1900, in Ross, North Dakota. The first Muslim cemetery and dedicated mosque were established in Cedar Rapids, Iowa, in the 1930s. The Syrian/Lebanese also developed a thriving written culture and had established a diverse range of newspapers and magazines by the 1920s.

While the peddling lifestyle allowed for freedom and wealth, many Syrian/Lebanese began to plant roots in cities such as Chicago, Detroit, and Toledo following World War I. A large proportion of the early

Ford autoworkers were Lebanese and other Arabs. Some Lebanese settled in the agricultural areas of central Illinois, where Lebanese names are still highly visible. It is said that the birth of mail-order houses, such as Sears, Roebuck and Company, is what finally put the Syrian/Lebanese peddlers out of business.

Second- and third-generation Lebanese Americans largely abandoned the retail and wholesale business niche. A large proportion of them received college educations, intermarried with other Americans, and melted into American society. They were, and continue to be, a highly successful ethnic group.

In 2000 nearly 40 percent of the estimated three million Arab Americans were of Lebanese origin. Almost one-third of them live in the Midwest, the majority in Michigan, Ohio, and Illinois. Some 25 percent of Lebanese are immigrants, and half came to the United States before 1980. Newer Lebanese immigrants are more likely to be Muslim than Christian and Druze. They are still settling in large numbers in the Midwest, especially in the Detroit area.

Sources and Further Reading: Anan Ameri and Dawn Ramey, eds., *The Arab American Encyclopedia* (1999); Alixa Naff, *Becoming American* (1985).

Louise Cainkar
University of Illinois–Chicago

Other Middle Easterners

Arabs began migrating to the United States in the late nineteenth century. They settled mainly in the urban areas on the coasts, as well as in some industrial cities in the Midwest. High industrial wages after 1910 attracted Arab immigrants to such cities as Chicago, Toledo, and Detroit as well as Dearborn, Michigan. Today greater Detroit is home to one of the largest Arab American communities in the United States, reputed to number over three hundred thousand members and still growing. The majority of Arab immigrants in the Midwest today come from Lebanon, Yemen, Syria, Palestine, Egypt, and, since the Gulf War, an increasing number of Iraqi immigrants as well. Virtually all nationalities and ethnicities of the Middle East are represented.

The first wave of Arab migrants arrived between the late 1800s and World War I. Most of them came to escape the economic and political changes in their homeland, and sought economic opportunity in the United States with the eventual goal of returning to their native land. The majority of these immigrants were Christian Lebanese and came from what was then greater Syria, now Lebanon. The second wave of migration began in 1948 and increased greatly with the Arab-Israeli war of 1967. These immigrants came from Egypt, Jordan, Lebanon, Syria, and Palestine. Some were forced to leave their countries in the Middle East due to political and economic uncertainties that followed the war, but most came to improve their prospects. From 1948 to 1979, 45 percent of Arab immigrants were women and more than 50 percent were between the ages of twenty and forty-nine; there was a marked increase in Muslim immigrants. Like most new immigrants, they preferred to live in areas that were inhabited by their compatriots and settled in areas that also offered employment opportunities. The 1980s and 1990s brought a smaller number of professionals and semiprofessionals from practically all fields. A majority originally came as university students and later settled near the universities they had attended.

By 2000 an estimated 299,107 Arabs, Chaldeans (members of a Christian ethnic group from Iraq), and Assyrians of first ancestry had settled in the Midwest. Arab immigrants tend to settle near their place of employment. They also locate at the heart of major cities, near the key points of commerce, or in ethnically mixed working-class neighborhoods. Cities with some of the highest numbers of Arab residents are Chicago, Columbus, Indianapolis, and, especially, Detroit and Dearborn. The Detroit auto industry and allied manufacturing opportunities have attracted Arab immigrants since early in the twentieth century. As their communities grew they relocated to other parts of the city or the suburbs.

Today, Arab Americans still living in major urban areas tend to hold retail and industrial jobs. Detroit and Dearborn were the destinations of many because they offered the largest concentration of ethnic Arabs, providing newcomers with family, friends, and a famil-

iar way of life. As the Michigan Arab population became established economically, the more prosperous joined the stream of Detroit and Dearborn residents moving to the growing suburbs. Dearborn became progressively more important as a staging area where new immigrants could learn English, assimilate to the American culture, and, if they succeeded, follow their predecessors into wealthier communities. But a fair number of Dearborn's old Arab families remained and provided the basis for a developing sense of community among new immigrants and old residents. Their neighborhoods often show clear visual signs of Arab settlement, from Middle Eastern grocery stores and restaurants to mosques, Islamic centers, and churches that offer both religious and community services.

Arab immigrants from Lebanon, Palestine, Yemen, and Iraq continue to locate in Dearborn; in 2000 the city had 29,344 people with Arab ancestry, 30 percent of the city's population. In Michigan, Arabic bilingual students constitute the second-largest student population with "limited speaking ability." This increase in children with limited English-language skills forced Detroit and Dearborn to institute bilingual/bicultural programs for Arab students. One of the significant accomplishments of these communities is the creation of a major social-services organization in the heart of Dearborn's Arab community, the Arab American Community Center for Social Services (ACCESS). It has developed outreach programs that primarily target the Arab American community in Michigan and is run by a predominantly Arab American staff. ACCESS offers outreach programs to educators, providing daily workshops that offer in-depth cultural-competency training to educators in public and private schools. They also host annual cultural events within the community, from concerts to art exhibitions.

In 2000 approximately 0.4 percent of the Midwest population was of Arab first ancestry, with the largest number residing in Michigan (103,303). This has been a significant increase since 1990, when the number of Arab first ancestry recorded for the Midwest was only 0.27 percent of the population, with the largest number also residing in Michigan (65,906). Although Detroit and Dearborn have always been considered the most popular locations for Arab settlement in the Midwest, there is a significant number of growing Arab American communities throughout the region.

Sources and Further Reading: Sameer Y. Abraham and Nabeel Abraham, eds., *Arabs in the New World* (1983); Ernest McCarus, ed., *The Development of Arab-American Identity* (1994).

Dwan Ossama El Kaoukji
University of Illinois–Chicago

Urban Native Americans

In the popular imagination, Native Americans are still associated almost exclusively with reservations. Yet cities throughout the United States—including Chicago, Detroit, Minneapolis, Cleveland, and many smaller midwestern cities—have vibrant Indian communities, many of which are still growing after fifty years of existence.

Until around 1940, the great majority of American Indians in the Midwest—including peoples known to European Americans as Chippewa, Ottawa, Potawatomi, Menominee, Winnebago, and Lakota—lived on reservations established during the nineteenth century. Then, beginning in the 1940s, a shift in federal Indian policy (from tribal "reorganization" in the 1930s to tribal "termination" and "job relocation" in the 1950s) coupled with economic factors (poverty on reservations and increasing employment opportunities in cities) resulted in large reservation-to-city migrations. Although some came for only a short time to earn quick money before returning home, many stayed, married, and raised families.

Unlike many other ethnic groups, urban Native Americans in the Midwest tended not to develop geographically bounded enclaves. In some of the largest cities, however, newly arrived Indian people did tend to gravitate to certain—often economically depressed, inner-city—neighborhoods, including Detroit's Cass Corridor, the Uptown-Edgewater area in Chicago, and Minneapolis's Franklin Avenue. This last neighborhood, commonly known by community members as "The Reservation," is where the American Indian Movement (AIM)—an activist movement that formed in the 1960s to improve the lives of Native Americans—originated. The conditions of poverty and related social problems that AIM and other organizations sought to alleviate continue to plague some urban Indian families. Others have achieved middle-class lifestyles and dispersed into more affluent urban neighborhoods and suburbs.

A key institution developed by Native Americans throughout the Midwest is the urban Indian center. At first, these were places offering informal assistance to new arrivals in the form of tips on housing and employment, short-term small loans, and social and cultural support. As urban American Indian communities have stabilized and grown, these centers have expanded and formalized their services. Furthermore, American Indian community leaders have developed a wide array of other more specialized institutions to serve the needs of urban Indian people, from drug and alcohol treatment facilities to educational programs and cultural centers.

Native Americans who migrated to midwestern cities during the third quarter of the twentieth century shared a sense of common cause that often transcended tribal differences, creating a "pan-Indian" culture. Urban powwows, which arose during the late 1960s, are one of the most visible expressions of this phenomenon. Tribal affiliations, however, remained important, and the last quarter of the twentieth century saw the beginnings of a new trend: a lessening of "detribalization" and a rise of "retribalization" as urban Indian people renewed connections to home reservation communities. This trend continues to bring increased vitality to urban Indian communities. In short, as they enter the twenty-first century, urban Native Americans in the Midwest persevere in retaining and strengthening both their "urbanness" and their "Indianness."

Sources and Further Reading: Edmund Jefferson Danziger, Jr., *Survival and Regeneration* (1991); Donald L. Fixico, *The Urban Indian Experience in America* (2000); Deborah Davis Jackson, *Our Elders Lived It* (2002); Terry Straus and Grant P. Arndt, eds., *Native Chicago* (1998).

Deborah Davis Jackson
Earlham College, Indiana

Latino/as

The 2000 U.S. Census defined *Latinos* as synonymous with *Hispanics*. Both terms refer to those Americans who identify themselves as originating in Spain, Spanish-speaking countries (including Mexico and Cuba), and Spanish-speaking territories of the United States (such as the Commonwealth of Puerto Rico). Although *latinos* is masculine (and *latinas* feminine) in Spanish, the label is often gender neutral in English. In this article, *Latinos* includes both men and women.

Latinos have been a part of the North American landscape since the early sixteenth century, when Spaniards began to colonize the territories that later became the states of Florida, Texas, New Mexico, Arizona, Colorado, and California. Mexican workers who began to establish themselves in Kansas, Nebraska, Iowa, and Missouri by the early 1900s were among the first Latinos to settle in large numbers in the Midwest. As many as one million Mexicans—professionals, ex-soldiers, peasants, political activists, skilled workers—fled across the U.S. border during the Mexican Revolution (c. 1910–1920). Many eventually found their way to farming regions and industrial centers in Minnesota, Wisconsin, Michigan, Indiana, and Illinois with the help of *enganchistas*, or labor contractors.

Puerto Ricans are more recent newcomers in this region. Puerto Rico became an unincorporated terri-

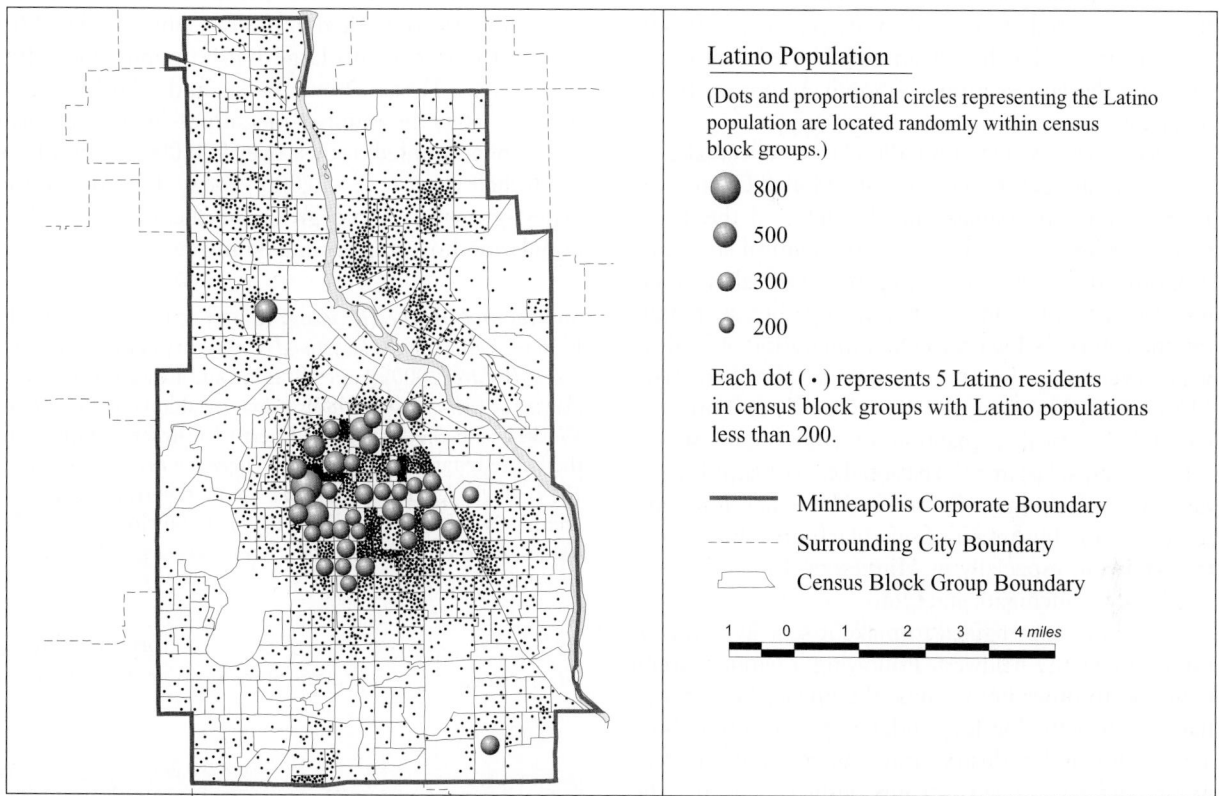

Latino Population

(Dots and proportional circles representing the Latino population are located randomly within census block groups.)

● 800

● 500

● 300

● 200

Each dot (·) represents 5 Latino residents in census block groups with Latino populations less than 200.

—————— Minneapolis Corporate Boundary

- - - - - - - Surrounding City Boundary

⬓ Census Block Group Boundary

1   0   1   2   3   4 miles

The Latino population in Minneapolis, 2000. Prepared by Margaret Popovich. *Source:* U.S. Bureau of the Census (2000).

tory of the United States soon after the Spanish-American War of 1898. The Jones Act of 1917 unilaterally conferred American citizenship on the islanders, facilitating their relocation to the U.S. mainland. They began arriving in the Midwest in sizable numbers in the 1940s in response to several "push" and "pull" factors. The Great Depression crippled the island's agricultural economy, leading to rising unemployment and labor unrest. In response, by the late 1940s the administration of Governor Luis Muñóz Marín launched an ambitious industrialization program known as Operation Bootstrap. At the same time, representatives of several midwestern farming, railroad, mining, and industrial companies began recruiting Puerto Rican workers. This influx coincided with an organized-labor campaign to persuade Congress to end the Bracero Program, an agreement started in 1942 to procure Mexican contract workers for the U.S. economy. Puerto Rican migrants fanned out over the region, finding their way to the well-established Mexican and Mexican American barrios of Detroit; Chicago; Gary; Lorain, Ohio; and Milwaukee.

Aside from Mexicans and Puerto Ricans, the Midwest has also attracted Latinos from Cuba and Central and South America. Cubans arrived in the Midwest under the auspices of the 1961 Cuban Refugee Assis-

tance Program, a federally funded relief agency that provided $1.4 billion to help Cubans relocate across the United States between 1961 and 1981. The first group came between 1959 and the missile crisis of October 1962 and included a disproportionate contingent of professionals and entrepreneurs bitterly opposed to the Cuban Revolution. The U.S. mainstream press quickly dubbed them the "Golden Exiles." Approximately three hundred thousand Cubans were airlifted to the United States in a string of "freedom flights" between 1965 and 1973. Destitute and working-class Cubans known variously as *marielitos* (refugees departing from the Cuban port of Mariel in 1980) and *balseros*, or rafters, comprise the most recent tide. Today the state of Illinois, led by Chicago, is home to the sixth-largest Cuban American community on the mainland, followed by smaller concentrations in Michigan, Ohio, Missouri, Indiana, Minnesota, Wisconsin, and Kansas.

The remaining Latino population in the Midwest is made up of Central and South Americans. They include intellectuals, students, politicians, and business owners who fled Colombia in the 1950s and 1960s to escape *La Violencia* ("The Violence"), a period of bloody political factionalism between rival Conservative and Liberal Parties. Political and social instability increased in the post-1970 years following the rise of the cocaine cartels and guerilla warfare. Nearly 500,000 Colombians reside legally in the United States and make up the largest group of South Americans in the Midwest.

Successive streams of middle-class intellectuals, activists, and indigenous peasants abandoned Guatemala, El Salvador, Nicaragua, and Honduras in the 1970s and 1980s in response to domestic political strife and economic dislocation. Church groups critical of American foreign policy in Central America began sheltering those turned down by U.S. immigration officials in what eventually became known as the Sanctuary Movement. The Chicago Religious Task Force on Central America, a coalition of church and social-action groups, became the national coordinator for this newest Underground Railroad. These developments led to the establishment of sanctuary sites throughout the Midwest, especially in Minnesota, Iowa, Wisconsin, Illinois, Michigan, and Ohio.

Latinos have struggled to make it socially and economically in the Midwest. Following a national trend common to other immigrants, the financially strapped have had to settle for dead-end, low-paying jobs in both agriculture and industry. Poverty, segregation, redlining, and restrictive covenants pushed them into the least desirable urban spaces burdened with severe infrastructural problems, such as inadequate social services, dilapidated housing, and underfunded schools. Xenophobic and nativist sentiments during the 1930s led to the large-scale repatriation or deportation of Mexicans and Mexican Americans across the United States. As a result, the *Mejicano* population in the states of Illinois, Indiana, Kansas, Michigan, Minnesota, Missouri, Ohio, and Wisconsin fell from 60,611 to 26,048 between 1930 and 1940, nearly a 60 percent drop.

Latinos have met these challenges by relying largely on extended families, resilient cultural traditions, and a strong survival ethos. Over the years, they have established churches, bilingual newspapers, small businesses, social clubs, and *mutualistas* (self-help organizations), as well as ethnically sensitive educational and health-care programs. Puerto Rican activists in Chicago founded the Young Lords Organization in the 1960s, a precursor of the Young Lords Party. Chicanos and Chicanas (Mexican American men and women) and Boricuas (Puerto Ricans and people of Puerto Rican descent) have rallied around a collective Latino identity to fight for jobs and political representation. In Detroit, both groups not only share the same community (Mexicantown), but they have also supported the creation of the Center for Chicano-Boricua Studies at Wayne State University, one of the oldest undergraduate ethnic-studies programs for Latinos and Latinas in the Midwest. In 1970 nearly 400,000 Latinos dwelled in Illinois, which ranked fifth among the states with large Latino populations after California, Texas, New York, and Florida. Two decades later, the number of Latinos in the state had more than doubled, to just over 900,000. By 2000 the figure had risen to 1,530,000. Today, Latinos are the fastest-growing ethnic group in the nation, with a population hovering around 45 million.

Sources and Further Reading: Robert Aponte and Marcelo E. Siles, *Latinos in the Heartland* (1994); Juan González, *Harvest of Empire* (2000); James B. Lane and Edward J. Escobar, *Forging a Community* (1987); Edwin Maldonado, "Contract Workers and the Origins of Puerto Rican Communities in the United States," *International Migration Review* 13 (Spring 1979); Felix M. Padilla, *Latino Ethnic Consciousness* (1985); Dennis N. Valdés, *Al Norte* (1991); Dionicio [Dennis] N. Valdés, *Barrios Norteños* (2000); Zaragosa Vargas, *Proletarians of the North* (1993).

Jorge L. Chinea
Wayne State University, Michigan

Out-Migration

For more than two hundred years, midwesterners have left home in order to find economic, cultural, and social betterment elsewhere. Importing outside technologies, ideas, and goods, many of the farms, small towns, and cities of the Midwest have continually exported both young and old who left in search of peoples and places they perceived as more conducive to their changing needs and desires: farmland out west; the attractions of city life on the coasts; and warmer, healthier climates in the Sunbelt. Knowing the history of midwesterners outside of the Midwest contributes to the understanding of life inside the Midwest by showing not only what the world beyond the horizon offered but also what the Midwest was not providing.

In the early and mid-nineteenth century, many families of the early Midwest took part in intraregional and westward movement, two frequently overlapping migratory patterns. Settled by people from New England, the Middle Atlantic states, and the Upland South—particularly New York, Pennsylvania, Maryland, Virginia, and Kentucky—Ohio and Indiana provided homes to people who later migrated to Illinois, Iowa, Missouri, the plains states, and beyond in search of available, productive farmland. The evolving Midwest of the nineteenth century functioned as a gateway to the west for a rapidly expanding United States.

Much of midwestern life has involved migration and the pursuit of economic opportunity: "moving out" oftentimes has meant "moving up." Beginning in the 1840s, many midwesterners followed the overland trails to gold-rush California, the widespread rumors of instant wealth having spread across the country. Others explored the Pacific coastal valleys in Oregon and California in search of fertile farmland.

As corporate capitalism restructured agriculture in the late nineteenth century, midwesterners increasingly migrated to regional cities and the booming urban centers of the Far West. In short, large corporate landholdings and advancements in science and technology—which made knowledge, supplies, and equipment more expensive while at the same time eliminating jobs—rendered small family farms economically unviable. Such widespread change forced many midwesterners to leave their plows in the field for jobs in town. As farm families left the countryside—and local social and economic networks—for hopefully more secure futures in cities, they bypassed small towns dependent on their business, foreshadowing the long-term abandonment and impoverishment of much of the rural Midwest in the late twentieth century.

Economic changes also have shaken one-time thriving regional cities. Midwestern urban centers that prospered in the early and mid-twentieth century by developing industrial and manufacturing bases experienced dramatic economic displacement in the decades following World War II. Facing foreign competition, rapid and expensive technological change, a lack of diversified industries, and a shrinking population of employers and workers (who relocated to Sunbelt states where light industrial and high-technology industries flourished), the industrial Midwest from Cleveland to St. Louis became popularly known as the Rust Belt.

Midwesterners have emigrated for other reasons, including a persistent admiration for the cultural sophistication and educational opportunities "back East." Defending Iowa history and culture in the 1920s, midwestern writer Ruth Suckow lamented that Iowa's intellectuals desperately flocked to New York and other East Coast cities—rather than remaining in the Midwest—to find people, places, and issues worth studying. Iowans had many local colleges, Suckow noted, "And they did very well—if we did not have the money to go East to school." The regional self-perception and national opinion that the Heartland is hopelessly uncultured, unexciting, and uninteresting has made the urge to get away a central characteristic of midwestern identity.

By the early twentieth century, midwesterners were streaming to America's growing cities not only for culture and college but also for lives promising abundant recreational opportunities and modern consumer amenities. As Robert S. and Helen Merrell Lynd observed in *Middletown* (1929) and *Middletown in Transition* (1937), their classic studies of 1920s and 1930s Muncie, Indiana, the growth of a national consumer culture introduced various goods and services—including radios, movies, syndicated periodicals, and automobiles—that dramatically altered the routines and expectations of everyday life. Major cultural change was underway, specifically an intense struggle between traditional life rooted in local identity and the "opposed pride" of resonating and being in step with the big people and the smart set in the outside world of the new and modern.

Exposed to the stark differences between town and country through expanding media and increasingly affordable inventions, many midwesterners sought to escape the monotony and drudgery of small-town and farm life for easier, more comfortable lives. In addition to running water, electricity, and recreation, city life provided greater access to the latest fashions and a tangible closeness to the glamorous lifestyles of the rich and famous. In the end, day trips and vacations by automobile—and in later decades by air travel—relocated many midwesterners permanently to cities and to other parts of the country, heightened mobility having resulted in one-way migration.

This consumer culture contrasted environmental landscapes as well as lifestyles. Inventing a sense of midwestern placelessness based on the generally flat terrain of the Midwest, it commodified mountains, oceans, and exotic sights, provoking an outward search for environmental amenities believed to be more aesthetically pleasing, physically healthy, and conducive to leisure and recreation. "I had lived in a country where the long, flat landscape reached out to the sky across the cornfields," one midwesterner, who migrated to California in the late nineteenth century, remembered. "I wanted to look at the mountains."

Many midwesterners historically have perceived the social world of the Midwest as parochial, competitive, and intolerant, providing another powerful impetus for leaving. Well documented in such early-twentieth-century works of regional literature as Sinclair Lewis's *Main Street* (1920), Sherwood Anderson's *Winesburg, Ohio* (1919), and Edgar Lee Masters's *Spoon River Anthology* (1915), many imagined the midwestern small town as overexerting social control through family and community on individuals who sought the growing personal autonomy, mobility, and privacy of twentieth-century America. As the Lynds noted, while the small town favored and protected mainstream values, typical jobs, and traditional diversions—all of which did not threaten the existing social order—the politically radi-

The Iowa Picnic held each summer throughout most of the twentieth century in Bixby Park, Long Beach, California, c. 1935. Historical Society of Long Beach, P-5710-3.

cal individual, the artist, or "the person with a flair for the unusual" migrated to larger cities, magnets for Americans desiring greater diversity of cultural interests and opportunities for forming selective—instead of established or obligatory—personal relations.

Not only "odd personalities" sought liberation from seemingly repressive moral codes and clearly delineated class and gender lines. In the early twentieth century, many young farm women set out for cities across the country, leaving behind lives that offered too few opportunities and too much isolation, hard labor, and patriarchal values and violence. Leaving home for increased independence and individuality has allowed midwesterners to break away from their pasts and begin anew.

World War II prompted one of the largest population redistributions in American history. Midwesterners were at the heart of this movement, migrating to the Sunbelt—the southern band of states stretching from Florida in the Southeast to California, Arizona, and Nevada in the Southwest—for defense-industry jobs and for military service. Many wartime workers and servicemen and -women who witnessed the opportunities for better lives in Sunbelt states did not return home to the Midwest. In the postwar decades, the communications, tourism, and high-tech industries in booming Sunbelt cities, bolstered by defense spending and consumer demand, offered better-paying jobs. Midwestern agricultural and industrial bases continued to shrink while television glamorized life in cities like San Diego, Miami, and Dallas. Sunbelt destinations offered new versions of work, play, and community in warm climates with plentiful sunshine. In particular, postwar Southern California and the suburban ranch-style house, featuring a year-round patio, a barbeque grill, and a private backyard, embodied the ideals of the middle-class "good life" for many Americans. Midwesterners were leaving behind not only the Rust Belt, but also the "Frostbelt" and the "Snowbelt."

By the 1940s and the 1950s, many elderly midwesterners moved seasonally or permanently to retirement communities in the Sunbelt. Florida, nicknamed the "Afterlife for Ohio," witnessed the relocation of many Ohioans to retirement villages and mobile-home parks in the Tampa, St. Petersburg, and Orlando areas. The expansion of Bob Evans Farms, a popular chain of restaurants serving home-style food in Ohio and surrounding states, paralleled these migrations in later decades, opening the first of many Florida stores in the 1980s. In the postwar Southwest, residents of Indiana, Illinois, Missouri, and Iowa led midwestern migration to such "retirement new towns" as Sun City in the Phoenix area and the Leisure World developments of southern California.

The Midwest-to-Sunbelt movement, however, began well before the mid-twentieth century. As early as the late nineteenth century, midwesterners, many of them retired farmers and merchants seeking semitropical climates for health, comfort, and year-round recreation, migrated to southern California. In the 1870s, a group of Hoosiers formed the Indiana Colony and settled Pasadena, trading the ice storms of Indiana for the southern California sun.

In the following decades, midwesterners continued

to migrate to other southern California communities to escape their cold winters and sweltering summers. By 1930 at least 150,000 native Iowans lived in California. So many of them resided in or regularly visited Long Beach that Californians dubbed this burgeoning city "Iowa by the Sea." Evidence suggests a similar midwestern mania for warmer climates in Arizona and Florida existed during the early decades of the twentieth century.

Despite the revolt against the farm or the small town, midwesterners have tended to look back nostalgically at their past. Hundreds of thousands of midwesterners who migrated to southern California in the early and mid-twentieth century organized and attended popular annual state-society picnics (the Iowa Associations of Los Angeles and Long Beach sought to promote the community spirit shared by those who came from the same state) that featured songs and speeches celebrating such memories of the old home state as the beauty of the pastoral countryside and tall corn, and the self-reliance of the hard-working farmer. While many migrants brought with them old-fashioned morals and distinct political traditions, they were not re-creating their former lives or communities by forming these associations. Instead, this remembered Midwest provided an emotionally comforting version of the world they left behind—a life to which few actually wanted to return—to temper preoccupations wrought by rural-to-urban migration and a critical transformation in popular ideas about work and leisure. As reported in the *Long Beach Independent-Press-Telegram* of August 13, 1961, at a recent picnic in the town, one Iowa native responded to the question of whether or not she would ever move back to the old home state: "Go back? Never. I'm glad to be from Iowa. It's a good state to be from." The Midwest was a good place to be from, but California—offering sunshine, thrills, and jobs—was a better place to live.

Not all midwesterners had the desire—or the socioeconomic means—to leave the region in the first place. Many retired midwesterners have survived on Social Security and modest pensions, unable to relocate to Florida or Arizona. Others have opted to stay for the familiarity of their hometowns and for close proximity to family and friends. And as long commutes, pollution, rising housing costs, crowding, and social anonymity have increasingly endangered Sunbelt dreams over the last several decades, others have returned for the clean air, affordability, accessibility, and face-to-face community of the small towns and cities of the Midwest.

Midwesterners who have stayed behind have faced the problems wrought by decades of out-migration. The exodus of young people, especially those with college and advanced degrees, has created a brain drain of the cutting-edge knowledge, leadership, and creativity vital to economic development. The emigration of younger generations, coupled with the departure of retirees, has undercut tax bases and public services, weakened political representation and power, reduced the number of Main Street and other local businesses, and eroded community morale.

"When I got out of the service," one midwesterner recalled of his return from World War II, "people said 'What the hell you come back here for?'" Today, younger generations of midwesterners have heeded this advice, and continue to seek out more varied, comfortable lifestyles in hip, high-tech East and West Coast cities: Boston; New York; Washington, D.C.; Seattle; the San Francisco Bay area; Los Angeles; and such Sunbelt cities as Atlanta and Austin. Like many before them, these midwesterners-on-the-move cite weather, job opportunities, casual manners, social freedom, and a culture of risk-taking as attractive features unavailable in the Midwest.

In recent years, government officials and business leaders have proposed a variety of programs aimed in part at stemming regional out-migration. A good example is Michigan Governor Jennifer Granholm's "Cool Cities'" initiative (2003), which was designed to revitalize downtown areas in order to attract new businesses and residents as well as encourage entertainment and cultural opportunities.

Sources and Further Reading: Carl Abbott, *The Metropolitan Frontier: Growth and Politics in the Sunbelt Cities* (1993); Carl Abbott, *The New Urban America: Cities in the Modern West* (1981); Harry Carr, *Los Angeles: City of Dreams* (1935); Andrew R. L. Cayton and Susan E. Gray, *The American Midwest: Essays on Regional History* (2001); Richard O. Davies, *Main Street Blues: The Decline of Small-Town America* (1998); Richard O. Davies, Joseph A. Amato, and David R. Pichaske, eds., *A Place Called Home: Writings on the Midwestern Small Town* (2003); Robert V. Hine and John Mack Faragher, *The American West: A New Interpretive History* (2000); Robert S. Lynd and Helen Merrell Lynd, *Middletown: A Study in Modern American Culture* (1929); Robert S. Lynd and Helen Merrell Lynd, *Middletown in Transition: A Study in Cultural Transition: A Study in Cultural Conflicts* (1937); James H. Madison, ed., *Heartland: Comparative Histories of the Midwestern States* (1988); Randall M. Miller and George E. Pozzetta, eds., *Shades of the Sunbelt: Essays on Ethnicity, Race, and the Urban South* (1988); Denise S. Spooner, "A New Perspective on the Dream: Midwestern Images of Southern California in the Post–World War II Decades," *California History* 76 (Spring 1997); Ruth Suckow, "Iowa," *American Mercury* 9 (Sept. 1926); Kenneth J. Winkle, *The Politics of Community: Migration and Politics in Antebellum Ohio* (1988).

Drew T. Meyers
University of Michigan

Table 3. Census Demographics—Ancestries in the Midwest in Terms of Absolute Numbers and Percentages of Total Populations, according to the Census 2000

The Midwest as a Whole:

Census Ancestry Group	Number	Number	Census Ancestry Group	Number	Percentage
Arab	289612	.42	Lithuanian	185287	.27
Armenian	36210	.05	Norwegian	2231168	3.2
Austrian	175148	.25	Polish	3392525	4.9
Brazilian	10783	.02	Romanian	99691	.14
Canadian	115145	.17	Russian	446933	.65
Croatian	163491	.24	Scotch-Irish	813857	1.2
Czech	625683	.91	Scottish	1006460	1.5
Danish	477406	.69	Serbian	67953	.10
Dutch	1640367	2.4	Subsaharan African	319564	.5
English	5409663	7.9	Swedish	1592709	2.3
Finnish	296092	.43	Swiss	315961	.5
French	2030113	3.	Turkish	15559	.02
German	17115507	24.9	Ukrainian	188167	.27
Greek	261752	.38	USA	4273361	6.2
Hungarian	447384	.65	Welsh	415203	.60
Iranian	28486	.04	West Indies	69132	.10
Irish	7587767	11.0	Other Ancestries	11719819	17.0
Italian	2628533	3.8	TOTAL	68868198	100.00

Illinois

Census Ancestry Group	Number	Percentage	Census Ancestry Group	Number	Percentage
Arab	52798	.4	Lithuanian	87294	.7
Armenian	7958	.1	Norwegian	178923	1.4
Austrian	44937	.4	Polish	932996	7.5
Brazilian	3093	.0	Romanian	24308	.2
Canadian	15332	.1	Russian	121397	1.0
Croatian	43613	.4	Scotch-Irish	126963	1.0
Czech	123708	1.0	Scottish	150255	1.2
Danish	59632	.5	Serbian	17893	.1
Dutch	195847	1.6	Subsaharan African	73194	.6
English	831820	6.7	Swedish	303044	2.4
Finnish	19108	.2	Swiss	37505	.3
French	267089	2.2	Turkish	4298	.0
German	2440549	19.7	Ukrainian	47623	.4
Greek	95064	.8	USA	569102	4.6
Hungarian	55971	.5	Welsh	51769	.4
Iranian	8184	.1	West Indies	27286	.2
Irish	1511569	12.2	*Other Ancestries*	*3601078*	29.0
Italian	744274	6.0	TOTAL	13248253	

Indiana

Census Ancestry Group	Number	Percentage	Census Ancestry Group	Number	Percentage
Arab	11680	.2	Brazilian	967	.0
Armenian	1424	.0	Canadian	7840	.1
Austrian	8555	.1	Croatian	12380	.2

Table 3. Continued

Indiana (Continued)

Census Ancestry Group	Number	Percentage	Census Ancestry Group	Number	Percentage
Czech	12299	.2	Romanian	7606	.1
Danish	12244	.2	Russian	19007	.3
Dutch	134700	2.2	Scotch-Irish	79932	1.3
English	540079	8.9	Scottish	100264	1.6
Finnish	4952	.1	Serbian	9238	.2
French	148544	2.4	Subsaharan African	22104	.4
German	1377902	22.7	Swedish	58175	1.0
Greek	18711	.3	Swiss	35567	.6
Hungarian	35715	.6	Turkish	1208	.0
Iranian	1476	.0	Ukrainian	8118	.1
Irish	655530	10.8	USA	730331	12.0
Italian	141486	2.3	Welsh	36392	.6
Lithuanian	10051	.2	West Indies	3632	.1
Norwegian	34174	.6	*Other Ancestries*	*962637*	15.8
Polish	183989	3.0	TOTAL	5589916	

Iowa

Census Ancestry Group	Number	Percentage	Census Ancestry Group	Number	Percentage
Arab	4432	.2	Lithuanian	2572	.08
Armenian	294	.0	Norwegian	166667	5.38
Austrian	4026	.1	Polish	32704	1.06
Brazilian	271	.01	Romanian	965	.03
Canadian	2810	.09	Russian	7685	.25
Croatian	3432	.11	Scotch-Irish	41407	1.34
Czech	51508	1.67.	Scottish	43402	1.4
Danish	66954	2.16	Serbian	889	.03
Dutch	134076	4.33	Subsaharan African	6991	.23
English	277487	8.96	Swedish	95337	3.08
Finnish	2413	.08	Swiss	16300	.53
French	75501	2.44	Turkish	411	.01
German	1046153	33.79	Ukrainian	2021	.07
Greek	5754	.19	USA	196807	6.36
Hungarian	3366	.11	Welsh	22841	.74
Iranian	709	.02	West Indies	941	.03
Irish	395506	12.77	*Other Ancestries*	*251575*	8.12
Italian	49449	1.6	TOTAL	3096503	

Kansas

Census Ancestry Group	Number (2000)	Percentage (2000)	Census Ancestry Group	Number (2000)	Percentage (2000)
Arab	6785	.25	Canadian	3295	.12
Armenian	488	.02	Croatian	6312	.24
Austrian	5815	.22	Czech	18021	.67
Brazilian	337	.01	Danish	15145	.57

Table 3. Continued

Kansas (Continued)

Census Ancestry Group	Number	Percentage	Census Ancestry Group	Number	Percentage
Dutch	61178	2.28	Russian	16903	.63
English	289938	10.82	Scotch-Irish	51879	1.94
Finnish	1933	.07	Scottish	50339	1.9
French	82501	3.08	Serbian	585	.02
German	695442	25.95	Subsaharan African	9205	.34
Greek	4145	.16	Swedish	64308	2.4
Hungarian	3903	.15	Swiss	14018	.52
Iranian	2004	.08	Turkish	380	.01
Irish	309181	11.54	Ukrainian	2577	.1
Italian	50729	1.9	USA	237358	8.86
Lithuanian	2073	.08	Welsh	21882	.82
Norwegian	29773	1.11	West Indies	1796	.07
Polish	34695	1.3	*Other Ancestries*	*507298*	18.9
Romanian	911	.03	TOTAL	2679577	

Michigan

Census Ancestry Group	Number	Percentage	Census Ancestry Group	Number	Percentage
Arab	116331	1.07	Lithuanian	30977	.29
Armenian	15746	.15	Norwegian	85753	.79
Austrian	23605	.22	Polish	854844	7.87
Brazilian	2488	.02	Romanian	26857	.25
Canadian	46824	.43	Russian	71015	.65
Croatian	19407	.18	Scotch-Irish	130282	1.2
Czech	40754	.38	Scottish	224803	2.07
Danish	44267	.41	Serbian	8709	.08
Dutch	480774	4.43	Subsaharan African	51435	.47
English	988625	9.1	Swedish	161301	1.49
Finnish	101351	.93	Swiss	24700	.28
French	489240	4.5	Turkish	2261	.02
German	2028210	18.68	Ukrainian	46350	.43
Greek	44214	.41	USA	517701	4.77
Hungarian	98036	.9	Welsh	50609	.47
Iranian	4673	.04	West Indies	11135	.1
Irish	1067474	9.83	*Other Ancestries*	*1978584*	18.22
Italian	450952	4.15	TOTAL	10859658	

Minnesota

Census Ancestry Group	Number	Percentage	Census Ancestry Group	Number	Percentage
Arab	13923	.23	Czech	85056	1.38
Armenian	1152	.02	Danish	88924	1.44
Austrian	17483	.28	Dutch	99944	1.62
Brazilian	652	.01	English	309802	5.01
Canadian	6926	.11	Finnish	99388	1.61
Croatian	8460	.14	French	202728	3.28

Table 3. Continued

Minnesota (Continued)

Census Ancestry Group	Number	Percentage	Census Ancestry Group	Number	Percentage
German	1806650	29.23	Scottish	62152	1.01
Greek	10619	.17	Serbian	4296	.07
Hungarian	12279	.2	Subsaharan African	43628	.71
Iranian	2500	.04	Swedish	486507	7.87
Irish	552172	8.93	Swiss	23140	.37
Italian	111270	1.8	Turkish	1154	.02
Lithuanian	5633	.09	Ukrainian	14356	.23
Norwegian	850742	13.76	USA	142500	2.31
Polish	240405	3.9	Welsh	21677	.35
Romanian	5364	.09	West Indies	3991	.07
Russian	35513	.57	Other Ancestries	522631	8.45
Scotch-Irish	46370	.75	TOTAL	6181742	

Missouri

Census Ancestry Group	Number	Percentage	Census Ancestry Group	Number	Percentage
Arab	12927	.24	Lithuanian	5571	.1
Armenian	1545	.03	Norwegian	40887	.76
Austrian	11135	.21	Polish	90448	1.68
Brazilian	603	.01	Romanian	3189	.06
Canadian	6248	.12	Russian	25839	.48
Croatian	8941	.17	Scotch-Irish	92706	1.72
Czech	23856	.44	Scottish	83047	1.54
Danish	18207	.34	Serbian	1685	.03
Dutch	99948	1.86	Subsaharan African	26140	.49
English	528935	9.82	Swedish	55774	1.04
Finnish	3261	.06	Swiss	21909	.41
French	195335	3.63	Turkish	1191	.02
German	1313951	24.39	Ukrainian	6228	.12
Greek	12088	.24	USA	587082	10.9
Hungarian	13694	.25	Welsh	34187	.64
Iranian	2267	.04	West Indies	4658	.09
Irish	711120	13.2	Other Ancestries	1039730	19.3
Italian	176209	3.27	TOTAL	5387527	

Nebraska

Census Ancestry Group	Number	Percentage	Census Ancestry Group	Number	Percentage
Arab	4696	.24	Dutch	38523	1.97
Armenian	330	.02	English	163651	8.36
Austrian	3404	.17	Finnish	1427	.07
Brazilian	177	.01	French	44835	2.29
Canadian	1498	.08	German	661133	33.77
Croatian	2367	.12	Greek	3161	.16
Czech	83462	4.26	Hungarian	2740	.14
Danish	52470	2.68	Iranian	561	.03

Table 3. Continued

Nebraska (Continued)

Census Ancestry Group	Number	Percentage	Census Ancestry Group	Number	Percentage
Irish	229506	11.72	Subsaharan African	5195	.27
Italian	42979	2.2	Swedish	84294	4.31
Lithuanian	3215	.16	Swiss	8596	.44
Norwegian	39536	2.02	Turkish	263	.01
Polish	62475	3.19	Ukrainian	1944	.1
Romanian	885	.05	USA	76910	3.93
Russian	11002	.56	Welsh	10374	.53
Scotch-Irish	24964	1.27	West Indies	753	.04
Scottish	23173	1.18	*Other Ancestries*	*220130*	11.24
Serbian	765	.04	TOTAL	1957736	

North Dakota

Census Ancestry Group	Number	Percentage	Census Ancestry Group	Number	Percentage
Arab	1042	.13	Lithuanian	265	.03
Armenian	177	.02	Norwegian	193158	23.75
Austrian	1138	.14	Polish	17700	2.18
Brazilian	66	.01	Romanian	316	.04
Canadian	1115	.14	Russian	22514	2.77
Croatian	295	.04	Scotch-Irish	6674	.82
Czech	12541	1.54	Scottish	8011	.99
Danish	9188	1.13	Serbian	92	.01
Dutch	9095	1.12	Subsaharan African	1051	.13
English	31560	3.88	Swedish	31966	3.93
Finnish	3474	.43	Swiss	1749	.22
French	25078	3.08	Turkish	110	.01
German	282058	34.67	Ukrainian	3815	.35
Greek	605	.07	USA	15495	1.91
Hungarian	2802	.34	Welsh	1660	.2
Iranian	161	.02	West Indies	237	.03
Irish	49346	6.07	*Other Ancestries*	*50218*	6.17
Italian	5328	.66	TOTAL	813468	

Ohio

Census Ancestry Group	Number	Percentage	Census Ancestry Group	Number	Percentage
Arab	54656	.47	English	1046671	8.95
Armenian	3665	.03	Finnish	18817	.16
Austrian	27017	.23	French	271423	2.32
Brazilian	1457	.01	German	2866565	24.5
Canadian	16619	.14	Greek	50609	.43
Croatian	41812	.36	Hungarian	193951	1.66
Czech	61640	.53	Iranian	3927	.03
Danish	18103	.16	Irish	1445668	12.36
Dutch	200850	1.72	Italian	675749	5.78

Table 3. Continued

Ohio (Continued)

Census Ancestry Group	Number	Percentage	Census Ancestry Group	Number	Percentage
Lithuanian	23970	.21	Swedish	72369	.62
Norwegian	41537	.36	Swiss	70302	.6
Polish	433016	3.7	Turkish	3159	.03
Romanian	26017	.22	Ukrainian	47228	.4
Russian	73863	.63	USA	981611	8.39
Scotch-Irish	165741	1.42	Welsh	132041	1.13
Scottish	197437	1.69	West Indies	11375	.1
Serbian	16859	.14	*Other Ancestries*	*1873298*	16.01
Subsaharan African	65250	.59	TOTAL	11699513	

South Dakota

Census Ancestry Group	Number	Percentage	Census Ancestry Group	Number	Percentage
Arab	1407	.16	Lithuanian	287	.03
Armenian	72	.01	Norwegian	115292	13.14
Austrian	1277	.14	Polish	11527	1.3
Brazilian	93	.01	Romanian	249	.03
Canadian	554	.06	Russian	9372	1.07
Croatian	270	.03	Scotch-Irish	7521	.86
Czech	15618	1.78	Scottish	7898	.9
Danish	20112	2.29	Serbian	117	.01
Dutch	35655	4.07	Subsaharan African	1731	.2
English	53241	6.07	Swedish	29707	3.39
Finnish	3921	.45	Swiss	3085	.35
French	21864	2.49	Turkish	54	.01
German	307309	35.04	Ukrainian	875	.1
Greek	733	.08	USA	29181	3.33
Hungarian	982	.11	Welsh	3587	.41
Iranian	201	.02	West Indies	181	.02
Irish	78379	8.94	*Other Ancestries*	*86740*	9.89
Italian	7541	.86	TOTAL	877136	

Wisconsin

Census Ancestry Group	Number	Percentage	Census Ancestry Group	Number	Percentage
Arab	8935	.14	French	205975	3.18
Armenian	3359	.05	German	2289585	35.35
Austrian	26756	.41	Greek	15449	.24
Brazilian	579	.01	Hungarian	23945	.37
Canadian	6084	.1	Iranian	1823	.03
Croatian	16202	.25	Irish	582316	8.99
Czech	97220	1.5	Italian	172567	2.66
Danish	72160	1.11	Lithuanian	13379	.21
Dutch	149777	2.31	Norwegian	454726	7.02
English	347854	5.37	Polish	497726	7.68
Finnish	36047	.56	Romanian	3024	.05

Table 3. Continued

Wisconsin (Continued)

Census Ancestry Group	Number	Percentage	Census Ancestry Group	Number	Percentage
Russian	32823	.51	Turkish	1070	.02
Scotch-Irish	39368	.61	Ukrainian	8032	.12
Scottish	55679	.86	USA	189283	2.92
Serbian	6825	.11	Welsh	28184	.44
Subsaharan African	13640	.21	West Indies	3147	.05
Swedish	149977	2.32	*Other Ancestries*	*625900*	9.66
Swiss	59090	.91	TOTAL	6477169	

Source: Census 2000. QT-P13. Ancestry: 2000. Data Set: Census 2000 Summary File 3 (SF 3)—Sample Data.

Notes: The Ancestries listed are selected from Census categories presented in the cited work. "Other Ancestries" is a Census designation and not simply a residual category. As there are additional ancestries not listed here, the individual rows will not add up to the total listed. Calculations are taken out of total ancestries rather than total population as multiple ancestries can be reported. State-level data is used.

Society and Culture

Language

SECTION EDITOR
Dennis R. Preston

Section Contents

Overview

It may surprise readers of this encyclopedia to discover that, just as the Midwest is remarkably varied in its physical and cultural environments, it is and has been home also to an enormous variety of languages and to considerable variation in its English. That last point may seem most peculiar because midwesterners themselves, as well as those who caricature them, tend to think that they are normal, ordinary, white-bread Americans, but that is no truer of their language than the suggestion that the Midwest is a relatively flat plain of small towns and villages. This section treats, therefore, not only the variety of languages of the Midwest but also how those languages vary internally, including particularly the varieties of English of the region. Because linguistics, the scientific foundation of this section, is a young science, it is impossible to report on every language and every variety of every language in the Midwest, but the studies on which these entries are based were done in midwestern communities and are exemplary, if not exhaustive, studies of midwestern languages and varieties.

The Midwest has an especially rich history of Native American languages, some long vanished, some with a fairly robust and continuing existence, some displaced outside the area but still alive, and some experiencing remarkable revivals. "Native American Languages" provides an overview of the Native American groups that once inhabited the region and is followed by three essays on its major linguistic families—Algonquian, Iroquoian, and Siouan—and by shorter sketches of Miami, Ojibwe, and Winnebago.

The first Europeans to enter the region that became the Midwest were French, and, although they left behind a rich heritage of place-names (see "Geographic Names"), the language was short-lived in the area, and the only remaining cultural enclaves of former French speakers celebrate their heritage with foods and holidays but not with the language (see "French").

After the French, English speakers came from nearly all the eastern colonies with the exception of those of the far South. Settlers from western New England and upstate New York planted the seeds of what was to become the northern variety of English in the Midwest, and settlers from the middle colonies formed the eventual midland variety. Finally, English-speaking settlers from the Upland South gave the lower Midwest its distinctly southern speech characteristics.

Figure 1 shows that the major boundary of northern speech reaches just into the northeastern corner of Ohio. Later work shows that this speech region extends throughout northern Indiana and Illinois, Michigan, Wisconsin, Minnesota, northern Iowa, and the Dakotas. This speech region of the Midwest is primarily the result of immigrants from areas 1–6 in figure 1. Settlers from areas 7–11 are responsible for the dialect area of the Midwest that has come to be known

Foreign newsstand. Farm Security Administration–Office of War Information Photograph Collection, Library of Congress, Prints and Photographs Division, LC-USF346-001359-Q-C DLC.

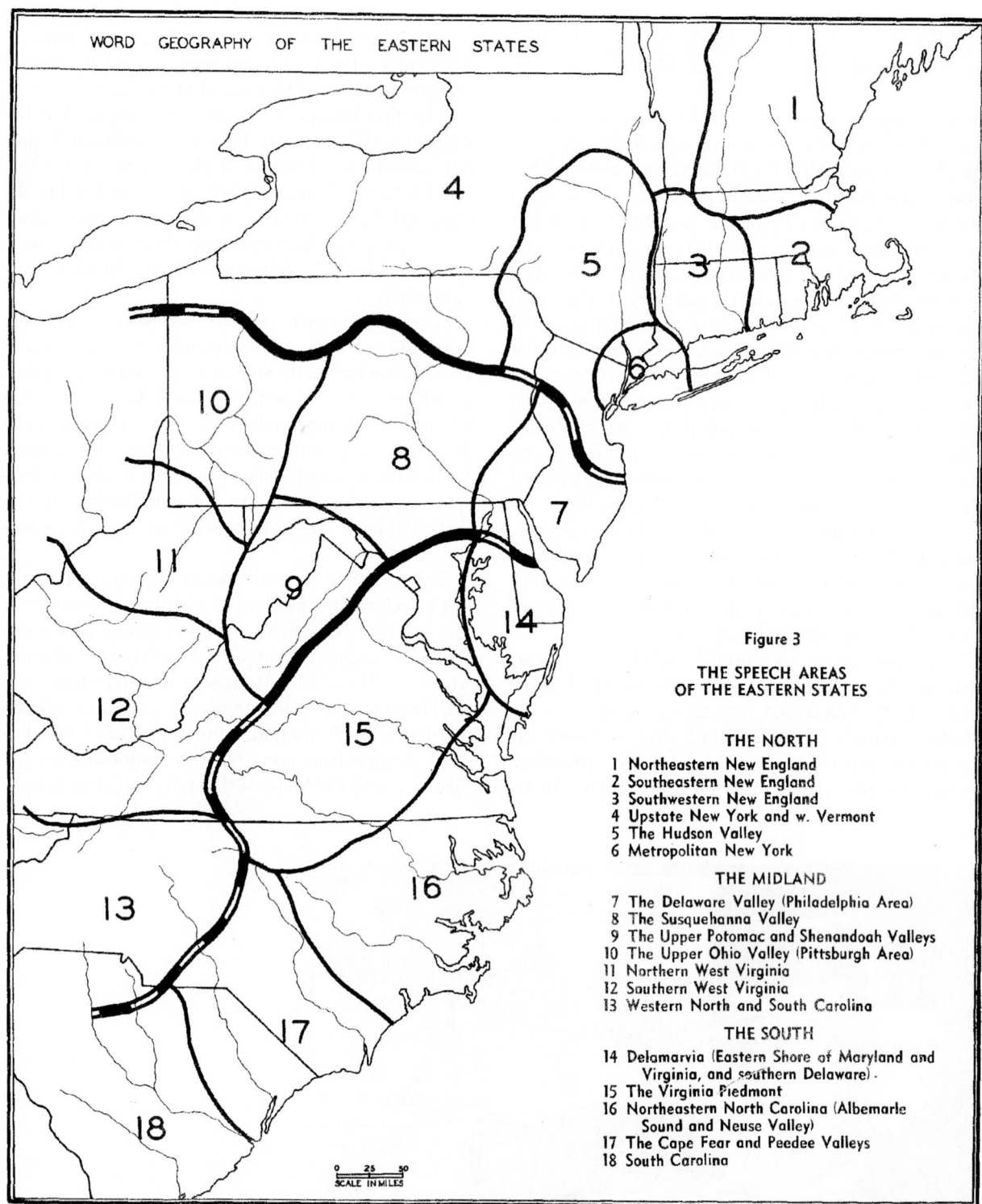

WORD GEOGRAPHY OF THE EASTERN STATES

Figure 3

**THE SPEECH AREAS
OF THE EASTERN STATES**

THE NORTH

1 Northeastern New England
2 Southeastern New England
3 Southwestern New England
4 Upstate New York and w. Vermont
5 The Hudson Valley
6 Metropolitan New York

THE MIDLAND

7 The Delaware Valley (Philadelphia Area)
8 The Susquehanna Valley
9 The Upper Potomac and Shenandoah Valleys
10 The Upper Ohio Valley (Pittsburgh Area)
11 Northern West Virginia
12 Southern West Virginia
13 Western North and South Carolina

THE SOUTH

14 Delamarvia (Eastern Shore of Maryland and
    Virginia, and southern Delaware)
15 The Virginia Piedmont
16 Northeastern North Carolina (Albemarle
    Sound and Neuse Valley)
17 The Cape Fear and Peedee Valleys
18 South Carolina

0   25   50
SCALE IN MILES

Figure 1. The eighteen dialect areas of the East Coast, showing the major tripartite division into North, Midland, and South. *Source:* Hans Kurath, *A Word Geography of the Eastern United States* (1949) figure 3, np.

as the North Midland, and settlers from areas 12 and 13 and some other southern areas eventually formed the speech area of the Midwest known as the South Midland.

Figure 2 is an even more detailed view of the American dialects of the eastern United States. A and B indicate the northern area; C is roughly the North Midland, and D is the South Midland, although parts of southeastern Ohio, southern Indiana, southern Illinois, and southeastern Missouri are south of D, indicating even greater southern influence in the speech there. A survey of the linguistic features of these subregions of the Midwest is provided in the next three entries in this section: "Pronunciation of English," "Dialect Vocabulary," and "Dialect Grammar." Other Americans have left their mark on the English of the

Midwest, but they are discussed after some earlier-arriving non-English-speaking immigrant groups.

In the nineteenth century, a large number of immigrants to the Midwest included farm and city dwellers from Scandinavian and German-speaking countries. Their languages have survived only in religious enclaves (see "Religious German"), but they were once widespread with their own schools, newspapers, and home-language churches. In spite of their languages' disappearance, they have had some influences on the pronunciation, vocabulary, and even the grammar of local English. Residents of such cities as Milwaukee still can be "by" somebody's house (rather than "at" it) as a result of the German preposition *bei*. The doubtless Scandinavian-influenced substitution of *d* and *t* for English *th* sounds is celebrated in the Upper Peninsula

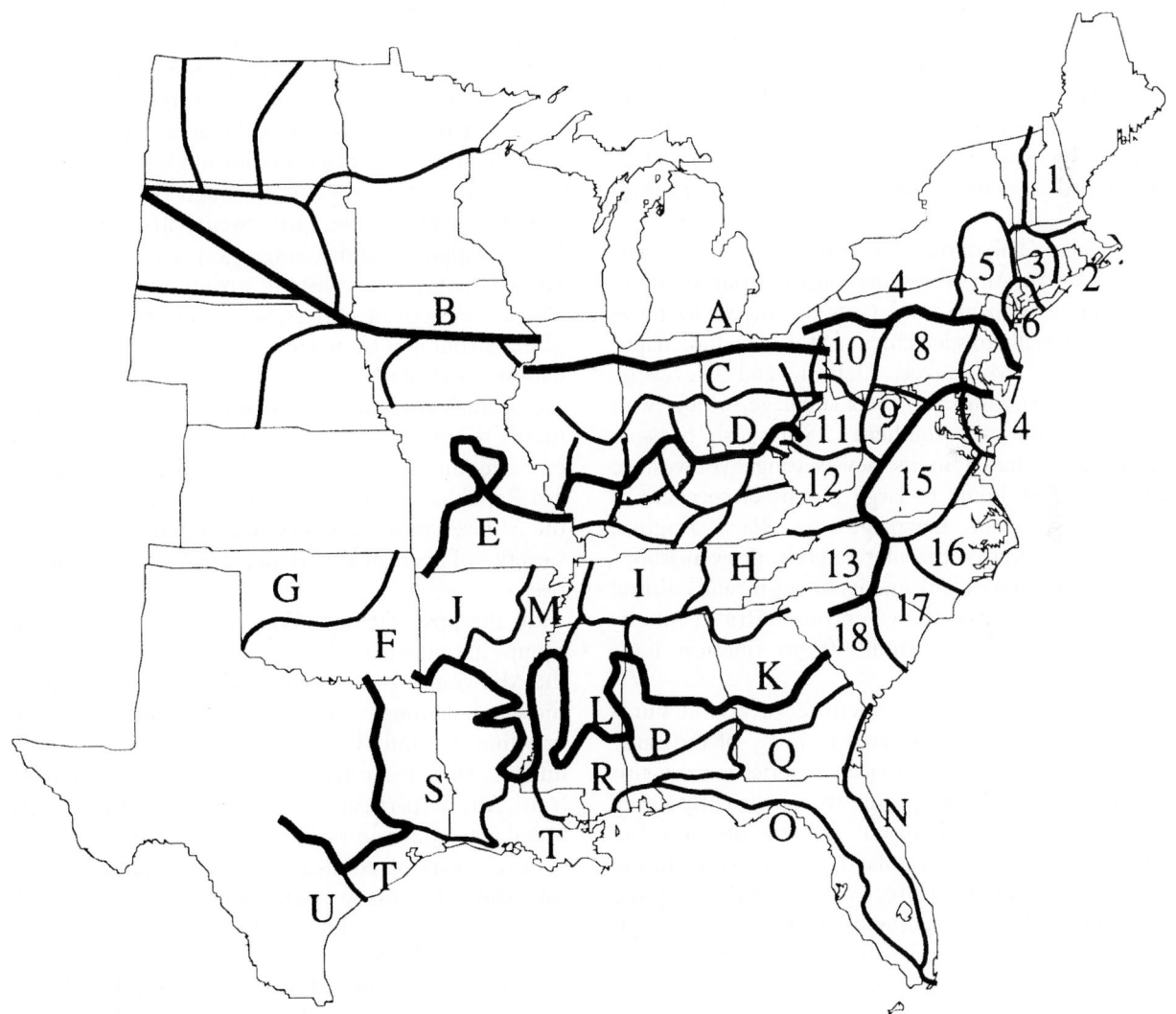

Figure 2. The dialects of the eastern United States. *Source:* Donald M. Lance and Stuart Kingsbury, eds., "Variation in American English," in *American Pronunciation* (12th ed., 1994) 352.

of Michigan on bumper stickers that invite one to "Just Say Ya To Da UP, Eh," and the radio entertainer Garrison Keillor has made the Norwegian word *lutefisk* well known far beyond his Minnesota home.

Later in the nineteenth century, many immigrants from Poland to Bulgaria in eastern Europe and from Greece to Portugal in southern Europe came to the Midwest. They often lived in isolated communities (for example, coal towns) or ethnic neighborhoods in larger cities. Like groups of Germans and Scandinavians these communities generally supported schools, various print media, and church services in their home languages. Most of these languages have died out in the third generation. Some eastern European languages have had a recent small revival as a result of a new wave of immigrants following the breakup of Soviet-dominated eastern Europe in the 1990s.

These eastern and southern European languages have left their imprint on midwestern English, particularly, perhaps, in words for foods and cooking. Surely many a midwesterner lives within shopping distance of some eastern European neighborhood and will have learned one of the "k" words for sausage (e.g., Polish *kielbasa*, Hungarian *kolbasz*). Even the ubiquitous Italian *pizza* has a midwestern identity in *Chicago deep-dish*.

In the first half of the twentieth century, large numbers of African Americans, particularly from Arkansas, Mississippi, Alabama, and Georgia, began to move north, especially to such cities as St. Louis, Indianapolis, Chicago, Milwaukee, Detroit, and Cleveland. They brought with them their language, which, with its many affinities to southern U.S. English, has survived and mutated in its new setting. Midwestern cities are now home to large groups of speakers of African American Language (or Black English, African American Vernacular English, or even Ebonics, as it has been called), and its linguistic and cultural features are explored in two entries: "African American Vernacular English" and "African American Language."

In the middle of the twentieth century, large numbers of Appalachians migrated to many of the same northern cities in which African Americans were also recent arrivals. This migration was particularly heavy into southeastern Michigan due to the wartime airplane- and vehicle-manufacturing industries in the 1940s, and it continued after World War II during the boom of the American automobile industry. Although second-generation Appalachian Michiganders have lost their south midland speech characteristics, at one time their speech patterns were very noticeable and led to prejudice against them. Their presence in the area is remembered by the unofficial name of the northeast section of the Michigan city of Ypsilanti—

Ypsitucky. Appalachian southerners have established outposts in such other industrial areas as Akron, Ohio, and their trek to the northern Midwest was noted in Bobby Bare's country hit of 1963 entitled "Detroit City," which contained the plaintive words

> Some folks think I'm big in Detroit City
> But by day I make the cars, and by night I make the
> bars
> Dreamin' of them cotton fields at home.
> I want to go home, I want to go home,
> Oh, how I want to go home.

Racial identity and social isolation contributed greatly to the African American immigrants' retaining their older speech patterns, while the Appalachian immigrants were more quickly integrated, and soon adopted the new Michigan dialect.

In the 1960s, particularly as a result of federally funded resettlement programs, large numbers of Mexican Americans, primarily Texas residents, began to settle in the Midwest. Today they can be found in cities and towns throughout the area, and there is a lively Spanish presence on radio and television and in print media in the region. Although bilingual education programs in the early twenty-first century no longer support Spanish-language preservation in the United States, the constant stream of Mexican and Mexican American settlers, some not speakers of English, encourages language survival. Enriching the situation, particularly in such larger cities as Chicago, are Spanish-speaking groups who formerly came primarily to urban northeastern or Florida locations (for example, immigrants from Puerto Rico, the Dominican Republic, and Cuba). Spanish-language groups in the Midwest and the interesting contact among their varieties of Spanish are discussed in three separate entries.

In the post–Vietnam War era a number of Asian groups have come to the United States, and, although the Midwest does not equal California in the size of those populations, some groups, including the Hmong in Minnesota and Wisconsin, have had a considerable impact. Most recently, refugee children and families from Africa, particularly the Horn of Africa, have found new homes in various parts of the Midwest.

After years of political turmoil in Haiti, it is not surprising that many speakers of pidgin and creole languages, one of which is Haitian French, can be found in the Midwest; other minor languages, some almost gone from their homelands, are still spoken in parts of the Midwest, and they are included in the entries in this section of the encyclopedia. The Midwest is also home to numerous users of American Sign Language (ASL), a language of the deaf.

Because English clearly dominates the language scene of the Midwest, several entries provide greater detail about the dialect subdivisions of the area briefly outlined above. English in the Midwest is, however, not differentiated solely by dialect regions and ethnic groups; its social breadth is much wider. "Language and Society" discusses the linguistic differences reflected in gender, social class, profession, ethnicity, and the rural/urban division. "Conversational Narratives" deals with midwestern modes of storytelling; "Slang," with slang, metaphor, and turns of phrase in midwestern English; and "Geographic Names," with the patterns of personal, geographic, and institutional naming.

One wonders, in the face of this richness of variety, why the English of the Midwest is so unremarkable in the American linguistic landscape. With perhaps the recent exception of putative Minnesota talk in the movie *Fargo*, midwestern English is not often caricatured in popular culture, and its speakers are thought to be ordinary users of the language. Some of the dominant myths about midwestern English appear to be that the Midwest is the place where speakers have no dialect; that it is the home base for national-news-announcer English, and that it is the locus of a kind of American English standard variety—General American.

All these myths are demonstrably untrue. First, if the word *dialect* refers to regionally (and sometimes socially) differentiated varieties of a language, then everyone speaks a dialect; there are no dialect-free areas. This is how linguists use the word. To them, dialect suggests neither a standard nor a nonstandard variety, although in popular use it is often confused with the notion of nonstandard language. Second, there is no academy of news-announcer English based in the Midwest; at the beginning of the twenty-first century the three major television network announcers were Dan Rather (CBS), a Texan; Peter Jennings (ABC), a Canadian; and Tom Brokaw (NBC), a South Dakotan, the last being the only one with midwestern speech credentials. Third, "Standard English" in America appears to be a matter of status and education: higher-status, better-educated speakers (in every region) speak a local English that is standard simply by virtue of class position. Listen, for example, to congressional proceedings on C-Span to hear the many regional varieties of U.S. Standard English.

The myths of midwestern English are perhaps strongly rooted in an even more overarching myth—the "Heartland" myth, one that encompasses ethnicity, religion, politics, the general cultural climate, and more. Midwesterners are thought to be strong, brave, polite, hard-working, self-effacing, self-sufficient, generous, friendly, Protestant, white, normal, average,

and boring. They are the mythical creatures who populated such 1950s popular culture vehicles as "Leave It to Beaver." It makes no difference that the Heartland myth is made up of stereotypes that often widely diverge from reality; it is a strong one, and its relationship to a standard (but not prissy), unremarkable, ordinary, dialect-free English is a straightforward one. When asked about good English in America, a Michigan respondent said

[I]f you have such a thing as called standard English other than textbook English, it would probably be the language that you're hearing right now. As you listen to the Midwestern.

Asked to draw maps of where language differences exist in the United States, respondents provide representations like figure 3. The Michigander who drew this map believes that an area very much like the Midwest of this encyclopedia is the home of "midwestern english (normal)," although he had some doubts about Indiana. Many such respondent hand-drawn maps identify the Midwest as the home of "no accent" and "correct," "average," and "normal" English. The people who entered such comments on their maps are from all over the United States, not just the Midwest, as figure 4 shows, in which a South Carolinian respondent notes that the Midwest "doesn't have [an] accent."

When asked directly about language status (i.e., "correctness") Michiganders rated the fifty states, New York City, and Washington, D.C., as shown in figure 5 (where 1 = "least correct" and 10 = "most correct"). Pennsylvania, Connecticut, Colorado, and Washington are the only non-midwestern states that scored in the 7.00–7.99 range. Michiganders obviously center correctness on the Midwest, giving themselves the only mean score rating that fell in the 8.00–8.99 range, and giving four other midwestern states 7.00–7.99 ratings.

From a linguistic point of view, Standard English in America is not regionally based. The better-educated, higher-status people in every area are speakers of Standard English, although all have local variants of pronunciation, vocabulary, and even grammar. It is mostly upper midwesterners who pronounce *bag* so that it sounds like *beg* (or even *big*), midwesterners who say "My shoes need shined" and fail to distinguish between the vowels of *caught* and *cot*, and southern midwesterners who say "you all" (not southern "y'all"). But these local idiosyncrasies do not prevent them from being speakers of Standard English any more than the New Yorkers' propensity to "stand on line" (not "in line") or the New Englanders' often-noted vowels and *r*-loss in the much caricatured "Pahk the cah in Hahvahd Yahd."

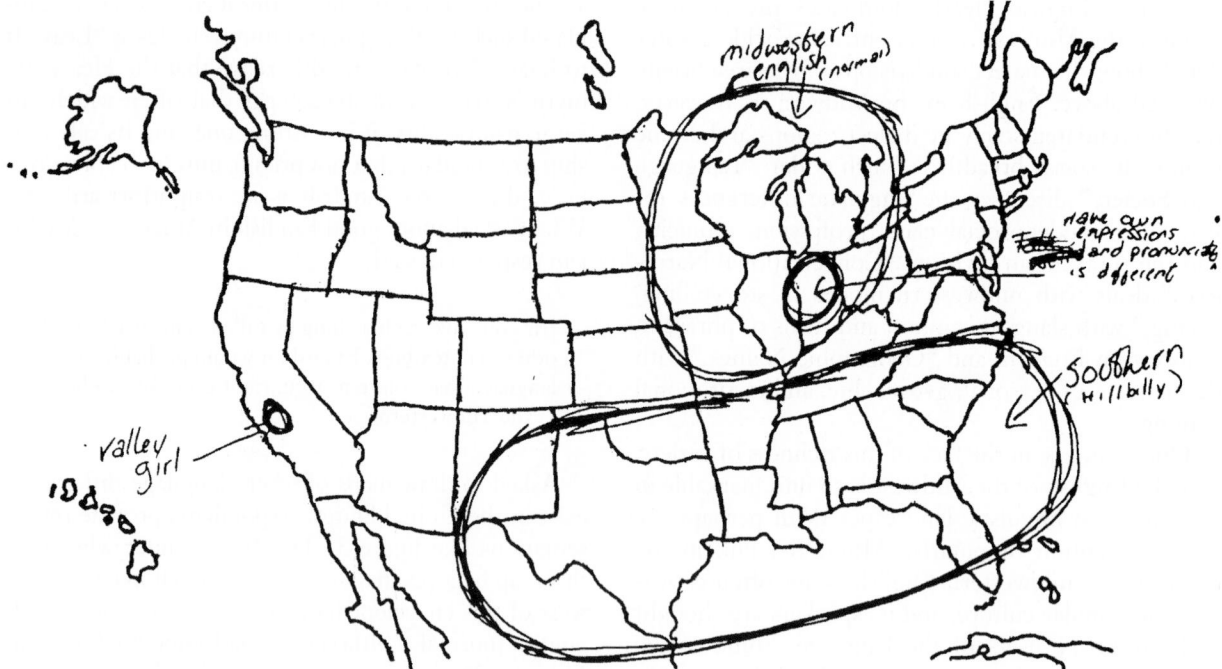

Figure 3. A Michigander's hand-drawn map of U.S. dialect areas. *Source:* Preston (1996) 307.

Figure 4. A South Carolinian's hand-drawn map of U.S. dialect areas. *Source:* Preston (1996) 310.

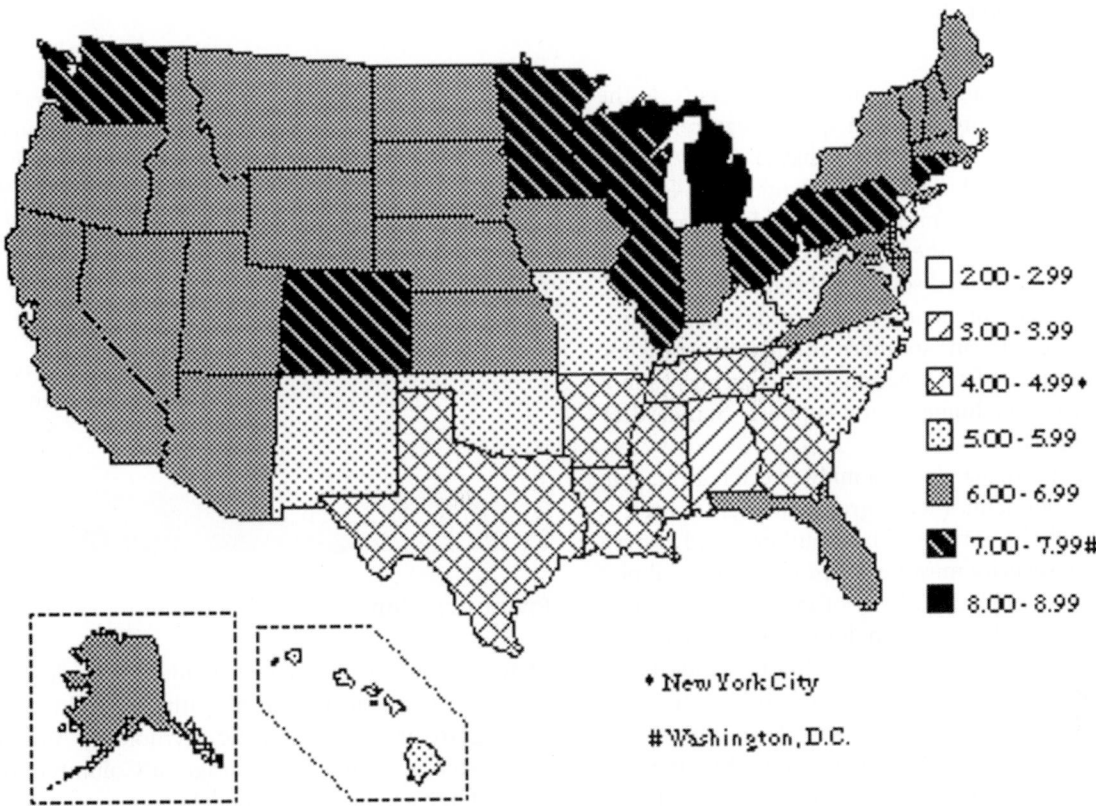

Figure 5. Ratings of "correct English" by 147 respondents from southeastern Michigan (1 = "least correct"; 10 = "most correct"). *Source:* Preston (1996) 312.

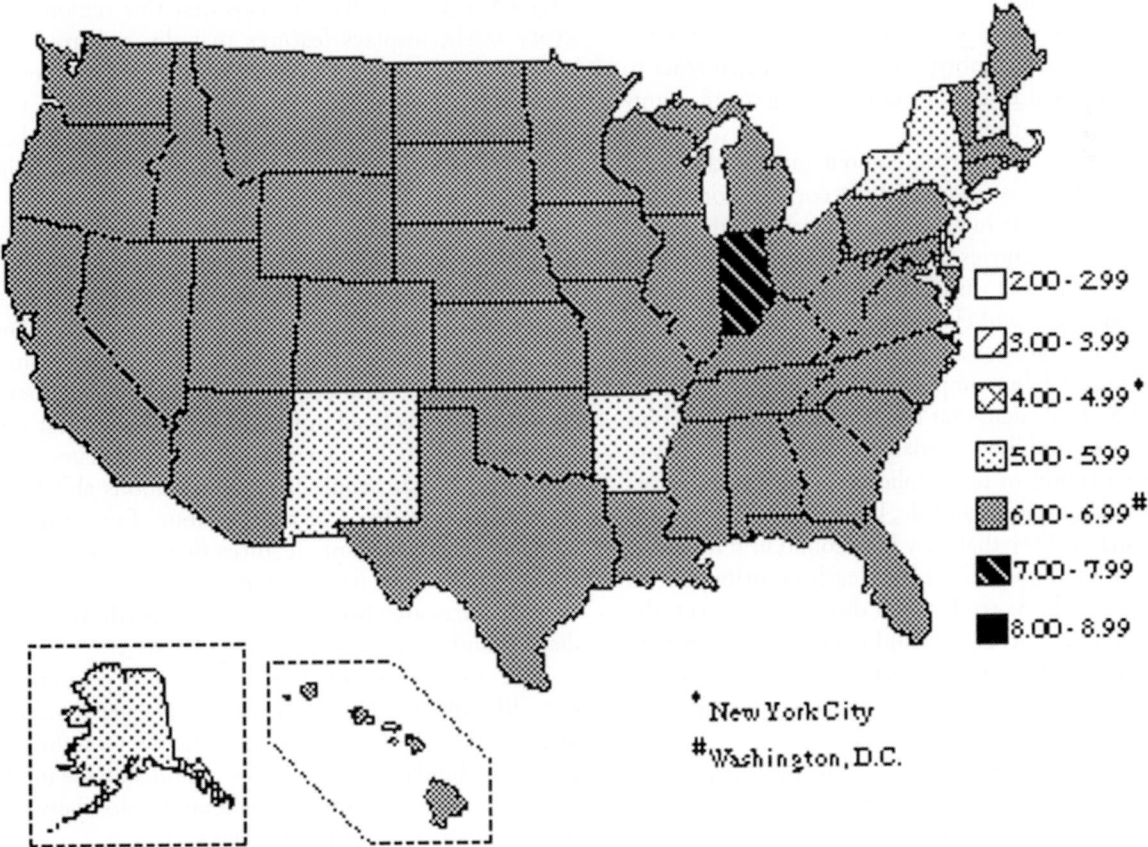

Figure 6. Ratings of "pleasant" English by 123 respondents from southern Indiana (1 = "least pleasant"; 10 = "most pleasant"). *Source:* Preston (1996) 316.

Yet another example of linguistic diversity is the prominence of many southern speech features in the southern edge of the Midwest (that is, areas around and even south of D in figure 2). As figures 3, 4, and 5 suggest, Americans generally do not admire southern English. Even the southerner who outlined the speech areas in figure 4 called southern English "very slow" and "hard to comprehend." This breeds a kind of linguistic insecurity in southern-influenced speakers, who, in the face of such national caricaturing, cannot believe that their home region supports Standard or correct English.

Southern Indiana is such a midwestern region, and, indeed, respondents there agree that their speech is not particularly correct. This southern midwestern linguistic insecurity must be added to the general picture, but these most southern of midwesterners have apparently found a value in local speech that their northern cousins do not share. Although they know that their speech is not correct, it is by far the most *pleasant* of all U.S. varieties. When 123 southern Indiana residents were asked to rate the states for language pleasantness, they provided the results shown in figure 6. This looks very much like the Michigander's notion of language correctness, and it may point to a general fact about two major attitudes to language, both in place in the Midwest: Those who believe their language correct spend their linguistic capital on that; others (including minority speakers, perhaps) react to criticism of their English by emphasizing the pleasantness of their language.

What is most remarkable about most midwestern English is that it is *imagined* to be correct, normal, or standard, and that myth is pervasive throughout the country. As the entries in this encyclopedia show, English is enormously varied throughout the region, not only in ethnicity and class structure and in such other social areas as gender and specialization, which might all be expected, but simply in its geographic distribution. It is clear, then, that the linguistic Midwest joins other features of the Heartland in the American desire to have a center of uncomplicated values and performances, language included. Those who seek such a center may believe that they have found it in the Midwest, and their quest for it has clearly contributed to a powerful myth. As readers will discover, however, the myth, though worth study and contemplation, has no foundation in the uniformity or the *standardness* of English, or in the monolingual character of the region.

Sources and Further Reading: Harold B. Allen, *The Linguistic Atlas of the Upper Midwest*, 3 vols. (1973–1976); Frederic G. Cassidy, ed., *The Dictionary of American Regional English* (1985); Ed Finegan and John Rickford, eds., *Language in the USA* (2004); Tim Frazer, ed., *Heartland English* (1993); Hans Kurath, *A Word Geography of the Eastern United States* (1949); Donald M. Lance, "Variation in American English," in John Samuel Kenyon, *American Pronunciation*, ed. Donald M. Lance and Stuart A. Kingsbury, 12th ed., expanded (1994); Nancy Niedzielski and Dennis R. Preston, *Folk Linguistics* (2000); Dennis R. Preston, "Where the Worst English Is Spoken," in Edgar Schneider, ed., *Focus on the USA* (1996); Edgar Schneider, ed., *Focus on the USA* (1996).

Dennis R. Preston
Michigan State University

Varieties of English

Pronunciation

Many Americans associate "Standard American English" or "General American" with the Midwest. According to national linguistic mythology, American newscasters are trained in Chicago or Columbus, or in Iowa. They are taught to model their pronunciation on that of the American Heartland, rather than on the clearly identifiable regional varieties of the Northeast or the South. Yet a close study of the pronunciation of English in the Midwest reveals that this region, like every other, displays features that diverge from the popular conception of General American pronunciation. Moreover, the very notion of "midwestern English," insofar as it suggests a unified dialect spoken from Ohio to the Dakotas, from Michigan to Missouri, has very little basis in fact.

To begin, there are clear divisions between the pronunciation of most European American midwesterners and that of most African American midwesterners. Some areas of the Midwest have also received many Appalachian immigrants, who in some cases continue to sound more southern than other midwesterners. Anyone who has lived in the Midwest knows that it is not difficult to tell a Clevelander from a Cincinnatian, or to distinguish people from Minneapolis and Indianapolis, on the basis of speech alone. Furthermore, while there are certainly features that are common to the speech of most, if not all, midwesterners, many of these features are also found in other North American dialects and are not specifically midwestern.

The diversity of modern midwestern pronunciation, like many other aspects of midwestern speech, originated with the European settlement of the region. The fundamental phonetic regional divide in the Midwest corresponds to the general division between Inland North and North Midland speech.

The Inland Northern region extends along the Great Lakes from western New York to southeastern

Wisconsin, and farther west to parts of northern Iowa, Minnesota, and the Dakotas. The major Inland North cities are Syracuse, Rochester, Buffalo, Cleveland, Toledo, Detroit, Chicago, Milwaukee, and Minneapolis-St. Paul. Pronunciation in this region bears many similarities to that of southwestern New England (Hartford, Connecticut, and Springfield, Massachusetts).

The North Midland region covers the wider belt of territory between the Inland North and the Ohio River, from central Ohio to central Illinois, and farther west to southern Iowa, northern Missouri, and eastern Nebraska and Kansas. The major North Midland cities are Columbus, Dayton, Cincinnati, Indianapolis, Peoria, Des Moines, Omaha, St. Louis, and Kansas City. North Midland pronunciation is similar in many respects to that of the southern Mid-Atlantic region (extending from southern New Jersey through southeastern Pennsylvania to Maryland and Delaware). The Inland North/North Midland divide is most clearly discernible in the eastern half of the Midwest, where the two streams of settlement remained distinct. Farther west, in parts of Iowa, Minnesota, and the Dakotas, where diverse settlers intermingled and influenced one another, the divide is not sharp, constituting a gradual transition zone rather than a clear boundary.

Political boundaries do not necessarily reflect linguistic boundaries: Rarely does pronunciation change noticeably when we drive across a state line. Areas outside the Midwest, such as western New York, are phonetically midwestern and there are regions within the Midwest that belong to neither the Inland North nor the North Midland speech areas. Examples of the latter are found all around the geographic margins of the Midwest. Eastern Ohio around Youngstown has more in common with the Pittsburgh, Pennsylvania, area than with nearby Cleveland, while southeastern Ohio, around Athens and Marietta, shares more linguistic affinity with the Appalachian South than with the rest of Ohio. Southern-sounding speech can also be heard across much of southern Indiana, Illinois, Missouri, and Kansas, a broad transition zone between midwestern speech and the southern varieties of Kentucky, Arkansas, and Oklahoma called the South Midland. Another transition zone covers the western parts of Kansas, Nebraska, and the Dakotas: There is no clear boundary between the pronunciation of these states and the western speech of Montana, Wyoming, and Colorado or, indeed, of Washington, Oregon, and California.

Returning to the pronunciation of the majority of European American midwesterners, the features that uniquely and consistently characterize the Midwest are relatively few. On the one hand, midwesterners pronounce their r's in *star* and *start*, voice their inter-vocalic t's (so that *bitter* sounds like *bidder*), and make no difference between the vowels of *hand* and *command*, or *gas* and *pass*. These features make them sound North American, and therefore different from speakers of Standard Southern British English, but they do not help to distinguish the Midwest from most other parts of North America: The same features could be identified with Canada or the West. A further similarity with Canadian and western speech is that most midwesterners distinguish only a minimal set of vowels before *r*. Unlike in most of the eastern United States or England, *Mary, merry,* and *marry* are all homonyms in the Midwest, having the vowel of *met* rather than the vowels of *mate, met,* and *mat,* respectively. *Forest* and *forced,* and *hurry* and *her,* also contain the same vowel sounds. On the other hand, most midwesterners, unlike most southerners, do distinguish short *i* and short *e* before nasal consonants: *pin* and *pen,* and *him* and *hem,* have different vowels, though this feature, too, is shared with all North American varieties outside the South. Most midwesterners also distinguish all vowels before *l,* so that *fool* and *full, feel* and *fill,* and *fail* and *fell* are all different words.

Nevertheless, midwesterners do not agree on many other aspects of pronunciation. Among the general public, discussions of pronunciation differences usually focus on individual words that people notice when listening to speakers from other towns. Some of these are aligned with the Inland North–North Midland division. Particularly well known are variables such as whether you pronounce *greasy* to rhyme with *easy* or *fleecy,* whether you rhyme *route* with *boot* or *bout;* whether you pronounce an *r*-sound in *wash* and *Washington;* and whether *room, roof,* and *root* have the vowel of *boot* or *book.* These items can tell us a great deal about settlement history and undoubtedly play some role in our ability to determine where people come from on the basis of the way they talk. However, the primary factor in this ability comes from a more systematic level of language that involves phonetic shifts in the pronunciation of whole classes of words. These, in turn, are related to fundamental differences in the number of contrasts maintained in the sound system of each dialect.

At this level, the most important division in midwestern speech concerns whether or not you make a distinction between a relatively bright-sounding short-*o* of words such as *cot, stock, Don, sod,* and *collar,* and a longer, darker vowel (with the lips noticeably rounded) in words like *caught, stalk, dawn, sawed,* and *caller.* In the Inland North, this distinction is generally maintained, as in most of the eastern and southern United States and most of England. In the North and South Midland it is less stable. In many Midland communities it is in fact disappearing, though its status varies from one city to another. In general, older midlanders maintain a clear distinction between *cot* and *caught*, while many younger midlanders have lost it, like people in Canada, the West, western Pennsylvania, and eastern New England. In areas where midlanders do maintain the distinction, they often disagree with Northerners on which words have the *cot*-vowel, and which the *caught*-vowel. The most consistent difference is that for midlanders the word *on* rhymes with *dawn*, while for northerners it rhymes with *Don*. Similar but less geographically consistent variation occurs in other words that feature these sounds: How do you say *launch*, *beyond*, *honk*, *fog*, *hog*, *log*, *doll*, *watch*, and *water*?

The preservation of the *cot-caught* distinction in Inland North speech underlies a remarkable development called the Northern Cities Vowel Shift. This is a chain shift: a coordinated series of changes in the pronunciation of two or more vowels, so that the distinctions between the vowels are maintained, but all of the vowels simultaneously change their quality. The quality of a vowel is mostly determined by the position of the tongue during its articulation. The space available to the tongue is a continuum, ranging from the high-front region of the mouth (used for vowels like the long-*ee* of *seed*), to the low-central region (the short-*o* of *sod*), to the high-back region (the long-*u* of *pool*). Within the limits of this space, vowels can be articulated in relatively higher, lower, farther front, or farther back positions; their exact place of articulation is one of the principal ways in which English dialects differ. The Northern Cities Vowel Shift is a systematic rotation of six vowels that makes the speech of cities like Buffalo, Cleveland, Detroit, and Chicago sound very different from that of cities farther south. The vowels involved are: the short-*a* of words like *stack*, pronounced higher in these Inland North cities than in the rest of the Midwest, something like *stay-ack*; the short-*o* of words like *stock*, which is farther front, sounding to many non-Northerners a little like *stack*; the vowel of *stalk*, which sounds like *stock*; the vowel of *stuck*, which sounds like a shorter version of *stalk*; the short-*e* of *bed*, which sounds like *bud*; and the short-*i* of *bid*, which can sound a little like either *bud* or *bed*. Not all northerners display the full set of these changes, and the shift is more advanced in some speakers than in others, but its general effect on northern speech is unmistakable. It has created a unique dialect that is remarkably uniform from western New York to Milwaukee. Although some of its effects can also be heard as far west as the Twin Cities, it does not extend southward into the North Midland.

The Midland displays its own set of vowel shifts that make it sound different from the North, and in some ways more similar to the South. In particular,

the long-*u* and long-*o* of *boot* and *boat* are articulated farther forward than in the North. This can be heard by comparing the pronunciation of these vowels before the letter *l* and in other contexts, because a following *l* tends to pull vowels backward. In the North, there is relatively little difference between the vowels in pairs of words like *too* and *tool*, or *code* and *cold*: They are all pronounced quite far back in the mouth (though long-*u* has begun to shift forward among younger northerners). In the Midland, by contrast, while *tool* and *cold* have back vowels, *too* and *code* are pronounced in the central region of the mouth, almost as in Southern British English. Midlanders also pronounce the diphthong of words like *cow*, *south*, and *down* farther forward in the mouth than northerners, with the first part of the diphthong sounding like the vowel in *cat*. Northerners use a darker, more retracted vowel in these words, with the first part of the diphthong sounding more like *cot*. This difference is reversed for words like *star* and *start*: Here it is northerners who have the brighter, more advanced vowel, and midlanders the darker, more retracted vowel. Finally, while northerners pronounce the long-*a* of *lake* as a monophthong in a relatively high, tense position, perhaps sounding to midlanders a little like *leak*, midlanders use a lower, more open and diphthongal vowel, though not as low or open as that in the South, which Northerners might hear as *like*.

What, then, are we to make of the belief that midwestern speech is the closest thing Americans have to a standard version of their language? To begin, "midwestern speech" is not a particularly useful term in classifying American dialects at the level of pronunciation because the Midwest, while it may be a unified entity in many other ways, is not a single linguistic region. Rather, it comprises two main dialect areas, Inland North and North Midland (and even a bit of South Midland), that share certain phonetic features but differ on many others. Furthermore, one of these areas, the Inland North, exhibits a set of changes in vowel articulation that make its speech sound quite different from what most Americans would identify as standard or "General American" English. The pronunciation of most of the North Midland is closer to being what many Americans would consider an unmarked, nonregional variety, but it has no greater claim to this status than the vast area in which western varieties are spoken, from Denver and Phoenix to Los Angeles and Seattle. The more important fact is that we all have an accent, regardless of where we come from, and that while we may prefer the sound of one accent over another, there is no scientific basis for asserting that one pronunciation is "better" or "more correct." On the contrary, accents are one of the many ways in which we demonstrate to people around us our membership in a community: They help to maintain a sense of local identity.

Sources and Further Reading: Harold B. Allen, *The Linguistic Atlas of the Upper Midwest,* 3 vols. (1973–1976); Robert E. Callary, "Phonological Change and the Development of an Urban Dialect in Illinois," *Language in Society* 4 (1975); Timothy C. Frazer, ed., *"Heartland" English* (1993); John S. Kenyon and Thomas A. Knott, *A Pronouncing Dictionary of American English* (1944); Hans Kurath and Raven I. McDavid, Jr., *The Pronunciation of English in the Atlantic States* (1961); William Labov, *Principles of Linguistic Change,* vol. 1, *Internal Factors* (1994); William Labov, *Principles of Linguistic Change,* vol. 2, *Social Factors* (2001); William Labov, Sharon Ash, and Charles Boberg, *Atlas of North American English* (2005); Albert H. Marckwardt, "Principal and Subsidiary Dialect Areas in the North-Central States," *Publications of the American Dialect Society* 27 (1957); Charles Kenneth Thomas, *An Introduction to the Phonetics of American English* (1947).

Charles Boberg
McGill University, Montreal, Canada

Vocabulary

The vocabulary of the Midwest is as diverse as its people. The Midwest is not a homogeneous, uniform area, not in geography, not in settlement history, and not in language usage. In fact, there is no consensus about what constitutes the Midwest. Allan Metcalf takes us on a tour of all states and regions of the United States in his book *How We Talk: American Regional English Today* (2000), but not once does he even mention the Midwest. The closest the *Dictionary of American Regional English (DARE)* comes is using the term *Upper Midwest* (defined as North and South Dakota, Nebraska, Minnesota, and Iowa), taken from Harold Allen's *Linguistic Atlas of the Upper Midwest* (1973–1976), part of the Linguistic Atlas Project that studied the entire United States. To cover the whole area defined here as Midwest, one must also include most of *DARE*'s North Central region (Wisconsin, Michigan, Illinois, Indiana, Ohio; it also includes Kentucky), and the northern part of the Central region (Nebraska, Kansas, Missouri; also Oklahoma and Arkansas).

It is generally considered that the Midwest as defined for this encyclopedia contains three of four major U.S. dialect divisions, the North, the North Midland, and the South Midland, running roughly east to west through the Midwest, reflecting the original settlement patterns of immigrants from the East Coast westward. The North–North Midland boundary runs roughly through the northern parts of Ohio, Indiana, and Illinois; the North Midland includes

most of Iowa and Nebraska. The South Midland is mostly to the south of the Midwest but traditionally includes the southernmost parts of Ohio, Indiana, Illinois, and a large part of Missouri. Words like *pail* (North)/*bucket* (Midland); *sweet corn* and *corn on the cob* (mostly North and North Midland)/*roasting ears* (Midland); *sick to one's stomach* (North; also North Midland)/*sick at one's stomach* (Midland); and *darning needle* 'dragonfly' (North)/*snake feeder* (mostly North Midland)/*snake doctor* (South Midland) reflect this division within the Midwest.

This is not to say that each dialect area has its specific terms, exclusive only to it; rather, each area has a combination of terms that makes it unique. *Snake feeder* is also used in the South Midland, although its heaviest usage is in the North Midland; *sick to one's stomach* is used very heavily in the North, but both it and *sick at one's stomach* are used in the North Midland. These terms are used in the Midwest. Their usage stretches from the East Coast westward, cutting through the Midwest and continuing on, following the paths of the original settlers. Many vocabulary items are also used farther south than the Midwest, such as *roasting ears* and *sick at one's stomach*.

Other terms whose usage can be traced from the East Coast to the West include *belly-flop* 'to coast on a sled face down' in the North and North Midland, and *belly-buster* in the North Midland and South Midland; *green pepper* in the North and North Midland (while *mango* is used in this sense chiefly in the noncoastal Midlands, especially in Ohio, Indiana, Illinois, Iowa, and Missouri); and *eaves trough* and *eaves spout* through the North and North Midland, although *gutter* (used in the South and South Midland as well as in the North Atlantic states) is more commonly used in western Ohio, Indiana, Illinois, and northern Missouri; Pennsylvania *spouting* carries over into eastern Ohio, and to a much lesser extent to other Midwest states. *Four corners* 'a crossroads, a place where two roads cross' is used in New England and New York, then shows up again in the Midwest and the West. *Farmer*, a derogatory term for 'a rustic, countrified, awkward, or rude person', also follows the North and North Midland areas from the East Coast across the country. This is a term used mainly by younger, educated speakers. *Farmer match* 'a wooden match that can be struck on any rough surface' is used in upstate New York, Pennsylvania, and West Virginia, as well as in the Midwest; it is especially common in western Illinois, Iowa, and Minnesota. *Fishing worm* is found throughout the Midland area, while *dew worm* is in the northern states as far west as Minnesota and Iowa.

In the course of its settlement, the Midwest became home to many non-English-speaking immigrant groups. The Midwest accounted for large numbers of

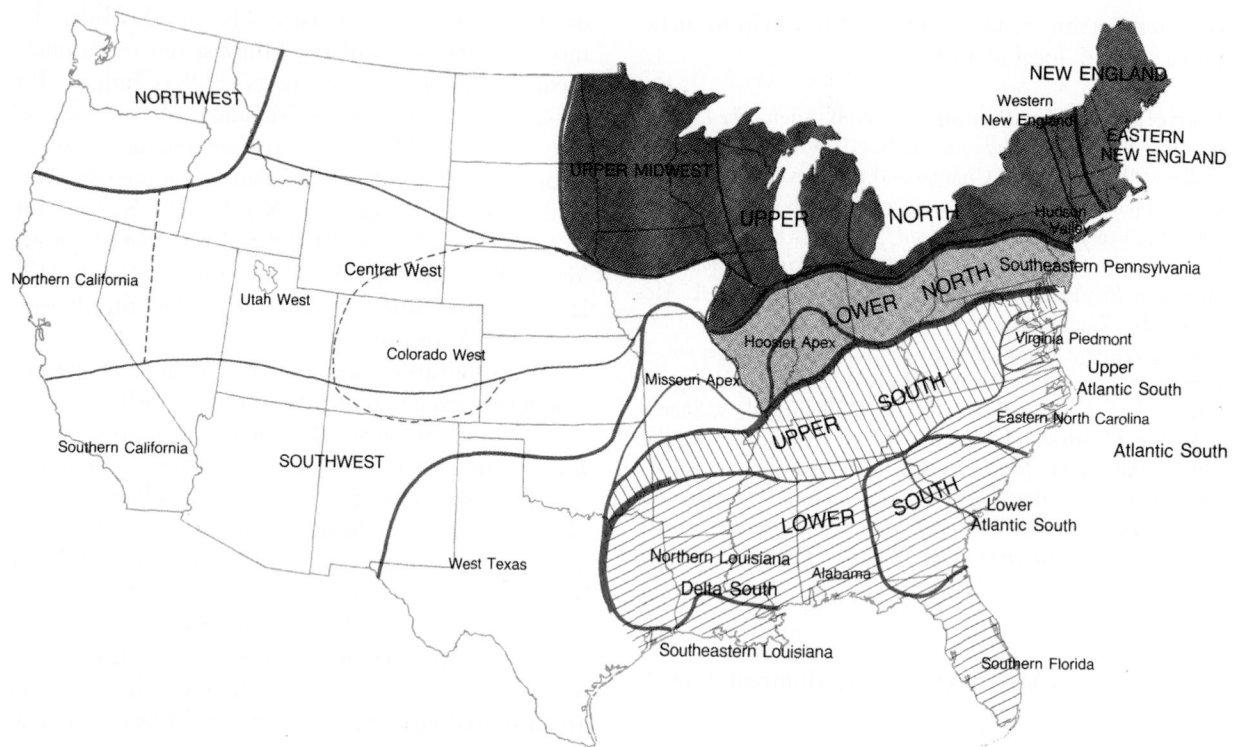

The regional vocabulary of American English, showing both the diversity within the Midwest and the Midwest's connections to other areas. *Source:* Craig M. Carver, *American Regional Dialects: A World Geography* (1987).

Norwegians, Swedes, Danes, Finns, Poles, Germans, Russians, Czechs, French, Italians, and Dutch, to give an incomplete list. Their influence can still be felt today: In the area of food items, Wisconsinites eat *brats, czarnina, kringle, krumkake,* and *wurst;* Minnesotans (well, not all of them) eat *lefse* and *lutefisk, sandbakkels* and *rommegrot;* Michiganders eat *balkenbry, erwten soup,* and *paczki;* North Dakotans eat *fruit soup;* and Nebraskans eat *runzas.*

Some terms are used more frequently in the Midwest than elsewhere in the United States. *Bismarck* 'jelly doughnut', a term that originated in Chicago at the bakery in the Hotel Bismarck, has spread strongly throughout the Midwest and somewhat beyond. *Long john* 'an oblong or rectangular pastry, filled with cream or jelly and often frosted' is quite common. According to the files of *DARE*, a term for the grassy strip between the sidewalk and the curb, *boulevard,* shows most of its usage in the Midwest, as does *terrace,* although the latter is not as common. There were also several responses of *treelawn* in the Midwest, especially in northeastern Ohio. A common grass bug, black with red markings, is called a *box-elder bug* in the upper Midwest states and Wisconsin and Illinois, or, more descriptively, a *democrat bug,* especially in Kansas, Mis-

souri, Nebraska, and Iowa. In the largely Republican countryside of these states, the name may well have derived from the fact that, as one person told *DARE,* the insect "was viewed as a pesky outsider that seemed to serve no useful purpose and just got in the way." An outdoor toilet may be a *biffy* or a *shanty. Burr oak,* not the type of oak tree itself but the name, is concentrated in the Midwest but has spread to some neighboring states as well. The bowfin (a freshwater fish) is called a *dogfish.* A jocular and frequently derogatory term for a Catholic is *cat-licker.* A pastry of sweetened yeast dough or pie dough with a sweet filling or topping is the Bohemian or Czech *kolacky.* A *maintainer* is a person who keeps roads in good shape. A game of tic-tac-toe, or such a game that is tied, is called *old cat* or *one old cat,* while a children's chasing game, probably from a Swedish game, in the Midwest is termed *last couple out.* To latch onto, to appropriate, can be to *grab onto.* To *pooh out* is to fail, grow weak or tired, to come to nothing. *Owly* means irritable, cross, or angry. *Fresh fried potatoes* are raw potatoes thinly sliced and fried, while *American fried potatoes* are boiled potatoes sliced and fried. If you want to ask if someone understands, you can say *siehst du?* If you want to avoid a dirt road, which can be very dusty, you can take an *oil mat* or *oil mat road*. And only in the Midwest, especially in Minnesota, do you hear *ish!* as an expression of disgust.

Some terms present in the Midwest are used almost exclusively in the northern band of states, that is, Michigan, Wisconsin, Minnesota, and the Dakotas: *baga* 'rutabaga or Swedish turnip', *hot dish* 'a casserole or main dish, frequently one taken to a potluck', *lawyer* 'burbot (a freshwater fish)', *pin cherry* 'a small shrubby cherry tree', *putz* 'to fool around, to waste time', *schafkopf* and *sheepshead* 'a card game', *shine* 'to hunt at night using a bright light, to attract and temporarily immobilize game or fish with a bright light', *Norski* 'a person of Norwegian descent', *northern* 'a freshwater game fish', and *Christmas fool* or *julebakk* 'a costumed person who goes from house to house at Christmas time asking for treats and drink' where such a group of people might be given *julekake* 'a sweetened bread with candied or dried fruits'.

Other terms used mainly in the Midwest are found mostly in its Midland area: *carry-in (dinner)* 'a potluck meal', *black man* 'a children's outdoor game', *goose-drownder* 'a heavy rain', and *hedge* and *hedge apple* 'Osage orange'.

Still other terms appear chiefly in one or two states or even parts of a state, or a city. *Dope* 'a dessert topping' appears mainly in Ohio. As a term for 'a paved road' *hard road* is used chiefly in central and southern Illinois. A *mud boat* 'a low sled, frequently with runners, used for hauling stones, logs, or other heavy loads' is found in Ohio, Indiana, and Illinois. *Pat* 'partridge, ruffed grouse' is a Michigan term, as is *lunch roll* for the above-named *long john*. *Doodinkus* 'a thingamabob' is said in Kansas and Nebraska. Nebraskans also call a 'small barren hill that looks chopped up' a *chophill*. A *hodag* 'a ferocious imaginary animal' is known mostly in Wisconsin. A *leaky roof* or *leaky road* is a term in Missouri for 'a small branch railroad'. In the southern part of Indiana what was mentioned above as a *carry-in dinner* is a *pitch-in dinner*. The Canadian term *bluff* 'a clump of trees growing on an open area or prairie' has slipped over the border into North Dakota and Wisconsin.

As society became more urban and suburban, words dropped out of active vocabularies and were replaced by words that named items and concepts in a different world. While many midwesterners may not recognize *darning needle, fishing worm, nearside horse, fruit cellar,* or, used as a call to pigs, *pooey*, they do recognize vocabulary items not known a hundred years ago. A term with heavy usage in the Midwest is *semi* 'a very large truck used to haul freight'. All vehicles must stop when the *stop-and-go light* turns red. Take advantage of shopping bargains at *Crazy Days* or *Maxwell Street Days*. Run to a *pony keg* 'convenience store' in Cincinnati, Ohio, for items you forgot to purchase. All language is always changing, never static. The vocabulary, regional or not, reflects the influences at work on the language. The Midwest is no exception.

Culture, folklore, history, and geography are inseparable from language usage and vocabulary of any country or region, as the terms given here demonstrate. Although the Midwest is not homogeneous, it is unique. The vocabulary with which midwesterners define themselves deserves mention, including Hoosier, Buckeye, Jayhawk, Cornhusker, Hawkeye, Cheesehead, and Yooper.

Sources and Further Reading: Harold Allen, *Linguistic Atlas of the Upper Midwest* (1973–1976); Frederic G. Cassidy and Joan Houston Hall, eds., *Dictionary of American Regional English*, vol. 2 (1985); James Ciment, ed., *Encyclopedia of American Immigration* (2001); Robert Ford Dakin, "The Dialect Vocabulary of the Ohio River Valley," 2 vols., Ph.D. diss., University of Michigan (1966); A.L. Davis, "A Word Atlas of the Great Lakes Region," Ph.D. diss., University of Michigan (1948); Timothy C. Frazer, ed., *"Heartland" English* (1993); Donald M. Lance, "Variation in American English," in John Samuel Kenyon, *American Pronunciation*, eds. Donald M. Lance and Stuart A. Kingsbury, 12th ed., expanded (1994); Allan Metcalf, *How We Talk: American Regional English Today* (2000); Luanne von Schneidemesser, *An Index by Region, Usage, and Etymology to the Dictionary of American Regional English* (1993–1999); Walt Wolfram and Natalie Schilling-Estes, "Regional Dialects," in *American English: Dialects and Variation* (1998).

Luanne von Schneidemesser
University of Wisconsin–Madison

Grammar

Regional dialects in the Midwest are distinguished by grammatical, vocabulary, and pronunciation features. What is normally called *grammar* includes what linguists call *syntax* (the arrangement of words in sentences) and *morphology* (word forms, especially affix forms, which determine concepts like tense, aspect, or plural). While both syntax and morphology show some regional variation, they are also affected by education and literacy. Prior to the eighteenth century, few attempts were made to standardize the grammar of English. Eventually, however, authorities began to claim that only certain grammatical forms were "correct." These "prescriptive" grammarians—grammarians who try to tell which forms are "right" or "wrong"—began to stigmatize such features as multi-

ESL (English as a Second Language) literacy instruction. Ohio Historical Society, P30 AL00053.

ple negation (e.g., "we don't have none of them"), which had been part of English throughout its history. Multiple negation was commonly used by established authors such as Geoffrey Chaucer (fourteenth century) and William Shakespeare (sixteenth and seventeenth centuries).

By the nineteenth century, prescriptive grammars had become part of school curricula. At the same time, especially in the United States, more formal education became the norm. Although dialects were established on the East Coast well before the rise of prescriptive grammarians, the interior settlements showed the effects of schooling and prescriptivism. Especially in the northern tier of states, which inherited a concern for scriptural literacy as an element of salvation, areas farther west or later settled are likely to show more standardization and less grammatical variation.

Besides education, the other variable affecting grammar is settlement history, which also affects pronunciation and vocabulary. Linguistic geographers agree that the regional English of the Midwest is largely determined by the extension of older dialect areas on the East Coast. For this reason, Wisconsin, Michigan, northern Ohio, and northern Illinois are part of what is variously called by dialectologists the Inland North or the Upper North—which originates in New York State and western New England—while Indiana, central Ohio, central Illinois, southern Iowa, and Missouri have been called part of the Midland, which originates in Pennsylvania. Parts of Missouri, southern Illinois, southern Indiana, and southern Ohio are part of the South Midland or Upland South, which originates in Virginia, the Carolinas, Kentucky, and Tennessee. These relationships become less clear as we move farther west—in this case, Minnesota, Iowa, the Dakotas, Nebraska, and Kansas share some features

with eastern areas but for reasons mentioned earlier, the features themselves are harder to find.

This relationship to eastern varieties is especially clear from responses to the Linguistic Atlas surveys, which were conducted around the middle of the twentieth century and included respondents born during the middle and late nineteenth century. These samples, especially those taken in rural areas, included a large number of older informants with limited formal education and often no more than basic reading skills. This preponderance of grammatical dialect differentiation among less-educated speakers is reflected in studies of eastern states as well. While a large number of vocabulary items separate New York (Inland North) from most of Pennsylvania (largely Midland), only a half dozen or so grammatical items show the same distribution. Most are nonstandard forms of irregular (usually Old English "strong") verbs: *see* versus *seen* for the past tense of *see*, *dove* versus *dived* (past tense of *dive*), *clim* versus *clum* (past tense, *climb*). In each pair, the first is Northern/New York State; the second, Pennsylvania/Midland. Dialects were also distinguished by *hadn't ought* versus *oughtn't*; invariant *be*, as in "How be you?" (New York, from New England); and *got awake* (Pennsylvania, from Pennsylvania German).

Because New Yorkers tended to move due west, we find *see, dove, clim, hadn't ought,* and *How be you?* in the northern settlement areas of Michigan, Wisconsin, Minnesota, and in northern Illinois and Ohio. The Midland forms *seen, dived, clum, oughtn't,* and *got awake* appear in those parts of Ohio, Indiana, and Illinois where more settlers came from Pennsylvania and the southern uplands, as well as in areas of Illinois, Iowa, and Nebraska, where Ohio emigrants were prominent.

To some extent, settlement history does indeed predict the distribution of regional forms. The Linguistic Atlas survey records *see* in Northern Ohio and in Michigan and Wisconsin; *clim* in Michigan, Wisconsin, and Minnesota; *dove* shares about the same regional distribution. However, age and other factors become variables. Atlas responses of *see* and *clim*, for example, are recorded only among the oldest respondents—in interviews, we need to remember, given no later than the middle of the twentieth century. A generation or so later, these forms would rarely be heard. By the same token, the Midland forms *clum* and *dived* have been confined to those areas most affected by Pennsylvanian and upland southern settlement: Illinois, Indiana, Ohio, and Missouri.

Seen, however, behaves somewhat differently. Among atlas informants, it appears all over the Midwest, apparently (in the northern areas) at the expense of *see*; it is not simply confined to the same Midland areas as *clum* and *dived*. Although speculative, two possible explanations present themselves. First, many irregular verbs in English display a long-standing tendency to collapse the past tense and past participle forms: *eat*, *ate*, eaten become eat, *ate*, *ate*; hence, "I've ate a lot of candy lately." The past participle *seen* for many speakers replaces the past tense *saw*.

The explanation may be found in differences among and within states. Education was stressed more strongly in northern areas of the Midwest. In Illinois, a number of free public high schools were scattered throughout the northern part of the state by 1860; at the same time, very few had been established in southern Illinois, even though that part of the state was originally settled (mostly by southerners) at least a generation earlier. For this reason, the nonstandard form *see* has been replaced by Standard English *saw* in northern settlements more rapidly than its Midland counterpart *seen*. Without a nonstandard competitor, *seen* has apparently spread into northern areas, replacing *see*.

This education difference has also led to the longer apparent survival of nonstandard forms in the lower Midwest, again, Illinois, Indiana, Ohio, and Missouri, especially in the rural, southern parts of these states. Other irregular verbs that have collapsed the past tense and past participle are *be* ("you was there"—usually called "invariant *was*"), *come* ("he come over yesterday"), *done* ("he done it"), *wear* ("I'm wore out"), *swim* ("I swum the river yesterday"), and *write* (I've wrote a lot of letters); still others form the past tense or participle by analogy with regular verbs, such as *blowed* ("the wind blowed and blowed") or *throwed* ("I got throwed in jail"). While none of these examples shows a particular regional distribution in the East, among midwestern Linguistic Atlas informants they are most common in the Midland areas of the lower Midwest.

The same fate has faced what is called *a*-prefixing ("let's get that fan a-goin"). Once widespread in English, it has receded steadily with the advance of education and literacy. In the eastern United States, it was rare among "cultured" and urban informants and most common in Appalachia. In the Midwest, it was least common in the northern areas. As recently as the 1970s, it was more common in central than in northern Illinois, and unknown in the larger cities. When used at all it was in the context of joking, high stress, or with children.

The *a*-prefixing phenomenon also serves to illustrate yet another complicating element in the geography of midwestern grammar. Public education was common in the so-called upper Midwest of the Dakotas, Iowa, Nebraska, and most of Minnesota from the beginning of European American settlement. For this reason, Linguistic Atlas surveys find fewer nonstandard verb forms in these northern, trans-Mississippi states. For one thing, *a*-prefixing is rare here. The same is true of invariant *was*, *throwed*, past tense *eat*, past tense *run*, and even *ain't*—all of these are more likely to be heard in the older states (Wisconsin, Michigan, Illinois, Indiana, Ohio, Missouri), and none of them has any particular regional identification in the East. Even those nonstandard verb forms that are definitely northern in origin, *clim*, past tense *see*, and *be you going?* are rare if occurring at all in the upper Midwest.

It is important to remember too that many parts of the Midwest were settled by Europeans who valued formal education but did not speak English as a mother tongue. Those areas that were heavily settled by Germans (Wisconsin, Iowa, the Dakotas, the St. Louis area of Missouri, northern Illinois) and Scandinavians (Wisconsin, Minnesota) saw English learned in schools and textbooks rather than from neighbors who spoke a nonstandard dialect of English. This is another reason we find fewer nonstandard verb forms in the upper Midwest and in the cities.

Despite pressures for standardization, some Midland features have survived and seem well on the way to becoming established, perhaps even spreading into former northern areas. While Standard English uses an infinitive between a verb of volition and the past participle ("the grass needs to be mowed") or a particle ("the cat wants to come in"), some dialects omit the infinitive ("the grass needs mowed," "the cat wants in"). The latter construction has been recorded in Scotland and northern Ireland as well as in Pennsylvania and Appalachia, and is very likely a result of Scotch-Irish migration. This feature is well established in those parts of Illinois, Ohio, Indiana, Iowa, and Missouri affected by migration from Pennsylvania and Appalachia. Expressions such as "the program needs funded" appear in local newspapers, suggesting that these constructions are becoming part of literate discourse, while "the cat wants in" seems to be spreading northward.

At the same time, the Midwest exhibits other grammatical features that can often be traced to word-for-word translations of Finnish, German, Norwegian, or Swedish. Particularly in the Iron Range of Minnesota but in other areas as well, we can hear *Do you want to go with?* ("Do you want to go with me?"), *Do you want to go Hibbing?* ("Do you want to go to Hibbing?"), *I didn't go prom* ("I didn't go to the prom").

Decades after the English-speaking settlement of the rural Midwest came the migration of African Americans from the rural South to the industrial cities of the Great Lakes—Detroit, Cleveland, Gary, Toledo, Chicago, and others. Their Black English vernacular dialect included some of the forms already mentioned, like invariant *was*, but it also had deep southern dialects features such as double modals ("we might could go") or perfective *done* ("I done told you kids to go to bed"). Many of these features are also found among rural whites. Perfective *done*, in fact, is still used in the Midwest in former fishing communities along the Illinois and Mississippi Rivers. But other features are more exclusively found among African Americans and may be of African Creole origin, such as habitual *be* ("she be reading to us all the time") or perfective *been* ("I been knowed that all this time"). The origin of features like *be* deletion ("They right here; we ready") are more problematic. Many languages—Russian is just one example—do not use the *be* verb in some contexts. But the *be* deletion may also be due to pronunciation. In dialects that in the past did not pronounce *r*, "we're tired" could easily become "we tired."

The origins and migration patterns of settlers played a critical role in forming the dialect geography of the Midwest. Formal education affected the frequency of nonstandard forms, especially in areas settled in the second half of the nineteenth century.

Sources and Further Reading: Virginia Glenn McDavid, "Verb Forms of the North Central States and Upper Midwest," Ph.D. diss., University of Minnesota (1956); Thomas E. Murray, "Appalachian/Ozarkian English on the Plains," *Kansas Quarterly* 22 (Fall 1990); Thomas E. Murray, "Positive Anymore in the Midwest," in Timothy C. Frazer, ed., *"Heartland" English* (1993); Roger W. Shuy, Walt Wolfram, and W.K. Riley, *A Study of Social Dialects in Detroit* (1968).

Timothy C. Frazer
Western Illinois University

Language and Society

Midwesterners think that their language to be General American or Standard English, and that it is the variety heard on radio and television. They identify with smaller geographic groups such as a town or a neighborhood and they also identify themselves by their gender, social class, profession, and, often, their ethnic group. None of these identities is exclusive, nor are they conscious. Normally several different identifications are expressed simultaneously. A male doctor from Milwaukee might use the formal term *drinking fountain* when he is at work. But when playing handball with a friend, he might use the local term, *bubbler*. In both places he is likely to indicate his gender by articulating his *s*'s in a retracted form, closer to his gums, and have lower vowels than the female doctors who work with him.

Social and ethnic varieties of language mix with regional varieties reflecting such factors as the age, gender, ethnic background, and occupation of the speaker. Professional people in general tend to speak a more prestigious variety throughout the region, while a

❖ Court Interpreters

The challenge of translation reveals the extent to which language is much more than a collection of words and grammar. Translation is not literal. Interpreters must account for cultural context and body language, including the proper interpretation of gestures and emotion. Nowhere is the complexity of language more obvious than in the flexibility and innovation required of a wide range of public institutions, including courts.

The doubling of Hmong and Hispanic populations in Wisconsin in the 1990s led to a major effort by the Office of State Courts to formalize the training, testing, and certifying of court interpreters for people who do not speak English or are deaf. When the governor vetoed funds allocated to implement the program, judges were left to rely on their own sense of a potential interpreter's qualifications. Guidance is provided by a code of ethics adapted from national standards and adopted by the Wisconsin Supreme Court in 2002. The code is a tribute to the nuances of language as a system of communication that goes well beyond a literal translation or a mimicking of a person's behavior. According to the code, "interpreters are required to apply their best skills and judgment to preserve, as faithfully as is reasonably possible and without editing, the meaning of what is said, including the style or register of speech, the ambiguities and nuances of the speaker, and the level of language that best conveys the original meaning of the source language."

Andrew Cayton
Miami University, Oxford, Ohio

more local variety is spoken by working-class people in both urban and rural settings, reflecting the greater social mobility of the professional class. Large urban areas such as Chicago, Detroit, Cleveland, Milwaukee, and the Twin Cities of Minnesota have multiple ethnic dialects. Many rural areas and small towns have a single ethnic dialect: Swedish in Chisago, Minnesota; Dutch in Holland, Michigan; German in the Hutterite Colonies near Frankfurt, South Dakota, and Strasburg, North Dakota; Finnish in Esko, Minnesota; and Hungarian in South Bend, Indiana.

In general, wherever the original European language was used for three or more generations, it evolved into an ethnic dialect. However, the increasing pace of social change since World War II, including the movement to large-scale agriculture, the demise of the family farm, the spread of hobby farms, and the consolidation of schools has eaten away at ethnic dialects as well as at ethnic rural communities. Nevertheless, ethnic dialects have left their mark on the region.

Among the ethnic terms in the Midwest are *lutefisk* 'a white fish cured with lye', and *lefse* 'a round white flour tortilla', from Swedish, Norwegian, and Danish; *sauna* 'steam bath', from Finnish; *sarma* 'cabbage leaves stuffed with rice and meat', from Serbo-Croatian; *potica* 'a rolled pastry filled with honey and walnuts', from Slovenian; *pirogi/pierogi* 'rectangular-shaped pies filled with meat, cabbages, cottage cheese, or apples', from Russian and Polish; *kaffeeklatch* 'a social gathering for conversation'; and *sauerkraut*, from German.

The tendency for long vowels, especially the *a* in "April" and the *o* in "Minnesota," to be monophthongal is distinctive of the western part of the Midwest and is also a vestige of the numerous ethnic dialects that have been spoken in the area. In the aforementioned Chisago, Holland, Strasburg, and the Hutterite Colonies, the voiced consonants /b d g v ð z/ devoice to /p t k f θ s/ in final position. Thus Strasburg, North Dakota-born Lawrence Welk, a bandleader with a popular television program from the 1950s through the 1970s, revealed his German ethnic dialect with his famous references to "boyS and girlS." Throughout Minnesota the phrase, "Do you want to go with" originated in the Swedish, Norwegian, Danish, German, and Finnish ethnic dialects. It also appears in other communities where any of these ethnic dialects were spoken.

Gender is also marked in speech, both stylistically and linguistically. Individual situations determine how strong gender marking is. Professionals at work or college students at school are in roles where gender normally does not play a significant role so there is little gender marking. In contrast, flirting brings out gender roles, which are reflected by the language. In general, women have higher off-glides in diphthongs than men and generally their vowels are higher, although this distinction is less in the Midwest than in the South, where women have higher voices. In general, women use fewer stigmatized forms such as *ain't* and fewer double negatives than men, who "drop their g's in -*ing* words" more often than women. But in a heated volleyball tournament or hockey game, women players often match men in both the quality and quantity of their cursing. Some traditional roles are maintained, which is reflected in the vocabulary. Generally, women know more color, sewing, and knitting terms and men know more car parts and hunting terms. Men tend to be more literal and project orientated while women tend to be more symbolic and relationship orientated.

Greater differences in speech persist between older men and women in rural working-class and farm families. Because these groups have little social and geographic mobility, most of them have lived their entire lives in the same area. The grammatical forms listed in *The Linguistic Atlas of the North-Central States* and *The Linguistic Atlas of the Upper Midwest* portray vocabulary differences between men and women as percentage differences, rather than as categorical differences. Among the dialect terms listed as being used more by women than men are *pit* (of a cherry), *shell* (of a pea), *darning needle* 'dragon fly', *firefly*, and *somersault*. Among those lexical terms more often used by men are *lightning bug* and *handspring*. Many of the old bachelor farmers do not refer to a male cow as a *bull* in the presence of a woman, but as a *gentleman cow*. Phonological differences between these older men and women include males pronouncing *soot* so it rhymes with *boot*, *with* so that the *th* sounds like the *th* in *the*, and slurring *hundred* so that the last syllable either sounds like *dirt* or the *d* is omitted and it rhymes with *nerd*. In contrast, older rural women pronounce *soot* so that it rhymes with *foot* and the *th* in *with* so that it sounds like the *th* in *thin*, and they clearly pronounce the *r* in *hundred*.

Nonstandard grammatical forms are used more often by the older rural men. Frequently, they use *give* as the preterit of *give* and *clumb* as the preterit of *climb*. They also use *who-all* as the plural interrogative of *who* and they *want off* a bus and get *sick to the stomach* and *die with* (rather than "from") something. Older rural women use the standard forms *gave* as the preterit of *give*, *climbed* as the preterit of *climb*, and *who* as the interrogative of *who*. When the time is appropriate, they *want to get off* a bus, and they *get sick at the stomach* and *die from* something.

Two types of age differences can be cited to account

for types of speech diversity in the Midwest. Changes have been taking place in English that reflect a change in values and attitudes in generational speech. Teenagers, as they separate from childhood, adopt special group terms, often from their favorite musical group. These terms tend to spread over the country. In addition, teenagers in smaller groups will have special terms or slang to identify their intimate group. With this type, there will be several groups with special language within a single school. These tend to be short-lived. The expression *quit dippin in my business*, which was popular in the late 1900s seems to be dead now. In contrast, many new technical terms such as *I/O* (for input/output; from computers), *meltdown* 'having a bad day' (from atomic reactor jargon), or *no fly zone* 'stay out' seem to be coming into the language but are used primarily by younger people. A few senior citizens when they are among themselves will still use *twenty-three skidoo* for *goodbye* or *sedan* for car. Each generation of teenagers wants to claim some group activities as their own and coin their own terms. Thus in northern Minnesota, a party out in the woods with much beer is called a *picnic* by people over seventy, a *beer bust* by those fifty to sixty, a *keg party* by those in their forties, a *kegger* by those in their thirties, and a *pit party* by younger people.

Language varies by profession or occupation. Professional people such as doctors, lawyers, and teachers use fewer stigmatized forms such as double negatives and *ain't*, and less frequently pronounce *singing* as *singin'*. They use regional and ethnic forms less often than working-class people and have a more Latinate vocabulary. Thus in Minnesota, a professional is less likely to ask a friend *Wanna come with?* instead of *Do you want to come with me?* than a working-class speaker. In general, class differences diminish with westward movement, until in western North and South Dakota there is little class dialect. However, occupational jargon is still used. Thus anywhere in the Midwest terms such as *headache* will be used by a lineman when he drops his tools from the pole, or *blow-up* will be used by a forest-fire firefighter when she sees a crown fire, and a *powder monkey* will utter *Fire in the hole!* just before he sets off explosives.

Conversational patterns in the Midwest generally seem halfway between the East Coast and the South. On the one hand, the length of time between alternating speaker turns is longer than in the East Coast but shorter than in the South. Thus midwesterners often seem brusque and impolite to southerners and uninvolved to easterners. On the other hand, midwesterners are often considered uninvolved yet stoic because they have less variation in pitch than southerners and less volume in their speech than easterners. They tend to be perceived as honest because they

are usually more direct with few indirections in their speech.

The interaction of varieties of English in the Midwest is demonstrated by patterns in the Upper Peninsula (U.P.) of Michigan and the Iron Range of northeastern Minnesota. In these places, ethnic varieties amalgamated with regional and social patterns to form a combination of regional and social dialect. During their settlement period, European workers were imported to work in the mines and lumber camps. The largest ethnic group was Finns, followed by Germans, Swedes, and Norwegians. The first generation of workers kept their native language for social activities, but used a pidginlike variety of English in mixed ethnic groups such as at work. Frequently, women knew only their native language because outside activity was handled by their husbands. As a result, the children of this first group learned English from one another rather than from their parents, so a nonstandard language developed. The following ethnic terms represent the vocabulary of the everyday speech in the Iron Range and the U.P.: *pasty* (Welsh) 'a meat turnover'; *polenta* (Italian) 'a type of boiled cornmeal with tomato sauce', the only type of cornmeal dish found on the range; *potica* (Slovenian), a pastry; *sarma* (Serbo-Croatian), often called pigs in a blanket; and of course Finnish *sauna*. *Moyaka*, often called Finn soup, seems to be unique to the area. The term is unknown in Finland. Other new words and phrases were coined. The miner *takes the pail to work* and his wife *makes the pail*, even if he made his own lunch and took it in a paper bag. *Dumps* refer to either large piles of nonmagnetic ore or overlay from the opening of a mine, in which case it might be the best part of town. The *drys* are the changing rooms at work.

Pronunciation reflects the language of the large number of Finnish, Germanic, and Slavic immigrants. There is a devoicing of final consonants so that *and* is pronounced like *ant*. In these areas devoicing is so strong that *ing* often sounds like it has a *k* at the end, as in *runningk*. There are syntactic patterns that originated in the immigrant stage, such as *Wanna go show?* for *Do you want to go to the show?* or *We went Detroit* for *We went to Detroit*. While women do have these features, they usually have them in fewer numbers than men. Those Rangers and Yoopers who want to leave the area or who have professional jobs there sound like educated people from the Twin Cities or Milwaukee. Those who want to remain in the area, especially if they are working class, maintain the dialect, reflecting their social class, gender, ethnicity, and occupation.

Sources and Further Reading: Harold B. Allen, *The Linguistic Atlas of the Upper Midwest*, 3 vols. (1973–1976); Michael D. Linn, "The Development of Dialect Patterns in the

Upper Midwest, *Kansas Quarterly* 22 (Fall 1990); Albert Henry Marckwardt, *Linguistic Atlas of the North-Central States* (1976); Daniel Naslund, "The /s/ Phoneme: A Gender Issue," master's thesis, University of Minnesota (1973); Deborah Tannen, *That's Not What I Meant* (1986).

Michael Linn
University of Minnesota–Duluth

African American Vernacular

The language variety known as African American Vernacular English (AAVE) or Ebonics refers to the vernacular speech of native-born African Americans residing primarily in working-class areas of large cities such as Chicago, Detroit, and Philadelphia. Originating in the southern United States, AAVE was taken to northern cities by migrating blacks. Studied increasingly since the 1960s, AAVE has many linguistic characteristics that distinguish it from the typical speech of most white Americans. Despite ongoing heated debates over its origins, future, and sociopolitical and cultural dynamics, AAVE is a distinct variety of English. Its features are found in urban African American speech across the country. Walter Wolfram laid the groundwork for investigation of AAVE in the Midwest, and current research has confirmed and elaborated his findings.

The pronunciation of AAVE often is its most conspicuous feature. Among its features are the reduction of consonant clusters at the ends of some words so that *test* and *left* are often pronounced *tess* and *lef;* use of the sounds [d] and [v] in place of the *th* sound in words like *there, they* (*der, dey*) and *brother* (*bruhver*); use of the sound [f], or sometimes [t] or nothing at all, in place of the other *th* sound as in *moth* (*mof*), *nothing* (*nuttin*), and *with* (*wi*); absence or weakening of the [r] and [l] sounds in words such as *car* (*cah*) and *person* (*puhson*), *well* (*weh*), and *myself* (*mysef*). These features are also used by middle-class African Americans when they style-shift to the vernacular for sociocultural identification. The deletion of [r] was much more frequently observed among men than women in both middle and working classes.

There are also distinctive vowel sounds in AAVE. For example, the vowel /i/ in *feet* and *read* may become the shorter, lax /i/ vowel, causing the words to sound like *fit* and *rid*. On the one hand, some diphthongs (two-part vowels) may become monophthongs (one-part vowels). Thus sounds such as /ay/ in *mine* may be pronounced *mahn*. On the other hand, some monophthongs are pronounced as diphthongs so that the *i* in *kid* and the *ea* in *head* sound more like *ee* and *ay*, yielding *keed* and *hade*, respectively.

The speech of urban white upper midwesterners is currently undergoing a series of vowel changes called the Northern Cities Chain Shift (NCCS), which is affecting some vowels, including the *a* in *bat*. Speakers of AAVE appear not to be participating in the NCCS. Thus, while a working-class white Detroiter might say *end* for *and* (rhyming with *mend*), black Detroiters continue to pronounce the word with the vowel of *hat*.

One of the best-documented grammatical markers of AAVE is that it often does not require the suffix *-s* to indicate third-person agreement in the present tense of verbs or the marking of plurals or possessives on nouns. Hence we get, "I seen how *he try* to get a job, *he try* to get a trade" (third person); "Plus these kids, these orphanage *kid* . . . " (plural); and "Every day . . . I normally see my cousin, or go *my uncle or somebody house*" (possessive). This option is taken most frequently when these grammatical distinctions are signaled elsewhere in the sentence or discourse.

Other distinctive AAVE characteristics pertain to its syntax and semantics. One such feature is the "zero copula," which refers to the absence of the *be* verb in statements such as "Yeah, he all right." This feature has often been at the center of the debate over AAVE's origins because the zero copula is frequent in African and Caribbean English but not in other British or American English dialects. William Labov observes about the AAVE present tense copula: "Wherever standard English can contract, [AAVE] can delete," meaning that any sentence that may include forms such as *I'm, he's,* or *it's* allows for shortened forms *I, he, it* in AAVE grammar. However, this rule does not account for all of the AAVE zero copula constructions. The deletion principle also affects such AAVE sentences as "I be home soon," where the underlying future-tense contraction *'ll* has been deleted. This *be* differs in meaning from AAVE "habitual be" that occurs in such sentences as "I think those busses be blue." That sentence would be rendered in Standard English as "I think those busses are usually blue."

AAVE has the verb markers *bin, BIN* and *don,* which have functions with no exact equivalents in colloquial Standard English. Preverbal *bin* is used to indicate past reference but also implies continuation of the action into the present as in, "I bin keeping him ever since eighty-three." Stressed *BIN* indicates that the action was complete in the remote past, as in "He BIN gone," which states emphatically that the subject has been gone for a long time. The *don* marker, in constructions such as "Most of them don moved out," not only marks a perfect aspect, as in Standard English *have* but may carry emphatic or emotive nuances as well. The usages of *bin*, *BIN*, and *don* seem to remain in AAVE to convey semantic subtleties that are difficult to express syntactically in mainstream English.

Multiple negation, or negative concord, is another noticeable feature of AAVE, although it is not unique to this variety. The sentence "Boy cain't stay no boy for nothin' but a minute," in which there are three negative elements where Standard English would use only one, is an example of multiple negation. Experts note that multiple negation occurs much more frequently in AAVE than in other nonstandard varieties.

The multifaceted arguments surrounding AAVE are politically and emotionally charged. Regardless of AAVE's linguistic ancestry or current direction, however, the speech of the urban poor in African American–dominated communities continues to operate with distinct rules of pronunciation and grammar and to enrich the linguistic diversity of English in the Midwest.

Sources and Further Reading: Walter Edwards, "Phonetic Differentiation between Black and White Speech in East-Side Detroit," *Word* 41 (Aug. 1990); Walter Edwards, "Aspectual də in African American vernacular English in Detroit," *Journal of Sociolinguistics* 5 (Aug. 2001); Walter Edwards, *African American Vernacular English in Detroit* (forthcoming); Lisa Green, "Aspect and Predicate Phrases in African American Vernacular English," in Salikoko S. Mufwene, John R. Rickford, Guy Bailey, and John Baugh, eds., *African-American English: Structure, History and Use* (1998); William Labov, *Language in the Inner City* (1972); William Labov, *Principles of Linguistic Change: Internal Factors* (1994); Walter Wolfram, *A Sociolinguistic Description of Detroit Negro Speech* (1969).

Walter F. Edwards
Wayne State University, Michigan

African American Language

African American Language (AAL) is characterized not only by patterns of grammar and pronunciation, but also by distinctive words and styles of speaking shared by African Americans from all walks of life. Further, many of AAL's words and phrases have crossed over into mainstream use and enrich the language of all Americans.

"Talking black" is often associated with rapidly evolving slang. A common core of words and phrases that crosses boundaries of age, gender, and social class, however, has been around for more than half a century. This common core is called black semantics. It is derived from the experience of Africans in America and functions as a bond of group solidarity expressed through language use. Examples are *kitchen* 'the hair at

the neckline', typically the most *nappy* 'tightly curled' part of black hair; *high yella*, *red/redbone*, *light-skinnded/light-skinned* 'light-complexioned African American'; *nose open* 'totally and vulnerably in love'; and *ashy* 'whitish or greyish appearance of black skin due to wind or cold exposure'.

Although Wolof, Mandingo, and other African languages and cultural patterns did not survive enslavement intact, some words and phrases did survive and have become household words in America. For instance: *tote* 'to carry', from Kikongo, *tota*; *cola* as in *Coca-Cola*, from Temne, *kola*; *banjo*, from Kimbundu, *mbanza*; *banana*, from Wolof and Fulani, *banana*; and *jazz*, from Mandingo, *jasi*. There are also loan translations, expressions in which the literal meaning of the original language is retained, but not the word or phrase itself. The most well-known example in American English is the word *bad* when it is used to refer to something that is "good." In Mandingo, the phrase is *a ka nyi ko-jugu*, which means literally "it is good badly," that is, something is so "good" that it's "bad"!

Other phrases that have crossed over from AAL into mainstream white America include *high five* (from phrases in several West African languages, meaning, literally, 'put your hand in my hand' to show agreement and affirmation of something a speaker has said); *hit on* (romantic talk, most often from a man to a woman to spark her interest in him); *hip* (from Wolof, *hepi/hipi* 'be aware of what's happening').

The black church is a rich source of black semantics because it has not had to compromise black language and culture. Examples of linguistic-cultural idioms and expressions from the church: *on time* (referring to psychological, not clock, time), *sista/brotha* (generic terms for any African American), proverbs such as "God don't like ugly" and "What go round come round."

Black music, from field hollers and work songs during enslavement to hip-hop in contemporary times, has always been central to black reality and thus constitutes yet another major force in the development of black semantics. The musicians' way of life; their artistic contributions to black culture; and the dramatic, flamboyant way they present themselves (*stylin* and *profilin* in AAL) make them linguistic trendsetters in the black speech community. The jazz tradition gave us *gig*, *funky*, *goin through changes*. Rhythm 'n' blues artists contributed *r-e-s-p-e-c-t* and *git on the good foot* 'correct whatever needs improving'. Hip-hop created a broader audience for old sayings like "The blacker the berry, the sweeter the juice" (applauding black skin color) and "Tryin to make a dolla outa fifteen cent" (bemoaning the economic plight of many African Americans).

Forced to use their version of English in the multi-

What Are Our Immediate Goals?

1. To mobilize five million Negroes into one militant mass for pressure.

2. To assemble in Chicago the last week in May, 1943, for the celebration of

"WE ARE AMERICANS – TOO" WEEK

And to ponder the question of Non-Violent Civil Disobedience and Non-Cooperation, and a Mass March On Washington.

15,000 Negroes Assembled at St. Louis, Missouri
20,000 Negroes Assembled at Chicago, Illinois
23,500 Negroes Assembled at New York City
Millions of Negro Americans all Over This Great
Land Claim the Right to be Free!

FREE FROM WANT!
FREE FROM FEAR!
FREE FROM JIM CROW!

"Winning Democracy for the Negro is Winning the War for Democracy!" — A. Philip Randolph

World War II inspired African Americans to demand civil rights at home as well as abroad. Courtesy A. Philip Randolph Institute, Washington, D.C. and The Library of Congress Manuscript Division, African American Odyssey, LC-MSSMISC ODY0808.

lingual enslavement community, Africans created a counterlanguage, assigning alternate and sometimes oppositional meanings to English words. The coded, derisive terms for European Americans, such as *ofay, Miss Ann, Mr. Charlie*, came out of this practice as did negative terms for African Americans who act as spies and agents for European Americans, such as *Uncle Tom, Aunt Jane*, and the expression "run and tell that."

The Biblical phrase *promised land* was appropriated during the twentieth-century Great Migration of blacks. Two major centers in the Midwest, Chicago and Detroit, drew large numbers of blacks seeking both jobs and escape from U.S.-style apartheid in the South. Chicago was dubbed *Chi-town*. Detroit, the automotive capital of the world, was called *Motor town*, which in the 1960s was shortened to *Motown* by record-company founder and entertainment entrepreneur Berry Gordy. Detroit's automobile plants were renamed *the plantations* because blacks were assigned the hardest, dirtiest and most potentially dangerous jobs there—as had been the case on the plantations of the South.

Talking black also involves discourse modes such as signification/signifyin, a style of talk in which a speaker puts down—signifies on—a person. This lin-

guistic practice involves hyperbole, irony, indirection, metaphor, humor, and deployment of the semantically or logically unexpected. Although signifyin is tantamount to a *dis* (a put-down, or expression of disrespect), it is sociolinguistically acceptable because it is a well-known, long-established verbal tradition, with socioculturally defined rules and linguistic norms that African Americans share.

For example, in a *beauty shop* (AAL for "hairdressing salon") in Chicago around October 2000, Keisha, a *beautician* (AAL for "hairstylist") inquires about the hairstyle Towana, her customer, wants: "Hey girl, whatcha want today?" Before replying, Towana removes her hat, and Keisha exclaims: "Damn, girl, you waitin' for slavery to roll back around?!" Towana and other women nearby laugh heartily at Keisha's signifyin question, which is, of course, not a question at all, but a commentary that conveys two messages in a humorous way: (1) criticism of the *nappy* condition of Towana's hair (i.e., extremely tightly curled, wooly, impossible to comb) and assertion of its dire need of some work, and (2) acknowledgment that during enslavement, black hair in its natural, unstyled, uncombed, unstraightened state was acceptable, but slavery ended nearly 140 years ago and neither its recurrence nor the hair norms of that era are possible today.

There are two types of signification. One is the ritualized tradition of verbal play in which speakers level the dis at a person's mother (and occasionally at other relatives). Historically, this was referred to as "The Dozens" or "playin the Dozens." Today it is often referred to as "snappin" or "yo momma jokes." Like, "Yo momma so dumb she thought a quarterback was a refund!" This verbal game is played by social intimates, and one of its crucial rules is that the "insult" hurled at the mother or other relative must not be literally, objectively true. If it is, then this is no longer a game. The objective is to best one's opponent with one's verbal skills until, eventually, the opponent runs out of verbal comebacks. The game tests a person's ability to maintain his or her cool, or grace under pressure. It undoubtedly dates to African sources; analogues have been found in several African cultures, such as this from the Efik ethnic group in what is now known as Nigeria: "You are a child of mixed sperm."

The other type of signification is a dis leveled at a person, rather than his/her mother or other relatives. Although this kind of signifyin can be "light" (that is, verbal play, as in the beauty salon exchange), it is often "heavy" (that is, social critique). A classic example is revolutionary 1960s black leader Malcolm X's opening use of signifyin in the opening of a speech to a black audience: "Mr. Moderator, Brotha Lomax, Brothas and Sistas, friends and enemies." Because we do not usually begin a speech by addressing our enemies, Malcolm's signifyin statement let his audience know that he knew that hostile forces were in their midst. (And indeed, he was later assassinated by some of his own people while giving a speech.)

Other discourse modes are: call-response, tonal semantics, narrativizing, proverb use/proverbializing, and testifyin. In all they show that the language repertoires of African Americans in the Midwest and elsewhere are not only rich and varied but tied to their historical connections both to the American South and to Africa.

Sources and Further Reading: John Baugh, *Black Street Speech* (1983); Joseph Holloway and Winifred Vass, *The African Heritage of American English* (1993); Thomas Kochman, *Black and White Styles in Conflict* (1981); Sonja Lanehart, *Sista Speak! Black Women Kinfolk Talk About Language and Literacy* (2002); Marcyliena Morgan, *Language, Discourse and Power in African American Culture* (2002); John Rickford and Russell Rickford, *Spoken Soul* (2000); Geneva Smitherman, *Black Talk: Words and Phrases from the Hood to the Amen Corner*, rev. ed. (2000); Geneva Smitherman, *Talkin and Testifyin: The Language of Black America* (1977).

Geneva Smitherman
Michigan State University

Narratives

Bits of life history are part of the fabric of every conversation. As they talk about their experiences, people draw on and reinforce ideas about who they are and what their social world is like. This article focuses on conversational narratives by one set of white, middle-class people from northern Indiana, exploring how their ideas about the nature and function of language color their style in their stories. These people's narratives differ in some ways from narratives by northeasterners and southerners described in other studies. We will explore in depth, in one particular context, how conversational narratives can function as part of the process through which people evoke and create a sense of place—in this case a midwestern place—as they talk. Whether or not the midwesterners and the talk described here are typical of white, middle-class midwesterners and their talk or (less likely) of midwesterners and midwestern speech in general, remain open questions because comparative research has not been published.

Data for the study consisted of sixty-four narratives of personal experience that arose in conversations among family and friends in Fort Wayne, Indiana. They are the kinds of anecdotes that Americans tell everywhere: about such things as meeting one's spouse, getting in trouble as a child or adolescent, embarrassing misunderstandings or mistakes, or memorable successes. The Fort Wayne stories were typically framed as lessons about good luck, proper social behavior, or (more commonly for men's stories than women's) personal skill. Unlike the stories by New Yorkers and other Northeasterners that were the data for other studies of conversational style, the Fort Wayne stories were not very interactive. Once the teller took the conversational floor for a narrative, other people were relatively silent. They provided supportive cues, verbal and nonverbal, that they were listening and interested, but they tended not to interject with suggestions about how particular events should be interpreted or what the overall point of the story should be. They left the responsibility for the meaning of the events to the person who was telling the story rather than actively "co-constructing" the narrative the way audiences elsewhere sometimes do.

The Fort Wayne stories were also full of very specific details that were not immediately relevant to the unfolding narrative. Experiences that for the purposes of what was suspenseful or unusual about the story, could have occurred anywhere, were identified as having happened "out by Homestead High School" or "in the Rolling Hills Addition" or "at the Hollandin Hotel in Cleveland, Ohio." Stories that were timeless in their effects were referenced to "the day after

❖ Conversational Narrative: A Courtship Story

This is a transcription of a conversational narrative told by a young woman. Courtship stories like this are common in settings where meeting a mate is a key event in a successful life; personal anecdotes like these help perpetuate that idea. The story reinforces traditional American ideas about love. The storyteller frames the event as the result of a series of accidental events so that the outcome seems to be the result of fate rather than human design.

You want to know how I met this guy?

OK—we went, OK—we were in high school, me and these two other girls were going to see *Oh, God.* Opening night we went to the movie theater, opening night you know we got to—We got there a little bit late. The line was way back; by the time we got up to the box office, they were sold out. Depression set in.

So we were walking back to the car in the parking lot you know, and as we were walking back to the car I saw a friend that I know from church. So I stopped—it was a male friend—so I stopped and said "How are you?" And he just happened to be with this other guy, and, uh, so you know, we stood there and talked for a little while, and that's about all there was to it. Then we talked about like maybe going to the movies with them, but then we split and went our own way.

Listener: Right.

Well [laughs] then it turned out, that—uh—couple days later well the next Sunday I saw this friend that I knew at church, and he goes "You remember that guy I was with?" And I go "Well yeah," cause you know it was dark and everything, "Yeah, yeah, kinda remember him." "Well he wants to go on a date with you."

So we got it set up for a blind date, and uh I happened to know this girl that he was—that Duane was dating and so we um, we went out on a blind date and all that stuff.

That's how I met him

Source: Barbara Johnstone, Carnegie Mellon University, Pennsylvania

---

Valentine's Day," "in 1949 when I started college," or "about nine o'clock one night." Movies that were the incidental background for other events (meeting a new boyfriend, getting into a car wreck) are identified by name: "We were going to see *Oh, God*"; "Laura and I were going to see *Gone with the Wind.*" People unknown to a teller's audience were sometimes referred to with first and last names: "Let's see, his name was Louie Moore"; "And so Bobby Jones, who was usually the ringleader . . . came over." And events that frame stories were described in detail, these descriptions sometimes making up half of the transcribed text. The felt need for extra detail is especially clear in several stories in which tellers said "I forget his name" or "Let's see, now what was his name?" in repeated attempts to call to mind the names of characters whose names their audiences would not have recognized in any case.

Setting is an essential component of stories, literary or conversational. The term *orientation* has been used for the clauses in conversational narratives that provide the setting. To conform with hearers' general expectations that speakers provide only the right amount of relevant information, we might expect storytellers to provide just as much orientation as would be necessary to inform audiences about the settings in their stories, no more details than necessary for hearers to figure out the crucial background information, and no

details extraneous to the story's theme. Why, then do many of the Fort Wayne personal-experience stories include far more orientational material than should be necessary?

Details force hearers to engage with speakers by using their imaginations to construct alternative worlds or call to mind familiar worlds. There are differences among storytellers and groups of storytellers, however, in what can constitute an appropriate world for a story. In Fort Wayne, the world reflected in personal-experience stories must be the real, familiar, local world, even when the story's events could in fact have taken place anywhere. This is a correlate of local beliefs about the nature of storytelling as it relates to truth.

All tellings of the past are fictions, in the sense that all tellers make choices about what to present and how to present it most effectively. The line between what counts as "fact" and what counts as "fiction" is culturally drawn, and a teller's responsibility to be "factual," and how that responsibility is carried out, depends on how the social cohort defines factualness, on the culturally defined genre of the telling, and on the immediate social and rhetorical contexts.

For Fort Wayne's storytellers, recountings of personal experience must in principle be verifiable by other witnesses to those events. A person who tells good stories is someone to whom interesting things have happened, not someone who is good at making up or performing stories. For middle-class white Fort Wayners, a person perceived as dressing up ordinary events in gifted talk would be regarded with suspicion. To be perceived as valuable, personal narratives must be tied to real places and times in the local world. Tellers must display the fact that their stories are about actual, named people, and about things that really happened. The Fort Wayners used details to show that they were following their rule that stories are to be (or to appear to be) about things that really happened and that could be factually verified.

The idea that conversational narratives are factual reports of events that actually happened reflects mainstream American ideas about language and its relationship with "reality." In this view, language reflects preexisting meanings. Stories translate events into words; they re-create history. For people who imagine language this way, the events recounted in stories were actually discrete and actually occurred in the order in which they are reported; the meaning of the story was already there as the events happened, and storytellers are like cameras that capture life without analyzing it. It follows from this set of ideas that the best way of deploying language would be the most literal way: the way that reflects the facts in the most direct way possible. Self-consciously artistic verbal performances have a place in this literalist ideology of language, but it is a special, set-aside place. "Everyday" conversations are not the stage for displays of verbal skill.

Accordingly, the sounds and structures of everyday talk do not function as a resource for the construction and display of local identity the way they do in some other parts of the United States. In the American South, nonstandard speech, though stigmatized there as elsewhere as rural, uneducated, and low class, is a powerful resource for signaling nuances of personal and regional identity. Partly because southern speech stands out so clearly, the speech of southern whites gets media attention, through the country-western music industry and in television shows and movies, in a way that no other variety of American English does. Southern speech is also central to some of the most canonical American literature. Paradoxically, then, the ability to use features of this socially stigmatized minority variety is a way of getting heard: the South has a distinctive and noticeable voice.

In northern Indiana, by contrast, nonstandard speech may sometimes sound rural, but it does not appear to be symbolically associated with localness or region, or, accordingly, to function as a resource for the construction of local identity. In the Fort Wayne conversational stories, nonstandard grammar is very rare.

With the exception of fairly frequent reversals of transitivity in the pairs *sit/set* and *lay/lie* (so that *sit* might be used with a direct object and *set* might not), there are only occasional stories with any nonstandardness at all. One teller employed *a*-prefixing, for example ("a-runnin'"); one said "I says" and one, "I seen"; and two used a slightly nonstandard *at* as a verbal complement with *find* or *pick up*, as in "Where did I pick that guy up at?" Very little if any of this nonstandardness appears to be strategic, a resource for characterization or personal identification.

This reflects the more general fact that Midland midwestern speech like that of the Fort Wayners is an unmarked and largely unremarked variety. It is the "General American English" aimed at by radio and television announcers and television and movie characters about whom scriptwriters do not want to make any particular social point. There is no "local color" literature or music that draws on Midland speech forms the way Uncle Remus tales or country music draw on Southern forms. (This distinguishes the linguistic Midland from the northern linguistic area of the Midwest, including Michigan, Wisconsin, Minnesota, and the Dakotas, where local-sounding speech can sometimes act as a resource for creating a local sense of place.) Fort Wayners rely on local physical details to create a sense of place in their stories; they do not use regional-sounding speech for this purpose, because local speech forms are not symbolically linked to region. Precisely because Fort Wayners speak the variety of English that dominates in the economic and symbolic marketplace, they cannot use the sounds and structures of speech to express regional identity.

Sources and Further Reading: Barbara Johnstone, "Community and Contest: Midwestern Men and Women Creating Their Worlds in Conversational Storytelling," in Deborah Tannen, ed., *Gender and Conversational Interaction* (1993); Barbara Johnstone, *Stories, Community, and Place: Narratives from Middle America* (1990); Barbara Johnstone, "Variation in Discourse: Midwestern Narrative Style," *American Speech* 65 (Fall 1990); William Labov and Joshua Waletzky, "Narrative Analysis: Oral Versions of Personal Experience," *Journal of Narrative and Life History* 7 (1997); W.J.T. Mitchell, ed., *On Narrative* (1981); Livia Polanyi, *Telling the American Story: A Structural and Cultural Analysis of Conversational Storytelling* (1985); Deborah Schiffrin, "How a Story Says What It Means and Does," *Text* 4 (1984); Deborah Tannen, "New York Jewish Conversational Style," *International Journal of the Sociology of Language* 30 (1981); Deborah Tannen, *Talking Voices: Repetition, Dialogue, and Imagery in Conversational Discourse* (1989); Katherine Galloway Young, *Taleworlds and Storyrealms* (1987).

Barbara Johnstone
Carnegie Mellon University, Pennsylvania

Slang

The popular folk-characterization of midwestern English as relatively bland and colorless is well articulated by one of the laypeople interviewed in the educational video *American Tongues* (1986). The speaker, himself a midwesterner, says the language is "straight English" that comes "right out of the dictionary," and describes it further as having "no colloquialisms" and "no uniqueness." Although such perceptions cannot be dismissed out of hand—they do, in fact, dictate the reality of many Americans—a great deal of empirical evidence suggests that the slang and other unconventional words and phrases used in the English of the Midwest help render it as interesting and distinctive as the English used anywhere in the United States.

This distinctiveness, however, is often misrepresented by popular how-to manuals that purport to teach their readers "how to talk midwestern." The authors of such guides typically prescribe such folksy-sounding constructions as *woulda, coulda,* and *shoulda* (for "would have," "could have," and "should have," respectively); *gonna, wanna, liketa, useta,* and *oughta* (for "going to," "want to," "like to," "used to," and "ought to"); or *kinda* and *sorta* ("kind of," "sort of"). Other similar advice includes that the final syllable of *Missouri* and *Cincinnati* be pronounced *uh* rather than *ee;* that the *-ing* of words like *nothing, something, fishing,* and *working* be replaced with *-in'* (*nothin', somethin', fishin', workin'*); and that speakers comment frequently on the changeability of the weather ("if you don't like the temperature, just wait thirty minutes"). Again, the linking of speech patterns like these to the Midwest constitutes a powerful cultural stereotype—and again, one that influences what many Americans believe to be true (because ideas grounded in illusion are just as powerful as those grounded in fact), so it cannot be ignored—but the reality is that such features mark general stylistic informality rather than any specific regional dialect. Indeed, they occur so regularly throughout all colloquial American English that it is impossible to identify them even quantitatively with any one geographic area.

The other major stereotype about midwestern speakers, particularly those who are older and rural, is that they describe life's circumstances almost entirely through the use of quaint aphorisms. "He's the highest man on the totem pole" and "It's no skin off my nose," in fact, are often described as "midwestern folk sayings," as are "Beggars can't be choosers," "He's a wolf in sheep's clothing," "There's more than one way to skin a cat," "Don't count your chickens before they hatch," and a host of similar expressions. But once again, there is no empirical evidence to support this folk perception. Some of these sayings may be more popular in the Midwest than in other places—"He's the tallest hog at the trough," for example, is more likely to be heard in Illinois than in New Jersey or Arizona or Florida—but such proverbial wisdom is expressed in one form or another throughout American (as well as all other varieties of) English.

What, then, is unique about midwestern English? If we accept that this variety of the language is actually a patchwork of overlapping subvarieties loosely identified with corresponding, overlapping sections of the Midwest (the plains, the upper Midwest, the Ohio and Upper Mississippi River Valleys, the eastern and western Midwest, and so on), the answer is a great deal indeed. According to the *Dictionary of American Regional English (DARE),* many older speakers, especially, may describe a torrential rainfall as *raining pitchforks and nigger babies* in the Eastern and Central Midwest (elsewhere in the country, such downpours are variously described as *raining pitchforks and bullfrogs, pitchforks and darning needles, pitchforks and sawlogs, pitchforks and grindstones,* and *pitchforks and barn shovels*). When someone fails, does poorly, grows weak or tired, or backs out of an agreement, he or she is often said to *poo(h) out* in the northern and eastern Midwest (this may be a variation of the more common *poop out*). And chiefly in those states bordering the Mississippi River, the slippery elm tree (*Ulmus rubra*) and white elm tree (*Ulmus americana*)—both of which, when cut or burned green, spew copious amounts of sap—is called a *piss elm* (with *elm* sometimes pronounced as two syllables, *ell-um*).

Again according to *DARE,* if something such as a tree or a building is tipping or slanting or out of plumb in much of the eastern Midwest, speakers may describe it as *leaning toward Fisher's* (the same building or tree in Indiana may also be *leaning toward Cooper's;* elsewhere in the country it is *leaning toward Perkins's, leaning toward Jones's,* or *leaning toward Sawyer's*). A once-popular children's game in which a long stick was used to flip up and then hit a shorter stick was called *knick-knock* between the Mississippi and the Ohio Rivers. A large sum of money can be referred to as *the bucks* or *big bucks* (as in, "John just got a new job; he's really in the bucks now") everywhere except the southern half of Kansas and Missouri. And the freshwater clam *Fusconaia flava* is known in the upper Mississippi Valley as a *pigtoe* and in the Ohio Valley as an *Ohio River pigtoe.*

Everywhere language reflects the diversity of midwesterners. From the many online dictionaries and glossaries that chart the evolution of such subcultures and lifestyles, we learn that cyclists use *pooch polo* to describe the swinging of a frame pump to dissuade a pursuing dog. *Mud duck* occurs among members of adolescent street gangs to characterize an unattractive female (the phrase should not be confused with the *mud duck* used elsewhere in the Midwest as well as farther south and east, which refers to any of a variety of ducks otherwise known as *coots*). Many older gay males in the Midwest describe their peers' backsides with *spare tire*. Drug dealers and users, especially in the larger urban areas of the central Midwest, often use *222* to refer to methamphetamine, and *Joe Friday(s)* to refer to one or more Quaaludes (known more widely as *Ludes*; according to the Indiana Prevention Resource Center at Indiana University, *Joe Friday* derives from *714* being both the numeric code imprinted on Quaalude tablets and the badge number of the eponymous character from the popular 1950s television series *Dragnet*).

It is almost impossible to know how current such terminology is, however. One of the hallmarks of slang is that, as a linguistic fad, it tends to be ephemeral. This is especially true of the slang used by subcultures engaged in illicit or socially unacceptable activities. The members of these subcultures must often communicate with one another while simultaneously concealing their activities from the authorities, potential marks, or society at large; thus they have a vested interest in keeping their specialized language a secret. None of the terms cited in the previous paragraph appear in any of several of the most comprehensive dictionaries of modern American slang, including the *Dictionary of American Slang*, *A Dictionary of Slang and Unconventional English*, and the *Random House Historical Dictionary of American Slang*. By the time they are included in future editions, they will most likely have become obsolete, at least among the groups that used them originally.

The currency of slang and other unconventional language used by broader cross-sections of midwesterners is often easier to document, though establishing the precise sociocultural origins of such words can still be difficult. Most, in fact, are probably lost to history, though some can be traced most immediately to the East and West Coasts. Cities such as New York, San Francisco, and Los Angeles have long been recognized as trendsetting hubs of creation in the worlds of fashion and hairstyle; less well known is that they often serve as progenitors of linguistic fads as well. In the late 1980s, *doughnuts* was being used to mean 'dollars' on the West Coast; but by the early 1990s the term had migrated inward at least as far as the central Midwest, where it was adopted as a sign of being "cool" by many college students (who then abandoned it by the mid-1990s, the word by then presumably having lost its luster of chic). Similarly, *three-tie* in much of the East Coast business world in the early 1980s referred to a person wearing suspenders and a tie. The term quickly fell out of use, but it was discov-

ered again within a few years on college campuses from central Ohio to eastern Kansas.

Some midwestern folk speech is directly traceable to ethnic settlement patterns. Chiefly throughout many heavily German-settled areas of the Midwest, for example, *liver sausage* (a translation of the German *Leberwurst*) is used to describe the food known elsewhere as *braunschweiger*, *liverwurst*, or *hog-head sausage*. *Klatch*, also sometimes spelled *clatch*, *clotch*, *clutch*, *glutch*, *klatsch*, *klot(s)ch*, or *klutch*, is a verb that means 'to participate in a coffee gathering' (another translation, from the German *Klatsch* 'gossip', the word is known more commonly in the phrase *coffee klatch*, which refers to a gathering that features coffee and conversation). *Schnickelfritz* (also with many variant spellings, but most often *shnickelfritz* and *snicklefritz*) can be used to describe a rowdy or mischievous child (the etymology of the word is uncertain, but is believed to involve the German *Schnickel/Schniggle* 'little boy's penis' and the common German name *Fritz*, which passed into general usage during World War I after the military began using it as a derogatory slang term to describe anything or anyone German). Especially in Minnesota and Wisconsin, which are areas known to have been heavily settled by Scandinavians, porridge or pudding that has cream as the principal ingredient is called *rommegrot* (the Norwegian word is *rømmegrøt* 'cream porridge'). And in French-settled regions primarily west of the Mississippi River, from Minnesota and the eastern Dakotas to Missouri and eastern Kansas, the terms *pomme blanche*, *pomme de prairie*, and/or *pomme de terre* (literally, 'white apple', 'prairie apple', and 'ground apple', respectively) can refer to the edible tubers of the plant *Psoralea esculenta* (known more commonly as the breadroot scurf pea), and sometimes to the plant itself.

Of course midwesterners have also created their share of unconventional English by adapting to new purposes words and phrases already in the language (as with *three-tie* and *doughnuts*, mentioned above). This is especially true of midwestern adolescents, who, like their peers everywhere, are the foremost originators and users of such language as the natural result of attempting to exert their autonomy from adult authority and mark the boundaries of their age-defined group. In the 1980s, students at The Ohio State University appear to have coined, among many other terms, *junior* 'an odd person', *Russell* 'one who teases severely', *sport* 'to lend money', *sugardale bologna* 'bad breath', *W. C. Steakhouse* 'a person lacking a suntan', and *zovrako syndrome* 'the condition of having an unzipped fly'. These words and phrases are no longer as popular as they once were—many, in fact, no longer seem to be used at all—but most could be heard on larger college campuses in the central Midwest at least through the mid-1990s.

A great deal more remains to be done in the recording of midwestern slang and folk speech (as well as in how that slang and folk speech are perceived, both inside and outside the Midwest, and how those perceptions affect the way midwesterners and their language are treated), but the research so far has revealed that this language is anything but plain. Its vitality and complexity mirror the vital and complex needs of its users, and because those needs are changing constantly, so too is the language. In fact, the only certainty concerning the slang, metaphors, and other unconventional turns of phrase used in the Midwest is that they will continue to remain as interesting as the people who use them.

Sources and Further Reading: Frederic G. Cassidy, ed., *Dictionary of American Regional English*, vol. 1, *A–C* (1985); Frederic G. Cassidy and Joan Houston Hall, eds., *Dictionary of American Regional English*, vol. 2, *D–H* (1991) and vol. 3, *I–O* (1996); Center for New American Media, *American Tongues* (1986); Robert L. Chapman, ed., *Dictionary of American Slang* (1998); Stuart Berg Flexner, *I Hear America Talking* (1976); Stuart Berg Flexner, *Listening to America* (1982); Stuart Berg Flexner and Anne H. Soukhanov, *Speaking Freely: A Guided Tour of American English from Plymouth Rock to Silicon Valley* (1997); J. E. Lighter, ed., *Random House Historical Dictionary of American Slang*, vols. 1 (A–G; 1994) and 2 (H–O; 1997); Eric Partridge and Paul Beale, eds., *A Dictionary of Slang and Unconventional English*, 8th ed. (1984).

Thomas E. Murray
Kansas State University

Geographic Names

Midwest geographic names are products of three primary naming traditions. The first was established by the early French explorers, the second commemorated historical and national figures and events, and the third resulted from "progressive pioneering," where an original name was given many times over in memory of homes and farms left behind in the eastern states or Europe.

The first of these naming patterns runs south and north and consists of the many French names found throughout the Mississippi River Valley, from below New Orleans, Louisiana, to St. Cloud, Minnesota, and beyond. These names generally follow the waterways of the region and they extend from the Mississippi and the Ohio Rivers along their tributaries through the Great Lakes and the upper Midwest. The influence of the French naming tradition is easy to underestimate because many of the names have been so changed in form or translated into English that they are not easily recognized as French. We can gather a general sense

Table 1. French Place-Names in the Midwest

State	Number of names	State	Number of names
Michigan	293	Ohio	96
Illinois	248	North Dakota	91
Minnesota	219	Nebraska	77
South Dakota	202	Wisconsin	59
Missouri	186	Iowa	54
Indiana	164	Kansas	44

Source: René Coulet Du Gard, *Dictionary of French Place Names in the U.S.A.* (1986).

of the depth and extent of French names in the Midwest from table 1.

René Coulet du Gard, who compiled the data in table 1, has a very broad definition of French names and we would have to refine these raw numbers considerably before we could draw any firm conclusions. Even so, from the gross number of entries alone, we can make several observations: first, the sheer number of French names in the Midwest (more than 1,700), considerably more than from any other language except English, and second, their uneven distribution. The relative abundance in South Dakota and unexpected paucity in Wisconsin are particularly striking.

French names were brought to the Midwest from two directions: a small number from the lower Mississippi Valley and the majority from French Canada, initially by the *coureurs du bois* and the *voyageurs*, explorers, hunters, trappers, and traders who used the lakes and streams of the Midwest as their highways into the interior in the seventeenth and eighteenth centuries. With the exception of the priests who often accompanied them, these were wanderers and transients who depended upon the waterways for their very survival. Thus, most of the names were related to riverine features and water travel. Among the early names were those of streams, such as *Rivière aux vases* 'slimy river' (Missouri) and *Rivière aux Ecorces* 'bark river' (Michigan), and lakes, such as *Lac du Flambeau* 'lake of the torches' (Wisconsin) and *Lac bois blanc* 'lake of the white wood' (Minnesota).

Many French names related to conditions of travel. Some, such as *detour*, meaning a circuitous route, especially a horseshoe bend in a river, as in Grand Detour, Illinois, and *portage*, where canoes and supplies had to be carried overland from one navigable waterway to the next, as in Portage (Wisconsin, Ohio, Michigan, and elsewhere), are known to most Americans. Many others have disappeared from the general vocabulary and now exist only as geographic names, their meaning opaque to modern readers. The French term *ance* referred to a little bay or cove that marked the shoreline; it has left its trace in L'anse, Michigan. *Presque* was a peninsula, 'a near island'; the place-name Presque Isle occurs in Michigan and several other states. A *traverse* was a place where canoes, instead of hugging the shoreline, could cut safely across the mouth of a bay or a bend in a river, thereby shortening the journey. The name has left its mark in Traverse City and Grand Traverse, both in Michigan.

Two names of great importance to seventeenth-century travelers are largely unknown today. *Racine* 'root' (Illinois, Ohio, Wisconsin, and elsewhere) designated a spot on a river so overgrown with roots and branches that passage was difficult or impossible. The most confusing of the French names to contemporary ears is surely *Embarrass*. Embarrass Rivers in Minnesota, Wisconsin, Illinois, and elsewhere take their name from the common noun *embarrass*, which meant 'an obstruction in a river', often a pile of uprooted trees and other debris that made navigation hazardous. (The equivalent early American term, now largely unknown as well, is *raft*.)

Other French names in the Midwest include *Eau Claire* 'clear water' (Wisconsin), *Des Plaines* 'at the maples' (Illinois), *Terre Haute* 'high land' (Indiana), *Fond du Lac* 'end of the lake' (Wisconsin and Illinois), *Detroit* 'the strait' (Michigan and Illinois), and *Vermil(l)ion* 'bright orange' (Michigan, Minnesota, and elsewhere) for the red clay used by Native Americans as paint.

The early French names have been treated inconsistently by English speakers. Some, such as *Prairie du Chien* 'meadow of the dog' (Wisconsin), *Pointe aux Pins* 'point of the pines' (Minnesota), and *Prairie du Rocher* ' meadow of the rocks' (Illinois) have been retained in their full French forms; others, such as *Lac Superior* and *Isle au Boeuf* (Missouri), have been partially relexified with the more familiar and similar-sounding English equivalents *lake* and *island*, respectively, while others, such as *La Rivière des Feves* 'river of beans', now Fever River, Illinois, have been completely translated and their French origin obscured to the point of opacity.

The French naming system in the Midwest is now only an artifact, replaced by two evolving naming systems brought by American and European settlers. These two naming patterns, which were quite minor in the eastern states, were developed into the dominant ones that characterize American geographic naming to this day. Unlike the French, Americans were interested in establishing and naming political subdivisions such as counties and townships.

Much of the Midwest was named in the first half of the nineteenth century. This great expanse of territory needed thousands of names and settlers had a group of national heroes, especially from the American Revolu-

tion and the War of 1812, from which to choose. Towns, townships, and counties were named in honor of naval officers Stephen Decatur and Oliver Hazard Perry. General Andrew Jackson lent both his name and his nickname "Old Hickory" to counties, townships, and settlements; there was even an occasional Hermitage, from the name of Jackson's plantation near Nashville, Tennessee. Commemorative naming reached back to the Revolution and even to Christopher Columbus himself. Each state has a number of Washingtons, Adamses, Jeffersons, and Franklins. Washington was especially favored: Indiana has forty-seven townships named Washington and Ohio has forty-three. Signers of the Declaration of Independence figure prominently as well, especially Charles Carroll, of Carrollton, and John Hancock.

Battles were also celebrated: Concord and Bunker Hill from the American Revolution, Valparaiso from the War of 1812, Buena Vista and Cerro Gordo from the Mexican War, and, later, Corinth and Iuka (both in Mississippi) from the Civil War. Above all, there was Union. Indiana alone has thirty-five townships named Union and Ohio has twenty-eight. Contemporaries such as Martin Van Buren, Henry Clay, John C. Calhoun, and Stephen Douglas were honored, along with Revolutionary War heroes Francis Marion and George Rogers Clark, and Europeans who had helped win the Revolution, including Johann DeKalb, Casimir Pulaski, and, especially, the Marquis de Lafayette and his estate near Paris, Lagrange.

Perhaps the ultimate in commemorative naming was reached in January 1825, when the Illinois legislature created eight new counties all named for men who had achieved fame in the era of the American Revolution: Patrick Henry, John Adams, John Hancock, Henry Knox, Hugh Mercer, Israel Putnam, Joseph Warren, and Philip Schuyler. The seat of Adams County was named Quincy and the town common was named John's Square, thereby appropriating the complete name of John Quincy Adams.

This intense commemorative naming led to the linking of names in unpredictable but interesting ways. Valparaiso in Porter County, Indiana, is named for the city in Chile, off the coast of which Captain David Porter, namesake of the county, engaged the British fleet in the War of 1812. The seat of DeWitt County, Illinois, named for New York governor DeWitt Clinton, is Clinton, and Moultrie County, Illinois, named for William Moultrie of the Revolution, has as its seat Sullivan, likely named for the battle of Sullivan's Island, the site of Moultrie's victory in Charleston Harbor.

Commemorative naming on this scale was previously unknown, and it was extended to ordinary citizens as well as to major regional and national figures, a uniquely American innovation. In laying out new towns, it quickly became customary to name a community for the person who owned the town site or who was an early settler or postmaster. These names established the pattern that was followed by the rest of the country and which remains a dominant naming pattern today.

The other major naming pattern that was established in the Midwest was personal rather than nationalistic and provided a means of maintaining ties with families and farmsteads left behind. For the first time on such a grand scale, new communities were named for old communities; towns in the Midwest were named for former homes in the East or South. This had been a very minor naming pattern in America, and such names, called transfer names, were often marked with "New"—New Britain and New London in Connecticut, and even New England itself. But namers in the Midwest largely dispensed with "New" and the names were given over and over again as succeeding waves of settlers rolled westward. Wyoming, originally a New York name, was transferred to the Wyoming Valley of Pennsylvania, from where it was transferred to Wyoming, Ohio, and then to Wyoming, Illinois. Aurora, for Aurora, New York, was brought first to Ohio, then to Indiana and to Illinois, and then taken to points farther west. Sometimes the journey of a name was short. A part of east-central Illinois was settled by migrants from Ohio, who named their newly established twin cities Champaign, for their former home, Champaign County, Ohio, and Urbana, for the seat of Champaign County, Ohio.

Allen Walker Read calls such naming "progressive pioneering" and notes the case of Aaron Street, who emigrated from Salem, New Jersey, and founded Salem, Ohio. He then moved farther west and founded Salem, Indiana. Street's son then moved across the Mississippi River and founded Salem, Iowa. Elsewhere Read has called the connections created by this network of transferred names "gossamer threads," which bind new names to old names and new places to old places, and which served to unify the country and maintain connections between families and communities, however distant.

Before leaving this brief account of names in the Midwest, two auxiliary or secondary naming systems deserve mention: native names and names resulting from the establishment of foreign and domestic colonies.

In the Midwest, American Indian names were not a significant part of the naming system. Those that do occur are not Native American names per se, but commemorative, county and township names given by Europeans for a tribe or a person who once may have lived in the area. The various Osceolas scattered throughout the Midwest and named for the Seminole

leader provide one example. By the second half of the nineteenth century, however, honoring an American Indian was not nearly as important as honoring a colonial figure or the owner of the town site. This is somewhat ironic when we consider that all of the state names in the Midwest are derived from native sources: Illinois, from the Illinois confederacy, with a French suffix and meaning 'the people'; Indiana, a coined name presumed to mean 'land of the Indians'; Iowa, from the Iowa or Ioway tribe; Kansas, from a Siouan word likely meaning 'the people of the south wind'; Michigan 'great lake'; Minnesota 'cloudy' (perhaps 'blue') water; Missouri, perhaps meaning 'people of the big canoes'; Nebraska 'flat water'; Dakota 'an alliance of friends'; Ohio 'great river'; and Wisconsin, probably a Menomini word whose meaning is disputed.

European immigrants often brought names with them. Among their contributions to the midwestern landscape are Hanover, Sweden, Berlin, New Glarus, Upsala, New Ulm, and Strasburg.

Naming in the Midwest in the nineteenth century reflected the growing Americanization of the country, especially the growing confidence of the people in themselves and their ability to create a new nation and a growing sense of a secure, dignified, and illustrious past. The naming patterns established in the early Midwest quickly became not only quantitatively but qualitatively different from those of the eastern states. Their success is measured by the fact that the patterns that are characteristic of present day naming in all parts of the country, especially commemorative names and transfer names, were established first in the Midwest.

Sources and Further Reading: Ronald L. Baker and Marvin Carmony, *Indiana Place Names* (1975); Edward Callary, ed., *Place Names in the Midwestern United States* (2000); René Coulet du Gard, *Dictionary of French Place Names in the U.S.A.* (1986); Larry L. Miller, *Ohio Place Names* (1996); Allen Walker Read, *America: Naming the Country and Its People* (2001); Virgil J. Vogel, *Indian Names in Michigan* (1986); Virgil J. Vogel, *Indian Names on Wisconsin's Map* (1991); Virgil J. Vogel, *Iowa Place Names of Indian Origin* (1983).

Edward Callary
Northern Illinois University

Native American Languages

The symbolic importance of the Midwest's Native American languages to the general population is shown by the use of words from those languages to name all of the midwestern states except Indiana, which honors Native Americans in another way. To American Indians of the Midwest, their languages are not only means of communication but unique carriers of their ancestral cultures and as such are themselves precious cultural artifacts.

Around thirty of the more than three hundred North American indigenous languages were once spoken or are still spoken in the Midwest, representing five distinct language families, groups of historically related languages: Algonquian, Caddoan, Iroquoian, Kiowa-Tanoan, and Siouan. The indigenous languages of the Midwest today are languages in crisis; extensive social change and government policies of eradication have led to their replacement by English as the dominant language in most Native American communities. Few children now learn their ancestral languages in the home. The loss of the languages is keenly felt by the Native American peoples who are struggling to revitalize them.

The languages likely to have been spoken in the Midwest at the time of first European contact are shown, along with their family membership, in map 1. Defining a language can have linguistic dimensions and historical/political dimensions. Linguistically, if two individuals, each speaking in their own tongue, cannot understand each other well, they are speaking separate and mutually unintelligible languages. If they understand each other well, they are speaking different dialects of the same language. Because the degree of mutual comprehension can vary, determining whether two language varieties are separate languages or dialects can be difficult. If the peoples speaking the varieties are separate historically and politically, their language varieties may be considered distinct languages even though they are mutually intelligible.

Some of the midwestern languages, such as Menominee and Shawnee, are mutually unintelligible with all other languages and show little internal dialect variation; their status as distinct languages is clear. Others, such as Sauk, Fox, and Kickapoo, are largely

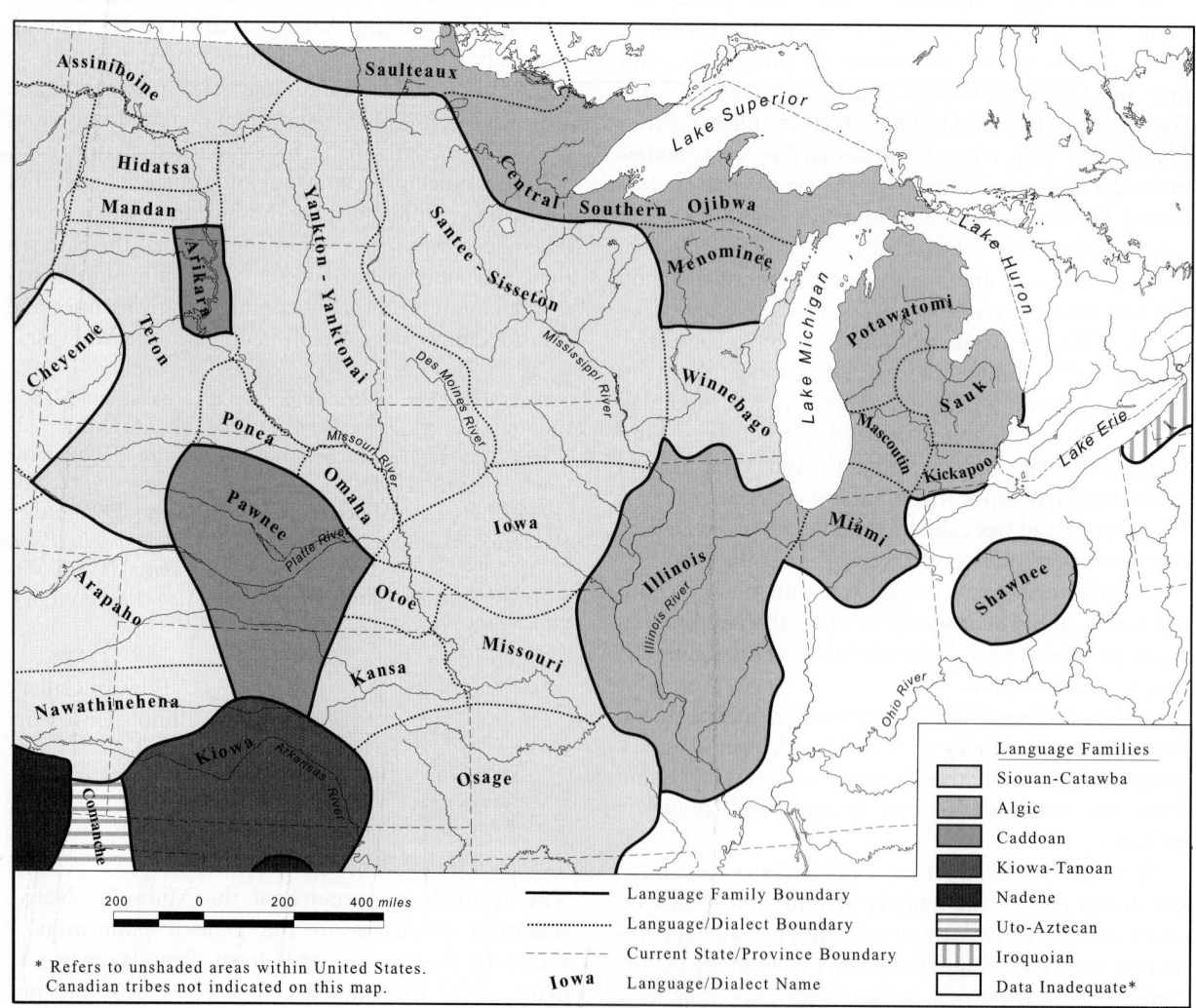

Map 1. Native American language families. Prepared by Margaret Popovich. *Source:* Ives Goddard, ed., *Handbook of North American Indians,* vol. 17 (1996).

mutually intelligible with each other and can be treated for descriptive purposes as dialects of a single language, Sauk-Fox-Kickapoo, which has no common name in either the languages themselves or in English. Historically and politically, however, the peoples speaking these language varieties are distinct and so their ways of speaking can also be given status as distinct languages. Another example is Sioux, or Dakota, language names that cover distinct dialects that for historical and political reasons may be treated as distinct languages: Sisseton-Santee (Dakota), Yankton-Yanktonais, and Teton (Lakota). In other cases, adjacent communities may speak mutually intelligible varieties but be connected through a chain of many such relationships to geographically distant communities speaking language varieties that are not mutually intelligible. Ojibwe is an example of such a continuum or chain of dialects, and its major dialect groups can be treated as separate languages even though there are not clear boundaries between them.

In the eighteenth century, the area that became the Midwest was occupied mainly by Siouan- and Algonquian-speaking peoples, with the Siouan-speaking peoples concentrated in the area west of the Mississippi and running across Minnesota and Wisconsin to Lake Michigan. Elsewhere Algonquian-speaking peoples predominated, but the languages of the peoples of the Ohio River Valley, with the exception of the Algonquian-speaking Shawnee, were not recorded and their exact affiliation is unknown. In southern Kansas lived the Kiowa, speaking a Kiowa-Tanoan language, and north of them in Nebraska, the Pawnee, and in South Dakota, the Arikara, both speaking languages of the Caddoan family. It is likely that speakers of other languages were also present before recorded contact with Europeans, such as the Algonquian language Cheyenne, later found farther west. There are other languages, such as Michigamea and Erie, for which we have names but not enough documented words to be certain of their linguistic affiliation.

Following initial contact with Europeans, many tribes changed locations or were dispersed, many ultimately exiled to other locations in the region or to present-day Oklahoma, others to Canada or Mexico. Speakers of some Eastern Algonquian languages came from New England and New York, and speakers of Ottawa came from the North. Speakers of Iroquoian languages (Huron and Wyandot from the North, and Seneca from the East) relocated into the Ohio region soon after contact with Europeans in their homelands. Speakers of another Iroquoian language, Oneida, were relocated from New York to Wisconsin in the mid-nineteenth century.

The languages are grouped into language families on the basis of extensive similarities in sounds, vocabu-laries, and sentence and word-building patterns. Some of the basis for the assignment to a language family can be seen in table 2, a sample comparison of two words across some of the midwestern languages. Even though these two words represent but a tiny part of the evidence for a language classification, the basic division as well as some subgrouping of languages within families can be seen. The best explanation for extensive similarities that exist between certain languages is that these languages are descended from a single common ancestral language, itself no longer spoken. Each of the languages of the Midwest descends from such an un-

Table 2. Two Words in Some Indigenous Languages of the Midwest

	"five"	"tobacco"
Algonquian		
Sauk-Fox-Kickapoo		
Fox	nya:nanwi	nese:ma:wa
Kickapoo	niananwi	neθe:ma:
Menominee	nianan	nɛʔnema:w
Miami	ya:lanwi	ahse:ma
Ojibwe group		
Ojibwe (Southern Central)	na:nan	asse:ma:
Ottawa	na:nan	sse:ma:
Potawatomi	nyanən	sema
Shawnee	nya:lanwi	laθe:ma:
Caddoan		
Arikara	šíhUx	na:wlškánuʔ
Pawnee	sihuks	ra:wiska:ruʔ
Iroquoian		
Oneida	wísk	oyú:kwaʔ
Siouan		
Sioux (Dakota)		
Santee (Dakota)	záptą	čʰą dí
Teton (Lakota)	záptą	čʰą lí
Assiniboine	záptą	čʰą ní
Dhegiha		
Omaha	sáttą	nínǐži
Ponca	sáttą	niní
Kansa	sáttą	nǫnú
Osage	sáttą	nanúhü
Chiwere-Winnebago		
Iowa/Otoe	θa:tʰą	ra:nʸį
Winnebago (Ho-chunk)	sa:čą́	ta:ní

For comparative purposes, different ways of indicating vowel length have been replaced by the sequence of vowel-colon: a:, etc. Capital vowel symbols represent voiceless vowels.

Sources: Leonard Bloomfield, *Menomini Lexicon* (1975); David J. Costa, personal communication; Ives Goddard, "The Languages of the Plains: Introduction," in William C. Sturtevant, ed., *Handbook of North American Indians* 13 (2001); Ives Goddard, ed., *Leonard Bloomfield's Fox Lexicon* (1994); Karin Michelson and Mercy Doxtator, *Oneida-English English-Oneida Dictionary* (2002); Kennth L. Miner, comp., *Winnebago Field Lexicon* (1992); Paul Voorhis, *Kickapoo Vocabulary* (1988).

recorded ancestral or proto-language, now known only through scholarly methods of comparison of the daughter languages within each family. Some of the families belong to larger groups: Algonquian belongs in a larger Algic family with two languages spoken on the Pacific coast in California, and Siouan, in a larger Siouan-Catawban family, along with several southeastern languages.

The indigenous languages of the Midwest are severely endangered. Under pressure from the increasingly dominant language, English, the percentage of each population speaking the language has diminished. Of the thirty or so languages of the Midwest, two-thirds are either extinct, being no longer spoken anywhere in the world as a mother tongue, or are spoken as a mother tongue by fewer than 100 people, none of them children. Only three of the other languages have more than 1,000 mother-tongue speakers, including some children. The languages with the largest number of speakers are Sisseton-Santee (Dakota), with around 600 speakers (with closely related Teton [Lakota], spoken west of the Midwest, having 5,000), Kickapoo, with more than 1,500 (nearly all outside the region), and all of the midwestern dialects of Ojibwe taken together, with perhaps 10,000 speakers, most of whom live in Canada. Other Canadian dialects of Ojibwe not represented in the Midwest account for at least an additional 20,000 speakers.

In the last decades of the twentieth century, the reduction in the number of speakers became a matter of great concern for American Indian communities. Nearly every community with a language still spoken has arranged for the teaching of the language in local schools. Numerous projects have created or spread writing systems, written school language lessons and readers, and recorded oral lessons, with increasing reliance now placed on new media such as the compact disk and the Internet. For some languages, a small group of "language warriors"—activists who did not grow up as fluent speakers—have learned the languages as second languages; practice them with their families; use them in tribal ceremonies, language lunch tables, and summer camps; and work to further document and promote them in the communities. The more widely spoken languages such as Dakota and Ojibwe are taught at tribal and community colleges and at public universities and colleges. Academic linguists have worked with communities and elderly speakers, and with older written records, to document the languages in dictionaries, grammars, and collections of oral traditions. Where there are only a few remaining speakers of a language and resources are limited, it may be difficult to keep language classes and programs going despite the hopes of individuals, as has

Table 3. Menominee Sisters and Brothers

System 1 (distinguishing relative age)

my younger sister or brother	næhsēh
my older brother	næqnæh
my older sister	nemēh

System 2 (distinguishing relative sex)

my brother (man speaking), my sister (woman speaking)	nekoqsema
my brother (man speaking)	nēmat
my sister (woman speaking)	nētekæh

been the case for the Sauk language. Many communities without living languages prefer to view them as not extinct but merely sleeping, and work to relearn them, basing their lessons on the documents of the languages created by speakers of previous generations, most often as recorded by European missionaries, travelers, anthropologists, and linguists.

While the last speaker of Miami-Illinois died in the 1980s, Miami language activist and linguist Daryl Baldwin has relearned his ancestral Miami language from extensive written documentation beginning in the eighteenth century, as organized and interpreted by linguist David Costa. Baldwin aims to reawaken the language by using it as an everyday language with his children, who are becoming a new generation of native speakers. He has organized summer immersion courses for the now widely dispersed Miamis and distributed oral language lessons on tapes and compact discs.

Each language has a distinct system for encoding meaning in words and word-building elements, and direct equivalencies between words in different languages do not always exist. In Ojibwe, there are no simple words equivalent to English verbs describing motions such as run, walk, fly, crawl, wade, swim; each Ojibwe verb contains two main ideas each represented by a separate word part; the initial part indicates a direction or a manner of motion, and the final part indicates the type of motion, thus *bimoode* 'crawl by/past', *biidoode* 'crawl this way', *ondoode* 'crawl from a place', *gizhiiyoode* 'crawl fast', each containing an element *-oode* 'crawl', which is not a complete word by itself, but which combines with adverbial initial elements to make words or word stems.

Menominee kin terms form another striking example. Corresponding to the two English terms *brother* and *sister* are six Menominee terms, given in table 3. There are two ways of identifying siblings. One way makes a distinction of relative age: There is one term for a younger brother or sister, but there are distinct terms for an older brother and an older sister. The other way makes a distinction for relative sex: There is a single cross-sex term for a female's brother and a male's sister, but distinct terms for a male's brother and for a female's sister. This set of terms is also used for one kind of cousin (for the children of one's mother's sister and one's father's brother); distinct terms are used for cousins related in another way (the children of one's mother's brother and one's father's sister).

Sources and Further Reading: Lyle Campbell, *American Indian Languages* (1997); Ives Goddard, ed., *Languages*, vol. 17 of William C. Sturtevant, ed., *Handbook of North American Indians* (1996); Ives Goddard, "The Languages of the Plains: Introduction," in William C. Sturtevant, ed., *Handbook of North American Indians*, vol. 13, *Plains*, ed. Raymond J. De-Mallie (2001); Leanne Hinton and Ken Hale, eds., *The Green Book of Language Revitalization in Practice* (2001); Marianne Mithun, *The Languages of Native North America* (1999); Douglas R. Parks, "Caddoan Languages," in William C. Sturtevant, ed., *Handbook of North American Indians*, vol. 13, *Plains*, ed. Raymond J. DeMallie (2001); Shirley Silver and Wick R. Miller, *American Indian Languages* (1997).

John D. Nichols
University of Minnesota–Twin Cities

Algonquian

The majority of the indigenous languages of the Midwest belong to the Algonquian family, which includes some thirty languages once or now spoken by Native American peoples from North Carolina north through the middle states and New England to the Maritime Provinces and Labrador, west through Canada and the Midwest across the Great Lakes and the Great Plains west to the Rockies and north to Hudson Bay. Distantly related to the Algonquian languages are Wiyot and Yurok of northern California, which are grouped together with Algonquian in a larger Algic family.

A likely location for the ancient homeland of the Algic-speaking peoples is the Plateau region, with a later Algonquian homeland located farther east, one study placing it between Georgian Bay and Lake Ontario some three thousand years ago. The proto-Algonquian language spoken then, ancestral to all of the Algonquian languages, is known only through scholarly reconstruction based on comparison of the sounds and words of its daughter languages that have been documented in writing.

There are six main groups of midwestern Algonquian languages: Menominee, Miami-Illinois, Ojibwe, Potawatomi, Sauk-Fox-Kickapoo, and Shawnee. Menominee, a single language with little dialect variation, has long been spoken in eastern Wisconsin. Although there are now only a small number of elderly speakers, an active tribal teaching program exists, as does a joint tribal–University of Wisconsin research program building on considerable earlier documentation. Miami-Illinois identifies tribal varieties of a language once spoken south of Lake Michigan in Indiana and Illinois, and later in Kansas and Oklahoma. There are now vigorous revitalization activities underway building on extensive written records.

Ojibwe is spoken over a large area of Canada and the Great Lakes states in more than a hundred communities. A chain of overlapping dialects, its southern varieties spoken in the Midwest and adjacent regions of Canada, are Central Southern Ojibwe, generally known as Ojibwe (Ojibwa, Ojibway) or Chippewa, spoken in Minnesota, Wisconsin, the Upper Peninsula of Michigan, and Ontario, and Ottawa (Odawa), spoken on the Lower Peninsula of Michigan and on Manitoulin Island and west to Sault Ste. Marie in Ontario. Northern Ojibwe and other varieties of Southern Ojibwe are spoken in Canada. Closely related to Ojibwe is Potawatomi, once spoken to the south of the Great Lakes, now spoken by around fifty elderly speakers in Kansas, Michigan, Oklahoma, Ontario, and Wisconsin.

A group of languages formerly spoken across the western Great Lakes region centering on southern Michigan and Wisconsin, Sauk-Fox-Kickapoo includes two tribal dialects of a single language, Fox (Mesquakie), now spoken in Iowa, and Sauk, spoken in Oklahoma and, until recently, in Kansas, as well as a closely related language, Kickapoo, now spoken in Coahuila, Mexico, by a band that migrated there in the mid-nineteenth century, and in Kansas, Oklahoma, and Texas. Shawnee, documented as spoken in Ohio at the time of the European invasion, now has several hundred speakers in Oklahoma.

Some of the Algonquian languages of the East have also been spoken in the Midwest. Speakers of three languages of the Delaware group of Eastern Algonquian languages, Mahican, Munsee, and Unami, these last two also known as Delaware, moved into the region that became the Midwest from New York, New Jersey, and Pennsylvania after initial European contact. Mahican was last known to be spoken in Wisconsin in the 1930s, and, as a mother tongue, Unami was still spoken at the beginning of the twenty-first century in Oklahoma. A small number of Munsee speakers live in Ontario, but Munsee was formerly also spoken in Wisconsin, Kansas, and Oklahoma. Of the dozen or so other Eastern Algonquian languages, only Maliseet-Passamaquoddy (New Brunswick and Maine), Micmac (the Maritime Provinces and Quebec), and Western Abenaki (Quebec) are still spoken as first languages.

Spoken across Canada from Quebec to Alberta are several languages of the Cree group (including Cree, Montagnais, Naskapi, and Atikamekw), each with many thousands of speakers. On the Great Plains are spoken Arapaho (in Montana, Wyoming, and Oklahoma), Blackfoot (in Montana and Alberta), and Cheyenne (in Montana and Oklahoma), with some children still speaking the latter two languages.

Something of the rich structure of Algonquian languages can be suggested by the following description of Ojibwe verbs. Each verb is built around a stem carrying its basic meaning. Inflectional prefixes and suffixes added to the stem index the person, number, obviation (a category distinguishing main from secondary third-persons), and gender of subjects and objects, verb mode, and negation. Thus a single stem can occur in many thousands of possible inflected forms. A few examples of forms of the stem *waabam-* 'see someone' are: *niwaabamaa* 'I see her/him', *giwaabamigonaadog* 'he/she must be seeing you and me', *waabamaasiwadwaa* 'if you (singular) don't see them', and *waabamigooyaambaan* 'had I been seen'. Verbs are further inflected with prefixes for tense/aspect and other categories. Verb stems can themselves be complex, containing an initial root and one or more final elements identifying actions, states, instruments, or relationships, along with optional nounlike or classifying medial elements; the root may also be reduplicated (a doubling up of part of a word). An example of a complex stem is *aayaazhawaakosidamaw* 'lay a stick-like thing across something over and over for someone' with root *aazhaw-* 'across' reduplicated with *aay-* adding the 'over and over' meaning, medial element *-aako-*, a classifier for sticklike objects, a final element *-sid* specifying an action 'lay or place something inanimate', and another final element *-amaw* (or *-aw*) adding a relationship to another person, 'do it for someone'.

Many Algonquian tribes used pictographs to record sacred texts and rites. Sound-based writing was introduced by seventeenth-century missionaries using letters of the alphabet. Modifications of several of the writing systems they created remained popular among a number of tribes; some evolved into syllabaries or mixed alphabetic-syllabary systems. Popular in the late nineteenth and early twentieth centuries, these writing systems were used by the Fox, the Kickapoo, the Ottawa, the Potawatomi, and the Sauk, and even spread to the Siouan-speaking Winnebago. These and English-orthography-based writing systems were used to compose letters and to record sacred texts and rites. Some continue in local use, but newer orthographies based on the sound patterns of each language are often used in the growing number of dictionaries, grammars, and textbooks, and by trained language teachers and students, although they may not have been adopted by older speakers.

Current publications in and about Algonquian languages are listed in a newsletter, *Algonquian and Iroquoian Linguistics*, published at the University of Minnesota; much current research appears in the annual *Papers of the Algonquian Conference*, published at the University of Manitoba. Updated information can be found on Internet pages, many sponsored by tribes or institutional language programs.

Sources and Further Reading: Leonard Bloomfield, "Algonquian," in Harry Hoijer, ed., *Linguistic Structures of Native America* (1946); Leonard Bloomfield, *The Menomini Language* (1962); Laura Buszard-Welcher, "Language Use and Language Loss in the Potawatomi Community: A Report on the Potawatami Language Institute," in David Pentland, ed., *Papers of the Twenty-Eighth Algonquian Conference* (1997); David Costa, *The Miami-Illinois Language* (2002); Ives Goddard, "The Algonquian Languages of the Plains," in Raymond J. DeMallie, ed., *Handbook of North American Indians*, vol. 13, *Plains* (2001); Marianne Mithun, *The Languages of Native North America* (1999); Ives Goddard, "Central Algonquian Languages," in William C. Sturtevant, ed., *Handbook of North American Indians*, vol. 15, *Northeast*, ed. Bruce G. Trigger (1978); Ives Goddard, "Eastern Algonquian Languages," in William C. Sturtevant, ed., *Handbook of North American Indians*, vol. 15, *Northeast*, ed. Bruce G. Trigger (1979); Richard Rhodes and Evelyn Todd, "Subarctic Algonquian Languages," in William C. Sturtevant, ed., *Handbook of North American Indians*, vol. 6, *Subarctic*, ed. June Helm (1981); Paul Voorhis, *Introduction to the Kickapoo Language* (1974).

John D. Nichols
University of Minnesota–Twin Cities

Iroquoian

Among all the Siouan and Algonquian-speaking nations of the Midwest, there is only one Iroquoian-speaking group, the Oneidas, who live near Green Bay, Wisconsin. However, the Oneidas are not indigenous to this area. They are relatively recent immigrants from New York State, where they had resided near Oneida Lake. During the American War of Independence, the Oneida Nation, one of the members of the historical Iroquois Confederacy, together with half of the Tuscaroras, supported the American patriots while the rest of the Confederacy—the Mohawks, Onondagas, Cayugas, Senecas, and some Tuscaroras—sided with the British in Canada. At the end of the war, the Oneidas in New York were guaranteed possession of six million acres of their homeland. As of 1788, the state of New York started to acquire Oneida land in more than thirty treaties until a remnant of the Oneidas owned only 32 acres in 1842.

In 1823 the Oneidas in New York started to seek a

new home in Wisconsin, under the influence of Eleazar Williams, an Episcopal lay preacher. A small group settled there in 1823, having acquired four million acres from the Menominee, an amount President James Monroe considered excessive and reduced to 500,000 acres. In 1838, by which time about 650 Oneidas had relocated to Wisconsin, their reservation was reduced again, to just over 65,400 acres. Today the Oneidas live on a checkerboard reservation of which several thousand acres are owned by the tribe; the reservation is interspersed with property owned by non-Indians. Of the 12,000 registered Oneidas in Wisconsin, only a few thousand live on the reservation; the rest reside nearby.

The Oneida language has been sparsely documented in historic documents, such as word lists or religious materials. But it has been extensively documented by Floyd G. Lounsbury, whose linguistic analysis of the Iroquoian languages remains unsurpassed; his description of Oneida has provided the basis for most Iroquoian linguistic study today (carried out to a large extent by his students). Lounsbury began his study of Oneida in 1939–1940, when he was placed in charge of a project, sponsored by the University of Wisconsin and carried out under the Works Projects Administration, that employed bilingual Oneidas to write down texts in Oneida. Approximately eight hundred pages of written material resulted from this project.

In 1996 Professor Clifford Abbott of the University of Wisconsin at Green Bay published the first extensive dictionary of Oneida, incorporating some of Lounsbury's material as well as his own work on Wisconsin Oneida. A companion to the Wisconsin Oneida dictionary is a recent dictionary of the Ontario dialect. The number of Wisconsin Oneida speakers, about two hundred when Lounsbury began his study of Oneida, has now dwindled to a mere handful, probably fewer than ten fluent speakers. The Oneidas are anxious to preserve Oneida for future generations. The tribal school system has introduced language instruction from pre-Kindergarten through Grade 12. In addition a group of traditionalists perform ceremonies in Oneida at the longhouse, and the tribe's government supports a language-preservation project, with a staff of eight, within its Cultural Heritage Division. Some streets and buildings in the community have signs with Oneida names.

Oneida words are typically complex, being composed of several component parts. The word *Onn^ yote?a:ká:* or *Onyote?a:ká:* 'People of the Standing Stone', which is the name the Oneida use for themselves, may serve as an example. (The symbol ^ in these examples is a nasalized vowel, similar to *en* in French, and the symbol ? is a glottal stop, found in the English exclamation *uh-oh*.) It is composed of five

parts. The first is a prefix *o-* 'it', followed by the root- *nvy-* 'stone'. Next comes a verb root *-ot-* 'be standing', which is followed by a suffix *-e?*, indicating that the verb describes a state as opposed to an action. Finally, the ending *-a:ká:* adds the meaning 'people of'.

As might be expected, the direction of influence between English and Oneida has been one-sided, with Oneida having little, if any, influence on English. However, one notable Iroquoian term is present in the vocabulary of the Midwest, and that is the name *Ohio*, which is Iroquoian in origin and means 'a great river'. The names of two other states and one Canadian province are Iroquoian: *Kentucky* 'on the plain', *Tennessee* (which comes from Cherokee, the only Southern Iroquoian language, and was the name of a village), and *Ontario* 'a great lake'. The name *Canada* is also Iroquoian; it means 'town, village'.

Sources and Further Reading: Clifford Abbott, ed., *An Oneida Dictionary* (1996); Jack Campisi, "Oneida," in William C. Sturtevant, ed., *Handbook of North American Indians*, vol. 15, *Northeast*, ed. Bruce G. Trigger (1978); Floyd G. Lounsbury, *Oneida Verb Morphology* (1953); Karin Michelson and Mercy Doxtator, *Oneida-English/English Oneida Dictionary* (2002).

Karin Michelson
University at Buffalo, The State
University of New York

Miami

The Miami language (Myaamia iilaataweenki) is a member of the Algonquian linguistic family. Some of its closest relatives are Kickapoo, Meskwaki, Ojibwe, and Shawnee. Miami is grouped together with the Illinois language as different dialects of the same language. In the eighteenth and early nineteenth centuries, Miami-Illinois was widely spoken in the region south of Lakes Erie and Michigan. Loss of homelands, a forced removal in 1846, and boarding schools all contributed to social fragmentation, which led to the eventual dormant state of the language by the early 1960s. Two major Miami communities exist today in Indiana and northeastern Oklahoma. The Indiana Miami, who are the descendants of those exempted from the 1846 removal, were terminated as a tribe in 1897, while the Oklahoma Miami, who are the descendants of those removed, have retained their federal status and maintain tribal offices in Miami, Oklahoma.

Not much occurred in the way of language revival or reclamation after the passing of the last speakers of Miami in the early 1960s. During that period there was an assumption that the language "became extinct without a scientifically accurate orthography having been worked out for it." Beginning in 1988, University of California–Berkeley graduate student David Costa began to determine what was known of the language among modern community members and in unpublished manuscripts. His trips led him to Oklahoma, Indiana, Washington, and other places across the country reported to have documentation on Miami-Illinois. These efforts proved fruitful, as Costa's work showed that the Miami-Illinois language was well recorded in written form for nearly three hundred years by linguists, missionaries, and hobbyists alike. Without speakers but with thousands of pages of manuscripts, Costa began to reconstruct Miami-Illinois morphology and phonology. His 1994 dissertation became the foundation of contemporary Miami communities' efforts to reclaim an important link to their ancestral and social identity, their heritage language.

Starting in 1995, the Miami communities in Oklahoma and Indiana developed a plan for a language-reclamation effort. This effort was initiated by tribal members who believed that the preservation of Miami culture, beliefs, and values would best be maintained through the context of their traditional language. Having no real models to follow, they began by organizing summer workshops and camps for children and adults, creating language lessons, and developing interactive software, learning a great deal along the way. This effort has produced a handful of children who have had exposure to the language since infancy and can understand and speak a functional language.

The Miami communities have begun to reconnect and reinforce their heritage in a way not experienced for many years. Those leading this community effort have come to realize some important and unexpected lessons from the venture. Language reclamation at any level is an important process that reestablishes the people's identity as Miami, and this has provided a means for the community to begin healing from the effects of the past. Recently, Chief Floyd Leonard observed young Miami children playing behind him and speaking the language at the annual Miami Nation powwow held in Miami, Oklahoma. The words they were using may have been few, but the unique interaction they were experiencing through their heritage language will be essential in shaping their identities as young Miami children.

Sources and Further Reading: Charles Callender, "Miami," in William C. Sturtevant, ed., *Handbook of North American Indians*, vol. 15, *Northeast*, ed. Bruce G. Trigger (1978); David J. Costa, *The Miami-Illinois Language* (2003).

Daryl Baldwin
Miami University, Ohio

Ojibwe

The Ojibwe language, a member of the Algonquian family, is the most widely spoken indigenous language of the Midwest. It is a continuum of local dialects, varying in details of pronunciation, word and sentence structure, and vocabulary from community to community. Its main groups of dialects are equivalent to separate languages, although the overlapping features make clear boundaries difficult to draw. Its main midwestern varieties are Central Southern Ojibwe, usually just called Ojibwe (Ojibwa, Ojibway, or Chippewa), spoken in Minnesota, Wisconsin, and the Upper Peninsula of Michigan, in which the people are called the Anishinaabe and the language is called Anishinaabemowin; and Ottawa (Odawa) spoken in the Lower Peninsula of Michigan and in Ontario, in which the people are called the Nishnaabe and the language is called Nishnaabemwin. They are grouped together with two Canadian varieties, Saulteaux and Eastern Ojibwe (Algonquin) in a Southern Ojibwe group. Northern Ojibwe includes two other Canadian varieties, Severn (River) Ojibwe and Northern Algonquin. Ojibwe was widely used as an intertribal *lingua franca* in the Great Lakes area and on the upper Mississippi River through the nineteenth century.

While there may be as many as thirty or forty thousand speakers of Ojibwe, there are probably under a thousand in the Midwest, where first-language speakers are middle-aged or elderly. However, there are many community-based programs and language classes promoting its maintenance and revitalization, as on the Mille Lacs Reservation in Minnesota, where the band teaches Ojibwe as a second language in its schools, sponsors a weekly language table at which elders and learners converse and tell stories (contributing a nickel when they use an English word), runs a language and culture camp where short-term immersion experiences are available, and produces language textbooks and recordings. Ojibwe is one of the most widely taught North American languages with courses available at many schools and more than thirty colleges and universities.

A written language since the seventeenth century, Ojibwe employs a variety of alphabetic writing systems as well as, in Canada, a shorthand-based syllabary with unique geometric and curvilinear characters. In 1996 many language teachers from the Midwest and central Canada met in Toronto and agreed on a standard writing system; most Ojibwe reference and course books now use it. *Oshkaabewis Native Journal*, published at Bemidji State University in Minnesota, is devoted to stories in the language and articles about it.

Sources and Further Reading: Maude Kegg, *Portage Lake*, ed. John D. Nichols (1991); John D. Nichols and Earl Nyholm, *A Concise Dictionary of Minnesota Ojibwe* (1995); Richard Rhodes, *Eastern Ojibwa-Chippewa-Ottawa Dictionary* (1985); J. Randolph Valentine, *Nishnaabemwin Reference Grammar* (2001).

John D. Nichols
University of Minnesota–Twin Cities

Siouan

The languages of the Siouan family were once spoken over a great deal of the western Midwest, as well as in parts of the Southeast and the Western Plains. Iowa, North and South Dakota, and Kansas are named in Siouan languages for Siouan tribes, while Minnesota and Nebraska are named in Siouan languages for rivers within their boundaries, and Missouri has the Algonquian name of still another Siouan tribe.

Siouan consists of Crow-Hidatsa, Mandan, Mississippi Valley Siouan, and Southeastern Siouan. The closest relatives of Siouan are the Catawban languages of the Carolinas. The Siouan languages of the historical Midwest are the languages of Mississippi River Valley Siouan (MVS), which has three subbranches: Dakotan, Dhegiha, and Winnebago-Chiwere.

There are five Dakotan dialects: Santee-Sisseton, Yankton-Yanktonais, Teton, Assiniboine, and Stoney. In the now canonical view of Santee-Sisseton speakers there are seven allied Dakota tribes—the Mdewakanton, the Wahpekute, the Wahpeton, and the Sisseton (the four Santee-Sisseton or Santee groups); the Yankton and the Yanktonais; and the Teton. The unallied and complexly divided Assiniboine and Stoney were reckoned separate in this view, and, for that matter, the nominal Teton tribe actually has seven major divisions—Brules, Sans Arcs, Sihasapa, Minneconjou, Two Kettles, Oglala, and Hunkpapa.

Dhegiha speakers are divided among five tribes: the Ponca, the Omaha, the Kansa (or Kaw), the Osage, and the Quapaw (or Arkansas), but the Ponca and the Omaha speak dialects of the same language, so there are only four languages. The Quapaw have lived out of the Midwest to the south since before contact with Europeans. Winnebago-Chiwere consists of two languages, the shared language of the Ioway, Otoe, and Missouria tribes, and Winnebago (*see* "Winnebago").

Of the Santee-Sisseton Dakota, there remain in the Midwest groups termed the Mdewakanton (in four small reservations in southern Minnesota), the Sisseton-Wahpeton (in South Dakota at Sisseton-Wahpeton and in North Dakota at Spirit Lake), and the Santee (in South Dakota at Flandreau and Nebraska at Santee). Both the Yankton (in South Dakota at Yankton) and the Yanktonais (in South Dakota at Crow Creek) remain, too. The Dhegiha Omaha and the Northern Ponca are in Nebraska; the Winnebago are in Wisconsin, Minnesota, and northeastern Nebraska; and part of the Ioway are in Kansas. The other former residents, including the Southern Ponca, have been relocated to Canada, to the western Dakotas and Montana, and to Oklahoma.

All groups now within the Midwest are culturally robust, though use of their languages has declined and in some cases has been eliminated in favor of English. Of the groups still in the Midwest, the Dakota and the Winnebago use their languages fairly actively. Among the Omaha fluency is restricted to elders, and this is increasingly true even of the Dakota and the Winnebago. The Ioway and the Ponca, still in the Midwest, appear to have lost their languages.

MVS languages have moderately complex phonologies. The sound inventory of the MVS languages includes *p t č* (like English *ch*) *k* (produced without the usual puff of air that follows them in English); *b d ǰ* (like English *j*) *g*; *ph th čh kh* (sounds produced very much like English *p t ch k*); *pp tt čč kk* (lengthened consonants, as in Italian); *pʔ tʔ čʔ kʔ* (ejectives, in which the sounds of *p t č k* are accompanied by a popping sound produced by releasing air from below the larynx); *s š* (like English sh) *x* (like German *ch*); *z ž* (like *s* in *measure*) *ɣ* (like *x*, but voiced—with vibration of the vocal cords); *sʔ šʔ xʔ* (again with explosive release of air from below the larynx); *w, m n, h,* and *ʔ* (a glottal stop, like the sound between the two parts of *huh-uh*). There are usually five plain vowels *a e i o u* and three nasalized vowels *ą į ų* (like French vowels with following *n*). In lieu of both *r* and *l* there is a single sound from the set *r, l, d,* or *ð* (like English *th* in *this*) instead. Clusters of consonants are quite restricted in form and occur mostly at the beginning of words—*bðá* 'smell', *šną* 'bare', TE *pté* 'buffalo', but TE *yámni* 'three'. Examples are all from Omaha-Ponca unless identified as Teton (TE).

Sound symbolism occurs in these languages; for example *ðišnúde* 'pluck' has *š*, a sound deemed diminutive, while *ðixðúde* 'pull large thing out' has *x*, a sound deemed augmentative. The expected combination *xn* becomes *xð* in actual pronunciation. Nasal vowels may cause sounds before them to become nasal; compare TE *blé* 'I go' with *mní kte* 'I will go', where the future particle *kte* causes *e* to become *i*, in turn causing *bl* to become *mn*.

Accent is typically on the first or second syllable of a word. Accent is often pitch accent, though not in Dakotan. In Siouan pitch accent, a series of higher-pitched syllables is followed by a series of lower-pitched ones. The last higher-pitched vowel is marked with an acute accent, as in *ðišnúde* above. In monosyllables, the higher-lower sequence is telescoped to produce a falling-pitch-contour.

Verbs and to some extent nouns often have a pattern of alternating final vowels (typically *a ~ e*) controlled by the following element—*ðé* 'go' versus *ðá ži* 'not go'. Additional vowels participate in some languages; for example, *e ~ i* in Teton in the example of 'I will go' above.

The MVS languages all prefer the constituent order subject-object-verb, with the definite article 'the' following its noun, and require various modifying particles without exact parallels in English, for example:

Maštíge i   akha ttáde khe
Rabbit RESPECT the   ground the

athą   bi   ama
he-trod-it PROXIMATE REPORTIVE

"The Rabbit trod the ground."

Dhegiha, however, has a strong tendency to move subjects or objects to a position after the verb in running text:

É di aðá   bi   ama   Maštíge
that to he-went PROXIMATE REPORTIVE Rabbit

"Rabbit went there."

In these examples *i*, glossed RESPECT, is an optional mark of respect for a mythical character; *bi*, glossed PROXIMATE, indicates that the subject is currently a focus of attention in the discourse; and *ama*, glossed REPORTIVE, indicates that the sentence is represented in the context as traditional knowledge.

A very small set of grammatical prefixes exist for nouns, mainly possessor indications on some possessed nouns, for example, *wi-négi* 'my-uncle' from *negí* 'uncle'. In contrast, verbs are more elaborately prefixed. The subject and object of the clause are indicated in that way, and there are other prefixes that help to identify the nature of the object—*dábe* 'see' (direct object), *gídábe* 'see for one' (indirect object), *gittábe* 'see one's own' (possessed object), *kkittábe* 'see oneself' (reflexive object)—or indicate other sorts of relationships, *ádąbe* 'look upon'. There is another group of prefixes called instrumentals that indicates with certain verbs the manner in which the action is accomplished (by hand, mouth, striking, pushing, etc.), for example, from *-se* 'sever' come *ðisé* 'pull off', *ðasé* 'bite off', *gasé* 'strike off', *basé* 'saw off', and so forth.

Siouan verbs have four general patterns of agreement using two basic series of pronominal inflections—an agent or actor series, and a patient or acted-on series. Active intransitive verbs agree with their subject using an agent pronoun—*a-tʔé* 'I-die'. So-called stative intransitives, which serve in place of adjectives, agree with their subject using a patient pronoun—*ą-šį* 'me-fat', that is, 'I am fat'. Transitive verbs agree with their subject and object using the agent and patient series, respectively—*ą-ðá-ną̨ą* 'me-you-hear', that is, 'you hear me'. There are also what might be called experiencer verbs that agree with the party experiencing something using a patient pronominal, but which also take or imply an associated noun—*hí ą-wą̨žeða* 'legs me-tired', that is, 'my legs are tired'.

Verbs may incorporate nouns—especially body parts, *žú-ttą* 'flesh-have', meaning 'mature'. As a result of such incorporated elements, sometimes old and now obscure in nature, subjects and objects are often indicated by infixation—that is, by placing the pronominals within the verb instead of before or after it. For example, *žú-he* 'wade' yields *žú-a-he* 'I wade'.

Verbs are subject to various verb-verb compounding processes, including motion-verb compounding to indicate complex patterns of movement—*aí-aðe* 'come-go', that is, 'to depart'. Various other modifications are made by an accompanying auxiliary, for example, *ną̨ží ną̨ží* 'rain stand', that is, 'keep on raining' ('rain' and 'stand' are homophones) or *ną̨ží thi-ðé* 'rain arrive-move', that is, 'start to rain'. Several elements marking subject may exist in a verb as a result of this compounding. Both processes—compounding and multiple-subject marking—are exhibited in *gá-ða* 'he wants', *k-ką́-bða* 'I want'. Sometimes, as here, the meanings of the individual elements in the compound are obscure.

The characteristic pattern of noun formation in Siouan is to make nouns out of whole clauses—*wasábe* 'something-that-is-black', that is, 'black bear', *nâb uðíxða* 'finger it-encircles', that is, 'ring'. In this form the final *-e* of *ną̨bé* 'finger' is lost. This is also the basis of much of the syntax, as relative clauses are made in the same way—*šį́gažįga ppahága ídaðe ðįkhe* 'child first she-bore-it the', that is, 'the one who had given birth to a child before'.

The legacy of the Siouan languages in English has been mostly in the sphere of place-names. Loanwords such as *Mankato*, from Santee *Mąkhá-tho* 'earth-blue', that is, 'Blue Earth', or loan translations like adopted French *Platte* (River) 'flat', from Ioway-Otoe *ní-braske* 'water-flat', that is, 'Flatwater', are common in the Midwest. The latter, this time as a loanword, is also the source of Nebraska. Specialist common nouns like teepee, borrowed from Dakota *thípi* 'dwelling' are rarer, but the influence of the Siouan languages in the Midwest has been an enduring one.

Sources and Further Reading: Franz Boas and Ella Deloria, *Dakota Grammar* (1941); Franz Boas and John R. Swanton, "Siouan (Dakota)" *Bulletin of the Bureau of American Ethnology* 40 (1911); Raymond DeMallie and Douglas Parks, "Sioux, Assiniboine, and Stoney Dialects: A Classification," *Anthropological Linguistics* 34 (1992); James Owen Dorsey, "The ȼegiha Language," *Contributions to North American Ethnology* 6 (1890); Bruce Ingham, *English-Lakota Dictionary* (2001); Stephen Return Riggs, *Dakota Grammar, Texts, and Ethnography*, ed. James Owen Dorsey (1973); David S. Rood, "Siouan," in Lyle Campbell and Marianne Mithun, eds., *The Languages of Native America: Historical and Comparative Assessment* (1979).

John E. Koontz
University of Colorado

Winnebago

The Winnebago are an indigenous people of Wisconsin. Their language is part of the Winnebago-Chiwere branch of Mississippi Valley Siouan (MVS; *see* "Siouan"). The native name is Hochank (*Hoocą́k*), representing 'big voice', or 'big fish', that is, 'sturgeon', or perhaps 'big camp-circle', depending on what meaning we assume for the element *hoo-*. The English name *Winnebago* is of Algonquian origin; compare Potawatomi *winpyeko* 'people of the dirty water', a reference to the fetid water of Lake Winnebago. The Wisconsin Winnebago now prefer their native name for English use, sometimes spelling it Ho-Chunk.

Scholars debate the prehistoric connections of the Winnebago. Paul Radin associated the Winnebago with the Woodland Effigy Mound culture (A.D. 800–1300) of southern Wisconsin and adjacent areas. Robert Hall argues for the Oneota Lake Winnebago focus (A.D. 1250–1600). The Winnebago simply say that they originated at *Moógašúč* 'Red Banks', probably a location on Green Bay.

The Winnebago perhaps first encountered Europeans—the French—with the Nicollet Expedition in 1634, which found them living in large horticultural villages in the vicinity of Lake Winnebago and Green Bay. Disasters led to depopulation and a wandering lifestyle. In a series of treaties from 1829 they were dispossessed of their lands and forced westward into Minnesota; only the so-called Disaffected Bands remained in Wisconsin.

After the Sioux uprising in 1862, the peaceful Minnesota Winnebago were relocated to Crow Creek in Dakota Territory. The deportees, about 2,000 in number, found themselves at odds with the neighboring Dakota and starving in a harsh environment. After nearly 600 died that winter, the rest fled to the friendly Omaha in Nebraska. This arrangement was formalized in 1865 and 1874, producing the current Winnebago Reservation in Nebraska.

The Wisconsin holdouts survived there despite repeated deportations to Nebraska and were recognized as the Ho-Chunk Nation in 1963, with headquarters at Black River Falls, Wisconsin. In 1974 there were about 2,500 individuals enrolled—listed as legally recognized members of the tribe—in Nebraska and another 2,500 in Wisconsin and Minnesota.

Winnebago remained the first language of most Winnebagoes up through the period of urbanization ushered in by World War II. Loss in favor of English has increased since then. In 1995 there were perhaps 250 speakers, mostly among the older generations.

Winnebago is in most respects a typical Siouan language. The sounds of the language are *b ǰ* (like English *j*) *g d* (often written *t*); *p č* (like English *ch*) *k*; *pˀ čˀ kˀ* (ejectives, in which the sounds of *p č k* are accompanied by a popping sound produced by releasing air from below the larynx); *s š* (like English *sh*) *x* (like German *ch*); *z ž* (like *s* in measure) *ɣ* (like *x*, but with voicing—vibration of the vocal cords); *sˀ šˀ xˀ* (again with explosive release of air from below the larynx); and *w r m n h ˀ* (a glottal stop, the sound between the two parts of *huh-uh*) *a e i o u ą į ų* (short vowels) *aa ee ii oo uu ąą įį ųų* (long vowels). Vowels with a hook under them are nasalized (like French vowels with following *n*). Winnebago has contrastively placed pitch accents. Each word has a higher-pitched section followed by a lower-pitched section. The last higher-pitched vowel is marked with an acute accent.

Winnebago literature encompasses genres similar to those of adjacent Native American languages, including histories and *waikâ* 'myths'. The myth cycles of *Wakją́kaga* 'Trickster', *Wašč̣igéga* 'Rabbit' (or 'Hare'), and others have been recorded by Radin. Here is an example sentence from a Rabbit story recorded by William Lipkind:

> *Woogų̆ ra   piǐaˀų*
> Creation the I-perfect-it
>
> *huúįgigi   ra*
> he-made-me-[his-kin]-come the
>
> *hanąą̆č tuuxúruk   šąną.*
> I-have-completed-it ASSERTION
>
> 'I have completed all of the perfecting of Creation for which He [my Grandfather] sent me.'

As in other Siouan languages, the definite article (form *the* meaning) follows its noun.

Winnebago is unlike other MVA languages in that

it does not have two sets of sentence-final particles like the assertion marker *šáną* in this example, one for male speakers, and one for females. A single series of forms occurs instead.

Sources and Further Reading: Davis S. Brose, "Late Prehistory of the Upper Great Lakes Area," in William C. Sturtevant, ed., *Handbook of North American Indians*, vol. 15, *Northeast*, ed. Bruce G. Trigger (1978); Robert L. Hall, *The Archeology of Carcajou Point, with an Interpretation of the Development of Oneonta Culture in Wisconsin* (1962); William Lipkind, *Winnebago Grammar* (1945); Nancy Oestreich Lurie, "Winnebago," in William C. Sturtevant, ed., *Handbook of North American Indians*, vol. 15, *Northeast*, ed. Bruce G. Trigger (1978); Kenneth L. Miner, "Dorsey's Law in Winnebago-Chiwere and Winnebago Accent" *International Journal of American Linguistics* 45 (1979); Paul Radin, *The Winnebago Tribe* (1990).

John E. Koontz
University of Colorado

African, Middle Eastern, Asian, and Pacific Languages

Arabic

Over the course of the last one hundred years, waves of immigrants from the Middle East have arrived in the Midwest, with the largest numbers settling in the metropolitan Detroit area. This population has maintained the essential elements of Arab culture: the importance of family and social ties, the primacy of religion, the entrepreneurial tradition, and the use of the Arabic language.

In the late nineteenth century, a lack of economic opportunity spurred large numbers of mostly single men from present-day Lebanon and Syria to come to Detroit in search of employment in the manufacturing and automotive industries. The majority were Christians of the Maronite, Melkite, and Syrian Orthodox faiths who clustered into ethnic enclaves and established an entrepreneurial presence.

The Immigration Act of 1924, which imposed strict quotas on immigration, slowed the flow of Middle Eastern arrivals to the Detroit area dramatically. Immigration was also discouraged by the Great Depression and World War II. Following the war, however, the second major wave of Middle Eastern immigration began. This wave intensified after the passage of the Immigration Act of 1965, which removed the quota system as part of the 1960s civil rights movement. Also, the 1953 Refugee Relief Act, which recognized the refugee as a type of immigrant, increased the number of Palestinian immigrants wishing to escape the political turmoil surrounding the establishment of the state of Israel in 1948.

This second wave of immigrants was made up of families in search of educational opportunities, a better economic life, and relief from war and human rights abuses. Refugees from the Lebanese Civil War of the mid-1970s, the Arab-Israeli War of 1976, Israel's invasion of Lebanon in 1982, the Iran-Iraq War of the 1980s and the Persian Gulf War of 1991 came to the Detroit metropolitan area. Unlike those of the

Arabic storefront. Photo by Roman Nitze. Courtesy Al-Quds Market, 4920 Scioto Darby Rd., Hilliard, Ohio 43026.

first wave, the majority of these immigrants were Muslim, coming from Lebanon, Palestine, Jordan, Yemen, and Iraq. Also included were the Chaldeans, Christians from northern Iraq who spoke a dialect of Aramaic. They were drawn to the growing Middle Eastern community in Detroit by the promise of familiar surroundings.

Political instability and socioeconomic deterioration in the Middle East continue to add to the number of immigrants to the Detroit area. A diversity of nationalities and religious beliefs has led to the formation of Middle Eastern subcommunities. But in general, the Arab-American population falls into three major occupational groupings: well educated professionals such as doctors and engineers; independent business owners, especially shopkeepers; and factory workers. The neighborhood of Salina, in Dearborn, which is home to the Ford Motor Company Rouge Plant, has been an Arab-American community for more than fifty years.

Like many minority groups in the United States, Arab subcommunities are geographically concentrated. Their cumulative population in the Detroit area is estimated at three hundred thousand, although the exact number is hard to determine. The development of community organizations has mirrored population growth. Today each subcommunity or "village" is supported by a wide range of organizations and associations. There are more than eighty Middle Eastern organizations in the metropolitan Detroit area. They address human service needs and provide places of worship, media outlets, and arenas for professional development and political involvement. They share concern for charity and social assistance, the preservation of community ties and cultural heritage, as well as helping people to become successful members of American society. The Arabic language, used extensively within these organizations, provides social cohesion and greater accessibility to services for the Arab American community as a whole.

A spirit of pan-Arabism that emphasizes the common themes of family, religion, entrepreneurship, and language transcends organizations and neighborhoods. Arabic is the primary foreign language in the community, and the Arab-American people of metropolitan Detroit recognize Arabic as a vital mark of ethnic identity, a cultural identifier that provides unity to the subcommunities. While English is the primary means of adaptation to life in the United States and is necessary for education and social advancement, Arabic remains the vehicle for cultural preservation.

Religious organizations in the Detroit metropolitan area take the lead in the maintenance of the community's cultural heritage and do so by offering worship services in Arabic. Religious leaders function as spokesmen for their communities. Men often meet in local coffeehouses, which provide an Arabic-language arena in which to share their views about current issues. Local shops conduct business in Arabic, and storefronts advertise their merchandise in Arabic script. Social-welfare programs provide an Arabic-speaking staff, including professional caseworkers who specialize in issues of immigration and naturalization, deportation, and cultural-adaptation problems, including translation assistance and job-training programs. There are employment agencies, health clinics, organizations that facilitate the sponsorship of refugees, and neighborhood drop-in centers all catering to the Arabic-speaking population of Detroit. Many in the area subscribe to Arabic-language periodicals, which include numerous newspapers and magazines that report on developments in their ancestral homelands. There are weekly broadcasts in Arabic on several local radio stations, reporting news and playing traditional music. Also, there are television news and entertainment programs in Arabic on local cable-access stations. The issue of language preservation is important because the community has a strong belief in the notion that language shapes one's perception of the world.

While many doubt the possibility of being a true member of the Arab community without knowing Arabic, most members of this community speak English, and most children of immigrants are fully bilingual, using Arabic in the home and in social interactions and English in school. Test scores routinely show children know English better than Arabic. As generations pass, fewer and fewer Arab Americans are maintaining their Arabic language ability, and as a result their bond with the Arab community is weakening. There is an increasing reluctance to self-identify as an Arab American due to a recent rise in anti-Arab sentiment. Many young people are moving toward the use of the local standard of English as a mark of their assimilation. For now, however, there remains a strong and vibrant presence of Arabic speakers in the metropolitan Detroit area and other parts of the Midwest.

Sources and Further Reading: Sameer Abraham and Nabeel Abraham, eds., *Arabs in the New World* (1983); Anan Ameri and Dawn Ramey, eds., *Arab American Encyclopedia* (2000); Aleya Rouchdy, ed., *The Arabic Language in America* (1992); United Way Community Services of Metropolitan Detroit, *Arabic-Speaking Peoples of Metropolitan Detroit* (1974); United Way Community Services of Metropolitan Detroit, *Middle Eastern Community of Metropolitan Detroit: 1998 Directory of Organizations* (1998); United Way Community Services of Metropolitan Detroit, *The Mosaic of Middle Eastern Communities in Metropolitan Detroit* (1999).

Marianne Lingg
University of Michigan

Armenian

Armenian has been spoken in the large industrial cities of the northern Midwest since the turn of the twentieth century. Armenians principally settled in Madison and Racine, Wisconsin; Grand Rapids, Michigan; Chicago, and Cleveland. In 1910, of the Armenian American population of 23,938, only 2,195 were in the Midwest, half of whom lived in Chicago. By 1920 the Midwest population was 5,545 foreign-born Armenians, out of a total U.S. population of 37,647.

After World War I, the flourishing automobile industry made Detroit one of the largest settlements of Armenians in the United States. The Armenian colony of 337 in 1910 quintupled to 1,692 by 1920. Armenians came to the Midwest largely because of higher wages. The Armenians' country of origin tended to be Turkey, with smaller groups from Egypt, Cyprus, and Palestine. Still smaller groups also came from Russian Armenia, but these eastern Armenians were considerably fewer and settled largely in the St. Louis area.

The Armenian migration at first was of a surprisingly literate people: 76 percent could read, compared to 74 percent for eastern European Jews, 99 percent for Finns, and 46 percent for southern Italians. Initially the migrants were single, young men. But many soon arranged for Armenian women to be sent to become their wives. By 1930 Armenian community life was firmly established in the northern Midwest. The Eastern (Russian) Armenian group in the lower Midwest was having more difficulties, which may be explained by the rural backgrounds of the Eastern Armenians, compared with those from the large towns and cities of Turkey and Egypt.

The Armenian language is historically most closely related to Greek, but this relationship must have been rather ancient, for there were, even by A.D. 400, no obvious similarities between the languages. Armenian has certain typological similarities with the easternmost Indo-European languages, those spoken in northern India and, especially, Iran. There are certain Caucasian influences in Eastern (Russian) Armenian, where several interesting consonants, particularly those pronounced with glottal accompaniment, can be found.

There are two principal dialects of Armenian, and both are represented in the Midwest. The Armenian speakers of the eastern dialect come largely from Iran and Russian Armenia. The western dialect is known elsewhere, especially in Turkish Armenia and in Beirut, Jerusalem, and Cairo, whither Armenians migrated from Turkey beginning in the early Middle Ages. The differences between the two dialects are quite systematic, though not automatically obvious. Hence an Eastern Armenian migrant in the St. Louis area would at first have trouble understanding the speech of a Western Armenian migrant in the northern Midwest. The differences are primarily in pronunciation and in the formation of verbs. The differences between the verb formations can quickly be grasped and understood, and not much practice is needed. The pronunciation differences are more complex. Eastern Armenian reflects conservatively the pronunciation of Classical Armenian. Western Armenian, however, has made significant changes. Where the eastern dialect has a /p/, the Western dialect has /b/; and where the eastern dialect has a /t/ or a /k/, the western dialect will have a /d/ or a /g/. This is confounded by a further reversal; where the eastern dialect has a /b/, /d/, or /g/, the western dialect will have /p/, /t/, or /k/. Thus the eastern-dialect word *gort* 'frog' is pronounced *kord* in the western dialect.

The smaller dialects of Turkish and Russian Armenian have been largely lost in the speech of the second generation, most of whom speak a rather uniform western dialect such as is taught in Armenian schools. Third-generation Armenians know little of their language. Saturday schools and the few day schools make an effort to preserve the language and traditions, but though such traditions as food, religion, and dance are passed along, language skills are pretty much lost.

Source and Further Reading: Robert Mirak, *Torn between Two Lands: Armenians in America, 1890 to World War I* (1983).

John A. C. Greppin
Cleveland State University, Ohio

Chinese

The Chinese-speaking population in the Midwest is relatively sparse and mainly concentrated in the larger cities. According to Census 2000, 175,061 people over the age of five living in the Midwest reported Chinese as their home language. Two-thirds of them live in the states of Illinois, Ohio, and Michigan. More than half of those who claim to be ethnically Chinese are foreign-born. Little is known about the percentage of ethnic Chinese who speak Chinese and how many are literate in Chinese.

The first Chinese speakers arrived in the 1860s–1870s. Many left jobs in railroad construction and mines in California and agriculture in the South to escape discrimination and to find better economic opportunities. These settlers, most whom were originally from Guangdong province in southern China, spoke Cantonese, Toishanese, and other southern Chinese dialects. They mainly lived in Chicago and St. Louis, creating the only two prominent Chinatowns in the Midwest, and worked in restaurants, laundries, groceries, and (in St. Louis) cigar making.

From 1882 until 1943, Congress officially prohibited most Chinese from emigrating to the United States through the Chinese Exclusion Acts. Following the repeal of these acts, and particularly a modification of immigration law in 1968, there was a second wave of mass Chinese immigration, with immigrants coming not only from Guangdong and southern China, but also from Taiwan, Hong Kong, and other parts of mainland China. This wave of immigration continues to this day. In the Midwest, the Chinese-speaking population spread, both from concentrated urban settlements to more diffuse affluent suburbs and throughout the states in the region. The newer immigrants brought with them varieties of Chinese that are phonologically and grammatically distinct from one another (as different as French is from Italian). Although Cantonese is still quite common in Chinese communities, other dialects (most predominantly Mandarin, but also others) are spoken.

This small but constant influx of Chinese-speaking immigrants helps maintain the Chinese language in the Midwest. Chinese-language newspapers and radio and television programs are produced in urban areas with large Chinese settlements (especially Chicago and St. Louis). Chinese community churches in urban and suburban areas are common, and frequently feature services in either Cantonese or Mandarin, or both. Chinese schools, predominant in Chinese immigrant communities worldwide, are also available, where children learn to read and write Chinese characters (which are the same in all Chinese dialects), speak in either Mandarin or Cantonese, and become familiar with other aspects of Chinese culture.

At the same time, however, within individual families there is frequently a language shift over approximately three generations: the first generation speaking mostly Chinese; the second a combination of Chinese and English; and, finally, the third generation shifting to English only.

Sources and Further Reading: Huping Ling, *Surviving on the Gold Mountain* (1998); Eleanor Wong Telemaque, *It's Crazy to Stay Chinese in Minnesota* (2000); Sau-ling Cynthia Wong, "The Language Situation of Chinese Americans," in Sandra Lee McKay and Sau-ling Cynthia Wong, eds., *Language Diversity, Problem or Resource?* (1988).

Ashley M. Williams
University of Michigan

Horn of Africa

Immigrants from the Horn of Africa (Ethiopia, Eritrea, Somalia, Djibouti, and adjoining parts of Sudan) have arrived in the Midwest in significant numbers since the mid-1970s, with the largest numbers arriving after 1991. These immigrants speak a variety of languages. Those from Somalia all speak Somali (Cushitic). Most from Eritrea speak Tigrigna/Tigrinya. Most from Ethiopia speak Amharic (Semitic) and/or Oromo (Cushitic), while others have different languages, including Nuer and Anywa (Nilo-Saharan) communities from Ethiopia/Sudan. All but the Nilo-Saharan languages have verb-final grammar and no sound like the English *th*, so they share some struggles learning English.

The numbers of people in immigrant communities in various states are difficult to estimate. Populations are fluid and some of the statistics collected are suspiciously high. Across the Midwest, the total number of immigrants from the Horn probably does not exceed 150,000. The greatest concentrations are in Minnesota where the Twin Cities metropolitan area is home to the largest populations of Somalis, Oromos, and Anywa in the United States. Additional thousands from the Horn live in other parts of Minnesota. Other midwestern communities numbering over 1,500 include Somalis and Eritreans/Ethiopians in Columbus, Ohio; Ethiopians around Chicago; Ethiopians and Somalis in St. Louis; Nuer in Omaha; and Ethiopians in Kansas City.

People in concentrated language communities create a variety of ways to use their languages in social spheres. Frequently, these will include community associations and churches or mosques. These institutions use the language for culturally familiar functions, serve as venues for selling literature in the language, and generally strengthen ethnic and community identity. The Oromo church in Minneapolis has published a hymnal, for example.

When there are enough speakers of a language, radio and even television broadcasts are possible. In the Twin Cities, there is programming in Somali, Oromo, Amharic, and Tigrigna as well as ethnic-related programming in English. Some community associations produce newsletters, which are often bilingual, and/or maintain websites almost entirely in English.

School districts have hired community liaisons and made various efforts to meet the needs of students who do not yet speak English well, notably in Minneapolis for Oromo and Somali; Columbus for Somali; and Omaha and Lincoln, Nebraska, for Nuer.

Many communities want schools to teach their children to read. Amharic and Tigrigna, with their unique script, have achieved notable success only in the Eritrean school in the Twin Cities. The Somali community in Columbus has received approval to open a charter school.

As is common, many immigrant children are not learning their parents' languages well. Community support is often decisive in language retention.

Peter Unseth
Graduate Institute of Applied Linguistics and
SIL International, Dallas, Texas

Korean

Koreans are currently one of the largest immigrant groups in the United States. The majority are from metropolitan areas in Korea and are participants in an urban-to-urban migration pattern.

Generational classification of Koreans is very important in establishing an immigrant identity. Korean Americans classify themselves as first generation, 1.5 generation, or second generation depending on their age of arrival in the United States. The first generation consists of people born in Korea who have emigrated as adults, while the second generation includes U.S.-born descendants of Korean immigrants. The third category, the 1.5 generation, involves immigrants who were born in Korea but left there before the age of eighteen. Linguistically, the classification of generation helps determine Korean Americans' use of English and Korean. In the 1.5 and second generation, the Korean language is acquired and maintained at home through private and informal education.

The Korean language ranks eleventh out of more than three thousand languages spoken around the world in number of speakers. It is often classified as a member of the Altaic language family, with its closest ties being to Japanese. After the Korean War (1950–1953), the dialect varieties of Korean used in North Korea and South Korea greatly diverged. The two varieties are still mutually intelligible despite increasing differences in vocabulary.

Hangul ('the Great Writing'), the Korean writing system, was invented in the fifteenth century by King Sejong. Before Hangul, Chinese characters were used exclusively. Thus the Chinese influence on Korean is seen in loanwords and the continuous use of characters as well as letters in newspapers. Hangul consists of forty letters: ten vowels, eleven compound vowels, fourteen basic consonants, and five double consonants.

The vocabulary of Korean is comprised of Sino-Korean words (about 60 percent), pure Hangul words (about 35 percent), and loanwords (about 5 percent). Of the loanwords, approximately 90 percent are from En-glish. The basic word order of Korean is Subject-Object-Verb (SOV), but the subject is often dropped if it can be understood in the context. Therefore, Korean is classified as a situation- or discourse-oriented language. In terms of morphology, Korean is an agglutinative language, one that relies heavily on affixes and grammatical indictors known as particles placed after rather than before words. One other definitive characteristic of Korean is honorifics; social factors such as age, sex, and social class determine the degree of politeness used in language, and this politeness is expressed in grammatical forms as well as vocabulary choice.

The Midwest has a small but steadily increasing number of Korean immigrants. Illinois has the largest population of ethnic Koreans at more than fifty thousand. Chicago is the only city in the Midwest that has an established "Koreatown."

The English loanword *pan pizza*, which refers to the deep-dish pizza found in Chicago, is one indicator of midwestern influence on Korean. The emergence of subsequent U.S.-born generations will surely change the use of Korean by Korean Americans.

Sources and Further Reading: William Bright, ed., *International Encyclopedia of Linguistics* (1992); Nam-Kil Kim, "Korean," in Bernard Comrie, ed., *The World's Major Languages* (1990); Hansol H. B. Lee, *Korean Grammar* (1989); Ho-min Sohn, *The Korean Language* (1999).

Hikyoung Lee
Korea University, Seoul, Korea

Pacific

In Census 2000, 6.3 percent of individuals who identified themselves as a member of the category "Native Hawaiian and Other Pacific Islander," either alone or along with another racial category, resided in the Midwest. The 55,364 Native Hawaiian and Other Pacific Islanders represent just 0.1 percent of the total population of the Midwest. Nationwide, 0.3 percent of respondents identified themselves as wholly or partly Native Hawaiian or Other Pacific Islander.

The majority of Pacific Island immigrants come from areas where English is an official language, namely, Hawai'i, American Samoa, Guam, the Federated States of Micronesia, and the Marshall Islands. These individuals typically have solid English-language skills and tend to arrive alone or with immediate family only. Furthermore, there are dozens of different languages spoken by Pacific Islanders in the Midwest. These languages are not mutually intelligible because their histories diverged centuries ago and their homelands are thousands of miles apart.

Opportunities to use Pacific Island languages outside of the immediate family are thus rare, and continued use of the Pacific Island language by second and later generations who remain in the area is atypical. Pacific Islanders are more likely to live in urban areas than rural ones. In the Midwest's largest city, Chicago, 0.2 percent of its population self-identified as Native Hawaiian and Other Pacific Islander.

There are notable instances of continued use of languages indigenous to the Pacific Islands in the Midwest, however. These tend to be part of established social networks such as local faith communities. A congregation of the Church of Jesus Christ of Latter-day Saints in Davenport, Iowa, offers interpretation for Marshallese speakers at worship services. Chamorro speakers in Milwaukee meet in social groups affiliated with the Roman Catholic Church. Nonetheless, for most Pacific Islanders in the Midwest, Pacific Island languages are spoken only in the home.

Although many in the Midwest may never be closely acquainted with an individual of Pacific Islander heritage, some Pacific Islander and, in particular, Samoan last names are well known. As of 2003, several individuals of Samoan heritage played professional football for midwestern teams, including Brandon Manumaleuna of the St. Louis Rams.

Jason Roberts
University of Wisconsin

Pidgins and Creoles

A "pidgin" variety is a new language developing from a first-generation encounter between a dominant and a subordinate population group and then used for purposes of trade or political mediation. The grammar in such a language typically shows certain sound-system substitutions and a variety of simplified forms in noun, verb, and article use, together with vocabulary choices that combine influences from the dominant language and the subordinate language. The language may also show certain patterns from any history of pidginization from either or both of the contributing languages. A "creole" variety of the new language shows a rapid expansion of vocabulary and a more complex grammar in the second and following generations. Examples of creoles now found in the Midwest may be drawn from Jamaican (English-based) and Haitian (French-based):

Jamaican:
Dem a waak an luk roon. / "They are walking and looking around."
A wa im go ina palitiks, im neva waan no moni. / 'Why did he go into politics, he didn't lack money.'

Haitian:
Konbyen ou vann sa a? E sila a? / "How much do you sell this one? And this one?"
Dye pou proteje u. / "May God protect you."

The major pidgins and creoles in the continental United States in addition to Haitian French Creole and Jamaican Creole include some mostly extinct American Indian varieties, the Mexican Spanish variety called Pachuco, Gullah (found in the Sea Islands of the coasts of South Carolina and Georgia), and Hawaiian Pidgin English. In the Midwest, there were Michif, a French and Cree pidgin found in North Dakota, and a pidginized form of Unami, a Delaware dialect originally spoken by Swedes, Dutch, and English in New York, Delaware, and Pennsylvania and perhaps known in some Delaware settlements as members of the tribe moved to the Ohio Country in the second half of the eighteenth century.

The compelling story of pidgins and creoles in the twenty-first-century Midwest centers on population movements and the high mobility of creole speakers in cities and small towns. In recent years, the population of creole speakers has expanded noticeably. Census researchers have discovered a 114 percent increase in Afro-Caribbean speakers (mostly speakers of Jamaican Creole and Haitian French Creole) in the 1990s in Columbus, Ohio, with a total of 1,825 for the year 2000, and an 80 percent increase with a total of 633 in Lansing-East Lansing, Michigan. In smaller cities, there is a similar finding: Benton Harbor, Michigan, shows a 69.1 percent increase with a total of 788, and St. Cloud, Minnesota, shows a 144 percent increase with a total of 44 speakers. Evidence thus indicates that creole speakers are continuing to move into the Midwest and will do so in the future.

Sources and Further Reading: Michel DeGraff, "Empirical Quicksand: Probing Two Recent Articles on Haitian Creole," *Journal of Pidgin and Creole Languages* 14:2 (1999); Claire Lefebvre, "The Tense, Mood, and Aspect System of Haitian Creole and the Problem of Transmission of Grammar in Creole Genesis," *Journal of Pidgin and Creole Languages* 11:2 (1996); Peter Patrick, "Variation and the Mesolect in Jamaican Creole," in *Georgetown University Round Table on Languages and Linguistics* (1999); Allan Taylor, "Indian Lingua Francas," in Charles Ferguson and Shirley Brice Heath, eds., *Language in the USA* (1981).

Thomas S. Donahue
San Diego State University, California

Sub-Saharan Africa

Sub-Saharan Africa is a region of considerable linguistic diversity. There are about two thousand languages spoken in the region, about 30 percent of the world's languages. Most of the languages are not written and are spoken by only several thousand people. Only twenty languages have more than five million speakers.

Based on the findings of Joseph Greenberg, the languages of Africa are classified into four language families: (1) Afroasiatic, (2) Nilo-Saharan, (3) Niger-Congo, and (4) Khoisan. Afroasiatic languages are spoken in the Sahara, northeast Africa, and the Horn of Africa, with pockets in East Africa. Languages such as Amharic, Tigrinya, Berber, Arabic, and Hausa belong to this family. These languages share several features, including case and verb conjugations. Nilo-Saharan languages stretch from the upper Nile Valley to the Sahara and include such languages as Songhai in West Africa and Luo and Maasai in East Africa. These languages, which mostly have Subject-Verb-Object (SVO) word order, mark gender, and are tonal.

Niger-Congo is one of the largest phyla in the world in terms of the number of languages. It extends from west Africa to East Africa and South Africa. Features of this group include the extensive use of tones, the classification of nouns into groups, rich verbal inflections and derivations, and mostly SVO word order. Examples of such languages are Wolof in Senegal; Akan in Ghana; Yoruba in Nigeria; Bantu languages such as Kiswahili (also known as Swahili), spoken in East and central Africa; and IsiZulu (or Zulu), spoken in South Africa. Khoisan languages are found in South Africa, Botswana, and Namibia with pockets in Angola, Zimbabwe, and Tanzania. One of the distinguishing features of Khoisan languages is that they share complex consonants, including an impressive inventory of clicks, consonants produced by suction activity of the tongue.

Two relatively new language families in Africa are Malayo-Polynesian and Indo-European. Malayo-Polynesian languages spoken on the island of Madagascar belong to the same stock as Malay, Indonesian, Tagalog, and languages of Papua New Guinea and other Pacific islands. Malagasy is the most widely spoken language in Madagascar. The sole Indo-European language spoken only in Africa is Afrikaans, in South Africa and Namibia. This language shares much of its vocabulary with the Dutch of the immigrants who settled in the region.

Midwestern immigrants from Sub-Saharan Africa are both diverse and few in number. In Africa, most grew up in environments where learning more than one language is the norm. The languages with sizable populations of speakers in the Midwest are Swahili, IsiZulu, Hausa, Wolof, Bamanankan, Amharic, Yoruba, Oromo, Somali and Akan. Various universities offer these languages for students, and in some school districts, high schools and grade schools provide opportunities for American children to learn them. Television and radio broadcasts are monitored mostly from foreign media outlets such as the British Broadcasting Corporation (BBC), Channel Africa (South Africa), and Deutchwelle. Voice of America broadcasts programs in Amharic, Kinyarwanda, Kirundi, Hausa, Oromo, Tigrigna, Swahili, Isindebele, and Chishona. The Minneapolis Telecommunications Network broadcasts Somali and Oromo programs.

Sources and Further Reading: Joseph Greenberg, *The Languages of Africa* (1963); Barbara Grimes, ed., *Ethnologue*, 14th ed. (2000).

Deogratias Ngonyani
Michigan State University

South Asia

There are an estimated sixteen hundred–plus linguistic varieties in South Asia, some accorded language status, others considered dialects. In the Midwest, some of these are spoken by individuals of South Asian background, whether they or their predecessors emigrated directly from South Asia, came into the United States from African nations following changes in citizenship laws, or arrived from the Caribbean or South America. All four South Asian language families—Indo-Iranian, Dravidian, Tibeto-Burman, and Austronesian—are found in the Midwest, and the seven South Asian languages in the top twenty languages in the world with most mother-tongue speakers (Hindi-Urdu, Bengali, Panjabi, Bihari, Telegu, Tamil, and Marathi) are well represented.

Data from the 1990 and 2000 U.S. censuses long-form survey questions about "Language Spoken at Home" show the following varieties in use: Assamese, Bengali, Bihari (i.e., Bhojpuri, Magahi, or Maithili), Dravidian (including Coorgi and Tulu), Gujerati, Hindi, Kannada, Malayalam, Marathi (and Konkani), Nepali, Oriya, Panjabi, Rajasthani (and Bhili), Sanskrit, Sindhi, Sinhalese (and Maldivian), Tamil, Telegu, Tibetan, and Urdu. In 1990 nearly 117,500 midwestern speakers used at least one of twenty-eight South Asian languages. Of these, 60,225 reported Hindi or Urdu, two historically intertwined varieties with great structural similarities but differences in vocabulary and social function, Urdu being associated with Muslims and, increasingly, Hindi with Hindus. Third most numerous was Gujerati at nearly 21,000, followed by Bengali, Kannada, Malayalam, Marathi, Panjabi, Tamil, and Telegu, each reported in the thousands, and several hundred Nepali, Oriya, Sindhi, and Sinhalese speakers.

The Census 2000 responses show impressive numeric increases, recording twenty-six of the thirty-one South Asian language labels reported in the United States. Nearly 104,000 responses are Urdu or Hindi. In 2000, with Hindi and Urdu counted separately, more midwesterners of South Asian background reported Urdu than Hindi, suggesting a higher percentage of Muslims to non-Muslims. Of these approximately 45,000 Urdu speakers, most live in metropolitan Illinois, Indiana, Michigan, and Ohio, four of the top ten U.S. states for Muslim population. Gujerati speakers, at nearly 42,000, were again third most numerous. Few speakers of South Asian languages live in the more rural states of Iowa, Minnesota, North Dakota, and South Dakota. Overall, however, South Asian languages have not undergone the dramatic language decline experienced within other immigrant groups.

South Asians in the United States tend to look for marriage and business partners among others of similar ethnolinguistic heritage—an important factor in replenishing pools of speakers, ensuring South Asian language use in important domains, and promoting the vitality of South Asian languages. At home, the South Asian language of origin might be used among adults and between first-generation adults and children, while children might speak the South Asian language or English with one another, or might code-switch. Another language might be used as *lingua franca* in heterogeneous groups, as well as Sanskrit or Persianized Urdu for ritual purposes.

A northeastern Indiana social gathering for *Nav Ratri* provides an example of how such linguistic plurality plays out. One hundred and fifty people attended the festive event. The Gujerati- and Sindhi-speaking hosts spoke their respective languages among themselves. Standard Hindi was the *lingua franca* for mixed South Asian groups from northern India, Indian English was in use with mixed groups from southern India, while American English was the choice for socializing in groups that included non–South Asians.

Sources and Further Reading: Bhadriraju Krishnamurti, Colin P. Masica, and Anjani K. Sinha, *South Asian Languages: Structure, Convergence and Diglossia* (1986); M.C. Shapiro and H.F. Schiffman, *Language and Society in South Asia* (1981); B.L. Simon, personal communication (2002); U.S. Bureau of the Census, "Language Spoken at Home," *Census 2000,* www.census.gov/mp/www/spectab/language spokenSTP224.xls (2000); U.S. Bureau of the Census, "Language Spoken at Home and Ability to Speak English for United States, Regions and States: 1990," *Census '90* CPH-L-133 (1990).

Beth Lee Simon
Indiana University–Purdue University, Indianapolis

Mainland Southeast Asia

Refugees from the mainland Southeast Asian countries of Cambodia, Laos, and South Vietnam arrived in the United States in large numbers following the defeat of their U.S.-supported governments in the 1970s and 1980s. They are predominately ethnic Khmer (Cambodian), Lao, Hmong, and Vietnamese, but the group also includes members of smaller minority groups from within these three countries. In all, 1,342,532 mainland Southeast Asians came to the United States as displaced war refugees between 1975 and 1998. Other mainland Southeast Asians have also come to the United States as immigrants, but they are numerically overshadowed by these large refugee groups.

Although refugees from mainland Southeast Asia and their American-born descendants, taken as a whole, are not as numerous in the Midwest as they are in other parts of the country, especially the West, the settlement patterns of particular groups have made a distinctive addition to the character of this region. This is especially true of urban areas in Minnesota, Wisconsin, Illinois, and Michigan. Members of one group, Hmong Americans, live in greater numbers in Minnesota and Wisconsin than in any other part of the country except California. The number of Mutual Assistance Associations—community-based self-help organizations—in a state-by-state count made in 2000 roughly reflects the location of self-identified mainland Southeast Asian communities in the Midwest. There were sixteen in Minnesota; fifteen in Wisconsin; six in Illinois; one or two each in Iowa, Kansas, Michigan, and Ohio; and none in Indiana, Missouri, Nebraska, North Dakota, and South Dakota.

While the languages Vietnamese and Khmer have an ancient historical connection, the modern languages are quite dissimilar. Vietnamese is a tonal language like Chinese, in which the "melody" of words can make different meanings, for example, whereas Khmer is atonal. The other two major languages of this group, Lao and Hmong, are related neither to each other nor to Vietnamese or Khmer. The cultures of the four groups are, similarly, quite distinct. It should therefore not be surprising that these four mainland Southeast Asian communities in the United States are also quite distinct, and the people are separated by language and culture much as they were in their homelands. There are a number of Khmer communities in Ohio, primarily in Columbus, but there are no Hmong communities at all. In neighboring Michigan, the opposite picture holds: There are a number of Hmong communities, primarily in Detroit, but there are no Khmer communities.

The Hmong, the Khmer, and the Lao maintain compact and distinct communities whereas the Vietnamese are more integrated into the larger society. For those who have converted to Christianity, churches also contribute to community maintenance. The relatively greater cohesion of these communities allows for the possibility of language maintenance into the second and third generations and accounts for the higher proportion of "linguistically isolated" people as identified by the census and by the public schools. However, as more Americans of mainland Southeast Asian descent are born, the familiar pattern of language shift to English in the younger generations is occurring.

Sources and Further Reading: Courtland Robinson, *Terms of Refuge* (1998); Southeast Asia Resource Action Center, *Southeast Asian American Mutual Assistance Association Directory* (2000); Keith St. Cartmail, *Exodus Indochina* (1983).

Martha Ratliff
Wayne State University, Michigan

Polish district. Library of Congress, Prints and Photographs Division, LC-USW3-007044 D.

European Languages

Balto-Slavic

Baltic

The contemporary Baltic languages, a branch of the Indo-European language group, now consist of the East Baltic languages Latvian (about 2 million speakers worldwide) and Lithuanian (about 3.5 million speakers). West Baltic, including Old Prussian and other dialects, has been extinct since around 1700. (Estonian is not Indo-European, but is part of the Finno-Ugric group.)

The Baltic languages, particularly Lithuanian, have long attracted the interest of linguists because of their archaic structure and vocabulary. Both languages have six cases in the noun system, largely preserved from Proto-Indo-European. The verb system is not as conservative, having undergone a number of modifications and innovations compared to Proto-Indo-European.

Baltic shows more similarities to the Slavic languages than to any other Indo-European group. The reasons for this have intrigued linguists for over a century; geographic proximity of the two groups has led to borrowings between Baltic and Slavic, but there was probably also a period of Balto-Slavic unity after the breakup of Proto-Indo-European, eventually developing into separate Baltic and Slavic groups.

At present, the Baltic languages are taught at few institutions. The scholarly study of Baltic languages and literatures has been carried on by interested individual scholars, and linguists were among those who participated in the formation of the Association for the Advancement of Baltic Studies in 1968.

The Midwest is the home of thousands of immigrants, and their descendants, from what are now the independent Baltic states of Latvia and Lithuania. There are more than 600,000 Americans of Lithuanian background, predominantly in and around Chicago. The Lithuanian language has been one of the principal bonds uniting the community, and, thanks to the efforts of religious and civic leaders, a number of Lithuanian cultural institutions have been established in Chicago. Among these are the Balzekas Museum of Lithuanian Culture, with genealogical and historical holdings; *Draugas*, the only Lithuanian-language daily newspaper outside Lithuania; and the endowed chair in Lithuanian studies at the University of Illinois–Chicago, which offers a doctoral program in Lithuanian literature. The Upton Sinclair novel

The Jungle (1906) describes the life of Lithuanian Americans working in the Chicago meatpacking industry.

There are some 50,000 Latvian American speakers of Latvian in the United States. The study of Latvian as an academic subject was established in the 1960s at Western Michigan University. In 1998 this program, including a library of 12,000 Latvian books, was transferred to the Scandinavian Studies Program of the University of Washington in Seattle.

Archival materials on both Lithuanian and Latvian are housed at the University of Minnesota's Immigration History Research Center.

One problem facing the Latvian and Lithuanian communities in America is language retention. A recent study at the University of California at Los Angeles (UCLA) on bilingual speakers of English and Lithuanian points out the tendency of many American speakers of Lithuanian to incorporate a great deal of English vocabulary and syntax into their Lithuanian. The 1991 independence of the Baltic states from Soviet control has greatly improved overseas communication and travel. Whether the language of Baltic Americans and that of Balts overseas will now grow closer remains to be seen.

Sources and Further Reading: Terje Mathiassen, *A Short Grammar of Latvian* (1997); Terje Mathiassen, *A Short Grammar of Lithuanian* (1996); David F. Robinson, "Baltic Languages," in Harry B. Weber, ed., *Modern Encyclopedia of Russian and Soviet Literature*, vol. 2 (1978); William R. Schmalstieg, "The Baltic Languages," in Anna Giacalone Ramat and Paolo Ramat, eds., *The Indo-European Languages* (1998).

David F. Robinson
The Ohio State University–Columbus

Czech

Mass Czech migration into the Midwest began in the 1850s. Perhaps 90 percent of these immigrants were

Railroad advertisement in Czech. Kansas State Historical Society, HE.10, ATSF.Doc PRO.1875.

literate. They founded newspapers that became the foundation of Czech communities as well as sources of information about land and settlement. Initially, men were more likely to be bilingual than women.

Czech Americans set out to create a grassroots culture and to educate their children in music and literature. Theatrical plays were staged in the national, fraternal, or *sokol* halls that were built in most of the Midwest communities. Several Czech American writers and many notable journalists wrote in Czech. Initially, knowledge of and fluency in the Czech language was the basis of Czech American ethnicity. Whenever Czechs settled in ethnic communities or neighborhoods, they supported Czech language schools or, later, Sunday schools in the halls or churches.

The Omaha Czech weekly *Pokrok západu*, the "Czech University" of Nebraska, very quickly published a translation not only of the Homestead Act, but also of the constitution of Nebraska, excerpts from the U.S. Constitution, and laws and regulations concerning naturalization and the rights of U.S. citizens. These translations were sent to the old country, where they educated the Czech politicians and influenced the demands of the Czech political parties in Austro-Hungary. Ultimately, they inspired the Czech and Slovak public to ask for political democracy, at the price of destruction of the Austro-Hungarian Empire in 1918.

The written form of Czech used in the periodicals is the standard literary form (*spisovná čeština*). Throughout the twentieth century, Czechs increasingly borrowed from English, especially for objects tied to the American life. For example *corn* in American Czech is *korna*, *car* is *kára*, *barn* is *barn*. *Stodola* (a Czech-style barn for the storage of grain and hay that does not house any animals) is only applied to a grain-storage shed.

Because many townships settled by Czechs came from the same locality, their expressions contain lexical and grammatical differences that point to their ancestral dialects. Widespread literacy and exogamy have leveled these differences, however. Often a Moravian town would be adjacent to a township with descendants of a Bohemian ancestry. Intermarriages leveled the majority of local traits, and grammatical dialectalisms from different regions appear side by side in the speech of members of the same family (as in Rossville, Kansas). The Czech spoken in the United States today does not exhibit any marked dialectal differentiation. The spoken form is most often the supradialectal colloquial form Common Czech (*obecná čeština*).

At the beginning of the twenty-first century, only recent immigrants or people over forty are conversant in Czech. The latter rarely speak it outside the home. Czechs celebrate their ethnicity through festivals, music, and food rather than through language.

Sources and Further Reading: Thomas Capek, *The Cechs in America* (1969); Karel Kučera, *Český jazyk v USA* [Czech language in the USA] (1990); Leoš Šatava, *Migrační procesy a české vystěhovalectví století do USA* [Migration processes and the Czech emigration to the USA] (1989).

Míla Šašková-Pierce
University of Nebraska–Lincoln

East Slavic

One of the three divisions of the Slavic branch of Indo-European, along with West and South Slavic, East Slavic comprises *Belarusian* (*B[y]elorussian* or *White Russian*), *Russian*, and *Ukrainian*. *Carpatho-Rusyn* (*Rusyn* or *Ruthenian*), spoken in eastern Slovakia, gained official recognition in Slovakia in 1995. It is regarded by some linguists as a branch of Subcarpathian Ukrainian, as are *Lemko* dialects of southeastern Poland.

All of the East Slavic languages are known in the Midwest. From the 1870s to World War I, Ukrainians, Rusyns, and Lemkos from Austria-Hungary and Ukrainians and Belarusians from the Russian Empire immigrated for economic reasons. Although most numerous in the Mid-Atlantic region, they formed sizable enclaves in industrial cities such as Cleveland and Youngstown, Ohio; Detroit; Chicago; and Minneapolis.

It is difficult to get a clear picture of the immigrants' language because they did not always have a strong sense of linguistic identity. Because all East Slavs traced their culture back to the medieval state of Kievan Rus, they tended to call their own languages "Rus(s)ian" while using differentiating labels for the others. This, together with the fact that only the Russians had a nation-state, led to terminological confusion when emigration began in earnest. Moreover, U.S. immigration and census officials treated all the languages as "Russian" or labeled incomers according to country of origin (for example, "Austrian") as "Slavic unspecified," or "Slavish." Language identity was more clearly established for the Russian "First Wave" or "White" refugees after the Revolution of 1917, which included russophones of other ethnic/cultural groups, for example, Cossacks, as well as some Ukrainian speakers.

Although assimilationist pressures were strong, language maintenance among the East Slavs was fostered by institutions such as churches and mutual-aid societies. Ukrainian and Rusyn publications appeared in the United States from the 1890s, either in the vernacular or in hybridized "Russian"; Belarusian publications began appearing in the 1920s. Nevertheless, by the third generation the communities were almost completely anglophone.

East Slavic languages were revived in the Midwest after World War II by "displaced persons" from the Soviet Union, including "Second Wave" Russians, Ukrainians, and Belarusians. While a shift to English has again occurred, many of the institutions founded by this wave of immigrants continue to promote their linguistic heritage through publications, broadcasts, church camps, so-called Saturday schools, and other efforts. In addition, the Russian linguistic presence in the Midwest has recently been strengthened by immigrants of the "Third Wave," primarily Soviet Jews, which began in the 1970s, and by the post-Soviet economic emigration. While mostly russophone, these last waves have included some speakers of Ukrainian and Belarusian (as first or second languages), as well as members of other ethnicities (e.g., Armenians) with proficiency in Russian. The 2000 census lists 96,508 individuals in the Midwest five years of age or older who speak Russian at home—up from 32,371 in the 1990 census; this represents 13.7 percent of the national total of Russian speakers aged five and older. The largest populations in midwestern states were in Illinois (38,053), Ohio (16,030), and Michigan (11,701).

Sources and Further Reading: David R. Andrews, *Sociocultural Perspectives on Language Change in Diaspora* (1999); Véra M. Henzl, "Slavic Languages in the New Environment," in Charles A. Ferguson and Shirley Brice Heath, eds., *Language in the USA* (1981); Paul Robert Magocsi, *Our People: Carpatho-Rusyns and Their Descendants in North America* (1994); Vladimir C. Nahirny and Joshua A. Fishman,

"Ukrainian Language Maintenance Efforts in the United States," in Joshua A. Fishman, *Language Loyalty in the United States* (1966).

Daniel Collins
The Ohio State University–Columbus

South Slavic

Speakers of South Slavic languages, the Slavic subgroup located originally in the Balkan peninsula of southeastern Europe, constituted a major source of Slavic immigration to the Midwest. The languages present problems of enumeration owing to political and social developments in the late twentieth century that redefined language boundaries. Whereas in the mid-twentieth century, one had only to count Slovenian, Serbo-Croatian, Bulgarian, and Macedonian as South Slavic languages, the breakup of Yugoslavia in the 1990s, beginning with Slovenian independence in 1991, has led to claims for separate language status for Serbian, Croatian, and Bosnian, largely for political and national reasons and not strictly on linguistic grounds.

Moreover, despite significant differences between Macedonian and Bulgarian, widespread and official recognition of a separate Macedonian language occurred only in the first half of the twentieth century, and, in any case, careful distinctions among these languages and their speakers have not always been made by immigration officials. Nonetheless, characterizing

Macedonians in Springfield, Ohio, 1940. Immigration History Research Center, University of Minnesota, IM000029.

the languages by the preindependence fourfold division provides a useful point of reference, though recent U.S. censuses have recognized Croatian ethnicity as distinct from Serbian, while also having a general "Yugoslavian" label.

All of these languages are represented in the Midwest, and Croatians, Slovenes, and Serbs, in that order, constitute their most numerous speakers. Immigration began in the mid-nineteenth century and was most intense later that century and into the early twentieth century. A significant portion of South Slavic immigrants, like all Slavic groups, gravitated to rural mining and urban industrialized areas, so that the Midwest, with its various mining concerns (Ohio coal, Michigan copper, and Minnesota iron) and manufacturing centers drew large numbers. Chicago had the largest population of Serbo-Croatian-speaking immigrants; Cleveland, the greatest number of Slovenes; and Detroit, the highest number of Bulgarians (of whom some might now be called Macedonians). Census figures for 1990 reveal that nearly 40 percent of Americans of South Slavic descent live in the Midwest, with the highest concentrations in Illinois and Ohio.

Relatively little linguistic research exists on the effects of contact with English on South Slavic languages in the United States, but familiar patterns of borrowing, code-switching, and, ultimately, language loss occur with South Slavic as well. Of those South Slavic Americans in the Midwest now, only a small percentage have maintained the homeland language, and the classic pattern of language loss in the third generation is evident throughout the region.

Religion played an important role at first in the preservation of the languages. In the early years of immigration, Slovenian and Croatian communities held Catholic masses in the respective languages, and Serbian settlements regularly had Orthodox services in Serbian, though eventually English began to prevail. Similarly, ethnic clubs and other social organizations were, and still are, important fixtures in the various communities, providing an avenue for the perpetuation of the language, especially among older speakers.

Ethnic-language newspapers were common in the late nineteenth century and into even the mid-twentieth century, but most have now ceased publication. Cleveland is home still to a Slovenian newspaper, and the official News Digest of the Serbian Orthodox Church of America and Canada is published in South Holland, Illinois. There are some indications of revival of interest in South Slavic linguistic heritage among Americans of South Slavic descent, but the languages' future is not bright.

Sources and Further Reading: Nikolay G. Altankov, *The Bulgarian-Americans* (1979); Branko M. Colakovic, *Yugoslav Migrations to America,* Ph.D. diss., University of Minnesota (1970); George Prpic, *Croatian Immigrants in America* (1971); Rudolph M. Susel, "The Perpetuation and Transformation of Ethnic Identity among Slovene Immigrants in America and the American-born Generations: Continuity and Change," in Irene Portis Winner and Rudolph M. Susel, eds., *The Dynamics of East European Ethnicity outside of Eastern Europe* (1983).

Brian D. Joseph
The Ohio State University–Columbus

Slovak

According to the 1990 U.S. census, there were 1,882,897 people of Slovak ancestry in the United States. The states with the largest Slovak communities, in order, are Pennsylvania, Ohio, Illinois, New York, New Jersey, California, and Connecticut. Slovaks settled particularly in the industrial cities of Cleveland, Chicago, New York, Kansas City, and Pittsburgh.

The beginning of the mass Slovak immigration to the Midwest started in the 1880s. Until 1918, the year of the creation of Czechoslovakia, Slovakia was a part of Hungary, within the Austro-Hungarian Empire. Slovak immigrants tended to be poor and without much formal education. Agents of American mining companies and steamship lines in Slovakia encouraged mass emigration, and, as a result, one-fifth of Slovaks emigrated and often reemigrated to the United States between 1880 and 1920.

The low motivation of many Slovaks to learn English and their desire to engage in Slovak American organizations slowly changed as settlements became permanent. In their neighborhoods, Slovaks built *sokol* and *orel* halls for gymnastic events that offered space for theatre performances, book clubs and libraries, Slovak language classes for subsequent generations of Slovak children, and English classes for new arrivals. Newspapers, after experimentation with Hungarian spelling, Slovak dialects, and Czech, have used a literary form of Slovak as codified by Ludovít Štúr in 1843—*spisovná slovenčina.* Some Protestant churches used Czech in their publications until the 1960s. These periodicals dealt with the North American continent and its political institutions and offered announcements of cultural events and the publication of books. The language of American Slovaks exhibits frequent borrowings from English, especially for objects that are tied to American life and technology.

The spoken language of Slovak Americans reflects regions from which immigrants came. The Northeastern Slovaks accepted jobs in the meatpacking plants of Chicago and Kansas City. The Central Slovakian miners searched for jobs in the mines around Pittsburgh and the steelworks of Detroit.

Although Slovak associations used Slovak language into the 1960s, today it is mostly people over forty who are conversant in Slovak. The decline in language use slowed after the 1989 fall of Communism and the ensuing freedom to travel, as well as the economic difficulties in Slovakia in the 1990s, bringing a renewal to Slovak ethnic life in cities such as Chicago, Pittsburgh, and Cleveland.

Sources and Further Reading: Gregory C. Ference, "Slovak Immigration to the United States in Light of American, Czech, and Slovak History," *Nebraska History* 74 (Fall/Winter 1993); Imrich Minár, *Americkí Slováci a Slovensko: 1880–1980* [American Slovaks and Slovakia: 1880–1980] (1994).

Míla Šašková-Pierce
University of Nebraska–Lincoln

Polish

An estimated 1.8 million Poles emigrated to the United States between 1885 and 1972. This number is an educated guess. Until World War I and the creation of an independent Poland, U.S. immigration authorities lumped Poles with people from the German, Russian, and Austro-Hungarian Empires that occupied the historical lands of the Polish kingdom. Like many other European emigrants, Poles wanted to escape poverty and political oppression as well as avoid the military drafts of the three occupying empires.

Wisconsin, Illinois, and Missouri had the largest Polish agricultural settlements, and beginning in the 1880s cities in and near the Midwest had the largest influx of Polish workers. Chicago, Milwaukee, Buffalo, Detroit, Gary, Cleveland, Pittsburgh, St. Louis, and other cities were the destination of 90 percent of the immigrants.

Polish political immigrants founded newspapers that used the literary form of Polish (see table 4). Subsequent immigrants used these periodicals for communication that supported efforts to form ethnically homogeneous Polish communities. In many of these communities people came from the same region in Poland and kept their dialects. The linguistically unifying force, however, was the Catholic Church, which organized parochial schools in which nuns taught in Polish. Parochial schools contributed to the preservation of Polish traditions and helped in the spread of literacy and language. The level of literacy of Polish male immigrants before World War I was in the sixtieth percentile, lower for women; through parochial education and mandatory school attendance, the level of literacy of the second generation reached that of the U.S. population as a whole.

Because of foreign occupation, Poles were used to cultural self-sufficiency, and they had little trouble perpetuating their language and culture in the Midwest. Theatrical plays, either by Polish writers or by Polish-language writers born in America, were staged in the fraternal or parish halls. Knowledge of and fluency in the Polish language and the exercise of the Catholic faith were the bases of Polish American ethnicity.

Throughout the twentieth century, the written language of Polish Americans exhibited increasingly frequent borrowings from English, especially for objects

Table 4. Polish-Language Newspapers by City

State/City	Number of Papers in City's History	Number still Publishing in 2005
Illinois	**21**	**5**
Chicago	21	5
Indiana	**3**	**0**
Gary	2	0
South Bend	1	0
Michigan	**10**	**2**
Bay City	1	0
Detroit	6	2
Grand Rapids	2	0
Orchard Lake	1	0
Minnesota	**3**	**1**
St. Paul	1	1
Winona	2	0
Missouri	**3**	**1**
St. Louis	2	1
Union/Washington	1	0
Nebraska	**1**	**0**
Omaha	1	0
Ohio	**17**	**4**
Cleveland	10	3
Toledo	7	1
Wisconsin	**11**	**1**
Milwaukee	7	0
Pulaski	1	1
Stevens Point	3	0
Total	**69**	**14**

Source: http://www.polishroots.org/newspapers/newspapers.htm, August 3, 2005.

that are tied to the American life. American Polish *haiwej* 'highway' (Polish *szosa, autostrada*), *dragi* 'drugs' (Polish *narkotiki*), and *kontraktor* 'contractor' (Polish *kontrahent*) are examples.

At the beginning of the twenty-first century, American Polonia, a term that describes the general community of people of Polish origin, has been partially assimilated through exogamy and the lack of new émigrés. However, in cities such as Chicago, Detroit, and St. Louis, an influx of immigrants has created new communities that use Polish as their language. They are literate and they come from different regions in Poland, but their public communications do not exhibit marked dialectal differentiation. Except for these newly arrived immigrants, however, the intergenerational transmission of Polish as a mother tongue has ceased. Polish Americans in the Midwest keep their ethnicity alive through festivals, music, and food rather than through language.

Between 1800 and 1950 between six hundred thousand and one million Jews immigrated to the United States from the Polish territories. Although their mother tongue was Yiddish, many spoke Polish as well. However, because Polonia was defined as Roman Catholic, Polish Jews congregated with other Jews rather than with other Poles and produced plays, newspapers, and books in Yiddish.

Sources and Further Reading: John J. Bukowczyk, ed., *Polish Americans and Their History* (1996); Helena Znaniecka Lopata, *Polish Americans*, rev. ed. (1994).

Míla Šašková-Pierce
University of Nebraska–Lincoln

Finno-Ugric

Finnish

Between the 1860s and the 1920s, some 360,000 Finns immigrated to the United States. Poor young rural people mostly, little schooled but energetic and remarkably literate, they tended to settle in the Midwest. Men worked as miners, lumberjacks, railroad builders, and farmers, women as maids, cooks, and in light industry. They showed fierce language loyalty and dotted the Great Lakes region with hundreds of Finn villages.

The immigrants maintained Finnish—and learned little English—but their children began a shift to English. The parents spoke only Finnish at home. Typically, the oldest child, monolingual before reaching school, suffered greatly learning English and did his or her siblings the favor of speaking English with them at home before they went to school. The home then be-

Cover illustration for *Lukukurta American Suomalaisille Lapsille*, a Finnish American reader for children, 1923. Immigration History Research Center, University of Minnesota. IM600078.

came generationally bilingual: The parents spoke Finnish to the children, who spoke English to one another and to their parents, and only the eldest of the children retained an active knowledge of Finnish. The third generation, generally English-speaking monolingual, learned Finnish, if at all, through formal education.

There is little support now for maintaining Finnish in the Midwest. The Finnish subculture, once lively with churches, athletic clubs, workers' societies, choirs and theatre groups, cooperative stores, dairies and banks, and dozens of Finnish newspapers, withered around World War II, when the second generation, educated and Americanized by the U.S. school system, left their villages for more varied jobs. The newspapers have folded and the clubs and societies have gone under or shifted to English. Finnish is dying out. There are minor exceptions, such as the little community of Esko near Duluth, Minnesota, where even some third-generation Finns grow up speaking fluent Finnish.

According to census data, the number of people

speaking Finnish at home in the United States in 1990 was 54,350, which is 2.4 times the number of foreign-born Finns, 22,313. For each state, by multiplying the number of foreign-born Finns by 2.4 we can get a rough estimate of the number of Finnish speakers: Michigan, 2,664; Minnesota, 2,318; Illinois, 1,267; Ohio, 914; Wisconsin, 825; Indiana, 470; Missouri, 208; Iowa, 156; South Dakota, 55; Nebraska, 31; and Kansas and North Dakota, 19 each.

American Finnish vocabulary is partly archaic, partly English-influenced through thousands of loanwords. The morphology of Finnish is rich: The equivalent of "I am not sure whether to leave or not" is one word, *Lähtisinköhän?*, composed of five morphemes: *läht + isi + n + kö + hän*. Finnish morphology is quite resistant to English influence but not to attrition.

Beyond the word *sauna*, Finnish's contributions to the English language are minimal. The Finnish sound system, lacking voiced stop consonants (for example, English *b d* and *g*), affricates such as *ch* and *j* (as in *church* and *judge*), *th*-sounds, and word-initial consonant clusters such as *play* and *slip*, influences the English pronunciation of some third-generation Finns. If you meet a person, then, who is "comin' fum up nort and lookin' for a chop in Tulut, Tetroit, Levelant or Sicaco," chances are she or he is of Finnish origin.

Sources and Further Reading: Eloise Engle, *Finns in North America* (1975); Pekka Hirvonen, "The Finnish-American Language Shift," in Jussi Niemi, Terence Odlin, and Janne Heikkinen, eds., *Language Contact, Variation and Change: Joensuu University Studies in Languages* (1998); Frances Karttunen, "Finnish in America: A Case Study in Monogenerational Language Change," in B. G. Blount and M. Sanches, eds., *Sociocultural Dimensions of Language Change* (1977).

Pekka Hirvonen
University of Joensuu, Finland

Hungarian

After sporadic immigration following the aborted Hungarian Revolution and War of Independence in 1848–1849, the first massive wave of Hungarian immigrants to the Midwest arrived between the 1870s and World War I. The immigrants were poor peasants from Hungary who became miners or industrial workers. Five smaller waves followed: those who came between the two world wars; those who immigrated under the Displaced Persons Act after World War II; the "freedom fighters" who left Hungary after the 1956 Hungarian Revolution; those who came from communist Hungary in the 1960s–1980s; and those who left Hungary or a neighboring country after the

demise of Communism in 1989. Many of the later immigrants were highly educated professionals.

The pre–World War I immigrants created sizable Hungarian ethnic neighborhoods. Cleveland's Hungarian population exceeded 43,000 by 1920, constituting 18 percent of the city's foreign-born population. In the mid-twentieth century an estimated 113,000 greater Clevelanders were of Hungarian birth or origin. However, Hungarian ethnic communities had all but vanished by 2000. For instance, South Bend, Indiana Hungarians numbered about 10,000 in 1932 and more than 5,000 in 1970, but the Hungarian-language churches, radio broadcasts, and associations have all died along with the old-timers' U.S.-born children and the 1956 freedom fighters.

According to the 2000 U.S. census, in Ohio there were 6,064 foreign-born Hungarians (compared to 8,431 in 1990), 193,951 people of Hungarian ancestry (the 1990 number was 218,145), and 11,859 people who spoke Hungarian at home (18,219 in 1990). Hungarian was used in the home by 4,851 people in Michigan (7,712 in 1990), 4,270 in Illinois (5,772 in 1990), 1,744 in Indiana (2,999 in 1990), 982 in Wisconsin (1,572 in 1990), and several hundred elsewhere in the Midwest. The disparity between the 1990 and 2000 data shows the rapid assimilation of Hungarian Americans.

Through World War II, many Hungarian churches, schools, and newspapers thrived in more or less self-contained neighborhoods where interaction, let alone intermarriage with outsiders, was shunned. By the end of the twentieth century, all such Hungarian communities, including the Buckeye Road neighborhood in Cleveland, the Delray section of Detroit, and Rum Village in South Bend, had ceased to exist. Hungarian communities today survive in a social and symbolic, not a geographic, sense. Hungarians by birth or descent living scattered in suburbs occasionally gather for social or cultural events hosted, for instance, by the Hungarian American Cultural Center in Taylor, Michigan; the American Hungarian Reformed Church in Allen Park, Michigan; or Magyar Baráti Közösség in Lake Hope State Park, Ohio. While the written and printed word was "the strongest cohesive force in Hungarian language life in the United States" in the 1960s, today telephones and the Internet have assumed that role.

All varieties of Hungarian spoken in the Midwest show the impact of English in pronunciation, grammar, and vocabulary. For instance, the consonants *p t k* are often followed by a puff of air or "aspirated" as they are in English; number agreement may be violated (for example, *mikor fiatal voltunk* 'when young-singular we-were' for standard Hungarian *mikor fiatalok voltunk* 'when young-plural we-were'); and hundreds of English words and expressions have been borrowed, such as *káré* 'car', *bakszi* 'box', *meridol* 'get married', and *vonatot cserél* 'change trains'.

Hungarian-accented English is an unmistakable feature of those who immigrated after puberty, for example, word-initial stress on *development*. U.S.-born Hungarians speak the English of their social class. Hungarian speakers have not influenced English in the Midwest in any way other than enriching the stock of surnames with *Kovacs*, *Nagy*, *Nemeth*, *Sabo*, and *Toth*, among others.

Sources and Further Reading: Linda Dégh, "Hungarians," in Robert M. Taylor, Jr., and Connie A. McBirney, eds., *Peopling Indiana* (1996); Joshua A. Fishman, *Hungarian Language Maintenance in the United States* (1966); Éva V. Huseby-Darvas, *Hungarians in Michigan* (2003); Susan M. Papp, *Hungarian Americans and Their Communities of Cleveland* (1981); Albert Tezla, ed., *The Hazardous Quest* (1993).

Miklós Kontra
Hungarian Academy of Sciences, Budapest

Germanic

Danish

Danish immigrants brought their language to the Midwest in the nineteenth century. By 1900 approximately ninety-six thousand Danes lived in the region, with the largest concentrations in Iowa, Minnesota, Wisconsin, Illinois, and Nebraska. Danish was initially the language of homes, churches, schools, cultural clubs, farms, and unions. The publication of more than two hundred nineteenth-century Danish periodicals and the fifty Danish music clubs that performed at Chicago's World's Fair in 1893 attest to the prevalence of Danish in the period.

Not only were Danish immigrants a small minority in the Midwest, they migrated primarily for economic rather than religious reasons. Perhaps for these reasons, in comparison with other Scandinavian immigrant groups, Danes were relatively more open to embracing English. Second-generation Danish Americans were most likely bilingual in Danish and English, as is typical of an immigrant-minority language group. By the third and fourth generation, however, English was the dominant language. Naturally, language use and the pace of change varied from community to community. Around 1890, Pastor Kristian Anker, principal of the Danish folk high school in Elk Horn, Iowa, emphasized, "Vi har Danmark som vort fædreland, men vore børn har Amerika.' [We have Denmark as our fatherland, but our children have America.]

Nevertheless, several generations later, the numerous active Danish American cultural clubs and social organizations throughout the Midwest demonstrate the importance of a dual identity. The vast majority of midwestern Danish-Americans today are monolingual speakers of English, but some Danish words, including greetings, songs, and words associated with celebrations, are commonly used. The bilingual newspaper *Den Danske Pioneer/The Danish Pioneer* (established in 1872) reports on the lives of Danish Americans, shares news from Denmark, and advertises Danish American activities throughout the United States. In addition, Danish-language courses are available at various levels: Skovsøen, Concordia College's Danish Language Village in Minnesota, offers immersion summer programs for children aged seven to eighteen; the Danish American Athletic Club in Chicago offers gymnastics and Danish-language lessons; and several midwestern universities offer Danish courses.

One typical feature of English in Minnesota and Wisconsin is that speakers often end sentences with *with* as in, "I am going to the store. Do you want to come with?" Grammatically, questions ending in *with* are perfectly well formed in Danish. We cannot attribute this similarity to the singular influence of Danish, however, because such questions are also well formed in other Germanic languages, including Swedish and Norwegian. It is therefore difficult to see any Danish influence on English independent of that of other Germanic languages.

Sources and Further Reading: Enok Mortensen, *Danish-American Life and Letters: A Bibliography* (1945); Erik Helmer Pedersen, *Drømmen om Amerika* (1985).

Britta Jensen
University of Cambridge, United Kingdom

Dutch

The majority of nineteenth-century Dutch immigrants to the United States settled in the Midwest. In 1847 two groups of orthodox Protestants left the Netherlands for religious and economic reasons. The largest group went to Michigan and founded Holland. The smaller group went to Iowa and founded Pella. A third Dutch settlement was Alto, Wisconsin. In 1848 a group of Roman Catholic immigrants settled in the Little Chute area of Wisconsin.

Later, many Dutch immigrants joined their compatriots in these early settlements (and their surroundings), whereas others went to the big American industrial towns. Consequently, Dutch immigrants settled in the Chicago area and in towns such as Grand Rapids or Kalamazoo, Michigan. In addition, the earliest settlements gave rise to a whole series of "daughter colonies," such as Lucas and Vogel Center in the Cadillac region in Michigan or Orange City in Sioux County, Iowa.

Protestants and Roman Catholics diverged sharply when it came to maintaining their language. Protestants were attached to Dutch whereas the Roman Catholics switched to English much more rapidly. Among Protestants, Dutch has been retained for a remarkably long period of time. Even today, there are still quite a few third- and fourth-generation immigrants who speak Dutch fluently.

American Dutch has evolved over the past century and a half. However, unlike many other immigrant languages, it does not have many loanwords. Among the majority of Dutch, the wish to keep their ethnic language pure has always been widespread. There is a notable exception, though. In Grand Rapids, a highly mixed code, called Yankee Dutch, came into existence at the end of the nineteenth century; at present, this variety of Dutch is extinct. However, English influence may be pervasive in other parts of the language (for example, in syntax), although in a way that cannot easily be detected by the nonlinguist. Moreover, American Dutch has also changed because it has rarely been spoken on a regular basis during the last few decades. Thus many present-day speakers (nearly always in their sixties or older) have lost their grip on the grammatical "details" of Dutch. Nevertheless, the majority of the ethnic Dutch continue to hold their language in high esteem.

Sources and Further Reading: Jacob van Hinte, *Netherlanders in America* (1985); Jaap van Marle and Caroline Smits, "American Dutch: General Trends in Its Development," in P. Sture Ureland and Iain Clarkson, eds., *Language Contact across the North Atlantic* (1996); Caroline Jeannine Martine Smits, *Disintegration of Inflection* (1996); Robert P. Swierenga, *Faith and Family* (2000); Philip E. Webber, *Pella Dutch* (1988).

Jaap van Marle
Free University, Amsterdam, The Netherlands

Immigrant German

The Midwest is home to the largest numbers and highest percentages of German-speaking immigrants to the United States; by some measures, they constitute the largest group in the region. German speakers have been arriving since roughly 1830. This flow of German speakers slowed only around the turn of the twentieth century, due to restrictions on immigration and other factors. The Midwest, though, has remained a destination for German speakers in smaller numbers up to the present, including the arrival of displaced persons after World War II and Pennsylvania German–speaking Anabaptists.

In cities such as Cincinnati, Milwaukee, and St. Louis, speakers of different dialects often formed neighborhoods, which led to a lessening of salient dialect differences over generations. The opposite hap-

German birth announcement, 1819. Mahoning Valley Historical Society. Fraktur no. 1369B.

pened in rural areas where members of the same village(s) in Europe settled together. In extreme cases, like that of East Franconian in Haysville (Dubois County), Indiana, such migration from compact, homogeneous areas resulted in the retention of almost every characteristic of the home dialect five or six generations after immigration.

At its peak (1890–1900), German was the predominant language in numerous areas across the region, spoken natively by about a third of the population of some states. Today, aside from recent immigrants and Old Order Amish/Mennonites, the oldest people in formerly German-speaking areas often still know some variety of German, but few use it regularly.

Defining "German" is hardly straightforward. Dialects from every corner of German-speaking Europe can be found in the Midwest, as well as many "twice-transplanted" varieties from eastern and southern Europe, like the so-called Black Sea German and Volga German dialects, which are especially widespread in the Dakotas, Nebraska, and Kansas. Many German dialects are not mutually intelligible with Standard German or with one another, from Swiss (spoken, e.g., in New Glarus, Wisconsin) or Bernese (in Adams County, Indiana) to Pomeranian; dialects from what is now northern Poland (especially in central Wisconsin); or East Frisian Low German, from the area near the Dutch border (especially in Iowa). In many such communities, speakers of these varieties also command what we might call "American Standard German."

American Standard German developed loosely on the written European standard of the late nineteenth century, incorporating numerous established English loanwords, a few of which, like *Farm*, have become part of European German. This variety is well attested in the thousands of German-language newspapers (including dozens of dailies) and thousands of books published in German across the region, and the vast German-language creative literature of the Midwest from that era. A leveled-out spoken form was used, particularly in urban areas. This colloquial German with regional coloring appears to have been taught in schools and used in religious services and functions from social clubs to businesses. Those who still speak such varieties often first learned them in catechism classes, Saturday schools, or even in German-language schools (public and parochial), which survived into the 1930s.

After well over 150 years, language contact has left clear marks on midwestern German dialects, most obviously in vocabulary. A widespread set of loanwords appears across many dialects, often showing similar morphology. Aside from new concepts, cultural terms, and so forth—*County, Sheriff, Prairie, Hickory*—some loanwords replaced viable native German terms, like *Fence* (typically feminine, plural *-en*, for *Zaun*, masculine), or *Creek* (masculine or feminine, plural *-s*, for *Bach*, usually masculine but feminine in some dialects). Native words also often changed in meaning, so that *gleichen* 'to resemble, be like' (an irregular verb) shifts to mean 'to like' and becomes a regular verb in most American dialects: *Wir haben dich immer gegleicht* 'we always liked you'.

In grammar, the picture is more complex. Take the change of front-rounded (or "umlauted") vowels in *grün* or *schön* by which they come to be pronounced much like English *green* and *Shane*. Because English lacks these German vowels, it seems natural to assume that this reflects English influence. In fact, in most parts of the German-speaking world, this change had happened long before immigration, so that these pronunciations were typically imported rather than developed. Likewise, where Standard German has four cases (nominative, accusative, dative, genitive) for nouns and pronouns, many German American dialects have only two (nominative and oblique, or "nonnominative"). These reduced systems were usually native to the imported dialects. Even in those few dialects where we know that reductions took place, the seeds of the change certainly came from Europe.

Also characteristic of the Midwest are the effects of German on regional English dialects (found also in southeastern Pennsylvania). *To cook* in the meaning 'to make coffee' or 'to boil' is patterned after German *kochen* and attested largely in the Midwest. Many (especially upper) midwesterners use *by* to mean 'at', as in "We had dinner by grandmother's house last night," a usage almost certainly connected to German *bei* 'at'. In wider areas, *once* is commonly used much like German *mal*, for example, *Come here once!* 'Komm mal her!'

The transition from German to English in the Midwest has been long and hotly contested. Scholars generally see the shift as a consequence of the rise of anti-German sentiments during and after World War I. But the shift to English was well underway far earlier: The ebb in German immigration had stemmed the influx of new monolingual speakers; the German-language press and publishing industry had been in decline since around 1900; and in states such as Illinois and Wisconsin, nineteenth-century legislation restricted foreign-language-medium instruction. Finally, increasing centralization of governmental and private domains diminished local control in ethnic communities, making English ubiquitous, and restricting German increasingly to use only with family and neighbors. While that transition is virtually complete, the language leaves a variety of traces in the Midwest today.

Sources and Further Reading: Karl Arndt and May E. Olson, *German-American Newspapers and Periodicals, 1732–1955*, 2nd ed. (1965); Leopold Auburger, Heinz Kloss, and Heinz Rupp, eds., *Deutsch als Muttersprache in den Vereinigten Staaten*, Teil 1, *Der Mittelwesten* (1979); Frederic Cassidy and Joan Hall, eds., *Dictionary of American Regional English* (1985–2002); Kathleen Neils Conzen, *Immigrant Milwaukee, 1836–1860* (1976); Glenn Gilbert, ed., *The German Language in America* (1971); Joseph Salmons, ed., *The German Language in America: 1683–1991* (1993).

Joseph Salmons
University of Wisconsin–Madison

Religious German

Pennsylvania German thrives as the co–first language, alongside English, of an estimated one hundred fifty thousand Amish and Old Order Mennonites across the Midwest. The rapid growth of these separatist Anabaptist communities has established the Midwest as the geographic and demographic hub of Pennsylvania German (superseding Pennsylvania itself, with approximately fifty thousand speakers).

Pennsylvania German—also known as Pennsylvania Dutch, though it is, in fact, a variety of German—is not a religious language restricted to the domain of church liturgy but, rather, is used for everyday conversation and business among community members. The association of the language with religion stems both from its origins in Lutheran and Reformed communities in colonial Pennsylvania and from its current status as a first language only in Amish and Old Order Mennonite communities. The history of Pennsylvania German in the Heartland is best understood by considering the history of the Anabaptist groups.

The first Amish settlement in the Midwest was established in 1809 in Holmes County, Ohio, by families from Somerset County, Pennsylvania. Earlier in the decade Mennonites had begun to settle in Columbiana County, Ohio. From 1840 through the 1860s major Amish settlements, each with several hundred people, were established in Elkhart and Lagrange Counties, Indiana; in Johnson County, Iowa; and near Arthur, Illinois. During this same time a new stream of European Amish immigrants—totaling approximately three thousand—arrived in the Midwest. Many of them established their own settlements, for example, in Adams and Allen Counties, Indiana, where Bernese Swiss and Alsatian dialects of German unrelated to Pennsylvania German are spoken today. Some nineteenth-century European Amish immigrants joined the midwestern Amish settlements, but their numbers were not great enough to have significant impact on the language. Throughout the nineteenth century Amish families in the Midwest exhibited a high degree of mobility within the region and relatively little contact with Amish in Lancaster, Pennsylvania. This aided in the establishment of a distinct midwestern Amish identity marked in part by a homogeneous regional dialect.

Today the largest Amish communities in the Midwest are in Holmes County, Ohio (with more than twenty-five thousand Amish, it ranks first in the world); Elkhart and Lagrange Counties, Indiana; Geauga County, Ohio; and Arthur, Illinois. Other major settlements include those in Daviess County, Indiana; Jamesport, Missouri; Buchanan County, Iowa; Harmony, Minnesota; and Cashton, Wisconsin. Midwestern states with the largest populations of Amish are Ohio, Indiana, Wisconsin, and Michigan—the latter two the beneficiaries of scores of new settlements since 1980. Old Order Mennonite communities in Indiana, Iowa, and Missouri are fewer and smaller than the Amish.

The ability of these communities to maintain Pennsylvania German in the face of long-term, intense cultural pressure from the surrounding English-speaking society stems from their religious commitment to live as a separate (nonproselytizing, strictly endogamous), rural-oriented society that places a premium on face-to-face interaction, simplicity, and communal mutual aid as markers of their Christian faith. These religious convictions, which support the maintenance of Pennsylvania German for most in-group communication (with English used mostly for out-group interactions), also account for certain restrictions that the Amish and Old Order Mennonites place on the use of modern telecommunication and transportation technologies such as phones and cars.

Literacy and literature in Pennsylvania German are extremely limited. New Order Amish in Holmes County, Ohio, have aided in the translation of the New Testament into Pennsylvania German (completed in 1995), and this in turn has led to a fledgling body of literature in the language, including a collection of Bible stories for children and some religious poetry. An archaic form of Standard German has a limited role in worship services in Amish churches. Preachers quote from Luther's German translation of the Bible, and the songbook dates from seventeenth-century Europe. But aside from these limited domains, literacy in midwestern Pennsylvania German-speaking communities is exclusively in English—a direct result of the consensual practice among Amish that instruction in Amish schools be entirely in English.

The Pennsylvania German language emerged in

the period between the 1680s and the Revolutionary War when approximately eighty thousand German-speaking immigrants—most from the southwestern part of German-speaking Europe: Baden, Würtemberg, Alsace, Switzerland, and, especially, the Palatinate—arrived in colonial Pennsylvania. The mixing and leveling of the features from their respective dialects resulted in a unique New World variety of German that strongly resembles Palatinate dialects with some influence from Alemannic as well.

Pennsylvania German inherited from its European inputs a sound system with no front-rounded vowels, thus *Küh(e)* 'cows' sounds, in Pennsylvania German, like the English word *key*. Another notable but more recent development in the grammar is its reduced case system. For example, dative pronominal forms (*mir, dir, ihm*) have been replaced with the accusative (*mich, dich, ihn*). Pennsylvania German syntax generally preserves German word order with the finite verb in second position in main clauses (for example, *No hott er ihne gsagt* 'Then he told them') and in final position in subordinate clauses (for example, *Wu sie ihn gsehne henn*, 'When they saw him').

Although Pennsylvania German has maintained its character as a dialect of German, two hundred years of intense contact with an English-speaking society have left unmistakable imprints on the language. In the verb system progressive and future forms have emerged and expanded to match the English system. English loanwords can be noted in any conversation and may include such unnecessary borrowings as *because, some, teach, farm,* and *pig*. It is difficult to measure precisely the amount of borrowing, but impressionistic reports suggest that midwestern speakers borrow more English words than their Pennsylvania counterparts.

The development of Pennsylvania German in midwestern Amish communities has diverged from that of Pennsylvania speakers in other ways as well. Midwestern Amish retain a trilled *r*-sound in words like *Ohre* 'ears' and have innovated a change in the vowel sound of words like *Deitsch* 'German' that has come to resemble the vowel in the English word *dad*. Midwestern Pennsylvania German speakers know that these differences separate them from speakers of Pennsylvania origin.

The Amish population has doubled approximately every twenty years since 1950. The continued growth and vibrancy of these communities ensure that Pennsylvania German will play a prominent role in the Midwest for the foreseeable future.

Sources and Further Reading: Karen M. Johnson-Weiner, "Group Identity and Language Maintenance," in Kate Burridge and Werner Enninger, eds., *Diachronic Studies on the Languages of the Anabaptists* (1992); Steve Hartman Keiser, "The Origins and Maintenance of Dialect Differentiation in Midwestern Deitsch," in William Keel and Klaus Mattheier, eds., *German Language Varieties Worldwide* (2003); Donald B. Kraybill, *The Riddle of Amish Culture*, rev. ed. (2001); Mark Louden, "Linguistic Structure and Sociolinguistic Identity in Pennsylvania German Society," in James Dow and Michèle Wolff, eds., *Languages and Lives: Essays in Honor of Werner Enninger* (1997); Mark L. Louden, "Patterns of Sociolinguistic Variation in Pennsylvania German," in Joseph C. Salmons, ed., *The German Language in America, 1683–1991* (1993); Silke Van Ness, "Pennsylvania German," in Ekkehard König and Johan van der Auwera, eds., *The Germanic Languages* (1994).

Steven Hartman Keiser
Marquette University, Wisconsin

Norwegian

According to Census 2000, 1.6 percent of the American population reported themselves to be of Norwegian ancestry, and the Norwegian language was ranked as the 53rd most common non-English language in the United States.

But because more than half of the Norwegian American population lives in the Midwest, they have enjoyed a more dominant position in the region. In Wisconsin they are the fourth-largest ethnic group, while in North Dakota, South Dakota, and Minnesota they are the second largest. These states are strongholds of the Norwegian language. As late as 1990, Norwegian, with sixteen thousand speakers, was the second-largest European heritage language in Minnesota, only surpassed by German. In 2000, Norwegian, with close to three thousand speakers, was the third largest minority language in North Dakota; only Spanish and German had more speakers.

While Norwegians started arriving in the Midwest in the 1830s, the main era of emigration took place between the 1860s and the start of World War I. Most of the approximately seven hundred thousand emigrants settled in the Midwest. Quite a few found a new home in cities like Madison, Minneapolis, and Chicago, but the majority lived in rural Wisconsin, Minnesota, and North and South Dakota.

The Norwegian immigrants' strong tendency to cluster in rural areas turned out to be a benefit for language maintenance. In many places, they established social networks based on ethnicity where the local Norwegian dialects were used by third and in some cases even fourth generations as well as by the original immigrants and their children.

Shortly after their arrival in the Midwest, Norwegian Americans started to form a variety of religious and secular institutions and organizations important for both the transition into a new society and the maintenance of their immigrant culture and language. The Lutheran Church played an important role in the struggle to keep the language alive. For many decades the Norwegian language was used in church, thus giving it authority as a "*lingua sacra.*" Many parochial schools provided training in reading and writing Norwegian. The church's need for educated personnel led to the founding of Norwegian American colleges such as Luther College in Iowa (1861) and St. Olaf College in Minnesota (1875). Another important institution for the use and maintenance of the language was the Norwegian American press. More than four hundred newspapers printed in Norwegian existed at one time or another in America. Papers like the *Decorah-Posten* (Iowa), *Minneapolis Tidende,* and *Skandinaven* (Chicago) had a circulation comparable to the largest newspapers in Norway; in fact *Skandinaven* had at one time a larger circulation than any newspaper printed in Norway.

With World War I and the end of mass immigration, Norwegian started to lose ground. By the end of World War II, most churches had changed from Norwegian to English, and the large midwestern Norwegian American papers had disappeared or were about to disappear. The last one, *Decorah-Posten*, ceased publication in 1972. Because the majority of Norwegian speakers today are older, the Norwegian language in America is on the verge of extinction. In 2000 only fifty-five thousand (twenty thousand in the Midwest) reported speaking Norwegian at home. Thirty years earlier, more than 600,000 claimed Norwegian as their mother tongue.

The traditional Norwegian-American language diverges from contemporary Norwegian in several ways due to various changes the language has undergone on each side of the Atlantic. The majority of rural midwesterners who still speak Norwegian use a dialect that is easy to trace to an exact location in Norway, and sometimes their speech contains archaic traits that are starting to be rare in Norway. On the other hand, the Norwegian American language has been strongly influenced by English. In the sound system, the Norwegian rounded vowel *y*, a sound not found in English, is often replaced with the unrounded counterpart *i*, a sound found in both languages. The "American *r*" is another sound that is quite common in Norwegian American speech, where it is competing with the Norwegian "tongue-tip *r*" or "uvular r." In the inflectional system the most common result of years in exile is the tendency toward system simplification. Most Norwegian dialects have a more complex system of inflection with more irregular patterns than English. In the spoken Norwegian American language, the large, regular inflectional classes tend to get bigger while the rarer and irregular ones are being abandoned.

The influence of English is most obvious in the vocabulary. Hundreds of English words are employed in the speech of Norwegian Americans. Quite a few refer to concepts encountered in the American experience, like *street, turkey, engine, saloon,* and *sidewalk.* But the borrowing is by no means limited to these kinds of words; hardly any semantic field has been protected from this process. Even terms referring to family relations, like *ma, pa, aunty, grandma,* and *cousin,* are borrowed. Some of these English words are fully adapted to Norwegian; they are pronounced and inflected as if they were "true" Norwegian words. Other words are only partially, if at all, integrated into the Norwegian sound and inflection system.

The influence of Norwegian (or, rather, Scandinavian) on English is minimal, limited to a few words and phrases like *lutefisk* (a fish delicacy) and *uff da* (an all-purpose expression commonly used to express mild displeasure, as in "Uff da, I forgot my keys!"). However, the Norwegian language in America has had a great importance internationally within the field of linguistics. It was the subject of Einar Haugen's path-breaking linguistic study published in 1953, which to a great extent laid the foundation for modern research on bilingualism.

Sources and Further Reading: Einar Haugen, *The Norwegian Language in America* (1953; reprint, 1969); Botolv Helleland, ed., *Norsk språk i Amerika* [Norwegian Language in America] (1991); Odd S. Lovoll, *The Promise Fulfilled* (1998); Odd S. Lovoll, *The Promise of America* (1984); Sture Ureland, *Global Eurolinguistics* (2001); Sture Ureland and Iain Clarkson, *Language Contact across the North Atlantic* (1996).

Arnstein Hjelde
Östfold University College, Norway

Swedish

Many people associate the first Swedish presence in the Midwest with the characters of *The Emigrants* (1951), Vilhelm Moberg's novel set in the 1840s. However, large-scale Swedish emigration only began after 1850, with the largest numbers arriving around 1870, in the 1880s, around 1905, and, finally, in 1923. The emigrants came from all over Sweden, particularly the south, and went to the Midwest because its landscape and climate resembled their home country's. Despite their rural background many obtained industrial and domestic jobs, making Chicago temporarily the second-largest Swedish-speaking city in the world. Other major settlements included Rockford, Illinois, and Minneapolis.

Although millions still identify themselves as Swedish Americans—about 2.9 million people claim Swedish as their first ancestry (nearly 4 million, as one or more of their ancestry categories)—very few speak Swedish today. Its use in churches and schools is almost nonexistent, although it is taught at some traditionally Swedish colleges like Augustana, in Rock Island, Illinois; Gustavus Adolphus, in St. Peter, Minnesota; and North Park, in Chicago, as well as at a few major universities. Of five remaining Swedish newspapers in the United States, only one midwestern paper survives, Chicago's *Svenska Amerikanaren Tribunen.*

Forty years ago, Swedish speech, especially in isolated communities like Bishop Hill, southwest of Chicago, included archaic words and structures from the speakers' regions of birth. Today, archaisms are rare. However, first-generation immigrants usually retain their regional Swedish accent. The English influence, though, is strong in lexicon and grammar, affecting even the core of the language, such as prepositions, pronouns, and numerals. Notable is the conversational use of English *yes* and *no;* of *and, but,* and *or* as linking words; and of "fillers" like *well, like, I see,* and *you know.* When alternative Swedish grammatical constructions exist, those closest to English are preferred, including the passive voice. Nouns like *store, farm, apartment,* and *depression;* adjectives like *nice;* adverbs like *still* and *even;* and verbs like *rent, spend,* and *join* have replaced Swedish equivalents. Native words adopt English meanings, for example, *go to America* becomes *gå till Amerika,* with a verb meaning 'walk' in Standard Swedish. An "American Swedish mode" has thus evolved, distinct from home-country usage. Even the phrase *Språkar du svenska?*—'Do you speak Swedish?'—marks a speaker who does not live in Sweden, where everyone says *Talar du svenska?*

When using English, older speakers in particular may be recognized by certain Swedish-sounding vowels; by pronouncing *th* in words like *Duluth* and *father* as [t] and [d], respectively; by failing to differentiate between *y* and *j* in word pairs like *Yale-jail;* and occasionally by their "sing-song" intonation. The choice of lexical or grammatical alternatives such as that between different English relative pronouns may also reflect Swedish usage. The phrasal verbs *come with* and *go with* used without objects (for example, *I'm going downtown. Do you want to come with?*), often heard in the Midwest, may derive from Swedish *kom med* and *gå med,* perhaps reinforced by parallel constructions in German. A similar background sometimes leads to overlap with closely related languages, as in a food name like *lutefisk,* which is generally used in its Nor-

wegian form. A genuine national heritage is preserved in the Swedish songs sung at the Midsummer and Lucia Festivals.

Sources and Further Reading: Nils Hasselmo, *Amerikasvenska* (1974); Folke Hedblom, "Bishop Hill Swedish after a Century," in Evelyn Scherabon Firchow, Kaaren Grimstad, Nils Hasselmo, and Wayne A. O'Neil, eds., *Studies for Einar Haugen* (1972); Staffan Klintborg, *The Transience of American Swedish* (1999); Lars Ljungmark, *Den stora utvandringen* (1965); P. Sture Ureland, "Maintenance, Language Contact and Convergence among the American Swedes 1968–1996," in P. Sture Ureland, ed., *Global Eurolinguistics* (2001).

Staffan Klintborg
Blekinge Technical Institute, Sweden

Yiddish

Yiddish arose as the indigenous vernacular of Ashkenazic Jewry approximately one thousand years ago. Ashkenazic Jewry includes the Jewish civilization that was born, grew, and flourished in central and eastern Europe, and later expanded to form new communities on several continents around the world. By the end of the nineteenth century, Ashkenazic Jewry had grown to constitute the majority (approximately 90 percent) of the Jewish population in the world. Just before the start of World War II and the genocide perpetrated by Nazi Germany, the number of Yiddish speakers in the world was estimated at eleven to thirteen million.

Large-scale migration of Yiddish speakers to North America began during a late nineteenth-century period of anti-Jewish pogroms in Eastern Europe. The heaviest area of settlement was on the East Coast, primarily New York. Settlement of Yiddish-speaking Jews in the Midwest was of three main types. The largest numbers came to major urban areas like Chicago, Cleveland, and Detroit, where they rapidly outnumbered the established German-speaking Jewish community. Additionally, Jewish agricultural communities arose near major urban centers. Finally, individual Jews settled in scattered small towns, typically working as pharmacists, peddlers, or owners of dry-goods stores. Although the major Ashkenazic population centers were in New York and Europe, the Midwest also entered into Jewish perceptual geography. Life in Jewish urban centers such as Chicago was seen as normal and familiar, whereas the far Midwest was seen as exotic terrain in the American Ashkenazic imagination, for example in the portrayal of Jews in the Dakotas in the writings of Ayzik (Isaac) Raboy.

A number of social, educational, and political structures supported the use of Yiddish for several generations of Ashkenazic Jews in the Midwest. Yiddish-language schools for children, run by organizations such as the Arbeter-Ring and the Farband, were established in major cities. The Yiddish theatre flourished, especially in Cleveland, Detroit, and Chicago. An active Yiddish press found new homes in Chicago and Cleveland. Yiddish radio programming served several generations of avid listeners in the mid-twentieth century. For a large sector of American Ashkenazic Jews, Yiddish language maintenance has shown the generational pattern typical of immigrant groups in America, ranging from full fluency among the immigrants to vestigial knowledge of the language among the third generation. In Hasidic and traditionally observant communities, however, Yiddish continues as the vibrant language of everyday life across all generations.

The influence of English on spoken and nonnormative Yiddish in America is most prominently lexical, although some syntactic influences may also be observed. Widespread loanwords include *yuzn* 'to use', *vatshn* 'to watch', and *vinde* 'window'. Reanalysis and adaptation to Yiddish structure are common; thus, singular *bizne* is formed from plural *bizne-s* from English 'business'. Nonstandard usage includes frequent literal borrowing from English; for example, *vartn far* from English 'wait for' (normally Yiddish uses *vartn* + preposition *af*).

The Yiddish influences on English must be distinguished as two distinct phenomena. The language shift from Yiddish gave rise to a specifically Jewish variety of English. This Jewish English is characterized in all levels of language structure, including intonation, word order, and vocabulary. By contrast, the Yiddish influences in general American English, though widespread, are mostly seen in the vocabulary, for example, *glitch*, *chutzpah*, *maven*. The few exceptions to this generalization are well known; for instance, the word order referred to by linguists as "Yiddish movement" (for example, *This song I like*).

Sources and Further Reading: Joshua A. Fishman, *Yiddish in America* (1965); Yudl Mark, "Yidishe anglitsizmen," in *Yorbukh fun Amopteyl* (1939); Sol Steinmetz, *Yiddish and English*, 2nd ed. (2001); Max Weinreich, *History of the Yiddish Language* (1980).

Neil G. Jacobs
The Ohio State University–Columbus

Greek

Greek

The Greek language has been a part of midwestern culture ever since its speakers immigrated to the region in the middle of the nineteenth century. Over the past 150 years, they have established some 120 communities across the Midwest, resulting in the second-largest regional concentration of Greeks in the United States after the Northeast.

Greeks have avidly maintained and promoted their language. Greek schools were quickly established in association with the local Greek Orthodox parishes, which in the Midwest belong to one of four separate metropolises of the Greek Orthodox Archdiocese of America: Chicago, Denver, Detroit, or Pittsburgh. Several schools in larger cities such as Chicago, Detroit, Cleveland, Columbus, and Kansas City, during the first half of the twentieth century, offered a comprehensive education using Greek as the primary language of instruction. After World War II, however, the Greek schools changed into afternoon tutoring schools whose sole purpose was the instruction of Greek. According to the website of the archdiocese (whose seat is in New York) there are currently thirteen such schools with active links, most of them offering only one teaching session per week.

Today the midwestern Greek community is in the process of language death. There are very few monolingual speakers left and they are quite advanced in age. The most fluent speakers of both English and Greek are middle-aged. Many of them are not speakers of Standard Greek but of their particular dialect (for example, Cretan, Northern Greek, Peloponnesian, etc.). This is because they, or their parents (from whom they learned the language), are first-generation immigrants who did not receive an extensive Greek education, and they learned the language before 1975. During that period the standard for Modern Greek was a dying variety (*katharevousa*) that was inaccessible without extensive schooling.

Members of the younger generations (people up to forty years old) have various levels of competence in Greek. Most of them have a very limited knowledge of the language because most of the schools offer classes for preteen children only. Those who are able to converse with any success have typically maintained close contact with relatives in Greece and use a mixture of dialectal, *katharevousa*, and standard forms but have very limited reading and writing skills.

This process of language death is irreversible because the influx of native Greek speakers has all but ceased, and the majority of those who come to the Midwest do so in order to receive a postsecondary education. Although these individuals spend a considerable number of years in a particular area, very few of them become part of the local community, mostly because they cannot converse with their Greek American peers in Greek. However, these students often provide a valuable service to the local communities by teaching Greek in language schools.

Sources and Further Reading: Charles C. Moskos, *Greek Americans: Struggle and Success* (1980); Theodore Saloutos, *The Greeks in the United States* (1964); Alice Scourby, *The Greek Americans* (1984).

Panayiotis A. Pappas
Simon Fraser University, Burnaby, Canada

Romance Languages

French

The overwhelming number of French names for towns and cities in the Midwest are found along rivers and lakes. French trappers and hunters (called *voyageurs*, one of many French words borrowed into English) were sent to America primarily to work for French fur companies, not to settle there. Indian wars, such as the Black Hawk War in 1832, drove them back down the Illinois and the Mississippi Rivers, while the invention of the steamboat brought waves of farmers from the East, most of whom cut down the trees that hunters needed so badly. As a result, many of the French trappers left for Canada or went back home to France. Their legacy today consists largely of place-names, some of which have been anglicized to the point of being unrecognizable as French. We are not likely to guess that the town of Bob Ruly, Michigan, derives its name from the French, *Bois Brûlé*. More frequently, some names remain close to the original French spellings but have long since lost their French pronunciations—Des Plaines, Terre Haute, Detroit, and Pierre.

If the French have been in the Midwest since 1606, why are there so few French speakers in the region today? To begin with, the French plan to establish a New France in the Americas was primarily reserved for conservative Catholics who were steered to Louisiana and Canada. French progressives or liberals, such as the Huguenots, were excluded from the Catholic enclaves, and their language was quickly absorbed by the English-speaking colonists with whom they were obliged to intermingle, in the Midwest as in other parts of the country. By 1803 Napoléon Bonaparte had little interest in overseas possessions and needed money to support wars in Europe, so he sold the Louisiana Territory to the United States, ending the French political presence.

Since that time, America has witnessed a very low rate of immigration from France. By 1970 some 2 million Americans claimed French as their native tongue but only a fraction of them reported using it in their households. The U.S. census of 1970 showed only Michigan and Illinois as having from 50,000 to 150,000 mother-tongue speakers of French, with Minnesota, Wisconsin, and Ohio having from 25,000 to 50,000. Other midwestern states had fewer. Although more recent census figures do not report mother-tongue usage, there is every reason to suspect that the number of French speakers in the Midwest has decreased. The 1990 U.S. census found less than 0.001 percent of the Midwest population reporting that they even spoke French, much less used it as their mother tongue, and the 2000 U.S. census records only 213,197 people over five years of age in the twelve midwestern states as people who speak French at home, over half of them in Illinois, Michigan, and Ohio.

Roger W. Shuy
Georgetown University, Washington, D.C.

Italian

Italian in the Midwest is best viewed as a variety of dialects on the one hand, and as social and regional variations of the standard language on the other. The dialects and the standard varieties date from primarily two periods of immigration: 1890–1920 and 1960–present. The greatest numbers of Italians were from the south and Sicily. Italians grouped together, as had other immigrant groups before them, in close communities. However, there was also some subgrouping among Italians themselves, for example, Baresi with Baresi, because of discrimination and intra-Italian relationships originating in the homeland, where competition and hostility between regions was—and is—common.

Although the Italian presence was strongest in large cities, newcomers also settled in rural communities where they could find work that responded to their needs and experience, including the mining areas of the Mesabi Range in Minnesota and central and southern Illinois. Where Italians from different regions grouped together, a certain syncretism both of customs and of language occurred.

Differences among the dialects and the varieties of the standard language are striking. Even among newcomers to the Midwest, who found themselves in contact for the first time with those from other areas of Italy, these differences are raised as points of humor and indications of social level. With reference to syntax, there is the difference in the position of the possessive adjective within the noun phrase. In Standard Italian, the possessive adjective occurs before the noun, for example, *mia figlia* 'my daughter'. In contrast, the dialects of the southern mainland typically place the possessive adjective unstressed after the noun, for example, *figlia mia*. There are also morphological differences with regard to the pluralization of nouns. In Italian, noun plurals are formed by reserving

-*i* for masculine nouns, for example, *cognato* 'brother-in-law' but *cognati* 'brothers-in-law', *mese* 'month' but *mesi* 'months'; and -*e* for certain feminine plurals, for example, *cognata* 'sister-in-law' but *cognate* 'sisters-in-law'. For other feminine nouns, however, the plural is also -*i*, for example, *lezione* 'lesson' but *lezioni* 'lessons'. In some dialects of the southern mainland, however, the plurals are typically formed through a phenomenon known as metaphony. This is a process whereby an original final -*u* or -*i* will "raise" an original stressed *é* to *í*, for example, *mési > mísë* 'months (masculine plural)', but not in *mése > mésë* 'month (masculine singular)'; and an original stressed *ó* to *ú*, for example *nóvu > núvë* 'new (m sg)', *nóvi > núvë* 'new (m. pl.)', but not in *nóva > nóvë* 'new (feminine singular)' or *nóve > nóvë* 'nine'. Thus the singular/plural contrast is no longer signaled by the final vowel in these dialects, but, rather, by the quality of the stressed vowel: *mésë* 'month' versus *mísë* 'months'. In the same way, gender is no longer communicated in these dialects via a final vowel as in Standard Italian, but, rather, by the quality of the stressed vowel: *núvë* 'new (m. sg.)' versus *nóvë* 'new (f. sg.)'.

The most important differences are in vocabulary and pronunciation. With respect to vocabulary, the three essential categories are: (1) the major differences between northern and southern Italy, (2) vocabulary items peculiar to each region subject to historical influence, and (3) influences from the exceedingly strong impact of English. As examples of vocabulary separating the north and the south, the following few can be cited, respectively: *brigidino* versus *pizzella* 'a small spiced waferlike biscuit'; *prendere* versus *pigliare* 'to take'; *donna* versus *femmina* 'woman'; *cattivo* versus *malo* 'bad', *molto* versus *assai* 'much', *ora/adesso* versus *mo* 'now'.

Vocabulary differences among regions are also due to invasions of Italy after the initial period of Romanization. Thus Sicilian is heavily influenced both by Arabic, for example, *tabbútu* 'coffin', *malasénu* 'warehouse', and by French, especially Norman, for example, *arré(ri)* 'again' (cf. French *arrière*), *vuccería* (cf. French *boucherie*) 'marketplace'. The dialects of the southern mainland, especially Calabria and Lucania, are typically very conservative in their retention of original Latin vocabulary, for example, *cras > crai* 'tomorrow' as opposed to the more common later Romance creation *domani* 'tomorrow'. The borrowings from English largely reflect the period of U.S. immigration coincidental with the advent of new inventions. Thus, we have *telephone > telefúni* rather than *teléfono*, *car > carru* rather than *mácchina*, *sidewalk > sàjudawókku* rather than *marciapiede*, and *gasoline > gasolína* rather than *benzina*.

Pronunciation also preserves a striking contrast among the immigrants from the various regions.

Northern dialects offer an array of differences ranging from *pang* for *pane* 'bread' in Bolognese, where final *n* is regularly changed to *ng*; to *paze* for *pace* 'peace' in the dialect of Vicenza, where *c* before *i* or *e* is realized as *z* [ts]. Also characteristic of the dialects of the north, especially of Piedmont and Lombardy, are the front-rounded vowels similar to those of French in *poco > peu* 'little' and the uvular *r* like the *r* of French and German, labeled in Italian the *erre moscia* 'lazy *r*'. Tuscan dialects are immediately identified by their characteristic "*Gorgia Toscana*." This separates Tuscan from the other dialects of Italy by the change of *c*, whenever it occurs between vowels, to *h*. Thus we have Standard Italian *dico* 'I say' pronounced as *diho*, and *Michele* 'Michael' as *Mihele*. This is so embedded in the dialect that it is also realized in loanwords from English, for example, *Cocacola > Cohahola*, and across word boundaries, for example, *la Cocacola > la hohahola* and *Mihele, ti diho he . . .* for *Michele ti dico che . . .* 'Michael, I tell you that . . .'.

The dialects of the south and Sicily are prominently represented in the Midwest and share a number of characteristics. There is a process, commonly called nasal assimilation, whereby historically [p] is changed to [b] after [m], for example, *tempo > tembu* 'time', *campo > cambu* 'field'; or [t] is changed to [d] after [n], for example, *tanto > tandu* 'so much', *santo > sandu* 'saint'. Related is a further assimilation whereby [b] is changed to [m] after [m], for example *piombo > kyummu* 'lead', *gamba > yamma* 'leg'; or [d] is changed to [n] after [n], for example *quando > quannu* 'when'. Also shared by these dialects is the typical change of *pi* to *ki*, for example *pieno > kinu* 'full', *piangere > kyaññere* 'to cry'; and of *bi* to *gi*, for example *bianco > (g)yangu* 'white', *biondo > (g)yunnu* 'blond'.

Descendants of the first wave of immigrants have largely been assimilated into the mainstream of American life. For this reason, the earlier forms of the dialects are gradually being lost to English, just as in Italy they are being displaced by Standard Italian.

Instruction in Italian is offered in the major midwestern universities and in many suburban school districts, as well as by thriving centers (for example, the Italian Cultural Center of Chicago). Italian-language radio stations exist (for example, 1430 AM and 1530 AM in Chicago), but locally produced Italian newspapers are not available as they were early in the twentieth century.

Sources and Further Reading: Martin Maiden and M. Mair Parry, eds., *The Dialects of Italy* (1997); Michael L. Mazzola, *Proto-Romance and Sicilian* (1976); Humbert S. Nelli, *From Immigrants to Ethnics* (1983); Humbert S. Nelli, *Italians in Chicago, 1880–1930* (1970); Gerhard Rohlfs, *Grammatica storica della lingua italiana e dei suoi dialetti: Fonetica* (1966);

Gerhard Rohlfs, *Grammatica storica della lingua italiana e dei suoi dialetti: Morfologia* (1968); Andrew Rolle, *The Italian Americans: Troubled Roots* (1980); Giovanni E. Schiavo, *The Italians in Missouri* (1975).

Michael L. Mazzola
Northern Illinois University

Caribbean Spanish

The Midwest has attracted Caribbean peoples for more than half a century. Their specific motives for immigration vary, depending on national circumstances. Puerto Ricans came to solve their economic problems and have established important communities in Youngstown, Cleveland, and Lorain, Ohio; Chicago; and Detroit. Cubans who tended to settle in Detroit were fleeing their government, while Dominican nationals came to North Dakota and Iowa for both economic and political reasons.

Rural Caribbean Spanish speakers with little or no formal education established these communities, but their descendants have obtained a higher level of education in the United States. Although the first to relocate were monolingual or Spanish dominant, levels of Spanish proficiency vary dramatically within the other generations. In fact, the linguistic situation is a continuum, with a Spanish-dominant first generation at one extreme and an English-dominant younger generation at the other.

The interactions in Spanish at home vary, but English is the dominant language in outside environments, although various religious denominations hold their services in English, in Spanish, or in a combination of both, and public schools in the region offer Spanish classes. The community has access to Spanish newspapers, most with a clear Mexican flavor, and national Spanish television networks, some of which transmit very popular Latin American shows.

People in a Hispanic community in northwestern Indiana reported speaking more English but with no decrease of Spanish use. In general, however, language shift has advanced more in the Midwest than in other parts of the United States with significant Hispanic populations. John J. Attinasi describes it as a stage in bilingualism with English having a greater influence.

Caribbean Spanish in the Midwest preserves features found in the islands' rural areas. Changing word and syllable final -*s* to an -*b* sound or deleting it altogether, and changing -*n* to velar nasal [*ng*] at the end of a syllable or a word are some of the pronunciation characteristics preserved from these Spanish dialects. However, other features seem to reflect English influence: for example, an American English–like [*r*] sound.

Moreover, within some communities, different narrative styles are used. Among Puerto Ricans in Cleveland, younger and older speakers have different ways of presenting a story. Younger speakers who have more contact with English and a higher education, construct more direct and less-elaborated narratives. Older, less-educated speakers, have greater contact with Spanish, and construct narratives with strategies used in Puerto Rican Spanish (that is, more elaborated narratives with more evaluations, the historical present tense, and more directly-reported speech).

The differences between Caribbean and U.S. Caribbean Spanish are the result of contact with English and with other Spanish dialects as well as the internal developments of the languages themselves. U.S. Hispanic communities have a heterogeneous mix of language use and linguistic strategies to convey their meaning and signal their bicultural identity.

Sources and Further Reading: Robert Aponte and Marcelo Siles, *Latinos in the Heartland: The Browning of the Midwest* (1994); John J. Attinasi, "Hispanic Attitudes in Northwest Indiana and New York," in Lucía Elías-Olivares, ed., *Spanish Language Use and Public Life in the United States* (1985); Diane R. Uber, "Narrative Strategies and Social Identity in Puerto Rican Spanish," in Sheila Embleton, ed., *Linguistic Association of Canada and the United States Forum XXIV* (1998).

Michelle Ramos-Pellicia
The Ohio State University–Columbus

Mexican Spanish

The rich complexity of Mexican Spanish in the Midwest reflects a long history of immigration, migration, segregation, discrimination, deportation, neglect, struggle, cultural renaissance, and recontact. The sociohistorical realities of Mexican and Mexican American Chicano communities are embodied in the diverse language practices of their members. Due primarily to labor-recruiting practices and "chain migration," the Spanish of central and southern Mexico predominates in the Midwest.

Central Mexican Spanish is characterized by several pronunciation features, most notably the pronunciation of an *r* at the end of a syllable so that it sounds somewhat like the *sh* in English *shut*; the full pronunciation of the /y/ sound, in such words as *Mayo* 'May'—a sound deleted in some other varieties—or even a pronunciation of this *y* so that it sounds a bit like the *z* of English *azure*; the reduction or even deletion of vowels that are not strongly stressed, so that a word like *habla* 'speaks', which has weaker stress on the second *a*, may have a final sound that sounds a bit like the *a* in English *sofa*, while most varieties of Spanish preserve the /a/ quality; and full pronunciation of the /s/ sound at the end of syllables, while many nearby varieties of Spanish weaken or even delete this sound, so that a word like *chicas* 'girls' might sound like *chica*.

The Midwest has attracted and continues to attract Mexicans and Mexican Americans from border states of the U.S. Southwest, especially Texas and California. This adds to the heterogeneity of Mexican Spanish in the Midwest, given that northern Mexican Spanish predominates in the American Southwest.

The lexicon of Mexican Spanish is characterized by the use of several specific types of words: archaisms, words no longer in common usage; regionalisms, words used predominantly or exclusively in Mexico and its zone of influence; nahuatlisms, words borrowed from Nahuatl, an indigenous language of Mexico; and colloquialisms, or popular expressions. Archaisms include the use of *¿mande?* 'what?' in place of *¿cómo?*; and regionalisms include *güero* 'blonde, fair complexioned', *bolillo* 'Caucasian', *pinche* 'damned, cursed', and the wide variety of words and expressions derived from *chingar* 'to have sexual intercourse'. Nahuatlisms include *popote* 'drinking straw' and *escuincle* 'small child, brat', among others. Colloquialisms include *híjole* (an expression of surprise); *úpale* (said when lifting heavy objects); *ándale* 'let's go, that's okay, I agree, you're welcome'; *no más* 'only, just' (as in *No más quería platicar contigo*, "I just wanted to talk to you"); *mero* 'just, right' (as in *Está en el mero centro*, "It's right in the middle of town"); and *padre* 'super, cool'.

Like most U.S. Spanish varieties, Mexican Spanish has been influenced by English in the form of anglicisms, or words borrowed from English, and codeswitching, that is, the alternating use of two languages, in this case Spanish and English. Anglicisms reported by Eva Mendieta and Isabel Molina in their lexical study of Spanish in northwestern Indiana include household words such as *closet* 'closet', *yarda* 'yard', and *suich* 'light switch'; words describing clothing such as *overol* 'overalls', *suéter* 'sweater', and *siper* 'zipper'; and work-related words such as *lonch* 'lunch' and *mopear* 'to mop'. Examples of English loanwords from Stanley Tsuzaki's dialectological study of Detroit, Michigan, include *quora* 'quarter', *hotdog*, and *high school*, among many others. Like Mexican Spanish in the Southwest, many anglicisms found in the rural Midwest are related to farming and farm work. However, in the urban Midwest, anglicisms reflect the industrial character of the region. Tsuzaki documents the following borrowings and extension of meanings of Spanish words in Detroit: *general labor*, *factoría* 'factory', *boila* 'boiler', and *Great Lakes Steel*.

The practice of code-switching, while often considered "a degradation of Spanish" by both Spanish speakers and outsiders, is generally considered by linguists to evidence high levels of bilingual competence and sensitivity to the linguistic competence and language preference of coparticipants in conversation. Marcia Farr and Juan C. Guerra noticed that Mexican teens leading a Catholic catechism in a Chicago neighborhood combined Spanish and English to ensure that all the pupils, including Spanish-dominant and English-dominant children, understood the religious lesson. In her study of code-switching in Detroit, Michigan, Holly Cashman provides several examples, including the following interaction involving Leticia and Bob, two co-workers in a bakery:

> L: Okay Bob see you tomorrow. *¿Llevas tus lentes verdad?* ("You have your glasses right?")
> B: Yep.
> L: Okay? Okay.
> B: Bye.

Code-switching may relate to the competence or language preference of the speakers, or it may be used to highlight turns in conversation by switching languages as a monolingual might use changes in pitch, volume, or tone of voice. In the above example, Leticia switches from English to Spanish to draw attention to her shift from closing the conversation to initiating a brief side conversation about whether or not Bob remembered his glasses.

Another effect of prolonged contact with English and the subordinate position of Spanish in schools and in the workplace is the shift from Spanish to English across generations. Although the residential and employment segregation of Mexicans throughout both the rural and urban Midwest in the first part of the twentieth century led to the uninterrupted transmission of Mexican Spanish in the region across generations, in the World War II era, Spanish was actively discouraged throughout the United States. Mexicans and Mexican Americans were pressured to assimilate to Anglo-American culture, especially through the use of English. Students were discouraged from speaking Spanish at school, and many parents, having experienced discrimination and deportation during the Great Depression, spoke only English to their children.

However, the Mexican American civil rights movement of the 1960s and 1970s led to a cultural renaissance and ethnic pride that promoted native language rights and the maintenance of Spanish. Maintenance has been promoted by the density of the Mexican population in a given area and the isolation resulting from poverty and lack of formal education, as well as by the presence of Hispanic Americans and Spanish monolinguals in U.S.-born speakers' network of contacts, including friends, family, co-workers, and neighbors with whom they interact on a regular basis. The continued immigration of Spanish-dominant and Spanish-monolingual Mexicans in the urban and rural Midwest has led to a situation of recontact in which English-dominant and English-monolingual third- and fourth-generation Mexican Americans interact with Spanish-monolingual and Spanish-dominant Mexicans in school, at work, and in the community, thus leading to the acquisition of Spanish for use outside the home.

Spanish-language media thrive in Chicago, which boasts the largest Mexican population in the Midwest. Mexicans and Mexican Americans in Chicago may choose between two local Spanish-language television stations (owned by the major networks Univisión and Telemundo), more than three locally produced weekly newspapers in Spanish (including *El Día* and *La Raza*, which circulate nationally), and many radio stations. While Chicago dominates the Spanish-language media in the Midwest, many areas outside Chicago have weekly newspapers in Spanish. Weekly Spanish-language or Spanish/English-bilingual newspapers in Minneapolis, Kansas City, Milwaukee, and Detroit (which has two) boast circulations of over ten thousand each.

Sources and Further Reading: Holly Cashman, "Being Bilingual: Language Maintenance, Language Shift, and Conversational Code-Switching in Southwest Detroit," Ph.D. diss., University of Michigan (2001); René Cisneros and Elizabeth Leone, "Mexican American Language Communities in the Twin Cities: An Example of Contact and Recontact," in Lucía Elías-Olivares, ed., *Spanish in the U.S. Setting* (1983); Marcia Farr and Juan C. Guerra, "Literacy in the Community: A Study of Mexicano Families in Chicago," *Discourse Processes* 19 (Jan.–Feb. 1995); John Lipski, *Latin American Spanish* (1994); Eva Mendieta, "Actitudes y creencias en la comunidad hispana del noroeste de Indiana," *Hispanic Linguistics* 9 (Fall 1997); Eva Mendieta, "Índices de mantenimiento del español en el noroeste de Indiana," *Southwest Journal of Linguistics* 13:1–2 (1994); Eva Mendieta and Isabel Molina, "Caracterización léxica del español hablado en el noroeste de Indiana," *Southwest Journal of Linguistics* 19 (Dec. 2000); Stanley M. Tsuzaki, *English Influences on Mexican Spanish in Detroit* (1970).

Holly R. Cashman
Arizona State University

Other Varieties of Spanish

The Spanish imprint on the Midwest is obvious in the names of many places in the region, especially in the area that was part of the province of Alta Louisiana (High Louisiana) in the eighteenth century. Beyond names, however, the Spanish language does not have a major historical legacy. Rather, most of its influence is contemporary and reflects recent migration patterns. Although Basque people, many of whom speak Spanish in addition to Basque, are present in the Midwest, most Spanish speakers are from Latin America.

Central and South American (CSA) Spanish has become important in the Midwest, as in the rest of the country, although it does not match the impact of Mexican, Cuban, or Puerto Rican (MCPR) Spanish. The largest groups of Hispanic immigrants in the Midwest, besides MCPR speakers, are from Guatemala, El Salvador, and Colombia. Many Hispanic immigrants have settled in the big cities of the Midwest, such as Chicago, which has one of the largest concentrations of CSA Spanish speakers. The Colombian community in Chicago is formed mainly of *costeños* (from Colombian coastal regions), who are generally well integrated into city life. There are also Spanish settlements from Honduras, Nicaragua, Peru, Ecuador, and other CSA countries. Outside major cities, the presence of CSA Spanish in the Midwest is small but growing. In 2000 the Midwest had only 5 percent of the total CSA Spanish population in the United States.

The Spanish dialects of these communities can be distinguished very well from other Spanish dialects, and their speakers tend to be very proud of such differences. It is easy to distinguish a Colombian or Peruvian accent from the Mexican, Cuban, or Puerto Rican ones. The differences are in several lexical items (*aguacate* 'avocado' in Mexican Spanish is *palta* in Peruvian Spanish, for instance), pronunciation, and aspects of morphology and syntax. Although speakers generally understand one another's dialects, some cultural differences are hard to ignore. Tacos and tortillas, very popular among Mexicans, are foreign food for Colombians or Ecuadorians. Whereas tequila, distilled from agave, may be the Mexican national beverage, its counterpart in Peru is pisco, distilled from grapes. Overall, however, similarities outweigh differences, and CSA Spanish speakers normally have to make a conscious effort to distinguish themselves from other Spanish speakers in order to preserve their own identities.

Sources and Further Reading: Peter Duignan and L. H. Gann, *The Spanish Speakers in the United States* (1998); Carlos Fernández-Shaw, *Presencia española en los Estados Unidos* (1987).

Miguel Rodríguez-Mondoñedo
University of Connecticut

Other Romance Languages

Romanian (or Rumanian) speakers live in many European countries including Moldavia, Yugoslavia, Ukraine, and Hungary as well as in Romania. Romanian communities in the Midwest are most common in Michigan, Ohio, Illinois, and Indiana. Detroit has one of the largest Romanian communities in the United States.

Some Romanians from the Midwest have become distinguished Americans. Brigadier General George Pomutz, a Romanian immigrant from Hungary, was a member of the Fifteenth Iowa Regiment during the Civil War. Mircea Eliade, distinguished service professor at the University of Chicago, was a scholar in the humanities. In addition, Romanians have published several periodicals in the Midwest, in both English and Romanian.

For most of the twentieth century, the Romanian language declined in the United States because new Romanian immigrants were scarce and the cultural assimilation of the descendants of earlier migrants was rapid. According to the U.S. Census Bureau, the number of Romanian speakers in the United States decreased by around forty thousand from 1920 to 1970. The fall of the Soviet Union and the Ceausescu regime in Romania, however, reversed this decline by making emigration easier. In the 1980s, the number of people in the United States reporting the use of Romanian in their homes rose from 24,058 to 53,493. These immigrants and the descendants of earlier immigrants honor their distinctive heritage by celebrating their ancestral roots. There are several Romanian-studies associations in the Midwest.

Catalan is the language spoken in Catalunya (Catalonia), a region in northeastern Spain. Because Spanish governments once worked hard to suppress the language in favor of Spanish, most Catalonians also speak Spanish very well. Indeed, they are easily confused with Spanish speakers. While Catalonian immigrants have blended with people from other parts of Spain, there are some Catalonian communities, especially in California and New York. Catalonian communities in the Midwest are small, although there are vital ones in Chicago and Detroit. Some universities in the Midwest, including the University of Illinois and Indiana University, have Catalan Studies programs.

There are other Romance languages spoken in the Midwest, such as Friulian (a language from northeastern Italy that has flourished in Chicago and southern Michigan). We can say the same about Corso (a language from Corsica, a former Italian island, now part of France); Sardinian (from the Italian island Sardinia); and other languages and dialects from the Italian peninsula. But there is no substantial presence of other Romance languages in the Midwest, such as Occitan (southern France), Galician (northwestern Spain) or Romansch (southeastern Switzerland); or of any Romance creole like São Tomense (São Tomé Island, from Portuguese), Mauritian (Mauritius Island, from French), Palenquero (Colombia, from Spanish), Chabacano (Philippines, from Spanish), Papiamentu (Netherlands Antilles, from Portuguese), and Haitian (Haiti, from French), among others.

Sources and Further Reading: S. Beck, "The Study of Romanian Americans," in Paul Quinlan, ed., *The United States and Romania* (1988); Carlos Fernández-Shaw, *Presencia española en los Estados Unidos* (1987); Vladimir Wertsman, ed., *The Romanians in America, 1748–1974* (1975).

Miguel Rodríguez-Mondoñedo
University of Connecticut

Folklore

SECTION EDITOR
James P. Leary

Section Contents

Overview

Folklore is at once a word with peculiar origins and meanings, a complex and evolving system of traditional artistic practices within cultural groups, and a field of study—all of which have significance within the American Midwest.

William J. Thoms, an English gentleman-scholar, first fused *folk* with *lore* in 1846. A romantic nationalist who equated the artistic soul of England with the traditional expressions of its common people, Thoms discarded the Latinate term *Popular Antiquities* that had been used previously to encompass "manners, customs, observances, superstitions, ballads, proverbs, etc.," in favor of "a good Saxon compound, Folklore—the Lore of the People." His neologism took hold quickly and, by the late nineteenth century, was recognized around the world.

Thoms's restrictive notion of folk as European peasants, however, has been abandoned for a broader, more fluid conception that includes anyone who participates in a cultural group. Individual midwesterners, for example, typically belong to several shifting, sometimes overlapping, cultural aggregations. A young African American man or woman in Detroit might be, by turns, a college student, a line worker in an auto plant, a hip-hop devotee, a member of a Baptist choir, a long-suffering Tigers fan, a weekend hook-and-line fisher, or a cook possessing family recipes. An elderly Finnish couple in northern Minnesota might be or have been coffee klatsch regulars, avid gardeners, rag-rug weavers, accordionists, ardent Socialists, pious Lutherans, farmers, or, respectively, a miner and a shirt-factory seamstress. Disparate and fragmentary though they are, the ethnic, occupational, and recreational groups within which any midwesterner mingles each have what Thoms deemed lore: shared words, phrases, stories, songs, tunes, customs, beliefs, crafts, and related traditional activities that artfully express the experiences of their members.

Missionaries, traders, soldiers, government officials, naturalists, and adventurers regularly chronicled the folklore of the Midwest's indigenous peoples from the seventeenth through the nineteenth century. In his memoirs Lamothe Cadillac (1718; reprint, 1947) writes of his experiences in the western Great Lakes country during the 1690s. Marred by notions of European superiority and reckless speculations—"all these tribes are descended from the Hebrews and were originally Jews"—Cadillac's chapters on "customs" and "traditions" nonetheless include valuable early accounts of songs, ceremonies, and such mythological stories as the earth's formation on a great turtle's back. While non–Native American chroniclers generally shared Cadillac's prejudices, a handful like the German ethnologist Johann Georg Kohl, who visited northern Wisconsin in 1855, were truly enlightened. Inspired by the Grimm Brothers' inquiries into the folklore of German peasants, Kohl's *Kitchi-Gami: Life among the Lake Superior Ojibway* (1860; reprint, 1985) was the Midwest's first comprehensive, even-handed presentation of a culture's folklore.

In the early nineteenth century—when the Midwest was regarded in turn as the "West," the "Northwest," and, eventually, the "Old Northwest"—curious travelers and ideologically fervent outsiders alike emphasized the unruly frontier nature of folk traditions emerging amongst the region's immigrant and old-

Paul Bunyan and Babe the Blue Ox. Courtesy Minnesota Office of Tourism.

stock American populace. Some, exceeding Cadillac, were moved by narrow conviction to condemnation. The Methodist preacher and New Englander Alfred Bronson, incensed in 1822 by supposedly "foreign" yet well-established customs of fellow citizens, "proclaimed a war of extermination" on the traditional Sunday markets of French Catholics in southern Michigan: "it raised a great fuss among the French who from time immemorial had thus broken the Sabbath, and, after market, gone to mass, then to the horse-races in the afternoon, and fiddled and danced and played cards at night." Encountering raucous frontier pastimes of English, Irish, Welsh, upland southern, and Yankee lead miners at Uncle Abe Nichols's Mineral Point, Wisconsin, tavern in 1837, Alexander Pratt, as quoted in Yoder (1969), was similarly scandalized:

> Such a sight as presented itself to our view we never saw before or since. It seemed that the miners were in the habit of assembling there on Saturday nights to drink, gamble, and frolic until Monday morning.... One man sat back in a corner, playing a fiddle, to whose music two others were dancing in the middle of the room. Hundreds of dollars were lying upon the tables.

Worse yet, "among the crowd were the principal men of the Territory—men who held high and responsible offices."

The settlers themselves, however, were for the most part neither indignant moralists nor ceaseless carousers. Their reminiscences typically favor domestic prowess and pleasant diversions wherein young and old, women as well as men, appreciate both subsistence and social skills—the worth of a tasty dish and a well-told tale, of a deft stitch and a nimble dance step. Oliver Johnson's memories of life in central Indiana in the 1830s extol spinning wheels no less than hunting know-how:

> All bed clothes, towels, table cloths, and women's stockins was linen. Mother spun her own thread for sewin. If we wanted a fish line, mother spun that, too.... A favorite way of huntin turkeys was with a caller. We made it from a flat bone of the second joint of a turkey wing. It took experience to make "turkey talk" on one of these callers.

Elizabeth Margaret Chandler of Tecumseh, Michigan, likewise valued practicality and play, writing in 1832: "I was at a quilting last week. There were about twenty girls besides myself and in the evening about the same number of men." To the northeast in Calhoun County, A.D.P. Van Buren celebrated an 1840 "quilting frolic; the girls attending in the afternoon, the boys coming in the evening," after having done their particular chores, for singing and games.

Frequently judged by early chroniclers as illustrating either the savagery and vice, or the civility and virtue, of people living close to nature, midwestern folklore has just as often been associated with the region's distinctive landscape, waters, plants, and animals. Legends of European newcomers, for example, emphasized the familiar and the exotic. Cincinnati's German and Irish Catholics, as in the Old World, reported the Virgin Mary and healing springs on local hilltops. Norwegians and Poles occasionally regarded the trolls, water sprites, and household spirits of home as persisting in rural Wisconsin. And Anglo-Protestants in southern Illinois invoked the fertile Nile and biblical Joseph by calling the confluence of the Ohio and the Mississippi Rivers "Egypt," a place where, as in the pharaohs' day, food was found amidst famine: "As a result of the 'winter of the deep snow' (1830–1831) not all of the corn in northern and central Illinois was harvested. Then a late spring was followed by a killing frost . . . which ruined the immature corn. Southern Illinois, however, had a plentiful supply of corn." Yet there were also encounters with hitherto strange creatures: giant catfish, lurking panthers, stinging mosquitoes, noxious skunks, and mysterious reptiles. In the 1830s the Nowlin family of Wayne County, Michigan, was troubled while cutting hay by "vexatious and annoying" snakes, supposedly poisonous "blue racers" that "would go like a streak of blue." Old-timers in the upper Mississippi Valley continue to talk about blue racers, although mostly with tongue in cheek to bamboozle gullible youngsters and city people. In contrast, the typical environmentally oriented stories of Woodland Indians—more properly considered myths than legends because of their focus on the world's formation by sacred beings—have concerned the primordial exploits of characters like Wenabozho, who formed islands in Lake Superior, acquired tobacco for the people, discovered uses for wild rice and maple sugar, gave the birch its features, caused ducks to waddle and the grebe to have red eyes, and plenty more.

Wenabozho is one of several midwestern figures canonized within the nation's pantheon of folk heroes. But not without considerable alteration. Intrigued by Henry Rowe Schoolcraft's 1839 publication of Ojibwe narratives heard in the Upper Peninsula of Michigan, the Harvard-based linguist and poet Henry Wadsworth Longfellow replaced the name of Wenabozho, a supernatural Algonquian figure, with that of Hiawatha, an actual leader of New York's Iroquoian confederacy. The resulting *Song of Hiawatha* (1855) also abandons the rough charm of oral tellers for prettified language, avoids the original's bawdy and roguish aspects, invents Minnehaha as a conventionally European love interest, and adopts the meter of the Finnish epic poem the *Kalevala*. The author of *Evangeline* (1847) and *The Courtship of Miles Standish* (1858), Longfellow was undeniably a creative artist fashioning what he hoped would be lasting contributions to a distinctively American literature. Yet his *Hiawatha* has been touted falsely in schools and mass media as an authentic rendering of American Indian folklore.

Such legendary midwesterners as Mike Fink, Johnny Appleseed, Jesse James, and Paul Bunyan have likewise enjoyed national prominence abetted by poetic license. A crack shot, the brawling, hard-drinking, boasting Fink led keelboat crews on the Ohio and Mississippi Rivers prior to being killed in a feud around 1823. John Chapman (1774–1845) moved west from Massachusetts, earning the nickname "Appleseed" for establishing nurseries in Ohio and Indiana. Missourian Jesse James (1847–1882), Civil War guerilla and postwar robber, ranged throughout the Midwest, inspiring stories and songs casting him mostly as a gallant Robin Hood. Paul Bunyan, who may or may not have been an actual French Canadian woodsman, figured in a handful of tall tales circulating in the upper Midwest by around 1900. Although the folklore concerning each was, to varying degrees, esoteric, bloody, raunchy, and racist, a succession of artists, ideologues, and entrepreneurs nonetheless contrived antiseptic, romantic narratives linked to broad nationalist themes. In novels, plays, films, paintings, statues, and promotions, consequently, Fink personifies bumptious frontier individualism; Appleseed, the peaceful rendering of wilderness into farmland; James, tragic border conflict; and Bunyan, capitalist dreams of powerful, cheery, compliant toilers. Walt Disney, a midwesterner gone Hollywood, was arguably the most successful peddler of censored, nostalgic, and homogenized products masking as the real stuff of folklore. In the post–World War II era of cold war and conformity, his widely distributed films and books, notably *Walt Disney American Folklore* (1956), cast Hiawatha, Mike Fink, Johnny Appleseed, and Paul Bunyan as cuddly heroes and marketable commodities for all Americans, children especially, to admire and consume.

Frequently altered, harnessed to national uniformity and purpose, authentic folklore is, to the contrary, stubbornly protean, highly localized, and sustained by particular groups. No folk hero or song or dance or craft or festival fully embodies the culture of any region, let alone of all Americans. Neither do midwesterners, or any other Americans, align their identities exclusively with region and nation. With regard to ethnicity, for example, the Midwest can be very roughly characterized as African American and upland southern white along its southern border;

Woodland Indian, French, and Nordic to the north; and German, Irish, Yankee, and Yorker across its broad middle and nearly everywhere else, with all of those peoples, plus Italians, Jews, Slavs, and, since the late twentieth century, Asians and Hispanics in its cities. Consequently, cultural pluralism or what has come to be called multiculturalism—the persistence and coexistence of diverse communities in a given place—has been just as important in the region as assimilation to an Anglo-Protestant "mainstream" purporting to be "100% American." And while citizens of the Reverend Alfred Bronson's ilk have always "proclaimed a war of extermination" on cultural traditions other than their own, most have combined curiosity with tolerance.

In 1853 an Irish woman in Green County, Wisconsin, wrote in her diary that her family debated where to spend the Fourth of July. Should they stay in "Irish Hollow"; visit the French settlement at Belleville; "take a look at the nearby Dutch" (Germans); or travel to New Glarus, where "we can look at the Swiss, if we can't understand them"? Deciding on the Swiss, they were soon charmed by a reenactment of Wilhelm Tell shooting an apple from his son's head and "Swiss wrestlers" as well as "Swiss dances in the dining room of the hotel." The dancers were especially compelling: "Round and round the couples would glide, while at certain intervals in the music the men would stamp their feet and emit wild whoops." Perhaps the visitors even joined in, if not that year, then the next? Some 150 years later dancers of Irish, Norwegian, and Swiss descent continue to whoop and stamp in the nearby Hollandale community hall to the strains of German-Bohemian polka bands. Although some midwesterners are well aware of these particular ethnic strands, most regard what they have come to call "old-time music" as part of their common heritage.

Because divisions between ethnic communities in the Midwest have been more permeable than impassable, the region's folklore exemplifies not only pluralism but also creolization—a creative process through which the cross-pollination of several distinctive cultural forms results in a vigorous hybrid. Some participants in one or another midwestern cultural scene have perpetually crossed over and back, exchanging and blending recipes, jump-rope rhymes, handwork patterns, jokes, and a good deal more. Woodland Indians and French settlers swapped tales, Norwegian and Anglo-American fiddlers traded tunes, African Americans and Irish tried each other's dance steps. Once associated solely with a particular group, some forms of folk culture are now seen in neighborhoods, cities, even states as symbolic of a broader shared identity. Hence in certain midwestern locales, citizens need not be Scandinavian, German, Anglo-Celtic, Cornish, Macedonian, Slovenian, or

African American to claim deep connections with Minnesota talk, Wisconsin bratwurst, Missouri fiddling, Upper Peninsula pasties, Cincinnati chili, Cleveland-style polka, or Chicago blues.

Sometimes maintaining, sometimes blurring ethnic and other cultural borders, the folklore of midwesterners asserts more rigid distinctions between states. Ardent rivalries and disparaging nicknames have been entrenched since the territorial era. When the Presbyterian missionary Zenas Eddy traveled to Wisconsin's lead-mining district in 1845, he encountered a motley assemblage "representative of the western states, called in the unique nomenclature of this region *Hoosiers, Wolverines, Badgers, Suckers, Buckeyes,* etc." Referring to folks from Indiana, Michigan, Wisconsin, Illinois, and Ohio, these names, in turn, declare residents to be uncouth rustics, small yet fierce and gluttonous beasts, drunken robbers, fair-weather friends, and backwoodsmen. Illinoisans abandoned Sucker, just as Missourians disavow the disparaging "Puke," yet several states pugnaciously identify with once-derisive terms. Wearing slurs with pride may lessen their sting, yet midwesterners are particularly inventive in catcalling across state lines. Minnesotans refer to Iowa as "Baja Minnesota." People from Illinois taunt Wisconsin "Cheeseheads," while Wisconsinites uncharitably deem their neighbors "FIBs" (Fucking Illinois Bastards). And residents along the northern banks of the Ohio River hold themselves superior to the "Briers" and "Kentuckians" on the other side. Jokes abound. Why do they play football on grass in Iowa? So the cheerleaders can graze. What's printed on the bottoms of whisky bottles in Kentucky? Open other end. What separates a Cheesehead from a Blockhead? The Mississippi River. Ruthless though their interstate verbal duels may be, midwesterners close ranks when assailed as dull flatlanders, striking back through folk humor at stereotypical aggressive New Yorkers, bragging Texans, and trendy Californians.

Certainly the contributions of midwestern scholars and institutions to the study of folklore rival those of any American region. Folklore, as a discipline, combines social scientific dedication to empirical field research with humanistic appreciation of artistic cultural expressions. Since the late nineteenth century folklorists have interviewed, recorded, photographed, and otherwise documented the life histories, performances, events, and objects of participants in midwestern cultural groups. Based in universities and public agencies, they have presented their work through publications, exhibits, events, and media productions.

In 1907 Stith Thompson, a student at the University of Wisconsin, was moved to study folklore by an English professor, Arthur Beatty. Thompson subsequently offered folklore courses at Indiana University in the early 1920s, established a summer Folklore Institute in 1942, then presided over America's initial folklore Ph.D. in 1953. Although Thompson's own work looked beyond the region, his students and colleagues profoundly shaped our understanding of midwestern folklore. Richard M. Dorson explored the relationship between traditional stories, region, and nation in *Bloodstoppers and Bearwalkers* (1952) and *Land of the Millrats* (1981), based, respectively, on field research in the forested Upper Peninsula of Michigan and industrialized northern Indiana. Warren Roberts investigated the origins, patterns and makers of folk crafts and architecture in *Log Buildings of Southern Indiana* (1984) and *Viewpoints on Folklife* (1988). And Linda Dégh, through the journal *Indiana Folklore* and a series of essays published as *Narratives in Society* (1995), identified the interplay of pluralism and creolization in thriving legend traditions of ethnically diverse urban midwesterners. Their pioneering efforts, inspiring several generations of students, were paralleled in Detroit, where Emelyn Gardner and Thelma James collaborated with working-class students—mostly immigrants' children—on fieldwork projects that resulted in the Wayne State University Folklore Archive's founding in 1939.

Folklore study persists at Indiana University, as well as through interdisciplinary programs at the University of Wisconsin and The Ohio State University, where Francis Lee Utley launched folklore classes in the 1930s. Wayne State's pioneering archive was acquired in 2003 by the Michigan Traditional Arts Program at Michigan State University, which operates a museum, produces an annual folklife festival, and helps community organizations document their own folklore.

Such outreach-oriented or "public folklore" efforts took hold in the Midwest in the 1930s with support from Depression-era federal programs. Field researchers—some toting bulky sound-recording equipment—captured the voices, lives, and cultural traditions of former slaves in Indiana, Chicago's diverse working poor, Ojibwe Indians in northern Wisconsin, Great Lakes sailors, and more, resulting in guidebooks, crafts cooperatives, and public art. World War II travel restrictions and the McCarthy period's unease with anything combining populist, pluralist, and progressive politics ended such activities from the 1940s through the 1960s. In the 1970s, however, a trio of federal agencies—the Office of Folklife Programs at the Smithsonian Institution, the Folk Arts Program at the National Endowment for the Arts, and the American Folklife Center at the Library of Congress—fostered the renewal of state folklore programs throughout the Midwest.

The entries in this section of the encyclopedia circumscribe and sketch the region's folklore, moving from considerations of forms—architecture, arts and crafts, foods, festivals, music and dance, song, and oral narratives—to observations on their relationship with groups distinguished by shared ethnicity or occupation or recreational pursuits.

Sources and Further Reading: Karel D. Bicha, "From Where Come the Badgers?" *Wisconsin Magazine of History* 76 (Winter 1992–1993); Walter Blair and Franklin J. Meine, *Half Horse, Half Alligator: The Growth of the Mike Fink Legend* (1933); Richard M. Dorson, *American Folklore* (1959); Richard M. Dorson, "Illinois Egyptians," in Richard M. Dorson, ed., *Buying the Wind* (1964); Oliver Johnson, *A Home in the Woods: Pioneer Life in Indiana; Oliver Johnson's Reminiscences of Early Marion County* (1951; reprint, 1978); Marsha MacDowell and Ruth D. Fitzgerald, *Michigan Quilts* (1987); Deborah Neff and Phillip B. Zarrilli, *Wilhelm Tell in America's "Little Switzerland," New Glarus, Wisconsin* (1987); John Nowlin, *The Bark Covered House; or, Back in the Woods Again* (1875; reprint, 1937); Milo Milton Quaife, ed., *The Western Country in the 17th Century: The Memoirs of Lamothe Cadillac and Pierre Lieite* (1718; reprint, 1947); Henry Rowe Schoolcraft, *Algic Resource: Indian Tales and Legends* (1839); Stith Thompson, *A Folklorist's Progress: Reflections of a Scholar's Life* (1996); William Thoms, "Folklore," [1846] in Alan Dundes, *The Study of Folklore* (1965); Paton Yoder, *Taverns and Travelers: Inns of the Early Midwest* (1969).

James P. Leary
University of Wisconsin–Madison

Folk Architecture and Landscape

Landscape is an interpretation of the land shaped by ever-changing variables. The landscape artist paints a scene colored by weather, lighting, seasonal change. The landscape architect manipulates natural features of a plot of ground to enhance its attractiveness and use. The folklorist and cultural geographer codify and map sections of earth by regional cultural imprint. Thus, landscape is a continuing process of humankind's imposition of form, order, control, and meaning on the land.

The natural landscape of the Midwest has great diversity, including prairie, lakes, and woodlands, the Great Lakes maritime region; major river ways and minor tributaries; and, in the southeast, what amounts to foothills of the southern highlands. These areas attracted human inhabitants of all kinds, of whom the Native Americans were first, followed by the early Anglo-European voyageurs and explorers who opened the interior trade and travel routes that allowed penetration of the wilderness by pioneers. All these inhabitants interpreted and manipulated the natural landscape to meet their physical and spiritual needs, leaving behind the diverse material cultural representations of their presence that distinguish the midwestern vernacular landscape.

The town square is a product of both multicultural antecedents and the division of virgin land into gridlike sections, townships, and city blocks. Sold into private ownership, the land became dotted with structures of human occupation and use such as the I-house, with its central hall flanked by first- and second-floor rooms, the bi-level bank barn and the Great Lakes fish tug, with its covered deck and gill nets. The builders and users of these structures—and those of the Native Americans who preceded them—are remembered by shrines and grave markers, by both sacred and secular representations of what a community holds most dear.

These and all other traditional elements of the midwestern landscape are cultural ideas converted through knowledge and acquired skills passed down informally through generations into recognizable yet constantly varied forms. The Anglo-European settlers moving into the Midwest brought with them what they could from their previous homes. Fiction abounds with tales of travel by covered wagons filled with household goods and assorted family members. Laura Ingalls Wilder wrote of such trips in her Little House series of children's novels. Who can forget Jack, the family's brindle bulldog, trotting loyally alongside the wagon as it lumbered out of the Big Woods of Wisconsin and crossed the sweeping prairies of Minnesota, Iowa, and Missouri before coming to a stop in Kansas?

When the Ingalls family selected a homesite near the Verdigris River, Pa immediately set about building a house of round logs. The wagon held all the tools he required, his mind all the knowledge, his hands all the skill. Unlike modern-day folk who are plunged unprepared into pioneer life in PBS specials or for the weekend at a local living-history museum, Pa and Ma and the girls possessed all the competencies that real pioneers needed to survive.

Wilder wrote vivid stories of pioneer life, but the great majority of inhabitants left no written record of their experiences. They did, however, leave all sorts of cultural objects on the land that can be read for insight into their forgotten lives and the lives of those who followed. And because the meaning of cultural objects changes as they cycle through periods of active use, alteration, abandonment, reclamation, reconstruction, rethinking, and reuse, they reveal quite a bit about their subsequent users.

Many of the Ingallses' homesites, for example, survive in one form or another. At Mansfield, Missouri, the house Laura and her husband Almanzo built in 1913 remains carefully preserved as it was in 1957, the year of Laura's death. At Pepin, Wisconsin, Laura's birthplace, a small frame building houses a museum of local history, while a recently built log cabin can be found at the "Little House Wayside" several miles out of town. Yet another homesite is found at Walnut Grove, Minnesota, which honors its pioneer family with the Wilder Museum; a pageant based on the Little House books; and, two miles outside of town, the remains of the Ingalls family's dugout home.

Mansfield honors its daughter by maintaining her house as an inviolate public shrine, but the village of Pepin is not so lucky. There a generic log cabin was built to betoken Laura's birth and the Ingallses' residence in the Big Woods. These examples illustrate how landscape, as an interpretation of the land, is manipulated to celebrate a community's unique identity. This is the objective of "cultural heritage tourism," which the website of the National Trust for Historic Preservation defines as traveling to see and understand the places, objects, and deeds that accurately capture the narratives of people past and present.

In what other ways does landscape as interpretation lend it new meanings? Heritage tourism is strongly aligned with the American historic preservation movement, of which the National Trust is the largest not-for-profit organization. Among the first strategies toward saving an endangered historic property is to add it to the National Register of Historic Places. Overseen by the Department of the Interior, the National Register is a collection of cultural resources—town squares, family farms, national historic sites, cemeteries, iron bridges, ships and shipwrecks, privately owned homes, and much, much more—that the federal government deems worthy of preservation.

In 1994 Sauk Centre, Minnesota, successfully petitioned to list its Main Street, the original commercial corridor in the Stearns County town of approximately 3,900 people, in the National Register. Because of the town's association with Sinclair Lewis, its Main Street has been recognized by the National Register as America's Main Street, a profoundly influential symbol of the American small town. Writing in *Preservation*, the magazine of the National Trust, Adam Goodheart describes Lewis's literary Main Street as "a place in the geography of the national soul." Once hated by his neighbors for attacking them so cruelly in *Main Street*, Sinclair Lewis is now revered as Sauk Centre's hometown hero with his restored boyhood home (on Sinclair Lewis Avenue) and an interpretive center.

As a collection of artifacts carefully assembled to convey a particular story, the interpretive center or museum is an important manifestation of the cultural landscape as interpretation. It comes in several types.

Compiled sites are assembled from a variety of structures and objects. These include multiacre outdoor living-history museums dotted with relocated and reconstructed buildings that illustrate a carefully constructed narrative of the regional past. Prime examples are Old World Wisconsin, near the town of Eagle, and Conner Prairie at Noblesville, Indiana. America's largest museum of rural life, Old World Wisconsin interprets the state's immigrant experience with seventy relocated and reconstructed traditional structures representing the state's Danish, Finnish, Norwegian, Polish, German, Anglo, and African American traditions. At Conner Prairie, visitors are invited to experience life played out on four different historic stages: an 1816 Indian camp, an 1836 pioneer village, the 1836 William Conner estate, and an 1886 rural community.

Replica sites are reconstructed from surviving archeological evidence. At Grand Portage National Monument, on the shore of Lake Superior in extreme northeastern Minnesota, a stockade wall and a great hall and kitchen complex have been reconstructed over their original archeological footprints. The site is significant for its association with the Great Lakes fur trade, and costumed interpreters reenact period traditions of the Native Americans, French voyageurs, and Anglo employees of the fur agents who rendezvoused here each summer.

Authentic sites, such as Fort Totten at Bismarck, North Dakota, remain relatively intact and in situ. Constructed as a military post in 1867, Fort Totten evolved into an Indian boarding school, an Indian health-care facility, a reservation school, and, since 1960, a North Dakota State Historic Site. The history of Fort Totten is one of repeated adaptation to new uses, all of which are reflected in the site's interpretation. Adaptive use continues into the present day with the conversion of the original officer's quarters into an inn whose guests, like costumed museum personnel, PBS pioneers, and those restoring historic homes, must interpret their own modern-day lives within the context of the cultural landscape of the past—and vice versa.

As a carefully manipulated cultural landscape, the museum and historic site is both familiar and exotic. As visitors pass through the entrance stile or gate, they willingly exchange the modern landscape of gated rural subdivisions and urban sprawl for a liminal one of the past, both time-out-of-time and place-out-of-place. A few hours later, they emerge from the dirt-covered acres dotted with regional, ancestral log cabins, one-room schoolhouses, and double-crib barns. Assured by museum promotional literature that their experience has been an authentic representation of the past, they climb into their air-conditioned cars and reenter the contemporary midwestern landscape. First stop, McDonald's.

If museums and historic sites are liminal landscapes, how much more so are those under water. Consider the 448-square-mile Thunder Bay National Marine Sanctuary and Underwater Preserve (NMS/UP) headquartered at Alpena, Michigan. Established in 2000 as one of thirteen National Marine Sanctuaries, NMS/UP protects an estimated 116 historically significant Lake Huron shipwrecks ranging from nineteenth-century wooden side-wheelers to twentieth-century steel-hulled steamers. Strewn about on the lake's bottom, buried in silt and accumulated debris, the shipwrecks are both relatively untouched, unaltered graveyards of human lives and an unopened archive of Great Lakes maritime history and commerce. A surreal landscape of accident created by human error, the breakdown of ships, and the clash of weather and water, the NMS/UP awaits further discovery, exploration, and research.

The hitherto inaccessible and therefore unexplored collection of cultural resources located under water has in recent years been guaranteed a measure of protection and conservation by legislative action patterned on successful efforts at land conservation on the part of individuals and not-for-profit agencies such as the Land Trust Alliance (LTA), which maintains a Midwest office at Lansing, Michigan. Recent dialogue on the future of land conservation has included the protection of cultural features of the land plus the traditional competencies and performances underlying their construction and use.

Recognition and documentation of the unique cultural features of the landscape is the first step toward an overall conservation plan. A prime example of such documentation is found in Monroe County, Indiana, where the 6,000-acre Maple Grove Road Rural Historic District, listed on the National Register of Historic Places in 1998, is recognized as one of the state's most intact traditional landscapes. Significant features include dry rock fences built by Irish craftsmen, a large stone I-house built in 1832, rural frame churches, the modest house of environmentalist and author Rachel Peden, roads that have been in use for well over one hundred years, and field patterns that have remained relatively unchanged for at least as long. Even as contemporary housing divisions filled with starter castles penetrate the district, and as proposals for the new Interstate 69 corridor pose an additional threat to its integrity, the landscape continues to be revered for its distinct composition, aesthetics, and historicity.

In summary, the traditional cultural landscape of the Midwest is an interpretation of human impact on the land. It is a way of viewing the characteristic material features created and left by generations of occupants from prehistoric times to the present. Ever changing, landscape can provide valuable evidence of past human lives and of people's interaction with the land, particularly in the absence of written documentation. Most significantly, however, landscape reveals volumes about the way the past is used in the present, about the way humans impose form, order, control, and meaning on the land.

Sources and Further Reading: Henry H. Glassie, *Folk Housing in Middle Virginia* (1975); Adam Goodheart, "This Side of Main Street," *Preservation* (Mar./Apr. 2002); John Brinckerhoff Jackson, *Discovering the Vernacular Landscape* (1984); John Brinckerhoff Jackson, *A Sense of Place, a Sense of Time* (1994); John Stilgoe, *Common Landscape of America, 1580 to 1845* (1982); Laura Ingalls Wilder, *Little House in the Big Woods* (1953).

Joanne Raetz Stuttgen
Martinsville, Indiana

Bank Barns

Bank barns have been central to countless midwestern farmsteads. This type of barn evolved from the simple rectangular structures early settlers had known in Europe. These were single-level threshing barns built directly on the ground with a central threshing floor and areas for grain storage at either end. Inside, sheaves of ripened grain were stored. Their gable roofs were supported by mortised-and-tenoned timber structural systems that included four transverse framing systems, or "bents." Two of these were situated at the end walls, while the two interior bents divided the barn into three spaces or "bays." The grain was threshed with flails on the floor of the central bay with its wide double doors at each end in the long walls. The doors could be opened to create a through breeze that blew the dust and chaff away leaving the grain, which was stored in bins in the barn. Later, New England farmers sometimes modified these barns by adding cattle stalls at one end to shelter young stock, poultry, and the oxen or horses used for tilling the fields. The simple New England barn was carried into parts of the Midwest, where it was used for primarily wheat farming early in the mid-nineteenth century.

Later, because of better growing conditions farther west and insect-infestation problems, wheat farming in the Midwest declined, and diversified agriculture, often centered on dairying, became prevalent. As a result, many of the grain barns were jacked up and a masonry basement was constructed under the structure where the cows were kept in stanchions. To reach the upper floors of the barn an earthen ramp, or bank, was built on one side leading up to the doors, hence the name *bank barn*. New barns incorporated this basement level.

During the twentieth century, bank-barn construc-

Early Wisconsin bank barn. Courtesy William Tishler collection.

tion evolved further because of changing agricultural technology. Modifications included fastening the outward-swinging doors together so that they could be opened more easily by sliding them along a metal track, since the through breeze necessary for threshing the grain was no longer needed. This type of door eliminated the need to shovel snow away to open the traditional outward-swinging doors. Also, the advent of threshing machines eliminated the need for traditional threshing by hand with a flail. As tractors and other farm machinery became prevalent, they were often stored in the central bay because the ramp provided easy access to the upper floor.

An important advancement in bank-barn design occurred early in the nineteenth century with the development of the gambrel roof. This provided a larger volume of storage space, enabling hay to be piled higher in the enclosed hayloft. Like the older grain barns, early versions of gambrel-roof bank barns were framed with mortised-and-tenoned timbers supported by heavy upright posts. Subsequent structural systems were devised with the upright supports to the sides, providing a larger unobstructed space—important for storing and moving large machinery.

Surviving bank barns in the Midwest are important reminders of the region's past.

Sources and Further Reading: John Fraser Hart, *The Look of the Land* (1975); Allen G. Noble, *Wood, Brick, and Stone* (1984); Thomas Durant Visser, *Field Guide to New England Barns and Farm Buildings* (1997).

William Tishler
University of Wisconsin–Madison

Fish Tugs

The fish tug has remained the largest, sturdiest, and most powerful of Great Lakes commercial fishing vessels since the last half of the nineteenth century. A "sea boat" compared to others, notorious for causing seasickness, it became the most visibly distinctive fishing-boat type on the lakes during the twentieth century. Common features of the tug from Lake Superior to Lake Ontario reflect the fierce nature of the midwestern snowbelt's fall–spring weather and confirm long communication and exchange across the lakes and along their shores. The tugs' primary type of fishing gear, the gill net, recalls generations of precontact fishing Indians of the upper lakes, whose survival through winter depended on it.

Gill nets have remained most effective for capturing prize species, like whitefish and lake trout, in deeper, offshore waters for more than a thousand years. Compared to canoes and inshore sail- and row-boats, steam-powered wooden vessels built like harbor tugs, and sometimes operated as such when not fishing, removed some risks during the best times, but worst weather, for offshore fishing. Generally more than fifty feet long, designed by fishers working with marine architects and built in shipyards, early steam-tugs required substantial investment and large fishing crews. As wind, sleet, frozen fog, and snowstorms iced up gear, fishers covered work spaces on deck, linking structures to the pilothouse. Responding quickly to advances in petrochemical engines and downturns in fishing stocks, boat builders built smaller versions of the tugs, for smaller crews, in the early 1900s. The tug name and some hull features persisted, but these new cousins also pulled characteristics from smaller inshore sail- and gas-powered boats.

By the 1920s and 1930s, the classic fish tug form emerged, with its "full bluff bow"; buxom bilge; pleasant sheer; shallow rounded forefoot to mount ice and break it with the weight of the boat; overhanging stern counter, often with a rounded fantail shape; and distinctive, massive, "single-concept superstructure." Stretching the length and breadth of the boat, the superstructure entirely enclosed the work space, protecting four main interior spaces: a spare, raised wheelhouse aft or amidships; a massive engine abaft amidships surrounded by passageways connecting work spaces; a forward net-lifting and fish-picking work station with powered net-lifter and fish-box storage; and a stern net-setting space, sometimes with a protectively raised deck.

For protection from ice, metal sheathing covered wooden hulls, usually ribbed and planked heavily with oak until the 1940s. From lengths of thirty-two to thirty-eight feet during the 1930s, tugs (generally powered by diesel) lengthened into forty- and fifty-foot ranges after World War II, with beams near a third the length, and drafts of four to five feet. With scarcities of oak and shipyard customers, fish tugs after World War II were built of steel, often with squarer, broader sterns and Veed and chined bottoms. While steel versions have quicker, less comfortable rides than their rollier, rounder-bottomed wooden forerunners, fishers prefer their improved stability, lower maintenance, and durability in ice and rocky shoals. Upper lakes fishers observe that Lake Michigan tugs, built for "laying on the net" and breaking ice, are heavier, deeper, and narrower than the broader, flatter-bottomed, and shallower Lake Erie tugs, which have been most adapted for trawling since the 1950s.

Dwindling in numbers with increased restrictions on gillnetting, fish tugs are increasingly invisible in the cultural landscape. As in their beginnings, they again are outnumbered by smaller inshore commercial fishing craft. Yet they remain the boat type most readily identifiable with the Great Lakes maritime region, and their persistence reminds us of the importance of the Great Lakes to midwestern sustenance, trade, and transportation.

Sources and Further Reading: Robert C. Grunst, "Boats, Nets and Rigs: Early Twentieth Century Commercial Fishing on Lake Michigan," *Michigan History* 77 (July/Aug. 1993); Robert C. Grunst, "Farsighted Designs: The Fish Tug *Johanna* and Trends in the Upper Great Lakes Fishery," *Inland Seas* 53 (Summer 1997); Robert C. Grunst, "The Swan, the Elk, and the Shark," *Inland Seas* 50 (Spring 1994); A. B. McCullough, *The Commercial Fishery of the Canadian Great Lakes* (1989); Frank Prothero, *The Good*

Years: A History of the Commercial Fishing Industry on Lake Erie (1973).

Janet C. Gilmore
University of Wisconsin–Madison

Grave Markers

One of humankind's oldest folk traditions is the custom of marking the final resting places of the dead with symbolic objects. Grave markers manifest themselves in a variety of ways, ranging from homemade wooden crosses to huge marble mausoleums that cost a million dollars or more to construct. Just as human beings build "cities of the living" in which dwellings and other buildings are located in close proximity to one another, people also create "cities of the dead" in which large numbers of graves and memorial markers are clustered together.

Grave markers in the Midwest are in many ways similar to those found in other parts of the United States. The vast majority of grave markers in the Midwest date from the past two centuries, with stone being the most commonly used material. While midwestern grave markers often reflect general styles and mortuary trends observable elsewhere, there are still interesting differences. These are evident in the "spirit houses" of Woodland Indians; in small rural burial grounds like those in Kansas and Nebraska; and in much larger urban graveyards such as Bellefontaine Cemetery in St. Louis, Missouri, and Graceland Cemetery in Chicago, Illinois. In southern Indiana, one sees wrought-iron and cast-iron grave crosses in many of the communities settled by Bavarian and other German immigrants.

One of the best-documented areas in the Midwest for grave markers is Door County, Wisconsin. Most of the truly distinctive markers found there date from the 1800s and early 1900s, and they reflect a number of prevalent styles. Among the many motifs are the weeping willow, the funeral urn, an upraised hand with the index finger pointing upward, an open book, crosses, angels, doves, lambs, flowers, logs, and obelisks of all sizes. An extremely common tombstone motif is the handclasp, a rather ambiguous symbol that may be interpreted as a gesture of welcome (into the next world) or a sign of departure (from the earthly world).

Even when midwesterners purchase commercial grave markers, they often erect them in traditional ways that are strikingly different from those of mainstream society. The descendants of Canaan Moravian Brethren who settled on the prairies of southeastern North Dakota use modern, laser-etched tombstones but these large granite markers are placed flat on the grave rather than in an upright position. Furthermore, males are buried on one side of the cemetery, females on the other. A wide, grassy path runs between the two cemetery halves, physically separating the male and female sections.

Local legends are associated with numerous midwestern cemeteries and grave markers. There is even a fair share of folk humor to be found in cemeteries throughout America's Heartland. Such humor perhaps is not entirely surprising when considering somber reminders such as this epitaph: "Remember friend, as you pass by, / As you are now, so once was I. / As I am now, you soon will be / So prepare for death and follow me." Beneath one such inscription, a young passerby allegedly wrote in chalk: "To follow you I'm not content / Because I'm not quite sure just where you went!"

Sources and Further Reading: John Gary Brown, *Soul in the Stone* (1994); John M. Kahlert, *Pioneer Cemeteries: Door County Wisconsin* (1981); Richard E. Meyer, ed., *Cemeteries and Gravemarkers: Voices of American Culture* (1992); Richard E. Meyer, ed., *Ethnicity and the American Cemetery* (1993).

Timothy J. Kloberdanz
North Dakota State University–Fargo

I-Houses

The I-house is a form of vernacular architecture found throughout the Midwest, especially in rural areas. Cultural geographer Fred B. Kniffen, who first identified this house type, says, "The I-house was first so named in 1936 in recognition of the Indiana, Illinois, or Iowa origin of many of its builders in prairie Louisiana." The I-house is considered a folk type because, like folktales, the basic form has remained the same as variations developed in it as it spread geographically. It was also a product of folk knowledge; that is, the plan for the house was carried into the Midwest not in written or printed form but in the minds of settlers.

Kniffen described the basic characteristics of the I-house in one of the original studies of the type: "But these qualities all I-houses unfailingly had in common: gables to the side, at least two rooms in length, one room deep, and two full stories in height." The house, in frame or brick, usually had chimneys on one or both gable ends and was generally symmetrical. Variation occurred in the number of upstairs front windows and in additions on the back as well as in decorative details such as Victorian gingerbread. The I-house in the Midwest usually has a central doorway, three or five windows on the second floor in front, and a central hallway.

Settlers from the British Isles patterned the I-house after a traditional English house type brought to the United States. Well established in the Middle Atlantic region by the late seventeenth century, it spread by migration into the Midwest and the South in the nineteenth century, eventually reaching as far west as Iowa and Texas. Complicated by local conditions and influences from other cultural settlement patterns, the spread of the I-house was by no means a simple process. For instance, cultural influences from New England were dominant across the northern tier of Ohio, Indiana, and Illinois, whereas the southern edge of this area experienced influence from the Middle Atlantic. As a result, examples of houses that combined traits from the two cultural regions could be found. Also, the same cultural source could follow different paths but end up at the same place.

Folk architecture is a cultural expression and, as such, can have symbolic meaning, which can be interpreted much as a narrative or other verbal expression can. In fact, the meaning of the midwestern I-house can be better understood by studying it in the context of other kinds of expressions, such as family history and personal narratives. The story Ohio farmer Bob Glasgow tells about the building of his family's I-house in 1842 illustrates this point:

My grandfather had a fancy for cattle, and his first wife died, and he was riding around one evening looking for some more cattle. And he went above Hamilton [and bought some cattle from a man there]. So the man said, "Where you live?" And he told him. So he said, "You better stay all night," and he said, "and you can go home in the morning." He said, "Appreciate it." So he stayed. Well, there was a young lady there looked pretty prosperous. So he went back in a couple of weeks, and by golly he talked something besides cattle.

So the old man asked him, says, "What kind of a house have you got?" Well, he said he had, described it, had a log house right in there, four rooms and by a spring, told him about it, tried to brag it up pretty nice. "Ah," he said, "my daughter's used to a nicer home than that." Said, "You let me draw the pattern for a house, plan," and said, "you build the house and alright." So Grandpa come home and built the house.

Glasgow told this story standing outside the house while talking to two folklorists. He added, "And this is it. And he built the house, and they got married, and she had ten children. There's been twenty-two births, four weddings, and, I believe, it's been five deaths in that house."

As Kniffen has said and folklorist Henry Glassie has reiterated, the I-house connotes the economic success and "agrarian stability" of the middle-class farmer. Glasgow's story suggests an additional meaning mentioned by material-culture scholar Alan Gowans: "[Traditional houses] are metaphors of the traditional Western concept of marriage, as the founding of a landed family in a *joint* enterprise." Bob Glasgow's description of his grandmother as looking "pretty prosperous" links human and house together symbolically and supports the visual metaphor of marriage. The story is clearly from the masculine point of view in making the woman part of the man's property. It indicates that Glasgow's grandfather had to have physical proof of his agrarian stability, of his middle-class status, before his prospective father-in-law would give him permission to marry his daughter. The replacing of a log house with a frame one at a certain point in the growth of a family farm was a traditional pattern. The house had symbolic value as an ideal even before it was built; behavior and object affected each other in planning, building, and living in the house. A status symbol of that society is reflected in the courtship behavior, which is in turn symbolized by the house and carried down in family tradition by the oft-repeated story. Glasgow's comment about births, weddings, and deaths in the house indicates that the generations-old house represents the cycle of life for his family.

The stories and behaviors associated with the Glasgow I-house in Adams County, Ohio, were continued across the southern part of the Midwest from the nineteenth century into the twentieth. As people moved west, establishing farms and building log houses, then replacing them with I-houses, they carried the same symbolic cultural meanings with them—meanings that became a part of the agrarian consciousness, linking family history and region even into the twenty-first century.

Sources and Further Reading: Henry Glassie, *Pattern in the Material Folk Culture of the Eastern United States* (1968); Alan Gowans, "The Mansions of Alloways Creek," in Dell Upton and John Michael Vlach, eds., *Common Places: Readings in American Vernacular Architecture* (1986); Fred B. Kniffen, "Folk Housing: Key to Diffusion," in Dell Upton and John Michael Vlach, eds., *Common Places: Readings in American Vernacular Architecture* (1986); Howard Wight Marshall, *Folk Architecture in Little Dixie: A Regional Culture in Missouri* (1981); Patrick B. Mullen, *Listening to Old Voices: Folklore, Life Stories, and the Elderly* (1992); Warren Roberts, *Log Buildings of Southern Indiana* (1984); Dell Upton and John Michael Vlach, eds., *Common Places: Readings in American Vernacular Architecture* (1986); Michael Ann Williams, *Homeplace: The Social Use and Meaning of the Folk Dwelling in Southwestern North Carolina* (1991).

Patrick B. Mullen
The Ohio State University–Columbus

Sacred Sites and Shrines

From prehistoric times to the present, sacred sites have marked the midwestern landscape, the hills and waters of the region matching dwellers' beliefs about sacred space. Some sites became sacred based on the belief of their being conducive to communing with the divine, and others because a revered event occurred in the place. Some sites became sacred due to ceremonial use and lost that sacredness when the ceremony's location changed. Some midwestern cultural groups mark sacredness in the landscape ostentatiously and others minimally.

The oldest sacred sites in the Midwest are earthworks created by native peoples. Although most were destroyed by European American farmers working the land, hundreds still exist. The earliest are conical burial mounds in the Ohio River Valley region dating from 1000 B.C.E., the largest being Miamisburg Mound, in Miamisburg, Ohio. Sophisticated geometric earthworks that enclosed ceremonial spaces were built in the same area after 200 B.C.E., such as the Newark Earthworks, near Newark, Ohio. Representational effigy mounds dating from C.E. 500 figure most prominently in Wisconsin, although the most spectacular is the monumental Serpent Mound near Peebles,

An Ojibwe spirit house. Photo by Jim Leary, 2002.

Ohio, and impressive clusters are in Effigy Mounds National Monument near Marquette, Iowa. Flat-topped pyramid mounds dating from C.E. 1000–1200 were ceremonial centers. The premier midwestern temple mound is the impressive Monk's Mound in Cahokia, an important center of Mississippian culture near Collinsville, Illinois.

Physical markers do not identify most of the sacred ceremonial sites of the Midwest's Woodland and Plains Indians. These sites are diverse, including quarries, such as the quarries at Pipestone National Monument at Pipestone, Minnesota; bodies of water, such as Coldwater Springs and Minnehaha Falls in Minneapolis; burial sites, such as Huron Indian Cemetery in Kansas City; and mythic or legendary sites, such as Sleeping Bear Dunes near Empire, Michigan.

European immigrants to the Midwest constructed churches, chapels, and shrines that evoked the sacred places of their homelands, such as the Wexford Immaculate Conception Church, built in the 1860s near Harpers Ferry, Iowa, by Irish immigrants from County Wexford. Some were built as the result of a vow, like Our Lady of Consolation shrine in Leopold, Indiana, built by three native Belgians who survived imprisonment as Union soldiers in the Civil War. The most flamboyant public shrine is the block-long Grotto of the Redemption in West Bend, Iowa, constructed by a German immigrant priest during the early twentieth century. Father Paul Dobberstein embedded local and exotic minerals into the grotto's cement for an eclectic effect that other regional artists copied. Many midwesterners, especially newer immigrants like Tibetan Buddhists or traditional Hmong, construct private sacred spaces like household altars.

Kitschy or serious, secular shrines throughout the Midwest pay homage to the economic base of the area. The Corn Palace in Mitchell, South Dakota, is a shrine to one of the Midwest's great crops. Other tributes to key midwestern resources include the Lumbermen's Monument in Iosco County, Michigan; the Hoard Dairy Shrine in Ft. Atkinson, Wisconsin; the four-story fiberglass muskie in Hayward, Wisconsin; and the twelve-foot concrete egg in Mentone, Indiana.

Sources and Further Reading: Robert A. Birmingham and Leslie E. Eisenberg, *Indian Mounds of Wisconsin* (2000); Lisa Stone and Jim Zanzi, *Sacred Spaces and Other Places: A Guide to Grottos and Sculptural Environments in the Upper Midwest* (1993); David Hurst Thomas, *Exploring Ancient Native America: An Archaeological Guide* (1994).

Anne Pryor
Wisconsin Arts Board, Madison, Wisconsin

Town Squares

In many midwestern communities, the town square provides a key fulcrum for the organization of everyday public life. It serves as a central space through which significant official and unofficial displays and performances give meaning and form to local, regional, and national culture. As such, town squares provide a fertile field and ready starting point for understanding the spatial dramatization of local culture.

The concept of the central plaza has been well documented. Setha M. Low suggests that what midwestern observers would recognize as the common pattern of gridiron streets surrounding a central square can be traced through a continuous development of planning models reaching back to the agora designed by the Greek Hippodamus around 470 B.C. While the form of the central square finds multiple expressions throughout the further expansion of colonial interests over centuries, the function of the square has varied considerably, from military (the Roman *castrum*), to aesthetic (the Italian *piazza*), to commercial and social (the French *bastide*).

Midwestern town squares, central to a grid of streets, most often have New England precedents harkening in turn to earlier English patterns in which dense towns with small lots were surrounded by larger farm plots and a horizon of commons land including pastures and woodlots. Yet whereas New England greens were often open, common spaces for activities ranging from grazing to games to military maneuvers, their midwestern successors function differently. Although what locals in Stevens Point, Wisconsin, refer to as "The Square" was platted by New England Yankees, it has been associated since the nineteenth century with Polish settlers who established a thriving farmers' market while surrounding the square with family taverns and a prominent building featuring a bulbous eastern European dome. Elsewhere midwesterners have frequently filled in central spaces with that ever-important public edifice, the county courthouse.

In 1999 folklorists documented the various meanings of the Monroe County, Indiana, courthouse square over time and across the experience of multiple groups. Similar to squares throughout the Midwest, the Monroe County square, with its historic 1908 Beaux Arts courthouse, includes war memorials and other official core symbols of significant events, local to national. Moreover, it plays a primary role as a locus for cultural expression ranging from mainstream arts-and-crafts festivals to seasonal celebrations, musical events, and parade stands. As a site for political and civic expression it celebrates the central role of law in public life; organizes civic duties such as taxpaying,

A town square in Illinois. Library of Congress, Prints and Photographs Division, FSA-OWI Collection, LC-USF34-063644-D DLC.

land transfers, and public hearings; and provides a visible platform for individual and collective political protest.

While the most visible and official uses of the courthouse square suggest its focal role in local culture, the Monroe County study discovered that this meaning is not universally shared. Elder African Americans reported that the square was not, historically, a place for them to gather, as it was for whites. Similarly, rebellious or "alternative" adolescents cruising in cars or skateboarding have preferred to hang out in other downtown locations of their choosing, where they feel less hassled. Hence, while the town square spatializes important cultural beliefs and practices, understanding what's "off the square" may contribute just as much to a comprehensive understanding of local culture.

Sources and Further Reading: Setha M. Low, *On the Plaza* (2000); John W. Reps, *Town Planning in Frontier America* (1969); Scott Russell Sanders, "On Loan from the Sundance Sea," *Preservation* 53 (July–Aug. 2001); David A. Taylor, "Indiana Field School Explores Life 'On the Square,'" *Folklife Center News* 22 (Fall 2000).

Philip B. Stafford
Indiana University–Bloomington

Folk Arts and Crafts

The folk arts and crafts of the Midwest include forms of material culture created throughout the region that are traditional in nature, learned informally, and based in a shared aesthetic. Whether Odawa black ash baskets or Norwegian rosemaled bowls, African American quilts or Hmong *paj ntaub,* Armenian lace doilies or Slovak wheat weavings, miniature logging sleds or intricate examples of sailors' knotwork, hand-tied fishing flies or carved duck decoys, all are the products of long-standing traditions, passed from father to son, grandmother to granddaughter, old hand to young apprentice. They are the most recent versions of many similar artifacts that have been fashioned over the years using common materials and techniques learned from others. At once old and new, these artistic expressions are further shaped by a consciousness of community standards that value consistency with an established norm while allowing some degree of individual variation to satisfy the need for personal expression and to meet the demands of changing cultural context. Thus, the folk arts and crafts of the Midwest are the results of a subtle balancing act between continuity and creativity, between the past and the present, between the individual and the group. Consequently, each work is richly symbolic and deeply meaningful because it carries both the authority of successive generations of artists and the approval of the contemporary community.

Midwestern folk arts and crafts reflect many of the defining characteristics of the Great Lakes and the Northern Plains. They are rooted in the natural resources of the region, in its woods and waters, in its clay and stone, and in its crops and livestock. They are as diverse as the many peoples who have settled America's heartland, from the original Native American inhabitants, through the European immigrants who flocked to the region during the late nineteenth and early twentieth centuries, to the African Americans, Hispanics, and Asians who have come to the area more recently in search of jobs and freedom.

The Midwest's earliest inhabitants, the Native Americans, relied upon the abundant natural resources the land offered to meet many of their most basic needs. The woodlands of the northern Great Lakes provided birch bark and basswood for Ojibwe canoes and fish decoys. The wildlife of the region yielded fur and feathers for both everyday clothing and such special dance regalia as Menominee moccasins and Ojibwe deer-toe jingles. And the Midwest's golden fields of corn provided not only food for Native American people but also raw material for Oneida corn-husk dolls.

The European immigrants who came to the Midwest in the late 1800s and early 1900s were attracted by the same fertile farmland and rich woodlands that earlier supported Native Americans, as well as by the numerous industrial jobs that the region's growing cities offered. Once settled, they began to fashion homes, barns, articles of clothing, and household furnishings according to patterns first learned in the old country. German settlers in Wisconsin constructed *Fachwerk*, or "half-timbered," dwellings, while Finns in Minnesota utilized the state's abundant timber to construct tightly fitted *saunas*. Dutch immigrants to western Michigan and Iowa followed Old World precedents by making wooden shoes for use in the garden and the fields. And in major urban centers like Chicago, Illinois, and Cleveland, Ohio, Polish immigrants transformed colored paper into decorative *wycinanki* and Ukrainians created intricately decorated Easter eggs, called *pysanky*, using the age-old wax resist dyeing technique.

During this same period, lumbermen and hunters, fishers and farmers transformed the tools of their trades into things of beauty. Czech basket makers in northeastern Wisconsin used the same black ash as their Native American counterparts to fashion large feed baskets for hauling hay and silage to animals in the barnyard. Duck hunters along the Mississippi flyway crafted decoys and hunting skiffs for use in pursuing the waterfowl that migrated through the region each fall. Anglers throughout the Midwest carved trout and musky decoys for ice fishing on frozen lakes and tied a seemingly endless assortment of fishing flies for casting in free-flowing streams. Lumberjacks in the north woods of the upper Great Lakes turned their woodworking skills to both practical pursuits and pastimes such as carving wooden chains, balls in cages, and even bucksaws in bottles.

More recently, African Americans from the Deep South, Hispanics from both Mexico and the Caribbean, and emigrants from the Middle East and Southeast Asia have added their music and dance, crafts and customs to the rich and diverse mix that characterizes the Midwest. Quilters from throughout the American South brought distinctive "string" and "strip" quilting techniques, clearly reflective of their African heritage, north to the Heartland when they migrated to the region's urban centers in search of jobs made more plentiful by the demands of two world wars. Similarly, Hispanics from Mexico, Puerto Rico, and the American Southwest, often introduced to the Midwest as migrant farm workers, have brought carnival masks, piñatas, and paper flowers to enrich the region's many community celebrations. In addition, Hmong immigrants who came to cities throughout the Midwest from their native Laos following the Vietnam War introduced their colorful needlework and elaborate traditional clothing into the region's multicultural mosaic. Arab Americans, too, have introduced their distinctive foodways, musical instruments, and clothing traditions to urban centers like Detroit and Dearborn, Michigan.

Times have changed considerably in the years since the first European settlers came into contact with the Native American inhabitants of the Midwest. As might be expected, the region's folk arts and crafts have changed as well, evolving gradually in response to such forces as individual creativity, the availability of new materials, changes in technology, and larger forms of social and cultural change. Yet, despite these changes, many midwestern folk arts and crafts continue to be practiced to this day.

At the most basic level, some degree of change is inevitable as folk arts and crafts are passed along from one artist to another. Stored in the memories of masters and apprentices and communicated orally or by example, a particular form of basket or woven belt is no more likely to be replicated exactly than an individual folktale or legend is expected to be retold word for word. These small, "passive" changes, rather than being regarded negatively, are valued in most communities as signs of the individual artist's presence within the tradition.

Folk artists and craftspeople throughout the Midwest have also sought to introduce more "active" kinds of change into their traditional art forms. Master artists like Leif Melgaard, a Norwegian American woodcarver from Minneapolis, and Betty Piso Christenson, a Ukrainian egg decorator from Suring, Wisconsin, attempted to improve, modify, or vary their designs both in order to further the tradition and in order to demonstrate their creativity and skills.

Other midwestern artists have chosen to replace older materials and technologies with new ones in response to changes in their own circumstances or to the myriad technological changes that have occurred during recent decades. Hmong artists recently arrived in the region have replaced bamboo, which they typically used in baskets in their native Laos, with materials as unusual as plastic pallet-binding strips retrieved from work sites. Finnish rag-rug weavers in Michigan's Upper Peninsula have occasionally substituted plastic bread wrappers for fabric strips in order to produce waterproof mats. Similarly, the advent of chain saws in the lumbering woods of the region's northern tier of states gave rise to a whole new genre of folk art, suggesting that the introduction of a new power tool can itself generate a new form of expression, related to earlier forms like whittling and hand carving in some ways, but also dependent in style upon the advantages and limitations of the tool itself.

While the various active and passive changes introduced by midwestern traditional artists into their work are certainly significant, larger variations resulting from cultural and social changes imposed upon the artists by contemporary American life may have had an even greater effect on the folk arts and crafts of the region. For example, although certain folk arts continue to be practiced without interruption over long periods of time, the unimpeded flow of any one folk-art form from one generation to the next is becoming increasingly the exception rather than the rule. Similarly, the likelihood of there being several artists within one community who continue to practice the same art form is dwindling. Instead, in most communities, a few individuals commit themselves to preserving their art forms, keeping them alive as part of their heritage and as a resource in case others might take an interest. As a result, interruptions in the continuous flow of midwestern folk arts and crafts have occurred periodically. Consequently, later artists have sometimes sought to revitalize or revive their traditions by conducting research and experimenting on their own until they are again able to produce the temporarily "lost" art form. This commitment to preserving and perpetuating the folk arts and crafts of the Midwest speaks strongly to the role that these seemingly simple forms of expressive culture play in the lives of residents of the region.

Although shaped and reshaped by the forces of change, the folk arts and crafts of the Midwest continue to play a significant role in the life of the region. Rather than fulfilling everyday functions, these traditional arts now provide practitioners ways of acknowledging their heritages; celebrating their communities; and expressing their ethnic, regional, and occupational identities. Thus, midwestern artists do not fashion Potawatomi cradleboards and Norwegian mangle boards because modern baby carriers and electric irons are not available to them. Instead, they continue to create these time-honored objects because of their importance as symbols—symbols of ethnic identity, of religious belief, and of a commitment to the "old ways." Similarly, many of the region's retired loggers, hunters, and fishers make use of their newfound leisure to recall the central experiences of their lives in wood, metal, or paint. Lumberjacks, fishers, and farmers fashion models of their logging skids, fish tugs, and steam tractors to remind themselves of the work that they valued and the way it was done in the old days.

As a result of their traditional nature, the folk arts and crafts of the Midwest combine elements of continuity and consistency—which link them to the past—with aspects of creativity and change—which join them to the present and the future. As a result of their grounding in ethnic, regional, occupational, and religious groups that share systems of belief and aesthetics, midwestern folk arts and crafts reflect a sense of community despite their creation by individuals.

Rooted in the past yet responsive to the present, reflective of both common values and individual creativity, the folk arts and crafts of the Midwest have served as symbols central to the lives of residents of the region for generations. Their beauty and meaning, their resiliency and richness, argue strongly for their continuing presence for years to come.

Sources and Further Reading: Simon Bronner, *Chain Carvers: Old Men Crafting Meaning* (1985); Joanne Cubbs, ed., *Hmong Art: Tradition and Change* (1985); C. Kurt Dewhurst and Marsha MacDowell, eds., *Michigan Folk Art, its Beginnings to 1941* (1976); C. Kurt Dewhurst and Marsha MacDowell, eds., *Rainbows in the Sky* (1978); Willard B. Moore, Marion J. Nelson, Colleen J. Sheehy, and Thomas Vennum, Jr., *Circles of Tradition: Folk Art in Minnesota* (1989); Marion Nelson, ed., *Material Culture and People's Art among the Norwegians in America* (1994); Steven Ohrn, ed., *Passing Time and Traditions* (1984); Robert T. Teske, ed., *From Hardanger to Harleys* (1987); Robert T. Teske, ed., *Wisconsin Folk Art: A Sesquicentennial Celebration* (1997); Nicholas Curchin Vrooman and Patrice Marvin, *Iron Spirits* (1982).

Robert T. Teske
Milwaukee County Historical Society,
Milwaukee, Wisconsin

Baskets

Native peoples of the Midwest, especially in the upper Midwest, continue to make baskets and related containers of woven, coiled, or plaited natural materials. The southwestern Ojibwe—whose scattered reservations extend from the eastern tip of the Upper Peninsula of Michigan westward to North Dakota's Turtle Mountains—are noted for birch-bark baskets used to process and store maple sugar and wild rice, but their repertoire has included coiled sweetgrass baskets, "melon-shaped" baskets of woven willow or stiff inner basswood bark, and market and kettle baskets plaited from pounded black ash.

Black-ash baskets—often fitted with a white-ash handle and adorned with dyed and twisted strips—are likewise actively made by Odawa, Oneida, Potawatomi, and, especially, Ho-Chunk peoples. Among the Ho-Chunk, who reside primarily in central Wisconsin, men have traditionally selected and felled "basket trees," quartered them, then pounded segments with the blunt side of a poleax until the wood separates into strips. Women subsequently trim strips to desired widths, then fashion the baskets. Their knowledge is attributed to revelations by the ash tree's generous spirit at a critical time when Ho-Chunk women needed ways to earn money. As Lila Greengrass Blackdeer recounted in 1994, a young woman "went and lived outside and those four days she dreamt about the ash wood, the ash tree, and how . . . to prepare it and so forth. And then when she came home that's when they started." Since the late nineteenth century, Ho-Chunk women have secured income through basket sales from roadside stands, trading posts, and gift shops, while making baskets as gifts and as personalized expressions of their cultural identity.

Mostly male midwesterners of European heritage have likewise practiced basket-making traditions. Initially their durable constructions from local materials satisfied neighbors' utilitarian needs. Across the region's lower tier Anglo Americans like Hocking County, Ohio's, Dwight Stump and Joseph Westfall of Howard County, Missouri, relied on white oak to create round-rod and flat-splint baskets for sewing notions, eggs, apples, laundry, and as picnic hampers. Czechs in Wisconsin's Manitowoc and Kewaunee Counties relied on pounded-ash baskets to make the aforementioned forms plus baskets for picking mushrooms and carrying chopped hay to young cattle. Elsewhere Germans and Swiss, including Amish and Mennonites, as well as Poles and Finns have made baskets of birch bark, cedar, willow, and even rye straw. The post-1975 influx of Southeast Asian refugees into the Midwest has included skilled Hmong basket makers. Lacking bamboo, some, like Tong Kay Moua of Eau Claire, Wisconsin, have fashioned market baskets from plastic pallet-binding strips retrieved from his son's industrial job.

The numbers of traditional basket makers have steadily dwindled in the Midwest because their handiwork cannot compete monetarily with cheaply manufactured metal or plastic containers. Those who persist seldom do so primarily for money. Rather, their motives may include a sense of responsibility for sustaining a valued elder's skill, the necessity for "something to do" in spare time, the pleasure of creating heirlooms for loved ones, and pride in their particular cultural heritage.

Sources and Further Reading: Rosemary O. Joyce, *A Bearer of Tradition* (1989); Carrie A. Lyford, *Ojibwa Crafts* (1943); Howard Wight Marshall, "Mr. Westfall's Baskets: Tradi-

Longaberger Basket headquarters.
Courtesy Longaberger Company's
Home Office,
Newark, Ohio.

tional Craftsmanship in Northcentral Missouri," *Mid-South Folklore* 2 (Summer 1974); Robert T. Teske, ed., *From Hardanger to Harleys* (1987).

James P. Leary
University of Wisconsin–Madison

Knotwork

Fashioning rope into decorative and useful objects using knots is an occupational art shared by maritime workers worldwide. In the Midwest, maritime culture thrives along the Great Lakes coasts and the shorelines of rivers and waterways. Here, workers in the merchant marine, the coast guard, and the navy, on river boats, barges, tugs, and rescue vessels, and in shore operations like marinas and net sheds—may take up fancy knotwork, or "marlinespike seamanship."

Knot tying is an essential skill among maritime workers, typically taught by a mentor or other more experienced mariner. Classic how-to books such as *The Ashley Book of Knots* (1944) add to their repertoires. By repeatedly practicing, using knots in everyday situations, and teaching others, they hone their skills.

Mariners embellish personal tools such as knives, keys, ice chisels, and flashlights with lanyards and coverings of knots for easier handling and to make them distinctive from others' tools. They make numerous other articles from rope and knots, such as shaving brushes, hammocks, picture frames, belts, and ditty bags.

Decorating the workplace with knotted art is a way that mariners express their shared sense of community. On a vessel, knotwork may be employed to cover railings and steering wheels. Ships' bells are outfitted with elaborate bell ropes.

Co-workers mark rites of passage such as retirements by making and giving displays of nautical knotted items such as knotboards or plaques. Commemorating the honored person, they use knots and knotwork in a symbolic way to express their shared experience as mariners. Knotboards may be found at coast guard stations and maritime museums throughout the Midwest.

Sources and Further Reading: Clifford W. Ashley, *The Ashley Book of Knots* (1944); Raoul Graumont and John Hensel, *Encyclopedia of Knots and Fancy Rope Work*, rev. ed. (1952); LuAnne Gaykowski Kozma with Jay C. Martin and Janet C. Gilmore, *Marlinespikes and Monkey's Fists* (1994).

LuAnne Gaykowski Kozma
Michigan State University Museum

Quilting and Needlework

Until the mid-twentieth century, when it became much more common for women to be employed outside the home and low-cost ready-made textiles became widely available, virtually every young woman learned sewing as a requisite for creating clothing as well as items for decorative, ceremonial, and ritual uses. Indigenous peoples in the Great Lakes region were especially noted for their fine beadwork, embroidered porcupine quillwork, and fingerweaving. When steel needles, commercial fabric and thread, and other sewing equipment became available, Native American women, like later pioneer settlers and immigrants to the region, also engaged in quilting, rag-rug weaving, embroidery, ribbonwork, tatting, lace making, crocheting, rug hooking, cutwork, felting, and many other needlework techniques. Depending on the individual's regional, religious, occupational, ethnic, or cultural background, the textiles were produced in different formats, styles, and techniques and for distinct purposes.

One of the most ubiquitous forms of needlework to be found in the Midwest has been quilt making. A quilt is essentially a rectangular-shaped textile made by sewing, usually, three layers of fabric together. The variations on how this basic form is constructed and decorated are seemingly endless. Likewise, the reasons why quilts are made and how they are used are also tremendously varied. Quilts have been made and used most extensively for bed coverings, but they are also used for any everyday purpose requiring a blanket or rectangular fabric. Quilts are also made as fundraisers, instruments to effect social change, such as the AIDS memorial quilt, and as means to commemorate

❖ **Quilting and the Community**

Raisings, logging-bees, husking-bees, quilting-bees and the many other occasions in which the word bee was used to indicate the gathering of the settlers to render gratuitous aids to some neighbor in need, originated in, and was confined to new settlements. It was merely the voluntary union of the individual aid and strength of an entire community to assist a settler in doing what he was unable to accomplish alone. Hence by bees the pioneers raised their houses and barns, did their logging, husked their corn, quilted their bed coverings, and enjoyed themselves in frolic and song with the girls in the evening.

Source: A. D. P. Van Buren, "Raisings and Bees among Early Settlers," in *Pioneer Collections, Report of the Pioneer Society of the State of Michigan,* vol. 5 (1883) 296; quoted in Marsha MacDowell and Ruth D. Fitzgerald, eds., *Michigan Quilts: 150 Years of a Textile Tradition* (1987) 5.

important personal, family, community, and national occasions, such as quilts made in response to the 9/11 terrorist attacks. Lastly, some quilts are made to express to others the maker's personal, creative ideas about color, texture, pattern, shape, and form.

Every community in which quilting occurs not only recognizes when a textile is a quilt but also sets evaluative standards. These standards vary depending on such factors as family, ethnicity, occupation, and region. In some situations, fastidious workmanship is a primary criterion; in other communities it might be how well the quilt has honored the memory or the work of an individual.

Tens of thousands of individuals in the Great Lakes region have been connected to quilting in one way or another—as artists, teachers, collectors, quilters, quilt teachers, quilt owners, or quilt scholars. Hundreds of exhibitions of quilts have occurred at schools, religious centers, community buildings, state and county fairs, powwows, quilt shops, museums, and at landmark events such as the World's Columbian Exposition in 1893 in Chicago. Some exhibitions, like those once hosted by the *Detroit News* at the National Guard Armory in Detroit, the Sears National Quilt Contest at the 1933 World's Fair in Chicago, and the Quilt Nationals at the Dairy Barn Southeastern Ohio Cultural Arts Center have been instrumental in raising the awareness in individuals of quilting.

Individuals and organizations have engaged in quilt-history documentation efforts on statewide and local levels in the Midwest. These efforts have yielded important collections of data as well as exhibitions and publications. Important public collections are housed regionally at the Henry Ford Museum (Dearborn, Michigan), the Illinois State Museum, and the Great Lakes Quilt Center/Michigan State University Museum.

Sources and Further Reading: Ricky Clark, George W. Knepper, and Ellice Ronsheim, *Quilts in Community* (1991); Ellen Kort, *Wisconsin Quilts: Stories in the Stitches* (2001); Marsha MacDowell, ed., *African American Quiltmaking in Michigan* (1997); Marsha MacDowell, ed., *Great Lakes, Great Quilts* (2001).

Marsha MacDowell
Michigan State University

Rag Rugs

Rag-rug weaving is a tradition in many cultures of the world. It arrived in the Midwest with settlers from the Upland South and Europe. Today, rag-rug weaving is especially viable as a family and ethnic tradition among Amish, Mennonites, and Finnish Americans, descendants of settlers from the Upland South and the Amana Colonies. It is also embraced by a world of craftspeople with whom it is not traditional.

Crafted from a wide variety of used materials, traditional rag rugs are prime examples of recycling. Over time they evolved from rugs covering an entire floor to smaller throw rugs. The most common patterns, "hit and miss," "striped," and "banded," are not limited to the Midwest, but discrete regional and ethnic variations do exist. Looms are two-harness and locally hand crafted or manufactured; fewer four-harness looms are used today.

Weavers are most often women who learned as children and returned to weaving as adults, but men also weave and some are loom makers. Couples also turn to rug weaving in retirement; the man weaves while the woman prepares rags and designs the rugs. Traditional weavers are actively supported by their communities and families, who collect and prepare rags, warp looms, tie fringe in completed rugs, and who themselves are consumers. Weavers often sell rugs from their homes but also at local art fairs, in gift shops, and for fundraisers and relief sales.

Despite waxing and waning in popularity, traditional rag rugs are acknowledged as an unbroken family and community tradition.

Sources and Further Reading: Geraldine Niva Johnson, *Weaving Rag Rugs* (1985); Bonnie J. Krause and Cynthia R. Houston, "Bits and Pieces: The Southern Illinois Tradition in Rag Rugs," *Mid-American Folklore* 21 (Spring 1993); Janet Meany and Paula Pfaff, *Rag Rug Handbook* (1988).

Yvonne R. Lockwood
Michigan State University

Wood Carving

One of the most common folk arts of the Midwest is wood carving. Most midwestern communities include carvers who craft a range of pieces, and local carving clubs are commonly found in both rural and urban areas of the region. Wood-carvers frequently give their pieces to family members and friends, sell them at craft fairs, or display them at home, county and state fairs, carving competitions, and local art exhibits in libraries and community centers.

Mask and doll carving has a long and vibrant history within American Indian communities, and the Midwest's immigrant and ethnic groups have all brought intricate carving traditions into the region. Scandinavian relief carving can be found on altars in churches where immigrants settled. German or Swiss chip carving adorns chests, boxes, and other wooden items treasured as family heirlooms. Carvers who make wooden canes dressed up with figures and motifs common within African American traditional culture work throughout the Midwest, and African American cane carvers from Missouri have had their work prominently featured in studies of American folklife.

Ethnic influences remain as important facets of contemporary carving, but popular figures and styles of carving currently reflect localized influences. Popular figures include farm and domestic animals, wildlife, old boots, tools, replicas of antiques, chains, puzzles, decoys, and walking sticks. Carvers work in a variety of representational modes including caricatures, realistic renderings, models, dioramas, relief, abstract motifs, and natural forms.

Carvers work with an array of woods yet prefer wood that is soft enough to carve easily but rigid enough to hold detail. Some choose well-recognized carving woods such as tupelo gum and basswood, and others opt to carve a range of woods such as butternut, poplar, catalpa, and pine. Those who work with woods with little character in the grain frequently paint their work, and others struggle with hard woods that show off a rich grain that they leave exposed in their pieces.

Some wood-carvers make a distinction between "whittling" and "carving" by explaining that whittlers use only pocket knives but carvers use knives, chisels, rotary power tools, and even chain saws. Many carvers do not necessarily view themselves as artists, and it is common to hear carvers describe their work as simply "cutting off anything that isn't supposed to be there." This self-effacement belies some incredibly intricate artistry, and most carvers use their pieces as conversation-starters for sharing their rich perspectives on life in their communities.

Historically, carving has been a highly gendered activity. Many young boys first learn to carve wood from a father, grandfather, or other relative. Frequently they lose interest in carving but then pick up the art once again upon retirement. Although women have carved wood throughout the region's history, it has been more common for women to paint decoys or other carvings that their husbands crafted. Currently, there is an increasing interest in carving among women, and their work is often featured at shows throughout the Midwest.

Sources and Further Reading: Simon J. Bronner, *The Carver's Art: Crafting Meaning from Wood* (1996); Paul W. Parmalee and Forrest Loomis, *Decoys and Decoy Carvers of Illinois* (1969).

Gregory Hansen
Arkansas State University–Jonesboro

Foodways

The Midwest is an area of good, hearty eating. Meat and potatoes country. Meals of all-white food, more plain than fancy. The land of casseroles and Jell-O salads. Much of this picture is stereotype, of course, especially in this time of global franchising. But in terms of traditional eating, there's enough truth to legitimate the image. And, in any case, regional foodways are not just a collection of recipes but also ideas about food, erroneous or not.

Establishing absolute boundaries of a culinary region is quite impossible. There is nothing that all midwesterners—and only midwesterners—eat in common. Rather, midwestern foods are those of the many communities—ethnic, occupational, local—that constitute the Midwest. What's more, state or regional boundaries never dictate cultural boundaries. Bie-

❖ **O, Lutefisk**

E. C. "Red" Stangland

May be sung to the tune of "O Tannenbaum."

O Lutefisk . . . O Lutefisk . . . how fragrant your aroma
O Lutefisk . . . O Lutefisk . . . you put me in a coma
You smell so strong . . . you look like glue
You taste yust like an overshoe
But Lutefisk . . . come Saturday
I tink I'll eat you anyvay.

O Lutefisk . . . O Lutefisk . . . I put you by the doorvay
I vanted you to ripen up . . . yust like dey do in Norvay
A dog came by and sprinkled you . . .
I hit him vid an army shoe
O Lutefisk . . . now I suppose
I'll eat you as I hold my nose.

O Lutefisk . . . O Lutefisk . . . how vell I do remember
On Christmas Eve how we'd receive . . .
Our big treat of December
It vasn't turkey or fried ham . . .
It vasn't even pickled Spam
My mudder knew dere vas no risk . . .
In serving buttered lutefisk.

O Lutefisk . . . O Lutefisk . . . now everyone discovers
Dat Lutefisk and lefse makes . . .
Norvegians better lovers
Now all da vorld can have a ball . . .
You're better dan dat Yeritol
O Lutefisk . . . vid brennevin [Norwegian brandy]
You make me feel like Errol Flynn.

Source: E. C. "Red" Stangland, *Uncle Torvad's Norwegian Memories* (1978).

rocks, also called runsa or runza (a savory yeasted pastry of Volga Deutsch origin stuffed with beef and cabbage), are common in Nebraska but lap over into Iowa and Kansas. Butter tarts (individual-sized pastries filled with custard, sometimes including currants, raisins, or nuts) are a specialty of Ontario, Canada, but are also traditional in parts of eastern Michigan along the Canadian border. Ingredients of booya vary, but this stew exists from Minnesota to southern Indiana.

Still, it is possible to make a number of generalizations about traditional food and the ways that midwesterners eat. In this area you can find fresh, high-quality ingredients not far from the field, stockyard, or lake, prepared expertly but simply. There is an emphasis on meat, especially pork, except in locales like Omaha and Chicago where, for historic reasons, beefsteak reigns supreme. Throughout the region, but especially across the northern half, fish is a dietary staple. Consumption of milk and milk products is probably higher per capita in the Midwest than elsewhere in America.

How do such culinary generalizations, as well as the many more localized food traditions, develop? Two factors are most significant: physical environment and history, particularly immigration history. Both factors are complex and highly interrelated, and their persistent interaction is critically important.

The varied physical environment of the Midwest produces unique wild foods traditional to local foodways. Thimbleberries grow in limited pockets in Michigan's Upper Peninsula and are a favorite of residents across the upper Midwest. From southern Indiana to Kansas the wild persimmon grows in unattended pastures, along fences, and at the edge of woods, and its sweet orange fruit is highly coveted for cooking and eating. Wild cranberries, one of three fruits native to North America, grew abundantly in Wisconsin's marshes. Today's domesticated varieties, descendants of these wild berries, have appeared on settlers' tables in sauces, baked goods, and beverages since the early nineteenth century. Similarly, wild blueberries abound in forest patches and disturbed areas with plenty of sunlight and dry, sandy soil. Berrying was a major seasonal activity for the area's Native American people, and families across the northern Midwest's cutover forests enjoy berry-picking outings as much as the resulting harvest.

Other fruits, although cultivated across the nation, have become identified with the Midwest. With the felling of forests in the 1800s, farmers planted fruit trees, especially apple, and soon orchards appeared throughout the region. Apple cider is an all-time favorite, and making apple butter is an old tradition still maintained in midwestern kitchens. Sour-cherry orchards, established by early homesteaders in north-west Michigan, spawned a range of foods and traditions—preserves, dried cherries, juice, pies—maintained in local family foodways and prized throughout the region. Families flock to apple and cherry orchards in summer and fall to stock up. Fruit pies are stereotypically associated with the Midwest for the very reason that they are one of the most popular foods, not only eaten for dessert and snacks but regarded by many to be best for breakfast. Pie-making, eating, and -throwing contests are popular components of county and state fairs.

Corn farming extends throughout most of the region, its productivity rivaled only in the adjacent Great Plains. As one might expect, a nice ear of boiled or roasted corn, slathered with butter, minutes away from the field where it grew, is one of the great midwestern culinary treats. A roadside truck loaded with ears of corn for sale is a common sight in season. A frequent part of seasonal family meals, corn is also the centerpiece of community events—corn roasts and boils—held by churches, service organizations, and fraternal orders. And it's no coincidence that the corn dog (invented as the "cozydog" in Springfield, Illinois, in the 1940s) and cornflakes (invented by the Kellogg company in Kalamazoo, Michigan, in the late 1800s) both originated in the Midwest, and that corncob jelly is a traditional specialty in Indiana.

Because corn is excellent feed for pigs, a good proportion of the nation's hogs are raised and butchered in the region, too. When winter comes and pigs are slaughtered, country ham, bacon, and many kinds of sausage are prepared in kitchens, sheds, and butcher shops across the Midwest. Pork roast is the frequent centerpiece of Sunday dinners, with applesauce its common side dish. Whole pigs are spit-roasted at community and extended-family events. Some chefs split a fuel-oil tank in two, install a spit, and mount it on wheels, making an enclosed roaster that can be towed anywhere. For a fee, professionals will come and cook a pig. Barbecue, too, is plentiful in homes, restaurants, and at community festivals or cook-offs. In northern cities of the Midwest it is often the province of African Americans, who have a long barbecue tradition.

The pork chop—grilled, fried, baked, or smoked—also constitutes a popular home and restaurant meal. A favorite lunch all across Iowa, Illinois, Indiana, and parts of neighboring states is the tenderloin sandwich: a slice of pork tenderloin (conscientious cooks slice their own) pounded very thin (the thinner the better) and dipped in flour (some add a bit of cornmeal for crunch) before frying. It is commonly eaten on a hamburger bun with the usual sandwich condiments. At dinner, the same tenderloin becomes an entree with mashed potatoes. Size is important: a tenderloin should extend beyond—even far beyond—the bun. In eastern Wisconsin, a traditional specialty is the Butterfly Pork Chop: a similar boneless slice of pork pounded flat, grilled, and served in a sandwich. In Indiana there's even pork cake, traditionally made at Christmas, a moist spice cake with ground pork or finely chopped salt pork in the batter.

In the northern half of this region, the site not only of the five Great Lakes but of countless smaller lakes, rivers, and streams, fish takes center stage. Fish was a crucial resource for both the Native American population and the people of the frontier who intruded on them. Commercial fishing is important to the regional and local economies of Michigan, Wisconsin, Minnesota, and Ohio, and sport fishing continues to be one of the most popular pastimes. Ice fishing and smelting are major seasonal activities. Fish is an important part of the daily diet as well as the centerpiece of special events including Lenten fish fries; Christmastime lutefisk dinners held as fund-raisers; and festivals celebrating fish sandwiches, catfish, trout, smelt, and even generally disdained species such as carp and eelpout.

Midwesterners use a wide variety—whitefish (the main commercial catch); lake, brook, and rainbow trout; perch; pike; pickerel; mullet; catfish; muskellunge; sturgeon; chubs; suckers; and smelt and salmon (both introduced from salt water)—prepared in an even wider variety of ways: fried, baked, pickled, boiled, steamed, grilled, and planked. Fish that aren't eaten immediately are preserved. Drying is less common today than it was historically, but individuals still can and pickle fish. Most important of all is smoking, both a commercial and a private enterprise. Smoked lake trout, chubs, and whitefish are popular but even suckers, little used otherwise, are good. Private smokehouses range from elaborate, custom-built structures to the more common gutted refrigerators. Individual taste and creativity govern the selection of fish and the source of smoke, the length of time allowed for curing and the strength of the salt solution, the heat and duration of the smoking process.

Fish boils are important group activities around the Great Lakes, much like the pig roasts farther south. An organization or extended family will set a huge pot atop a campfire (or, more common these days, a propane burner) and fill it with water for boiling large chunks of fish, potatoes, and onions. Some cooks add tomato juice. A combination of local fish varieties is thought best. Fish boils are the most institutionalized in Door County, a peninsula in northeastern Wisconsin. Anglers host smaller events, often cooking the day's catch in camp. At home, a fish boil is usually women's work. But at larger communal events—fish for over a hundred is not uncommon—men usually take over.

The region's significant Catholic population, especially in the larger cities, has enhanced the emphasis on fish. The Friday fish fry is an important institution throughout much of the area. Restaurants and a wide variety of organizations offer a Friday-night special, often all-you-can-eat. The battered, deep-fried fish (cod, whitefish, and, best of all, lake perch) is most often served with french fries, coleslaw, tartar sauce, and a roll, though side dishes can vary considerably. With relaxed church strictures on Friday, meat eating had little, if any, effect on the popularity of Friday fish fries; besides, there is no clear correlation today between attendees and religious affiliation.

Hunting is a way of life in the Midwest. Game is most plentiful in the region's northern reaches, and hunters from Indiana, Ohio, and Illinois make pilgrimages in droves, especially during deer season. Deer is incorporated into many regional dishes: pasty, Swedish potato sausage, jerky, Italian *cudighi*, Italian pork sausage, Christmas mincemeat, German sauerbraten, stew, steaks, roasts, barbecue, and burgers. Waterfowl hunters also flock to the region's wetlands and flyways in season, hoping to bag their limit. Roast stuffed goose and duck, sometimes smoked, enjoyed at any time, are a special treat at Christmas. Other coveted game is associated with specific locales. Muskrat in season is the center of many family, restaurant, and club dinners in Monroe, Michigan, where it has been the town's symbol since the early twentieth century.

How midwesterners use the abundance from lake and woods, field and pasture, depends greatly on the culture they and their forebears brought to the area. It is from this interaction that current foodways developed. Midwesterners owe thanks to the original Native American inhabitants for having first cultivated corn, among other crops. Perhaps the best examples of Native American influence on midwestern foodways are maple syrup and wild rice. A large number of small-scale maple-syrup producers exist in Michigan, Wisconsin, and Minnesota, working with better tools, perhaps, but otherwise harvesting sugar much as Native Americans did before Europeans arrived. Wild rice, growing in northern lakes in Minnesota and Wisconsin (as well as Ontario) and hand harvested, is now a favored ingredient in gourmet and homey dishes. Its popularity has spawned commercial growers, mostly outside of the region, who farm and mechanically harvest "paddy rice." Morels, large wild mushrooms, are another seasonal favorite that Native Americans showed to settlers.

Many of the people who originally settled this area came from, or at least paused long enough in, New York, New Jersey, and Pennsylvania to absorb the cooking and eating patterns of the British, German, and Dutch colonists. Immigrants coming directly from northern Europe, especially Germans, Scandinavians, and Irish, soon followed. Many of the features that define the Midwest's traditional foodways are due to this early northern European–especially German— influence. Some of this influence is general, affecting food preferences, cooking styles, and taste combinations. For example, the emphasis on pork probably relates to the heavy settlement of Germans during the formative period; the traditions of later arrivals bolstered this pattern. Similarly, the influx of Scandinavians, with a high per-capita milk consumption, probably shaped the Midwest's love of dairy products.

In another process, ethnic foods transformed into regional specialties. Pasty, the dough-encrusted meat-and-root-vegetable dish of the Cornish, has become a hallmark of Michigan's Upper Peninsula where it is known as U.P. pasty. By the late nineteenth century, new waves of immigrants were enriching the cuisine with their diverse styles. Macedonian immigrants, for example, lent their traditional cooking know-how to create the famous Cincinnati chili and Michigan's coney, both of which are today considered midwestern, not ethnic. This process continues to the present day as immigrants from all continents settle in the region.

Culture is always changing, evolving; so, too, are food and foodways. The Midwest continues to beckon settlers who bring with them new resources, ingredients, and cuisines. Sometimes a process of adoption, adaptation, or amalgamation occurs; new foods, such as U.P. pasty and Cincinnati chili, may be integrated into family, community, and, finally, regional foodways. But while food traditions are quick to adapt and change, they can also resist change and be tenaciously maintained. Thus, newer traditions coexist with those from earlier times. No matter how we describe midwestern food traditions today, one thing is certain: The picture will look somewhat different in the future.

Sources and Further Reading: John Bennett, "Food and Culture in Southern Illinois," *American Sociological Review* 7 (Oct. 1942); Linda Keller Brown and Linda Mussel, eds., *Ethnic and Regional Foodways in the United States* (1984); Janet Gilmore, " 'Pretty Hungry for Fish': Fish Foodways among Commercial Fishing People of the Western Shore of Lake Michigan's Green Bay," *Midwestern Folklore* 29 (Spring 2003); Harva Hachten, *The Flavor of Wisconsin* (1981); Anne R. Kaplan, " 'It's All from One Big Pot': Booya as an Expression of Community," in Theodore C. Humphrey and Lin T. Humphrey, eds., *"We Gather Together": Food and Festival in American Life* (1988); Anne R. Kaplan, Marjorie A. Hoover, and Willard B. Moore, *The Minnesota Ethnic Food Book* (1986); Katherine S. Kirlin and Thomas M. Kirlin, eds., *Smithsonian Folklife Cookbook* (1991); Timothy Lloyd, "The Cincinnati Chili Culinary Complex," *Western Folklore* 40 (Jan. 1981); Yvonne R. Lockwood and William G. Lockwood, "Pasties in Michigan," in Stephen Stern and John

Allan Cicala, eds., *Creative Ethnicity* (1991); Raymond Sokolov, *Fading Feast* (1981); Thomas Vennum, Jr., *Wild Rice and the Ojibway People* (1988).

Yvonne R. Lockwood
Michigan State University

Anne Kaplan
Minnesota Historical Society,
St. Paul, Minnesota

Catfish

Six of the eight North American edible catfish species (*Ictaluridae*) are common in the Midwest. There is little evidence, historical, archaeological, or ethnographic, that catfish were an important traditional food among midwestern Native American people, with the exception of the Arikara, the Hidatsa, and the Mandan of the northern plains, and also the Cherokee of the southeast.

Fishing for catfish is associated with the stereotype of a lazy fellow relaxing by a riverbank or pond with a homemade pole. Popularly believed to be scavengers, catfish are not considered fit food by many people, especially farm families. In an early description of the Mississippi River, explorer Captain Frederick Marryat proclaimed that "it contains the coarsest and most uneatable of fish, such as the cat-fish." Mark Twain wrote "the catfish is a plenty good enough fish for anybody."

The enormous size that some catfish species achieve has inspired monster and horror legends about extremely large catfish, some of which involve the fish swallowing tackle, livestock, or even boats and humans. Legendary monster "cats," often bearing names, such as Cutoff John, live in cutoffs and oxbows and tempt local fishermen for generations. Humorous midwestern tall tales feature catfish appearing at a farmer's pump looking for water during a drought or a large catfish so weighed down with tackle from previous encounters that it was sold as scrap metal.

Catfish fries and festivals are public events in some midwestern communities, such as Petersburg, Indiana, and Potosi, Wisconsin. Potosi's annual Firemen's Catfish Festival cooks 2,400 pounds of catfish and includes a parade and the crowning of Little Miss Catfish.

Sources and Further Reading: Linda Crawford, *The Catfish Book* (1991); Dick Kaukas, "What Really Lives in the Ohio? 'Sure We Have Monsters Down There,' " *Louisville [Ky.] Times* (Sept. 6, 1980); Jens Lund, *Flatheads and Spooneys: Fishing for a Living in the Ohio River Valley* (1995).

Jens Lund
Washington State Parks and
Recreation Commission

Church Dinners

The Midwest calendar is filled with Lutheran lutefisk dinners, Catholic fish fries, and other church-sponsored meals, events that offer a feast of home-style regional specialties plus a large helping of camaraderie. Popular throughout the region, church dinners serve as fund-raisers and as carriers of community identity and tradition. These repasts—not all of them technically dinners—are low-key, low-priced local affairs fueled by word of mouth and by repeat business.

Church picnics and socials date to pioneer days, when group functions centered around parishes and schools. They are not unique to the Midwest, but nowhere do they better mirror a region's ethnic and agricultural diversity. Descendants of European settlers serve hearty foods like German pork hocks, Cornish pasties, and Norwegian meatballs. African American parishioners prepare fried chicken and collard greens for homecoming dinners, and Mexican Americans share tamales and tortillas at monthly potlucks. Regional dishes are the highlight at Missouri ham suppers, Iowa corn boils, and church functions in Minnesota, where hot dishes (the local name for casseroles) feature wild rice. From an annual turkey-and-dressing dinner at St. John the Baptist in Payne, Ohio, to St. Hagop's Armenian lamb-stew picnic in Racine, Wisconsin, church dinners express the region's meat-and-potatoes image and its varied cultural heritage.

Ethnic food at church dinners can also be a symbol. At St. Hagop's, "madagh" is the main course and the name of the event, observed in memory of Armenians massacred in 1915 by the Turkish government. The heirs, survivors who came to Wisconsin, gather to bless the stew and to honor their heritage. Traditionally containing lamb—a symbol of sacrifice—madagh is now made with more easily procured beef (an example of how church suppers, as living tradition, adapt to their environment while retaining essential meaning). Open to the public, the picnic supports parish programs and encourages outsiders to participate in its celebration of community. Like the food at many church fund-raisers, madagh is served family style and delivered to shut-ins, highlighting such midwestern values as community cohesiveness and Christian charity.

Church dinners can be small, private, and casually organized, or they can be gigantic public affairs managed by committees. Menus, exotic to those who have had little contact with ethnic fare, are frequently supplemented with more familiar dishes. At one congregation's annual German dinner, for example, organizers offer a choice of pork hocks, wieners, or smoked sausages.

Meal preparation is volunteer, communal, and labor-intensive. Job assignments often parallel gender roles and/or life stages. One Ohio native says, "When I was serving at these meals, the younger women poured coffee and offered warm-ups. Men set up chairs and washed dishes. Wrapping silverware was a task for the very young or very old. Some people go from that task through all the others and back to it again. My Mom says when they ask her to wrap silverware instead of make dressing, she's going to quit!"

By offering from-scratch, affordable fare in a sociable setting, church dinners reflect such Heartland traits as honesty, frugality, stamina, and friendliness. In an age when fewer families cook ethnic or regional dishes at home, and local culinary customs are dying out nationwide, church dinners play a key role in the survival and cultivation of treasured midwestern food traditions.

Sources and Further Reading: Terese Allen, *Wisconsin Food Festivals* (1995); Eleanor Arnold, ed., *Feeding Our Families* (1983); Theodore C. Humphrey and Lin T. Humphrey, eds., *"We Gather Together": Food and Festival in American Life* (1991); Anne R. Kaplan, Marjorie A. Hoover, and Willard B. Moore, *The Minnesota Ethnic Food Book* (1986).

Terese Allen
Madison, Wisconsin

Lutefisk

Lutefisk is a cod or ling that has been either air- or kiln-dried until it becomes stockfish, a sort of hardened fish jerky that can be kept for years in a cool, dry place. Prior to being served, the stockfish is soaked first in fresh water for eight to ten days, and then in a freshwater and hydrogen-peroxide solution for five days before being boiled or baked. Properly prepared, lutefisk should be translucent but still firm. Lutefisk may be served with bacon or pork drippings, white sauce, mustard sauce, melted butter, or even melted goat cheese. Traditional side dishes accompanying lutefisk include boiled potatoes, rutabagas, corn, green peas, coleslaw, and lefse and other flatbread. Lutefisk is also available in microwaveable frozen dinners for those who relish the dish's taste but not the work involved in its preparation.

Lutefisk suppers abound in the upper Midwest from October through December, often hosted by Lutheran churches or by chapters of the Sons of Norway. Lutefisk-related humor is also extremely popular and plentiful, including lutefisk jokes, bumper stickers, cheers, and songs. In October 2000 an anonymous petition suggesting that Ole the Viking, the traditional mascot of Augustana College in Sioux Falls, South

Ojibwa wild rice gathering in Minnesota. Courtesy Minnesota Office of Tourism.

Dakota, be replaced by a lutefisk appeared on campus bulletin boards just in time for homecoming. Later that fall, northland Ford dealers ran a television ad throughout the upper Midwest declaring that it was hard to tell what was better: a monthly payment of $185 on a Ford Ranger XLT or "not having to eat lutefisk for supper." The commercial's tagline—"If you don't live around here, you just don't get it"—neatly encapsulates that area's complex love/hate relationship with this Scandinavian specialty.

Sources and Further Reading: Anne R. Kaplan, Marjorie A. Hoover, and Willard B. Moore, *The Minnesota Ethnic Food Book* (1986); Gary Legwold, *The Last Word on Lutefisk* (1996); Astri Riddervold, *Lutefisk, Rakefisk and Herring in Norwegian Tradition* (1990).

Debbie A. Hanson
Augustana College, Illinois

Wild Rice

Wild rice (*Zizania aquatica* or *palustris*), actually not a rice but an aquatic grass seed, has grown naturally for millennia in shallow lakes and rivers of the so-called rice district of northwestern Ontario and northern Minnesota and Wisconsin. Rich in protein-producing carbohydrates and minerals, wild rice has been known for its food value for centuries, and American Indians, especially the Ojibwe, have been its principal harvesters since before contact with Europeans. Traditionally as well as currently, Indians set up family rice camps next to the ripening beds in late summer. To collect the grains, canoes—formerly of birch bark, today of aluminum—are poled through the fields and stalks are bent over gunwales and beaten with sticks into the boat. Brought back to shore, the rice is sun

dried, parched in kettles, "danced" in a pit to break the chaff (husks) from the kernels, and winnowed (by tossing in the air so that the wind blows away the chaff). It is then ready to be stored for food.

Wild rice played a key role in the fur trade, often sustaining Indians and traders alike through brutal winters. Today, Ojibwe people serve it as a complement to venison or walleye. A cultural identifier, it is found at feasts, wakes, and powwows, where it is sold at concession stands.

Since the 1960s wild rice has been cultivated commercially, but connoisseurs insist that cultivated rice lacks the flavor of natural lake rice, and Indian people view such "paddy rice" as culturally inappropriate.

Sources and Further Reading: Alfred E. Jenks, "The Wild Rice Gatherers of the Upper Great Lakes: A Study in American Primitive Economics," *Nineteenth Annual Report of the Bureau of American Ethnology, 1897–98* (1899; reprint, 1977); Thomas Vennum, Jr., *Wild Rice and the Ojibway People* (1988).

Thomas Vennum, Jr.
Smithsonian Institution, Washington, D.C.

Folk Festivals and Celebrations

For midwesterners, the traditional folk festival may be defined as an occasional event that celebrates special aspects of life within the community. It may include food and drink, music and dance, costumes and other material culture, that are traditionally known to the participants and serve to mark the event. Taken as a whole, the performance of the folk festival may be considered a social performing folk art.

The Midwest is literally rife with festivals that celebrate all manner of life and work. Harvest festivals, for example, mark the end of the growing season in traditional farming communities. After the onset of the period of modernization in the Midwest, the traditional harvest festival evolved into local and state-sponsored fairs, such as the one depicted in *State Fair* (1932), Phil Stong's famous novel set in Iowa. Farmers exhibit their best produce, finest animals, exemplary sewing, and contest-worthy desserts. Farming families return home bearing ribbons to hang on kitchen walls–reminders through the winter of a successful harvest season. The Cory (Indiana) Apple Festival, the Circleville Pumpkin Show in Ohio, and the Old Tyme Corn Boil in Lewis, Iowa, are examples of typical harvest-celebration festivals.

Festivals, celebrations, and festival behavior are human efforts to connect people and cultures while creating trust. Festivals may range in scale and complexity from a single focused event to a comprehensive carnival. The traditional quilting bee, threshing bee, or bluegrass festival connects people and creates trust by working to reach common understanding. Just as traditional folk festivals such as dance parties, picnics, and barn raisings rely upon enduring relationships within small communities, the contemporary "folk" festival brings people together within the context of a complex heterogeneous society. In the transition from a rural homogeneous culture to a multicultural urban society, the midwestern folk festival continues to celebrate the breadth of community-based knowledge and skill while presenting the diverse heritage of the community to a public audience.

Ethnic communities and neighborhoods come together similarly in a festival fashion to celebrate, marking their common interests—whether at the Bill Monroe Bluegrass Festival in Bean Blossom, Indiana, or the Bucyrus (Ohio) Bratwurst Festival—through community food, music, and dance. While European, Asian, and African American communities have a relatively short history in America from the time of settlement to the beginning of the twenty-first century, American Indian communities have a long history in the region, marked by significant movement and interaction among different national or tribal groups. Each individual ethnic and community group focuses on its own special qualities through the festival event and behaviors.

Throughout their settlement history, the region's diverse peoples have tried to establish their American identity while simultaneously affirming their ties to their home cultures. Festivities in the region are typically organized around known behavior, such as ethnic foodways and European national holidays. Midwestern kitchens are known for delights that hail from Ireland, Italy, Germany, France, Poland, Scandinavia, and the Baltics. Norwegian Independence Day (May 17), Finnish Independence Day (December 6), and Estonian Independence Day (February 24) are celebrated in upper Midwest communities in recognition of national independence and the local emigrants' connection to the old country. A visit to Cedar Rapids, Iowa, reveals the strong, and recent, Czech traditions that are celebrated there. Travelers to the Upper Peninsula of Michigan will often hear the Finnish language spoken by older residents who emigrated from Finland during the last generation. The Swedish-Finnish residents of Brevort, Michigan, celebrate "the Mid-Sommar Festival" with bonfires and a "mid-sommar pole" much as people do in Sweden, Finland, and Norway.

Folklorists have long debated the essential nature and definition of the folk festival. The whole festival is composed of many folklore genres including rituals and traditional games, and the material folk-culture genres such as crafts, costume, and cookery. For Richard M. Dorson, one of the founders of folklore studies in the United States, the overall complexity of the traditional folk festival defines it as "a social folk custom." Folklorist Robert J. Smith reaffirms that the festival provides "a unified context . . . [for] the genres that occur within it." Folkorist Beverly J. Stoeltje notes that the "discipline of folklore has seen a resurgence of interest [in the festival] with a strong emphasis on the current social significance of traditional celebrations." Stoeltje points out contemporary community festivals "reflect the diversity of American traditions" and that ethnic celebrations, religious fiestas, and festivals connected with region or occupation "encapsulate elements of relevant shared experience in public presentation." For both indigenous peoples and those who immigrated to the Midwest, the element of sharing vital experience in a public festival presentation continues to be an important ingredient in regional life. One is reminded of such sharing in Willa Cather's writing about the Nebraska frontier and the Russian and Czech pioneers in *My Ántonia* (1918).

The traditional folk festival underwent significant change and alteration during the latter half of the twentieth century. Folklorists and anthropologists observe that with the growth of mass culture, people have found it more difficult to understand themselves and their society in fundamental terms as they did in traditional communities. The traditional folk festival of a homogeneous society has largely given way to a fabricated "folk" festival of mass-culture society. With the growing tide of mass culture during the past fifty years, there has been tremendous growth in created or fabricated festivals. Whether for commercial or nostalgic reasons or both, the emergence of these synthetic festivals has blurred the distinctions between traditional authentic folk festivals and popular festivals conceived as folk. The blurring of this distinction has led to confusion on both the folk and the popular levels of understanding. Stoeltje has suggested that "Scholars as well as the general public and public institutions have rediscovered festivity, and the term *festival* has been adopted by many of the burgeoning popular events that share few generic features." She concludes, "Events which *do* share such features, however, rarely use the term to name the event."

While these distinctions are important to scholars who attempt to study and analyze our contemporary society, the distinctions are probably less relevant to the people of the Midwest who employ festivals and festive behavior to celebrate their collective lives. Midwesterners continue to invent new ways to celebrate their lives and the culture of their communities. The fact that neighborhoods, cities, regions, and interest groups have created festivals means that while people will have less intimate intuitive knowledge about the specific event, they will persist in finding ways to celebrate through festive behavior. The Reynoldsburg (Ohio) Tomato Festival and the Covered Bridge Festival in Parke County, Indiana, are largely created festivals that a contemporary population encounters and celebrates in ways that they intuitively bring to them.

Examples of the transition between authentic folk festivals and invented or created folk festivals can be found everywhere on the landscape. For approximately seventy years, a portion of the African American population in Columbus, Ohio, gathered at Franklin Park, a large urban park on the east side of the city, on Sundays and holidays for day-long get-togethers when people could cook, picnic, meet other people, and share. When this traditional venue was appropriated for a 1992 international floral exhibition, the black community invented a new street festival for its people to attend. Called Coming Home, the festival was intended to supplant the preexisting use of the urban park as a place for people to picnic and gather. The new festival was created, or contrived, and yet it embodied some of the rich traditional elements of African American life within the framework of the festival: music and dance, food and eating, making crafts, and wearing costumes. The black community made the new festival function with respect to the traditional folk interests of the community. The name *Coming Home* in some ways suggested to the community that the act of the folk festival was an effort to combine the old with the new. This act of synthesis, combining the old with the new, melds the folk festival in its traditional form with the mass-culture folk festival.

Federal sponsorship has encouraged statewide folk festivals in the Midwest. Each summer on the Mall in Washington, D.C., the Smithsonian Institution presents the Annual Smithsonian Folklife Festival. Initiated in 1967, the event is a national festival that asserts the ability of people to engage one another and appreciate one another's abilities and tasks. Midwestern states have often been the highlighted focus of the Smithsonian Festival, and Michigan, Ohio, Iowa, and Wisconsin used the national festival as an impetus to bring the festival event back to the home state. Since the mid-1980s, the Museum at Michigan State University has presented an annual folklife festival that grew out of Michigan's experience as part of the Smithsonian's national event.

As the distinction between traditional folk festivals and created folk festivals blurs in the tide of contemporary mass culture, ordinary citizens remain committed to the harmony of the festival amid a larger and complicated world. The Midwest has historically witnessed significant immigration from regions both inside and outside the nation. At the beginning of the twenty-first century, as at the end of the nineteenth, the population of the region is made up of people who still identify strongly with their roots—where they came from or where their immediate family originated. Some people came from other regions of the United States and some came from another country; together they share a common goal of making a life in the Midwest. They celebrate not only their historical roots and heritage, but also their contemporary goals and identities through festivals. People's use of the festival to celebrate their culture attests to the strength of the traditional folk-festival form within midwestern society. From the region's many indigenous peoples to the Danes who settled Danetown in western Iowa at the end of the nineteenth century, to the Somalians who settled in central Ohio at the end of the twentieth century, and to the Hmong who settled in Minnesota, people brought their community traditions to the Midwest, continued them, and, ultimately, shared them with neighbors. The many folk festivals and celebrations in the Midwest are a fundamental means through which the region's heterogeneous peoples persist in showing one another where they come from and who they are.

Sources and Further Reading: Jan Harold Brunvand, "Customs and Festivals" in Jan Brunvand, ed., *The Study of American Folklore: An Introduction*, 2nd ed. (1978); Richard M. Dorson, "Introduction: Concepts of Folklore and Folklife Studies," in Richard M. Dorson, ed., *Folklore and Folklife: An Introduction* (1972); Richard Kurin, *Smithsonian Folklife Festival* (1998); John F. Moe, "The 'American Surprise': Reflections on the Meaning of Encounter, Discovery, and the Columbiad Quincentenary," in Ruth D. Fitzgerald and

Yvonne R. Lockwood, eds., *1992 Festival of Michigan Folklife* (1992); John F. Moe, "Folk Festivals and Community Consciousness: Categories of the Festival Genre," *Folklore Forum* 10 (Spring 1977); John F. Moe, "Meaning in Community Events: An Ice Cutting Festival in Michigan," in Kurt Dewhurst and Yvonne R. Lockwood, eds., *Michigan Folklife Reader* (1987); Leslie Prosterman, *Ordinary Life, Festival Days* (1995); Robert J. Smith, *The Art of the Festival* (1975); Robert J. Smith, "Festivals and Celebrations," in Richard M. Dorson, ed., *Folklore and Folklife: An Introduction* (1972); Beverly J. Stoeltje, "Festival in America," in Richard M. Dorson, ed., *Handbook of American Folklore* (1983).

John F. Moe
The Ohio State University–Columbus

Julebukk (Christmas Masquerade)

Imported to the upper Midwest by nineteenth-century Norwegian immigrants and spelled in a variety of ways (*yulebuck, julbok, julebakk*) after most Norwegian Americans had forgotten its literal meaning, *julebukk* (Christmas goat; pronounced *yul-uh-book*), with pre-Christian origins, refers to Halloween-like masquerading during *romjul* (December 26–31). The name derives from the goat's head, which is usually made of wood; complete with horns, beard, and a string to open its jaw; and mounted on a pole; an example is on display at the Vesterheim Museum, in Decorah, Iowa. The object was traditionally carried by the leader of the heavily disguised, often raucous, group that used to go from house to house expecting inhabitants to guess their identities and serve them refreshments. Once identified, the masqueraders removed their disguises, usually characterized by cross-dressing and reversals such as shoes worn on the wrong feet, clothing worn inside-out or backward, or nightgowns and underwear worn in public.

Also attested in England, Scotland, Ireland, Sweden, Germany, and Austria (and among North American immigrants from these countries), Christmas masquerading may have first functioned to ward off evil spirits. In preindustrial Norway the custom's sampling of yuletide fare served to enforce the critical norm of timely and correct year-end food preparation. Among the midwestern Norse immigrants, julebukking remained functional, permitting a necessary emotional release from the sharply defined social expectations of isolated, homogeneous communities while simultaneously revitalizing these essential social and work networks. The once widespread practice of "going julebukk" declined during the 1930s and 1940s, giving way to the increasing mobility and standardization of the American lifestyle, but a limited version of the practice has since the 1970s experienced a revival among some of the region's Norwegian Americans.

Sources and Further Reading: Henry Glassie, *All Silver and No Brass: An Irish Christmas Mumming* (1975); Kathleen Stokker, *Keeping Christmas: Yuletide Traditions in Norway and the New Land* (2000).

Kathleen Stokker
Luther College, Iowa

National Folk Festival

The National Folk Festival, founded by Sarah Gertrude Knott in St. Louis in 1934, was America's first multicultural folk festival. Knott, a recreation leader from western Kentucky trained in community dramatics, was influenced by existing southern Appalachian folk festivals and exhibitions of ethnic culture and arts in eastern and midwestern cities, as well as by antimodern reform movements of the time, which used folklore activities as remedies for the lack of "wholeness" and "authenticity" they saw in modern American life.

In its early years, the festival moved annually to a new city and presented a series of stage performances of folk music and dance, along with subsidiary exhibitions or demonstrations of folk arts-and-crafts traditions. After World War II, the festival featured presentations of recreation-center folk-dance ensembles, which Knott had encouraged as a way of bringing "wholesome" recreation activities based on folk traditions into modern people's lives. In 1970 Knott left the festival organization, which after several years named Joseph Wilson of Tennessee as its new director in 1976, and renamed itself the National Council for the Traditional Arts (NCTA) to indicate its new and broader sense of responsibility.

From 1971 to 1982 the festival was held in suburban Washington, D.C., but in 1983 it began moving to a new site every three years. The NCTA also began partnering with local organizations to produce the festival and to build support for permanent, locally produced festivals on the National Folk Festival model. Local coproducers have taken an active role in shaping festival programs during its three-year residency in their community, and the festival has left behind strong presentations in most of its recent host cities.

Three of those sites—Bath, Ohio (1983–1985), Dayton, Ohio (1996–1998), and East Lansing, Michigan (1999–2001)—were midwestern, as were several sites for earlier National Folk Festivals: St. Louis (1934, 1947–1955), Chicago (1937), Cleveland (1946), and Milwaukee (1968). Thus twenty-two of those sixty-three presentations took place in the Midwest, and the festival has presented a significant number of midwestern folk performers and craftspeople.

Sources and Further Reading: T.J. Jackson Lears, *No Place of Grace* (1981); Timothy Lloyd, "Whole Work, Whole Play, Whole People: Folklore and Social Therapeutics in 1920s and 1930s America," *Journal of American Folklore* 110 (Summer 1997); David E. Whisnant, *All That Is Native and Fine* (1983); Joe Wilson, *The National Folk Festival: 1934–1936* (1988).

Timothy Lloyd
American Folklore Society, Columbus, Ohio

Powwows

Powwows are found in American Indian communities across the United States and Canada, but in the Midwest they provide an especially important link to Native American traditions. Many of the essential aspects of the contemporary powwow come out of earlier rituals and dances found among Indian peoples in the Midwest, creating a foundation for the modern celebration that is rooted in the past.

The word *powwow* comes from the Algonquian Indian language family and originally referred to a healer or a ceremony for healing. Today it refers to an essentially secular celebration held by Indian people, from one tribe or many, involving drumming, singing, dancing, and feasting. Powwows are public events similar to other community and ethnic festivals that provide a public display of culture.

Powwows can best be described as a series of ever-widening circles, with the drum at the center. The drum is the heartbeat of the powwow, the hub around which everything else revolves. The drum is surrounded by a circle of singers, men and boys who both drum and sing. They may also be surrounded by a circle of women singers. Powwow songs are sung in unison, either in an Indian language or in vocables, simple syllables that can be shared by speakers of many different Native American languages. A circle of dancers surrounds the drum and singers. Categories of dancers are distinguished both by their specific attire ("outfits" or "regalia") and by their dance styles, including men's traditional, grass, and fancy and women's traditional, jingle-dress, and fancy. Spectators encircle the dancers, and the final outer circle is the traders or vendors, selling foods and crafts.

The powwow may be either contest, in which drums and dancers compete for cash prizes, or traditional, in which there is no competition. On reservations powwows are held on powwow grounds or in community centers; in urban areas they are held in Indian centers, rented halls, parks, campgrounds, fairgrounds, college arenas, and churches. The Midwest is home to many well-known powwows, including the Mesquakie Indian Powwow, held in Tama, Iowa, each year since 1915, and Indian Summer, a large, urban contest powwow held in Milwaukee, Wisconsin. The powwow season in the Midwest begins in late winter

Native American dancers at the Grand Portage Powwow, Minnesota. Courtesy Minnesota Office of Tourism.

and early spring with celebrations sponsored by college and university Indian-student organizations, continues through summer with tribal powwows held on home reservations, and extends into early fall with powwows sponsored again by colleges and by urban Indian organizations. Particularly in the summer, many Native American families follow the "powwow circuit" as singers, dancers, and traders.

Native American traditions in the Midwest have been particularly influential in the development of the contemporary powwow. The drum dance originated among the Sioux and spread to the upper Great Lakes tribes, providing the large dance drum now common to powwows. The war dance and the grass dance of the eastern plains tribes form the basis for men's dance styles seen today. The jingle-dress dance came through the vision of a Chippewa man and spread to all Native peoples. These contributions have shaped and defined the American Indian powwow.

Sources and Further Reading: Tara Browner, *Heartbeat of the People: Music and Dance of the Northern Powwow* (2002); Luke Eric Lassiter, ed., *Powwow: Native American Performance, Identity, and Meaning* (2003); Thomas Vennum, Jr., *The Ojibwa Dance Drum: Its History and Construction* (1982).

Susan Applegate Krouse
Michigan State University

Queen Contests

Many communities throughout the Midwest sponsor a contest to choose a "queen," a young woman to represent the community. Such contests became particularly popular beginning in the 1930s. Often the queen competition is part of a community festival emphasizing such midwestern specialties as cheese, corn, chips, ice, and walleyes. Organizers and participants insist that the contest is not a "beauty pageant" but, rather, is designed to choose a young woman who exemplifies what the community believes is best about itself: talent, friendliness, commitment to the community and its values, upward mobility. Candidates are often immediate high school graduates and the prizes awarded usually consist of scholarship money for postsecondary education.

Candidates are ordinarily sponsored by local businesses. Once selected, they spend time together preparing for the pageant and are then presented to the community as a group in the local newspaper and at the pageant. In this way, a queen contest shares some elements with a debutante presentation. A few queen contests are connected with national programs (Miss America or Miss USA), and in these cases, judging is by professionals associated with those programs. Otherwise, pageant judges are almost always people from outside the community—often friends or business associates of the organizers—who base their selection on locally established criteria that frequently emphasize a private interview as well as a public talent presentation, evening-gown competition, and onstage question session.

The winners—a queen and one or more princesses—travel to festivals in other communities to ride in their parades and attend their queen pageants. In some cases the queen attends other noteworthy events in her own town. She is expected to be able to talk intelligently and pleasantly about her town, and to project an image of wholesomeness that will reflect positively on her community.

Sources and Further Reading: Colleen Ballerino Cohen, Richard Wilk, and Beverly Stoeltje, eds., *Beauty Queens on the Global Stage* (1996); Robert H. Lavenda, *Corn Fests and Water Carnivals* (1997).

Robert H. Lavenda
St. Cloud State University, Minnesota

Mennonite Relief Sales

Since the mid-1950s, Mennonites, Mennonite Brethren, Amish, and others from the Anabaptist tradition from around North America have raised money for overseas projects through what have become known as relief sales. Fifteen of the thirty-two sales in the United States are held in Mennonite communities in all but perhaps one of the states of the Midwest.

The two-day events include an auction and food sales generating more than four million dollars every year for Mennonite overseas missions such as those sponsored by the Mennonite Central Committee. They are also a rich and festive display of Mennonite aesthetics, bringing together diverse congregations and providing family and old friends a time and place to socialize.

In a manner similar to the barn raisings and threshing dinners held when Mennonites were primarily agrarian, volunteers contribute thousands of hours in preparation. Church sewing circles quilt year-round, woodworkers craft furniture in their workshops, and weeks before the sale, churches prepare food. The sale is a way for Mennonites to serve locally in a worldwide ministry.

While each relief sale is unique, influenced by region and ethnicity, traditional arts such as music, food, and quilts are central to all. Traditional Mennonite a cappella four-part-harmony hymn-singing opens many of the sales, and in the middle of some auctions, the audience is led in a brief hymn-sing.

Indiana Mennonite quilt relief auction. Photo by Erin Roth.

Food varies with immigration settlement patterns. Mennonites and Mennonite Brethren in North and South Dakota, Minnesota, Nebraska, and Kansas adopted many Russian foodways during their several-generation stay in Russia. Borscht (cabbage-beet soup), *zweibach* (salty dinner-roll), and *verenika* (a cottage cheese–filled dumpling) are some of the foods available at the Kansas Relief Sale. Mennonite foodways in Midwest states farther east are influenced by their Swiss and German heritage, better known for shoofly pie, apple butter, and pork tenderloin.

Some of the larger sales—in Indiana and Kansas—auction nearly three hundred quilts every year—some selling for as much as ten thousand dollars. Beautifully made quilts draw buyers from all over the country, many who are not Mennonites. Quilters typically occupy front-row seats at the auctions to record each sale, noting which colors and patterns bring the highest price, gathering information for their next quilt. Most quilts indicate the maker, donor, or church group, but Amish quilters at the Daviess County Relief Auction in southern Indiana donate theirs anonymously, a practice reflecting the value of humility. As more women work outside the home, the sale's quilts have begun to change. Today there are more wall hangings, which are much smaller than full-sized quilts, and some machine-printed quilts. Traditionalists like the Michiana (Goshen, Indiana) Relief Sale quilt committee will not accept machine-quilted products for auction.

The auction includes playful exchanges between auctioneer and bidders, many of whom the auctioneer knows personally. Many sales begin by auctioning a loaf of bread after an opening prayer. In Kansas, each year the same man buys the first loaf for approximately a thousand dollars, demonstrating the importance of the donation made, not the item sold.

The relief sales beautifully demonstrate the cultural and religious values of the Mennonite communities of the Midwest, evidence of their strong sense of community and commitment to service.

Sources and Further Reading: Robert S. Kreider and Rachel Waltner Goosen, *Hungry, Thirsty, a Stranger: The MCC Experience* (1988); Harry Lowen and Steven Nolt with Carol Duerksen and Elwood Yoder, *Through Fire and Water: An Overview of Mennonite History* (1996); Judy Schroeder Tomlonson, *Mennonite Quilts and Pieces* (1985); Norma Jost Voth, *Mennonite Foods and Folkways from South Russia* (1990).

Erin Roth
University of Maryland
Baltimore County

Seasonal Displays

During occasions of festivity, religious observation, or commemoration known as holidays, and at related events such as celebrations of the life cycle, homes and other buildings are customarily adorned with evergreens, flowers, fruits, vegetables, ribbons, drawings, candles, signs, and many other items. This national and even international phenomenon is very much a part of midwestern culture.

Perhaps because of the region's agrarian heritage, its four distinct seasons, and its citizenry's cultivation of community, more than a few midwesterners decorate their homes and yards throughout the entire year. The display of "harvest" fruits and vegetables is appropriate from September through November. At Halloween, pumpkins are carved into jack-o'-lanterns and images of witches, ghosts, bats, and otherworldly or nocturnal creatures are added, but these are removed shortly after October 31 while the Indian corn, squash, and uncarved or painted pumpkins generally remain through Thanksgiving before giving way to the evergreens and electric lights of Christmas and the menorahs of Hanukkah. Some people display wreaths for all the holidays, or they add and subtract various holiday symbols on a single wreath as appropriate: a red ribbon and a heart in February, a green ribbon and a shamrock in March. After the Easter symbols of rabbits, eggs, and perhaps a specifically Christian item, flowers and flags are most common through May and the summer holidays from Memorial Day through Flag Day, the Fourth of July, and Labor Day.

In addition, people create displays for such important sporting contests as high school basketball's "March Madness" and the fall clashes of traditional college football rivals like the Ohio State University and the University of Michigan. Midwesterners have also fashioned public displays in wartime, encircling trees with yellow ribbons or facsimiles during the Gulf War and, before that, during the period when American citizens were held hostage in Iran.

People decorate homes and yards for births, birthdays, homecomings, and retirements. People in the Midwest largely embrace the idea that they constitute "America's Heartland," and patriotic displays are many. In the wake of the terrorist attacks on the United States on September 11, 2001, for example, American flags were creatively displayed on homes and cars, along with red, white, and blue electric bulbs, and these were joined by displays regarding the United States' actions in Iraq beginning in 2003.

Decorating for holidays, rituals, and other festivals and celebrations, while a very old custom, is enjoying a widespread growth in contemporary American society, in terms of both when decorations are displayed as well as what the decorations are. The contexts they reflect and the range of meanings they express are as varied as the population itself. We can say, however, that holiday decorations have become a year-round phenomenon and a major form of popular culture.

Sources and Further Reading: Jack Santino, *All Around the Year* (1994); Jack Santino, *Halloween and Other Festivals of Death and Life* (1994); Jack Santino, "Yellow Ribbons and Seasonal Flags: The Folk Assemblage of War," *Journal of American Folklore* 105 (Winter 1992).

Jack Santino
Bowling Green State University, Ohio

Folk Music and Dance

Folk music and dance, sometimes accompanied by song, have thrived and intertwined in the Midwest for centuries. Still common amid such local seasonal and life-cycle events as harvest festivals, winter revelries, and weddings, music and dance traditions nowadays also serve as recreational pastimes and public expressions of cultural heritage.

From the late 1600s through the mid-1800s European American chroniclers observed that the Midwest's Algonquian and Siouan peoples relied on voices, rattles, jingles, and hand drums to accompany dances for peace, war, spears, scalps, prisoners, and slaves; for begging, greeting, medicine, courting, marriage, death, and mourning; for green corn, beans, buffalo, bear, deer, and otter; for warriors, women, women warriors, and *berdache*, or men-women. Eventually defeated in battle and confined to reservations, the region's American Indians nonetheless transformed old dances and invented new ones, sustaining significant elements of their culture in the intertribal powwow. Through "traditional dances" men sustain the vigorous movements of hunters and warriors, while women's stately steps perpetuate connections with Mother Earth. Male and female "fancy dances," meanwhile, permit youngsters to leap and spin, shaking shawls, feather bustles, and jingles. Accessible to the general public, yet neither choreographed nor staged, powwows are paralleled by "shows" through which the Midwest's Native American peoples have displayed their culture to outsiders since the late nineteenth century.

Ojibwe and various Siouan peoples from the region participated in "Wild West" troupes organized by Buffalo Bill and others, while Ho-Chunk performed—along with Berbers, Sami, and Michigan lumberjacks—at Chicago's "Columbian Exposition" World's Fair of 1893. During the decades that followed, Indian encampments and regularly scheduled programs proliferated at fairgrounds, reservations, and parks throughout the region. The still-vibrant Stand Rock Indian Ceremonial, for example, commenced in the 1920s at Wisconsin Dells when members of the local

Lion's Club convinced Ho-Chunks to entertain tourists drawn by the area's scenic beauty. Early-twenty-first-century displays of such music and dance are organized mainly by the performers themselves, often adjacent to casinos or, billed as "dance-theater," on stages formerly reserved for ballet.

English, French, Irish, and Scottish immigrants—whether arriving via the Ohio River, the Great Lakes, or from Canada—brought fifes, drums, fiddles, and footwork to fur-trade and military outposts, lumber camps, farms, and burgeoning towns. Brisk marches and "fiddle tunes"—jigs and reels in AABB format—compelled militia, woodsmen, New Year's revelers, and harvest hands to promenade, step-dance individually, or form squares at a caller's behest. Vivid descriptions of rustic dances and noted fiddlers abound in nineteenth-century reminiscences and histories. A. Banning Norton's *History of Knox County, Ohio* (1862), for example, lauds fiddler Seeley Simpkins:

> He was a great favorite with the squaws and papooses, by reason of his uncommon musical talent. He could mimic the sound of varmint or human, surpassed the lute of Orpheus, and outwhistled all creation. He furnished music for early musters, and when it took four counties to make a regiment he gave a challenge to outwhistle any man among them. He frequented race tracks, and drew crowds and supplied hoedowns on demand.

Dan Emmett, born in 1815 and one of Simpkins's youthful neighbors, went on to fame as a military drummer, old-time fiddler, and minstrel show performer credited with such celebrated compositions as "Turkey in the Straw" (1834), "Old Dan Tucker" (1843), and "Dixie" (1860).

An avid tune collector, Emmett included a jig attributed to Simpkins and a "Genuine Negro Jig" as numbers forty-seven and forty-eight in one of his notebooks. Howard Sacks suggests the tune may have come from Thomas Snowden, a neighbor of both Simpkins and Emmett. Born a slave in Maryland, Snowden was freed and settled in central Ohio in 1828. A fiddler and whistler like Simpkins, with a great store of tunes, Snowden founded a family band that entertained black and white dancers on fiddle, guitar, banjo, and bones throughout the nineteenth century.

Long before ragtime, the blues, jazz, and gospel began to flourish in midwestern cities, free blacks and former slaves, influenced by and affecting white repertoires, introduced decidedly African American note bending and hip shaking on riverboats and throughout the region's southern hinterlands. Former slave George Taylor Burns of Evansville, Indiana, interviewed by Works Progress Administration field-

workers in the 1930s, regularly passed by a showboat, *The Banjo*, while working as a deckhand on *The Gray Eagle* in the 1850s: "The captain would keep the calliope playing, and the roustabouts, all of them Negroes, would be out on the deck dancing and shouting." Another former slave, George Morrison, recalled "a square dance that was held near St. Joseph, Indiana, one summer afternoon." During a lull, "the fiddler played a hoedown . . . and George did his best to interpret a dance that the slaves performed on the plantation." Perhaps this was at one of the square dances "in German Catholic settlements around St. Joe" attended by ex-slave George Thomas. Indeed, fiddler Tom Collins, erstwhile a flatboat operator from 1849 to 1873, "noted German fiddlers and African American fiddle and banjo players," including "numerous instances of both African Americans and whites singing, dancing and playing music in and around Ohio River towns and on the boats that plied the river."

Parallel cross-cultural musical interchanges occurred all along the Midwest's northern border where métis and Native American peoples created asymmetrical "Indian tunes" like "Red River Jig" on fiddle to accompany hybrid steps. Mike Page, a Turtle Mountain Ojibwe whose father fiddled and jigged after buffalo hunts, speculated on the process in an interview with Nicholas Vrooman:

> They used to play the Red River Jig. That came from the late 1700s . . . some Frenchman, or Irish or Scottish was playing this violin. And they probably seen . . . some Chippewas from Minnesota over here, or the Cree Indians from Canada . . . do this dance, this Indian dance . . . Yeah, they do mix. There's a lot of Indian in me, I'll say, when I'm playing. It's like I feel some Indian in me and other nationalities.

Known north of the Canadian border from James Bay to Alaska, the "Red River Jig" tradition also extends along Lake Superior's southern shore through northern Minnesota to eastern North Dakota.

Nor were cross-fertilizations fundamentally different across the agrarian Heartland extending from Ohio to eastern Kansas, Nebraska, and the Dakotas. Although Anglo-American square-dance tunes and steps sometimes dominated, they were often combined with the round-dance music of Germanic, Nordic, and Slavic immigrants. In places like Posen, Michigan, along Lake Huron, nineteenth-century settlers of Yankee stock mingled with German and Polish immigrants to form a common repertoire of jigs, reels, polkas, waltzes, and *obereks*. The thirty performers sketched in "Fiddlers We Have Known" (1932), a handwritten manuscript by P. T. Gillett of Antigo,

Wisconsin, included several Irish, a "Scotch Canuck," "a Frenchman," "a real old Yankee," several "Kentucks, a few Czechs or "Bohemians," and numerous Germans "come north to work in the woods." Each had his special repertoire; nonetheless, "the music seemed to be of the same class. Much of Irish and Scotch extraction. The round dances seemed to have come mostly from the German and Bohemian and local ¾ time songs." More recently and farther west, musicians like Dwight Lamb of Onawa, Iowa, near the Missouri border, made a 1999 recording on the Rounder label that mingled his family's accordion-driven Danish couple-dance pieces with Anglo-American fiddle tunes percolating up from Missouri.

Before the early-twentieth-century emergence of the guitar to accompany a lead fiddle, a second fiddle, a banjo, the occasional piano, a hammered dulcimer, or a button accordion were common backup instruments in various communities. Settlers of English extraction brought the trapezoidal hammered dulcimer to the region, Michigan especially, in the mid-nineteenth century, while "Volga Germans" established the related *hackbrett* on the Kansas prairies. The far more ubiquitous accordion, interweaving with fiddles at many a house party, was just as often played solo or was combined with brass and reed instruments in emerging midwestern polka bands.

Prominent in cities extending east to west from Youngstown to Omaha, and north to south from Minneapolis to St. Louis and Cincinnati, polka music likewise thrives in the upper Midwest hinterlands wherever non-Anglo-Europeans hold cultural sway. While many bands have tended toward one or another ethnic style in accordance with their locale's particular cultural concentration, others have embraced several sounds, since the 1930s especially. During that era Minnesotan "Whoopee John" Wilfahrt, steeped in the German and Czech dance melodies of his native New Ulm, widened his audience by playing Scandinavian and minstrel show tunes. Similarly, the Viking Accordion Band from Albert Lea, located in southern Minnesota, and led by Leighton "Skipper" Berg, added German and Czech pieces to an erstwhile Nordic repertoire. Wisconsin's Frank Kuczynski, a Polish accordionist, became "Pee Wee King" while fusing his old-time sound with country music and, eventually, rock 'n' roll. And North Dakotan Lawrence Welk blended Volga German melodies with sweet jazz and pop.

Technological change invariably abetted cultural crossovers. Folk music and dance in the Midwest, occurring initially in homes, barns, and rustic bowers, found its way into community dance halls and, in the early twentieth century, onto radio and records. The self-described "oldest station in the nation," Wisconsin Public Radio, launched in 1917 by University of Wisconsin physics students, soon featured live broadcasts of Ho-Chunk, Irish, and Norwegian traditional performers. In 1924 Chicago's WLS inaugurated the "National Barn Dance," a homey Saturday-night musical-variety show whose decidedly Anglo-American tilt was occasionally counterbalanced by Little German Bands, Scandinavian dialect singers, and Swiss yodelers. The "Barn Dance" quickly spawned similar programs regionally: on KDAL (Duluth), KMA (Shenandoah, Iowa), KMOX (St. Louis), WCKY (Cincinnati), WDAY (Fargo), WIBC (Indianapolis), WJMS (Ironwood, Michigan), WNAX (Yankton, South Dakota), WTMJ (Milwaukee), and many others. Commercial recording companies—like Gennett of Richmond, Indiana, and Paramount of Port Washington, Wisconsin—also emerged in the 1920s, waxing old-time fiddlers, transplanted southern "hillbillies," blues and gospel performers come north, and polka bands aplenty. Columbia, Victor, and other commercial labels were especially active in Chicago, recording not only the aforementioned groups and genres but also Irish pipers, Greek *bouzoúki* players, pluckers of the zitherlike Lithuanian *kankle*, and more.

Assisted by technology, regional folk music and dance have also been afflicted by xenophobic, pietistic, and temperance movements. In post–Civil War Chicago, as in other industrial communities with diverse populations, such organizations as the Socialist Labor Party and the International Working People's Association sponsored parades, picnics, and dances. The antiforeign *Chicago Tribune* of 1885 derided a typical event: "Every variety of step might have been witnessed yesterday. The 'Bohemian dip,' the 'German lunge,' the 'Austrian kick,' the 'Polish romp,' the 'Scandinavian trot.'" In 1913 Anglo-American urban reformers crusaded against Chicago's combination tavern–dance halls, which doubled as working people's social clubs, equating them with alcoholism, godless immorality, and even white slavery. Heralded by a succession of blue laws, the onset of Prohibition curtailed public occasions for midwestern folk music and dance. Dance-hall culture rebounded vigorously, however, with the Volstead Act's repeal.

The interim period, 1919–1933, witnessed manipulations of midwestern folk traditions by both right- and left-wing Anglo-American activists. In 1924, nostalgic for the fiddle and hammered dulcimer accompanying square dances of his youth, but also disturbed by what he regarded as the African American and Jewish tainting of the era's prevailing music, Detroit industrialist Henry Ford sought to "replace the jazz dances popular in the cities with the more graceful steps." His solution was to sponsor an old-time string band and, through Ford dealerships, a series of old-time fiddlers' contests that would supplant supposedly degenerate foreign influences with Anglo-American purity. Jane Addams, an equally meddlesome albeit less sinister reformer, was part of the coalition condemning Chicago dance halls. Her solution for the immigrant newcomers served by her settlement-house movement was a series of sedate international exhibitions—begun from 1921 to 1930 in such cities as Cleveland, Detroit, Duluth, Flint, Minneapolis, and Omaha—wherein cultural outsiders might sit politely sipping lemonade in genteel auditoriums as successions of authentically costumed ethnic dancers executed short programs of choreographed steps on a distant stage.

Happily, few Ford contestants shared his ideological warp, while exhibition dancers seldom saw contradictions in shucking their old-country garb to dance to some crossover band in a beer hall. Still the revival and display movements championed, respectively, by Ford and Addams made their mark. Organizations of old-time Anglo-American and Scandinavian fiddlers, Finnish *kantele* players, Serbian and Croatian tamburitzans, Slovenian button-box clubs, and the like abound, as do seasonal culture shows like Milwaukee's Holiday Folk Fair, where troupes of well-trained folk dancers assert their heritage and entertain the curious. Indeed, the region's recent Hmong immigrants, encouraged to participate yet lacking a distinctive Old World folk-dance tradition, fit in by fusing Lao court dances with break-dance moves.

Sources and Further Reading: Ronald L. Baker, comp., *Homeless, Friendless, and Penniless* (2000); Allen H. Eaton, *Immigrant Gifts to American Life* (1932); Paul Gifford, *The Hammered Dulcimer* (2001); P. T. Gillett, "Fiddlers We Have Known" Local History Special Collection, Antigo (Wisconsin) Public Library (1932); Reginald Laubin and Gladys Laubin, *Indian Dances of North America* (1977); James P. Leary and Richard March, *Down Home Dairyland* (1996); Gerald Milnes, *Play of a Fiddle* (1999); Bruce C. Nelson, "Dancing and Picnicking Anarchists? The Movement below the Martyred Leadership," in David Roediger and Franklin Rosemont, eds., *Haymarket Scrapbook* (1986); Howard Sacks, "From the Barn to the Bowery and Back Again," *Journal of American Folklore* 116 (Summer 2003); Nicholas Vrooman, *Turtle Mountain Music* (recording and booklet, 1984); Ann Wagner, *Adversaries of Dance* (1997).

James P. Leary
University of Wisconsin–Madison

Fiddling

On an April Saturday night in Chicago in 1924, an old-time fiddler inaugurated the WLS "National Barn Dance," the dominant country music radio show prior to World War II. In the following weeks, the unknown

OLD TIME FIDDLERS' CONTEST

COMING TO

THE MAJESTIC THEATRE
MARCH 17th and 18th
THIRTY DOLLARS IN PRIZES

That's the inducement held out to the old time fiddlers to try their luck at the Majestic Theatre on Wednesday and Thursday, March 17 and 18. There are only two rules. One is that the contestants must be over 50 years of age and the second is that they must play by ear only. The use of music in this contest not allowed. The contest will be held both nights and competent judges will award the prizes. An entrance blank is printed below. Fill out now and mail at once. Get in on the money.

ENTRANCE BLANK
OLD TIME FIDDLERS' CONTEST

Name ....

Address ....

Phone No.......................... Age...............

Below list the titles of the three numbers to be played in the contest.

1. ....

2. ....

3. ....

Mail this blank to
Old Time Fiddlers' Contest
MAJESTIC THEATRE
Rice Lake, Wis.

Fiddling contest in Rice Lake, Wisconsin, 1926. Courtesy Rice Lake Chronotype.

fiddler was identified in Chicago papers only as "Timothy Cornrow" from "Ioway," a pseudonym. Later historians claimed he was Tommy Dandurand, a streetcar operator from a French-Canadian settlement in nearby Kankakee County. However, Timothy Cornrow could have been one of twenty other fiddlers from four midwestern states who appeared on the show during its first months. In 1927 Tommy Dandurand and his WLS Barn Dance Gang recorded thirteen old-time tunes in an archaic regional style with a lead fiddler playing the melody to the accompaniment of a chording second fiddler and a square-dance caller. No other fiddling of this type can be heard on commercial recordings. Historical documents and the memories of folk fiddlers born early in the twentieth century, like Les Raber of Hastings, Michigan, attest to the onetime strength of this midwestern tradition.

The sounds of the Midwest's traditional fiddlers have frequently been drowned out by newer styles of fiddling popularized through mass media. Nonetheless, half of the first country fiddlers to make commercial records in 1922 and 1923 were midwesterners, including Illinois native William B. Houchens of Dayton and John Baltzell of Mt. Vernon, Ohio. Especially noteworthy is Jasper "Jep" Bisbee of Paris, Michigan, who was born in 1843, making him the earliest-born fiddler on phonograph records.

Besides finding outlets in the new mass media, old-time fiddlers attracted attention in the 1920s through a wave, peaking in 1926, of highly publicized fiddle contests. John Baltzell was named "Champion of Ohio, Indiana and Kentucky," while Missourian W.H. Elmore of West Baden, Indiana, was crowned "Champion of Dixie" (actually, southern Indiana, Kentucky, and Tennessee). Tom Croal, an Irish fiddler from Sauk County, Wisconsin, took first in a Milwaukee contest a month before Leizime Brusoe, a French-Canadian émigré to Rhinelander, Wisconsin, won the Midwest Championship in a field of more than one hundred fiddlers in Chicago. Concurrent contests were held in Michigan, Missouri, Iowa, and the Dakotas.

Fiddling was ubiquitous in North America, and local traditions, especially those connected with social dancing, were strong in the Midwest in the early twentieth century. But as old-time fiddling's place in the spotlight faded, and as mass-mediated country music became more professionalized, the public face of fiddling acquired a southern hue. In eastern and central portions of the Midwest, most professional and semiprofessional fiddlers embraced such new commercial styles as bluegrass and western swing. Only western radio stations continued to broadcast the older traditional tunes—breakdowns, hornpipes, and quadrilles for square dancing; waltzes and schottisches for round dancing. Happy Jack O'Malley was a long-time favorite on WNAX in Yankton, South Dakota, while Casey Jones could be heard for twenty years on KFNF in Shenandoah, Iowa, and Bob Walter held forth on KMMJ in Grand Island, Nebraska, into the mid-1950s.

Midwestern fiddlers with roots deep in local and family traditions did most of their playing for community dances, for informal musical gatherings, or simply for personal pleasure. In the 1930s, Library of Congress fieldworkers made few forays to the Midwest but still recorded such local masters as Patrick Bonner of Beaver Island, Michigan; Otto Rindlisbacher of Rice Lake, Wisconsin; and Mr. Mitchell and Indian Tom in Mitchell, South Dakota. The urban folk music revival of the 1960s and 1970s stimulated another batch of field recordings. Young aficionados discovered gifted old-timers like Ward Jarvis of Athens, Ohio; Bill Big-

ford of Portland, Michigan; Stella Elam of Greenfield, Illinois; and Lotus Dickey of Paoli, Indiana. Only a few post-World War II midwestern fiddlers saw their artistry and tunes disseminated through commercially issued albums. Two titles from Rounder Records epitomize this rare achievement: *Indiana Fiddler*, a 1984 LP featuring John W. Summers of Marion, Indiana, and *Joseph Won a Many-Coated Fiddle*, a 1999 CD by Dwight Lamb of Onawa, Iowa.

Midwestern fiddlers have always produced a wide array of sounds reflecting the cultural diversity of the region. Fiddles first arrived with the *habitants* of New France. Dancing master M.B. Brouillette, born in 1810, the grandson of a pioneer, fiddled in Wabash Valley towns. French traditions lived on in twentieth-century Missouri in the playing of Joe Politte of Old Mines and Lloyd Lalumondiere of St. Genevieve. The fiddle early became a favorite in American Indian and métis communities. A founder of Davenport, Iowa, Antoine LeClair, born in 1797 to a Canadian father and Potawatomi mother, played a three-string fiddle. Big Chief Henry Hall of Wichita, Kansas, recorded commercially in Dallas in 1929, while Joe Cloud of Odanah, Wisconsin, recorded for the Library of Congress 1938. In the 1980s, on the Turtle Mountain Chippewa Reservation, Fred Allery and Mike Page were recorded for the North Dakota Arts Council.

African Americans were also some of the earliest fiddlers in the region. In the 1830s, Nelson Perry played for public dances in Chicago, and William Taylor, a barber in St. Paul, headed a popular dance orchestra in the Minnesota Territory in the 1840s. A published list of twenty-four contestants at an Indianapolis contest in 1909 noted that Edward Cambron and Clay Brown were "colored." Bill Katon, an influential black fiddler in Missouri, played on WOS in Jefferson City, Missouri, in the 1920s. Howard Armstrong made some of the earliest recordings of black string-band music when he arrived in Chicago from Tennessee in 1933.

Other immigrant and ethnic communities have maintained strong fiddle traditions as they settled into new homes in the region. Leonard Finseth of Mondovi played many Norwegian tunes at dances in western Wisconsin, while Thea Arndt Clark and Jorgen "Alfred" Blagen are among the Norwegian fiddlers from rural Iowa whose tunes have been revived by Beth Hoven Rotto of Decorah. In 1924, Edwin Johnson immigrated to St. Paul, Minnesota, where he played music at house parties in the growing Swedish community. His grandson, Paul Dahlin, now leads a large, fiddle-dominated *Spelmanslag* (Musicians Club) at the American-Swedish Institute in Minneapolis.

Perhaps the most prominent style of traditional fiddling in the Midwest today is Irish fiddling. Chicago persists as a vital destination for Irish immigrants, including many fiddlers, and is the birthplace of two internationally celebrated Irish fiddlers. John McGreevy became a master of the distinctive style from County Sligo, and touring artist Liz Carroll is recognized for an expressive virtuosity that remains firmly centered in the sound of traditional Irish fiddling.

At the start of the twenty-first century, there are probably more active fiddlers in the Midwest than at any time in the past. Most are attracted to repertoires and styles that are not distinctively regional, but widely disseminated through mass media. A few unheralded contemporary fiddlers are shepherding older tunes and forgotten regional traditions into the new century. A number of thriving ethnic music traditions rely on fiddlers to conserve older sounds and create new styles that bridge the gap between Old and New Worlds. This short survey, regrettably, has not brought deserved attention to the Polish, Finnish, Scottish, Romany, South Slavic, South Indian, and Hispanic fiddlers who continue to play throughout the Midwest.

Sources and Further Reading: Nicholas Carolan, *A Harvest Saved* (1997); R.P. Christeson, ed., *The Old-Time Fiddler's Repertory*, 2 vols. (musical score; 1973, 1984); James Leary, ed., *Medicine Fiddle: A Humanities Discussion Guide* (1992); Michael Loukinen, prod. and dir., *Medicine Fiddle* (video, 1991); Philip Martin, *Farmhouse Fiddlers* (1994); Howard L. Sacks and Judith Rose Sacks, *Way up North in Dixie* (1993); *Traditional Irish Music in America: Chicago* (CD, 2001); Paul L. Tyler, "The True Story of 'Dickey's Discovery': Thoughts on Lotus Dickey's Fiddling," in Nancy C. McEntire, Grey Larsen, and Janne Henshaw, eds., *The Lotus Dickey Songbook* (1995).

Paul L. Tyler
Old Town School of Folk Music,
Chicago, Illinois

Garage Rock

The amateur garage band likely reigns as the most widespread grassroots form of group music-making in the Midwest over the past forty years. The essence of this style is a "combo" with electric guitar and bass, drum set, electric keyboard, and vocals that plays rock music in a rough, energetic manner. Although beginning rock bands have been found throughout the United States, garage-rock authorities see the tradition as having particular vitality in the Midwest. Isolation from the record-industry bases on either coast, enhancing the impact of local and regional bands, is

the primary reason given for vibrant garage-rock scenes across the Midwest. Instead of seeking national popularity by being signed to a large record label, garage bands have emphasized the joys of musical performance at the neighborhood level—whether in practices and home recording sessions in suburban basements and garages or playing for peers at schools, youth centers, and house parties.

Regional qualities of midwestern garage rock during its 1960s heyday include unique venues where bands played for various events such as Catholic Youth Organization dances in cities with large Catholic populations like Milwaukee, Chicago, Detroit, and Cleveland, or summer dances held in resort areas like northern Indiana's Lake Tippecanoe and Indiana Beach. They were also found in the many small recording studio/record labels that allowed amateur rock bands to make singles that sometimes received regional or national airplay, for example, Soma in Minneapolis and Cuca in Sauk City, Wisconsin. While changes can be seen in midwestern garage rock from the 1960s to the present (now bands are writing their own material and there is more female participation), continuation of the neighborhood context is evident in the multiband "basement shows" that occur in the home of a band member and the rite of passage of entering a Battle of the Bands at a local school.

Garage rock and "garage-punk" have been used as labels for raw, amateurish rock recordings, typified by one-hit wonders made in the mid-1960s by American bands that imitated British groups in ascendancy at the time. The *Nuggets* 1960s garage-rock compilation features numerous Midwest bands from Mankato, Minnesota, to Mansfield, Ohio. Subsequent revivals of rough, less commercial rock allowed midwestern punk and alternative rockers to move from local garage band to national recording artists (for example, Devo of Akron, Ohio, and the Replacements of Minneapolis, Minnesota). While the tradition of amateurs forming garage bands continues, professional bands playing in a "garage" style have frequently been heard in Midwest rock clubs since the 1990s.

Sources and Further Reading: Archive International, *Highs in the Mid Sixties*, vol. 4, *Chicago*; vol. 5, *Michigan*; vol. 9, *Ohio*; vol. 10, *Wisconsin* (1983); Classics Records, *Cuca Rock 'n' Roll Story* (CD, 1996); Hugh MacLean and Vernon Joynson, *An American Rock History*, pt. 3, *Chicago and Illinois, 1960–1992*; pt. 4, *Indiana, Iowa and Missouri, 1960–1993*; pt. 5, *Minnesota and Wisconsin, 1960–1997* (2000); Soma Records, *Big Hits from Mid-America: The Soma Records Story, 1963–1967* (2 CDs, 1998).

Peter Roller
Alverno College, Wisconsin

Polka

The polka, a couples dance in ¾ time, was in vogue in much of Europe during the second half of the nineteenth century, a period when many immigrants from Europe settled in the Midwest. Thus they brought with them an affinity for the polka dance and its associated music. Once in America, several central European ethnic groups continued to emphasize polka music and dancing in the festive events of their communities. In some cases, their continuing devotion to polka in the United States outstripped that of their conationals in the homeland. Germans, Czechs, Swiss, Poles, and Slovenes have been the most active in perpetuating polka traditions in the Midwest. Many Swedes, Norwegians, Danes, Finns, Belgians, Dutch, Ukrainians, Italians, Croatians, and other European Americans also identify with and participate in polka activities, and musicians from those groups have made significant contributions to midwestern polka.

The nineteenth-century polka craze also entered Mexico from Europe, and Mexican musicians in Texas interacted with musical German, Polish, and Czech immigrants there to shape the polka style of the Texas-Mexican *conjuntos* (bands). During the twentieth cen-

tury Mexican Americans migrated to many areas of the Midwest, bringing the *conjunto* style of polka music and dancing with them.

Recordings of polka music from the Midwest can be found among early 78 rpm discs produced at the beginning of the twentieth century. The earliest recordings reveal a diverse array of instrumentation and performance styles. Polkas were played, for example, by large brass bands, by solo accordionists, by fiddle and concertina duos. The labels on the discs frequently were in languages other than English, and often the music differed little from its European antecedents. After several decades of gestation in the midwestern environment, distinctive American polka traditions began to emerge by the late 1920s. The 1930s, 1940s and 1950s proved to be the key decades in which the music played by influential bands became the models that defined several distinct American polka styles. Each style evolved a standard instrumental line-up, a core repertoire, and a distinct set of musical aesthetics. Although each polka tradition is different, mutual influences are common both in the music and dancing.

The styles' names refer to ethnic groups. The five most widespread are Czech or "Bohemian," German or "Dutchman," Mexican, Polish, and Slovenian. A core constituency of dancers and players from the particular ethnic group are influential in each of the polka "scenes;" however, people from a variety of ethnic backgrounds participate as dancers or musicians in each polka style as well. In addition to their ethnic names, most polka styles have also developed an American geographic identity and are supported by many of the European American ethnic groups that live in the particular area. For example, Slovenian-style polka is often called "Cleveland-style" or sometimes "Milwaukee-style"; Czech is called "Nebraska-style"; and Dutchman is called "Minnesota-style." In terms of extensive multiethnic participation, the exception is Mexican polka, which typically is played at dance events where the dominant language is Spanish and relatively few non-Mexicans participate.

The most influential musicians who established the paradigm for four of the widespread polka styles in the 1930s through the 1950s were midwesterners. "Whoopee John" Wilfahrt and Harold Loeffelmacher, both of New Ulm, Minnesota, were renowned for the Dutchman style while Romy Gosz of Manitowoc, Wisconsin, and Ernie Kucera of Fremont, Nebraska, were celebrated performers of the Bohemian or Czech style. Perhaps the best-known polka musician of the twentieth century is Frankie Yankovic of Cleveland, Ohio, who shaped the Slovenian style; "Li'l Wally" Jagiello of Chicago was a pioneer in spreading the most popular style of Polish

Frankie Yankovic, polka king. Courtesy Ida Yankovic.

American polka. Key midwestern figures in more eso-teric polka styles include Viola Turpeinen, an accordionist from upper Michigan, who plays Finnish polka, and the Skertich Brothers from the Calumet region of northern Indiana and Illinois, for Croatian polka.

Squeezeboxes are essential instruments in most polka traditions, especially the button accordion, the piano accordion, and the Chemnitzer concertina. At the same time as the polka fad was sweeping Europe in the mid-nineteenth century, it so happened that inventors in several European countries were fashioning these new mechanized musical instruments that produced sound by forcing air through free reeds, tongues of metal surrounded by a frame. With the help of bellows springs, levers, and reed blocks, it became possible for one musician to sound like a small ensemble, playing melody and harmony on the right hand and bass notes and rhythmic chords with the left. Manufacture and sale of squeezeboxes made the instruments widely accessible at a time when polkas were all the rage. The squeezebox-polka association remains. A majority of polka bands use an accordion or concertina.

As polka styles have continued to evolve since the 1960s, midwestern musicians and dancers have continued to have tremendous influence. In the early 1960s Chicagoan Eddie Blazonczyk created a modernized Polish polka sound known as "Dyno" or "Push." The appearance of this musical style was accompanied by the emergence, originally in Chicago, of the "Polish hop" style of dancing to it. The Polish hop, also called "Chicago hop," emphasizes vertical motions and jitterbug-derived hand dancing and is done in double time to the music. The popularity of Dyno and hop-style dancing soon spread to Polish American communities nationwide, overwhelming the eastern Polish American polka style that had been the dominant Polish sound as far west as Detroit and Cleveland, having originated in the East Coast states.

Adherents of Frankie Yankovic's style from Ohio, Wisconsin, and Illinois, including Joey Miskulin, Roger Bright, Verne Meisner, Steve Meisner, and Joey Tomsick, have perpetuated and elaborated this music. The button-box revival, another trend on the midwestern Slovenian scene since the 1970s, a retraditionalizing movement, has brought back strong interest in the diatonic button accordion.

Virtuoso concertina players from the upper Mississippi River Valley, Karl Hartwich and Brian Brueggen, revolutionized the Dutchman style in the 1980s inspired by the less orchestrated, more spontaneous music of their mentor Sylvester Liebl. While still using brass and reed instruments, Hartwich and Brueggen placed even greater emphasis on the Chem-nitzer concertina as the chief melodic voice in the Minnesota sound.

Younger Czech or Bohemian musicians, like Mark Vyhlidal in Nebraska and Mark Jirikovec in Wisconsin, are sustaining their particular regional styles within that polka scene, and northern Minnesota, Wisconsin, and Michigan remain the point of origin of most Finnish American polka.

Sources and Further Reading: Victor Greene, *A Passion for Polka: Old-Time Ethnic Music in America* (1992); Charles Keil and Angeliki V. Keil, *Polka Happiness* (1992); James P. Leary, "The German Concertina in the Upper Midwest," in Philip V. Bohlman and Otto Holzapfel, eds., *Land without Nightingales* (2002); James P. Leary and Richard March, *Down Home Dairyland: A Listener's Guide* (1996); Richard March, *Deep Polka: Dance Music from the Midwest* (CD, 1998).

Richard March
Wisconsin Arts Board, Madison, Wisconsin

Qeej

The Hmong came to the United States as refugees from Laos beginning in 1975, settling in particularly large concentrations in the Minneapolis-St. Paul metropolitan area, in cities throughout Wisconsin, and in greater Detroit. The *qeej* (pronounced *keng*), a musical and ritual instrument, is an easily recognized visual symbol of Hmong identity.

It is widely held in Hmong culture that words can be "spoken" by musical instruments. The qeej, a traditional wind instrument made of bamboo and wood, plays the most serious texts, long memorized funeral prayers that seek to console the soul of the deceased as that soul returns to the ancestors.

When the first Hmong families arrived in the Midwest, few American funeral parlors were able to accommodate the time or space needed for their traditional funerals. In the late 1980s, Hmong-owned funeral homes were opened, including two in St. Paul, Minnesota, contributing to a growth of interest among young people in musical and other aspects of "the Hmong way."

Hmong funerals also include a self-accompanied acrobatic dance called *dhiam qeej tawj qeej* (jumping qeej, spinning qeej). The dance is a metaphorical depiction of the journey to the ancestors. The basic moves have entered secular life, too; competitions are routinely held for the best dancers, especially during New Year festivities.

As the twenty-first century commences there has been a blossoming of classes in qeej, often taught as a secular performance genre. Serious students are sometimes introduced to the ritual repertoire. Elder players are finding their skills appreciated once again.

Sources and Further Reading: Amy Catlin, "The Hmong and Their Music: A Critique of Pure Speech," in John Michael Kohler Arts Center, *Hmong Art: Tradition and Change* (1986); Catherine Falk, "Upon Meeting the Ancestors: The Hmong Funeral Ritual in Asia and Australia," *Hmong Studies Journal* 1 (Fall 1996); James P. Leary, "Joua Bee Xiong, Hmong Musician," in James P. Leary, *Wisconsin Folklore* (1998).

Cliff Sloane
Seattle, Washington

Irish Dance

Irish dance is an international phenomenon. Midwestern cities, however, particularly Chicago, Detroit, Cleveland, and Milwaukee, have long been bastions of schools, organizations, and individuals promoting this tradition. The popularity of *Riverdance* in the mid-1990s brought media attention to the art form and demonstrated the strength of Irish dancing in the Midwest since one of its stars, Michael Flatley, hailed from Chicago.

Irish dancing was brought into the Midwest in the early 1800s by Irish immigrants, many of them laborers on canals and railroads. This dancing was informal and social, found at weddings and holiday celebrations as well as at any Irish gathering. Stereotypes associated it with drinking and fighting. Formal schools and *feiseanna* (competitions) were established at the beginning of the 1900s but tended to be found only among Irish-American communities in urban areas, particularly Chicago. The first dance classes were held there in 1904 by Philadelphia-born, Irish-bred John McNamara. The first midwestern *feis* (competition) was held there in 1912, and an influential volume of Irish tunes was collected there by Captain O'Neill and published in 1913. The Chicago World's Fair of 1933 included an "Irish Village" that presented Irish dance to the general public.

Other cities began establishing dance schools in the 1940s and 1950s, and the 1990s witnessed a phenomenal increase in interest. Today, almost every major city can claim dance schools officially registered with An Comisiun (the Irish Dancing Commission) in Ireland. Midwestern branches of the Gaelic League as well as Irish American cultural organizations sponsor events supporting Irish dance.

Irish dance can be divided into three formats: step dance, sets, and *ceili*. Step dancing features elaborate, frequently percussive footwork in which the upper body and arms are held straight while the legs and feet move to the rhythm of the music. Dances are classified by rhythm: jigs (treble meter), reels (duple time), and hornpipes (duple time). Soft-soled shoes are worn for most jigs and reels; hard soles are used for hornpipes, treble jigs, and treble reels. Step dancing, now iconic of Irish culture, was developed in the late 1700s through the 1800s by dance masters who traveled throughout Ireland, teaching and performing.

Set dancing ("country sets") developed in the late 1700s from French quadrilles and native Irish steps, and are similar to American square dances. In the 1920s, they were considered foreign by Irish nationalists and banned from official dance schools. A revival of sets began in the early 1970s, and they have since regained popularity.

Ceili refers to both social dance events and specific group dances. Developed by the dance masters, they range from easy dances that can be performed at informal gatherings to complex, intricate figures with demanding footwork. *Ceili* events are held in many larger cities in the Midwest on a weekly basis.

A large number of accredited teachers and events are now based in the Midwest, allowing Irish dance to become a thriving activity that attracts Irish Americans as well as individuals having no Irish heritage. The Midwest today boasts a number of professional Irish dance companies, numerous champion dancers and dance schools, and a phenomenal number of youngsters learning the tradition.

Sources and Further Reading: Brendan Breathnach, *Folk Music and Dances of Ireland* (1971); Helen Brennan, *The Story of Irish Dance* (1999); John P. Cullinane, *Aspects of the History of Irish Dancing in North America* (1991); Donal O'Sullivan, *Irish Folk Music, Song and Dance* (1952).

Lucy Long
Bowling Green State University, Ohio

Folk Song

Folk song is a generic term for songs passed on by folk tradition. Indigenous and immigrant peoples in the Midwest have longstanding, varied, continuously vital folk-song repertoires that include both lyric songs emphasizing sentiments and ballads presenting narratives.

In the late nineteenth century Francis J. Child, a Harvard professor of modern languages and a founder of the American Folklore Society, published an influential multivolume compendium, *The English and Scottish Popular Ballads* (1882–1898), including 305 distinctive songs soon dubbed "Child ballads." Set in late-medieval/early Renaissance Britain, occasionally

❖ Chicago Bound

1. When I left out of Georgia in 1934
   My baby she begged me "daddy please don't go"
   But I left that town, you know I left that town
   When I left out of Georgia, you know I was Memphis bound

2. Well I stayed in Memphis until 1939
   The woman I was loving she didn't pay me no mind.
   Then I left that town, you know I left that town
   When I left out of Memphis, you know I was St. Louis bound

3. I didn't need no steam heat by my bed
   The little girl I had kept it cherry red.
   But I left that town, you know I left that town,
   When I left St. Louis, you know I was Chicago bound

4. I'm gonna tell you something that you all should know,
   Chicago is the best place I ever know
   I'm gonna stay in this town, I'm gonna live in this town
   I'm gonna live in Chicago, it's the greatest place around.

Source: "Chicago Bound" words and music by James Lane. Copyright 1965 (Renewed) by Arc Music Corporation (BMI). All rights reserved. Used by Permission. International Copyright Secured.

humorous, but more often preoccupied with tragic love, murder, incest, and the supernatural, Child ballads concentrate on a single episode, tell their story in dramatic fashion marked by dialogue, and favor an impersonal approach with little or no intrusion of the narrator's point of view. Thus, in a version of "The House Carpenter" collected in the 1930s by Mary O. Eddy in Canton, Ohio, a lady leaves her husband and baby to sail with a demon lover, after which she dies despairing as the boat sinks. The verses offer no platitudes but merely conclude with "And her mourning was heard no more."

Charmed by the possible persistence of ancient British ballads amid local singers, Child's disciples, mostly Anglophile college professors, worked actively over the next half century to document and publish compendiums spanning North America and including the Midwest: Earl J. Stout, *Folklore from Iowa* (1936); Charles Neeley and John W. Spargo, *Tales and Songs of Southern Illinois* (1938); Eddy, *Ballads and Songs from Ohio* (1939); Emelyn E. Gardner and Geraldine J. Chickering, *Ballads and Songs of Southern Michigan* (1939); Henry M. Belden, *Ballads and Songs Collected by*

the *Missouri Folklore Society* (1940); Paul G. Brewster, *Ballads and Songs of Indiana* (1940); and Harry Peters, *Folksongs out of Wisconsin* (1977, based on field research by Helene Stratman-Thomas in the 1940s).

Not surprisingly, these ballad hunters encountered other forms of narrative folk songs, among them "broadside" and "native American" ballads. The former, originating in England, Ireland, and Scotland, but also circulating in America, are named for their occasional printing on a single-sided handbill, or broadside. Set amidst the simultaneous disruption of Old World village life and emergence of industrialized cities and global empires, broadside ballads characteristically chronicle the experiences of wandering soldiers, sailors, criminals, and lovers both faithful and capricious. Many commence with "Come all ye" invocations and more than a few are "goodnights," supposedly the last words of miscreants facing execution. "The Flying Cloud," widely sung throughout the Midwest but particularly in lumber camps and on Great Lakes vessels, involves an Irish apprentice who runs off to sea, where his misdeeds as a slaver and pirate result in hanging.

So-called native American ballads do not emanate from American Indians but are narrative folk songs composed in North America, albeit with recourse to earlier tunes, plots, and rhetorical devices. Of those originating in America, most found in midwestern tradition date from 1850 to 1950, but the oldest such ballad, "Springfield Mountain," regarding a farmhand's death by snakebite, goes back to the 1760s. Murders; crimes; outlawry; tragedies; disasters; the experiences of pioneers, sailors, and lumberjacks; and moralizing conclusions typify this group of ballads. The origins of many, like "The Jam on Gerry's Rock," are unknown, yet singers in Wisconsin, Michigan, North Dakota, and elsewhere have all claimed that this log-drive disaster occurred locally. Others are based indisputably on actual events. "Jesse James" and "Cole Younger" chronicle post–Civil War Missouri bank robbers; the lumberjack ballad "The Flat River Girl" is based on an unrequited love affair in 1872 near Greenville, Michigan. The words, tunes, singers, composers, and cultural background of lumber camp and Great Lakes ballads are especially well documented through the works of a trio of folklorists: Franz Rickaby, *Ballads and Songs of the Shanty-Boy* (1926); Earl C. Beck, *Songs of the Michigan Lumberjacks* (1941); and Ivan Walton, *Windjammers: Songs of the Great Lakes Sailors* (2002).

The privileged status scholars bestowed on English-language ballads and midwesterners of Anglo-American heritage, however, slights equally worthy and numerous ballads sung by other peoples and in other languages. Indeed the putative English and Scottish ballads identified by Child were, in many cases, internationally circulating narrative folk songs that had crossed cultural and linguistic borders for centuries. Immigrants predictably brought such ballads to the Midwest. In the late 1930s and early 1940s, Sidney Robertson Cowell, Alan Lomax, and Helene Stratman-Thomas all made sound recordings for the Archive of American Folksong at the Library of Congress that included a northern Minnesota Finnish version of Child's "The Twa Brothers," a Milwaukee German rendition of "Lord Lovel," an Icelandic counterpart of "Clerk Colvill" from Washington Island in Lake Michigan, and more. And despite the English tilt of broadside and native American ballad categories, Minnesotan M. C. Dean, a retired sailor and logger and an active singer, included a preponderance of ballads illuminating the Irish immigrant experience in *The Flying Cloud and One Hundred and Fifty Other Old Time Songs and Ballads* (1922).

Dean's version of "The Roving Irishman" commenced with "Oh I am bound for Wisconsin, that's right among the Dutch / And as for conversation, it won't be very much," thus heralding ballads employing "broken-English" comically to chronicle the intercultural experiences of midwestern immigrants. Such German or "Dutchman" songs as "They Say I'm a Dutchman (And Ain't Got No Schtyle)" about a frumpy newcomer's attempts to court "American girls," or "Dunderbeck's Machine," wherein a sausage maker grinds up "all the neighbors cats and dogs," have been widely sung throughout the region. And Scandinavian comic-dialect ballads like "Ole Olson the Hobo from Norway" and "Swede from Nord Dakota" abound in the upper Midwest: "Aye bane a big Swede from Nord Dakota, / Vorked on a farm for about vun year. / Aye come down to Minnesota, / Yust to see da big state fair."

African Americans attracted to midwestern cities in the post–Civil War era also performed and composed what scholars term "blues ballads." Based around a stable narrative core, yet comprised of recurrent "floating verses" sung in shifting sequences, blues ballads have a less linear, more improvisational approach to storytelling than their Anglo- and European American counterparts. The region's most celebrated blues ballad—known variously as "Staggerlee," "Stackerlee," and "Stagolee"—emerged in St. Louis in the late nineteenth century and concerns a gun-toting "bad man" who terrorizes black folks and defies white authority.

Mexican Americans from south Texas, especially, brought their ballads or *corridos* to the Midwest with the onset of the Great Depression. Such exemplary performers as Silvano Ramos and Daniel Ramirez made commercial recordings in Chicago, including "El Corrido de Texas," issued in 1929 and widely sung from Wisconsin's apple orchards to Michigan's sugar-beet fields.

Esos trenes del T.P.	Those trains of the Texas and Pacific Railroad
Que cruzan por Louisiana,	Which cross Louisiana,
Se llevan los Mexicanos	They take the Mexicans
Para el estado de Indiana.	To the state of Indiana.

While ballad stories fully considered dramatize the cultural pluralism characterizing midwestern life, lyric folk songs embody emotions, attitudes, and customary practices. In 1893 Alice Cunningham Fletcher's *A Study of Omaha Music* offered our first full glimpse of an American Indian people's ancient and evolving tradition. Lullabies and songs of courtship, healing, greeting, and, especially, *hay lush ka* (warrior songs) persist among the Omaha, with parallels among many midwestern Indian nations. Warrior songs, frequently incorporated into powwows, extend from the War of 1812, when numerous tribes under Tecumseh allied with England, to the twenty-first-century invasion of Iraq. A still-circulating Ho-Chunk song from World War I declares that "The Ho Chunk boys went across the water / Germany was defeated."

Early French settlers brought folk songs aplenty. Juliette Kinzie's *Wau-Bun, The Early Days in the Northwest* (1857) mentions French voyageurs singing in the 1830s as they paddled canoes on the Fox River between Portage and Green Bay. French songs still resounded a century later in such settlements as Vincennes, Indiana, Prairie du Rocher, Missouri, Baraga, Michigan, and Somerset, Wisconsin and among the Turtle Mountain Métis of eastern North Dakota. Likewise, Laura Ingalls Wilder's *Little House in the Big Woods* (1932) reveals that, between 1860 and 1890, her fiddling "Pa" was one of many pioneers bringing Anglo-American lyric folk songs like "Old Grimes" from, in his case, New York to successive dairying and windswept homesteads in Wisconsin, Kansas, Minnesota, and the Dakota Territory: "Old Grimes's wife made skim-milk cheese / Old Grimes, he drank the whey / There came an east wind from the west / And blew old Grimes away."

Other European immigrants establishing communities in the nineteenth century similarly sustained old-country folk songs, adapted venerable lyrics to new surroundings, and composed original verses in traditional modes concerning their experiences and fantasies. Around 1900 Croatians and Slovaks in cities and hinterlands combined English lines with the original to remake "*Ja Sam Sirota*" ("I'm an Orphan") into an immigrant's lament: "I'm an orphan boy, come from Illinois / Have no mother, have no father, I'm an orphan boy," a song I heard sung in the late 1970s and early 1980s by assorted Slavs in northern Wisconsin, Milwaukee, and Chicago. In contrast, Wladyslaw Polak, a Polish immigrant to Chicago's North Side, performed the cheery, boastful "Children in Squares" (1928): "Here in the United States / The girls are after me/Swarming over me like flies" (*Songs of Migration and Emigration*, sound recording & booklet, 1976). Walloon Belgians arriving on Lake Michigan's western shores in the 1850s preferred abundant food and drink to multiple lovers:

Nos-estans quites po l'Amerique.	We are setting out for America.
I nos faut foute one cole.	We are going to get drunk.
Nos f'rans peter l'djambon.	We shall treat ourselves to ham.

Similarly optimistic paeans to midwestern opportunity and plenty combined with nostalgic anthems to abandoned homelands in constituting songs favored by ethnic singing societies and related musical organizations. Besides traditional songs, such groups typically included recited poems, original numbers, and highly arranged choral pieces in their performances. Singing clubs often afforded expressions of democracy in opposition to an undemocratic Old World class order. This was a main goal of Wilhelm Wagner when he established a *Sangerbund* in Freeport, Illinois, in 1855. Most common among German Americans, singing societies have also been widespread among other Germanic midwesterners (Swiss especially) as well as those of Baltic, Nordic, and Slavic heritage. Post–World War II Latvians and Lithuanians relied particularly on folk songs to maintain their ethnic identity and rally against Soviet occupation of their homelands.

The Midwest's Welsh depart from secular singing-society patterns to engage in *Gymanfa Ganus* (song fests) held mostly in Methodist and Presbyterian churches throughout ethnic enclaves across rural Ohio, Wisconsin, and Iowa. German and Nordic Lutherans in particular have composed new songs, most strikingly in the case of Finnish Apostolic Lutherans in the Lake Superior hinterlands, where song makers receive verses through visions.

Largely absent from singing societies and churches, immigrant songs accentuating anger and despair regarding dangerous working conditions, poor pay, awful food, and xenophobia frequently merged with the musical protests of agrarian and industrial workers. A parody of "Ta-Ra-Ra Boom Ti-Ay" composed by the Swedish immigrant and Industrial Workers of the World (IWW) minstrel Joe Hill was widely sung by itinerant threshers on midwestern prairies: "I worked for a farmer threshing wheat / Twenty-four hours on hands and feet. / When the moon was shining bright, / He kept us working day and night." When hirelings sabotage equipment, the farmer wises up by raising pay, cutting hours, and improving meals: "Now he works from spring till fall / And has no accidents at all." Arthur Kylander, a Finnish IWW organizer from Hibbing, Minnesota, composed "Lumberjakki" as an organizing tool in the Lake Superior region. Labor poems and songs were especially prominent in urban centers like Chicago, where the IWW was founded in 1905. A decade later Ralph Chaplin composed "Solidarity Forever," arguably America's best-known labor song, to the tune of the "Battle Hymn of the Republic." There are also antilabor songs, such as "Flag of Blue, White, and Red" (c. 1965), collected in central Missouri, which speaks of "Idle men and a roving band, [who] strike the tools from a miner's hand." Still, one can't say much about the extent of these songs because they have been little studied.

African Americans have made the most celebrated contributions to the region's lyric folk songs, especially as exponents of the continuously evolving blues and gospel genres that, through eloquent chronicling of hard times and good news, have enthralled audiences and performers throughout the nation and the world. Less known are poignant, kindred compositions of recent immigrants, like that of Eau Claire, Wisconsin's, Joua Bee Xiong, who drew upon traditional prosody and his refugee experiences to fashion something "pretty much from this country": "When I go to school / There is nobody to support me / I have to struggle by myself and suffer." One of many new midwestern folk songs in Hmong.

Sources and Further Reading: Cecilia Ray Berry, *Folk Songs of Old Vincennes* (1946); Cecil Brown, *Stagolee Shot Billy* (2003); *Corridos and Tragedias de la Frontera* (CD and booklet, 1994); M. C. Dean, *The Flying Cloud and One Hundred and Fifty Other Old Time Songs and Ballads* (1922); Mary O. Eddy, *Ballads and Songs from Ohio* (1939); G. Malcolm Laws, Jr., *American Balladry from British Broadsides* (1957); G. Malcolm Laws, Jr., *Native American Balladry*, rev. ed. (1964); James P. Leary, "Dialect Songs Among the Dutch," *Midwestern Folklore* 31 (Spring, 2005), James P. Leary, *Wisconsin Folklore* (1998); James P. Leary and Richard March, *Down Home Dairyland* (1996); James P. Leary and Richard March, "Farm, Forest, and Factory: Songs of Midwestern Labor," in Archie Green, ed., *Songs about Work* (1993); Dorothy Sara Lee and Maria LaVigna, eds., *Omaha Indian Music: Historical Recordings from the Fletcher/LaFlesche Collection* (LP, 1985); Francoise Lempereur, ed., *Anthologie Du Folklore Wallon*: Les Wallons d'Amerique, *Les Wallons d'Amerique* (LP and booklet, 1981); Harriet Pawlowska, ed., *Merrily We Sing: 105 Polish Folksongs* (1961); Andreas V. Reichstein, *German Pioneers on the American Frontier* (2001); Richard K. Spottswood, ed.,

Songs of Migration and Emigration (LP and booklet, 1976); Kenneth Swanson, "Music of Two Finnish Apostolic Lutheran Groups in Minnesota: The Heidemanians and Pollarities," *Student Musicologists at Minnesota* (1970); Laura Ingalls Wilder, *Little House in the Big Woods* (1932; rev. ed., 1953); Wisconsin Dells Singers, *Traditional Winnebago Songs* (cassette, c. 1990).

W. K. McNeil
Ozark Folk Center, Mountain View, Arkansas

James P. Leary
University of Wisconsin–Madison

Blues

At the beginning of the twentieth century, a new African American song form called blues spread from the southern United States in to the Midwest. Although contemporaries of that period recognized similarities between blues and other African American song styles including spirituals, ballads, work songs, and hollers, the term *blues* itself and the style it designated were not in common usage before that time. Initially blues came in many formats either sung a capella or with instrumental accompaniment, or even as an instrumental style. As a vocal form, it expressed both individual and social concerns and was used for self-expression, to comment on black community life or as a preferred soundtrack for weekend dances.

Initially disseminated by riverboat and railroad workers who commonly returned south, it was spread by itinerant guitar players who crisscrossed the Midwest. For example, blues promoter W.C. Handy (1873–1958), the first composer to use the term *blues* in a song title, first heard two such guitarists in St. Louis in 1892. They sang a piece called "East St. Louis" that included verses common to the blues tradition. Further east along the Ohio River, former minstrel Tom Fletcher (c. 1873–1954) heard two similar guitarists playing bottleneck or knife-style blues in 1900. He also noted the popularity of blues in the riverfront cafés where amateur and professional piano players pounded out their versions of the blues. Ma Rainey, the first to perform blues onstage, first heard blues sung in a small town in Missouri in 1902. Already a tent-show veteran, Rainey added blues to her stage act, which traveled throughout the Midwest and the South. Ironically, Handy and Rainey were called, respectively, the father and mother of blues, yet neither invented it. But they did recognize its value and help to popularize and standardize the form. Although shunned by the church and by so-called respectable folk, and despite its negative reputation as lower-class music, blues flourished as working-class entertainment along the Mississippi

Delta to Chicago corridor and outward to other cities with substantial black populations, such as Detroit, Kansas City, and Cleveland, becoming a fixture of midwestern African American life.

By the second decade of the twentieth century blues was firmly entrenched as popular culture, first on the stage, then as sheet music, and finally in 1920, on phonograph recordings when Cincinnati-born Mamie Smith (1883–1946) recorded "Crazy Blues," launching what would be termed the "race record" industry. Several midwestern companies entered this business, including Gennett, located in Richmond, Indiana, and Paramount, which began as a chair company in Grafton, Wisconsin, then relocated in Chicago. Other record companies—Vocalion, Okeh, Columbia, and, later, Bluebird and Decca—also recorded blues talent in Chicago, including artists such as the Indianapolis-based piano-guitar duo Leroy Carr (1905–1935) and Scrapper Blackwell (1903–1962), who enjoyed great success. They, like most blues artists in the Midwest, were born in the South and came north as part of the African American Great Migration. St. Louis, the major gateway city to Arkansas and Mississippi, was particularly rich in blues talent. Many southern-born piano players, including Roosevelt Sykes (1906–1984), Peetie Wheatstraw (1902–1941), and Walter Davis (1912–1963), worked the café, rent party, and speakeasy circuit developing a popular piano-guitar duet style. While St. Louis was a thriving blues town, musicians still went to Chicago to record, but by the late 1930s Chicago also developed its own club circuit, characterized by southern-born customers patronizing clubs that featured southern-born artists. In this manner part of African American Chicago remained an outpost of Mississippi Delta culture.

Farther west, in Kansas City, musicians also came from the South, including Oklahoma and Texas. Blues stalwarts Jimmy Rushing (1903–1972) and Jay McShann (b. 1916), for example, were born in Oklahoma. Blues shouter Wynonie Harris (1915–1969) came from Omaha, Nebraska, a wide-open territory town with its own black nightlife. But Kansas City remained the most wide-open city, at least during the reign of political boss Tom Pendergast. He kept the clubs open and the liquor flowing until 1938, an atmosphere conducive to blues and musical creativity. Kansas City natives included boogie pianist Pete Johnson (1904–1967), big-voiced Big Joe Turner (1911–1985), and saxophonist Charlie Parker (1920–1955). Jesse Stone, who hailed from Atchison, Kansas, also worked in Kansas City before moving east to become the primary architect of rhythm and blues (R & B). Together Kansas City musicians created a blues-based dance music that combined boogie, blues, jazz, and R & B, a major branch of the midwestern blues tradition distinct from the Delta-derived styles of St. Louis, Chicago and Detroit.

World War II curtailed recording activity but accelerated the migration from the South to the Midwest as African Americans found work in factories in Chicago, St. Louis, and Detroit. Immediately after the war new independent record labels such as King in Cincinnati and Aristocrat, later named Chess, in Chicago sprang up, catering to the desires of relatively affluent black consumers. The new blues, termed rhythm and blues in the late 1940s, enjoyed great success with artists like Chess's Muddy Waters (1915–1983) and Gary, Indiana's, VeeJay label's Jimmy Reed (1925–1976) becoming major recording stars. Guitarist John Lee Hooker (1917–2001) was born in Clarksdale, Mississippi, and moved first to Cincinnati, where he sang with several gospel quartets, before moving on to Detroit. Detroit's Hastings Street was a blues mecca teeming with small clubs featuring piano players and electric bands. There, Hooker was discovered playing house-rent parties to supplement his day job; his first record, released in 1948, went to Number 1 on the R & B charts. St. Louis, Missouri, and East St. Louis, Illinois, also maintained a vibrant blues community through the 1950s supporting artists like Clarksdale's Ike Turner (b. 1931) and fellow Mississippian Little Milton Campbell (b. 1934).

Indeed, pockets of blues activity sprang up wherever Delta culture took root, in Toledo and Cleveland, in Flint, Milwaukee, Minneapolis, and Waterloo. In the twenty-first century, blues still remains vital to the Midwest and central to the cultural tourism of the city of Chicago. As a form of popular music, blues draws thousands of fans to more than forty-five major blues festivals scattered across every midwestern state. And as ethnic expression, blues continue to be part of African American culture both in more modern forms of African American dance music and as part of a traditional heritage that continues to connect midwestern blacks to their southern roots.

Sources and Further Reading: David Honeyboy Edwards, as told to Janis Martinson and Michael Robert Frank, *The World Don't Owe Me Nothing* (1997); Nathan W. Pearson, Jr., *Goin' to Kansas City* (1987); Henry Townsend, as told to Bill Greensmith, *A Blues Life* (1999); Steven C. Tracy, *Going to Cincinnati* (1993).

Barry Lee Pearson
University of Maryland–College Park

Quinten Lotus Dickey (1911–1989)

A prolific composer of ballads and lyrical songs and a vigorous fiddle player and singer, Lotus Dickey per-

formed for audiences throughout Indiana, the Midwest, and the nation after being discovered and promoted by folklorists and folk-song enthusiasts in Bloomington, Indiana. His life was like a ballad—full of action, romance, tragedy, and poetry.

In 1911, Marion and Sarah Jane Dickey were anticipating a move from Muncie and what Marion perceived as the perils of the industrial revolution to rural Orange County, Indiana. Sarah was pregnant, and when Lotus was born, Marion chose the names Quinten Lotus for their fifth child; he chose Lotus from a passage in the *Bhagavad-Gita* that describes the lotus blossom as a symbol of purity and transcendence. A few months later, the family relocated on forty acres in a one-room log home on a dirt track named Grease Gravy Road. The living conditions were difficult for everyone but Lotus, who had never known anything different. He flourished in southern Indiana, drawing from nature and his own spiritual yearnings to compose songs and poetry. Although Lotus graduated with honors from Paoli High School in 1929, he could not afford further schooling. He worked in a basket factory near Paoli and continued to live on the family farm. In 1943 he married Dorothy Johnson, who had come to Indiana from the mountains of Kentucky. The stress of poverty and a large family was too great for Dorothy, who returned to her family after the birth of their eighth child. Lotus turned to music for solace. His creative output—more than three hundred songs at the time of his death—reveals a gift for rhyme and attention to detail, deep religious faith, and a complex and insightful worldview, with melodies alternately jaunty or haunting.

Lotus is remembered each year at the Lotus World Music and Arts Festival in Bloomington and at the Lotus Dickey Hometown Reunion in Paoli.

Sources and Further Reading: Dillon Bustin, "The Virtues of Lotus Dickey: 'Sitting at the Feet of Lotus,'" *Country Dance and Song* 20 (Mar. 1990); Nancy C. McEntire, Grey Larsen, and Janne Henshaw, eds., *The Lotus Dickey Songbook* (1995); Paul Tyler, "The True Story of 'Dickey's Discovery,'" in Lotus Dickey: *Fiddle Tunes from Orange County, Indiana*, vol. 1 (1992).

Nancy Cassell McEntire
Indiana State University

Gospel Music

The meaning of the term *gospel music* varies in American society. For African Americans, since the 1930s the term has referred to religious music that emerged in urban contexts following the massive influx of migrants from the rural South during the Great Migration surrounding World Wars I and II. Initially distinguishable from the Negro spiritual only by its instrumentation, gospel music has become the predominant musical expression in present-day African American worship.

First accompanied by only acoustic instruments, mainly piano, gospel music is now commonly heard with a range of instruments from electric organ, synthesizer, and rhythm section (bass guitar and drums) to saxophones, trumpets, lead guitar, and strings. Although much of the gospel music literature is composed, frequently other forms of hymnody are rearranged or reinterpreted through a system of aesthetic values that unifies all forms of African American music. Characterized by overlapping call-response, varying timbres, vocal and instrumental melismas, extensive melodic and textual repetition, parallel vocal harmonic movement, as well as a strong polyrhythmic foundation, gospel music comes alive through the performance dynamic, which utilizes the musical score as a mere point of departure.

For African Americans, gospel music was born in Chicago, the city that welcomed gospel pioneers Thomas Dorsey (1899–1993), Mahalia Jackson (1911–1972), and Roberta Martin (1907–1969) as part of the Great Migration. In 1932, Thomas Dorsey, viewed as the "father of gospel music," and a group of other seminal figures (Sallie Martin, Theodore Fry, Magnolia Lewis Butts) joined forces to found the National Convention of Gospel Choirs and Choruses for the express purpose of promoting this emergent genre. The original nucleus of two hundred participants now attracts an audience of thousands; it continues to meet annually in various cities across the United States for a week-long celebration of gospel music instruction and performance. The Dorsey Convention, as it is sometimes called, has served as a model for the creation of over a dozen similar organizations, including the largest, founded in 1968 by Grammy Award–winning James Cleveland in Detroit.

During gospel music's formative stage in the first third of the twentieth century, three distinct musical types forged the transition from the spiritual to what is now commonly referred to as "traditional" gospel music. First was the gospel hymn style pioneered by Methodist minister Charles Albert Tindley (1851–1933); second, the rural gospel style, which mirrors the rural blues genre and was typically performed by itinerant solo musicians who accompanied themselves on guitar or harmonica; and third, the holiness-Pentecostal style, strongly rooted in the Church of God in Christ, with its broad array of instrumental accompaniment including jugs, mandolins, trombones, and trumpets and a demonstrative style of worship that included religious dance.

Dorsey's designation as the father of gospel music results from his innovative blending of components from these three transitional gospel music forms, his role in creating interest and support for the genre through his leadership of the National Convention of Gospel Choirs and Choruses, and his prolific output of over five hundred compositions, including his most well-known, "Precious Lord" (1932), which was sung at the funerals of President Lyndon Johnson, Mahalia Jackson, and Martin Luther King, Jr. Performed by soloists and ensembles, choirs and quartets, gospel music embraces such perennial favorites as the Caravans and the Roberta Martin Singers, both groups that started in Chicago, as well as more contemporary artists whose sound often closely parallels that of current secular music—Kirk Franklin, Andraé Crouch, Yolanda Adams, Take 6, and the Gospel Gangstas.

Although the gospel music genre has been well defined within African American culture for approximately sixty years, a related yet distinct concept of gospel music also exists among white Americans. With its grounding in the nineteenth-century gospel hymn as popularized by such writers as Ira Sankey (1840–1908), of the famed Moody-Sankey evangelistic team, and Fannie Crosby (1820–1915), who penned several thousand gospel hymn texts, including the cross-cultural favorite "Blessed Assurance," the aesthetic value system as well as the majority of the repertoire associated with gospel music performance among white Americans is distinct from that of blacks. Called variously inspirational or contemporary Christian music in *Billboard* magazine, industry designations for gospel music as performed by whites also include labels such as bluegrass or southern gospel.

The concept of gospel music cannot be narrowly defined; the developmental trajectories of gospel music within the African American and white communities are both distinct and interrelated. The perception and marketing of the two expressions have been profoundly influenced by the racial and cultural politics of the region and the nation. As these musical forms evolve, so do the musicians who perform them as well as the principles that govern their interpretation.

Sources and Further Reading: Mellonee Burnim, "The Black Gospel Music Tradition: A Complex of Ideology, Aesthetic and Behavior," in Irene V. Jackson, ed., *More Than Dancing* (1985); Don Cusic, *Sound of Light* (1990); Harry Eskew and Paul Oliver, "Gospel Music," in Stanley Sadie, ed., *The New Grove Dictionary of Music and Musicians* (1980); C. Eric Lincoln and Lawrence H. Mamiya, *The Black Church in the African American Experience* (1990); Paul Oliver, *Songsters and Saints: Vocal Traditions on Race Records* (1984); Bernice Reagon, ed., *We'll Understand It Better By and By: Pioneering African American Gospel Composers* (1992).

Mellonee Burnim
Indiana University–Bloomington

Hiski Salomaa (1891–1957)

Born in 1891 at Kangasniemi, Finland, Hiski Salomaa arrived in the United States in 1909 hoping, like so many of his compatriots, to earn a living in the "Golden Land." He settled first in the Copper Country of Michigan, where he became known as a master tailor by Finnish and American customers.

He also earned a reputation as a singer and composer, first performing in family circles and on festive occasions, then on the stages of "Finn Halls" in the Midwest and beyond. Columbia Records of New York asked Salomaa to record some of his best-known songs, and eighteen were issued on 78 rpm recordings between 1927 and 1931, with accompaniment by such well-known Finnish American groups as Hänninen's Orchestra, Wäinö Kauppi's Orchestra, and Antti Kosola's Orchestra.

There were many singers among Finnish Americans who settled in the Midwest, and what separates Hiski Salomaa from such rivals as Arthur Kylander, Elmer Lamppa, or Leo Kauppi are his witty compositions about the lives of Finnish Americans. Salomaa based his humorous songs on actual situations, good and bad. The boastful swagger of itinerant workers dominates "*Lännen lokari*" ("The Logger of the West").

> Here is the Logger of the West's brushwoods
> I have been everywhere . . .
> I have sailed on seas and gone to continents . . .
> And everywhere those wild girls remember.

A sharp pen is evident in the immigrant housemaid's lament "*Tiskarin polkka*" ("Dishwashers Polka"):

> Those hags are yelling, drinking and eating
> Here I am only washing the dishes
> The coffee is nearly boiling over
> 'Cause I can't fly after everything.

Salomaa's compositions also drew masterfully upon Finnish folk-song tradition, connecting immigrant audiences with their distant homeland. His logger and housemaid are joined by memorialized wanderers and sweethearts of the old country. "Remulan häät" (Weddings at Remula) recalls

> When Matti of Remula was dancing at weddings
> Then all week he polkaed and waltzed
> They even made a new floor for the living room
> And they had six brides and bridegrooms.

Hiski Salomaa returned to Finland several times, and "The Logger of West" introduced *Metsäradio* (Logger Radio) on National Radio of Finland. He died on July 7, 1957, in New York.

Sources and Further Reading: "Hiski Salomaan kootut teokset 1927–1931," trans. Juha Niemelä, *SIBCD* 4 Siboney (1991); Olavi Larjamaa, interview by Juha Niemelä, Vehmaa, Finland (2000); Heikki Palaskari, "Lännen lokari," *Kansanmusiikki* 2 (1983).

Juha Niemelä
University of Turku, Finland

Singing Societies

Singing societies exist throughout the United States, but they originated in the Midwest and have been a prominent feature of midwestern towns and cities. German American singing societies were first founded in the 1830s and were the model for other groups such as Slovenian, Norwegian, and Polish Americans who sang songs celebrating an ethnic homeland along with American favorites. Many singing societies belong to regional and national networks of similar societies, holding annual conventions where choirs perform in a mass ensemble. One such German American singing festival held in Cincinnati in 1870 brought together eighteen hundred singers and an audience of twelve thousand; a concert hall was constructed to accommodate them.

The heyday of the singing society was the late nineteenth and early twentieth centuries, a time when social clubs such as the Elks, the Knights of Columbus, and the Masons were a significant part of middle- and working-class social life. By the mid-twentieth century many singing societies had folded because of dwindling membership, but most urban areas in the Midwest continue to have one or more active groups. For example, the Swedish Club of Detroit, the Nordkap Chorus of Minneapolis, the Swiss Singing Society of Milwaukee, the Zarja Singing Society of Cleveland, the Eintracht Singing Society of Dayton, and the Germania Männerchor of Evansville, Indiana, all continue to perform, host social events, and attract new members. Singing societies have ranged in size from small neighborhood groups to large institutions with nearly a thousand members and their own club hall. Because they host festivals and dances, singing societies have been important in fostering local dance bands. They have also provided a gathering space for informal singing and social activities such as card playing, celebration of ethnic foodways, festivals, and weddings. They remain important institutions for passing on and creating knowledge of an ethnic heritage, and for sharing the pleasures of music and social company.

Sources and Further Reading: Alan Burdette, "'Ein Prosit der Gemütlichkeit': The Traditionalization Process in a German American Singing Society," in Philip V. Bohlman

A Welsh Gymanfa Ganu in Wisconsin. Photo provided courtesy Wisconsin Historical Society, WHi-7180.

and Otto Holzapfel, eds., *Land without Nightingales* (2002); Suzanne Gail Snyder, "The Männerchor Tradition in the United States," Ph.D. diss., University of Iowa (1991).

Alan R. Burdette
Indiana University–Bloomington

Folk Narrative

Although the forms of midwestern folktales are universal, settlement patterns, historical circumstances, occupations, and the physical environment contributed to a blend of folk narratives unique to the Midwest. Chandler Gilman accurately portrays the heterogeneity of midwestern storytelling in *Legends of a Log Cabin* (1835) when he introduces his narrators as a Native American, a Frenchman, a backwoodsman, an Englishman, a Yankee, an African American, and a Methodist circuit rider. Already at this early date Gilman observed that midwestern folk narrative is a patchwork of tales from various cultures: ethnic, regional, religious, and occupational, among others. Besides identifying some major contributors to midwestern folktales, Gilman, in re-creating a social context in a log cabin, also recognized that storytelling is a process, not just texts.

As in other regions, the earliest known midwestern oral narratives are myths and other tales of Native Americans. In Michigan's Upper Peninsula, Richard Dorson (1952) collected secular versions of ancient Native American myths of the trickster Wenabozho, who is not only a lecher or clown but also the creator of life and ruler of the earth. Although most European settlers generally did not borrow and adapt Native American tales, Native Americans profoundly influenced at least one type of narrative recounted throughout the Midwest, place-name legends, and Native Americans freely borrowed and adapted European tales.

Early French travelers, traders, missionaries, and settlers mingled with Native Americans, adapting many aspects of Native American cultures—including narratives of the human-eating Piasa Bird in the Illinois and Mississippi River area. French, settling in what was then upper Louisiana, established towns throughout the Midwest and told *contes* they brought with them about 'Tit Jean as well as legends of the *loup garou* (werewolf), *lutin* (diminutive night riders, and sometimes groomers, of horses), *chasse galerie* (phantom canoe), and *feu follet* (will-o'-the-wisp). Joseph Médard Carrière (1937) collected contes about the hero 'Tit Jean from French descendants living in Old Mines, Missouri, and Marie Caroline Watson Hamlin (*Legends of le Détroit*, 1884) published legendary accounts of the loup garou, *le feu follet*, and *la chasse galerie*. These migratory legends told in the old French villages incorporate familiar motifs from France, such as disenchantment of a werewolf by drawing blood,

❖ **Italian Storyteller Clementina Todesco**

As a youngster, Clementina Todesco worked long hours in her Alpine village, planting and harvesting crops, caring for her father's cows, and helping prepare dinner for family members and friends who gathered in the evenings in the warmth of the stables. Here men repaired farm implements, and women busied themselves in the *filo*, the spinning of hemp from flax on spindles. Others gossiped, shared folk cures, disciplined children, engaged in courtship, and even told magic stories. Esteemed local raconteurs spun tales of fear of abandonment arising from living in families with stepmothers, common in these villages where women's childbirth mortality rate was high.

Folktales dramatized familial loyalty, respect for hierarchies, and resourcefulness. In the stable, Clementina learned her craft. Years later, when she emigrated to the United States with her husband and her daughter Bruna, she brought her tales with her. The family followed the common occupational trails, first to New York City for construction; then to Export, Pennsylvania, to the coal mines; then, finally, to Detroit, for construction again. The location for storytelling became the kitchen table, where the family would gather before bedtime. When the children were grown, Clementina recounted personal-experience narratives about World War I, when her village became a base for the Austrian army as it battled the Italians in the Alps. Stories of starvation and brutality replaced stories of abandonment by stepparents. Clementina's immigrant voyage evolves in her later years into another journey, following the retirement trail to Arizona. Clementina's life as an immigrant storyteller in the Midwest served as the basis for Elizabeth Mathias and Richard Raspa's ethnographic study *Italian Folktales in America* (1985).

Richard Raspa
Wayne State University, Michigan

Elizabeth Mathias
Charlottesville, Virginia

Sources: Luisa Del Giudice, ed., *Studies in Italian American Folklore* (1993); Frances M. Malpezzi and William M. Clements, *Italian-American Folklore* (1992); Dorothy Noyes, *Uses of Tradition: Arts of Italian Americans in Philadelphia* (1989).

but often they are specifically set in familiar midwestern locales. French Canadians whose families moved to the Upper Peninsula of Michigan from Quebec Province in the 1880s and 1890s to work in the lumber camps recounted the same kinds of contes and legends to Dorson.

Contes, called märchen by folklorists and fairy tales by others, are folktales involving magic, wonders, and unpromising heroes who win fame and fortune, normally out of all proportion to the deed, in an unreal world of improbable characters and creatures. The unpromising hero is kind, shrewd, or, in most cases, just plain lucky. After the American Revolution, Scotch-Irish storytellers brought Jack tales, their versions of 'Tit Jean tales, across the Alleghenies into the southern parts of Ohio, Indiana, Illinois, and, later, Missouri. Other settlers from western Pennsylvania and Maryland followed the Ohio River into Ohio, Indiana, and Illinois, bringing with them similar narratives, including many humorous tales influenced by British and Irish traditions but nurtured in the New World.

During this period and throughout the next century, the humorous tall tale—often dealing with the outdoors (hunting, fishing, rough weather, fertile soil, big crops, fabulous animals)—was very popular among hunters, fishers, farmers, boatmen, and others living on the Midwest frontier. As Ernest W. Baughman (1966) shows, motifs of humorous lies and exaggera-

tion have been the most popular ones in North America. Many of Baughman's tall-tale motifs deal with the legendary midwestern logger Paul Bunyan, who quickly passed from a folk hero of loggers to a mass-culture hero of all Americans; however, printed texts of Bunyan's exploits in juvenile literature fail to capture the tall tale's art, which lies in its manner of telling, not especially in its content. Ore boats on the Great Lakes and steamboats on rivers spawned tall stories, too. Along the great rivers, comic legends were told of keelboatmen and ring-tailed roarers, especially about Mike Fink, hero of midwestern boatmen. Roger Welsch's collection (1972) of tall tales from the Great Plains clearly shows that international narratives have been adapted to regional climate, topography, and conditions and that the tall-tale tradition is still alive in the Midwest.

Other humorous midwestern folk narratives include jokes about animals, married couples, drunks, lazy people, ethnic and regional groups (often incorporating age–old motifs of the wise and foolish), the clergy and religious figures, occupational groups, and contemporary pastimes such as golf. James P. Leary's representative collection of jokes from the upper Midwest (2001) illustrates that many midwestern jokes were brought from Europe and have versions throughout the United States, but in the Midwest they have been adapted to people, places, occupations, and events of the region. Dialect jokes about the Scandinavian stock characters Ole and Lena and their Finnish counterparts Eino and Toivo are especially representative of contemporary ethnic humor in the upper Midwest.

African Americans moving north before and especially after the Civil War brought with them all kinds of narratives, including many animal tales, in which animals talk and act like humans, though generally there is some connection between the personality of an animal in a tale and the actual animal. Animal tales often deal with a clever animal tricking a stupid animal or are etiological, explaining physical or behavioral characteristics of a particular animal, such as an Indiana variant of "Dog Loses His Patent Right," which explains why dogs examine each other under their tails. Though many old-time animal tales have been supplanted by children's storybooks and animated cartoons, off-color jokes about animals are very popular in the Midwest.

Around the beginning of the nineteenth century, Yankees and Yorkers joined the movement west by way of the Great Lakes and settled first in Ohio and Michigan, then in the northern parts of Indiana and Illinois, and finally in Wisconsin and Iowa. These settlers spoke English and easily mingled with one another, swapping tales among themselves as well as with other groups living in the region. At the same time, Germans by way of Pennsylvania began pouring into the Midwest from Ohio to Missouri, adding yet another body of lore and a third European language to the already diverse body of midwestern folk narrative. By 1850 Germans accounted for over half of the foreign-born population in some midwestern states, and they spun tales, first in their native language and later in English, of coming to the Midwest, of pioneer preachers and priests, of place and personal naming, and of witches and the devil, among other kinds of narratives.

What Gilman didn't know in 1835 was that migration to the Midwest would remain constant throughout the nineteenth and the twentieth centuries. Many folktales, including more Old World märchen, were brought to the Midwest directly from Europe from 1880 to 1920 by another wave of English, Scottish, Welsh, Cornish, and Irish immigrants, as well as by a considerable number of Scandinavians, Poles, Italians, Lithuanians, Hungarians, and other immigrants from southern and central Europe, who settled in the region to work in mills, mines, farms, and factories. Susie Hoogasian-Villa (1966) published a hundred of these Old World tales that she collected between 1940 and 1942 from Armenians working in or about the auto industry in Detroit. At that time most of her informants had lived twenty or thirty years in the Midwest, but the tales, retaining Armenian or Turkish names and places, show very little localization to the Midwest. At the same time, but in the small coal-mining community of Blanford, Indiana, Anthony Milanovich (1971) collected similar Old World magic tales from Serbian immigrants. Sometimes, these Old World märchen and novelle (much like märchen, though longer, more realistic, and more romantic) are transformed into jokes or legends, more familiar forms of contemporary midwestern oral narratives. Thus, one novella found throughout the Midwest, "The Taming of the Shrew," usually is collected as a joke, and another novella, "The Seemingly Dead Revives," reported in several midwestern states, generally is collected as a legend. Apparently, märchen and novelle must transform into other genres to survive, for today in the Midwest, as in other places, märchen and novelle can't compete with mass media, which exploit the same formulas and serve the same needs as the old folktales.

In the twentieth century, more immigrants from Europe, Asia, and Mexico brought with them still other bodies of narrative in other languages, such as the tales of the Hmong of Laos in Minnesota and of Mexican Americans and other Spanish speakers in East Chicago and other midwestern cities. Earlier, many midwestern tales were collected in rural areas or small close-knit communities unified by language and, often, national origin; however, today in midwestern cities there are many folk groups, each unique in its retention of folk narratives and assimilation of other narrative traditions. Anecdotes and tales of some of these ethnic groups and steelworkers in Gary—as well as in neighboring cities of East Chicago, Hammond, and Whiting—in Dorson's *Land of the Millrats* (1981) deal with the urban experiences there: crime on the streets, flight from the city, and working conditions in the steel mills.

Today, along with jokes, legends—oral prose narratives set in this world in the recent past with humans as main characters and regarded as fact by the people who pass them along—are the most popular forms of midwestern folktales. Legends may be sacred or secular, but because of settlement history, most midwestern legends are secular, though saint's legends and other religious legends have been collected in the Midwest from Orthodox and Roman Catholics. Most midwestern legends fall into one of four general groups: supernatural and religious, personal, place, and modern (also called urban-belief tales). Personal legends of famous midwesterners, local eccentrics, and outlaws have been especially popular. Each state has its heroes, but legends of some heroes, such as the outlaw Jesse James, are spun from Missouri, where he was born, north to South Dakota, where he escaped from robbing a bank in Minnesota, and east to Indiana, where allegedly he had several hideouts.

Personal legends are stories about others told in third person. Personal-experience stories told in first person are called memorates. Memorates were first defined as single-episodic narratives of a personal encounter with the supernatural, but American folklorists now call all personal experience tales memorates. Many family stories, easily collected today in the Midwest, are either legends or memorates. Dorson's sagamen in *Bloodstoppers and Bearwalkers* boast about their strength, endurance, and cleverness in personal-experience tales from the Upper Peninsula. Family legends, memorates, and oral history comprise the raw material for an account of Wisconsin farm life in Roger E. Mitchell's monograph (1984). Besides settlement history and occupations, the physical environment also has had an impact on contemporary midwestern legends and memorates. Larry Danielson (1990), for instance, examines commonplace stories about tornados in the Midwest and their relation to regional consciousness and identity. Especially common are short matter-of-fact narratives describing striking and unusual consequences of a tornado, sometimes sprinkled with a bit of humor, such as an account of an airborne police car caught in a Kansas twister. A more somber family legend tells of a woman sucked up the chimney by a tornado.

Märchen, novelle, animal tales, jokes, myths, legends, and memorates—universal genres found in other regions of the United States as well as in other countries—are the main forms of midwestern folk narratives. Although various national/ethnic, regional, and occupational groups brought with them the folk narratives of their countries, regions, and occupations, once settled in the Midwest they shared, borrowed, adapted, and blended the imported material to new settings and situations and created new stories inspired by historical circumstances, occupations, and the physical environment in the region. The Native American heritage; the transplantation, acculturation, and blending of various European, Asian, southern, Yorker, Yankee, African American, and Hispanic cultures in a new environment; and the agricultural and industrial experience contributed to a body of folk narratives that we may term "midwestern."

Sources and Further Reading: Ronald L. Baker, *Hoosier Folk Legends* (1982); Ernest W. Baughman, *Type and Motif Index of the Folktales of England and North America* (1966); Joseph Médard Carrière, *Tales from the French Folk-Lore of Missouri* (1937); Larry Danielson, "Tornado Stories in the Breadbasket: Weather and Regional Identity," in Barbara Allen and Thomas J. Schlereth, eds., *Sense of Place: American Regional Cultures* (1990); Richard Mercer Dorson, *Bloodstoppers and Bearwalkers: Folk Traditions of the Upper Peninsula* (1952); Marie Caroline Watson Hamlin, *Legends le Détroit* (1884); Susie Hoogasian–Villa, *100 Armenian Tales and Their Folkloristic Relevance* (1966); James P. Leary, *So Ole Says to Lena* (2001); Anthony Milanovich, "Serbian Tales from Blan-

ford," *Indiana Folklore* 4 (1971); Roger E. Mitchell, "From Fathers to Sons: A Wisconsin Family Farm," *Midwestern Journal of Language and Folklore* 10 (Spring/Fall 1984); Roger Welsch, *Shingling the Fog and Other Plains Lies* (1972).

Ronald L. Baker
Indiana State University

Dialect Jokes

Traditional humorous narratives featuring the regional-, or class-, or "native"-language inflected dialect of a stock character in juxtaposition with Standard American English define the essence of dialect jokes. Such jokes emerged in the Midwest out of white–American Indian contact as the former portrayed the latter via monosyllables and malaprops. In Wisconsin, the name Sheboygan, for example, was attributed facetiously to a chief disappointed in his wife's delivery of yet another son: "Ugh, she boy 'gain!" Lower midwesterners likewise have long imitated the speech of southern "hillbillies" or "briers" crossing the Ohio River as economic migrants, while white folks' jocular mimicry of African American patois persists.

Used by cultural outsiders to signal difference and unease, dialect jokes also connote commonality and affection for cultural insiders. Comic tales with an added and dropped *h* still echo among Cornish in upper midwestern mining communities: a tool handle supposedly either "hoak, hash, or helm" is actually "'ickory." Meanwhile those of Norwegian and Swedish descent savor updated tales of Ole and Lena rendered in their ancestors' "broken English": Ole scoffs at George W. Bush's boast of an Ivy League education, "Yah, vell, aye been to yail too."

The polyglot culture of Indian and immigrant farmers, fishers, loggers, and miners extending from the Upper Peninsula of Michigan through northern Wisconsin and Minnesota has particularly fostered the egalitarian exchange of dialect stories by raconteurs adept at shifting from Cornish to Finnish to French to Italian to Ojibwe to "Scandihoovian" to Slavic contributions to their region's shared vernacular. Indeed, fieldwork in Michigan's "Upper Peninsula" inspired Richard Dorson to proclaim the dialect story a "new form of American folklore."

Sources and Further Reading: Richard M. Dorson, "Dialect Stories of the Upper Peninsula: A New Form of American Folklore," *Journal of American Folklore* 61 (Apr.–June 1948); James P. Leary, *So Ole Says to Lena* (2001); George T. Springer, *Yumpin' Yimminy* (1932).

James P. Leary
University of Wisconsin–Madison

❖ The Lank

I understand that when old Luigi first came over from Italy, he was put on the job in the mine with Heikki as his partner. Heikki was an experienced miner. He had been in this country maybe ten years or so. And there was some communication problem between these two immigrants from different countries.

But at one point, Heikki was holding up that big old drilling machine, and he wanted to brace it. So he pointed at a board that was leaning up against the wall of the stope. And he said, *"Luigi, give it for me that 'lank."* Well, Luigi didn't know what he was talking about. But wanting to be helpful, he picked up a pickax and he handed it over.

And Heikki said, *"No, no, I don't want that pickax. Give it that 'lank."* Luigi looked around and picked up a dynamite box and handed that over. *"No, no, don't give it the box. Give it the 'lank."*

Well, this went on for some time with Heikki struggling to hold that drilling machine, until through the process of elimination, Luigi finally handed him the plank. And Heikki took it and braced the machine. And he said, *"Yah, that's what I wanted was that 'lank."*

When Luigi finally found out what it was that Heikki had been asking for, he got rather irritated and excited, and he jumped up and down. And he said, *"Whatsa matter you? You been this country ten, fifteen years and already you can'ta say planka?"*

Heikki is a common Finnish name and immigrant Finnish Americans typically were unable to conjoin two consonants at the beginning of a word, while Italian immigrants often ended words in a vowel. This joke has been widely told in mining communities from Michigan to Minnesota. Performed by the Finnish American storyteller Oren Tikkanen, Calumet, Michigan, March 1984; recorded by Michael Loukinen.

The Swede in the Hoghouse

This Swede went and got drunk and couldn't find his way into the house. So he got down into the hoghouse and opened up the door and lay down in the straw and went to sleep. And he woke up. He thought somebody was sleeping alongside him. It was a big sow.

So he poked it with his elbow and said, *"Ar du Svensk?"*

And the old sow says, *"Norsk, norsk."*

Performed by the Swedish American storyteller Edwin Pearson; recorded by folklorist Jim Leary, Maple, Wisconsin, 1987. "Ar du Svensk" means "Are you Swedish?" The sound "Norsk, norsk" may suggest a pig's grunts, but the words mean "Norwegian, Norwegian"—and so this dialect story connotes the upper midwestern rivalries between Swedes and Norwegians.

Source: James P. Leary, ed., *So Ole Says to Lena: Folk Humor of the Upper Midwest* (2001) 66.

Monsters and Tall Tales

Monster and tall-tale narratives emphasize the element of the unique, the unfamiliar, the grotesque, and the dangerous found in both the Midwest's pioneer settlement conditions and its contemporary, industrial environment. The monster of these tales may be a realistic or an imaginary creature. It may resemble other humans or animals, their antecedents or their hybrids. Viewed as a marvel or a prodigy, the monster is extraordinary, abnormal, or alien, most often in terms of its huge size, its fearsome appearance, or its terrifying behavior. The tales take the forms of sighting accounts, adventurous personal experiences, quest narratives, legends, jokes, tall tales, and hoaxes.

The most common monster tales for the frontier family involved the understandable attack of the panther, that is, the enormous cat. Panther-panic narratives persist to this day. Legends about humans who transform into wolves likewise recur throughout the region, especially in the Great Lakes and Mississippi Valley areas, where comparable French and Native American traditions merge in regionally distinct tales of human-animal transformers who terrorize, enact revenge, or devour the living. Nineteenth-century legends about a Grosse Pointe werewolf in Michigan leave their marks around Lake St. Clair, while 1990s tales of Elkhorn's Bray Road Beast in southern Wisconsin report a werewolf who frightens motorists, thwarts burglars, and even endorses a congressional candidate. In northern Wisconsin, Rhinelander's Hodag, a dog covered by a horsehide made into the shape of a prehistoric dinosaur, began as a lumberjack tall tale and hoax in the 1890s and lives on as a mythical community icon.

Tales of sea serpents or lake-dwelling monsters, also widespread throughout the Midwest, further manifest all of the narrative patterns in service to the community and its local economy. Civic boosterism motivates the Alkali Lake Monster in Nebraska and Ohio's South Bay Bessie, also known as the Lake Erie Monster, to tale tellers in northeastern Ohio from Toledo to Huron to Vermilion. Churubusco, Indiana, has a five-hundred-pound snapping turtle known as Oscar, the Beast of 'Busco, once said to have swallowed a cow. A Turtle Days festival continuously commemorates this creation of local observation, tall-tale telling, native American tradition, and newspaper hoaxing from its 1949 inception to the present day in what residents proclaim "the world's biggest celebration for a turtle."

Midwestern humanlike monsters often resemble the prehistoric hominoids commonly known in the Northwest as Bigfoot. These become Momo in eastern Missouri, the Big Muddy Monster of southern Illinois, and the Sister Lakes Monster in Michigan. The humanoid animal known in Ohio as the Loveland Frog sometimes resembles a frog, sometimes an iguana, and bears some resemblance to the Creature from the Black Lagoon, from a popular horror film of the 1950s.

The best-known human monster in the Midwest is the giant Paul Bunyan. The predominant literary evidence portrays Bunyan as a sympathetic, sentimental, and lovable character, sharing with the folk tradition the tall-tale tendencies toward amusement through exaggeration and overstatement.

Sources and Further Reading: Richard Mercer Dorson, *Bloodstoppers and Bearwalkers: Folk Traditions of the Upper Peninsula* (1952); John A. Gutowski, "The Beast of 'Busco: An American Tradition," *Midwestern Folklore* 24 (Spring/Fall 1998); Daniel Hoffman, *Paul Bunyan: Last of the Frontier Demigods* (1952).

John A. Gutowski
Saint Xavier University, Illinois

State Jokes

Jokes told by midwesterners address many of the common experiences and shared anxieties of living in the various regions of the Midwest. A great deal of midwestern humor comes in the form of numskull jokes, those that attribute extreme stupidity to particular groups. Although numskull jokes are not exclusive to the region, the ethnic diversity and geography of the different states in this region have led to the creation of jokes that are uniquely midwestern.

For example, Ronald L. Baker (1986) notes that Kentuckian jokes are very popular in southern Indiana. "These jokes told by contemporary Hoosiers permit a reversal of roles, allowing Hoosiers to discount their southern roots and identify more closely with other northerners, who often feel superior to southerners." Similarly, in Ohio there are several jokes about Kentucky "Briers" and West Virginians, in which the people from the states directly south of the Ohio River are characterized as dirty, uneducated, and often racist hillbillies who have uncommon difficulty trying to figure out even the simplest things.

Farther north, where the numskull jokes have tended to target ethnic stereotypes, the jokes express different anxieties. As immigrants came into the Midwest, especially into northern Indiana and the states of the upper Midwest, they experienced economic competition and cultural change, and in the past jokes targeting such groups as the Poles and the Irish have expressed hostility toward these apparent threats.

Swedes and Norwegians are prominent ethnic groups in Minnesota, Wisconsin, and Michigan's Upper Peninsula, and there is a joke cycle in these areas featuring Ole and Lena, stock characters who fulfill the numskull role of bumbling newcomers and also demonstrate the significant influence that Scandinavians have had on the culture of the region, including new dialects, the temperance of the Lutheran church, and the introduction of different foods. Similarly, the high population of Finns in these areas has led to the emergence of a joke cycle with the stock characters Eino, Toivo, and Helvi. The Finnish presence is so prominent in the Michigan's Upper Peninsula that "Yoopers," inhabitants of this area, are often characterized in jokes as embracing their Finnish heritage by speaking "Finglish," having saunas, and eating Finnish foods.

The numskull jokes in midwestern states have recently begun to focus on university rivalries, so that people from The Ohio State University, for example, place University of Michigan students and graduates in the role of the fool, and vice versa. Sports rivalries are also a prevalent theme in interstate jokes, where the ultimate insult among sports fans occurs when teams such as the Hoosiers from Indiana or the Cornhuskers from Nebraska are presented in the jokes as athletically inferior to their rival teams.

In addition, in Wisconsin there is a cycle of jokes targeting "FIBs" (Fucking Illinois Bastards), an in-state term referring to "intruders" from Illinois with their aggressive big-city mentality. These jokes not only address a rivalry between neighboring states, they draw on the stereotypes of the different lifestyles of the inhabitants of each state. Clearly, the different types of state jokes provide a glimpse of the unique experience of living in the diverse states and regions of the Midwest.

Sources and Further Reading: Ronald L. Baker, *Jokelore* (1986); James P. Leary, ed., *So Ole Says to Lena*, 2nd ed. (2001).

Sheila Bock
The Ohio State University–Columbus

James Douglas "J.D." Suggs (1887?–1955)

James Douglas "J.D." Suggs, a raconteur of traditional African American folk tales and folk songs, was born in Kosciusko, Attala County, Mississippi, either on March 10, 1887, as he reported to folklorist Richard Dorson, or on March 9, 1886, according to Suggs's death certificate at the Michigan Department of Health. Suggs came from racially mixed family lines of African, European, and American Indian descent.

Suggs began his long and varied work life as a county prison guard in 1907 before joining the Rabbit Foot Minstrel Show, which traveled from Alabama to North Dakota. He played semiprofessional baseball from 1908 to 1909 and worked out of Memphis as a brakeman for the Illinois Central Railroad. Working as a sandhog in 1912, he helped build the Harland Bridge on the Mississippi River before returning to Mississippi, where he was employed as a cook and nurse on the Bishop plantation.

Suggs joined the massive migration of African Americans who left the South to settle in the urban North. He moved his family to Chicago in 1940, then to Vandalia, Michigan, in 1947 before settling in Calvin Township in 1950, where he worked construction. At the time of his death, June 19, 1955, Suggs lived in Niles, Howard Township, Michigan. His daughter Martha, editor of *Suggs Black Backtracks*, established the Suggs Underground Railroad Museum in Vandalia.

Among the most prolific and charismatic storytellers in African American folklore, Suggs told Dorson 170 oral narratives including animal stories; "Old Marster and John" tales; slavery, hoodoo, and Jim Crow tales; and traditional folk songs. Two of his most important, archetypal tales are "Nicodemus from Detroit" and "The Mermaid."

Sources and Further Reading: Richard M. Dorson, "The Astonishing Repertoire of James Douglas Suggs," *Michigan History* 40 (June 1956); Richard M. Dorson, "Negro Folksongs in Michigan from the Repertoire of J.D. Suggs," *Folklore and Folk Music Archivist* 9 (Fall 1966); Richard M. Dorson, *Negro Folktales in Michigan* (1956); John F. Moe, "'Your Life Is a Book': The Artistic Legacy of Elijah Pierce," in Norma Roberts, ed., *Elijah Pierce: Woodcarver* (1992).

John F. Moe
The Ohio State University–Columbus

Supernatural Legends

Folk narratives focusing on otherworldly topics constitute the realm of supernatural legends. Although the line between "natural" and "supernatural" may be drawn differently for different individuals, groups, and time periods, folklorist Wayland D. Hand's 1971 subject categorization of American folk legends is still a useful place to begin. Hand notes that legends about the paranormal are global yet have distinctive regional patterns in the United States. What is unique about midwestern supernatural legendry is the extent to which the region has drawn international, national, and other regions' stories within its own borders.

Although Hand debated whether Native American legends should be considered in his classification system, these stories are strands in the complex fabric of midwestern beliefs. Legends about a cannibal ghost, known among Ojibwe throughout the upper Midwest, highlighted people's fears of meeting, or becoming, the "windigo." Legends about "bearwalks" or "bearwalkers" described evil shape-shifters. Archie Megenuph, a Potawatomi from Michigan's Upper Peninsula, told folklorist Richard Dorson in the 1940s: "There were five or six bearwalks here from Wisconsin. We shot them. They can't kill a white man but they can kill Indians, so we had to get them first. . . . The Chippewas [Ojibwe] and the Winnebagoes [Ho-Chunk] go in for that still—they're pagans." Megenuph's comments, possibly tongue in cheek, indicate a dialectic of belief that folklorists Linda Dégh and Andrew Vázsonyi note as the hallmark of most legend-telling sessions.

Hand reports that European immigrants brought stories of some "creatures of lower mythology" with them—fairy folk, trolls, vampires, and werewolves—that reveal distinctive ethnic settlement patterns, belief structures, and social interaction in the Midwest. French settlers told the old stories of *le loup garou*, or "*le roup garou*," the werewolf, along the Detroit River, connecting them to Missouri Creoles and Louisiana Cajuns. The werewolf legends of métis tellers in Michigan's Upper Peninsula merged the Old World with the New as they told of men who could shapeshift into wolves, dogs, oxen, or bears.

Traditional legends about midwestern witches, although not as common as they once were, follow the classic European American pattern in which an old

❖ The Roup Garou

Old Sarah [Champain] was very sick all the time, she was choking. Every night she took ill and had to go to bed, when a great big *ghibou* [owl] came and perched on her clothes line. It came the same hour every night. It is unusual, you know, to see an owl right in the city. Mrs. Champain got the doctor and the priest but they couldn't tell her what was wrong.

The clothes line ran right out under the window—she was in an upstairs apartment—right next to my aunt's house. The door of my aunt's room was open in the summer, and she would see the owl when she went to take the clothes in. She told her nephew to kill the *ghibou* because he would get the chickens. So he takes a shotgun and shoots the *ghibou*. He sees it flop over, puts the gun away, and goes to pick up the *ghibou*, to cut it up for a feather duster. But he can't find it. He goes round the house to the highway, down the trail—the building was set up on the hill—and sees old Mrs. Lozon, lame trying to crawl up the hill. She'd been perfectly all right the day before, but now she could hardly walk. Charlie Lottie picked her up in a rig and took her over to one of her sisters. She never got over it—she stayed there till she died.

The man, Jimmy Vallier, ran back, all excited and numb, crying, "That was no *ghibou*, that was a *roup-garou*!" Jim said he was afraid to follow after Mrs. Lozon because she might do something to him, to keep her secret. My aunt laughed and said, "That was only a *ghibou*; I saw it right out the door." My aunt changed her mind later, though.

And do you know, when Mrs. Lozon died, old Sarah got better right away.

Note: *Loup garou* is standard French for werewolf. *Roup garou* is a dialectical variation used in St. Ignace.

Collected by Richard M. Dorson from Jane Goudreau, of French Canadian and Chippewa descent in St. Ignace, Michigan.

Source: Reprinted by permission of the publisher from *Bloodstoppers and Bearwalkers: Folk Traditions of the Upper Peninsula* by Richard M. Dorson, p. 75, Cambridge, Mass: Harvard University Press. Copyright 1952 by the President and Fellows of Harvard College; Copyright 1980 by Richard M. Dorson.

woman makes her neighbors' milk cows go dry and their butter not churn. Likewise, both European and American Indian legends persist and sometimes intertwine regarding sorcerers who affect victims with potent charms. Contemporary legends about witches' covens, neopagans, and Satanic cults, and rumors of Church of Satan–owned corporations and businesses, currently of national import, impact the Midwest. When folklorist Bill Ellis interviewed teenagers, including in Ohio and Indiana, about their own stories of using the Ouija board to call up the Devil, he found that these informal initiations have more in common with other ritualized play forms than with Satanic abuse.

Migration of African Americans from the South; Hispanic Americans from the Southwest; and immigrants from Asia, the Middle East, and southeastern Europe to the Midwest may also account for the vibrancy of supernatural legend–telling. Dorson felt that he had "struck gold" in western Michigan when African American tellers spoke to him of the Devil as trickster, conjurer, voodoo, or hoodoo, and of witch riding in the 1950s. More recently, folklorist Mark Glazer reports that the traditional southwestern Hispanic legend "The Devil at the Dance" (in which a young girl chooses a handsome stranger with a cloven hoof as dance partner to her peril) has also been recorded in Ohio and Indiana, "home of middle America . . . where such legends, beliefs and related folklore may well have been unexpected until re-

cently." Dorson also recorded evil-eye narratives from "a spectrum of ethnics" in his Gary, Hammond, and East Chicago, Indiana, fieldwork in the 1970s. One account represents the Mediterranean mosaic in the urban heartland: "And also I had a sister who had beautiful eyes, beautiful. So some Armenian lady said, 'Oh, boy, what beautiful eyes!' just like that, without saying mashallah [May God protect you]. My sister had her eyes operated on twice, and almost went blind afterward."

When Hand wrote, "Ghostlore and the realm of the dead remain a persistent and inexhaustible source of folk legend, and there have been in recent years many modern innovations on old themes" he was referring to the widest web of supernatural legends in the Midwest. Traditional ghost stories have been reported from every midwestern state, making the region a "Haunted Heartland" whose landscape marks personal and collective memories. Accounts of personal experiences with death warnings are probably the most widespread "memorates" of the supernatural. In one example, an Indiana housewife speaks of an elderly neighbor who always used to come over to see the children in her family when she was young. One day their mother saw the old lady come up the walk so "all us kids ran to the door, and Grandma Newman wasn't there." They learned the next day that she had died.

Although folklorist Jan Harold Brunvand notes that few contemporary legends contain supernatural themes, those that do are well known in the Midwest.

His own study of versions of "The Vanishing Hitch-hiker" shows that the legend of a young girl returned from the dead who disappears after a driver picks her up is probably the most famous of the stories that blend modern car culture with international ghostly themes. Chicago historian Ursula Bielski notes the connection between the widespread legend and Chicago-area stories of "Resurrection Mary" (in which a ghost of a young woman, killed on her way home from a dance hall in the 1930s and buried in Resurrection Cemetery, haunts Archer Avenue). Whatever the attitudes toward legendary accounts, supernatural lore is characterized by its density, its variety, and its prevalence in the Midwest.

Sources and Further Reading: Ronald Baker, *Hoosier Folk Legends* (1982); Ursula Bielski, *Chicago Haunts* (1998); Jan Harold Brunvand, *The Vanishing Hitchhiker* (1981); Richard Mercer Dorson, *Bloodstoppers and Bearwalkers: Folk Traditions of the Upper Peninsula* (1952); Richard Mercer Dorson, *Land of the Millrats* (1981); Richard Mercer Dorson, *Negro Folktales in Michigan* (1956); Mark Glazer, introduction to "Evil and the Devil in Folklore," ed. Mark Glazer, special issue, *Contemporary Legend* 4 (1994); Wayland D. Hand, ed., *American Folk Legend* (1971); Beth Scott and Michael Norman, *Haunted Heartland* (1985).

Janet L. Langlois
Wayne State University, Michigan

Wenabozho

Also known as Manabozho, Manabus, Nanabush, Nanapush, and Wenebojo, Wenabozho is a hero and trickster of Cree, Menominee, Mesquakie, Ojibwe, Potawatomi, and other Algonquian-speaking peoples. Wenabozho is not only a serious mythological being who shape-shifts; battles with underwater spirits; fashions the earth; gives plants and animals their characteristic features; and favors his people with fire, maple sugar, tobacco, and their most sacred spiritual teachings, but also a comic buffoon whose wanton adventures emphasize cunning, the fragility of the social order, and the necessity of laughter in a dangerous, often chaotic, world.

Wenabozho was first introduced extensively to non-Algonquian peoples by Henry Rowe Schoolcraft, an Indian agent in Sault Ste. Marie, Michigan, who heard traditional stories from, among others, his mother-in-law, Ozhaagaskodewekwe, of the LaPointe, Wisconsin, Ojibwe. Schoolcraft's portrayal of what he dubbed "the Indian Hercules" inspired Henry Wadsworth Longfellow's celebrated epic poem, although Longfellow substituted the Iroquoian name *Hiawatha*. A minor presence in mainstream American literature, Wenabozho persists as the major figure in a formal cycle of tales told in the Ojibwe medicine lodge. He is also sustained through everyday narrative associations as elders acquaint youngsters with explanations for the grebe's red eyes and stooped back, the birch tree's black streaks, the kingfisher's tuft, the landscape's features, indeed, with the construction of the natural world. And he has been transported by artful Native American storytellers, educators, and activists into tales of the fur trade, the lumber camp, the modern world: confounding missionaries and psychiatrists, battling Paul Bunyan, offering a uniquely American Indian voice of humorous sagacity.

Sources and Further Reading: Victor Barnouw, *Wisconsin Chippewa Myths and Tales* (1977); Henry Rowe Schoolcraft, *Algic Researches*, 2 vols. (1839); Christopher Vecsey and John F. Fisher, "The Ojibwa Creation Myth: An Analysis of Its Structure and Content," *Temenos* 20 (1984).

James P. Leary
University of Wisconsin–Madison

Ethnic Folklore

Ethnic folklore is a resource for understanding the cultural life of the Midwest. Serious interest in documenting midwestern ethnic folk traditions did not begin until the early twentieth century. At that time, southern and eastern European immigrants migrated from the densely populated East Coast where finding a job was difficult and living conditions were squalid. Though their intent was to work in the automobile factories of Detroit, the steel plants of Gary, or in the mines in southern Ohio, the immigrants did not plan to stay in America. They wanted to earn enough money to go back to their villages, where they would buy land and live a comfortable life.

This initial purpose changed when the newcomers decided to make their homes in this country. They lived in enclaves among their own kind, however; their customs and traditions conflicted with those of the established Anglo Americans. The general feeling existed that the strangers threatened basic American values with their peculiar behavior and their nationalistic loyalties. Though Anglos could never define the threat except in xenophobic terms, social workers and scholars viewed racial and prejudicial implications inherent in the mainstream attitudes.

Social activists worked to understand the cultures of these peoples, eliminate pernicious stereotypes, and show that the immigrant ethnics could contribute to the "American mosaic." For example, in the 1920s,

Marie Hall Ets, a social worker at the Chicago Commons settlement house, befriended an Italian housekeeper, Rosa Cavalleri. Ets discovered that Rosa was a gifted storyteller and that she narrated her traditional tales at other settlement houses, women's clubs, and universities in Chicago. During their thirteen-year friendship, the social worker transcribed Rosa's life history detailing her childhood in Italy; her youth with her husband, who worked in the iron mines of Union, Missouri; and her latter years as a widow in the sprawling Chicago slums. Ets also produced Italo-English dialect translations of the fairy tales that Rosa had learned in her village and later performed before American audiences. Rosa's life narrative and stories were as important as the works of any creative artist. Ets believed that they contained a wealth of historical detail and original perception that folklorists and anthropologists would later find invaluable for researching the period.

An example of an academic activist was Emelyn Elizabeth Gardner, a Wayne State University folklore professor who decided to document the folklore that circulated in Detroit's ethnic enclaves. She believed that ethnics were a hidden resource and that the children of these immigrants, particularly the American-born women, could collect information that would document historical and cultural traditions. During the early 1940s, Gardner visited the Detroit high schools, talked to the young female students, and met with their immigrant parents. Through her status as a "University Professor," she encouraged them to send their daughters to Wayne State. There they learned the techniques of interviewing and taking down the spoken word. The results were Polish, Italian, Armenian, Finnish, Greek, Yugoslavian, and Jewish collections that formed the basis of the Wayne State University Folklore Archives where students and scholars have studied Detroit's ethnic folk traditions for more than sixty years.

These examples show how dedicated individuals have documented immigrant folklore with the intention of giving the newcomers a "voice" and preserving materials for research.

During the ensuing years, as Americans began to view ethnicity less as a threat and more as a status symbol reflecting one's "roots," folklorists became interested in identifying newer forms created by succeeding generations and describing the processes that sustained ethnic traditions in urban and rural areas.

Due to its proximity to the Indiana University Folklore Institute, Gary, Indiana, became a proving ground for ethnic folklore in an urban industrial setting. Gary, located on the wetlands of the Grand Calumet River, began constructing steel plants around 1906 and attracted unskilled European immigrant labor. In the 1960s, folklore professor Linda Dégh researched the Hungarian Protestant steel and oil workers and collected traditional tales, beliefs, songs, and customs that had long died out in the "Old Country." In her view, the living Hungarian peasant folk tradition consisting of archaic forms and new elements had continued to survive because its flexibility allowed for the assimilation of traditions from other ethnic groups and mainstream culture. The Gary Hungarian folk retained their peasant outlook by adapting it to the northwestern Indiana environment. She reports, for example, that when she asked a retired laborer about the existence of mermaids in the area, he replied that such creatures could never survive in the icy waters of Lake Michigan. Mermaids flourished, he continued, in the warmer Florida Gulf. In another example, Dégh describes two elderly Hungarian women from the old quarter who lived far apart in the suburbs. They spent hours on the telephone gossiping about their non-Hungarian neighbors, soap operas and situation comedies, and Gary political personalities. Transforming their talk into traditional narratives, they communicated and comforted each other in their lonely existence.

Richard Dorson, director of the Folklore Institute at Indiana University, extended his research in Gary to the Calumet Region, which included the major ethnic groups living in the city and the surrounding area. Following the thinking in the 1970s, Dorson viewed ethnicity as a series of strategies that ethnic groups devised to emphasize those aspects of their culture they wished to employ in their maneuvering to find a place within an urban multiethnic society. He formulated organizing principles that ethnic peoples like Serbs, Mexicans, Croatians, Puerto Ricans, African Americans, and southern Whites manipulated to portray themselves to the nonethnic world and to each other.

For example, Gary Mexican Americans put on festivals with food, dancing, music, and crafts to present to the region a unified "public" face that emphasized all that was good in Mexican culture. However, when it came to issues that were important for the group's "historic" survival in the area such as racial prejudice, bilingual education, or illegal aliens, they lobbied politicians for just laws, conducted protests against racial oppression, and created folk plays to keep the political topics alive among their own compatriots. On a more "private" level, Mexican Americans of Gary told fairy tales and supernatural legends, prepared national and regional dishes, and practiced local traditions that members from the different states and villages would recognize. In this way they, like other Gary ethnics, could represent themselves as acceptable to Americans through their public celebrations. However, these groups could protect the survival of the most intimate and personal aspects of their culture through their political efforts, and the observance of their private traditions behind closed doors.

In the less congested villages and towns of the Midwest, folklorists have attempted to show how ethnics adapted their traditions to fit a regional pattern. An example of rural midwestern multiethnic regionalization of a traditional foreign item occurred in Michigan's Upper Peninsula with the introduction of the Cornish meat and vegetable turnover called pasty (pronounced *pass-tee*). Cornish tin miners came to the state during the 1840s to help develop the iron- and copper-mining industries that were appearing in the north. Folklorist Yvonne Lockwood explains that the English-speaking Cornish with their mining background became supervisors and, later, models of American behavior for the unskilled Finnish and Italian immigrant laborers who arrived during the mid-1800s. Cornishmen had always considered pasty an ideal food to take to work: It was small enough to carry around and its mixture of meat and vegetables made it a delicious lunch. The Finns and Italians adopted pasty as a work food and changed the ingredients, preparation, size, and accompaniments. The transmission from the Cornish to the Finns and the Italians blurred its origin because the latter two ethnic groups had dough-enveloped specialties that were similar to pasty and could have mistaken it for a regional version of one of their own. Consequently, the Cornish viewed pasty as Cornish, the Finns saw it as Finnish, and the Italians stated that it was Italian. As it gained popularity outside home, church suppers, and other social events, pasty entered the mass media through restaurants, in-jokes portrayed in newspaper cartoons, and mock competitions (e.g., the First Annual Pasty Throwing Contest) to become the Upper Peninsula's most distinctive specialty dish.

A contrasting example of an indigenous creation of a multiethnic regional folk genre is the Dutchman band. The Dutchman band has characterized the musical tradition in the rural areas of central Wisconsin, southern Minnesota, the eastern Dakotas, northeastern Iowa, and northwestern Illinois for more than fifty years. The Dutchman band arose out of German- and Czech-speaking immigrant cultures and fermented in an upper Midwest pluralistic regional setting. As musical expression, the Dutchman band consists of a rhythm section of tuba and drums and a melodic concertina "pushing and pulling" the dance tune. The music has a distinctive German melodic emphasis, strong military rhythms, and "round true notes."

Folklorists James Leary and Richard March have studied the genre from a variety of perspectives. They traced how the Dutchman band arose out of the concert-band and house-party musical traditions; analyzed the musical style itself, with its clear melodies and measured vocal phrasing; and showed the influences that German involvement in the two World Wars had on the genre. In addition, Leary and March discussed seminal figures like "Whoopee John" Wilfahrt and Harold Loeffelmacher from New Ulm, Minnesota, and current innovators like Brian Brueggen and the Mississippi Valley Dutchmen. They analyzed their styles of presentation from the way they played their instruments to the "looks" that they conveyed according to current fashion. These looks consisted of rural frumpiness in the 1910s, the sophisticated merry burgher in 1920, urbane Europeans by 1930, comic German-American rubes in the 1930s and 1940s, and central European rustic cool in the 1980s. More importantly, Leary and March showed that the Dutchman genre survived because its performers have assimilated big band, country, and jazz musical styles and mass-media marketing paraphernalia without compromising the same "square" sounds that locals recognize as Dutchman.

An example of ethnic group adaptation to a particular region is the German settlement in southwestern Illinois. Germans immigrated during the decades before the Civil War looking for farms and jobs in slavery-free states. Once German in language, food, custom, and behavior, this region now has a few threads of the original surviving lore. However, the German descendants still behave in a manner that non-Germans identify as German. Anthropologist John M. Coggeshall catalogs the distinctive characteristics of this regional ethnic group. When Illinois Germans talk, they speak in a "sing-songy" voice and impose Germanic grammatical structures on English sentences, like "it was down by the log house laying." Germans tend to be financially conservative, are homeowners, and have the habit of entering their domiciles through the back door. Food traditions consist of traditional German foods like homemade sausages, potato pancakes, German potato salad, and specialty cookies. They also show a preference for meat, potatoes, vegetables, beer, bread, noodles, and dumplings. Their eating habits are routine: German Americans eat the same dishes on the same day every week throughout the year except on holidays. Other distinctive characteristics include holiday customs like shooting in the New Year and celebrating St. Nicholas's Day on December 6, singing folk songs like the "Schnitzelbank Song," dancing traditional mixers like the Grandpa Dance at weddings, parties, and get-togethers, and playing card games like klepper or solo. Coggeshall suggests that these Illinois Germans act and behave without any awareness of their German heritage except when outsiders encounter them and notice that they are "peculiar."

Ethnic groups in the Midwest have retained their identity by adapting to their multiethnic urban and rural environments. This process of culture change will continue to operate within the older established communities and it will affect the folk traditions of exotic newcomers such as Afghans in Nebraska or Somalis in Iowa. Folklorists from arts organizations and universities are documenting the lore of the old and new arrivals. Through oral history projects, community studies, documentary films, radio programs, festivals, and exhibits, folklorists are creating an information database that will be important for those who want to know what direction ethnic folklore will take in the Midwest.

Sources and Further Reading: John M. Coggeshall, "'One of Those Intangibles': The Manifestation of Ethnic Identity in Southwestern Illinois," *Journal of American Folklore* 99 (Apr.–June 1986); Larry Danielson, ed., *Studies in Folklore and Ethnicity* (1978); Linda Dégh, "Approaches to Folklore Research among Immigrant Groups," *Journal of American Folklore* 79 (Oct.–Dec. 1966); "Two Old World Narrators in Urban Setting," in *Kontakte und Grenzen* (1969); Richard Mercer Dorson, *Land of the Millrats* (1981); Marie Hall Ets, *Rosa: The Life of an Italian Immigrant*, 2nd ed. (1999); Linda Dégh, Susie Hoogasian-Villa, *100 Armenian Tales and Their Folkloristic Relevance* (1966); Americo Paredes and Ellen J. Stekert, eds., *The Urban Experience and Folk Tradition* (1971); Harriet M. Pawlowska, ed., *Merrily We Sing: 105 Polish Folksongs*, rev. ed. (1983); Stephen Stern and John Allan Cicala, eds., *Creative Ethnicity* (1991).

John Allan Cicala
Mount Saint Mary College, New York

Easter Eggs

The decorating of eggs is thousands of years old and has roots in the pre-Christian nature-based sun ceremonies of many European horticultural and agricultural peoples. These ceremonies—emphasizing the naturalistic trinity of fire, water, and air—were held in the spring, and the egg, due to its inherent essence of life, became associated with spring themes of renewal, life after death, and fertility. Symbolic designs and colors were applied to eggs to convey spiritual beliefs and worldviews closely tied to the land. With the advent of Christianity, egg decorating and its associated worldview blended well with Easter celebrations. The tradition of elaborately decorating Easter eggs remains particularly strong among midwestern peoples of Ukrainian, Czech, Slovak, Polish, and Russian heritage who have sustained a sense of spirituality and a worldview that remains closely tied to nature.

There are two broad categories of Easter eggs and both are included in Easter baskets to be blessed at church services. One kind is cooked, simply decorated, and eaten as part of the Easter feast ending the forty-day Lenten fast, and one is raw or only a shell, elaborately decorated and made for artistic and spiritual purposes rather than for consumption.

The eggs in this second broad category take many forms and reflect a high degree of symbolism and artistry. Some are made using the batik (wax-resist) method of repeated and alternating applications of wax to a raw egg followed by repeated and alternating dye baths beginning with the lightest color and ending with the darkest, resulting in intricate designs of numerous colors. Every color and every design has a meaning. An eight-pointed star represents the Son of God; birds, the fulfillment of wishes or human souls; ribbons, water and everlasting life; dots, stars; ladders, prayer; roosters, the Resurrection; wheat, fertility and a bountiful harvest. Red represents fire and happiness; white, purity; orange, wisdom; blue, air and good health; brown, earth and fertility. Some eggs are decorated by using a needle or other sharp object to scratch designs onto the surface of an egg dyed a single color.

Ukrainian Easter eggs, Bathgate, North Dakota. Image provided courtesy North Dakota Council on the Arts. Photo by Katrina Callahan.

Other eggs, called *slamenky* in Czech, are decorated with pieces of wheat, barley, and oat straw split, ironed, and cut into geometric shapes and applied to the egg to create richly beautiful designs of varying golden hues.

These ornate eggs may be blessed by priests and buried by farmers in the corner of fields in the belief that the spiritual fertile power of the egg will transfer to the soil, ensuring a bountiful harvest. Some are placed in barns to supernaturally aid the calving season, while others are placed in windowsills to protect against storms. Still others are given as gifts wishing health, wealth, and happiness. The Ukrainian word for Easter eggs, *pysanky*, is derived from *pysaty*, "to write." The Easter egg artist's worldview and culture, written in colorful symbols on the egg, renders it a folk icon.

Sources and Further Reading: Troyd Geist, *From the Well-spring* (1997); Christopher Martin, *Prairie Patterns* (1989); Venetia Newall, *An Egg at Easter* (1971); Steven Ohrn, ed., *Passing Time and Traditions* (1984).

Troyd A. Geist
North Dakota Council on the Arts

Ethnic Saturday Schools

So-called Saturday schools emerged in the 1940s among post–World War II European refugees. While such schools sprang up all over the country, they were densely clustered in the Midwest (in Chicago, Cleveland, Detroit, Milwaukee, Minneapolis, Indianapolis, and Kalamazoo). They were founded by highly educated, nationally self-conscious, and politically aware newcomers, who lived "in exile" from "Soviet-dominated or occupied homelands." In addition to Balts (Latvians, Lithuanians, and Estonians), other refugee groups (Hungarians, Ukrainians, Armenians, and Poles, for example) also established Saturday schools as part of an overall strategy to preserve national culture and foster ethnic solidarity "until the homeland is again free" and return was possible.

Saturday schools were first staffed by volunteers, typically those who had been leaders, intellectuals, or cultural workers in the homeland and who welcomed a break from their initial menial jobs in the United States as janitors, dishwashers, and housekeepers. Parents supported the schools financially. Over time, national ethnic organizations coordinated curricula, provided some funding, and recognized outstanding achievement.

Saturday schools educate children in the language, history and politics, culture, and religion of the homeland. They encourage membership in performing troupes prominently featuring folk music, dance, customs, and clothing. They foster social relationships. As Latvians quip: "Let's get together; let's marry."

In the early years, the cultural heritage that was a living reality for the immigrating generation came alive on Saturday mornings to teach offspring how to live as "exiles." After the collapse of the Soviet Union, the mission shifted. Offspring (albeit in decreasing numbers) now learn how to be "long-distance nationals," individuals deeply committed to life in the United States but knowledgeable about and actively involved in the ancestral homeland.

Sources and Further Reading: Ethnic Heritage and Language Schools in America, developed by Elena Bradunas, comp. and ed. Brett Topping (1988); Stephan Thernstrom, ed., *The Harvard Encyclopedia of American Ethnic Groups* (1980).

Inta Gale Carpenter
Indiana University–Bloomington

Paj Ntaub

Like their relatives in their Southeast Asian homeland of Laos and in communities scattered throughout the world, Hmong Americans begin to learn how to make *paj ntaub* (meaning "flower cloth" and pronounced *pan dow*) at a very young age. A variety of patterns, motifs, and needlework techniques, including appliqué, reverse appliqué, and embroidery, are used in creating the colorful textiles. Mastery of the techniques and expansion of the repertoire of designs and motifs usually takes years, and expert craftsmanship is valued within the community. The basic elements of Hmong clothing are the same for all Hmong; the names of Hmong subgroups correspond to variations in the basic outfits. For instance Blue Hmong wear blue batiked skirts, White Hmong wear white skirts, and Striped Hmong wear black jackets with large appliquéd and embroidered bands on the sleeves.

When war and political unrest in the 1970s caused a dislocation of the Hmong from their homeland and resettlement in other countries, women also employed their portable needlework skill to create items for sale. Influenced by resettlement workers, *paj ntaub* artists began to use new color schemes and to create products such as wall hangings, pillow covers, quilts, and other items that would be attractive to this new market.

In the Midwest, where thousands of Hmong resettled, traditional Hmong clothing is still worn by women at weddings, by babies, by the deceased at funerals and burial, and by young Hmong at their annual community New Year's celebrations and cultural showcases. *Paj ntaub* artists also sell their work in galleries, craft cooperatives, and art fairs in the Midwest.

Sources and Further Reading: C. Kurt Dewhurst and Marsha MacDowell, eds., *Michigan Hmong Arts* (1983); John

Michael Kohler Arts Center, *Hmong Art, Tradition, and Change* (1986); Marsha MacDowell, *Stories in Thread: Hmong Pictorial* (1989).

Marsha MacDowell
Michigan State University

Quillwork

Quillwork is a Native American weaving or sewing technique that applies porcupine or sometimes avian quills to regalia or everyday objects. Seeds, shells, and quills preceded and persisted alongside European trade beads. Quills are embroidered or applied to animal hides, birch bark, or other materials. This practice appears most prominently in the Great Lakes region but extends through the plains and even on into the Northwest Coast. The eastern porcupine exists from the Atlantic to Wisconsin and north into Canada, and the use of quills requires their careful removal from the dead porcupine, cleaning, sorting, and often dyeing them before use. It is customary to use tools such as a compass, tweezers, scissors, knife, and an awl to prepare the quills, to mark designs, and then to insert the quills.

The actual constructing techniques of preparation and application of porcupine or bird quills require that they be soaked in warm water or, as in earlier times, softened by putting them in the mouth. In some traditions, the quills are flattened by pulling them through the teeth. Traditional tribal motifs provided the designs for quillworkers. The primary specific techniques are wrapping, plaiting, telescoping (often also involving other materials such as sweetgrass), beading, knotting, and tufting.

Contemporary quillwork is most common on birch-bark boxes in the Great Lakes region, on dance regalia in the plains, or on bags or other ceremonial objects in Alaska. Protected access to porcupines is an important natural resource policy issue for many Native American artists, and this has led to special collecting permits for quillwork artists in states such as Michigan and Wisconsin.

Sources and Further Reading: Lois Sherr Dubin, *North American Indian Jewelry and Adornment: From Prehistory to the Present* (1999); Christian F. Feest, *Native Arts of North America* (1980); Bryan Sentance, *Art of the Basket* (2001).

C. Kurt Dewhurst
Michigan State University Museum

Rosemaling

The second half of the nineteenth century was the period of greatest migration from Norway to the upper Midwest. Among the traditions the immigrants brought with them was rosemaling, decorative painting of stylized flowers and scrolls, with occasional figures. Originally painted onto the interior walls of peasant homes in Norway, rosemaling also adorned furniture, such as the *Amerika trunks* the immigrants used for storing valuables over their ocean voyages to the New World.

Besides immigrant trunks, most rosemaling in the upper Midwest is the product of either of two American revivals. The first began about 1930, when a Stoughton, Wisconsin, Norwegian immigrant named Per Lysne began decorating wooden furniture items with rosemaling for sale. In an attempt to fit the American scene, his work used brighter colors than the centuries-old Norwegian rosemaling. His success stimulated others to take up the form, which now was chiefly painted not on interior walls of homes, but primarily onto wooden furniture and accessories.

Vesterheim, the Norwegian American Museum in Decorah, Iowa, provided much of the spark igniting the second revival, beginning in the late 1960s. Vesterheim sponsored a national exhibition of rosemaling in 1967 and began inviting Norwegian masters to the museum to give workshops to grassroots rosemalers. The masters influenced participants to create within the conventions of Norwegian regional styles while increasing their technical abilities as painters.

Rosemaled Amerika trunks and other items have been prominently displayed in Norwegian American homes in the upper Midwest since frontier days. Early in the twenty-first century, in Norwegian areas of the Midwest, one also sees rosemaling in public settings such as stores and churches. Expressive of Norwegian heritage, rosemaling is also valued by peoples of diverse backgrounds who appreciate decorative painting.

Source and Further Reading: Philip Martin, *Rosemaling in the Upper Midwest* (1989).

Philip Nusbaum
Minnesota State Arts Board

Workers' Folklore and Cultural Traditions

Variously termed workers' folklore, occupational folklife, laborlore, industrial folklore, factory folklore, or simply folklore from the working folk, workers' cultural traditions generally refer to informal knowledge or work technique communicated in expressive cultural forms such as speech, poetry, music, song, painting, sculpture, stories, jokes, celebrations, and rituals as well as in makeshift or homemade tools and the artifacts of work itself. Each term carries different assumptions about what is the appropriate scope and object of attention—tradition, ideology, aesthetics, or artifacts—but all terms illuminate forms of expression and representation embedded in or commenting on the work setting, work process, or workers' experience.

Early approaches to the study of workers' cultural traditions established the primacy of collecting and cataloging these forms, especially speech and song. Where ethnographic context is scarce, for early sources of labor song in particular, benchmarks of traditionalism and popularity are primarily indicated from journalistic accounts and memoirs, multiple reprintings of chapbooks such as the *Little Red Songbook* (first edition 1909), by the Industrial Workers of the World (IWW), and media productions like the recorded coal-mining songs treated in Archie Green's *Only a Miner* (1972). Increasingly, histories of labor or work have added useful context and descriptions of cultural traditions. In fact, the culture of the IWW has come to serve as a touchstone for early-twentieth-century workers' cultural traditions, owing to the organization's reputation for song and story as well as the solidarity of its members. "An injury to one is an injury to all" remains a popular slogan of the IWW. It is perhaps from this IWW context that the current terms *workers' folklore* and *workers' culture* acquire their class and industrial connotations.

More contemporary ethnographic approaches explore the meaning of traditional expression in terms of membership and identity, or in terms of the status of individuals and groups accommodating or resisting larger impersonal production processes or political economy. Jack Santino's *Miles of Smiles, Years of Struggle: Stories of Black Pullman Porters* (1989) provides a key, oft-told narrative about union leader A. Philip Randolph's refusal of a bribe from the Pullman Company—the so-called blank check story—that illustrates rank-and-file solidarity. By contrast, a study of production welders who fashion miniature sculpture from scrap materials on the job illuminates worker alienation. Folklorist Richard Mercer Dorson's *Land of the Millrats* (1981) considered the civic, ethnic, and occupational crucible of an urban region around Gary, Indiana, that included narratives of steel workers. Some scholars of work have broadened their inquiries to include organizational culture, leveling labor/management opposition and building upon management theories of performance and leadership style as vernacular aesthetics.

Although workers' cultural traditions are ubiquitous and the lenses with which we view them varied, a midwestern perspective is discernable for particular industries, occupations, and the unique conditions of their development. Regional characterizations and sensibilities are rooted in expansive landscapes, vast natural resources, extensive waterways and transportation networks, diverse immigrant communities, and myriad interrelated occupations. In *The Nine Nations of North America* (1981), Joel Garreau noted that industrial parts from seventeen midwestern manufacturers were in use on the production line at Ford's Rouge River Plant. In the nineteenth century communities and cultures rode the boom and bust of such extractive industries as coal, petroleum, copper, limestone, and iron; harvesting hardwoods, softwoods, and pulpwood; farming on small and large scales; and fishing the Great Lakes and major rivers. The cultural traditions of mining, logging, and fishing have all been documented, with particular attention to speech, stories, songs, customs, and their meanings. Timothy Lloyd and Patrick Mullen's exemplary *Lake Erie Fishermen* (1990) for example focuses on themes of work, tradition, and identity.

Manufacturing and other value-added processes built upon this extractive primacy. The region gave the world the automobile and a variety of other manufactured products, including rubber, steel, glass, and machine tools, to name a few. Processing of the region's timber and pulpwood gave rise to furniture factories and lumber, paper, and pulp mills. Labor in the factories was a varied mix of extremely skilled work, such as the design and building of dies and tooling, to unskilled toil that used men and women as interchangeable parts on the moving assembly line, itself a midwestern species of work management that has come to be called "Fordism," after the production process developed at the Ford Motor Company. If worker alienation is a pervasive theme of production work (by no means a midwestern phenomenon) its expression in "work-on-the-side"—sometimes referred to as "homers" or "government jobs"—demonstrates creativity and capacity beyond rationalization. Examples abound: poetry writing in paper mills, sewer-tile statuary in tile works, multilayered paint chips from auto plants fashioned into jewelry, discarded Harley Davidson engine parts welded into commemorative retirement sculptures, ejection-mold plastics resembling a "black cobra" revived as abstract sculpture.

While company sanction of such secondary production varies, some companies, such as the Harley Davidson Motor Company in Milwaukee, have addressed issues of worker alienation in restructuring the company for greater employee involvement. Workers at Harley Davidson enjoy a widespread reputation in business circles as team members who are especially proud of their history and role in reclaiming a local, family-built company. Many employees own Harleys and set standards of design and taste through customization, and the company reserves parking prominently along the front of the main building to display these "rolling sculptures." Even in such progressive companies, traditional skills and creativity prevail, especially in tool and die shops, millwright shops, and other shops where production values are enhanced through problem solving, innovation, and design. One worker in the company's machine repair shop, nicknamed "Yooper" because he hails from Michigan's Upper Peninsula, has a reputation for his ingenuity and dexterity with hand-made, special-purpose tools.

Social dynamics of work relations—between workers and employers, employers and unions, and among workers—are complex and hardly contained by formal or contractual arrangements. The so-called government jobs identify an aesthetic of subversion. Other forms of subversion, of course, include sabotage, and one narrative with a version set in the Indiana stone quarries tells of day laborers shortening their shovel handles to equalize a reduction in wages. More pervasive informal work-group hierarchies managed and maintained by verbal skill, stereotype, and evaluations of the good or bad worker represent another expressive dimension in a work setting. So do expressions about work outside of production, such as the slogans and illustrations relevant to work emblazoned on hard hats worn in the steel mills in Chicago/Gary and Cleveland. An autoworker's murals painted on factory or lunchroom walls or a mural painted for striking Hormel meatpackers in Austin, Minnesota, demonstrate further meanings. Such public displays valorize their subject, as evident in Diego Rivera's *Detroit Industry* murals of 1932. In the case of the Hormel meatpackers, Mike Alewitz's 1986 mural depicting the struggle of an unauthorized, grassroots union that opposed concessions by its local was later sandblasted and erased, symbolic of defeat.

Industrial development in the Midwest has been a major force in the shaping of the region and its identity; no less so the agricultural base of the Midwest, which made the region a logical and dominant manufacturer of such products as tractors and other agricultural implements, as well as fertilizers and chemicals for planting, growing, and harvesting crops. The region's abundant dairy products, along with fruit, vegetable, and grain harvests gave rise to creameries, cheese factories, cereal plants, canning and processing facilities, flour mills, breweries, and industrial centers transforming crops into ethanol and other chemicals. Hence James P. Leary's *Wisconsin Folklore* (1998) includes essays on the jargon, customs, and stories of apple pickers, pickle packers, and brewers. Getting products to market or raw materials to mills required the special skills of a myriad of transportation occupations, including railroad workers, sailors and long-

shoremen, warehousemen and teamsters, truck drivers and shipbuilders, each with their cultural traditions.

The Midwest's cities and towns, mines and forests, farms and factories attracted thousands of immigrants from foreign countries and other areas of the United States, giving the large cities and small towns of the region a potent mixture of ethnic and religious cultures that affected the resultant workers' culture. On the Iron Range in northern Minnesota, a retired taconite miner spends his time carving wood figures based on fellow workers, arranged in dioramas—Jukie (Croatian), Hank (English), and Primo (Italian) as one example—that are "ethnically correct" and expressive of the ethnic character of the Iron Range and of an ideal of interethnic cooperation among the miners. In ethnic joke cycles like the upper Midwest's Ole and Lena stories, occupational lore authenticates setting. But workers' culture is also more than ethnic culture, because it includes work-related customs and practices that are shared by more than the workers of one ethnicity. Pasty in the Upper Peninsula of Michigan, for example, is meat and root vegetables encased in dough turnover—a meal-in-one. Cornish in origin, it was carried into the mines by Cornish miners and soon taken up by co-workers of different ethnic groups. It has since spread beyond the workers' ethnic group, beyond iron and copper mines, to become a regional food, adapted and adopted by everyone.

Just as pasty jumped the boundary of the mines to become a staple meal in a number of northern Great Lakes workplaces, other workers' cultural traditions combine occupational and ethnic strands to address larger regionally shared experiences. The title story of Archie Green's *Calf's Head and Union Tale* (1996) has been collected or cast in many locales, yet the version set amid the 1916 Minnesota Iron Range miner's strike powerfully articulates a union stance against strikebreakers that has become sacred in the community's history. When a striking miner's wife cannot afford the cheapest purchase in a unionized meat market, the sympathetic butcher renders a "union calf's head" into a "scab calf's head" by knocking "out two bits worth of brains." Another version of this tale collected elsewhere was performed for folklorist Ben Botkin as an "old-fashioned street corner spiel" according to Green. In an earlier era, soapbox or street-corner orators, performing a form of public discourse blending working-class radicalism with traditional song and story, brought class consciousness, strike news, and story and song from far and wide. Routinely converging on Chicago's Bughouse Square, near the railroad's "main stem" to and from the wheat fields and other work sites throughout the Midwest, soapboxers made Chicago the Midwest's center of free-speech activism. Slim Brundage, a Bughouse regular, was also a "founder and janitor" of Chicago's "college of complexes," an institution for radical working-class poets, philosophers, and other counterculture figures.

Many aspects of workers' lives, however, transcend local or regional characterizations altogether. Beliefs that work is a necessary evil; that workplace tools and materials should be used for "government jobs" or "homers"; that competent workers are led by incompetent "superiors"; and that workers will always be "screwed" arguably constitute a prevailing American workers' worldview.

The recent phenomenon of globalization with effects of "restructuring," "outsourcing," and "downsizing" has had an impact, directly and indirectly, on most American workers and many industries. In the Midwest, globalization encompasses other trends already reshaping the region's industrial and agricultural character: deindustrialization, weak unions and a beleaguered labor movement, the growth of agribusiness, and the influx of new immigrants. The network of industrial and mercantile centers of the Midwest, particularly along the Great Lakes and major rivers, has come to be seen as a Rust Belt. But with the conversion to many new economies, including service and technology as well as revived industries, workers have also changed. Hmong, Mexican, Bosnian, Tibetan, Russian, Lao, and other new immigrant workers in midwestern industries today are reminiscent of the older immigrant/ethnic mix in the factories of the late nineteenth and early twentieth centuries. It remains to be seen how the cultural traditions of new ethnic and immigrant groups and the work traditions of new technologies and new work settings and dynamics will interact with the older regional determinants to reshape the workers' cultural traditions of the Midwest.

Sources and Further Reading: Tristram Potter Coffin and Hennig Cohen, eds., *Folklore from the Working Folk of America* (1973); Richard M. Dorson, *Land of the Millrats* (1981); Joel Garreau, *The Nine Nations of North America* (1981); Archie Green, "American Labor Lore: Its Meanings and Uses," *Industrial Relations* 4 (Feb. 1965); Archie Green, *Calf's Head and Union Tale* (1996); Archie Green, "Industrial Lore: A Bibliographic-Semantic Query," in Robert H. Byington, ed., *Working Americans* (1978); Archie Green, *Wobblies, Pile Butts, and Other Heroes* (1993); Michael Owen Jones, introduction to "Works of Art, Art as Work, and the Arts of Working—Implications for Improving Organizational Life," *Western Folklore* 43 (July 1984); Joyce L. Kornbluh, ed., *Rebel Voices: An IWW Anthology* (1988); James P. Leary, *So Ole Says to Lena*, 2nd ed. (2001); James P. Leary, *Wisconsin Folklore* (1998); Timothy Lloyd and Patrick Mullen, *Lake Erie Fishermen* (1990); Yvonne R. Lockwood, "The Joy of Labor," *Western Folklore* 43 (July 1984); Robert S. McCarl, Jr., "Occupational Folklife: A Theoretical Hypothesis," in Robert H. Byington, ed., *Working Americans* (1978); Bruce E. Nickerson, "Factory Folklore," in Richard M. Dorson, ed., *Handbook of American Folklore* (1983); Franklin Rosemont, ed., *From Bughouse Square to the Beat Generation: Selected Ravings of Slim Brundage—Founder and Janitor of the College of Complexes* (1997); Jack Santino, *Miles of Smiles, Years of Struggle: Stories of Black Pullman Porters* (1989).

Tom Walker
Washington, D.C.

John Beck
Michigan State University

Yvonne R. Lockwood
Michigan State University

Paul Bunyan

A gigantic logger of Herculean strength and remarkable ingenuity, Paul Bunyan was born of the early-twentieth-century midwestern imagination and is now recognized internationally as one of the nation's most enduring folk heroes. Writers, artists, and ordinary Americans have incorporated the fictive imagery of Paul Bunyan into manifold cultural forms including advertisements, opera, children's books, paintings, statues, festivals, and oral traditions. He has become an icon of the first order, eminently useful for thinking about American attitudes toward work, nature, and both regional and national identity.

Paul Bunyan emerged from the logging country of Minnesota, Wisconsin, and Michigan, first from the pen of journalist James MacGillivray, whose "Round River Drive" essays appeared in Midwest newspapers in the first decade of the twentieth century. It was advertising executive William B. Laughead, however, who brought Bunyan to life on a grand scale when, in 1914, he combined logging folklore he had heard in a Minnesota logging camp with his own artistic renderings of the demigod's persona to launch a public relations campaign for the Minneapolis-based Red River Lumber Company. Laughead's stories and drawings followed in the tradition of American tall tales, depicting the larger-than-life Bunyan—and an ensemble cast of equally fantastic and humorous characters—as capable of removing entire forests with a single swing of an ax and creating the Great Lakes to water his immense Babe the Blue Ox. The image of Bunyan was purposely never copyrighted because Red River management wanted to encourage adoption of the image outside of the industry in order to enhance the company's public name recognition. Consequently, the giant logger moved quickly from his regional origin to the national scene in popular and elite literature and art for adult and juvenile audiences, always serving to represent American rugged individualism, hard work, entrepreneurial ambition, and mastery over nature.

The icon's greatest impact, however, was on the people of the Midwest, particularly from the 1920s through the 1950s when a declining timber industry and emergent tourist economy produced widespread nostalgia for the region's frontier past. Live performances by Bunyan impersonators and storytellers were common at reunion picnics, youth camps, and community festivals. Colossal statues, postcards, murals, and booklets of tales gave the tradition material permanence. Loggers themselves recognized Bunyan as a corporate fabrication, management's attempt to inculcate a work ethic of superproductivity; thus Bunyan served as a free-enterprise antidote to the revolutionary spirit of Joe Hill, martyred hero of the twentieth-century labor movement. Nonetheless, woodsworkers attempted to reclaim Bunyan for their own. Some told stories to test the credulity of those unfamiliar with their occupational culture; others added Bunyanesque attributes to narratives about living timber workers, describing the extraordinary feats of strength exhibited by Otto Walta, a Finnish American logger in Minnesota. Stories and images of Bunyan appeared frequently in midwestern labor publications, where editors used the popular icon to characterize both regional pride in occupational heritage and the collective power of organized workers. Most recently, Bunyan has been used to comment on the often tragic environmental legacy of logging. He has appeared as a repentant logger in children's books, and as a victim of Native American vengeance for misuse of Indian lands, clubbed with a walleye by culture hero Wenabozho on an Ojibwe reservation sign. A statue of Bunyan was also used prominently in the film *Fargo* (1996) as a foreboding symbol of terror and greed in the midwestern heartland.

Sources and Further Reading: Richard M. Dorson, "Paul Bunyan in the News, 1939–41," *Western Folklore* 15 (Jan., July, Oct. 1956); Daniel G. Hoffman, *Paul Bunyan: Last of the Frontier Demigods* (1983); Michael Karni, "Otto Walta, Finnish Folk Hero of the Iron Range," *Minnesota History* 40 (Winter 1967); Robert E. Walls, "The Making of the American Logger: Traditional Culture and Public Imagery in the Realm of the Bunyanesque," Ph.D. diss., Indiana University (1997).

Robert E. Walls
University of South Carolina–Columbia

Flatboats

A very old form of boat found throughout Europe, the rectangular flatboat is distinguished for its simple, economical construction, the responsiveness of its design to individual taste, good performance, and its stability and ability to transport generous loads in shallow, smooth inshore waters. Immigrants, readily shaping trees into planks, found it the answer to moving goods to and within America's Heartland. Fishing flatboats, shapely, sturdy, and swift, "the most boat for the buck," perpetuate the best of the Midwest's flatboat heritage and still prove the utility of the concept on midwestern rivers.

Although they are widely called johnboats, flatboat is the preferred term among "river rats" on the upper Mississippi. Fishers and builders continue to co-create variations of the type throughout the Ohio, Mississippi, and Missouri river systems. Prevalent as mass-produced aluminum stock boats, the standardized forms owe their shapes to successful flatboats designed and built by people who find them "the best working boat by far" on midwestern rivers.

The boat's flat bottom is sometimes slightly rockered toward stern and bow. Depending on the boat's use, the flared sides vary in width, measured from top-rail to chine (18'–24' on the upper Mississippi, 14' in southeastern Missouri), and generally taper toward the bow, sometimes to the stern. Flat stern and bow pieces rake slightly outward and give the boat its squared ends. Upper Mississippi commercial fishing and musseling flatboats are largest (16'–28' long by 4'–6' bottom beam, flaring to 6'–8' topside), reflecting heavier catches and bulkier gear. Shorter flatboats (10'–16') are popular for hunting, trapping, and sport-fishing on the lower Ohio and upper Mississippi systems, for upper Mississippi ice fishing, and for Ohio-system musseling (14'–20'). Ozark johnboats, built for shallow, fast-running, and eddying streams, are distinctively narrowest (2'–3' bottom beam) for their length (14'–26' median range). Once important for transportation and subsistence fishing, they are now essential for sociable, festive gigging for rough fish.

Often shaped upside down around forms or key ribs, then upturned and fit with (remaining) ribs, custom seating, steering, and stowage, flatboats have varied in woods and metals through time depending on availability, cost, durability, and preference. Wooden flatboats persist because of cost and comfort, but heavy-gauge rivetless aluminum versions are popular for the upper Mississippi's largest flatboats, lasting longer and requiring less maintenance. Once rowed, poled, sailed, and then outfitted with engines, most early twenty-first century boats feature 25 to 65 horsepower outboards. Commercial vessels can plane impressively at good speeds even with a ton of fish, while Ozark boats, still poled or propelled by small 1.5 to 10 horsepower motors, can outmaneuver more heavily powered competitors.

Sources and Further Reading: Howard I. Chapelle, *American Small Sailing Craft: Their Design, Development, and Con-*

River folk on the Ohio in the 1940s. Photographer unknown. Courtesy Sarah Weaver Clark.

struction (1951); Malcolm L. Comeaux, "Origin and Evolution of Mississippi River Fishing Craft," *Pioneer America* 10 (June 1978); Dana Everts-Boehm, *The Ozark Johnboat: Its History, Form, and Functions*, ed. C. Ray Brassieur and Howard Wight Marshall (1991); Jens Lund, *Flatheads and Spooneys* (1995).

Janet C. Gilmore
University of Wisconsin–Madison

River Folk

During the 1820s, travel writer Timothy Flint described a variety of homemade houseboats plying the inland rivers, but not until the late nineteenth century did accounts of a distinctive subculture of nomadic Mississippi and Ohio River Valley river dwellers appear in literature. In the early and middle nineteenth century, some riverbanks remote from larger settlements were settled by poor squatters, some of whom made their living outside of the law. This precipitated the stereotype of the savage "flathead," named after an ugly catfish species known for dwelling in rivers' deepest mud holes. The most distinctive river folk subculture lived in houseboats on the rivers. By the early twentieth century it numbered in the thousands, and during the Depression its ranks swelled to more than fifty thousand.

Seeming colorful to outsiders, the river folk subculture was noted in numerous late-nineteenth- and early-twentieth-century magazine articles and travel accounts. Ben Lucien Burman traveled along the rivers in the 1920s and 1930s and wrote five novels, three nonfiction books, and numerous articles about the river folk, publicizing them to the general population. Burman's accounts romanticized the river folk, as did many of the articles and travel accounts. Some of the popular writings probably referred to their homes as "houseboats," but the derogatory term, "shanty boat," appeared more often. During the 1930s, Ernest Theodore Hiller conducted a sociological study of this population, published as an *Illinois Studies in the Social Sciences* monograph in 1939.

Some houseboat families lived on the rivers for generations. Others, especially during the Depression, had been land dwellers but were forced onto the river by hard times. A few artistic and intellectual people were also attracted to the romance of nomadic river life, such as artist and writer Harlan Hubbard and his musician wife, Anna, who floated on the Ohio and Mississippi during the late 1940s.

Most nomadic river folk were whites of an ethnic composition similar to that of the Appalachian population. Descriptions of them were often stereotypical and the derogatory term "river rat" was used for both the nomads and other poor riverbank dwellers. Negative aspects included larceny and laziness, but positive traits noted were self-sufficiency, hospitality, honesty, strong family ties, and closeness to nature. The most common occupation was commercial fishing, but making and repairing fishing gear, trapping, driftwood gathering, shake splitting, boat building, moonshining, musseling, chair bottoming, root and herb gathering, basket weaving, stove-wood sawing, willow-furniture making, and commercial photography were also observed. Families tied up away from town sometimes put in squatter gardens. Other aspects of their culture noted were "colorful" speech and a propensity for storytelling, singing, and playing traditional music on stringed instruments.

Houseboats floated downstream, but some were able to hitch rides upstream from friendly towboat captains. The more active commercial fishers among river folk had motored skiffs, which they could use to move their houseboat.

During the 1950s, the nomadic river population disappeared as sanitation and tie-up laws, and wakes made by larger barge trains, made life on the river impractical. Some of their descendants still live near the rivers making their living from seasonal fishing, musseling, and trapping, thus perpetuating aspects of river folk culture.

Sources and Further Reading: Ben Lucien Burman, *Big River to Cross* (1940); Ben Lucien Burman, *Children of Noah* (1951); Harlan Hubbard, *Shantyboat: A River Way of Life* (1977); Jens Lund, *Flatheads and Spooneys* (1995); Jens Lund, "Nomadic Architecture," in Robert E. Walls and George H. Schoemaker, eds., *The Old Traditional Way of Life* (1989).

Jens Lund
Washington State Parks and
Recreation Commission

Worker Poets

Midwestern worker poets follow a long tradition of recording the struggles and satisfactions of various occupational lives, including logging, farming, maritime, and industrial jobs. In recent years, worker poets use blank verse as well as more conventional rhyme and meter to speak to and for their work communities.

Such poetry often portrays real places and events. William N. Allen, who worked as a woodsman in Wisconsin and published under the name "Shan T. Boy" in the nineteenth century, chronicled the lives of loggers in such poems as "Shanty Boy on the Big Eau Claire." More recently, Peter L. Webber has self-published his recollections of logging in poetry and prose often nostalgic and peppered with political commentary.

Many poems about work do not so much tell a story as describe a situation or evoke emotion. Poetry about the hardships of certain occupations can be used to rally a community to action. The late nineteenth century saw a flourishing of songs and poems written by and for industrial workers in the Midwest and published by the labor press. The Industrial Workers of the World, established in Chicago in 1905 and known as Wobblies, produced many poets. Ralph Chaplin wrote the American labor movement anthem "Solidarity Forever!" while he lived in Chicago. Carlos Cortez, born in 1923 in Milwaukee to a Mexican Wobbly father and a German pacifist Socialist mother, continues to write about the labor movement, asking "Where Are the Voices?" who "paid . . . with their lives to bring / The extra hours of leisure time / That working fools like you and me now enjoy?"

Worker poetry is directed to its own community and is more likely to be appreciated for expressing shared ideas, not original insights. For example, poems about fishers on the Great Lakes and major midwestern rivers present them as resourceful and independent people. Autoworkers detail the repetitiveness and alienation caused by line work. Daryl Scanland of Michigan writes: "I put up with the noise / the stench and the heat / Like a joke that's not very funny / For a piece of blue paper at the end of the week / Oh, the things I do for money."

The line can waver between poets who write of their experience as workers and university-trained poets who use their work experience as subject matter for their craft. Philip Levine's memories of growing up and working in Detroit have distinguished him in his university career as "working class." Jim Daniels of Michigan, currently at Carnegie-Mellon University, has written labor poems that have inspired other writers in the auto industry. Michael Carey, trained at the University of Iowa, spends his summers crop farming and his winters teaching and writing poetry about farming.

Worker poets might read their poems at co-op meetings or work-related gatherings, or print them in local publications. Poets in industrial settings may post their work around the plant for other workers and even management to see. Worker poetry in the Midwest, as elsewhere, is community-based and community-directed art, produced for people who will recognize and value conventional ideas, vernacular language, and common occupational experiences and causes.

Sources and Further Reading: Leon Chamberlain, ed., *Labor Pains: Poetry from South East Michigan Workers* (1991); Clark D. Halker, *For Democracy, Workers, and God* (1991); Lake Shore Kearney, *The Hodag and Other Tales of the Logging Camps* (1928); Jens Lund, *Flatheads and Spooneys* (1995).

Ruth Olson
University of Wisconsin–Madison

Recreational Folklore

Much of traditional culture—music, dance, story-telling—is experienced as recreation. While a broad range of activities is a part of the recreational folklore of the Midwest, particular forms especially reflect the region's identity. Hunting, fishing, boating, skiing—many midwestern pastimes are connected to the resources of the region. Season is a marker of recreational life in the Midwest. Winter, for example, brings with it an abundance of amusements that celebrate the season: ice fishing, sturgeon spearing, cross-country skiing, and sports such as curling and hockey. Many other activities are inspired by ethnic traditions and particular places. Former ways of life, especially food gathering, have now become hobbies or passions, done for pleasure rather than necessity. Often recreational hunters and fishers are maintaining longstanding family traditions.

Many kinds of hunting exist in the Midwest—squirrel, rabbit, deer, bear, duck, turkey, quail, grouse, and other fowl—and each carries with it stories, traditional lore and skills, knowledge of equipment and place; all in all, the stuff of folklore. But deer hunting, in the fall of the year, has generated the most lore and perhaps the greatest connection to place.

In Wisconsin alone, typically more than six hundred thousand people hunt deer each November. Deer hunting in the northern parts of states like Michigan, Wisconsin, and Minnesota becomes a major preoccupation. Churches gear up for Hunters' Suppers that will help them raise funds to sustain projects for the rest of the year. Motels are filled up months in advance. Downstate, activities for "hunters' widows" are advertised—from bus trips to the Mall of America to an evening out with male dancers such as the Chippendales. Local radio shows help to build "buck fever" with call-in programs, anecdotes about previous hunting seasons, and songs about hunting. Da Yoopers, a musical group from the Upper Peninsula (U.P.) of Michigan, use hunting and other common regional activities as themes for their music. Two now-classic songs get lots of playtime around hunting season: Da Yooper's "Second Week of Deer Camp" and "The 30-Point Buck" by Bananas at Large.

Many hunters enact family rituals annually at deer camp. Hunting-camp traditions are often rich and deep—from card playing and storytelling to rituals like kissing a mounted deer head for luck, or cutting off a shirttail when a hunter misses a shot. Youngsters also learn hunting skills at camps—knowledge of the animal, proper use of guns, and "reading" place, which often includes knowing local names of places.

Hunting camps, typically deer camp and duck camp, usually offer rustic living conditions and are used just a few weeks a year. Hunting camps can range from tiny shacks or trailers with a wood-burning stove and an outhouse to more elaborate seasonal homes complete with TV antenna, indoor plumbing, and electricity. Interiors may be decorated with posters or reproductions of hunting scenes, mounted heads, and plenty of hooks for outdoor clothing. Hunting camps commonly include bunk beds and fold-out couches to create multiple sleeping spaces. The central social feature is a table, where hunters gather to eat, talk, play cards, and partake of liquid refreshment. Another common feature is the camp log, kept year to year, which gives a daily account of events—weather reports, records of game shot, or successful tomfoolery. Such semipublic documents provide camp rules, define the characters of the camp members, and establish the patterns for their interactions. Camp logs build relationships over time while preserving and passing on local place-names and the peculiar vernacular of hunting and fishing.

Mert Cowley, the "Jack Pine Poet," has described a number of hunting traditions within the Midwest, including hunting camps, a tradition that he believes is threatened. Fewer hunters take time off to "camp" during hunting season and fewer have access to these seasonal shacks. Cowley has produced two books of poetry about deer hunting, mostly based on true events. His poems offer humor and advice, telling stories of inexperienced or inattentive hunters, braggarts who meet their come-uppance, terrible camp cooks, and fantastic inventions in aid of the hunter, from inflatable boots to the ultimate deer stand. Elsewhere, he describes another model of hunter—the serious, sober, respectful user of natural resources who loves and values traditional knowledge and culture.

Many people who hunt also fish, and just as most hunters hunt more than one type of animal, most anglers fish for many kinds of fish. The Midwest's plentiful waterways are rich in species and offer many types of fishing: angling for pan fish, like crappies and bluegill; bass and musky fishing; trolling for walleyes; ice fishing; sturgeon spearing in the winter. Even rough fish are fair game. Some are celebrated in festivals, such as the International Eelpout Festival in Walker, Minnesota.

Fishing can include solitary pursuits like fly fishing as well as public competitions. Perhaps the most glamorous fishing in the Midwest is for the muskellunge, or musky. Called "the fish of ten thousand casts," this feisty game fish is prized for its size and fight. Although found throughout the Midwest, in part because of stocking efforts in some states, muskies prefer moderate water temperatures and thus are relatively rare compared to their relative, the northern pike. The equipment, knowledge, and passion involved in musky fishing create a rich cultural environment, and the stories and lore of musky fishers and their guides prove this.

Many anglers mark the seasons by the type of fishing they do. Ice fishing, for example, is an important recreational activity in the upper Midwest. It demonstrates a region so heavily invested in winter that it can sustain towns and roads on ice just for the pleasure of fishing. Some keep it simple, traveling out to the ice with an ice auger, "tip-ups" (devices that indicate when a fish is on the line by popping up a flag), and a bucket to sit on. Others rely on ice shanties that often remain out all season, as long as the ice is not "rotten." In either case, seasoned ice fishers recognize the importance of a common culture: good fishing etiquette; numerous stories of great catches or great disasters; knowledge about the fish they strive to catch; and an understanding of the ice itself.

Smelting is another fishing activity that defines the upper Midwest. Smelting occurs in the spring during the smelt runs, when these fish leave the deeper water to spawn in the shallow water near shore. In restaurants and homes, people look forward to the season of smelt, when these small fish are fried and eaten without being deboned. Once plentiful, the number of smelt has diminished and most of the smelt provided to taverns and restaurants now come from commercial fisheries. Still, during spring nights, people gather on the beaches of Lake Superior and Lake Michigan to scoop up the little fish as they come near shore. The smelt fishers wade into the lake and use strainers or nets to ladle the fish into buckets. On the shore, bonfires and beer await. One of the pleasures of smelt fishing is frying up the catch immediately on the beach. For many families, smelting is an annual event. Some people symbolically mark the beginning of the smelting season by biting the head off their first smelt and throwing it back into the lake. Within the Midwest, the pronunciation of the name of this activity provides a clue to even more regional distinctiveness. In Milwaukee, the word *smelt* is commonly pronounced *schmelt*, a nod to the city's German heritage.

The region's abundant waterways also support a variety of boating activities. Speedboats and other pleasure craft, ski boats, charter fishing boats, sailboats, and more are common on midwestern lakes and rivers. Numerous lakes and rivers sustain houseboat communities, either for vacationers or for more permanent residents. Canoers and kayakers can also find plentiful opportunities for exploring. The Boundary Waters of northern Minnesota, for example, have historically attracted serious canoers. Various federally recognized "Wild and Scenic Rivers" such as the Au Sable in Michigan and the St. Croix in Wisconsin and Minnesota are enjoyed by canoers and kayakers.

With the prominence of the Great Lakes, the Mississippi and the Ohio Rivers, and other important lakes and rivers, it is small wonder that many industries related to the recreational life of the waterways developed in the Midwest. These range from small lure companies in people's basements to larger, well-known operations. Evinrude outboard motors from Milwaukee and Chris-Craft boats and Heddon lures from Michigan are good examples of smaller enterprises that became icons in water-related recreation.

Midwesterners also have a passion for their sports teams. Professional and college teams—such as the Green Bay Packers, the Chicago Bulls, the Michigan Wolverines, and the Ohio State Buckeyes—provide reasons for regional celebrations, and, in general, team rivalry serves community building. Football season, especially, creates a plethora of related celebrations, such as tailgating parties. Tailgaters gather hours before a game to prepare and serve food and drinks from the back of their vehicles. For example, Packer tailgating activities feature a Carnival-type atmosphere. A couple of the more famous characters who regularly appear at Lambeau Field tailgating parties include St. Vince (named after the legendary Vince Lombardi) and Packalope (with antlers on his football helmet). A roaming polka band entertains the masses, and people sometimes break into a brief polka. Some people even bring couches and televisions to watch the game in the parking lot after the lucky ticket holders have gone inside.

Taverns play an important part in the recreational folklife of the Midwest, where professional sports can be watched in the company of other fans, and where softball and bowling leagues are generated for the more physically active. Taverns also sponsor indoor sports like darts, shuffleboard, and duck pins, a modified bowling game. Taverns in the upper Midwest tend to be social gathering places for families. Wisconsin's European immigrants, for example, influenced that state's particular brand of tavern culture. During the nineteenth century many German immigrants and their families enjoyed Sunday afternoons in local taverns with a number of amusements: music, dancing, food, conversation, and card games.

One such traditionally popular card game is euchre. In many midwestern taverns, standing games regularly occur. Leagues and tournaments abound. The specialized vocabulary associated with the game can indicate some of its connection to the ethnic and occupational heritage of the region: "don't send a boy to the mill," "crossing the creek," "Dutchman's point," and "in the barn." Variations in the game, superstitions, and other related euchre customs crop up across the Midwest and may be adopted elsewhere as information travels through tournaments or across the Internet.

Other games such as sheepshead or clabber may not be well known outside particular areas within the Midwest. Clabber, a distinctly regional game played in southwest Indiana in and around Evansville, is similar to euchre. However, it has its own set of terms—"I got a Dad" (run of face cards) or "call a mule" (four jacks). Clabber leagues play throughout the winter in taverns in this mostly German American community. Sheepshead, or *Schafskopf*, another passionately regional card game, is strongly associated with the German American community in eastern Wisconsin. Sheepshead is typically played with three to five players, although two-, six-, and even seven-player versions exist. In Milwaukee, the five-handed version is most common. Again, the game has its own unique vocabulary and rules. For example, a "mauer" is a player who passes the opportunity to pick the blind despite having a powerful hand.

Other types of recreational activities also reflect ethnic heritage, for example, the Italian lawn-bowling game of bocce, found throughout the Midwest, and the related Belgian tradition of feather bowling, where balls are rolled toward a feather, in Michigan. More recent immigrants to the Midwest such as the Hmong are instituting games such as *tuaj lub*, Hmong top spinning, where competitors try to knock their opponents' tops from a specified playing surface.

Although some instances of recreational folklore detailed here can be found elsewhere in the country, each is integrally connected with the Midwest's distinctive peoples, places, resources, and seasons.

Sources and Further Reading: Mert Cowley, *A Hundred Hunts Ago: Seasons of the Past* (1996); Mert Cowley, *In Camps of Orange* (1993); Mert Cowley, *The Ultimate Stand: Poetic Tales of Deer Hunting from the Pearly Swamp Camp* (1990); Robert Lavenda, *Corn Fests and Water Carnivals* (1997); James P. Leary, "Wisconsin Tavern Amusements," in James P. Leary, ed., *Wisconsin Folklore* (1998); Ruth Olson, "A Good Way to Pass the Winter: Sturgeon Spearing in Wisconsin," in Marshall Cook, ed., *Wisconsin Folklife: A Celebration of Wisconsin Traditions* (1998); Bill Roberts and Rob Pavey, *The Heddon Legacy* (2002); Jeffrey L. Rodengen, *Evinrude, Johnson and the Legend of OMC* (1992); Jack Savage and Anthony Mollica, *Chris-Craft Boats* (2001); Eli Singer, *The Musky Chronicles* (2001).

Ruth Olson
University of Wisconsin–Madison

Car Customizing

The historic epicenter of car customizing is southern California, where even today modified car culture is the most developed. But second in importance is the Midwest, centered in southern Michigan and northern Ohio, where a cultural emphasis on cars developed alongside the automotive industry.

Henry Ford may be considered the first hot-rodder. In addition to building Model Ts, he also stripped them down and hopped them up to race the bigger and more expensive cars of his competitors. Then, most of the emphasis on automobile modification had to do with increasing speed.

Street rods were a corollary of these hot rod dragsters. Cars were rebuilt to drive on the street, using the same performance-enhancing techniques and according to the same developing visual aesthetic. Soon hot rod pioneers were scattered across the country, and hot-rodder culture began to take shape in this prewar period.

Customized car show. Photo by Bill Lockwood. Courtesy Michigan State University Museum.

The intermingling of young men from all over the country during World War II did much to spread interest in modifying cars. In the prosperity of the immediate postwar period, young men had money to pursue their dream cars. Construction skills acquired through working on aircraft came in handy. Aviation fuel tanks were made into bodies of dragsters. Airplane wing-flap hydraulic systems were adapted to lower cars.

It was in this environment that the flowering of the street rod took place. By the early 1950s, custom-car clubs had been established throughout the Midwest, drag races and other events were being staged, and pilgrimages were being made to the Bonneville Salt Flats in Utah.

What made hot-rodders "hot-rodders" was not just their cars but the development of a distinct subculture—clubs, plaques hung from cars and jackets emblazoned with club insignia, hangouts at corner gas stations and favored drive-ins, jargon filled with vocabulary unintelligible to the ordinary person on the street, even particular tastes in music and clothes. A particularly important aspect of this subculture was the development of a shared automotive aesthetic. Although everyone wanted a car different from every other, this was always achieved within the bounds of an ever-evolving group aesthetic. With time, this culture would divide into a number of overlapping and closely related subcultures.

The custom car began to evolve from the street rod in the 1930s, but its heyday began in 1949 with the introduction of cars featuring fenders integrated into the body. The distinction has become formalized today, and car shows usually distinguish between pre-1949 "street rods" and post-1949 customs or "street machines."

But the difference is not simply the year of manufacture; more important is the difference of emphasis. Street rodders tend to stress performance whereas customizers stress appearance. The street rodder uses a variety of techniques to lighten the car and make it go faster. Early customizers used lead to achieve the desired flowing forms, even if it added weight. While the street rodder strips the vehicle to make it lighter, the customizer does so for reasons of aesthetics. He—and, increasingly, she—"noses" (removes hood ornaments), "decks" (removes trunk ornaments), "frenches" (removes headlight and tail-light rims), and removes the other clutter such as door handles, maker's insignia, and ornamental chrome. He may "chop" (lower the top by cutting out a section), "section" (cut a horizontal section out of the body), or "channel" (drop the body below the frame rails) to achieve the desired low, sleek look. She may or may not improve the engine.

Low riders, yet another category of modified vehicle, emphasize the suspension system, the defining characteristic being a hydraulic system whereby the car can be lowered and raised at will, tilted, bounced up several feet off the pavement, and even made to dance. Associated with the Mexican American community, this subculture first developed in the barrios of southern California during the early postwar period. It became significant throughout the Midwest in larger communities such as Chicago, Detroit, Milwaukee, and Minneapolis, as well as in smaller cities where low-rider clubs, builders, and individuals participate in local Mexican American festivals. Despite the strong association with Mexican Americans, there are African American low-rider clubs in some cities, and most Mexican American clubs have an Anglo member or two.

Car modifiers are organized into a number of clubs that vary greatly. Some emphasize engine performance, others customizing, and still others a combination of the two. Many, including all those affiliated with the National Street Rod Association (NSRA), restrict membership to owners of pre-1949 street rods. A few are even more restrictive: Chrysler products only, or just 1940 Fords. Low-rider clubs are restricted to low riders. Some clubs are localized and independent, whereas others are affiliated with one or another of the national associations.

NSRA is the largest and most influential of the national organizations. It was founded in 1970 and has grown to more than fifty-two thousand members. National offices are in Memphis, Tennessee, and the headquarters of the North Central Division are currently in Plainfield, Illinois. Special emphasis is put on safety, on bettering the reputation of street rodders among the general public, and on lobbying to contest motor-vehicle legislation that adversely affects street rodders. Other national associations include the International Show Car Association (which emphasizes "show cars" rather than "drive cars"), the KKO8 (which emphasizes custom cars), and Good Guys (which limits membership to 1972 cars or older).

There is an annual round of events that provide occasions to meet, talk cars, admire one another's handiwork, celebrate, swap spare parts, learn of new techniques and products, and reaffirm social ties. Some such gatherings are very large, including the northern regional show of the NSRA in Kalamazoo, Michigan, and the national Good Guys show held annually in Columbus, Ohio. Participants attend from across the region and beyond. Autorama is a profit-generating hot rod and custom show that has been held annually in Detroit since 1953. Sponsored by the Michigan Hot Rod Association, originally to raise money to build a drag strip, it is one of the relatively few winter events in the Midwest for custom and hot rod enthusiasts. It has become one of the principal indoor shows in the nation. Much newer, and even larger, is the Woodward Dream Cruise, established in 1995. Over one million viewers now gather annually to watch some thirty thousand cars cruise along sixteen miles of Woodward Avenue from Detroit through the northern suburbs. It is the "world's largest one-day auto event." In addition there are a great number of smaller shows, most commonly day- or weekend-long events at which cars are exhibited and prizes are awarded according to category. Usually there is a public address system over which music is played by a DJ from a local "oldies" station supported by car enthusiasts.

Many activities at these events are nostalgic of the 1950s. There may be a dance, often a sock hop, inevitably with music of the 1950s and 1960s. There might be an Elvis look-alike contest or prizes for the best dress of the period. Contests or games are often held involving muffler-rapping and flame-throwing (in which an extension is put on the exhaust pipe with a spark plug wired to ignite escaping gas). Low-rider shows include hopping and car-dancing contests.

Cruises are smaller and more frequent, modeled on the practice of youths to "cruise" Main Street, stopping at a favored drive-in to eat, flirt, and visit with other cruisers. The Woodward Dream Cruise is a nostalgic reenactment. Once cruises were seen as a minor social problem with local laws prohibiting the practice, special police assigned to hassle cruisers, no-U-turn signs posted at the customary ends of cruise routes, and fifteen-minute limits imposed by some drive-ins.

Car modification continues to thrive in the Midwest. Today many more midwesterners own a modified car (many, more than one) than ever owned them in the 1950s. Street rods and custom cars continue to be a source of inspiration for Detroit automakers. They have always borrowed heavily both performance developments and stylistic innovations but have now produced entire cars—the Plymouth Prowler, the PT Cruiser—with street-rod configuration. But car modification has, of course, changed. Computer-chip technology and unitized bodies of modern cars are not conducive to backyard rebuilding at a grassroots level. As car modifiers continue to take as their raw material the same vintage automobiles their predecessors did, there has been a steadily decreasing number of cars left to modify. Hence a whole industry grew up to replace any and all body parts in fiberglass replica—even an entire car body in many of the more popular models, either stock or already chopped. Although purists strongly resist the use of any other than original metal parts, one way or another people continue to build street rods and custom cars.

Sources and Further Reading: Dean Batchelor, *Dry Lakes and Dragstrips: The American Hot Rod* (2001); Bo Bertilsson, *Classic Customs and Lead Sleds* (2001); John DeWitt, *Cool Cars, High Art: The Rise of Kustom Kulture* (2001); Albert Drake, *Hot Rodder! From Lakes to Street: An Oral History* (1993); Pat Ganahl, *The American Custom Car* (2001); Pat Ganahl, *Hot Rods and Cool Customs* (1995); Tom Medley, *Hot Rod History*, 2 vols. (1994); Michael Karl Witzel and Kent Bash, *Cruisin': Car Culture in America* (1997). An important source of information on car-modification culture is specialist magazines, including *Car Craft, Custom Rodder, Hot Rod, Low Rider, Popular Hot Rodding, Rod and Custom, Rodder's Journal,* and *Street Rodder*.

William Lockwood
University of Michigan–Ann Arbor

Duck Decoys

The Mississippi Flyway—a major zone for millions of waterfowl during their seasonal migration—runs through a vast section of America's Midwest. The flyway's ecosystems feature rivers, streams, swamps, and potholes that provide wetlands and cover for ducks and geese during their migratory flights. Areas along the flyway have been renowned by hunters, and the sport has spawned a folk art that is an icon of midwestern wetlands, the duck decoy.

American Indians first crafted decoys from reeds, grasses, and other fibers at least two thousand years ago, and the form and function of their decoys influenced the development of wooden decoy construction by the early nineteenth century. By the early twentieth century, hunters in the Midwest used hand-carved wooden decoys as well as rigs of live ducks to attract waterfowl when hunting. Although duck hunting provided fresh game for home consumption, the sport grew exponentially with the development of market hunting as hunters harvested thousands of birds for restaurant owners and milliners. The rise of market hunting precipitated not only a boom in duck decoy carving but also the depletion and extinction of various species of waterfowl. As market hunting was tamed by the nascent conservation movement and live rigs were outlawed by the 1930s, wooden decoys were in such great demand that hand-carved items were in competition with mass-produced models. Factory-made wooden decoys, in turn, were replaced by models made of fiberboard, rubber, and eventually plastic. By mid-century the handmade wooden decoy came to be recognized as an objet d'art.

As collectors began to appreciate the aesthetic qualities of decoys, carvers began making decorative decoys in addition to the working decoys that they hunted over or sold to other shooters. Decorative carving has now developed into an intricate and highly complex art, and the decorative style of carving was crystallized by the 1970s in the writing of Richard LeMaster of Chillicothe, Illinois. LeMaster developed precise ways and set standards for woodworkers to create highly realistic carvings. A plethora of books, magazines, videos, seminars, and other teaching aids have been largely developed from his systemization of decorative carving. These resources have inspired countless carvers, and they have led to the popularity of high-speed rotary carving tools, wood-burners, and a burgeoning technology designed to give carvers an edge when they enter wood-carving competitions. Curiously, although decorative bird carving in the Midwest has become more popular than the crafting of actual decoys made for hunting, antique working decoys carved prior to World War II are now the most highly prized collector's items. The highest price for a decoy paid in 2000 was $684,500, for a working goose decoy made by A. E. Crowell.

Although few hunters continue to shoot over hand-carved decoy rigs, the surge in duck decoy and bird carving has created an interest in decoys and the paraphernalia associated with duck hunting in the Midwest. With environmental threats to the region's rivers and wetlands, duck hunting is highly restricted, and the sport is regarded as endangered. In these respects, the duck decoy has come to symbolize memories of past hunts, time spent in a home workshop, and a reminder of the consequences of overdevelopment and careless management of wildlife resources.

Sources and Further Reading: Alan G. Haid, *Decoys of the Mississippi Flyway* (1981); Richard LeMaster, *Waterfowl: The Artist's Guide to Anatomy, Attitude, and Color* (1983); Paul W. Parmalee and Forrest Loomis, *Decoys and Decoy Carvers of Illinois* (1969).

Gregory Hansen
Arkansas State University–Jonesboro

Fly-Fishing

Fly-fishing involves fishing with an insectlike lure that floats on or just above the water surface to attract fish, and it is practiced today on rivers around the world. Fly-fishing has been especially popular in the Midwest due to the prevalence of cold, quality trout waters. The tradition is especially strong on the "blue ribbon" trout streams of the upper Midwest, such as the Au Sable, the Pere Marquette, and the Big Two Hearted.

The earliest records of fishing can be traced to almost seven thousand years ago through an ancient gorge, the predecessor to the hook, that was found in France. However, it was Izaak Walton, author of *The Compleat Angler* (1653), who contributed what has come to be known as the most revered treatment of fly-fishing. By the end of World War II, the interest in fly-fishing exploded, with over 4.5 million fly-fishers in the United States at the turn of the century and a population that is growing about 10 percent annually.

Fly-fishing has been practiced along rivers and streams in the Midwest for generations. While most fly-fishers have learned to fish in family or community situations, river guides have also played a significant role in the development of the tradition. Even though there have been many changes to the equipment used in fly-fishing, there are still three primary ways to fly-fish: from the banks of a river or stream, in waders in a river or stream, or in a boat or other floatable device.

River or stream trout fishing usually means fishing along the "edges" where the water meets a rock, a tree limb, or a log: areas where fish can find food and shelter in moving water. Fish conserve energy in these slow currents while feeding in adjacent fast water. The successful fly-fisher is a student of fish behavior.

Historically, the boats created for fly-fishing reflect a combination of regional cultural influences, practical function, and individual creativity. Boats such as wooden canoes; Au Sable, Pere Marquette, and Jordan riverboats; and, more recently, driftboats have become appreciated by both scholars and practitioners as an important part of the rich material culture of fishing.

The tying of flies for fly-fishing is still a well-established tradition, and it is directly related to place. River guides, bait-shop owners, and other fly-fishers have created flies with local names related to their favorite river, and flies are often named to honor a local person or the original maker, such as the "Ernie Borcher Special" and the "Earl Madsen Skunk Fly" from the Au Sable River in Michigan. In recent years, however, the availability of information regarding entomology related to fly-fishing and the availability of new materials has resulted in a wide array of new forms of both handmade and commercially made flies.

The Midwest is the home to some of the foremost businesses that produce fly-fishing equipment. Perhaps best known are the Shakespeare Rod and Reel Company of Kalamazoo, Michigan; the Paul Young Company of Detroit, Michigan; and Scientific Anglers of Midland, Michigan.

Sources and Further Reading: Eric Leiser, *The Complete Book of Fly Tying* (1977); John Merwin, *The New American Trout Fishing* (1994); Holly Morris, ed., *A Different Angle: Fly Fishing Stories by Women* (1995); Paul Schullery, *American Fly Fishing: A History* (1999).

C. Kurt Dewhurst
Michigan State University

Spearfishing Decoys

In the upper Midwest fishing decoys are an essential element of spearing fish through lake ice, a centuries-old method of subsistence fishing, in North America first practiced by Native Americans. The essentials of spearfishing have not changed much over centuries. A spearfishing decoy is an object resembling a fish and weighted so that it sinks when lowered through a hole cut in lake ice. The decoy "swims" when its line is manipulated ("jigged") by the fisher. The decoy is intended to lure a fish that, once attracted, can be speared. Upper Midwest Native American fishers either crouch next to a fishing hole and cover themselves and the hole with blankets, or fish under small, portable teepeelike structures. European Americans usually fish from small "fish houses" (or "ice houses" or "shanties"). These structures admit scant external light; rather, light refracted through lake water and emitted through the hole glows like a television screen in a darkened room. As a result a fisher can see into the hole in the ice, but fish cannot see out.

Fishers agree on little regarding the most effective decoy. Some say that a carrot or aluminum foil rolled into a ball is as effective as anything. Spearfishing decoys resembling living fish, however, are the most common. Typically made of wood, fish decoys are also created from metal and plastic. Most decoys are constructed with adjustable fins to affect the way each swims. Although small factories have produced fish decoys, most are homemade. Wooden fishing decoys are generally painted to make them appear more realistic and, presumably, more interesting to real fish. Yet others have painted markings unlike anything in nature. Some fishers espouse elaborate theories on which colors of decoys are most effective according to water temperature and clarity.

While winter fishing is widely practiced, most who engage in winter fishing use other means than spearing. In many places spearing is illegal, or illegal to non-indigenous people. However, where it is legal, committed spearfishing enthusiasts continue their tradition with zeal. In the early twenty-first century, there are voluntary associations of spearfishing enthusiasts that work with the legal system to preserve the right to spear fish through the ice, while providing locations where those who share an interest in spearing can get together. In many cases, spearfishing has evolved from a solitary subsistence activity to one enacted by groups of people whose main goal is sociability.

In the latter decades of the twentieth century, there emerged a group of spearfishing decoy collectors who hailed decoys as art objects. To collectors, spearing decoys are not only utilitarian objects, but also symbolic ones representing a prior way of life. Many collectors attend outdoor collectibles shows, events at which spearfishing decoys, along with items such as antique shotgun shells, sporting-related magazines, and fishing rods are bought and sold. These shows are to collectors what spearfishing trips are to fishers: occasions to enact their shared interest. The interest in collecting has created a market not only for antique decoys. The presence of collectors has stimulated the growth of a market for contemporary "artistic" spearfishing decoys that are built for use in spearfishing but whose elevated price prevents them from being placed in water.

Sources and Further Reading: Art Kimball and Brad Kimball, *Fish Decoys of the Lac du Flambeau Ojibway* (1988); Art Kimball, Brad Kimball, and Scott Kimball, *The Fish Decoy*, 3 vols. (1986); Jay A. Leitch, *Darkhouse Spearfishing across North America*, 2nd ed. (2001); Philip Nusbaum, "Spear Fishing and Spear Fishing Decoy Collecting: Connected, Yet Different Experiential Worlds," *New York Folklore* 19 (Summer/Fall 1993).

Philip Nusbaum
Minnesota State Arts Board

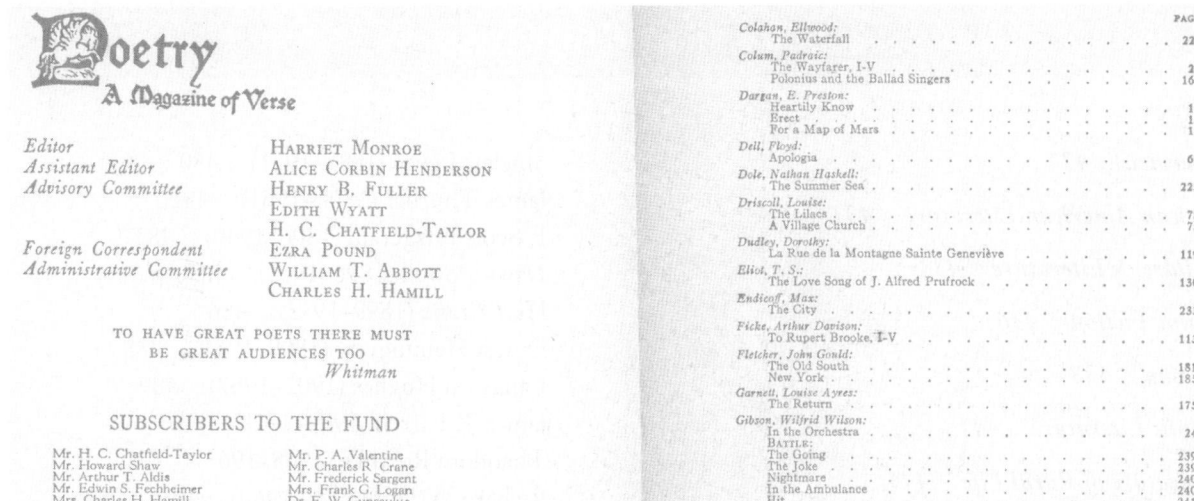

Literature

SECTION EDITOR
Timothy B. Spears

Section Contents

Overview

In 1924, the first issue of the *New Yorker* appeared on newsstands with the now famous proviso that it was "not edited for the old lady in Dubuque." Wondering how the new offering would play in the heartland, *Time* magazine sent a copy to one of its midwestern readers, who retorted, "The editors of the periodical you forwarded are, I understand, members of a literary clique. They should learn that there is no provincialism so blatant as that of a metropolitan who lacks urbanity."

Pitched at the height of the modernist era, this skirmish over the cultural identity of Dubuque, Iowa, reveals some of the primary themes and tensions that have informed the literary history of the Midwest. As early as the 1830s, when newly arrived migrants such as James Hall and Caroline Kirkland portrayed to eastern readers the hardships and beauties of the western frontier, midwestern writers and editors struggled to identify and promote the prospects of a regional literary culture. In 1833, Hall announced in his newly formed *Illinois Monthly Magazine*, "The literature of the West is still in its infancy, and we trust that we are not unconscious of the responsibility which rests on those who attempt to direct it." Nearly forty years later, the Midwest still seemed to lack a viable literary tradition. In the preface to *The Hoosier School-Master* (1871), Edward Eggleston explained how difficult it was for midwesterners to see themselves in American literature, remembering from his own reading experience that "the manners, customs, thoughts, and feelings of New England country people filled so large a place in books, while our life, not less interesting, not less romantic, and certainly not less filled with humorous and grotesque material, had no place in literature." Eggleston's realist novel was the first of several groundbreaking views of midwestern life to appear in the final decades of the century—for instance, E.W. Howe's *The Story of a Country Town* (1883); Joseph Kirkland's *Zury: The Meanest Man in Spring County* (1887); Hamlin Garland's *Main-Travelled Roads* (1891); and Mark Twain's Mississippi River writings, including "Old Times on the Mississippi" (1875) and *Adventures of Huckleberry Finn* (1884)—all of which portray rural and frontier experience and garnered positive reviews from eastern critics. But while these works gave the Midwest a literary voice, their subject matter tended to confirm the perception that the region lacked intellectual and aesthetic resources capable of sustaining an indigenous literary culture.

For a brief period, it appeared as though Chicago might become a cosmopolitan hub to rival East Coast cities. Beginning in the 1890s and spanning more than two decades, the Chicago Literary Renaissance generated city-defining novels such as Henry Blake Fuller's *The Cliff-Dwellers* (1893) and Theodore Dreiser's *Sister Carrie* (1900); innovative, vernacular poetry like Edgar Lee Masters's *Spoon River Anthology* (1915) and Carl Sandburg's *Chicago Poems* (1916); lyrically introspective fiction like Willa Cather's *Song of the Lark* (1915) and Sherwood Anderson's *Winesburg, Ohio* (1919); several literary journals; and a wealth of first-rate journalism. However, Chicago's moment as the region's self-proclaimed literary capital did not last. Ambitious young writers who had left their small-town and rural homes—or, as one critic put it, "revolted" from them—to launch careers in the city departed Chicago in the 1910s and 1920s for bigger places, in particular New York, the headquarters for most of the nation's publishers. In 1926, critic H.L. Mencken, who had earlier championed Chicago literature, lamented in *Prejudices: Fifth Series* that the city's creative forces were "in decay." Edgar Lee Masters agreed and, writing to a friend from his new home in

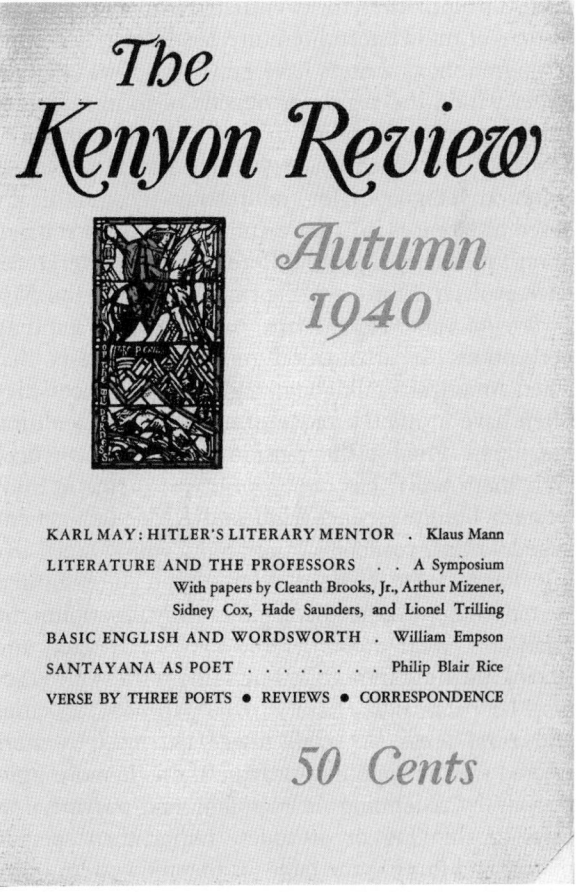

Cover of an early issue of *The Kenyon Review*. First Published in The Kenyon Review—Autumn 1940, OS vol. II, no. 4. Copyright The Kenyon Review.

New York City (in a letter now housed at Chicago's Newberry Library), he blamed "the village mind which curses Chicago in every department of life" for the exodus of writers from the city.

The inclination to equate Chicago with Dubuque, and the region as a whole with provincialism, derived from the Midwest's geographical location, its distance from eastern cities (New York, Boston, and Philadelphia), and its historical association with mainstream, commercial values. By no means unique to the American context—consider, for instance, the cultural differences, both real and imputed, that separate London, Paris, or Beijing from their hinterlands—the opposition between "provincial" and "metropolitan" perspectives nonetheless offers a useful framework for thinking about the development of midwestern literature. First of all, the two poles highlight the larger, social-historical forces that have shaped the contours of American regionalism and established hierarchical relations between urban centers and smaller cities or rural areas. Despite their subjective, relative meanings, the terms underscore a material gap in cultural conditions, differences that have had a decisive impact on where writers have chosen to live and work. Indeed, up until the late twentieth century, the social history of midwestern literature has largely been one of migration, as writers have gravitated toward cities, either within the region or outside of it, in search of employment, community, and intellectual stimulation. Secondly, "provincial" and "metropolitan" provide a common language for addressing geographically based differences in culture and power, and a starting point for examining how different regional literatures have evolved. Moreover, their appearance in the *New Yorker*—as value-laden terms, based on long-standing perceptions of urban/rural relations—suggests that when Americans talk about regional differences they often have in mind a range of economic and cultural inequities. Finally, the tension between "province" and "metropolis" has been a principal theme in midwestern literature since Hall and Kirkland first engaged eastern readers on the realities of western living. Particularly during the late nineteenth century, writers addressed this theme literally by describing the relation between the hinterland and urban society and tracing the migration (often by some restless protagonist) between them. Later, as the gap between cities and rural areas or small towns narrowed, writers treated the metropolitan-provincial divide more figuratively by redefining metropolitan and provincial as ways of thinking or attitudes (rather than specific places) and turning the table (as the midwestern critic of the *New Yorker* did) to show how a "metropolitan" perspective may in fact be provincial. In fact, this ironic approach informs several groundbreaking literary texts published in the years surrounding the *New Yorker*'s first appearance. In Sinclair Lewis's *Main Street* (1920), F. Scott Fitzgerald's *The Great Gatsby* (1925), and Ernest Hemingway's *In Our Time* (1925), the view from the provinces becomes the basis of a modernist sensibility—a tendency toward irony, self-consciousness, stylistic innovation, and reconstituting mythic themes—suggesting that Dubuque had more to do with the development of a cosmopolitan literary consciousness than some New Yorkers imagined. Or, put in terms that the Iowan-raised realist Hamlin Garland used in his 1894 manifesto *Crumbling Idols*, "Provincialism (that is to say, localism) is no ban to a national literature."

As many of the entries in this section attest, literature written in and about the Midwest continues to highlight place-specific features. From Jane Smiley's portrayal in *Moo* (1995) of Iowa skies "meeting the flat of the land" to poet James Wright's images of Ohio factory-towns, the landscapes that appear in much recent midwestern literature are readily identifiable places, while the people who move through these spaces—be they German American farmers or African American steelworkers—are connected to one another (or not) by the social and economic transformations that shaped the region (e.g., industrialization and deindustrialization, civic boosterism and rural degradation, immigration and urban migration). In this regard, the "middleness" associated with the Midwest refers not just to the region's geographic position, its modulated topography, and its representative character (as being "typical" of American society), but also to the sense that the Midwest has been the epicenter of modernizing forces that have recast the nation's culture. This sense of being connected to larger social forces, though not as acute as the retrospective historical consciousness that distinguishes southern writing, permeates much of the region's literature and gives it a distinctly modern stamp. Whether or not midwestern writing is more place-specific than other regional literatures, there is little doubt that the region's diverse cultural landscapes are well reflected in a body of literature that, by virtue of this diversity, seems uniquely representative of the American whole.

Not surprisingly, then, midwestern literature is filled with linked images and relative meanings. So the view of Nebraska in Willa Cather's *My Ántonia* (1918) is from New York City looking back through the narrator's memory, while the Chicago neighborhood that Sandra Cisneros describes in *The House on Mango Street* (1984) reminds the novel's young bilingual heroine of Mexico. In *American Indian Stories* (1921), Zitkala-Sa describes her transition from the Yankton reservation in South Dakota to the Indian Manual Labor Institute in Wabash, Indiana, as a journey across "the great circular horizon of the Dakota prairies" to "broken English," a drive toward assimilation that frayed her ties to home yet enabled her writing about Sioux culture. The relation between Native American and European American culture is also central to Louise Erdrich's North Dakota novels, written more than half a century later. However, in such works as *The Beet Queen* (1986) Erdrich pushes past the issue of coercive assimilation to dramatize the complex interweavings and mixed bloodlines that join the Chippewa (Ojibwe) peoples to the descendants of European immigrants. Perhaps the best-known example of the yoked identity that often emerges in midwestern fiction is the final paragraph of *The Great Gatsby*, where Nick Carraway (a Minnesota native) stands on Long Island and imagines Gatsby's (and the nation's) dream to be "somewhere back in that vast obscurity beyond the city, where the dark fields of the republic rolled on under the night."

The essays gathered here, thematic and author-specific, cover almost one hundred fifty years of midwestern literature. Although comprehensiveness in a volume like this is impossible, the entries as a whole are meant to acknowledge the contributions of midwesterners who remained in the region to write about their homes and writers who left the region but whose work in some fashion reflects their midwestern roots. While the author entries (arranged chronologically by birth date) focus on individual poets, fiction writers, playwrights, and essayists, the thematic essays (organized alphabetically) consider genres, historical trends, and ideas that the shorter biographical entries cannot fully address. Comprising a range of interpretive approaches and historical perspectives, the section is a guide for integrating and synthesizing the great variety of midwestern literature.

For all the attention given to literature as an art form that is primarily enjoyed or studied through the solitary act of reading, the public, institutional dimensions of literary culture have also had a significant impact on midwestern society. As Christine Pawley notes in her essay, since the nineteenth century, midwesterners have been committed to developing and sustaining a vital print culture. Besides being socially efficacious, this commitment has helped create a culture in which midwestern literature is tangibly alive. Annual celebrations such as the National Tom Sawyer Days, held in Hannibal, Missouri, since 1956, and the Riley Festival in Greenfield, Indiana, honoring the poet James Whitcomb Riley, attract tourists and generate revenue but also draw attention to local history and perhaps even inspire literary work (the Riley Festival features a poetry-writing contest). Gatherings like the Nebraska Storytelling Festival in Omaha, Nebraska (first held in 1987), and the Great Lakes Folk Festival in Lansing, Michigan, showcase literature's oral traditions alongside other creative arts and within various ethnic/cultural traditions. More academically oriented events, emphasizing critical as well as creative writing, include the Willa Cather Annual Spring Conference in Red Cloud, Nebraska (begun in the late 1990s), and the James Wright Poetry Festival in Martins Ferry, Ohio (begun in 1980). Even these scholarly celebrations of midwestern writing contain a certain amount of civic boosting.

Literary boosterism in the Midwest dates to the nineteenth century, when periodicals such as *The Illinois Monthly Magazine* simultaneously staked out the new country and promoted it as a fitting subject for American literature. Often complementing the educational efforts of local literary societies and fledgling colleges and academies (in the 1820s and 1830s Cincinnati played a key role in such efforts), these early publishing ventures were aimed at creating belletristic cultures similar to those that existed in eastern cities. At the same time, they also represented efforts to establish autonomous cosmopolitan literary centers in the Midwest. Nowhere was this ambition more dramatically developed than in late-nineteenth-century Chicago, where a robust publishing industry, including several daily newspapers, a deep pool of writing talent, and a well-endowed urban elite boomed the city's literary reputation. During the early twentieth century, *The Dial* (1880–1919), *The Friday Literary Review* (1909–1932), *Poetry: A Magazine of Verse* (1912 to the present), and the avant-garde *Little Review* (1914–1919) became literary journals of national note. In 1893, two recent Harvard graduates, inspired by the example of highly aesthetic book designs in England, founded Stone and Kimball, which competed with New York publishers until its demise in 1905. Literature also found a home in the city's foreign-language press and in African American journals like *The Defender* (1905 to the present) and *Negro Story* (1944–1946), which both dealt in varying degrees with the politics of race and published such writers as Richard Wright, Langston Hughes, and Gwendolyn Brooks.

Similar initiatives took place in other midwestern cities. In St. Louis the literary journal *Reedy's Mirror* (1891–1920), edited by the forward-thinking William Marion Reedy, was the first to publish Edgar Lee Masters's *Spoon River* poems. During the early twentieth century, in Indianapolis, publisher Bobbs-Merrill became the chief source of noteworthy Hoosier writing. In Iowa City, John T. Frederick founded *Midland: A Magazine of the Middle West*, which from its first number in 1915 to its dissolution in 1933 served as a literary voice for the agrarian and small-town Midwest. In praising the fiction of Willa Cather and O.E. Rølvaag and promoting young writers like Iowan

Ruth Suckow, the journal gave final expression (as literary historian Ronald Weber has noted) to the rural regional movement in the Midwest. After the *Midland* failed, Frederick became the director of the Chicago-based Illinois Writers Project (part of the New Deal's Federal Writers Project). There, he worked closely with writers Nelson Algren, Jack Conroy, and Richard Wright in the collection of urban and industrial folklore—material that informed Algren and Wright's fiction and in fact already figured in Conroy's work, for instance, his 1933 novel *The Disinherited*, illuminating working-class life in the Missouri coal-mining region.

As a nonpaying, loosely academic journal, *Midland* was by no means the last of its genre. Over the course of the twentieth century, the Midwest hosted countless literary periodicals, several of which are still in operation and boast distinguished publishing records: *The Prairie Schooner*, founded in 1926 at the University of Nebraska in order to "change the view of the Midwest as a literary wasteland"; *New Letters*, an "international" quarterly established in 1934 and affiliated with the University of Missouri; *The Kenyon Review*, founded in 1939 at Kenyon College in Ohio under the direction of the southern poet and critic John Crowe Ransom; *The Antioch Review*, established at Ohio's Antioch College in 1941 with a liberal political agenda; *TriQuarterly*, begun in 1958 and affiliated with Northwestern University in Evanston, Illinois; the *Iowa Review*, founded at the University of Iowa in 1970 with the goal of publishing literature that is "local but not provincial." Today, these journals remain conscious of their midwestern roots and continue to publish the work of midwestern writers, but their mission differs from that of the *Midland* as they imagine their pages and the region itself as home to literature from across the nation (and world). Their success affirms Hamlin Garland's contention that provincialism is no ban to a national literature, though not in the terms that he imagined.

In this regard, the development of English department curricula and creative writing programs at colleges and universities had a major impact on the cultural status of midwestern literature. Prior to 1920, American literary texts were seldom included in college-level English classes. However, as American literature became an acceptable field of study during the 1920s, midwestern literature attracted attention from scholars such as Ralph L. Rusk, whose *Literature of the Middle Western Frontier* appeared in 1925, and Vernon L. Parrington, whose influential work in American Studies, *Main Currents in American Thought*, published in 1930, located the Jeffersonian tradition in the literature of the "Middle Border." The emergence of midwestern literature as an object of study and the

occasion for scholarly conferences and organizations such as the Society for the Study of Midwestern Literature (established in 1971 at Michigan State University) has helped to construct the region's image in the public eye and to define the Midwest's place in American history.

The academy likewise played a crucial role in reorienting the career paths of writers. While during the late nineteenth and early twentieth centuries many American writers learned their craft—and paid the bills—by working for newspapers and mass-market periodicals, by World War II, serious writers were more likely to find jobs on university and college faculties. In the Midwest, where the connection between journalism and literary work was quite strong (William Dean Howells, Dreiser, and Hemingway all started in the newspaper business), the focus of literary culture gradually shifted from city to campus. Leading the way in this transformation was the University of Iowa's Writers' Workshop, founded in 1934. In setting an academic curriculum for educating writers and by granting advanced degrees (in particular, the now famous M.F.A.), the workshop established a model that was subsequently embraced by universities across the country.

The increased connection between higher education and midwestern letters is reflected in the work of Saul Bellow and Rita Dove, two of the region's most celebrated contemporary writers. Bellow, who graduated from Northwestern University in 1937 and then began a graduate program in anthropology at the University of Wisconsin—only to drop out of the program and concentrate on fiction writing—has served on the faculty of several universities, including the University of Minnesota and the University of Chicago. Moreover, *The Dean's December* (1982) and *Ravelstein* (2000) explore a range of philosophical issues within the context of academic life. The link between poet Rita Dove's writing career and the academy is even more explicit. In 1977, Dove earned an M.F.A. from Iowa's Writers' Workshop. Four years later, she started teaching creative writing at Arizona State University and in 1989 she moved to the University of Virginia, where she now holds a chaired professorship in the English department. Although it is difficult to assess the impact that academic training and professionalization have had on the literature itself, there is no doubt that many midwestern writers now address their readers from a different cultural position than their predecessors did. So while in 1902 the popular Indiana novelist Booth Tarkington discussed the special character of his "Middle West" in *Harpers' Monthly*, a century later such observations by regional writers are more likely to be found in specialized academic journals like *TriQuarterly*.

Though the case for literary regionalism is harder to make now than it was a century ago, writing about and in the Midwest remains a local affair. Jane Hamilton's 1993 novel *A Map of the World* is not about globalization but, rather, small-town life in Wisconsin, and while Garrison Keillor and Larry Woiwode followed their careers to New York City, they have both returned to their homes in Minnesota and North Dakota to write fiction about the worlds of their youth. For the would-be and practicing writer, much of the Midwest remains a remarkably supportive, democratic environment. In Minneapolis, where writers and readers can visit the Loft (the "nation's largest and most comprehensive literary center"); or at Cleveland State University's Poetry Center, where the public has participated in workshops since 1962; or in Detroit, where the Broadside Press carries on the activist tradition established in the mid 1960s by poet Dudley Randall and fellow participants in the Black Arts Movement; or at poetry slams throughout the region, literary culture continues to develop hand in hand with local communities.

Sources and Further Reading: Maurice Beebe, "What Modernism Was," *Journal of Modern Literature* 3 (July 1974); Andrew R.L. Cayton and Susan E. Gray, eds., *The American Midwest: Essays in Regional History* (2001); Philip A. Greasley, ed., *Dictionary of Midwestern Literature*, vol. 1, *The Authors* (2001); Bill V. Mullen, *Popular Fronts: Chicago and African-American Cultural Politics, 1935–46* (1999); Marcia Noe, ed., *Exploring the Midwestern Literary Imagination: Essays in Honor of David D. Anderson* (1993); Ralph L. Rusk, *The Literature of the Middle Western Frontier*, 2 vols. (1925); Carl S. Smith, *Chicago and the American Literary Imagination, 1880–1920* (1984); Timothy B. Spears, *Chicago Dreaming: Midwesterners and the City, 1871–1919* (2005); Booth Tarkington, "The Middle West," *Harper's Monthly* 106 (Dec. 1902); Julius E. Thompson, *Dudley Randall, Broadside Press, and the Black Arts Movement in Detroit, 1960–1995* (1999); Ronald Weber, *The Midwestern Ascendancy in American Writing* (1992); Stephen Wilbers, *The Iowa Writers' Workshop: Origins, Emergence, and Growth* (1980); Ben Yagoda, *About Town: The New Yorker and the World It Made* (2001).

Timothy B. Spears
Middlebury College, Vermont

African American Literature

For much of their twentieth-century life, African American fiction and poetry have been children of the cities. This does not necessarily mean that the significant works are set only against the backdrop of the great urban centers of the Midwest or Northeast (more to the point, of New York and Chicago). To suggest so is to ignore the grand achievements of Jean Toomer, Sterling Brown, Zora Neale Hurston, Ernest J. Gaines, Alice Walker, and countless others through the last century and into this one. These are writers who created important fiction and poetry set in the small-town or rural South as minority figures when the weight was on works set in urban America. Yet the urban context predominates as the site for the exploration of political and social issues. Themes related to migration, disruption, and personal alienation are vigorously demonstrated in the context of cities. During the last half of the twentieth century, however, a growing number of midwestern writers sounded the notes of affirmation and the heroic.

The period 1910–1950 was a time of dramatic industrialization in the Midwest and the most dramatic resettling of African Americans to its cities. More than fifty thousand African Americans entered Chicago within eighteen months beginning January 1916. In 1917, at least five times as many black Americans lived in Detroit as lived there in 1910. Four times as many lived in Cleveland in 1920 as lived there in 1910. With the change of setting and a changing emphasis in literature, especially the naturalistic efforts in fiction, came a change of artistic emphasis among African American artists. What follows are brief explorations of selected works of poetry and fiction that captured most effectively the transformation of midwestern cities and the African American population—Richard Wright's *Native Son* (1940), early poems by Gwendolyn Brooks and Robert Hayden, the Cleveland stories of Chester Himes, Langston Hughes's *Not without Laughter*; and Toni Morrison's *The Bluest Eye* (1970). These works are either set during the 1910–1950 period or were published during that time.

Before this period, much of African American literature was tied to a rural or small-town setting. This includes the rich body of nineteenth-century slave narratives, as well as much early poetry. Indeed, the achievement of Paul Laurence Dunbar, born in Dayton, Ohio, is marked by his pastoral celebrations of the hearth and home and less by his romantic musings of interior states. Charles Chesnutt was a native of North Carolina who lived most of his life in Cleveland. Like Dunbar, Cleveland-born Chesnutt, in his first tales, collected in the important *The Conjure Woman* (1899), made extensive use of regional dialect. Later writers would be challenged to shape a black literary voice not bound to the pastoral or gently mocking human foibles.

The Harlem Renaissance (1918–1940) was a period in which black creative arts, especially musical theatre, blues, jazz, and poetry, enjoyed great popularity. At its extreme, the body of literary works from this period emphasized the notion of the city—the promised land—as a context for rampant sexuality, good times, and hot jazz. Despite notes of disillusionment, the myth of Harlem prevailed through the 1930s. This myth was predicated on the optimism and confidence of youth, on an apparent urgency to reject the staid manners and attitudes of an older generation, and on the romantic notion that spontaneous passion could free one from the humdrum problems of everyday life. Liberation was a place.

Dismissing the Harlem Renaissance as urban pastoral, Richard Wright entered the literary landscape in dramatic fashion. His collection of southern stories, *Uncle Tom's Children* (1938), foretold the arrival of a different sensibility. Shaped as much by his close study of Marxism and naturalistic fiction as his own lived experience in the Deep South, Wright's view of Western civilization placed the isolated individual at the center, developing a consciousness/identity in the face of antagonistic and concrete forces. When brought to the urban setting—"machine city"—as Wright would have it, the experience was harshened. In *Native Son*, Wright's most important sustained fiction, the South Side of Chicago is an overwhelmingly bleak setting.

In very important ways, Wright's concern with confinement, interracial sexuality leading to violence, and pursuit to exile or death became an effective prototype for African American fiction for a generation. Indeed, black fiction began to be popularly described as the plight of the black (male) victim. Yet later interpretations of the novel would define Bigger's isolation less in racial terms than in the terms of existentialism. Bigger's plight was after all the plight of Modern Man. As Wright noted in his essay "Literature of the Negro in the United States," "the Negro is America's metaphor." In "How Bigger was Born" and his important introduction to the classic sociological study of Chicago *Black Metropolis*, Wright moves toward a schema emphasizing class versus race exclusively. At the same time, it would be impossible to erase the fact that his first novel spoke to the depths of racial division.

It can be argued that Wright and his peers at the South Side Writers Club would usher in the second Chicago renaissance of the century. This group consisted of writers such as poets Margaret Walker and Frank Marshall Davis as well as playwright Theodore Ward. Whether a collective aesthetic prevailed during that period is still to be explored; however, it is clear that Wright's shade of urban realism had its impact. That it was born in the shadow of the migration experience and friction along the color line is a salient part of its legacy.

In less than a decade, Wright's harsh Chicago was tempered by Gwendolyn Brooks's poems of the "unheroic" kitchenette communities amid the South Side of Chicago. Brooks is not at odds with the city. Born in

Kansas and reared in Chicago, she crafted early poems that were wry, often poignant. Her city would be won over through sheer toughness, wit, and imagination (read improvisation). She was awarded the Pulitzer Prize for Poetry in 1950 for her second volume, *Annie Allen* (1949). Perhaps the signature poems in her earlier project were the sonnets contained in "The Motherhood" section of that volume, as well as the portrait of the dandy in "Sundays of Satin Legs Smith." These are poems well controlled, characterizing the range of responsibility for mothers, the assumptions of too-proper readers, and a figure disdaining self-inspection. Gwendolyn Brooks would serve as an effective generational bridge figure as she mentored members of the Black Arts Movement more than twenty years later. Her later poems have a sharper political cutting edge, though the generous gestures to the working class of Chicago are not lost. She was appointed poetry consultant to the Library of Congress for the year 1985–1986.

In many of his first poems, Robert Hayden related the experience of growing up in Detroit on the eve of the Depression. Hayden grew up in an area dubbed Paradise Valley. As affirmative in tone and power as those of Gwendolyn Brooks, Hayden's early poems never slip to easy satire or a long wail about life in the city. His first volume, *Heart-Shape in the Dust* (1940), contained a number of poems—especially, "Bacchanale" and "Shine, Mister?"—that relate the experience of Detroit laborers. Hayden would produce several of the most important poems on the African American experience in the English language: "Frederick Douglass," "Runagate, Runagate," and "Middle Passage." At the same time, he kept his compass true to his early years in Paradise Valley. In the series Elegies for Paradise Valley in his *American Journal* (1978), Hayden would extend his earlier sympathetic tone across broadly ranging sketches of Detroit. He was appointed poetry consultant to the Library of Congress for the two-year period 1976–1978.

Although Chester Himes is noted for the searing naturalism of his earliest novels, such as *If He Hollers, Let Him Go* (1945) and *The Primitive* (1955), his earliest fiction consisted of short stories written during and shortly after his incarceration in the Ohio State Penitentiary. While in prison he published his first story, "What Red Hell?" (1934) and after his release on parole began to write prolifically. The early stories set in the Midwest appeared in *Esquire*, *Abbott's Monthly Magazine*, *Coronet*, and *Bronzeman*. Works such as "Salute to the Passing" (1939) chronicled generational conflicts, and his less naturalistic works laid a foundation for later writers from the region such as Cyrus Colter and Ronald Fair.

Not without Laughter (1930) by Langston Hughes

and *The Bluest Eye* by Toni Morrison are growing-up novels set for the most part in Lawrence, Kansas, and Lorain, Ohio, respectively. Though published nearly forty years apart, both novels deal with personal histories that bring into sharp relief attitudes shaped in the South and the expectations of empowerment in the northern city. Sandy, the protagonist in the Hughes novel, absorbs the values of his small town, moving between the generous and sympathetic views of Aunt Hager, his grandmother, and the harsher, more secular represented by Harriet and the male laborers. Eventually he will leave for Chicago with his mother in search of his father, Jimboy. Like the Richard Wright of *American Hunger* (1977), Sandy finds both a colder place and the lure of literacy.

Pauline and Cholly are the parents of Pecola in the Morrison novel; they have married in Kentucky and come north to seek work. Sadly, the North is also the site for conflict, loneliness, abuse, and, eventually, temporary madness. Morrison's Lorain was a small city to which many men like Cholly were attracted by the booming steel mills. Morrison's use of idiom defines the small African American community as one of transplanted southerners. But it is her use of a communal voice that heightens the reader's sense of a small, tightly knit, and ultimately accepting community. When Mrs. MacTeer gathers with her neighbors to talk about the arrival of a roomer to the MacTeer home, when the neighborhood women gather and talk about incest in the Breedlove home and Pecola's pregnancy, the reader senses a chorus of voices moving to the same rhythms. Values are shared, fears dramatized. A community takes shape.

The Midwest was central to the force of the Black Arts Movement during the late 1960s. Largely a cultural nationalist movement that emphasized poetry and one-act plays, nearly every major city in the region was a site for poetry and theatre groups. Indeed, the movement was far more national in scope than the Harlem Renaissance some forty years earlier. As the journals *Crisis* and *Opportunity* were so important to the earlier movement, *Black World*, edited monthly from Chicago by Hoyt Fuller and his staff, was equally important to the Black Arts Movement. All major writers of the period published there. Other, smaller literary journals based in the region included *Free Lance*, *Vibration* (both based in Cleveland), and *Confrontation* (Athens, Ohio). Midwestern writers who contributed significantly during this period and beyond included, among many others, Mari Evans, Etheridge Knight, Haki Madhubuti, Nikki Giovanni, Eugene Redmond, and Calvin Hernton. Rita Dove is a well-known recent writer whose work *Thomas and Beulah* was honored with a Pulitzer Prize in 1987. She was appointed poet laureate of the United States in

1993 (a designation that had changed a few years earlier from poetry consultant to the Library of Congress).

If the African American experience was depicted as primarily southern and rural in the nineteenth century, it would diversify to include both the large- and the small-city Midwest well before the last century's end. The heart of the country contained it all.

Source and Further Reading: Bernard Bell, *The Afro-American Novel and Its Tradition* (1987).

John McCluskey, Jr.
Indiana University–Bloomington

Children's Literature

Midwestern writers have produced a wide range of works for children: memoirs like Luther Standing Bear's *My Indian Boyhood* (1922); fantasy fiction like Carl Sandburg's *Rootabaga Stories* (1951), Jane Louise Curry's Abáloc novels, and L. Frank Baum's Oz books; historical fiction like Laura Ingalls Wilder's Little House books, Richard Peck's stories of Grandma Dowdel, Louise Erdrich's *The Birchbark House* (1999), and Maude Hart Lovelace's Betsy-Tacy books; picture books by Kevin Henkes and Sarah Stewart; and books set in the present, like M. E. Kerr's *Deliver Us from Evie* (1994), Marion Dane Bauer's *Foster Child* (1977), Zibby Oneal's *The Language of Goldfish* (1980), and Virginia Hamilton's *Plain City* (1993).

Important children's magazines have come from the region. Among the most influential was *The Little Corporal* (1865–1875), which mixed morality and fact in stories, poems, and nonfiction. Twentieth-century readers were entertained and edified by *Child Life* (1921–), *Highlights for Children* (1946–), and *Ebony, Jr!* (1973–1985). One of the best late-twentieth-century magazines was *Cricket* (1973–), whose blend of splendid illustrations and fine writing for elementary school–aged children launched a handful of similar magazines for readers from infancy to college.

Midwestern writers have made important contributions to children's books. Newbery Award winners include Ellen Raskin (from Wisconsin), Irene Hunt (Illinois), Christopher Paul Curtis (Michigan), Richard Peck (Illinois), and Virginia Hamilton (Ohio), who also won the Wilder Award. Iowan Mildred Wirt Benson wrote the first Nancy Drew book on Edward Stratemeyer's outline. L. Frank Baum, who lived in Chicago, wrote the first successful American fantasy series.

Exploring universal themes, midwestern writers for

Laura Ingalls Wilder. Photo © Laura Ingalls Wilder Memorial Society, DeSmet, S.D.

children combine a strong sense of place with often-quirky characters, in works that celebrate the region. The famously broad midwestern landscape is a major element in many works: The physical setting frequently turns the plot, and the landscape is a tangible presence. Prairie often receives this kind of treatment. Standing Bear's *My Indian Boyhood* (1922) is as filled with a sense of far horizons and limitless sky as are Wilder's Little House books. But the coal country of Hamilton's *M.C. Higgins, the Great* (1974) is as carefully described; and the Mississippi River almost becomes a character in Samuel Clemens's *Tom Sawyer* (1876) and in Mary Calhoun's Katie John books (1960s).

The books frequently display great pride in place. On the classroom map in *Chrysanthemum* (1991), by Kevin Henkes, a bright star highlights Madison, Wisconsin, Henkes'—and Chrysanthemum's—home. As written by Benson, Nancy Drew is "a true daughter of the Middle West" who sees the beauty in farmland, in *The Secret of the Old Clock* (1930). There are wonders here. In Curry's Abáloc novels, the landscape is literally magical: Prehistoric Astarlind, a land of goblins

and talking wolves, leaves its traces in the midwestern landscape, and a ravening force of evil lies bound beneath the hills of eastern Ohio. Less overtly magical are the prairies in a number of books. Here, the prairies are, in Wilder's words, "enormous sky and . . . land you couldn't see to the end of. Everything was so fresh and clean and big and splendid." When the narrator of Louise Erdrich's *The Range Eternal* (2002) looks into the fiery heart of the family stove, the "Range Eternal" emblazoned on the stove's front becomes "the range of the buffalo . . . the deer range . . . the wolf range and fox range"—the vast prairies of North Dakota, where there is room to run. Wilder contradicts the sense that all prairies are alike, noting in *By the Shores of Silver Lake* (1939) the "enormous silence" of the South Dakota prairie, lacking on the Kansas prairie; caught in that silence one moonlit winter night, Laura feels herself "part of the wide land, of the far deep sky" and slides along the moonpath on the ice to a wondrous encounter with a prairie wolf.

The landscape also can threaten. Overshadowing M. C. Higgins's Ohio house is the spoil heap left from coal mining, which will one day bury his home. Dorothy Gale's Kansas as conceived by Baum is a gray, "unromantic" place where a farmer can wear himself out struggling against weather that withers crops and people.

On weather hinges the story in a number of works. It is the stuff of tall tales; it is the device that moves the plot. So cold is Flint, Michigan, in Christopher Paul Curtis's *The Watsons Go to Birmingham—1963* (1995) that a boy kissing his reflection in a car mirror sticks to the glass. A South Dakota farmer entering his stable on a sunny April day finds a blizzard raging before he leaves, in Wilder's *The First Four Years* (1971). Many works set in the northern plains share the theme of winter held at bay. When Windigo howls around the corners of the house in Erdrich's *Range Eternal*, it is deflected by the warmth of the family and of their stove. Deep Valley's social pace quickens as "a sort of defiance" against winter's dreariness, in Lovelace's *Betsy Was a Junior.*

In a number of works, weather is a plot device. Blizzards are especially useful here: The heirs in Ellen Raskin's *The Westing Game* (1978) are isolated by snow as they start to solve their mystery; Buhlaire Sims loses her way during a whiteout in Hamilton's *Plain City* (1993) and thereby meets the father she had been told was dead; the Ingalls family struggles to survive in *The Long Winter* (1940). The sometimes-melodramatic weather of summer also can steer a plot. Dorothy makes her first visit to Oz courtesy of a cyclone, in *The Wizard of Oz* (1900); an unexpected rainstorm leads to Nancy Drew finding an important clue, in *Secret of the Old Clock*. In Kerr's *Deliver Us from Evie*, a fundamentalist Christian family sees the flooding Mississippi River as a sign that it is following the wrong moral path, ending the romance budding between the eldest daughter and the book's narrator. Often, weather brings characters together. When a January thaw floods the camp Buhlaire's father shares with other homeless people in Hamilton's *Plain City*, she has her chance to help him and to shape a closer relationship. The whites and the Arickarees form a bond while fighting the cold and snow, in *The Willow Whistle*, by Cornelia Meigs (1931); Almanzo Wilder courts Laura Ingalls by bringing her across the snowy prairie in his showy sleigh, in *These Happy Golden Years* (1943).

The small towns dotting the midwestern landscape are well represented in these books, with authors of two minds about small-town culture. The tradition of small town as small-minded is upheld by several writers, who point to the fact that everyone in a small town knows—and tells—everything that goes on: Learning that details of a special night out have been reported to his family, Parr Burrman notes succinctly in Kerr's *Evie*, "Living in a small town sucks!" In these places, Buhlaire realizes, "People like to put everybody neatly into place. . . . Anybody doesn't want to do what they do, does something different or acts different . . . they're going to talk about them. Maybe even shun them." The small-town folks of Richard Peck's *A Long Way from Chicago* (1998) are "hayseeds and no-'count country people" who are shocked at the thought of a Chicago girl playing the Virgin Mary in the Christmas pageant, in *A Year Down Yonder* (2000). Lesbian Evie Burrman is unwelcome in her community after she begins an affair with the daughter of a prominent family; her lesbianism, Evie's parents decide, is the "fault" of the other, more sophisticated, girl. Suburbs sometimes replace small towns as centers of provincial thinking: A suburbanite in Stella Pevsner's *Would My Fortune Cookie Lie?* (1996) dismisses going into Chicago to visit museums or to attend cultural events because "[p]eople out here don't do that stuff"; Carrie Stokes's mother downplays her daughter's mental breakdown in Oneal's *Language of Goldfish* (1980) because "[p]eople in Northpoint did not have crazy children."

In other works, small towns have a less distasteful reputation. After all, Buhlaire admits, they are essentially no different from other places; the kind of things that jar people's lives happen in "backwater places," just as they do in larger towns. In Green Town, Illinois, in Ray Bradbury's *Dandelion Wine* (1957), the mundane details of everyday life spin into something extraordinary; and the little Illinois town in Peck's works is a hotbed of romance and intrigue. There is, apparently, little reason to go anywhere else. Betsy Ray, convinced that the "Great World" is more im-

pressive and important than little Deep Valley, Minnesota, finds as she tours Europe in *Betsy and the Great World* (1952) that Europeans envy her for living not far from Minnehaha Falls; Paris, she is assured in *Heaven to Betsy* (1945), isn't half as nice as Deep Valley. In Sarah Stewart's *The Journey* (2001), all that Hannah sees or does in Chicago is simply an extension of what she has experienced already in her intimate Amish community.

What saves small towns in many books praising them is their people. There is a solidness to some characters: Nancy Drew is logical and level-headed; Dorothy Gale has great natural dignity because "I'm only a little girl from Kansas, and we've got more dignity at home than we know what to do with." More often, midwesterners are individual to the point of eccentricity. Some are born special: An African goddess becomes the ancestor of the Perry family in Hamilton's *The Magical Adventures of Pretty Pearl* (1983). Others owe their eccentricities to the Midwest's tradition of tall talking. Baum's Oz is populated by creatures like a tall-tale gone askew: Jack Pumpkinhead, growing his own replacement heads; the Wogglebug, who expanded after being magnified under a microscope. In Carl Sandburg's *Rootabaga Stories* (1922, 1923), two skyscrapers produce a free-running child in the form of a railroad train, and the Huckabuck family's burning popcorn field covers their farm in deep drifts of popcorn. Larger-than-life prankster Grandma Dowdel, of Peck's *Long Way from Chicago* and *A Year Down Yonder*, is, Peck points out, "the American tall tale in a Lane Bryant dress." More common are eccentrics like those in Ellen Raskin's books: the Figg family, practicing its own religion, and Sister Figg Newton, literally tap-dancing through life in *Figgs and Phantoms* (1974); or the eccentric millionaire and his oddball heirs in *Westing Game*. Elizabeth Brown's passion for books rules her life and overwhelms her house, in Stewart's *The Library* (1995).

Many characters in the books are white, though Standing Bear and Erdrich have written about Native Americans and Curtis and Hamilton have written almost exclusively about African Americans. Nonwhite characters are most often found in works set in cities. The heart of Pevsner's *Fortune Cookie* is the relationship between the white and Asian Chicagoans; Curtis's books tend to be set in and around Flint, Michigan. Prejudice is most often a factor when the setting is a small town, past or present. Ma Ingalls has nothing good to say about the Native Americans the family encounters on the prairies in the 1870s. In 1963, the Watsons worry about racism only when they go to Birmingham, Alabama. In the 1930s, Bud, in Curtis's *Bud, Not Buddy* (1999), witnesses overt racism only in little Owosso, Michigan, which urges "Our Negro

Friends" to "Kindly Don't Let the Sun Set on Your Rear End in Owosso." In the present, M. C. Higgins's father is prejudiced against a Melungeon family, with their indistinct race and their "witchy" six-fingered hands.

Weather, small-town life, and prejudices notwithstanding, these writers tend to celebrate the Midwest in all its faults and quirkiness. After all, what better place to hail from? Asked, "Are you of royal blood?" by a haughty princess, Dorothy Gale says it best: "Better than that. . . . I came from Kansas."

Sources and Further Reading: Barbara Bader, *American Picturebooks from Noah's Ark to the Beast Within* (1976); Robert Bator, *Signposts to Criticism of Children's Literature* (1983); Eleanor Cameron, *The Green and Burning Tree* (1969); Beverly Lyon Clark, *Kiddie Lit* (2003); Dana L. Fox and Kathy G. Short, eds., *Stories Matter: The Complexity of Cultural Authenticity in Children's Literature* (2003); R. Gordon Kelly, ed., *Children's Periodicals of the United States* (1984); Cornelia Meigs, Anne Eaton, Elizabeth Nesbitt, and Ruth Viguers, *A Critical History of Children's Literature*, rev. ed. (1969).

Pat Pflieger
West Chester University, Pennsylvania

Crime Fiction

For most of the twentieth century, crime fiction was derided as pulp fiction, published in cheap paperbacks with lurid covers and sensational titles intended to be consumed and discarded like fast food. The genre focused almost exclusively on plots dealing with sex and corruption in urban areas. Writers specialized in evoking a sordid underworld in which heroes as well as villains regularly defied social conventions. Crime stories were about respectable people only to the extent that the stories exposed their respectability as a hollow shell. Almost always set in New York City, Los Angeles, or Miami—places where people supposedly drank, cursed, and behaved in ways that respectable midwesterners ignored, at least in public—crime fiction emphasized the importance of personal morality rather than public citizenship. It has grown in importance as a form of popular fiction, and the Midwest has been its home, too.

Crime stories were not new. Mark Twain had dabbled in the form in works such as *The Tragedy of Pudd'nhead Wilson* (1894) and *Tom Sawyer Detective* (1896). But in the middle of the twentieth century, pulp fiction constituted a burgeoning semiunderground industry. Crime novels predominated, although other subgenres, including science fiction,

westerns, and adventure stories, also flourished. Authors such as Mickey Spillane became minor celebrities by affecting the attributes of their fictional heroes. Among those who sought to transcend formulaic plots and stock characters were Dashiell Hammett and Chicago-born Raymond Chandler. Hammett's Sam Spade was the iconic private investigator, a hero whose behavior verged all too close to that of the villains and who lived by a private code of conduct in which loyalty to one's partner matters more than loyalty to institutions. Chandler's major contribution was a lush prose style brimming with memorable similes. Chester Himes, who was born in Missouri and grew up in Ohio, used the crime genre to explore issues of race, although he did not set his books in the region.

The cachet acquired by Hammett and Chandler was enhanced by Hollywood movie adaptations, including *The Thin Man* (1934) and *The Maltese Falcon* (1930). Film noir was an established genre by the late 1940s, and directors such as Alfred Hitchcock took crime stories and produced intricate and subtle tales of mystery and intrigue. In the 1950s and 1960s, commercial television validated the acceptability of crime stories. Insatiably hungry for plots and characters that worked within the confines of a weekly format, writers and producers flooded the airwaves with detectives. No less important was the impact of the cultural and political revolutions of the 1960s and early 1970s. As public distrust of government and other civic institutions grew in the wake of the civil rights movement, the Vietnam War, and the Watergate scandal, the cynical ethos of crime novels seemed increasingly plausible. Crime fiction attracted younger authors eager to write the kind of book they liked to read: fast-paced novels with familiar characters who told "the story behind the story."

One of the major themes of such fiction in the late twentieth century was the idea that crime was omnipresent, even in the American Heartland. Many authors also found crime novels a congenial format for exploring questions of personal identity, alienation, and diversity. In addition to entertaining readers, the books were a kind of plot-driven muckraking journalism. If the novels rarely told readers something new, they presented a large audience with very concrete information about corporate corruption, child abuse, domestic violence, illicit sexuality, and government incompetence. They personalized social ills that contradicted images of the Midwest as a safe, homogeneous region free from the problems that beset New York or Los Angeles.

Perhaps the most successful author of midwestern crime novels is Sara Paretsky. Born in Kansas on June 8, 1947, she moved to Chicago after graduation from the University of Kansas. Unable to find a job with a

PhD in history from the University of Chicago, she earned an MBA. and spent a decade as a marketing manager for an insurance company. In her early thirties, Paretsky fulfilled her lifelong ambition to write a novel when she created the witty private investigator V. I. Warshawski. The Warshawski books were enormously successful, in no small part because of their unabashed feminism and their exposés of corporate greed and cultural intolerance. Paretsky was named *Ms.* magazine's 1987 Woman of the Year and won several awards, including the 1996 Mark Twain Award for Distinguished Contribution to Midwest Literature.

Paretsky both honored and subverted the conventions of crime fiction. Warshawski is a variation on the stereotypical Sam Spade detective. She lives alone, has prickly relationships with the police, frequents a bar where she imbibes scotch, is a devoted Cubs fan, and often finds herself in physical altercations with bad guys. However, Warshawski gives as good as she gets. Unlike the stock females of earlier crime novels, she is a strong woman who takes care of herself and is not afraid of her sexuality. And while V.I. is loyal to her friends, she embraces social issues that go well beyond her own life. She is proud of her ethnicity—her Italian mother and her Polish father—and is deeply committed to civil rights and feminism. A child of the 1960s, she confronts crimes that usually revolve around corporate malfeasance or social problems. The novels are successful despite their convoluted plots. Recreating the texture of a place through the accumulation of telling details, Paretsky reveals Chicago as rich, complex, and distinctive.

Less prominent novelists have created something similar for other midwestern cities. Cincinnati native Jonathan Valin captures the underworld of his hometown as a shadowy collection of bars and dark alleys in a series featuring private investigator Harry Stoner. Cleveland in Chicago-born Les Roberts's tales of Milan Jacovich is no cheerier. Both writers describe worlds in which individuals must be true to themselves, for they can reliably depend on no one else. Eugene Izzi's *The Criminalist* (1998) features detective Dominick DiGrazia and his partner Janice Constantine working a case involving ruined reputations and despair in the very nasty streets of Chicago. Gory and sensational psychosexual crimes permeate Richard Montanari's tales of Cleveland detective John Salvatore Paris. The seamier side of Detroit gets its due in Loren D. Estleman's stories of Amos Walker. (Estleman also traces the history of twentieth-century Detroit in seven novels focusing on organized crime, the automobile industry, and Motown.)

Detroit is the setting for several novels by Elmore Leonard, who grew up in the Motor City. Taking a job with an advertising agency in 1949, Leonard indulged his passion for writing and eventually became one of the most successful pulp fiction authors of the twentieth century. He initially specialized in westerns, most notably *Hombre* (1961), which were often adapted into movies. In the late 1960s, Leonard switched to crime novels distinguished by snappy dialogue, droll humor, and a colorful array of low-life characters whose criminal plans tended to go hilariously awry. While Leonard set his books in a variety of settings, including south Florida, he featured Detroit in *Fifty-Two Pickup* (1974), *The Switch* (1978), *City Primeval* (1980), and *Killshot* (1989), among others. Like Sara Paretsky, Leonard was a brand name in the 1980s and 1990s. Despite his fondness for Detroit and his skill at evoking the city through dialogue, Leonard's reputation is national.

Authors with loftier literary aspirations tend to focus on the moral consequences of a crime rather than on its solution. In *Mr. White's Confession* (1998), a story of the 1939 murders of two dance-hall girls in St. Paul Robert White's quarry is the nature of memory and love. His book is a meditation on truth and its eventual triumph. In *A Simple Plan* (1993), Scott Smith explores the destructive ramifications of the impulsive decision of three Ohioans to keep the $4.4 million dollars they find in a crashed plane and divide it after a year of silence.

More common are books that center on the lives of characters in well-defined locations. Detroit native Steve Hamilton's first manuscript won a contest sponsored by the Private Eye Writers of America and St. Martin's Press. His protagonist, Alex McKnight, is a former Detroit detective who moved to the Upper Peninsula after he was shot and his partner killed. Against his inclinations, the moody McKnight finds himself investigating crimes involving friends and acquaintances in and around Sault Ste. Marie. Revealing a Midwest that is anything but homogeneous and homey, Hamilton populates McKnight's world with a diverse cast of secondary characters, including an Ojibwa Indian named Vinnie Red Sky LeBlanc.

More often than not, midwestern crime fiction features characters whose race, sexuality, gender, or religion tends to be subsumed within their larger commitment to domesticity and community. In the Marti MacAllister novels, Eleanor Taylor Bland, a native of Boston, writes about life in a fictional multicultural city called Lincoln Prairie, Illinois, located on Lake Michigan just north of Chicago. MacAllister is an African American woman who worked as a cop in the Windy City for a decade. She moved her family to Lincoln Prairie when her husband was killed in the line of duty. Her partner in the multicultural Midwest is a taciturn traditionalist named Matthew "Vik" Jessenovik, who has more trouble adjusting to Marti's gender than to her race. The two cops are personally loyal to each other and respect each other's ethnic identities. Most of the crimes they encounter involve the plights of children, the elderly, and marginal members of society. MacAllister confronts racism and sexism as well as social change, including the growing Hispanic presence in her city. But her major interest lies in ensuring a decent family life for her own children as well as those without parents she meets in her work. Marti is no Sam Spade or V. I. Warshawski. She is a devoted mother who lives in a nice house with a good second husband and children who care about each other.

Claire Watkins is a deputy sheriff in Fort St. Antoine, Wisconsin, in a series by Mary Logue. Like MacAllister, Watkins is a former big-city cop (Minneapolis in this case), who fled with her daughter after the killing of her police officer husband. Small-town Wisconsin, to no one's surprise, has its share of unscrupulous citizens, including real estate developers who want to trash the local ecosystem and fathers who force their young daughters to have sex with them. Yet Claire does find some degree of peace in her new home. She starts a new relationship, resolves her feelings about her husband's death, makes new friends, and develops a sense of doing good in the world.

Across the Mississippi River in eastern Iowa lives the fictional deputy sheriff of Nation County, Carl Houseman. Created by Donald Harstad, a retired Iowa deputy sheriff with thirty years' experience, this popular series is straightforward in its concentration on investigative procedures. Houseman investigates sensational crimes involving vampires, group sex, and other things rarely associated with rural Iowa. Houseman and his wife communicate with each other in passing while he spends much of his time with an attractive and sympathetic female FBI agent. Nation County has more excitement than is plausible. (At one point almost the entire sheriff's office is wiped out.) The same thing is true in the small fictional town of Falls City, Nebraska, where author David Wiltse's former Secret Service agent Billy Trees operates after returning home suffering from trauma over the death of his partner. He meets old friends and gets wrapped up in the shooting of two high school teachers. Falls City is a place that nurtures Irish characters like Trees and harbors a multitude of secrets that belie its calm exterior.

By the early twenty-first century, few places in the Midwest were without their own crime series. Paul L. Gaus uses mysteries to explore the world of the Amish living in east-central Ohio. Michael Craft's Mark Manning is a former Chicago journalist living with his gay lover in a small Wisconsin town. Taken together, these and similar novels make the obvious point that crime is everywhere, that nothing is what it seems, and that evil lurks even in farmhouses. Their more important contribution is their evocation of distinctive places in which recognizable human beings struggle with personal demons and social problems by depending on their own grit and wit as well as the kindness of friends and neighbors. Despite its formulaic plots and sensationalism, crime fiction offers entertaining windows into life in the multiple recesses of the American Midwest.

Sources and Further Reading: Mike Ashley, ed., *The Mammoth Encyclopedia of Modern Crime Fiction* (2002); Woody Haut, *Neon Noir* (1999); John Muncie and Eugene McLaughlin, eds., *The Problem of Crime*, 2nd ed. (2001); Geoffrey O'Brien, *Hardboiled America: Lurid Paperbacks and the Masters of Noir*, rev. ed. (1997).

Andrew Cayton
Miami University, Oxford, Ohio

Drama

The Midwest is often conceived of in the American psyche as an undramatic place. However, the region has played a central role in American theatre since its rise in the mid-nineteenth century; it has exhibited a strong connection to realism and has proven particularly hospitable to women and African American playwrights. Some of the central conflicts of the Midwest—surviving on the land, staying or going, fitting in or not fitting in to the community—mirror the fundamental American struggle to sustain a viable new culture.

Mark Twain and William Dean Howells are the first major playwrights from the region whose works feature midwesterners seeking opportunity in the East. Their collaboration, *Colonel Sellers as a Scientist* (1887), is a delightful romp, as is Twain's *Is He Dead?* (1898). Howells's three dozen plays are wide ranging and effective, especially *A Counterfeit Presentment* (1877) and his one-act comedies.

Noteworthy at the turn of the century were Augustus Thomas and George Ade. Thomas, born in St. Louis, is remembered for "state" plays like *Alabama* (1891) and *In Mizzoura* (1893) and popular comedies. Ade made significant contributions to American musical theatre and with comic dramas such as *The Country Chairman* (1903) and *The College Widow* (1904), set in Crawfordsville, Indiana.

William Vaughn Moody, like Ade from Indiana, showed great promise with two masterpieces, *The Great Divide* (1906) and *The Faith Healer* (1909), before dying tragically at an early age. *The Faith Healer* can be regarded as the first important drama set in the Midwest and embodying its ethos and values.

The earliest American female playwrights originated from the Midwest, achieving success in the first third of the twentieth century. Among them were Zona Gale, Susan Glaspell, Rachel Crothers, and Zoë Akins. Gale, from Wisconsin, won the Pulitzer Prize in 1921 for *Miss Lulu Bett*, while Rachel Crothers of Illinois achieved an unmatched string of successes on Broadway from *The Three of Us* in 1906 to *Susan and God* in 1937. Crothers's *Expressing Willie* (1924) pits unpretentious midwestern values against the idle rich of Long Island, while her *As Husbands Go* (1931) takes place in Dubuque, Iowa.

Glaspell grew up in Iowa and went on to become associated with Eugene O'Neill and the Provincetown Players. Her probing plays include *Trifles*, which evokes both midwestern rootedness in the land and outlaw violence of the West; *Alison's House*, set like many of her plays in the Midwest, won the Pulitzer Prize in 1931. Akins, of Missouri, became famous for "society plays" like *Déclassé* (1919) and won a Pulitzer Prize for her dramatization of Edith Wharton's *The Old Maid* (1935).

The only play to come directly out of Maxwell Anderson's college experience in North Dakota, *White Desert* (1923) evokes the harsh realities of that wintry landscape. Donald Marquis of Illinois, known primarily as a humorous columnist, wrote several plays, including *The Old Soak* (1921), his most successful stage work.

Langston Hughes, the first major African American dramatist, was born in Joplin, Missouri; lived in Lawrence, Kansas; and went on to become a leading figure of the Harlem Renaissance. Following *Mulatto* (1930), in the mid-1930s he wrote several evocative midwestern plays for the Gilpin Players at Karamu House in Cleveland. Later he shifted focus to New York, paving the way for arguably the most significant group of African American playwrights from any region.

American theatre of the 1920s and 1930s featured a great deal of collaboration, much of it centered on George S. Kaufman. Kaufman collaborated productively with Marc Connelly on a series of plays, including *Merton of the Movies* (1922), set in Simsbury, Illinois. He worked with novelist Edna Ferber on *Dinner at Eight* (1932) and *Stage Door* (1936). With Ring Lardner, like Ferber a humorist from Michigan, Kaufman created *June Moon* in 1929. Lardner wrote a number of short dramatic pieces in his own right. Lewis Beach, born in Saginaw, Michigan, achieved some success with *The Clod* (1916) and, especially, *The Goose Hangs High* (1924).

The Front Page (1928), written by Ben Hecht and Charles MacArthur, grew out of the playwrights' experiences working as newspaper reporters in Chicago. *The Front Page* has been made into at least three films. Hecht and MacArthur also collaborated on *Twentieth Century* (1932), set on the Twentieth Century Limited train en route from Chicago to New York. Another significant Illinois play, *Abe Lincoln in Illinois* (1938), was written by Robert Sherwood.

The 1930s saw the rise of Thornton Wilder, one of America's premier novelists and playwrights, born in Wisconsin. *Our Town* (1938) evokes the Midwest in many respects, with allusions to works by Edgar Lee Masters, Sinclair Lewis, and Sherwood Anderson. *Pullman Car Hiawatha* (1931), one of his pathbreaking one-acts, begins in New York and arrives by train in Chicago a half hour later. Other plays, like *The Long Christmas Dinner* (1931), deal with traditional American rituals associated with midwestern values. Several later plays are set in the Heartland.

Also active in the 1930s was Paul Osborn from Indiana, whose *Morning's at Seven* (1939), winner of a Tony Award, is still performed with some regularity. Ohioan James Thurber's lone theatrical venture, *The Male Animal* (1940), cowritten with Elliot Nugent, proved one of the most successful comedies of this period.

Although musical theatre from the Midwest dates from Augustin Daly's adaptation of Twain's *Roughing It* (1872–1873) and L. Frank Baum's *Wizard of Oz* (1903), the World War II years witnessed a boom in film musicals set there: *The Wizard of Oz* (1939); *Meet Me in St. Louis* (1944), directed by Vincent Minelli and, like *Wizard*, starring Judy Garland; and *State Fair* (1945), set in Iowa. *St. Louis Woman* (1946) features African American experience and music by Johnny Mercer performed by Pearl Bailey and others. These and other midwestern musicals, like *The Music Man* (1957), based on Meredith Willson's upbringing in Iowa, continue to be performed, filmed, and updated.

In the 1940s, three major playwrights—Tennessee Williams, Arthur Miller, and William Inge—began to establish themselves, all with significant midwestern ties. Williams spent twenty formative years in the region and studied playwriting at the University of Missouri and the University of Iowa. Over a dozen of his plays are set in the St. Louis area, including *The Strangest Kind of Romance* and *The Long Goodbye*. Several were performed by the Mummers, a St. Louis theatre group with which Williams was actively involved. The most famous of Williams's midwestern plays, *The Glass Menagerie* (1945), evokes the gritty working-class feel of industrial St. Louis, along with its fascination with glamour and decay. He returned to the same area for his late play *A Lovely Sunday for Creve Coeur* (1979).

Born of Jewish parentage in New York, Miller spent a life-changing period at the University of Michigan, where he won the Avery Hopwood Award for Playwriting. Both *The Man Who Had All the Luck* (1944) and *All My Sons* (1947) are set in the Midwest, and *Death of a Salesman* (1949) evokes the region as a nostalgic contrast to gritty New York.

William Inge is considered by many the "dean" of midwestern playwrights, based on his four Broadway hits, *Come Back, Little Sheba* (1950), *Picnic* (1953), *Bus Stop* (1955), and *The Dark at the Top of the Stairs* (1957), all of which were successful as films. After Inge moved to New York, with the exception of the Oscar-winning screenplay for *Splendor in the Grass* (1961), a popular film set in Kansas starring Natalie Wood and Warren Beatty, his plays were not successful. Regional legend still attributes Inge's suicide in 1973 to his being divorced from his Kansas roots.

Another particularly successful play of the 1950s was *Inherit the Wind* (1955), written by Jerome Lawrence and Robert E. Lee, two Ohioans. Although based on the famous Scopes "Monkey" Trial of 1925 in Tennessee, the script is deliberately set in a more generalized "small town."

The 1950s saw the emergence of a whole new generation of talent. Particularly important were African American artists such as Lorraine Hansberry, Charles Gordone, Mari Evans, Adrienne Kennedy, and August Wilson. Hansberry became the first black woman to have a play on Broadway, *A Raisin in the Sun* (1959). Set in her native Chicago, this play has since become an American classic in its depiction of African American family life.

Charles Gordone was the first African American to receive the Pulitzer Prize for drama, for *No Place for Somebody* in 1970. Mari Evans, also from Indiana, wrote several plays in the 1970s, including *Eyes* (1979), an adaptation of Zora Neal Hurston's *Their Eyes Were Watching God*. Adrienne Kennedy, from *Funnyhouse of a Negro* (1964) through more recent works like *The Ohio State Murders* (1992) and beyond, has established herself as a poet of the theatre, whose demanding works create their own lyrical landscape.

August Wilson, born and raised in the midwestern fringe of western Pennsylvania, has become one of America's leading playwrights. Major works date from his residency in St. Paul, where he wrote *Ma Rainey's Black Bottom* (1984), set in Chicago, and *Fences* (1987) and *Piano Lesson* (1990), both winners of the Pulitzer Prize. His searing theatrical examinations of African American life often play out against the backdrop of the Great Migration and cultural intersections of North and South.

Another group from the same generation was energized by the antiestablishment ethos of the Vietnam War era. Megan Terry, "mother of American feminist drama," created the first rock musical, *Viet Rock*, in 1966 but left New York to found the Omaha Magic Theatre and has since gone on to write more than sixty plays in her adopted home. Maryat Lee, born and raised in the Cincinnati area, became disillusioned with elitist and commercial trends in contemporary theatre and moved to West Virginia, where she established EcoTheater. This approach relies on amateur players and dramatizes oral histories, aiming at authenticity in a specific community. Chicago-born Jack Gelber is chiefly known for *The Connection* (1959), an aleatory, counterculture play featuring street-wise drug addicts that shocked and energized Broadway in the decade following.

David Rabe (b. 1940), from Dubuque, Iowa, emerged with explosive energy in the early 1970s with his Vietnam trilogy featuring a midwesterner who encounters a disorienting world. *Sticks and Bones* (1971), the second play, focuses on Ozzie and Harriet, "typical" American parents, and their failure to understand the trauma experienced in Vietnam by their eldest son, David.

Another Vietnam veteran, Lanford Wilson, has written an important series of plays set in his native Missouri: *5th of July* (1978); *Talley's Folly* (1982), which won the Pulitzer Prize; and *Talley and Son* (1985). All three plays focus on family, landscape, and continuity. *The Mound Builders* (1975) involves anthropology and the Native American legacy that undergirds contemporary American life in the Mississippi Valley.

Sam Shepard (b. 1943), often thought of as a western playwright, was born and spent his early years in Illinois. *Chicago* (1966) and other early plays are set there, and *Buried Child* (1978), winner of the Pulitzer Prize in 1979, employs quintessentially midwestern tropes of growth, decay, and rebirth through cyclical nature.

Larry Shue's untimely death was a tragic loss for American theatre. His early one-act, *Grandma Duck Is Dead* (1968), is set in a central Illinois college town, and *The Nerd* (1984), his first major hit, seems likewise distinctly midwestern.

In the exciting theatrical scene in Chicago in the 1960s and 1970s, *Sexual Perversity in Chicago* (1976) established David Mamet as a fresh new voice. *The Duck Variations* (1976) and other one-acts are set either in Chicago or in midwestern resort areas; *Lakeboat* (1981) is an example. His most important work of this phase is *American Buffalo* (1977), a classic of the American theatre. Like Rabe and Lanford Wilson, Mamet arose from the Midwest and has since broadened his perspective to other areas of the country.

The newer generation of playwrights includes a number of energetic artists whose future remains still in formation. Emily Mann has written on a variety of documentary topics, including *Still Life*, based on interviews with three people in Minnesota in the summer of 1978. David Auburn's *Proof* won the Tony Award and the Pulitzer Prize in 2001. Many younger playwrights flourish now in cities like Minneapolis, Chicago, Cleveland, and Detroit. The Midwest continues to generate genuine theatrical talent that feeds into mainstream American culture. The range of significant playwrights the Heartland has produced gives ample testimony to the vitality of its culture and its centrality to American habits of thinking and self-definition.

Source and Further Reading: Walter J. Meserve, *An Outline History of American Drama* (1994).

David Radavich
Eastern Illinois University

Ethnic Literature

The history of ethnic literature in the Midwest is long and, due to ongoing immigration into the region, continually developing. But what constitutes "ethnic literature"? Does the term describe works written by first-, second- or third-generation immigrants but that do not address ethnicity explicitly—such as those by David Mamet, Stanley Elkin, Nelson Algren, Carl Sandburg, John Muir, or Lucien Stryk? Does it pertain to works written by people who are neither immigrants nor children of immigrants but who do write explicitly about ethnicity—such as Willa Cather, Stuart Dybek, or Upton Sinclair? What about literature by or about Native or African Americans? Indeed, the meaning of the term *ethnicity* itself is subject to considerable popular and critical debate. In the United States today, "ethnic" is commonly used to signify difference from White Anglo-Saxon Protestantism; for example, "ethnic immigrants" or "ethnic minorities" are typically conceived of as those who are not WASPs. This includes, of course, all "people of color"—a term generally used to refer to groups that historically have been considered to be racialized minorities in the United States—thereby creating additional ambiguity surrounding the concept of race vis-à-vis ethnicity.

For the purposes of this entry, "ethnic literature" can be defined as writing that focuses on ethnic experience and identity. An ethnic group will be understood along the lines commonly employed by contemporary ethnic theorists: as "a named human population with myths of common ancestry, shared historical memories, one or more elements of common culture, a link with a homeland and a sense of solidarity among at least some of its members." Separate entries exist in this volume for Native American and African American literatures.

Perhaps the most useful way to examine ethnic literature as a whole, despite the diversity of writers and groups represented, is to identify several dominant themes that appear in a wide range of works. Two of the most prominent stem from the reasons for which ethnic midwesterners came to the region originally: to settle and establish farms or to find work in urban centers. Ole Edvart Rølvaag (1876–1931) is probably the most notable example of a writer who explores the promises and perils of immigrant farm life in the Midwest. Rølvaag, author of the prairie trilogy consisting of the epic masterpiece *Giants of the Earth* (English translation, 1927), *Peder Victorious* (1929), and *Their Father's God* (1931), chronicles the experiences of Norwegian immigrant farmers during the late nineteenth and early twentieth centuries. Using the characters of Per and Beret Hansa as contrasts, Rølvaag illustrates how the 1870s South Dakota frontier was a liberating space filled with potential for some immigrants and an isolating and formidable place for others. Rølvaag juxtaposes the lure of the American dream with the cost of cultural alienation that can result from leaving one's homeland. He shows how life in America's fertile "breadbasket" is also subject to the cruelty of nature, signified by blizzards, plagues of locusts, and deprivation.

Herbert Krause (1905–1976), emulating but also departing from Rølvaag, casts a slightly different eye on the settlement of the prairie as he focuses on German American farmers in *Wind without Rain* (1939) and *The Thresher* (1946). Krause similarly depicts the forces of nature as violent and unforgiving, but these forces are matched by the parochialism of ethnic midwestern farm towns that have little tolerance for people who do not conform to community expectations. Finally, Willa Cather, although neither "ethnic" nor midwestern by birth (she was born to non-immigrant parents in Virginia), penned the most widely read renditions of immigrants on the prairie in her novels *O Pioneers!* (1913) and *My Ántonia* (1918). Cather casts the landscape as a character in itself in *O Pioneers!* as she parallels the maturation of Alexandra Bergson, the Swedish immigrant protagonist, with the taming of the frontier from wilderness to farmland. *My Ántonia*, populated by a strikingly multiethnic cast of Bohemian, Russian, Italian, French, and Scandinavian immigrant farmers, considers how memory and nostalgia can help temper cultural conflicts and harsh realities on the prairie.

The Midwest is not solely agricultural, however,

and urban centers play as important a role as the farm in the region's ethnic literature. Rapid industrialization at the end of the nineteenth century drew an influx of immigrants to midwestern cities—most notably, to Chicago—to find work in factories. For Jewish author Saul Bellow (1915–2005), the city and its ethnic neighborhoods functioned as much as a character as they did a setting. Eight of his twelve novels, ranging from his first, *Dangling Man* (1944), to his most recent, *Ravelstein* (2000), are set in Chicago. Most of his novellas and short stories focus on the city, and much of his autobiographical writing comments upon his experience as a Jewish immigrant growing up in the polyethnic neighborhoods of Chicago's northwest side. If Cather is responsible for authoring the most widely read novels about the ethnic midwestern prairie, then her counterpart for the ethnic midwestern city is surely Bellow.

The list of authors who draw extensively upon Chicago includes other such notable figures as Jewish authors Studs Terkel (b. 1912), Bette Howland (b. 1937), and Maxine Chernoff (b. 1962); Irish American writers Finley Peter Dunne (1867–1936), James T. Farrell (1904–1979), and Andrew Greeley (b. 1928); Mexican Americans Sandra Cisneros (b. 1954) and Luis J. Rodríguez (b. 1954); Greek American Harry Petrakis (b. 1923); and Ukrainian American Mike Royko (1932–1997). Upton Sinclair, although not himself a midwesterner, famously exposed the dangers of Chicago and its meatpacking industry for eastern European immigrants in his novel *The Jungle* (1906).

Other midwestern cities figure prominently in ethnic literature as well. Fannie Hurst (1885–1968), German American and Jewish, introduced the reading public to socially, politically, and financially conservative St. Louis. Les Roberts (b. 1937) depicts east-side Slovenian Croatian Cleveland through the eyes of Milan Jacovich, the protagonist of his detective series. Ruth Seid (whose pseudonym is Jo Sinclair; 1913–1995) captured the changing nature of multiethnic and multiracial neighborhoods in Cleveland and Detroit between the Depression and the Cold War. But Chicago stands out as the focal city of ethnic literature in the Midwest.

Agendas for social reform are often linked to the portrayal of urban life in midwestern ethnic literature. This is not surprising given that immigrant laborers during the Gilded Age continually battled exploitation by industrialists, and their activism left a legacy for subsequent generations. In addition, many ethnic authors identify with the condition of the oppressed—whether rooted in class, gender, or ethnicity—and give voice to these concerns in their writing. For instance, Tillie Olsen (born c. 1912), the daughter of Jewish socialists who emigrated from Russia in 1905, grew up in a politically radical Jewish community in Omaha and brings this political stance to her writing. As an early feminist working-class author, Olsen focuses (most notably in her first collection of stories, *Tell Me a Riddle*, 1962) on poor, often immigrant, working women who struggle to sustain and create meaningful lives in stifling environments. Her novel *Yonnondio: From the Thirties* (1974) investigates the ways in which the double yoke of poverty and gender cripple both a mother and a daughter as they move with their family through low-wage jobs in Wyoming mines, South Dakota tenant farms, and Chicago urban meatpacking houses. Olsen also advocates strongly for women writers specifically, as is demonstrated by her collection of essays, *Silences* (1978), and her republication of the long-neglected *Life in the Iron Mills*, written by Rebecca Harding Davis in 1861. Through these efforts, Olsen provides an important model and spokesperson for other ethnic midwestern authors who are committed to using their writing to challenge class and gender norms that disempower significant portions of society.

Studs Terkel, also Jewish and one of the region's most popular writers due in part to his long tenure (1953–1998) as host of a radio show for WFMT in Chicago, similarly uses the pen to agitate for social reform. He was born in New York City but moved to Chicago at about age eight and has never left. Terkel, who adopted the name Studs in admiration for Irish American James T. Farrell's *Studs Lonigan* trilogy (1935), uses oral history as his primary means of social critique. In such works as *Division Street: America* (1967), *Working: People Talk about What They Do All Day and How They Feel about What They Do* (1974), and *Race: How Blacks and Whites Think and Feel about the American Obsession* (1992) Terkel laments what Bellow has described as Chicago's "brutal materialism" while fighting for economic equality and championing the dignity of society's most marginalized members. Terkel's work demonstrates how, to borrow from his fellow midwestern writer Richard Wright, "words" can be used as "weapons" to combat social ills.

With equal power, Mexican American writers and activists Sandra Cisneros, Luis J. Rodriguez, and Ana Castillo use "words as weapons." Cisneros, in her highly acclaimed collection of vignettes *The House on Mango Street* (1984), is among the first Chicana writers to depict in fiction the unique facets of midwestern (as opposed to southwestern) Mexican American life. Based in part on Cisneros's experiences growing up in a Chicago barrio, *The House on Mango Street* examines the triple liability faced by those who are discriminated against on the basis of class, gender, *and* ethnicity. Cisneros rejects victimization by creating Chicana characters whose strength and hope conquer societal barriers.

Rodríguez's work serves as a counterpoint to Cisneros's focus on women in that he confronts the challenges faced by young Mexican American men in the Midwest. Through poetry and prose, and most specifically in his gang memoir *Always Running* (1993), Rodríguez explores the similarities and differences between the distinctly urban experience of Chicanos in Los Angeles and Chicago and those in more rural southwestern border towns. But it is Castillo who wields the most combative weapon through her writing. Her novel *The Mixquiahuala Letters* (1986), which considers women's roles and identities in Mexico and the United States, marked her as a leading Chicana feminista writer, but *Massacre of the Dreamers: Essays on Xicanisma* (1994) is Castillo's most politically charged work. Castillo coins the term *Xicanisma* to describe the unique struggles of Chicanas who, being neither white nor black but brown, fall outside liberation movements grounded in the black/white racial paradigm that dominates American society.

Bharati Mukherjee, born in Calcutta, India, in 1940, also depicts the experience of women who fall outside America's racial binary. In her novel *Jasmine* (1989), set in contemporary Iowa, Mukherjee portrays the difficulties of adjustment experienced by an Indian immigrant as she moves from the patriarchal culture of her homeland to craft a new sense of self and of place in the United States. In so doing, Mukherjee provides a foundation for a growing body of recent immigrant writers from Southeast Asia—Hmong, Vietnamese, Filipino—who are now making the Midwest their home.

Finally, no entry on ethnic midwestern literature would be complete without reference to Garrison Keillor, the contemporary writer who is probably most responsible for the image of ethnic midwestern life held by those outside the region. In his writings and weekly *Prairie Home Companion* radio show (1974–1987 and 1993–present), Keillor playfully and poignantly depicts the mind-sets, mores, and mannerisms of Norwegian Lutherans and German Catholics in a small rural community in Minnesota. His weekly monologues deftly capture the ethnic dialects, foodways, cultural practices, and religious tensions and beliefs of rural townspeople and farm communities. In offering a sophisticated rendition of the human dramas that take place in all people's lives, regardless of where they live or with what ethnic group they may affiliate, Keillor joins the large group of writers cited here whose work importantly illustrates how the stereotypically homogeneous Midwest is in fact a site of considerable heterogeneity.

Sources and Further Reading: Philip A. Greasley, ed., *Dictionary of Midwestern Literature*, vol. 1, *The Authors* (2001);

John Hutchinson and Anthony D. Smith, eds., *Ethnicity* (1996); Werner Sollors, *Beyond Ethnicity: Consent and Descent in American Culture* (1986).

Heather Hathaway
Marquette University, Wisconsin

Literature of Rural Life

The federal government doesn't puzzle much over what "rural" might mean as a word or signify as an idea. Rural is simply the adjective that modifies the locale to which the government delivers mail (RFD) and electricity (REA). Our Bureau of the Census, slightly more scrupulous, defines rural America as any area, together with the region around it, under twenty-five hundred in population, areas known to their inhabitants as "out in the country." Any literary critic or historian would probably agree, then, that "rural literature" is what is written in and about that area of our nation. For a critic of midwestern rural literature, however, rural literature is not simply about any countryside. Region to region, "the rural" denotes something profoundly different in feel and content. William

Willa Cather. Nebraska State Historical Society, Photograph Collection, W689-766.

Faulkner, Marjorie Kinnan Rawlings, and Eudora Welty, for instance, strike a tone about the South that is different from Sarah Orne Jewett's and Jane Brox's about the Northeast; and John Steinbeck, David Mas Masumoto, and William Saroyan strike a different tone about California's Central Valley than Linda Hasselstrom, Louis Bromfield, Josephine Johnson, and Willa Cather do about the Midwest. Midwestern rural literature has a different tone, spirit, and perhaps even content. Midwestern rural literature has always been and continues to be mainly about a profound clash of values about life on the farm as it differs from and conflicts with life in the city. This is qualitatively different from southern literature, for instance, which has as its leitmotif the question of race, or California literature, which has as its focus the twin questions of assimilation and disruption of the natural world.

This conflict, of course, is not only the stuff of myth, it's the stuff of comedy, parody, and the coastal amusement that fuels such visions as *The Beverly Hillbillies* or Saul Steinberg's infamous map of the United States on which the Midwest hardly exists. By such a measurement, Midwesterners are thought to be ill-educated hicks by nature and choice, even as they long to escape the confines of their parochial rural experience, to which a particularly unkind fate has damned them. Sinclair Lewis and Hamlin Garland would spring to most minds as good examples of this response.

For another view of midwestern character, it's worth taking a look at Grant Wood, mainly a painter but sometimes a writer. In *American Gothic* (1930), he creates an image that almost every American would admit to knowing, probably understanding; in this painting, he apparently captures the flat, uninteresting quality of midwestern life at its most obvious. It's an image, almost everyone supposes, of a farmer and his wife standing in front of their simple abode in their simple clothes holding their simple tools. This "simple" image stirs deep love in many people; it strikes repulsion in the hearts of others; museumgoers flock to see it in the Art Institute of Chicago, an urban setting displaying an essential rural scene. But, of course, it's not a painting of a farmer and his wife, but one of a small-town businessman in Eldon, Iowa, and his daughter. He's taken off his day uniform (his collar) and he's working outdoors as a hobby. It may well be a simple life that's being portrayed, but not in the way it seems. It's about two people who live in the Midwest happily and by choice; they like their house, they like their surroundings. For better or worse, they do not wish to be on Broadway.

Wood's image, in its mythic if misunderstood power, catches a central truth about the midwestern experience and, consequently, about the literature of the Midwest: its deeply and inescapably ambivalent

nature. However many folks respond openly to what they think is the straightforward honesty of the presentation of the man and his daughter, just as many are pained and repulsed. Just as many respond positively to the presentation of vitality and beauty in that scarcely varying landscape as wish to escape it. Indeed, one might transfer this ambivalence of responses to midwestern literature itself. That is to say, as many people respond sympathetically to the starkness and power of midwestern life presented in, say, Willa Cather and Liberty Hyde Bailey as respond with the disgust of Sinclair Lewis and Meridel LeSueur.

In his passionate and forthright essay *Revolt against the City* (1935), Grant Wood decries what he calls "the domination exercised over art and letters and over much of our thinking and living by Eastern capitals of finance and politics . . ." and he lauds the "present revolt" against the East. His argument at its most interesting is the claim that this revolt results from widespread contemporary recognition that the East is actually colonial, subject to European domination, parochial; and that the "interior of the country," that is, the Midwest, is where it is possible for people to return and discover or rediscover real American values, what he baldly claims are "frontier virtues." "Central and dominant in our midwestern scene," he goes on, "is the farmer," characterized by independence, individualism, and conservatism. Indeed, Wood claims, "the life of the farmer, engaged in a constant conflict with natural forces, is essentially dramatic."

What Wood helps us to grasp, then, with his passionate and quaintly time-bound argument, is that midwestern rural literature has at its core this profound clash of values that has characterized georgic literature from its first appearance in Hesiod and Virgil, through eighteenth-century English poets like James Thomson, to the Romantics (especially William Wordsworth in a poem like "Michael"), and on into its American Jeffersonian guise and its rural midwestern flourishings. Whatever the reader's emotional response to the literature may be, midwestern rural literature is inherently georgic, that is to say, about the farm.

The georgic (the word derives from the Latin word for farmer) is a literary form or mode, which can also be called a literary impulse, that emerges when appropriate cultural conditions prevail, as they certainly have and do in the Midwest. Among the main concerns of the georgic are the nature of farmwork, the differences between time on the farm and time in the city, and the struggle of the farmer/writer to define his personal experience as valid in contrast to supposedly more public urban experience. Since early days, another characteristic of the georgic has been the sense of alienation from the larger culture that it projects:

Farmers distrust those whose lives are not bound to land and time the way their own lives are. This presumption can be seen as an ongoing dialectic between joy and despair, between stasis and change; on the farm, one is always dealing with the tension between entropy—the tendency of human culture and human life to fall apart or run down or lapse—and the inarguable permanence of the cyclic natural world. The georgic's underlying feeling of anxiety arises from the irresolvability of these issues.

Willa Cather's *My Ántonia* (1918) is in its essence a positive georgic. Ántonia Shimerda and Jim Burden arrive in rural Nebraska under warm wraps in the same horse-drawn wagon, and in late middle-age Jim writes the story of their intertwined lives. Ántonia, beautiful, strong, dominant, powerful, grows up used to hard work but parochially bound by the unforgiving terms of her life. She senses the beauties of the Nebraska landscape, and her own physical beauty seems utterly natural in it. Jim, seemingly finer and certainly of a different social class, ends up as a successful railroad lawyer. When, many years later, he returns to rural Nebraska and spends time on the family farm with Ántonia, her quiet husband, and her houseful of vivacious but well-behaved children, he is left feeling nostalgic and wistful. Has his worldly success been too dearly bought? Would he have been happier staying in his small town, lawyering there, living the simpler life that has so fulfilled Ántonia even as it has coarsened her body? There is an acknowledgement on Jim's part that, wealth and power aside, Ántonia in her rural neighborhood has lived a more meaningful life. With "a new kind of strength in the gravity of her face," Ántonia Shimerda is a quintessentially georgic hero.

In his much more recent nonfiction prose work *Great Possessions* (1990), a georgic account of contemporary Amish farming practices, David Klein openly rejects the world of the city and the struggles of contemporary industrial agriculture, and, like a psalmist, sings a hymn of praise to agricultural life on his large, traditionally farmed homestead in northeastern Ohio. Framed and structured, as such works often are, by the turning of the seasons, the book deals with a specifically modern aspect of the midwestern georgic, the threat to the environment. Like Virgil, Klein manages to tell his readers how to farm: Here's when and how to plant; to harvest; to let the land lie fallow; here's how to raise a good crop without poison or fertilizer. He is passionate about the wildlife that thrives on his farm even as it is banished from the environmentally threatened farms of his technologically more "advanced" neighbors. It is a book that makes a large claim for the rural life: It is better than an urban life, and only by remaining old-fashioned and untechnological can it avoid environmental degradation.

In her novel *Q Road* (2002), Bonnie Jo Campbell creates a rural story about the contemporary farm and those who work it, facing impossible financial demands, under threat from the urban sprawl of the ever-advancing city and the folks who flee its degradation and ruin. These are particularly georgic themes; rats and roaches, the georgic claims, are urban. Campbell's heroine is a young woman named Rachel Crane, who carries a .22 rifle slung over her shoulder; knows how to skin a skunk; is as familiar with the land she and her husband struggle to make a living farming as were the Potawatomi who farmed it only two hundred years ago; and whose language is as salty as her behavior is passionately given over to preserving a vision of life she instinctively understands is both precious and precarious. It is clear, in Campbell's vision, that Rachel's farm, indeed the very nature of rural experience itself, is under threat and that the force that will destroy it is not the economy, or the pull of the city, or the failure of the farmers' collective will. If the farm disappears as a source of radical simplicity and naturalness, it will be because of the inherent and contradictory hatred for the natural, rural world held by refugees from the city who want rural simplicity without rural naturalness.

One such person, Elaine Shore, sits across Q Road from the farm, drinking her morning coffee, gazing out on the lawn she forces her husband to sweep clean every day of the debris that blows onto it from Rachel's activities in her fields and gardens. Elaine has a vision of the perfect future, and it will arrive when the farm is completely developed and those nasty outbuildings, especially the barn, are torn down; when the road is paved, when the township board has regularized garbage pickup; when the zoning board has managed to get rid of rural chaos and disorder. Rachel senses her neighbor's antagonism without understanding its source, and, when her 140-year-old barn burns down, confronts the task of rebuilding it and maintaining the farm in an ever-more-perilous environment without ever comprehending the nature of the forces arrayed against her and her family.

In heightened form, Rachel confronts what has almost always been the struggle of rural Midwest literature, and if Bonnie Jo Campbell is the voice of the georgic of the future, the suburbs will not prevail, and rural midwestern literature will remain by definition what it has always been: radical, counter, rebellious, willful, and strikingly independent. On the other hand, if Campbell is wrong, all such literature may become an exercise in (or tribute to) nostalgia.

Sources and Further Reading: Thomas L. Altherr, "'The Country We Have Married': Wendell Berry and the Georgic Tradition of Agriculture," *Southern Studies* 2 (Summer

1990); Karla Armbruster and Kathleen R. Wallace, eds., *Beyond Nature Writings: Expanding the Boundaries of Ecocriticism* (2001); Lawrence Buell, *Writing for an Endangered World: Literature, Culture, and Environment in the U.S. and Beyond* (2001); Ian Marshall, *Peak Experiences: Walking Meditations on Literature, Nature and Need* (2003); John Murdoch, "The Landscape of Labor: Transformations in the Georgic," in Kenneth R. Johnston, Gilbert Chaitin, Karen Hanson, and Herbert Marks, eds., *Romantic Revolutions: Criticism and Theory* (1990); Gary Snyder, "Ecology, Literature, and the New World Disorder," *ISLE: Interdisciplinary Studies in Literature and Environment* 11 (Winter 2004).

Thomas Bailey
Western Michigan University

Literature of Small-Town Life

According to William Gass, the Midwest is "a dissonance of parts and people" but "a consonance of Towns." The importance of midwestern small-town literature in American culture is striking. Historically, small towns played a vital role in the mainly agrarian economy and culture of the region. And they produced an inordinate number of writers whose works in the first part of the twentieth century transcended regionalism to achieve national prominence.

In pioneer days, the literary life of the Old Northwest was predictably sparse. The harsh imperatives of survival and the onerous labor of clearing the land or extracting its mineral wealth preoccupied most citizens. "Our people, perhaps, have as yet no literature because they have nothing to say. They are busy living, doing, growing. The age of reflection and imaginative reproduction has not yet arrived," observed the *Western Messenger*, an early literary paper in Cincinnati.

The earliest novel about a midwestern town—or rather, settlement—was Caroline Kirkland's *A New Home—Who'll Follow?* (1839). The eastern-educated Kirkland drew good-humoredly on her experiences in the newly founded village of Pinckney, Michigan. The novel caused a sensation back east, where people were hungry for news of life on the frontier. It sparked a different kind of sensation among Kirkland's backwoods neighbors, who made life so unpleasant that Kirkland retreated to New York City, where she wrote two mediocre sequels, *Forest Life* (1842) and *Western Clearings* (1845).

Kirkland's novel possessed several traits that would replicate themselves in future specimens of midwestern small-town literature. First, there was the backlash from townsfolk who imagined that they were portrayed in an unflattering light. Second, there was

Kirkland's use of reportorial realism mingled with satire to evoke character and setting. She depicted frontier life unromantically and criticized the pressures for conformity in pioneer society. In midwestern small towns people might tolerate eccentricity, but they shunned anyone deemed a heretic, an infidel, "radical," or deviant.

The first wave of midwestern small-town novels crested in the 1870s and 1880s. These were tinged with pessimism and bitterness over the cultural aridity of village life (a continuing theme in subsequent works) or disillusionment with the depressed agricultural conditions in the West, which threatened the economic stability of the market towns that depended on the farm trade. In Missourian E. W. Howe's *The Story of a Country Town* (1883) the residents of Twin Mounds hoped to grow rich with the new country but found themselves sinking into poverty and idleness.

Another midwestern rural realist was Joseph Kirkland, a Chicago lawyer and son of Caroline Kirkland. His *Zury: The Meanest Man in Spring County* (1887) is a shrewdly drawn character study showing the hard-eyed materialism needed to prosper in the Midwest. Kirkland's portrait of small-town ways in Illinois through the eyes of the title character is contrasted with the sophisticated perspective of the New England schoolmarm who becomes his wife.

In American literary history Kirkland would perhaps be better remembered for urging his friend Hamlin Garland to portray in stories the exploited farm people he had observed on a trip to South Dakota in 1887. Garland, who had grown up in Wisconsin, Iowa, and the Dakotas and "backtrailed" to Boston, returned from his visit infused with the zeal of a convert, determined to tell people in the East the truth about the situation. The stories, collected in *Main-Traveled Roads* (1891), shattered illusions about the nobility of farm life, depicting it as hard and brutish, a "long and wearyful" road that "has a dull little town at one end and a home of toil at the other." There was a populist message in the stories of farmers crushed by debts to town bankers and moneylenders. William Dean Howells, then the most influential critic in America and herald of the new realism, wrote: "If any one is still at a loss to account for that uprising of the farmers of the West . . . let him read *Main-Travelled Roads*, and he will begin to understand."

Howells's good friend Samuel Clemens praised E. W. Howe's grim novel as a truthful picture of village life as he had known it in Hannibal, Missouri. Angered by the excesses of capitalism, Clemens set several of his own novels and stories in small towns to illustrate the soul-warping effects of the age's prevailing greed and fraud, from *The Gilded Age* (1873) with its portrait of Colonel Sellers, the quintessential midwestern town boomer and conman, to *The Man That Corrupted Hadleyburg* (1900), which indicted small town people's self-serving moral blindness.

Still, small towns had their literary defenders, who painted them as places where the folks were folksier—friendlier, more egalitarian—than the harried, mongrelized denizens of the wicked, grimy cities. Their writings struck a popular nerve. Native-born urban Americans, most of them raised on farms and in villages, were anxious about the upheavals wrought by industrialization, urbanization, and immigration and recalled with rosy nostalgia the stability and community of small-town life. The "home town" gave nineteenth-century Americans a sense of roots, even as they escaped it to seek opportunity in the cities.

Garland had sounded this emotional note in his story "God's Ravens." A reporter returns to his home town in Wisconsin to escape the terrible city. At first he is critical of the narrow gossip and conformity, but he changes his mind after he faints in the street and the townspeople aid him and heap kindnesses on him and his family.

A typical rural attitude is more realistically expressed in Willa Cather's *O Pioneers!* (1913) when the farmwoman heroine's childhood friend who has moved to the city tells her that the freedom she so envies in cities is hollow. There are thousands of rolling stones like him that die anonymously and alone.

Though deeply attached to her home town, Red Cloud, Nebraska, Cather was no small-town sentimentalist; in stories and novels like "The Sculptor's Funeral" (collected in *The Troll Garden*, 1905) and *My Ántonia* (1918), she flays the petty-mindedness of village society, the lack of culture, of beauty.

The most prominent literary champions of the village were Zona Gale and Booth Tarkington. Gale, who quit her job as a reporter in New York and returned to her Wisconsin home town, wrote short stories about life in *Friendship Village* (1908), where "togetherness," a warm neighborliness, enveloped any unfortunate soul who got into some kind of respectable trouble. The Hoosier author Booth Tarkington launched a long career with *The Gentleman from Indiana* (1899), in which the hero, like Gale, chucks a New York newspaper job after becoming disillusioned with "the rush and fight and scramble to be first, to beat the other man," of city life. He becomes editor of a country paper in Plattville, Indiana. The friendly townspeople prove their sterling worth by helping him expel the roughnecks at a nearby crossroads, and he finds contentment among "the beautiful people."

But a literary counterreaction against midwestern small towns began to build. Christened in 1920 "the revolt from the village" by the literary editor of *The Nation*, Carl van Doren, this movement reflected lib-eralized morals and manners among intellectuals and the urban young, who claimed the freedom of the city and rebelled against the notion that virtue, religion, and sound Americanism could be found only in small towns and on farms.

The opening shot in the revolt from the village was Edgar Lee Masters's *Spoon River Anthology* (1915). Masters, who had grown up in Lewistown and Petersburg, Illinois, wrote a sequence of free-verse portraits of small-town folk inspired by people he had known in his home towns. His unifying conceit was that these characters were speaking from the grave, exhuming the truth about lives of quiet desperation twisted by village taboos and the need to maintain a front of respectability.

Although he claimed never to have read *Spoon River Anthology*, Sherwood Anderson was clearly inspired by Masters's approach when he wrote *Winesburg, Ohio* (1919), a group of linked stories about buried lives in an Ohio town. Anderson, who grew up in Clyde, Ohio, envisioned his characters (some of them based on displaced small-towners whom he met in the city) as lonely grotesques, spiritually deformed by thwarted love.

Winesburg, Ohio trains a light on the inner lives of these characters, but Anderson's next book, *Poor White* (1920), dramatizes the social consequences of industrialization, which he contended had vitiated closeness to the land, craftsmanship, and sense of community in small towns. More a poetic meditation than a novel, *Poor White* meshed with 1920s intellectuals' attack on "Fordism"—mass production of standardized products sold by mass-market advertising that engendered standardized thinking and mindless consumerism.

In Sinclair Lewis's *Main Street* (1920), the Ford car is ironically held up as the pinnacle of American civilization in the all-powerful opinion of the citizens of Gopher Prairie, Minnesota. Lewis, a rebel born, escaped his home town of Sauk Centre, Minnesota, for Yale University and New York City, where he worked in publishing and dreamed of writing the definitive Great American Novel about small-town life. In *Main Street* he delivered.

Gopher Prairie was intended as a synecdoche of standardized American life, its Main Street the continuation of Main Streets everywhere. Lewis was an acute satirist of the great middle—the Midwest, the middle class, the national mediocrity. *Main Street* was a sensation, the most talked-about novel of the watershed year. The argument it touched off was in part shouted across the cultural divide between country and city, the old America and the new; it also partook of a more serious mood of self-criticism as the nation assumed its place as a world-class economic power in the post–World War I era.

Published the same year as *Main Street* were two intelligent novels about village rebels. Floyd Dell, a Greenwich Village poet, novelist, and editor, drew on his boyhood in Davenport, Iowa, a river town of more than usual cultural diversity. His novel *Moon-Calf* (1920) is about a young man whose thrashings for self-realization beat against the bars of his home town until he flies away to Chicago, art, and freedom. Zona Gale in *Miss Lulu Bett* (1920) abandoned togetherness to paint a portrait of a spinster who breaks with her family's suffocating expectations to find happiness in marriage with an outsider.

Eventually, the revolt from the village ran its course. In the 1930s, with the economic system collapsing and farms and towns hurting, the narrow-mindedness of the Widow Bogart in Gopher Prairie seemed of minor importance. Small-town preservation, rather than debunking, was part of the salient folk revival of the decade. Pennsylvania-born Conrad Richter's trilogy—*The Trees* (1940), *The Fields* (1946), *The Town* (1950)—tells the story of an Ohio town from frontier times through a generational chronicle of the early hardships and ultimate material success marked by the disillusionment of a pioneer family.

The country changed after World War II and novels reflected this. In the Midwest and elsewhere many towns were swallowed by urban sprawl or withered away with the decline of farming. In any event, they had long ago lost their provincialism as, for better and for worse, they became linked to the mass cultural grid by radio and television and tied to the cities by improved transportation links. The anomic suburbs replaced small towns in our literature as thwarters of spiritual and emotional growth.

If no longer as controversial as in the 1920s, small towns continue to provide a natural literary ecosystem in which a rooted set of characters may dramatically intertwine. A mellower yet unsentimental attitude toward them has set in, expressed in Minnesota-born Garrison Keillor's *Lake Wobegon*—a long way from Minnesota-born Sinclair Lewis's *Gopher Prairie*. Yet small towns in fiction continue to reflect a peculiarly American ambivalence between nostalgia and rebellion, between the need for roots and the impulse to mobility. And young people continue to leave them in search of themselves—like George Willard in *Winesburg, Ohio*.

Sources and Further Reading: Lewis Atherton, *Main Street on the Middle Border* (1966); R. Carlyle Buley, *The Old Northwest: Pioneer Period 1815–1840*, 2 vols. (1950); Everett Carter, *Howells and the Age of Realism* (1954); David M. Cook and Craig G. Swauger, *The Small Town in American Literature* (1969); James DeMuth, *Small Town Chicago* (1980); Hamlin Garland, *Crumbling Idols*, ed. Jane Johnson (1960); Parke Dixon Goist, *From Main Street to State Street* (1977);

Anthony Channell Hilfer, *The Revolt from the Village, 1915–1930* (1969); Richard Lingeman, *Sinclair Lewis: Rebel from Main Street* (2002); Richard Lingeman, *Small Town America: A Narrative History, 1620–The Present* (1980); Page Smith, *As a City upon a Hill* (1966).

Richard Lingeman
The Nation, New York

Literature of Urban Life

Many of the midwesterners singled out in this volume as major authors have written with special force and passion about American city life, including William Dean Howells, Theodore Dreiser, Carl Sandburg, Vachel Lindsay, Sherwood Anderson, Sinclair Lewis, Willa Cather, Hart Crane, F. Scott Fitzgerald, James T. Farrell, Nelson Algren, Richard Wright, Gwendolyn Brooks, Saul Bellow, Lorraine Hansberry, Studs Terkel, and David Mamet. Among these, most who pay attention to midwestern urbanism, in particular, have written about (and often in) Chicago, the region's literary capital. Any discussion of the urban literature of the Midwest must center on Chicago, which dominates the region's canon of urban scenes, characters, and language.

The transformation of hinterlanders into city people, for instance, is perhaps most memorably figured as a set of train journeys to and within Chicago: George Willard's at the end of Anderson's *Winesburg, Ohio* (1919) and Carrie Meeber's at the beginning of Dreiser's *Sister Carrie* (1900); Wright's entry from the South at the beginning of *American Hunger* (1977) and the last, fateful rides of Studs Lonigan and Frankie Machine, dead-end scions of immigrant-ethnic families, in Farrell's *Judgment Day* (1935) and Algren's *The Man with the Golden Arm* (1949). In "Chicago" (1916), Sandburg personifies the city as an industrial worker "flinging magnetic curses amid the toil of piling job on job"; in *Lucy Gayheart* (1935), Cather's heroine embodies Chicago as a center of high culture. Gwendolyn Brooks fitted the traditional poetic forms of ballad and sonnet to the southern-inflected language and stories of black migrants to the urban North; David Mamet, a fellow South Sider, invented a new kind of highly stylized theatrical diction that articulates the meaning in the lonely transactions of city life. Sandra Cisneros's portraits of a neighborhood in Chicago offer a kind of abstraction between the clean lines of realism; Stuart Dybek's stories about a similar neighborhood, by contrast, evoke the experience of ordinary city life with startling accuracy even when they venture well into the heightened realm of the extraordinary and the surreal.

A bird's-eye view of Chicago, 1874. Library of Congress, Geography and Map Division, g4104c pm001492.

One could make similar (if shorter) lists for midwestern cities other than Chicago, but the Midwest's place in the development of urban literature is to a large extent encapsulated in Chicago's contributions to the development of a tradition of letters equipped to address urban modernity: the Chicago renaissance, Chicago realism, the literary journalism of Finley Peter Dunne and Mike Royko, and the Chicago School of Sociology.

Even as we recognize the impressive quality and quantity of writing about Chicago and other cities in the region, it is still difficult to argue that midwestern urban literature is radically distinct in form and content from the larger body of American urban literature. That may be, in part, because cities in different regions are often more like one another than they are like the nonurban parts of their respective regions, and affinities between midwestern and nonmidwestern cities often transcend regional differences. The cities that have provided the subjects, settings, and contexts for midwestern urban literature do not share many exclusive attributes other than significant remove from an ocean coastline and relative youth in comparison to East Coast cities. The large-scale historical processes

that have shaped midwestern urbanism and presented the region's writers with their great urban subjects are for the most part not unique to the Midwest. The nineteenth century's master trinity of industrialization, immigration, and urbanization may have breathed life into most midwestern cities and their literatures, but those same processes also profoundly shaped cities in the East, the northern tier, and the West. Moving forward into the latter part of the twentieth century, deindustrialization, ghettoization, suburbanization, the arrival of new immigrants from Asia and Latin America and the Caribbean, and other processes that define the latter-day history of the cities of the Midwest are also by no means unique to the region. If we cannot, then, identify absolutely distinctive qualities of midwestern urbanism and its literature, we can at least take note of tendencies that amount to a regional inflection, a certain urban midwestern feel.

First, we can read for midwestern specificity identifiably regional versions of general processes and events not exclusive to the region. For instance, in the case of folk migrations from south to north, black migrants to the urban Midwest tended to come from the central Deep South, especially Mississippi. The works of Wright and Brooks bear the marks of that particular flow of people (in the same way that parallel stories of black migration to New York often trace the flow from the Carolinas and Georgia, or Los Angeles stories trace the flow from Texas and Arkansas). Similarly, the migration of working-class whites from Appalachia to cities like Cincinnati and Detroit inflects Harriette Arnow's masterpiece, *The Dollmaker* (1954).

Second, the writing of the urban Midwest bears evidence of the region's complex attitude toward the concentration of cultural authority on the East Coast (and, since the rise of Hollywood, the West Coast). One can find that attitude—a blend of regional pride, preemptive reverse snobbery, anxiety of influence, and a quiet but firmly held conviction that American life is lived most uprightly and authentically in the Heartland—most clearly expressed in East Coast novels by Midwesterners that stage a return to the author's hometown at the moment of truth. Perhaps the most famous example is a passage near the end of Fitzgerald's *The Great Gatsby* (1925) in which the narrator recalls long-ago train rides from Chicago's Union Station to St. Paul through "my middle-west," journeys that made him "unutterably aware of our identity with this country." Those intensely regional memories provide him with a comforting perspective on his New York story of Jay Gatsby and the intimidatingly rich, stylish company in which he moved. "I see now," he concludes, "that this has been a story of the West, after all—Tom and Gatsby, Daisy and Jordan and I, were all Westerners, and perhaps we possessed some deficiency in common which made us subtly unadaptable to Eastern life." Or maybe the deficiency lies in the shallowness and decadent falsity of eastern life.

To take a more recent example, the same complex attitude animates the revelatory return to "St. Jude"—which bears a suspicious resemblance to St. Louis—at the end of Jonathan Franzen's Pulitzer Prize–winning novel *The Corrections* (2001). Three midwesterners who went east to New York and Philadelphia in search of their fortunes are called home to spend one last excruciating Christmas with their terminally bourgeois mother and dying father. The grown-up sons and daughter feel a shamed sense of defeat in returning to Franzen's cartoonishly provincial Midwest of inedible 1950s-style cooking and insufferable bridge-table pieties, but a hint of ecstatic possibility also animates their journey back to the heart of things. One son, Chip, surprises everyone by eventually staying for good in the Midwest, shedding his leather-pantsed affectations of chic, his get-rich-quick schemes, and his old life as a sexually desperate literary theorist and Internet confidence man. He makes long-delayed repairs to his parents' house and takes up with one of his father's neurologists, eventually settling down with her

in Chicago. At novel's end, Chip is teaching at a private high school and raising twin daughters—and, since the complex exchange between interior and coast continues, rewriting his screenplay for a movie producer back in New York.

A third tendency of midwestern urban writing is a self-conscious awareness of its own middleness. Take, for example, the work of Elmore Leonard, a long-time resident of the Detroit area who is widely considered to be the finest living writer of crime fiction in English. Leonard started out writing westerns in the 1950s, but during the urban crisis of the late 1960s he switched to contemporary crime fiction. Several of his earliest and best urban novels are set in Detroit, but over time his characters and stories have migrated to Florida (and eventually to Hollywood and more exotic locales). His Detroit stories are acutely conscious of the middleness of their geographic and mythic situation, suspended between the frontier traditions of the Old West and the emergent possibilities of Sun Belt boom towns. These novels' protagonists look backward and westward as they try to live up to the examples set by movie gunfighters, but they also look forward and southeastward as they scheme to make a big score and flee to a place in the sun in Florida, far from the hard facts of life in a Rust Belt metropolis. One can trace the arc of Leonard's career as well as the contours of American popular fiction's map of the nation in the lives of characters like Ernest "Stick" Stickley, Jr., a laconic fellow from Norman, Oklahoma, who has seen enough movies to know that a man's gotta do what a man's gotta do. Over the course of two novels, *Ryan's Rules* (1978) and *Stick* (1983), he steals cars and commits armed robberies in Detroit, does hard time at Jackson after attempting to hold up Detroit's biggest department store, then heads to Florida, where he becomes entangled with low-life drug dealers and a high-class eastern woman—a Boston-educated stock market analyst from New York named Emma.

These three literary tendencies—regional twists on more general subjects, a complicated relationship with coastally based cultural authority, and self-conscious middleness—take root in the region's historical progression from periphery to center to a curious combination of both. A century ago, the young industrial cities of the Midwest were emergent capitals of American life. Not only did they play an outsize socioeconomic role as burgeoning centers of manufacturing and population, but the westering of American language and letters seemed to promise that they would become cultural and literary capitals, a status that H. L. Mencken had already claimed for Chicago by 1920. Their stories would become the nation's stories. To some extent, this is exactly what happened: Midwestern cities have contributed mightily to the sustained literary outpouring from the region, and they continue to do so. But book and magazine publishing have remained largely headquartered on the East Coast, which has also retained a disproportionate share of the oldest and most distinguished institutions of culture, especially universities. The movie and television industries, too, are concentrated on the coasts. These conditions have encouraged many midwesterners with writerly ambitions to leave home, physically and psychically, to make their fortunes, even when their subjects and language remain powerfully midwestern. Also, in the last fifty years, the Midwest's maturing urban centers have been significantly supplanted in the public imagination by fast-growing Sun Belt cities—Los Angeles, Las Vegas, Atlanta, and the like—that embody for many people the urban shape of things to come. This may help to explain why the writing of midwestern cities has become increasingly elegiac since the mid-twentieth century, and why the once-important notion of "the next big Chicago novel" has become quaint.

Elegiac or visionary, inward-turning or outward-reaching, the literature of the urban Midwest continues to manifest familiar tendencies. To take one among many possible current examples, Keith Gandal's novel *Cleveland Anonymous* (2002) begins when the narrator and his foster sister lose their virginity to each other as the Cuyahoga River catches fire in 1969. The fire, a spectacular historical event with wide-reaching period resonances (pollution, deindustrialization, civic malaise), also carries a powerful regional specificity: The Cuyahoga catching fire is, without question, a Cleveland thing, and a Cleveland thing is a midwestern thing. Later, coastal anxiety and self-conscious middleness come into play as the narrator moves to San Francisco and then to New York. Along the way, he falls in with fellow hometown expatriates who have formed a "self-help" group, Cleveland Anonymous, whose members gather in bars to consider their curious situation: so far from home among strangers, yet so at home among their kind in the big city.

Sources and Further Reading: Sidney Bremer, *Urban Intersections* (1992); Carla Cappetti, *Writing Chicago* (1993); Graham Clarke, ed., *The American City: Literary and Cultural Perspectives* (1988); Blanche Gelfant, *The American City Novel* (1954); Farah Jasmine Griffin, *"Who Set You Flowin'?" The African-American Migration Narrative* (1995); Catherine Jurca, *White Diaspora* (2001); Richard Lehan, *The City in Literature* (1998); Carlo Rotella, *October Cities* (1998); Carl Smith, *Chicago and the American Literary Imagination, 1880–1920* (1984); David Starkey and Richard Guzman, eds., *Smokestacks and Skyscrapers* (1999).

Carlo Rotella
Boston College

Native American Literature

Midwestern Native American nations have a rich heritage of oral literatures that includes, but is not limited to, songs, narratives, ceremonies, and oratory. Native American cultures and histories challenge the concept of a midwestern literature because the traditional territories of many American Indian nations extend beyond state, regional, or national boundaries. Some Indian nations, previously located in the Midwest, moved westward under pressure from enemy tribes and settlers. The federal government also forcibly removed tribes from their ancestral lands. Consequently, a tribal approach to Native American literature can be more appropriate than a regional one.

This essay is focused primarily on literature by Indian authors who grew up in and wrote about the Midwest. From the mid-nineteenth to the mid-twentieth century, most of the books that Indian authors published were life histories, which they either narrated to editors or wrote themselves. Native American life histories usually combine tribal myths, history, and personal experience. Among the most popular is *Black Hawk, an Autobiography* (1833). Black Hawk (a Sauk), who lived from 1767 to 1838, narrated his life history to Antoine LeClair, who translated it; John B. Patterson edited the book in final form. Two Ho-Chunk siblings from Wisconsin narrated their life stories to anthropologists: *The Autobiography of a Winnebago Indian* (1926) is the account Sam Blowsnake told to Paul Radin. Blowsnake is also known as Big Winnebago and Crashing Thunder. *Mountain Wolf Woman, Sister of Crashing Thunder* (1961) is the life story of Mountain Wolf Woman, narrated to Nancy Oestrich Lurie.

Native authors also wrote autobiographies. One of the earliest authors is George Copway, born in 1818. Though raised as a traditional Ojibwe at Rice Lake, Ontario, Copway converted to Methodism and became an apprentice missionary in Michigan. He was subsequently sent to school in Jackson, Illinois, and then became a missionary in Wisconsin, Minnesota, and Ontario. Copway later immigrated to the United States, where he lectured on Ojibwe culture and Indian causes. He is best known for *The Life, History and Travels of Kah-ge-ga-gah-bowh* (1847), republished in 1850 as *The Life, Letters and Speeches of Kah-ge-ga-gah-bowh*. Copway died in 1869. Later in the nineteenth century, Andrew Blackbird (Odawa), who lived from 1822 to circa 1887, wrote *History of the Ottawa and Chippewa Indians of Michigan . . . and Personal Family History of the Author* (1887), a tribal and personal history.

Native authors began writing fiction in the nineteenth century. Simon Pokagon (Michigan Potawatomi), who lived from 1830 to 1899, was one of the earliest to write a romance: *O-gî-mäw-dwe Miti-gwä-kî* (*Queen of the Woods*; 1899). Mrs. C.H. Engle, wife of Pokagon's lawyer and close friend, probably assisted in writing the book, which her husband published. It combines a nostalgic reminiscence for the lost golden age of the Potawatomi with fiery attacks on alcohol. It also contains a section on the Potawatomi language.

The most widely read midwestern Indian author of the early twentieth century is Charles Eastman (known as Ohiyesa, a name that he used from four years after his birth in 1858 until his death in 1939). Eastman spent most of his youth in what is now Minnesota, leading the life of a typical Santee Dakota warrior in training. He later attended Beloit College in Wisconsin and Knox College in Galesburg, Illinois. In 1887, he received his B.S. from Dartmouth College in Hanover, New Hampshire, and in 1890, his M.D. from Boston University. He and Elaine Goodale Eastman, whom he married in 1891, coauthored many books on Indian life and issues. Throughout his career, Eastman attempted to serve as a bridge between the Indian and non-Indian worlds. Among his most influential books are *Indian Boyhood* (1902), an account of his life as a traditional Santee Dakota that was written for children, and *From the Deep Woods to Civilization* (1916), a moving description of his experiences in the non-Indian world. The Eastmans chronicled the lives of Indian leaders in *Indian Heroes and Great Chieftains* (1918). They also wrote *Wigwam Evenings* (1909) and *Red Hunters and Animal People* (1904), collections of stories. *The Soul of the Indian* (1911) is Eastman's attempt to explain American Indian philosophy and religion from a Dakota point of view. *The Indian To-day* (1915) surveys Indian history, Native American contributions to the United States, and reservation life.

An important political and literary voice of this period is Gertrude Simmons Bonnin, born on the Yankton Nakota Reservation, in what is now South Dakota, in 1876. In her writing, she used the name *Zitkala-Ša*, Lakota for "Red Bird." She attended two Quaker schools in Indiana: White's Manual Labor Institute and Earlham College. She taught at Carlisle Indian School in 1899. A talented violinist, she studied at the New England Conservatory in Boston from 1900 to 1901. For much of her life, Zitkala-Ša was a political activist; she worked with the Society for the American Indian and later founded the National Council of American Indians. Although she was Nakota, she worked with the Dakota language and oral traditions. Her *Old Indian Legends* (1901) contains her reinterpretations of Dakota stories. Her most important book is *American Indian Stories* (1921), which includes three memorable autobiographical essays: "Impressions of an Indian Childhood," "The School Days of an Indian

Girl," and "An Indian Teacher among Indians." Originally published in the *Atlantic Monthly* (1900, 1902) and *Harper's Magazine* (1901), they chronicle her traditional Sioux childhood, rebellion at school against assimilation, growing sense of self, and disillusionment with the Indian educational system. The volume also includes original stories and the essay "America's Indian Problem." In addition, she collaborated with William F. Hanson in 1913 to create the *Sun Dance Opera*, first performed in 1938, the year of her death.

Until the mid-twentieth century, Indian authors published few creative books. Much of their writing during this period appeared in newspapers and journals. One of the few to publish a novel was Ella Deloria, who lived from 1889 to 1971 and is primarily known as an anthropologist and linguist. Born on the Yankton Nakota Reservation, she was raised on the Standing Rock Reservation, also located in South Dakota. She grew up speaking Dakota, Lakota, and Nakota. Deloria attended Oberlin College and Columbia University, from which she graduated in 1914. While at Columbia, she worked with the anthropologist Franz Boas, collecting material on South Dakotan Indian languages and ethnography. She is best known for *Dakota Texts* (1932). Her *Speaking of Indians* (1944) describes the impact of the reservation system on traditional Dakota culture. During the 1940s, she completed the ethnographic novel *Waterlily*, not published until 1988. Told from a woman's perspective, *Waterlily* vividly portrays nineteenth-century Sioux life.

By the mid-1970s, a new generation of highly sophisticated Native American writers had emerged. The most prolific is Gerald Vizenor. This versatile, White Earth Ojibwe author has written autobiography, fiction, nonfiction, poetry, and literary criticism. Vizenor grew up in Minneapolis, where he was born in 1934. He graduated from the University of Minnesota in 1960. Formerly a social worker and journalist, Vizenor is professor emeritus of American Studies at the University of California, Berkeley. In his writings, Vizenor examines both the history of the Ojibwe and the struggles of Native American people in contemporary, often urban, society. A skilled satirist, he frequently uses the figure of the trickster as a compassionate observer of society. Among his best books using these themes are *The People Named the Chippewa* (1984), *Earthdivers: Tribal Narratives on Mixed Descent* (1981), *Griever: An American Monkey King in China* (1987), and *The Heirs of Columbus* (1991). *Interior Landscapes: Autobiographical Myths and Metaphors* (1990) is a moving and humorous portrayal of episodes in his life. Vizenor's *Matsushima: Pine Islands* (1984) demonstrates his mastery of haiku. His *Narrative Chance* (1989) and *Manifest Manners: Postindian Warriors or Survivance* (1994) are important discussions of his theories of Native American literature.

Another important writer is Ray A. Young Bear (Meskwaki). Although his nation's name is usually spelled *Mesquakie*, Young Bear prefers *Meskwaki*. Born in Marshalltown, Iowa, in 1950, Young Bear was raised on the Meskwaki Settlement near Tama, Iowa, where he still lives. He studied writing at Pomona College, the University of Iowa, and Iowa State University. Young Bear initially thought out his work in Meskwaki before translating it into English. In *Black Eagle Child: The Facepaint Narratives* (1992), he describes his goal as "creative emulation of thought through the extraordinary, tragic, and comedic stories of an imagined midwestern tribal experience." Critics have praised his striking command of images and language, his celebration of Meskwaki traditions, and his analyses of political and cultural issues. *Winter of the Salamander: The Keeper of Importance* (1980) is divided into four sections based on the seasons. It includes such topics as both loss and survival of cultural tradition, family, loneliness, addiction, and racism. More polished than its predecessor, *The Invisible Musician* (1990) is organized around four bilingual transcriptions of Meskwaki songs that deal with love, veterans, and celebration. It also contains themes present in *Winter of the Salamander.* Young Bear's most recent book is *The Rock Island Hiking Club* (2001), a collection of poems. Here, Edgar Bearchild, Young Bear's alter ego and a spiritual seeker, wittily and perceptively recounts his experiences in and observations of the fictional Black Eagle Child Settlement.

In *Black Eagle Child*, Edgar Bearchild narrates his experiences and comments on settlement life. The book is both a coming-of-age story and a powerful examination of contemporary life in the settlement. *Remnants of the First Earth* (1996), a sequel, describes Bearchild's further adventures and observations on Native American life and emphasizes the crucial role that storytellers play as keepers of memory and symbols of moral and social tribal culture.

A talented author who has achieved popular and critical attention is Susan Power (Yanktonai Dakota), who was born in 1961 and raised in Chicago. She has spent considerable time on the Standing Rock Reservation, the original home of her mother, Susan Kelly Power. The author, who now lives in St. Paul, received her B.A. degree from Harvard/Radcliffe, her J.D. from Harvard Law School, and her M.F.A. from the University of Iowa. *The Grass Dancer* (1994) interweaves Sioux folklore, history, and contemporary experience. The novel describes the efforts of two lovers, Charlene Thunder and Harley Wind Soldier, to make peace with the ghosts of the old ways while they contend with the living. Power's *Roofwalker* (2002), which is divided into "Stories" and "Histories," focuses more on Chicago and the lives of urban Indians. It also includes experiences that she and her mother have had in Chicago and elsewhere.

E. Donald Two-Rivers, born in 1945, focuses much of his writing both on urban Indians in Chicago and on his early life as a Sein River Ojibwe in Senape, Ontario. In 1961, when he was sixteen, Two-Rivers moved to Chicago with his parents and siblings. He and his family moved in 2002 to Green Bay, Wisconsin. Although he worked for many years as a machinist, Two-Rivers became artistic director of the Red Path Theater Company, for whom he wrote and produced plays. In his poetry, plays, and fiction, Two-Rivers forcefully voices his resistance to injustice and the harshness of life for rural and urban Native American people, the homeless, and workers. His stories in *Survivor's Medicine* (1998) vividly portray the impact on Indians of racism and poverty at the same time that they affirm Native American survival through the healing power of laughter. *Briefcase Warriors: Stories for the Stage* (2001) contains six plays that illuminate the complex lives of urban contemporary Indian life. Although his characters talk fast and live hard, they also laugh to survive. In *Powwows, Fat Cats, and Other Indian Tales* (2003), Two-Rivers creates tender and tough poems that tell it like it is. In his work, he combines comedy with cultural commentary.

Many Ojibwe authors have emerged in the last decade. *Stories Migrating Home: A Collection of Anishinaabe Prose* (1999), edited by Kimberly Blaeser, showcases many of these talented writers. Ojibwe authors include Kimberly Blaeser; Lise and Heid Erdrich, sisters of Louise Erdrich; Gordon Henry, Jr.; Winona LaDuke; Jim Northrup; Denise Sweet; Mark Turcotte; and David Treuer. Two other Native American authors reared in the Midwest are Roberta Hill (Oneida) and Elise Paschen (Osage). Through their writings, midwestern American Indian authors have greatly expanded our understanding of their tribal cultures and histories. Their books are significant contributions to Native American and American literatures.

Sources and Further Reading: Kimberly M. Blaeser, *Gerald Vizenor: Writing in the Oral Tradition* (1996); Louis Owens, *Other Destinies: Understanding the American Indian Novel* (1992); Catherine Rainwater, *Dreams of Fiery Stars* (1999); A. LaVonne Brown Ruoff, *American Indian Literatures* (1990); James Ruppert, *Mediation in Contemporary Native American Fiction* (1995); Jace Weaver, *That the People Might Live* (1997); Norma Wilson, *The Nature of Native American Poetry* (2001); Raymond Wilson, *Ohiyesa: Charles Eastman, Santee Sioux* (1983); Ray A. Young Bear, *Black Eagle Child: The Facepaint Narratives* (1992).

A. LaVonne Brown Ruoff
University of Illinois–Chicago

Nonfiction Literature

Midwestern writers tend to be acutely aware of the contrast between how they, as insiders, see the place about which they're writing and how outsiders either don't see it or see it through stereotypes of the Midwest as a place where all land is flat and farmed, where the people live uncomplicated, provincial lives and exhibit traditional values (i.e., they are hard-working, honest, practical, friendly). Midwestern writers of midwestern places push against these stereotypes. In the words of Kent C. Ryden,

> Collectively, contemporary midwestern nonfiction writers go to the big blank space in the center of the American cultural map, adopt small portions of it for themselves, and fill in all the details they can, annotating it thickly with the events of past and present human lives, drawing in the specifics of contour and ground cover, trying to make their writings, in [Michael] Martone's words, "a map more detailed than the thing it represents."

A stunning example of the tendency to fill in the emptiness that some see in the center of the country is *PrairyErth (A Deep Map)*, published in 1991, in which William Least Heat-Moon lovingly, methodically explores Chase County, in the Flint Hills of eastern Kansas. Like most midwestern writers of midwestern places, Heat-Moon confronts the inadequacy of the outsider's vision of this place. While standing atop centrally located Roniger Hill, he observes: "For years, outsiders have considered this prairie place barren, desolate, monotonous, a land of more nothing than almost any other place you might name, but I know I'm not here to explore vacuousness at the heart of America. I'm only in search of what is here, here in the middle of the Flint Hills of Kansas."

Heat-Moon structures PrairyErth according to the twelve grids of the county, one each for the U.S. Geological Survey maps. He walks Chase County "grid by topographic grid, digging, sifting, sorting, assembling shards . . . up to down, right to left," providing a "thick description" of the place that includes journal entries; lists (140 ways to spell Kansas, different types of hawks, an inventory of the personal possessions of a Dunkard preacher); a hornbook of testimonies about the Kaw Indians; weather reports; "a couple of dozen gleanings" from the *Strong City Leader-News* from the past century; histories of past and present Chase Countians; geological investigations; and profiles of Chase County communities in the form of the *New Yorker*'s On the Town.

Heat-Moon admits that he has only told a portion

of what he knows about Chase County's natural and human history: "Ninety-nine-point-nine to the ninth decimal of what has ever happened here isn't in the book. Its two hundred thousand words are my nutshell." By extension, other "unmapped" parts of the Midwest are just as complex, compelling, full, thick.

Like Heat-Moon, Aldo Leopold, the author of *A Sand County Almanac; with Essays on Conservation from Round River* (the almanac was originally published in 1949, one year after Leopold's death; *Round River*, from which several essays were taken, was published in 1953), fills a "blank" midwestern space with close observation of what is there—in Leopold's case, for the purpose of setting forth an ecological philosophy and ethic. Leopold was born in Burlington, Iowa; went to school in the East; then worked for the U.S. Forest Service in the Southwest. In 1933, he returned to the Midwest when he accepted a position as the nation's first professor of game management at the University of Wisconsin. Two years later, he bought 120 acres of depleted, sandy soil in central Wisconsin. This sand farm is the subject of the almanac essays. Part 2 of the book includes sketches about "some of the episodes in my life that taught me, gradually and sometimes painfully, that the company [American culture] is out of step." Part 3 contains philosophical essays, such as "The Land Ethic," in which Leopold calls for humans to see themselves not as "conqueror[s] of the land-community" but as "plain member[s] and citizen[s] of it."

Whether meditations, narratives, or parables, the almanac essays dramatize the issues that Leopold grapples with in "The Land Ethic" and other essays in parts 2 and 3. For instance, in "November: Axe-in-Hand," Leopold writes that November is an ideal time to thin out his woodlot because then one has a "clear view of treetops . . . [and can see] if any, needs felling for the good of the land." Leopold's definition of a conservationist is not written with a pen but an axe, and concerns what one is thinking about while chopping or deciding what to chop. He then proceeds "to analyze, ex post facto, the reasons behind my own axe-in hand decisions"—an analysis he finds disconcerting. When a white pine and a red birch are crowding each other, Leopold confesses that he always cuts the birch to favor the pine. Why? He planted the pine; the birch "planted itself." Birches are abundant; pines are scarce. Pines live longer, stay green all winter, and shelter Leopold's beloved grouse. But the birch feeds the grouse. Leopold keeps pushing to understand his bias. "Does the pine stimulate my imagination and my hopes more deeply than the birch does? If so, is the difference in the trees, or in me?" He concludes that his decision is subjective: while "I love all trees, I am in love with pines." Then, he examines the effects of his bias. Removing the birch will create more inviting circumstances for the pine weevil to lay her eggs in the pine's leader. During a droughty summer, the loss of the birch's shade will increase water loss for the pine. If the birch's limbs rub the pine's terminal buds, the latter will be deformed. Now, the choice of which tree to remove isn't as clear. What we should strive for, says Leopold, is "skill in the exercise of bias."

Other midwestern works about midwestern places that also provide thick descriptions or deep maps of seemingly empty places and that counter the stereotypes of the region are Loren Eiseley's *The Immense Journey* (Nebraska), Linda Hasselstrom's *Between Grass and Sky: Where I Live and Work* (South Dakota), Sue Hubbell's *A Country Year: Living the Questions* (Missouri), Kathleen Norris's *Dakota: A Spiritual Geography* (South Dakota), and Scott Russell Sanders's *Staying Put: Making a Home in a Restless World* (Ohio and Indiana).

Given the popular associations of the Midwest as a place of small towns, farms, and wild places, the significant body of literature about midwestern urban industrial people and places is easily overlooked. Three works can stand to exemplify the character and range of the nonfiction writing about one midwestern city, Chicago.

Jane Addams came to Chicago in 1889, along with college friend Ellen Starr, to found Hull-House. Through this experiment in collective living, the worker-residents at Addams's settlement house sought to educate, advocate for, and ultimately empower their neighbors in the impoverished neighborhood near Halstead and Polk Streets.

In *Twenty Years at Hull-House* (1910), part autobiography, part social theory and call to activism, Addams presents a Chicago that was still raw and new: "Fifteen years ago the State of Illinois, as well as Chicago, exhibited many characteristics of the pioneer country in which untrammeled energy and an 'early start' were still the most highly prized generators of success." By 1890, most of the residents of Chicago were immigrants. Yet Chicago lagged behind other modern industrial nations, as well as New York and Massachusetts, in passing labor laws because such laws "ran counter to the instinct and tradition, almost to the very religion of the manufacturers of the state, who were for the most part self-made men."

In *Twenty Years at Hull-House*, in *Spirit of Youth and the City Streets* (1909), and in other collections of essays, Addams presents a side of the city often ignored or forgotten. For instance, following the spectacular Chicago World's Fair of 1893, the city was hit by an economic depression, a smallpox epidemic, and "thousands of destitute strangers [were] stranded in the city." Addams and her co-workers strove to ameliorate the situation but "our best efforts were most inade-

quate to the situation." Most remarkable, Addams's portrayals of her neighbors reveal her deep insight into what motivated them, whether juvenile delinquent, corrupt cop, factory owner, striking shoe-factory worker, political boss, or tenement dweller. And like Heat-Moon and Leopold, Addams provides a thick description of a small spot on the map, the urban neighborhood in Chicago where she lived.

Like Addams, Richard Wright, who was born in 1908 in Roxie, Mississippi, and died in 1960, in Paris, focuses on a particular neighborhood in his autobiography—in Wright's case, the South Side of Chicago. The first part of *Black Boy (American Hunger)*, published as *Black Boy* in 1945, concerns Wright's youth and coming of age in the segregated South. The second part, published posthumously in 1977, concerns Wright's 1927 migration from Memphis to Chicago. When Wright arrived in his Promised Land, he was immediately disappointed: "My first glimpse of the flat black stretches of Chicago depressed and dismayed me, mocked all my fantasies." Indeed, Wright saw a hostile landscape: "There were no curves here, no trees; only angles, lines, squares, bricks and copper wires. . . . Each person seemed to regard the other as a part of the city landscape." The substandard housing, difficulty in obtaining and keeping employment, and the racism that Wright encountered in Chicago differed little from what he had known in the South. Even the Communist Party, in which Wright initially found hope, "honor and glory," so disillusioned him with its racism and anti-intellectualism, that Wright eventually broke with it.

In the 1960s, Studs Terkel (b. 1912) went citywide to obtain "a cross section of urban thought" because there was no one street or neighborhood in Chicago where people of different ethnic, racial, and income levels lived together. "I guess I was seeking some balance in the wildlife of the city as Rachel Carson sought it in nature," he wrote. In *Division Street: America* (1967), the first in his series of oral histories, Terkel presents the results of his seventy interviews with ordinary or "noncelebrated" Chicagoans—the schoolteacher, homemaker, landlady, cop, nun, architect, cabdriver, steelworker, corporate vice president—and their thoughts on civil rights, the atom bomb, automation, God, the Vietnam War, "the nature of the city itself," and in many cases, the individual's sense of powerlessness.

Division Street opens with the words of Florence Scala. As a child, Scala benefited from the programs at Hull-House; as a teenager, she volunteered there. In the 1960s, Scala, who had lived all but a couple of her forty-seven years on the same block, was concerned with the loss of neighborhood and stability brought by urban renewal and public housing. When the city announced in 1961 its intent to demolish the entire community near Hull-House so that the University of Illinois could locate a branch campus there, she fought the decision and the corrupt influences behind it. Nonetheless, in 1965, the city demolished Hull-House and the surrounding area. As a result of her unsuccessful fight for her neighborhood, Scala concludes that Jane Addams's vision no longer seems alive.

Although there is a Division Street in Chicago, Terkel uses the name metaphorically. Division Street is Chicago and Chicago is America. Dave Williamson, who traded his North Shore suburban, professional life for a position at the Ecumenical Institute "in the heart of the city's black West Side ghetto," voiced the sentiments of many Chicagoans in Division Street, indeed, in other U.S. cities, when he says: "Yes, the city's a threat. It's a horrible threat to all mankind. And yet it's the most beautiful thing there is. There's more creativity going on in the city than anywhere else in the world. Unless a person allows himself the privilege of living deeply in the city, he's missing a great deal of life." Whether their subject is an urban or a rural place, midwestern writers of nonfiction tend to "annotat[e] it thickly," revealing the complexity of the terrain, the history of the place, and the people who live there.

Sources and Further Reading: Jane Addams, *Twenty Years at Hull-House* (1910); William Least Heat-Moon, *PrairyErth (A Deep Map)* (1991); Aldo Leopold, *A Sand County Almanac; with Essays on Conservation from Round River* (1949; reprint, 1953); Kent C. Ryden, "Writing the Midwest," *Geographical Review* 89 (Oct. 1999); James R. Shortridge, *The Middle West* (1989); Studs Terkel, *Division Street: America* (1967); Kenny J. Williams, "'Creative Defiance': An Overview of Chicago Literature," *Midwestern Miscellany* 14 (1986); Richard Wright, *Black Boy (American Hunger)* (1945).

Lisa Knopp
Goucher College, Maryland

Poetry

The Midwest poetry "renaissance" centered in Chicago in the years before World War I signaled the region's coming-of-age in literary terms. Harriet Monroe's influential *Poetry: A Magazine of Verse* forced the American modernists—Ezra Pound, T. S. Eliot, H.D., and William Carlos Williams—into awareness of the middle of the country as they sought outlets for their work. The triumvirate of populist poets who achieved fame and large followings in this period—Carl Sandburg (born in Galesburg, Illinois), Vachel Lindsay (Springfield, Illinois), and Edgar Lee Masters (Garnett, Kansas)—brought the democratic and open-form impulse of Walt Whitman to bear on a typically realist concern with "ordinary people." Masters's brilliant and influential collection *Spoon River Anthology* (1915) is credited with bringing the achievement of this generation of midwestern writers to national attention. In the heady atmosphere of modernist experimentation and the more general American poetic renaissance—when serious poetry stretched to embrace, at once, the minimalist productions of the imagists, the philosophical "observations" of Marianne Moore, and the epic/historic ambition of Pound's *Cantos*—for a brief time the inclusive rhythmic chants of these midwestern bards had a serious audience. But although *Poetry* has published continuously since its founding in 1912, and although two other of the nation's most enduring and important literary institutions are also midwestern—the Iowa Writers Workshop, founded at the University of Iowa in 1936; and the *Kenyon Review*, founded in 1939 at Kenyon College in Gambier, Ohio—Chicago, Iowa City, and central Ohio remain outposts to Boston and New York; and Sandburg, Lindsay, and Masters are hardly read anymore.

Perhaps as a result, contemporary poets born or transplanted to the middle of the United States are reluctant to claim an essential midwestern inheritance and are quick to point out the obvious plurality of the region's culture. Nevertheless, it is interesting to group contemporary poets with midwestern roots or ties by the degree of their identification with the region. Some groupings are superficially easy to make: poets born abroad, who came to the United States as adolescents or young adults, such as Carl Rakosi (Callman Rawley), Lucien Stryk, Charles Simic, Liesel Mueller, and Li Young Lee, who write in English and who have come to know a speech cadence and directness that is midwestern but whose work defies regional (or even national) classification; or African American poets, such as Maya Angelou (born in St. Louis), Gwendolyn Brooks (Topeka), Paul Laurence Dunbar (Dayton), Nikki Giovanni (Cincinnati), and Robert Hayden (Detroit), who were born in the Midwest but who have a national identity based on race rather than region. In a group by himself, perhaps, is Dave Etter, born in the Northwest but now regarded as the most successful inheritor of the Sandburg/Lindsay tradition of Illinois populist verse.

A much larger group of well-known poets were born in the Midwest but left as young adults and never returned. T. S. Eliot is the prototype: born in St. Louis (though into a solidly New England family), he headed east to Harvard and then to London, where he remained for the rest of his life. One may find traces of

Poetry
A Magazine of Verse

Editor	HARRIET MONROE
Assistant Editor	ALICE CORBIN HENDERSON
Advisory Committee	HENRY B. FULLER
	EDITH WYATT
	H. C. CHATFIELD-TAYLOR
Foreign Correspondent	EZRA POUND
Administrative Committee	WILLIAM T. ABBOTT
	CHARLES H. HAMILL

TO HAVE GREAT POETS THERE MUST
BE GREAT AUDIENCES TOO
Whitman

SUBSCRIBERS TO THE FUND

Mr. H. C. Chatfield-Taylor
Mr. Howard Shaw
Mr. Arthur T. Aldis
Mr. Edwin S. Fechheimer
Mrs. Charles H. Hamill
*Mr. D. H. Burnham
Mrs. Emmons Blaine (2)
Mr. Wm. S. Monroe
Mr. E. A. Bancroft
Mrs. Burton Hanson
Mr. C. L. Hutchinson
Mrs. Wm. Vaughn Moody
Mr. Wm. J. Calhoun
Miss Anna Morgan
Mrs. Edward A. Leicht
Mrs Louis Betts
Mrs. George Bullen
Mrs. P. A. Valentine
*Deceased

Mr. P. A. Valentine
Mr. Charles R. Crane
Mr. Frederick Sargent
Mrs. Frank G. Logan
Dr. F. W. Gunsaulus
Mrs. Emma B. Hodge
Mr. Wallace Heckman
Mr. Edward B. Butler (2)
Mr. Robert Metz
Mrs. Bryan Lathrop
Mr. Martin A. Ryerson
*Mrs. La Verne Noyes
Mrs. E. Norman Scott (2)
Mr. Wm. O. Goodman
Mrs. Charles Hitchcock
Hon. John Barton Payne
Mr. Thomas D. Jones
Mr. H. H. Kohlsaat

[i]

The June 1915 issue of the most influential poetry journal in the Midwest. The Poetry Foundation.

the Midwest in his work—the concern with everyday speech and characters, the Mississippi River images in "The Dry Salvages"—but that work is international in diction, in reference, in audience, and in reputation. Others in this group might include Kay Boyle (St. Paul), Hart Crane (Garrettsville, Ohio), Jean Garrigue (Evansville, Indiana), Horace Gregory (Milwaukee), Allen Grossman (Minneapolis), Richard Howard (Cleveland), Weldon Kees (Beatrice, Nebraska), Kenneth Koch (Cincinnati), Archibald MacLeish (Glencoe, Illinois), Marianne Moore (Kirkwood, Missouri), Kenneth Rexroth (South Bend, Indiana), Frederick Seidel (St. Louis), Sara Teasdale (St. Louis), Mark Van Doren (Hope, Illinois), David Wagoner (Marsillon, Ohio), and Yvor Winters (Chicago).

Another small group of successful twentieth-century poets was born in the Midwest but made careers elsewhere, carrying with them a cadence of speech and a stockpile of images from their native region. These poets express themselves in a variety of styles but never stopped identifying themselves as midwestern. Several members of the above group may also show traces of their origins, of course; such distinctions can never be absolute and we all remain products of our native place, whether we want to or not. Amy Clampitt (New Providence, Iowa) expressed this idea trenchantly in "Local Genius": "all that / utilitarian muck down underfoot, / brown loam, debris of

grassroots packed / thicker than anywhere else on the planet—/ soil, so much of it that the central fact // must be, after all, not SPACE but DIRT, / forever present as the sense of guilt / washday alone can hope to expiate." Poets like Clampitt, Richard Eberhart (Austin, Minnesota), Carolyn Forché (Detroit), Jane Kenyon (Ann Arbor), Philip Levine (Detroit), John Logan (Red Oak, Iowa), William Matthews (Cincinnati), Theodore Roethke (Saginaw), and Jean Valentine (Chicago) came out of the Midwest to achieve great national success without relinquishing a recognizably midwestern idiom. James Tate (Kansas City, Missouri) and Mary Oliver (Cleveland) can serve as contemporary exemplars of this group. Tate, who has taught for many years at the University of Massachusetts at Amherst, verges on the postmodern foregrounding of the LANGUAGE poets and has affinities with surrealism, but his language and imagery, in often ironic and playful juxtaposition to these abstract tendencies, is thoroughly down-home. The final lines of "Late Harvest" are an almost-too-obvious example:

The prairie chickens
do not seem to fear
me; neither do the
girls in cellophane
fields, near me, hear me
changing the flat tire

on my black tractor.
I consider screaming
to them; then, night comes.

The objects in the poem are ordinary and identified with the Midwest ("prairie chickens" gives it away), and yet the poem is about the speaker's perception of these elements; the surreal vision makes use of that regional specificity but reaches toward an international artistic movement. The implied commentary on the scene is not about fixing location, but transcending it. Oliver, who has taught for several years at Bennington College in Vermont, has taken her experience with the beleaguered Ohio natural environment and extrapolated it into an urgent call for all to see and feel the distress of the land and its creatures, and an Emersonian admonition to take from nature (rather than from industry or even culture) spiritual sustenance and guidance. While she writes often of New England and the sea, her experience of a relatively rural and frontierlike Ohio lies behind. She has in common with many of these poets the preoccupation with the animal life, broad sky, resonant light, extreme weather, and seasonal drama of the region; and with several others—Bly, Forché, Levine, for example—the belief that poetry can express political ideals and catalyze change. Her most urgent voice summons the individual to a prayerful awareness of nature, as in "In Blackwater Woods": "Look, the trees / are turning / their own bodies / into pillars // of light, / are giving off the rich / fragrance of cinnamon / and fulfillment, . . . / To live in this world // you must be able / to do three things: / to love what is mortal; / to hold it // against your bones knowing / your own life depends on it; / and, when the time comes to let it go, / to let it go."

A final group of poets were born in the Midwest and have remained there, making careers and reputations of largely midwestern materials. Masters, Sandburg, and Lindsay are perhaps the best-known twentieth-century members of this list, but in the nineteenth century Ella Wheeler Wilcox prospered as a temperance writer, spiritualist, and love poet from her home in rural Wisconsin; and James Whitcomb Riley wrote regional dialect poetry so beloved (and so prolifically) that Indiana made a holiday of his birthday. These careers demonstrate the risk poets take in avoiding the East and West Coast epicenters of literary activity: their reputations have waned, or have lagged far behind their achievement in poetry. Even to list contemporary poets in this group is inherently misleading: The recognizable names are those who have, at last, received the recognition their work has long deserved. Lorine Niedecker, born in Fort Atkinson, Wisconsin, in 1903, lived on Black Hawk Island in Lake Koshkonong, Wisconsin, most of her life. Her

plainspoken, crystalline, epigrammatic lyrics were rediscovered in the early 1980s. Jim Harrison (born in 1937 in Grayling, Michigan) writes short, imagistic verse drawn from the beautiful and rural northern Michigan landscape where he has lived nearly all his life. Robert Bly, born in western Minnesota of Norwegian stock, returned home after Harvard and navy service and has had a rich and varied career as poet, editor, translator, and gender theorist, as well as mentor to younger poets. John Frederick Nims (Muskegon, Michigan) has written highly crafted, classical lyrics in the context of an academic career, most recently at the University of Illinois at Chicago Circle. James Wright (Martins Ferry, Ohio) is considered a major poet in a remarkable generation of poets, and since his death in 1980 his reputation has steadily risen.

Like Wright, Mona Van Duyn (Waterloo, Iowa) has made universal meaning from relatively local materials. Having lived most of her adult life in St. Louis, Van Duyn was poet laureate of the United States (1992–1993) and has won nearly every major poetry award offered in this country, but she remains little known in the larger world. Her poems range across all possible subject matter, in the context of a quotidian domestic life marked by the joys and sorrows of marriage, motherhood, time, work, and love. While her allusions span all of English literature, many of her poems are plainspoken, with images drawn from the objects, facts, and circumstances of life in the middle of the United States. She can convey the local speech convincingly, as in "Nine": "That was my grandfather, nearly went to prison, / I'm your grandmother and he was my grandfather, so / you must say. In the Old Country, and they was poor / and then if they could get to a big town some way, / why you see they could buy things cheaper." And she can make poetry, as midwestern poets often do, of the evocative names of towns. "A Small Excursion": "Take a trip with me / through the towns in Missouri. / Feel naming in all its joy / as we go through Braggadocio, Barks, Kidder, Fair Play, / Bourbon, Bean Lake, / and Loose Creek." In "The Cities of the Plain" she takes on the region's social conservatism, again in a matter-of-fact tone and language:

Their sex life was their own business,
I thought, and took some of the pressure off women,
who were treated, most of the time, as merely
a man's way of producing another man.
And there were plenty of the other kind—
the two older girls got married when they wanted to.
The riot in front of our house that evening,
when a gang of young queers, all drunk and horny,
threatened to break in, yelling
for the two strangers, our guests, handsome
as angels, to come out and have some fun,

was not intelligently handled by my husband,
to say the least. . . .
"Two little virgins," he told them. "Now, fellows,
wouldn't that be nicer, and more fun?"

Recognition has come slowly to Van Duyn, no doubt in part due to her decision to locate herself and her work outside the nation's literary capitals. For her and for other poets less physically committed to the Midwest, the region has nonetheless provided an inheritance of language and idiom, of complex and troubled natural beauty, and of individuals who transcend and transform—and sometimes embody—the most negative stereotypes of the region's homogeneity and provincialism.

Sources and Further Reading: Amy Clampitt, *The Collected Poems of Amy Clampitt* (1999); John Knoepfle, "Crossing the Midwest," in John Gordon Burke, ed., *Regional Perspectives: An Examination of America's Literary Heritage* (1973); Vachel Lindsay, *The Poetry of Vachel Lindsay* (1984); Mary Oliver, *New and Selected Poems* (1992); Kevin Stein and G. E. Murray, eds., *Illinois Voices* (2001); Lucien Stryk, ed., *Heartland: Poets of the Midwest* (1967); James Tate, *Selected Poems* (1991); Mona Van Duyn, *Selected Poems* (2002); Sylvia Griffith Wheeler, ed., *In the Middle: Ten Midwestern Women Poets* (1985); James Wright, *Above the River* (1990).

Brett C. Millier
Middlebury College, Vermont

Print Cultures

During the nineteenth century, as industrialization transformed the United States from an agrarian society dominated by East Coast, English-speaking Protestants to a continental power with a population vastly expanded not only in numbers but in diversity, a variety of print cultures helped to produce and reproduce the "Midwest" as a geographic region that claimed a distinct cultural, social, and political identity. Print-capitalism, argues Benedict Anderson, contributed to the formation of regions and nations as "imagined communities," encouraging people to see themselves as members of groups beyond the face-to-face. The development and diffusion of any print culture depends in part on an interplay between print production and distribution technologies and the groups and individuals who control them. The white settlers who colonized the lands that came to form the Midwest brought with them the knowledge and technology for producing newspapers and pamphlets to support the development of the churches; schools; and financial, commercial, and government institutions that were the

building blocks of their emerging communities. Competing groups who sought to stamp localities with their beliefs and ideas contended over print as they struggled for control over the region's economic resources. And at the same time, they imported printed publications that helped maintain links between the old and the new ways of life; through writing and reading, migrants maintained a sense of their continuing identities as "farmers," "Pennsylvanians," "Norwegians," "Czechs," "Catholics," or "Presbyterians." Thus, while some print publications carried out a consolidating function, knitting people together in their mind's eye as midwesterners, others helped to keep them apart.

The ability to read became an essential skill for all Americans, and universal literacy a social and political imperative that was realized through technological developments like railroad transportation, mass paper production, and printing techniques as well as through middle-class institutions like schools, colleges, and libraries and government agencies that included a federal postal service with nationwide reach. Bureaucratization and standardization in the world of work required managers and employees to comprehend operating manuals, policies, and procedures. Print mediated between government and citizens, too, through instructions, rules, and regulations. Advertisements in mail-order catalogs and periodicals, on product labels and in flyers, directed the consumer's gaze to an imagined world of endless plenty, disconnected from the finite stock of tangible goods occupying space in local stores. Farmers read journals and manuals that instructed them in the intricacies of new agricultural techniques. Political and issue-oriented groups like those advocating temperance and women's suffrage communicated strategies and motivated one another through print. Print was also a source of pleasure and information for individuals and families as stories conveyed in the pages of novels, newspapers, and magazines supplemented, and in some cases supplanted, those related orally by personal acquaintances who were keepers of the communal memory.

Even the smallest midwestern towns boasted their own locally compiled and printed newspaper—and often more than one. Originally the mouthpieces of political parties, as the nineteenth century wore on, newspapers like the *Emporia Gazette* of Emporia, Kansas, assumed the role of community booster, stressing local business opportunities and cultural advantages. At the same time, a system of "exchanging" news items with papers in other regions facilitated a wide geographic coverage and made it possible for people living in villages like Osage, Iowa, as well as in cities like Chicago or Bismarck to imagine themselves as "Americans" as well as "Midwesterners." Through the development of such imagined communities, print channeled midwesterners' consciousness from a local to a national horizon—and back again. Newspapers and magazines also provided the base for other imagined communities that crossed geographical borders while reinforcing boundaries based on gender, class, occupation, ethnicity, race, and religion. For many midwestern farmers, subscribing to one or more of the region's myriad farm journals was an occupational practice that persisted through the twentieth century. Newspapers also helped migrants resist assimilation and maintain ethnic ties. While the big cities of Minneapolis and Chicago were major centers of Scandinavian publishing, so were some smaller ones such as Decorah, Iowa, which circulated a Norwegian-language newspaper, the *Decorah-Posten*, throughout the Midwest and beyond during the second half of the nineteenth century. For African Americans migrating north during the first half of the twentieth century, the *Chicago Defender* provided a voice and a forum for the imagined community of "the Race," as did *Streetwise* for the Chicago's homeless later in the same century.

Churches were among the first organizations to establish networks of print in the Midwest, both by importing texts and through local production. All denominations used books and periodicals to consolidate congregations of the faithful in frontier settlements as well as to communicate with their imagined communities across the region and beyond. They also used print to attract newcomers. In Prairie du Chien, Wisconsin, Roman Catholic missionary Joseph Cretin printed materials for Native Americans in their own language during the late 1830s. But Protestants, too, were keen to proselytize among indigenous peoples, and the ownership and distribution of religious texts in Native American languages became a matter for anxiety between rival groups of Christians. Even within denominations, published materials constituted a site of contest: In the second half of the nineteenth century, for instance, "traditionalist" Catholics and "accommodationists" (led by Archbishop John Ireland of St. Paul) played out their differences vis-à-vis each other as well as Protestantism through an extensive national Catholic publishing industry that produced not only devotional works but also newspapers, periodicals, and fiction.

A force for standardization in midwestern print culture was the public school. In 1836, William Holmes McGuffey copyrighted the first of his famous *Readers*. These textbooks would eventually sell more than one hundred twenty million copies in a variety of editions and transmit Protestant values of hard work, thrift, and civic virtue across the nation, but especially in the Midwest and the South. *McGuffey Readers* established a pattern for educational content as well as publishing profitability that attracted many imitators as the century wore on. An educational publishing industry

formed that standardized the production not only of texts but also of readers—those generations of teachers and students who passed along an educational conveyor belt that for most started and ended with elementary education (often in one-room rural schools). For an elite minority the process extended to a state university or normal school or to one of scores of private religious institutions. Yet the influence of the public education system did not go uncontested. For many nineteenth-century German immigrants, for example, control over the language and content of instruction was of deep political concern. They fiercely defended their right to maintain parochial schools with their own curriculum and teaching materials against attacks by the anglophone political establishment that included the 1889 passage of Wisconsin's Bennett Act, requiring public and private school instruction to be in English.

By the end of the nineteenth century, state regulation of teaching texts and methods and the 1862 Morrill Land Grant Act had helped to establish a system of education that rested on a massive body of official publications along with prescriptions on how to read them. During the Progressive Era (lasting from about 1890 to 1920) midwestern public universities created connections and built alliances that cemented their cultural and political influence throughout their states. The "Wisconsin Idea," for example, expressed the university's mission to serve all the state's citizens. Extension classes and traveling libraries channeled reading materials that included novels and stories as well as informational books and pamphlets to people of all ages in even the remotest rural areas. A typical career path for midwestern women university graduates led them to states farther west, where as teachers and librarians, they transmitted mainstream cultural practices to the latest generation of "pioneers." From the 1920s on, the federal- and state-supported agricultural extension system took on the task of educating rural people in a gendered division of work and leisure that assigned farm women to "homemaking" groups while it simultaneously expanded their opportunities for building social and information networks with women across the state, the region, and the nation.

When antebellum Yankee pioneers began to settle the Midwest, they brought with them a model for institutionalizing the sharing of books—the public library. The same leading families who established local banks, schools, churches, and voluntary and fraternal organizations like the Masons also formalized cooperative groups for the circulation of reading materials based on subscription or the purchase of shares. By the 1870s, midwestern states were passing legislation that enabled municipalities to set up free libraries. Some communities converted local subscription collections into public libraries. Elsewhere, women's study clubs were the moving force in establishing free collections. From the 1890s until 1917, the Carnegie Corporation consolidated the public library movement by providing matching grants for the building of over sixteen hundred public libraries. About half went to midwestern communities (Indiana alone built 165 Carnegie libraries), a reward for the value they placed on books and reading and for the political drive needed to compile the required grant application. The resulting buildings were significant for their prominent location on Main Street, their imposing architecture, and for an internal design that shaped work practices and patron experiences for decades, reinforcing a gendered division of librarians' tasks and responsibilities yet facilitating service to specific clienteles including immigrants and young people.

But although some librarians demonstrated a desire and capability to serve people of different interests and backgrounds, professional practice did little to diversify collections. Public libraries' early founders—those leading pioneer families and women's clubs—were predominantly of English-speaking, Protestant origin, and library collections reflected their interests, beliefs, and values. As a result, Catholics and non-English-speaking immigrants tended to avoid public libraries. At the same time, the emerging library profession emphasized uniform collecting, classifying, and cataloging practices that left little room for regional, ethnic, or linguistic variation. In the early twentieth century, for example, Minneapolis publisher H. W. Wilson began to produce aids to library collection development and reference services, starting with the *Cumulative Book Index* in 1898. Influenced by these convenient though homogenizing aids to professional practice, for most of the twentieth century librarians ignored small-press publications, especially those that represented beliefs and attitudes that they defined as outside the mainstream. Library service to ethnic minorities focused on assimilation rather than the celebration of cultural difference. Library service to everyone stressed the importance of "useful information" rather than reading fiction for pleasure, even though public-library patrons expressed a strong preference for the latter. Yet for the last three decades of the twentieth century, two midwestern librarians led a practical protest against these pressures to conformity. At the Hennepin County Library in Minnetonka, Minnesota, Sanford Berman argued for local cataloguing practices to provide more comprehensible access to the public library's holdings, while at Wisconsin's State Historical Society, James P. Danky gradually built up a unique collection of those ephemeral and alternative-press materials that most librarians ignored.

While early print-culture boundaries reflected broadly defined identities of class, gender, religion, race, and ethnicity, by the end of the twentieth century shifting demographics and new technologies had contributed to a segmentation of markets for printed materials and other media that was designed to deliver to advertisers audiences precisely defined by their purchasing preferences. Such segmentation, rather than welding readers together into an imagined community by emphasizing common aspects, tends to drive them apart. Locally based print communities continue to thrive, but often based on lifestyle preferences for genres—late-twentieth-century comic-book readers of Iowa City, for instance—rather than the broader class and ethnic identities of the previous era. Concentration of the publishing industry into a handful of multinational corporations has increased the standardization of many types of publication. Yet as Janice A. Radway's study of midwestern consumers of that quintessentially mass-produced print genre—the "formula" romance—indicates, readers adopt and adapt cultural practices to suit themselves. And digitization provides new scope for contest over texts, whether mediated by paper or by electronic device, as producers and consumers struggle for control over the fixed nature of print.

Sources and Further Reading: Benedict Anderson, *Imagined Communities* (1983); James P. Danky and Wayne A. Wiegand, eds., *Print Culture in a Diverse America* (1998); Sally Foreman Griffith, *Home Town News* (1989); Carl F. Kaestle, "Standardization and Diversity in American Print Culture, 1880 to the Present," in Carl F. Kaestle, Helen Damon-Moore, Lawrence C. Stedman, Katherine Tinsley, and William Vance Trollinger, Jr., eds., *Literacy in the United States* (1991); Joanne E. Passet, *Cultural Crusaders* (1994); Christine Pawley, *Reading on the Middle Border* (2001); Matthew J. Pustz, *Comic Book Culture: Fanboys and True Believers* (1999); Janice A. Radway, *Reading the Romance: Women, Patriarchy, and Popular Literature* (1991); Abigail A. Van Slyck, *Free to All* (1995); Ronald J. Zboray, *A Fictive People* (1993).

Christine Pawley
The University of Iowa

Major Writers

Mark Twain (1835–1910)

The writing of Mark Twain (the pseudonym of Samuel Langhorne Clemens) demonstrates an often uneasy relationship to the Midwest of his boyhood. At the time of Twain's birth in 1835, Missouri was still the frontier; small towns like Florida and Hannibal were "a sort of

Mark Twain in a photograph from 1907. Library of Congress New York World-Telegram & Sun Newspaper Photograph Collection, LC-USZ62-112065.

realism, and would have been impossible without the thorough knowledge of a native Missourian. Critics' reviews have run the gamut, from William Dean Howells, who praised his authenticity; to Arnold Bennett, who considered him "a divine amateur"; to Van Wyck Brooks, who theorized that "the humorist was the victim of an environment that crushed out the artist in him," and cited the influences of his Presbyterian mother and the censorship of his wife, Olivia, as central factors in stifling his creativity. Central to such disagreements is the traditional privileging of eastern writers, a tendency still active in some literary circles. Twain himself was not immune to such criticism. While his tales focused on vernacular characters and broad humor, often burlesquing the literati, he coveted and cultivated their readership and friendship, ultimately measuring his success against their standards.

This critical debate aside, the influence of the Midwest on his imagination is clear. The Mississippi River, the heart of the Midwest, functioned as a touchstone for Twain's creative efforts. It figures prominently in *Life on the Mississippi* (1883), *Tom Sawyer*, and *Huck Finn*. *Life* celebrates Twain's apprenticeship as a cub pilot; in it, he represents the Mississippi as a powerful physical force. In some places he describes its sheer beauty; in others, he delineates the dangers of taking the river for granted. The Mississippi serves as a controlling metaphor for life itself; both can hold incredible beauty and bounty, and also bring grief and pain.

> The face of the water, in time, became a wonderful book—a book that was a dead language to the uneducated passenger, but which told its mind to me without reserve, delivering its most cherished secrets as clearly as if it uttered them with a voice. And it was not a book to be read once and thrown aside, for it had a new story to tell every day.

Both *Tom Sawyer* and *Huck Finn* are set in the mythical St. Petersburg (a thinly disguised Hannibal). Walter Blair's 1960 study *Mark Twain and Huck Finn* details the real-life places and people Twain used in creating *Huck* and the earlier novel, *Tom Sawyer*. Tom, Huck, and Becky Thatcher depict youth and adolescence in an idyllic river-town setting. However, Twain's paeans to boyhood on the Mississippi challenge the notion of childhood innocence. Every nostalgic scene of midwestern boyhood is juxtaposed against an example of boyish nightmare. In *Tom Sawyer*, Tom bamboozles his chums into paying to whitewash a fence, trades for chits to earn a Sunday School Bible, and dazzles Becky with his boyish athletics. But these idyllic memories often ride uneasily upon a substrate of human ignorance, greed, and fear. In the midst of a boyish prank, Tom and Huck witness

fringe to the prairies." But the Hannibal of 1844—far from the "drowsy" place of Twain's subsequent memory—was a burgeoning town. Industries and social institutions flourished, including everything from slaughterhouses and distilleries to churches and schools; its port served as a hub for heavily loaded steamboats; and Hannibal was a major stopover on the overland route west to the goldfields in 1848.

Growing up in Hannibal situated Twain at the crossroads between East and West, North and South. He left Missouri at age seventeen, returning seldom and at widely spaced intervals, but his childhood experience became the driving force of his creative energies. However, critics have seldom agreed on whether that influence was beneficial or detrimental to his artistic development. Minnie M. Brashear, in her early study (1934), hails Twain as a son of Missouri, believing his early childhood essential to his development as a writer; biographer Ron Powers (1999) agrees. Clearly Twain's study and careful use of dialect in *The Adventures of Tom Sawyer* (1876) and *Adventures of Huckleberry Finn* (1884) stem from his commitment to a murder, are threatened by Injun Joe, and become lost in a cave with the murderer.

The same balancing act is integral to *Adventures of Huckleberry Finn*, where navigating the river becomes a metaphor for navigating life. Huck fakes his own death to escape an abusive father and anticipates living a free and easy life on the river; but this pastoral vision of Eden is immediately complicated by Huck's collusion in the escape of a runaway slave. In this novel, the river signals freedom from social constraints—"you feel mighty free and easy and comfortable on a raft"—while each return to land reinforces Huck's pangs of conscience. Sections of the novel contain idyllic descriptions of the river's beauty; yet evidence of the river's dangerous power abounds. Images of Huck and Jim floating down the Mississippi alternately smoking, swimming, and talking are juxtaposed against the sinking of the *Walter Scott*, the "Raftman" chapter containing Dick Albright's horrific story of setting his dead child adrift on the river, and the destruction of the raft in a storm. The Mississippi gives, and it takes away; its dangerous shoals and sandbars mirror the dangers posed by "civilization" shown in the river towns Huck and Jim encounter.

In Twain's late works, the Mississippi goes underground; although masked, its influence remains prevalent, represented in other times and places. His later, darker tales borrow from his knowledge of river piloting to tell stories of navigating the macrocosm of the universe and the microscopic world. Throughout a long career, Mark Twain foregrounded his midwestern experiences, using them both as literal plot devices and as more metaphorical figures. He memorialized the dialects, people, and places of his childhood, creating the definitive image of the Midwest that endures to the present day.

Sources and Further Reading: Howard G. Baetzhold and Joseph B. McCullough, eds., *The Bible According to Mark Twain* (1995); Minnie M. Brashaer, *Mark Twain: Son of Missouri* (1934); Justin Kaplan, *Mark Twain and His World* (1974); Justin Kaplan, *Mr. Clemens and Mark Twain* (1966); Leland Krauth, *Proper Mark Twain* (1999); Joseph B. McCullough and Janice McIntire-Strasburg, *Mark Twain at the Buffalo Express* (1999); Milton Meltzer, *Mark Twain Himself* (1960); Ron Powers, *Dangerous Water* (1999).

Janice McIntire-Strasburg
St. Louis University

William Dean Howells (1837–1920)

William Dean Howells is probably the most notable midwestern writer who didn't want to be one. Howells was born in 1837. For much of his youth and early career, he groomed himself—insofar as this was even possible in the Western Reserve—to become an author whose graces would be recognized by the literati of New England. When his first poem was accepted by the *Atlantic Monthly* in 1860, his rapture knew no bounds. This entry into the citadel of culture was a portent, and Howells knew it. "The truth is," he appealed, "there is no place quite so good as Boston— God bless it! and I look forward to living there some day—being possibly the linchpin in the hub." Before long that prophecy would almost become true.

Besides romantic poems, young Howells also authored a campaign biography for another midwesterner by the name of Abraham Lincoln. Republican victory in the election of 1860 afforded the Ohioan a patronage appointment in the diplomatic service, and he assumed the American consulship at Venice shortly thereafter. From Europe, Howells sent back vignettes of the Italian picturesque, the serial appearance of which in the Boston *Advertiser* kept him within the sights of the Brahmin literary elite. Collected later in *Venetian Life* (1866) and *Italian Journeys* (1867), Howells's travel sketches earned him the cultural credentials he would need in place of a diploma from Harvard. Soon after his repatriation, Howells joined Boston's flagship *Atlantic Monthly* in 1866, and, just five years later, he rose to become that magazine's chief editor and literary arbiter.

For the next ten years, Howells was in an extraordinary position to redefine the contours of American literary life. With the prestige of the *Atlantic* behind him, he opened the pages of that journal to a wider range of writers, including Mark Twain and Henry James, two of his lifelong friends who otherwise had nothing much in common. Through his own creative work—an outpouring of fiction, reviews, parlor theatricals, and miscellaneous commentary—and the significant encouragement of others, Howells championed the virtues of literary realism, which he defined as "nothing more and nothing less than the truthful treatment of material." Though frequently derided by later critics as morally timid and sexually squeamish, Howells in his own day scandalized many readers because of his willingness to tackle subjects like divorce (*A Modern Instance*, 1882), the corruption of business ethics (*The Rise of Silas Lapham*, 1885), social inequality (*A Hazard of New Fortunes*, 1889–1890), and interracial marriage (*An Imperative Duty*, 1892). To the genteel, his material seemed commonplace and dingy; but Howells deliberately valorized "the dialect, the language that most Americans know—the language of unaffected people everywhere." Maintaining those artistic priorities while seeking acceptance from the literary establishment of New England strained Howells's democratic sensibilities. Although the author knew that he could never go back to live in the midwestern world from which he had exiled himself, he never completely abandoned the frontier values of simplicity and social equality that he had imbibed during his Ohio boyhood. In novel after novel, Howells contrasts the freedom and spontaneity of characters from western or rural backgrounds with the staid conventionality of eastern city-dwellers whose social veneer, however smooth, cannot conceal their invidious snobbery. In fact, the author's favorite target was none other than Boston, a city, he remarked in *A Chance Acquaintance* (1873), "that would rather perish by fire and sword than be suspected of vulgarity."

Not anticipating that cataclysm, Howells transferred his publishing allegiances in the middle 1880s to the New York house of Harper and Brothers, with whom he established lucrative contractual relations that continued until his death. Besides occupying the "Editor's Study" in *Harper's Magazine*, he authored dozens of novels and numerous volumes of criticism, poetry, travel writing, and autobiography over the span of his tenure with the firm.

For all its vitality, New York impressed upon Howells a growing sense of social discord in American life. As the materialistic frenzy of the Gilded Age was reaching its crescendo, in 1888 Howells confessed to an expatriated Henry James,

I'm not in a very good humor with "America" myself. It seems to me the most grotesquely illogical thing under the sun; and I suppose I love it less because it won't let me love it more. I should hardly like to trust pen and ink with all the audacity of my social ideas; but after fifty years of optimistic content with "civilization" and its ability to come out all right in the end, I now abhor it, and feel that it is coming out all wrong in the end, unless it bases itself anew on a real equality.

Howells's skepticism assumed narrative form in his greatest book, *A Hazard of New Fortunes*, which began its serial run in *Harper's Weekly* the following year. New York exposes Howells's characters to brutal new facts—forms of poverty that can no longer be viewed as picturesque, inequalities of status that make a mockery of democratic principles, the real power of capital to blight whatever it touches. The novel exemplifies the corruption of American ideals in the career of the Dryfoos family, whose fortunes change when natural gas is discovered on their Indiana farmland. With their newfound wealth they migrate to New York, where money brings power; but exercising that power betrays the simple Christian values of the rural heartland they have left behind.

Howells lived another thirty years, but he never wrote another novel equal to *A Hazard of New Fortunes*. At his memorial service in New York City on May 12, 1920, the *New York Times* noted that an "outpouring of representative men and women in the world of American letters" crowded the solemn chapel to pay their respects. "But, as if by common consent, those in charge of the arrangements had decided that Howells's place in both literature and life was too well established and too adequately granted to require further stress," and so no eulogy was offered. Surely Howells, secure within his coffin, would have known that the newspaper got it wrong.

Sources and Further Reading: Michael Anesko, *Letters, Fictions, Lives* (1997); Edwin H. Cady, *The Realist at War* (1958); Edwin H. Cady, *The Road to Realism* (1956); Edwin H. Cady and Louis J. Budd, eds., *On Howells* (1993); John W. Crowley, *The Mask of Fiction* (1989); W. D. Howells, *A Chance Acquaintance* (1873; reprint 1971); W. D. Howells, *Criticism and Fiction* (1891); W. D. Howells, *Selected Letters*, ed. George Warren Arms (1979); Kenneth S. Lynn, *William Dean Howells: An American Life* (1971); Elsa Nettels, *Language, Race and Social Class in Howells's America* (1988); "Simple Rites: Mark Howells Funeral," *New York Times* (May 13, 1920); Henry Nash Smith and William M. Gibson, eds., *Mark Twain–Howells Letters*, 2 vols. (1960).

Michael Anesko
The Pennsylvania State University

James Whitcomb Riley (1849–1916)

James Whitcomb Riley, the "Hoosier Poet," embodied the values that Gilded Age Americans wanted to find in the Midwest. He began his professional life on the medicine-show circuit, hawking "Doc" McCrillus's Blood Purifier, and he never lost his knack for selling. He gave the public exactly what it craved: images of a pastoral Indiana countryside peopled by unsophisticated "Hoosiers" such as "Little Orphant Annie" and the "Raggedy Man." John Singer Sargent painted his portrait, Anna Pavlova's dance company interpreted his poems, and in 1915 the U.S. Secretary of the Interior called for the observance of James Whitcomb Riley's birthday as a national holiday. More than any other poet, Riley epitomized the Indiana that Americans were eager to claim as their nation's Heartland.

Riley was born and raised in Greenfield, Indiana, the son of Elizabeth Marine and Rueben A. Riley. After quitting the medicine show, he worked as a roving sign-painter and then, for many years, as a journalist at the *Indianapolis Journal*, where many of his early poems appeared. His published volumes included *The Old Swimmin' Hole and 'Leven More Poems* (1883), *The*

Boss Girl (1885), *Afterwhiles* (1887), *Old-Fashioned Roses* (1888), *Pipes o' Pan at Zekesbury* (1888), *Rhymes of Childhood* (1890), *The Flying Islands of the Night* (1891), *Green Fields and Running Brooks* (1892), *Poems Here at Home* (1893), *Armazindy* (1894), *A Child-World* (1896), *The Rubaiyet of Doc Sifers* (1897), *Home-Folks* (1900), and *The Book of Joyous Children* (1902). He maintained a lifelong relationship with the Bobbs-Merrill publishing house in Indianapolis, although he constantly sought acceptance from prestigious journals, like the *Atlantic Monthly*, that shunned him. Like many midwesterners, Riley felt marginalized by eastern publishers, but he sought support (and provided it for others) through the Western Association of Writers.

His work is philosophically antimodern, celebrating pastoral pleasures in poems such as "The Old Swimmin' Hole" and "When the Frost Is on the Punkin":

> The strawstack in the medder, and the reaper in the
>   shed;
> The hosses in theyr stalls below—the clover over-
>   head!—
> O, it sets my hart a-clickin' like the tickin' of a clock,
> When the frost is on the punkin and the fodder's in
>   the shock!

However, even as his poems express old-fashioned values, their calculated commercial appeal roots them in the nascent advertising industry. Riley promoted his publications with national tours sponsored by the Redpath Lyceum Bureau; in "opera houses" from Peoria to Portland, he performed his familiar poems to great acclaim. His shows reassured, more than they challenged, his audiences. As the *Kansas City Star* put it, in a review of an 1897 performance: "Mr. Riley, happily, has not changed since he was here last. There is the same droll, humorous expression that we laughed at some years ago . . . and those who laughed heartiest were those who heard him before—who knew exactly what was coming."

Although he marketed himself as a squeaky-clean small-town boy, Riley's private life was complicated. He was a lifelong problem drinker, and his biographer Elizabeth J. Van Allen even suggests that the surreal imagery in his one play, *The Flying Islands of the Night*, was inspired by alcoholic hallucinations. His relationships with women were often tortured and he never married, although his poems idealize women as citadels of virtue. His self-promotion sometimes backfired, as in 1877, when he engineered the "discovery" of a lost Edgar Allan Poe manuscript, "Leonainie," which was secretly written by Riley. His ostensible point was to show how the Eastern establishment would embrace anything by Poe while rejecting new work by midwesterners like himself. But when the hoax was discovered, it did lasting damage to his wholesome reputation. He managed these private inconsistencies by presenting himself to the public as a "child-man," a kind of Hoosier Peter Pan who scorned adult conventions.

Riley was dismissed—perhaps too hastily—by the generation of modernists that followed him, although his poems are still regularly reprinted in children's anthologies. And his poems still have the power to fascinate: Even as they radiate sentimentality, they also vent anxieties (about class, urbanization, and "authenticity") generated by his historical moment. In an era when class gaps were widening, his most famous poem, "Little Orphant Annie," describes a lower-class girl who came to work in the middle-class Riley home:

> An' Little Orphant Annie says, when the blaze is
>   blue,
> An' the lamp-wick sputters, an' the wind goes woo-
>   oo!
> An' you hear the crickets quit, an' the moon is gray,
> An' the lightnin' bugs in dew is all squenched away,—
> You better mind yer parents, an' yer teachers fond an'
>   dear,
> An' churish them 'at loves you, an' dry the orphant's
>   tear,
> An he'p the pore an' needy ones 'at clusters all about,
> Er the gobble-uns'll git you
> Ef you
> Don't
> Watch
> Out!

In Riley's poems, lower-class "Hoosiers" are treated with an ambivalent nostalgia. Orphant Annie may speak of "gobble-uns," but she ultimately acts as a performer for her middle-class listeners who like to be thrilled but not threatened. The rural Midwest was industrializing, and, in a mobile society, people were perhaps getting harder to "read." Riley's characters, by contrast, are "readable" because they are types; they seem to solve the problems of social instability by offering a vision of Hoosierdom that every turn-of-the-century American (rich and poor, westerner and easterner) could understand, not intellectually but emotionally. Riley's lively mix of sentimental images and manageable "gobble-uns" represented the region to the rest of the nation. It was a Midwest of swimming holes and golden autumns, and readers across the country felt at home there.

Sources and Further Reading: William Lyon Phelps, ed., *Letters of James Whitcomb Riley* (1930); James Whitcomb Riley, *Complete Poetical Works of James Whitcomb Riley* (1993); Angela Sorby, "Performing Class: James Whitcomb Riley's

Poetry of Distinction," *MLQ: A Journal of Literary History* 60 (June 1999); Elizabeth J. Van Allen, *James Whitcomb Riley: A Life* (1999).

Angela Sorby
Marquette University, Wisconsin

Charles Waddell Chesnutt (1858–1932)

African American short-story writer, novelist, and essayist Charles Waddell Chesnutt was born on June 20 in Cleveland, Ohio, in 1858. He was the son of Ann Maria (Sampson) and Andrew Jackson Chesnutt, mixed-race African Americans from Fayetteville, North Carolina, who were among a group of free blacks who left North Carolina by wagon train in 1856 for a better life north of slavery. In 1866, after the Civil War ended, the family returned to Fayetteville, where Andrew opened a grocery store with the help of Waddell Cade, a white landowner who was probably his father.

Charles's youth and young manhood were spent in the South during the embattled years of Reconstruction, an era that marked his life and work. Beginning in 1867, when he was nine, Charles attended Howard School, a flagship free public school built for black children with money from the Freedmen's Bureau. The failure of his father's grocery store put pressure on Charles to help support his family, and at sixteen, he became a pupil-teacher at Howard, launching a career as an educator that lasted several years.

During this period of growth, frustrated with his inadequate formal schooling, Charles began a course of self-education, keeping a journal and studying Latin, German, French, algebra, ancient history, rhetoric, and British and American literature. But in some respects, self-education only intensified the young man's frustrations, as racial barriers made him feel "cut off," as he put it in his journal in 1880, from "cultivated society" and "almost every source of improvement." By that time, married (to Susan Perry, a Howard teacher, in 1878) and already a father, Chesnutt was principal of the State Colored Normal School in Fayetteville, North Carolina, and organist, choirmaster, and Sunday school superintendent at Fayetteville A.M.E. Zion Church.

Blue-eyed and light-skinned, Chesnutt had once considered leaving Fayetteville and living as a white man. But he rejected a life of passing and determined to make his way up the social and economic ladder as an African American. While in his twenties, Chesnutt began thinking about retracing his parents' migration to the North to escape the "blot" of racial prejudice and "show to the world," as he wrote in his journal, "that a man may spring from a race of slaves, and yet far excel many of the boasted ruling race." His literary ambitions received a jolt when he read the former carpetbagger Albion Tourgee's best-selling novel *A Fool's Errand* (1879), about the Reconstruction South. Tourgee's success persuaded Chesnutt that the post-emancipation racial world he knew intimately could capture the interest of northern audiences. In 1883, after a brief stint in New York City as a reporter for Dow, Jones & Company, he returned to Cleveland and took work in the accounting department of the Nickel Plate Railroad Company. It was in Cleveland that Chesnutt, who also trained as a lawyer, made his literary career.

In 1887, the year Chesnutt passed his Ohio bar exam, the *Atlantic Monthly* published his story "The Goopherd Grapevine." It was the first work by an African American to be published by the *Atlantic Monthly*, and it was Chesnutt's first important work of fiction. Set in rural North Carolina, the story introduced its white audience to African American folk culture, including "conjuration," in the storytelling of the protagonist, Uncle Julius McAdoo, a former slave who uses his recollections of plantation life to outwit his white employer, a businessman newly arrived from Ohio. Other "conjure stories" followed and, in March 1899, Houghton Mifflin published *The Conjure Woman*, Chesnutt's first short-story collection.

That fall, Houghton Mifflin published Chesnutt's second short-story collection, *The Wife of His Youth and Other Stories of the Color Line*. In these stories, Chesnutt aimed to examine a problem his conjure tales did not address: the moral and psychological conflicts of the mixed-race upper class, people like Chesnutt who lived close to the color line in a northern city, modeled on Cleveland, after the Civil War. Chesnutt showed how this group of African Americans dwelled in a social and spiritual no-man's-land between the races, where there was no easy resolution for their internal conflicts. Praised by the white novelist and respected critic William Dean Howells, these stories drew sharp criticism from other critics for dealing with the highly charged subjects of miscegenation and racial violence.

About this time, Chesnutt closed the prosperous stenographic business he had started earlier to pursue his dream of becoming a full-time writer and lecturer. Within six years, he published three novels, *The House behind the Cedars* (1900), a story of passing; *The Marrow of Tradition* (1901), about the Wilmington, North Carolina, race riot of 1898; and *The Colonel's Dream* (1905), about a failed effort to address racial problems in one postwar Southern town. At the same time, his short stories and essays appeared in various journals, including a controversial three-part essay in the *Boston*

Evening Transcript, called "The Future American," in which Chesnutt argued that the solution to America's race problem was racial amalgamation. This was a view he advanced in the face of severe criticism from both sides of the color line until the end of his life. Alongside W.E.B. DuBois, Chesnutt was also an activist seeking political and economic rights for blacks, although he refused to endorse a 1910 public statement by DuBois attacking Booker T. Washington. In 1913, he persuaded Cleveland mayor Newton Baker to oppose a bill prohibiting interracial marriage in Ohio (the bill was defeated), and in 1917 he successfully enlisted the Chamber of Commerce to ban D.W. Griffith's film *The Birth of a Nation* from being shown in Cleveland. He also supported women's suffrage.

By the 1920s, Chesnutt had achieved the stature of a much-admired writer and scholar among African Americans. In 1928, the NAACP awarded him its Spingarn Medal for his "pioneer work as a literary artist depicting the life and struggles of Americans of Negro descent." That year, he completed his final novel, *The Quarry*, which was not published until 1999. He died at home in 1932.

Sources and Further Reading: William L. Andrews, *The Literary Career of Charles W. Chesnutt* (1980); Richard Brodhead, ed., *The Journals of Charles W. Chesnutt* (1993); Charles W. Chesnutt, *Stories, Novels, and Essays* (2002); Helen M. Chesnutt, *Charles Waddell Chesnutt: Pioneer of the Color Line* (1952); Frances Richardson Keller, *An American Crusade* (1978); Joseph R. McElrath, Jr. and Robert C. Leitz III, eds., *To Be an Author: Letters of Charles W. Chesnutt, 1889–1905* (1997); Joseph R. McElrath, Jr., Robert C. Leitz III, and Jesse S. Crisler, eds., *Charles W. Chesnutt: Essays and Speeches* (1999).

Jennifer Fleischner
Adelphi University, New York

Hamlin Garland (1860–1940)

During a productive and varied literary career, Hamlin Garland published almost fifty volumes of fiction, poetry, plays, and essays. For fifty years he was an important figure in American literary culture. His reputation rests chiefly on his short fiction written before 1895, particularly on his innovative volume of short stories, *Main-Travelled Roads* (1891), and on his autobiographies, *A Son of the Middle Border* (1917) and *A Daughter of the Middle Border* (1921). In these volumes, Garland demonstrated that it had at last become possible to deal with the American farmer in literature as a human being instead of seeing him simply through the veil of literary convention. By creating new types of characters, and writing with an unmatched compas-

sion, sympathy, and understanding, Garland hoped not only to inform readers about the realities of midwestern life but to touch the deeper feelings of a nation.

Through his fiction, and especially in *Main-Travelled Roads*, Garland became a principal spokesman for nineteenth-century agrarian society. Faithful to his instinct for telling the truth, he used particular settings in the Midwest to bring to his readers the problems that men and women in crude surroundings had to face and solve in order to survive. He succeeded in dramatizing the severe restrictions of prairie life, with its loneliness and drudgery, and suggested the waste of finer values exacted by that life. And he was one of the first novelists to view skeptically the conventional American belief in the purity, wholesomeness, and freedom of life on the farm.

Born in 1860 on a small farm near West Salem, Wisconsin, Garland was the second of four children. He remembered his dominant father, Richard Garland, as a stern military disciplinarian who continually moved his family westward to various family farms in Wisconsin, Iowa, and the Dakota Territory—from certainty to uncertainty; from a modest, comfortable home to a shanty—in search of a better life, and who refused, despite setbacks, to accept a life of ease. Garland was drawn to his mother, Isabelle McClintock Garland, who accepted her husband's migratory nature with quiet resignation, despite the sufferings and hardships of the moves. Watching his mother's plight left Garland with a particular tenderness toward women—a tenderness that he transformed into a recurring theme in his fiction, in which he dealt with the isolated and beaten farm wife.

His early years on the farm were difficult, and he gradually developed an intense dislike for farmwork and yearned for a better life away from the prairies of the "Middle Border" (Garland's usual term for the Midwest). After his graduation from Cedar Valley Seminary ("seminary" was a western name for any school offering an advanced degree) in Osage, Iowa, in 1881, Garland left home for the first time to travel, returning briefly to South Dakota, where his family had moved, and leaving shortly afterward to teach school for a year in Illinois. He again returned to South Dakota in the spring of 1883 to stake a claim, but had no intention of remaining a farmer. Then, in the fall of 1884, he made the most crucial decision of his personal and artistic career: Possessing approximately one hundred dollars and (what later proved to be useless) letters of introduction, he set out for Boston, the intellectual and literary center of the country. But though he abandoned the life of farming, his early experiences, combined with later visits back to the Midwest, where he saw his family's and other farmers' plight from a different angle, influenced his best fiction.

Garland's reading of Henry George's *Progress and Poverty* (1879) in 1884 confirmed his own experiences of farm life and quickly converted him into an advocate of the single tax. In 1892, he spent considerable time lecturing and writing on behalf of the single tax and campaigning for Populist candidates in cities throughout the Midwest. But, disappointed in the reception of his literary work, he resolved to move to Chicago in 1893, where he published his first book of poetry, *Prairie Songs* (1893); another book of short stories, *Prairie Folks* (1893); his literary manifesto, *Crumbling Idols* (1894), in which he continued his campaign for realism and impressionism in American literature; and his most ambitious novel, *Rose of Dutcher's Coolly* (1895). However, with the defeat of the Populist Party in 1896 and his continued disappointment with the reception and sales of his work, Garland turned to the mountain West for new material, producing dozens of Rocky Mountain romances and advocating for more humane treatment of Native Americans.

In the 1910s, Garland again changed his angle of vision, reverting to the Middle Border where he began. As his fiction began to decline, he felt the need to deal more directly and fully with the major events of his own life. Consequently, from 1916 until his death in California on March 4, 1940, he produced two multivolume autobiographies. The first chronicled the pioneering of the Midwest through his family history; the second collected his literary logs, based on his diaries and letters, and recorded his impressions of the leading figures of the day. Clearly, the most important of these memoirs was *A Son of the Middle Border* (1917), which was instrumental in his being awarded a Pulitzer Prize in 1922 for its sequel, *A Daughter of the Middle Border*.

Garland's first major autobiographical effort, however, was not *Son*, but, rather, *Boy Life on the Prairie* (1899). The collection is both an informative account of the painful realities of western farm life in the 1870s and a nostalgic attempt to dwell on the lost world of Garland's boyhood. However, the past to which Garland returns in *A Son of the Middle Border* is a more private one than the generational history that he had presented in *Boy Life on the Prairie*. Portraying the Middle Border as a child might have experienced it and from which he escaped—only to remain attracted to it—Garland shows how he finally assuaged his guilt by financially rescuing and resettling his parents and discovering himself as a writer. Ironically, he also realized that his self-discovery and success as a spokesman for the Middle Border had emerged from his rejection of the West. Garland was thus able to evoke his sense of

loss and yet realize that he could never lose his emotional identification with the Middle Border—an identification that remained as strong as his rebellion against it.

Sources and Further Reading: Jean Holloway, *Hamlin Garland: A Biography* (1960); Robert Mane, *Hamlin Garland: L'homme et l'oeuvre (1860–1940)* (1968); Joseph B. McCullough, *Hamlin Garland* (1978); James Nagel, ed., *Critical Essays on Hamlin Garland* (1982); Keith Newlin, *Hamlin Garland: A Bibliography, with a Checklist of Unpublished Letters* (1998); Keith Newlin and Joseph B. McCullough, eds., *Selected Letters of Hamlin Garland* (1998); Donald Pizer, *Hamlin Garland's Early Work and Career* (1960).

Joseph B. McCullough
University of Nevada–Las Vegas

Edgar Lee Masters (1868–1950)

Edgar Lee Masters was born in 1868 in Garnett, Kansas, and was raised in the downstate Illinois county seats of Petersburg and Lewistown, two villages that provided him with both the setting and much of the

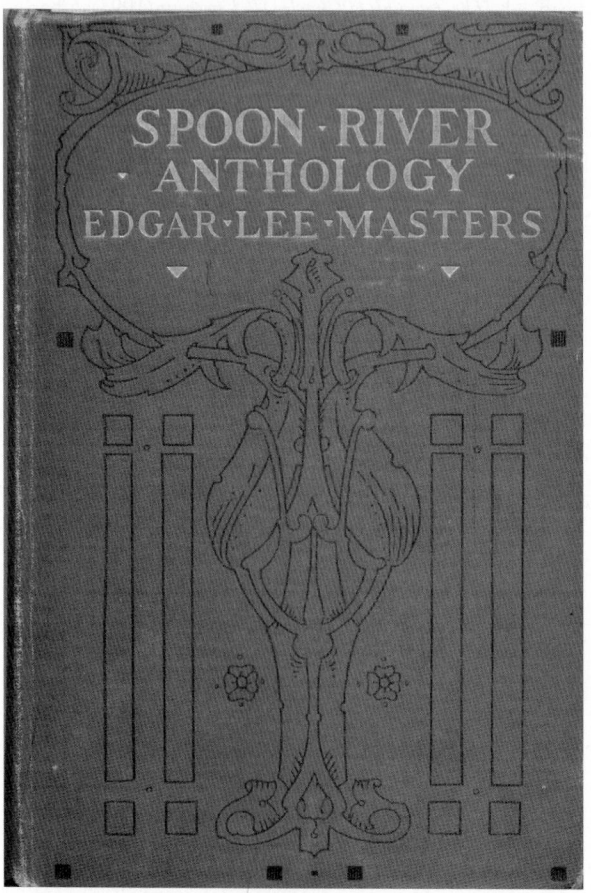

Cover from Edgar Lee Masters's *Spoon River Anthology* (1915).

information for his enduring masterpiece of small town life, *Spoon River Anthology* (1915). Petersburg was in the heart of the Lincoln country, two miles below the dam at New Salem on the Sangamon River. Lewistown was on the prairie, a day's ride to the northwest across the Illinois and Spoon Rivers.

Masters's education consisted of several years of uneven learning in Petersburg's elementary schools, graduation from the Lewistown high school (from which he was often absent), and two semesters in the preparatory unit of nearby Knox College in Galesburg. An additional six months of home study under the tutelage of a lawyer in Lewistown provided Masters with enough professional training to pass the Illinois bar exam in 1891. A year later, he followed the example of thousands of other young people uncomfortable with the constrictions of village life and went to Chicago.

Over the next two decades, Masters married the daughter of a Chicago railroad baron; became a law partner of Clarence Darrow and an intimate of Mayor Carter Harrison and presidential aspirant William Jennings Bryan; and self-published a dozen books of poetry, plays, and political essays. In 1915, with the encouragement of his St. Louis editor-friend William Marion Reedy, Masters published with the Macmillan Company the book that made him world famous, *Spoon River Anthology*.

Few other books of American poetry before or since had the impact of this collection of short poems telling how people in the fictive village of Spoon River had lived and died in the half century between the Civil War and the Great War. The poems were presented as epitaphs, but they were far different from the rhymed verses that visitors to cemeteries usually found on tombstones. Many of Masters's epitaphs contained shockingly frank personal details written in free verse, itself a departure from the norm. His unquiet dead spoke candidly of unhappy marriages, blighted aspirations, early and unglamorous deaths of children, murder, abortions, village tyrants, hypocritical churchmen, class warfare, and false appearances. Masters's villagers destroyed their minds with whisky, served time in the prison at Joliet, frequented brothels in Peoria, and awakened with self-loathing and guilt. When their physical and mental torments became too great, they committed suicide, men and women alike. And always, they gossiped. The village, Masters said, knows what's in everybody's closet, including all its skeletons.

That the characters Masters described were often based on real people or composites of real people added to the verisimilitude of his poems. Their collective effect was to shatter many of the popular, sentimental stereotypes of village life on which Henry Wadsworth Longfellow, John Greenleaf Whittier, and other genteel writers had built their reputations. Older readers, especially those who were comfortable with such stereotypes, were shocked by Masters's matter-of-fact writing on previously forbidden subjects. At the same time, many younger writers recognized a new direction in American literature.

Sherwood Anderson stayed up all night reading *Spoon River Anthology* shortly before beginning *Winesburg, Ohio*; *Main Street* author Sinclair Lewis remarked on the importance of the Masters anthology in his 1930 Nobel Prize speech; Thornton Wilder alluded to one of Masters's epitaphs in *Our Town*—and this list of other writers he influenced could easily be extended to include other short-story writers, novelists, dramatists, and, of course, poets. Masters had hit upon a universal truth without actually articulating it: All of us live in a metaphorical village. It is peopled with those who shape us and are, in turn, shaped by us. The population of this mythical village is relatively small, but it is this easily understood subtext of *Spoon River Anthology* that is partly responsible for its worldwide appeal, even in cultures far different from the Illinois Corn Belt that produced it.

Unfortunately, *Spoon River Anthology* would be Masters's only outstanding achievement. He often claimed that his 1920 poetry epic *Domesday Book* was his best work, but few agreed with this estimate, and after publishing several undistinguished novels and miscellaneous volumes of poetry, he returned to free-verse epitaphs in *The New Spoon River* (1924). Long-windedness and the inclusion of personal political and social opinions marred this book, and only a handful of readers found it superior to the first *Spoon River*. During the 1930s, Masters attracted public attention with his biography *Lincoln: The Man* (1931) and with his own life story, *Across Spoon River: An Autobiography* (1936). The former painted Abraham Lincoln as a cold-blooded tyrannical ogre, turned his assassin into a hero, and drew some of the stiffest criticism ever leveled at an American biography; Masters's autobiography was too candid for some readers and too self-serving for others in addition to being incomplete.

The judgment of influential eastern critics was particularly difficult for Masters to deal with, especially when they praised the verse of fellow poets Robert Frost, Edwin Arlington Robinson, and Carl Sandburg. Masters's chronically abrasive personality also alienated many. Such disharmonies notwithstanding, Masters moved from Chicago to New York City in 1923 following a costly divorce from his first wife. He remarried and published forty books after *Spoon River Anthology*—histories, biographies, poems, and plays—but became increasingly insular and antisocial and spent his final productive years in New York's Chelsea

Hotel, estranged from both his second wife and the times. In his last book, *Along the Illinois* (1942), he returned to many of the central Illinois subjects of his earlier works. Masters died in a Pennsylvania nursing home in 1950 and was returned to Illinois for burial in Petersburg's Oakland Cemetery, also the final resting place for several of those whose lives he had transformed into art in *Spoon River Anthology*.

Sources and Further Reading: John T. Flanagan, *Edgar Lee Masters: The Spoon River Poet and His Critics* (1974); Edgar Lee Masters, "The Genesis of Spoon River," *American Mercury* 28 (Jan. 1933); Edgar Lee Masters, *Spoon River Anthology: An Annotated Edition*, ed. John E. Hallwas (1992); Hilary Masters, *Last Stands* (1982); Ronald Primeau, *Beyond Spoon River* (1981); Max Putzel, *The Man in the Mirror: William Marion Reedy and His Magazine* (1963); Herbert K. Russell, *Edgar Lee Masters: A Biography* (2001); John H. Wrenn and Margaret M. Wrenn, *Edgar Lee Masters* (1983).

Herbert K. Russell
Carbondale, Illinois

Booth Tarkington (1869–1946)

It took Booth Tarkington a while to settle into the Midwest as the principal locale of his fiction and his home for half of each year. He was born in Indianapolis in 1869, the only son of a family well established in the city and state. He was sent East to prep school (Phillips Exeter), returned to study for a couple of years at Purdue, and then completed his education at Princeton in 1893. He returned again to live in his parents' house while he worked hard at novels and plays. Success came all at once when *McClure's* serialized his first two novels, *The Gentleman from Indiana* and *Monsieur Beaucaire* in 1899 and 1900.

Tarkington remained in Indianapolis for a few more years, marrying the daughter of a local banker and serving a term in the state legislature. In 1904 he left with his family for Europe, and for the rest of the decade he lived in Capri, France, and occasionally in New York. He diligently enlarged his first success with eight books of fiction and a half dozen plays. But his mother died in 1909; his marriage was unraveling; he started to worry, with reason, about his drinking; and he was beginning to tire of the tricks of his trade. In 1911 Tarkington went back to Indianapolis and moved into the house in which he had grown up.

In this first passage of his career Tarkington sometimes wrote historical romances (e.g., *The Two Vanrevels*, 1902) in the manner of *Monsieur Beaucaire*, a comedy set in eighteenth-century England. In other novels (e.g., *His Own People*, 1907) and in plays (*The*

Man from Home) he put solidly decent Americans in Europe, where they foiled designs on their innocence. Except for *In the Arena* (1905), sketches of political corruption, when he wrote of contemporary America he used the conventions of local color (Hamlin Garland was one of the enthusiastic readers of his first novel for *McClure's*) and melodrama to enliven his fiction and resolve its plots. He later wrote to a friend that his writing had grown flaccid. "I was perishing, I think, and hardly knew that I had anything in me that *wasn't* perishing."

Back in the Midwest Tarkington found two restorative themes. In *Penrod* (1914), *Seventeen* (1916), and two succeeding collections of Penrod stories, he made a midland urban idyll of tree-lined streets and substantial houses in which young men of good family practiced the harmless pranks and endured the temporary travails of boyhood and adolescence. At the same time, in other books Tarkington began to look closely at what else was happening in these cities. In a suite of four novels—*The Turmoil* (1915), *The Magnificent Ambersons* (1918), *Alice Adams* (1921), and *The Plutocrat* (1927)—he considered the effects of a force he called Bigness on the midland city to which he had returned. He wrote of the puzzle and promise of immigrant faces on the streets; of industry fouling the city center with smoke; of the automobile taking affluent families out of the smoke into new suburbs; and of the literal and figurative decline of grand houses—post–Civil War mansions degenerating into boardinghouses and the lodges of fraternal orders, the prominent families of bankers, lawyers, and landowners being pushed aside by the developers of suburbs and the owners of factories.

Tarkington was of two minds about these changes. *Penrod* had made nostalgia an important source of his popularity, and his novels almost always include scenes or memories of the harmonious life of his own privileged past. At the same time, while his plots record the exhaustion of the old patriarchs and the shallowness of some of the strivers who hustle to succeed them, he also acknowledges the vibrant possibilities of growth. He entrusts these possibilities to young men from good neighborhoods and good families. Alice Adams and her family, for example, fail in their attempt to rise from the shabby house of a man on salary. But George Minafer, scion of the collapsed Ambersons, mends his arrogant ways after he is hit by a car, and buckles down to effect the retrieval of his fortunes by going to work in an automobile factory.

These novels in the middle of his career brought Tarkington eminence as well as popularity. *The Magnificent Ambersons* and *Alice Adams* won Pulitzer Prizes, and several times in the 1920s his name appeared high on lists of distinguished Americans. He wrote fifteen books of fiction after 1927, the year in which he collected three of his novels about Bigness into a trilogy he titled *Growth*. All his fiction was first serialized in popular magazines, and many of his novels became movies, most notably *Alice Adams*, *The Magnificent Ambersons*, *Monsieur Beaucaire* (twice), and *Presenting Lily Mars* (first published in 1933).

Although his popularity remained high until the end of his life in 1946, Tarkington's standing in American letters declined after the 1920s. He continued to set most of his novels in a midland city, which he imagined as an arena of social change and the residence of sensibilities that moderated its baneful effects. But his allegiance to these attitudes and values created biases that show even in his best fiction—in the account of an immigrant ward boss in *In the Arena*, for example, in the caricatures of African Americans in the *Penrod* books and the strong novels of the 1920s, in the patronizing note that runs almost to the end of the complicated story of Alice Adams's simple ambition to marry well. For that reason, except for these novels, most of Tarkington's writing is interesting now primarily as an index of the feelings and opinions of the large audience of middling taste that he entertained for almost half a century. But almost every Tarkington novel contains at least one scene in which, as good writers do, he surprises. Sometimes he catches attention simply by his skill, his acute observation, and the assurance of his unobtrusive style. Just as often he surprises by rising into recognitions that the pursuit of happiness does not work out for everyone, and that before they earn their modestly happy endings, even the right people have something to learn about how rectitude can confine, and privilege can enervate.

Sources and Further Reading: Keith J. Fennimore, *Booth Tarkington* (1974); Susanah Mayberry, *My Amiable Uncle* (1983); Dorothy Ritter Russo and Thelma L. Sullivan, *A Bibliography of Booth Tarkington, 1869–1946* (1949); Julian Street, "When We Were Rather Young," *Saturday Evening Post* 105 (Aug. 20, Nov. 19, Dec. 17, 1932); Booth Tarkington, Letter to Julian Street (May 5, 1921), Princeton University Library Manuscripts Division; Booth Tarkington, "As It Seems to Me," *Saturday Evening Post* 114 (July 5, 12, 19; Aug. 2, 9, 16, 23, 1941); Booth Tarkington, *The World Does Move* (1928); James Woodress, *Booth Tarkington: Gentleman from Indiana* (1956).

Donald Gray
Indiana University–Bloomington

Theodore Dreiser (1871–1945)

When Carrie Meeber, age eighteen, boards the train from Columbia City, Wisconsin, for Chicago in the opening paragraph of Theodore Dreiser's *Sister Car-*

Theodore Dreiser, 1933. Photo by Carl Van Vechten, Library of Congress, Prints and Photographs Division, LC-USZ62-42486.

rie, the reader is told that the "threads which bound her so lightly to girlhood and home were irretrievably broken," her concern now only for "what Chicago might be." Carrie's decisive journey out of the rural Midwest was Dreiser's as well, and with it came a fresh direction for both midwestern literature and American writing as a whole, turning it from country and small-town life to the attractions and uncertainties of the urban metropolis.

The year of *Sister Carrie*'s publication, 1900, saw the appearance of Maurice Thompson's popular historical romance *Alice of Old Vincennes* and an equally popular volume of James Whitcomb Riley's nostalgic verse, *Home-folks*. Dreiser shared with Thompson and Riley an Indiana boyhood but little else. The Indiana where Dreiser was born in 1871 was one of family scandal and small-town poverty that he abandoned for the life of a journalist and a magazine editor, first in Chicago, St. Louis, and Pittsburgh, eventually in New York. In later life he would cast a warm glow over his Indiana past in his travel book *A Hoosier Holiday* (1916) and the autobiographical account *Newspaper Days* (1931), but in his fiction his eye was kept steadfastly on the urban territory ahead.

As a result, much of the familiar landscape of midwestern writing is absent in Dreiser's work. There is little that recalls the fictional worlds of Hamlin Garland or Willa Cather or Sherwood Anderson, and even Chicago gives way in his work to the greater metropolis of New York. In *Sister Carrie*'s second half Carrie flees with her married lover George Hurstwood to New York following his theft of money from the Chicago saloon that he manages, and Dreiser turns to the contrast between the two cities. Compared to the life of vigorous possibility offered by Chicago, New York is oddly indifferent to human aspiration. In New York Hurstwood spirals downward in failure to eventual suicide while Carrie is lifted to the heights of an acting career and a grand apartment.

In an interview Dreiser said that his aim as a writer was "to tell about life as it is . . . the facts as they exist, the game as it is played!" It was the truth-telling quality of *Sister Carrie*, including its sexual openness and insistence on the mysterious ebb and flow of life that baffles understanding, that would deeply influence later writers. At the time of the book's publication, however, it influenced hardly anyone. Doubleday, Page had agreed to publish the work, but when the firm's senior partner opposed publication and Dreiser insisted the company honor its oral agreement, the book appeared with little publicity. Only 456 copies were sold in the first two years and Dreiser received a paltry $68.40 in royalties. Heartened by the novel's successful publication in England, he sought an American publisher to reissue it, and finally in 1907 a new firm, B.W. Dodge, brought out a fresh edition. *Sister Carrie* now drew wide critical approval and sold well.

Dreiser was a successful editor of New York–based magazines like the *Delineator* when he returned to the Midwest in *Jennie Gerhardt* (1911), the story of an attractive young girl who drifts from Columbus, where her mother works as a hotel cleaning woman, to Cleveland and Chicago, the pawn of men of higher station. Jennie's past is treated with more detail than Carrie's, and unlike Carrie she doesn't rise in the world, leaving her lovers behind. She is a figure "born to yield, not seek," as the novel has it, as against the dreamy, self-absorbed Carrie, and Jennie is clearly the more sympathetic figure, a tragic heroine of sorts. In an early study of Dreiser, the critic F.O. Matthiessen said that "the whole book gives the sense of being solidly planted in the Middle West." This is true not so much in the thinly sketched settings of Columbus, Cleveland, and Chicago as in Dreiser's use of his family history in Indiana, especially his wounded sense of poverty and social inferiority set against the teasing nearness of comfort and success.

In his next work Dreiser turned to that latter world in an ambitious trilogy based on the life of the financial tycoon Charles Yerkes. For the middle volume, *The Titan* (1914), he revisited Chicago for research on Yerkes's manipulation of the gas and public transportation business, there developing friendships with Floyd Dell, Maurice Browne, Sherwood Anderson, Edgar Lee Masters, and other members of the city's literary renaissance. For the figure of Frank Cowperwood Dreiser grafted some of his own Chicago experience of the time to what he learned of Yerkes's career, adding sexual adventures to Cowperwood's ruthless pursuit of power. Chicago as a place is lightly portrayed in the story, as against its tangled business dealings, and Cowperwood never comes to life with the vividness of *Sister Carrie*'s Hurstwood. The strongest case for the novel was made by H.L. Mencken, who held that Dreiser had "thrown overboard all the usual baggage of the novelist," especially that catering to sentimental "heart interest," and in Cowperwood had created a hero who is "no hero at all but merely an extraordinary gamester—sharp, merciless, tricky, insatiable."

Still ahead for Dreiser after *The Titan* was his most famous and successful novel, *An American Tragedy* (1925), in a career that extended to his death in California in 1945. He had long since left behind any narrow identification as a midwestern writer, turning back to the region for material only in travel and autobiographical writing. His legacy in fiction was to American writing as a whole, yet his starting point was the Midwest, as his fellow midwesterner Sinclair Lewis recognized. In his address after winning the Nobel Prize in 1930—an award many thought should have gone to Dreiser—Lewis looked back to the turn of the century when *Sister Carrie* had come "to housebound and airless America like a great free Western wind, and to our stuffy domesticity gave us the first fresh air since Mark Twain and Whitman."

Sources and Further Reading: Richard Lehan, *Theodore Dreiser: His World and His Novels* (1969); Richard Lingeman, *Theodore Dreiser: An American Journey, 1908–1945* (1990); Richard Lingeman, *Theodore Dreiser: At the Gates of the City, 1871–1907* (1986); F.O. Matthiessen, *Theodore Dreiser* (1951); Ellen Moers, *Two Dreisers* (1969); Donald Pizer, ed., *Critical Essays on Theodore Dreiser* (1981); Donald Pizer, *The Novels of Theodore Dreiser* (1976); Jack Salzman, ed., *Theodore Dreiser: The Critical Reception* (1972); W.A. Swanberg, *Dreiser* (1965).

Ronald Weber
University of Notre Dame, Indiana

Paul Laurence Dunbar (1872–1906)

Born in Dayton, Ohio, to ex-slaves in 1872, Paul Laurence Dunbar became the foremost African American poet of his generation. His father, Joshua Dunbar, escaped from slavery in Kentucky on the Underground Railroad and went to Canada, but eventually returned to the United States to settle in the Miami Valley area of Ohio. His mother, Matilda Murphy, had been a house slave on a Kentucky plantation when the Emancipation Proclamation declared her free. When Dunbar was four years old, his parents divorced. Although uneducated, his mother memorized poems that she had heard and regularly recited them to Paul. Dunbar was born in a world where literary talent was associated with white ancestry. He took great pride in the fact that his family line was of all African ancestry. To use a description from his poem "Dely," he wasn't "no mullatter"; he was "pure cullud." Prior to Dunbar's time, the intellectual or literary talent of African Americans was attributed to their mixed blood.

The Miami Valley area of Dayton, Springfield, Xenia, and Wilberforce, Ohio, turned out to be a rich area for nurturing Paul Laurence Dunbar's creative arts. Unlike larger urban areas where neighborhoods were more segregated, the Miami Valley area during the turn of the century was a place where Dunbar could mingle with and benefit from his white contemporaries. Dunbar attended Dayton's Central High School, where he excelled. Although the only black in his class, he was president of his class and of the literary society and a member of the debate team. His classmates included Orville and Wilbur Wright, whose family employed his mother. Before graduating from high school, Orville Wright and Dunbar worked together on *The Tattler*, a community newspaper that Wright printed and Dunbar edited and circulated. Although Dunbar graduated from Central High School with great promise, he then had to take a job as an elevator operator.

His big break came when he was asked to read his poetry before a convention of the Western Association of Writers, held in Dayton in 1892. A favorable review helped convince Dunbar that he should self-publish his first collection, *Oak and Ivy* (1893). His reputation spread to the point that he was asked to recite poetry at the World's Columbian Exposition in Chicago, where he met such notable black leaders as Frederick Douglass, Ida B. Wells-Barnett, and Mary Church Terrell. An even bigger break came with the publication of his second book of verse, *Majors and Minors* (1896), a collection that white Toledo benefactors subsidized. Well-known novelist and critic William Dean Howells favorably reviewed the collection and wrote an introduction to Dunbar's next collection, *Lyrics of Lowly Life* (1896).

In 1898, Dunbar married African American poet and journal writer Alice Ruth Moore, who had a master's degree from Cornell University. For a while the couple lived in Washington, D.C., where Dunbar worked for the Library of Congress. Although first hailed as a marriage akin to that of Robert and Elizabeth Barrett Browning, the Dunbar poets began to have marital troubles. The marriage did not last due to class differences between the two and Paul's increasing alcoholism. Paul returned to Dayton, where his mother helped nurse his tuberculosis. He died in 1906 at age thirty-three, but not before he had written twelve books of poetry, over one hundred short stories, a play, and five novels.

One of Dunbar's most famous poems is "We Wear the Mask," about the double life, the life of "grins and lies" that African Americans live due to their hyphenated existence as African and American. A major trope in African American literature, mask-wearing figures prominently in Dunbar's poetry. For instance, in "Sympathy" (1899), although caged, a bird masks its predicament and sings. The poet asserts that he knows "why the caged bird sings"—a line that would later become the title of Maya Angelou's autobiography.

"Ode to Ethiopia" and "The Colored Soldiers," a poem inspired by his father's service in a black cavalry regiment during the Civil War, celebrate pride in one's ancestry and honor for one's country. Other poems celebrate everyday activities: a woman singing ("When Malindy Sings"), a woman baking bread ("Dinah Kneading Dough"), and a man courting his lady ("A Negro Love Song"). The latter poem's refrain, "Jump back, honey, jump back," became a popular folk rhyme. With its emphasis on everyday activities and the folkways of his community, Dunbar's dialect poetry made him famous.

The white reading public of Dunbar's day praised the dialect poems as authentic representations of Negro speech and favored these poems over those Dunbar wrote in more formal English. Later, during eras of black nationalism such as the Harlem Renaissance and the Black Arts Movement, black critics accused Dunbar's dialect poetry of being sentimental and falsely stereotypical of black voices. These critics argued that dialect poetry limits the range of emotions to humor and pathos. Thus, they saw the dialect poems as plantation pastorals of a romanticist. Due to a renewed interest in vernacular and expressive cultures, more recent criticism argues that Dunbar's poems are much more sophisticated in tone and theme than previously thought.

Other than poetry, Dunbar wrote fiction, referring to his short stories as "Ohio Pastorals." Set in white communities in Ohio, these stories, like his dialect poems, raise debates about assimilation and accommodation. His best-known novel, *The Sport of the Gods* (1902), deals with a black family that tries to make it in a northern city but in the end returns to the rural South. From Dunbar's modest beginnings, he earned enough respect for Atlanta University to confer upon him an honorary master's degree and enough fame to ride in two presidential inauguration parades—William McKinley's in 1901 and Theodore Roosevelt's in 1905. His canon earned him the title of poet laureate of African Americans. Despite the controversy surrounding his dialect poetry, there are many African American schools and public facilities named for him, and Dunbar's Dayton home became the first state memorial in Ohio honoring an African American.

Sources and Further Reading: Eleanor Alexander, *Lyrics of Sunshine and Shadow* (2001); Houston A. Baker, Jr., *Singers of Daybreak* (1974); Felton Best, *Crossing the Color Line* (1996); Gossie Harold Hudson, "Paul Laurence Dunbar: The Regional Heritage of Dayton's First Black Poet," *Antioch Review* 34 (Summer 1976); John Keeling, "Paul Dunbar and the Mask of Dialect," *Southern Literary Journal* 25 (Spring 1993); Jay Martin, "'Jump Back Honey': Paul Laurence Dunbar and the Rediscovery of American Poetical Traditions," *Bulletin of the Midwest Modern Language Association* 7 (Spring 1974); Jay Martin and Gossie H. Hudson, eds., *The Paul Laurence Dunbar Reader* (1975); Esther Nettles Rauch, "Paul Laurence Dunbar," in Valerie Smith, Lea Baechler, and A. Walton Litz, eds., *African American Writers* (1991).

Valerie Lee
The Ohio State University–Columbus

Willa Cather (1873–1947)

A midwestern bird of passage, Willa Cather grew up in Nebraska and then moved away. She was born in Back Creek, near Winchester, Virginia, in 1873. When she was ten years old, her parents followed other members of the Cather family and uprooted to Webster County, Nebraska, eventually settling in Red Cloud. Critics and biographers agree that the move west was the single most traumatic, inspiring, and indelible experience of Willa Cather's life. Today, Red Cloud hosts the Willa Cather Pioneer Memorial and Educational Foundation, and Cather-related sites are major tourist attractions in the tiny agricultural town, a few miles north of the Kansas border. Main Street of Red Cloud still resembles the Hanover, Black Hawk, Moonstone, Haverford, and other fictional locations Cather drew from memories of her childhood hometown.

"The only thing very noticeable about Nebraska," we learn from an immigrant to the state in *My Ántonia*, "was that it was still, all day long, Nebraska." *My Ántonia* (1918) is Cather's most famous novel, drawn from her own experiences of moving to the Midwest, narrated by a character who makes a similar uprooting.

According to this narrator, "There seemed to be nothing to see" on the Nebraska frontier in the 1880s. "There was nothing but land; not a country at all, but the material out of which countries are made." The materials that fascinated Cather and that recur in her novels include the mobility of those who settled; the diversity of their origins; the ways in which the setting of the Midwest contributed to the formation of an American empire; and the effect of landscape, exile, and migratory experience on the character of those who settled the region. Her very fine literary treatment of the Midwest in the early twentieth century led one critic to claim in astonishment that Cather's work amounted to "a triumph of mind over Nebraska." Her work, in many ways, demonstrates that art is not endemic to any particular human experience but is the result of an attitude of mind toward any experience.

Including *My Ántonia*, Cather wrote six major novels set in the Midwest. Her success at making art of midwestern materials earned her an early reputation as an elegiac; the label is not quite accurate. Although never systematically satirical (as was the case with her contemporary Sinclair Lewis), Cather was more adept at locating aesthetic strands in midwestern habits of mind and action. Quite often, her theme is one of survival and more—of transcendence of the local forces that would delimit the future of ambitious spirits. *The Song of the Lark* (1915) tells the story of a gifted young woman's escape from a provincial Colorado town. Inspired by a mentor who tells her "the world has to be got back and forth," Thea Kronborg comes to profitably associate her own impatience with ambition. "She believed that what she felt was despair," Cather asserts, "but it was only one of the forms of hope." *O Pioneers!* (1913) takes place in the agricultural community of Hanover, Nebraska, a little town in the 1880s "trying not to be blown away" by the howling winds of a midwestern winter. The main character, Alexandra Bergson, achieves "a new consciousness of the country . . . almost a new relation to it," which makes her a successful farmer but does not alleviate a recurring desire to escape the confines of her homestead. *One of Ours* (1922) is set one generation away from the pioneer era, allowing one character to have "watched the farms emerge one by one from the great rolling page where once only the wind wrote its story." Nonetheless, his son is eager to leave the farm, finding death in battle preferable to life as a farmer. *A Lost Lady* (1923) looks back at the pioneer era from the vantage point of a town called Sweet Water, bypassed by the railroad, beset by crop failures, with a population adjusting to a future that "no longer looked bright." The struggles of the present generation, summed up by the titular character's desire "to get out of this hole," are consciously enacted against the backdrop of heroic pioneers and settlers, those who had developed the town "of which great things were expected."

Misfortune, in Cather, is never material from which to draw satire alone; more often it is the source of reappraisal and deep resolve. This is certainly the case in *The Professor's House* (1925), where Godfrey St. Peter draws on his memories of a traumatic move to Kansas ("No later anguish, and he had had his share, went so deep or seemed so final") as he works to resign himself to the necessity of uprooting himself once again. Finally, in *Lucy Gayheart* (1935), perhaps her most poignant novel, Cather tells the story of another restless young woman in the Midwest who desires to "get away from this frozen country and these frozen people," but who is successful only in going to her death with these ambitions. As the novel opens, "the townspeople still talk of Lucy Gayheart," but her life, and the town's memory of her, do not amount to very much: "life goes on," Cather shrewdly narrates, "and we live in the present." More than any American novelist of her time or since, Cather captured the truth of human struggle on the midwestern canvas—a truth that is marked by great success, but realized at the cost of much anguish and much individual sacrifice.

In 1891, Willa Cather left Red Cloud to attend the University of Nebraska. She graduated in 1895. In 1896, she took an editorial job in Pittsburgh and relocated to that city. She would never live in Nebraska again. Ten years later she moved to New York City, where she maintained a permanent address until her death in 1947. While her family stayed in Red Cloud, Nebraska, and went to rest, finally, in the family cemetery plot there, Willa Cather is buried in Jaffrey, New Hampshire, a favorite destination of hers for writing.

Sources and Further Reading: Anonymous, *The Nation* (25 Sep. 1920); Sharon O'Brien, *Willa Cather: The Emerging Voice* (1987); Ann Romines, ed., *Willa Cather's Southern Connections: New Essays on Cather and the South* (2000); John N. Swift and Joseph R. Urgo, eds., *Willa Cather and the American Southwest* (2002); Robert Thacker and Michael A. Peterman, *Willa Cather's Canadian and Old World Connections* (1999); Joseph Urgo, *Willa Cather and the Myth of American Migration* (1995).

Joseph R. Urgo
The University of Mississippi

Ole Edvart Rølvaag (1876–1931)

Ole Edvart Rølvaag was born in 1876 on the northern Norwegian island of Dønna and wrote in his native language. With his seven novels, many short stories, all set in the Midwest, and a wide range of nonfiction, he is the best known of the many midwestern writers who wrote in Norwegian and were published by presses in the upper Midwest. Rølvaag and other Norwegian American writers also wrote for the many Norwegian-language newspapers and journals published all over the Midwest. Long before he was "discovered" and translated into English, Rølvaag was well known to the midwestern Norwegian American community as a writer, orator, and educator.

Rølvaag came to the United States in 1896 and first settled in eastern South Dakota. He had only a primary school education and worked as a farmhand to pay back the cost of his ticket and to save money for further schooling, eventually at St. Olaf College in Minnesota, where he so impressed his teachers that he was awarded a scholarship for further study in Norway in 1905–1906 and a teaching position at the college. By then he had decided that he was a writer.

A novel of immigrant life, 1927. Cover of HarperPerennial 1999 edition of *Giants in the Earth: A Saga of the Prairie* by O. E. Rølvaag. Reprinted by permission of HarperCollins Publishers Inc.

His first book, published in 1912, is an epistolary novel, *Amerika-breve* ("America Letters," translated as *The Third Life of Per Smevik*, 1971). The letters, beginning with the protagonist's arrival in August 1896 and concluding in July 1901, tell the story of the education and acculturation of a young immigrant in northeastern South Dakota. His second novel, *Paa glemte veie* ("On forgotten paths"), published in 1914, has not been translated. The main setting is the same imaginary South Dakota Township as in *Amerika-breve* but with some of the central action set in the prairies of Saskatchewan. It is an uneven work but has descriptions of the land and accounts of man pitted against the land that are as powerful as any in western fiction.

Rølvaag used the pseudonym Paal Mørch for his early fiction but published his third novel, *To tullinger* ("Two fools"), in his own name in 1920. It was revised and translated as *Pure Gold* in 1930. It is a powerful, naturalistic novel of greed set in a Minnesota farm community. The two protagonists, a playful and loving young couple in the opening chapter, gradually give in to their growing lust for money, eventually selling all they have in order to add to their growing store of paper currency in high denominations, worn in canvas belts under their clothes. After their death, a direct consequence of their avarice, their filthy clothes, including the money belts, are thrown on a fire. The story of *The Boat of Longing* (1933; first published as *Længselens baat* in 1921) moves back and forth between a northern Norwegian island and Minneapolis. The immigrant protagonist is a potential artist but too weak in character to realize his gifts.

His next novel, *I de dage* ("in those days"), was published in Oslo in 1924. Rølvaag had wanted to reach a wider audience than was possible through his Minneapolis publisher, Augsburg Publishing House. Although their reader's report was enthusiastic, the Norwegian publishers were reluctant to publish a thick novel by an unknown American and agreed to print the first half and await the response before deciding whether to publish the second part, *Riket grundlægges* ("The founding of the kingdom"). The two parts were published as one novel in New York in 1927, as *Giants in the Earth*.

Giants in the Earth is the first volume of a trilogy that also includes *Peder Victorious* (1929) and *Their Fathers' God* (1931), both first published in Norway, as *Peder Seier* and *Den signededag*. The protagonists, Beret and Per Hansa Holm, enter the novel with their children, traveling in a covered wagon from Fillmore County, Minnesota, to the present Minnehaha County in South Dakota in 1873. The novel tells the story of the founding and growth of a settlement, focusing on suffering and loss as much as on adventure and success. The main characters are a loving yet mis-matched couple. Beret is deeply religious and is concerned with the soul and with eternity, while Per is an adventurous spirit always ready to take a chance where he sees an opportunity to get ahead. In his imagination he sees their great farm even before the first piece of soil is broken: "A divine restlessness ran in his blood; he strode forward with outstretched arms toward the wonders of the future, already partly realized." The novel ends with Per's death in a snowstorm as—urged by Beret—he tries to go on skis to bring back a pastor for a sick friend and neighbor.

Beret; their youngest son, Peder; and his Irish-American wife, Susie, are the central characters of the two other volumes of the trilogy. The religious theme of the first volume is played out in the conflict-ridden relationships among the pragmatic Peder and his devout Lutheran mother and his equally devout Roman Catholic wife. The two novels focus on Peder, beginning with his early childhood and concluding with his unsuccessful attempt to begin a career in politics in 1896. By the time he wrote his last two books, Rølvaag realized that there would be no lasting midwestern ethnic culture and literature in the Norwegian language, and the concluding novel in the trilogy bears witness to his pessimistic concern for the development of the second and third immigrant generations.

Rølvaag several times insisted that he was an American writer using the Norwegian language and not a Norwegian diaspora writer, as for instance in his book of polemical essays *Concerning Our Heritage* (1922, translated into English in 1998). The fragments of an autobiography he wrote just before his death in 1931 are in English, suggesting that he may have been planning to write in that language in the future. While most of Rølvaag's characters are Norwegian Americans, his books tell of experiences shared by many inhabitants of the Midwest in the late nineteenth and early twentieth centuries.

Sources and Further Reading: Einar Haugen, *Ole Edvart Rølvaag* (1983); Theodore Jørgenson and Nora O. Solum, *Ole Edvart Rølvaag: A Biography* (1939); Ann Moseley, *Ole Edvart Rølvaag* (1987); Orm Øverland, *The Western Home* (1996); Paul Reigstad, *Rølvaag: His Life and Art* (1972); Harold P. Simonson, *Prairies Within* (1987); Gerald Howard Thorson, ed., *Ole Rølvaag: Artist and Cultural Leader* (1975).

Orm Øverland
University of Bergen, Norway

Sherwood Anderson (1876–1941)

Sherwood Anderson, a writer whose most influential book was a collection of loosely related short stories entitled *Winesburg, Ohio*, was born in Camden, Ohio, on September 13, 1876. Camden was a small but prosperous town about thirty miles west of Dayton. Anderson's father, Irwin, was an indifferent harness maker who was happiest when playing his cornet. The Anderson family moved to Clyde in northern Ohio in 1880.

Sherwood grew into a restless young man, perpetually in search of employment. Indeed, he was always in motion, moving from job to job and wife to wife. Unsurprisingly, the midwesterners in his stories are usually unhappy souls who yearn for human connection and emotional sustenance. Satisfaction in relationships with other people is ephemeral at best.

After his mother, Emma, died in 1895, Anderson went to Chicago, labored in a warehouse, and took business classes. He volunteered during the Spanish-American War in 1898–1899. After attending Wittenberg Academy in Springfield, Ohio, Anderson got a job writing copy for the Long-Critchfield Agency in Chicago. Later he became president of the United Factories Company in Cleveland and the Anderson Manufacturing Company in Elyria, Ohio. Anderson and his wife, Cornelia, had three children (Robert, John, and Marion).

A successful businessman who enjoyed playing golf and spending time with his children, Anderson was nevertheless dissatisfied with his predictable life. He sought solace in work and writing. In 1914, he and Cornelia were divorced. Anderson gave up business to devote himself to writing and returned to Chicago, the cultural capital of the Midwest. His goal, he said, was "not to make a success, but to give myself an interest in life." *Windy McPherson's Son* (1916) and *Mid-American Chants* (1918) won attention, but it was *Winesburg, Ohio* (1919) that made Anderson famous. Critics loved it, although it sold only three thousand copies in the first two years.

Anderson called the characters in *Winesburg* "grotesques" because they were distorted by the tension between their expectations of happiness and the reality of loneliness. Winesburg is a small Ohio town like the ones in which Anderson grew up. The book is a series of short stories linked by their reference to the same town and the frequent appearance of the young journalist George Willard. Because the tales are so connected, Anderson's book has the feel of a novel, narrated by Willard. Willard is a sensitive young man with whom many people feel comfortable enough to talk about their lives. The people live in a world suffused with religious fanaticism and sexual repression. But *Winesburg* does not caricature its characters or present midwestern towns as wastelands. Anderson was particularly apt at conveying a sense of the mood of small-town life. In *Winesburg*, plot is less important than the accumulation of details, or moments, into a coherent sense of the rhythms of a distinctive place.

In the last story, George Willard experiences a fleeting instance of connection with Helen White, a friend home from college. They wander around town, then sit at the fairgrounds and kiss each other. "They had for a moment taken hold of the thing that makes the mature life of men and women in the modern world possible." Later, Willard leaves for a city (probably Chicago) with a sense of sudden nostalgia for the town that is already "but a background on which to paint the dreams of his manhood."

Poor White, a novel published in 1920, traces the rise and decline of the Midwest through the story of Hugh McVey, a Missourian who settles in Bidwell, Ohio, and becomes an inventor. It is the story of possibility and creativity transformed into an emphasis on the material and the practical. The residents of a small town who once "were to each other like members of a great family" become so obsessed with progress and materialism that they lose their "native energy and strength" and neglect "art and beauty."

Anderson's fiction, which poured out in a torrent in the early 1920s, was often lumped with the satirical novels of Sinclair Lewis. It was a comparison Anderson rejected. He was less interested in condemning small-town life than in lamenting what progress had done to it. "Real life," wrote the perpetually busy Anderson in a memoir of his childhood, "people never stood still. Nothing in America ever stands still for very long." To think otherwise is to live an illusion. The realism and economy of Anderson's short stories and novels influenced a new generation of writers that included William Faulkner and Ernest Hemingway. After the publication of the best-selling *Dark Laughter* (1925), Anderson tended to write autobiography as well as social criticism.

In 1925, Anderson's life changed yet again when he visited the town of Marion in southwestern Virginia. He fell in love with Eleanor Copenhaver, who became his fourth wife. Two years later Anderson moved to Marion, bought a home, and remained there for the rest of his life. In addition to his writing, he published and edited two local newspapers. In the 1930s, Eleanor, a strong labor activist, and Anderson worked to unionize miners in Harlan County, Kentucky. Anderson died on March 8, 1941. A toothpick he swallowed at a party perforated his intestine and led to deadly peritonitis.

Sherwood Anderson was amazingly prolific, largely because he was so restless. He wrote as if he was writing to keep himself busy and the world at bay. At his death, he was the author of eight novels, four short-story collections, three books of poems and plays, three volumes of autobiography, and more than three hundred essays. In addition, his estate included some eleven hundred pieces of unpublished fiction and journal entries.

Over time, Anderson's reputation has been eclipsed by those of Faulkner, Hemingway, and others. Today, critics consider him primarily a regional writer. Nonetheless, his combination of nostalgia and realism expertly evokes small midwestern towns in the early twentieth century while it reflects on the ravages of time and warns against the danger of confusing material with spiritual progress.

Sources and Further Reading: David D. Anderson, ed., *Critical Essays on Sherwood Anderson* (1981); Sherwood Anderson, *Poor White* (1920); Sherwood Anderson, *The Portable Sherwood Anderson*, rev. ed. (1972); Malcolm Cowley, introduction to Sherwood Anderson, *Winesburg, Ohio* (1976); Richard O. Davies, *Main Street Blues* (1998); N. Bryllion Fagin, *The Phenomenon of Sherwood Anderson* (1973); Kim Townsend, *Sherwood Anderson* (1987); Ray Lewis White, *The Achievement of Sherwood Anderson* (1966).

Andrew Cayton
Miami University, Oxford, Ohio

Carl Sandburg (1878–1967)

Carl Sandburg wrote of the Midwest for five decades. His earliest journalism appeared between 1909 and 1912 in Milwaukee newspapers that promoted moderate, "constructive" Wisconsin socialism. After he moved to Chicago, he made his living as a journalist for the *Chicago Daily News*, covering local labor events; from 1913 until 1918 he also wrote under pseudonyms for the Chicago-based *International Socialist Review*. His poems often focused on the plain folk of midwestern cities and small towns. His two-volume *Abraham Lincoln: The Prairie Years* (1926) emphasized the great president's midwestern experience and attitudes. From the 1930s until the 1960s, largely because of his Lincoln biography, which grew to six volumes, Sandburg became a national figure, lecturing, befriending, and advising major liberal politicians and making guest appearances on prominent radio and television shows. On these occasions, he presented himself as still a child of the Midwest, where he was born in 1878. Finally, in *Always the Young Strangers* (1953), he told the story of his upbringing in Galesburg, Illinois.

Much of Sandburg's early journalism and poetry was deeply engaged with public-policy issues, especially labor-management relationships, collective bargaining, and strategies for social change. This work was typically written for a particular cause, under varying ideological commitments and constraints, and it typically stressed the oppression of the "people" by bosses, capitalists, and corrupt politicians. The "people" were not differentiated by region, midwestern or otherwise. That is to say, in this early work, class relationships were determinative.

Chicago Poems (1916) was Sandburg's first exploration of urban Midwest values and circumstances. Here he wrote distinctively about Chicago's working class, emphasizing within some sixty poems the quiet dignity and occasional heroism of people who worked tough jobs under tough circumstances. The immigrants from abroad as well as the migrants to the city from midwestern small towns were the essence of Chicago, Sandburg argued. In "Chicago," the title poem of the collection, he depicted the city as, among other things, "Hog Butcher for the World," "Stormy, husky, brawling, / City of the Big Shoulders." These were probably the best-remembered lines that Sandburg ever wrote; they are still heard in schoolrooms and are sometimes uttered by announcers of NFL games involving the Chicago Bears.

Sandburg returned to Chicago as his subject a few years later in "The Windy City," the long opening poem of *Slabs of the Sunburnt West* (1922). In a number of ways, this second effort to define Chicago is superior: It is more detailed, it gets down to careful images of Chicago's particular look, it captures the ever-

Carl Sandburg. Records of the Redpath Chautauqua Collection, Special Collections Department, University of Iowa Libraries, Iowa City, Iowa.

changing character of the industrial city. But "The Windy City" never received the sort of attention that "Chicago" received.

Sandburg continued to depict Chicago and a few other urban places, but over the years his Midwest became primarily the rural Midwest, a land of small towns and farms. *Cornhuskers* (1918) included a substantial number of lyrics about rural places and rural folk, as did each of his subsequent volumes. These poems argued for the continuing existence of a rural folk culture, as yet relatively untouched by industrialization and urbanization; and rural locales became metaphors for stable values, warm human relationships, wise outlooks, and simple pleasures. "I am the prairie, mother of men," Sandburg had his personified land say in "Prairie," the long opening poem of *Cornhuskers*. Near the end of that poem, he said, "O prairie mother, I am one of your boys."

Much of Sandburg's understanding of Abraham Lincoln proceeded from a sense that the president, too, was a child of the prairies. Indeed, the basic argument of *The Prairie Years* was that Lincoln was the avatar of Midwest culture, that all the values and understanding of human aspirations that he brought to the presidency were a consequence of his Midwest experience. Sandburg wrote persuasively of the nineteenth-century Midwest, including a great deal of detail about the land and its folk, arguing that Lincoln's sense of freedom and equality arose largely, if not exclusively, from its soil. Lincoln's character, he led his readers to conclude, fundamentally derived from his roots among the Midwest folk.

In 1936, Sandburg published a long poem titled *The People, Yes*, which included quite a bit of anecdotal material illustrating the wit and wisdom of midwestern and other American plain people. In 1939, he added to *The Prairie Years* his four-volume *Abraham Lincoln: The War Years*, which won the Pulitzer Prize for history. At this point in his career, Sandburg was a national figure. But he was a national figure who was seen by his audiences, according to numerous newspaper and magazine accounts, as a Midwest man, a child of the prairies who had grown up in hardscrabble circumstances and through hard work had risen to great heights. Sandburg, of course, did not discourage these descriptions of his Lincolnesque qualities.

Sandburg's public persona in the middle of the twentieth century was tied to public understandings of the nature of midwesternness, understandings that he had had a hand in fostering. The reading public could have expected, then, that his autobiographical *Always the Young Strangers* (1953) would be more of the same. It was not. This, Sandburg's last major publication (he died in 1967), told a far more complicated and crosshatched story of life in Galesburg, Sandburg's home-

town, between the early 1880s and the late 1890s. A son of Swedish immigrants, Sandburg wrote of how he had grown up among people from many countries and cultures, how he had learned the hard lessons of getting an education and doing without and working, all the while trying to appreciate the gifts he had been given and the pleasures of a small-town childhood. One of the finest accounts of a Midwest childhood ever published, *Always the Young Strangers* was a stunning and complex ending to Sandburg's long interest in things midwestern.

Sources and Further Reading: Harry Golden, *Carl Sandburg* (1961); Penelope Niven, *Carl Sandburg: A Biography* (1991); Carl Sandburg, *The Complete Poems of Carl Sandburg* (1970); Philip R. Yannella, *The Other Carl Sandburg* (1996).

Philip R. Yannella
Temple University, Pennsylvania

Nicholas Vachel Lindsay (1879–1931)

Nicholas Vachel Lindsay was born on November 10, 1879, in Springfield, Illinois, the son of Vachel Thomas and Esther Catharine (Frazee) Lindsay. Lindsay attended Hiram College from 1897 to 1900 without graduating and subsequently studied drawing at the Art Institute of Chicago (1901–1903) and the New York School of Art (1903–1904). In 1906 Lindsay undertook a walking tour from Florida to Kentucky, an account of which was later published as *A Handy Guide for Beggars* (1916), and during the summer of the same year he toured Europe with his parents. Failing to achieve any measurable degree of success as a poet or pen-and-ink artist in New York City, Lindsay returned, in 1908, to the family home in Springfield, where over the next four years he further articulated his aesthetic of beauty and visionary social philosophy in a series of *War Bulletins*; a cultural-literary miscellany, *The Village Magazine*; and a substantial number of poems (most notably, the miscellany *Rhymes to Be Traded for Bread*), pamphlets, and illustrations. In the summer of 1912, Lindsay set out on an extended walking tour of the United States. Though he fell short of his projected itinerary, eventually returning to Springfield from Los Angeles, Lindsay's tramp provided the basis for *Adventures while Preaching the Gospel of Beauty* (1914), the highlight of which is his account of working the summer wheat harvest in Kansas.

In 1913, Lindsay achieved his first popular success as a poet with the publication of "General William Booth Enters Heaven" in Harriet Monroe's influential *Poetry: A Magazine of Verse*, an auspicious debut that attracted the admiration of, among others, William Butler Yeats and led in turn to the publication of Lindsay's first collection of poems, *General William Booth Enters Heaven and Other Poems* (1913). Beyond the publication of *The Congo and Other Poems* (1914), *The Chinese Nightingale and Other Poems* (1917), and *The Collected Poems* (1923; revised in 1925), Lindsay's reputation was further augmented by his annual public recitation tours that covered the full sweep of the United States. In 1925, at the age of thirty-eight, while residing in Spokane, Washington, Lindsay married Elizabeth Conner. Four years later, Vachel Lindsay, together with Elizabeth and their children (Susan Doniphan and Nicolas Cave), established residence in Lindsay's paternal home in Springfield, where, exhausted by his life on the road and his audience's greater interest in his role as poet-performer than poet-reformer, he died, an apparent suicide, on December 5, 1931.

Central to Lindsay's work, whatever the medium, is a socially ameliorative vision of America that is firmly grounded in a Jeffersonian agrarian ideal and that found expression in the populist and agrarian movements in the American Midwest during the late nineteenth and early twentieth centuries. Such a vision is most directly, though elusively, set forth in Lindsay's "Gospel of Beauty," in which he advocates a "new localism" based on the beautification of the American "home and neighborhood" in accordance with the democratic principles set forth in the Declaration of Independence and Lincoln's Gettysburg Address. Insulated from the corrupting influences of the East, the small-town Midwest represented, in Lindsay's estimation, the most fertile, generative setting for the cultivation of the "new localism." More specifically, Lindsay viewed his hometown of Springfield as the ideal prototype for his projected scheme of local improvement, the various stages of which are charted in those three poems that Lindsay felt best expressed his "Gospel of Beauty": "The Proud Farmer," "The Illinois Village," and "The Building of Springfield."

Throughout his poetry, Lindsay enlists any number of former and contemporary historical figures in support of his millenarian vision—Francis of Assisi, Thomas Jefferson, Ralph Waldo Emerson, Walt Whitman, Andrew Jackson, Alexander Campbell, John P. Altgeld, William Jennings Bryan, Theodore Roosevelt, Woodrow Wilson, and his own father and maternal grandfather—nearly all of whom assume a mythic dimension commensurate with the idealism of Lindsay's vision. Two of the most notable heroes in Lindsay's mythography are Abraham Lincoln, the most illustrious citizen of Lindsay's hometown and the subject of one of Lindsay's most poignant poems, "Abraham Lincoln Walks at Midnight," and John Chapman ("Johnny Appleseed") whose legend, as celebrated in such poems as "In Praise of Johnny Apple-

seed," served as a defining touchstone for Lindsay's vocation and career as a public poet. Like Chapman, Lindsay's self-appointed vocation was nothing less than the "seeding," albeit metaphorically, of America, and, like Chapman, too, such a vocation was transacted "on the road." Like Theodore Dreiser, Frank Norris, Sinclair Lewis, and fellow Illinois poets Edgar Lee Masters and Carl Sandburg, Lindsay recognized and challenged such social problems as industrialism, urban blight, and the exploitative tactics of big business and big government and likewise regretted such perceived ills as materialism, consumerism, and secularism. Yet Lindsay, no less than Walt Whitman, maintained his faith in the perfectibility of human institutions and foresaw a future republic invigorated and sustained by democratic ideals.

Though often dismissed as a visionary naïf, a mere versifier who traded on bombast and the crowd-pleasing "barbaric yawp," a vaudeville evangelist, and a populist who long outstayed his welcome, Lindsay, in contrast to the more fashionable modernist poetic advocated by Ezra Pound, persistently played true to an unsophisticated popular-populist aesthetic, and as an unembarrassed enthusiast and visionary bardic emissary, he resembles such poets as Whitman and Allen Ginsberg. Moreover, Lindsay is perhaps America's greatest, and certainly its most impassioned and unrelenting, vagabond poet and one of America's most notable acolytes of the open road. Equally memorable as one of America's legendary poet-performers, through his energetic and highly dramatic recitations Lindsay extended the provenance of poetry from the printed page to the public arena of performance art. Finally, however, Lindsay is best remembered as a self-proclaimed representative of the Midwest—its landscapes, history, people, and promise.

Sources and Further Reading: Dennis Camp, "Vachel Lindsay," *Dictionary of Literary Biography*, vol. 54 (1987); John T. Flanagan, ed., *Profile of Vachel Lindsay* (1970); John E. Hallwas and Dennis J. Reader, eds., *The Vision of This Land* (1976); Mark Harris, *City of Discontent* (1952); Ann Massa, *Vachel Lindsay: Fieldworker for the American Dream* (1970); Edgar Lee Masters, *Vachel Lindsay: A Poet in America* (1935); Eleanor Ruggles, *The West-Going Heart* (1959); Robert F. Sayre, introduction to Vachel Lindsay, *Adventures, Rhymes and Designs* (1968).

Michael Wentworth
University of North Carolina–Wilmington

Sinclair Lewis (1885–1951)

America's first winner of the Nobel Prize for Literature, Sinclair Lewis often used the setting of the Midwest in his writings to speak to his concerns about America as a whole. Lewis's best-known novels were written in the 1920s, although he used this region throughout his career, creating several fictional midwestern towns—Gopher Prairie, Zenith, and Grand Republic—in order to critique American society. His novels explore various aspects of society, including small towns in *Main Street* (1920); business in *Babbitt* (1922) and *Dodsworth* (1929); medicine in *Arrowsmith* (1925); religion in *Elmer Gantry* (1927); feminist concerns in *The Job* (1917) and *Ann Vickers* (1933); fascism in *It Can't Happen Here* (1935), marriage in *Cass Timberlane* (1945); and race relations in *Kingsblood Royal* (1947). Through his understanding of middle-class hopes and aspirations, a keen ear for ordinary speech, and a zest for social satire, Lewis portrayed middle-class, middle-western America, and in doing so caused great controversy, received strong critical acclaim, and sold very well. As E. M. Forster noted, "Whether he has 'got' the Middle West, only the Middle West can say, but he has made thousands of people all over the globe alive to its existence, and anxious for further news."

Lewis was born in 1885 in the small town of Sauk Centre, Minnesota, and felt from an early age that small-town life was so stifling that he had to leave and experience more of the world. His pre-1920s books treat such themes as the potential for freedom and adventure that America holds and show how often that potential is dampened by small-minded people and institutions that seek to maintain the status quo. Lewis's first novel, the juvenile adventure *Hike and the Aeroplane* (1912) as well as his later *The Trail of the Hawk* (1915) focus on pioneering efforts in air transportation. The need for adventure is also present in *Free Air* (1919), loosely based on an automobile trip across the Midwest that Lewis and his wife took in which they encountered rutted and muddy roads, bad food, and car breakdowns. Lewis was criticized by Minnesota authorities for this unflattering portrayal, but he noted that he was only presenting the reality of traveling by automobile.

With *Main Street*, Lewis achieved his artistic potential, creating a novel that still has great relevance. The protagonist, Carol Kennicott, a St. Paul librarian, marries a doctor and moves to his hometown of Gopher Prairie, Minnesota. Because her husband is a professional man, Carol is expected to exist primarily as the doctor's wife, supporting his endeavors and bearing his children. Carol finds the town ugly, dirty, and shabby, with a rigid social hierarchy. The business and professional class look down upon immigrants and farmers and expect newcomers to fit into traditional patterns of behavior. Lewis revealed strong feminist sympathies, showing the limited choices available to women at the beginning of the twentieth century and

how frustrating it was for them to be thinking human beings with only a very small stage on which to exercise their intelligence. This novel, part of the "revolt from the village" literary movement, shows Gopher Prairie's development over the course of twenty years, seen primarily through Carol, but also through her husband Will, the librarian Vida Sherwin, the disillusioned lawyer Guy Pollack, the hired girl Bea, Bea's radical carpenter husband Miles Bjornstam, the frustrated artistic tailor Erik Valborg, and their neighbors. *Main Street* was one of the best sellers of the 1920s because of its frankness in challenging American ideas about the small town as a place for neighborliness, good feeling, and virtue.

Two years later, Lewis published *Babbitt*, a study of a middle-aged, middle-class businessman in the Midwest. The portrayal of the everyday life of a businessman capitalized on the excessive consumerism of the 1920s under the presidencies of Warren G. Harding and Calvin Coolidge. Lewis did copious research for this novel, visiting midwestern cities and attending meetings of such business clubs as the Rotary and the Elks, as well as chambers of commerce. With a careful ear, he picked up slang, rhythms of speaking, and the discourse of "boosterism." His critique of this obsessively capitalist culture and the incipient fascism it can engender distressed many readers, but it too became a best-seller, giving the world the term *Babbitt*, a synonym for the average man whose life is defined by his business.

The metropolis of Zenith in *Babbitt* represents the growing cities of the Midwest, whose character was defined by business and industry. It is also the city where Lewis's corrupt minister Elmer Gantry appears to try to provide a solution for a pernicious spiritual malaise. Because the soul of Zenith seems to be business, retiring industrialist Sam Dodsworth leaves there so that he can see more of the world and experience art and culture.

Many of Lewis's 1930s novels are set on the East Coast, but in the 1940s Lewis returned to the Midwest both literally and in fiction to create his last midwestern city, Grand Republic, a place not as striving as Zenith, but with a more settled history. Judge Cass Timberlane often thinks in romantic terms of the pioneers who founded the city, but Lewis shows that these older cities are also mired in deep-seated prejudices with an agenda of maintaining a superficially ordered society. In *Cass Timberlane*, Lewis confronted sexual and gender stereotyping in this city where apparently ordinary marriages mask highly dysfunctional families. In *Kingsblood Royal*, Grand Republic becomes a battleground as notions about race and class are challenged by the protagonist, who discovers that he has a black ancestor.

Sinclair Lewis loved the Midwest and loved America but was highly critical of how societal forces stifled people's ability to enjoy life. His novels, as Sheldon Grebstein notes, serve as his "warning that if we have created only a high material culture without an equally high sense of beauty and decency and tolerance for individual differences, we have failed utterly." Lewis died in 1951. His writings continue to be important for exposing the dichotomy between the American Dream and the reality of American life, and for encouraging Americans to make American ideals a reality.

Sources and Further Reading: David D. Anderson, "Sinclair Lewis and the Midwestern Tradition," in Michael Connaughton, ed., *Sinclair Lewis at 100: Papers Presented at a Centennial Conference* (1985); Martin Bucco, *Main Street: The Revolt of Carol Kennicott* (1993); Maxwell Geismar, "Sinclair Lewis: The Cosmic Bourjoyce," in *The Last of the Provincials: The American Novel, 1915–1925* (1947); Sheldon Grebstein, *Sinclair Lewis* (1962); James M. Hutchisson, *The Rise of Sinclair Lewis, 1920–1930* (1996); George Killough, ed., *Minnesota Diary, 1942–46* (2000); Richard Lingeman, *Sinclair Lewis: Rebel from Main Street* (2002); Sally E. Parry, "Gopher Prairie, Zenith, and Grand Republic: Nice Places to Visit, but Would Even Sinclair Lewis Want to Live There?" *Midwestern Miscellany* 20 (1992); Mark Schorer, *Sinclair Lewis: An American Life* (1961).

Sally E. Parry
Illinois State University

James Thurber's boyhood home, Columbus. Courtesy Thurber House.

James Thurber (1894–1961)

Summarizing James Thurber's life is as precarious as explaining humor itself. The temptation to dwell on the preciosity of early 1900s midwestern culture, or his quirky family members, or his own physical and mental difficulties, can trivialize the work, which is what brings us to Thurber, one of the few canonical figures in American humor. His life and times may have been harder than many, yet his genius prevailed by twisting reality "to the right into humor rather than to the left into tragedy." He became the first major American writer whose reputation (agonizing as this was for him) was based on short pieces.

In his 1933 autobiography, *My Life and Hard Times*, Thurber took liberties with his midwestern roots: He was born on December 8, 1894,

> in the blowy uplands of Columbus, Ohio, in a district know as "the Flats," which, for half of the year, was partially underwater and during the rest of the time was an outcropping of live granite, rising in dry weather to a height of two hundred feet. This condition led to moroseness, skepticism, jumping when shots were fired, membership in a silver cornet band,

and, finally, a system of floating pulley-baskets by means of which the Thurber family was raised up to and lowered down from the second floor of the old family homestead.

The book recounts the most memorable events of his college years living in and commuting by trolley from what is now the Thurber House, a literary center in the restored Victorian house his family rented from 1913 to 1918. It is here that "the ghost got it," sockets "leaked" electricity, and alarms were heard in the night.

Thurber's childhood included two enduring influences: his mother's uncanny memory and eccentric and dramatic sense of humor, and a severe eye injury caused by an arrow while "playing" William Tell, which left James blind in one eye and, decades later, overtook his other eye. Owing to this, his school days began with a certain frailty and introspection. However, with the recognition of his writing and drawing abilities, his years at East High blossomed with honors, including class presidency.

At his hometown Ohio State University, he struggled with subjects like botany and military drill, but found professors to hone his appetite for literature. There he met Elliott Nugent, whose theatrical gifts and energy redirected Thurber's unchanneled creativity. Thurber wrote for OSU's newspaper, edited its humor magazine, and created plays and songs for the dramatic club. Without earning a degree, he left the university. The army rejected him because of his eyesight, and Thurber departed for Paris for a year before returning to Columbus, where he began his first column, "Credos and Curios"—an admixture of commentary, parody, cultural observation, and humor—for the *Columbus Dispatch*.

While writing for the Scarlet Mask Club, OSU's dramatic group, Thurber met Althea Adams; they married, and eventually returned to France. Before Thurber joined the *New Yorker* in 1927, he'd worked at a musical comedy, a novel, the Paris edition of the *Chicago Tribune*, a book-length parody of best sellers, and other freelance projects, many of which proved frustrating.

E. B. White arranged Thurber's first meeting with editor Harold Ross, who had just started the *New Yorker*. Thurber was hired as managing editor and, so he claimed, worked his way down to writer. In 1929, he and White published *Is Sex Necessary?*, a parody of popular sex and psychology books. Thurber provided spontaneous pencil sketches that White inked. This inspired Thurber to submit drawings to the magazine, which eventually published hundreds of his cartoons and spot illustrations. Thurber's artwork, at his peak, powered national advertising campaigns, appeared on clothing and tableware, and illustrated dust jackets and books. He was so profligate with his drawings that he often bragged that if someone stretched out all his drawings they'd create "a mile and a half of lines." As his eyesight failed, he created pictures with white chalk on black paper or by using a Zeiss jeweler's loupe to magnify his work (he called himself a welder from Mars). His sight failed completely, in 1951, after a series of stressful operations.

Thurber divorced Althea after twelve difficult years. He soon married Helen Wismer, who, for most of their twenty-six years together, was also his business manager, editor, helpmate, "seeing-eye wife," and nurse. Between 1930 and 1961, Thurber published nearly thirty books (several more were published posthumously), showcasing the unparalleled breadth of personal essays, memories, journalism, profiles, parodies, and fables, and scores of stories such as "The Catbird Seat" and "The Secret Life of Walter Mitty," two of the most anthologized pieces of modern fiction. He also published five children's books and saw three of his works produced on Broadway: *The Beast in He; The Male Animal;* and a revue, *A Thurber Carnival*, which won a Tony Award. His subjects were equally broad: photography, bicycling, Antarctica, colloquialisms, dogs, soap operas, science—he addressed each

with a calm plainspokenness that could be mistaken as inherently midwestern: he underplayed the ironic, allying himself with the curious general reader.

Although Thurber resided in New York, Connecticut, Bermuda, and France, Columbus remained the well-spring for much of his best work. "In the early years of the nineteenth century," he wrote in *My Life and Hard Times*, "Columbus won out, as state capital, by one vote over Lancaster, and ever since then has had the hallucination that it is being followed, a curious municipal state of mind which affects . . . all those who live there. Columbus is a town in which almost anything is likely to happen and in which almost everything has."

Encroaching blindness plagued his last decade, as did the *New Yorker*'s changing attitudes and staff. Partly because of his eidetic memory, much of Thurber's later work revels in wordplay and restless interior monologues preoccupied with McCarthyism, the preternatural, America's linguistic slovenliness, and the "darkening" of humor.

Thurber collapsed one evening in Manhattan: A large tumor was discovered and removed from his brain. After a month-long coma, he succumbed to respiratory failure on November 2, 1961. His remains are buried in Columbus.

Sources and Further Reading: Harrison Kinney, *James Thurber: His Life and Times* (1995); Harrison Kinney, ed., *The Thurber Letters: The Wit, Wisdom, and Surprising Life of James Thurber* (2002); James Thurber, *People Have More Fun Than Anybody*, ed., Michael J. Rosen (1994); James Thurber, *The Thurber Album* (1952); James Thurber, *The Thurber Carnival* (1945); James Thurber, *The Years with Ross* (1959).

Michael J. Rosen
Founding Literary Director,
Thurber House, Columbus, Ohio

F. Scott Fitzgerald (1896–1940)

F. Scott Fitzgerald is one of the major fiction writers in English in the twentieth century, remarkable for his American novels and short stories, which express profound social insight in a lucid, often witty style. He is unique among modern novelists for mixing a lyricism inspired by his favorite poet, John Keats, with a skeptical vision inherited from Frank Norris and Theodore Dreiser. In such novels as *The Great Gatsby* (1925), *Tender is the Night* (1934) and the unfinished *The Love of the Last Tycoon* (1941), Fitzgerald shows an ambivalent enthusiasm for new American commercial culture vying with a nostalgia for inherited manners.

The dramatic tension between money and manners

❖ **The Great Gatsby**

One of my most vivid memories is of coming back West from prep school and later from college at Christmas time. Those who went farther than Chicago would gather in the old dim Union Station at six o'clock of a December evening, with a few Chicago friends, already caught up into their own holiday gayeties, to bid them a hasty good-by. I remember the fur coats of the girls returning from Miss This-or-That's and the chatter of frozen breath and the hands waving overhead as we caught sight of old acquaintances, and the matchings of invitations: "Are you going to the Ordways'? the Herseys'? the Schultzes'?" and the long green tickets clasped tight in our gloved hands. And last the murky yellow cars of the Chicago, Milwaukee & St. Paul railroad looking cheerful as Christmas itself on the tracks beside the gate.

When we pulled out into the winter night and the real snow, our snow, began to stretch out beside us and twinkle against the windows, and the dim lights of small Wisconsin stations moved by, a sharp wild brace came suddenly into the air. We drew in deep breaths of it as we walked back from dinner through the cold vestibules, unutterably aware of our identity with this country for one strange hour, before we melted indistinguishably into it again.

That's my Middle West—not the wheat or the prairies or the lost Swede towns, but the thrilling returning trains of my youth, and the street lamps and sleigh bells in the frosty dark and the shadows of holly wreaths thrown by lighted windows on the snow. I am part of that, a little solemn with the feel of those long winters, a little complacent from growing up in the Carraway house in a city where dwellings are still called through decades by a family's name. I see now that this has been a story of the West, after all—Tom and Gatsby, Daisy and Jordan and I, were all Westerners, and perhaps we possessed some deficiency in common which made us subtly unadaptable to Eastern life.

Source: F. Scott Fitzgerald, *The Great Gatsby* (1925) 211–12.

in Fitzgerald's work was likely based in his experience of his own family. Though his father, Edward Fitzgerald, had little money or business acumen, he was descended from Maryland aristocrats related to F. Scott Key, author of "The Star-Spangled Banner." Fitzgerald's father went from Maryland to the West, to Chicago and then St. Paul, and in 1890 married Mary McQuillen, whose father owned a successful wholesale grocery business. Francis Scott Key Fitzgerald was born in 1896, following the infant deaths of two sisters. Fitzgerald explained his ancestry to novelist John O'Hara: "I am half black Irish and half old American stock with the usual exaggerated ancestral pretensions. The black Irish half of the family had the money and looked down upon the Maryland side of the family who had, and really had, that certain series of reticences and obligations that go under the poor old shattered word 'breeding'."

Fitzgerald adapted to eastern life in attending the Newman School in Hackensack, New Jersey, a Catholic prep school for boys. Visits to New York City kindled in him a love for its grandeur and for certain stars he saw in films. A key mentor was Father Cyril Sigourney Webster Fay, who gave Fitzgerald a sense of belonging, accepting Fitzgerald's Catholic and Irish character and encouraging his sense of uniqueness, all qualities that had been of ambiguous merit to the young Fitzgerald, though Fitzgerald essentially left the church when he left the school. He attended Princeton from 1913 to 1917. He did not graduate, withdrawing at one point due to poor grades and not returning after a stint in the army, which stationed

him in Alabama. There he met his future wife, Zelda Sayre, the daughter of a prominent Montgomery judge. She refused to marry him at first because he had little money, but she agreed when his first novel, *This Side of Paradise* (1920), set at Princeton, was accepted by Scribner's. The most financially successful of all his novels, it made Fitzgerald a literary celebrity, intoxicating him with a sense of early completion that he later regretted as false, though he never renounced the romantic intensity of the time.

His marriage was exciting but difficult, and its early struggles are reflected in his second novel, *The Beautiful and Damned* (1922). It was a marriage rife with competitive tensions, complicated by the alcohol abuse of both parties. Zelda was obsessed with realizing her own artistic talents, which were largely unfulfilled, though she published a novel, *Save Me the Waltz* (1932). She was eventually beset by serious mental illnesses that became more debilitating through the 1930s, and her decline exacted a heavy emotional and financial toll on Fitzgerald, who tried to provide her with the best care possible, in Europe, Baltimore, and, finally, North Carolina. Fitzgerald wrote, "I left my capacity for hoping on the little roads that led to Zelda's sanitariums."

Through his early period of fame and some fortune, Fitzgerald became typecast as a documentarian of the Jazz Age youth culture of the 1920s in ways that his reputation did not overcome in his own lifetime. He indeed published many short stories about young love, such as "Winter Dreams" and "Bernice Bobs Her Hair," that manipulate an idiom of popular magazine fiction, but he also wrote such stories as "May Day" (set against the New York City riots of 1919), "Absolution" (a dazzling prototype of *The Great Gatsby*), and "Babylon Revisited" (in which a young father confronts a wasted youth and a lost family), which approach the intensities of his novels.

The Great Gatsby, published in 1925, remains his tour de force and a major fable of American identity, as Gatsby, a dashing but "meretricious" midwestern self-inventor, comes to a bitter end while pursuing a lost love among the mansions of Long Island. From the perspective provided by this New York tragedy, narrator Nick Carraway regards the West with some longing; as St. Paul is lauded in Fitzgerald's story "The Ice Palace" as a "three generation town," so in *The Great Gatsby* the Midwest has an ancestral authenticity lacking in New York's commercial world of brokers and the newly rich. As Carraway says,

> I am part of [the Midwest], a little solemn with the feel of those long winters, a little complacent from growing up in the Carraway house in a city where dwellings are still called through decades by a family's name. I see now that this has been a story of the West, after all—Tom and Gatsby, Daisy and Jordan and I, were all Westerners, and perhaps we possessed some deficiency in common which made us subtly unadaptable to Eastern life.

Fitzgerald's next novel, *Tender Is the Night* (1934), describes the rise and fall of an American psychiatrist, Dick Diver, who studies and works in Switzerland. Diver, who has a southern, semiaristocratic heritage, marries a patient, Nicole, who is of new, industrial Chicago money. Although the novel lacks the concision of *Gatsby*, its gradually unfolding, achronological structure provides detailed insights into American characters and shows Fitzgerald's style at its greatest maturity. His last novel, *The Love of the Last Tycoon*, focuses on a Hollywood producer (inspired by Irving Thalberg) who struggles to be a successful corporate manager with the conscience of an artist. Despite Fitzgerald's meticulous outline, the novel was unfinished when Fitzgerald died of a heart attack, in Hollywood, in late 1940. He was forty-four; he is buried, along with his parents; Zelda (who died in 1948); and their only child, Scottie, in Rockville, Maryland.

Sources and Further Reading: Matthew Bruccoli, *Some Sort of Epic Grandeur: The Life of F. Scott Fitzgerald* (1981); F. Scott Fitzgerald, *The Letters of F. Scott Fitzgerald*, ed., Andrew Turnbull (1963); *F. Scott Fitzgerald Centenary*, http://www.sc.edu/fitzgerald/ (1997, update 2002); John T. Irwin, "Compensating Visions: *The Great Gatsby*," *Southwest Review* 77 (Autumn 1992); Andre Le Vot, *F. Scott Fitzgerald: A Biography* (1983); James R. Mellow, *Invented Lives* (1984); Arthur Mizener, *The Far Side of Paradise* (1951); Arthur Mizener, *Scott Fitzgerald and His World* (1972).

Phillip L. Beard
University of Maryland

Dawn Powell (1896–1965)

Born in Mount Gilead, Ohio, in 1896, Dawn Sherman Powell had a fragmented childhood. Powell's father, a traveling salesman, frequently left his wife and three daughters alone, and when Dawn was seven, her mother died. The girls were shuttled to various relatives until Dawn was eleven, when her father remarried. One day, Powell's stepmother burned all the stories she had written, so Powell ran away to live with an aunt in Shelby, Ohio, where she stayed until going to Lake Erie College. Immediately after graduating, she moved to New York City.

Powell, who called herself a "permanent visitor" in New York City, married Joseph Gousha and they had a son, Jojo, who was mentally and physically damaged from birth. The cost of his care gave Powell impetus to write constantly, producing sixteen novels as well as short stories, magazine articles, movie scripts, and dramas. She developed a following of admirers, including Ernest Hemingway (who called Powell his favorite living writer), E. E. Cummings, John Dos Passos, and Edmund Wilson. Powell played as hard as she worked, holding forth at Greenwich Village's Hotel Lafayette, much as Dorothy Parker held sway at Midtown's Algonquin Hotel.

But Powell was outsider and insider in both the Midwest and New York. In her haunting memoir "What Are You Doing in My Dreams?" (1963) Powell wrote: "It's as if the day I left Ohio I split in two at the crossroads, and went up both roads, half of me by day here in New York and the other half by night with the dead in long-ago Ohio." Powell's novels are rooted in this dualistic outlook.

Individually, the novels focus on the lives of everyday people; as a body of work, they trace the movement from the provinces to the city. "Coming as I do from many generations of small-town American people," Powell wrote, "I am basically interested in the problem of the provincial at home and in the world, in business, love, and art. I would like to portray these Americans as vividly as Balzac did his French provincials at home and in Paris." The characters are outsiders in these towns, reflecting Powell's own "outsider" feeling among relatives reluctant to care for three orphan sisters.

Powell's Ohio background wrapped itself around her life in Greenwich Village, informing her outlook and her writing. Although critics divide Powell's novels into an Ohio cycle of five novels published between 1928 and 1934 and a New York cycle published between 1936 and 1964, Powell's diaries evidence a continual tension between her midwestern background and her New York present. Her Ohio novels feature glittering glimpses of the Big City; her New York novels feature midwesterners trying to overcome their "low beginnings." Excepting Powell's largely forgettable first novel, *Whither* (1925), set in New York City, her early works—five novels written between 1928 and 1934—are set in Ohio. Drawing upon Powell's memory, the novels move from the rural Ohio of 1900 in *The Bride's House* (1929) into small towns in *She Walks in Beauty* (1928) and *The Tenth Moon* (or its working title, *Come Back to Sorrento*) (1932) and into the factory town in *Dance Night* (1930).

Although these first novels were published in the wake of the "revolt from the village" movement, which reached its peak in the 1920s with the publication of Sinclair Lewis's *Main Street* (1920) and *Babbitt* (1922), Powell's Ohio novels do not properly belong to this movement because they neither satirize nor idealize the small-town life. Powell is not seeking to redeem America, to save it from encroaching urbanization, but, rather, to set down the stories of people's inner struggles. "In the Ohio books I was not interested in making up romances, but in archaeology and showing up people and places that are or have been familiar types, but were not acceptable to fiction, because of inner wars in their nature that make them confused human characters instead of standard fiction black and white types—good, bad, strong, weak."

In writing *The Story of a Country Boy* (1934), she moved into unknown territory: the burgeoning suburbs of the 1930s. While writing the novel, she visited Ohio, and found that the world she remembered had utterly changed: There is not the anxious "striving" to be like society that used to characterize the Ohio little towns. Their possessions are more truly a gauge of their financial stations than the city person's possessions, which are merely a testimony to glibness with creditors. Powell "moved out" of Ohio into her contemporary New York novels.

Midway through her career, after developing a following with her sharply satiric, fast-paced New York novels, Powell published *My Home Is Far Away* (1944), a novel devoid of satire set in slow-moving early-twentieth-century Ohio. In it, Powell lays bare the raw truth of her "bastardized life" as she called it, in an effort to explain herself and the compulsion driving her ambitious female characters, who fear that failure might force them to return home. The women are infused with a stoicism that reflects Powell's own calm visage, at odds with the strife of her life. This autobiographical novel reveals the fragmented youth that gave birth to the strong woman. *My Home Is Far Away* has sold more copies since its reprinting in 1995 than it did in the previous fifty years.

After decades of obscurity, nearly all of Powell's works are back in print, both individually by Steerforth Press and in a two-volume Library of America collection. Powell will likely be best remembered for her biting New York satires. But within every sharp-tongued Gotham protagonist is a midwesterner scared to go home. After Powell's death in 1965, Edmund Wilson wrote, "She was really an old-fashioned American woman not far from the pioneering civilization: strong-willed, stoical, plain-spoken, not to be imposed upon." It is this midwestern view that informs and enriches her body of work.

Sources and Further Reading: Tim Page, *Dawn Powell: A Biography* (1998); Tim Page, ed., *Diaries of Dawn Powell* (1995); Tim Page, ed., *Selected Letters of Dawn Powell, 1913–1965* (1999); Tim Page, ed., *Dawn Powell, Novels, 1930–1942* (2001); Tim Page, ed., *Dawn Powell, Novels, 1944–1962* (2001); Marcelle Smith Rice, *Dawn Powell* (2000); Harry Redcay Warfel, *American Novelists of Today* (1951); Edmund Wilson, "Dawn Powell: Greenwich Village in the Fifties," in *The Bit between My Teeth* (1965).

Marcelle Smith Rice
North Carolina State University

Hart Crane (1899–1932)

To those born and bred in it, the city rarely looks glamorous. But to the writer who comes to the city from elsewhere, it is the overwhelming and almost barbaric energy of the city that seems so compelling. No one insisted upon the vitality of the modern city as fervently as Hart Crane in *The Bridge* (1930), an "epic of America" that was truly an homage to New York City.

Harold Hart Crane was born in 1899 and raised in Garrettsville, Ohio, a small town near Cleveland, and he left for New York City almost as soon as he could. At seventeen, he used his parents' messy divorce as the occasion for him to be sent to New York for the private tutoring that would help enroll him in Columbia University. This unlikely proposition made sense to his father, a prosperous manufacturer who packaged expensive chocolates, and his mother, a Chicago-born would-be actress. From 1916 on, Crane shuttled back and forth between Cleveland and New York, in a pattern of uprootedness that persisted through his short life.

When he was in Cleveland, he worked as a menial in his father's outlet stores, ostensibly learning the family business at the entry level. When he was in

New York, he worked as a copywriter for mail-order catalogs and advertising agencies, while making friends in the intellectual and artistic subculture that was inventing American modernism. But New York was essential for another reason. Since 1919, Crane had known himself to be a gay man in a homophobic culture. The urban spaces of New York offered a social milieu and a degree of anonymity that he could not expect to find elsewhere.

Crane would repay the city handsomely for its hospitality. In the fifteen interlinked poems of *The Bridge*, New York is identified with a distinctly American modernism that embraced the future and that celebrated the machine. Unlike the London from whose center T. S. Eliot viewed a collapsing civilization in *The Waste Land* (1922)—hallucinatory falling towers and "unreal cities"—Crane's New York was rapidly erecting skyscrapers with equipment that itself seemed ready to soar: "All afternoon the cloud-flown derricks turn." Even when Crane turned pessimistic, as in the late-night subway ride of "The Tunnel," he portrayed not just the harrowing descent of a near-empty car rocketing at speed underground but its inevitable ascent aboveground to river's edge.

Crane's modernist poetry was makeshift, cobbled together from unlikely sources, yet streamlined, the poetic equivalent of a backyard hot rod. It displayed his engagement with the European avant-garde of Eliot, but it also reflected such popular art as the silent film and the advertising pitch. Crane's opening "Proem" teases its readers with glimpses of the Brooklyn Bridge that is the poem's guiding "star." Like an advertiser preparing an audience to be receptive to a product, Crane first establishes a condition of crisis and then discovers the bridge to be a symbolic solution. In "The River," he uses such filmic techniques as montage, cross-cutting, and fade-ins and fade-outs—devices sanctioned by a "dream-sequence" that initiates one of the rare moments in the epic when Crane revisits the Midwest. He returns as one twice-enclosed: in the unreality of a dream, and as a passenger cocooned in a steel railroad coach. In a climactic moment he throws open the coach window and leans toward the Mississippi River. This is staged as a triumph and a breakthrough, though it is remarkable that so simple a gesture required so elaborate a production. In one of the last poems written for the sequence, "Indiana" (1929), a mother's wheedling voice urges her son not to set off as a vagabonding sailor but to remain by her side and care for her in old age.

In New York Crane found alternatives to a midwestern parochialism that he had indicted in his earlier work. In "Porphyro in Akron"—its very title suggesting discord—Greek immigrants who gather immigrant friends about them represent a vitality that

Crane sets against the conventional image of a single rose cultivated for display in a stereotypically neat front yard. In "For the Marriage of Faustus and Helen," Crane counters a banal geography that is recognizably Cleveland (the Euclid Avenue trolley, the giant-size Sherwin-Williams paint billboard) with an extravagant vision of modern beauty that celebrates orgiastic dancing to jazz. Crane's "Helen" is an anomalous figure, at one point compared to an airplane pilot and described as a "religious gunman." As Crane matured as a poet, he needed to interject into his work, more or less invisibly and silently, instances of homosexual desire. In 1924, he met the man who would be the great love of his life, Emil Opffer, a New York merchant marine from a family of literary journalists. For Opffer, he fashioned the six poems that he entitled *Voyages* (1924–1925), an extraordinary souvenir of their too-brief affair. When the Brooklyn Bridge appears in Crane's long poem, it serves as a coded reference to their love, especially in its ecstatic final section, "Atlantis."

Published in 1930, *The Bridge* met with mixed reviews, underscoring a dilemma that—along with a deepening alcoholism—helps explain Crane's diminishing productivity in his later years. Ever since *Voyages*, and in short lyrics like "The Wine Menagerie" that were collected in his first book (*White Buildings*, 1926), Crane had been struggling to present himself more openly as a homosexual. However, when he successfully applied in 1931 for a Guggenheim Fellowship, the project that he proposed was an extended sequence on the Aztec culture of Mexico. The gulf between his intricately personal poetry of homosexual desire (several poems written, few published) and the public poetry of his Aztec sequence (few poems even written) he did not live to resolve. In April 1932, he was returning home after the unexpected death of his father to a family estate vastly diminished by the stock-market collapse when he jumped from the deck of an ocean liner into the Florida seas. A witness spotted him swimming strongly for a moment, until he disappeared beneath the waves.

Sources and Further Reading: Edward Brunner, "'The Farewell Day Unkind': The Fragmentary Poems of Hart Crane's Last Five Years," in H. Daniel Peck, ed., *The Green American Tradition* (1989); Hart Crane, *O My Land, My Friends*, eds., Langdon Hammer and Brom Weber (1997); Hart Crane, *The Poems of Hart Crane*, ed., Marc Simon (1986); Tim Dean, "Hart Crane's Poetics of Privacy," *American Literary History* 8 (Spring 1996); Clive Fisher, *Hart Crane: A Life* (2002); Thomas A. Yingling, *Hart Crane and the Homosexual Text* (1990).

Edward Brunner
Southern Illinois University–Carbondale

Ernest Hemingway (1899–1961)

Although he was born (in 1899) and raised in the Chicago suburb of Oak Park, Ernest Hemingway's relation to the Midwest remains largely unexplored. An expatriate from his mid-twenties until his death in 1961, Hemingway was a self-taught, multilingual intellectual who developed a Spanish sensibility and could pass for a native in several foreign cultures. He was also an international celebrity and generational spokesman whose fiction, almost always set outside of America, focused on non-midwestern specific concerns: modern alienation, European wars, existential angst, and the codes by which individuals could maintain their dignity in an increasingly dehumanized world. To critics, he is preeminently a modernist author whose minimalist prose style, innovative dialogue techniques, and achievements in the short story made him one of the most influential writers of the twentieth century. Yet this cosmopolitan was indeed a midwesterner, and the values that informed his life and art reflect the cultural milieu of his formative years.

Hemingway's family was respectably middle class. His father was a physician who insisted on competence and professionalism; his mother an energetic and ambitious professional musician; and his grandfather a former Union army officer who founded the local YMCA and helped establish Oak Park, a village conceived and developed as a wholesome alternative to urban Chicago. Socially conservative but politically progressive, Oak Park revered Theodore Roosevelt and the town's ethos emphasized rugged individualism, civic responsibility, honesty, hard work, self-sacrifice, and self-improvement. Young Hemingway internalized these values, but he also bridled under them. In the other locus of his youth, the family cottage on Walloon Lake in northern Michigan, he learned to hunt and fish and was exposed to the marginalized existences of Ojibwas, lumberjacks, and drifters. The traits associated with Hemingway and his fictional heroes derive mainly from these midwestern settings: the love of outdoorsmanship, the code of honor, personal integrity, pride in one's craft, professional competence, unflinching honesty, understatement, sympathy for underdogs, self-reliance, and a sense of social obligation.

Hemingway frequently transmuted his own life into art. The fiction set in the Midwest—short stories that usually feature his youthful persona, Nick Adams—takes place during the author's childhood and adolescence and is mainly set in the hills, forests, lakes, fishing streams, and small towns of northern Michigan. Some stories depict characters on the fringes of society: the waitress who is raped on a dock in "Up in Michigan"; the punch-drunk ex-fighter and his black companion in "The Battler"; the prostitutes, drifters, and Native Americans of "The Light of the World." Other stories bring together Hemingway's two midwestern worlds. In "Indian Camp," young Nick falls from the security of his middle-class life as he witnesses a primitive cesarean section and a suicide, and senses his own mortality. In "The Doctor and the Doctor's Wife," Nick observes the violence of the lower-class world impinging upon the social order, leading to an intimation that violence itself lies simmering beneath Oak Park's middle-class respectability. In "Soldier's Home," another Hemingway surrogate returns home disillusioned from the war to a town in Oklahoma resembling Oak Park and is unable to reintegrate himself back into conventional society.

Hemingway avoided using the Midwest as the setting for a significant novel. As he fashioned his worldly public image, he increasingly expressed bitterness toward the region he had physically left behind forever, partly due to conflicted feelings about his domineering mother and his depressive father, and partly because he felt that the world that had formed him had left him vulnerable to the vagaries of the emerging modern age. As he shaped his cosmopolitan identity, he symbolically tried to exorcise his midwestern one. In "The End of Something," the formerly vibrant lumbering Michigan town of Hortons Bay is now a ghost town. In "Big Two-Hearted River," the once thriving town of Seney, Michigan, is but a skeleton: "Even the surface had been burned off the ground." In "God Rest You Merry, Gentlemen," Kansas City (Missouri) is described by what it no longer is: "In those days the distances were all very different, the dirt blew off the hills that now have been cut down, and Kansas City was very like Constantinople."

Hemingway never wrote about Oak Park in his fiction, but this absence signifies a powerful if impalpable presence. When Jake Barnes of *The Sun Also Rises* (1926) turns from the modern wasteland and immerses himself in the ancient ritual of Spanish bullfights to find a meaningful sense of order; when Frederick Henry in *A Farewell to Arms* (1929) deserts the Italian army in a war in which honor, glory, and courage have lost all meaning; when Robert Jordan of *For Whom the Bell Tolls* (1940) goes to Spain to fight against Franco and, facing death, considers himself lucky to be able to sacrifice his life to save his comrades, they all act as figurative sons of Oak Park. And when Hemingway, galvanizing support for the Loyalist cause in Spain, publicly announced "fascism is a lie told by bullies," he spoke the language of his hometown's beloved Roosevelt.

In the final Nick Adams story, "Fathers and Sons" (1933), the protagonist, now older and himself an author, is driving with his own young son and reminiscing about his father and his youth. He thinks that if he could write about it "he could get rid of it. . . . But it was still too early for that." He resents his father but, when questioned by his own son, his memories turn nostalgic and he fills with pride. Although they live far from Dr. Adams's tomb, the boy wants to visit and, in the end, Nick relents: "I can see we'll have to go." In this symbolic representation of the author's ambivalent feelings toward the region that shaped him, we can intuit the bulk of the iceberg that lay below the surface of his articulated consciousness, the mostly omitted portion of his early experiences. For Hemingway, the Midwest to which he never did return would remain a clean, well-lighted place, a normative center of ethical value that could brace him against a changing modern world gone terribly awry.

Sources and Further Reading: Carlos Baker, *Ernest Hemingway: A Life Story* (1969); Scott Donaldson, ed., *The Cambridge Companion to Ernest Hemingway* (1996); Ernest Hemingway, *The Short Stories of Ernest Hemingway* (1953); Kenneth S. Lynn, *Hemingway* (1987); James R. Mellow, *Hemingway: A Life without Consequences* (1992); James Nagel, ed., *Ernest Hemingway: The Oak Park Legacy* (1996); Michael Reynolds, *Hemingway*, 5 vols. (1986–1999); Linda Wagner-Martin, ed., *A Historical Guide to Ernest Hemingway* (2000); Philip Young, *Ernest Hemingway: A Reconsideration*, rev. ed. (1966).

Robert Paul Lamb
Purdue University–West Lafayette, Indiana

Langston Hughes (1902–1967)

Riding a train from Cleveland to Toluca, Mexico, after his graduation from high school, Langston Hughes (1902–1967) wrote "The Negro Speaks of Rivers." Hughes was visiting his father because he made such a visit a precondition for paying for college. Although his father, James N. Hughes, was an African American man born and educated in the United States, he left the country because legalized segregation restricted his business opportunities. Langston had not seen his father in over a decade. The poem itself, its circumstances of production, and this pivotal moment in Hughes's life reveal much about Hughes's relationship to the Midwest. In his autobiography, *The Big Sea* (1940), Hughes talks about seeing the Mississippi River and its significance for African Americans. He thinks of slavery and how being "sold down the river was the worst fate that could overtake a slave in times of bondage." In the poem, he links this particular river to ancient rivers in Africa, the Euphrates and the Nile. The Mississippi River becomes associated with freedom and possibility through its "singing." Degrada-

tion is transformed into victory. Hughes had the ability to see issues of global significance in particular local features and geography, and his experience of the Midwest revolved around transition and transformation. Growing up he moved constantly, living in such places as Joplin, Missouri; Lawrence, Kansas; Lincoln, Illinois; and Cleveland. In the essay "Ten Thousand Beds," Hughes uses sleeping in one's own bed as a synecdoche for being at home. However, his ease in sleeping in numerous beds demonstrates that he is at home anywhere. He says, "quite early in life I got used to a variety of beds from the deep feather beds of the country to the studio couches of the town, from camp cots to my uncle's barber chair in Kansas City elongated to accommodate me. If strange beds had been given to upsetting me, I would have lost many a good night's sleep in my life. And there is nothing I like better than to sleep."

His first novel, *Not without Laughter* (1930), is set in Stanton, Missouri, and suggests that even home has its upsetting aspects. Hughes explores not the geographical divisions of waterways in the Midwest but the social divisions of color lines. Those color lines force Sandy's father Jimboy to work as a migrant laborer to stay partially employed. They consign Sandy's grandmother Hagar to life as a washerwoman. Sandy re-

Langston Hughes. Library of Congress, Prints and Photographs Division, LC-USW3-000697-D.

flects on a local gathering place, Cudge's, and thinks, "That must be the reason why poverty-stricken old Negroes like Uncle Dan Givens lived so long—because to them, no matter how hard life might be, it was not without laughter." Cudge's is a pool hall and it is significant as a place where people can enjoy life and escape the burdens of the color line. Such color lines are exposed as permeable in *The Big Sea*, where Hughes discusses his ancestry as African, Jewish, Scottish, French, and Cherokee. Although *Not without Laughter* started as an autobiography, the family situation in the novel is very different from Hughes's own. In his actual autobiography, Hughes repeatedly refers to his grandmother as an Indian. Hughes explains that "nobody ever cried in my grandmother's stories. They worked, or schemed, or fought. But no crying. When my grandmother died, I didn't cry, either." His real-life grandmother expresses an independent stoicism of the frontier. African Americans forfeit such stoicism to not only endure life but also enjoy it. Not at all stoic, the fictional grandmother in *Not without Laughter* clings to her religious beliefs for meaning and enjoys spirituals.

Hughes's father is an exception to the rule because he "hated Negroes." American individualism and the economic promise of the American dream fuel his father's repudiation of people who do not focus on acquiring and investing money. Hughes highlights the fact that his father uses his mobility to escape racial oppression in the United States and to exploit Mexican and Indian workers in Mexico. Mexican descendants in the United States are disinherited even when born in the United States because of the complicated racial policies that systematically dispossessed people of color. While the parallel between Mexicans and African Americans is implicit, Hughes's discussion of solidarity with eastern European students at Central High School in Cleveland is very explicit. He builds identification with dispossessed and disinherited people in the Midwest and throughout his travels; the Midwest becomes a representative locale for chaos and conflict. In Cleveland, immigrants from Russia, Poland, Italy, and Hungary educate Hughes about the Russian Revolution, Communism, Socialism, and workers' rights. His immigrant classmates inform his evolving political consciousness. They also elect him to positions in school government because in an environment where the largest division was between Jew and Gentile, "they would compromise on a Negro, feeling, I suppose, that a Negro was neither Jew nor Gentile!"

On his summer vacation after his sophomore year, Hughes worked in Chicago while staying with his mother, an experience that changed his perception of immigrants. Unlike Cleveland, where Hughes was able to build friendships with immigrants, in Chicago a group of boys assaulted him as he walked through an ethnic neighborhood. Instead of promoting class solidarity over and against racial divisions, Chicago seemed to generate conflict and perpetuate the cowboy versus Indian mentality that could also take the form of native versus foreigner or white versus black. In "The Streets of Chicago," Hughes explains that these streets "were then, and have remained to this day, more interesting and exciting to me than any stage show or western shoot 'em-ups. Almost every time I have walked down a Chicago street, I have seen some sort of excitement, sometimes violent, sometimes humorous, sometimes a combination of both." If stereotypical portrayals of the western frontier repress the contributions of African Americans, American Indians, and immigrants, then as a city Chicago seems to be a place where such diversity returns with a vengeance. In the return of a repressed diversity, the western frontier's stereotypical cultural contact is replaced with Chicago's more subtle cultural conflict.

Hughes wrote for the *Chicago Defender* from the 1940s to the early 1960s. His best-known columns featured the character of Jesse B. Semple. Semple was an everyman character without intellectual pretensions. He was a man trying to make sense of the world, and in asking apparently simple questions he asked complex questions about racism, democracy, and American society. Hughes was an artist who found global significance within the currents of midwestern communities at the same time that he participated in shaping a midwestern literary and cultural scene even when the Midwest ceased to be his physical home.

Sources and Further Reading: Emily Bernard, ed., *Remember Me to Harlem* (2001); Henry Louis Gates, Jr., and K. A. Appiah, *Langston Hughes: Critical Perspectives Past and Present* (1993); Langston Hughes, *The Big Sea* (1940); Langston Hughes, *Not without Laughter* (1930); Arnold Rampersad, ed., *The Collected Poems of Langston Hughes* (1995); Arnold Rampersad, *The Life of Langston Hughes*, 2nd ed., 2 vols. (2002); Steven C. Tracy, *Langston Hughes and the Blues* (1988); C. James Trotman, ed., *Langston Hughes: The Man, His Art, and His Continuing Influence* (1995).

Kimberly J. Banks
University of Missouri–Kansas City

James T. Farrell (1904–1979)

James T. Farrell, a writer who was hailed as a major new voice in American literature during the 1930s, has long since fallen out of favor with the critics and, unfortunately, has been relegated to the status of a writer of secondary importance. Most of his gigantic output of novels, short stories, and criticism is out of print today and therefore seldom taught and studied. Yet his true place in American literature is not a small one, for Farrell was a pioneer in ethnic literature and urban fiction, producing a massive series of novels and short stories that were not only exceptionally high in literary quality but also strongly influenced important writers as diverse as Richard Wright, Norman Mailer, and William Kennedy. Very few American writers knew the city as well as Farrell, and even fewer were able to make better literary use of the city. Farrell's *Lonigan Trilogy* and *O'Neill Pentalogy* remain major works of the American urban imagination.

Like Theodore Dreiser, who deeply affected him as a young writer, Farrell (1904–1979) wrote compellingly of his own lived experiences as a person coming from what he called the "plebian origins" of a working-class family. Like James Joyce, Marcel Proust, and Sherwood Anderson, writers who strongly influenced Farrell throughout his career, he centered his work in a rich sense of place and time. The core of Farrell's enormous literary output—he published over fifty books during his lifetime and left a score of unpublished manuscripts at his death—is the sequence of his novels envisioning the world of working-class Irish Catholic people living in Chicago from the early part of the twentieth century to the middle of the Great Depression. Farrell handles this critically important slice of American history very differently from his contemporaries. Whereas John Dos Passos focused broadly on the nation in his *U.S.A.* trilogy, Farrell drew a much more sharply focused and intimate portrait, depicting an Irish Catholic neighborhood on the South Side of Chicago. And whereas Richard Wright described a nearly identical piece of Chicago geography as a nightmarish racial ghetto, Farrell drew his picture of the South Side ambivalently, lovingly detailing its many beauties while also being careful to criticize its negative features, most notably its narrowness. Better than any other major American writer, Farrell understood the ethnic neighborhood, a community held together by a common history rooted in generally accepted religious, social, and political beliefs.

Two especially remarkable features of Farrell's novels are their coherence and depth. Written over a fifty-year time span, his four cycles of novels essentially tell one basic story, becoming what Farrell would describe late in his career as one continuous work. *Studs Lonigan* is a trilogy that dramatizes the life of a working-class young man who never fully understands his urban environment and therefore is victimized by its worst tendencies. This trilogy is balanced by the O'Neill pentalogy, which focuses on a young man who is from the same environment but who employs his existential consciousness and free will both to utilize the best features of that environment and to transcend its

liabilities. Whereas Studs Lonigan's narrative is a classic story of American failure, a downward spiral to psychic disintegration and death, Danny O'Neill's story is an archetypal success tale, an ascent from poverty and misunderstanding to the achievement of selfhood. The Bernard Carr trilogy extends O'Neill's narrative, dramatizing his development as a leftist intellectual and writer in New York. Farrell's final series of novels, *A Universe of Time*, returns to the Chicago setting of the earlier novels and centers on Eddie Ryan, who in most respects is an autobiographical portrait of Farrell as a young man.

Like Theodore Dreiser, Carl Sandburg, and Sherwood Anderson, Farrell is an unmistakably midwestern writer who was acutely aware of the fact that he was part of a regional literature that had broken free of the constraints of the romantic and genteel traditions of the East. His Chicago, while quite different from Dreiser's metropolis and Sandburg's brashly energetic city, is essentially a midwestern city, lacking a rich past but endowed with midwestern space and vigor. Farrell's naturalism, therefore, is often softened and complicated by the open vistas of sky, lake, and parks that sometimes inspire and even transform his heroic characters. And Farrell's plain, midwestern diction, like Anderson's language, can be beautifully lifted in surprisingly lyrical moments.

Although primarily noted for his novels, Farrell was also an accomplished short-story writer, publishing twenty-two collections of short fiction from *Calico Shoes and Other Stories* (1934) to *Judith and Other Stories* (1973). His stories are often Chekhovian in form and outlook, economically crafted and rooted in the apparently small details of life. They also may be compared to James Joyce's short fiction, for they usually generate surprisingly rich moments of revelation, distilling extraordinary meanings from mundane circumstances.

Farrell also produced important works of cultural and literary criticism throughout his career, most notably *A Note on Literary Criticism* (1936), *Reflections at Fifty and Other Essays* (1954), and *Literary Essays* (1976). Farrell's fiercely independent mind saw critical weaknesses in leftist political theory long before other American critics drew away from Stalinism. His integrity as an artist produced throughout his career a healthy suspicion of ideologies from the left and the right. It is also notable that Farrell was one of the first American critics to hail William Faulkner as an important writer and one of the first white writers to draw attention to the significance of Richard Wright's work. And his essays on Dreiser are still regarded as important studies.

Like Dos Passos, John Steinbeck, and Thomas Wolfe, who began their careers with much critical praise in the 1930s and 1940s but then were demoted in importance by later generations of critics, Farrell needs to be reassessed as an artist and thinker. A balanced estimate of his work and place in American literature is long overdue.

Sources and Further Reading: E. M. Branch, *James T. Farrell* (1971); Charles Fanning, *The Irish Voice in America* (1990); Dennis Flynn, ed., *On Irish Themes* (1982); Blanche H. Gelfant, *The American City Novel* (1954); Alan M. Wald, *James T. Farrell: The Revolutionary Socialist Years* (1978).

Robert Butler
Canisius College, New York

Theodore Roethke (1908–1963)

Theodore Roethke, one of the major American poets of the twentieth century, wrote several poems that vividly evoke the Midwest he grew up in, among them "Mid-Country Blow," "In Praise of Prairie," and "Highway: Michigan." But Roethke, who was born in Saginaw, Michigan, on May 25, 1908, and who wrote a coarsely funny "Saginaw Song," was no local-color versifier, nor was he a regional poet in any conventional sense. The greenhouse world he knew as a child was to become, however, along with its immediate surroundings, the central place of his creative imagination, to which he returned again and again. Poems such as "Cuttings," "Cuttings (*later*)," "Root Cellar," "Weed Puller," "Transplanting," and "Flower Dump" reveal a specialized, intimate knowledge of nature utterly unique in American poetry. In *The Lost Son and Other Poems* (1948) the greenhouse also becomes a region of the self, invested with primal fears as well as powers of growth, decay, and regeneration. Roethke's created poetic world is one of ongoing organic, psychological, and spiritual processes.

On both sides of his family Roethke was of German immigrant stock. His paternal grandfather, Wilhelm Roethke, had emigrated from Germany to America in 1872 with his wife and three sons, and, starting out, he bought twenty-two acres of land in west Saginaw on which he established a market garden. The lumber boom that made Saginaw prosperous had begun and, doing well, Wilhelm soon was able to build a greenhouse. In Roethke's childhood the greenhouse became the center of a domain covering some twenty-five acres, a quarter of a million feet of it under glass, and "The William Roethke Greenhouses"—the German surname became Americanized as "Rett-key"—could advertise itself as "the largest and most complete floral establishment in Michigan." When in his poetry Roethke returned to his midwestern roots, it was to the greenhouse world created by his grandfather, maintained by his father, and in which he worked as a boy. It was a world unto itself, extending to a game preserve and to the field and the woods beyond, "the last stand of virgin timber in the Saginaw valley," Roethke later recounted. The greenhouse itself he recalled as "both heaven and hell, a kind of tropics created in the savage climate of Michigan, where austere German Americans turned their love of order and their terrifying efficiency into something truly beautiful."

The most recurrent underlying theme in Roethke's poetry is the need of the self to assimilate fear in the process of its development. In the greenhouse poems, fears are associated not only with the world beyond the greenhouse but with the greenhouse itself and, at its center, the father, at one stage in the lost son's rite of passage referred to as "Father Fear." In his frequently anthologized "My Papa's Waltz," Roethke recalls with love, fear, and humor how his father would romp with him and waltz him off to bed. In the "Lost Son" there is a return to the greenhouse and a passage through a dark night of fear that enables the lost son to assimilate his fears and to experience, at dawn, a healing stillness of the spirit.

A psychologically oriented critic might find in Roethke's relationship with his father a source of fears that plagued him throughout his life. Clearly, Otto Roethke's prolonged illness and painful death at home from cancer, in April 1923, had a devastating impact on his son, already shaken by the suicide of his uncle Charles Roethke in February. Later bouts of mental illness probably derive in part from an emotionally ambivalent relationship to his father, cut off early. His mother, Helen Huebner Roethke, also from a Saginaw German immigrant family, is less a presence in his early poetry, but after her death in 1954 she became the inspiration of a major sequence, "Meditations of an Old Woman." In the Lost Son sequence it is three female workers in the greenhouse, Frau Bauman, Frau Zeiler, and Frau Schwarze, who are transformed into the protective female geniuses of the place in "Frau Bauman, Frau Schmidt, and Frau Schwartze." Being a poet, Roethke changes "Frau Zeiler" to "Frau Schmidt" for rhythmical purposes. Later, Beatrice O'Connell, whom he married in 1953, became another important female presence in his work and inspired several joyous, humorous love poems.

After high school, Roethke enrolled at the University of Michigan at Ann Arbor, where he took a bachelor's degree and, in 1929, entered the Law School. Dropping out after one semester, he took graduate courses in literature over the next two years, at Michigan and then at Harvard, and by 1930 poems of his had begun to appear in print. By summer 1931 the impact of the Depression had made itself increasingly felt and Roethke abandoned his doctoral plans. Turning to teaching, he took a position in the English Department at Lafayette College and began a career that led to his becoming the most renowned poet-teacher of his generation. His later teaching posts were at Michigan State College, Pennsylvania State University, Bennington College, and, from 1947 to his death on August 1, 1963, the University of Washington.

Roethke's first book, *Open House* (1941), won him critical acclaim, but it was *The Lost Son and Other Poems* (1948) that established him as one of the most gifted contemporary American poets. The journey of the self encountering its fears continued in *Praise to the End!* (1951), *The Waking* (1953), *The Exorcism* (1957), *Words for the Wind* (1958), his volume of children's poems, *I Am! Says the Lamb* (1961), and his posthumous *The Far Field* (1964), in which he returns for the last time to the greenhouse, to the father, and to the "far field" beyond the greenhouse. Roethke's body now lies buried in Saginaw, in Oakwood Cemetery, alongside the remains of his mother and father. The greenhouses are gone.

Sources and Further Reading: Theodore Roethke, *The Collected Poems* (1966); Theodore Roethke, *On the Poet and His Craft*, ed., Ralph J. Mills, Jr. (1965); Allen Seager, *The Glass House: The Life of Theodore Roethke* (1991).

Frank Kearful
Bonn University, Germany

Richard Wright (1908–1960)

Richard Wright's characters do for South Side Chicago what James Joyce's characters do for Dublin. They map out the territory as well as any cartographer. Wright was born in 1908 on Rucker's Plantation near Natchez, Mississippi, to Nathaniel Wright, an illiterate sharecropper, and Ella Wilson Wright, a schoolteacher. All four of his grandparents had been slaves. Marked by poverty, racism, and fear, Wright's childhood was a litany of misfortunes: His father abandoned the family when young Richard was six years old; his mother suffered a paralytic stroke; the mother kept moving around, once leaving Richard and his brother in an orphanage; they were always hungry; young Richard set the house ablaze; a white deputy sheriff killed his Uncle Hoskins because he was becoming too prosperous; and Richard's grandmother used her religion to brutally whip him and damn him to hell. Critics have remarked that Wright's traumatized childhood was more a blueprint for the making of a criminal than for an artist. Wright survived all the

Richard Wright. Library of Congress, Prints and Photographs Division, LC-USW3-030283-D.

hardships, managing to piece together eight or nine years of education.

He moved to Chicago during the Great Migration of the 1920s and worked as a postal clerk and for the Federal Writers' Project. He joined the John Reed Club, the literary group sponsored by the Communist Party. In 1939, he married a classical dancer of Russian Jewish descent and in 1941 divorced her for Ellen Poplar, a Jewish Communist Party organizer. By 1944, he had left the Communist Party. Believing that there was less racism in France, Wright went to Paris, where he met intellectuals such as Simone de Beauvoir and Jean-Paul Sartre. He died in Paris in 1960 at the age of fifty-two.

Wright wrote several collections of short stories and novels, including *Uncle Tom's Children* (1938), a collection of stories about southern racism; *Black Boy* (1945), his well-known autobiography of his childhood; *The Outsider* (1953), an existentialist work; *White Man, Listen!* (1957), a collection of essays; and *Eight Men* (1961), another collection of stories. Chicago provides the setting for Wright's posthumously published novels *Lawd Today!* (1963) and *American Hunger* (1977), as well as for *Native Son* (1940). Wright states in "How 'Bigger' Was Born," his preface to *Native Son*, that he wanted the novel to be "so hard and deep that [readers] would have to face it without the consolation of tears," unlike the experience of reading *Uncle Tom's Children*.

Native Son tells the story of Bigger Thomas and his family's maladjustment to their restrictive Chicago environment. The story opens with Bigger and his brother trying to kill a cornered rat, a foreshadowing of Bigger's fate. Their vermin-infested one-room kitchenette, a type of housing where several families share the same bathroom, is too small for Bigger's sister to maintain any sense of modesty. Bigger's mother wants him to get what she perceives as a good job, and so he takes a job as a chauffeur for a wealthy white family, the Daltons.

One night, Bigger brings home a drunken Mary Dalton. Worried about her intoxicated state, he takes her up to her bedroom. Mary's blind mother senses she is home and walks in the room. Frightened because he is a black man in a white woman's bedroom, Bigger smothers Mary's muffled moans so that her mother will think she is sleeping. When the mother leaves the room, Bigger discovers that he has suffocated Mary. Panicking, he takes the body down to the basement and stuffs it in the furnace, decapitating her so that she will fit. When the family and news reporters finally realize that Mary is missing, perhaps kidnapped, they first suspect her Communist boyfriend. It does not occur to them that Bigger is smart enough to have written the ransom note. Once the authorities start to look for him, Bigger begins hiding. While evading capture, he kills his black girlfriend, Bessie. The news media discuss him as a beast at bay. When finally captured, Bigger must stand trial for killing Mary. Although his Communist lawyer tries to show Bigger as a product of a racist environment, the jury convicts him. Although condemned to death, Bigger gains a greater sense of himself, taking responsibility for his actions, bringing him a certain type of freedom.

As an American novel, *Native Son* jointly reflects Wright's encounters with the politics and urban theories of post–World War II University of Chicago sociologists and the midwestern naturalism in the writings of Theodore Dreiser, James T. Farrell, Stephen Crane, Sinclair Lewis, and Frank Norris. As a black protest novel, *Native Son* challenges white benevolence and racism. Although Bigger's family is no longer in an oppressive southern environment, their lives are circumscribed in South Side Chicago, where restrictive housing covenants keep them segregated. Rather than the Promised Land of spirituals, Wright's Chicago was a seven-mile black metropolis where 90 percent of the black population lived in kitchenette buildings and hosted rent parties to make ends meet.

The author Margaret Walker, Wright's friend, points out that Chicago was two cities for Wright and other rural blacks who migrated north. At night, the city offered entertainment for those blacks expecting a faster-paced and less segregated life. Many musicians, including Duke Ellington, Cab Calloway, and Count Basie, entertained white and black audiences in such places as the Savoy Ballroom. Ella Fitzgerald and others sang at the Regal Theatre. During the day, as Walker notes, racism was more apparent, as whites and blacks rode the elevated trains "with poker faces and no overt hostility but a studied indifference."

Wright's fiction describes a world where the relationships between blacks and whites are bitter. He captures the anger of racial oppression. His essay "Blueprint for Negro Writing" demonstrates his concern for the future of black American literature. Throughout his life Wright wrote about native sons who were treated as second-class citizens and outsiders in their own nation.

Sources and Further Reading: David Bakish, *Richard Wright* (1973); Robert Butler, *The Critical Response to Richard Wright* (1995); Carla Cappetti, "Sociology of Existence: Richard Wright and the Chicago School," *MELUS: The Journal of the Society for the Study of the Multi-Ethnic Literature of the United States* 12 (Summer 1985); Michel Fabre, *The World of Richard Wright* (1985); Maryemma Graham, ed., *Richard Wright: A Special Issue* (1986); Keneth Kinnamon, ed., *New Essays on Native Son* (1990); Hazel Rowley, *Richard Wright: The Life and Times* (2001); Margaret Walker, *Richard Wright: Daemonic Genius* (1988).

Valerie Lee
The Ohio State University–Columbus

Nelson Algren (1909–1981)

Born in 1909, Nelson Ahlgren Abraham grew up in Chicago and became one of its best-known naturalistic writers. The only son of a Swedish Jewish machinist and his German Jewish wife, he won the first National Book Award (1950) for *The Man with the Golden Arm* (1949), which became a breakthrough film for Frank Sinatra. Algren was soon known as a "Chicago writer" and was hailed for his portraits of life on Division Street.

Algren's political stance was initially formed by experience outside Chicago. He attended the University of Illinois, graduating in journalism (1931). Thrust into the Great Depression, he found both jobs and ideals scarce. He hitchhiked and hopped freight trains to the South, spending time in New Orleans, then drifted to the Rio Grande Valley with a con man who set him up as the fall guy in a crime. His early experiences shattered Algren's ideals: He felt that everything he had been told was wrong, that social institutions had lied to him. Like the Russian novelist Maksim Gorky, his hero, he saw literature as something that challenged institutions through its compassionate humanism.

He returned to Chicago determined to write, taking his experiences to the Writers' Circle at the Jewish People's Institute. Algren modeled himself partially on his peripatetic paternal grandfather, a Swede who converted to Judaism and, later, Socialism. When sending out manuscripts, however, he dropped "Abraham" for "Algren," feeling that the Midwest allowed him freedom in self-fashioning. Soon he submitted to *Story*, which bought a piece and expressed interest in more work. At the John Reed Club, he heard fellow naturalists Richard Wright and James T. Farrell speak.

His publication in *Story* led Vanguard Press to give Algren a one-hundred-dollar advance on a novel. He returned to the Southwest to write about life on the skids. After four months of research in Texas, Algren was ready to return when he stole a typewriter, was arrested, and spent a month in jail awaiting trial. Texas gave him an education in boredom, racism, and gratuitous cruelty. Back in Chicago, Algren finished *Somebody in Boots* (1935), a picaresque road novel. Like much proletarian fiction of the era, it is marred by didactic broadsides; but parts occur in Chicago, and it shows an ear for dialogue and hints of his lifelong themes: personal betrayal and the failure of love. Algren then worked five years as an editor for the Works Progress Administration's Illinois Writers' Project, deepening his knowledge of Chicago; he also edited a leftist magazine, *The New Anvil*. Meanwhile, he wrote the story of Bruno Bicek, a Polish boxer in a Chicago slum who turns to crime and murder after allowing gang-member friends to rape his girl. Algren's characters now were mostly from the Division Street neighborhood he insistently inhabited: Poles, boxers, and card players.

After serving in the U.S. Army (1942–1945), Algren began his most productive decade. His work was collected in *The Neon Wilderness* (1947), which contains such celebrated stories as "Design for Departure" and "A Bottle of Milk for Mother." In 1947 he met Simone de Beauvoir; they spent vacations together for the next four years before their unusual affair ended. During this period he was writing *The Man with the Golden Arm* (1949), his best novel and the first serious treatment of drug addiction in American literature. The story of card dealer and morphine addict Frankie Machine, his wife Sophie, his mistress Molly, and his friend Sparrow explores betrayal and predation, self-sacrifice and love. The novel shifts in tone from bleak, urban despair to humor and midwestern

grotesquerie. It established Algren as a major writer and, because it was a "neighborhood novel," confirmed Chicago as the most important locale of 1950s naturalism. Critics hailed its complex female characters, its symbolism, the credible determinism, and the poetic diction. It is also a compendium of drug information and introduced the phrase "monkey on his back." The 1955 film, directed by Otto Preminger for United Artists, though it was the first to break the Production Code ban on portraying drug use, was sanitized and served Sinatra's blossoming career. In the novel, Frankie commits suicide, but in the film Sophie's death frees him to leave town with Molly.

Algren's 1951 prose poem, *Chicago: City on the Make*, recalls Carl Sandburg but won Algren no friends, as it traces the psychobiography of urban hustler–dom rather than heroic labor. Superimposing past and present, Algren created a historic montage in highly metaphoric language. *A Walk on the Wild Side* (1956), though it repeats some themes of *Somebody in Boots*, is Algren's other major novel. Cass, another young, illiterate Texan, drifts to New Orleans and involvement in a sex show. Though Cass and other characters exist on the thinnest of margins, Algren still finds meaning, even comedy, in their lives. Deemed nihilistic by some critics, the novel won younger admirers and broke the barrier for later films such as *Midnight Cowboy* (1969) and *Easy Rider* (1969). Much of Algren's writing in the 1960s and 1970s was journalism, which was collected in *The Last Carousel* (1973). On assignment for *Esquire* in 1974, Algren went to Paterson, New Jersey, to research the murder trial of boxer Rubin "Hurricane" Carter. *Esquire* dropped the story, but Algren stayed on. He died of a heart attack in 1981, before his excellent account, *The Devil's Stocking* (1983), appeared. Other posthumous works are *America Eats* (1993) and *Nonconformity: Writing on Writing* (1994).

During his life, Algren was praised by Richard Wright, Carl Sandburg, and Ernest Hemingway. After his death, Studs Terkel predicted that his writings would outlast those taught in academia. Ross Macdonald wrote that the intensity of Algren's feeling and the accuracy of his thought made him the most important questioner of democracy in his day. He was a significant predecessor to writers ranging from Saul Bellow to Raymond Carver and David Mamet. Among Chicago writers he stands in the first rank.

Sources and Further Reading: Simone de Beauvoir, *The Force of Circumstance*, trans. Richard Howard (1965); Martha Heasley Cox and Wayne Chatterton, *Nelson Algren* (1975); H.E.F. Donohue, *Conversations with Nelson Algren* (1964); Betina Drew, *Nelson Algren* (1989); James R. Giles, *Confronting the Horror* (1989); James A. Lewin, "A Jew from East

Jesus: The Yiddishkeit of Nelson Algren," *Midamerica* 21 (1994); Robert C. Rosen, "Anatomy of a Movie Junkie," in Gerald Peary and Roger Shatzkin, eds., *The Modern American Novel and the Movies* (1978); Arthur Shay, *Nelson Algren's Chicago* (1988).

William Marling
Case Western Reserve University, Ohio

Wright Morris (1910–1998)

Born in Central City, Nebraska, Wright Morris was the only surviving child of Will and Grace Osborn Morris. His mother's death within a week of his birth in 1910 rendered him "half an orphan," as he put it, and precipitated an emotional distance between himself and his father. In time, this led him to a series of meditations on being and identity, some including literary doubles, giving much of his work a haunted quality. Inheriting his father's wanderlust, he relished solo road trips, including a "photo-safari" in 1940–1941, when he traveled extensively across the United States to photograph American structures and objects in which human meanings were imbedded. His adventitious rediscovery of Nebraska when he was in his

Writer-photographer Wright Morris's *Reflection in Oval Mirror, Home Place, 1947.* Photo by Wright Morris, Collection Center for Creative Photography © Arizona Board of Regents, LC-DIG-cwpb-05620 DLC.

thirties set the main themes for his mature work, in which energy is derived from a confluence of memory, imagination, and meditation on the mysteries of time.

Morris is of particular interest to considerations of regionalism for two reasons: first, his identity as a borderland westerner-midwesterner born on the hundredth meridian, a point he emphasizes frequently; second, his dual career as writer and photographer. Regarding the latter, Morris began with mixed intentions, a challenge he resolved early by pairing photographs with word sketches and short narratives. During the Depression, the idea of "photo-text" was widespread, but Morris was unique in creating *both* photographs and words. His career began with a photo-text entitled "The Inhabitants," which was exhibited at the New School for Social Research, published in *New Directions 1940*, and expanded into *The Inhabitants* (1946).

Morris published more than thirty books of fiction, photo-text, and criticism. His first of nineteen novels, *My Uncle Dudley*, appeared in 1942; his last, *Plains Song*, in 1980. His most important book of criticism was *The Territory Ahead* (1958), in which he both placed himself inside American literary tradition and asserted his independence from it. There he criticized many canonical American writers for their subjection to nostalgia for the mythic past—a crucial theme in all his work.

Clues to Morris's conception of the Midwest are found in his introduction to an edition of Sherwood Anderson's *Windy McPherson's Son* (1965). There he emphasizes the centrality of Chicago for midwestern imaginations by recalling the maps that used to hang on the walls of railroad stations: The lines converged on the city like spokes toward a hub. Morris also draws a broad distinction between Anderson's world and his own: Whereas Anderson's characters *walk* from place to place, Morris's are creatures of the automobile and the mobility and mores associated with it.

Morris's regionalism is most clearly found in five or six novels, two photo-texts, and one of his three memoirs. A pivotal work is *The Home Place* (1948), in which Morris combined photographs, most of which he had taken at his Uncle Harry and Aunt Clara's dilapidated Nebraska farm, and a written text in which Harry and Clara serve as fictional characters. Morris uses the tension between fictional narrative and factual photographs as a thematic subtext to support a spirited defense of personal privacy. Considered mythically, the photographs in *The Home Place* generalize the experience of rural life as experienced on American frontiers across time.

In several works that followed, Morris seemed intensely aware of his midwestern roots, but he exercised skepticism toward rural virtues and values. In the novel *The World in the Attic* (1949), for which his editor disallowed photographs, Morris combines two motifs—the "revolt from the village" and the return of the (Nebraska) native—and probes the "home-town nausea" on the other side of nostalgia.

Morris's bleakest look at the Midwest is found in the powerful *The Works of Love* (1952), which he worked on for six years following his father's death—exaggerating both his father's life and his own. Dedicated in part to Sherwood Anderson, the novel begins "[w]est of the 98th Meridian" and ends in Chicago, with protagonist Will Brady falling to his death in a sewage canal. That Brady is dressed for his department store role as Santa Claus suggests his failed desire for transcendence.

Perhaps the two greatest works of Morris's career were the comic novel *The Field of Vision* (1956) and its sequel, *Ceremony in Lone Tree* (1960), both of which are critical of midwestern American civilization: Morris's particular targets are narrow-mindedness, fear of risk, and nostalgia for the past. *The Field of Vision* develops its critique from a bullfight arena in Mexico, where Gordon Boyd, along with his "psychological adviser" and another odd patient, encounters some old Nebraska friends, including the woman Boyd had avoided marrying many years before.

Most of the characters from *Field* (along with many new ones) are carried into *Ceremony in Lone Tree*, set in a jittery Nebraska just after real-life mass murderer Charles Starkweather (in the novel renamed Munger) has been captured. *Ceremony* reconsiders the satire of the earlier novel, as Morris more compassionately explores the motives of the characters, who have come together ostensibly to celebrate Tom Scanlon's ninetieth birthday. The novel manages both to criticize outdated reliance on the western frontier myth as a source of heroism and to honor the myth's motivational power.

Finally, after two decades of novels set mostly outside the Midwest, Morris returned to the Nebraska setting in *Plains Song* (1980), a novel based loosely on his Aunt Clara (in this account named Cora Atkins) and her niece, Sharon Rose. The novel is a bittersweet paean to women in American social history, from the perspective of three generations of women. Its basic themes are the perennial attraction of the home place amid cultural change and the potential for women as agents of freedom and meaning.

Some of the essential autobiographical elements of Morris's Midwest are found in the photo-text *God's Country and My People* (1968), and they are explored more fully in his first memoir, *Will's Boy* (1981)—books of special interest because they provide perspective from Morris's approaching old age. Morris died in 1998. His honors include three Guggenheim fellowships (two in support of his photography), the National Book Award for *The Field of Vision*, and the American Book Award for *Plains Song*.

Sources and Further Reading: James Alinder, ed., *Wright Morris: Photographs and Words* (1982); Roy K. Bird, *Wright Morris: Memory and Imagination* (1985); G. B. Crump, *The Novels of Wright Morris* (1978); Leon Howard, *Wright Morris* (1968); Robert Knoll, ed., *Conversations with Wright Morris* (1977); David Madden, *Wright Morris* (1964); Sandra S. Phillips and John Szarkowski, *Wright Morris: Origin of a Species* (1992); Joseph J. Wydeven, *Wright Morris Revisited* (1998).

Joseph J. Wydeven
Bellevue University, Nebraska

Studs Terkel (b. 1912)

No one has done more to expand the midwestern literary tradition and its library of voices than Studs Terkel. Called the "inheritor of the unfinished business of Chicago realism, through the province of oral history" by noted poet Michael Anania, Terkel was included among thirty-five Illinois authors (from the "Chicago School") whose names were etched into the frieze of the Illinois State Library when its new building was dedicated in 1990.

Born Louis Terkel in New York on May 16, 1912, his life spans nearly an entire century. He has observed it, recorded it, interpreted it, and lived it. His father, Samuel, a Jewish tailor, and his mother, Anna (Finkel), a seamstress, moved the family to the Midwest in 1922 and opened a rooming house at Ashland and Flournoy on the near West Side of Chicago. From 1926 to 1936 they ran another rooming house, the Wells-Grand Hotel, at Wells Street and Grand Avenue, where young "Studs" (renamed after author James T. Farrell's famous character Studs Lonigan) was essentially oriented to working-class life along with his brothers.

Arguably, Terkel became America's best interviewer, and, certainly, one of its best talkers by listening to the stories of retired firemen, Wobblies, merchant seamen, and the Great-Unheard-From in the lobby of the Wells-Grand. From his daily conversations with these men and the occasional passersby at Bughouse Square, Terkel was already seeking, in his own words, to gather "history from the bottom up."

He attended the University of Chicago, where he received a law degree in 1934. He was no Clarence Darrow, however, and chose not to pursue a career in law but turned to acting instead. However, he was influenced enough by the University of Chicago's Sociology Department to seek out Philip Hauser, its chairman, in doing research methodology for what became his first oral-history book, *Division Street, America*.

Studs sustained himself by playing gangster roles in radio soap operas during the Depression, and he acted in agitprop theatre (a worker's theatre movement of the 1920s and 1930s, influenced by the mobile street theatre popular in Russia) with the famed Chicago Repertory Group, appearing in *Waiting for Lefty*. Terkel went on relief first with the Federal Emergency Relief Administration and then joined the Works Progress Administration's Illinois Writers' Project, where he excelled as a radio scriptwriter from 1935 to 1942, when the project folded. He was also one of the pioneers of labor radio in the Midwest who helped form the American Federation of Radio Artists (AFRA) in 1937. In 1939 he married Ida Goldberg, and they had one son.

After a year in the air force, he returned to writing radio shows and ads. In 1944, he landed his own show, called the *Wax Museum*, on WENR. As a liberal disc jockey and radio announcer for the Independent Voters of Illinois he reached an even broader audience on WCFL, Chicago's voice of labor. From the 1940s through the 1960s Terkel was among many producers at educational and noncommercial radio stations in the Midwest who were experimenting with the new forms of voicing and production made possible by analog tape. But it was through the improvisational *Studs' Place* in 1949 that Terkel made the greatest contributions to what has been called "Television Chicago style."

Studs' Place, which first aired during November 1949, took its place (along with *Garroway at Large* and *Kukla, Fran and Ollie*) in broadcast history. Set in a tavern (like *Cheers*) with Studs as proprietor, it featured an improvisational style that became the signature of Chicago television. However, by 1951 Studs's path was overshadowed by Wisconsin senator Joesph McCarthy's Communist witch hunt. Terkel's name appeared in "Red Channels: The Report of Communist Influence in Radio and Television" (1950), for he had signed Communist petitions in the 1930s and 1940s. Thus sponsors backed out of his show and he was blacklisted for a couple of years. Although his television career ended in 1951, within a year he would be writing and producing for radio again. In addition, Terkel would go on to star in films like John Sayles's *Eight Men Out* (1987).

In 1952, Terkel began working for WFMT, first producing the *Studs Terkel Almanac* and then *The Studs Terkel Show*, primarily to give exposure to folk culture and its music. Both broadcasts reached not only a midwestern audience but also a national cable audience in 200 cities and 30 states, in addition to 161 international stations via the Armed Forces Network. As the on-air host for forty-five years of *The Studs Terkel Program*, and because he was nationally syndicated, his interviews were eventually compiled into spoken-word programs and special radio documentaries including *Born to Live* (1962), which won the 1962 Prix Italia radio documentary prize; *This Train* (1963), an account of the Freedom Ride to Washington, D.C.; and *Hard Times: An Oral History of the Great Depression*.

Through his oral-history books Terkel helped define the "common man" typically found working in the Rust Belt. More than any other of his books, *Working* (1974) broke through to the stage and screen and was the subject of a teaching guide by Rick Ayers. As a member of the Illinois Labor History Society, Terkel took on the role of a voice for Midwest labor. He befriended Ed Sadlowski, a young steelworker who had won a rank-and-file victory over the candidate supported by Steelworkers' president I. W. Abel. In *Hard Times* (1970) Terkel explored the essential "Three Strikes" as his oral-history informants remembered the 1936 United Automobile Workers (UAW) sit-down, the Memorial Day Massacre at Republic Steel in 1937, and the 1940 UAW strike at Ford in Detroit.

On September 29, 1997, President Bill Clinton awarded the prestigious National Humanities Medal to Terkel for his lifetime of achievement, dubbing him "America's oral historian." In 1999, the Illinois Humanities Council launched the Studs Terkel Humanities Service Award to honor participation in the humanities by citizens of Illinois.

Like Nelson Algren, Terkel looked beyond the postcard Chicago into the real Chicago and thus reinforced the city's identity, in *Division Street: America* (1967) and *Chicago* (1986). Terkel never labeled himself an "oral historian" and preferred to call what he was doing "guerilla journalism." However, he is considered an innovator in modern ethnographic research.

The national exposure lost to him during the 1950s blacklisting was regained as he won the Pulitzer Prize for *The Good War* (1984), and published another dozen or so best-selling books, including *Working, American Dreams: Lost and Found* (1980), *Race* (1992), *Coming of Age* (1995), *My American Century* (1997), *The Great Divide* (1998), *Will the Circle Be Unbroken?* (2001), and *Hope Dies Last* (2003). Terkel was formally recognized again on May 16, 2002, when Studs Terkel Day was proclaimed by Mayor Richard Daley and the City of Chicago. His career is documented in his archives at the Chicago Historical Society, where he has been Distinguished Scholar in Residence since 1998.

Sources and Further Reading: Michael Anania, *In Plain Sight* (1993); James T. Baker, *Studs Terkel* (1992); Nathan Godfried, *WCFL: Chicago's Voice of Labor, 1926–78* (1997).

Alan H. Stein
New Orleans

Robert E. Hayden (1913–1980)

Born Asa Bundy Sheffey in 1913, Hayden was adopted by William and Sue Ellen Hayden, changing his name to Robert Earl Hayden. Hayden grew up in Detroit's Paradise Valley neighborhood, which, during his youth, changed from a mixed community populated by African Americans and eastern and southern European immigrants to an overwhelmingly black ghetto as African American migrants poured in, primarily from the Deep South, to work in the factories of Detroit. Paradise Valley was also the heart of a thriving black entertainment district centered on the blues and jazz clubs of Hastings Street. Poor health, especially eye problems; domestic violence; and much conflict with his religious foster parents dogged Hayden's childhood. The disapproval of his father promoted a strong feeling of sinfulness in him. This sense of sinfulness, which deepened as his sexual attraction to men became clearer to him, as well as a religious bent that went both with and against his parents' evangelical Christianity, profoundly marked Hayden's poetry and life.

Hayden attended Detroit City College (now Wayne State University). After graduating in 1936, he worked on the Federal Writers' Project (FWP), a job that provided him his first serious opportunity to systematically investigate African American history and culture. Following his tenure at the FWP, he served as editor and critic for the *Michigan Chronicle*, a pro-labor Detroit subsidiary of Sengstacke Enterprises and probably the most important black newspaper in Michigan at the time. While working at the FWP and for the *Chronicle*, he became active in the lively political and artistic milieu of the Communist left in Detroit, participating in the Detroit branch of the John Reed Clubs and reading his poetry at political demonstrations and at union meetings and rallies. The publisher of the *Chronicle*, Louis Martin, encouraged Hayden to publish his poetry, arranging for the printing in 1940 of a collection of Hayden's radical poetry, *Heart-Shape in the Dust*. Also in 1940 Hayden married Erma Morris—and essentially repressed his homosexual desires.

Hayden left the newspaper to attend graduate school at the University of Michigan, receiving a master's degree in English in 1944. Under the direction of the noted British poet W. H. Auden, an assistant professor in the Michigan English department during the early 1940s, Hayden wrote a group of poems that engaged the history of African Americans in the United States, particularly their arrival in the slave era and their formation as a people with a coherent identity. As part of this project Hayden wrote some of his most famous poems, including "Middle Passage" and "The Ballad of Nat Turner," winning the Hopwood Award

in 1942. During this time, Hayden joined the Baha'i faith (a religion emphasizing the spiritual unity of humanity), moving away from both his earlier radical politics and his parents' Christianity while retaining the notion of a universalist rejection of racism and an attachment to spirituality.

The Fisk University English Department hired Hayden in 1946, and he remained at Fisk for more than two decades. In the late 1960s, he returned to the English Department at the University of Michigan, his institutional base for the rest of his life. Hayden published eight books of poetry after his appointment at Fisk. While he gained some attention, particularly among black artists and intellectuals, as a first-rate poet who wrote in a vein much influenced by the high modernists, he did not really achieve a substantial national reputation until the publication of *Selected Poems* in 1966. That same year he became a lightning rod for artistic and intellectual debates within the African American community after a famously contentious exchange with the poet Melvin Tolson at the 1966 Fisk Negro Writers Conference. In that exchange, Hayden proclaimed his allegiance to a universalist artistic credo, wishing to be known as a "poet," not a "Negro poet." Tolson claimed that such a universalism was impossible and such a desire, a retreat before racism. Thereafter, Hayden was taken by some Black Arts Movement militants to embody old-fashioned assimilationism—though many writers of the movement greatly admired Hayden's historical poems and his craftsmanship. In 1976, Hayden became the first African American to be appointed consultant in poetry to the Library of Congress (a forerunner to the current position of national poet laureate). He died in 1980.

Hayden is justly famous for his powerful historical poems as well as for his technical skill. His ability to modulate between abstraction and evocative detail while suggesting a restrained emotion that might at any moment overwhelm the poem's structure, the poem's speaker, the poet, and the reader makes his more personal lyrics a moving reading experience. However, a less considered aspect of Hayden's work is the degree to which he documented and memorialized the Great Migration to the industrial Midwest. In his early work, such as "Sunflowers: Beaubien Street," he invoked the transposition of the history and culture of black people in the rural South to the urban setting of Paradise Valley. Later, near the end of his life, in a more direct and less ornate manner than characterized his early work, Hayden elegized not only his childhood but the original neighborhoods where the black migrants to the urban North first lived, communities like Paradise Valley with its vibrant Hastings Street music scene that had been virtually obliterated by so-called urban renewal or urban decay (or both). In particular, Hayden's "Elegies for Paradise Valley" evokes a virtually lost midwestern world, a world marked by an intense northern version of Jim Crow segregation but also by a dynamic secular and sacred culture. It directly engages, for the first time since his earliest published poetry, the feelings of homoerotic desire and sinfulness that shaped much of Hayden's young emotional life. This poetic series locates the speaker, a young Robert Hayden, in the powerful loves and hates, pleasures and terrors, of a boy growing up in a world that he recalls lest the reader forget:

> Where's mad Miss Alice, who ate from garbage cans?
> Where's snuffdipping Lucy, who played us 'chunes'
> on her guitar? Where's Hattie? Where's Melissabelle?
> Let vanished rooms, let dead streets tell.

Sources and Further Reading: Laurence Goldstein and Robert Chrisman, eds., *Robert Hayden: Essays on the Poetry* (2001); James C. Hall, *Mercy, Mercy Me* (2001); Robert Earl Hayden, *Collected Poems*, ed., Frederick Glaysher (1985); Pontheolla T. Williams, *Robert Hayden: A Critical Analysis of His Poetry* (1987).

James Smethurst
University of Massachusetts–Amherst

Saul Bellow (1915–2005)

Saul Bellow's fiction derives directly from both European and midwestern literary traditions. Like William Dean Howells, Theodore Dreiser, and Sherwood Anderson, he has worked against the dehumanizing influence of technology, rationalism, naturalism, and absurdism. Chicago is his enduring symbol, of both the American ideal of progress and the deadly legacy of modernism. He told Joyce Illig in 1973 that

> All of civilized mankind is entering this peculiar condition in which we were pioneers. That's why Chicago is significant. We experienced it before the others did. We experienced the contemporary condition before others were aware of it. . . . Chicago is, I believe, the symbol of it. In Chicago, things were done for the first time, which the rest of the world later learned and imitated. Capitalist production was pioneered in the stockyards, in refrigerator cars, in the creation of the Pullman, in the creation of farm machinery, and with it also certain urban political phenomena which are associated with the new condition of modern democracy. All that happened here. It happened early.

Born in Lachine, Montreal, Canada, on June 10, 1915, Saul was the fourth child of Abraham Bellow and Lescha "Liza" Bellow, both of whom had immigrated from St. Petersburg, Russia, in 1913. In 1924, the family left Lachine for the tenements of Humboldt Park, Chicago, which in the 1920s boasted a population of about 225,000. Saul attended Lafayette School, Columbus Elementary School, and Sabin Junior High and then graduated from Tuley High School on Chicago's northwest side in 1933. That year he entered the University of Chicago, and he transferred to Northwestern University in 1935. For much of his life Bellow taught at the University of Chicago, and in 1976 he won the Nobel Prize for Literature. He died on April 5, 2005.

Within the white androcentric world of Bellow's novels there are a disturbingly predictable number of misogynistic and racial stereotypes, and only one female protagonist. Many of the books hinge upon failed male/male relationships. In *Dangling Man* (1944) and *The Victim* (1947), Joseph and Asa suffer increasing alienation as they search somewhat unsuccessfully for sustaining moral truths in the face of nightmarish Chicago conditions. *The Adventures of Augie March* (1953), Bellow's ebullient portrayal of 1930s Chicago, owes even its Mexican adventure to Bellow's Tuley High School exposure to Nathan Gould, a notable Chicago-based Trotskyite. Augie March is a Cervantesque picaro, whose fictional landscape is woven of Dreiserian realism, Whitmanesque catalogs, Dickensian character portraits, vernacular language, Bellovian homily, and scenes from the old Chicago ethnic neighborhoods. *Seize the Day* (1956) features the absurd hero Tommy Wilhelm, who discovers the charlatanism of the commercial world as well as the literal holiness of the human heart in an epiphanic moment in the Chicago subway. *Henderson the Rain King* (1959), a dreamscape of Africa, is an elaborate transcendental parody of the modern hero, modern philosophy, and Hemingwayesque literary formulas. *Herzog* (1964), his masterwork, depicts Moses Herzog, an embattled Chicago academic whose romantic impulses—sexual, spiritual, and intellectual—are severely tested in 1960s Chicago. Bellow's summa on the Chicago condition of late modernity, it foregrounds Chicago politics and vivid downtown scenes. In *Mr. Sammler's Planet* (1970), Mr. Sammler, a fastidious Polish-Oxonian displaced person and Holocaust survivor, believes that civilization is being threatened again by destructive 1960s hippies. Now in his old age, he prays over Elya Gruner's body, and finally understands that all human beings are accountable for one another because each knows the value of a human life: "For that is the truth of it— that we all know, God, that we know, that we know, we know, we know." *Humboldt's Gift* (1975), Bellow's 1970s portrait of Chicago, features Charlie Citrine, a

Chicago writer with a taste for gangland excitement and pneumatic young women, who seeks to retrieve the poetic gift he has almost lost. In Chicago, he observes, you could truly "examine the human spirit under industrialism" in all its agony and nightmare. He must continue to exert the equal sovereignty of the human imagination over modern science. The miracle of a small crocus growing out through the cracks of the Chicago pavement convinces him that much of the spirit is still there despite the urban nightmare. *To Jerusalem and Back* (1976) shows Bellow's neoconservative ambivalence about the Jewish state. *The Dean's December* (1982) features Albert Corde, a Chicago academic, who travels to Budapest with his Romanian wife. This tale of two cities compares a decaying Fascist Europe to a decaying democratic America, noting both cultures' broken political systems, doomed underclass populations, inhuman prison systems, failed intellectual elites, and dishonest media. *More Die of Heartbreak* (1987) is full of misogynistic love lore, botched loves, fatal forays into sex and romance, and crackpot sexual philosophizing. It registers Bellow's comic despair over the modern impasse in heterosexual relations. *A Theft* (1989) further describes the hijinks of the heterosexual human pair in what Bellow now calls gogmagogsville—a frightening jungle of ethnic others. It focuses on the theft of the human heart and the classic evasions of the male lover. *The Bellarosa Connection* (1989) features an unnamed memory freak who mourns his loss of human love, his lifelong amnesia with regard to the Holocaust, and his lost Jewish soul. *The Actual* (1997) is the ironic story of Harry's unrequited adolescent love for Amy Wustrin, his "actual," in whom he has invested half a century of longing. *Ravelstein* (2000) is a fictional autoethnography in which Chick (Saul Bellow) memorializes the now departed Ravelstein (Allan Bloom, Bellow's colleague at the University of Chicago). This Chicago-based book shows Chick gradually accepting Ravelstein's legacy to him of their shared Russian Jewish origins, voices, and Jewish moral anxiety.

It was Chicago and the Midwest that fired Saul Bellow's imagination, provided his landscapes and characters, and shaped his antimodernist social philosophy. While Dreiser's career as a Chicago-based writer inspired him to draw on this material, it was James Joyce's use of Dublin to describe the modern moment that really inspired Bellow to see in the ethos of Chicago all the manifestations of modernity that thrilled and appalled him.

Sources and Further Reading: James Atlas, *Bellow: A Biography* (2000); Joyce Illig, "An Interview with Saul Bellow," *Publisher's Weekly* (Oct. 22, 1973); *Saul Bellow Journal* (bian-nual); *Saul Bellow Society*, http://www.saulbellow.org (update, 2003).

Gloria L. Cronin
Brigham Young University, Utah

Gwendolyn Elizabeth Brooks (1917–2000)

Gwendolyn Brooks was poet laureate of Illinois from 1968 to 2000. A self-proclaimed Chicagoan, Brooks was actually born in Topeka, Kansas, on June 7, 1917, to native-born, middle-class Kansans David Anderson Brooks and Keziah Corinne Wims. David and Keziah were married in 1916, and their union produced two children, Gwendolyn and her brother Raymond, who was sixteen months younger. The family relocated to the South Side of Chicago when Gwendolyn was five weeks old.

Before Gwendolyn was five, her mother was encouraging her creativity by having her rehearse recitations for their church programs. Both parents supported Gwendolyn's budding writing talent, her mother by completing most of the domestic chores to give Gwendolyn ample time to write, and her father by providing her with a writing desk that included space for her book collection, which he revered as much as his daughter did. Gwendolyn began writing poetry by the age of seven and compiling her creations in a composition notebook by age eleven. She was delighted when her mother happily prophesied that Gwendolyn was destined to become the "*lady* Paul Laurence Dunbar." She wrote at least a poem or two a day, and her first published poem was "Eventide," which appeared in *American Childhood* magazine (1930). By 1934, she had published more than seventy-five poems in the *Chicago Defender's* "Lights and Shadows" poetry column, and soon after she compiled her first unpublished manuscript, *Songs after Sunset* (1935–1936).

Brooks was educated in public schools on the South Side of Chicago and graduated from Forrestville Elementary School, Englewood High School (1934), and Wilson Junior College (1936). At an early age, she was an avid reader and patron of the neighborhood library. Her favorite works included Countee Cullen's anthology *Caroling Dusk* (1927), which introduced Brooks to many writers of New York's Harlem Renaissance, and poet Langston Hughes's *The Weary Blues* (1926), which influenced Brooks to write about ordinary black folk, much as Hughes had done throughout his life. Additionally, Brooks broadened her literary repertoire to include the works of E. E. Cummings, T. S. Eliot, and Ezra Pound.

In 1938, when they were both twenty-one, mutual

friends introduced Brooks to fellow poet Henry Low-ington Blakely II at a youth council meeting at the local YWCA. Following a two-year courtship, the two married and moved into the first of several kitchenette apartments in Chicago's South Side community of Bronzeville, known as the Black Belt because of its high concentration of black residents. Gwendolyn and Henry had two children, Henry III (b. 1940) and Nora (b. 1951).

As Brooks was striving for literary maturity during the 1930s and 1940s, she was able to hone her poetic skills by being in the company of highly acclaimed writers like Richard Wright and Margaret Walker, both of whom lived in Chicago for brief periods as they worked on a project called "The Negro in Illinois" (1936–1942), under the auspices of the Works Progress Administration's Federal Writers' Project. By 1941, Brooks had formalized her writing instruction by joining a writers' group that included poets Margaret Burroughs, William Couch, and Margaret Danner. The group met at the South Side Community Arts Center and was led by Inez Cunningham Stark, a fashionable North Side socialite, critic, lecturer, president of the University of Chicago's Renaissance Society (1936–1940), and patron of *Poetry* magazine.

During her life, Brooks published more than twenty books, including poetry, prose, fiction, and autobiography. Her first poetry collection was *A Street in Bronzeville* (1945). In May 1950, she was awarded the Pulitzer Prize for her second collection, *Annie Allen* (1949); she was the first black writer to win the prize. Her one novel, *Maud Martha*, was published in 1953; she also published two children's books, *Bronzeville Boys and Girls* (1956) and *Children Coming Home* (1991), and two autobiographies, *Report from Part One* (1972) and *Report from Part Two* (1996).

Brooks remains highly acclaimed for her adroitness in merging character vignettes developed from Chicago's Bronzeville community and intertwining those stories with the complex structures of European poetic forms like the sonnet, folk and literary ballads, terza rima, and rhyme royal. Some examples of these prosodic and metrical techniques are visible in poems like the "The Gay Chaps at the Bar" sonnet series and "The Anniad." Additionally, she honed the rhythmic flow of form with rhetorical strategies like anaphora, alliteration, epistrophe, and polyptoton in poems like "the mother," "The Lovers of the Poor," and "In the Mecca." Although Brooks was not as form conscious in her post-1967 poetry, often employing free verse to tell a succinct story, she still manipulated story and structure with the flourish of schemes of repetition, such as anadiplosis and epanalepsis, in place of strict metrical lines.

In her poetry, Gwendolyn Brooks expresses the universal human condition. She looked at her all-black community of Bronzeville and, in poems like "kitchenette building," wrote about the life-wrenching poverty and oppression that threatened to suffocate its residents, yet she was a humanist whose vision was sufficiently broad to see and articulate the ills that afflicted the world. While Brooks was a regionalist who wrote about the ever-raging fires of racism that held economic and social equality at bay for black Americans, especially in her own community of Bronzeville, she was also a universalist who, in poems like "The Chicago *Defender* Sends a Man to Little Rock," addressed the dire racial and social conditions in America that have long been fueled by the nation's racial ambivalence. Later poems like "Medgar Evers" and "Malcolm X" suggest her commitment to the civil rights struggles of the 1960s and the impact of the new black cultural consciousness on her poetic direction.

Gwendolyn Brooks's many honors and awards confirm the stature she earned as one of America's most acclaimed poets. She died in Chicago on December 3, 2000.

Sources and Further Reading: B.J. Bolden, *Urban Rage in Bronzeville* (1999); Gwendolyn Brooks, *Blacks* (1987); Gwendolyn Brooks, *Report from Part One* (1972); St. Clair Drake and Horace Cayton, *Black Metropolis*, rev. ed. (1962); D.H. Melhem, *Gwendolyn Brooks: Poetry and the Heroic Voice* (1987).

B.J. Bolden
Chicago State University

J.F. Powers (1917–1999)

Few fiction writers of high critical standing have published so little or worked in such narrow range as J.F. Powers. His half-century career resulted in just two novels and three collections of short stories, nearly all of them about Catholic priests pursuing their temporal careers as midlevel managers of the church. A Catholic himself, Powers presents his clerical figures in a gently ironic light, as neither saints nor sinners, caught between belief in both realms and the immediate business of the here and now. From their divided state emerges both amusing comedy and the underlying suggestion that they are stand-ins for similar, if less apparent, conflict within all men at all times.

Born in Jacksonville, Illinois, in 1917, James Farl Powers finished high school in Quincy, worked at various jobs in Chicago, and took night courses at Northwestern University. Influenced by the pacifism of Dorothy Day and the Catholic Worker movement, he was a conscientious objector during World War II. In the 1950s he took his wife, the writer Betty Wahl, and five children to Ireland (the subject of a rare nonclerical story, "Tinkers"), thereafter dividing his time for some years between Ireland and the Midwest. Eventually he settled in Minnesota, teaching creative writing courses at St. John's University until his death in 1999.

The upper Midwest provides the setting for most of Powers's fiction, a rural and small-town world with the Twin Cities and Chicago shimmering just beyond. But it is the human comedy within the region's rectories, retreat centers, and chancery offices that holds center stage—a human comedy that is also a muted spiritual drama. In "Prince of Darkness," Father Ernest Burner, at forty-three the sole member of his seminary class without his own parish, dreams of such ascendancy, his mother serving as housekeeper, yet does everything possible to scuttle his appointment. In a final scene his hopes are dashed yet again when the archbishop gives him a letter—which he isn't supposed to open until the following day but opens at once—that tells him he is to remain an assistant pastor, and adds the admonition: "I trust that in your new appointment you will find not peace but a sword." In "Zeal," a bishop aboard a train suffers the company of an intrusive, inexhaustible priest guiding a group of the faithful on a European tour. Escaping the priest after an especially trying evening, the bishop enters his Pullman car and "slept well that night, after all, but not before he thought of Father Early still out there, on his feet and trying, which was what counted in the sight of God, not success. *Thinkest thou that I cannot ask my Father, and he will give me presently more than twelve legions of angels?*" In a final scene the bishop abandons his own plans for a leisurely trip and takes up the burden of shepherding the touring faithful.

What the bishop acts upon and what Father Burner must yet discover is a spiritual life that comes down to remaining out there, on your feet, trying. Saul Bellow, a Powers admirer, remarked of the novel *Morte D'Urban* (1962) that it seemed to reduce faith to something "shadowy, more like obscure tenacity than spiritual conviction." Certainly there is little talk among Powers's priests of saving souls, let alone deep expressions of religious belief; what there is instead is, at best, a midwestern style of low-key religious persistence. In *Morte D'Urban*, which won a National Book Award, Father Urban, a popular traveling preacher in the otherwise dim Order of St. Clement, is reduced to helping start a rural Minnesota retreat house, a dismal task he yearns to escape but never fully abandons until, to his surprise, he is elevated to the thankless job of carrying on as the order's provincial. In the story "Priestly Fellowship," a garrulous pastor recalls during a rectory evening with young curates a shining moment from his seminary days when he had asked a theological stumper: "How can we make sanctity as attractive as sex?" And recalls the answer he had gotten:

" 'Just have to keep trying.' Not much of an answer. Nobody remembers it—just the question."

Over two decades after publishing his first novel, Powers published *Wheat That Springeth Green* (1988), a work that places the spiritual effort to keep trying within the context of contemporary changes in the Catholic Church. Well received by critics and nominated for a National Book Award, the novel created only a modest stir among readers, and at the time of his death Powers's reputation rested largely with his exact, vividly realized short stories in which clerical characters make funny, foolish, and occasionally moving efforts to negotiate between the demands of God and humankind. In "Keystone," priests wonder whether "godlessness" should be capitalized; in "Bill," a pastor seeks in vain to discover the surname of a new curate; in "Farewell," a bishop escapes the lethargy of retirement when he finds himself in demand as a substitute for pastors who are sick or—in one instance—AWOL.

Beside such typical stories should be placed "Lions, Harts, Leaping Does," a story first published in 1943 and appearing in Powers's initial book, *Prince of Darkness and Other Stories* (1947). Here the veil of comedy is absent and Powers presents in direct fashion internal religious experience. As life slips from him, Father Didymus, once an eminent Franciscan preacher, seeks spiritual peace yet remains "beset by the grossest distractions"—distractions, he realizes, that are "indelible in the order of things: the bingo game going on under the Cross for the seamless garment of the Son of Man: everywhere the sign of the contradiction, and always." He recalls Good Friday services during which he carried a crucifix along the communion rail for people to kiss, "and afterwards in the sacristy wiping the lipstick of the faithful from the image of Christ crucified." It is within such signs of contradiction, though never again so directly and solemnly expressed, that Powers found his lifelong subject.

Sources and Further Reading: Fallon Evans, *J. F. Powers* (1968); John V. Hagopian, *J.F. Powers* (1968); Ross Labrie, *The Catholic Imagination in American Literature* (1997); Michael Paul Murphy, "J.F. Powers: The Burden of an American Catholic Writer," Ph.D. diss., University of Minnesota (1980); J. F. Powers, *The Presence of Grace and Other Stories* (1962); J. F. Powers, *Look How the Fish Live* (1975).

Ronald Weber
University of Notre Dame, Indiana

Ray Bradbury (b. 1920)

Born in Waukegan, Illinois, in 1920, Ray Douglas Bradbury has retained strong creative bonds with his midwestern roots through six decades as a master of

❖ The Martian Chronicles

The ship came down from space. It came from the stars and black velocities, and the shining movements, and the silent gulfs of space. It was a new ship; it had fire in its body and men in its metal cells, and it moved with a clean silence, fiery and warm. In it were seventeen men, including a captain. The crowd at the Ohio field had shouted and waved their hands up into the sunlight, and the rocket had bloomed out great flowers of heat and color and run away into space on the *third* voyage to Mars! . . .

The rocket landed on a lawn of green grass. Outside, upon this lawn, stood an iron deer. Further up on the green stood a tall brown Victorian house, quiet in the sunlight, all covered with scrolls and rococo, its windows made of blue and pink and yellow and green colored glass. Upon the porch were hairy geraniums and an old swing which was hooked into the porch ceiling and which now swung back and forth, back and forth, in a little breeze. At the summit of the house was a cupola with diamond leaded-glass windows and a dunce-cap roof! Through the front window you could see a piece of music titled "Beautiful Ohio" sitting on the music rest.

Around the rocket in four directions spread the little town, green and motionless in the Martian spring. There were white houses and red brick ones, and tall elm trees blowing in the wind, and tall maples and horse chestnuts. And church steeples with golden bells silent in them.

The rocket men looked out and saw this. Then they looked at one another and then they looked out again. They held to each other's elbows, suddenly unable to breathe, it seemed. Their faces grew pale. . . .

. . . [The captain said,] "This town out here looks very peaceful and cool, and so much like Green Bluff, Illinois, that it frightens me. It's too *much* like Green Bluff." . . .

. . . The captain looked as if he wanted to go sit under a shady apple tree. "We're strangers here. We want to know how this town got here and how you got here."

"Are you census takers?" [asked the woman.]

"No."

"Everyone knows," she said, "this town was built in 1868. Is this a game?"

"No, not a game!" cried the captain. "We're from Earth."

"Out of the *ground*, do you mean?" she wondered.

"No, we came from the third planet, Earth, in a ship. And we've landed here on the fourth planet, Mars—"

"This," explained the woman, as if she were addressing a child, "is Green Bluff, Illinois, on the continent of America, surrounded by the Atlantic and Pacific oceans, on a place called the world, or sometimes, the Earth." . . .

Source: Ray Bradbury, "April 2000: The Third Expedition," in *The Martian Chronicles* (1950) 49–50, 52, 55.

fantasy and science fiction. His memories of life in Waukegan inform many of his best stories and anchor such mainstream masterpieces as *Dandelion Wine* (1957) and *Something Wicked This Way Comes* (1962). In fact, his wide-ranging international reputation as a prose stylist has its basis in the various childhood hopes and fears awakened during his Midwest youth. Through his father (Leonard Bradbury), he is a tenth-generation American, and he was part of the fourth Bradbury generation raised in Waukegan. By contrast, his mother (Esther Moberg Bradbury) was Swedish, arriving in America with her family as a young girl. Bradbury's close identification with this rich cross-section of midwestern family life and values survived brief relocations to Arizona in 1926 and 1932 and a permanent move to Los Angeles in 1934 as his father searched for work. Bradbury graduated from Los Angeles High School in 1938 and supported himself by selling newspapers from a corner stand until early 1942, when he began to develop a reputation as a unique new talent writing offbeat stories for the weird, detective, and science fiction pulps.

By the late 1940s, Bradbury had outgrown the pulps and was placing stories with a number of America's mainstream magazines. Over the next decade he earned two O. Henry Awards and four Best American Short Story selections, and published some of his most enduring book-length fiction, including his novelized story cycles *The Martian Chronicles* (1950) and *Dandelion Wine* (1957); such story collections as *The Illustrated Man* (1951), *The Golden Apples of the Sun* (1953), and *The October Country* (1955); and his only sustained science fiction work, the expanded novella *Fahrenheit 451* (1953). *The Martian Chronicles*, more speculative fable than science fiction, along with three popular 1960s *Life* magazine essays on space exploration, established his reputation as a lay spokesperson for the space age. From the early 1960s, his output of stories diminished as he turned more to speaking engagements and to the dramatization of many of his best stories. Over his career, Bradbury has published more than four hundred stories, and the majority remain available through anthologies, textbooks, and his own story collections. His numerous awards include the

2000 National Book Foundation Medal for Distinguished Contribution to American Letters.

Bradbury's stories often defy genre classification, but many of his locales are midwestern and his characters typically share his midwestern roots. "The Lake" (1944), his first self-acknowledged breakthrough story, is set on the shore of Lake Michigan. "The Big Black and White Game" (1945), which marked his first appearance in a major American magazine (*The American Mercury*), draws on childhood memories of Wisconsin's Lake Delavan. In "The Third Expedition" (also known as "Mars Is Heaven!," 1948), the most famous of his Martian chronicles, Bradbury's Martians project the illusion of a 1920s Illinois town. But there is a deeper connection to the Heartland informing all his fiction. In large part, his aesthetics and motivation derive from his close association with the small circuses and carnivals that were once a hallmark of midwestern life. The carnival experience, like the cinema of Bradbury's youth, brought the outside world and all its possibilities to Waukegan. His defining carnival experience was a late summer 1932 encounter with Mr. Electrico, whose staged admonition to "Live Forever!" came just as the young Bradbury had to deal with the violent death of his uncle in a Waukegan bank robbery. A further conversation with Mr. Electrico focused Bradbury on a lifelong goal: to fulfill the admonition by becoming a writer of lasting impact.

The first twenty years of Bradbury's career were arguably the most creative in terms of prose fiction, and his most sustained efforts during that period involved the creation of his mythological Green Town stories and novels, set firmly in the Illinois of his youth. *Dandelion Wine* (derived from a larger but still unpublished Green Town novel, at present in progress as *Farewell Summer*) won a 1957 Midland Author's Award and was praised by critics as a true chronicle of the bedrock American experience just prior to the Great Depression. The terrain of Green Town is Bradbury's Waukegan, and the ravine that cuts through the town becomes one of Bradbury's best-known dark places: a "softly blowing abyss" where a "million deaths and rebirths" happen every hour. Like the Midwest itself, it is a borderland full of transitions as town and nature vie for control of the landscape. For Bradbury's youthful protagonist, the ravine triggers both self-awareness and a deeper understanding of the human condition. *Something Wicked This Way Comes* represents Bradbury's most fully developed statement of his midwestern values. The dark carnival at the center of this novel conflates all the characters and sideshows he encountered in his youth, and inverts them to form the basis for a most unconventional horror novel. The literary treasures of Green Town's library and the soul-enslaving carousel focus the battle between good and evil; eventually, laughter emerges as the great leveling device in the carnival of life.

The strange circus worlds that periodically broke up the routines of Bradbury's midwestern youth provided core metaphors that underlie his entire approach to literature. Not surprisingly, within the fabric of his poetic prose is a constant critique of fixed ideas that have become too serious or one-sided. Bradbury's impulse is to carnivalize subjects and ideas—including the very genre traditions in which he writes. This is apparent in three detective novels—*Death Is a Lonely Business* (1985), *A Graveyard for Lunatics* (1990), and *Let's All Kill Constance!* (2002)—as well as in *From the Dust Returned* (2001), a novel that expands on the supernatural Illinois family that populates some of his best early weird tales with characters named after his own Waukegan relatives. From the beginning, Bradbury's career transcended his regional roots, but the landscapes, characters, and sentiments of his fiction continue to reflect fundamentally midwestern connections to family and place.

Sources and Further Reading: Steven Aggelis, ed., *Conversations with Ray Bradbury* (2004); Harold Bloom, ed., *Ray Bradbury* (2001); Ray Bradbury, *Dandelion Wine* (1957; repaginated paperback, 1976); Jonathan R. Eller and William F. Touponce, *Ray Bradbury: The Life of Fiction* (2004); Marvin E. Mengeling, *Red Planet, Flaming Phoenix, Green Town* (2002); Robin Reid, *Ray Bradbury: A Critical Companion* (2000); William F. Touponce, *Ray Bradbury and the Poetics of Reverie*, 2nd ed., rev. (1998); Jerry Weist, *Bradbury: An Illustrated Life* (2002); Sam Weller, *The Bradbury Chronicles: The Authorized Biography of Ray Bradbury* (2005).

Jonathan R. Eller
Indiana University–Purdue University,
Indianapolis

Kurt Vonnegut (b. 1922)

Born in 1922 into the prosperous German American society of Indianapolis, Kurt Vonnegut experienced as a youth how World War I made his family reject their German heritage and how the Depression ruined their financial basis. With his architect father withdrawing into a private world and his mother succumbing to depression, Vonnegut went to Cornell University to study biochemistry and soon evaded impending academic failure by joining the army. When he returned home for Mother's Day in 1944 before being shipped to Europe, he found that his mother had committed suicide the night prior to his arrival. That December, he was taken prisoner at the Battle of the Bulge and brought to Dresden, where he survived the firestorm of the Allied bombardment in the subterranean meatlocker no. 5 of the city's slaughterhouse. Upon his return to the United States, he married and studied anthropology in Chicago. But again he did not finish, because his thesis was rejected as "unprofessional," and only in 1971 would the faculty award him the master of arts degree, accepting his novel *Cat's Cradle* (1963) in lieu of a thesis. From 1947 onward, he worked as a publicist for General Electric in Schenectady, New York, and after he had sold some stories to the big weeklies he moved to Cape Cod and made writing his full-time profession. He tried for many years before he accomplished his breakthrough, and many a traumatic experience still awaited him: In 1958 his beloved sister Alice and her husband died, and he adopted three of their orphaned sons; in 1970 he separated from his wife and left his home for New York. When in 1972 his son Mark suffered a schizophrenic breakdown, the old fear that insanity might run in the family resurfaced; after his own attempt at suicide in 1984, Vonnegut checked himself into a sanitarium.

Vonnegut's oeuvre comprises fourteen novels, three short-story collections, plays, and several volumes of essays and speeches. While it constitutes a broad narrative panorama of life in the United States from the 1950s till today, it is also an attempt at autotherapy through literary exorcism, since Vonnegut's themes refer back to the child's experience of the Depression, the young man's trauma of the Dresden holocaust, and the mature adult's encounters with insanity and death. Time and again Vonnegut returns to the Midwest of his youth, as when he debunks Indiana's Hoosier mythology; denounces the small town of Rosewater, Indiana, as a medley of "shithouses, shacks, alcoholism, ignorance, idiocy and perversion" (in *God Bless You, Mr. Rosewater*, 1965); and has his characters either unanimously deride the representative Midland City, Ohio, as "the asshole of the Universe" (*Breakfast of Champions*, 1973) or dismiss it as an inhospitable place "where people weren't doing all that much with their lives anyhow" (*Deadeye Dick*, 1982). His scathing portraits of life in the Midwest are part of his general criticism of U.S. politics and economics, and together with his unmasking of the failure of the American Dream and his partisanship for the poor, they hark back to the decline of his family. His attacks against irresponsible scientists whose inventions endanger the world derive from his disillusioning experiences at General Electric, and his radical pacifism is indebted to his Dresden experience. His depictions of disturbed father-son relationships mirror his own problems; the threat of schizophrenia that haunts his protagonists points back to his mother's suicide, his son's mental illness, and his own bouts with insanity; and his self-definition as a "Christ-worshiping agnostic" (*Palm*

Sunday, 1981) is grounded in his family's tradition of German *Freidenkertum*. But while he treats all existing religions as Rube Goldberg inventions, he creates ever-new religious systems, from the "Church of God the Utterly Indifferent" in *The Sirens of Titan* (1959) to Bokononism in *Cat's Cradle*, thus illustrating Starbuck's insight in *Jailbird* (1979) that "we are here for no purpose, unless we can invent one."

Vonnegut's apprentice novel, *Player Piano* (1952), a traditional dystopia about a computer-controlled world, has achieved new topicality. *The Sirens of Titan*, long misread as a mere space opera, is now recognized as a brilliant parody of the ideology of progress in the name of human self-sufficiency. The bestselling *Cat's Cradle*, which tells about the end of the world caused by irresponsible science, is an accomplished humorous apocalypse. *Slaughterhouse-Five* (1969), a daringly innovative attempt at exorcising the trauma of the Dresden firebombing, combines science fiction motifs, metafictional strategies, and elements of popular culture to circle the unspeakable horror of mass extermination; it is one of the most influential narratives of postwar literature. In such later works as *Galápagos* (1985) or *Bluebeard* (1987) Vonnegut's narrators become ever more garrulous, and *Timequake* (1997) is a collage about the impossibility of writing a novel, in which Vonnegut resurrects the failed science fiction writer Kilgore Trout, who served as Vonnegut's alter ego in some of his previous tales.

Vonnegut is an experimental writer whose fictions have gained both a mass readership and academic recognition; someone whom the youthful counterculture of the 1960s celebrated as a guru of the new consciousness as expressed in the antitechnology stance of *Cat's Cradle*; someone a bourgeois audience enjoyed because he battled for the little man, believing that "love may fail, but courtesy will prevail"; and someone postmodern critics have praised for his narrative innovations. This unique impact is due to the unusual mixture of his sentimental plea for mutual understanding and "common decency," as in *Slapstick* (1976), which would certainly "play in Peoria," with his cynical evocation of a meaningless world in which the individual is nothing but "a victim of a series of accidents." His combination of the jokes of early radio comedians, the slapstick humor of Laurel and Hardy, the lyrics of well-known pop songs, and the jingles of famous advertisements, on the one hand, with extremely complex plot and time structures, epistemological explorations, and the demanding strategies of metafictional historiography, on the other hand, makes Vonnegut's novels into texts that a mass audience can read as entertainment but that his academic critics can analyze as demanding artifacts. It is this tension that belatedly caused a hesitant academia to take the clown of Armageddon seriously, elevating the former science fiction hack into literary celebrity.

Sources and Further Reading: Lawrence R. Broer, *Sanity Plea*, rev. ed. (1994); Jerome Klinkowitz, *Kurt Vonnegut* (1982); Jerome Klinkowitz and Donald L. Lawler, eds., *Vonnegut in America* (1977); Leonard Mustazza, ed., *The Critical Response to Kurt Vonnegut* (1994); Leonard Mustazza, *Forever Pursuing Genesis* (1990); Peter J. Reed, *Kurt Vonnegut, Jr.* (1972); Peter J. Reed, *The Short Fiction of Kurt Vonnegut* (1997); Peter J. Reed and Marc Leeds, eds., *The Vonnegut Chronicles* (1996).

Peter Freese
University of Paderborn, Germany

William Gass (b. 1924)

William H. Gass was born in Fargo, North Dakota, in 1924, the son of William Bernard Gass and Claire Sorensen Gass. His aesthetic sensibility was shaped in a childhood that he remembers as unhappy and damaging; he was schooled early by his father in the art of hate. The elder Gass, a World War I veteran, moved the family to Warren, Ohio, where he taught mechanical drawing and played minor league baseball. Gass remembers his father as a bitter, right-wing bigot, a man who was disappointed with life; his alcoholic mother he recalls as a passive woman, "a puddle of silence." Before his childhood ended he had decided to become a writer. Gass earned a doctorate in philosophy from Cornell University in 1954; he taught philosophy at Washington University in St. Louis for thirty years before retiring in 1999. Among his most important works are three novels, *Omensetter's Luck* (1966), *Willie Masters' Lonesome Wife* (1968), and *The Tunnel* (1994); two short-story collections, *In the Heart of the Heart of the Country* (1968) and *Cartesian Sonata* (1998); and seven works of nonfiction: *Fiction and the Figures of Life* (1970), *On Being Blue* (1976), *The World within the Word* (1978), *Habitations of the Word* (1984), *Finding a Form* (1996), *Reading Rilke: Reflections on the Problems of Translation* (1999), and *Tests of Time* (2002).

Across five decades, Gass's fiction and essays have limned the limits of hatred; trusting honest hatred more than false love, by his own admission Gass writes to get even. Almost without exception his characters are utterly unlikable, and this is by design; word men and word women, they lead deflected and defeated lives, their only defense a well-turned phrase or carefully planted word bomb. His essays, while often brilliant, are just as often screeds. Yet his writing is oddly compelling, in part because of his inventive use of language. As a prose stylist, Gass is almost without peer.

His writing is ironical, irreverent, self-referential, perverse, and at times, as in *The Tunnel*, deeply disturbing.

Gass writes at the intersection between philosophy and literature. Although he is a true child of the Midwest, and his fiction often *appears* to be set there—along the banks of the Ohio in *Omensetter's Luck*, or "fastened to a field" in "In the Heart of the Heart of the Country"—Gass is an *antirealist*. He claims to have set *Omensetter's Luck* in a river town in the 1890s precisely because he knew nothing of that time or place; both the geographical region and the river refer to nothing outside the work itself, no world outside the word. Similarly, "In the Heart of the Heart of the Country" is not an account of life in a small midwestern town. It is, rather, a formal negation of W. B. Yeats's poem *Sailing to Byzantium*. His *metafiction* is a working out of philosophical and literary theories; character is central, plot is not. Gass creates fictional characters who themselves create fictional figures, as in *Omensetter's Luck*. (Omensetter is himself a fictional construct created wholly by the words, perceptions, and anxieties of fellow characters.) Methodologically, his fiction begins with a name of some character or a story title; at times, as in the story "Mrs. Mean," these are the same; what follows is the unpacking of the meaning of that name, in this case the meaning of *mean*.

Gass explores self-referential philosophical themes in his fiction, in particular the problem of evil. Mrs. Mean, whose character matches her name, is the incarnation of average, everyday evil absorbed into daily life. The contagion of evil in "Mrs. Mean" carries through to the meanness of *The Tunnel*, a novel thirty years in the making. As always in Gass, plot is kept to a minimum and is a consequence of character: Having completed his book *Guilt & Innocence in Hitler's Germany*, William Frederick Kohler, distinguished professor of history at an Indiana university, sits in his chair, intending to write an introduction. Blocked, he writes instead a history of history, a *metahistory*—a history of the historian-as-liar, lout, and loser. Fearing his wife will discover it, he hides the new manuscript by slipping it into the pages of his book. Meanwhile, he digs a tunnel out from the basement of his house. Kohler is Mean with the volume turned up. His mother was a drunk, his father a verbally abusive bigot. He is a textbook case of an "unreliable narrator." His excavations replace the objective with the subjective, the public with the private, the innocent with the guilty; like the members of the PdP (Party of the Disappointed People) he is a meanie, a fascist of the heart. Only language does not lie: Notice, says Kohler, that lover is mostly spelled by using over, and sex is two thirds ex. Kohler, plumber of the depths, is himself a word man, and Gass (the word *Gasse* is German for "alley") has so cleverly matched structure to prose that for the first fifty pages of the book readers hit the wall in a series of false starts. Kohler and his readers are trapped at the end of moral history; the book is a total word war.

As an essayist and theorist, Gass hasn't changed his mind in forty years. He believes that philosophy is fictional, and fiction philosophical. Novelists and philosophers share an obsession with language; both are cut from the same conceptual cloth. Neither the philosophical nor the fictional world is more real than the other. Though there are differences between the two—philosophers tend to employ abstract nouns and verbs, while novelists fill in the blanks of proper names—both create verbal worlds, engaging in an "ontological transformation" whereby all objects, real or imagined, must conform to our ways of thinking; must conform, that is, to our words. Both we and the world we inhabit are fictional. As a formalist Gass insists that to understand the deep structure of the world—and the thin line separating reality from the representation of reality—one needn't consult the periodic table; a thesaurus will do as well.

Sources and Further Reading: Robert Alter, "The Leveling Wind," *New Republic* 212 (Mar. 27, 1995); Swen Birkerts, "One for the Angry White Male," *Atlantic Monthly* 275 (June 1995); Elizabeth W. Bruss, *Beautiful Theories* (1982); H. L. Hix, *Understanding William H. Gass* (2002).

Gary Percesepe
Wittenberg University, Ohio

Robert Bly (b. 1926)

Though he is well known as a translator of Pablo Neruda and Rainer Maria Rilke and many other modern poets from Europe and South America, Robert Bly's own poetry begins deep in the American Midwest, where Bly was born in 1926. His first book of poems was called *Silence in the Snowy Fields* (1962), and it set the terms for much of his long and productive career. The poems contain references to, and scenes from, Ohio, Wisconsin, and Iowa, not to mention "the pale lakes of Minnesota," which is his home state. His ideas about poetry are informed by his readings in medieval mystics like Jacob Boehme and modern thinkers like Carl Jung. Bly is a paradoxical combination of modern urbanity and deep ruralism. But it is the spirit of the Midwest that one breathes in when reading Bly, and that spirit has never been forsaken by him.

Silence in the Snowy Fields announced a new approach to contemporary poetry. Gone were the rational, tightly structured poems favored by the so-called academic poets, many of whom were teaching in universities and working under the influence of T.S. Eliot. Instead, Bly and others were devoted to the possibilities of what he came to call the "deep image," a poetic evocation of experience through sensory renditions of quiet moments and intense, often spontaneous reflection. Many of these early poems are written in short sections, as the discontinuities of experience are summoned and resolved through images that are often natural and mysterious at once. "Driving toward the Lac Qui Parle River" begins like this:

> I am driving; it is dusk; Minnesota.
> The stubble field catches the last growth of sun.
> The soybeans are breathing on all sides.
> Old men are sitting before their houses on car seats
> In the small towns. I am happy,
> The moon rising above the turkey sheds.

The field knowledge, if we may call it that, here joins the promise of incipient illumination, as a moment of quietness and completion contains a strong hint of renewal. The landscape is nearly without personal communication, in a world marked by "solitude covered with iron," but at the end a laconic image suggests that secrets can be shared, along with human warmth. The poem concludes: "When I reach the river, the full moon covers it. / A few people are talking, low, in a boat."

The early poems of Bly are rich with a sense of midwestern space, a space marked by openness and the pioneering history of people driven by stern values. Human habitation has created a rich culture in this space, though often its exterior appearances suggest deprivation and denial. A central part of the culture of the Midwest is a strong Protestant sense of self-reliance and social propriety. Bly, however, is more like a radical Protestant, one whose theological musings lead to a need to go beyond the boundaries of habit and routine. Very often his poetry praises the ability of the imagination to make fruitful leaps of association, yet the poems contain a moral sense that reaffirms a sense of duty and place. It is largely through and against the strictures of duty and place that Bly's spiritual longings are profiled. In a poem called "Uneasiness in Fall," he says, "This sloth is far inside the body, / The sloth of the body lost among the wandering stones of kindness." The Protestant tradition of self-examination never operates far from Bly's imagination.

In one of the prose sections of his *Selected Poems* (1986), Bly speaks of how his first poems were written out of a despair that he "couldn't quite bring into the house." He eventually decided not to publish these first attempts, and it was through *Silence in the Snowy Fields* that he domesticated and ruralized those early emotional intensities. But these intensities soon took another form, when Bly faced the developing conflict in Vietnam and became an antiwar activist, devoting all his poetic energy to bringing about an end to that military action. During the two decades after publication of his first book, Bly tried to join his theories about lyric poetry with a passionate antimilitarism to create a wholesale condemnation of many of the accepted values of American life. One could relate Bly's antiwar activism to a strain of isolationism in midwestern politics, especially in its combination with a mistrust of federal bureaucrats and the modernizing rationalism of centralized government. Since the end of the Vietnam War, in 1975, Bly has seldom retreated from his stance as a poet addressing highly controversial political issues.

In 2000, Bly was named the annual recipient of the Distinguished Artist Award of the McKnight Foundation, the largest private funder of the arts in Minnesota. The booklet celebrating this award had as its cover a photograph of Bly pushing open the screen door of a log cabin set in the woods. Though Bly gained national recognition for his lectures and appearances promoting his views on the psychology of men and the need to reactivate a mythical consciousness, his life is centered in the rural midwestern landscape where he was born. In "The Night Abraham Called to the Stars," he returns again to the imagery of his early, silent fields:

> We stand in the onion fields looking up at the night.
>
> My heart is a calm potato by day, and a weeping
> Abandoned woman by night. Friend, tell me what to
>   do,
> Since I am a man in love with the setting stars.

After the stars set the sun will rise, and we can sense that Bly is again, and still, looking for the right thing to do and think. He is rather like a midwestern pioneer, looking for an open space beneath the stars where he can establish a new sense of community.

Sources and Further Reading: Robert Bly, *Eating the Honey of Words: New and Selected Poems* (1999); Robert Bly, *The Night Abraham Called to the Stars: Poems* (2001); Robert Bly, *Selected Poems* (1986); McKnight Foundation, *Robert Bly: Distinguished Artist* (2000).

Charles Molesworth
Queens College, City University of New York

James Wright (1927–1980)

Born and raised in Martins Ferry, Ohio, James Wright was the son of Dudley and Jessie (Lyons) Wright.

James was born in 1927, so his early years coincided with the Great Depression, which hit working-class families especially hard in Martins Ferry, an industrial town across the Ohio River from Wheeling, West Virginia. While the Wrights fared better than many in the area, the psychological impact of poverty would become a central theme in Wright's poetry, as would the destructive effects of industrialism on the American landscape. His poetry often expresses anger about greed and cruelty, while finding solace in nature and in unexpected acts of human nobility.

After high school, Wright served two years (1946–1948) with the U.S. Army in occupied Japan. After his discharge, he completed degrees in English at Kenyon College (B.A., 1952) and the University of Washington (Ph.D., 1959), where he studied creative writing under poet Theodore Roethke. Wright's Ph.D., however, was in English literature; he wrote a dissertation on Charles Dickens and thereafter taught literature, not writing. He married Liberty Kardules, also from Martins Ferry, in 1953; they would have two sons, Franz, born in 1953, and Marshall, born in 1958, before divorcing in 1962.

In 1954 Wright won the Yale Series of Younger Poets award, chosen by W. H. Auden, for his first book, *The Green Wall* (1957), which was followed by *Saint Judas* (1959). These books reflected the dominant formalism of post–World War II American poetry in their verbal density, abstraction, and irony. While certain poems succeed in evoking the isolation of Wright's Ohio characters and a sense of their social milieu, most of Wright's early poetry has not proven durable despite its technical virtuosity.

Wright reevaluated his work in the late 1950s and sought new influences and forms. Personal and professional developments accelerated this change. Wright began teaching in 1957 at the University of Minnesota in Minneapolis, a city that he disliked and where he succumbed to clinical depression, partly because his marriage was failing. Yet he also established a crucial and enduring friendship at this time with poet Robert Bly, who advocated devotion to imagery, literal or surrealistic, and the reading of modern European and Latin American poets as a tonic to the academicism of American verse. These ideas profoundly affected Wright, who often visited Bly's farm near Madison, Minnesota, where the poets worked on translations as well as their own writing.

The marked transition between Wright's second and third books has occasioned much discussion among literary scholars. *The Branch Will Not Break* (1963) turned from Wright's earlier formalism to embrace vivid imagery, geographical specificity, and, for the most part, free verse rather than traditional poetic forms. Wright identifies his settings through environmental detail and reference by name to places in Ohio and Minnesota. Ohio poems, consistently bleak in tone, predominate at first; these include "Two Poems about President Harding" and the much-anthologized "Autumn Begins in Martins Ferry, Ohio." A movement from despair to transcendent joy in nature occurs as Wright shifts from Ohio to the Minnesota prairie, as in "To the Evening Star: Central Minnesota" and "A Blessing," an evocation of two horses that has become the most beloved of Wright's poems. The epiphanies in these poems gain credibility because they emerge from a spiritual struggle to feel at home in nature, in one's own body, and in the medium of poetry.

In 1966 Wright accepted a professorship at New York's Hunter College, where he taught for the rest of his life. He married Annie (Edith Anne) Runk in 1967. His next books, *Shall We Gather at the River* (1968); the Pulitzer Prize–winning *Collected Poems* (1971), which included an extensive selection of new poems; and *Two Citizens* (1973) further developed his experiences in Minnesota and Ohio, but with a renewed focus on private and public griefs. Three themes prevail in these books: loneliness, the dark side of American history, and the dislocation of Americans from their local landscapes. Several poems focus on racial violence and the legacies of conquest, such as "On a Phrase from Southern Ohio" and "A Centenary Ode: Inscribed to Little Crow, Leader of the Sioux Rebellion in Minnesota, 1862," which should be counted among Wright's finest achievements.

In his later work Wright tried to come to terms with Ohio and the Midwest. Several poems express admiration for people in Depression-era Ohio who exhibited kindness and courage despite their travails. Notable among these are "A Flower Passage," which memorializes a man who made his living recovering bodies from the Ohio River, and "The Old WPA Swimming Pool in Martins Ferry, Ohio," dedicated to Wright's father and other men who built the pool to give their children a safer place to swim. Descriptions of pollution, scarification of land, and violence still occur, but Wright manages to find beauty even in loss.

Wright's feeling for Ohio was also affected by his European travels. His last two books, *To a Blossoming Pear Tree* (1977) and the posthumous *This Journey* (1982), mainly consist of poems set in Europe, most memorably in Italy, whose landscapes enabled Wright to see his native land, as well as his own poetry, in a more generous light. A conciliatory tone resounds throughout Wright's late poems, which are notably confident, given his earlier doubts about the power of poetry to soothe spiritual and psychological distress.

Wright developed cancer of the tongue and died in 1980, soon after completing the manuscript of *This Journey*. His influence extends beyond the Midwest but is perhaps most evident in the work of midwestern poets like Dan Gerber, Bruce Weigl, and Jim Daniels. He remains one of the most popular twentieth-century American poets. *Above the River: The Complete Poems* (1990) compiles all of Wright's books along with translations and prose poems. Also worthwhile are *Collected Prose* (1983), which includes autobiographical sketches and critical essays, and *The Delicacy and Strength of Lace* (1986), Wright's correspondence with Native American novelist Leslie Marmon Silko. Martins Ferry, Ohio, maintains Wright's memory with an annual poetry festival in his honor. Similar events are held occasionally at the University of Minnesota.

Sources and Further Reading: Robert Bly, *Remembering James Wright* (1991); David C. Dougherty, *James Wright* (1987); Andrew Elkins, *The Poetry of James Wright* (1991); Frank Graziano and Peter Stitt, eds., *James Wright: A Profile* (1988); William S. Saunders, *James Wright: An Introduction* (1979); Dave Smith, ed., *The Pure Clear Word* (1982); Kevin Stein, *James Wright: The Poetry of a Grown Man* (1989); Peter Stitt and Frank Graziano, eds., *James Wright: The Heart of the Light* (1990).

William Barillas
University of Wisconsin–La Crosse

Philip Levine (b. 1928)

Philip Levine, one of America's best and most honored poets, was born in 1928 and raised and educated in Detroit. Since leaving Wayne State University, Levine's address has changed many times. He attended both the Iowa Writers' Workshop and Stanford University and taught for many years at Fresno State University. Besides living in Spain for long periods of time, as he became well known in the literary world he taught at various universities and has lived part of each year in New York City.

Levine is one of a fairly rare breed of poets from the Midwest who have established national and international literary reputations. A list of some of the others might include Carl Sandburg, Edgar Lee Masters, Vachel Lindsay, Gwendolyn Brooks, Theodore Roethke, Robert Hayden, James Wright, Robert Bly, and Rita Dove. While it would be difficult to posit a midwestern school or style of poets and/or poetry, each of these poets can be associated with a key midwestern place: for instance, Sandburg with Chicago; Masters, Spoon River; Wright, Martins Ferry, Ohio; and Bly, the Minnesota farm country.

Levine's place is Detroit. The world as the poet has internalized it is centered in the city of his youth. As he has described it, it is a place filled with intolerance, inequality, and anti-Semitism. This place has ignited a vision of fury and lamentation in Levine that he has dramatized in the language and imagery of his poetry. He centers this vision in the grimy factories, weed-strewn vacant lots, and dilapidated neighborhoods of Detroit. This place, this city, this world is secular and materialistic and it is ravaged by the selfishness and greed of the industrialists and politicians and other citizens who control it.

If Levine's vision sounds radical, it is, for he has long been attracted to anarchism and views the Spanish anarchists as heroes who fought against the state's oppression of the worker. However, Levine is first and foremost a poet, so he does not engage in political rhetoric. In poems such as "They Feed They Lion" (1972), "What Work Is" (1991), "Fear and Fame" (1991), and "A Walk with Tom Jefferson" (1988) he shows industrial workers in action and dramatizes the conflict that he feels between the workers and those who exploit them.

Levine grounds his poems in evocative memories of key moments in his life, especially his experiences as a factory worker in and around Detroit. While he is anything but provincial, his persona is an earthy, simple, straightforward midwestern tough guy: someone very close to the poet, who has shared much of his imaginative life. In his key poems, Levine imagines hard industrial labor as somehow redemptive, as part of the human endeavor to survive against the negative forces of nature and the crimes of state-sponsored oppression.

It was in the factories of Detroit that the poet met the workers who changed his life. Levine's imaginative remembrance of these workers inspired one of his most powerful poems. As he has said, " 'They Feed They Lion' is their poem. The rhythm, grammar, and details are theirs, as I remembered them fifteen years later, in 1968 when the country seemed to be hanging on the edge of civil war with millions of insulted people ready to burn their prisons. I tried to pay my small homage." Levine's empathy for the workers' dignity, courage, and honor in the midst of hell is integral to the vision that he renders in "They Feed They Lion."

In the poem, the workers' sense of the world's horror and beauty and the poet's rage at the terrifying energy that devours human hopes and aspirations merge. The lion is the final and crucial reference in each of the five stanzas. The poet says he was influenced by a passage in Christopher Smart's "Jubilate Agno," where the lion roars itself into being. He might also have been moved by the lions of the twenty-second psalm:

"Ravening and roaring lions / open their mouths wide against me." The psalmist envisions a dying man confronted by his enemies. And the man cries out, "My God, my God, why hast thou forsaken me?"

Levine does not directly address the Lord in his poem, but the voice of "They Feed They Lion" does convey the wonder and terror of the human spirit confronted by an ineffable force. Levine's lion symbolizes an awesome power that both creates and destroys. Born of grass, slime, acid, trees, fences, and old cars, this kingly lion is a raging force that makes all the earth's creatures holy and yet devours them, their hopes and ideals.

Many of Levine's best poems have strong narrative and dramatic elements, so that the reader feels as if he or she has experienced what the poet writes about. His long poem "A Walk with Tom Jefferson" is set in a ruined Detroit neighborhood near Briggs Stadium, the old major league stadium of the Detroit Tigers baseball team. Tom is a black worker and war veteran. He loves gardening; is a loyal family man; and endures despite terrible hardships caused by forces beyond his control, such as the death of his only son in the Korean War. Tom's ruined neighborhood is returning to its natural state with weeds, wild dogs, and Dog-man, a human animal on the loose.

Detroit provides Levine with a setting, an enveloping action, a way of life, a myth. Tom Jefferson, who shares the name of an American icon and slaveholder, is a common man, a laborer, who refuses to be defeated by the social, economic, and political forces that conspire against him. He embodies for the poet a bedrock humanity. Tom is "six feet of man, unbowed."

At the poem's conclusion, the poet shifts the focus back to himself as a youthful laborer in Detroit: "Still a kid / when I worked nights / on the milling machines / at Cadillac Transmission. . . ." He is struck by all that the "Amazing earth" has given to himself and others. The poem ends with a sense of mystery and wonder at all that has transpired in the interaction between man and the earth. Philip Levine has traveled far from Detroit but as a poet he has never left the city of his birth.

Sources and Further Reading: Christopher Buckley, ed., *On the Poetry of Philip Levine* (1991); Philip Levine, *The Bread of Time* (1994); Paul Mariani, "Keeping the Covenant: A Look at Philip Levine's 'A Walk with Tom Jefferson,'" *Kenyon Review* 11 (Fall 1989); Gary Pacernick, "Philip Levine: Prophet of Oneness," in *Memory and Fire* (1989); Gary Pacernick, "Staying Power: A Lifetime of Poetry, an Interview with Philip Levine," in *Meaning and Memory*, ed., Gary Pacernick (2001).

Gary Pacernick
Wright State University, Ohio

Lorraine Vivian Hansberry (1930–1965)

Born in Chicago in 1930 to Carl Augustus Hansberry, a successful real estate broker, and Nannie Perry Hansberry, a schoolteacher, Lorraine Hansberry was the youngest of four children. Carl Hansberry was from Mississippi, where he had attended Alcorn College, and Nannie was the college-educated daughter of a Tennessee minister. As a middle-class family, the Hansberrys were active in social and political circles. Their friends included such notables as actor, singer, and activist Paul Robeson; jazz musician Duke Ellington; athletes Joe Louis and Jessie Owens; and Harlem Renaissance poet Langston Hughes. An uncle, William Leo Hansberry, was a distinguished professor of African American history at Howard University. Yet the family's social and economic class did not shield them from experiencing bitter incidents of racial strife when they moved from South Side Chicago to another neighborhood where housing covenants restricted black mobility, creating a "Black Metropolis." Because Carl Hansberry worked with real estate, the Hansberrys had first-hand knowledge of housing discrimination. The family's efforts in the late 1930s to move to a white neighborhood would become the seed for Lorraine Hansberry's most famous play, *A Raisin in the Sun* (1959).

When the family moved, Lorraine was eight years old. During one of the more intense moments of racial strife, someone threw a brick through the family's living room window, narrowly missing Lorraine's head. The Illinois courts evicted the Hansberry family from the white neighborhood. In 1940, Carl Hansberry and the NAACP won a landmark Supreme Court housing case (*Hansberry v. Lee*) that repealed the restrictive covenants, but enforcement of the law did not follow. Determined to bring about change, Hansberry, a Republican, ran unsuccessfully for Congress in a city known for its Democratic leadership. Disillusioned, he left Chicago for Mexico, where he died in 1946.

From 1944 to 1948 Lorraine attended Chicago's Englewood High School, and she then went to the University of Wisconsin. She left college to work for Robeson's newspaper, *Freedom*. While working on a picket line, she met her future husband, Robert Nemiroff, a Jewish activist and intellectual. Later in life, Lorraine divorced Nemiroff, but she named him her literary executor.

Hansberry's writings show her interest in race, class, and gender issues. While speaking to the winners of a writing contest sponsored by the United Negro College Fund, she coined the phrase "young, gifted, and black," a characterization that later resonated throughout black communities. Hansberry felt it important to claim all of her identities, and in letters to a lesbian periodical, *The Ladder*, she disclosed her sexual orientation as a lesbian. After Hansberry's death

from cancer at age thirty-four in 1965, Nemiroff compiled her writings in a collection he entitled *To Be Young, Gifted and Black: Lorraine Hansberry in Her Own Words* (1969). Although Hansberry wrote other plays, including *The Drinking Gourd* (1960), *The Sign in Sidney Brustein's Window* (1964), *Les Blancs* (1972), and *What Use Are Flowers?* (1972), *A Raisin in the Sun* remains her signature work.

First performed on March 11, 1959, at the Ethel Barrymore Theatre in New York City, *A Raisin in the Sun* was an immediate success. Its production marked the first time a play by a black woman appeared on Broadway. In addition to Sidney Poitier, the cast included many actors who would later become well known: Ruby Dee, Ossie Davis, Claudia McNeil, Louis Gossett, Jr., and Diana Sands. The play had a run of over five hundred consecutive performances and earned the New York Drama Critics Circle Award for Best Play of the Year. Hansberry became the youngest American, the fifth woman, and the first black playwright to win the award.

The play's family, the Youngers, Lena (Mama), Walter Lee (Brother), Beneatha (Sister), Ruth (Walter's wife), and Travis (Walter and Ruth's son), live in South Side Chicago in a kitchenette, a one-room apartment where different families share a bathroom. Lena's dream is to move her family to better housing. After receiving the needed money from her deceased husband's insurance policy, she gives it to Walter Lee to make the down payment. Having his own ambitions that extend beyond his job as a chauffeur, Walter Lee loses a significant portion of the money in a business deal, and now the family must decide how it will realize its dreams. Complicating the situation is the fact that each family member has a personal dream. Politically active, Beneatha wants money to go to medical school. Ruth has to deal with another pregnancy. Walter Lee is trying to define his manhood in a city that has not turned out to be the mecca he thought it would be. The play discusses the politics of "dreams deferred"—a reference to "Harlem," a poem by Langston Hughes. The poem ponders whether dreams deferred "dry up like a raisin in the sun." At the end of the play, Walter Lee is tempted to take an offer from the white representative of the neighborhood association who wants to pay the Younger family *not* to move in.

A Raisin in the Sun later became a film (1961), a musical (1973), and the most anthologized play by an African American author. However, during the Black Arts Movement (1965–1975), some criticized the play for its integrationist impulses, unfavorably comparing it to Richard Wright's *Native Son* (1947). Although both works take place in South Side Chicago and chronicle the lives of black families, especially black men whose dreams extend beyond their chauffeur status and who feel trapped by their racist environments, some of Hansberry's critics accused her of trying too hard to write an everyman story. Hansberry argued that her play uses the specificity of black life in South Side Chicago to tell an honest story.

Although leaving their southern roots was not easy for many blacks, desegregating the neighborhoods of midwestern urban cities proved just as challenging. In what has become an American classic, Hansberry chronicles the emotional turmoil of living in restrictive environments.

Sources and Further Reading: Steven R. Carter, *Hansberry's Drama* (1991); Anne Cheney, *Lorraine Hansberry* (1984); Harry J. Elam, Jr. and David Krasner, eds., *African American Performance and Theater History* (2001); Richard M. Leeson, *Lorraine Hansberry: A Research and Production Sourcebook* (1997); Robert Nemiroff, *To Be Young, Gifted, and Black* (1969); Margaret B. Wilkerson, "Lorraine Hansberry," in Valerie Smith, Lea Baechler, and A. Walton Litz, eds., *African American Writers* (1991); Margaret B. Wilkerson, "The Sighted Eyes and Feeling Heart of Lorraine Hansberry," *Black American Literature Forum* 17 (Spring 1983).

Valerie Lee
The Ohio State University–Columbus

Toni Morrison (b. 1931)

For the stature she has achieved, and her contributions to American literature, Toni Morrison, Nobel laureate (1993) and recipient of numerous national and international literary prizes, ranks among the Midwest's most notable writers. Since 1957, she has held several academic positions, including appointments at the State University of New York at Albany and Princeton University. A leader in African American literature's recent movement into the center of American thought, her seven novels give eloquent testimony to the power of black art. Perhaps because Morrison's artistic roots are firmly planted in southern black expressive culture (a river that never runs dry), in spite of her catholic interests, breadth of knowledge, and worldliness she grounds her novels in black southern culture yet otherwise connects most to the Midwest where she grew up. One midwestern characteristic in her writing is her skillful use of seasonal and climate changes (striking in that region) and their influences on those who live there.

In the late nineteenth century, Morrison's parents and grandparents were sharecroppers in Greenville and Birmingham, Alabama (on her mother's side), and in Georgia (on her father's). By then, the failure of sharecropping, Ku Klux Klan outrages, Jim Crowism, and the wanton lynching of blacks in the 1880s and 1890s had made life in the South intolerable for tens of thousands of African Americans. So, in the early 1900s, Morrison's kin joined the grassroots black exodus, a migration of former slave families from the South to the North, the Midwest, and the West that began in the 1880s. The migrants fled poverty and racism with hopes for education, economic solvency, and dignity for themselves and their children. Morrison's relatives settled in the Midwest.

Toni Morrison, the second of four children, was born Chloe Anthony Wofford on February 18, 1931, in Lorain, Ohio, to George and Ramah Wofford. The racial violence in her father's youth in Georgia left him with a lasting distrust of white people but did not destroy his will to achieve a better life. In Ohio, he worked in shipyards and steel mills, sometimes at three jobs simultaneously. Ramah Wofford did domestic work. Ramah was more tolerant of whites than her husband, always optimistic about better relations between the races. George and Ramah Wofford gave their children a strong sense of their own value on their own terms, a defining trait in Toni Morrison's life and career. Everyone in Lorain was poor, racial hostility was less overt and less oppressive than in the South, and, almost unique to the Midwest, white migrant and white immigrant ethnic groups and African Americans maintained separate communities with little open hostility between them. The young Woffords understood the reality of racism but did not permit it to impoverish their dignity.

In general, black migrants to Lorain found a better life in the North. Morrison grew up in a close-knit three-generation family that placed high value on group loyalty and women's centrality to its social and personal cohesion. Once finding herself with four generations of women of her clan together, Morrison noted the deference the others paid to her great-grandmother. Such experiences reinforced the value of black women in the community for her and influenced her portrayal of women in her novels.

Although no longer in the South, Morrison's elders assured preservation of the heritage of black culture that defined and sustained them through good and bad times by passing on to their children the lore, music, language, myths, and rituals they valued. First among these were the stories. Women and men in Morrison's family told thrilling and terrifying ghost stories; her mother used a dream book to decode dream symbols, and signs; and jokes, visitations, and ways of knowing outside of western cosmology filled their children's days and nights. They lived close to nature and knew that animals talked and humans could fly like birds.

In high school, the great European writers, French, Russian, and English, impressed young Chloe. Later, at Howard University (where she changed her name to

Toni Morrison), she majored in English, minored in classics, and performed in the Drama Club. She received a bachelor of arts degree in 1953; after receiving a master of arts degree from Cornell University (1955), she married and divorced, taught, worked as an editor, raised two sons, and in 1970 published her first novel.

Morrison's first two novels, *The Bluest Eye* (1970), in which a young black girl believes she is ugly and that her ugliness will disappear if she secures blue eyes, and *Sula* (1973), which focuses on black women's friendships that fall apart in a male-dominated world, are set in the Midwest—the first in Lorain, the second in a fictitious city. In her third novel, *Song of Solomon* (1977), she expands her geographic range and returns a midwestern young black man to the South to recover his roots. Her fourth, *Tar Baby* (1981), the first of three to bypass the Midwest, takes place on an offshore non-U.S. owned island where Morrison explores the dynamics of race, class, and gender. In her fifth, *Beloved* (1987), the action moves between the South and the Midwest, focusing on history, memory, black pain, and the struggle for healing during Reconstruction. The sixth, *Jazz* (1992), the second without a Midwest connection, is set in the 1920s and surveys the journey north and east (rather than west) and its outcome for southern black migrants unprepared for life in New York City. The seventh, *Paradise* (1998), critiques the disastrous effects of black nationalism in the late-twentieth-century civil rights era in an all-black town in Oklahoma.

Morrison's fiction embraces the richness of many cultures. In her writings she weaves together images from artistic expressions that originate in African, African American, European, American Indian, and Eastern epistemologies. Her stories appeal to a broad section of the American public and to readers on every continent. Her genius is her ability to create richly textured narratives based in African American experiences but representative of the universal condition. The themes she pursues unite in the search for the meaning of humanity through the prism of blackness in white America.

Sources and Further Reading: William L. Andrews and Nellie Y. McKay, eds., *Toni Morrison's Beloved: A Casebook* (1999); Jan Furman, *Toni Morrison's Fiction* (1996); Henry Louis Gates, Jr. and K. A. Appiah, eds., *Toni Morrison: Critical Perspectives Past and Present* (1993); Missy Dehn Kubitschek, *Toni Morrison: A Critical Companion* (1998); Jill Matus, *Toni Morrison* (1998); Valerie Smith, ed., *New Essays on Song of Solomon* (1995); Danille Taylor-Guthrie, ed., *Conversations with Toni Morrison* (1994).

Nellie Y. McKay
University of Wisconsin–Madison

Gerald Vizenor (b. 1934)

At first it may seem a misnomer to call Gerald Vizenor a "Midwest author." Though Vizenor's childhood and early career were spent in the region where he was born in 1934, his time in Japan while in the army from 1952 to 1955 also looms large. This influence stretches from volumes of haiku to novels like *Griever: An American Monkey King in China* (1987). And Vizenor left Minnesota in 1983, before producing the bulk of the prodigious literary output or the theoretical work on which his reputation as a leading Native American writer and thinker largely rests. Applying to Vizenor a phrase tinged with a foundational notion of place as origin runs counter both to his sustained critique of any kind of essential Indianness—whether in anthropology, academic Native American studies, or popular culture images—and to his own sense of his life. Vizenor foregrounds the role of "chance" in his unconventional autobiography, *Interior Landscapes: Autobiographical Myths and Metaphors* (1990), an often third-person collection of "self-imaginings" that resists the typical narrative logic of a life story.

But on second thought, given Vizenor's love of irony and play, the label Midwest author makes sense. The term *Midwest*, designating this middle region as "west" compared to the East coast but distinct from the western frontier, echoes the similarly ironic term "Indian," which is imbued with a perspective that mistakes the Americas for India. To use one of his own words, Vizenor's work can be read as "postindian." Its exuberantly prolific diversity, akin to the immense diversity of historical tribes and contemporary Native American cultural practices, challenges the static singularity of the word *Indian*, which, according to Vizenor, covers the "absence" of its lack of a real referent.

To call Vizenor a Midwest author is also to play with place. Describing a Midwest characterized by the process of (dis)placement, Vizenor locates the future of Native American peoples in creative redeployment, as suggested by the unique vocabulary he has coined to designate the cultural position of Native Americans. "Survivance" and "sovenance" combine *survival* and *sovereignty* with the more active *resistance*; "manifest manners" equates the damaging "manners," or stereotyped representations of authenticity to which Natives conform, with the ideological doctrine of manifest destiny that supported the colonization of America. Vizenor's Midwest is a kind of "crossblood," to use another of his trademark terms, combining the Scandinavianism of his third-generation Swedish American mother and the Anishinaabe heritage of his mixed-blood Chippewa father, the White Earth Reservation, and the city of Minneapolis that he experienced as a child shuttled between relatives and foster care after his father's murder when he was two years old. Vizenor's Midwest, then, far from being rooted in a traditional or tribal place characteristic of the work of many Native American authors, resembles what he calls "a postmodern tribal bloodline."

Indeed, *The People Named the Chippewa: Narrative Histories* (1984) asserts that culture itself is "invented" through the stories that people tell about themselves, and the stories that Vizenor's characters tell about themselves in his many works undermine any attempt to place them (or him) within a single tradition or genre. Instead, culture and place have more to do with one's state of mind than where one resides. For Vizenor, the common stereotyping of Indians as tied to particular landscapes, or "mother Earth," limits Native American identity. Thus the characters in *The Heirs of Columbus* (1991) trace their heritage to the White Earth Reservation but set up a utopian community in Point Assinka, Washington, open to everyone with a conducive worldview. This novel, like much of Vizenor's work, blurs the boundaries between past and future, fiction and nonfiction—understood both as history (Christopher Columbus as Mayan Jew) and autobiography (Vizenor's own trajectory from Minnesota to the West Coast and Berkeley)—to rework stable categories and concepts in new ways. The resulting comic play unsettles boundaries through the productive "transmotion" of the trickster, a recurrent figure throughout Vizenor's work. Vizenor's emphasis on motion, rather than "settling," seems at odds with popular understandings of the Midwest, which usually signifies tradition, stability, rootedness, community, and old-fashioned values. In *Survival This Way: Interviews with American Indian Poets* (1987), Vizenor tells Joseph Bruchac, "the characters I admire in my own imagination and the characters I would like to make myself be break out of things. They break out of all restrictions. They even break out of their blood."

But while Vizenor's work challenges the conventional meanings of the Midwest, it does not reject the Midwest: Disrupting the stereotype of Indians as tied to *one* place does not discount the importance of place altogether. Tying together his themes of storytelling, invention, and motion, place becomes for Vizenor both imaginative and traditional, something "greater than reality." Vizenor's warriors of survivance move physically from the Minnesota reservation to Bureau of Indian Affairs offices, New Mexico, university settings, and China; they move culturally from challenging Chinese totalitarianism to performing laser light shows, gene therapy, coffee scams, and gambling for unleaded gasoline in What Cheer, Iowa. In this way, Vizenor's stories participate in the ongoing construction of the Midwest as an imagined place.

By creating imaginary landscapes Vizenor attempts not to escape from harsh realities but to pursue "an idea of the comic, that the adventures of living and the strategies of survival are chances," which can build a new kind of community: "[y]ou can't act in a comic way in isolation. You have to be included. There has to be a collective of some kind." Vizenor's use of humor grows out of Native American storytelling traditions, but the way that he envisions humor as a matter of resilience, of finding the comic in the "things [that] just happen," also seems constitutive of the Midwest, from the humor found in the absurdity of weather fronts dropping the temperature forty degrees in an hour's time to the everyday struggles faced by Garrison Keillor's Lake Wobegon folk. Vizenor's creative reimagining of a fluid, fabulous midwestern Heartland, like his reimagining of Native American tradition as postmodern theory, is, as he describes humor, "a positive, compassionate act of survival, it's getting along."

Sources and Further Reading: Joseph Bruchac, *Survival This Way: Interviews with American Indian Poets* (1987); Gerald Vizenor, *Darkness in Saint Louis Bearheart* (1978); Gerald Vizenor, *Fugitive Poses* (1998); Gerald Vizenor, *Manifest Manners: Postindian Warriors of Survivance* (1994); Gerald Vizenor, *Shadow Distance* (1994); Gerald Vizenor and A. Robert Lee, *Postindian Conversations* (1999).

Christopher R. Nelson
Oregon State University

Garrison Keillor (b. 1942)

By 1990 or so, Garrison Keillor's fictional Lake Wobegon in Minnesota had become the small town that for millions of Americans epitomized the culture, climate, history, and range of human types that characterize the Midwest. Keillor established this imaginary midwestern town as the quintessential American home place by using it as the setting for most of the oral stories he narrated on live radio variety shows, the most famous of which was *A Prairie Home Companion*, which debuted in 1974 in St. Paul, and gained a national radio audience in 1980.

Born in Anoka, Minnesota, in 1942, the third of six children, Gary Edward Keillor grew up in then semirural Brooklyn Park, now a bedroom community of Minneapolis. Though his fundamentalist family frowned on writers and entertainers and college educations, Keillor was already determined to be a writer when he was only thirteen and chose the pen name Garrison. He attended the University of Minnesota, where he majored in English, edited the literary magazine, and took his first job in radio at the university station, primarily because his father had refused to pay for his education and he needed the money. In 1970 he was living on a farm near Freeport, Minnesota, with his first wife and infant son, and trying to write while supporting his family by working at the first station of what grew into Minnesota Public Radio. He wanted to escape radio work by breaking into the *New Yorker*, and as soon as he started selling his first stories and sketches to that magazine, he quit his radio job. But in the meantime he had started writing rube jokes and sketches to tell on the air, eventually setting them in Lake Wobegon, which he modeled on Freeport and other nearby towns in Stearns County. The time he stole from the typewriter to speak into a microphone turned out to be well invested because his greatest achievement is his vernacular style, a cross between spontaneous oral narrative and the studied verbal artistry of the *New Yorker* writers he worked so hard to join. His mastery of this hybrid art is best symbolized by the Grammy awarded for his reading of his first novel, *Lake Wobegon Days* (1985), as the best spoken-word recording of 1987.

In his humorous radio monologues of the 1980s Keillor customarily offered Lake Wobegon as "the little town that time forgot, that the decades cannot improve." It sheltered its citizens from the harried life of the cities, suburbs, and shopping malls and evolved into a pastoral retreat where the values of the past were still alive. This evolution had much to do with Keillor's gradual movement beyond jokes and satirical send-ups of midwestern people and small-town culture in the early 1970s and toward an empathic celebration of his home state, people, and region. Lake Wobegon ultimately became a fully imagined place and even attained the status of myth through Keillor's detailed depiction of regional culture and characters. For his weekly monologue he affected a Stearns County voice, and his narrative pose as a shy, slow-talking exile and frequent visitor to his idealized American town resembled the pose of cracker-barrel philosopher.

Keillor's oral and written burlesques of commercial and public service announcements, his doggerel verse, and his tall tales link him to literary comedians of the late nineteenth and early twentieth centuries. But the Lake Wobegon tales, with their elegiac strains and careful attention to homely detail, also recall the sentimental realism of nineteenth-century local-color writers. His frequent satire of small-town insularity recalls early twentieth-century regionalists such as Sherwood Anderson and Sinclair Lewis. Yet Keillor is seldom so syrupy as the local colorists, nor so bitter as Anderson and Lewis could be. On air, he uses a rustic accent and slow delivery for recounting cozy episodes, but he switches to the citified accents of a professional radio announcer to maintain his tonal balance.

The people of Lake Wobegon are mainly descendants of Norwegian Lutheran and German Catholic immigrants, with a sprinkling of Sanctified Brethren—fundamentalists who resemble Keillor's family. The town motto is "'*Sumus quod sumus*' (We are what we are)." These are plain-living, plain-talking, ordinary folks, not "paradise people." "Left to our own devices," Keillor wrote in *Lake Wobegon Days*, "we Wobegonians go straight for the small potatoes. Majestic doesn't appeal to us; we like the Grand Canyon better with Clarence and Arlene parked in front of it, smiling. We feel uneasy at momentous events."

In 1987, after thirteen years of weekly performances, exhausted and feeling the strain of being a celebrity whose personal life was the subject of the daily news, Keillor brought the show to an end, saying he was leaving Minnesota. He had recently married a Dane, and the couple left for what turned out to be a brief time in Copenhagen and almost five years in Manhattan. During this period of exile from Minnesota, Keillor tried to abandon his familiar midwestern subject matter and experimented with other nonmidwestern matters and voices. But ultimately, though he would write more frequently in this period about how Minnesota was a "repressive" place, his life as a prodigal son in New York taught him "*Ich bin ein* Minnesotan." By 1993, he had resurrected *A Prairie Home Companion* and was once more broadcasting live from St. Paul.

His self-exile from the Midwest was foreshadowed by a string of characters who in a number of ways resembled their creator. Johnny Tollefson of *Lake Wobegon Days* and *Wobegon Boy* (1997) and Francis With of *WLT: A Radio Romance* (1991) both tried to escape their constricted small-town lives via writing or radio work. The anonymous author of "95 Theses 95," which condemns the blandness, narrowness, and hypocrisy of the town in *Lake Wobegon Days*, also speaks for Keillor. That the narrator and the point-of-view character of so many Lake Wobegon stories on air and in print should be associated with such prodigal and rebellious sons became ever clearer in the years after Keillor ended *A Prairie Home Companion* in 1987. In *Lake Wobegon Summer 1956* (2001) there was yet another rebellious adolescent protagonist, but this time he was not Johnny, Francis, or Anonymous, but was named Gary Keillor. The author's command and range of genres, moods, subjects, and themes was wider and freer than ever before—and he was home.

Sources and Further Reading: Judith Yaross Lee, *Garrison Keillor: A Voice of America* (1991); Peter A. Scholl, *Garrison Keillor* (1993); John Skow, "Lonesome Whistle Blowing," *Time* (Nov. 4, 1985).

Peter Scholl
Luther College, Iowa

David Mamet's first major dramatic success, *American Buffalo* (left to right: Joshua Hutchinson, David Gianopoulos, Mike Hagerty). Directed by Andrew Barnicle, Laguna Playhouse, Laguna Beach, California, May 29–July 1, 2001. Photo by Ed Krieger.

David Mamet (b. 1947)

David Mamet is Chicago's primary playwright, although his professional association with the city was limited to the first decades of his career and his significance extends to contemporary theatre in general. The settings, language, and concerns of his work (including screenplays, novels, essays, and poetry) reflect the region's influence and contribute to Chicago's public identity and mythology.

Mamet was born in Flossmoor, Illinois, in 1947 and grew up in Chicago's suburban "New South," a sign of his family's upward mobility, since his Ashkenazi grandparents had settled on the city's Euclid Avenue. His father, a labor lawyer, and his mother (born Silver), a teacher, were divorced when David was ten, causing his transfer from Rich Central High to the Francis Parker School, where he acted, besides doing radio and television shows for an uncle who was head of broadcasting on Chicago's Board of Rabbis. As a teenager he took workshops from Viola Spolin at the Hull House Theatre and bused tables at Second City, the improvisational theatre that, under Spolin's son, Paul Sills, established the genre's format. Mamet's studies at Goddard College in Vermont (1965–1969) necessitated jobs in and around Chicago that inspired his future plays, whether their subject concerned the merchant marine (*Lakeboat*, 1970) or a real estate agency in Lincolnwood (*Glengarry Glen Ross*, 1983). His college education also began a lifelong connection with Vermont.

If there ever was a Great American Novel, Mamet believes it was of the northwestern frontier, the stories of survival written by the children of immigrant settlers—Willa Cather's *My Ántonia* (1918) and *O Pio-*

neers! (1913), O. E. Rølvaag's *Giants in the Earth* (1927), Theodore Dreiser's *An American Tragedy* (1925)—a tradition carried on by second-generation artists like Saul Bellow in *The Adventures of Augie March* (1953). Hence, Mamet prefers F. Scott Fitzgerald's Basil Lee stories about his poverty-stricken childhood in St. Paul to *The Great Gatsby* (1925), or Ernest Hemingway's stories about Nick Adams in the Michigan tales to his novels. For the nice, Jewish middle-class boy, Hemingway's macho persona was a role model. For the fledgling writer, the Nobel Prize winner's limpid, pared-down style appealed for being the workingman's product of a struggle equal to the protagonists'. Still, Hemingway's recoil from didacticism clashes with the Jewish-inspired mentor-protégé relationships in Mamet's drama.

His professional career started with the 1970 production of *Lakeboat* by the Theatre Workshop at Marlboro College, Vermont, where he took up teaching. Upon returning to Goddard he and some students founded the St. Nicholas Theatre, which under his administration (1973–1976) was relocated to Chicago, where it developed into a leading Off-Loop venue helping to turn the city into a hub for resident theatre. In contrast to the Organic Theatre, which hosted Mamet's *Sexual Perversity in Chicago* (1974) and whose loose style recalled the 1960s' hippie approach, the St. Nicholas set professional standards unprecedented for the alternative scene, but without forgoing a democratic structure. Such community principles, still deemed typical of the Chicago theatre, go back to Jane Addams and Ellen Gates Starr, founders of Hull-House. Their ideals were passed on by Spolin and her son, who schooled Mamet in the virtues of verbal theatre and bare stages, an approach reflected in his episodic early plays. References to local landmarks (e.g., the zoo, Marshall Field's, *The Tribune*, the relaxation of fire codes in the 1970s) root these plays in the city without limiting their relevance. His first major success, *American Buffalo* (1975), in which small-time crooks plan the heist of a coin, is (despite its realistic language) less a slice of life than an allegory of the shoddy American business ethic, set in the mythical city of gangsters. Mamet's social critique became even more outspoken in his take on the car industry, *The Water Engine* (1977), which exposes the Social Darwinism underlying the ideology of Chicago's 1933 Century of Progress exhibition.

American Buffalo was coproduced by the St. Nicholas and Stage Two of the Goodman Theatre, where Mamet became associate director and artist-in-residence during Gregory Mosher's leadership (1978–1985). Together they contributed to the revival of its producing company, turning the institution into a nonprofit organization and shifting its affiliation from the Art Institute of Chicago to DePaul University's School of Drama. During this period, Mamet wrote and produced several important plays, though not all premiered in Chicago. For instance, the revision of *Lakeboat* opened in Milwaukee (1980) and the Pulitzer Prize–winning *Glengarry Glen Ross* in London (1983) before playing at the Goodman. In the mid 1980s, Mamet seemed to reorient himself. After cofounding Chicago's New Theater Company in 1985, he affiliated the company with Cambridge's American Repertory Theatre, which coproduced his adaptations of Anton Chekhov's *The Cherry Orchard* (1985) and *Uncle Vanya* (1988). While Mosher became artistic director of Lincoln Center Theater, New York, in 1985, Mamet's New York University clinics in Vermont (1986) led to the establishment of the Practical Aesthetics Workshop, later renamed the Atlantic Theater Company. As he has grown older, Mamet has glanced backward: Thus he combined his previously published one-acters, *The Disappearance of the Jews* (1983) and *Jolly* (1989), with the newly written *Deeny* into *The Old Neighborhood* (1997), in which his alter ego returns to Chicago to close out some unfinished business with his sister, pal, and former girlfriend. Similarly, in *The Cryptogram* (1994) he comes to terms with the divorce of his parents.

While Mamet's artistic activities have outgrown their origins—with worldwide productions, publications, and movie screenings—what remains is Chicago's impact, beginning with a theatre community that prizes the virtues of integrity and reciprocal development. No less important is the tradition of intellectual radicalism exemplified by Thorstein Veblen, Clarence Darrow, Robert Maynard Hutchins, and Studs Terkel, and reflected in plays like the controversial *Oleanna* (1991), which mixes gender issues with reflections on higher education. Finally, there is the picaresque tradition of gangsterism, which Mamet has mined theatrically (*American Buffalo* and *The Water Engine*) and cinematographically (*The Untouchables*, 1987; *House of Games*, 1987; *Things Change*, 1988; *Homicide*, 1991; *Hoffa*, 1992; *Lansky*, 1998). By combining all of these strands, Mamet's work proves as diverse and great as the city he hails from.

Sources and Further Reading: C.W.E. Bigsby, *David Mamet* (1985); Dennis Carroll, *David Mamet* (1987); Chicago Public Library, *Resetting the Stage* (1990); Anne Dean, *David Mamet: Language as Dramatic Action* (1990); Leslie Kane, ed., *David Mamet: A Casebook* (1992); Leslie Kane, ed., *David Mamet in Conversation* (2001); David Mamet, *A Whore's Profession* (1994); Jeffrey Sweet, *Something Wonderful Right Away* (1978).

Johan Callens
Free University of Brussels
(Vrije Universiteit Brussel), Belgium

Charles Johnson (b. 1948)

Charles Richard Johnson was born in 1948 in Evanston, Illinois, into an extensive African American family whose elder members adhered to the values of integration and self-help. Those values informed Johnson's youth and adolescence, and one sees shades of them in his writing, which challenges rigid definitions of racial identity and simultaneously celebrates how African Americans have freed themselves creatively and spiritually from such limitations.

Johnson attended Evanston Township High School and recalls that he and his friends rejected bigotry and racial divisiveness. He carried this integrationist ethos with him to Carbondale, Illinois, in 1966, when he enrolled at Southern Illinois University (SIU). When he arrived, as part of a wave of African American students mostly from the Chicago area, the university was changing from a relatively harmonious institution into an increasingly acrimonious environment marked by political and racial unrest. Although Johnson largely ignored this upheaval at first, he was eventually drawn into campus politics. Around this time he also heard a speech by Amiri Baraka, who was visiting SIU to bring the message of the Black Arts Movement that he had helped found in 1965. Baraka's challenge to the audience to take black art back to black people inspired Johnson to draw his first book of cartoons, *Black Humor* (1970). He followed this work with a second collection, *Half-Past Nation Time* (1972). Both books mock rigid racialized notions of American identity, poking fun equally at white racists and black militants.

After publishing these drawings, Johnson wrote six apprentice novels in the space of two years while he was doing graduate work in philosophy at SIU. In 1972 he forged a relationship with the writer John Gardner, who was then teaching creative writing in Carbondale. Working under Gardner's careful supervision, Johnson developed his ideas about philosophical fiction and produced his first published novel, *Faith and the Good Thing* (1974). On the strength of this novel and with Gardner's strong support, in 1976 Johnson joined the creative writing faculty of the University of Washington. Although he has fully embraced Seattle as his adopted home, his midwestern roots continue to manifest themselves in his fiction.

Johnson's two best-known novels, *Oxherding Tale* (1982) and *Middle Passage* (1991), are set respectively in South Carolina and on the route of the transatlantic slave trade; however, he has never written a novel that did not reference southern Illinois or Chicago. Two of his novels are set primarily in the Midwest and typify the region's symbolic significance to him. *Faith and the Good Thing* is the story of Faith Cross, an eighteen-year-old African American who leaves her Georgia home for Chicago in search of some elusive object or experience, the "Good Thing" on which she plans to build an ideal existence. Robbed and raped on her first night in the city, she drifts into a life of drug use and prostitution, emerging from the depths of this despair only to enter a loveless marriage that almost destroys her. As these events play out against the backdrop of Chicago's South Side, the city represents the racial injustice, outrage, and violation that Faith must overcome in order to find her ideal life. Interestingly, in his efforts to transcend Chicago, Johnson takes up the task of revising a seminal work of Chicago fiction: Theodore Dreiser's *Sister Carrie* (1900); intent on rejecting notions of determinism, especially the idea that race can somehow be a limiting or determinative factor for individuals, he moves his heroine, Faith, through a series of experiences that resemble Carrie Meeber's exploits in Chicago, then finally twists the ending of his story away from the unresolved dissatisfaction that marks Carrie's fate.

At the novel's end, Faith flees Chicago for her Georgia home and for spiritual liberation, a move that reinforces Johnson's negative view of the city. For much of Johnson's fiction, Chicago and the Midwest represent attitudes and experiences that his protagonists must separate themselves from in order to overcome their narrow-mindedness about racial and personal identity formation. The pattern of flight does not always hold up. In fact, in "Alethia," a short story written after *Faith and the Good Thing*, the narrator, who grew up on Chicago's South Side and left it behind, must return and face his past in order to escape the sense of victimization that plagues him. Nevertheless, even in this instance where the return is essential, the legacy of the South Side is a burden that the protagonist bears.

Johnson foregrounds the Chicago setting again in his fourth novel, *Dreamer* (1998). This text chronicles the 1966 Campaign to End Slums of Martin Luther King, Jr., his effort to improve housing conditions for African Americans in Chicago. In this story of Chaym Smith, King's body double who comes to understand the minister's philosophy through his attempts to become his "twin," the South Side is both the symbol of gut-wrenching poverty and the site of mental and spiritual liberation. As the narrator, Matthew Bishop, attempts to guide Smith through his transformation, he reflects on both the oppression he sees in Chicago's ghetto neighborhoods and the resilience of former generations of blacks who beat those apparently insurmountable odds to create a place for themselves in Chicago society. Johnson weaves a thinly veiled account of his uncle William Johnson's life into the text, citing him as the model of one who "made a way out of no way" for himself and his family. With this celebration of William Johnson and his generation, Johnson effectively comes full circle in his understanding of his home region and his family, embracing once again the integrationist, self-help ethos that characterized his childhood home and his family.

Although Johnson balks at the classification "midwestern writer," in the tradition of other great midwestern authors he has deeply identified with the region. Indeed, the Midwest has proven integral to his efforts to transform readers' understandings of racial and personal identity.

Sources and Further Reading: Michael Boccia, "An Interview with Charles Johnson," *African American Review* 30 (Winter 1996); James Dorsey, *Up South: Blacks in Chicago's Suburbs, 1719–1983* (1986); Jonathan Little, *Charles Johnson's Spiritual Imagination* (1997); William R. Nash, *Charles Johnson's Fiction* (2002); William R. Nash, "A Conversation with Charles Johnson," *New England Review* 19 (Spring 1998); James R. Ralph, Jr., *Northern Protest* (1993).

William R. Nash
Middlebury College, Vermont

Jane Smiley (b. 1949)

Although born in Los Angeles, California, in 1949, Jane Smiley moved with her mother to St. Louis when she was one year old. Her father divorced her mother when Jane was four and she grew up never knowing him. Inspired by her newspaper editor mother's and her grandparents' love of reading, she developed an early interest in literature and writing. Smiley graduated from Vassar College in 1971 having decided only in her senior year that she wanted to write, and she was awarded a doctoral degree in English from the University of Iowa in 1978. Concurrent with her appointment as an assistant professor at Iowa State University, Smiley published her first work, *Barn Blind*, in 1980, a novel expressing the isolation of an Illinois farm wife and mother following the death of one of her four children, a death that may have been related to the mother's passion for her horses. Jane Smiley has three children and has been married and divorced three times. In 1996, Smiley left Iowa State and moved her family to an oceanside home on California's Monterey Peninsula in 1996. She was awarded the National Book Critics Circle Award in 1991, and in 2001 she was inducted into the American Academy of Arts and Letters.

Smiley's novels are studies in genre and form. While *Moo* (1995) is a farcical comedy and *A Thousand Acres* (1991) is a tragedy of Shakespearian dimensions, Smiley also has written detective fiction (*Duplicate Keys*, 1984); romance (*The All-True Travels and Adventures of Lidie Newton*, 1998); domestic drama (*Barn Blind*, 1980, and *At Paradise Gate*, 1981); biography (*Charles Dickens*, 2002); epic (*The Greenlanders*, 1988); novellas (*Ordinary Love and Good Will*, 1989); short stories (*The Age of Grief*, 1987, and *Life of the Body*, 1990); nonfiction (*Catskill Crafts: Artisans of the Catskill Mountains*, 1987, and *The True Subject: Writers on Life and Craft*, 1993); and a horse-racing novel (*Horse Heaven*, 2000). The novel *Good Faith* (2003) is a satire on the greedy and sex-driven 1980s. She is also an in-demand essayist who writes on such diverse topics as President Bill Clinton's extramarital affair and American motherhood.

Often labeled a "midwestern writer," Smiley refrains from embracing that distinction. However, the label persists—for example, the blurb on the cover of *Horse Heaven* categorizes Smiley as "the Balzac of the late 20th-century Midwest"—because many of her novels are set in the midwestern landscape, either literally or psychologically. The repeated themes of the domestic or the agrarian, ecological concerns, and disappearing ways of life that appear in her novels illuminate the farming crisis of the Midwest as well as the values of rural family life in the region. In particular, Smiley delves beneath the pervasive stereotypes associated with the region, exposing depth of character and experience.

A Thousand Acres, Smiley's Pulitzer Prize–winning revision of *King Lear*, details the midwestern agricultural crisis of the 1970s and 1980s. In a 1998 essay, Smiley explains that *A Thousand Acres* was written about a "specific" historical moment, "when land values were so high that any farmer who might die and leave the farm to his children would risk their losing the farm, or part of it, to high inheritance taxes. That this moment was followed by the crash of the midwestern farm economy was understandable." In the novel, Smiley pronounces the dangers of attempting to subdue and control the land as patriarch Larry Cook does in procuring more and more land and maintaining an intricate drainage system. His labor, he believes, entitles him to master his own destiny as well as the destinies of his family members. Dividing up the farm between two of his daughters, Cook attempts to stave off crippling inheritance taxes, yet it becomes clear that he does not expect his daughters to be able to control the land. As his daughters strive to manage the farm, Cook is infuriated by his own obsolescence. The land's indifference to Cook is the one betrayal he cannot countenance. Cook then sabotages the farm, perhaps to prove his power, a futile gesture in the wake of the farm's failure. Smiley suggests that the land is not, in fact, subject to the farmers.

Much of Smiley's midwestern work examines what lies "below the level of the visible." Just as the Cooks' farm is arable because of the tiles beneath the earth, the hidden core of *Moo* is Earl Butz, the grotesquely obese pig concealed at the center of the university. *Moo's* huge cast of characters, initially recognizable as a variety of different university and midwestern types, contain sometimes startlingly surprising depths to their personalities. The university ultimately contradicts the initial impressions of Cecelia Sanchez, a new faculty member, who finds the place "eerie," "flat," "quiet," "provincial," and "bland." However, behind the veneer of polite distance lies intrigue, passion, commitment, and absurdities. As Smiley reveals the often unrecognized complexities of midwestern university life, the contradictions swell and burst, much like Earl Butz the pig.

At the heart of many of Smiley's midwestern novels is the figure of the isolated male and his inability to connect with others. *A Thousand Acres's* Larry Cook, *Good Will's* Robert Miller, and even *Moo's* Loren Stroop attempt to control their land and their families, clinging to a vision of themselves as independent and perhaps heroic, a role that may no longer be possible in the newly anonymous corporate-farmed Midwest. With the collapse of the male role in Smiley's novel, the central female characters find their patterns of life in disarray as well. From Kate Karlson (*Barn Blind*) to Lidie Newton (*The All-True Travels and Adventures of Lidie Newton*), Smiley's women find that the traditional roles of womanhood no longer work, especially when husbands die, farms fail, and fathers fall short of their daughter's needs. In short, Smiley's characters, feeling the land shift beneath their feet, must reconstruct their visions and beliefs in order to survive.

Sources and Further Reading: Jonis Agee, "Jane Smiley: Location and a Geographer of Love," *Great Plains Quarterly* 21 (Fall 2001); David Brauner, " 'Speak Again': The Politics of Rewriting in *A Thousand Acres*," *Modern Language Review* 96 (July 2001); Mary Paniccia Carden, "Remembering/Engendering the Heartland: Sexed Language, Embodied Space, and America's Foundational Fictions in Jane Smiley's *A Thousand Acres*," *Frontiers: A Journal of Women Studies* 18 (May–Aug. 1997); Becky Faber, "Women Writing about Farm Women," *Great Plains Quarterly* 18 (Spring 1998); Steven G. Kellman, "Food Fights in Iowa: The Vegetarian Stranger in Recent Midwest Fiction," *Virginia Quarterly Review* 71 (Summer 1995); Carl D. Malmgren, "The Lie of the Land: Heartland Novels by Smiley and Kinsella," *Modern Fiction Studies* 45 (Summer 1999); Neil Nakadate, *Understanding Jane Smiley* (1999); Jane Smiley, "Not Just a Pretty Picture," in Mark C. Carnes, ed., *Novel History* (1998).

Sarah Appleton Aguiar
Murray State University, Kentucky

Rita Dove (b. 1952)

The year 1993 proved miraculous for the State of Ohio: Rita Dove from Akron, Ohio, became poet laureate of the United States, and Toni Morrison from Lorain won the Nobel Prize. Rita Dove had previously won a Pulitzer Prize, for her Akron, Ohio–based *Thomas and Beulah* (1986). Though moored in native ground, Dove should not be defined as a regional writer but, instead, as a major voice who cherishes a locale and its people, and who writes from within the culture, rather than drawing it as odd, humorous, or idiosyncratic.

Rita Dove testifies that her beginning memories come out of her experiences in Akron. "I'm not going to write about Paris and try to make it my own. Akron is my own." Though she graduated from Miami University in Oxford, Ohio, and from the Iowa Writers' Workshop, she spent a formative year in Germany. Her local and global views are best summarized in the two fundamental speeches she delivered in 1995 as part of her poet laureate's duty, as described in *The Poet's World* (1995). They envision both "the poet in the world" and "the world in the poet."

Loosely based on the lives of her maternal grandparents, *Thomas and Beulah* (1986) is Dove's masterpiece that straddles her local and global concerns. The double sequence of forty-four poems depicting a couple's, a city's, and a country's life between the Great Migration and the civil rights movement is unified, if not in time, then in action and location. The poems are all set in Akron—which in Greek means "the highest point." The genius loci of Dove's home-

Rita Dove. Courtesy Heinz Family Foundation and Jim Harrison, photographer.

town is thus the ground and the vanishing point of her writing, and it is embodied in the image of the airship Akron hovering over the city, which Dove imaginatively boards to write her poetry.

Dove was born in Akron in 1952, the daughter of the first African American chemist, who, in the 1950s, broke the race barrier in the Goodyear Tire and Rubber Company. Her father, Ray, gave her his chemist's sense of science, and her mother, Elvira, gave her a gift for storytelling. With two younger sisters and an older brother, Rita Dove grew up protected, in a supportive but also stern environment. Her grandparents were blue-collar workers who moved north from the South during the Great Migration. A first-generation sense of achievement motivated her to carry that earned respect further. As a child Rita was encouraged to read and took advantage of the offer. In seventh grade she began learning German. In 1970, she was invited to the White House as a Presidential Scholar, before attending Miami University as a National Achievement Scholar. Dove graduated from Miami summa cum laude with a degree in English in 1973 and then studied at the University of Tübingen. In terms of craft, Rita Dove's knowledge of the German language has been one of the biggest influences on her work.

An encounter with the poet and translator John Ciardi convinced Dove that authors could exist in real life. She joined and subsequently graduated from the University of Iowa Writers' Workshop in 1977. Her teachers included Stanley Plumly, Marvin Bell, Louise Glück, Bill Matthews, and Carolyn Kizer. While a graduate student in Iowa, she met the German writer Fred Viebahn; they married in 1979, and their daughter Aviva was born in 1983.

Since 1982, Rita Dove's poetry has earned her prestigious fellowships, and honorary doctorates. Among other honors, she was granted a Portia Pittman Fellowship in 1982 and was chosen by Robert Penn Warren for a 1986 Lavan Younger Poet Award. She received a 1987 General Electric Foundation Award, the 1988 Ohio Governor's Award in the arts, and a Literary Lion citation from the New York Public Library in 1990; Sara Lee and Heinz Awards followed. From 1993 to 1995 Dove was U.S. poet laureate. She taught creative writing at Arizona State University from 1981 to 1989, and since then has served as Commonwealth Professor of English at the University of Virginia in Charlottesville.

Appearances in national magazines and anthologies had already won acclaim for Dove when she published her first poetry collections, *The Only Dark Spot in the Sky*, and *The Yellow House on the Corner*, both in 1980. *Museum* followed in 1983, containing her well-known poem "Parsley," which recounts the massacre by General Trujillo of Haitian blacks for their failure to pro-

nounce the letter *r* in the Spanish word *perejil* (parsley). Her lyric epic, *Thomas and Beulah*, appeared in 1986. Other publications include a book of short stories, *Fifth Sunday* (1985), and the poetry collection *Grace Notes* (1989) as well as the bildungsroman *Through the Ivory Gate* (1992). *Selected Poems* (1993) punctuated her election as poet laureate.

A verse drama, *The Darker Face of the Earth*, adapting the Oedipus conflict to an antebellum setting, was published in 1994 and has been performed worldwide since 1996. Dove's poetry collection grew with *Mother Love* (1995), a lyric sequence that explores the function of the Demeter and Persephone myth as well as the sonnet form. In 1999, *On the Bus with Rosa Parks* followed, a poetic sequence on segregation and desegregation in the Deep South. After a long pause Dove published her *American Smooth* (2004).

Rita Dove's oeuvre stands out for its creative variety and thematic complexity, and most of all for its border-transcending reach. She combines history with family and individual histories, enriching the commonplace with legendary moments. Her language is precise, her imagery vibrant. In all, three major features define the ethical and aesthetic essence of her writing: the magic of linguistic and visual imagination, the polyphony of voices, and her standpoint beyond temporal-spatial and cultural fixations that allows a revised artistic freedom.

Sources and Further Reading: Houston Baker, "Rita Dove: Grace Notes," *Black American Literature Forum* 24 (Autumn 1990); Ekaterini Georgoudaki, "Rita Dove: Crossing Boundaries," *Callaloo* 14 (Spring 1991); Arnold Rampersad, "The Poems of Rita Dove," *Callaloo* 9 (Winter 1986); Therese Steffen, *Crossing Color* (2001); Helen Vendler, *Soul Says* (1995).

Therese Steffen
University of Basel and University of Zurich

Louise Erdrich (b. 1954)

Born in Little Falls, Minnesota, in 1954, Karen Louise Erdrich was raised in Wahpeton, North Dakota, on land that once belonged to the Wahpeton-Sisseton Dakota and was home to a Bureau of Indian Affairs boarding school, where her parents taught and which her Ojibwe grandfather attended. She is a member of the Turtle Mountain Chippewa Nation of North Dakota. She attended Dartmouth College, where she met her future husband, Michael Dorris (1945–1997). After various jobs teaching poetry, editing a Boston Indian Council newspaper, and earning a master's degree from Johns Hopkins University, Erdrich returned to Dartmouth in 1980 as writer-in-residence. The next year she married Dorris, who became her literary agent and collaborator.

In 1982 Erdrich made an impressive literary debut with "The World's Greatest Fisherman," a short story that won the Nelson Algren Award. She submitted the story at Dorris's urging, after "barricading" herself in the kitchen while Dorris, incapacitated with a bad back, encouraged her writing and revising from the floor. The next year her story "Scales," which incorporated her own job experience at a highway weigh station, was selected for *The Best American Short Stories, 1983*. Both stories became chapters in Erdrich's inaugural book, *Love Medicine* (1984; it was revised and expanded in 1993). *Love Medicine* received numerous awards, including the National Book Critics Circle Award. Although usually classified as a novel because of recurring characters and development, it challenges the definition with independent, nonlinear and multiple-voiced narratives. Erdrich expanded the genre further with subsequent volumes that continue her first book's story, themes, and characters: *The Beet Queen* (1986), *Tracks* (1988), *The Bingo Palace* (1994), *Tales of Burning Love* (1996), *The Last Report on the Miracles at Little No Horse* (2001), and *Four Souls* (2004).

Each of these novels is set in the Midwest and illustrates challenges for contemporary American Indians. Erdrich presents traditional Ojibwe beliefs and practices, Roman Catholic adaptations, alcoholism, desperation, and survivals. The novels do not have protagonists in the traditional literary sense, but present a tribal community seeking ways to continue and persist against various forces of opposition. In the cycles of life, characters are born and die; they leave the reservation but most try to return. Their survival is aided by a dark humor. Among the memorable characters are Fleur, the paragon of tribal endurance and strength; Nanapush, the incarnation of the Ojibwe trickster; Pauline/Sister Leopolda, a perverse woman trying to purge herself by becoming a nun; Marie, a matriarch to the tribe; Lulu, a contemporary trickster; Lipsha Morrissey, a young man coming of age; Lyman Lamartine, a tribal entrepreneur; Jack Mauser, a pursuer of love; and Father Damien, a woman disguised as a priest.

The landscape is a constant factor that shapes their culture and defines who they are. In *The Last Report on the Miracles at Little No Horse*, Nanapush uses the term *Anishinaabeg*, the historical and traditional name of the Ojibwe/Chippewa, and explains: "Every feature of the land around us spoke its name to an ancestor. Perhaps, in the end, that is all that we are. We Anishinaabeg are the keepers of the names of the earth. And unless the earth is called by the names it gave us humans, won't it cease to love us? And isn't it true that if the earth stops loving us, everyone, not just the Anishinaabeg, will cease to exist?"

Tracks, in particular, addresses the diminishing Indian land base in the Midwest. The year of its publication Erdrich coauthored an essay with Dorris, for the *New York Times Magazine*, titled "Who Owns the Land?" In it they outline the specific land swindle on the White Earth Chippewa Reservation.

> What followed [the Indian Appropriations Bill of 1906] was a land-grab orgy so outrageous that to this day local people, regardless of ethnic heritage, speak of it with a sense of bewildered shame. Threatened, duped, or plied with drink, many Chippewa signed away their deeds with an X or a thumb print. . . . The effect on the band was devastating. While lumber companies clear-cut millions of dollars' worth of pine from forests located within White Earth, dispirited and broken Indian families clustered ten or more to single-room cabins on the allotments left to them.

This description fits the scenario of *Tracks*, in which some characters lose their land allotments. Although the particularities are consistent with the White Earth Chippewa in Minnesota, the situation could have, and has, happened to many indigenous peoples.

In addition to the cycle of novels set in North Dakota, Erdrich has authored three collections of poetry, *Jacklight* (1984), *Baptism of Desire* (1989), and *Original Fire: New and Selected Poems* (2003). *The Blue Jay's Dance: A Birth Year* (1995) is a memoir of her mothering, her writing life in New Hampshire, and her longing for the horizon of the Midwest. *Books and Islands in Ojibwe Country* (2003) is a lyrical journey through language and place. She has also written a children's book based on an Ojibwe traditional story, *Grandmother's Pigeon* (1996), and two young adult novels, *The Birchbark House* (1999), and its sequel, *The Game of Silence* (2005), which both include her own illustrations. *The Antelope Wife* (1998) is Erdrich's one novel that does not carry over characters from the other works. Its primary setting is Minneapolis/St. Paul and its characters are urban Ojibwe Indians.

Although Erdrich and Dorris collaborated, only two books appear with both of their names credited. *Route Two* is a limited-edition travelogue of a family journey across the northern plains. The novel *The Crown of Columbus* (1991) was written in recognition of the Columbus quincentenary.

In a 1985 essay for the *New York Times Book Review*, "Where I Ought to Be: A Writer's Sense of Place," Erdrich explains, "We can escape gravity itself, and every semblance of geography, by moving into sheer space, and yet we cannot abandon our need for reference, identity or our pull to landscapes that mirror our most intense feelings." Erdrich's literary landscapes are grounded in the Midwest. She now lives in Minnesota, where she owns an independent book store and has continued writing. Each new novel in the North Dakota saga sheds new light on the previous works and keeps the storytelling alive in the oral tradition.

Sources and Further Reading: Gloria Bird, "Searching for Evidence of Colonialism at Work: A Reading of Louise Erdrich's *Tracks*," *Wicazo Sa Review: A Journal of Indian Studies* 8 (Fall 1992); Allan Chavkin and Nancy Feyl Chavkin, *Conversations with Louise Erdrich and Michael Dorris* (1994); Louise Erdrich, "Where I Ought to Be: A Writer's Sense of Place," *New York Times Book Review* (July 28, 1985); Louise Erdrich and Michael Dorris, "Who Owns the Land?" *New York Times Magazine* (Sept. 4, 1988); P. Jane Hafen, " 'We Anishinaabeg Are Keepers of the Names of the Earth': Louise Erdrich's Great Plains," *Great Plains Quarterly* 21 (Fall 2001); Sidner Larson, "The Fragmentation of a Tribal People in Louise Erdrich's *Tracks*," *American Indian Culture and Research Journal* 17 (1993); Louis Owens, "Erdrich and Dorris's Mixedbloods and Multiple Narratives," in Louis Owens, ed., *Other Destinies: Understanding the American Indian Novel* (1992); Greg Sarris, "Reading Louise Erdrich: *Love Medicine* as Home Medicine," in *Keeping Slug Woman Alive* (1993), ed. Greg Sarris; James D. Stripes, "The Problem(s) of (Anishinaabe) History in the Fiction of Louise Erdrich: Voices and Contexts," *Wicazo Sa Review: A Journal of Indian Studies* 7 (Fall 1991).

P. Jane Hafen
University of Nevada–Las Vegas

Sandra Cisneros (b. 1954)

Historically known for its European and African American migrations, in the 1910s Chicago's demographic landscape changed when Mexican immigrants began to respond to the labor needs of World War I. Although large numbers of deportations would hinder the growth of the Mexican community during the Depression, Mexican immigration resumed in the labor shortages of World War II and the following years. In those postwar years, Puerto Ricans would migrate to Chicago in large numbers for the first time. These two Hispanic populations would settle in different neighborhoods of Chicago.

Raised on the West Side of Chicago in an ethnically diverse neighborhood, critically acclaimed poet and novelist Sandra Cisneros is considered a major voice of Latina literature in American letters. Cisneros has often stated that she carries a legacy of the Chicago literary tradition by acknowledging the influences of fellow Chicago writers Carl Sandburg and Gwendolyn Brooks in the development of the first stages in her writing. Born in 1954 and growing up in the time of the civil rights movement of the 1960s, she was able to tune in to the myriad experiences, perspectives, and voices that distinguished the multiethnic. As the only daughter of a Mexican father and Mexican American mother in a family that included six brothers, she was the first family member to leave home. She journeyed into the world of poetry and fiction (at a young age) at the University of Iowa Writers' Workshop in the 1970s. Upon returning to her native Chicago, though, Cisneros dedicated her time to teaching at the Latino Youth Alternative High School in order to mentor and encourage Latino youth in the arts. Drawing from this experience and her formal training, she published her first major critical success, *The House on Mango Street*, in 1984; it won the Before Columbus Foundation's American Book Award.

The novel presents Cisneros's portrayal of urban Mexican and Mexican American migratory experiences in the Midwest. Hailed by scholars, this work has become required reading in high schools and universities across the United States. Emblematic of urban diversity, Cisneros's first book of fiction dramatizes the presence of European American, Mexican, Puerto Rican, Chinese, and European cultures in contact with one another in the city of Chicago. Although the protagonist, Esperanza Cordero, is a young Latina coming of age, her experiences are also representative of other youngsters growing up in a twentieth-century American city.

Although *The House on Mango Street* is a fictional portrayal of a working-class barrio, its setting bears a strong resemblance to Cisneros's native Chicago. It is a work as much about sound as it is about place. In fact, Cisneros incorporates vernacular speech in her work by paying close attention to urban voices just as Carl Sandburg and Gwendolyn Brooks did in their writing. Cisneros's linguistic experimentation also stems from her juxtaposition of the English and Spanish languages. In *Latina Self-Portraits*, she says, "[My mother] has a working-class Chicago voice that is the antithesis of my father's voice. My father is very much the lyrical voice in my writing." Cisneros is well aware that the combination of colloquial English and lyrical Spanish forms an essential component of her poetry and fiction.

In her first collection of poetry, *My Wicked, Wicked Ways* (1987), Cisneros moves into another stage of her writing in the literary persona of the independent woman who celebrates her travels throughout the world through her romantic relationships. This work alludes to places—streets, stores, and people—taken from the actual city of Chicago as well as many historical cities in Europe. Cisneros travels throughout this geographical landscape to exemplify her strong identification with place and space in a rapidly changing world. Yet the reader is also introduced to the Chicago neighborhood of Cisneros's youth in a section called "1200 South/2100 West."

In *Woman Hollering Creek* (1991) and *Loose Woman* (1994), Cisneros broadens her demographic spectrum by situating her stories between the United States and Mexico along the border region of Texas. Cognizant of the hardships of immigration and migration between Mexico and the United States, Cisneros traces the history behind these social movements through the genealogical portrait of the Reyes family in her recent novel, *Caramelo* (2002). Here Cisneros travels between Chicago, San Antonio, and Mexico City to create a dialogue among major metropolises of the Americas and a vibrant portrayal of the cosmopolitan city of the twentieth century. Richly layered in characters and action, the plot unravels three generations of Reyeses. The protagonist, Lala (Celaya) Reyes, is the youngest of seven and the only daughter of a Mexican-born carpenter, Inocencio Reyes, and his Mexican American wife, Zoila. Cisneros not only captures the nuances of a Mexican and Mexican American family in cultural conflict—and does so with humor—but she also pays homage to an important era in Mexican cul-tural history, the Golden Age period (1935–1955), through her references to historical figures and enter-tainers.

Cisneros has received fellowships from the National Endowment for the Arts and the MacArthur Foundation and a Lannan Foundation Literary Award, and she leads writing workshops in the Guadalupe Cultural Center in San Antonio, Texas, where she makes her new home. In 2004 Vintage Books published *Vintage Cisneros*, a collection of excerpts from her fiction and poetry. This native daughter of Chicago has redefined the Midwest as a leading ethnic cosmopolitan writer of the twenty-first century.

Sources and Further Reading: Héctor Calderón and José David Saldívar, *Criticism in the Borderlands* (1991); Annie Eysturoy, *Daughters of Self-Creation* (1998); Bridget Kevane and Juanita Heredia, *Latina Self-Portraits* (2000); Deborah Madsen, *Understanding Contemporary Chicana Literature* (2000); Ellen McCracken, *New Latina Narrative* (1999); Sonia Saldívar-Hull, *Feminism on the Border* (2000).

Juanita Heredia
Northern Arizona University

Arts

SECTION EDITOR
Barbara Groseclose

Section Contents

Overview

To consider the Midwest as a breeding ground for creativity in the production of architecture, the visual and decorative arts, and music, one must take into consideration more than a summary of its constituent parts. Probing beyond the "catalog" approach to makers and their creative offerings, however, suggests that the operative assumption could be something like "region imprints artists and/or art." An inquiry on this fundamental level would lead to a search for evidence—physical? metaphysical?—of what a regional "imprint" might be. And there is a practical question involved: How does the mobility of the American population affect the notion of something being "midwestern"—say, if the artist is born in the Midwest but spends a significant portion of her career elsewhere? These questions force an "overview" of the Midwest and its arts to coalesce into something broader and more profound than a summary: Is there a difference between art forms/styles/subjects in the Midwest and those produced anywhere else in the country? These are all difficult and complex questions and they have no obvious answers. A related issue that can be more easily, or at least more substantively, addressed has to do with what particular claim the Midwest has on the development of the arts in the United States.

Most historians agree that the Midwest's claim to being an influence nationally in the arts can best be made in two areas: music and architecture, with a bow to decorative arts as well. Because two of the greatest names in American architectural history—Frank Lloyd Wright and Louis Sullivan—are well known as midwesterners, a stake on national influence in terms of architecture might be construed to be purely modern. And, in this case, one might expand the list to three names, in order to include the mature career of the chief exponent of the International Style, Mies van der Rohe, who was in Chicago beginning in the 1930s. In truth, a midwestern history of building should be considered from its inception with the indigenous peoples, whose uses of local materials, especially certain woods, linked the necessity of shelter with beauty in regionally specific ways. In spirit the indigenous structures were models for buildings of extraordinary ingenuity and adaptability erected by the many immigrant groups who oftentimes displaced the Native American communities on what was then the frontier in the late eighteenth and early nineteenth centuries. The log cabins of the Scandinavians who farmed the heavily timbered upper Midwest, the fortified clay and frame houses and barns of the German-Russians on the plains, the sod houses made famous in early photographs of the Czech settlers in Nebraska—these and other vernacular structures not only retain the flavor of the immigrants' origins but also respond to the terrain and materials of the North American continent's interior in memorable ways.

During the nineteenth century, as the frontier

Taliesin by Frank Lloyd Wright, 1925, Spring Green, Wisconsin. Courtesy The Frank Lloyd Wright Archives, Taliesin West, Scottsdale, AZ.

moved farther west and the "middle" Midwest—Indiana, Illinois, Ohio, Missouri—became more densely populated and urban, the standard styles of architecture then prevalent in the Northeast, neoclassicism and Gothic revival among them, were used for public buildings and grand domestic dwellings alike. Pattern books showing the plans of structures built by establishment architects in the Boston and Newport areas gave nineteenth-century midwesterners an opportunity to adopt these ideas in their own houses, an architectural heritage that, along with borrowed town-planning patterns carried to the Western Reserve by settlers from New England, further identified parts of the Midwest with New England.

That midwestern architecture retained a distinctive and local quality nevertheless can be attributed to the genius of Frank Lloyd Wright. Wright's move from Wisconsin to Chicago in 1887 launched a career founded on the design of startlingly original and regionally specific single-family dwellings, such as the Robie House (1909), collectively known as the Prairie school of architecture. Wright's idea was to "anchor" his dwellings, as he termed it, to the plains, stretching low roofs across flat terrain, shadowing interiors with cantilevered eaves, and opening the floor plan so that the inhabitants moved unimpeded through the supremely serene interiors. Further, when Wright pioneered what he called "Usonian" houses, he modified some of these ideas in order to make them available in "affordable" buildings, as seen, for example, in those he built for Herbert Johnson in Wisconsin (1939, 1950). One might make an artificial but not entirely indefensible leap from Wright's imaginative midwestern designs to the visionary novelties of Buckminster Fuller, whose Wichita House (1945) was inspired by midwestern farm buildings modified for mass-produced living units.

Tellingly, public buildings in the Midwest also are characterized by structural and design innovations; the most globally significant of these structures is the skyscraper. For many, the "birth" of the skyscraper, that original and unmatched contribution of America to world architecture, took place in Chicago. The now-destroyed Marshall Field Wholesale Store (1887) in Chicago, by Henry Hobson Richardson, provided the groundwork for some of the design and technical features of the skyscraper, a contribution that accounts, perhaps, for the spread of the Richardsonian Romanesque style over the Midwest. In Chicago, too, William Le Baron Jenney erected the nine-story Home Insurance Building (1885), which, it is claimed, was the first metal frame–construction building. The Home Insurance Building constituted a technical achievement that paved the way for the dramatic climax of cagelike construction clad in glass recognized around the world as the quintessential statement of Mies van der Rohe's International Style and expressed most formidably in his Lake Shore Drive apartments (1948–1951) in Chicago. Important transitional developments of the skyscraper—like the lavish organic ornamentation and vertical articulation of St. Louis's Wainwright Building (1891), by Louis Sullivan, and the narrative historicism of the Nebraska State Capitol (1932), by Bertram Goodhue—also unfolded in the Midwest. Finally, and not surprisingly, midwestern architectural firms have been the source of many of the world's tallest buildings: the Sears Tower in Chicago (1976) and the Jin Mao Tower in Shanghai (1998), by Skidmore, Owings & Merrill, and New York's iconic World Trade Center (1976–2001), by Minoru Yamasaki and his associates.

Creative use of local materials and invention in terms of form—arguably the hallmarks of the architecture produced in the Midwest that influenced the rest of the country—also show up as distinctive characteristics of the decorative arts. The author of the "Decorative Arts" overview essay postulates that artists in the Midwest have a stronger connection to the land and to products of the land than may be found in other parts of the country. While this claim may be debatable, it does help to differentiate exemplary arts like pottery and furniture produced in the Midwest from their counterparts originating elsewhere in the United States. And such a hypothesis permits a link to be discerned between these utilitarian decorative arts of the Midwest and the freewheeling, occasionally practical, and always materially oriented pieces of visual artists working in three dimensions, like Minnesota sculptor Siah Armajani and Ohio's Ann Hamilton, who creates assemblages.

As in the relationship of midwestern architecture to its national counterparts, the dominant site for the impress of midwestern music on the national scene is Chicago. There are those who might see the Windy City as the endpoint of a jazz narrative begun down South and moving through Kansas City and St. Louis. In this progression, one might draw a line from Earl "Fatha" Hines, Louis Armstrong, and others playing on Chicago's South Side during the 1920s through the swing years of the 1930s to the avant-garde era of the second half of the twentieth century. Others might acknowledge Chicago as a transition point, especially for artists who would go on to play in the Northeast, and rank Kansas City as Chicago's peer as a breeding ground for musicians whose names became household words thanks to radio and recordings. In this case, names like Count Basie, who got his start as a bandleader in Kansas City, would arise. A strong dissenting voice can be cast against Chicago and in favor of Detroit as the musical garden where jazz flowered. The names of Detroit's great players—Jean Goldkette, the

Jones brothers, Kenny Burrell—no longer retain a national cachet in the way that names like Count Basie and Earl "Fatha" Hines continue to do, but the city's clubs attracted the country's finest modernists, like Miles Davis, for playing dates of varying length, and its emphasis on—make that its love of—music for several decades may have been the generative impulse for the place of Motown in national music history.

Deciding whether art forms in the Midwest are different from those in other parts of the country can be problematic. Regional arts often have qualifying adjectives ready-made in the public mind: for example, "gothic" southern literature or "austere" New England church interiors. "Californian" has even become an adjective in its own right, summoned to identify the characteristics of everything from certain rock music harmonies to styles of performance art. The term *Midwest*, though carving a region out of the North American interior larger than all other such geographic circumscriptions, usually carries associations neither stereotypical nor archetypal when linked with the arts.

To be sure, there is an exception, a glaring and well-known one, but in this instance the connotations of qualifying an art form with the adjective referring to region are not aesthetically based. Grant Wood's *American Gothic* (1930) stands, to many people, as a quintessentially "midwestern" painting. In fact, almost any regionalist painting is likely to be termed midwestern, but if the sober miens of Woods's farmers or, say, the down-home piety of John Steuart Curry's believers in *Baptism in Kansas* (1928) conjure up an image of the Midwest, it is not style to which the term alludes but content. "Midwestern" and "regionalist" have become synonymous accounts for the often-repeated calumny that midwestern painting can be identified with plainness, seriousness, agrarianism, and an utter lack of sophistication. Midwestern in these terms, then, equates with parochial. *American Gothic, Baptism in Kansas*, and many similar paintings spring from a particular historical moment in post–World War I American art circles, a time pitting rural against urban in a cultural contest of wills among artists and critics. It was a contest in which geography was claimed not simply as a component of a given aesthetic value system but as its determinant. Despite popular opinion, in other words, the paintings of Wood, Curry, and other regionalists have to do much more with particular art-historical issues of time rather than place.

The time and place that fostered the idea of midwestern parochialism through regionalist paintings and similar visual images also saw the deeply cosmopolitan jazz of Chicago and Kansas City rise to national dominance and the international reputation of Frank Lloyd Wright bloom. And if one looks at the visual arts of the Midwest in the decades bracketing the two World Wars, it is not agriculture or religion that "identifies" regional imagery at all but, rather, abstractions in welded steel or funkiness in pictorial imagery in the contemporary era (as in the work of Richard Hunt or Jim McNutt) and European—particularly French—academicism in the nineteenth century (for example, the art of Kenyon Cox).

The truth of the matter is that there are no unique regional characteristics of style or content pertaining to the fine arts in the Midwest (that's true for other parts of the country too, though it is not always admitted). Some proclivities, like the interest in local material and in innovation, have already been cited. There are, as the example of *American Gothic* demonstrates, misperceptions and misrepresentations as well. Certain special conditions inform and shape the arts produced in the Midwest, and these relate both to the influence of the region on national artistic development and to the issues of "regional imprint."

The first of these is historical. In some places it has been less than a century since what is now regarded as "middle" geographically was "west" or frontier. The consequences of this change are everywhere present in both scholarly and popular narratives of the region's artistic production. In painting, for instance, genre scenes depicting the activities of boatmen on the Missouri River before the Civil War as painted by George Caleb Bingham were lauded by East Coast audiences as true "frontier" scenes, while only eighty years later portrayals of ordinary Missourians like those Thomas Hart Benton painted became fodder for attacks on midwestern "provincialism."

Second, the Midwest has a distinctive, though not unique, sociological formation. The shift from west to Midwest, from pioneer to provincial, is only one manifestation of a region always in flux, a condition magnified by a transitory and highly diverse population. Pioneers from Europe, like the Swiss and Germans who settled Wisconsin or the Scandinavians who spread over Minnesota, joined an already diverse indigenous population. Later, immigration from the southern states, like African American musicians who came up the Mississippi River from New Orleans to St. Louis or Kansas City, added to the mix. The immense cultural diversity of the region became the source of both new and hybrid forms of art. While the most obvious instance of hybridity can be found in musical forms like rags—music composed and produced in the Midwest blending African rhythms and European harmonics—midwestern visual arts have continually demonstrated the effects of demographic fluidity. Beginning with the various minor European sculptors of the mid-nineteenth century who brought methods of casting and carving to a part of the country not heavily endowed with opportunities for training or disseminating three-dimensional art, and flourishing most vividly with the various photographers, designers, and architects who brought the pedagogical and aesthetic proclivities of Germany's influential Bauhaus when they were forced out of Europe in the 1930s, the Midwest has been a cosmopolitan intersection of ideas and cultures having a profound effect on the region's and the nation's artistic heritage.

How important is it to judge an artist, or a work of art, by location? What is learned by asking who is a midwestern artist? To put it another way, what are the stakes in claiming a regional appellation? In the case of, say, Henry Holmes Smith—born in Illinois, educated in Chicago and Columbus, and an esteemed teacher of photography at Indiana University and elsewhere—the answer is based purely on geographic continuity (that his work and teaching might be described as "highly innovative" would be a factor also likely to associate him with the Midwest). Astonishingly, as the "Photographers and Photography" overview points out, most of the major American photographers of the twentieth century were either born or raised in the Midwest, a list that includes artists as diverse pictorially and stylistically as Gertrude Kasebier and Edward Steichen or Edward Weston and Lewis Hine. In addition, very nearly every major Farm Security Administration (FSA) photographer was born or worked in the Midwest, from Walker Evans to Russell Lee. Yet because they did not remain in the region as Smith did, not one of them has been termed a midwestern artist, although the FSA sent many of these same photographers back to the region to document effects of the Depression and attendant catastrophes. It seems clear, therefore, that in the case of photography, residence has played a greater role in assigning "midwestern-ness" than birthright.

Despite a celebrated career elsewhere, could someone like, say, the sculptor David Smith, who was born in the Midwest and retained only limited ties to the region (in his case, the connection between working as a welder in Indiana and his innovative use of welding as a sculptural technique), be identified with the region just on the basis of technique? Then the criteria for "midwestern artist" might involve more than continuous residence in the region, something ineffable, randomly available or discernible, and surely unmeasurable: the formative potency of a region. The painter Robert Indiana must have put some credence in this idea, since he changed his surname from the mundane Clark to Indiana after taking up residence in New York. While Indiana has made an overt statement of origin, other examples of a regional formative influence are less publicly available. For example, a contemporary performance artist, Laurie Anderson, who grew up in the Midwest, uses semiautobiographical narrative like that employed by midwestern storytellers in her highly urbane pieces, a feature that has usually gone unnoticed but is not obviated by the prevailing critical tendency to interpret her work as "universal."

Conversely, there are artists who were raised elsewhere in the world but who have made some or all of their career in the Midwest. In this case the appropriateness of a midwestern appellation must reside in the uses to which region has been put or the relevance of region to the production or dissemination of the work. For example, the freeborn Robert Duncanson chose to work in antebellum Cincinnati and Detroit instead of his home state of New York because there were commissions forthcoming not only for a person of color but also for landscape painting in the Ohio River Valley. Harvey Littleton, a contemporary glass sculptor from New York and founder of the studio glass movement, trained at the Cranbrook Academy of Art in Michigan and, shortly after joining the art faculty of the University of Wisconsin, made use of the midwestern glass industry, especially in Toledo, Ohio, to explore the possibilities of the material as a fine arts form unconnected to decorative functions.

If, sometimes, the effects of region are obvious and in other instances they are buried, nonetheless region is a part—only a part, to be sure, and to greater or lesser degrees—of the rich creative brew from which art is made. It is safe to say, however, and it is saying a lot, that for a visual, architectural, or musical artist to be of the Midwest—born there, raised there, resident there—counts.

Sources and Further Reading: H. Allen Brooks, *The Prairie School: Frank Lloyd Wright and His Midwest Contemporaries* (1972); Gerald Early, *One Nation under a Groove: Motown and American Culture* (1995); William Gerdts, *Art across America: Two Centuries of Regional Painting, 1710–1920*, vol. 3 (1990); Donald Megill, *Introduction to Jazz History* (1993); Marion Nelson, *Art Pottery of the Midwest* (1988); New Art Association (Chicago, Ill.), *New Art Examiner,* Midwest edition (1980–1985); W. Jackson Rushing, ed., *Native American Art in the 20th Century* (1999); G. E. Kidder Smith, *Architecture of the United States*, vol. 3 (1981); Robert Stearns, ed., *Illusions of Eden: Visions of the American Heartland* (2000).

Barbara Groseclose
The Ohio State University–Columbus

Architecture: Traditional Native American Forms

Home to a large number of Native American cultures, the Midwest includes people from both the Algonquian and the Siouan language families. The eastern

Ho-Chunk Mat Lodge. Nebraska State Historical Society, Photograph Collection, 970.1 N117n p57.

portion of the region, or the western Great Lakes, is the territory of the Ho-Chunk, or Winnebago; the Chippewa, or Ojibwa; the Menomini; the Potawatomi; the Kickapoo; the Mesquakie, or Sac; and the Fox. Mid Ohio and the central states of Indiana and Illinois include the Shawnee, the Miami, and the Illinois. Farther west, in the portion of the Midwest bordering the plains that is sometimes referred to as the Prairie Plains, are the Yankton, Yanktonai or Nakota, and Santee Dakota; the Iowa, Missouria, Kansa, Otoe, Pawnee, Ponca, and Omaha; and a portion of the Osage peoples. Each of these cultures, like people throughout indigenous North America, developed architecture that combined available materials with the needs dictated by environment, social structure, and worldview. Given the great diversity of Native American peoples in the Midwest, variety is apparent in architecture, but many factors remain constant. Wood was the primary building material, and houses were microcosms of the world, reflective of the organizing principles of daily life and of the universe at large.

Because of the wealth of trees in much of the area, houses were generally constructed of bent or angled wooden frames covered with bark, brush, or woven reed mats. In the Great Lakes region, for example, the Menomini, the Ho-Chunk, and the Chippewa sewed cattails together with root or plant fiber to create mats that averaged four or five feet long and perhaps two feet wide. The pithy stalks of the plants were not only readily at hand but also provided good insulation. Other house coverings came from strips of bark, up to six feet long and a foot or two wide, that were cut from trees during the spring when sap was flowing, with

birch a favorite of many people. Whether bark or mats were used, the separate coverings overlapped each other to provide adequate protection from the elements. Additional linings might be used on the home's interior for further insulation in colder weather. As it became available, canvas was also sometimes used both as an exterior and as an interior covering.

In addition to availability of materials with which to build, Native American cultures developed housing in accord with their worldviews and social structure. Circular in floor plan, bentwood frames for single-family dwellings that might average between twelve and fifteen feet in diameter could be expanded for elliptical or rectangular ceremonial lodges to hold large groups of people, while smaller one-person structures were used for some ritual specialists' needs as well as for temporary hunting shelters. Larger longer-term village locations generally took advantage of the wealth of rivers and lakes in the Midwest.

While caves and rock shelters were undoubtedly previously occupied, the earliest constructed housing types known from the Midwest are those from the archaeological past. Especially notable structures were built by the early agriculturalists of the Woodlands era, approximately 1000 B.C.E. to C.E. 1000, and the following Mississippian period, from 1000 to 1600. The Adena culture of the Ohio River Valley region and the Hopewell of Ohio and Illinois, in particular, are known as Mound Builders who used earthen mounds as burial locations. People were often interred with elaborate offerings of both raw materials such as shell and mica, much of which had to be obtained through trade, as well as sculpted art forms, including pipes. Based on postholes revealed through excavation, Adena houses are assumed to have been circular in plan, between twenty and seventy feet in diameter, with roofs that may have been conical, the entire house shape mirroring the Adena burial mounds, which reached as high as seventy-one feet in height. Small villages of a few such houses were probably composed of related families. Hopewell houses from perhaps 100 B.C.E. to C.E. 500, in contrast, are generally assumed to have been rectangular in floor plan. These structures, shaped like many Hopewell mounds, may have been flatter roofed than their Adena counterparts. Both types of houses were constructed of wooden frames of posts and either bent saplings, for roof foundations of Hopewell structures, or posts leaning from the circular enclosure toward the central fire pit as the framework for the Adena houses. Each was undoubtedly covered with brush or bark.

Larger-scale communities of the later Mississippian era were more heavily dependent upon agriculture, which now included significant production of corn, originally introduced to North America from Mesoamerica. Extensive agriculture required that villagers develop more sedentary lifestyles, and effective crop production made heavier populations possible in compact areas. With increasing populations and the requirements brought by agriculture and organized building, planting, and harvesting, more complex social organizations are evident. Various Mississippian sites in Illinois and Missouri, for example, included large-scale earthen mounds as the bases for structures that were either temples or houses for an elite leadership. Monks Mound at Cahokia, near East St. Louis, Illinois, was the biggest mound north of Mexico, rising one hundred feet high with its base measuring approximately one thousand by seven hundred feet. Site planning is evident with large plaza spaces, undoubtedly for public use and for ceremonies. The metropolis of Cahokia itself was home to perhaps twenty thousand people living in a six-square-mile area. Most Cahokians lived in smaller, rectangular floor-plan structures with thatched roofs, reconstructions of which are based on the kinds of houses that European explorers encountered in parts of the Midwest and Southeast during the seventeenth century.

Specialized structures are apparent in the archaeological record from at least the Hopewellian era through the Mississippian period. Of particular importance are wooden-frame and probably brush-covered buildings that were places where the deceased received elaborate preparation for burial. Some of these charnel houses may also have been considered temples and were elevated on mounds much like temples Europeans found in parts of the Southeast during the sixteenth and seventeenth centuries.

From the archaeological past to more recent times, Native American people of the Midwest selected locations for their villages based on access to good hunting areas as well as fertile soil for agriculture. Rich waterways of the region provided important means of transportation and access for trade. The basic house type, regardless of its specific covering, was circular or oval in floor plan. Saplings forming the outer circle were bent toward the dome-shaped roof in many examples with horizontal stringers tied to the uprights for additional support. A centrally placed smoke hole and a doorway, usually rectangular, both provided necessary ventilation. Generally, men and women had specific places within lodges, and children observed rules not only of location but also of activities or ways of movement within the home.

By the time of European contact and undoubtedly well before, most of the people of the Midwest moved for hunting and gathering purposes but retained strong ties to specific areas, returning there annually, especially at times of harvest. Bentwood frames for houses might be left standing while the village traveled during parts of the year, taking with them the rolled mat or bark coverings. Mats were then reused at other camps as well as upon the return to the permanent village. Fall gathering of wild rice brought larger groups together in the western Great Lakes, while harsh winters frequently required that limited numbers of people camp together.

Permanent community size was most frequently small but there were exceptions; the Miami of present-day Wisconsin had much larger villages, reflective of a more highly structured society that resembled a chiefdom; seventeenth-century French explorers reported one village on the Fox River as home to perhaps twenty thousand people. Villages like this had undoubtedly grown with an influx of refugees from farther east who fled not only Europeans but also the powerful Iroquois Confederacy. For much of the seventeenth and eighteenth centuries, and into the nineteenth, the Native American people of the Midwest were caught between these forces to the east and an inability, in most cases, to move farther west because of the strength of plains people such as the Lakota.

Among some western Great Lakes peoples, the preferred winter lodge was conical in form, composed of a series of poles that leaned against a foundation tripod. Similar to the plains-style teepee, this style of lodge was generally covered with horizontal rolls of bark or mats held in place by additional poles placed against them leaning toward the central supports. Just as the dome-shaped wigwam could be expanded, so could the conical form through the addition of a ridgepole simultaneously supported by the tripod poles spaced regularly underneath it and additional poles leaning against that foundation. Such homes were most frequently extended- or multiple-family dwellings. Summer temperatures and the accompanying humidity brought other architectural forms into use for many people of the Midwest. Some were rectangular in floor plan and were covered by bark. Rectangular ramadas or open-sided sun shades were also important additions for the heat of summer.

Native peoples who inhabited the farthest western portions of the Midwest or the Prairie Plains shared various cultural traits with those of the high plains cultures. Many of these peoples, however, remained strong agriculturalists who, while they might leave their permanent villages to hunt buffalo and gather wild plants, returned to sow, maintain, and harvest their crops. The Kansa, Otoe, Missouria, and Iowa peoples of present-day Kansas, Missouri, and Iowa used teepees or skin tents as shelters, as they did the other types of wooden-frame lodges found to the east. However, the Kansa, Iowa, Missouria, and Otoe also built earth lodges. Circular in floor plan, such structures averaged forty feet in diameter, as recorded by early explorers. The lodge floor was excavated some three feet into the earth below ground level and surrounded the central fire pit. When covered with earth, the domed structure blended into the environment and provided good insulation against the varied climate. Some earth lodge villages were large, averaging between forty and seventy structures, while at least one Kansa village contained 120 such homes.

The Yankton, Yanktonai, and Santee Dakota peoples of Minnesota and the eastern portions of North and South Dakota and the Caddoan-speaking Pawnee of Kansas and Nebraska also exhibit architectural features known from the plains. Teepees or conical skin tents, egg-shaped or oval in floor plan, were built with doorways facing toward the east, the direction of the rising sun as well as the direction away from the prevailing westerly winds of the plains. Pawnee earth lodge architecture is among the most complex in its known associations with cosmology and worldview. Entry into Pawnee semisubterranean lodges was through an angled tunnel-like ramp that opened to the east. Regular houses generally had four central support posts while the larger lodges of leaders and ritual specialists had eight or ten. Like earth lodges elsewhere, other smaller supporting saplings and crossmembers of wood formed the frame, which was subsequently covered in earth. An opening in the roof, the smoke hole, was necessary for ventilation but also connected the people in the lodge to the supreme deity in the skies above. The most sacred space within the lodge, as was the case for many Native American cultures of the plains, was in the rear or western portion, where an altar was kept. East was not only the direction of the rising sun, but also that of Morning Star, deemed male. West was Evening Star's direction, that

of woman. Morning Star and Evening Star are the parents of the first Pawnee people, and the entry of the sun through Morning Star's doorway every morning shining light toward the rear of the lodge, or Evening Star's space, reenacts the first union that brought the Pawnee into the world. Such rich narratives of the indigenous peoples of North America tie many daily activities, including the manner of building houses, to cultural origins and proper ways of behavior.

Sources and Further Reading: David S. Brose, "The Woodland Period," in David Brose, James A. Brown, and David W. Penny, eds., *Ancient Art of the American Woodland Indians* (1985); Raymond J. DeMallie, ed., *Plains*, vol. 13 of William C. Sturtevant, ed., *Handbook of North American Indians* (2001); Peter Nabokov and Robert Easton, *Native American Architecture* (1989); Stewart Rafert, *The Miami Indians of Indiana* (1996); Bruce G. Trigger, ed., *Northeast*, vol. 15 of William C. Sturtevant, ed., *Handbook of North American Indians* (1978); Bibloine Whiting Young and Melvin L. Fowler, *Cahokia: The Great Native American Metropolis* (2000).

Joyce M. Szabo
University of New Mexico

Architecture: The Long Nineteenth Century

The built environment of the Midwest is crucial for understanding the architectural development of the United States. The region is home to one of the richest varieties of vernacular architecture in the nation, not surprising given the many immigrant groups that made their way west during the nineteenth century. National trends were quickly established in the Midwest, resulting in many fine examples of the various revival styles common to the architecture of the nineteenth century. The development of the tall building must be understood through the work of the Chicago school, led by innovators such as Louis Sullivan. Whether reflecting local traditions, adapting national styles, or suggesting new directions, the architecture of the Midwest is central to the story of built America.

The cultural landscape of the Midwest was shaped by the rectangular grid system created by the Northwest Land Ordinance of 1785 (expanded in 1796). Drafted by Thomas Jefferson, the act mandated that land be divided into six-mile-square townships, which were in turn subdivided into smaller units of various sizes. These basic units could be grouped together as counties, and the counties combined to form the different states. This grid formed most of the boundaries and connections between built spaces throughout the Midwest, visible today in straight roads, fences, and planted tree lines. Buildings and town plans tended to respond to this grid system in the same orderly manner. The grid pattern is one of the most distinctive characteristics of the Midwest when viewed from above.

Settlers brought their own cultural traditions of building, and the Midwest was the site of many distinctive vernacular forms. Early examples would be the buildings of the French settlers along the Mississippi River at sites such as Ste. Genevieve, Missouri, and Cahokia, Illinois. This architecture is distinctive for its use of closely spaced upright logs placed on a timber sill (*poteaux-sur-sole*), with the gaps between posts filled with mixtures such as clay and grass, and for high-peaked roofs with large overhanging eaves. A good example is the reconstructed Cahokia Courthouse (1737).

Perhaps the most common vernacular house type in the Midwest is the I-house, an adaptation of a traditional house type from the British Isles. Examples are common in the rural areas of most midwestern states, but especially in Illinois, Iowa, Missouri, and Indiana. There are several variations, but the basic form is a house with side gables, one-and-a-half or two stories high, one room deep, and two rooms wide. The lower floor usually has an entrance hall separating the rooms with a central staircase. These houses were decorated in a variety of styles, depending upon when they were built, from Federal, Greek, and Gothic to Victorian gingerbread styles.

German immigrants introduced the greatest variety of European vernacular styles throughout the Midwest. By the middle of the century, German settlements were established around the Great Lakes and along the Ohio, Mississippi, and Missouri River Valleys. These settlers came from diverse backgrounds and traditions, and what they built reflected the character of these origins. Given their wide distribution, these groups also responded to different landscapes, levels of settlements, and interactions with existing populations. Thus, German American vernacular architecture varied extensively. The use of stone and brick was widespread because they were familiar materials from every region of Germany, but settlers from the more heavily wooded areas of southern and western Germany often used logged construction in the upper Great Lakes region. The most distinctive German style is seen in Missouri and central and eastern Wisconsin, where half-timbered, or *Fachwerk*, construction was used by immigrants from Pomerania, Brandenburg, and Saxony. Developed in their home regions because of wood shortages, the technique continued in their new settlements despite the abundance of timber. An excellent surviving example of Fachwerk is the well-preserved Petsch Barn (c. 1850) in Lebanon, Wisconsin.

Several other European groups could be highlighted in a survey of midwestern vernacular styles. In the areas around Lake Michigan, Belgian Walloon farmers built distinctive redbrick farmhouses (frame structures were typical in the region) with attached outdoor bake ovens. Log construction (usually with squared timbers) was widely used in the upper Midwest by immigrant populations, including Norwegian and Swedish settlers in Iowa, Minnesota, and the Dakotas, and Czech groups in Kansas, Nebraska, Iowa, and South Dakota. In the plains states, mixed German-Russian immigrants from the Volga and Black Sea regions easily adapted to the harsh conditions found in the western Midwest. Unlike the temporary sod houses commonly built by the first generation of settlers, their buildings were constructed of clay mixed with manure, straw, and water, which was then combined in a variety of framing techniques to form sturdy houses, farm buildings, churches, and meeting halls.

Surviving examples of these vernacular structures are rare. Settlers in the region tended to quickly adapt their traditional building forms to contemporary styles. Such changes ranged from covering log construction with milled sidings to completely replacing older structures with new ones exhibiting the modern styles made popular through pattern books and the increasing availability of architectural professionals. The typical house, capitol, or courthouse of the period followed the latest style, with classical and Gothic revivals dominant in the first half of the century and a wide variety of other historical forms popular after 1850.

Pattern books such as Asher Benjamin's *The American Builder's Companion* (1806), Andrew Jackson Downing's *Architecture of Country Houses* (1850), and Alexander Jackson Davis's *Rural Residences* (1837) had a major impact on the spread of these styles throughout the country. They typically illustrated a variety of decorative features and floor plans, easily adaptable to local conditions. Especially important in rural areas were plans published in such magazines as the *American Agriculturist* (midcentury) or *Wallace's Farmer* (1879–1929).

Builders made use of sawed lumber, factory bricks, regionally quarried stone, and manufactured components. Increasing standardization and the relative affordability of these components made "high"-style architecture accessible to most inhabitants of the Midwest. By the second half of the century, marble and limestone were being quarried in places such as Carthage, Missouri; Cold Spring, Minnesota; and

Burlington, Indiana. St. Louis was a major center of production for architectural ornamentation in terra cotta and iron. And every decent-sized town seemed to have a woodworking enterprise to produce milled lumber and decorative work. The commercial availability of these elements served to unify the architecture of the Midwest, eliminating much of the local vernacular and cultural traditions.

The standardization of lumber made possible perhaps the most far-reaching advance in construction practice in the nineteenth century, the development of the balloon frame in the 1830s. Balloon-frame construction, still in common use today, consists of regularly sized studs, joists, and rafters nailed together to form the frames for roofs, walls, ceilings, and floors. Affordably manufactured wire-cut nails replaced the earlier hand-produced spikes and dowels. In the nineteenth century, the frame was sheathed with boards, which were then covered with various materials, such as clapboards, stucco, or shingles. This system quickly replaced the traditional heavy-beamed construction in wood using intricate joinery and made possible (economically and technologically) the rapid expansion of settled regions. The term was in common use by 1835 in Chicago, and it is likely that the development of light framing systems was widespread throughout the Midwest by that time.

Designs inspired by ancient Greek and Roman classical architecture were especially popular for public buildings such as banks, churches, courthouses, and capitols; and classical fragments, especially columns and pilasters, were applied as ornamentation on both rural and urban houses. An excellent example of the Greek Revival style is the Ohio State Capitol (1838–1861), designed primarily by Thomas Cole and A.J. Davis. By midcentury, various forms of Gothic revival were the most popular styles. It was most commonly used for churches and houses, though in the latter, Gothic elements were often combined with other forms, such as Italianate features. The Fort Street Presbyterian Church in Detroit (finished 1855) is a good example of an urban version of Gothic revival, while the Pioneer Gothic Church (1857) in Dwight, Illinois, can represent the many small-town Carpenter Gothic churches throughout the Midwest.

Many other styles could be listed as part of the fashion parade that was nineteenth-century high-style architecture. Commonly used styles included Italianate, Queen Anne, Octagon, Eastlake, and Egyptian. Of particular interest in the Midwest was the Richardsonian Romanesque style, an adaptation of the round-arched masonry construction, visually heavy forms, and overall clarity of the buildings of the Boston architect Henry Hobson Richardson. This style was a particular favorite for courthouses, city halls, and other municipal structures. In Indiana, for instance, the style was used for a dozen county courthouses, including a particularly fine example in Rochester, the Fulton County Courthouse (1896), designed by A. William Rush. A few buildings by Richardson himself were built in the Midwest, including the influential Marshall Field Wholesale Store in Chicago (1887; demolished 1930).

Technological innovation is also an important element of the story of architecture in the nineteenth century. Two major bridges highlight the engineering advances. The Eads Bridge (1874) at St. Louis, designed by James B. Eads, was the first major steel structure in the country, anticipating the widespread use of steel by about fifteen years. At Cincinnati, the Roebling Suspension Bridge (1864) was a precursor to John A. Roebling's more famous design for the Brooklyn Bridge (1883).

Chicago, New York, and Philadelphia were key centers for the development of steel-frame construction, which, combined with inventions such as the Otis Safety Elevator, made construction of the tall building feasible. The Chicago designers of this new building type tended to have stronger engineering backgrounds than the New York architects, and this led to a distinctive style called the Chicago school. Which building was the first to use steel-cage construction is still being debated, but it is clear that Chicago designers such as William Le Baron Jenney and John Wellborn Root were pioneers in working out the basic elements of this new type of structure. Their buildings are noted for a rejection of historical ornament, a visual relationship between the hidden skeletal framework and the outer cladding, and a strong sense of openness due to the use of large-scale windows.

Louis H. Sullivan, with his partner Dankmar Adler, articulated the functionalist aesthetic of the early modern architecture and the tall building. Famous for its often misquoted statement that "form ever follows function," his essay published in 1896, "Tall Office Building," was a major starting point for the debates surrounding the new building type. His ideas about the relationship between appearance and function were fully explored in the Wainwright Building (1891) in St. Louis, also notable for Sullivan's organic terra-cotta decorations. His later work is highlighted by a number of richly decorated small-town banks throughout the Midwest, including the National Farmer's Bank (1908) in Owatonna, Minnesota, and the People's Savings and Loan Association (1918) in Sidney, Ohio. Sullivan was a major influence on the young Frank Lloyd Wright, who worked in his office from 1888 to 1893.

Chicago was also the site of the most public reaction against the modernism emerging at the end of the century. Visitors to the 1893 World's Columbian Exposition on Chicago's South Side were greeted with architecture seemingly taken directly out of ancient Rome. "The White City," as it was quickly named, centered on several large structures unified by a common style of grand classical ornament as well as by clearly organized plans. Known stylistically as Beaux Arts architecture, these structures served as models for numerous public buildings throughout the country, perhaps most strikingly in the many large state capitols built in the decades around 1900. Cass Gilbert's Minnesota State Capitol (1893–1904) is representative of the type, especially with its rich complement of sculptural and painted decorations. The unity and organization of the Columbian Exposition also inspired an interest in urban renewal projects, a phenomenon known as the City Beautiful movement, which transformed many cities across America, including sections of Chicago, Cleveland, and Kansas City.

Sources and Further Reading: Kathryn Bishop Eckert, *Buildings of Michigan* (1993); John S. Garner, ed., *The Midwest in American Architecture* (1991); David Gebhard and Gerald Mansheim, *Buildings of Iowa* (1993); Cyril M. Harris, *American Architecture: An Illustrated Encyclopedia* (1998); Frederick Koeper, *Illinois Architecture from Territorial Times to the Present* (1968); Leland Roth, *American Architecture: A History* (2001); David H. Sachs and George Ehrlich, *Guide to Kansas Architecture* (1996); Susan W. Thrane, *County Courthouses of Ohio* (2000); Dell Upton, ed., *America's Architectural Roots* (1986); Dell Upton, *Architecture in the United States* (1998).

Jeff Ball
Adrian College, Michigan

Architecture: 1918 to the Present

By the close of World War I, the modern movement in midwestern architecture known as the Prairie school was expiring. Frank Lloyd Wright was now preoccupied with new buildings in California and Japan. His mentor Louis H. Sullivan was in his final years, building a handful of small but extraordinary buildings in rural towns, such as his Farmers and Merchants Union Bank (finished 1920) in Columbus, Wisconsin. A few tried to continue the progressive spirit of Sullivan, as seen in George G. Elmslie's Capital Building and Loan (1922, demolished 1968) in Topeka, Kansas. However, most architecture built in the Midwest during the 1920s reflected the historical eclecticism and emerging art deco style evident throughout the United States at this time. The distinct regionalism of the earlier Chicago and Prairie schools was for the most part gone.

Two New York architects, John Mead Howells and Raymond M. Hood, were chosen in an international competition to build the Chicago Tribune Tower (1925). Their building, ornamented with many medieval motifs, was typical of major skyscrapers of this time in that it incorporated a theatrical and distinctive crown to distinguish its corporate client on the skyline of the city. Toward the end of the decade, overt historical eclecticism gave way to the decorative, machine-age modernism of art deco, as seen in Holabird and Root's Chicago Board of Trade Building (1930). This was a period when larger midwestern cities were being embellished with central, landmark skyscrapers, such as Cleveland's Terminal Tower (1930) by Graham, Anderson, Probst, and White. A skyscraper tower by Bertram Grosvenor Goodhue even distinguished the Nebraska State Capitol (1932) in Lincoln, one of more original buildings to be built in the Midwest during this period.

Michigan had emerged as America's center for automobile production. Albert Kahn was a prolific architect of many of the automobile factories built in the Detroit area. With the Ford River Rouge Plant (1938) in Dearborn, Michigan, Kahn built an enormous industrial complex that handled the breadth of automobile production from steel production to final assembly. Such steel and glass buildings as the Glass Plant (1922), with its spare, functional, single-story design, were some of the most advanced factory buildings in the world. For European modernists, factories were talismans of modern design with lessons for all building types. For Kahn, factories were just factories. For more traditional building types, he retreated to standard historical styles as seen in his mansion (1929) for Edsel Ford at Grosse Pointe Shores, Michigan, which was inspired by the historic architecture of the English Cotswolds. As the automobile was radically transforming the American landscape, Henry Ford created Greenfield Village (opened 1929) in Dearborn, an outdoor museum of historic buildings that were dismantled and moved from their original locations (such as the Wright Brothers' bicycle shop brought from Dayton, Ohio) and re-erected in Ford's enclave, celebrating the past before the past became asphalted over by the new automobile culture.

After placing second in the Chicago Tribune Tower competition in 1922, the Finnish architect Eliel Saarinen immigrated to the United States in 1923. One of his greatest contributions to the architecture of the Midwest is a series of buildings that Saarinen built between 1924 and 1943 for the unique educational institution of Cranbrook Academy of Art in Bloomfield Hills, Michigan. Buildings such as his Kingswood School for Girls (1931) reflect a modernist distillation of geometry, a reverential feel for traditional materials, an arts and crafts celebration of details, and an awareness of Wright's prairie architecture. Saarinen's carefully crafted and reserved modernism influenced a younger generation, particularly when he was president of Cranbrook from 1932 to 1946.

As America plunged into the Great Depression, Chicago staged a World's Fair to celebrate the city's centennial, the Century of Progress Exposition (1933–1934). The classical splendor of Chicago's earlier World's Columbian Exposition (1893) was abandoned in favor of an architectural image of modern progress. The Travel and Transportation Building (by Bennett, Burnham, and Holabird) was a theatrical exercise in modernism with its faceted walls and exposed structure. George Fred Keck's House of Tomorrow provided fairgoers with a glimpse of an imagined future where one could live in a twelve-sided steel-framed house that contained both a garage for one's car and a hangar for one's airplane. However, the immediate future was not as promising for most because construction dropped off dramatically during the Depression. A few major monuments of the Streamline Moderne were built in the Midwest during the Depression, like the Cincinnati Union Terminal (1933) by Fellheimer and Wagner (Roland A. Wank, chief designer) and the Butler House (1937) in Des Moines by Kraetesch and Kraetesch. Also, New Deal programs, such as the Public Works Administration, did

stimulate the construction of important works of public architecture across the Midwest, from post offices to schools, often in a spare, stripped classical style.

In the late 1930s, as Frank Lloyd Wright was entering his seventies, his career underwent a revival with such commissions as the Johnson Wax Administration Building (1939) in Racine, Wisconsin. For Johnson Wax, Wright rethought the corporate headquarters as a low, enclosed, streamlined building, focusing inward on a great work space with its unique forest of structural columns: a shrine to work in the middle of the Depression. With such residences as the Goetsch-Winkler House (1939) in Okemos, Michigan, Wright presented his vision of the Usonian house, which updated his earlier prairie houses and would influence suburban houses in the decades to come.

One of the most significant events in midwestern architecture during this period was the arrival in Chicago of the German architect Ludwig Mies van der Rohe. Mies was one of most celebrated architects of European modernism (the International Style) and had been the last director of the Bauhaus in Germany before it closed in 1933. In 1938, Mies became director of the architecture program at the Armour Institute (now the Illinois Institute of Technology; IIT). At IIT, Mies helped to transform the direction of American architectural education away from the classical traditions of the French Beaux-Arts system to a more focused study on the modern demands upon design

Ford Motor Company's River Rouge Plant, Dearborn, Michigan, 1927. Library of Congress, Prints and Photographs Division, Detroit Publishing Company Collection, LC-D414-K3461.

that had been addressed by the Bauhaus. Mies was able to demonstrate his ideas as he designed a new campus for IIT, beginning in 1939. Mies's spare, reductive, factorylike boxes of steel, brick, and glass that he built for IIT created an approach to architecture that forsakes an overt reverence for the past in favor of modern structural refinement with unencumbered universal spaces within.

On the one hand, Mies adapted his vision of elegant glass and steel boxes to the skyscraper when he built two apartment towers (1948–1951) at 860–880 North Lake Shore Drive in Chicago. These austere, transparent modern towers with floor-to-ceiling glass and flat roofs dramatically contrast with the masonry-sheathed masses of prewar skyscrapers with fanciful tops and ornament. On the other hand, the rational statement of the structural frame of these towers seemed to be an intriguing return to the earlier skyscrapers of the Chicago school. Mies would go on to build other glass-box skyscrapers, which established this as one of the dominant approaches for urban America in the postwar era. Skidmore, Owings & Merrill, a firm that was founded in Chicago, did much to spread the Miesian image of skyscraper design, although its buildings tended to be flashier and slicker in their use of structure and materials, as seen in the Inland Steel Building (1958) in Chicago. By the 1960s, the Miesian approach to skyscraper design was becoming redundant. Some skyscrapers began to assert individuality through a greater emphasis upon innovative and dramatic structure, more sculptural form, and unprecedented height, as seen in Chicago with the John Hancock Center (1969) and the Sears Tower (1974), both by Skidmore, Owings & Merrill.

For the boom in house construction that followed World War II, Buckminster Fuller, Jr. promoted a radical vision of what the American house could be in his circular Dymaxion Dwelling Machine, a prototype of which was produced by Beech Aircraft in Wichita, Kansas, in 1946. Fuller encouraged factories that had been producing such machines of war as bombers to convert to the production of prefabricated aluminum houses. However, most postwar suburban houses in the Midwest would be built of traditional materials by contractors, in a variety of styles that had now become national, from ranch to Cape Cod.

Suburbs were proliferating outside major cities as Americans became more dependent upon cars in their daily lives and the American landscape was being forever altered by the construction of new interstate highways. In Edina, Minnesota, Victor Gruen Associates built the first fully enclosed shopping mall. Rather than travel to downtown Minneapolis, suburbanites could now drive to the much more convenient shopping center of Southdale (1956), with its acres of free parking surrounding a safe, enclosed, climate-controlled environment with dozens of stores. In Des Plaines, Illinois, the first franchised McDonald's drive-in was unveiled in 1955, with its distinctive golden arches luring car-borne midwesterners to partake of rapidly produced hamburgers and french fries. Some major corporations built horizontally rather than vertically in the more expansive suburbs, an impressive example of which is General Motors Technical Center (1958) in Warren, Michigan, by Eliel and Eero Saarinen.

As the suburbs flourished, the answer to declining sections of midwestern cities was often drastic urban renewal projects that eradicated many older neighborhoods in favor of what was perceived to be bold new architectural visions. St. Louis lost several blocks of its historic architecture along the riverfront of the Mississippi so that a heroic new monument to westward expansion, the Gateway Arch (1947–1966, by Eero Saarinen) could be erected in a large urban park. Massive public-housing projects often attempted to replace decaying ghettoes with new modern high-rises. However, such projects as the sixteen-story towers of the Robert Taylor Homes (1962, Chicago Housing Authority), stretching for about two miles along Chicago's South Side, did not solve but only compounded problems of poverty, crime, and racial segregation.

By the 1970s, many midwestern downtowns were being renewed with reflective, glass-sheathed buildings that included large enclosed public spaces that were both pleasing and impressive, such as the Crystal Court in Johnson/Burgee's IDS Center (1973) in Minneapolis and the soaring atria of John Portman's Renaissance Center (1977) in Detroit. The 1980s saw a burst of corporate construction, now enlivened with a postmodern flirtation with more traditional forms, as seen in the two towered Procter and Gamble Headquarters (1985) in Cincinnati by Kohn Pedersen Fox.

Columbus, Indiana, acquired a major work of modern architecture when Eliel and Eero Saarinen built the First Christian Church (1942) in this rural community. This stimulated interest in Columbus in new buildings by major architects. The local Cummins Engine Foundation offered to cover the architects' fees if significant architects were chosen to design selected schools, public buildings, and churches. This encouraged construction in this small prairie town of dozens of buildings by a who's who of American contemporary architects.

Beyond the work of Frank Lloyd Wright, one of the most intriguing houses responding to the midwestern prairie is Bruce Goff's Glen Harder House (1972) near Mountain Lake, Minnesota, with its swooping roof covered with orange carpet, built for turkey farmers. Utilizing the midwestern agrarian vernacular, Laurence Booth transformed a lowly farm outbuilding into a simple summer home in his "Chicken Coop" (1988) near Lake Bluff, Illinois. A much more urban assertion of regionalism can be seen in the Harold Washington Library in Chicago (1991, by Hammond, Beeby, and Babka), which monumentally alludes to the earlier buildings of the Chicago school.

In recent years, the Midwest has been distinguished by a series of visually arresting new landmark buildings for museums and art centers by some of the world's most celebrated architects, like Peter Eisenman's Wexner Center for the Arts (1989) at The Ohio State University in Columbus, Frank Gehry's Weisman Art Museum (1993) at the University of Minnesota in Minneapolis, I. M. Pei's Rock and Roll Hall of Fame (1995) in Cleveland, Tadao Ando's Pulitzer Foundation for the Arts (2000) in St. Louis, Santiago Calatrava's Quadracci Pavilion for the Milwaukee Art Museum (2001), and Zaha Hadid's Rosenthal Center for the Contemporary Arts Center in Cincinnati (2003). The Midwest continues to be receptive to the daringly new and to its own regional expressions in architecture.

Sources and Further Reading: Federico Bucci, *Albert Kahn: Architect of Ford*, trans. Carmen DiCinque (1993); Robert Judson Clark and Andrea P. A. Belloli, eds., *Design in America* (1983); Columbus (Indiana) Area Chamber of Commerce, *A Look at Architecture*, rev. ed. (1980); Kathryn Bishop Eckert, *Buildings of Michigan* (1993); John S. Garner, ed., *The Midwest in American Architecture* (1991); David Gebhard and Gerald Mansheim, *Buildings of Iowa* (1993); David Gebhard and Tom Martinson, *A Guide to the Architecture of Minnesota* (1977); Phyllis Lambert, ed., *Mies in America* (2001); William Allin Storrer, *The Frank Lloyd Wright Companion* (1993); John Zukowsky, ed., *Chicago Architecture and Design, 1923–1993* (1993).

Craig Zabel
The Pennsylvania State University

William Le Baron Jenney (1832–1907)

William Le Baron Jenney was born in 1832 in Massachusetts and was educated in Paris at the École Centrale des Arts et Manufactures. There he studied Continental innovations in metal construction and fireproofing. He later served as a major in the Corps of Engineers in the U.S. Civil War. Jenney died in 1907.

Often faulted for his too pragmatic and pedestrian attitude toward form and rarely listed among the great American architects, Jenney is nonetheless called the "Father of the Skyscraper" and "Founder of the Chi-

cago School," in part for his innovations in structure and construction but also because many luminaries of the Chicago school trained in his office, including Daniel Burnham, Louis Sullivan, William Holabird, and Martin Roche.

Jenney came to Chicago in 1867 and set up the practice Jenney, Schermerhorn, and Bogart. He worked on important urban projects, such as the railroad suburb of Riverside (with Frederick Law Olmsted and Calvert Vaux), and Chicago's boulevard and park system. However, Jenney's most significant achievement was his development of metal-frame construction and fireproof building systems. Jenney's first purely skeletal building was the nine-story Home Insurance Building (1885), where the cast iron and Bessemer steel frame is clad by a nonbearing glass curtain wall. In Jenney's Fair Store (1892) and Second Leiter Building (1891), the constructional system is further systematized so that all members are uniform I-beams, allowing great economy and ease in construction. Jenney's Manhattan Building (1891) uses a skeletal metal frame and curtain wall to rise to a height of sixteen stories.

Sources and Further Reading: Theodore Turak, "The École Centrale and Modern Architecture: The Education of William Le Baron Jenney," *Journal of the Society of Architectural Historians* 29 (Mar. 1970); Theodore Turak, "William Le Baron Jenney, a Nineteenth Century Architect," Ph.D. diss., University of Michigan (1966); Theodore Turak, "William Le Baron Jenney: Teacher," *Threshold: Journal of the School of Architecture* 5/6 (Fall 1991).

Jacqueline Gargus
The Ohio State University–Columbus

H. H. Richardson (1838–1886)

In his brief life, Henry Hobson Richardson succeeded in clarifying and refining architectural objectives of the preceding generation and setting the groundwork for the modernist ambitions of the generations to come. Born in Louisiana in 1838, Richardson studied at Harvard University and the École des Beaux Arts in Paris, returning from Paris after the Civil War to practice in New York. In 1874, he moved his family and practice to Boston, where he often collaborated with landscape architect Frederick Law Olmsted. Richardson died in 1886.

Richardson's first important commission was the Church of Unity in Springfield, Massachusetts (1869). Commissions for other churches followed, most importantly Trinity Church (1877) in Boston. Trinity Church launched him to international prominence and inspired the influential style of Richardsonian Romanesque, which spread throughout the United States in the 1880s. Richardson's work is distinguished by its handling of historical forms with a tough, elemental feel for geometry, a heightened sense of materiality and polychromy, and playful asymmetries. Richardson designed many libraries, ranging in style from the "pyrotechnic quality" of early works, like the Winn Memorial Library (1879) in Woburn, Massachusetts, to the simple and powerful play of massing at Crane Memorial Library (1881) in Quincy, Massachusetts, or the Glessner House (1887), Chicago. Richardson's personal favorite among his buildings was the Allegheny County Courthouse, Pittsburgh (1885), but his most influential work was perhaps the unprecedented Marshall Field's Wholesale Store (1887) in Chicago, a vast, arcuated, seven-story stone block that helped define strategies for articulating facades of the Chicago School.

Sources and Further Reading: Henry-Russell Hitchcock, *The Architecture of H. H. Richardson and His Times* (1966); James F. O'Gorman, *H. H. Richardson: Architectural Forms for an American Society* (1987); Jeffrey Karl Ochsner, *H. H. Richardson, Complete Architectural Works* (1982).

Jacqueline Gargus
The Ohio State University–Columbus

Dankmar Adler (1844–1900)

Dankmar Adler was born in 1844 in Stadt Lengsfeld, near Eisenach, Germany, and moved with his family to Detroit in 1854. After learning architectural rendering with a local firm, Adler worked briefly for Chicago architect-engineer Augustus Bauer. Between 1862 and 1865 he served in the Civil War. Afterward, he worked for O. S. Kinney as a draftsman and foreman. In 1871 he started an eight-year partnership with Edward Burling, in which Adler was chief designer and supervisor of construction. The firm was active in rebuilding Chicago after the great fire of 1871. In 1879 Adler started his own practice, and Louis Sullivan began working in it as a draftsman. The Central Music Hall (Chicago) dates from this year, a pivotal work for the future Adler & Sullivan partnership, founded in 1883. The Central Music Hall exemplified the acoustic principles that determined the unobstructed layout of the auditorium and combined retail stores and offices in a six-story building. The firm developed these features in subsequent theatre projects, most notably the Auditorium Building in Chicago (1890).

Adler & Sullivan led the Chicago school of architecture in developing the steel-frame skyscraper. This new building type made up the bulk of the firm's com-

missions. Their most important works in the Midwest include the Wainwright Building (St. Louis, 1890), the Schiller Building (Chicago, 1892), the Union Trust Building (St. Louis, 1893), the St. Nicholas Hotel (St. Louis, 1893), and the Stock Exchange Building (Chicago, 1894). It is generally believed that Adler handled the business affairs and engineering problems and Sullivan composed harmonious elevations and unified decorative schemes.

The Adler & Sullivan partnership was dissolved in 1895. Working briefly for the Crane Elevator Company, Adler returned to independent architectural practice in 1896, with his last work dating from 1899. He died in 1900.

Sources and Further Reading: Charles E. Gregersen, *Dankmar Adler: His Theatres and Auditoriums* (1989); Hugh Morrison, *Louis Sullivan: Prophet of Modern Architecture* (1935); Robert Twombly, *Louis Sullivan: His Life and Work* (1986).

Lauren Weingarden
Florida State University

Burnham and Root

The organizational ability of Daniel Burnham (1846–1912) and the superbly talented architects he hired made Burnham and Root the country's leading firm in the engineering, planning, design, and construction of skyscrapers between 1886 and 1903. John Wellborn Root (1850–1891) created the most lithic and sculptural of the Chicago school's tall office buildings (Rookery, 1888; Monadnock Building, 1893). Charles Atwood, Root's replacement at D. H. Burnham and Company after Root's untimely death in 1891, designed the Reliance Building (1895), the period's only steel-frame skyscraper to eliminate almost all suggestions of the traditional masonry wall. Its triangular site, rippled surfaces, and powerful cornice made Frederick P. Dinkelberg's neoclassical Flatiron Building (1902) for the Burnham firm even more famous internationally than Root's Masonic Temple (1892), the first of the world's tallest skyscrapers to be highly touted as such. For Marshall Field's (Chicago, 1902), then for Selfridge's (London, 1906) and Wanamaker's (Philadelphia, 1911), the Burnham firm created the prototype of the modern department store as a consumerist pleasure palace. After his administration of the 1893 World's Columbian Exposition helped launch the City Beautiful movement, Burnham's plans for Cleveland (1903) and San Francisco (1905) allied Beaux-Arts urban design with the progressive movement, while those for two Philippine cities (1905) linked it to America's recent imperialism. Coauthored with Edward H. Bennett, Burnham's landmark Plan of Chicago (1909) inspired Chicagoans to carry out during the next three decades projects whose scope and scale (e.g., fifteen miles of lakeshore parks) that no other American municipality undertook. The plan thus crowned the one career most emblematic of the city where organizational and technological modernity arrived sooner and was more pervasive than anywhere else.

Source and Further Reading: Thomas Hines, *Burnham of Chicago* (1979).

Edward Wolner
Ball State University, Indiana

Holabird and Roche

The architectural firm of Holabird and Roche was established in 1881 when William Holabird (1854–1923) made Martin Roche (1855–1927) a partner in the firm he had founded in 1880. In 1929 the firm was taken over by Holabird's son, John Augur Holabird, and John Welborn Root, Jr., the son of Daniel Burnham's partner at Burnham and Root. From 1945 to 1957, the firm was known as Holabird, Root, and Burgee (the third partner being John Henry Burgee). While Roche was a native of Chicago, educated at the Armour Institute of Technology (now the Illinois Institute of Technology), Holabird studied at West Point and had only come to Chicago from New York in 1875.

Like many members of the Chicago school, Holabird and Roche met while working in the architectural office of William Le Baron Jenney. Hence it is not surprising that their most innovative work involved the skyscraper. The firm designed many important skyscrapers and hotels in the Chicago area, such as the Tacoma Building (1889; since demolished), the Old Colony Building (1894), the Marquette Building (1895), the La Salle Hotel (1909), the Palmer House (1923), and the Stevens Hotel (1925). Distinctive features in their work are the straightforward, rational expression of orthogonal steel framing and a preference for the "Chicago window," a compound system of fenestration that makes use of a large inoperable central window while still providing natural ventilation by means of smaller, operable side windows. The firm was very successful, and during the latter decades of the nineteenth century it had a hand in from 5 to 10 percent of all new construction in Chicago.

Sources and Further Reading: Robert Bruegmann, *The Architects and the City* (1997); Robert Bruegmann, *Holabird &* *Roche, Holabird & Root: An Illustrated Catalog of Works* (1991); Robert Bruegmann, "The Marquette Building and the Myth of the Chicago School," *Threshold: Journal of the School of Architecture* 5/6 (Fall 1991).

Jackie Gargus
The Ohio State University–Columbus

Louis H. Sullivan (1856–1924)

Louis Henry Sullivan was born in Boston, Massachusetts, in 1856. In 1872 he entered the Massachusetts Institute of Technology as a "special student" in the architecture department. Here he studied classical design under Robert Ware and Eugene Letang. Seeking more practical experience, Sullivan left "Tech" in June 1873 to apprentice in Richard Morris Hunt's New York City architectural office. Unable to employ him, Hunt sent Sullivan to the Philadelphia firm of Frank Furness and John Hewitt, where he worked as an apprentice draftsman until November.

Wainwright Building (St. Louis) by Adler and Sullivan, 1891. Library of Congress, Prints and Photographs Division, Historic American Buildings Survey, HABS, MO, 96-SALU, 49-1.

From Philadelphia Sullivan went to Chicago to join his parents and to take part in the city's building boom that followed the 1871 fire. Immediately upon his arrival he was hired as a draftsman in the office of architect-engineer William Le Baron Jenney. In October 1874 he sought additional formal training at the École des Beaux-Arts in Paris. In April 1875, again disillusioned with classical training, Sullivan left the école to travel through southern France and Italy. He returned to the United States in May.

Back in Chicago, Sullivan began to freelance as a decorative designer and draftsman. Beginning in 1879 he worked for Dankmar Adler, and in 1883 they established the firm of Adler & Sullivan, a partnership that lasted twelve years. The firm became a leader in the Chicago school of architecture, enabling Sullivan to achieve national acclaim as a designer of the steel-frame skyscraper.

The Auditorium Building (now Roosevelt University; 1890), the firm's first large project, demanded innovative planning and construction for multiple uses, including a hotel, theatre, and rental offices. While the exterior was built with traditional load-bearing masonry walls, its ten-story interior construction anticipated the skyscraper's fireproofed metallic skeleton. If the building's exterior remained eclectic, its interiors evinced Sullivan's artistic originality. Here his personal style of ornament, derived from botanical studies and John Ruskin's interpretations of medieval motifs, permeated the public spaces. Intertwining networks of scrolling contours and tendrils and radiating leaf patterns, rendered in gilt reliefs and stenciled frescoes and oak-wood carvings, embellished ceilings, capitals, spandrels, and beams. In the Auditorium Theater, broad acoustical arches, spanning its entire width, hallmarked Adler's engineering skills and Sullivan's decorative skills. Incandescent light bulbs inserted in bands of gold relief ornament combined to diffuse a golden light throughout the vast, unobstructed ground story and balcony tiers.

Sullivan's novel skyscraper design involved a clear articulation of its internal cagelike construction and a three-part division of its rectangular mass. Sullivan first realized this scheme in the Wainwright Building in St. Louis (1890). Unbroken vertical piers, rising from a two-story base, unify and accentuate the skyscraper's soaring height, terminated by an ornamented attic story. Recessed spandrels of terra-cotta relief ornament reinforce both the vertical dimension and the logic of pier-and-lintel construction. Herein Sullivan formulated a prototypical skyscraper design, which he described in his landmark essay "The Tall Office Building Artistically Considered" (1896).

In this essay Sullivan treated both the practical and the technical aspects of the skyscraper and its philosophical function. In the first half he explained the three-part composition as the rational solution to housing retail and bank facilities in the base and uniform office cells in the shaft, while the attic story marked where "the circulatory system [of mechanical equipment] completes itself, and makes its grand turn, ascending and descending." Up to this point Sullivan concurred with his Chicago school colleagues' practices and pronounced his celebrated axiom "form follows function."

In the second half of the essay, Sullivan explained how he sought to go beyond these utilitarian solutions and attributed the skyscraper with a spiritual-organic meaning. Sullivan now justified the exaggerated verticality as an expression of the tall building's "emotional appeal." He also devised a corresponding symbolism based on Ralph Waldo Emerson's transcendentalist ideals and Walt Whitman's poetry and prose. Sullivan claimed that the poet/artist's task was to reveal, through an art based on nature, the creative spiritual forces permeating all things natural and humanmade. The material world and rational faculties, such as the geometric masses and structural grid of a building, comprised the "objective." Conversely, the immaterial and emotional faculties, expressed in ornament, comprised the "subjective." These dialectical forces, he maintained, were manifestations of a generative cosmic force that he called the "Infinite Creative Spirit." For Sullivan, the ornamented skyscraper functioned as a metaphor for that spirit.

The Guaranty Building (Buffalo, 1896) exemplifies what Sullivan called "an image of poetic art: utilitarian in foundation, harmonious in superstructure." The entire geometric framework is sheathed in terra-cotta relief ornament, which marks steel-cage construction and enhances the ascending and descending directions of the piers and arches. Sullivan completed the Guaranty Building just after he and Adler ended their partnership (1895), due to an economic depression. From that time, Sullivan's commissions steadily declined. This was due in part to his Chicago clients' new taste for classical revival architecture, monumentally displayed in the "White City" of the 1893 Chicago World's Fair. In his own design for the fair, the Transportation Building, Sullivan enveloped the entire building in crimson-hued ornament of multicolored stenciled patterns. And for the main entrance, called the "Golden Doorway," he adorned concentric half-circle arches with gilt-relief ornament to create a radiant halo of golden light.

The Schlesinger & Mayer Department Store (now Carson Pirie Scott) in Chicago (1904) and eight midwestern rural town banks (1906–1920) are among the works Sullivan completed during the last decades of his career. Except for the rounded tower entrance, Sullivan's design for the Schlesinger & Mayer store translates the vertical skyscraper into the horizontal dimensions that dominate the twelve-story elevations. In the upper stories, post-and-lintel construction was enveloped in white tiles with bands of green tiles that define the windows and the superimposed floors. In contrast to this rationalist restraint, the entire base and the display windows were adorned in cast-iron reliefs of Sullivan's lush botanical ornament, painted with the verdant hues of sun-dappled foliage.

Sullivan experienced personal as well as financial hardships during these last decades. Having married Mary (Margaret) Azona Hattabaugh in 1899, Sullivan auctioned his personal library and household furnishings in 1909 in order to finance her fledgling acting career in New York City. The couple divorced in 1916. In financial ruin, Sullivan was forced to move his office from the Auditorium Building Tower (which his firm had occupied since 1888), and eventually he had to give up office space altogether. He also suffered from chronic illness, to which historians attributed a decline in his talent. He died in 1924.

His rural bank buildings counter this assessment of decline. Faced with new building and economic conditions, Sullivan translated the skyscraper's solutions into a building type that served small-town agrarian communities. For the exteriors, Sullivan emphasized the solitary rectangular mass, which echoed the open, "democratic" layout of the banking hall. In the National Farmers' Bank (1908) in Owatonna, Minnesota, for example, a single half-circle arch window spans the entire width of each elevation that forms a massive cube of interior space. As in the other banks, Sullivan faced the elevations with tinted bricks that created an overall reddish-brown hue, and he framed the entrance and windows with green-glazed terra-cotta ornament. These complementary colors produced such a radiant effect that local residents dubbed them the bank "jewel boxes." Sullivan extended this polychromy to the interiors with color harmonies suggestive of sunlit landscapes, explaining that he wanted to make "the out of doors—indoors."

In retrospect, Sullivan viewed the Chicago World's Fair as a sign of America's failure to realize a naturalized architectural expression. This, together with his professional decline, compelled him to assume the role of educational and social reformer, writing caustic indictments of cultural materialism and revival style architecture. His major written works from this time are *Kindergarten Chats* (1901–1902; revised 1918), *The Autobiography of an Idea* (1924), and *A System of Ornament According With a Philosophy of Man's Powers* (1922–1923). In these writings, Sullivan repeated the philosophical ideas set forth in "The Tall Office Building Artistically Considered." However, later modernist designers and critics ignored Sullivan's or-

nament and polychromy, the primary attributes of what he called "the true, the Poetic Architecture." Identifying him as the "prophet of modern architecture" (the subtitle of Hugh Morrison's influential book), they mistook "form follows function" as a creed for structural realism as an end in itself. Yet Sullivan's naturalist aesthetic endured in the Midwest. Frank Lloyd Wright, Sullivan's draftsman from 1888 to 1893, led the next generation of progressive midwestern architects, known as the Prairie school. Wright extended Sullivan's organic theory and ornamental design into the open plans of his prairie houses and, thereby, into the International Style.

Sources and Further Reading: Larry Millet, *The Curve of the Arch* (1985); Hugh Morrison, *Louis Sullivan: Prophet of Modern Architecture* (1935); Sherman Paul, *Louis Sullivan: An Architect in American Thought* (1962); Joseph Siry, *The Chicago Auditorium Building* (2002); Paul Sprague, *The Drawings of Louis Henry Sullivan* (1979); Louis H. Sullivan, *The Autobiography of an Idea* (1924); Louis H. Sullivan, *Kindergarten Chats (Revised 1918) and Other Writings* (1947); Robert Twombly, *Louis Sullivan: His Life and Work* (1986); Lauren S. Weingarden, *Louis H. Sullivan: The Banks* (1987).

Lauren Weingarden
Florida State University

Cass Gilbert (1859–1934)

The architect Cass Gilbert was born in 1859 in Zanesville, Ohio, and attended public school in St. Paul, Minnesota. After studying with William R. Ware at the Massachusetts Institute of Technology and traveling in Europe, he worked for the prominent American Beaux-Arts firm of McKim, Mead & White in New York City. In 1882 Gilbert returned to St. Paul to begin his own architecture practice, and he partnered with James Knox Taylor from 1884 until 1892. The Mediterranean Romanesque style characterized his campus buildings, such as Finney Chapel (1908), Bosworth Hall (1931), and Fairchild Chapel (1931) at Oberlin College in Ohio. Neoclassicism supplied his symbols of art and government for the U.S. Customs House in New York (1907); the U.S. Supreme Court in Washington, D.C. (1935); the Allen Art Museum at Oberlin (1917); and the St. Louis and Toledo art museums. Gilbert's neo-Gothic Woolworth Building (1913) pioneered a new building type, the skyscraper. Woolworth's pyramidal spire rising to fifty-five stories inspired many later cathedrals to capitalism and helped create the New York City skyline.

Before moving his practice to New York around 1899, Gilbert received national recognition when he was awarded the commission for the Minnesota State

Capitol building. The classical dome resting on a drum with paired columns commands the highest point in the axial Beaux-Arts landscape site designed for the capitol. In 1900 Gilbert also produced the Endicott Building in downtown St. Paul, and in 1908 he won a competition to design the master plan for the University of Minnesota's Minneapolis campus. Typical of the City Beautiful movement, the campus plan included thirty buildings forming a linear central mall, a tunnel under Washington Avenue, a campanile, a monumental staircase, promenades, and landscaping to link the campus to the Mississippi River. Gilbert's plan guided the university's development until 1950. He also proposed master plans for the University of Texas and the City of New Haven that demonstrated in the public domain his ideals of civic unity. Cass Gilbert died in Brockenhurst, England, in 1934.

Sources and Further Reading: Geoffrey Blodgett, *Cass Gilbert: The Early Years* (2001); Barbara S. Christen and Steven Flanders, eds., *Cass Gilbert, Life and Work* (2001); Sharon Irish, *Cass Gilbert, Architect* (1999).

Kay Bea Jones
The Ohio State University–Columbus

Frank Lloyd Wright (1867–1959)

Frank Lloyd Wright was born in Richland Center, Wisconsin, in 1867. His father, William Carey Wright, moved from job to job and eventually departed from the family when Frank was a teenager. Frank was much closer to his mother, Anna Lloyd Jones Wright, and her family, the Lloyd Joneses, Unitarians from Wales who had settled on farms near Spring Green, Wisconsin. The hard work and the closeness to nature that he experienced on his relatives' farms provided strong lessons for Wright as he grew up. Another early influence was his mother's introduction of the Froebel kindergarten method to Wright, which helped to develop his feeling for abstract geometry.

In 1886 Wright briefly studied engineering at the University of Wisconsin in Madison before moving to Chicago in 1887 to begin work in the architectural office of Joseph Lyman Silsbee, a designer of Shingle Style buildings. The concentrated and electric urban energy of modern Chicago at first was a shock to the young Wright with his rural background. He emerged as a precocious draftsman and soon moved to the architectural office of Adler & Sullivan, a leading firm in the city's progressive approach to skyscraper design that has come to be known as the Chicago school. The ideas of his new master, Louis H. Sullivan, had a pro-

found impact on the shaping of Wright's architectural ideals, particularly Sullivan's quest to define a democratic, organic, functional, honest, and contemporary architecture, particularly for the Midwest.

In 1889 Wright married Catherine Lee Tobin and began to build his own home in Oak Park, a suburb west of Chicago. After Wright left Adler & Sullivan in 1893, he expanded his Oak Park home (1895) and attached a studio (1898). It was from there that Wright developed a thriving architectural practice that would become the cornerstone of the Prairie school of architecture. The single-family house was Wright's premier building type. These houses were shrines to family life and suburban retreat romantically integrated with their environments. Prime examples include the Ward W. Willits House (1903) in Highland Park, Illinois, and the Frederick C. Robie House (1909) in Chicago. A central chimney core anchors these prairie houses, from which the principal spaces pinwheel in an open plan out toward nature; the interiors are abstractly contained by generously fenestrated screenlike walls and sheltering low roofs with cantilevered eaves. Traditional architectural styles are eschewed, as Wright takes his cues from nature, particularly the strong level horizontal of the Illinois prairie. However, these houses are not typically out in the country, but usually contained within the rectangular grid of the lots and streets of Chicago and such suburbs as Oak Park. The most discernible foreign influence on Wright's prairie houses came not from Europe but from Japan, which Wright visited in his first trip abroad, in 1905. The custom-designed furniture, art glass, and integrated lighting created an Arts and Crafts totality while accepting the realities of the emerging machine age.

From 1900 to 1909 Wright built numerous prairie houses across the Midwest and some extraordinary nonresidential designs, such as Unity Temple (1908) in Oak Park. He had created a regional and organic approach to midwestern architecture, whose buildings were also some of the most radical works of modern architecture in the world. However, his marriage was crumbling and he desired recognition beyond the Midwest. In 1909 he abandoned his family and, scandalously, traveled to Europe with Mrs. Mamah Borthwick Cheney, the wife of one of his former clients. In 1910 Ernst Wasmuth of Berlin published a magnificent portfolio of Wright's work that would introduce some new modern architects in Europe to the extraordinary buildings that Wright had designed, primarily for the American Midwest.

After returning to the United States, Wright retreated from suburban Chicago to the Wisconsin farmlands of his youth and in 1911 began to build a new home and studio, Taliesin, on a hill near Spring Green, for himself and his mistress. In 1914 Mamah

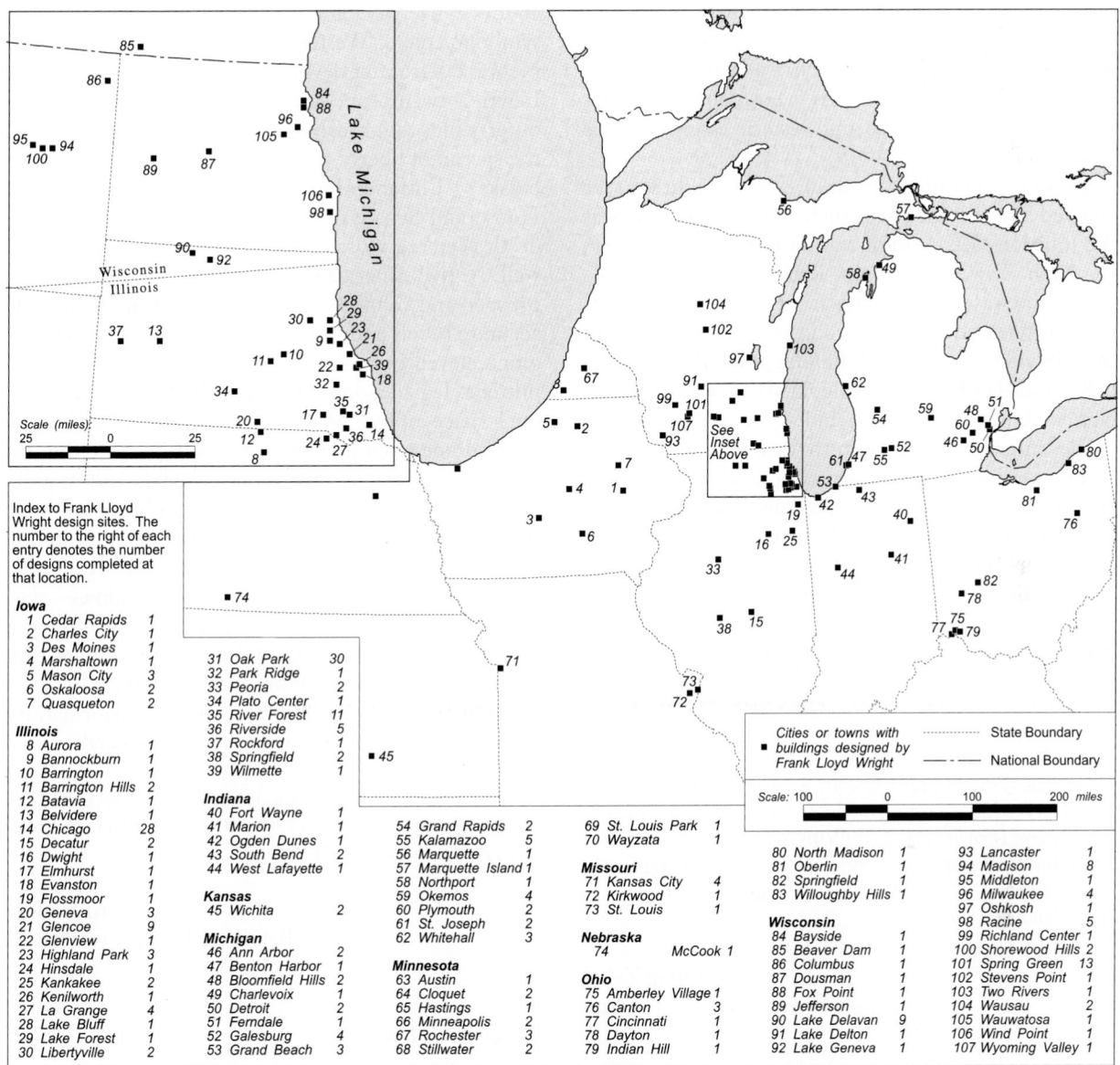

Index to Frank Lloyd Wright design sites. The number to the right of each entry denotes the number of designs completed at that location.

Iowa
1 Cedar Rapids	1
2 Charles City	1
3 Des Moines	1
4 Marshaltown	1
5 Mason City	3
6 Oskaloosa	2
7 Quasqueton	2

Illinois
8 Aurora	1
9 Bannockburn	1
10 Barrington	1
11 Barrington Hills	2
12 Batavia	1
13 Belvidere	1
14 Chicago	28
15 Decatur	2
16 Dwight	1
17 Elmhurst	1
18 Evanston	1
19 Flossmoor	1
20 Geneva	3
21 Glencoe	9
22 Glenview	1
23 Highland Park	3
24 Hinsdale	1
25 Kankakee	2
26 Kenilworth	1
27 La Grange	4
28 Lake Bluff	1
29 Lake Forest	1
30 Libertyville	2

31 Oak Park	30
32 Park Ridge	1
33 Peoria	2
34 Plato Center	1
35 River Forest	11
36 Riverside	5
37 Rockford	1
38 Springfield	2
39 Wilmette	1

Indiana
40 Fort Wayne	1
41 Marion	1
42 Ogden Dunes	1
43 South Bend	2
44 West Lafayette	1

Kansas
| 45 Wichita | 2 |

Michigan
46 Ann Arbor	2
47 Benton Harbor	1
48 Bloomfield Hills	2
49 Charlevoix	1
50 Detroit	2
51 Ferndale	1
52 Galesburg	4
53 Grand Beach	3

54 Grand Rapids	2
55 Kalamazoo	5
56 Marquette	1
57 Marquette Island	1
58 Northport	1
59 Okemos	4
60 Plymouth	2
61 St. Joseph	2
62 Whitehall	3

Minnesota
63 Austin	1
64 Cloquet	2
65 Hastings	1
66 Minneapolis	2
67 Rochester	3
68 Stillwater	2

| 69 St. Louis Park | 1 |
| 70 Wayzata | 1 |

Missouri
71 Kansas City	4
72 Kirkwood	1
73 St. Louis	1

Nebraska
| 74 | McCook 1 |

Ohio
75 Amberley Village	1
76 Canton	3
77 Cincinnati	1
78 Dayton	1
79 Indian Hill	1

80 North Madison	1
81 Oberlin	1
82 Springfield	1
83 Willoughby Hills	1

Wisconsin
84 Bayside	1
85 Beaver Dam	1
86 Columbus	1
87 Dousman	1
88 Fox Point	1
89 Jefferson	1
90 Lake Delavan	9
91 Lake Delton	1
92 Lake Geneva	1

93 Lancaster	1
94 Madison	8
95 Middleton	1
96 Milwaukee	4
97 Oshkosh	1
98 Racine	5
99 Richland Center	1
100 Shorewood Hills	2
101 Spring Green	13
102 Stevens Point	1
103 Two Rivers	1
104 Wausau	2
105 Wauwatosa	1
106 Wind Point	1
107 Wyoming Valley	1

Cities or towns with ▪ buildings designed by Frank Lloyd Wright

State Boundary
National Boundary

Scale: 100 0 100 200 miles

Scale (miles) 25 0 25

Frank Lloyd Wright buildings in the Midwest. Prepared by James DeGrand. *Source:* http://www.franklloydwright.org/index .cfm?section=research&action hework; William Allin Storrer, *Frank Lloyd Wright: A Complete Catalogue*, 3rd ed. (2002).

Borthwick and others died in a horrific arson/murder at Taliesin. Wright rebuilt Taliesin after this tragedy, and rebuilt it again after another fire in 1925. Nestled beneath the crown of the hill, Taliesin is a rambling complex of low-hipped roofs, native stone and plaster walls, long horizontals, and generous windows. The quarter century after 1909 saw a decline in Wright's productivity as he became embroiled in scandals, a disastrous second marriage, lawsuits, and debt. Many of his most important works during this period were built far from the Midwest, such as a series of concrete-block houses in southern California and the Imperial Hotel (1923, demolished 1968) in Tokyo. His personal life finally stabilized with his marriage to

his third wife, Olgivanna, in 1928, but then the beginning of the Great Depression evaporated many promising projects that had come Wright's way.

In 1932 Wright founded the Taliesin Fellowship, an educational venture in architecture and related arts, which provided Wright with a community of apprentices. At first centered at Taliesin in Wisconsin, Wright built a winter home for the fellowship called Taliesin West (begun 1938), near Scottsdale, Arizona. Wright also began to update his approach to the single-family house radically in his Usonian houses, beginning with the first Jacobs House (1937) in Madison, Wisconsin, an economical single-story house that turns its back to the street in favor of the backyard terrace and garden. Wright experimented with a modular organizing grid, gravity heating in the concrete floor slab, and unorthodox sandwich walls in these flat-roofed, wood and brick houses, whose obsessive horizontality maintained the midwestern essence of his earlier prairie houses.

From 1936 until his death in 1959, Wright's career enjoyed a renaissance with such major commissions as the Johnson Wax Administration Building (1939) and Research Tower (1950) in Racine, Wisconsin. Although he was now building across the United States, he continued to assert a strong regional response to the Midwest through such buildings as his second Jacobs House (1948) in Middleton, Wisconsin, a semicircular house with large windows to the south that nestles into an earthen berm to the north.

Frank Lloyd Wright created a modern, regional, and organic approach to architecture that first crystallized in the Midwest and ultimately had a profound impact on the development of modern architecture throughout the United States and beyond.

Sources and Further Reading: H. Allen Brooks, *Frank Lloyd Wright and the Prairie School* (1972); Herbert Jacobs with Katherine Jacobs, *Building with Frank Lloyd Wright* (1978); Neil Levine, *The Architecture of Frank Lloyd Wright* (1996); Bruce Brooks Pfeiffer, *Frank Lloyd Wright*, ed. Yukio Futagawa: vols. 1–8, *Monograph*; vols. 9–11, *Preliminary Studies*; vol. 12, *In His Renderings* (1984–1988); Meryle Secrest, *Frank Lloyd Wright* (1992); William Allin Storrer, *The Frank Lloyd Wright Companion* (1993); Frank Lloyd Wright, *An Autobiography* (1977); Frank Lloyd Wright, *Studies and Executed Buildings* (1986).

Craig Zabel
The Pennsylvania State University

Bertram Goodhue (1869–1924)

Born in Pomfret, Connecticut, and schooled at home, Bertram Grosvenor Goodhue moved to New York City in 1884 to work as an apprentice at the architecture firm of Renwick, Aspinwall, and Russell. Following his apprenticeship, in 1891 Goodhue joined the Boston firm of Ralph Adams Cram and began refining a style of neogothic ecclesiastical architecture visible in such buildings as St. Bartholomew's Church and St. Thomas Church in New York City and Rockefeller Chapel at the University of Chicago.

The Nebraska State Capitol in Lincoln (1920–32) was Goodhue's most powerful and expressive midwestern building, even if it was due as much to Hartley Burr Alexander's iconography as it was to a design that solidified Goodhue's national reputation. A political Progressive and a professor of history and philosophy at the University of Nebraska, Alexander scripted a symbolic epic of Western values and their bearing on Nebraska's frontier development. Hence, sculptor Lee Lawrie's twenty-one incised panels on the capitol's outer wings vigorously depict the widening cycles in the spread of liberty from the Athens of Solon to Nebraska's "Entrance into the Union" in 1867. In the House and Senate chambers Alexander ordered Hildreth Meiere's mosaics and friezes into epic cycles as well: Native Americans, the French, and the Spanish prosper and founder in their turn. Ethnographically accurate reliefs and inscriptions commemorate the region's eleven Indian tribes and invoke the epic's intermittent elegiac moods. The inscribed walls and octagonal space of the War Memorial Room under the tower dome attempt a lyric of heroic death. Other inscriptions gravely endow pioneer reliefs and mosaics with a sense of manifest destiny, the political keystone of the epic. Visible from within a radius of ten miles, Goodhue's titanic tower—all stressed verticality, thickened corners, and deeply inset windows—suggests an archaic mural density and the reverberant scale of epic events, visual and narrative thunder thus conjoined in the one region of the country where the sense of epic turbulence, of sweeping transformations in territory and culture, was most pronounced.

Sources and Further Reading: Frederick C. Juebke, ed., *The Nebraska State Capitol* (1990); Richard Oliver, *Bertram Grosvenor Goodhue* (1983).

Edward Wolner
Ball State University, Indiana

Chicago School

Chicago, with its pivotal location for the production and distribution of goods, the apocalyptic fire that destroyed much of its manufacturing and commercial core in 1871, and the need to recoup the millions of dollars that European and eastern investors had poured into its development since the 1830s, was an ideal place for venturesome young architects like Daniel H. Burnham, Louis H. Sullivan, John Wellborn Root, Solon Beman, William Holabird, Martin Roche, Jens Jensen, and Frank Lloyd Wright. In Chicago's epic rebuilding, which was an urbanized and highly technological version of Frederick Jackson Turner's frontier crucible, architects and landscape architects confronted new building types (the multistory loft, the wholesale store, the retail department store, the tall office building); the novel engineering problems of erecting these structures in unstable subsoil conditions; the shift from masonry buildings to ones framed in iron and then in steel; and the unprecedented problems and promises of metropolitan park design and modern city planning. These challenges pushed even those Chicagoans who had graduated from eastern schools into largely self-taught, highly creative careers that the more elaborate professional protocols in force on the East Coast might have constricted or in some cases snuffed out.

Initially, William Le Baron Jenney was the key figure. Most of the younger designers benefited from formal and informal associations with this older man, a French-educated Civil War engineer whose rapid construction and repair of bridges under the time imperatives of battlefield conditions prepared him and the architects he taught to meet the demanding construction schedules for commercial buildings in downtown Chicago. His Home Insurance Building (1885) was the first high-rise erected on a metal frame. His two department stores on State Street (Siegel, Cooper and Company and the Fair Store (1892), which employed faintly classicizing ornament and the unprecedented expanses of glass this new building type needed to illuminate large open interiors, set the terms of development used in the State Street department stores later designed by Chicago's other major firms. Even Jenney's Paris-inspired designs in the 1870s for three West Side parks and their connecting boulevards were the point of departure for Jens Jensen's creation of parks with indigenous or prairie landscapes.

For several reasons, Jenney and the architects who followed him were able to make the Loop America's workshop in technological and organizational modernity. In the 1880s the swelling number of managerial employees in industry forced them to move from factory compounds to downtown offices to make more efficient use of the lawyers, accountants, and bankers they required for their expanding industrial enterprises. Their demand for more office space in the Loop occurred at the same time as new technologies made taller office, loft, and retail buildings possible. The telephone; the telegraph; and advances in fireproofing, heating, ventilation, lighting, and sanitation were as necessary as the steel frame and elevator for the development of the earliest skyscrapers. Simultaneously, Chicagoan George A. Fuller developed the single-contract system that increased the efficiency, quality, and cost controls for large-scale construction: Rather than the developer or architect negotiating separate contracts with masons, carpenters, plumbers, bricklayers, glaziers, and demolition teams, one contractor handled every aspect of construction and subcontracting.

Robert Bruegmann's *The Architects and the City* (1997) has overturned the once orthodox modernist view that Chicago's tallest and largest buildings expressed structure and pioneered modern architecture while New York's towers deemphasized structural expression in favor of theatrical versions of traditional styles. This modernist view unknowingly compared apples with oranges. The most prominent Manhattan skyscrapers were corporate headquarters requiring more lavish treatments to heighten corporate identity, while in Chicago entirely speculative office buildings, for which such treatments were irrelevant, predominated. Further, out-of-town developers with no civic pride in Chicago pushed the Chicago architects toward relatively severe designs to maximize profits in order to attract the best class of tenants. Still further, the canonical loft buildings cited by modernist historians were located on less valuable land on the Loop's periphery because they mixed retail, wholesale, and light-manufacturing functions; the least prestigious and expensive of the tall building types, they thus received the most stripped-down treatment. Finally, Chicago's buildings, often cubical masses, looked more rationalized than Manhattan's thinner and more fanciful towers because they rose from larger, nearly square sites on a regular grid, not from lower Manhattan's narrow plots on irregular streets.

Meeting the financial, structural, functional, and aesthetic demands of new types of commercial buildings in one of the world's fastest-growing cities enabled the Chicago architects to bureaucratize architectural practice itself well before firms in any other city did so. Daniel Burnham and John Wellborn Root, Dankmar Adler and Louis H. Sullivan, and William Holabird and Martin Roche divided labor between designers and planners and greatly expanded the size of their firms through the many clerks, secretaries, draftsmen, and engineers they hired in order to handle the unprecedented variety and complexity of new building types and the rapidly increasing number of commissions that the regional and national scope of their practices demanded.

The uniquely high concentration of distinctly modern building types in the Loop and the ruthless elimination from it of churches, temples, clubs, and civic buildings because of its skyrocketing land values and commercial possibilities created sooner and more completely than in any other downtown the most purely modern cityscape in the world. Within and outside it, moreover, Chicagoans confronted the problems of modern landscape architecture, urban design, and city planning well before reformers in other cities tackled them in such various and comprehensive ways. George Pullman and Solon Beman planned the company town of Pullman late in the 1870s, and Sullivan proposed in 1891 the earliest theory of zoning to solve the problems posed by ever taller skyscrapers. Holabird and Roche not only produced the largest number but also the most influential, the most stylistically unified, and the most subtly varied group of buildings in the Loop. Over the next two decades Frank Lloyd Wright's prairie houses radically redefined suburban living, just as his unrealized ideas for industrialized housing could have remade workers' urban neighborhoods. Daniel Burnham's administration of the 1893 World's Fair catalyzed the nationwide City Beautiful movement, and his 1909 masterwork, the Plan of Chicago, decisively influenced the city's development into the 1930s.

Sources and Further Reading: Robert Bruegmann, *The Architects and the City* (1997); Thomas Hines, *Burnham of Chicago* (1979); Arnold Lewis, *An Early Encounter with Tomorrow* (1997); Robert Twombly, *Louis Sullivan* (1986).

Edward Wolner
Ball State University, Indiana

Prairie School

In the first two decades of the twentieth century, a style of architecture—the Prairie school—appeared in the American Midwest that departed from conventional and historical designs. The Prairie school style is seen in buildings that are primarily residential and have prominent low-pitched roofs of either open gable or hipped form with broad eaves, emphasizing a horizontal massing in one- and two-story structures when viewed from the street. Adding further emphasis to the horizontal lines are casement windows grouped together and placed high in the walls and just below the eaves, creating a visual separation between roof and façade and making the roof seem to hover above the spaces below. Inside, a living room or a master bedroom sometimes will have an inclined ceiling that follows the slope of the roof, creating greater interior volume. A feature in such rooms is a large brick or stone fireplace whose dimensions are wider than they are high. Interior spaces tend to flow from one room into another without the compartmentalization so common to dwellings of the Queen Anne or Colonial Revival styles. Ornament is minimal. But when exhibited in the stained glass of casement windows, the terra-cotta capping pilasters, and stone urns atop garden walls, it is kept simple and geometric. The style can also be found in small commercial and institutional buildings, such as banks and libraries, but it predominates in residences.

The architect who is best known for his practice in the Prairie school style is Frank Lloyd Wright. Wright was influenced by Louis H. Sullivan, with whom he apprenticed in Chicago, and by the British arts and crafts movement of the late-nineteenth century, accounts of which had circulated in architectural magazines. However, Wright was a virtuoso, and his residential designs, first appearing in the suburbs of Chicago, were unique. By 1900 Wright had acquired a following. Because of the number of young architects who followed his example, each exhibiting variations in design of his or her own, a stylistic movement or school of design ensued. Among these architects were George Elmslie, whom Wright had first met in Lyman Silsbee's office, and Elmslie's later partner, William Purcell; Marion Mahoney and Walter Burley Griffin, both of whom had been in Wright's employ; and others who shared Wright's concepts and occasionally collaborated with him or worked in his studio, including George Maher, Robert C. Spencer, Jr., William E. Drummond, Hugh Garden, George Dean, and Barry Byrne, to name the better known. The style remained regional as it expanded beyond the suburbs of Chicago to Peoria, Springfield, and Quincy, Illinois; to Milwaukee and Madison, Wisconsin; to Mason City and Des Moines, Iowa; and to Minneapolis and Owatonna, Minnesota, among the many towns and cities known for buildings in the Prairie school style.

The legacy of the Prairie school is that it liberated architecture from the slavish imitation of building styles of the past and the rather old-fashioned proportions of tall, narrow, and angular Victorian-period buildings. The new style emphasized nature as seen in natural landscapes with contoured grounds with foliated cover. The horizontal lines of roofs and windows echoed the prairie below. Earth tones in subtle shades of gray, green, and brown were chosen for walls and trim. Natural light and ventilation were environmental concerns addressed by the style. By the 1920s, however, the International Style of modernism had overtaken the regional phenomenon known as the Prairie school.

Sources and Further Reading: H. Allen Brooks, *The Prairie School* (1972); Henry Russell Hitchcock, *In the Nature of Materials* (1942); Grant C. Manson, *Frank Lloyd Wright to 1910* (1958).

John S. Garner
University of Illinois–Urbana-Champaign

Mies van der Rohe (1886–1969)

All but one of the office building projects that Mies van der Rohe designed in Berlin from the mid-1920s through the mid-1930s subordinated structural expression to the play of reflections on glass skins. Born Ludwig Mies van der Rohe in Germany in 1886, the architect moved to the United States in 1937. All of his North American high-rises, however, abandoned sheer glass walls in order to emphasize structure and skyscraper verticality, the result of living in Chicago (1938–1969) and observing Chicago school skyscrapers. At Promontory Apartments (1949), Mies reproduced in concrete the projecting structural columns and recessed windows used on many Chicago school buildings that he had seen in the seven years he worked in the Loop. While no building code prevented full exposure of the one-story steel cage for the canonical Farnsworth House (1951), expressing high-rise frames of steel was more complicated. For the breakthrough apartment towers at 860–880 Lake Shore Drive (1948–1951), Mies projected vertical I-beams in front of horizontal steel panels below the windows. This nonstructural surface grid symbolized the actual steel structure that code requirements buried in concrete fireproofing, just as Chicago school architects had found various ways to express metal frames encased in terra cotta or brick. Further, Mies's I-beams emphasized verticality exactly as the non-load-bearing piers on many Chicago skyscrapers had done. In each of his later high-rises Mies echoed the thickened corners of the Chicago buildings by revealing the curtain-wall edges for the tower's full height.

The architect Ludwig Mies van der Rohe. Library of Congress, New York World-Telegram and Sun Newspaper Photograph Collection, LC-USZ62-116647.

The majestic Seagram Building (New York, 1958) was Mies's most radical and refined transformation of Chicago's skeletal, vertical, and emphatically cornered skyscrapers. Mies died in 1969.

Sources and Further Reading: Phyllis Lambert, ed., *Mies in America* (2001); Franz Schultze, *Mies van der Rohe* (1985).

Edward Wolner
Ball State University, Indiana

Buckminster Fuller (1895–1983)

Born in Milton, Massachusetts, in 1895, R. Buckminster Fuller, Jr., was the son of Richard Buckminster and Caroline Wolcott (Andrews) Fuller. In the tradition of his patrician New England family, he attended Milton Academy (1904–1913) and Harvard University (1913–1915), but failed to graduate and served instead as a junior officer in the U.S. Navy during and after World War I. In 1917 he married Anne Hewlett, who studied at the New York School of Applied Design and was the daughter of a New York architect. The Fullers had two children, Alexandra and Allegra.

After turbulent years as a young adult, Fuller found purpose in his life as a designer of products for "universal citizens." He devised the term *4-D*, for "four-dimensional thinking"—involving time instead of only space, and thinking of the consequences for humanity rather than only personal gain. He was a pioneer of prefabricated housing. Recognizing that low-cost efficiency depended on weight reduction, he introduced his Dymaxion House in 1927. A metal and glass structure suspended from a central mast that included central air-conditioning and vacuuming, it was light enough to be airlifted to any site. This requirement of portability was a fundamental component of Fuller's commitment to bettering humankind through design revolution. His Dymaxion Car, a nineteen-foot, three-wheeled, streamlined "omni-directional plummeting device" created from aircraft parts was a sensation at the 1933 Chicago World's Fair. When it crashed during a demonstration for investors, his interest in automobile design waned, and his interest in mass-produced housing intensified during the post–World War II housing shortage. Fuller was inspired by midwestern farm structures as a source for affordable family dwellings and he began to turn grain bins into houses. His designs from the early 1940s for "Dymaxion Deployment Units," or DDUs, produced of corrugated steel structures from the Butler Manufacturing Company (Kansas), were transformed into the Wichita House project by 1945, and were constructed with the assistance of the Beech Aircraft Corporation.

In 1946 *Fortune* magazine featured Fuller Houses Inc., describing these cornerless cottages as "modern igloos" with the testimony of a South Bend, Indiana, customer; the company received more than thirty-five thousand unsolicited orders. Fuller's inventions, however, were better than his business methods, and production soon ceased.

In 1948 he turned to lecturing and was hired as professor of architecture at Black Mountain College, North Carolina. There he focused his attention on spanning large spaces and invented the geodesic dome, a construction that could be dropped from airplanes and would be able to provide housing for all peoples. By 1951 Fuller was recognized as a visionary, received a position at the Massachusetts Institute of Technology, and began speaking tours on campuses around the world. His most famous project remains the three-quarter-sphere, two-hundred-foot-high dome designed for the United States Pavilion at Expo '67 in Montreal, the largest geodesic structure in the world upon its completion. During the 1970s Fuller continued his public-speaking circuit, captivating audiences with his marathon lectures and revolutionary ideas, increasingly convinced that the earth's resources are limited and humanity's time is short. He died in 1983.

Sources and Further Reading: R. Buckminster Fuller, *Education Automation* (1962); Karen Goodman and Kirk Simon, "Buckminster Fuller: Thinking Out Loud," *American Masters* (television program, 1996); Martin Pawley, *Buckminster Fuller* (1992).

Thelma Rohrer
Manchester College, Indiana

Minoru Yamasaki (1912–1986)

Born in Seattle, Washington, in 1912, Minoru Yamasaki was the son of first-generation Japanese immigrants, and he followed his uncle in becoming an architect. He graduated from the University of Washington, received a master's degree from New York University, and worked for New York firms Shreve, Lamb and Harmon, designers of the Empire State Building, and Harrison, Fouilhoux and Abramovitz, designers of Rockefeller Center. In 1945, at the age of thirty-three, he became chief designer for Smith Hinchman & Grylls in Detroit, and in 1955 he established his own firm, Minoru Yamasaki Associates Inc. (MYA), which continues today with its main office located in Rochester Hills (Detroit), Michigan.

Yamasaki's work consists of modern minimalist forms, in which he has increasingly blended structural simplicity with technological innovation and added graceful elements. His Pruitt-Igoe Housing project, in St. Louis (1955), received professional acclaim for efficiency but was eventually demolished by city officials, in 1972. Recognized successes include the Lambert-St. Louis Airport Terminal (1956); the McGregor Memorial Conference Center, Wayne State University, Detroit (1958); and the Standard Federal Building, Fort Wayne, Indiana. In 1962 he began work on his largest project, the World Trade Center in New York, resulting in two 110-story towers (1,368 feet tall) of self-supporting steel tubes that were recognized as the tallest buildings in the world upon their completion in 1976. The towers were destroyed in the terrorist attacks of September 11, 2001. Later projects include the Rainier Bank Tower (1977), Seattle, and works across the United States, Saudi Arabia, and Japan. Yamasaki died in 1986.

Sources and Further Reading: Vivian M. Baulch, "Minoru Yamasaki, World-Class Architect," *Detroit News*, http://www.detnews.com (accessed June 2003); Paul Goldberger, *The Skyscraper* (1989); National Geographic Society, *The Builders: Marvels of Engineering* (1992).

Thelma Rohrer
Manchester College, Indiana

Siah Armajani (b. 1939)

Artist Siah Armajani has played a crucial role in defining contemporary ideas about sculpture, architecture, and their potential interactions, particularly in art for public places. Born in Tehran, Iran, in 1939, he came to the United States in 1960 to attend Macalester College in St. Paul. He settled in Minneapolis and became a U.S. citizen in 1967. Armajani's artworks began to attract attention in the late 1960s and the 1970s, when many artists sought to break down the boundaries among different kinds of art making while simultaneously proposing a new, more active engagement with viewers. As interest in—and funding for—public art burgeoned in the late 1970s and the 1980s, he became a leader in this field. Whether intended for art venues or public places, Armajani's projects usually involve structures that viewers are invited to enter, move through, and use. Although he employs recognizable architectural materials and elements and refers to the familiar forms of bridges, houses, and towers, he consistently challenges viewers' expectations regarding functionality, interior or exterior spaces, and private or communal uses. Among his best-known works is the Irene Hixon Whitney Bridge (1988), a walkway incorporating a text by poet John Ashbery that spans a

Minneapolis's Irene Hixon Whitney Bridge, by Siah Armajani. Chris Gregerson Stock Photography, Image no. 1684.

major highway to link the Walker Art Center's Minnesota Sculpture Garden with a city park in another Minneapolis neighborhood. Internationally renowned, Armajani's art can be found in numerous major museums and at public sites throughout the United States and Europe. His work is particularly well represented in the Midwest at such museums as the Walker and the Art Institute of Chicago and in permanent public projects in Minneapolis, Beloit (Wisconsin), Iowa City, and several other communities.

Sources and Further Reading: San Armajani, Jean-Christophe Ammann, and Margrit Suter, *Sian Armajani* (1987); Siah Armajani, *Contributions anarchistes/Anarchistic Contributions 1962–1994* (1994); Janet Kardon, *Siah Armajani: Bridges, Houses, Communal Spaces, Dictionary for Building* (1985); Calvin Tompkins, "Profiles: Open, Available, Useful," *New Yorker* 66 (Mar. 19, 1990).

Ann Bremner
The Ohio State University–Columbus

SOM (Skidmore, Owings & Merrill)

The firm of Skidmore, Owings & Merrill (SOM) was founded in Chicago in 1939 when engineer John Merrill (1896–1975) joined the practice established in 1936 by architects Louis Skidmore (1897–1962) and Nathaniel Owings (1903–1984). All three had studied at the Massachusetts Institute of Technology.

After World War II, SOM became the world's foremost purveyor of International Style office towers and quickly grew to become the largest architectural practice in the United States. Many designers at SOM were also among the most innovative American architects practicing at the time. Lever House, New York

(1952), by Gordon Bunshaft (1909–1990), anticipated Ludwig Mies van der Rohe's Seagram Building in exploring the ways that modernist themes such as the expression of skeletal structure, glass enclosure, and roof gardens could be used in the design of an urban skyscraper. Perhaps Bunshaft's most striking building was the Beinecke Library (1963), at Yale, in which glazing is made of thin, translucent sheets of marble. SOM designers Bruce Graham (b. 1925), Walter Netsch (b. 1920), and Myron Goldsmith (1918–1996) likewise took the notion of the glass and steel Miesian box to new refinement in buildings like Netsch and Graham's Inland Steel Building (1957), Chicago, or Goldsmith's Republic Newspaper Building (1971), Columbus, Indiana. SOM is responsible for the design of some of the tallest buildings in the world, including the John Hancock Tower (1970), Chicago, at 1,129 feet; the Sears Tower (1976), Chicago, at 1,450 feet; and the Jin Mao Tower (1998), Shanghai, at 1,378 feet.

Sources and Further Reading: Albert Bush-Brown, *Skidmore, Owings & Merrill* (1983); Wilfried Wang, ed., *SOM Journal* (2001).

Jacqueline Gargus
The Ohio State University–Columbus

Decorative Arts

The decorative arts of the Midwest go beyond the aesthetic excellence exemplified by the likes of Cincinnati's Rookwood Pottery (1880–1960), the architectural design and furniture of Minneapolis's Purcell and Elmslie (1909–1922), and the utilitarian products such as furniture of the so-called western communities of the Shakers and the many communities of Amish that produced (and still do) breathtaking quilts—they tell the story of the Midwest in its people's search for pragmatically useful forms that were as beautiful to look at as they were to use. The decorative arts of the Midwest smack of the pragmatism that has so often been seen as a defining characteristic of the midwestern Heartland. It seems fitting that the decorative arts have been the avenue for artistic excellence in the Midwest—objects made from materials readily available such as clay, which could be dug from the hills, and wood, which was even more abundant. Could it be that artists in the Midwest have a stronger connection to the land and the products of the land itself, and the decorative arts became an extension of this? It is certainly true that the decorative arts produced in the Midwest, especially in the late nineteenth and early twentieth centuries, helped to launch the United States into the international art scene and created a defining moment in the development of an American art. The decorative arts tradition continued in the Midwest throughout the twentieth century through the "Studio Craft Movement," begun with the New Bauhaus (1937–1944) in Chicago, which stressed the relationship between art and life and the idea of equality among art forms.

The American decorative arts phenomena began with the Philadelphia Centennial Exposition of 1876, at which not only artists but the general public were exposed to art objects from countries around the world. Immediately, art societies and clubs were founded across the country and magazines and books were published that extolled the many benefits of the arts. The British publications *Magazine of Art* and *Art Journalist* created American editions, and new American publications such as *Art Amateur, Art Interchange,* and *Art Age* all guided the American public in the creation of aesthetic objects for their home. Household decoration became nothing short of a craze, and books such as Charles Locke Eastlake's *Hints on Household Taste* (published in eight American editions between 1868 and 1872), George Ward Nichols's *Art Education Applied to Industry* (1877), Clarence Cook's *The House Beautiful* (1878), Harriet Prescott Spofford's *Art Decoration Applied to Furniture* (1878), Edith Wharton's *The Decoration of Houses* (1897), and Elsie de Wolfe's *The House in Good Taste* (1913) fueled the decorative arts fires. Nichols's wife, Maria Longworth Nichols, founded the internationally acclaimed Rookwood Pottery.

The ideals of the British arts and crafts movement were introduced at the Philadelphia Centennial Exposition and were particularly influential in the American Midwest. This movement was founded in England by the Oxford art historian and philosopher John Ruskin and spread by his student William Morris in the belief that the reform of art would occur only through social reform and, hence, art and life could not be considered separately. Many of the centers of the decorative arts in the Midwest, such as Jane Addams's Hull-House (founded in 1889) in Chicago, combined art and social reform. Addams felt that education in the production of handicrafts, pottery, textiles, bookmaking, metalwork, and woodworking, to name but a few decorative arts media, could provide the new immigrant population of the United States with a dignified and spiritually and monetarily rewarding occupation—and make them good, productive citizens as well. This endeavor was echoed across the Midwest in many settlement houses and centers, though none so successfully as Hull-House.

American arts and crafts philosophers followed the ideals of Morris except for the fact that they did not shun the machine but used it as just another tool to create successfully designed, aesthetically pleasing objects, which, because they used available industrial technology, could be afforded by the masses; hence the philosophy of the arts and crafts movement was spread farther afield to more individuals. This unique philosophical twist was especially prevalent in the American Midwest where, perhaps because of an inherent pragmatism, the best American arts and crafts designs were copied, manufactured, and marketed to the public. The furniture designs of American arts and crafts purists Roycroft and Gustav Stickley were copied and produced using industrial means by the Grand Rapids Furniture Company in Michigan.

One interesting aspect of the decorative arts of the American Midwest is that a whole realm of decorative arts came out of religious communities, specifically Amish and Shaker. These religious communities were those of the western Shakers of Indiana and Ohio as well as Amish enclaves still in existence in the midwestern states of Indiana, Ohio, and Kansas. Both groups exemplified the arts and crafts ideals of the wedding of art and life, in the hand production of only functional objects, and in the production of these objects in an aesthetically pleasing manner. The Shakers believed that their designs originated in heaven and that angels transmitted the specific patterns to them on earth. The late art historian Robert Hughes noted that "the quilt is where the desire for beauty and the moral scorn for extravagance used to intersect."

The Shakers, or "Shaking Quakers" as they were known, came to the American colonies from Manchester, England, in 1774 and settled in various communities in the East. Timothy D. Rieman writes that "spirituality, as defined by the Church ministry, directed all aspects of the Shakers' lives, including the design and construction of furniture." In 1880 Joseph

Meacham, who succeeded Mother Ann Lee as the leader of the Shakers, wrote a text entitled *Way Markers*, which outlined the rules governing Shaker-made design; the following is an excerpt: "All work done, or things made in the church for their own use ought to be faithfully and well done, but plain and without superfluity. All things ought to be made according to their own order and use.... We have a right to improve the inventions of man so far as it is useful and necessary, but not to vain glory or anything superfluous."

While Shaker design was regulated by the leaders of the church, there was some regional variation in the aesthetic. In general, objects, specifically furniture, from the western communities, those in Ohio and Indiana, used primarily woods that were native to the area, and the design was slightly less refined. Despite this regional variation, all objects tended toward the "plain and simple" design.

Amish design has many similarities to Shaker, not the least in the fact that community doctrine guided the outcome of aesthetic endeavors. The majority of Amish quilts from all communities favor somber colors and simple geometric patterns that are the direct stylistic antithesis of the lavish fabrics and flamboyant designs of Victorian crazy quilts. This can certainly be read as adherence to the "Ordnung" and a rejection of the worldliness or showiness of mainstream American culture.

The Amish quilts from Lancaster County, Pennsylvania, are considered the masterpieces of Amish quilt design for the saturation of the dyes used in their textiles, the intricate detail of the actual quilting stitches, and the large geometrical blocks of colors that make up the overall design. Quilts created by the midwestern Amish favor more sober colors with a great deal of black, are less intricately quilted, and have less minimal design, instead using smaller textile pieces and playing with variations of traditional American quilt patterns such as Baskets, Log Cabin, and Baby's Blocks. Midwestern Amish quilts do not have the large geometric central focus that the Lancaster County quilts do, instead favoring smaller, repetitive patterns. They were also primarily made of cotton, rather than the wool of the Lancaster County quilts, which did not allow for the intensity of color saturation.

The late nineteenth and early twentieth centuries were certainly the pinnacle of achievement for the decorative arts in the Midwest but this tradition did not go away. The ideals of the German Bauhaus (1919–1933); the importance of craftsmanship; the unity of art, architecture, and design; and the idea that together these elements could change society for the better were brought to the United States and the Midwest by the immigration of many European artists to the urban centers of the United States after World War I. The formation of the New Bauhaus in Chicago (1937–1944) and Cranbrook Academy (1937–present) in Bloomfield Hills, Michigan, continued the idea that art and life are intimately connected and that all arts are equal.

Sources and Further Reading: Whitney Chadwick, *Women, Art, and Society*, 2nd ed. (1996); Sharon Darling, *Chicago Furniture* (1984); Barbara Floyd and Julia Baldwin, *The Noble Craftsman We Promote* (1999); Robert Hughes, *Amish: The Art of the Quilt* (1993); Wendy Kaplan, *"The Art that is Life": The Arts and Crafts Movement in America, 1875–1920* (1998); Metropolitan Museum of Art, *In Pursuit of Beauty: Americans and the Aesthetic Movement* (1986); Timothy D. Rieman, *Shaker: The Art of Craftsmanship* (1995); Davira Taragin, *Contemporary Crafts and the Saxe Collection* (1993).

Janette Knowles
Ohio Dominican University

Quilts

The earliest quilts documented in the Midwest were eastern quilts traveling westward with the settlers. In the early nineteenth century, quilts were commonly composed of small blocks, with many of the block designs bearing names meaningful to the settlers, for example, Churn Dash or Windmill. Their colors coincided with the dye techniques developed by the textile manufacturers of the time. The strong, acid colors of mineral dyes were developed in the 1820s. In 1829 turkey red, a fast red dye, became available. Mauve dye was discovered in England in 1856, leading to the development of bright aniline dyes. By the middle of the nineteenth century, midwestern quilts were made with American textiles in these colors.

By 1850 immigrants to the Midwest from a variety of European countries had settled close to one another. Some, like the Scandinavians, had no tradition of quilting, but learning from their neighbors they, too, made quilts. Women were the quilt makers, and the activity was both a creative and a social outlet for them during which they exchanged patterns, fabric, labor, and news; their quilts became canvases on which they expressed their concerns about wars, loss of family members, and religious beliefs. In 1846 the Stearns and Foster Company of Ohio began marketing batting to fill quilts. The sewing machine, marketed in 1856, facilitated quilt making. Simpler bedcovers known as "comforters" were sewn to make quick bedding for bitter winters. These were constructed of clothing scraps or sales representatives' woolen samples and tied together with yarn. Quilting reflected the tastes of the times, and in the late 1800s Victorian design ethic dictated great embellishment and rich textiles.

In the twentieth century, published quilt patterns were widely available. Notable designers included Carrie Hall of Kansas, Ruby McKim of Missouri, and Marie Webster of Indiana. Many intricate quilts were produced across the Midwest. Mary Schafer in Michigan and Grace Snyder in Nebraska did significant work. The Century of Quilts contest at the 1933 Chicago World's Fair received extensive publicity.

Quilts made from printed feed sacks became both a rural and an urban phenomenon in the 1930s and 1940s. The federal government sponsored Works Progress Administration projects in the 1930s to create employment in hard times; in Milwaukee, women involved with this program made quilts for orphanages.

Two cultures produced unique styles. In Minnesota and the Dakotas in the 1800s, missionaries taught the Sioux women to quilt. Their early quilts were traditional "white women's" designs, but an indigenous style developed in the twentieth century; Native American women began piecing the traditional Lone Star quilt pattern with solid bright colors on a white background, creating an easily identifiable quilt they called the Indian Star. And as eastern Amish families moved westward toward Iowa in 1846, their quilts changed from diamonds and bars in dark colors to brighter colors sewn into small, traditional quilt blocks. Bear Paws and Pieced Baskets became favorites.

After World War II, inexpensive, factory-made bedding became preferable to homemade covers. The patriotic fervor of the U.S. bicentennial in 1976 renewed interest in quilting. Many of the quilts made since 1976 are small, intended to be displayed as art.

Source and Further Reading: Helen Kelley, *Dating Quilts* (1990).

Helen Kelley
Minneapolis

The Arts and Crafts Movement

Although the arts and crafts movement originated in England, one of its strongest manifestations took place in the Midwest, where several of the most important figures and workshops in the movement were based, among them architect Frank Lloyd Wright and ceramist and Rookwood Pottery founder Maria Longworth Nichols.

The arts and crafts movement was a response to the adverse effects of the ramifications of the Industrial

Art Nouveau vase decorated with the Rookwood Glaze, Cincinnati, 1902. Ohio Historical Society, M00228.

Revolution on both the quality of the design of goods produced and the quality of working conditions of the industrial laborer. The movement sought to wed the design and production processes so that one person was responsible for the creation of a work from start to finish, and his or her humanity and hand were inseparable from the final crafted object. It was believed that this would instill a sense of pride in the object that would spill over into the life of the person who produced it and ultimately lead to a more successful aesthetic object as well as a new sense of dignity in the life of the maker through handwork. Individuals would no longer be mere machine tenders or cogs in the industrial mechanism, but skilled artisans whose stylistic signature was completely individual. John Ruskin was the leading philosopher of this movement but it was his student, William Morris, who attempted to put the philosophy into practice. Both called for the abandonment of factories in favor of a guild system, inspired by that of the medieval era, in which individuals would create handmade goods. Unfortunately and ironically, these handmade goods were so expensive to produce that they were unaffordable by the masses and subsequently undermined the sentiments of social reform that were so important to the ideals of the arts and crafts movement.

The movement followed the sentiments of social and design reform but, from the beginning, saw the machine as less of an enemy and more a tool to be used to bring the movement's ideals, aspirations, and superior aesthetic products to the masses in order to ensure its widespread promulgation. In 1901, in a Hull-House lecture entitled "The Art and Craft of the Machine," Frank Lloyd Wright discussed the "effective utilization" of the machine to spread the ideals and aesthetics of the arts and crafts movement. The Midwest became the most influential American arts and crafts center precisely because of its enthusiastic use of the machine. The heart of the movement in the Midwest was Chicago—the location of Jane Addams's social-reform center and artisan workshop, Hull-House; Frank Lloyd Wright; the influential Chicago Arts and Crafts Society (founded at Hull-House in 1897); and the periodical largely responsible for spreading the ideals and design aesthetic of the movement, *House Beautiful* (which began publication in 1896). Hull-House, founded in 1889, epitomized the highest ideals of the British arts and crafts movement. Located in one of the poorest neighborhoods in Chicago, it provided a place where local immigrants could take classes in various handicrafts, domestic sciences as well as American civics. The Chicago Arts and Crafts Society worked out of Hull-House to teach the immigrant populations handicrafts, ranging from needlework to metalsmithing, so that they could earn a livable and respectable wage and become productive members of their newly chosen country.

Wright was one of the founding members of the Chicago Arts and Crafts Society. He was concerned with three major elements in his designs—function, affordability, and harmony with nature, all of which could be traced to the original ideals of the British arts and crafts movement and which found life in his Prairie school architecture.

Chicago and its surrounds were home to several other important arts and crafts entities, such as Oscar Lovell Triggs's Industrial Art League and the Bohemian Guild of Arts and Crafts as well as Hyde Park's Blue Sky Press, which was modeled after William Morris's Kelmscott Press and produced hand-printed and -bound artists' books.

Pottery was the most important aspect of the arts and crafts movement in the Midwest, partially due to the presence of rich clay deposits in significant portions of many midwestern states. Maria Longworth Nichols's Rookwood Pottery of Cincinnati; Weller and Roseville Potteries in Zanesville, Ohio; Mary Chase Perry Stratton's Pewabic Pottery in Detroit; University City Pottery in University City, Missouri; and the work of Susan Frackleton in Milwaukee, all began under the influence of the ideals and aesthetic of the British arts and crafts movement. Many of them, like Rookwood and Pewabic, were formed to provide a responsible, profitable, and dignified vocation for women outside of teaching and domestic labor. All eventually used mechanization in some aspect of production to reduce the cost of the final product.

The production of furniture was another important aspect of the arts and crafts movement of the Midwest and much of it took place in Grand Rapids, Michigan, which was known as "Furniture City." The Charles P. Limbert Company, the Grand Rapids Chair Company, and the Michigan Chair Company specialized in taking the design elements of the arts and crafts style to produce furniture using mechanization. While working-class consumers could not afford an original handcrafted Stickley, they could afford a well-designed and well-made production piece by one of these industries, and so the taste for the arts and crafts style was spread even farther.

Many other midwestern cities were home to other kinds of arts and crafts industry; Chillicothe, Ohio, for instance, had the book production of Dard Hunter, and Cambridge City, Indiana, had Overbeck Pottery. This is testimony to the fact that handwork and, in the arts and crafts movement, the art of the hand are woven into the fabric of midwestern life.

Sources and Further Reading: Patricia Fidler, *Art with a Mission* (1991); Barbara Floyd and Julia Baldwin, *The Noble Craftsman We Promote* (1999); Wendy Kaplan, "*The Art that is Life*": *The Arts and Crafts Movement in America, 1875–1920* (1987); Sheila Schwartz, ed., *From Architecture to Object* (1989).

Janette Knowles
Ohio Dominican University

Marion Mahony Griffin (1871–1961)

The first woman in the United States to be licensed as an architect (in 1898), Marion Mahony Griffin was also an artist, renderer, designer, landscape architect, and planner whose professional life spanned fifty years and included work in the United States, Australia, and India. During the early years of her career, she contributed to the development of the Prairie school of architecture and she is considered the most gifted architectural renderer of that time. With her husband, architect Walter Burley Griffin, she forged a long-term creative partnership that integrated their personal lives, social concerns, and professional interests.

Born in Chicago in 1871, Mahony was the second child and eldest daughter of educator, poet, and journalist Jeremiah Mahony and Clara Hamilton (Perkins) Mahony. Her mother, a member of the influential Chicago Woman's Club, became certified as a school principal after the death of her husband, when Mahony was eleven years old. Mahony attended public schools in Winnetka (Hubbard Woods) and Chicago and experienced a culturally vibrant, progressive, and nurturing home life during her childhood. Encouraged by family friend and local philanthropist Mary Wilmarth, she followed her cousin, Dwight Heald Perkins, to the Massachusetts Institute of Technology (MIT), where she studied under Constant Desire Despradelle, one of the first graduates of the École des Beaux Arts to come to the United States to teach. In 1894 Mahony became only the second woman (after Sophia Hayden) to graduate from MIT's four-year architectural program. She returned to Chicago and worked briefly for her cousin before joining the Frank Lloyd Wright studio in 1896. Her thesis project, "An Artist's Home and Studio," may have influenced Wright to combine his home and workplace in Oak Park. Mahony was an important figure in Wright's office, responsible for many decorative designs including art-glass windows, furniture, light fixtures, fireplaces, and garden ornaments. Her beautiful, Japanese-inspired drawings, which featured dramatic viewpoints and integrated architecture and nature, were instrumental in promoting the work of Wright. Mahony was responsible for more than half the drawings produced for Wright's famous *Wasmuth Portfolio*, one of the most influential architectural publications of the twentieth century. Along with Wright and Jane Addams, she was one of the founding members of the Chicago Arts and Crafts Society. After Illinois passed legislation making it the first state to regulate the architectural profession, Mahony was among the first group to take the licensing exam. During this period she completed one known independent project, the All Soul's Church in Evanston, Illinois (1901; since demolished).

Mahony met Walter Burley Griffin, a graduate of the University of Illinois whose primary interest was landscape architecture, when he joined Wright's office in 1901. Griffin worked for Wright until 1906, when he left to establish an independent practice. Mahony continued to work for Wright in various capacities until 1909. During Wright's extended trip to Europe in 1909–1910, Mahony worked as chief designer for Herman von Holst, a Beaux-Arts classicist who had taken over the Wright practice. She completed several of Wright's designs and several of her own. The David Amberg House in Grand Rapids, Michigan (1909); the Adolph Mueller House in Decatur, Illinois (1910); and a design for a house for Henry Ford (1913) are attributed to Mahony. She invited Griffin to act as landscape architect on several Decatur projects, and in 1911, after a courtship that included nature explorations, Mahony and Griffin married and Mahony assumed a role in Griffin's office. Their most important project is the Rock Crest/Rock Glen development in Mason City, Iowa, for which Mahony executed a brilliant aerial perspective of the entire subdivision. In 1912 Griffin won the international competition for Australia's new federal capital, Canberra. Mahony's extraordinary drawings, consisting of fourteen panels and one large plan executed in exotic photo dyes and watercolor on satin, were instrumental in securing the prize for the Griffin entry.

In 1914 Mahony and Griffin moved to Australia so that Griffin could supervise the construction of Canberra. The couple established a home and Griffin established a practice with offices in Sydney and Melbourne. Mahony continued to participate actively in the Griffin practice. Important Australian projects include numerous residential designs for their Castlecrag development (1921–1933), Newman College at the University of Melbourne (1915–1918), the Capitol Theatre (1921–1924), and Café Australia (1916). Mahony, a pacifist, pursued interests in anthroposophy (a social philosophy founded by Rudolf Steiner), education, and theatre and produced a series of exquisite drawings, the Tree Studies, which delineated native Australian species. During a lengthy trip home to Chicago in the early 1930s, she completed a mural, *Fairies and Woodland Scenes* (extant), as a gift to the graduating class of the Armstrong School in Rogers Park, where her sister taught.

In 1935 Griffin was invited to India to design a library for Lucknow University; when he obtained other projects, Mahony joined him. A period of intense creativity followed. Their numerous commissions included residences and the complete design (sixty buildings) of the United Provinces Exhibition of Industry and Agriculture (1936). Together they produced designs for more than a hundred projects. Upon Griffin's sudden death in 1937, Mahony declined a partnership and teaching position. After supervising the construction of the Pioneer Press Building, she went back briefly to Australia before returning to Chicago.

There she was honored by the local architectural community in 1940 at a meeting of the Illinois Society of Architects, but she never established an independent practice. She prepared town-planning schemes for her friend Lola Maverick Lloyd. Plans for the World Fellowship Center (New Hampshire, 1942) and the towns of Hill Crystal–Rosary Crystals (near Boerne, Texas, 1943) were abandoned upon Lloyd's death. In 1945 Mahony submitted entries to both the *Chicago Tribune* Chicagoland Prize Home Competition and the *Chicago Herald-American* Better Chicago Contest. In the late 1940s she completed a manuscript, "The Magic of America," an unpublished, four-volume memoir of her life that includes detailed discussions of the Griffins' work. Although the collaborative nature of her work with Wright and Griffin makes Mahony's individual contributions difficult to identify, she pioneered the active participation of women in the design professions. Her superlative renderings and drawings continue to be architectural and artistic treasures without equal. She died in 1961.

Sources and Further Reading: Susan Fondiler Berkon and Jane Holtz Kay, "Marion Mahony Griffin, Architect," *Feminist Art Journal* 4 (Spring 1975); Elizabeth Joy Birmingham, "Marion Mahony Griffin and the Magic of America," Ph.D. diss., Iowa State University (2000); Marion Mahony Griffin, "The Magic of America," manuscript, New York Historical Society, microfilm edition, Art Institute of Chicago (n.d.); "Marion Lucy Mahony Griffin," in Rima Lunin Schultz and Adele Hast, eds., *Women Building Chicago, 1790–1990* (2001); Janice Pregliasco, "The Life and Work of Marion Mahony Griffin," in *The Prairie School: Design Vision for the Midwest* (1995); Anna Rubbo, "Marion Mahony Griffin: A Portrait," in Jenepher Duncan, ed., *Walter Burley Griffin: A Re-View* (1988); Jeff Turnbull and Peter Y. Navaretti, eds., *The Griffins in Australia and India* (1998); Anne Watson, ed., *Beyond Architecture* (1998).

Pamela J. Hill
Des Plaines, Illinois

William Gray Purcell (1880–1965) and George Grant Elmslie (1871–1952)

Purcell and Elmslie worked together as architects from 1910 to 1922. Born in Scotland, Elmslie moved to Chicago in 1884 and began to apprentice as a draftsman for architectural firms, eventually becoming Louis H. Sullivan's chief assistant. Purcell was born in the Chicago suburb of Oak Park and already knew the work of Frank Lloyd Wright and Sullivan well at the time he entered Cornell University's architectural program. Purcell and Elmslie became fast friends during Purcell's brief tenure with Sullivan.

Building for both the commercial and residential markets, Purcell and Elmslie were the most productive Prairie school architects. There are Purcell and Elmslie buildings in twenty-two states, primarily in the Midwest. In the thriving agrarian and industrial economy before the Depression and world wars, they defined a regional identity for the Midwest that was resistant to East Coast influences. That definition is their legacy.

What distinguished Purcell and Elmslie was their ability to conceptualize a desired building as the expression and purpose of a local community. Campaigning for an American architecture as the organic expression of historically specific communities, Purcell and Elmslie fought hard against the classical and Gothic revivalism then in vogue. They argued that it was in the factories where use determined form that a truly American architecture already existed.

These modernist convictions did not go so far as to condemn ornament as a crime, however. Purcell and Elmslie were contractors for the most talented craftspeople of the Midwest, and for this reason are associated with the arts and crafts movement. Yet their value lies in what they brought to the modernism of their time. Their residential homes, such as the 1913 Edna S. Purcell House in Minneapolis, or the larger and more dramatically sited Bradley Home (1911–1912) in Woods Hole, Massachusetts, are known for their open interiors. In the Purcell House, the ceiling is a consistent height throughout and extends along a single axis. This spacious simplicity is varied by different floor levels that structure a variety of living areas and views across them, allowing for both intimacy and openness.

Purcell and Elmslie's arguments for a truly American architecture were received well in the Midwest. Building in the first two decades of the twentieth century, they had as clients midwestern merchants who thrived in an economy of agricultural and industrial health in the region. Self-reliant and resistant to East Coast influences, they had faith in enterprise, ingenuity, and the expression of local democratic values, and they trusted Purcell and Elmslie to help them articulate what they believed to be specific to their own business aims and lifestyles. The Merchant's Bank of Winona (1911–1912), Minnesota, exemplifies how they determined their own modern architecture. In a small midwestern town, the bank was nearly as important symbolically as the church, but there was no adequate architectural representation of its function for the community. Beaux-Arts classicism lent banks an imposing authority, and only recently Sullivan's gigantic vault (1908) in Owatonna, Minnesota, had symbolized the function of a bank. Their aim was to represent the bank as the place of business for a vibrant community with the thought that the bank should not overbearingly declare authority or restricted access. Indeed, later Purcell and Elmslie banks included a fireplace and a community meeting room.

They worked hard so that their clients understood architectural design as a collaborative and conceptual process involving both the client and the firm. Long before corporate identity was understood as a marketing tool, Purcell and Elmslie were the first architects to consider such things as advertising, sales psychology, packaging, consumer response, and employee behavior. An indication of the extent to which the architects worked closely with their clients to define identities is that they designed checks for the banks they built, and even private residences had custom-designed stationery.

Elmslie was the ornament designer for Sullivan's buildings, and was solely responsible for the elaborate National Farmer's Bank of Owatonna. Purcell and Elmslie describe the role of ornament in their own work as something that begins from the start, organically, as a part of the structure of the building. By its purposeful elaboration of design problems and meaning, and by its disposability, ornament assists in the conceptualization of an idea. From the beginning of a project, thumbnail ornament sketches were filed away as a record of the evolution of the idea. Unlike Mies van der Rohe's "less is more" modernism of the International Style, Purcell and Elmslie stood behind ornament as articulating the singular idea of the work throughout the process of design.

Both men regarded themselves as part of an architectural movement and were important advocates of their own and others' work, publishing in the *Craftsman*, *Western Architect*, and *Architectural Record*. This period of regional confidence disappeared, however, just prior to the Depression years. It was not simply a matter of economics, as there was also a shift in the circulation of architectural ideas in print media. Several of the magazines that Purcell and Elmslie wrote for, both separately and together, relocated to the East Coast and began to shift their address to that audience. In 1910 *House Beautiful*, which had been a strong advocate of the Prairie school architects, moved east and by the end of World War I was promoting the American colonial style rather than any truly innovative architectural ideas. By 1922 the independently wealthy Purcell was no longer able to subsidize the struggling firm and could see no future for progressive architecture in America. Elmslie continued, with few commissions. Elmslie died in 1952 and Purcell in 1965.

Sources and Further Reading: H. Allen Brooks, *The Prairie School* (1972); David Gebhard, ed. *Work of Purcell and Elmslie, Architects* (1965); Larry Millett, *The Curve of the Arch* (1985); Craig Zabel, "George Grant Elmslie," in Craig Zabel and Susan Scott Munshower, eds., *American Public Architecture* (1989).

Catherine Spaeth
Purchase College, New York

Charles Eames (1907–1978) and Ray Eames (1912–1988)

Charles Eames (1907–1978), of St. Louis, Missouri, and Ray Kaiser (1912–1988), of Sacramento, California, met at the Cranbrook Academy of Art in Bloomfield Hills, Michigan, in 1940. As an architect, Charles Eames won notice from Eliel Saarinen, architect and director of Cranbrook, and he received a fellowship to study there in 1938. By the end of the year, Saarinen appointed Eames as an instructor of design. Ray Kaiser came to Cranbrook from New York, where she had studied with painter Hans Hoffman and dancer Martha Graham. The two were married in Chicago in 1941, beginning what is now recognized as the most successful design partnership of twentieth-century America. Their work has meant something to nearly everyone in the United States. They are well known among architects for their Case Study House; among filmmakers for their films; among curators and educators for their multimedia exhibition installations and slide lectures; and in graphics for their textiles, logos, and processes that anticipated desktop publishing. Finally, it is difficult to imagine anyone living in the United States who has never sat in one of their chairs in a school, airport, office, or lobby. The work of Charles and Ray Eames is both so ubiquitous that it is

A 1945 Eames chair. Vitra Design Museum Weil am Rhein. Photo by Thomas Dix.

nearly invisible and so singular that the Eames lounge chair is the status symbol of American modernism.

What the Eames lounge chair symbolizes is the casual lifestyle of the American post–World War II middle class. It is not the machine of high modernism but combines the Victorian coziness of wood and overstuffed leather with well-machined swivels and bracing supports. Accustomed to apartment living and to entertaining guests without the help of servants, a new and well-educated class was drawn toward a personalized modernism of low-maintenance pleasure and comfort.

Such a modernism of warmth and comfort owes its debt to midwestern tradition, most notably that of the Arts and Crafts Movement at the Cranbrook Academy of Art. At Cranbrook, the standardization of industrialism was regarded as a social danger, and artists believed that they could remedy this by attending to the beauty of ordinary things. The philosophy of the Cranbrook Academy was instrumental in shaping an American attitude in favor of designing for the good life where modern technology is apparent and enjoyed, as opposed to an international aesthetic of the machine for living in a "brave new world."

It could also be said that hands-on practicality and a collaborative respect for the skills of others are midwestern traits that shaped the optimism of Eames design. At the age of ten, Charles Eames was working with heavy machinery to help support his family in St. Louis. While in high school he worked at the Laclede Steel Mill, which began to rely on his drawing skills to convey engineering solutions. It was this experience in a steel mill that earned Eames a scholarship to study architecture at Washington University.

Although Eames never earned his degree, his determination soon paid off. Reading *Architectural Forum*, Cranbrook president and renowned architect Eliel Saarinen admired Eames's St. Mary's Cathedral (1935–1936) in Helena, Arkansas. Saarinen kept an eye on this promising architect, and when Eames built the Meyer House (1936–1938) in Huntleigh Village, Missouri, Saarinen offered him a full scholarship to Cranbrook.

It is their designs for molded plywood that first secured the reputations of Charles and Ray Eames. While at Cranbrook, they began to research prototypes for military medical field splints under government contract and in collaboration with local industry. Their success resulted from the unusual extent to which they were involved with experiments in production at the Detroit-based Evans Woods Products Company. The Eameses' hands-on involvement with all dimensions of their work, from production to sales, is also evident in the relationship the pair maintained with the Herman Miller Furniture Company, based in Zeeland, Michigan, and still carrying the Eames line of furnishings. Their whimsy and sheer love of visual

pleasure in arrangements of the Herman Miller showrooms drew much attention.

Charles and Ray were unusual in that they had high regard for vernacular traditions. This is most evident in the Max de Pree House (1954) in Zeeland, Michigan, which drew upon the architecture of early Michigan settlers. Borrowing from local tradition to build for a colder climate, they designed the house to be built by local craftsman-woodworker immigrants from Holland.

Such a passion for local traditions tended toward visual excess. Perhaps the most influential aspect of the Eameses' design for modern American living was an allowance for the clutter of interesting things. Their own home was full of tumbleweeds, kachina dolls, and paper butterfly kites, which they referred to as "functional decoration." Visual excess became their trademark, and their films, such as *Tops* (1969), are extraordinary essays in movement and color. Their toys, such as the famous *House of Cards* (1952, 1953), are a joy to look at, and all the more so in that they provoke the making of one's own world as a place of movement and color. This practice extended as well into their design of major educational exhibitions, which often emphasized the sheer pleasure of the natural and scientific world. In an interview, asked whether a designed object could exist only for the sake of pleasure, Charles Eames replied, "Who would say that pleasure is not useful?"

So valuable were the Eameses' ideas and practices to the industrialized modern world that a developing nation sought their aid in protecting the beauty of local craft traditions from the cheapening tendencies of industrialized modernism. This collaborative respect and their ethical aesthetics resulted in Charles and Ray Eames's 1958 "India Report," for Prime Minister Jawaharlal Nehru of India, which led to the creation of India's National Institute of Design in Ahmadabad.

Sources and Further Reading: Donald Albrecht, ed., *The Work of Charles and Ray Eames* (1997); Eames Demetrios, *An Eames Primer* (2001); Pat Kirkham, *Charles and Ray Eames* (1995); John Neuhart, Marilyn Neuhart, and Ray Eames, *Eames Design* (1989); UCLA Arts Council, *Connections: The Work of Charles and Ray Eames* (1976).

Catherine Spaeth
Purchase College, New York

Warren MacKenzie (b. 1924)

Warren MacKenzie was born in 1924 to Fred and Adelaide MacKenzie in Kansas City, Missouri. He studied at the School of the Art Institute of Chicago, where he met Alix Kolesky, a fellow student in ceramics; they married upon her graduation in 1947 and he graduated the next year. From 1950 to 1952 they apprenticed with the influential potter Bernard Leach in St. Ives, England. Working in the Leach tradition, they became committed to the idea of making utilitarian ceramics of simple beauty. In 1953 the couple purchased a farm near Stillwater, Minnesota, to establish a studio. That year Warren MacKenzie also began teaching ceramics at the University of Minnesota, where he taught until his retirement in 1990. MacKenzie has exhibited his work at such venues as the Walker Art Center (1954, 1961); the Art Institute of Chicago (1959); the Everson Museum in Syracuse, New York (1979, 1989); the Renwick Gallery in Washington, D.C. (1979); and the Victoria and Albert Museum in London (1986). Most of his sales, however, have been directly from his studio in Stillwater, where he maintains a small, self-service showroom. He prices his work modestly to encourage an understanding of his work as genuinely intended for use. MacKenzie is credited with being a father of the "Mingei-sota" style of ceramics; this refers to a style and accompanying philosophy of Japanese folk arts (*mingei*) known for a commitment to utility and direct expression. His influence, while deeply felt in the upper Midwest, extends internationally as he continues to exhibit and teach in South America, Asia, Europe, and the United States.

Sources and Further Reading: David Lewis, *Warren MacKenzie: An American Potter* (1991); Robert Silberman, "Down-to-Earth Idealist," *American Craft* 49 (June/July 1989); Gerry Williams, "Warren MacKenzie: Potter's Potter," *Studio Potter* 19 (Dec. 1990).

Jeanne Quinn
University of Colorado–Boulder

Tobey Furniture Company

In 1865 Tobey Furniture Company founder Charles Tobey and his brother Frank united with established Chicago furniture manufacturer F. Porter Thayer, enabling Tobey to become a manufacturer and dealer. The company (which began in 1856 and endured to 1954) survived the 1873 financial panic and ensuing three-year depression by purchasing inventory of failing furniture stores. Tobey furnished some of Chicago's newest hotels after the 1871 fire, producing Louis XIV, Louis XV, and Louis XVI reproductions; furniture in the arts and crafts, art nouveau, and French art moderne styles; and tall case clocks. It sold furniture from more than two hundred international companies, becoming an industry leader marketing factory-made arts and crafts furniture.

In spring 1900 Tobey's mission furniture premiered, setting the stage for the New Furniture collection designed by Gustav Stickley. Introduced in fall 1900 and inspired by contemporary British designers and objects from California's missions, the New Furniture included approximately seventy-five oak pieces. It was available in three stains with a dull-wax finish: Tyrolean green, gunmetal gray, and grayish-brown "weathered oak." Stickley sold the same collection in his catalog. By December 1900 Stickley left Tobey, displeased at serving as an anonymous supplier.

In 1901 Tobey introduced the New Furniture in weathered oak in oak, ash, and mahogany finishes. The patented Tobey Chair also debuted, a streamlined version of the Morris chair (which had an adjustable back) that had both an adjustable back and a sliding seat. In 1902 the affordable Russmore line premiered, marketed as durable, simply designed furniture with a deep-brown sheen. The same year, designer Joseph Twyman mounted an exhibition of William Morris fabrics at the Tobey store.

Sources and Further Reading: David M. Cathers, *Furniture of the American Arts and Crafts Movement* (1981); Sharon Darling, *Chicago Furniture* (1984); New York Arts & Antiques, *Nineteenth Century Furniture* (1982).

Jennifer Janna Baron
Tinker Swiss Cottage Museum
Rockford, Illinois

The American Encaustic Tile Company

The American Encaustic Tile Company was founded by F. H. Hall in Zanesville, Ohio, in 1875 to create ceramic tiles for domestic and commercial interiors. The company set out to use the rich clay resources of southeastern Ohio to make tiles that would compete with those being imported in large numbers from England. Hall extolled the virtues of the rich and abundant clay deposits in Ohio and received the financial backing of two New York capitalists, Benedict Fischer, who would later become president of the company, and G. R. Lansing. The Philadelphia Centennial Exhibition of 1876 featured many European tile industries that created works according to the philosophy of the arts and crafts movement and its call for simple, healthful, and well-designed functional objects. This resulted in the founding of many tile companies in the United States in 1878 and for the corporate expansion of the American Encaustic Tile Company that year.

The company began by making only encaustic tiling, resulting from a process in which decoration is inlaid into the clay and fired but left unglazed. This technique originated in the Middle Ages in monastic potteries and was used mainly for flooring, as were the tiles created by the American Encaustic Tile Company. By the 1880s glazed tiles that exhibited a strong stylistic debt to the arts and crafts movement were being created. Herman Carl Mueller, a sculptor who trained in Munich and Nuremburg, was brought into the firm in 1887 to raise the artistic standards of its wares. He designed several lines of modeled or bas relief tiles based on classical themes from ancient Greece and Rome and Renaissance Italy, which were often grouped to make a single architectural assemblage.

The American Encaustic Tile Company was always drawn in two directions: keeping up with aesthetic developments in the international world of art pottery, and selling to the commercial market. After earning aesthetic kudos for its work in the early 1880s, the company expanded and continued making tiles equal in quality to the imports of centuries-old European companies, winning commissions such as the tiling of New York's Holland Tunnel. At the same time, important figures in the development of the American art pottery movement played a role in the growth of the company. Frederick Hurten Rhead (1880–1942), an English-born and -trained potter and ceramic designer who was one of the most important figures in the spread of the ideals of the British arts and crafts movement in pottery to the United States, became research director of the company about 1920. The firm consistently experimented with surface treatments to keep abreast of aesthetic developments of the art pottery movement, but its efforts were conservative ones geared toward marketability and commercial success rather than aesthetic merit.

After making glazed earthenware tiles for the commercial market through the 1920s, the American Encaustic Tile Company closed in 1935, like so many other ceramic industries unable to recover from the Depression.

Sources and Further Reading: Cooper-Hewitt Museum, *American Art Pottery* (1987); Alice Cooney Frelinghuysen, "Aesthetic Forms in Ceramics and Glass," in Doreen Bolger, ed., *In Pursuit of Beauty: Americans and the Aesthetic Movement* (1986).

Janette M. Knowles
Ohio Dominican University

Rookwood Pottery

Rookwood Pottery was very important in the development of the American art pottery movement and brought with it the first international recognition of ceramic work from the United States. The American art pottery movement came to Cincinnati, Ohio, when a group of young, socially prominent women, including the founder of Rookwood Pottery, Maria Longworth Nichols, inspired by the rhetoric of the British arts and crafts movement and its aesthetic elevation of functional objects, began experimentation in ceramic overglaze decoration. Their experimentation led to the formation of the Cincinnati Pottery Club, organized by Mary Louise McLaughlin, who with Nichols studied at the Cincinnati School of Design. McLaughlin developed what was known as the "Cincinnati Limoges" technique, or the *process barbotine*, in which colored liquid clays or "slips" were painted onto the body of the ceramic form while it was still "green," or unfired. The Cincinnati Limoges technique allowed for painterly designs to be preserved under the glaze.

Nichols never received an invitation to join the Cincinnati Art Pottery Club. Nichols instead founded Rookwood Pottery, which evolved into this country's most successful art pottery, producing wares from 1880 through 1960. At the heart of Nichols's philosophy was the principle of the British arts and crafts movement, that objects should be both beautiful and useful. Rookwood grew from an experimental studio endeavor to a commercial pottery, always trying to avoid the artistic pitfalls associated with larger industrial potteries where aesthetics mattered less than economics.

Rookwood specialized in surface decoration. Decorators were given prethrown forms and worked at creating surface decoration that harmonized with the form. Rookwood's international reputation was made on the strength of its naturalistic underglaze depictions, often of botanical forms. These early works exhibited the importance of *japonisme* on Rookwood's surface designs as well as the forms themselves. Rookwood designers studied the art of Japan as well as japonisme found in contemporary French ceramics. The Japanese designer and porcelain painter Kataro Shirayamadani worked at Rookwood from 1887 to 1948.

Rookwood's continual experimentation with forms and glazes had many unpredictable results, such as "Goldstone," in which crystals appeared randomly on the surface of the vessel, and "Tiger's Eye," in which the surface of the vessel appeared to be coated in soft gold. In 1884 Laura Fry began experimenting with the application of colored slip via mouth atomizer, a process in which diluted pigment is misted onto the surface of the vessel. This allowed for the most thorough integration of surface decoration and background form achieved to date. Rookwood designers also created wares influenced by traditional ceramics of China and Persia and responded to contemporary developments in aesthetics such as art deco. The continual experimentation in form would not protect the pottery from the financial devastation of the Depression, and though Rookwood's name was still used on wares until 1948, it never fully recovered.

Sources and Further Reading: Cooper-Hewitt Museum, *American Art Pottery* (1987); Anita Ellis, *Rookwood Pottery: The Glorious Gamble* (1992).

Janette M. Knowles
Ohio Dominican University

Libbey Glass

The Libbey Glass Company of Toledo, Ohio, was founded in 1888 as the W.L. Libbey & Son Company. During the first half of the twentieth century it was the most important glass tableware company in the Midwest. William L. Libbey and his son, Edward D. Libbey, had joined the New England Glass Company, of Cambridge, Massachusetts, in the 1870s. In 1878 the Libbeys took over the factory, reorganizing it as the New England Glass Works, Wm. L. Libbey & Son Props. They specialized in colored artistic glasses and elaborately cut glass. However, the cost of bringing in fuel and union demands made glass manufacture in the East increasingly expensive, and in 1888 the younger Libbey, owner since his father's death in 1883, decided that he would move west. In Ohio natural gas was abundant, and backers in Toledo offered Libbey a free glasshouse site as well as lots for workers' housing. The factory in Ohio started operations in August 1888. Fortunately, more than a hundred experienced employees made the move to Toledo with Libbey and the company was profitable by 1891.

In 1893 Libbey built a glass factory on the grounds of the World's Columbian Exhibition in Chicago, and this became one of the most popular sights of the fair, establishing the Libbey name nationally. One outstanding exhibit at the fair was a dress made of spun-glass fibers that was presented to Princess Eulalie of Spain with great fanfare. Many pressed-glass souvenirs were made in Chicago, but of more importance for publicity were the cut-glass pieces that the company turned out in great numbers at the turn of the century. These were time-consuming and expensive to make, but they could be sold at a large profit and were extremely fashionable from the 1890s until World War I.

The company also blew glass blanks for lightbulbs for Edison General Electric. The supervisor of this process was Michael J. Owens, a glassblower from West Virginia who became one of Libbey's most valued employees. Owens was a practical glassmaker who

was constantly trying to better the process, and in the 1890s he perfected a semiautomatic blowing machine to produce lightbulbs. In 1896 Libbey, Owens, and associates formed the Toledo Glass Company to take advantage of this machinery and continued to work on an automatic bottle-blowing machine that was finally patented in 1903. Eventually, this machine was the genesis of the company now called Owens-Illinois Inc. A few years later, Owens developed the Colburn process for producing flat glass automatically, which was equally innovative and cost efficient. This led to the formation of the Libbey-Owens Sheet Glass Company, now Libbey-Owens-Ford.

In 1924 Libbey patented the "Safedge" tumbler, which had a rim that resisted chipping. In the 1930s the Libbey company pioneered machine-made stemware, inexpensive decorated glass, and mass-produced colored glass. In 1936 Owens-Illinois purchased Libbey glass and ran it as a subsidiary and, later, as a division, but in 1993 the tableware company became independent again. Since the 1950s Libbey has been a major manufacturer of mid-priced glass for the home, all of it mass produced.

Sources and Further Reading: Carl U. Fauster, *Libbey Glass since 1818* (1979); Albert C. Revi, *The Encyclopedia of American Cut and Engraved Glass* (2000).

Jane Shadel Spillman
The Corning Museum of Glass, New York

Grand Rapids Furniture Company

In the late 1800s and early 1900s several enterprises were named the Grand Rapids Furniture Company, but the most notable was founded in Grand Rapids, Michigan, in 1902. Preceded by the New England Furniture Company, producer of inexpensive bedroom and dining suites, the Grand Rapids Furniture Company made dining room suites, library tables, and desks in Austrian arts and crafts and English revival styles. The name New England Furniture Company was changed to Grand Rapids Furniture Company in 1902 when new owners acquired the company. Production under the new title did not begin for several years.

After several years of litigation over who had controlling interest and management changes, in 1907 the new Grand Rapids Furniture Company began production. Like its predecessor, it turned out midpriced dining furniture, but its products changed from the heavily ornamented and painted styles of the previous century to a more streamlined appearance, initially offering Sheraton and Modern English styles. Ornamentation was limited to plain woodcuts in the Sheraton line. The Modern English line was simpler still, with the only ornamentation being crisscross bracing on dining chairs.

In 1908 the company changed its advertising approach from simply providing its address with images of products to adding text that attempted to convince retailers and consumers that its furniture was worth buying. Ad copy said that the company's products were "well made (and) well designed by experts and at right prices." In December 1908 the company announced that it would add a full line of library suites including tables, desks, and bookcases. The company was lauded by at least one trade journal for excellence in design and construction as well as range of prices.

During the winter of the 1908–1909 furniture season, it launched its Old English collection. They expanded it for the 1909 midsummer season. It featured furniture with a warm brown finish and "characteristic sixteenth century style." Designers traveled to England and Europe to study original pieces on which the collection was based.

In the spirit of the times, a 1916 ad stated that the company's products had the "indefinable 'spirit' of good furniture" and that the era was the "age of real Art, the only age in history when true Art could be commercialized." Affordability was stressed, as it would be into the 1920s.

During World War I, the company was one of fifteen Grand Rapids furniture factories that united to form the Grand Rapids Airplane Company. One-third of each factory was given over to production of the Handley-Page bomber.

In the early 1920s the Grand Rapids Furniture Company made a high-end line of Duncan Phyfe furniture in mahogany with rosewood panels. In the late 1920s it turned to international design consortium Contempora to produce a line of chairs.

The Grand Rapids Furniture Company experienced brief production in the late 1930s and 1940s. By 1950 only the name remained. Brower Furniture Company, a manufacturer of retail-store, hotel-dining-room, and dormitory furniture acquired the company in 1957.

Sources and Further Reading: Christian Carron, *Grand Rapids Furniture* (1998); *Grand Rapids Furniture Record* (Jan. 1907, June 1907, Sept. 1908, June 1909, Aug. 1916, July 1916, Sept. 1916, July 1922, Nov. 1922); Z. Z. Lydens, ed., *The Story of Grand Rapids* (1966).

Jennifer Janna Baron
Tinker Swiss Cottage Museum
Rockford, Illinois

Popular Music

Ragtime, blues, jazz, and music of the recording firm known as Motown exemplify the richness of African American contributions to midwestern culture. Several significant movements were situated in midwestern cities that at one time or another had thriving African American nightlife in districts where venues for live music flourished. Not only did the participants succeed in entertaining local audiences, but they also produced lasting music that had international impact.

During the 1890s a combination of Caribbean rhythms and the compositional form of European marches brought ragtime its vitality and charm, epitomized by Missouri-based composers Scott Joplin and Tom Turpin. It was spread by live music, sheet music, and piano rolls.

By the beginning of the twentieth century it was evident that the enormously varied rhythms, highly expressive pitch bending, and imaginative manipulations of tone quality in West African singing had been applied to English poetic forms in the American South to create the blues, as in the music of Robert Johnson and Charley Patton. Then, during the 1940s and 1950s, its electric form became better known, and Mississippi natives were recorded with bass and drums in the genre called Chicago blues, best known in recordings by Muddy Waters. This music was rediscovered and widely disseminated during the 1960s and 1970s by white musicians and singers.

The repertory of ragtime mixed with the ingredients of brass band music, the blues style, and pop music of the 1890s to result in jazz, the most complex of African American contributions, and many of the great African American jazz instrumentalists and blues singers from the South actually refined and recorded their best music in the Midwest. A major center for jazz during the 1910s and 1920s was Chicago. For example, some of the earliest recordings were made in 1923 at a studio in Richmond, Indiana, by New Orleans native Joe Oliver and his all-star band, who were performing regularly in Chicago at the time. Louis Armstrong's best recordings were made in Chicago during the late 1920s, including his collaborations with Pittsburgh native Earl Hines, an influential pianist who remained in Chicago long after most others had relocated to New York. Hines had significant impact with his own big band that was based there. As a bandleader during the 1940s, he hired many modern jazz stars-to-be, including Dizzy Gillespie, Charlie Parker, Billy Eckstine, and Sarah Vaughan.

African Americans from the South were not the only prominent musicians in Chicago during the

Bill Monroe performs at the 1965 Newport Folk Festival. Photo by Diana Davies, courtesy Center for Folklife and Cultural Heritage, Smithsonian Institution.

1920s. A cadre of white musicians including Bud Freeman, Jimmy McPartland, Frank Teschemacher, Dave Tough, and Eddie Condon developed an influential small-group style that historians refer to as "Chicago School" or "Chicago Style." Benny Goodman and Gene Krupa, white musicians who were born and raised in Chicago, became giants of big-band swing in the 1930s.

Chicago and Detroit offered opportunities for live performance as well as recording. Consistent and high-paying employment was also available in nonmusical jobs that lured musicians and nonmusicians alike from the South to big cities in the North. In later years, Chicago was the source of outstanding urban blues recordings by southern African Americans such as Muddy Waters in the 1940s and Howlin' Wolf in the 1950s, and Detroit became the base for John Lee Hooker from 1948 to 1956.

During the latter half of the twentieth century, Chicago birthed two avant-garde movements in African American music. Alabama native Sun Ra was based in Chicago in the 1950s and early 1960s. The Association for the Advancement of Creative Musicians (AACM), founded in 1969 and spearheaded by Richard Abrams, led to the internationally acclaimed Art Ensemble of Chicago, the band called Air, composer-saxophonist Anthony Braxton, and other important avant-garde artists.

Detroit was important, too. The city contributed to the birth of big-band dance music during the 1920s with popular white bands under the Jean Goldkette booking organization, such as the Casa Loma Orchestra. McKinney's Cotton Pickers, a black Detroit band, posed serious competition for the early New York–based big bands of Fletcher Henderson and Duke Ellington. The Great Lakes region also played a role in early combo jazz. For example, influential jazz cor-

netist Bix Beiderbecke, a Davenport, Iowa, native, appeared throughout Indiana, Michigan, and Illinois during the 1920s, playing at college fraternity parties, on lake excursion boats, and at summer resorts. He also graced the ballrooms of Detroit briefly as a member of the Goldkette organization.

Detroit continued to be an important center for distinctive African American music. Rock and roll had come from the American South during the 1950s as a blend of rhythm-and-blues style and country-and-western music with some Caribbean derivatives. Then, a new form of pop music, neither entirely rock nor rhythm-and-blues, originated in Detroit with the many artists assembled by Berry Gordy, Jr., at his Motown recording studios, as documented by the 2002 film *Standing in the Shadows of Motown.* The instrumentalists, particularly pianists Earl Van Dyke, Joe Hunter, and Johnny Griffith, guitarists Eddie Willis, Joe Mesina, and Robert White, bassists James Jamerson and Bob Babbitt, and drummer Benny Benjamin invented their own unique accompanying style that set the pace for numerous singers who had fused gospel and blues approaches (Smokey Robinson, Marvin Gaye, Stevie Wonder, The Supremes, The Temptations, the O'Jays, the Jackson Five, and others).

By the time the pop music of the Motown studios became world renowned, an entire string of outstanding modern jazz musicians had already emerged from Detroit. So many important modern jazz figures had arrived in New York from there by the late 1950s that their brand of bebop soon became designated by some musicians and journalists as the "Detroit School": Kenny Burrell, Thad Jones, Hank Jones, Elvin Jones, Tommy Flanagan, Curtis Fuller, Pepper Adams, Donald Byrd, Louis Hayes, Yusef Lateef, Paul Chambers, Doug Watkins, Barry Harris, and others. They and other outstanding jazz musicians had come from a thriving performance scene in the city that was assimilating bebop during the 1940s and had produced stars who were already influential on the national scene: Milt Jackson, Lucky Thompson, Wardell Gray, Frank Foster, and Frank Rosolino are among the best known.

Kansas City, Missouri, provided the site for a particularly energetic musical environment, immortalized in the 1955 film and 1959 television series *Pete Kelly's Blue*s and in the 1996 film *Kansas City*. It served as a central relay station and gathering place for southern and southwestern jazz and blues musicians, so much so that, despite geographical borders that might otherwise classify it with the Midwest, the Kansas City music scene of the 1920s and 1930s is ordinarily referred to as "southwestern style." Dynamic centers of music for nightlife already were fertile in Dallas/Fort Worth, Omaha, Oklahoma City, and St. Louis. But musicians from all over the South and these other cities were attracted ‚to Kansas City in particular. It even brought some from the East Coast, like Count Basie. As in Chicago, this was partly facilitated by the relaxed enforcement of vice laws in Kansas City, particularly during Prohibition. The wild entertainment atmosphere there was friendly to musicians seeking employment, with the city's abundant dance halls hosting many after-hours opportunities.

During the swing era of the 1930s and 1940s, the confluence of talent in Kansas City, Missouri, ultimately developed the national prominence of Kansas City–based bands led by Count Basie, Andy Kirk, and Jay McShann and the blues singers Jimmy Rushing and Joe Turner. It identified a style of big-band swing music that was less elaborate than concurrent New York styles. There was an emphasis on freewheeling improvisation with accompaniments based mostly on chord progressions, from blues and such pop songs as "I Got Rhythm" and "Honeysuckle Rose." Simple, repeating riffs supplied horn backups and often the tunes themselves. The resulting format almost conveyed the attitude of a big combo instead of a small orchestra. It was known for generating pronounced swing feeling. It also produced a founder of modern jazz, saxophonist Charlie Parker.

Jazz and blues continued developing during the 1920s and 1930s in African American entertainment districts of midwestern cities, as jazz had in New Orleans before the 1920s and blues had in the Mississippi Delta during the late nineteenth century and the first half of the twentieth century.

Several caveats should be considered when contemplating attributions of style causality to any given region. First, vice and hedonism did not necessarily cause this music. They merely continued to support performance opportunities. The settings where musicians could mature were fueled by the Midwest's long and excellent traditions of church music and school music, combined with the demands of dance halls for particularly lively, syncopated music. The high-quality, resident symphony orchestras that existed in most midwestern cities increased the abundance of teachers for budding young instrumentalists; and town bands and school bands have been common in the Midwest since at least the end of the nineteenth century.

Second, for most musicians in dance bands, the music provided employment as well as an outlet for creativity within an existing style. But for some it was also the opportunity to innovate. New music was invented primarily by the talent, hard work, and tenacity of a few very unusual individuals, such as saxophonist Parker in Kansas City, Missouri, and trumpeter Miles Davis in East St. Louis, Illinois, who became arguably the most important jazz bandleader of the 1950s, 1960s, and 1970s. For their tenacity to pay off, the creators had to have opportunities to try out their inventions in public. For instance, Parker played with summer resort bands in the Ozarks, then with dance bands and at jam sessions in Kansas City while learning his craft. Davis initially played with dance bands around St. Louis but developed the most distinctive parts of his style after relocating to New York. In other words, these sites and their atmosphere are not necessarily the cause of the distinctive talent that arose in the region but, rather, part of the channeling of that talent.

Third, family influence is a key factor. For example, Parker's father and Davis's mother were musicians. Just being in an urban area with numerous nightclubs is not sufficient for innovation to occur.

Fourth, the talent that allowed such geniuses to assimilate diverse sounds and synthesize new approaches can exist anywhere, and it is portable. For instance, though Parker initially imitated saxophonist Buster Smith, who was temporarily based in his hometown, an important part of his style also derived from incorporating the advances of Toledo, Ohio, native Art Tatum while that pianist was performing in New York. Though Lester Young was briefly available as a live model in Kansas City, Parker learned Young's style primarily by memorizing solos from commercial recordings. Similarly, though Davis initially studied trumpeters from his own hometown region, significant sources for his style also included South Carolina native Dizzy Gillespie and Cleveland, native Freddie Webster, whose style Davis studied firsthand in New York. Parker was an equally important influence on Davis.

Finally, we must not neglect the fact that a single energetic entrepreneur such as Gordy, the founder of Motown, or Leonard Chess, of Chicago's pivotal recording firm documenting southern blues singers, can draw together talent from diverse regions, and that such talent might not be from there or ultimately live there. The music was merely recorded there. Not knowing the details, we could accidentally conclude that the site of the distinctive sound was actually the origin of it.

Rather than being the site of any one particular style that reflected something uniquely midwestern, the region was second home to several kinds of music, all of which had substance and international impact. Missouri was an incubator for ragtime as Detroit was for the brand of pop music associated with Gordy. And although the contributions of white musicians were significant, particularly in the Chicago jazz combos and the Detroit big bands of the 1920s, the most distinctive kinds of music in the twentieth- and early twenty-first-century Midwest reflected African American contributions.

Sources and Further Reading: Lars Bjorn, *Before Motown: A History of Jazz in Detroit, 1920–1960* (2001); Michael Erlewine, ed., *All Music Guide to the Blues,* 2nd ed. (1999); Mark C. Gridley, *Jazz Styles: History and Analysis,* 8th ed. (2003); William Howland Kenney, *Chicago Jazz* (1993); Karl Koenig, ed., *Jazz in Print (1856–1929)* (2002); Joe Mosbrook, *Cleveland Jazz History,* 2nd ed. (2003); Leroy Ostransky, *Jazz City: The Impact of Our Cities on the Development of Jazz* (1978); Nathan Pearson, *Goin' to Kansas City* (1987); Ross Russell, *Jazz Style in Kansas City and the Southwest* (1971); Allan ("Dr. Licks") Slutsky, *Standing in the Shadows of Motown* (1989).

Mark C. Gridley
Heidelberg College, Ohio

Rags

Ragtime was a uniquely American musical form that appeared on the music scene around 1897 and remained the dominant popular style until approximately 1917. It was actually a vital and energetic invention that combined something of the rich rhythmic complexity of African music and the melodic and harmonic legacy of the classical European traditions. It was truly revolutionary in its impact and is the basis of all American popular music that followed, including jazz, swing, and rock and roll.

The essential elements of a rag—a term of uncertain origin—are the continuous use of syncopation over a regular, two-beat rhythmic foundation in the basic structure of a three- or four-theme march. Although there were originally rag songs and dances, a rag is now generally considered to be primarily a composition for the piano, despite the fact that ragtime was played by every conceivable combination of instruments and by bands and orchestras.

Ragtime was especially popular in the Midwest, which produced most of its significant composers and the majority of the era's publications. The first published rag, "The Mississippi Rag" by William Krell, came out of Chicago in 1897. However, many scholars consider this to be a cakewalk rather than a true rag and credit Theodore H. Northrup, also of Chicago, with the first idiomatic, fully developed rag. That was "The Louisiana Rag," also from 1897.

One of the most important centers of early ragtime development was Cincinnati, home to several ragtime musical inventors of note, including actor and songwriter Robert S. Roberts. His 1897 composition "The Pride of Bucktown" contained many complicated and original rhythmic devices that would later be used by more famous ragtime composers like Scott Joplin.

Joplin and his Sedalia, Missouri, publisher John Stark really established the viability of ragtime with the publication of his masterpiece, "The Maple Leaf Rag," in 1899. It was an enormous success both commercially and artistically and defined the rag as a classical musical form. Missouri produced more rags than any other state. The illustrious list of Missouri classic rag composers begins with Tom Turpin, owner of the famous St. Louis red-light district Rosebud Saloon. His "Harlem Rag," appearing in 1897, was the first rag publication by a black composer. His pupils included the legendary Louis Chauvin, whose sole published composition, "Heliotrope Bouquet" was transcribed by Scott Joplin in 1907, and Joe Jordan, whose 1909 hit "That Teasin' Rag" was recorded in 1917 as "The Original Dixieland One-Step." Others in Stark's stable of quality ragtime writers included James Scott of Carthage, Missouri, and Artie Matthews, whose 1915 number "The Weary Blues" (originally "The Pastime Rag #8") was the first jazz number performed in the White House.

The last important ragtime phenomenon, known as "novelty piano," was also initiated in the Midwest. It was developed and exemplified in the early 1920s by Zez Confrey, who hailed from Peru, Illinois. His arrangement of piano rolls for the QRS Company in Chicago resulted in such extremely popular hits as "Kitten on the Keys" (1921), "Stumbling" (1922), and "Dizzy Fingers" (1923).

Sources and Further Reading: Rudi Blesh and Harriet Janis, *They All Played Ragtime* (1950); David Jasen and Gene Jones, *That American Rag* (2000); David Jasen and Trebor Tichenor, *Rags and Ragtime* (1978); Terry Waldo, *This Is Ragtime* (1976).

Terry Waldo
New York, New York

Jazz

The black New Orleans cornet player Freddie Keppard might have been the first musician to record any jazz, but the recording deal fell through for reasons that remain unclear. Some scholars conjecture that the recording company regarded his music as too "dirty" for the general public. Others suggest that Keppard was worried that recording would allow others to plagiarize his style. As a result, jazz first reached the ears of the general listening public after 1917, when a white New Orleans group, the Original Dixieland Jazz Band (ODJB), began issuing recordings such as "Livery Stable Blues." It is somewhat ironic that the ODJB style was the first to be widely heard, because the band's style is usually regarded as a simplification of the black music of the Crescent City.

The transmission of jazz via recordings and radio was so quick that it was taken up and disseminated by innovative talent almost simultaneously in every middle-sized northern city. Some jazz musicians carried the music north by working the Mississippi riverboats. Louis Armstrong describes disembarking from the Dixie Belle in St. Louis in 1920 and finding local bands there trying—with only moderate success—to play in the style he knew from New Orleans. However, the often-repeated story that New Orleans jazz came north on the riverboats is an exaggeration. In 1917 the ODJB had already made a sensation in New York, and Keppard had played in Los Angeles as early as 1914. Musicians traveled in every direction, by various means of transportation.

However, there is no doubt that by 1920 Chicago was rapidly becoming a kind of northern jazz nexus. In 1923 Armstrong was making history there playing second trumpet with Joe "King" Oliver on the city's South Side. Others heard there included influential clarinetists Sidney Bechet and Jimmy Noone and pianist Earl Hines. In his autobiographical *Really the Blues* (1946), the white clarinetist Milton "Mezz" Mezzrow documents the profound effect of this new black jazz on young white musicians who flocked to hear it. These years not only saw the flowering of black jazz as a national music, but they also marked the beginning of white jazz in the Midwest.

Among those who made great names for themselves was trumpeter Leon "Bix" Beiderbecke, whose music—like that of other white players—spread through the Midwest as touring bands played clubs, colleges, and universities, where they inspired locals. One figure who early caught the fever was Indiana's Hoagland Howard "Hoagy" Carmichael, the composer of great American popular songs such as "Stardust." It was during these years that the small Gennett record company made history in Richmond, Indiana, by recording the musicians—black and white—that crisscrossed the Midwest.

Other white musicians who cut their jazz teeth on Chicago's South Side included drummer clarinetist Benjamin "Benny" Goodman and his drummer Gene Krupa. Although Goodman was to acquire the label "King of Swing" in the 1930s, much of his style reflected the work of the black arranger Fletcher Henderson, who took Armstrong's new "swinging" way of playing solos and adapted it for an entire ensemble.

Even in the rock music era, Chicago never entirely lost its jazz aura, although it was eclipsed for a time by the blues scene that burgeoned in the city's South Side after World War II. Well into the 1950s one could still find major South Side jazz clubs functioning as home bases for local musicians as well as those passing through. Chicago bred major figures such as Johnny Griffin, the spectacular saxophone player who returned year after year to celebrate his birthday playing at the Jazz Showcase on the city's North Side. In the 1960s, Chicago became the hub of the African American avant-garde jazz movement, inspired by figures like Lester Bowie, Henry Threadgill, and Muhal Richard Abrams. In the early twenty-first century, their music and that of a younger generation of avant-gardists could still be heard in Chicago clubs like the Velvet Lounge.

Second only to Chicago in defining northern jazz history was Kansas City (Missouri). By the 1920s, one white Kansas City band—the Coon-Sanders Nighthawks—had already acquired national fame for its radio broadcasts. But the city's seminal decade was the 1930s, when, under political boss Tom Pendergast, it became a wide-open town. In the 18th and Vine Street neighborhood, jam sessions often ran all night long and half the next day. Its legendary status is outstripped only—if at all—by Basin Street in New Orleans. Among the rising Kansas City stars were bandleaders Benjamin "Bennie" Moten, William "Count" Basie, and Jay McShann. Mary Lou Williams made her name there as an arranger with Andrew "Andy" Kirk. Famous saxophone players who got started in Kansas City included Benjamin "Ben" Webster, Lester Young, and Charles "Charlie" Parker, who later helped found the modernist movement known as bebop in New York. Most typical of this era was the driving blues- and riff-based music that became the basis of the swing craze of the 1930s.

One early musician who made his reputation in Chicago actually got his start in Detroit—Charles "Doc" Cook. Indeed, Detroit boasts a jazz history almost as rich as any midwestern city's. A major figure of the 1920s was Jean Goldkette, whose band made its home at the Graystone Ballroom and employed such budding white jazz stars as violinist Giuseppe "Joe"

Venuti and the Dorsey brothers—Thomas (Tommy) and James (Jimmy). Goldkette's umbrella musical corporation controlled some twenty bands operating throughout the Midwest, one of which evolved into the famous Casa Loma Orchestra. Goldkette also helped to organize and manage (William) McKinney's Cotton Pickers, one of the premier black big bands of the era, which was founded in Springfield, Ohio. And not far north was Toledo, the home of Art Tatum.

In the black Detroit of the 1940s, the intersecting neighborhoods known as Black Bottom and Paradise Valley were centers of jazz energy. The bars and theatres there nurtured a staggering list of talents who would eventually populate nearly every major jazz ensemble in the country, including the Jones brothers—pianist Henry (Hank), trumpeter Thaddeus (Thad), and drummer Elvin—pianist Thomas "Tommy" Flanagan, saxophonists Yusef Lateef (born William Evans) and Park "Pepper" Adams, composer Donald Byrd, vocalist Betty Carter (born Lillie Mae Jones), trombonist Curtis Fuller, and harpist Dorothy Ashby.

Guitar innovator Kenneth "Kenny" Burrell and bass player Paul Chambers both hail from Detroit. Among its legendary clubs, the Blue Bird stands out. In 1948 it became a home of the new modernism, attracting celebrated players from around the country such as Miles Davis (who lived in the St. Louis area), who came to play there and often stayed for extended periods. But the real attraction of the Blue Bird was the freedom it offered the younger musicians who would soon leave the nest and help make Detroit famous.

In Indianapolis, a one-mile stretch of road called "Indiana Avenue," just northwest of the city center, was once filled with jazz clubs, bistros, and theatres that served as a training ground for such modern-jazz trombonists as James "J.J." Johnson and Locksley "Slide" Hampton. Trumpeter Frederick "Freddie" Hubbard and guitarist John "Wes" Montgomery are from Indianapolis. Indiana Avenue is still honored as a local jazz cradle.

In Columbus, Ohio, Mount Vernon Avenue on the city's east side was the musical hub. Among the many who have traced their jazz roots to the city's east side are vocalist Nancy Wilson, saxophonist Royal "Rusty" Bryant, trumpeter Harry "Sweets" Edison, and the legendary multi-instrumentalist Rahsaan Roland Kirk (born Ronald Kirk). With the help of players like Donald "Don" Patterson and Henry "Hank" Marr, Columbus helped give the Hammond B-3 organ its status in jazz. In short, jazz was disseminated at almost the same time in virtually every urban area of the Midwest.

Sources and Further Reading: Garvin Bushell, *Jazz from the Beginning* (1988); Ted Gioia, *The History of Jazz* (1997); Barry Kernfeld, ed., *The New Grove Dictionary of Jazz* (1996); Mezz Mezzrow and Bernard Wolfe, *Really the Blues* (1972); Gunther Schuller, *Early Jazz* (1968); Gunther Schuller, *The Swing Era: The Development of Jazz, 1930–1945* (1989); Marshall Stearns, *The Story of Jazz* (1967); Richard M. Sudhalter, *Lost Chords* (1999).

Lee Brown
The Ohio State University–Columbus

Scott Joplin (1868–1917)

Although Scott Joplin, born in 1868, was from the town of Texarkana, on the Texas-Arkansas border, his fame is linked to St. Louis and, especially, Sedalia, Missouri. Indeed, Joplin's identification with Sedalia inspired its nickname, the "Cradle of Classic Ragtime," and created a permanent connection between the Midwest and ragtime music.

Joplin's parents, a former slave and a free-born black woman, played musical instruments and probably provided him with his earliest instruction. Later, a German musician, generally assumed to have been Julius Weiss, provided Joplin with formal training and

A Scott Joplin rag, 1904. Prepared by John Stark & Son, St. Louis, MO.

encouraged his taste in art music. While still in Texarkana, Joplin became a professional musician, playing the piano and singing, as well as offering instruction in piano, mandolin, and guitar.

Little is certain about Joplin's whereabouts in the 1880s, but it is known that, after a brief stay in Sedalia, Joplin was in St. Louis by 1890. There Joplin was influenced by ragtime pianist-composer Tom Turpin, who was known as the "Father of St. Louis Ragtime." After traveling to Chicago in 1893 to play with a band at the World's Columbian Exposition, where he observed the growing popularity of ragtime, Joplin returned to Sedalia in the mid-1890s. Joplin furthered his musical education there at the George R. Smith College for Negroes; he also taught piano and composition, influencing the young ragtime composers Arthur Marshall and Scott Hayden, and played ragtime at the Maple Leaf Club. Another important Sedalia connection was with music publisher John Stark. After selling his first two ragtime compositions outright for a small fixed sum, he entered into a deal with Stark in which he was paid a royalty of one cent per copy sold. The first rag published under this deal was the *Maple Leaf Rag* (1899), named after the club, which sold over half a million copies by 1910 and which afforded Joplin a steady, if modest, income. Stark and Joplin referred to the rags he wrote after *Maple Leaf Rag* as "classic rags," hoping that they would be received seriously as art music. The skill of Joplin's composition indeed raised his rags beyond the level of most.

While he achieved success with his rags, Joplin yearned to write serious works for the stage. His first such work, the ballet-tableau *The Ragtime Dance*, was premiered in Sedalia in 1899 to little success. After returning to St. Louis in 1901, he formed the Scott Joplin Opera Company, which premiered his ragtime opera *A Guest of Honor* (1903), the score to which is lost. It, too, was unsuccessful. Although he continued to write rags, Joplin moved to New York with the purpose of composing works for the stage and finding a publisher for those works. In 1910 he completed the opera *Treemonisha*, which was never staged in the composer's lifetime. Other works for the stage from this period are lost. Joplin died in 1917.

His work experienced a revival in the 1970s, and in 1975 *Treemonisha* was given a well-received production by the Houston opera. In 1976 Joplin received a posthumous Pulitzer Prize.

Sources and Further Reading: Edward A. Berlin, *King of Ragtime* (1994); Susan Curtis, *Dancing to a Black Man's Tune* (1994); Peter Gammond, *Scott Joplin and the Ragtime Era* (1975).

Jim Lovensheimer
Vanderbilt University, Tennessee

Hoagy Carmichael (1899–1981)

Born in Indiana in 1899, Hoagland Howard "Hoagy" Carmichael remained attached to his midwestern roots throughout his career. Indeed, his songs often evoked his childhood home—"Can't Get Indiana off My Mind" (1940), for instance, or "Lazy River" (1931) recall Carmichael's background. His nostalgic portraits of Indiana, or of characters found there ("Little Old Lady," 1936; "Small Fry," 1938), are more prominent in his songs than the usual romantic topics, and even Mitchell Parish's reflective lyrics to "Star Dust" (1929), Carmichael's most popular tune, evoke the past as well as a lost love. Other lyricists provided him with images of small-town life in America, and many of his songs express a regionalism that first gained popularity in his work.

Carmichael's musical training was minimal—early instruction came from his mother, who, although formally untrained, played for the local movie house and favored ragtime and popular songs, and from Reginald Alfred DuValle, a pianist who, after the Carmichaels moved to Indianapolis in 1916, taught Carmichael the fundamentals of jazz. While at Indiana University, Carmichael formed a jazz band, and he learned from the jazz players who passed through Bloomington. Among them was cornetist Bix Beiderbecke, with whom Carmichael developed a close friendship that lasted until Beiderbecke's tragic death in 1931, at age twenty-eight, from alcohol-related causes. In fact, one of Carmichael's first known compositions, the jazz piece "Riverboat Shuffle," was written for Beiderbecke and was recorded by his group, the Wolverines, in 1924.

Carmichael left Bloomington for New York in 1929, and while there he wrote songs and played and recorded with such jazz greats as Louis Armstrong, Paul Whiteman, Benny Goodman, and the Dorsey brothers, among others. Carmichael's relationship with early jazz is recalled in his two autobiographies, *The Stardust Road* (1946) and *Sometimes I Wonder* (1965), both of which also suggest that this relationship diminished after Beiderbecke's death. At that point, Carmichael's musical interests moved toward mainstream popular music, a shift that was abetted by his move to Hollywood around 1935.

There Carmichael found a niche as an actor in films and television, usually playing a fictionalized version of himself. He continued to write songs and collaborated with lyricists like Johnny Mercer ("Skylark," 1941; "In the Cool, Cool, Cool of the Evening," which won an Academy Award in 1951); Frank Loesser ("Heart and Soul," 1938); and Stu Gorrell ("Georgia on My Mind," 1930). The different styles of his lyricists are reflected in the differing styles of the tunes that he created for them, and thus it is hard to define a "typical" Carmichael style beyond the wistfulness that permeates many of his ballads. Yet the subject matter of his songs, whoever the lyricist, most often looks back to the past and an often idealized rusticity. Indeed, before Carmichael generally stopped composing in the 1960s, two of his last pieces, composed for orchestra, were titled "Brown County in Autumn" (1949), an impression of an area of Indiana, and "Johnny Appleseed" (1962), an evocation of the man known for sowing apple seeds throughout the Midwest. He died in 1981.

Sources and Further Reading: John Edward Hasse, *The Works of Hoagy Carmichael* (1983); Rick Kennedy, *Jelly Roll, Bix and Hoagy* (1994); Richard M. Sudhalter, *Stardust Melody* (2002).

Jim Lovensheimer
Vanderbilt University, Tennessee

Earl "Fatha" Hines (1903–1983)

One of the great figures in jazz piano, Earl "Fatha" Hines was also one of its most enduringly gifted and innovative. Born near Pittsburgh, Pennsylvania in 1903 to a musical family, Hines studied cornet and piano with his parents as a boy, later continuing his piano studies with a classical teacher. He began playing professionally while quite young, first around Pittsburgh and then touring and recording with singer Lois Deppe's big band. In 1924 Hines moved to the musical hotbed of Chicago, home to many of the most important players in jazz, including Joe Oliver, Louis Armstrong, and Jelly Roll Morton. While there, Hines worked and toured extensively with Carroll Dickerson's orchestra, a top-flight band featuring Armstrong, with whom Hines became close. The two also gained valuable experience with Erskine Tate's Vendome Orchestra, a theatre-pit band that played light classics as well as jazz, film, and other popular music. In 1927 Armstrong and Hines took on the direction of the Dickerson band for a while, after which Hines joined clarinetist Jimmy Noone's band. A high point of this period was in 1928, when Hines played a vital role in Armstrong's small recording band, producing some of the greatest classics of early jazz on disc. His innovative approach, featuring "trumpet style" soloing in the right hand and sophisticated offbeat playfulness in the left, is famously highlighted on these recordings.

For the next twenty-seven years Hines led a series of big bands, starting with a more than ten-year stint at the elegant Grand Terrace ballroom in Chicago; his orchestra gained national prominence through live radio broadcasts there. Hines's groups featured many of the finer singers and players of the era and successfully made the extraordinary transition from 1920s jazz to 1930s swing and beyond. Seminal young be-boppers Dizzy Gillespie, Charlie Parker, and Sarah Vaughan worked with him in the early 1940s. As the big band era declined later in that decade, however, Hines was obliged to seek other paths and returned to small-band formats. He played with Louis Armstrong's All Stars and then led his own groups in the early 1950s; from then up until the mid-1960s he led a Dixieland-style house band in San Francisco, an ultimately disheartening experience. But in 1964, thanks to a series of solo and trio performances in New York, Hines gained fresh critical praise and embarked on a fruitful autumnal career, recording some of his finest music and touring extensively until the end of his life in 1983.

Source and Further Reading: Stanley Dance, *The World of Earl Hines* (1977).

Graeme M. Boone
The Ohio State University–Columbus

Count Basie (1904–1984)

One of the great swing pianists and bandleaders, Count Basie represents a high point of the "Kansas City style" that so influenced jazz beginning in the 1930s. Born William Basie in Red Bank, New Jersey, in 1904, Basie played the drums and took piano lessons as a boy. A quick learner, he was soon working as a pianist in local venues and absorbing all he could from local musicians as well as those passing through on their way to or from New York. In 1924 he made the leap to Harlem, where he befriended leading jazz players, including the pianists Fats Waller and Willie "the Lion" Smith. He also landed the pianist's spot in a performing troupe that toured widely, giving him his first taste of Kansas City. As he recalled many years later, "it was one of the most fantastic sights I've ever seen in my life. . . . There we were, way out there in the middle of nowhere, . . . and wham, we were coming into a scene where the action was greater than anything I'd ever heard of."

In 1927 Basie settled in Kansas City when a tour broke up there. At that time he discovered the great southwestern bands that would change his life: the Blue Devils, with their pervasive bluesiness and collaborative improvisational intensity, and Bennie Moten's Kansas City Orchestra, the most stylish African American big band in the region. Basie played with both groups in short order and ended up staying with Moten for several years. Then in 1935, drawing on personnel from both bands, Basie landed an ongoing gig with his own group at Kansas City's Reno Club, complete with radio broadcast. This led to national exposure and a tour to New York, where the band settled after 1936, becoming one of the most idolized bands of the swing era. The Basie Orchestra was distinctive in its hard-swinging Kansas City style and in the brilliance of so many of its players, including tenor saxophonist Lester Young, drummer Jo Jones, and singer Jimmy Rushing. Basie's playing was an essential component of their sound too, with rock-solid comping and an instantly recognizable, witty sparseness that flew in the face of the excesses of stride piano style.

The personnel of the band evolved, and the swing landscape was changing too, especially after World War II, when many factors combined to spell the end of the big band era. Basie's orchestra disbanded twice (1948, 1950) and then re-formed in 1952, finding success in extensive touring and recording and creating a permanent niche for its own brand of big band swing, marked by the contributions of gifted arrangers, including Neal Hefti and Quincy Jones, and occasionally fronted by superb singers, including Joe Williams and Frank Sinatra. Until his death in 1984, Basie was an elder statesman of jazz, beloved around the world, and to this day his band continues to thrive under the leadership of others.

Source and Further Reading: Count Basie with Albert Murray, *Good Morning Blues* (1985).

Graeme M. Boone
The Ohio State University–Columbus

Peter Schickele (b. 1935)

Peter Schickele is a composer, broadcaster, and musical humorist. Born in Ames, Iowa, in 1935, he grew up listening to Everly Brothers and Spike Jones records. He studied composition at Swarthmore College, the Aspen Music School, and the Juilliard School. In 1957 he presented his first "discoveries" of works by P.D.Q. Bach, whom he describes as "the last of Johann Sebastian's 20-odd children, also the oddest" and a composer whose "plagiarism [was] limited only by his faulty technique." A very successful concert career followed of Schickele presenting musical parodies under P.D.Q.'s name, many of them documented on recordings for Vanguard and Telarc. In 1976 he published *The Definitive Biography of P.D.Q. Bach, 1807–1742?* and the book has gone through eleven printings.

As a humorist, Schickele uses puns, slapstick, sound effects from bizarre ad hoc instruments (presented as musicological discoveries), musical inside jokes (evi-

dent in some of his titles), and stylistic parody and collisions. His "serious" music has its critics, disappointing many of those coming from the P.D.Q. Bach angle, as well as those who expect music of contrasting weight and importance. In 1991 Schickele strongly cut back on his P.D.Q. appearances in order to concentrate on composition. The following year he began to channel some of his humor to the syndicated radio show *Schickele Mix*. This program takes a freewheeling, at times stream-of-consciousness approach to musical fundamentals, backed up by examples that range from obscure cowboy ballads to seventeenth-century dances by Michael Praetorius.

An eclectic and a polymath, Schickele has also made arrangements for pop singers and has written film, television, and Broadway scores.

Sources and Further Reading: Richard Kostelanetz, "Peter Schickele," in *On Innovative Music(ian)s* (1989); Janice A. Leroux, "Two Shots That Changed My Life: An Interview with Peter Schickele," *Music Educators Journal* 70 (Nov. 1983); Peter Schickele, *The Definitive Biography of P.D.Q. Bach, 1807–1742?* (1976); Peter Schickele, *Peter Schickele Presents An Evening with P.D.Q. Bach (1807–1742)* (1965; CD 1999).

Arved Ashby
The Ohio State University–Columbus

Motown

Motown (or the "Motown Sound") is the name commonly given to a style of music as well as a group of record labels founded by Berry Gordy, Jr., in 1959 and headquartered in Detroit, from their founding until the company moved to Los Angeles in 1970. The story of Motown is a story of black capitalism, of midwestern managerial precision and factory-style assembly-line production, of middle-class black uplift, and of the possibilities for crossover cultural production in the prointegration atmosphere of the civil rights era. It is also the story of many wonderful singers, musicians, songwriters, and producers who worked together to create the most popular and economically successful independent record company of the 1960s.

Berry Gordy, Jr., was born in 1929 in Detroit to a successful middle-class black family. His grandfather and his father had each owned their own businesses. Berry Gordy, Sr., had achieved a level of financial success in Georgia that caused him to worry about white retaliation and so he moved his family to Detroit in 1922. There he established a painting and construction business along with a grocery store that he named after

The storefront of the Motown sound. Courtesy Motown Historical Museum Collection.

Booker T. Washington. His wife, Bertha, cofounded the Friendship Mutual Insurance Company. Berry Gordy, Jr., grew up in an ambitious family with diversified business interests and a demonstrated capacity to invest and succeed in a wide range of enterprises.

With this family history it might be surprising that Gordy would choose entertainment as his field. But there can be little doubt about his drive to succeed in this area. Gordy's first entry into entertainment was as a boxer. Although successful, he quickly realized that he boxed at too light a weight to achieve the recognition and financial rewards that he desired. His next entrepreneurial venture, 3-D Record Mart–House of Jazz, stuck too closely to Gordy's own interest in the more complex styles of jazz to succeed as a local record store. After it failed, Gordy went to work for the Ford Motor Company. While working in the upholstery department of the Ford-Lincoln plant, Gordy penned his first entertainment success as a songwriter, "Reet Petite," which was a hit in 1957 for Jackie Wilson. Gordy soon quit the Ford plant and followed up his previous hit with "Lonely Teardrops," also for Wilson.

Branching into talent management and record production, Gordy attended an audition by a group called the Matadors. Their lead singer, Smokey Robinson, agreed to change the act's name to the Miracles, and in 1958 they hit the charts with "Got a Job." The royalty income from these initial successes, combined with an eight hundred dollar loan from his family, enabled Gordy to establish Tamla Records and Jobete Publishing as the first two branches of what would soon be known as Motown Records. Robinson's songwriting skills, his way of turning a clichéd phrase inside out

and matching it with a simple, hummable melody, were the basis for an astounding number of hits. Motown's first national hit, however, was written by Gordy. Entitled "Money (That's What I Want)," it rendered clear the drive for success that shaped the history of Motown.

This drive found its most dramatic implementation in the Motown system of record production. Gordy's ability to spot talent combined with Motown's unique placement as the first successful independent record company located in Detroit and specializing in rhythm-and-blues (R&B) to ensure a steady flow of highly motivated and highly skilled individuals into the Motown system. Drawing from his experience on the assembly line, Gordy separated out the different factors that contributed to the production of hit records. Proven songwriters competed to have their material recorded by the best singers, whose records, in turn, were produced by the hottest production teams. Access to the best talent in each division was determined solely by the marketplace success of each individual component. By the mid-1960s, the songwriting and production team of Brian and Eddie Holland and Lamont Dozier was dominating the nation's airwaves, creating twenty-five Top 10 hits before leaving the company in the late 1960s. Instructed to create recordings that would sound good on car radios, Holland-Dozier-Holland's success probably peaked when one of their productions, "Can't Help Myself" by the Four Tops, replaced another, "Back in My Arms Again" by the Supremes, at the top of the pop charts in June 1965. Laying down the unstoppable beats and carefully written charts for all of these hits were the Funk Brothers, featuring James Jamerson, Benny Benjamin, Earl Van Dyke, and Robert White, among other veterans of Detroit's jazz and R&B scenes. These team members contributed to Top 10 hits by Stevie Wonder, Marvin Gaye, the Temptations, Mary Wells, Martha Reeves and the Vandellas, and Edwin Starr, in addition to the Miracles, the Supremes, and the Four Tops.

Gordy's emphasis on maintaining the quality of Motown's output was not limited to the company's recordings. With his ambitions directed at the most mainstream tastes in America, Gordy hired Harvey Fuqua to oversee artist development. Working within this "company charm school" were Maxine Powell, the director of a local modeling school, whose job it was to ensure the public poise of Motown's young performers, and the famous dancer Cholly Atkins, who choreographed their smooth, trademark moves. Like the company itself, the charm school enacted and enforced solid middle-class values of respectability and decorum.

Cultural critic Gerald Early has argued that Motown changed American culture by virtue of Berry Gordy's insistence that "*his* performers be able to sell the company's songs to whites and that *his* performers be able to play at the better-playing white venues." According to Early, Gordy wanted to erase the boundary that separated black performers out into the segregated R&B charts and demonstrate that black as well as white singers could succeed in the field of pop. Motown's dominance of the pop charts from 1963 into the 1970s proved that a highly disciplined market-oriented approach to cultural production could desegregate the airwaves and the recording industry's pop charts. In light of these accomplishments, Early claims that "Motown stands as the most shining hour of the American black in popular culture." But if popular culture produces public economic and political effects as well as private moments of pleasure, what have been the long-term effects of Motown's success? According to history professor Suzanne Smith, Motown was the largest black-owned business in the United States in 1973, but by 1998 it was a wholly owned subsidiary of a white-managed and largely white-owned corporate conglomerate. Perhaps, as the long struggle to achieve full civil rights and racial equality continues, it will be motivated by memories linked to the sounds of an earlier America. If so, perhaps that struggle will in the future challenge, rather than adopt, the mainstream, middle-class, white-dominated cultural values that were both the vehicle of Motown's success and the guarantee of its final ownership.

Sources and Further Reading: Gerald Early, *One Nation under a Groove* (1995); Nelson George, *Where Did Our Love Go? The Rise and Fall of the Motown Sound* (1985); Berry Gordy, Jr., *To Be Loved* (1994); Suzanne Smith, *Dancing in the Street: Motown and the Cultural Politics of Detroit* (1999); Brian Ward, *Just My Soul Responding* (1998).

Barry Shank
The Ohio State University–Columbus

Painting

In the days of riverboat travel, St. Louis and Cincinnati were the principal outposts of culture in the Midwest. They were also the first centers of midwestern painting. St. Louis, which is close to the juncture of the Mississippi and the Missouri Rivers, served as the headquarters of the artists who first recorded what was then the western frontier—such as Indian painter George Catlin and George Deas, a painter of frontier scenes. George Caleb Bingham also worked in this region. Bingham led an itinerant life, but he spent long sojourns in St. Louis, and there he created his most ambitious genre painting, *The Verdict of the People* (1854–1855). By the time of the Civil War, several artists not only used St. Louis as a base but chose to settle there, including Carl E. Wimar, a painter of Native Americans, and Joseph Rusling Meeker, known for romantic marsh scenes, who became active in art organizations in the city.

Cincinnati, located farther up the Mississippi River system, on the Ohio River, also became a major art center at an early date. In the 1830s, the sculptor Hiram Powers started his career there. In subsequent decades, Cincinnati served as home to several major landscape painters, including Worthington Whittredge, Alexander Wyant, William Louis Sonntag, and African American artist Robert Duncanson. All these figures received patronage from the wealthy merchant and ardent abolitionist Nicholas Longworth, who in 1848 commissioned Duncanson to create murals for his home (now the Taft Museum).

With the arrival of the railroad in the 1860s, culture began to expand rapidly across the Midwest and art academies were created surprisingly quickly in nearly every western city. Cincinnati, which had an early start, became a center of serious art training. In the later nineteenth century, the central figure of Cincinnati art-life was Frank Duveneck, who studied in Munich and then returned to Cincinnati, where he played an active role as a teacher at the Cincinnati Fine Arts Academy. Another notable figure was Henry Farny, a skilled painter of Indians, who served as founder and director of Cincinnati's Art Students League. Because of such figures, Cincinnati became the first training ground of a number of noted American painters who pursued their later careers elsewhere, including illustrator Robert Blum, mural painter Kenyon Cox, and expatriate Salon painter Elizabeth Nourse. In addition to such young aspirants, a good many talented figures made Cincinnati their home, at least briefly. For example, noted American impressionist John H. Twachtman worked in a variety of locations, but frequently returned to Cincinnati, his hometown.

One indication of increasing midwestern prosperity was the rapid spread of art academies, which by the end of the nineteenth century existed in nearly every midwestern city. Among these were the McMicken School, Cincinnati, created in 1866, which was reorganized and renamed the Cincinnati Fine Arts Academy in 1887; the Chicago Academy of Design, founded in 1869, renamed the Art Institute of Chicago in 1882; the Indiana School of Art, formed in 1877 and headed by John Farmington Gookins; the Saint Louis School of Fine Arts, established in 1879 and headed by Halsey Cooley Ives; the Minneapolis School of Fine Arts, created in 1886 and headed by Stephen Arnold Douglas Volk; the Kansas City Art Institute, founded in 1887 and dominated by two conservatives, George Van Millet and John Douglas Patrick; the Des Moines Academy of Art, established in 1891 and soon taken over by Charles Atherton Cumming, who renamed it after himself; and the Columbus Art Students League, created in 1910 under the leadership of Alice Schille. Omaha formed an academy in 1891 and lured one of Thomas Eakins's pupils, J. Laurie Wallace, to teach there.

The more progressive cities took up impressionist styles. St. Louis, for example, became home to Dawson Watson and Frank Nudersher, and Indianapolis boasted a group championed by the writer Hamlin Garland, the "Five Hoosier Painters"—William Forsythe, Richard Gruelle, Otto Stark, Theodore Clement Steele, and John Otis Adams. One of these figures, Steele, created an art colony in Brown County that attracted additional impressionist painters, many of them from Chicago. Even remote areas often embraced progressive styles. For example, the Swedish community of Lindsborg, Kansas, supported the postimpressionist painter Sven Birger Sandzen, who had studied in Stockholm with Anders Zorn and lived for several years in Paris. Sandzen came to Lindsborg in 1894 to teach at Bethany College and remained there until his death.

On the whole, modernism developed late in the Midwest, but major modern painters did emerge there, in Cleveland and Chicago. Cleveland's heyday as an art center occurred in the early decades of the twentieth century, which was also the period of the city's most rapid growth. The rival leaders of the Cleveland painting establishments were Frederick Carl Gottwald and Henry Keller, both of whom taught at the Cleveland Institute of Art. Gottwald was a diehard conservative, but Keller encouraged modernist experimentation and was a major influence on young artists, including the famous modernist visionary Charles Burchfield.

One of the most interesting Cleveland painters, William Sommer, stood somewhat outside the art establishment, supporting himself as a lithographer. Though academically trained, Sommer became a convert to modernism around 1914 and employed the innovations of Paul Cézanne, the cubists, and the fauves to render humble Ohio scenes of horses and cows in pastoral settings. Because of its industrial base Cleveland also became a center of innovative work in modern industrial design, a newly invented field. For example, Viktor Schreckengost not only pursued painting throughout his career, but designed trucks, children's toys, dinnerware, printing presses, light fixtures, bicycles, and dozens of other items.

Chicago also reached its high point in the early years of the twentieth century, although, given its great place in the history of modern architecture, most of its painting was surprisingly academic. While the Art Institute of Chicago can boast illustrious students, such as Thomas Hart Benton and Georgia O'Keeffe, the faculty of the school consisted of conservative, academically trained figures, such as the portraitist Louis Betts, and for the most part the school turned out commercial illustrators. Three of the best Chicago painters moved elsewhere in search of more interesting subject matter—Walter Ufer, Victor Higgins, and E. Martin Hennings all started their careers in Chicago but eventually settled in Taos, New Mexico. They all made their first trips to the Southwest under the sponsorship of Carter Harrison, Chicago's mayor and a major art patron.

Chicago's most significant modern painter was Manierre Dawson, also a structural engineer. Largely self-taught as an artist, Dawson was trained as an engineer at the Armour Institute of Technology and during the period of his greatest paintings was employed by the Chicago architectural firm of Holabird and Roche, which had produced some of the earliest Chicago skyscrapers. In 1910 Dawson created a group of nonobjective paintings that appear to have been the first purely abstract paintings produced anywhere. Shortly thereafter, Dawson traveled to Europe, where he visited Gertrude Stein and viewed the work of Cézanne. When the Armory Show visited Chicago in 1913, Dawson befriended Walter Pach, one of the project's organizers, and arranged to show one of his works in the exhibition. In 1914 he had a one-man show at the Milwaukee Art Institute. But in 1914

Dawson also married, and to support himself decided to take up fruit farming in Michigan. The demands of supporting a family and managing a farm soon curtailed his artistic production, and he essentially ceased to exhibit or promote his work. Today, while his accomplishments are solidly documented, Dawson remains a relatively little known figure whose role in inventing abstract art has yet to receive widespread recognition.

While the Midwest had produced major artists earlier, the 1930s was certainly the high point of art in the Midwest. During this period, three midwestern artists, Grant Wood, Thomas Hart Benton, and John Steuart Curry, achieved national fame. In addition during this period, imagery distinctive to the life and landscape of the Midwest began to be featured in midwestern painting. The idea of grouping these three artists into a movement first occurred to the art dealer Maynard Walker, who managed to sell this concept to Henry Luce, the creator of *Time* magazine. In 1934 *Time* devoted its first issue with color illustrations to the painters of the American scene, placing Benton's self-portrait on the cover. Much of what was newsworthy about the story was the notion that one could actually make art out of midwestern subject matter, since up to that time the Midwest had been almost synonymous with cultural desolation. The belief that simple farms and farmers could be the subject of serious art was new and iconoclastic. For a decade the three held their position at the forefront of American art. In the early 1940s, however, the tide of popular feeling turned against their work. Benton, Curry, and Wood did not work alone. Their move to the Midwest spurred a brief renaissance, and during the 1930s the Midwest gave birth to a surprising number of gifted painters. Contrary to popular conception, these figures were not all white Anglo-Saxon Protestants but had a variety of cultural backgrounds. Aaron Bohrod, for example, was a midwestern Jewish regionalist. They were also politically diverse, ranging from conservatives, like Curry, to card-carrying Communists, like Joe Jones.

One of the most interesting of these figures was John Rogers Cox, who was appointed the first director of the Sheldon Swope Art Gallery in Terre Haute, Indiana, when he was in his twenties. During his brief tenure, Cox acquired superb paintings by Grant Wood, Thomas Hart Benton, Edward Hopper, Reginald Marsh, Raphael Soyer, and other notable figures. Cox's own painting *Gray and Gold* (1942), his second picture in oils, was a sensational success when he exhibited it in the *Artists for Victory Exhibition* at the Metropolitan Museum, and shortly afterward it was acquired by the Cleveland Museum of Art. Encouraged by this triumph, Cox quit his job as museum director to paint full time, but he never again equaled his first triumph and by the late 1940s had lapsed into obscurity.

While Cox's rise and fall was particularly dramatic, the same pattern can be observed in the career of dozens of midwestern artists of the period. A case in point is Raphael Gleitsman of Akron, Ohio, who produced a small group of remarkable paintings in the late 1930s, notably *The White Dam* (1939), now owned by the Cleveland Museum of Art. Wounded during World War II, Gleitsman produced a few gloomy, surrealist cityscapes during the 1940s but was unable to find adequate patronage, and in the 1950s he became discouraged and abandoned painting altogether. Shortly before his death in 1995, he burned most of the paintings in his possession. One of the few regionalist masters whose reputation survived into the 1950s was Ivan Albright of Chicago. While Albright's work was realistic, its existential qualities made it popular during an age largely dominated by abstract styles.

Since the 1930s, much art has been created in the Midwest, but little of it can be seen as distinctively regional in character. Much of it simply echoes the work of the leading international art centers, such as New York, and the most successful "midwestern artists," such as Richard Anusciewicz, Robert Indiana, and Roy Lichtenstein, have been the ones who moved to New York City. One of the few midwestern movements to receive more than local attention has been the "Hairy Who" group in Chicago, who have produced garish paintings with imagery reminiscent of comic books and other popular art forms. On the whole, however, the art world has become international rather than local. Most midwestern art no longer has a midwestern character, and it is marketed not locally but to a national and international audience.

Sources and Further Reading: Henry Adams, *Thomas Hart Benton* (1989); Henry Adams and Randy J. Ploog, *Manierre Dawson* (1999); Darrell Garwood, *Artist in Iowa* (1944); William Gerdts, *Art across America*, 3 vols. (1990); Patricia Junker, *John Steuart Curry* (1998); William H. Robinson and David Steinberg, *Transformations in Cleveland Art, 1796–1946* (1996).

Henry Adams
Cleveland Museum of Art

Folk Art

Folk art comprises material culture, two-dimensional works, and crafts produced by individuals who continue living traditions and learn their art in an informal, oral tradition. Some forms of folk art are specific to an ethnic community, while others—for example, boatbuilding, instrument making, wood carving, and textile production—descend from widely dispersed guild and shop traditions. In the Midwest, Germanic-Swiss and Anglo-Irish artists have long fashioned furniture, guns, coverlets, quilts, and clocks based on European predecessors but made from locally available materials. Asian and European needleworkers, typically residing in and near cities, draw on their home cultures to produce fine embroideries for ceremonial and domestic purposes. Split-oak basket-making tradition has persisted among Appalachian rural communities. Pottery, a vital folk craft in other areas of the United States, has been largely a factory- and studio-based activity in the Midwest, except for sewer-tile human and animal figures produced by factory workers in the tile industry. Midwestern folk art collections sometimes include material created for recreational and commercial purposes, such as ship mastheads, cigar-store Indians, advertising signs, whimsies, and weathervanes. Some of this material is anonymous.

Defining folk art is problematic because there are sharply opposing schools of thought on the subject. On the one hand are the museums and collectors who initiated the field in the early twentieth century, and on the other are folklorists and experts in material-culture studies. Herbert W. Hemphill, Jr., a pioneering collector and curator, advanced the still-persuasive idea that folk art is timeless and reflects humanity's earliest, less conscious stages of creative awareness. He emphasized artists' social isolation, lack of art education, and uniqueness of vision: "the inner world they paint (or sculpt or make of other materials) is theirs alone and does not come to them through cultural associations and the study of art and its history." Folk art has been subject to a critical language that in other contexts would be understood pejoratively, including praise for its awkwardness, distortion, charm, and innocence. At various times, professionals have defined folk art as naive, self-taught, outsider, visionary, primitive, and vernacular.

Folklorists draw a very different picture of folk art, which they often call "traditional art." For this group, the focus on objects is itself a misguided approach to the field. They define folk or traditional arts as including the performing arts—music, dance, and storytelling. Rather than isolated, unique products of an individual creative personality, folk arts are properly understood as "rooted in time and place and [as] expressions of the shared aesthetics, values and meanings of a cultural community," as folklorist Betsy Peterson describes them. Creativity is important, but the art must be informed by and judged according to values held by people who share a common language, ethnicity, occupation, religion, or region. In addition, whereas the museum/collector view implies that folk artists learn incidentally or by unfettered inspiration, folklorists attend to the process of cultural transmission. They define a process of informal, one-to-one mentorship that takes place among family members or community residents as they go about their everyday life. Folklorists also challenge the museum definition of folk art genres. Art historian John Vlach, for example, argues that easel painting is not folk art. In his view, the itinerant and other untrained painters valued by museums were not attempting to convey a distinctive "folk" vision and aesthetics but in fact emulated the values of academic painting. Therefore, their work is not "folk" but failed fine art and should be judged accordingly.

Many midwestern folk artists have received the prestigious National Heritage Fellowship Award from the National Endowment for the Arts. Designed along the model of Japan's recognition of "national living treasures," the NEA Heritage Fellowships honor those practitioners of living traditions who are at the highest level of excellence and authenticity.

Sources and Further Reading: Charles Camp, *Traditional Craftsmanship in America* (1983); Ricky Clark, George Knepper, and Ellice Ronsheim, *Quilts in Community* (1991); Herbert W. Hemphill, Jr., and Julia Weissman, *Twentieth-Century American Folk Art and Artists* (1974); Rachel Nash Law and Cynthia W. Taylor, *Appalachian White Oak Basketmaking* (1991); Jean Lipman and Tom Armstrong, eds., *American Folk Painters of Three Centuries* (1980); Philip Martin, *Farmhouse Fiddlers* (1994); Betsy Peterson, *Changing Faces of Tradition* (1996); John Vlach, *Plain Painters* (1988).

Judith Rose Sacks
Kenyon College, Ohio

George Caleb Bingham (1811–1879)

Born in Virginia in 1811, George Caleb Bingham as a youth moved to Missouri, where, aside from a few years in the East and three years (1856–1859) in Dusseldorf, Germany, he was to remain for the rest of his life. In a painting career marked by acclaim from his native region as well as nationally, he would become known as "the Missouri artist." He has also been called "the Whig artist of Missouri" because he not only served as a Whig state legislator from 1848 to 1850 but also enthusiastically campaigned for the party until it ceased to exist after the Civil War.

Bingham began as a portraitist in Jefferson City, Missouri, with only minimal training in his craft. In 1837 he acquired some instruction in painting at the Pennsylvania Academy of Fine Arts in Philadelphia, which gave him the confidence to try his hand at portrait painting in Washington, D.C., from 1840 to

1844. It was upon his return to Missouri, however, that he began the work that made him famous: scenes depicting the activities of boatmen on the Missouri and the Mississippi Rivers and scenes picturing the American electoral process, from campaigning to the announcing of election results. *The Jolly Flatboatmen* (1846), which many eastern viewers thought represented the essence of raw-boned western exuberance, was the first to bring him success. His mid-century election "trilogy"—*County Election* (1854), *Verdict of the People* (1854–1855), and *Stump Speaking* (1856)—established him as one of America's nineteenth-century masters in oil. Many of Bingham's canvases were purchased by the American Art Union, located in New York, which reproduced them in engravings and distributed them to its nearly ten thousand–strong membership. Bingham died in 1879.

Sources and Further Reading: Nancy Rash, *The Painting and Politics of George Caleb Bingham* (1991); Michael Shapiro, ed., *George Caleb Bingham* (1990).

Barbara Groseclose
The Ohio State University–Columbus

Robert S. Duncanson (1821–1872)

A freeborn person of color, Robert S. Duncanson worked as an artist in mid-nineteenth-century Cincinnati, where he formed the locus of an Ohio River Valley group of American landscape painters. Freed from slavery around 1790, the Duncanson family of tradesmen moved north to Fayette, New York, where Rob-

ert was born, about 1821. The Duncansons then moved to Monroe, Michigan, around 1830, where Robert learned the family trade of house painting. Robert aspired to become an artist, however, and he moved to Cincinnati, "the Athens of the West," about 1840.

The bustling economic and cultural life of Cincinnati provided a fertile ground for Duncanson to work painting "portraits . . . historical and fancy pieces." Throughout the 1840s, he traveled between Cincinnati and Detroit as an itinerant painter, securing commissions from anyone who would employ an artist of color. Duncanson's earliest datable painting, *Portrait of a Mother and Daughter* (1841), indicates the style of his work in his debut exhibition in 1842. In 1848 the Reverend Charles Avery, an abolitionist minister, commissioned Duncanson to paint *Cliff Mine, Lake Superior* (1848), launching Duncanson's career as a landscape painter.

Duncanson and fellow Cincinnati landscape painters William Louis Sonntag and Worthington Whittredge were the preeminent Cincinnati landscape painters at midcentury. During the 1850s, Duncanson produced some of his finest landscapes of midwestern scenery, including *Blue Hole, Flood Waters, Little Miami River* (1851), *Western Forest* (1857), and *Landscape with Rainbow* (1859), earning him the reputation as "the best landscape painter in the West." Duncanson also worked closely with James Pressley Ball, an African American daguerreotype photographer. In 1855 Ball, with Duncanson's assistance, released a monumental antislavery panorama that toured the northern states.

On the eve of the Civil War, Duncanson created his "great picture," *Land of the Lotus Eaters* (1861), to tour

Blue Hole, Little Miami River, by Robert Scott Duncanson, 1851. Cincinnati Art Museum, Gift of Norbert Heermann and Arthur Helbig, Accession no. 1926.18.

the United States and Europe with the aspiration to secure an international reputation. Modeled on Frederic E. Church's *Heart of the Andes* (1859), Duncanson's vast tropical landscape was inspired by Alfred, Lord Tennyson's epic poem of the same title. Following the outbreak of the Civil War, in 1863 Duncanson exiled himself to Canada. The artist remained in Canada for two years and exerted a considerable influence on Canadian landscape painting before continuing on his journey to Europe. In the British Isles he exhibited his paintings in several cities, earning the recognition that he sought from the London *Art Journal*, which praised Duncanson as a "master."

Upon his return to Cincinnati in 1867, Duncanson exhibited a series of Scottish landscapes, among the finest being *Ellen's Isle, Loch Katrine* (1871). About this time family and friends began noting the artist's psychotic behavior; he believed that the spirits of past artists possessed him. The severity of Duncanson's mental illness led to his collapse in October 1872, as he was hanging an exhibition in Detroit. He died shortly thereafter.

Source and Further Reading: Joseph D. Ketner, *The Emergence of the African American Artist: Robert S. Duncanson, 1821–1872* (1993).

Joseph D. Ketner II
Brandeis University, Massachusetts

Lilly Martin Spencer (1822–1902)

Lilly Martin Spencer, christened Angélique Marie, was born in Exeter, England, in 1822 to Gilles and Angélique LePetit Martin and spent most of her youth in Marietta, Ohio. Her artistic ability appeared early and was encouraged by her family and community. In 1841, accompanied by her father, she moved to Cincinnati to pursue a career as a painter. This young, vital town offered a hospitable environment for artists. Community leaders were working to build their city's cultural reputation and were inclined to provide generous support and patronage. Spencer received an offer from merchant Nicholas Longworth to fund a trip to Europe, although she opted to remain at home. In 1844 she married Benjamin Rush Spencer and four years later they moved to New York City. Lilly Spencer was the breadwinner—her husband minded their seven children and helped in the studio—and the larger city would provide more commissions for still life and portraits. In New York, she trained at the National Academy of Design and was made an honorary member in 1850. As a female professional painter in antebellum America Spencer was unique, but she was continually frustrated by the constraints of family, gender, and patronage. Her more ambitious works, like the large allegory *Truth Unveiling Falsehood* (1869), while praised by critics, did not sell. It was her domestic genre scenes that established her reputation. Charming, homey images such as *Shake Hands?* (1854) were viewed as appropriate subjects for a female painter and were widely disseminated by the Art Union to an eager audience. Spencer died in 1902.

Sources and Further Reading: Robin Bolton-Smith and William H. Truettner, *Lilly Martin Spencer, 1822–1902: The Joys of Sentiment* (1973); Elizabeth Johns, *American Genre Painting: The Politics of Everyday Life* (1991); Wendy Jean Katz, *Regionalism and Reform* (2002).

Nora Kilbane
The Ohio State University–Columbus

Frank Duveneck (1848–1919)

Frank Duveneck was born in Covington, Kentucky, in 1848 to working-class German-Catholic immigrants Bernard and Katherine Siemers Decker. Frank's father died soon after and Katherine married Joseph Duveneck. In 1869, following work as an apprentice church decorator, Frank Duveneck left to study in Germany at Munich's Royal Academy. A top student, he was drawn into the circle of Wilhelm Leibl and Wilhelm Diez, who espoused an innovative painting style influenced by Spanish and Dutch seventeenth-century art. Duveneck's style was soon characterized by a dark palette; loose, energetic brushstrokes; *alla prima*, or direct application of paint with very little preparatory drawing; and subjects chosen from the city's streets. *Whistling Boy* (1871) is typical of this style.

Traveling frequently between America, Germany, and Italy, Duveneck became a leading figure in American art, influencing the direction of American painting by introducing the "Munich school" style and subject matter to a large circle of American art students, known as the "Duveneck Boys," who were drawn to his charismatic teaching. Duveneck also worked closely in Europe with William Merritt Chase, John Singer Sargent, and James McNeill Whistler. After working in Italy, his own style began to lighten considerably and to include landscapes and etchings. In 1888, following the death of his wife, Elizabeth Boott, Duveneck returned to Cincinnati, where he continued, until his own death in 1919, to be an influential teacher, primarily at the Cincinnati Art Academy. Among his many awards and honors, he was given a solo exhibition at the 1915 San Francisco Panama-Pacific International Exposition. His life with the Duveneck Boys is fictionalized in William Dean Howells's *Indian Summer* (1885).

Sources and Further Reading: Josephine Whitney Duveneck, *Frank Duveneck: Painter-Teacher* (1970); Robert Neuhaus, *Unsuspected Genius* (1987); Michael Quick, *An American Painter Abroad* (1987).

M. Melissa Wolfe
The Ohio State University–Columbus

John Twachtman (1853–1902)

John Twachtman was born in 1853 in Cincinnati to Frederick and Sophia Droege Twachtman. After study at the Ohio Mechanics' Institute and the McMicken School of Design, Twachtman followed fellow Cincinnatian Frank Duveneck to Munich, Germany, in 1875, studying at the Royal Academy until 1877. He traveled with Duveneck in Germany and Italy as one of the "Duveneck Boys," learning the "Munich school" style of depicting people of the streets with a direct and vigorous application of paint. Twachtman returned to Cincinnati in 1878 but was discouraged by the city's conservatism. In the following years he moved among Cincinnati (which was also the hometown of his wife, Martha Scudder), New York, and Europe. In 1880 he taught with Duveneck in Florence, Italy, and from 1883 to 1885 he studied at the Julian Academy, Paris. Around 1883 he began to abandon his early style in favor of simplified designs and a more tonal palette, a response to his encounters with the Hague school, expatriate James McNeill Whistler, and French *plein air* painting. In 1889 he settled in Greenwich, Connecticut, and taught at the Art Students League and the Cooper Union Institute in New York.

Twachtman adopted an impressionism that emphasized subtle tonal relationships, quiet nature, and asymmetrical design achieved through layers of thin glazes. Opposed to prevailing conservative tastes, he was one of the "Ten American Painters," an influential group who broke ties with the Society of American Artists in an attempt to revitalize American art. Late in life, Twachtman painted again with Duveneck in Gloucester, Massachusetts, reintroducing the more vigorous style, though with a heightened palette, of his early years. He died in 1902.

Sources and Further Reading: Richard Boyle, *John Twachtman* (1979); Lisa N. Peters, *John Henry Twachtman: An American Impressionist* (1999).

M. Melissa Wolfe
The Ohio State University–Columbus

Kenyon Cox (1856–1919)

Kenyon Cox was born in Warren, Ohio, in 1856. His father, Jacob Dolson Cox, served as governor of Ohio, U.S. secretary of the interior, dean of the Cincinnati Law School, and president of the University of Cincinnati. His mother, Helen Finney, was the daughter of evangelist Charles Grandison Finney, a professor at and president of Oberlin College. While staying with relatives in Cincinnati, the young Kenyon began to study art. He ultimately spent five years in Paris training under Carolus-Duran, Alexandre Cabanel, and Jean-Léon Gérôme. He returned to the United States in 1882 and ten years later married Louise Howland King. Although Cox was well respected as a painter, his favorite subject, the idealized, classical nude, was rejected by American audiences and he had few patrons, so he turned to teaching, illustration, and art criticism. He finally found his true niche as a muralist. By the 1890s, numerous civic buildings were incorporating ambitious decorative programs into their décor, and Cox's restrained, orderly, classicizing style was perfectly suited to the intellectual, allegorical content and symmetrical compositions required of these large-scale public works. A steady flow of these lucrative commissions kept Cox in contact with his midwestern roots as he completed murals for the state capitols of Minnesota, Iowa, and Wisconsin; a number of public libraries; courthouses; and two lunettes at Oberlin College in honor of his parents. He died in 1919. Always outspoken, Cox championed the academic tradition in his writings on art, in his exhibition reviews, and, most particularly, in his vehement attacks on the modernist movements, which he saw as threatening the very core of artistic practice.

Sources and Further Reading: H. Wayne Morgan, ed., *An American Art Student in Paris: The Letters of Kenyon Cox, 1877–1882* (1986); H. Wayne Morgan, ed., *An Artist of the American Renaissance: The Letters of Kenyon Cox, 1883–1919* (1995); H. Wayne Morgan, *Kenyon Cox, 1856–1919: A Life in American Art* (1994).

Nora Kilbane
The Ohio State University–Columbus

Alice Schille (1869–1955)

Alice Schille was an important early proponent in the Midwest of modernism. Through the regular exhibition of her innovative work at museums throughout the region, Schille brought to the Midwest a visual record of her discerning study of the European avant-garde. Accordingly, she introduced a new aesthetic vocabulary to a generation of admirers. She also instilled these experiences in the imaginations of the many students that she instructed at the Columbus Art School from 1904 to 1948. To quote William Robinson, assistant curator of the Cleveland Museum of Art, "in retrospect, Schille was clearly one of the earliest American artists to assimilate European modernism and to bring its influence to the United States."

Born in Columbus, Ohio, in 1869, Schille studied at the Columbus Art School from 1891 to 1893 and then traveled to New York to augment her training. There she enrolled at the Art Students League and also studied at William Merritt Chase's New York School of Art from 1897 to 1899. In 1903 she traveled to Paris for instruction at the Academie Colarossi and for private study.

Although she returned to Columbus in 1904 to commence teaching at the Columbus Art School, she revisited France each summer until the outbreak of World War I in 1914. During this decade, she witnessed the major 1907 retrospective of Paul Cézanne's work in Paris and visited the studio of Gertrude Stein, where she met Pablo Picasso and was profoundly influenced by his work and that of Henri Matisse. These influences began to be seen in her work as early as 1909. That year, Schille exhibited some of the first examples of pointillism by an American artist at the Pennsylvania Academy of Fine Arts, and soon thereafter she began showing such works at the annual watercolor exhibitions of the Art Institute of Chicago and with the Society of Western Artists (SWA). The SWA held its exhibitions at major museums in the Midwest, including those in Detroit, St. Louis, Chicago, Cleveland, Cincinnati, and Indianapolis. Schille also had numerous one-person exhibitions at the Columbus Art Association (1912), the Columbus Gallery of Fine Arts (1921, 1923, 1926, and 1932) and the Cincinnati Art Museum (1911 and 1915). A series of postimpressionist watercolor paintings earned her the first prize at the Society of Western Artists in 1913. In 1915 the eminent art instructor and artist Arthur Dow awarded her the first prize for watercolor at the Pennsylvania Academy of Fine Arts. That year she also won a gold medal in this medium at San Francisco's Panama-Pacific Exposition.

After the outbreak of World War I, Schille spent the next several summers in the art colonies of Gloucester, Massachusetts, and Santa Fe. Encouraged by her American peers, she then fully embraced modernism. In 1917 the pioneering dealer Charles Daniel exhibited her work in New York, and Ferdinand Howald, an astute collector of modernism from Columbus, purchased three of her pointillist beach scenes.

Throughout her life, Schille delighted in travel. After World War I, she resumed exploring European sites and also visited more exotic locales. Always visually alert, she incorporated local motifs and designs within her constantly evolving and eclectic watercolors. She died in 1955.

Sources and Further Reading: William H. Gerdts, *Alice Schille* (2001); James M. Keny, "The French Experience: Alice Schille's Artistic Legacy," *Timeline* 5 (Feb./Mar. 1988); William H. Robinson, "Alice Schille Watercolors," *American Art Review* 13 (Apr. 2001).

James M. Keny
Keny Galleries, Columbus, Ohio

George Bellows (1882–1925)

Though he claimed that his life began after leaving the Midwest for a career in New York, George Wesley Bellows was in many ways a product of his past. Born in Columbus, Ohio, in 1882 to traditional, Methodist parents, Bellows was raised in a conservative climate. His father hoped that his son might follow his own career as a builder and contractor, while his mother imagined her son as a future Methodist bishop. The young Bellows, however, had his own life plan: Before he was old enough to read or write, he had decided to become an artist.

While his early talent was nurtured by teachers, Bellows was ridiculed by peers at school who considered male artists sissies. Consequently, the young Bellows became preoccupied with proving his masculinity by participating in competitive sports. What he lacked in natural talent he made up for with sheer force of will; in both high school and college, Bellows was better known as an athlete than an artist. As a student at The Ohio State University, he was touted as a basketball phenomenon, while his baseball skills brought Bellows offers from professional teams. Nonetheless, he still considered himself essentially an artist and, at the age of twenty-two, a year short of graduation, he left Ohio State and headed east to pursue a career in art.

As a student of Robert Henri at the New York School of Art, Bellows abandoned his earlier genteel manner, influenced by the illustrations of Charles Dana Gibson and Howard Chandler Christie, to focus on the city's seamy side. In keeping with Henri's emphasis on real life subjects, Bellows and other artists associated with Henri, including William Glackens, George Luks, Everett Shinn, and John Sloan, immersed themselves in urban street life. Some of Bellows's better-known paintings show violent boxing matches, tenement kids bathing on the banks of the Hudson River, and the newly excavated pit created for the construction of Pennsylvania Station. Such gritty urban subjects combined with a dark palette and vigorous style led critics to call this group the Ashcan School of artists.

While collectively the group opposed conservative art-world standards, Bellows personally appealed to audiences with both traditional and modern tastes. He was well received at conservative institutions such as the National Academy of Design and the Pennsylvania Academy of Fine Arts. At the same time, Bellows was praised by a younger generation of critics who found his down-to-earth muscular style ideally suited to the industrial landscape. His "all-American" image as a midwestern athlete only fueled what one scholar has called his "meteoric rise [to fame]." More so than most of his colleagues, who were steeped in urban experience, Bellows observed the city freshly, from a visitor's point of view. Bellows died in 1925.

Sources and Further Reading: Marianne Doezema, *George Bellows and Urban America* (1992); Charles H. Morgan, *George Bellows: Painter of America* (1965); Michael Quick, Jane Myers, and Marianne Doezema, *The Paintings of George Bellows* (1992).

Elizabeth Lee
Dickinson College, Pennsylvania

Regionalism in Painting

"Regionalism" has become the most strictly focused of any art-historical term applied to twentieth-century American painting. By the middle of the 1930s, the popular press identified as regionalist any depictions of work-a-day life in the rural Midwest. This narrow definition was due primarily to the abrupt success of John Steuart Curry, Thomas Hart Benton, and Grant Wood. By coincidence, they set a collective precedent for farm subjects at the very beginning of the Great Depression as the term "American Scene" became current among art critics.

Curry led the way in the fall of 1928 when he sent *Baptism in Kansas* to be exhibited at the Corcoran Gallery of Art in Washington, D.C. *New York Times* critic Edward Alden Jewell praised it and Gertrude Vanderbilt Whitney soon bought it for the brand new Whitney Museum of American Art. Just before the stock market crash at the end of October 1929, Curry completed his even more famous *Tornado over Kansas* (1929), which depicted a farm family rushing into their tornado cellar in the face of a twister. This dramatization of rural heroics appealed to a crisis-

stricken urban audience from the moment it appeared in the rotogravure section of the *New York Herald Tribune* in 1931 up to its ready association later with the opening episode of the 1939 movie *The Wizard of Oz*.

In late 1929 a New York gallery exhibited over one hundred mainly watercolors and drawings of rural labor that Benton had painted the previous year on a swing through the Deep South from Appalachia to Texas. *Boomtown* (1928), the big attraction of the show, explodes with the hit-it-rich force of the American Dream. Its dynamics anticipate Benton's rapid succession of murals, including his melodramatic histories of Indiana and Missouri for the Chicago Century of Progress Exposition of 1933–1934 and the Missouri State Capitol, respectively.

Wood's singular *American Gothic* and his first fantasy farmscape, *Stone City, Iowa*, appeared at the very end of 1930. Constant parodies of the staring couple, of their on-guard pitchfork and carpenter-Gothic house, have amused an American public in search of national identity and confounded any attempt to define the painting's relevance to regionalism.

The so-called triumvirate of the short-lived movement exploited local subject matter from their native states of Kansas, Missouri, and Iowa in varying degrees. Although willing to stray far from the boundaries they themselves set for regionalism, they and their supportive critics managed to restrict its membership. Their antiurban sentiments, intensified by the Depression, negated the city as an authentic region. Therefore, such New York localists as Edward Hopper, Reginald Marsh, Isabel Bishop, and the Soyer brothers could never qualify. Oddly enough, neither did painters belonging to regions other than that of the upper Mississippi basin. Southern regionalists Robert Gwathmey, John McCrady, Peter Hurd, and Alexander Hogue, for example, were relegated to the margins of regionalism. New England painters Stephen Etnier and Lauren Ford—and even Clarence Carter of southern Ohio—lacked the proper, if arbitrary, geographic credentials. As for West Coast painters, they were mostly beyond the sights of a Northeast-dominated American art world.

Wood, Benton, and Curry credited the anti-industrial, antiurban polemics of the southern agrarian writers led by John Crowe Ransom and Allen Tate with stimulating their own regionalist theories. But marked differences of opinion toward the city, industrial mechanization, and the ultimate purposes of regionalist art as a national school distinguished them from one another. Having lived in Chicago and Paris, and following visits to New York and Munich, Wood dismissed metropolitan experiences as inconsequential to the regionalist artist of the Midwest. He particularly reproached cubist origins of abstract art, the so-called School of Paris, as a detached, cosmopolitan bohemianism to avoid. But then he ironically adapted basic characteristics resembling cubism to the design of his mature compositions.

In 1935, the same year that Wood published his personal manifesto, *Revolt against the City*, Benton departed for Kansas City, Missouri, after almost twenty-five years in New York. While he too intensified his personal attack on cosmopolitanism, he could not deny the excitement of his own city subject matter. Nor could he take a definite stand in accepting or rejecting machine technology, alternating at will between celebration and doubt. He loved steam engines and their billows of thick, black smoke, which flatten out as bold, abstract shapes in numerous paintings.

Benton's dramatization of America's frenzied transformation into an urban-industrial, engine-paced society had little in common with Wood's stolid aversion to the advancement of industrial mechanization onto the fields of his ornamental farmscapes. In only one painting does Wood permit electrification and engines and it is a violent tragedy: *Death on Ridge Road* (1935). A city limousine passing a slow-moving car is about to collide with a devilish red truck hurtling over the hill above.

Curry, in contrast to the agrarian preferences of Wood, painted much of what his Iowa compatriot qualified as "violent extremes of weather, primitive conflicts between beasts, and the fundamental religious fanaticism and fears of the Kansas farm people." Sublime confrontations culminate in his mural for the Kansas Statehouse in Topeka, *The Tragic Prelude—John Brown* (1937–1942), complete with insane fanaticism, death, tornado, and prairie fire. In anger he engaged in social criticism and political protest much more overtly than regionalism would seem to permit as he depicted a runaway slave in *The Fugitive* (1935) for an antilynching exhibition and *Law versus Mob Rule* (1937), a mural in the United States Department of Justice Building, Washington, D.C.

In contrast to Wood's guardian matriarchs and Benton's glamour girls, Curry's stalwart mothers alternate with an image of young, fair-haired innocence. Through her he alerts the viewer to injustice, attacks on individual freedom, and, in *Parade to War: Allegory* (1939), entry into war.

Although they enjoyed the fame of epitomizing regionalism, in retrospect Wood, Benton, and Curry seem less capable of maintaining total allegiance to the Midwest than other relatively obscure artists of the region, for example, Edwin Fulwider of Indiana. To one extent or another, especially in their woman imagery and abstract manipulations of nature, or in their mimicry, satire, caricature, social criticism, and protest, the premier trio of Midwest regionalism demonstrate a strong tendency toward modern independence.

Sources and Further Reading: Charles C. Alexander, *Here the Country Lies* (1980); Matthew Baigell, *The American Scene: American Painting of the 1930s* (1974); Thomas Hart Benton, "American Regionalism: A Personal History of the Movement," *University of Kansas City Review* 13 (May 1951); James M. Dennis, *Renegade Regionalists* (1998); Alan Gussow, *A Sense of Place: The Artist and the American Land* (1971); Merrill Jensen, ed., *Regionalism in America* (1951); Karal Ann Marling, *Wall to Wall America* (1982); Marlene Park and Gerald E. Markowitz, *Democratic Vistas* (1984).

James M. Dennis
University of Wisconsin–Madison

Grant Wood (1891–1942)

The Iowa artist Grant Wood is famous for his painting *American Gothic* (1930) depicting a pitchfork-armed, rural couple guarding their carpenter-Gothic house, a painting that has prompted numerous parodies. Born in 1891 near Anamosa, Iowa, Wood moved with two brothers, his sister Nan, and their mother to Cedar Rapids upon their father's death in 1901. Following high school, Wood attended evening courses at the School of the Art Institute of Chicago before serving in an army camouflage unit in 1918. During his early career, metalsmithing, carpentry, interior designing, and teaching high-school art accompanied his work as a painter of local landscapes, backyard scenes, flower still lifes, and portraits. Some of his later impressionistic street scenes, fountains, and medieval doorways, painted in France; Sorrento, Italy; and Munich, Germany, were exhibited in Paris in 1926. He exchanged many paintings with his Cedar Rapids patron, a mortician, in return for a studio apartment in the mortuary's carriage house, where he lived with his mother before moving to Iowa City in 1934 to become an art professor at the University of Iowa. He died in 1942.

The linear style of *American Gothic* and *Stone City, Iowa* (1930) also stemmed from northern Renaissance and *Neuesachlichkeit* paintings he saw in Germany during his last visit abroad in 1928. Precise forms rendered over a grid of diagonals characterized his paintings, drawings, lithographs, book illustrations, and a series of murals for the Iowa State University library done throughout the 1930s. His fanciful farmscapes alternated with the witty *Daughters of Revolution* (1932), *Adolescence* (1933), *Dinner for Threshers* (1934), and *Parson Weems' Fable* (1939) as he shared the leadership of Midwest regionalism with Thomas Hart Benton and John Steuart Curry.

Sources and Further Reading: Wanda Corn, *Grant Wood: The Regionalist Vision* (1983); James M. Dennis, *Grant Wood: A Study in American Art and Culture* (1975); Brady M.

Grant Wood Art Festival, Stone City, Iowa. Iowa Division of Tourism.

Roberts, James M. Dennis, James Hornes, and Helen Mar Parkin, *Grant Wood: An American Master Revealed* (1995).

James M. Dennis
University of Wisconsin–Madison

Archibald J. Motley, Jr. (1891–1981)

Archibald J. Motley, Jr., was born in 1891 into a Creole family in New Orleans. Although his parents soon moved to Chicago, the family kept strong ties to their southern heritage. Motley graduated from the School of the Art Institute of Chicago. In 1929, one year after becoming only the second African American artist to receive a solo exhibition in New York City, Motley was awarded a Guggenheim Fellowship to study in Paris for a year. Returning to Chicago in 1930, he exhibited widely and to notable acclaim throughout the 1930s and 1940s. Motley became the most significant Midwest representative of the "Negro renaissance," a cultural rebirth of urban African American communities that achieved its pinnacle in Harlem. He died in 1981.

Motley is best known for his portraiture and for genre scenes of urban African American life. Upon his return from Paris, he translated his images of Parisian nightlife into depictions of Bronzeville, the African American community in Chicago in which he lived. Typical of his highly stylized, syncopated compositions is *Gettin' Religion* (1948), with its intense color contrasts, signature red tones, and compressed space. *Mending Socks* (1924) is an equally typical example of his portraiture. This depiction of his eighty-two-year-old grandmother is both a sensitive narrative portrait and a genre image of middle-class African American life. In 1933 Motley succinctly described his intentions as an artist, stating, "It is my earnest desire . . . to express the American Negro honestly and sincerely, . . . and to bring about a more sincere and brotherly . . . understanding, between him and his white brethren."

Sources and Further Reading: Sharon F. Patton, *African-American Art* (1998); Jontyle Robinson and Wendy Greenhouse, *The Art of Archibald J. Motley, Jr.* (1991); Robert Stearns ed., *Illusions of Eden* (2000).

Nannette V. Maciejunes
Columbus Museum of Art, Ohio

Charles E. Burchfield (1893–1967)

Charles Burchfield is considered one of the preeminent American painters of the twentieth century. Born in Ashtabula Harbor, Ohio, in 1893, Burchfield grew up in the small town of Salem, Ohio, where he developed a deep love of nature through the nearby woods and hollows. In his youth he also began compiling the journals he would keep throughout his life, filled with memorable passages detailing his personal artistic struggle. From 1912 to 1916, he studied at the Cleveland School (now Institute) of Art, originally intending to become a commercial illustrator. The artistic milieu of Cleveland, shaped by such modernists as Henry Keller and William Sommer, exerted a profound influence on Burchfield's decision to become a painter, his choice of watercolor as a medium, and his lifelong willingness to experiment with that medium.

After graduation and a brief enrollment at the National Academy of Design in New York, Burchfield returned to Salem in November 1916 to paint independently while working as an accounting clerk. It was at this time that he began to paint the memories and moods of his childhood, including such masterpieces as *Church Bells Ringing, Rainy Winter Night* (1917).

In 1921 Burchfield moved to Buffalo, New York, to work as a wallpaper designer at M. H. Birge and Sons. There he raised a family and lived until his death. In 1929 the Frank K. M. Rehn Galleries in New York became his representative and Burchfield quit his job to paint fulltime.

In the 1920s Burchfield began to receive acclaim for his innovative use of watercolor and for his ability to capture what the artist later described as the "great epic poetry of the Midwest American life." Many critics saw his work as the visual counterpart to the literary regionalism of such writers as Sherwood Anderson. His images of rural and small-town America propelled Burchfield to national fame as one of the founders, along with Edward Hopper, of the "American Scene." It was at this time that museums began to acquire Burchfield's paintings, beginning with the Brooklyn Museum of Art's 1921 purchase of *February Thaw* (1920). In 1930 the new Museum of Modern Art in New York selected Burchfield as the first American artist to receive a solo exhibition, focusing on his early, 1916–1918 watercolors. In 1944 the Albright Gallery in Buffalo gave Burchfield his first major retrospective, followed in 1956 by a retrospective at the Whitney Museum of American Art in New York. He died in 1967. The Metropolitan Museum of Art in New York honored him with a retrospective in 1984.

In the early 1940s, Burchfield began to paint large-scale expressionist landscapes, exemplified by works such as *The Four Seasons* (1960). His early watercolors were the foundation for this new body of work. Reviving the spirit of fantasy characteristic of his early work, Burchfield pasted blank strips of paper to existing watercolors and reworked their compositions to create new works, which he called "reconstructions." This distinctive process became Burchfield's hallmark and is the technique with which he is still most closely identified.

Sources and Further Reading: John I. H. Baur, *The Inlander* (1982); Charles Burchfield, "On the Middle Border," *Creative Arts* 3 (Sept. 1928); Nannette V. Maciejunes and Michael Hall, eds., *The Paintings of Charles Burchfield* (1997); J. Benjamin Townsend, ed., *Charles Burchfield's Journals* (1993); Nancy Weekly, *Charles E. Burchfield: The Sacred Woods* (1993).

Nannette V. Maciejunes
Columbus Museum of Art, Ohio

Ivan Albright (1897–1983)

Ivan Le Lorraine Albright gained national attention between the two world wars as a painter of aging, eerily lit figures and faded, tattered still-life objects rendered in minute detail. Sometimes labeled "Magic Realism," Albright's bizarre imagery and obsessive technique constitute a dark variant of midwestern regionalism. The artist's father, Adam Emory Albright, was a successful painter of sunny, impressionistic rural subjects who moved his family to various locations in greater Chicago following Ivan's birth in North Harvey, on the Illinois city's southern border.

Albright and his twin, Malvin (pseudonym, Zsissly), were born in 1897 and graduated from the School of the Art Institute of Chicago in 1923. By 1929 both had studios built in the western suburb of Warrenville. There many of Ivan's best-known paintings were produced, including *Into the World There Came a Soul Called Ida* (1929–1930), typical in its depiction of a pathetically aged subject (in reality the model was a local housewife of twenty); the inclusion of *vanitas* motifs (mirror, flowers), reminders of life's transience; and its skewed perspective. The 1940s marked the apogee of Albright's fame, capped by the appearance of his painting *The Picture of Dorian Gray* (1943–1944) in the MGM film adaptation of Oscar Wilde's novel.

In 1946 Albright married newspaper heiress Josephine Medill Patterson Reeve and soon after moved to Chicago, where he remained until relocating to Woodstock, Vermont, in 1963, where he resided until his death in 1983. His later works include a compelling series of self-portraits (1981–1983) that unsparingly document the effects of aging during his final years.

Sources and Further Reading: Art Institute of Chicago, *Ivan Albright*, by Courtney Graham Donnell et al. (exhibit cat., 1997); Michael Croydon, *Ivan Albright* (1978); Hood Museum of Art, *Ivan Albright: The Late Self-Portraits*, with essays by Richard R. Brettell and Phylis Floyd (exhibit cat., 1986).

David Stark
The Art Institute of Chicago

John Steuart Curry (1897–1946)

Born near Dunavant, Kansas, in 1897, John Steuart Curry is best known for his narrative depictions of rural life in the state, such as *Baptism in Kansas* (1928) and *Tornado over Kansas* (1929), and he is typically characterized as a regionalist (along with Thomas Hart Benton and Grant Wood) or as an "American

Thomas Hart Benton's *Cradling Wheat*, 1939.
© T. H. Benton and R. P. Benton Testamentary
Trusts/UMB Bank Trustee/Licensed by VAGA,
New York, NY; UAM, UCSB, Ken Trevey
Collection.

Scene" painter. He studied at the School of the Art Institute of Chicago from 1916 to 1918 and in 1919 joined the studio of Harvey Dunn in Tenafly, New Jersey. After seven years as an illustrator around New York, Curry traveled to Paris and studied with Russian academician Vasily Shukhayev. After returning to the United States in June 1927, Curry began producing nostalgic scenes of Kansas life at his art colony studio in Westport, Connecticut.

In 1936 Curry became the country's first university artist-in-residence, at the University of Wisconsin, Madison, and he held this appointment until his death in 1946. The position, which linked a famous artist with rural citizens interested in producing art, was an example of the "Wisconsin Idea"—an initiative to foster the intellectual, economic, social, and moral development of the state. Between 1936 and 1938, Curry completed mural cycles for the Departments of Justice and the Interior in Washington, D.C., with New Deal patronage. In 1937 he was commissioned to paint murals for the Kansas Statehouse in Topeka. This cycle was to portray the history of settlement on the plains, featuring his unforgettable image of John Brown, but the work was ill received by the public and never fully completed.

Sources and Further Reading: Patricia Junker, *John Steuart Curry: Inventing the Middle West* (1998); M. Sue Kendall, *Rethinking Regionalism* (1986); Laurence E. Schmeckebier, *John Steuart Curry's Pageant of America* (1943).

Wendy Koenig
The Ohio State University–Columbus

Thomas Hart Benton (1889–1975)

One of the best-known American artists of the twentieth century, Thomas Hart Benton painted scenes of the central Midwest in the style called regionalism. Born in 1889 in Neosho, Missouri, Benton studied at the School of the Art Institute of Chicago and in Paris, worked and taught in New York from 1912 to 1935, and spent the remainder of his life in Kansas City. Teaching at the Kansas City Art Institute from the mid-1930s to 1941, Benton was an influential spokesperson for a uniquely American form of modern art attentive to the people and landscapes of the Midwest, a region that he described in 1935 as "the least provincial area in America."

Benton's major works include four ambitious historical murals painted during the 1930s: *America Today* (1930–1931, for the New School for Social Research in New York City), *The Arts of Life in America* (1932, for the library of the Whitney Museum of American Art in New York City), *A Social History of the State of Indiana* (1933, now owned by Indiana University, Bloomington), and *A Social History of the State of Missouri* (1936, painted for the House of Representatives Lounge at the state capitol in Jefferson City, Missouri). These dynamic and brightly colored paintings were based on Benton's first-hand observation of American life and legend, from the industry and arts of Indiana to the folktales and political culture of Missouri. Like his fellow regionalist painters Grant Wood and John Steuart Curry, Benton also produced many individual paintings and prints of midwestern subjects, including *Threshing Wheat* (1938–1939). His later work included *Independence and the Opening of the West*, a mural he painted for the Truman Library in Independence, Missouri, from 1959 to 1966. Benton died in 1975.

Sources and Further Reading: Henry Adams, *Thomas Hart Benton: An American Original* (1989); Thomas Hart Benton, *An Artist in America*, 4th ed. (1983).

Erika Doss
University of Colorado–Boulder

Clyde Singer (1908–1999)

Clyde Singer was born in 1908 in Malvern, Ohio. From 1931 to 1932 he attended the Columbus Art School (now the Columbus College of Art and Design) in Ohio, where he was influenced by George Bellows's work in the Columbus Gallery of Fine Arts (now the Columbus Museum of Art). He continued his training at the Art Students League in New York from 1933 to 1934, where he studied with several important American painters, including Kenneth Hayes Miller and John Steuart Curry. Singer's decision in 1934 to return to Malvern to paint was met with Curry's endorsement, "Oh, you're going home to paint the American Scene! Good." Working from his Malvern studio, Singer garnered numerous national awards, including the Harris Silver Medal at the Art Institute of Chicago's annual exhibition for his work *Sandy Valley* (1934). In 1941 he executed a mural in the post office at New Concord, Ohio, for the Treasury Relief Art Project. Throughout his life, he remained an active painter of both Ohio and New York City subjects, the latter inspired by annual sketching trips. In 1940 he became the assistant director and curator of the Butler Institute of American Art in Youngstown, Ohio, a position he held until his death in 1999.

Singer was an important "American Scene" painter of the Midwest. His realistic, and at times gently satiric, depictions of the everyday spectacle of city and small-town life comprise a rich portrait of the world he knew. His work from the 1930s and 1940s, such as *Street People* (1936), is arguably his most historically significant.

Sources and Further Reading: M. J. Albacete, *Clyde Singer's New York* (1989); Elizabeth McClelland, "Little Bits of History: Clyde Singer, American Scene Painter," *Timeline* 13 (Nov./Dec. 1996); Robert Stearns, ed., *Illusions of Eden* (2000).

Nannette V. Maciejunes
Columbus Museum of Art, Ohio

Robert Indiana (b. 1928)

Born in New Castle, Indiana, in 1928 and adopted by Earl and Carmen Clark, Robert Indiana (né Robert Clark) spent most of his childhood in or near Indianapolis and graduated as class valedictorian from Arsenal Technical High School in 1946. He attended the School of the Art Institute of Chicago under the G.I. Bill, majoring in painting and graphics, and won a travel fellowship to Scotland, completing his bachelor of fine arts degree with courses from the University of Edinburgh. Clark eventually landed in New York City, and in the late 1950s he moved into the studios located at Coenties Slip, which also housed artists Ellsworth Kelly and Agnes Martin. During this period Clark changed his name to Robert Indiana, in honor of his birth state, and worked to integrate his longstanding interest in poetry and language into his paintings, all assemblages and sculptures.

Like his New York neighbors Jasper Johns and Robert Rauschenberg, Indiana often used found objects in his works, such as wood pieces from demolished buildings. Such objects were used to produce his "Herms," beam sculptures loosely based upon sacred pillars mythologically associated with the trial of Hermes. These works typically incorporated numerals and words, as did his paintings, which often referred to political events, American writers such as Walt Whitman and Herman Melville, autobiographical details, or elements of Americana. His most recognizable work was developed between 1964 and 1966: the famous *LOVE* word painting. This motif was subsequently translated into sculptural form by the artist and has been frequently appropriated by other artists and designers since its first appearance.

Sources and Further Reading: Robert Indiana, *Retrospective 1958–1998* (1998); Susan Elizabeth Ryan, *Robert Indiana: Figures of Speech* (2000).

Wendy Koenig
The Ohio State University–Columbus

Jim Nutt (b. 1938)

Born in 1938 in Pittsfield, Massachusetts, Jim Nutt graduated from the School of the Art Institute of Chicago in 1965. Part of a group of artists known as Chicago imagists, Nutt, along with Art Green, James Falconer, Gladys Nilsson, Suellen Rocca, and Karl Wirsum, exhibited under the collective name "Hairy Who" between 1966 and 1969. Following this period, Nutt continued to work as a painter, showing in group exhibitions in Chicago and other American venues, as well as in one-man shows in the United States and

Holland. He and other Chicago imagists were brought to national prominence, in part, through the efforts of the Phyllis Kind Gallery in Chicago.

Nutt shared with other members of the Hairy Who an interest in popular culture, comic books, low humor, and wordplay, and his figurative works often feature characters with exaggerated sexual parts and deformed limbs and have titles that act as puns, such as *Miss Sue Port* (1967–1968), which is a play on "support," or *She's Hit* (1967), which becomes a scatological phrase if the division of the letters is shifted. Nutt has frequently employed a technique of painting with bright colors on Plexiglas, which creates a shiny surface reminiscent of mass-culture publications and effectively removes all surface texture. In many works, Nutt has included comic-style motion marks, narrative frames within frames, and an overlapping technique to indicate spatial relations. His paintings play with feelings of attraction and repulsion and typically exhibit a mood of erotic tension and menacing drama.

Sources and Further Reading: Patricia Hills and Roberta K. Tarbell, *The Figurative Tradition and the Whitney Museum of American Art* (1980); Tony Knipe, ed., *Who Chicago? An Exhibition of Contemporary Imagists* (1980).

Wendy Koenig
The Ohio State University–Columbus

Gladys Nilsson (b. 1940)

Born in 1940 in Chicago, Gladys Nilsson graduated from the School of the Art Institute of Chicago in 1962. Along with other "Chicago imagists," including Jim Nutt and Karl Wirsum, Nilsson exhibited under the collective banner of the "Hairy Who" at the Hyde Park Arts Center in Chicago, at the San Francisco Art Institute, and at the Corcoran Gallery of Art in Washington, D.C., between 1966 and 1969. Following this period, Nilsson continued to work with paint and watercolor, showing in both group and one-person exhibitions all over the United States. She was associated with the Phyllis Kind Gallery in Chicago and her work is represented in the Museum of Modern Art and the Whitney Museum of American Art in New York as well as the Art Institute of Chicago.

Nilsson's work reveals an interest in the metamorphosis of form, and her dense, dynamic compositions are filled with irregular, seemingly organic shapes that multiply before the viewer's eyes. Like other members of the Hairy Who, Nilsson was attracted to popular culture and language play, reflected in works such as *Enterprize Encountered by the Spydar People* (1969), which was inspired by the television series *Star Trek*. Her works appear as games of association that grow in several directions in a cumulative fashion and exhibit a sense of fear of emptiness. Her pastel and softly modulated colors differentiated her work from that of other Hairy Who artists, as did her occasional references to traditional history in titles such as *Bottacelle Series* and *3 Graces and the Virgin Spring*.

Sources and Further Reading: Jonathan Fineberg, *Art since 1940* (1995); Tony Knipe, ed., *Who Chicago? An Exhibition of Contemporary Imagists* (1980); Museum of Contemporary Art, Chicago, *Chicago Imagist Art* (1972).

Wendy Koenig
The Ohio State University–Columbus

Gladys Nilsson's *Cake*, 2002. Courtesy Jean Albano Gallery, Chicago, Ill.

The Hairy Who

The "Hairy Who" was the name adopted by a group of "Chicago imagist" artists working from 1966 to 1969, including Jim Nutt, Gladys Nilsson, James Falconer, Suellen Rocca, Art Green, and Karl Wirsum, all of whom attended the School of the Art Institute of Chicago. While there is no underlying stylistic unity in the work of the Hairy Who, its members shared certain similar interests, including an admiration for "outsider" art, such as the work of self-taught painter Joseph Yoakum from the South Side of Chicago; an attraction to products of popular culture; and a propensity to play with language and spelling. Many of the works produced by the group are characterized by an abundance of figurative and organic, asymmetrical shapes; the use of unmodulated and intense color; and a carefully finished surface that exhibits no evidence of the artist's "hand."

The Hairy Who exhibited as a group for four years, holding three shows (in 1966, 1967, and 1968) at the Hyde Park Arts Center, located in the University of Chicago community on Chicago's South Side. Two additional exhibitions were held outside of Chicago (in 1968 and 1969), the former at the San Francisco Art Institute; and a sixth and final show was held at the Corcoran Gallery of Art in Washington, D.C. In their third exhibition, the group displayed their interest in accentuating cultural elements typically absent from the "fine" art exhibits by covering the walls of the gallery with flowered linoleum, hanging yellow price tags from their works, and exhibiting actual comic books and toys alongside their art. Further, the artists often produced collaborative exhibition catalogs in the form of comic books. For example, the Corcoran catalog featured "sci-fi he-man figures" on the front and back covers, and the word "cat-a-log" is written as a rebus, using the visual symbols of a cat and a log. In some works, such as Karl Wirsum's *Screamin' J. Hawkins* (1968), which refers to a well-known blues singer, words or phrases accompany figurative imagery, clashing patterns, and brilliant colors. Although the compositions are often crowded and complex, individual elements retain a comic book's clarity of definition and a sense of flatness against a simple background color.

The Hairy Who inspired the formation of other exhibition groups at the Hyde Park Art Center, such as the "Nonplussed Some," which included artist Ed Paschke; the "False Image"; and "Marriage Chicago Style." Following the period of the group shows at Hyde Park, the focus of the Chicago imagist movement shifted to Phyllis Kind's Chicago-based commercial gallery, which expanded upon the opening of its New York branch in 1975. This development, in addition to the support of critics like Whitney Halstead, Franz Schulze, and Dennis Adrian, helped bring the work of the Hairy Who and other imagists to the attention of a national audience.

Sources and Further Reading: Jonathan Fineberg, *Art since 1940* (1995); Tony Knipe, ed., *Who Chicago? An Exhibition of Contemporary Imagists* (1980); Museum of Contemporary Art, Chicago, *Chicago Imagist Art* (1972).

Marsha Morrison
University of Louisville, Kentucky

Contemporary Native American Art

Contemporary Native American art encompasses a broad spectrum of traditions and media generally divided into two categories: contemporary Native American traditional art and contemporary Native American fine art.

Native American traditional artists produce art that is deeply rooted in the long-standing tradition of a particular culture (in the Midwest, primarily the Woodlands and some plains cultures). Natural materials that were part of their environment influenced these indigenous cultures. Woodland traditions grew out of the abundance of plant and animal life surrounding them. Consequently, they produced objects created from woods, bark, and plant fiber and, later, beaded items and ribbon work. Their decoration often included images of flowers and plant life indigenous to the area.

Work being made today by contemporary Native American traditional artists, such as baskets and clothing, generally draws on styles and designs handed down from one generation to the next. As the tradition is passed along, individual artists influence how that tradition changes and how it reflects change within the culture.

Contemporary Native American fine art encompasses an even broader range of traditions, mediums, and cultures. Native American artists today are making films, doing installation and performance work, and creating political painting and other types of personal expression that reflect the long history and heritage of the indigenous artists as well as a contemporary experience. They are influenced by and are influencing traditions usually associated with European cultures, such as painting, sculpture, and printmaking. Moreover, Native American fine artists are collaborating with other indigenous peoples to explore similarities and differences in expression and experiences. The combination of cultural traditions provides a greater range for individual expression. Current Native American art can be political in its message and often reflects the conflict between the Native American and European American, or white, perspective. The rich and varied types of art and artists working today are a reflection of the great diversity among indigenous peoples and the environmental influences of more urban lifestyles.

In the past fifty years, there has been a strong movement by contemporary Native American fine artists to compete in the mainstream art market. Artists such as Allan Houser and TC Cannon, rather than conforming only to the traditional artwork usually associated with American Indian art, began creating and encouraging others to create art that drew from their experience as Native American artists in a very personal and individual way, rather than conforming only to the traditional artwork usually associated with American Indian art.

One of the most pivotal exhibitions bringing attention to the Native American fine artists was Shared Visions, developed by the Heard Museum in Phoenix, Arizona, in 1991. This exhibition, curated by Margaret Archuleta, documented and established the momentum of the Native American contemporary fine art movement in an effort to bring attention and recognition to contemporary Native American fine artists by the mainstream art world.

Museums and art organizations such as the Heard Museum and the San Francisco Museum of Contemporary Arts and artists like Jaune Quick-to-See Smith (a Flathead) and Sara Bates (Cherokee) have written about and curated many exhibitions contributing to a greater understanding of Native American art and the appreciation of native cultures as living cultures.

In 1999 the Eiteljorg Museum of American Indians and Western Art in Indianapolis, established a program to promote and reward contemporary Native American fine artists. This program is unique in the United States. Every other year, a distinguished artist and five fellows are each awarded twenty thousand dollars; the museum purchases work for its permanent collection, produces a catalog, and presents a major exhibition. This unprecedented program has honored such artists as George Morrison (Chippewa, Truman Lowe (Ho-Chunk), and Kay WalkingStick (Cherokee) as well as important First Nations (Canadian) artists such as Robert Houle (Saulteaux) and Shelley Niro (Bay of Quinte Mohawk). In the last fifteen years, the efforts to integrate Native American artists into the fabric and interpretation of American art by museums and organizations has produced thought-provoking perspectives on the representation of indigenous peoples.

Sources and Further Reading: Margaret Archuleta and Rennard Strickland, *Shared Visions: Native American Painters and Sculptors in the Twentieth Century* (1991); Gerald McMaster, *Reservation X* (1998); W. Jackson Rusing III, *After the Storm: The Eiteljorg Fellowship for Native American Fine Art* (2001); Kathleen McManus Zurko, ed., *We the Human Beings* (1992).

Jennifer Complo McNutt
Eiteljorg Museum of American Indian and
Western Art, Indianapolis

Photographers and Photography

The beginnings of photography in the United States were advanced by the astonishing rapidity with which the Midwest took to the new medium, first in daguerreotypes and later in the proliferating variety of techniques that eventually led to the photographs we know today. In 1846, on a thin plate of silver-coated copper, the first known photograph of Abraham Lincoln was made by daguerreotypist N.H. Shepherd in Springfield, Illinois. In Cincinnati, painter Thomas Faris opened a daguerreotype studio in 1841, and African Americans James F. Ball and Thomas C. Ball opened theirs in 1847. Eight 6½ × 8½ inch daguerreotypes creating a panorama of the Cincinnati waterfront made by Charles F. Fontayne and William S. Porter were displayed at the Crystal Palace Exposition in London in 1851.

Mid-nineteenth-century Ohio can be singled out as the site of much experimental photographic art. In 1851 the collodion wet-plate process began another chapter in the history of photography. Using this process, Ambrose Cutting made a thin negative on glass that appeared as a positive when placed on a dark background. Photographer Marcus A. Root, of Granville, Ohio, who wrote *The Camera and the Pencil* (1864), considered to be the first history of photography published in the United States, described it as an "ambrotype," a name that stuck. In 1856 in Gambier, Ohio, Kenyon College professor Hamilton Smith, using the collodion wet-plate process, patented the making of photographs on thin iron plates, later marketed as "melainotypes" by Smith's colleague, Peter Neff of Cincinnati. Victor Griswold patented a similar product, marketed as a "ferrotype," which he manufactured in Lancaster, Ohio. After a brief patent dispute, both Smith's and Griswold's plates became commonly known as tintypes.

Despite the predominance of men in the field, there were also professional women photographers, some of whom advertised their first names only with initials—W.A. Reid of Quincy, Illinois, and L.C. Gillet of Saline, Wisconsin, for example. Others, like Mrs. H.P. Harvey of Maquoketa, Iowa, and Mrs. H.E.

Nebraska Gothic, by Solomon Butcher, 1886. Nebraska State Historical Society, Photograph Collection, RG2608.PH:000000-001048.

Rainheld of Fort Atchinson, Wisconsin, may have felt it expedient to identify their marital status. Myra B. Rush of Olney, Illinois, advertised her full name. Most of the women were portraitists. The specialty of Belle Johnson, of Monroe, Missouri, was portraiture of cats.

Lewis Wickes Hine, born in Oshkosh, Wisconsin, bridged the nineteenth and twentieth centuries in the history of American photography. His sensitive images of immigrants at Ellis Island, child laborers in cotton mills, and steel workers atop the unfinished Empire State Building blurred the distinction between a photograph as document and as art; the latter characteristic, often called pictorialism, was an especial feature of the Midwest.

In 1903 pictorialist photographers Louis Fleckenstein of Faribault, Minnesota, and Carl Rau of La Crosse, Wisconsin, organized the Salon Club of America. Its membership included J. W. Schuler of Akron; sisters W. and G. Parrish of St. Louis; Julius Field of Wisconsin; and Herbert A. Hess of Crawfordsville, Indiana. Clarence H. White, who resided in Newark, Ohio, and Edward Steichen, who was born in Luxembourg and whose career in photography began as a youth in Milwaukee, became founding members of the Photo-Secession of Alfred Steiglitz (1902), which established photography as an art form.

Photogravures by Gertrude Käsebier of Damascus, Iowa, and those of other members of Photo-Secession appearing in Steiglitz's *Camera Work* (1903) stimulated the publication of fine photographs in magazines and in books. The first two volumes of *Portraits from North American Indian Life*, by photographer Edward S. Cur-

tis of Whitewater, Wisconsin, were described by the *New York Herald* of June 16, 1907, as "the most gigantic undertaking in the making of books since the King James edition of the Bible."

By 1902 Bert and Elmer Underwood of Oxford, Illinois, were publishing over 7 million photographic stereoviews and 300,000 stereoscopic viewers a year, widely used for entertainment and enlightenment in Victorian parlors; but the mass market for published photographs was realized on November 23, 1936, when all 466,000 copies of the first issue of *Life* magazine sold out at once. *Look* magazine, founded in 1937 by Gardner Cowles, Jr., in Des Moines, had a circulation of 5,006,000 by 1957.

Under the direction of Roy Emerson Stryker, who was born in Great Bend, Kansas, the Farm Security Administration's images of the Depression of the 1930s were intended for publication in newspapers and magazines. Among the photographers who worked for the FSA were Walker Evans of St. Louis; Russell Lee, born in Ottawa, Illinois; Gordon Parks of Fort Scott, Kansas; John Collier, Jr., of Detroit; John Vachon of St. Paul; and Esther Bubley, a native of Superior, Wisconsin. Ralph Steiner of Cleveland, a member of the New York Photo League, was cinematographer on the classic documentary films *The Plow That Broke the Plains* (1936) and *The River* (1937). Berenice Abbott, born in Springfield, Ohio, famous for her cityscapes of New York, was also distinguished for her resurrection of the work of French photographer Eugene Atget. Notable twentieth-century documentary and photojournalists include W. Eugene

Smith of Wichita; Wright Morris of Central City, Nebraska; Eliot F. Porter of Winnetka, Illinois; David Douglas Duncan of Kansas City, Missouri; Arthur Siegel, born in Detroit; and Chicagoans William Ashford Garnett and Wayne Miller.

In 1937 Chicago became the most important center of photography in the Midwest when Lázló Moholy-Nagy founded the New Bauhaus, which became part of the Institute of Art and Design of the Illinois Institute of Technology. Among its teachers and students were Harry Callahan of Detroit, Ray Metzker of Milwaukee, and Edmund Teske of Chicago.

In 1952 Minor White, born in Minneapolis, began publication of *Aperture*, the influential quarterly of photography. In 1962 White joined Nathan Lyons, founder of the Society for Photographic Education, whose purpose was to include the study of photography in institutions of higher education. John Szarkowski, born in Ashland, Wisconsin, replaced Edward Steichen as curator of photography at the Museum of Modern Art in New York City, where through his writings and exhibitions he educated photographers, students, and critics to appreciate a photograph both as art and as artifact.

The Midwest, as photographed by established professional "outsiders," was often pictured quite differently by local commercial and amateur "insiders," but their combined images documented the transition of the Midwest from the "Breadbasket" to the "Industrial Heartland" of America.

As early as 1904 the National Cash Register Company of Dayton, Ohio, commissioned the famous photographer of the American frontier William Henry Jackson, then a partner in the Detroit Publishing Company, to photograph its operation for personnel training and corporate advertising. Subsequent artists were attracted to the industrial and mechanical forms. Charles Sheeler photographed the Ford plant at River Rouge. Edward Weston, of Highland Park, Illinois, a founding member of Group f/64 in California, captured the abstractions of the Armco steel plant in Ohio. Margaret Bourke-White photographed the industrial mills of Cleveland and the storage tanks of the Standard Oil Company. These images became icons of the industrial Midwest, but in the 1960s the changing social and economic scene began to reflect different images.

Walker Evans's photographs of the industrial Heartland published by *Fortune* in 1961 were titled "People and Places in Trouble." Art Sinsabaugh's panoramic photographs of Illinois and Indiana farmlands for Sherwood Anderson's poetic *6 Mid-American Chants* (1964) foreshadowed urban sprawl. Michael Lesy's *Wisconsin Death Trip* (1973) illustrated the seamy side of earlier life in the Midwest with prints from glass-plate negatives made in 1890–1910 by Charles van Schaick of Illinois. Chauncy Hare's *Interior America* (1978) documented the sterile interiors of homes of alienated families in the Ohio communities of Wintersville, East Liverpool, Mingo Junction, Steubenville, and Cincinnati. Photographer Michael Williamson and journalist Dale Maharidge's *Journey to Nowhere: The Saga of the New Underclass* (1985) pictured the Midwest as a "rustbowl," postulating that the nation's economic and social problems originated in Ohio and Michigan. Personal statements were expressed by Jack Welpott, born in Kansas City, Missouri, who collaborated with Judy Dater to produce *Women and Other Visions* (1977), and by Chicago's Anne Noggle, whose self-portraits documented the sagging flesh of old age in her book *Silver Lining* (1983).

Bruce Davidson of Oak Park, Illinois won the first National Endowment for the Arts grant in photography for his documentation of a Harlem street, *East 100th* (1968). Other Midwest-born photographers include Chicagoans Barbara Crane, Joseph Jachna, Wynn Bullock, Judith Golden, Betty Hahn, Bevans Davies, Charles Gatewood, and Eve Sonneman; Barbara Morgan (Buffalo, Kansas), Ralph Eugene Meatyard (Normal, Illinois), Scott Hyde (Montevideo, Minnesota), Will McBride (St. Louis), Kenneth Josephson (Detroit), Don Worth (Hays Center, Nebraska), Joan Callis (Cincinnati), Nicholas Nixon (Detroit), Jo Deal (Topeka, Kansas), Carollota Copron (Blue Earth, Minnesota), and Keith Smith (Tipton, Indiana).

Technological innovations and developments in the Midwest have ranged from the tintype to the hologram. Using magnesium flares, Charles Waldack of Cincinnati took the first photographs inside Mammoth Cave (1866); Cleveland photographer James F. Ryder introduced negative retouching to the Midwest (1902). In 1895 N. S. Amstutz of Cleveland described a technique for sending an engraving ready for the printing press, which led to the transmission of photographs by wire. The electronic strobe light was developed in 1931 by Harold Edgerton of Fremont, Nebraska. The Electrophot, invented by Thomas Rhamstine of Detroit, was the prototype of the Weston exposure meter (1932). In 1944 Chester Carlson, at the Battelle Research Institute in Columbus, improved his invention of the first dry photocopier, which, in 1959, became the 914 Xerox. In 1960, at the University of Michigan, Emmett Leith and Juris Upatnieks demonstrated the first practical use of lasers in the creation of transmission holograms.

In 1962 John Glenn, born in Cambridge, Ohio, using a Minolta Optiper automatic 35 millimeter camera he purchased in a drugstore, took the first hand-held photographs of Earth from space. On June 20,

1969, Neil Armstrong of Wapakoneta, Ohio, made the first portrait of a human being standing on the surface of the moon—that of fellow Apollo 11 astronaut Edwin "Buzz" Aldrin.

A symposium and exhibit titled "Digital Photography," held at the University of Minnesota, and the appearance of the magazine *Photo Electronic Imaging*, published by the Professional Photographers of America in 1991, confirmed the arrival of a new generation of image makers, including Nancy Burson, a native of St. Louis, who became one of the first important internationally known artists in the field of photoelectronic processing.

In a time of dissolving forms, technologies, and philosophies, classic dialogues on photography continue. Photographer Robert Fichter, in a rejection of traditional "straight" photography, wore a T-shirt imprinted with the legend "Weston is Dead!" Detroit-born Jerry Uelsmann, maker of composite silverprints, posted a sign on the door of his darkroom announcing that nineteenth-century combination-print-makers "Robinson and Rejlander Live!" Both Fichter and Uelsmann are former students of Henry Holmes Smith, a native of Bloomington, Illinois, and, later, a professor of photography at Indiana University.

The issue of art and morality, raised in England in 1857 over Oscar Rejlander's allegorical photograph *Two Ways of Life*, which included seminude models, surfaced in the American Midwest in 1990 when local law-enforcement officials unsuccessfully tried to ban Robert Mapplethorpe's sexually explicit photographs from display at the Contemporary Art Center in Cincinnati.

The aesthetic, philosophical, and academic influences of photographers, educators, and technologists born, raised, and educated in the Midwest have shaped the history of photography in America and the world.

Sources and Further Reading: Herbert Amelunxsen, Stefan Iglhaut, and Florian Rotzer, eds., *Photography after Photography: Memory and Representation in the Digital Age* (1996); Kathleen Collins, ed., *Shadow and Substance* (1990); Edward S. Curtis, *Portraits from North American Indian Life* (1972); Robert Doty, *Photo-Secession* (1960); Catherine Evans, "Inside and Outside: Midwest Photography in an Emerging Culture," in Robert Stearns, ed., *Illusions of Eden: Visions of the American Heartland* (2000); Jonathan Green, *American Photography: A Critical History, 1945 to the Present* (1984); Sadakicki Hartmann, *The Valiant Knights of Daguerre* (1978); Diana Emery Hulick with Joseph Marshall, *Photography: 1900 to the Present* (1998); Beaumont Newhall, *The History of Photography: From 1839 to the Present*, 5th ed. (1982); Miles Orvell, *American Photography* (2003); Theodore Peterson, *Magazines in the Twentieth Century* (1958); Floyd Rinhart and Marion Rinhart, *The American Daguerreotype* (1981); Robert Stearns, ed., *Illusions of Eden* (2002); John

Szarkowski, *Looking at Photographs* (1973); Robert Taft, *Photography and the American Scene: A Social History, 1839–1889* (1938); Alan Trachtenberg, *Reading American Photographs* (1989); John Waldsmith, *StereoViews* (1991); Claudia Watson, "Teaching through the Eye," *Timeline* (Nov. 2003).

Robert W. Wagner
The Ohio State University–Columbus

Farm Security Administration Photography

The Farm Security Administration (FSA) photographs of life in the United States during the years 1935 to 1943 remain the single most important visual legacy of that time for the nation and certainly for the Midwest. The FSA collection provides the most comprehensive view of American life during that eight-year period bounded by severe drought and economic depression on one end and America's participation in World War II on the other. Among the thousands of photographs in the collection are myriad images of lifestyles on rural farms and small towns across the Midwest.

In 1935 Rexford Tugwell, one of the members of Roosevelt's "Brain Trust," decided that for some of the controversial programs of the New Deal to succeed they would need the help of a public relations team. He named Roy Stryker, one of his former students from Columbia University, as head of the Historical Section and charged him with communicating the plight of the rural poor and the work of government programs to members of Congress and the American middle class in order to alleviate that poverty. Originally located in the Resettlement Administration (it was renamed the Farm Security Administration in 1937) and finally coming under the auspices of the Office of War Information (OWI) in 1942, the Historical Section employed eighteen photographers throughout the course of its existence. Six photographers took the majority of photographs of the Midwest between 1937 and 1943. Over the course of the eight-year existence of the Historical Section the photographers altered their focus away from Depression poverty toward the depiction of small-town life and the more patriotic, celebratory images needed for public support of the war.

Very few of the photographs from the Midwest became enduring national icons, although many are well known and have been widely circulated. The Midwest photographs provide a panorama of activities and livelihoods from the mid-1930s to the early 1940s, encompassing farming, rural and urban poverty and hardship, small-town parades and picnics, small factories changing over to war production, people sitting on porches, people bowling, kids playing, families gathered for dinner, and, of course, rehabilitation projects. Though a few of the images have been touted as fine art, the photographs are of most value as vernacular images, pictures that represent indigenous, ordinary, everyday activities and people in a specific historical time and place. Stryker was fond of saying that there is "not a single shot of Wall Street, and absolutely no celebrities" in the entire file. In distinguishing how his photographers differed from photojournalists, he said, "Newspictures are the noun and the verb; our kind of photography is the adjective and the adverb." As such we can appreciate the Midwest photographs best as natural and social landscapes. The photographers gave us a visual memory of the countryside not yet overrun by suburbs and highways. They depicted how individual farmers cleared and plowed their fields and sowed and harvested corn, wheat, and tomatoes, and how families tended dairy farms in Minnesota and Wisconsin before mechanization. The photographs remind us of the erosion and flooding along the Ohio River in 1937. The photographers moved in on their subjects to give us close-ups of how the community came together at harvest times and in crisis, the men loaning out their equipment and their bodies to help one another, the women baking and sewing together. The Midwest collection contains remarkable images of social landscapes disrupted by rural poverty in Iowa, farmers meeting bank officials at the edge of their property with pitchforks, and foreclosed farmers moving into shantytowns along the Mississippi in Dubuque. In depicting the separate shopping and eating establishments for blacks and whites they give evidence of a past social landscape the remnants of which are still with us.

As styles and practices of photography changed it was increasingly common for the photographers to shoot in series, or "photo-essays," and these have proven of great value to the study of life during that time because, taken together, they give a much more well-rounded image of activities and places than a single image ever could. Some of the better-known series from the Midwest include Jack Delano's 1943 multistate series on freight trains and Esther Bubley's 1943 cross-country Greyhound bus trip, both of which depict the Midwest readying for war. Other fascinating midwestern series are Russell Lee's Minnesota Logging Camp of 1937 and John Vachon's 1938 essay of street scenes, architecture, and small-town business activities in Omaha. Equally fascinating are lesser-known series such as Lee's February 1937 Closing Out Sale, on Indiana farmer Frank Sheroan's situation. As Robert Reid notes in *Back Home Again*, farm auctions "reached their peak in February as sellers anticipated the property tax assessment due on the first of March." Another series (176 photographs) by Vachon in July 1940 covers the migrant workers who traveled from Florida and Arkansas to Berrien County, Michigan, for the fruit-picking season. The photographs depict whole families working in the field, workers attending open-air movies on Saturday night, and the police monitoring the workers on their nights off. At the end of the season's work in one town we see scenes of families packing up the truck to move on. Such series offer tangible evidence of the difficult choices and conditions people faced in the Depression years. In the fullness of photographs representing the Depression, everyday activities of urban and rural life, and the regions' contributions to World War II, the Midwest photographs of the FSA collection testify to enduring lifeways and yield robust regional memories and identity.

The FSA-OWI photographs are available online through the Library of Congress American Memory website (http://memory.loc.gov/ammem/fsowhome. html), where *America from the Great Depression to World War II* contains around 165,000 negatives and transparencies from the FSA-OWI file and can be searched in a number of ways, including by proper names of both people and places. There are also several books that reproduce individual state collections of the photographs.

Sources and Further Reading: Carl Fleischhauer and Beverly Brannan, eds., *Documenting America, 1935–1943* (1988); Carl Mydans, *Ohio: A Photographic Portrait, 1935–1941* (1980); Robert Reid, ed., *Back Home Again: Indiana in the Farm Security Administration Photographs, 1935–1943* (1987); Robert Reid, *Picturing Minnesota, 1936–1943* (1989); Herbert K. Russell, *A Southern Illinois Album* (1990); Constance Schulz, ed., *Bust to Boom* (1996); Roy Stryker and Nancy Wood, *In This Proud Land* (1973); John M. Zielinski, *Unknown Iowa* (1977).

Catherine L. Preston
University of Kansas

Aaron Siskind (1903–1991)

Aaron Siskind was born in New York City in 1903, earned an undergraduate degree in literature at City College, and worked as an English instructor in the New York City public school system from 1926 to 1949. In 1929 Siskind received his first camera, as a honeymoon gift. He joined the New York Workers Film and Photo League in 1932. In 1936 it was reorganized as the New York Photo League; Siskind remained a member until 1941. In 1950 he worked as a part-time instructor of photography at Trenton College, New Jersey. He taught photography with Harry Callahan at Black Mountain College in Berea, North

Carolina, in 1951. He was hired that year as professor of photography at the Institute of Design in Chicago and held that position until 1971. He taught at the Rhode Island School of Design from 1971 to 1976. Siskind died in 1991.

As founder of the documentary photography unit of the New York Photo League, Siskind organized and worked on projects such as The Harlem Document. Having grown dissatisfied with documentary photography, Siskind made a breakthrough in 1944 while photographing on the docks at Gloucester, Massachusetts. He photographed an abandoned work glove, pointing his camera straight down, eliminating perspective, and creating an image that was simultaneously an evocative object and an abstraction. Siskind felt that "for some reason or other there was in me the desire to see the world clean and fresh and alive, as primitive things are clean and fresh and alive. The so-called documentary picture left me wanting something. . . . For the first time in my life, subject matter, as such, had ceased to be of primary importance. Instead, I found myself involved in the relationships of the objects, so much so that these pictures turned out to be deeply moving and personal experiences."

As a photographer, Siskind was a terrific painter. He adopted the modernist position, an uncompromising acceptance of the characteristics of his medium. He was, in fact, good friends with the first-generation abstract expressionists such as Willem de Kooning and Franz Kline, to whom he would later dedicate a portfolio.

It was in Chicago, teaching at the Institute of Design, that Siskind internalized the discovery he'd made on the Gloucester docks and began making the images he is most recognized for. Initially he photographed swimmers diving into Lake Michigan, single figures silhouetted against a white sky, not unlike the abandoned work glove, gestural and evocative. Following his assertion of the photograph as a two-dimensional surface, he began photographing flat surfaces, such as the sides of buildings. He moved closer and closer until his camera focused on small areas of urban surface, offering a pentimento or trace image of fragmentary images revealed by the abrasions of time and weather. Siskind's images are located at the boundary between chaos and meaning, and perhaps record the instant when chaos became meaning for him.

Sources and Further Reading: Jonathan Green, *American Photography: A Critical History, 1945 to the Present* (1984); Colin Naylor, ed., *Contemporary Photographers,* 2nd ed. (1988).

Lawrence Jasud
University of Memphis, Tennessee

Henry Holmes Smith (1909–1986)

Henry Holmes Smith, born in Bloomington, Illinois, in 1909, was a lifelong midwesterner. He attended State Normal College in Bloomington from 1927 to 1929 and 1930 to 1931, the School of the Art Institute of Chicago from 1929 to 1930, and the Ohio State University from 1932 to 1933, graduating with a bachelor of science degree in 1933. He taught photography at the New Bauhaus School of Design in Chicago from 1937 to 1938, worked as an independent photographer in Chicago from 1934 to 1946, and taught photography at Indiana University in Bloomington from 1947 to 1977. He died in 1986.

Smith organized two important national conferences. The first, in 1956, focused on interpreting the photograph and was attended by such important photographers as Minor White, Van Deren Coke, Ralph Eugene Meatyard, and Ralph Hattersley, among others. In 1962 he organized "Problems in Photographic Education." These conferences led directly to the 1963 founding of the Society for Photographic Education, which became the primary professional organization for university photography teachers. Smith served as its vice chairman from 1963 to 1967 and was a member of the board of directors.

As a member of the first post–World War II generation of university photography teachers, Smith's influence proliferated through some of his best students, who became teachers in turn. Among them were Jerry Uelsmann, Betty Hahn, Jack Welpott, and Robert Fichter. All important photographers and influential teachers, their styles were so individual and varied that no common influence is discernible. Rather than turning out copies of himself, Smith brought out the best and unique qualities in his students.

According to Fichter, "Henry's favorite question to his graduate students when I was there was: 'What should a photograph look like?' When you answered, he would just laugh and walk off." This attitude was contrary to the commonly held belief that photography enjoyed some special and direct relationship with reality. Making photographs that were other than a faithful and transparent description of visual experience was a betrayal of photography's essential nature. Clearly, Smith had little use for this attitude.

In his own work, Smith was equally unconventional. He worked in cliché-verre, making his negatives with syrup and water on glass plates, and printing them on black-and-white photo paper, or Dye Transfer Matrix film. The resulting matrices were printed with varied colors and in varying combinations to produce numerous variations of the same basic images. The final images, entirely abstract, suggested mythic archetypes, which Smith identified variously as Castor and Pollux, giants, the phoenix, or kings and queens. His work, like that of his students, resists easy characterization. Although the work itself is not widely known, Henry Holmes Smith's ideas and approach continue to influence succeeding generations of young photographers.

Sources and Further Reading: Howard Bossen, *Henry Holmes Smith: Man of Light* (1983); Jonathan Green, *American Photography: A Critical History, 1945 to the Present* (1984); Colin Naylor, ed., *Contemporary Photographers*, 2nd ed. (1988).

Lawrence Jasud
University of Memphis, Tennessee

Harry Callahan (1912–1999)

Harry Callahan was born in Detroit in 1912 and attended public school in Royal Oak, Michigan. He studied engineering at Michigan State College in East Lansing from 1931 to 1933 and went to work for Chrysler Motor Parts in 1934 (and then General Motors in 1944–1945). Callahan became interested in photography in about 1938, and was essentially self-taught.

In 1946 Laszlo Moholy-Nagy hired Callahan to teach photography at the Institute of Design in Chicago, where he taught until 1961. In 1951 he also taught at Black Mountain College in North Carolina. In 1961 he was hired to teach photography at the Rhode Island School of Design, where he remained until 1977. Throughout his life, Callahan won many awards and honors, including a Guggenheim Fellowship in 1972. He died in 1999.

As the story has it, Harry Callahan was working in the accounting department at Chrysler when he joined the Detroit Camera Club in order to pursue his interest in photography. In 1941 the club invited Ansel Adams to visit and show his work. This experience opened Callahan's eyes to the potential of photography. "His photographs and attitude freed me and made me realize that I didn't have to photograph the 'Grand Landscape' to make a good picture—that had already been done." Callahan turned his camera toward the people, events, and things of his daily life.

The Institute of Design was essentially the Bauhaus, a progressive German design school, transplanted to America. Moholy-Nagy's view of photography was that it was simply another medium to be explored to discover its characteristics and potentials, the camera just another kind of pencil or brush.

This approach became the foundation of Callahan's photographic work for the rest of his life. The product

of a keen visual intelligence, constant effort, and an unwavering faith that the resulting photographs would tell him what to do next, Callahan's work evolved steadily in sophistication, elegance, and depth over the next fifty years. Its beauty lies in its direct evocation of fundamental human experience and an elegant simplicity reminiscent of Shaker design.

Together with his colleague Aaron Siskind, at both the Institute of Design and the Rhode Island School of Design, Callahan profoundly influenced generations of students. Many went on to become teachers themselves and some of the most important contemporary American photographers. Among them are Ray K. Metzker, Emmett Gowin, Joseph D. Jachna, and Kenneth Josephson.

Sources and Further Reading: Harry Callahan, *Water's Edge* (1980); Jonathan Green, *American Photography: A Critical History, 1945 to the Present* (1984); Colin Naylor, ed., *Contemporary Photographers*, 2nd ed. (1988).

Lawrence Jasud
University of Memphis, Tennessee

Art Sinsabaugh (1924–1983)

Although born and raised in New Jersey, Art Sinsabaugh (1924–1983) is inextricably linked to the Midwest. Sinsabaugh came to Chicago in 1946 to study at the Institute of Design, where he was a student of Harry Callahan and, later, served on the faculty. This experience imbued Sinsabaugh with a strong foundation in abstract design and a love for environments.

In 1952 Sinsabaugh became acutely aware of the "unbelievable infinite detail" on the horizon. A twelve-by-twenty-inch banquet camera subsequently provided the ideal tool for capturing his vision, enabling him to produce large-format contact prints, which he cropped to evoke the sweeping vistas he saw in nature. Sinsabaugh captured the rhythms of human life through the forms—buildings, silos, highways, homes, skyscrapers, trees, and gravestones—that punctuate the midwestern landscape.

The evolution of his mature style coincided with his move downstate, where he served as a professor of photography at the University of Illinois from 1959 until his death. His two largest series—the Midwest and Chicago Landscape Groups—preserved a record of the changing Heartland. Sinsabaugh's images formed a perfect complement to Sherwood Anderson's poems in *6 Mid-American Chants/11 Midwest Landscapes* (1964) and illustrated Chicago's 1964 "Comprehensive Plan."

Sinsabaugh was recognized with numerous national

awards and fellowships from the Illinois Arts Council, the Graham Foundation, the Guggenheim, and the National Endowment for the Arts. His works are in many prestigious collections, including the Art Institute of Chicago and New York's Museum of Modern Art. His archive is housed at the Indiana University Art Museum.

Sources and Further Reading: Greg Daugherty, "Found Horizon: Art Sinsabaugh and the American Landscape," *Professional Photographer* 105 (Nov. 1978); Keith Davis, *American Horizons: The Photographs of Art Sinsabaugh* (2004); Allan Porter, "Art Sinsabaugh," *Camera* 6 (June 1972).

Nanette Esseck Brewer
Indiana University Art Museum, Bloomington

Sculpture

The Woodland Native American cultures in Ohio, Indiana, Michigan, and Illinois produced the first known sculpture in the Midwest. These cultures had a rich tradition of sculpture in stone, wood, bone, shell, and clay from at least the Late Archaic period (beginning about 4000 B.C.E.). Best known today are their elegant bird and banner stones and pipe bowls. The skill and artistic quality of these carvings would not be equaled by settlers of European descent until well into the nineteenth century.

During the early settlement of the Midwest by immigrants from the East Coast or Europe, a handful of artisans opened shops in the more populated areas and used their talents to make functional objects such as grave markers, decoys, weathervanes, decorative carvings for household and religious objects, and commercial signs such as cigar-store "Indians." An illustration of an early, skillful midwestern artisan can be seen in Thomas R. Reding of Salem, Indiana. Although originally trained as a cabinetmaker, Reding, during an 1833 cholera epidemic in Salem, turned to making sandstone-slab gravestones. These stones typically had shaped tops with relief carving of urns, willows, and birds coupled with incised inscriptions in both script and block letters. His trade born of necessity became his lifelong business.

In the Midwest, the production of European-type bronze and marble statuary could not provide a livelihood for sculptors unless an area had a sizable city with a sufficiently stable and wealthy population base to provide commissions to keep sculptors busy in their workshop. Until this condition was met, the best-known artists from the Midwest often sought not only their training but also their livelihood in Europe. Unlike painters, sculptors could not easily travel from

State Soldiers and Sailors Monument by Bruno Schmitz, 1902, Indianapolis. Library of Congress, Prints and Photographs Division, LC-D4-70022 DLC.

town to town with their materials and equipment to find work. Moreover, specialized training and equipment were necessary to produce marble and bronze statuary. Not until the last quarter of the nineteenth century did the climate for sculpture significantly change, although less populated areas lacked the conditions to produce sculpture well into the twentieth century.

In 1823 Frederick Eckstein, who had studied at the Academy in Berlin, settled in Cincinnati. One of his young protégés was Hiram Powers, brought by his family to Cincinnati from Vermont. Powers, employed at Watson's Clock Factory carving clocks, showed a talent for modeling and inventing mechanical devices and was hired to make wax effigies and automatic contrivances for *The Regions*, a large commercial installation in Cincinnati based on Dante's descriptions of hell. In 1829, under the patronage of Nicholas Longworth and encouraged by Eckstein, Powers went to study in Italy, the mecca of marble sculptors. He opened a studio in Florence where he produced, until his death, marble portrait busts of American statesmen and of the well-to-do as well as statuary of allegorical subjects.

Unlike the early gravestone artisans who chiseled directly into stone, European-trained sculptors modeled their statuary and busts in wax or clay that was subsequently copied in plaster and marble by others. Plaster busts of popular Americans often earned more revenue for the sculptor than the original commission had. Expatriate sculptors in Italy became the norm. Italy attracted sculptors with its abundance of skilled marble workers, its wealth of Renaissance sculpture, its low cost of living, and its large audience of buyers. By 1850 visits to American sculpture studios in Italy were popular with tourists.

In the second half of the nineteenth century, many of the sculptors who found work and a home in Midwest cities were immigrants: Norwegian-born Jacob Fjelde in the Twin Cities of Minnesota, Prussian-born Julius T. Melchers of Detroit, Italian-born Louis Rebisso of Cincinnati, and Danish-born Herman Matzen of Cleveland. Some of these men came as artisans, some arrived fully trained as sculptors, and some came to teach in newly established art schools. Others were like Leonard Volk, born in New York State, who moved with his father, a stonemason, to Illinois, then studied art in St. Louis and later in Europe, through the patronage of Stephen Douglas, before settling in Chicago in 1857. His son Douglas Volk became the first art director of the Minneapolis School of Art in 1886.

The Midwest's most famous citizen, Abraham Lincoln, also made the reputation of many a sculptor. If the sculptor's bust or statue of Lincoln had popular appeal, the demand for copies could make him not only famous but rich. The 1842 patent law permitted a sculptor to patent his work and have it cast or carved to order. Volk became famous for his mask of Lincoln cast from the latter's face while he was in Springfield in 1860, as well as for hands and busts of Lincoln made after his assassination.

The devastating Chicago fire of 1871 slowed down art production there for about ten years, but by 1890 the city was thriving again. The most notable sculptor was Lorado Taft, who not only employed legions of Midwest sculptors in his studio, many of them women, like Janet Scudder from Terre Haute and Bessie Potter Vonnoh from St. Louis, but also played a crucial part in Chicago's World's Columbian Exposition of 1893, seen by more than twenty-seven million people. The exposition exhibited Beaux-Arts-style sculpture that was sent to the fair as one-sixth-sized models to be enlarged in Chicago. Although European art, especially French and German, was the stylistic model for sculpture in the 1890s and the early twentieth century, the subject matter was frequently American and the size monumental. Subjects included not only famous statesmen but also allegorical subjects, such as Taft's *Fountain of the Great Lakes* (1913) and Native Americans, like his 48-foot-high *Black Hawk* (1911).

From 1876 until the end of World War I, the most important source of income for sculptors became civic commissions for public monuments and buildings. In 1905 B. F. Ferguson donated one million dollars to commission monuments for Chicago's public parks. In the larger cities, these monuments were elaborate buildings, obelisks, columns, and fountains, surrounded by or encrusted with sculpture. Sculpture was also needed for newly built statehouses that were modeled on the neoclassical buildings of Washington, D.C. Sculptors for these projects came from not only the Midwest but also Europe and New York City. Cities selected a sculptor based on small models that were later enlarged in plaster and sent, after approval of the city, to a bronze foundry or to a carver to be completed and shipped by rail or steamer to their final location. Although the American Brass Company of Chicago was a common foundry choice in the 1890s, a Midwest sculptor might send his work to Paris or Philadelphia for casting. A full-length, life-size or larger figure sculpture was sand cast in bronze using many molds that would be assembled later into the figure. The resulting bronze, sometimes weighing as much as 34,000 pounds, was mounted on a stone pedestal. Such massive monuments would have been impossible for an inland city before the advent of railroads.

The number of sculptors employed by the Columbian Exposition and other expositions, like the 1904 World's Fair in St. Louis, created a shortage of experienced sculptors. The largest monument in the Midwest was Indianapolis's Soldiers and Sailors Monument, begun in 1888 by German architect Bruno Schmitz. The 314-foot-high obelisk-shaped monument surrounded by a large circular plaza and fountains called for numerous bronze sculptures. Unable to recruit enough American sculptors capable of carrying out all the ambitious plans for the monument, Schmitz eventually brought in Rudolph Schwarz, a Vienna-trained sculptor who had worked for Schmitz in Berlin. Schwarz had huge blocks of stone brought directly to the site, where he carved them himself. After the completion of the monument in 1902, Schwarz remained in Indianapolis the rest of his life doing a limited amount of work because, unlike other sculptors of the era, he did his own carving and, later, his own casting. By employing a lost-wax casting method that traditionally had been used only for small bronzes, he was able to make lighter, more accurate casts than sand-casting methods produced. The 11-foot-high, 8,000-pound bronze *Governor Pingree* (1903) in Detroit is an example of his lost-wax casting.

The demand for commemorative statues reached its apogee around 1900. By 1925 even a former student of Taft's, Janet Scudder, would condemn the commissioning of public monuments as an art form that was blighting American cities. Despite the establishment of art schools and sculpture studios like Taft's, midwestern artists continued to go to the East Coast and Europe to both train and work. Midwestern sculptors born in the waning years of the century would be among the first American sculptors to reject the premises of Beaux-Arts naturalism and, later, its workshop production methods. Some, like Chicagoan John H. Storrs, experimented with European modernism, making abstract sculpture as early as 1920. Although he lived in France as much as possible, Storrs returned to Chicago in the 1930s to make sculptures like his aluminum *Ceres* (1930), which surmounts the Chicago Board of Trade Building. Others, like North Dakotan John B. Flannagan, William Zorach, a Russian immigrant from Cleveland, and Cleveland-born Hugo Robus, carved rudimentary and simplified masses directly into stone or wood but never embraced the geometric or organic abstraction of European modernism.

Paul Manship from St. Paul, the most famous and financially successful of this generation, straddled the old and the new. He adhered to the traditional techniques of modeling in plaster for transformation into bronze that he learned in New York from beaux-arts sculptor Solon Borglum, an ex-cowboy who grew up in Fremont, Nebraska, and was known for his animal sculptures. But from his study of preclassical Greek sculpture, Manship developed a distinct new style of simplified smooth forms embellished with stylized linear ornament that came to be known as art deco. In 1928 the Lincoln National Life Insurance Company of Fort Wayne, Indiana, commissioned *Abraham Lincoln–The Hoosier Youth*, a 12-foot bronze outdoor work. His sculpture in Rockefeller Plaza, New York City is his best known today.

While artists born in the Midwest migrated to Europe and the East Coast, Europeans, hired as teachers and for other artistic projects, migrated to the Midwest. In 1923 Eliel Saarinen and his wife and son Eero emigrated from Finland to Bloomfield Hills, Michigan, to build Cranbrook Academy of Art, and in 1930 Swede Carl Milles became resident sculptor there. At Indiana University, France's Robert Laurent, a direct stone carver, came to teach sculpture in 1942. Hungarian Laszlo Moholy-Nagy from the Bauhaus arrived in Chicago to direct the Institute of Design. The impact of the Institute of Design can be seen on the next generation of sculptors like fabric sculptor Claire Zeisler; George Rickey, known for his moving stainless-steel, geometric sculptures; and Richard Lippold, known for his dramatic steel-wire constructions.

Unlike Manship's generation, the sculptors that were born between 1900 and World War I would adopt and transform European modernism in a dramatic fashion. Men like Lippold, Charles Biederman, Theodore Roszak, and David Smith all trained briefly in the Midwest before going east. Unlike Manship, these men all approached sculpture from a painter's perspective rather than a sculptor's. Their early inspiration was European painters like Piet Mondrian or Pablo Picasso, not sculptors like Auguste Rodin, Emile Bourdelle, or Constantin Brancusi. Often their first sculptures were relief structures. They found meaning and beauty in industrial materials, geometric structures, and technology that had brought the Midwest prosperity with its railroads, mills, and manufacturing plants.

Smith, more than any other sculptor of his generation, understood that the properties of steel could lead to a whole new type of sculpture where lines and planes of steel could replace the bronze, stone, and wood masses of traditional sculpture. In the 1950s, Smith's welded steel work, shown throughout the Midwest, initially inspired several generations of sculpture students, such as John Chamberlain, David von Schlegell, Richard Hunt, and Michael Todd.

A contemporary of Chamberlain, Donald Judd developed nonrepresentational sculptures of industrial materials that were known for the extreme clarity of their forms, volumes, and colors. These sculptures in part grew from the lifelong love he developed for the open, uncluttered spaces of the Midwest that he experienced as a child growing up in Omaha, Kansas City,

Missouri, and Des Moines and spending summers on his grandparents' farm in Excelsior Springs, Missouri. In later life he built his home and studio in the open spaces of Marfa, Texas.

Steel sculpture provided new possibilities for a public art that could be modern and be outdoors. Three landmark works were put up in the late 1960s that set the tone for public sculpture the way the Columbian Exposition had in 1893: Eero Saarinen's *Gateway Arch* (1966), a 630-foot stainless steel arch in St. Louis; Pablo Picasso's 50-foot-high Cor-Ten steel head of a woman (1967) in Chicago; and Alexander Calder's red-painted steel stabile *La grande vitesse* (1969) in Grand Rapids, Michigan. All three works became icons for their respective cities. Throughout the remainder of the twentieth century, outdoor sculpture, often funded partially by city, state, and/or federal funds, appeared in newly formed sculpture parks, city plazas, and airports and in front of corporate headquarters throughout the Midwest. The Chicago Picasso was fabricated at a nearby steel company by industrial steelworkers who had the skill as well as the equipment to lift, cut, bend, shape, and weld enormous pieces of steel plate into an enlarged version of Picasso's maquette for the sculpture. Only artists as famous as Calder and Picasso could hope to receive a commission to fabricate such enormous, expensive sculptures. Initially most metal sculpture was built by welding together preexisting shapes. Art schools and universities did not offer the training or equipment for their students or faculty to do otherwise. Some sculptors, like Claes Oldenburg, made fanciful drawings that showed everyday objects, like baseball bats or spoons, as enormous outdoor sculptures. Many years later, fabricators made his depictions into the Chicago *Bat Column* (1976) and *Spoonbridge and Cherry for Minneapolis* (1988). Others, like Chicagoans Richard Hunt and Jerry Peart, put together their own industrial shops to make outdoor pieces. But by the 1970s, many large midwestern universities had fine arts departments with equipment and faculty capable of making large outdoor steel sculptures. The universities attracted sculptors from elsewhere to teach the hundreds of art students who enrolled each year.

With the sculptors and equipment available, outdoor sculpture parks and exhibitions as well as commissions for civic and corporate sculptures sprang up throughout the Midwest. One of the more unusual projects was the 1976 Nebraska Bicentennial Committee's placement of outdoor sculptures at highway rest stops along the Nebraska portion of Interstate 80. Throughout the rest of the century, outdoor sculpture parks would be built by numerous private individuals, such as the Harry Lynde Bradley family in Milwaukee; by museums, such as the Sheldon Art Museum at the University of Nebraska in Lincoln; by nonprofit groups such as those that founded Laumeier Sculpture Park in 1976 in St. Louis; and by corporations like General Mills Inc. in Minneapolis. By 2002 nearly all the art museums in the Midwest had sculpture gardens to complement their indoor galleries.

Although the initial impetus for the revival of outdoor sculpture after World War II came in the form of steel sculpture, many other types of outdoor sculpture have been made in the last fifty years. As large metal sculpture came to be associated with business and civic interests, much the way the nineteenth century's commemorative bronzes were, younger artists in the 1970s began making sculptures that were designed to enhance a particular landscape and to speak to some facet of the local culture of the area. Sometimes these works, made of temporal materials, were intended to last for a limited amount of time and then be dismantled or simply disintegrate in the weather. At other times, the works were intended to last but needed maintenance in the form of landscaping or replacement parts like light fixtures or periodic weatherproofing. Sculptures often served a useful purpose by doubling as shelters, bridges, or furniture.

While there have always been women sculptors, successful women sculptors were unusual until the 1970s, when young women, as well as men, began setting the trends in new types of outdoor sculpture. Donna Dennis's *Mad River Tunnel* (1981), now dismantled, was a small wooden building suggestive of an entrance to a tunnel in Dayton, Ohio. Martin Puryear's sculpture at the Nathan Manilow Sculpture Park in University Park in Chicago consists of paths and boardwalks through a marshy field that culminate at a bronze bench beneath a hedgerow. Siah Armajani of Minneapolis is best known for a sculpture that functions as a pedestrian bridge used to enter the Walker Art Museum's outdoor sculpture garden, and he has constructed a reading garden in Omaha and a book store in Cincinnati as well as another bridge for the General Mills Corporation. Dale Eldred is well known in Kansas City for his light works. The City Beautiful program in Dayton, Ohio, brought artists on a regular basis to make temporary outdoor installations around the city in the 1970s. Other midwestern cities also brought in artists to design special installations. One of the more unusual ones was the 1974 earth sculpture of Kansas City (Missouri)–born Robert Morris in Grand Rapids, Michigan, where he transformed an eroded hillside in a recreation area into a mammoth geometric earthwork. In addition, the Midwest has a number of works by self-taught artists, like Samuel Dinsmoor's *Garden of Eden* installation (1907–1929) in Lucas, Kansas, and Fred Smith's *Concrete Park* (1950–1964) in Phillips, Wisconsin.

Although outdoor sculpture garnered the most public attention and the bulk of the government and corporate money, a more personal kind of sculpture appeared in the Midwest. Sculptors for these works drew inspiration from lowbrow American culture and depicted easily recognized and often banal objects, like food, such as hamburgers and corn on the cob; signage; city apartment buildings; ordinary middle-class people; cartoon characters; tools; toilets; and toys. These artists used domestic materials like Styrofoam, cloth, wood, discarded objects, paint, and plastic as well as durable metals. Their creations were often both amusing and naughtily sexual. People labeled these sculptures pop, funk, or imagist art, depending on whether they were made in New York, San Francisco, or Chicago. The images, like many of the artists, often had roots in the Midwest and the art was widely collected in the Midwest. Like the steel sculptors, most of these sculptors were painters who saw sculpture as paintings that came off the wall. Many of the pieces had an implied narrative. A few of the better-known popular-culture artists from the Midwest were Oldenburg, Robert Indiana (aka Robert Clark), Roy Lichtenstein, Karl Wirsum, H. C. Westermann, Tom Wesselman, William Wiley, Duane Hanson, Judy Chicago (aka Judith Cohen), Roger Brown, and Jim Dine. Oldenburg, Indiana, Brown, Wirsum, Wiley, and Westermann all attended the School of the Art Institute in Chicago. Dine, Lichtenstein, and Wesselman received their art training in Ohio, while Hanson attended Cranbrook Academy of Art in Michigan.

Another sculptor from the Midwest who also relies on very common everyday objects and words and actions for his subject matter is Bruce Nauman, who spent most of his youth and his college years in Wisconsin. Sound, video, moving objects, and flashing neon signs of Nauman's works invade the viewer's space aggressively. In his work one feels that everyday American life is spinning out of control. Nauman, like Wiley, Westermann, and Chicago, practiced in California. Oldenburg, Hansen, Wesselman, Dine, Indiana, and Lichtenstein migrated to the East. Wirsum and Brown remained in Chicago; Westermann worked and lived on both coasts as well as in Chicago. Like Americans in all walks of life, American sculptors move to those areas where they think their chosen careers might flourish. Whether they lived in the Midwest all their life, migrated to the Midwest or migrated from the Midwest, midwestern sculptors have played a major role in American culture through their sculptures and public monuments.

Sources and Further Reading: Ira J. Bach and Mary Lackritz Gray, *A Guide to Chicago's Public Sculpture* (1983); Dennis Barrie, Jeanie Huntley Bentley, Cynthia Helms Newman and Rosp, eds., *Artists in Michigan, 1900–1976: A Biographical Dictionary* (1989); Board of Commissioners of the State of Indiana's Soldiers and Sailors Monument, *1st*, *2nd*, and *3rd Report* (1887, 1888, 1890); Porter Butt, *Art in Wisconsin* (1936); Rena Neumann Coen, *Painting and Sculpture in Minnesota, 1820–1914* (1976); Holliday T. Day, with contributions by Dore Ashton and Lena Vigna, *Crossroads of American Sculpture* (2000); Arthur Hopkin Gibson, *Artists of Early Michigan* (1975); Mary Sayre Haverstock, Jeanette Mahoney Vance, and Brian Meggitt, eds., *Artists in Ohio, 1787–1900* (1900); Franklin Mead, *Heroic Statues in Bronze of Abraham Lincoln* (1932); Zenobia Ness and Louise Orwig, *Iowa Artists of the First Hundred Years* (1939); Ann Nolan and Keith A. Buckley, *Indiana Stonecarver* (1984); Ernestine Rose, *The Circle* (1971); Eero Saarinen, *Eero Saarinen on His Work* (1962); Esther Sparks, "A Biographical Dictionary of Painters and Sculptors in Illinois, 1808–1945," 2 vols., Ph.D. diss., Northwestern University (1971); Theodore Stempfel, Sr., *Ghosts of the Past* (1935); Joseph Stuart, ed., *Index of South Dakota Artists* (1975); Lorado Taft, *History of American Sculpture* (1903); Lorado Taft, *Modern Tendencies in Sculpture* (1921).

Holliday T. Day
Indianapolis

Cast and Constructed

There was no regionalist movement for sculpture in the Midwest as there was for painting, which enjoyed popular success in the early twentieth century through such major figures as Thomas Hart Benton, Grant Wood, and John Steuart Curry. There is no particular theme that carries through sculpture produced in the Midwest. Geographical separation from the coasts has allowed modern midwesterners the ability to cultivate their own opinions and follow their own rules, so to speak. Not tied to the constraints of ideologies that rule the edges of the United States, artists and the general population of the region have been able to pick and choose what trends they would or would not like to follow and how to do so. And vernacular art, with its strong wood-carving and mixed-media traditions, has always coexisted with more traditional methods of sculpture in the Midwest. Such methods—public sculpture projects and art-school traditions of cast and constructed sculpture—flourish in a region full of pride.

In the nineteenth and the early twentieth centuries, professionally trained artists in the Midwest were schooled in European styles; instructors had either come directly from Europe or were trained in Europe. At that time, midwestern media did not differ from media in other parts of the country. After 1850 sculptors began to use foundries, originally constructed to cast cannons or utilitarian objects, for making sculpture. Sculptures of the late 1800s and early 1900s were generally modeled in plaster and cast in bronze or carved from marble.

In the nineteenth century, neoclassical revival traditions prevailed as America looked to the world of ancient Greece for models of political systems, art, and architecture. The classical concept of the beautiful human body was combined with North American subject matter to produce portraits of such notables as Abraham Lincoln or Black Hawk. Great expositions that happened in midwestern cities—such as the World's Columbian Exposition in Chicago in 1893 and the World's Fair in St. Louis in 1904—with their grand buildings, fountains, and public sculpture and the preparatory assignments that brought many artists to the cities for great amounts of time, were significant avenues of exposure to Beaux-Arts styles for artists in America and particularly for those in the Midwest. Sculptors were inspired by the grand buildings and monumental sculptures and the ways that architects and sculptors worked together for the overall design. This partnership was utilized for public spaces as well as private buildings.

A midwestern tradition of cast-bronze public sculpture parallels the outdoor sculpture park environments popular with many midwestern vernacular artists. Since the nineteenth century, with interest waning and renewing at various times, public sculpture has been particularly prevalent in many major metropolitan areas—Chicago being the prime example in the Midwest.

During the nineteenth and the early part of the twentieth century, Lorado Taft became the greatest proponent of traditional sculpture in the Midwest, and his influence spread internationally. Born in Illinois, he studied in Europe and the United States and, eventually, became an instructor himself in Chicago. Influential for his sculptures as well as his teaching and writing, he hoped to create a great museum of sculpture in Chicago. His monumental, heroic sculptures were cast in bronze or carved marble and were often used for public spaces. Clearly an advocate of classical sculpture, he was aware of but avoided the modernist abstract impulses of Europeans. Taft's opposition to abstraction and the onset of modernism in general is not to be taken as a sign of popular artistic opinion of the Midwest at the beginning of the twentieth century.

In the 1930s and 1940s, major shifts in sculpture occurred across the United States and western Europe. While cast sculpture was still being used for public commissions, artists began to learn how to weld and how to use welding in their repertory of techniques, and they utilized mechanisms that allowed sculptural forms to move and began to turn to found objects as viable sources of materials for their sculpture. The technique of welding allowed for greater dimension and variability in sculpture, and midwestern artists recognized the opportunities for change and a broader technical vocabulary that would allow them to expand their ideas.

Richard Hunt has been a major Midwest proponent of open-form welding. Born and raised in Chicago, he was influenced by the welded sculpture of Spaniard Julio Gonzales and Indiana-born sculptor David Smith, an artist who was changing the face of sculpture in America during the formative years of Hunt's art education. Hunt would scour junkyards for materials—copper, iron, aluminum, steel, machine parts—welding them into abstract shapes that retain a connection to nature—animal, plant, human. Through his work and his teaching Hunt has played an important role in the history of art and sculpture in Chicago and the nation.

Additive types of sculpture—like the welding of Hunt—became more and more commonplace as the twentieth century progressed and as art markets evolved that demanded a certain number of objects. This kind of sculpture was also much easier to produce in a studio, where a sculptor did not have to rely on the large machines and materials necessary to cast sculpture in a foundry. A Chicago artist who combined old traditions with new and reflects the individualist tendencies of the Midwest is H. C. Westermann. Born in Los Angeles, he studied at the School of the Art Institute of Chicago and lived and worked in Chicago, where he made a significant contribution to the artistic flavor of the city and the region. While he was a master wood-carver, his sculptures were usually constructed and embellished rather than completely carved. He also incorporated found objects and materials. Other innovative sculptors born and raised in part in the Midwest, like William T. Wiley and Bruce Nauman, cite Westermann's irreverence, humor, and maverick approach to art making as major influences on their own work.

While constructed sculpture—a general designation for three-dimensional objects built with an additive process, whether it be welded metal, found object accumulations, or other—can be produced at almost any time and anywhere, cast sculpture requires particular conditions to be realized. The actual techniques of cast sculpture have not changed for hundreds of years; while new materials are being used for casting—not just bronze and iron but also plaster, resin, metals, and more—the actual task of carrying out the casting has not changed. Even today, sculptors—in the Midwest and beyond—have to rely on a foundry to cast their work, and so major cast sculptures are still usually the product of a commission.

There are notable midwestern artists making innovations in the field of cast sculpture. Carolyn Ottmers, a sculpture professor at the School of the Art Institute of Chicago for the last decade, makes multiple cast forms inspired by both the natural and the urban landscape. Her objects—cast with a variety of materials including concrete, wax, paper, rubber, glass, aluminum, and iron—represent a desire to experiment. Her presence and influence in the Midwest have promoted opportunities for artists, especially women, in the field of cast sculpture. In addition, programs like the internationally recognized Arts/Industry Program, a joint effort of the John Michael Kohler Arts Center in Sheboygan, Wisconsin, and the Kohler Company in Kohler, Wisconsin, give recognition to the region. Since 1974 the Arts/Industry Program has allowed hundreds of artists to create new work in residencies that give them access to major industrial foundry processes.

Sources and Further Reading: Tom Armstrong et al., *200 Years of American Sculpture* (1976); Jan Garden Castro, "Richard Hunt: Freeing the Human Soul," *Sculpture* 17 (May/June 1998); Holliday T. Day, with contributions by Dore Ashton and Lena Vigna, *Crossroads of American Sculpture* (2000); Jane McCarthy and Laurily K. Epstein, *A Guide to the Sculpture Parks and Gardens of America* (1996); Lynne Warren, ed., *Art in Chicago 1945–1995* (1996).

Lena Vigna
John Michael Kohler Arts Center, Wisconsin

Lorado Taft (1860–1936)

Lorado Taft was born in Elmwood, Illinois, in 1860, and his family moved to Champaign after his father, Don Carlos Taft, earned a post at Illinois Industrial University (after 1885 known as the University of Illinois). Throughout his career Lorado displayed an intense loyalty to both the university and the hometown of his youth. He was introduced to art by John Milton Gregory, regent of the university and founder of its art gallery. Taft graduated in 1879, received a master of literature degree in 1880, and continued his studies at the École des Beaux Arts in Paris in the atelier of Augustin Dumont from 1880 until 1883. Impervious to the avant-garde developments in Paris during his stay, Taft advocated a conservative, academic approach to sculpture in his practice and in his later lectures. Upon returning to America in 1885, Taft married Carrie Louise Scales, settled in Chicago, and set himself to the task of awakening an appreciation of sculpture in his compatriots. He described his *Fountain of the Great Lakes,* dedicated near the Art Institute of Chicago in September 1913, as a pivotal work in his career. This bronze group with five female figures spilling water from tilted shells was an important sign of the changing cultural scene in Chicago during the early twentieth century and resulted, in part, from a rise in public interest in civic beautification. In 1919 Taft was appointed nonresident professor at the University of Illinois; his annual lectures on sculpture attracted large audiences. He also taught courses at the Art Institute of Chicago and the University of Chicago, and his *History of American Sculpture* (1903) remains a standard text in the field. Taft died in 1936.

Sources and Further Reading: Timothy J. Garvey, *Public Sculptor: Lorado Taft and the Beautification of Chicago* (1988); Lorado Taft, *The History of American Sculpture* (1903); Allen Stuart Weller, *Lorado in Paris* (1985).

Wendy Koenig
The Ohio State University–Columbus

David Smith (1906–1965)

David Smith, world famous for his welded-steel sculptures, grew up in the agricultural communities of Decatur, Indiana (his 1906 birthplace), and Paulding, Ohio. After graduation from Paulding High School, a summer spent working as a welder at the Studebaker plant in South Bend, Indiana, and a year of study at Ohio University, Smith moved to the East Coast in 1926. In New York City he encountered the ideas of cubism. In 1933 he made his first welded-steel and iron sculpture, *Agricola Head.* In 1955, while visiting Indiana University, he completed ten of eleven *Forgings,* thin vertical sculptures made from steel bars and ranging from sixty-seven to ninety inches in height. The next year he made *History of Leroy Borton* to honor LeRoy Borton, an Indiana metalworker who worked in the shop where Smith made *Forgings.* Following his stay in Bloomington, Smith returned to his home in Bolton Landing, New York, where he continued to work until his death in an auto accident in 1965. Between 1932 and 1965 Smith made more than seven hundred sculptures. His adventurous experimentation with a wide range of styles, techniques, and materials; his complex imagery; his lively combinations of forms and linear elements; and his invention of unusual surface treatments for sculpture set Smith apart from his peers as a pioneer in the development of twentieth-century sculpture. His stainless steel *Cubi* sculptures (1961–1965), with their distinctive calligraphic surfaces, are his best-known works. He said that his sacrifices to be a pioneer sculptor were akin to the hardships his ancestors endured to settle in the wilderness of the Midwest.

Sources and Further Reading: Holliday T. Day, with contributions by Dore Ashton and Lena Vigna, *Crossroads of American Sculpture* (2000); Rosalind E. Krauss, *The Sculpture of David Smith—A Catalogue Raisonné* (1977).

Holliday T. Day
Indianapolis

Harvey K. Littleton (b. 1922)

Known for promoting artist-produced glass and initiating the studio glass movement, Harvey K. Littleton espoused the value of an individual artist's freely exploring glass as a material for artistic expression, and he sought ways to make glass available as a medium outside of the industrial tradition of factory produc-

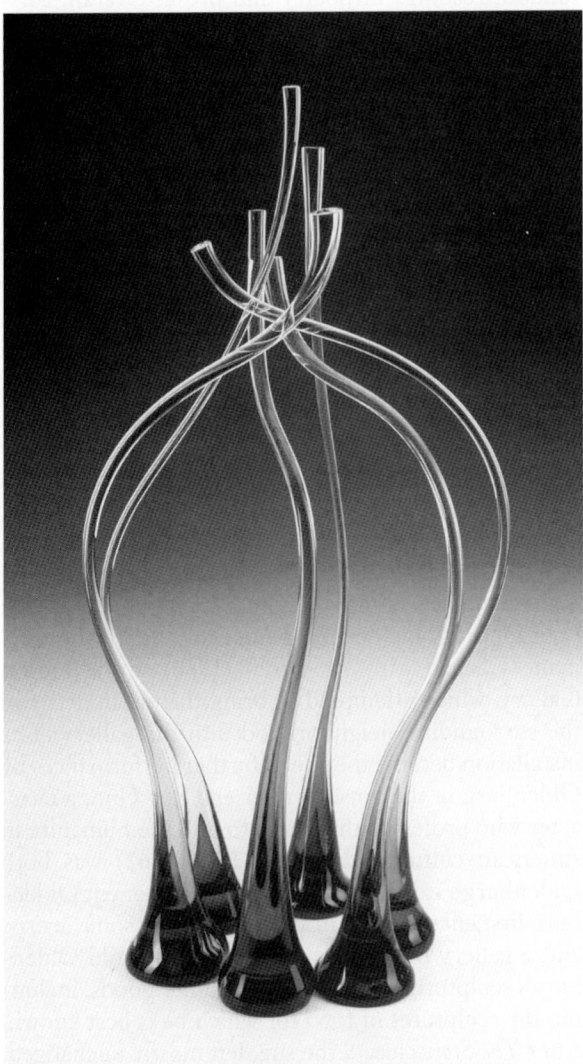

Harvey K. Littleton's *Implied Movement*, 1986. Smithsonian American Art Museum, Washington, D.C./Art Resource, NY, ART189109.

tion. He was born in 1922 in Corning, New York, where his father was a physicist in the glass industry. He studied at Brighton School of Art in England in 1945 and earned an undergraduate degree in design at the University of Michigan in 1947. He received a master of fine arts degree in 1951 from Cranbrook Academy of Art in Bloomfield Hills, Michigan, a creative environment that included noted teachers Charles Eames and Eero Saarinen. In 1951 Littleton joined the art faculty of the University of Wisconsin, Madison, to teach ceramics. A decade into his appointment, he successfully convinced the Toledo Museum of Art in Ohio to hold two glass-art workshops. The 1962 workshops explored how artists might create glass-studio equipment suitable for solo use and then explore techniques for blowing glass. In 1963 Littleton established a glass-art education program, the first ever in a university, at the University of Wisconsin, which subsequently produced a generation of studio glass artists and teachers, including Dale Chihuly, Bruce Chao, Fritz Dreisbach, Henry Halem, Kent Ipsen, Gene Koss, Marvin Lipofsky, Tom McGlauchlin, and many others. Littleton retired in 1977. He currently lives and works in Penland, North Carolina, where he is pioneering a technique for creating prints utilizing glass plates, which he dubs "vitreography."

Sources and Further Reading: Joan Falconer Byrd, *Interview with Harvey K. Littleton;* Nanette L. Laitman, Documentation Project for Craft and Decorative Arts in America (2001); Harvey Littleton, *Glassblowing: A Search for Form* (1971); William Warmus, "A Fire in the Studio: Harvey Littleton," *Glass* (Autumn 1998).

Richard Harned
The Ohio State University

H. C. Westermann (1922–1981)

Horace Clifford "H.C." Westermann, Jr., was born in Los Angeles in 1922. After graduating from high school he moved to the Pacific Northwest, where he worked in the logging industry. In 1942 he enlisted in the U.S. Marine Corps and was stationed aboard the USS *Enterprise.* He died in 1981.

Although Westermann did not come to the Midwest until 1947, when he enrolled in the School of the Art Institute of Chicago, his work bears the distinctive outlook and spirit of tolerance that defines that region. Westermann refused to submit to the ideological agendas of any of the avant-garde movements of the time, allowing him to create works of art that synthesized various approaches in an eclectic but highly original manner. For instance, in his 1965 sculpture *A Piece from the Museum of Shattered Dreams*, Westermann combined his love of wood carving and American folk art with the prosaic objects of everyday life admired by pop artists (the object represented in his sculpture resembling a cooked ham) and the conceptual incongruities typical of surrealism (shark fins protruding from the base of his sculpture for no apparent reason). In Westermann's work middle American ingenuity meets avant-garde shock and surprise.

Westermann's art has been included in many prestigious national and international exhibitions. It can be found in public and private collections in both the United States and Europe. In 1961 Westermann and his wife moved to Brookfield Center, Connecticut, where he lived until his death in 1981.

Source and Further Reading: Lynne Warren and Michael Rooks, eds., *H.C. Westermann* (2001).

Steven Hunt
The Ohio State University–Columbus

Richard Hunt (b. 1935)

Richard Hunt was born in Chicago in 1935. In 1957 he graduated from the School of the Art Institute of Chicago with a bachelor of arts degree in art. In his early work Hunt developed a profound technical virtuosity in the medium of welded-steel sculpture, placing himself in a tradition that can be traced back to Pablo Picasso. At that time Hunt's work was distinguished by open, flowing, linear forms that hover between abstraction and figural imagery, and he was one of only a very few African American artists who were exploring and extending the formal vocabulary of modernist art.

After a retrospective exhibition at the Museum of Modern Art in New York in 1971, which secured his status as a major artist, Hunt became interested in the possibility of creating large outdoor public sculptures that could be experienced by a wide audience. In 1977 he was commissioned to create a work to memorialize Martin Luther King, Jr., at the King Memorial in Memphis. The resulting sculpture, titled *I Have Been to the Mountain*, is made of welded steel and incorporates the functions of altar and playground furniture. Children (and adults) are routinely seen climbing on it. Hunt's unique contribution to the concept of public sculpture in this and other works is to bring the members of a community together not just by sacralizing the memory of a place or person but by creating opportunities for those members to discover one another anew through a specific shared experience.

Source and Further Reading: Elsa Honig Fine, *The Afro-American Artist* (1982).

Steven Hunt
The Ohio State University–Columbus

Performance Art

Performance art in the United States has many close ties with the Midwest, both through its early practitioners and in its later exhibition. It developed out of the multimedia musical performances of John Cage at Black Mountain College in North Carolina. Those performances, beginning in 1952, involved not only audio components, typically consisting of silence meant to heighten the audience's awareness of its own audible presence, but also some recorded sound and random readings of poetry and prose. Overall, early performance art embraced multiple art forms, all of which were largely based on a time-limited experience. Because the art form lacked a salable object beyond documentary photographs and videos, in contrast to painting and sculpture, performance art tended to occupy the fringes of the New York gallery scene. Indeed, such works were often presented in alternative spaces or even in the street.

It is notable that some of the most important early performance artists were born, raised, or trained in the Midwest. Claes Oldenburg (b. 1929), the son of a Swedish diplomat, spent his early years in New York and Oslo until he moved to Chicago with his family at the age of seven. Except for his years of undergraduate study at Yale in the late 1940s, Oldenburg remained in Chicago until 1954, working as a reporter and taking classes at the Art Institute of Chicago alongside nationally known local artists H.C. Westermann and Robert Indiana. After Oldenburg arrived in New York City in 1956, his environmental installations/performances began with *The Street* (1960) at the Judson Gallery, which attempted to bring the urban decay of the surrounding neighborhood into the gallery. The installation became the site of further performances by Oldenburg in the guise of alter ego Ray Gun, a character who professed the desire to find the humanity in American culture. *The Store* (1961–1962) was both Oldenburg's storefront studio, an arrangement Oldenburg first encountered in Chicago among some artists, and a gallery of sorts that exhibited and sold Oldenburg's sculptures of common consumer goods, including the sculptures of food for which he is best known. After *The Store* closed, the site, left mostly unchanged, became the venue of a series of Ray Gun performances in the back room.

Oldenburg's attachment to what can be called a

Gesamtkunstwerk, or a total work of art, which includes multiple media to create a complete environment, has its roots in not only European modernism but also the early-twentieth-century American architecture of Frank Lloyd Wright, whose homes and buildings were very visible in the Chicago area. Wright's desire to create a total environment, complete with furniture and windows, that was in harmony with its surroundings is not very different from Oldenburg's decision to embrace the environment outside the gallery as a backdrop for his performances.

Another artist whose interest in language and the body has led him to performance art is Bruce Nauman. Born in Fort Wayne, Indiana, in 1941, Nauman remained in the Midwest to study at the University of Wisconsin between 1960 and 1964. Further rejecting the New York gallery scene, Nauman moved to California, where he studied for a master of fine arts degree at the University of California at Davis with the sculptor Robert Arneson. Nonetheless, Nauman's approach was always more conceptual than sculptural, as is evident in the 1966–1967 performance *Eating My Words*, in which Nauman ate his sculpture of the word *words*. Such linguistic play forms the basis of works like his 1966–1967 *Waxing Hot*, a photograph in which Nauman's hands are visible polishing a sculpture of the word *Hot*. Ultimately, Nauman's turn to video culminates in installations like *World Peace (Received)* (1996), shown through December 2003 at the St. Louis Art Museum, a work in which a group of five video monitors is positioned around one stool and each monitor shows a different person discussing world peace while running through all of the pronoun possibilities of one or more people speaking and one or more people listening.

Another midwesterner, Laurie Anderson, grew up in Chicago and has embraced language as one material for her performances. A self-proclaimed storyteller, Anderson weaves long, humorous, semiautobiographical tales not unlike Garrison Keillor's. Her musical abilities have augmented the stories, beginning with street performances like *Duets on Ice* (1974–1975), in which she played half of a violin duet wearing ice skates embedded in blocks of ice in the middle of July while a tape recording of the other half of the duet played inside the violin. The performance ended when the ice melted. By the late 1970s, Anderson's performances had developed into elaborate spectacles complete with songs, stories, and electronic gadgets for modifying her voice and projecting images on the stage behind her. In *United States*, a two-night performance held at the Brooklyn Academy of Music in 1983, Anderson explored the theme of communication, including a segment entitled *Hello Looks Like Goodbye*, where she posed a dilemma encountered when considering what sorts of signs should be painted on the outside of a spaceship. As she points out, a person holding her arm up in a wave meant to signify hello looks just like a person who is waving good-bye. Taking her cue from semiotics in this piece, as in others, Anderson demonstrates why any communication system based on oppositions can fail.

By the late 1980s, performance art festivals were cropping up in major cities around the world, including a very important one in Cleveland. Inaugurated in 1988 and running until 1999, the Cleveland Performance Art Festival showcased established artists as well as local artists who were just starting out. Some years the festival extended to twelve weeks, and at the end of twelve years it had shown more than a thousand performance artists from across the world. Not only did the festival attract people already familiar with performance art, but it also drew a wide local audience. As the Cleveland Performance Art Festival prepares its online archive compiled from the twelve festivals, it will further extend that audience.

Sources and Further Reading: Gregory Battcock and Robert Nickas, eds., *The Art of Performance* (1984); RoseLee Goldberg, *Performance: Live Art since 1960* (1998); Doug Hall and Sally Jo Fifer, eds., *Illuminating Video* (1990); Mary Emma Harris, *The Arts at Black Mountain College* (1987); Leslie Hill and Helen Paris, *Guerilla Performance and Multimedia* (2001); Janet Kardon, *Laurie Anderson: Works from 1969 to 1983* (1983); Michael Kirby, *Happenings* (1965); Barbara Rose, *Claes Oldenburg* (1970); Joan Simon, Neal Benezra, and Kathy Halbreich, *Bruce Nauman* (1994).

Eileen Doyle
The Ohio State University–Columbus

Ann Hamilton (b. 1956)

Ann Hamilton was born in Lima, Ohio, in 1956. She received a bachelor of fine arts degree from the University of Kansas in 1979 and graduated with a master of fine arts in sculpture from Yale University in 1985. In 1999 she represented the United States at the Venice Biennale, one of the most prestigious exhibitions of contemporary art.

Hamilton's work falls within the field of installation art—multimedia sculptural environments that occupy one or more rooms. Her contribution has been to develop a unique vocabulary of forms, including copious amounts of everyday objects, videotaped images, recorded sound, and live performers. In the installation titled *malediction* (1991), Hamilton covered the floor of the first of two rooms with wine-soaked linens that emitted a pungent aroma. In the adjacent room she sat at a large refectory table repeatedly molding

Malediction, by Ann Hamiliton. Courtesy the artist and Sean Kelly Gallery, New York. Photo by D. James Dee.

small pieces of bread dough into concave forms using the inside of her mouth and then placing them in a large woven casket. As viewers traversed these rooms, they heard a recording of Walt Whitman's *Song of Myself* and *The Body Electric*.

In *malediction*, Hamilton's use of bread, wine, and routinized action brings to mind a life of meditative quietude and humility. Despite its apparent lack of specificity, however, *malediction* elicits nostalgia for a specific place and time—a place like the Midwest, and a time prior to the disruptive transformations of modernity. Hamilton's achievement in this and other works is to force us to acknowledge both the depth of our longing for such a place and time and our inexorable historical distance from it.

Source and Further Reading: Joan Simon, *Ann Hamilton* (2002).

Steven Hunt
The Ohio State University–Columbus

Glass

The Midwest is widely recognized as the birthplace of contemporary American glass sculpture as a result of two workshops held during March and June of 1962 at the Toledo Museum of Art in Ohio. These workshops led directly to a proliferation of glass-art education programs at institutions of higher learning, first in the Midwest region and then throughout the United States. At first just a handful, thousands of artists are now involved in the creation of glass sculpture worldwide.

The workshops at the Toledo Museum were designed to demonstrate how artists might shrink glassblowing equipment from the impersonal scale and automation of the factory environment to an intimate one suitable for use by individual artists. Discussions were initiated to dispel the mindset that glass could only be made by people specializing in areas like design, craft, manufacture, or marketing and that no one person could make glass from start to finish. The sessions in Toledo were led by Harvey Littleton, a ceramics professor from the University of Wisconsin at Madison. Norman Schulman, head of the ceramics workshop at the Toledo Museum School, put together the small glass studio in a museum garage, using some equipment gleaned from the Libbey Glass Company factories and hand tools from the museum's collection. The studio's glass furnace was not hot enough to melt the glass. Dominick Labino, at the time vice president for research at the Johns Manville Fiber Glass Corporation and an avocational student in museum art classes, was consulted to help solve technical difficulties and did so by providing easy-to-melt glass marbles used to make fiberglass.

Once the glass melted, it became apparent that no one really knew how to make forms with it. Harvey Leafgreen, a sixty-nine-year-old retired glassblower from Libbey Glass, demonstrated essential, almost forgotten, handworking techniques that Edith Franklin, a member of the first workshop, described as magical. Participants were excited with the potential of glass art, and this excitement led to the second seminar in June, where the knowledge of how artists might work with the glass was expanded. In 1966 the Toledo Museum built a permanent glass studio. Until he was ninety-two, Leafgreen kept coming to the Toledo Museum studio to make blown glass for friends.

Dominick Labino, the man with the marbles, was an inventor of glass compositions, processes, and machines for forming glass fibers. He held more than sixty U.S. patents and hundreds of foreign ones. In June 1962 he built his own glass studio at home, and he retired three years later to devote his full time to creating his own glass art. This work ranged from recreating ancient techniques, notably that used for Egyptian hollow sand-core vessels from 1500 B.C., to casting architectural-scale, multicolored glass relief panels in which the glass chemistry itself played a part in creating abstract patterns inside the work.

In October 1966 the Toledo Museum held the Toledo Glass National, a competitive exhibition of creative work in glass. Labino won jury awards for two of his blown works. Reflecting an explosion of interest in the activity of making glass, there were forty-eight entrants in the exhibition. The museum purchased work by seven participants in the show for its permanent collection. In 1968 Labino published an influential book, *Visual Art in Glass*, in which he described the history of glass material as a medium for visual art, illustrated how creative artists might build their own studio to make glass, and challenged them to make sculpture from glass. Labino died in 1987.

Harvey Littleton went on from the Toledo workshops to establish an influential glass-art education program at the University of Wisconsin. His interest in glasswork was more with the freestanding sculptural potential of the material than with its utility as a vessel, and his enthusiasm for seeing glass become a material for use in artistic expression was infectious. Many of Littleton's first students went on to become leaders in the field of glass sculpture: Dale Chihuly, who taught at the Rhode Island School of Design and started the influential Pilchuck Glass School in Washington State, is now well known for his monumental,

colorful glass sculpture. Fritz Dreisbach, a sort of Johnny Appleseed of glass, in 1971 founded the Glass Art Society, an organization devoted to advancing glass arts worldwide. Dreisbach traveled from his home in Ohio to every corner of the country, presenting workshops on glassblowing, chemistry, and sculpting and networking with anyone interested in the material. Henry Halem, a professor at Kent State University in Ohio and the first president of the Glass Art Society, is known for his abstract relief sculptures made from architectural and painted glass. Tom McGlauchlin was director of the glass program at the Toledo Museum from 1971 to 1984 and is known for his work in the tradition of abstract sculpture. Marvin Lipofsky started important glass programs in California. Lipofsky makes his inventive glass sculpture during visits to factories around the world, creating forms utilizing molds from the production lines and then further refining them back in his studio by cutting and polishing. According to the society, these artists' students, and their students' students, were instrumental in developing over a hundred glass-education programs. These programs still have a significant concentration in the Midwest. There is a trend of growth in new community workshops devoted to providing glass facilities to the public.

The wave of artists producing their own glass since 1962 is called the studio glass movement. This was initially understood as being a crafts movement: The word *glass* implies that what is important is what the piece is made of, or how it might be used, in contrast to terms like *art* or *sculpture*, which might be more apt to reflect a dedication to content and what a piece is about or might mean.

Glass artists show work in venues ranging from crafts fairs to galleries to museums, and museums and collectors in the Midwest have made an important impact on the field. Beginning in 1966, the Toledo Museum held national biennial exhibitions for new studio glass movement work, culminating in 1972 with *American Glass Now*. The Leigh Yawkey Woodson Art Museum in Wausau, Wisconsin, created *Americans in Glass* exhibitions in 1978, 1981, and 1984. The studio glass movement was clearly a worldwide phenomenon by the time of the 1979 exhibition *New Glass*, which was a survey of work being made worldwide. *New Glass* was organized by the Corning Museum in New York with participating museums including the Toledo Museum; the Renwick Gallery of the National Collection of Fine Arts in Washington, D.C.; the Metropolitan Museum of Art in New York; and the Fine Arts Museums of San Francisco. The Corning Museum defined the exhibition in this way: "This exhibition is about a profound change taking place in the history of glass: after 35 centuries of utilitarian use—

from containers and window panes to television tubes and laser transmitting fibers—glass has become the amorphous substance from which functionless art is made."

The *New Glass Review* of the Corning Museum continues as an annual competition in which a changing jury selects one hundred of the most innovative glass artworks to publish from images of glass sculpture submitted by the now thousands of artists, worldwide, who are using this material. Exhibitions of glass sculpture attract huge audiences; the viewers are compelled to examine glass for the exquisite beauty at its core and to seek meaning beyond its functionality.

Artists' access to glass technology and widespread sharing of techniques for working with glass material, begun in the Midwest, resulted in a blending of the role of designer with those of manufacturer and craftsperson. This has allowed glass to be conjoined with other media, and it clearly is now being widely used and appreciated as a material for artistic expression.

Sources and Further Reading: Corning Museum, *New Glass* (1979); *Glass Art Society Journal* (annual); Dominick Labino, *Visual Art in Glass* (1968); Leigh Yawkey Woodson Art Museum, *Americans in Glass* (1978, 1981, 1984); Toledo Museum of Art, *American Glass Now* (1972).

Richard Harned
The Ohio State University–Columbus

Fiber and Installation Art

Sometimes, because so much attention is paid to the East and West Coasts, midwesterners are given an opportunity to experiment. Fiber and installation art are two areas in which they have done so. Artists working with fiber, while not obviously confined to the Midwest, would find a cultural and geographical climate in that part of America that suits the laborious processes of their work. Cultural traits that generally characterize the Midwest include practicality, a strong work ethic with a focus on the well crafted, and a necessary attachment to the land. Geographically, cold and long winters have historically necessitated the pursuit of indoor activities. While these characteristics have certainly been modified by urbanization, modernization, and the "march of progress," some values have managed to persevere beyond time and have an effect on contemporary life in the Midwest. In this region where the traditions and values of so many European cultures have molded a regional character, individualism is combined with hearty work and craft traditions, providing a nurturing environment for fiber-related art.

Most techniques associated with fiber—such as knotting, sewing, and winding—are lengthy processes that become markers of time and memory. As a handicraft or technique for producing functional objects, fiber traditions such as basket making and rug weaving are found throughout the United States, with various regions providing their own character. There are also instances of people looking to cross the boundary that was seen as existing between artist and artisan. For example, in the late 1800s and early 1900s, members of the Bauhaus and the arts and crafts movements, to name just two, looked to abolish the distinctions between craftsperson and artist, a trend based on movements in architecture, the production of furniture and functional objects, and fiber traditions.

The dialogue concerning what is "craft" and what is "art" has continued into the beginning of the twenty-first century and has been given a strong voice by fiber artists who choose to use craft techniques such as crocheting, knitting, sewing, and weaving to deal with contemporary art issues, including notions of space, feminism, process, the body, time, and memory. In contemporary art, "fiber" has become a broad designation that includes a variety of techniques and materials. Many feminist artists in the 1970s used these techniques subversively and expanded the boundaries for fiber-based art. In recent years, it has also turned into one of the gray areas of contemporary art—practiced both by artists who are specifically trained as textile artists and by those considered mainstream contemporary artists.

Several midwestern contemporary artists have played major roles in the development of fiber art, expanding or eliding its boundaries and bringing recognition to the region. Cincinnati-born Claire Zeisler (1903–1991) was an innovator in fiber sculpture in the Midwest. She began making experimental weaving pieces in Chicago in the 1960s, eventually developing them into three-dimensional structures. Other Chicago artists, such as Anne Wilson and Joan Livingstone, have strong fiber backgrounds and use them to make work that comments on the history of their materials and the creative processes as well as on the body, notions of transformation, and issues of femininity. As teachers at the School of the Art Institute of Chicago, Wilson and Livingstone have experimented with new ideas and new technologies in the field of fiber, and they translate a sense of exploration to their students.

While installation art in the Midwest has not always been associated with fiber traditions, the intersection of the two has produced some of the most innovative work of the 1990s and has focused attention on ground-breaking artists utilizing innovative practices that cross boundaries of art making. The idea of "total art environments" is not particular to the contemporary era (some argue that even the Lascaux caves of France are site-specific installations); the term *installation art* really came to mainstream prominence in the early 1990s. Unlike the typical art experience, where an object is presented for contemplation and a physical and psychological distance is maintained between object and viewer, installation art is utilized to break down preexisting barriers. Audience participation and the relationship of object to space are important elements, as is the desire to subvert the "hierarchy" of other art forms and the prevailing ideologies of institutions.

Installation art often stresses and muddies the ideas of time and physical passage. All types of media are often combined, as stereotypes about "art" are challenged. Installation art is different from an "art installation," which is the presentation of works of art in a space, manipulated by the curator more than the artist. With installation art, by definition the artist is responsible for all elements of the presentation and is on site to complete the piece or present definitive instructions as to how objects, videos, and other elements are to fit within the space. Meaning becomes much more subjective and must be "completed" by the viewer. Installation art provides many different avenues through which a viewer (who becomes more of a "visitor") is able to experience the work—part of the intention being a focus on the individual meaning that the viewer can bring to the work in addition to that intended by the artist.

A major boost to the field of installation art has come from institutional venues and artist-run spaces across the Midwest that have supported artists who choose to work as installation makers. Smaller art centers such as the John Michael Kohler Arts Center in Sheboygan, Wisconsin, and the Kemper Museum of Art in Kansas City, Missouri, and larger museums such as the Indianapolis Museum of Art and the Museum of Contemporary Art in Chicago have either engaged installation artists for site-specific projects or acquired installation works as a part of their collection.

Ann Hamilton, a pioneering installation artist, combines her background in fiber with her desire to make art that can be experienced by more than just the visual sense. Her multimedia installations often include sound, video or photography, objects, and live participants. Hamilton is very interested in the tactile—mixing various types of materials and emphasizing the notion of "touch" as a site for experience. A native of Ohio, Hamilton returned there after attending school and teaching in other parts of the United States. She has said that qualities impressed upon her as a part of her Midwest upbringing—pragmatism, perseverance, and the importance of craftsmanship—continue to be significant in her role as artist and teacher. Hamilton's influence transcends the boundaries of the Midwest but it also marks the region as an innovative place for fiber.

For several years, Gerhardt Knodel has been a driving force in contemporary fiber in the Midwest. While he attended school on the West Coast, he has been working in the Midwest for several years as artist-in-residence, head of the fiber department, and now as director at the Cranbrook Academy of Art in Bloomfield Hills, Michigan. His fabric installations play with ideas of space, architecture, light, and the malleability of cloth. His influence on colleagues as well as students has contributed to an enduring legacy for exploring the possibilities of fiber and installation in the Midwest.

Sources and Further Reading: Nicolas De Oliveira, Nicola Oxley, and Michael Petry, *Installation Art* (1994); Milwaukee Art Museum and University Art Museum, University of Wisconsin–Milwaukee, *Fiber R/Evolution* (1986); Museum of Contemporary Art, San Diego, *Introducing Installation: A Legacy from Lascaux to Last Week* (1997); Sarah Campbell Blaffer Gallery, University of Houston, Texas, *American Fiber Art* (1980); Lynne Warren, ed., *Art in Chicago 1945–1995* (1996).

Lena Vigna
John Michael Kohler Arts Center, Wisconsin

Cultural Institutions

SECTION EDITOR
Erika Doss

Section Contents

Overview

The words *culture* and *midwestern* are rarely linked in American popular consciousness. Indeed, New York has been considered the cultural capital of the United States since the nineteenth century. Yet, to paraphrase poet Carl Sandburg, the Midwest functions as the "big shoulders" on which the culture of the nation rests.

Mirroring the Midwest's cultural diversity and working from an expansive understanding of culture itself, the "Cultural Institutions" section (organized alphabetically) is purposefully sweeping and inclusive. Thematic essays and entries (also alphabetically organized) consider the broad range and significance of institutions that collect, preserve, transmit, display, and interpret culture in the Midwest, from museums, libraries, theatres, historical societies, and opera houses to parks, zoos, arts councils, literary societies, and sites of cultural tourism. These include major museums ranging from the Art Institute of Chicago to the Nelson-Atkins Museum of Art in Kansas City, Missouri, as well as cultural centers from the Guthrie Theatre (Minneapolis) and the Rock and Roll Hall of Fame (Cleveland) to the Serpent Mound Historical Center (Locust Grove, Ohio), the St. Louis Symphony Orchestra, Greenfield Village (Dearborn, Michigan), the Baraboo Circus World Museum (Wisconsin), and the Youngstown Historical Center of Industry and Labor (Ohio).

As such a list indicates, midwestern cultural institutions vary from set physical spaces such as museums and public memorials (including the Mother Jones Memorial [1936] in Mt. Olive, Illinois, and Chicago's 1967 Picasso sculpture) to temporary structures and seasonal events such as festivals and fairs (including the spectacular 1893 World's Columbian Exposition in Chicago and Milwaukee's Summerfest, an annual music festival that is one of the largest in the Midwest). Providing culture with a base of support, cultural institutions emerge, contain, direct, and are transformed by ever-changing and increasingly comprehensive understandings of culture itself. Active in the role of creating community and providing forms of civic, social, and political cohesion and identity, cultural institutions may also reinforce or perpetuate problems of racial, class, ethnic, and gender division.

Given these assumptions, questions pertinent to this section are those of midwestern distinctiveness amid recognition of culture's dynamic, elusive, and often conflicted character. What, for example, is unique about midwestern cultural institutions as compared to those of other regions of the United States? What, in fact, does culture mean in the Midwest, and what impact have changing understandings of the arts and humanities had on the growth and transformation of the region's cultural institutions? Speculating on such questions, this section of *The American Midwest* features twelve themes divided by medium and topic: major art museums; mid-tier art museums; history museums and other sites; memorials and monuments; libraries and literary organizations; zoos, botanical gardens, and natural history museums; music organizations; theatre groups; dance companies; cultural philanthropy; cultural tourism; cultural controversies; and public sculpture.

The first Ferris wheel, World's Columbian Exposition, 1893, Chicago. Reprinted from *Official Views of the World's Columbian Exposition* (Chicago: Gravure Co., 1893).

Museums are among the Midwest's best-known cultural institutions; indeed, Chicago's Art Institute and Field Museum, Detroit's Institute of Arts, and Cleveland's Museum of Art have long been considered national, not just regional, treasure houses for their superb collections of world art. In large part, their establishment corresponded with the economic growth of their midwestern communities and the financial success and materialistic accumulations of wealthy midwestern merchants. Built to house the paintings, sculptures, antiquities, and anthropological artifacts that Gilded Age elites collected from around the globe, museums helped to display and legitimate the vast fortunes of their founders. Chicago department store magnate Marshall Field, for example, wrote a one million dollar check to create the Field Museum in 1894; Toledo, Ohio, industrialist Edward Libbey, owner of the Libbey Glass Company, largely funded Toledo's Museum of Art, founded in 1901; Cleveland artist-entrepreneur Jeptha Wade, president of Western Union Telegraph, donated the land on which the Cleveland Museum of Art was built in 1916; and Kansas City newspaper mogul William Rockhill Nelson, along with wealthy heiress Mary Atkins, provided bequests for the Nelson-Atkins Museum of Art, which opened in 1933. The art these magnates collected often formed the core of midwestern museums: Detroit newspaper publisher James E. Scripps donated seventy old master paintings (including a Peter Paul Rubens) to Detroit's first art museum in 1889; the Milwaukee Art Museum and Minneapolis's Walker Art Center owe their origins to the cultural largesse of local industrialists (Wisconsin meatpacker Frederick Layton and Minnesota lumber baron Thomas Walker, respectively); and Chicago society figure Bertha Honoré Palmer (the wife of wealthy Chicago merchant and hotelier Potter Palmer) left her important collection of impressionist paintings to the Art Institute of Chicago on her death in 1918.

Midwestern culture followed midwestern capital. The first museum to be established in the trans-Allegheny region was founded in Cincinnati in 1820 following the city's spectacular economic success as a transportation hub and meatpacking center. Originally opened as a science and natural history museum, the Western Museum charged visitors twenty-five cents (half price for children) to gape at its collection of stuffed birds, reptiles, fossils, and shells as well as Roman coins, Egyptian mummies, medieval reliquaries, and "500 specimens of fine arts." Soon, however, financial woes (lacking a generous donor, the museum was organized as a stock company, with members owning shares) and public apathy led the museum to develop more sensational entertainments, including tableaux of local murderers. One of its most popular exhibits was the Infernal Regions, a theatrical depiction of hell modeled after Dante's *Divine Comedy* and John Milton's *Paradise Lost*, which featured mechanical wax figures that jumped out at visitors while emitting horrible shrieks and cries. Designed by Hiram Powers, a local artist who left Cincinnati in 1834 and went on to design important sculptures including *The Greek Slave* (1843), the Infernal Regions was so popular that an electric fence was constructed to keep visitors from touching the wax effigies. Despite such showmanship, the Western Museum fell into disrepair and closed in 1867. It had a lasting impact, however, as subsequent midwestern cultural institutions recognized the importance of sound financing, attracting audiences with interesting and innovative exhibits, and cultivating local and regional support.

In addition to legitimizing the tastes and collections of the wealthy, midwestern museums were also organized as institutions of cultural enlightenment. In the late nineteenth century, the Midwest joined the rest of the country in building many celebrated museums, following the belief that cultural institutions were key places where American citizens—especially the millions of immigrants who were flocking to the United States at this time—could be instructed about the nation's cultural, social, and political values. The 1893 World's Columbian Exposition, a six-month fair erected on 686 acres of swampy marshland seven miles from Chicago's downtown Loop, functioned as a primary school of instruction for its twenty million visitors. Divided into two sections—a dazzling "White City" of neoclassical buildings containing hundreds of artistic and industrial exhibits, and a midway featuring rides (including the first Ferris wheel), shops, and ethnographic displays—the Chicago exposition announced America's cultural supremacy, celebrated national unity (the Civil War had ended less than thirty years earlier), and consecrated an emergent modern era, all on the shores of Lake Michigan. Its all-white, neoclassical architecture expressed turn-of-the-century assumptions of white Anglo-Saxon supremacy and deemed ancient Greece and Rome the pinnacles of world art and culture. Its ethnographic exhibits on the midway, where villages of nonwhite and non-Western "natives" were placed on display and deliberately contrasted with the culture displayed in the White City, reinforced notions of social Darwinism and the supposed evolutionary differences between savagery and civilization. Its rituals of nationalism—the "Pledge of Allegiance" was written expressly for the Chicago fair—instructed visitors about American patriotism. The fair also displayed a great deal of midwestern art and culture, including the first major exhibition of prehistoric artifacts from the region.

The refined aesthetics of the 1893 World's

Columbian Exposition, and its assumptions that culture was a moral and social force that could elevate and educate the general public, beautify and civilize the nation, and inspire proper civic behavior, greatly influenced the style and substance of cultural institutions throughout the Midwest, including museums and libraries. Chicago's Art Institute (1893); St. Louis's Art Museum (1907); Cleveland's Museum of Art (1916); and the Butler Institute of American Art in Youngstown, Ohio, all followed the Chicago fair's neo-classical architectural model. (The Butler Institute, which opened in 1919, was the first American art museum completely dedicated to American art.) Similarly, libraries in Columbus, Ohio (1901), Waukegan, Illinois (1903), and Sheboygan, Wisconsin (1904), were among the many public libraries built in a neo-classical style in the early twentieth century, and number among the more than 600 midwestern libraries financed by wealthy industrialist Andrew Carnegie between 1886 and 1919. Indeed, America's first Carnegie library opened in Fairfield, Iowa, 1893, and more than half of the Carnegie libraries built in the United States were located in the Midwest. Like the backers of the World's Columbian Exposition and the founders of multiple midwestern museums, Carnegie viewed libraries as primary cultural institutions that could socialize and civilize American immigrants and educate citizens about core, shared national values.

Importantly, midwestern cultural institutions have undergone significant changes as their regional economies and populations have transformed in recent decades. Youngstown, Ohio, for example, owed its considerable economic development in the nineteenth and twentieth centuries to plentiful natural resources such as coal, ore, and wood, and to its ideal location in the Mahoning River Valley in northeastern Ohio. The discovery of rich veins of Brier Hill black coal in 1844 helped dramatically transform the quiet rural village into a booming industrial landscape; between 1846 and 1872, eleven blast furnaces were built in Youngstown and another ten in surrounding areas. By 1918 Youngstown was second only to Pittsburgh in steel production in the United States. With capital came culture, and Youngstown's citizens saw the development of parks (including the 450-acre Mill Creek Park, designed by Frederick Law Olmsted in 1891, and the Franklin Park Conservatory and Botanical Gardens, designed in 1895); museums (the Butler Institute of American Art, founded by Youngstown industrialist Joseph G. Butler and constructed in the Beaux-Arts style by the architectural firm of McKim, Mead & White); libraries (Youngstown's Main Public Library was designed by Charles F. Owsley in 1907 following a $50,000 gift from Andrew Carnegie); and

historic homes (the Mahoning Valley Historical Society, founded in 1875, includes the Arms Family Museum of Local History, located in Greystone, the turn-of-the-century arts and crafts home of Youngstown elites Wilford and Olive Arms).

After World War II, the American steel industry began to dramatically decline and Youngstown's economy stagnated. Between 1977 and 1982, many of the area's major steel mills closed, tens of thousands of citizens lost jobs, and Youngstown's population steadily decreased (from about 168,000 in 1960 to just 82,000 in 2000). Faced with the threat of their own extinction amid such deindustrialization, yet refusing to abandon their civic mission, the leaders of Youngstown's cultural institutions began to reconsider their presence and purpose in the community. The Butler, for example, opened two new museum branches in the nearby towns of Salem and Howland, Ohio, cosponsored summer music festivals with Youngstown State University, and increased its educational outreach. In 2003 the museum initiated an After-School Youth Studio Art Honors Program, with the goal of mentoring aspiring visual artists in area high schools. Likewise, Youngstown's Mill Creek Park has expanded to include more than 2,600 acres of gardens, drives, hiking paths, a golf course, a restored mill, and a nature education center.

Other cultural institutions emerged in Youngstown that directly addressed its working-class history as "Steel Town U.S.A." In the 1980s, the Ohio Historical Society created the Youngstown Historical Center of Industry and Labor, a 32,000-square-foot museum with exhibitions, classrooms, archives, and a research library focused on the Mahoning Valley's iron and steel industries. Postmodern architect Michael Graves designed the $3.9 million building and incorporated local industrial and religious architectural forms (turrets that resemble steel-mill stacks and a roofline that echoes the arched roof of nearby St. Columba's Catholic Church). A permanent exhibition titled By the Sweat of Their Brow: Forging the Steel Valley features equipment and tools from local factories (including a blooming mill, where steel ingots were shaped for further processing, and a steelworkers' locker room) and personal mementos donated by former laborers (including photographs and clothing); the exhibit also includes a full-scale recreation of a company-built worker house. Opened in 1992, Youngstown's historical center chronicles the rise and fall of the steel industry in the Mahoning Valley and, especially, foregrounds the history and meaning of working-class culture.

The Plains Art Museum in Fargo, North Dakota, is another example of a regional cultural institution that has developed in response to changing midwestern demographics. The museum dates to the mid-1960s, when it was housed in an old post office building in bordering Moorhead, Minnesota, and was called the Red River Art Center. In 1975 it adopted its present name and in 1997 reopened in a renovated warehouse (originally owned by the International Harvester Company) in Fargo, the largest city in North Dakota. Its name change and move into a larger building reflect regional transformations in eastern North Dakota and west-central Minnesota. Originally established in the 1870s by the Northern Pacific Railroad, Fargo grew as an agricultural and transportation hub; noted architect Cass Gilbert designed the city's passenger depot in 1898. Originally inhabited by Plains Indians, Fargo's first European American settlers were mostly farmers from Scandinavia and Germany. Eager to attract homesteaders to the region to ensure financial support for its railroad, Northern Pacific advertised large-scale farms of 1,000 acres on either side of its route along the Minnesota-Dakota border, especially along the Red River Valley. These late-nineteenth-century "bonanza farms" were highly successful and are remembered today at Bonanzaville, a living-history museum of forty restored regional buildings and 400,000 artifacts managed by the Cass County Historical Society in West Fargo. The restored buildings include a train depot, a dry-goods store, a blacksmith's forge, a newspaper firm, and the U.R. Next Barber Shop, built in 1900 in Buffalo, North Dakota.

In the decades following World War II, North Dakota, like much of the Midwest, saw the decline of both the railroad and its rural population. While agriculture remains central to the state's economy, Fargo has especially developed as a financial, commercial, medical, and cultural center, which includes North Dakota State University, the North Dakota Repertory Theater, the Fargo-Moorhead Symphony Orchestra, and the Plains Art Museum. A 56,000-square-foot facility with 9,000 square feet of exhibition space, classrooms, studios, offices, a library, a café, and a large, skylighted atrium that doubles as a performance space, the museum often features exhibits of regional artists and especially pursues educational outreach with its Rolling Plains Art Gallery, a semitrailer converted into a mobile art museum that visits schools and communities throughout North Dakota and Minnesota. Located in downtown Fargo, the museum is the most visible sign of the North Dakota city's changed civic identity from railroad hub to culture capital. In 1977 the city honored its agricultural and Native American history by winning a $20,000 matching grant from the Art in Public Places Program of the National Endowment for the Arts (NEA) and commissioning artist Luis Jiménez to create a large fiberglass sculpture ti-

tled *Sodbuster*. The memorial, which portrays a stout homesteader guiding an ox-drawn plow through soil that exposes buried artifacts such as the potsherds of former Indian inhabitants, was originally placed near Fargo's Northern Pacific railroad depot and was donated to the Plains Art Museum in 1992.

Memorials and monuments, like museums and other cultural institutions, clearly reflect changed and changing midwestern identities. Dedicated in 1965 and still the tallest monument in America, St. Louis's Gateway Arch commemorates the 1803 Louisiana Purchase and the addition of midwestern and western territories to the continental United States, while its stainless steel design and unique tramway system celebrate the space age and St. Louis's status as a modern midwestern city. Likewise, *La Grande Vitesse* in Grand Rapids, Michigan, pays tribute to that city's civic beautification and urban renewal. Grand Rapids was the first city in America to request NEA funding for public art, and the gigantic, red-painted steel sculpture, designed by Alexander Calder and dedicated in 1969, was paid for with a $45,000 NEA grant and $85,000 in private funds. Initially greeted with bemusement and hostility because of its abstract style and steep price tag, the sculpture has now become a well-known symbol for Grand Rapids and its design is seen on everything from city letterhead to the sides of garbage trucks. George Segal's sculpture *The Steelworkers* was similarly controversial when unveiled in downtown Youngstown in 1980. Featuring an open hearth from the Brier Hill steel mill and two life-size bronze figures modeled on workers at that mill, Segal intended the sculpture as an appreciation and celebration of "the human spirit" of ordinary, working-class laborers. Yet it was erected at a moment when Youngstown's mills were closing, and many locals reacted bitterly; the sculpture was repeatedly vandalized. In the early 1990s, it was dismantled and moved to the Youngstown Historical Center for Industry and Labor, where it was split into two parts (the hearth was placed outside and the sculptures inside the museum). Perhaps over time, Youngstown will more readily reckon with its earlier civic and cultural identity as a midwestern steel-making capital.

Differences in cultural identity account for the popularity of midwestern cultural tourism in various religious communities, such as the Amish in eastern Ohio and northern Indiana, and the Amana Colonies in Iowa. Cultural tourism is especially evident in midwestern locales that claim unique identities. Cleveland, for example, claims to be the city where rock and roll originated and in 1995 opened the Rock and Roll Hall of Fame and Museum (designed by architect I. M. Pei), which now receives a million annual visitors. Seymour, Wisconsin, claims to be the home of the hamburger (invented in 1885 and celebrated with an annual Burger Fest and in the city's Hamburger Hall of Fame), while Des Plaines, Illinois, claims to be the home of the first drive-through McDonald's (opened in 1955). And Ripon, Wisconsin, claims to be the birthplace of the Republican Party (an event dating to 1854 and celebrated in the town's Little White School House museum), although Jackson, Michigan, and Crawfordsville, Iowa, also vie for the title. Issues of cultural identity often play a central role in midwestern civic controversies, from debates over alleged Viking relics in Minnesota arund 1900 to those over art exhibitions in Cincinnati in the early 1990s. Clearly, "culture" has undergone dramatic change and transformation in recent decades yet remains a vital force in the Midwest.

Sources and Further Reading: John Beardsley, *Art in Public Places: A Survey of Community-Sponsored Projects Supported by the National Endowment for the Arts* (1981); Whitfield J. Bell, Jr., *A Cabinet of Curiosities: Five Episodes in the Evolution of American Museums* (1967); Steven Conn, *Museums and American Intellectual Life, 1876–1926* (1998); Andrea Stulman Dennett, *Weird and Wonderful: The Dime Museum in America* (1997); Erika Doss, *Spirit Poles and Flying Pigs* (1995); Theodore Jones, *Carnegie Libraries across America* (1997); Sherry Lee Linkon and John Russo, *Steeltown U.S.A.* (2002); Robert W. Rydell, *All the World's a Fair* (1984); Carl Sandburg, *Chicago Poems* (1916).

Erika Doss
University of Colorado, Boulder

Cultural Controversies

Occupying a crucial geographic and symbolic position as America's Heartland and repository of cultural values, the Midwest figures prominently in national battles over culture, its meaning, and the right to define it. Recent controversies—involving an alleged Viking relic, American Indian sports mascots, a gay photographer, and the public school science curriculum—offer a snapshot of the multiple claims on communities' identity, revealing competing understandings of place, history, and belonging that make up the Midwest. Conflicts often erupt over the objects and images chosen to define the history of places because stories assumed by many to be precious and shared open bitter and painful memories for others. Other controversies turn on the role of culture in the present and future of communities.

Since 1898, controversy has swirled around a thirty-one-inch-long, two-hundred-pound slab of

The contested Kensington Runestone. Minnesota Historical Society, MHS Location no. MD6.7k r16, neg. no. 61074.

graywacke unearthed by Olof Ohman, a Swedish immigrant, on his farm near Kensington, Minnesota, a small town 150 miles northwest of Minneapolis. The stone, now displayed at the Rune-Stone Museum in Alexandria, Minnesota, carries carved inscriptions purported to be of medieval Swedish origin. Translated into English, the inscription reads:

8 Goths and 22 Norwegians on exploration journey from Vinland over the West We had camp by 2 skerries one days journey north from this stone We were and fished on day After we came home found 10 men red with blood and dead Ave Maria Save from evil, Have 10 of our party by the sea to look after our ships 14 days journey from this island Year 1362.

Hjalmar Holand, a Scandinavian American resident of Ephraim, Wisconsin, who purchased the stone from Ohman in 1907, interpreted the inscriptions to mean that a Viking expedition reached what is now the Midwest during the fourteenth century, arriving near present-day Kensington, Minnesota, where ten of them were killed by hostile Native Americans. Holand advanced his theories in several articles and a book, *Norse Discoveries and Explorations in America, 982–1362* (1969). While the academic establishment doubted the authenticity of the inscriptions, Holand's theory gained popularity among Scandinavian immigrants in Minnesota and has incited more than one hundred years of debate over who has the right to define the prehistory of the Americas. Mainstream archaeologists consider the Kensington Runestone a hoax. However, a committed fringe of lay historians contest the authority of orthodox archaeology. The controversy pits avocational archaeology buffs against a firmly entrenched academic establishment. Individuals and organizations such as the Institute for the Study of American Cultures (ISAC) have undertaken extensive epigraphic and material analysis and have published their work independently, on the Internet, and in specialist journals committed to the study of Norse exploration of North America before Columbus and to theories of "intercontinental diffusion," which posit transoceanic connections among the ancient Americas, Asia, Africa, and northern Europe.

Racism may motivate some in the diffusionist community, who argue that what remains in the archaeological record of prehistoric North America is not the work of indigenous cultures, but was built by Norse explorers, ancient Canaanites, and Phoenicians. However, diffusionist theories have the support of some Native American scholars, such as Standing Rock Sioux writer Vine Deloria, Jr., who harshly criticizes the standard histories of European and Native American relations. Deloria has chastised the academic establishment for its uncritical acceptance of the Bering Strait hypothesis, which maintains that Native Americans first entered North America via a land bridge from Siberia between seventy thousand and eleven thousand years ago, and which Deloria describes as a "fictional doctrine that places American Indians outside the realm of planetary human experiences."

Indeed, racism, or accusations of such, is at the heart of many midwestern cultural controversies. In recent years, the use of Indian images by sports teams has become a flashpoint for community conflict. Native American images are employed by countless small-town high schools, college teams such as the University of Illinois Fighting Illini, and professional franchises such as the Cleveland Indians and the Kansas City Chiefs. Like the numerous Native American names of the Midwest, Native American sports mascots are an important part of non–Native Americans' sense of place and history. Such images connect these midwesterners to local history and instill feelings of membership in a community of fans.

Native American activists counter that such images are cartoonish misrepresentations. Most offensive to them are the halftime and between-innings antics of mascots, such as the University of Illinois's "Chief Illiniwek" or the Cleveland Indians' "Chief Wahoo." Activists argue that associating American Indian images with sports teams is an invidious theft of cultural agency that denies contemporary indigenous people control over their own images and raises difficult questions of power and representation as well as a legacy of dispossession and racism that stings as Native Americans still fight for the recognition of treaty rights centuries after the European conquest of the Americas.

Many non–Native American fans counter that images and costume performances are not malicious insults but honorific celebrations of America's Indian heritage. However, this argument is wearing thin in many locales. Dartmouth College, Stanford University, Syracuse University, and many other higher-education institutions outside the Midwest have abandoned their Native American mascots in favor of less offensive and more generic characters. While the University of Illinois, the Cleveland Indians, and the Kansas City Chiefs have remained steadfast in their adherence to longstanding tradition, they have become objects of protest and censure by many indigenous and nonindigenous midwesterners. Currently, at least three schools in the Big Ten Conference will no longer allow Chief Illiniwek to perform at home games. The Minneapolis *Star-Tribune* and newspapers in Portland, Oregon; Salt Lake City, Utah; and Seattle, Washington, have editorial policies against publishing "Indian" team names, referring instead to the team by city. A recent accreditation report recommended that the University of Illinois retire Chief Illiniwek out of respect for Native Americans.

The power of visual images figures prominently in many recent controversies. In 1990 Cincinnati became a flashpoint in the culture wars that shook the American art world and resulted in the downsizing of the National Endowment for the Arts (NEA). Cincinnati is no stranger to controversy: In the 1950s local businessman Charles Keating (later indicted during the savings and loan crisis) founded Citizens for Decent Literature and attempted to ban *Playboy* magazine; in the 1970s the city brought suit against adult-magazine publisher Larry Flynt; and in 1990 the city protested the Perfect Moment, a retrospective exhibition of the work of American photographer Robert Mapplethorpe (1946–1989), organized by the Institute of Contemporary Art (ICA) at the University of Pennsylvania. The exhibition featured more than 150 photographs of flowers, portraits, and nudes as well as the "X-Portfolio," which depicted homosexual acts. Fresh from recent tussles with the NEA over a $15,000 grant awarded to New York artist Andres Serrano (indirectly, through the Southeast Center for Contemporary Arts' Awards in the Visual Arts program), right-wing critics mounted an openly homophobic media campaign tarring Mapplethorpe as a "pedophile" and a "Nazi." Conservative politicians soon joined the fray as Representative Dick Armey (Republican, Texas) and one hundred members of Congress sent a letter of protest to the NEA, which had awarded the ICA a grant of $30,000 to underwrite an exhibition budget of more than $200,000. The Perfect Moment was scheduled to travel to the Corcoran Gallery of Art in Washington, D.C., and the Contemporary Arts Center (CAC) in Cincinnati. The Corcoran, which received no NEA funds directly related to the exhibition, canceled the exhibition.

In advance of the scheduled April 1990 opening in Cincinnati, the CAC and the Mapplethorpe estate filed suit to determine whether, under Ohio law, the photographs would be considered "obscene" or be found to possess "artistic merit." An Ohio judge refused to make an advance ruling. At the opening, the exhibition was protested by Citizens for Community Values, a local conservative Christian organization. CAC director Dennis Barrie refused to remove seven controversial photographs and became the first museum director arrested for the exhibition of obscene material. Cincinnati police closed the gallery for one hour while the exhibition was videotaped for evidence. A federal judge blocked county officials from confiscating material or interfering in the exhibition while charges were under consideration. The CAC and Barrie were indicted for misdemeanor charges of "pandering obscenity, and of illegal use of a minor in nudity-oriented material." The CAC faced a $10,000 fine; Barrie faced $2,000 and jail time. However, after a ten-day trial in which ten expert witnesses analyzed Mapplethorpe's photographs, Barrie and the CAC were acquitted following just two hours of jury deliberation.

The CAC's and Barrie's acquittal in Cincinnati was a Pyrrhic victory. At the national level, events in Cincinnati had dramatic reverberations. Conservative critics, recognizing the power of culture in defining community values, argued that they were "losing the war for America's culture" to an antifamily and antireligious "gay agenda." An amendment authored by Senator Jesse Helms (R, North Carolina) proposed new guidelines for the NEA that would have prohibited use of NEA funds for the "dissemination, promotion, or production of obscene or indecent materials or materials denigrating a particular religion." The proposal did not pass, but an appropriation bill cut a symbolic $45,000 from the NEA budget—representing Serrano's $15,000 grant and the $30,000 ICA grant. Following the 1994 election of a Republican majority to Congress, Newt Gingrich's Contract with America restructured the NEA, cut its budget by 40 percent, and placed restrictions on how federal funds could be spent by arts organizations. A House bill mandating that the NEA be defunded by 1997 failed in the Senate. However, six members of Congress were added to NEA's national council, resulting in a loss of autonomy in the grant-making process.

Since the landmark *Brown v. Board of Education* case of 1954, which found the principle of "separate but equal" segregation in state services unconstitutional, the Midwest has been at the center of a number of national controversies in educational access and curriculum. In response to a general trend in American public education toward a standardized curriculum and testing, the Kansas State Board of Education in 1997 appointed four committees, including one in science, to establish the content of statewide assessment tests used to measure student and school success. The science standards committee met with opposition from supporters of intelligent design, a theory that allows for microevolution (changes within species) but holds that the tremendous complexity of life requires a guiding force. Advocates of intelligent design maintain an antievolutionist, rather than pro-creationist, stance. Shortly before the board of education was scheduled to vote on the committee's proposed standards, one board member put forth an alternative proposal that challenged the primacy of evolutionary theory. Members of the standards committee and the public debated the compatibility of science and religion. In August 1999, the board passed (6–4) a compromise document that omitted the topics of evolution and cosmology from the state's science curriculum. The adoption of these new standards gave local school boards authority to decide how biology would be taught.

The new standards brought the state notoriety in the national and international press. Many scientists and educators warned that the deemphasis of evolution would put Kansas students at a disadvantage when they applied to colleges or jobs. Many Kansans feared that potential employers would pass over a state that appeared in thrall to religious conservatives. Critics of the new standards feared that teachers would downplay evolutionary theory in response to local pressure, but no community mandated the teaching of alternatives (as in previous cases in Arkansas and Louisiana). The school board of Pratt, Kansas, considered adopting an intelligent-design biology textbook, but ultimately did not.

Science standards were a prominent issue in the 2000 Kansas Board of Education elections. Governor Bill Graves disapproved of the decision and encouraged voters to replace the board members who had voted for the new standards. Three conservative candidates, including the incumbent chairwoman, were defeated in primary elections. In February 2001, the new board approved 7–3 a new document drafted by the original standards-writing committee restoring the concept of macroevolution, the big bang, and the age of the Earth to the standards. Evolution was one of the unifying concepts on the science assessment tests at the end of that school year. As the 2000 Kansas School Board elections demonstrate, cultural controversies illuminate the importance of the local in relation to the national. Local controversies, emerging from local disagreements and formed by local factors, are often bellwethers of national issues.

Sources and Further Reading: Richard Bolton, ed., *Culture Wars: Documents from the Recent Controversies in the Arts* (1992); Vine Deloria, Jr., "Indians, Archaeologists, and the Future," *American Antiquity* 57 (Oct. 1992); Vine Deloria, Jr., *Red Earth, White Lies* (1995); Carol Spindel, *Dancing at Halftime* (2002); Mark K. Stengel, "The Diffusionists Have Landed," *Atlantic Monthly* 285 (Jan. 2000); Brian Wallis, Marianne Weems, and Philip Yenawine, eds., *Art Matters* (1999); Stephen Williams, *Fantastic Archaeology* (1991).

Bill Anthes
Carnegie Mellon University
Pittsburgh, Pennsylvania

Cultural Philanthropy

Cultural philanthropy combines public and private assistance to support a community's social and cultural organizations and institutions, including the arts, libraries, historical societies, and education. In the Midwest, beginning in the last quarter of the nineteenth century, cultural philanthropy took a particular form, which Peter Dobkin Hall identifies as federationist and associational. This form of cultural philanthropy was characterized by a commitment to cooperative community action, combining the interests of government, business, and wealthy individuals in a stable, economically healthy community to create an institutional hybrid, a quasi-public commitment to support cultural institutions for the public good. It requires, in general, broad public participation rather than exclusive reliance upon the largesse of a small group of wealthy individuals. It also emphasizes arts education as both a means of and an end to cultural participation. The midwestern approach is pragmatic and communal, emphasizing cooperation in the creation of a vital cultural life that serves the interests of the broader community.

Why and how did this particular form of cultural support arise in the Midwest? Most of the Midwest's earliest European settlers were transplants from New England and the Mid-Atlantic states, who brought with them values of hard work and social conservatism. By the mid-nineteenth century, the promise of land and opportunities for work attracted waves of immigrants, especially from northern Europe, who swelled the populations of midwestern cities emerging at strategic transportation points. With industrialization and urban growth came turmoil: Labor conflicts erupted in many cities, and in some places local government was corrupt and machine-dominated. Business leaders, in particular, became anxious that bedrock institutions—the family and the church—were losing their power to "civilize" and stabilize communities. Moreover, new immigrants brought with them different languages and customs, which some believed might undermine "American values." Helen Lefkowitz Horowitz points out that it was in this context that civic leaders—wealthy industrialists and business barons in cooperation with local government—"turned to cultural philanthropy, not so much to satisfy personal aesthetic or scholarly yearnings as to accomplish social goals. Disturbed by social forces they could not control and filled with idealistic notions of culture, these businessmen saw in the museum, the library, the symphony orchestra, and the university a way to purify their city and to generate a civic renaissance."

These ideas about philanthropy were an outgrowth of social Darwinist theories, in particular those of the British political economist Herbert Spencer, which were embraced by the American industrialist Andrew Carnegie. In Carnegie's view, true philanthropy involved economic empowerment, not a handout but a hand up. Nor was philanthropy the exclusive domain of the rich; Carnegie believed that everyone could contribute something toward the civic good, even if it was only volunteering time. For civic leaders in midwestern cities, Carnegie's view affirmed an impulse toward social reform that was locally controlled, promoted by business leaders in partnership with municipal government, and broadly based.

Although a community-support approach remains a general feature of midwestern cultural philanthropy, it takes different forms depending upon local conditions. In the westernmost states—Kansas, Nebraska, North Dakota, and South Dakota—cultural philanthropy tends toward the conservative, reflecting local attitudes and economic conditions. These states are largely rural, with small populations and widely separated towns, and they have few large private foundations or endowments. To bring cultural activities across vast spaces requires cooperation among and contributions from business and civic leaders, usually in federation with a similar leadership structure in neighboring communities. The Nebraska Cultural Endowment, for example, was the first state-funded endowment for both the arts and the humanities. In 1998 the state legislature set aside five million dollars, and when matched from other sources, the income from investment earnings is made available to support programs of the Nebraska Humanities Council and the Nebraska Arts Council.

Cooperation also extends across state lines, for example, through such organizations as the Heartland Arts Fund, which at the beginning of the twenty-first century served fifteen midwestern state arts agencies. Its grants help large and small communities pay for touring shows, including dance, music, and theatre. Another cooperative effort was Artrain USA, which began in 1971 as a short-term outreach program of the Michigan Council for the Arts to take art to communities statewide that did not have access to museums. It was incorporated as a nonprofit in 1975 in order to offer its traveling exhibitions nationwide. Artrain USA couldn't function without the cooperation of railroad companies, which donate equipment and crews to run the train from state to state, nor would it succeed without the commitment of local communities, which must raise funds to offset about 20 percent of the expenses associated with a tour stop.

In the major industrial centers of the Midwest, cultural philanthropy sprang from the impulses of a wealthy elite to make their cities more livable. They recognized that wealth brought with it civic responsibilities to act for the public good. They were equally aware that safe, clean cities with a vibrant cultural life attracted new businesses, which helped insulate local economies from boom-bust business cycles. Initially their attitude was paternalistic, governed by a sense of noblesse oblige. In Chicago, between 1871 (the year of the Great Chicago Fire) and 1900, this philanthropic urge produced the city's great cultural institutions—the Chicago Art Institute, the Field Columbian Museum, the Chicago Symphony Orchestra, and the Newberry and John Crerar Libraries. Even here, however, the cultural explosion was not accomplished strictly through individual gifts but, rather, through the willingness of the well-to-do and well connected to work cooperatively to attain common goals.

This led to new ways of supporting culture, ways not dominated exclusively by profit or reliant upon a single donor. A case in point is the way in which the University of Chicago was funded. Originally a Baptist-supported college, it was faltering when a group of civic leaders approached John D. Rockefeller, a devout Baptist, in 1887. Rockefeller pledged six hundred thousand dollars if another four hundred thousand dollars could be raised from other sources. It was an early and important instance of the "matching" or "challenge grant" concept that governs much philanthropy, private or public, today.

In Minnesota, progressive politics, pragmatism, and a populist value system shaped the response of cultural philanthropists. Geographically isolated, with long, hard winters, its communities took local responsibility for their own cultural activities as a way of bringing people of diverse backgrounds together. Communal consensus required pragmatic solutions. Art education and formal training were seen as integral to the state's cultural life, and support for them evolved late in the nineteenth century, in part as a response to demands for more industrial arts training. This growing demand led to the formation of the Minnesota State Arts Society in 1903. According to the society's bylaws, it sought "to advance the interest of fine arts, to develop the influence of art in education, and to foster the introduction of art in manufacture." By the early twentieth century, Minnesota was recognized for its innovation in promoting a statewide arts-education program.

Minnesota's business leaders were early supporters of civic and cultural institutions. In a kind of enlightened self-interest, their contributions extended beyond their private fortunes to involve their companies, establishing a regional tradition of corporate funding for arts and culture. One example was the Five-Percent Club, initiated in the 1960s by Kenneth Dayton of Dayton-Hudson Corporation, headquartered in Minneapolis-St. Paul, which pledged 5 percent of its before-tax profits to support a range of civic and cultural organizations. Dayton urged other business leaders to follow suit, and many did and continue to do so. Corporate funding is a double-edged sword, however. In the late twentieth century, corporate America shifted footing to a more globally based economy, and many once-local businesses were merged into multinational corporations. They no longer claimed allegiance to specific communities, altering the nature and commitment of corporate funding. This has had a dramatic impact on support for many cultural institutions, which had come to rely on funding from their local business communities.

Another innovation in public philanthropy was the regional arts council, which emerged nationwide in the 1970s following the founding of the National Endowment for the Arts. Minnesota was one of the first to adopt statewide regional arts councils, where counties were grouped into regions and a locally controlled regional council was given the responsibility of allocating state funds to cultural organizations and institutions within its boundaries. The regional-council model puts decision making and control of cultural activities into local hands. Politically it was important because it seeded development of cultural organizations in rural parts of the state that might not otherwise have had access to funds. That encouraged widespread public support for the arts, in particular from lawmakers in rural constituencies. Many other states subsequently followed Minnesota's lead, establishing in-state regional arts councils to administer public funds locally. State humanities councils, established following passage of the 1965 National Foundation on the Arts and Humanities Act, provide another layer of cultural support, funding programs in libraries, museums, and schools that advance a community's understanding of its history and traditions and open up public dialogue on sensitive social, cultural, and political issues.

Cleveland produced two additional philanthropic innovations in the early twentieth century, the Community Chest/United Way and the "community trust." Both grew out of the reform efforts of the city's Chamber of Commerce and were concerned as much with support for social programs and education as they were with culture. The Community Chest emerged from a chamber study of the fund-raising problems of seventy-three local charities, which were competing for donations from the same small pool of donors. In 1913 the chamber created a new organization, the Cleveland Federation for Charity and Philanthropy, which supported fifty-three charitable organizations. Its biggest innovation was to broaden the base of donors by soliciting small contributions from every stratum of society. The federation, later known as the Community Chest, and then as the United Way, made a coordinated annual appeal to all residents, allowing donors to either select particular organizations or permit the governing board to distribute their contributions.

The Cleveland Foundation was created a year later as the nation's first community trust. It was conceived by Frederick H. Goff, president of Cleveland Trust Company, as a single large endowment created from many gifts, large and small, with a broad range of charitable purposes. It would be administered professionally and limited in geographic scope to serving the residents of Cleveland, with distribution overseen by a board of public and private trustees. Goff's concern was to free the wealth tied up in irrevocable wills—characterized by Sir Arthur Hobhouse as "the dead hand"—that dictated how endowment money was used, even when the endowment's original purpose had become obsolete. A community trust, by contrast, would allow philanthropists to designate the purposes of their bequests without tying them in perpetuity to any single institution. By the late twentieth century, community foundations dedicated to supporting local concerns had become major features of public-private philanthropy nationwide. In 2000 there were 560 community foundations nationwide, and 9 of the 25 largest, based on assets, were located in the Midwest.

Indiana provides an example of a public-private initiative in the creation of community foundations. In 1990 the Lilly Endowment, the private foundation of the Eli Lilly family and among the largest private foundations in the United States, launched the Giving Indiana Funds for Tomorrow (GIFT) initiative to help communities establish local foundations. GIFT grants provided money for administration, thus encouraging organized, local fund-raising efforts. By 2002 there were ninety-five community foundations in Indiana, with more than one billion dollars in assets. Indiana also adopted the regional model and has twelve in-state regions, each with its own cultural plan and local advisory council. Together, the community foundations and regional councils point toward the major cultural philanthropic trend of the twenty-first century—a move toward strong local support and control, which has spread beyond the Midwest to become a national model.

Sources and Further Reading: Robert H. Bremner, *Giving: Charity and Philanthropy in History* (1994); Michael Conforti, ed., *Minnesota 1900* (1994); Daniel M. Fox, *Engines of Culture* (1995); Peter Dobkin Hall, *Inventing the Nonprofit Sector and Other Essays on Philanthropy, Voluntarism, and Nonprofit Organizations* (1992); Charles H. Hamilton and Warren F. Ilchman, eds., *Cultures of Giving* (1995); Helen Lefkowitz Horowitz, *Culture and the City* (1976); Robert L. Payton, *Philanthropy: Voluntary Action for the Public Good* (1988); Diana Tittle, *Rebuilding Cleveland* (1992).

Dinah Zeiger
University of Colorado, Boulder

Cultural Contributions of Fraternal Organizations

At the height of their popularity in the 1920s, there were some 800 differently named fraternal organizations in the United States. Their thirty million members, more than a quarter of the country's 105 million inhabitants, made the country a haven of fraternal orders. Many of the 800 organizations were nationwide entities. The best known and the largest was the Freemasons, which many other fraternal groups often used in part as a model. Many had unusual names, and their members were known as Odd Fellows, Elks, Buffaloes, Beavers, Eagles, Owls, and Red Men, to name but a few.

Given their prevalence, some of their words and expressions became a part of American culture. The term *blackballed* is derived from Freemasons' voting with a white or black ball (cube); a single black ball barred a proposed candidate for membership, hence he was "black balled." Being "on the level" morally also comes from Freemasonry. The all-seeing eye, the unfinished pyramid, and other symbols on the back of the U.S. dollar bill are a Masonic cultural contribution. Some fraternal orders, like the Freemasons, founded homes for their aged members; Shriners built hospitals for crippled children; and the Loyal Order of Moose created a home for orphaned children in Mooseheart, Illinois, in the heart of the Midwest. Scottish Rite Freemasons built large stone edifices called temples in many American cities, including some in the Midwest. Many of these temples had large auditoriums available for community gatherings. The Elks built golf courses for members; like the Eagles, they also provided clublike facilities where members could drink beer with fellow lodge "brothers."

Many fraternal orders, but not all, offered economic security by providing life and burial insurance, which aided their members before the days of company pensions and Social Security. During the Great Depression of the 1930s, many fraternal groups became extinct, but others, especially some fraternal benefit organizations, continued to prosper, among them the Aid Association for Lutherans, founded in Appleton, Wisconsin, in 1902; the Lutheran Brotherhood, organized in 1917 in Minnesota; Modern Woodmen of America, formed in Lyons, Iowa, in 1883; and Woodmen of the World, founded in 1890 in Colorado. Some became multi-billion-dollar entities and are thriving to this day.

From 1880 to 1920, the heyday era of American fraternal orders, more than twenty million immigrants landed in America. The Midwest had its share of immigrants who needed to be integrated into American society, and midwestern fraternal societies and others that functioned as branches of organizations first formed in the eastern states helped to assimilate these new Americans culturally. Of the 800 fraternal orders, approximately 120 had their headquarters in midwestern states. Many of these 120 groups had ethnic roots, and some also had denominational ties. The Midwest attracted an unusually large number of immigrants with similar backgrounds who thus felt at home in these fraternal societies.

A couple of decades before and after 1900, when America was largely rural, fraternal societies were often the only places where individuals could realize social prestige. In numerous lodges, members adorned themselves in colorful regalia, impressing their neighbors in public parades. Such participation was especially important in rural small towns, where fraternal members gained prestige by impressing neighbors, particularly nonmembers; as lodge brothers, they knew signs, passwords, and secrets that nonmembers did not. But as America became increasingly urbanized, the social prestige of belonging to a fraternal organization waned: In the new context of anonymity, it is difficult to impress strangers.

Sources and Further Reading: Charles Merz, "Sweet Land of Secrecy: The Strange Spectacle of American Fraternalism," *Harper's Monthly Magazine* (Feb. 1927); Alvin J. Schmidt, *Fraternal Organizations* (1980); Alvin J. Schmidt, *Oligarchy in Fraternal Organizations* (1973); Alvin J. Schmidt and Nicholas Babchuk, "Trends in U.S. Fraternal Associations in the Twentieth Century," in *Voluntary Action Research*, David Horton Smith, ed. (1973); Albert Stevens, ed., *Cyclopedia of Fraternities* (1907).

Alvin J. Schmidt
Illinois College

Rotary International

Rotary International is a global organization of business and professional people who provide humanitarian service, encourage high ethical standards in all vocations, and help build good will and peace in the world. The object of Rotary is to encourage and foster the ideal of service as a worthy enterprise. It seems only appropriate that this organization devoted to community service should have originated in the Midwest. Paul Harris founded Rotary in a meeting with three young businessmen in Chicago in 1905. By 1910 there were sixteen Rotary clubs in the country, linked as an organization called the National Association of Rotary Clubs. Two years later, the name was changed to International Association of Rotary Clubs, as Rotary spread to Winnipeg, Canada, and then England, Ireland, and Scotland. In 1922 the name was shortened to Rotary International.

With midwestern friendliness, Rotary members from the beginning have referred to one another by first names. Name tags (sometimes indicating a member's nickname) have also been a custom at Rotary for nearly a hundred years. This spirit of easy friendship informs the organization's attitude toward service.

The name *Rotarian* derived from the fact that members took turns, or rotated, holding meetings in their places of business, though soon they met in various hotels and restaurants, thus further rotating their places of fellowship. The organization's emblem became the rotary wheel, a symbol of civilization and movement. The final, international design of the wheel (containing twenty-four cogs and six spokes, with a keyway in the center) was adopted in 1922.

As an example of the impact of Rotary today, in Illinois alone there are seven districts, and in District 6490 (located in mideastern Illinois) there are fifty-five Rotary clubs, with the membership of each ranging from twenty-five to three hundred. There are more than 1,200,000 members of Rotary worldwide. Clubs help their communities on projects concerning schools, parks, roadsides, food banks, literacy, and habitats, to name a few. Internationally, Rotary currently works to eliminate polio everywhere and to promote peace among peoples.

Sources and Further Reading: Jeffrey A. Charles, *Service Clubs in American Society* (1993); David C. Forward, *A Century of Service* (2003).

George W. Wolf
Hudson, Illinois

State Arts and Humanities Councils

Most state arts and humanities councils date from the early 1970s, following passage of the 1965 National Foundation on the Arts and Humanities Act, which established two independent federal agencies, the National Endowment for the Arts (NEA) and the National Endowment for the Humanities (NEH). By law, the NEA allocates 40 percent of its grant funds to state and regional arts agencies, which then distribute the monies to cultural organizations, ranging from dance troupes to local museums. State humanities councils receive an annual congressional appropriation through the NEH, which they use to leverage state, individual, corporate, and foundation support at the local level. For example, the South Dakota Humanities Foundation, formed in 1987, raises funds independently, investing them in an endowment that makes the interest available for humanities council programs statewide. Humanities grants typically sustain cultural institutions, such as museums, libraries, colleges, public television and radio stations, and individual scholars working in fields like history, literature, and religion.

Support for the arts and humanities reflects the particular concerns and character of the Midwest. State funding tends to be conservative, which has forced cultural agencies to cooperate in unusual ways, fostering strong collaborative and public-private partnerships. For example, the Indiana Arts Commission Cultural Trust Fund, created by the state legislature in 1997, taps financial resources outside the commission's official budget, augmenting rather than replacing public funding to ensure a local, private base of support. Midwestern arts and cultural organizations typically feature a decentralized structure, with decision making pushed down to the local level. Minnesota pioneered a unique structure that has since been copied in many other states, dividing the state into eleven regions, each with a regional arts council receiving a direct appropriation from the legislature. Local arts organizations within each region then allocate the funds.

Long before officially designated arts and humanities councils appeared, the Midwest inaugurated the concept of matching public dollars with private dollars to support the arts. The philosophy behind matching anticipates not only a broader base of financial support but also a wider appeal to a greater range of citizen tastes. Increasingly, state arts and humanities councils jointly benefit from the matching concept. The Nebraska legislature, for example, launched the first state cultural endowment in 1998 with a five-million-dollar endowment to support both the arts and the humanities. When matched from other sources, the income from earnings supports programs of the Nebraska Arts Council and the Nebraska Humanities Council.

Cooperation extends across state lines, as well, through regional arts organizations that coordinate touring performances and visual exhibitions. Mid-America Arts Alliance, formed in 1972, was one of the first regional agencies. From its inception, it drew on private foundations as well as public funds to support traveling exhibitions, performing-arts touring programs, and artist residencies, an idea that later spread nationwide. Humanities councils likewise tap into national networks to support such projects as traveling exhibitions from the Smithsonian Institution.

Dinah Zeiger
University of Colorado–Boulder

YMCA and YWCA

During the late nineteenth and early twentieth centuries, urban reformers concerned with the deleterious effects of industrialization lobbied for the creation of organized programs that stressed physical exercise in a wholesome Christian atmosphere for the working class. Attempting to replace the evil influence of the saloon, the dance hall, and the boardinghouse, reformers created alternate spaces for America's young workers. Two urban institutions, the Young Men's Christian Association (YMCA) and the Young Women's Christian Association (YWCA), were central to this social movement.

Although administratively separate organizations, the YMCA and the YWCA share a similar heritage and purpose. Both originated in Great Britain in the mid-nineteenth century in response to a population shift of young people caused by industrial and urban growth. The YMCA, founded as a prayer group in 1844 in London, quickly expanded and attracted young men from the merchant class, offering them an alternative to the morally questionable leisure activities of the city. A group of American men first visited a YMCA when they attended the London World's Fair in 1851. Believing that American churches were failing to protect young male migrants from the evils of the city, this group organized the first American YMCAs in Boston that year and in New York City the following year. Throughout the 1850s, YMCAs flourished and spread across the urban North, from the East Coast to the Midwest.

On the eve of the Civil War, more than two hundred city associations operated in the United States. In 1861 northern YMCAs formed the U.S. Christian Commission to provide relief work for soldiers and sailors and in so doing attracted popular praise. With this new support, city associations began to construct buildings that reflected the needs of their constituents. The first building designed specifically for YMCA use was constructed in New York City in 1869. The New York plan was used as the model for city associations across the country. However, the first dormitories for young men were introduced by the Chicago YMCA in 1867 and by the Dayton, Ohio, and Milwaukee YMCAs in 1887. By the 1890s, the emphasis on athletic and recreational activities as useful character-building tools was so great in the local YMCAs that existing buildings and new construction were adapted to include gymnasiums, bowling alleys, swimming pools, and locker rooms. With large physical facilities to maintain and dozens of activities, clubs, and classes to run, the YMCA had been transformed from a small evangelical organization intent on saving young men from the vices of the city to an urban institution resembling the corporations whose directors sat on the YMCA board.

The YWCA came to America from Great Britain during the tumultuous years preceding the Civil War. Inspired by a religious revival that swept urban America in 1857 and 1858, Protestant women were encouraged to save their sisters who were in "moral danger." To nineteenth-century social reformers, the city presented special challenges for the young woman forced by familial or financial circumstances to live on her own. They feared that a young woman would become a victim and ultimately an employee of the vice industry. Because of the inequitable wage structure that forced women into low-paying jobs, many social reformers believed that women were particularly vulnerable to the financial advantages that both organized and casual prostitution offered. Thus the YWCA had a special mission to protect the minds, bodies, and reputations of young women alone in the city. Local churchwomen organized YWCAs in seven American cities, including Cincinnati, Cleveland, and St. Louis, during the 1860s. Over the next few decades, the female constituency of numerous city associations raised funds to construct YWCA buildings that included housing, cafeterias, employment bureaus, classrooms for vocational training, gymnasiums, and, during the early decades of the twentieth century, swimming pools.

Both the YMCA and the YWCA faced a wide array of issues as the population and spatial structure of the city changed throughout the twentieth century. As the number of young, native-born white Protestant men and women, the traditional constituency of both organizations, decreased and the numbers of European immigrants and African American southern migrants grew, the associations were constantly under pressure to adapt their programs. The YWCA established fifty-five International Institutes in cities across the United States to meet the specific needs of immigrants. Located in immigrant neighborhoods, they contained recreational facilities as well as employment bureaus and classrooms. The race issue was more difficult, however. In most cases, city association boards established separate "branch" organizations for the African American population. Usually underfunded and underrepresented on the citywide board, the African American branches seldom had equal recreational facilities. On several occasions, YMCA city associations allowed their African American members to use the YMCA pool only before its annual cleaning.

The national YWCA passed the Interracial Charter in 1946 and encouraged local associations to reorganize their branches on a "metropolitan" basis—that is, by location, not by race or ethnicity. For instance, the St. Louis YWCA examined each program, club, committee, and facility and reported in 1950 that every aspect, including the swimming program, was completely integrated. However, post–World War II suburbanization and white flight from America's aging inner cities created a branch structure for both the YMCA and YWCA that reflected the nation's racial divide. While the YWCA continued to advocate social reform, particularly in its campaign to eliminate racism, during the 1970s the YMCA abandoned its traditional agenda to build strong Christian men and began to attract entire families to join its fitness centers and swimming clubs. In many American cities, including those of the Midwest, the YMCA and the recreation center are synonymous.

Sources and Further Reading: John Donald Gustav-Wrathall, *Take the Young Stranger by the Hand* (1998); C. Howard Hopkins, *History of the Y.M.C.A. in North America* (1951); Nina Mjagkij and Margaret Spratt, eds., *Men and Women Adrift: The YMCA and the YWCA in the City* (1997); Clifford Putney, *Muscular Christianity: Manhood and Sports in Protestant America, 1880–1920* (2001); Mary S. Sims, *The YWCA: An Unfolding Purpose* (1950).

Margaret A. Spratt
California University of Pennsylvania

Cultural Tourism

Though our society is inundated with supposed proof that most popular-culture history and offbeat historical sites are relegated to the most high-profile coastal centers (New York and Los Angeles, primarily), the facts do not quite support that. Those places may be the movie, television, and finance capitals of the world and the places where celebrities tend to display their most infamous behavior. But to really understand the heart and soul of American pop culture, one must journey to the heart and soul of America, to the Midwest.

Most people typically plan their summer vacations, road trips, and weekend escapes with an eye on big-name attractions, whether they're visiting in the Midwest or anyplace else. Amusement parks and popular restaurants are one sort of destination, but lesser-known sites and landmarks can make a visit to the Midwest as interesting and exciting as anything one might find in New York or Los Angeles.

Chicago is an obvious regional destination rich in history and culture, but instead of the Sears Tower, Marshall Field's, or Wrigley Field, a cultural tourist might first visit the most mythical of Chicago landmarks, the site of the Great Chicago Fire, 558 Dekoven Street. According to legend, the fire was started by a cow that belonged to an Irishwoman named Catherine O'Leary. She ran a neighborhood milk business from the barn behind her home, and after carelessly leaving a kerosene lantern in the barn following her evening milking, a cow kicked it over and ignited the hay on the floor. No proof of this story has ever been offered, but the legend took hold in Chicago and was told around the world. Regardless of how the fire started, on Sunday evening, October 8, 1871, Chicago was a city in flames. The blaze burned homes and shops and left 300 people dead and 500,000 homeless. Firefighters brought the fire under control the next day, but only with the help of a rainstorm. Ironically, today the site of the fire's origin, marked by a statue, is occupied by the Chicago Fire Department's Training Academy.

Another notable pop culture site in Chicago is the spot where a famous political event took place. On September 26, 1960, 70 million U.S. viewers tuned in to watch Senator John F. Kennedy of Massachusetts and Vice President Richard M. Nixon in the first-ever televised presidential debate. It had a decisive impact on the outcome of the 1960 election, and had Kennedy not emerged from that debate as the clearly perceived winner, many believe he almost certainly would not have gone on to capture the White House later that year. The event took place at WBBM-TV, located at 630 North McClurg Court in Chicago, and a plaque in the building's lobby acknowledges the event.

An explosive moment? Yes, but not nearly as powerful as what happened at the site of the Joseph Regenstein Library at the University of Chicago (1100 East 57th Street). It was there, on December 2, 1942, that Enrico Fermi supervised the design and assembly of an "atomic pile," a code word for a device that in peacetime would be known as a nuclear reactor. The bronze memorial *Nuclear Energy*, by famed sculptor

The *Field of Dreams* baseball diamond, Dyersville, Iowa. Iowa Division of Tourism.

Henry Moore, is situated on the west edge of the twelve-acre site of the library, marking the exact spot where Fermi and other scientists achieved the first controlled, self-sustaining nuclear chain reaction. Tourists to Chicago could go on to visit the site of the St. Valentine's Day Massacre or the place where outlaw John Dillinger was ambushed and killed, but they also might want to head north in the Midwest and lighten things up a bit.

If the Nicollet Mall Pedestrian Shopping Area (Seventh Street and Nicollet Mall) in Minneapolis looks familiar, it is with good reason. For the opening title sequence of *The Mary Tyler Moore Show*, one of the most enduring shots in television history was created there: Mary flinging her tam into the air with that big, carefree smile on her face. Today, a bronze statue capturing Moore in mid toss can be found near the exact site where she originally twirled in the opening montage. (The house where she lived is located at 1204 Kenwood Parkway in Minneapolis.)

"The day the music died," words from Don McLean's 1971 classic "American Pie," refer to another midwestern site of pop culture significance—the spot where Buddy Holly's plane crashed. The site is located off State Road 20, north of Clear Lake, Iowa. The Winter Dance Party Tour was planned to cover twenty-four cities in a short, three-week time frame, and Buddy Holly would be the biggest headliner. It was the dead of winter and the tour bus carrying him and others had heating problems when they arrived at the Surf Ballroom in Clear Lake, Iowa, on February 3, 1959. They were cold and tired. So harsh was the situation that Buddy decided to charter a plane for the group. Dwyer Flying Service was called, and it charged thirty-six dollars a person for a single-engine Beechcraft Bonanza. At the last minute, Waylon Jennings gave his seat up to the Big Bopper, who was ill and had a hard time fitting comfortably into the bus. When Holly learned that Jennings wasn't going to fly, he said, "Well, I hope your old bus freezes up." Jennings replied, "Well, I hope your plane crashes." Tommy Allsup flipped Ritchie Valens for the remaining seat and Valens won. The plane took off just after 1:00 A.M. from Clear Lake and had not gotten far from the airport when it crashed, killing all onboard. The Surf Ballroom is still open in Clear Lake and pays tribute to the musicians with a historic-site marker out front.

On another midwestern musical note, Detroit is home to the Motown Museum, located at 2648 West Grand Boulevard. The famous, soulful sound known as Motown was born in the very brick structure that today houses the museum. Marvin Gaye, Smokey Robinson, Diana Ross and the Supremes, Stevie Wonder, the Jackson Five—all got their starts there under the orchestration of Motown Records impresario Berry Gordy, Jr. Today, visitors can see their sheet music and music studio equipment, including the piano used by all the greats. Photographs and gold records adorn the walls, and original costumes are also on display.

On a final musical note, while other regions boast some major Elvis Presley sites, only the Midwest can lay claim to the location of the King's final concert. It happened at Market Square Arena, 300 East Market Street, in Indianapolis. Presley gave his last concert there, on June 26, 1977. Twenty-five years later a commemorative plaque was placed there (the marker is in a gravel parking lot where the arena stood before being demolished). A time capsule encased within it holds Presley memorabilia, including a scarf of Presley's and a bootlegged recording of one of his last shows. A bronze plaque reading "Ladies and Gentlemen, Elvis has left the building" sits atop a stone column, repeating the words that announcer Al Dvorin would say at the end of each of Presley's shows.

In the southern Midwest, a site of immense cultural significance can be found in St. Joseph, Missouri, at the Pony Express Museum, located at 914 Penn Street. Only in the Midwest can one find the original stables of the famed Pony Express, which was devised to provide the fastest mail delivery between St. Joseph and Sacramento, California. The service was active from April 3, 1860, to late October 1861. The Pony Express ran day and night, and 183 men are known to have ridden for the organization during its eighteen-month existence. Four hundred horses were purchased to stock the Pony Express route—thoroughbreds, mustangs, pintos, and Morgans were often used across about 165 stations. The total trail length was almost two thousand miles, and it ran through the present-day states of Missouri, Kansas, Nebraska, Colorado, Wyoming, Utah, Nevada, and California.

As Neil Young bitterly documented in his musical diatribe "Ohio," on May 4, 1970, U.S. National Guardsmen opened fire on students demonstrating against the Vietnam War at Kent State University in Ohio. The National Guard had been sent in to prevent riots and regain control of the campus but began shooting after some of the students started throwing rocks. More than sixty shots were fired, and when the dust had settled four students were dead. Seeing American troops firing on American students was shocking, and it led many citizens to rethink their views on the war. The Kent State campus was shut down and twenty thousand students were sent home. Within the next two weeks, more than five hundred campuses around the country would shut down as millions of students took to the streets to protest the Kent

State murders and the invasion of Cambodia. Plaques have been laid at the sites in Kent State's Prentice Hall parking lot and surrounding area where the students were shot.

Tourists who are property owners may want to visit the Homestead National Monument in Beatrice, Nebraska. After all, it was there where the concept of landownership was born. The Homestead Act of 1862 was one of the most significant and enduring events in the westward expansion of the United States. By granting land to claimants, it allowed nearly any man or woman a chance to truly experience the American Dream. President Abraham Lincoln signed the Homestead Act, which declared that any citizen (or intending citizen) could claim 160 acres—one-quarter of a square mile—of surveyed government land. Claimants had to "improve" the plot with a dwelling and grow crops. After five years, if the original filer was still on the land, it was his or her property, free and clear. One of the first partakers of this opportunity was a man named Daniel Freeman, a Union scout from Iowa. The Homestead National Monument is located on the site of Freeman's original land claim.

These are but a few of the unique pop-culture landmarks that help validate the cultural significance of the Midwest. There are many more to be visited in the Heartland, where American popular culture always has been—and always will be—alive and well.

Sources and Further Reading: Richard F. Bates, *The Great Chicago Fire and the Myth of Mrs. O'Leary's Cow* (2002); Scott L. Bills and Shirley Bills, "Kent State/May 4," *Echoes through a Decade* (1988); Kenneth E. Foote, *Shadowed Ground*, rev. ed. (2003); Ross Miller, *American Apocalypse: The Great Fire and the Myth of Chicago* (1990); Beverly Narkiewicz and Lincoln S. Bates, *Uncommon and Unheralded Museums* (1991); Dave Walker, *American Rock and Roll Tour* (1992).

Chris Epting
Huntington Beach, California

African American Planned Communities and Recreational Resorts

The establishment of all-black towns presents a unique example of an African American ethnography of autonomy. In the years after the Civil War, black-initiated independent settlements in the Midwest took two forms. The best-known examples of planned independent villages were Nicodemus, Kansas (1877); Boley, Oklahoma (1904); Robbins, Illinois, southwest of Chicago (1917); and Lincoln Heights, Ohio, north of Cincinnati (1926). By 1940 more than seventy urban black communities had a combined population of over ten thousand. But by the 1950s, with the impact of civil rights legislation and the national shift toward racial integration, most of these all-black towns were only a memory.

A second variety of black settlements uniquely associated with the Midwest is the recreational village of the early twentieth century. Black resorts constituted a self-help response to the exclusion of the expanding African American middle class from public and private recreational facilities, notably in the cities of Chicago and Detroit. Recreational villages also offered performance venues for a rising black professional class. At their peak, black resorts featured performers such as Louis Armstrong, Count Basie, Dinah Washington, Sammy Davis, Jr., and Della Reese.

Cooperative resort communities flourished in the Great Lakes area, especially in southern Wisconsin and east-central Michigan. Particularly notable were Idlewild and Lake Ivanhoe. About two hundred miles west of Detroit, on the edge of forestland bought from a railroad company, Idlewild or the "Black Eden" was considered the first and most famous of the black resorts there. Early purchasers of lots at Idlewild included National Association for the Advancement of Colored People (NAACP) leader W.E.B. DuBois, Chicago surgeon Daniel Hale Williams, and cosmetologist Madame C.J. Walker. Lake Ivanhoe, founded near a segregated white resort at Lake Geneva in southeastern Wisconsin in 1926, was the brainstorm of black Chicago businessmen. Lake Ivanhoe's streets bear the names of famous African Americans and historically black colleges and universities, such as Dunbar, Fisk, and Tuskegee.

The black utopian dream—of both permanent black settlements and resorts—declined because of the Great Depression, and, ironically, the enforcement of fair-housing laws in the 1950s and 1960s. They also suffered from an unmet need for jobs, goods, and services—including temporary housing and personal services such as barbering, banking, and mortuary services. By the time of the civil rights movement, prospects for the small, organized black recreational village were bleak. The most promising goal for many black utopians was to pass their passion for the recreational village to a younger generation with enough money to tour and purchase a second home.

Sources and Further Reading: Samuel Gonzales, "A Black Community in Rural Wisconsin," master's thesis, University of Wisconsin (1972); Thomas Knight, *Sunset on Utopian Dreams* (1977); Lewis Walker, *Black Eden* (2002).

Richard Ralston
University of Wisconsin–Madison

Amish and Mennonite Communities and Villages

The Old Order Amish (henceforth "Amish") are one of the most visible religious minorities in North America, especially in the Midwest. Large Amish populations are found in Ohio (49,000), Pennsylvania (42,000), and Indiana (33,000). Among Anabaptist sects, the Amish are among the most conservative in terms of lifestyle, while the Mennonites are the most numerous. The majority of Mennonites in North America are not as visibly identifiable as the Amish; that is, most do not dress or groom themselves in a distinctive way or place limitations on the use of technology. Outward signs of Amish identity include distinctive dress and grooming, use of the horse and buggy, and maintenance of the Pennsylvania German dialect (also known as Pennsylvania Dutch), and these have generated the Amish tourism industry.

Tourism and other forms of commercialism involved with marketing the Amish have been steady over the last hundred years, and business enterprises that cater to tourists interested in the Amish take many forms. Perhaps most common are those focused on "Pennsylvania Dutch" cuisine. For most outsiders, tourists and businesses alike, the terms *Amish* and *Pennsylvania Dutch* are interchangeable, despite the fact that historically most Pennsylvania Dutch (i.e., Pennsylvania Germans) are not of Amish or Mennonite background. In any case, most tourism in Amish communities features restaurants that offer "Pennsylvania Dutch" or "Amish" home-cooked dishes, often served family style.

Other tourist enterprises in Amish areas feature guided tours on roads past Amish farms. In a few cases, entire outdoor museums showcasing Amish farm life have been established. Some museums, which are often run by Mennonites, give an in-depth view of Amish faith and life against the broader background of Anabaptist history. These museums (e.g., Menno-Hof in Shipshewana, Indiana; the People's Place in Intercourse, Pennsylvania) are really more like interpretive centers and are much less commercially oriented.

Many Amish are indifferent to such tourism and do their best to live their lives in accordance with their faith. They may see the effects of tourism, such as increased traffic on country roads, as inconvenient. Being photographed is particularly troublesome because Amish faith interprets visual representations of humans, including photographs, as graven images.

Whether tourism benefits the Amish is an open question. Some people argue that increased revenues from tourism help all residents of Amish-populated areas. Others point to the fact that some Amish are themselves employed in the tourist enterprises. Other Amish are proprietors of cottage industries that sell crafts such as quilts and furniture to non-Amish customers. Whatever positive or negative effects tourism has on the Amish, it is a fact of life that most Amish living in larger settlements have come to accept.

Sources and Further Reading: Donald B. Kraybill, *The Riddle of Amish Culture*, rev. ed. (2001); Donald B. Kraybill and Carl F. Bowman, *On the Backroad to Heaven* (2001); David Luthy, "The Origin and Growth of Amish Tourism," in Donald B. Kraybill and Marc A. Olshan, eds., *The Amish Struggle with Modernity* (1994).

Mark L. Louden
University of Wisconsin–Madison

Branson, Missouri, and Country and Western Music

Established in the early 1880s, and named for R. S. Branson, its first postmaster, Branson, Missouri, has become known as "the nation's newest music capital." True, a majority of people who visit the Ozark town today do so to attend music shows, but long before it became noted as a music stop it had been a favorite destination for tourists. Initially, visitors came for fishing; then, in 1907, Harold Bell Wright's highly successful novel *Shepherd of the Hills*, which was set in the community, brought a great influx of curiosity seekers. With the creation of Lake Taneycomo in 1913 and Table Rock Lake in the 1950s the town became greatly appealing to outdoor enthusiasts.

Branson's ascendancy as a country music mecca began in the 1960s when Hugo and Mary Herschend opened Silver Dollar City, a small crafts village that also featured music, atop Marvel Cave. This "sideshow," which was originally intended to entertain visitors awaiting entrance into the cave, became so popular that it eventually expanded to two sites, with the one in Pigeon Forge, Tennessee, now known as Dollywood. Although it was advertised that music from a century ago was performed at the city, much more recent music was also heard. Today Silver Dollar City still pays homage to old-time music with several festivals devoted to traditional music and dance scattered throughout the year.

Sources and Further Reading: Arthur Frommer, *Branson!* (1995); Lee N. Godley and Patricia M. O'Rourke, *Daytrip Missouri*, 3rd ed. (2000); Robert L. Ramsay, *Our Storehouse of Missouri Place Names* (1973).

William K. McNeil
Ozark Folk Center
Mountain View, Arkansas

Celebrity Memorial Sites

One of the Midwest's best-known celebrities is movie actor and popular icon James Dean. Born in 1931 in Marion, Indiana, Dean spent many of his formative childhood years in the farming community of Fairmount, Indiana, where he lived with family relatives after his mother died. Dean himself died at age twenty-four when the car he was driving (a Porsche Spyder) collided with another vehicle on a California highway. He had just completed his third movie, *Giant*, with Rock Hudson and Elizabeth Taylor. Today, thousands of fans and devotees flock year-round to Dean's gravesite in Fairmount's Park Cemetery and other locations associated with him in life. The city also hosts a festival each September in his honor. On September 30 a memorial service is held for him at the Back Creek Friends Meeting followed by a procession to his grave. Fairmount's claim to Dean is marked by the James Dean Memorial Park, the James Dean Memorial Gallery, the Fairmount Historical Museum's exhibition of Dean memorabilia, and other sites associated with Dean's life. Other events held in his honor include a dance and birthday party in February and the James Dean Fans Weekend in July.

Also memorialized in the Midwest is early rock-and-roll star Buddy Holly. He, along with J. P. "Big Bopper" Richardson and Ritchie Valens, died in an airplane crash near Clear Lake, Iowa, on February 3, 1959, which has come to be known as "the day the music died" through the popular song "American Pie" by Don McLean. Holly was twenty-two years old. The crash site is marked by a small stainless steel guitar with three stainless steel records and four trees. A tribute is held every February at the Surf Ballroom in Clear Lake, Iowa, the site of Holly's final gig.

Singer and Rock and Roll Hall of Fame inductee Otis Redding died in a plane crash in Lake Monona, Madison, Wisconsin, on December 10, 1967, at age 26. A memorial to Redding is included in the rooftop garden overlooking the lake at the Monona Terrace Community and Convention Center in Madison.

Sources and Further Reading: Scott Freeman, *Otis! The Otis Redding Story* (2001); John Goldrosen and John Beecher, *Remembering Buddy: The Definitive Biography of Buddy Holly*, rev. ed. (1994); James F. Hopgood, " 'Back Home in Indiana' " in Walter R. Adams and Frank A. Salamone, eds., *Anthropology and Theology* (2000).

James F. Hopgood
Northern Kentucky University

Festivals

The Midwest is home to a great number of festivals, ranging from large urban spectacles to patriotic commemorations, ethnic heritage and hobbyist events, and community celebrations put on by local businesspeople. While these festivals may address different audiences, many share certain features. All are the product of a dual organization. That is, one small set of

---

❖ Wisconsin Death Trip

In the early 1970s, Shaker Heights, Ohio, native Michael Lesy became fascinated with a cache he found in the Wisconsin State Historical Society of some three thousand glass-plate negatives made between 1890 and 1910 by Charles Van Schaick, a town photographer who worked in Black River Falls, Wisconsin. Lesy began reading spools of microfilm that preserved the state's small-town turn-of-the-century newspapers and records, including *The Badger State Banner*, published by the father-and-son editorial team of Frank and George Cooper. He had originally planned to splice together pictures and texts to create a short movie, but the high costs of filmmaking led him to produce, instead, the photo-history book *Wisconsin Death Trip*. First published in 1973, Lesy's book became an instant classic and has since spawned its own subindustry.

Refusing the easy, uncomplicated nostalgia of a romanticized midwestern past, *Wisconsin Death Trip* juxtaposes haunting late-nineteenth-century photographs of dead babies, inmates in Wisconsin's state mental asylum, and uncomfortably posed families with disturbing written accounts of suicide, arson, bank failure, alcoholism, unemployment, and outbreaks of diphtheria. Like much of America, Wisconsin was wracked by economic depression during the 1890s, and *Wisconsin Death Trip* examines the darker side of the midwestern American dream.

Lesy's visual record of an unsettling Midwest has inspired novelists like Stewart Onan, whose book *A Prayer for the Dying* (1999) is set in an eerie nineteenth-century Wisconsin landscape beset by pestilence and fire; musicians like Static-X, whose 1999 debut album was titled *Wisconsin Death Trip*; and, also in 1999, writer/director James Marsh's award-winning feature film *Wisconsin Death Trip*.

Erika Doss
University of Colorado, Boulder

people takes on as a year-round or nearly year-round activity the planning and organization of the festival and then calls on a much larger group of people to assist in the actual implementation of the festival itself. These latter are the people who ensure the smooth operation of the parade; who pour the beer in the beer garden; who direct traffic, take tickets, remove garbage, sell food, and much more. Frequently, they are the face of the festival to the third set of people involved with festivals—the attending public.

Fundamentally, festivals are a form of celebration, and at base they celebrate the community that participates in them, whether it is a small town in Minnesota, the Czechfest in Decorah, Iowa, a Fourth of July celebration in Kansas, a Memorial Day parade in Indiana, or a blues festival in Chicago. What is significant about the community created by a festival is that it is an undemanding form of community—no one is required to attend a festival, and no one is required to stand up and be counted or swear allegiance to the town, city, ethnic group, or other intentional community represented. But by attending, participants are able to indicate their voluntary acceptance of membership in the community, whether it be country music fans, an ethnic group, U.S. residents generally, or the town or city they live in. Festivals celebrate belonging in a society in which belonging is seen as both voluntary and problematic. They provide a physical form to the imagined communities that underlie them. That is, for country music fans, attendance at the WE Fest in Detroit Lakes, Minnesota, gives them a sense of physically belonging to a like-minded community of people that they could only imagine, not feel, prior to attending. The same, actually, is true in small towns—it is the community festival that gets people out experiencing their joint membership in the community in ways that do not regularly occur and that moves community membership from an idea to a physically experienced phenomenon. In the context of community-based festivals, the issue of community membership is never entirely straightforward. The festival may not always be open to everyone, or different groups in a town or city may feel that the festival is not a place where they are welcome. In small towns, it is often young men or recent immigrants to the community who feel that there is nothing in the festival for them, or that they are not welcome.

For the organizers of festivals, there is another level of meaning: Through their participation, they are able to demonstrate both their capacity to act successfully in the world and their commitment to the community the festival represents. The people who organize the St. Paul Winter Carnival are not only putting on a large urban festival under usually harsh conditions,

they are also demonstrating their commitment to St. Paul and its residents as well as their own organizational skill. This is particularly the case in small towns, where festival organizers are unpaid volunteers whose reward comes through the satisfaction of a job well done and the thanks of the community.

Festivals are also a form of diversion, of entertainment, and here it is clear that the particularities of any community are expressed in what qualifies as entertainment. This is most obvious in festivals designed for very specific communities—the Columbus (Indiana) Bluegrass Festival, say, or the Chicago Blues Festival—where the entertainment is predetermined, so to speak, by the nature of the community. But in community festivals with a diversity of events, specific events are designed to appeal to a variety of entertainment interests within the community. Thus, while a great many small-town festivals feature a parade, the specific units that make up the parade vary from place to place. Similarly, a street dance is found in many community festivals, but the particular kind of music featured will be to the taste of the people that the organizers expect to attend.

Community festivals tend to be nonprofit organizations, or dedicated to returning any profits to the community in the form of improvement projects or donations to community organizations. Connected with many festivals, however, is a wide range of community voluntary organizations; often the festival is their major fund-raiser for the year. Thus, from volunteer fire department to Lions Club to youth baseball to public library to church and arts groups, the community's organizations sell food or beverages, services, entertainment, clothing, handicrafts, and more. The festival itself generates the revenue it needs to continue from year to year from donations, fund-raising events, and admission charges associated with one or more festival events. In recent years, festivals of all kinds have increasingly sought sponsorships from corporate or business sources, enabling them to remain vital while providing valuable publicity for the sponsoring companies.

What makes midwestern festivals midwestern? Midwestern festivals tend to avoid excess and are generally well controlled, reflecting rather than challenging the values of their perceived communities. While they may lack the ecstatic highs of other festivals, they also lack the riotous dangers that some festivals may pose.

Sources and Further Reading: Frederick Errington, "Reflexivity Deflected: The Festival of Nations as an American Cultural Performance," *American Ethnologist* 14 (Nov. 1987); Robert H. Lavenda, *Corn Fests and Water Carnivals* (1997); Robert H. Lavenda, "Festivals and the Creation of Public

Culture: Whose Voice(s)?" in Ivan Karp, Christine Mullen Kraemer, and Stephen D. Lavine, eds., *Museums and Communities* (1992); Greta Pratt, *In Search of the Corn Queen* (1994); Sheldon Smith, "The Re-establishment of Community: The Emerging Festival System of the American West," *Journal of American Culture* 8 (Fall 1985); Beverly Stoeltje, "Festival in America," in Richard Dorson, ed., *Handbook of American Folklore* (1983).

Robert H. Lavenda
St. Cloud State University, Minnesota

Greenfield Village

A ninety-acre living-history museum, Greenfield Village was founded in Dearborn, Michigan, by Henry Ford in 1929 to feature his extensive collections of motor vehicles, locomotives, and airplanes. One of the most popular historical visitor attractions in the Midwest, the village (along with the Henry Ford Museum) richly interprets material and technological progress in the United States. Featuring more than eighty historic buildings relocated to a re-created village setting, Greenfield Village is recognized as a pioneer American museum for its influence on historic preservation in America. The original idea for Greenfield Village was guided by Henry Ford's personal vision of American history and his passion for celebrating and understanding the "great men" of American agriculture, transportation, and manufacturing. Hence the village features midwestern sites such as Orville and Wilbur Wright's home and cycle shop from Dayton, Ohio; the Harry Firestone Ohio farm; and Eagle Tavern of Clinton, Michigan, alongside other American buildings such as Thomas Edison's New Jersey Menlo Park Laboratory.

In recent years, Greenfield Village has grown beyond Ford's personal vision to present a history of ideas and American ingenuity that have shaped America and the Midwest. Attention has been given to providing a broader representation of the life of farm families, the experience of black slavery and the Underground Railroad, and urban industrialization.

Greenfield Village is now part of what has been renamed "The Henry Ford"—a combination of the museum, the open-air historic village, an IMAX theatre, Ford Rouge Factory tours, and a variety of other entertainment experiences.

Source and Further Reading: Kathryn Bishop Eckert, *Buildings of Michigan* (1993).

C. Kurt Dewhurst
Michigan State University Museum

Halls of Fame

Halls of fame have been described as "museums with a personality," dealing with specific men and women and their particular achievements in fields like sports and other popular pastimes. Victor Danilov traces the origin of halls of fame to Europe at the end of the eighteenth century, where they began as tributes to national heroes. They evolved in American popular culture into institutions honoring everything from quilts to football. Halls of fame generally are tied to specific locations, commemorating activities or people associated with place, but their location may be the result of other factors. For example, USA Roller Sports provides space for the Roller Skating Hall of Fame in its national headquarters and museum in Lincoln, Nebraska.

The Midwest is home to an unusual number and variety of halls of fame: Michigan ranks third nationally in sheer numbers, with thirteen halls and sites, followed by Wisconsin, with thirteen halls at eight separate sites. They range from the quirky, like the Hamburger Hall of Fame in Seymour, Wisconsin, and the Quackery Hall of Fame in Minneapolis, which features the world's largest collection of medical devices that pretended to cure illnesses, to the serious, like Inventure Place, the National Inventors Hall of Fame in Akron, Ohio, an interactive museum honoring inventions and inventors. Halls of fame may commemorate activities that were or are part of local history, like the Circus Hall of Fame in Peru, Indiana, where several circuses had winter quarters, including the Ringling Brothers Circus, in the late nineteenth and early twentieth centuries. Economic factors may also play a part. For example, the bidding to win the Rock and Roll Hall of Fame was fierce, but it ended up in Cleveland when a public-private partnership combining state, city, county, and local corporations and foundations provided sixty-five million dollars of the ninety-two-million-dollar cost of the building. It draws more than one million visitors a year, making it the most popular hall of fame in the United States at the beginning of the twenty-first century.

The popularity of halls of fame, gauged by attendance figures, is fed by Americans' nearly insatiable curiosity about celebrities of all kinds, from sports figures to inventors. As Danilov points out, with increased leisure time and more disposable income, people want to travel and see the sights, whether historic or cultural. Halls of fame allow people to relive memories and pay homage to heroes while learning more about their particular interests, as, for example, at the National Motorcycle Hall of Fame in Sturgis, South Dakota. Some feature a simple wall of plaques and pictures, like the Route 66 Hall of Fame in Mc-Clean, Illinois, which is located in a truck stop. Others have evolved far beyond collections of photographs and objects and may include interactive exhibits that invite the public to participate, like the National Agricultural Center and Hall of fame in Bonner Springs, Kansas, with more than thirty thousand agricultural implements and a re-created FarmTown U.S.A. featuring an entire rural town.

Sources and Further Reading: Victor J. Danilov, *Hall of Fame Museums: A Reference Guide* (1997); Paul Soderberg and Helen Washington, eds., *The Big Book of Halls of Fame in the United States and Canada* (1977).

Dinah Zeiger
University of Colorado–Boulder

Major Amusement Parks

During the nineteenth century, amusement parks emerged in the Midwest as "trolley parks" at the end of electric trolley lines, or as ventures modeled on New York's Coney Island. Among the traditional amusement parks in the Midwest were Chicago's Cheltenham Beach and Riverview; Cincinnati's Coney Island; Cleveland's Euclid Beach; Geauga Lake in Aurora, Ohio; Kansas City, Missouri's Electric and Forest Parks; St. Louis's Forest Park Highlands; and Sandusky's Cedar Point. Chicago's 1893 World's Columbian Exposition introduced the essential elements of amusement parks: ornate architecture and brilliant lights, exotic locales, a midway, and the use of engineering and technology for fun and spectacle. Walt Disney's father was a laborer at the 1893 exposition, and America's foremost amusement park entrepreneur (born in Chicago and raised in Marceline, Missouri) was strongly influenced by midwestern culture and its amusement venues.

Traditional parks reached their zenith around 1920 and declined precipitously by 1940 due to wars and rising urban property values. Social conditions (the baby boom, increased income and leisure time, more automobiles, and the growth of suburbia) coincided with the creation of Disneyland (California) in 1955. Harnessing electronics, plastics, exotic sectors, and lavish landscaping, today's theme-park industry is largely managed by conglomerates. In the Midwest, Six Flags dominates with four parks: Great America (Gurney, Illinois), Six Flags St. Louis, Worlds of Adventure (Cleveland), and Wyandot Lake (Columbus, Ohio). Paramount owns Kings Island near Cincinnati. Cedar Point in Sandusky, Ohio, is the Midwest's gem. In operation since the 1870s (and now owned by Cedar Fair LP), the lakeside park has successfully transformed itself with thrill rides while preserving elements of its traditional past.

Sources and Further Reading: Judith A. Adams, *The American Amusement Park Industry* (1991); David W. Francis and Diane DeMali Francis, *Cedar Point* (1988); Gary Kyriazi, *The Great American Amusement Parks* (1976).

Judith Adams-Volpe
University at Buffalo
State University of New York

The Rock and Roll Hall of Fame and Museum

Atlantic Records cochair Ahmet Ertegun and lawyer Suzan Evans established the Rock and Roll Hall of Fame Foundation in 1983 in New York City. On August 5, 1985, a board of twenty-one members, including Cleveland native and New York disc jockey Norm N. Nite, was then assigned to determine where to construct the building—which would honor the music industry's greatest contributors and influences through collections, archives, interactive computers, and film clips.

Cleveland city officials lobbied hard, beating out competitors that included New York City and Los Angeles. Clevelanders used credible facts in rock and roll's early history for their arguments. Disc jockey Alan Freed first used the term *rock 'n' roll* to describe the rhythm-and-blues records he was playing on his Cleveland-based radio program *The Moondog Rock & Roll House Party.* Freed also orchestrated what many believe to be the first bona fide rock concert, the Moondog Coronation Ball, at the Cleveland Arena. In addition, Cleveland was well known within the industry as a proving ground for new records as well as for successful national artists such as the O'Jays, Bobby Womack, James Gang with Joe Walsh, the Raspberries with Eric Carmen, Chrissie Hynde of the Pretenders, Devo, and others.

Thus, the Rock and Roll Hall of Fame and Museum opened in Cleveland on September 1, 1995, at 1 Key Plaza, on the lakefront. Since then, the hall of fame has received more than 5.5 million visitors from around the world. Although there are a few permanent exhibits, such as Dedicated to the One I Love, honoring influential disc jockeys like Freed, Wolfman Jack, and Casey Kasem, many exhibits and special programs vary on a regular basis to encourage visitors to return. Among the most popular of these have been the John Lennon Exhibit and In the Name of Love: Two Decades of U2.

The Rock and Roll Hall of Fame and Museum, Cleveland. © Gail Meese/Meese Photo Research.

Source and Further Reading: Deanna R. Adams, *Rock 'n' Roll and the Cleveland Connection* (2002).

Deanna R. Adams
Mentor, Ohio

The United States Air Force Museum

The United States Air Force Museum at Wright-Patterson Air Force Base near Dayton, Ohio, is the world's largest and oldest military aviation museum. Featuring more than four hundred aircraft and missiles and thousands of artifacts throughout more than ten acres of indoor exhibit space, the museum is the Midwest's largest free tourist attraction, welcoming 1.2 million visitors a year. It serves as the air force's national museum, projecting air force history through aircraft, artifacts, sensory exhibits, entertaining special events, and informative educational programs.

Begun in 1923, the museum has grown through numerous capital expansion phases. From the Wright Military Flyer to the YF-22, the museum's aircraft connect the Wright Brothers' era to today's stealth-fighter age. The museum boasts a vast collection of presidential aircraft, including SAM (Special Air Mission) 26000, a Boeing 707 that served as President John F. Kennedy's plane. The museum features galleries containing aircraft, exhibits, and artifacts designed to explore in depth the stories of America's military air arm in World War I, World War II, the

Korean War, the Vietnam conflict, and recent operations. Museum exhibits incorporate customized mannequins and special-effects lighting to create a historically authentic setting, capturing drama and appealing to emotion.

Source and Further Reading: Nick P. Apple and Gene Gurney, *The Air Force Museum*, 7th ed. (1999).

Christopher McGee
Wright Patterson Air Force Base, Ohio

World's Fairs

World's Fairs, spectacles of industrial, agricultural, and national progress, originated with London's 1851 Crystal Palace Exhibition and had proliferated around the world by the end of the nineteenth century. Midwestern cities hosted some of the most important World's Fairs ever held in the United States. Clustered around the beginning of the twentieth century, the Chicago World's Columbian Exposition (1893), the Omaha Trans-Mississippi and International Exposition (1898), and the St. Louis Louisiana Purchase Exposition (1904) celebrated the productivity of midwestern agriculture and industry and underscored the centrality of the region to the ongoing reconstruction of the American nation after the Civil War. A generation later, during the Great Depression, Chicago's Century of Progress Exposition (1933–1934) and

Cleveland's Great Lakes and International Exposition (1937) formed crucial links in the chain of World's Fairs that stretched coast to coast and north to south in an effort to hasten America's recovery from the crash of 1929. Following World War II, despite successful fairs in Seattle (1962), New York (1964–1965), and Spokane (1974), the Midwest became something of a black hole for World's Fairs. With the World's Fair medium losing popularity to theme parks and electronic media, the Knoxville International Energy Exposition (1984) struggled to make ends meet, and Chicago could not overcome internal political divisions over a proposal to host a fair in 1992 commemorating the five hundredth anniversary of Columbus's landfall in the New World.

The success of the first generation of World's Fairs held in the Midwest was due to their proximity to the Civil War. Between 1861 and 1865, more than six hundred thousand Americans died in a war that pitted region against region. Reconstructing the United States proved no easy task, especially as industrialization and recurrent economic depressions threatened war between social classes. Coming on the heels of the Philadelphia Centennial Exhibition (1876) and held against the backdrop of some of the worst industrial violence in America's history, the World's Fairs held in Chicago, Omaha, and St. Louis are best understood as cultural responses to the growing anxieties of middle-class Americans about the future of the country. Each of these fairs was organized by powerful consortia of local civic leaders, state political and economic authorities, and national political leaders who sometimes vied with one another for the privilege of hosting a World's Fair in their particular city.

Competition was especially fierce when the U.S. Congress announced that it would decide which city would be chosen to host the fair celebrating the Columbian quadricentennial. When Chicago's business interests anted up five million dollars at the last minute, Congress selected Chicago over New York City and over other regional competitors like St. Louis. The results were impressive. More than twenty million Americans visited the fair, stood in awe of its neoclassical architecture, and delighted in riding the Ferris wheel to a height of over 250 feet above the fairgrounds. With this fair, Chicago came of age as the hub of an inland railroad and agricultural empire. The manifold legacies of this fair, not the least of which are Jackson Park and the Museum of Natural History, made that city the pride and envy of the Midwest and stimulated civic leaders in other cities to emulate and improve upon the Chicago example.

Right after the close of the Chicago fair, the business community in Omaha, Nebraska, jumped on the World's Fair bandwagon and organized a small-scale copy of the Chicago exposition. Intended to boost Omaha's importance to the economic development of the region and nation, the fair also played host to a massive Indian Congress that began as an effort to educate white Americans about the different cultures of the Plains Indians but quickly degenerated into a wild west show. The Omaha Trans-Mississippi and International Exposition appeared to be headed toward economic ruin when America's war with Spain began in 1898. By the time it closed, the fair had become the site for a nationwide victory celebration that helped turn the attention of Americans everywhere toward the dazzling prospects of overseas markets for America's agricultural and industrial surpluses.

It was precisely the potential for exporting those surpluses of the Midwest to foreign markets that, together with the centenary of the Louisiana Purchase, inspired the 1904 St. Louis fair. The fair took form in the context of the national debate about the rightness of U.S. involvement in quelling the bloody Philippine Insurrection, and the primary focus of the fair quickly became winning public support for American occupation of the Philippine Islands, deemed vital for American economic penetration of Asia. Over a thousand Filipinos were put on display at the fair, joining hundreds of other people from around the world who were organized into displays purportedly illustrating the progress of humanity from "savagery" to "civilization." Like other World's Fairs, the St. Louis fair, with its enchanting "Meet Me in St. Louis, Louis" theme song, made the Midwest more cosmopolitan and helped integrate its economies into the broader world economy. Perhaps because of its scale (the St. Louis fair was the biggest world's fair ever in size, covering 1,272 acres) and attendance numbers (some fourteen million visitors), no other midwestern city felt it could match St. Louis's accomplishment. Indeed, the St. Louis extravaganza was the last World's Fair in the region until the 1930s, when a worldwide crisis in capitalism rejuvenated interest in the World's Fair medium.

Planning for a major fair in Chicago actually began in the mid-1920s. But it was the collapse of the stock market and the ensuing economic debacle that lent urgency to the dreams of Chicago business leaders Charles and Rufus Dawes, who sought to create a fair that would rival the World's Columbian Exposition in importance. With the help of the National Research Council, which fixed the focus of the fair on the contributions of science to America's national progress; leading architects, who abandoned neoclassical designs in favor of a more streamlined aesthetic; and a fan-dancer named Sally Rand, Chicago's exposition authorities succeeded in organizing a wildly popular exposition during the darkest days of the Great Depression. Its 1933 run so impressed President Franklin D. Roosevelt that he personally intervened to persuade Chicago's business leaders to renew their fair for another year. It was this exposition that inspired succeeding fairs around the nation, including a smaller one in Cleveland and the 1939–1940 New York World's Fair with its World of Tomorrow theme.

Cleveland's Great Lakes and International Exposition (1937) is often ignored in histories of the Great Depression. True, the fair was not as large and did not last as long as other expositions, but it too put countless people to work in the Depression and organized exhibit palaces that reminded visitors of the value of American corporations to the economy. If its architecture had an unsettling *fascist moderne* quality to it, this fair nonetheless underscored the deep involvement of the United States in international currents of cultural and political expressions.

For about a hundred years, World's Fairs left their mark on the Midwest. They left behind parks and museums that still exist today. No less important, they became sites of memory that informed the imaginations of millions. More than anything, they made the Midwest an economically and politically integrated part of the American nation and its expanding quest for overseas markets. The enormous financial losses incurred by Expo 2000 in Hannover, Germany, will probably deter midwestern cities from becoming World's Fair sites in the immediate future, but to the extent that Americans may once again require the visible reassurances offered by the World's Fair medium, there is every reason to think that a future midwestern World's Fair—perhaps one that would help find solutions to pressing planetary issues of inequitable wealth distribution, ecological collapse, and biological/nuclear terror—will someday be held.

Sources and Further Reading: John E. Findling and Kimberly D. Pelle, eds., *Historical Dictionary of World's Fairs and Expositions, 1851–1988* (1990); Robert W. Rydell, *All the World's a Fair* (1984); Robert W. Rydell, *World of Fairs: The Century of Progress Expositions* (1993); Robert W. Rydell, John E. Findling, and Kimberly D. Pelle, *Fair America* (2000).

Robert W. Rydell
Montana State University–Bozeman

Dance Companies

Dance exists as part of a larger whole—of the world, of the United States—and on many levels, from Kansas to Wisconsin, Ohio to Michigan, and Illinois to Iowa. It exists as transformations and relocations of other regional parts of the country, and it exists in its own right, with beats and pulses, swings and jumps, and with different forms and histories. The Ohio Ballet, for instance, founded in 1968 and first called the Chamber Ballet, grew out of the University of Akron's Dance Institute. The founding members of the Chamber Ballet were all students in the university, and a cooperative and symbiotic relationship still exists between the Ohio Ballet and the university. The Milwaukee Ballet, ranked among the top ten ballet companies in the nation, is also part of the Wisconsin Arts Board's Touring & Arts in Education offerings, and each year its audience numbers exceed eighty thousand. Often accompanied by the Milwaukee Ballet Orchestra, Milwaukee Ballet's repertoire ranges from the great classics to contemporary works. The Milwaukee Ballet School is ranked among the nation's top five ballet schools. Other professional or semiprofessional ballet companies in the Midwest include the Cincinnati Ballet, Columbus's Ballet Met, the Dayton Ballet, the Chicago City Ballet, and the Joffrey Ballet of Chicago.

The growth and development of regional ballet companies reflects the interest and desire for ballet training and ballet productions in the United States. As Richard Kraus, Sarah Chapman Hilsendager, and Brenda Dixon note, the term *regional ballet* is usually applied to companies that consist chiefly of nonsalaried dancers and directors. Supportive services are often provided by local community organizations that value having the arts present in their neighborhoods. Regional ballet companies provide performance opportunities to local dancers and help to promote local interest in ballet. A list of the top of semiprofessional and regional ballet companies and schools of the Midwest would include Canton (Ohio) Ballet, Cincinnati Ballet, Columbus Youth Ballet, Ballet Arts Minnesota (Minneapolis), Children's Ballet Theatre (Lansing, Michigan), Omaha Theater Company Ballet, and Ballet North of metropolitan Kansas City, Kansas.

The State of Wisconsin's support for dance companies typifies midwestern interest in the art. The Connolly Dance Company, located in Madison, is made up of five dancers whose purpose is to share the art of dance with the broadest possible audience. Milwaukee boasts the Danceworks Performance Company, established in 1997, a twelve-member company that offers direct and accessible concerts, including Dancing through the Decades, a look at Wisconsin history through dance. K & K Capoeira integrates capoeira and other African forms of martial dance, affirming strength and self-worth in their workshops and residencies. The Kanopy Dance Company, a professional dance company based in Madison for more than twenty years, tours nationally, offering residencies, lecture-demonstrations, and classes in modern-dance technique and choreography. The Ko-Thi Dance Company of Milwaukee offers dance performances and workshops to students in grades K–12. Based in Monona, Wisconsin, the Wisconsin Dance Ensemble's Dance in School program teaches third-, fourth-, and fifth-grade students ballet and jazz through a three-week program that culminates in a performance showcase.

At the beginning of the twentieth century, as ballet was experiencing a resurgence, it not only established itself as a viable art form but gave other forms of dance something established to transform or rebel against. The other category that dance is often too dichotomously divided into is modern dance. Modern dance is one of those "other forms of dance" that rebelled against ballet. Its progenitor, Marie Louise Fuller, later known as Loie Fuller, was born in Fullersburg, Illinois, in 1862. A temperance advocate and actress, Fuller had little formal dance training and was "not much of a dancer," according to Joseph A. Mazo. However, Fuller transformed the audience's response to movement by filling the stage with flowing movements created by her large illuminated skirts and billowing cloth. Fuller's ingenious performances with light and cloth captured not only the spirit of an age becoming familiar with electricity but also a spirit of unbridled movement through the billowing and rippling of her costumes.

Inspired by Loie Fuller's movement, Isadora Duncan, born in San Francisco in 1878, pioneered a new type of expression rebelling against the limb-based, upright, pulled-in expression of classical ballet. Though Duncan studied classical ballet as a child, she broke from its externalized, formalized structure, believing that dance was an expression of inner ideas and impulses originating from the solar plexus. Duncan's debut in Chicago in 1899 was not successful, but she made her way to Europe where she performed in Paris in 1900 to a much more appreciative audience.

Isadora Duncan's movements grew from her need to express her inner life through movement. Duncan's unconventional life, her teachings, and her dances expressed the conflicting and changing spirit of the times. Her work allowed the next generation of modern dancers—Martha Graham, midwesterners Doris Humphrey and Charles Weidman, and others—to create a world of innovative dance that not only provided a contrast to the world of ballet but eventually allowed many dance forms to be appreciated and analyzed for their formal and expressive qualities.

Doris Humphrey, an innovative modern dancer born in Oak Park, Illinois, in 1895, received her first dance training in Chicago. After working with Ruth St. Denis and Ted Shawn in the Denishawn Company, Humphrey joined forces with Charles Weidman, forming her own company and school. Humphrey strove to find a basic dance built upon her theory that all movement existed between the arcing continuum of balance and unbalance, fall and recovery, motionlessness and motion.

Another native midwesterner was Katherine Dunham, born about 1914 in Chicago. Dunham is an example of a dancer and choreographer whose work destroys the either-or categorization of dance as ballet or dance as modern. Dunham was trained as both a dancer and an anthropologist, and she wove dance and anthropology together, creating pieces informed by her fieldwork in Haiti and other areas of the African diaspora. Dunham respected the diversities of cultures. Sally Banes writes that without a specifically feminist agenda Dunham "unearthed a distinctive social role for African American women—one that had to do with a tradition, with long roots perhaps traceable back to West Africa, of matrifocal family life that has in the past 400 years systematically invested woman with far more power than the dominant Euro-American Protestant kinship structure." Dunham established her own school in Chicago in 1931. She was director of ballet for the Negro Unit of the Federal Theatre in 1938 and directed choreographing and dancing in films. Dunham formed her own company that traveled the United States and Europe.

Though the beginnings of modern dance were not warmly received in Chicago, today the Midwest is the home to hundreds of progressive and experimental dance companies. Founded in 1980 by Mary Verdi-Fletcher, Dancing Wheels is an innovative dance company paving new roads for dancers and choreographers (accomplishing what the early modern dancers did during their day). Based in Cleveland, it is one of the world's first integrated dance companies composed of professional dancers with and without disabilities. It reaches more than 125,000 people around the world each year through lecture/performances, community classes and workshops, residencies, and main-stage concerts.

Kraus, Hilsendager, and Dixon state that the historical development of dance as a cultural form in American society has been marked by the increasing inclusion of dance as a medium of education in American schools and colleges. The rationale for dance education is that it not only promotes healthy, sensitive physical bodies but also nurtures cultural and aesthetic values. Children educated by dance become the future audiences attending professional, regional, and experimental dance concerts.

Margaret H'Doubler, born in Beloit, Kansas, in 1889, was a pioneer of dance education. Educated at the University of Wisconsin–Madison and at Teachers College at Columbia University, H'Doubler taught dance as part of the physical education program at the University of Wisconsin. She integrated dance into the physical education curriculum, emphasizing creativity rather than strict technique. H'Doubler felt that every child had the right to know how to achieve control of his or her body in order to use it as a communicative means. "Even if he can never carry his efforts far enough to realize dance in its highest forms, he may experience the sheer joy of the rhythmic sense of free, controlled, and expressive movement, and through this know an addition to life to which every human being is entitled."

The emphasis on dance in education has gone in and out of favor. However, it is significant that it was a midwestern state that first granted bachelor and master degrees in dance. In 1926, the University of Wisconsin became the first college to grant degrees in dance. By the late 1950s, emphasis was being placed less on dance as an aesthetic, physical experience and more on nondance physical conditioning. In the 1960s and 1970s, there was a renewed interest in dance education. Today dance is being offered as a cross-cultural and education enrichment experience to children across the United States.

People have their own ways of dancing, learned by instruction or imitation. The ways that people acquire their abilities to dance in the Midwest are as varied as the states of the region. For observers or participants, dance has a way of creating and uniting communities. Indiana Folk Dance, the Lira Ensemble, the Trinity Irish Dance Company, Folk Dance Council of Chicago, the Dance Improvisation Group, the Royal Scottish Dance Society–Central Iowa Branch, the Ragamala Music and Dance Theater, the Latin & Argentine Tango Club of Detroit, North Dakota Folk Dance, and Classical Middle Eastern Dance are a few of the many dance organizations in the Midwest promoting respect for dance and diversity.

Dance of the Midwest is reflected in multiple histories, dance forms, abstractions, and styles. Dance of the Midwest is versatile. And as the wheat of the Heartland sways—even when there is no wind—so the people of the Midwest dance, even when they are not moving.

Sources and Further Reading: Sally Banes, *Dancing Women: Female Bodies on Stage* (1998); Isadora Duncan, *The Art of the Dance*, ed., Sheldon Cheney, rev. ed. (1977); Isadora Duncan, *My Life* (1927); Havelock Ellis, *The Dance of Life* (1923); Margaret H'Doubler, *Dance: A Creative Art Experience* (1940); Deborah Jowitt, *Time and the Dancing Image* (1988); Richard Kraus, Sarah Chapman Hilsendager, and Brenda Dixon, *History of the Dance in Art and Education*, 3rd ed. (1991); Joseph A. Mazo, *Prime Movers* (1977); Cobbett Steinberg, ed., *The Dance Anthology* (1980); Ellen Switzer, *Dancers! Horizons in American Dance* (1982).

Jennifer S. Holmes
Whittier College, California

History Museums and Other Sites

The Midwest is home to many kinds of history museums, mirroring the diversity of the region and its people, economy, and politics. The variety of museums includes large state historical societies, restored communities, historic houses, and volunteer-run local historical societies. These museums can be private nonprofit organizations, state or other government-supported agencies, or an amalgamation of private and publicly funded agencies. Midwestern museums and historic sites cover a wide range of topics, including industrial history; labor history; communal societies; homes of the rich and famous; rural life; and general local, regional, and state histories.

Several statewide historical agencies in the Midwest have more in common with one another than they do with those in other regions. By and large, midwestern statewide agencies are fairly large, perform a number of functions, and operate a system of sites throughout their respective states. The Ohio Historical Society (OHS), the largest of these agencies in terms of the number of properties and acreage owned, is typical of midwestern historical societies. As its website notes, OHS was founded in 1885 as the Ohio Archeological and Historical Society, centered in the state capital of Columbus, where it is still located. Since that time, it has grown from one site in the capital city to more than sixty sites around the state. OHS, like many other statewide organizations, also includes the state archives and the state historic preservation office. The Columbus site houses the administrative offices; a museum (with exhibits on Ohio history, archaeology, and natural history); archives/library, the Ohio Historic Preservation Office; and the Ohio Village, a reconstructed mid-nineteenth-century rural Ohio community. While OHS performs several functions for the state of Ohio, it is a private, nonprofit organization that receives more than half of its income from the government. Its site system includes history, archaeology, and natural-history sites ranging in size from the restored Zoar Village in northeastern Ohio to the Armstrong Air and Space Museum in Wapakoneta.

Several other midwestern statewide historical agencies are nearly the size of OHS; according to its website, the State Historical Society of North Dakota with fifty-six properties runs a close second in the number of sites

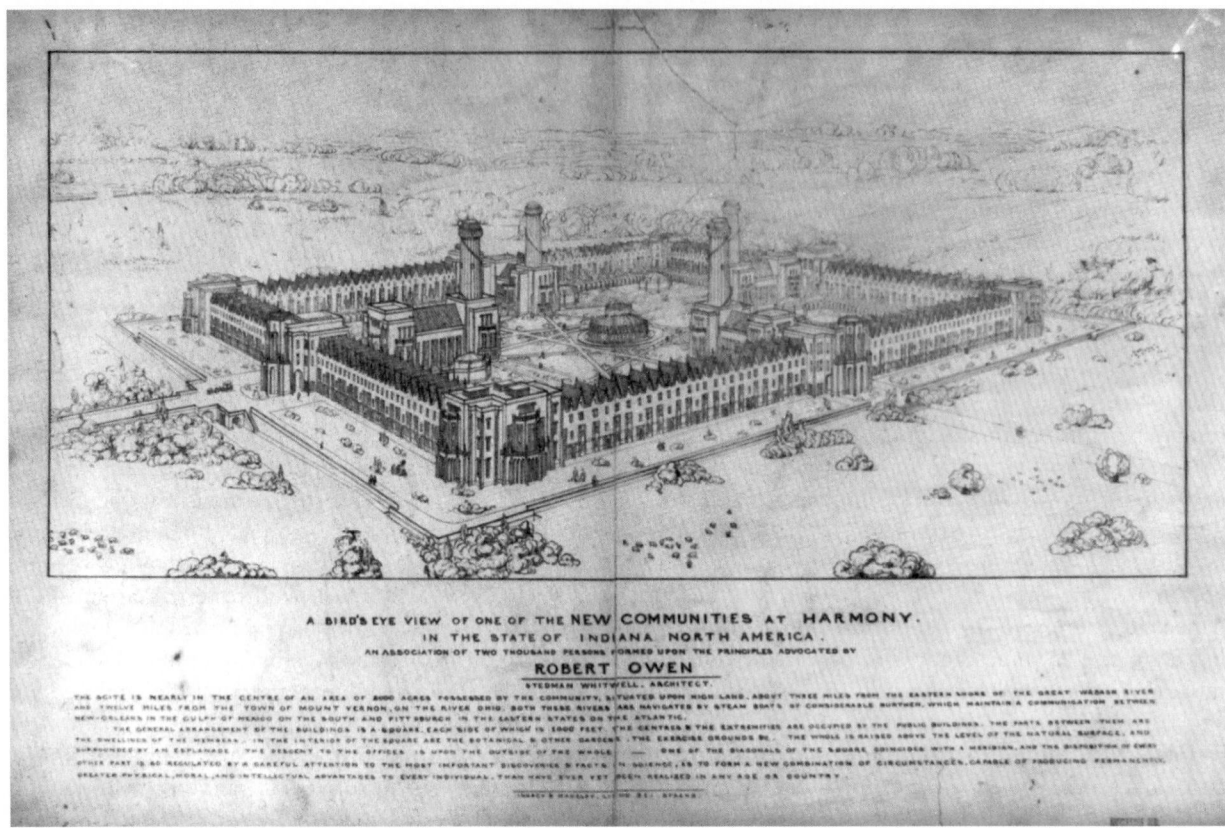

A BIRD'S EYE VIEW OF ONE OF THE NEW COMMUNITIES AT HARMONY.
IN THE STATE OF INDIANA NORTH AMERICA.
AN ASSOCIATION OF TWO THOUSAND PERSONS FORMED UPON THE PRINCIPLES ADVOCATED BY
ROBERT OWEN

Robert Owen's secular utopian commune, New Harmony, Indiana. Library of Congress, Prints and Photographs Division, LC-USZ62-1045.

it owns and operates. Other large state organizations include the Nebraska State Historical Society, the Minnesota Historical Society, and the Wisconsin Historical Society. Besides their main sites, these large historical societies operate a wide variety of museums and other historic and archaeological sites in their respective states. Their websites provide information on the organizations and their associated properties. North Dakota, for example, operates, among other sites, Camp Hancock in Bismark, Chateau de Mores in Medora, and the Gingras Trading Post in Walhalla. The Wisconsin Historical Society has its headquarters in Madison and operates properties such as the outdoor living-history site Old World Wisconsin and the late-nineteenth-century Victorian cum arts and crafts mansion Villa Louis. Taken together, these state historical societies provide visitors many opportunities to explore the Midwest's history, culture, archaeology, and natural history.

Among other kinds of museums located in the Midwest is the outdoor museum. The prototype for outdoor museums is Greenfield Village in Dearborn, Michigan. Developed in the 1920s by automobile magnate Henry Ford, and located near the site of his original factories, Greenfield Village brings together buildings from various parts of the United States. Some of the structures on the property include the Wright Brothers' Dayton, Ohio, bicycle shop and Thomas Alva Edison's Menlo Park, New Jersey, laboratory. Greenfield Village inspired a number of other facilities that contain structures brought in from sites elsewhere, such as Ohio's Hale Farm and Village in Bath. Hale Farm consists of early-nineteenth-century buildings from different parts of Ohio's Western Reserve that are placed around a village green in an attempt to re-create the New England town plan that was prevalent in that section of Ohio. Another midwestern museum site based on the Greenfield idea is Old World Wisconsin. There, buildings once located elsewhere in the State of Wisconsin were brought together at this 576-acre site near Milwaukee. Old World Wisconsin is a living-history site that depicts life among the ethnic groups that settled Wisconsin in the nineteenth century, including Germans, Norwegians, and New England Yankees. Indiana's Conner Prairie, near Indianapolis, grew up around the home of an early Indiana settler, William Conner. Over time, the museum site expanded to encompass other nineteenth-century Indiana structures that were moved to the property. These are just a few of the largest outdoor museums in the Midwest, which tend to focus on rural nineteenth-century life, which in many ways remains the image of the region in the popular imagination.

Geographic opportunities and attitudes regarding religious tolerance in the nineteenth-century Midwest encouraged a number of communal societies to establish homes in the region. The Shakers, for example, settled in Ohio at Shaker Heights in Cleveland and South Union near Cincinnati; however, little remains of those communities. Other communal societies did leave the legacy of their built environment behind, and these sites are now operated as museums. New Harmony, Indiana, preserves the legacy of two very different communal societies: the pietistic Rappites, or Harmonists, and Robert Owen's secular utopian commune. The Rappites, who migrated to the United States from Germany, established their society in southern Indiana in 1814. Eleven years later, the Rappites sold their property in Indiana to Scottish reformer Robert Owen and moved to their new home in what is now Ambridge, Pennsylvania. A religious group from the same area of Germany as the Rappites formed a communal society in eastern Ohio, about twenty miles south of Canton, which they named Zoar. Led by Joseph Biemeler, the Zoarites settled in their new home in 1817. They lasted as a communal society until they dissolved in 1898. The Ohio Historical Society website notes that eight original and two reconstructed buildings are operated as a museum; the site includes the Zoarites' symbolic garden, with flower beds forming the Zoar star (one of the society's symbols) radiating out from a large tree of life in the center that is surrounded by twelve smaller trees, representing Christ's apostles. The Amana Colonies in Iowa are the result of another pietistic communal society that originated in Germany, known as the Community of True Inspiration. The Amana colonists originally settled in 1842 near Buffalo, New York. They quickly outgrew their original settlement, and in 1855 laid out the new village of Amana in Iowa. In 1932 Amana dissolved the communal society and became a profit-sharing corporation with the Amana Church Society. Today, the Amana Heritage Society operates several of the original Amana communal buildings as museums.

Nearly every community large and small in the Midwest operates some kind of local history museum. Museums that focus on large metropolitan areas include the Chicago Historical Society, the Western Reserve Historical Society in Cleveland, Cincinnati Museum Center, the Milwaukee Public Museum, and the Detroit Historical Museum. (Cincinnati Museum Center houses history, natural history, and children's museums as well as an Omnimax theatre and the Cincinnati Historical Society Library.) Local historical societies abound in the Midwest; no matter the size, they provide the visitor with a glimpse into the past of the community they serve.

One important facet of midwestern life and culture that is steadily gaining attention by museums is industrial history. Greenfield Village was one of the earliest midwestern museums to look at the manufacturing of automobiles as an integral American industry. The legacy of the automobile is also preserved at the Auburn-Cord-Duesenberg Museum in Auburn, Indiana, the Indianapolis Motor Speedway Hall of Fame, and the R.E. Olds Museum in Lansing, Michigan. Minnesota, which is home to the Mesabi Range, known for its iron ore, has several facilities focusing on the iron-extraction industry, including the Ironworld Discovery Center, the Minnesota Museum of Mining, and the huge Hull Rust Mahoning Mine. The iron ore mined in Minnesota made its way to the iron and steel mills of the United States.

One of the few American museums dedicated to the history of the ferrous industries is Ohio's Youngstown Historical Center of Industry and Labor. This museum, which features a building designed by prominent postmodernist architect Michael Graves and a sculpture, titled *The Steelworkers*, by artist George Segal, highlights the impact of the iron and steel industries on Youngstown and other Mahoning Valley communities. Objects on display at the historical center include workers' tools and clothing and "last heats," the last batches of steel produced at nearby regional mills before they were closed.

In Minnesota, the once-burgeoning flour-mill industry is represented by Minneapolis's Pillsbury A Mill and the Archer Daniel Midlands Grain Elevators. The remnants of an important industrial company town in Illinois, Pullman, can still be visited in south Chicago.

The Midwest has been home to numerous notable Americans. The nation's presidents are represented by many sites, including the Harry S Truman home in Independence, Missouri; the Rutherford B. Hayes home and museum in Fremont, Ohio; the James A. Garfield home in Mentor, Ohio; the Gerald R. Ford library at the University of Michigan, Ann Arbor, and museum in Grand Rapids, Michigan; the William Howard Taft historical site in Cincinnati; the Herbert Hoover historical site in West Branch, Iowa; the Warren G. Harding home in Marion, Ohio; and the Benjamin Harrison home in Indianapolis. Ulysses S. Grant is represented in Ohio's Grant Birthplace in Point Pleasant and his boyhood home in Georgetown as well as his home in Galena, Illinois. Abraham Lincoln is the best-represented president, with sites in Springfield, Illinois (including the only home he actually owned); the reconstructed New Salem, Illinois, Lincoln City, Indiana (the Lincoln Boyhood National Memorial); and Fort Wayne, Indiana (the Lincoln Museum).

Other museums pay tribute to other famous midwestern citizens. African American poet Paul Laurence Dunbar's home is a museum in Dayton, Ohio, and the homes of various writers from the region have been preserved. Frank Lloyd Wright's home and studio in Oak Park, Illinois, is among several museums honoring the noted American architect; Oak Park features the largest collection of Wright-designed buildings and houses, with twenty-five structures built between 1889 and 1913. Wright is also represented by the Robie House in Chicago; the Dana-Thomas House in Springfield, Illinois; and Taliesin, his home, school, and workshop located near Spring Green, Wisconsin. Jane Addams's Hull-House in Chicago is now a museum dedicated to the work of the settlement house movement and its famous founder. Among several sites in the Midwest associated with abolitionist John Brown is the John Brown House in Osawatomie, Kansas, which sits on the site of the famous antislavery conflict, the Battle of Osawatomie.

People from a great variety of ethnic groups settled in the Midwest and their presence is felt in sites throughout the region. Native American heritage is preserved and presented at sites like Iowa's Hopewellian Toolesboro Mounds and Museum; the Pipestone County Historical and the Mille Lacs Indian Museums in Minnesota; the Oneida Nation Museum near Green Bay, Wisconsin; and the Marquette (Michigan) Mission Park and Museum of Ojibwa Culture. African American sites include major museums such as the National Afro-American Museum in Wilberforce, Ohio, and Detroit's Museum of African American History. European immigration history is examined in museums such as the American Swedish Institute in Minneapolis, the Frankenmuth (Michigan) Historical Museum (which concerns Germans), and Chicago's Polish Museum of America.

Source and Further Reading: Suzanne Winckler, *The Great Lakes States* (1989).

Donna M. DeBlasio
Youngstown State University, Ohio

America's Black Holocaust Museum

America's Black Holocaust Museum, located at 2233 North 4th Street, Milwaukee, was founded in 1988 by a lynching survivor, James Cameron. The museum's purpose is to challenge popular assumptions about racial progress. The specific impetus for the museum was Cameron's near-lynching experience as a teenager in Marion, Indiana, where he narrowly escaped a mob that killed two other men accused of robbery, rape, and murder. His personal experience is included as a permanent video exhibit in the museum and suggests how routinely lynchers circulated rumors about African Americans and used them to perpetrate acts of vigilante terrorism.

America's Black Holocaust Museum houses both traveling and permanent exhibits. Among the permanent exhibits are slave artifacts from Africa and the United States collected by the founder; artwork, writings, murals, and an exhibition called *The Middle Passage: A Voyage to Slavery;* and a lurid reproduction of the interior of a slave ship in the entryway. Also displayed are permanent photo exhibits on general black-life subjects (e.g., black Milwaukee judges).

America's Black Holocaust Museum has achieved regional fame well beyond its modest dwellings in south Milwaukee. Though not a truly comprehensive repository of African American heritage and culture, the museum's exhibits focus on some of the ugliest pages in U.S. history: the private denial of rights and security publicly promised to America's citizens.

Sources and Further Reading: Black Holocaust Museum website, www.blackholocaustmuseum.org.; James Cameron, *A Time of Terror: A Survivor's Story* (1982); Angela Davis, "Rape, Racism and the Myth of the Black Rapist," in Angela Davis, ed., *Women, Race, & Class,* (1981); Walter White, *Rope and Faggot* (1969).

Richard Ralston
University of Wisconsin–Madison

Baraboo Circus World Museum

In the late nineteenth and early twentieth centuries, Wisconsin, with more than a hundred traveling tent shows, became widely known as "The Mother of the Circus." Most significant among the circus families were the Ringling brothers of Baraboo, who in 1884 formed what would become the best-known circus worldwide. Their wildly successful circus wintered in Baraboo until 1918; they bought the Barnum & Bailey Show in 1907 and merged the two in 1919. John Kelly, attorney for the Ringlings for thirty years, envisioned a circus world museum and facilitated the state's acquisition of the Ringling winter camp in 1959; the Circus World Museum (CWM) is still owned by the State Historical Society of Wisconsin. Since 1960 it has been run by Circus World Foundation, a nonprofit educational foundation.

The mission of CWM is to collect, preserve, and present circus history and culture, particularly as an integral part of the Midwest's cultural history. Because "you have to see it to believe it," the museum features summertime circus performances and exhibitions. It has facilitated the research of countless cultural and art historians, moviemakers, and individuals with a personal interest. The museum's research center and library are one of the nation's most comprehensive archives for circus posters, flyers, books and articles, memorabilia, and photographs.

Today more than two hundred antique circus wagons and show vehicles are a part of this collection. Restored at the museum's own restoration center, the wagons are put to use every year in the museum's pinnacle event, Milwaukee's Great Circus Parade. This two-hour re-creation of an old-time circus parade features wagons (including cage-wagons, steam calliopes, and spectacle floats), wild animals, performers, and an eye-popping forty-horse-hitch and wagon.

Sources and Further Reading: Robert Bogdan, *Freak Show: Presenting Human Oddities for Amusement and Profit* (1988); Molly Cone, *The Ringling Brothers* (1971); Fred Dahlinger, Jr., and Stuart Thayer, *Badger State Showmen* (1998).

Leslie Umberger
John Michael Kohler Arts Center, Wisconsin

The Billy Sunday Museum

Located in the village of Winona Lake, Indiana, the Billy Sunday Museum represents the historic capstone to this once popular and recently revived vacation and conference destination. Situated on a lawn first made famous by turn-of-the-twentieth-century Chautauquas that drew people from Chicago and other midwestern towns along the Winona Inter-Urban Railway, the museum re-creates Billy Sunday's world through a collection of displays, exhibits, and memorabilia. The museum's centerpiece is a replica of the Billy Sunday Tabernacle, a structure located in Winona Lake that, in its 1920s heyday, annually played host during the summer conference season to crowds of well over seven thousand. Although not nearly as imposing as the original, the scaled-down tabernacle along with its recorded sounds of Sunday's fire-and-brimstone preaching transport the visitor to the early twentieth century when millions filled the pews of similar structures throughout America to see and hear the famous evangelist. Born in Iowa in 1862 and converted to Christianity in 1886 while playing professional baseball for the Chicago White Stockings, by the early twentieth century Sunday had become a national celebrity for his dynamic preaching style and political outspokenness. Such status afforded him the financial wherewithal to make Winona Lake home for his family and the organizational base for his evangelistic activities. For three decades following Sunday's death in 1935, Winona Lake continued to serve as a conference center for regional and national religious organizations. The Billy Sunday Museum thus serves as both a memorial to one of America's most famous evangelists and a testament to Winona Lake's legacy as an epicenter of midwestern evangelical Protestant culture.

Sources and Further Reading: Lyle W. Dorsett, *Billy Sunday and the Redemption of Urban America* (1991); William G. McLoughlin, Jr., *Billy Sunday Was His Real Name* (1955).

Darren Dochuk
University of Notre Dame, Indiana

Birthplace of the Republican Party

The dispute over the birthplace of the Republican Party is primarily semantic: What constitutes a "birthplace"? Listed chronologically, Crawfordsville, Iowa; Ripon, Wisconsin; and Jackson, Michigan—all midwestern towns—can claim the status of natal home. The Republican Party is, in its origins, essentially midwestern.

In the stormy politics of the 1850s, the established political parties were confounded by the issue of slavery and how to respond to the movement for abolition. Thus Whig Party defectors met to discuss these issues in February 1854 in Crawfordsville, but without starting a new party or using the word *republican*. But on March 20, 1854, fifty-four of the one hundred voters of Ripon, Wisconsin, met and after long debate decided to start a new party and adopt the name *Republican*. The following July saw the first statewide convention dedicated to an antislavery platform, in Jackson, Michigan. That these events occurred over wide distances within the same brief period of time indicates that a groundswell of public opinion in the Midwest was building and that an antislavery party would at some point and in some place be inevitable.

Thus Ripon can claim priority in starting a party and calling it "Republican," and Jackson can base a claim on being the first town to host a statewide party meeting. As each town seems respectful of the facts of the other's claim, it is for the observer to decide what a birthplace is.

Source and Further Reading: Dennis McCann, "Ripon's Grand Old Party Ties," *Milwaukee Journal Sentinel* (2 July 1998).

Geoffrey Thrumston
Boulder, Colorado

Children's Museums

There is a plethora of children's museums in the Heartland of America that focus on midwestern life and experience. Equally important, the Midwest has been a hub of national children's museum conferences.

The Association of Children's Museums (ACM) has held its annual conference in the Midwest several times. InterActivity, the ACM conference, was held in Minneapolis in 1996 with the theme "Building for the Future." Indianapolis hosted ACM's InterActivity 1997, "Transforming the Learning Landscape." At InterActivity 2001, in St. Louis, the ACM unveiled its vision of bringing children and families together in a new kind of "town square" where play motivates lifelong knowledge. This concept complemented the conference's focus on "Children's Museums Creating a Sense of Place." Many children's museums of the Midwest embody these learning and experiential themes, focusing on the uniqueness of the region and helping to revitalize midwestern cities.

Notable among children's museums in the region is the Children's Museum of Indianapolis, which features ten galleries, was founded in 1925, and is the fourth oldest in the world. Covering global culture, science, and history, its midwestern focus encourages visitors to follow the trail of pioneers, excavate an archaeological dig, and play on an Indy 500 racecar. It also contains a collection of more than thirty-nine thousand American objects spanning two hundred years, including African American objects. Many other large midwestern cities host children's museums. The Chicago Children's Museum on Lake Michigan attends to Illinois themes and houses a three-story climbing schooner, a mini Chicago cityscape, and a waterway exhibit in which children manage a dam and irrigate farmland. Not far away, in the suburb of Wilmette, is the Kohl Children's Museum. This museum opened in 1985 and is one of the busiest museums in the Midwest, drawing more than two hundred thousand visitors annually. The Minnesota Children's Museum in St. Paul has many interactive exhibits and activities, such as Habitat, which lets toddlers explore four Minnesota habitats.

Other midwestern cities house children's museums with a midwestern flavor. The Omaha Children's Museum introduces kids to life in that midwestern city with a model of Omaha's landmark structures. The Madison (Wisconsin) Children's Museum, founded in 1980, has an exhibit called the Milking Parlor; through it, kids explore Wisconsin's dairy industry with a visit to the barn, where they dress in overalls and brush, groom, and milk cows. In Bettendorf, Iowa, the Children's Museum merged with the city's Center for the Cultural Arts and became the Family Museum of Arts and Science. St. Louis's popular Magic House is a children's museum founded in 1975 and housed in the three-story Victorian home of George Lane Edwards, the director of the 1904 St. Louis World's Fair.

Source and Further Reading: Jackie Trescott, "Museums for Kids Growing by Leaps and Bounds," *Washington Post* (May 1, 2001).

Kathleen FitzCallaghan
Boulder, Colorado

Historic Homes

Many houses in the Midwest have been preserved as museums commemorating famous people, providing a glimpse of nineteenth-century life or illustrating architectural innovations such as the Midwest's own Prairie school of architecture.

Insights into the lives of American presidents abound in the restored houses of William Henry Harrison (Vincennes, Indiana), Abraham Lincoln (Springfield, Illinois), Ulysses S. Grant (Galena, Illinois), James A. Garfield (Mentor, Ohio), Rutherford B. Hayes (Fremont, Ohio), Benjamin Harrison (Indianapolis), William Howard Taft (Cincinnati), Herbert Hoover (West Branch, Iowa); and Warren G. Harding (Marion, Ohio). Harrison's, Hayes's and Taft's homes include political memorabilia.

Frank Lloyd Wright built his first house in Oak Park, Illinois, in 1889, and by 1909 in his attached studio he had produced hundreds of horizontal Prairie school houses with open-space plans, banded leaded-glass windows, and integral furniture. Other Wright homes in the Midwest open to the public include the Meyer May House (1908) in Grand Rapids, Michigan; his later home and studio, Taliesin (1911 and 1925), in Spring Green, Wisconsin; and the expansive Dana-Thomas House (1905) in Springfield, Illinois. Prairie school origins can be seen in H. H. Richardson's Glessner House (1887) in Chicago and George W. Maher's Pleasant Home (1897) in Oak Park. Prairie architects Purcell and Elmslie designed the captivating Purcell House (1913) in Minneapolis.

Midwestern industrialists built some of the most impressive nineteenth-century mansions, including the stunning Second Empire Hegeler-Carus mansion (1874) in LaSalle, Illinois; the stone Queen Anne Copshaholm (1895–1896) in South Bend, Indiana; and the regal Flemish Renaissance Pabst Mansion (1892) in Milwaukee. St. Louis's Samuel Cupples finished the forty-two-room 1888 Richardsonian Romanesque home he owned with Tiffany glass, but he was exceeded by the Dodge family in Rochester, Michigan, whose one-hundred-room English Tudor Meadow Brook Hall (1929) is now part of Oakland University. The National Trust's Brucemore in Cedar Rapids, Iowa, a twenty-one-room 1884 Queen Anne mansion, interprets industry, architecture, and the rich cultural life of the early 1900s. James J. Hill's baronial mansion

The Harry S Truman Library and Museum, Independence, Missouri. L. D. Jones/Courtesy Harry S Truman Library.

(1891) in St. Paul survives as a witness to another late-nineteenth-century industrialist's wealth.

Historic homes comprise a timeline of midwestern architectural history from Pierre Menard's 1802 French colonial home in Kaskaskia, Illinois, to Herbert Johnson's 1937 Wright-designed Wingspread in Racine, Wisconsin. The early-nineteenth-century Greek revival style fashioned Ohio landmarks like the Follett House (1837) in Sandusky, the McClintock House (1838) in Chillicothe, and the Perkins Mansion (1837) in Akron. The square, bracketed Italianate style of the 1849 Tower Grove House in St. Louis charts the Midwest's enormous nineteenth-century growth, while Gilded Age Parisian elegance characterizes the 1872 Alexander Ramsay House in St. Paul. Victorian exuberance defines the Solomon Comstock House (1882) in Moorhead, Minnesota, in contrast to the rough-stone Romanesque-style Newcomb-Stilwell Mansion (1891) in Quincy, Illinois.

The homes of poets Carl Sandburg (Galesburg, Illinois), Paul Laurence Dunbar (Dayton, Ohio), and James Whitcomb Riley (Indianapolis) are preserved along with those of writers Ernest Hemingway (Oak Park, Illinois), Harriet Beecher Stowe (Cincinnati), Eugene Field (St. Louis), James Thurber (Columbus, Ohio), Zane Grey (Zanesville, Ohio), and Ernie Pyle (Dana, Indiana). Inventors and innovators are celebrated in the homes of Charles Lindbergh (Little Falls, Minnesota), Thomas Edison (Milan, Ohio), Scott Joplin (St. Louis), and William Mayo (LeSueur, Minnesota).

Sources and Further Reading: H. Allen Brooks, *The Prairie School: Frank Lloyd Wright and His Midwestern Contemporaries* (1972); Cyril M. Harris, *American Architecture: An Illustrated Encyclopedia* (1998); Alice Sinkevitch, ed., *AIA Guide to Chicago* (1993); William Allin Storrer, *The Architecture of Frank Lloyd Wright*, 2nd ed. (1978); Suzanne Winckler, *The Smithsonian Guide to Historic America*, vol. 6, *The Great Lakes States* (1989).

Vincent L. Michael
School of the Art Institute of Chicago

Historical Forts That Are Now Museums

The turbulent military history of the Midwest is well represented by archaeological sites, preserved or reconstructed buildings, and restored fortifications and military posts. These physical reminders of the region's military past span the eighteenth to the twentieth centuries and today play a prominent educational and commemorative role in presenting the early history and culture of the Midwest.

The locations selected for forts track the advance of European American traders, soldiers, and settlers as they moved into the region, fought among themselves and with Native American groups, and ultimately confirmed the Midwest as part of the United States. Most military posts established before the late nineteenth century were at important points on the major waterways that provided convenient transportation in the days before railroads and automobiles. Military posts were often at critical choke points—river portages, straits, or harbors—that were also important to the fur trade, settlement, and commerce. After 1796, forts on the Great Lakes provided border defense along the boundary with Canada.

Relatively few midwestern forts survived their period of military use intact or in their original form. A few were the nucleus of larger cities—Detroit, Cincinnati, Chicago, St. Louis—and were lost in the course of urban growth. Most midwestern forts were constructed of perishable materials, such as wood and earth, which quickly deteriorated when not maintained by a garrison. Few were substantial structures of stone or brick like the massive forts guarding the nation's harbors. Today, most midwestern forts are commemorated only in local museums, represented by a few surviving artifacts. Substantial numbers of fort sites have been preserved as archaeological areas or memorials within state or local parks, where their history is interpreted through exhibits and signage. A few have been reconstructed as educational complexes, while a number have been preserved complete or in part with their original buildings and walls carefully restored, maintained, and interpreted.

Interest in the history and preservation of old military posts developed soon after the passing of the frontier period in individual states. As early as 1827, a few people in Detroit advocated the preservation of Fort Shelby, which dated to the American Revolution and the War of 1812. The walls of Fort Shelby succumbed to urban growth, but the United States centennial of 1876 saw an increase in interest in things historical. Many forts of the more western states were only being established during the Indian Wars, while in 1875 the more antiquated Fort Mackinac, Michigan, became the center of the country's second national park, and one of its oldest buildings was preserved largely because of its historical significance. Fort Mackinac and its buildings became part of Michigan's first state park in 1895, thereby enabling its preservation as the Midwest's first fort museum.

Those forts that remained in public hands were the most likely to survive relatively intact. Fort Snelling, Minnesota, and Fort Wayne, Michigan, were active army posts well into the 1960s, resulting in significant architectural survivals. Likewise, the more substantial buildings of many later forts on the eastern Great Plains had twentieth-century utility. Missouri, Kansas, Nebraska, and the Dakotas all have military architecture at posts established from the Civil War through the Indian Wars. Most of the long-serving posts include twentieth-century military architecture as well.

Initial antiquarian interest in local history and the preservation of historic forts got an added boost during the years of the Great Depression, when a number of midwestern forts were reconstructed or restored as public works projects by the Works Progress Administration and the Civilian Conservation Corps. The post–World War II era saw increasing interest in local history and museums. The United States bicentennial and the growth of the preservation movement encouraged restoration of surviving buildings or even the reconstruction of entire complexes on their original sites. These impulses corresponded with the development of travel and cultural tourism as major leisure pursuits as combined better roads and increased disposable income sent midwesterners and other Americans in search of physical evidence of their country's past. More sophisticated techniques of restoration, exhibition, and public education converted many underused or sterile fort buildings into educational complexes. In the 1960s and 1970s, many fort museums adopted the increasingly popular technique of "living history," which peopled the posts with uniformed or costumed demonstrators to enhance the visitors' experience and understanding.

The size and complexity of fort museums dictate that many be administered by state or federal agencies. Some smaller sites, often only a single surviving building, are administered by county governments or local historical societies and not-for-profit organizations. Websites exist for most midwestern fort museums to provide both historical and current information.

The diversity of midwestern fort museums allows most of the region's historical themes to be explored. Colonial French and British influences and the American Revolution are interpreted at Fort Chartres, Illinois, and Fort Michilimackinac in Michigan. The Indian Wars of the 1790s are addressed at Fort Recovery, Ohio, and Fort Massac, Illinois, while the War of 1812 is represented in Ohio (Fort Meigs), Michigan (Fort Mackinac), Missouri (Fort Osage), and Indiana (Fort Knox). Following the War of 1812, the United States took control of the upper Mississippi Valley region. Surviving buildings of Forts Howard, Winnebago, and Crawford (Wisconsin) and larger complexes at Minnesota's Fort Snelling and Nebraska's Fort Atkinson cover that period. Michigan's Fort Wilkins focuses on the protection of mining in the 1840s, while Detroit's Fort Wayne interprets border tensions with British Canada. Expansion up the Missouri River system and onto the Great Plains and the Indian Wars of the later nineteenth century are perhaps the best represented. Many of these forts have been preserved, including several in Kansas (among them Scott, Hays, and Larned), Nebraska (Hartsuff, Kearney, Robinson, Sidney) and North Dakota (Abercrombie, Abraham Lincoln, Buford, Totten). Even

Fort Mackinac, Michigan, is largely restored to its later days as a national park post in the 1880s.

Sources and Further Reading: William T. Alderson and Shirley Payne Low, *Interpretation of Historic Sites*, rev. ed. (1985); American Association of Museums, *The Official Museum Directory, 2003* (2002); Jay Anderson, *Time Machines: The World of Living History* (1984); Eugene T. Petersen, *Mackinac in Restoration* (1983); Robert B. Roberts, *Encyclopedia of Historic Forts* (1988).

Brian Leigh Dunnigan
University of Michigan–Ann Arbor

Horicon Marsh

Horicon Marsh, located in Dodge County, Wisconsin, is the largest freshwater cattail marsh in the United States, spanning thirty-two thousand acres. It is both a state wildlife area and a national wildlife refuge. It has been designated a "Wetland of International Importance" and a "Globally Important Bird Area." Horicon Marsh is also a unit of the Ice Age National Scientific Reserve, serving as an example of an extinct glacial lake.

In 1846, a dam was constructed to flood the marsh for shipping. Disputes with surrounding landowners led to its removal twenty-three years later, returning it to a wetland. The resulting abundance of waterfowl lured market hunters who harvested ducks for commercial sale. By the turn of the century ducks had nearly disappeared from Horicon Marsh.

From 1910 to 1916, the marsh was ditched and drained in an attempt to farm the peat soil. Failure of this effort led to its abandonment, resulting in peat fires that burned on and off for twelve years. These fires ignited spontaneously as the organic material decomposed under the summer sun. As a result, the marsh was destroyed.

Today, Horicon Marsh is a restored wetland ecosystem. Efforts began in 1927 when the State of Wisconsin started purchasing land. Horicon Marsh was originally established for ducks with later management programs focusing on endangered species. Today, biologists are emphasizing management of the marsh as a wetland ecosystem. Two hundred thousand Canada geese stop at the marsh in their fall migrations, and more than 268 species of birds have been recorded at Horicon, plus numerous mammals, fish, insects, and plants.

Among the best times to view wildlife at Horicon Marsh are spring, from mid-April to the end of May, and from mid-September to the end of October.

Sources and Further Reading: Janet Battista, "Quaternary Geology of Horicon Marsh," master's thesis, University of Wisconsin (1990); Mary K. Judd, *Wisconsin Wildlife Viewing Guide* (1995); Daryl Tessen, ed., *Wisconsin's Favorite Bird Haunts*, 4th ed. (2000).

William K. Volkert
Horicon Service Center, Wisconsin

Indian-Run Museums

American Indian–run museums and cultural centers throughout the Midwest display the arts, material culture, and history of Native Americans in order to remember the past and shape contemporary experiences. These museums often present their histories as survival under oppression as well as vitality in the face of adversity. Indian-run museums are often located on tribal lands, where they present displays to facilitate tribal education, develop tourist revenue, and serve as community resource centers hosting events such as powwows and ceremonies as well as retail centers that help promote tribal artists. They may serve as repositories of historical materials (often loaned by tribal members), archives of tribal records, personal histories, and photographs. Many indigenous communities have regained custody of sacred objects and materials held in other museums through the Native American Graves Protection and Repatriation Act of 1990 (NAGPRA). Some of these items are displayed in tribal museums, while others have been returned to sacred conditions or to the families who would have inherited them. Indian-run museums have flourished since the 1970s in response to increasing political awareness. Attendance at these museums has risen as a result of heightened public interest in American Indian history. Currently there are more than fifty such museums in the Midwest, including the Ojibwe Abinoojiiyag Center in Lac du Flambeau, Wisconsin; the Millelacs Indian Museum in Onamia, Minnesota; the Turtle Mountain Chippewa Heritage Center in Belcourt, North Dakota; and the Shawnee and Woodland Native American Museum, owned by the Shawnee Nation United Remnant Band, in Bellfontaine, Ohio.

Source and Further Reading: Nancy J. Fuller and Suzanne Fabricius, "Tribal Museums," in Mary B. Davis, ed., *Native America in the Twentieth Century: An Encyclopedia* (1994).

Bess Reed
University of Louisville, Kentucky

The National Music Museum

The National Music Museum was founded in 1973 to preserve the musical heritage of the nation and world and to facilitate teaching and research on music. It has rapidly become one of the world's largest and most valuable music-related archives and collections of musical instruments and music artifacts. At present the museum contains more than ten thousand American, European, and non-Western musical instruments from most of the world's cultures and historical periods. Seven hundred fifty representative instruments are displayed in eight galleries. Only a handful of institutions elsewhere rival the museum's collections.

The museum is housed in a modern twenty-thousand-square-foot climate-controlled facility on the campus of the University of South Dakota in Vermillion. It was founded as a partnership between the university, which provides staff and facilities, and the museum's board of trustees and is a non-profit corporation.

The museum houses a concert hall for performing and recording music using historical instruments, an extensive specialized library, study areas, storage facilities, and a laboratory for the conservation and restoration of the instruments. The facility has become a focal point for research and regularly hosts visiting scholars from around the world as well as prestigious national and international conferences.

Highlights of the collection include rare grand pianos dating to the eighteenth century; seventeenth-century English, Flemish, German, French, and Portuguese harpsichords; seventeenth- and eighteenth-century woodwind instruments; and the world's most extensive collection exemplifying the American band movement of the late nineteenth and early twentieth centuries. The museum is the world's preeminent center for historical studies of the saxophone, clarinet, and brass instruments. The National Music Museum is fully accredited

by the American Association of Museums and is recognized as a Landmark of American Music by the National Music Council.

Barry Donald Mowell
Broward Community College, Florida

Native American Mound Sites

Large raised mounds and earthworks were built throughout the Midwest and the Southeast by Native Americans from 1800 B.C. to A.D. 1500. While the oldest known mounds in the United States are in Watson Brake, Louisiana (3400–3000 B.C.), the earliest mounds in the Midwest were built by the Adena (1100 B.C.–A.D. 200) in the rich woodlands near the Mississippi and Ohio Rivers (Early Woodland period). The Adena, hunters and gatherers with limited agriculture, buried their dead in large conical mounds often containing a log crypt. They were sometimes in use for over a century and contained subsequent burials above the original crypt as well as cremated remains. The largest Adena burial mound in the Midwest, at Miamisburg, Ohio, measures nearly nine hundred feet in circumference and was originally more than ninety feet high.

Beginning in the Ohio River Valley around A.D. 200 and spreading north and west, the Middle Woodland period, characterized by the increasingly agricultural Hopewell culture, created geometric earthworks and burial sites that appear to have functioned as social and cosmological maps. Artisans of this culture created some of the most beautiful pieces of art in ancient North America. One of the most elaborate sites is outside Newark, Ohio. An octagon and square that probably functioned as a lunar observatory are preserved at

Cahokia, one of the largest Mississippian culture cities in pre-Columbian North America. Courtesy Cahokia Mounds State Historic Site.

the Mound-builders Country Club. Serpent Mound, near Peebles, Ohio, is a quarter-mile-long snake effigy. Long attributed to the Adena, recent carbon dating indicates that it was probably built by a nearby village of the Fort Ancient culture (c. A.D. 1000–1600). The snake's head is a flaring Y surrounding a large oval that may represent its eye or a stolen bird's egg. Its form may represent the appearance of Halley's Comet in A.D. 1066. Its jaws may have been used as sight lines marking the solstices, reflecting interest in the calendar year. Extraordinary Late Woodland effigy mounds can also be found in Wisconsin, at High Cliff State Park, and in Iowa, at Effigy Mounds National Monument.

The Late Woodland period was characterized by the Mississippian culture (A.D. 900–1700), which spread from the Southeast across Indiana and Illinois all the way to Iowa. Cahokia (A.D. 700–1450), near East St. Louis, Illinois, was a huge Mississippian center (with a peak population of about twenty thousand) incorporating up to fifty towns, making it one of North America's largest pre-Columbian urban sites. Mississippian communities appear to have been influenced by Mesoamerican practices, which included temple-topped rectangular mounds surrounding large plazas, social stratification, maize agriculture, and human sacrifice. A palisade enclosed the political and religious center at Cahokia, including the plaza and Monks Mound (about one hundred feet high), which was crowned by a temple. Elites were buried in some mounds with the bodies of retainers. Many mound sites along the periphery of the Woodland culture far from the Mississippian heartland built platform mounds and maintained trade ties with the great Mississippian cities. All the Woodland cultures and the earthworks they built linked religion, political organization, and cosmology together. The mounds they raised, whether to harbor the dead or mark the movements of the heavens, are sacred.

Sources and Further Reading: Robert A. Birmingham and Leslie E. Eisenberg, *Indian Mounds of Wisconsin* (2000); Warren K. Moorehead, *The Cahokia Mounds* (1922); W. N. Morgan, *Prehistoric Architecture in the Eastern United States* (1980); Jessica E. Saraceni, "Redating Serpent Mound," *Archaeology* 49 (Nov.–Dec. 1996).

Bess Reed
University of Louisville, Kentucky

Presidential Commemoration Sites

Commemoration of midwestern presidents, beginning with Abraham Lincoln, represents a shift in power to the region. Of the fifteen presidents from Lincoln to Herbert Hoover, the Midwest produced nine. The area's presidents and first ladies have been commemorated with preserved homes, statues, funerary monuments, and presidential libraries, the last being a national institution first developed in the Midwest.

After Lincoln died from an assassin's bullet on April 14, 1865, his remains were placed on a train for the 1,700-mile journey to his hometown of Springfield, Illinois. Along the route, hundreds of thousands of mourners viewed Lincoln's body. The sixteenth president's role in saving the Union and ending slavery, and his eloquence on the Civil War's meaning, assured Lincoln a place equal to George Washington's in the landscape of public memory. Mary Todd Lincoln insisted that the first national monument to her husband be constructed as part of his grave in a Springfield cemetery. The monument features a 117-foot obelisk rising out of a large base containing a crypt. It was dedicated in 1874, ten years before the larger obelisk dedicated to Washington was completed in Washington, D.C. For a time, the monument's visitors could climb a staircase to the top and look out windows at a panorama of the surrounding area, giving tourists a physical experience of Lincoln's cultural apotheosis. The tomb itself could only be viewed from the outside through an iron grate. But when the monument was reconstructed in 1930, the staircase was closed and the crypt was rebuilt to allow visitors. Within the crypt's marble chambers visitors can read Lincoln's speeches and view his tomb with its epitaph by Secretary of War Edwin Stanton, "Now He Belongs to the Ages." Like the Lincoln Memorial in Washington, D.C. (completed in 1922), the monument commemorates the Union's salvation, but Lincoln's Gettysburg and Second Inaugural Addresses recorded in the crypt foreground the issues of race and equality in national identity.

Lincoln's preserved home in Springfield is part of a block of buildings re-created to display mid-nineteenth-century life, and it presents Mary and Abraham Lincoln's upper-middle-class domesticity as part of the moral structure on which his political leadership was built. In Lincoln City, Indiana, are the remains of one of Lincoln's boyhood cabins, his mother's grave, and a memorial visitors center. The site constructs Lincoln's character as a product of his tragedy-laced frontier life. Of the additional Lincoln monuments in the region, the most significant artistically is a standing bronze by Augustus Saint-Gaudens in Chicago's Lincoln Park.

Although no other midwestern president can match Lincoln's extensive commemoration, their memorials are often impressive. Ulysses S. Grant's tomb is in New York City, but his birthplace is preserved in Point

Pleasant, Ohio. William Taft's Cincinnati birthplace is similarly preserved, although he is buried in Arlington National Cemetery. Also in Ohio are the homes (or plaques marking where the homes once stood) and graves of Rutherford Hayes, James Garfield, William McKinley, and Warren Harding. The Garfield monument in Cleveland is a 180-foot Romanesque tower that contains Memorial Hall, with a statue of the assassinated president and the flag-draped caskets of James and Lucretia Garfield. In Niles, Ohio, the McKinley Memorial Library commemorates another assassinated president with a museum and a colonnaded sculpture court. The McKinley Memorial Library has a public lending library, not to be confused with the institution of the presidential library discussed in this entry. The Harding Memorial in Marion, Ohio, encircles the graves of Warren and Florence Harding with a massive Doric colonnade.

Rutherford and Lucy Hayes's son, Webb Hayes, created the first presidential library in order to honor his parents, a privately administered neoclassical library containing an archive and museum, next to the Hayes mansion in Fremont, Ohio. It was completed in 1914, and Franklin D. Roosevelt used it as a model to construct his presidential library in Hyde Park, New York (completed in 1940), but with an important difference—FDR's library is administered by the federal government's National Archives. Every president since Roosevelt, and even his predecessor Hoover, has had a hand in designing a privately built and federally administered presidential library as a memorial to himself. The destruction and disbursement of earlier presidents' records provided an important rationale for creating an institution to preserve presidential materials.

In addition to the Hayes Library, the Midwest is home to the Herbert Hoover Presidential Library and Museum in West Branch, Iowa; the Harry S Truman Library and Museum in Independence, Missouri; the Dwight D. Eisenhower Library and Museum in Abilene, Kansas; the Gerald R. Ford Library in Ann Arbor, Michigan; and a separate Ford Museum in Grand Rapids. The unprecedented access to records that presidential libraries give has created an explosion of scholarship that has profoundly affected the understanding of the presidency. Most presidents are buried at their libraries, and their preserved homes are usually nearby. Presidential libraries draw hundreds of thousands of tourists annually to their museum displays of history and presidential lives, and each has unique features. For instance, inside the Truman Library is Thomas Hart Benton's mural *Independence and the Opening of the West*, which frames the entry to a 94 percent–scale replica of Truman's Oval Office. There is an implied parallel between the settling of the West and the preservation of the American way of life from

the Oval Office during the cold war. In 2001, the Truman Library opened a new exhibit on Truman's presidency that examines such issues as the decision to drop the atomic bomb and the tension between civil liberties and national security, sometimes using interactive multimedia theatres. Similarly, the Eisenhower Library has created new displays that examine World War II and the cold war through the life of "Ike." Although first ladies are given display space in their husbands' libraries, in 1998 the National First Ladies' Library opened in Canton, Ohio, in the restored home of Ida McKinley.

From Lincoln's obelisk to presidential libraries, there has been a shift in presidential commemoration, from relatively abstract symbols to archives that preserve presidential materials as well as museums that feature interactive computer-controlled video displays.

Sources and Further Reading: Benjamin Hufbauer, "The Father in the Temple: Memory and Masculinity in Presidential Commemoration," Ph.D. diss., University of California (1999); Pat Hyland, *Presidential Libraries and Museums* (1995); Rachel M. Kochmann, *Presidents: Birthplaces, Homes and Burial Sites*, 9th ed. (1994); Merrill D. Peterson, *Lincoln in American Memory* (1994); Kirk Savage, *Standing Soldiers, Kneeling Slaves* (1997); Frank L. Schick, *Records of the Presidency* (1989); Curt Smith, *Windows on the White House* (1997).

Benjamin Hufbauer
University of Louisville, Kentucky

Re-created Heritage Villages

Re-created heritage villages consist of structures from the early settlement landscape that have been gathered in from a surrounding community in modern times to form an artificial village. The primary reason these villages have been re-created and currently operate is to preserve historic structures or cultural heritage. They are not historic sites but may include historic structures. The structures are not on their original foundations and the village may consist of buildings from different areas and different periods of time. Authentic historic structures have been preserved and assembled in a manner that replicates the village style and atmosphere of an earlier period in history. The urban reflection of a village or town indicates an inclusion of those structures that represent the institutions of community; that is, churches, one-room schools, general stores, blacksmith shops, railroad depots, or log homes. These sites act as community-heritage banks that illustrate various aspects of community life from days past, and they provide local residents a greater sense of belonging to their community and heritage in a world experiencing rapid globalization.

Though re-created heritage villages can be found throughout the United States, the Midwest is home to more than seventy-five such sites. The era portrayed by each village may vary from site to site and structure to structure, but the period most prominently represented in the re-created heritage villages of the Midwest is the latter part of the 1800s and the early half of the 1900s. Many of these sites hold festivals celebrating the cultural background of early European immigrants to the region.

The majority of re-created heritage villages were developed during the 1960s and 1970s. The average re-created heritage village has about twenty heritage structures and is operated as a nonprofit enterprise. Many sites have volunteers who assist in the display of heritage or the operation of the village. Volunteers at some sites dress in the attire of the era and provide visitors with a living-history experience. The re-creation of the village atmosphere is portrayed in the furnishings, artifacts, and décor of each structure. The level of adherence to strict codes of authenticity varies from village to village, but each site provides visitors with a unique kind of heritage tourism experience. Many sites offer community events, historical reenactments, traditional crafts, and other forms of entertainment or activities. Some villages are in their early reconstruction stages while others are well developed with an extensive tourism agenda.

Examples of re-created heritage villages are Billie Creek Village at Rockville, Indiana; Bonanzaville at Fargo, North Dakota; Heritage Hill at Green Bay, Wisconsin (featuring the French heritage of the community of La Baye and a 1905 Belgian farm); Midway Village at Rockford, Illinois; Pella Historical Village at Pella, Iowa; Village of Yesteryear at Owatonna, Minnesota (featuring the St. Wenceslaus of Moravia Church built in 1891); and White Pine Village at Ludington, Michigan.

Sources and Further Reading: Royal Berglee, "Heritage Tourism and Re-created Heritage Villages in the American Midwest: A Geographic Analysis," Ph.D. diss., Indiana State University (2000); Joslyn Green, *Getting Started: How to Succeed in Heritage Tourism* (1993).

Royal Berglee
Morehead State University, Kentucky

Religious Museums and Collections

With a rich and varied history of religious belief, midwestern states boast a large number of religious museums, archives, collections, and shrines that commemorate immigrant faiths and the central role that religion has played among Americans of all kinds. While the overwhelming majority of these institutions are Christian, both Protestant and Roman Catholic, there are many collections of artifacts of religions other than Christianity that detail the important links among ethnicity, race, and religion in the Midwest. Indeed, many religious collections are the product of immigrant groups, including the Lithuanian Museum, Chicago; the Swedish American Museum, Chicago; the Norwegian-American Historical Association, Northfield, Minnesota; El Museo Latino, Omaha; the Romanian Ethnic Art Museum, Cleveland; and the Ukrainian Museum-Archives, Cleveland.

Protestant museums and collections include the Billy Graham Center Museum, Wheaton, Illinois; the Museum of Amana History, Amana, Iowa; the Mennonite Heritage Museum, Goessel, Kansas; the Minnesota Conference Archives, United Methodist Church, Minneapolis; the Concordia Historical Institute (Lutheran), St. Louis; and the Friends (Quaker) Meeting House, Mount Pleasant, Ohio.

Roman Catholic museums, archives, and collections include the Teutopolis Monastery Museum, Teutopolis, Illinois; the Archives–Archdiocese of St. Paul and Minneapolis; the Old St. Ferdinand's Shrine, Florissant, Missouri; the Museum of the Western Jesuit Missions, Hazelwood, Missouri; and the Marian Library, University of Dayton, Ohio. The many grottoes built by several Catholic priests in Illinois, Iowa, and Wisconsin in the early twentieth century are helpfully documented in *Sacred Spaces and Other Places.* Noteworthy collections of Jewish culture include the Spertus Museum, Chicago; the Hebrew Union College–Jewish Institute of Religion, Skirball Museum, Cincinnati; and the Temple Museum of Religious Art, Cleveland.

The opportunity to study non-Christian and para-Christian religions is supported by several unusual collections: the Museum of Ancient Artifacts, Chicago, dedicated to the study of occult and psychic phenomena; the Wings of Love—Healing Arts Museum, Clinton, Michigan; and the Lentz Center for Asian Culture, Lincoln, Nebraska.

Religious individuals, groups, and organizations of importance in American history are often well represented in midwestern collections, including the Billy Sunday Museum and Home, Winona Lake, Indiana; the Willard House (Women's Christian Temperance Union Museum), Evanston, Illinois; the Joseph Smith Historic Center, Nauvoo, Illinois; the Iowa Masonic Library and Museum, Cedar Rapids; the Carry A. Nation Home Memorial, Medicine Lodge, Kansas; the Gospel Music Hall of Fame and Museum, Detroit; the Adventist Heritage Center, Berrien Springs, Michigan; the Great Plains Black Museum, Omaha; the

African American Museum, Cleveland; the Shaker Historical Society, Shaker Heights, Ohio; and the Museum of Woodcarving, Shell Lake, Wisconsin.

Sources and Further Reading: The Official Museum Directory, 32nd ed., vol. 1 (2001); Lisa Stone and Jim Zanzi, *Sacred Spaces and Other Places* (1993).

David Morgan
Valparaiso University, Indiana

State and Local Historical Societies

State and local historical societies are cultural institutions devoted to the collection, preservation, and dissemination of the local history of a place—a state, county, community, or region of the Midwest. While the desire to remember, preserve, and celebrate the past is universal, the historical societies of the Midwest are shaped by the unique history of the region. Midwestern historical societies participate in the ongoing process of defining a collective regional identity by representing the past in documents, artifacts, historic sites, and public events.

Historical societies in the Midwest vary widely in their size, activities, budgets, and relationship to state or local government, but their institutional histories have elements in common. The rationale for founding a state or local historical society springs from the founders' recognition that early documents, sites, and residents are being lost along with the history they represent. Pride of place and interest in local history also motivate societies' founders. Sesquicentennials or centennials for the founding of communities or states can also prompt the founding of historical societies.

Historical societies of all sizes may go through cycles of founding, disbanding, and reorganizing until a stable membership base forms to maintain the society. The history of the Historical Society of Michigan offers such an example. The society was founded in 1828 by men from New England or the Middle Atlantic states, many of whom were members of historical societies in their prior home states. The society became dormant between 1841 and 1847, was reorganized in 1857 by officers of the Detroit Young Men's Society, and folded once more in 1861. It was reorganized again in 1874 in Lansing, and continues to function today.

A central element of any historical society's mission is the collection and preservation of historic documents and data. Societies make the data from these collections accessible in a variety of forms. Many societies make these collections available in a library or archive. Most societies publish newsletters or journals as one of the benefits of membership. *Relatively Seeking* is the Cherokee County (Kansas) Genealogical-Historical Society's semiannual newsletter, and journals are published by state historical societies in Nebraska, North Dakota, Iowa, and Michigan. Publications provide a way to disseminate historical data like marriage or burial records. They also provide a place for articles on local history. Books are another popular publication as well as a potential source of revenue for the society; the Greene County (Missouri) Historical Society, for example, published *The Civil War Letters of Albert Demuth and Roster of the Eighth Missouri Volunteer Cavalry* (1997). Websites provide another way for a society to make documentary resources and publications available; so, for instance, the Burlington (Wisconsin) Historical Society publishes an online list of marriages in the Burlington vicinity.

Preserving the physical traces of the past—artifacts, historic buildings, and historic sites—is another activity of state and local historical societies in the Midwest. Through the identification and exhibition of artifacts and sites representative of the history of their locale, societies participate in defining a collective historical identity. Some shared themes can be found in the physical preservation efforts of historical societies across the Midwest, evidenced by a perusal of historical society websites. The pioneer heritage of the locale is one such theme, exemplified in "pioneer log cabin" displays that may feature a separate physical structure, such as the log cabin maintained by the Lee County (Illinois) Historical Society, first built as the Old Settlers Memorial in 1894, or a pioneer cabin exhibit in a historical society museum like the display of the La-Porte County (Indiana) Historical Society. Other common themes in historical society artifacts and sites include the natural environment, Native American groups in the area, local participation in wars, the agricultural heritage, and the homes or belongings of prominent citizens. Historic homes also serve as headquarters and museums for some societies. The Jacob Van Orden mansion is the home of the Sauk County (Wisconsin) Historical Society as well as an active museum and venue for public events.

Along with these shared themes, a historical society's physical representations of the past highlight events, people, and sites that set their locale apart from other areas. The Minnesota Historical Society operates the North West Company Fur Post as a living-history museum to commemorate the importance of the fur trade in the state. The Nebraska State Historical Society maintains historic sites for famous citizens like Willa Cather and President Gerald Ford. The Washington County (Minnesota) Historical Society maintains the Warden's House of the Minnesota Territorial Prison as a museum to represent the prison's role in local history. The Floyd County (Iowa) Historical Society Museum celebrates Charles City as the birthplace of the gasoline-driven tractor. An area's identification with a popular imaginary history can also be used by a society to represent its locale. For instance, the Kansas Historical Society sells *Wizard of Oz* memorabilia alongside Kansas pins and books on Kansas history in its gift shop.

Historical society programs of all kinds represent and perpetuate local history in the service of collective identity. These activities include a lecture like "Finding Lewis and Clark: Old Trails, New Directions," delivered at the 2003 annual meeting of the South Dakota State Historical Society, or the exhibit Jewish Heritage in Wayne County by the Wayne County (Ohio) Historical Society. Online databases can make accessible a society's holdings, such as the battle flag collection of the Ohio Historical Society. Assistance in teaching state and local history is another service societies can offer. The Nebraska State Historical Society offers teaching materials, National History Day assistance to students, and a teacher-training institute, while the Wisconsin Historical Society offers an online curriculum for "An Overview of Cultural Periods in Wisconsin Archaeology." Workshops on historic foodways, crafts, and agricultural techniques and even sports clubs playing vintage baseball, like the St. Croix Base Ball Club of the Washington County (Minnesota) Historical Society, increase a society's visibility in the community while providing information on local history.

Sources and Further Reading: Joseph A. Amato, *Rethinking Home* (2002); Alan R. Havig, *A Centennial History of the State Historical Society of Missouri, 1898–1998* (1998); Carol Kammen, *On Doing Local History*, 2nd ed. (2003); Alfred E. Lemmon, "Trans-Mississippi States," in H. G. Jones, ed., *Historical Consciousness in the Early Republic* (1995); Philip P. Mason, "Trans-Mountain States," in H. G. Jones, ed., *Historical Consciousness in the Early Republic* (1995); Charles Phillips and Patricia Hogan, *A Culture at Risk: Who Cares for America's Heritage?* (1984); Frederick L. Rath, *Local History, National Heritage* (1991); Lana Ruegamer, *A History of the Indiana Historical Society, 1830–1980* (1980).

Barbara Truesdell
Indiana University–Bloomington

Underground Railroad Sites and Museums

The Underground Railroad operated from the early 1820s through the end of the Civil War. A unique, secret, or semisecret, northern operation, the railroad offered help in the way of transportation, food, clothing, and medical aid to runaway slaves fleeing to free-

Freedom Stairway, Ripley, Ohio. Ohio Historical Society, SC1591 AL01171.

dom in Canada. For railroad workers, the law and slave hunters posed barriers to helping slaves. The railroad is historically important because it represents a spontaneous, clandestine, illegal, charitable activity carried on by blacks and whites in an era of slavery.

The Midwest played a significant role in the Underground Railroad's operation because of its location and the willingness of its people to help. A number of people and sites significant in railroad history are remembered throughout the Midwest. In Kansas, for instance, visitors can stroll through John Brown Memorial Park in Osawatomie, and more adventurous travelers may explore John Brown's Caves and Museum three miles west of Nebraska City, Nebraska. In Indiana, the Levi Coffin home is in Fountain City. Cincinnati is home to the Freedom Center, a museum that focuses on topics concerning the railroad, slavery, and the quest for freedom. By their participation in the railroad, midwesterners demonstrated their ideological opposition to slavery, uniting people to challenge existing legal and social constructs in America. The importance of the railroad in the Midwest illustrates people's religious codes, their good will, and their belief in ideals espoused in the Declaration of Independence. Today, Underground Railroad sites serve as a reminder of past injustices, action to right wrongs, and a desire to help those in need.

Sources and Further Reading: Charles L. Blockson, *Hippocrene Guide to the Underground Railroad* (1994); Donna DeBlasio and Marcelle R. Wilson, *Historic and Architectural Resources of the Underground Railroad in Ohio* (2001).

Marcelle R. Wilson
Youngstown State University, Ohio

Libraries and Literary Organizations

Settlers who moved into the Midwest replicated, within the limits of frontier life, the libraries and literary organizations from their past. At the heart of such institutions was the goal of ensuring an educated and cultured populace, and also, by providing an alternative to more dangerous and unproductive paths, a means to assure communities with good moral character. While initially based on established northeastern models, the Midwest put its own stamp on the pace and direction of library development locally, regionally, and nationally, culminating in the late twentieth century with Chicago serving as a locus not only for libraries and the library profession as the seat of the American Library Association but for literary organizations in the form of Oprah Winfrey's book club.

It is not easy to generalize the development of libraries and literary organizations across the Midwest because settlers clustered in various regions at different times and according to ethnicity and points of origin. Even so, institutions based on New England prototypes predominated, particularly social or subscription libraries, which served members who bought stock or paid subscription fees. For example, in 1804 the Western Library Association in the Town of Ames, Ohio, undertook an original bit of fund-raising to acquire a book collection of history, religion, and fiction by arranging for local men to catch raccoons and send the skins to Boston for sale, thus originating the popular name "Coonskin Library." Social libraries also benefited specific vocational groups in trade centers such as Chicago, Cincinnati, and St. Louis, where mercantile libraries based on similar ones in New York, Boston, and Philadelphia were established to serve the working class in the 1830s and 1840s.

The moral imperative of early libraries in the Midwest should not be underestimated, nor should the influence of women in disseminating literary culture. In many communities, Sunday school libraries provided the only book collections, however modest. The Young Men's Association Library founded in Chicago in 1841, which served as the city's chief circulation library until the fire of 1871, stated as one of its objectives "to foster intellectual activity and improvement; [and to] provide a retreat which would keep young

---

❖ **One Aspect of Unity in a Small-Town Community**

It began with a lumbering bookmobile coming to Ashland, Missouri (pop. 1,950), twice a month in the 1980s. By 1996, Ashland and southern Boone County readers had increased their withdrawals from one thousand in 1990 to nearly seven thousand in 1996. This led the Library Board to park the old 1968 Gerstenslanger Bookmobile permanently in the Baptist Church parking lot. This dinosaur became a beloved town feature.

In the 1990s, Ashland's library check-out rate grew so much that the Library Board felt the town was ready to be home to a branch library. A vacant downtown building was rented and modestly remodeled. On July 29, 2000, some 150 citizens (ranging in age from about seven to older than seventy) arranged themselves in an old-fashioned bucket brigade that stretched more than 150 yards between the bookmobile and the new library. For four hours, book tote after book tote was passed, moving nearly five thousand items into the new space. Not a book was misplaced in this summer exercise of community support for this new expression of Ashland's town pride.

Beginning with a small, part-time staff and at first open only twenty hours a week, the library has now expanded to being open six days a week (fifty-two hours) with three and a half permanent staff positions. Sitting at one of the reading tables after school, you can hear and feel the buzz of local school kids, parents with young children, seniors chatting over checkers or chess, and continual conversation and interaction among librarians and town folks of all ages.

Asking a librarian "What role do you play here?" evoked "Well, let's see . . . We have to be teachers, mothers, older sisters and brothers, study-hall monitors, reference sources, computer technicians, disciplinarians, exam proctors and . . ." "mind readers!" the librarian across the room added. Several parents nodded in agreement with this array.

This small-town library is not only a source of pride for Ashland but also a font of unity in this community.

Kit Salter
Peckham & Wright Architects, Columbia, Missouri

men in their unemployed hours from idling in barrooms or at card tables."

The Women's Christian Temperance Union (WCTU) was a force in places such as Kendall County, Illinois, where the WCTU Reading Room served as a cultural center that provided lectures and debates, declamations, readings, and music "to renew the youth of the aged, while putting the youth and children in a position to acquire social graces under adult supervision." Improvement in elocution, composition, and debate were stated as Reading Room objectives, and the WCTU expressed hope that these activities would "[call] young men away from the four enticing fiery halls that we see by our doorsteps."

While nearly 60 percent of social libraries were located in the Northeast by 1876, a single state, Michigan, had more than half of the "ladies' libraries" through the turn of the century. Although social library registers from early in the nineteenth century show predominantly male membership, by 1900 libraries for women outnumbered libraries for men five to one. In Kalamazoo, Michigan, the Ladies' Library Association formed in 1852 to maintain a library "to afford and encourage useful and entertaining reading; to furnish literary and scientific lectures; and [to provide] other means of promoting moral and intellectual improvement," among other things. The Ladies' Library Association Reading Room influenced the intellectual life of the town through a lecture series and a subscription library and was the only library in town until a public library was created in 1872.

The dominance of social libraries through the first half of the nineteenth century overlapped the establishment of tax-funded public libraries, free to all rather than serving only specific subscriber groups able to afford membership. The rise of public libraries was facilitated by many factors, including the spread of free public education, industrialization, urbanization, and the progressivist philosophy popular up until the Civil War: that humans possessed rational capacity and had the natural right to acquire knowledge. Libraries provided an institutional means through which everyone could achieve individual intellectual potential, and such self-improvement was considered an effective hedge against societal ills. New York enacted the first state law in 1835 to fund school-district libraries, charging government with the responsibility to provide free library service through taxation, to provide state aid to libraries, and to recognize them as educational agencies. School-district library laws followed in states of the Midwest, superseded by enabling state laws for public libraries throughout the region in the 1870s and 1880s.

Public libraries were founded across the Midwest beginning with the Cincinnati Public Library in 1853,

funded through a revision of the school law of the state of Ohio. Others followed: Detroit in 1865; Cleveland in 1869; Indianapolis, Kansas City (Missouri), Chicago, Lincoln (Nebraska), and Milwaukee in the 1870s; and St. Louis in 1893. Library building received a substantial boost from 1886 to 1919 when industrialist and philanthropist Andrew Carnegie donated over forty-one million dollars to establish public libraries nationwide. The Midwest was a primary beneficiary of Carnegie's largesse, with libraries established in 633 communities at a cost of nearly fourteen million dollars. Further library development, especially in rural areas and communities with populations of less than ten thousand, was assisted by federal funding through the Library Services Act of 1956 and the Library Services Construction Act of 1964.

As tax funding of public libraries became standardized across the country in the late nineteenth century, midwestern libraries and librarians made their mark on the development of library services in ways that reached beyond their immediate communities. In 1890, the Cleveland Public Library became the first large public library to adopt an open-access policy, following an initial practice limiting access only to library officials. The Wisconsin Library Commission, established in 1895, advised the state's free libraries and communities planning to establish libraries in book selection, cataloging, and library management. The *Library Journal* stated in January 1897 that Wisconsin had become "not only a library model to the other states of the west, but an example to many of the eastern states where the library movement has never taken such a strong foothold or awakened such general interest." By the end of the century, library commissions had also been established in Ohio and Indiana, operating in an advisory capacity across the states and controlling traveling libraries, which numbered fifty-six in Ohio by the end of 1897.

Midwestern libraries also provided outreach beyond their central buildings by creating branches such as the one at Chicago's Hull-House in 1890 and deposit stations such as those at Cleveland's Fire House Number Two and even on the fireboat *Clevelander*, as well as in Dayton, Ohio, at the National Cash Register Company. In 1910, the Minneapolis Public Library created a reading room for the unemployed, many of them immigrants, in an area of the city where men lived in cheap hotels and flophouses, while Evanston, Illinois, and Hibbing, Minnesota, served people in outlying areas by means of library buses. In 1915, Hibbing boasted the first bus that patrons could actually enter. It was heated by a coal-burning stove and served a diverse clientele including populations of Finnish, Irish, and Serbian immigrants. Outreach to rural areas was furthered in the 1950s and 1960s by federal funding through the Library Services Act and Library Services Construction Act.

William Frederick Poole, a former librarian of the Boston Athenaeum, made his mark on three important midwestern libraries: the Cincinnati Public Library, the Chicago Public Library, and the Newberry Library. He took over directorship of the Cincinnati Public Library in 1869, and during his five-year tenure oversaw the preparation of a card catalog; created a simplified loan system; and opened the reading rooms on Sunday, a first for a large municipal library. When he left Cincinnati, the library was considered second in stature only to Boston's. As director of the Chicago Public Library from 1874 to 1887, Poole bought German and French literature to serve the needs of immigrants and bolstered the popular-fiction collection, countering the prevailing notion that it was the duty of libraries to provide only materials that would lead to readers' self-improvement. In 1885, Poole went so far as to question the "public" nature of the New York Public Library because it did not cater to Socialists, Communists, anarchists, and persons of foreign birth: "We have these same classes in Chicago . . . and they give us no trouble. The public library has no better friends than the foreigners, for we give them the books they want to read in their own languages. The socialists and communists are all friends of the library, for we give them the books they want." Although Poole's ideas did not gain immediate currency with other library leaders of the time, his advancement of intellectual freedom came to be an important part of American Library Association doctrine in 1939 in its Library Bill of Rights.

Poole was appointed librarian of the Newberry Library in 1887 and set about creating a collection for the "use of earnest and advanced students . . . a scholar's library." The Newberry reference and research collection focuses on history, literature, philosophy, and music. With the Chicago Public Library providing popular materials and the Newberry resources in the humanities, a third collection, the John Crerar Library, opened to the public in 1897. In his bequest, John Crerar, a Chicago merchant and railroad executive, stipulated that the materials in the library be "selected with a view to create and sustain a healthy moral and Christian sentiment in the community, and that all nastiness and immorality be excluded"; specifically, "dirty French novels and all skeptical trash and works of questionable moral tone." The trustees of the library unanimously decided to maintain it as a scientific reference library, covering social, pure, and applied sciences.

From the early days of settlement through the early days of the public library movement, midwesterners have recognized the power of the word and have had faith in its ability to transmit culture. Questions about what constituted proper, self-improving reading concerned those who compiled social library collections in the first half of the nineteenth century as it did librarians throughout the twentieth century. In 1879, the ALA adopted the motto "The best reading for the largest number at the least cost," and at the ALA annual conference in Chicago in 1893, a prescriptive five-thousand-volume collection of books recommended for public libraries—one that omitted many popular writers of the day—was disseminated. Poole had questioned the wisdom of denying taxpayers the books they wanted to read, and by the 1920s librarians were less inclined to consider "light reading" deleterious to the public.

The tension between giving the people what they want and giving them what they need continues to play itself out, most notably in the controversy surrounding Oprah's Book Club. Oprah Winfrey's syndicated daytime television talk show, originating in Chicago, focuses on the value of self-improvement much as literary organizations throughout the history of the Midwest have, even though her brand is more a manifestation of personal spirit than morality. Her show is viewed primarily by women, and through her book club, which began in 1996, Winfrey personally recommended books and featured their authors on her show. Her recommendations triggered a publishing phenomenon, with each book she chose becoming a best seller, and her book club has had many imitators in the Midwest and nationally. But she was also slighted by critics who questioned the merit of her choices. In other words, she was taken to task for not recommending the "right" books, and in one instance, evoking the image of an important cash crop of the Heartland, was accused of having taste that "ran heavily to middlebrow corn." Whether or not Winfrey's selections were the right ones, the discussion about the importance of intellectual activity, reading, and its relationship to self-improvement is deeply rooted in the regional history of literary organizations.

Sources and Further Reading: George S. Bobinski, *Carnegie Libraries: Their History and Impact on American Public Library Development* (1969); Paul Dickson, *The Library in America* (1986); Evelyn Geller, *Forbidden Books in American Public Libraries, 1876–1939* (1984); Allen Kent and Harold Lancour, eds., *Encyclopedia of Library and Information Science* (1968); Haynes McMillen, "The Distribution of Libraries throughout the U.S.," *Library Trends* 25 (July 1976); "Oprah's Influence," *Report/Newsmagazine* 29 (Apr. 29, 2002); Daniel Ring, "Outpost of New England Culture: The Ladies Library Association of Kalamazoo, Michigan," *Libraries and Culture* 32 (Winter 1997); Elizabeth W. Stone, *American Library Development, 1600–1899* (1977); Mary Faith Thomas, "The Development of Literary Activities and Library Services in Yorkville, Illinois, from 1864–1915," *Illinois Libraries* 79 (Winter 1997); Wayne A. Wiegand, "Tunnel Vision and

Blind Spots: What the Past Tells Us About the Present; Reflections on the Twentieth-Century History of American Librarianship," *Library Quarterly* 69 (January, 1999); Wayne A. Wiegand and Donald G. Davis, Jr., *Encyclopedia of Library History* (1994); Howard W. Winger, ed., *American Library History: 1876–1976* (1976).

Thomas Riedel
Regis University, Colorado

Book Clubs

Though people have always read collectively, formal book clubs in the Midwest proliferated in close association with the women's club movement (1880–1920). Many of these clubs "were an attempt at 'civilizing' and imposing a class structure on a relatively unformed Midwest society," says historian Anne Ruggles Gere. In response to prejudice, midwestern African Americans, Jews, and other groups formed reading clubs of their own during this period. Chicago was and continues to be home to several institutions that have supported book clubs, such as the Great Books Foundation, which was incorporated in 1947 after Robert Maynard Hutchins and Mortimer Adler brought the Great Books program to the University of Chicago. Another Chicago-based club facilitator is the American Library Association. Its nationwide "Let's Talk About It" book discussion program, begun in the 1980s, directs readers to common texts chosen by scholars. And the Association of Book Group Readers and Leaders, based in suburban Chicago, has served as an information clearinghouse since 1995. The largest club to originate in the Midwest has been Oprah Winfrey's televised book club, begun in 1996. Produced in Chicago, this club has been credited with increasing the popularity of book clubs in general and African American book clubs in particular. In the past decade, city-wide book clubs have also flourished. Some midwestern affiliates of the Center for the Book at the Library of Congress have played a role in club promotion.

Sources and Further Reading: Anne Ruggles Gere, *Intimate Practices* (1997); Rachel Jacobsohn, *The Reading Group Handbook* (1994); Elizabeth McHenry, *Forgotten Readers* (2002).

K. D. Trager
Indiana University–Bloomington

Carnegie Libraries

Andrew Carnegie spent forty-one million dollars for the construction of 1,679 public libraries in the United States, of which more than 600 were built in the Midwest. In civic motivation, architecture, and impact, midwestern Carnegie libraries were not noticeably different from those in other regions of the country. Except for North Dakota, most states already had libraries that were founded by charitable groups such as the Young Men's Christian Association or, more frequently, the Ladies' Library Association. Women often were instrumental in local library establishment by lobbying civic leaders to ask Carnegie for a library. Whether initiated by men or by women, the push for Carnegie libraries came from the middle class.

Motives for the establishment of Carnegie libraries varied. Middle-class women viewed a library as an agency of social control that would save workers from

A Carnegie library, Brazil, Indiana. Jay Small Postcard Collection, Indiana Historical Society, neg. no. P391.

the saloons, while men often couched their support in terms of civic boosterism. Everywhere, library dedications evidenced local pride and boosterism. In East Liverpool, Ohio, five thousand people turned out for one that included tightrope walkers and tumblers. Library dedications were a mélange of entertainment, community bonding, and civic jubilee.

Building design usually followed a style known as Carnegie Classic. This architecture was a product of the classical revival school and not an innovation of Carnegie's. While there were departures from this style—Beaux-Arts architecture in Ohio; the Prairie school style in Wisconsin; or an innovative radial design in Fargo, North Dakota—it is estimated that 50 percent of the libraries were Carnegie classic, or its variant, classical revival. Building materials were locally or regionally derived, such as locally kilned bricks, Indiana limestone, South Dakota quartzite, or Marathon County (Wisconsin) granite.

Critics have lodged a number of complaints about Carnegie libraries. Some have argued that they were overbuilt. More seriously, Carnegie libraries never became "people's universities." Book collections were small and usually oriented toward children or women. The buildings exuded a cold and forbidding presence, and the librarians often insisted on genteel behavior.

Nevertheless, Carnegie libraries might best be measured by their long-term social and physical accomplishments. Perhaps Carnegie's lasting contribution was the creation of permanent buildings with designated rooms for a variety of readers. In the Midwest, where interest in public libraries was slow to emerge, few communities had library buildings before Carnegie. More importantly, Carnegie libraries created public space that was devoted to middle-class users and that met middle-class demands for educational opportunity. It was in a Carnegie library (Robinson, Illinois) where James Jones, the son of a dentist, studied the canons of American literature, and where Ernest Hemingway (Petoskey, Michigan), the son of a doctor, composed his war experiences. For an era that had limited means of entertainment, Carnegie libraries provided recreation and expanded the educational vista for the sons and daughters of the middle class who dwelled on the middle border. Carnegie libraries created a more complex culture that served to expand the minds of the middle classes and enhanced their ability to think, write, and dream.

Sources and Further Reading: George Bobinski, *Carnegie Libraries* (1969); Theodore Jones, *Carnegie Libraries across America* (1997); Daniel J. Macleod, *Carnegie Libraries in Wisconsin* (1968); Abigail Van Slyck, *Free to All* (1995).

Daniel F. Ring
Oakland University, Minnesota

Literary Centers

Several centers in the Midwest have become radial points for the world of literature, among them Woodland Pattern Book Center in Milwaukee; the Sherwood Anderson Literary Center in Elyria, Ohio; the Loft in Minneapolis; Thurber House in Columbus, Ohio; the Ragdale Foundation in Lake Forest, Illinois; and the Mary Anderson Center in Mount St. Francis, Indiana. They serve not only writers and readers in their communities but also people interested in related literary journeys. These centers provide forums for authors and readers of contemporary literature and make workshops, mentor programs, art exhibits, performances, and related arts available to the public.

Woodland Pattern Book Center, located in Milwaukee's Riverwest neighborhood, was founded in 1979 and is known for its presentation of new and emerging writers and community outreach through its collaborative and diverse programming. It is a literary center committed to presenting new literature in the nonacademic and nontheoretical context of its working-class neighborhood. Woodland Pattern makes small-press and cross-cultural books available to the public, especially materials difficult to obtain in the Milwaukee area. Throughout its history, Woodland Pattern has hosted hundreds of diverse writers and artists and offered its audiences opportunities to engage with the literary performing arts through artists' residencies and educational activities.

In Elyria, Ohio, the Sherwood Anderson Literary Center, an affiliate of the Lorain County Historical Society, encourages "people who enjoy reading and writing to engage more completely in the creative process and to experience the adventure that its discoveries yield." Inspired by the work of Ohio-born author Sherwood Anderson, the center promotes an understanding of his life and work while also offering a variety of writing- and reading-oriented activities that encourage individual writing processes and stimulate creative processes in general.

The Loft, founded in 1974 in Minneapolis, is one of the nation's best-known literary centers. Its mission is to foster a writing community, the artistic development of individual writers, and an audience for literature. It seeks "to recognize and encourage cultural diversity and pluralism in its membership and in all of its programs." The center offers, among other things, classes and workshops for writers, special programs for readers, mentoring for writers, grants and awards for writers, and two bimonthly publications—*Speakeasy* and *A View from the Loft.*

Columbus's Thurber House was founded in 1984 in writer James Thurber's former home to celebrate his life and work and to support literary endeavors of all kinds. It offers book readings; writing workshops; used-book sales; book-related art exhibitions; a bookstore/museum shop; writing classes for children; an annual prize for American humor writing; and residencies for writers, playwrights, and journalists.

The Ragdale Foundation, located in the house built as a summer retreat in 1897 for prominent architect Howard Van Doren Shaw, describes itself as "a place where writers and artists of all kinds can find uninterrupted time to work." Founded in 1976, Ragdale overlooks a fifty-acre nature preserve in Lake Forest, Illinois, and provides room for up to two hundred resident creative artists at a time.

Located on the grounds of a Franciscan friary in Mount St. Francis, Indiana, the Mary Sanderson Center makes available to resident artists a quiet, four-hundred-acre retreat space. The center, founded in 1989, is named for the nineteenth-century actress who originally owned the property. It offers full and partial fellowships and hosts special events open to the public.

Sources and Further Reading: Philip A. Greasley, ed., *Dictionary of Midwestern Literature*, vol. 1 (2001); Western Literature Association, *A Literary History of the American West* (1998).

Jennifer S. Holmes
Whittier College, California

The Newberry Library

Local businessman Walter Loomis Newberry left funds to create a public library for frontier Chicago upon his death in 1868. By the time his widow died, in 1887, Chicago already had a downtown public library, so the fledgling Newberry Library served the city's North Side with a "universal" range of noncirculating publications. When the John Crerar Library was founded in 1896, it agreed to focus its collection on science and technology, leaving music and the humanities for the Newberry and business for the Chicago Public Library, an emphasis still apparent at the Newberry and the Crerar.

The Newberry is known for its stunning collection of more than 300,000 maps, preserved in the Hermon Dunlap Smith Center for the History of Cartography, with special strength in the discovery and exploration of the Americas and the American West. The stately 1892 Romanesque revival edifice by Chicago architect Henry Ives Cobb today houses more than 1.5 million titles and 5 million manuscripts, accessible to any interested readers over age sixteen. Ground-floor gallery exhibitions highlight the library's diverse collections, including Chicago literature and history, American Indian history and literature, linguistics,

and the French Revolution. The Dr. William M. Scholl Center for Family and Community History promotes social history, while the library's genealogical holdings attract over half of its readership. The D'Arcy McNickle Center for the History of the American Indian sponsors conferences and publications, and the Center for Renaissance Studies is a premier midwestern resource. Public programs include a resident music ensemble, lectures, tours, and partnerships with regional universities and scholars.

Source and Further Reading: Dominic Pacyga and Ellen Skerrett, *Chicago: City of Neighborhoods* (1986).

Vincent L. Michael
School of the Art Institute of Chicago

Woodland Pattern Book Center

Woodland Pattern Book Center is a community-based arts center located in Riverwest—a working-class, racially mixed neighborhood that presents cross-cultural books, readings, workshops, art exhibits, and music performances in Milwaukee. Founded in 1979, it is the only Milwaukee arts organization presenting contemporary literature to the general public on a continuous basis.

Woodland Pattern is known for the presentation of new (experimental) and emerging writers, its community alliances, and its inclusive approach to programming. Its efforts in this regard have increased audiences across cultural boundaries, encouraging innovative and genre-bending new literature. Woodland Pattern is unique in that it sells books, making contemporary literature available, with an emphasis on small-press publications and poetry. The actual selling of books is combined with an unusual number and unusual types of activities, including educational classes, film screenings, music performances, readings, exhibitions, workshops, installations, community-based service, and conferences/symposiums.

Throughout its history, Woodland Pattern Book Center has hosted hundreds of diverse writers and artists, both emerging and renowned. Artists such as Sherman Alexie, Amiri Baraka, Sandra Cisneros, Li-Young Lee, Wang Ping, Leslie Marmon Silko, and Derek Walcott have presented their work to audiences at Woodland Pattern.

Sources and Further Reading: Jack Hirschman, ed., *Art on the Line: Essays by Artists about the Point Where Their Art and Activism Intersect* (2002); Tom Tolan, *Riverwest* (2003).

Jennifer S. Holmes
Whittier College, California

Major Art Museums

The growth of art museums in America followed the growth of wealth. Thus, the first group of major American art museums was concentrated on the East Coast, in New York, Hartford, Philadelphia, and Baltimore. The second great cluster of such museums developed in the Midwest, reflecting the region's extraordinary industrial growth in the later nineteenth century. The first wave of these midwestern museums was largely located along the shores of the Great Lakes—in Buffalo, Cleveland, Toledo, Chicago, Milwaukee, and Detroit, where easy transport and access to iron ore led to the growth of iron and steel making and many related industries. The center of this industrial region was Ohio, which was also a center of major art collecting. With six major institutions (one each in Cleveland, Toledo, Youngstown, and Columbus and two in Cincinnati), Ohio probably has more major art museums than any state except New York. The Cleveland Museum of Art, which was created in 1913 through the bequests or donations of four civic leaders, became the richest art-buying institution in the world in the 1950s, when Leonard C. Hanna (a nephew of industrialist Mark Hanna) left it a bequest of some fifty million dollars. This first wave of museum creation in the Midwest occurred from 1890 to 1920. It was followed in the 1930s by a second wave

that produced museums in cities such as Kansas City (Missouri), Omaha; and Wichita.

Cincinnati's cultural development occurred earlier, however, due to its early-nineteenth-century success as a port city. British writer Frances Trollope created the city's first "museum" in the 1830s, whose main attraction was a life-size tableau representing Dante's Inferno, created by sculptor Hiram Powers. The Cincinnati Art Museum was an outgrowth of the Woman's Art Museum Association of Cincinnati. In 1880 Charles West gave a major gift for the creation of an art museum, in 1881 the museum was incorporated, and by 1886 the building for it was constructed. Originally modeled on the Victoria and Albert Museum in London, with its emphasis on the decorative and industrial arts, the museum shifted to a "classical" art museum model that emphasized collecting original works of art, organizing its collection in a survey of art history, and curating (or managing) its collection with a staff of trained museum professionals and art historians. Daniel Burnham designed several extensions to the museum building.

Around the turn of the nineteenth century, the classical museum model especially evolved in the Midwest, in large part through the influence of the architecture of the 1893 Chicago World's Fair and the Art Institute of Chicago. The origins of the Art Institute's museum can be traced back to an art school founded in 1866, the Chicago Academy of Fine Arts, which changed its name to the Art Institute of Chicago in

The Art Institute of Chicago. Photo by Sathyan Sundaram.

1882. In 1893, at the time of the World's Fair, the Art Institute persuaded the fair managers to partly subsidize the cost of constructing a new building on Michigan Avenue at Adams Street. Supported by the wealthy citizens of Chicago, the museum quickly assembled impressive collections, and, due to the influence of the World's Fair, it provided a model that was imitated across the United States, particularly in the Midwest. The Toledo Museum of Art, for example, was created in 1901 and the St. Louis Art Museum in 1907. Like Chicago's Art Institute, St. Louis's museum was an outgrowth of an international exposition, the St. Louis World's Fair of 1904, and it occupied a building originally constructed for the fair. Interestingly, its original source of financial support was a public referendum, making it the first publicly funded art museum in the United States. Minneapolis, which had had an active art society for some thirty years, founded its Art Museum in 1911 and opened a classical building, designed by McKim, Mead & White, four years later.

By the early twentieth century, it had become common for midwestern business magnates to leave bequests for the creation of an art museum. Edward Drummond Libbey, the most innovative glassmaker of his time, left his fortune to create the Toledo Museum of Art in 1901. In 1927, Thomas Barlow Walker, who had assembled a large collection of representational paintings, created the Walker Art Center in Minneapolis. In 1933, James Edmundson, a pioneer of Des Moines, Iowa, who was born in a log cabin, died at the age of ninety-five and left a large bequest to create the Des Moines Art Center. In 1928, Sara Joslyn, the widow of the richest man in Nebraska, Omaha newspaper magnate George Joslyn, established the Society of Liberal Arts, which in turn created the Joslyn Art Museum. In 1915, William Rockhill Nelson, owner of the *Kansas City Star*, left a bequest to create an art museum. His funds were combined with those of a prosperous widow, Mary Atkins, and in 1933, the Nelson-Atkins Museum of Art opened in Kansas City, Missouri. In 1915, the widow of Roland P. Murdock, owner of the *Wichita Eagle*, left a bequest to create an art museum for Wichita. In 1927, Charles Phelps Taft of Cincinnati, the half brother of U.S. president William Howard Taft, bequeathed the Taft house as a museum, and it opened to the public as the Taft Museum in 1932. The museum is a kind of midwestern equivalent to the Frick Collection in New York, with notable paintings by Rembrandt and Frans Hals as well as such nineteenth-century canvases as John Singer Sargent's portrait *Robert Louis Stevenson* and James Whistler's early masterpiece *At the Piano*.

Early midwestern art museums, such as the first building of the Cincinnati Art Museum, reflected a Romanesque style. By 1900, however, the neoclassical architecture of the 1893 Chicago World's Fair became the midwestern norm. The first of these structures was the neoclassical design of Chicago's own Art Institute. Several architects who had worked for the World's Fair were soon called upon to build or add to art museums elsewhere, as Daniel Burnham did in Cincinnati. Cass Gilbert designed the St. Louis Art Museum. McKim, Mead & White designed the Minneapolis Institute of Arts in 1911 and the Butler Institute of American Art in Youngstown in 1919. In other cases, local architects followed the World's Fair model, as was the case with the Cleveland Museum of Art, designed by Hubbell and Benes in 1916.

The neoclassical model remained the norm until the 1930s, although later examples were more severe in style, like, for instance, the new building of the Detroit Institute of Arts, designed by Paul Cret in 1927, or the Nelson-Atkins Museum of Art, designed by Wright and Wright in 1933. In the post–World War II era, however, major midwestern art museums followed the model of New York's Museum of Modern Art. The most faithful follower of this model was the Walker Art Center, which in 1969 sold off the nineteenth-century collection of its founder and replaced it with modern art, at the same time replacing its original Moorish-style building with a "white box" designed by Edward Larrabee Barnes. Other art museums added modern wings to their original neoclassical buildings. For example, Barnes designed an addition to the Carnegie Museum of Art in Pittsburgh that was completed in 1974 and an addition to the Wichita Art Museum in 1975; Buffalo's Albright-Knox Art Gallery added a wing designed by Gordon Bunshaft of Skidmore, Owings & Merrill; the Minneapolis Institute of Art added a new entrance by the Japanese modernist Kenzo Tange; and the Cleveland Museum of Art added two successive wings designed by Byers Hays (1954) and Marcel Breuer (1971). Modern architecture also became the preference of newly created institutions, such as the Sheldon Memorial Art Museum and Sculpture Garden in Lincoln, Nebraska, which commissioned a building by Philip Johnson in 1963. Older institutions sometimes remodeled galleries in a modern style, as did, for example, the Nelson-Atkins, which hired the West Coast modernist architect John Yeon to design several dramatic installations.

During their early years, many midwestern art museums were chiefly concerned with public education and exhibitions. But collecting art was an increasing concern. Chicago was a leader in building a great collection. In 1906 it acquired El Greco's *Assumption of the Virgin* on the advice of Mary Cassatt; in 1922 Mrs. Potter Palmer left her French impressionist masterpieces to the museum; and in 1933 the museum received a substantial bequest from Martin A. Ryerson that included old masters and contemporary paintings, prints, textiles, and decorative arts. Through a variety of sources the museum has continued to receive major gifts and bequests and to make major art purchases up to the present day.

The Toledo Museum of Art began collecting from its inception, because the Libbey gift specified that 50 percent of it be devoted to art acquisition. Because of this directive, the museum has continued to build its collection and remains one of the world's most powerful art-buying institutions. By the 1930s, art collecting had become the major goal of most midwestern museums. Cleveland acquired nine extraordinary medieval objects from the Guelph Treasury in 1931. The museum's real growth as a collection, however, occurred in 1957, when Hanna's bequest made it the most richly endowed museum in the world for art purchases.

Indeed, the most dramatic growth of midwestern collections occurred just after World War II, when Europe had not yet rebuilt its industry and the dollar was strong. Toledo, for example, tripled the size of its collection under the leadership of Otto Wittman, who joined the staff as curator and associate director in 1946 and served as director from 1959 to 1977. Wittman's single most notable purchase was *The Agony in the Garden* by El Greco, one of the master's greatest works, acquired in 1946, and Wittman acquired notable works from the Dutch seventeenth century and the French eighteenth century, two fields that were then somewhat out of fashion. Similarly, Sherman Lee at the Cleveland Museum of Art purchased major works by figures such as Caravaggio, Velázquez, and Poussin, and also put together an encyclopedic collection of Asian art. Lawrence Sickman, at the Nelson-Atkins Museum of Art in Kansas City, presided over major old masters purchases by figures as varied as Petrus Christus and Caravaggio. But his most notable contribution was the acquisition of remarkable Chinese paintings that came on the market after the Communist takeover of China in 1949 and that nicely complemented the Chinese archaeological objects he had acquired for the museum in the 1930s. While it lacked major acquisition funds, the St. Louis Art Museum also grew in this period as a result of the generosity of Morton May, who collected German expressionist painting, and Joseph Pulitzer, who collected paintings of the School of Paris. One of the most notable gifts was Henri Matisse's *Bathers with Turtle*, which Pulitzer had acquired from the "Degenerate Art" sale organized by Adolf Hitler.

Other midwestern museums chose to focus on American art, including the Butler Institute in Youngstown, Ohio, founded in 1919, the first museum devoted entirely to American art. A similar course was followed by the Wichita Art Museum. In the period from 1935 to 1962, Elizabeth Stubblefield put together an exceptionally fine collection of American painting with funds from the Roland P. Murdock bequest. Her first purchase was *Kansas Cornfield* by Kansas regionalist painter John Steuart Curry, and the collection contains strong examples of American realism by Winslow Homer, Thomas Eakins, and Edward Hopper. During roughly the same period, Norman Geske put together a fine American collection with funds from the Hall bequest for the Sheldon Memorial Art Museum in Lincoln, Nebraska. Edgar P. Richardson, who served as director from 1945 to 1962, also put together a major collection of American painting for the Detroit Institute of Arts.

The rapid growth of collections that continued through the 1970s has slowed today because of the rising cost of art and new legal restrictions on art exports and the sale of smuggled antiquities. Instead, educational programs and activities have taken on new importance, as midwestern art museums respond to increasing public interest in culture and the arts. Only a generation ago, art museums did not exist in many midwestern cities. Now they are regarded as a fact of life, something no major city could do without.

Sources and Further Reading: Michael Churchman and Scott Erbes, *High Ideals and Aspirations: The Nelson-Atkins Museum of Art, 1933–1993* (1993); Martin Friedman and Lucy Flint-Gohlke, *Walker Art Center: Painting and Sculpture from the Collection* (1990); Julia P. Henshaw, ed., *A Visitor's Guide: The Detroit Institute of Arts* (1975); Osmund Overby, *The Saint Louis Art Museum: An Architectural History* (1987); Millard F. Rogers, *Masterpieces from the Cincinnati Art Museum* (1993); Elois Spaeth, *American Art Museums: An Introduction to Looking* (1975); Kristie C. Wolferman, *The Nelson-Atkins Museum of Art: Culture Comes to Kansas City* (1993); James Wood and Debra N. Mancoff, *Treasures from the Art Institute of Chicago* (2000).

Henry Adams
Cleveland Museum of Art

Mid-Tier Art Museums

Many mid-tier midwestern art museums were founded by community members who recognized the educational impact and cultural value of such institutions. Indeed, public education is central to the purpose of many of these museums, as is evident in their mission statements.

A few of these statements are strikingly activist, such as the declaration of the South Bend Regional

Santiago Calatrava's addition to the Milwaukee Art Museum. By permission of Anthony M. Orum.

Museum that it seeks "to preserve the power of art to secure us, challenge us and change us" or of the John Michael Kohler Arts Center (Sheboygan, Wisconsin) that calls on "the power of the arts to inspire and transform the world." For some, the transformational power of art is implicit in a dramatic museum building. Santiago Calatrava's addition to the Milwaukee Art Museum (2001) soaring over Lake Michigan holds this sort of spiritual potential as do Cesar Pelli's designs for expanding the Madison (Wisconsin) Arts Center. Other museums aim to reach a broader public by diversifying the cultural bases of their collections to more fully reflect their local communities. Indeed, midwestern art museums have been in the vanguard of building user-friendly interactive centers and offering programs specifically oriented toward family-friendly and regionally relevant visits.

The earliest of these museums were established between the 1870s and the 1930s. Though currently located in urban centers, mid-tier midwestern art museums are located most typically in cities that did not mature until the mid to late twentieth century. Their collections contain thousands of objects. There is great variation in the size of their staff, though staffs of all sizes are often supplemented by as many as hundreds of volunteers. The museums are most often the offspring of a band of local citizens, not a single donor. Their collections are often strongest in nineteenth- and twentieth-century American art, including regional and local artists. Their holdings feature late-nineteenth- and twentieth-century European art along with a smattering of folk, American Indian, Meso-American, and Asian

art. Another driving force behind the creation of museums was expositions and World's Fairs. A group of women in Columbus, Ohio, were reportedly inspired by the Philadelphia Centennial Exposition of 1876 and formed the Winckelmann Society, where they met to read and discuss J. J. Winckelmann's *History of Art*. Within a couple of years, many of these women were instrumental in founding what is today the Columbus Museum of Art. However, it was the Chicago World's Columbian Exposition of 1893 that spurred the federal government to see the economic value in promoting American culture. And it was in Chicago that women stepped forward to create their own pavilion to showcase the contributions of women of the world to art. Women frequently kept mid-tier art museums and the art schools often affiliated with them afloat until wider community support could be cultivated. The founders of the earliest institutions were white but were by no means always people of great wealth, and frequently included members of the middle class such as merchants, bankers, and teachers. These museums often began by providing such educational opportunities as lectures, art lessons, and exhibitions, usually showcasing the work of their students and instructors. Historian Steven Conn reminds us that "because many scholars of museums have not investigated thoroughly, or taken seriously, the intellectual foundations of museums, they seem to miss not only that knowledge was always understood to be what museums had to offer but also that knowledge was what they were charged to create and what they were obligated to provide to a visiting public."

As teaching institutions, many mid-tier museums

recognize, either consciously or unconsciously, the importance of relating their collections to their visitors' life experiences. The civil rights and women's movements paved the way for diversifying the collections of older institutions and opened opportunities in newer institutions. Recent collection additions and exhibitions include more works by women and underrepresented artists as well as past and current artists from the local community or region. School programs bring thousands of children into museums for interdisciplinary tours. Similarly, the Internet has become a popular way for mid-tier art museums to provide lesson plans and even virtual tours to teachers, parents, students, and homeschoolers. Scholarly exhibitions that unapologetically explore the unique nature of artistic expression in the Heartland are being nurtured by many mid-tier art museums.

The Columbus Museum of Art, the Taft Museum in Cincinnati, and the Dayton Art Institute exemplify mid-tier museums in Ohio. Museums in Michigan include the Flint Institute of Arts and the Grand Rapids Art Museum, which promises to "expand the way people think about art and how it affects their lives." The Fort Wayne Museum of Art (Indiana) has committed a design team to building an interactive education exhibition to explain some basics of art and art museums. In Illinois, the Rockford Art Museum has especially invested in a family interactive exhibition, the Creation Station. In Wisconsin, there are at least three mid-tier art museums, in Milwaukee, Madison, and Sheboygan. Other midwestern mid-tier art museums include the Joslyn Museum in Omaha; the Wichita Art Museum of Kansas; Iowa's Des Moines Art Center and the Davenport Museum of Art; the Kemper Museum of Contemporary Art in Kansas City, Missouri; and the Minnesota Museum of American Art in St. Paul. The Dakotas boast several small public museums, such as the Plains Art Museum in Fargo and the North Dakota Museum of Art in Grand Forks, whose mission includes the promise "to seek out artists who transform the materials of the plains and prairies into visual language which illuminates the past, present and future of rural America."

Most mid-tier art museums in the region are private nonprofit institutions with self-perpetuating boards of trustees and the ability to respond quickly to changes in their communities. The diversification in their collections and the aggressive stances many of them have taken in their mission statements promise change and relevance.

Sources and Further Reading: Edward P. Alexander, "The American Museum Chooses Education," *Curator* 31 (March, 1998); American Association of Museums, *Excellence and Equity* (1992); American Association of Museums, *Museums for a New Century* (1984); Steven Conn, *Museums and American Intellec-*

tual Life, 1876–1926 (1998); Joel J. Orosz, *Curators and Culture* (1990); Michael Parsons, "Integrated Curriculum and Our Paradigm of Cognition in the Arts," *Studies in Art Education* 39 (Winter, 1998); David N. Perkins, *The Intelligent Eye* (1994).

Barbara Zollinger Sweney
Columbus Museum of Art, Ohio

The Butler Institute of American Art

Opened in 1919 in Youngstown, Ohio, by steel industrialist Joseph G. Butler, Jr., the Butler Institute of American Art was the first museum in the country dedicated to the collection and exhibition of American art. Within twenty-four hours of a 1917 fire that destroyed Butler's first collection, he had appointed McKim, Mead & White to construct the Beaux-Arts building, its style symbolically reflecting his interest in a similar renaissance of culture in the area. In 1916 Butler had stated that "'Americanization' is the battle cry. . . . Seventy percent of our population in Youngstown is of foreign birth. . . . The newly arrived foreigner can be helped by inviting him to see something which will please and interest him before he can read English. . . ." Later he stated, "We lead the world in genius for invention. . . . There is no reason why we cannot . . . do so . . . for art and literature." Until 1981 the institute was directed by Butler's son Henry Audubon (1927–1934) and grandson Joseph G. III (1934–1981). The strength of its early-twentieth-century collection is deeply indebted to Clyde Singer (curator, 1940–1998). Jurists for the museum's National Mid-Year Exhibition, begun in 1935, have included Charles Burchfield, Reginald Marsh, John Steuart Curry, Edward Hopper, and Leo Castelli.

The Butler Institute is most notable for its comprehensive collection, including nearly every major American movement, style, and artist. It is highlighted by Winslow Homer's *Snap the Whip* and contains exceptional works by Fitz Hugh Lane, Albert Bierstadt, William Merritt Chase, John Singer Sargent, Marsh Hopper, Adolph Gottlieb, and Romare Bearden. It also includes works by a group of modernist painters called "The Eight" (Robert Henri, George Luks, William Glackens, John Sloan, Everett Shinn, Maurice Prendergast, Ernest Lawson, and Arthur Bowen Davies). Its collections of impressionism, western painting, and prints are especially strong.

Sources and Further Reading: Joseph G. Butler, Jr., "The Small Museum" (BIAA Archives); Joseph G. Butler, Jr., *Recollection of Men and Events* (1925); Irene S. Sweetkind, ed., *Master Paintings from the Butler Institute of American Art* (1994).

M. Melissa Wolfe
The Ohio State University–Columbus

Cranbrook Academy of Art

Officially established in Bloomfield Hills, Michigan, in 1932, Cranbrook Academy of Art occupies the physical and conceptual core of an educational community that today includes an academy of science, an art museum, and elementary and preparatory schools. Its founder, newspaper magnate George G. Booth, actively promoted the ideals of the arts and crafts movement and believed that good design could enrich modern life, which had been impoverished by the effects of industrialization. Booth envisioned a center, similar to the American Academy in Rome, where visiting artists could participate in the free exchange of ideas. Utopian communities had a long history in America, particularly in the Midwest, but none offered a suitable architectural model. For this Booth turned to Finnish architect Eliel Saarinen, known for his scrupulous attention to detail. The commission resulted in a number of important buildings as well as coordinated carpets, furniture, table settings, and other decorative objects. As president of the academy, Saarinen oversaw the hires of a number of influential teachers, including Harry Bertoia, Maija Grotell, Arthur Nevill Kirk, Carl Milles, Eero Saarinen, and Maja Wirde. From the beginning, students took no classes but were encouraged to develop their own aesthetic sensibilities in consultation with established artists, a pedagogical philosophy that endures. Today, ten resident artists and designers and an architect advise approximately 145 students. It is therefore difficult to identify characteristics of a Cranbrook "school," though notable graduates include Charles Eames, Florence Knoll, Duane Hanson, Jack Lenor Larsen, Wallace Mitchell, Ed Rossbach, and Toshiko Takaezu.

Source and Further Reading: Robert Judson Clark and Andrea P. A. Belloli, eds., *Design in America: The Cranbrook Vision, 1925–1950* (1983).

Kirk Ambrose
University of Colorado–Boulder

Intuit: The Center for Intuitive and Outsider Art

Originally associated with the art of asylum inmates, and later celebrated by Jean Dubuffet as *art brut* (raw art), "outsider art" now describes a wide range of work by self-taught or partially trained artists marginalized by the historical canon or the art market, including folk and ethnic artists, the homeless, and the incarcerated. Situated outside the New York art world, Chi-

cago, like Milwaukee, has long been an important midwestern center for outsider art, and Intuit: The Center for Intuitive and Outsider Art has been one of its primary venues since it was founded there in 1991. Initially called the Society for Outsider, Intuitive and Visionary Art (SOIVA), Intuit was launched as a nonprofit organization by the joint efforts of artists, collectors, art dealers, and businesspeople to recognize the work of artists uninfluenced by popular aesthetic trends, who pursued unique personal visions. Since its first major exhibit in December 1991, Thrift Store Paintings, curated by Los Angeles artist Jim Shaw, Intuit has organized numerous shows by self-taught American and European artists; been instrumental in restoring the work and living environment of Chicago outsider artist Henry Darger; opened a bookstore (Visions) and a study center; developed outreach and training programs teaching educators how to integrate intuitive art into their curriculums; organized tours to local visionary environments; and sponsored lectures, readings, and panel discussions on the history, theory, and practice of intuitive and outsider art. In these multifarious ways Intuit has lived up to its mission to promote public awareness and appreciation of art outside the mainstream.

Sources and Further Reading: Jeff Cory, "Intuit Celebrates 5 Years," *Outsider* 1 (Summer 1996); Michael D. Hall and Eugene W. Metcalf, Jr., eds., *The Artist Outsider* (1994); Vera L. Zolberg and Joni Maya Cherbo, eds., *Outsider Art: Contesting Boundaries in Contemporary Culture* (1997).

Melinda Barlow
University of Colorado–Boulder

John Michael Kohler Arts Center

Established in 1967, the John Michael Kohler Arts Center is one of the Midwest's largest and most diverse contemporary arts centers. John Michael Kohler, the center's namesake, purchased the Sheboygan (Wisconsin) Union Iron and Steel Foundry and founded Kohler Company in 1873; today's center stems from his patronage.

The Kohler Arts Center works closely with Kohler to support the arts. Since 1974, the company's Arts/Industry program has made Kohler's industrial facilities and technologies available to artists to create new works in long-term residencies. Both Kohler and the Arts Center hold collections of work by artists in this program.

The Kohler Arts Center also has a deep commitment to the work of self-taught and folk artists. Its most renowned collection concentrates on work by self-taught artists, predominantly from the Midwest, with particular attention to bodies of work that were initially envisioned as part of a cohesive environment but could not be preserved as such. It generates approximately twenty original exhibitions and four performing-arts series annually and develops major interdisciplinary commissions and educational programs.

In recent decades, Kohler Foundation Inc. (an affiliate of Kohler Company) has been committed to the preservation of folk architecture as well as environments and objects by midwestern vernacular and self-taught artists. This enterprise began in 1977 when the Wisconsin Arts Board asked the Foundation to join it and the National Endowment for the Arts to save Fred Smith's Wisconsin Concrete Park, in Phillips, Wisconsin, from destruction. Since then, the Foundation and the John Michael Kohler Arts Center have orchestrated the conservation of numerous arts environments in Wisconsin and elsewhere, which are conserved and subsequently gifted to local governments or not-for-profit organizations. It is internationally recognized as a leader in vernacular art preservation.

Sources and Further Reading: Michael Feldman and Diana Cook, *Wisconsin Curiosities* (2000); Betty-Carol Sellen and Cynthia J. Johanson, *Self Taught, Outsider, and Folk Art* (2000).

Leslie Umberger
John Michael Kohler Arts Center, Wisconsin

Kansas City Art Institute

The Kansas City Art Institute is a private, independent, fully accredited four-year college of art and design offering the bachelor of fine arts degree in art history, ceramics, design, fiber, illustration, painting, photography and new media, printmaking, and sculpture. Enjoying a strong national reputation, the Institute attracts students and faculty from around the country and from abroad. The oldest cultural institution in Kansas City, Missouri, the school grew out of a sketch club founded in 1885, and it opened in 1888 as the Kansas City Art Association and School of Design. It was reincorporated in 1907 as the Fine Arts Institute of Kansas City and assumed its current name in 1920. After occupying temporary quarters in a succession of different downtown buildings, the school moved in 1928 to its present midtown location: a scenic twelve-acre campus adjacent to the Nelson-Atkins Museum of Art and the Kemper Museum of Contemporary Art. Thomas Hart Benton, the Missouri-born

leader of the midwestern regionalist art movement, taught painting at the school from 1935 to 1941. Other prominent faculty members have included painters John Douglas Patrick, Ernest Lawson, Wilbur Niewald, and Warren Rosser; sculptors Dale Eldred and Jim Leedy; and ceramist Ken Ferguson. Animator Walt Disney attended Saturday children's classes at the school and was later awarded an honorary degree. Other noted Kansas City Art Institute alumni include multimedia artist Robert Rauschenberg, sculptor Robert Morris, painters John Steuart Curry and Keith Jacobshagen, ceramists Akio Takamori and Richard Notkin, graphic designer April Greiman, and photographer Thomas Barrow.

Sources and Further Reading: Milton S. Katz, *The Kansas City Art Institute: A Centennial History, 1885–1985* (1985); Mazee Bush Owens and Frances S. Bush, *Kansas City Art Institute and School of Design* (1964).

David Cateforis
University of Kansas

Minneapolis College of Art and Design

The Minneapolis College of Art and Design has sought a balance between fine arts training and career preparation since its founding as the Minneapolis School of Fine Arts in 1886. Its parent organization, the Minneapolis Society of Fine Arts, was a citizens' group organized three years earlier to "advance the knowledge and love of art" by establishing the art school and a museum, which would open in 1915 as the Minneapolis Institute of Arts.

Douglas Volk and Robert Koehler, the art school's first directors, developed a curriculum based on the French academic paradigm of drawing from casts and life models. Renamed the Minneapolis School of Art in 1910, the school offered a broader course that included the applied arts of handicraft and design under Mary Moulton Cheney. Interior design, fashion, and photography were added in the 1930s.

The school transformed itself in the 1950s under Wilhelmus Bryan into a four-year institution with a liberal arts curriculum. Accredited in 1960, it was rechristened as the Minneapolis College of Art and Design in 1970. In that year the Society of Fine Arts engaged Japanese architect Kenzo Tange to develop an arts complex for its several components; Tange's building offers a flexible and open plan for studios and a gallery.

In its second century MCAD continues to address evolving artistic and professional demands, adding a master of fine arts degree and a high-tech-oriented bachelor of science in visualization to its established programs in fine arts and the design professions.

Sources and Further Reading: Jeffrey A. Hess, *Their Splendid Legacy* (1985); "History of the College," *Minneapolis College of Art and Design Alumni Directory* (1990); Eileen Michels, *An Architectural View, 1883–1974* (1974).

Thomas O'Sullivan
Carleton College, Minnesota

The Minneapolis Institute of Arts

In 1883 twenty-five civic-minded arts patrons founded the Minneapolis Society of Fine Arts. The group's stated purpose was "to advance the knowledge and love of art." Beginning in 1889, members of the society exhibited works in a one-room gallery in the downtown Minneapolis Public Library; they opened the Minneapolis Institute of Arts in 1915. Housed in a neoclassical building designed by the architecture firm McKim, Mead & White, the institute showcases an extensive collection of approximately one hundred thousand objects. Encompassing works of art through the ages and from around the world, the institute provides an in-depth look at the highest caliber of artistic achievement to hundreds of thousands of visitors each year. It is organized into seven major collecting areas: the art of Africa, Oceania, and the Americas; Asian art; decorative arts, sculpture, and architecture; paintings; photography; prints and drawings; and textiles. In 1974 adjoining buildings housing the Children's Theatre Company and the Minneapolis College of Art and Design were added, furthering the institute's standing as a major arts center. From 1988 to 1998 the Minneapolis Institute of Arts expanded and grew, dramatically increasing the number of works on view in its galleries. In addition, membership has grown from three hundred members at the turn of the nineteenth century to more than twenty-six thousand today.

Sources and Further Reading: Sandra L. Hoyt, ed., *Treasures from the Minneapolis Institute of Arts* (1998); Sandra LaWall Lipschultz, *Selected Works: The Minneapolis Institute of Arts* (1981).

Lara Roy
Walker Art Center, Minneapolis

Native American Art Centers

Although not as well known for Native American art venues as Oklahoma and the Southwest, the Midwest boasts a wide variety of centers for the collection, preservation, study, and practice of Native American art.

Archaeological sites include the Great Serpent Mound in Adams County, Ohio, and Cahokia Mounds State Historic Site near Collinsville, Illinois. A number of smaller sites include museums and interpretive centers. The Dickson Mounds Museum in Lewistown, Illinois, features rotating special exhibits of Illinois River Valley and Mississippian art and culture.

Among the largest collections of Native American material in the Midwest are those at the Field Museum of Natural History in Chicago and the Detroit Institute of Art. The Ohio Historical Center in

The Eiteljorg Museum, Indianapolis. Courtesy The Indianapolis Star and Matt Dial.

Columbus and the Minnesota Historical Society in St. Paul also contain important collections. The Eiteljorg Museum of American Indian and Western Art in Indianapolis houses a major collection of plains and southwestern art and offers a fellowship for Native American Fine Art, a prestigious award for contemporary Native American artists. Among the small museums is the Oscar Howe Art Center, named for the Dakota painter, in Mitchell, South Dakota, which exhibits traditional and contemporary art from the northern plains region.

A number of art centers are associated with Native American community organizations serving the ethnically diverse Native American populations of large cities. In Minnesota, the Two Rivers Gallery, located in the Minneapolis American Indian Center, is a prominent example; it exhibits contemporary Native American art from across North America as well as interpretive exhibitions of Native American history and culture. In Wichita, the Mid-America All-Indian Center Museum is a multipurpose organization that provides social services for urban indigenous peoples and functions as a center for the preservation and practice of Native American art and culture.

Other centers are affiliated with Native American colleges and universities. In Keshena, Wisconsin, the College of Menominee Nation is home to the Culture Institute, which organizes summer institutes and pow-wows. The Haskell Indian Nations University in Lawrence, Kansas, is home to the Cultural Center and Museum, which serves as a gallery and study center for Native American and Alaskan indigenous cultures. Additionally, Haskell Indian Nations University sponsors the annual Haskell Indian Art Market.

Reservation museums and community centers tend to focus on the art and culture of a particular nation or reservation community. Examples include the Journey Museum in Rapid City, South Dakota, which interprets the art and culture of the Lakota peoples (as well as the Anglo-American pioneer experience). Other examples include the Oneida Nation Arts Program in Wisconsin and Five Nations Art in Mandan, North Dakota. The Mille Lacs Indian Museum in central Minnesota interprets the history, culture, and art of the Mille Lacs Band of Ojibwe. The Nokomis Learning Center in Okemos, Michigan interprets the history, culture, and arts of the Ojibwa, Odawa, and Potawatomi nations. In Kyle, South Dakota, the Lakota Fund, which raises money for Native American–owned small-business development on the Pine Ridge Reservation, includes the Arts and Crafts Marketing Program.

Sources and Further Reading: Patricia Pierce Erikson, "Encounters in the Nation's Attic," Ph.D. diss., University of California (1997); Tom Hill, "Woodland Cultural Centre Museum," *Muse* 12 (Fall/Nov. 1994); Moira Simpson, "Native American Museums and Cultural Centres," in *Making Representations: Museums in the Post-Colonial Era* (1996); Smithsonian Institution, *Tribal Museum Directory* (1998).

Bill Anthes
Carnegie Mellon University,
Pittsburgh, Pennsylvania

New Art Examiner

Between 1973 and 2002, the nonprofit journal *New Art Examiner* served as a vital document and outlet for the artistic community of Chicago and the Midwest. Published by the Chicago New Art Association and founded by Chicago-based critics Derek Guthrie and Jane Addams Allen, the *New Art Examiner* issued its first number, an eight-page newspaper-style tabloid focused on the Chicago art scene, in October 1973. Several cycles of expansion and retrenchment followed until publication ceased with the May/June 2002 issue. At first, the journal grew in both size and scope, and in 1984, the publication switched to magazine format. It positioned itself as an alternative to such magazines as *Art News, Art in America,* and *Artforum,* concentrating on artists, exhibitions, and critical issues in the Midwest and other regions often underrepresented in the mainstream art press. By 1980, the magazine had editorial offices in Washington, D.C., and Philadelphia as well as in Chicago, and additional offices (in Richmond, Virginia; Houston; Dallas; Boston; New York; Los Angeles; and even London) appeared sporadically on the masthead in the 1980s. The offices outside Chicago closed in the early 1990s, but a network of regional editors and correspondents facilitated coverage in much of the Midwest—Illinois, Indiana, Michigan, Minnesota, Missouri, Ohio, Wisconsin—and elsewhere. For most of its history, the *New Art Examiner* published eleven issues a year (cut back to six in 2001), with subscription numbers varying between 2,500 and 4,500. Along with feature articles and columns, the magazine offered an extensive reviews section, which was particularly significant in nurturing regional arts criticism.

Sources and Further Reading: "Editorial," *New Art Examiner* 12 (Oct. 1984); Derek Guthrie, "Editorials: From the Publisher and Staff," *New Art Examiner* 18 (Apr. 1991); Kathryn Hixson, "Editorial," *New Art Examiner* 28 (May/June 2001); Deanna Isaacs, "Back to the Brink," *Chicago Reader* (May 10, 2002).

Ann Bremner
The Ohio State University–Columbus

School of the Art Institute of Chicago

The founding intention of the School of the Art Institute of Chicago was to both exhibit and teach art and thereby bring a degree of culture to a city that at the time was more often associated with commerce and industry, lumber and meat. Begun under the leadership of a group of Chicago artists in 1866, the school continues, incorporated with a major art museum, as one of the largest private art schools in America.

The school has evolved from a professional fine arts "museum school" to a college of art that, in addition to the time-honored study of painting, sculpture, and printmaking, embraces new media, electronic arts, design, and transdisciplinary fields such as visual and critical studies. Graduate programs in art history, theory and criticism, writing, arts administration, historic preservation, art therapy, and art education provide students with the knowledge and skills to both present, interpret, and preserve art, architecture, and design and advance the arts and help shape visual culture. In support of these diverse programs, the school provides unique study collections and resources, from the Ryerson and Burnham Libraries, first established in 1901, to the Video Data Bank, the Gene Siskel Film Center, the Fashion Resource Center, the Joan Flasch Artists' Book Collection, and the Roger Brown Study Collection.

Though midwestern, the School of the Art Institute of Chicago draws its student body from across the country and around the world. Twenty percent of its 2,500 students are from Illinois; the balance of students represent all the other states and forty other countries.

Sources and Further Reading: Roger Gilmore, ed., *Over a Century* (1982); Peter C. Marzio, "A Museum and a School: An Uneasy but Creative Union," *Chicago History* 8 (Spring 1979).

Shanna Linn
School of the Art Institute of Chicago

Self-Taught and Vernacular Art

The Midwest has been a particularly fertile ground for vernacular art production. In both rural and urban areas, diverse objects, images, edifices, and environments have been created without regard to mainstream art-world fashions or concerns, focusing instead on personal beliefs and interests. Vernacular art falls within the broader category of art by the self-taught, referring to art that draws on a personal vision. Ranging from religious grottoes to oeuvres investigat-ing personal experience and beliefs, "vernacular" art expresses the native language of a place.

Place, specifically home ground, is central in vernacular art. Settled primarily by people of northern and eastern European ancestry, the Midwest's vernacular art reflects the religious and ethnic heritages of these groups—folktales and legends from Germany and Scandinavia, and folklore about the trades and industries these immigrants pursued, such as farming, fishing, and logging. People proud of their hard-won farms, homes, and other accomplishments produced patriotic signs and sculptures that paid tribute to their adopted homeland and have been popular.

Much of the vernacular art in the Midwest is site-specific, that is, oriented to particular local places and communities. Examples include religious grottoes such as Father Paul Dobberstein's Grotto of the Redemption (1901–1954) in West Bend, Iowa, and Father Mathias Wernerus's Dickeyville Grotto and Holy Ghost Park (c. 1924–1930) in Dickeyville, Wisconsin. Made from concrete inlaid with shells and exotic rocks from underground caves, these grottoes were built as inviting environments whose natural qualities would engage the senses and open visitors to spiritual encounters.

More personalized vernacular art environments reflect the close relationships artists have with local places. Fred Smith found his yard to be fertile ground for his Wisconsin Concrete Park (c. 1948–1964) in Phillips, Wisconsin, as did Carl Peterson for his Environmental Garden (1917–1937) in St. James, Minnesota. Smith, a retired lumberjack, eventually made more than two hundred sculptures with subjects ranging from Ben Hur and Paul Bunyan to forest creatures and livestock. Wisconsin proved to be particularly fertile ground for vernacular art environments, eventually including works by Mollie Jenson of River Falls and Nick Engelbert of Hollandale.

Levi Fisher Ames of Monroe, Wisconsin, decided to make his environment portable. Influenced by Wisconsin's many circuses and sideshows in the late nineteenth and early twentieth centuries, he carved his own impressive menagerie of domestic, wild, and mythic animals and, carefully encasing each in a glass-fronted folding box, would travel to fairs to exhibit them in a tent and tell stories about each. Drawing on folk styles of woodcarving and his rich imagination, Ames depicted creatures of legend and lore from the lumberjack camps such as the legendary fire-breathing Hodag.

Self-taught artists are by no means unique to the Midwest, yet the region has been home to many. "Self-taught" refers to the artists' lack of formal training and to works not originally intended to address the concerns of the art world. Like most artists, self-taught artists are influenced by era and place, the social and political framework of their lives, and the realities of their mental and physical health. Distinguished from folk artists by having a singular rather than communal or traditional vision, self-taught artists are best known for unique visions and passions.

Joseph Yoakum traveled with the circus and later lived for many years in Chicago. Heavily influenced by the nomadic lifestyle of circus folk, Yoakum blended the places he visited with the landscapes of his imagination, creating unique landscapes through a process of "spiritual unfoldment." Visited often by Chicago artists who would become known as the Hairy Who and the Imagists, Yoakum influenced the visual culture of the Midwest.

Henry Darger, also from Chicago, held a menial job and attended church regularly but lived a reclusive personal life. Darger created a five-thousand-page autobiography in addition to an epic saga (some fifteen thousand pages in fifteen volumes), illustrated with hundreds of large-scale watercolors and collages. This astonishing body of work, discovered after his death, was executed entirely in solitude. His saga, "The Story of the Vivian Girls . . . ," told of a bloody war between the enslaved Vivian sisters and the evil Glandelinians.

While some have conflated vernacular and self-taught modes of production with "outsider art"—on the assumption that all art created outside of the mainstream art world is somehow outside of any common culture—this drastically limits genuine understanding of the work by divorcing it from its context.

Sources and Further Reading: John Beardsley, *Gardens of Revelation* (1995); Colin Rhodes, *Outsider Art* (2000); Lisa Stone and Jim Zanzi, *Sacred Spaces and Other Places* (1993); John Michael Vlach and Simon J. Bronner, eds., *Folk Art and Art Worlds* (1986).

Leslie Umberger
John Michael Kohler Arts Center, Wisconsin

Taliesin

Frank Lloyd Wright (1867–1959) named his house in Spring Green, Wisconsin, Taliesin after an ancient Welsh bard whose name means "shining brow." Taliesin (sometimes known as Taliesin North) wraps around a hill's brow, providing views of a surrounding valley settled in the 1860s by Wright's Welsh maternal family, the Lloyd-Joneses, eighteen miles from his birthplace, Richland Center. Wright discovered the hill while working on the Lloyd-Jones farmsteads—located south of the Wisconsin River in the state's Driftless Area—during the summers when he was between ages eleven and eighteen.

Wright returned to the Jones Valley to begin Taliesin for himself and a mistress, Mamah Borthwick (1869–1914), after leaving his first home, studio, and marriage in Oak Park, Illinois. An excellent example of Wright's "organic architecture," Taliesin's construction includes local limestone and low-angled roofs meant to evoke the Driftless Area's stone outcroppings and hills, and Wisconsin River sand in the stucco to suggest its sandbars. Wright used Taliesin as his architectural sketchbook, changing it continuously from 1911 until his death.

Two fires destroyed Taliesin's living quarters: The first, in August 1914, was set by a servant, Julian Carlton, who then murdered seven people there with a hatchet, including Borthwick, while Wright was away; electrical problems caused the second fire, in April 1925. Wright rebuilt the structure each time.

Wright eventually acquired the six hundred acres of the Jones Valley, which includes five Wright-designed buildings, three of them originally designed for family members. He left the estate to his widow, Olgivanna Lloyd Wright (1897–1985), and their Taliesin Fellowship, a community of architectural apprentices established in 1932.

Sources and Further Reading: Curtis Besinger, *Working with Mr. Wright: What It Was Like* (1995); Narciso G. Menocal, ed., *Taliesin 1911–1914, Wright Studies*, vol. 1 (1992); Kathryn Smith, *Frank Lloyd Wright's Taliesin and Taliesin West* (1997).

Mary Keiran Murphy
Taliesin Preservation, Incorporated, Wisconsin

University Art Museums

With its strong public research universities, the Midwest is home to an impressive array of university art museums, many of which are leaders in their fields at the national level and in their region. They mount ground-breaking exhibitions, publish important scholarship, hold significant collections, pioneer new museum practices, and build world-class facilities designed by renowned architects. In short, they serve as dynamic and influential institutions within their region as well as within their universities. Their status as public institutions—publicly held, publicly funded (if only partially), and accountable to citizens as well as alumni—separates them from their counterparts in other regions, where museums at private universities and colleges tend to dominate the field.

In the past two decades, university art museums from Ohio to Minnesota have ceased playing second fiddle to art departments and have emerged as powerful cultural institutions that link campus life with their broader communities. Museums such as the Wexner Center for the Arts at The Ohio State University, the Krannert Art Museum at The University of Illinois–Urbana-Champaign, the Spencer Museum of Art at the University of Kansas–Lawrence, the Frederick R. Weisman Art Museum at the University of Minnesota–Twin Cities, the University of Michigan Museum of Art in Ann Arbor, and the Elvehjem Museum of Art at the University of Wisconsin–Madison are among the top in the region.

Today, university art museums straddle the border between the academy and the community. As universities continue to realize that public support depends on serving that public, their art museums have grown in stature as vital to that audience. Like their counterpart public museums, university art museums are following trends in becoming gathering places where lively and entertaining learning programs are offered for students and faculty, families, and a wider public. Yet because of their position within the academy, these museums are not always bound by the blockbuster mentality of larger museums and can present research-based exhibitions or ones dedicated to more specialized topics that reflect faculty research. Because university art museums are based within large teaching and research institutions, they have been pioneers of interdisciplinary and cross-disciplinary exhibitions, an emphasis also now noticeable more broadly among museums.

In the Midwest, university art museums are important venues for contemporary art because not every sizeable metropolis has a contemporary art museum. For instance, the Wexner Center for the Arts in Columbus, part of Ohio State, focuses on the national and international contemporary art scene, while the Columbus Museum of Art presents an encyclopedic overview of world art. With exhibitions, film, and performing-art departments, the Wexner offers a lively roster of programming that makes it a prominent force on and off campus. Noted architect Peter Eisenman designed its building, which opened in 1989.

Because of their responsiveness to regions, university art museums are often important venues for locally based artists, who are often ignored by larger public museums. Therefore, university museums become important repositories for the work of university faculty and other artists from the state. The Frederick R. Weisman Art Museum at the University of Minnesota holds a significant collection of the work of the international ceramist Warren Mackenzie, who taught in Minnesota's Art Department. The Weisman has become an attractive venue for exhibitions, due in part to the bold design of its new building, which opened in 1993. Designed by Frank Gehry, who went on to de-

sign the Guggenheim in Bilbao, Spain, the Weisman building promotes the notion of fresh thinking on a college campus.

Sources and Further Reading: American Association of Museums, *The Official Museum Directory, 2002* (2001); Frederick R. Weisman Art Museum, *The Frederick R. Weisman Art Museum at the University of Minnesota* (1993); Wexner Center for the Visual Arts, *Always Subject to Change* (1999).

Colleen J. Sheehy
University of Minnesota

Walker Art Center

Among the most influential museums of contemporary art in the United States, the Walker Art Center originated in the collections of Thomas Barlow Walker, a lumber magnate who established the Northwest's first public art gallery in 1879, based on his own collections of old master paintings, archaeological artifacts, and Chinese jade. By 1927, the Walker Art Gallery had moved into a new, thirty-five-room facility on its present site adjacent to downtown Minneapolis. Its name officially changed to the Walker Art Center in 1940 and innovative programs of exhibitions and educational opportunities were introduced. The commitment to contemporary art by which the Walker would come to be identified was solidified in the 1940s and 1950s, in part by deaccessioning older works from the core collection and acquiring masterworks by twentieth-century American and European artists, and is further exemplified in its publishing, beginning in 1946, *The Everyday Art Quarterly: A Guide to Well-Designed Products.* Following the move into a considerably larger facility designed by Edward Larrabee Barnes in 1971 (expanded in 1984), the Walker's programs in film and performing arts expanded dramatically, as did its commitment to large-scale outdoor sculpture on the building's terraces as well as in the adjacent eleven-acre Minneapolis Sculpture Garden, maintained since 1988 with the Minneapolis Park and Recreation Board. In 1998, Walker was among the first museums to establish a department in digital art. The Walker's building has been significantly renovated and expanded by the Swiss firm Herzog & de Meuron.

Sources and Further Reading: Walker Art Center, *Walker Art Center: A History* (1985); Walker Art Center, *Walker Art Center: Painting and Sculpture from the Collection* (1990).

Bill Horrigan
The Ohio State University

Music Institutions and Organizations

Music institutions in the Midwest developed almost entirely after the start of the nineteenth century. Alexis de Tocqueville observed that the scarcity of artists in America was due to the fact that most of the energy of its inhabitants was directed at conquering the new land. This was certainly true of music and music institutions in the early Midwest. Settlers in Ohio, Indiana, and other parts of what was then the Far West had little time to devote to the finer things in life, and such pursuits were generally considered frivolous and effete.

Much of the earliest musical activity consisted of unaccompanied group singing in churches and singing societies. Singing masters are known to have conducted vocal groups in Cincinnati and Marietta, Ohio, and other villages as early as 1802. By the late 1810s, two musical organizations—the Harmonical Society and the Euphonical Society—were operating in Cincinnati. In Indianapolis, one of the most notable church choirs was the fifty-voice ensemble that sang at the Second Presbyterian Church, where Henry Ward Beecher was pastor from 1839 to 1847.

Instrumental music was slower to develop. Pianos were scarce, although flutes and fiddles were more widespread. Players were mostly self-taught and music was heard predominantly at dances and social gatherings. As the region became more settled and towns and villages grew, stage entertainment became increasingly popular, with occasional concerts given by musicians playing instruments such as spinets, vir-

ginals, and violas. Instruments became more numerous during the nineteenth century and more children received musical instruction.

Not surprisingly, music institutions gained a foothold first in the larger towns. In Milwaukee, the Beethoven Society was formed in 1843 and performed both choral and orchestral concerts. By the time Cleveland was incorporated, in 1836, singing schools and brass bands were flourishing there. There were music schools and private music teachers in Chicago as early as 1835. The first formal musical organization in that city was the short-lived Old Settlers' Harmonic Society (1835–1836). One of the earliest U.S. orchestras, the Philharmonic, was founded in St. Louis in 1838.

Musical activity increased as the nineteenth century progressed. When Jenny Lind, the popular Swedish soprano, toured the United States in the early 1850s, she brought classical music to large numbers of Americans, including midwesterners, and paved the way for tours by other European artists. Composer-conductor Walter Damrosch, conductor Theodore Thomas, and other impresarios sought to spread the gospel of classical music throughout the land. By the middle of the nineteenth century, larger cities began to organize resident symphony orchestras, operas, operettas, and the like. A handful of these are still in existence.

Many of the early music institutions were clustered in the northern part of the region. Milwaukee developed into something of a music center due to the large number of German and Scandinavian immigrants, who fostered an appreciation of the arts. By the end of the nineteenth century the city had forty-nine groups

The National Music Museum in Vermillion, South Dakota. Photo by South Dakota Tourism.

performing choral music. The Arion Musical Club, founded in 1876, and the Milwaukee Liederkranz (1878) are still active. Choral music was also strong in Minneapolis and St. Paul. The Schubert Club of St. Paul, founded in 1882, is still active, sponsoring recitals, commissioning new musical work, and organizing educational projects. The St. Paul Symphony performed the first symphony heard in Minnesota sometime in the mid-1800s. Chicago's first orchestra, the Philharmonic Society, performed from 1850 to 1868. The Chicago Orchestra was founded in 1891 and renamed the Chicago Symphony Orchestra in 1912.

Other midwestern cities saw a rise in musical pursuits in the second half of the century. The St. Louis Choral Society was founded in 1880. Chamber music, introduced to St. Louis as early as 1807, spawned many organizations, including the Philharmonic Quintet Club (1878–1897) and the Mendelssohn Quintet Club (1882–1899). The Indianapolis Mannerchor was founded in 1854, and the Indianapolis Matinee Musicale (originally the Ladies Matinee Musical), founded in 1877, is still active.

A number of choral groups sprang up in Detroit during this period, including Harmonie (founded in 1849) and the Detroit Philharmonic Society (1855). While the present Detroit Symphony Orchestra was not founded until 1914, groups going by that name appeared in Detroit as early as 1875. Few formal music institutions existed in Kansas City, Missouri, before the twentieth century. Operas, concerts, and plays, presented by touring companies, were performed at the Coates Opera House, built in 1870. Several choral groups were started late in the nineteenth century, including the Oratorio Society (1897–1917), which had one thousand members at its peak.

Grand opera became one of the most exclusive and fashionable forms of entertainment in the Midwest in the late nineteenth century. After the opening of the Metropolitan Opera House in New York City in 1883, postseason touring companies performed in leading American cities. Opera performances in the larger midwestern metropolises of Chicago, St. Louis, and Cincinnati gave the upper crust in those cities the opportunity to emulate their social counterparts in New York. Milwaukee proudly claimed the only Polish opera company in the country. The Cincinnati Opera, the second-oldest continuing opera company in the United States, had its inaugural season in the band pavilion in the Cincinnati Zoological Gardens in the summer of 1920. The company performed there until 1972, when it moved to the Music Hall, its current venue.

In Chicago, Crosby's Opera House opened in 1865 with a stage large enough to accommodate a full-scale grand opera. Destroyed in the Chicago Fire of 1871, it was soon rebuilt. Light opera, operetta, and musical comedy predominated on Chicago's stages throughout the 1870s. Grand opera was revived in the early 1880s, with performances by New York touring companies. That city's first resident opera company, the Chicago Grand Opera Company, was formed in 1910. Until 1946 there were some seven opera companies in the Chicago area. The 4,000-seat Auditorium Theatre opened in the late 1880s and was the city's principal opera venue until 1929, by which time most opera performances were mounted at the 3,500-seat Civic Opera House. The Lyric Opera of Chicago was founded in 1954 as the Lyric Theatre of Chicago and is today one of the city's premier music institutions.

The 1860s and 1870s saw the construction of opera houses in Detroit, Cleveland, and Kansas City, Missouri. The Indianapolis Opera Company was founded in the 1880s to satisfy the local appetite for light opera and lasted for about ten years. After a long association with the Columbus Symphony Orchestra, Opera Columbus became a separate, independent institution in 1981.

The number and diversity of music institutions in the Midwest increased greatly after the turn of the century, when nearly every large midwestern city established its own symphony orchestra. The Minneapolis Symphony Orchestra was founded in 1903; it changed its name in 1968 to the Minneapolis Orchestra. The Indianapolis Symphony Orchestra, one of the nation's few year-round orchestras, was founded in 1929. The Columbus Little Symphony formed in 1951 and changed its name to the Columbus Symphony Orchestra two years later. The Cleveland Orchestra was founded in 1918. Today the Cleveland Orchestra and the Chicago Symphony Orchestra are widely regarded as among the finest in the world.

By the midpoint of the twentieth century, as the region prospered, midwesterners found themselves with more time and money to pursue the fine arts. Appreciation of cultural achievement increased, and civic leaders and philanthropists put more and more emphasis on the development of local music institutions. Musical culture was not confined to the large cities. High school and college orchestras brought classical music to many in the Midwest, and music institutions sprang up in smaller towns, some well outside the major metropolises. A number of regional orchestras active today in smaller communities were started between the 1910s and the 1930s, including the Green Bay (Wisconsin) Symphony Orchestra (founded in 1914); the Sioux City (Iowa) Symphony Orchestra (1915); the Omaha Symphony (1921); and the Fargo-Moorhead Symphony (1931), based in the adjacent communities of Fargo, North Dakota, and Moorhead,

Minnesota. The Des Moines Symphony, which began in 1937 as an adjunct of Drake University, is one of many institutions that have grown out of colleges and universities in the region.

Even opera, which typically attracts a more rarefied audience than other musical forms, thrives in smaller communities throughout the region. Such opera companies active today include Opera Illinois, based in Peoria; the Des Moines (Iowa) Metro Opera; the Whitewater Opera Company, in Richmond, Indiana; Opera Grand Rapids, in Michigan; the Springfield Regional Opera, in Missouri; and Opera Omaha.

With the burgeoning of music institutions in the Midwest in the twentieth century came a great number of specialized organizations. In addition to symphony orchestras and operas, the cities and towns of the Midwest are home to all manner of smaller, more specialized musical groups, including chamber orchestras, wind ensembles, early music ensembles, sinfoniettas, chorales, ethnic music associations, and pops and jazz orchestras.

Music education developed in tandem with music institutions generally, and many fine music academies are located in the Midwest. The College-Conservatory of Music is among the oldest, tracing its origins back to 1867 and the founding of the Cincinnati Conservatory of Music. It merged in 1955 with the College of Music of Cincinnati to become the College-Conservatory of Music, which became part of the University of Cincinnati in 1962. Two of the most important music schools in the country—the Cleveland Institute of Music and the Indiana University School of Music—were founded in the early 1920s.

Most major metropolitan areas, and many smaller ones as well, have youth symphonies, youth choirs, and other ensembles for musically talented young people. Some of these, like the Cleveland Orchestra Youth Orchestra, are adjuncts of larger symphonies. The Greater Twin Cities Youth Symphonies, which started in 1972 and comprises eight orchestras, is the largest youth orchestra organization in the country.

The history of music festivals in the Midwest dates to the late nineteenth century. The Cincinnati May Festival, established in 1873 by conductor Theodore Thomas, is the second-oldest music festival in the United States. The World's Columbian Exposition in Chicago (1893) and the Louisiana Purchase Exposition in St. Louis (1904), while not music festivals, featured many musical events. At the Chicago exposition, the operas of Richard Wagner and some of the orchestral concerts were poorly received. As a result, planners of the St. Louis exposition eleven years later emphasized band concerts. These included daily concerts by local and internationally known bands (John Philip Sousa's among them) as well as choral and orchestral concerts and daily recitals on what was then the largest organ in the world.

Music enthusiasts in the Midwest today support a large number of music festivals throughout the region. Ravinia Park, in the Chicago suburb of Highland Park, has been the site of an annual summer festival since 1906, and the Chicago Symphony Orchestra performs there summers. The Blossom Music Center, in Cuyahoga Falls, Ohio, opened in 1968 and is a regional performing-arts center as well as the summer home of the Cleveland Orchestra. Other festivals in the Midwest cover a wide range of musical genres and interests. The Madison Early Music Festival, sponsored in the summer by the University of Wisconsin–Madison School of Music, focuses on medieval, Renaissance, and baroque music. The Sonic Circuits Electronic Music Festival, one of the largest of its kind, was founded in Minneapolis in 1993 by the American Composers Forum. Since 1980, Detroit has been the site of what is purported to be the largest free jazz festival in North America. Originally called the Montreux-Detroit International Jazz Festival, the name has changed over the years, reflecting changes in corporate sponsorship. Two festivals devoted to ragtime music take place annually in Missouri: the Scott Joplin Ragtime Festival in Sedalia and the Theron C. Bennett Ragtime & Early Jazz Festival in Pierce. Since 1972, Davenport, Iowa, has paid homage to a great cornetist, composer, and native son with the annual Bix Beiderbecke Memorial Jazz Festival.

Sources and Further Reading: Dan Elbert Clark, *The Middle West in American History* (1966); *International Directory of the Performing Arts* (2001); Stanley Sadie and John Tyrrell, eds., *New Grove Dictionary of Music and Musicians*, 2nd ed. (2001); Kenneth R. Walker, *A History of the Middle West* (1972).

David Conrads
Shawnee Mission, Kansas

Lyric Opera of Chicago

Chicago had a resident opera company as early as 1910. Lyric Opera (founded in 1954 as the Lyric Theatre of Chicago) is considered one of the best opera companies in the United States. It has expanded from a three-week season to a span of eight productions in six months. The first general manager was Carol Fox (1954–1981). During her tenure, Bruno Bartoletti and Pino Donati were named co–artistic directors; after the death of Donati in 1975, Bartoletti continued as artistic director and principal conductor until 1999 (when he was succeeded by Sir Andrew Davis) and became music director laureate on his retirement.

European oriented (especially Italian) in its early years in both programming and casting, the company has become increasingly cosmopolitan in the tenures of Fox's successors, Ardis Krainik (1981–1997) and William Mason (1997 to the present). The increasing independence from the musical star system was exemplified by the cancellation of a contract with Luciano Pavarotti in 1989. Programs that have influenced diversification include the Lyric Opera Center for American Artists (founded in 1974 as an apprentice artist program); the Composer-in-Residence Program (1984; including Bright Sheng and Shulamit Ran among recipients to date); and Toward the Twenty-First Century, succeeded by American Horizons, both of which sponsored American and world premieres of operas by living composers.

Singers who have appeared at Lyric Opera include Maria Callas, Jussi Björling, Renee Fleming, Tito Gobbi, Christa Ludwig, and Samuel Ramey. Guest conductors have included Sir Georg Solti, Zubin Mehta, Dimitri Mitropoulos, and Michael Tilson Thomas.

Sources and Further Reading: Claudia Cassidy, *Lyric Opera of Chicago* (1979); Ronald Davis, *Opera in Chicago* (1966).

Susan M. Filler
Chicago

Chicago Symphony Orchestra

Theodore Thomas established the Chicago Symphony Orchestra in 1891. The orchestra performs from September to June at Orchestra Hall in Chicago and at the Ravinia Festival (see separate entry) during the summer.

On the death of Theodore Thomas in 1905, shortly after Orchestra Hall opened, his assistant conductor, Frederick Stock, was appointed music director. He held the position until his death in 1942, a term unequalled by any other music director. Stock initiated the orchestra's long history of recording and established the Civic Orchestra, the only training orchestra in the United States affiliated with a professional orchestra, coached and conducted by members and conductors of the Chicago Symphony.

Three music directors served brief terms after the death of Stock. Fritz Reiner held the position from 1953 to 1963, establishing the Chicago Symphony Chorus (conducted by Margaret Hillis) as a permanent partner of the orchestra. Jean Martinon held the position for five troubled years and was succeeded in 1969 by Sir Georg Solti. In twenty-two years as music director and five years as music director laureate, until

his death in 1997, Solti raised the orchestra to its greatest reputation through recording and, for the first time, foreign touring.

The tenure of Daniel Barenboim, who succeeded Solti as music director in 1991, has been marked by controversy about quality of performance, conducting, and repertoire. However, the introduction of principal guest conductors—Carlo Maria Giulini and Claudio Abbado (both during Solti's term) and Pierre Boulez (during Barenboim's)—has been a balancing influence in the orchestra's recent history. The Chicago Symphony Orchestra is known internationally for its recordings, especially since the time of Solti, and its recent attention to modern music is due to the influence of Boulez. Its civic outreach and educational efforts include the annual Marshall Field's Day of Music at Symphony Center, regular children's concerts, and chamber ensembles from the orchestra that visit schools for workshops and demonstrations of their instruments.

Sources and Further Reading: E. A. Johnson, "The Chicago Orchestra: 1891–1942," Ph.D. diss., University of Chicago (1951); P. A. Otis, *The Chicago Symphony Orchestra* (1924).

Susan M. Filler
Chicago

Cleveland Orchestra

One of the America's youngest major orchestras, the Cleveland Orchestra holds a firm position among the world's top symphonic ensembles. It is admired in particular for precision, balance, and attention to detail, characteristics that have been in place for more than sixty years, especially in its performance of works by Mozart, Beethoven, and Brahms. But Cleveland also excels in the gamut of orchestral repertoire, from works of the classical era to contemporary scores. Founded in 1918 by the Musical Arts Association, the ensemble has had seven music directors: Nikolai Sokoloff (1918–1933), Artur Rodzinski (1933–1943), Erich Leinsdorf (1943–1946), George Szell (1946–1970), Pierre Boulez (1970–72), Lorin Maazel (1972–1982), Christoph von Dohnányi (1984–2002), and Franz Welser-Möst (2002–present). Pierre Boulez served as musical supervisor between the tenures of Szell and Maazel. In 1931 the orchestra moved into its own home, Severance Hall, built largely with funds provided by Cleveland industrialist and philanthropist John L. Severance. It also maintains an al fresco summer facility, Blossom Music Center, in Cuyahoga Falls, about thirty-five miles south of Cleveland. During the late 1980s and early 1990s, Cleveland made more than one hundred recordings, with releases on the Decca/London, Deutsche Grammophon, EMI Classics, Sony Classical, Telarc, and Teldec labels. In addition to subscription programs at Severance Hall, the orchestra makes frequent appearances at New York's Carnegie Hall and around the globe as well as giving educational concerts and offering community performances in downtown Cleveland and to mark the birthday of Martin Luther King, Jr. In addition, it hosts the Cleveland Orchestra Chorus, Cleveland Orchestra Youth Orchestra, Cleveland Orchestra Youth Chorus, and Cleveland Orchestra Children's Chorus.

Source and Further Reading: Donald Rosenberg, *The Cleveland Orchestra Story* (2000).

Donald Rosenberg
Cleveland Plain Dealer

Grant Park Music Festival

Founded in 1935, Chicago's Grant Park Music Festival, a series of free concerts given from June to August, is the only remaining free, municipally funded, outdoor classical music series in the United States. In 1934 James C. Petrillo, founder of the Chicago Musicians' Union, was appointed to the Park Commission, and he convinced the then commission chairman, Robert Dunham, that a series of classical music concerts would benefit the city. In 1936 the Chicago Park District, together with the Chicago Federation of Musicians, financed these concerts in a band shell in the park directly south of the Loop. This continued until 1943, when the Chicago Federation of Musicians ended its funding. It was at this time, however, that a single resident orchestra was founded, the Grant Park Orchestra, under the direction of Nikolai Malko, who held that post until 1956. Other prestigious conductors, such as Irwin Hoffman, Leonard Slatkin, and Zdenek Macal, have subsequently held the post. In 1999 Carlos Kalmar was named the festival's principal conductor and James Paul the principal guest conductor.

A broad range of programs, often with works by contemporary American composers, is presented, featuring major artists. The Grant Park Chorus (founded by Thomas Peck) likewise participates in several concerts. In addition, the Grant Park Festival highlights the Lyric Opera Center for American Artists in one concert annually. In 2004 the festival moved to a new home in Chicago's Millennium Park.

Enrique Alberto Arias
DePaul University, Illinois

Marching Bands

"Seventy-six trombones led the big parade." Even if they don't know the context, many Americans can identify this famous line from Meredith Willson's 1957 musical *The Music Man*. Willson rooted his tale in the Midwest's rich connection between marching bands and its cities and communities. Long before the flash and presentation of a high school or college marching band at a football game, band music and the ensembles that produced it were central to midwestern identity. Marching bands not only entertained local, regional, or national audiences, they generated city revenues, created community pride, and gathered crowds to community festivals and political rallies.

Though the sackbut, a predecessor of the trombone, and trumpets had been around since the Renaissance, brass music's popularity has had a short life. By the nineteenth century, French, German, and eventually American innovations in instrument making led to improvements on existing models and the creation of new horns. New brass instruments were durable, could be heard a great distance, and, thanks to new designs, were quite portable. No longer was music restricted to the formality or geography of the orchestra hall. Brass music had a brasher sound and more common spirit that invigorated audiences beginning in the

A marching band in Mason City, Iowa. Iowa Division of Tourism.

mid-nineteenth century. Bands now played in park gazebos and on riverboat decks or marched in parades. Despite the current association of marching bands with high schools, most bands began as municipal or private organizations. By the 1850s and 1860s, the U.S. Army harnessed the popularity of the movement to lift troops' morale and to raise support and funds for the Civil War, a tactic it has continually employed.

Band music arrived in America with European immigrants in the early 1800s, gleaned out of polkas and waltzes, and was at first dismissed as an ethnic trapping of undesirable newcomers. Eventually this attitude melted away as American performers, composers, and instrument manufacturers gave band music a distinctly American flair. Gaining acclaim first on the East Coast, the new genre soon spread into the heart of the Midwest. East Coast pioneers in composing and directing Patrick S. Gilmore and John Phillip Sousa fueled the imaginations of generations of their midwestern counterparts. Karl L. King of Paintersville, Ohio, first gained renown under the big top playing baritone and composing pieces like "Barnum & Bailey's Favorite" (1913) for several traveling circus companies. In 1920 King took a position as director of the Fort Dodge (Iowa) Municipal Band, which he held for more than fifty years. During this time, King produced more than three hundred pieces and helped found the American Bandmasters Association and the Iowa Bandmasters Association, adding renewed professionalism to the occupation.

During the last half of the nineteenth century, towns of all sizes sought to attract and maintain municipal marching bands of their own. The quality of one's band was something to brag about and often incited heated rivalry. "No town or village . . . ," claimed an 1881 catalog of Chicago-based Lyon and Healy Band Instrument Company, "can pretend to have attained much progress in social esthetics which is not blessed with a good brass band." Many Americans came to believe what they were told and felt less civic pride without a marching band to welcome politicians, cheer heroes, or rouse crowds in the public event of a parade. Some communities even valued their bands as much as their schools or hospitals.

Bands sprang up throughout the Midwest during the second half of the nineteenth century and remained strong well into the twentieth century, when big bands, jazz, and rock and roll catered to new audiences. Though bands entertained audiences of all varieties, they also gave the members an artistic or social outlet. Bands often had their own recital hall or practice building, though some were known to rehearse in barns belonging to members. Specialty bands organized to entertain the public as well as to draw attention to themselves and their cause. Early volunteer fire departments often founded bands to fund the purchase of their own equipment. Suffragette societies and other groups of women founded all-female bands to show their equality with men; coed bands were quite rare. Ethnic groups also formed bands: African Americans, Native Americans, and, most well known in large cities, German polka bands. During the last decades of the nineteenth century, bands delighted local audiences, drew crowds from far distances, and even toured to reach a larger public.

As new forms of music took the place of bands on the East Coast, band music remained popular in the Midwest, but the region was not merely a stronghold for performing band music. Early in the development of the genre, American manufacturers of musical instruments settled in the Midwest to create and fuel the need supplied by so many local bands. Among the ranks were brass giants C. G. Conn of Elkhart, Indiana, founded in 1875, and the Cleveland firm of King Instruments, emerging eighteen years later. Since the late twentieth century, both companies have been part of the conglomerate United Musical Instrument Company (UMI), which operates plants in both original locations as well as in many other midwestern communities and supplies most American-made wind instruments.

Marching bands no longer draw huge crowds at political rallies, and few cities maintain municipal band halls, but they are still a mainstay of any parade. Due to the work of early bandmasters, by the 1930s bands began appearing in most school districts. During the twentieth century, high school marching bands came to far outnumber community bands of the century before. Youngsters dedicated to their music may even travel sizable distances to join a Drum Corps International marching team such as the Madison Scouts of Madison, Wisconsin, or the Quad Cities Cadets of Rock Island, Illinois. These groups rehearse rigorously during summers and travel across the country to compete in intense contests, ensuring the future of the marching band in the Midwest and keeping the spirit of rivalry alive and well.

Sources and Further Reading: Margaret Hindle Hazen and Robert M. Hazen, *The Music Men* (1987); Vincent Scuro, *Presenting the Marching Band* (1974).

Eugene R. H. Tesdahl
Chicago

Music Education

The Midwest has been a strong region for education in music, from elementary schools through higher education, stemming in part from its historical roots as a leader in programmatic and curricular development since the latter part of the nineteenth century. This strength likely stems from a number of variables—the overall support for education, including music education, by midwesterners; the desire of rural communities and small towns to have live music in the early twentieth century; and the cultural valuing of music by the diverse groups found in the Midwest.

Music classes began to appear in the public schools of large cities in the 1840s and 1850s, with state music-teacher associations beginning to organize in the 1870s. Music educators in the Midwest were instrumental in the establishment of MENC: The National Association for Music Education, hosting all but five of the national meetings held during its first thirty years, 1907–1936. The Midwest Clinic, an international band and orchestra conference held annually in Chicago since 1946, is considered the leading professional conference in the field. The National High School Orchestra camp, founded in 1928, led to the establishment of the Interlochen Center for the Arts (Michigan), which continues today as the nation's premier fine arts boarding school and summer fine arts camp.

Music education programs in the Midwest are characterized by general music classes taught by music specialists in elementary schools and choir programs offered in middle schools and high schools. Band programs are typically offered beginning in either fifth or sixth grade, and high school marching bands are essential parts of midwestern parades and football games. It is most common to see string orchestra programs offered in medium-size school districts of average socioeconomic level located near cities, with instruction beginning in the fourth or fifth grade. As in the rest of the nation, music education curricular offerings in high schools are predominantly performing ensembles, with non-ensemble classes, such as music theory and music history/appreciation, making up a small portion of the typical music program.

Music programs in midwestern colleges and universities have been models for other universities throughout the nation. At the end of the nineteenth century, normal schools, which focused on teacher training, were the prevalent institutions of higher education in the nation. An 1878 survey of normal schools nationwide indicated that more than a third of those offering vocal music were in the Midwest. Another sign of leadership is evident in the charter membership list of the National Association of Schools of Music (NASM), the national accrediting agency for music and music-related disciplines. About half of the charter institutions in 1928 were in the Midwest. Today, some of the most highly regarded collegiate

programs in music are found in the Midwest, including, for example, public institutions such as the University of Michigan and Indiana University, as well as private conservatories such as Oberlin College and the Cleveland Institute of Music. A fine professional education in music, as well as rich musical opportunities for non–music majors, can easily be found in the region's many colleges, universities, and conservatories of music.

Sources and Further Reading: Harold F. Abeles, Charles F. Hoffer, and Robert H. Klotman, *Foundations of Music Education,* 2nd ed. (1994); Edward B. Birge, *A History of Public School Music in the United States,* rev. ed. (1988); Michael L. Mark and Charles L. Gray, *A History of American Music Education,* 2nd ed. (1999); Camille M. Smith, "Access to String Instruction in American Public Schools," *Journal of Research in Music Education* 45 (Winter 1997).

Judith K. Delzell
Miami University, Oxford, Ohio

Paisley Park

Among the most unusual musical figures of the Midwest is Prince. Born Prince Roger Nelson in 1958 and performing under the names Prince, Jamie Starr, and the Artist Formerly known as Prince (among others), Prince has shown an allegiance to the Midwest by continually returning there, making his home there, and eventually building his dream production facility in Chanhassen, Minnesota, near Minneapolis. He is said to appreciate the anonymity that comes from being distant from the main centers of the music industry.

The Chanhassen facility is called Paisley Park and consists of three recording studios featuring state-of-the-art digital technology and a twelve-thousand-foot soundstage. It began as a warehouse that Prince purchased for $450,000 in cash in 1984. After substantial remodeling, it opened as a recording facility in 1987. Almost all of Prince's subsequent work has been recorded there, and the soundstage has been used for films (*Grumpy Old Men* and Prince's films and videos) and television commercials (for McDonald's and others). Paisley Park was closed to the public and again remodeled in 1996 and then reopened for use as a studio and production facility.

Source and Further Reading: Jon Bream, *Prince: Inside the Purple Reign* (1984).

Geoffrey Thrumston
Boulder, Colorado

Ravinia Festival

Outdoor music festivals in the United States began to proliferate in the nineteenth century and have become an important "alternative" season in the present day. In the Midwest, the tradition took hold with the Cincinnati May Festival in 1873. The World's Columbian Exposition in Chicago in 1893 gave a spur to such activities in that city, and the Grant Park Concerts were established on the lakefront just a few years before the Chicago Symphony made its summer home at Ravinia Park. The site, in Highland Park, Illinois, was created as an amusement park in 1904. In 1911 it became a summer venue for classical music, and opera was later performed there too. The Chicago Symphony Orchestra has made its summer home at the festival since 1936. Performances between June and early September also include piano and vocal recitals, chamber music, and popular and ethnic music.

The Ravinia Festival maintains a separate administration and music director from those of the regular season of the Chicago Symphony. The first music director, Seiji Ozawa, was appointed in 1964 and was succeeded by James Levine (1971–1993) and Christoph Eschenbach (1994–2003). James Conlon was appointed music director commencing with the 2005 season. The awkward discrepancy between administrations and music directors of the orchestra at different times of year has resulted in comparisons of concurrent music directors at least since the tenure of James Levine (concurrently with Sir Georg Solti); however, under their successors, Eschenbach and Daniel Barenboim, the arrangement has stabilized enough for the two directors to guest-conduct at each other's venues.

The executive directors (most recently Edward Gordon, Zarin Mehta, and Welz Kauffman) plan programming with the music director and recruit visiting artists, many of whom not only perform in concerts but give classes at the Steans Institute for Young Artists, which Gordon established in 1988. Many young musicians from the institute have gone on to international careers. The outgrowth of the institute is the Rising Stars series, which is based at Bennett-Gordon Hall at Ravinia Park during the off season.

Source and Further Reading: E. A. Johnson, "The Chicago Orchestra: 1891–1942," Ph.D. diss., University of Chicago (1951).

Susan M. Filler
Chicago

Saint Louis Symphony Orchestra

The Saint Louis Symphony Orchestra (SLSO), founded in 1880, is the second-oldest orchestra in the country; only the New York Philharmonic has endured longer. Among its most significant conductors have been Max Zach (1907–1921), who first shaped it into a truly professional ensemble; Rudolph Ganz (1921–1927); Vladimir Golschmann (1931–1958); Walter Susskind (1968–1975); Leonard Slatkin (1979–1996); and Hans Vonk (1996–2002).

Prior to Slatkin's tenure, the orchestra was known as a solid regional ensemble. By championing new music; building the orchestra's quality; making a series of acclaimed recordings; and touring the United States, Europe, and Japan, Slatkin helped the SLSO to achieve an international reputation for fine playing and innovation. Vonk refined the orchestra's playing and brought both a more beautiful sound and a new emphasis on the European classics. His career was cut short by a rare neurological disease; he resigned in April 2002. American conductor David Robertson was named the orchestra's next music director, with a contract taking effect in 2005. Robertson is celebrated for both his commitment to new music and his solid grounding in the standard repertoire.

After losing a 1989 bid to join the St. Louis Zoo and several museums in receiving taxpayer funding—it was perceived as elitist and out of touch—the SLSO launched a now-celebrated community outreach program that takes musicians out of Powell Symphony Hall and puts them in local schools and churches. The SLSO's endowment did not keep pace with its artistic achievements, however, and the orchestra approached bankruptcy in 2000 and 2001. Then the Taylor family, owners of Enterprise Rent-a-Car, put up a forty-million-dollar challenge grant—at that time the largest private gift to a symphony orchestra; the players made significant contract concessions; and the SLSO seemed to be winning its battle for survival while retaining its artistic quality.

Source and Further Reading: Katherine Gladney Wells and Gayle R. MacIntosh, *Symphony and Song* (1993).

Sarah Bryan Miller
St. Louis Post-Dispatch

Public Sculpture

Outdoor sculpture in the Midwest, as elsewhere, has evolved and enlarged in theme and concept over time.

Apart from occasional ornate gravestones and religious statuary, scarcely any public outdoor sculpture materialized in the region before the middle of the nineteenth century, unless the extensive prehistoric mounds found particularly in Ohio, Indiana, and Illinois are considered. A surge in sculpture in public spaces began in earnest after the Civil War ended; monuments and memorials honoring those who had fought in that war began to appear in courthouse squares and other prominent locations. The largest is the Indiana Soldiers and Sailors Monument in Indianapolis, completed in 1902, covered with huge sculpture groups in stone and surrounded with oversize bronze figures. For the most part, however, the Civil War is commemorated throughout the Midwest with single statues of soldiers in bronze or stone. Among others, the W.H. Mullins Company of Salem, Ohio, provided hundreds of these in cast iron, cast bronze, or sheet bronze over a metal alloy core. Subsequent wars produced similar commemorative statues, lessening in number after World War II and the controversial conflicts that followed, although in recent years efforts by various veterans' organizations have resulted in the dedication of numerous memorials throughout the Midwest.

Statues honoring individuals also appeared in the last third of the nineteenth century, where there were funds to support them. Public subscription was the most common method of securing the money to erect a monument, sometimes augmented by legislative appropriation. Military heroes were typical choices, followed by national or local political figures or historical personages. Abraham Lincoln has always been a popular subject in the Midwest, especially as both Indiana and Illinois stake some claim to him. Among the scores of effigies of our sixteenth president are George Grey Barnard's realistic rendition in downtown Cincinnati; Henry Herring's seated Lincoln in Indianapolis; Andrew O'Connor's standing Lincoln in Springfield, Illinois; Minnesota-born sculptor Paul Manship's *Abraham Lincoln, The Hoosier Youth* (1932) in Fort Wayne, Indiana; and the figures of Abraham and Mary Todd Lincoln in Racine, Wisconsin, by Frederick C. Hibbard. Many other presidents are represented in bronze; in his hometown, Cincinnati sculptor Charles Niehaus fashioned an image of James Garfield, and in Indianapolis, the rotund figure of Benjamin Harrison. The concept was carried to the extreme with the nation's best-known outdoor sculpture, the Mount Rushmore National Memorial in the Black Hills, featuring the colossal heads of four U.S. presidents created by Gutzon Borglum over a period of fourteen years ending in 1941. Something in the South Dakota air must inspire the manipulation of mountains; less than twenty miles away is the gargan-

tuan Chief Crazy Horse Mountain Memorial begun by Korczak Ziolkowski in 1947, still an ongoing project long after the artist's death in 1982. Commemorative images began to appear with increasing frequency in the twentieth century and, after a midcentury lull, continue into the present, in remembrance of the past and in celebration of current events. Native Americans have reemerged as a popular subject; George Carlson created *The Greeting* (1989), an oversized figure of a shaman, for the entrance to a museum of Indian and Western art in downtown Indianapolis.

Some sculptures of this category are more whimsical than commemorative: Town boosters often promoted symbolic figures as a means of increasing tourism. Minnesota boasts several gigantic human and animal statues; the oldest and most famous is the concrete statue of mythical lumberjack Paul Bunyan in Bemidji, dating to 1937, accompanied by Babe the Blue Ox. In the same spirit, in 1993, the town of Metropolis in southern Illinois commissioned a heroic statue of Superman to draw attention to its annual festival in honor of the comic book hero. In an interesting juxtaposition, the nearby Fort Massac State Park features a large bronze statue of real-life Revolutionary War hero George Rogers Clark.

Despite the fact that the Midwest boasted a large number of its own sculptors by the latter part of the nineteenth century, chiefly in Chicago and other urban centers, major commissions continued to be awarded to renowned artists from the East, who are well represented throughout the region. Boston's Daniel Chester French, for example, created his masterwork, *Republic* (1918), for Jackson Park in Chicago; his final work, *Beneficence* (1930), stands in Muncie, Indiana, a memorial to the Ball brothers of canning-jar fame. The establishment of the Art Institute of Chicago brought a number of talented artists to the Windy City, chief among them Lorado Taft, who went on to design the statues and facades for the World's Columbian Exposition of 1893. Many other sculptors came to exhibit their own creations or to assist Taft, including some prominent women, such as Janet Scudder, born in Terre Haute, Indiana. A decade later, the Louisiana Purchase Exposition in St. Louis provided similar opportunities for sculptors to display their works, among them Cyrus Edwin Dallin's *The Protest* (1903). Boston-based Dallin executed many heroic figures of Indians, several of which are in the Midwest, including *Signal of Peace* (1890) in Chicago's Lincoln Park and *The Scout* (1910) atop a hill in Kansas City, Missouri. A few years after that fair, German-born sculptor August Leimbach came to St. Louis, where he would eventually make his home; it was there that he was commissioned in the 1920s by the Daughters of the American Revolution to create twelve identical statues in honor of pioneer women. The *Madonna of the Trail* stands in each state along U.S. Route 40, including Ohio, Indiana, Illinois, Missouri, and Kansas.

As cities and towns established their identities, along with fine civic structures and lovely parks came an increase in aesthetic sculptures and resplendent fountains, such as *Genius of Water* (1871) in Cincinnati's Fountain Square and Chicago's Buckingham Fountain. Elegant public gardens usually included allegorical or purely decorative sculpture. With a modern twist, sculpture gardens have experienced a revival since the end of World War II. A number of them have sprouted throughout the Midwest: Several are associated with universities; some have been privately endowed by wealthy arts patrons; still others are funded by corporate foundations.

The rise of public art in the 1930s, aided by a number of New Deal programs, resulted from one of the earliest cries for art for the people, not simply for well-informed aesthetes. The movement faded in the 1940s when midwesterners, along with the rest of the nation, were too busy fighting World War II and, afterward, reestablishing a normal life. New ideas were afoot in the art centers of the East, but it took a while for them to reach most of the Midwest apart from Chicago and a few other urban centers. Little abstract public sculpture appeared in the Midwest before 1960, mainly in isolated hothouses such as Indiana's New Harmony or the Cranbrook Academy of Art outside Detroit or on college campuses and museum grounds.

Iowa State University's sculpture collection originated in the 1930s and has since benefited from the state's public art program begun in 1978. Several nationally renowned sculptors are represented; the signature piece of the campus is Andrew Leicester's terra cotta *G-nomes* (1992). The University of Nebraska in Lincoln in 1970 opened its Sheldon Sculpture Garden, which features pieces by such acclaimed artists as Mark diSuvero and Claes Oldenburg. The University of Chicago's outdoor sculpture collection is dominated by Lorado Taft's huge concrete work *Fountain of Time*, completed in 1922 and located on the site of the World Columbian Exposition's midway, and by Henry Moore's disturbing bronze abstract *Nuclear Energy* (1967). A number of midwestern universities have sculptors in residence. Ivan Mestrovic spent the last years of his productive life at Indiana's University of Notre Dame, which displays several of his brooding pieces.

Once the seeds were sown, many more large abstract works had enlivened the landscape by the 1970s. Art museums began to assemble permanent collections of outdoor pieces. The Walker Art Center in Minneapolis opened its sculpture garden in 1988 with Oldenburg's whimsical *Spoonbridge and Cherry*. The Indianapolis Museum of Art's signature piece is Robert Indiana's famed *LOVE* (1966), along with his ten *Numerals 0-9* (1980). Another version of *LOVE* stands amid the large collection of noted twentieth-century works at Wichita State University, which includes pieces by Henry Moore, Chicago sculptor John Kearney, and Indiana-born George Rickey. The Columbus Museum of Art features works by internationally renowned artists such as Rickey, Alexander Calder, and Henry Moore. British sculptor Moore, considered by many to have been the greatest sculptor of the twentieth century, is well represented throughout the Midwest. Indeed, the largest collection of his pieces outside of England is at the Nelson-Atkins Museum of Art in Kansas City, Missouri.

New movements for public art had begun to surface in the 1960s, and by the next decade many sculptors found work, often teaching classes but also creating permanent public art, through the Comprehensive Employment and Training Act and grants from state arts commissions funded by the National Endowment for the Arts. In the 1970s, the federal government through the General Services Administration began its Art in Architecture Program whereby 0.5 percent of the construction cost of new federal buildings goes toward art, which often has taken the form of sculpture. Midwestern examples include contemporary sculptures along Interstate 80 in Nebraska, installed in 1976, and Claes Oldenburg's *Batcolumn* (1977) outside Chicago's Social Security Administration Building.

Government funding for art, at least in the form of grants, has dwindled over the past few decades, but in many cases corporate money has taken its place. Early on, some corporations began to sprout sculpture outside their headquarters. In Sioux Falls, South Dakota, a ten-foot abstract piece has enlivened the Spitznagel Office Building since 1977. Some companies started corporate collections; food giant General Mills, for example, began to buy and display significant modern art in 1958 when it moved into new quarters in suburban Minneapolis. Others include Lincoln National Life Insurance's collection in Fort Wayne, Indiana, and sprawling discount retailer Meijer's (in its Frederik Meijer Gardens and Sculpture Park) in Grand Rapids, Michigan. Corporate funds have also helped the cause of public sculpture in civic spaces; one shining example is the city of Columbus, Indiana, world famous for its modern architecture, accompanied by equally modern sculpture. Its most renowned piece is Henry Moore's *Large Arch* (1971). Venues for corporate-sponsored art include shopping malls, considered by many social historians to be today's substitute for the town square. Detroit's J. L. Hudson Company hit upon the idea early; in the mid-1950s it installed works at its new suburban shopping centers.

Today's multipurpose malls often embrace art to draw in customers.

There is much movement for art in public places today, perhaps the result of several trends happening all at once and in symbiosis. A recent trend is community and collaborative art, which relies greatly on private resources—not simply cash, but materials and labor are donated. This concept has worked especially well when schools are involved; an artist works with the children, the parents, and community organizations, the end result being a piece of permanent contemporary art that has a sense of place. Bloomington, Indiana, artist Joe LaMantia has worked with hundreds of schools and community groups throughout Indiana and Illinois, often with funding from Young Audiences and Very Special Arts, two organizations devoted to introducing children to the arts.

Public art is often conceived in celebration of an event; for example, several recent outdoor sculptures resulted from a desire to celebrate the new millennium. Public art is also a means of expressing the identity of a place. There is no limit today as to where contemporary sculpture might be found in the Midwest—from a beach in St. Joseph, Michigan, where, among others, silhouetted against the sunset is Chicago sculptor Richard Hunt's fifty-foot stainless steel abstract *And You, Seas* (2002), to the exterior walls of the new Indiana State Museum, where ninety-two individual works represent each of the state's counties. Is there a uniquely midwestern art? While many regional sculptors address their surroundings in abstract works, like Thomas Scarff of Chicago, whose work often reflects Lake Michigan, or southern Indiana artists who work exclusively in native limestone, the public sculpture of the Midwest is as varied as its landscape and quintessentially American.

Sources and Further Reading: Tom Armstrong, ed., *200 Years of American Sculpture* (1976); Brooke Barrie, *Contemporary Outdoor Sculpture* (1999); Glory-June Greiff, *Remembrance, Faith and Fancy: Indiana's Outdoor Public Sculpture* (2005); Moira F. Harris, *Monumental Minnesota* (1992); Jane McCarthy and Laurily K. Epstein, *A Guide to the Sculpture Parks and Gardens of America* (1996); Louis G. Redstone, *Public Art: New Directions* (1981); Lorado Taft, *The History of American Sculpture* (1930).

Glory-June Greiff
Indianapolis

Effigy Tumuli

One of the largest examples of public sculpture in the Midwest is *Effigy Tumuli* (1985), in Ottawa, Illinois, about eighty miles southwest of Chicago. Commissioned to reclaim 150 acres of strip-mined land on a sandy bluff near Buffalo Rock State Park, artist Michael Heizer designed five huge earth mounds shaped as indigenous midwestern insects and reptiles: a turtle, a water strider, a catfish, a snake, and a frog. Best known for minimalist earthworks sculptures in Nevada such as *Double Negative* (1969–1970) and *Complex One* (1972–1974), Heizer retained his characteristic abstract style and huge scale in the *Effigy Tumuli* mounds, which are geometric and gigantic, ranging from 340 to 2,070 feet in length and from 10 to 18 feet in height. The mounds also pay homage to the Woodland Indians earth mounds once common in the central Midwest, such as the Serpent Mound near Peebles, Ohio (built circa A.D. 1000–1600), and the mound complex near Cahokia, Illinois (built circa A.D. 700–1450).

Effigy Tumuli is an example of contemporary land reclamation art. Despoiled by unregulated surface mining in the 1930s, the site was earmarked for reclamation when acid water runoff was found to be polluting the Illinois River and nearby fields. Landowners commissioned Heizer to regenerate and transform the site into a public sculpture park, managed by the Illinois Department of Conservation. While the mounds have largely eroded due to their having been poorly constructed atop a windswept bluff, *Effigy Tumuli* is an ideal site for observing both industrial devastation and local wildlife (deer, coyotes, Eastern meadowlarks) and contemplating issues of environmental responsibility.

Sources and Further Reading: Erika Doss, "Sculptures from Strip Mines," in Erika Doss, ed., *Spirit Poles and Flying Pigs*, (1995); Douglas C. McGill, *Michael Heizer: Effigy Tumuli* (1990).

Erika Doss
University of Colorado–Boulder

The Gateway Arch

The Gateway Arch springs from the St. Louis, Missouri, bank of the Mississippi River like a gleaming portal to paradise. The facts of the monument, known officially as the Jefferson National Expansion Memorial, are just as dazzling: Between February 1963 and October 1965, at a cost of thirteen million dollars, nearly 5,200 tons of stainless steel were assembled into a 630-foot-high, 630-foot-wide catenary arch, a "dynamic" and "upward thrusting" form according to its designer. The arch is part of a national park site, and it features a unique tramway system, designed by Dick

Bowser, that conveys people to a small observation deck at its pinnacle. It is the tallest monument in the United States, surpassing even the Washington Monument, and was erected as a tribute to President Thomas Jefferson, whose 1803 Louisiana Purchase symbolized an expansion of the physical boundaries, as well as the limitless possibilities, of the United States.

The Gateway Arch was the first major solo commission of Finnish American architect Eero Saarinen (1910–1961), whose bold design was chosen as the winner of a national competition in 1947–1948. He was later recognized for his work on the TWA terminal at JFK International Airport in New York City and the Dulles International Airport near Washington, D.C., as well as for his line of modern furniture. With his futuristic monument, Saarinen paid fitting tribute to the pioneers who followed their own vision to explore and settle the North American continent a century before.

Sources and Further Reading: National Park Service, *Jefferson National Expansion Memorial,* http://www.nps.gov/jeff/ (July 2002); Aline B. Saarinen, ed., *Eero Saarinen on His Work* (1962).

Stephanie L. Taylor
New Mexico State University

La Grande Vitesse

Located in Grand Rapids, Michigan, Alexander Calder's *La Grande Vitesse* (loosely translated as "great swiftness") was the first public sculpture to be partially funded through a matching grant from the National Endowment for the Arts' Works of Art in Public Places Program, begun in the late 1960s. Calder (1898–1976) is best known for his mobiles, kinetic sculptures that move in response to environmental

conditions or human touch. The scion of a long line of artists—both his father and his paternal grandfather were well-known sculptors, and his mother was a painter—Calder earned a degree in engineering at the Stevens Institute of Technology in Hoboken, New Jersey, before pursuing training at the Art Students League in New York City. His ability to rationally reckon weights and balances obviously affected his approach to his work, but the resulting sculptures were anything but cold or mathematical. Rather, Calder's flamboyant, fun-loving personality is reflected in the bright colors and cartoonish shapes of his art.

La Grande Vitesse was installed in front of the city hall in Grand Rapids in 1969 and has since been adopted as a local icon. Such large-scale corporate and public commissions were prevalent late in Calder's career, due to his international reputation and the growth of federally supported grant programs in the arts. *La Grande Vitesse* is considered a stabile because of the immovable nature of its riveted steel parts. Calder's title, a play on the name of the sculpture's host city, also implies a swiftness that is belied by the actual scale of the enormous, forty-two-ton structure.

Sources and Further Reading: Alexander Calder, *Calder: An Autobiography with Pictures* (1966); Joan M. Marter, *Alexander Calder* (1991).

Stephanie L. Taylor
New Mexico State University

Lincoln Statues

Abraham Lincoln's significance as a midwestern icon is reflected in more than sixty heroic (life-size or larger) statues of him throughout the region. One of the earliest notable examples was sculpted by Larkin G. Mead,

La Grande Vitesse, by Alexander Calder, 1969, Grand Rapids, Michigan. Photo courtesy the Grand Rapids/Kent County Convention & Visitors Bureau.

Jr., for the Lincoln Tomb in Springfield, Illinois (1874). Augustus Saint-Gaudens's 1887 work in Chicago's Lincoln Park is widely considered the most artistic, followed closely by that of Daniel Chester French on the state capitol grounds in Lincoln, Nebraska (1912). In the early twentieth century, sculptors turned away from portraying Lincoln as an immortal statesman to celebrate instead his midwestern origins, in works like Charles J. Mulligan's *The Railsplitter* (Chicago, 1911), Lorado Taft's *Lincoln the Lawyer* (Urbana, Illinois, 1927), Leonard Crunelle's *The Captain* (Dixon, Illinois, 1930), and *The Hoosier Youth* by Paul Manship (Fort Wayne, Indiana, 1932). George G. Barnard's rough-hewn version (Cincinnati, 1917) took the trend to a controversial extreme and was criticized by Lincoln's son Robert, among others, as a crude caricature.

After World War II, new Lincoln statues continued to appear, including a fiberglass roadside attraction over sixty feet tall intended to draw tourists to Charleston, Illinois (1968). A few artists, like Abbott Pattison, attempted to express the Lincoln theme in semiabstract art (Springfield, Illinois, 1976), but the turn of the twenty-first century saw a resurgence of traditional commemorative works, including those of Lily Tolpo (Freeport, Illinois, 1992), Rick Harney (Bloomington, Illinois, 2000), and John McClarey (Vandalia and Peoria, Illinois, 2001).

Sources and Further Reading: F. Lauriston Bullard, *Lincoln in Marble and Bronze* (1952); Merrill D. Peterson, *Lincoln in American Memory* (1994).

Gerald J. Prokopowicz
East Carolina University, North Carolina

Notable Cemeteries

Historic cemeteries capture both the history of midwestern settlement and the aspirations of generations of midwestern Americans. The earliest cemeteries are those of first millennium Native American Mound Builders: the great ceremonial pyramids of Cahokia, near St. Louis, and thousands of effigy mounds throughout the Great Lakes and the Mississippi, Missouri, and Ohio river systems. The oldest non-Indian cemeteries, like St. James of the Sag in Illinois (1833), contain the remains of fur trappers, canal laborers, and other pioneers of the eighteenth and nineteenth centuries. Early small cemeteries still dot the Midwest along old plank roads or the trails of prairie schooners in the Great Plains, a poignant link to the past now often overrun by new commercial strips. Segregated even in death, sites like St. Louis's Father Dickson Cemetery memorialize the region's African Americans.

As the Midwest transformed from frontier prairie to industrial and agricultural giant, urban cemeteries were relocated for health concerns. The rural cemetery movement emphasized serene landscapes and stately architectural mausoleums in beautiful memorial parks like Cincinnati's Spring Grove Cemetery; St. Louis's Bellefontaine Cemetery, with its Wainwright tomb by Louis Sullivan; and Chicago's Graceland Cemetery, where politicians and industrialists repose beneath architectural styles that range from classical and Egyptian to modern. Cleveland's picturesque Lake View Cemetery features Tiffany stained glass and mosaics in the Wade Chapel and the stunning Garfield mausoleum, while Indianapolis's Crown Hill Cemetery, the fourth largest in America, offers a serene wooded repose for poets and politicians like Benjamin Harrison, James Whitcomb Riley, and Booth Tarkington.

Sources and Further Reading: James J. Farrell, *Inventing the American Way of Death, 1830–1920* (1980); Richard E. Meyer, ed., *Cemeteries and Gravemarkers* (1989); William Tishler, ed., *American Landscape Architecture* (1989).

Vincent L. Michael
School of the Art Institute of Chicago

Picasso in Chicago

Pablo Picasso (1881–1973), arguably the most important visual artist of the twentieth century, had an impact on Chicago's art scene despite the fact that he never visited the city. Prime examples of every phase of his celebrated career can be found in private and public collections there, including several important paintings on display at the Art Institute of Chicago. One of his earliest outdoor monuments—an untitled 50-foot-tall, 162-ton sculpture—has graced Daley Plaza in downtown Chicago since 1967. According to Picasso biographer Roland Penrose, the artist expressed delight that a city famous for gangsters was one of the first to ask him for a public sculpture when he was approached by a group of Chicago architects for this design in the early 1960s.

The monumental Chicago Picasso sculpture was fabricated from a 42-inch model of the design by the U.S. Steel Corporation in nearby Gary, Indiana. The finished work—made of the same Cor-Ten steel as the nearby Civic Center so that it would blend in with the plaza once it achieved the rust patina characteristic of this material—was revealed to the public on August 15, 1967.

Picasso ultimately refused to accept payment for his work on the Daley Plaza sculpture, choosing instead

A Civil War battle reenactment, Keokuk, Iowa. Iowa Division of Tourism.

to give it as a gift to the people of Chicago. While not universally appreciated (many question whether the artist intended to portray a woman or an Afghan hound), this monumental sculpture symbolizes Chicago's firm status as an international art center.

Sources and Further Reading: Roland Penrose, *Picasso: His Life and Work*, 3rd ed. (1981); William Rubin, ed., *Pablo Picasso: A Retrospective* (1980).

Stephanie L. Taylor
New Mexico State University

War Memorials

Befitting a region celebrated as the American Heartland, the Midwest contains a multitude of memorials commemorating America's military conflicts. From roadside markers, brass plaques, and granite monuments to museums, elaborate plazas, and enormous sports coliseums, thousands of war memorials populate the Midwest.

The erection of war memorials began in earnest in the 1880s, when many communities celebrated the twentieth and twenty-fifth anniversaries of the Civil War. Although all major American military conflicts from the Revolutionary War through the Gulf War have been memorialized, the Civil War (in which nearly a million and a half midwesterners served) and World War II dominate the landscape. The Wiscon-

sin Department of Veterans Affairs, for example, has cataloged more than 150 of the state's World War II memorials to date. From Ohio to South Dakota, however, memorials to the veterans of the Korean and Vietnam Wars are either recently dedicated or in development.

Home to the American Legion, Indianapolis claims more war memorials than any U.S. city other than Washington, D.C. Completed in 1902 to honor Indiana's Civil War veterans, the Soldiers and Sailors Monument stands 285 feet tall at the city center. Nearby, the neoclassical Indiana War Memorial anchors the six-square-block Veteran's Memorial Plaza. Two national memorials, the Congressional Medal of Honor Memorial and the U.S.S. Indianapolis Memorial, are found in proximity.

War memorials are prominent in all other midwestern cities and states as well. Chicago officially lists nearly three dozen memorials, including the National Vietnam Veterans Art Museum and Soldier Field, a football stadium. Opened in 1926, the 67,000-seat stadium commemorates the sacrifice of America's military personnel and contains a renovated 3,600-square-foot memorial.

The National Park Service of the U.S. Department of the Interior maintains four other major war memorial–related sites in the Midwest: Fort Larned and Fort Scott National Historic Sites in Kansas, Wilson's Creek National Battlefield in Missouri, and George Rogers Clark National Historic Park in Indiana.

Source and Further Reading: U.S. Department of the Interior, National Park Service, www.nps.gov/parks.

R. Dale Ogden
Indiana State Museum

Workers' Memorials and Labor Monuments

The two most significant labor centers in the Midwest are Illinois and Michigan. Important labor leaders, like John L. Lewis of the United Mine Workers, labor activist Mother Jones, and Eugene V. Debs of the American Railway Union, began their careers in Illinois. Michigan, with its large automobile industry, became home to the United Auto Workers in 1936. Labor monuments marked these states' active participation in supporting workers' rights. The Workers Memorial Statue, dedicated on April 28, 1992, on the lawn of the Illinois State Capitol in Springfield, represents an injured worker attended by a co-worker and a forward-looking figure representing the future of labor in the state. The Haymarket Martyrs Monument, dedicated on June 25, 1893, in Forest Home Cemetery in Forest Park, Illinois, commemorates the Haymarket Tragedy of 1886 and continues to function as an icon for the labor movement both nationally and internationally. The Mother Jones Monument, dedicated on October 11, 1936, in Mt. Olive, Illinois, consists of a granite spire flanked by two bronze statues of miners. And, finally, the Pullman Historic District, one of the earliest company towns, commemorates the origins of the nationwide railroad strike of 1894, when Eugene Debs organized the American Railway Union. Michigan features the Ford River Rouge Complex in Dearborn, constructed between 1917 and 1927 as an integrated-operations plant encompassing all the basic steps in automobile production. It was the site of many labor conflicts in the 1930s.

Sources and Further Reading: Melissa Dabakis, *Visualizing Labor in American Sculpture* (1999); Archie Green, "Labor Landmarks: Past and Present," *Labor's Heritage* 6 (Spring 1995).

Melissa Dabakis
Kenyon College, Ohio

Theatre Groups and Ensembles

Midwestern theatre groups descended from the diverse cultures carried by the wagons, railroads, and riverboats of early American migration. Like the agricultural products that drive the region's economy, theatre has often prospered, nearly always struggled for nourishment, and sometimes withered and died.

Traditional storytelling, accompanied by music and dance, is a major cultural medium in all human societies. Enacted stories prefigure historic records and propagate the myths celebrated in communal rites. Native American stories are the primary transmitters of tribal memories. Although they constitute native entertainments in midwestern America, they have been effectively displaced in popular culture by the European theatrical traditions that landed with the early settlers—the performance of stories that have been preserved in literature.

Puritan sentiments in early America were so strong that the first official license to produce a play was not granted until the turn of the eighteenth century. But once official barriers were withdrawn, theatrical companies developed rapidly. Between 1703 and the onset of the Revolutionary War, well-known English plays of all types, including opera, were presented in New York; Boston; Williamsburg, Virginia; and Charleston, South Carolina.

Theatre in the Midwest evolved following the American Revolution, when the completion of land acquisitions like the 1803 Louisiana Purchase opened the frontier west of the Allegheny Mountains. As ethnic multitudes spilled into the American interior, they ventured into a true wilderness of dense forests and wide plains. Without roads, the fastest and safest means of travel was by boat along the vast network of waterways that crisscross the continent. Consequently, the early midwestern theatre first flowered in the population centers that sprouted along those lakeshores and riverbanks.

Early American theatre was dominated by stock companies controlled by actor/managers who oversaw the organizations' artistic and financial affairs. Each actor had a "line of business" consisting of his or her "stock" of roles in the company's various productions, but the manager bore the added responsibilities of direction, design, personnel, budgeting, and publicity. There is evidence that the earliest productions west of the Alleghenies probably took place in Pittsburgh. The great steel town of the future was home to approximately one thousand settlers in 1790, when soldiers are thought to have produced Englishman Joseph Addison's *Cato*. Army forts were one of the few safe places for such gatherings, and William G. B. Carson notes in his book on frontier theatre that the first production of a play in the Midwest was also by soldiers—an unknown work performed in Detroit in 1798.

The California gold rush of 1849 attracted settlers even farther west, facilitated by the new technologies of the Industrial Revolution. Steam power, in particular, played a major role; travel time, especially for upstream journeys, was dramatically shortened when steamboats began to ply the rivers. Actor/manager Noah Miller Ludlow recounts the rigors faced by his theatre troupe in 1819, when it quit Nashville for the greener pastures of a new town called St. Louis, where professional theatre was unknown. The downstream trip to the Mississippi River was relatively easy, but the approximately 140 miles upstream to St. Louis was accomplished by "cordelling" their keelboats: tying long ropes to the shore by which six or eight strong men could pull the craft upstream. Ludlow and his wife finally gave up the struggle and waited for a steamboat to complete their journey. Some companies—especially those originating near New Orleans—chose to actually perform on the boats. Showboats eventually presented every sort of entertainment, including melodramas, variety acts, and the infamously racist minstrel shows. But the difficulties of travel motivated many companies to settle down and employ some local talent, finding success as a permanent part of the community. Some resident companies prospered, and by 1850 most major towns and cities of the Midwest had some type of theatre.

Although most of these stock companies had been formed in the East, their resident status and growing local identity made them the first truly "midwestern" ensembles. As their talent and repertory grew, so did their audiences, until many were able to attract famous actors to perform in their productions. The most successful companies employed those stars in the most fashionable plays of the day. However, they often did so without a contract with the playwright. The widespread piracy of popular dramas eventually caused a backlash among powerful writers and producers like Dion Boucicault, who established a new type of touring company—the "combination" company—that was facilitated by the burgeoning railroad system. These shows, originating primarily in New York, featured famous actors in highly publicized and completely packaged productions of the most popular plays. In a system that has changed little over the decades, the actors were typecast. Versatility was not essential in a company performing the same play every night. While combination companies protected the playwrights, they also contributed to the gradual erosion of local stock companies, which struggled to compete at a higher level of literary, technical, and promotional sophistication. Eventually, powerful eastern producers recognized that the profitability of a tour was enhanced if it could make the maximum number of stops on a continuous route between the largest cities, playing longer engagements where justified. At the end of the nineteenth century, New York producer Charles Frohman combined forces with theatre owners across the country to form a "syndicate" that effectively monopolized the business for a quarter century. The big New York productions only played in syndicate playhouses and those houses booked only syndicate shows. The result was a predatory but effective domination of the best plays, directors, stars, actors, designers—and the best markets, including those in the Midwest. The touring New York production dominated popular theatre through two world wars, though increasingly squeezed by competition from talking motion pictures. Management excesses were eventually brought under control following the advent of the actors' labor union, Actors' Equity Association, which assured working conditions for touring actors and ultimately dominated the professional stage by establishing a "closed shop" in 1924.

In the 1950s, diverse elements began to merge into a regional theatre "movement" that, while not limited to the Midwest, did find many of its most dramatic success stories there. In 1951, Dallas entrepreneur Margo Jones wrote *Theatre-in-the-Round*, a manifesto that urged the talented and ambitious theatre practitioners of America to gather their talents, create great theatre, and make it an integral part of their community. Theatre people were attracted to her ideas because of the constant struggle to make a living in a most demanding, competitive, and insecure industry. In addition, local arts aficionados—particularly in communities that housed progressive university theatre schools—realized that their most talented actors and designers were being siphoned off into the New York theatre industry. Many leaders felt that these local talents should be able to remain in their hometowns and make a decent living while simultaneously elevating the cultural atmosphere of the community. Good theatre was as important as good libraries and museums.

The idea that local communities deserved recognition as culturally significant entities was an important concept driving the regional theatre movement. Although it initially arose because talented artisans needed to secure an outlet for their ideas, it was also partly a reaction against New York theatre and what were sometimes viewed as overly liberal eastern ideals. Therefore, midwestern theatre could generally be defined as reproducing the region's agricultural heritage: home grown and locally consumed, while inspired—and occasionally restricted—by conservative midwestern values.

Another important component of the regional theatre movement was its emancipation from the profit motive that drove the New York theatre, with its excessive ticket prices, restricted tours, extravagant salaries, and powerful unions. If cultural organizations were valuable community assets, a rationale could be developed justifying their operation as nonprofit, tax-exempt entities. Regional theatres could survive—

even flourish—without the money woes that had traditionally plagued the industry, especially if their civic value justified subsidy by entities like the Ford Foundation, the Rockefeller Foundation, the National Endowment for the Arts, or state and local philanthropic organizations. The Ford Foundation established a successful service organization for such theatres, the Theatre Communications Group, to provide assistance in areas ranging from casting and management to fund-raising and subscriptions.

Some of these new resident theatres grew from entirely local roots. The Milwaukee Repertory Theatre is the oldest regional theatre in the Midwest. It originated in 1954 as the Fred Miller Theatre, named for the head of Miller Brewing. Founded by Mary John, the theatre succeeded initially by offering a varied season featuring stars appearing in plays that had been proven on Broadway. In 1963, John A. McQuiggan transformed the company into a nonprofit organization known as the Milwaukee Repertory Theatre, and in the late 1960s the company moved into a new arts center in central Milwaukee.

In Cincinnati, the Playhouse in the Park was founded in 1960, when a 125-year-old shelterhouse in Eden Park was saved from demolition and a new stage was installed with seats for 166. Now known as the Thompson Shelterhouse Theatre, it has been expanded to more than 220 seats. The playhouse was so successful that an additional facility was added in 1968: the 629-seat Robert S. Marx Theatre. With two full-time theatres, the Playhouse in the Park was able to expand its offerings to include innovative productions including those of the Living Theatre of Julian Beck and Judith Malina. In 1987, the Lois and Richard Rosenthal New Play Prize was instituted as an annual award for new dramatic works of high quality, drawing up to eight hundred submissions each year.

Cleveland is home to two historically important companies. The oldest regional theatre company in America, the Cleveland Play House, occupies a facility built in 1927 that now contains four theatres. The company is known for commissioning new plays through its Next Stage Festival of New Plays and for its aggressive children's theatre program. Also in Cleveland, the Great Lakes Theatre Festival has grown from a summer Shakespeare theatre into a year-round organization. Founded in 1962 by Arthur Lithgow, the festival originally performed in a high school auditorium. Vincent Dowling, a veteran of Dublin's famed Abbey Theatre, became artistic director of the festival in 1976, expanding the company's repertory and importing fresh talent from across the country. In 1982 the Great Lakes Theatre Festival became part of the comprehensive Playhouse Square Complex in downtown Cleveland.

While many of the new resident companies have depended upon university talent to fill supporting positions, some might never have appeared but for the early influence of academe. The Goodman Theatre in Chicago was originally a gift to that city's art institute, where an acting/design training center was established in 1925. Chicago's oldest resident theatre, the facility was donated to the Art Institute of Chicago in 1925 as a memorial to playwright Kenneth Sawyer Goodman. The Goodman flourished as a resident company under Thomas Wood Stevens, but during the Depression the Art Institute was forced to transform it into a drama school to make ends meet. Under the leadership of Maurice Gnesin, the school was eventually recognized as one of the nation's premier theatre conservatories. In 1957, John Reich took over the academy and introduced guest stars into the student productions. The training program gradually diminished in importance until 1969, when the Goodman became a professional Actors' Equity resident theatre (in 1977, it became a nonprofit organization). The Goodman is also heavily involved in community outreach programs, providing free admission for area high school students with pre/post-performance classroom discussions.

Missouri Repertory Theatre (MRT) in Kansas City also originated within a university environment. It was founded in 1964 by Patricia McIlrath as the Summer Repertory Theatre of the University of Missouri at Kansas City, presenting two plays in a two-week season. The original theatre was a 500-seat, wood-frame structure that relied upon inadequate exhaust fans for ventilation. McIlrath was initially motivated by the need to expose her students to the rigors of professional theatre. She accomplished her goal by hiring visiting professionals and community veterans to accompany a core of advanced students and technicians. MRT was a true repertory company from the outset, with a single acting company performing in a rotating group of plays. In 1967 the company was affiliated with Actors' Equity Association, and in 1968 it became Missouri Repertory Theatre. MRT has now grown into a year-round theatre presenting a full slate of plays and operating with a multimillion-dollar budget.

Also in Missouri, the Repertory Theatre of St. Louis grew out of the theatre department at Webster College, where in the early 1960s construction of the technically advanced Loretto-Hilton Center enabled the company to achieve early success. The theatre center houses a highly flexible auditorium with variable seating configurations. In addition, its capacity can be expanded from a minimum of 500 seats to as many as 1,200. Ironically, the theatre's fortunes have proven as variable as its physical plant. The first three seasons, the company performed a complex mix of recognized classics in rotation. They also initiated a series of touring productions and a children's theatre program. This schedule proved exhausting and expensive. A simplified season failed to cover expenses and the company was forced to close for a year in 1970–1971. David Frank was brought in to turn things around, and by 1973 the theatre had produced a surplus. A generous matching-funds grant from the Ford Foundation finally put the company on firm financial ground. An era of artistic unevenness eventually resulted in the disbanding of the resident acting company in 1980, and the theatre was named the Repertory Theatre of St. Louis. Attendance and critical reception continued to fluctuate, but additional income from the small Studio Theatre and experimental Rep's Lab, combined with a redefinition of the artistic director's responsibilities, resulted in a continuation of quality theatre at the Rep.

Perhaps the most famous midwestern regional theatre is the Guthrie Theatre in Minneapolis/St. Paul. Sir Tyrone Guthrie, a well-known director who was disaffected with New York theatre, chose the area in 1960 after a hard-fought competition among several cities seeking to acquire his ambitious venture. An impressive new facility was built to house the company, which has experienced uneven success following its celebrated opening season in 1963. Guthrie's departure after three years left an artistic vacuum that was filled by a succession of directors whose artistic and business talents proved erratic. A new facility, with a planned opening in 2006, will replace the company's oft-renovated original building and provide three theatres in a convenient downtown location.

Funding, facilities, and subscriptions continue to be major issues for nearly all of these organizations, and many fail each year. But as long as the artists need to perform and the communities believe in the benefits of their endeavors, the Midwest will remain a vibrant creative center for the performing arts in the United States.

Sources and Further Reading: Gerald M. Berkowitz, *New Broadways* (1997); William G. B. Carson, *The Theatre on the Frontier* (1965); Tyrone Guthrie, *A New Theatre* (1964); Mary C. Henderson, *Theater in America* (1993); Glenn Hughes, *A History of the American Theatre, 1700–1950* (1951); Margo Jones, *Theatre-in-the-Round* (1951); Noah Miller Ludlow, *Dramatic Life as I Found It* (1880); Steven Samuels, ed., *Theatre Profiles 12* (1966); Sol Smith, *Theatrical Management in the West and South for Thirty Years* (1968); Garff B. Wilson, *Three Hundred Years of American Drama and Theatre*, 2nd ed. (1982); Joseph Wesley Zeigler, *Regional Theatre: The Revolutionary Stage* (1973).

E. James Zeiger
Denver, Colorado

Alternative and Experimental Theatre Groups

Alternative and experimental theatres are definitively fringe phenomena, often elusive but seldom reclusive in the predominately conservative Midwest. Some companies qualify as "experimental" because of their minimalist, avant-garde, or postmodern production values. "Alternative" theatres often produce the dramas of ethnic or gender-based minorities. Artists who work outside the mainstream usually gravitate to cities, where they form creative partnerships; significantly impact the development of new plays; and often cultivate appreciative audiences from ethnic, social, and political strata that may be marginalized by mainstream theatres. Such groups are naturally prone to extremes of success or failure, with some surviving long enough to become cultural institutions.

One such is Chicago's Steppenwolf Theatre Company, founded in 1974. The fully professional company numbers more than thirty artists working in a permanent two-theatre complex. They are known for ensemble works in which established and emerging playwrights are able to develop their scripts in a stimulating creative environment. Some notable examples are Tug Yourgrau's *The Song of Jacob Zulu*; Ntozake Shange, Joseph Shabalala, and Eric Simonson's *Nomathemba*; and Steve Martin's *Picasso at the Lapin Agile*.

Other established experimental theatres in the region include Chicago's Neo-Futurists, the Twin Cities' Frank Theatre and 15 Head, and Milwaukee's Wind-Up Dolls.

In St. Paul, the Penumbra Theatre Company is a year-round African American ensemble. Founded in 1976, it has won recognition for promoting playwrights like August Wilson and for artistic explorations of the human condition from an ethnic perspective. Other theatres include Latino Chicago, Plowshares Theatre Company in Detroit, and Unity Theatre Ensemble in St. Louis.

Sources and Further Reading: Robert Brustein, *Dumbocracy in America* (1994); James Roose-Evans, *Experimental Theatre from Stanislavsky to Peter Brook* (1984); James Schevill, *Break Out! In Search of New Theatrical Environments* (1973).

E. James Zeiger
Denver, Colorado

Chautauquas

Theodore Roosevelt called Chautauqua "the most American thing in America." He might as correctly have said it was the most midwestern thing in Amer-

A late-nineteenth-century traveling Chautauqua troupe, Iowa. Records of the Redpath Chautauqua Collection, Special Collections Department, University of Iowa Libraries, Iowa City, Iowa.

ica. Though the Chautauqua movement began in upstate New York and spread throughout the United States and even abroad, it was most successful in the Midwest, where it drew its largest audiences and developed its most characteristic programs as an annual summertime tent show of culture, education, inspiration, and entertainment. It is also from the Midwest, after an absence of nearly fifty years, that the summertime Chautauqua has returned.

It began as a summer school for Sunday school teachers. In 1874 John Heyl Vincent, a Methodist minister, and Lewis Miller, an Akron, Ohio, businessman, gathered a group of forty teachers on the shores of Lake Chautauqua, New York, for two weeks of study. Within a few years, hundreds of people were going to Chautauqua for courses in history, literature, and science as well as religion. By 1900 they came by the thousands, and a permanent lakeside village grew up to accommodate the crowds. The Chautauqua Literary and Scientific Circle was organized, and correspondence courses were created for those who wanted more and for those who lived afar. The circle sponsored a "book-a-month" club, which by 1900 had a membership of 2.5 million. Most were midwesterners, who knew how very far removed the Corn Belt was from urban, back-East culture.

As early as 1888, lakeside Chautauquas had been established in Ohio, Michigan, and Iowa, and by 1900 there were 200 so-called permanent sites. All that was required was for a town to build an open-air pavilion in a grove or by a lake, hire some lecturers and musicians, and then invite the public. The hunger for culture in rural America was acute, and nowhere was it more intensely felt than in the Midwest.

In 1904 two businessmen, Keith Vawter and Roy Ellison, found a way to satisfy this hunger and make a fortune in the bargain. Employing the talent of the Redpath Lyceum Bureau, they secured contracts from 15 towns to host Chautauquas under large brown tents. Within a decade, the tent, or circuit, Chautauqua was big business. The Redpath Chautauqua alone traveled to 250 communities. Other Chautauqua companies provided standard programs to some 2,400 hamlets across the country. The majority were midwestern villages that offered nothing more than a vacant lot near Main Street and civic-minded business owners willing to put up the cash to guarantee a certain number of season-ticket sales. The Chautauqua company got the profit from all single-ticket sales, ending the season with very hefty profits. The peak year was 1924, when Chautauquas traveled to nearly 10,000 towns and an estimated 40 million people attended.

Well-advertised programs of culture and uplift gave audiences in remote places a taste of learning. The typical Chautauqua week brought audiences music, inspirational oratory, and dramatic readings. Travelogue lectures accompanied by glass slides and, occasionally, motion pictures brought people who had almost no opportunity for travel a glimpse of the larger world. Occasionally a professor of science gave an illustrated talk about the mysteries of nature. There were craft programs and dramatics for children. The idea of a week of refinement and uplift sold the required minimum number of season tickets at from $7 to $10, and sometimes for as little as $2.50 each. The tent just off Main Street served as a billboard and drew even more single-ticket holders who paid from 25 to 50 cents for each event they chose to attend.

Curiosity drew many, but name talent drew even more. For twenty-five years William Jennings Bryan brought in the biggest crowds, going out on the circuit even after becoming U.S. secretary of state. Thousands came year after year to hear his "Prince of Peace" address and were mesmerized by his voice, even if they were not challenged by the content. Dr. Russell H. Conwell delivered his "Acres of Diamonds" speech 6,000 times to demonstrate that real treasure is to be found at home and not in some remote place. He told his audiences: "Get rich. Money is power and power ought to be in the hands of good people." Even at best, the intellectual content of Chautauqua lectures was not high. The music was better and gave rural audiences a taste of symphonic works and even opera. After 1924 Chautauquas began to contain more and more entertainment: Broadway plays, magicians, comedians, impersonators. They also began to be taxed as entertainment, much to the disappointment of the managers who were thereby exposed as the entrepreneurs they were. By the end of the decade, people were finding better entertainment elsewhere, and 1932 was the last season for the circuit Chautauquas.

When the tent Chautauqua returned in the 1980s it was as a public humanities program. In North Dakota, Everett Albers, executive director of the North Dakota Humanities Council, established the Great Plains Chautauqua Society. He persuaded the National Endowment for the Humanities and the state humanities councils in Kansas, Nebraska, and the Dakotas to join together to send scholars out to towns like those served by the old Chautauquas. There they have conducted programs of historical characterization, portraying famous Americans like Thomas Jefferson, W. E. B. Dubois, Mark Twain, Walt Whitman, Henry David Thoreau, Louisa May Alcott, Elizabeth Cady Stanton, Frederick Douglass, and Nathaniel Hawthorne. After speaking in the costume and diction of their characters, scholars take audience questions in character, answering with passages from the letters and diaries they know intimately. These humanities Chautauquas are designed to promote critical thinking about American culture and are offered to the general public free of charge. Within a decade, Chautauquas had returned to Missouri, Illinois, Ohio, Iowa, and Oklahoma. Then, like the old Chautauquas, the revival spread across the nation. Most states now hold humanities Chautauquas on an occasional basis and all have sponsored programs of historical characterization. Audiences for these new programs are large, though nowhere as large as for the old Chautauquas. Nevertheless, in a time of ubiquitous entertainment, the modern circuit Chautauqua offers the public programs of authentic history and careful scholarship.

Sources and Further Reading: Victoria Case and Robert Ormond Case, *We Called It Culture* (1948); Joseph E. Gould, *The Chautauqua Movement* (1961); Theodore Morrison, *Chautauqua: A Center for Education, Religion, and the Arts in America* (1974); Jeffrey Simpson, *Chautauqua: An American Utopia* (1999); John E. Tapia, *Circuit Chautauqua* (1997).

George Frein
University of North Dakota

Comedy Clubs and Groups

The Midwest participated in the national boom of comedy clubs in the mid-1970s and 1980s that grew out of television's *Saturday Night Live* (*SNL*) and its smart brand of humor. With young people alive to comedy, and cable TV capitalizing on the trend, each state in the Midwest opened several comedy clubs. Those that have lasted typically feature stand-up comedians, a nightclub format, or an amateur night. Some clubs offer competing teams of improvisers who take suggestions from the audience. Midwestern college towns are especially likely to have a strong comedy club, with smaller cities like Grand Forks, North Dakota, no exception.

Even before the rise of this comedy phenomenon, the Midwest had supplied the nation with a disproportionate number of important comedians, including Johnny Carson (Corning, Iowa), Phyllis Diller (Lima, Ohio), David Letterman (Indianapolis), Richard Pryor (Peoria, Illinois), Lily Tomlin (Detroit), Robin Williams (Chicago), and Jonathan Winters (Dayton, Ohio) to name only a few. The additional hundreds of comedians who have come out of The Second City in Chicago testify to the fertile ground the Midwest has provided for American comedy.

Of all the comedy institutions in the Midwest, arguably the most influential has been The Second City, because of its tradition of satirical comedy, its high standard of sketch comedy, its working-class appeal, and the sheer number of its alumni who have achieved stardom. Essentially theatre, The Second City has a distinct style and mission. Started by a group of students interested in theatre at the University of Chicago, the Compass Theatre (parent to the Second City) had a unique intellectual commitment. Mike Nichols and Elaine May, prominent Compass actors, could as easily improvise on Nietzsche as on the experience of a first date. However, this incisive comedy was never intended to exclude the working class. David Shepherd, a Compass producer, spoke of founding a political cabaret for the working class. Rooted in this tradition, The Second City aimed at a comedy that was affordable, accessible, and inclusive. Its location in Chicago, known for its vibrant working class and democratic values, nurtured the growth of this experimental theatre. It soon became clear that comedy could thrive there. Against the midwestern traditions of stability, normalcy, and fundamental decency, the comic could create disruptive, deviant, and mischievous entertainment.

The Second City has developed a unique style of comedy that is at once satirical and democratic. By presenting sketches on social and political topics of the day, it engages audiences in their own world. Most evenings after the sketch presentation, the audience participates directly in the show by giving suggestions for the actors to improvise.

Because the sketch itself is developed through improvisation, the actors depend on ensemble work, rather than a star system. The artistic use of improvisation accounts in part for the longevity of The Second City. From its beginning (1959), Paul Sils, one of its founders, brought to rehearsals a wealth of theatre games developed by Viola Spolin, his mother and the foremost expert in improvisation. Sils used the games to generate ideas, form ensembles, and keep work fresh. The high level of ensemble work and the imaginative thinking demanded by the games set the standard still practiced in the sketch preparation. At The Second City, a show develops over a year with a team of actors and a director; by contrast, *SNL* skits are prepared in less than a week.

The spread of The Second City to Toronto, Detroit, Cleveland, and Las Vegas and the contributions of its alumni attest to its influence. A brief list of alums of the Compass Theatre and The Second City would include Dan Aykroyd, Alan Alda, Jane Alexander, Alan Arkin, John Belushi, Shelley Berman, John Candy, Chris Farley, Tina Fey, Shelley Long, Anne Meara, Bill Murray, Gilda Radner, Joan Rivers, Martin Short, and Jerry Stiller. Career highlights of a few alums reflect a common path from The Second City to prominence in television or film.

John Belushi (1949–1982), born in Chicago, acted at The Second City and was cast for *SNL* (1975–1979), where he influenced a generation with his characters in "Samurai Warrior," "Cheeseburger, Cheeseburger," and "Killer Bees." His movies included *Animal House*, *The Blues Brothers*, *Neighbors*, and *Continental Divide*.

Gilda Radner (1946–1989), born in Detroit, was in the first cast of Toronto's Second City and the first cast of *SNL*. Her characters, Roseanne Roseanna Dana, Lisa Loopner, and Baba WaWa, established her comic genius, and her prominence in both casts helped equalize gender roles. Her credits included a Broadway show, *Gilda Live*, and several movies, including *The Woman in Red* and *Witch's Night Out*.

Bill Murray, born in Wilmette, Illinois, in 1950, joined the Second City Chicago company in 1973 and in 1976 took Chevy Chase's place on *SNL*, where his writing earned him an Emmy Award. He became a comic movie star through such films as *Ghostbusters*, *Tootsie*, *Little Shop of Horrors*, *Groundhog Day*, and *Rushmore*.

Betty Thomas, born in St. Louis in 1948, was a waitress and then an actor at The Second City. Thomas went into television, garnering an Emmy for her performance as Officer Lucy Bates in the series *Hill Street Blues*. She became a director for such films as *Dr. Dolittle*, *Private Parts*, and *The Brady Bunch Movie*.

Chris Farley (1964–1997), born in Madison, Wisconsin, graduated from Marquette University and performed at Improv Olympic before joining The Second City in Chicago in 1989. One of his famous Second City characters, Matt Foley, motivational speaker, became a mainstay for him on *SNL* when he joined that show in 1990. He became a comedy star in such movies as *Tommy Boy*, *The Coneheads*, *Billy Madison*, and *Almost Heroes*.

When asked why the Midwest has produced so many successful comedians, Kelly Leonard, a producer from The Second City in Chicago, said, "It's their everyman quality. A midwestern comedian knows how to relate to the average person in the audience, how to engage the audience in comedy." Though comedians may not be known for being well-adjusted themselves, midwestern comedians have used the stability of midwestern society as a background upon which to develop their own unconventional views of reality. Given the success of comedy clubs and The Second City, midwesterners appear to enjoy their disarming comic reflection. Contributions to comedy continue to enrich the spectrum of democracy that the Midwest has cast across the nation.

Sources and Further Reading: Suzanne Lavin, "Women and Comedy in Solo Performance," Ph.D. diss., University of Colorado (1996); Sheldon Patinkin, *The Second City* (2000); Viola Spolin, *Improvisation for the Theatre* (1963); Jeffrey Sweet, *Something Wonderful Right Away*, 3rd ed. (1996).

Suzanne Lavin
Denver, Colorado

Guthrie Theatre

The Guthrie Theatre was founded by Sir Tyrone Guthrie, who had become disenchanted with Broadway theatre's high costs and limited production opportunities. In 1959 he met with Oliver Rea and Peter Zeisler to devise an alternative theatre that would create a resident regional theatre by uniting superior literature and talent with a deserving community. After a spirited competition, Minneapolis/St. Paul was chosen. Money was raised statewide, enabling the completion of a new theatre designed by Ralph Rapson that featured over fourteen hundred seats and an innovative stage developed by designer Tanya Moiseiwitsch. Though the theatre opened in 1963 with twenty-two thousand season subscriptions and impressive advance ticket sales, the Ford Foundation helped cover the first six years of operating losses.

Smaller venues nearby were used for alternative or experimental productions beginning in 1968, when the Other Place began experimenting with new plays, including *Red Cross* by Sam Shepard, *Little Murders* by Jules Feiffer, *Silence and Landscape* by Harold Pinter, and *Winners* by Brian Friel. Guthrie's 1968 main-stage production of *The House of Atreus* brought the theatre renewed honor and attention via a national tour. But after Guthrie and the original production team left the organization, artistic decisions were often questioned, attendance fell sharply, and deficits grew. The Guthrie has survived many financial crises to remain one of the most remarkable success stories of the regional theatre movement, and the new millennium found planning underway for a new, three-theatre complex to be built on the west bank of the Mississippi River.

Sources and Further Reading: Tyrone Guthrie, *A New Theatre* (1964); Stephen Joseph, ed., *Actor and Architect* (1964); Bradley G. Morison and Kay Fliehr, *In Search of an Audience* (1968); Joseph Wesley Zeigler, *Regional Theatre: The Revolutionary Stage* (1973).

E. James Zeiger
Denver, Colorado

Popular Outdoor Drama

Despite a brief history of temporary airdome (open-air) theatres located on vacant lots in many midwestern cities and towns from the 1890s until World War I, the current phase of outdoor drama dates nationally from 1937 with the premiere of Paul Green's *The Lost Colony* in North Carolina. In 1970, one of the most prominent current historical dramas, Green's *Trumpet in the Land*, opened near New Philadelphia, Ohio. Typical of many outdoor productions, both Green plays depict historical events from their locales. The former treats the story of Walter Raleigh on Roanoke Island, and the latter, the oldest outdoor drama in the Midwest region, the story of David Zeisberger, a Moravian missionary who, with a small group of Delaware Indians, established Ohio's first settlement, Schoenbrunn, in the Tuscarawas Valley during the American Revolution.

According to the Institute of Outdoor Drama, as of 2002 there were some two dozen similar outdoor venues in the Midwest, all operating during the summer months. The majority, devoted to the production of Shakespearean plays aimed at a populist audience, can be found in Illinois, Indiana, Iowa, Michigan, Minnesota, Missouri, Nebraska, and Ohio. A few specialize in religious subjects. The more unusual and regionally oriented are those site-specific amphitheatres that specialize in historical subjects by combining drama, dance, music, and spectacle. This phenomenon is a late phase of the American civic pageantry movement prominent from 1910 through the 1920s.

The early life of Abraham Lincoln, for example, can be experienced at Lincoln City, Indiana, where *Young Abe Lincoln* covers Lincoln's life in the Indiana Territory from 1816 to 1830; for the years 1831–1837, Theatre in the Park in New Salem, Illinois, offers *Abraham!*. Other notable dramas in the region include *Blue Jacket* (Xenia, Ohio), based on the struggle for freedom among Shawnee Indians, Ohio settlers, and African slaves during the American Revolution; *Tecumseh* (Chillicothe, Ohio) by Allan Eckert, one of the most prolific authors of historical dramas, the story of the Shawnee Indian leader's lifelong effort to protect his homeland (the Scioto River Valley of southern Ohio) from white settlers; *City of Joseph Pageant* (Nauvoo, Illinois), on early Mormon history; *Fragments of a Dream* (Walnut Grove, Minnesota), based on the life of Laura Ingalls Wilder, whose books about life on the plains in the 1870s inspired the television series *Little House on the Prairie*; and *Beacon on the Rock* (Marquette, Michigan), a musical based on the life of early settlers of the Upper Peninsula.

Predating all permanent outdoor venues in the Midwest, however, and uniquely different in aim from most, is the St. Louis Municipal Outdoor Theatre (known as the MUNY), which opened in 1919 in Forest Park with the intention of presenting comic opera and operetta with local performers on a massive stage and with seating totaling 9,500 (today the capacity is 12,000). After a few years the policy changed to that of importing stars to augment local casts, and today the MUNY is nationally acclaimed for its excellent musical comedy seasons.

Sources and Further Reading: Landis K. Magnuson, *Circle Stock Theater* (1995); Jere C. Mickel, *Footlights on the Prairie* (1974); William L. Slout, *Theatre in a Tent* (1972); Don B. Wilmeth, ed., *Cambridge Guide to American Theatre* (1996).

Don B. Wilmeth
Brown University, Rhode Island

Walking the dog Theater, Inc.

Walking the dog Theater, Inc. of Beloit, Wisconsin is a nonprofit organization, cofounded in 1997, that has given more than two hundred performances and more than forty workshops throughout Australia, New Zealand, Europe, and North America. Walking the dog Theater Inc. draws from music, poetry, architecture, painting, movement, and other moments of human infinite potential to create elaborate inner individual and collective experiences. The company has adapted *Hamlet* and performed other works such as *The Happy Man's Shirt*, *Blue Arches*, *The Holy Man*, and *Walking the dog*. This theatre group especially explores interrelationships between various disciplines such as drama and eurythmy, an art of movement that focuses on an awareness of the whole human being as an instrument of artistic expression. Walking the dog's productions involve live and often original music, storytelling, and movement. Working from the relatively central position of Beloit, this company brings in artists from around the world and takes their performances to far and wide locations, creating a wheel of links and interconnections. Implied in the synthesizing capacity of the Midwest is the ability to draw from both coasts to produce something uniquely midwestern.

Sources and Further Reading: Rudolph Steiner, *Art as Seen in the Light of Mystery Wisdom*, 2nd ed. (1997); Rudolph Steiner, *An Outline of Esoteric* (1997).

Jennifer S. Holmes
Whittier College, California

Zoos, Botanical Gardens, and Natural History Museums

Botanical gardens, natural history museums, and zoological gardens are all about the physicality of location even as they provide documentation, education, and recreation. Collecting specimens—skeletons, skins, eggs, nests, dried plants, minerals, rocks, and fossils, as well as living animals and human artifacts—was a well-established practice reaching far back into human history, but it gained unprecedented popularity in the eighteenth and nineteenth centuries, an era of imperial expansion. Like other federal expeditions throughout the nineteenth century, the Lewis and Clark Expedition of 1803–1806 intensified interest in the natural history of North America even as resettlement of Native Americans made the region accessible to scientific investigation on European terms. Charles Willson Peale's museum in Philadelphia displayed artifacts from the ancient Ohio mounds in the early nineteenth century, while the American Antiquarian Society in Worcester, Massachusetts, reluctantly maintained a mummified body from a cave in Kentucky that reinforced expectations of the unexpected.

New World specimens were originally raw materials sent to Europe for intellectual processing, but after the colonial period, nationalistic naturalists sought to maintain the record of discovery in North America by systematically recording and publicizing the types and distribution of plants and animals along the continuously receding frontier. Settlers following the river valleys and crossing the Great Lakes counterbalanced their sense of discovery by carrying familiar objects with them, including favorite flowers and trees, hoping to tame the indigenous landscape. River towns grew quickly, and with prosperity came aspirations for a cultural life that would be both useful to residents and a demonstration to visitors of the quality of western intellectual and social life. New immigrants also brought community patterns and aspirations from more than one European homeland and they, too, created diverse institutional patterns and priorities as private patronage and civic pride endorsed the study of natural history as part of an emerging regional identity in the middle states.

Botanical gardens provided an important regional expression, often featuring the best of local specimens as well as exotics compatible with local climate conditions. Specialized gardens, long useful for providing and testing herbal remedies and spices, proved important to acclimatizers who sought to relocate potentially profitable as well as ornamental species from around the world. Transplanted Europeans typically carried with them plants that would help them adapt to North America. Leading intellectuals like Thomas Jefferson encouraged naturalists John Bartram and his son William to expand their botanical gardens through exploration and exchange as a way of documenting the variety of native species. Before 1820, Thomas Nuttall, curator of the botanical garden at Harvard University, explored the Mississippi and Missouri River Valleys to collect specimens for educational and medical school purposes. Midwestern residents pursued a familiar pattern of medical school gardens, private herbal gardens, and commercial suppliers. There were few examples of the stylized, picturesque gardens of the eighteenth century, although traces are to be found in places like Henry Shaw's estate near St. Louis. He started at mid-nineteenth century with such a plan in mind, but under guidance from naturalist friends, including William J. Hooker of Kew Gardens near London, his Missouri Botanical Garden became not only a well-known public park but also a research facility whose library was rich in rare reference books and whose herbarium had extensive holdings for serious study. Botanical gardens could be features of urban parks, sometimes established in conjunction with other facilities like the Culture Gardens, part of the complex of institutions for art and science that now constitute University Circle in Cleveland.

As land-grant universities were established following the 1862 and 1890 Morrill Land-Grant Acts, they expanded their agricultural mission in relationship to state experiment stations, they established gardens,

The flight cage at the 1904 St. Louis Louisiana Purchase Exposition. Saint Louis Zoo archives.

more or less ornamental and practical, as part of their responsibility, and by the early twentieth century often worked in conjunction with programs in landscape architecture as well. The research of Wilhelm Miller at the University of Illinois complemented imaginative productions of contemporary architects like Frank Lloyd Wright as the latter built homes and public buildings that reflected the distinctive landscape of the prairies. Miller's experiment station circular, *The Prairie Spirit in Landscape Gardening* (1915), provided a grassland symbol for a discussion that also included ponds, dunes, lake bluffs, ravines, woods, wetlands, and riverbanks of the middle states. His and others' emphasis on native species coincided as well with a country life movement under Theodore Roosevelt that emphasized the moral and aesthetic values of farm and small-town life. This situated outlook was also explicit in the new field of ecology, which was fundamentally formulated in the Midwest. Leaders in the movement included Stephen Forbes of the Illinois Natural History survey, who studied lakes as macroorganisms, and Henry Cowles, who patterned life cycles along the sand dunes on the southern shores of Lake Michigan while a faculty member at the University of Chicago. Frederic and Edith Clements detailed succession patterns on the prairies of the central states in order to document the relationship among plants, climate, and geography, and Victor Shelford at the University of Illinois studied freshwater marine organisms in a similarly ecological way.

Encouraged by the emphasis on naturalistic settings, common plants, and local landscapes that characterized the research and presentation at leading midwestern botanical gardens, many added arboretums around the turn of the century as a way to address issues of forestry and conservation. Not all botanical gardens were university related; Fernwood

Botanical Garden and Nature Preserves in Niles, Michigan, for example, grew from a combination of community and private sponsorship. Conservatories, however, were intended as greenhouses to create an artificial environment for more exotic species from warmer climates. By the twentieth century, botanical institutions made clear their philosophy that a professional garden was art and science, not simply nature.

Natural history collections available to the general public superseded generations of private "cabinets" held by wealthy individuals and related indirectly to a broader audience whose tastes were framed by a range of activities from lyceum lecturers to passing animal shows. Just as major coastal cities had societies of naturalists, so too did Cleveland, Cincinnati, St. Louis, Chicago, and Milwaukee as they grew into metropolitan areas. An early effort was the small collection created by Charles Alexander Lesueur in the utopian community of New Harmony, Indiana, intended as a resource for teaching and research for those who were part of William Maclure's "boatload of knowledge." Early ventures in aspiring towns like Flint, Michigan, and Indianapolis were short-lived, unable to rely on a stable community of local naturalists. Cincinnati, the "Queen City of the West," made the most sustained antebellum efforts through its Western Academy of Sciences, clearly an effort to follow the Philadelphia Academy of Natural Sciences, but limited financial resources and expertise left little trace of them. The Academy of Science of St. Louis, in the 1850s and beyond, had somewhat greater success with active amateur naturalists like George Engelmann, working at a critical junction through which much western exploration took place. Its natural history collection was destroyed by fire in 1869, an unfortunate precursor to the Chicago Academy's loss in 1871. The academies of science in Davenport, Iowa; Madison, Wisconsin; St.

Paul; and elsewhere also published reports on local archaeology, botany, geology, and paleontology in the later nineteenth century. The enthusiasm for building collections by state and local societies proved easier to initiate than sustain, and most required subsidies. The alternative was finding a major patron, like Marshall Field, whose sponsorship underwrote a new natural history museum for Chicago (not affiliated with that of the local Chicago Academy of Sciences) based on various collections made available after the World's Columbian Exposition in 1893. Thus wealthy patrons in Chicago provided the resources that made the Field Columbian Museum into a research facility (affiliated in some fields with the University of Chicago), a public exhibition hall, and an educational center. Its model was the American Museum of Natural History, which it at first surpassed in size. Enthusiasm for natural history among the people of Milwaukee, initiated by Increase A. Lapham, soon had competition from a German society whose combined collections ultimately became the Milwaukee Public Museum (housed with a public library); in many instances, too, historical societies housed natural history (and especially anthropology and archaeology) artifacts. By the 1880s, cities as well as states became partners in such organizations, which had often started as voluntary associations.

As science was regularized into the college curriculum, colleges and universities established study collections for their students, typically natural history objects that reflected the particular interests and expertise of the faculty alongside standardized specimens and teaching aids from museum suppliers. The myriad small colleges across the Midwest emulated the pattern at eastern predecessors, while the expanding state universities dealt with much larger holdings, often gathered in conjunction with state natural history surveys and with the enthusiastic support of a university president interested in science. One of the best examples is the University of Nebraska in Lincoln, opened in 1871, where consistent support from faculty and students sustained a high level of research publication and public exhibition.

Traveling and established menageries anticipated the formulation of zoological parks (or gardens) in North America after the Civil War. Cincinnati's civic leaders established the Cincinnati Zoo in 1875, a year after the establishment of the widely promoted Philadelphia Zoo. Perhaps because zoos were a significant part of the "middle scape," providing opportunities for the middle classes with expanding leisure time to see and be seen, they were immediately popular. An accelerating number of zoos established a landscape safe for human observers, showing lions and tigers from faraway places and wolves and bears from a wilderness quickly receding from growing cities. Cincinnatians, many of them German immigrants

committed to liberal education, supported this new facility with their attendance. To purchase significant displays, however, zoo directors in Cincinnati, St. Louis, and elsewhere used publicity ("elephant campaigns") to raise public contributions. Patrons thus joined civic leaders and a general public in this particularly popular scientific exhibition. Zoos were founded across the country between 1875 and 1940, with about a third of them in the Midwest.

Typically zoos were established on city sites like Lincoln Park in Chicago, Como Park in St. Paul, and Washington Park in Milwaukee. In the twentieth century, as the new open-air landscaping modeled on Hamburg's Tierpark required more acreage, city zoos moved or had competitors built in suburbs like Brookfield, Illinois, and Apple Valley, Minnesota. These new and larger facilities often introduced small "petting zoos" where children far removed from rural life could get up close to farm livestock. Although exotic African, Asian, and Australian animals remained standard features, zoos moved away from an emphasis on domesticated exoticism and began to establish larger groups with fewer species, and with more North American species.

In the twentieth century, zoos began to undertake breeding programs, sometimes focused on rare breeds nearing extinction but equally often using their facilities to concentrate on local endangered species. No curator wanted the dubious distinction of the Cincinnati Zoo, where the last known living passenger pigeon died in 1914, and staff began to promote their facilities as a place of conservation. Expeditions to obtain rare wild animals were largely replaced by international exchanges among zoos. A widespread nature-study curriculum in pre-high school grades in the early twentieth century drew attention to local flora and fauna through the use of field trips. Adults participated in Audubon, wildflower, and preservation societies that encouraged the development of nature preserves in familiar locations—dunes, wetlands, original prairie, or forest bluffs—or in some fragile habitat of particular species. Their work and sensibility reflected a pattern of engagement with nature in the Midwest region even as a national nature preserve effort created new sites across the country. By the last half of the twentieth century, too, special projects focused on particular species, like the International Crane Foundation in Baraboo, Wisconsin; the International Wolf Center in Ely, Minnesota; and the Raptor Center in St. Paul.

Sources and Further Reading: John Grassy and Tom Powers, *Audubon Guide to the National Wildlife Refuges: Northern Midwest* (2000); Joel B. Hagen, *An Entangled Bank* (1992); Elizabeth A. Hanson, *Animal Attractions* (2002); Walter Hendrickson, "Science and Culture in the American West," *Isis* 64 (1973); R. J. Hoage and William A. Deiss, eds., *New*

Worlds, New Animals (1996); Therese O'Malley and Marc Treib, eds., *Regional Garden Design in the United States* (1995); Joel Orosz, *Curators and Culture* (1990); Ronald Rainger, Keith R. Benson, and Jane Maienschein, eds., *The American Development of Biology* (1988); Michael S. Shapiro, ed., *The Museum: A Reference Guide* (1990); Ronald C. Tobey, *Saving the Prairies* (1981).

Sally Gregory Kohlstedt
University of Minnesota

Cleveland Cultural Gardens

The Cleveland Cultural Gardens are a unique group of nationality gardens running through Rockefeller Park from Superior Avenue to St. Clair Avenue along Martin Luther King, Jr. Boulevard. Aiming to link and celebrate Cleveland's diverse ethnic populations and to promote global peace and unity, the garden chain extends over a mile and includes landscaped grounds, memorials, and portrait busts dedicated to the city's Czech, German, Greek, Hungarian, Irish, Italian, Jewish, Lithuanian, Polish, Russian, Ukrainian, and Yugoslavian citizens, among others. Two gardens, the Shakespeare Garden (1916) and the Hebrew Garden (1926), preceded the rapid succession of gardens developed during the 1930s, whose building was aided by federal funds provided by the New Deal's Works Progress Administration. An estimated $1,250,000 was expended from the 1930s to the 1950s to develop the bridges, stone walls, pathways, statuary, plaques, and elaborate plantings that make up the gardens. Following a 1939 dedication ceremony, attended by thirty-five thousand people, the gardens were declared a "living embroidery" of the ethnic heritage of Cleveland. By the mid-1950s, they featured more than fifty statues, busts, and plaques of figures including Marie Curie (in the Polish Garden), Antonín Dvořák (Czech Garden), Friedrich von Schiller (German Garden), Chaim Nachman Bialik (Hebrew Garden), and Imre Madách (Hungarian Garden). Recently refurbished and partially conserved, the Cultural Gardens remain a beautifully landscaped urban park frequented by picnickers and bicyclists. Each summer the One World Parade celebrates Cleveland's rich history of ethnic diversity, and participants march through the garden chain in traditional costumes.

Sources and Further Reading: Clara Lederer, *Their Paths Are Peace* (1954); Brian Pfeiffer, "Cleveland Culture Gardens, Story 1," Cleveland Public Radio, WCPN (22 Nov. 2002).

Keith Sorensen
Cleveland

Field Museum

A world-class museum of natural history and anthropology in Chicago, the Field Museum's mission is to collect, preserve, and exhibit specimens; to perform collections-based research; and to provide public education. With a one-million-dollar gift from retail magnate Marshall Field, a group of Chicago business leaders and philanthropists established the museum in 1893. A colleague inspired Field's generosity, in part, by arguing that the museum would serve as a unique educational resource for the Midwest. Initially intended as a memorial of the 1893 World's Columbian Exposition, the nucleus of its disparate collections was obtained from exposition exhibits. By 1905 its focus had narrowed to anthropology, botany, geology, and zoology. Growth was slow and fraught with problems while the museum occupied temporary quarters in Jackson Park. In 1921, after relocation to a permanent home at the south end of Grant Park, the museum entered a decade characterized by dramatic growth; higher attendance; and extravagant, far-flung collecting expeditions to Mesopotamia, Malaysia, Patagonia, and elsewhere. Activity slowed during the Depression, a time of low spending and high attendance. Following World War II, the museum expanded its staff, revised many of its exhibits, and inaugurated a period of intensified scientific activity that continues to the present. The museum's research library and its collection of approximately twenty-one million specimens constitute one of the world's premiere centers for systematic biology and anthropology studies. *Fieldiana*, the museum's scientific journal, publishes original research on these collections. The museum captured international attention with the 1997 acquisition of Sue, the world's most famous dinosaur.

Sources and Further Reading: Field Columbian Museum, *An Historical and Descriptive Account of the Field Columbian Museum* (1894); Logan Ward, *An Explorer's Guide to the Field Museum* (1998).

Paul Brinkman
University of Minnesota

International Crane Foundation

The International Crane Foundation (ICF) is a private, nonprofit organization in Baraboo, Wisconsin, devoted to the study and preservation of cranes. Founded in 1973 by Cornell University biologists George Archibald and Ron Sauey, the ICF acts as a crane research and breeding facility and as a public educator and advocate on behalf of cranes and their habitats. It is supported through grants, individual memberships, and visitor fees.

The ICF's preservation efforts are centered around a breeding program and periodic reintroduction of cranes into the wild. The population of approximately 110 cranes has enabled reintroductions in twenty-two countries under the auspices of the ICF or proxy organizations. The ICF is a founding member of the Whooping Crane Eastern Partnership, which since 2001 has used ultralight airplanes to lead young cranes along a migratory route from Wisconsin to Florida. The foundation also supports crane research by making its facilities available to conservationists and biologists and by underwriting conferences and publications. As the only institution of its kind devoted specifically to cranes, it serves as a locus for those with professional interests in the study of cranes.

Notwithstanding that focus, the ICF's work and advocacy extend to broader conservation issues. Its educational outreach programs stress the relationships among wildlife, habitat, and humans. While these programs are local to the upper Midwest, the foundation's relationships with other conservation societies in the United States and abroad, its role as a provider of advanced professional training, and the wide-ranging nature of its charges give it a legitimately global sphere of influence.

Sources and Further Reading: Barbara Katz, *So Cranes May Dance* (1993); Peter Matthiessen, *Birds of Heaven* (2001); Gretchen Schoff, *Reflections: The Story of Cranes*, ed. David H. Thompson (1991).

Matthew Lavine
University of Wisconsin–Madison

Lincoln Park Zoo

Established in 1868, Chicago's Lincoln Park Zoo is the oldest zoological garden in the Midwest. After unexpectedly receiving two swans from New York's Central Park Menagerie, the commissioners of Lincoln Park reluctantly authorized the creation of a small zoo that eventually encompassed thirty-five acres of the lakefront park. By the early twentieth century, the zoo was one of Chicago's most popular attractions, drawing tens of thousands of visitors every weekend. Like many midwestern zoos, Lincoln Park unabashedly favored recreation and entertainment over science and education, catering to a local family audience and welcoming all visitors free of charge.

After World War II, the zoo's national profile increased dramatically. In 1949 director Marlin Perkins inaugurated the nation's first zoo-based television program, *Zoo Parade*, often broadcasting live from Lincoln Park and introducing the zoo's biggest "celebrities," like Bushman the gorilla, to millions of viewers nationwide. Through the 1960s and 1970s, the zoo continued to enjoy both professional and popular acclaim, especially for its unusual Farm-in-the-Zoo, an urban re-creation of a midwestern farm. In 1995 the city ceded control of the zoo to the Lincoln Park Zoological Society, a nonprofit organization originally founded in 1959 to raise funds for the zoo's capital projects. While such privatization of zoos is increasingly common, the continuation of Lincoln Park's longstanding policy of free admission has distinguished it as one of only a handful of free American zoos and has guaranteed its perennial popularity—with some three million visitors annually in the early twenty-first century.

Sources and Further Reading: Marlin Perkins, *My Wild Kingdom* (1982); Mark Rosenthal, Carol Tauber, and Edward Uhlir, *The Ark in the Park* (2003).

Jeffrey Hyson
Saint Joseph's University, Pennsylvania

Missouri Botanical Garden

The Missouri Botanical Garden in St. Louis was the private vision of an English immigrant from Sheffield, David Henry Shaw, who established and sustained a landscape that was originally modeled on eighteenth-century picturesque estates. With advice from William Jackson Hooker of Kew Gardens, near London, Shaw gradually developed a botanical garden on his country estate in collaboration with local naturalist and physician George Engelmann. After 1859 the incorporated Missouri Botanical Garden was managed by a board of trustees and became a place for public recreation. Simultaneously, the dried specimens collection and growing library led to informal ties to small but aspiring Washington University in St. Louis. In 1885 Shaw endowed a chair in botany at the university, thus emphasizing the research role of the Missouri Botanical Garden. Under William Trelease, a graduate of Harvard who had studied at Harvard Herbarium with leading North American botanist Asa Gray and was director from 1889 to 1912, the garden attained an international reputation. Nineteenth-century visitors to the Midwest—like English author Charles Kingsley, botanist Joseph Hooker, and American novelist Mark Twain—all described this natural wonder as the "Gateway to the West."

George Moore, director from 1912 to 1953, developed the garden for local visitors. Struggling during the Depression and World War II, the botanical garden survived, but staff found it difficult to maintain both the public gardens and the research collections. Since 1972, and under the direction of Peter Raven, the garden has expanded its research considerably and has also developed extensive walkways, a dramatic conservatory, and such specialized areas as a Japanese garden. At the beginning of the twenty-first century, the extensive herbarium and library are housed in the new Monsanto Center, and the staff are engaged in a significant number of international research projects involving the digitization of data and conservation programs.

Sources and Further Reading: William Barnaby Faherty, *A Gift to Glory In: The First Hundred Years of the Missouri Botanical Garden (1859–1959)* (1989); Kim Kleenman, "The Museum in the Garden: Research, Education, and Display at the Missouri Botanical Garden," Ph.D. diss., Union Institute (1997).

Sally Gregory Kohlstedt
University of Minnesota

Religion

SECTION EDITOR
Peter W. Williams

Section Contents

Overview

The first major factor in accounting for the development of religion in the Midwest is the region's relatively recent settlement by European Americans. Unlike that of the eastern seaboard and the southwestern states, the European presence in the Midwest during the age of colonization (the seventeenth and eighteenth centuries) was minimal. The major presence was French, confined largely to the Detroit area and the Mississippi Valley and never large enough in numbers or power to result in a permanent contribution to the region's religious configuration. Most especially, the absence of a powerful colonial presence was responsible for the corresponding absence of an "establishment of religion"—that is, an "established church" economically supported by a government that demanded compulsory attendance of the populace and that in turn expected political support from religious leaders. Anticipating the First Amendment to the U.S. Constitution, the first article of the Northwest Ordinance of 1787 provided that "No person, demeaning himself in a peaceable and orderly manner, shall ever be molested on account of his mode of worship or religious sentiments, in the said territory."

Unlike Puritans in New England, Anglicans in much of the South, Quakers in Pennsylvania, Spanish Catholics in the Southwest, and French Catholics in Quebec, no single religious group ever enjoyed even theoretical hegemony in the region. The result was something of a religious *tabula rasa*, a blank slate on which religious identity and practice would have to be constructed from scratch by a plethora of players who from the beginning occupied as close to a level playing field as had ever been seen in the European American experience.

In addition, the rapid dispossession of the Native American peoples of their lands ensured that their religions, which were inseparable from their broader cultures, would follow them into exile. In a few cases, such as the shamanic prophecies of Tecumseh's brother Tenskwatawa, Native American religion took on some new content. Such activities, however, proved brief in duration as American Indians yielded to the European American advance, and nothing that could be called an enduring new religion, such as the Peyote cult of the West or the Gaiwi'io of upstate New York, arose in the middle part of the new nation. The region's religious future was closely linked to its political, economic, and cultural future, which lay in the hands of people of European birth or ancestry.

The second decisive factor in the making of the region's religious landscape was, accordingly, immigration from Europe and migration from other parts of the United States. Successive waves of newcomers entering the region from the widest variety of cultural backgrounds ensured that the new region would be simultaneously religiously intense and diverse. Although the Midwest is often depicted as blandly homogeneous, its religious history suggests a very different characterization. By following the pattern of immigration, we can easily discern the growth of a strikingly diverse pattern of religious settlement that continued to change as newcomers and relatively established settlers were continually forced to come to terms with one another.

French Catholics were the first to establish themselves, but their presence was not to prove very significant in the long run. Not surprisingly, it is in areas that still bear French names, such as Detroit's St. Anne Catholic parish, where remnants of their early settlement can be found. Early French clergy certainly played an important role in the establishment of the region's religious and educational institutions: Père

The Islamic Center of Greater Toledo. © Gail Meese/Meese Photo Research.

Jacques Marquette accompanied Louis Joliet down the Mississippi; Gabriel Richard helped establish what would become the University of Michigan and himself became that territory's first delegate to Congress; and Edward Sorin, CSC (Congregatio Sanctæ Crucis; Congregation of the Holy Cross), founded what is now the region's (and perhaps the nation's) premier Catholic institution of higher learning—the University of Notre Dame in South Bend, Indiana. Nevertheless, the French presence never attained the critical mass necessary to ensure a more lasting influence. As Irish and German Catholics began to enter the region in ever-increasing numbers, their dominance over regional Catholic life inevitably followed. (Notre Dame's remarkable football squads, for example, have never been known as "The Fighting Frenchmen.")

As French influence north of the Ohio River waned with the arrival of thousands of citizens of the new United States, that of their long-time rivals, the British, increased, even though their presence was now manifested by those arriving directly from New rather than old England. As English and Scottish settlers left the Atlantic states, they brought with them their religious cultures, which are still visible in the Congregational churches dotting the northern sector of the region, including that part of Ohio named for its Connecticut founder, Moses Cleaveland, and those of the Presbyterians, more usually found farther south along the lines of settlement from Pennsylvania and Virginia. Other denominations of British origin soon followed; as the saying had it, the Baptists came on foot, the Methodists on horseback, and the Episcopalians in parlor cars.

The competition from popular denominations was intense as the Methodists, for example, applied their highly effective tactic of commissioning circuit riders to spread the word among scattered settlers not yet ready to support a settled clergy. In response, the more elite Congregationalists and Presbyterians devised their Plan of Union, which forbade competition and encouraged cooperation between these sister denominations of Calvinist origin. Within a short time following the Civil War, however, all these denominations had become sufficiently established to erect great brick or stone houses of worship in the medieval fashion along the grand boulevards of the larger cities—Chicago's LaSalle, and Detroit's Woodward and Cleveland's Euclid Avenues—as well as on the innumerable Church Streets of smaller towns.

The "new immigration" that began in the middle of the nineteenth century and lasted until World War I disrupted transoceanic crossings brought still more religious variety to the region. The upper Midwest, though settled by considerable numbers of Catholics and Methodists, rapidly became a prime site for Scan-

dinavian relocation. These Oles and Lenas, now the subject of good-humored nostalgia on Garrison Keillor's *Prairie Home Companion*, were overwhelmingly Lutheran, as were large numbers of German speakers who populated the "German triangle" delimited by Cincinnati, St. Louis, and Milwaukee. Although united by religion, these Lutherans were nevertheless divided by language and other cultural attributes, and the Lutheranism of the era between the Civil War and World War I was fragmented into countless larger or smaller groups based on various combinations of region, ethnicity, and theology. Even as these differences eroded and most of the region's Lutherans, like their counterparts elsewhere in the nation, aggregated into three major groupings—the Evangelical Lutheran Church in America (ELCA) and the smaller, more conservative Missouri and Wisconsin Synods—such states as Wisconsin, Minnesota, Iowa, Missouri, and the Dakotas retained their claim to be the Lutheran "heartland" of the New World.

Complicated and potentially conflict-inducing juxtapositions of religion and ethnicity were also characteristic of three other major religious traditions whose numbers were greatly expanded by the ongoing immigration from southern, central, and eastern Europe as well as from Scandinavia. The distinctive domes of Eastern Orthodox churches began to mark settlements of Greeks, Ukrainians, Russians, Serbs, and others who came attracted by opportunities for brutal but relatively remunerative work in the stockyards, factories, and mines of Great Lakes cities and their environs. Forced at first to worship at whatever Orthodox church might be at hand, these newcomers soon split into ethnically homogeneous parishes as clergy arrived and church buildings could be financed. Irish hegemony in the Catholic community was now challenged by a feisty German Catholic presence as well as by new arrivals from what are now the independent nations of Poland, Hungary, Slovakia, Slovenia, and Lithuania. Demands for equality of representation in the ranks of the clergy and the episcopate and the erection of ethnic parishes and even dioceses were met with reluctantly by the Vatican, and occasionally led to actual schism among the Poles. By the time of World War I, however, a new policy of assimilation and the uniform use of English, prompted by both external social pressures and an internal drive toward centralization of authority, put an effective quietus on such demands for ethnic pluralism within a common framework of belief and worship.

Jews also found opportunity in the Midwest. Cincinnati was a major point of Jewish settlement from early in the nineteenth century, and that community's aspiring merchants and professionals blended in easily with their German-speaking gentile counterparts. The city on the Ohio River later became the national focus of the Reform movement within Judaism, as Bavarian immigrant Isaac Mayer Wise utilized his magnificent Moorish-Gothic temple on Plum Street as a base for the beginnings of an educational and organizational infrastructure for his assimilation-minded compatriots. The new immigration would later bring many Jews of other backgrounds—Yiddish-speaking Orthodox and antireligious political radicals—to the region, but never in the way that New York City continued to attract and retain these "unwashed" upon whom their by-now English-speaking Reform-minded coreligionists looked with deep ambivalence. Major Jewish communities arose in virtually all of the region's great (and most of its smaller) cities, and department stores with Jewish names such as Lazarus appeared, reflecting the origins of the region's Jewry more in the commerce-minded German immigrants of the mid-nineteenth century than in their alternately more radical- and tradition-minded coreligionists of a later era. The tenor of midwestern Judaism has generally been unobtrusive and assimilation minded, seldom productive of the distinctive, vibrant, and sometimes raucous subcultures associated with New York.

What was perhaps the greatest of the social upheavals of the twentieth century brought throngs of African American sharecroppers and small-town dwellers from the South to the urban centers of the Midwest in vast numbers, originally to replace the young white men who left industrial jobs to serve in World War I. These migrants brought with them the distinctive brands of evangelical Protestantism that had nurtured them in the South—Methodist, Baptist, and "sanctified" (Holiness and Pentecostal) churches. The latter were usually led by minimally educated men and occasionally by women who felt called by the Holy Spirit to rent a storefront to conduct highly emotive and performative services on Sundays while holding day jobs during the week. Some, such as Jesse Jackson, followed the paths of fellow black Baptists elsewhere—Martin Luther King, Jr., in the South, Adam Clayton Powell, Jr., in Harlem—by linking the prophetic teachings of the Hebrew and Christian Bibles to contemporary political and social crises.

Although most of these ventures remained within the broad parameters of traditional Christianity, other African Americans, alienated by the associations of Christianity with European American culture, stepped beyond Christian boundaries to invoke the name of Allah, finding Islam a religious tradition more clearly aligned with people of color. The careers of the early leaders of the Nation of Islam—W.D. Fard, who laid the seeds of the movement while selling silk goods door-to-door in 1930s Detroit; Elijah Muhammad (né Poole), his successor, who helped the movement grow

to national dimensions; and the young Malcolm X (known early on as "Detroit Red," even though he actually hailed from the Lansing area)—all had their roots in the Great Lakes region even as these leaders extended the movement to New York, Boston, and beyond.

The impulse for social change was by no means confined to minority religious communities. The organized movement to abolish slavery took shape in Ohio in the 1830s as former students of Cincinnati's Lane Seminary relocated to Oberlin and fanned out from there, making converts to the cause and organizing antislavery societies in towns throughout the region. The reform impulse was also manifest in the utopian and communitarian societies that flourished in the nineteenth-century Midwest: Ohio's Shaker communities and Zoar, Indiana's New Harmony, and Iowa's Amana. The Seventh-day Adventists brought health and dietary reform as they resettled from New England to Battle Creek, Michigan. The crusade against the evils of alcohol grew to national proportions through the influence of two Ohio-founded organizations, the Anti-Saloon League and the Women's Christian Temperance Union. The "Social Gospel" was preached by Washington Gladden in Columbus and implemented by Samuel "Golden Rule" Jones in Toledo. In the twentieth century, Reinhold Niebuhr cut his ethical teeth as pastor of a German parish in Detroit, where he gained first-hand knowledge of big-city issues of race and labor that would inform his later theological reflections. Charles Coughlin, Detroit's "radio priest" of the 1930s, became the voice of urban populism from his Royal Oak pulpit until he strayed into the unacceptable territory of anti-Semitism.

Religious conservatism has also flourished in the Midwest. In the 1830s, Lyman Beecher, the president of Lane Seminary who saw most of his student body desert the institution over the slavery issue, led revivals and preached fervently against the Catholic menace as he sought to gain evangelical support for his venture in clerical education. Later in the nineteenth century, Chicago became a national center of revivalism, as Dwight L. Moody and, later, Billy Sunday gained national reputations for their preaching—and, in Sunday's case, antimodernist diatribes. Although Billy Graham was originally from the South, the Baptist revivalist grew into a national figure based in Minneapolis, with a research center in his name at Wheaton College near Chicago. In addition, considerable numbers of rank-and-file Protestants in the region's mainline denominations—Baptists, Congregationalists, Disciples of Christ, Lutherans, Methodists, Presbyterians—self-identified as evangelicals even as their national leadership began to shift in a more liberal direction in the 1960s. Indiana's Quakers also shaped an evangelical identity for themselves during the nineteenth century as their Philadelphia counterparts became more and more identified with peace and reform.

During the later twentieth century, the religious identity of the region grew even more diverse as demographic patterns continued to change. Appalachians who had migrated to the region's industrial centers during World War II continued to resettle after the war, bringing countless Baptist, Holiness, and Pentecostal churches to Ohio, Indiana, and other states where jobs and kinfolk who had preceded them in their northward trek awaited. The new popularity of evangelicalism among the middle classes, which began to take shape during the 1970s, resulted in the erection of large churches, even megachurches, along the region's main transportation arteries such as the interstate beltways that encircle its major cities.

The Immigration Act of 1965 (also called the Hart-Cellar Act) triggered a very different migration pattern by smoothing the path for South Asians in particular to come to the United States. The result has been, in the Midwest as elsewhere, a proliferation of newcomers from the Indian subcontinent, including many highly educated professionals as well as motel proprietors seeking opportunity for their children. The result, often visible alongside the evangelical megachurches on the interstates, has been a blossoming of Hindu temples and Islamic mosques, which have married Asian traditions with New World necessities such as educational and cultural programs that had never been needed in societies permeated by these traditions.

The Midwest, in short, has over two centuries come to host—and, occasionally, give rise to—a panoply of religious communities representative of those of the entire nation. The difference lies in their patterns of distribution and subsequent regional influence, which correlate with regional configurations of ethnicity, education, and even health care. No single group, in short, religious or ethnic, has ever concentrated enough power to exert regional or even subregional hegemony in its influence on public policy and culture. Lutherans—the closest to a distinctive regional group—have been balanced by Catholics and Methodists and have been spread out over extensive but thinly populated territory. Catholics and Methodists, major players throughout much of the region, have lacked the focus that overwhelming Irish ethnicity has given Catholics in the Northeast and which the reinforcement of other purveyors of a regional evangelical culture has lent Methodists in the South. To be sure, particular groups do exist in great concentrations and exert great influence on the "micro" level, including the Dutch Reformed in the Grand Rapids, Michigan, and Pella, Iowa, areas; the

Amish in Holmes County and Welsh Presbyterians in Gallia County, Ohio; and Polish Catholics in Hamtramck, Michigan. Although such concentrations may play a major role in, say, who represents Grand Rapids in the U.S. House of Representatives, the Grand Rapids Dutch and the Poles of Hamtramck may well offset each other in races for Michigan's Senate seats and governorship.

On the whole, the Midwest has set a good national example of how religious diversity may exist in an atmosphere of reasonable harmony. Counterexamples, of course, can be readily cited, such as the dominance of the Ku Klux Klan in 1920s Indiana politics, but the short-lived nature of this phenomenon—as well, perhaps, as Indiana's atypically southern brand of culture—may make this a rule-illustrating exception. Chicago, where Irish Catholicism has played a major role in creating a civic ethos, has also provided a base for the ecumenically minded Italian American Joseph Cardinal Bernardin as well as for Baptist activist Jesse Jackson. The city's hosting of the path-breakingly ecumenical World's Parliament of Religions in 1893 as well as its current configuration of national-class theological seminaries linked collegially in a local consortium are also excellent examples of a regional inclination toward pragmatic acceptance of diversity and even, at times, an ability to turn its presence to mutual advantage.

Sources and Further Reading: Philip Barlow and Mark Silk, eds., *Religion and Public Life in the Midwest: Heartland as Common Denominator* (2004); Thomas D. Hamm, *The Transformation of American Quakerism* (1988); James W. Lewis, *The Protestant Experience in Gary, Indiana, 1906–1975* (1992); Robert F. Martin, *Hero of the Heartland* (2002); John T. McGreevey, *Parish Boundaries* (1996); Tetsuo Scott Miyakawa, *Protestants and Pioneers* (1964); L. C. Rudolph, *Hoosier Zion* (1963); Jonathan D. Sarna and Nancy H. Klein, *The Jews of Cincinnati* (1989); Charles Shanabruch, *Chicago's Catholics: The Evolution of an American Identity* (1981); Leslie Woodcock Tentler, *Seasons of Grace* (1990); Peter W. Williams, *Houses of God* (1997).

Peter Williams
Miami University, Oxford, Ohio

Regional Profiles

Chicago

In 1673, at the end of the prairie, Père Jacques Marquette, SJ, and Louis Jolliet crossed a swampy lowland the Potawatomi called *Checagou*, or "skunk," in reference to the wild garlic growing in marshlands along

Lake Michigan. Though the great prairie is long gone, its influence is found throughout Chicago from its style of architecture to its vacant lots, still called prairies. Jean Baptist Point du Sable, a French speaker from Santo Domingo, built the first permanent dwelling in 1779, and the U.S. Army established Fort Dearborn in 1803. The state of Illinois incorporated the town of Chicago in 1833 and the city in 1837.

Chicago has since grown into the hub of the Midwest, known for its beef, pork bellies, and big shoulders. Chicago is also a crossroads for religions spilling out of traditional forms and into public life. Chicago religion, intra- or nondenominational, is about interfaith dialogue, the communion of communions. The World's Parliament of Religions, waves of urban revivals, a strong Catholic presence, and synergy among schools of religion support this crossroads claim. Religion in Chicago has been characterized by a lively pluralism.

Liberal Protestants called the World's Parliament of Religions into being for seventeen days at the World's Columbian Exposition in 1893, drawing thousands from around the world. The exposition, itself an extraordinary event, showcased a new relationship between space and electricity, embodied in the great Ferris wheel on the Midway, Chicago's answer to the Eiffel Tower in Paris. University of Wisconsin professor Frederick Jackson Turner presented his frontier theory of American history. Newspaper reports were distributed widely; one headline reporting on the parliament featured Swami Vivekananda introducing Hinduism and yoga to the West. While interfaith dialogue had begun, liberal Protestant assumptions were more present than were representatives of the world's religions. Only one Muslim attended and he was a convert to Islam.

British reporter and moral reformer William T. Stead arrived in Jackson Park the day after the fair closed. But he was able to see, in the fine temporary palaces, the possibility of what the city might become, so he gathered a number of people and asked what they would say "if Christ came to Chicago." Jane Addams attended, though she already had an answer in Hull-House (1889), one of the first settlement houses in the United States. Dwight L. Moody, the great urban revivalist, had been answering the question since his arrival in 1856. He organized Sunday schools, the Young Men's Christian Association, and huge evangelical gatherings. Billy Sunday, a baseball player converted at the Pacific Garden Mission, wrote another Chicago chapter in the history of American revivalism. In the 1920s, evangelist Paul Rader's Chicago Gospel Tabernacle reached out over radio waves. Billy Graham, educated at Wheaton College and known for passionate oratory and honest bookkeep-

ing, built a worldwide mission. Nondenominational evangelism flows through the massive Willow Creek Community Church, which began in an old movie theatre, using 1970s music for its worship; Willow Creek has since expanded to 155 acres in South Barrington where a reported seventeen thousand plus attend weekend services.

Episcopalians met in Chicago in 1886, approving what became known as the Chicago-Lambeth Quadrilateral, an approach to Christian unity based on four essentials: scriptures, creeds, sacraments, and the historic episcopate. These four essentials representing Christian teaching, faith, worship, and authority are considered to be the foundations of the visible church. Episcopalians signed an accord with Chicago Catholics in 1986. Mutual association is typical of the city. One of Abraham Lincoln's famous attempts to discern the will of God in the Civil War can be found in his September 13, 1862, reply to a memorial from "Chicago Christians of All Denominations," asking the president to issue a proclamation of emancipation.

The headquarters of the Evangelical Lutheran Church in America is in Chicago; that of the Women's Christian Temperance Union (WCTU), in Evanston. During Prohibition in the 1920s the WCTU had its hands full with "Bugs" Moran and Al "Scarface" Capone (who used the "Gangsters Bible," a parchment-paged tenth-century Argos lectionary, as an oath book).

The Nation of Islam, led by Minister Louis Farrakhan, has its headquarters at Mosque Maryam (once a Greek Orthodox church) on Chicago's South Side. Its most famous convert, Muhammad Ali (né Cassius Clay), kept a mansion in Kenwood seventeen blocks from the mosque. Founded by W. D. Fard, the organization was moved in 1934 from Detroit to Chicago by Elijah Muhammad. The "indigenous" Muslims of the Nation of Islam are by far the largest group of Muslims in Chicagoland.

In 1971, the Reverend Jesse Jackson founded Operation PUSH (People United to Save Humanity). It has developed into the Rainbow/PUSH Coalition, which seeks to realize the American Dream for "workers, women and people of color" by registering voters, mediating labor disputes, and lobbying for affirmative action. The U.S. offices of the Baha'í faith are in Wilmette.

Though Protestants played a leading role, Chicago's story is distinctively ethnic, immigrant, and Catholic. A seemingly endless number of parochial schools exist in Chicago, as any radio listener will attest from the list of school closings on the morning of a severe snowstorm. Given their minority status in American history as well as normative claims about the church's role in salvation, Catholics often maintained a sometimes self-imposed distance from other religious communities. Even the liberal James Cardinal Gibbons of Baltimore, when asked to make the opening prayer at the World's Parliament of Religions, wondered what to pray for and was uncertain of the efficacy of his invocation, given the diverse multitudes (he recited the Protestant version of the Lord's Prayer). That said, Catholics have played a central role in the life of Chicago, and they have done so confidently and with unusual openness, as in the XXVIII International Eucharistic Congress (1926) in Soldier Field on the Chicago lakefront.

Open academic exchanges with other theological seminaries also describe Catholics in Chicago. Catholic Theological Union (1968), the largest Roman Catholic school of theology and ministry in the United States, through its diverse mix of men, women, lay and religious, Catholic, Jewish, and Protestant faculty continues the spirit of Vatican II. A like spirit emerged in "The Challenge of Peace: God's Promise and Our Response" (1983), a pastoral letter written by Joseph Cardinal Bernardin and the National Conference of Catholic Bishops. Its powerful support of "nuclear pacifism" resounded beyond parish and diocese. Many Methodists, Presbyterians, and Lutherans wrote their own letters. *Christian Century*, a liberal Protestant weekly based in Chicago, made this conversation public.

Immigrants drawn to the city have made monumental contributions. The Irish rebuilt the city after the Great Chicago Fire of 1871 and became known for their political savvy and clout. A biography of former mayor Richard J. Daley is titled *American Pharaoh* (2000). Theodore Dreiser, American novelist and author of *Sister Carrie* (1900), the son of a devout German Catholic immigrant father, moved from Indiana to Chicago at age fifteen to work as a hack journalist and writer of urban stories. Prolific writer and Catholic priest Andrew Greeley was born of Irish parents. Bohemians, Czechs, Greeks, Italians, and Lithuanians brought their worship. Ashkenazic Jews settled along Maxwell Street and later moved to Skokie, where they established a rabbinical college. It is widely known that Serbs and Croats have long shared neighborhoods and attended each other's weddings. By the 2000 census, more Chicagoans claimed Polish ancestry than any other, followed by Irish and Germans. Other ethnic Catholic communities include Belarusian, Chaldean, Marionite, Melkite, Roman, Ruthenian, Syro-Malabar, Syro-Malankar, and Ukrainian.

In the early twenty-first century, Hispanics and Asians were the fastest-growing groups in Chicago. Hispanics, in the old Czech neighborhood of Pilsen, celebrate Holy Week with a procession and a graphic reenactment of Christ's crucifixion. It is a tourist at-

traction as popular as the Chinese New Year's festival featuring dancing dragons and fireworks on Wentworth, though with a different tone. There are seventy-seven mosques in the greater metropolitan area, as well as Islamic centers, schools, and foundations in Bridgeview, Lombard, and Villa Park. Two ornate Hindu temples have gone up in the western suburbs of Lemont and Aurora, and a dozen smaller Hindu sites of worship exist. Zen Buddhist translator D. T. Suzuki of Japan worked in Chicago after the first parliament. In 2001, Zen practitioners promoted Kamakura-style archery as a form of meditation. The Yellow Pages list a dozen Buddhist temples serving Japanese, Cambodian, Laotian, and Vietnamese communities. Jains and Sikhs are present, as is a Zoroastrian fire temple. In autumn of 2000, when the Tiki Lounge on 53rd Street closed, notes were left at a makeshift shrine out front thanking the establishment's Afro-Caribbean voodoo madame and requesting her forwarding address.

The World Council of Churches first met in Amsterdam (1948), but American awareness dates from the Second Assembly in 1954 at Evanston. Many denominations, including Eastern Orthodox, were represented, though Catholics were not. However, Catholic-Protestant dialogue grew in the 1960s when Catholics learned biblical criticism and Protestants, church history. A trend in relocating denominational seminaries from rural areas into the city created synergy among schools, faculties, and students. The Lutheran School of Theology moved from a remote site to Hyde Park, where it shares a building with the Presbyterians of McCormick Theological Seminary and with Jesuits.

The University of Chicago Divinity School is a center of modernism in bible study and theology, a home for innovative approaches to the academic study of religion, and an anchor for thinking about religion in public. In the early 1890s, John D. Rockefeller, a devout Baptist who had made a fortune in the oil business, founded the University of Chicago, drawing upon the resources of the local Baptist Theological Union as well as the talents of William Rainey Harper, the university's first president. In the twentieth century, the social history perspectives of faculty members Shirley Jackson Case and Shailer Mathews led to conflict with fundamentalists. Process theology, in which Creation and God evolve, provoked new ideas on the existence of evil. Historian of religions Mircea Eliade, through a descriptive, neutral approach, shaped the way that religion is taught in public schools and universities across the country.

Nondenominational in character, the Divinity School includes Catholic faculty and students and a center for Jewish studies. Islam is also represented. A

Great Books program led some to say that at Chicago, a Jew (Mortimer Adler) and a Presbyterian (Robert Maynard Hutchins) taught Catholic theology (St. Thomas Aquinas) to Baptists. The school plays a central role in the life of the university, and many faculty hold joint appointments in other academic departments. In 1998, the Institute for the Advanced Study of Religion at the Divinity School was renamed the Marty Center, after prominent professor Martin E. Marty, and dedicated to the study of religion in public life.

The number of schools of religion in Chicago is second only to that in Rome, Italy. The Seventh-day Adventists have an academy. Unitarian Universalists study at Meadville/Lombard Theological School. The Norwegian-Danish Free Church has Trinity Evangelical Divinity School in Deerfield. Seabury-Western Theological Seminary (Episcopal) and Garrett-Evangelical Theological Seminary (United Methodist) are in Evanston. Many seminaries interact in the Association of Chicago Theological Schools. Religious bodies founded the American Islamic College and Benedictine, DePaul, Dominican, Franciscan, and Loyola Universities. Elmhurst College (famous for Reinhold and H. Richard Niebuhr) is affiliated with the United Church of Christ; North Central is United Methodist; and North Park is Evangelical Covenant (where Swedes began the Christian Business Men's Committees in 1930).

Religion in Chicago is forever spilling out of its traditional forms. Whether practiced in Frank Lloyd Wright's influential Unity Temple in Oak Park or the First United Methodist Church, atop an eighteen-story Loop skyscraper, religion in Chicago is dynamic and it is big. Coach Phil Jackson's Zen philosophy, published in the best-selling *Sacred Hoops* (1996), guided Michael Jordan and the Chicago Bulls to victory by reminding them that while basketball players cannot share the ball, they can share a philosophy of defense.

The second Parliament of the World's Religions in 1993, whose planning committee represented more world religions than did the entire parliament of 1893, epitomizes the dynamism and size of religion in Chicago. Despite comparisons of the centennial parliament, which met in the huge McCormick Place Convention Center, to a boat show, its influence persists. One program, the Metropolitan Chicago Interreligious Initiative, with its congregation exchanges and open houses, is a model for activities in Vancouver, San Francisco, New Delhi, and Cape Town. A port of call, Chicago is a crossroads for religions streaming out of traditional forms and into public life.

Sources and Further Reading: William Cronon, *Nature's Metropolis: Chicago and the Great West* (1991); Diana Eck, *Encountering God* (1993); Thomas Wakefield Goodspeed, *A History of the University of Chicago* (1972); Melvin G. Holli and Peter d'A. Jones, eds., *Ethnic Chicago*, 4th ed. (1994); Lowell W. Livezey, ed., *Public Religion and Urban Transformation* (2000); William G. McLoughlin, *Modern Revivalism* (1959); Donald L. Miller, *City of the Century* (1996); William T. Stead, *If Christ Came to Chicago!* (1894).

John Kloos
Benedictine University, Illinois

Iowa

The rich religious history of Iowa, a quintessential midwestern state, began with the Sioux, Winnebagos, Oneota, Sacs, Foxes, Potawatomi, Mascoutin, Ioway, and many other American Indians. When these peoples were obliterated or removed in the nineteenth century, their names were appropriated as labels for towns and counties. Frenchmen brought Catholicism as well as trade goods in the late 1600s and 1700s. But it was only with the arrival of citizens of the United States in the 1800s that the current religious landscape of Iowa began to emerge.

Soon after the visit of circuit rider Peter Cartwright in 1834, Methodists built the first house of worship in Iowa, a log structure erected in Dubuque, where the first service was held on July 25, 1834. The meeting-house was "raised without spirits of any kind," one of the congregants proudly noted. Ever since, Methodists have exerted a powerful influence on religion, society, and politics in Iowa. Several institutions of higher learning were begun by Methodists: Morningside College, Cornell College, Iowa Wesleyan College, and Simpson College, named in honor of an abolitionist bishop, Matthew Simpson. The influence of Iowa Methodism has also extended beyond the state's borders. In the fall and winter of 1873–1874 Phineas Bresee, a Methodist preacher, conducted an extraordinary revival at Red Oak, which touched the entire town and affected the young preacher with an experience of the Holy Spirit. A decade later, forced into bankruptcy by the flooding of a mine in which he held stock, Bresee headed for Los Angeles and eventually formed the Church of the Nazarene.

In 1835 Roman Catholics completed a church in Dubuque, designed by Father Samuel Mazzuchelli, thereby laying the foundation for a significant network of churches, schools, and hospitals that began to take shape under the direction of Mathias Loras, Iowa's first Catholic bishop. Roman Catholics settled initially in the northeastern section of the state but then expanded well beyond that with the arrival of German Catholics in the 1840s and 1850s.

Iowa's Religious Diversity

Religious Preferences in 1895

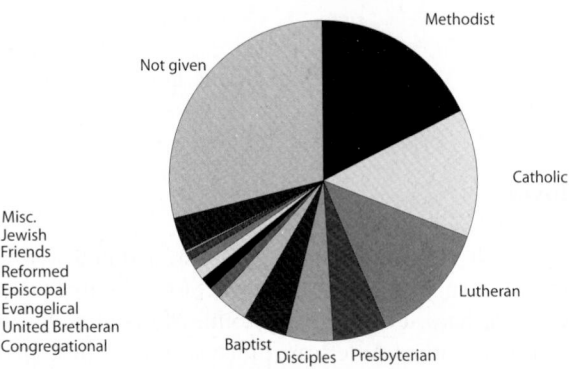

Religious Adherents in 2000

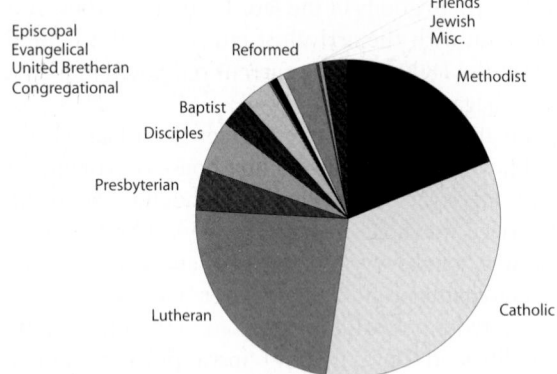

Changes in religious affiliation in twentieth-century Iowa. Prepared by Sathyan Sundaram. *Source:* Richard Jensen, *The Winning of the Midwest* (Chicago: University of Chicago Press, 1971), p. 86, table 5; American Religion Data Archive, "RCMS State Report (Iowa)," http://www.thearda.com/RCMS/2000/State/19.htm.

Various social experiments and utopian schemes, some of them motivated by religious principles, have taken root, however briefly, in the loamy soil of Iowa. Abner Kneeland, jailed for blasphemy and driven from Boston in 1838, founded a short-lived colony called Salubria, in Van Buren County. The Mormons, another sort of communitarian group, traversed Iowa and established a camp at Council Bluffs in 1846 as a way station on their journey to the promised land of Salt Lake City. In 1850 a group of Hungarians arrived in Decatur County with plans to build a city called New Buda. More recently, in the mid-1970s, the followers of Maharishi Mahesh Yogi, propagator of Transcendental Meditation, purchased the defunct Parsons College in Fairfield and turned it into the Maharishi University of Management.

Because of their strong communal ties and their tireless industry, the Community of True Inspiration has enjoyed the greatest success and longevity of any communal group. A band of Pietist Germans initially sought refuge in Ebenezer, New York, near Buffalo, but soon removed to the verdant, undulating hills along the Iowa River and there built six communal villages, all named Amana (with various distinguishing prefixes), and a seventh, designated Homestead by the railroad. Although the society surrendered its communalism in favor of a modified form of capitalism in 1932, members of the Amana Society still cling to their simple worship, superb craftsmanship, and, in many cases, plain-style dress that visitors often confuse with the Amish of Indiana, Ohio, and Lancaster County, Pennsylvania.

If the Germans of the Community of True Inspiration have left their mark, other religious groups have punctuated the Iowa landscape with their church buildings. Tall steeples pierce the prairie sky, rising from structures that are both architecturally spectacular and ethnically distinctive. The construction of a church announced that immigrants meant to stay, but it also provided employment for craftsmen and artisans, and an impressive building served as a kind of billboard advertising their skills.

German Catholics, with their long tradition of elaborate worship, constructed splendid Gothic churches throughout the state, especially in the northeast at Dyersville, New Vienna, Guttenberg, and Petersburg. Irish immigrants left numerous testaments to their piety, including New Melleray Abbey near Dubuque and St. Joseph's Church in Elkader. French-speaking Catholics settled in St. Donatus. Czech immigrants constructed St. Wenceslaus in Spillville, modeled on the Church of St. Barbara in Kunta Hora, Czechoslovakia. The composer Antonín Dvořák spent the summer of 1893 in Spillville, played the organ for church services, and composed much of his famous elegy to America, *Aus der Neuen Welt*, known as the *New World* Symphony.

Protestant immigrants brought different religious sensibilities to Iowa, including worship centered around preaching rather than the mystery of the sacraments. Such distinctions affected everything from clergy-parishioner relations to architecture. Compare, for example, the florid accoutrements in the Basilica of St. Francis Xavier, erected in 1888 by German Catholics in Dyersville, with the simple lines of the Nazarene Church in Burlington, built by German Lutherans in 1868, or the clapboard austerity of the Zoar Reformed Church, constructed by German Reformed near Baxter.

Other Protestant groups have thoroughly shaped their communities. Swedish Lutherans settled in

Ogden and Norwegians in Sheldahl and Decorah, where the Reverend Ulrick Koren of Washington Prairie Lutheran Church lured Luther College away from its original site in Wisconsin to a lovely parcel of land on the edge of town. Welsh Congregationalists settled in Johnson County, just south of Iowa City; Mennonites established a presence in Kalona; and Danes found a home in Elk Horn and Kimballton. And it is impossible to imagine Marion County without the Dutch, who settled Pella in 1847 under the guidance of the Reverend Henry Scholte, who doubled as a real estate agent.

Most of Iowa's religious history has been dominated, at least until recently, by the mainline Protestant denominations, especially Lutherans and Methodists, with smatterings of Presbyterians, Congregationalists, Baptists, and Disciples of Christ. The Baptists formed their first congregation at Long Creek, near Burlington, in 1834; Presbyterians gathered at Sugar Creek, in Lee County, two years later. The Society of Friends (Quakers) established their first meeting at Salem in 1835 and organized meetings around the state at Earlham, Cumming, and West Branch, which produced Iowa's only U.S. president, Herbert Hoover, a Quaker. In 1837 Episcopalians came to Davenport, where they eventually established the Iowa Christian Home as a hospital for the sick and the needy, but Episcopalians have never established themselves as a major presence in the state, claiming less than one percent of the population in 1990.

In 1838 Asa Turner and Julian A. Reed, two Congregationalist ministers, formed a church in Iowa, a country that Turner found "so beautiful that there might be an unwillingness to exchange it for the paradise above." Concerned about the incursions of Mormons into the territory, Turner appealed to Congregationalist authorities back east for missionaries. Twelve men from Andover Theological Seminary's class of 1843 heard the call and became known as the "Iowa Band." A few years later another Congregationalist minister heeded a different call. It was to Josiah Bushnell Grinnell, an abolitionist preacher in New York City, that Horace Greeley issued his famous dictum "Go West, young man, go West!" Grinnell settled in the town that now bears his name, helped to establish a college, and remained active in the fight against slavery, even to the point of inviting John Brown to preach in church while Brown was planning his raid on Harpers Ferry. The most obvious legacies of the Christian Church (Disciples of Christ), first organized in Lee County in 1836, are Drake University and the mainline Protestant journal *Christian Century*, whose earlier incarnation was the *Christian Oracle*, first published in Des Moines in 1884.

The religious history of Iowa includes colorful characters. After Billy Sunday's religious conversion and retirement from professional baseball he became an itinerant preacher. In January 1896 the Iowa-born evangelist held his first revival at the opera house in Garner and then began barnstorming throughout the Midwest. But the flamboyant evangelist did not always meet with success on what he referred to, often disparagingly, as the "Kerosene Circuit." A rather unavailing visit to Eddyville persuaded Sunday that the "most low, God-forsaken town he was ever in was Eddyville, Iowa, and Morehead, Minn." Sunday's sentiments provoked a spirited response from the editor of the Eddyville *Tribune*, who asserted that in Eddyville "the actual infidels to God, as we understand the term, do not exceed five."

Another religious development in Iowa was even less edifying. In March 1887 Henry F. Bowers and six associates gathered in Clinton to form the American Protective Association, an anti-Catholic nativist organization. Members of the association subscribed to the notion that Roman Catholics were plotting to undermine American democratic institutions and that Catholics were subservient to a "foreign potentate." The American Protective Association propagated these ideas throughout the Midwest, especially in rural areas, and claimed that half a million members had pledged never to vote for a Catholic, go on strike with a Catholic, or hire a Catholic when a non-Catholic was available.

Ida B. Wise Smith was also consumed by hatred, but a hatred directed against the liquor traffic rather than Roman Catholics. Smith, an ordained minister in the Disciples of Christ denomination, was a schoolteacher in Des Moines who went on to become a crusader for social reform—for women's suffrage, to improve the welfare of children, and to outlaw cigarettes and liquor. "I love God, my country, and little children," Smith declared once, summarizing her views. "I hate the liquor traffic and abhor all vice." Smith, together with other religious crusaders such as the Reverend Claud N. McMillan of Sioux City, sought to eradicate vice from the state. Smith served as the president of the Iowa chapter of the Women's Christian Temperance Union (WCTU) for twenty years and became national president of the WCTU in 1933, the year the Eighteenth Amendment to the U.S. Constitution was repealed.

Where have the religious energies gone? In an odd way, the popular Iowa politician Harold E. Hughes epitomized the changes in Iowa's religious configuration over the final decades of the twentieth century. Hughes was a truck driver and alcoholic from Ida Grove who found religion in the form of Methodism, mended his ways, and became both a politician and a

Methodist lay preacher. Elected governor three times as a Democrat, Hughes won election to the U.S. Senate in 1968, briefly ran for president in 1972, and then retired from the Senate after one term because he wanted to devote his energies to an evangelical religious organization, Fellowship Foundation.

The Hughes analogy cannot be pushed too far, in part because his politics differed sharply from those of the religious right, but Hughes's movement from mainline Methodism toward a form of evangelicalism reflected larger cultural shifts. Church adherence within mainline denominations, including the Roman Catholic Church, has declined steadily since the mid-1960s in favor of evangelical churches, most of them located in the suburbs. In Des Moines, the rapid growth of First Assembly of God, First Federated Church, and Westchester Evangelical Free Church, which relocated from Highland Park to the northwestern suburbs in 1970, underscores this reconfiguration of Protestantism away from the mainline toward evangelicalism.

The evangelicals of Iowa, like those across the nation, have not confined their activities to churches. Politically conservative evangelicals, together with conservative Catholics, contributed to the defeat of incumbent Democratic senators Dick Clark and John Culver in 1978 and 1980, respectively. As David Yepsen of the Des Moines *Register* has pointed out, evangelical activists in Iowa have made it virtually impossible for any Republican politician in the state to countermand their positions on major issues, especially their opposition to abortion.

The entry of evangelicals—especially women—into the political arena, moreover, signaled the resumption of a long tradition of moral activism in Iowa history. Whereas mainline Protestants had dominated the social-reform movements in Iowa around the turn of the twentieth century, that mantle has been assumed by evangelicals, who mobilized to defeat a 1992 ballot initiative guaranteeing equal rights to women. Evangelical political fervor in Iowa ebbed somewhat in the succeeding decade, in part because of the growing religious pluralism of the population and in part because of greater mobilization on the left, drawing on the state's long tradition of progressivism.

In a way, the best indication of the importance of religion in Iowa life lies quite apart from partisan politics and denominational statistics. This index becomes visible in Iowa communities every summer during RAGBRAI, the *Register*'s Annual Great Bicycle Ride across Iowa. As cyclists from around the country (and the world) roll into towns along the route they encounter signs advertising a variety of church suppers—spaghetti or roast beef or fried chicken, along with generous helpings of vegetables, salad, corn on the cob, homemade pie, and that trusty midwestern staple, hotdish. Everyone seems to benefit from this arrangement. Hungry riders get fed; church people work together and may wind up with a few extra dollars to repair the roof or purchase new tires for the church van.

This page from Norman Rockwell's sketchbook serves as a reminder that the old-fashioned church supper has survived into the twenty-first century, that the sturdy midwestern values of community and hospitality might well be endangered by sociological and demographic changes but have not disappeared altogether. Like Americans generally, Iowans are devoutly religious, even though the patterns of religious affiliation have changed markedly over the course of the state's history, and especially in the last decades of the twentieth century. The momentum may have shifted from the mainline to evangelicalism and now to other expressions of pluralism, and the box social may have given way to the church banquet or the fund-raising telethon in some communities, but religion remains a vital part of Iowans' lives.

Sources and Further Reading: Randall Balmer, *Mine Eyes Have Seen the Glory*, 3rd ed. (2000); Diane L. Barthel, *Amana: From Pietist Sect to New World Community* (1984); Cyrenus Cole, *Iowa through the Years* (1940); Federal Writers' Project, *The WPA Guide to 1930s Iowa* (1986); Harold E. Hughes, *Man from Ida Grove* (1979).

Randall Balmer
Columbia University, New York

Michigan

The historian Sidney Mead once observed that the "central theme" of the Midwest's religious history has been the "trying out" of a multitude of religious traditions. "Into the pot," he wrote, "has gone every sect and sectarian view of Christendom, plus Judaism, and representatives of all the world's religions." No single midwestern state quite lives up to Mead's generalization of course, but one comes close: Michigan. Long an economic powerhouse, Michigan has been a magnet for migrants from around the United States and around the world, resulting in a society that continues to be culturally complex and religiously dynamic to this day.

Yankees, from New England or of New England descent, enjoyed a certain cultural dominance in Michigan beginning with its statehood in 1837. Michigan was one of the earliest destinations for the massive "Yankee exodus" kicked off by the opening of the Erie Canal in 1825. Yankees founded most of the towns in southern Michigan outside of Detroit, and Michigan's early politics and economy were largely controlled by New Englanders and New Yorkers. Not surprisingly, Yankee religion predominated in early Michigan. Congregationalists, Presbyterians, Methodists, Baptists, and Episcopalians established congregations in the state by the late 1820s. As a result, a kind of Yankee religious ethos developed that, despite denominational rivalries, encouraged cooperation on such issues as public education, social reform, and, in some cases, joint worship. One of the earliest Protestant bodies in the state was the First Protestant Society of Detroit, founded in 1816 by Presbyterian John Monteith. A model of Yankee ecumenicalism, the society brought together Presbyterians, Congregationalists, Episcopalians, and Methodists and lasted several years, until the individual denominations had enough members to establish their own churches in the city.

The Michigan frontier attracted the full range of Yankee religion. In addition to the mainstream, "alternative" Yankee religions made the state home. The first Universalist congregation was established near Detroit in 1829, and from there Universalism spread to most of southern Michigan. By 1843, twenty-two Universalist societies existed. Unitarians appeared in the state in the late 1840s, followed closely by Swedenborgians and Spiritualists. One Michigan city in particular became a haven for alternative Yankee religions. Battle Creek by the early 1850s played host to Universalists, Hicksite Quakers, and Swedenborgians and had one of the largest Spiritualist communities in the Midwest. Perhaps because of this tolerance, the city also attracted Seventh-day Adventists, who for decades made it the headquarters of their denomination.

Relations between members of the mainstream and alternative Yankee traditions were sometimes strained and theological controversy among them was common; and yet, an overarching Yankee ethnicity bound these people together and gave them a sense of cultural preeminence and entitlement. Their position did not go unchallenged, especially with the rise of European immigration in the middle of the nineteenth century. Many immigrant groups maintained strong religious and ethnic ties with the Old World and resisted assimilation into Michigan's dominant Yankee culture. Perhaps the most successful of these were the Dutch. In 1847, the Reverend Albertus C. van Raalte led a group of Dutch immigrants to western Michigan. In Michigan, they hoped to restore the Reformed faith to its original purity, and thus, soon after founding the city of Holland, they established the independent Classis Holland and the First Reformed Church of Holland. The Dutch quickly expanded throughout the

area, including into Grand Rapids, where the Second Reformed Church was established in 1849. Despite later schisms, the Dutch Reformed tradition thrived in Michigan, and strong vestiges of Dutch culture can still be found in the state.

Even more disturbing than the Dutch for Michigan's Yankees was the arrival of large numbers of Roman Catholics. Roman Catholicism, of course, had long been established in Michigan. French Catholic missionaries had been active in the region for over 150 years before the American period, and Detroit's St. Anne's parish (1704) boasts of being the second-oldest documented continuously operating parish in the United States. And yet, by the time of statehood, the small numbers of French Canadian or Native American Catholics then living in Michigan were considered economically and politically insignificant by the arriving Yankees and often were the objects of their ridicule. However, Catholic immigration, beginning in the 1830s and 1840s and accelerating after the Civil War, completely changed the demography of the state. Detroit was the most popular destination for this immigration, but all of Michigan's cities felt its impact to some degree. By 1906, around half of all churchgoers in Grand Rapids were Roman Catholic. Catholic immigration also radically changed the ethnic composition of the state. Irish and German Catholics, who arrived during the antebellum period, were later joined by large numbers of Poles, Hungarians, Czechs, Belgians, Slavs, and Italians in the second half of the nineteenth century. Irish domination of the church hierarchy in Michigan was frequently offset by the development of strong ethnic parishes, such as Detroit's Polish parish, St. Albertus, led by the charismatic (and ultimately schismatic) Father Dominic Kolasinski.

By the end of the nineteenth century, the Catholic presence in Michigan was formidable. Led by a series of strong-willed bishops, the church invested heavily in infrastructure, building churches, schools, colleges, and hospitals. Thus, in addition to the sheer number of Catholics in the state, the very landscape had been changed. Moreover, despite continuing ethnic rivalries within the church, Catholics were banding together to become a political force, first at the local level and then statewide. Catholic growth inevitably engendered a Protestant backlash that ranged from temperance crusades and a "Social Gospel" movement aimed at urban Catholics to the popularity of nativist political parties, such as the American Protective Association, and the rise of terrorist organizations, including the Ku Klux Klan and the Black Legion.

Emblematic of the tensions between Protestants and Catholics in Michigan was the battle over education. For many non-Catholics, public schools, which began to proliferate in Michigan in the 1830s, were seen as the key transmitters of the values of American democracy. For many Catholics, however, public schools taught a veiled Protestantism, making parochial schools necessary to perpetuate their religious traditions. Attacks against the parochial school system in Michigan started in the early nineteenth century, and the conflict became acute when a constitutional amendment making public school attendance mandatory was introduced in the state legislature in 1920 and 1924. By allying themselves with other religious groups that maintained parochial schools (German Lutherans, Christian Reformed, Seventh-day Adventists), and by flexing their own considerable political muscle, Michigan's Catholics handily defeated the amendment both times it appeared on the ballot.

Unquestioned Yankee dominance in Michigan was a thing of the past by the first decades of the twentieth century. Not only did foreign immigration continue, but from 1880 to 1910 the major sources of domestic migration to the state had shifted away from New York and New England. Now the majority of migrants came from Pennsylvania, Ohio, Indiana, Illinois, and Wisconsin; and in the two decades before 1940 this migration drew from all the southern states as well. The cultural mix of the state was thus transformed yet again. New or hardly represented denominations such as the Church of God, the Church of the Nazarene, and the Reorganized Church of Jesus Christ of Latter Day Saints now became strongly established.

The new migration catalyzed the rise of new religious movements, of which fundamentalism had the greatest impact. Grand Rapids' Wealthy Street Baptist Church, led by the Reverend Oliver van Osdel, became a national headquarters for this movement. In 1917, van Osdel gathered thirteen other like-minded Baptist congregations into the Grand River Valley Baptist Association, which would be instrumental in the formation of the national General Association of Regular Baptist Churches. Attacking modernism wherever they found it, the association Baptists sought to bring all Christians back to the importance of personal conversion and a literal belief in premillennialism. This "fundamentalist crusade" would in time have an impact not only on other Baptist congregations, but on other denominations as well.

As unsettling as the cultural flux of the first half of the twentieth century was for many Michiganders, others found it liberating. Nowhere was this better illustrated than in the development of African American religious communities, especially in Detroit. Small numbers of African Americans, some brought by the Underground Railroad, began settling in Michigan before the Civil War. In Detroit in 1836, thirteen former slaves founded the Second Baptist Church, reputed to be the oldest African American congregation

in the Midwest. Second Baptist was followed in 1839 by the Bethel African Methodist Episcopal (AME) Church and by St. Matthew's Protestant Episcopal Church, organized in 1846. By the turn of the century, each of these churches had spun off several new Detroit congregations.

Black church life in the city was revolutionized by the massive African American exodus from the South in the first half of the twentieth century. Not only did mainstream black denominations experience a dramatic increase in members, but the number of storefront fundamentalist, Holiness, Pentecostal, and Independent churches exploded. Although African Americans found grinding poverty and pervasive discrimination in Detroit, they also found the freedom to experiment with their Christianity, or to reject it altogether. Detroit became one of the strongholds of the Moorish Science Temple and the birthplace of the Nation of Islam. Founded by W. D. Fard in 1930, the Nation of Islam achieved national prominence under the leadership of Elijah (Poole) Muhammad, a former Georgia sharecropper who migrated to Detroit to work in the auto industry.

Today, Michigan's religious scene continues to diversify. The number of non-Christian religions has grown, along with Christian groups such as the Amish and Hispanic Catholics. In the nineteenth century, the only significant non-Christian religion in the state was Judaism; at the end of the twentieth century, there were dozens. When the Nation of Islam temple in Grand Rapids disbanded after the death of Elijah Muhammad in 1975, many of its members simply became orthodox Muslims worshiping at the local Islamic center. Ethnic Islam in Michigan dates back to 1919, when one of the first mosques in the United States opened to serve the Lebanese population of Dearborn. Since that time, and especially after the loosening of immigration regulations in 1965, the number of Michigan's Muslims has soared; there are now some forty mosques and Islamic centers in the Detroit area alone. The year 1965 also marked the arrival of Hindus, Buddhists, Sikhs, Baha'is and Asian Christians, including Vietnamese Catholics and Korean Presbyterians. While strongly ethnic in character, some of these groups have begun to attract a few American converts, although they are in competition with indigenous non-Christian options such as New Age and neopaganism.

Despite Michigan's religious diversity, some generalizations can be made. In gross terms, Michigan can be divided into two cultural regions: Detroit and its hinterland. Most of Michigan outside of Detroit—especially rural Michigan—is still preponderantly populated by white Protestants. This reflects the strong early settlement of Yankees in the region, as well as the later immigration of Dutch and German Protestants. Detroit, on the other hand, long the preferred destination for large numbers of European Catholics and African American Protestants, forms a strong cultural counterpoint to the rest of the state. Religious distribution, in fact, correlates fairly well with the polarization of political attitudes often manifested in the tense relations between liberal-leaning Detroit and the rest of Michigan, which tends to be moderately to strongly conservative.

Michigan's polarized religious geography can perhaps best be appreciated when contrasted to that of other midwestern states. Ohio, for example, with its several large, religiously diverse cities, exhibits none of the center/periphery cultural dynamic as does Michigan. The opposite extreme is Iowa: Never having developed the major metropolitan centers that attracted large-scale Catholic or African American migration, white Protestantism still predominates there statewide. Of all the midwestern states, Michigan is most like Illinois, with its religiously diverse major metropolitan core, Chicago, surrounded by a largely rural and mainly white Protestant periphery.

Sources and Further Reading: James D. Bratt and Christopher H. Meehan, *Gathered at the River* (1993); Claude Andrew Clegg III, *An Original Man* (1998); Susan E. Gray, *The Yankee West* (1996); David M. Katzman, *Before the Ghetto* (1973); Sidney Mead, "In Search of God," in John J. Murray, ed., *The Heritage of the Middle East* (1958); George Pare, *The Catholic Church in Detroit, 1701–1888* (1951); Robert P. Swierenga and Elton J. Bruins, *Family Quarrels in the Dutch Reformed Churches in the Nineteenth Century* (1999); Leslie Woodcock Tentler, *Seasons of Grace* (1990); N. Gordon Thomas, *The Millennial Impulse in Michigan, 1830–1860* (1989); JoEllen McNergney Vinyard, *For Faith and Fortune* (1998); Linda S. Walbridge, *Without Forgetting the Imam* (1997).

Brian Wilson
Western Michigan University

Major Themes

Revivalism

Evangelicalism and revivalism played crucial roles in the development of midwestern regional culture. Today, the Midwest is in many ways the center of evangelicalism in the United States, and possibly the world, playing host to numerous evangelical organizations, institutions, and publishing houses, a large contingent of which lies in cities such as Grand Rapids, Michigan; Chicago, Illinois; and St. Louis, Missouri.

Gallup polls from the 1980s suggest that as many as 40 percent of people residing in the Midwest could be considered evangelicals, though their precise number is difficult to determine, in part because "evangelical" and "born again" have differing meanings according to various scholars and religious practitioners.

Evangelicalism refers to a particular version of Protestantism that emphasizes a literal interpretation of the Bible and a personal relationship with God. In the most general sense, evangelicals are those who adhere to three basic beliefs: (1) The Bible is the inerrant Word of God; (2) Christ is divine; and (3) Christ's life, death, and physical resurrection make possible the salvation of the human soul. In addition, most self-described evangelicals call themselves "born again," by which they mean that at a specific place and time they repented their sins and sought salvation by turning their life over to God and establishing a personal relationship with Jesus. This experience, which is often very emotionally powerful, is the moment at which a person becomes "saved" and Jesus enters into their life in the form of the Holy Spirit. Evangelicalism in this sense refers to a particular style of Christianity that emphasizes not just belief but active religious practice and an interactive personal relationship with Jesus, the incarnated Son of God. Most evangelicals believe that God wishes for all people to have the same relationship with Jesus as they do, and therefore they actively seek to share their version of Christianity with others.

Revivals are mass meetings where large groups of evangelicals gather to worship God, save souls, and reform societal norms in accordance with Biblical standards. Evangelicalism and revivalism are related terms, and in many ways evangelical Christianity is an institutionalized form of the type of Christian worship found in the revivalist setting. A revival is typically characterized by intense religious experience and emotionally charged sermons, often delivered by an itinerant preacher who travels throughout the country from one revival meeting to the next. A key component of the message of revivalism is the urgency of acting upon belief in order to transform both the self and the world.

Evangelicalism emerged during a series of revivalist movements between 1720 and 1740 referred to as the Great Awakening. The Great Awakening shaped the beliefs of the first English-speaking settlers of the region that became the Midwest. Theologian Jonathan Edwards (1703–1758); the founder of Methodism, John Wesley (1703–1791); and transatlantic itinerant preacher George Whitefield (1714–1770) are the three people most commonly associated with the Great Awakening. The message of the Great Awakening was that anyone could have a relationship with

God irrespective of the church. A wide array of revival meetings was held throughout the colonies over roughly twenty years. These efforts resulted in numerous converts, which led to the rise of new churches, churches that were built to sustain and institutionalize the particular style of worship from the revivalist setting that today we call evangelicalism.

Between 1800 and 1840 a better organized revivalist movement, later called the Second Great Awakening, had a major impact on the development of the Midwest. Numerous seminaries and evangelical institutions such as Oberlin College arose that taught the theology of Edwards and the intense style of preaching characteristic of revivalism. These teaching centers produced a wave of missionaries and itinerant preachers instructed in techniques to convert souls and to discipline people in lives of holiness, which led to the production and cultivation of revivalist religious experiences in the church setting. The most prominent figure in this movement was itinerant preacher and president of Oberlin College Charles Finney (1792–1875). Finney systematically developed connections between emotion and belief, which in turn led to an increased emphasis upon religious affect in the church and revival setting. More efficient forms of the printing press made possible mass productions of Bible tracts and other religious publications. Largely lay-led organizations connected believers through various evangelical publications, uniting disparate and dispersed individuals into a collective revivalist movement throughout the country. Revivalism helped some denominations to grow in prominence in the Midwest, particularly the Baptists and Methodists, who became the largest Protestant denominations in the country during the nineteenth century.

The well-organized revivalist efforts of the Second Great Awakening significantly shaped the hearts and minds of the first settlers of the Midwest. In the evangelical vision of history, the United States was a "New Jerusalem," the place chosen by God that would pave the way for earth to become a heavenly place fit for Jesus to return to and rule. Westward expansion was part of a divine plan for the nation, a belief referred to in secular terms as manifest destiny. In the nineteenth century, the area now called the Midwest was the "West," and those who first entered the area from the East were in pursuit of their own version of the American dream, a dream informed by the basic tenets and beliefs of evangelical Christianity. Typically these people were a mix of mostly farmers, businessmen, missionaries, and preachers. Accompanying many was their evangelical faith, specifically the belief that the providence of God would protect and lead them to safe settlement in the relatively unknown "promised land" that lay ahead. Gradually people clustered,

towns arose, and churches were built, often with the assistance of people formally trained in evangelical seminaries and universities.

Revivalism flourished in the Midwest during the early nineteenth century, particularly in the form of camp meetings, which were large tent revivals that lasted anywhere from a few days to several weeks. Camp meetings virtually brought life to a standstill in the surrounding areas, drawing in entire communities to participate in an "experimental" form of religious worship. The Methodist doctrine of sanctification was a basic tenet of most revivalist preachers. This essentially put the emphasis of religious praxis on holiness, a second blessing beyond conversion. This belief led to an emphasis upon more pronounced, ecstatic behaviors interpreted to be manifestations of the power of God. Common religious practices in camp meetings included ritualized laughter, barking, and people falling to the ground shaking and trembling.

By the mid-nineteenth century revivalism waned and camp meetings were held less frequently, but evangelicalism grew to become a defining characteristic of midwestern regional culture. The bombastic style of preaching and strong affect of the revivalist setting became institutionalized in churches throughout the region, and colleges such as Oberlin continued to be the primary training grounds for evangelicals. Missionary organizations and lay-led social reform groups also arose during the time, providing evangelicals with common religious and moral concerns. By the late nineteenth century the Midwest had become the center of evangelicalism in the United States, and evangelicalism in turn became a defining characteristic of the region.

Also in the late nineteenth century, the Industrial Revolution was drawing large numbers to urban areas, forcing a redrawing of boundaries in the public sphere, and as in earlier times of great socioeconomic change, many evangelicals called for revival. This is not to say that the revivalist efforts of the late nineteenth century were primarily reactionary. However, many sermons delivered at the time drew upon people's fears that materialism would overtake the nation and supplant what they believed were its Christian foundations. A rapid influx of immigrants at the time also caused many people to think that they would lose their jobs or be forced to take lower wages. Anti-Catholic sentiment was particularly high among many evangelicals. Darwinism also posed a serious threat to evangelical theology, and this led many theologians and preachers to reject science in favor of maintaining a belief that the Bible was the inerrant word of God.

The revivalist message of this era drew upon much of the nervousness many people felt from changes in the public sphere, and it particularly appealed to those who moved to urban centers from more rural areas. Itinerant preachers like Dwight L. Moody (1837–1899) and Billy Sunday (1862–1935) were the best-known revivalist figures of the time. Moody virtually perfected the art of revivalism, creating techniques that would be employed by revivalists in the years to come, including Sunday, whose influence continued into the early twentieth century, after Moody's death. Moody advertised heavily and constructed elaborate arenas for his meetings, including the eight thousand–capacity Tabernacle building in Chicago, the city where he also founded the Moody Bible Institute. By the late nineteenth century Chicago was competing with New York City in size and industry, and many evangelical groups along with Moody made Chicago their home, transforming it into the center of evangelicalism, a role that in many ways it continues to play today.

The steady influence of urbanization and industrialism combined with the rise of science, the secular university, and a large influx of non-Protestant Americans to diminish the influence of evangelicalism in the early twentieth century. Revivalism declined considerably, and evangelicals were gradually pushed to the periphery in the public sphere. By the 1910s, evangelicalism began to be associated with fundamentalism, a movement that emphasized the inerrancy of the Bible and rejection of Darwinism and liberal theology. Fundamentalism in many ways polarized evangelicals against mainstream secular society.

Evangelicalism in the early to mid-twentieth century became a more cohesive national movement through the establishment of organizations such as the National Association of Evangelicals and Youth for Christ, both of whose homes are in Chicago, and today evangelicalism continues to have an important influence in the Midwest. Wheaton College rose to prominence in the 1950s to become the intellectual center of evangelicalism and today plays host to the Institute for the Study of American Evangelicals. Numerous publishers, missionary groups, and other evangelical organizations clustered in the area surrounding Wheaton, and places like Grand Rapids, Michigan, are homes to similar evangelical universities and institutions such as Calvin College and Zondervan Publishing. In recent years evangelicals have emerged from the shadow of the pejorative media image of fanaticism placed upon them in the 1920s to reassert their voice in the public sphere. In politics, evangelicalism has become almost synonymous with conservativism, especially with regard to issues such as Creation science, abortion, and prayer in schools.

In recent years, Billy Graham (b. 1918) and the Promise Keepers, among others, have given a different public face to evangelicalism, and their successes at gaining converts have led many to suggest that the nation is currently in the midst of another mass revival movement. A broad resurgence in interest in religion in what we might call the post–September 11 era has bolstered evangelicalism even further as an increasingly higher number of Americans seek greater meaning in their lives through participation in various religious communities. This is particularly the case in the Midwest, the world home of evangelicalism. Evangelicalism and revivalism thus have been influential from the time of the nineteenth-century camp meetings to the present, and it appears that this religious movement will continue to flourish and define the character of the region for years to come.

Sources and Further Reading: Randall Balmer, *Mine Eyes Have Seen the Glory* (2000); Jonathan M. Butler, *Softly and Tenderly Jesus Is Calling* (1991); Michael O. Emerson and Christian Smith, *Divided by Faith* (2000); Ellen Eslinger, *Citizens of Zion* (1999); Harriet A. Harris, *Fundamentalism and Evangelicals* (1998); Robert H. Krapohl, *The Evangelicals: A Historical, Thematic, and Biographical Guide* (1999); Edward J. Larson, *Summer for the Gods* (1997); George M. Marsden, *Fundamentalism and American Culture* (1980); Leigh Eric Schmidt, *Holy Fairs* (1989); Peter J. Wosh, *Spreading the Word* (1994).

David Passiak
Princeton University, New Jersey

Ethnicity

Nineteenth-century migration from northern and western Europe introduced a number of new ethnic groups to the Midwest, many of whom brought Western religious traditions with them. The most prominent groups were ethnic Catholics such as Italian, Irish, and German. Catholics had been an important presence in the region since the arrival of French explorers and missionaries in the seventeenth century. Although small in number, the French left a legacy in place-names such as Prairie Du Chien, Wisconsin, and Lac qui Parle, Minnesota, and educational institutions such as the University of Notre Dame (1834).

By 1850, there were more than five hundred thousand Germans in the United States, and a significant portion of them were in the Midwest. More affluent and better educated than other immigrants, German Protestants and Catholics formed a triangle of German communities from Cincinnati to St. Louis to Milwaukee. Germans were deeply attached to their language and tradition, bringing both into their churches and schools. Immigrant Catholics in particular, however, confronted efforts to Americanize them through public education and social reform. German Lutherans dealt with similar issues. Of the estimated six million Lutherans in the United States, 56 percent reside in the Midwest. One Lutheran denomination, the Lutheran Church-Missouri Synod (LCMS), was founded by German Saxon immigrants in 1847. Until the end of World War I, the LCMS remained largely German in makeup and language.

Ethnic churches in the Midwest became places where immigrants maintained traditions and established communities. Particularly troubling were Catholic fears of Protestant-dominated public education. This was not simply an Irish concern. Throughout most of the nineteenth century, Catholics in places like Detroit and Chicago frequently felt that bishops and other religious leaders from different ethnic backgrounds failed to understand their needs and concerns. In Milwaukee, Catholic leadership decided that obedience to Roman Catholicism superseded ethnic solidarity. Archbishops in Cincinnati curtailed the use of German in their churches and schools.

Many immigrants sought out the numerous organizations that combined ethnic and religious identity. Ukrainian, Polish, and Slovak immigrants of what is called the second wave of immigration (from 1880 to 1914) were particularly attracted to these organizations. Some reflected church influence, such as the Polish Roman Catholic Union. In effect, Poles equated their ethnicity and their religious identity. Balancing ethnicity and religion was often a tricky business. Although the Chicago archdiocese attempted to adapt to different needs and had German-speaking priests and schools, Archbishop George Mundelein also encouraged the use of English.

As ethnic communities vied for space and resources from the church, dominant groups moved out and were replenished by new immigrant groups. Italians replaced Germans and Irish, which led to conflict over ethnic clergy, language problems, and political power.

Some immigrants started churches that would validate the importance of their ethnicity. The Polish National Church used Polish instead of Latin. Poles, Italians, and other eastern and southern European immigrants arrived in the second wave of nineteenth-century immigration. Poles were intensely devoted to the institutional church. Many who immigrated eventually became farmers, but many more settled in urban centers. For centuries, Poles joined their nationalism to their religion, and so in the United States they, like the Germans, sought to maintain a distinct national ethos, preserving their language in churches and schools.

The same was true of Orthodox immigrants and later Greek Orthodox immigrants who settled in the Midwest, most prominently in Chicago. By the close of the twentieth century, there were more than one million Orthodox immigrants in the United States. Other ethnic Orthodox immigrants included Ukrainians, Albani-ans, and Romanians. Unlike Catholics, who since Vatican II have been able to hold services in different languages, Orthodoxy still has the majority of its services in the original language.

Two distinct ethnic groups exemplify different paths of cultural adaptation. The Dutch Reformed are an example of the persistence of ethnic identity and Italian Protestants are an example of a loss of ethnic identity. Dutch Protestants, specifically the Dutch Reformed Church, created ethnic congregations and settled in isolated rural communities. Like their German counterparts in Milwaukee, they formed separate congregations in an attempt to resist Americanization.

Nowhere is the loss of ethnic identity more evident than in the history of Italian Protestants, many of whom were part of American Pentecostal churches like the Assemblies of God and were most prominent in urban centers such as Chicago. Many of these Protestants were converts and therefore required a changed worldview from reliance on clergy to a non-clerical idea. Those Italians who left Catholicism weakened links to the Italian community, which equated being Catholic with being Italian. Italian Protestants were grafted onto the American Protestant organizational structure and in the process began to assimilate rapidly. The demise of Italian Protestant congregations was inevitable, given the abandonment of the Italian language, their one distinctive feature, in the second generation. Currently, there are fewer than a dozen Italian Pentecostal churches in the Chicago area, and those with Italian services are even rarer.

Another predominantly Catholic immigrant group that has seen substantial growth in the region and has also had to confront the realities of engaging a divided religious community is Hispanic Americans. Most Spanish-speaking people in the Midwest are of Mexican descent, though there is a substantial population of Puerto Rican immigrants in major urban centers like Chicago. With the tremendous growth of evangelical/Pentecostal churches in Hispanic communities, the percentage of Catholics has fallen from close to 80 percent to 65 percent in the second generation. As the population continues to expand, the diversification of religious practices is likely to continue.

The first waves of Middle Eastern immigrants arrived in the early twentieth century and comprised mostly Christians and Muslims from Lebanon, Syria, and Egypt. Communities in Michigan and Illinois, chiefly in urban areas, survive to this day and include thriving populations of Muslims from Egypt, Pakistan, and Saudi Arabia. A religion with roots in Iran has also made inroads into the Midwest: The Baha'i temple in Wilmette, Illinois, is the largest in the United States and was built largely with help from immigrant followers.

Varieties of Hinduism are represented in the Midwest. In the Chicago suburbs are temples dedicated to specific gurus, transplanted by immigrants who were the gurus' followers in India. In Iowa, practitioners of the Maharishi Mahesh Yogi's Transcendental Meditation (TM) relocated some years ago to found Vedic City, a community dedicated to TM teachings. There are also communities of Hindu-derived religions in suburban Chicago, where a Jain temple was built in the early 1980s, and in Michigan, where the Sikh community has grown to such an extent that there are now specializations in Sikh studies at the University of Michigan. Hindu temples vary from multideity temples meant to serve as worship centers and gathering places for major festivals of various gods to temples dedicated to movements like Swaminarayan or Balaji.

Among Asian immigrants, there are several strains of Buddhism, Christianity, and animism. Vietnamese immigrants have brought their distinctive brand of Theravada Buddhism as well as several varieties of Christianity. There are Vietnamese-language Catholic churches as well as a significant representation of Vietnamese in the Protestant denomination the Christian Missionary Alliance. Laotian and Hmong immigrants are represented most in urban areas of Wisconsin and Illinois, respectively. Laotian Buddhist temples can be found in Illinois and Wisconsin. The Hmong, who settled in Wisconsin and Minnesota in the mid-1970s, are predominantly animist and have brought their unique customs of funeral practice and health care management with them, often causing a clash with local cultures not used to the highly shamanistic nature of Hmong religion. At the end of the twentieth century, there were twenty-four thousand Hmong in the Twin Cities area alone.

Sources and Further Reading: Catherine Albanese, *America: Religions and Religion*, 3rd ed. (1999); John Bodnar, *The Transplanted* (1985); Helen Rose Ebaugh and Janet Saltzman Chafetz, *Religion and the New Immigrants* (2000).

Arlene M. Sánchez Walsh
Azusa Pacific University, California

Higher Education

In the Midwest, as in the rest of the United States, most higher educational institutions were under religious auspices until the twentieth century. Even public institutions were frequently led by minister-presidents until well into the 1800s.

The reasons for establishing postsecondary institutions under explicit religious auspices were varied. The Midwest was seen by many Protestants as the battleground with Catholics for domination of the new republic. For Roman Catholics, higher educational institutions anchored the church's presence and served as centers for pastoral activity. Concern to transmit ethnic cultures also prompted institutional establishment. By 1870, at least twenty-one religiously affiliated colleges had been founded in Illinois and another thirteen in Iowa.

Prior to the Civil War, mainline Protestants dominated the field. Congregationalists were among the major proponents of higher education. Throughout the region, institutions such as Oberlin, Beloit, and Knox Colleges testified to the educational drive of missionaries who came to evangelize the West. Methodists, because of a theology that emphasized personal religious experience over formal learning, had initially shown little interest in colleges. However, the need to train clergy, coupled with the desire to establish themselves on a par with other Protestant groups, promoted sponsorship after the 1830s. At least thirteen midwestern colleges were begun, including DePauw, Northwestern, Baker, Ohio Wesleyan, and Hamline. During this same era, Baptists were also active in collegiate formation. Having entered into cooperative agreements with other denominations, they took the lead in creating at least five colleges, including Denison, Franklin, and Hillsdale.

Presbyterians established midwestern colleges. Beginning with Hanover in 1827, they founded Coe and what is now the University of Dubuque, as well as Blackburn, and partnered with Congregationalists in forming Illinois College and Knox. The Episcopal Church created three colleges by the mid-1850s. The missionary bishop Philander Chase was instrumental in establishing a seminary that would become Kenyon College, as well as Jubilee College. These were followed by Racine College. An American-founded denomination, the Disciples of Christ, also was among the first to create colleges. It began Columbia, Hiram, and Eureka prior to the Civil War.

Only a small number of Roman Catholic schools developed in the early nineteenth century. One of the first was St. Xavier College in Cincinnati, founded as the Athenaeum of Ohio and chartered in 1831. Another was St. Louis University, established by the local bishop in 1818 but taken over by the Jesuits and formally established in 1832. A land bequest in north-central Indiana resulted in the creation of Notre Dame in 1842, though the college was a de facto primary school throughout its early years. A few women's colleges, such as St. Mary's at Notre Dame, were also founded.

Pre–Civil War religious colleges, while denominationally related, generally did not have strong sectarian ties. Many were the creations of religious entrepreneurs rather than denominational ventures. Most were quite small: The average enrollment in Ohio's religious colleges in 1859 was eighty-five students. Fragile in resources, many failed.

By the last years of the nineteenth and the first of the twentieth century, many secular institutions were choosing lay presidents. The same process of secularization was at work in religious colleges. Schools such as Oberlin, Franklin, and Ripon gradually became more secular and eventually disaffiliated from the sponsoring religious bodies.

New religious colleges differed from their predecessors. As immigration from non-anglophone Europe increased, many were created to transmit ethnoreligious cultures. These denominations as well as new, more conservative American religious groups accounted for the majority of new foundations. Those institutions established by older, mainstream churches tended to be tied more closely to the sponsoring religious body.

Many of these characteristics are exemplified by the wide array of Lutheran colleges. The second great wave of German immigration brought more than 1.2 million Germans to the United States by 1860 and led to a greater interest in ethnic preservation. The Lutheran Church Missouri Synod became an educational leader, sponsoring at least nine regular and teacher's colleges prior to World War I, including Concordia Teachers and St. John's.

Migration in the late nineteenth and early twentieth centuries brought more than two million Swedes to the United States. Clergy education was an immediate need. Seminaries and academies quickly turned into colleges, so that by 1900 there were at least three midwestern colleges with a Swedish Lutheran culture, including Augustana, Gustavus Adolphus, and Bethany. During this same era, Swedish Baptists founded Bethel and the Swedish Covenant Church established North Park.

This same period witnessed Norwegian immigration, though in smaller numbers. At least seven colleges were founded by the end of World War I, including Luther, St. Olaf, and Augustana. The still smaller Danish and Finnish immigrations resulted in the formation of at least two colleges, Dana and Grand View, by Danes and Suomi by Finns. The concentration of Lutheran groups in the Midwest made the region the dominant center for Lutheran education in America, with at least twenty-two colleges.

Dutch groups who came to the Midwest in the late nineteenth century founded several colleges to transmit Reformed theology and Dutch culture. The Reformed Church in America established Hope and Northwestern (Iowa) Colleges, while the Christian Reformed Church founded Calvin.

Though radical reformation groups had typically opposed higher education in Europe, immigration shifted this pattern. Mennonites started at least four midwestern colleges, including Bethel and Goshen. The Church of the Brethren established at least eight more, such as Ashland, Manchester, and Plattsburg.

During the latter part of the nineteenth century the bible college, with its emphasis on practical education for ministry, emerged as a new element on the religious higher educational scene. The largest midwestern examples are Baptist and Central Bible Colleges in Missouri and Moody Bible Institute in Chicago.

Two other conservative American-founded denominations were also significant. The Reorganized Church of Jesus Christ of Latter Day Saints built Park and Graceland colleges, while the Seventh-day Adventists established a college at Battle Creek, Michigan, which would later become Andrews University, as well as Union College.

Twentieth-century Protestant college formation was done disproportionately by conservative groups. Missouri Synod Lutherans took over Valparaiso University in 1925, turning it into their flagship institution. The Association of Regular Baptists did the same with Cedarville College in 1953. Among the most prolific sponsors of higher education has been the Church of the Nazarene, establishing Olivet, Mt. Vernon, and Mid-America, two of them after 1960.

Roman Catholic higher education burgeoned after the Civil War, a testimony both to the growing Catholic population and to its prosperity. During this period, many Catholic institutions reconfigured themselves from the six-year German *Gymnasium* model to the four-year baccalaureate. These tended to emphasize professional education, including of women. In addition, communities of religious women established numerous colleges. Typical of these are Mount Mary College and the College of St. Catherine, the largest Catholic women's college in the United States. Financial constraints forced many to close or merge with large institutions.

By the end of the twentieth century, Catholic colleges and universities had become the dominant form of religious higher education in the Midwest. The sixty plus Catholic colleges and universities in the region in 2001 ranged in size from small liberal arts colleges like Benedictine, Presentation, and Notre Dame of Ohio, which enroll fewer than a thousand students, to DePaul University in Chicago, whose more than twenty thousand students make it the largest Catholic institution in the United States. Many of the schools that have managed to survive and prosper have done so as a result of moves to coeducation as well as innovative programming for adult and nontraditional students. The greatest number of American Catholic colleges are located in the Midwest.

Religious ministry to students at secular institutions has taken a variety of forms. The Young Men's Christian Association has been important, as has the Young Women's Christian Association, first organized at the Illinois State Normal School in 1873. Intervarsity Christian Fellowship has been disproportionately active in midwestern schools. Many groups also established college chaplaincies. These included the Melvin Catholic Club, begun at the University of Wisconsin in 1883, and the Hillel Foundation for Jewish students, first established at the University of Illinois in 1923.

The story of the relationship between religion and higher education in the Midwest is perhaps the most diverse in the United States. A rich array of ethnoreligious traditions motivated the formation of a wide variety of postsecondary institutions and agencies. In addition, nineteenth-century awareness of the potential of the Midwest for evangelization spurred attempts to establish schools as integral parts of the competition for souls.

Sources and Further Reading: Harold Buetow, *Of Singular Benefit* (1970); "Catholic Universities and Colleges," in Michael Glazier and Thomas J. Shelly, eds., *The Encyclopedia of American Catholic History* (1997); Philip Gleason, *Contending with Modernity* (1995); William J. Ringenberg, *The Christian College* (1984); Frederick Rudolph, *The American College and University* (1962); Richard W. Solberg, *Lutheran Higher Education in North America* (1985).

F. Michael Perko
Loyola University, Chicago

Race

"Race" is a concept subject to constantly evolving meanings, and the concentration here on interactions of religion with "blackness" and "whiteness" should not obscure the fact that race is a matter of great complexity for midwesterners and the entire nation.

The few African Americans resident in midwestern states during the earliest years of the republic grappled with the same kind of segregated church seating and racially discriminatory practices experienced by blacks nationwide. In Missouri, religious observances of African American slaves were sometimes subject to strict oversight by their white masters. Elsewhere in the Midwest, the formal prohibition of slavery contained in the Northwest Ordinance of 1787 could not mask the general hostility of whites to the presence of blacks in their midst, a hostility often formalized in laws, as in Ohio's Black Codes, enacted as early as 1804. Racial discriminatory attitudes were more pervasive among midwestern whites in the first half of the

nineteenth century than was an antislavery attitude. Even Oberlin College president Charles Finney, who believed that slavery was a sin, opposed racial integration in church pews.

These racially discriminatory practices sparked departures of African Americans from mixed-race churches and the formation of separate black churches. In the 1820s, John Berry Meachum formed an African Baptist Church in St. Louis with the assistance of two white Baptists. Black Baptist churches were formed in Illinois in the same decade, also with the help of sympathetic whites. In Cincinnati, African Americans formed a congregation of the African Methodist Episcopal Church (AME) in 1823. The formation of several black Baptist regional associations and the strenuous efforts of AME missionaries helped black churches to strengthen their community ties and to expand further throughout the Midwest.

However, many people strongly committed to human rights for African Americans questioned whether all-black congregations were the most suitable way to realize the universal, non–racially oriented message that they found in Christianity. Frederick Douglass in 1848 called the separate black churches "negro pews, on a higher and larger scale," maintaining that the black denominations provided an unfortunate confirmation of the regrettable, artificial construct of race. Instead of maintaining separate organizations, African Americans should witness within mixed-race churches on behalf of a real freedom and equality for all.

Some midwesterners agreed. In 1836, the Chillicothe, Ohio, presbytery recommended exclusion from communion for anyone advocating segregation of African Americans in churches, until such persons repented of their stance, and black abolitionist John Malvan's protest led in 1838 to an antisegregation policy in Cleveland's First Baptist Church. AME bishop and Ohioan Daniel Payne consistently supported the admission of white ministers and members into his denomination, on the grounds that it had been founded as a protest against the color bar and not as an exclusive refuge for African Americans. Payne also worked unsuccessfully to reunite black and white Methodists following the Civil War. In 1864, during the initial flush of optimism following emancipation, midwestern Baptists established an integrated missionary society, the American Baptist Free Mission Society. William P. Newman, a black Baptist pastor from Cincinnati, wrote, "We want a union of the . . . white and black . . . that shall revolutionize the religious and political sentiments of this country," arguing for establishing a "great equal-rights and gospel organization with the name of the American Baptist Anti-Caste Missionary Convention."

For several reasons, such sentiments proved mostly evanescent. The growth of separate black denominations and the formation of new ones, such as the Colored Methodist Episcopal Church in 1870 and the National Baptist Convention in 1895, continued unabated. Resurgent racism after the Civil War helped to squelch race-unifying sentiments among midwesterners, but African American Christians also found that separate black churches played an indispensable role in nurturing black culture and community, and hence insisted on their retention. Strongly conscious of the plight of millions of recently freed African Americans, midwestern blacks sought to unify with their southern neighbors. The Northwestern and Southern Baptist Convention, founded in 1864, played an important role in this regard. Reunion with whites took a distant second place to these newfound ties with the freed people of the South.

From 1880 to 1930, midwestern clergy associated with the "Social Gospel" movement, both white and black, did much to advance the cause of racial equality. Washington Gladden, a Social Gospel–oriented Congregationalist pastor in Columbus, Ohio, from 1882 until his death in 1918, showed growth in interracial outreach over his long tenure. In the 1880s, he had been largely concerned with conciliating white southerners, but he formed lasting friendships with black pastors and by the early 1900s had become a thoroughgoing social reformer with a firm and outspoken commitment to racial equality. Similar stands were taken by other Social Gospel advocates, such as Congregationalist pastor Charles Sheldon in Topeka, Kansas, and AME minister (later bishop) Reverdy Ransom, an Ohio native.

Racism nonetheless persisted among white church people. A newly resurrected Ku Klux Klan found wide support during the 1920s among mainline Protestant clergy and laity for its antiblack, anti-Catholic, and prohibitionist message in some midwestern states. Hundreds of Indiana Methodist, Baptist, Presbyterian, and Disciples of Christ clergy joined the Klan prior to the 1924 elections, while only a few white clergy opposed it. African Americans remaining in predominantly white churches during the early twentieth century found it difficult to cope with racial prejudice. Amy Robbins, a black member of the Reorganized Church of Jesus Christ of Latter Day Saints in Battle Creek, Michigan, was one layperson who in 1946 decided to hold religious meetings in her home after more than four decades of often painful experiences as one of very few blacks in a predominantly white congregational setting.

The "Great Migration" of southern blacks in the first half of the twentieth century brought millions of refugees to cities such as Chicago, Detroit, and Cleveland. This massive movement strengthened both the cultural importance and the pragmatic political power of northern black churches and their clergy. Southern migrants provided a receptive audience for a revived race consciousness preached by Jamaican immigrant Marcus Garvey in the 1920s: "Up you mighty race, you can accomplish what you will." Several messianic nationalist movements influenced by Garvey, including the Moorish Science Temple, the Nation of Islam, and the Hebrew Israelites, built a strong base in midwestern cities such as Chicago. Garvey explicitly worshipped a black Christ, but later messianic nationalists tended to repudiate Christianity as too tainted by idolatry of whiteness and its adherents' willingness to tolerate human rights abuses, strongly affirming the goodness of black people, who were seen, in the words of Nation of Islam leader Elijah Muhammad (né Elijah Poole), as "the original race." The Nation of Islam originated in Detroit in the early 1930s as a result of the preaching of an itinerant peddler, W. D. Fard, and the leadership of one of his Detroit converts, Elijah Muhammad.

Black Christian clergy also attracted many southern migrants with their strongly race-conscious messages. In 1927, William E. Guy, an AME pastor in Springfield, Illinois, wrote that "Christianity is hanging in the balance" because of the struggle with segregation. Yet if the black man "[will] exemplify this Christian religion to the world, . . . Almighty God will exalt him to a place of unquestioned supremacy among the sons of men."

During the civil rights movement of the 1940s to the 1960s, most mainline Protestants belatedly committed themselves to racial equality and racial integration. The first black United Methodist bishop assigned to a predominantly white area was James S. Thomas, who was appointed to head the Iowa Annual Conference in 1963. Previous black United Methodist bishops had supervised mainly black congregations. Also in 1963, the Commission on Religion and Race of the National Council of Churches devised a "Midwest strategy" in support of the civil rights bill, successfully mobilizing Protestant, Catholic, and Jewish clergy and laity to lobby the region's mostly Republican congressional delegations. Together with the efforts of labor unions and the National Association for the Advancement of Colored People (NAACP), this concerted effort by church people convinced midwestern members of Congress to vote overwhelmingly for the Civil Rights Act of 1964. Martin Luther King, Jr.'s, ill-starred 1966 Chicago campaign, which sought to end slums, promote open housing, and ensure civil rights, ran afoul of Mayor Richard J. Daley's subtle opposition and cooptation. No less problematic were lukewarm support by influential white clergy such as Catholic

Archbishop John Cody and the active opposition of King's black Baptist rival, Joseph H. Jackson, pastor of Olivet Baptist Church on Chicago's south side.

The civil rights revolution of the 1960s, however, produced fewer concrete changes in religious institutions than in other aspects of American life. Some predominantly white evangelical Protestant church groups apologized for condoning racist acts in the past and have reached out to black Christian counterparts. The predominantly white National Association of Evangelicals and the National Black Evangelical Association have agreed to hold future meetings jointly. AME, AME Zion, and Christian Methodist Episcopal churches have participated in ecumenical organizations such as the National Council of Churches, and they have also held periodic merger discussions with the predominantly white United Methodists. These discussions have not yet resulted in any firm agreements. Despite such welcome initiatives, Martin Luther King's statement that the eleven o'clock hour on Sunday morning is the most segregated hour in America still holds true.

Sources and Further Reading: Stephen W. Angell and Anthony B. Pinn, eds., *Social Protest Thought in the African Methodist Episcopal Church, 1862–1939* (2000); Joan L. Bryant, "Race and Religion in Nineteenth Century America," in Peter W. Williams, ed., *Perspectives on American Religion and Culture* (1999); Barbara J. Fields, "Ideology and Race in American History," in J. Morgan Kousser and James M. McPherson, eds., *Region, Race, and Reconstruction* (1982); James F. Findlay, Jr., *Church People in the Struggle* (1993); Roger D. Launius, "A Black Woman in a White Man's Church: Amy E. Robbins and the Reorganization," in Judith Weisenfeld and Richard Newman, eds., *This Far by Faith: Readings in African-American Women's Religious Biography* (1996); Leon F. Litwack, *North of Slavery* (1961); Carleton Mabee, *Black Freedom* (1970); Leonard J. Moore, *Citizen Klansmen* (1991); James M. Washington, *Frustrated Fellowship: The Black Baptist Quest for Social Power* (1986); Ronald C. White, Jr., *Liberty and Justice for All: Racial Reform and the Social Gospel, 1877–1925* (1990).

Stephen W. Angell
Earlham School of Religion, Indiana

Reform

Midwesterners have long contested the connection between religion and social reform. Within this crucible of religious pluralism, the region's residents have developed widely conflicting opinions about religion's ability to alleviate pressing social problems. Since the mid-nineteenth century, these competing attitudes have been evident in debates over alcohol, abolition, poverty, war, and other social issues. The history of religion and reform in the Midwest is thus a tale of spiritual diversity, impassioned disagreement, and uneasy coexistence.

The pluralistic religious culture that has typified the Midwest emerged in the early 1800s. Settlers carried with them an eclectic assortment of religious beliefs and practices and made the region a spiritual hothouse. During the 1830s and 1840s, the Mormons were driven out of Kirtland, Ohio, and Nauvoo, Illinois, before they finally found their Zion in Utah. For the most part, however, migrants enjoyed a great deal of liberty to practice religion. The Midwest was particularly fertile ground for Protestant Christians, notably Methodists and Baptists accustomed to evangelizing on the nation's western borders. The region also attracted congregants of well-established churches, including the Congregational, Episcopalian, and Presbyterian denominations. Moreover, religious communitarians, such as the Amana Society, which took root in eastern Iowa in the 1850s; and the Amish, who established small communities in Ohio and Wisconsin, found that in the Midwest they were able to practice their religion in relative freedom. Finally, in the second half of the century, German Catholics and Scandinavian Lutherans crossed the Atlantic and settled in Illinois, Wisconsin, Iowa, Minnesota, and the Dakotas. The region thus became a sanctuary for an exceptional collection of Christian traditions.

One consequence of this diversity was that midwesterners often had profoundly different opinions about social reform. Evangelical Christians often believed that social activism was key to their spiritual salvation. More ritualistic Christians, including many ethnic Catholics, however, often argued that reform undermined the moral authority of the church. Such critical theological disagreements kept many religious midwesterners at odds with one another over a wide variety of social issues.

One issue that religious-minded midwesterners fought over was the consumption of alcohol. Evangelical Christians first rallied behind prohibition because they associated liquor with crime, family violence, destitution, and poor work habits. As early as the 1850s, religiously motivated settlers helped to enact new laws and constitutional amendments that prohibited liquor consumption in Ohio, Michigan, Iowa, and Indiana. The Midwest also became fertile ground for private religious organizations devoted to prohibition after the Civil War. Both the Women's Christian Temperance Union (1874) and the Anti-Saloon League (1893) emerged in Ohio, founded chapters throughout the region, and continued to agitate for national prohibition into the next century.

Not every devout midwesterner felt that prohibition offered a cure for the nation's social problems.

Main Street, Amana, Iowa, c. 1910. The Amana Colonies in Iowa were established in 1855. Photo by Friedrich Oehl. Courtesy Amana Heritage Society.

German Catholics in Wisconsin were suspicious of intertwining religion and secular activism and often saw prohibition as either a form of anti-Catholic nativism or an attack on their cultural values. Although the Midwest became a center of temperance reform during the nineteenth century, prohibition remained a contentious issue in the region until the 1930s.

Many pious midwesterners disagreed over the troubling issue of slavery in the United States. Abolition often enjoyed support among the region's religious leaders. Several evangelical religious organizations and colleges, including Oberlin College in Ohio and Knox College in Illinois, became bastions of abolition in the region during the 1830s and 1840s. The Midwest also boasted some of the most vocal antislavery religious leaders of the era. The journalist and Presbyterian minister Elijah P. Lovejoy became an abolitionist martyr when a mob killed him in Alton, Illinois, in 1837. In 1859, John Brown, who had spent much of his life in Ohio and Kansas, earned national notoriety when he claimed to be God's agent and attacked the federal arsenal at Harpers Ferry, Virginia, in an attempt to provoke a slave rebellion.

On the eve of the Civil War, the Midwest had become a vital center of abolition in the United States. Yet the complexity of midwestern religion meant that not every spiritually motivated inhabitant supported emancipation as fervently as Lovejoy or Brown. Many people, in fact, viewed abolition as a radical threat to social harmony and religious freedom. Catholics and German Lutherans denounced abolition for the same reason they criticized temperance reform: They be-

lieved that congregants should remain wholly devoted to the church and largely disengaged from the world's social problems beyond looking out for the material needs of their coreligionists.

Religious-minded midwesterners' attempts to limit liquor consumption and to bring an end to slavery remade two-party politics throughout the region. Religious affiliation became a crucial factor in determining partisan loyalties. For the most part, pietistic Christians who believed that they could only gain salvation by purifying the world around them, such as the Methodists, supported the Republican Party because of its strong stance on abolition, temperance, and other moral issues. However, members of more ritual-oriented denominations, including many ethnic Catholics who feared that social activism would distract congregants from the theological activities of the church, often supported Democrats who opposed the expansion of government power. In Ohio, Illinois, Wisconsin, and other midwestern states, pietistic voters typically outnumbered ritualists and helped ensure that reform-minded Republicans would continue to dominate regional politics into the twentieth century.

Reform continued to divide religious-minded midwesterners when they debated growing urban poverty during the late nineteenth and the twentieth centuries. After the Civil War, some devout midwesterners, many of whom had cut their teeth fighting for prohibition and abolition in the decades before, focused on a new set of social issues that accompanied the rise of big cities and urban industrialization. In response to poverty, many ministers championed the "Social Gospel," an activist theology based on the notion that Christians had a moral obligation to reform society and to help the urban poor. The Social Gospel found some of its most ardent advocates among Protestant ministers in the Midwest. Congregationalist clergy members, such as Washington Gladden and Josiah Strong in Ohio, George D. Herron in Iowa, and Charles Sheldon in Kansas, were some of the leading lights in the Social Gospel. Some midwestern Catholics also took up the charge to reform society. Religiously minded academics at colleges and universities across the Midwest also contributed to this new spirit of reform. University of Wisconsin economist and Episcopalian Richard T. Ely articulated a philosophical framework for social reform rooted in Christian principles. These spiritually motivated reformers had a lasting influence on the Midwest and the nation into the twentieth century.

By the 1910s, however, many pious midwesterners had begun to question the optimistic theological premises underlying the Social Gospel. In some cases, Methodists and members of other denominations became weary of reform-minded theology and longed for a return to more fundamental religious concerns. In 1905, Chicago minister Amzi C. Dixon argued that the church had no place in modern politics and should concentrate on improving the spiritual lives of its members. Around the same time, Iowa evangelist Billy Sunday electrified audiences with his assault on the Social Gospel and his attacks on liquor and political radicals. Critics also questioned social reform from the left. Beginning in the 1920s, Reinhold Niebuhr, an ethics professor at Union Theological Seminary in New York who had come of age in Missouri and spent thirteen years as a pastor in Detroit, argued that the theological tenets that informed the Social Gospel were no longer applicable. During the 1910s, Dixon, Sunday, Niebuhr, and other skeptical midwestern religious leaders raised significant questions about the lasting theological and spiritual costs of widespread church efforts to reform the world's problems.

The Great Depression challenged midwesterners to reassess their positions on church involvement in the secular world. At the local level, urban churches of almost all denominations addressed the desperate need of their members. In Chicago, churches and private religious organizations established soup kitchens, held fund-raisers, and organized clothing drives to assist poor, unemployed congregants. The colossal scope of the nation's economic turmoil, however, taxed such institutions to their limits and many clergy eagerly supported Franklin D. Roosevelt's federal welfare programs. Even Chicago Catholics, who had long been hostile to government relief on theological grounds, became convinced that federal programs could help assuage the problems of poor city dwellers.

At the same time, the region produced several of the nation's most influential socially conservative spiritual leaders who questioned Roosevelt's New Deal policies. In the 1930s, Gerald B. Winrod, a Baptist minister from Wichita, Kansas, filled his sermons with anti-Semitic attacks on New Deal programs. Father Charles E. Coughlin, a Catholic priest from Royal Oak, Michigan, who had once admired Roosevelt and his New Deal programs, increasingly used his national radio network, which reached an estimated forty million listeners at its height, to vilify the New Deal as a Communist plot. The popularity of such conservative spokespeople suggests that religiously based criticism of New Deal social programs was widespread in the Midwest.

Since the end of World War II, religious belief has continued to shape how many midwesterners have viewed social reform. Many residents of the region disagreed about American military involvement in Vietnam during the 1960s and 1970s. The conservative evangelical Church League of America, headquartered in Wheaton, Illinois, supported military escalation to prevent the spread of Communism in Southeast Asia. At the same time, however, religious-minded reformers from a range of denominations increasingly criticized President Lyndon B. Johnson's wartime policies. A number of pacifist clergy and churchgoers marched with student protestors at Wisconsin, Iowa, and the region's other universities to end the war. In 1970, a cohort of thirty-nine Methodist clergy argued that the United States was on the brink of military dictatorship. Two years later, former seminarian and South Dakota senator George McGovern opposed American involvement in Vietnam on moral grounds during an unsuccessful presidential campaign. The heated reaction to Vietnam demonstrated that deep theological divisions continued to separate many of the region's residents when it came to questions of social reform.

Ultimately, the story of religion and reform in the Midwest from the nineteenth century through modern times remains a tale of incredible spiritual diversity. Time and again, members of different denominations disagreed with one another about the need for social reform. The Midwest's religious geography has continued to evolve in ways that guarantee that church involvement in the secular world will remain a contested issue. Most important, an increasing number of non-Christians have settled in the region and have added to its religious diversity. Many Muslims now call the Midwest home. Detroit, in fact, boasts one of the largest Islamic populations in the country, and Muslims have established mosques throughout the region. Although many Jews have long inhabited the Midwest's major cities, some have also relocated to smaller rural communities such as Postville, Iowa. Furthermore, Hmong refugees from Laos who practice the Ua Dab faith have settled throughout Wisconsin and Minnesota. The arrival of such groups, along with the continued presence of a remarkable range of Christians, ensures that the Midwest will remain a spiritually diverse region in which people from different religious traditions will continue to debate contentious social issues, such as U.S. foreign policy, abortion, and cloning.

Sources and Further Reading: Sydney E. Ahlstrom, *A Religious History of the American People* (1972); Stephen G. Bloom, *Postville* (2000); Robert S. Ellwood, *The Fifties Spiritual Marketplace* (1997); Robert S. Ellwood, *The Sixties Spiritual Awakening* (1994); Jon Gjerde, *The Minds of the West* (1997); Nathan O. Hatch, *The Democratization of American Christianity* (1989); Richard Jensen, *The Winning of the Midwest* (1971); Paul Kleppner, *The Cross of Culture* (1970); James Brewer Stewart, *Holy Warriors* (1976); Ronald C. White, Jr. and C. Howard Hopkins, *The Social Gospel* (1976).

Eric J. Morser
Shippensburg University, Pennsylvania

Architecture

Midwestern religious architecture reflects the ethnic and religious diversity of the region and highlights the beliefs of the communities that have erected buildings to accommodate their worship.

Native American burial mounds and earthworks constitute the earliest religious building in the region. Archaeological examination of examples in all twelve midwestern states has yielded much information about the lives, beliefs, and death rituals of several pre- and post-Columbian groups. More than one hundred mounds remain in the Cahokia site near East St. Louis, Illinois, built by the Mississippian culture between C.E. 700 and 1400. This site includes the largest earthwork in North America, the terraced Monk's Mound, over 92 feet high and sixteen acres in size. Wisconsin is home to some four thousand mounds, many of them effigy mounds in the shape of birds, animals, and humans. Other significant examples are the Great Serpent Mound in Adams County, Ohio, which winds 1,348 feet in length and was built between 800 B.C.E. and C.E. 100, most likely by the Adena culture, and the geometrical earthworks in nearby Mound City built later by the Hopewell culture.

The next period of permanent religious building began in the early nineteenth century as settlers migrating to the Midwest erected modest log churches, which they soon replaced with more substantial churches. Old St. Ferdinand Shrine near St. Louis in Florissant, Missouri, built in 1834, incorporated the log walls of the earlier church built on the site within its brick façade. With its bell cupola and steeple, round-arch door and windows, small rose window, inscribed cross, and dentil fringe, the church projects a sense of transcendence and stability.

The small log-cabin chapel erected by the Holy Cross brothers in the early 1830s near what is now

Oak Ridge Lutheran Church, Hamar, Norway (relocated from Minnesota). Photo by Knut Djupedal. Courtesy The Norwegian Emigrant Museum's Photo Archives.

South Bend, Indiana, was replaced with a small Gothic church in the 1840s and the large Gothic revival Basilica of the Sacred Heart, featuring a cruciform plan with a 273-foot-long nave, a chancel, seven apsidal chapels, and a vaulted ceiling, in 1893. Such a progression indicated both the growing financial stability of the University of Notre Dame and the desire of Catholic leaders to identify with their European heritage. Similar efforts to replicate European buildings occurred among German immigrants in Iowa and Minnesota, who employed German architects. Assumption Church in St. Paul, with its twin Romanesque clock towers reportedly based on Munich's Ludwigskirche, was designed by Joseph Reidl, court architect for the ruling Wittelsbach family in Bavaria.

Churches of early Protestant settlers replicated on a small scale the colonial churches familiar to their congregations. By 1816, Baptists in Franklin County, Indiana, had replaced their log meetinghouse with the Little Cedar Grove Church, built on the colonial meetinghouse model. This two-story brick building featured an entry centered in the long wall and flanked by two windows and a sanctuary open to the roofline with a balcony on three sides. When the Congregationalists of Oberlin College decided to replace their small chapel, they chose to build a "plain church" representative of their New England Calvinist heritage. This rectangular brick meetinghouse with modest Greek revival elements contained a large, acoustically innovative sanctuary designed for the college's president and renowned preacher, Charles Grandison Finney.

In 1830, Joseph Smith and his followers arrived in eastern Ohio and within the year began construction of a temple for the new religious group, the Church of Jesus Christ of Latter-day Saints, or Mormons. The Kirtland Temple, a two-story building featuring a stuccoed façade, pointed arch windows and a classical entry, had one floor devoted to educational needs and another to worship. As the Mormons continued westward, they erected more buildings, including another temple in Nauvoo, Illinois. Although the Nauvoo Temple was destroyed in 1850, its recent reconstruction has created a religious landmark of great significance to Latter-day Saints, who visit the site to pay homage to their nineteenth-century predecessors.

Urban growth in the late nineteenth century launched a period of monumental religious construction as congregations of all types vied to claim a place in changing city landscapes. Cincinnati's unique Reform Jewish Plum Street Temple featured both Moorish and Gothic elements, with a vaulted nave, a clerestory, side aisles, transepts, and stained glass windows, and with an exterior combining Gothic pointed arches with Moorish elements such as two slender towers resembling minarets. Across the street is St. Peter-in-Chains Cathedral, a Greek revival Catholic church modeled after a Greek temple. Nearby stands the quarried-stone–faced Covenant-First Presbyterian Church, which melds both Gothic and Romanesque elements. Such a blend of architectural styles came to characterize the religious landscapes of most midwestern cities during the final quarter of the century and indicated growing urban diversity.

By 1900, immigrants from southern and eastern Europe brought new styles to this architecturally diverse landscape. In Cleveland, Russian Orthodox immigrants erected the impressive St. Theodosius Cathedral, built on a Greek cross plan and featuring both Byzantine and Romanesque elements, the most striking of which is the central onion dome surrounded by twelve smaller ones, representing Jesus and the apostles.

This period also saw development of a new Protestant worship space, the auditorium sanctuary, an amphitheater-like room with sloped floors and curvilinear seating radiating upward from the elaborate stage housing a pulpit, choir, and organ. Hundreds of such churches throughout the Midwest—like Manistee, Michigan's, First Congregational, designed by William Le Baron Jenney, and Minneapolis's Wesley Methodist Episcopal, designed by Warren H. Hayes—owe their existence to the economic prosperity of the 1880s and 1890s and the movement of wealthy city residents to new residential areas.

Rural religious buildings remained modest. Architectural pattern books sanctioned by Protestant denominations strongly influenced midwestern buildings with their championing of the Gothic revival style. Among the many modest Gothic churches are the Danske Evangelist Lutheran Kirke, built by Danish settlers in Denmark, Kansas, in 1880. Though only vaguely Gothic in form, the three white clapboard prairie churches depicted in Dorothea Lange's famous photograph taken near Winner, South Dakota, also illustrate typical rural churches. These small buildings proved highly functional, and as Jewish immigrants moved into the upper Midwest, particularly northern Minnesota, they occasionally purchased them for refurbishment as synagogues.

In the twentieth century, renewed interest in the Gothic revival style resulted in the erection of many new churches, including architect Ralph Adams Cram's St. Paul's Episcopal Cathedral in Detroit and Fourth Presbyterian Church in Chicago. Soon, however, a modernist aesthetic, indicating congregations' embrace of science and technology, became influential. Frank Lloyd Wright's Unitarian church, Unity Temple, in Oak Park, Illinois, combined new construction technologies and Japanese architectural motifs. By the 1950s, Finnish architects Eero and Eliel Saarinen had built important buildings in the Midwest, including Minneapolis's Christ Church Lutheran, a rectangular building with a semidetached tower and a boxlike nave illuminated by natural light that dramatically floods the chancel through a slender floor-to-ceiling window. The modernist aesthetic is also apparent in Wright's flying-saucer-like Annunciation Greek Orthodox Church in Wauwatosa, Wisconsin; Marcel Breuer's St. John's University Chapel with its monumental bell banner hovering like a sail over the prairie in Collegeville, Minnesota; and the nautiluslike Temple of the Reorganized Latter Day Saints in Independence, Missouri.

Twentieth-century immigrant groups have influenced the religious landscape of the Midwest. Among the earliest mosques in the United States was the Mother Mosque of Cedar Rapids, Iowa, built in 1934 by Lebanese Muslims. This modest storefront building remains an important landmark for Muslims. With growing Muslim populations, all midwestern cities now boast mosques, which are typically identified by a slender minaret, used to call the faithful to prayer—an Islamic architectural symbol as evocative as the Christian steeple. An exception is the Mosque Maryam in Chicago, a Byzantine-style building with a large central dome, originally erected as a Greek Orthodox church but purchased by the Nation of Islam in 1972. Temples erected by Buddhist immigrants from Vietnam, Cambodia, and Laos, with the traditional pagodas and inverted arches of East Asian architecture, also exist in many midwestern metropolitan areas. Hindu temples in the region include the Hindu Temple of Greater Chicago, a religious complex containing two temples; the Sri Rama temple, built in the south Indian style of the Chola dynasty (C.E. ninth–thirteenth centuries) and boasting an eighty-foot *gopuram*, or entrance tower; and the smaller Ganesha-Shiva-Durga temple, built in the style of the Kalinga dynasty (first century B.C.E.). These many types of religious buildings attest to the pluralism that has long characterized midwestern religious architecture.

Also new to midwestern church architecture are Protestant megachurches, featuring large auditoriums with state-of-the-art theatrical technologies and family-oriented social spaces including food courts and recreation arcades. Modeled after the Willow Creek Church in South Barrington, Illinois, their mission is to make attending church as familiar and comfortable as possible.

Sources and Further Reading: Foster Armstrong, Richard Klein, and Cara Armstrong, *A Guide to Cleveland's Sacred Landmarks* (1992); Robert A. Birmingham and Leslie E. Eisenberg, *Indian Mounds of Wisconsin* (2000); Marilyn J.

Chiat, *America's Religious Architecture* (1997); Jeanne Halgren Kilde, *Church Becomes Theatre* (2002); George A. Lane, *Chicago Churches and Synagogues* (1981); Peter W. Williams, *Houses of God* (1997).

Jeanne Halgren Kilde
Macalester College, Minnesota

Publishing

The religious newspaper was understood by many people to be a key way to communicate to the masses migrating into the nineteenth-century Midwest. One minister expressed this sentiment well in the Circleville (Ohio) *Religious Telescope:* "A well conducted religious periodical is like a thousand preachers, flying in almost as many directions, by means of horses, mail stage[coach]s, steam boats, rail road cars, ships, . . . offering life and salvation to the sons of men in almost every clime." Spectacular growth in religious publishing occurred in the 1830s. Cincinnati became a hub for the distribution of printing supplies and more efficient presses, and by 1840 no fewer than forty thousand weekly or biweekly papers were in circulation.

These papers typically featured secular news as well as theological matters and news of particular local congregations, denominational concerns, or voluntary societies. In addition to English-language periodicals sponsored by Protestant denominations, many foreign-language papers, primarily German and Scandinavian, served immigrant communities. They promoted both the preservation of ethnic traditions and assimilation into the swiftly changing majority culture. Whatever the language or religion, periodicals were often directed at very specific audiences. *Die Deborah,* for example, was for women who were slower to learn English than their husbands. Men read Rabbi Isaac Mayer Wise's *American Israelite,* the oldest Jewish newspaper in America.

Religious periodicals played a part in transforming midwestern society. Publications such as the *Catholic Telegraph* challenged the Protestant press to assist working people struggling against the abuses of railroad companies. Editors also had much to say about temperance and public education, generally dividing along Protestant and Catholic lines. The printed page was used to engage a political battle over slavery from moral and religious grounds well before the outbreak of the Civil War. By the middle of the nineteenth century, however, a new form of communication was arguably as influential as the religious periodical—the novel.

Harriet Beecher Stowe's *Uncle Tom's Cabin* (first serialized in the *National Era* and then published as a novel in 1852) was written in Maine, but it might not have been written at all were it not for her exposure to radical antislavery efforts during her fourteen years in Cincinnati. Despite its flaws, noted by northern and southern, black and white reviewers alike, *Uncle Tom's Cabin* influenced many white Northerners to change their minds about slavery. It also marked a turning point in religious leaders' attitudes toward novels. No longer an oxymoron, Christian fiction became central to religious publishing.

What *Uncle Tom's Cabin* did for slavery, Charles Sheldon's novel *In His Steps* did for the didactic writings of the father of the "Social Gospel," Washington Gladden of Columbus, Ohio. This popular religious novel, whose influence has recently been extended to the present day, reflects some of the complex social, political, and religious changes that the United States was experiencing in the late 1800s. *In His Steps* was originally read to Sheldon's congregation in Topeka, Kansas, in the fall of 1896 and was then serialized in the *Advance*, a Congregational weekly. The story revolved around a spiritually stagnant minister and congregation who were revitalized by asking the question "What would Jesus do?" The question was not relegated to some spiritual realm but applied to the town and country's moral, social, political, and economic problems. Sin was viewed as institutional as well as personal. Sheldon tried to sell *In His Steps* to two major publishers in Chicago, the McClurg Company and Fleming H. Revell. Both turned him down. Revell was founded by the son-in-law of Chicago's famous evangelist Dwight L. Moody, and the rejection of the novel by Revell may prefigure what some have called "the Great Reversal" wherein evangelicals downplayed corporate social action, in part out of fear that it somehow supplanted or detracted from the personal saving work of Jesus Christ.

For good or for ill, the marketplace has influenced the religious publishing culture, its relationship to individualism, and the mission of publishing companies. This influence is sometimes magnified among evangelicals. When fundamentalists split from the mainline denominations in the 1920s, a huge vacuum was created for Sunday school materials, magazines, and books from their theological perspective. New companies were formed and some older companies repositioned themselves to fill this void. Zondervan Publishing House and the William B. Eerdmans Publishing Company began as small, family-owned concerns primarily serving the Dutch Reformed from their home bases in Grand Rapids, Michigan. But they expanded to capture a share of the northern evangelical market in the 1930s. In 1988, Harper & Row (now Harper-Collins), a major trade company with an ecumenical religious division that includes New Age titles, ac-

quired Zondervan. Critics wonder what happens to the religious mission of a company that is controlled by stockholders in an open market, or even by a privately held company that places an undue emphasis on profit.

Much more could be said about midwestern religious publishing companies with great local or national influence. The premier periodicals of liberal and evangelical Protestantism (the *Christian Century* and *Christianity Today*, respectively) are both based in or near Chicago. Crossway Books in Wheaton, Illinois, launched the best-selling novel by Frank Peretti *This Present Darkness* (1986), which unleashed a whole new genre of books about spiritual warfare. Christian romance novels have proliferated. Kenneth Taylor's paraphrase of the Bible for his children (resulting in *The Living Bible* and the subsequent founding of Tyndale House Publishers) changed the way many think about the Bible. The influence of Willow Creek Community Church near Chicago, the subsequent development of an association of "seeker churches" which collaborates with publishing companies to market its curriculum, has changed the way many clergy think about the church.

Sources and Further Reading: Joel A. Carpenter, *Revive Us Again* (1997); P. Mark Fackler and Charles H. Lippy, eds., *Popular Religious Magazines of the United States* (1995); John F. Ferré, "Searching for the Great Commission: Evangelical Book Publishing since the 1970s," in Quentin J. Schultze, ed., *American Evangelicals and the Mass Media* (1990); John F. Ferré, *A Social Gospel for Millions* (1988); Thomas F. Gossett, *Uncle Tom's Cabin and American Culture* (1985); George M. Marsden, *Fundamentalism and American Culture* (1980); Martin E. Marty, "Protestantism and Capitalism: Print Culture and Individualism," in Leonard I. Sweet, ed., *Communication and Change in American Religious History* (1993); Martin E. Marty et al., eds., *The Religious Press in America* (1963); Wesley Norton, *Religious Newspapers in the Old Northwest to 1861* (1977).

Douglas Milford
Wheaton College, Illinois

Specific Traditions and Communities

African American Religious Movements

Most African Americans in the nineteenth-century Midwest were Methodists and Baptists. Because of racism, they worshiped separately. In Cincinnati, African Americans were forbidden to shout in the churches, and in 1823 an African American man died while trying to stifle a shout in church. This led to an

African American exodus from the Methodist Episcopal Church and the formation of an African Methodist Episcopal (AME) congregation, pastored by James King, a slave from Lexington, Kentucky, who was permitted to hire his time.

Also in the early 1820s, Richard Allen, founder of the AME Church, sent his first missionary to black settlements in Ohio, and soon many African American ministers, including David Smith, William Paul Quinn, and Jarena Lee were proselytizing in Chillicothe, Zanesville, and Columbus, making Ohio an area of strength for the AME Church. Paul Quinn, beginning in 1836, planted African Methodism in such states as Illinois and Missouri.

Black Baptists also found the Midwest fruitful ground. Some of the earliest black Baptist associations were formed there, including the Providence Association in southeastern Ohio in 1834; the Union Association in southwestern Ohio in 1836; the Wood River Association (later the Western Convention) in 1839, centered in Illinois but embracing far-flung churches in Wisconsin and Kansas; and the Amherstburg Association, which included churches in Michigan and Canada West.

Ohio was an important center of African American education. Some of the earliest leaders in the Midwest were educated at Oberlin College, including John Mifflin Brown, a preacher later elevated to bishop in the AME Church. A significant milestone was reached in 1856 when AME bishop Daniel A. Payne founded the institution that would later be known as Wilberforce College near Xenia, Ohio. While AME clergy later founded other schools, mostly in the South, Wilberforce was universally regarded as that church's flagship educational institution.

Early African American religious movements differed in the forcefulness with which they advocated antislavery principles. Samuel Davis of the Amherstburg Association spoke very directly in 1843, urging African Americans no longer to "submit in silence to our accumulated wrongs." The AME Church adopted a more muted stance when it rejected a radical abolitionist plank at its 1856 General Conference in St. Louis, accepting Richard Robinson's judgment that the strong statement was useless because "every colored man is an abolitionist, and slaveholders know it." Many black Methodists and Baptists threw themselves into "uplifting the race," especially in the South after emancipation. Ohio AME bishop Daniel Payne visited his birthplace, Charleston, South Carolina, when it fell to Union forces and helped organize AME churches in the South.

Like their colleagues in other regions, many black ministers in the Midwest played an active part in politics. AME minister Benjamin Arnett, a powerful force in Ohio politics and church affairs, was elected to the Ohio legislature in 1886. Becoming a bishop in 1888, he was a confidante of President William McKinley. Hiram Revels, an AME minister in several midwestern states, accompanied a Missouri regiment south during the Civil War to Mississippi. In 1870, he became the first African American elected to the U.S. Senate. Revels's election was engineered by Jesse Boulden, formerly a pastor of Chicago's Zion Baptist Church.

With the collapse of Reconstruction in the 1870s, some southern blacks saw the Midwest as a haven from white supremacy. Benjamin "Pap" Singleton, an AME layman from Tennessee, helped to organize an exodus of African Americans to Kansas in 1879. Some of the "Exodusters" founded all-black towns such as Nicodemus, while others settled in existing cities such as Topeka.

In 1863, nine-year-old Augustus Tolton, a native of Missouri, was whisked by his mother across the Mississippi River to Springfield, Illinois, to escape the effects of civil war. Becoming the first American priest of unmixed African descent when ordained in Rome in 1886, Tolton returned to Illinois to pastor a church in Springfield, then went on to found a black Catholic church in Chicago before his premature death in 1897. In the past century, African American Catholics have grown in number to 2.3 million nationwide as of 2003, largely due to conversions. One such convert is Wilton Gregory, bishop of Belleville, Illinois, the first African American to be elected president of the U.S. Council of Catholic Bishops.

The "Social Gospel" received staunch support from some Chicago AME ministers such as Reverdy Ransom and Richard R. Wright, Jr. Ransom, who founded the Institutional AME Church in 1901 to provide social services to the poor throughout the week, wrote that his church was designed "to level the inequalities and bridge the chasms between rich and poor." Other, more conservative AME ministers ensured that the Chicago stays of Ransom and Wright were short-lived. But successful black Baptist and Methodist pastors soon found that they had to copy Ransom's actions, while leaving aside his rhetoric. This effort was encouraged by the onset of the "Great Migration" in the early 1900s, a major exodus of southern blacks seeking to escape human rights violations and to embrace economic opportunities in cities such as Chicago, Detroit, and Cleveland.

Two old-line churches that successfully accommodated the realities of this massive influx were Chicago churches: Olivet Baptist and Pilgrim Baptist. Olivet's membership increased from six hundred in 1902 to twelve thousand three decades later, largely because its pastors, most notably Lacy K. Williams, ascertained community needs and instituted social-service programs designed to meet those needs. Pilgrim Baptist Church, pastored by the dynamic J. C. Austin, was involved in many political and social activities, including the National Association for the Advancement of Colored People (NAACP) and the back-to-Africa movement of Marcus Garvey. It is most noted for its pioneering gospel chorus, led by renowned Chicago jazz musician Thomas Dorsey. Austin and Williams were bitter rivals, with Williams holding the coveted presidency of the National Baptist Convention, U.S.A., Inc. African American Methodist churches in the North grew by 85 percent during the Great Migration, and northern black Baptist churches grew by an even larger 151 percent, cementing Baptist predominance among African Americans in the Midwest.

The old-line black Methodist and Baptist churches did not meet the needs of all the new migrants. A startling variety of new religious movements catered to their needs, often meeting in low-rent storefront space. The modern-day Pentecostal movement, beginning at Azusa Street in Los Angeles in 1906, found plentiful converts among African Americans in the Midwest. Particularly successful was the racially mixed Pentecostal Assemblies of the World, headquartered in Indianapolis, professing worship of "Jesus only." The trinitarian Church of God in Christ also won many adherents. An eclectic Spiritualist movement, combining voodoo and communication with the dead with more conventional Catholic and Protestant elements, found a home among African Americans in such cities as Chicago, Detroit, and Kansas City, Missouri. Mother Leafy Anderson, who traveled from Chicago to New Orleans about 1920 and started Spiritualist congregations in both locations, is often identified as the founder of this tradition.

Many new religious movements were non-Christian. The Moorish Science Temple, founded by Timothy Drew, better known as Noble Drew Ali, expanded quickly from its East Coast origins to be centered in Chicago by the late 1920s. Declaring that his followers were not "Negroes," but rather "Moorish Americans," Ali combined black nationalism, Christian revivalism, and some Muslim elements in his teaching. After Ali's violent, mysterious death in Chicago in 1929, several small warring sects sought to build upon his heritage. The most successful turned out to be the Lost-Found Nation of Islam, led by Elijah (Poole) Muhammad. The Nation of Islam was founded in Detroit in 1931 by W. D. Fard, a salesman of mysterious origins. After his disappearance three years later, Muhammad assumed leadership of the movement. He taught that African Americans, descended from the tribe of Shabazz, had lost their knowledge of God and self, including their true identity as practitioners of Islam. His strong self-help message, combined with a militant black separatist ideology, appealed strongly to many black midwesterners, including a young man reared in Nebraska, Wisconsin, and Michigan: Malcolm Little, later Malcolm X. After Muhammad died in 1975, the Black Muslim movement suffered more division, but its most prominent branch, the Nation of Islam headed by Louis Farrakhan, is still headquartered in Chicago.

The Midwest has continued to nurture religiously based African American movements for social change. A campaign enlisting Martin Luther King, Jr., to end segregation and racial discrimination in Chicago in 1966 achieved less dramatic results than the campaign in Selma, Alabama, the previous year, but Operation PUSH and the Rainbow Coalition, strongly supported by black churches and headed by Jesse Jackson, were headquartered in Chicago and spearheaded advances in political and economic freedoms in the years after King's death. In 2001, the Baptist Ministers' Conference of Cincinnati was a key supporter of a boycott against the city of Cincinnati, protesting police, housing, and economic discrimination.

Sources and Further Reading: Hans A. Baer and Merrill Singer, *African-American Religion in the Twentieth Century* (1992); Randall Burkett, "The Baptist Church in Years of Crisis: J. C. Austin and Pilgrim Baptist Church, 1926–1950," in Paul E. Johnson, ed., *African-American Christianity* (1994); Cyprian Davis, *The History of Black Catholics in the United States* (1992); Carol V. R. George, "Widening the Circle: The Black Church and the Abolitionist Crusade, 1830–1860," in Timothy E. Fulop and Albert J. Raboteau, eds., *African-American Religion* (1997); C. Eric Lincoln, *The Black Muslims in America*, 3rd ed. (1994); Daniel Payne, *History of the African Methodist Episcopal Church* (1969); R. C. Ransom, "The Institutional Church," in Stephen W. Angell and Anthony B. Pinn, ed., *Social Protest Thought in the African Methodist Episcopal Church, 1862–1939* (2000); Milton C. Sernett, *Bound for the Promised Land* (1997); James Melvin Washington, *Frustrated Fellowship* (1986).

Stephen W. Angell
Earlham School of Religion, Indiana

Amish and Mennonites

Mennonites and Amish form a sectlike branch of Christianity with intellectual roots in the New Testament church combined with a unique sixteenth-century European heritage. In a worldwide population exceeding one million, nearly three hundred thousand people are affiliated with established congregations in the twelve states of the American Midwest, where roughly 43 percent identify as Amish, and the rest as Mennonite.

Many Mennonites and Amish in Ohio and adjacent states stem from origins in Pennsylvania, where in the late seventeenth century their German and Swiss ancestors began to arrive and settle in North America. Rapid expansion in the nineteenth century brought additional numbers to the Midwest, where they were later joined by others coming directly from Switzerland, Germany, Alsace, and even Russia and the Ukraine. Whether known as Amish or as Mennonites, these migrants carried with them an ethical rather than a sacramental form of Christianity with a foundation in Anabaptism.

The Anabaptist movement developed in Switzerland in the 1520s with a call for literal obedience to the teachings of Christ and an emphasis on the New Testament rather than the established church as the basic authority for everyday life. Adherents argued for separation of church and state, and they formed communities of believers who espoused an ethic of love that (for most groups) meant rejecting violence in all aspects of life. Based upon a voluntary confession of faith, their practice of adult baptism (with its implied rejection of infant baptism) led others to label them as Anabaptists (meaning rebaptized) and brand them as heretics. Seen as a challenge to established authority, they were vigorously persecuted, and thousands were executed. Flight from persecution combined with missionary zeal to spread the movement into Germany, the Netherlands, and elsewhere.

The writings and influential leadership of Menno Simons, a Dutch Catholic priest who became an Anabaptist in 1536, led to the use of his name by many Anabaptists of the sixteenth century and later. Similarly, the Amish received their name from Jakob Amman, an Anabaptist leader who in 1693 advocated stricter practices to bring about a renewal of church life. Since Amman's time the Amish and the Mennonites have followed distinctive paths that nonetheless continue to overlap in many ways. Typically more open to change, many Mennonites have roots in stricter Amish traditions.

Despite a shared foundation of Anabaptist beliefs and practices, Amish and Mennonite communities today express many divisions often bewildering to the outsider. Donald B. Kraybill and C. Nelson Hostetter collapse this diversity into three groups—traditional, transitional, and transformational—with many shades of difference within each category.

Traditional groups concentrate on preserving their religious and cultural ways and are very cautious about engaging the larger culture. Typical traits include the use of horse-drawn transportation and a very selective use of technology, using a special dialect such as Pennsylvania German, wearing distinctive clothing, preserving older forms of worship and ritual, practicing nonresistance, preferring occupations in agriculture and related enterprises, and even referring to themselves as Old Order. The best example of a traditional group is the Old Order Amish, found in large numbers in Ohio and Indiana, with lesser numbers elsewhere in the Midwest as far west as Kansas.

Like the Old Orders, transitional groups generally ordain lay pastors, forbid divorce and the ordination of women, and discourage higher education; but they allow greater freedom regarding other traits characteristic of the Old Orders. They allow ownership of automobiles, use electricity, and actively engage in evangelism. Transitional groups include the Amish Mennonites, Beachy Amish, and Conservative Mennonites—names that suggest movement away from Old Order identity and practices.

Transformational groups have moved even further from sectlike Mennonite roots and toward becoming almost indistinguishable from many other Protestant groups in the United States. They support higher education—with colleges like Bethel in Kansas, Bluffton in Ohio, and Goshen in Indiana. They often hold professional jobs, participate in mainstream activities including politics, operate large church organizations, accept modern technology and a much broader base of individual expression, emphasize involvement in peacemaking and social justice, and in general are fully engaged in the larger social and cultural milieu. The prime example of a transformational group is the Mennonite Church USA, formed in 2002 through a merger of two previous groups. This new expression of the Mennonite heritage also includes small but increasing numbers of urban populations with Hispanic and African American identities.

Sources and Further Reading: Cornelius J. Dyck, ed., *An Introduction to Mennonite History* (1993); John A. Hostetler, *Amish Society* (1993); Donald B. Kraybill and C. Nelson Hostetter, *Anabaptist World USA* (2001); Levi Miller, *Our People: The Amish and Mennonites of Ohio* (1992); Steven M. Nolt, *A History of the Amish* (2003); Calvin Redekop, *Mennonite Society* (1989); Theron F. Schlabach, *Peace, Faith, Nation* (1988).

Carl R. Jantzen
Miami University, Oxford, Ohio

Baptists

The Baptists are the largest family of Protestants in the United States. They had thirty-six million members in 1996, divided into a multitude of denominations.

The Baptist movement originated in the radical wing of the English Reformation of the seventeenth century. Baptists believed that no one could be considered a true Christian without a conscious, adult profession of faith, and a corresponding baptism. They formed voluntary congregations consisting of true Christian believers, insisting that these congregations were the essence of the true church. The local congregation determined true teachings and ordained its leaders. All structures beyond the local congregation were merely advisory. Traditionally, Baptists have believed in a strict separation of church and state, and in the freedom of all believers to determine Biblical truth for themselves, a concept known as "soul liberty."

Baptist congregations were established throughout the American colonies during the colonial period, and after a slow beginning grew to become the third-largest Protestant group after the Congregationalists and the Presbyterians. Their growth accelerated during the nineteenth century because of their expansion into the frontier areas of the Midwest, the South, and the Southwest. The Baptist form of organization was uniquely suited to frontier conditions. Because the church did not insist on a formally educated, full-time clergy, itinerant Baptist preachers gathered congregations wherever like-minded individuals could be found. Baptists expanded into the Midwest early in the nineteenth century through two routes, one through the Great Lakes region, and the other through the Ohio, Mississippi, and Missouri River basins.

Slow to form national organizations, Baptists began to form cooperative organizations to advance home and foreign missions, moral reform, and the production of Bibles and other publications. Tensions over slavery caused southern Baptists to break ties with their northern counterparts in 1845 and establish the Southern Baptist Convention (SBC). Northern Baptists formed a unified organization, the Northern Baptist Convention (NBC), in 1907, eventually known as the American Baptist Churches in the U.S.A. These northern Baptists founded many of the first wave of Baptist congregations in the Midwest as well as educational and social-service organizations; among them the antecedents of the University of Chicago.

The Northern Baptists were divided by theological liberalism during the late nineteenth century. Two groups of midwestern conservative congregations left the NBC during the first half of the twentieth century: the General Association of Regular Baptist Churches in 1932, and the Conservative Baptist Association of America in 1947, both headquartered in suburban Chicago. In Minnesota, conservative Baptist leader William Bell Riley was influential, and the state was also the longtime home of the Billy Graham Evangelistic Association.

European immigrants helped to shape the Baptist tradition in the Midwest. Swedish Baptists in the upper Midwest formed the Baptist General Conference in 1852 and organized Bethel College and Seminary in St. Paul, Minnesota. German Baptists formed the North American Baptist Conference in 1865 and established their college and seminary at Sioux Falls, South Dakota. Both groups initially cooperated with the NBC, but they joined other conservatives in pulling away from the group in the twentieth century. There are also smaller groups of Russian and Ukrainian Baptists in the upper Midwest and Canada.

Baptists in America have split many times over doctrine and practice, into groups of Regular (Calvinist), General (Arminian), Free-Will, Separate, and Primitive Baptists. Many of these groups, which have been particularly active in Appalachia and the Upland South, found their way into the southern regions of Ohio, Indiana, Illinois, and Missouri. Often, they consist of small conventions of like-minded congregations. One group, the General Association of General Baptists, has its headquarters in Poplar Bluff, Missouri, and its college in Oakland City, Indiana. Another group, the Seventh-Day Baptist General Conference, has its headquarters in Janesville, Wisconsin.

The SBC is the largest Baptist denomination in the United States, with around sixteen million members. Historically, the only midwestern state with a strong Southern Baptist presence was Missouri, but since 1950 the SBC has expanded dramatically, with congregations throughout the region. In the southern Midwest, they have become numerous. A major Southern Baptist seminary is located near Kansas City. A nineteenth-century offshoot from the Southern Baptists, the Landmark Baptists, has congregations in Missouri and Kansas.

With a combined membership of fourteen million members, the various African American Baptist organizations are the largest denominational family within that community. After the Civil War, former slaves did not wish to worship with white Baptists, and so they formed their own local congregations. Many of these congregations joined in creating the National Baptist Convention of the USA Inc. in 1895. A division within this denomination over organizational issues led to the formation of the National Baptist Convention of America in 1915, and a further split in 1961 resulted in the founding of the Progressive National Baptist Convention Inc. Although these groups are strongest in the South, many African American Baptist congregations were established in the Midwest during the twentieth-century "Great Migration" of African Americans. A number of these Baptist congregations hold dual memberships in one of the African American denominations and either the American Baptist Church or the SBC.

Baptists predominate only in Missouri, where one-third of the religious population was Baptist at the end of the twentieth century. Their numbers ranged from 10 to 15 percent in Illinois, Indiana, Ohio, Michigan, and Kansas, and five percent or less in the other midwestern states.

Sources and Further Reading: Nancy Tatom Ammerman, *Baptist Battles* (1990); Robert Baker, *The Southern Baptist Convention and Its People, 1607–1972* (1974); William H. Brackney, *The Baptists* (1988); Lawrence B. Davis, *Immigrants, Baptists, and the Protestant Mind in America* (1973); Bill Leonard, ed., *Dictionary of Baptists in America* (1994); H. Leon McBeth, *The Baptist Heritage* (1987); C. Eric Lincoln and Lawrence Mamiya, *The Black Church in the African-American Experience* (1990); James E. Wood, Jr., ed., *Baptists and the American Experience* (1976).

Mark Granquist
Gustavus Adolphus College, Minnesota

Buddhists

Due to national immigrant settlement patterns and the relative cultural conservatism of the region, the Midwest has always lagged behind the West Coast in numbers of Buddhist sympathizers, adherents, and institutions. Even so, Buddhism in the Midwest has made significant contributions to the overall development of Buddhism in the United States. The Buddhist presence in the region has grown steadily over the last century.

The World's Parliament of Religions, held in Chicago in 1893 in conjunction with the World's Columbian Exposition, brought representatives of Asian Buddhist traditions to national attention. Anagarika Dharmapala, a Ceylonese Buddhist reformer influenced by the Theosophical views of Colonel Henry Olcott and Madame Helena Blavatsky, made a memorable impression at the parliament. During his stay in Chicago, at a public lecture sponsored by the local Theosophical Society, Dharmapala presided over the first formal conversion to Buddhism on American soil, that of Charles T. Strauss, a New York businessman of Jewish background. A local branch of Dharmapala's international Maha Bodhi Society opened in Chicago in the years following his second visit to the United States in 1897. The Theosophical Society, which in 1926 located its headquarters in Wheaton, Illinois, just west of Chicago, continues its interest in Buddhism to the present time.

Another Buddhist representative at the 1893 parliament was the Japanese Zen monk Soyen Shaku. At the parliament, Soyen met Paul Carus, editor of his own Open Court Publishing Company in LaSalle, Illinois, southwest of Chicago. For several years following the parliament, Carus published numerous articles about Buddhism written by prominent Buddhists and liberal Christians, part of a national interest in Buddhism during that period. Carus invited Soyen to join him, but Soyen instead recommended one of his lay students, D. T. Suzuki, who spent his time at Open Court translating and writing works on Buddhism and other topics. Suzuki would later become a major figure in Zen Buddhism's popularity in the United States during the 1950s.

The release of internees from military "relocation centers" throughout the United Stats brought tens of thousands of Japanese Americans to the Midwest between 1943 and 1950. Many eventually returned to their homes on the West Coast, but significant numbers remained to swell the small Japanese American communities in the region. In Chicago, the number of Japanese residents jumped from 390 in 1940 to nearly 11,000 in 1950. Chicago and Cleveland have the only temples in the Midwest affiliated with the Buddhist Churches of America (BCA), the oldest Buddhist denomination in the country (California alone has forty-three BCA temples). Midwest Buddhist Temple in Chicago was founded in 1944; the Cleveland Buddhist Temple, in 1945. Four more Japanese temples representing other Buddhist traditions were established in Chicago between 1944 and the 1960s.

The next large influx of Asian American Buddhists to the Midwest began with the immigration-reform legislation of 1965 and continues to the present time. Buddhist immigrants and refugees, and their American-born offspring, are adapting Buddhist traditions from China, Korea, Southeast Asia, and other Asian homelands to the American context. Twelve Thai Buddhist temples have been established in five midwestern states—six in Illinois; three in Michigan; and one each in Missouri, Wisconsin, and Kansas (California has twenty-five Thai temples). Wat Phothikaram, a Laotian Buddhist temple established in Rockford, Illinois, in 1982, gained notoriety due to harassment from some local elements in the 1980s, as captured in the documentary film *Blue Collar and Buddha* (1988). The Asian American Buddhist presence in the Midwest tends to concentrate in the larger metropolitan areas, although families can also be found in nonmetropolitan places.

Non-Asian midwesterners continue to show interest in Buddhism, especially its Zen and Tibetan traditions. Every state in the Midwest except North Dakota has at least one Buddhist meditation group listed in the 1998 *Complete Guide to Buddhist America*, with Illinois (51) and Wisconsin (23) leading the list of 142 groups in the region. Here the Midwest lags behind both coasts: California alone has 199 groups in the guide; New York State and Massachusetts, a combined 133.

Buddhism's influence on the Midwest is difficult to gauge precisely, but the religion's national visibility and popularity during the 1990s certainly extended to this region through books, magazines, the Internet, entertainment, the media, and education. Virtually every community college, four-year college, and university in the region offers courses that include Buddhism as a topic. Schools with major programs in the scholarly study of Buddhism include the University of Chicago, the University of Wisconsin, Northwestern University, and the University of Michigan.

Local associations representing a variety of Buddhist groups and traditions have formed around the country since the 1980s. These include the Buddhist Association of Southwest Michigan and the Buddhist Council of the Midwest, the latter centered in Chicago but listing groups in several midwestern states in its directory. Such associations typically celebrate the diverse expressions of Buddhism and seek to educate the larger public about the religion. National and international networks within specific Buddhist traditions also have representation in the Midwest, such as the Council of Thai Bhikkhus in the USA, representing the largest monastic body in Thailand and the United States; the Association of Soto Zen Buddhists, from one of two main branches within Japanese Zen Buddhism; and somewhat looser networks of meditation groups inspired by the style of *vipassana*, or "insight," meditation found in the Theravada branch of Buddhism.

In 1993 in Chicago, the second Parliament of the World's Religions commemorated the centennial of the original World's Parliament of Religions. In one hundred years, Buddhism in the Midwest had evolved from a foreign curiosity to an established local religion. Eight Buddhist organizations from the Midwest were listed as cosponsors of the 1993 parliament, and three local Buddhist leaders served on the parliament's board of trustees—a Thai Buddhist monk, a Japanese BCA minister, and a European American meditation teacher.

Sources and Further Reading: John Henry Barrows, ed., *The World's Parliament of Religions*, 2 vols. (1893); Rick Fields, *How the Swans Came to the Lake*, rev. ed. (1992); Paul David Numrich, "How the Swans Came to Lake Michigan: The Social Organization of Buddhist Chicago," *Journal for the Scientific Study of Religion* 39 (June 2000); Paul David Numrich, "Local Inter-Buddhist Associations in North America," in Duncan Ryuken Williams and Christopher S. Queen, eds., *American Buddhism* (1999); Paul David Numrich, *Old Wisdom in the New World* (1996); Masako Osako, "Japanese Americans: Melting into the All-American Melting Pot," in Melvin G. Holli and Peter d'A. Jones, eds., *Ethnic Chicago*, 4th ed. (1995); Thomas A. Tweed, *The American Encounter with Buddhism, 1844–1912* (2000).

Paul David Numrich
Loyola University, Illinois

Christian Science and New Thought

The well-organized Christian Science church and the loosely affiliated congregations of New Thought began to grow rapidly in the upper Midwest beginning in the last two decades of the nineteenth century. They were made popular through well-publicized testimonies of physical healing and personal success found in books and periodicals. They attracted thousands of disenfranchised but generally optimistic and progressive Protestants, thus staking out a small but influential religious niche in industrial cities and towns.

The scriptural-centered Church of Christ, Scientist, was founded in 1879 by New Hampshire native Mary Baker Eddy (1821–1910) in Boston, inspired by the teachings of her book *Science and Health* (1875). This book explored the idea that Jesus's teachings revealed to everyone a scientific spiritual means for healing the sick and reforming the sinner. An early significant association of Eddy's in the 1860s was with Phineas Quimby, a magnetic mesmerist from Maine whose secular therapeutic insights into the mind/body connection were an important source of New Thought and mind cure ideas concerning healing. Eddy's approach was radically theological, and after trying to recast Quimby's interests into a Christian framework, by the late 1860s she claimed to have discovered the decisive curative power of a spiritual understanding of the scriptures. In 1881 Eddy chartered the Massachusetts Metaphysical College in Boston, whose graduates went on to establish institutes and academies in the Midwest in Milwaukee (1884); Chicago, Cleveland, and Detroit (1886); Kansas City (1887); and Minneapolis (1891). Students joined local associations that together constituted the membership of the National Christian Scientist Association (NCSA), which held two of its four national meetings in Chicago (1888) and Cleveland (1889) before Eddy adjourned it and disbanded much of the organization in 1889, reorganizing and centralizing the church administration in Boston in 1892.

Between 1890 and 1920 the largest percentage of Christian Science congregations in the United States was in the Midwest. In 1906 more than 300 congregations were located in the Midwest, holding nearly half of all services in the country. By 1950 the midwestern states had more than 750 congregations and were holding nearly a third of all services in the United States. By 2000 the church had contracted to fewer than 380 congregations.

Christian Science arrived in Chicago in 1883 through Bradford Sherman, who had great success as a public practitioner/healer. Others followed, including Caroline and Gideon Noyes, who helped establish the first Christian Science church there in 1886. Eddy herself taught a class in Chicago in 1884 and returned in 1888 to attend the NCSA convention. The Midwest also provided many important teachers and national lecturers. Best known is Edward Kimball, a Chicago businessperson who achieved national and international prominence as a lecturer and teacher of Christian Science.

The first church built solely for Christian Science worship services anywhere in the world was in Oconto, Wisconsin, in 1886. By 1897 Christian Scientists in Chicago and other cities began to build commodious churches as part of a nationwide building campaign. The Midwest also supported an independent elementary school for Christian Scientist children, the Principia, established in St. Louis in 1898 and expanded by the 1930s to include a four-year liberal arts college with a campus in Elsah, Illinois.

Many teachers in the New Thought movement had been associated with Eddy. Emma Curtis Hopkins, from Eddy's 1883 graduating class, in 1886 began forming her own Christian Science institutes in Chicago, Detroit, and St. Paul, where her consideration of comparative religions and Eastern mysticism set her apart from the Christian emphasis of Eddy's theology. She also started a publication, *The Christian Metaphysician* (1887–1897), and taught classes in her version of "Mental Science." Her students subsequently founded other metaphysical New Thought organizations in the Midwest, the largest being Charles and Myrtle Fillmore's Unity School of Christianity in Kansas City, Missouri.

By 1889 the Fillmores were publishing their own harmonial metaphysical magazine, *Modern Thought*, and establishing a school and a prayer ministry called Silent Unity. Attracting thousands of adherents, Silent Unity continued to grow beyond its local ministry in Kansas City and by 1920 had established a large headquarters at Lee's Summit, Missouri. In 1966 an Association of Unity Churches was established as a separate organization to provide services for these local congregations.

Creating a centralized organization to support cooperation between local and regional New Thought groups was difficult, though conventions were held in Chicago (1903), St. Louis (1904), Omaha (1911), and Detroit (1913). By 1914 the establishment of the International New Thought Alliance (INTA) created a federation of New Thought organizations, with fourteen yearly conferences held in the Midwest through the 1950s. By 2002 twenty-five New Thought churches—nearly one-third of New Thought congregations in the nation, including Unity, Divine Science, and Religious Science churches—were registered with the INTA in the Midwest.

Sources and Further Reading: Charles Braden, *Spirits in Rebellion* (1984); Stephen Gottschalk, *Rolling Away the Stone* (2006); Stephen Gottschalk, "Christian Science and Harmonialism," in Charles H. Lippy and Peter W. Williams, eds., *The Encyclopedia of the American Religious Experience*, vol. 2 (1988); Stephen Gottschalk, *The Emergence of Christian Science in American Religious Life* (1973); Gail Harley, "New Thought and the Harmonial Family," in Timothy Miller, ed., *America's Alternative Religions* (1995); Paul Eli Ivey, *Prayers in Stone* (1999); J. Stillson Judah, *The History and Philosophy of the Metaphysical Movements in America* (1967).

Paul Ivey
University of Arizona

Eastern Orthodox Christians

The origins of Eastern Orthodox Christianity in North America are associated with Alaska and California. Nevertheless, the Midwest played a crucial role in the growth of Orthodoxy in the late nineteenth and early twentieth centuries.

The largest group of Slavic immigrants to the United States prior to World War I was Carpatho-Russians (also known as Rusyns) from the Carpathian Mountains area in the Austro-Hungarian Empire who worked in the coal mines and steel mills of eastern Ohio and western Pennsylvania. Carpatho-Russians were Eastern Catholics (or Uniates). Although they were administratively integrated into the Roman Catholic Church in the sixteenth century, they were permitted to retain their Byzantine liturgy and other Orthodox traditions, including married priests.

As Carpatho-Russian emigrants began to organize parishes in the United States, they encountered opposition from American Roman Catholic priests and bishops who tried to force them to join the Latin Catholic parishes. These tense relations resulted in the conversion of tens of thousands of Carpatho-Russian clergy and laity to the Russian Orthodox church of their ancestors. The leader of this movement was Father Alexis Toth of the St. Mary Parish in Minneapolis. After his death in 1909 he was called the "father of Orthodoxy in America."

Thus it was not accidental that in 1905 Bishop Tikhon of the Russian Orthodox Missionary Archdiocese—the future patriarch of the Russian Orthodox Church—established the first American Orthodox seminary in Minneapolis. Unlike the Orthodox seminary in Sitka, Alaska, the new St. Platon's Seminary conducted classes in both Russian and English as well as liturgical services in English and Church Slavonic.

Since the 1890s, Greek immigrants from the Ottoman Empire and the Kingdom of Greece had streamed en masse into the United States, spurred by

St. Josephat's Basilica, Milwaukee.
Wisconsin Department of Tourism.

oppression and poor economic conditions at home. Unlike Slavs, Greeks concentrated in large urban centers, where they set up independent small businesses. Chicago soon had a flourishing "Greek town," the remains of which still exist along Halsted Street, with an Annunciation parish and a priest from Greece.

In the early 1900s, the Midwest played a decisive role in organizing the religious life of Orthodox Romanian and Serbian immigrants. The first Romanian Orthodox parish was founded in 1904, in Cleveland. Twenty-five years later, scattered Romanian communities held a congress in Detroit and formed a North American Romanian Orthodox diocese. In 1938, Bishop Polycarp Morusca purchased land in Grass Lake, Michigan (near Jackson), and built Vatra Romanesca ("Romanian home"), a spiritual center for his far-flung diocese. The early Serbian Orthodox parishes in Chicago; Kansas City, Kansas; and Steubenville, Ohio belonged to the multiethnic Russian Orthodox Archdiocese, but in 1921, in the wake of the Communist revolution in Russia, they established an independent diocese subordinated to the Serbian Patriarchate in Belgrade. In 1927, Bishop Mardarije Uskovich founded St. Sava Monastery near Libertyville, Illinois, to serve as the center of his diocese.

In the late twentieth century, the Midwest became home to the world headquarters of the most ancient of all Eastern Christian churches—the the Assyrian Church of the East. The community of Orthodox Assyrians (also known as Nestorians) was formed in the mid-second century in upper Mesopotamia and spread throughout Iraq, Iran, Syria, Lebanon, North America, Australia, and India. Until 1933, the Patriarch of the Assyrian Church resided in Baghdad, but after the end of the British mandate in Iraq, a clash between Assyrians and Iraqi troops (who suspected Assyrians of supporting the British enemy) ended in massacre and the further scattering of community. The Iraqi authorities stripped Patriarch Mar Simon XXIII of his citizenship and expelled him; he went into exile in America. Since 1994, the residence of the current patriarch, Mar Dinkha IV, has been located in Morton Grove, near Chicago.

The monastic tradition has always been emphasized in the Orthodox Church. Today, the Romanian Orthodox women's Monastery of the Dormition in Rives Junction, Michigan, is not only an important religious center but also a spiritual retreat welcoming numerous visitors (Orthodox and not Orthodox alike).

Currently, the proportion of Eastern Christians in the Midwest population varies from 0.02 percent in North Dakota to 0.5 percent in Illinois. Chicago is by far the center of Orthodox Christianity in the Midwest, with more than thirty parishes of various Orthodox churches in the city (including nearly seventy in the metropolitan area) and five residing Orthodox bishops. Other significant communities of Orthodox Christians are in Detroit, Cleveland, Toledo, and Minneapolis.

Sources and Further Reading: John Erickson, *Orthodox Christians in America* (1999); Thomas Fitzgerald, *The Orthodox Church*, student ed. (1998); George Michalopulos and Herb Ham, *The American Orthodox Church* (2003); Archimandrite Serafim, *The Quest for Orthodox Unity in America* (1973); Mark Stokoe with Leonid Kishkovsky, *Orthodox Christians in North America, 1794–1994* (1995).

Alexei Krindatch
Patriarch Athenagoras Orthodox Institute,
Berkeley, California

Episcopalians

The Episcopal Church (Protestant Episcopal Church in the United States of America) is a branch of the Anglican Communion, a worldwide family of churches that descend from the Church of England, use the *Book of Common Prayer*, and participate in the Lambeth Conference. The Archbishop of Canterbury is the communion's symbolic leader but has no jurisdiction over provinces.

Because of its origins in Great Britain, the Episcopal Church in North America suffered during the American Revolution. Following the Revolution, Episcopalians concentrated on the eastern seaboard, with no coherent national strategy for western expansion until 1835. Western evangelism prior to that time was the result of the individual efforts of lay and clerical Episcopalians, such as Philander Chase. In 1835, however, the denomination's General Convention began to appoint missionary bishops for the Northwest and the Southwest, who were to be its chief evangelists on the frontier. They organized congregations, recruited clergy, and established diocesan structures.

The first bishop of the Northwest was Jackson Kemper. His responsibilities included Missouri, Indiana, Iowa, Wisconsin, Nebraska, and Kansas. Episcopalians eventually gained sufficient resources to organize individual dioceses. Wisconsin organized in 1859 and selected Kemper as bishop. He was replaced as missionary bishop the following year by John Talbot, who referred to himself as "Bishop of All Outdoors."

Educator James Lloyd Breck founded Episcopal seminaries in Wisconsin (Nashotah House, 1842) and Minnesota (Seabury, 1860; Seabury-Western in Chicago since a 1933 merger). Much of the financial support for new missions came from the fund-raising activities of women's circles.

The members of the high church party (so called because of high emphasis on church polity) recalled the response to pro-British involvement during the Revolution and urged against any stance on slavery. Northern evangelicals supported abolition in muted tones until the 1850s. During the Civil War, the General Convention of 1862, with representation only from the North, criticized the Confederacy. When the war ended, southerners dissolved the General Council of the Confederate States and rejoined the General Convention.

During the colonial era, the Society for the Propagation of the Gospel supported missionary work among Native Americans in western New York. When European immigration pushed tribes west, missionaries followed, with their most active work in Wisconsin, Minnesota, and South Dakota. Bishops Henry Whipple of Minnesota and William Hobart Hare of South Dakota were leading advocates of ministry to

and by Native Americans. Emmegabowh, an Ottawa who served in Minnesota, was the first Native American Episcopal deacon (1859) and priest (1867).

Episcopalians struggled over the relative importance of conversion and sacramental grace. Evangelical Episcopalians in Ohio believed in a conscious adult embrace of faith, which could take the form of a dramatic conversion. "Advanced high church" or "Anglo-Catholic" Episcopalians, centered in Wisconsin and Illinois, added an emphasis on the sacraments to the high church stress on episcopacy. They rejected conversion as an emotional "works-righteousness" that undermined the efficacy of baptism. In 1869 Bishop Henry Whitehouse brought charges against evangelical priest Charles Cheney of Chicago for omitting the word *regeneration* from the baptismal service. When Whitehouse convicted Cheney in church courts, Cheney joined with Bishop of Kentucky George Cummins to form a separate Reformed Episcopal Church (1873).

The departure of unhappy evangelicals did not end strife. Anglo-Catholic clergy clashed with authorities, who often represented older, high church views. The high church faculty of Nashotah House blocked approval of the elections of Anglo-Catholic James DeKoven as bishop (1874, 1875). Arthur Ritchie, the Anglo-Catholic rector of the Church of the Ascension, Chicago, introduced the Benediction of the Blessed Sacrament over the objections of high church bishop William McLaren. Anglo-Catholic members of the Companions of the Holy Savior, whose number included Nashotah House faculty, converted to Roman Catholicism following the General Convention's decision to open pulpits to Protestant guest preachers (1907).

Some dioceses (originally units the size of states) subdivided in order both to deal with increasing numbers and to accommodate greater diversity of opinion. In the 1870s the dioceses of Illinois, Ohio, Michigan, and Wisconsin divided.

As the church grew, the Midwest became important to the denomination nationally. In 1886 the Episcopal Church's General Convention met in Chicago. That convention gave its name to the Chicago Quadrilateral, an important ecumenical statement. Thereafter, conventions met frequently in the Midwest (Minneapolis, 1895; Cincinnati, 1910 and 1937; Detroit, 1919 and 1961; and Cleveland, 1943).

Some wealthy families, such as the Proctors of Cincinnati's Proctor and Gamble corporation, provided financial resources for the Episcopal Church's ministry. Female Episcopalians, such as Ellen Gates Starr of Hull-House, provided much of the leadership for the church's social ministry.

Growth in numbers continued through the 1920s but stalled during the Depression. Following World War II the denomination enjoyed a spurt of suburban growth. Richard Emrich, Bishop of Michigan, provided important leadership in that expansion.

During the 1960s Episcopalians were both active in and divided by the civil rights movement. The divisions were evident at the 1969 General Convention in South Bend, Indiana, which supported a multimillion dollar special program for minority empowerment, but rejected demands by the Black Economic Development Fund for reparations. Episcopalians worked for civil rights behind the scenes. In 1966 Bishop James Montgomery of Chicago brokered a fair-housing agreement between Chicago officials and Martin Luther King, Jr.

The first midwestern bishop of African heritage was Quinton Primo, Jr. (Suffragan Bishop of Chicago). In 1988 Herbert Thompson, Jr., of southern Ohio became the first African American diocesan bishop in the Midwest.

Midwestern Episcopalians were both supportive and critical of the 1976 decision to ordain women to the priesthood and the episcopate. The Diocese of Quincy in Illinois has remained opposed to the ordination of women. In contrast, the Diocese of Indianapolis elected Catherine Waynick as bishop in 1997.

Four of the ten sessions of the General Convention between 1976 and 2003 met in the Midwest (Minneapolis, 1976 and 2003; Detroit, 1988; and Indianapolis, 1994). Frank Tracy Griswold III, former Bishop of Chicago, became the Episcopal Church's presiding bishop in 1998. The 2003 convention approved the election of V. Gene Robinson as bishop of New Hampshire. Robinson is a divorced man with a same-sex partner. Some dioceses, including Quincy and Springfield in Illinois, were vocal opponents of the decision; others supported it.

Sources and Further Reading: Owannah Anderson, *400 Years: Anglican/Episcopal Mission among American Indians* (1997); Diana Hochstedt Butler, *Standing against the Whirlwind* (1995); Mary Sudman Donovan, *A Different Call* (1986); Charles R. Henery, ed., *Beyond the Horizon* (1986); David L. Holmes, *A Brief History of the Episcopal Church* (1993); Catherine Prelinger, ed., *Episcopal Women* (1992); Robert W. Prichard, *A History of the Episcopal Church*, rev. ed. (1999); Gardiner H. Shattuck, Jr., *Episcopalians and Race* (2000).

Robert W. Prichard
Virginia Theological Seminary

Friends (Quakers)

Quakerism, the belief system of the Society of Friends, was one of the radical sects that emerged from the English Civil War of the 1640s. The first known Friends to cross the Ohio River were Zebulon Heston and John Parrish, Quakers from Pennsylvania who visited the Delaware tribe in what is now eastern Ohio in 1773. In 1777 and 1778 a small party of North Carolina Friends led by Thomas Beals, a Quaker minister, made similar visits.

Significant Quaker settlement began in the 1790s, as Friends moved into the Ohio Valley from two directions. Quakers whose roots were in the Delaware Valley, Maryland, and northern Virginia began to settle in eastern Ohio, often after residence in southwestern Pennsylvania. Friends from Virginia and the Carolinas settled mostly west of the Scioto River, in southwestern Ohio. Friends first settled in the Indiana Territory, near Richmond, in 1806. By 1813 enough had settled west of the Appalachians that they formed their own organization, Ohio Yearly Meeting of Friends. After the War of 1812, migration continued at such a pace that in 1821 another yearly meeting in Indiana was formed. Perhaps twenty-five thousand Friends were living in the two states. By 1860 more Friends lived in Indiana than in any other state of the union.

These Friends did not escape the conflicts and schisms faced by Quakers in the East. In 1828 both Ohio and Indiana yearly meetings split, in what is known as the Hicksite Separation. It pitted supporters of the Long Island Quaker minister Elias Hicks against his opponents, who were known as Orthodox Friends. Hicks advocated the primacy of the traditional Quaker doctrine of the Inward Light; his opponents accused him of denying the authority of scripture and the divinity of Christ. Ohio Yearly Meeting split almost evenly, while Orthodox Friends in Indiana outnumbered Hicksites about four to one. Both groups faced another round of schisms in the 1840s and 1850s. Some Hicksite Friends, drawn to radical reforms such as abolition, women's rights, and nonresistance, separated to form meetings of what they called Congregational or Progressive Friends, especially in Ohio. Orthodox Friends divided over the teachings of the English Quaker minister Joseph John Gurney, who urged them to emphasize doctrines that were similar to those of non-Quaker evangelicals and to join with them in good works. Primitive Friends, who became known as Wilburites after their leader John Wilbur, resisted such views as compromising Quaker distinctiveness. They were few in Indiana, but probably were a majority in the Orthodox Ohio Yearly Meeting.

Quakers followed the general trend of white movement west after 1820. Friends from New England and New York settled in southeastern Michigan. Relatively few Friends settled in Illinois. More crossed into the Iowa Territory after 1840, mostly Gurneyite Friends, who formed a yearly meeting there in 1863. Similarly, Gurneyite Friends in Kansas were numerous enough to form a yearly meeting there in 1872.

Before the Civil War, Quakers set themselves apart from their neighbors in various ways. Their worship lacked pastors and was based on silence. They followed a "plain" way of life, with distinctive dress and speech, such as using "thee" and "thou." They refused to perform any kind of military duty. They were supportive of American Indians and African Americans. Many were involved in the Underground Railroad and sent protests to state legislatures against discriminatory laws. Rural black settlements were disproportionately found near Quaker communities.

Midwestern Friends showed striking diversity after the Civil War. Gurneyites, who were probably 80 percent of them, embraced revivalism, gave up the plain life, began to call pastors, and made thousands of converts from non-Quaker backgrounds. Increasingly, Gurneyites were indistinguishable from other Protestants. Hicksite Friends retained older forms of worship, but they dwindled in numbers and also gave up most of their outward differences. By 1900 Wilburite Friends were calling themselves Conservatives. They clung most closely to older Quaker ways.

In the twentieth century, midwestern Friends moved in different directions. For Gurneyite, or pastoral Friends, the Midwest was their heartland, home to the denominational headquarters of Friends United Meeting in Richmond, Indiana. Pastoral Friends also experienced fundamentalist/modernist tensions after 1900 that led to the formation of a separate body that is now known as Evangelical Friends International. After many years of decline, Hicksite Friends stabilized in number after World War II, but are now nearly all urban, disproportionately found in college and university towns. Conservative Friends have also declined in number, and eastern Ohio remains their stronghold.

Sources and Further Reading: Hugh Barbour and J. William Frost, *The Quakers* (1988); Errol T. Elliott, *The Quakers on the American Frontier* (1969); Thomas D. Hamm, *The Transformation of American Quakerism* (1988); Rufus M. Jones, *The Later Periods of Quakerism* (1921); James H. Norton, "Quakers West of the Alleghenies and in Ohio to 1861," Ph.D. diss., Case Western Reserve University (1965).

Thomas D. Hamm
Earlham College, Indiana

German and Dutch Reformed Churches

Continental Calvinism arrived in the Midwest during the early nineteenth century under the patronage of two denominations, the Reformed Church in the United States and the Reformed Church in America.

The former traced its roots to the Rhenish Palatinate, the latter to the Netherlands. The Dutch Reformed immigrants, many of them religious refugees, tended to maintain a distinct identity. The German Reformed immigrants, mostly economic refugees, in time blended in more thoroughly with the broader American culture.

In 1803 ministers sent by the Synod of the Reformed German Church in the United States of America first conducted services north of the Ohio River among settlers from Pennsylvania and North Carolina. The Reverend Samuel Weyburg claimed the honor of preaching the first Protestant sermon west of the Mississippi River, in present-day Cape Girardeau County, Missouri. In 1819 the Classis of Ohio was organized with five ministers, fifty congregations, and 1,800 communicants. Four years later, responding to the need to ordain more ministers and the difficulties of attending meetings east of the Appalachians, this body reconstituted itself as the Evangelical Reformed Synod of Ohio (popularly known as the Western Synod). A shortage of trained ministers for the many isolated congregations combined with vigorous debates on the merits of evangelistic practices associated with the Second Great Awakening to create competing tendencies among the German Reformed churches. While all the members professed adherence to the doctrines of the Heidelberg Catechism, many ministers and laypeople embraced much of the revivalist enthusiasm of the period and promoted greater cooperation with other Protestant denominations. Another faction, particularly strong among more recent immigrants, preferred to maintain more traditional forms of Reformed worship. Still others embraced the high-church liturgical ideas of the Mercersburg Theology movement within the Eastern Synod of the German Reformed church.

In 1863, the Heidelberg Catechism's tercentennial, the Western Synod effected a union with the older Eastern Synod to form the Reformed Church in the United States. As German immigration continued, the denomination grew. New congregations and classes were organized and new regional synods created for those who spoke mostly German. Hungarian Reformed congregations and classes were also organized. Ohio remained the stronghold of the German Reformed church in the Midwest; 60 percent of church members in the region belonged to Ohio congregations in 1934.

Long active in the ecumenical movement, the Reformed Church in the United States merged with the Evangelical Synod of North America in 1934 to form the Evangelical and Reformed Church, which in turn joined the Congregational Christians in 1957 to form the United Church of Christ. A few dissident congregations of Russian Germans, centered in the Dakotas and Nebraska, refused to join the new body and assumed the denominational name. In 2002 they opened a new theological school, Heidelberg Seminary, in Vermillion, South Dakota.

The Reformed Protestant Dutch Church in North America (since 1867 known as the Reformed Church in America) arrived in the Midwest in 1837 when settlers from New York established a congregation in Fairview, Illinois. Ten years later immigrants from the Netherlands founded Holland, Michigan, and Pella, Iowa. These two colonies continued to attract immigrants for several decades. Other Dutch churches soon appeared in Wisconsin, Illinois, Indiana, and Ohio.

Dutch Reformed polity embraced the Heidelberg Catechism as one doctrinal standard alongside the Belgic Confession and the Canons of Dort. Strict adherence to the latter documents and language differences precluded affiliation with German Reformed churches. The earliest Dutch immigrants tended to be orthodox Calvinist religious dissenters wary of liberal theological trends, government intrusions, and liturgical innovation. They resisted Americanization. However, because their leader, the Reverend Albertus C. Van Raalte, regarded links to the broader culture as both necessary and desirable, new arrivals accepted a union with the older Dutch Reformed churches on the East Coast.

Sensing a lack of orthodoxy in the eastern churches, a few western Michigan congregations seceded in 1857. Other congregations followed during the 1880s, reacting to the Dutch Reformed synod's refusal to condemn membership in secret societies. In 1890 the secessionists agreed to call themselves the Christian Reformed Church. Subsequently, immigrants from the dissenting churches in the Netherlands gravitated to the Christian Reformed Church, while those from the state church gravitated to the Reformed Church in America. Most Dutch settlements in the Midwest supported congregations from both denominations. One clear distinction between the two major Dutch Reformed bodies has been the Christian Reformed church's official endorsement of parent-controlled Christian elementary and secondary schools. The Reformed Church in America has tended to leave education to parental discretion and the public school system.

Membership of the two major denominations in the Midwest reached parity by 1900, with each exceeding two hundred thousand by midcentury. The Christian Reformed Church suffered two significant secessions in this period, one during the 1920s over the doctrine of common grace, the ability of sinful humans to reflect divine goodness (Protestant Reformed Church), and another beginning in the 1980s in reaction to synodical decisions supporting the ordination of women as ministers and elders (United Reformed Church). In recent years, the Reformed Church in America and the Christian Reformed Church have begun cosponsoring churches in more sparsely settled areas of the region.

German and Dutch Reformed churches formed in every midwestern state coincidentally with the distribution of their constituent ethnic groups. Denominational nodes developed in areas of ethnic concentration—for the Germans, the vicinities of Canton, Cleveland, and Dayton, Ohio, and Sheboygan, Wisconsin; for the Dutch, western Michigan, Chicago, and the southeastern and northwestern corners of Iowa. Denominational offices and publishing houses arose in these locales, as did colleges and seminaries. For the German Reformed church, the latter included Heidelberg College, Central Theological Seminary (later merged with Eden Seminary in St. Louis), and the College of the Mission House (now Lakeland College). For the Reformed Church in America, they were Hope College and Western Theological Seminary in Holland, Michigan, as well as Central College and Northwestern College in Iowa. The Christian Reformed Church founded Calvin College and Seminary in Michigan, Dordt College in Iowa, and Trinity Christian College in Illinois.

Sources and Further Reading: James D. Bratt, *Dutch Calvinism in Modern America* (1984); David Dunn, ed., *A History of the Evangelical and Reformed Church* (1961); James I. Good, *A History of the Reformed Church in the U.S. in the 19th Century* (1911); Robert E. Grossman and Norman C. Hoeflinger, eds., *You Shall Be My People* (1996); Louis H. Gunnemann, *The Shaping of the United Church of Christ* (1977); Henry S. Lucas, *Netherlanders in America* (1989); Robert P. Swierenga and Elton J. Bruins, *Family Quarrels in the Dutch Reformed Churches in the 19th Century* (1999).

Robert Schoone-Jongen
Calvin College, Michigan

Hindus

In the first half of the nineteenth century such transcendentalist authors as Ralph Waldo Emerson and Henry David Thoreau were aware of the existence of Hinduism, as classic Hindu texts began to be translated into Western European languages. An awareness of Hinduism slowly grew until the 1893 World's Parliament of Religions that was sponsored in connection with the Chicago World's Columbian Exposition. Swami Vivekananda (1863–1902) attended the parliament and made a tremendous impression on those in

Hindu Temple, St. Louis, Missouri, was
constructed between 1990 and 2000.
The Hindu Temple of St. Louis.

attendance with his speeches. He traveled throughout
the United States and England on a speaking tour
before returning to Calcutta in 1897 to establish
the Ramakrishna Mission. Following in his footsteps
in 1930, a monk of the Ramakrishna Mission established the first Hindu institution in Chicago, the
Vivekananda Vedanta Society of Chicago. The Hinduism taught by the Vivekananda Vedanta societies
focuses on the practical discipline of yoga as well as intellectual inquiry into the ultimate unity of all existence and human nature. Vivekananda's Vedanta societies were the first of several forms that Hinduism has
taken in the Midwest.

The growth of Hinduism in the Midwest reflects
general patterns of emigration from India to the
United States. Changes in the Immigration Act of
1965 led to a sharp rise in the number of people emigrating from India to the United States, and to an accompanying rise in the practice and presence of Hinduism. Between 1820 and 1960, only 13,607 people
emigrated from India to the United States. Between
1961 and 1990, however, there were 442,109 emigrants, and more than 363,000 emigrants between
1991 and 2000.

Chicago, Detroit, Minneapolis-St. Paul, and
Cincinnati, as well as a few smaller cities, were among
the first cities to host various Hindu organizations that
emerged in the United States before the late 1970s
and the 1980s. These organizations included the Self-
Realization Fellowship, founded in 1925 by Parama-
hansa Yogananda; the Transcendental Meditation
movement, established by Maharishi Mahesh Yogi;
and the widely known "Hare Krishna" movement formerly known as the International Society for Krishna
Consciousness. Prior to the marked increase in Indian
immigrants beginning in 1965, most of these move-

ments attracted non–South Asian followers. As the
size of South Asian communities grew in the Midwest,
however, the established Hindu organizations soon
found that their membership included South Asian–
born Hindus alongside ethnic white Americans.

With the increase in South Asian immigrants has
come a different form of Hinduism, well known in
India but new to the midwestern states. This type of
Hinduism is practiced in temples as well as in homes,
at private shrines or altars, and revolves around a daily
or weekly *puja* (worship) service, which is a ritual of
worship for the deities enshrined in the temple or
altar. This type of worship is sometimes led by ordained priests and is traditionally rooted in sixteen rituals (it is rare to find all sixteen undertaken in a person's life, even in India). South Asian communities
have undertaken rigorous fund-raising throughout
cities of all sizes in the Midwest to establish temples
and to perform the puja services.

Larger urban centers, such as Chicago and Detroit,
often have several Hindu temples, sometimes divided
along geographical lines reflecting different geographical traditions in India. According to the Pluralism Project, developed by Diana L. Eck at Harvard
University, the greater metropolitan area of Chicago
alone hosts twenty-nine Hindu organizations, not all
of them located in temples. The wave of temple construction that has spread throughout the Midwest first
emerged in urban areas in the late 1970s, and it continues vigorously today in smaller cities throughout
the region. The most elaborate temples are often of
south Indian design, although temples constructed in
the north Indian style are not lacking.

The scale of the temple often reflects the resources
a community can bring to bear; regardless of scale,
however, the process of establishing a temple is long

and involved. The Hindu Temple of Greater Chicago, located in Lemont, Illinois, began planning in 1977 and conducted the inauguration ritual for its first deity in 1984. In Kalamazoo, Michigan, the Indo-American Cultural Center and Temple bought a building that had housed a Protestant church in the mid-1990s. It renovated the interior of the building, began to use it formally as a temple in late 1997, and in 2001 ritually installed a spectacular array of deities. There are temples scattered throughout the Midwest, often in unexpected places and small towns.

In India, Hindu temples are the loci of a wide array of social activities. Similarly, Hindu temples in the United States serve a variety of functions. For individuals of South Asian descent, identifying as a Hindu today signifies some degree of cultural, and occasionally national, identity along with the religious affiliation. It is thus natural that, along with weekly puja services, temples also host music and dance performances; offer lectures, "Hindu Heritage" courses for younger members of the community, language lessons, and reenactments of Hindu classics (such as the *Ramayana*); and serve as resources for ritual services that require a priest.

The community involved in the planning of a temple must also wrestle with the difficult question of how inclusive of regional and devotional differences they will be. Particularly in smaller urban areas, geographical and sectarian variations central to Hinduism in India are swept away in the spirit of ecumenism. Just as Hindus have replicated the worship practices of India in temples in the Midwest, so too is Hinduism engaged in the process of becoming "American." It is not uncommon to find the list of Hindu festivals commonly celebrated at Hindu temples expanded to embrace quintessentially American holidays. One vivid example of this appears at the Hindu Temple of Greater Chicago, which celebrates a Mother's Day Puja each May.

Sources and Further Reading: Harold Coward, John R. Hinnells, and Raymond Brady Williams, eds., *The South Asian Religious Diaspora in Britain, Canada, and the United States* (2000); Diana L. Eck, "'New Age' Hinduism in America," in Nathan Glazer and Sulochana Raghavan Glazer, eds., *Conflicting Images* (1990); C. T. Jackson, *Vedanta for the West* (1994); Mark Juergensmeyer, *Radhasoami Reality* (1991); E. Viswanathan, *Am I a Hindu?* (1992); Raymond Brady Williams, *A New Face of Hinduism* (1984); Raymond Brady Williams, *Religions of Immigrants from India and Pakistan* (1988); Raymond Brady Williams, ed., *A Sacred Thread* (1992).

Carol S. Anderson
Kalamazoo College, Michigan

Holiness and Pentecostal Church

Members of the Methodist Church began to "come out" as Holiness advocates in the 1880s because of the perceived rigidity of leadership and a lack of emphasis on holy living after conversion. One of the first breakaway groups was the Church of God in Anderson, Indiana, founded by Daniel S. Warner in 1880. Organized around Holiness principles, the Church of God is today one of the largest Holiness denominations in the Midwest.

By 1895, much of the Holiness ranks were filled by rural Methodists. Traveling evangelists stressed modest dress, opposed anything that smacked of entertainment, and denounced the alleged coldness and formality of the Methodist Church. Holiness endured problems with leaders such as Benjamin Hardin Irwin, who was discredited because of public drunkenness in 1900. Racial segregation led African Americans to establish their own churches. William Fuller founded the Fire Baptized Holiness Church of God of the Americas in 1908 and moved the denomination's headquarters to the South. Today, aside from the Church of God in Anderson and a couple of other Holiness denominations, the strength of the movement has shifted from the Midwest to the South.

Pentecostalists broke away from the Holiness movement and stressed the operation of spiritual gifts as described in the New Testament, including shouting, screaming, speaking in tongues, falling into trances, dancing, and laughing. Pentecostalism took hold of many midwesterners and their churches at the turn of the twentieth century. One of the more intriguing churches was Alexander Dowie's Christian Catholic Church in Zion City, Illinois. By 1900, Zion City was holding all-day healing services on Sundays. In 1901, Dowie proclaimed himself to be Elijah and sought to restore the role of the Apostle to Christianity. Zion City soon diminished under the weight of Dowie's prophetic claims.

In the meantime, in Topeka, Kansas, Charles F. Parham began to formulate one of the theological foundations of the Pentecostal movement. Parham singled out speaking in tongues as the initial evidence of having received the baptism of the Holy Spirit. He founded the Bethel Bible School, site of one of the most memorable Pentecostal outpourings after midnight on New Year's Eve in 1900.

By 1910, Chicago had become the strategic center of the worldwide spread of Pentecostalism. Utilizing Chicago's vast immigrant population, Pentecostal churches like William Durham's North Avenue Mission and Dowie's Zion City sent missionaries throughout the world. In 1908, two Italian immigrants, Luigi

Francescon and Giacomo Lombardi, founded Pentecostal churches in the United States, Brazil, Argentina, and Italy. Before venturing outside the United States, Francescon established the first Italian American Pentecostal congregation in the country, which continues to exist today. Two Swedish immigrants from the Midwest, Daniel Berg and Gunnar Vingren, founded Pentecostal churches in Brazil in the 1900s.

Like the Holiness movement, Pentecostalism experienced fragmentation early on over theological and racial tensions. Of particular note were the Oneness controversy and the national problem of segregation. Probably no Pentecostal group was more affected by these two divisions than the Missouri-based Assemblies of God. This denomination was born in Hot Springs, Arkansas, in 1914, when white ministers left the Church of God in Christ, a mixed black and white body led by Charles H. Mason. Almost immediately after its founding, the Assemblies of God lost nearly half of its congregations and many of its influential leaders to a theological breakaway group of Oneness Pentecostals. Oneness held to a Unitarian view of the Trinity. Oneness became a staple of the movement in the Midwest; two of its largest denominations, the United Pentecostal Church and the Pentecostal Assemblies of the World, are headquartered in Missouri and Indiana, respectively.

Today, if the Midwest is any indication of trends across the country, the Pentecostal movement continues to make inroads into what still is traditionally ethnically rooted mainline Protestantism. The historical view of Pentecostalism as a black/white phenomenon has been complicated by Pentecostalism's reach into Hispanic American, Asian American, and African American communities. Indeed, the Assemblies of God's growth during the 1990s, from more than 400,000 adherents to 2.5 million adherents, strongly suggests that Pentecostalism will continue to play an important role in the Midwest.

Sources and Further Reading: Vinson Synan, *Holiness-Pentecostal Tradition,* 2nd ed. (1997); Grant Wacker, *Heaven Below* (2001).

Arlene Sánchez Walsh
Azusa Pacific University, California

Islam

Islam has had a relatively short yet major impact on the midwestern religious landscape. Substantial numbers of Muslims arrived in North America as slaves. Approximately 15 to 20 percent of Africans forcibly brought to the Americas were Muslims. Some Muslims tried to maintain their Islamic identity by refusing to drink alcohol or eat pork. In the twentieth century, many descendants of these first Muslims have tried to recover their lost religious heritage. In the 1940s, major midwestern cities saw the establishment of Muslim African American institutions, such as the Moorish American Science Temple Movement, followed by those associated with the Nation of Islam. Today, roughly a third of all Muslims in the United States are African American.

Middle Eastern Muslims began arriving in the Midwest in the late nineteenth century. The majority

Baha'i temple. Illinois Department of Commerce and Community Affairs.

of them were unskilled laborers from what is today Syria and Lebanon. Many were single men who had no intention of staying permanently. They often segregated themselves and tended to live on the border of African American neighborhoods, especially in Chicago and Detroit. Some became migrant workers, traders, and peddlers. Because many found work in the automobile industry, the area around the Ford plant at Dearborn, Michigan, became a major center of Muslim settlement. Many of these individuals began to organize for social interchange and to maintain a sense of ethnoreligious identity. Islam was thus important socially as well as religiously. Eventually, mosques and Islamic centers began to dot the midwestern architectural landscape.

The first mosque in North America was constructed in Ross, North Dakota, in 1900. It and subsequent mosques were an attempt, in part, to legitimize Islam within the American context, particularly to Jews and Christians, who could be readily identified with their churches and synagogues. Detroit; Toledo, Ohio; and Cedar Rapids, Iowa also saw the construction of some of the earliest mosques in America. For the most part, relations between Muslims and their non-Muslim neighbors have been peaceful.

A second wave of immigration occurred in the 1960s, brought on by the Immigration Act of 1965, also known as the Hart-Cellar Act. Whereas earlier emigrants had primarily been unskilled laborers, many of the newer migrants were skilled workers, and many came from the non-Arab Islamic world, including Pakistan and Malaysia. A third wave of emigration has included Muslims who moved to America in order to escape various political and religious problems.

Within the Midwest are Muslims of all ethnicities and nationalities, representing all sects, including Sunni, Twelver, Ismaili, Ahmadiyya, and Sufi. Because extended familial relations and commitments are essential to many Muslims, it was only natural that many later Muslim emigrants to America would settle in areas where there already existed a large community. Places with large Muslim populations, such as Detroit, Chicago, Toledo, and Cedar Rapids, continue to attract immigrants.

The Midwest has been an important region for the development of Islamic institutions in North America. During the 1950s and 1960s, a large number of Islamic foreign students came to study in the United States; many of them settled permanently. In 1963 a group of such students met at the University of Illinois at Urbana-Champaign in order to establish the first Muslim Student Association of the United States and Canada (MSA). Its headquarters until 1975 was in Gary, Indiana. This organization is the central body of all Muslim students in North America. In 1982 the MSA was incorporated into a larger, umbrella organization of Islamic institutions known as the Islamic Society of North America (ISNA). Today, this institution is located in Plainfield, Indiana, a western suburb of Indianapolis.

The events of September 11, 2001, have had a tremendous impact on Islam in the American landscape in general, and the midwestern one in particular. On the one hand, the rights of many innocent Muslims have been curtailed simply because of their ethnicity or religious background, and 9/11 will continue to have significant repercussions on the ways in which non-Muslims perceive Muslims. On the other hand, federal investigations have focused on a number of extremist mosques and Muslim organizations in large urban centers, including those in the Midwest.

One thing is certain: As Islam continues to grow in the Midwest, it will play an ever greater role in the region, as it will in North America generally.

Sources and Further Reading: Yvonne Yazbeck Haddad, ed., *The Muslims of America* (1991); Asad Husain and Harold Vogelaar, "Activities of Immigrant Muslim Communities in Chicago," in Yvonne Yazbeck Haddad and Jane Idelman Smith, eds., *Muslim Communities in North America* (1994); Steve A. Johnson, "The Muslims of Indianapolis," in Yvonne Yazbeck Haddad and Jane Idelman Smith, eds., *Muslim Communities in North America* (1994); C. Eric Lincoln, *The Black Muslims in America* (1973); Linda S. Walbridge, *Without Forgetting the Imam* (1997).

Aaron Hughes
University of Calgary, Alberta, Canada

Judaism

Because Jews arrived in the Midwest from a variety of countries, they created a diversity of Jewish religious expression.

Historically, the practice of Judaism in the West has been tightly controlled by non-Jewish governmental authorities. Jews who found their way to the United States, however, encountered an unprecedented situation. In the colonies and the early republic, there was little if any governmental control over Jewish religious or social life. Synagogues were voluntary institutions, governed by rules and bylaws of their own making and financed by the dues or voluntary contributions of their members. Rabbis were hired and fired by lay leadership boards. Members who disagreed with how the liturgy was conducted, who disliked the rabbi, or who had disputes with congregational policy were perfectly free to leave and create their own rival congregation. The result was the emergence of diverse, creative, and innovative Judaisms in the United States

The Plum Street Temple, Cincinnati, Ohio, was built from 1864 to 1866. Library of Congress, Prints and Photographs Division, Historic American Buildings Survey, HABS, OHIO, 31-CINT, 12-5.

that were unlike anything then or now elsewhere in the world.

The creation of a typical American style of Judaism took place mainly in the Midwest and the South. To be sure, there were established Jewish communities along the eastern seaboard as early as the colonial period. But these communities, made up largely of Jews of Spanish or Dutch heritage, were small and highly assimilated. The real foundation of American Judaism was laid by immigrants from the German-speaking lands of central Europe who arrived in North America during the first half of the nineteenth century. For a number of social and, especially, economic reasons, these German Jewish immigrants very often chose not to settle in the established cities east of the Appalachians, but migrated west into the Midwest and South. There, free of any preestablished Jewish communities or governmental regulation, they proceeded to reinvent their Judaism to fit their new circumstances.

The first choice, of course, was whether to maintain Jewish practice at all. Given the widely scattered and sparse settlement of Jews in the Midwest, the cre-

ation of synagogues and other Jewish communal institutions was at first out of the question—the requisite population mass simply did not exist. Most Jews did, however, maintain a kind of Jewish ethnic identity and practiced Jewish rituals, to a greater or lesser extent, at home. Only by the 1830s and 1840s were there sufficient numbers of Jews in places like Chicago, Cincinnati, Cleveland, Detroit, or St. Louis to make possible the chartering of institutions like synagogues or burial societies. Some Jews refrained from joining such synagogues and societies and essentially disappeared from the Jewish community. Others became active members.

Once a congregation was established, the question arose as to the nature of the liturgy to be performed. In the early years of the German Jewish migration, the only Judaism known to most migrants was traditional Orthodoxy, and so most early Jewish congregations in the Midwest were traditional in practice. By the 1840s, however, many immigrants were familiar with the Reform Judaism that had taken shape in Germany in response to Jewish legal emancipation. The Reform movement, though hardly monolithic, greatly simplified the liturgy; translated what remained of the service from Hebrew into the vernacular (in this case German); encouraged the delivery of well-crafted and spiritually uplifting sermons; demanded churchlike decorum; and in numerous other ways encouraged Jewish worship to conform to the highest standards of Lutheran religiosity.

While such innovation and reform were severely resisted by rabbinical and governmental forces in Europe, no such restraints existed in America. The result was that most midwestern synagogues had, by the middle of the nineteenth century, adopted at least some measure of Reform Judaism. The process was not always easy, and the history of synagogues in the Midwest during this period is one of factionalism, splittings, and recombinations. The first congregation in Cincinnati was organized by English Jews in 1824 and was Orthodox. In 1840 German immigrants founded a second Orthodox synagogue, which gradually adopted Reform practices and liturgy. A few years later two more German Orthodox synagogues were founded. By 1907 these later two had liberalized and then merged as a Reform congregation. Detroit saw a similar process. The first congregation was founded in 1850 as an Orthodox synagogue. In 1861 it went Reform, with its dissident members breaking away to found a new Orthodox congregation.

Other factors were at work as well. Jews from different parts of Europe often had different rituals and customs, and they brought with them European nationalistic prejudices. Thus the Cleveland community began with two German Orthodox congregations, both of which eventually drifted to Reform. In 1866 Hungarian Jewish immigrants, uncomfortable in the "German" synagogues, founded their own "Hungarian" congregation. A few years later Polish and Lithuanian Jews joined together to create a synagogue more to their own liking.

In the years following the Civil War and Reconstruction, the United States experienced a tremendous wave of immigration from southern and eastern Europe. Within this wave were a large number of eastern European Jews, who came to America directly out of what were still essentially medieval societies. This migration began in 1881 and continued until strict new American immigration policies went into effect in 1924. Overall, some 2.5 million traditional, Yiddish-speaking, eastern European Jews arrived during these decades, entirely overwhelming the 250,000 or so by now highly Americanized German Jews. The eastern Europeans found the established "German" synagogues, with their churchlike pews, mixed male and female seating, organ music, English-language prayers, and uplifting sermons, to be utterly alien. The eastern Europeans immediately proceeded to recreate for themselves the communal institutions they knew from the Old World: small and intimate Orthodox synagogues, kosher butchers, social associations, orphan asylums, mutual aid societies, Yiddish newspapers and theatres, and the like. While most stayed in the East, especially in disembarkation port cities like New York and Boston, many found their way west. By establishing their traditional Orthodox synagogues and a variety of corresponding social and religious institutions, these immigrants changed drastically the Jewish landscape of the larger cities of the Midwest.

Despite this influx of eastern European Jewish orthodoxy, the Midwest remained the heartland of American Reform. A number of Reform rabbinical conferences, for example, were held in Cleveland, in 1855, 1870, and 1874. In the wake of such conferences, a number of reformist rabbis issued a statement of principles for American Reform, the so-called Pittsburgh Platform of 1885. Four years later, in 1889, a meeting in Detroit ended with the founding of North America's first formal rabbinic professional organization, the Central Conference of American Rabbis. This organization held its first national conference in Cleveland the following year. These meetings produced other results as well. After the 1855 conference, two Ohio Reform rabbis, Isidore Kalisch of Cleveland and Isaac Mayer Wise of Cincinnati, put together the first American Jewish prayer book, called *Minhag America* (The American Rite). Of even greater significance was the founding of the Union of American Hebrew Congregations (an umbrella organization for Jewish congregations) in 1873 in Cincinnati, which

was followed two years later by the establishment of North America's first rabbinical seminary, Hebrew Union College, also in Cincinnati. The result was that while Orthodox and its more flexible Conservative counterpart remained centered in New York, the Reform movement had its center in the Midwest. It is thus not surprising that when the Reform movement decided in the mid-1930s to update its 1885 Pittsburgh Platform in order to take into account recent developments—especially the rise of Nazism in Europe and the creation of a new Jewish population center in British Palestine—it issued the statement at a meeting in Columbus, Ohio (1937).

In the decades following World War II, the differences between "German" and "Russian" Jews began to fade as the descendants of the eastern European immigration assimilated into American life and all Jews found common cause in recovering from the Holocaust, dealing with assimilation and intermarriage, and supporting the new State of Israel. At the same time, the growth of national Jewish organizations, whether religious or secular, has established a certain organizational and cultural uniformity across North America. Finally, as Jews of all backgrounds move into the professions, and move to wherever their education, jobs, or lifestyle takes them, the demographic character of the Jewish community in America is becoming more homogeneous. At the same time, some communities developed particular characteristics due to certain settlement patterns. Skokie, Illinois, is known for its large and active Holocaust survivor community, and Cleveland, Ohio, has an unusually large Hasidic population because of the transplantation there of the Telz Yeshiva, one of the only Hasidic organizations to survive the Holocaust essentially intact.

Jewish communities in the Midwest today are gradually losing their distinctive quality. Newer Jewish religious and spiritual movements, like "Renewal Judaism," are making themselves felt in the Midwest in the same way they are in other parts of the country. As a result, there are in the Midwest today a bewildering variety of ways in which Jews can express their ethnic and religious identities.

Sources and Further Reading: Gerhard Falk, *American Judaism in Transition* (1995); Sue Fishkoff, *The Rebbe's Army* (2003); Karla Goldman, *Beyond the Synagogue Gallery* (2001); Jeffrey S. Gurock, *American Jewish Orthodoxy in Historical Perspective* (1996); Dana Evan Kaplan, *American Reform Judaism* (2003); Jonathan D. Sarna, *American Judaism* (2004); Jack Wertheimer, ed., *Jews in the Center* (2000); Jack Wertheimer, *A People Divided* (1997).

Peter J. Haas
Case Western Reserve University, Ohio

Latino/a Religion

Latino/a religion constitutes an amalgam of distinct Latin American folk and institutional patterns mixed into the cultural patterns of ritual observance fostered in U.S. churches. As in Latin America, Catholicism represents the dominant affiliation by birth and practice. As its impact varies in Latin American nations, it varies in midwestern communities, depending upon the inroads made by Protestants as well as the survivals of pre-Columbian and African traditions.

In the Midwest, as in the nation as a whole, Mexican Americans constitute the largest Latin American–origin subgroup—having lived and worked in the region since the early twentieth century. Since around 1920, seasonal migrant streams from Texas have fed Michigan, Ohio, Minnesota, and the eastern Dakotas. Migration directly from central Mexico has constituted another element in the influx; this wave has followed similar migration patterns. Puerto Ricans migrated from the Caribbean to Michigan and Illinois fields and factories beginning in the late 1940s, promptly settling in cities such as Detroit and Chicago. Cuban exiles fleeing the Revolution led by Fidel Castro generally arrived first in Miami, then in the mid-1960s and early 1970s were increasingly resettled under federal auspices in midwestern cities and towns, especially Chicago and Detroit. The 1980 Mariel boatlift brought a renewed influx, which included larger numbers of Afro-Cubans. During the past two decades, arrivals from Central and South American countries have spiked migration to the region's cities.

Whether Latino/as entered through cities, towns, or farms they quickly encountered the extensive apparatus of midwestern Catholicism. Some male and female religious personnel came from abroad, including dozens of Mexican priests and nuns persecuted during the Mexican Revolution. For the most part, however, the newcomers lacked an immigrant clergy. The first Mexican church in the Great Lakes region emerged in 1920 in Detroit, after Bishop Michael Gallagher brought in a priest from Monterrey, Mexico, to minister to immigrant workers scattered near automobile assembly plants. During the 1920s, parishes formed in Chicago; St. Paul, Minnesota; Kansas City, Missouri; Toledo, Ohio; Milwaukee; Gary, Indiana; and other cities, where they anchored fledgling communities. Following a debilitating decade of poverty and population decline in the 1930s, the renewed influx beginning in the 1940s boosted older settlements and led to the expansion of the parish network. Local parishes, along with the national hierarchy, have increasingly advocated on behalf of undocumented workers while implementing a wide range of social initiatives to alleviate the problems brought about by migration.

Church leadership has remained largely in non-Hispanic hands, even in cities such as Chicago where Latino/as constitute an ethnic plurality. Despite intermittent ethnic tensions, cultural interchange among parishioners of diverse origins, and between them and non-Latino clergy, have led to increased understanding of the importance of the *Virgen de Guadalupe*—the mestiza (Spanish-Indian) patroness of Mexico—as well as other elements of popular Catholicism imported from Latin America and the U.S. Southwest.

Mexican religious holidays include the December commemoration of *Guadalupe*, *Las Posadas* on Christmas, and the *Vía Crucis* (Stations of the Cross) featured during the Easter pageant. Caribbean Catholicism differs in many religious particulars—saints, holidays, and organizational aspects. Cubans have their own patroness, *Nuestra Señora de la Caridad del Cobre* (Our Lady of Charity), and have developed their own patterns of observance. Similarly, Chicago Puerto Ricans formed their own organizations with strong church ties, notably the *Caballeros de San Juan*, which was very active in the 1950s and 1960s. Interestingly, in those North Side neighborhoods where Latino/as from Mexico, Puerto Rico, and elsewhere live together, several Chicago parishes reflect a melding of practices, observing jointly the holidays, saints, and subcultures of Mexican, Caribbean, and Central American coreligionists.

The Latino/a emergence in Protestant congregations has witnessed a shift from the larger mainline denominations—mainly Methodist, Baptist, Presbyterian, and Congregationalist—to Pentecostal and other evangelical congregations. These faiths tend to be very decentralized and smaller in size, allowing for the ascendance of ministers who conduct religious services exclusively in Spanish. The burst in popularity of Protestantism among Latino/as in the Midwest parallels its growth throughout Latin America. At present, storefront churches are visible in most of the region's urban Hispanic neighborhoods. They are patronized by the whole range of subgroups, perhaps most notably by Puerto Ricans in Chicago.

In recent years, fierce competition over Latino/a congregants between Protestants and Catholics has softened into ecumenicalism, and coalitions have arisen for social causes, such as those involving Guatemalan and other Central American refugees. During the 1980s, the sanctuary movement in the Midwest saw many churches in the larger cities seeking to shield refugees from deportation back to hostile regimes. Similarly, concern for the poor both in Latin America and the United States bred an adherence to liberation theology, especially among activist clergy seeking to bring about both ecclesiastical and social change. Among the laity there has arisen a tendency to see religion as a partner in community empowerment.

The Midwest serves as a laboratory for observing the full range of Latino/a religion and ethnicity. The region's long history of European immigration led to an earlier and more sustained growth of Roman Catholic institutions than in the historically isolated Southwest, the regional homeland of Mexican Americans. Even the syncretic observance of Catholic and African rites, known as *Santería*, based on practices of the Yoruba people of present-day Nigeria (but considerably modified over many generations) has been imported to the urban Midwest by some of the Cuban *marielitos* arriving in the 1980 boatlift. *Santería* followers adhere to secret initiation, divination, and healing rituals. Some Puerto Ricans, notably in Detroit and Chicago, have also become adherents, and though they may still consider themselves Catholic, they patronize barrio shops called *botánicas* that sell religious articles for home altars.

Latino/a religion in the Midwest has flourished since the days of the pioneer parish communities of the 1920s. Today, in Catholic churches and Protestant congregations, as well as in locales geared to the practice of syncretic religiosity, Latino/as are breaking away from the static homogeneity and cultural strictures of pre–Vatican II Catholicism.

Sources and Further Reading: Jay P. Dolan and Gilberto M. Hinojosa, eds., *Mexican Americans and the Catholic Church, 1900–1965* (1994); Jay P. Dolan and Jaime R. Vidal, eds., *Puerto Rican and Cuban Catholics in the U.S., 1900–1965* (1994); Andrés G. Guerrero, *A Chicano Theology* (1987); Eugenio Matibag, *Afro-Cuban Religious Experience* (1996); Moises Sandoval, *On the Move* (1990); Dennis N. Valdés, *Barrios Norteños* (2000).

David A. Badillo
Bronx Institute, Lehman College, New York

Latter-Day Saints (Mormons)

Dozens of religious groups since 1830 have traced their origins to the authority of Mormon prophet Joseph Smith. Two have sustained numerical significance. The Church of Jesus Christ of Latter-Day Saints, exiled to the West in the 1840s and headquartered in Salt Lake City, boasts an expanding membership approaching 12 million. Nearly half of them reside in the United States and almost 360,000 in the Midwest, ranging from around 55,000 in Missouri to about 5,000 in North Dakota. The Reorganized Church of Jesus Christ of Latter Day Saints (in 2001 renamed the Community of Christ) is based in Independence, Missouri, with an American membership of 100,000, two-thirds of them in the Midwest. The two churches have experienced contrasting transfor-

mations redefining their respective natures, but they share an increasingly global consciousness and a midwestern heritage.

Although born in New York and widely identified with Utah, the movement's formative years—and its initial and crucial transformative years—unfolded in the Midwest. Indeed, the Reorganized Church, along with additional tiny branches of the movement led by James J. Strang and others, never did surrender its midwestern homeland. Even Utah-based Mormonism returned to the region in the latter decades of the twentieth century, enjoying a 32 percent increase in midwestern membership between 1990 and 2000.

For all its continuities, the numerically dominant stream of Mormonism may be seen as developing in four stages. The first arose in upstate New York, where the young Joseph Smith, disturbed by sectarian agitation, experienced visions of God, Jesus, and angels. He received ancient records of Hebrew immigrants to the New World, translating them with divine help into the Book of Mormon, which complemented the Bible. He was ordained to the restored and solely authorized priesthood, once a casualty of an apostate Christianity. By divine direction, as he understood it, he also organized, in 1830, a new church, the restoration of primitive Christianity. These elements com-

Temple of the Church of Jesus Christ of Latter-Day Saints, Kirtland, Ohio, 1833–1836. Library of Congress, Prints and Photographs Division, Historic American Buildings Survey, HABS, OHIO, 43-KIRT, 1-4. Photo by Carl F. Waite.

prised the early self-understanding of Mormonism, which promptly attracted dozens, then hundreds, of converts.

Between the birth of the church and the death of its founding prophet, Mormonism moved to the Midwest—and was transformed. Establishing centers at Kirtland, Ohio, and western Missouri, and then at Nauvoo, Illinois, hundreds of adherents became thousands, prophetically beckoned to gather to these centers. They strove to absorb dozens of Smith's revelations, which changed Mormonism from a church into a still-Christian but half-Hebrew church-kingdom. The movement eclipsed other denominations' metaphorical understanding in its aspiration to establish a literal, Christianized New Israel, complete with a promised land, patriarchs, temples, economic communalism, polygamy, political theocracy, and an enduring millennial consciousness.

The extraordinary changes and increasing adherents spawned internal and external alarm. Mormon leaders were driven from Kirtland in 1837 and all Mormons from Missouri by 1839, under threat of extermination. Smith was murdered near Nauvoo in Carthage, Illinois (1844), and the Mormons were expelled from the state in 1846.

The second stage began when Brigham Young led the dramatic exodus of many Mormons to the Rocky Mountains, where they developed their kingdom in magnified form during the next half century. A third of the Latter-Day Saints did not follow, many rejecting the transformed Mormonism that had developed in Nauvoo. By the late 1850s, scattered bands of followers had "reorganized," united by their hostility to polygamy, to doctrinal innovation, to temple rites, to gathering physically to establish a literal Kingdom of God, and to Brigham Young. For a century, the Reorganized Church, led by Smith's son and his descendants and headquartered at Plano, Illinois; Lamoni, Iowa; and, finally, Independence, Missouri, understood itself as the true heir of Joseph Smith's restoration of original Christianity. Since the 1960s, however, the church has—at the cost of schism—moved dramatically toward a liberal Protestantism and away from traditional Mormon understandings.

Its better-known cousin in the West underwent a second transformation, inaugurating, between 1890 and 1907, Mormonism's third stage, which endured for much of the twentieth century. Almost become an ethnic entity unto itself through two generations of geographic and social isolation, the church, under federal pressure, surrendered polygamy, along with the theocratic character and isolationist economics that had dominated Utah Territory. With great travail, the church also seated Mormon apostle Reed Smoot as a U.S. senator from the new state of Utah. This political

and social accommodation enabled the Latter-Day Saints, before midcentury, to find a comfortable role in the nation.

The movement's fourth stage surfaced in the 1960s and began to mature in the latter decades of the twentieth century into what some see as a new world religion. A Mormon "perestroika"—an all-encompassing administrative program called Correlation—began to fashion the immense, expanding, contemporary church, subject to a global program of reorganization, coordination, and bureaucratization and a simplification of doctrine, curricula, and purpose that points to Mormonism's emerging shape for the twenty-first century. This church has a three-pronged mission: "to proclaim the gospel," "to perfect the Saints," and "to redeem the dead" by performing vicarious ordinances for those who once lived on the earth.

Are Mormons Christian? The answer depends on what one means by the term *Christian*, which branch of Mormonism one contemplates, and which stage of the movement one considers. The Missouri-based Community of Christ has from its inception as an independent organization, and especially since the 1960s, been less distant from traditional Protestantism than has its more radical cousin in Utah. The Church of Jesus Christ of Latter-Day Saints headquartered in Salt Lake City is indisputably Christian in its self-consciousness and its devotion to the figure of Jesus Christ. Mormonism regards Christ as God's firstborn in the spirit and his only begotten in the flesh. His unique, vicarious sacrifice enabled salvation for all who have faith in his name and who obey the laws and ordinances of the gospel.

Mormons are not Christians, however, if by that term one means those in the great historic tradition that honors the fourth-century consensus forged and enforced at Nicea and the creeds that followed in its wake. It is this tradition that Joseph Smith described as apostate from the pure and original church that he sought to restore. In addition to introducing extrabiblical scripture, the Mormon prophet in the antebellum Midwest distinguished his movement by developing practices and doctrines—including polygamy and private temple rites suggesting the possibility of deification for resurrected humans in the eternities—sharply at odds with those of traditional Christianity. Although the Latter-Day Saints have much in common with other Christians, Mormon Christianity is more and other than merely one additional Christian denomination.

Sources and Further Reading: Leonard J. Arrington and Davis Bitton, *The Mormon Experience*, 2nd ed. (1992); Philip L. Barlow, *Mormons and the Bible* (1991); Paul M. Edwards, *Our Legacy of Faith* (1991); Edwin Scott Gaustad and Philip

L. Barlow, *New Historical Atlas of Religion in America* (2000); Klaus Hansen, *Mormonism and the American Experience* (1981); Sterling McMurrin, *The Theological Foundations of the Mormon Religion* (1965); Jan Shipps, *Mormonism: The Story of a New Religious Tradition* (1985); Jan Shipps, *Sojourner in the Promised Land* (2000).

Philip Barlow
Hanover College, Indiana

Lutherans

Approximately 70 percent of America's nine million Lutherans live in the Midwest, a part of a large belt of Lutheran settlement that extends from Pennsylvania through the Great Lakes region to the Great Plains. In a number of midwestern counties, especially in the upper Midwest, Lutherans form the largest single religious group and have had a notable impact on not only the religious life of the region, but also its social and cultural patterns. Almost all the major Lutheran denominations have had their headquarters in the Midwest, and most of the major Lutheran institutions are found in this region.

Most Lutherans trace their ethnic roots to immigrants who came to the United States from northern Europe, especially Germany and Scandinavia. The first Lutherans in the Midwest were descendants of

Bethel Chapel, a Lutheran Church north of Kearney, Nebraska. Solomon D. Butcher, 1903. Nebraska State Historical Society, Photograph Collection, RG2608.2623.

Germans who had immigrated to America during the colonial period. These Lutherans, who settled in Ohio, Indiana, and Illinois, had, for the most part, assimilated into American culture and used English in their worship. They formed regional synods (groupings of congregations) affiliated with eastern Lutheran groups such as the General Synod and the General Council, which merged in 1918 to become the United Lutheran Church in America.

These English-speaking Lutherans would in turn be inundated by waves of Lutheran immigrants who formed a part of the massive immigration to the United States in the middle to late nineteenth century. The first large-scale immigration was of Saxon Germans who came to Missouri and in 1847 formed the German Lutheran Synod of Missouri and Other States, headquartered in St. Louis (now known as the Lutheran Church Missouri Synod). This group of conservative Confessional Lutherans left Europe as a protest against religious changes in Germany, and its members were not inclined to join together with the English-speaking Lutherans of the General Synod and the General Council, whose Lutheranism the Missourians saw as suspect. Differences of language and theology kept many of these immigrant Lutheran denominations formally separate from one another, although there were many ways in which they worked together informally. Other groups of immigrant Germans also came to the United States and formed their own denominations. The Joint Synod of Ohio was formed in 1818, the Wisconsin Synod was founded in 1850, and the Evangelical Lutheran Synod of Iowa and other States was founded in 1854. In 1872 several of these synods established a joint organization called the Synodical Conference, but this group was almost immediately torn apart by theological disputes.

Scandinavian immigrants coming to the Midwest also formed their own ethnic denominations. Many of these groups were also divided internally by issues of theology and church structure, so that there were often several immigrant denominations in each ethnic community. Swedish immigrants formed at least five ethnic denominations, but only the largest of these, the Augustana Synod, was Lutheran. Founded in 1860, the Augustana Synod had its headquarters in Rock Island, Illinois, but was a national denomination. Norwegian immigrants were divided into as many as five separate Lutheran denominations. Most of these groups united to form the Evangelical Lutheran Church in 1917, with dissenting Norwegians forming the Evangelical Lutheran Synod and the Lutheran Free Church. All of these groups had their headquarters in Minnesota. Danish Lutherans formed two different denominations, the United Evangelical Lutheran Church and the American Evangelical

Lutheran Church, both of which had their main strength in Iowa and Nebraska.

Early Lutheran immigrants tended to settle in rural areas, while groups coming later in the century, who arrived after most of the good land was already taken, settled either in mining and logging areas or in major cities, such as Minneapolis, Milwaukee, Chicago, St. Louis, Detroit, and Cleveland. Finnish immigrants predominated in the mines and logging areas around Lake Superior. One group of Finnish Lutherans formed the Suomi Synod, and a second group eventually joined the Missouri Synod. Still other pietistic Finns formed Apostolic Lutheran congregations. Lutherans from Slovakia formed two different groups, one a part of the General Council, and the other a part of the Missouri Synod. Icelandic Lutherans, centered around North Dakota and Manitoba, formed their own ethnic synod within the General Council. After 1945, Estonian, Latvian, Lithuanian, and Hungarian Lutheran refugees formed small ethnic denominations or synods in exile.

As these immigrants settled in the Midwest, they formed rich ethnic subcultures, of which their religious organizations were a major component. Beyond the formation of Lutheran congregations and synods, these immigrants founded schools, academies, colleges, and seminaries as well as hospitals, nursing homes, and orphanages. Scores of major midwestern colleges, such as St. Olaf College and Valparaiso University, and hospitals such as Passavant Hospital, Chicago, and the Lutheran Hospital in St. Louis, trace their origins to these immigrant beginnings. Each denomination had its own publishing ventures, which produced books and newspapers for the faithful, first in the immigrant languages and later in English, including Augsburg Fortress Publishers and Concordia Publishing House. Camps and outdoor centers were established by the score. Midwestern Lutherans were also busy spreading their beliefs through mission activities, both in the United States and in countries around the world.

The immigrant era for midwestern Lutherans drew to a close after World War I with federal immigration restrictions. Although transition to full American citizenship was the goal of most groups, the changes involved could be wrenching for these ethnic denominations. The principal difficulty was the language transition, the switch from the use of the immigrant language to the use of English in worship and denominational business. Although this transition happened gradually, by 1940 most Lutherans had made the change to English, though older members still wondered aloud if Lutheranism could really work in this new language. Speeding the language transition along were acculturation of second- and third-generation Lutherans, the rise of nativist sentiment after World War I, and the end of mass immigration.

With this transition to the widespread use of English, the continued existence of all the ethnic Lutheran denominations was called into question, and midwestern Lutherans began to think about merging some or all of the groups into a larger American Lutheran denomination. Still, theological and structural differences among the groups were a barrier, and the process of merger dragged out through the 1940s and 1950s. The Iowa, Ohio, and Texas synods merged in 1930 to form the American Lutheran Church (1930–1960), which in turn merged with the Evangelical Lutheran Church and a Danish group to form another American Lutheran Church (1960–1988). The Augustana Synod merged with the United Lutheran Church in America, the Suomi Synod, and another of the Danish groups to form the Lutheran Church in America (1962–1988).

Though it participated in some early merger discussions, the Lutheran Church Missouri Synod decided not to enter either of the two new denominations, although it did for a while establish ties with the American Lutheran Church. In the late 1960s the Lutheran Church Missouri Synod took a strongly conservative path, and a dispute over the denominational seminary in St. Louis led to a split within the synod, with moderate dissidents forming the Association of Evangelical Lutheran Churches (AELC) in 1976. The AELC merged with the Lutheran Church in America and the American Lutheran Church in 1988 to form the Evangelical Lutheran Church in America (ELCA).

Currently, 95 percent of American Lutherans are members of two denominations centered in the Midwest. The ELCA, headquartered in Chicago, has 5.1 million members, while the Lutheran Church Missouri Synod, with its offices in St. Louis, has 2.6 million members. The next-largest group, the Wisconsin Evangelical Lutheran Synod, headquartered in Milwaukee, has 400,000 members and is by far the largest of the remaining smaller Lutheran denominations. The ELCA is usually counted as a mainline Protestant denomination, while the Missouri and Wisconsin Synods generally take much more conservative positions on theological and social issues.

Midwestern Lutheran groups have had an important effect on the Midwest beyond their own communities, especially through their educational and social-service agencies. Although they tend to be underrepresented in national politics, Lutherans have been influential in midwestern politics, especially in the upper Midwest. Lutherans have perceptibly influenced the social and cultural life of many midwestern communities, and they have the numbers to continue to be influential in the future.

Sources and Further Reading: G. Everett Arden, *Augustana Heritage* (1963); Walter A. Baepler, *A Century of Grace: A History of the Missouri Synod, 1847–1947* (1947); L. DeAne Lagerquist, *The Lutherans* (1999); Fred W. Meuser, *The Formation of the American Lutheran Church* (1958); E. Clifford Nelson, *Lutheranism in North America, 1914–1970* (1972); E. Clifford Nelson, *The Lutherans in North America* (1975); E. Clifford Nelson and Eugene Fevold, *The Lutheran Church among Norwegian Americans*, 2 vols. (1960); John H. Tietjen, *Which Way to Lutheran Unity?* (1966); R. C. Wolf, ed., *Documents of Lutheran Unity in America* (1966).

Mark Granquist
Gustavus Adolphus College, Minnesota

Methodists

Methodists are followers of the religious tradition established by the English preacher John Wesley, who lived from 1703 to 1791. Today in the United States, the United Methodist Church is the largest denomination of Wesleyan origin and is the second-largest Protestant denomination, with more than eight million members. The Methodists are the largest Protestant denomination in Iowa and either the second or third largest in the other midwestern states, competing with the Baptists and the Lutherans.

The Methodists began with John Wesley's quest to live a more fulfilling Christian life. The movement grew steadily in England during the middle of the eighteenth century, and made its way to North America. By the time of the American Revolution, there were several hundred members located exclusively in the Middle Atlantic States. Despite the Methodists' association with the Church of England they survived the Revolution and began growing again.

Resisting Wesley's desire to keep the Americans under his control, American Methodists at the Christmas Conference of 1784 declared themselves a new denomination and founded the Methodist Episcopal Church. Following English precedents, they established an itinerant clergy led by bishops and superintendents. Most of the power was reserved to the bishops and other high church officials and the vote of the ordained clergy. Under the leadership of Francis Asbury, the American church grew spectacularly. Membership reached sixty thousand in 1800, two hundred thousand by 1820, and was over one million by the 1850s, when the Methodist Episcopal Church had become the largest Protestant denomination in the United States.

Methodism was well suited to compete in the wide-open religious environment of the new republic. Methodist clergy were all itinerant preachers, riding a circuit on horseback to form new congregations and check on existing ones. The early Methodist clergyman was recruited based on his ability to preach effectively rather than his formal education, which rival denominations often required.

Methodists had two distinct advantages that led them to become the leading denomination in most of the midwestern states by 1840. First, Methodists preached an Arminian free-will theology that claimed that each individual had the capacity through his or her own free will to achieve salvation. This theology contrasted with the Calvinism preached by their two chief competitors, the Baptists and the Presbyterians, which claimed that because salvation was predetermined from birth, individual volition did not matter. In an egalitarian society (at least for white men) in which people could go as far as their talents and ambitions would take them, the free-will theology made more sense.

The Lake View Methodist Episcopal Church, 1911, Tripp County, South Dakota. Fred Hultstrand History in Pictures Collection, NDIRS-NDSU, Fargo, 2028.011.

Second, Methodists embraced the revivalism of the Second Great Awakening. While other denominations debated the legitimacy of the raucous, outdoor evangelical revivals known as camp meetings, the Methodists wholeheartedly committed themselves to such events. Held regularly throughout the year, these meetings consisted of several days and nights of non-stop preaching and praying. They became known for the loud and boisterous behaviors of the congregants.

In order to keep up with the Presbyterians, the Methodists founded dozens of colleges, despite their traditional disdain for a college degree as a requirement for ministers. The Methodists founded McKendree College in Illinois in 1828, Indiana Asbury (now Depauw University) in Indiana in 1837, Ohio Wesleyan in 1842, Northwestern in 1851, and many others. The Methodists were also among the strongest supporters of Sunday schools and compulsory public education.

The biggest crisis of nineteenth-century Methodism was over slavery and the sectional issue. When a call for immediate abolitionism arose in the 1820s and 1830s, church officials did everything they could to silence it, including banning any discussion in the General Conference. But in the 1844 General Conference, the issue came to a head.

One of the bishops, James Andrew, inherited several slaves through marriage. Northern members protested, saying that they would not be supervised by a slaveholding bishop. Andrew, himself a moderate, tried to free his slaves but his native South Carolina did not allow manumission and the slaves did not want to be recolonized in Liberia. The conference overwhelmingly approved a compromise in which Andrew would not perform any of his Episcopal duties until he had disposed of his slaves. Southern delegates, however, walked out rather than accept the compromise and formed the Methodist Episcopal Church, South. Both sides ardently supported their respective sections in the Civil War.

As a faith strongest in small towns and rural areas, Methodism was relatively late in recognizing the problems caused by industrialization and urbanization. However, as the problems became more severe, northern conferences began denouncing some of the worst excesses of industrialism and labor exploitation. They supported legislation outlawing child labor, for example. In 1908 the Methodist Episcopal Church; the Methodist Episcopal Church, South; and three African American Methodist denominations joined the Federal Council of the Churches of Christ in America, an association of denominations trying to confront the social ills of early-twentieth-century America. The council adopted a social creed that clearly resembled the Social Creed of Methodism, is-

sued earlier that year by the northern conference. Nevertheless, Methodism would never fully adapt to the increasingly urban nation.

Methodism's single greatest contribution to American political and social life was its support for restrictions on the consumption of alcoholic beverages. Methodists in all regions of the country were staunch supporters of the nineteenth-century temperance movement as it shifted its focus from personal responsibility and state prohibition to a constitutional amendment. The founder of the Anti-Saloon League of America was a Methodist, as was Frances Willard, founder and longtime leader of the Women's Christian Temperance Union.

The church has grown steadily more inclusive, with lay representation in the General Conference beginning in 1872, women eligible to be delegates to the General Conference in 1892, and women gradually becoming ordained clergy in the twentieth century. In 1980 Marjorie Matthews was ordained as the first woman bishop of the church. Northern and southern churches began working toward reunion as early as 1916, although it was not until 1939 that the Methodist Episcopal Church; the Methodist Episcopal Church, South; and the Methodist Protestant Church joined to form the Methodist Church. The denomination's growth crested in the 1950s and 1960s, with eleven million members in 1968 when the United Methodist Church was formed by the union of the Methodist Church with the Evangelical United Brethren and Evangelical Association. Since then, membership has declined to eight million in the United States.

Today, the church continues to preach the gospel and get involved in what it considers to be worthwhile charitable endeavors. Like so many other American institutions, the church continues to struggle with contemporary issues, such as nuclear power, the environment, the rights of gays within the church and society, abortion, and AIDS (acquired immunodeficiency syndrome). Methodists are as divided as the rest of American society over these controversial issues.

Sources and Further Reading: Sidney Ahlstrom, *A Religious History of the American People* (1963); Stanley Ayling, *John Wesley* (1979); John Boles, *The Great Revival, 1787–1805* (1972); Emory Stevens Buck, ed., *The Story of American Methodism*, 3 vols. (1964); Roger Finke and Rodney Starke, *The Churching of America* (1992); Elizabeth Nottingham, *Methodism and the Frontier* (1941); William Warren Sweet, *Methodism in American History* (1932).

Douglas Montagna,
Grand Valley State University, Michigan

Native Americans

The Native American populations of midwestern states have varied widely in language and culture, as well as in religion. In the Hopewellian (500 B.C.E.–C.E. 400) and Mississippian (C.E. 700–1500) epochs, the time periods of the great earthworks found in Cahokia in Illinois and the Serpent Mound in the Ohio Valley, native peoples prospered in this region and seem to have shared some basic religiocultural practices.

However, by the eighteenth century, great diversity in American Indian cultures had developed. Iroquoian, Algonquian, and Siouan linguistic groups were present, and Great Lakes/Riverine, northern Plains, and central Plains cultural groups inhabited this region. Some American Indian nations had lived in midwestern lands for many centuries prior to the colonial era, while others migrated to and from these lands before and after colonial times. All Native American cultures changed, and many nations relocated as contact with European colonials brought new challenges, such as disease, warfare, and religious missions, to indigenous peoples of the region. Notably, nations who went westward to the northern and central Plains (including the Mandan and the Hidatsa peoples) were culturally transformed by the arrival of the horse in the Americas. Further geographic relocations of indigenous groups occurred after the United States became a nation and acquired a larger land base by implementing policies of allotment (restriction of land possession only to acculturated Native American peoples) and removal (expulsion to or restriction of Indians to newly established reservations). Because of the great concentration of government-created reservation lands in Oklahoma, many Native Americans were displaced from their original midwestern homes.

However culturally diverse the Native American people of the Midwest were, and remain, their traditional religions do share certain elements. The Shawnee, Miami, Potawatomi, Ojibwa, Winnebago, Menomini, Osage, Iowa, Oto, Pawnee, and Hidatsa peoples, among others, have similar traditional cosmologies that include belief in a tripartite and interrelated universe. In this view, three levels of being exist: the upper world (the sky, sun, and stars); the this-world (the earth upon which human beings, plants, and animals live); and the lower world (below the earth or in the waters). Each cosmic level is reverenced, and each is understood to have the potential to influence the inhabitants of the others. Another shared traditional religious orientation is the belief in the enspiritedness of the beings of all three realms. The sacred power that enspirits things (called *orenda* in the Iroquoian languages, *manitou* in the Algonquian languages, and *wakan* in the Siouan languages) is potentially present in all beings but can manifest itself specifically and noticeably in certain beings, including human beings, animals, plants, forces of nature, and features of landscape.

The mythologies of the peoples indigenous to the Midwest reflect and sacralize the varied geographies of the Midwest. An origin myth of the Menomini of Wisconsin tells of the emergence of two bears from land along the mouth of the Menominee River; these two bears became the first human beings. Myths of this type acknowledge the sacrality of particular locations to particular people. Also, many Native Americans tell a similar story of the earth's creation by an animal (an elk, a muskrat, a duck, a frog, a turtle, a water beetle) who dives beneath primordial waters and brings up earth, which then becomes stable land. Rather than emphasizing a particular sacred site, this type of myth illustrates the interrelation of the three levels of being.

Although religious rituals performed by peoples indigenous to the Midwest vary greatly, certain forms and themes appear in the rituals of agricultural societies, while others are found in those of hunting societies. Many agricultural societies performed rituals ensuring and celebrating fecundity. In contrast, many hunting and gathering societies performed rituals to ensure proper respect for the sacred power present in the animals hunted and in the substances gathered. Nations who arrived on the central Plains and embraced horse culture and bison hunting performed rituals in which the animal was praised and hunting success was requested. Individualistic rituals such as the vision quest (in which a person establishes a relationship with a particular sacred power) were more often practiced in these types of societies.

Religious specialists, or shamans and/or medicine people, are also present (although in distinctive cultural forms) in American Indian nations of the Midwest. These people are noted in their societies for their abilities to heal through ritual practice, to cure sickness by administering herbal remedies, and/or to preside over public rituals. Religious specialists having particular relationships with sacred powers have always been consulted in matters of warfare, hunting, planting, migrating, and interpreting dreams. In some nations, people who were not religious specialists nevertheless participated in medicine societies—organizations of those cured by a certain type of medicine, or of those sharing a relationship with a certain sacred power. The most notable medicine society in all of Native America may be the *Midewiwin*, or Great Medicine Society, an institution of the Ojibwa, Menomini, Potawatomi, Winnebago, Kickapoo, Sauk, and Fox nations.

The Midwest has been the place of origin of many

❖ "Come, Holy Spirit, Heavenly Dove"

(A comparison of an original poem by the English pastor and hymn writer Isaac Watts with the version in the 1910 Ojibwe Hymnal reveals the ways in which Native Americans have reinterpreted Christian sentiments in accord with their spiritual heritage.)

Isaac Watts (1707)	Ojibwe Hymnal (1910)	(Re)Translation (late 20th century)
Come, Holy Spirit, heavenly Dove, With all Thy quickening powers; Kindle a flame of sacred love	Ondashan, Kichi Ochichag, Widokawishinam, Atoniu sagiiwewin Ima nindeinang	Come here Great Spirit, Help us Put it there, love [to love, treasure people] There in our hearts
In vain we tune our formal songs In vain we strive to rise; Hosannas languish on our Tongues, And our devotion dies.	'Na eji-gotugiziyang Oma aking ayayang; Nin kichi bejiwimin su Ishpiming wi-jayang	Look how miserable we are Here as we are on earth We are very slow in our doing [to go] Up there, in heaven, where we Want to go.
And shall we, Lord, for ever be In this poor dying state? Our love so faint, so cold to thee, And thine to us so great?	Anawi nindinend amin Nagumotagoyun; Nind anamiawininan Nonde ko takisin.	We think vainly of that, that you are sung to; Our prayers Cool too soon.*
Come, Holy Spirit, heavenly Dove, With all thy quickening powers; Come, shed abroad a Savior's Love, And that shall kindle ours?	Ondashan, Kichi Ochichag, Widokawishinam, Moshkinaton nindeinang Iu sagiiwewin.	Come here, Great Spirit help us, Fill it, our heart, With that love.

* = (Larry Cloud Morgan, an Ojibwe spiritual leader who seriously considered becoming a Roman Catholic priest earlier in his life, had translated this stanza, after some difficulty, as follows: As we are thinking, = As we sing, = Our Prayers = Touch beautiful places in us. Morgan died in Minnesota in 1999.)

Source: "Table 2.3: Come, holy spirit, heavenly dove, p. 59," from *Ojibwe Singers* by Michael McNally, copyright 2000 by Oxford University Press, Inc. Used by permission of Oxford University Press, Inc.

important Native American religious movements in response to colonialism and intercultural encounters. The pan-Indian movement initiated in the early nineteenth century by the Shawnee prophet Tenskwatawa and his brother Tecumseh originated in Ohio and Indiana. Other prophets of midwestern significance have included Neolin of the Delaware, Kanakuk of the Kickapoo, and Patheske of the Winnebago.

Today, the Native Americans remaining in the Midwest, while predominantly Christians, celebrate their traditional cultural and religious heritage (and simultaneously practice outreach to the larger populace) by erecting cultural centers and reviving indigenous languages. Some midwestern nations have attempted to improve economic conditions by using their sovereign status to operate bingo halls, casinos, and tax-exempt stores, and by encouraging tourism and education on Native American issues through powwow sponsorship. Powwows have become popular venues in which to solidify pan-Indian identity; indeed, many of the most popular intertribal powwows in the nation are held in midwestern states.

Sources and Further Reading: Raymond J. DeMallie, ed., *Plains*, vol. 13 of William C. Sturtevant, ed., *Handbook of North American Indians* (2001); Brian M. Fagan, *Ancient*

North America (1991); James Mooney, *The Ghost Dance* (1996); Lawrence E. Sullivan, ed., *Native American Religions* (1989); Bruce G. Trigger, ed., *Northeast*, vol. 15 of William C. Sturtevant, ed., *Handbook of North American Indians* (1978).

Lisa J. M. Poirier
Miami University, Oxford, Ohio

Presbyterians and Congregationalists

By some accounts, the opening scene of the story of Presbyterians and Congregationalists in the Midwest actually begins in Schenectady, New York, in the office of the Reverend John Blair Smith, president of Union College, when he met with Congregationalist frontier missionary Eliphalet Nott. From their discussions a plan began to unfold, a plan that would meet the pressing need for pastors and evangelists on the developing frontier of the Western Reserve. Neither the Presbyterians nor the Congregationalists could separately meet the demand to establish churches in the new communities springing up in Ohio and elsewhere on this new frontier. Both Churches were Calvinistic in doctrine, so the only obstacle to a cooperative effort was their differing form of church government.

Congregationalists espoused the autonomy of the local congregation and generally employed a system of democratic rule within the church, while Presbyterians held to a representative form of government in which elders ruled over the church in a tier of courts termed the session (for the local congregation), the presbytery (regional), the synod (larger regional or state-wide), and, lastly, the General Assembly (national). Under the developing plan, a minister from one denomination could pastor a congregation of the other denomination. The discipline of offending members was to be handled by committees consisting of members of both groups; unresolved disputes were then referred to similarly constituted regional councils. From the Presbyterian side, Jonathan Edwards, Jr., ultimately brought the motion before the general assembly of his church to effect what became known as the Plan of Union (1801), in which the two denominations agreed to work together, thus allowing pastors, churches, and laity to effectively operate simultaneously as both Presbyterians and Congregationalists.

From the high priority placed upon education by both denominations, Plan of Union schools and colleges were soon in preparation to match the westward advance, with Western Reserve College (Ohio, founded in 1826), Illinois College (1829), and Knox College (Illinois, 1837) as well as Beloit College (Wisconsin, 1846), Grinnell College (Iowa, 1846), and Rockford College (Illinois, 1847) among the resulting institutions. Separately, the Congregationalists went on to either found or influence the establishment of colleges including Oberlin in Ohio in 1833; Marietta (Ohio, 1834); Ripon (Wisconsin, 1851); Wheaton (Illinois, 1860); and some eleven other schools in the Midwest. The Presbyterians too were active in the establishment of Wabash College (Indiana, 1832), Monmouth College (Illinois, 1853), Lincoln University (Missouri, 1866), Wooster College (Ohio, 1866), Emporia College (Kansas, 1882), and at least another eighteen institutions throughout the Midwest. Presbyterians also played a significant role in education at the elementary level as well, as illustrated in the prodigious success of William Holmes McGuffey's series of "eclectic readers."

For a time the Plan of Union worked well, with its greatest success occurring in the Midwest. The subsequent planting of churches under the plan now seems phenomenal, if judged only by critics of the plan. Under one estimate, "no less than 2,000 churches of Congregational origin [were] estimated to have become Presbyterian" in the New York and Ohio regions. But the shortcomings of the plan were unforeseen. Organizationally, the Presbyterian system took precedence in the outworking of church discipline. Both denominations also had members who were straying from the established forms of Calvinism and it became easy for each to see these errors as arising from the other camp. While the stricter Congregationalists voiced their qualms over the revivalist methodologies of Presbyterian Charles Grandison Finney, conservatives among the Presbyterians charged the New Haven theology of Nathaniel Taylor and Lyman Beecher with being a form of Pelagianism, or human "self-salvation." These tensions precipitated a division of the Presbyterian Church in 1837 along conservative "Old School" and progressive "New School" lines. That division marked the effective end of the Plan of Union, although the New School Presbyterians did not officially quit the arrangement until 1852.

Presbyterian seminaries established in the Midwest included Lane, in Cincinnati (1829); McCormick, in Chicago (1851); the German Presbyterian school in Dubuque (1852); and, finally, Omaha (1891). Interestingly, Lane Theological Seminary was founded through a donation made by Ebenezer Lane and his brother, an offer initially made to the Baptists. Headed by Beecher, the school operated under a manual-labor plan to reduce expenses, but the shortfalls of that system were soon evident. McCormick Seminary, formerly the Theological Seminary of the Northwest, was founded through the generosity of Cyrus H. Mc-

Cormick, who donated more than one hundred thousand dollars from his estate. It was said that civilization moved westward thirty miles a year due to McCormick's invention of the mechanical reaper; so, too, the western advance of the Presbyterian Church was equally in his debt.

Abolitionist sympathies were strongly evidenced throughout the Midwest among both Presbyterians and Congregationalists. The Reformed Presbyterian Church, a small denomination with regional strength in Illinois and Ohio, was arguably the first to take a clear stand, declaring in 1802 that no slaveholder could be a member in good standing. Congregationalist Oberlin College, under the leadership of Theodore Dwight Weld, was a forerunner in accepting African American students and other schools soon modeled its example. The Beecher family, which included Calvin Stowe, husband of Harriet Beecher, should also be noted as leading abolitionists within the Congregationalist fold.

The Presbyterian Church in the U.S.A., by far the largest of the Presbyterian denominations, did not come to a strong stance against slavery until the 1860s. In large part this was because the slavery issue had become but one aspect of the larger debate within the church that had begun in the 1830s between the Old School and New School factions. The New School was decidedly antislavery, while the Old School in the heat of the larger debate found itself on the defensive. Only with the reunion of 1869 did the Presbyterian Church in the U.S.A. truly come to a resolved position against slavery.

No sooner had that reunion taken place than new controversies began. The heresy trials of theologian Charles Briggs and preacher David Swing were indicative of unresolved tensions between the Old School and the New School. These trials were precursors of the later unfolding of the fundamentalist/modernist controversy of the 1920s and 1930s, which was played out in the Midwest in the seminaries and colleges of both Presbyterian and Congregationalist Churches. J. Oliver Buswell, Jr. (then president of Wheaton College), and other conservatives in the Chicago area took leading roles in the formation of the Orthodox Presbyterian Church (1936) and, subsequently, the Bible Presbyterian Church (1938). Much of the later growth of these smaller denominations took place in the Midwest.

In 1958 the United Presbyterian Church of North America (UPCNA) found its way into a union with the older Presbyterian Church in the United States of America. The UPCNA had been formed in 1858 and was a denomination that existed almost entirely within the Midwest and western Pennsylvania. The newly united church took the name United Presbyterian Church in the United States of America (UPCUSA) and continued as such until a further merger with the southern Presbyterian denomination, the Presbyterian Church in the United States, in 1983 created the Presbyterian Church (U.S.A.).

That pending union led its critics to form the denomination known as the Evangelical Presbyterian Church. From a meeting in St. Louis in 1980, Bartlett Hess, pastor of Ward Presbyterian Church in Livonia, Michigan, along with Andrew A. Jumper, senior pastor of Central Presbyterian Church in St. Louis, and the pastors of some forty other churches began to work toward the establishment of this new denomination. Their departure was based upon concerns over the doctrinal direction of the mother church, the UPCUSA.

Throughout the later nineteenth and twentieth centuries, Presbyterians looked for leadership primarily in their centers in Philadelphia and the South. By contrast, the truly important events in Congregational history in the twentieth century occurred in the Midwest. The way was first paved by the Oberlin Statements of 1871 and the Ohio Association's Commission Creed of 1881. Then in 1913, a national meeting in Kansas City, Missouri, produced a declaration that marked a decisive turn away from the Calvinism that had historically been a part of Congregational theology, now supplanted by the Social Gospel of the progressive movement. Following a series of mergers in 1927 and 1931, the resulting Congregational denomination finally merged in 1957 with the Evangelical and Reformed Church at a meeting in Cleveland, Ohio, resulting in what is now called the United Church of Christ. Eden Seminary in St. Louis by this union became a part of the Congregational story.

More traditional Congregationalists departed prior to that union, in 1955, to form the National Association of Congregational Christian Churches, which is based in Oak Creek, Wisconsin, while the more theologically conservative Congregationalists had already left in 1948 to form the Conservative Congregational Christian Conference, headquartered in St. Paul, Minnesota. While Presbyterian centers have gravitated back to Philadelphia; Louisville, Kentucky; and Atlanta, Congregationalists of all stripes have moved from their historic East Coast roots in Connecticut and New England to become a set of denominations well grounded in the Midwest.

Sources and Further Reading: Randall Balmer and John R. Fitzmier, *The Presbyterians* (1994); Albert E. Dunning, *Congregationalists in America* (1894); Joseph H. Hall, *Presbyterian Conflict and Resolution on the Missouri Frontier* (1987); J.F. Hinkhouse, ed., *One Hundred Years of the Iowa Presbyterian Church* (1932); A.T. Norton, *History of the Presbyterian*

Church in the State of Illinois (1879); James R. Rohrer, *Keepers of the Covenant* (1995); L. C. Rudolph, *Hoosier Zion* (1963); E. B. Welsh, *Buckeye Presbyterianism* (1968); J. William T. Youngs, *The Congregationalists* (1998).

Wayne Sparkman
Presbyterian Church in America Historical
Center, St. Louis, Missouri

Restorationists and Campbellites

The "restoration movement" is an indigenous religious movement that emerged in the eastern United States in the early nineteenth century. Restorationism is a form of Christian primitivism that seeks to restore the doctrines and practices of early Christianity. Because its early leaders, Barton Warren Stone and Thomas Campbell, gave their names to the movement, it is often called the Stone-Campbell movement and its followers are called Campbellites.

Barton Warren Stone, a Presbyterian preacher in eastern Kentucky, was instrumental in leading the major Cane Ridge camp meeting in 1801. Criticism by other clergy led Stone and several associates to leave the Presbyterians and form their own fellowship. By 1820 Stone had several thousand followers in Kentucky and adjacent states who used the name *Christian* exclusively.

Thomas Campbell was a Presbyterian minister who migrated from Ireland to Pennsylvania in 1807. Controversy over his relationship with other denominations led him to leave the Presbyterians. In 1809 Campbell and several followers formed the Christian Association of Washington, Pennsylvania, and in 1811, a separate congregation called the Brush Run Church, near Washington. When Campbell's family joined him shortly thereafter, his son Alexander became a leader.

Within a short time, numerous congregations began to call themselves Christian, Church of Christ, or Disciples of Christ. Their restorationist emphasis led them to adopt adult baptism by immersion and the weekly observance of the Lord's Supper. Scottish immigrant Walter Scott became an associate of the Campbells in the 1820s and was instrumental in the spread of the movement into Ohio.

By the 1830s, individuals and congregations in Stone's "Christian" movement and the Campbells' "Disciples" movement were aware of similarities between the organizations. They started to coalesce into one movement, although a branch of Stone's Christian movement remained aloof from this merger.

By the Civil War, the Campbellites had an estimated membership of over 190,000. Scholars have often noted that the movement found its greatest strength in the border states. Rapid expansion spread the movement throughout Ohio, Indiana, Illinois, and Missouri, as well as in Kentucky and Tennessee.

After the Civil War, tensions within the movement led to divisions. While the splits were not strictly sectional, what became the Disciples of Christ was stronger in the North, especially in the Ohio-Indiana-Illinois region. In the upper tier of southern states from Kentucky to Arkansas and westward to Texas, another group used the name *Church of Christ* exclusively. Theological modernism was one issue in this division, but issues directly related to restorationist ideals were central. The Churches of Christ generally emphasized restorationism more strongly and were opposed to extracongregational organizations and the use of instrumental music in worship.

Within the Disciples movement, continuing controversies over theological liberalism and matters of church government eventually led to another schism. By the late 1920s, a group sometimes deemed "independents" had coalesced. They opposed the trend within the Disciples movement toward a more formally organized denomination. Between the 1920s and the 1970s, the independents became a distinct group, often referred to simply as "Christian churches" or "independent Christian churches." In the 1960s, the Disciples went through a process of "restructuring" and organized the denomination today known as the Christian Church (Disciples of Christ).

Today, although churches of all three branches of the movement are found throughout the country, there are clearly regional patterns. The Disciples and the independent Christian churches are generally strong throughout Midwest, except for the northern prairie and plains region. The Churches of Christ still find its largest strength in the region from Tennessee westward to Texas.

Certain midwestern cities have become important centers of the Disciples movement and the independent Christian churches. The headquarters of the Christian Church (Disciples of Christ) is in Indianapolis, Indiana, as is one of its major seminaries, the Christian Theological Seminary. The Board of Publication of the Christian Church (Disciples of Christ) is in St. Louis, Missouri. Standard Publishing in Cincinnati, Ohio, supplies literature and periodicals for the independent churches. Cincinnati Bible College and Seminary, founded in 1924, was one of the first schools to serve the independent Christian churches. Ozark Christian College in Joplin, Missouri, was also an early independent Bible college. In Cincinnati and Joplin, the presence of these schools led other organizations that serve the independent churches to locate nearby, creating regional centers of influence.

The early churches of this movement were part of a process that historian Nathan Hatch has called the "democratization of American Christianity." The idea of challenging established religious authorities may have appealed to the individualism of the early settlers in the Midwest. "Christians" and Disciples preached a sensible, rational religion that eschewed both mysticism and theoretical theology; this message no doubt appealed to the pragmatism of midwestern minds.

Today, most major metropolitan areas in the Midwest have all three of the branches of the restoration movement. Because the Churches of Christ remains a predominantly southern movement, congregations of the Christian Church (Disciples of Christ) and the independent Christian churches are the most numerous throughout the Midwest. Like many so-called mainline American denominations, the Disciples of Christ have sustained significant losses in membership over the past several decades. Among the independent "Christian" churches, many small-town and rural churches are struggling to sustain membership, but overall the group has seen marked growth due to a number of megachurches in large metropolitan areas.

Sources and Further Reading: Leroy Garrett, *The Stone-Campbell Movement* (1981); Winfred E. Garrison and Alfred T. DeGroot, *The Disciples of Christ*, rev. ed. (1958); Nathan O. Hatch, *The Democratization of American Christianity* (1989); Richard T. Hughes, *Reviving the Ancient Faith* (1996); Lester G. McAllister and William E. Tucker, *Journey in Faith* (1975); James B. North, *Union in Truth* (1994); Richard M. Tristano, *The Origins of the Restoration Movement* (1988); Henry E. Webb, *In Search of Christian Unity* (1990).

Mark S. Joy
Jamestown College, North Dakota

Roman Catholics

The Roman Catholic Church has played an important role in the shaping of social and cultural life in the American Midwest since the eighteenth century, when Catholic faith and identity took firm root in the region. Nearly one in four midwesterners is Roman Catholic. Illinois and Wisconsin, each more than 30 percent Catholic, have the largest blocs. Minnesota, North Dakota, South Dakota, Michigan, Nebraska, and Ohio, where Catholics comprise between 20 and 25 percent of the populations, also have significant numbers. Smaller percentages, ranging from 13 to 18 percent, are found in Indiana, Kansas, Missouri, and Iowa.

Individual dioceses also vary in size. Chicago is the leading Catholic archdiocese in the region, with a Catholic population of more than two million, or over

41 percent of the total population of the two northeastern Illinois counties of Cook and Lake. In contrast, in the Ozarks of southwestern Missouri, the sixty thousand Catholics in the counties of the Diocese of Springfield/Cape Girardeau constitute just over five percent of the total population. Although urban workers make up a large number of the Catholic populace, the Catholic Church is also strong in heavily agricultural states, such as Nebraska, North Dakota, and South Dakota.

Roman Catholic religious beliefs, rituals, and language have provided a point of contact among heterogeneous groups. To a large extent, the Roman Catholic Church has been an essential player in encouraging community cohesion in a diverse region. More specifically, Catholicism's role in the shaping of the Midwest can be characterized in four ways: organizational, spatial, cultic, and communitarian.

From 1805 forward, the Midwest was continually divided and subdivided into new ecclesiastical jurisdictions. Often the first stage of independent diocesan existence was the creation of a vicariate apostolic—a kind of interim administrative unit presided over by a prelate called a vicar apostolic. This was the arrangement in Kansas, Nebraska, and the Dakotas. Sometimes the creation of dioceses predated statehood, such as the Diocese of Milwaukee. More commonly, however, when statehood was conferred, separate dioceses conforming to state and county boundaries (for the most part) were created.

In the second half of the nineteenth century, two events stimulated population growth and development. First, the advent of heavy industry transformed the cities, especially Chicago, Cleveland, Milwaukee, and Detroit. The huge demand for unskilled labor brought millions of European immigrants, many of whom were Catholic, to these cities. Second, the transcontinental railroad and the expansion of rail traffic transformed the Great Plains. Diocesan growth continued throughout the twentieth century, slowed by the Great Depression and World War II but picking up steam again after the war. Eventually, deindustrialization slowed and even halted the growth of new Catholic jurisdictions in the 1970s.

The Roman Catholic Church created its distinctive administrative machinery. Various offices managed the diverse affairs of the diocese: education, social welfare, and internal church affairs (the chancery). In the period since Vatican II (1962–1965), reorganizations of these bureaucracies addressed new needs: liturgical life, ethnic concerns, women's issues, and various outreach programs of the diocese, including counseling and immigrant relocation.

The establishment of a diocese gave a scope and a structure to church life. Diocesan administrators over-

St. Francis Xavier Catholic Church, c. 1900. Minnesota Historical Society, MHS Location no. E97.7r4, neg. no. 71553.

saw the establishment and management of parishes, schools, and other church-sponsored agencies. Bishop Edward Dominic Fenwick, a Dominican priest and the first bishop of Cincinnati, was a strong leader who pressed hard for church expansion. German-speaking Catholics turned to the archbishops of Milwaukee, John Martin Henni, Michael Heiss, Frederick X. Katzer, and Sebastian G. Messmer, for guidance. Those who favored a more accomodationist approach to American life and culture looked to St. Paul archbishop John Ireland. More rugged pioneer bishops included another German speaker, Martin Marty, who headed the Vicariate of the Dakotas until it was broken into separate dioceses.

The rank of cardinal, an official elector of the pope and a signal honor to a Roman Catholic bishop and his diocesan city, was not conferred on a midwestern prelate until Archbishop George William Mundelein of Chicago received a scarlet hat in 1925. Other midwestern prelates soon became members of the College of Cardinals, including all of Mundelein's successors in Chicago (Samuel Stritch, Albert Meyer, John P. Cody, Joseph Bernardin, and Francis George). Bishops in Detroit Edward Mooney, John Dearden, Edmund Szoka, and Adam Maida received the honor. St. Louis has had three cardinals, John Glennon, Joseph Ritter, and John Carberry.

Midwestern bishops occasionally formed a phalanx for their particular issues at the meetings of the National Catholic Welfare Conference (NCWC), the chief lobbying arm of the American bishops in Wash-

ington, D.C. During the 1930s, Archbishops Samuel Stritch of Milwaukee, Edward Mooney of Detroit, and John T. McNicholas of Cincinnati formed a close working relationship with the NCWC, emphasizing concerns such as economic justice, labor unions, foreign policy, and the care of immigrants as part of their agenda for the larger American church. Midwestern Catholic bishops continued to weigh in on pressing social issues. Joseph Cardinal Bernardin of Chicago took a major role in crafting the response of the American Catholic hierarchy to the military buildup of Ronald Reagan's presidential administration. The same administration's economic policies came under scrutiny when Milwaukee archbishop Rembert G. Weakland chaired the writing and public discussion of "Economic Justice for All," a pastoral letter critical of the neoconservative emphasis on laissez-faire economics.

Although all denominations constructed churches and other institutions, the Roman Catholic Church was by far the most ambitious builder in the region. These structures generally provided space for worship, educational needs, social welfare, or residences for professional church workers, including convents, religious houses, and monasteries. Cathedrals, the largest and most prominent of church buildings, were always located in the heart of cities.

Catholic cathedrals vary in size and elegance depending on the locale and the availability of resources at the time of their construction. Cincinnati's St. Peter in Chains Cathedral was first built in the 1840s and later enlarged. St. John the Evangelist Cathedral in Milwaukee was begun in 1848 and completed in 1852. When Archbishop John Ireland sought to erect his massive Cathedral of St. Paul in St. Paul, he received huge infusions of cash from railroad mogul and personal friend James J. Hill. The massive Cathedral of St. Louis, with a Byzantine interior and Romanesque exterior, was built in 1907 to replace the old French church along the river. Large cathedral buildings were a point of pride for smaller dioceses as well. In 1916 Bishop Thomas O'Gorman of Sioux Falls, South Dakota, erected the lavish St. Joseph Cathedral on a hill overlooking the city.

Many Catholic churches favored the neo-Gothic style, with its soaring spires and arched interiors, or the Romanesque style, with its huge bell towers and magnificent tympanum. Many churches began as small, wood-framed buildings and then "graduated" to more permanent and elaborate structures. German-speaking Catholics often moved quickly to build permanent brick buildings, which were elaborately decorated, and create large space for choirs, pipe organs, and even orchestras. Stained-glass windows, many of them created by European studios, were imported to add elegance. Many churches contained marble floors, walls, and altars.

Convents and monasteries shared an increasing tendency toward the elaborate as their membership grew in size and complexity. Benedictine monasteries in St. Meinrad, Indiana, and Conception Abbey in Missouri replicated the techniques of monastic building found in Europe. In the 1960s, however, a starkly modernist design by architect Marcel Breuer was employed at St. John's Abbey in Collegeville and established a new pattern for monastic structures. The convents of the major teaching sisterhoods shared the same history. The Dominican Sisters of Sinsinawa constructed an elaborate new motherhouse in 1964 on the crest of a magnificent hill overlooking the Illinois-Wisconsin boundary.

Training facilities for men studying for the priesthood are a feature of the Catholic built environment. St. Francis Seminary, erected in 1856 on the shore of Lake Michigan, is the oldest seminary building still in use in the Midwest. In 1917 Archbishop Mundelein completed Quigley Preparatory Seminary on Rush Street in Chicago. After World War I he spent millions erecting St. Mary of the Lake Seminary in rural Area, Illinois, in Lake County. Area gratefully renamed itself Mundelein in the prelate's honor, and on thousands of rural acres a minicity of colonial Georgian buildings arose, dominated by a New England–style meetinghouse chapel. Mundelein built his own personal residence on the property, a virtual replica of George Washington's Mount Vernon. St. Louis

erected Kenrick Seminary during the Glennon years, and Polish seminarians were sent to Saints Cyril and Methodius Seminary in Orchard Lake, Michigan. German-speaking candidates for the priesthood were welcomed at the Pontifical College of the Josephinum in Columbus, Ohio.

After the liturgical reforms of Vatican II, Catholic architecture in the Midwest changed to adapt to evolving liturgical needs. New church designs abandoned the traditional cruciform church style for a more semicircular format that brought worshippers nearer to the altar for closer participation in the Mass and sacraments. Striking new designs created baptismal pools, modernistic bell towers, geodesic domes, and church interiors devoid of traditional statuary and with special chapels where the reserved Sacrament was not readily visible in the church. Cathedrals in contemporary styles include the Cathedral of the Risen Christ (1967) in Lincoln, Nebraska and the Cathedral of Our Lady of Guadalupe (2001) in Dodge City, Kansas.

Catholic rituals mark sacred time and space. On Ash Wednesday, the opening of Lent, Chicagoans wait in long lines at the downtown church of St. Peter's in the Loop to receive the blessed ashes on their foreheads. In rural Catholic villages like St. Nazianz, Wisconsin, and in monasteries the popular Corpus Christi processions take place several weeks after Easter. Christmas and Easter have rituals refracted through the ethnicity of the celebrants. Polish Catholics in Detroit, Milwaukee, and Chicago share a Christmas wafer called "oplatki" and construct tombs for the body of the crucified Christ on Good Friday. Latino Catholics transform city spaces in their popular celebrations of Our Lady of Guadalupe in December and public processions on Palm Sunday and during Holy Week.

One of the most famous outpourings of popular devotion in the Midwest occurred in June 1926 when George Cardinal Mundelein hosted an international Eucharistic Congress in Chicago. Prelates and laity from all over the world converged on the Windy City. Huge public demonstrations were held in Soldier Field, including a dramatic candlelit rally held in the presence of the papal legate, Archbishop Giovanni Bonzano. The climax of the weeklong celebration was an elaborate outdoor procession held on the grounds of the archdiocesan seminary.

Other devotional practices found their midwestern expressions. The practice of honoring the Virgin Mary took a myriad of forms. One of the most interesting shrines is the Grotto of the Redemption, a series of nine elaborate shrines built by the single-minded labor of Father Paul Dobberstein, a priest in West Bend, Iowa. Dobberstein promised the Virgin Mary that he would build a shrine to her honor if she helped him recover from a bout of pneumonia. Healed from his malady, Dobberstein began building his shrine in 1912 by collecting rocks from all over the country, along with bits of tile and glass. He continued until, literally, the day of his death in 1954.

Other midwestern locations contain covelike devotional sites, including Dickeyville, Wisconsin, and the campus of the University of Notre Dame. Marian shrines exist in Illinois—Belleville's Our Lady of the Snows and Marytown in Libertyville. The Chicago-based Order of the Servants of Mary promoted the highly popular Novena to the Sorrowful Mother out of their cavernous Basilica of Our Lady of Sorrows on Jackson Boulevard in Chicago. Thousands of devotees crammed the services held frequently during the darkest years of the Great Depression and World War II.

Devotions to other saints were also a part of the fabric of religious life. Devotion to St. Anne, the mother of the Virgin Mary, was very popular in Detroit, where a church named in her honor became a regional shrine in 1910. Healings associated with saint's relics took place at the Detroit shrine and also at a shrine to Mary north of Milwaukee called Holy Hill. One of the most notable midwestern healers was the saintly Detroit Capuchin Father Solanus Casey. From his post at St. Bonaventure Monastery, Casey ministered to thousands of beleaguered Detroit Catholics.

Historically, the Catholic church in the Midwest began its mission reaching out in an undifferentiated way to people of all groups. As the numbers of migrants to the river ports and early industrial centers of the region grew, ethnic differentiation occurred. German-speaking Catholics, from a variety of areas in Europe, began to clamor for their own churches and schools. In the 1830s local Catholics formed Holy Trinity Church in the Over the Rhine area of Cincinnati. In Milwaukee in 1846, St. Mary's Church for Germans, destined to become one of the centers of German life in America, was founded by the women's St. Anne's Society. In older areas like St. Louis; Vincennes, Indiana; and Dubuque, Iowa, French-speaking Catholics made their presence felt through separate church membership.

The church/school tandem, always urged by Rome and by bishops and then ordered as normative in 1884 at the Third Plenary Council of Baltimore, had a dynamic impact on the presence of the Catholic church in the Midwest. The staffing of these schools was almost exclusively the province of teaching orders of sisters, brothers, and priests. Important Midwest-based teaching orders include the School Sisters of Notre Dame, the Sinsinawa Dominicans, the Sisters of St. Joseph of Carondelet, the Society of Jesus, the Fathers and Brothers of the Holy Cross, and the Brothers of Christian Schools.

Midwestern parishes created bonds of community in large and often bewildering cities. Likewise, churches also provided a cement for cities and rural communities. Historian Kathleen Neils Conzen, regarding the heavily German and rural Stearns County in Minnesota, speaks of "the trinity of farm, family, and church . . ." and of communities of "strongly religious culture, in which life was ordered by the rituals, the teaching and community leadership, and the social activities fostered by the church, and in which parishes could proudly count the role of the religious vocations they had provided."

Catholic communitarian identity shifted as ethnicity waned following World War I and federal immigration restriction in the early 1920s. Parish organizations for youth and adults had been strong for many years, but new translocal umbrella organizations took root that forged an even greater sense of Catholic identity. Among them was the Holy Name Society, an association of Catholic professional men that formed in virtually every midwestern diocese. Councils of Catholic Women also began to form in most dioceses during the Progressive era and increased during the 1920s and 1930s. Both groups sponsored study clubs and speaker's bureaus staffed by the growing cadre of Catholic professionals.

Sports leagues were intensely popular among Catholic youth. One of the most popular organizations that developed in the 1920s and 1930s was the Catholic Youth Organization organized by the charismatic Bishop Bernard J. Sheil, auxiliary of Chicago. Sheil's emphasis on athletic competition and his sponsorship of boxing matches, day camps, and other events provided an enormous boost to Chicago's efforts to deal with its youth. Sheil's formula was widely emulated.

Social issues found a host of eloquent Catholic clerics and laypeople who were willing to press causes. One of the most famous was Monsignor John A. Ryan, a priest of the Archdiocese of St. Paul, who was for many years the leading Catholic social theorist and thinker. Although he spent his professional career in Washington, D.C., at the Catholic University of America, Ryan's midwestern roots were revealed in his deep appreciation of the Populists of Minnesota, such as Ignatius Donnelly. One of Ryan's successors at the National Catholic Welfare Conference was another midwesterner, Monsignor George Gilmary Higgins of Chicago, who was active in labor affairs and workers' rights almost up to his death in May 2002. Monsignor (later Bishop) Francis Haas of Milwaukee won a sterling reputation as a labor mediator in Wisconsin and as an adviser to President Franklin Delano Roosevelt in the 1930s. Perhaps the most famous public voice of Catholic social teaching was the "Radio Priest" Charles E. Coughlin, who broadcast a popular radio show from his Shrine of the Little Flower in Royal Oak, Michigan.

Midwestern Catholic leadership was felt in the reform of the Catholic liturgy. Three Midwest-based priests, Benedictine father Virgil Michel, Jesuit Gerard Ellard, and St. Louis convent chaplain Martin Hellreigel, met at the Benedictine monastery of St. John in Collegeville, Minnesota, and spearheaded a major program of reform calling for a rejuvenation of earlier Catholic liturgical practices linked to a renewed Catholic concern for social justice. Chicago became an important center of liturgical reform, especially under the leadership of Monsignor Reynold Hillenbrand, rector of St. Mary of the Lake Seminary in Mundelein. At the same time he urged liturgical reform, Hillenbrand ran labor schools and did street preaching in Oklahoma. Out of these stirrings came larger groups with a midwestern flair: The Chicago Catholic Interstudent Action organization brought together an alliance of teenagers to discuss the liturgy and social action, and the Christian Family Movement, directed by a Chicago couple, Patrick and Patty Crowley, found fertile soil in the Midwest with its emphasis on family life and social action.

Catholic communitarianism was part of the Civil Rights movement in the decades after World War II. As African Americans began to arrive in sizable numbers to take industrial jobs in midwestern cities, Catholic reaction was mixed. In some cities, on the one hand, aided by black Catholic leaders such as Daniel Rudd, Lincoln Valle, and others, strong efforts were made to convert African Americans to Catholicism by the use of separate churches, catechetical programs, social services, and Catholic schools. The conversion strategy was deployed in large cities like Chicago and Milwaukee where parishes and schools exclusively for African Americans were established. St. Monica Parish on Chicago's increasingly African American South Side was turned over to the missionary Divine Word Fathers, who ran a popular school and parish for black Catholics. The same community established the only seminary for African American men, at Bay St. Louis, Missouri. Other religious orders such as the Capuchins devoted themselves to working with black Catholics. In Milwaukee, St. Benedict the Moor Mission was created in 1908 by laypersons Lincoln and Julia Valle in the city's small black district. Eventually the mission was taken over by the Capuchins. They expanded the modest building and created a highly successful boarding school that attracted black youth from all over the nation.

On the other hand, the growth of black populations precipitated tensions in fluid urban neighborhoods. African Americans' desire for new homes in white areas brought about an angry response from white Catholics who also objected to black requests for admission into white parishes and schools. Catholics were often in the forefront of people resisting any efforts at integration, sometimes violently, as in the case of Cicero, Illinois, and Chicago's segregated Visitation Parish. In Milwaukee, racial integration of the city's old German Catholic bastions took place with comparatively little opposition; however, blacks never ventured south into the Brew City's heavily Polish areas.

Midwestern Catholic leaders were at the forefront of the efforts of racial justice. Clerics such as Chicago priests Daniel Cantwell and Anthony Vader and James Groppi of Milwaukee were well known for their work in the African American community. Religious orders such as the Sinsinawa Dominicans took in African American postulants. Black priests such as Herman Porter, a Sacred Heart father; Rollins Lambert and Kenneth Briggs of Chicago; and Joseph Perry and Marvin Knighton of Milwaukee joined the ranks of the priesthood. African American clergy served as bishops of midwestern dioceses: Moses Anderson and Joseph Perry as auxiliaries of Detroit and Chicago, and Wilton Gregory first as an auxiliary and then as the first African American to head a diocese in the Midwest when he was appointed to Belleville, Illinois, in 1993.

Catholicism in the Midwest continues to find itself in the midst of changing demographic patterns. The tremendous growth of the Hispanic, mostly Mexican, population has brought a new dimension to midwestern Catholic identity. Swelling Hispanic communities have taken over many parishes once dominated by Polish, German, Italian, and other European Catholics. Asian Catholics are also carving a niche for themselves with the emergence of churches for Vietnamese, Koreans, Hmong, and others.

In many urban communities, however, the once highly visible church is contracting. Chicago, Detroit, Milwaukee, St. Louis, and Cleveland have all undertaken highly controversial parish closures and downsizing as church memberships can no longer sustain the financial and personnel demands of the community. The closure of urban schools and churches has been complemented with expansion and construction in suburbs and exurbs. Traditional Catholic commitment to urban centers has been maintained, sometimes by creatively appealing to new urban denizens (regentrification). Some church properties have sold portions of unused church buildings for condominiums and recreation centers. In Davenport, Iowa, a former Carmelite convent is now a luxury hotel. In Chicago, a former Catholic grade and high school are now swanky condominiums. As the population shifts to the Sunbelt and the West, Catholicism in the Midwest has lost some of its clout. In the 1990s Los Angeles surpassed Chicago as the single largest archdiocese in the United States.

Sources and Further Reading: Patrick Henry Ahern, *Catholic Heritage in Minnesota, North Dakota, South Dakota* (1964); Steven M. Avella, *In the Richness of the Earth* (2002); Steven M. Avella, *This Confident Church* (1992); Kathleen Neils Conzen, *Foundation of a Rural German-Catholic Culture: Farm and Family in St. Martin, Minn., 1857–1915* (1977); William L. Crozier, *Gathering a People* (1989); William Barnaby Faherty, SJ, *Dream by the River* (1997); Mary Kevin Gallagher, ed., *Seed Harvest* (1987); Michael J. Hynes, *History of the Diocese of Cleveland* (1953); Edward Kantowicz, *Corporation Sole* (1983); Terrence G. Kardong, OSB, *Beyond Red River* (1988); Sister M. Aquinata Martin, *The Catholic Church on the Nebraska Frontier* (1937); John McGreevy, *Parish Boundaries* (1996); Sister Mary Carol Schroeder, *The Catholic Church in the Diocese of Vincennes* (1946); Ellen Skerrett, *Chicago's Neighborhoods and the Eclipse of Sacred Space,* (1994); Ellen Skerrett, *The Irish Parish in Chicago* (1981); Leslie Tentler, *Seasons of Grace* (1990); Mary Lethert Wingerd, *Claiming the City* (2001).

Steven M. Avella
Marquette University, Wisconsin

Seventh-Day Adventists

Seventh-Day Adventists are a Protestant denomination whose organization and early growth took place in the Midwest. The name highlights two distinctive beliefs: expectation of a literal, premillennial second coming ("advent") of Christ, and observance of the Sabbath on the seventh day of the week (Saturday). Adventists are evangelical in holding that eternal life cannot be merited but is received only as a free gift through faith in Christ. They rest from ordinary work on the Sabbath as an outward expression of the believer's inward spiritual rest in Christ's gift of salvation (Heb. 4:1–3, 9–10) and in obedience to the Ten Commandments (Exod. 20:8–11).

Adventist origins go back to the Millerite movement that climaxed in the Northeast in 1844. In the 1850s many Adventists migrated to Michigan, Illinois, Iowa, and Minnesota. Adventist cofounders Joseph Bates, James White, and Ellen G. White and others crisscrossed the region by rail and on foot, winning adherents throughout the Midwest.

When four businessmen in Battle Creek, Michigan, offered to erect a publishing house, the fledgling denomination located its headquarters there in 1855. For almost a half century, Battle Creek remained the institutional center of Seventh-Day Adventists. The SDA Publishing Association, chartered in 1861, and the General Conference, organized in 1863, moved to Washington, D.C., in 1903.

A third Adventist institution in Battle Creek, the Health Reform Institute, opened in 1866 and was renamed Battle Creek Sanitarium in 1876. The term *sanitarium* connoted an institution that used surgery and physical, diet, and exercise therapies but eschewed the use of drugs. From the 1890s to the onset of the Depression in 1929, the sprawling medical complex directed by J. H. Kellogg, M.D., was perhaps the most famous American health resort.

The success of Battle Creek Sanitarium led to the establishment of other health care institutions. Notable in the Midwest are Hinsdale Medical Center in suburban Chicago; Charles F. Kettering Memorial Hospital and Medical Center near Dayton, Ohio; and Shawnee Mission Medical Center near Kansas City, Kansas. In 1895, the sanitarium launched a school of medicine, the American Medical Missionary College (AMMC) in Chicago. Fifteen years and 194 graduates later, Adventists started another college of medicine (now Loma Linda University) in southern California and the AMMC merged with the medical school of the University of Illinois.

The efforts of the Battle Creek Sanitarium to develop practical applications of the nutritional philosophy of cofounder Ellen G. White had a major impact on the midwestern food industry. J. H. Kellogg's promotion of flaked cereals in place of bacon and eggs for breakfast led to the founding of the Toasted Corn Flake Company (now the Kellogg Company) by his brother, W. K. Kellogg. The exploding popularity of flaked cereals profoundly changed Americans' breakfast habits, spawned a new industry, and gave grain growers an expanding market for their corn, wheat, and oats. Other midwestern food companies that trace their conceptual impulse to the Adventist nutritional philosophy include International Nutrition Labs of Mt. Vernon, Ohio, which pioneered the manufacture of soy-based milk substitutes, and Worthington Foods of suburban Columbus, Ohio, which developed technology for making meat substitutes from vegetable protein sources.

A fourth Adventist institution, Battle Creek College (founded in 1874), became the forerunner of a worldwide educational system of more than 6,000 schools serving more than one million students, represented in the Midwest by three tertiary schools (Union College in Lincoln, Nebraska; Andrews University in Berrien Springs, Michigan; and Kettering College of Medical Arts in Kettering, Ohio); 18 secondary schools ("academies"); and some 180 elementary schools.

When Adventists entered the Midwest in the mid-nineteenth century, they worked in the cities but made a greater impact on the people in rural areas and small towns. In the twentieth century, youth from these rural churches attended Adventist colleges and helped spread the Adventist movement all over the world, but most did not return to their rural origins. The result was the aging, shrinking, and even disbanding of many rural congregations. As the twenty-first century began, Adventism was still strong in the Midwest, but the region was no longer the numerical center of gravity for the now global denomination. Adventists in 2002 constituted about 942 congregations with 124,000 members in the Midwest, as compared with 900,000 members in North America and 12 million in the world.

Two area headquarters offices are located in the Midwest: Mid-America Union Conference in Lincoln, Nebraska, and Lake Union Conference in Berrien Springs, Michigan. Ohio is part of the Columbia Union Conference with headquarters in Columbia, Maryland.

Sources and Further Reading: George R. Knight, *A Brief History of Seventh-day Adventists* (1999); Gary Land, ed., *Adventism in America*, rev. ed. (1998); Richard Schwarz and Floyd Greenleaf, *Light Bearers: A History of the Seventh-day Adventist Church* (2000); *Seventh-day Adventist Encyclopedia*, 2nd rev. ed., 2 vols. (1996).

Jerry Moon
Andrews University, Michigan

Shakers and Other Communitarian Groups

Charles H. Lippy defines communitarianism as the "conviction that the shared life offers opportunities not only for attaining personal spiritual purity but also for promoting social change." For two centuries a variety of groups—from religious, philosophical, or practical motives—have pursued a communitarian ideal in the Midwest. The first to do so were the Shakers.

Between 1805 and 1824 the Shakers founded four communities in Ohio and Indiana (and two in Kentucky). Apart from short-lived West Union, Indiana, plagued by endemic disease, the communities were a success for much of the century. The believers sought lives of celibate perfection and unity in gender-separated communal dwellings and workshops. They farmed thousands of acres of land, introduced some of the earliest purebred livestock in the Midwest, and sold a variety of goods to the outside world. The first books the Shakers published on their history and theology came from the Midwest. Aggressive proselytizing brought controversy, but at its height Union Village, Ohio, claimed about six hundred members. By the time of the Civil War, however, male membership had begun to decline, and the Industrial Revolution

had weakened the communities' economic base. Beginning in 1889, the three Ohio settlements were sold. North Union was subsumed into the Cleveland suburb of Shaker Heights, and in 1912 Union Village became a retirement home.

Four of the other numerically significant communitarian groups to settle in the Midwest in the nineteenth century were immigrant German pietists seeking greater freedom. In 1805 George Rapp and his followers, the Harmonists, settled in Pennsylvania. Needing more land and better access to markets, the group bought land in southern Indiana and moved in 1815. Harmonie, Indiana, became a prosperous town of small manufacturing enterprises, surrounded by large-scale communal farming. The Harmonists held all property in common. They lived in small "families" and held celibacy as an ideal (not always met, as married couples were not separated). Following their leader's dictates, the Harmonists sold their land and buildings and returned to Pennsylvania in 1825.

The Harmonists' town was taken over by secular utopian Robert Owen. After attempting to implement his vision of the ideal socialist working community at his textile mill in New Lanark, Scotland, Owen took his dream to America, where he founded New Harmony, Indiana. Never an economic success, the settlement gained fame for the people it attracted. Social reformers such as Frances Wright were joined by scientists, among them William Maclure and Thomas Say, and a mixed group of idealists and opportunists. New Harmony became known for its innovations in childhood education and for the Workingman's Institute and Library, a model for adult education.

In 1817 another pietistic group, three hundred in number and led by Joseph Bimeler, founded Zoar, Ohio. They practiced community of resources, not from ideals but from economic necessity. They lived in single-family homes and abandoned celibacy after attempting it for a brief period. Communal farming and production continued until 1898, when property was divided.

Yet another group of pietistic immigrants came from Germany in 1842, settling first in New York. From 1855 through the early 1860s, the Inspirationists moved to Iowa and founded the seven towns of the Amana Colony. Families lived in houses owned by the community. They farmed, cooked, and ate in common and operated a variety of community industries. In 1932 the colony was reconstituted as a joint stock corporation. Many modern descendants still practice their religion without its communal forms, and the towns are best known as a tourist attraction (a trait shared by several other reconstructed communitarian settlements).

Another non-German pietist community, begun in

1846 and lasting until 1861, was Bishop Hill, Illinois, built by followers of Swedish charismatic Eric Janson.

The fourth and last communitarian pietists to immigrate to the Midwest were the Hutterites, who settled in North and South Dakota and Canada beginning in the 1870s. Today thirty-six thousand members inhabit more than four hundred small communities and live much as their ancestors did. They hold land and possessions in common, work and eat together, but live in nuclear family units.

The next surge of communitarianism in the Midwest began in the counterculture of the 1960s and the 1970s. Some groups, such as the Jesus People of Chicago, were religiously based. Many others based communities on secular principles of equality, commonality of goods, and concern for a "natural" lifestyle. One recent offshoot of the communitarian impulse is the 1990s cohousing movement, which encompasses a spectrum of groups with ecological, spiritual, or pragmatic goals and which has spread into many midwestern states.

Sources and Further Reading: Karl J.R. Arndt, *George Rapp's Harmony Society, 1785–1847* (1965); Arthur Bestor, *Backwoods Utopias*, 2nd ed. (1970); Rosabeth Moss Kanter, *Commitment and Community* (1972); Charles H. Lippy, "Communitarianism," in Charles H. Lippy and Peter W. Williams, eds., *Encyclopedia of the American Religious Experience*, vol. 2 (1988); Bertha H.M. Shambaugh, *Amana, the Community of True Inspiration* (1908; reprint, 1988); Stephen J. Stein, *The Shaker Experience in America* (1992).

Dawn E. Bakken
Indiana University–Bloomington

Spiritualism

Spiritualism was an interdenominational religious movement begun in 1848 that flourished until roughly World War I. Spiritualists posited that the living could remain in contact with the dead via mediums, most often women, who served as conduits between this world and the next.

With the telegraph, the telephone, and photography, communication cut across both time and space, and Spiritualism was for many the epitome of technological innovation of the age. The Midwest embraced Spiritualism in both the domestic seance and the trance lecture, where itinerant mediums would deliver spirit-inspired lectures to large audiences. Uprooted from more traditional forms of religious expression, midwesterners were willing to give consideration to experimental movements such as Spiritualism.

In 1858 Chicago hosted Emma Hardinge (later Britten), one of the most influential mediums of the century. In 1860 the transcription of her lecture series was published as *Six Lectures on Theology and Nature*. This work contains many of the theological elements that made Spiritualism a distinctive and radical movement in its day, including the denial that hell existed. Chicago was an active center for Spiritualist lectures, with a local lawyer, Russell Green, organizing weekly meetings at Kingsbury Hall. The William T. Stead Memorial Center had a seance room, where at the end of the century the prolific medium Mrs. Cecil M. Cook would conduct much of her work.

Spiritualist books were published in Chicago and Cincinnati. Ohio boasted three Spiritualist weekly newspapers, Indiana at least two, and Illinois another one before the Civil War. Subscriptions to the Boston weekly *The Banner of Light* were abundant in Ohio and Illinois. The Mississippi Valley Spiritualists Association was very active in Clinton, Iowa, holding annual camp meetings and publishing its program in a journal. Registries of Spiritualists in the middle of the nineteenth century put the total number of believers in the Midwest at 586,000.

Wisconsin was a hotbed of Spiritualist activity, with Governor and former U.S. senator Nathaniel P. Tallmadge at the helm of the movement. Tallmadge was responsible for Abraham Lincoln's introduction to Spiritualism, although Lincoln was never convinced of the phenomenon. The politically progressive movement that consulted history's great minds for advice and deceased kin for solace caught the imagination of midwesterners from all ranks of society.

Sources and Further Reading: John W. Edmonds and George T. Dexter, *Spiritualism* (1853); Emma Hardinge, *Six Lectures on Theology and Nature* (1860).

Cathy Gutierrez
Sweet Briar College, Virginia

Unitarians and Universalists

The Unitarian Universalist Association (UUA) celebrated its fortieth anniversary in 2000. Before 1960 Unitarians and Universalists belonged to separate traditions. Both developed out of New England Protestantism and were counted "liberal," but they differed in focus.

Unitarianism developed among educated, urban Congregational communities and took its early shape under the leadership of William Ellery Channing of Boston in the first quarter of the nineteenth century. It focused on rational beliefs about God, rejecting the divinity of Jesus, and a positive view of human nature. William Greenleaf Eliot began missionary work in St.

Louis in 1852. He created the Western Unitarian Conference to provide support for new churches and to serve as a channel for greatly needed funds from eastern Unitarians.

In the mid-1860s Unitarians went through a denominational crisis over whether member churches should declare a theistic (basically Christian) belief system. The Christian side won and those with more radical views left to form other bodies. The Western Unitarian Conference maintained this focus until Jenkin Lloyd Jones became its secretary in 1875. His missionary efforts focused on ethical religion, not theology. His success roused opposition led by Jabez Sunderland of Michigan and Jasper Douthit of Illinois, who believed that ethics could not be considered religion without reference to and worship of God. Each side had its periodicals: *Unity*, published by Jones, and *The Unitarian*, published by Sunderland. This "Western Controversy" troubled eastern churches too until it was settled by small changes to the Constitution of the National Unitarian Conference in 1894.

Liberal shifts continued, however. A typical example is Kansas City, Missouri, where Leon Birkhead changed All Souls Unitarian Church into the Liberal Center in the 1920s. The rationalist focus of Unitarianism may have reached its peak with Unitarian participation in the Humanist Manifesto, published in 1933. Birkhead was one of the signers. Curtis Reese and John Dietrich, both midwestern Unitarians who converted from more conservative denominations, were leaders in the humanist movement.

Universalism had its origin even earlier than Unitarianism, in evangelical communities that objected to the Calvinist doctrine that only some people will be saved. Religious people who found this inconsistent with God's love formed communities in a number of localities and came together as an organization in 1793. The Winchester Profession, which declared the importance of the scriptures, the saving work of God, and the value of a holy life, was first accepted in 1803 and was reaffirmed throughout the nineteenth century.

Although Unitarians and Universalists produced many leaders of the women's rights movement, their record on ordaining women was spotty until the mid-twentieth century. Michigan-born Universalist Olympia Brown was one of the first women ordained in a regular denomination, in 1863. She served churches in Massachusetts, Connecticut, and Wisconsin. Caroline Bartlett, a Wisconsin native, served the Unitarian People's Church in Kalamazoo, Michigan, from 1889 to 1898 and made it famous for its outreach work.

In the early twentieth century the two traditions began moving closer together. Unitarian John Haynes Holmes and Universalist Clarence Skinner were col-

leagues in the development of greater social commitment on the part of liberal churches. Skinner's Declaration of Social Principles in 1917 marked a move in Universalist circles away from concern for universal salvation to the importance of improved social welfare for all. By the 1940s the limitations of small size and the strength of shared values encouraged lay members of the two traditions to form a fellowship movement, which led in 1953 to the Council of Liberal Churches. Sharing resources such as publications, the members moved to the formation of the Unitarian Universalist Association in 1961.

The Unitarian Universalist Association is a small denomination whose members are often found at the forefront of social justice issues. The UUA *Principles and Purposes*, first approved in the 1980s and revised in 1995, affirms the value of every person, the search for truth, and spiritual growth; the right of conscience; respect for the environment; and the importance of work for peace and justice. Of 218,404 members worldwide, 210,640 live in the United States; 42,438 of them are in the twelve midwestern states in 199 congregations, located primarily in urban and suburban communities. Members may be Christians or pagans, humanists or spiritual seekers, who find fellowship in like-minded small groups within the cherished diversity of the larger congregation.

Sources and Further Reading: Charles H. Lyttle, *Freedom Moves West* (1952); David Robinson, *The Unitarians and the Universalists* (1985); Warren R. Ross, "The Unitarian Universalist Association at 40," *UU World* (Sept./Oct. 2001); Cynthia Grant Tucker, *Prophetic Sisterhood* (1990).

Ellen Roberts Young
Las Cruces, New Mexico

Institutions

Hebrew Union College–Jewish Institute of Religion

Founded in 1875, Hebrew Union College (HUC) is the oldest Jewish theological seminary in the United States, training rabbis and scholars of Judaica. It has led the development of Reform Judaism as a liberal religious philosophy and as a movement. In 1972 HUC ordained the first American woman rabbi, Sally Jane Priesand.

HUC is one fruit of an Americanized Judaism that grew in the nineteenth-century Midwest. In 1873 a convention in Cincinnati, then the capital of Jewish America and known as "a sort of paradise for the Hebrews," created the Union of American Hebrew Congregations (UAHC; now the Union for Reform Judaism). The congregational union's principal project was to support a school to provide American-trained rabbis to meet the unique needs of American Jews. A gift of ten thousand dollars from Henry Adler, a layman in Lawrenceburg, Indiana, made the project a reality.

The college was first located on West Sixth Street in downtown Cincinnati. In 1912 the campus moved to its present location on Clifton Avenue, near the University of Cincinnati, with which HUC has long cooperated academically.

As an institution, HUC has grown beyond its Ohio roots. In 1950 it merged with the Jewish Institute of Religion of New York (founded in 1922 by Rabbi Stephen S. Wise as a nondenominational liberal seminary), giving it a permanent New York City presence (and its hyphenated official name). A branch was established in Los Angeles in 1954 and in Jerusalem in 1963. All four campuses now ordain rabbis.

The Reform movement's schools for the cantorate, education, and Jewish communal service are at the three newer HUC campuses, which have gained parity in influence within the movement. Although other institutions of Reform Judaism are now headquartered in New York City, the Cincinnati campus continues to be an important center of scholarship. The American Jewish Archives and American Jewish Periodical Center make it a mecca for research on American Jews and Judaism.

Isaac Mayer Wise served as HUC's first president until his death in 1900. Successive presidents have been Moses Mielziner (interim, 1900–1903); Gotthard Deutsch (interim, 1903); Kaufmann Kohler (1903–1921); Julian Morgenstern (an Illinois native who was the college's first American-born president, 1921–1947); Nelson Glueck (a native Cincinnatian, 1947–1971); Alfred Gottschalk (1971–1996); Sheldon Zimmerman (1996–2000); and David Ellenson (since 2001).

Sources and Further Reading: Samuel E. Karff, ed., *Hebrew Union College–Jewish Institute of Religion at One Hundred Years* (1976); Michael A. Meyer, *Response to Modernity* (1995); Jonathan D. Sarna and Nancy H. Klein, *The Jews of Cincinnati* (1989).

Amy Hill Shevitz
California State University–Northridge

Lane Theological Seminary

In the late 1820s Ebenezer and William Lane, New Orleans merchants, contributed funds to found a Presbyterian seminary that would Christianize and civilize the West. On February 11, 1829, the Ohio General Assembly granted a charter to the Lane Theological Seminary. Elnathan Kemper, his father, and his brothers donated land for the site on Walnut Hills, just outside of Cincinnati.

In late 1832 Lyman Beecher, one of the most prominent ministers in America, accepted the presidency of Lane. Under President Beecher, Lane favored "new school" initiatives including revivalism; cooperation with other denominations; and the advocacy of social reform movements such as temperance, missions, and Sabbath reform.

In early 1834 the students decided, against the advice of Beecher, to debate whether slavery should be abolished immediately and whether the American Colonization Society should be supported. After eighteen nights of discussion, the majority decided in favor of immediatism and against colonization. Following the debates, the students began to work in schools in

Lane Theological Seminary, Cincinnati, Ohio. Cincinnati Museum Center—Cincinnati Historical Society Library.

the black sections of Cincinnati and advocate for anti-slavery. The trustees and faculty, concerned that these actions would harm the seminary, instituted regulations forbidding these activities and even the discussion of slavery. Seventy-five students, under the leadership of Theodore Dwight Weld, withdrew from the seminary and became known as the Lane Rebels.

Efforts by Beecher and others ensured Lane's continuation. Prominent alumni of Lane include Jonathan Blanchard, president of Knox College and Wheaton College; Josiah Strong, author of *Our Country* (1885); and John Gregg Fee, founding president of Berea College.

In the early 1930s declining enrollment and finances led to the merger of Lane with McCormick Theological Seminary in Chicago. The Lane Seminary Trustees maintain an office in Cincinnati.

Sources and Further Reading: Lawrence T. Lesick, "The Founding of the Lane Seminary," *Cincinnati Historical Society Bulletin* 37 (Winter 1979); Lawrence T. Lesick, *The Lane Rebels* (1980).

Lawrence T. Lesick
Wilmington College, Ohio

University of Chicago Divinity School

The Divinity School is fully integrated into the workings of the University of Chicago as one of its professional schools. Its polity is comparable to that of the schools of law and medicine in relation to the university. As a professional school it has contributed to what educators there traditionally have called "a learned ministry." For that reason, the school has provided relatively small but notable programs for preparing ministers.

Most of the energies of the Divinity School since the mid-twentieth century, however, have gone into programs more conducive to work in the humanities and social science divisions of the university. Particularly, this has meant a concentration in research in and training for what has come to be called religious studies.

The Divinity School was very much a product of midwestern outlooks and ambitions. The prestigious theological schools that dated back to colonial times, Harvard, Yale, Princeton, and others, were all on the East Coast. Clergy and especially theological scholars in the South and the developing Far West were trained in New England, New York, and New Jersey, and they often appeared to be importers of alien religious outlooks. The same was true in the Midwest, but by the end of the nineteenth century the region had the population, resources, needs, and ambition to train its own children—they were then almost all sons—and take

care of its own. In that setting some Baptists founded the Morgan Park Seminary of the Baptist Theological Union, which became the Divinity School of the University of Chicago in 1892. The founding president, William Rainey Harper, a Yale-trained Ohioan who taught Semitic languages, lured prime candidates in many disciplines and gave encouragement to the midwestern school. The university was host to schools of thought such as pragmatism and it pioneered in sociology. It was no surprise therefore that founding Divinity School professors stressed practical theology, embraced theological modernism, and focused on the social environment of people in biblical and early Christian eras.

The Divinity School has always had an international reach. In its early years it trained many missionary-scholars who taught overseas. It also attracted students and faculty from Europe and Asia. Typical of its pioneering efforts in these directions was the appointment of Joseph M. Kitagawa, a Japanese-born Anglican priest and world-renowned expert on Buddhism, as dean from 1970 to 1980.

It would be foolish to try to isolate distinctively midwestern elements in the theology and religious studies that issued from Chicago. Many of its scholars in recent decades, such as Paul Ricoeur, Mircea Eliade, and, briefly, Paul Tillich, were European imports, and there was nothing provincial about the scholars who came to Chicago from all over America. Also, through the years the Divinity School became notable for its devotion to process theology, history of religion, hermeneutical and phenomenological accents, and, consistently, historical research. None of these are conceptually region-specific.

Still, Chicago remains the only large private-university divinity school in the Midwest. It naturally has influence on academic, religious, and cultural affairs within a several-hundred-mile range of Chicago, influence that surpasses that of non-midwestern centers of religious inquiry.

Sources and Further Reading: Conrad Cherry, *Hurrying toward Zion* (1995); Bernard E. Meland, ed., *The Future of Empirical Theology* (1969); Richard J. Storr, *Harper's University: The Beginnings* (1966).

Martin E. Marty
University of Chicago, Illinois

University of Notre Dame

The University of Notre Dame, which dates its beginnings to the arrival in November 1842 of the French missionary priest Edward F. Sorin and a handful of religious brothers, was fortunate in the timing and loca-

Altar, Basilica of the Sacred Heart, University of Notre Dame. University of Notre Dame.

tion of its founding. The Indiana-Michigan border region stood on the threshold of rapid development, and the infant institution in Indiana four miles south of the state line grew along with the area, profiting especially from early rail connections with Chicago and its burgeoning Catholic population. Its history can be divided into three epochs of roughly a half century each.

Father Sorin dominated the first, serving as president of the college until 1865 and guiding his successors until his death in 1893. A man of expansive vision, he took advantage of its early presence in a developing area to make Notre Dame the base from which the priests, brothers, and sisters of his religious community, the Congregation of Holy Cross, extended their apostolic works throughout the country. The college, always the centerpiece of the project, gradually assumed greater independence and stature. Like all nineteenth-century Catholic colleges, it was a combined secondary-collegiate institution. College-level work improved in scope and quality after the Civil War, but Notre Dame was still bottom heavy with college preparatory students in 1900, when its overall enrollment of 700 made it one of the nation's largest Catholic colleges.

Between Father Sorin's death and World War II, Notre Dame moved decisively toward true university status. At the same time, its fame in football gave it unprecedented national visibility and nurtured a fanatical following among its real and "subway" alumni. Academically, prep-level students were eliminated, curricular offerings expanded, scholastic standards upgraded, organizational procedures modernized, and foundation support successfully pursued. Prospective faculty members among the Holy Cross community were sent off for doctoral training, and many lay faculty were hired, including an important sprinkling of European refugee professors. By 1940, enrollment had neared 3,300 and graduate work was well established at the master's level, along with a few solid doctoral programs in the natural sciences.

Thanks to these developments and to its experience in war-related research projects, Notre Dame was poised to participate fully in the post–World War II boom in higher education. Three Holy Cross priests provided able leadership. Systematic fund-raising and academic expansion began in the presidency of Father John J. Cavanaugh (1946–1952), but the real breakthrough came under Father Theodore M. Hesburgh, in whose thirty-five-year term (1952–1987) dozens of new buildings were erected, academic quality was improved, women were admitted to the formerly all-male institution, and juridical control was transferred from the Congregation of Holy Cross to an autonomous lay board of trustees. Under Father Edward A. Malloy (1987–2005), who aspired to make Notre Dame a leader among the nation's research universities, the annual operating budget exceeded six hundred million dollars; doctoral degrees were offered in twenty-three fields; and more than 11,000 undergraduate, graduate, and professional students populated the 1,250-acre campus.

Father Sorin might find the statistics overwhelming, but the reality accords with the vision he projected 160 years ago.

Sources and Further Reading: Robert E. Burns, *Being Catholic, Being American*, 2 vols. (1999–2000); Arthur J. Hope, *Notre Dame: One Hundred Years*, rev. ed. (1978); Marvin R. O'Connell, *Edward Sorin* (2001); Thomas J. Schlereth, *The*

University of Notre Dame: A Portrait of Its History and Campus (1976).

Philip Gleason
University of Notre Dame, Indiana

Wheaton College

Wheaton College is the most prominent liberal arts college of American Protestant evangelicalism. The Wesleyan Church founded Illinois Institute in 1852 in the town of Wheaton, thirty miles west of Chicago. After financial struggles, it was reestablished in 1860 as nondenominational Wheaton College by Congregationalist minister Jonathan Blanchard. Blanchard dedicated the school to radical reform causes, including temperance; equal rights for women; Sabbatarianism; and, especially, abolition and anti-Masonry.

During John Blanchard's son Charles's presidency, Wheaton became a charter member of the nation's first regional accrediting agency and the leading liberal arts college in the emerging fundamentalist movement. This new national constituency made Wheaton one of the nation's fastest-growing colleges in the 1930s, and the area around it one of the main centers of the movement.

Wheaton's best-known graduate, evangelist Billy Graham (class of 1943), caused great controversy in fundamentalism when he cooperated with nonfundamentalist Protestants in his urban revival crusades. This controversy helped to divide fundamentalism into a separatist wing that retained the name *fundamentalism* and a more inclusive wing that called its members "evangelicals." Wheaton followed Graham into the evangelical wing of the movement.

Wheaton's greatest strength has always been the high caliber of its students. Its graduates have for years gone on to earn doctoral degrees at rates comparable to the nation's most elite liberal arts colleges, and its alumni have become some of evangelicalism's most prominent theologians, writers, missionaries, and organization builders. In 2002, Wheaton enrolled 2,400 undergraduate and 450 graduate students from all fifty states and twenty-nine countries.

Sources and Further Reading: Paul M. Bechtel, *Wheaton College: A Heritage Remembered* (1984); Michael S. Hamilton, "The Fundamentalist Harvard: Wheaton College and the Continuing Vitality of American Evangelicalism, 1919–1965," Ph.D. diss., University of Notre Dame (1994); Richard T. Hughes and William B. Adrian, eds., *Models for Christian Higher Education* (1997).

Michael Hamilton
Seattle Pacific University, Washington

Major Figures

The Beecher Family

The Beecher family exemplifies the piety, industry, and activism of the New Englanders who flocked to the Midwest in the early decades of the nineteenth century. Lyman Beecher and several of his children made remarkable contributions to both religious and secular life in the United States.

A Connecticut native and Yale College graduate, Lyman Beecher (1775–1863) accepted the presidency of Cincinnati's Lane Theological Seminary after serving in pulpits in New York and New England. A leader in the wave of religious revivals that swept the nation between 1790 and 1840, Beecher was celebrated for his eloquence as a preacher and his success as an organizer of voluntary associations. Because of his positions on slavery and moral reform, Beecher stirred controversy wherever he went. Returning to the East in his old age, he died at the home of his son, the Reverend Henry Ward Beecher, in Brooklyn, New York, in 1863.

Beecher's son Edward (1803–1895) studied at Yale and at Andover Seminary, where he became a member of the "Yale Band," a group of Presbyterian missionaries determined to bring religion and higher education to the West. He was a founder of Illinois College, which he served as president for fourteen years. Organizer of the first antislavery society in the state, his *Narrative of the Riots at Alton* (1837), which described the brutal murder of abolitionist minister Elijah P. Lovejoy by an Illinois mob, became one of the key documents of the antislavery movement. Beecher resigned from Illinois College in 1844, and moved back to the East Coast to pastor Boston's Salem Street Church. He returned to Illinois in 1855, becoming pastor of the First Congregational Church in Galesburg. In 1871 he moved to Brooklyn, New York, and devoted the remainder of his life to writing on theological subjects.

Beecher's son Henry Ward (1813–1887) graduated from Amherst College in 1834 and entered Lane Theological Seminary. Like his father and brother, he combined evangelical preaching with social activism. Beecher's reputation as a preacher brought him nationwide fame. For a decade, he served congregations in Lawrenceburg and Indianapolis, Indiana. In 1847 he became pastor of Plymouth Congregational Church in Brooklyn, New York, one of the largest congregations in the United States, where he spent the rest of his career. Although his life was tinged with personal scandal, Beecher remained an extraordinarily influential spokesman on religious and political subjects. His brother Charles (1815–1900) served as pastor of the

Second Presbyterian Church in Fort Wayne, Indiana, and other churches in the Midwest.

Beecher's daughters Isabella (1822–1907) and Catharine (1800–1878) were as accomplished as their brothers. Isabella, who married John Hooker in 1841 and resided in Hartford, Connecticut, fought for property rights for married women as well as for female suffrage. An early advocate of women's education and a leading domestic reformer, Catharine through her writings helped to redefine the public and private roles of women. In 1837 she organized the Ladies Society for Promoting Education in the West, and she was a moving force in the founding of schools and colleges in Iowa, Illinois, Ohio, and Wisconsin.

Harriet Beecher Stowe (1811–1896) is the best-known child of this remarkable family. During the two decades she lived in Cincinnati, Harriet encountered firsthand the evils of slavery. Her best-selling novel *Uncle Tom's Cabin*, first published in 1851, was instrumental in moving Northerners to support abolition. In addition to bearing and raising seven children, Harriet was a prolific writer, inspired teacher, and ardent social activist. She returned to New England in 1855, where she continued her successful writing career.

Sources and Further Reading: Marie Caskey, *Chariot of Fire: Religion and the Beecher Family* (1978); Joan D. Hedrick, *Harriet Beecher Stowe: A Life* (1994); Milton A. Rughoff, *The Beechers: An American Family in the Nineteenth Century* (1981); Stephen H. Snyder, *Lyman Beecher and His Children* (1991).

Peter Dobkin Hall
Harvard University, Massachusetts

Joseph Bernardin (1928–1996)

Widely considered the most influential U.S. Roman Catholic official during the last quarter of the twentieth century, Joseph Cardinal Bernardin helped to steer the church through many public convulsions.

Joseph Bernardin was born in 1928 in Columbia, South Carolina, to Italian immigrants, and earned degrees from St. Mary's Seminary and Catholic University, after which he served as a priest in Charleston, South Carolina, and as Archbishop of Cincinnati from 1972 to 1982. Bernardin revealed an emerging social conscience when he coauthored a pastoral letter condemning the Vietnam War in 1966. He led the U.S. Conference of Catholic Bishops in producing the pastoral letter "The Challenge of Peace: God's Promise and Our Response" in 1983, which addressed the moral dimensions of nuclear war.

In 1982, Bernardin was appointed archbishop of Chicago, the largest U.S. Roman Catholic diocese at the time. Bernardin provided a model of how to offer constructive religious perspectives on pressing issues, such as AIDS (acquired immunodeficiency syndrome), public education, abortion, and capital punishment. In 1993, Bernardin received national attention when a former student accused him of sexual abuse. Following his accuser's retraction of the charges, Bernardin won acclaim for his forgiving spirit.

Near the end of his life, Bernardin waged a courageous battle against cancer, and his account of his struggle, *The Gift of Peace* (1997), taught parishioners how to overcome personal challenges with dignity. He died on November 14, 1996, at the age of sixty-eight.

Sources and Further Reading: Eugene Kennedy, *My Brother Joseph* (1997); Alphonse P. Spilly, ed., *Selected Works of Joseph Cardinal Bernardin* (2000); A. E. P. Wall, *The Spirit of Cardinal Bernardin* (1997).

Jeffrey B. Webb
Huntington College, Indiana

Peter Cartwright (1785–1872)

Peter Cartwright, a longtime Illinois Methodist preacher and presiding elder, is best known today for *The Autobiography of Peter Cartwright* (1856), in which he colorfully describes his life as a Methodist circuit rider.

The stern demeanor of the Methodist Episcopal minister Peter Cartwright, pictured here with his wife in the mid-1860s, captures the determination and commitment that made Cartwright the most famous itinerant preacher in the nineteenth-century Midwest. Library of Congress, Prints and Photographs Division, LC-USZ62-95736.

Cartwright was born in Virginia in 1785 and was converted at the famous Cane Ridge, Kentucky, revivals in 1801. He was a circuit rider in Kentucky and Indiana before finally moving to Illinois in 1824, where he served as a presiding elder until the Civil War. His autobiography recounts his efforts to establish Methodism in the Old Northwest. At every turn, he was opposed by preachers from competing denominations, infidels, and drunken rowdies intent on disrupting revival meetings. Cartwright was a lifetime opponent of slavery, although he was equally critical of abolitionists.

In his autobiography, he expressed a mixture of satisfaction and regret at the success of Methodism over the course of his lifetime. Cartwright felt that the church had strayed from its original simplicity and stress on preaching and conversions and had become too refined and sophisticated. In addition to his clerical career, he was a two-time Illinois Democratic state legislator and was defeated by Abraham Lincoln when he ran for the U.S. Congress in 1846. He died in 1872.

Source and Further Reading: Peter Cartwright, *The Autobiography of Peter Cartwright*, ed. William P. Strickland (1856).

Douglas Montagna
Grand Valley State University, Michigan

Episcopal leader Philander Chase. Library of Congress, Prints and Photographs Division, Daguerreotype Collection, LC-USZ62-109898.

Philander Chase (1775–1852)

When Philander Chase arrived in Ohio in 1817, the Episcopal Church had no plans to extend ministrations to the West. Chase raised his own financial support, created new congregations, and established diocesan structures. He became the first Episcopal bishop west of the Allegheny Mountains and was the founding president of the first midwestern Episcopal college.

Chase, who was born in New Hampshire in 1775, joined the Episcopal Church while he was a student at Dartmouth College. He became a priest in Albany in 1799 and served as a missionary and minister in New York, New Orleans, and Hartford before moving to Ohio. In 1818 Chase organized a diocesan convention, which adopted a constitution and elected him bishop. He was consecrated in Philadelphia in 1819.

There were no funds for a bishop's salary. An appeal to the Episcopal General Convention in 1820 brought only temporary relief. Chase supported himself by becoming the president of Cincinnati College from 1821 to 1823. His experience convinced him that Episcopalians needed their own institution. He raised money in England, including contributions from Lord Kenyon and Lord Gambier, and persuaded the diocesan convention to support the 1824 founding of Kenyon College, of which he became president.

In 1831 faculty members criticized Chase's leadership style. He resigned as president and bishop and moved his family to Michigan. He remained there until 1835, when Episcopalians in Illinois elected him bishop. Repeating his experience in Ohio, he raised funds for a new school, the ultimately unsuccessful Jubilee College. Chase served as presiding bishop at the General Conventions of 1847 and 1850. He died in 1852.

Sources and Further Reading: Diana Hochstedt Butler, *Standing against the Whirlwind* (1995); Philander Chase, *Bishop Chase's Reminiscences*, 2 vols. (1847); Robert W. Prichard, *A History of the Episcopal Church*, rev. ed. (1999).

Robert W. Prichard
Virginia Theological Seminary

Charles Edward Coughlin (1891–1979)

During his heyday in the 1930s, Father Charles Coughlin was perhaps the most famous and controversial ecclesiastical figure in the United States.

A native of Ontario, Canada, where he was born in 1891 and ordained in 1916, Coughlin moved to the United States in 1923, taking up duties as a parish priest in Detroit. In 1926 he was asked by Bishop Michael J. Gallagher to create a new parish in the suburb of Royal Oak. The parish was dedicated to St. Thérèse of Lisieux, "the Little Flower of Jesus." As part of fund-raising efforts, Coughlin began a series of radio broadcasts that fall. By 1930 his radio program, *The Golden Hour of the Little Flower*, had been picked up by the Columbia Broadcasting System (CBS) and was being heard by an estimated forty million listeners.

Audiences found Coughlin compelling because of his compassion for people suffering from the Depression and his articulate defense of workers' rights. Coughlin also was not afraid to promote specific reforms, championing a series of radical monetary policies including the abandonment of the gold standard. Coughlin initially supported Franklin Delano Roosevelt. His support unrequited, he turned against the president and his policies.

In 1934 the priest helped to found the populist National Union for Social Justice and began publication of a rabidly anti–New Deal weekly newspaper, *Social Justice*. Alarmed by his growing radicalism, Gallagher's successor, Archbishop Edward Mooney, silenced Coughlin for a time, although popular pressure brought him back to the airwaves in 1938. Coughlin's broadcasts became increasingly anti-Semitic, filled with theories of global Jewish conspiracies allying Bolsheviks with Jewish bankers. More than once, Coughlin's *Social Justice* featured Adolf Hitler on the cover and praised National Socialism.

With America's entry into World War II in 1941, Coughlin's support began to erode. The federal government, threatening sedition charges, pressured Mooney to silence Coughlin, which he finally managed to do later that year. Choosing obedience, Father Coughlin returned to life as an anonymous parish priest in Royal Oak. Nearly four decades later, in 1979, he died in obscurity.

Sources and Further Reading: Alan Brinkley, *Voices of Protest* (1982); Donald I. Warren, *Radio Priest* (1996).

Brian Wilson
Western Michigan University

W. D. Fard (1877?–?)

Details of the life of Wallace D. Fard (also known as Wallace Ford, Wallace Dodd Farrad, and Master W. Fard Muhammad) are notoriously difficult to ascertain. Although some records claim that Fard was born in Mecca, Saudi Arabia, in 1877, Federal Bureau of Investigation files state that his parents were Hawaiian, or British and Polynesian, and that he was born in either Portland, Oregon, or New Zealand in 1891. He lived in Los Angeles in the 1920s, owned a restaurant, and served time at San Quentin. He was best known as W. D. Fard.

Fard's public life began in 1930 in Detroit, Michigan. There he preached a unique form of American Islam influenced by many contemporary currents in African American religious thought, including Moorish Science, Ahmadiya Islam, and Garveyism. In Detroit, Fard presented himself as an Arab immigrant from Mecca and made his living as a peddler of "Oriental" goods to the African American public. Fard also preached his religious message, which soon made him a popular speaker. He met Elijah Poole around 1931, renaming Poole Elijah Muhammad and appointing him "supreme minister." After suffering baseless persecution by local police, Fard "disappeared" from Detroit in 1934. Nothing is known of his life after that.

Fard was the foundational source of the doctrines that Elijah Muhammad proposed after becoming the sole leader of the Nation of Islam (NOI). Muhammad continued to refer to Fard as "Allah in person," "the Mahdi," "our Lord and Savior," and "the Messiah" throughout his tenure as supreme minister of the NOI. In the 1990s, Muhammad's son and successor, Wallace Muhammad (also known as Warith Deen Muhammad), attempted to disavow Fard's mythic status, opining that Fard was probably an Ahmadiya Muslim.

Sources and Further Reading: Claude Andrew Clegg III, *An Original Man* (1997); Edward E. Curtis IV, *Islam in Black America* (2002); Elijah Muhammad, *The True History of Master Fard Muhammad* (1996).

Lisa J. M. Poirier
Miami University, Oxford, Ohio

Clarence LaVaughn Franklin (1915–1984)

Born in Sunflower, Mississippi, in 1915 and raised in neighboring Cleveland, Clarence LaVaughn Franklin experienced conversion and, at age sixteen, accepted a call to the ministry during a revival at his family's church, St. Peter's Rock Baptist. After a stint as a circuit rider, Franklin accepted a call in 1939 by the New Salem Baptist Church in Memphis, Tennessee. His dynamic preaching enlarged the congregation considerably, and he began a widely popular weekly radio broadcast that mixed sacred themes with social and political commentary. In 1944 the Friendship Baptist Church in Buffalo, New York, called him to the pulpit. He experienced a similar success as a preacher there and established the first black-run radio program in that city. In 1946 he moved to Detroit's New Bethel Baptist Church, where he remained until his death in 1984.

Franklin's Detroit career marked him as among the most important preachers of his generation in the Afro-Baptist tradition. A "whooper" who chanted major parts of the sermon, Franklin also preached a message that addressed with equal power matters of faith and political and social concerns. The appeal of his preaching increased the congregation to more than three thousand paid members; a local radio station broadcast his Sunday evening service live; and some seventy-four of those sermons were recorded and sold nationally. He was a major figure on the national gospel circuit. Politically active, Franklin urged his congregation to participate, and he led a major "March for Freedom" in Detroit in June 1963. An integrationist, Franklin also proudly proclaimed the uniqueness of African American cultural traditions. His daughter, Aretha Franklin, became one of the most popular and accomplished singers of her generation.

Sources and Further Reading: C. L. Franklin, *Give Me This Mountain*, Jeff Todd Titon, ed. (1989); Nick Salvatore, *Singing In A Strange Land: C. L. Franklin, the Black Church, and the Transformation of America* (2005).

Nick Salvatore
Cornell University, New York

Andrew M. Greeley (b. 1928)

Born to Grace and Andrew Greeley in Oak Park, Illinois, in 1928, Andrew M. Greeley knew early in his life that his vocation was the priesthood. After earning his licentiate of sacred theology degree from St. Mary of the Lake Seminary, he was ordained in May 1954 and entered into parish work with the Archdiocese of Chicago. Early in his career, Greeley worked on issues involving Catholic youth and families but increasingly turned to interpreting the impact of changing cultural mores on the church as an institution. Such interests led him to enter the University of Chicago in 1960, from which he earned both a master of arts and a doctorate in sociology.

As a sociologist, Greeley has been affiliated with the National Opinion Research Center and other prestigious bodies. In addition, he has published scholarly works such as *The Education of Catholic Americans* (with Peter H. Rossi, 1966); *The Catholic Priest in the U.S.: Sociological Investigations* (1972); *Catholic High Schools and Minority Students* (1982); *The Dilemma of American Immigration: Beyond the Golden Door* (with Pastora Cafferty, Barry Chiswick, and Teresa Sullivan, 1983); and *Catholic Schools in a Declining Church* (1972).

While earning a strong reputation as an intellectual, Greeley's artful prose won him additional plaudits and considerable notoriety. The priest served in editorial capacities with *Concilium* and other journals but also enjoyed success as a popular writer. After composing a novel and a book of poetry in the late 1970s, Greeley published *The Cardinal Sins* (1981), the first of many best-selling novels that also included *Virgin and Martyr* (1985) and *An Occasion of Sin* (1991), an adroit balance of sensationalism and critique of power in the modern American church. These and many of Greeley's novels cultivate themes of immigration and accommodation, ecclesiastical power and its abuse, tensions between faith and desire, and the intersection of powerful secular institutions and the Catholic Church.

Sources and Further Reading: Allienne R. Becker, *The Divine and Human Comedy of Andrew M. Greeley* (2000); Andrew M. Greeley, *Confessions of a Parish Priest* (1986).

Timothy Dean Draper
Waubonsee Community College, Illinois

John Ireland (1838–1918)

John Ireland, a native of County Kilkenny, Ireland, born in 1838, energetically promoted Americanism within the national Catholic community and built influential Catholic educational, social, and religious institutions in the Archdiocese of St. Paul, Minnesota.

Ireland immigrated with his family to the United States and eventually settled in St. Paul. Educated for the priesthood in France, he was ordained in 1861. During the Civil War, he volunteered as an army chaplain with the Fifth Minnesota Regiment. Ireland became coadjutor bishop of St. Paul in 1875 and in 1884, its bishop. In 1888 he became St. Paul's first archbishop, an appointment he held until his death in 1918.

An eloquent orator, Ireland called for the Americanization of immigrants, Catholic cooperation with public schools, and the establishment of a national Catholic University. Within his own diocese he built or helped build the College of St. Thomas (1885), St. Thomas Seminary (1894), St. Catherine's College (1905), the Cathedral of St. Paul (1915), and the Basilica of St. Mary (1915). These institutions symbolize his attempts to develop an educated Catholic elite whose presence in the halls of political and economic power would make a Catholic difference in American society. Ireland's participation in national attempts to Americanize the Catholic Church was cut short by

Pope Leo XIII's apostolic letter "Testem Benevolentiae" (January 1899), which condemned the so-called heresy of Americanism.

Sources and Further Reading: John Ireland, *The Church and Modern Society*, 2 vols. (1896–1904); Marvin R. O'Connell, *John Ireland and the American Catholic Church* (1988).

Patrick W. Carey
Marquette University, Wisconsin

Jesse Jackson (b. 1941)

Born in Greenville, South Carolina, to Helen Burns and Noah Robinson in 1941, Jesse L. Jackson was adopted by his stepfather, Charles Jackson, in 1957. Interested in playing football, Jackson attended the University of Illinois for a year, leaving when he realized that an African American had little chance of becoming a quarterback there. Jackson transferred to North Carolina Agricultural and Technical College (NCA&T) and graduated in 1964. While at NCA&T, he married Jacqueline Lavinia Brown and became involved in the Civil Rights movement. Jackson returned to Illinois in 1964 to attend Chicago Theological Seminary and was ordained a Baptist minister in 1968.

In Chicago Jackson worked for the Southern Christian Leadership Conference (SCLC), spearheading Operation Breadbasket from 1966 to 1971. In 1971 he left the SCLC and founded his own organization, People United to Save Humanity (PUSH; the full name was later changed to People United to Serve Humanity). Jackson continued his work in civil rights and politics, founding a sister organization to PUSH, the National Rainbow Coalition, in order to make reforms in the Democratic Party. He sought the Democratic presidential nomination in 1984 and 1988 and moved to Washington, D.C., in 1989.

Jesse Jackson continues to be active in the struggle for human rights domestically and worldwide. In the 1990s he assisted with democratic reforms in several countries, and achieved the release of U.S. soldiers held in the former Yugoslavia. In 2000 Jackson was awarded the Presidential Medal of Freedom. His son, Jesse L. Jackson, Jr., serves as a Democratic representative from the Second Congressional District of Illinois.

Sources and Further Reading: Marshall Frady, *Jesse: The Life and Pilgrimage of Jesse Jackson* (1996); Charles P. Henry, *Jesse Jackson: The Search for Common Ground* (1990); Karin L. Stanford, *Beyond the Boundaries* (1997).

Lisa J. M. Poirier
Miami University, Oxford, Ohio

Jenkin Lloyd Jones (1843–1918)

Born in Wales in 1843, Jenkin Lloyd Jones grew up on a farm in Wisconsin. He served in the Civil War and then attended Meadville Seminary in western Pennsylvania, graduating in 1870. He served churches in Illinois and Wisconsin and became secretary of the Western Unitarian Conference in 1875, for which he traveled extensively. In 1882 he became minister of Fourth Unitarian Church in Chicago. He renamed it All Souls Church and then changed its name and focus again in 1905, to Abraham Lincoln Center. This remained his base until his death in 1918.

In 1878 Jones founded *Unity* magazine, which became the voice of his "ethical" form of Unitarianism, which opposed requiring any creedal statement by the denomination. His slogan for the magazine, "Freedom, Fellowship and Character in Religion," printed on the masthead, was all the affirmation he thought necessary for a liberal religious community. This put him in conflict with Unitarians who felt that a Christian basis was necessary. The resulting "Western Controversy" was settled at the National Unitarian Conference in 1894.

Jones served as executive secretary, under the leadership of Presbyterian Henry Barrows, for the World's Parliament of Religions held in September 1893 in conjunction with the World's Columbian Exposition in Chicago. He also chaired the hymn committee, which chose "universal" hymns from the Christian repertoire for this interfaith gathering. At the same time, Jones convened a gathering of liberal religious leaders from which the Congress of Liberal Religions developed, linking Unitarian, Universalist, independent, and Ethical Culture fellowships. *Unity* was the official publication of the congress, and Jones its driving force until his death in 1918.

Sources and Further Reading: Charles H. Lyttle, *Freedom Moves West* (1952); David Robinson, *The Unitarians and the Universalists* (1985).

Ellen Roberts Young
Las Cruces, New Mexico

Dominic Kolasinski (1838–1898)

Born in the town of Mielec, in what is now Poland, in 1838, Dominic Kolasinski was ordained in 1864 and, after emigrating to the United States, fostered Polish ethnic identity in late nineteenth-century Detroit. Kolasinski served in the St. Albertus Parish of Detroit's east side, a working-class community of Polish immigrants.

Parish trustees, who worked with Kolasinski to build the largest Roman Catholic church in Michigan at the time, grew suspicious of Kolasinski's management of parish funds and, fueled by accusations of sexual indiscretion, complained to Bishop Caspar Henry Borgess of Detroit. Kolasinski was summarily dismissed in 1885, an outcome that many in the Polish community believed to be too severe. Kolasinski instructed his parishioners to protest his dismissal, tapping into Polish ethnic resentments against Borgess, a German. Kolasinski's resistance, which included a parish militia and large-scale demonstrations, led to Borgess's decision to excommunicate Kolasinski's supporters.

In 1886 Kolasinski returned from a short stint in Dakota Territory to start an independent Roman Catholic congregation. He gathered more than ten thousand worshippers and began building a new church some four blocks from his former church. Wary of clerical authority, the Sweetest Heart of Mary Church insisted on certain "democratic" principles, such as elections of priests and extension of the vote in congregational elections to women. Diocesan efforts to curtail these excesses eventually failed, and the democratic principles even worked against Kolasinski himself when he could not get the church to vote out trustees who were limiting his control over church finances.

Kolasinski died in April 1898, leaving a legacy of resistance to diocesan authority among an increasingly energized Polish immigrant community.

Sources and Further Reading: Lawrence D. Orton, *Polish Detroit and the Kolasinski Affair* (1981); Leslie Woodcock Tentler, *Seasons of Grace* (1990).

Jeffrey B. Webb
Huntington College, Indiana

Martin E. Marty (b. 1928)

Martin Marty, Fairfax M. Cone Distinguished Service Professor Emeritus at the University of Chicago, is a leading expert on religion in America. A media personality (appearing on *Nightline* and the PBS *News Hour*); an avid reader; the author of more than 50 books and nearly 4,500 articles; and a senior editor (of *Christian Century* and *Context*), Marty has lectured at six hundred campuses. The University of Chicago's Martin Marty Center promotes religion in public life, electronically publishing his weekly column, "Sightings."

Born in 1928 in West Point, Nebraska, Martin E. Marty was educated at Concordia College in Milwau-

kee, Concordia Seminary in St. Louis, and the University of Chicago. In the tradition of his teachers Jerald C. Brauer and Sidney E. Mead, Martin writes on religion in the American republic. The multivolume *Modern American Religion* (1986, 1990, 1996) extends *Pilgrims in Their Own Land* (1984) and *Righteous Empire* (1970; National Book Award, 1972) through the twentieth century. Central themes include social forces shaping religion, and religious traditions informing American culture.

Pastoral work has dominated Martin's career, yet this Lutheran was an observer at Vatican II and marched for civil rights at Selma, Alabama. Through interfaith meetings and open conversations, Marty coaxes religion into public life. Typical are his direction of the Public Religion Project (for Pew Charitable Trusts) and the Fundamentalism Project (for the American Academy of Arts and Sciences). As a teacher, Martin has modeled to generations of scholars how to be faithful in a plural world. He was awarded the National Humanities Medal in 1997, and on February 5, 1998, he celebrated his seventieth birthday with five hundred guests at the Chicago Historical Society. A creative writer and contemplative napper, Martin Marty is a highly productive public scholar.

Sources and Further Reading: "Martin Marty," *Contemporary Authors* Online (2001); Martin E. Marty, *Modern American Religion*, 3 vols. (1986–1996); Martin E. Marty and Jerald C. Brauer, eds., *The Unrelieved Paradox* (1994).

John Kloos
Benedictine University, Illinois

John T. McNicholas (1877–1950)

Born in Ireland in 1877, John T. McNicholas emigrated to the United States with his family in 1881 and settled in southern Ohio. He entered the Dominican Order at St. Rose's Priory in Springfield, Kentucky in 1894, became a priest in 1901 and received additional education at Minerva University in Rome, Italy.

After a short tenure in Ohio, McNicholas became, successively, a professor at the Catholic University of America in Washington, D.C., National Director of the Holy Name Society in New York City, and a professor in Rome. Appointed bishop of Duluth, Minnesota, in 1918, he was named archbishop of Cincinnati in 1925. Like many of his colleagues in the American Catholic hierarchy at that time, McNicholas was an autocrat who ruled his archdiocese with a tight hand.

In Cincinnati, McNicholas became a vocal advocate for workers. But his great passion was Catholic education. He built dozens of parish schools and worked to obtain state aid for them from the Ohio legislature. He also envisioned a great Catholic university in Cincinnati. In 1928 he received a charter for the Athenaeum of Ohio, a university that gathered four local Catholic colleges on a single campus. In 1935 McNicholas added a graduate school to the enterprise. He assisted Pope Pius XI in drafting a 1938 encyclical on Catholic education and was to become archbishop of New York until the pontiff's sudden death put an end to those plans.

In the 1940s, McNicholas turned his attention to Catholic education on the national level. He served two terms as chair of the education committee of the National Catholic Welfare Conference and was president of the National Catholic Educational Association from 1946 to 1950. He died in 1950 at his residence in College Hill, Ohio.

Sources and Further Reading: Steven M. Avella, "John T. McNicholas in the Age of Practical Thomism," *Records of the American Catholic Historical Society of Philadelphia* 97 (Mar.–Dec. 1986); Maurice E. Reardon, *Mosaic of a Bishop* (1957).

Timothy Walch
Hoover Presidential Library,
West Branch, Iowa

Dwight Lyman Moody. Library of Congress, Prints and Photographs Division, LC-USZ62-122752.

Dwight L. Moody (1837–1899)

Born in Northfield, Massachusetts, in 1837, Dwight Lyman Moody was baptized Unitarian, attended school to age thirteen, worked in Boston selling shoes at seventeen, and received full membership in a Congregational Church in 1856. That year he moved to Chicago, where his warm personality and self-taught business skills would make him the first name in urban revivalism. Moody recruited his first Sunday school class, which met in a converted saloon. He led Young Men's Christian Association (YMCA) volunteers in aiding wounded Civil War soldiers. Never ordained, Moody served as a lay pastor at the Illinois Street Church, which would become the Chicago Avenue Church and, later, Moody Memorial Church.

A successful tour of Britain (1873–1875) with singer-composer Ira D. Sankey launched Moody's pulpit career. His charisma and organizational skills at staging events were virtually unrivaled. Fame made it possible to reestablish himself in Northfield and to return twice to Britain.

In a plain style Moody told audiences that God wished to save everyone ready to accept the gift of grace. Harry Moorehouse, the "Boy Preacher" of England, inspired this message. Direct, heartfelt, and theologically unsophisticated, Moody would rescue individual souls, not engage in social welfare. His mission reached migrants newly arrived from farms more than Catholics from eastern and southern Europe.

In 1887, Moody and some of his supporters founded the Chicago Evangelization Society to train what Moody termed "gapmen" to do mission work in the city. After Moody's death in 1899, the Chicago Evangelization Society was renamed the Moody Bible Institute of Chicago.

Sources and Further Reading: Henry Warner Bowden, *Dictionary of American Religious Biography*, rev. ed. (1993); James F. Findlay, *Dwight L. Moody, American Evangelist, 1837–1899* (1969); Bernard A. Weisberger, *They Gathered at the River* (1958).

John Kloos
Benedictine University, Illinois

William Nast (1807–1899)

The father of the German-language movement in American Methodism was born into a family of Lutheran pastors and minor officials in Stuttgart,

Württemberg, in 1807. When William Nast trained for the Lutheran ministry at Tübingen University, his roommate was David Friedrich Strauss, who later published a notorious, rationalistic biography of Jesus. The rationalistic atmosphere, which stimulated Strauss, discomforted Nast, who left after two years.

In 1828 Nast came to America. After years of consulting Lutheran and Methodist clergy in America about salvation, he experienced conversion in 1835 at a Methodist revival in Ohio. That year, officials of the Methodist Episcopal Church appointed Nast as a missionary to the Germans of Cincinnati. The movement he created during a long career in Ohio consisted, at its zenith, of some sixty-three thousand adult members and a much larger number of affiliated people. It included six colleges, two seminaries, orphanages, hospitals, a home for the elderly, and a deaconess program.

Most German Methodists in the United States resided in the Midwest, especially in Ohio, Illinois, Iowa, and Missouri. The movement spread back to Germany in the 1850s. German Methodist churches declined in America following the ebb of new German immigration about 1890 and the trauma of World War I.

Nast published dozens of books but was better known as the editor of *Der Christliche Apologete*. Beginning this religious newspaper in 1839, he served as editor until his son Albert succeeded him in 1892. William Nast died in 1899.

Sources and Further Reading: Paul F. Douglass, *The Story of German Methodism* (1939); Adam Miller, *Experience of the German Methodist Preachers* (1859); Carl Wittke, *William Nast: Patriarch of German Methodism* (1959).

Robert Frizzell
Northwest Missouri State University

Kathleen Norris (b. 1947)

Although Kathleen Norris did not grow up in the Midwest, she spent her childhood summers visiting her grandparents in Lemmon, South Dakota. Norris was born in Washington, D.C., in 1947. Following college at Bennington in Vermont and a period in New York City, where she married fellow poet David J. Dwyer, she accepted an inheritance and moved to her grandmother's house in 1974 to connect with her roots and deepen her writing.

Norris has written both poetry (*The Middle of the World*, 1981; *Little Girls in Church*, 1995; and *Journey*, 2001) and autobiographical reflections (*Dakota: A Spiritual Geography*, 1993; *The Cloister Walk*, 1996; and *Amazing Grace*, 1998). Her work focuses primarily on her spiritual journey, which began with her return to her grandmother's house and her grandmother's Presbyterian church in South Dakota, places that centered her "in the middle of the world." Although Norris did not abandon her Presbyterian ties, her religious journey was complicated through her association with Benedictine monasteries. She became an oblate, or lay associate, in 1986. Through this rich religious mosaic, Norris found the key to understanding her Dakota heritage and herself in this midwestern land.

In *Dakota*, Norris describes her move to South Dakota and her visits to monasteries as pilgrimages to a desert—a place of silence and isolation, a place at the ends of the earth. The marginality of the Dakotas, the harsh weather, and the economic devastation are painful reminders of human limits and sources of self-knowledge.

Sources and Further Reading: David W. Landrum, "Community and Coherence in the Poetry of Kathleen Norris," *Christianity and Literature* 46 (Spring–Summer 1997); Kathleen Norris, "Places and Displacement: Rattlesnakes in Cyberspace," in Mark Vinz and Thom Tammaro, eds., *Imagining Home* (1995); Michele Potter, "*Dakota: A Spiritual Geography*, Revisited," in Nancy Owen Nelson, ed., *Private Voices, Public Lives: Women Speak on the Literary Life* (1995).

Lynn Ross-Bryant
University of Colorado–Boulder

Mary O'Connell (Sister Anthony) (1814–1897)

Mary O'Connell was born in Limerick, Ireland, in 1814 and emigrated to the United States about 1825. After a convent education in Massachusetts, she entered the Sisters of Charity in Emmitsburg, Maryland, and took the name Sister Anthony.

She began her nursing career in Cincinnati, Ohio, in 1854 and soon became head of St. John's Hospital. The hospital won great respect among non-Catholics in the city and the state and was one of the first Catholic teaching hospitals in the nation. Sister Anthony also established a Cincinnati province of the Sisters of Charity and numerous orphanages, asylums, and hospitals for the poor.

The proximity of Cincinnati to the first Union encampments led to Sister Anthony's involvement in the Civil War. With other sisters of her order, Sister Anthony cared for the wounded at Shiloh, Stone River, Murfreesboro, and many other battles. For more than two years she also served in Union army field hospitals near Nashville.

In 1865 Sister Anthony returned to Cincinnati and her work as a hospital administrator. She received substantial donations from the non-Catholic community in Cincinnati and used these funds to expand St. John's Hospital and establish an infant and maternity house in 1873.

Sister Anthony continued to direct these institutions until her retirement in 1880. She remained active in the work of her religious order until her death in 1897. She is buried on the grounds of the motherhouse that she helped to establish in 1852.

Sources and Further Reading: Mary Denis Maher, *To Bind Up the Wounds* (1999); Ursula Stepsis and Dolores Liptak, eds., *Pioneer Healers* (1989).

Timothy Walch
Herbert Hoover Presidential Library,
West Branch, Iowa

Charles Fox Parham (1873–1929)

Born in Muscatine, Iowa, in 1873, Charles Fox Parham was the third of William M. and Ann Maria Parham's five children. A supply pastor for a Methodist Church for two years, Charles Parham began an independent ministry (1895), married Sarah Thistlethwaite (1896), and with his wife founded the Beth-el Healing Home in Topeka, Kansas (1898), as part of his faith-healing ministry.

Influenced by Frank Sanford's Shiloh community in Maine, Parham believed that the return of Jesus would be hastened through *xenolalia*—the speaking of previously unknown foreign languages as a divine gift for evangelism. Parham became the first person to articulate the distinctive doctrine of Pentecostalism—that "speaking in tongues" is the "initial evidence" of the baptism of the Holy Spirit. Starting a Bible school in an abandoned mansion, Parham encouraged his students to seek tongues while in foreign mission service. Evangelist Agnes Ozman and others first manifested this phenomenon on January 1, 1901. Historians generally acknowledge this event as the beginning of modern Pentecostalism.

Parham spent several years as an evangelist, founded the Apostolic Faith movement, and started a Bible college in Houston, Texas, in 1905. There he allowed an African American, William Seymour, to attend his lectures by sitting outside the classroom. Invited to Los Angeles, Seymour became the leader of the Azusa Street Revival (1906–1909), an event that triggered the worldwide propagation of Pentecostalism.

Dogged by scandal and ill health and alienated from the Azusa revival, Parham spent his remaining years as the leader of the Apostolic Faith movement. He died in Baxter Springs, Kansas, in 1929.

Sources and Further Reading: Robert Mapes Anderson, *Vision of the Disinherited* (1979); James R. Goff, Jr., *Fields White unto Harvest* (1988); Sarah Parham, *The Life of Charles F. Parham* (1985).

Barry Hamilton
Northeastern Seminary, New York

John Baptist Purcell (1800–1883)

Born in Mallow, Ireland in 1800, John Baptist Purcell stepped off a steamboat in November 1833 to begin his tenure as bishop of Cincinnati—a city with but a single Catholic church amid its 30,000 residents. Purcell, who was trained in Mount St. Mary's Seminary in Maryland and the Sulpican Seminaries in Issy and Paris, France, had been ordained a priest in Notre Dame cathedral in Paris in May 1826 and consecrated a bishop a month before his arrival.

The explosive growth in the number of Catholics and parishes under Bishop Purcell led to his appointment as archbishop of Cincinnati by Pope Pius IX in 1850. By the time Purcell celebrated his golden jubilee as a priest, Cincinnati's Catholic population alone had reached 150,000 and was served by forty parishes.

Archbishop Purcell became the driving force behind the creation of Catholic schools. He was also a powerful apologist for the American Catholic Church, as he demonstrated in his defense of American church-state separation at the First Vatican Council and in his many public debates with local Protestant leaders. (The most famous was with Alexander Campbell in 1837.) Purcell was an ardent supporter of the Union during the American Civil War, a somewhat controversial position repudiated by many Catholics.

Purcell's final and most infamous battle, however, was neither ecclesial nor political, but financial. For decades, the diocese had safeguarded deposits made by parishioners skeptical of the then unregulated banking system. In 1878, a $140,000 accounting discrepancy was discovered. Although the archbishop was not directly involved, public opinion held him responsible, in part because Purcell's brother, Father Edward Purcell, had managed the diocese's financial affairs.

Archbishop Purcell died five years later, in 1883.

Sources and Further Reading: Jay P. Dolan, *The American Catholic Experience* (1992); Gerald P. Fogarty, ed., *Patterns of Episcopal Leadership* (1989); Mary Agnes McCann, *Archbishop Purcell and the Archdiocese of Cincinnati* (1918).

Michael Epperson
University of Chicago, Illinois

Gabriel Richard (1767–1832)

Gabriel Richard was one of the best-known Catholic priests in the Midwest before the Civil War. Born in Saintes, France, in 1767, Richard entered the Sulpician Order as a young man. In 1792, alienated by the anticlericalism of the French Revolution, Richard emigrated to Baltimore, Maryland, and taught at St. Mary's Seminary. The priest was then sent to Illinois, where he labored as a missionary for six years before being reassigned to Detroit in 1798.

Richard distinguished himself there as a parish priest, a supervisor of missionaries, and, perhaps most importantly, as an educator. By 1808 Richard had founded six elementary schools and two academies for girls in and around Detroit. That year, he installed Michigan's first printing press, publishing elementary textbooks, religious tracts, and Michigan's first newspaper, the short-lived *Michigan Essay; or, Impartial Observer.* Richard also participated in the founding of the forerunner of the University of Michigan in 1817.

Having proven his loyalty to the United States during the War of 1812, Richard was elected a nonvoting delegate to the U.S. House of Representatives in 1823, the only priest to serve in Congress until 1970. His tenure was limited to one term, however, and his effectiveness was undermined by ongoing conflicts with some of the trustees of his own parish. It was perhaps because of these conflicts that Richard was not elevated to bishop when the Diocese of Detroit was established in 1827.

Father Richard died in the Detroit cholera epidemic of 1832.

Sources and Further Reading: Dolorita Mast, *Always the Priest* (1965); George Pare, *The Catholic Church in Detroit, 1701–1888* (1951); Frank B. Woodford and Albert Hyma, *Gabriel Richard, Frontier Ambassador* (1958).

Brian Wilson
Western Michigan University

William Bell Riley (1861–1947)

Born in Green County, Indiana, to Branson and Ruth Jackson Riley in 1861, William Bell Riley grew up on his family's Kentucky farm. After graduating from Hanover College and Southern Baptist Seminary, Riley pastored churches in Lafayette, Indiana (where he met and married Lillian Howard); Bloomington, Illinois; and Chicago. In 1897 Riley became pastor of Minneapolis's First Baptist Church, which he transformed into a "soulwinning center," with 3,550 members at his 1942 retirement.

Riley's ambitions transcended his church. Alarmed by theological liberalism in the churches and Darwinism in the schools, in the 1920s this theological archconservative organized the national fundamentalist movement. Prodigiously energetic, Riley founded the World's Christian Fundamentals Association, led the fundamentalist campaign to control the Northern Baptist Convention, and stumped the country against evolution (while also editing fundamentalist periodicals and writing innumerable books and pamphlets). As the fundamentalist crusades failed, a bitter Riley responded to these defeats and to the New Deal, which he hated, by writing diatribes against the "Jewish conspiracy."

Riley presided over Northwestern Bible School of Minneapolis, which he founded in 1902 and which by the 1940s included a seminary and college. Hundreds of Northwestern graduates pastored churches in the upper Midwest. They remained remarkably loyal to their school and to their leader; with their help, in 1936 Riley masterminded a fundamentalist takeover of the Minnesota Baptist Convention.

The first great leader of American fundamentalism, William Bell Riley's most important legacy was his midwestern empire, which served as the prototype of contemporary personality-based fundamentalist organizations. He died in 1947.

Sources and Further Reading: Marie Acomb Riley, *The Dynamic of a Dream* (1938); Charles Allyn Russell, "William Bell Riley: Organizational Fundamentalist," in Russell, *Voices of American Fundamentalism: Seven Biographical Studies* (1976); William Vance Trollinger, Jr., *God's Empire* (1990).

William Vance Trollinger, Jr.
University of Dayton, Ohio

Walter Scott (1796–1861)

Walter Scott, a founding member of the Disciples of Christ, was born in Moffat, Scotland, on October 31, 1796. He was the son of Presbyterian parents, Mary Innes and John Scott, and studied music at the University of Edinburgh. After graduating in 1818, he emigrated to the United States and taught Latin at a grammar school on Long Island.

Scott grew restless and moved to Pittsburgh, where he became an assistant at George Forrester's academy. A nominal Presbyterian reformer, Forrester had united two independent congregations into a Christian Church. Forrester introduced Scott to the Haldanean reform movement of the 1790s, which emphasized the authority of scripture, and convinced him that infant baptism was unwarranted and that immersion rather than sprinkling was the correct form of baptism.

When Forrester drowned in the Allegheny River in 1820, Scott, who was already in charge of the academy, took over his mentor's church. He also developed a lifelong friendship with Alexander Campbell. In 1826 he moved to Steubenville, Ohio, and became a traveling evangelist for the Mahoning Baptist Association. It was around this time that he also developed a primitive and rational plan of salvation, which rested on the scriptural order of the New Testament: (1) faith in Christ, (2) repentance from sin, (3) baptism, to symbolize both faith and repentance, (4) remission of sin, (5) the gift of the Holy Spirit, and (6) eternal life. This simpler plan of salvation removed the Calvinist tenets of recounting the conversion experience and the congregational vote for church membership, thus paving the way for thousands of conversions.

Scott's ancient gospel spread swiftly throughout the Midwest and, together with Campbell's New Testament restorationism, marked the demise of the Mahoning Baptist Association and the beginning of the Campbellite movement and the Disciples of Christ.

Scott died in 1861.

Sources and Further Reading: William Baxter, *Life of Elder Walter Scott* (1874); William A. Gerrard, *A Biographical Study of Walter Scott, American Frontier Evangelist* (1992); William A. Gerrard, "Walter Scott: Frontier Disciples Evangelist," *Lexington Theological Quarterly* 21 (Apr. 1986).

Michael Sletcher
Yale University, Connecticut

Abba Hillel Silver (1893–1963)

Rabbi of Cleveland's Congregation Tifereth Israel (1917–1963), a prominent Reform congregation known simply as "The Temple," Abba Hillel Silver was a nationally known advocate for social justice and Zionism.

Born in Lithuania in 1893, Silver came to the United States at the age of nine. He was educated at the University of Cincinnati and Hebrew Union College, where he was ordained in 1915. In the 1940s, as chair of the American section of the Jewish Agency Executive, Silver presented the case for Jewish statehood at the United Nations. He was also responsible for the strategy that convinced President Harry S Truman to support Jewish claims in Palestine and, eventually, to recognize the State of Israel.

For Silver, Zionism was more than a cultural or humanitarian effort; as early as the 1920s, he advocated Jewish political sovereignty in Palestine. An exceptional orator and effective writer, Silver generated sympathy among Americans for Zionism and Israel. Tough and politically savvy, he preferred militancy to diplomacy, which brought him into conflict with other Zionist leaders. As a result, he resigned from formal positions in 1949, though he continued his personal lobbying. He died in 1963.

Silver was a maverick within Reform Judaism, which until the late 1930s was on record against Zionism, and his bold position was particularly anomalous in the Midwest, where anti-Zionism was especially strong. But Silver saw Reform Judaism's prophetic universalism and Zionism's Jewish particularism as complementary, joining Jewish values and the life of the Jewish people.

Sources and Further Reading: Marc Lee Raphael, *Abba Hillel Silver* (1989); Melvin I. Urofsky, *American Zionism from Herzl to the Holocaust* (1975).

Amy Hill Shevitz
California State University–Northridge

Joseph Smith (1805–1844)

Joseph Smith had his earliest distinctive spiritual experiences in upstate New York, where his farming family had migrated in 1816 from his 1805 birthplace in Sharon, Vermont. Scarcely educated but keenly intelligent, the boy grew perplexed over religious differences among revival preachers and family members. In 1820 he experienced a vision of God and Jesus, who instructed him to join none of the churches. Subsequent revelations led to his production of *The Book of Mormon*, the reception of exclusive religious authority, and organization of a new church in 1830.

The balance of Smith's dramatic career unfolded in the Midwest, where he sought to restore not only Christianity in its primitive, pristine state, but also the ancient order of human and divine relations through the establishment of the literal kingdom of God on earth. Smith privately taught and practiced polygyny in the pattern of Old Testament patriarchs. The church-kingdom he envisioned entailed the physical gathering of dispersed converts into communities where they could learn to become one in heart and in society, build temples to administer the sacred ordinances of salvation, and usher in the return of Christ. Followers gathered by the hundreds in Kirtland, Ohio; western and northern Missouri; and Nauvoo, Illinois. But the prophet and his followers encountered persistent criticism. Opponents tarred and feathered Smith in Ohio, imprisoned him in Missouri, and in 1844 murdered him in Illinois.

While he lived, Smith functioned not only as church leader and prophet but also as translator, healer, husband, father, colonizer, politician, city planner, real estate agent, social reformer, architectural consultant, farmer, banker, treasure-hunter, fugitive, prisoner, and lieutenant general of an independent militia. Within two years of his death, more than half his followers fled their midwestern homes under duress, migrating to their eventual refuge in the Rocky Mountains. Dozens of smaller groups, however, claim Smith as their founder. The most significant of these is the Community of Christ, headquartered in Independence, Missouri.

Sources and Further Reading: Richard L. Bushman, *Joseph Smith and the Beginnings of Mormonism* (1984); Donna Hill, *Joseph Smith: The First Mormon* (1977); Dean Jessee, ed., *Personal Writings of Joseph Smith*, rev. ed. (2002); Lucy Mack Smith, *Biographical Sketches of Joseph Smith the Prophet* (1853).

Philip Barlow
Hanover College, Indiana

Edward Anders Sövik (b. 1918)

Edward Anders Sövik has been a fellow of the American Institute of Architects since 1967. He has won numerous awards for his outstanding building designs, working out of his practice in Northfield, Minnesota, from 1949 until his retirement in the late 1990s.

Born in Kikungshan, China, in 1918, Sövik was the son of Norwegian Lutheran missionaries. He studied art and English at St. Olaf College, Northfield, Minnesota, where he earned a bachelor of arts degree (1939); painting at the Art Students League in New York City (1939–1940); and theology at Luther Theological Seminary, St. Paul, Minnesota (1940–1942). Following service in the navy as a pilot during World War II, Sövik studied architecture at Yale University, receiving his degree in 1949.

Sövik primarily designed churches for both Protestant and Roman Catholic communities. He developed a particular approach to worship space, best articulated in his book, *Architecture for Worship* (1973). Two primary influences on his original church design were the International Style movement in architecture and the liturgical renewal movement. Simplicity, flexibility, and hospitality are hallmarks of Sövik's designs. Sövik sought to design churches for multipurpose use that could easily accommodate changes in worship patterns. His reflections on church design have been published in more than seventy journal articles and book chapters.

Sövik has had a significant influence on the design of approximately four hundred church-related projects in the United States, including Trinity United Methodist Church in Charles City, Iowa; St. James Lutheran Church in Lake Forest, Illinois; and the renovation of Saints Peter and Paul Cathedral in Indianapolis, Indiana.

Sources and Further Reading: Edward A. Sövik, *Architecture for Worship* (1973); Mark A. Torgerson, "Edward Anders Sövik and His Return to the 'Non-church,'" Ph.D. diss., University of Notre Dame (1995).

Mark A. Torgerson
Judson College, Illinois

James J. Strang (1813–1856)

Born in Scipio, New York, in 1813, James J. Strang grew up in the "Burnt-Over District" of western New York, a region renowned for revivalism. Strang was precocious, charismatic, intelligent, selectively idealistic, and breathtakingly ambitious. His extraordinary diary, penned between the ages of nineteen and twenty-four, discloses both a desire to devote his life to the service of humankind and a drive for "royalty and power" to rival even "Cesar [*sic*] or Napoleon."

Years later Strang discovered a vehicle—Mormonism—that he believed held the potential to help him realize his goals. Four months before Joseph Smith's 1844 assassination in Illinois, Strang was baptized. One month after Smith's martyrdom, Strang produced a letter (apparently forged) indicating Smith's desire that Strang succeed him. Strang also avowed angelic ordination, adopted Smith's authority as a prophet of God, dug up and translated brass plates into new scripture, denounced (though he later practiced) polygamy, and crafted a complete and thoughtful framework for government and human relations. In the process, and often temporarily, he attracted prominent Mormons who had renounced their allegiance to Brigham Young, the leader of the westward-moving Mormon majority. Strang established a community of about twenty-six hundred followers on Beaver Island in Lake Michigan, had himself crowned king, and ruled there for almost ten years until disgruntled followers took his life in 1856.

A handful of disciples still honor him. Among the more intriguing religious figures of the nineteenth-century Midwest, Strang presents the paradox of the Earnest Imposter. He sought greatness by attempting to fashion, by whatever means necessary, a compelling and benevolent model of human society.

Sources and Further Reading: Lawrence Foster, "James J. Strang: The Prophet Who Failed," *Church History* 50 (June 1981); Mark A. Strang, ed., *The Diary of James J. Strang*

(1961); Wingfield Watson, ed., *The Revelations of James J. Strang* (1856).

Philip Barlow
Hanover College, Indiana

Billy Sunday (1862–1935)

Born in Ames, Iowa, in 1862, William Ashley "Billy" Sunday spent his childhood living with his mother and grandfather until his impoverished relatives sent him to an orphanage. He left the orphanage in his teen years and worked odd jobs around the state until his athletic prowess, especially his running speed, earned him a baseball contract with the Chicago White Stockings, with whom he played until 1891. While in Chicago in 1886 Sunday was converted to evangelical Christianity at the Pacific Garden Mission, and soon afterward joined the Jefferson Park Presbyterian Church, where he met and eventually married Helen Amelia Thompson.

Under the auspices of the Young Men's Christian Association (YMCA), Sunday began his work as a

Billy Sunday, 1908. Archives of the Billy Graham Center, Wheaton, Ill.

part-time evangelist while he played baseball in Chicago, Pittsburgh, and Philadelphia. Retiring from professional sports, Sunday did advance planning for itinerant revivalist J. Wilbur Chapman in 1893. When Chapman accepted the pastorate of Bethany Presbyterian Church in Philadelphia in 1895, Sunday struck out on his own on what he called the "kerosene circuit" of small towns, beginning with an evangelistic campaign in Garner, Iowa, on January 7, 1896.

Sunday used vaudeville antics to attract attention. Speaking in a folksy, salty vernacular, he often taunted his audiences. Especially during World War I, Sunday trotted out patriotic and nativist rhetoric, arguing that "Patriotism and Christianity are synonymous terms." He routinely condemned alcohol, gambling, and licentiousness but cared little for the niceties of theology. "I don't know any more about theology than a jack-rabbit knows about ping-pong," he would say, "but I'm on my way to glory." Sunday, feisty to the end, spent his final years at Winona Lake, Indiana. He died in Chicago in 1935.

Sources and Further Reading: Lyle W. Dorsett, *Billy Sunday and the Redemption of Urban America* (1991); Douglas Frank, *Less Than Conquerors* (1986); Robert F. Martin, *Hero of the Heartland* (2002); William G. McLoughlin, *Billy Sunday Was His Real Name* (1955); Mark A. Noll, Nathan Hatch, George Marsden, David Wells, John Woodbridge, eds., *Eerdmans' Handbook to Christianity in America* (1983).

Randall Balmer
Columbia University, New York

David Swing (1830–1894)

David Swing was born in Cincinnati, Ohio in 1830. After graduating from Miami University in Oxford, Ohio, he studied at Lane Seminary in Cincinnati. From 1853 until 1866, Swing was principal of a preparatory school associated with Miami.

Gaining a reputation as a preacher, Swing became pastor of the Westminster Presbyterian Church in Chicago in 1866. Swing had a way with words and his sermons exuded a creative, liberal spirit. Westminster Church became Fourth Presbyterian Church in 1869 and, after a new building was erected following the Great Fire of 1871, emerged as one of the most influential churches in the city. (A third building, designed by Ralph Adams Cram and completed in 1914, sits on Michigan Avenue across from the Hancock Tower.)

Conservatives worried about Swing's liberal ideas. In 1874 theologian Francis L. Patton of McCormick Seminary accused the poetic preacher of heresy, and his subsequent trial before the Chicago Presbytery attracted national attention. Critics were displeased with Swing's humanism, thinking he strayed from the Westminster Confession on sin, atonement, and damnation. The "professor," as friends and followers called him, had emphasized human ability in hopeful sermons on the experience of personal freedom and its uses.

Acquitted of all charges, Swing nevertheless resigned from Fourth Presbyterian in 1875 and formed a nondenominational congregation called Central Church. Swing's new church, which after 1880 was housed in the Central Music Hall, was very successful. As popular as ever, Swing toured the country, speaking in every state as well as in Alaska.

A charismatic preacher rather than a rigorous thinker, David Swing made an ancient faith intelligible to modern minds. He died in 1894.

Sources and Further Reading: Henry Warner Bowden, *Dictionary of American Religious Biography*, rev. ed. (1993); Joseph F. Newton, *David Swing: Poet-Preacher* (1909); David Swing, *Truths for To-Day*, 2 vols. (1874–1876).

John Kloos
Benedictine University, Illinois

Tenskwatawa. Ohio Historical Society.

Tenskwatawa (1775–1836)

Tenskwatawa, born in 1775 as the younger brother of the Shawnee leader Tecumseh, lost his father in battle and was abandoned by his mother. During his youth, Tenskwatawa was known as Lalewethika ("rattling sound") because of his idle boasting. The loss of an eye in a childhood bow-and-arrow accident and alcohol abuse as an adolescent damaged his early reputation among the Shawnee people.

In 1804 or 1805, Lalewethika fell ill and was believed dead, but he emerged from his sickness having experienced a vision of a peaceful and prosperous spirit world. Changing his name to *Tenskwatawa*, "The Open Door," he embarked upon his new role in guiding all American Indian nations to earthly happiness and otherworldly paradise. He preached abstention from internecine warfare, promiscuity, and alcohol and advocated a return to precolonial lifeways, which included renunciation of European American technologies.

Tenskwatawa's message spread to many nations, including the Ottawa, Seneca, Wyandot, Kickapoo, and Miami. His advice to join with the British in Canada against the Americans appealed to many whose lands had been taken by the U.S. government. From 1805 to 1809, Tenskwatawa led this intertribal movement, but

after the Treaty of Fort Wayne, in which vast amounts of land in Illinois and Indiana were ceded to the United States, Tenskwatawa's religious movement lost ground to Tecumseh's military leadership. Defeat at the Battle of Tippecanoe in 1811 brought about further loss of faith in Tenskwatawa, who lived in exile in Canada for a decade before returning to the United States, accepting removal, and leading his small band of remaining followers to Kansas. He died in 1836.

Sources and Further Reading: R. David Edmunds, *The Shawnee Prophet* (1983); James H. Howard, *Shawnee! The Ceremonialism of a Native Indian Tribe and Its Cultural Background* (1981); John Sugden, *Tecumseh: A Life* (1998).

Lisa J. M. Poirier
Miami University, Oxford, Ohio

D. Elton Trueblood (1900–1994)

David Elton Trueblood was born in 1900 near Indianola, Iowa, the son of Samuel J. Trueblood and Effie Crew. After graduating from William Penn College in 1922, he did graduate work at Brown University and Hartford Theological Seminary before receiving a graduate degree of bachelor of systematic theology from Harvard University in 1926 and a doctorate in philosophy from Johns Hopkins University in 1934. Appointments to the faculties of Guilford College, Haverford College, and Stanford University, where Trueblood served as chaplain and became a national figure, led him in 1946 to Earlham College in Richmond, Indiana, where he taught until his retirement in 1966. A lifelong Quaker, Trueblood was active in numerous Quaker organizations. He died in 1994.

Trueblood was one of the best-known and most widely read religious and devotional writers of the post–World War II period. His first book intended for a nonacademic audience, *The Predicament of Modern Man* (1944), won considerable attention for its depiction of what he called "our cut-flower civilization"—beautiful, but dying because it had lost connection to its roots. In this and subsequent books Trueblood advocated self-discipline and Christian commitment as the solutions to the problems that the United States faced in the cold war years. To this end he founded the Yokefellow movement. Nondenominational, its devotees worked for spiritual renewal and transformation. Trueblood considered himself an evangelical, but he eschewed fundamentalism. His repudiation of Quaker pacifism in the 1950s and steadfast defense of Richard Nixon until 1974 made him controversial in Quaker circles.

Sources and Further Reading: James R. Newby, *Elton Trueblood* (1990); D. Elton Trueblood, *While It Is Day*, 2nd ed. (1974).

Thomas D. Hamm
Earlham College, Indiana

Carl Ferdinand Wilhelm Walther (1811–1887)

Born in Germany on October 25, 1811, Carl Ferdinand Wilhelm (C.F.W.) Walther became a leading American Lutheran leader, responsible for the establishment of the second-largest denomination of American Lutherans today.

A Lutheran pastor in Saxony, Walther was upset with religious changes in Germany, and joined a group that immigrated to Missouri in 1839. Walther became prominent when he successfully argued in the 1841 "Altenburg Debate" that the immigrants constituted a church. In 1847, they organized the German Lutheran Synod of Missouri and Other States (now the Lutheran Church Missouri Synod). Beyond his work as pastor of Trinity Lutheran Church in St. Louis from 1841 until his death, Walther served the Missouri Synod as president (1847–1850, 1864–1878); as a professor at Concordia Seminary, St. Louis (1850–1887); and as editor of several church periodicals.

It was as a theologian that Walther put his stamp on the Missouri Synod (and other American Lutherans). Walther held a staunchly conservative and confessional Lutheranism based on a strict interpretation of sixteenth-century Lutheran confessional documents, and he opposed what he saw as the more liberal or "unionistic" Lutheranism of other Lutheran groups. He and the Missouri Synod held that before they could enter into fellowship (union) with other Lutheran groups, they would have to come into complete doctrinal agreement, something rarely achieved.

In 1872 Walther organized the Synodical Conference as a general organization for conservative Lutheran groups in America, but the organization fell into theological dispute, and Walther spent many of the remaining years of his life arguing with other American Lutheran theologians about points of doctrine. Walther died on May 7, 1887.

Sources and Further Reading: Lewis W. Spitz, Sr., *The Life of Dr. C.F.W. Walther* (1961); Theodore G. Tappert, ed., *Lutheran Confessional Theology in America, 1840–1880* (1972).

Mark Granquist
Gustavus Adolphus College, Minnesota

Daniel S. Warner (1842–1895)

Born in Wayne County, Ohio, in 1842, Daniel Sidney Warner was the fifth of six children of David and Leah Warner. After serving in the Union Army, Warner attended Vermillion College and Oberlin College, both in Ohio. While teaching school, he was licensed to preach by the West Ohio Eldership of the Churches of God (Winebrennerian).

After serving as a pastor, evangelist, and home missionary in Nebraska, Warner was ejected from the Winebrennerian ministry in 1878 for his advocacy of entire sanctification, the doctrine of a second work of grace favored by the Wesleyan holiness movement. He made a "Covenant with God" to reject sectarianism and call out the "Church of God." After a brief time in the Northern Indiana Eldership of the

Churches of God (Winebrennerian), Warner published *Bible Proofs of the Second Work of Grace* (1880). The next year he renounced membership in the Indiana Holiness Association and formed the first congregation of a reformation movement in Beaver Dam, Indiana (1881). Warner edited a newspaper called *The Gospel Trumpet* and conducted extensive revival campaigns, mostly in the Midwest.

Notable for his profound vision and distinctive synthesis of nonsectarian primitivism and Wesleyan holiness, Warner is regarded as the originator of the Church of God concept of the restoration of the New Testament Church, a leading figure in what his contemporaries called "come-outism." The Church of God movement emerged from the revival meetings of Warner and his associates. The church is headquartered in Anderson, Indiana. Warner died in 1895 in Grand Junction, Michigan.

Sources and Further Reading: Barry L. Callen, *It's God's Church* (1995); Melvin E. Dieter, *The Holiness Revival of the Nineteenth Century*, 2nd ed. (1996); Thomas A. Fudge, *Daniel Warner and the Paradox of Religious Democracy in Nineteenth-Century America* (1998).

Barry W. Hamilton
Northeastern Seminary, New York

Rembert G. Weakland (b. 1927)

Rembert G. Weakland, born in Patton, Pennsylvania, on April 2, 1927, was the ninth bishop of the Roman Catholic Archdiocese of Milwaukee, serving from 1977 until his retirement in 2002. Archbishop Weakland was not a diocesan priest, but a Benedictine monk. He joined the Benedictines in 1945 and eventually served as the worldwide head (abbot primate) of the order from 1967 to 1977.

Weakland was one of the last U.S. bishops appointed by Pope Paul VI. As the lengthy papacy of John Paul II took the Catholic Church in a more conservative direction, most observers considered Weakland one of the few remaining liberals in the U.S. hierarchy. He was a consistent voice in support of economic justice, most prominently as the chair of a committee of U.S. bishops who drafted the 1986 "Economic Justice for All: Pastoral Letter on Catholic Social Teaching and the U.S. Economy." He also allowed an open discussion within the archdiocese on abortion, thus earning the ire of the Vatican. Weakland's mandatory 2002 retirement was marred by revelations of payments to a former male lover.

Weakland was not originally from the Midwest. However, his skeptical view of laissez-faire capitalism continues the tradition of midwestern prelates' support for Catholic social teaching as an alternative to both unbridled capitalism and socialism. In this, Weakland followed in the footsteps of other prominent midwestern bishops such as Edward Cardinal Mooney of Detroit, Samuel Cardinal Stritch of Milwaukee and Chicago, and Archbishop John T. McNicholas of Cincinnati.

Source and Further Reading: Paul Wilkes, *The Education of an Archbishop* (1992).

Robert B. Shelledy
University of Wisconsin

Theodore Dwight Weld (1803–1895)

Born in Hampton, Connecticut, in 1803, Theodore Dwight Weld was the son of the Reverend Ludovicus and Elizabeth Clark Weld. In 1826 he experienced a religious conversion under the influence of a prominent revivalist, Charles G. Finney. This led to a commitment to various reforms, including temperance and the manual labor movement. In 1832, after conversation with abolitionists Elizur Wright, Charles B. Storrs, and Beriah Green, he became convinced of the necessity of the immediate abolition of slavery.

As a student at Lane Theological Seminary in 1834, he organized and facilitated the Lane Debates, a series of discussions over eighteen evenings that led the majority of students to endorse the immediate abolition of slavery and condemn the principles of the American Colonization Society. When the trustees and faculty of Lane Seminary, then headed by Lyman Beecher, ordered the students to cease their antislavery activities, the majority of these "Lane Rebels" left the seminary and became involved in the antislavery movement. Weld became an agent for the American Antislavery Society and trained most of that organization's early agents. He also wrote *The Bible against Slavery* (1837) and *American Slavery as It Is* (1839). The latter was a compilation of the horrors of American slavery and sold more than a hundred thousand copies.

In 1838 Weld married Angelina Grimke, a prominent abolitionist and early feminist. He ceased involvement in reform movements after 1844 and spent the remainder of his life as an educator. Weld died in 1895.

Sources and Further Reading: Robert H. Abzug, *Passionate Liberator* (1980); Benjamin P. Thomas, *Theodore Weld, Crusader for Freedom* (1950).

Lawrence T. Lesick
Wilmington College, Ohio

Isaac Mayer Wise (1819–1900)

Rabbi of Cincinnati's Congregation B'nai Jeshurun for more than fifty years, Isaac Mayer Wise is widely regarded as the founder of American Reform Judaism.

Born in Steingrub, Bohemia, in 1819, Wise had both a traditional Jewish education and some university training, though the actual status of his rabbinic ordination is unclear. He immigrated to the United States in 1846 and served as rabbi in Albany, New York. In 1854 he was hired by B'nai Jeshurun. Cincinnati's was then the third-largest Jewish community in the United States, after those in New York City and Philadelphia.

From his Cincinnati base, Wise promoted the development of a modern Judaism that expressed the essential compatibility of Jewishness and Americanness. His major goals were a union of Jewish congregations, a common prayer book, and a college to train American rabbis.

In 1854 Wise started a weekly newspaper, the *Israelite* (now the *American Israelite*), which linked American Jews by providing news from all over the country and which urged them toward moderate religious reform. In 1857 he issued *Minhag America*, soon the most widely used prayer book in American Judaism. In 1873 he inspired lay leaders of Cincinnati congregations to spearhead the formation of the Union of American Hebrew Congregations (UAHC; now known as the Union for Reform Judaism). The UAHC sponsored the first permanent Jewish theological school in America, the Hebrew Union College in Cincinnati, of which Wise was president from its founding in 1875 until his death in 1900.

Congregation B'nai Jeshurun is now known as the Isaac Mayer Wise Temple.

Sources and Further Reading: Michael A. Meyer, *Response to Modernity* (1995); Sefton D. Temkin, *Creating American Reform Judaism* (1998).

Amy Hill Shevitz
California State University–Northridge

Education

SECTION EDITOR
Kate Rousmaniere

Section Contents

Overview

The popular image of the one-room country schoolhouse as the embodiment of education in the Midwest is only one dimension of a complex story. Indeed, the characteristics of midwestern schooling are remarkably diverse. The distinctive regional themes of education in the Midwest have emerged from dynamic tensions among conflicting positions on local and centralized control of schooling, traditional and innovative curricular ideas, and vocational and intellectual purposes of education.

Demographic diversity has also shaped elementary and secondary education in the region for more than two centuries. Some of the nation's most densely populated urban school districts as well as some of its most geographically expansive rural districts are in the Midwest. The region has a range of culturally homogeneous schools, from predominantly white rural and suburban schools to predominantly African American urban schools to schools designed specifically for Native American students, ethnic identity groups, and religious communities. Historically, the Midwest has fostered innovation, including the nineteenth-century readers of William Holmes McGuffey and the progressive ideas associated with John Dewey's early-twentieth-century work with experimental education at the University of Chicago's Laboratory School.

And while we tend to think of the Midwest as homogeneous, it was the great racial and cultural diversity of midwestern city schools that led to some of the major legal landmarks in racial desegregation, including the U.S. Supreme Court decision *Brown v. Board of Education of Topeka, Kansas* (1954, 1955). The persistent movement of peoples into and around the region has directly shaped the character of its schools as districts have adapted in a variety of ways to the influx of populations from Europe, Central America, and Asia; religious minority populations from abroad; and internal migratory waves of African American, Appalachian, and Latin American populations from southern regions of the country.

Higher education in the Midwest has also been marked by great diversity of purpose and form, and it has made a profound impact on American culture as a whole. Through the nineteenth century, midwestern states supported the establishment of land-grant and agricultural colleges, teacher-training institutions, and large state universities as well as private and religiously based colleges. Both public and private institutions were oriented toward expanding trades, professions, and culture in a new region. This purpose has continued into the modern era with a wide array of institu-

tions, from small liberal arts to religiously based institutions to large universities with professional and technical expertise. The cultural identity of higher education across America is popularly associated with "Big Ten" universities and their boosterish blend of athletics and academics.

Across elementary, secondary, undergraduate, and graduate education, then, the Midwest has played a defining role in the development of American educational institutions and ideas. Superficially, midwestern education may seem less dynamic than education in other parts of the United States, but it actually has been the site of some of the most significant turning points in American educational history. The "Education" section examines the breadth of educational initiatives in the region with introductory essays that survey the history and characteristics of midwestern rural and urban education and distinctive intellectual and social movements linked with educational reform. Six other survey essays introduce studies of specific aspects of midwestern higher education, elementary and secondary education, teachers and administrators, progressive and reform movements, multicultural education, and multiculturalism.

The charter documents of education in the Midwest—the Land Ordinance of 1785 and the Northwest Ordinance of 1787—outlined the cultural as well as the economic and political development of the territory north of the Ohio River. The Northwest Ordinance stated that "religion, morality, and knowledge being necessary to good government and the happiness of mankind, schools and the means of education shall forever be encouraged." The Land Ordinance called for the creation of six-mile-square townships divided into thirty-six sections. The sixteenth section, which fell closest to the center of the township, was set aside for a public or common school for the community's children. This act thus transferred the decentralized, local model of schooling from colonial New England into the interior of North America. Because the ordinances were general statements, the individual states created from the Northwest Territory had to deal with the details of public education. For the most part, legislators left control in local hands. By the middle of the nineteenth century, district schooling, locally funded and managed by representatives of the community, was particularly popular in sparsely populated rural communities. The diverse architecture, curriculum, classroom practice, and teacher models developed in these rural schools coalesced into the powerful iconography of American education as pastoral, community based, and traditional.

Rural schooling was never as peaceful or idealized as it may seem in retrospect, however. Nineteenth-century rural schools were often isolated and primitive

Built in 1902 as the administrative center of the St. Louis World's Fair, Brookings Hall is now the administration building of Washington University. Courtesy Joe Angeles/ WUSTL Photo.

buildings where young men and women teachers had little preparation and constructed the course of study around eclectic collections of available books. The emphasis on local control led to persistent conflict over curriculum, school funding, and district policy. Rural educators argued that such ideological battles were the necessary price for self-governed local school systems that they believed were the signatures of a democratic society. By the early twentieth century, many other educators disagreed, arguing that the traditional one-room schoolhouse with a governing board of local farmers was inefficient, unprofessional, and sectarian. They advocated instead the consolidation of small districts into one large district with graded elementary and secondary education, a common curriculum, and a systematized and centralized management funded by district and state financing.

Despite the disappearance of the one-room country schoolhouse, local control has remained a consistent thread in school policy across the region. Today, midwestern states have a larger number of school districts than any other region of the country, and they rely more heavily on local property tax to fund public schools, leading to serious financial inequities. Legal challenges to school funding formulas have been mounted in midwestern state courts, beginning in the 1970s in Michigan and Kansas and continuing through the early twenty-first century in Ohio. But the powerful tradition of local control makes it difficult for legislatures to consolidate districts or centralize public-school finances. Indeed, it encourages local educational initiatives, including private and parochial schooling and discrete educational programs for immigrant and linguistic minorities, as well as legal decisions that are the foundation of home schooling, school vouchers, and educational provisions for religious groups such as the Amish.

While rural communities wrestled over the issue of local control, midwestern cities moved swiftly to centralized school administrative structures in the late nineteenth century. In Chicago, Cleveland, and Detroit, administrators addressed the challenges of their economically and culturally diverse populations by developing large city school bureaucracies and systems of management. Late-nineteenth-century city school superintendents such as William T. Harris in St. Louis and Albert G. Lane in Chicago expanded their urban district operations to include secondary, vocational, and adult education as well as kindergartens. They also helped to develop professional structures for school personnel. Some of these systems were unique: The schools of Gary, Indiana, became world famous due to Superintendent William Wirt's "platoon system," which organized daily activities into a rotation among regular classes and a wide range of extracurricular activities. The reform impulse continued into the

1980s and 1990s, when Chicago introduced local school councils controlled by voting parents, and Milwaukee and Cleveland introduced city-wide school voucher plans in an attempt to improve educational opportunities.

Early-twentieth-century school reformers in rapidly growing midwestern cities saw education as the key to creating cohesive civic communities. These educators affiliated with the labor, social settlement, alcohol temperance, agricultural reform, and women's club movements and used both informal and formal education to further their cause of expanding and improving public services to children. Social progressives such as Jane Addams in Chicago played a significant role in expanding education beyond classrooms and into public playgrounds, vacation schools, civic and arts education, and community programs for immigrant and poor children. Reformist political leaders in Ohio such as Toledo mayor Samuel Jones and Cleveland mayor Tom Johnson put school reform at the center of their urban reform initiatives to expand the tax base and social services so as to make cities more responsive to citizens' needs. Elementary teacher Margaret Haley organized the nation's first teachers' union, in early-twentieth-century Chicago, in order to defend public funding for schooling and promote teachers' occupational rights. The great popularity of teacher education institutes in the Midwest furthered the development of child-centered and socially oriented teaching practices.

The Midwest was the site of some of the nation's most innovative curricular reforms. Beginning in the mid-nineteenth century, educators across the region redesigned curricula from an emphasis on esoteric knowledge to more practical content areas that related to students' learning interests and abilities. Francis W. Parker became known as "the father of progressive education" because of his progressive teacher education practices in the Cook County Normal School in Chicago in the late nineteenth century.

Parker inspired John Dewey, who applied his progressive educational philosophies at the Chicago's Laboratory School. Dewey argued that the classroom should be a model community of learning, and that children learned best with hands-on, experiential activities. His ideas, which formed the core of what became known as the progressive education movement, advocated child-centered education, manual work, projects, and creative expression. Other progressive curricular movements across the Midwest introduced the kindergarten and the junior high school as well as developed manual training, vocational and agricultural education, and the arts.

Higher education in the Midwest originated in a complex array of institutional structures that ultimately influenced the shape of higher education across the United States. Private religiously affiliated colleges were the first higher education institutions north of the Ohio River, introduced in the early nineteenth century for the dual purpose of spreading Christianity and boosting young towns. The changing needs of developing communities led these institutions to shift from a classical intellectual curriculum to more practical subjects such as agriculture, engineering, and teaching, as well as religious education. Although some of these institutions featured only a fragment of what we now think of as four-year higher education, they provided the first advanced education for men from rural and frontier communities. Women were invited into some of these early institutions, and many communities established private academies for women in order to educate future mothers and teachers.

The Northwest Ordinance's call for public education and the general commitment to the economic and moral development of the region encouraged states to charter universities. Ohio established Ohio University in 1804 and Miami University in 1809. Public higher education expanded dramatically when President Abraham Lincoln signed the 1862 Morrill Land-Grant Act, which provided federal money to establish public colleges that taught agriculture, mechanics, and military tactics as well as the established curriculum. Morrill funds transformed former agricultural and teacher-training schools into universities and helped to start up new institutions. By the end of the nineteenth century, the midwestern public college had emerged as a symbol of democratic higher education. Open to men and women, immigrants and African Americans, the colleges were inexpensive; committed to community development; and offered an array of liberal arts, professional, and technical education.

By the early twentieth century, large state universities housed a variety of activities and cultures. The rapid development of competitive sports led to the founding in the 1890s of a governing intercollegiate body known as the Big Ten that came to symbolize the cultural identity of midwestern state universities. A lively college student culture developed in these institutions with the development of the profession of student affairs and the founding of a number of national fraternities and sororities. These innovations encouraged cocurricular and leadership opportunities for new generations of college students and further expanded the social impact of midwestern higher education.

Midwestern students were also involved in political activities. In the 1930s, midwestern university students led nationwide Socialist and pacifist student organizing. In the 1960s, they played critical roles in the antiwar and free speech movements, and the deaths of four students at an antiwar protest at Ohio's Kent State University in May 1970 came to symbolize university unrest over the Vietnam War. Midwestern state universities remain in the limelight of contemporary politics. Beyond affiliations with the Republican and Democratic Parties, student activists in recent years have focused on gay and lesbian rights, feminism, antiracism, pacifism, labor rights for graduate students, local community relations, and greater diversity in curricula and admissions. Midwestern students have also participated in religious movements such as the Campus Crusade for Christ.

Beyond state universities, the Midwest has multiple higher education models. Small private liberal arts colleges dot the landscape, some retaining part of their origins as religious institutions. The University of Chicago originated in millionaire John D. Rockefeller's initiative to create a leading research institute. A commitment to practical skills led to the founding of agricultural and technical educational institutions and the development of research and professional education in state universities. Such pragmatism also drove the establishment of what became junior colleges, which were designed to separate less academically capable and more vocationally oriented students from the new competitive universities. All these ventures reflected their founders' attempts to introduce traditional education into the Midwest and simultaneously create new models of higher education.

Racial, ethnic, and religious diversity in midwestern higher education was first addressed by religiously affiliated colleges that opened their doors to African American and women students, in part to promote their religion and in part to increase their enrollment in the underpopulated region. Oberlin College, founded in northern Ohio in 1833, accepted African American and women students as part of its religious mission. Other colleges, including Grinnell in Iowa and Earlham in Indiana, had abolitionist ties. Four historically black colleges were founded in midwestern states in the mid-nineteenth century, including Wilberforce (now Central State University), founded in Ohio in 1856 by the Methodist Episcopal Church, and Missouri's Lincoln University, which was founded by African American Civil War veterans. By the late nineteenth century, a number of state universities were admitting women and ethnic and racial minorities, leading to some dynamic enrollment shifts, such as in the University of Illinois, which in the early twentieth century attracted over one-third of all Chinese students in American higher education. Religious minorities, too, have furthered the development of higher education in the Midwest. Catholics, excluded from many of the elite private colleges of the East Coast because of their religion, had by the late nine-

teenth century developed a number of higher-education opportunities in institutions founded by different orders, including the University of Notre Dame and DePaul University. The commitment to make extra efforts to include diverse students in midwestern higher education was affirmed by the University of Michigan's 2003 Supreme Court case on affirmative action.

The educational opportunities available to midwestern multicultural students of all ages have expanded since the early nineteenth century. Although minority ethnic and cultural groups were originally excluded from standard public schooling, they demonstrated remarkable resilience in their struggles for education. Some communities, such as the Chinese, Native American, African American and Mexican American, were relegated to segregated schools. Over time, those groups fought successfully to be included in mainstream public education and to continue their own locally controlled schooling that fostered their cultural identity. Religious minorities, such as the Amish, Lutherans, and Catholics, had from the beginning set up their own systems of educational programming to protect their personal religious and cultural traditions.

The underside to cultural cohesion is forced segregation, and the legal challenge to racially segregated schools originated in the Midwest with the 1954 Supreme Court decision in *Brown v. Board of Education*. The *Brown* decision in no way settled the problem of racial segregation in schools, and midwestern cities have been the site of some of the most complicated legal cases over continued racial segregation. Chicago; Milwaukee, Wisconsin; and Cleveland and Dayton, Ohio, among others, still struggle with racial equity issues and have adopted a variety of policy initiatives, including magnet and charter schools and voucher programs, in attempts to mediate ongoing residential segregation and economic inequality between white and multicultural groups.

Midwestern educational history, then, is far more dynamic and contentious than the popular iconography of the little red schoolhouse would have it. Across all educational levels, midwestern education has been marked by two often opposing forces: independence and community. A passion for independent institutions was fostered by those pioneers who moved west to seek religious, cultural, and economic freedom. Independent farmers on isolated prairies sought to control their own school districts; religious minorities sought to create their own school systems; and refugees from the slaveholding South and other oppressive societies sought to create their own havens for independent learning. The strong tradition of independence from a standard system continued in the early twentieth century progressive movements for innovative curriculum and in contemporary policies for local control of schooling.

Simultaneously, midwestern education has been marked by an emphasis on building community—whether that be a collection of farm families, the residents of a newly formed village, or a mixed group of immigrants in cities. Central to the midwestern vision of education has been the importance of civic education, work values, and community responsibility. Localism, after all, can be seen both as isolation from other communities and as a commitment to building a cohesive community. The vibrancy of universities; the dynamic developments of elementary and secondary curriculum; and the tensions raised by multiculturalism, progressivism, political reform, and urban-rural conflict retain the common theme of a struggle to nurture different types of social and cultural communities in the American Midwest.

Sources and Further Reading: Mary Hurlbut Cordier, *Schoolwomen of the Prairies and Plains: Personal Narratives from Iowa, Kansas, and Nebraska, 1860s–1920s* (1992); Lawrence A. Cremin, *The Transformation of the School: Progressivism in American Education, 1876–1957* (1971); Wayne E. Fuller, *The Old Country School: The Story of Rural Education in the Middle West* (1982); Roger L. Geiger, ed., *The American College in the Nineteenth Century* (2000); Michael W. Homel, *Down from Equality: Black Chicagoans and the Public Schools, 1929–1941* (1984); Paul H. Mattingly and Edward W. Stevens, Jr., eds., *"Schools and the Means of Education Shall Forever Be Encouraged": A History of Education in the Old Northwest, 1787–1880* (1987); Robert McCaul, *The Black Struggle for Public Schooling in Nineteenth-Century Illinois* (1987); Christine A. Ogren, "Where Coeds Were Coeducated: Normal Schools in Wisconsin, 1870–1920," *History of Education Quarterly* 35 (Spring 1995); Timothy L. Smith and Donald E. Pitzer, *The History of Education in the Middle West* (1978); David B. Tyack, *The One Best System: A History of American Urban Education* (1974); Wayne Urban and Jennings Wagoner, Jr., *American Education: A History* (2004).

Kate Rousmaniere
Miami University, Oxford, Ohio

Rural Education

One reason why the one-room schoolhouse has remained such a prominent symbol of life in the rural Midwest is that states in the region developed as Americans in general were gradually coming to terms with the notion of free, tax-supported, common schools. Because most trans-Mississippi states established free school systems upon achieving statehood and older states gradually adopted free school systems during the 1840s and 1850s, two unprecedented dynamics were playing out at roughly the same time. First, the Midwest became the laboratory for implementing the separation of church and state (the East Coast states had a long history with established churches), and, second, the Midwest struggled with the creation of free school systems.

These two developments were symbiotic. The

Students at a public school in Oxford, Ohio, c. 1910. Courtesy Smith Library of Regional History, Oxford, Ohio.

Midwest, and to a lesser degree the trans-Appalachian South, represented a potential harvest of souls for established religious denominations. Pietistic religious groups, especially the Methodists and Baptists, made huge inroads in these areas. By 1840 these previously quite small religious groups had become the largest denominations in the country, thanks to their rapid growth in the Midwest and the South.

Unlike the South, however, the Midwest struggled to establish free schools along with free churches. This proved to be a contentious undertaking. Calvinist denominations, mainly Presbyterians and Congregationalists, sought to provide leadership for the quickly spreading common-school concept. In fact, most of the Midwest's first state school officers were Calvinist clerics. The prospect of their taking control of school curriculum did not please many rural folk. As a consequence, free state school systems headed by Calvinist clerics were often resisted fiercely by Methodists and Baptists, who enjoyed a numerical majority.

One Methodist legislator in Indiana was so disenchanted at the prospect of a state school system run by Calvinists that he boldly proclaimed that he wanted etched into his gravestone "Here lies an enemy of free schools." Faced with this kind of hostility in the Hoosier state, the Reverend Caleb Mills wrote concerning his successor as Indiana's chief state school officer, "Let him be elected by popular vote, or appointed by Executive authority, or chosen by joint ballot of the Legislature, the question would be immediately asked by thousands, not is he qualified, but is he Presbyterian?"

In the end, although state school systems were established, rural and small town residents insisted on a great deal of local control. This local-control ethic has lingered in the region and, consequently, rural school consolidation and other state education department initiatives have often been strenuously, and successfully, resisted. In the post–Civil War South, by contrast, Northerners established state school systems that developed considerable power, allowing less local control than in the Midwest.

As midwestern states adopted the common-school concept, rural dwellers gradually formed school "districts." Criteria for the creation of districts varied from state to state, but it often required little more than a petition signed by the majority of residents in a particular vicinity, asking to be declared a school district complete with the power to levy a school tax. Once this request was granted, an election was held to determine three school board officers, usually a president, a clerk, and a treasurer. The board, together with the taxpaying residents of the new district (those who owned property), then began to plan for the construction of a schoolhouse large enough for the chil-

dren in the new district. Each year the board had to attend to such matters as maintaining the schoolhouse; supplying fuel and instructional materials (such as maps, globes, and school desks); and hiring the teacher. Supplying textbooks was a pivotal school board duty as early as the 1880s and 1890s in many states west of the Mississippi. Older areas dismissed the call for free textbooks (that is, shifting the burden of supplying books from individual families to the school board) until well into the 1900s and 1910s.

Because of loose criteria, school districts often assumed unusual geographic configurations. As residents moved in and out of the district, these boundaries frequently caused hard feelings because many families found themselves closer to the school in a neighboring district than they were to their own. One of the duties of the county superintendent of schools was to field requests by families to join another school district. If their attempts to locate their farms in another school district failed, parents could still petition the neighboring school board asking that their children be admitted as "outside scholars." These requests were so common that almost every rural school board had to determine a policy stating whether it would admit outside scholars free, with a tuition charge, or not at all.

Rural students studied from textbooks that were often passed down from older siblings to younger ones and sometimes even further, from parents or even grandparents to their children and grandchildren. In fact, school textbooks were often considered family heirlooms. In time, the necessity of texts for school became a political issue. Books were expensive and not all families could afford them. The Mandan, North Dakota, *Pioneer* reported in 1873 that "many children throughout the state are kept from schools because of the cost of books." The Farmers Alliance and its Populist political party lobbied for free textbooks in all public schools. Nebraska and other trans-Mississippi midwestern states were among the first to turn this policy into state law.

Although rural schools are often touted as having been bastions of basic education and staunch proponents of the three Rs (reading, 'riting, and 'rithmetic), the reality is that their pupils were inoculated with religious and moral instruction, character-building efforts, and racial-ability assessment. In addition to reading and grammar, many nineteenth- and early-twentieth-century readers also taught children lessons about the deficiencies of Native Americans, blacks, and sometimes Catholic Americans. William Holmes McGuffey, a Presbyterian minister, was the author of the nation's leading nineteenth-century textbook reading series. Through his books McGuffey taught several generations why some families were rich and some were poor, why women properly aspired to household endeavors, why Irish Americans were prone to drink, and why it was almost impossible to civilize American Indians. Interestingly, the McGuffey Readers included such practice spelling words as *Presbyterianism* but never *Methodism* or *Catholicism*.

Textbooks were a requirement for school attendance because so much of the rural school experience was predicated on a form of instruction known as recitation pedagogy. This was a style of teaching and learning that almost exclusively included reading and then reciting literary passages, speeches, poems, geographic lists, science definitions, and mathematical equations from memory. Flawless recitations were a sign that lessons had been mastered. It was not until the first two decades of the twentieth century that this instructional approach began to fall out of favor. Evidence indicates that it lingered much longer in the one-room schools of the Midwest.

It is common today to claim that our summers-off school calendar is a by-product of our agricultural past. Actually, until about the first and second decades of the twentieth century, schooling occurred in two terms: winter and summer. Spring and fall were too work-filled to hold school sessions. Gender dynamics grew out of these circumstances. Male teachers were more common for winter sessions and female teachers for summer sessions until the early twentieth century. During winter sessions, older male students, sometimes well into their twenties, would attend school. School boards thought that it was imperative to have a male teacher to control the older boys during winter session. Older boys were less likely to attend in the summer and thus female teachers were more desirable for these sessions. Because men were paid from 30 to 50 percent more than women, it was difficult for male teachers to find work for summer sessions.

Women gradually came to dominate the ranks of elementary teachers, and they still represent about 80 percent of the nation's total. But it was not until the final days of one-room schools, in the middle of the twentieth century, that married women were employed in any large numbers. Prior to that, most women quit teaching as soon as they married—in part out of local custom and in part because of local marriage bans for women. And there were quite severe restrictions placed on the lives of these unmarried women. In a rural Minnesota district, a female teacher was fired in 1915 for riding down the main street of a small town on the back of a motorcycle with her arms around the man driving it. Another Minnesota teacher was fired in 1918 because she was seen sitting on a hotel bed with a man at a local Halloween party.

As these occurrences suggest, the history of rural education in the Midwest is intimately tied to the values of the local community. One district might close school for three weeks during potato-picking season, while the district nearest it would not. A Wisconsin county superintendent expressed complete exasperation in his diary when he traveled many hours by horse and buggy to observe a distant school. Much to his dismay, when he arrived he discovered that school was not in session because it was a Catholic holiday.

Sometimes Catholic/Protestant dynamics played themselves out around the local school. In Chippewa County, Minnesota, a local district allowed the Women's Christian Temperance Union to use the schoolhouse for its meetings at no charge—until the balance of power on the board shifted in favor of the local Catholics. After that, the temperance group had to pay a rental fee to use the building. In one North Dakota school, Catholics were dismissed at two o'clock on Fridays so that the remaining Lutheran students could have Sunday school.

More often than not, local values included a high tolerance for corporal punishment. Indeed, this classroom management practice was a veritable fixture of the one-room school experience. The 1881 diary of Anna Webber in rural Kansas provides an excellent example. As she took her first teaching position, she confided to her diary that she did not believe in corporal punishment, thinking that it was not a proper way to motivate kids to learn. A few weeks into the term she wrote, "I have no serious difficulties but the mischievous little rascals are into some mischief half the time." A couple of weeks after that episode, she wrote, "I had to keep two scholars after school this evening, and that is not all I did for them, the little rascals." Still later, "I had the pleasure of giving one little chap a whipping."

In a rural district in Minnesota the school board "moved and seconded and carred [*sic*] that the teacher has liberty to use a switch." Another teacher not only possessed the warrant of the board to use the switch, he proudly hung twelve of them from his desk, each of a different thickness to be used depending on the severity of a student's transgression. There are several instances of severe beatings meted out by teachers, though these were generally rare. Still, corporal punishment was a predictable feature of the rural school experience across the Midwest.

With the refinement of the internal combustion engine, rural one-room schools were gradually closed, although a few remain open today. Tractors meant fewer people were needed to work the land, and cars (and buses) meant that families could take their children farther from home to attend school. In some locales there is currently only one school for the entire county. In recent years, however, the wisdom of doing away with rural schools has been called into serious question.

Sources and Further Reading: John Mack Faragher, *Sugar Creek* (1986); Barbara Finkelstein, *Governing the Young* (1989); Wayne E. Fuller, *The Old Country School* (1982); Andrew Gulliford, *America's Country Schools* (1984); David R. Reynolds, *There Goes the Neighborhood* (1999); Paul Theobald, *Call School* (1995); Paul Theobald, "Country School Curriculum and Governance," *American Journal of Education* 101 (Feb. 1993); Paul Theobald, "The Role of the Common School Concept in the Religious Crusade for the West," *Journal of Religion and Public Education* 18 (Fall 1991); David B. Tyack, "The Tribe and the Common School" *American Quarterly* 24 (Mar. 1972); David B. Tyack and Elisabeth Hansot, *Managers of Virtue* (1982).

Paul Theobald
Wayne State College, Nebraska

Ronald S. Rochon
University of Wisconsin–La Crosse

Urban Education

Americans tend to believe that urban schools represent the most vexing problems in contemporary education. This is no less true of city schools in the Midwest than in other parts of the United States, and it is especially true of schools in the region's largest metropolitan centers.

Historically, midwestern cities have been centers of innovation in education. But they have also been troubled by funding inequities, segregated schools, and persistent patterns of underachievement among inner-city students. Beginning in the 1980s, however, education became an important dimension of urban revitalization campaigns. This new focus infused energy into efforts to reform what had come to be seen as virtually unresponsive institutions, and led to new hope for the thousands of children who attend them.

Since the late nineteenth century urban schools in the Midwest have benefited from visionary leaders, many of whom came to exert considerable influence on the national stage. Among the most important educational figures of the early years was William T. Harris, who served as superintendent of the St. Louis Schools from 1869 until 1880 and later became U.S. commissioner of education. Harris was one of the first system-building superintendents of his era, but he had many well-known counterparts in other cities of the region. Albert G. Lane was an important leader in Chicago during the 1890s, when the system expanded rapidly in response to booming population growth. During the twentieth century, Frank Cody played a similar role in Detroit, as did Milton Potter in Milwaukee. In each of these cases, the leaders of these districts initiated substantial expansion of their schools'

capacity, establishing comprehensive high schools and municipal colleges and defining professional standards of conduct and accomplishment for school personnel. They led the development of bureaucracy as a characteristic of urban school systems, and they distanced the schools from the problems that characterized city politics.

The turn of the twentieth century was a colorful era of education reform. Figures such as Samuel "Golden Rule" Jones in Toledo, Ohio, and Victor Berger in Milwaukee, Wisconsin, made improvement of the schools an important element of their populist and Socialist urban-betterment regimes. Progressive education innovations, such as "vacation schools," vocational programs in the high schools, and field trips to community institutions, also became commonplace. The schools of Gary, Indiana, became world famous due to Superintendent William Wirt's "platoon system" for organizing daily activities in each school, rotating children between regular classes and a wide range of extracurricular activities. In nearby Chicago, progressive educators Francis W. Parker and John Dewey exerted considerable influence, and in 1909 their friend Ella Flagg Young became one of the first women to serve as superintendent of a major urban school district. The rapidly expanding Midwest urban schools were leaders in innovation.

Beginning in the 1920s, many of the region's city school systems entered into a prolonged period of stability in leadership and organizational character, cementing what in certain respects was a golden age of urban education. As the population base of the larger cities leveled off, educators became less preoccupied with continuing expansion and focused instead on gradual improvements in the quality of education, especially expanding access to secondary and higher education. It was an era characterized by high levels of public confidence in the schools, as the bureaucratic rules and standards established in the earlier period helped to ensure wide access to the schools and at least the perception of equity in the outcomes. Despite financial hardships during the Great Depression of the 1930s, public support remained high.

As larger numbers of youths graduated from high school, approaching 50 percent by 1950, the education system came to be seen as a vital engine of economic development, providing opportunities for advancement to children from all segments of the population. At the same time, many schools were still viewed as neighborhood institutions, and teachers and administrators who worked in them over the years came to assume an endearing familiarity. Large numbers of local women and men took positions as educators, deepening ties between the schools and the cities' various communities. It was a time of considerable consensus about the purposes of public education and widespread public confidence in the Midwest's urban schools.

This situation began to change dramatically during the period following World War II. It was in these years that a grand migration to suburbia started in most of the region's largest cities. Pressured by severe housing shortages in the central cities, and encouraged by public policies that stimulated road building and guaranteed cheap private transportation, city residents began flocking to new suburban developments on the fringes of urban areas. These migrants were disproportionately young, middle class, and upwardly mobile. They also were overwhelmingly white, partly because of discrimination that discouraged blacks from buying homes in suburban areas. And as whites moved to suburbia, the populations of the central cities became older, poorer, and darker.

Because of this process, the proportion of central-city populations that was white diminished each decade after 1950. African Americans migrated from the South in large numbers in the middle of the twentieth century and constituted nearly 40 percent of the overall population in the Midwest's ten largest cities by 1980. Immigration also led to a significant increase in the number of Hispanics after 1970 in Chicago, Detroit, and other cities. Poverty levels increased significantly among all groups of city residents in the closing decades of the twentieth century, and particularly among African Americans. In Chicago, some 11 percent of central-city residents and 18 percent of central-city blacks were poor in the mid-1970s; by 1990 the figures had jumped to almost 20 percent and 34 percent, respectively.

This process had an almost immediate impact. Schools serving areas with large concentrations of poor, minority students generally were highly segregated. As a rule, they exhibited a host of problems, including lower attendance, more discipline issues, and higher teacher turnover. Academic achievement was also sharply lower in these schools.

Beginning in the 1950s, questions of racial equity became major policy issues facing urban school districts in the Midwest. Led by civil rights groups such as the National Association for the Advancement of Colored People (NAACP), protests focused on the poor quality of inner-city schools. Racial segregation and inequity became important issues, and midwestern cities were in the forefront of these controversies. In *Brown v. Board of Education*, the U.S. Supreme Court ruled in 1954 that laws requiring the segregation of public schools were unconstitutional, setting in motion a massive campaign to desegregate schools across the country. Schools in Topeka, Kansas, were formally integrated, as were their counterparts in Kansas City and St. Louis, Missouri, as well as a number of other midwestern cities.

Eventually, conflict over desegregation and equity spread to most major metropolitan areas in the region, even those where legally mandated segregation did not exist. In some cities these disputes led to legal challenges to local school district policies and, eventually, court-mandated desegregation plans. Cleveland, Ohio; Detroit; Milwaukee; and Minneapolis, Minnesota, struggled with this general pattern of events in the 1960s and 1970s along with a number of other cities. The impact of these developments was decisive. By the early 1970s, white students were less than half of all students in most big-city school systems. By 1980 whites represented fewer than one in five students in the region's largest public school systems. Despite desegregation plans, schools remained highly segregated, closely mirroring patterns of residential segregation in urban areas across the region. In general, the region's urban schools were marked by high levels of racial and ethnic isolation and significant disparities in educational outcomes from the 1960s onward.

Chicago illustrated these trends, even though it did not receive a court-mandated desegregation plan until 1980. Non-Hispanic whites constituted less than 20 percent of students in the city's public schools at that time, and in 1990 they were barely 10 percent. This made meaningful integration, particularly in the system's large high schools, a virtual impossibility. The story elsewhere was similar. By 1973 the landmark *Millikan* decision, focusing on a sweeping desegregation plan in Detroit, had foreclosed the possibility of judicially mandated desegregation plans across urban-suburban district lines. As a result, the racial profile of schools on either side of big-city district lines became increasingly stark. By the end of the century a small minority of urban public school students were white, an even smaller—though growing—portion of suburban students were black, and the prospects for change were minimal.

It was in the 1980s, however, that the most recent manifestations of school reform first became evident. They have taken a variety of forms. In 1987 Mayor Harold Washington of Chicago called an education summit of the city's various education, business, and community groups to discuss ways of reforming the public schools. The meeting led to a sweeping package of reform legislation creating local school councils controlled by voting parents and breathing new life into urban education. With new resources pledged by the state legislature, schools began to improve. A second round of reform measures was adopted by Mayor Richard M. Daley in 1995, increasing Chicago's commitment to improving the schools. Before long,

Chicago-style school reforms were being implemented, to one degree or another, in other big cities. Following the leadership of Mayor Dennis Archer, Detroit elected a new school board dedicated to improving the schools—and then voted the board out just a few years later. Despite improvements, significant problems remain.

Other cities have taken different routes to reform. Minneapolis has focused on working closely with teachers to foster greater professionalism and higher student achievement. In Milwaukee, an experimental voucher plan was launched with state assistance, and improvements were made to the city's public schools. A similar plan was started in Cleveland and met legal challenges. The constitutionality of these and other voucher programs was upheld by the U.S. Supreme Court in 2002. Both of these programs drew national attention but involved relatively small numbers of students. They have been credited with stimulating progress in the public schools of each city, although these institutions continue to lag behind their suburban counterparts. By and large, the two voucher programs have not led to dramatic improvements in student achievement. In other cities the political will to organize sustained campaigns over school reform has seemed to wax and wane. In certain places, such as St. Louis, protracted legal battles over desegregation continued into the 1990s, sapping civic resolve to focus effort and resources on improving the city's schools.

Today, urban schools in the Midwest exhibit many of the problems associated with big-city education systems across the country. Saddled with disproportionate numbers of poor and minority students, often beset with a weakened tax base and facing declining public confidence in the wake of political battles of the 1960s and 1970s, school districts have responded creatively. Chicago has represented one strategy of reform, with Detroit and other cities following its lead. Milwaukee and Cleveland have charted a different path to reform, but even the controversial voucher plans led to improved public support for the public schools in some instances. Creative student-exchange programs between urban and suburban schools have existed on a small scale in St. Louis and Milwaukee for many years, and expanding such initiatives may be a way to stimulate even more telling advances in the years ahead. The challenges to urban schools are manifold, and it will require all of the inventiveness and resources of the next generation of educators to overcome them.

Sources and Further Reading: Ronald D. Cohen, *Children of the Mill* (1990); Mary J. Herrick, *The Chicago Schools* (1971); Jeffrey E. Mirel, *The Rise and Fall of an Urban School System* (1993); William J. Reese, *Power and the Promise of School Re-* *form* (1986); John L. Rury, ed., *Urban Education in the United States: A Historical Reader* (2005); John L. Rury and Frank A. Cassell, eds., *Seeds of Crisis* (1993); Jon C. Teaford, *Cities of the Heartland* (1993); Mary Vander Weele, *Reclaiming Our Schools* (1994); Amy Stuart Wells and Robert L. Crain, *Stepping over the Color Line* (1997).

John Rury
University of Kansas

Intellectualism

From the 1820s through the 1960s, the guiding ideas of the midwestern educational establishment passed through three stages. First, from the 1820s to the 1890s, the midwestern academy founded its institutions upon the development of a particular regional culture. Second, between the 1890s and the 1920s, midwestern academics sought and achieved considerable national influence. Third, building on their intellectual legacy, midwesterners subtly shaped post–World War II technological inquiry and innovation.

In the first stage, a largely Protestant, middle-class culture that disliked hierarchy and promoted local autonomy underlay the structure of higher education. As egalitarian, production-minded, and future-oriented people shaped the curriculum and the students of midwestern higher education, manual labor programs and coeducation demonstrated the distinct forging of a regional intellectualism in the midwestern academy. During the second stage, this intellectualism, embracing the natural sciences, brought about a high production of scientists in the late nineteenth and early twentieth centuries, the same period when the midwestern academy flowered. Finally, this regionally specific intellectualism contributed to the development of the Silicon Valley high-technology center of northern California, a place that owed its distinct corporate culture to midwestern experiences and ideas.

In the early to mid-1800s, a college-educated, elite class often had less to do with planting midwestern colleges than farmers, town promoters, and local ministers. The resulting variety of supporters, localities, and religious ideas within the decentralized structure of midwestern higher education shaped the region's intellectualism. Most midwestern state legislatures freely gave college charters to individuals and religious groups. This pattern contrasted with the East and the South, where less denominational diversity and the colonial legacy of established, state-supported churches slowed college construction. In the Midwest, native midwesterners along with people from the mid-Atlantic, southern, and New England states served as college founders, presidents, and professors. They created a variegated landscape of higher education with much local autonomy and experimentation.

This intellectual climate led to a regionally specific curriculum and student population. During the late 1820s and the 1830s, a manual labor movement spread nationally through American higher education. Borrowing from European educational theorists, Americans in all regions adapted manual labor programs to schools and colleges so that students could engage in productive efforts and defray their education costs. Manual labor students primarily worked a few hours each day on school farms; they also staffed print shops and made barrels and brooms. Supporters believed that manual labor programs would build moral character, bind together future leaders and laborers, provide useful exercise leading to sound health, and teach students a manual trade from which they could benefit after graduation.

By 1840, however, most schools outside the Midwest had abandoned manual labor, often in favor of gymnastics or military drills. New England collegiate leaders, dedicated to a classical curriculum, had never fully embraced the program. Elite southern college students, who associated manual labor with a degraded class status and even enslavement, sabotaged their programs in some instances, breaking tools or refusing to work. When sponsors realized that manual labor was a financial drain rather than a boon, they jettisoned the programs.

In the Midwest, though, while college administrators knew that these programs were unprofitable, their interest in and sustained commitment to manual labor underscored a belief in democratic access to education, a desire to erase class distinctions, and the goal of useful, forward-looking lessons. Midwestern schools held on to their programs and even began new ones after 1840. In the 1850s, the United Brethren in Christ instituted manual labor at Otterbein College in Ohio and Western College in Iowa to help poor students and keep their college students closely tied to the largely agricultural denominational members. The manual labor movement of the early and mid-nineteenth century segued into scientific agriculture programs at land-grant universities in the later 1800s.

These manual labor programs represented a revolt against the dominant northeastern U.S. classical curriculum, best characterized by the Yale Report of 1828, which defended traditional intellectual training that taught "the *discipline* and the *furniture* of the mind." Many midwesterners instead favored the "physical, intellectual, and moral" education of the whole person. Midwesterners were more interested in planning the future than in honoring the past glories of the Greeks and Romans. Beyond manual labor, midwestern deviations from the classical curriculum included annual re-

ligious revivals that displaced course work, the replacement of Latin language study with biblical Hebrew, and, of crucial importance, an emphasis on the natural sciences, a result of sexual coeducation.

Coeducation at the collegiate level, with significant intellectual ramifications, not only began in the Midwest, it became a regional norm. By 1860 two dozen midwestern colleges (and a few in upstate New York and western Pennsylvania) were admitting women alongside men, while no coeducational colleges existed in New England or the South. In the late nineteenth century, coeducation was still most likely to appear in the Midwest, in both private and public higher education. Of the first eight state universities to admit women by 1870, seven were midwestern. The first fully coeducational modern research university was the University of Chicago, founded in 1890. Overall, from the denominational college to the state university to the research university, midwesterners consistently embraced collegiate coeducation. Often, the farmers and townspeople who founded these colleges were Methodists or members of rural or marginal religious groups that appealed particularly to the middle classes. These founders were unconcerned about European educational traditions and the exclusivity of their educational institutions. They were comfortable with letting men and women, who worked together on farms and in households, learn together in classrooms.

Because women's education in the late eighteenth and early nineteenth centuries moved away from the classical curriculum found in many men-only schools and emphasized the natural sciences instead, when midwestern college leaders embraced coeducation, they also diminished the classical curriculum and enhanced their science offerings. As the natural sciences became pronounced at coeducational colleges, other schools followed suit; even at all-male midwestern schools, the scientific curriculum gathered steam.

The long-range significance of these curricular changes became apparent in 1952 when R. H. Knapp and H. B. Goodrich investigated the baccalaureate provenance of eighteen thousand American scientists to discover what institutions produced, as a percentage of their alumni, the most graduates who went on to receive a doctorate in science. The authors found that during the late nineteenth and early twentieth centuries, the top scientist-producing schools were mostly small liberal-arts colleges clustered heavily in the Midwest and started or operated by Protestant denominations such as Methodists, Presbyterians, Dutch Reformed, Quakers, Norwegian Lutherans, Mennonites, and the Disciples of Christ.

The intellectualism of the academy in the Midwest that fostered manual labor and coeducation in the early and mid-nineteenth century led directly to the emphasis on the natural sciences and the production of scientists. The values that underlay these patterns—practicality, productivity, egalitarianism—defined that intellectualism. The early-nineteenth-century midwestern society that wanted college graduates to know manual labor from experience evolved into a society that did not mind if college graduates took jobs that involved getting their hands dirty. Students at midwestern colleges, Knapp and Goodrich concluded, generally came from middle-class families that perceived the vocation of scientist as a useful, worthwhile occupation with a sufficiently high class status, while eastern college students from more elite backgrounds considered the scientist's class status socially regressive. Eastern colleges offered sound scientific instruction but had fewer students interested in becoming scientists.

This production of scientists from small colleges occurred at the same time that midwestern universities were at the height of their influence. The apex of midwestern intellectual culture occurred from the 1890s through the 1920s, when many of the brightest academic minds influenced national discourse. Charles Beard, Carl Becker, Vernon Parrington, Arthur Schlesinger, and Frederick Jackson Turner dominated the field of history. Economics professor Thorstein Veblen, a Wisconsin native who grew up in Minnesota, offered trenchant social criticism as he challenged dominant classical economic theories. John Dewey, Veblen's one-time colleague, first experimented with his revolutionary ideas about education while working at the Universities of Michigan and Chicago.

One of the more important and surprising influences of this regional propensity for the production of scientists was Robert Noyce's influence on the work culture of Silicon Valley. In the 1940s Noyce was a Grinnell College (Iowa) physics major taught by Grant Gale. Gale, a Wisconsin native, had contacted his boyhood friend John Bardeen, a Bell Laboratories engineer who cocreated the transistor. Bardeen sent Gale some transistors, and Noyce was a party to the first academic instruction in the world involving transistors as a rural Iowa undergraduate in 1948. When Noyce entered the Massachusetts Institute of Technology for graduate work that fall, his new professors knew nothing about transistor technology. Noyce continued his work with transistors and, in 1959, created the first integrated circuit, or microchip, on silicon.

During his years with Fairchild Semiconductor and, after 1968, the Intel Corporation he cofounded, Noyce helped to create a work culture in Silicon Valley that differed drastically from the East Coast corporate system of privilege, seniority, and hierarchy. Noyce based his corporate culture on a midwestern small-town emphasis on social equality, non-ostentation, hard work, and a Congregational model that emphasized local control. (Grinnell and the Noyce family were Congregationalists.) In Tom Wolfe's words, "Not only would there be no limousines and chauffeurs, there would not even be any reserved parking places." Noyce's workplace, democratic and decentralized, prized experimentation and innovation. Noyce matured in a midwestern culture that valued these traits. He then transported this regional intellectualism to the West. The result was not just new technology, but a new place in the American mental landscape.

A regional ethos stamped midwestern intellectual academic culture. An early focus on values and norms supporting manual labor programs and coeducation promoted the study of the natural sciences and the emergence of scientists in the late nineteenth and early twentieth centuries. Today, midwestern intellectuals continue to shape ideas and institutions well beyond the bounds of the region.

Sources and Further Reading: Leslie R. Berlin, "Robert Noyce and Fairchild Semiconductor, 1957–1968," *Business History Review* 75 (Spring 2001); Richard Hofstadter and Wilson Smith, eds., *American Higher Education* (1961); R. H. Knapp and H. B. Goodrich, *Origins of American Scientists* (1952); Doris Jeanne Malkmus, "Capable Women and Refined Ladies: Two Visions of American Women's Higher Education, 1760–1861," Ph.D. diss., University of Iowa (2001); Earle D. Ross, "The Manual Labor Experiment in the Land Grant College," *Mississippi Valley Historical Review* 21 (Mar. 1935); Timothy L. Smith, *Uncommon Schools* (1978); Kenneth H. Wheeler, "The Antebellum College in the Old Northwest: Higher Education and the Defining of the Midwest," Ph.D. diss., The Ohio State University (1999); Tom Wolfe, "Two Young Men Who Went West," in Tom Wolfe, *Hooking Up* (2000).

Kenneth H. Wheeler
Reinhardt College, Georgia

Social Movements

Throughout the nineteenth and twentieth centuries, the Midwest nurtured a multitude of social movements, many of which, while varying in their membership, goals, and tactics, shared a belief in education as a means to bring about social change. Organizations and associations affiliated with the labor movement, the social settlement movement, temperance, agricultural reform, progressivism, and the women's club movement used both informal and formal education to further their causes. These movements turned to education in three significant ways. Through participation in social reform, members acquired new skills, learned a new consciousness that shaped political and social identities, and sought to educate the public. Social educational activism in the Midwest resulted from a combination of democratic beliefs, a dominant ideology of social reform Christianity, and a tradition of local and personal independence.

Much of the social reform grew out of the larger progressive movement of the early twentieth century. Using science, education, and regulation to improve the lives of Americans, progressivism challenged laissez-faire government and sought to revitalize democracy. Progressives acted on a belief in positive environmentalism, which posited the idea that environment, not innate character, shaped a person's moral behavior. Their varied agendas maintained a common thread: a firm belief in education as a means to bring about social change. Recognizing the mass media and other publicity tactics as valuable educational tools, progressives sought to shape public opinion to support their goals.

These progressive social agendas were intricately linked with the progressive education movement, which supported child-centered education and other pedagogical innovations. Both social reformers and school reformers saw education as central to a democratic social movement. Progressive education experiments at John and Alice Dewey's laboratory school at the University of Chicago and Francis W. Parker's Chicago Normal School rested on the belief that new ways of learning would serve to create a community in which children grow up to be active political participants. Extending beyond the responsibility of voting, political participation would include deliberation over the definition of the public good, efforts to form government policy, and communal inquiry into social problems. In Winnetka, Illinois, in the early 1920s, administrators and teachers developed a highly successful progressive education that engaged students in individualized learning and an intensive study of community life through participation in self-government, organized clubs, and a labor union. Such curricula led students to engage broader questions of social organization. Teachers in progressive schools in Winnetka also shared power with administrators as they conducted investigation in their own classrooms, collectively determined schoolwide needs, and debated school curriculum and policy.

Other midwestern social movements drew closely on progressive educational ideas. The settlement-house movement was the most notable of these. The first settlement house was founded in New York in 1886, but the most famous, Hull-House, opened in Chicago in 1889. Some settlements were religiously oriented, while others, such as the Northwestern University Settlement, were sponsored by universities. Though their agendas varied, all sought to address problems of urban industrialism and immigration through both formal and indirect education. The settlements offered study groups in topics as wide ranging as English literature and labor matters. They served as a location for college extension courses and as a force of Americanization through English-language and housekeeping classes for recent immigrants. Through informal education, the movement also sought to break down barriers between middle-class residents and their neighbors. In so doing, they helped to teach the former about the problems of urban industrial life and the traditions of their immigrant neighbors. The majority of settlement workers were women, and the movement proved instrumental in teaching them new political skills and identity that had far-reaching consequences. As residents learned about their poor and ethnic working-class neighbors, they began to lobby for child-labor and social-insurance legislation. Their successes played a significant role in the transition to the welfare state.

The women's club movement also played an important role in moving women from the domestic sphere into the public world of political activism. The club movement was strong in cities, growing out of literary clubs established after the Civil War. The Wednesday Club in St. Louis; the Chicago Women's Club; the Atheneum in Kansas City, Missouri; and the Wednesday Afternoon Club in Milwaukee, Wisconsin, began as clubs devoted to the study of literary works but soon expanded their interests to include current social questions.

One important goal of the clubs was to educate women for public life. Members learned public-speaking skills as well as parliamentary procedure and business practices, which served them well as they moved into civic and political associations with men. They increasingly used their resources to educate the public about social causes such as child labor, smoke abatement, and kindergartens. Though they shared an ideology of domestic feminism, clubs varied in the extent to which they supported full suffrage for women. Nonetheless, club life helped women to perceive themselves as active political participants, and many club members went on to support the suffrage movement. Once women's suffrage was attained nationally with the ratification of the 19th amendment to the U.S. Constitution in 1920, women's clubs helped to educate women in the practical details of their new right. In Chicago, the interracial Alpha Suffrage Club distributed lists of candidates, made recommendations, circulated directories of voting locations, and instructed women how to use the voting machine. The club also sponsored speakers, and frequently candidates appeared to outline their platforms.

The Women's Christian Temperance Union (WCTU) was also based on public education—about alcohol. Beginning in Ohio in 1873, the Women's Crusade against saloons and their patrons spread throughout the region, giving rise to the Women's Christian Temperance Union; eventually it became the largest national organizer of women in the nineteenth century. Though it enjoyed its greatest successes in small towns, the WCTU was popular in rural areas and cities alike. Initially using evangelical tactics of prayer and moral suasion, the WCTU adopted an educational agenda to spread its message about the dangers of alcohol to home life. Lacking the ballot, women relied on education through mass meetings and other publicity tactics. They distributed literature and contributed temperance columns to local newspapers. State chapters of the WCTU also published their own papers, such as the *Signal* in Illinois, the *Alliance* in Ohio, and the nationwide *Union Signal*. In addition to educating the public about temperance matters, the organization also served as an educational forum for many women who had little experience in public life. It helped women to form a collective identity around the need to protect their homes from the dangers of saloons and alcoholism. Gaining public-speaking skills and experience in the business of organizing, women in local chapters and the national association soon began to move their agenda of home protection into politics. Their WCTU experiences taught many women about the necessity for women's suffrage to protect their homes, their children, and their communities effectively.

The organized labor movement had a similar strategy of educating workers, particularly with the goal of mobilizing them, and the general public. Through newspapers sponsored by national unions and local papers published by labor activists, workers learned about political issues and union activities in other regions; shared experiences and opinions on a variety of matters related to labor relations and politics; and read book reviews and commentary by labor leaders, academics, and political figures. Prominent national papers were located in the Midwest, including the *Firemen's Magazine*, the official publication of the Brotherhood of Locomotive Firemen based in Terre Haute, Indiana, and the nation's largest circulating Socialist paper, the *Appeal*, based in Girard, Kansas. Union organizing offered further education in practical matters like recruitment, finances, and negotiation and grievance procedures. During strikes workers' identity deepened as they gained increased awareness of labor issues, cooperatively challenged management,

and provided material and moral support to fellow strikers.

The labor movement also established more formal educational programs and institutions. It distributed leaflets, pamphlets, and books, particularly with the help of Indiana-born Julius Wayland's Socialist press, which commissioned and published in 1905 the original edition of Upton Sinclair's *The Jungle*, a fictional exposé of working conditions in the Chicago meatpacking industry. Unions and working-people's organizations sponsored lyceums and discussions as well as formal classes. Socialists in Chicago, Milwaukee, St. Louis, and other midwestern cities opened Sunday schools to educate their children about Socialist principles and the problems of capitalism. The National Women's Trade Union League opened the Training School for Women Organizers. Established in Chicago in 1914, it was the first full-time national labor program in the country. In Duluth, Minnesota, Finnish workers created Work People's College, an institution devoted to training radical editors, teachers, and agitators. Supported in its early years by Socialists, it later was patronized by the International Workers of the World, which had a strong presence in the midwestern agriculture and lumber industries.

Because farming has figured prominently in the midwestern economy, it is not surprising that agricultural reform movements have been strong in the region. Founded in 1867, the Patrons of Husbandry, popularly known as the Grange, was established as a social and educational organization. With membership and leadership strongest in the Midwest, the Grange and, later, the Farmers' Alliance provided education in the economics of agriculture. These organizations sponsored cooperatives, and farmers gained significant knowledge of and experience in cash and credit systems; marketing, purchasing, and production; and the significance of legislation to their livelihood. They also served political ends by pressuring state and federal governments to be more responsive to farmers' educational needs. Through newspapers, bulletins, and annual meetings, farm families shared knowledge and sought to overcome their social isolation. These organizations helped farmers to realize that their personal troubles were public issues, leading many into political activism.

The Grange and the Farmers' Alliance worked to make practical scientific knowledge available to farmers. Agricultural and mechanical colleges, supported by the 1862 Morrill Land-Grant Act, by the 1880s operated experiment stations that responded to farmers' demands that land-grant colleges offer concrete information and pragmatic advice. Pressures from state farmers' organizations forced state universities in Wisconsin and Minnesota to redesign their programs.

Consequently, land-grant universities and the U.S. Department of Agriculture (USDA) sponsored farmers' institutes—public meetings of several days' length where academics, bureaucrats, and respected farmers and teachers gave talks, mounted exhibits, and led discussions. Such pressures led to the Smith-Lever Agricultural Extension Act in 1914. This act built on the popularity of the institutes by encouraging the formal organization of outreach activities in land-grant colleges throughout the Midwest and in the USDA.

Though reform movements in the Midwest generally used education to further their goals, rural and urban reformers clashed over the agendas of some social movements. In the early twentieth century, an effort spearheaded by urban progressive leaders sought to revitalize what they perceived as an ailing rural society. The country life movement sought to create new institutions that would recognize the distinctive nature of agrarian life and provide the resources and infrastructure required to help farmers modernize their practices. At the heart of the movement was a commitment to agricultural education at the elementary and high school levels and to rural school consolidation. While urban progressives viewed these changes as necessary to ensure that agricultural regions remained productive and attractive to youth, who were fleeing the countryside in search of greater opportunities, farmers were more skeptical. Desiring to preserve local control of their one-room schoolhouses, farmers in Iowa attacked consolidation efforts, and only six states adopted agricultural curricula. Farmers maintained that agricultural education would limit their children's opportunities to choose their own livelihoods.

The range of issues and diversity of membership in various reform movements, like the country life movement, illustrates the heterogeneity of the region and its people. The central role of education methods in these movements suggests their commitment to a long American tradition of using education to achieve social change.

Sources and Further Reading: Jane Addams, *Twenty Years at Hull-House* (1990); Richard J. Altenbaugh, *Education for Struggle* (1990); Ruth Bordin, *Woman and Temperance* (1981); Lawrence Cremin, *American Education: The Metropolitan Experience, 1876–1980* (1988); Lawrence Cremin, *The Transformation of the School* (1961); Anne Ruggles Gere, *Intimate Practices* (1997); Arthur S. Link and Richard L. McCormick, *Progressivism* (1983); Donald B. Marti, *Women of the Grange* (1991); David R. Reynolds, *There Goes the Neighborhood* (1999); Anne Firor Scott, *Natural Allies* (1991).

Laura Westhoff
University of Missouri–St. Louis

Higher Education

Because the first American colleges were in the original British colonies, most histories of higher education depict important educational developments as beginning in the East and then moving west. The Midwest, however, spawned several important innovations and movements within higher education that spread outward to other regions. Some firsts in the Midwest include racially integrated colleges; coeducation; interuniversity organized athletics (the "Big Ten"); the flourishing of public higher education; the introduction of "service" to the now tripartite mission of universities (teaching, research, and service); the origins of student affairs; and the first community college.

Many town founders desired a college to help boost their new community and to further a Christian influence. The various denominations had an interest in founding colleges for training the clergy and influencing the community. Between 1800 and 1820, the number of new colleges was small, but after 1820 the number of denominational colleges exploded, and a significant number of them were in the Midwest. Ohio was an especially popular locale because of its religious

The Administration Building (Old Capitol) at the University of Iowa. Kent Photo Collection, Special Collections Department, University of Iowa Libraries, Iowa City, Iowa.

diversity and geographic centrality. Although these small colleges were founded by particular denominations, most were not rigid, sectarian institutions. The president was most likely a minister of the founding church, but few required that all faculty and students be of that faith.

In the decades before the Civil War, the changing needs of a growing nation and the visions of various educational reformers prompted experimentation and gradual change in the college curriculum. While the classical foundation persisted, colleges began instructing students in English and adding more useful or practical subjects. Some liberal arts colleges added a spattering of courses that would be recognized today as engineering, agricultural, and civics education. In addition, a handful of special purpose colleges was founded that focused on agricultural, normal, or "mechanical" (engineering) education. Thus, the multipurpose college began—an institution where students prepared for an increasing variety of adult professions with a combination of liberal arts and practical training.

Individual colleges sometimes had distinctive missions that inspired particular innovations. Two such colleges were Oberlin (founded in 1833) and Antioch (1852) in Ohio. Both were inspired by Christian missionary zeal and abolitionist sentiments. Both institutions admitted African American students and provided the first racially integrated higher education in the United States. They were also the first coeducational colleges in the nation. Although women's education began on the East Coast, inspired in part by the desire to train women for two acceptable professions—teaching and missionary work—the model of educating women and men together began at Oberlin College in 1837.

Today we would call these denominational colleges private institutions. Public higher education has a slightly different history. Under the provisions of the Land Ordinance of 1785 and the Northwest Ordinance of 1787, which mandated the encouragement of "schools and the means of education," the first states created north of the Ohio River established public colleges. Ohio chartered Ohio University in 1804 and Miami University in 1809 while Indiana founded Indiana University in 1820. Prior to the Civil War, most of the early public colleges were small and resembled the private colleges in purpose and mission, and most states were not generous with their resources. However, in 1862 President Abraham Lincoln signed the first Morrill Land-Grant Act, which provided federal dollars to establish public colleges that taught agriculture, mechanics, and military tactics in addition to the established curriculum. Although Morrill funds went to every state, the East remained dominated by private higher education, the defeated South was slow in developing research universities, and the not-yet-settled West was well behind the Midwest, where public higher education became the dominant model.

Morrill funds embellished preexisting state colleges such as the University of Wisconsin, which had been founded in 1848; started brand-new institutions, including Indiana's Purdue University in 1874; and turned former agricultural schools into universities (thus the Agricultural College of the State of Michigan, established in 1855, eventually became Michigan State University). For a variety of reasons, the midwestern states invested in public higher education—not only land-grant colleges but other state institutions (including, for example, both the University of Iowa, founded in 1847 as the State University of Iowa, and the land-grant Iowa State University, created in 1858 as the State Agricultural College and Model Farm) as well as a growing number of normal schools for teacher training. As a result, the midwestern public college became symbolic of democratic higher education—open to all, experimental, and expansive. Collectively, they were commonly dubbed "democracy's colleges." These institutions were generally coeducational, had a few African American students, and remained inexpensive. Yet even as some public institutions grew more prosperous and became more elite, no aspect of American culture more aptly represented the ideal of democratic higher education than the midwestern public college.

The democratic mission of the midwestern university included involvement in the public schools. In the Midwest it became clear that democracy's colleges needed "democracy's high schools." By the 1870s most midwestern states had established public common schools (grades 1–8), but high schools were rare and varied considerably in quality. President James Angell of the University of Michigan established a plan whereby faculty would certify various public high schools if they had acceptable academic standards. In return, the university would admit any graduate of the certified schools. This created statewide standards in high schools and prompted the state to take over supervising secondary education. Variations on this basic idea were instituted in many states. Further, state sponsorship of normal (teacher-training) schools and education departments in state universities complemented such developments by providing teachers and principals for the newly created or newly certified schools.

During the latter half of the nineteenth century a profound transformation occurred in higher education. Some colleges, which emphasized undergraduate education and faculty as teachers, remained colleges, but other institutions developed into universities. Although the criteria for what officially constitutes a university are not concrete, typically the presence of graduate and professional schools and an emphasis on faculty research denote university status. Although research universities were being built in the East, one of the first visionaries of the university movement was Henry Tappan, who was appointed first president of the University of Michigan in 1851. In his 1851 book *University Education*, Tappan outlined his plan to build a university based on the German model. At the heart of this endeavor was hiring faculty members to do research and adding graduate training to the mission of the institution. Unfortunately, the regents of the University of Michigan were not persuaded and Tappan was eventually fired, but during the 1870s Michigan and other state institutions of the Midwest began building large research universities.

Like other progressive Americans at the turn of the twentieth century, midwestern university builders were captivated by the potential and wonder of science, which, it was believed, could cure many social ills. In this milieu, universities occupied a unique niche. As research institutions, they were making discoveries that would improve lives. As graduate institutions, they were preparing the scientists, social workers, doctors, and other expert professionals who would take their knowledge into the community to improve it.

Nowhere was this new mission of universities—to improve the society of which they were part—more developed than at the University of Wisconsin (UW). President Charles Van Hise (1903–1918) is largely credited with institutionalizing the "Wisconsin idea," which suggested that anything of concern to the political, economic, or social well-being of the state of Wisconsin was of concern to the university. This impulse translated into tangible benefits such as cures for cow diseases and ways to measure butterfat in milk, both of which helped to save Wisconsin's dairy industry. There were also UW faculty advising the governor and making social policy. Thus faculty added another element to their role. Now they were teachers, researchers, *and* service providers. Although this movement was best personified at Wisconsin, other universities followed suit as the notion that university-generated knowledge should be useful to society became accepted and even expected.

The growth of universities in the late 1800s inspired fear of the loss of the social cohesiveness associated with smaller campuses. Widespread urbanization and a backlash against women's success at universities and their forays into new social and professional roles created a public concern that American men were becoming soft.

Not coincidentally, intercollegiate sports captured the public's imagination as a remedy to both problems. A student at The Ohio State University might not know all other students, but he or she could rally behind the scarlet-and-gray banners and cheer the Buckeyes. At the same time, the fierce competition and rough nature of sports, especially football, demonstrated the best of American manhood. Although Harvard and Yale are credited with the first intercollegiate competition (a boat race in 1852), interest in athletics grew faster and sports were consuming more energy and resources at midwestern universities by the turn of the twentieth century. The phenomenal growth of sports and various scandals regarding the integrity and safety of football prompted universities in the Midwest to organize the first intercollegiate athletic association—the Intercollegiate Conference of Faculty Representatives, founded in 1895 and eventually known as the Big Ten. Ironically, institutions that had failed at earlier attempts to meet and coordinate on academic matters successfully organized around athletics.

Private universities also grew in the Midwest. Among the most notable was the University of Chicago, founded in 1890 with generous donations from John D. Rockefeller. Its first president was the young and brilliant William Rainey Harper. Harper's skills, which included a knack for enticing accomplished scholars to Chicago, and Rockefeller's money built a strong university in a very short time. Only eight years after opening to students, the university was recognized as one of the twelve best in the country when it became one of the founding members of the Association of American Universities.

Women's professional presence in midwestern higher education was furthered in the early twentieth century at the coeducational University of Chicago. The professions of social work and student affairs flourished, and under the leadership of Marion Talbot, the university's first dean of women, the professional position of dean evolved through a network of other officials around the country. In 1915 Lois K. Mathews of the University of Wisconsin wrote the first book in the profession that eventually became student affairs; it was entitled, *The Dean of Women*.

Community colleges developed out of Harper's concern that his and other universities needed to focus on research, leaving other institutions to concentrate on less academically oriented students. Harper believed that great universities should teach only advanced students and that faculty should concentrate on research and graduate education. Therefore, he wanted freshmen and sophomores to enroll elsewhere before entering the University of Chicago. He reasoned that the less serious students would leave college after earning an associate's degree. Working with a nearby high school, Harper succeeded in creating the first junior college, in Joliet, Illinois (1901). Several of Harper's presidential peers supported the idea of jettisoning freshmen and sophomores, but that strategy proved costly, both in lost revenue and in lost support from community members and state legislatures. Universities retained the model of graduate education in addition to a full four-year undergraduate program, but the idea of junior colleges—as distinct institutions—caught on. The first junior colleges concentrated on the transfer function of preparing students to enter a four-year institution. Slowly, junior colleges began to change their emphasis to their terminal function and offered two-year, vocationally oriented programs that required no further schooling. The 1947 Truman Commission Report recommended that these "community colleges" emphasize service to local populations and offer a mixture of transfer and terminal (associate's degree) programs.

Midwestern colleges and universities, in sum, have been pioneers in many respects, responsible for important innovations in organization, student life, and mission.

Sources and Further Reading: Merle Curti and Vernon Carstensen, *The University of Wisconsin: A History*, vols. 1 and 2 (1949); Roger L. Geiger, ed., *The American College in the Nineteenth Century* (2000); Thomas Wakefield Goodspeed, *A History of the University of Chicago* (1916); Allan Nevins, *The State Universities and Democracy* (1962); Jana Nidiffer, *Pioneering Deans of Women* (2000); Earle Dudley Ross, *Democracy's College* (1942); Frederick Rudolph, *The American College and University* (1990); Lincoln Steffens, "Sending a State to College," *American Magazine* 67 (Nov. 1908–Apr. 1909); John Sayle Watterson, *College Football: History, Spectacle, Controversy* (2000).

Jana Nidiffer
University of Michigan

Academic Freedom

The Midwest has figured prominently in the development of academic freedom in both public schooling and higher education in the United States. Academic freedom is the right of teachers and students to study without restriction on their views. The idea began in German universities as *Lehrfreiheit* and *Lernfreiheit*—freedom to inquire and publish and to learn—and later came to define the "true" (research) university in the United States. Today it pertains to all higher education but is more controversial in public schooling. Academic freedom is balanced by academic *responsibility*—to not be biased, propagandize, or advocate outside of one's academic competence.

Academic freedom requires institutional support. Tenure recognizes the right of teachers to their positions once competence is demonstrated and unless they lose their effectiveness, neglect their duties, or violate the law. Tenure upholds the principles of experience, through seniority, and professionalism, or informed judgment. Standards for appointment, advancement, and reward are other supports of academic freedom.

Some misunderstandings exist about academic freedom and tenure. Tenure does not guarantee lifetime employment; it is a seniority principle. Neither does tenure prevent the dismissal of incompetent teachers—so long as due process is followed. And academic freedom does not excuse teacher misbehavior in the classroom.

In earlier times, restrictions on academic freedom resulted from doubting religious authority. Today, because of their implications for values, the social (and sometimes scientific) studies are the more likely object of attacks on academic freedom. In public schooling, social restrictions on teachers, book banning, and censorship of curricular materials and student speech (and now Internet use) have been common. In Kansas in 1999, the state board of education removed references to evolution from its science standards. (A new board restored the material in 2001.) Several Midwest cases have reached the U.S. Supreme Court and thus have become national standards. *Tinker v. Des Moines* (1969) affirmed the student right to symbolic speech by wearing antiwar armbands. *Hazelwood School District* (1988), from Missouri, allowed student newspapers to be regulated for educational purposes.

Economists John R. Commons at Indiana University and Edward R. Bemis at the University of Chicago were dismissed in the 1890s because of their unorthodox economic views, and Richard T. Ely at the University of Wisconsin was "tried" but cleared in a nationally significant declaration of academic freedom that has been called the "Wisconsin Magna Carta." During the 1950s, investigations into Communism led to administrator and faculty dismissals, the administering of loyalty oaths, and censorship of speakers and student publications at the University of Chicago, Olivet College in Michigan, and The Ohio State University.

Although some observers believe that academic freedom is so well established that it needs no special protection, the midwestern experience warns that it is always vulnerable.

Sources and Further Reading: Howard K. Beale, *A History of Freedom of Teaching in American Schools* (1941); Richard Hofstadter and Walter P. Metzger, *The Development of Academic Freedom in the United States* (1955); Robert M. MacIver, *Aca-*

demic Freedom in Our Time (1955); David Rubin, *The Rights of Teachers* (1984).

Robert R. Sherman
University of Florida (Emeritus)

Community Colleges

Community colleges originated in the Midwest, although a great deal of their development occurred in California. The first public two-year college was Joliet Junior College in Illinois, organized as a result of negotiations between the president of the University of Chicago and the principal of Joliet Township High School and established in 1901. Many early junior colleges were private institutions, although by the mid-1940s there were about equal numbers of private and public junior colleges. Junior college development in midwestern states was uneven, especially strong in Illinois, Kansas, Michigan, and Missouri, less so in Minnesota and Wisconsin, and very weak in Indiana and Ohio. Community colleges now offer a wide range of students the opportunity to enter higher education.

In 1947 the Truman Commission on Higher Education proposed using the name community college, and since the 1960s almost all two-year colleges have been called community colleges. In the 1960s and the 1970s, public community colleges experienced tremendous growth in number of institutions and enrollment. By the early 2000s, nationally about a third of all colleges and universities were community colleges, and about half of all college students were enrolled at community colleges.

Early junior colleges in the Midwest focused on both general education and the preparation of students for careers; students transferred to four-year colleges and universities or entered careers. Teaching, especially at the elementary school level, was a popular career choice. Many early junior colleges in the Midwest were in small or midsize towns, where schools often welcomed elementary school teachers with a junior college education. Junior colleges offered towns and cities the opportunity to claim a college as their own and allowed parents to send their children to a local college. Midwestern junior colleges were often part of a local school district until the 1960s and 1970s in many states, but by the 1980s states were assuming such responsibility. Transfer and career preparation functions remain important, and the colleges also often offer a variety of continuing and community education programs.

Historically, student transfer rates to four-year colleges and universities have been uneven, even among community colleges in the same town or city, although in general community college students intending to earn a bachelor's degree are less likely to do so than those students who begin at a four-year institution. Faculty members were often drawn from local secondary schools. In the 1960s faculty unionization began at Michigan community colleges, and it then spread to other midwestern states. During the 1970s community college faculty members increasingly came to the institutions from graduate school, and fewer and fewer were from secondary schools. At about the same time, institutions began to appoint more part-time professors and fewer full-time faculty. Often, part-time community college professors teach at two or more institutions.

Sources and Further Reading: Arthur Cohen and Florence B. Brawer, *The American Community College*, 3rd ed. (1996); John H. Frye, *The Vision of the Public Junior College, 1900–1940* (1992); Edward Gallagher, "The Potent Bacillus," *Michigan Academicus* 17 (Fall 1997); Stephen G. Katsinas, J. Leland Johnson, and Lana G. Snider, "Two-Year College Development in Five Midwestern States: An Introduction and Overview," *Community College Journal of Research and Practice* 23 (Jan.–Feb. 1999); Robert Pederson, "The St. Louis Conference: The Junior College Movement Reborn," *Community College Journal* 65 (Apr.–May 1995).

Philo Hutcheson
Georgia State University

Fraternities and Sororities

College fraternities and sororities have flourished in the Midwest since their arrival in 1833. Colleges and universities committed to cocurricular learning and student development welcomed Greek-letter organizations for their contributions to campus life. In 1963 there were 497 campuses with fraternities and/or sororities in the United States and Canada. By 2002 832 campuses hosted fraternities and sororities, 213 of them in the Midwest. Additionally, 48 of 101 fraternity and sorority headquarters are in the region, 24 in Indianapolis alone.

The North-American Interfraternity Conference represents sixty-seven men's fraternities, eighteen of them founded at midwestern institutions. Miami University in Oxford, Ohio, was home to the first fraternity founded west of the Alleghenies, Beta Theta Pi (1839), and was the founding site of four others. Women's Greek-letter organizations blossomed after the Civil War. Eight of the twenty-eight sororities in the National Panhellenic Conference were founded in the Midwest, the first at Monmouth College (Illinois) in 1867. Of the twenty-four members of the National Association of Latino Fraternal Organizations, three were founded in the Midwest, two at the University of Iowa and one at Indiana University.

Of the nine historically black fraternities and sororities in the National Pan-Hellenic Council, two were founded in the Midwest: Kappa Alpha Psi (Indiana University, 1911) and Sigma Gamma Rho (Butler University, 1922). By the mid-1920s, chapters were established both at historically black colleges in the region and at research universities where African Americans were enrolled.

Sources and Further Reading: Jack Anson and R.F. Marchensani, eds., *Baird's Manual of American College Fraternities*, 20th ed. (1991); Edward G. Whipple, ed., *New Challenges for Greek Letter Organizations* (1998).

Barbara J. Tootle
Columbus, Ohio

Historically Black Colleges and Universities

Slavery, segregation, and migration north shaped black colleges in the Midwest. Before emancipation allowed for the creation of black colleges in the South, midwestern black colleges provided education to free African Americans. One of the most successful institutions was Wilberforce University, established at Tawana Springs, Ohio, in 1856 by the Methodist Episcopal Church. Wilberforce was created because blacks were excluded by law from education in the South and excluded by de facto segregation in the North. In 1863 the African Methodist Episcopal (AME) Church purchased the school and it remains involved in its operation today. Ohio's other black college is Central State University, which began as the state-sponsored Combined Normal and Industrial Department of Wilberforce. Because of its state affiliation, the department officially left Wilberforce in 1951 and became Central State College.

Missouri's Lincoln University was founded at the end of the Civil War. Unique in its creation, Lincoln was established by black Civil War veterans. Located in Jefferson City, Lincoln became a state-sponsored institution in 1879 and was greatly affected by the 1954 *Brown v. Board of Education* decision prohibiting segregation. The institution responded to the landmark ruling by opening its doors to students of all backgrounds.

Harris-Stowe State College in St. Louis, Missouri, which traces its roots back to 1857, resulted from a merger between the white Harris Teacher's College (the original campus) and the black Stowe Teacher's College. In 1954 the two institutions became one in an effort to comply with *Brown*. The city of St. Louis

thought it wise to integrate teacher training as an example for public-school students and parents.

During the early twentieth century blacks began to migrate north in greater numbers. Employment and higher wages were important pulls but Jim Crow segregation may have been the greatest impetus. While legalized segregation was the norm in all aspects of southern life, separation in the North was less overt. The North also offered superior public educational facilities. With increased wages, blacks were able to send their children to school, and within a short time multiple generations of blacks were attending college.

Black colleges in the Midwest are unique in that they were for the most part established or reconstituted by African Americans. Most important, unlike those of their counterparts in the South, the curriculum and governance of midwestern black colleges were not altered by white northern industrial philanthropy. Among the reasons cited for northern capitalists' funding black colleges in the South were the need to train workers for a developing industrial economy and to create a political climate favorable to investment—one that accommodated segregation but provided some economic hopes for blacks. In the North, where there was no legalized segregation and where industrial economies were already well established, there was no need for industrial philanthropists to influence black education in the same way. Thus black colleges in the Midwest, for the most part, enjoyed a greater degree of freedom from outside tampering than their southern counterparts.

Sources and Further Reading: Ronald Butchart, *Northern Schools, Southern Blacks, and Reconstruction* (1980); Daniel C. Thompson, *Private Black Colleges at the Crossroads* (1973).

Marybeth Gasman
University of Pennsylvania

Liberal Arts Colleges

The founding of midwestern liberal arts colleges during the nineteenth century was a collective community endeavor. Popular zeal for education, combined with the difficulties of traveling long distances to attend established institutions, resulted in a proliferation of small liberal arts colleges by 1900. These local colleges were deeply rooted in the social and economic fabric of community life, and their strong regional ties defined their missions, their curricula, and the types of students they educated.

Early colleges enjoyed a broad base of local financial support. They often received many small contributions from nearby residents, for whom the college served as a symbol and a source of local pride and prosperity. Frontier towns vied for the honor of hosting a college, which brought prestige and economic stimulus to a region and helped establish a town's identity. Many colleges initially had few financial resources and little prospect of offering a full-fledged liberal arts curriculum, yet their founders were not deterred. Some opened their institutions with as few as a dozen students.

The diversity of midwestern liberal arts colleges reflects the pioneering spirit common to the men and women who were part of the movement westward. Some colleges had abolitionist ties, such as Grinnell College in Iowa and Earlham College in Indiana. Others, including Wilberforce University in Ohio and Lincoln University in Missouri, were established to educate African Americans. Oberlin College in Ohio inaugurated coeducational higher education by admitting women as students. In the 1920s, Antioch College in Ohio implemented a progressive experiment combining liberal education, work experience, and social training for its students.

The most active college founders were religious denominations. Presbyterians founded Indiana's Wabash College for men in 1832 and Nebraska's Hastings College in 1882. In the mid-1800s, brothers of the Congregation of the Holy Cross inaugurated in Indiana the college later called the University of Notre Dame while the Sisters of Charity began what became St. Mary's College in Kansas. Lutherans were responsible for St. Olaf College in Minnesota and Augustana College in South Dakota, and Baptists founded Denison University in Ohio and Hillsdale College in Michigan. Today, some colleges retain their sectarian roots while others are independent of religious affiliation.

Widespread educational opportunity was part of an egalitarian impulse that characterized the Midwest during the early days of its settlement. Gaining admittance to college was relatively easy, and many students came from humble family backgrounds. Geographical proximity and modest fees meant that even families of little means could access education at the local college.

By the end of the nineteenth century, with the rise of large land-grant and research universities offering practical curricula and graduate study, liberal arts colleges defined their educational niche through their commitment to undergraduate teaching and dedication to a broad, liberal curriculum. Today, each midwestern liberal arts college has its own distinctive qualities arising from both the impulse of its founding and the shaping influence of its regional ties. Many of these colleges enjoy national reputations and draw students and faculty from across the country.

Sources and Further Reading: Christopher J. Lucas, *American Higher Education: A History* (1994); David B. Potts, " 'College Enthusiasm!' as Public Response: 1800–1860," in Lester F. Goodchild and Harold S. Wechsler, eds., *The History of Higher Education*, 2nd ed. (1997); Frederick Rudolph, *The American College and University* (1990).

Auden D. Thomas
Indiana University–Bloomington

Professional Education

In the early twentieth century historian Frederick Jackson Turner described the Midwest region as a modern industrial colossus such as the world had never seen before. Granary of the nation, the greatest railroad center in the world, a mining frontier and "huge industrial organism," a complex inland maritime highway of commerce: The vast, landlocked "Middle Border" (as writer Hamlin Garland called it in his memoirs) in the center of the nation was a study in evolutionary history, from pioneer settlement to the industrial energy released by diversification, consolidation, and systematization. At the pinnacle of the midwestern colossus was a system of professional schooling institutionalized in state universities—the crown of public education in each Midwest state—and private universities such as the University of Chicago.

In the nineteenth century, state universities were established in Michigan, Wisconsin, Minnesota, Illinois, Ohio, Iowa, Missouri, and Kansas. Michigan and Wisconsin excelled first. Turner recognized that the large university of the Midwest, representing the diversified and maturing history of the region, would make an enduring contribution to the formation of knowledge and professional life in America. This contrasts with the attention later paid by writers to Main Street mediocrity and hucksterism.

The state universities all began in fits and starts as provincial fledgling institutions caught up in largely political controversies over location, pedagogical mission, organization of colleges, recruitment of students, and relationship to sectarian and proprietary educational institutions. The Morrill Land-Grant Act of 1862 provided some stability by funding public universities with a reliable income while charging them with expanding the educational mission to include academic training in agriculture, vocations, and industrial skills. Presidents James Burrill Angell of the University of Michigan and William Watts Folwell of the University of Minnesota favored a model of an expanding but coherent marketplace of an institution. They sought a "uni-versity" in which all subjects were given value as a science and where anyone could pursue an interest at an advanced level, including applied, clinical, and research training. Especially in midwestern institutions adopting an electives system, undergraduate education was increasingly perceived as preprofessional rather than general.

From the beginning, students in the Midwest were more occupationally minded and older than those in classical programs in the East. They came from a relatively broad band of middle-class families. Additionally, the cohort of midwestern state university presidents in the later nineteenth century was mostly common in origin compared to its members' wellborn eastern counterparts. This fact, and the increasing legitimacy of applied engineering and new technologies, led the presidents to favor programs in emerging "sciences" including the expanding specialties in engineering and medicine as well as programs in pedagogy, forestry, and home economics. In turn-of-the-century Iowa, the graduate "pharmacist" began replacing the home-grown, job-trained "druggist," "chemist," and "apothecary." Change and reform did not happen without controversy and a fight as the older practitioners entrenched themselves in state professional associations and argued that a college education was both too expensive and unnecessary to gain valuable experience. Ironically, pharmacy schools did not fare well as physicians gained control over prescription writing and pharmaceutical companies soon dominated the market with their research and patents.

The resources massed in the complex university corporation gave it a decisive advantage over single-mission institutions in attracting support for growth. The highly publicized 1910 Flexner Report on "Medical Education in the United States and Canada" condemned substandard facilities in professional training as a public threat and a scandal. Flexner declared the city of Chicago, with its proliferation of proprietary schools, "the plague spot of the country" and thereby furthered the growth of more regulated professional schools in state universities.

In the late nineteenth century, the Johns Hopkins University in Baltimore, Maryland, initiated the German model of research seminars and investigation for the advanced training of doctoral candidates. An increasing number of faculty members at the leading midwestern institutions, including Turner himself, received their doctorates at Johns Hopkins. However, while drawing on its strengths, the large midwestern institution departed in important ways from the German model's elite higher learning and inferior technical training. By combining practical, clinical, research, and professional training under one roof, the midwestern universities succeeded at popular professional training and investigation. Occupational medicine investigating the hazards of the workplace, for instance, was first developed as a professional specialty in a midwestern institution.

In respect to size, the midwestern university was usually larger than European and East Coast institutions. Its purpose was to prepare a large number of average students for work in the world rather than a few, best privileged students for matriculation in the civil service. Indeed, in contrast to the politically insulated, mandarin German state, midwestern institutions were continually influenced and pressured by proprietary, moneyed, and political interests in society, a subject Thorstein Veblen successfully lampooned in *The Higher Learning in America: A Memorandum on the Conduct of Universities by Business Men* (1918) by caricaturing William Rainey Harper at the University of Chicago as a "captain of erudition."

Professional schools in the Midwest were continually in political, social, and academic flux. They confronted questions about whether a state or region needed expensive schools and duplicate programs; which and how many students to admit; what role the community should be given in policy questions; and how to reconcile different standards for professional performance for expert researchers, investigators, and teachers in the academy versus worldly practitioners in the marketplace. But common to all schools was the belief that professional schooling had traditionally been biased against women except for teaching and social work, against the working class because of monetary expense, and against minorities and African Americans at all levels.

Frederick Jackson Turner's description of the Midwest resonates a century later by embracing the nation. The pervasive system of professional training has succeeded in nurturing a dominant culture of professionalism in American life. While making efforts to address historical failures, professionals persist in anguishing over the profound problems of competence, accountability, and public trust in the largest economy in the world.

Sources and Further Reading: Burton J. Bledstein, *The Culture of Professionalism* (1976); Thomas Neville Bonner, *Medicine in Chicago, 1850–1950*, 2nd ed. (1991); Abraham Flexner, *Medical Education in the United States and Canada* (1910); Stow Persons, *The University of Iowa in the Twentieth Century* (1990); Winton U. Solberg, *The University of Illinois, 1894–1904* (2000); Richard J. Storr, *Harper's University: The Beginnings* (1966); Frederick Jackson Turner, *The Frontier in American History* (1920; reprint 1976); Thorstein Veblen, *The Higher Learning in America: A Memorandum on the Conduct of Universities by Business Men* (1965); Laurence R. Veysey, *The Emergence of the American University* (1965).

Burton J. Bledstein
University of Illinois–Chicago

State Universities

While the flagship institutions of higher learning in the New England and Middle Atlantic states have long been the private, independent universities, the defining characteristic of higher education in the Midwest has been the predominance of public, state-supported universities. Though every state today has a mixture of public and private schools at all levels, the concept of public support of education was an inheritance of the American Revolution and the emerging belief that every American should have the opportunity to realize his or her potential, regardless of family income or status.

In 1787, the U.S. Congress approved the Northwest Ordinance as a plan by which the new nation could grow through the addition of new states "equal in every respect" to the thirteen already in the union. Though written for the territory north and west of the Ohio River, the ordinance set precedents for the orderly expansion of the nation.

Not only did the Northwest Ordinance establish what has been called the most liberal colonial policy in the history of the world, it laid the foundation for support of education in the territories and future states, the belief being that if democracy and enlightened self-government were to prevail, an educated citizenry was essential. Indeed, if settlers were to take up lands in the new West beyond the Ohio River, educational opportunities for their children would have to be assured.

It was Article Three of the Northwest Ordinance that stated, "Religion, morality, and knowledge, being necessary to good government and the happiness of mankind, schools and the means of education shall forever be encouraged." But should those schools be private and church-related, like almost all the eastern colonial colleges and universities, or should they be public and nonsectarian? The answer initially proved to be a mixture of each. In the more than two centuries that have elapsed since the passage of the great ordinance, hundreds of private, often church-related colleges and universities have sprung up across the land, many in the twelve states of the Midwest. Indeed, even the earliest of the midwestern state universities combined religion with public support, blending the sectarian traditions of the colonial colleges of the East with the expectations of public support and control in the West.

Congress said in 1787 that schools should be encouraged. It led the way, reserving two grants of land in 1792 for the support of academies or other institutions of higher learning in the Northwest Territory, one in the Ohio Company lands of what is now southeastern Ohio, the other in the lands of the Symmes Purchase in the Miami River valleys of southwestern Ohio. From these two grants would emerge the Midwest's first two state universities, Ohio University in Athens, chartered in 1804, and Miami University (named for the area's principal Native American tribe) in Oxford, chartered in 1809. It was no accident that the earliest presidents of both schools were clergymen, or that daily attendance at chapel was expected of both faculty and students. Indeed, ten of the first twelve presidents of Miami (including all of the first seven) were clerics, and not until 1954 was chapel attendance discontinued, though two chapel buildings on the Oxford campus are still used for special services, weddings, and funerals. While religion may not have played as important a role at other midwestern state universities, it had a presence on many campuses that persists to this day.

The inheritance from the colonial colleges on the Eastern Seaboard could be seen in many other ways: architectural styles of campus buildings; curricula; departmentalization of subject matter; degree requirements for undergraduates and graduates; and the emergence of professional programs in law, medicine, and other fields. Yet as state universities proliferated in the Midwest through the nineteenth and twentieth centuries and as their enrollments and financial resources grew, they developed their own styles and modes of operation reflecting diversity as well as commonality.

A leader among the new state schools was the University of Michigan, founded in 1817 at Detroit and moved to Ann Arbor in 1837. In 1850 it became the first public university to be controlled by regents elected by the voters of a state.

Most state universities of the Midwest today are governed by boards of trustees appointed by the governors of their states who are in turn elected by and responsible to the voters. In some states, boards of regents (or curators) have been established to provide coordination among state schools, with each of these retaining its own board of trustees (as in Ohio since 1963) or actual governance (as in Wisconsin since 1971, where twenty-six campuses are governed by a single board of regents). Almost all of the midwestern state schools are funded by annual or biennial state legislative appropriations; tuition, fees, and room-and-board charges (where applicable) collected from students; income from endowments; contributions from alumni, former students, and friends; and grants from federal and state agencies as well as foundations for the support of research and special programs. A number of factors, such as the ratio of in-state and out-of-state students, whether campuses are residential or commuting, and the nature and comprehensiveness of programs help to determine the relative proportion of income distribution among the several schools in each state. Most campus chief executive officers are presidents, while academic divisions in the main are headed by deans. The primary goals of virtually all institutions are teaching, research, and public service, while their principal priorities are the development of human resources and the discovery and dissemination of knowledge through research and publication.

While they all have much in common, diversity is certainly also a hallmark of the state universities. Most grant doctorates, but some have programs leading only to master's or baccalaureate degrees. Some with prestigious academic programs are selective in admissions; others accept nearly all high school graduates who apply. Some, such as the University of Missouri and the University of Wisconsin, have established university systems with multiple comprehensive campuses offering undergraduate, graduate, and professional degree programs. Others, such as Ohio's, assure both access and choice at lower cost through two-year branch or regional campuses, attracting large numbers of students of all ages and serving much the same role as the nation's community colleges. Many of the largest campuses began or were identified as agricultural and mechanical (A&M) colleges under the terms of the Morrill Land-Grant Act of 1862, by which the federal government granted to each state thirty thousand acres of public land for each senator and representative to found such schools. Included among these are The Ohio State University at Columbus; Purdue University at West Lafayette, Indiana; Michigan State University at East Lansing; Kansas State University at Manhattan; the University of Missouri at Columbia; the University of Nebraska at Lincoln; North Dakota State University at Fargo; Iowa State University at Ames; the University of Minnesota at Twin Cities; South Dakota State University at Brookings; the University of Illinois at Urbana-Champaign; and the University of Wisconsin at Madison. Comprehensive flagship campuses that antedated the A&M colleges include the University of Michigan at Ann Arbor, Indiana University at Bloomington, and the University of Iowa at Iowa City.

Another large group of state universities in the Midwest began as normal schools or state teachers' colleges. Examples are Bowling Green and Kent State Universities in Ohio; Ball State and Indiana State Universities in Indiana; Illinois State University and Northern, Southern, Eastern, and Western Illinois Universities; Winona, Mankato, St. Cloud, Moorhead, and Bemidji State Universities in Minnesota; Mayville and Valley City State Universities in North Dakota; and Emporia and Pittsburg State Universities in Kansas.

Two midwestern state universities serve predominantly African American student bodies: Chicago State University in Illinois and Central State University in Ohio. Two have been repeatedly cited for academic excellence as "Public Ivys": Miami University and the University of Michigan. At least four were once municipal universities: Cincinnati, Akron, Toledo, and Youngstown Universities, all in Ohio. One has an enrollment of only 705 students—Mayville in North Dakota. Another has an enrollment on its central campus of more than 47,000—Ohio State at Columbus. Many have sororities and fraternities. Most have residence halls. Almost all offer intercollegiate athletic programs as well as intramural sports. All have valuable libraries. Some of the largest have emerged among the nation's foremost research universities. Most are fully computerized. Most require the American College Test (ACT) or Scholastic Aptitude Test (SAT) for admission. Most have students from across the nation and the world. In sum, a wealth of opportunity exists in the universities of the twelve midwestern states for the intellectual, social, and cultural enrichment of the more than one million students enrolled in their courses of study.

A question arose in the early twenty-first century about whether or not that opportunity will continue to exist for all students who wish to enroll in the years ahead because of serious reductions in state legislative appropriations and rising levels of student tuition and fees. Determined to keep their doors open to the greatest possible number of students, midwestern state universities are resolved to keep alive the pledge of the Northwest Ordinance that "the means of education shall forever be encouraged."

Sources and Further Reading: Barron's Educational Series, *Profiles of American Colleges* (1999); William Donohue Ellis, *The Ordinance of 1787* (1987); Edward B. Fiske, *The Fiske Guide to Colleges* (2002); Richard Moll, *The Public Ivys* (1985); National Association of State Universities and Land-Grant Colleges, "State Cutbacks, Higher Costs Boost Tuition at Public Universities," National Association of State Universities and Land Grant Colleges *Newsline* (Nov. 2002); James A. Rhodes, *A Short History of Ohio Land Grants* (1955); Phillip R. Shriver, "America's Other Bicentennial," *The Old Northwest: A Journal of Regional Life and Letters* 9 (Fall 1983); U.S. News and World Report, *America's Best Colleges* (2002).

Phillip R. Shriver
Miami University, Oxford, Ohio

Student Activism

Student political activism has long thrived in the Midwest. In the 1930s, midwestern university students joined in the first mass student protest movement in American history. During the peak years of student activism, Communist and Socialist students mobilized at least five hundred thousand collegians (about half the American student body) in strikes and educative activities against war and on behalf of governmental programs for students and the poor, federal aid to education, academic freedom, racial equality, and the abolition of military recruiting on campuses. The key leader in the movement was the American Student Union, founded by a number of disparate groups in Columbus, Ohio, in 1935.

Although the popular image of 1960s student radicalism centers on the East and West Coasts, some of the major political events of the decade happened at or were related to midwestern universities. The Student Peace Union of the early 1960s was based at midwestern colleges and universities. Students for a Democratic Society (SDS) had its origins at the University of Michigan, where student Tom Hayden penned the founding document of SDS at its national convention in 1962 in Port Huron, Michigan. Called the "Port Huron Statement," the document reflects the emerging conflict between students raised in the conservative comfort of the Midwest and a political world with which they disagreed.

During the 1964 Freedom Summer organized by the Student Nonviolent Coordinating Committee (SNCC), eight hundred students trained for up to two weeks at Western College (later incorporated into Miami University) in Oxford, Ohio, in pacifist methods of promoting voter registration for African Americans in the South. Soon after the first students left Ohio for Mississippi, three disappeared. Michael Schwerner, Andrew Goodman, and James Chaney were driving to investigate a burned-out church in Mississippi when they were murdered. The publicity from the murders helped further the enforcement of the 1964 Civil Rights Act.

Midwestern state universities, especially some in Michigan and Wisconsin, were the site of some of the largest student protests against the Vietnam War. As students' outrage about the war increased later in the 1960s, so too did the intensity of the protests, culminating in violent police repression of protesting students at the Democratic National Convention in Chicago in 1968. On May 4, 1970, protestors at Kent State University in northern Ohio were fired upon by the National Guard. Four students were killed. In August of the same year, the death of one person in the bombing of a University of Wisconsin building proved to be the death knell of campus radicalism.

Since 1970, student activism at the many colleges and state universities of the Midwest has broadened to include protests demanding that universities divest their stock holdings in South Africa and demonstrations in support of the anti-sweatshop movement. There is also activism around gay and lesbian rights; feminism; antiracism; pacifism; and in response to university policies on affirmative action, labor rights for graduate students, and local community relations. In the late 1990s and early 2000s, secondary and elementary students and their parents in Illinois, Michigan, and Ohio joined nationwide moves to protest required high-stakes standardized testing.

Sources and Further Reading: Robert Cohen, *When the Old Left Was Young* (1993); James Miller, *Democracy Is in the Streets* (1987); Linda McCants Pendleton, "High Voltage Protest," *Rethinking Schools* 13 (Summer 1999); Tony Vallela, *New Voices: Student Activism in the 80's and 90's* (1988).

Kate Rousmaniere
Miami University, Oxford, Ohio

University of Chicago

Founded in 1890 and opened in 1892, the University of Chicago quickly established its reputation as one of the premier academic institutions in the Midwest and a leader among the new research universities beginning to reshape American higher education at the turn of the twentieth century. Today, with an endowment of more than three billion dollars, an enrollment of more than twelve thousand students, and numerous Nobel laureates among its faculty, the University of Chicago enjoys a worldwide reputation for academic research as well as for graduate, undergraduate, and professional education. Located in Hyde Park, south of downtown Chicago, the university attracts students and faculty from throughout the United States and abroad to its sheltered urban campus. Gothic quadrangles, reminiscent of the ancient English universities of Oxford and Cambridge, represent the dominant architectural motif, but more modern buildings, including designs by Eero Saarinen and Ludwig Mies van der Rohe, proclaim the university's ties to its own city's architectural heritage.

The university's connection to Chicago and the Midwest extends beyond architecture, however, to encompass its spirit and identity. Although the nineteenth-century eastern academic establishment initially scoffed at Chicagoans' plans to create a leading research university in the heart of the Midwest, derision soon turned to admiration. Led by a dynamic young president, William Rainey Harper, the University of Chicago quickly recruited faculty from other universities across the country and instituted a wide variety of innovative programs. Millionaire philan-

Bird's-eye view of the University of Chicago. Library of Congress. American Memory, Prints and Photographs Division, Panaromic Photographs Collection, LC-USZ62-53407 DLC.

thropist John D. Rockefeller provided the bulk of the funding for the new undertaking, but large contributions came from local supporters as well. The guidance and support provided by trustees recruited from among Chicago's business elite ensured the university's place among the city's most prized civic institutions. Just as visitors gaped at the wonders of Chicago's World's Columbian Exposition, staged in 1893, educators marveled at the audacity of the academic enterprise taking shape along the midway.

By the early decades of the twentieth century the University of Chicago's leadership in a number of fields was undisputed. The physical sciences and the newer social sciences in particular flourished. While Chicago physicists unlocked the secrets of space, time, and matter, sociologists, economists, and political scientists conducted research aimed at ameliorating the worst of the conditions they found in the laboratory provided by the city's infamous industrial yards and immigrant neighborhoods. Meanwhile, wealthy Chicagoans continued to support the university, believing in the importance of promoting an institution commensurate with the greatness of their city.

In 1929 the youthful, charismatic, and controversial Robert M. Hutchins became the University of Chicago's fifth president, instituting a period of significant development for the institution. During Hutchins's tenure, the university's undergraduate college became known for its distinctive curriculum, featuring classic texts, small discussion sections, and comprehensive examinations.

During the second half of the twentieth century and into the twenty-first, the University of Chicago has continued to be an important presence in the city and beyond. A leader among academic institutions and

host to a plethora of cultural attractions, the university's international reputation confirms Chicago's status as a world city.

Sources and Further Reading: Mary Ann Dzuback, *Robert M. Hutchins: Portrait of an Educator* (1991); Edward Shils, "The University, the City, and the World," in Thomas Bender, ed., *The University at the City* (1988); Richard J. Storr, *Harper's University* (1966).

Sarah V. Barnes
Boulder, Colorado

Women's Colleges

The midwestern states have a rich history of seminary and collegiate education for women.

Before the Civil War, the region north of the Ohio River benefited from the female seminary movement, which peaked between 1830 and 1860. Young women brought their East Coast training to start schools in the likeness of their alma maters, Mount Holyoke, Troy Seminary, and others, laying the foundation for women's college.

Private funding supported most single-sex women's education through the nineteenth century. In Illinois, 29 female seminaries were chartered in the antebellum years, including Rockford Female Seminary, which was founded by Mount Holyoke Female Seminary (renamed Mount Holyoke College in 1888) graduates and which would educate social activist Jane Addams. In Ohio between 1831 and 1851, some 30 seminaries were incorporated specifically for females and at least 116 for males. A few Ohio seminaries aimed at achieving status equal to that of men's colleges. In Cincinnati alone 10 female seminaries existed in 1836, including Western Female Institute, founded by Catharine Beecher, sister of novelist Harriet Beecher Stowe, in 1833.

In some states, public funding supported women's education. In Michigan, the legislature established branches of the state university with a provision that each would have an institution for the education of females. Six female seminaries were incorporated in this way. In Indiana, county seminaries mandated by the state in 1818 were never successful and were sold by midcentury.

Coordinate colleges and normal schools provided other models of single-sex education for women. With a sharp decline in male enrollments during the Civil War, the University of Wisconsin established a coordinate college for women in 1867 that lasted until the university went coeducational in 1871. Normal schools were first introduced to the Midwest in 1849; by 1879, there were more than one hundred normal schools in the region, attended overwhelmingly by women.

Although many antebellum female seminaries were short-lived, they laid the groundwork for collegiate education. They proved women's mental and physical capacity to learn and gained public support for educating women. After the Civil War, coeducation at state universities became the rule rather than the exception. By the mid-1870s, seminaries were being redefined as either high schools or colleges. In these years, several notable women's seminaries were elevated to collegiate status.

Women's colleges thrived through the twentieth century. By the 1980s, however, the women's movement, economic need, and political pressure led many all-male colleges to open their doors to women, and women's colleges found it equally expedient to open their doors to men. With the exception of the Catholic women's colleges, no single-sex colleges remain in the midwestern states. Several prominent Catholic women's colleges have maintained their commitment to single-sex education, including Ursuline in Ohio, Alverno in Milwaukee, and St. Catherine in Minnesota.

Young women graduates of eastern women's colleges such as Mount Holyoke and Troy Seminary were the threads connecting midwestern women's collegiate history with that of sister schools in the East. In the antebellum years, they came determined to elevate women's education to equal that of men. While coeducation became the norm for women in the Midwest, several notable women's colleges, including Catholic colleges, have contributed significantly to the history of women's single-sex higher education.

Sources and Further Reading: Mabel Newcomer, *A Century of Higher Education for American Women* (1959); Barbara Solomon, *In the Company of Educated Women* (1985); Thomas Woody, *A History of Women's Education in the United States,* vols. 1 and 2 (1966).

Roberta Wollons
Indiana University–Northwest

Elementary and Secondary Education

"Education," Wayne E. Fuller reminds us, "was the Midwest's birthright." The congressional commitment to education in the Land Ordinance of 1785 and the Northwest Ordinance of 1787—the idea that "religion, morality, and knowledge, being necessary to good government and the happiness of mankind, schools and the means of education shall forever be encouraged"—has long been a cornerstone of the region's commitment to civic culture and economic progress.

The states were slow to implement the vision of the ordinances, however. Ohio was the first to enact a public education law, in 1821. Indiana followed in 1824, Illinois in 1825, Michigan in 1837, and Missouri in 1839. The laws were supported by midwestern professional educators and reformers, such as Illinois's Newton Bateman; Indiana's Caleb Mills; Michigan's Isaac Crary and John Pierce; Ohio's Ephraim Cutler, Nathaniel Guilford, Samuel Lewis, William Holmes McGuffey, Joseph Ray, and Calvin Stowe; and Wisconsin's Michael Frank. All advocates of state-supported education, they differed on what kind of schools required governmental support and what form that support should take.

Throughout the early nineteenth century, the difference between public and private schooling in the Midwest was blurred. "Public" education provision included academies, charity schools, common schools, district schools, German schools, high schools, Roman Catholic schools, seminaries, subscription schools, town schools, union-graded schools, and ward schools. There was no commonly agreed upon systemic definition of elementary and secondary schooling other than recognition of the state's role in supporting elementary education. Democrats tended to favor local township control of district schools while Republicans and Whigs supported state-sponsored common-school reform with a state-level superintendent of common schools.

Secondary schooling was rare in the nineteenth-century Midwest. In 1890 Cincinnati had two public high schools; Chicago, Detroit, and St. Louis, one each. The public high school, hierarchically above the common school and, like the latter, organizationally graded based on educational accomplishment, replaced the increasingly unpopular academy, a state-incorporated, tuition-charging institution viewed by Republicans and Whigs as aristocratic, as the means for "diffusion of knowledge in general and the higher branches in particular." The free public high school's popularity occurred through achievement of political equality, social efficiency, and social mobility purposes. As late as 1890, only 1.6 percent of enrolled students in the United States were in high school.

Increasingly, nineteenth-century midwestern states established free public elementary and secondary education requiring school districts to open schools for certain periods of each year and to fund these schools by tax revenue derived from communities-at-large rather than by the previous rate system, in which parents had paid a certain rate for their children's attendance at school. This state legislation in Iowa (1846), Wisconsin (1848), Indiana (1852), Illinois (1855), Minnesota (1858), Kansas (1861), Nebraska (1867), and Michigan (1869) served as a precursor to post–Civil War legal battles over public school funding through state-mandated communitywide property-tax revenue, perhaps best represented by the Michigan State Supreme Court case *Stuart et al. v. School District No. 1, Kalamazoo, Michigan* (1874).

Democrat Charles E. Stuart opposed the efforts of Kalamazoo Whigs to establish a tuition-free high school on the consolidated Union School's third floor. Dedicated in February 1859, Kalamazoo's Union School included a high school course of instruction embracing "all the branches usually taught in the best class of male and female academies." Funding for this "crown" of Kalamazoo's public education system would derive from communitywide property-tax revenue, not, as Stuart desired, from the tuition fees of students able to afford them.

At Kalamazoo's 1867 annual town meeting, Stuart urged elimination of the free high school. The Republican-dominated school board disregarded Stuart. Opposed to centralized control of Kalamazoo's public schools as well as the funding method, Stuart lost his circuit court lawsuit and, subsequently, his Michigan State Supreme Court appeal. Majority opinion in Stuart's appeal reasoned that because Michigan's constitution and laws did not prohibit school districts from teaching knowledge or restricting the grade of instruction offered, the right of school authorities to levy taxes for the support of public high schools was affirmed. The *Stuart* decision resulted in confirmation of the common-school reformers' ideal of the locally controlled district school replaced with a state-regulated, free, graded elementary school topped by a free, graded secondary high school, also state regulated. This case became the basis for state taxation codes in all midwestern states.

Although critiques of tax-funded education remained strong, common-school reform became widespread toward the end of the nineteenth century. Gradually, midwesterners viewed a state-regulated, free public school system as the appropriate means for assuaging social dislocations resulting from immigration, industrialization, and urbanization. Public education took a variety of forms, including evening schools for adults and normal schools for elementary school teachers-to-be.

In post–Civil War St. Louis, Missouri, the student population grew from 266 to 55,870 between 1840 and 1880. Correlated with St. Louis's total population, these figures suggest that in the decade 1840–1850, St. Louis's public education system schooled one in fifty of the city's population; by 1880, it was "one out of every six or seven persons," and the system was well on its way to becoming a preeminent social institution. However, the social structure of public schools in St. Louis during this period reveals sharp contrasts in the attendance patterns of pupils. The sons of professionals had the lengthiest attendance records, including in the public high school, while the children of businesspeople, white-collar workers, and the working class largely confined their attendance to elementary school.

Part of the discussion about public education revolved around the content of that education, with some educators promoting academic work while others, like St. Louis's Calvin M. Woodward of Washington University promoted in-school manual education programs. This debate over the curricular content of St. Louis public schools occurred simultaneously with Superintendent William Torrey Harris's (1868–1880) dictum that short periods of formalized academic instruction, not in-school manual training programs, would bring about individual and social betterment. Following his St. Louis superintendency, Harris would serve the Benjamin Harrison, Grover Cleveland, William McKinley, and Theodore Roosevelt administrations as U.S. commissioner of education.

In 1887 the U.S. commissioner of education complimented midwestern advocates of public elementary and secondary schooling: "While the density of the population in the North Central States is less than one-third of that in the North Atlantic States . . . the people of the former group have nearly equalled, and in some cases surpassed, those of the latter in the development of their public schools." Midwestern preeminence in the provisioning of public elementary and secondary schooling would endure during the progressive era of the early 1900s, as elementary and secondary schooling came to be viewed as social correctives for an increasingly ethnically diverse, urbanized society. The Midwest was the location for some of the innovations in the elementary and secondary school model, for example, the junior high school, which was pioneered in Columbus, Ohio, in 1909 as a three-year program centered on early adolescence. Also introduced in the early-twentieth-century Midwest was the comprehensive high school combining academic and vocational studies, following the defeat of Chicagoan Edwin G. Cooley's plan for separate industrial schools. Child-centered progressive education had midwestern roots too, in Carleton Washburne's Winnetka, Illinois, plan of individualized instruction and William Wirt's Gary, Indiana, "platoon system."

These elementary and secondary schooling innovations were at odds with the traditional one-room country school; urban school reformers often referred to this discrepancy as "the rural school problem." To late-nineteenth-century educators like Ohio-born Burke A. Hinsdale, the "little red schoolhouse" had outlived its educational purpose. In their demands for centralization, efficiency, and standardization in public school provision, professional educators viewed country schools as costly; unlike large urban schools, they were "individualistic, inefficient, and chaotic." The answer to this rural school problem: school consolidation. Prior to World War II school consolidation triumphed in the Midwest, reducing the proportion of one-room schools in Indiana between 1918 and 1936 from 67.2 percent to 39.1 percent. After World War II a declining rural population finished them off.

Race became another factor in midwestern elementary and secondary schools throughout the twentieth century. Segregated schools in the Midwest were the source of some of the most significant court cases on school desegregation. To this day midwestern cities house highly segregated school systems. The 1954 U.S. Supreme Court decision in *Brown v. Board of Education* against de jure public school segregation, in part based on the all-black Monroe Elementary School in Topeka, Kansas, was offset two decades later by the Court's ruling in *Milliken v. Bradley* (1974). The Warren Burger Court (1969–1986) ruled that de facto segregation in the Detroit, Michigan, public schools could not be remedied by multidistrict solutions, for example, interdistrict busing. The *Milliken* decision essentially blocked city-suburban desegregation throughout the Midwest. Scholars involved in Harvard University's Civil Rights Project reported in *A Multiracial Society with Segregated Schools* (2003) that "apartheid" schools, "where enormous poverty, limited resources, and social and health problems of many types are concentrated," educate one-fourth of black students in the Midwest. Lingering problems like apartheid schools in midwestern cities have encour-

aged some people to redefine the "public" in "public education."

The redefinition of contemporary midwestern public education has raised a myriad of issues for elementary and secondary schools: bilingual education, charter schools and school voucher programs, increased regulation and standardization, and teacher certification and teacher quality issues, for instance. Bilingual education programs in the Midwest include teaching English as a second language to immigrant children from rural Southeast Asia in Wisconsin and recognition of bilingual culture and home language in teaching standard English, addressed in *Martin Luther King Junior Elementary School Children et al. v. Ann Arbor School District* (1979). The U.S. district court reasoned that school language, including "black English," was a means of achieving equal educational opportunity.

Charter schools and school voucher programs are viewed as means to redefining public elementary and secondary schooling. Public "chartered" schools, alternatives to local and state educational bureaucracies, originated in Minnesota (1992); in 2001 they numbered 1,988 in thirty-five states. School voucher programs permitting parents and students to spend their portion of public school funds in schools they favor, private or public, were initiated in two cities: Cleveland, Ohio, and Milwaukee, Wisconsin.

Increased regulation and standardization issues affect not only public elementary and secondary school curricular concerns, but teacher certification and teacher quality issues. Much of the controversy over increased regulation and standardization in midwestern public elementary and secondary schools focuses not on what is taught but on how what is taught is assessed. In the 1990s Chicago's Mayor Richard M. Daley stated that Chicago public school children would need to achieve a predetermined score on the Iowa Test of Basic Skills, a nationally normed achievement test, prior to proceeding to the next grade level. The Iowa Test of Basic Skills compared pupil achievement against a national sample of same-grade students. Children from Chicago's minority, poor neighborhoods "were . . . asked to perform at the same levels . . . as students from affluent and traditionally mainstream backgrounds." Known as "high-stakes testing," standardized achievement testing has become a popular means of measuring the results of schooling, evinced in President George W. Bush's No Child Left Behind Act (2001) requiring states to test children in mathematics and reading annually in grades three through eight. Beginning in 2005, federal legislation encouraging states to accent student standardized test scores in overall education improvement.

Teacher certification and quality issues have a long

history in the Midwest. The nineteenth-century Midwest was a leader in establishing normal schools for the training of elementary teachers and in recognizing education as legitimate university-level study through the establishment of university chairs of pedagogy. This focus on teacher certification issues continues to the present day; the Holmes Group (1986–1996), a consortium of research universities with a focus on graduate-level teacher education, and the Ohio Governor's Commission on Teaching Success (2001–2003), which emphasized quality teachers, are two examples. Neither group overlooked, moreover, the working conditions of teachers, a concern with a midwestern history dating back to the organization of the Chicago Federation of Teachers (1897), a predecessor of the American Federation of Teachers (1916).

Over the past century and a half, midwestern elementary and secondary schools have faced enormous challenges in implementing the rhetoric of Article Three of the Northwest Ordinance (1787). Implementing that "birthright" fully remains the central challenge.

Sources and Further Reading: Lee Anderson, Nancy Adelman, Kara Finnigan, Lynyonne Cotton, Mary Beth Donnelly, and Tiffany Price, "A Decade of Public Charter Schools. Evaluation of the Public Charter Schools Program: 2000–2001 Evaluation Report" (U.S. Department of Education, Nov. 2002); Richard B. Boone, *Education in the United States: Its History from the Earliest Settlements* (1890); Lawrence A. Cremin, *American Education: The Metropolitan Experience, 1876–1980* (1988); Erica Frankenberg, Chungmei Lee, and Gary Orfield, *A Multiracial Society with Segregated Schools* (2003); Wayne E. Fuller, *The Old Country School* (1982); David F. Labaree, *How to Succeed in School without Really Learning* (1997); Paul H. Mattingly and Edward W. Stevens, Jr., eds., *"Schools and the Means of Education": A History of Education in the Old Northwest, 1787–1880* (1987); William J. Reese, *The Origins of the American High School* (1995); John L. Rury, *Education and Social Change* (2002); Selwyn K. Troen, "Popular Education in Nineteenth Century St. Louis," in B. Edward McClellan and William J. Reese, eds., *The Social History of American Education* (1988); Wayne Urban and Jennings Wagoner, *American Education: A History* (2000).

Malcolm B. Campbell
Bowling Green State University, Ohio

Agricultural and Vocational

Although educators historically have thought of the origins of major reforms in education in the United States as occurring in the New England states, several key developments began with movements in the Midwest. Certainly reforms that furthered the develop-

ment of industry, home arts, and the science of farming in elementary, secondary and higher education originated in the Midwest.

Two major congressional acts that heavily enriched education in the Midwest were the Morrill Acts of 1862 and 1890. The first Morrill Act (or Land-Grant College Act), passed by Congress in 1861 and signed by President Abraham Lincoln in 1862, granted states large areas of land to sell, the proceeds from the sale of which were to be invested and the income used to establish colleges of agriculture and the mechanical arts. The Morrill Act led to the founding of land-grant colleges that in turn produced many of the advances in American agriculture during the 1900s. One of these colleges, Michigan State University, founded in 1855 as Michigan Agricultural College, was the first state school to offer courses in agriculture for credit, serving as a model for land-grant colleges and universities founded later in the United States.

In 1890 Congress passed the second Morrill Act. It more than doubled the first act's federal contribution to higher education by allowing more students to attend college and affected colleges and universities by withholding grants from states that denied admission to land-grant schools for racial reasons. These two acts also encouraged the development of home economics programs, or "domestic studies," in both secondary and higher education.

During the 1800s, public schools began to offer vocational education under such names as manual training and mechanical arts. In 1880 Calvin M. Woodward, dean of the O'Fallon Polytechnic Institute at Washington University, opened the Manual Training School in St. Louis, Missouri, the first school of its kind in the United States. The Manual Training School provided a three-year secondary program that divided the curriculum equally between mental and manual labor. Woodward supported this division because he believed that the goal of the school was not job preparation but preparation for life in an industrial society. Arguably, this was the origin of what we now call vocational education.

In 1914 the Smith-Lever Act, signed into law by President Woodrow Wilson, introduced extension programs in home economics to improve the quality of home life. These programs provided for the dissemination of practical information to farmers and homemakers by establishing extension programs organized through cooperation among the land-grant colleges, the states, and the federal government. This act provided dollar-matching federal funds to the states for farm- and home-demonstration work and complemented the progress seen in the first and second Morrill Acts. Of underlying significance, the act strengthened the role of the farmer by recognizing the farm family's importance at a time when farmers were experiencing problems brought on by increased industrialization.

The Smith-Hughes Act of 1917, known as the Vocational Education Act, provided funds to support the teaching of agriculture, industrial arts, and home economics in secondary schools and financed job training. The act confirmed the acceptance of vocational education as a necessary part of schooling, leading to a rise in the number of vocational programs offered; extracurricular clubs and organizations such as 4-H, Future Homemakers of America, and Future Farmers of America; and work/study programs in schools across the nation.

Sources and Further Reading: Lawrence A. Cremin, *American Education: The Metropolitan Experience* (1988); Linda Eisenmann, *Historical Dictionary of Women's Education in the United States* (1998); Herbert M. Kliebard, *The Struggle for the American Curriculum, 1893–1958* (1987).

Susan Clark Studer
California Baptist University

Art

In late-nineteenth-century Chicago, two schools founded under progressive principles by Francis W. Parker and John Dewey promoted creative expression and imagination in learning. Dewey's Laboratory School at the University of Chicago organized its program around "occupations," including weaving, carpentry, cooking, sewing, and the arts.

While these initiatives remained unusual, by the 1920s a concern for teaching art as part of daily living gradually supplanted the study of art masterpieces. In the 1930s, Melvin Haggerty, dean of the College of Education at the University of Minnesota, advocated art instruction in the schools aimed at elevating community taste rather than training the talented few. He organized a five-year project to introduce art into the schools of Owatonna, Minnesota. The project placed primary emphasis upon the applications of art to problems in daily living. Edwin Ziegfeld directed the Owatonna Project after Haggerty's death, and his work influenced his widely adopted text *Art Today: An Introduction to the Fine and Functional Arts* (coauthored with Ray Faulkner and Gerald Hill; 1942).

Post–World War II population growth and suburban expansion fueled a demand for teachers met in part by teacher education programs in art and music. Spurred by the success of the Soviet Union's space program in the late 1950s, educators sought more disciplined approaches to curriculum reform. Graduate

instruction in arts education also developed in many universities, with programs that have attracted students from many countries.

Today, the Midwest follows the pattern of the nation as a whole, with reductions of arts programs in major cities where school districts serve large populations of minority students, while in the more affluent suburbs serving a predominantly white population they continued to flourish. Throughout the twentieth century, curriculum initiatives in the arts were more likely to serve the everyday needs of individuals than cultivate refined or elitist tastes.

Source and Further Reading: Arthur Efland, *A History of Art Education* (1990).

Arthur Efland
The Ohio State University–Columbus

Curriculum

Curricular development in the Midwest has always paralleled national educational trends. It also has reflected cultural conflict related to questions of ethnicity, religion, social change, and political power. Yet no factor has loomed larger than the divergence between urban and rural school districts.

Through the nineteenth century, the urban school curriculum (usually grades 1–8) resembled that of America's early common, or public, schools: penmanship, spelling, reading, mathematics, geography, history, and morals. The standard method of teaching, recitation, required students to memorize and declaim prose and poetry. Reforms such as "unification" combined curricular strands (spelling, reading, composition, handwriting, and literature) into a single course (English).

The late nineteenth century ushered in more change. Although trustees and superintendents wielded great influence, they consulted with teachers, educators, and experts. Two St. Louis, Missouri, educators—Susan Blow and Calvin M. Woodward—advocated kindergartens and vocational training, respectively, to help students adapt to industrialized society. These innovations were also intended to minimize class differences and racial prejudices, and to mediate tension between "native" white and immigrant populations. A third St. Louis educator, William Torrey Harris, believed that education should serve to develop a child's interests and that the curriculum should comprise the "five windows of the soul": math, history, grammar, geography, and literature.

Reforms also evolved from the "platoon system," instituted in the Gary, Indiana, schools in 1908 by Superintendent William Wirt. The plan, which rotated students around the school instead of keeping them in one classroom, exemplified efficient school management and enabled the addition of physical education, fine arts, and vocational classes. The post-elementary curriculum grew further with the debut of the junior high school in Cleveland, Ohio; Sioux City, Iowa; Chicago; Kansas City, Kansas; and other cities. These districts introduced specialized classes such as biology, algebra, and theatre.

In urban districts with large non-English-speaking populations, many children could not understand their teachers. During the 1890s, Milwaukee's German immigrants demanded German-language instruction. St. Louis; Minneapolis-St. Paul, Minnesota; and Des Moines, Iowa, also confronted this issue. After 1900 most urban districts added Americanization and citizenship classes. Many educators adopted the view of John Dewey, University of Chicago professor and founder of its Laboratory School, that citizenship signifies participation in public life as well as voting and patriotism.

The challenge of educating immigrants was especially strong in Chicago, where the conflicting demands of Russian and Polish Jews, Italians, Czechoslovakians, Germans, and Irish Catholics created issues that University of Chicago president William Rainey Harper addressed in the Harper Report (1898). Harper called for remedial classes, individual instruction, and further curricular unification. In addition to Harper, Hull-House founder Jane Addams, social activist Florence Kelley, school superintendent Ella Flagg Young, and John Dewey pressed for a learning-by-doing curriculum incorporating activities that came to be associated with the progressive education movement, including manual work and creative expression.

Meanwhile, rural schools tended to lag behind their urban counterparts in resources and innovation. Students studied reading, drawing, printing, and numbers, and they recited interminably.

During the late nineteenth century, two national initiatives reflected concerns about the decline of agrarianism and strongly affected rural schools. In 1895 the National Education Association appointed a committee to evaluate country schools. The committee suggested that the rural curriculum fueled antagonism between farm families and the rising urban middle class by marginalizing agrarian values. It urged educators to connect the rural curriculum to life on the farm. Subsequently, in 1908 President Theodore Roosevelt appointed the Country Life Commission, chaired by Cornell horticulturalist Liberty Hyde Bailey. Its purpose would be to reconcile the increasingly separate cultures of agricultural and industrialized regions. The commission concluded that the rural curriculum should emphasize agriculture. Depending heavily on Bailey's Rural Text-Book series, rural teachers would emphasize agricultural study until the Dust Bowl era. When rural schools were consolidated into township districts, their curriculum more closely resembled those of urban schools.

After World War II, cold war imperatives altered the curriculum nationwide, with new approaches to math, science, and social studies and new courses in life adjustment and citizenship. While following the national consensus on curriculum revision, Chicago; Omaha, Nebraska; Topeka, Kansas; and other cities struggled with integration, which affected the curriculum because schools began to marginalize disadvantaged students through "tracking." Similarly, in North Dakota and South Dakota, school leaders faced the issue of educational equity among Native American students.

Since the 1960s, midwestern school districts have kept pace with schools nationwide. The U.S. government report *A Nation at Risk* (1983) and the middle school movement have been extremely influential. Some regions have faced unique issues, such as the Kansas state school board's 1999 vote to remove evolution from its science curriculum, a decision subsequently reversed. In 2002 the Ohio state school board considered adding the theory of intelligent design to its science curriculum.

Midwestern urban and suburban high schools are largely comprehensive, offering academic, occupational, and business classes. Debate and forensics programs thrive, having never been eliminated as they were in the East and the West. While cycling through occasional reforms in reading, writing, and mathematics instruction, midwestern elementary and middle schools maintain a traditional subject curriculum. Standardized state tests increasingly dictate teachers' approaches to the curriculum, and it remains to be seen whether testing will influence the next round of curricular reforms.

Sources and Further Reading: Mary Hurlbut Cordier, *Schoolwomen of the Prairies and Plains* (1992); Lawrence A. Cremin, *The Transformation of the School* (1961); Edward A. Krug, *The Shaping of the American High School*, vol. 1, *1880–1920* (1969); William J. Reese, ed., *Hoosier Schools* (1998); David R. Reynolds, *There Goes the Neighborhood* (1999); Paul Theobald, *Call School* (1995).

Claudia Keenan
Emory & Henry College, Virginia

Early Childhood

The education and care of children from birth to age eight has been important in the Midwest for two centuries. Many early-education initiatives were pio-

Students in the TriCounty Head Start program in Waterloo, Iowa. Courtesy MEandV.com.

neered in the region, beginning with German immigrants who brought kindergartens to the United States.

From the 1830s through the 1870s kindergartens were introduced in Columbus, Ohio; Watertown, Wisconsin; Detroit, Michigan; Milwaukee, Wisconsin; and LaPorte, Indiana. German was the language of instruction in these private kindergartens, such as the one opened by Margarethe Schurz in her home in Watertown in 1856. William and Eudora Hailmann opened several English-speaking private kindergartens and training schools in the Midwest to replace German-speaking schools. Susan Blow established the first public school kindergarten in 1873, with the approval of St. Louis, Missouri, school district superintendent William Torrey Harris. Kindergarten founders often established educational communities, like the Chicago Kindergarten Club, which in the 1880s met monthly to discuss educational problems and listen to cultural and educational talks.

Almost as influential was the Laboratory School for young children run by John Dewey at the University of Chicago from 1896 to 1903. Students there were encouraged to pursue their interests through self-study and individual and class projects.

Many women rose to prominence as supervisors and administrators of kindergartens and nursery schools and as faculty members in normal schools and colleges in the Midwest. Ella Flagg Young, the general supervisor of Dewey's school, later became the Chicago superintendent of schools and as such was the first woman superintendent of a large urban school system in the country. Alice B. Temple chaired the Department of Kindergarten-Primary Education in the University of Chicago College of Education and coauthored a book on unified kindergarten and first grade teaching.

In the early twentieth century, two major research institutes, the Iowa Child Welfare Research Station at the University of Iowa and the Merrill-Palmer Institute of Detroit (now part of Wayne State University), examined the mental, social, physical, and nutritional development of two-to-six-year-old children and the education of their parents. They also provided instruction in homemaking and childcare skills. The University of Minnesota Institute of Child Development later joined this work.

Federally funded programs for three- and four-year-olds supported other ventures in early childhood education, including the Emergency Nursery Schools (1930s) and the Lanham Act Centers (1940s). The founding of Head Start in 1965 led to "Planned Variation" Head Start models still in use, including the Behavior Analysis Model of Donald Bushell, Jr., and High/Scope, developed by David Weikart and his colleagues in Ypsilanti, Michigan.

The Midwest has sustained the preparation of a cadre of committed professionals who implement developmentally appropriate practice in early childhood education programs. It has continually supported the quality care and education of young children by originating research-based and experimental programs.

Sources and Further Reading: V. Celia Lascarides and Blythe F. Hinitz, *History of Early Childhood Education* (2000); Barbara Ruth Peltzman, *Pioneers of Early Childhood Education* (1998); Alan R. Sadovnik and Susan F. Semel, eds., *Founding Mothers and Others* (2002); Agnes Snyder, ed., *Dauntless*

Women in Childhood Education (1972); Leslie R. Williams and Doris Pronin Fromberg, eds., *Encyclopedia of Early Childhood Education* (1992).

Blythe Simone Farb Hinitz
The College of New Jersey

Gender and Sexuality

Gender and sexuality in midwestern schools have enjoyed a dynamic history marked by cycles of polarization, depolarization, and repolarization. People commonly regard polarization, the division of an issue into opposites, as natural when discussing gender and sexuality. For example, many believe that "opposite" sexes exist, and that homosexuality stands in opposition to heterosexuality. Similarly, people think of sex as biological, and gender as the social organization of biology into the polar opposites of masculinity and femininity. Even the words describing sexual desire have a dynamic history, as seen in the shifts from *sexual preference* to *sexual orientation* to the now preferred term *sexuality*.

As the history of midwestern schools reveals, social forces have created an environment in which gender and sexuality are anything but static or purely oppositional. As in the rest of the United States, immigration was one of the social forces that structured gender and sexuality and forcibly replaced indigenous American Indian institutions. But unlike the rest of the United States, the insular German, Dutch, Scandinavian, and Polish ethnic communities in rural midwestern areas, who typically taught schoolchildren in their native language, and, to a lesser extent, the ethnic enclaves in large urban areas preserved their indigenous institutions and national heritages. Some of the preserved heritage included conservative northern and northwestern European Protestant and Catholic attitudes toward gender and sexuality. Even these attitudes, however, were marked by depolarization and repolarization as the rural and urban ethnic enclaves responded to pressures to assimilate and as national tensions about sex and gender rumbled through the nation's Heartland.

As common schooling began in the mid-1800s, midwestern schools enrolled female and male students together, bypassing traditions of single-sex schooling in eastern states and ushering in a period of gender depolarization. New England women's seminaries produced hundreds of teachers who traveled to the Midwest eager to establish common schools, recruit students, and otherwise enjoy a level of independence unmatched by previous generations. These women teachers demonstrated skill and toughness in demanding circumstances, although they commanded only one-third to one-half the wages of men teachers. Consequently, communities throughout the region enthusiastically hired women teachers.

Gender in midwestern schools became repolarized as more women taught and men abandoned the profession. The few men who remained in schoolwork entered the emerging realm of administration. Schoolwork became so gender polarized by 1910 that men held nearly every school superintendency while women accounted for around 80 percent of teachers. Although most women teachers nationwide were single, divorced, or widowed, many rural midwestern schools retained women teachers after they married, preferring instructional continuity and professional experience. If communities tolerated married women teachers, though, they required male superintendents to be married, a persistent pattern today.

As the nineteenth-century women's movement gathered strength, women began winning elected county superintendencies, signaling a period of gender depolarization. In 1869 Julia Addington, an Iowa teacher, became the first woman elected county superintendent in the nation. By 1930 women held the majority of county superintendencies in six midwestern states. They occasionally held state superintendencies, and, as in the case of Ella Flagg Young of Chicago, superintendencies of large urban school systems.

After World War II, however, midwestern schools experienced sharp gender repolarization. The proportion of women superintendents dropped steeply. Married women displaced single women teachers. Largely male administrative organizations trivialized the contributions of women educators by publishing articles on the important role of the administrator's wife. Meanwhile, communities enlisted school administrators into campaigns to rid schools of homosexual teachers in a backlash movement following the 1948 publication of Indiana University researcher Alfred Kinsey's landmark volume *Sexual Behavior in the Human Male.* Gender repolarization also appeared at the student level, revealing post–World War II anxieties about gender and sexuality. Schools pushed girls into home economics courses, where they learned household and marriage skills. They steered boys into manual training programs, science and math courses, and athletics.

In the 1950s worries about youthful sexuality led schools to institute family-life courses. These courses taught young people to adhere to narrowly defined gender roles, abstain from sex, and plan their life around marriage and heterosexual families. These courses supplanted the earlier social hygiene courses in high schools, and they typically were taught in sex-segregated classrooms. Four decades earlier, Young had instituted the nation's first such social hygiene/sex education courses in Chicago.

The 1960s and 1970s sexual revolution prompted a new examination of sex education in midwestern public schools. Concerns about teenage pregnancy, sexually transmitted diseases, and the supposed moral decline of youth reached an all-time high. During this time, a majority of parents surveyed favored sex education in public schools. However, as in the South, grassroots activism by politically savvy white evangelical Protestants resulted in many midwestern school districts authorizing only programs that focused on premarital abstinence and the prevention of sexually transmitted diseases.

The baby boom generation came of sexual age in the 1960s and 1970s, stimulating community attempts to control their sexuality and challenges to gender norms. Contraction of the traditional midwestern economy that had been based on heavy industries such as steel and auto manufacturing further fueled the expansion of New Right policies of moral traditionalism into public schools; midwestern state legislatures responded to the pressures of the New Right and revised acts authorizing sex education. Many forbade the distribution of birth control in public schools and allowed parents to withdraw their children from sex education programs. Additionally, schools instituted dress codes to control gender expression of students. Some schools suspended or even expelled boys with long hair.

After the 1969 Stonewall Rebellion in New York City, a grassroots gay and lesbian liberation movement emerged. Lesbian and gay teachers began resisting job discrimination by coming out, organizing lesbian and gay teachers' groups, or bringing lawsuits against districts that dismissed lesbian and gay teachers. In response, singer Anita Bryant and California senator John Briggs led a national backlash movement to prevent the employment of homosexual teachers. Following a protracted battle in which an Iowan activist threw a pie in Bryant's face, California and some municipalities across the country eventually offered legal protection for lesbian and gay school workers. To this day, however, most do not.

The 1991 publication of a federal report on high suicide rates among lesbian, gay, bisexual, and transgender (LGBT) youth shifted national attention from teachers to students. Federal guidelines were issued to prevent harassment of LGBT students. However, in 2000 a Wisconsin study of students, parents, and teachers revealed continuing harassment of them. Citing this study, Senators Russ Feingold (D-Wisconsin) and Paul Wellstone (D-Minnesota) cosponsored a bill to study the implementation of federal antiharassment guidelines. Meanwhile, students around the Midwest have resisted victimization by starting gay-straight alliances at their schools, establishing LGBT history curricula, and organizing gay-straight proms, efforts for which increasing numbers are receiving recognition and even scholarships to colleges and universities.

Currently, gender and sexual polarization and depolarization seem to coexist. Although gay-straight alliances are proliferating in high schools across the Midwest, LGBT teachers have job protection in relatively few states. Minnesota and Wisconsin account for two of only fourteen U.S. states (and the District of Columbia) that currently ban discrimination based on sexual orientation. As midwestern women university students fill increasing proportions of seats in previously male disciplines such as medicine, business, and law, momentum builds for single-sex schooling. Gender and sexuality, then, remain central to the social organization of schooling in the Midwest.

Sources and Further Reading: Jackie Blount, *Destined to Rule the Schools* (1998); John D'Emilio and Estelle B. Freedman, *Intimate Matters*, 2nd ed. (1997); Karen M. Harbeck, *Gay and Lesbian Educators* (1997); Jeffrey P. Moran, *Teaching Sex* (2000).

Sine Anahita
Iowa State University

Jackie M. Blount
Iowa State University

Literacy

Literacy, defined as the ability to read and write, has played a central role in the development of the Midwest. More than the acquisition of practical skills, literacy is a means through which people debate and inculcate core values.

The Midwest emerged as literacy was becoming widespread in North America and Europe. Despite the persistent popularity of speeches, songs, and folktales, the region flourished in an age of reading and writing. The growing numbers of schools and the explosion of newspapers, magazines, and books created a public immersed in print. In 1840, 85 to 98 percent of white residents of the midwestern states were functionally literate, a little below rates in the Northeast but somewhat higher than those in the South. Because reading and writing were so important in the transmission of culture, the kind of literacy taught in schools was highly controversial. Native-born Protestant Americans insisted on a standard version of the English language. Many immigrants and southerners resisted efforts to teach a standard English. Like other immigrants and Native Americans, Germans saw control of language as a key to the survival of their culture and insisted on bilingual education.

English literacy defined nineteenth-century cultural wars. A top priority of the boarding school education of Native American children was fluent English reading, writing, and speaking. For immigrant children as well, English language literacy was part of the citizenship process. Despite the formation of private and parochial schools, immigrant and Native American children often paid the price of ridicule and embarrassment as well as the loss of culture even as they entered school in a new country where they yearned to practice a new language.

Nevertheless, many midwestern cities provided alternative models of literacy until World War I and immigration restriction in the 1920s. Many people beyond Protestant, native-born middle-class citizens intuitively understood that the nature of functional literacy varies from place to place. A rancher or farmer on the Great Plains needed different skills than a factory or office worker in a crowded city on the Great Lakes.

Despite the development of a mass uniformity in English literacy in the twentieth century, midwesterners have learned to use language to function in multiple contexts. With modernity, literacy offered occupational and personal freedom as well as the rights of citizenship.

Late-twentieth-century adult (age sixteen and older) literacy levels as defined by years of schooling are similar across the midwestern states. On average, 21 percent of the population achieved grade 12 or less; 34 percent earned a high school diploma or equivalent; 28 percent achieved some college; and 16 percent earned a bachelor's degree or higher. Today, literacy levels of adults in the Midwest states are slightly higher than the national average. Further, compared to adults nationally (85 percent), a higher percentage of midwestern adults (93 percent) reported that English was the only language they learned before school. This high incidence of English as the first and often only oral language in part explains the slightly higher literacy levels of adults in the Midwest.

Although some studies have shown a decline in literacy in the United States, other researchers have argued that the definition of literacy has expanded in the twentieth century to include information technology and media literacy, suggesting that the apparent decline may be more aptly expressed as a raising of the bar.

Sources and Further Reading: David W. Adams, *Education for Extinction* (1995); William Gilmore-Lehne, "Literacy," in Mary Kupiec Cayton, Elliott J. Gorn, and Peter W.

Williams, eds., *Encyclopedia of American Social History, vol. 3* (1993); Carl F. Kaestle, *Literacy in the United States* (1991).

Jacqueline K. Peck
Kent State University, Ohio

Private Schools and Academies

The Land Ordinance of 1785 set out specific ways that settlers should support education by providing that land be set aside, the rents from which would fund schools. This legislation, along with the Northwest Ordinance of 1787, was a landmark in stating the importance of universal education. Yet in practical terms, it accomplished little, because the set-aside lands generally were too poor to garner much rent. When money was collected, it was often diverted toward other projects, such as building railroads and canals. A state-regulated, tax-supported system of free public education for all children did not come into effect in most midwestern states until the 1840s and 1850s. Where there was education outside the home prior to the establishment of the state system, it occurred in a private school or academy.

In the early nineteenth century, it would have been hard to distinguish a public school from a private school. Parents of scholars in town- or district-sponsored schools would have paid in some way for their children to attend. The school might have been a "subscription school," meaning that parents paid a fee for each child attending, or families might have paid by boarding the teacher with them for a few weeks at a time. Most children who received formal schooling in the early nineteenth century did so in some version of a private school or academy.

Some private schools and academies in the nineteenth-century Midwest were famous in their day. The well-known advocate of female education Catharine Beecher established academies in Ohio and Wisconsin. Mount Holyoke Female Seminary in Massachusetts sponsored institutions in Ohio and inspired the founding of many other schools that educated women and trained them to be teachers of the children on the new frontier. Wilberforce University (Ohio) originally opened in 1856 as a private academy for African Americans from the South who could not get schooling there. Various religious groups, particularly Roman Catholics, also founded private schools due to fears that the expanding public education system excluded their religious views.

As the public school system grew in the late nineteenth century, the academies either folded into the public school system as high schools, continued as elite private schools, became the foundation for colleges and universities, or ceased to exist altogether. In the Midwest in 2001–2002, private schools educated 11.2 percent of children, slightly more than the national average. Most of those schools are at the elementary level. Overwhelmingly, the private schools are Catholic; 64 percent of private school attendees in the Midwest are in Catholic schools. The next single largest type of private school is Lutheran, which accounts for 11 percent of all midwestern private school students. The introduction of voucher programs in the 1990s in Milwaukee, Wisconsin, and Cleveland, Ohio, heralded the potential growth of private academies with public funding.

Sources and Further Reading: Nancy Beadie and Kimberley Tolley, eds., *Chartered Schools* (2002); Carl F. Kaestle, "Public Education in the Old Northwest: 'Necessary to Good Government and the Happiness of Mankind,'" *Indiana Magazine of History* 84 (Mar. 1988).

Margaret Nash
University of California–Riverside

Special Education

Since its inception special education has been synonymous with social reform, and midwestern reform often targeted persons with disabilities. In 1837 Ohio

❖ Campus Video Communications Project Is Underway

The Missouri School for the Deaf is implementing a new system to provide two-way video communications for its staff and students, both on and off campus.

To this end, the school will be distributing a series of D-Link "I2Eye" personal videoconferencing units (also called Video Phones) to selected personnel and locations around the campus. Each unit will be delivered with a 13" TV. Deaf staff will also receive a "Phone Flasher" to be used with the D-Link. These units will be connected through a new, separate "Video Network." Parents and colleagues off campus with compatible equipment will be able to place calls to these units.

Deaf users will also be able to use their V-Phones to place and receive Video Relay calls using Sprint VRS. Video Relay Services is a system that works in much the same way as TTY Relay; the deaf user can place a video call to a VRS operator, who will then place a voice call to a hearing individual and interpret between the two in real time.

Source: Missouri School for the Deaf, "Campus Video Communications Project Is Underway," *Here's What's Happening at MSD!* 9 (Nov. 11, 2003).

became the first state in the region to establish a publicly supported school for blind students, followed by Indiana in 1847 and Illinois in 1848. Their purpose was to extend the right to education to a "class" generally believed incapable of learning to become self-sufficient.

Settlement workers, a strong force for reform in the Midwest, often worked through schools. At Chicago's Hull-House, Jane Addams pressed for services for children with physical impairments or chronic health conditions. In Cleveland, Ohio, in 1900, a volunteer society collaborated with Alta House Settlement to establish the region's first day school for children with physical impairments. Three decades before federally mandated early intervention, agencies like the Society for Crippled Children provided special preschools. This agency, formally established at the 1927 Rotary International Convention in Belgium, began as a network of Ohio Rotary Clubs lobbying for legislation for children with physical disabilities. The 1919 "Ohio Plan," which encouraged the creation of special treatment for disabled children, was expanded by other states to include schools.

Special education's history reflects the contrast in the Midwest between densely populated urban centers and vast rural areas. A major factor in successive states' adoption of the centralized residential school model for students with sensory impairments was that the total number of these students was relatively low. By contrast, as early as the 1870s Chicago, Detroit, and Cleveland had formed special classes for "unrulies" and "backward" students, children requiring speech correction, and those with chronic health conditions—all associated with, or ascribed to, urban problems: poverty, immigration, and crowded classrooms. In 1910 Chicago became the first school district in the United States to offer speech-correction services, followed by state mandates in Illinois, Iowa, Michigan, Minnesota, Missouri, Ohio, and Wisconsin.

Special education programs for students identified as gifted and talented began in the Midwest in 1920 with the establishment of the nation's longest-continuing gifted education program, Cleveland's Major Work. Several midwestern universities, notably the University of Illinois, accorded this often-neglected area of special education an important place on their faculties' training and research agendas.

While the residential training school was the dominant model for blind and deaf students until the 1970s, there were notable exceptions. In Chicago in 1900, Frank Hall sent one of his teachers, John Curtis, to help establish day classes for blind students, a model to which Robert Irwin in Cleveland added "sight-saving" (low-vision) classes. Parent activism in Wisconsin and Ohio brought legislation mandating day classes, intended to equip deaf children with speech, rather than sign language, in order to adapt them to hearing society. This philosophy ran counter to that of the residential schools, strongly linked to deaf culture. The sometimes bitter conflict between "deficit" and "difference" conceptions of deafness continues today.

Special education's development was also spurred by scientific advance. By 1900 most midwestern states had institutions for "feebleminded" people, which served as centers for both the training of special educators and research. In the diagnostic clinic at the Faribault, Minnesota, institution, Frederick Kuhlman developed new psychometric measures. The first school-based psychoeducational clinic was in Chicago's Department of Scientific Pedagogy and Child Study, formed in 1899.

The Iowa Child Welfare Research Station, which by the 1920s had emerged as a leading center for research in child development, provided a training ground for scholars later known for their pioneering research on exceptional patterns in children's learning and social behavior. Among the most notable was Newell C. Kephart, later of Purdue University, who developed a widely used diagnostic and remedial system. Another whose research greatly influenced special education practices was Alfred E. Strauss, who studied learning problems of brain-injured children in an experimental unit he established in 1941 at the Wayne County Training School in Northville, Michigan, and later at the Cove Schools in Racine, Wisconsin, and Evanston, Illinois.

Growing awareness of the psychological needs of children and youth linked educators with mental health professionals and the emerging juvenile justice system. William Healy founded the Juvenile Psychopathic Institute in Chicago, later called the Illinois Juvenile Research Institute. In 1924 Karl Menninger, cofounder with Healy and others of the American Orthopsychiatric Association, opened the Menninger Foundation's Southard School for emotionally disturbed children in Topeka, Kansas. Other residential treatment centers established in the 1920s include Starr Commonwealth in Albion, Michigan, which created affiliates in Battle Creek and Detroit, Michigan, as well as in Van Wert and Columbus, Ohio. Under child psychologist Bruno Bettelheim, the Sonia Shankman Orthogenic School was founded in 1944 at the University of Chicago, while at Detroit's Pioneer House Fritz Redl and David Wineman demonstrated group therapeutic interventions for youth presenting highly challenging behaviors.

In 1952, through Illinois special education director Ray Graham's efforts, the University of Illinois's Institute for Research on Exceptional Children was established. Under Samuel Kirk, this interdisciplinary research and training center was the prototype for the American Association of University Affiliated Programs for Persons with Development Disabilities (now AUCD) recommended by President John F. Kennedy's Blue Ribbon Panel on Mental Retardation. Throughout the 1960s and 1970s, midwestern universities strove to meet the rapidly growing demand for well-trained special education teachers, therapists, and diagnosticians.

Several organizations important in special education's development had midwestern origins. In 1923 the Council for Exceptional Children held its first convention in Cleveland. Plans to form the organization that became the American Speech-Language-Hearing Association were initiated in 1925 in an Iowa City living room. The Association for Children with Learning Disabilities was formed on April 6, 1963, at a meeting in Chicago's La Salle Hotel, the name suggested by Kirk. The Association for Retarded Citizens (ARC) began as a network of parents whose children were excluded from school.

In recent years, the disability rights movement has flourished in the Midwest. Minnesota's Senator Hubert Humphrey led the fight for the national legislation that culminated in 1972 with the passage of Free Appropriate Public Education, especially Section 504, which was reauthorized in 1990 as the Individuals with Disabilities Education Act. University of Minnesota scholars were early leaders of the inclusive schooling movement later known as the Regular Education Initiative. In 1974 the organization later called TASH held its first meeting in Kansas City, its mission to support the right of people with severe disabilities to participate fully in school and community life.

Sources and Further Reading: Barbara Aiello, "Especially for Special Educators: A Sense of Our Own History," in June B. Jordan, ed., *Exceptional Child Education at the Bicentennial* (1977); R. H. Bremner, *Children and Youth in America: A Documentary History, vol. 2, 1866–1932* (1970); Harlan Lane, *The Mask of Benevolence* (1992); Philip L. Safford and Elizabeth J. Safford, *A History of Childhood and Disability* (1996); R. C. Scheerenberger, *A History of Mental Retardation* (1983); Geraldine T. Scholl, ed., *Foundations of Education for Blind and Visually Handicapped Children and Youth* (1986); Margaret A. Winzer, *The History of Special Education* (1993).

Philip L. Safford
Case Western Reserve University, Ohio

William Holmes McGuffey (1800–1873)

William Holmes McGuffey, a minister and educator born in 1800, compiled his famous readers for schoolchildren while serving as a member of the faculty at Miami University in Oxford, Ohio, during the 1830s.

❖ McGuffey Readers

Written by William Holmes McGuffey, a professor at both Miami and Ohio Universities, and published in Cincinnati, the McGuffey Readers were the most successful textbooks in nineteenth-century America. In addition to teaching basic skills, the readers promoted middle-class notions of character and personal morality, as in this excerpt.

"No Excellence without Labor" is as good a commencement motto as "Labor Omnia Vincit [hard work conquers all things]," the favorite motto for a hundred years.

The education, moral and intellectual, of every individual must be, chiefly, his own work. Rely upon it, that the ancients were right; both in morals and intellect, we give the final shape to our characters, and thus become, emphatically, the architects of our own fortune. How else could it happen that young men, who have had precisely the same opportunities, should be continually presenting us with such different results, and rushing to such opposite destinies?

[O]bserve the mediocre plodding his slow but sure way up the hill of life, gaining steadfast footing at every step, and mounting, at length, to eminence and distraction, an ornament to his family, a blessing to his country.

The best seminary of learning that can open its portals to you, can do no more than afford you the opportunity of instruction: but it must depend, at last, on yourselves, whether you will be instructed or not, or to what point you will push your instruction.

And of this be assured, I speak from observation a great truth: THERE IS NO EXCELLENCE WITHOUT GREAT LABOR. It is the fiat of fate, from which no power of genius can absolve you.

Source: William H. McGuffey, *The Fourth Eclectic Reader: Containing Elegant Extracts in Prose and Poetry from the Best American and English Writers with Copious Rules for Reading and Directions for Avoiding Common Errors* (1838). Courtesy the McGuffey Museum, Miami University, Oxford, Ohio.

His desire to spread education and religion throughout the new region of the Midwest inspired him to compile a new set of school readers, geared toward the children of America's Heartland. He amassed materials, edited and arranged them according to levels of difficulty, and in 1836 and 1837 published the four volumes that comprised the McGuffey Eclectic Readers series (two additional volumes were added years later). These books grew in popularity over the years, and by the end of the century the readers had gone through countless editions and sold tens of millions of copies, doing especially well in the developing communities of the Midwest and the South.

The readers taught children how to spell, read, and write, and they also offered a set of values, beliefs, and ways of behaving. Just sampling titles that the readers anthologized gives a sense of their emphasis: "The Greedy Girl," "Beware the First Drink," "The Insolent Boy," "True Courage," "Consequences of Idleness," "Advantages of Industry," and "Religion the only Basis for Society." Learning the McGuffey lessons was an act of faith for Victorian children—that education would elevate them morally, refine them culturally, and advance them socially. The readers provided a blueprint for building middle-class American lives centered on evangelical morality and bourgeois earnestness while ignoring controversial issues such as slavery, immigration, and workers' rights.

McGuffey moved on from Miami to Cincinnati College, Ohio University, and finally the University of Virginia. He died in 1873. The influence of his readers, however, lived on into the twentieth century, as men as different as Henry Ford and Clarence Darrow—both raised on the McGuffeys—testified to their power to shape young minds.

Sources and Further Reading: Elliott J. Gorn, *The McGuffey Readers* (1998); Richard Mosier, *Making the American Mind* (1965); Wayne Urban and Jennings Wagoner, Jr., *American Education: A History* (1996).

Elliott J. Gorn
Brown University, Rhode Island

Teachers and Administrators

Midwestern teachers and administrators have played a defining role in the development of American school structure and politics. Rural midwestern culture prioritized local control of schools, and teachers and administrators have long faced the particular conditions of strong community influence. In the great cities of the Midwest, teachers at the turn of the century organized the first American teachers' unions. The work of midwestern teachers and administrators, then, can be characterized as a long struggle to balance local control with centralized control, and teachers' rights with community rights.

The earliest schooling in the Midwest was local, or district, schooling. The district system of schooling located control of education at the school-district level. Generally, schools were small, serving as few as two to four families. As a result, states had hundreds of districts, each with its own board of education elected from the local citizenry. Men dominated school board membership throughout the nineteenth century, with only two recorded instances of women as school board members in the entire Midwest. Local boards of education had limited control over school curriculum, in part due to the lack of free textbooks for students, who would supply their own books, such as Noah Webster's *Elementary Spelling Book* or one of William Holmes McGuffey's readers, often handed down the generations in a family. The school board visited a school to oversee instruction, discipline, and attendance and to supervise the teacher, although rural school board members most often neglected this job. The hiring of the teacher was the school board's most important and influential job.

Because midwestern schooling was tied to local tradition and practice, there was a wide range of commitment to public schooling. Some communities cared greatly about schooling and invested money and time toward the maintenance and operation of a one-room school. Beyond providing sufficient financial support, parents and community members helped to paint the schoolhouse, build outhouses, clean and tend the school and its yard (if, indeed, there was a yard beyond prairie grass and dirt), and arrange for firewood for fuel. Those schools having public support could be in close proximity to schools in other communities that did not display as much concern for public schooling. Teachers' salaries, professional support, and guidance were thus dependent on the local community.

The decision to hire a teacher often was influenced by testaments to the moral character of the applicant, the board's acquaintance with or relationship to the teacher, and consideration of the grade of teaching certificate held by the aspiring teacher. The gender of the teacher also determined hiring decisions. While men dominated the midwestern schoolhouse in 1800, women entered teaching in large numbers after 1830. Estimates of the percentage of female teachers in the Midwest range from 82 percent in 1850 to a lower estimate of 58 percent in 1880. Although data differ by historical accounts, intraregional differences within the Midwest existed, with the northern states of Michigan and Wisconsin feminizing earlier than the southern states of the region, such as Missouri.

Because of the lack of district supervision in rural areas, teaching was an individual enterprise. A lone schoolteacher typically had complete control over her or his rural one-room school and scholars who could range in age from four to the late teens. Predominantly using the recitation method of instruction, teachers taught the three Rs and a bit more: grammar, penmanship, spelling, geography, and history. Teachers also disciplined students, including the use of corporal punishment.

Teachers' education in the nineteenth century was haphazard, in part because of the great geographic distances between schools, teachers, and teacher education institutions. County teacher institutes, annual seminars lasting from a few days up to six weeks, were popular in the Midwest after 1870. Controlled and offered locally by the county superintendent, these institutes aimed to teach the subject areas and pedagogy, although their effectiveness in helping teachers improve their teaching is questionable. Because teaching licenses had to be renewed annually, attendance at county institutes often allowed teachers to renew their license without having to take the examination again. For many teachers in the nineteenth century, the only form of teacher training was attendance at county institutes. A few rural teachers were able to attend early teacher education schools, called normal schools, which many midwestern states offered in state and private institutions. By the 1890s every state but Ohio had at least one state normal school, and the Midwest was second only to the East in founding state normal schools. In the twentieth century the normals grew into teachers' colleges and, eventually, more generalized institutions for higher education.

States created the position of county superintendent in the mid- to late 1800s as a way for the state to monitor, control, and standardize local education efforts. County superintendents examined and licensed teachers; distributed state monies to local districts; visited schools and kept records of school population, children in attendance, and conditions of schoolhouses; and adjusted school-district boundaries. The presence of superintendents in the educational hierarchy was an effort to centralize control of local public schools and to control teachers' work in those schools.

The developing hierarchy of state and district school administrative positions was designated for men, while women remained in the lower-paying and lower-status classroom. This reflected traditional gender dynamics and led to increased tension between the two groups. Male superintendents often disassociated themselves from the ranks of female teachers by creating professional associations, such as the Department of Superintendence of the National Education Association. In the twentieth century, the development of specific graduate-level university programs to prepare school administrators created further distinctions between teachers and administrators. These programs often limited women's enrollment so that the gender divide remained and became supported by a supposedly scientific standard of professionalism. These efforts legitimized the administrator's work and further institutionalized the division between administrators and teachers.

Midwestern women, however, were not wholly absent from the position of superintendent, especially as women won school suffrage after the turn of the twentieth century. By 1900 more midwestern states granted women school suffrage than states in any other region. Women could vote in school-related elections in Illinois, Iowa, Kansas, Michigan, Minnesota, Nebraska, North Dakota, Ohio, South Dakota, and Wisconsin, as well as in fourteen other states in the union. Using their newly won right, women voted women into the position of superintendent, and by 1910 27 percent of local and county superintendents in the Midwest were women, well above the representation of women in the Northeast and the South, but still below the 34 percent female representation in the West. By 1930 the combined percentage of local and county female superintendents in the Midwest peaked, at 40 percent. After World War II, women superintendents in the Midwest (and around the country) declined for two reasons. First, states tightened their control over the superintendency by making it a position appointed by educational and political authorities. Second, in an effort to make rural schools more efficient, rural school districts were consolidated. Nationwide, the number of school districts declined from 104,000 in 1947 to 59,000 in 1956. Both appointed positions and school consolidation favored men as administrators and valued professional authority over local determination.

While hundreds of rural school districts reflecting local tradition existed throughout the Midwest, teachers in urban centers such as Chicago, St. Louis, Minneapolis, and Detroit had very different work experiences. Like their rural counterparts, urban teachers often found themselves isolated in their classrooms, with little direct daily supervision by or assistance from either colleagues or supervisors. Because of the size of city schools and the development of business-type models of school systems designed to educate thousands of students efficiently, however, supervisors were standard parts of urban educational systems. City supervisors infrequently visited classrooms, but when they did they often required teachers to demonstrate that they had been following the prescribed course of instruction exactly, even though this was rare given the realities of overcrowded classrooms, limited resources, and diverse student bodies.

Urban teachers in the Midwest developed formal means of collective action as a way to resist centralization and administrative reform, leading to the first organized teachers' associations and unions in the country. The teacher unionism that arose in large midwestern cities such as Chicago; Milwaukee, Wisconsin; and St. Paul, Minnesota, between 1897 and 1920 emerged out of a similar aversion to centralized control and professional authority displayed in the rural areas of the Midwest. The Chicago Teachers Federation, one of the largest teachers' unions of the era, successfully fought to secure pensions and tenure, increase wages, and involve teachers in decision making. Its success encouraged teachers in other regions of the country to unionize. Led by Margaret Haley, the federation counted up to half of Chicago's teachers as members, most of them female elementary teachers. The federation allied itself with male trade unions and local community organizations to secure voting blocs. It also worked closely with teacher-friendly school boards and administrators, including Ella Flagg Young, superintendent of the Chicago city schools and eventual president of the National Education Association. The Chicago Teachers Federation helped elect her to that position.

Although rural and urban educators shared their antipathy toward centralized control, unionization remained predominantly an urban phenomenon. Rural teachers were much more disposed not to join a union but to join the National Education Association, which espoused a professional ideology rather than trade unionism until after World War II and the start of collective bargaining.

In the postwar years, teachers' unions again became active in some midwestern cities, in particular Chicago, St. Paul, and Minneapolis. The unions mediated discussions between teachers and the school system in a more formal and organized manner than had been true in the past. Whereas early in the twentieth century teacher unionism pitted local teachers and the community against a centralized administration, by the 1960s collective bargaining had recognized and legitimized teacher unionism as an organized element within the field of education. But with collective bargaining, teachers' unions maintained fewer ties to local trade unions and community groups and more to centralized authority, with which unions could bargain to win material gains and professional prerogatives. Teachers' unions, once a voice for local control and decision making, had become part of the establishment and in direct communication primarily with the centralized board of education, not community members.

Centralization of control, be it through appointed superintendents, collective bargaining, or consolidated school districts, not only limited women's participation in school administration and circumscribed teachers' roles in school affairs, but it also had similar effects on the local community's role in educational matters.

Consolidation of school districts made participation in school matters more difficult and less likely for rural people. No longer did a district's citizenry have direct control over hiring a teacher or managing a schoolhouse. Rather, professional experts—usually male administrators—held tight reins on a consolidated school and its personnel, which had expanded to include subject-area specialists and numerous support staff to tend to students' psychological and vocational needs. Professional experts, not local community members or even teachers, would determine those needs.

Sources and Further Reading: Jackie M. Blount, *Destined to Rule the Schools* (1998); Edward Eggleston, *The Hoosier School-Master* (1984); Wayne E. Fuller, *The Old Country School* (1982); Myrna J. Grove, *Legacy of One-Room Schools* (2000); Paul Mattingly and Edward W. Stevens, Jr., eds., *"Schools and the Means of Education Shall Forever Be Encouraged": A History of Education in the Old Northwest, 1787–1880* (1987); Marjorie Murphy, *Blackboard Unions* (1990); Joel Perlmann and Robert A. Margo, *Women's Work? American Schoolteachers, 1650–1920* (2001); Dina L. Stephens, "The Role of County Superintendents in Rural School Reform in Late Nineteenth Century and Early Twentieth Century Wisconsin," Ph.D. diss., University of Wisconsin (1996); Paul Theobald, *Call School* (1995).

Laurie Moses Hines
Kent State University–Trumbull

Teacher Education and Normal Schools

Early approaches to teacher education included the efforts of the National Board of Popular Education, which between the mid-1840s and mid-1850s selected young women in the East to take a short training course conducted by Catharine Beecher, a prominent advocate of education for women, before heading to frontier schools in the Midwest. Midwestern educators soon began to import other methods of teacher training from the East.

By the 1850s, teachers' institutes were widespread in the Midwest. Teachers' institutes usually lasted several days and presented a program of discussions of teaching methods and speeches by prominent educators. While institutes provided opportunities for practicing teachers to update and improve their methods, school reformers also sought more permanent, preservice means for professional development. In response, some private colleges and academies created teacher-education courses. Between 1857 and 1865, the State of Wisconsin subsidized academies and colleges that trained teachers. Private seminaries devoted to educating teachers, which appeared in the East in the 1820s, spread quickly to the Midwest; among the first was one in Illinois in 1837.

Modeled on Prussian and French institutions, some of these teacher seminaries were called normal schools, a translation of the French term *école normale*, which was used for schools imparting the norms, or standards, of teaching. Some normal schools were private and others were municipal, but the state-run normal school was the most common and enduring type throughout the United States. The first state normal school opened in Massachusetts in 1839, and the East had several state normals before the first midwestern one appeared, in 1853 in Ypsilanti, Michigan. During the 1850s and the 1860s, the Midwest was second only to the East in its enthusiasm for founding state normal schools. In 1857 Illinois ambitiously opened its State Normal University in a town that was soon called Normal, and during the 1860s state normal schools opened

The vocational aspects of a normal school education. Chicago Historical Society, *Chicago Daily News*, DN-0067959.

in Winona, Mankato, and St. Cloud, Minnesota; Emporia, Kansas; Platteville and Whitewater, Wisconsin; and Peru, Nebraska. By the 1890s every midwestern state but Ohio had at least one state normal. With seven by 1900, Wisconsin had the most state normal schools in the Midwest; nationally, only Massachusetts, New York, and Pennsylvania had more. The Iowa State Normal School in Cedar Falls would remain that state's only state normal, and Ohio would not establish state normals until the 1910s. These states were unusual probably because their private multipurpose colleges were influential teacher educators and in Ohio many students attended private normal schools.

State normal schools usually offered between one and three years of study and granted various degrees or certificates in pedagogy. Before the late nineteenth century, the schools' official focus was on the preparation of teachers for the common, or public, schools. Students brushed up on academic subjects in addition to learning how to teach. Instruction in pedagogy, a brand-new concept in the early nineteenth century, evolved decade by decade as professional knowledge expanded. Into the 1870s the education courses listed in most schools' catalogs were simply "methods," or perhaps "theory and art of teaching." Psychology and the science of education or pedagogy appeared in catalogs later in the 1870s, and school economics and school law soon followed. By the end of the century, many midwestern normals followed the lead of Illinois State Normal University and adopted the Herbartian approach to teacher training. Developed in the early nineteenth century by the German philosopher Johann Friedrich Herbart, this approach stressed systematic lesson planning according to five concrete steps, which served as "five windows" into the soul of the child. Observation and practice teaching were also integral to normal-school training. Most normals had "model," or "practice," elementary schools where students spent a significant amount of time observing the methods of advanced normal students and full-time "critic" teachers before doing any teaching themselves. In addition, literary societies, the most popular and long-lived student associations, allowed students to study and debate current issues in education and other fields. At the end of the nineteenth century, the representatives of different schools' literary societies competed against one another in debate leagues.

Some normal-school leaders were not content to only train elementary-level teachers. Within a few decades of opening, many state normals began to add the preparation of high school teachers and administrators to their offerings.

Many students and their families had an even broader conception of the purpose of a normal school. Although most state governments were reluctant to allow normal schools to offer a general college education and normal-school leaders felt pressure for their graduates to serve the public schools, many citizens, especially in the Midwest, viewed state normal schools as an attainable form of general higher education, closer to home. Thus state normal schools unofficially made higher education available to the children of farmers and others who could not afford colleges and universities. Normal schools were coeducational and enrolled large numbers of women, who were not very welcome at colleges and universities at the time.

As normal schools grew, some state universities also began to educate teachers. The Midwest was distinctive in that many of its universities, including Indiana University and the Universities of Wisconsin, Iowa, Missouri, and Kansas, established "normal departments" in the 1850s, 1860s, or 1870s. Most of these departments had a limited life span because of education's low prestige and the popularity of the separate normal schools.

By the 1880s many universities—in the Midwest and throughout the country—began to conduct research in the field of education, and by the turn of the twentieth century, many universities had schools or colleges of education that offered teacher education, but prioritized research. This approach to teacher education ultimately affected normal institutions, which first became four-year college-level institutions, still officially focused on teacher education and by the 1930s had symbolically changed their names to "teachers college." These former normal schools continued to seek higher status, expanding to become state colleges in the 1940s and the 1950s and, later, state universities.

Thus, in the Midwest as in the United States as a whole, teachers in the early twenty-first century receive their education in universities or colleges, often in the shadow of research or other courses of study.

Sources and Further Reading: John I. Goodlad, Roger Soder, and Kenneth A. Sirotnik, eds., *Places Where Teachers Are Taught* (1990); Charles A. Harper, *Development of the Teachers College in the United States* (1935); Jurgen Herbst, *And Sadly Teach* (1989); Jurgen Herbst, "Nineteenth-Century Normal Schools in the United States: A Fresh Look," *History of Education* 9 (1980); Carl Kaestle, *Pillars of the Republic* (1983); Christine A. Ogren, "'A Large Measure of Self-Control and Personal Power': Women Students at State Normal Schools in the Late-Nineteenth and Early-Twentieth Centuries," *Women's Studies Quarterly* 28 (Fall/Winter 2000); Christine A. Ogren, "Where Coeds Were Coeducated: Normal Schools in Wisconsin, 1870–1920," *History of Education Quarterly* 35 (Spring 1995).

Christine A. Ogren
University of Iowa

Teacher Unions

Teacher unions thrive today in public school districts of the Midwest. The American Federation of Teachers (AFT) and the National Education Association (NEA) bargain collectively with employers, local school boards, over wages, hours, and working conditions. At a time of relative decline in union membership nationally, teacher unions stand out as vibrant, growing organizations that aggressively speak to current issues of educational reform, especially teacher accountability.

Since its inception in 1916, the AFT, referred to as "the Union," has been aligned with the broader labor movement, the American Federation of Labor (AFL) and, later, the merged AFL-CIO. Three teacher organizations in Chicago and one in Gary, Indiana, founded the AFT. Charles B. Stillman (1885–1948), a Chicago high school teacher, served as the first AFT president. The AFT emerged after the Chicago Teachers Federation, a militant union of women elementary teachers, was forced to abandon its labor affiliation by the Chicago Board of Education.

The NEA, widely known as "the Association," has its roots in a professional association formed in 1857 by professors and educational philosophers. By the end of the century it included administrators from large urban districts. But teachers, who were mostly women, were not recognized as members by the NEA's male, non-teacher leadership until the 1910s. At that point most beginning teachers joined the NEA, as did administrators. The organization continued to be male dominated and administrator led until the 1960s, when the NEA began acting like a union, that is, participating in collective bargaining. During those years classroom teachers took control of the NEA from school administrators.

While the AFT looked to big-city, pro-union teachers, the NEA, which has always been much larger than the AFT in terms of membership, attracted teachers in areas where labor unions were weak. For much of its history the NEA viewed unions as unprofessional, encouraging potential members to join their professional association instead. A proposed merger with the AFT in the 1970s fell apart when the NEA refused to join the AFL-CIO. Since the 1990s AFT locals in Cincinnati and Toledo, Ohio; Minneapolis/St. Paul, Minnesota; and, most recently, Chicago have led in efforts to reform the educational labor force from within. The NEA has become focused nationally on fighting efforts to privatize public schools; it also opposes teacher accountability measures tied to high-stakes testing of students. The organizations continue to talk merger. Since October 2001 they have been engaged in the NEAFT Partnership, in which they promote common themes but act as independent organizations.

Some observers note a new teacher unionism based on collaboration with school boards instead of confrontational collective bargaining. Others contend that the power, control, and financing of education are all being questioned in the current context of educational reform, high-stakes testing, threats of school privatization, and a globalizing world economy. Within the parameters of a rapidly changing educational world, the NEA and the AFT, possibly together and possibly in new ways, will continue to seek power and a voice for classroom teachers.

Sources and Further Reading: Stephen Cole, *The Unionization of Teachers* (1969); Marshall O. Donley, *Power to the Teacher* (1976); Marjorie Murphy, *Blackboard Unions* (1990); Wayne J. Urban, *Gender, Race, and the National Education Association* (2000).

Kathleen A. Murphey
Indiana University–Purdue University,
Fort Wayne

Margaret Haley (1861–1939)

Margaret Angela Haley was an elementary school teacher in Chicago who led what became the first American teachers' union. Born in 1861 in northern Illinois to Irish immigrants, Haley taught in one of Chicago's poorest school districts for sixteen years be-

Margaret Haley. Chicago Historical Society, ICHi-23302.

fore she joined the Chicago Teachers' Federation, an organization founded in 1897 and led by women elementary teachers for the purposes of protecting their pensions and improving working conditions in city schools. Most elementary teachers worked in underfunded, overcrowded schools and had little or no voice in their school management or curriculum design. Most threatening to teachers were repeated cuts in their salaries and pensions by the powerful Chicago School Board, many of whose members were affiliated with major power-brokering corporate entities in the city and the state.

In her forty years as the paid business representative of the federation, Haley fought for improved teachers' salaries and benefits in Chicago and other midwestern states. She also allied the federation with other midwestern reform organizations that fought for more democratic political processes, reformed labor laws, women's suffrage, tax reform, and closer state monitoring of private corporations. In 1902 she engineered the federation's affiliation with the Chicago Federation of Labor, thereby effectively linking teachers with the powerful Chicago labor lobby. The Chicago Teachers' Federation became Local 1 of the newly formed American Federation of Teachers in 1916.

Haley's scope was national educational reform, but her focus remained on Chicago, where she spent her career fighting to improve Chicago's schools for teachers and students. She died in 1939.

Sources and Further Reading: Robert L. Reid, ed., *Battleground: The Autobiography of Margaret Haley* (1982); Kate Rousmaniere, "Progressive Education and the Teacher: Margaret Haley's Vision," in Alan R. Sadovnik and Susan Semel, eds., *Founding Mothers and Others* (2002); Wayne J. Urban, *Why Teachers Organized* (1982).

Kate Rousmaniere
Miami University, Oxford, Ohio

Ella Flagg Young (1845–1918)

Ella Flagg Young, born in Albany, New York, in 1845, moved to Chicago in her youth and later became arguably the most accomplished school leader of her time. She studied to become a teacher in a high school normal program. Then she commenced a remarkable career, rising rapidly through the Chicago teaching ranks to become a principal in her fourth year. She held two other principalships before assuming an assistant superintendency. At age fifty Young enrolled in the newly created doctoral program at the University of Chicago, where she studied with John Dewey and supervised his laboratory school. The university published her dissertation, *Isolation in the Schools* (1900), an incisive critique of industrialized education and a call for democratic schooling in the service of society. A popular professor, Young taught a number of education courses at the university. In 1905 she accepted the principalship of the Chicago Normal School, and a few years later, when the Chicago superintendent resigned, supporters forwarded her name for the position. In 1909 the board approved her unanimously, making her the first female superintendent of a large city school district and the highest paid woman in the nation. A year later teachers voted her into the presidency of the National Education Association, and again she was the first woman to hold such a position. She resigned from the superintendency in 1915 because of deep board divisions. Three years later, in 1918, she died in the flu pandemic. She left the bulk of her estate to her life partner, Laura Brayton.

Sources and Further Reading: John T. McManis, *Ella Flagg Young and a Half-Century of the Chicago Public Schools* (1916); Joan K. Smith, *Ella Flagg Young* (1979).

Jackie M. Blount
Iowa State University

Progressivism and Reform

As the Midwest's population and economy grew in size and global reach in the late nineteenth century, its citizens grappled over how to educate their children. By the 1920s coalitions of progressive reformers had rationalized and extended the common schools into bureaucratic systems that schooled children and most adolescents in a variety of academic and nonacademic topics. In the post–World War II era, however, school reformers from many quarters challenged "progressive" structures and practices, condemning them variously as permissive, unequal, exclusive, and ineffective. Today the Midwest has a mosaic of educational arrangements, governed sometimes loosely, sometimes tightly, by local, state, and federal authorities.

Midwestern progressives, a diverse lot that included middle-class men and women as well as upper- and working-class adherents, were confident that people could solve social problems through an expansion of government institutions and the application of scientific principles. Progressivism in education extended the school's mission to health, family and recreational life, political participation, and vocational pursuits; embraced the new social sciences of psychology, sociology, and education in school governance and classroom pedagogy; and accommodated growing numbers of students from various cultural and class backgrounds.

Some precursors of progressive education, such as St. Louis, Missouri's public kindergartens and manual training school; and agricultural education for rural teachers in Wisconsin, date to the 1870s. Nevertheless, progressivism in midwestern education began in earnest in the 1890s, a decade punctuated by economic depression and political unrest. In response to burgeoning enrollments of students new to the urbanizing Midwest, reform encompassed three themes. Elite reformers—business executives and professional men—sought to centralize school governance and rationalize operations according to "social efficiency." Grassroots coalitions of women's groups, trade union and Socialist Party leadership, and organized grade-school teachers wanted the schools to meet what they, not the social efficiency advocates, perceived as the manifold educational needs of working-class students and their families. Reformers sought to change the tenor of teaching from authoritarian delivery of an esoteric curriculum to strategies that sought to match the curriculum to students' social and psychological development.

To reformers trying to build a new social order, schools were an attractive site for improvement: They shaped dispositions for work and citizenship, yet they stood largely outside of elite control. Locally elected politicians and their appointees essentially ran the schools, and in the reformers' view this interfered with running the schools according to business and professional principles. Armed with the slogan "keep the schools out of politics," reformers whom historian David Tyack has termed "administrative progressives" used their influence in state legislatures to embark on mostly successful campaigns to transfer control of urban schools from partisan school boards to smaller, administratively centralized boards where cosmopolitan elites could set broad policies and select professionally trained superintendents. Cities across the Midwest made the shift. The Cleveland and Toledo, Ohio; St. Louis; and Milwaukee, Wisconsin, school boards centralized in the 1890s. Detroit and Chicago followed in 1916 and 1917, respectively.

Reforms sweeping American businesses guided many of the new educational administrators. Like factories, the schools should be governed according to scientific management, with the students as raw material and the teachers as workers. Departments of educational administration trained the new leaders, and university presidents, professors, and superintendents often circulated between university and public school systems. Andrew Draper, for example, left the Cleveland schools superintendency for the presidency of the University of Illinois.

Education professors, many of whom believed that the school's goal was to help the population perform the tasks of an unequal society more efficiently and with less strife, surveyed school systems and made recommendations. In the early 1900s the University of Chicago's John Franklin Bobbitt began to differentiate the public school curriculum according to the perceived ability of each class of individuals. In the cities, social efficiency reformers built larger, more cost-effective schools, developed Americanization programs for immigrants, and by the 1920s were using intelligence tests to categorize students for programs in college preparation, living skills, or vocational or commercial education. Meanwhile in the rural Midwest, reformers consolidated school districts.

This new leadership did not, however, put an end to politics in schools. Administrative progressives were not immune to corruption, and grassroots activists blunted many elite measures and established school practices of their own. In cities ranging from the polyglot Chicago to the largely immigrant Milwaukee and more native-born Kansas City, Kansas, grassroots progressives insisted that public schools be responsive to non-elite demands. Penny lunches, vacation schools, playgrounds, and social centers were instituted as local activists prodded school systems to provide impoverished children with meals, safe places to play, and summer excursions. Social centers even turned some schools into places for political organizing.

Grassroots progressives had various reasons for advocating these policies. For middle- and upper-class leaders of women's clubs and settlement houses such as Chicago's Jane Addams or Milwaukee's Lizzie Kander, activism in education meant participating in the public sphere, caring for the poor, and maintaining concern for the family. For Social Democratic politicians such as Milwaukee's Victor and Meta Berger, grass roots' reforms protected workers' children from the excesses of capitalism during the struggle for a Socialist state. For "Social Gospelers" such as Toledo mayor Samuel Jones, free meals and textbooks put the Golden Rule into practice. For elementary school teachers such as Chicago's Margaret Haley and Catherine Goggin, such efforts represented solidarity with organized labor, with teachers providing quality education and workers supporting teacher demands for better pay and school conditions.

Other progressive reformers changed classroom pedagogy to instruction based on child and adolescent development that educated for participation in democratic processes and flexibility in an evolving economy. Francis W. Parker, principal of Chicago's Cook County Normal School from 1883 to 1899, first popularized progressive pedagogy through that institution's practice school, in which the school was organized as a "model home" that incorporated art, nature study, and student experiences into the academics. This new spirit of teaching was extended by Parker's contemporary John Dewey, who founded the University of Chicago's Laboratory School in 1896 and directed it until 1904. For Dewey, the school served as a miniature community: Each child's emerging talents contributed to the school community, and the school educated others through its interactions with the wider society. In the early twentieth century progressive pedagogy took its place alongside the more pervasive social efficiency reforms in midwestern schools.

By the early 1950s, progressive public schooling meant education for a wide social life, a differentiated curriculum, expert control, and a modicum of child-centered instruction, and this progressivism was mirrored in some private and parochial schools. From the reams of data on the psychological health of young children disseminated by the Iowa Child Welfare Research Station to the assortment of "mental hygiene" films emanating from the Coronet Studios of Glenview, Illinois, midwestern education meant much more than academics. The downplaying of the disciplines, however, particularly in the guise of "life-adjustment" education after 1945, vexed many public intellectuals who placed academic rigor at the heart of education. In *Educational Wastelands* (1953), University of Illinois history professor Arthur Bestor condemned educators for trying to meet the vague needs of youth (properly the family's domain) and sought a renewed focus on intellectual development and Western cultural heritage. Educational responses to the cold war reinforced Bestor's concerns and bolstered the natural sciences, mathematics, and foreign languages in secondary schools.

The growth of the Midwest's progressive system of public schools contained, rather than ameliorated, large-scale inequalities of access and resources, whereby students who were African American or another ethnic minority, working class, female, or disabled had fewer opportunities. Activists seeking to extend quality education to all stepped up their demands after 1950, beginning with opposition to racially segregated schools. For African Americans, educational inequalities were particularly glaring. In the southern Midwest segregation was legally sanctioned, and in the Great Lakes cities to which many African Americans had migrated authorities segregated school systems on social efficiency grounds, which alleged that enrolling black students in white schools was educationally disruptive whereas "neighborhood" schools were more effective. In Kansas, Oliver Brown and twelve other parents filed suit in 1951 against Topeka's system of racially segregated elementary schools, which formed the lead case for the landmark *Brown v. Board of Education* (1954, 1955) decision.

In the cities of the upper Midwest, the struggle to desegregate the schools crested in the 1960s and 1970s. Civil rights activists led school boycotts, sit-ins, and freedom schools, and they blocked the school buses and construction equipment used to maintain segregated schools. They demanded equal access, improved facilities, a pluralist curriculum, and high standards in predominantly African American schools. Lawsuits resulted in federal rulings that forced school districts and states to dismantle segregated systems. Responding to racial segregation in Detroit, the U.S. Supreme Court's *Milliken v. Bradley* (1974) decision limited the scope of desegregation to city school districts.

Growing school enrollments in relatively affluent suburban districts after 1950 changed the contours of socioeconomic inequalities in public education beyond a divide between cities and poorer rural districts. Most large cities in the Midwest lost population and industry in the late twentieth century, often to the suburbs. The high costs and racial discrimination in suburban housing markets meant that students in big-city schools were more likely to be poorer and hail from racial or ethnic minority backgrounds than their suburban counterparts. Urban school systems saw their traditional sources of support erode: the enrollment of middle-class and upwardly mobile working-class students, the big-city tax base, and the backing of organized labor. The locus of control shifted from school districts to state departments of education, and no single suburban district assumed regional educational leadership as the city systems once did.

In the 1990s state-level centralization brought with it increased curriculum requirements backed by frequent standardized testing. It did not, however, lead to equity of resources among districts. Rural and urban school districts joined together in several states to demand equal school funding, but with mixed results. In the 1990s courts in Minnesota and Wisconsin upheld their funding systems whereas Missouri and Ohio courts ruled theirs unconstitutional.

In midwestern public high schools, female enrollment rates often edged male. But the shift from elite to mass secondary education brought with it policies that offered girls' educational opportunities that did not keep pace with boys', because enrollments in scientific, commercial, industrial, vocational, and home economics programs were often sex-typed. The women's movement of the 1960s broadened women's educational options, and federal initiatives in the 1970s extended this trend. Schools across the Midwest made changes, among them increased female enrollment in advanced science and mathematics courses, better women's athletic programs, and more women moving into educational administration. For children with disabilities too, the 1970s marked a turning point—via pressure at local, state, and federal levels—that increased access to schools and mainstream classrooms. Yet, as with racial desegregation, full inclusion of women and students with disabilities remained difficult to implement completely. Schools in Indiana excluded AIDS (acquired immunodeficiency syndrome) patient Ryan White in the mid-1980s, and enrollments of female and minority students at Chicago's Washburne Trade School remained low through the 1990s.

Recent reforms in midwestern school governance have led away from the structures that administrative progressives erected a century ago. Several urban school systems have witnessed forms of democratic localism reminiscent of the early Progressive Era. From 1988 in Chicago, and extending to other cities, local school councils consisting of parents, teachers, and residents make educational decisions that were previously the purview of central administrations. City politicians have also regained authority in public school affairs, with mayors in Chicago (1995) and Cleveland (1998) appointing school boards and superintendents. Also growing in popularity are school reforms that shift authority in public education to market mechanisms such as charters and vouchers. Despite the growing acceptance of parental choice school reforms in the cities and the rise of homeschooling throughout the Midwest, the "one best system" of progressive public education nevertheless remains well ensconced—even vibrant—in most of the suburbs, where a plurality of midwesterners live.

Sources and Further Reading: Barbara Beatty, *Preschool Education in America* (1995); Lawrence A. Cremin, *The Transformation of the School* (1964); Ira Katznelson and Margaret Weir, *Schooling for All* (1985); Herbert M. Kliebard, *The Struggle for the American Curriculum, 1893–1958*, 2nd ed. (1995); James T. Patterson, *Brown v. Board of Education* (2001); Diane Ravitch, *The Troubled Crusade* (1983); William J. Reese, *Power and the Promise of School Reform* (1986); Ken Smith, *Mental Hygiene* (1999); David B. Tyack, *The One Best System* (1974); David Tyack and Larry Cuban, *Tinkering toward Utopia* (1995).

Jim Carl
Cleveland State University, Ohio

Progressive Education

Progressive education, a widespread and important effort to change American schools in the twentieth century, originated in the Midwest. In the last decade of the nineteenth century the founders of the movement rejected the dominant educational practices of the day, and established educational institutions in Chicago that focused on the needs and interests of children.

This educational reform was part of a larger progressive movement that was prominent in midwestern politics and social policy at the turn of the twentieth century. While they differed in many ways, in general progressives held a positive view of human nature and saw ignorance and misunderstanding as the source of social conflict; therefore education was crucial for social reform.

Advocates of progressive education argued that education should begin with the curiosity and desire to learn that are natural in all children. The role of the teacher was to guide that curiosity rather than to dictate a preestablished curriculum. They saw children as developing and changing as they matured; accordingly, the schools needed to adapt themselves to the changing needs and abilities of their students. Progressives believed that education could take place in many settings and that the schools should not be isolated from the educational opportunities offered outside their walls. They took a broad view of education, maintaining that it involved not only learning from books but also learning from activities; they valued manual training as well as reading Shakespeare. The "whole child"—emotional and physical development as well as intellectual needs—should be the focus of a progressive classroom. Academic subjects should be coordinated in ways that showed children the connections among subjects. Schools should be organized, as much as possible, as democratic institutions and model communities. In this way, they would provide models for organizing the larger society.

Francis W. Parker, called the "father of progressive education" by John Dewey, came to Chicago in 1883 as head of the Cook County Normal School after establishing a record of educational reform in Quincy, Massachusetts. In Cook County's practice school Parker instituted a number of progressive practices. Reading and writing, for example, were taught through leaflets that the children wrote. Science was taught with many field trips. When Dewey moved to Chicago, he was impressed with Parker's school and enrolled his own children there before he established his laboratory school at the University of Chicago. In 1901 Parker founded a school that bears his name and is still an important part of the educational scene of Chicago.

John Dewey was the primary philosopher of progressive education. He joined the faculty of the University of Chicago in 1894 and with his wife, Alice, established its Laboratory School in 1896. In *The School and Society* (1900), he outlined progressive educational principles and argued that they were the key to social reform. Schools, he argued, should be constituted as "embryonic communities." "When the school introduces and trains each child of society into membership within such a little community . . . we shall have the deepest and best guaranty of a larger society which is worthy, lovely, and harmonious."

Informal and formal education were central to the mission of serving the needs of the immigrant neighbors of Jane Addams's Hull-House. That settlement's educational efforts included nursery schools for children and a "Plato Club" for adults. Dewey was a frequent visitor at Hull-House and credited Addams with helping him to form the framework for progressive education.

Even before the full development of progressive education in Chicago, parts of what would become the progressive program had been developed elsewhere in the Midwest. In St. Louis, Missouri, Calvin M. Woodward of Washington University was critical of the schools for continuing to pursue the outmoded goals of "gentlemanliness and culture." Accordingly, he established the Manual Training School at the university, which opened its doors in 1880. Its curriculum was divided between mental and manual labor. Woodward's was not, however, a vocational school. Rather, it sought to establish a liberal learning approach to manual training—one that would be useful to all students regardless of their future occupations. Cities such as Cleveland and Toledo, Ohio, and St. Paul, Minnesota, instituted manual training. Best known was the work in Menomonie, Wisconsin, and surrounding Dunn County, where an extensive program was instituted in the early 1890s.

Progressive education was important in other midwestern cities. The schools of Gary, Indiana, gained an international reputation during the 1907–1938 tenure of Superintendent William Wirt (who had studied with Dewey). Gary schools were structured in such a way that students alternated among classroom instruction, laboratory work, shop instruction, and recreation. While one group was in a laboratory or shop, another group would occupy the classroom. In this way the "platoon system" made very effective use of valuable classroom space. The schools stayed open later to serve as community centers, and Gary had an extensive program of adult education. When Dewey and his daughter Evelyn visited Gary in 1915 they were deeply impressed by its varied program. Other observers, however, were much more impressed with the cost efficiency of the platoon system, and it was this feature that others tried to imitate.

The wealthy Chicago suburb of Winnetka was another well-known center for progressive education that combined progressive features with an efficient use of classroom time. Under the leadership of Carleton W. Washburne (who came to Winnetka in 1919) the "Winnetka Plan" featured individualized instruction in the "tool" subjects—reading, math, and spelling. Stu-

dents learned these subjects by advancing at their own pace through sequential texts, moving from one to the next after passing a test. If they did not pass the test, they were directed to work on the kinds of problems that had given them difficulty. This form of programmed learning allowed children to move through the curriculum at their own pace.

By the 1950s there was a strong reaction against progressive reforms and a successful popular demand for more traditional practices—a return to "basics." In this atmosphere, progressive education suffered a rapid decline.

Sources and Further Reading: Jane Addams, *Twenty Years at Hull-House* (1910); Ronald D. Cohen, *Children of the Mill* (1990); Lawrence A. Cremin, *The Transformation of the School* (1961); John Dewey, *The School and Society* (1899; reprint, 1956); Katherine Camp Mayhew and Anna Camp Edwards, *The Dewey School* (1936); Marie Kirchner Stone, "The Francis W. Parker School," in Susan F. Semel and Alan R. Sadovnik, eds., *"Schools of Tomorrow," Schools of Today* (1999); Carleton W. Washburne and Sidney P. Marland, Jr., *Winnetka: The History and Significance of an Educational Experiment* (1963); Arthur Zilversmit, *Changing Schools* (1993).

Arthur Zilversmit
Lake Forest College, Illinois

John Dewey (1859–1952)

Although he was not originally from the Midwest, much of the work that made philosopher and educator John Dewey famous took place in Michigan and Illinois. Born in Burlington, Vermont, in 1859, Dewey grew up in a pietistic, liberal Congregational household. He developed an interest in Hegelian philosophy and the new science of psychology as ways of bridging the troublesome gap between reason and will in traditional Calvinist theology. Over time Dewey transformed his early religiosity into a scientific- and secular-based faith in the possibilities of American democracy, egalitarianism, and community. In the 1890s and 1900s at the University of Chicago, Dewey developed and elaborated a child-centered philosophy of education designed to connect the growth of the individual with the welfare of the community.

Dewey's parents both grew up in rural Vermont and they spent most of their adulthood in Burlington, where Dewey's father ran grocery and tobacco shops. Family circumstances were comfortable. Dewey studied at the University of Vermont and upon graduating in 1879 became a teacher in Oil City, Pennsylvania, remaining long enough only to decide to continue his study of philosophy. He did so first in private study

John Dewey. Chicago Historical Society, *Chicago Daily News*, DN-0087487.

and then in 1882 at the Johns Hopkins University, a new institution of higher education based on the German model of research.

At Johns Hopkins Dewey was exposed to the new world of German empirical scholarship, including the new science of experimental psychology. Though he never entirely abandoned his idealism, he saw psychology as a way of exploring the emotional substratum that organically undergirded and held together rational thought. Over time, his interest in human desire and motivation—the will—propelled him in the direction of experimentalism (or instrumentalism), as his new philosophy came to be called. Influenced by evolution as a model, Dewey came to believe that all knowledge represents evolving attempts to solve real-life problems. Whether any absolute truth existed was a moot point. Humans could only pursue contingent solutions to problems that allowed successful functioning in particular social and cultural environments.

So successful was Dewey at Johns Hopkins that his mentor recommended him to the philosophy department at the University of Michigan in 1884. At that time, Michigan not only valued the investigative, experimental research model; the institution also laid heavy emphasis on service to community institutions,

particularly schools. While at Michigan Dewey had frequent contact with teachers and administrators and began to formulate some of the rudiments of the child-centered models of education that he would elaborate later at the University of Chicago. In 1887 Dewey also published *Psychology*, one of the first psychology texts in the country, which focused on the important developments of the German experimental school.

Dewey taught at Michigan and chaired the philosophy department there until 1894, with the exception of academic year 1888–1889, which he spent at the University of Minnesota. When William Rainey Harper wanted to hire faculty at the new university at Chicago, he invited Dewey to become professor of philosophy. Harper's reputation for valuing both research and experimentation in education lured Dewey. Seeing social and economic democracy as the truest form of Social Christianity (then a flourishing movement in Chicago), Dewey dedicated his time and energies to nurturing social experiments, including the settlement house Hull-House, where he served as trustee. So close did Dewey and his wife, Alice Chipman Dewey, become to its founder Jane Addams that they named their daughter after her.

Early in his tenure at Chicago Dewey asked Harper for a laboratory in which to try out his educational ideas, just as other scientists might use laboratories to test hypotheses. Though Dewey's Laboratory School was never lavishly supported by the University of Chicago, it was of great significance nonetheless. Begun in 1896 with a handful of students and faculty, it grew to include 33 faculty and staff and 140 students by the time Dewey left in the early 1900s. Dewey's Laboratory School was the first such facility in an American university. In viewing education as a researchable subject, Dewey also sought to elevate the status of teachers as professionals. His philosophy department included both psychology and pedagogy as components, and he lobbied Harper for a separate department of pedagogy.

In *The School and Society* (1900), *The Child and the Curriculum* (1902), *How We Think* (1910), and *Democracy and Education* (1916) among other works, Dewey discussed some of the principles from which the Laboratory School operated. Like nineteenth-century German educational reformers Friedrich Froebel and Johann Pestalozzi, Dewey saw the child as naturally desirous of learning. In an integrated curriculum centered around projects and questions about which children had natural curiosity, students would learn as a matter of course and without resort to authoritarian measures designed to give them the "will" to learn. Dewey's curriculum also emphasized the degree to which the child was by nature a social being—a member of a community who would grow best by identifying his or her own interests with those of the community. The contrast with traditional methods of learning was stark: Obedience-centered learning focusing on traditional subjects and utilizing recitation, reading, and writing versus a developmentally appropriate curriculum tapping into the child's natural motivations, focused on cultural and industrial learning, and involving the child in collaborative, project-centered work.

Dewey left Chicago in 1905 after disputes over curriculum with Harper, whose authoritarianism had begun to bother Dewey. Dewey would spend the next forty-seven years of his distinguished career at Columbia University in New York. His work continued to deal with the philosophical issues that he saw as most important to American life—education, politics, ethics. Ever the pragmatist, Dewey was instrumental in forming the American Federation of Teachers in 1916. When he died in 1952, he was something of an icon. One of the primary catalysts behind the Chicago school of pragmatism, this philosopher of growth, transformation, progress, and possibility left his fellow citizens a legacy that still wields considerable influence—a philosophy born in New England but transformed and indelibly colored by life in the urban Midwest at the turn of the century.

Sources and Further Reading: John Dewey, *The Early Works, 1882–1898*, Jo Ann Boydston, ed. (1972); John Dewey, *The Later Works, 1925–1953*, Jo Ann Boydston, ed. (1981); John Dewey, *The Middle Works, 1899–1924*, Jo Ann Boydston, ed. (1976); Andrew Feffer, *The Chicago Pragmatists and American Progressivism* (1993); Herbert M. Kliebard, *The Struggle for the American Curriculum, 1893–1958* (1995); Jay Martin, *The Education of John Dewey: A Biography* (2002); Alan Ryan, *John Dewey and the High Tide of American Liberalism* (1995); Robert Westbrook, *John Dewey and American Democracy* (1991).

Mary Kupiec Cayton
Miami University, Oxford, Ohio

Francis W. Parker (1837–1902)

Francis W. Parker was born on October 9, 1837, in the village of Piscataquog, New Hampshire. Determined to teach despite family tragedies that interfered with his schooling, he worked his way through Mt. Vernon Academy and secured teaching positions in small New Hampshire towns. In 1859 he went to Carrollton, Illinois, to become principal of the county's only district school.

After the Civil War, Parker became principal of North Grammar School in Manchester, New Hamp-

shire, and successfully instituted near total regimentation, only to realize that he was destroying the children's natural drive to learn. In search of new approaches, he was elected principal of the First District School in Dayton, Ohio, in July 1868, where the "object teaching" of Swiss educator Johann Heinrich Pestalozzi had already been introduced. Despite conflicts with conservative community members, Parker was appointed principal of the new normal, or teacher-training, school in September 1869. Following the death of his first wife in December 1870, he decided to go to Germany to study progressive pedagogical theory. After two years in Germany, he returned in the winter of 1874–1875 just as the Quincy (Massachusetts) School Committee was seeking a trained superintendent to whom they were willing to give total control to solve the schools' problems. After four years the results of Parker's work were publicized by committee member Charles Francis Adams, Jr., as "The New Departure in Education" and became nationally known as the "Quincy method."

Now an irrepressible crusader for progressive education, Parker became primary school supervisor in Boston in 1880 in order to take on even more entrenched conservative forces and, as he said, to make change a bit easier for his successors. His summer teacher institutes at Martha's Vineyard were documented by Lelia Patridge in *Talks on Teaching* (1882), and his contacts there with Chicago teachers led to his becoming principal of the Cook County Normal School in Chicago in 1883. His insistence on freeing children to learn naturally and joyfully, and on educating teachers to help them do so, pitted him against conservatives at every biennial budget meeting of the school board, and in 1899, subdued too by his wife's losing battle with cancer, he accepted the offer of Anita McCormick Blaine to endow a private institute in which he could fulfill his vision of comprehensive progressive teacher education.

The combination of a weak economy and the determination of President William Rainey Harper of the University of Chicago to incorporate Blaine's million-dollar endowment into his new university delayed the opening of Parker's "Chicago Institute" and resulted in 1901 in a mutually unhappy merging of John Dewey's devoted University of Chicago Elementary School teachers with Parker's equally devoted Cook County Normal School teachers. The conflict was only resolved after Parker's death in March 1902, through an additional endowment from Blaine for the work of the Parker teachers under Flora J. Cooke in what would become the Parker School, still in existence today. Parker died with his vision of a truly progressive school unfulfilled.

Sources and Further Reading: Jack K. Campbell, *Colonel Francis W. Parker* (1967); Ida Cassa Heffron, *Francis Wayland Parker* (1934); Francis W. Parker, *Talks on Pedagogics* (1894).

Kate Cruikshank
Lilly Library, Indiana University–Bloomington

Consolidation

School consolidation refers to the merger of two or more schools into a single larger institution. It is often accompanied by the centralization of school administration into a larger school board or other administrative body, in many cases on a countywide basis. School consolidation was a trend throughout the United States in the first half of the twentieth century and was especially prevalent in the rural Midwest, as locale after locale witnessed the replacement of small one-room schoolhouses and tiny school systems with larger consolidated school districts.

School consolidation resulted from a variety of changes both in the theoretical underpinnings of American education and in American society itself. Perhaps most significantly, the increased specialization inherent in a modern industrial society mandated both a lengthening of the span of time that young people were spending in school and an increased focus on vocational training that could prepare young people to take their place in an increasingly mechanized industrial and agricultural workforce.

Accordingly, the almost continuous upward trajectory of high school enrollment in the United States in the first half of the twentieth century encouraged the movement to consolidate students into larger schools that could serve the diverse needs of both college-bound students and those who desired training that could help them to enter skilled labor occupations. Consolidation also reflected the ideas of progressive educators, who favored larger schools because their expanded budgets, facilities, and staffs offered more specialized faculties, greater vocational and practical training, and a wider array of school services such as health supervision and occupational guidance.

The process of school consolidation in the Midwest and elsewhere has often been arduous. State governments, which were providing an increased share of educational funding in the early twentieth century, tended to favor consolidation as a means to cut long-term operating costs. But practical problems, like the difficulty of transporting students on the often poor roads of the rural Midwest and the high costs of providing buses and building new facilities, often combined with local resistance to undermine consolidation.

Ohio lawmakers passed a series of consolidation measures between 1894 and 1914, but to little avail. In 1924 5,500 one-room schoolhouses remained in the state, and as late as 1935–1936 Ohio contained about 900 school districts with no high school. Iowa became the scene of national and even international attention in 1913 because of its coordinated campaign to consolidate rural school districts, which succeeded in the closure of 2,663 rural schools. But Iowa abandoned the plan in 1923 and saw little further consolidation until after World War II.

While consolidation was more common in states such as Indiana, Kansas, and Minnesota in the 1920s, the real decline of small school districts did not come until the Great Depression, when the loss of local tax revenue and other financial problems caused the closure of many small schools. School consolidation efforts have continued since World War II despite opposition from supporters of local autonomy.

Sources and Further Reading: Alan Peshkin, *The Imperfect Union* (1982); David R. Reynolds, *There Goes the Neighborhood* (1999); Robert Shreve, *History of Ohio's County Boards of Education, 1914–1989* (1989).

Kevin P. Bower
University of Cincinnati, Ohio

Desegregation

Although many people think that racial segregation is peculiar to the states of the old Confederacy, racial separation is most severe in the midwestern states. Using U.S. census data for 2000, the Lewis Mumford Center found that six of the ten most segregated cities in the United States were in the Midwest. More important, it was in this region that civil rights activists met two of their greatest defeats, the first in Chicago, Illinois, and the second in Detroit, Michigan.

After 1954, when the U.S. Supreme Court found separate schools to be inherently unequal, the movement to bring about the desegregation of schools advanced slowly until 1964, when Title VI of the U.S. Civil Rights Act gave the Office of Education in the Department of Health, Education, and Welfare (HEW) the power to require integration without a trial. Using their newfound authority, federal officials successfully confronted school districts throughout the South where segregation had been required by law.

But in 1965, when HEW tried to force Chicago schools to desegregate, the federal officials failed. Although there was evidence that African American stu-

❖ *Brown v. Board of Education* **Timeline**

The U.S. Supreme Court's decision in *Brown v. Board of Education of Topeka, Kansas,* 347 U.S. 483 (1954), 349 U.S. 294 (1955) declaring "separate but equal" public schools unconstitutional was only the beginning of school desegregation in Topeka. As this timeline reveals, the process mandated by the decision was hotly contested for decades.

1951	Oliver Brown files suit on behalf of his daughter, Linda Brown Smith.
1954	*Brown* ruling declares segregation unconstitutional.
1955	In second *Brown* decision, the U.S. Supreme Court leaves implementation of desegregation to lower courts because of differences in local circumstances but orders them to proceed "with all deliberate speed."
1955–1961	Topeka's desegregation plan is implemented.
1964	U.S. Civil Rights Act is passed.
1966	Kansas public schools are reorganized.
1970	School boycott/riot occurs (April 17–30).
1970–1971	Proportional representation is implemented in High School.
1973	*Johnson v. Whittier* seeks monetary damages of $200 million for inequalities in facilities on behalf of all Black children who had attended elementary and junior high schools in East Topeka and North Topeka between 1963 and 1973.
1974	U.S. Department of Health, Education, and Welfare (HEW) investigates Civil Rights Act compliance.
1975	Class-action status for Johnson is denied.
1976	HEW ends complaint and accepts long-range plan.
1979	Second HEW investigation opens; *Brown* is reopened to redefine "desegregation."
1986	District court finds for the defendant.
1989	District court findings are reversed.
1994	U.S. District Court for the District of Kansas approves Unified School District No. 501's third desegregation proposal.

Source: Adapted from Raymond Wolters, *The Burden of Brown: Thirty Years of School Desegregation* (1984) and Paul E. Wilson, *A Time to Lose: Representing Kansas in Brown v. Board of Education* (1995).

dents attended separate schools in the city, HEW officials could not persist amidst the resulting controversy. This failure marked the beginning of the end of HEW's influence in school desegregation. In 1969 President Richard Nixon announced that HEW would rely on court trials rather than bureaucratic decisions; the court trials were much slower.

Despite the withdrawal of effective HEW intervention, lawyers for the National Association for the Advancement of Colored People's Legal Defense Fund (LDF) won *Keyes v. Denver School District* in 1973, which required a northern city to desegregate its schools despite the absence of explicit statutes requiring segregation. The LDF lawyers argued that officials in the school district caused segregation with techniques such as manipulation of attendance zones, appointment of teachers, and the selection of school building sites. The following year, LDF lawyers suffered a significant defeat in *Milliken v. Bradley*, which involved Detroit, Michigan.

In *Milliken*, LDF lawyers asked the U.S. Supreme Court justices to require some fifty-two suburban school districts, whose student populations were about 81 percent white, to integrate their students with the Detroit city schools, whose student populations were about 70 percent African American. Lower-court judges had agreed that they could not bring about integration if they limited desegregation to the city because many schools would retain nearly all black populations. The Supreme Court justices did not attend to this problem. Contending that the LDF lawyers had not shown that public officials caused the segregation, the justices found no legal reason to correct it by ordering what was called a metropolitan plan.

After *Milliken*, lawyers found it difficult to desegregate midwestern schools because many districts follow city or town boundaries. The situation was different in many southern states because there school districts encompassed entire counties, which made a metropolitan plan possible. But in the Midwest, several smaller, independent districts often surrounded a city school district. City or state officials aggravated this situation. In Columbus, Ohio, officials allowed school districts outside the city school-district boundaries to remain independent after the city extended such things as water and sewer services or annexed the land.

The U.S. Supreme Court offered some hope for metropolitan desegregation in 1976 in a ruling about housing in Chicago. *Hills v. Gautreaux* led to a decision ordering the U.S. Department of Housing and Urban Development to join with the Chicago Housing Authority to locate public housing in areas outside the municipal boundaries. But this decision did not change housing patterns enough to alter school integration. Nevertheless, successful school desegregation plans appeared in Indianapolis, Indiana; Dayton, Ohio; and Flint, Michigan.

In the mid-1970s, scholars and policy analysts argued over the extent to which desegregation plans exacerbated white flight from cities to suburbs. The problem was difficult to resolve because economic shifts aggravated white flight. Factories closed as the Midwest became the Rust Belt. When people relocated, they tended to buy homes in suburban communities rather than in the cities. Though it was not clear that white people left their urban homes to avoid busing, the percentage of white people in cities fell because white people had more alternatives for housing than black people did.

In 1972 the U.S. Congress offered federal support for magnet schools to reduce the need for cross-district busing. A magnet school was a building in a depressed or African American area that offered a unique curriculum in hopes of attracting middle-class or white students. Cities including Cincinnati, Ohio, accepted magnets as the only type of acceptable desegregation.

An interesting controversy arose in the 1990s about the effectiveness of magnet schools to reduce racial segregation. Christine Rossell used information from twenty school districts to determine that magnets in a system with the most voluntary control, such as Cincinnati, offered the most racial integration. Using exactly the same data, Brian Fife came to the opposite conclusion. He claimed that systems with magnets in addition to a coercive court order, like Dayton, offered the most integration.

In 1986 the U.S. Supreme Court allowed school districts across the nation to end desegregation plans. The decision, *Riddick v. School Board of the City of Norfolk, Virginia*, allowed courts to declare a school district to be unitary, allowing it to return to neighborhood schools. By 1991 the proportion of schools with more than half minority students had returned to the level for 1971, just before the Court made its first busing decision.

In the Midwest, school district officials proclaimed these changes as beneficial, yet they aggravated the racial separation in schools. Cleveland's desegregation plan began in 1976 and ended in 1998. According to the Mumford Center's 1999–2000 analysis, released from court supervision, the Cleveland elementary schools experienced the most rapid increase in racial segregation of students in the United States. Columbus; Milwaukee, Wisconsin; and Minneapolis, Minnesota, also experienced rapid increases in school segregation during the same decade. In 2002 federal courts released the Dayton schools from their desegregation plan.

Sources and Further Reading: James Coleman, *Trends in School Segregation: 1968–1973* (1975); Paul R. Dimond, *Beyond Busing* (1985); Brian Fife, *Desegregation in American Schools* (1992); Gregory S. Jacobs, *Getting Around Brown* (1998); Jeffrey Mirel, *The Rise and Fall of an Urban School District* (1993); Gary Orfield and Susan E. Eaton, *Dismantling Desegregation* (1996); Christine H. Rossell, *The Carrot or the Stick for School Desegregation Policy* (1990); Rosemary C. Salomone, *Equal Education under Law* (1986).

Joseph Watras
University of Dayton, Ohio

Finance

Although school finance equity is a contested issue nationally, the extremely fragmented local governance structures of the Midwest make it an especially thorny problem in the region. More than two hundred years after the Northwest Ordinance of 1787, most states in the region still struggle with how to fund schools without creating wide disparities among wealthy, average, and poor communities.

When the Northwest Territory—the heart of today's Midwest—was settled in the late eighteenth century, American schools were financed in a haphazard fashion. A mixture of private, public, and parochial schools was supported by tuition, local taxes, and in-kind contributions to teachers such as housing and farm produce. Thus the passage by the U.S. Congress of the Land Ordinance of 1785 established an important precedent by setting aside in every township a 640-acre section of land to be used to support education. Although the proceeds from renting out these sections were inadequate for funding schools fully, they made it clear that the government valued education and would pay for it.

However, it took most of the nineteenth century to obtain legislation providing adequate tax support for public elementary and secondary schools. Statutes in support of elementary schools were passed well before similar legislation for secondary ones, and the battle over mandatory local property taxes for education was bitterly fought. Ohio, Indiana, and Illinois, with large southern populations who were accustomed to minimal educational provisions, passed such laws later than the other midwestern states, most of whose settlers had come from New England and New York, long pioneers in public education. Nonetheless, by the early twentieth century publicly funded schools were the norm throughout the region.

However, by this time professors of school administration had identified a problem that still haunts American education: school finance inequity. When schools are supported by local property taxes, wealthy communities develop well-financed systems while poor ones struggle just to keep their doors open. Early school finance experts recommended that states pay a significant portion of the cost of education through minimum foundation programs, which are designed to insure that everyone, even in poor or poorly funded districts, has access to a basic education. This approach was widely adopted throughout the Midwest. It did not solve the problem because large inequalities persisted. In the early 1970s, poor districts across the United States began to challenge the constitutionality of such systems. In October 1971, with *Van Dusartz v. Hatfield*, Minnesota became the second state in the nation to declare its school finance system unconstitutional.

Litigation in this area continues. As of 2002 the constitutionality of the school finance system had been challenged in most midwestern states. The plaintiffs lost almost all these cases. It is likely, however, that poor districts will challenge these finance systems again, for most midwestern states share two characteristics associated with significant school finance inequality. First, in the average midwestern state the state government contributes just 44 percent of funds for education, compared with 47 percent nationally. Second, the typical midwestern state has 463 school districts, compared with 290 nationally. This combination of a low state share and fragmentation into a larger number of districts guarantees major inequality among districts. It is likely, therefore, that the future holds more battles over school finance equity for the Midwest.

Sources and Further Reading: Vern Brimley, Jr., and Rulon R. Garfield, *Financing Education in a Climate of Change*, 8th ed. (2002); Carl F. Kaestle, *Pillars of the Republic* (1983); Allan R. Odden and Lawrence O. Picus, *School Finance: A Policy Perspective*, 2nd ed. (2000); Austin D. Swanson and Richard A. King, *School Finance: Its Economics and Politics*, 2nd ed. (1997).

Frances Fowler
Miami University, Oxford, Ohio

Homeschooling

Historically, homeschooling was normal practice, not only in the Midwest but across the United States. Geographically isolated farm families and religious communities, such as the Amish and the Mennonites, practiced homeschooling. In recent years, midwestern parents have increasingly turned to homeschooling for other reasons.

Homeschooling is legal in all states, and many of the legal decisions that are the foundation of homeschool parents' rights were generated in the Midwest. In *Wisconsin v. Yoder* (1972), the U.S. Supreme Court upheld an Amish family challenge to compulsory education based on their right to religious freedom. In *Mazanec v. North Judson–San Pierre School Corporation* (1985), a federal district court ruled that parents have the right to educate their children at home, even though the primary teacher in the case was a Mennonite mother with an eighth-grade education. In *Newstrom v. Minnesota* (1985), the Minnesota Supreme Court ruled that the teacher qualification component of the compulsory attendance law was unconstitutional. On the strength of such parent-friendly court decisions, the Midwest has become a very homeschool-friendly region of the country.

The growth of homeschooling in the Midwest reflects the national expansion of homeschooling since the 1960s. Reasons parents give for homeschooling children today include concerns with school violence, drug use in schools, and disagreements over public school curriculum. Exact numbers of homeschooled children are unknown; however, estimates range from 1 to 3 percent of school-age children.

Sources and Further Reading: David Gerger, "No Place Like Home," *U.S. News and World Report* (June 19, 2000); Patricia Lines, "Home Schooling Comes of Age," *Educational Leadership* 54 (Oct. 1996).

Pamela B. Riegle
Ball State University, Indiana

Testing

Educational researchers, teachers, and students in the Midwest have played a major role in both the development and the critique of educational testing. Henry Chauncey, founder of the Educational Testing Service (ETS) and the person responsible for making SAT (Scholastic Aptitude Test) a household word, first learned about the new field of psychological testing while a student at The Ohio State University in the 1920s. Chauncey's belief was that testing could help objectively identify talent in people regardless of their circumstances. The SAT was designed in 1926 to measure the verbal and mathematical reasoning abilities, or aptitude, of college-bound students.

While ETS became ensconced on the East Coast, Iowa became the home for competing versions of standardized tests. The test that would become the Iowa Test of Basic Skills (ITBS) in 1955 was initially developed in 1935 for elementary and secondary students with the purpose of helping teachers identify students' academic strengths and needs and thereby improving instruction. Its founder, University of Iowa psychology professor E. F. Lindquist, also developed the American College Test (ACT), an achievement test designed to measure students' readiness for post-secondary education. The ACT remains the dominant college admissions test for schools in the Midwest, while the SAT is the primary test of the two coasts.

In the school accountability reform movements of the 1980s and 1990s, states across the country increased the number of standardized tests required of students and intensified the weight of test results—what is often called "high-stakes testing" because of the repercussions on schools whose students perform poorly on tests. Many of the critics of such developments were based in the Midwest. In Milwaukee, the progressive educational journal *Rethinking Schools*, founded in 1986, developed a national readership with its articles critical of standardized testing. In a middle-class suburb of Columbus, Ohio, parents organized in the late 1990s to protest the Ohio Proficiency Test.

Organized resistance to tests reached a crescendo in Chicago in the 1990s when parents, teachers, students, and community leaders protested the misuse of the ITBS for student retention and promotion decisions; the use of high school standardized tests for teacher and school accountability; and the general proliferation of testing, tests, and test-prep-as-curriculum. Demonstrations and boycotts led to the elimination of standardized test data from teachers' grade books, and parent protests led to modifications of grading, promotion, and retention policies.

Sources and Further Reading: Nicholas Lemann, *The Big Test: The Secret History of American Meritocracy* (1999); Susan Ohanian, "National Test Resistance Grows," *Phi Delta Kappan* (Jan. 2001); George N. Schmidt, "Teachers for Social Justice to Hold May 12 Protest against Iowa Test," *Substance: The Newspaper of Public Education in Chicago* (May 2003); "Why the Testing Craze Won't Fix Our Schools," *Rethinking Schools* 13 (Spring 1999).

Kate Rousmaniere
Miami University, Oxford, Ohio

Vouchers and Charter Schools

Charter schools and vouchers, two of the most controversial educational policies in the United States at the beginning of the twenty-first century, originated in and maintain a powerful presence in the Midwest. Charter schools are public schools established through contractual agreements that allow them exemptions from specified state and local regulations. Under school voucher programs, the state gives students a financial voucher to use for payment to any nonpublic school.

Minnesota established the first charter schools in the United States, in 1991. In 2003 forty-one states, including all but three in the Midwest, had charter school laws. Although legislation varies from state to state, all specify who may start a charter school, the level of funding, staffing credentials, accountability, student services, and exemptions from state and local educational legislation.

The charter school concept grew out of the site-based management movement as a process for teachers to offer alternative curricula in public schools and was promoted by the school choice movement, with its arguments favoring accountability and competition. Proponents believe that charter schools address the needs of individual students better than traditional public schools because the students and parents choose the school and therefore are committed to it. Opponents point out that many states do not hold charter schools to the same level of accountability as regular public schools, and that the competition model does not apply because charter schools are often smaller than public schools or so specialized that comparisons are difficult.

Vouchers are the most controversial of the current school-policy proposals. They were first used by southern states to allow white students to attend private schools as part of massive resistance to desegregation. In the 1990s the debates surrounding the use of vouchers revolved around the market model as a way to address the needs of students underserved by the traditional school systems. Two American cities that permit the use of vouchers are in the Midwest. In both Cleveland, Ohio, and Milwaukee, Wisconsin, vouchers are reserved for low-income families and may be used at either public or private schools. The most controversial part of the voucher movement is the use of tax revenue to pay tuition to private religious schools. Opponents of vouchers claim that this use of public funding violates the separation of church and state in the First Amendment to the U.S. Constitution. Supporters of vouchers claim that religious schools will not necessarily use the funds for religious instruction. In the 2002 U.S. Supreme Court case *Zelman v.*

Simmons-Harris, the Court declared that the use of vouchers at religious schools in Cleveland did not violate the separation of church and state and was therefore constitutional.

Supporters of both charter schools and vouchers claim that parents have the right to choose the schools their children attend and that these alternative approaches to education will increase the quality of traditional public schools through competition. Opponents charge that the competition model does not hold up under scrutiny and that public funds would be better spent improving traditional public schools.

Sources and Further Reading: Thomas L. Good and Jennifer S. Braden, *The Great School Debate* (2000); Joe Nathan, *Charter Schools: Creating Hope and Opportunity for American Education* (1996); John F. Witte, *The Market Approach to Education* (2000).

Deanna Michael
University of South Florida–St. Petersburg

Multicultural Issues

The Midwest in the nineteenth century was "a multicultural mosaic of peoples" living in homogeneous communities that preserved family and ethnic traditions, languages, and customs. The inhabitants of these communities migrated from New England and the Upland South along with immigrants from northern and western Europe. The Midwest offered seemingly unlimited opportunities for economic, social, and political progress. Despite their differences, early settlers offered a cultural model rooted in the values of white, Protestant, middle-class people that continues to dominate the region. The successful implementation of that model ultimately required the assimilation of many peoples, the segregation of others, and the nearly total expulsion of the region's indigenous population. One major instrument used to impose cultural dominance was the common (public) school.

As immigrants streamed into the upper Midwest from Germany, the British Isles, Scandinavia, and eastern Europe, they encountered educational reformers who viewed the one-room school as an outpost of civilization "at the West." One-room district schools reinforced Anglo-American beliefs. The ideology promulgated by the district schools reinforced the superiority of American Protestant culture and morality as being essential to republican government. During the nineteenth century, the pervasive use of the McGuffey Readers in district schools was a key element in the inculcation of a middle-class macroculture.

Often referred to as "Schoolmaster to the Nation," William Holmes McGuffey (1800–1873) was the proprietor of subscription schools in Ohio and Kentucky and a professor of ancient languages at Miami University (Ohio). In 1836 the first Eclectic Readers, compendiums of stories and aphorisms that encouraged hard work, Christian principles, allegiance to country, and good deeds, were published. Wildly popular, more than 122 million readers were sold between 1836 and 1920. The readers attempted to standardize the English language by instructing pupils (and teachers) in correct pronunciation and usage. They also included Bible passages and literary selections from American and British writers such as John Greenleaf Whittier, Washington Irving, William Wordsworth, and William Shakespeare, thus establishing an American canon.

While codifying the white Anglo-Saxon Protestant macroculture, the McGuffey Readers and their imitators portrayed Native Americans pejoratively, failed to include African Americans whatsoever, accused overweight little girls of the sin of gluttony, and disparaged the Pope. Their usage in public schools drew complaints from ethnic and religious minorities and heated debates developed over the issue of whether one group had the right to impose its values on everyone else's children. Resistance to the imposition of a dominant Protestant culture formed in urban areas of the Midwest such as Cincinnati, Ohio, and St. Louis, Missouri. Catholics, Norwegian Lutherans, and others objected not only to the McGuffey Readers but also to the required reading of the Protestant (King James) Bible instead of the Douay Bible. Religious controversies were persistent and not limited to doctrine and such debates continue in contemporary education. In *Wisconsin v. Yoder* (1972) the U.S. Supreme Court ruled that the right to live a traditional way of life supersedes the state's right to require Amish children to attend school beyond the eighth grade.

In general, native-born Protestants insisted upon English-only education in public schools. Although students in Cincinnati were allowed to alternate lessons in English and German, compromise was the exception. With the passage of such laws as the Edwards Act (1889) in Illinois and the Bennett Act (1889) in Wisconsin, English was declared to be the unofficial language of instruction in public and private schools. After World War I and the passage of the Immigration Act of 1924, there was a decline in ethnic identity as European Americans and other ethnic midwesterners felt pressured to Americanize.

Native Americans had already experienced a similar process. The case of the Menominee nation is illustrative of "deculturization"—the process of eliminating the culture of a conquered people and replacing it with the dominant culture. The first European contact with the Menominee occurred during the seventeenth century, when French fur traders and Jesuits came to the upper Midwest. By the early nineteenth century, much of their land had been ceded in a series of treaties with the United States. By midcentury, their population decimated by disease, the Menominee were confined to a reservation in northern Wisconsin. Parochial schools, which had been established as a result of Jesuit missionary efforts, coexisted alongside public government-funded schools. Children were forcibly removed from their homes in an attempt by the government to "civilize" the tribe by eliminating the "savage." Sent away to boarding schools, children were forced to speak English, wear "western" clothing, and cut their hair. Older students were sent to Carlisle Indian School (Pennsylvania) or United States

Indian Industrial Training School (also known as the Haskell Indian Institute) in Lawrence, Kansas.

In the middle of the twentieth century, the Menominee territory was stripped of its status as a reservation and designated Menominee County, which resulted in the closing of the Bureau of Indian Affairs public school. Menominee children continued to attend local public elementary schools, but high school students had to travel to nearby Shawano, Wisconsin. With the movement toward Indian self-determination during the 1960s and the 1970s, the Menominee gained greater control over school policies and curriculum. In the twenty-first century, Native Americans who attend public schools continue to cite cultural genocide and racism as contributing to high school dropout rates, however.

While Native Americans experienced expulsion

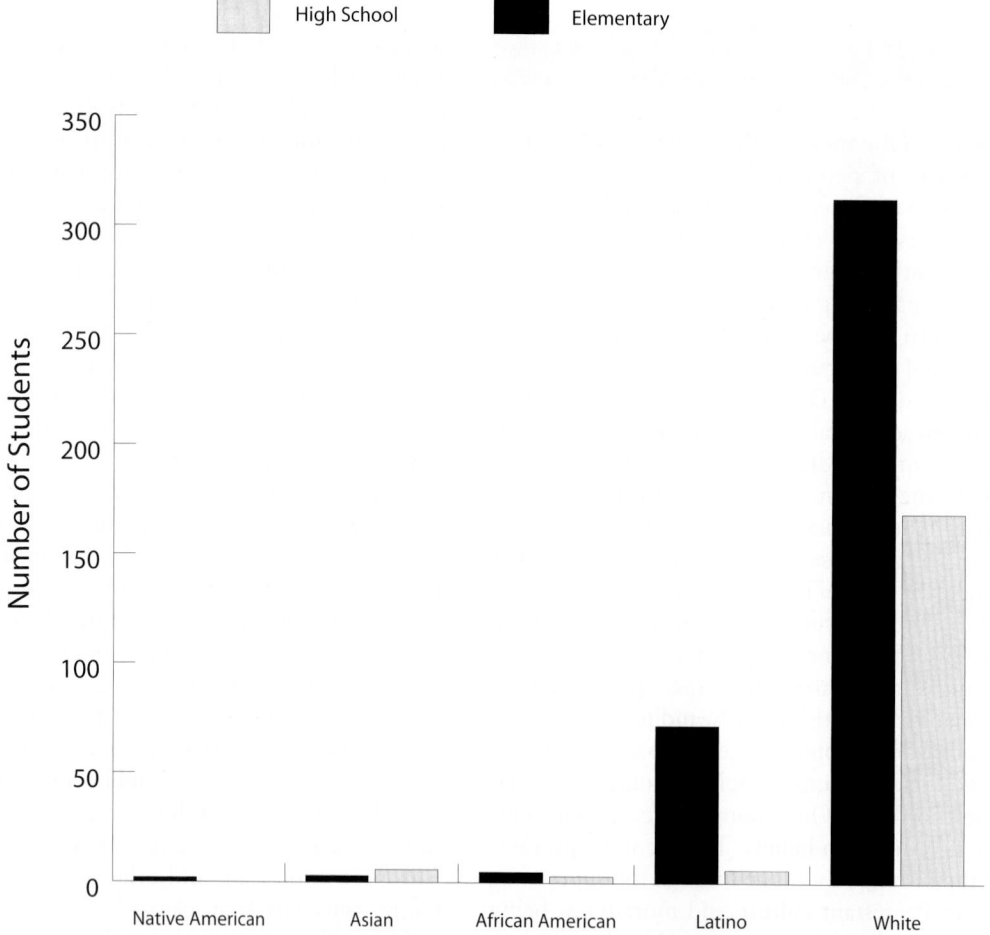

Postville, Iowa, School Enrollment by Race, 2001–2002

The late-twentieth-century spike in the Hispanic population in Postville, Iowa, shows the renewed diversity of schools in rural communities. Prepared by Sathyan Sundaram. *Source:* National Center for Education Statistics, *CCD Public School Data for the 2001–2002 School Year,* District ID 1923340 (2003).

and deculturization, African Americans were met with *de facto* segregation and restrictive black codes. In the early nineteenth century, there were numerous settlements of free blacks in the Midwest, often consisting of several hundred residents. Thousands of black southerners fled the South. Denied access to education by the southern caste system, blacks pursued education as a means of empowerment and a path to self-determination. Often victims of both *de facto* and *de jure* school segregation, they introduced new institutional forms to the Midwest such as manual labor institutes. In so doing, they experimented with racial integration and coeducation. The Union Literary Institute and the Woodstock Manual Labor Institute are two examples of that educational experimentation.

The Union Literary Institute, in Randolph County, Indiana, was founded in 1846 by abolitionist Quakers and free blacks who had migrated from North Carolina, Ohio, and Kentucky. The curriculum consisted of basic skills (reading, writing, and ciphering) as well as manual (vocational) training. Boarding students—some of whom came from as far away as Cincinnati; Indianapolis, Indiana; and Tennessee—worked for four hours a day on the adjacent farm in exchange for room and board. Although most students were black, whites also enrolled, making it an early example of racial integration in the Midwest. When the black population scattered, the school became a district school until it closed in the early 1920s.

Prior Foster, a free black from Ohio, and his brothers founded the Woodstock Manual Labor Institute in Addison, Michigan, in 1846. Combining academic instruction with manual arts and agricultural practices, the institute taught fugitive and free blacks until 1865. It has been referred to as the first school in the Northwest Territory to be operated by blacks. Both Woodstock and the Union Literary Institute are testaments to African American faith in education as a means of racial and personal uplift. The Midwest is also home to two historically black institutions, both located in Wilberforce, Ohio: Wilberforce University (founded in 1856) and Central State University (founded in 1887).

Between 1915 and 1940, a "Great Migration" of African Americans left the rural South bound for urban centers such as Chicago and Detroit. As they pressed for social, political, and educational equality, the growing debate over access to education was argued before the courts. In *State of Missouri ex rel. Gaines v. Canada* (1938), Lloyd Gaines sued successfully for admittance to the University of Missouri Law School. The case specifically attacked the pervasive practice of awarding out-of-state tuition scholarships to black graduate students rather than allowing them to attend white institutions. In a decision largely ignored by the South, the court ruled that states had to provide equal educational opportunities *within* the state, setting the stage for future legal challenges to discrimination at the graduate and professional education level. Another case that originated in the Midwest would have far-reaching national implications. In *Brown v. Board of Education* (1954, 1955) a unified U.S. Supreme Court ruled that separate education was inherently unequal. As midwestern states attempted to comply with the *Brown* decision, urban areas often resorted to court-ordered busing to achieve racial desegregation.

More recently, Asian immigrants have struggled with issues of education and acculturation. After the end of the United States' war with Vietnam, Southeast Asians who had collaborated with the United States could no longer safely remain in Laos, Cambodia, or Vietnam. Resettlement efforts brought small groups of refugees such as the Hmong, members of a nomadic mountain tribe, to midwestern cities such as Milwaukee, Wisconsin, and St. Paul, Minnesota. This initial resettlement was followed by a secondary migration largely consisting of members of extended families that set up cultural and racial clashes between European Americans and Southeast Asian immigrants. The town of Wausau, Wisconsin, is a case in point. Proclaimed by the 1980 United States census to be the most ethnically homogeneous city in the nation, less than 1 percent of Wausau's forty thousand residents were nonwhite. In 1978 the Lutheran Immigration and Refugee Service sponsored a few dozen Hmong refugees. By 1994 the Hmong community had grown to more than four thousand, resulting in the need for additional schools and English-as-a-second-language services, prompting taxpayer revolts, and culturally redefining the city.

The midwestern multicultural mosaic continues to evolve in response to both national and regional population changes. Nationally, the increasing Hispanicization of the United States (where in 2000 66.1 percent of Hispanics were of Mexican origin) will contribute to whites becoming a racial minority in the twenty-first century. Regionally, increasing urbanization and the decline and disappearance of rural spaces will transform the landscape. In the midst of social and cultural change, midwesterners will once again be confronted with redefining the meaning of community.

Sources and Further Reading: David Wallace Adams, *Education for Extinction: American Indians and the Boarding School Experience, 1875–1928* (1995); Malaika Adero, *Up South* (1993); James A. Banks and Cherry McGee Banks, *Multicul-*

tural Education: Issues and Perspectives (2001); Roy Beck, "The Ordeal of Immigration in Wausau," *Atlantic Monthly* 273 (Apr. 1994); Andrew R. L. Cayton, "The Anti-Region," in Andrew R. L. Cayton and Susan E. Gray, eds., *The American Midwest: Essays on Regional History* (2001); Wayne E. Fuller, *The Old Country School* (1982); Andrew Gulliford, *America's Country Schools* (1984); Carl F. Kaestle, *Pillars of the Republic* (1983); Nicholas Lemann, *The Promised Land* (1991); Charles Lindquist, *The Antislavery–Underground Railroad Movement in Lenawee County, Michigan, 1830–1860* (1999); Shawn Francis Peters, *The Yoder Case* (2003).

Jayne Beilke
Ball State University, Indiana

African Americans

The battle over African American education in the Midwest has largely focused on the issues of access and equality. Initially educational access emerged as a point of contention for students. African Americans, individually and collectively, have equated education with racial uplift, but historically they often had to fight whites' ideas concerning what type of education best suited northern blacks. The efforts of black churches and civil rights organizations in fighting for education underscore the idea that education of African Americans has largely been a communal enterprise.

African Methodist Episcopal churches, black Baptist churches, and white Quakers took responsibility for African American education before and during the Civil War. By the end of Reconstruction, African Americans in most midwestern states, excluding Missouri (considered by many to be a southern state), were entering public schools at some level alongside white students. African American religious groups took the lead in establishing African American education in Evanston, Illinois; Indianapolis, Indiana; St. Paul, Minnesota; Detroit, Michigan; and throughout Ohio, Illinois, and Iowa. In cities and river towns with substantial increasing African American populations, officials enforced "whites only" clauses and refused to tax black property owners; this in turn excluded African Americans from public schools.

During Reconstruction and the early Jim Crow period, some states barred African American students from primary schools but accepted them in a number of newly established secondary schools. Only Missouri barred blacks at every grade level. Other states, like Indiana, left the question of racial desegregation up to local politicians and school boards. As African American parents and local black communities pushed to have their children enrolled in public schools, states such as Ohio, Michigan, and Iowa separately taxed

African Americans' property and maintained separate black public schools. Undeterred, African Americans persistently challenged racial segregation in public schools. The best-known cases of African American legal resistance to racially segregated schools occurred in Chicago (1865); Muscatine and Keokuk, Iowa (1868, 1875); Detroit (1869); and Alton, Illinois (1897–1908).

In rural areas and towns with small numbers of African Americans, black children generally attended white primary schools. This was especially the case in North Dakota and South Dakota, where the African American populations in both states remained minuscule. Predominantly and majority African American towns in Iowa, Illinois, Ohio, and especially Kansas established viable schools for black children but fought local white residents over control of school boards. By the late nineteenth and early twentieth centuries, most states had passed legislation outlawing racial segregation in public schools. However, Indiana continued to yield to local school officials; Kansas instituted its "first-class city law," which permitted cities with more than fifteen thousand residents to maintain racially segregated primary schools; and Missouri maintained a solid color wall.

During the first four decades of the twentieth century, the history of African American education shifted almost exclusively to the urban Midwest. The "Great Migration" of southern blacks north of the Ohio River led local school officials and white parents to explore subtler means of keeping the schools racially segregated. Three types of racial segregation flourished after 1900: (1) legal, or *de jure* segregation, in Missouri and Kansas; (2) sanctioned practices of segregation, called *de facto* segregation, in which segregated residential patterns were used to justify segregated schools, in Indiana; and (3) *de facto* segregation, such as the "transfer system" and gerrymandering of school districts in Ohio, Nebraska, Illinois, Michigan, Iowa, Minnesota, and Wisconsin. In Chicago, the transfer system allowed white students to move from one district to the next while black students were locked into districts with poorly maintained schools. While some African Americans in Chicago; Indianapolis; Detroit; Cleveland, Ohio; and Milwaukee, Wisconsin, challenged segregated schooling, other African Americans fought to maintain racially segregated schools in an attempt to provide job security for African American teachers.

For many African American parents, students, and teachers, *de jure* and *de facto* segregation had at least one major benefit—caring, culturally sensitive, and competent African American teachers. Some black communities fought for black teachers' access to black, and later racially integrated, classrooms. When district administrators desegregated schools, they customarily replaced African American teachers with European American teachers. In many cases, African American communities endorsed racial segregation in schools if African American teachers maintained their jobs. Usually debates concerning African American teachers' access to the classroom grew out of questions about the quality of education. African American teachers wanted to teach black children, while some white teachers viewed their time in black schools as paternalistic charity work. Both African American and European American teachers in all-black or majority black schools entered classrooms with a variety of qualifications and varying interests in black educational and social advancement. But African American teachers often enhanced their curricula to address some of the educational and cultural needs of African American students, and they served their students beyond the basic teaching requirements despite being paid less than their white counterparts.

The question of racial segregation in schools came to a head in 1954 with the first *Brown v. Board of Education* case in Topeka, Kansas. Although the *Brown* decision prohibited racial segregation in schools throughout the country, the response to *Brown* in most midwestern cities was a move toward more subtle *de facto* segregation through redistricting and transfer policies.

In the post-*Brown* years, desegregation strategies, which included busing, have changed the racial demographics of schools, particularly in the urban Midwest, making them even more segregated. As European American parents have moved their children to suburban and private schools, urban schools have become overwhelmingly resegregated. Some African American educators responded to failures of desegregation with the development of Afrocentric schools. In the 1990s, Afrocentric schools that emphasize a neo-pan-African curriculum have gained support in Detroit, Chicago, and Milwaukee. While supporters laud these schools for their culturally relevant curricula, critics accuse Afrocentrists of self-segregation and myth making. In either case, the influence of Afrocentric schools on African American education has yet to be determined.

Sources and Further Reading: James C. Carper, "The Popular Ideology of Segregated Schooling," *Kansas History* 1 (Winter 1978); Hal Chase, "You Live What You Learn," in Bill Silag, ed., *Outside In: African Americans in Iowa, 1838–2000* (2001); Jack Dougherty, "'That's When We Were Marching for Jobs,'" *History of Education Quarterly* 38 (Summer 1998); William D. Green, "Race and Segregation in St. Paul's Public Schools," *Minnesota History* 55 (Winter 1996–1997); Michael W. Homel, *Down from Equality*

(1984); Robert McCaul, *The Black Struggle for Public Schooling in Nineteenth-Century Illinois* (1987); Judy Jolley Mohraz, *The Separate Problem* (1979); William W. Stephenson, "Integration of the Detroit Public School System during the Period 1839–1869," *Negro History Bulletin* 26 (Oct. 1962–1963).

Richard M. Breaux
University of Iowa

Katrina M. Sanders
University of Iowa

Appalachians

Geographers define Appalachia as the region running along the Appalachian mountain range from New York to Mississippi. Appalachians are people born in this area. Urban Appalachians are their descendants and relatives who have moved away but whose ancestry lies within the region. More than three million mostly white Appalachians moved from rural Appalachian counties between 1940 and 1970 seeking employment in midwestern "port of entry" cities such as Akron, Cincinnati, Columbus, and Dayton, Ohio; Detroit, Michigan; and Chicago.

In addition to contending with negative stereotypes exemplified in such labels as "hillbilly," "redneck," and "trash," first-, as well as second-, third-, and fourth-generation rural and urban Appalachians contend with marginalization in the educational system. Appalachian values of kin loyalty, strong neighborhood affiliation, and an affinity for specific people rather than goals are often positioned as pathologies. Thus, a high number of Appalachian youths feel disconnected to school and eventually drop out. In fact, in some cities, Appalachians experience a much higher dropout rate than other racial and/or ethnic groups.

Achieving success in public education in part requires Appalachians to take up middle-class school identities that conflict with culturally and ethnically meaningful ones. Many Appalachian youths who are successful in public education cite the impact of teachers who push and expect them to excel. Those who leave public education find success in completing General Educational Development (GED) requirements in community-based, community-run educational programs that draw on Appalachian values.

Sources and Further Reading: Rebecca Eller-Powell, "Teaching for Change in Appalachia," in Etta R. Hollins, Joyce E. King, and Warren C. Hayman, eds., *Teaching Diverse Populations* (1994); Henry D. Shapiro, *Appalachia on Our Mind* (1978); Patricia Timm and Kathryn Borman, "The Soup Pot Don't Stretch That Far No More," in Max-

Vital Statistics: Education in Appalachian Ohio

Factor	State	Mean Appalachian Districts	Appalachian Districts High	Low
Total Average Daily Membership (ADM)	2,953	1,868	9,054	317
Ohio Works First	3.43%	8.92%	22.92%	0.00%
Median Income	$31,169	$25,810	$37,898	$17,891
Expenditure per Pupil	$7,547	$6,980	$9,267	$5,229
Effective Operating Mills	26.91	23.63	32.99	20.00
Authorized Operating Mills	45.66	34.19	61.80	20.00
Pupil Attendance Rate	94.95%	94.48%	98.60%	92.2%
Drop-Out Rate	10.56%	12.71%	44.30%	0.00%
Property Valuation Per ADM	$10,813	$7,927	$24,925	$25,677
Regular K–12 Pupil Teacher Ratio	16.13	16.24	22.10	13.10
Average Teacher Salary	$44,266	$38,149	$50,059	$28,153

Note: All data are from fiscal year 2002 (school year 2002–2003) except Median Income [per State Return], which is from calendar year 2000. All district averages exclude three island districts and College Corner as outliers and Monroe Local due to data problems. Median Income [per State Return] replaces Average Income [per Federal Return] used in previous CORAS Vital Statistics reports.
Source: Coalition of Rural and Appalachian Schools, "Vital Statistics for the Ohio Appalachian School Districts, Fiscal Year 2002," http://www.coras.org/character.html.

ine Seller and Lois Weis, eds., *Beyond Black and White: New Faces and Voices in U.S. Schools* (1997); Thomas E. Wagner, "Urban Schools and Appalachian Children," *Urban Education* 12 (Oct. 1977).

Tammy Ann Schwartz
Miami University, Oxford, Ohio

Asian Americans

Midwestern attitudes toward the education of Asian Americans were formed in part by the particular conditions of immigration of different groups, exemplified by the Chinese. In Chicago in 1894 about thirty Chinese children were enrolled in the first public school for Chinese in the Midwest. In 1890 there were 567 Chinese in Chicago; most of them were young men who worked in restaurants, laundries, and grocery stores. They did not form a colony; instead, they scattered throughout the city. The fact that they sent their children to one school indicates segregated schooling.

Due to common Anglo-American suspicions that Chinese women were engaged in prostitution, American missionaries took on their education. Among the first of these efforts was the Chinese Mission in Chicago, in which Anglo-American women taught English, home economics, and child rearing. The mass education of adult Chinese men in Chicago was launched by the Young Men's Christian Association in

1897 and by 1926 there were twelve YMCA Sunday schools serving more than three hundred men.

In 1905 the U.S. government mandated a census of Chinese residents to screen out illegal immigrants. Chinese in the United States responded by starting a legal defense fund and establishing Chinese schools. The education of Chinese by Chinese in the Midwest started in 1906 when the Chinese minister to the Americas, Dr. Ting-Feng Wu, came to Chicago to inaugurate six Chinese-language schools. Teachers were hired from China with funding from Chinese businesses in Chicago. All Chinese school-age children were required to attend after-school Chinese language schools. By the mid-1920s, about one in twelve high school–aged Chinese children in Chicago were in school or college. In small towns across the Midwest, Chinese children were a small minority and usually attended integrated schools. The tradition of Chinese-language weekend schools still widely exists today in the Midwest and elsewhere.

The midwestern Chinese advocacy of education in the early twentieth century led to massive changes in Chinese American life. One-third of Chinese students in the United States during this period attended college in Illinois. The students in higher educational institutions were in the pipeline of teachers for the Chinese-language schools in the area and greatly increased the number of Chinese Americans in academic and professional fields in subsequent years.

Japanese Americans who were interned during World War II were permitted to enter higher education institutions in the Midwest, and many settled in the Midwest after graduation.

After the Family Reunion Act, or Immigration Act, of 1965, the populations of Chinese and Asians in general increased in the Midwest. Asian American children were able to attend integrated public schools following the U.S. Supreme Court's decision in *Brown v. Board of Education* (1954, 1955). After the Vietnam War, Southeast Asian refugees were adopted by church groups in the United States and settled in midwestern small towns. Many of their children had difficulties in school, but gradually, in the 1990s, some began entering higher education institutions.

Sources and Further Reading: Ting C. Fan, "Chinese Residents in Chicago," master's thesis, University of Chicago (1926); Carol Huang, "The Soft Power of U.S. Education and the Forming of a Chinese-American Intellectual Community at Urbana-Champaign from 1905 to 1954," Ph.D. diss., University of Illinois (2001); Gary Okihiro and Leslie A. Ito, *Storied Lives* (1999); Paul C. P. Siu, *The Chinese Laundryman*, ed. John Kuo Wei Tchen (1987).

Carol Huang
Southern Illinois University–Edwardsville

Bilingual

Bilingual education refers to the utilization of two languages for content instruction, and it is an educational tradition deeply rooted in the Midwest. Bilingual education has a variety of sometimes conflicting rationales, such as promoting academic success among limited-English proficient (LEP) students; introducing LEP students to English; and preserving indigenous and minority languages and cultures, thus encouraging a positive self-image. Dual-language instruction is also sometimes used as a means of enriching the curriculum. Two-way bilingual programs, for instance, use mixed classes of English-proficient and LEP students to encourage both groups' fluency in two languages. Transitional bilingual education for language minorities is currently the most common type of program.

The Midwest was the epicenter of bilingual education in the nineteenth and early twentieth centuries. Ohio was the first state to pass permissive legislation regarding German-English education in the public schools, in 1839; a year later Cincinnati initiated a program that would become a national model. The Germans established a number of private German-English schools throughout the country, but they had enough political influence in many midwestern communities to have bilingual programs implemented in many public elementary schools as well. By 1900

German-English programs in public elementary schools could still be found in Illinois, Indiana, Ohio, Minnesota, and Michigan. Because of its ethnic diversity, the Midwest also hosted a variety of nonpublic schools that cultivated the languages of Poles, Scandinavians, and other—primarily European—immigrant groups. However, the nativism that accompanied the United States' entry into World War I created a movement for an English-only society, leading many midwestern states to either restrict or forbid foreign languages in public and parochial elementary schools. For decades after the Great War, bilingual education remained largely absent from the educational landscape, even after the U.S. Supreme Court found in its 1923 *Meyer v. Nebraska* decision that restricting nonpublic schools from teaching foreign languages was unconstitutional.

Although there were a number of factors that led to a renewed interest in bilingual education in the decades that followed World War II, perhaps the most important was a growing concern in the 1960s for providing language minorities, particularly Spanish-speaking populations, with equal educational opportunities in American schools. This concern led to the passage of the Bilingual Education Act—Title VII of the Elementary and Secondary Education Act—in 1968, which provided federal funds for bilingual programs. In 1974 the Court found in *Lau v. Nichols* that failure to assist LEP students violated Title VI of the Civil Rights Act of 1964; the Court, however, did not explicitly mandate bilingual education. Other courts have used the Equal Educational Opportunities Act of 1974 to promote bilingual education, as in *Castañeda v. Pickard* (1981).

State governments too became increasingly concerned about providing LEP children—many of them from Latin America and Asia—with equal educational opportunities, and several began to pass legislation regarding bilingual education. With the exception of Nebraska, all midwestern states either specifically mandated bilingual education or allowed for programs designed to assist LEP students.

Sources and Further Reading: Theodore Andersson and Mildred Boyer, *Bilingual Schooling in the United States* (1976); Donna Christian and Fred Genesee, eds., *Bilingual Education* (2001); James Crawford, *Bilingual Education: History, Politics, Theory, and Practice*, 3rd ed. (1995); Anita Garcia and Cynthia Morgan, "A 50-State Survey of Requirements for the Education of Language Minority Children," *READ Abstracts Research and Policy Brief* (Nov. 1997); Heinz Kloss, *The American Bilingual Tradition* (1998).

Paul J. Ramsey
Indiana University–Bloomington

Mexican Americans

Mexican migration to the Midwest began in the early 1900s when demand for labor in railroad and manufacturing industries and seasonal agricultural work spurred migration northward. In general, settlement in the Midwest was more urbanized than in the Southwest, though many Mexican migrants shifted between rural and urban locations in search of greater stability. Estimates of urban settlement range from less than 40 percent in some states to more than 80 percent in others. Mexican neighborhoods, or *colonias*, appeared in large urban centers such as Kansas City, Kansas, and Detroit, Michigan; midsized cities such as St. Paul, Minnesota; and small towns such as Emporia, Kansas. By the mid-1920s, more than one hundred thousand Mexicans were living in the Midwest.

The arrival of Mexicans in the Midwest coincided with the northward migration of African Americans and the arrival of other immigrants to the region, particularly southern and eastern Europeans. Mexicans were sometimes viewed as simply one more immigrant group although, unlike their European counterparts, discrimination against Mexicans continued through the twentieth century.

World War I–era educational measures such as IQ (intelligence quotient) testing and Americanization campaigns contributed to the creation of separate classrooms and schools for Mexican American children. A school for Mexicans opened in Topeka, Kansas, in 1918 and the Fort Madison, Iowa, public school district created a "Mexican Room" in the early 1920s. Such facilities were ostensibly created to teach American customs and English, but often they became a dead end. More typical was the experience of the children of some twenty thousand Mexicans in Chicago in the 1920s who attended school with the children of European and African Americans because of residential patterns.

Nonenforcement of compulsory school-attendance laws, poverty, bullying and teasing of Mexican children by white pupils in integrated settings, and discrimination by white teachers contributed to low levels of educational achievement. Children of migrant families in rural areas faced additional inequities—greater poverty, inconsistent or no access to schools, and few legal protections. Elva Treviño Hart's poignant memoir *Barefoot Heart: Stories of a Migrant Child* (1999) illuminates the trials of migrant farmworkers in Minnesota in the mid-twentieth century.

The Chicano *movimiento* of the 1960s and 1970s, War on Poverty programs, and passage of the Bilingual Education Act of 1968 contributed to improved educational opportunities. New strategies also emerged. An alternative high school in Milwaukee—Centro Cultural Educativo Chicano-Boricua—integrated Mexican and Puerto Rican history and culture. The Migrant Tutorial Program in St. Paul offered academic enrichment for migrant children. El Centro de la Causa provided tutoring, college recruitment, and language classes in Chicago's Pilsen area. And during the late 1960s and early 1970s students at the University of Illinois–Chicago Circle and the University of Wisconsin–Madison protested for Latino/a curriculum and more Latino/a student admissions. Desegregation efforts at the kindergarten through twelfth-grade (K–12) level, though often framed in terms of blacks and whites, also contributed to enhanced educational opportunities for Mexican Americans.

Education today continues to pose a challenge for first-, second-, and even third-generation Mexican American children in the Midwest. They perform at lower levels than their peers on most standard measures. In-school role models such as Hispanic teachers and counselors remain scarce. In addition, Mexican American youth are disproportionately clustered with other Hispanic and African American students in urban schools and increasingly in suburbs, far from the resources available to most suburban white youths. Moreover, Mexican American adults over the age of twenty-five are less likely to have completed high school than white and African American adults. A particular challenge for rural areas concerns the continued growth of a population with whom few officials in the Midwest have experience, either in bilingual education or in efforts to promote diversity sensitivity.

Midwestern Mexican Americans face both advantages and challenges in entering a part of the country where a history of discrimination against them was less entrenched than in the Southwest. New opportunities were tempered by discrimination and, alternatively, by the relative invisibility of Mexican Americans in a region that viewed race relations primarily in "black and white" terms. Additionally, although Mexican Americans in the Midwest formed mutual aid societies and, later, civil rights and militant organizations, these organizations and the communities they depended upon for support began much later in the Midwest than in the Southwest. The deep roots that provided a foundation for widespread Chicano political, legal, and educational activism in the Southwest are still in the process of formation in the Midwest.

Sources and Further Reading: Robert Aponte and Marcelo E. Siles, "Winds of Change: Latinos in the Heartland and the Nation," *Statistical Brief* 5 (1997); Gary Orfield, Mark Bachmeier, David R. James and Tamela Eitle, *Deepening Segregation in American Public Schools* (1997); Felix M. Padilla,

Latino Ethnic Consciousness (1985); Dennis N. Valdés, *Barrios Norteños* (2000).

Victoria Maria MacDonald
Florida State University

Teresa Garcia
University of Iowa

Native Americans

Native American education began long before contact with white civilizations. Native American parents and elders took great care to teach their children the basic skills they needed to become productive adults. Formalized schooling did not exist; Native American children were taught by example and through trial and error. Boys learned the skills necessary to become capable hunters, warriors, and political and spiritual leaders. Girls were taught how to farm, sew, cook, and care for children. All Native American children learned the oral history and traditions of their respective tribes and most were instructed in the artistic traditions of their communities.

Native Americans were first exposed to European education beginning with the arrival of French Catholic, or Jesuit, missionaries in the Great Lakes region in the middle and late 1600s. These missionaries, while focused on spreading Christianity, also made efforts to instruct Native Americans in basic French language skills. Few in number and widely dispersed, missionaries had an uneven impact. By the end of the French and Indian War in 1763, most of the Jesuits had left the region.

Beginning in the 1750s and continuing through much of the nineteenth century, attempts to educate Native Americans were led by Christian missionary societies. The first missionaries to establish permanent settlements in the region were German Moravians. In 1772 they and some of their Delaware Indian converts built the towns of Gnadenhutten and Schoenbrunn in what is now east-central Ohio.

Militia destroyed these settlements and massacred the inhabitants. But missionaries resumed their work as the United States asserted its sovereignty over the Ohio Country. Quakers, Presbyterians, Baptists, Catholics, and others were active throughout the Midwest. Missionaries built schools and established agricultural-training programs. The Wyandots of Ohio received both formal schooling and agricultural instruction from Methodist missionaries.

These efforts often met with limited success. Most mission schools, such as the Quaker mission to the Shawnee, suffered from poor attendance. And while some missions, such as Isaac McCoy's mission to the Potawatomi in the 1820s, were able to convert their students to Christianity, many Native Americans remained true to their cultures and refused to accept a new faith.

After the Civil War, the federal government began to take a more active role in Native American education. Still, the United States made only minimal efforts to honor its treaty obligations to provide resources and services for education. Day schools operated on most reservations, but their success was uneven. With the 1879 opening of Carlisle Indian School in Pennsylvania, a movement to place Native American students in government-funded boarding schools was born. Several boarding schools soon opened throughout the Midwest, including schools at Mt. Pleasant, Michigan; Tomah, Wisconsin; and Pipestone, Minnesota, and the noted Haskell Indian Institute in Lawrence, Kansas. By the 1890s, the government viewed boarding schools as the most effective way to educate Native American students.

Life in the boarding school system was extremely difficult for Native American children. While some midwestern reservations had their own boarding schools, many students were forced to relocate hundreds of miles from their homes. It was not uncommon for a Sioux student such as South Dakota-born and future actor and author Luther Standing Bear to attend the Carlisle Indian School in Pennsylvania. Aside from being removed from their parents and community, these children were subjected to countless efforts to eradicate their cultural beliefs. Boarding schools were intended to make Native American students more like whites. Teachers and administrators at the schools sought to destroy, sometimes through force, any connections these students had with their tribal cultures. Ojibwe students at both the Haskell Indian Institute and Flandreau Indian School in South Dakota had to cut their hair and wear uniforms, and they were forbidden to speak the Ojibwe language.

Native American students at boarding schools typically received basic education in reading, writing, arithmetic, and history as well as vocational training. This vocational training typically included agricultural training for boys and sewing and general household training for girls. Some students were also "outed," meaning that they were made to live and labor with white families near the school in order to further assimilate them into white culture. Students often rebelled against these efforts. Large numbers of Ojibwe students ran away from the boarding schools. Arson was also a common form of resistance. Two girls, one Sioux and the other Menominee, attempted to burn down buildings at the Carlisle Indian School. A more covert means of resisting assimilation was to speak Native American languages and observe tribal customs in private.

In the 1960s, Native Americans challenged government education policies. Reservation communities soon gained more control over their schooling systems. Boarding schools virtually disappeared and were replaced with local reservation schools. Colleges serving Native Americans, such as Haskell Indian Nations University in Kansas, also opened after World War II. In cities such as Detroit and Minneapolis, urban Indians have struggled and continue to struggle in predominantly white schools, facing obstacles to learning such as biases in learning systems and prejudice from students and teachers. Despite improvements in Native American education, much remains to be done.

Sources and Further Reading: David Wallace Adams, *Education for Extinction* (1995); Robert F. Berkhofer, Jr., *Salvation and the Savage* (1976); Brenda J. Child, *Boarding School Seasons* (1998); David H. Dejong, *Promises of the Past* (1993); Vine Deloria, Jr. and Daniel R. Wildcat, *Power and Place* (2001); Donald L. Fixico, *The Urban Indian Experience in America* (2000); Joane Nagel, *American Indian Ethnic Renewal* (1997); Margaret Connell Szasz, *Education and the American Indian*, 3rd ed. (1999).

Michael L. Cox
Amanda, Ohio

Religious Schooling

The story of religiously affiliated kindergarten through twelfth-grade (K–12) schooling in the Midwest is largely the story of immigration. Because successive waves of immigrants established their own schools, the Midwest has been disproportionately rich in schools sponsored by a wide variety of religious groups coming from a broad array of ethnocultural backgrounds.

In the first half of the nineteenth century, some Protestant denominations established schools in the absence of any other institutional options. The first common, or public, schools were mostly the product of mainstream anglophone Protestants who sought to make the nation godly through schooling. These were pan-Protestant and English speaking in character. Non-anglophone Protestants founded schools to maintain their languages and heritages, while Catholics and Jews moved to establish educational networks and systems to preserve and transmit their own unique religious cultures.

Among the anglophones, Presbyterians were among the earliest to create schools, following considerable debate over whether the most appropriate educational sponsor was the church or the state. In the period between 1846 and 1870, conservative "old school" Presbyterians established a small number of schools. Toward the end of this period, various parishes also created a small number of schools with German, French, and Spanish as the language of instruction in order to evangelize newly arriving immigrants.

The most extensive Protestant religious education efforts have been Lutheran. The Missouri Synod accounted for the greatest number. As soon as German Lutherans arrived in the 1830s, they began the process of school development to counter what they viewed as dangerous rationalist tendencies and to transmit their religious culture. These schools, modeled on the German *Volkschule* and *Gymnasium*, quickly attracted pupils both because they were religious and because they were frequently superior to fledgling public schools. By the end of the century, both elementary and secondary schools had been established in St. Louis, Missouri, and Milwaukee, Wisconsin. In the mid-twentieth century, there were more than 1,400 elementary schools and preschools with nearly 160,000 students; there were also numerous community high schools. Most were in Illinois, Michigan, and Wisconsin.

Two other Lutheran bodies also invested heavily in parochial education. Various groups of Scandinavian origin, largely centered in the upper Midwest, created schools for reasons comparable to those of the Missouri Synod. By the twentieth century, these had merged into the American Lutheran Church. Deeply committed to parochial education as well has been the ultraconservative Wisconsin Evangelical Lutheran Synod, founded in 1850. Its strength has been mostly in midwestern states with significant German populations, particularly Wisconsin, Illinois, and Indiana.

A combination of theological and ethnic concerns also drove the formation of Calvinist day schools. Reform theology coupled with the desire to maintain Dutch culture and language promoted the formation of religious educational institutions under the auspices of what later became the Christian Reformed Church in America. School formation was so difficult, however, that by 1900 there were only about fourteen schools, seven of them in Grand Rapids. The greatest impetus came when the theology of Abraham Kuyper, a Dutch theologian who advocated active engagement with the wider world, was transplanted to America in the last years of the nineteenth century. Although Calvin College's preparatory school at Grand Rapids, Michigan, was the only such secondary school until 1915, over a short time span comparable schools were established in Michigan, Illinois, and Iowa. Around that time, regional and national school organizations sprang up, providing overarching educational structures for these schools that were generally sponsored by organizations or parents' groups rather than churches.

Small numbers of schools have also been founded by radical reformation sects such as the Church of the Brethren and the Mennonites. The former established elementary and secondary schools in Brethren strongholds in Ohio and Iowa. Among those representing the latter group were ethnic German immigrants from Russia especially concerned about maintaining their religious and linguistic traditions. Beginning in Kansas in the 1870s and later extending into Minnesota and other areas of Mennonite settlement, they created both parochial and advanced preparatory schools.

An American-founded denomination that has invested heavily in religious education is the Seventh-day Adventists. Although they came late to educational sponsorship, largely because of their belief that an imminent Second Coming would make such institutions superfluous, they gained ground quickly. Early educational formation was centered around Battle Creek, Michigan, the denominational center. By the early 1870s, at least one school had been established there. Over the next twenty-five years numerous others were created in Missouri, Wisconsin, Kansas, Minnesota, Indiana, Iowa, and Illinois, a number of them in denominationally sponsored health sanatoriums. By the early years of the twentieth century, several intermediate and industrial schools had been established and, by midcentury, a number of high schools. The 1980s witnessed elementary schools and high schools educating more than sixty-eight thousand students, remarkable in a denomination with around six hundred thousand members.

A more recent phenomenon has been the emergence of the independent Christian day school. These institutions, sponsored by evangelical churches or local Christian school societies, burgeoned in the second half of the twentieth century, numbering between five and six thousand nationally and educating around one million students.

Easily the largest number of religious schools in the Midwest has been Roman Catholic. Desire to sustain Catholic life together with a felt need for the preservation of ethnic cultures drove midwestern Catholics first to attempt to reach accommodations with civil society about the education of Catholic children and finally to create their own schools. The development of Catholic schooling mirrored migration patterns, which eventually brought Catholics into the region in large enough numbers to create their own schools. A massive influx of German immigrants into the Ohio Valley, for example, eventually resulted in the establishment of parochial schools in eight of Cincinnati's ten parishes by 1850. In Chicago, with a largely Irish Catholic population, there were four or five schools established by midcentury. In Michigan, Detroit's mostly Irish and French Catholic community had also established institutions by then.

The first great period of Catholic school growth occurred between the Civil War and the early 1930s. The immigration of European communities of religious sisters, or the establishment of American ones, provided a cheap educational labor supply. Allied to this was the desire of non-English-speaking immigrants to preserve their ethnic heritage. Thus communities such as the Felicians and the Sisters of St. Casimir staffed schools in Chicago and Detroit oriented toward the strengthening of Polish and Lithuanian culture, while the School Sisters of St. Francis, a German group, were strong among Milwaukee's Catholic immigrants. The decision by the American Catholic bishops in 1884 to require the establishment of a school in every parish also exercised a driving force. The result was an increase in Catholic school enrollments by a thousand times or more over an eighty-year period.

The ethnic character of such schools eventually brought them into conflict with the mainline public educational establishment. Attempts to force the use of the King James Bible in the public schools, together with the passage of laws in Illinois and Wisconsin in 1889 that mandated English as the language of instruction in all schools and, in the latter case, public school attendance as well, convinced Catholic leaders as it did German Lutherans of the hostility of the anglophone Protestant mainstream, and the consequent necessity of establishing separate schools. Lutherans joined with Catholics in Wisconsin and Illinois in 1890 to defeat the Republican Party, which had passed the restrictive laws bringing parochial schools under state control. These battles exacerbated the tension between church and state over parochial schooling that exists to the present day in struggles over school vouchers in states such as Minnesota and Ohio. The fact that so much of the attendant controversy occurred in the Midwest testifies to the strength of religious K–12 schooling in the region.

The second major era of Catholic school expansion came in the thirty years following World War II. Growing Catholic prosperity coupled with suburbanization fueled the founding of new parishes and schools. Between 1945 and 1950 in the Archdiocese of Chicago alone there was an increase of thirty thousand pupils, and between 1950 and 1965 Catholic high school enrollments more than doubled. To handle this rapid growth, many midwestern dioceses created the role of superintendent of schools and established central school offices.

Changes in Catholic culture encouraging educa-

First parochial school in St. Louis, Missouri. Library of Congress, Prints and Photographs Division, Historic American Buildings Survey, HABS, MO, 96-SALU, 24-1. Photo by Theodore LaVack.

tional assimilation together with the decreasing number of religious sisters resulted in a precipitous decline in religious school enrollments after 1965. Between 1980 and 2000 Catholic school enrollments rebounded somewhat, largely as a result of the influx of Hispanic immigrants. By 2001 among the largest networks of Catholic schooling were those of Chicago, the most extensive in the nation; St. Louis; and Cleveland, Ohio.

As early as 1853, a Jewish congregation in Chicago established a day school. At least two other Chicago synagogues had established elementary schools before the Civil War, and comparable institutions, such as Cincinnati's Talmud Yelodim Institute (1849) and Hoyoth (1855) were to be found in other midwestern cities with high Jewish concentrations. The real growth in Jewish education occurred after World War II. Fueled by strong leadership, signal events like the Shoah (the Holocaust) and the foundation of the State of Israel, postwar immigration, relative economic prosperity, and the deterioration of supplementary education, Jewish day schooling multiplied rapidly. Jewish high schools came into existence in significant numbers. One of the most important phenomena of the late twentieth century was the creation of considerable numbers of schools under the auspices of Reform and Conservative congregations. In the Midwest, the greatest growth in Jewish day schooling occurred in metropolitan areas with large Jewish populations such as Chicago, Detroit, and Cleveland.

More recently, a small number of day schools have been established under Muslim auspices. Initial efforts came in Chicago with school formation by the Nation of Islam. Subsequently, mainstream Islamic schools have grown up there, as have schools in cities such as

Detroit with large Muslim populations. These schools teach a general education curriculum supplemented by Koranic and Arabic studies.

Diverse as these institutions are, similar factors drove most of their development. Virtually all were the product of popular desire to preserve and promote the religious and ethnic culture of a particular community. Most began once immigrant groups had achieved a basic level of economic prosperity and organizational ability that allowed school formation. All implied, to greater or lesser degrees, a tacit rejection of the values of the mainstream culture, symbolized by the public school. The comparative richness of the Midwest in such institutions is testimony to its unique ethnic and religious diversity.

Sources and Further Reading: Richard J. Altenbaugh, ed., *Historical Dictionary of American Education* (1999); Harold A. Buetow, *Of Singular Benefit* (1970); James C. Carper and Thomas C. Hunt, eds., *Religious Schooling in America* (1984); William J. Reese, "Soldiers for Christ in the Army of God: The Christian School Movement in America," *Educational Theory* 35 (Spring 1985); James W. Sanders, *The Education of an Urban Minority* (1977); August C. Stellhorn, *Schools of the Lutheran Church, Missouri Synod* (1963).

F. Michael Perko
Loyola University, Chicago, Illinois

Amish

The Amish, descendants of sixteenth-century Swiss Anabaptists, migrated to the United States in the eighteenth century. They sought religious freedom and a simple life rooted in farming and farm-related skills.

Old Order Amish eschew modern conveniences, dress, technology, and secular life; New Order Amish are somewhat more assimilated, culturally and economically, but individual communities of both groups determine their own practices. Amish congregations settled first in Pennsylvania, then migrated to Ohio and Indiana.

As farmland close to original settlements became scarce and expensive, the Amish resettled in other states or developed new means of income, such as tourism and small enterprises. Today, Amish settlements abound in all midwestern states except Nebraska and North and South Dakota. The Amish's chosen way of life in rural areas, based on strict observance of Christian religious principles, sets them apart as communities. They actively seek separation from the secular world, drawing boundaries between their religious community, their non-Amish neighbors, and the state, and following the biblical injunction from Romans 12:2 (King James Version), "And be not conformed to this world."

Small, rural, one-room Amish schools for kindergarten through eighth grade (K–8), taught by young Amish men and women with only an eighth-grade education themselves, transmit Amish religious values along with language and mathematical skills deemed necessary to carry on the economic, cultural, and spiritual life of their communities. The Amish reject worldly values, such as competition, individualism, self-emulation, and hierarchical organization, which they often find perpetuated, along with studies of history, science, and hygiene, in large public schools. In the landmark 1972 case *Wisconsin v. Yoder*, Amish won the right to educate their youth only through the eighth grade due to the Amish belief that further education teaches children the ways of secular society, from which the Amish seek to shield their children. The *Yoder* decision freed Amish teenagers from schooling to work in Amish farming communities. The case symbolizes religious liberty, granted by the First Amendment, and is the culmination of Amish challenges to state educational law since 1914.

The Amish had largely accommodated to public, rural, one-room schools until the 1950s, when rural public schools began consolidating at a greater rate, destroying the small country schools the Amish valued. The movement to form their own schools started then in earnest; it continues today. Of the 33,866 U.S. children attending Amish schools during the 2001–2002 school year, 20,595 lived in midwestern states. Two-thirds of all Amish schools, teachers, and pupils reside in Pennsylvania, Ohio, and Indiana.

Amish communities in the Midwest appear to their neighbors to be parallel cultural, economic, and spiritual communities whose main purpose is to teach, live, and model religious principles in the home, the school, the church, and the community, apart from the modern world that surrounds them and in tune with the values of the local Amish settlement. Amish education is synonymous with socialization into and perpetuation of the Amish religion and way of life. It serves as a thriving alternative model of education and a striking example of First Amendment protection of a minority religious community's educational vision.

Sources and Further Reading: Sara E. Fisher and Rachel K. Stahl, *The Amish School* (1986); John A. Hostetler and Gertrude Enders Huntington, *Amish Children: Education in the Family, School, and Community*, 2nd ed. (1992); Donald B. Kraybill and Marc A. Olshan, eds., *The Amish Struggle with Modernity* (1994); Thomas J. Meyers, "Education and Schooling," in Donald B. Kraybill, ed., *The Amish and the State* (1993).

Kathleen A. Murphey
Indiana University–Purdue University,
Fort Wayne

Jewish

By the 1840s there were Jewish congregations throughout the Midwest, especially in the larger communities of Cincinnati, Ohio; Detroit, Michigan; St. Louis, Missouri; and Chicago. These congregations ran Sunday schools modeled after those found in Protestant congregations or joined with the entire Jewish community in an attempt to sustain a communal Sunday school. There were also attempts at founding and maintaining Jewish day schools, which are full-time Jewish parochial schools. By the end of the Civil War, the number of Jewish day schools had dwindled tremendously, probably due to both the high costs of such endeavors and the general American trend toward public education.

Probably the greatest midwestern contribution to Jewish education was the creation of Hebrew Union College in Cincinnati, Ohio. Founded in 1875 to train Reform rabbis, it is the oldest institution of Jewish higher learning in America.

During the early decades of the twentieth century Bureaus of Jewish Education began to be established in Cleveland, Ohio; Cincinnati; Chicago; Detroit; and throughout the Midwest. These communal agencies attempted to regularize the curricula of the congregational Hebrew schools and Sunday schools; help with the recruitment, training, and retention of teachers for these programs; and raise the profile of Jewish education in the community. Currently, Cleveland and Chicago are homes to Jewish colleges originally founded as Hebrew teacher-training institutions.

The 706,000 Jews who live in the Midwest today support hundreds of congregational Hebrew schools and Sunday schools, dozens of day schools, and any number of family and adult learning programs.

Sources and Further Reading: Judah Pilch, *A History of Jewish Education in America* (1969); Jack Wertheimer, "Jewish Education in the United States," in *American Jewish Yearbook* (1999).

Rabbi Samuel K. Joseph
Hebrew Union College, Ohio

Lutheran

Lutheran Church–supported education has been a small but consistent presence in the Midwest. Lutheran schooling reflects the organizational structure of the Lutheran Church into synods, associations of self-governing Lutheran congregations. Basic sources for funding Lutheran schools are the congregation, tuition and fees, development income, fundraising, and some state and federal income. Increasingly, however, Lutheran schools are tuition driven.

The number of schools maintained by the largest Lutheran body, the Evangelical Lutheran Church in America, has remained relatively small. The Lutheran Church Missouri Synod (LCMS) maintains the greatest number of schools, with the significantly smaller Wisconsin Lutheran Synod a distant second. The Missouri Synod was founded in 1847 by twelve congregations seeking a more conservative affiliation. The church body, currently known as the LCMS, founded schools as an all-important means of ensuring the orthodoxy of future generations.

The first Lutheran schools in America were founded by Swedish, Dutch, and German settlers in the colonial mid-Atlantic states. Beginning in 1820, religious dissidents from Germany and Scandinavia who had settled in the Midwest for religious freedom and economic opportunity opened schools.

Lutheran immigrants who wanted to perpetuate their language and culture gathered in clusters scattered over the plains, villages, and forest clearings and along the rivers of what are now Ohio, Michigan, Indiana, Illinois, Wisconsin, Minnesota, and Missouri. It was there that they established congregations, schools, colleges, seminaries, foreign-language newspapers, publishing houses, and other social and cultural agencies. Migrants from the Middle Atlantic states, many of whom were Lutheran, joined the new immigrants. It was not uncommon in these settlements to find a Lutheran parochial school housed in a log cabin.

The twenty-five-year period following the formation of the new Missouri Synod was one of rapid growth. By 1872 the synod had grown from the original 12 charter congregations to 446, and the number of schools grew from 14 to 472 and experienced steady growth until the Great Depression. After World War II there was a resurgence in parish schools. The rising birthrate fed a steady growth in enrollments, necessitating the construction of new schools.

By 1961 LCMS schools had expanded in number to 1,323, a high-water mark. However, this growth did not change the schools' purpose, at least not in the early 1960s. Parish schools remained the congregation's preferred vehicle of serving members' children. The Missouri Synod continued to view conversion as a learning process rather than a moment of rebirth.

The growing numbers of non-Lutheran and non-Christian students in Lutheran schools, a result of concerns about the quality and curricula of public schools, have caused a reexamination of means and ends in Lutheran schooling. Interaction with nonchurch families has muddied the historic role of the Lutheran school, raising questions about the purpose of Lutheran schools. How far can a traditional curriculum be reformed before it no longer reflects a distinctively Christian Lutheran school?

The fact that Lutheran schools face challenges similar to those of their public counterparts demonstrates that they are no longer out of the cultural mainstream. Indeed, religious pluralism suggests that student populations are likely to become more multidenominational or less church affiliated as the twenty-first century unfolds.

Sources and Further Reading: Walter H. Beck, *Lutheran Elementary Schools in the United States* (1939); William A. Kramer, *Lutheran Schools—15 Crucial Years* (1975); William C. Rietschel, *An Introduction to the Foundations of Lutheran Education* (2000).

William C. Rietschel
Concordia University, Illinois

Roman Catholic

Among the first explorers in the westward expansion that swept across the Midwest were Catholic missionaries, who often established makeshift schools for settlers' children or for the conversion of Native Americans. Most of these early schools, dependent upon their founders, were short-lived.

A notable early effort, however, was that of Father Gabriel Richard, who came to Detroit in 1798 and established his first school in 1802. He organized a system of education that included both elementary and secondary schools for boys and girls. Technical and vocational training was offered as well as the basic "four Rs" (reading, 'riting, 'rithmetic, and religion). Having brought the first printing press to Michigan, Richard published a series of textbooks, which gained considerable circulation. He even tried to gain public funding for his schools. His laudatory efforts did not survive, with one exception. Richard is credited with helping to establish the University of Michigan. In 1817 he served as its first vice president and as one of its two initial professors along with its president, the Reverend John Monteith, a Presbyterian minister.

Catholic leaders' commitment to religious education intensified in the nineteenth century. Edward Fenwick, the first bishop of the Cincinnati diocese, which stretched to parts of Michigan, Wisconsin, Indiana, and Illinois, was instrumental in establishing numerous schools. Samuel Mazzuchelli, a Dominican, established parishes and schools throughout Wisconsin, Illinois, Iowa, and Michigan, as well as a college, over a thirty-four-year period beginning in 1830.

These educational pioneers, as well as their successors, were often dependent upon European religious orders who came to the United States to do varied work, including schooling. These orders of priests and nuns included Franciscans, Dominicans, Vincentians, Benedictines, Jesuits, Presentations, Poor Clares, School Sisters of Notre Dame, School Sisters of St. Francis, and many others.

St. Louis, Missouri, emerged as a resource center for Catholic education. The first viable Catholic high school in the Midwest was founded there along with the initial seminaries in the region. The Sisters of the Sacred Heart, having arrived in 1818, began three decades of work that initiated free universal education with outreaches to all economic levels and races in the city. Also in 1818, the Jesuits established St. Louis Academy, which developed into what are today St. Louis University High School and St. Louis University. These were the first permanent Catholic high school and college in the Midwest. With the city of St. Louis as an anchor, many religious orders branched out to spread Catholic education.

Societal pressures aided the Catholic schooling impetus. In the 1840s, fierce sentiment against immigrants, who were mostly Catholic and poor, caused them to look to their schools as a means to escape prejudice and retain their ethnic customs and identity. Furthermore, the public schools' insistence on using the Protestant version of the Bible gave additional cause for Catholics to segregate educationally. Germans were leaders among the ethnic groups in establishing their own Catholic schools in Ohio, Kansas, Illinois, Missouri, Minnesota, and Wisconsin.

The growth of Catholic schools initiated systematic organization. In 1879 Bishop Joseph Dwenger of Fort Wayne proposed a centralized diocesan system under a single board of control to coordinate curriculum, teacher qualifications, textbooks, and other issues. Eventually this central system became a national model.

Midwestern bishops led the Third Plenary Council of Baltimore of 1884, which recommended the centralized system and further mandated the growth of Catholic education. Such a demand added financial pressure to the parish. Archbishop John Ireland of St. Paul, Minnesota, sought a solution through the so-called Faribault Plan, which ignited calls for public financing of religious schools. Under the plan, the Catholic school was rented to the local public school board for use during the day but offered religious instruction before and after normal school hours. Secular leaders argued that this was public support of religious education, while many religious contended that it weakened the intent of the Third Plenary Council. Even though this arrangement lasted only a year, it ignited a controversy that was eventually addressed by the pope.

The Catholic education initiative extended to higher education. Notable midwestern institutions of higher learning include St. Louis, Notre Dame, Dayton, Marquette, Loyola, Detroit, Creighton, and DePaul Universities. Indiana's St.-Mary-of-the-Woods College, established in 1840, is the nation's oldest Catholic liberal arts college for women. These colleges eventually expanded to become universities encompassing graduate and professional schools, stimulating the Catholic environment in numerous ways. In 1909 Marquette was the first Catholic college in the nation to offer a summer session, primarily for pedagogical training of Catholic teachers, and it was soon followed by others. Today, DePaul is the largest Catholic university in the United States.

Enrollment peaked for Catholic schools in the mid-1960s. In 1932–1933, the Archdiocese of Chicago, historically the largest in the United States, had 387 elementary and secondary schools enrolling 180,810 students. By 1964–1965, there were 524 schools serving 366,171 pupils. But by 2000, Chicago had fallen to 336 schools with 131,054 students. Financial pressures intensified as the number of religious faculty dwindled at a tremendous rate in the late 1960s and the 1970s. Criticism of Catholic education from within the church added to the decline. Most notable was Joseph Cardinal Ritter of St. Louis questioning whether the investment in the Catholic school system had been wise.

Modern issues in Catholic education reflect the changing character of education in the region. In cities such as Detroit and Chicago, poor and minority students constitute a majority of students in many Catholic schools because they offer a relatively inexpensive and highly structured alternative to overcrowded and underfunded urban public schools. Catholic schools have also played a major role in the debate over the public funding of nonpublic schools through school vouchers. In 2002 the U.S. Supreme Court upheld the use of vouchers in Cleveland, Ohio, where more than 95 percent of those vouchers were used for sectarian schools, many of which are Catholic.

Today, Catholic schools emphasize academic quality, discipline, personal attention, social justice, and faith development as they serve a diverse student population. While in some parts of the Midwest new Catholic schools have recently been opened, the financing of Catholic schools, particularly in urban areas, is an enduring concern.

Sources and Further Reading: William E. Brown and Andrew M. Greeley, *Can Catholic Schools Survive?* (1970); Very Rev. J. A. Burns and Bernard J. Kohlbrenner, *A History of Catholic Education in the United States* (1937); Charles G. Herbermann, Edward A. Pace, Condé B. Pallen, Rt. Rev. Thomas J. Shahan, and John J. Wynne, S.J., eds., *The Catholic Encyclopedia* (1913); Thomas C. Hunt, Ellis A. Joseph, and Ronald J. Nuzzi, eds., *Handbook of Research on Catholic Education* (2001); National Catholic Educational Association, *NCEA/Ganley's Catholic Schools in America* (1976–2000); *The New Catholic Encyclopedia* (2002); Joseph M. O'Keefe, ed., *Catholic Education at the Turn of the New Century* (1997); F. Michael Perko, ed., *Enlightening the Next Generation* (1988).

Paul M. McInerny
Whitefish Bay, Wisconsin

Sports and Recreation

SECTION EDITOR
Robin F. Bachin

Section Contents

Overview

Visitors to Tommy Bartlett's Thrill Show in the Wisconsin Dells know they are getting something few other places in the nation now offer. The athletic water skiers, both male and female, dressed in sparkling sequins and satin, dazzle audiences with their daring flips, nimble jumps, and symmetrical human pyramids. The attraction is the oldest of its kind in the nation, dating back to 1952, and attests to the importance of midwestern sport enthusiasts who pioneered not only the sport of water skiing but also the popularity of ski shows like this one. The ubiquity of lakes in the Midwest, both Great and small, meant that waterskiing was destined to become as popular as cross-country skiing, a sport introduced by Scandinavian settlers because it was so well suited to the flat prairie landscape. Bartlett's Thrill Show, in short, highlights the central roles that climate, topography, ethnic sporting practice, and the rise of commercial leisure have played in shaping regional sport history.

Sports have always played an important part in structuring social relations. From the games of Native Americans to the outdoor winter sports of Scandinavian immigrants, the Midwest took on distinctive patterns of leisure and recreation. Unlike in the South, where gambling and blood sports helped to define the rigid racial and social structure of slave culture, sports and recreation in the Midwest often have extended opportunities for preserving cultural traditions and for penetrating ethnic and racial boundaries. Attitudes toward sports in the Midwest also differed from those in New England, where sports were often frowned upon or avoided as mere idleness.

Among Native Americans like the Algonquians, sport was woven into the fabric of daily life. Athletic games were associated with harvest festivals, healing ceremonies, and fertility rites. Foot races, ball throwing, and stickball (lacrosse) allowed Native Americans to enact on the athletic field the larger contests that structured tribal diplomacy. Tribes also made skating and sleighing, activities adapted to the climate and topography, into forms of recreation. In addition, sports provided a nexus of cultural exchange among Indians and whites. Some white youths learned hunting skills through bow and arrow contests held with Native Americans in Indian schools.

Indeed, the features of the midwestern landscape that encouraged trade among Native Americans as well as Europeans and European Americans also contributed to the region's patterns of sport and recreation. The proximity to four of the five Great Lakes, the confluence of river systems, and the vast forests of the frontier meant that hunting, fishing, and logging would be the foundations for survival in the territory. Yet on the frontier, the distinction between labor and leisure was less stark than in New England or the South. The qualities associated with "taming" the frontier, including courage, physical prowess, and competitiveness, also shaped early sporting contests. Hunting and fishing not only provided sustenance for frontier families but also became vehicles for showcas-

Memorial Stadium, University of Nebraska, Lincoln, 1923. Rick Anderson Enterprises.

ing masculinity. Women's work also shaped midwestern recreation. Métis daughters (girls of mixed Indian and European parentage) learned the art of maple sugaring from their Indian mothers and created spring festivals to celebrate the season and sample their wares.

German and Scandinavian immigrants who settled in the Midwest in the middle of the nineteenth century tied together work and recreation. The same skill and hard work necessary for clearing timber, plowing prairies, and raising dairy cows could be showcased in wood-chopping and milking competitions. These contests were not frivolous amusements, but instead reflected the determination and belief in improvement that many settlers brought with them. Competition had a utilitarian component, as it encouraged participants in this emerging agricultural economy to improve the skills they needed to ensure economic success.

Frigid winters and steamy summers contributed to the rise of outdoor sports to suit the weather. Native Americans used snowshoes as a means of crossing the snowy regions of the upper Midwest, and introduced the practice to white migrants from New England and the upper South. By the late nineteenth century, snowshoeing had emerged as a popular form of recreation, as clubs formed to help bring people together for social functions during the difficult winter months. Swedish and Norwegian immigrants helped move ice skating and skiing from practical forms of mobility to popular recreational activities. By the early twentieth century, the Midwest was the leading region for cross-country skiing. Similarly, speed skating and ice dancing began in competitions held by Scandinavians.

In the summers, residents of the Midwest sought out sandy lakeshores and shady forests as a respite from the heat and humidity. The upper Midwest alone boasts over 37,000 inland lakes, and each of these, as well as the rivers connecting them, became popular destinations for fishing, canoeing, and other water sports. Similarly, the dense pine and hardwood forests beckoned hikers and campers in search of shade during sweltering summers. Pioneering conservation efforts in the Midwest ensured that forests would be preserved for recreational purposes. Landscape architect John Nolen's 1909 plan for protection of Wisconsin's scenic places led to the preservation of wilderness areas such as Devil's Lake State Park. Thanks to the efforts of Iowan Aldo Leopold, the federal government began creating National Forests in 1924, giving impetus to preservation efforts nationwide. In 1961, Wisconsin became the first state to pass an Outdoor Recreation Act, which set aside over 580,000 acres for the state's conservation and recreation programs. The Midwest's leadership in linking

environmental conservation with recreation highlights the central role outdoor activity has played in shaping regional identity.

The importance of the landscape in shaping recreational activities fueled the rise of vacation destinations. As Marguerite Shaffer points out later in this section, the Midwest lacked the spectacular natural features that transformed other locales into resort areas. Yet the same economic and demographic transformations that shaped patterns of travel and tourism in the rest of the nation in the middle of the nineteenth century also contributed to the development of vacation sites along the Great Lakes and throughout the region. The rise of a market economy, and the transportation and communication revolutions that followed, created new wealth along with new opportunities for spending it. Already by the 1860s, resort hotels dotted the shorelines of the Great Lakes. Steamships, then railroads carried people from across the nation to these destinations, either en route to other venues or as their final stop. Many of the hotels started as hunting lodges and evolved into more elaborate resorts. In addition, the health reform movement that began in the middle of the century led many Americans to Michigan's Battle Creek Sanitarium and others like it, touting water cures, fresh air treatment, diet reform, and exercise, Dr. John Harvey Kellogg promised patients therapeutic rejuvenation. Soon patient C. W. Post opened his own spa, utilizing the same nutritional plans and exercise regimens popularized by Kellogg. By the turn of the twentieth century, Post and Kellogg's son, W. K. Kellogg, made breakfast cereal into a national commodity and sites promoting health and wellness into vacation hot spots. Immigrant groups, too, added to the variety of spa and resort offerings. Many resorts in Minnesota and Michigan's Upper Peninsula incorporated saunas into their design, providing guests with the traditional "sweat bath" introduced by Finnish immigrants.

Health reform was part of the larger process of social reform that characterized the Progressive Era at the turn of the twentieth century. As the nation became more urban, and family farming gave way to large-scale industry and factory labor, numerous reformers championed outdoor activity and organized play as vehicles for improving the physical and moral condition of Americans. Proponents of organized play argued that "wholesome" outdoor recreation offered an alternative to the lure of the saloons, billiards halls, and theatres that were so pervasive in American cities and that attracted the nation's youth. Chicago led the nation in constructing playgrounds, following the establishment of a special park commission charged with creating small parks in crowded wards throughout the city. The small parks included ball fields, swimming and wading pools, and field houses equipped with boys' and girls' gymnasia, showers, and libraries. Each park employed two trained play supervisors, and the director of the Special Park Commission was a trained physical educator, Edward B. DeGroot. When the Playground Association of America held its first annual convention in Chicago in 1907, President Theodore Roosevelt hailed Chicago's playgrounds as "one of the most notable civic achievements of any American city."

Immigrants influenced the character of urban sport and recreation. German "turners" (from *turnvereine*, or gymnastics clubs), Czech *sokols (gymnastic societies)*, and the Polish Falcons (a national organization devoted to physical fitness) offered alternative spaces for gathering and social activities that helped maintain links to ethnic culture. In cities such as Cincinnati, St. Louis, Chicago, and Milwaukee, these athletic clubs hosted gymnastic and track and field competitions, and served as important sites for family and community gathering outside the workplace. In addition, churches, temples, and ethnic and religious youth groups, including the Catholic Youth Organization and the B'nai B'rith Association, began sponsoring sports teams by the first decades of the twentieth century. These clubs had the dual effect of both preserving ethnic ties and promoting Americanization at a time when sports came to play an increasingly important role in shaping leisure and recreation among Americans nationwide.

The Midwest played a central role in organizing and promoting intercollegiate sports. Many of the small, sectarian colleges that dotted the landscape of the region introduced athletic clubs and varsity sports competition at the time of the Civil War. Larger state schools initiated athletic programs, often hiring athletic directors from eastern universities. The creation of the Western Conference (later called the Big Ten) in 1895 signaled the importance of midwestern collegiate sports, especially football. The first president of the University of Chicago, William Rainey Harper, called the athletic field "one of the University's laboratories and by no means the least important one." Harper and other promoters of collegiate sports linked athletics directly to manhood and morality, and invoked the rhetoric of "muscular Christianity" to articulate the central role competitive sports played in promoting the best attributes in college students. Supporters of college athletics highlighted how the values and discipline learned on the athletic field would have important applications within the classroom and in society at large.

Women were included in these prescriptions for participation in collegiate sport, though the issue of competition was a more delicate one. The Midwest was important in shaping women's sporting opportunities because the region played a pioneering role in promoting coeducation in the nineteenth century. Both Oberlin and Antioch colleges began admitting women before the Civil War, and in 1870, the University of Michigan became the first large state school to become coed. The University of Chicago was founded in 1890 as a coeducational research university, and soon after inaugurated the first program incorporating competitive athletics for women. Most advocates of women's athletics argued that the focus should be on the "corrective" aspects of individual exercise. Proponents also explained that cooperation rather than competition should be the emphasis of women's sports. Still, by the turn of the twentieth century, women competed in golf, tennis, swimming, rowing, baseball, and basketball, though under modified rules.

Midwestern universities took the lead in integrating collegiate sports at a time when a gentlemen's agreement to exclude African Americans pervaded college athletics. Black athletes had played football at the University of Iowa since 1895. Star athletes including right tackle Fred "Duke" Slater, lineman Calvin Jones, broad jumper Edward Gordon, and wrestler Simon Roberts led Iowa to numerous successes in their respective sports. Yet blacks still faced discrimination both on and off the field. In the 1930s, Ozzie Simmons quit the Iowa football team as a result of racial taunting, and in 1969, sixteen black football players boycotted the team to protest the treatment of fellow black players and push for more black coaches.

In addition to collegiate sports, organized youth sports have played a significant role in shaping race relations and promoting community identity in the Midwest. Indiana's obsession with high school basketball illustrates not only the importance of the game in fostering local pride, but also its potential for promoting racial understanding. In Indianapolis, a city with a long history of segregation, the all-black Crispus Attucks Tigers basketball team delivered the city its first state championship in 1955 under the leadership of star player Oscar Robertson. A white student recalled that the success of the Attucks team brought a sense of "pride to the whole city which I think helped break down a lot of the color barriers because those kids belonged to Indianapolis." The zeal for basketball from both black and white residents forced a reexamination of race relations in the city, and according to Richard B. Pierce, made the players "agents of change."

The enthusiasm that fostered participation in organized youth sports and collegiate athletics in the Midwest also shaped the rise of professional sports. Indeed, the Midwest has played a pivotal role in the history of professional sports in America in large part because it stands at the nexus of transportation systems, communication networks, northern and western migration, and economic markets both east and west. Although the birthplace of the national pastime may have been the playing fields of New York and New Jersey, the first professional baseball franchise, Harry Wright's Red Stockings, was formed in 1869 in Cincinnati. The Civil War and increased mobility set the stage for club players from the East to relocate to the Midwest with the promise of pay. The founding of the Red Stockings quickly spurred the nationalization and professionalization of the game. In 1876, eight professional teams joined together to form the National League of Professional Base Ball Clubs. The business of sport, with control in the hands of owners rather than players, had begun.

The commercialization of sport extended beyond the playing fields. Intimately connected with the rise of professional sports was development of sporting goods manufacturing as big business. Although bat and ball manufacturing was established, Albert G. Spalding's sporting goods company did more to promote the commercial and professional character of baseball than almost any other sponsor of the game. When Cincinnati organized the first professional baseball team in 1869, Spalding launched baseball as a major commercial venture. He opened his athletic gear manufacturing enterprise in Chicago, and quickly served a national market. Moreover, it was Spalding's initiative that led to the formation of the National League. Spalding's handbooks on the official rules of baseball, codified by the National League, became not only the standard guides for the game but also vehicles for promoting sales of his products. Chicago's Ashland Manufacturing Company was founded in 1913 to develop innovative ways to use the by-products of the meatpacking industry, headquartered on the South Side of Chicago. Ashland produced tennis racquets, string, and other products such as surgical sutures. One year later, when Thomas E. Wilson became president (the name of the company was changed to Wilson Sporting Goods in 1931), the company began focusing exclusively on the production of athletic equipment. Chicago thus became the headquarters of sporting goods manufacturing for the nation.

Both Spalding and Wilson played important roles not only in promoting professional baseball but also in anticipating the rise of professional football as a lucrative industry. Both companies supplied collegiate football teams with balls, helmets, and jerseys, and even worked with legendary coaches such as Walter Camp and Knute Rockne to design innovative equipment. When company-sponsored football teams emerged in the mill towns and steel yards of the Midwest, Spald-ing and Wilson competed for that market. These company teams joined together to form the American Professional Football Association, which became the National Football League in 1922. Of the original eleven teams, all but one, the Rochester (New York) Jeffersons, were from the Midwest. George Halas's Decatur (Illinois) Staleys, which morphed into the Chicago Bears in 1921, was the first of many regional powerhouse professional football franchises.

If professionalization helped expand the market for sports, it also shut down opportunities for some players. Once professionalism overtook the game of baseball, racial discrimination became more rigid. The professional leagues had no formal policy restricting African American players because they did not need one. Instead, member clubs maintained a gentlemen's agreement whereby no club would sign black players. Yet the gentlemen's agreement did not prevent African Americans from playing professional baseball. Many black baseball players enjoyed successful careers in semipro ball and in the various clubs that barnstormed throughout the nation. In 1920, Andrew "Rube" Foster founded the Negro National League in Chicago and made black baseball a successful enterprise throughout the nation. The Midwest, then, not only launched professional baseball and banned blacks, it was where black baseball emerged as a lucrative business venture.

The Midwest also was the region where female athletes had one of the few opportunities to play for pay. Chicago Cubs owner and chewing gum magnate Philip K. Wrigley created The All American Girls Baseball League (AAGBL) in 1943, when the future of major league baseball was threatened by World War II. Wrigley recruited some of the best softball players in the Midwest, many of whom had recently taken jobs in wartime industries and now played for their company teams. Teams such as the Racine (Wisconsin) Belles, Kenosha (Wisconsin) Comets, Fort Wayne (Indiana) Daisies, and Rockford (Illinois) Peaches began by playing a hybrid of softball and baseball. By the time of the league's demise in 1954, though, they were playing regulation major league baseball.

Yet the AAGBL was not the first time women had been paid to play. Women had been playing baseball for pay, especially in the Midwest, since the 1870s. The first game between professional women's barnstorming teams was in Springfield, Illinois in 1875. Despite the belief that this game was merely a publicity stunt, it set the stage for women playing on professional teams, including earning spots on men's teams. In 1907, Alta Weiss became the star pitcher for the semipro Vermilion Independents of Cleveland. Similarly, Toni Stone played second base for the Negro American League's Indianapolis Clowns in 1953, a time when the Clowns were the top-ranked team in the league.

The connection between professional sport and publicity continued to grow throughout the twentieth century as more sophisticated media outlets, from radio to television to cable to the Internet, broadcast athletic events across the country and later around the globe. The line between sports star and media celebrity began to blur as professional athletes were used to market everything from sneakers to breakfast cereal. No one epitomized this phenomenon more than Michael Jordan, the star forward of the Chicago Bulls, whose image was more recognizable worldwide than those of national leaders. In the 1990s, schoolchildren in China ranked Jordan as one of the two greatest figures of the twentieth century (the other was Zhou Enlai, a leader of the Communist Revolution and former prime minister). Because Jordan epitomized American culture around the world, professional sports became a pre-eminent symbol of America. By the late 1990s, Jordan's persona was linked less to his own team and more to the companies he endorsed, especially Nike. As historian Walter LaFeber explained, "Wearing his Nikes, Jordan's image flew around the world and across geographical boundaries that seemed increasingly to be almost meaningless lines on a map."

The local pride and regional attachments that have nurtured sport in the Midwest since the seventeenth century clearly have given way to transnational phenomena that have transformed sport into a dominant global industry at the start of the twenty-first century. Yet even as sport has become highly commercialized, less rooted in place, and more clearly shaped by multinational media conglomerates, it still maintains a powerful hold on local communities throughout the Midwest, as well as the rest of the nation. High school basketball, collegiate wrestling and hockey, and weekend ice fishing, camping, and hunting trips continue to be important activities that structure the lives of many midwesterners. Although professional sports and the worldwide media attention it has received have done much to diminish regional distinctiveness, the daily sporting experiences of midwesterners throughout the region keep alive the time-honored athletic and recreational traditions that have made the Midwest such a unique sporting landscape.

Sources and Further Reading: Gai Ingham Berlage, *Women in Baseball: The Forgotten History* (1994); Susan K. Cahn, *Coming on Strong: Gender and Sexuality in Twentieth-Century Women's Sport* (1994); Andrew R.L. Cayton and Susan E. Gray, eds., *The American Midwest: Essays on Regional History* (2001); Richard O. Davies, *America's Obsession: Sports and Society Since 1945* (1994); John Mack Faragher, " 'More Motley than Mackinaw': From Ethnic Mixing to Ethnic Cleansing on the Frontier of the Lower Missouri, 1783–1833," in Andrew R.L. Cayton and Fredrika Teute, eds., *Contact Points: American Frontiers from the Mohawk Valley to the Mississippi, 1750–1830* (1998); Gerald R. Gems, *Windy City Wars: Labor, Leisure, and Sport in the Making of Chicago* (1997); Elliott Gorn and Warren Goldstein, *A Brief History of American Sports* (1993); Walter LaFeber, *Michael Jordan and the New Global Capitalism* (1999); James H. Madison, ed., *Heartland: Comparative Histories of Midwestern States* (1988); David R. McMahon, "Remembering the Black and Gold: African Americans, Sport Memory, and the University of Iowa," in Stephen G. Wieting, ed., *Sport and Memory in North America* (2001); Richard B. Pierce, "More than a Game: The Political Meaning of High School Basketball in Indianapolis," in Patrick B. Miller and David K. Wiggins, eds., *Sport and the Color Line: Black Athletes and Race Relations in Twentieth-Century America* (2004); Benjamin G. Rader, *American Sports: From the Age of Folk Games to the Age of Televised Sports*, 3rd ed. (1996); Steven A. Riess, *Sport in Industrial America, 1850–1920* (1995); David K. Wiggins, ed., *Sport in America: From Wicked Amusement to National Obsession* (1995).

Robin F. Bachin
University of Miami, Florida

Early Sports and Recreation

Though daily life in the early Midwest necessarily focused on survival, sports and recreation were important aspects of pioneer culture as settlers sought respite from their toils. Some recreational activities took place in conjunction with social or work gatherings, others were extensions of protective or survival skills. Some were means to educate the young in necessary skills, others were purely for enjoyment. Recreation occurred year round, but was most common during the agricultural year's slack time of late fall and early winter or on days set aside for enjoyment.

Local in nature, most pioneer recreation rarely distinguished between participants' roles or between competitors and spectators. Organization was nonexistent or informal, and rules were unwritten and varied according to local practices.

Despite sometimes extensive interaction between American Indians and European settlers, little direct cultural transference occurred between the groups with regard to sports. Recreation was simply another piece of the cultural baggage settlers brought with them. They normally adapted familiar activities, although some who migrated from more settled areas may have taken part in survival-related recreation for the first time. It does not appear that any new sports were specifically "created" after the pioneers' arrival.

Ballplay of the Dakota on the St. Peters River in Winter, by Seth Eastman, 1848. Oil on canvas. Acquisition in memory of Mitchell A. Wilder, Director, Amon Carter Museum, 1961–1979. Amon Carter Museum, Fort Worth, Texas.

Physical strength and dexterity played important roles in pioneer sports, many of which were connected with defense or survival skills. Sport thus became a pleasurable pastime and a method to measure one's worth. Events like shooting matches, fighting, and horse and foot races were all examples of contests that could train the young or hone the survival skills of their elders.

Shooting matches were extremely popular and occurred throughout the year. Typically a target was attached to a tree or post, and shooters took three shots from varying distances. Prizes included cash, whiskey, or beef; an early Indiana settler recalled beef shoots in which marksmen shot for shares of a butchered cow. Equally important to most marksmen (and they were almost always men) was the pride inherent in being the "crack shot" in the area.

Though modern prizefighting was unknown, fights and wrestling matches were common. "Bully" fights in which a local tough picked a fight joined "friendlier" matches meant to settle who was the "best man." Both drew crowds of spectators backing (and occasionally betting on) their man. Other than prohibiting weapons, there were few rules and custom allowed kicking, gouging, biting and "stomping upon a fallen victim." Much the same was true for wrestling matches, although they could also be friendlier affairs at social gatherings. Ideally the battles did not result in lasting grudges, and combatants and spectators alike adjourned as friends, as in the famous case of a young Abraham Lincoln's match with "bully" Jack Armstrong in Illinois.

Speed of foot, both human and horse, was an obvi-

ous source of competition. Many gatherings featured foot races to determine the swiftest. Allied with these were other games analogous to modern track and field events. These included "Jumping the Bar," which was akin to modern high jumping, and early versions of pole vaulting.

Horse racing was perhaps the most popular sport during the first half of the nineteenth century. Races ranged from informal contests for bragging rights to organized "meets" complete with prize money. The sport's popularity grew from its long practice combined with an intense sense of competition and pride in one's livestock.

Informal match races usually took place along dirt roads or across farm fields and were held on the spur of the moment or at gatherings like militia musters or July 4th celebrations. The steeds were usually "saddle nags or plow ponies" ridden bareback by proud owners along distances from a few hundred yards to a quarter mile or longer. Most were "match races" between two horses, but occasionally a larger field competed. The spectacle seldom failed to thrill the crowd.

More formalized race meets were held on designated racecourses, often ovals, and offered purses. The first recorded race in what became the Midwest may have been an 1801 event in Cincinnati that lasted two days and earned the winner a $50 prize. The meet quickly grew to a three-day fair with a sweepstakes prize of $500. By 1840, many other towns featured racetracks. The horses that ran on these tracks were many cuts above the nags of earlier times. Horse breeding, long a Southern tradition, swiftly gained ground in the Midwest as blooded stock became available in most areas. Indianapolis newspapers carried ads for a number of stud horses in the 1830s, including one whose lineage was traced back to the famous Godolphin Arabian. Harness racing, later to be wildly popular in the Midwest, was rarely seen during the pioneer period.

Early settlers eagerly sought escape from their isolation by combining work and social functions into events such as husking bees or house and barnraisings. At such gatherings work skills, like survival skills, morphed into recreation with a purpose. Log rolling was a popular work sport that combined strength and speed. After trees were felled and stripped, two teams armed with hand spikes were chosen. Logs were rolled to a specified spot, where they were lifted to erect a cabin. Rollings to clear land continued beyond the log cabin era. Teams rolled unwanted logs to a spot and lifted them onto a pile. The first team to hoist their final log was the winner and the logs were set afire. Related skills were shown in wood chopping contests in which individuals or teams competed in felling and trimming trees.

The highly developed American sense of competition turned even mundane activities into sport. Corn huskings were coed, intergenerational contests that took place in a party atmosphere. Teams of men and women, adults and children, competed to remove the husk from the ears of corn. Though there were seldom prizes for the winners, there were rewards. Finding a rare red ear of corn sometimes earned the finder a kiss or, for the men, perhaps a "pull" from a bottle of whiskey.

Hunting and fishing were sometimes recreational as well as food-gathering activities. Small groups gathered for wolf, squirrel, or coon hunts, as much for sport as for procuring meat or fur. Hunts were also important avenues for educating the young in necessary survival skills. This was especially true in Native American cultures, which supplied children with small bows and arrows with which to practice for the future.

Not all sporting activities were directly related to work or defense. Some, like pitching quoits, were meant for amusement—sport for sport's sake. Two versions of quoits appeared in the region that became the Midwest. One mirrored the eastern game of tossing an iron ring toward a stake, similar to pitching horseshoes. In the other, quoit pitchers hefted a boulder or flat stone onto their shoulders and threw it to a designated spot. This version of the game, associated with the Indiana frontier, more closely resembles the Native American practice and may be one of the few examples of cultural transference; it is similar to today's shot put. Similar was the game of Long Bullets (not to be confused with the Native American gambling game of Moccasin and Bullet), which was played with an iron ball. Hard evidence about the game is sparse, but it appears to have been played by two teams who tried to prevent their opponents from throwing or rolling the "bullet" across their goal line. How widely the game was played is unknown.

Such ball games did not play a significant role in pioneer culture, at least among adults. This was in sharp contrast to Native Americans, who participated in games (often accompanied by gambling) similar to modern soccer, lacrosse, volleyball, and field hockey. A 1796 account described a game of "football" in Ohio in which a male team competed against a female team, a rarity. The idea was to drive the ball (probably a deer hide stuffed with hair) between the opponents' goal. Men were restricted to using only their feet to touch the ball, while women were allowed also to use their hands. Lacrosse, the most widely known Native American sport still practiced, was played throughout the Great Lakes area. One account claims more than 2,000 Miami Indians gathered to take part in a game.

The early Midwest was also a scene of blood sports such as cockfighting and gander pulling. Typically in cockfighting a ring was cleared and the agitated birds battled each other until one died or managed to flee. Even crueler was gander pulling. With feathers plucked and neck greased, a gander was suspended by its feet from a tree limb. A succession of riders took turns attempting to pull off the bird's head to win a prize. Shooting matches sometimes featured live geese or turkeys as targets. These "sports" were common enough to inspire laws designed to restrict them. An 1807 Indiana territorial law levied fines for any person who "shall cause to fight any cock or cocks, for money . . . or shall promote or encourage any match, or matches of cock fighting."

A trait shared by many pioneer pastimes was gambling, which one historian described as "in the blood of the time." Gambling was widespread as wagers, friendly and otherwise, were placed on horse races, footraces, billiards, and cockfights. Nearly every sort of contest was a potential venue for betting. Though it appears most wagering was as much for entertainment as profit, a strident anti-gambling movement formed in reaction as religious groups and reformers sought to outlaw it. Indeed, most laws concerning horse racing or cockfighting were meant more to inhibit gambling than prohibit it.

One of the few direct recreational transfers from Native Americans to pioneers was a form of gambling called Moccasin and Bullet. Later simply called Bullet, it was an early version of a shell game practiced by many tribes and eagerly taken up by settlers. In the game, a dexterous "tout" would gather the players around and show them a large bullet and four to six moccasins. The bullet was skillfully (and deceptively) placed under one of the moccasins, and players bet on which one nestled it. The game was very popular among wagering pioneers, as were various card games and billiards. Billiard tables, usually found in an inn or tavern, were a presence by the first decade of the nineteenth century. Contemporary descriptions of the games are rare, but it likely resembled modern pocket billiards.

As always, children found time to play. In addition to typical childhood games, they were more likely than adults to take part in ball games. Versions of games similar to baseball were played throughout the Midwest, among them Rounders, Town Ball, and One Old Cat. Children emulated adults by competing in footraces or wrestling matches. Boys were indoctrinated into their grown-up roles as providers through shooting matches, hunting, and fishing. Seasonal activities like swimming and ice skating probably also involved competition.

Though some of these childhood activities were coed, there was usually a clear separation of the sexes as females were expected to attempt less strenuous activities thought more in keeping with their delicate natures. Much the same held true for adults. Women occasionally took part in sporting activities. More often they were spectators or provided food.

Pioneer sports may have been limited by time and circumstance, but they did lay the groundwork for the future. The love of competition, exaltation of physical prowess, and eagerness for recreation exhibited during the era set the stage for the sporting boom, both participatory and spectator, which began in the late nineteenth century.

Sources and Further Reading: Melvin Adelman, *A Sporting Time* (1986); John R. Betts, *America's Sporting Heritage, 1850–1950* (1974); John Dizikes, *Sportsmen and Gamesmen* (1981); Carl Russell Fish, *The Rise of the Common Man* (1937); Jennie Holliman, *American Sport (1785–1835)* (1931); Jack Larkin, *The Reshaping of Everyday Life, 1790–1840* (1989); William S. Parker, "Pioneer Life," *Indiana Magazine of History* 3 (Mar. 1907); Francis Philbrick, ed., *Laws of the Indiana Territory, 1801–1809* (1930); Jerry Jaye Wright, "A History of Sports, Games, and Amusements Among Pioneer Cultures in Indiana, 1670–1820," Ph.D. diss., The Ohio State University (1980).

Timothy Crumrin
Conner Prairie Museum, Fishers, Indiana

Ice-Skating

By 1882, three distinct forms of ice-skating had emerged in the Midwest: fancy-show, figure-sport, and speed. Fancy arrived in 1865, when two young theatrical-skaters demonstrated their acrobatic-dance skills at the first covered ice rink in America.

Like forty other natural-air rinks built in the northern climate, Chicago's Wabash Avenue Skating Rink served as the first ice-theatre for Chicagoans Clarence

Synchronized skating: Oxford, Ohio, Ice Crystals, 2004. Midwest Media Inc.

"Callie" Curtis (1846–1905) and Erastus "E.T." Goodrich (1846–1933). By 1873, Callie and E.T. toured their ice-pantomime skills in Europe, successfully competing for theatre engagements with the famous Jackson Haines (1840–1875), who had inspired them with his final 1864 Chicago performance. They executed better figures than ice-dancer Haines, who hated to be restrained by official figure competitions that required the etching of twenty-six shapes and figures on the ice. Like Haines, Curtis never left Europe, but Goodrich returned to live in Chicago and tour midwestern theatres on roller skates as part of the touring Broadway hit *Humpty Dumpty*.

Midwestern women also became prominent fancy ice-show performers. Mabel Davidson's (Minnesota) ice family toured Europe from 1895 to 1909, and Nellie Dean (Chicago) partnered with Callie Curtis from 1867 to 1873. In 1865, Chicago was a launching pad for the world's first "Skatorial Queen," Carrie Augusta Moore from Concord, Massachusetts, who toured Europe in 1873 and paved the way for Mabel Davidson's 1896 tour of London and Paris.

By 1882 to 1884, amateur speed-skating emerged to become more popular when Norway's Axel Paulsen toured Minnesota, New York, and Canada, inspiring many proud Scandinavian immigrants who had settled in the Midwest. One hundred years later, Olympic gold-medal speed-skaters Eric Heiden, Bonnie Blair, and Dan Jansen would emerge from the same midwestern landscape rooted in Scandinavian speed-skating traditions.

Although amateur figure-skating became an official competitive sport in 1867, its lack of theatrical flair bored most spectators. Both speed- and figure-skating, however, satisfied amateur purists who abhorred the exhibitionist nature of fancy-skating. Nonetheless, by 1915, amateur figure-skating administrators willingly promoted the entertainment aspects of professional fancy in an effort to boost falling interest in figure. Gradually figure incorporated more flash and dance into official amateur competitions.

Since professional fancy offended amateur purists, and figure was considered boring, speed- and distance-skating would become an American strength from 1879 to 1915. Chicago's John Ennis was one pure "frontier skater" who would not offend amateur sportsmen promoting "the strenuous life." In the winter of 1876–1877, Ennis bested Eugene Millard of Cincinnati, Ohio, in a six-day, 500-mile match. This distance event set the stage for the predominance of speed-skating in the Midwest and throughout the nation, until the fancy show reemerged around 1915.

Sources and Further Reading: Franz Biberhofer, *Chronik des Wiener Eislaufvereines* (1906); Fritz Reuel, *Das Eissportbuch* (1928); Laurence Senelick, *The Age and Stage of George L. Fox, 1825–1877*, expanded ed. (1999); Western Skating Association, *Skater's History on Ice and Roller Skating* (1916).

Paul J. DeLoca
Greensboro, North Carolina

Native Americans

Whether Ojibwa or Miami, Ioway or Lakota, native cultures in what is now the Midwest revolved around cultivating, collecting, or preserving food. When not planting corn, stalking game, or netting fish, people enjoyed playing games whose popularity continues today.

Native sports were more than recreation and entertainment. Games educated the young, settled disputes, and earned respect for individual players. Footracing, canoeing, swimming, dice games, and stickball formed an important part of daily activities in native villages and kept members physically fit. Often, family members would play drums and sing songs to encourage contestants.

Particularly popular among Great Lakes tribes during the winter months was "Snow Snake." Participants dug a small trench in the snow and drenched it with water, creating a long icy gutter. They then thrust special wooden spears or "snakes" down the trench. The object was to push their snake further than others. In addition to keeping young boys physically active, the game honed the skills they would need in the summer months for hunting and waging warfare.

Probably the most famous of native sports, lacrosse, Bagatowé, or "Little Brother of War," served several important functions. As early as the sixteenth and seventeenth centuries, European missionaries and traders described lacrosse as field hockey played with a hooped stick and a small ball made of wood, leather, or even carved stone, on a field ranging in size from a few hundred feet to several miles between villages. Men played with bent sticks, the hoops of which originally represented the female anatomy. Women got their chance to exert themselves physically and to vent their frustrations with the opposite sex in "double ball," a game similar to lacrosse. They played it using straight sticks and two small leather, sand-filled sacks, which represented the male reproductive organs.

Lacrosse matches were usually friendly if violent contests between different clans or ages of men within a tribe. Sometimes, however, villages pitted themselves against one another to settle points of honor. In these cases, lacrosse was an alternative to a deadly battle.

Gambling was also a popular pastime. Many tribes wagered on games of bone or wooden dice. Today, this tradition persists in the more than one hundred casinos and bingo parlors operated by native tribes in the Midwest. These establishments generate billions of dollars each year for regional tribes and bands, helping to improve roads, fund medical clinics, and endow educational scholarships.

In the twenty-first century, sport remains central to most native tribes. The world's best lacrosse players are often native Americans, and we owe the modern sport of hockey to early native lacrosse players. Most controversial is the widespread use of mascot names such as "redmen," "chiefs," or "warriors," which many people see as demeaning the cultural heritage of Indians. However, some native communities such as Lac du Flambeau, Wisconsin, take pride in these monikers as symbols of their rich athletic tradition.

Sources and Further Reading: Stewart Culin, *Games of the North American Indians* (1973); Andrew McFarland Davis, *Indian* Games (1886); Joseph B. Oxendine, *American Indian Sports Heritage* (1995); Thomas Vennum, *American Indian Lacrosse* (1994).

Eugene R. H. Tesdahl
Boulder, Colorado

Lacrosse

Lacrosse developed as a ball game played by indigenous peoples around the Great Lakes and throughout eastern North America. Players used webbed sticks to carry, pass, and shoot a small ball, attempting to score more goals than their opponents. Traditionally, only men played lacrosse in contests in which the size of teams and the playing area, equipment, and objective might vary markedly. The sport had important spiritual components, reinforced social organization, and was associated with combat.

Seventeenth-century French missionaries described the sport. For much of the eighteenth century, Europeans watched and wagered on matches, eventually engaging in competitions against Native Americans. This fascination in part accounts for the successful attack by Indians on Fort Michilimackinac in 1763 under the guise of a lacrosse match. By the early nineteenth century, European Americans were playing the game among themselves, systemizing it in 1867.

Lacrosse did not attract public interest until after the Civil War when traveling exhibitions became popular, both for the novelty of sport and the representations of Indian players as wild and uncivilized. In the final decades of the nineteenth century, Americans rapidly institutionalized lacrosse, organizing in succession intercollegiate play, a national amateur association, and an intercollegiate association.

Lacrosse has enjoyed growing popularity and wider diffusion over the course of the twentieth century. Women began playing the sport shortly before the turn of the century. More recently, an indoor version of lacrosse, box lacrosse, has become a professional sport. A professional outdoor lacrosse league was started in 2001. Native Americans continue to play lacrosse. The sport has fostered the rediscovery of cultural heritage and the validation of ethnic identity.

Sources and Further Reading: Donald M. Fisher, *Lacrosse: A History of the Game* (2002); Robert Lipsyte, "Lacrosse," *New York Times Magazine* (June 15, 1986); Thomas Vennum, *American Indian Lacrosse* (1994).

C. Richard King
Washington State University

Skiing

Skiing in America first took hold in the Midwest thanks to Norwegian immigrants who brought ski-jumping and cross-country ski running from their homeland. The sport was so popular that, in 1905, the National Ski Association of the United States (NSA) was founded in Ishpeming in the Upper Peninsula of Michigan.

Though Norwegian clubs offered cross-country excursions and competitions, jumping was the main attraction. Towns vied to attract better jumpers from Norway with employment guarantees. On meet days, up to 10,000 spectators could be on hand to watch the "knights of the air" fly down the chutes from wooden and steel towers. Early ski-jumping style was set by the brothers Hemmetsveit, who eventually represented Red Wing, Minnesota. Jumps were measured for length and marked for style, and the events were covered, sometimes entirely in Norwegian, in the NSA's annual magazine, *The Skisport*.

As skiing spread over North American snow country in the 1920s and 1930s, the Midwest's predominance declined. New forms of skiing, downhill and slalom, imported from the European Alps, provided more excitement and speed.

After World War II, entrepreneurs at places like Caberfae and Boyne Mountain, both in Michigan, brought Alpine skiing to the region, something brewer Frederick Pabst had tried to do unsuccessfully in the 1930s. The star attraction at Boyne was Olympic gold medalist and stylist supreme, Stein Eriksen.

The Midwest continues to provide early Alpine

training for future Olympians while contributing a major pool of Nordic competitors and offering recreational skiing venues.

Sources and Further Reading: E. John B. Allen, "The Modernization of the Skisport: Ishpeming's Contribution to American Skiing," *Michigan Historical Review* 16 (Spring 1990); William F. Stark, *Heiliger Huegel Ski Club, 1935–1996* (1995); Helen M. White, "Ski-Sport Heroes from Norway," in *The Tale of a Comet and Other Stories* (1984).

E. John B. Allen
Plymouth State University, New Hampshire

Snowshoeing

Once used as a practical tool to traverse the deep snows of the upper Midwest, the snowshoe has evolved from a means of transportation to a form of recreation.

The snowshoe is thought to have originated in central Asia about 6,000 years ago. Migrants brought it across the Bering Land Bridge to North America. Ancestors of Native Americans from Alaska and Canada perfected the original solid wooden slab design and created a laced frame shoe that is still used today. The modified shoe helped tribes move camp and hunt for food in deep snow.

Snowshoeing as a recreational pastime took hold in the late 1800s. Clubs were formed in Minnesota, Michigan, and Wisconsin to enjoy the sport as a means of visiting friends. Night tramps and Sunday outings to members' homes for meals were popular pastimes.

Interest in snowshoe racing surfaced in the early 1900s and made the sport a featured event at winter festivals. Today racing in the Midwest has become very popular. The United States Snowshoe Association (USSSA), the official governing body for the sport of snowshoe racing as recognized by the U.S. Olympic Committee, holds regional events in Michigan and Wisconsin as qualifiers for its annual competition in New York. The Special Olympics also provides snowshoe racing opportunities in several midwestern states.

Sources and Further Reading: Jim Joque, "Running on Snowshoes," *Silent Sports* 19 (December 2002); Gene Prater and Dave Felkley, eds., *Snowshoeing*, 4th ed. (1997); Mark Stensaas, "Shoes on the Snow," *Lake Superior Magazine* 20 (Oct.–Nov. 1998).

D. E. Malone
Bloomington, Illinois

Urban Sports

The emergence of midwestern sports was closely connected to the rise of cities, which provided the needed population and many of the necessary venues for sport, ranging from rivers and streets to private clubs, semipublic arenas, and stadiums. Voluntary class, ethnic, and racial associations facilitated sport participation among members, entrepreneurs commercialized sports, municipalities regulated morality and controlled access to public space, and politicians got involved in the business of sports.

Before the Civil War, the sporting fraternity was comprised of a male bachelor subculture that enjoyed violent and gambling sports as well as rural pastimes such as group hunts in nearby woods. Saloon owners organized dogfights, cockfights, rat killings, pigeon shooting contests, and boxing matches. Municipalities tried to restrict amusements by barring billiards, bowling, and boxing, with mixed results. In 1859, the first American billiards championship was held in Detroit. The most popular sport then was harness racing, which started as impromptu matches on city streets between middle-class citizens racing their own carriages. In 1839, Cincinnati opened the Buckeye Course for harness racing, and one year later the Chicago Sporting Club held heat races for trotters.

A more uplifting sporting culture emerged around mid-century, justified by a positive sports creed that appealed to the middle class by claiming that clean sport built character, good morals, and sound health in young men. They learned to become muscular Christians at the YMCA. The first midwestern Y was established in Chicago in 1858 by the evangelist Dwight Moody. Clean sport was also advocated for women by female reformers such as Catharine Beecher and Frances Willard, who advocated exercise for women to promote beauty, grace, and fitness in future mothers. In 1845, two women's gymnastic academies opened in Chicago, and by the end of the century colleges and universities included physical culture programs for women.

Several ethnic groups brought sporting traditions. The Scots' Caledonian societies promoted physical culture and a sense of community. The first German American *turnvereine* were established in 1848 in Louisville and Cincinnati to promote noncompetitive gymnastics and calisthenics. Turner halls were community centers for political debates, theatre, social gatherings, and concerts where German culture was sustained. Members supported workingmen's interests, Republican or Socialist politics, and physical education.

The new sport ideology encouraged the formation of sports clubs that facilitated competition and helped maintain separate social classes. Cricket, played in the 1840s, was the first team sport, but was supplanted in the 1850s by the simpler and faster game of baseball, considered a positive force in promoting health, morality, and manliness. After the Civil War, the sport boomed, led in 1869 by the undefeated Cincinnati Red Stockings, the first openly professional baseball club, which had been organized by local boosters.

Aquatic sports clubs became popular by the 1850s in cities with navigable rivers and lakes. The region's first two boat clubs were Chicago's Pioneer Boat Club, organized in 1853, and the Ivanhoe Boat Club that opened in Cleveland two years later. In 1858, Chicago had its first sailing regatta on Lake Michigan. Twelve years later, the Chicago Yacht Club, the Midwest's most elite aquatics club, was organized. The prestigious Chicago-to-Mackinac-Island race began in 1898.

Municipalities reacted to the scarcity of public recreational space after the Civil War by constructing large suburban parks, beginning with Frederick L. Olmsted's South Parks system in Chicago in 1869. However, it was inaccessible to inner city residents. Reformers in the late 1890s responded with the small parks movement to help immigrant children assimilate, reduce juvenile crime, and improve public health. Chicago became a national model by constructing several small parks in the early 1900s and implementing Daniel Burnham's Chicago Plan of 1909, which sought to preserve the lakefront as a series of parks and beaches. However, population growth outpaced park construction, and ethnic rivalries over contested park space led to fights and even riots. During the Depression, when millions had unwanted free time, programs like the Works Progress Administration (WPA) repaired and expanded public sports facilities, including pools, ball fields, and skating rinks and ski courses in numerous cities.

The most impressive municipal recreation projects were public stadiums. Chicago's Soldier Field was opened in 1924 at a cost of $6.5 million. In 1927, 104,000 attended the Dempsey–Tunney "long count" championship fight, paying a record $2.6 million at the gate. However, the largest crowd was 120,000 spectators at the 1937 interscholastic football championship. In 1931, Cleveland's $2.5 million, 71,189-seat Municipal Stadium was opened to promote the city, generate revenue, and provide a regular home for the Indians.

Midwestern industrial cities were hotbeds of baseball, with six major league teams and several minor league teams. Amateur and semiprofessional baseball were extremely popular. Companies often sponsored teams to advertise themselves and to promote worker loyalty. A 1915 intercity championship game in Cleveland was attended by over 100,000 people. Widespread participation made midwestern metropolises excellent producers of future major leaguers.

Spatial limitations produced new ball games. Softball was invented in 1887 in Chicago. Residents continue to use a sixteen-inch softball, although a twelve-inch ball is used elsewhere. In narrow streets, youths played stickball and pinners or "ledge," a game in which a rubber ball was bounced off a stoop.

Social class was a major influence in urban sport until after World War II. The affluent had the leisure time and discretionary income to organize sports clubs to facilitate competition and separate themselves from lower-status folk. The most prestigious sports organizations were in Chicago, such as the Chicago Yacht Club and the Chicago Athletic Club. The Chicago Golf Club, organized in 1893, opened the nation's first eighteen-hole course and hosted the U.S. Open in 1897. By 1900, metropolitan Chicago had six golf courses.

In the late nineteenth century, thoroughbred racing was the dominant equine sport. Chicago became the regional center of thoroughbred racing after the opening of prestigious Washington Park in 1884, although Cincinnati and St. Louis were also important sites. However, racing was connected to gambling, the underworld, and corrupt politicians, and was often banned. Chicago's tracks were closed in 1905, although off-track betting continued. Some courses reopened in the early 1920s and employed evasive oral betting schemes. In 1927, Illinois legalized pari-mutuel betting, and thoroughbred racing boomed.

The middle-class sporting life took off in the late nineteenth century because of the influence of the positive sports creed, free time and incomes, and access to sporting sites, especially parks. Athletes often organized to promote their pastimes, like cyclists who rode the large front wheel and tiny rear wheel "ordinary." In 1879, aficionados organized the Chicago Cycling Club, the second in the nation, which held races and tours and pressured local governments to protect cyclists' rights. In the 1890s, the new British safety bicycle with its equal-sized wheels liberated young women by transforming sports clothing and enabling them to ride wherever they chose. Manufacturers sponsored races to demonstrate their products, including the Chicago-to-Pullman race on Memorial Day that drew some 400 competitors. African American Major Taylor of Indianapolis won the world one-mile sprint championship in 1899. In 1915, the Chicago Coliseum hosted the city's first six-day race, the winner completing more than 2,500 miles.

Working-class sport was limited by working hours,

income, and accessibility. However, Sunday blue laws were liberally enforced, and unions, religious organizations, and employers sponsored sport to promote a sense of community. The Pullman Company was the first major corporation to promote workers' sports. The Pullman Athletic Association, which was established in 1881, recruited British artisans who were experienced cricketers, soccer players, and oarsmen, and hosted professional regattas and national amateur championships. Welfare capitalism programs in the 1910s often promoted participatory and spectator sports. The Pennsylvania Railroad sponsored the Columbus Panhandlers, boilermakers who played football on Sundays, traveling to distant games on railroad passes. In 1920, industrial squads including the Decatur Staleys and the Green Bay Packers joined the new midwestern-based All American Football Conference (later the National Football League). Even during the Depression nearly half of Chicago's factories had sports programs, including men's and women's softball and bowling. The New Deal enhanced working-class athletic opportunities through agencies like the Public Works Administration that built hundreds of ball fields and other athletic facilities.

Billiards and bowling were very popular because of accessibility, sociability, and opportunities for gambling. In 1909, nearly half of Chicago's 7,600 saloons had a pool or billiards table. The coming of Prohibition resulted in a record 2,244 licensed poolrooms because of a need to replace saloon culture. The largest and most elegant poolrooms were located downtown, like Detroit's 142-table Recreation Room, the largest in the country. However, most inner-city poolrooms, usually considered dens of iniquity, had only a few tables.

Bowling was a regional sport played in dimly lit German saloons until the 1890s when it separated from taverns. In 1895, Moses Bensinger of the Brunswick Company founded the primarily midwestern American Bowling Congress, which held its first national tournament in Chicago in 1901. Women began bowling in the 1910s, once the sport lost its identification with the sporting fraternity, and a national women's league began in St. Louis in 1916. The sport boomed in the 1920s when it gained a reputation as good, cheap fun, providing street corner youth with a social and athletic outlet. Chicago alone had about 500,000 bowlers. The largest alleys were in the Central Business District, and the rest on commercial streets in white ethnic neighborhoods. Bowling moved to suburbia after the war, where larger alleys and automatic pinsetting appealed to homemakers, who comprised nearly 40 percent of the patrons. Televised bowling became very popular, beginning in Chicago in the 1950s. The sport declined in the 1960s,

but as late as the 1970s, metropolitan Cleveland had over 100,000 sanctioned league members.

Ethnic sports allowed newcomers to display prowess, gain respect, and maintain a sense of ethnic identity, while becoming Americanized. Irish newcomers first became known as boxers, which reflected their traditional male bachelor subculture, and baseball players, though by the 1880s, the Gaelic Athletic Association organized traditional Irish games to promote ethnic pride. But the Irish mostly focused on American sports and, by the turn of the century, organized neighborhood social and athletic clubs to facilitate play. In 1865, Bohemians established the first American *sokol* in St. Louis to promote physical culture through gymnastics and fitness drills and sustain their native culture. Eastern and southern European immigrants arrived with no sporting heritage and had no interest in athletics. However, the second generation was sports mad and participated in sports like boxing and basketball that fit in with their environment at settlement houses and city parks. Youth workers there used sports to promote morality, character, and Americanization, and to refute negative stereotypes. Inner-city boys dominated basketball, one of the few sports second-generation girls could play, participating in ethnic leagues whose seasons were highlighted by inter-ethnic contests like Chicago's annual Catholic Youth Organization–B'nai B'rith All-Stars exhibition game.

Self-defense was a valuable skill for inner-city youths, who often got into fights with other ethnics. Youths were trained at boxing gyms, settlement houses, and the Catholic Youth Organization (CYO), organized in Chicago in 1930 by Bishop Bernard J. Sheil to draw young Catholics back to the church. Amateur boxing flourished early in the century, but prizefighting was widely proscribed, including in Chicago from 1905 until 1926. Boxing champions like Cleveland's Johnny Kilbane, Chicago's Barney Ross, Cincinnati's Ezzard Charles, and Detroit's Joe Louis were ethnic heroes who demonstrated their groups' manliness and courage.

African Americans encountered discrimination at private clubs, semipublic facilities like the YMCA, and public parks and beaches. The 1919 Chicago Race Riot occurred after an African American youth drowned in Lake Michigan when he was hit by white youths throwing stones. Excluded from professional sports, African Americans organized their own traveling teams, which became important community institutions. The most eminent was the American Giants, co-owned by former star pitcher Rube Foster, who organized the Negro National League in 1920. They played near Comiskey Park, which from 1933 was the primary site of the East–West All-Star game, a major social event. Chicago was also the home base of the Harlem Globetrotters.

The most significant development in recent midwestern urban sport is municipal support for professional franchises. This began in 1953 when the Boston Braves moved to Milwaukee's publicly financed County Stadium. Such assistance blossomed in the 1970s as cities, led by Indianapolis, built stadiums and arenas to keep or attract professional teams, support economic growth, and improve their public image. Chicago revamped Soldier Field in 2003 at a cost of over $600 million.

Sources and Further Reading: David J. Bodenhamer and Robert G. Barrows, eds., *The Encyclopedia of Indianapolis* (1994); Chicago Recreation Commission, *The Chicago Recreation Survey, 1937,* 5 vols. (1937–1940); John J. Grabowski, *Sports in Cleveland: An Illustrated History* (1992); John Gurda, *The Making of Milwaukee* (1999); Richard Lindberg, *The Armchair Companion to Chicago Sports* (1997); Wilma Pesavento, "Sport and Recreation in the Pullman Experiment, 1880–1900," *Journal of Sport History* 9 (Summer 1982); Steven A. Riess, *City Games: The Evolution of American Urban Society and the Rise of Sports* (1989); John Schleppi, "'It Pays': John H. Patterson and Industrial Recreation at the National Cash Register Company," *Journal of Sport History* 6 (Winter 1979); The Survey Committee of the Cleveland Foundation, *Cleveland Recreation Survey,* 5 vols (1920).

Steven A. Riess
Northeastern Illinois University

1927 Dempsey–Tunney Fight

The most famous moment in the history of boxing occurred on September 22, 1927, in the seventh round of the heavyweight championship bout between William Henry "Jack" Dempsey (1895–1983) and Gene James Joseph Tunney (1898–1978) at Chicago's Soldier Field. Over one hundred thousand were at ringside, including screen actors Charlie Chaplin, John Barrymore, and Douglas Fairbanks. Grantland Rice, Damon Runyon, and Paul Gallico headed a long list of Jazz-Age sports writers. The fight was transmitted to 1,200 newspapers over 145,000 miles of Associated Press–leased wires, a company record. The spectacle was heard worldwide by an estimated one hundred million radio listeners.

When a violent flurry of punches by Dempsey, the "Manassa Mauler," put Tunney on the canvas, NBC announcer Graham McNamee shouted excitedly, "Tunney is down! Tunney is down!" Referee Dave Barry delayed his count until Dempsey moved to a neutral corner. Ten radio listeners dropped dead of heart attacks because of the excitement. The "long

count" meant that Tunney was not counted out at ten but had nearly sixteen seconds to get to his feet. Tunney, the "Fighting Marine," won the fight in a controversial ten-round decision.

Tunney made a record million dollars for thirty minutes' work, and promoter Tex Rickard enjoyed a $2.6 million gate. Chicago mayor Big Bill Thompson thought the fight made Chicago into a national sports center. For years, fans argued about a fight in which the guy who got knocked to the canvas managed to win in the end.

Sources and Further Reading: Bruce J. Evensen, *When Dempsey Fought Tunney* (1996); Roger Kahn, *A Flame of Pure Fire* (1999); Randy Roberts, *Jack Dempsey: The Manassa Mauler* (1979).

Bruce J. Evensen
DePaul University, Illinois

Harlem Globetrotters

Formed in Chicago, this world-famous black basketball team has long combined sports and entertainment.

Owner, promoter, and coach Abe Saperstein (1902–1966) transformed a local black semipro team, the Savoy Big Five, into the Harlem Globetrotters in 1927. The team had no connection to New York City. According to Saperstein, using the Harlem name associated the team with the cultural capital of black America, and the Globetrotter appellation suggested that the team "had been around."

Barnstorming around the Midwest, the Trotters began clowning in the mid-1930s to promote ticket sales to white audiences. Crowds loved the novelty of basketball clowning, which became a Globetrotter trademark. Saperstein also fielded a clowning Globetrotter baseball team in the 1940s and 1950s.

By mid-century, the Globetrotters claimed to be the nation's top sports attraction. Trotter games were sellouts everywhere, and the team was featured in popular movies like "Go, Man, Go" (1953). They demonstrated the quality of black basketball on national tours with the College All-Stars and by defeating the National Basketball Association (NBA) champion Minneapolis Lakers in several games in 1948 and 1949. The Trotters' success paved the way for the integration of the NBA, which Saperstein discouraged in order to retain control of black basketball. Several disgruntled star players left the Trotters in the 1950s and formed their own competing teams, such as the Harlem Magicians and the Harlem Road Kings. During the Civil Rights era, critics attacked basketball clowning for reinforcing negative black stereotypes, and some players charged Saperstein with paternalism.

When Saperstein died in 1966, the team was a multi-million-dollar business with four teams simultaneously traveling under the Globetrotter name. Currently owned by former player Mannie Jackson, the Harlem Globetrotters continue a long tradition of mixing sports and entertainment.

Sources and Further Reading: Ben Lombardo, "The Harlem Globetrotters and the Perpetuation of the Black Stereotype," *The Physical Educator* 335 (May 1978); Ron Thomas, *They Cleared the Lane* (2002); Dave Zinkoff, *Go, Man, Go* (1958).

Raymond A. Mohl
University of Alabama–Birmingham

Negro Baseball

Home to many great players and venerated teams, the Midwest played a central role in the history of Negro baseball.

In the late 1800s, several African American ballplayers competed on integrated professional teams. Bud Fowler, who broke an implicit color barrier when he joined a Massachusetts club in 1878, pitched for Stillwater, Minnesota, in the Northwestern League in 1884 and led clubs in most midwestern states prior to 1895. Moses Fleetwood ("Fleet") Walker starred for Toledo in the Northwestern League in 1883–1884 and played briefly for Cleveland in the Major's Western League. Six African Americans were on the 1892 Nebraska State League rosters, and six played for Adrian, Michigan, in 1895.

White hostility toward integrated teams was intense. In 1898, in Atchison, Kansas, pitcher Bert Jones was perhaps the last African American to compete on a white pro baseball team until 1947. By 1900, a gentleman's agreement among owners had established Major League Baseball as a white-only enterprise. Keeping blacks out of white pro ball created the golden age of Negro baseball.

Following the lead of eastern professional barnstormers, Michigan's Page Fence Giants toured the Midwest throughout the 1890s. The Leland Giants dominated Chicago semipro play around 1910, and the Indianapolis ABCs ruled the barnstormers. The powerful St. Paul Gophers pursued a heated neighborhood rivalry with the Minneapolis Keystones, while the legendary Kansas City Monarchs began touring.

In 1920, a host of quality teams and a huge fan base within the African American community created demand for a league with established schedules and set rosters. Chicago American Giants owner Andrew "Rube" Foster (1878 or 1879–1930) joined the Indianapolis ABCs' C. I. Taylor and other Negro team executives to found the Negro National League (NNL). The charismatic, competitive, and savvy Foster soon ruled the NNL as a virtual czar, and the soaring talents of several National stars elevated the league to the peak of professional baseball.

Future Hall of Famers Cool Papa Bell (St. Louis Stars), Oscar Charleston (Indianapolis ABCs), Ray Dandridge (Detroit Stars), and John Henry "Pop" Lloyd (Chicago American Giants) led their teams before cheering throngs of baseball fanatics.

Foster's death in 1930, the Great Depression, and the rise of rival eastern and southern leagues led to the decline of Negro baseball in the Midwest. Occasional triumphs continued, however. Though nearly forty, LeRoy Robert "Satchel" Paige (1906–1982), widely regarded as one of the greatest pitchers in history, led

---

❖ Andrew "Rube" Foster (1878 or 1879–1930)

Born in 1879 in the segregated community of Calvert, Texas, Andrew "Rube" Foster was the son of the Reverend Andrew Foster of the American Methodist Episcopal Church. Foster dropped out of school following the eighth grade, choosing to pursue a career in baseball. While still a teenager, the 6'1", 210-pound Foster acquired a reputation as a stellar pitcher. In 1903, he helped to lead the powerful Cuban X-Giants to the "colored championship of the world." The following year, he jumped to the rival Philadelphia Giants, whom he helped to guide to three straight titles.

Foster was considered the finest pitcher outside the white-only leagues. In 1907, he began managing the Chicago Leland Giants, who became the strongest team in black baseball. Following a power struggle with Frank Leland, Foster took control of the Leland Giants and renamed them the Chicago American Giants in 1911. Over the course of the next decade and a half, the team vied for supremacy outside organized baseball and traveled extensively. As Foster's playing career came to an end, he continued to skipper the Chicago American Giants to a series of "colored championship" crowns.

From his early days in Chicago, Foster had another vision: to create a black baseball league. In 1920, he became president of the Negro National League. But in 1926, mental illness, perhaps exacerbated by the unwillingness of organized baseball to discard its color barriers, resulted in his confinement at the Kankakee Asylum outside Chicago. He died in 1930. In 1981, Foster was named to the Baseball Hall of Fame.

Robert Cottrell
California State University–Chico

❖ Curt Flood

Curt Flood changed the face of professional baseball. In 1969, Flood was 32 years old, the first black man to play for the St. Louis Cardinals, and a star center fielder renowned for his defensive skills. When the Cardinals traded Flood to the Philadelphia Phillies, he refused to accept the decision. In January 1970, he filed suit against Major League Baseball, challenging the reserve clause that exempted the sport from antitrust laws. "After 12 years in the major leagues I do not feel that I am a piece of property to be bought and sold irrespective of my wishes," Flood wrote. "I believe that any system that produces that result violates my basic right as a citizen and is inconsistent with the laws of the United States."

In 1972, the U.S. Supreme Court found in favor of Major League Baseball on the ground that the sport ought to remain above the rules of ordinary competition. Free agency finally came to baseball in 1974, however, allowing players to exercise some control over their careers and escalating salaries to unimaginable sums. Flood enjoyed none of the bounty. His career had ended prematurely, as did his life when he died of cancer in 1997. Nevertheless, his impact was considerable. Columnist George Will eulogized Flood by saying that his refusal to accept the trade was to professional baseball what Rosa Parks' refusal to move to the back of a bus was to racial segregation.

Andrew Cayton
Miami University, Oxford, Ohio

the Kansas City Monarchs to two Negro World Series titles during the 1940s. Larry Doby (1923–2003) played for a New Jersey team before appearing with the Cleveland Indians in 1947 as the first Negro player in the American League, and the Kansas City Monarchs' Ernie Banks (b. 1931) joined the Chicago Cubs in 1953. All three were eventually inducted into the Baseball Hall of Fame.

Following Jackie Robinson's 1947 debut with the Brooklyn Dodgers, other Major League teams began signing African American players, and Negro baseball went into decline. In 1952, the Indianapolis Clowns, a barnstorming club promoted through racial stereotyping in dress and demeanor, sold the contract of a young Henry Aaron to the Boston Braves. A few midwestern squads toured during the 1960s, and the Clowns continued performing into the 1970s. Their disbanding ended the era of Negro baseball. The contributions of these players and teams are memorialized at the Negro League Hall of Fame in Kansas City, Missouri.

Sources and Further Reading: Phil Dixon and Patrick J. Hannigan, *The Negro Baseball Leagues 1867–1955* (1992);
Robert Peterson, *Only the Ball Was White* (1992); James A. Riley, *The Biographical Encyclopedia of the Negro Baseball Leagues* (1994).

R. Dale Ogden
Indiana State Museum

Roller Derby

Racing around a banked oval track on four wheels was just the beginning of what male and female teams endured to become the stars of Roller Derby during the Great Depression.

The offbeat sport originated in Chicago in 1935 when Leo Seltzer noticed Americans seeking entertainment from dance marathons and bicycle races. From the former publicist's original vision of couples skating around an oval track for up to twelve hours, new rules brought about a more aggressive style of teams competing against each other to score points.

The slamming, tripping, and elbowing drew up to a hundred thousand fans to Roller Derby in the 1940s and 1950s. Seltzer decided to move west to larger venues and soon had teams such as the Bay City Bombers packing stadiums and filling television screens on the weekends.

Names like Rosie, Babs, and Flowers and moves like "the whip" helped Roller Derby reach its peak in 1969. The trend was downward from there, and Roller Derby folded in 1973. It got a resurgence in late 1998 when Seltzer's son, Jerry, formed the World Skating League at Universal Studios in Orlando, Florida. Jerry Seltzer brought former boxers, speedskaters, and wrestlers to a program debuting on The Nashville Network. Roller Jam, performed on two-wheeled skates, mirrored its predecessor in some ways (such as speeds of up to 35 miles per hour) but not in its popularity. The Illinois Riot, the Nevada Hot Dice, and the Texas Rustlers were off the air by 2000.

Cindy Swavel
Bucyrus, Ohio

Sixteen-Inch Softball

Sixteen-inch softball was first played in Chicago in 1887 by several young men at the Farragut Boat Club. They used a boxing glove, rolled into a sphere and tied with its own strings, as a ball and a broomstick as a bat and played indoors in an area much smaller than a baseball field.

As the game became popular, players moved outdoors but retained the smaller field. Because it was easy to organize and play, softball attracted thousands of fans, and teams recruited some of the city's better athletes, including several major league baseball players. In Minneapolis, a different version of the game, which was played with a small medicine ball and allowed defense players to wear gloves, took root and eventually evolved into modern softball.

Sixteen-inch softball survived in Chicago, however, where it is as much a symbol of the city as deep-dish pizza and the Sears Tower. The game has spread beyond the city as well. In 2003, sixteen-inch softball leagues existed in Illinois, Iowa, and several other states.

Sixteen-inch softball is similar to standard slow-pitch softball. Pitchers are required to toss the ball to home plate with a visible arc. The game uses ten players on each side, including the nine positions of a baseball team and a "short" center-fielder, who plays behind secondbase. In general, the game requires less power and more finesse than regular softball. Placement is important when hitting the ball, and fielding is a bigger part of the game.

Henry De Zutter
Chicago, Illinois

Sporting Goods Manufacturers

Professional sports and the sporting goods industry emerged simultaneously in the late nineteenth century. The golden triangle of great American sports towns—Chicago, St. Louis, and Cincinnati—spawned some of the nation's best-known sporting goods manufacturers, including Spalding, Wilson, MacGregor, and Rawlings.

In 1876, professional baseball player Albert Goodwill Spalding and his brother Walter borrowed $800 from their mother to establish their first store on Randolph Street in Chicago. Betting that he could parlay his fame as a pitcher into a fortune, A.G. quit baseball following the 1877 season. The company grew quickly and soon became a leader in the sporting goods industry.

Numerous factors contributed to Spalding's success. First was Chicago's emergence as a commercial center. Second was his focus on brand labeling; Spalding's trademark appeared on every baseball put into official play from 1876 through 1976. Third, in 1889, the company changed its marketing strategy and established a direct mail catalog. Fourth, he diversified. In addition to making the first Major League baseball, Spalding manufactured the first American-made football, tennis ball, golf club, golf ball, volleyball, and the first "official" basketball.

Upon A.G.'s death in 1915, a trio of potential heirs

sought to fill the void: Wilson, MacGregor, and Rawlings. Wilson Sporting Goods Company was originally founded in 1913 in Chicago as Ashland Manufacturing, a company that was established to develop ways to use the by-products of the meatpacking industry. The company's original product line included surgical sutures and tennis racquet string. In 1914, Thomas E. Wilson, the company's young president, shifted the focus exclusively to sporting goods. Under Wilson's leadership, the company expanded through acquisitions and mergers. In 1924, Knute Rockne began a partnership with Wilson as a member of its Advisory Staff; in 1925, that partnership produced the first valve-inflated football. Previously footballs had a lump under the laces caused by the stem, whereas this new ball, nicknamed the "KR," eliminated that lump, allowing for a tight spiral throw. The introduction of

❖ Albert Goodwill Spalding (1850–1915)

Albert Goodwill Spalding was born near Byron, Illinois, and as a boy moved to Rockford, Illinois. He gained notice as a teenage pitcher for the Rockford Forest City baseball team when they beat nationally known teams. In 1871, Spalding was recruited to play for Boston in the National Association, the first professional baseball league. Spalding returned to Illinois in 1876 to play for William Hulbert's Chicago team and to assist Hulbert in the formation of the National League. Spalding was an important part of many powerful championship teams: as a league-leading pitcher for Boston and Chicago, as a manager in Chicago, and later, after Hulbert's death in 1882, as president of the Chicago National League team.

Spalding is perhaps best known for his pioneering role in sporting goods manufacturing. In 1876, Spalding opened a sporting goods store in Chicago that was the beginning of the A.G. Spalding and Bros. sporting goods empire. He was joined in the business by his brother J. Walter Spalding and later by his brother-in-law, William Thayer Brown. Spalding took advantage of every opportunity to gain an edge in business. He paid the National League to adopt the Spalding ball as the official league ball, which allowed him to dominate the market in baseball sales outside the league. He also published rule books for baseball and other sports that advertised his products.

Spalding opposed alcohol and gambling at the ball park and promoted baseball as a healthful, character-building, American sport. In 1888–1889, he organized an around-the-world tour of baseball exhibitions in fourteen countries. In 1908, a panel of notables picked by Spalding reported the Abner Doubleday story of the origin of baseball. In 1911, Spalding published a history of baseball, *America's National Game*.

David A. Goss
Indiana University–Bloomington

the KR contributed to the development of the modern passing game.

MacGregor Golf Company was originally founded in the late 1880s as Crawford, MacGregor, and Canby (CMC), a wooden shoe last company in Dayton, Ohio. Edward Canby, one of the founders, was introduced to golf on a trip to Europe. Convinced that the sport would be big in the United States, Canby, who bought the company and trademarked the name J. MacGregor (and later dropped the "J"), used his woodworking expertise to begin producing hickory shafts and persimmon heads. MacGregor grew to become one of the world's preeminent golf manufacturers, leading the industry with many firsts, including the introduction of a matching set of woods and irons in 1949.

Rawlings Sporting Goods Company was founded in St. Louis in 1898 by George Rawlings, a prominent local sporting goods retailer, and Charles Scudder. Although manufacturing was at first only a small part of the company's operations, by 1907, it had become Rawlings's exclusive focus. Rawlings has been an innovator in baseball equipment, such as the Bill Doak glove in 1920, the first to feature a pocket between the forefinger and thumb. In 1957, Rawlings created baseball's prestigious Gold Glove award, and in 1976, Rawlings replaced Spalding as the supplier of baseballs to both the National and American leagues.

Sources and Further Reading: Robert L. Burnes, *Fifty Golden Years of Sports* (1948); Jim Kaplan, ed., *MacGregor Golf* (1980); Jim Kaplan, ed., *Wilson Golf* (1981); Peter Levine, *A.G. Spalding and the Rise of Baseball* (1985); A.G. Spalding & Bros., *Spalding's Official Base Ball Guide* (1877–1939).

Jeremy T. Chrabascz
Indiana State Museum and Historic Sites

Organized Sports

The Midwest, home to some of the first organized sports teams in the United States, helped define organized sport.

Organized sport evolved in the nineteenth century, first in New York City, then in big American cities such as Chicago and Cincinnati. The contributions of the Midwest to organized sport include the first professional sports team, the 1869 Cincinnati Red Stockings baseball team. Later in the nineteenth century, the Midwest was at the center of the emergence of big-time college sport programs, especially football. College football programs are the most highly organized sports in college and university athletics departments, and they serve as the organizational model for all sports programs in schools and universities. These two organizational models of sport—professional and intercollegiate—continue to have an impact on how all Americans experience sport in the contemporary world.

Early organized sport was very different from the sporting tradition that preceded it, in large part because of population growth and industrial development. Technological developments and improved transportation also had a significant impact. Urban residents found it impossible to enjoy pastimes such as hunting and fishing, so they invented new forms of recreation, including team sports. The arrival of the telegraph made possible the almost instantaneous communication of sport results. The railroad followed the steamboat in transporting sports teams and journalists.

Other technological changes that affected American society had a more direct impact on sport. Mass production created inexpensive athletic equipment like bats and balls. Vulcanized rubber began to be used for bicycle tires, and the development of elastic and resilient rubber balls led to better golf and tennis balls. Photographic techniques improved significantly, and in 1872, Eadweard Muybridge made one of the first "moving pictures" of a trotting horse. The principle behind this process was eventually applied to celluloid film to create the moving picture that became the basis for newsreels and eventually televised sport.

Other inventions were applied directly to sport: the stopwatch, the percussion cap in starter pistols, the streamlined sulky, the modern bicycle (then known as the "safety cycle"), ball bearings, and artificial ice. Improved equipment continually changed the style of a sport. The invention of the sliding seat improved the rowing shell, the introduction of the rubber-wound gutta-percha ball necessitated the lengthening of golf courses, and the universal acceptance of the catcher's mask made baseball a safer sport.

Changes in American culture also influenced the ways in which Americans experienced sport. Americans began to use scientific thinking, or more rational thought processes, when considering the environment, people, and ideas. This shift from a traditional lifestyle—unchanging, unspecialized, male-dominated, and dependent on manual labor—to the modern one—dynamic, cosmopolitan, and technological—occurred between 1820 and 1870. Sport changed as society changed, and after 1870, Americans tended to organize their games in ways that historians call "modern." This modern approach to sport is still used today.

Organized sport has six characteristics: sport organizations, written rules, national and international competition, specialized roles, statistics and records, and public information. Organized sport is operated by organizations such as the National Football League (NFL) or the

National Collegiate Athletic Association (NCAA). All levels of sport are similarly governed, from the American Youth Soccer Organization (AYSO) through elite levels like the International Olympic Committee (IOC) and professional leagues. Organizations are where we go to find the rules of the game, and these rules are rationally created to improve games. Prior to the 1820s, there were no sport organizations, and the rules of games were locally determined (like playing tag or king of the hill). Since 1870, we have organized games into their modern form with written rules.

Another characteristic of organized sport is the national and international levels of competition. Prior to 1820, games were played only in one's community, whereas now we tend to organize popular games into national competitions like the Super Bowl, World Series, or NCAA Championships. Furthermore, organized sport is characterized by the specialized nature of the participants. Before 1820, fans and players were mixed; one was just as likely to be a player as a spectator. Now, however, athletes and fans tend to be separated, and the larger the sporting event, the more likely it is that the fans, players, referees, ticket takers, and other participants are separated by their roles in the event. Modern athletes are also highly specialized. Baseball pitchers do not play other positions. Football players no longer play both offense and defense, and further specialize by position.

Finally, organized sport keeps track of statistics and records. Winners and losers are recorded, and many statistics are kept on different aspects of the games. This information is made available through newspapers, radio, television, and now on the Internet.

One of the most significant contributions to organized sport was the development of the first professional baseball team. In 1868, the Cincinnati Red Stockings introduced knickerbockers (short pants) and red stockings and began a tradition in baseball uniforms that continues to this day. This same team became the 1869 Cincinnati Red Stockings Professional Base Ball Team, the first professional sports team. For the first time, players were placed under contract, primarily to overcome problems associated with gambling and sport. By paying players directly, major league baseball was able to minimize the influence of gamblers on the outcomes of games. Salaries were very good for the times, and the star player, George Wright, earned $1,400 for the season. The 1869 Red Stockings won sixty-five games and tied one, and were able to claim that they were the undisputed national champions. The overall success of the Red Stockings, based on signing players to contracts and professionalizing the game, helped set the stage for the development of the first professional baseball league, the National Association of Professional Base Ball Players.

Professional teams from all sports followed the example established by the Cincinnati Red Stockings.

College sports began during this same period of time. The first intercollegiate athletic contests were in the East, with Harvard racing Yale in rowing in 1852 and Rutgers playing Princeton in football in 1869. Unlike colleges in the East, where students had to fight for college sports, midwestern colleges were "born" with sports programs. Colleges and universities in Michigan, Ohio, Illinois, and Iowa founded during this time would eventually have some of the largest sports programs in the country.

Early track and field events were held at the University of Michigan, where open games took place in the 1880s. Iowa, Indiana, Ohio, Wisconsin, and Illinois soon followed this tradition. College football came of age as these universities developed, and Michigan's football team played such eastern colleges as Harvard, Yale, and Princeton in 1881. In 1890, the Western Intercollegiate Football Association was formed, composed of Iowa, Kansas, Missouri, and Nebraska.

The first college football bowl game, the Tournament of Roses, was played in 1902. The University of Michigan beat Stanford University 49–0, indicating the high quality of football in the Midwest. This contest was significant in that it was designed to be a game between a West Coast university and one from the South, East, or Midwest. Eventually the Rose Bowl grew to an extravaganza—the granddaddy of all bowl games. In the 1920s, Notre Dame established the model for the modern athletics program by signing the first national radio broadcast contract and becoming "America's Team" with fans from coast to coast.

Youth and high school sports organized in a similar manner to college and professional sports. Basketball tournaments were sponsored by Indiana YMCAs in the 1890s, and were followed by the formation of the Indiana High School Athletic Association in 1903 and the popular boys' high school basketball championship tournament in 1911. This tournament, which until the 1990s included all of Indiana's high school teams in one statewide division, was made famous by the film *Hoosiers* (1986). Similarly, recreational sports such as softball were first organized in the Midwest. The first national softball tournament was held in 1933 in conjunction with the Chicago World's Fair and included both men's and women's teams. The locally popular "Chicago" softball rules were used in the tournament, extending the influence of the Midwest over this national pastime. Regional pride was at stake in boys' football when midwesterners sent the Cook County championship teams to New York in 1902 and 1903, and lopsided victories of 105–0 and 75–0 demonstrated that midwestern high school sports were highly organized by the turn of the century.

Today organized sport in the Midwest is as popular as ever. The Ohio State University had the largest athletic budget in the country in 2003, and universities provide thousands of college students with the opportunity to compete, and spectators with the opportunity to watch. Professional sports such as basketball, baseball, football, and ice hockey are just as popular, and all areas of the Midwest are represented by professional teams. The Special Olympics, developed in the Midwest in the 1960s, provide opportunities to participate in a wide variety of sports for children and adults with physical and mental disabilities. Midwesterners of all ages continue to enjoy organized sport in its scholastic, professional, and amateur forms, and one can predict that organized sport will thrive in the Midwest for years to come.

Sources and Further Reading: Melvin Adelman, *A Sporting Time* (1986); John Rickards Betts, *America's Sporting Heritage, 1850–1950* (1974); Allen Guttmann, *From Ritual to Record* (1978).

Steve Estes
East Carolina University, North Carolina

Indiana Boys' High School Basketball

High school basketball, so closely identified with Indiana that it is known as "Hoosier Hysteria," was a defining element of the state's cultural landscape in the twentieth century. Ideally suited to agrarian, sparsely populated Indiana, basketball could be played during the farm boys' winter off-season and needed fewer players, less equipment, and smaller venues than football or baseball. To many Hoosiers, basketball became an object of the consuming interest usually reserved for wars or economic upheavals.

Basketball made its first appearance in the state within three years of the birth of the sport. The first scheduled game, played in Crawfordsville in 1894, featured Young Men's Christian Association (YMCA) teams, but it was quickly adopted as a high school sport. Interest in the sport led to the formation of the Indiana High School Athletic Association in 1903. High school teams became the focus of many communities. To don the school's uniform was to wear a badge of honor for most schoolboys. Rivalries were intense as community pride often depended upon the score of the last game or the size of the gym. Attesting to that rivalry and Hoosiers' regard for basketball is the fact that fifteen of the sixteen largest high school gymnasiums in the United States are in Indiana, including thirteen that seat over seven thousand people.

Much of Indiana's basketball lore is connected with the state's fabled tournament, which began in 1911 when twelve teams met to crown the state champion. (Appropriately, Crawfordsville High School won.) The tourney quickly expanded. By the 1920s, over 750 schools were competing for the ultimate prize in the single-class tournament. (Parochial and "colored" schools were excluded until the early 1940s.)

The 1950s were perhaps the golden age of the tournament. Attendance reached 1.5 million at a time when Indiana's population was approximately 4.6 million. In 1955, the legendary Oscar Robertson led Indianapolis Crispus Attucks to the championship in a game that featured two African American schools. But it was in 1954 that the most famous basketball game in Indiana history was played as Bobby Plump shot tiny Milan High School to the championship over Muncie Central. This David-vs.-Goliath struggle, which absorbed generations of fans, was later fictionalized in the film *Hoosiers*.

The largest crowd ever to see a high school basketball game, forty-one thousand, attended the 1990 state championship game featuring schoolboy phenomenon Damon Bailey. But generally, interest in high school basketball waned over the last two decades of the twentieth century as school consolidations and lifestyle changes took their toll. Another major contributor to the downslide was the controversial move to an enrollment-based, four-division tournament in 1998. By 2000, tourney attendance had dropped to under four hundred thousand.

Though it no longer holds the central place in Indiana life that it once did, high school basketball remains a crucial part of the state and its history. It is celebrated with its own hall of fame devoted to the game and legends like Oscar Robertson, Bobby Plump, John Wooden, and Larry Bird.

Sources and Further Reading: Donald E. Hamilton, *Hoosier Temples* (1993); Phillip M. Hoose, *Hoosiers, the Fabulous Basketball Life of Indiana* (1995); Herbert Schwomeyer, *Hoosier Hysteria, a History of Indiana High School Basketball* (1975); Bob Williams, *Hoosier Hysteria* (1982).

Timothy Crumrin
Conner Prairie Museum, Fishers, Indiana

Iowa Girls' Basketball

Today's basketball is played uniformly, based on standardized rules defined by a higher authority such as the National Collegiate Athletic Association (NCAA). But as the history of girls' basketball in Iowa demonstrates, that has not always been the case.

After James Naismith invented basketball for his

male students in 1891, girls immediately adopted it, slightly modifying the rules. They had five to ten players on a three-section court; players were restricted to one section, with three dribbles maximum, no physical contact, and a center jump after each field goal.

Girls' basketball became popular throughout the nation by the turn of the twentieth century. In Iowa, it emerged as a fixture of girls' sports in both rural and urban areas. The first Iowa high school girls' state tournament was held in 1920. At that time, many female leaders of women's athletic programs objected to competition for girls, finding it too demanding physically, and it involved only a limited number of girls. The Iowa High School Athletic Association (IHSAA) consequently decided to stop sponsoring girls' state tournaments. Some rural Iowa superintendents, coaches, and teachers rejected this decision and formed the Iowa Girls High School Athletic Union (IGHSAU), which continues today and is the oldest high school athletic association for girls in the country. When most high schools, including Iowa's urban schools, abandoned competitive basketball programs for girls, Iowa's rural schools maintained them because basketball did not seem too physical for people used to farm work and because it provided entertainment for rural communities.

Despite changes in the rules, such as the adoption of the two-court style in 1934, Iowa girls' basketball kept growing. In the 1950s, the state tournament even included festivities such as a fashion show, a Parade of Champions, bands, dancers, and drill groups performing in front of a sold-out crowd of perhaps fifteen thousand people and several national media. In 1951, the semifinals and the finals were broadcast on television. The boys' tournaments were not televised until 1952.

This success explains why the IGHSAU did not adopt the 1971 five-on-five rule, fearing that it would endanger the popularity of girls' basketball. It could not take that risk since the program's revenue allowed the association to finance fifteen other girls' sport programs.

In 1984, three Iowa high school girls filed a lawsuit against the IGHSAU, arguing that the two-court six-player style was not equal to boys' basketball and violated Title IX legislation because playing a different kind of basketball reduced their chances of getting a scholarship to attend college. To avoid a lawsuit, the IGHSAU allowed schools to choose their own format. Most urban schools chose five-on-five, most rural schools kept six-on-six. Despite its popularity, Iowa's six-player basketball ended in 1993 because cutting one of the two tournaments allowed the IGHSAU to save 38 percent of its athletic budget and use it to finance other girls' sport programs. More than the end of a sport tournament, it was the end of a local sport tradition and attraction that had become part of the state's popular culture, identity, and history.

Sources and Further Reading: Janice A. Beran, *From Six-on-Six to Full Court Press* (1993); Joanne Lannin, *A History of Basketball for Girls and Women* (2000); Shelley Marie Lucas, "Courting Controversy: Gender and Power in Iowa Girls' Basketball," Ph.D. diss., University of Iowa (2001).

Cécile Houry
University of Miami, Florida

Iowa Boys' Wrestling

Iowa, the pre-eminent wrestling state in the Midwest and perhaps the country, owes much of its wrestling success to the inspiration of its agrarian history. Even today, from the rolling cornfields of eastern Iowa to flatland farming in the western part of the state, consolidated rural schools send highly recruited athletes to the state high school wrestling tournament in Des Moines, the Iowa capital. Invariably, the event sells out for the weekend, topping seventy thousand in attendance.

More than a century ago, Iowa farm boys found in wrestling the sort of rugged individuality required of field hands working from sunrise to sunset. "It was hard work, farming, and it was natural that the hardy, tough nature of wrestling would draw people like that," said Mike Chapman, a wrestling historian, author of numerous wrestling books, and founder of the International Wrestling Institute & Museum in Newton, Iowa. Jessie Whitmer, who left an Iowa farm to win a National Collegiate Athletic Association (NCAA) title for the University of Iowa in 1997, talked about the hard work of baling hay and added, "You're throwing boys in wrestling with calluses on your hands."

Iowa has produced two wrestling icons, Frank Gotch (1878–1917) and Dan Gable (b. 1948). Gotch, handsome and hard-muscled, came off a farm near Humboldt in northwest Iowa to earn international acclaim by defeating George Hackenschmidt, nicknamed the "Russian Lion," for the world professional wrestling title on April 3, 1908, in Chicago. Three years later, a Labor Day crowd estimated at thirty-five thousand—including three hundred who came by train from Humboldt—turned out at Chicago's Comiskey Park to watch Gotch successfully defend his title.

Danny Mack Gable became Iowa's modern-day Gotch. Growing up in the industrial city of Waterloo, Gable possessed a fierce intensity that was almost palpable. He not only beat his opponents, he usually pinned them. He was unbeaten in high school and college until he lost the final match of his senior year (1970) at Iowa State University. Spurred by his defeat in the 142-pound class final of the NCAA Championships, Gable took aim at the 1972 Summer Olympics in Munich, where he pinned three of his six opponents and won a gold medal.

Injuries ended Gable's athletic career, but he saw in coaching an opportunity to rechannel his skills. His home state had three top-flight wrestling schools—Iowa, Iowa State, and Iowa State Teachers College (now the University of Northern Iowa)—but Iowa moved in quickly and made him an assistant coach and, in 1977, head coach. Fashioning teams that bore his trademarks of conditioning and aggressiveness, Gable became one of the most successful coaches in the history of intercollegiate athletics. In twenty-one years, his Iowa teams won twenty-one Big Ten titles and fifteen NCAA titles, including nine in a row from 1978 to 1986. In addition, Gable coached the 1984 U.S. Olympic freestyle team that won seven of ten gold medals.

Sources and Further Reading: Mike Chapman, *From Gotch to Gable* (1981); Mike Chapman, *Frank Gotch, World's Greatest Wrestler* (1990); Nolan Zavoral, *A Season on the Mat* (1998).

Nolan Zavoral
St. Paul, Minnesota

Softball

Softball originated on Thanksgiving Day 1887 as an indoor alternative to outdoor recreation. George Hancock invented the game and the original rules in the gymnasium of the Farragut Boat Club in Chicago, Illinois, where alumni of Yale and Harvard Universities had convened to learn the outcome of their schools' annual football game. Hancock started with a softer ball (not covered with leather), a bat, and four bases. This game was slower than baseball because of the larger ball, the slower pitching, and the rule against base stealing.

By 1888, the game had moved outside and was played on fields that were too small to accommodate a baseball diamond. In 1933, Chicago sporting goods salesman Michael J. Pauley organized the first national tournament, with Chicago-area businessmen raising money to host the event at the World's Fair. Fifty-five teams from sixteen states were invited. Eight of the teams were women's clubs. Women began to take part in the game because it was considered safer and slower than baseball. The first men's tournament champion was the local J. L. Friedman Boosters, who defeated a club from Detroit, Michigan. Teams had not been playing under a standard set of rules, so tournament officials declared "Chicago" rules would be used, which involved a sixteen-inch ball.

Today softball in the Midwest is enjoyed at all levels of play from amateurs to semipros to professionals. The Midwest Conference, which represents ten area colleges, held its first softball championship in 1979. The Midwest Senior Softball Club, which started in 1993, included seven clubs in 2002 with players ranging in age from fifty to over seventy. The Midwest Invitational Softball Tournament began in 1985 with participants from all over the United States and Canada. Each year the tournament rotates among Cleveland, Columbus, and Detroit.

Softball teams and tournaments can be found throughout the Midwest. The American Softball Association National Softball Hall of Fame was officially dedicated in Oklahoma City in 1973. The hall has more than three hundred members in two categories, players and nonplayers. It is just one of a number of halls of fame that have been created over the years to honor softball players. Softball has developed as a game for all ages because the diamond is smaller, the ball is larger, and with the addition of fast-pitch softball, the game can be enjoyed as either a purely recreational or highly competitive activity.

Sources and Further Reading: James Blair, "Life, Liberty, and a Nice Flat Infield," *Christian Science Monitor* (Apr. 1998); Tom Chiarella and Michael Segell, "The Real Summer Game," *Esquire* (May 1998); Bil Gilbert, "America's Favorite Game is the One Everybody Can Play," *Smithsonian* (Apr. 1996); Mark Marvel, "They Throw Like Girls," *Esquire* (July 1996).

Leslie Heaphy
Kent State University–Stark, Ohio

Special Olympics

The Special Olympics began in the Midwest with Chicago Park District summer programs geared toward children with mental retardation (MR). Funded by grants from the Joseph P. Kennedy, Jr. Foundation, the program grew out of the Kennedy family's experience with the mental retardation of Rosemary Kennedy, a sister of President John F. Kennedy. Rosemary's sister-in-law Eunice Kennedy Shriver's concern with the physical fitness of children with MR and their higher rates of obesity led her to launch a summer camp at her home in 1963. She worked with the Chicago Park District to stage a large, Olympic-style competition in one of their parks.

Opening ceremonies of the first Special Olympics were held at Chicago's Soldier Field in July of 1968 and brought together approximately one thousand athletes from the United States and Canada to compete in swimming and in track and field events. In 1968, the Kennedy Foundation established the nonprofit incorporation of the Special Olympics, which was later formally announced by U.S. Senator Ted Kennedy. Soon afterwards, the Special Olympics, Inc., expanded internationally to Canada and France. The original games at Soldier Field increased in size, and research began to document its benefits for participants. Special Olympics chapters were established across the country, and state-sponsored competitions that coincided with the larger Special Olympics began to take shape. The first winter games of the Special Olympics occurred in 1977.

Like the Olympics, the Special Olympics took on a four-year rotation in different locations around the world, with the Summer Games beginning this schedule in 1975 and the Winter Games beginning in 1977. Also like the Olympics, the games begin with a torch run, and bronze, silver, and gold medals are awarded to the first, second, and third place winners of each event. Unlike the regular Olympics, however, all other athletes receive ribbons in recognition of their participation. In addition, athletes' abilities are assessed so that they may compete with other athletes having similar abilities. Today, the Special Olympics include most of the same events as the Olympics.

Sources and Further Reading: Ana Bueno, *Special Olympics: The First 25 Years* (1994); James Haskins, *A New Kind of Joy* (1976); Chris Privett, "The Special Olympics: A Tradition of Excellence," *Exceptional Parent* 29 (May 1999); Edward Shorter, *The Kennedy Family and the Story of Mental Retardation* (2000).

Jan Sokol-Katz and Lorrie Basinger-Fleischman
University of Miami, Florida

Youth Leagues

Though youth in the Midwest have always played games, athletic pursuits became more organized in the late nineteenth century. Indeed, the Midwest became a national leader in youth sports at the turn of the twentieth century, with settlement house programs, playgrounds, park field houses, and interscholastic sports programs. Many towns and cities featured youth teams organized by age divisions such as juniors or "ponies."

Numerous organizations created baseball leagues for youth. In 1925, the American Legion, a military veterans' organization, began sponsoring baseball leagues for fifteen- to eighteen-year-old boys. A national championship followed a year later. Starting in 1939, Little League Baseball offered competition for younger boys. Its world championship is televised and features an array of regional and international teams. Pony League Baseball, founded in 1951, initially provided competitive ventures for boys of thirteen and fourteen years; it has since expanded to ages five through eighteen and includes girls.

Girls played baseball with skill and distinction. Alta Weiss pitched for semipro teams between 1907 and 1910, while others played on minor league teams or on all-female "bloomer girl" teams. Indeed, many well-known female athletes at the turn of the century hailed from the Midwest. A midwestern woman umpired minor league games for several years around 1910. Babe Didrikson, perhaps the most famous American female athlete of the twentieth century, played for the male House of David team from Benton Harbor, Michigan, in the 1930s, and Toni Stone played for the Kansas City Monarchs and Indianapolis Clowns in the Negro Leagues in the 1950s.

Little League formally revised its rules in 1974 to allow participation by girls, but most girls have chosen to play on interscholastic, park district, or club softball teams. Little League sponsored national softball competition for girls up to eighteen years of age. From 1943 to 1954, the best softball players became professional baseball stars in the All-American Girls Baseball League, which featured ten Midwest teams and drew nearly one million spectators in 1948.

The Midwest has long been a hotbed of football. When the University of Michigan played Harvard in 1881, the *Boston Herald* dismissed the midwesterners as unrefined backwoodsmen. Highly motivated teams from the universities of Chicago, Wisconsin, and Minnesota joined Michigan in persistent challenges to Eastern supremacy and demonstrations of the superiority of midwestern styles of play. High school teams finally settled the debate decisively when New York sent a team to Chicago in 1902 to meet the Cook County League champion, Hyde Park. Hyde Park featured speed over brute strength and won 105-0. When New Yorkers offered excuses, Chicago's North Division High School traveled to Brooklyn in 1903 and brought home a 75-0 victory. The popularity of youth football is perhaps best symbolized by Chicago's Prep Bowl, which matched Catholic and Public League champions in a city title game at Soldier Field. The 1937 contest drew around 120 thousand fans.

The Pop Warner football program, initiated in 1929 in Philadelphia, organizes local football and cheerleading leagues nationwide. Boys aged five to sixteen now may play flag football, while those between seven and sixteen can opt for the tackle variety. Local competitions culminate in regional and national championships. Tackle football is especially popular in the Midwest, with strong teams in Ohio and Illinois.

With the advent of basketball and volleyball in the 1890s, settlement houses and high schools soon formed leagues to organize fair play. By 1895, adult educators at the Universities of Wisconsin and Illinois formed state athletic associations to promote youth sports and set eligibility, age, and scholastic requirements. For those children who engaged in sports organized by the Young Men's Christian Association (YMCA), park districts, playgrounds, or churches, similar governing bodies enforced middle-class standards of decorum and sportsmanship.

Immigrant youth competed in clubs such as the German turners, Czech *sokols*, or Polish Falcons, which emphasized gymnastics and ethnic camaraderie. Religious sports networks, such as the Catholic Youth Organization (CYO) or the B'nai B'rith Youth Organization, promoted myriad activities that encouraged a sense of identity with the larger culture without jeopardizing a sense of community formed around religious and ethnic ties. The CYO, initiated in Chicago in 1930, claimed the world's largest basketball league, and its boxing program sent several working-class youth to the Olympics. Combined with the Golden Gloves boxing festival of the *Chicago Tribune*, it became a regional phenomenon that grew to national and international proportions as midwestern fighters challenged New Yorkers and, eventually, European opponents.

Interscholastic sports teams and local park district leagues offer competition for youth in many sports, while traveling club squads offer regional and national play in volleyball and soccer. The American Youth Soccer Organization, founded in 1964, services more than 650 thousand players nationally, while unaffiliated local soccer leagues swell that number considerably. Similarly, volleyball and basketball clubs offer age group competition for both boys and girls between the ages of ten and eighteen. Summer camps and leagues in each sport attract boys and girls who hope to develop skills, as well as elite players in search of college athletic scholarships.

Basketball has become the most popular youth sport, as even unorganized playground contingents meet in three-on-three competitions (three players per side), and traveling tournament organizers schedule city championships replete with street agents and local aficionados who hope to prosper by acting as recruiters. Basketball, however, transcends urban and rural boundaries. High school championship tournaments engender "March madness" each spring. In Indiana, boys' high school basketball is close to an obses-

sion for many fans. In Iowa the high school girls' tournament, initiated in 1920, surpasses the boys in popularity. The Illinois High School Athletic Association offers competition for wheelchair-bound players.

Athletes drawn to individual sports often choose track and field, gymnastics, tennis, or golf. National competition in the latter two activities is sponsored by junior associations, and the best players are often tutored in tennis and golf academies with hopes of a professional career. Female tennis players and gymnasts have often reached national prominence while still teenagers. Chicagoan Isadore Channels was the national African American tennis champion around 1930. The Czech *sokols* of the Midwest supplied the early American gymnasts of the 1920s and 1930s.

Less traditional sports have become equally regulated and commercialized. Skateboarding, motorcycle racing, roller blading, and snowboarding are now all televised as youthful competitors seek cash prizes. Still other sports remain largely amateur. North Dakota high schools sponsor karate and rodeo competition, and other upper Midwest towns and rural communities offer fishing derbies in warm weather and ice fishing during the winter.

Sources and Further Reading: Gerald R. Gems, *For Pride, Profit, and Patriarchy: Football and the Incorporation of American Cultural Values* (2000); Gerald R. Gems, *Windy City Wars: Labor, Leisure, and Sport in the Making of Chicago* (1977); Gerald R. Gems, *For Pride, Profit, and Patriarchy: Football and the Incorporation of American Cultural Values* (2000); Peter Levine, *A. G. Spalding and the Rise of Baseball* (1985); Dennis Read, "Noticing the Nontraditional," *Athletic Management* 13 (Oct.–Nov. 2001).

Gerald R. Gems
North Central College, Illinois

Intercollegiate Athletics

Intercollegiate athletics has long been a prominent feature of midwestern life, an activity universities and colleges use to promote themselves and foster community by giving people a reason to gather and cheer. The most obvious examples take place on autumn Saturday afternoons, from Columbus, Ohio, to Lincoln, Nebraska, and myriad places in between, when thousands of fans pack college football stadiums and millions more follow the action on television and radio. For many, this public ritual and spectacle is an important feature of their personal and community identities. Indeed, a handful of midwestern college football coaches and players have achieved legendary status:

❖ Amos Alonzo Stagg (1862–1965)

Amos Alonzo Stagg was the first professor of physical culture, football coach, and athletic director at the University of Chicago. The eastern transplant starred at Yale University in football and baseball. After a brief stay at the Springfield YMCA Training School, Chicago's President William Rainey Harper hired him as an associate professor in 1892.

He is known for helping to make college football in the Midwest a mass entertainment industry while advertising the University of Chicago. Harper had asked Stagg "to develop teams which we can send around the country and knock out all the colleges." At Chicago, Stagg did just that as he moved from player-coach in the 1890s, to "scientific" coach in the early 1900s, to celebrity coach by the 1920s.

While Stagg coached basketball and track, his celebrity came from producing 255 victories at Chicago and winning seven Big Ten titles in football before he was forced to retire at age 70 in 1933. More rigorous academic standards caused football to decline in the late 1920s and early 1930s. He moved to The College of the Pacific, coaching until he was again forced to retire at age 84, but not before he brought his new team back to Chicago, overwhelming his old team 32-0. Stagg then joined his son as coach at Susquehanna College and later at Stockton Junior College.

He finally retired at 98 years of age. His record of 314 wins remained the standard until Paul "Bear" Bryant surpassed him in 1982.

Ronald A. Smith
Pennsylvania State University–University Park

Knute Rockne, Red Grange, and Woody Hayes immediately come to mind.

Although college football is popular all over the region, different places have other passions. In Indiana, basketball is sacrosanct. In Iowa, college wrestling matches regularly draw over five thousand people. In Minnesota, college ice hockey is extremely popular. But intercollegiate athletics is not only about school and community spirit and vicarious glory. For institutions with big-time athletic programs, it is a multimillion-dollar-a-year industry frequently beset by corruption and hypocrisy. It also raises important issues about the appropriate relationship between higher education and the athletic experience, amateurism, academic integrity, gender equity, and race relations on campus.

Intercollegiate athletics was imported from the East, where it had, in turn, been imported from England. Oxford and Cambridge University students arranged intercollegiate athletic competitions as early as the 1820s. Approximately a generation later, a handful of American undergraduates, mostly young men from socially elite backgrounds, began organizing athletic contests. They rowed, played baseball, and later football, among other sports. They did so in response to a rigid curriculum and strict faculties, to relax, socialize, build a sense of community, and prove their manhood. Unsurprisingly, some educators questioned the intellectual and moral value of intercollegiate athletics—they thought it misdirected undergraduate energies—and challenged its existence. Eventually, though, administrators and alumni institutionalized and commandeered intercollegiate athletics, which was dominated by prestigious eastern schools for most of the nineteenth century.

Even before the last quarter of the nineteenth century, as interest in sport increased all over the country, midwestern colleges and universities were starting teams, nurturing school loyalty, and generally adopting eastern attitudes and customs. Kenyon College fielded a baseball team before the Civil War, and the University of Kansas had one soon thereafter. By 1878, the University of Michigan was playing football. Some of the nation's longest-running football rivalries—University of Minnesota–University of Wisconsin, University of Missouri–University of Kansas, University of Nebraska–University of Kansas, and Purdue University–Indiana University—commenced in the 1890s. And just five years after basketball was invented in 1891, Chicago defeated Iowa 15–12 in the first five-on-five intercollegiate men's basketball game.

Because intercollegiate athletics in the Midwest is played at different levels—from big-time to small-time and a few sizes in between—many athletic conferences operate in the region. The Big Ten, originally founded in 1895 and known as the Intercollegiate Conference of Faculty Representatives or the Western Conference, is the most prestigious, influential, and publicized. What began as an attempt to establish shared policies and practices limiting athletic eligibility to full-time students "who were not delinquent in their studies" has become a hugely successful enterprise. Indeed, for many people Big Ten football (and to a lesser extent men's basketball) defines midwestern intercollegiate athletics, though the conference also sponsors championships in twenty-four other sports, thirteen of them for women. All told, Big Ten universities now provide to 7,500 students more than $63 million annually in athletic scholarships. The annual athletic budget for a member school is in the $30–70 million range (and rising).

Contrary to conventional wisdom, most economists agree that virtually all of these programs lose money. Most sports fans and students at Big Ten schools do not seem to care, for their athletic teams have given them a great deal of pleasure over the years: national championships in virtually every sport, hundreds of All-American athletes, many thrilling games, and countless opportunities to bask in reflected glory.

Every place has its own athletic heroes, and the Midwest has an abundance of the intercollegiate variety. They can be found in every community. Still, a handful of intercollegiate athletic heroes, past and present, are known throughout the region. Sometimes this is solely because of their remarkable accomplishments, and sometimes because they exemplify cultural values that resonate with people.

More than seventy-five years after he played football for the University of Illinois, the modest and clean-living Harold "Red" Grange (1903–1991) is still glorified for scoring four touchdowns in the first twelve minutes of a 1924 game against the undefeated University of Michigan. The mild-mannered and deferential track star James Cleveland "Jesse" Owens (1913–1980) is similarly lionized for his performance on May 25, 1935, when as a sophomore at The Ohio State University, he broke three world records and tied a fourth at the Big Ten Championship. For many, the 1979 national championship basketball game between Indiana State University, led by senior forward Larry Bird (b. 1956), and Michigan State University, led by sophomore guard Earvin "Magic" Johnson, Jr. (b. 1959), was unusually dramatic, which helps explain why the game set a record for the largest television audience ever to watch a National Collegiate Athletic Association (NCAA) final.

As for prominent coaches, it would be difficult to find many people in the Midwest unfamiliar with the controversial basketball coach Robert "Bob" Knight (b. 1940), who was fired in 2000 after twenty-nine years at Indiana University. For a slightly older group, the same is probably true of Wayne Woodrow "Woody" Hayes (1913–1987), The Ohio State University's football coach for twenty-eight years. Born and raised in Ohio, both men were authoritarian, volatile, and successful: Hayes won 205 regular season games at Ohio State, thirteen Big Ten titles, four Rose Bowls, and three national championships. Knight won 661 games for Indiana, eleven Big Ten titles, and three national championships. Both also cultivated devoted followings and frequently exasperated fans and other onlookers. They elicited these responses partly because of some of the cultural values they articulated and personified: a commitment to discipline, perfectionism, hyper-competitiveness, and an outspokenness verging on boorishness.

Knute Rockne (1888–1931), arguably the most famous midwestern intercollegiate athletic icon, exhibited some of the same characteristics. A Norwegian immigrant, Rockne played football for Notre Dame University, graduating magna cum laude as an All-American end and becoming head football coach in 1918. As a coach, Rockne demonstrated remarkable creativity, an affinity for upsetting more highly regarded teams, and a genius for self-promotion, all of which helped little-known Notre Dame achieve national prominence. During his thirteen-year coaching career, Notre Dame had five undefeated seasons, won three national championships, and produced twenty first-team All-Americans. His lifetime winning percentage of .881 (105-12-5) suggests Rockne may be the greatest college football coach in history. More important for many midwesterners, especially Catholics, Rockne was the embodiment of the American Dream, an exemplar of ambition, hard work, and determination.

There is of course much more to intercollegiate athletics in the Midwest than big-time football and men's basketball. In addition to the twenty-seven Division I-A football programs (the NCAA's most elite and commercialized level), there are more than one hundred Division I-AA, Division II, and Division III football teams in the Midwest, as well as teams from schools that belong to the National Association of Intercollegiate Athletics (NAIA). And despite the media attention that football and men's basketball receive, and that women's basketball is beginning to garner, most student-athletes in the Midwest (and in the rest of the country) play in the so-called non-revenue or lower profile sports, including baseball, field hockey, golf, gymnastics, rowing, soccer, softball, swimming, diving, tennis, track and field, volleyball, and wrestling.

Nor is the focus the same in all divisions. As historian Murray Sperber puts it, "In Division I, the athletic department priority is to produce winning teams; in Division III, it is to allow athletes to develop as students." It is common to romanticize Division III athletics with its relatively paltry budgets: for instance, whereas the University of Michigan spent more than $47 million on intercollegiate athletics in 1997–1998, Kenyon College spent less than $1.2 million. Likewise, Division III athletes, who do not receive athletic scholarships and are often more committed to their studies than their Division I counterparts, are frequently lauded for playing for the love of the game. Yet a recent study has found that the big-time intercollegiate athletic paradigm, with its emphasis on winning and its patterns of recruitment, admissions, and coaching, is spreading to Division II and III institutions.

This phenomenon is perhaps most evident in women's intercollegiate athletics, which has grown tremendously in the last twenty-five years, largely due to the women's movement and the passage and implementation of Title IX of the Educational Amendments of 1972. The controversial Title IX (buttressed by the

Civil Rights Restoration Act of 1988) prohibits discrimination on the basis of sex in educational institutions receiving federal funding. More than any other legislation or policy, Title IX has spurred the creation of intercollegiate athletic teams and scholarship opportunities for women.

Midwestern college women participated in athletics long before Title IX. In the late nineteenth and early twentieth centuries, a handful of women college students formed clubs to play baseball, tennis, and croquet. More commonly, women physical educators organized sport for women, sometimes incorporating it into the curriculum. In 1898, under the guidance of Gertrude Dudley, the University of Chicago launched the first program of competitive athletics for women at a major university. A year before, women students at the University of Wisconsin were playing volleyball and soon thereafter ice hockey (1903) and baseball (1906). Basketball was particularly popular with many college women, although most physical educators thought the men's game was too rough and thus inappropriate for educated, middle-class women. Accordingly, they significantly modified its rules. It should be mentioned that many of these games were played within schools (frequently at women's colleges, out of public sight), rather than between them. This was because most women physical educators in the early twentieth century and beyond stressed the educational and recreational value of athletics (they believed that organized play was good for one's physical health and taught teamwork and fair play) and minimized what they thought was excessive (for women) individual accomplishment and highly intensive competition.

Times have changed. More than thirty years after Title IX, and more than twenty years after the NCAA began sponsoring women's intercollegiate athletics, its proliferation is remarkable. Concomitantly, the concerns of several generations of women physical educators have had their effect: in virtually every way, women's intercollegiate athletics now embraces the so-called men's model of competitive, commercialized sport. Most people view this as a positive development. As journalist Welch Suggs wrote in 2001, "All the studies, all the statistics, and all the signs say the same thing: There has never been a better time to be a female athlete in college." Perhaps, but gender equity has not been achieved. In general, female athletes still receive less scholarship aid than their male counterparts, women's athletics are still allocated less money for operating and recruiting expenses, and women's coaches are still paid far less than coaches for men's teams.

Gender inequity is only one of the problems bedeviling intercollegiate athletics in the Midwest and elsewhere. The list includes unethical recruiting, widespread academic abuses, a costly financial arms race, rampant commercialization, the exploitation of athletes (who are disproportionately African American) in revenue-producing sports, sporadic gambling and point-shaving scandals, occasional criminality, rabid boosterism, and an overemphasis on winning. All of these things undermine the primary mission of institutions of higher education. These are obviously not new issues; most have historically been endemic to big-time intercollegiate athletics. Virtually every school in the Midwest has experienced some or all of these problems, which can seriously damage an institution's integrity and reputation. "As many universities have discovered, publicity from intercollegiate athletics is a two-edged sword, generating attention and feel-good camaraderie when the teams are winning," notes Murray Sperber, "but when a scandal occurs, the sword swings back, drawing buckets of negative media coverage and public scorn."

Despite its problems, intercollegiate athletics remains a tremendously popular institution in the Midwest and an important source of regional identity, pride, and pleasure. Intercollegiate athletics is an amalgamation of ritualistic community celebrations, a way for students to develop as athletes and socialize, and a big business. It is part of the rhythm of many lives, a custom that links generations and perpetuates social values.

Sources and Further Reading: James E. Delany, "Commercialism in Intercollegiate Athletics," *The Educational Record* 78 (Winter 1997); Mary Jo Festle, *Playing Nice* (1996); Ellen W. Gerber, "Collegiate Sport," in Ellen W. Gerber, Jan Felshin, Pearl Berlin, and Waneen Wyrick, *The American Woman in Sport* (1974); Robin Lester, *Stagg's University* (1995); Patrick B. Miller, *The Playing Fields of American Culture* (2005); James L. Shulman and William G. Bowen, *The Game of Life* (2001); Ronald A. Smith, *Sports and Freedom* (1988); Murray Sperber, *Shake Down the Thunder* (1993); Murray Sperber, *Beer and Circus* (2000); Welch Suggs, "Female Athletes Thrive, but Budget Pressures Loom," *The Chronicle of Higher Education* (May 18, 2001).

Daniel A. Nathan
Skidmore College, New York

Big Ten Conference

The Big Ten, organized in January 1895 as the Intercollegiate Conference of Faculty Representatives, was born in response to the perceived problems, and the need for control, of intercollegiate athletics at the end of the nineteenth century. The presidents of the founding seven member institutions—Purdue University, Minnesota State University, Wisconsin State University, University of Illinois, Northwestern University, University of Michigan, and University of Chicago—met at the Palmer House in Chicago at the invitation of President J.H. Smart of Purdue. Indiana University and the State University of Iowa were admitted in 1899. In 1912, The Ohio State University joined the conference to make up the original Big Ten. The University of Chicago withdrew in 1946, and three years later Michigan State University took its place. The current composition of the Big Ten includes eleven member institutions, as Pennsylvania State University accepted an invitation to join the league in 1990.

The Big Ten is made up of ten publicly funded state universities and one private institution, Northwestern. All members are also members of the Association of American Universities. The eleven schools enroll more than 410,000 students, of whom over 7,500 participate in intercollegiate athletics. Big Ten student athletes have won over 1,250 individual NCAA titles and more than 185 team championships.

The Big Ten sponsors twenty-five sports and conference championships. Men's sports are baseball, basketball, cross-country, football, golf, gymnastics, soccer, swimming, diving, tennis, indoor and outdoor track and field, and wrestling. Women's sports include basketball, cross-country, field hockey, golf, gymnastics, rowing, soccer, softball, swimming, diving, tennis, indoor and outdoor track and field, and volleyball.

Members are free to compete as independents in sports not sponsored by the conference. For instance, five schools sponsor men's ice hockey teams, and three sponsor women's ice hockey. Among the less-practiced men's sports are rowing (at the University of Wisconsin) and fencing, volleyball, and lacrosse (at Ohio State and Penn State). Independent women's sports include water polo (at Indiana and the University of Michigan) and synchronized swimming (at Ohio State). In total, Big Ten members sponsor more than 250 intercollegiate varsity teams in over thirty-five sports. All members compete in women's and men's basketball, women's and men's golf, women's and men's tennis, women's cross-country, softball, women's swimming and diving, women's volleyball, men's football, and men's wrestling.

Football is clearly the king of Big Ten athletics. Stadiums at the University of Michigan, (capacity 107,501) and Penn State (107,282) are the largest collegiate arenas in the country. Ohio State's Ohio Stadium follows closely with a capacity of 101,568. Add other vast facilities like the University of Wisconsin's Camp Randall Stadium, Michigan State's Spartan Stadium, and Purdue's Ross-Ade Stadium, and it is easy to see how more than five and a half million fans attend Big Ten football home games each year.

Football attendance and revenues propel Big Ten Conference sports to the biggest of big business in intercollegiate athletics. According to the Equity in Athletics Disclosure Act reports of the member institutions for 2001–2002, revenues of the athletics departments at the eleven member universities totaled more than half a billion dollars, $507,056,626, while athletic expenditures were $443,291,935, for a surplus of almost $64 million dollars. Revenues from football, $237,913,260, represent about 47 percent of total revenues, while expenditures on football were reported at $96,829,403, or 22 percent of total expenditures. The excess of revenues over expenditures means football is the major revenue sport. For the reporting period, Big Ten athletics revenues were slightly greater than that of its nearest rival, the Southeastern Conference, which reported $504,306,220.

Big Ten sports fans attend the games for the competition and spectacle, but colorful figures and celebrated names have enhanced the lore of Big Ten athletics since its beginning. Football coaches include Amos Alonzo Stagg at the University of Chicago, Fielding Yost and Glenn E. Bo Schembechler at the University of Michigan, Robert "Bob" Zuppke of the University of Illinois, Wayne Woodrow "Woody" Hayes of Ohio State, and Joseph Vincent "Joe" Paterno of Penn State. Basketball coaches Robert "Bob" Knight and Branch McCracken at Indiana, Tom Izzo of Michigan State, and Frederick Rankin "Fred" Taylor at Ohio State all brought national championships to the Big Ten. Outstanding student-athletes have included John Jay Berwanger of the University of Chicago, Harold "Red" Grange of the University of Illinois, Mark Spitz of Indiana University, Nile Kinnick of the University of Iowa, Ron Kramer of the University of Michigan, Kirk Gibson of Michigan State University, Paul Giel of the University of Minnesota, Marty Riessen of Northwestern University, Jack Nicklaus and James Cleveland "Jesse" Owens of The Ohio State University, Kelly Mazzante of Penn State University, John Wooden of Purdue University, and Suzy Favor of the University of Wisconsin.

Sources and Further Reading: William Bowen and James Shulman, *The Game of Life: College Sports and Educational Values* (2001); James A. Michener, *Sports in America* (1976); "Playing for Dollars," *Orlando Sentinel* (Feb. 9, 2003); John Sayle Watterson, *College Football* (2000); Kenneth L. Wilson and Jerry Brondfield, *The Big Ten* (1967).

David A. Campaigne
University of South Florida

John R. Thelin
University of Kentucky

Big Twelve Conference

The Big Twelve Conference is made up of twelve member institutions located in seven states. The University of Nebraska, the University of Colorado, the University of Missouri, the University of Kansas, Kansas State University, and Iowa State University make up the North Division for football and men's and women's basketball. The South Division is made up of Texas A&M University, the University of Texas, Texas Tech University, the University of Oklahoma, Oklahoma State University, and Baylor University. Eleven institutions are publicly funded state universities, and Baylor is a private, religiously affiliated school.

The Big Twelve was organized in February of 1994, and competition began with fall sports in 1996. Conference headquarters are located in Dallas, Texas, the organizational site of one of its forerunners, the Southwest Conference. The Big Eight Conference merged with four members of the failing Southwest Conference in 1994 to form the Big Twelve Conference.

The Big Twelve traces its roots to the Midland Hotel in Kansas City, Missouri, where on January 12, 1907, representatives of the University of Kansas, the University of Missouri, the University of Nebraska, the State University of Iowa, and Washington University of St. Louis gathered to organize the Missouri Valley Intercollegiate Athletic Association (MVIAA). Iowa participated in football only and held dual membership in the Big Ten until it permanently affiliated with the Big Ten in 1911. In March 1907, Ames College (now Iowa State) and Drake University of Des Moines, Iowa, joined the conference. Over the next twenty years, Kansas State University and Grinnell College were added, the University of Oklahoma was admitted in 1920, and Oklahoma A&M (now Oklahoma State University) joined in 1925.

On May 19, 1928, six of the state universities formally reorganized the MVIAA. Kansas, Missouri, Nebraska, Oklahoma, Kansas State, and Iowa State retained the Missouri Valley name, but the conference was dubbed "The Big Six" by the media. This was modified to "Big Seven" with the addition of Colorado in 1947, and to "Big Eight" when Oklahoma State rejoined in 1957. In 1964, the designation MVIAA was dropped, and the league officially became the Big Eight Conference.

The Southwest Conference (SWC) was organized in Dallas in May 1914, and disbanded in 1996, when four Texas institutions joined the Big Twelve. Of the four, three were charter members of the SWC: the University of Texas, Texas A&M, and Baylor. The fourth, Texas Tech University, was a relative newcomer to the SWC, having joined in 1958. The SWC had been plagued by football recruiting scandals and NCAA sanctions for years, but the final blow to the conference came with the fast-growing popularity of the National Football League in Texas and the accompanying loss of attendance for private SWC schools in metropolitan Houston and Dallas.

Economics played a major role in the formation of the Big Twelve. The conference members are located in seven states whose population encompasses more than forty million people. This is important because the creation of the Big Twelve significantly increased the media and advertising exposure of the former Big Eight, and televised sports, especially college football, provide essential revenues for the operation of departments of intercollegiate athletics. More than 4,500 male and female student-athletes compete in twenty-one intercollegiate sports for the Big Twelve, and in 2003, the conference distributed $89 million to its member institutions.

The Big Twelve universities field teams in ten conference-affiliated men's sports—baseball, basketball, cross-country, football, golf, indoor track, outdoor track, swimming, tennis, and wrestling. All members participate in basketball, cross-country, football, golf, and indoor and outdoor track. Only three institutions compete in swimming (Missouri, University of Texas, and Texas A&M). The University of Texas has won all conference championships awarded, as well as five national championships since competition began in 1996. No member school participates in all ten men's sports.

Eleven women's sports are sponsored by the conference—basketball, cross-country, golf, gymnastics, indoor track, outdoor track, soccer, softball, swimming, tennis, and volleyball. All schools participate in basketball, cross-country, golf, indoor and outdoor track, and tennis. Three members (Iowa State, Missouri, and Nebraska) participate in all eleven sports sanctioned.

Since the founding of the Big Twelve, member institutions have won national championships in baseball (University of Texas), men's and women's cross-country (Colorado), football (Nebraska, Oklahoma, and Texas), men's golf (Oklahoma State), men's gymnastics (University of Oklahoma), women's indoor and outdoor track (University of Texas), skiing (Colorado, men and women; not conference-sanctioned), softball (University of Oklahoma), men's swimming (University of Texas), women's volleyball (Nebraska), and wrestling (Oklahoma State). Based on records reflecting results through the 2003–2004 academic year, Big Twelve members have won twenty-three national championships since 1996 and 174 national team championships since the formation of the NCAA.

Sources and Further Reading: James A. Michener, *Sports in America* (1976); Ronald A. Smith, *Play-by-Play* (2001); John Sayle Watterson, *College Football* (2000).

David A. Campaigne
University of South Florida

John R. Thelin
University of Kentucky

College World Series

The premier event in college baseball has been held in the Midwest since its inception in 1947. The first Series between the University of California–Berkeley and Yale University was held in Kalamazoo, Michigan. The Series was again held in Kalamazoo in 1948, then moved to Wichita, Kansas, for a year. In 1950, the Series moved to Omaha, Nebraska, and has been there ever since.

The Series has undergone many changes since its humble beginnings when two teams competed for the title. In 1947, only a couple of thousand fans watched the event. Now the tournament attracts more than 200 thousand fans and is shown live on television and the Internet to millions of viewers around the world. Now sixty-four teams are chosen to compete in the tournament, with eight teams competing for the national championship in Omaha. The format of the tournament has also come full circle. The first two Series featured a best-two-of-three games format. That was changed to a double-elimination format in 1949. The teams still play a double-elimination format to determine who will meet in the final, but the final was changed back to a best-of-three format in 2003.

The game has also gone through many changes. When the Series began, players used wooden bats and wore no helmets, and pitchers had to take their turn at the plate. Now the players use aluminum bats and wear helmets, and designated hitters swing the bat in place of pitchers. In the early days of the Series, a pitcher was expected to pitch the whole game. Now many relief pitchers are used, and a pitcher throwing a full game is more of a rarity. Also a rarity now is a shutout. Very seldom does a team not score a run during a game.

Rosenblatt Stadium has changed dramatically through the years. When the tournament first began there, the name of the facility was Municipal Stadium and seating capacity was about seven thousand. That number has more than tripled. The price of tickets has also gone up considerably, though the Series is still considered a bargain. Ticket prices ranged from $7 to $29 in 2003.

Over the history of the event, many famous people have played in the Series. Several have gone on to become stars in the major leagues, such as Barry Bonds and Roger Clemens. Others earned notoriety off the field. The most famous former Series player was George H. W. Bush, who became the forty-first United States president. In 2001, his son, President George W. Bush, became the first sitting president to visit the Series. He threw out the ceremonial first pitch and shook hands with the players.

Source and Further Reading: William C. Madden, *History of the College World Series* (2004).

W. C. Madden
Fishers, Indiana

Hockey at the University of Minnesota

Although many midwestern universities have rich hockey traditions and winning programs, perhaps none has been more prominent than the University of Minnesota's. Women's hockey has had a long-standing history at the university. A team played at Minnesota as early as 1917, wearing bloomers and playing at the Hippodrome at the State Fair Grounds. Since that time, teams organized sporadically until an official club team formed in 1974. In 1996, Minnesota native Laura Halldorson was hired to coach the team for its debut as a National Collegiate Athletic Association (NCAA) Division I program in 1997, leading the Golden Gophers to a 21-5-3 record during its inaugural season. By 2001, the NCAA organized the Women's Frozen Four (national championship), a tournament the Gophers qualified for in 2002. The success of the team and strong local support led to the construction of 3,400-seat Ridder Arena; 3,239 attended the opening game against St. Cloud State in 2002.

The men started a formal varsity program in 1921, attending their first NCAA championships in 1953 and subsequently winning at least five national titles. The program has traditionally relied on players born and trained in the state of Minnesota and has produced several notables who have gone on to successful professional careers, including Neal Broten, Mike Ramsey, and Reed Larson. One former Gopher, John Mariucci, who played in the National Hockey League, returned to Minnesota to coach the team between 1952 and 1966. Today the Gophers, members of the Western Collegiate Hockey Association, play their games at the 9,700-seat Mariucci Arena, renamed in his honor in 1987.

Playing on the 1954 team for Mariucci was John

Mayasich, regarded as one of the greatest amateur hockey players ever in the United States. Mayasich, whose jersey #8 was retired in 1998, is the university's all-time leading scorer with 144 goals and 154 assists in 111 games. He was also named to the NCAA's fiftieth anniversary team for his play during the 1953–1954 championships.

In 1972, the program hired Herbert P. "Herb" Brooks (1937–2003), who quickly turned the team into a national powerhouse. The Gophers won three titles under Brooks in 1974, 1976, and 1979. Brooks would later coach the Olympic gold-medal-winning team at Lake Placid in 1980, which featured eight University of Minnesota players on its roster.

The team won back-to-back NCAA Championships in 2002 and 2003. Attendance at the 2002 Championship game, held in St. Paul, set an NCAA tournament attendance record of 19,324, also a record crowd for a college hockey game in Minnesota. Despite the fact that other programs have won more national titles, the men's hockey program at Minnesota has consistently produced high-caliber teams and holds several NCAA records. They have qualified for at least twenty-seven NCAA Frozen Four tournaments, including a record thirteen consecutive tournaments between 1985 and 1997, and have the most wins in tournament history.

Sources and Further Reading: Ross Bernstein, *Frozen Memories: Celebrating a Century of Minnesota Hockey* (1999); National Collegiate Athletic Association, *Official 2002 NCAA Winter Championships Records* (2002).

Daniel S. Mason
University of Alberta–Edmonton, Canada

Notre Dame Football

The University of Notre Dame is the best-known Roman Catholic university in America, and that notoriety comes in large part from its success in intercollegiate football in the twentieth century.

Notre Dame football began in 1887, but it was not well organized. In the early 1890s, instructor James Kilvan attempted to get more order into the game by writing to Yale University's Walter Camp (1859–1925), the father of American football, asking Camp to "kindly furnish me with some points on the best way to develop a good Football team." In 1894, Notre Dame was invited by the University of Chicago's Amos Alonzo Stagg (1862–1965) to play in the first midwestern New Year's Day game, an 8-0 loss. Notre Dame won regularly when playing a number of small institutions but not as often against such Big Ten insti-

❖ Knute Rockne (1888–1931)

Knute Rockne was born in Voss, Norway, in 1888, and moved with his family to the multiethnic Logan Square district of Chicago, Illinois, when he was a child. A good track athlete as a youth, Rockne worked for the U.S. Post Office for several years before matriculating at Notre Dame in 1910, where he achieved modest fame as a football player and pole vaulter. He earned All-American honors for football in his senior year and helped launch Notre Dame to football prominence with a 35–13 victory over undefeated Army in 1913, as the Irish unveiled a precise, integrated passing attack to complement a powerful running game. After four years as an assistant coach, Rockne took over as head football coach and athletic director of Notre Dame in 1918.

In the next thirteen years at Notre Dame, Rockne led his teams to an unparalleled record of 105-12-5, a winning percentage of .881. In the process, he brought the relatively unknown midwestern school to national prominence. Its exciting brand of football helped shift power from the traditional eastern schools to the Midwest. Rockne also helped launch the nation's first coast-to-coast schedule of games in the 1926 season. His teams were undefeated in 1919, 1920, 1924, 1929, and 1930, as he showcased such stars as George Gipp and the Four Horsemen. A tireless promoter of football, Rockne's charisma fit exquisitely into the golden years of American sports. The nation mourned his death in an airplane crash over Bazaar, Kansas, on March 31, 1931.

Michael R. Steele
Pacific University, Oregon

tutions as the University of Michigan, Northwestern University, and Indiana University. Early on, Notre Dame was rejected several times for membership in the Big Ten.

In the 1910s, Notre Dame emerged as a preeminent football power. Five years after the composition of Notre Dame's famous Victory March calling for "Cheer, Cheer for Old Notre Dame," Notre Dame hired its first full-time coach, Jesse Harper, for the 1913 season. That year, the famous passing display of quarterback Charles E. "Gus" Dorais to, among others, end Knute Rockne (1888–1931), led to Notre Dame's stunning 35-13 victory over the West Point cadets. That game, in which 243 yards were gained through passing, gave national publicity to Notre Dame.

Notre Dame gained its greatest renown under Knute Rockne, who coached from 1918 through 1930. Under Rockne, Notre Dame won 105 games, had five undefeated seasons, and lost only twelve games in thirteen seasons, for an .881 winning percentage that ranks as the best of all time. One of Rockne's teams played before a record 120,000 spectators against Southern California in Chicago's newly constructed Soldier Field.

Notre Dame's success on the field led to its leadership in college sport broadcasting. Notre Dame began radio broadcasting in 1924. After World War II, when television came on the scene, Notre Dame began selling its exclusive rights to both radio and television. Had the National Collegiate Athletic Association (NCAA) not intervened in 1951 to limit TV coverage by creating a monopoly over TV broadcasting, Notre Dame would have led the nation in television revenue. In 1984, the U.S. Supreme Court ruled the NCAA TV contract an unconstitutional monopoly, allowing the open market to determine Notre Dame's true worth in football telecasting.

From the time of Rockne to the breakup of the NCAA monopoly, Notre Dame football continued to dominate intercollegiate football. Under Frank Leahy in the 1940s, Notre Dame won four national championships, while coaches Ara Parseghian, Dan Devine, and Louis Leo "Lou" Holtz won championships in the 1960s, 1970s, and 1980s. Notre Dame signed a multimillion-dollar TV contract with NBC in 1990, the only team in America that could secure a national network to telecast its games. As the twentieth century closed, Notre Dame turned the tables on the Midwest's major conference when it rejected a bid to become a member of the Big Ten.

Sources and Further Reading: Joe Doyle, *Fighting Irish* (1987); Gene Schoor, *100 Years of Notre Dame Football* (1987); Murray Sperber, *Shake Down the Thunder* (1993); Francis Wallace, *Notre Dame from Rockne to Parseghian* (1967).

Ronald A. Smith
Pennsylvania State University–University Park

Title IX

Passed by the United States Congress and signed by President Richard Nixon in 1972, Title IX of the Educational Amendments to the Civil Rights Act of 1964 was designed to encourage gender equity in education. The preamble states that "No person in the United States shall, on the basis of sex, be excluded from participation in, be denied the benefits of, or be subject to discrimination under any educational programs or activity receiving federal financial assistance." Regulations for the implementation of Title IX became effective on July 21, 1975. The act has had a profound impact on schools, colleges, and universities, most spectacularly in sports.

Enforcement of Title IX was minimal until the 1990s because of a lack of direction about how to proceed. In 1984, the U.S. Supreme Court ruled in *Grove City v. Bell* that school programs that did not directly receive federal aid were not affected by Title IX. Over a veto from President Ronald Reagan, Congress passed the Civil Rights Restoration Act in 1988, which reversed the Grove City decision. Various court challenges in the 1990s resulted in victories for women seeking enforcement of Title IX provisions.

The federal government, therefore, began to insist on compliance with a proportionality test adopted in 1979. This provision required that the gender breakdown in an institution's sports programs had to match the gender breakdown in the student body as a whole. Supporters viewed this as necessary to achieve gender equity, while critics complained that it was a quota system that promoted reverse discrimination against male athletes. Anger was especially strong among participants in nonrevenue sports such as wrestling and baseball, because they believe these athletes bore the brunt of the costs of compliance. They cite statistics such as the decline in the number of collegiate wrestling teams from 374 in 1980 to 229 in 2001.

Overall, however, Title IX has proved a boon to women athletes. High schools and universities have dramatically increased the opportunities and financial resources available to female students and added a wide variety of sports, including basketball, softball, volleyball, soccer, and precision ice skating. The increase in women in intercollegiate athletics in the last third of the twentieth century was 400 percent. Just under 400 women were student athletes at the University of Minnesota in 2002, representing half of the athletes on campus.

Title IX has had a major impact on the Midwest. In the midst of criticism of several members of the Big Ten for their failure to comply fully, the conference instituted a "Dream Big" campaign to highlight opportunities for female athletes. Although women's sports continued to lag behind men's, especially when viewed in terms of the revenue generated by football and basketball programs, there have been significant changes. In 2004, Indiana University offered twenty-four varsity sports, eleven for men and thirteen for women.

Controversy persists. If most people now support the idea of women's athletic programs, evidenced by the growing popularity of basketball, soccer, and golf, many remain staunchly opposed to the proportionality standard.

Sources and Further Reading: Jessica Gavora, *Tilting the Playing Field* (2003); Robert Mertzman, *Sports and Justice:*

Title IX and Gender Equality (video recording, 1999); Michael A. Messner, *Taking the Field* (2002).

Andrew Cayton
Miami University, Oxford, Ohio

Professional Sports

Professional sport came early to the Midwest. Yet for much of the nineteenth century, professionalism met with derision from middle- and upper-class Americans

<hr>

❖ **Sybil Bauer**

One of the greatest women swimmers in America and an Olympic champion, Sybil Bauer achieved numerous national and world records in the backstroke in the early 1920s. Bauer helped to promote competitive women's swimming at a time when many criticized women's athletics as counter to feminine and domestic roles in American culture. Sybil Bauer was born in Chicago on September 18, 1903, and learned to swim at age fifteen at Carl Schurz High School. She excelled in the sport and joined the Illinois Athletic Club (IAC), a leading team in aquatic sports. At the IAC, Bauer swam under the guidance of renowned Olympic swimming coach William Bachrach, along with teammate Ethel Lackie and star swimmer Johnny Weissmuller. Bauer entered Northwestern University and excelled in basketball and field hockey. She also served as the president of the Northwestern Women's Athletic Association (May 1925–February 1926) while swimming for the IAC.

Bauer earned acclaim as an outstanding backstroker, winning the National Amateur Athletic Union (AAU) Championships consecutively from 1921 to 1926 for the 100-yard backstroke and the National Championships for the 100-meter, 150-yard, and 220-yard backstroke. Bauer was also on the team of the world record and national championship freestyle relay. In 1924, Sybil Bauer won a gold medal in the Paris Olympics in the 100-meter backstroke. Bauer achieved the feat of being the first woman to best a man's existing world record in swimming: In a 1922 meet in Bermuda, Bauer lowered the world record time in the 440-yard backstroke by four seconds to beat Stubby Kruger's time. Her last swimming competition was the 1926 National AAU meet, where she repeated her title victories and also broke two of her own world records in the 300-meter and 200-yard backstroke.

Bauer, who was engaged to future television entertainer Ed Sullivan, became seriously ill in December 1926, and succumbed to cancer a few months later. Sybil Bauer was inducted in the International Swimming Hall of Fame in 1967 to honor her swimming achievements.

Linda J. Borish
Western Michigan University

who aspired to live up to the Victorian tenets of self-control, refinement, and deferred gratification. As the United States industrialized in the late nineteenth century, urban commercial recreation became more popular, as Victorian culture gave way to a consumer-oriented culture emphasizing self-fulfillment and instant gratification. Professional sport began to be accepted within the context of urban commercial recreation. The Midwest holds a central place in the development of professional sport, contributing organizations, teams (often established under corporate sponsorship), and innovations in rules and playing styles.

Why professional sport developed early in the Midwest is a question best addressed in terms of urbanization. Cities attracted young men and women from farms and villages in America as well as Europe. Single men found kindred spirits in urban taverns and saloons, where contests challenged men's physical strength and skill. Commercial amusements and sport were central to urban saloons, and in the nineteenth century, they were frequently sites of bare-knuckle prizefighting. In the mid-1850s, St. Louis stood out as a center of prizefighting in the Midwest. Eastern promoters and pugilists attracted thousands of working-class men to these fights, and purses could amount to as much as three hundred dollars, a year's wage for the average laborer. Following the Civil War, the Marquis of Queensbury rules brought boxing the imprimatur of gentility that the sport had previously lacked, and by the early 1880s, when champion John L. Sullivan toured the Midwest in a series of exhibition matches, middle- and upper-class men increasingly found in boxing legitimate commercialized sport.

Baseball emerged as America's national game and the country's first professional team sport in the mid-nineteenth century. Urban athletic and sporting clubs, inspired by new attitudes emphasizing exercise and genteel sport for middle- and upper-class men, established many of the early baseball teams. By the end of the Civil War, several eastern teams were paying players. In 1867, the Washington Nationals, with several professional players, toured the Midwest, arranging games from Cleveland to St. Louis. In Cincinnati, they played and soundly defeated a local team, the Red Stockings. The defeat convinced the Red Stockings of the benefits of hiring professional players, and in 1869, under the leadership of Harry Wright, the Cincinnati Red Stockings became the first all-professional sports team in American history.

The Cincinnati team folded following the 1870 season, and Wright left for Boston to form another professional baseball club. In 1871, he played a role in the creation of the first major professional league, the National Association. The new league contained teams from throughout the East and the Midwest, including

❖ Johnny Weissmuller (1904–1984)

Johnny Weissmuller was born in Freidorf, Hungary, on June 2, 1904. He and his family moved to the United States in 1905 and lived in Windber, Pennsylvania, for almost three years before moving to Chicago. Raised in the heart of Old Town, a German-American suburb of Chicago, Weissmuller represents the experiences of the so-called new immigrants settling in the area in the late nineteenth and early twentieth centuries. Weismuller participated in a number of German American activities, both in the city and in the rural outskirts where his grandparents lived, including pig-roasting ceremonies and yodeling contests.

He began swimming at Fullerton Beach in Lincoln Park at an early age and joined the Young Men's Christian Association swim team in 1916. In 1920, legendary swimming coach Bill Bachrach discovered Weissmuller and invited him to join the Illinois Athletic Club's swim team. Coached by Bachrach, Weissmuller began a career in competitive swimming, winning fifty-two national championship titles, five Olympic gold medals (in 1924 and 1928), and setting many world records before retiring from the sport in 1929.

In 1931, Weissmuller began the career he is best known for, as a cinema star playing the lead in *Tarzan, The Ape Man* (1932), a role he would reprise in twelve movies. In 1949, he began playing the character of Jungle Jim in a movie series. After suffering a stroke in 1977, Weissmuller's fifth wife, Maria, moved him to Acapulco, where he died of pulmonary edema on January 20, 1984.

Aldo J. Regalado
University of Miami, Florida

The National Football League (NFL) had its origins in the small mill towns and urban centers of the Midwest. Professional football emerged out of rivalries as cities competed for labor, for business, and for position within midwestern and emerging national markets. Urban boosters encouraged their small-town football teams to challenge teams from rival cities. The game spread into Ohio from its birth in western Pennsylvania, and by the early twentieth century, it had a foothold in towns like Akron, Cleveland, Youngstown, Massillon, and Canton. Professional football could be found in Michigan, Indiana, Chicago, and elsewhere in the Midwest where employers established industrial teams. But it was in Canton, Ohio, in 1920, where fourteen men representing ten clubs formed the American Professional Football Association (APFA), which would be renamed the NFL in 1922. Among those men was George Halas, who played a key role in professionalizing the sport. The former University of Illinois star became the central force in transforming the A.E. Staley Company industrial team into the Chicago Bears, a powerhouse in the early years of the NFL.

The Midwest dominated the new league. By the

Shoeless Joe Jackson. Chicago Historical Society, ICHi-19569.

the Chicago White Stockings and the St. Louis Brown Stockings. The National Association gave way to the National League of Professional Baseball Clubs in 1876. To soothe discontent, the new league banned Sunday games, gambling, and liquor sales at its ballparks. National League headquarters were in Chicago, and the league initially included teams there as well as in Cincinnati and St. Louis. By 1901, when the American League emerged, at one time or another the National League had included not only the original midwestern teams, but also clubs in Cleveland, Detroit, Indianapolis, Kansas City, and Milwaukee.

During World War II, women's professional baseball had a place in the Midwest in the form of the All-American Girls Professional Baseball League (AAGPBL). Organized by Chicago Cubs owner Philip K. Wrigley, the AAGPBL began play in 1943 with teams in Kenosha and Racine in Wisconsin, Rockford, Illinois, and South Bend, Indiana. By the time the league folded in 1954, ten teams had played in more than a dozen cities, including Peoria, Ft. Wayne, Milwaukee, Minneapolis, Grand Rapids, and Chicago.

end of the first season, fourteen clubs would field teams in the APFA. Twelve were from midwestern cities: Akron, Canton, Columbus, Cleveland, and Dayton in Ohio; Hammond and Muncie in Indiana; two Chicago teams, plus Decatur and Rock Island in Illinois; and Detroit, Michigan. The other two teams were in Buffalo and Rochester, New York. A few midwestern teams, like the Columbus Panhandles, barnstormed through the league as "road" teams, while others, like the Hammond Pros, Muncie Flyers, or Minneapolis Marines, played only limited league schedules. The NFL remained dominated by midwestern teams from small cities until the late 1920s. It would not be until 1925, when the New York Giants joined the NFL, that the league would enter the nation's largest market. When the Portsmouth (Ohio) Spartans moved to Detroit in 1934 and became the Lions, only the Green Bay Packers remained a small-market team.

A distinctively midwestern style influenced play in professional football. The University of St. Louis team probably threw the first forward pass in September 1906; within a month the Massillon Tigers, one of Ohio's top professional teams, were using it. By the late 1920s, the forward pass had become common in the NFL, with Benny Friedman of the Cleveland Bulldogs becoming the league's premier passer, eventually taking his game to the New York Giants from 1929 to 1931.

The National Basketball Association (NBA) also had roots in the Midwest. Basketball came to Indiana in 1892, shortly after it was invented in Springfield, Massachusetts. The game suited small towns and rural states and seemed to fit the agricultural cycle. Winter was the perfect time for games and spectator sports, and basketball required only a few players and venues sometimes as rustic as a barn. By the 1910s, barnstorming professional teams, like the Indianapolis Em-Roes, a team established by the Em-Roes Sporting Goods Company, were taking the professional game throughout the Midwest. In 1922, when the Fort Wayne Knights of Columbus played two games with the New York Original Celtics (champions of the East), the contests garnered national attention and professional basketball in the Midwest took a step forward.

The first professional league with national pretensions was the American Basketball League (ABL), established in 1925 by many of the same men associated with the NFL, including NFL president Joe Carr, who also served as president of the ABL. The league included teams in Cleveland, Chicago, Detroit, and Fort Wayne. The ABL collapsed during the Depression in 1931, but in 1935, teams established the Midwest Basketball Conference (MBC) composed of squads in Akron, Dayton, Pittsburgh, Buffalo, Chi-

cago, Indianapolis, and Windsor (Ontario, Canada). Much like the NFL Chicago Bears and Green Bay Packers, the ABL and the MBC each included midwest franchises with corporate sponsors. Frequently, these teams included on their rosters players from the company or the local community, and companies often created places on their payrolls for the players. These local connections brought teams closer to their fans, who found themselves cheering not only their teams, but their friends and fellow blue-collar workers, as well. The MBC became the National Basketball League (NBL) in 1937 and merged with the Basketball Association of America, an East Coast professional league, to become the NBA in 1949.

During the early days of professional basketball in the Midwest, the game underwent innovations and a different style emerged. Although the ABL survived only a few years, the league introduced several important changes to the game. The ABL was the first professional league to mandate the use of backboards, to prohibit the two-hand dribble, to fix schedules, and to require player contracts. The ABL also initiated the three-second lane. Aside from rules changes, the Midwest offered a new style of professional basketball. Traditionally, basketball was a game of ball control. Rules prohibited dribbling; only passes could advance the ball. The style fit in well with Victorian admonitions of self-control, and even after dribbling was permitted, ball control dominated the East Coast game. The midwestern game, inspired by players like John Wooden, who played with the Indianapolis Kautskys of the NBL and later coached at Indiana State University and led UCLA to ten national championships, was a faster and rougher style that emphasized the fast break and the jump shot. When the NBL eliminated the center jump after each basket in 1938, it proved perfect for the Midwest style. The Midwest game would eventually dominate the NBA.

The Midwest has also contributed to the development of professional soccer and hockey. From the inception of the American League of Professional Football in 1894, which included a St. Louis franchise, to the emergence of Major League Soccer (MLS) in 1996, more than six professional soccer leagues appeared in the United States, with most located on the East Coast. Prior to the MLS, significant leagues included the American Soccer League (ASL), established in 1921. Beginning in 1972, the ASL had Midwest franchises in Cincinnati, Chicago, Cleveland, Columbus, Detroit, and Indianapolis. When the ASL folded in 1983, the North American Soccer League (NASL) had already supplanted it as professional soccer's premier league. By the mid-1970s, the NASL consisted of twenty teams in four divisions, with Chicago, Minnesota, and St. Louis representing the Midwest before the league collapsed in 1984. Today, the MLS is well represented in the Midwest with teams in Chicago, Columbus, and Kansas City.

The National Hockey League (NHL) came to the Midwest in 1926, nine years after teams in Toronto, Montreal, and Ottawa established the league. Boston became the first U.S. city to field an NHL team in 1924, with franchises in Chicago and Detroit soon to follow. After expansion in 1967, the league placed teams in Minneapolis and St. Louis.

Individual sports were gaining in popularity among wealthy Americans by the turn of the century. In 1894, Chicagoan Charles Blair Macdonald joined members of several East Coast golf clubs to form the United States Golf Association. Macdonald built the first eighteen-hole golf course in the United States at the Chicago Golf Club, where the third U.S. Open championship was held in 1897. The U.S. Open became the most significant of professional golf's four major championships. In all, Midwest sites have hosted one-third of all U.S. Open championships, and today the Professional Golfers Association tour holds six to eight annual tournaments in the Midwest.

As professional sport integrated and became a multibillion-dollar bureaucratized and commercial business in the late twentieth century, the Midwest continued to play a significant role. When Larry Doby integrated the American League in 1947 by signing with the Cleveland Indians, for example, he had played professional baseball in the Negro Leagues, which had franchises throughout the Midwest. By creating new rules and styles, as well as contributing new leagues and franchises, the Midwest has been central to the development of professional sport.

Sources and Further Reading: Roger Allaway, Colin Jose, and David Litterer, *The Encyclopedia of American Soccer History* (2001); Andrew R. L. Cayton and Peter S. Onuf, *The Midwest and the Nation: Rethinking the History of an American Region* (1990); Stephen Fox, *Big Leagues: Professional Baseball, Football, and Basketball in National Memory* (1994); Warren Goldstein and Elliott J. Gorn, *A Brief History of American Sports* (1993); Elliott J. Gorn, *The Manly Art: Bare-Knuckle Prize Fighting in America* (1986); Todd Gould, *Pioneers of the Hardwood: Indiana and the Birth of Professional Basketball* (1998); David S. Neft and Richard M. Cohen, *The Football Encyclopedia: The Complete History of Professional Football from 1892 to the Present,* 2nd ed. (1994); Robert W. Peterson, *Pigskin: The Early Years of Pro Football* (1997); Benjamin G. Rader, *American Sports: From the Age of Folk Games to the Age of Televised Sports,* 4th ed. (1999); Benjamin G. Rader, *Baseball: A History of America's Game* (1992); John F. Rooney, Jr., *A Geography of American Sport: From Cabin Creek to Anaheim* (1974).

Brian Butler
University of Texas–Pan American

All-American Girls' Baseball League (AAGBL)

The All-American Girls' Baseball League (1943–1954) was a unique moment in women's sport history. The first women's professional baseball league attracted more than six hundred American, Canadian, and Cuban girls in teams located in the Midwest.

The league was a response to conditions created by World War II. By the start of the 1943 professional baseball season, more than three thousand minor leaguers had joined the service or taken war-related jobs. Only nine of twenty-six minor baseball leagues were able to field teams. Major league teams suffered losses as well, since most of the star players joined the war effort. In addition, gasoline rationing limited people's ability to travel and put a premium on local entertainment.

Philip K. Wrigley (1894–1977), the chewing gum mogul who owned the Chicago Cubs major league franchise, decided to create and manage a women's league to keep people interested in baseball. He recruited the best softball players and formed four teams located in medium-sized industrial cities around Chicago. Each team included sixteen players, usually in their late teens and early twenties, a coach, a business manager, and a woman chaperone to make sure that players behaved off the field. Stepping into a men's domain represented a threat to the established gender code and could therefore only be embraced if the players did not appear too masculine. This explains why uniforms emphasized gender more than practicality and why the spring training schedule included charm school classes.

Because it represented a unique athletic and financial opportunity for girls, the league was able to expand from four to ten teams. Rules were also modified over time, from a mixture of softball and baseball to baseball only, highlighting players' ability to master a male sport. In 1948, up to 910 thousand fans paid to attend games. Wrigley succeeded in selling his league because it maintained the players' femininity even as it showcased the girls' baseball skills. He also packaged it as a patriotic venture, organizing exhibition games at army camps.

As the United States recovered from World War II, attendance declined. The end of gasoline rationing gave people more freedom to travel to games. In addition, men were home, stimulating the renewal of major league baseball. The development of television provided alternative entertainment.

The league decentralized in 1951. Since each host city was left to assume full control of its team, there was no more national recruiting system and publicity campaign for the League. Finally, at a time when many Americans wanted a society with male providers and female homemakers, a women's baseball league seemed an anomaly. After the 1954 season, the league disappeared.

Until the late 1970s, the league was largely forgotten. With the popularity of the film *A League of Their Own* (1992), interest revived. In 1988, the National Baseball Hall of Fame officially acknowledged women's contribution to baseball history by displaying a "Women in Baseball" collection.

Sources and Further Reading: Gai Ingham Berlage, *Women in Baseball* (1994); Patricia I. Brown, *A League of My Own* (2003); Susan K. Cahn, *Coming on Strong* (1994); Merrie A. Fidler, "The Development and Decline of the All-American Girls Baseball League, 1943–1954," Ph.D. diss., University of Massachusetts (1976).

Cécile Houry
University of Miami, Florida

Indianapolis 500 and the Indianapolis Motor Speedway Hall of Fame

The Indianapolis Motor Speedway was the brainchild of Indianapolis business tycoons Carl G. Fisher, James A. Allison, Arthur C. Newby, and Frank H. Wheeler. They were the principal financial sponsors of the two-and-a-half-mile oval track built in 1909. On Memorial Day 1911, the Speedway hosted the inaugural Indianapolis 500 Mile Race.

The original surface, tarmacadam, was not designed for race cars, and in 1909, the track was resurfaced with 3.2 million paving bricks. An asphalt resur-

facing project was started in 1937, and new racing surfaces were laid down in 1976, 1988, and 1995. A three-foot-wide strip made out of the original bricks stands at the starting line as both architectural relic and historical symbol. While a sense of history is palpable at Indianapolis, the once grand wooden spectator stands have been replaced by modern steel and concrete structures.

The dimensions of the track attest to its reputation as the premier racetrack in the world. The front and back stretches measure five-eighths of a mile and the corners are banked at nine degrees and twelve minutes. Reserved seating tops 250 thousand spectators, but the infield (very similar to Louisville's Churchill Downs) can accommodate 150 thousand more.

The history of the Speedway is peopled by a succession of racing icons, ranging from the inaugural winner Ray Harroun to four-time winner A. J. Foyt, Jr., In the 1960s, when champion European Formula drivers such as Jack Brabham, Jim Clark, Graham Hill, and Jackie Stewart competed, their presence made the 500 the world's most talked-about auto race.

The Hall of Fame, built in 1956 and substantially expanded in 1976, is a dominating presence with its robust cement structure offset by an aesthetically appealing glass canopy. It is home to Ray Harroun's victorious 1911 racer ("The Marmon Wasp") and showcases A. J. Foyt's four champion cars.

Sources and Further Reading: F. M. Blunk, "Fate is His Co-Driver," *New York Times* (June 1, 1967); Scott A.G.M. Crawford, "The Indianapolis Motor Speedway Hall of Fame," *Journal of Sport History* 25 (Spring 1998); Scott A.G.M.

Indianapolis Auto Race (500) in 1928. Chicago Historical Society, *Chicago Daily News*, SDN-067644.

Crawford, "Raymond Harroun," in D. C. Porter, ed., *Biographical Dictionary of American Sports* (1995); Jan Shaffer et al., *Indianapolis 500 Media Fact Book* (1997).

Scott A.G.M. Crawford
Eastern Illinois University

NASCAR and the Indianapolis Speedway

The origins of stock car racing can be found in rural, southeastern America in the 1920s and 1930s. Regional groups representing rival drivers offered competitive races in which stripped-down and souped-up streetcars raced against one another. The sport did not become an organized sport until William "Bill" France, Sr., created the National Association for Stock Car Auto Racing (NASCAR) on December 12, 1947.

NASCAR's first national championship took place on June 19, 1949, in Charlotte, North Carolina. In 1959, a state-of-the-art race track opened in Daytona, Florida. Nevertheless, as late as 1990, stock car racing was still perceived as a quasi-outlaw, blue-collar sport with roots in the Old South. According to sports geographers John F. Rooney, Jr., and Richard Pillsbury, "NASCAR has attempted to nationalize its racing arena several times through the years, but was generally thwarted by the Midwest's traditional relations with local racing associations."

All of this changed dramatically when NASCAR successfully negotiated with the Indianapolis Speedway and arranged for the Brickyard 400 to take place on the world's most famous racing track in 1994. Literally overnight, stock car racing moved from the margins of American sport to command television audiences, commercial sponsorship, and spectator attendance. Everything conspired to make that first Brickyard a banner event for NASCAR. The winner of the inaugural race was the reigning glamour boy of stock car racing, Jeff Gordon. With a brightly colored race team known as the Rainbow Warriors and his matinee idol looks, Gordon gave the sport a touch of modernity. Much was made of the fact that, at heart, Gordon was a midwesterner. He was the Lizton, Indiana, high school prom king in 1989.

By 2001, the Brickyard 400 was so firmly established on the American sporting calendar that *USA Today* published a twelve-page special feature on August 3–5. Although the majority of Winston Cup races—the stock car annual championship to find the premier driver—are still found in the South, they have expanded significantly into the Midwest, including races in Michigan, Kansas City, and Joliet, Illinois.

Stock car racing at the start of the twenty-first century had impressive statistics. NASCAR was worth nearly $3 billion in television rights, and audiences for its regular telecasts were second in size only to those for National Football League games. The Brickyard 400 has also showcased important technological advances. In 2002, NASCAR embraced safer race track buffers and successfully installed "soft walls" made of concrete and foam that cushion the impact.

Although the Brickyard 400 does not threaten to usurp the Daytona 500 as NASCAR's most prestigious race, it has come to be seen as an important Midwest cultural celebration. Driver Kyle Petty described the Indianapolis Speedway thus: "Stock cars, Indy cars, school buses—and that would be a heck of a place for a school bus race—no matter what they run there, it's going to be big."

Sources and Further Reading: Scott A.G.M. Crawford, "Bill France" and "Jeff Gordon," in A. Markoe, eds., *The Scribner Encyclopedia of American Live—Sports Figures* (2002); Kathy Persinger, *The History of America's Greatest Stock Car Tracks* (2002); John F. Rooney, Jr., and Richard Pillsbury, *Atlas of American Sport* (1992).

Scott A.G.M. Crawford
Eastern Illinois University

Professional Baseball

Baseball, America's national pastime, grew out of European games like the British rounders and cricket. But professional baseball is an American phenomenon with its roots in the Midwest. A few early players took pay, but the first salaried team emerged in Cincinnati in 1869. Harry Wright, a native of England, was its manager, and his brother George was the shortstop and the highest salaried player at $1,400 a season. Investors led by Aaron Champion financed the team, which drew 179 thousand spectators, but earned less than two dollars that first year.

Before 1860, baseball was largely limited to the Northeast. But the Civil War changed that, as both Union and Confederate soldiers took the game home with them. By war's end, the game had a national following and was considered instrumental in national reconciliation. Its popularity also erased the stigma of professionalism. Before the war, players looked down on those who took pay. But "professional" eventually came to mean those who played the game at the highest level.

Perhaps because of the region's head start in professionalism, midwestern natives profoundly affected the game. More than half of the pioneers and executives in the National Baseball Hall of Fame were born in the Midwest, and many others worked there. William

OLD JUDGE
CIGARETTE FACTORY.
GOODWIN & CO., New York.

Charles Brynan, pitcher for the Des Moines Hawkeyes, 1888. Library of Congress, Prints and Photographs Division, LOT 13163-05, no. 433.

Hulbert, Chicago White Stockings owner, formed the National League in 1876. The American League was born in 1901 when Ban Johnson converted his minor Western League to a major league. Andrew "Rube" Foster, owner of the Chicago American Giants, organized the Negro National League in 1920, strengthening black baseball. Philip Wrigley, owner of the Chicago Cubs, founded the All-American Girl's Professional Baseball League in 1943, fielding teams in the Midwest.

Branch Rickey reintegrated the game by bringing Jackie Robinson to Brooklyn in 1947 after introducing

the farm system at St. Louis. William Louis "Bill" Veeck, Jr. (1914–1986) broke the American League racial barrier when he signed Larry Doby at Cleveland, also in 1947. Four years later, Veeck, more for promotion than progress, made history in another way by sending 3'7''? Eddie Gaedel to bat for the St. Louis Browns. Gaedel walked but was banned from further competition for lack of skill.

New technology found fertile ground in Midwest baseball. In 1930, the first regular season night game was held in Independence, Kansas, and the Kansas City Monarchs introduced portable lights to Negro baseball. In 1935, Cincinnati began playing at night and later became the first team to travel by airplane to away games. The Reds played Brooklyn in the first televised game in 1939.

Harry Wright is credited with introducing the now-traditional uniform when he outfitted players in knickerbockers. But not all innovations worked. Player and club owner Albert Goodwill Spalding missed in 1882 when he developed baseball uniforms color coded by position. The resulting rainbow embarrassed the players, ending the trial. Spalding organized baseball's first round-the-world tour in 1888 and is considered the first great sports equipment merchandiser.

On the diamond, the first major star was Mike "King" Kelly, whose nineteenth century Chicago Nationals fans called out, "Slide, Kelly, Slide!" The later shift from emphasizing defense and finesse scoring to power hitting was evident in the Midwest. Hack Wilson batted in a record 191 runs at Chicago in 1930. Roger Maris, born in Minnesota in 1934 and reared in North Dakota, hit sixty-one home runs in 1961 to break Babe Ruth's long-standing mark of sixty. St. Louis Cardinal Mark McGwire in 1998 became the first major leaguer to hit seventy home runs in a season. Cincinnati's Pete Rose's 4,256 career hits are the all-time record.

Johnny Vander Meer pitched consecutive no-hitters for Cincinnati in 1938. In 1968, Detroit's Denny McLain became the first modern pitcher with a 30-win season, earning the Cy Young Award as the American League's outstanding pitcher. The award honors Ohio native Young, who won 511 games and lost 316, both records. From Pete Gray, who lost an arm but played for the Cleveland Browns, to Zane Grey, better remembered for writing than hitting, midwestern athletes are prominent in professional baseball history.

But there were low periods. Baseball's biggest scandal occurred when gamblers allegedly bribed key White Sox players to throw the 1919 World Series, giving them the name "Black Sox." To restore credibility, Ohio-born Judge Kenesaw Mountain Landis

(1866–1944) became baseball's first commissioner. Nor did problems end with the Black Sox scandal. In 1920, Carl Mays threw the only pitch to kill a major leaguer, Cleveland shortstop Ray Chapman. Later in the century, Denny McLain and Pete Rose's off-field problems landed them in prison.

Still, baseball has long flourished in the Midwest. Thirteen cities have had big league baseball teams, 317 towns have had minor league franchises, and at least eight cities hosted forty Negro League teams, including eight from Cleveland. The Negro Leagues Baseball Museum is in Kansas City, Missouri. The National Collegiate Athletic Association and nonprofessional championships are determined annually in Omaha and Wichita. The House of David, a Michigan Jewish organization, sponsors a team that tours nationally.

Baseball always has been a game of boyhood dreams. Iowan Herbert Hoover realized this when he played at Stanford. Dwight Eisenhower is said to recall a youthful conversation with a friend about their ambitions. Ike wanted to be a professional baseball player like Honus Wagner. His friend wanted to be president. Neither dream came true, Eisenhower said.

So intertwined are baseball, dreams, and the Midwest that when the W. P. Kinsella novel, *Shoeless Joe*, was adapted for a movie, it was called *Field of Dreams* (1989) and set in an Iowa cornfield.

Sources and Further Reading: Paul Adomites et al., *Treasury of Baseball* (1994); Warren Goldstein, *Playing for Keeps* (1989); Frederick Ivor-Campbell, ed., *Baseball's First Stars* (1996); National Baseball Hall of Fame, *National Baseball Hall of Fame and Museum Yearbook* (1995); Robert Obojski, *Bush League: A History of Minor League Baseball* (1975); Harold Seymour, *Baseball: The People's Game* (1990); Jules Tygiel, *Past Time* (2000); Geoffrey C. Ward and Ken Burns, *Baseball: An Illustrated History* (1994).

Bob Rives
Wichita State University, Kansas

Professional Basketball

Basketball was invented in 1891 in Springfield, Massachusetts, and within the year had spread to most of the country through the YMCA and settlement houses. Basketball was particularly popular in the Midwest for a number of reasons. Geographer John Bale offers the "geographic thesis." The winter weather was not generally cold enough to produce consistent snow and freezing to make sports like skating, ice fishing, and skiing as popular as they were in the Northeast, nor was it warm enough to allow for longer outdoor seasons for things like football or baseball as in more southern climes. Thus, activity was pushed inside, and that fit nicely with the new sport of basketball. Another factor was the small size of teams, which meant that even the smallest rural area (which was much of the Midwest) could field a squad. The game also could be played in limited space and with rules modified as needed.

By 1910, many midwestern towns had formed teams, some of which were paid by local merchants. The distinction between professional and amateur was not always clear. In 1914, Frank Basloe's Globe Trotters from the Northeast toured the Midwest, playing teams throughout Illinois, Indiana, Wisconsin, and Ohio, and in 1916, the Basloe squad played as a professional team based in Fond du Lac, Wisconsin. With no other evening entertainment, basketball at any level became the top winter attraction.

In 1925, the American Basketball League (ABL) was formed with teams from Boston to Chicago. Midwestern teams were located in Chicago, Fort Wayne (Indiana), Detroit, and Cleveland. The teams were reflective of both their fans and their ownership. The Detroit team, owned by the *Pulaski Post*, reflected its Polish fan base and players. The Cleveland team, the Rosenblums, was owned by Max Rosenblum who had a department store, Rosenblum's, and used the team to advertise. Most of the players were professionals from the East, but Fort Wayne had some local players, which drew the support of Indiana fans. Pay was low and the fan base was not yet well developed or defined. In 1930, a team sponsored by Red Man Tobacco played as the Toledo Redmen.

During this period of time, Abe Saperstein (1902–1966) convinced a group of black former high school teammates from Chicago, who were playing as the Savoy Big Five before mostly black audiences, to take him on as their booking manager. The team first toured as Saperstein's New York (to imply sophistication) and then changed their name in the 1930s to Saperstein's Harlem Globe Trotters. The creation of an all-black team that played (and beat) white teams exemplified the high degree of racial segregation in professional sports, as well as the underlying (and often overt) tension that characterized race relations in the United States.

Beginning in the mid-1920s, many town teams in the Midwest began to bring in occasional outsiders from the larger region to play for them. By the 1930s, many of these teams had formed outstanding squads, some of which were affiliated with large businesses that employed them and sponsored the teams. Top teams included the Akron Firestone Nonskids, the Akron Goodyear Wingfoots, the Fort Wayne General Electrics, and the Indianapolis U.S. Tires. Other teams were sponsored by individuals or small businesses who did not employ them such as the Indianapolis Kautskys or the Chicago Duffy Florals. Many of the professionals were teachers and coaches who had played in college. In 1935, a number of these teams formed a semiprofessional league called the Midwest Basketball Conference.

Two years later a number of the teams restructured and renamed their league the National Basketball League (NBL). Joining this league was a squad from Oshkosh called the All-Stars; the next year, the Sheboygan Redskins joined the league. Even though Oshkosh was their home, the All-Stars played home games all over eastern Wisconsin, giving the team a statewide affiliation. During the life of the league, the top players in professional basketball played in the NBL cities; these included, at one time or another, Columbus, Cincinnati, Dayton, and Youngstown in Ohio; Whiting, Richmond, Hammond, and Anderson in Indiana; Minneapolis, Minnesota; Flint, Michigan; Kankakee, Illinois; Waterloo, Iowa; and the Tri-Cities of Illinois and Iowa.

The leading scorers of the early NBL were John Wooden from Martinsville, Indiana, who had starred at Purdue University and then achieved coaching greatness at UCLA, and Leroy Edwards of Indianapolis who played a year at the University of Kentucky before turning pro with the U.S. Tires team, then spending thirteen years with the Oshkosh All-Stars. Later stars included Bobby McDermott who played for Fort Wayne and Chicago, and George Mikan who led the Chicago Gears and the Minneapolis Lakers to NBL titles.

The Basketball Association of America (BAA) began in 1946 and lasted three years before merging with the NBL to form the National Basketball Association (NBA). Two BAA teams, the Detroit Falcons and the Cleveland Rebels, lasted only one year, and the St. Louis Bombers and Chicago Stags existed for one year after the BAA–NBL merger. The merger led to a stronger league, but Midwest teams were only in Fort Wayne, Indianapolis, Minneapolis, and Milwaukee by 1953. The Minneapolis Lakers dominated the league with George Mikan, but they moved to Los Angeles in 1960.

The Hawks moved from Milwaukee to St. Louis in 1955, and the Pistons moved from Fort Wayne to Detroit in 1957, the same year the Royals moved from Rochester to Cincinnati. Chicago returned to the league with a new team, the Packers, in 1961, but they moved two years later. In 1966 the Bulls joined the league in Chicago, and the Milwaukee Bucks entered the league in 1968, the same year the Hawks moved to Atlanta. Detroit's Pistons, led by Isiah Thomas, won the NBA title in 1989–1990. The Chicago Bulls led by Michael Jordan won the title in 1991–1993, after

which Jordan retired; the team again led the league from 1996 to 1998 with the "unretired" Jordan. Although professional teams in Chicago, Detroit, Minneapolis (Timberwolves), Milwaukee, Cleveland (Cavaliers), and Indiana (Pacers) continue the tradition of quality, the league is no longer as close to its local fan base as were the early NBA teams.

Sources and Further Reading: John Bale, *Sports Geography*, 2nd ed. (2003); Todd Gould, *Pioneers of the Hardwood* (1998); Zander Hollander and Alex Sachare, eds., *The Official NBA Basketball Encyclopedia* (1989); Michael Jordan with Mark Vancil, *For The Love of The Game: My Story* (1998); George Mikan and Joseph Oberle, *Unstoppable* (1997); David Neft et al., *The Sports Encyclopedia: Pro Basketball* (1975); Rodger Nelson, *The Zollner Piston Story* (1995); Robert Peterson, *Cages to Jump Shots* (1990); Richard Triptow, *The Dynasty that Never Was* (1997).

Murray Nelson
Pennsylvania State University–University Park

Professional Football

Whereas amateur football evolved out of soccer and rugby games played in the prestigious Ivy League universities during the 1880s, professional football was spawned in the athletic and social clubs of the Midwest. Sports competition among such clubs led them to offer outstanding athletes trophies, memberships, and finally money. The first recorded professional football player, three-time Yale All-American Walter "Pudge" Heffelfinger, was paid an astounding $500 under the table by the Allegheny Athletic Association in 1892 to help defeat archrival Pittsburgh Athletic Club. Three years later after a half-dozen more players were given secret payoffs, John Brallier became the first player to admit being paid when he received $10 for a game for the Latrobe (Pennsylvania) Athletic Association.

Pro football interest waned in western Pennsylvania at the beginning of the twentieth century, but in 1903, the semipro Massillon (Ohio) Tigers imported four Pittsburgh professionals to win the state championship. Over the next few seasons many teams imported and paid players. Particularly notable were Massillon and neighboring Canton, whose rivalry led to fully professional rosters and huge payrolls. In 1906, both teams spent themselves into bankruptcy. The season ended with unpaid players stranded in Ohio and various unproven charges of game-fixing. Pro football in Ohio retreated to a semipro level for the next few years. Only the Columbus Panhandles, manned by the six burly Nesser brothers, and the Shelby Blues and Akron Indians, with teams led by

George "Peggy" Parratt, a former Massillon quarterback, rose above the pack in Ohio during most seasons.

During this period, most cities and towns of consequence across the Midwest fielded at least one independent team. Usually a small admission was charged or sometimes a hat might be passed for donations. After the game, the proceeds would be shared among the players. On rare occasions when the outcome of a game loomed particularly large because of civic pride or fans' wagers, a "ringer" might be imported, but most of the players were local farmers and tradesmen, with a sprinkling of players who had college football experience. Among the more successful teams were those in Evanston (Illinois), Pine Village (Indiana), and Minneapolis.

Many town teams looked for better players. Massillon jumped back into pro football with a vengeance in 1915 by hiring for the Tigers most of Akron's best players plus several stars from outside Ohio. Archrival Canton responded with similar hirings. In November, Canton made a landmark move by paying Jim Thorpe, the most famous athlete in America, $250 for each of the Bulldogs' two games against Massillon.

Although the Bulldogs and Tigers split those two games, former All-American and Olympic hero Thorpe (1887–1953) earned his money by leading Canton to great seasons in 1916 and 1917, when the Bulldogs were considered by most the professional champions of the United States.

By becoming a professional, Thorpe lent legitimacy to professional football. Until then, despite its fans in the Midwest, most of the country either ignored pro football or found it somehow disreputable. Thorpe's hiring not only inspired many other teams across the Midwest to upgrade their lineups, it also caused many well-known former college players from outside the Midwest to try the professional game.

Proposals for a professional football league had been around for some time. Hammond, Pine Village, and Wabash formed a small Indiana league in 1917, but it lasted only one year. By 1919, soaring expenses caused by bidding for star players caused the Ohio teams to create a league. After meeting in Canton on August 20, the Canton Bulldogs, Akron Pros, Cleveland Tigers, and Dayton Triangles called for a meeting of the managers of the leading midwestern teams for the purpose of forming a professional league. On September 17, 1920, representatives from eleven midwestern teams met in Canton: the Akron, Canton, Cleveland, Dayton, and the Massillon Tigers from Ohio; the Hammond Pros and Muncie Flyers from Indiana; the Rock Island Independents, Decatur Stayleys, and Racine (Chicago) Cardinals from Illinois;

and the Rochester Jeffersons from New York. Although Massillon decided against fielding a team, the others formed the American Professional Football Association (APFL). Joining later were the Buffalo (New York) All-Americans, Columbus (Ohio) Panhandles, Detroit (Michigan) Heralds, and Chicago (Illinois) Tigers. Jim Thorpe was named league president.

The purpose of the league was to lower expenses. The team owners hoped to limit salaries by stopping players from jumping from team to team. To improve relations with colleges, they also pledged to stop using college players who still retained eligibility. However, the association had no way of enforcing its rules. By November, few mentions of the APFA could be found in newspapers.

At the owners' meeting in early 1921, most were ready to disband the league. President Thorpe did not even attend. Then Joe Carr, the manager of the Columbus Panhandles, took the floor and galvanized the room by proposing a stronger league structure. He was immediately elected president, a post he retained until his death in 1939. The APFA was renamed the National Football League (NFL) in 1922.

In its first few years, NFL membership was fluid. More teams failed than succeeded. New members included the Green Bay (Wisconsin) Packers, Minneapolis (Minnesota) Marines, and Racine (Wisconsin) Legion. Today, only the Packers survive. In fact, seven of the championship teams of the 1920s, are either no longer in operation or have moved to a different city.

In 1925, pro football got a big boost when halfback Harold "Red" Grange (1903–1991) joined the Chicago Bears. Along with Babe Ruth and Jack Dempsey, Grange was one of the superstars of sport in the 1920s. After completing his final season for the University of Illinois the previous Saturday, Grange took the field on Thanksgiving Day. It was the first time Wrigley Field ever sold out for football. Grange continued to draw huge crowds in a hastily arranged tour that included the remainder of the Bears' schedule plus numerous exhibitions. After the NFL season ended, Grange and the Bears continued into the South and ended with games on the West Coast in January. Not only did his tours give pro football a huge publicity boost, the money they raised literally saved some teams from bankruptcy.

The next year, Grange turned from the NFL's greatest friend to its greatest enemy when he and his agent Charles C. "Cash 'n' Carry" Pyle formed their own league, the American Football League (AFL). Many players and even one team, Rock Island, deserted the NFL. The new league placed teams directly opposite NFL teams in New York, Philadelphia, and

Chicago. As a counter to Grange's popularity, the NFL used the Duluth (Wisconsin) Eskimos as a road team with fullback Ernie Nevers, an All-American and Rose Bowl star, to attract fans. When the Grange League, as it was called, failed after one season, the NFL reduced its size in order to keep only profitable franchises. By the end of the decade, most of the NFL's founding teams were gone. The only small-town team to survive the Depression was the Packers.

The Green Bay Packers succeeded because they received strong civic backing. Other small-town teams succumbed to the Depression, but as 1929–1931 league champions, the Packers remained a strong gate attraction. Under innovative Coach Earl Louis "Curly" Lambeau (1898–1965), the Packers remained a power throughout the 1930s with titles in 1936, 1939, and again in 1944. Lambeau had long stressed the passing game, but his team really soared when receiver Don Hutson joined the Packers in 1935.

An even stronger franchise was the Chicago Bears, owned and coached by George Halas (1895–1983). One of the original NFL team managers with Decatur in 1920, Halas won his first NFL championship in 1921, when he moved that team to Chicago, where they became the Bears. He coached his final championship team in 1963. In the interim, the Bears hoisted championship banners in 1932, 1933, 1940, 1941, 1943, and 1946. Halas's Bears are credited with inventing the first modern T-formation, the basis of nearly all offenses in today's football.

Other midwestern cities have had great teams. The Cleveland Browns originated in the NFL rival, the All-America Football Conference (AAFC). After winning all four AAFC championships, the Browns moved to the NFL in 1950 and won three of the next six titles. The Detroit Lions' greatest seasons were 1952 and 1953, when they defeated the Browns in the championship game. The Minnesota Vikings have as yet to win a championship, but the team reached the Super Bowl four times.

Perhaps the most dominant midwestern team was the Green Bay Packers during the 1960s under legendary coach Vince Lombardi (1913–1970). With stars such as Paul Hornung, Bart Starr, and Willie Davis, the Packers won NFL titles in 1961, 1962, and 1965, as well as the first two Super Bowls.

Sources and Further Reading: Jim Campbell, *Golden Years of Pro Football* (1993); Bob Carroll et al., *Total Football II* (1999); Harold (Spike) Claassen, *History of Professional Football* (1963); Richard M. Cohen et al., *Scrapbook History of Pro Football* (1976); Tod Maher and Bob Gill, *The Pro Football Encyclopedia* (1997); David Neft, Richard M. Cohen, and Rick Korch, *The Football Encyclopedia* (1994); NFL Creative,

Official 2003 National Football League Record & Fact Book (2003); Robert W. Peterson, *Pigskin: The Early Years of Pro Football* (1997); Beau Riffenburgh, *The Official NFL Encyclopedia* (1986); Robert Smith, *Illustrated History of Pro Football* (1970).

Bob Carroll
North Huntingdon, Pennsylvania

Professional Hockey

For the past century, professional hockey has provided a welcome winter diversion for many midwesterners, who play at a variety of competitive levels and on different economic scales. Although the sport as we know it today was organized in Montreal during the late nineteenth century, openly professional hockey was first played in the Midwest and neighboring states. Cold winters provided an opportunity for the sport to flourish as it had in Canada, and the rugged sport of hockey appealed to the hard-working sensibilities of inhabitants of the region. Hockey was preceded by two other stick-and-skate sports, roller polo and ice polo, which were popular during the 1880s. Following some exhibition matches between polo teams and Canadian hockey teams, however, hockey was deemed to be a more exciting and vigorous sport and was taken up in earnest in the Midwest. Some observers credit the introduction of hockey to the Midwest to a game between University of Minnesota and the Winnipeg Victorias on February 18, 1895.

The sport quickly emerged as a popular entertainment spectacle in mining communities like Houghton, Michigan, whose Portage Lakes Hockey Club helped the town gain a reputation as the birthplace of hockey in the United States. However, since hockey was so new to the Midwest, few local athletes were playing the game at an advanced level. As a result, players were needed to fill out rosters of teams formed in Pennsylvania and Michigan, where crowds of up to 4,000 paid to see their local teams play. Because experienced players were paid to relocate from Canada (where leagues remained amateur through the beginning of the twentieth century), professional hockey owes its development to entrepreneurs in midwestern towns.

The first openly professional hockey teams operated out of Michigan's Upper Peninsula in the International Hockey League (IHL) between 1904 and 1907. The IHL featured five teams, including Pittsburgh, Pennsylvania; Houghton, Calumet, and Sault Ste. Marie, Michigan; and Sault Ste. Marie, Ontario. Pittsburgh was a geographic outlier, but had gate-sharing agreements that made the long train rides lucrative for the other league clubs and featured a commodious rink with artificial ice, a luxury at the onset of the twentieth century. The other league teams relied on cold weather for playing surfaces, but soon began building artificial ice rinks. Around the turn of the century, St. Louis built its own artificial rink and organized a four-team league that included teams from Michigan and Minnesota. This league was amateur, however, and it would be several decades before that city had professional hockey. Cleveland built the two-thousand-seat Elysium arena in 1907–1908, and in 1911, St. Paul built the Hippodrome.

Interest in early professional teams and the proliferation of rinks laid the groundwork for the home-grown talent who would go on to successful professional hockey careers. One early star was Francis "Moose" Goheen of White Bear Lake, Minnesota. Goheen starred for St. Paul of the professional American Hockey Association (AHA) during the 1920s and, despite efforts by National Hockey League (NHL, formed in 1917) teams to obtain his services, chose to play for the local Minnesota team during his prime. In fact, it has been suggested that the long-range goal of the AHA, which chose not to affiliate with the NHL, was specifically to develop U.S.-born and trained players. In the meantime, the NHL expanded to include several midwestern teams. In 1926, the Detroit Cougars (later the Red Wings) and the Chicago Blackhawks commenced operations, followed in 1934 by the short-lived St. Louis Eagles franchise. In all, minor professional teams and leagues have been in continuous operation since the 1920s and have included franchises in virtually every major urban center. In between the World Wars, the new International Hockey League (IHL) included teams from Toledo, Milwaukee, Muncie, and Akron, while the AHA featured clubs from Omaha, Wichita, Kansas City, St. Paul, and Duluth.

Indianapolis provides one example of the ongoing relationship between professional hockey and midwestern regional centers. Although the city's experiences are unique, they are indicative of the cyclical nature of ice hockey's popularity since the 1930s. The Indiana State Fairgrounds Coliseum was built in 1939 at a cost of one million dollars, and a franchise was entered in the International-American Hockey League (IAHL), which became the American Hockey League the following season. Called the Capitals, the team was a minor league affiliate of the NHL Detroit Red Wings. A crowd of 9,193 attended the opening game, and over the years the team featured Hockey Hall of Fame players Terry Sawchuk, Glenn Hall, and Alex Delvecchio on its roster. The team won the American Hockey League (AHL) championship twice before folding in 1952. Indianapolis has since had two IHL

teams, two Central Hockey League teams, and a World Hockey Association franchise. In all, the city of Indianapolis has had five different professional franchises playing in six different leagues over the past sixty years.

Today the Midwest features five National Hockey League franchises—the Columbus Blue Jackets, Detroit Red Wings, Chicago Blackhawks, St. Louis Blues, and Minnesota Wild—and continues to feature minor professional teams in most of its prominent urban centers. Not only did professional hockey first develop in the Midwest and establish ties with many communities, it continues to be a source of entertainment and civic pride for many people.

Sources and Further Reading: Kevin Allen, "The Origins of American Hockey," in Dan Diamond, ed., *Total Hockey* (1998); Donald M. Clark, "Early Artificial Ice," in Dan Diamond, ed. *Total Hockey* (1998); Ernie Fitzsimmons, "Minor Pro Hockey in the 1920s, 1930s, and 1940s," in Dan Diamond, ed., *Total Hockey* (1998); Daniel S. Mason, "The International Hockey League and the Professionalization of Ice Hockey, 1904–1907," *Journal of Sport History* 25 (Spring, 1998); Daniel Mason and Barbara Schrodt, "Hockey's First Professional Team: The Portage Lakes Hockey Club of Houghton, Michigan," *Sport History Review* 27 (May 1996).

Daniel S. Mason
University of Alberta–Edmonton, Canada

Professional Soccer

Midwestern soccer teams formed in the late nineteenth century around British athletic clubs, religious communities, and industrial sponsorship. These organizations depended on continual European immigration, native talent, and youth development programs. Enough interest developed that in 1901, Chicago White Sox owner Charles Comiskey attempted to form a professional league that featured clubs from Detroit, Chicago, Cleveland, Milwaukee, and St. Louis. The ambitious organization never got off the ground. Consequently, individual midwestern cities, rather than any regional effort, formed local soccer leagues with varying degrees of talent and professionalism throughout the 1900s.

Professional soccer involved individual clubs rather than leagues, except in St. Louis. Beginning in 1891, the St. Louis Major Professional League featured the city's top teams and nationally renowned players. One of its notable clubs, the St. Louis Ben Millers, all local boys, won the prestigious U.S. Open Cup in their 1920 tournament debut. The U.S. Open has been played annually since 1914 and is emblematic of the nation's best soccer club. The Catholic sodalities provided the impetus for St. Louis's soccer success and popularity. Most of the city's parishes sponsored soccer teams that drew players and fans who supported and nurtured the game.

Midwestern industries often sponsored professional teams. These company teams primarily provided employment, facilities, and equipment for a city's best players. During the Depression, most industries could no longer afford soccer expenditures, and many long-standing teams, such as the Chicago Bricklayers, Pullman Car Works, Detroit Packards, Akron Goodyears, and several others from Cleveland, Milwaukee, and St. Louis, folded.

Professional players then turned to ethnic clubs for financial backing. Some of the great professional ethnic teams of this era included the Chicago Spartans, Cleveland Slavics, Milwaukee Viennas, and the St. Louis Shamrocks. These clubs competed with surviving industrial teams such as Milwaukee's Pabst Blue Ribbons, Chicago's Manhattan Brewers, and Detroit's Holly Carburetors.

Regional professional league play began in 1946 when the North American Soccer Football League (NASFL) debuted. This midwestern pro circuit featured the Chicago Maroons, Chicago Vikings, Detroit Wolverines (later Detroit Pioneers), Pittsburgh Indians, St. Louis Raiders, and the Toronto Greenbacks. Detroit and Pittsburgh won titles in 1946 and 1947, respectively. Unfortunately, the league failed financially and folded after the 1947 championship.

Thereafter, professional soccer in the Midwest and United States slipped back into the murky area between amateur and professional. Many players found financial support or employment opportunities, but no professional league (excepting St. Louis) survived. This changed in the late 1960s with the advent of the North American Soccer League (NASL) and the Major Indoor Soccer League (MISL) in the late 1970s.

The NASL emerged from two rival soccer organizations that sought to capitalize on the interest created following England's 1966 World Cup win. Beginning in 1967, professional soccer franchises rose and collapsed in Chicago, Kansas City, Cleveland, Detroit, St. Louis, and Minneapolis. Although dominated by foreign players, the NASL engendered interest in both the indoor and outdoor game and created a massive youth organization. Most of these NASL franchises brought international stars to soccer pitches. St. Louis, however, remained true to its soccer heritage and relied primarily on native talent rather than international players to dominate its roster. Storied NASL franchises include the Chicago Sting, Kansas City Spurs, Minnesota Kicks (later Strikers), and the St. Louis Stars.

The Midwest also contributed to indoor soccer, with many cities promoting teams in the MISL. From 1978 to 1992, Chicago, Cincinnati, Cleveland, Detroit, Kansas City, Wichita, Minneapolis, and St. Louis competed for the league cup in this fast-paced, hybrid game, often played in hockey arenas. Like the NASL, the MISL added many talented foreign players. The St. Louis Steamers again led the way, often fielding St. Louis–born players. Other notable franchises included the Kansas City Comets, Wichita Wings, Cleveland Crunch (later, Force), and the Chicago Horizons.

In 1984, a second professional indoor league debuted, the American Indoor Soccer Association (AISA). Originally, the AISA served as a minor indoor league to the MISL. The Canton Invaders dominated the AISA championship for the first six years except in 1986–1987, when they finished second to Louisville. In 1990, the AISA became the National Professional Soccer League (NPSL) and, for a time, was the only viable professional soccer circuit in the United States. Midwestern clubs commanded the championships, including the Dayton Dynamo, Chicago Power, Cleveland Crunch, Kansas City Attack, Milwaukee Wave, Detroit Rockers, and the St. Louis Ambush. Other participating midwestern cities included Wichita, Cincinnati, and Columbus.

After the collapse of the NASL in 1984, outdoor professional soccer again returned to a semipro status. In 1996 the contemporary Major League Soccer (MLS) emerged as the latest U.S. outdoor professional soccer circuit. Unlike the NASL, the MLS rosters included mostly native-born players. Currently, franchises exist in Chicago, Kansas City, and Columbus. Of these, the Columbus franchise seems the most firmly established, primarily because the team owner paid for the construction of a 22,500-seat soccer venue. This stadium, rather than the mammoth football stadiums where most MLS teams compete, provides a more intimate setting for the fans.

Also in the 1990s, U.S. women's soccer witnessed unprecedented growth. Following the U.S. team's success in several World Cup finals and Olympic championships, a professional women's soccer league formed in 1998. The Women's Premier Soccer League (WPSL), while currently limited to the coasts, features many players who honed their skills in the Midwest.

Historically, professional soccer tends to ebb and flow, existing on the periphery of American sports fans' attention. Whatever the futures of the MLS and the WPSL, midwestern professional soccer tenaciously continues in local parks, indoor arenas, and sport stadiums as it has for the past century.

Sources and Further Reading: Roger Allaway, Colin Jose, and David Litter, *The Encyclopedia of American Soccer History*

(2001); Sam Foulds and Paul Harris, *America's Soccer Heritage* (1979); James Robinson, "The History of Soccer in the City of Saint Louis," Ph.D. diss., St. Louis University (1966).

Gabe Logan
Northern Illinois University

Heroes

Sports and sport teams developed on a more meritocratic basis in the Midwest than in the East. The realities of life in the region meant that social standing, so important in shaping sporting experiences in the East, had little role in structuring midwestern sport. Instead, talent was the most important factor in forming sport teams, opening new opportunities for those who might have been left out of sports circles back East.

The best and earliest example of this is the Cincinnati Red Stockings. Formed in 1869, the Red Stockings was the country's first professional baseball team. The club's president successfully raised money from local businesses to employ star players from eastern teams, emphasizing talent over status. The team won sixty-five games, one of which was a disputed tie/win, and was the only professional baseball team to go undefeated. They traveled over twelve thousand miles, taking the newly completed Transcontinental Railroad to California for exhibition games. By 1876, eight teams, including Chicago, Cincinnati, Louisville, and St. Louis, joined together to form the National League of Professional Baseball Clubs.

During these same years, football, particularly at the collegiate level, was growing in popularity. Football at the turn of the twentieth century was far different then we know it today. Before 1906, the forward pass was prohibited, and even after 1906, it was not widely used. It was a group of midwestern coaches, seeking greater financial returns from football, who implemented rule changes to make the game more fan-friendly, with long-scoring plays that would increase the chance of upsets.

Eastern fans received a taste of the cumulative effect of these rule changes when Knute Rockne's Notre Dame team upset top-ranked Army in 1913 with an offense based on the forward pass. The so-called western passing game was key in making football more appealing to fans. It also led to national recognition for Rockne. After starring for three years on the Fighting Irish roster, Rockne served as head football coach at Notre Dame. His death in a plane crash in 1931 was front-page news across the nation.

The 1920s would prove to be a golden age for spectator sports. The decade saw football stars like Harold "Red" Grange (1903–1991), who excelled for the University of Illinois. In the first game at Illinois's new stadium, Grange stunned the University of Michigan by scoring four touchdowns in the opening twelve minutes of the game, including a ninety-five-yard return of the opening kickoff. Grange's popularity expanded rapidly as newsreel footage enabled thousands of fans across the nation to see his exploits on the gridiron. Grange, unlike most other amateur athletes, elected to continue playing football as a professional, signing with the Chicago Bears and accompanying them on barnstorming tours. Grange capitalized on his enor-

Bob Gibson, Hall of Fame pitcher for the St. Louis Cardinals. National Baseball Hall of Fame Library, Cooperstown, NY.

mous popularity with commercial endorsements for sweaters, shoes, caps, and "Red Grange Chocolates."

James Cleveland "Jesse" Owens (1913–1980) was another stand-out athlete who began his career in the Big Ten. Owens established himself on the sport scene in his sophomore year at The Ohio State University. At the Big Ten conference meet in 1935, he established world records in the broad jump, 220-yard dash, and the 220-yard low hurdles. That same day he tied the world record in the 100-yard dash. Owens would repeat his triumphs on the international stage at the 1936 Summer Olympics in Berlin. There he debunked Adolf Hitler's ideas of Aryan supremacy by becoming the first African American athlete to win four gold medals, in the 100- and 200-meter sprints, the long jump, and the 100-meter relay. For his tremendous athletic achievements, Owens was named the sixth greatest athlete of the twentieth century by ESPN.

In many ways Gale Sayers (b. 1943) inherited Grange's mantle as the flashing halfback of the Chicago Bears. Following a collegiate career at the University of Kansas where he was twice named All-American, Sayers earned Rookie-of-the-Year honors in 1965. Sayers still holds the National Football League (NFL) record for most touchdowns in a game (six) and was named to the NFL's 75th Anniversary All-Time Team.

In the 1965 draft, the Bears used picks three and four to select Richard M. "Dick" Butkus (b. 1942) and Sayers. Considered by many to be the toughest, fiercest, and best linebacker ever, Butkus was also a two-time All-American during his collegiate career. Following his tenure at the University of Illinois, he would come to be known as the prototypical middle linebacker in the NFL. Possessing the speed to defend sideline to sideline, Butkus was most feared for his bone-crunching tackles.

The most recent in a long line of great Bears halfbacks, Walter Payton (1954–1999) is the second all-time leading rusher in the NFL with 16,726 yards and 125 touchdowns in his career. A seven-time All-Pro, "Sweetness" led the league in rushing five times and was twice named NFL Player of the Year. In 1985, he took the Chicago Bears to their only Super Bowl. Unstoppable on the gridiron, Payton died at the age of 45 from complications related to a rare form of liver cancer.

Leroy "Satchel" Paige (1906–1982) was the greatest pitcher of the Negro Leagues. Although he was in his early forties when he was signed by the Cleveland Indians in 1948, he helped lead that franchise to the World Series that year. Paige started in semipro leagues in his native Alabama before starring for Negro League teams in Kansas City, Cleveland, and

Pittsburgh, among other cities. Paige also faced white major leaguers on his numerous barnstorming tours that crisscrossed the country in baseball's off-season. Paige was an enormous drawing card and earned in excess of forty thousand dollars a season with his nationwide tours, more than most professionals earned.

Stanley F. "Stan "The Man" Musial (b. 1920) hit over .300 in his first seventeen seasons, playing the outfield and first base for the St. Louis Cardinals. Named league Most Valuable Player three times in his career, Musial won seven batting titles and completed his career with more extra-base hits than Babe Ruth. Musial's Cardinals won four pennants and the 1946 World Series over the Boston Red Sox.

"Mr. Cub" Ernest "Ernie" Banks (b. 1931) became the first National League player to win back-to-back Most Valuable Player awards in 1958 and 1959. Banks hit 512 home runs in his career, but is perhaps best known for his singular phrase "Let's play two," which best reflects his love of the game. Despite his personal success, Banks never played in the post season.

A star on the "Big Red Machine" teams of the 1970s, Peter Edward "Pete" Rose (b. 1941) is baseball's all-time hitting leader with 4,256. "Charlie Hustle" won two World Series with the Reds and a third with the Phillies in 1980. He was named World Series MVP and *Sports Illustrated* "Sportsman of the Year" for his sterling 1975 season. Rose would return to Cincinnati in 1984, where he was a player-manager through the 1986 season and, after he retired from playing, stayed on as manager through the 1988 campaign. Unfortunately, Rose's legacy and achievements have been tarnished by his sports gambling, which led to a lifetime suspension from all baseball activities. In his 2004 autobiography, *My Prison Without Bars*, Rose finally admitted to betting on baseball.

Hockey emerged as another major sport in the Midwest in the second half of the twentieth century. Czech-born Stanley "Stan" Mikita (b. 1940) played twenty-two seasons for the Chicago Blackhawks. Mikita was a member of the 1960–1961 Stanley Cup Champions. In the 1966–1967 season, he became the first player to win the Hart (MVP), Lady Byng (sportsmanship), and Art Ross (points) trophies in the same season, a feat he repeated the following year. He finished his career with more than five hundred goals and fourteen hundred points.

Mr. Hockey, Gordon "Gordie" Howe (b. 1928), is acclaimed as one of the greatest hockey players ever. In thirty-two seasons spanning six decades, Howe scored 1,071 goals and accumulated 2,589 total points. Howe was recognized for his all-around athleticism and deft scoring touch and was perhaps the most feared hockey player of his day. Howe was a seven-time MVP and six-time scoring champion for the Detroit Red Wings, with whom he spent twenty-five seasons.

Although initially lagging far behind football and baseball in popularity, basketball grew in importance over the last third of the twentieth century. One of the greatest players of this era was Oscar Robertson (b. 1938). Robertson was an All-American at Crispus Attucks High School in Indianapolis, where he led the team to consecutive state titles, the first ever for an all–African American team. From there, Robertson attended the University of Cincinnati, where he led the nation in scoring for three consecutive years. Robertson also starred on the 1960 USA basketball team, which brought home the gold medal. After graduation and his Olympics stint, he signed with the Cincinnati Royals, where he played until being traded to Milwaukee in 1970. Robertson was the all-time assist leader for the National Basketball Association (NBA) when he retired and was voted into the NBA Hall of Fame.

A key event for basketball in the Midwest and the nation was the 1979 National Collegiate Athletic Association (NCAA) championship game between Michigan State University and Indiana State University. Michigan State, led by Earvin "Magic" Johnson, Jr. (b. 1959), won the game over Larry Bird (b. 1956) and the Sycamores. Johnson, then only a sophomore, left Michigan State to join the NBA, where his rivalry with Bird was renewed. After losing to Bird and the Boston Celtics in the 1984 NBA finals, Magic and the Lakers avenged the defeat with victories in both the 1985 and 1987 finals. Their rivalry fueled the enormous growth and popularity of the NBA in the 1980s. Bird and Johnson would each be named NBA MVP three times.

The mantle of Bird and Magic was passed to another superstar playing in the Midwest, Michael Jordan (b. 1963). Considered to be the greatest basketball player ever and named by ESPN as "Athlete of the Century," Michael Jordan led the Chicago Bulls to six NBA championships. He captured five NBA MVP awards. He holds an NBA record of ten scoring titles, remains the NBA's scoring average leader, and is in the top-five for all-time points, steals, field goals, and free throws made. Jordan twice interrupted his career with retirements. After the first in 1993, he played outfield for the Birmingham Barons, the AA affiliate of the Chicago White Sox, where he batted .202 with three home runs. Jordan retired again after the 1997–1998 season, when he assumed a role as general manager and part owner of the Washington Wizards. He came out of retirement for the 2001–2002 and 2002–2003 seasons. Although Jordan's tremendous skills were still evident on occasion, he failed to lead the Wizards to the playoffs in either year.

Baseball in the Midwest enjoyed a resurgence in the 1990s. This trend peaked in the summer of 1998, as Samuel Peralta "Sammy" Sosa (b. 1968) of the Chicago Cubs and St. Louis Cardinal's first baseman Mark McGwire (b. 1963) chased the home run record of North Dakota native Roger Maris (1934–1985). After hitting twenty home runs in June, Sosa joined McGwire in the spotlight and by September the two had become good friends, each pushing the other to excel and rooting for each other in their regular press conferences. When McGwire hit his record-breaking sixty-second home run, he was met at home plate by Sosa, who loudly proclaimed the Cardinal slugger to be "The Man." Both men crushed Maris's record. McGwire ended the season with seventy home runs, Sosa with sixty-six.

The Midwest has also produced a number of world-famous athletes in individual sports. Jack Nicklaus (b. 1940), who holds a record of twenty major golf tournament titles, was the greatest golfer of his era and was named *Sports Illustrated*'s Athlete of the Decade of the 1970s. He was five times Professional Golfers of America's player of the year and was acknowledged as one of the ten greatest athletes of the century by ESPN.

Jackie Joyner-Kersee (b. 1962) dominated the sport of women's track and field and particularly its most demanding event, the heptathlon. Joyner-Kersee overcame poverty, discrimination, and asthma to achieve greatness. She holds the world record and the next five highest point totals in that event. After missing the gold medal in the 1984 Olympics by less then one second overall, she went on to win the gold in the next two Olympiads. She added a gold medal in 1988 and bronze medals in 1992 and 1996 in the long jump, to become America's most decorated track and field athlete.

Sources and Further Reading: Elliott J. Gorn and Warren Goldstein, *A Brief History of American Sports* (1993); Mike McGovern, *The Encyclopedia of Twentieth-Century Athletes* (2001); Benjamin G. Rader, *American Sports: From the Age of Folk Games to the Age of Televised Sports*, 4th ed. (1999).

Jonathan Mercantini
Canisius College, Buffalo, New York,

Broadcasting

Given the central role of sports in the development of broadcasting as a popular medium, it seems appropriate that the first ship-to-shore radio message in 1907 described the results of a yachting race on Lake Erie. The location is also fitting in light of the Midwest's role in sports broadcasting history.

Harry Caray, Chicago and St. Louis sportscaster. National Baseball Hall of Fame Library, Cooperstown, NY.

Although Pittsburgh radio station KDKA is credited with being the first commercial station to air a live sporting contest, in 1921, stations in Chicago, Detroit, Cincinnati, St. Louis, and Cleveland aggressively pursued sports coverage on radio. In 1925, WMAQ in Chicago convinced Chicago Cubs owner William Wrigley, Jr. (1861–1932), to allow the station to broadcast his team's home games. Seeing the impact those broadcasts had on home attendance—women became fans in such numbers that the Cubs offered special Ladies' Days—Wrigley invited any station to broadcast Cubs games, and soon five Chicago stations had taken him up on the offer. One of those stations, WGN, not only broadcast the Cubs, but also aired live coverage of the Indianapolis 500 and Kentucky Derby.

In Cleveland, former Indians outfielder Jack Graney (1886–1978) was hired by radio station WHK as the team's play-by-play announcer, thus beginning the practice that continues to this day of former athletes moving to the broadcast booth. Graney was also one of the first radio announcers to do telegraphic re-creations of his team's road games. This involved taking Western Union's basic play-by-play account of a game and turning it into a fully produced broadcast replete with sound effects of cheering crowds. In the mid-1930s, a young announcer for WHO in Des Moines named Ronald Reagan (1911–2004) ran into a common problem with telegraphic re-creations, when the wire account of a Cubs game was temporarily lost. The future president was forced to have the batter hit foul balls for over six minutes until the service was restored. It then turned out that the batter had been retired on the first pitch.

College football also became quickly popular with midwestern radio audiences. Even before KDKA's broadcast of the first baseball game, an experimental radio station at the University of Minnesota attempted in 1912 to broadcast by wireless telegraph a description of a university football game. The University of Notre Dame saw radio as a means to gain nationwide prominence. Echoing the Cubs' policy regarding radio, Notre Dame invited any station to come to South Bend and broadcast its football games. By the late 1920s, so many stations had done so that Notre Dame became, in effect, the first "America's team." By contrast, most Big Ten schools by the mid-1930s began selling the rights to their football games to local stations for sums that seem trivial in light of modern fees. In 1934, the University of Michigan received twenty thousand dollars from Detroit station WWJ for the rights to air its football games.

The conditions for early broadcasters were also often primitive compared to press boxes in modern stadiums. In the early days of WWJ's coverage of Michigan football, the announcers broadcast from seats in the stadium. Play-by-play announcer Pappy Tyson's statistician kept a rolled-up newspaper in his pocket to swat zealous fans who would jump up and block Tyson's view of the game.

Many of the Midwest radio stations that carried sports took advantage of both public policy and technology to reach broad audiences. The Federal Communications Commission had designated some radio outlets as "clear channel" stations, thus allowing them to broadcast at enhanced power unimpeded by stations on the same frequency. The reach of these stations was further enhanced by the phenomenon of sky waves, which allows AM radio signals to skip off the ionosphere at night and travel great distances. Thus, stations such as KMOX in St. Louis, WGN in Chicago, and WLW in Cincinnati (which for a few years had FCC authority to broadcast at 500 thousand watts, or ten times more than the power of contemporary stations) blanketed cities and rural areas from the eastern seaboard to the Rocky Mountains. The St. Louis Cardinals used the power of KMOX, combined with scores of station affiliates that also carried Cardinals games, to become, much like Notre Dame, extraordinarily popular with fans far removed from the team's home base. That popularity was further spurred by one of the most noteworthy sports broadcasters to emerge from the Midwest, Harry Caray (1914–1998). Caray's unabashed support of his Cardinals (which included vocal criticism of players who played poorly) resonated with fans across the listening audience. Caray spent twenty-five years broadcasting Cardinals games before moving to Chicago, where he first broadcast for the Chicago White Sox and then, most famously, for the Chicago Cubs on WGN television and radio.

A number of the radio stations that took the lead in sports coverage were joined in the late 1940s by co-owned television counterparts that recognized that sports programming would help the new medium attract an audience. In addition, this interest in sports was spurred by the fact that many of the first television sets were located in public establishments, especially bars and taverns. Given the heavily male clientele of such places, it is also not surprising that sports ranging from baseball and football to wrestling and roller derby were a staple of early television programming. The first sponsored broadcast aired by WLW's sister television operation, WLWT-TV, was the Golden Gloves amateur boxing tournament in 1948. Similarly, on its first day of operation in March 1948, WGN-TV telecast the Golden Gloves from Chicago Stadium.

The next month, WGN-TV broadcast an exhibition game between the Chicago Cubs and the Chicago White Sox, beginning a commitment to baseball broadcasting that continues to this writing. Later that year, WGN-TV aired Northwestern University and Chicago Bears football games. The announcer for virtually all of these WGN sports broadcasts was Jack Brickhouse, who would go on to broadcast Chicago Cubs games until 1982, when he retired and was replaced by Harry Caray. Brickhouse and Caray were recognized by the National Baseball Hall of Fame for "major contributions to baseball."

When Harry Caray joined the Cubs in 1982, WGN-TV was beginning to be carried by cable television systems across America. As Caray's voice had been amplified by the power of KMOX and its affiliate stations, Caray now took advantage of the newer broadcasting phenomenon of a "superstation" to gain status as a national icon. His work on Cubs' broadcasts elevated him from regional to national prominence, and his death in 1998 was mourned by baseball fans around the country.

The superstation concept that fostered Caray's national visibility is indirectly linked to another midwesterner, Cincinnati entrepreneur Powell Crosley, Jr. (1886–1961). It was Crosley who presciently recognized the advantages of combining media and sports ownership in 1934, when he added controlling interest in the Cincinnati Reds to his ownership of WLW radio. In the 1970s, Cincinnati native Ted Turner saw the advantages in owning media and sports properties and used the programming opportunities generated by his ownership of the Atlanta Braves and Atlanta Hawks to convince cable operators to carry his Atlanta television station WTBS. After Turner, other media companies, including Disney, Fox, and the Tribune, followed Crosley's vision and bought controlling interest in professional sports franchises.

Midwestern television stations also played a role in transforming professional football from a marginal regional sport to a hugely popular national game. Although college football was quickly popular with television viewers (so much so that the NCAA quickly instituted limits on the number of football telecasts), early attempts to air professional football had met with relatively little interest. In 1948, the Chicago Bears grossed fewer than five thousand dollars for the telecasts of its home games. In the early 1950s, when the Bears and Chicago (now Arizona) Cardinals assembled a network of eleven midwestern stations to televise their home games, the teams had to pay two of the stations to carry the games. The flagship station for the Bears–Cardinals network was Chicago's WBKB, owned by then-struggling ABC. An advertising executive noticed that the coverage of the network almost exactly mirrored the distribution area of a beer company he was promoting. He quickly convinced the beer company to buy significant time on the network. The beer company found the relationship extremely profitable, and when ABC was unable to provide the affiliate infrastructure to become further involved in professional football, the advertising company took the package to CBS. As one writer noted, this move "transformed professional football from a fringe curiosity to a mainstream television event."

Sources and Further Reading: Erik Barnouw, *The Golden Web: A History of Broadcasting in the United States, Volume II, 1933–1953* (1968); John R. Catsis, *Sports Broadcasting* (1996); George H. Douglas, *The Early Days of Radio Broadcasting* (1987); Michele Hilmes, *Radio Voices* (1997); Ron Powers, *Supertube* (1984); Curt Smith, *Voices of the Game*, rev. ed. (1992); Ronald A. Smith, *Play-by-Play* (2001); Murray Sperber, *Onward to Victory* (1998); Lawrence A. Wenner, ed., *Media, Sports, and Society* (1989).

Howard M. Kleiman
Miami University, Oxford, Ohio

Sports Writing

Sports writing assumed its modern form in the early twentieth century. Sports journalists in the Midwest contributed significantly to the development of modern trends in sports reporting, including the use of investigative techniques and the role of sports media as

❖ Soldier Field

Designed to be centers of commerce and symbols of civic pride as well as playing fields, sports stadiums are often the signature image of midwestern cities. Built in the 1920s, Soldier Field in Chicago could seat seventy-five to one hundred thousand people, covered seven acres, and was decorated with Doric colonnades that associated it with ancient Mediterranean cultures and complemented nearby landmarks such as the Field Museum of Natural History. Soldier Field was intended to be public space. Throughout the twentieth century, crowds attended football games, heavyweight boxing matches, religious revivals, concerts, circuses, and operas. Resisting a popular trend to replace stadiums, Chicagoans decided to remodel Soldier Field. Dedicated on September 27, 2003, the new version merged the traditional features with a contemporary framework so well that the *New York Times* named it one of the ten best architectural feats of the year.

Andrew Cayton
Miami University, Oxford, Ohio

promoters and sponsors of athletic events. Midwestern sports reporters were among the leaders in the development of sports writing from the more ornate "athlete as hero" style of the early century to today's more hard-edged and less adulatory brand of reporting.

The Sporting News became the "Bible of Baseball" under the direction of St. Louis sportswriter J. G. Taylor Spink (1888–1962). Spink became the editor of the sports weekly in 1914 and shifted the editorial focus of the magazine away from other sports to detailed coverage of baseball. His son, C. C. Johnson Spink, edited the publication from 1962 until its sale in 1977.

Midwestern sports writers Ring Lardner (1885–1933), James Isaminger, and Hugh Fullerton pioneered the field of sports investigative journalism when they uncovered the Black Sox scandal in the 1919 World Series. Lardner, born in Niles, Michigan, brought a strong midwestern sense of morality, mixed with an appreciation of vernacular speech to his sports writing for Chicago newspapers, including the Hearst-owned *Chicago Examiner*, in the years from 1907 to the early 1920s. His best-known newspaper work was done in his "In the Wake of the News" for the *Chicago Tribune*, and his newspaper experience informs the many short stories, e.g., "You Know Me Al" (1916), he wrote about baseball.

Arch Ward (1896–1955), sports editor of the *Chicago Tribune* for a quarter century, founded both Major League Baseball's All-Star Game and the College All-Star Football Game. The Notre Dame alumnus also played a major role in popularizing college football in the 1930s and 1940s.

Jerome Holtzman (b. 1926) of the *Chicago Sun-Times* and the *Chicago Tribune* is enshrined in the Writer's Wing of the Baseball Hall of Fame and is credited with inventing the save for relief pitchers. He also made a major contribution to the oral history of American sports journalism with his collection of interviews with sportswriters, *No Cheering in the Press Box* (1974).

Although Pulitzer Prize–winner Walter Wellesley "Red" Smith (1905–1982) became best known for his work for New York newspapers, the Wisconsin-born columnist began his career in Milwaukee and St. Louis. Sam Lacy (1903–2003) spent most of his career in sports journalism working for African American–owned newspapers in Washington, D.C., and Baltimore, but his columns in the early 1940s for the paper that would become the *Chicago Defender* laid the groundwork for Jackie Robinson to become Major League Baseball's first African American player.

Joe Falls (1928–2004) of the *Detroit News* and *Detroit Free Press*, Bob Broeg of the *St. Louis Post-Dispatch*, Hal McCoy of the *Dayton Daily News*, and Hal Lebovitz (1915–2005) of the *Cleveland Press* and *Cleveland Plain Dealer* are other veteran midwestern sports reporters who are best known for their baseball writing.

As sports journalism has moved toward adversarial reporting since the late 1960s, midwestern columnists and reporters have provided distinguished commentary and reporting. Bob Verdi (columnist) and Sam Smith (NBA basketball writer) are award-winning writers for the *Chicago Tribune*. Columnist Mitch Albom of the *Detroit Free Press* has gained fame outside sports journalism for his memoir *Tuesdays with Morrie* (1997). Sports reporter George Dohrmann of the *St. Paul Pioneer Press* won the Pulitzer Prize for beat reporting in 2000 for his coverage of academic fraud in the University of Minnesota's men's basketball program.

Sources and Further Reading: Joe Falls, *Joe Falls: Fifty Years of Sports Writing* (1997); Jerome Holtzman, *No Cheering in the Press Box* (1974); Murray Sperber, *Onward to Victory* (1998); Bob Verdi, *The Bob Verdi Collection* (1988); Jonathan Yardley, *Ring: A Biography of Ring Lardner* (1977).

Keith L. Cannon
Wingate University, North Carolina

Outdoor Recreation

The Midwest offers a considerable amount of outdoor recreation opportunities in both urban and rural settings. They range from team sports to activities en-

❖ Balloons

Balloons filled with hot air or gas have risen above the Midwest for almost two centuries, mainly as objects of exhibition. One of the earliest ascensions occurred in 1835 when Richard Clayton made the first flight in Ohio. By the mid-1800s, balloons were perennial attractions at state and county fairs.

In the 1880s, Missouri natives Samuel and Thomas Baldwin added a new dimension when they began to parachute from balloons. William Rogers, who billed himself as the "Black King of the Air," continued to tour the Ohio county fair circuit with his parachute and balloon into the 1920s.

Ballooning as a hobby sport became practical when the Federal Aviation Administration approved hot air balloon designs that allowed for the construction of sports balloons. Balloon rallies became popular in the late 1960s, and in 1970, the first National Hot Air Balloon Championship was held at Indianola, Iowa, now the site of the National Balloon Museum. Balloon rallies continue to attract spectators who, after almost two hundred years of lighter-than-air flight, seem never to tire of watching these colorful orbs ascend to the heavens.

Peter Hoehnle
Iowa State University

joyed in solitude, from instructional games for children to professional sports for adults, and from organized and structured forms of recreation with strict rules—and referees to enforce them—to casual pick-up games where fun is the focus and rules are considered merely guidelines. There are a variety of non-competitive and unstructured ways to enjoy outdoor recreation in the Midwest, as well.

Those who call this region "the land with 10,000 lakes," including four of the five Great Lakes, underestimate the importance of water. Wisconsin alone has approximately 15,000 lakes. Along with the Mississippi River, Missouri River, and countless other rivers, streams, and ponds, the lakes make water-related sports plentiful. Swimming is especially popular, an activity that encompasses a wide range of age and skill levels, and one that can be a competitive sport or a way to relax.

Other water sports include water skiing—an activity modernized by Minnesota resident Ralph Samuelson—boating, diving, surfing, fishing, kayaking, scuba diving, and canoeing. One of the country's premiere canoeing areas is located in the Boundary Waters Canoe Area Wilderness in Minnesota. Fishers of walleye will also find this region attractive. Other canoeing havens include the Niobrara River in Nebraska and the Middle Fork of the Vermilion River in Illinois. And although most water-related activity takes place off the shores of the mainland, the world's largest freshwater lake island houses Isle Royale National Park, a tree-intensive wilderness located in Lake Superior in Michigan. Visitors can hike, dive, and explore.

Sandy beaches also present a venue for volleyball and Frisbee. Disc golf tournaments are popular, in which participants mimic the game of golf using Frisbees and targets instead of the traditional club and ball. The Professional Disc Golf Association holds competitions in Iowa, Illinois, Michigan, Missouri, Ohio, Nebraska, and Wisconsin.

Other recreational activities associated with flight include kite flying and boomerang throwing. Although flying-object sports are generally thought to be solitary pursuits or casual activities enjoyed among friends, boomerang throwing is actually an international sport, with U.S. teams winning the majority of tournaments. In fact, Ohio boasts so many champions that the state is known as the Boomerang Capital of the World. Enthusiasts also live in Indiana, Illinois, and Michigan. The American Kitefliers Association, a nonprofit organization that promotes kite flying, currently offers events throughout most of the Midwest.

A significant number of outdoor pursuits involve throwing a ball, and these include football and baseball. There are professional teams in both football (National Football League) and baseball (American and National Leagues) throughout the Midwest, as well as collegiate play, with well-known football teams at The Ohio State University, University of Michigan, University of Illinois, Indiana University, University of Iowa, University of Notre Dame, University of Minnesota, Purdue University, University of Wisconsin, and Michigan State University. Collegiate play is also popular in baseball, softball, cross-country, track and field, and many other pursuits for both women and men.

Various sports—from football to baseball, softball, and T-ball, and from track and field to soccer—are also offered at schools, churches, and YMCAs. Many of these activities are enjoyed informally, as well, throughout parks and neighborhoods, and at scouting events, family reunions, and picnics. Other favorites include kickball, three-legged races, and freeze tag.

Although professional and collegiate basketball is played indoors, many three-on-three tournaments and pick-up basketball games are played outside in parks and similar venues. Yet another popular outdoor activity is soccer, an international sport that is played from the casual level to the professional. Still others enjoy tennis and golf, and the spectrum of those skill levels is as wide as that of soccer.

Much of Midwest topography is flat to hilly, which means that hiking opportunities are more plentiful than mountain climbing ones. Many hikers carry their supplies in a backpack, and they often incorporate camping into their recreational activity. Hardy campers stake their tents in winter months, while warmer weather entices more people to set up camp in state parks, on privately owned grounds, and in other venues.

For some, fishing is an important component of their experience, year-round, with walleye perhaps the most sought-after fish. Lake Erie contains so many walleye that it is known as the Walleye Capital of the World. Largemouth and smallmouth bass, as well as muskies, are often caught for sport, while crappies, perch, and catfish generally provide dinner. Besides these fish, northern pike, bullhead, carp, a wide variety of panfish—including bluegills, sunfish, yellow bass, and white bass—and an assortment of minnows attract the fishing enthusiast.

Other hikers and campers observe wildlife, hunt wildlife, or bird-watch. One of the most spectacular displays of nature occurs by the North Platte River in Nebraska each February when about four thousand sandhill cranes rise up to find food. American bald eagles can be spotted at the Cedar Glen Eagle Roost in Iowa and Illinois. Jersey County, Illinois, is the third largest roosting area for the bald eagle, and these birds can be spotted in the air from late November to early March in this locale. Those who love to track and observe wildlife can find elk, deer, badgers, porcupines, snowshoe hares, wild turkey, and bobcats in the Pigeon River Country State Forest in Michigan.

The Midwest has small mountains to climb, including High Point in Iowa, Taum Sauk Mountain in Missouri, and Eagle Mountain in Minnesota. Mountain biking is another activity for hilly terrain. According to the National Geographic Society, among the best spots for mountain biking are the hundred-mile Centennial Trail in Black Hills National Forest in South Dakota and the Pines and the Mines Mountain Bike Trail in the Upper Peninsula's Ottawa National Forest in Michigan.

Plenty of recreational activities have participants moving through the wilderness or through a city or town. Among them are horseback riding, roller or inline skating (inline skates were adapted for modern-day use by two brothers from Minnesota), skateboarding, jogging, and biking. For those wishing to bike along steep and glorious limestone cliffs, Spearfish Canyon Road in South Dakota is a treat. Other sites recommended by the National Geographic Society include Cedar Lake Loop in Shawnee National Forest in Illinois, Monroe and Brown Counties in Indiana, the Katy Trail in Missouri, and Ashtabula County in Ohio. Still other activities are confined to a precise square of lawn, like volleyball, badminton, archery, lawn bowling, croquet, and horseshoes.

Although many recreational activities can be enjoyed year round, some are more seasonal. When one thinks of summer, or at least more temperate weather, two of the world's best amusement parks (according to *Forbes*) are located in Ohio: Cedar Point, known as the Roller Coaster Capital of the World, and Paramount's King's Island, home of the world's first stand-up coaster. Cedar Point is also close to the Lake Erie Islands, where visitors can ride bicycles around the perimeters of the islands and enjoy boating and beach activities. Moreover, the Midwest boasts some of the finest fairs and festivals, ranging from county level to the State Fair, with food and music playing a prominent role.

Ready to bicycle in the Twin Cities in the 1890s. Minnesota Historical Society, MHS Locator no. GV3.81/r28, neg. no. 77385.

Winter sports also abound in the Midwest. Favorites include downhill snow skiing, cross-country skiing, ice skating, tobogganing, ice fishing, bobsledding, dog sledding, ice boating, ice hockey, snowshoeing, and snowmobiling. According to the Midwest Ski Areas Association, ski and snowboard training camps continue to grow in popularity, adding that snowboarding now accounts for 30 percent of activity in these camps. Racing camps are generally scheduled around Thanksgiving and Christmas holidays to prepare participants for the upcoming season, and skiing activities exist throughout much of the Midwest. Dogsledding camps are available in Minnesota and Wisconsin, and participants can sometimes stay in a yurt—an insulated structure of a canvas-covered wooden frame. Another more offbeat sport is skijoring, where a dog and a skier are harnessed together so that the dog can pull the participant on a cross-country skiing adventure. Snowshoeing is a growing activity in which some people participate recreationally and others race for sport.

Recreational activities that occur above ground are sky diving, parasailing, and hot air ballooning. Other activities take participants well below ground, like spelunking. Niagara Cave in Minnesota, one of the largest limestone caves in the Midwest, has hosted over three hundred ceremonies in its Wedding Chapel. The cave itself is named for a stream that falls approximately sixty feet. Another intriguing site is the Meramec Caverns located in Missouri. It houses the Stage Curtain, a seventy-foot-high cave formation that is the largest of its kind in the world. These particular cave visits are clean and pristine; for a down and dirty experience, there is the Marengo Cave in southern Indiana, a U.S. National Natural Landmark.

More information about recreational activities may be found at state offices of tourism and departments of natural resources. The wildernet (www.wildernet.com) and the National Park Service website (www.nps.gov) are also useful.

Kelly Boyer Sagert
Lorain, Ohio

Fishing

The Midwest can be viewed as a massive shallow trough scoured by successive glaciers, extending two-thirds to three-quarters of the distance between the Canadian border and the Ohio River. As a fortuitous result of the glaciers' journeys, the twelve states of the Midwest are replete with fishable waters. The Midwest contains four of the five Great Lakes, the Mississippi, Missouri, Ohio, and Wabash rivers, countless smaller riverine systems, and tens of thousands of natural lakes of glacial origin. Then there are the artificial reservoirs for flood and erosion control and hydroelectric power, municipal water reservoirs, farm ponds, and artificial lakes created for multiple uses. All of these waters offer heartland anglers sport and pan fishing opportunities unsurpassed in any other region in the continental United States. While the major waters of this region have provided commercial fish crops in the past and continue to do so to some extent, recreational fishing is a major feature of midwestern waterway usage.

Distant waters offer midwestern anglers Bunyanesque catches from Canadian lakes, Alaskan lakes and rivers, and ocean sites as varied as the letters in alphabet soup. Exciting sport and tasty catches are available, however, in every corner of this region for those who desire only short distances and brief periods devoted to piscatorial pursuits. As a result, angling can be accomplished before work, during noon breaks, and for any fraction of a weekend.

Midwest anglers fish at above-average levels of participation, according to the *2001 National Survey of Hunting and Fishing* conducted by the U.S. Fish and Wildlife Service. While national participation in some form of sport fishing totaled 16 percent in 2001 for Americans aged sixteen years and older, the rate is 17 percent for the Midwest east of the Mississippi River and 27 percent on the River's western side.

Midwestern fisheries illustrate humankind's capacity to construct desirable recreational environments. Fish hatcheries in the Midwest and elsewhere have supplemented natural populations of game fish for over a hundred years. Introduced fish species—the striped bass, coho salmon, splake, brown trout, catfishes, and hybrid sunfish, among others—have generated successful fishing environments in the Great Lakes, reservoirs, natural lakes, rivers, and streams. In addition, natural resources agencies in each state strive to expand access to public waters and improve lake and river habitats, while regulating sport fishing seasons, methods, and harvests to ensure sustainable fish populations in perpetuity.

The Great Lakes are renowned for offering the finest big game, fresh water fishing in the United States. Continual efforts are being made to control alien marine species, such as zebra mussels and snakeheads, which threaten the natives. Abating pollution requires constant vigilance. Lake Erie is a showcase example of successful cleanup efforts.

In short, recreational fishing has never been better. Once more "natural" (i.e., less regulated), perhaps, but the Midwest has never been so abundantly generous in fishing sites where successful fishing is within reach of almost everyone.

Sources and Further Reading: John Bailey et al., eds., *The New Encyclopedia of Fishing* (2002); Ira N. Gabrielson, ed., *The Fisherman's Encyclopedia*, 2nd ed. (1963); John F. Rooney, Jr., and Richard Pilsbury, *Atlas of American Sport* (1992); Michael J. Walker, ed., *Sport Fishing U.S.A.* (1971).

Richard L. Hummel
Eastern Illinois University

Golf

Golf has long been popular in the Midwest, but never to the same degree as in the South or the West. The main reason is cold weather. From November to March, golf can be played only sporadically, if at all. Despite the emergence of northern Michigan and Wisconsin as popular golfing destinations, most Americans associate golf with Florida, Texas, the Carolinas, Arizona, and California. Serious midwestern golfers regularly travel to the South and West to play famous courses in exotic locations.

In 2004, the Professional Golf Association (PGA) Tour made several stops in the Midwest, including such annual events as the Memorial Tournament in Dublin, Ohio; the Cialis Western Open in Lemont, Illinois; the Greater Milwaukee Open; and the Buick Open in Grand Blanc, Michigan. The Ladies Professional Golf Association (LPGA) also held several tournaments in the Midwest. Major competitions such as the U.S. Open (for both men and women) are periodically held on well-known courses in the region.

If anything is distinctive about golf in the Midwest, it is that the vast majority of courses are primarily intended for local players. Resorts designed to attract golfers from other parts of North America and the world are growing in number, but remain relatively rare. Whether as public facilities or as private or semi-private country clubs, golf courses are primarily gathering places for local men and women. Utilitarian and social in character, they are municipal and business centers.

State organizations encourage and regulate the game of golf within the parameters established by national bodies such as the United States Golf Association. The Wisconsin State Golf Association is typical. It brings together the members of almost four hundred courses and clubs, facilitates posting scores to determine handicaps, publishes a bimonthly magazine, and sponsors amateur and professional tournaments, including qualifying rounds for the men's U.S. Open and the U.S. Amateur Open, from May through September.

In keeping with the relatively low profile of golf in the Midwest, the region has produced only a handful

Minneapolis native Patty Berg, one of the founders of the Ladies' Professional Golf Association. Minnesota Historical Society, MHS Locator no. por/10543/p8, neg. no. 76421.

of famous golfers. The vast majority of legendary players, including Bobby Jones, Walter Hagen, Ben Hogan, and Mildred "Babe" Didrickson Zaharias grew up in the South. Still, the Midwest has made up in quality what it lacks in quantity. One such outstanding midwestern golfer is Tom Watson. Born in Kansas City, Missouri, in 1949, he led the PGA tour in the late 1970s and early 1980s.

The most successful golfer in the twentieth century was Jack Nicklaus. Born in Columbus, Ohio, on January 21, 1940, Nicklaus became a superb golfer, a prodigious driver as well as a master at course management. Nicklaus joined the PGA Tour in 1962. Over the next four decades, he won seventy-three tour events, including a record eighteen major tournaments, and finished second, fifty-eight times and third, thirty-six times. Nicklaus has also established himself as a premier golf course designer. While he maintains strong ties with Columbus, particularly with the Memorial Tournament, Nicklaus and his wife, Barbara, live in North Palm Beach, Florida.

Sources and Further Reading: John Feinstein, *A Good Walk Spoiled* (1996); Melanie Hauser, Liz Kahn, and Lisa D. Mickey, *Champions of Women's Golf*, ed. Nannette Sanson (2000); Jack Nicklaus, *Jack Nicklaus: My Story* (1997).

Andrew Cayton
Miami University, Oxford, Ohio

Hiking, Camping, and Canoeing

People hike year-round in the Midwest, enjoying pleasant summer strolls and tackling challenge-filled winter climbs in public parks and on private property. Much of the Midwest's topography ranges from flat to hilly, although Iowa High Point is 1,670 feet above sea level; Taum Sauk, Missouri, is 1,772 feet, and Eagle Mountain, Minnesota is, 2,301 feet.

The American Discovery Trail (ADT) offers a host of hiking options throughout the Midwest. ADT is over sixty-eight hundred miles long and transects fifteen states, seven of them midwestern. In Nebraska, explorers, Pony Express riders, and Mormon pioneers forged trails. In Kansas, hikers walk along the eye-catching Flint and Smoky Hills. Iowa, sculpted by massive glaciers, offers a gently rolling landscape, and Missouri contains the starting point of the Lewis and Clark expedition. ADT terrain in Illinois is of two varieties: glaciers flattened the north, while the southern portion remains hilly. Indiana, the Crossroads of America, also contains both terrains. Finally, Ohio's often wooded portion follows nearly half of the more than thirteen hundred miles of the Buckeye Trail that touches every section of the state. Besides ADT, hikers can utilize trails provided by the Rails-to-Trails Conservancy, where old railways are converted into trails for public use. All states contain converted trails; because these trails were former railroad beds, their inclines are gradual.

Many options also exist for paddle sport advocates, largely because of the Great Lakes and the Mississippi and Missouri Rivers. Some people leisurely canoe down picturesque waterways, while others associate canoeing with fishing. White-water rafting options range from family-friendly paddling adventures to fierce and challenging rapids for experts only. Other enthusiasts compete in marathon canoeing races, an elemental sport in which competitors canoe long distances over nearly flat water. Meanwhile, freestyle advocates choreograph canoe maneuvers in which the paddler focuses on the artistic representation of movements.

Canoeing seasons vary, depending upon the length of the warmer climate. In Minnesota, where the famous Boundary Waters draw dedicated canoeists, the season is fairly brief. In southern Missouri, where enthusiasts canoe by the Ozarks, the season is nearly year-round.

The American Canoe Association (ACA) divides the country into canoeing regions, and the Midwest consistently places first or second in the number of active canoeing participants. Many of the largest canoe manufacturers, especially those that build specialty watercraft, operate in the Midwest.

Significant camping options also exist, with campers staying in cabins and tents, in resort areas and in more primitive and natural locales. State parks provide campgrounds, and privately owned venues are also plentiful. Scouting programs, YMCAs, YWCAs, and churches frequently manage summer camps for children. The American Camping Association is located in Indiana.

Camping is often enjoyed in conjunction with hiking, canoeing, fishing, and other recreational activities. Guidebooks on outdoor recreation are available from state parks, tourism centers, bookstores, and online sites. Local and regional clubs also exist for each activity. Because of the four Great Lakes and the Missouri and Mississippi Rivers, the Midwest contains a unique spectrum of camping locations.

Source and Further Reading: Vici DeHaan, *State Parks of the Midwest* (1993).

Kelly Boyer Sagert
Lorain, Ohio

Hunting

The twelve midwestern states contain most varieties of game-dwelling habitats, including farm field edges, riparian waste cover, hardwood forests, pine woods, prairie marshes, and potholes, as well as the nation's largest freshwater lakes and river drainage systems. The major mid-continent migratory bird flyways, the Mississippi and the Central, cross the region from north to south. Thus, large, transient populations of waterfowl, ducks and geese, during their twice-yearly movements between nesting and feeding grounds create hunting opportunities equal to any other region in the continental United States. The Midwest also offers opportunities for hunting a variety of large and small game. The most abundant game animals in the region include whitetail deer, wild turkeys, cotton-tail rabbits, and squirrels.

Overall, hunting opportunities are better for large

Pheasant hunting in South Dakota. Mike Kuchera's South Dakota Guide Service, Inc.

and small game in the Midwest today than a century ago. American hunters' most popular big game animal, the whitetail deer, had nearly disappeared in the early 1900s. Due to intelligent restoration efforts and management practices, whitetail populations and geographical distribution have rebounded to unprecedented levels. At the present time all states in the Midwest have popular and successful whitetail hunting seasons. Whitetails coexist with humans to a highly compatible degree and have even become pests when pursuing their varied browsing among the ornamental plantings of suburban homes.

Another successful restoration of native game fauna is the reestablishment of the wild turkey to its original ranges. Other native species, such as the prairie chicken, have not fared so well, thus disappearing from the list of legal game birds. The ring-necked pheasant, an introduced species in the Midwest, achieved star status by furnishing exciting hunting opportunities and tasty table fare during the past seventy years.

Each of the twelve states regulates hunting seasons with an impressive and sometimes bewildering array of specifications regarding open season dates, allowable hunting methods, and legitimate game. The laws reflect each state's research on how to maintain sustainable populations of game species relative to the carrying capacities of the widely varying habitats.

The main challenge to midwestern hunters is finding places to hunt. Each state's wildlife agency can help locate public hunting grounds. The Internet offers easy access to regulations and hunting areas. Access to private lands requires personal contacts, increasingly difficult to arrange. Hunting clubs, leases, hunting guides, and other commercial hunting services are advertised in the many hunting magazines.

Midwest hunters hunt more than the national average, according to the *2001 National Survey of Hunting and Fishing* conducted by the U.S. Fish and Wildlife Service. Nationally, 6 percent of the population sixteen years and older took part in some form of sport hunting in 2001, compared with 7 percent in midwestern states east of the Mississippi and 12 percent in states on the river's western side. Although these percentages of hunters are unchanged or down a bit from 1991, millions of midwesterners pursue wild game afield, thus continuing to make a significant economic and cultural impact on the region into the foreseeable future.

Sources and Further Reading: Raymond R. Camp, ed., *The New Hunter's Encyclopedia*, 3rd ed. (1966); Byron Dalyrymple, *Complete Guide to Hunting Across North America* (1970); Eugene T. Petersen, *Hunters' Heritage* (1979); John F. Rooney, Jr., and Richard Pilsbury, *Atlas of American Sport* (1992).

Richard L. Hummel
Eastern Illinois University

Ice Fishing

While ice fishing is not peculiar to the Midwest, it is particularly popular in the region. It is a growing sport: In early twenty-first century Wisconsin, ice fishing accounted for close to one out of every four fish caught.

American Indians developed ice fishing to obtain food during the winter. Clearing a section of frozen lake and building a tent for cover, they would chisel a hole in the ice and lie flat beside it. Normally, they speared fish through the hole. Many of their tools and techniques are still employed by contemporary ice fishermen, although today people normally fish more for the sport than out of necessity.

Ice fishing has its own distinctive culture. Participants spend a good deal of time and money choosing both the best fishing sites and the proper tools and accessories, including ice saws, boots, clothes, and heaters. Experienced fishermen know to take sunscreen and sunglasses. They use sleds or snowmobiles to haul their equipment onto the ice, where they set up small shanties, often no more than six feet by six feet, with a bench or stools.

On some lakes, a group of shanties constitute a small, semipermanent village as long as the ice is thick enough to hold them. Much of the appeal of ice fishing is social. People gather around their ice holes to gossip and swap stories, often with the help of alcoholic beverages. Hardly an aerobic sport, ice fishing nevertheless requires considerable skill and endurance.

Sources and Further Reading: Al Lindner, Doug Stange, and Dave Genz, *Ice Fishing Secrets* (1998); Noel Vick, *Fishing on Ice* (1999).

Andrew Cayton
Miami University, Oxford, Ohio

Snowmobiling

Snowmobiling is a popular wintertime sport among many midwesterners. To provide for this activity, nearly five hundred miles of public snowmobile trails are available on state and county land. Additional trails for public use are made available by local snowmobile clubs on private land.

The idea for a power-driven sled originated in areas of heavy snowfall where the difference between life and death was the amount of time it took to transport an ill person to emergency care. Joseph-Armand Bombardier of Valcourt, Quebec, commonly referred to as the father of snowmobiling, invented in 1958 the kind of sport apparatus known today as a snowmobile. Yet Carl J. Eliason of Sayner, Wisconsin, received the first patent for such a machine in 1927, having used parts from a Ford Model T. With the development of smaller gasoline engines in the 1950s and the introduction of one- to two-passenger snowmobiles, a new recreational sport was born.

Snowmobilers generally ride close to home, traveling only thirty to seventy-five miles to favorite riding areas or trails. Snowmobile racing is also extremely popular. The World Snowmobile Association and other sanctioning bodies sponsor races throughout the year at popular resorts. The popularity of the sport has grown quickly; it now has its own Hall of Fame in St. Germain, Wisconsin, and is a significant factor in increased winter tourism in the Midwest.

Sources and Further Reading: Intertec Publishing Corporation, *Vintage Snowmobile*, vols. 1 and 2 (1996); Larry MacDonald, *The Bombardier Story: Planes, Trains, and Snowmobiles* (2001).

Alexander Cuenca
University of Miami, Florida

Vacationing and Tourism

In a July 1952, *Harper's* magazine essay extolling the ease of transcontinental airplane travel, Bernard DeVoto described his aerial view of the "Middle West" as a landscape he found monotonous, a checkerboard of rolling farmland punctuated by the Great Lakes and divided by the Mississippi River. DeVoto's description aptly positions the Midwest as a tourist destination. When one imagines a canon of national tourist attractions or vacation sites in the United States, the Midwest seems woefully devoid of any noted destinations. Chicago, the St. Louis Arch, the Mississippi River, and the Mall of America are more regional than national in stature. The Midwest boasts no Yellowstone National Park, no Disney World, no Las Vegas, no Statue of Liberty. Yet despite its seeming lack of tourist spectacle, the Midwest has played an integral role in the development of a national tourist infrastructure and economy. And what it lacks in spectacle it makes up for in thriving regional vacation spots and an established image as America's heartland.

Tourism and vacation travel developed in tandem with the expansion of regional and national commercial economies. The expanding market infrastructure that emerged to facilitate the exchange of goods paved the way for pleasure travel. Just as social, economic, and technological developments were transforming the nature of work, expanding commercial markets, and decreasing geographical distance, tourism became an elite pastime dependent on disposable income, increased leisure, and a canon of scenic and cultural attractions made accessible by an expanding transportation network.

In the early nineteenth century, as commerce flowed along the network of rivers and waterways throughout the Ohio and Mississippi valleys, immigrants and travelers boarded steamships that plied these waterways in search of new homes and new experiences. Noted European and American travelers curious about the society and character of the new republic's hinterland set out to discover and describe a vaguely defined area known as "the American interior." Traveling from Ohio to the Missouri River through what would later be called the Midwest, including the states of Ohio, Indiana, Illinois, Missouri, Michigan, Iowa, Wisconsin, and Minnesota, travelers such as Frances Trollope, Harriet Martineau, Charles Dickens, and Timothy Flint described the region as distinct from the East Coast and the South. Although set boundaries and destinations remained in flux, a series of noted sites and attractions came to define the region. These included the Ohio River valley, French settlements on the Mississippi, the English Prairie settlement in Illinois, the confluence of the Ohio and Mississippi Rivers, Native American earthworks and mounds, indigenous Indian tribes, prehistoric fossils, prairie land, native flora and fauna, as well as agricultural practices and social mores. Midwestern entrepôts such as Cincinnati and St. Louis emerged as celebrated stopovers. During his journey through the interior in 1842, Charles Dickens stopped in Cincinnati and remarked on the fine accommodations and the beauty of the riverfront city.

The rapid development of a national railroad network during the mid-nineteenth century shifted the locus and focus of pleasure travel in the Midwest. Luxury steamboats gave way to Pullman Palace Cars, and the river towns of Cincinnati and St. Louis gave way to the westernmost outpost of the expanding metropolitan economy—Chicago. Curiosity about the landscape and character of the Ohio and Mississippi valleys waned as packaged tours and the increased pace of railroad travel directed the attention of travelers to the more dramatic landscapes of the West. Recounting their cross-continent rail journeys, elite tourists often commented on the monotonous view of rolling farmland as they passed through the flat prairie states of the Midwest on their way to Colorado or California. Instead they turned their attention to the details of train travel, remarking on the wonders of Pullman car service while overlooking its midwestern origins.

Despite this shift in focus, the Midwest did not disappear from the tourist map. In 1869, after the completion of the first transcontinental rail lines, Chicago emerged as the central transfer point between the eastern and western rail networks. As the gateway between East and West, the city became the principal, if not the only, midwestern attraction for growing numbers of transcontinental tourists. Traveling from New York or Boston, tourists stepped off the train for a few hours or a day or two before transferring on to Omaha or St. Paul and beyond. Chicago was known for its broad streets and bustling commerce, and a trip to the Union Stockyards became obligatory. After the 1871 fire necessitated the complete rebuilding of the city, a series of modern hotels set the standard for first-class travel accommodations. The Tremont House, the Sherman House, the Drake Hotel, and the Palmer House were said to surpass East Coast competitors in luxury, comfort, and modern amenities. The success of cartographers Rand McNally & Company, established in Chicago in 1868, further linked the city to the growing national tourist infrastructure and economy.

The 1893 World's Columbian Exposition marked the culmination of Chicago's position as the pre-eminent midwestern tourist attraction at the turn of the century. Built to commemorate the four hundredth anniversary of Columbus's voyage to America, the fair celebrated American progress from its discovery to

Four yachts racing near Michigan City, Indiana, 1927. Chicago Historical Society, *Chicago Daily News*, SDN-066660.

the present. With its neoclassical white Court of Honor, colorful and exotic Midway Plaisance, replicas of Columbus's three caravels, the nation's first Ferris wheel, and vast displays of commerce, technology, art, and culture, the fair represented the apex of American accomplishment. An estimated twenty-eight million visitors came to Chicago to see the White City during the summer of 1893. Although only a temporary attraction, the fair solidified Chicago as a prominent national tourist destination. As long as the city remained at the heart of the nation's railroad network, Chicago remained the Midwest's foremost tourist spectacle.

In the twentieth century, the growing popularity and affordability of the automobile transformed the tourist experience, dramatically expanding the number of tourist sites and attractions and creating a more vibrant regional and local tourist and vacation infrastructure that repositioned sites across the Midwest as tourist destinations. The spectacle of national attractions and scenic wonders gave way to local and regional sites as tourists were freed from the predetermined destinations of railroad travel. As automobile touring became increasingly popular after World War I, prescriptive literature publicizing the landscapes of tourism began to promote historic sites, places associated with historic events, and the local color of particular places, in addition to the scenic attractions typically associated with railroad tourism. By chance and by design, automobile tourists sought out local color and regional history and character as they moved into the landscape, making their way from one destination to the next. During the 1920s, the Lincoln Highway was the most famous of a handful of new transcontinental roads that brought tourists through the heart of the Midwest on their way from New York City to San Francisco. Promoters of the highway encouraged tourists to follow the pathway of American pioneers and American progress.

Automobile tourists and summer vacationers sought out midwestern main streets, pioneer history, and outdoor recreation, and local communities became increasingly creative in their attempts to attract the growing tourist trade. In the winter of 1937, residents in Bemidji, Minnesota, constructed an eighteen-foot statue of Paul Bunyan and his blue ox Babe by the side of the highway in an effort to attract tourists to the first annual Paul Bunyan Winter Carnival. The Bemidji statue epitomized what historian Karal Ann Marling has documented as the emergence of the "roadside colossus" in the Midwest. The Corn Palace in Mitchell, South Dakota, constructed in 1921, boasted a façade decorated with ears of corn. Wall Drug established in Wall, South Dakota, in 1931, promised free ice water for thirsty tourists. Towns throughout the region vied for "world's largest" status:

the world's largest buffalo in Jamestown, North Dakota; the world's largest prairie chicken in Rothsay, Minnesota; the world's largest cow in New Salem, North Dakota; the world's largest bull in Audubon, Iowa; the world's largest six pack in La Crosse, Wisconsin; and the world's largest twine ball in Darwin, Minnesota. These are only a handful of the local oddities positioned throughout the Midwest to capture the attention of automobile tourists.

In addition to these tourist novelties, a number of noted regional vacation sites and summer retreats flourished along the lakes and rivers of northern Michigan, Wisconsin, and Minnesota. Places such as Minnehaha Falls, the inspiration for Henry Wadsworth Longfellow's *Song of Hiawatha* (1855), Mackinac Island, celebrated by Margaret Fuller and William Cullen Bryant, and the Wisconsin Dells, noted for its dramatic sandstone rock formations, had long attracted elite travelers in the mid-nineteenth century seeking fresh air, a healthy climate, and natural beauty. As lumber and mining industries waned in the early twentieth century, the northern Great Lakes region burgeoned as a summer playground. The arrival of automobile tourists and vacationers further stimulated the development of summer colonies and outdoor resorts. Although motels and tourist camps, along with golf courses and summer cabins, replaced the grand resort hotels, these locales, too, became increasingly dependent on the tourist trade.

With the decline of lumbering in northern Michigan at the turn of the twentieth century, railroads sought to revive their traffic by promoting the tourist trade. They financed large resort hotels such as the fashionable Grand Hotel on Mackinac Island and others in such places as Petoskey, Harbor Springs, and Charlevoix. The Grand Rapids and Indiana Railroad, one of the supporters of the Grand Hotel, advertised itself as "The Fishing Line," seeking to lure anglers and hunters to the region. By 1900, the Upper Peninsula was dotted with summer camps and resort towns. In 1911, a group of delegates from the fifteen counties that comprised the Upper Peninsula established a cooperative organization to support the construction of highways and to promote recreational attractions.

Similarly, in northern Wisconsin, businessmen and civic leaders turned to tourism in an effort to mitigate the effects of the declining timber industry. In 1922, a group of locals from Rhinelander, Wisconsin, organized the Northern Wisconsin Resort Association, which came to be known as the Wisconsin Land O' Lakes Association. The group initiated a massive publicity campaign in 1923 to promote the region, sending out brochures, road maps, and travel information to cities outside the state. Enthusiasts estimated that tourists spent almost one hundred million dollars in the state that year. Places such as the Wisconsin Dells, one of the older scenic resorts, expanded and prospered as increasing numbers of summer vacationers sought the spectacular sandstone gorges and canyons along the Wisconsin River and the cool waters and fresh breezes of Lake Delton and Mirror Lake.

Minnesota, "the land of 10,000 lakes," long touted by elite outdoorsmen as a hunting and fishing paradise, witnessed a similar expansion in the tourist trade. Lake Minnetonka, one of the many glacial lakes located west of the Twin Cities, emerged as a fashionable resort after the arrival of the railroad in the late 1860s. Elite pleasure seekers from Minneapolis, St. Paul, and other nearby cities relaxed at such grand hotels as the Lake Park Hotel constructed on the north shore in 1879; they toured the lake in such elegant steamboats as the City of St. Louis and socialized at such places as the Excelsior Casino, which boasted sweeping lakeshore views. By the early twentieth century, the fashionable resort hotels gave way to thriving summer colonies. In 1906, a group of Presbyterian Church members from Minneapolis established a summer community on Crane Island in Lake Minnetonka. By 1915, they had built fifteen family cottages. In the post–World War II era, the summer colonies that ringed the lake were transformed into year-round residences. Not limited to established lake resorts like that at Minnetonka, the growing interest in outdoor recreation spurred the expansion of summer colonies and tourist accommodations throughout the state.

Despite the expansion of leisure and recreation after World War II, and despite these thriving regional vacation and resort areas, the Midwest has consistently lagged behind other regions as a noted national vacation spot and tourist destination. However, what it lacks in dramatic tourist spectacle and renowned vacation retreats, it makes up for in symbolic presence. Known for its agricultural landscapes and its small-town main streets, the Midwest is widely celebrated as the nation's heartland. Tourists and vacationers, whether elite nineteenth-century travelers or the masses of twentieth-century automobile tourists, have long been attracted by this elusive quality.

Sources and Further Reading: Warren James Belasco, *Americans on the Road* (1979); Catherine Cocks, *Doing the Town* (2001); Mary Helen Dunlap, *Sixty Miles from Contentment* (1995); Frank Henry Goodyear, "Constructing a National Landscape," Ph.D. diss., University of Texas at Austin (1998); Neil Harris et al., *Grand Illusions: Chicago World's Fair of 1893* (1993); Drake Hokanson, *The Lincoln Highway* (1988); Karal Ann Marling, *The Colossus of Roads* (1984); Thomas J. Schlereth, *U.S. 40* (1985); Eileen Patricia Walsh, "The Last Resort," Ph.D. diss., University of Minnesota (1994).

Marguerite S. Shaffer
Miami University, Oxford, Ohio

Chicago-to-Mackinac Sailing Race

The Race to Mackinac is a world-renowned sailing competition that challenges the endurance, speed, and agility of three hundred boats and three thousand crew members. The 333-mile race from Chicago to Mackinac Island at the northern end of Lake Michigan is one of the world's longest freshwater races and is a hallmark of American inland sailing.

Racing began in 1898 when five members of the Chicago Yacht Club decided that, rather than taking the four-day steamer trip to Mackinac Island from Chicago, they would sail there. The five men supported the race with their own funds, and after a fifty-one hour journey, the yacht *Vanenna* was pronounced the winner. The second race was not held until 1904, when a committee at the Chicago Yacht Club established rules for the race and standardized the route. After the six-year hiatus, the "Mac" was held every year until 1917, when it was suspended due to World War I. It resumed in 1921 and has been held every year since.

The Mac is a handicapped race with several divisions. Monohull boats are scored under the U.S. Sailing Americap II handicap system, which allows boats of different sizes to compete against each other. Multihull boats compete under the Lake Michigan Performance Handicapped Racing Federation system. The race normally takes between forty and sixty hours to complete, depending on weather conditions, and ends at the lighthouse on Round Island, off Mackinac Island.

Sources and Further Reading: Pamela Lach and Thomas Piljac, *Mackinac Island: Island Frontier, Vacation Resort, Timeless Wonder* (1996); Sue Steward and Anthony Steward, *Top Yacht Races of the World* (2001); Deane Tank and Beverly Ford, eds., *The Tales of the Chicago to Mackinac Race, 1898–1998* (1998).

Alexander Cuenca
University of Miami, Florida

Door County

Door County is named for the usually stormy waterway, Death's Door (called *Port des Morts* by its seventeenth-century French explorers), which links Green Bay to Lake Michigan. Door Peninsula and the surrounding islands, including prominent Washington Island at its northern tip, form portions of Wisconsin's Brown, Kewaunee, and Door Counties. The Door, as it is commonly known, is blessed with uncommonly beautiful harbors and bays and encompasses rolling hills and valleys of great beauty. It also claims a number of fine freshwater beaches, and more state parks, lighthouses, and miles of shoreline (250) than any other county in the United States.

Once the hunting, fishing, and gathering homelands of Chippewa, Osawatomie, and other Native Americans, the Door became a producer of large quantities of freshwater fish, lumber, and farm products in the early nineteenth century. Those products were the work of Swedish, Norwegian, Finnish, English, German, and French settlers and the Native Americans who not infrequently assisted them, willingly or unwillingly, in their labors. In the nineteenth century, some of the inhabitants of the Door became ship builders and outfitters. Then as now, the center of the industry was Sturgeon Bay. In addition, farming families began to focus their efforts on the production of sour cherries, particularly Montmorency cherries, as well as apples and dairy products. Today the Door is the fourth largest producer of cherries in the United States.

In the late nineteenth century, the Door became a favorite boating, fishing, camping, and hunting resort area for midwesterners of means, especially residents of Illinois, Iowa, Indiana, and Wisconsin. In the 1920s and 1930s, visitors enjoyed water sports as well as theatrical and musical festivals. The most noteworthy among the latter are the Peninsula Players, with its marvelous woodland shore theatre facing Green Bay, and the Birch Creek Music Festival, housed in a fine old barn theatre just outside Fish Creek. The Peninsula Players Theatre, founded in 1935, is the oldest professional resident summer theatre in the United States and attracts actors from drama companies in London and New York, as well as Chicago, Minneapolis, Milwaukee, and other centers of the theatrical arts. The high school and college students who enroll in the Birch Creek summer programs work with musicians from the Milwaukee, Minneapolis, and Chicago symphony orchestras and primary jazz arts groups.

Famous for its fish boils, the Door supports a host of fine restaurants, interesting cafes, and fast food outlets. The peninsula is crowded with campgrounds, rental cottages, motels and hotels, condominiums, apartment complexes, and private homes. The Ridges, a plant sanctuary near Baileys Harbor provides spectacular "seminars in the wild," and The Clearing in Ellison Bay and Lawrence University's Björklunden in Baileys Harbor provide seminars on a wide range of topics. Ten public and private golf courses and several lengthy horse, biking, and hiking trails—like the Ahnapee State Trail—offer challenges to the athletically inclined. For others, a glittering array of galleries, museums, and shops of every description provide entertainment and enlightenment.

Sources and Further Reading: Norbert Blei, *Door Way* (1981); Hjalmar R. Holand, *History of Door County, Wisconsin*, 2 vols. (1993); Hjalmar R. Holand, *Old Peninsula Days*, 8th ed. (1959); M. Marvin Lotz, *Discovering Door County's Past* (1994); Roy Lukes, *Toft Point* (1998).

Denise A. Riley
Columbus State Community College, Ohio

G. Michael Riley
The Ohio State University–Columbus

Wisconsin Dells, Indiana Dunes, Ozarks, and Spas

Like their eastern counterparts, wealthy midwesterners sought the health-giving properties of mineral springs and spas in the nineteenth and early twentieth centuries. Railroads delivered them to places like Waukesha's Bethesda Spa or J. H. Kellogg's Battle Creek Sanitarium. Guests at Thomas Taggart's luxurious French Lick Springs in southern Indiana enjoyed its famous Pluto water, whose laxative effects inspired the motto "When Nature Won't, Pluto Will." Neighboring West Baden Springs, named after the German spa town of Wiesbaden, attracted celebrities to its casino, lush grounds, and enormous domed atrium built in 1902. Missouri claimed eighty-three mineral springs in 1892, while Michigan's spa city, Mount Clemens, offered vacationers bathhouses, hotels, and a distinct sulfurous odor. The iron and copper investors of northern Minnesota and Michigan's Upper Peninsula often returned from the East Coast with their families to enjoy the summer climate.

Originally established as a military outpost, Mackinac Island developed as a tourist destination after the fur trade declined in the 1830s. Composed of rock and relatively free of mosquitoes, the island provided relief from hay fever and asthma. Southern planters built summer homes to escape the heat, but left with the Civil War's onset. Wealthy Chicagoans revived tourism, and the island housed the nation's second national park, which became Michigan's first, Mackinac Island State Park, in 1895. Vacationers arrived on excursion boats from Buffalo, Cleveland, Chicago, and Detroit. As the number of passengers increased, railroad and steamship companies financed construction of the Grand Hotel, which first welcomed guests to its enormous front porch in 1887. Nearby Drummond Island, the thirty-five islands of the Les Chenaux chain, and Lake Erie's Put-in-Bay also attracted steamship travelers. Today, Mackinac Island visitors can stroll or take a carriage ride, but still cannot drive a car on the island.

In stark contrast to Mackinac Island, today's Wis-

Leaping the chasm at Stand Rock, Wisconsin, in 1886. Wisconsin Historical Society, WHi-2101.

consin Dells invites vacationers to golf, frolic at indoor water parks, attend water-ski shows, and visit the Circus World Museum while staying in one of the area's seven thousand hotel rooms or three thousand campsites. The Dells began attracting tourists in the 1870s when Henry Hamilton Bennett's photography lured visitors to the Wisconsin River's sandstone rock formations. Sightseers arrived via train to experience majestic scenery and traverse the path of earlier timber cruisers and fur traders. Railroad travel guides and train depots displayed Bennett's photographs, and his studio attracted tourists looking to purchase images. Bennett also sold people photos of their steamboat tours and named many rock formations. Promoters commercialized places while marketing nature's beauty. Along these lines, local officials changed the name of Kilbourn City to Wisconsin Dells in 1931 to attract additional tourists. Unlike the elite midwestern resorts of Lake Geneva and Mackinac Island, the Dells developed as a middle-class destination that emphasized comfort over elegance. Despite the Depression, tourist growth continued. After World War II, one ambitious entrepreneur brought wartime amphibious vehicles to the Dells, making Dells Duck tours a signature attraction.

Railroads also traversed the Missouri Ozarks in the 1870s and began transporting tourists from Kansas City and St. Louis. Tourist development remained slow, but Harold Bell Wright's 1907 novel *Shepherd of the Hills* publicized the region's people and landscape. That landscape, with its natural caves, springs, and sinkholes, was further transformed by the hydroelectric dams that formed Lake Taneycomo in 1913 and Lake of the Ozarks in 1929, one of the nation's last privately financed dam-lake projects. Human intervention to marshal the river for power transformed the Ozarks into a lake-based tourist destination in the nation's midsection. With the recreational potential of artificial lakes recognized immediately, tourists discovered shorelines filled with lodging and water-based activities. Formed in 1919, the Ozark Playgrounds Association conducted national and regional campaigns marketing Ozark vacations. As vacations became a middle-class ritual, Missouri's Ozarks attracted tourists to its new lakeside resort communities, transforming a formerly remote rural area into an extension of the white middle-class urban cultural landscape.

With informal segregation restricting vacation options for African Americans at spas, the Dells, and the Ozarks, Michigan's Idlewild developed as a resort community. Promoted by a white-owned Chicago real estate interest in the 1910s, *Chicago Defender* advertisements helped agents sell lots to middle-class African Americans. In 1921, the company turned the property over to the African American owners association. Famous musicians entertained vacationers into the 1960s, while author Charles Chesnutt, cosmetics mogul Madame C. J. Walker, boxer Joe Louis, and Chicago doctor Daniel Hale Williams helped promote the resort.

Accessibility enabled the Indiana Dunes to attract a diverse array of visitors from Chicago's Loop and South Side. The University of Chicago Settlement started a summer vacation school at the Dunes for children from the Back of the Yards neighborhood. Wealthy Chicagoans originally sought protection for the dunes, including the first head of the National Park Service, Stephen Mather. In 1911, landscape architect Jens Jensen led Saturday afternoon dunes walking tours, and twelve years later, Indiana established Dunes State Park. But the dunes as a recreation destination for the masses kick-started when utilities magnate Samuel Insull purchased the South Shore Line in 1925, promoting train trips that delivered anxious city dwellers directly to the dunes. Advertising posters enticed people to travel to this nearby escape along the railroad line with colorful portrayals of seasons, beaches, events, and destinations in train stations, Chicago "L" platforms, schools, and libraries. The railroad's outing bureau organized trips and another bureau promoted home sites, with communities like Ogden Dunes, Dune Acres, and Beverly Shores offering private retreats from the congested city. Like other vacation areas, promotion and accessibility were key elements in drawing visitors to the dunes. Highway improvements and increased automobile ownership also led tourists to Michigan's dunes. The battle over preserving Indiana's dunes launched in the 1910s culminated in 1966 when, after a decade of support from Illinois Senator Paul Douglas, portions were designated a national lakeshore.

Across the Midwest, tourist promoters and vacationers reshaped the landscape as technology, promotion, commercialization, and preservation helped transform areas into rustic escapes and sites of consumption for the growing vacationing populace.

Sources and Further Reading: A. C. Bennett, "A Wisconsin Pioneer in Photography," *Wisconsin Magazine of History* 22 (Mar. 1939); Ronald D. Cohen and Stephen G. McShane, eds., *Moonlight in Duneland* (1998); Jennifer Crets, "'The Land of a Million Smiles,'" in Andrew Hurley, ed., *Common Fields* (1997); Dells County Historical Society, *Others Before You* (1995); Kay Franklin and Norma Schaeffer, *Duel for the Dunes* (1983); Lynn Morrow and Linda Myers-Phinney, *Shepherd of the Hills Country* (1999); Milton D. Rafferty, *The Ozarks: Land and Life*, 2nd ed. (2001); Lewis Walker and Ben C. Wilson, *Black Eden* (2002).

Aaron Shapiro
University of Chicago

Media and Entertainment

SECTION EDITORS
James Schwoch and Mimi White

Section Contents

Overview

If the Midwest has a distinctive identity, it is not immediately clear that this readily extends to the area of Media and Entertainment. Indeed, for most people, the idea of media and entertainment immediately conjures up a range of individuals, texts, and artifacts that transcend regional identity to resonate at a national, even global, level. Moreover, in the United States, the most prominent center of media production is identified with Hollywood, California, the primary signifier of American film and television production, with New York holding an equally important, if less iconic, role. From this perspective, what the Midwest furnishes are the middle-American consumers of mainstream media produced elsewhere; the Midwest also represents American audiences through such typifying social science–based studies as "Middletown" (Muncie, Indiana), the implications of the classic question "Will it play in Peoria?", or the status of Columbus, Ohio, as a primary test market for consumer products. The Mid-

The Pabst, a Milwaukee movie palace. Library of Congress, Prints and Photographs Division, Historic American Buildings Survey, HABS, WIS, 40-MILWA, 33-1.

west has been a popular locale for feature films and TV series, from *Home Alone*, *Ferris Bueller's Day Off*, *Hoosiers*, and *American Splendor* to *That 70's Show*, *The Mary Tyler Moore Show*, and *Picket Fences*. In addition, for many people, media and entertainment have a sort of temporal immediacy—panoplies of contemporary stars, films, songs, programs, ads, and buzzwords that ceaselessly stream through commercial media channels, lacking any historical past and stripped of the particularities of regional production or reception. But some important aspects of media and entertainment are significantly regionalized in terms of the Midwest, and this regionalization has its own history. Identifiable organizations, individuals, and practices, such as Chess Records, Michael Moore, or agricultural journalism, emerge from a distinctly regional context but have the capacity to influence within and beyond those boundaries. If we think of New York and Hollywood as housing our most visible media celebrities and institutions, the Midwest, more than any other region of the United States, has been the historical key to circulating, distributing, and networking those celebrities and institutions into national and global prominence.

The major cities of the Midwest—Cincinnati, Cleveland, Columbus, Des Moines, Detroit, Indianapolis, Kansas City (Kansas and Missouri), Milwaukee, Minneapolis–St. Paul, Omaha, St. Louis, Wichita, and above all others, Chicago—have served as the most important transportation and communication hubs for the transmittal of goods, services, and information throughout the United States and, indeed, all of North America. Chicago as a media metropolis is a special case, and it probably is closer to New York and Los Angeles in terms of media history and national impact than it is to any other midwestern city. Like New York and Los Angeles, Chicago was at one time the undisputed center of film production; like New York and Los Angeles, it is the only other city in the U.S.A. that has always had direct network station ownership (rather than station affiliation) with the major TV networks; and like those two cities, Chicago historically has been a major force in media production, advertising, and recorded music. In significance and influence, Chicago ranks third behind New York and Los Angeles. But because Chicago does not so completely dominate the Midwest in the same way that New York and Los Angeles dominate their media landscapes, the distinctive achievements of other major Midwest media cities are also comparatively more visible. Thus, for example, Motown Records emerges in Detroit; Garrison Keillor's *Prairie Home Companion* comes out of Minneapolis; the influential regional network of Crosley television stations is based in Ohio; and *Better Homes and Gardens* is published by the Meredith Corporation in Des Moines. This metropolitan relationship between Chicago and the other major cities of the Midwest is a very distinctive feature of midwestern media and entertainment.

As is the case in finance, manufacturing, immigration, and a host of other American social phenomena, the central importance of Chicago and other major midwestern cities to national transportation and communication is key to understanding media and entertainment in the region. While the footlights of Broadway or the klieg lights of Hollywood may now mark the home territory of many American media figures, the Midwest historically has been the hub for circulation of those figures throughout the nation. Moreover, the Midwest was and is an enormously important market for media products as well as media research. And the roll call of American media stars with hometown roots or significant experience in the Midwest is a long and distinguished one.

In historical terms, the first manifestations of Midwest media were found in publishing, both newspapers and magazines. Midwest journalism in the early nineteenth century emerged both in growing cities and in rural areas, producing midwest journalists who became contemporaries of the major publishers of New York, Boston, and other eastern urban areas, as well as creating pioneers of agricultural and rural journalism. Cinema, radio, and recorded music arose in the Midwest in the last decade of the nineteenth century concomitant with the development of industrial society, the closing of the American frontier, and the transformation to an urban society across the United States. Although entertainment and feature film production had largely left the Midwest for Hollywood by the end of World War I (though it would return in the 1970s), radio broadcasting became a Midwest powerhouse through such stations as WLW Cincinnati, WCCO Minneapolis, KMOX St. Louis, WOW Omaha, WTMJ Milwaukee, and WGN, WLS, WMAQ, WBBM, and WCFL in Chicago. Many of these same stations led the Midwest into the television era after World War II. Midwest broadcasting produced numerous stars as well as pointed the way in standard program formats such as soap operas and talk shows.

Understanding media and entertainment means giving greater emphasis to the larger midwestern cities. Smaller cities and rural areas figure in the story of media and entertainment in the region, but it is the larger cities that have been, and continue to be, the most important spaces for stars, creators, audiences, and industries associated with media and entertainment. In the lives of many midwesterners, the appearances and performances of stars, major productions, and similar activities became associated with the "big city" experiences that could be found in the Midwest;

for many rural midwesterners, consuming media and entertainment as a part of the experience of visiting their nearby major city has been a commonplace practice for over a century. The various entries in this section testify to the depth and variety of Midwest media, to the impact of Midwest media stars, institutions, and audiences upon American media history, and to elements of Midwest media and entertainment that are witness to regional distinctiveness. While the five media streams focused on here—film, broadcasting, journalism, recorded music, and advertising (which includes publicity, public relations, and related aspects of popular culture)—intermingle and overlap, each is important in its own right. Thus, this section explores such issues as, for example, film production in Chicago, major broadcast outlets, large and small newspapers, Detroit and Motown, and Midwest ad agencies and their best-known contributions to popular culture.

The entries discussing film stars and broadcasting are among those exemplifying the depth and variety of Midwest media and entertainment. Entries on advertising, talk shows, and soap opera are among those demonstrating the national impact of Midwest media. The distinctiveness of Midwest media is notable in many entries, from discussions of the origins of agricultural journalism to analysis of the interplay between religion and broadcasting. Many of the entries and essays below discuss individuals who are prominent in their fields, and occasionally include a profile of a media personality of unique distinction.

The Midwest is a critical region for understanding not only media distribution but also media audiences and the exhibition of media; and it has produced many stars, directors, artists, corporate leaders, and other influential media figures. While many of these stars and institutions represent the mainstream, the Midwest also has a rich tradition of media diversity. Virtually every midwestern state saw African American newspapers begin in one or more of their cities in the nineteenth century. The *Chicago Defender* has a long history as one of the nation's most influential African American newspapers, and in 1975 WGDR-TV in Detroit became the first commercial TV station in the United States with African American majority ownership. The Midwest is a center of various forms of media production, and its media and entertainment reflect unique regional sensibilities. Whether Barry Gordy and Motown in Detroit, Irv Kupcinet and the celebrity culture of Chicago, broadcast giants like WLW Cincinnati, the rural and urban Midwest landscapes seen in so many feature films and TV series, or the Midwest market audiences of representative Columbus—all these examples, and many more, help us better understand media and entertainment in the Midwest. Perhaps this dual nature of being both regionally distinct and fully interwoven into national and global media and entertainment culture makes Midwest media and entertainment of particular value.

Finally, although this section may often speak more about the past than about the future, it is certain that Midwest media and entertainment will continue to show signs of regional distinctiveness into the twenty-first century. Pop music superstars with Midwest roots such as Madonna and Prince suggest that pop celebrities with national and global visibility will continue to emerge from the area, as did the many regional cinema and broadcast stars of past generations. Documentary filmmakers such as Michael Moore are achieving prominence and distinction through their productions by, among other things, reworking the documentary film medium in new terms for a new generation—and while the terms and conditions are strikingly different, Moore's new take on documentary filmmaking with, among other things, his own midwestern sensibilities harks back to Garrison Keillor's midwestern reworking of the radio medium in a previous generation. In sum, the Midwest in the twenty-first century will doubtless continue to be a distinct location for film and television production, an important and distinct market for media consumption, a birthplace of pop stars and media celebrities, and a supporter and innovator for the confluence of media and education.

The subsections and entries that follow are ordered alphabetically.

James Schwoch and Mimi White
Northwestern University, Illinois

Advertising

Historically, the advertising industry has been both economically and culturally centered on the East coast. Still, as a region, the Midwest has made important contributions to the advertising trade. Historians point to three major transformations in advertising in the early twentieth century: the establishment of the open contract system, the use of sex appeal, and the use of reason-why advertising. The first two came from New York City, but the last came straight out of the Heartland, from Albert Lasker of the Chicago-based Lord and Thomas Agency. The concept of reason-why, which argued that a specific rationale must be expressed in the advertisement to elicit purchasing, was uniquely suited to the morals, sensibilities, and rational values of the Midwest, and it helped to produce a number of notable advertising figures in the region.

One of them was Lasker, who worked in the advertising business for more than forty years. His importance to the industry was such that historian Stephen Fox dubbed the early portion of the twentieth century "The Age of Lasker." Lasker worked in concert at Chicago's Lord and Thomas Agency with legendary copywriter John E. Kennedy, who argued that advertising was simply "salesmanship in print." The two became famous as pioneers of reason-why advertising, and L&T became the largest agency in the country.

Lasker's work in advertising extended beyond the creation of theories and styles of advertising, eventually influencing social and cultural changes in the country. Through his advertising work for Lucky Strike cigarettes, Lasker helped to persuade Americans that it was socially acceptable for women to smoke in public. His efforts for Sunkist oranges made orange juice a beverage consumed throughout the day; as his slogan said, "Sunkist: it's not just for breakfast any more." Lasker also worked for the Republican Party and for the presidential campaign of Warren G. Harding. In 1941, he left the advertising business for other pursuits. Although no agency bears his name, his advertising legacy—that creatively drives a central idea—lasts to this day.

Yet Lasker was not the only midwestern ad executive to advance the state of advertising theory. It was while working in Detroit that Theodore MacManus, lead copywriter for General Motors, advanced the notion of advertising based on image and suggestion through his famed ad for Cadillac entitled "The Penalty of Leadership." Though penned nearly ninety years ago, the advertisement is still cited as one of the best of all time and hailed as the beginning of the use of soft-sell and impressionistic copy.

MacManus's work also left a lasting impression on a junior adman by the name of Leo Burnett. Burnett started his own agency in Chicago in 1935 and became a major advertising figure in his own right, creating such lasting figures as the Jolly Green Giant, the Pillsbury Dough Boy, Tony the Tiger, and the Marlboro Man. In addition, Burnett's work spurred what became known as the Chicago style of advertising. This style revolved around the consumer, used clear and effective language, and utilized imagery and copy that indicated a level of respect for the consumer. Burnett's ideas and campaigns had a lasting impact on both his agency, Leo Burnett Company, and the stature of Chicago as a major advertising city. He was posthumously named Ad Man of the Century by *Time* magazine.

Barbara Proctor, another significant advertising figure and one of the leading black female entrepreneurs of her generation, was not originally from the Midwest. In fact, her move to the region occurred largely by accident. On her way home from a job in Michigan, she stopped in Chicago and used the last of her travel

❖ Burma-Shave

In Minnesota in 1925, Clinton Odell's Burma-Vita Company changed the face of advertising with a novel roadside campaign featuring humorous jingles on signs that plugged its new brushless shaving cream, Burma-Shave. The last signs appeared in 1963.

These signs are not
For laughs alone
The face they save
May be your own
Burma-Shave

You can beat
A mile a minute
But there is
no future in it
Burma-Shave

Is he lonesome
Or just blind—
This guy who drives
So close behind?
Burma-Shave

On curves ahead
Remember, sonny
That rabbit's foot
Didn't save the bunny
Burma-Shave

Toughest whiskers
In the town
We hold 'em up
You mow 'em down
Burma-Shave

Altho insured
Remember, kiddo,
They don't pay you
They pay your widow
Burma-Shave

Heaven's latest
Neophyte
Signalled left
Then turned right
Burma-Shave

Angels who guard you
When you drive
Usually retire
at 55
Burma-Shave

A Man—A Miss
A Car—A Curve
He kissed the Miss
And missed the Curve
Burma-Shave

A beard that's rough
And overgrown
Is better than
A chaperone
Burma-Shave

If Crusoe'd kept
his chin more tidy
He might have found
A lady Friday
Burma-Shave

Ben met Anna
Made a hit
neglected beard
Ben–Anna split
Burma-Shave

We're widely read
And often quoted
But it's shaves, not signs
For which we're noted
Burma-Shave

Farewell, O verse
Along the road
How sad to know
You're out of mode
Burma-Shave

Source: Frank Rowsome, Jr., *The Verse by the Side of the Road* (1965).

funds to buy clothes, stranding herself in the city. Proctor worked there first as a freelance writer, then began writing for television, and later became a record company executive. In 1964, she joined Post-Keyes-Gardner Advertising, but six years later, after feeling limited to working only on the women's market, Proctor opened her own agency. Its name, Proctor and Gardner, combined her married and maiden names, a move she made because she believed clients would be more at ease if they thought she had a male partner.

Though she did not obtain a client for the first seven months, she soon had an impressive client list that included Sears Roebuck, E.J. Gallo Winery, and Alberto-Culver.

Proctor maintained a steadfast business philosophy in which she rejected accounts that she felt projected negative stereotypes about blacks and women or that would damage the community. Beyond advertising work, Proctor advocated government support for small businesses and organizations, such as operation

PUSH. In 1984, she was cited by President Reagan for her entrepreneurial accomplishments. Although she left the ad business in 1995, Proctor continues to be a tireless advocate of African American entrepreneurship and community building.

Thomas Burrell found his way into advertising in a unique manner. On a career aptitude test he took in high school, Burrell scored high in the categories of persuasion and creativity. Unsure what these results might mean for career aspirations, he sought out a guidance counselor, who told him they indicated an aptitude for writing advertising copy. Later, while enrolled at Roosevelt University in Chicago, Burrell began working in the mailroom of Wade Advertising, and he stayed on after college. During his years at Wade, Burrell had thoughts of starting his own agency. He and partner Emmett McBain (who later left the agency) did so in 1971.

As owner of his own agency, Burrell set out to convince corporate executives that African Americans had unique tastes and desires that, if properly appealed to, could lead to dramatic sales gains. Operating in Chicago also placed the Burrell agency in close proximity to some of the largest black-owned businesses in the country. Consequently, Burrell tapped the supportive entrepreneurial environment of the Chicago black business community in building his agency. Working for both black- and white-owned firms, Burrell pursued an advertising concept he called "positive realism." This concept involved placing blacks into realistic everyday situations in ads, and avoiding the stereotypical and demeaning situations of the past. The Burrell firm quickly became one of the leading black-owned agencies in the nation. Major Burrell clients included McDonald's, Coca-Cola, Ford Motor Company, and Johnson Publishing. Today the agency remains an industry leader, consistently winning awards for its creative work.

By the 1960s, the Midwest, and chiefly Chicago, was recognized by many in the industry as a major advertising center. And with the auto industry, Detroit also became an important advertising city. Yet unlike in Chicago, many of the firms that serviced the auto industry were not based in Detroit but were satellite offices of firms based elsewhere. By the 1980s, Minneapolis also contained advertising firms that were developing a national reputation for creativity and excellence. The region contained a concentration of some of the oldest and largest African American-owned agencies in the nation, among them Burrell Advertising, Vince Cullers Advertising, and Don Coleman Advertising.

Taken together, Chicago, Detroit, and Minneapolis transformed the Midwest into an advertising center second only to that of the East Coast. The three cities are today home to many of the nation's largest advertising agencies and are the source of some of the most award-winning and successful advertising created.

Sources and Further Reading: Edd Applegate, ed., *The Ad Men and Women* (1994); Draper Daniels, *Giants, Pigmies and Other Advertising People* (1974); Stephen Fox, *The Mirror Makers* (1984); John N. Ingham and Lynne B. Feldman, *African-American Business Leaders* (1994); Albert Davis Lasker, *The Lasker Story* (1963); Lawrence R. Samuel, *Brought to You By* (2001); Juliann Sivulka, *Soap, Sex, and Cigarettes* (1998); Juliet E. K. Walker, ed., *Encyclopedia of African-American Business History* (1999); Juliet E. K. Walker, *The History of Black Business in America* (1998).

Jason Chambers
University of Illinois–Urbana-Champaign

Broadcasting

Since the 1920s, broadcasting has been commonly understood to refer to radio's—and, later, television's—ability to transmit or to "cast" a signal "broadly" from a central transmission point to multiple points of reception. Broadcasting, in this technical sense, simply refers to a method of distributing sounds and images over the air. However, prior to the development of the mass media with which we are now familiar, the term "broadcasting" was primarily an agricultural concept that described the scattering of seed over a broad area, cast by hand, as opposed to seed sown methodically, in rows. The term's agricultural origin, in retrospect, might symbolically underscore and anticipate the centrality of America's Heartland to the imagination and codification of U.S. broadcasting in its most dominant form—commercial, national networking. The Midwest's imagined pastoral character has played a recurring and powerful role in the origination, development, and ongoing understanding of commercial network broadcast technology, its standardization, its program forms and appeals, and featured talent within American culture, from the 1910s to the twenty-first century.

In the early 1920s, the first attempts to define broadcasting utilized legal precedents of transportation and interstate commerce through which to imagine radio's relationship to region and nation. The Radio Act of 1927, for example, correlated wireless transmission of radio signals to transportation of goods or services to the market. This act required that each member of the Federal Radio Commission (later renamed the Federal Communications Commission, or FCC) must be a citizen of the United States and must represent one of five geographic zones, of which the fourth would include Indiana, Illinois, Wisconsin, Minnesota, North Dakota, South Dakota, Iowa, Nebraska, Kansas, and Missouri. From its earliest definition, therefore, broadcasting was conceptualized and codified as national in its scope of distribution but fundamentally local in its day-to-day service obligations.

In 1946 the FCC issued a report that specified the need for individual stations, whether network affiliates or independent, to be responsive to local interests. According to the Blue Book (so named for the color of its binding), station license renewal would now be premised on two factors: the station's use of local talent wherever possible, and the station's responsiveness to the specific interests of the public it served. Examples outlined in the report pointed to presumed differences in regional identity. While opera might be of interest in urban areas with a diverse public such as New York, for example, folk music was suggested as a more responsible choice for programmers in Missouri (as well as, ostensibly, a more logical outlet for local talent). The defining document of public service in broadcasting thus explicitly divided the postwar American audience between a Northeast corridor—fluent in national consumer ideals and "high" cultural taste—and a rural Midwest characterized by premodern, "vernacular" taste.

From the emergence of radio and television through the late 1950s, the Midwest was a thriving center for independent stations, the development of distinctive broadcasting talent and new program forms, and unparalleled experimentation with educational TV. Chicago, in particular, was a central hub of radio production and program form development. As broadcast historian Michele Hilmes observes, Chicago was the birthplace of the daily soap opera and of the talk show in the forms with which we are still familiar. Prior to the dominance of the major broadcast networks in radio of the 1930s, cities throughout the Midwest were also home to thriving independent stations and stations run by nonprofit organizations. Via stations such as Kansas City, Kansas's KFKB (for "Kansas Folks Know Best"), through radio personae such as Father Coughlin (broadcasting from suburban Detroit), and through country and western music programs and agricultural news programs, the region's early broadcast offerings were often populist in their appeal to listeners who learned to accept radio, in part, through its offering of such familiar sounds as the pulpit and dance hall. Radio was promoted, in this respect, as a new technological extension of conversations previously engaged in at the grain elevator or the Sunday social.

Midwestern universities also initiated educational radio and television stations and educational program services long before the institution of the Public Broadcasting Service (in 1969). It seems particularly symbolic that the first educational broadcast stations were, in the main, housed at major midwestern land-grant institutions—campuses founded through the Morrill Land Grant College Act, whose goal was to offer opportunities for higher education to those who had previously been unable to access it and obtain a college degree. Educational stations such as those at the University of Wisconsin, the University of Michigan, Iowa State University, and the University of Illinois offered university extension courses as early as the 1920s.

Perhaps most distinctive in this regard, the Midwest Program on Airborne Television Instruction (MPATI) was launched in the early 1960s. Based at Purdue University and financed by the Ford Foundation and private industry, the project coordinated courses from twenty regional colleges and universities to offer telecasts from airborne transmitters to middle schools throughout Indiana, Illinois, Ohio, Michigan, and Wisconsin (and parts of Kentucky) to offer courses that were otherwise unaffordable or unsupportable in local schools but were important for college-bound students. They included a range of courses from arithmetic to music.

The MPATI reflected the spirit of midwestern native and then-FCC Chairman Newton Minow's May 1961 challenge to leaders in the television industry to ally television service with the ethic of the New Frontier. Minow's now-famous 1961 "Vast Wasteland" address to the National Association of Broadcasters suggested that television, at its best, could be one of the most powerful forces for education in the modern age. Educational TV station extension courses and programs such as those offered by the MPATI gave broadcast media the potential to equalize previously inequitable distribution of educational resources—to redistribute educational and cultural capital to rural midwesterners. The legacy of these educational TV stations and projects lives on in the contemporary context in the form of public television and public access stations throughout the Midwest (many of which are still housed on university campuses) as well as in documentary filmmaking for television that is focused on the region.

For-profit television networking developed relatively gradually across postwar America, with the eastern seaboard interconnected to the Midwest and its spur extensions between 1948 and 1952. Until the late 1950s, NBC-TV operated a Central Division of the network with full production facilities located in Chicago. When the majority of all network production shifted to Hollywood and from live programming to filmed programming, midwestern cities were excised from the ability to "feed" the network—that is, the Midwest lost its prominence as a site of origination for prime-time network programming (though daytime and syndicated breakthroughs continued, as evidenced, for example, by *Donahue* and *Oprah*).

In radio, on the other hand, the Mutual Broadcasting System represented a Midwest-based network rival through the 1960s, when it shifted its focus to programming alone. Mutual's short history was marked by challenges to coastal network powers, including a complaint to the FCC that led to NBC's divestiture of one of its radio networks and ultimately to the formation of ABC. (Mutual's former stations are now part of the Westwood One radio networks.)

Throughout the 1950s, however, television network programs perceived to address midwestern sensibilities found a nationally enthusiastic audience, though they were often dismissed in the popular press and in industry publications for their Heartlander appeals. The country and western music program *Jubilee, USA* (ABC-TV, 1955–1961), for example, weekly portrayed the nation's rural Heartland as a positive, familial, restorative corrective to the anxiety, materialism, self-involvement, and distance from "real folk" presumed common in coastal and urban postwar American life. Traditional network centers of production in New York and Hollywood thus seized the opportunity to appeal to middle America throughout the tumultuous 1960s by featuring series helmed by celebrities such as Lawrence Welk (originally of Strasburg, North Dakota).

Welk's orchestra of "champagne music"-makers aired weekly on ABC from 1955 to 1971 and continues in syndication (typically carried by PBS stations) to this day. While Welk was consistently dismissed by television critics who implied that he was unbearably sincere and his music tastelessly amateurish (thus aligning the Midwest with questionable taste and residual populism), his program's highest ratings during the peak years of the late 1960s were recorded in eastern, urban, sophisticated Philadelphia. This implies that either Welk had a more urban and more broadly national appeal than otherwise considered, or that there were midwesterners everywhere across the country—in spirit, if not in locale.

In the 1970s, the prime-time imagination of the region and its people was urbanized and revised with *The Mary Tyler Moore Show*. The series was critically well regarded. Set in Minneapolis, a previously ignored, thriving midwestern metropolis, the program featured well-rounded characters who were socially savvy, fashionable, conversant with contemporary culture, and politically rather liberal. Grant Tinker's and Mary Tyler Moore's production company, MTM,

continued to feature such midwestern locales and challenges to conventional prime-time portrayals of midwestern identity through the early 1980s, with successful series such as *The Bob Newhart Show* and *WKRP in Cincinnati*. More recently, programs like *Picket Fences*, *ER*, and *Touched by an Angel* have featured midwestern settings and imagined the region and its people in diverse and engaging ways, while still associating it with a lack of pretense that harks back to earliest "folk" alliances of the radio era. Producers of the "reality TV" programming boom of the early twenty-first century have, for example, begun to audition midwestern participants because they are perceived to be more "real" and less careerist than volunteers from either coast.

Although broadcast media across the country have increasingly been incorporated into larger conglomerate media interests, this has had the dual effect of *both* undermining regional distinctiveness in broadcasting *and* encouraging new outlets for midwestern media production and expression. In 1978, for example, the Tribune Company's WGN television station in Chicago became a "superstation"—a local, independent station whose broadcast signal is delivered via satellite to cable systems all over the country. In effect, the superstation is "super" because what was once a Chicago-only, regional, independent television station featuring Chicago news, personalities, and sports is now a national television station that telecasts "Chicago-ness" to the broader nation (and to Canada, as well). WGN thus allows midwesterners to keep an eye on regional weather and sports teams from wherever they may be. It simultaneously "nationalizes" Chicago and re-localizes the television market within which WGN's viewers may live. WGN is now an important partner in the relatively new WB TV network. In radio, Minnesota Public Radio has a similar appeal and effect within the public broadcasting sphere, contributing significant programming to National Public Radio.

In conceptualization, policy, and business practice, then, U.S. broadcasting has been characterized by an ongoing tension and ambivalence between regional and national interests and identity. Place-identity also has been a powerful factor within broadcast content. At each of these sites, however—from licensing requirements to program content—there are two key, recurring tropes through which the Midwest and "midwesternness" typically have been imagined for both local and national broadcast audiences: as a predominantly rural region characterized by a populist ethic. "Populism" here refers to the Midwest as the locus of "real" Americans, a place-holder for an idealized agrarian and rural culture characterized by political conservatism, suspicion of the new, loyalty to tradition, religious fealty, and commitment to family (as heard and seen in key program genres, embodied by homegrown talent and stars, or represented by particular settings or subject matter). This is the Midwest imagined as the mythic American Heartland, symbolic of a residual culture to which the nation at large ritually desires to return—or to critique, depending on the tenor of the times.

Sources and Further Reading: Christopher Anderson, *HollywoodTV* (1994); William Boddy, *Fifties Television* (1993); Les Brown, *Les Brown's Encyclopedia of Television*, 3rd ed. (1992); James Carey, *Communication as Culture* (1992); Sydney Head, Christopher Sterling, and Lemuel B. Schofield, *Broadcasting in America*, 7th ed. (1994); Michele Hilmes, *Only Connect: A Cultural History of Broadcasting in the United States* (2002); Frank J. Kahn, ed., *Documents of American Broadcasting*, 3rd ed. (1978); Michael D. Murray and Donald G. Godfrey, eds., *Television in America* (1997); Christopher Sterling and John M. Kittross, *Stay Tuned: A Concise History of American Broadcasting*, 2nd ed. (1990).

Victoria E. Johnson
University of California–Irvine

The Chicago School of Television

Television in the Midwest traces its roots to experimental operations in the late 1920s and early 1930s in various cities, among them Milwaukee, Cincinnati, Iowa City, West Lafayette, and most notably, Chicago. However, it was not until the 1940s that television actually took hold, and under the guidance of two key individuals, Captain William Crawford Eddy and Jules Herbuveaux, it was Chicago that led the way in midwest TV growth.

A former naval officer and inveterate inventor, Eddy was hired to direct the development of Chicago's WBKB, owned by Paramount Pictures' subsidiary, Balaban and Katz theatres. It was licensed as one of six American television stations to operate during World War II. Eddy envisioned the Midwest, and especially Chicago, functioning as the network hub or nerve center for the rest of the country. At war's end, he anticipated network service up to forty hours weekly to small stations within a hundred-mile radius of Chicago at the rate of forty dollars per program. Ultimately, his plans called for an interconnection of stations within fifteen states between Chicago and the East Coast. But Eddy left WBKB in 1948, and subsequent management viewed his plans as too expensive. Notwithstanding, his pioneering efforts in programming and microwave relay transmission were important to television's early development.

On the programming side, NBC's Central Division Vice President Jules Herbuveaux and his WNBQ-TV program director Ted Mills set out to define television as a medium distinct from proscenium-based theatre or film. Taking a page from the days of Chicago radio, in which innovative formats and noncelebrity talent had proven successful, the programs they created with minimal facilities and minimal budgets were identified as being in the Chicago style. Nurtured in an idea-rich atmosphere, these low-key, almost casual programs easily mixed drama with reality by combining improvisation with theatrical elements drawn from Pirandello, *commedia del'arte*, and Chinese opera.

By Spring of 1950, thirteen of the twenty-five most popular series broadcast on Chicago's four stations were telecast on WNBQ. *Kukla, Fran & Ollie* and *Zoo Parade* had transferred from Eddy's WBKB. But others had been created by Herbuveaux's staff. One of the most representative of these offerings was Dave Garroway's *Garroway at Large* in which the host wandered the studio "bumping" into people and dramatic, comic, or musical situations. Studs Terkel's *Studs' Place* presented a true-to-life comedy-drama that focused on the lives of its principal characters. Referencing these Chicago School formats, on May 24, 1950, the trade paper *Variety* reported, "Here is none of your hit-or-miss programming. They all make fine video sense."

In 1953, Chicago provided thirteen network originations, but this number diminished quickly with the opening of coast-to-coast networks—a move contrary to Eddy's earlier thinking. To Herbuveaux's mind, as soon as the two coasts were linked, Chicago and the Midwest were no longer necessary. By the mid-1950s, the Chicago School was becoming a fond memory, giving way to big-star, high-energy network entertainments more typical of Broadway and Hollywood.

Sources and Further Reading: "Bill Eddy: Eyeing Chi as Tele Hub: Ready to Feed Area's Small Stations," *Variety* (Dec. 17, 1947); Bill Fay, "Top TV Town," *Collier's* (Mar. 17, 1951); Jules Herbuveaux, "Chi TV Parlays a Myth into B.O. Inventiveness," *Variety* 190 (May 27, 1953); "Highlights: '49–'50 Show Management Review," *Variety* (May 24, 1950); Joel Sternberg, "Chicago Television," *Quarterly Review of Film & Video* 16 (1999); Joseph H. Udelson, *The Great Television Race* (1982).

Joel Sternberg
Saint Xavier University, Chicago

Children's Programming

Children's broadcast programming in the Midwest dates back to the very early days of radio. As was true in other parts of the country, midwestern radio formats often centered around low-budget variety programming, clubhouse activities, and talent shows. Dramatic action-adventure stories in serial form took life in the larger cities, most notably Chicago. With access to more child talent than other Midwest cities, Chicago provided the networks and the country with highly successful long-running shows. Examples in this kid radio format included *Little Orphan Annie, Skippy, Captain Midnight, Terry and the Pirates, Dick Tracy, Jack Armstrong the All-American Boy, Tom Mix,* and the more educationally oriented *Quiz Kids.* As noted by Bill Thompson in his October 25, 1948, analysis of Chicago radio and television for *Broadcasting* magazine, these children's programs required bigger and better sound effects, so Chicago became headquarters for radio's first "noise" men, who developed many of the techniques later used in New York and Hollywood. In the same vein, Detroit's WXYZ offered a series of quality originations best represented by *The Lone Ranger* and the *Green Hornet* on the Mutual network and *Challenge of the Yukon* on the ABC network.

With the introduction of television in the late 1940s, children's programs often provided a way for local stations with limited facilities to begin production with minimal budgets. Throughout the Midwest, a number of locally produced variety and clubhouse

Stars of the *Kukla, Fran & Ollie* show. Courtesy Chicago Historical Society/Burr Tillstrom Copyright Trust.

shows made the transition from radio to television and mixed with puppet shows and cartoon shows as new stations came on the air. But as was typical in radio, the larger cities like Chicago led the way, often rivaling or exceeding program offerings from New York and Los Angeles in production quality and in critical acclaim. Midwest network offerings, although fewer in number, also proved to be highly successful.

One of the earliest of the Midwest shows and one of the most celebrated was *Kukla, Fran & Ollie.* Originally broadcast under the title *Junior Jamboree,* this long-running series first appeared in 1947 on Chicago's pioneer television station, WBKB. Utilizing puppet characters, including a bulb-nosed doll-like waif named Kukla and a gentle albeit curmudgeonly dragon named Ollie, puppeteer Burr Tillstrom's characters interacted Monday through Friday with their human counterpart, Fran Allison. The show was improvised, adult in tone, and unlike its network rivals *Howdy Doody* and *Rootie Kazootie,* often dealt with newsworthy issues on Tillstrom's mind, e.g., problems associated with environmental pollution. A mainstay in the Chicago School of Television, *Kukla, Fran & Ollie* remained on the air as a regular offering through August 1957. However, Tillstrom and his Kuklapolitans stayed in the national eye as television and stage performers until the puppeteer's death in December 1985.

Other network programs of note in the early 1950s included Detroit's *Soupy Sales,* with his White Fang and Black Fang puppet characters. Chicago's NBC outlet aired the long-running *Zoo Parade* from the city's Lincoln Park Zoo, *Watch Mr. Wizard* with Don Herbert, *Pet Shop* with its cute animals, *Ding Dong School* for pre-schoolers with Dr. Francis Horwich, various cartoon and fantasy offerings from Uncle Johnny Coons, and ABC-Chicago's *Super Circus* with ringmaster Claude Kirchner and vivacious blond band leader Mary Hartline. Also, making the transition from radio, the popular *Quiz Kids* with host Joe Kelly had a long network run on NBC and CBS. An early and highly successful program (1949–1951) that at one point rated sixth in the country behind Milton Berle's *Texaco Star Theater* and Ed Sullivan's *Toast of the Town* was NBC-Chicago's *Cactus Jim.* Working with a low budget, a fake beard, and a papier-mâché rock, former radio actor Clarence Hartzell and his replacement Bill Bailey portrayed grizzly old cowboys who would talk about the West between segments of western films.

In 1953, when national television network facilities utilizing coaxial cable were installed across the country, and television studios became more available on the two coasts, programs from cities other than New York and Los Angeles became afterthoughts. Midwestern children's programs left their respective network time slots and became almost exclusively local.

Notwithstanding this "demotion" in national status, many programs had long successful runs—for example, WGN-Chicago's *Garfield Goose and Friends*, *Ray Rayner and Friends*, and *Bozo's Circus* and from WOI-TV in Ames, Iowa, *The Magic Window*, the longest-running show in educational television history (1951–1994).

Today, children's programs exist principally as animated cartoon shows produced in cities outside the Midwest. Programs featuring comedy sketches and film segments surface occasionally but never in numbers comparable to previous years.

Sources and Further Reading: Tim Brooks and Earle Marsh, *The Complete Directory to Prime Time Network TV Shows, 1946–Present,* 5th ed. (1992); Frank Buxton and Bill Owen, *The Big Broadcast, 1920–1950,* rev. ed. (1972); Jeffery Davis, *Children's Television, 1947–1990* (1995); Stuart Fischer, *Kids' TV: The First 25 Years* (1983); Tim Hollis, *Hi There, Boys and Girls!* (2001); George W. Woolery, *Children's Television: The First Thirty-Five Years, 1946–1981, Part II* (1985).

Joel Sternberg
Saint Xavier University, Chicago

Corporate and Sponsored Film and Video Production

Corporate or sponsored films—produced by businesses, educational institutions, and governmental agencies for instructional or self-promotional purposes—existed as early as 1897. Historians have studied these films, their producers, and their corporate sponsors. The Midwest has been home to three major corporate and sponsored film producers—Jamison "Jam" Handy of Detroit, Reid H. Ray of St. Paul, and Byron Friend of Park Ridge, Illinois. Their productions spanned the twentieth century and provided films for all the major Midwest corporations.

Midwest corporate and sponsored films have contributed much to the film- and video-making processes. In 1911, International Harvester sponsored *Back to the Old Farm,* a film that incorporated the flashback and flash-forward techniques, and in 1953, it hired famous animator Ray Harryhausen to animate *A Man with a Thousand Hands.* These films were detailed in such midwestern film magazines as *Nickelodeon* (later *Motography*) and the premier corporate film magazine *Business Screen,* both published in Chicago.

As early as 1907, *Nickelodeon* reported that even single films from one company were reaching five hundred thousand people at a time when total attendance in the United States for commercial films was only twenty-five million a year. As well as being shown in house at their corporate sponsors, these films were and still are shown through educational systems, at organizational meetings, to religious groups, and often fill air time on local public access television. *Business Screen* reported in 1953 that viewing audiences for such films actually topped twenty million per week.

Over the years, midwestern corporate film sponsors have included all of the car manufacturers, all of the farm equipment manufacturers, the major breweries, and all of the Midwest insurance companies. Most of these businesses now have their own in-house production facilities. Communities also created sponsored films about themselves; as early as 1913 films were made to promote Akron (Ohio), Burlington (Iowa), and Oshkosh (Wisconsin).

Other midwestern organizations that still sponsor films and video productions include government facilities, schools (elementary through high schools), colleges, medical and health organizations, community agencies, and religious organizations. They produce films and videos for training, safety, product demonstrations, company news, documentaries, archival information, and teleconferencing. These production companies are excellent places for interested film and video production personnel to begin their careers. More than fifty corporate film and video production facilities currently operate in the Midwest, and their products now include video and digital productions.

Another facet of Midwest corporate film and video production is film education. All Midwest land grant universities have had film and video production units for many years. Those which tend to produce films and video of national merit, and in addition develop students whose work tends to garner national awards, are The Ohio State University, Indiana State University, Southern Illinois University–Carbondale, the University of Iowa, Iowa State University, and the University of Wisconsin.

Crucial to the history of film and video production in the Midwest is the American Archives of the Factual Film at Iowa State University. This collection now includes more than thirteen thousand catalogued films and can provide the interested scholar access to films produced as early as 1911. The collection also includes ancillary materials such as magazines, scripts, and letters, and is the central storehouse for corporate and sponsored films in the United States.

Sources and Further Reading: Diane Gayeski, *Corporate and Instructional Video* (1983); Walter J. Klein, *The Sponsored Film* (1976); Eugene Marlow, *Managing the Corporate Media Center* (1981); Daniel J. Perkins, "The American Archives of the Factual Film," *Historical Journal of Film, Radio and Television* 10 (1990); Daniel J. Perkins, "Sponsored Business Films: An

Overview 1895–1955" in *Film Reader* 6 (1985); Daniel J. Perkins, "The Sponsored Film: A New Dimension in American Film Research?" in *Historical Journal of Film, Radio and Television* 2 (Mar. 1982).

Daniel J. Perkins
University of Wisconsin–Eau Claire

Foreign-Language Radio

Foreign-language radio in the Midwest has always been as diverse as the immigrants to the region. Starting in the early 1920s, these stations represented cultural gathering spaces for German Americans, Polish Americans, Greek Americans, Swedish Americans, and other groups throughout the region. In 1937, stations in Illinois, Michigan, Ohio, and Wisconsin accepted foreign-language programming.

Most of these stations did not specialize in one language or ethnicity. A typical station programmed several hours a week in each of several foreign languages, and offered English-language news and programs during the remaining time. These stations were located in both large urban centers and small cities and towns. Languages represented over the years on Midwest ethnic radio have included (but not been limited to) Spanish, Greek, Ukranian, Polish, Swedish, Croatian, Latvian, French, Gaelic (Irish), Russian, Slovenian, Korean, Romanian, Finnish, Chinese, Arabic, Italian, Serbian, Hungarian, Farsi, Slovak, Portuguese, and Lithuanian.

The first Polish radio program on air in the United States was broadcast in Cleveland on WJAY in 1926. The program's first broadcast featured Paul Fout, a Polish singer and actor who had immigrated several years before. From 1927 on, the station regularly broadcast three weekly segments in Polish, including a weekly children's program featuring Polish American children performing music. Over the years, Fout became a radio personality, appearing on different Ohio stations until 1970. By 1930, Polish radio programming had also debuted in Chicago and Detroit.

Music and religion were two staples of Midwest ethnic radio. Programs often featured church choirs singing, church services, and other types of religious programming. By the late 1970s foreign-language radio was quite strong and diverse throughout the Midwest. In 1978 many different Greek programs were broadcast weekly in Chicago. In the same period in Cleveland, two stations were primarily aimed at African Americans and broadcast to other ethnic groups as well, including Hungarian, Polish, and Italian programs. Some stations were quite diverse; for example, in Cleveland in 1974, WXEN broadcast ethnic radio weekly in several different languages. In the

same period in Detroit, programs were broadcast in Greek, Polish, Spanish, and Macedonian, among other languages.

Today, Spanish radio is by far the largest foreign-language radio category. Generally these stations offer a variety of full-time Spanish-language programming. In Chicago, some Spanish stations broadcast music in Spanish from Latin America and the United States, while talk radio stations such as "La Tremenda" (AM 560) broadcast news and talk shows. One also finds in the Midwest programming in German, Polish, Korean, Russian, Bulgarian, Chinese, Serbian, Greek, and many other languages. Some programs are multilingual, such as the Hindi–Urdu–Punjabi "Desi Junction" on AM 1530 in Chicago. Foreign-language programs, on both FM and AM radio, continue to unite immigrant communities that have moved to disparate locations within cities and to promote cultural events, language retention, cultural continuity, and ethnic pride.

Sources and Further Reading: Theodore C. Grame, *Ethnic Broadcasting in the United States* (1980); Józef Migala, *Polish Radio Broadcasting in the United States* (1987); Derek W. Vaillant, "Sounds of Whiteness: Local Radio, Racial Formation, and Public Culture in Chicago, 1921–1935," *American Quarterly* 54 (Mar. 2002); Lubomyr R. Wynar and David Reith, *Ethnic, Nationality, and Foreign-Language Broadcasting and Telecasting in Ohio* (1981).

Devorah Heitner
Northwestern University, Illinois

Major Radio Stations

Although the question of who started the first U.S. radio station is still debated today, radio broadcasting began in the Midwest when Earle M. Terry transmitted signals from his physics lab at the University of Wisconsin in Madison in 1904. Since its beginnings, the medium has had a profound effect on the Midwest, the nation, and the world. "Broadcasting" was originally an agricultural term, meaning to sow seeds broadly instead of in rows. But when early midwestern radio stations aired crop and farm market reports, gave weather advisories, and kept farmers informed of up-to-date agricultural techniques, its meaning soon transformed. The noontime farm report remains a time of reverent concentration around many farm family tables across the Midwest.

American radio had another pioneer from the Midwest, WWJ Detroit. William E. Scripps founded WWJ in August 1920 as a way to expand the readership of his *Detroit News*. The station was one of the first to broadcast sports and political events, including the 1920 World Series between Brooklyn and Cleveland and the results of the 1920 presidential election. Transmitters in airplanes and trucks gave WWJ listeners the first traffic reports and on-the-spot reporting.

Following the *Detroit News'* example, the *Chicago Tribune* bought its own radio station in 1924, renaming it WGN for the paper's motto, World's Greatest Newspaper. Midwesterners tuned in for talk shows and sportscasts along with grain futures. During the 1950s, WGN, like many stations, expanded into television. Visual broadcasting gave new depth to coverage of Chicago Cubs games and entertainment programs such as the long-running *Bozo the Clown* show. As national regulation of radio took hold in the late 1920s and early 1930s, the Midwest also became home to many "clear channel" or fifty-thousand-watt radio stations, among the most powerful in the United States; and for a period of time, WLW Cincinnati was the only station in the country authorized to transmit at five hundred thousand watts, giving WLW coverage in all forty-eight states.

As towers became more powerful and stations expanded, some anchors became local and regional celebrities. Young Ronald Reagan of WHO Des Moines and later Harry Caray of WGN Chicago gained renown for their sportscasts. Sports were especially effective in creating listener loyalty. Fans identified stations as the homes of their favorite teams and identified with a city's sports teams even when they lived hundreds of miles away. Since 1951, listeners across the nation also tuned in to Paul Harvey and his *News and Comment*, making Paul Harvey News the largest one-person network in the world.

The Midwest was also home to some of the first manufacturers of radios. A joint venture of the U.S. Navy and General Electric in 1919, the Radio Corporation of America (RCA) of Indianapolis became a success overnight with a monopoly on American radios. Profiting by beating RCA prices that same year, Powel Crosley of Cincinnati converted his automobile accessories manufacturing company to make affordable radios. In Chicago, Zenith and Motorola became major electronics manufacturers, and the Harris Corporation of Ohio became an important supplier of transmitters. Along with many midwestern broadcasters, these manufacturers also expanded into the television industry after World War II.

In both broadcasting and manufacturing, radio and TV are still important in the American Midwest. Despite the growth of nationally syndicated shows, local radio remains an essential part of many communities. Radio and later television brought the rest of the world into midwestern homes. Broadcasting still links the rural heartland with the nation's urban centers, and along with news, sports, and music, it transmits a sense of midwestern culture and identity.

Sources and Further Reading: John R. Bittner, *Broadcasting: An Introduction* (1980); Robert L. Hilliard and Michael C. Keith, *The Broadcast Century* (1992); Curtis Mitchell, *Cavalcade of Broadcasting* (1970).

Eugene R. H. Tesdahl
Chicago

The Mutual Broadcasting System

One of the largest American radio networks had its origins in Midwest broadcasting. The Mutual Broadcasting System (MBS) began in 1934 as an interconnection between WGN Chicago, WOR Newark, WLW Cincinnati, and WXYZ Detroit for program exchange, and one of its first networked programs was WXYZ's *The Lone Ranger*. Organized without the system of central ownership and contracted affiliation found at CBS and NBC, MBS instead entered a number of cooperative exchange agreements with many stations across the nation in the late 1930s and 1940s. In several of these cases, other radio stations already affiliated with NBC and CBS took on MBS as a second network, using MBS programming as a backup to their primary network affiliation. Beyond *The Lone Ranger*, MBS did have other appealing programs, and its late-night dance band lineup was particularly popular. By the early 1950s, MBS had more station affiliates than any other radio network in the nation. However, counting the number of affiliates can be a misleading measure of importance: MBS typically lagged behind NBC, CBS, and ABC in other measures such as audience ratings, advertising revenue, and total transmitter wattage of all network-affiliated stations. The latter half of the 1950s saw difficult times for MBS. Efforts to create an MBS-TV network foundered, although WGN, WLW, and WOR all became major TV powers in their local markets. Crises in MBS management and a series of questionable MBS business practices saw many stations drop their MBS affiliation by the early 1960s. Nevertheless, especially in the period from 1935 to 1955, MBS rightly deserves consideration as a major national radio network, and it is the only major American commercial radio network to emerge from the Midwest.

Source and Further Reading: Michele Hilmes and Jason Loviglio, eds., *Radio Reader: Essays in the Cultural History of Radio* (2002).

James Schwoch
Northwestern University, Illinois

The National Barn Dance Radio Program

Nearly forgotten now, The National Barn Dance, aired from 1924 to 1971, was the most listened to hillbilly (later country) music radio variety program in the country through the 1930s and 1940s. The Federal Communications Commission then permitted fifty-thousand-watt clear channel radio stations that were aimed at rural audiences. WLS was broadcast from Chicago, started by Sears, Roebuck and Company, and named for the World's Largest Store. Originally called "The WLS Barn Dance," the show became the nation's favorite. In 1932, it moved to the Eighth Street Theater in Chicago; a year later, it was formally christened "The National Barn Dance" when the NBC radio network nationally broadcast a segment.

Early stars included Gene Autry and the singing duo of Lulu Belle and Scotty. Autry would go on to national fame in Hollywood; the latter would remain Midwest favorites. Later came comic George Gobel, balladeer Red Foley, and the singing comedy team of Homer & Jethro. Many others passed through for short stints, including the first solo country female star, Patsy Montana, and comic Pat Buttram. Unlike Nashville's Grand Ole Opry, The National Barn Dance struggled during the transition to television, and the WLS radio version ended in 1960. Another clear channel Chicago radio station—WGN, owned by the *Chicago Tribune* newspaper—took it over and tried various modifications until finally closing it down for good in 1971.

Sources and Further Reading: James F. Evans, *Prairie Farmer and WLS* (1969); Bill C. Malone, *Country Music U.S.A*, rev. ed. (1985); Cecil B. Sturges, "Behind the Scenes of America's Great Stations: When a Farmer Needs a Friend He Counts on WLS," *Radio Stars* (July 1934).

Douglas Gomery
University of Maryland

The Rise of the Radio Disk Jockey

The fictional disc jockeys of the sitcom *WKRP in Cincinnati* (1978–1982) spun tunes in a conservative Midwest city. Courting controversy by bringing musical hipness to midwestern ears, these characters represented the American disc jockey as a Promethean figure. The Midwest is situated between working-class taste and the more risky terrain of the record industry. Thus the Midwest audience is often imagined as culturally homogenous and isolated and the disc jockey as a cultural liberator and a threat, so

DJ Alan Freed, popularizer of the term "rock and roll." Courtesy www.alanfreed.com.

that a record "played in Peoria" may go on to mass distribution and popularity throughout the United States.

Indeed, the influence of the DJ is as unique as the locale of the radio stations dispersed throughout the nation. Unlike most film and television ventures aimed at national audiences, many midwestern record and media ventures, such as Motown (Detroit), King (Cincinnati), and Vee Jay and Chess (Chicago), could avoid the necessity of operating in Los Angeles or New York. As Gerald Early recognizes, without Detroit DJ voices like "Frantic" Eddie Durham of WCHB and Ken Bell of KJLB, "Berry Gordy would never have succeeded in seducing America with the Motown sound." This local influence precedes the rise of Motown. In the early 1960s, Detroit DJ Ed McKenzie told *Life* magazine, "if a big deejay in a key record-selling city such as Detroit, Chicago, Cleveland, or Pittsburgh was paid to play a record, it stood a good chance of hitting nationally."

Thus, the disc jockey functions in a symbiotic relationship with the recording industry, a fact that was clear by the end of the 1940s. With radio utilizing more recordings and less live talent, the demand for

DJs exploded. This demand intensified as the search for cheaper sources of "quality programming" expanded when national broadcast networks turned their attention and programming talents away from radio and toward television. By 1948, many record companies recognized that the way to sell records was via the person whom the audience accepted as the expert—the disk jockey.

Disc jockeys have always been somewhat ephemeral figures in American culture because they often live in a constant state of professional and personal flux. Examples include the most-heralded disc jockey in American history, Alan Freed. Freed claimed New York's WINS was responsible for his nationwide fame and, as a result of the Payola Scandals of the late 1950s, of his infamy. Yet it was in a well-traveled route through many Ohio cities, including Akron, Cincinnati, and Cleveland, that he honed and grew his act. Cleveland's WJW hosted Freed's initial "Moondog" persona, the wild eccentric whose rhythm-and-blues record-spinning made rock-and-roll part of the American vernacular. Midwestern metropolitan areas such as Cincinnati, Chicago, Detroit, and Milwaukee have routinely been positioned as breakout cities and test markets for American mass media. As John Jackson argues throughout his biography of Alan Freed, despite Freed's popularity among black audiences in Cleveland, it was only after attracting Cleveland's white audiences that the record industry noticed the nationwide potential of rhythm-and-blues as a genre. This media logic remains today as the midwestern disc jockey continues to be a key musical tastemaker. Whether lynchpin or liaison between the liberal coasts and the conservative heartland, the DJ will continue to thrive as long as cultural divisions between the geographic regions of the United States are salient to both media industries and audiences alike.

Sources and Further Reading: B. Bodec, "Disk Jockey Due For Sustained Run As Commercial Force in Local Radio," *Variety* (Jan. 7, 1948); Gerald Early, *One Nation Under A Groove* (1995); John A. Jackson, *Big Beat Heat* (1991); Wes Smith, *The Pied Pipers of Rock 'n' Roll* (1989).

Tim Anderson
Denison University, Ohio

The Rise of the Talk Show

The Midwest is the birthplace of the topical daytime television talk show—pioneered by Phil Donahue in Dayton, Ohio—and home to the most successful offspring of that birth, *The Oprah Winfrey Show*, based in Chicago. If Donahue is father of the genre, Winfrey is its queen. Charting the history of their programs reveals the intertwined development of television talk programming and American culture.

When Donahue was invited in 1967 to move his Dayton radio call-in show to television, the country was undergoing profound social and political upheaval. President Lyndon Johnson had declined to seek reelection amid widespread opposition to the Vietnam War, and many African Americans, women, and young people were calling for significant political change. Responding to the times, Donahue made political and social issues the focus of his program, brought the audience into the discussion, and laid the foundation for the issue-oriented, audience-participation talk show.

Tackling personal and political issues with his primarily female audience, Donahue also disproved the television industry's assumption that women had no interest in politics. Blending his passion for politics, his viewers' concerns as women, and his instincts as an entertainer, he explored issues such as gender inequality, women's reproductive health, sexuality, and consumer affairs from a liberal perspective. Feminist leader Gloria Steinem, a frequent guest, said Donahue "showed a view of the world in which women mattered." In 1974, *Donahue* moved to Chicago and went national, launching its host's reign as ruler of daytime TV.

His success invited imitation. One of those imitators became Donahue's most formidable competitor and eventually dethroned him. Oprah Winfrey was lured from a Baltimore talk show in 1984 to host *A.M. Chicago*, a half-hour program airing opposite *Donahue*. She surpassed his ratings within three months, and Donahue moved his show to New York City a year later. Renamed *The Oprah Winfrey Show* in 1985, the program went national in 1986 and won the top-rated talk show spot it has maintained ever since. In contrast to Donahue's more intellectual, issues-oriented approach, Winfrey emphasized emotional intimacy and self-revelation, including on-air confessions of her personal struggles. She formed a legendary bond with her audience and helped turn the genre into a form of public therapy.

Winfrey's popularity and profitability triggered an explosion of talk programs in the 1990s, such as *Ricki Lake* and *Jerry Springer*, that targeted younger viewers with increasingly outrageous topics and tactics. Winfrey and Donahue initially followed suit with more sensational content, despite mounting public criticism. Donahue succumbed to the competition and signed off in 1996. He returned in 2002 for a brief run on MSNBC, but his liberal politics were now out of step with a nation that had moved to the right. Winfrey, meanwhile, reinvented herself as an inspirational phenomenon. Since 1995, her program has become a platform for her psychospiritual, personal growth philosophy. Thus, a genre whose origins with Donahue embraced the feminist claim that the personal is political has, under Winfrey's tutelage, replaced the political with the personal.

Sources and Further Reading: Wayne Munson, *All Talk* (1993); Jane Shattuc, *The Talking Cure: TV Talk Shows and Women* (1997).

Janice Peck
University of Colorado–Boulder

Soap Operas

Cultural historians place the birth of soap operas at WGN Chicago in 1930, with the airing of *Painted Dreams*, written by Dayton, Ohio, schoolteacher Irna Phillips, proclaimed as the mother of daytime soap operas. Three years later, her network soap opera, *Today's Children*, established her philosophy of storytelling: love, family, and home. Frank and Anne Hummert, whose soaps never made it to television, ran a factory system of dialoguers, producing such favorites as *Ma Perkins, Just Plain Bill*, and *The Romance of Helen Trent*. Still others, groomed by Phillips to write for television, were Chicago advertising man William Bell and Northwestern University alumna Agnes Nixon. Their collaborations included *Guiding Light*, set in Springfield in an "unidentified midwestern state"; *As the World Turns*, set in Oakdale, Michigan; and *Another World*, set in nearby Bay City. Bell also served as head writer for *Days of Our Lives*, set in the midwestern town of Salem, before going on to create *The Young and the Restless* set in Genoa City, Wisconsin. According to *Another World*'s head writer, New Yorker Harding LeMay, Irna Phillips ". . . believed in the verities, apple pie, and motherhood, very midwestern values."

Radio soaps were quickly embraced by sponsors throughout the United States, and major Midwest soap sponsors included Procter and Gamble and many corporations in the food industry. These sponsors worked very closely with writers and producers on story lines, promotions, and market research. A number of soap operas' brightest stars were born and educated in the Midwest: Ruth Warrick, David Canary, and Julia Barr (*All My Children*); Kathryn Hays and Ellen Dolan (*As the World Turns*); the late, great Larry Gates and Jerry Ver Dorn (*Guiding Light*); and Deidre Hall and the late MacDonald Carey (*Days of Our Lives*).

Sources and Further Reading: The Museum of Television and Radio, *Worlds Without End: The Art and History of the Soap Opera* (1997); James Thurber, *The Beast in Me and Other Animals* (1948).

Mary B. Cassata
University at Buffalo
State University of New York

WCFL and Labor Radio

Radio station WCFL, created in 1926 by the Chicago Federation of Labor, was the nation's longest surviving broadcast outlet owned and operated by organized labor. The Voice of Labor originated as a listener-supported station, emphasizing popular entertainment and labor and public affairs programming. Throughout much of the period from 1926 to 1945, local labor groups throughout northern Illinois, Indiana, and southern Wisconsin used WCFL to convey information, analyses, and culture, thus breaking labor's dependence on business-controlled media. WCFL combined traditional entertainment formats (concerts, plays, festivals) with progressive social and political ideals. It produced programs that sought to address the economic and political needs and concerns of its ethnically diverse working-class population and enhance working-class culture and consciousness.

In the 1930s and 1940s, labor radio expanded as unions, especially those within the nascent Congress of Industrial Organizations, created programming for commercial stations throughout the Midwest and the nation. In 1949, the United Automobile Workers of America and the International Ladies' Garment Workers' Union established their own short-lived FM radio stations in Detroit and Cleveland, among other cities. WCFL survived well into the post–World War II era. But by the 1950s and 1960s, its labor programming succumbed to the dictates of commercial radio, and the station concentrated on generating profits for the local labor movement. Although it did become for a time the #1 Top-40 rock-and-roll station, its decline after 1970 led to its sale in 1978 and the demise of the dream of independent labor broadcasting.

Sources and Further Reading: Elizabeth Fones-Wolf, "Promoting a Labor Perspective in the American Mass Media: Unions and Radio in the CIO Era, 1936–56," *Media, Culture & Society* 22:3 (May 2000); Nathan Godfried, *WCFL: Chicago's Voice of Labor, 1926–78* (1997).

Nathan Godfried
University of Maine

Cinema

During the early years of motion picture production, there was a great deal of activity in the Midwest. Even though only a small amount of this silent film production has survived, the midwestern states offered some truly significant innovations during cinema's infancy.

One of the earliest movie pioneers was William N. Selig, who was born in Chicago in 1864. It was in this city that Selig founded the Mutoscope and Film Company, later called the Selig Polyscope Company, on April 9, 1896. Selig constructed his own movie projector and camera based on the Lumiere system and began shooting his first short subjects, which included slapstick comedies, and travel and industrial films.

Selig was brought to court by Thomas Edison for copyright infringement, but this eventually resulted in his joining forces with Edison to form the Motion Picture Patents Company in 1909. By then Selig had three studios: one in Chicago, another in New Orleans, and still another in Los Angeles. Selig's production of *The Count of Monte Cristo* (1908) is often cited as the first narrative film to be shot in Los Angeles. His *Damon and Pythias* (1908) is the first two-reeler produced in the United States, and the 1913–1914 production of *The Adventures of Kathlyn* is the first true movie serial.

Two of the screen's first western stars, "Broncho Billy" Anderson and Tom Mix, were among those who got their start in Selig productions. Although Selig continued to produce movies into the 1930s, he closed his studios in 1918. In 1947, he received a special

Oscar for being a pioneer in the developing art of motion pictures. He died the following year.

The aforementioned G. M. "Broncho Billy" Anderson, born Max Aronson, teamed with George K. Spoor to incorporate the Essanay Film Manufacturing Company in Chicago on February 5, 1907. The name of the studio derived from the first letters of Spoor's and Anderson's last names. Essanay was originally located at 501 Wells Street in Chicago, but in the Fall of 1909, its members and crew traveled west while filming *The Best Man Wins*, eventually settling in Niles, California, where Anderson starred in westerns for the next several years.

Essanay also employed several major film stars. Francis X. Bushman began his career there in 1911, and Buffalo Bill Cody began appearing in a series of authentic westerns in 1913 that realistically depicted pioneer life in the old west. Just as the new year of 1915 dawned, Essanay raided Mack Sennett's Keystone Studios and signed Charlie Chaplin to write, direct, and star in his own series of two-reel comedies by offering Chaplin a nearly tenfold salary increase. Chaplin's first Essanay film, appropriately titled *His New Job* (1915), was the only one shot in Chicago. He balked at the bitter cold winters, and the remainder of his Essanay films were shot in Niles. Chaplin left Essanay after only a year, and despite hiring comedian Max Linder in 1917, the studio went into a decline. Spoor bought out Anderson and released some of Chaplin's old outtakes, combined with separately shot footage, as new films. Essanay ceased production in 1918.

The Capital Film Company was incorporated on February 27, 1918, with backing from several Indiana

Scene from *Anatomy of a Murder* (1959). Copyright 1959, renewed 1987, Otto Preminger Films, Ltd. All Rights Reserved. Courtesy Columbia Pictures.

financiers. Capital was headquartered in Indianapolis, where, beginning in May of 1918, it began distributing films, including many produced by Selig. Capital ceased operating in 1924.

African American filmmakers emerged with the Lincoln Motion Picture Company in 1916. Formed by actor Noble Johnson and his brother George, the setup had Noble producing films in Los Angeles and George distributing them in Omaha. By the following year, the company created its own exchange, with films playing throughout African American neighborhoods in many major cities. The films produced by Lincoln dealt with black heroes overcoming odds through their own ambition as well as those featuring black sports or western heroes. The studio disbanded in 1923.

Another film company emerged using all-black casts for a series of slapstick comedies. Ebony Pictures Corporation was founded in April of 1918 by L. J. Pollard and Bob Horner. They began filming in Oshkosh, Wisconsin, and later built a studio in Fond du Lac, Wisconsin. By July of 1918, Ebony productions began integrating its casts, featuring black and white performers. The company's first two-reel film featured black actor Samuel Jacks as the star, with an all-white supporting cast. Despite its use of black actors in leading roles, the parts the actors played were stereotypical, and the white-owned company came under fire from the black press. It went out of existence in 1922. The Ebony-produced comedy *Spying the Spy* (1918) survives and is preserved in the National Film Collection at the Library of Congress.

William Steiner's Serial Film Company operated on the East Coast, but he did produce one film in Kenosha, Wisconsin. *Belle of Kenosha* (1923) starred several local Kenosha actors, but no print is known to survive.

The American cinema was flourishing in the 1920s, but nearly all of the films were being made on either coast, especially California. Some location filming occurred in the Midwest, but for the most part, the film industry shot on the west coast as the silent era ended and the Golden Age of Hollywood, the 1930s and 1940s, began.

During this Golden Age, midwestern moviegoers enjoyed the screen's offerings in some of the finest motion picture palaces in the country. Moviegoing in the Midwest was tremendous throughout the 1920s, 1930s, and 1940s, before the advent of television began closing some of the smaller theatres during the 1950s. The Wisconsin Theater in Milwaukee, the Michigan Theater in Detroit, and the Minnesota in Minneapolis were among the most beautiful movie palaces of their day. Many theatres were owned by the studios as franchise operations; Paramount, Fox, and

Warner Brothers all had movie theatres operating throughout the Midwest during this period. However, it should be noted that these theatres were not restricted to showing only films released by their own studios.

Along with the bigger cities, smaller towns throughout the Midwest had many theatres to accommodate the growing interest in movies. Racine (Wisconsin) had the Venetian, Rialto, Main Street, State, Crown, Capitol, Douglas, and Granada all operating at once. The Midwest also boasted smaller movie houses for small-town patronage including the Homer Theater in Hibbing (Minnesota), the Niles Theater in Anamosa (Iowa), the Campau Theater in Hamtramck (Michigan), and the Liberty Theater in Muncie (Indiana).

The Midwest is also noteworthy in regard to the distribution of motion picture equipment. Bell and Howell in Chicago was founded by projectionist Donald Bell and camera repairman Albert Howell in 1907. Their precision-built cameras and projectors purported to "take the flick out of flickers" and soon became widely used in the industry. Bell sold out his interest to Joe Hector McNabb in 1921, and by the following year, Bell and Howell began offering 16-millimeter and 8-millimeter equipment for amateur filmmakers and home movie enthusiasts.

Filmmaking briefly returned to the Midwest after World War II with Kroger Babb's Hallmark Productions. Organized in 1945 and located in Wilmington, Ohio, Hallmark productions were called Triple-E Presentations—for Enlightenment, Education, and Entertainment. However, the E that Hallmark truly represented was Exploitation. The company's films included titles like *Mom and Dad* (1948), a movie about childbirth that was screened separately for men or for women, and *Monika: The Story of a Bad Girl*, which was as exploitative as the title implies. Hallmark eventually moved to Los Angeles and stayed in business into the 1970s.

During the end of the silent era, nontheatrical film distribution emerged in the Midwest with Films Incorporated out of Wilmette, Illinois. Films Incorporated was founded in 1927 as Home Film Libraries, Incorporated. It was the first 16 millimeter distributor. These films were presented for home or school use. Initially only the smaller studio product was available, but by the mid-1930s, such major studios as Paramount and Universal saw the interest in 16-millimeter rental of their older films and offered Hicks the right to distribute from their backlog. In 1938, the company was purchased by Eric Haight, who changed the name to Films Incorporated. In 1941, 20th Century Fox offered the rights for its features to be distributed to the nontheatrical market. Films Incorporated was purchased by Encyclopedia Films in 1951, and in 1956,

Encyclopedia acquired the nontheatrical rights in perpetuity to all RKO features produced before 1948. Charles Benton acquired the company in 1968.

By the 1950s and 1960s, location filming became more common, including in the Midwest. Sidney Salkow's *Chicago Confidential* (1957) was among many films shot in the Chicago area. Vincente Minnelli's *Some Came Running* (1958) was filmed chiefly in Indiana. Otto Preminger's *Anatomy of a Murder* (1959) was set in Michigan and filmed in and around the Marquette area.

With the demise of the studio system, independent producers were once again able to get their films distributed. This became especially evident after 1960, when more low-budget independent productions were made to fill the popular drive-in movie theatres, nearly 40 percent of which were located in the midwestern states. Drive-in theatres were noted for pairing a major Hollywood feature with a rerelease or a lower-budget independent production. Triple features were not uncommon, with the third movie being a smaller, independent release. Minnesota-born Tom Laughlin, later of *Billy Jack* (1971) fame, shot one of his first films, *The Young Sinner* (1965), in Milwaukee. Small-time horror producer Herschell Gordon Lewis filmed some of his early slasher movies of the late 1960s and early 1970s in Chicago.

Low-budget horror film producers are often especially attracted to some of the woodsy areas of Wisconsin, even such recent productions as Jason Paul Collum's *5 Dark Souls* series, filmed in Racine during the mid- to late-1990s. That same Wisconsin city also hosted Jack Perez and Mick Wynhoff's *America's Deadliest Home Video* (1991), a highly unconventional production that inspired such noted Hollywood films as *Natural Born Killers* (1994) and *The Blair Witch Project* (1999).

By the 1980s, filming on location became the norm for Hollywood productions. Hence, many films were shot in the Midwest, from *The Blues Brothers* (1980), *Ferris Bueller's Day Off* (1986), and *The Color of Money* (1986), in Chicago to the more recent *Fargo* (1996) in Minnesota and North Dakota and *8 Mile* (2002) in Detroit.

Documentaries shot in the Midwest include such recent successes as Michael Moore's *Roger and Me* (1989) filmed in Flint, Michigan, and Chris Smith's *American Movie* (1999), which follows Milwaukee filmmaker Mark Borchardt's efforts to shoot one of his own independent productions. By the twenty-first century, the Midwest was noted not only for its various contributions to cinema's history but also for the many film festivals that afforded area moviegoers the opportunity to see movies produced outside the mainstream.

Filmmaking in the Midwest still continues, from major studio productions to low-budget independents. Scott Thompson's My Town Pictures has been successful since 1999 with a series of feature films shot in northwestern Wisconsin for national cable TV outlets. The casts consist of local community theatre performers, bringing filmmaking to those who would otherwise never have a chance to experience it.

The Midwest has a very rich cinematic heritage, going back to the earliest days of the moving picture and offering a variety of important contributions throughout film's history. Midwestern locations continue to appear in a variety of studio and independent film productions, and midwestern independent filmmakers continue to offer creative alternatives to the mainstream.

Sources and Further Reading: Charles Musser, *Before the Nickelodeon* (1991); Jay Robert Nash and Stanley Ralph Ross, *The Motion Picture Guide* (1985); David Robinson, *Chaplin: His Life and Art* (1985); Henry T. Sampson, *Blacks in Black and White* (1977); Anthony Slide, *The American Film Industry* (1986).

James L. Neibaur
Racine, Wisconsin

Cinema Exhibition: Picture Palaces, Movie Houses, and Drive-ins

Soon after projected motion pictures debuted in New York in April of 1896, their easily portable technology quickly enabled midwestern theatres, already the backbone of the nation's touring circuit, to become centers of American film exhibition. City vaudeville programs and tent shows at amusement parks featured brief film scenes of waves crashing on beaches and trains steaming through the countryside. The 1904 St. Louis World's Fair featured Hale's Tours, a program of travel films shown to viewers seated inside a gently rocking stationary train car. Traveling film exhibitors brought one-reel films and the latest Tin Pan Alley songs to small-town opera houses. The continuing popularity of films spurred thousands of nickelodeon storefront movie theatres to open after 1905 from Ashtabula, Ohio, to Anamosa, Iowa. Cowboy films and Charlie Chaplin comedies from the Chicago-based Selig and Essanay studios were popular, along with those of a dozen other producers. Many of the brightly colored movie posters adorning theatre fronts were produced by the Hennegan Company, Cincinnati show printers.

Chicago entrepreneurs Barney Balaban and Sam Katz entered the movie theatre business in the later

1910s and quickly rose to prominence by bringing a new affordable elegance to moviegoing. They built gigantic picture palaces, strategically located at central transportation centers across the city. Their theatres, like the 3,800-seat Chicago and 4,300-seat Uptown, offered programs that combined silent feature films, newsreels, and cartoons with elaborate musical stage revues, performances of the "mighty Wurlitzer organ," blissfully cool air conditioning in the summer, and fantastical Moorish, Mayan, French, or Aztec décor. In the 1920s, picture palaces opened in every midwestern city. Many of the impressive theatres, such as the Wisconsin Theater in Milwaukee, the Michigan in Detroit, and the Minnesota in Minneapolis, proudly proclaimed their cultural status in the region; others promoted the brand names of the great studios—the Paramounts in Des Moines, Omaha, and Sioux City, the Fox in St. Louis, the Loews in Akron and Canton. In a typical smaller city like Muncie, Indiana, sociologists Robert and Helen Lynd noted that "Middletown's" nine movie theatres had a major impact on local culture, with movie fan magazines the preferred reading of high school students and young housewives, and the leading theatre manager elected to the Rotary Club. Even the tiniest midwestern village had its own Bijou or Strand theatre, often operated as a family business. Perhaps 20 percent of small-town theatre managers were female, such as Gladys McArdle, who ran the 250-seat Owl Theater in Lebanon, Kansas.

The wild popularity of the new sound motion picture—"talkies," like Al Jolson's *The Jazz Singer* in 1927—broke attendance records at picture palaces that had been wired for sound. The Great Depression of the 1930s, however, squeezed palaces and small-town theatres alike. Nearly 40 percent of all movie theatres closed, at least temporarily. Movie houses trimmed expenses, ran double features, and promoted "bank night" cash contests and dishware giveaways to lure back cash-strapped customers. (These promotional practices are described in Indianan Jean Shepard's short story "Leopold Doppler and the Great Orpheum Theater Gravy Boat Riot.") During World War II, movie attendance reached its highest levels ever. Theatres held patriotic bond rallies, showed the latest war newsreels, and organized scrap drives for which children collected tin cans and bottles to earn free tickets to Saturday morning cowboy shows. The Midwest was home to 6,384 movie theatres, 30 percent of the national total, and 48 "art house" cinemas thrived in its urban centers, screening foreign films. The region also had 481 theatres for African Americans, who in the Jim Crow era were sometimes discouraged from entering white urban showplaces.

In the post–World War II period, television broadcasting began to change midwesterners' movie-going habits, as millions of young families purchased cars, moved out to the new suburbs, had several children, and stayed home to watch TV. The region's theatres fought back with lavish Hollywood color films presented in Cinerama and Cinemascope wide-screen formats, and expanded popcorn and candy concession stands in their lobbies. Drive-in theatres built on suburban farm land were a 1930s innovation that boomed in the 1940s. They featured a casual, come-as-you-are atmosphere, luring families and groups of teenagers to arrive at dusk to watch westerns, science fiction, and monster movies on gigantic outdoor screens, cavort on the swing sets, socialize, or make out in the privacy of their own automobiles. By 1957, the Midwest had 1,654 drive-ins, 36 percent of the nation's total.

The 1960s and 1970s saw nearly all of the older movie theatres close, but the following decades brought the opening of several thousand new multiplex cinemas located in suburban shopping centers. Preservationists have helped renovate numerous historic picture palaces to serve as performing arts centers vital to the region's cultural life, such as the Chicago, the Fox in St. Louis, the Ohio in Columbus, and the Playhouse Square theatres in Cleveland.

Sources and Further Reading: Richard Butsch, *The Making of American Audiences* (2000); Kathryn Fuller, *At the Picture Show* (1996); Kathryn Fuller-Seeley and George Potamianos, eds., *Beyond the Bowery: The Cinema in Rural America from Its Origins to the Multiplex* (2004); Douglas Gomery, *Shared Pleasures* (1992); Melvyn Stokes and Richard Maltby, eds., *American Movie Audiences* (1999).

Kathryn H. Fuller-Seeley
Virginia Commonwealth University

Directors

Chicago's Essanay Studio was a major producer of movies from 1907 to 1917, but filmmaking in the Midwest declined precipitously after Essanay's collapse. For a time, those with ambitions to direct feature films had to make their way to Hollywood or New York. Many midwesterners nonetheless have built successful Hollywood careers, including Illinois's John Sturges (*The Great Escape*), John G. Avildsen (*Rocky*), William Friedkin (*The French Connection*), Philip Kaufman (*The Right Stuff*), Andy and Larry Wachowski (*The Matrix*), and Robert Zemeckis (*Forrest Gump*); Indiana's Howard Hawks (*The Big Sleep*) and Robert Wise (*The Sound of Music*); Michigan's Sam Raimi (*Spider-Man*); Minnesota's George Roy Hill (*Butch Cassidy and the Sundance Kid*); Ohio's Wes

Craven (*Scream*); and Wisconsin's Jim Abrahams (*Hot Shots!*), David Zucker (*The Naked Gun*), and Jerry Zucker (*Ghost*). Francis Ford Coppola and Steven Spielberg are midwesterners by birth—from Detroit and Cincinnati, respectively—although they were raised elsewhere and their films show few if any traces of their origins.

Changes in production practice during the 1960s and state film commissions' encouragement of location shooting gave filmmakers the opportunity to make major studio pictures in their home states. John Landis filmed *The Blues Brothers* around his native Chicago, and Andy Davis shot many scenes of *The Fugitive* there as well. John Hughes, Michigan born and a long-time resident of Illinois, sets in Chicago and environs most of the movies he has directed, such as *Ferris Bueller's Day Off*, as well as the many films he has produced and/or written, such as *Home Alone*, directed by Chris Columbus, born in Pennsylvania but raised in Ohio. Indiana filmmaker David Anspaugh filmed his debut, *Hoosiers*, in Indiana.

Minnesotans Joel and Ethan Coen shot *Fargo* in Minnesota and North Dakota, and it remains the best movie evocation of certain aspects of the upper Midwest. Independents of lesser stature and skill but equal drive, such as Wisconsin's Bob Rebane (*The Giant Spider Invasion*) and Michigan's Gary Jones (*Mosquito*), make most of their films in their home states. Conversely, Michigan's Roger Corman and Minnesota's Tom Laughlin (creator of the *Billy Jack* films) relocated to other regions and introduced innovations in low-budget film production and distribution.

A strong midwestern strain of individuality manifests itself among filmdom's most famous mavericks and most indomitable studio directors. Some filmmakers' cosmopolitan public personae may have obscured their midwestern origins, but their works nonetheless show traces of their roots. Vincente Minnelli, renowned director of musicals and one of Hollywood's foremost visual stylists, was born, raised, and trained for the theatre in Chicago; his *Meet Me in St. Louis* has permanently colored viewers' notions of Midwest suburban life around the turn of the century. Orson Welles, born and raised in Kenosha, Wisconsin, with considerable time spent in Chicago as a youth, chose to adapt *The Magnificent Ambersons*, one of Booth Tarkington's three "Growth" novels about Indianapolis, for his second film project, in part because of resonances in the story with his own family history (after *Citizen Kane* had reworked some elements of Chicago tycoons' lives). Monty Python alumnus Terry Gilliam, famous for his feuds with producers, credits his childhood in Medicine Lake, Minnesota, for aspects of his particular cinematic vision. Missourian Robert Altman shot *A Wedding* in a Chicago suburb and *Thieves Like Us* throughout the Midwest.

The independent spirit also manifests itself in the way midwesterners already established in other artistic fields have turned to directing films, with varying degrees of success and duration. Actors who have moved behind the camera include Illinoisans Bob Balaban, Karl Malden, Bill Murray, Richard Pryor, and Gary Sinise (co-founder of the Steppenwolf Theatre Company); Iowans Stuart Margolin and John Wayne; Kansans Roscoe "Fatty" Arbuckle and Dennis Hopper; Michiganders Charlton Heston and George Peppard; Missourian Wallace Beery; Nebraskans Marlon Brando and early western star Hoot Gibson; Ohioans Burgess Meredith, Paul Newman, and Martin Sheen; and Wisconsin's Gene Wilder. Among Illinois playwrights, Sam Shepard has made two features, and David Mamet has enjoyed a prolific directorial career. Illinois dancer-choreographer Bob Fosse received three directing Oscar nominations, winning for *Cabaret*. Detroit's Berry Gordy (Motown Records founder) and Minnesota legend Bob Dylan each made one feature, and Minneapolis composer-musician Prince has directed three.

African American film began in the Midwest and continues to depend on directors from this region. In 1912, Chicagoan William Foster was making all-black films for ghetto markets. Nebraska's Lincoln Motion Picture Company, incorporated in 1916 by George Johnson and his actor brother Noble, was the first black-owned movie company, producing films extolling African American achievements. Chicago native Oscar Micheaux became the most enduring and revered African American film pioneer. Another Chicago native (educated at Ohio Wesleyan University), Melvin Van Peebles, literally and figuratively revolutionized black film in 1971 with his aggressive *Sweet Sweetback's Baadasssss Song*, which became a huge hit with black audiences and inspired other African American filmmakers. Also premiering in 1971 was another influential blaxploitation film, *Shaft*, by Kansan Gordon Parks, internationally regarded as a photographer before turning to filmmaking. The many current African American directors born and raised in the Midwest include Illinois's Robert Townsend (*Hollywood Shuffle*) and Reginald Hudlin (*House Party*), Michigan's Albert and Alan Hughes (*Menace II Society*), Ohioan Leslie Harris (*Just Another Girl on the I.R.T.*), and Wisconsin's Michael Schultz (*Cooley High*).

Documentary filmmaking has a notable heritage of Midwest directors. The father of American feature documentary filmmaking is Michigan's Robert Flaherty (*Nanook of the North*). His work inspired Iowan Ernest Schoedsack to make documentary features (like *Grass*) similarly set in exotic locales but with fictional narrative components (leading eventually to his totally fictional *King Kong*). In the early 1960s, D. A. Pennebaker of Illinois was among the first practitioners in America of cinema verité or Direct Cinema. Today, Michigan's Michael Moore carries on the documentary tradition in a more politically charged and sardonic mode (*Roger and Me, Fahrenheit 9/11*).

Midwesterners figure large in avant-garde filmmaking. Stan Brakhage, a towering figure in avant-garde film throughout the second half of the twentieth century, was born in Kansas City, Missouri, and spent 1969–1981 on the faculty of the School of the Art Institute of Chicago. Bruce Baillie, born in South Dakota, is renowned for combining lyrical and documentary elements in formally challenging ways, as in his *Mass for the Dakota Sioux*. Bruce Conner from Kansas is famous for using found footage to construct his films. James Benning crafts highly formalized works that use his Wisconsin surroundings to suggest and simultaneously deny narratives. His daughter, video artist Sadie Benning, became a sensation with her diary films using Pixelvision, a technology marketed as a children's toy.

Midwesterners have had a profound influence in animated film. After several decades in his Michigan birthplace and in Illinois and Ohio honing his drawing skills, Winsor McCay subsequently made the first American animated cartoons. The combined inventions of directors John Randolph Bray of Michigan and Earl Hurd of Kansas made the animated cartoon industry possible. Walt Disney, born in Chicago but relocated at age five to Marceline, Missouri, directed his first cartoons at his Kansas City, Missouri, studio. A strong midwestern influence can be seen most clearly in the rural settings of Disney cartoons and their emphasis on traditional values. A disproportionate number of classic cartoon directors have come from Kansas City, Missouri, including Ub Iwerks, Rudolph Ising, and Friz Freleng. Disney animator-directors Art Babbitt and Wilfred Jackson came from Omaha and Chicago, respectively, and their legacy continues in Iowan Ron Clements (*The Little Mermaid*). Lee Unkrich of Cleveland carries that tradition into computer animation with *Toy Story 2* and *Monsters, Inc.* Michigan's Art Clokey helped popularize clay animation and claymation, through his Gumby character, and Iowan Charles Bowers was not only an early cartoon animator but also devised a sophisticated form of object animation for his otherwise live-action comedy shorts.

Sources and Further Reading: Donald Bogle, *Toms, Coons, Mulattoes, Mammies, & Bucks*, 4th ed. (2001); Donald Crafton, *Before Mickey* (1982); Ephraim Katz et al., *The Film Encyclopedia*, 4th ed. (2001); P. Adams Sitney, *Visionary Film*, 3d ed. (2002); Kristin Thompson and David Bordwell, *Film History: An Introduction*, 2nd ed. (2003).

Richard J. Leskosky
University of Illinois–Urbana-Champaign

Essanay Film Studios

In the early years of the twentieth century, Chicago and the Midwest played a dominant role in filmmaking. The single most important studio connecting the Midwest to the early silent film era was Essanay Film Manufacturing Company. Founded in 1907, Essanay produced hundreds of early silent films. The studio's name phonetically combined the initials of its founders' last names, George Spoor and Max Aronson. Essanay is perhaps best remembered as the home of silent-era stars Gloria Swanson and studio co-founder and star G. M. "Broncho Billy" Anderson. Anderson (born Max Aronson) was the first cowboy action star in American cinema, starring in some four hundred action shorts under the "Broncho Billy" moniker while at Essanay, many of which he also wrote.

Essanay's most prominent star was Charlie Chaplin. Chaplin signed with the studio in 1915, just one year after the release of his first film, and received a record salary of $1,250 weekly. Although Chaplin was with Essanay for only a year and only a small percentage of the star's films were made with the company, it was with Essanay that his onscreen talents began to evolve. Essanay released one of Chaplin's greatest films, *The Tramp*, in 1915.

In 1916, Chaplin's departure and disputes between the company's founders led to the studio's decline. Essanay, like other studios, had established a presence in California to take advantage of that state's mild climate and reliable weather, which accommodated outdoor filmmaking. The company collapsed in 1918, by which time the U.S. filmmaking industry had permanently shifted its focus away from the Midwest.

Sources and Further Reading: William K. Everson, *American Silent Film* (1998); James L. Neibaur, "Chaplin at Essanay," *Film Quarterly* 54 (Fall 2000).

Barry Donald Mowell
Broward Community College, Florida

Feature Film Production

Early film production required access to chemicals and technicians that kept most major midwestern cities except Chicago from participating. The city on the lake produced original cinema beginning in 1896, when William Selig started his earliest film. In 1904, the Vitagraph Company opened a studio, as well. Starting in 1907, Essanay Studios produced numerous short comedies and westerns. At one point, their laboratory was based in a train car so that film could be developed immediately after shooting.

As inviting as Chicago was, it had one major drawback. Inconstant midwestern weather stymied cinematographers, who needed a great deal of light to expose early film stock. By 1914, sunny California attracted a mass of filmmakers, including Essanay, Selig, and Vitagraph. Selig folded in 1918, and Vitagraph merged with Warner Brothers in 1925. Essanay closed in 1917, despite helping to launch the career of Charlie Chaplin, because they could no longer compete with the bigger companies.

These big companies monopolized American film production for the next several decades. California had an added advantage with its varied landscapes offering deserts, mountains, marshes, and an ocean, all within an easy commute. A film set in the Midwest need not be shot in the Midwest when cheaper and closer would suffice. The major film studios—Universal, MGM, Fox, Columbia, Paramount, Warner Brothers, United Artists, and RKO—began to consolidate at this time. They built sets simulating almost any locale in the world. Sound added production requirements that made the studios even more insular. Stray noises could ruin a shot, and rerecording was impractical; if any shot could be done in the controlled environment of a studio, it was.

In the 1930s and 1940s, location footage was occasionally used, but that was unusual. *The Major and the Minor* (1942) was made partly in Wisconsin and on scenic Mackinac Island; Michigan was the setting for the Esther Williams swimfest, *This Time for Keeps* (1947). Exceptions like these tended to prove the rule that most major productions were studio-bound affairs.

The success of the studio system frustrated and nearly bankrupted independent producers by the late 1930s. As the studios bought up theatres across the country, they could crowd out a smaller film and keep it from ever being screened. This climate prompted several independent producers, including Disney and Sam Goldwyn, to mount an antitrust suit, *United States of America v. Paramount Pictures, Inc., et al.* in 1938. By the late 1940s, the studios were stopped from acquiring more theatres, and by the mid-1950s they were forced to sell off most of their theatre holdings. More producers began financing their own films, and the studios, no longer owning all productions outright, charged high overhead fees for use of their facilities. Technically, it was becoming easier to shoot films, and film laboratories began to crop up in most large cities. Suddenly, a location shoot, even with all the travel expenses involved, became economically feasible.

Realism also became important, since a public educated by World War II laughed at phony studio "locations." Producers, looking to satisfy audiences, began to shoot on location. Shots from Indiana, Chicago, and South Dakota crept into *North by Northwest* (1959), still mostly a studio production. Vincente Minnelli's *Some Came Running* (1958) was shot almost entirely in Indiana, a novelty at the time, and Otto Preminger's *Anatomy of a Murder* (1959) was set and filmed in Michigan.

Productions became increasingly independent and decentralized. With faster shipping, it became feasible to shoot nearly anywhere and have the developed film ready for viewing in a few days. Established stars seemed overly expensive when a film like *Easy Rider* (1969) could make millions with a very small budget. Producers began to look to smaller projects with easier returns and higher profits. Inevitably, this meant exploitation films.

A tremendous number of horror and exploitation films have been shot in the Midwest, starting in the mid-1950s, hitting full-stride in the late 1960s and early 1970s, waning a bit by 1980, but still continuing today. Low-budget horror films are a good way for a young filmmaker to be noticed by bigger concerns. Michigan native Sam Raimi's *Evil Dead* (1981) and *Evil Dead 2* (1987) are probably the best known of this group. Raimi did become a major director, unlike Herschell Gordon Lewis, whose Chicago-lensed films *The Wizard of Gore* (1970) and *The Gore Gore Girls* (1972) were strictly for those with iron stomachs.

By 1980, studio productions were the exception, not the rule. Big-budget productions like *The Blues Brothers* (1980) and *Ferris Bueller's Day Off* (1986) were shot almost entirely in Chicago. Indiana hosted sleeper hits like *Breaking Away* (1979) and *Hoosiers* (1986). Cult favorite *Somewhere in Time* (1980) used Mackinac, Michigan. Kevin Costner's classic *Field of Dreams* (1989) made filmmakers come to Iowa, while his *Dances with Wolves* (1990) showcased locations in South Dakota. Best Picture winner *Rain Man* (1988) was partly shot in Ohio and in rural Indiana.

The Minnesota-born Coen brothers, Joel and Ethan, started a small cinema dynasty beginning in 1984 with the underground hit, *Blood Simple*. Their sometimes violent, sometimes funny, skewed filmic world reached an apex with the Oscar-winning *Fargo* (1996), filmed largely in Minnesota. Independent production suits the Coens because their storytelling style flies in the face of Hollywood conventions.

Also of note are the works of Michigan native Michael Moore, whose documentaries from *Roger and*

Me (1989) to *Bowling for Columbine* (2002) to *Fahrenheit 9/11* (2004) tweak the nose of the corporate world from a uniquely Midwestern viewpoint.

Popular films, like *8 Mile* (2000), filmed in Detroit, continue to be made in the Midwest. However, the major productions are moving again. Despite efforts by film commissions in most midwestern states, producers have begun looking to Canada for its cheap labor and inexpensive studio space. Even *Blues Brothers 2000* (1998), a story set in Chicago, was shot mostly in Canada. But still, more movies are being shot in the Midwest than ever before, and with each state eagerly courting new productions, this trend shows no signs of dying out.

Sources and Further Reading: A. Scott Berg, *Goldwyn: A Biography* (1989); Ephraim Katz, *The Film Encyclopedia* (1979).

Eric Grayson
Indianapolis

Film Festivals

Over the last two decades, most large American cities have hosted a concentrated, periodic, or annual series of film screenings under a "festival" rubric, but the scope and ambition specific to each make further descriptive generalities hazardous. None of the Midwest's film festivals ranks among the top tier of those annually rated by the Paris-based International Federation of Film Producers Associations (FIAPF), the only global organization to officially rate festivals according to a minimum code of professional practices.

That distinction has more relevance to film professionals than to filmgoers, since traditionally one of a festival's values to its community abides in its function of giving viewers a chance to see nonmainstream work otherwise unlikely to be released in their regional markets. The fact that film festivals often begin in a populist cinephilia—in an individual's or a group's desire to bring movies they might have read about to their hometown—has a bearing on the virtual impossibility of identifying a reliable directory of events self-defining as a "festival," since they tend to flourish or expire according to the vagaries of leadership, volunteerism, and community peculiarities. While almost always originating in cinephilia (often among college and university students), film festivals of sustained presence in their initial iterations frequently evolve to attract substantial civic and corporate support, both as a way of symbolizing the city's or region's commitment to culture and of offering a mechanism to realize the social and marketing aspirations of its funders and eventual board members. In these respects, the Midwest's film festivals are no different from those in other parts of the world.

The Midwest's two oldest major annual festivals are the Chicago International Film Festival (begun in 1964) and the Cleveland International Film Festival (1977), both of which offer a mix of new foreign and domestic features, documentaries, shorts, animation, and live presentations and panels by filmmakers and professionals. Three of the country's oldest ongoing festivals for more experimental works are in the Midwest, each uniquely affiliated with a university community: Michigan's Ann Arbor Film Festival (begun in 1963); Ohio's Athens International Film and Video Festival (1979); and in Carbondale, Illinois, the Big Muddy Film Festival (1979). The University of Minnesota's veteran Film Society expanded in 1983 to sponsor the annual Minneapolis–St. Paul International Film Festival, and the Wisconsin Film Festival (1999) grew directly from the University of Wisconsin–Madison's strong film studies tradition. Most self-aware of its status as a specifically midwestern phenomenon is Indianapolis's Heartland Film Festival, established in 1991.

Source and Further Reading: *Variety Film Festival Guide* (Aug. 25–31, 2003).

Bill Horrigan
The Ohio State University–Columbus

Film Reviewing

Long known as a bastion of moderation and conservatism, the Midwest has nonetheless spawned two extremes in the realm of movie reviewing. The first is represented by the television program *Ebert and Roeper at the Movies*, which elevated film criticism to a new level of visibility and influence in the culture at large. Originally entitled *Sneak Previews*, the show was conceived by public television producer Thea Flaum in 1975 as a vehicle for the movie reviewers of Chicago's two daily newspapers, the *Tribune* and the *Sun-Times*. In 1981, the program severed its ties with public television and moved into syndication under the auspices of the *Tribune*. Buena Vista took over the show in 1986, changing its name to *Siskel and Ebert at the Movies*. Siskel and Ebert became national celebrities, appearing regularly on venues such as national nightly talk shows and the annual Oscar telecast. Following Siskel's untimely death in 1999 at the age of 53, Ebert chose Steve Roeper, a fellow writer at the *Sun-Times*, as his new on-air partner the following year.

The appeal of the TV show arose from a number of factors. Most importantly, it featured clips from contemporary films. Further, the "thumbs up or thumbs down" gesture from the hosts provided each review with a visual analogue to the star system employed by print reviewers and gave viewers an unforgettable signal for ascertaining the critics' recommendations on any given film. Finally, the visible rivalry between the two on-air personalities complemented the drama of the movies they were reviewing and reflected the ordinary person's sense that everyone has his or her own opinion about a movie. The two critics were not especially telegenic; Siskel was balding and Ebert was overweight. Yet audiences found common cause with these everyman figures in a way they might not have done with more glamorous screen presences. And the pair maintained a viewer-friendly approach to their topic. Siskel specialized in issues concerning the Hollywood industry. Ebert, who won a Pulizer Prize for his *Sun-Times* reviews, has kept up with what is new and noteworthy by regularly attending an array of international film festivals.

At the other extreme from the Midwest's popular television reviewer personalities is Jonathan Rosenbaum, critic for the alternative weekly newspaper, *The Chicago Reader*. With his New York University graduate training, his years in Paris attending screenings at its famed Cinemathèque, and his background as a university teacher, Rosenbaum is perhaps the most scholarly of all American movie commentators. His lengthy reviews have been collected in several volumes published by the University of California Press. Rosenbaum has also authored numerous other books on film-related topics.

A fervent advocate of the *auteur* presumptions that understand great movies as the creations of director-geniuses, Rosenbaum regularly champions alternative cinematic forms such as avant-garde and documentary. He also has special interests in French and Iranian film and in the work of Orson Welles. Though at times his reviews can be maddeningly arcane, serious movie buffs consistently look to him as the most knowledgeable authority on cinema whose writing appears in the popular media on a regular basis.

Sources and Further Reading: Roger Ebert, *The Great Movies* (2002); Jonathan Rosenbaum, *Movies as Politics* (1997); Jonathan Rosenbaum, *Placing Movies* (1995).

Virginia Wright Wexman
University of Illinois–Chicago

Minority and Alternative Cinema

While the Heartland may serve as the place for measuring the pulse of the nation, the lives of people of color in the region have remained largely untold or demonized in Hollywood cinema. Thus in the Midwest, many minority filmmakers work as independents who try to counter racist and sexist imagery by inserting their stories into the midwestern and national landscape. Much of their output appears on television and at film festivals.

Traditionally, Midwest filmmakers of color have made work that reflects the histories, challenges, and everyday living experiences of their sociocultural groups. Their narratives cover issues ranging from identity and nation to immigration, race relations, and the economy. African American media makers have provided the most work of all minority groups. The first U.S. black film company was based in Omaha. In 1916, actor Noble Johnson founded the Lincoln Motion Picture Company along with his brother George Johnson. However, the most prolific African American filmmaker to date began his work on the plains of Gregory County, South Dakota. Over his thirty-year career, author, director, screenwriter, producer, and distributor Oscar Micheaux made more than forty fictional films that explored African American life in the early twentieth century. Known as "race films" be-

Filmmaker Oscar Micheaux. Photo courtesy the South Dakota State Historical Society–State Archives.

cause they featured blacks, Micheaux distributed the films himself throughout the Midwest and across the United States. The best known of his existing works—many of which were lost—are *Within Our Gates* (1920) and *Body and Soul* (1925).

Chicano activists, such as the Midwest Chicano Mass Media Committee, began calling for a revisioning of film and television representations in the late 1960s. Mexican Americans converged around the need for community access to media, media industry employment, and alternative media portrayals. The Latino Consortium (housed for a period in Detroit), helped organize several PBS stations, including WKAR in East Lansing, Michigan, to carry the television program *Acción Chicano*.

Not unlike its national output, Midwest Native and Asian American film production has been limited. Historically, most Native and Asian American portrayals have come from Caucasian perspectives and been confined to westerns and re-creations of romanticized manifest destiny marches. Only in 1998 did the first feature-length narrative film by a Native American about Native Americans appear, *Smoke Signals*. However, films focusing on Native and Asian Americans in the Midwest circulate within educational and public broadcasting spheres and film festivals. Films like the *Last Stand at Little Big Horn* by Paul Stekler and James Welch (1992) and *Barrier Device*, directed by Grace Lee (2002), offer new and inside views of these groups.

And despite the odds, several native midwesterners of color have attained national and international recognition. For example, native Chicagoan Renee Tajima-Peña has made award-winning documentaries like *Who Killed Vincent Chin?* (1988) and *My America . . . or Honk if You Love Buddha* (1996). Milwaukeean George Tillman, Jr., wrote and directed the Hollywood films *Soul Food* (1997) and *Men of Honor* (2000). Wisconsin producer Dan Banda explores the lives of Mexican Americans in the Midwest through his *Mountain's Mist and Mexico* (1996) that has aired on public television's *P.O.V.* and Mexico-based TV channels. Banda's *Indigenous Always: The Legend of La Malinche and the Conquest of Mexico* (2000) received five Emmy nominations. Focusing on the life of the poor and disenfranchised, St. Louis native Henry Hampton became one of the pre-eminent documentarians to chronicle twentieth-century social and political movements. Some of his works include *Eyes on the Prize I* and *II* (1987, 1990), *The Great Depression* (1993), and *America's War on Poverty* (1995). Chicago filmmaker Yvonne Welbon tells award-winning stories about black women's lives. Her works include *The Cinematic Jazz of Julie Dash* (1992–1993), *Remembering Wei Yi Fang, Remembering*

Myself (1995), and *Living With Pride: Ruth Ellis @ 100* (1999).

Several annual film festivals showcase the work of marginalized Midwest filmmakers. The Black Harvest International Festival of Film and Video, the Chicano Latino Film Festival, and the Asian American Showcase are held annually in Chicago. Chicago also has hosted Reeling, the Chicago Lesbian and Gay International Film Festival for more than twenty years. In addition to Reeling, the Midwest annually hosts at least a dozen film and video festivals with significant programming featuring gay and lesbian themes and artists, including Ladyfest (Columbus, Ohio, and other locations), Reel Pride (Royal Oak, Michigan), and the Flaming Film Festival (Minneapolis). Regarding film collections and respositories, the Black Film Center Archive at Indiana University serves as one of the largest and few repositories of films about, produced by, and/or marketed to African Americans. Also, the National Black Programming Consortium, a nonprofit media arts organization based in Columbus, Ohio, distributes black programming to Public Broadcasting stations nationally and serves as a clearinghouse for black film and video. The Latino Midwest Collective promotes the production and distribution of its members' works from its Chicago home.

Sources and Further Reading: Donald Bogle, *Toms, Coons, Mulattoes, Mammies & Bucks*, 4th ed. (2001); Pearl Bowser and Louise Spence, *Writing Himself into History* (2000); J. Ronald Green, *Straight Lick* (2000); Chon Noriega, *Shot in America* (2000).

Beretta E. Smith-Shomade
University of Arizona

Movie Stars

In the 1930s and 1940s, the peak years of the studio system in the Hollywood film industry, producers would often preview a film in the town of Pomona, about fifty miles southeast of Los Angeles. Producers presumed that how a film played in Pomona is how it would play in America's Heartland. To them, Pomona's residents were representative of the thousands of midwesterners who immigrated westward—many to southern California towns—in the previous fifty years. Many film stars were part of that demographic of transplanted midwesterners. Harold Lloyd (from Burchard, Nebraska), John Wayne (Winterset, Iowa), Carole Lombard (Fort Wayne, Indiana), Jean Harlow (Kansas City, Missouri), and Judy Garland (Grand Rapids, Minnesota) had all moved from the Midwest to southern California with their families as children or adolescents. Other film stars were born in the Midwest but started performing professionally alone or with their families at a young age—work that took them all over the country, with them settled in no place until beginning film careers in Hollywood as young adults. Betty Grable (St. Louis), Ginger Rogers (Independence, Missouri), Lillian Gish (Springfield, Ohio), and Mary Astor (Quincy, Illinois) are examples of stars with midwestern roots who were on the stage or in vaudeville or dance travel circuits at an early age. Clark Gable (Cadiz, Ohio) traveled around the Midwest doing manual labor while simultaneously acting as handyman or performer in theatre companies before coming to Hollywood in the late 1920s.

Although some Midwest towns have claimed these stars as their own (e.g., Grand Rapids, Minnesota, has regular events commemorating native Judy Garland), it is difficult to identify any specific influence of midwestern culture in them or their star mythologies (in their lifestyles and values, types of roles, aspirations for fame, professional training, etc.) or to make claims for what generally characterizes stars with midwestern roots. Although Judy Garland played one of the most famous midwestern characters in literary and film fiction—*The Wizard of Oz*'s Dorothy Gale from Kansas—Jean Harlow typically played wisecracking women assumed to hail from the urban northeast. So did Ginger Rogers. (However, one of her best roles was in *The Major and the Minor* (1942) as midwesterner Susan Applegate, who, broke and sick of being exploited in New York, travels by train back to her home in Ohio disguised as a child.)

A number of Midwest natives who became film stars had their first training or performance experience while still living and studying in the Midwest. While filmmaking was centralized elsewhere (first in New York, then in Hollywood), many towns and cities in the Midwest had strong community or college theatre groups. Spencer Tracy (Milwaukee) debated at Ripon College, which inspired him to study acting in New York. Don Ameche (Kenosha, Wisconsin) studied law at the University of Wisconsin, but his excellence in college dramatics and summer stock made him change careers. Charlton Heston (Evanston, Illinois) was in plays at Northwestern University and worked in local Chicago radio. Paul Newman (Cleveland) sold the interest in his late father's sporting goods store to study drama at Yale, but his interest in acting had originated from theatrical experience at Kenyon College in Ohio and summer stock companies in Williams Bay, Wisconsin, and Woodstock, Illinois. Richard Widmark (born in Sunrise, Minnesota, and raised in Sioux Falls, South Dakota) acted in over thirty plays while attending Lake Forest College outside Chicago, even staying on

as drama instructor for two years after graduation. Julie Harris (Grosse Pointe, Michigan) began acting while in high school, as did Rock Hudson (Winnetka, Illinois) and James Dean (Marion, Indiana). Actor-director Orson Welles (Kenosha, Wisconsin) was directing the Woodstock (Illinois) Theater Festival while still in his teens.

Dean Martin (Steubenville, Ohio) had been a prizefighter and gambling house croupier before getting singing jobs in nightclubs in his hometown. Betty Hutton (Battle Creek, Michigan) and Doris Day (Cincinnati) sang on local radio before joining traveling swing bands while still teenagers. As with Martin, their singing led to major contracts with Hollywood studios. Theda Bara (Cincinnati) was promoted in her teens by Fox studio as an actress of mysterious origins—born "in the shadow of the pyramids"—but she had already appeared extensively on stage in Cincinnati and New York under her birth name of Theodosia Goodman.

Perhaps the backgrounds of midwestern natives Louise Brooks, Henry Fonda, and Marlon Brando exemplify what prepared and propelled so many in the region to seek performance careers in New York and Hollywood. Brooks (Cherryvale, Kansas) came from a respected, upper-middle-class family, and was encouraged in a dancing career by a mother whose frustrations as a small-town caretaker made her take refuge in the arts. Brooks received attention from choreographer Ted Shawn when he taught a modern dance class in Wichita; she left home at fifteen to join his troupe in New York. Brooks eventually derailed her own film career by rebelling against studio authority and sustained a life-long ambivalence toward the Midwest. While her harshest criticism concerned its sexual hypocrisy, her upbringing in an unpretentious environment might have sharpened her critical perceptions about the phoniness and manipulations needed for success in New York and Hollywood show business, about which she wrote with great wit and lucidity in her later years. Marlon Brando (raised in Omaha and Libertyville, Illinois), too, had a mother whose frustrations as housewife led to work in the arts, but she was also an alcoholic. The family's often unconventional behavior made them town outcasts, and Brando's inability to live in a conservative social climate without getting in trouble motivated his move to New York to study acting. Henry Fonda (born in Grand Island, Nebraska, and raised in Omaha) was encouraged as a young man in his twenties to participate in community theatre by Marlon Brando's mother. Fonda was almost immediately addicted to acting, and while he angered his politically liberal but culturally conservative father when he quit his safe clerkship to take up acting, he eventually won the support of both parents. He would later describe them as exemplifying a gentle, yet confident, midwestern social ethos. As an actor, Fonda would himself exemplify that ethos in such roles as Tom Joad in *The Grapes of Wrath* (1940) and Abraham Lincoln in *Young Mr. Lincoln* (1939).

More recent film stars from the Midwest—Bill Murray (Wilmette, Illinois), Brad Pitt (born in Oklahoma, raised in Springfield, Missouri), John Cusack (Evanston, Illinois), John Malkovich (Benton, Illinois), and Willem Dafoe (Appletown, Wisconsin)—share some similarities, certainly more so than the earlier generation of stars from the Midwest, in that they tend to choose roles that eschew the romantic, leading man for humorous but unconventional heroes or perverted villains. They have also stayed much more connected to their former region's cultural and social identities, with Cusack producing pictures set in Chicago (for example, *High Fidelity*, 2000) and Dafoe and Malkovich still retaining associations with independent theatre in the Chicago area.

Sources and Further Reading: Paul Alexander, *Boulevard of Broken Dreams* (1994); Marlon Brando, *Songs My Mother Taught Me* (1994); Louise Brooks, *Lulu in Hollywood* (1982); Henry Fonda with Howard Teichmann, *Fonda: My Life* (1981); Eve Golden, *Vamp: The Rise and Fall of Theda Bara* (1996); Peter Manso, *Brando: The Biography* (1994); Barry Paris, *Louise Brooks* (1989); David Shipman, *The Great Movie Stars*, 3 vols. (1989–1991).

Mary Desjardins
Dartmouth College, New Hampshire

Screenwriters

Although New York and Los Angeles have produced the bulk of screenwriters, many major ones have midwestern roots. And while it would be tempting to dismiss the work of these screenwriters as a large block of heartwarming tales and little else, the reality is far different. Midwestern screenwriters have composed a diverse array of stories, including crime dramas, horror plots, romances, and comedies.

In the early days of cinema, technology limitations required a filmmaker to be a jack-of-all-trades. Many directed, wrote, and acted in the same films. One of these early craftsmen was Allan Dwan, born in Toronto but educated at Notre Dame and employed at a number of Chicago firms, notably Essanay. An engineering major, Dwan was talented at solving technical problems and found himself drifting to California as more production moved there. Known mostly as a director, Dwan still wrote or cowrote over forty films,

including *Robin Hood* (1922), the Douglas Fairbanks swashbuckler. A major figure in early film, Dwan's career stretched into the 1960s.

Oscar Apfel had a long career as an actor, and came into movies about the same time as Dwan. The Cleveland native helped Cecil B. DeMille craft the script for *The Squaw Man* (1914), generally regarded as the first feature-length film shot in Hollywood. Apfel wrote and directed several other films, but returned to acting, appearing in many low-budget 1930s B films.

Throughout the 1920s, movies got bigger budgets and crews. Recognized authors and playwrights became hot commodities. Studios, turning out dozens of features per year, welcomed any talent, male or female. One such woman was Hoosier naturalist Gene Stratton-Porter. Famous for her *Limberlost* novels, Porter went to California in 1922 to begin adapting her works for the movies. In 1924 she was killed when her vehicle was struck by a streetcar. Porter's company did manage to produce *Michael O'Halloran* (1923), *A Girl of the Limberlost* (1924), and *The Keeper of the Bees* (1925) before her death.

Scandal plagued Chicago native Ring Lardner, Jr., despite his enormous talents. As an uncredited script doctor, he cowrote such classics as *A Star is Born* (1937) and *Laura* (1944). He won an Oscar for *Woman of the Year* (1942) and worked on Fritz Lang's classic *Cloak and Dagger* (1946) before running afoul of the House Un-American Activities Committee. Congress jailed a group of writers, directors, and producers known as the Hollywood Ten, including Lardner, for refusing to cooperate in an investigation of suspected Communist infiltration in Hollywood. Upon his release, Lardner was blacklisted and worked under various pseudonyms for many years. By the late 1960s, the climate had cooled enough that he could once again use his own name, and he wrote the screenplay for the highly successful *M*A*S*H* (1970).

Also blacklisted, though without as much publicity, was Chicago-born Waldo Salt. Writing from the late 1930s on, Salt's political troubles matured his work into a weary cynicism. He won Oscars for his screenplays for *Midnight Cowboy* (1969) and *Coming Home* (1978) and was nominated for his work on *Serpico* (1973).

As movies diversified and allowed more independent productions, a strange new kind of filmmaker emerged whose goal was to produce cheap films very quickly. The king of this style is Roger Corman, a lanky Detroit native with over two hundred films to his credit. Like the jack-of-all-trades filmmakers before him, Corman would write, direct, produce—anything to get the film finished. His writing credits range from *The Fast and the Furious* (1954) to the three-day quickie *The Terror* (1963) and the more modestly budgeted *Frankenstein Unbound* (1990). Even Corman's most dubious works usually contain moments of true quality, often because of his keen eye for young talent.

Key among Corman's talent pool was Francis Ford Coppola, also from Detroit. After working for Corman for a few years, Coppola wrote and directed *Dementia 13* (1963), which Corman produced. The film, while effective, suffered from a cheap, slapdash feel, but it earned Coppola enough clout to write the screenplays for *Patton* (1970) and *The Godfather* (1972), which he also directed. His screenplay for *The Conversation* (1974) is today considered a suspense classic. Still known mostly as a director, Coppola has continued to write screenplays for many of his films, including *Godfather II* (1974), *Apocalypse Now* (1979), *The Cotton Club* (1984), and *The Rainmaker* (1997). In many ways, Coppola has come full circle from Corman's approach, producing some of the most big-budget features of the last thirty years.

Director-writers Jerry Zucker, Jim Abrahams, and David Zucker, all from Wisconsin, created a laugh-a-minute spoof of disaster films with *Airplane* (1980). *The Naked Gun* (1988) expanded their TV cop show send-up, *Police Squad!* (1982). They also skewered Elvis films with *Top Secret!* (1984).

A twisted insanity also pervades the work of Joel and Ethan Coen, born in Minnesota. From their sleeper, *Blood Simple* (1984), the brothers have gone on to write films like *Raising Arizona* (1987), *Barton Fink* (1991), the award-winning *Fargo* (1996), *The Big Lebowski* (1998), and *O Brother, Where Art Thou?* (2000). They tend to favor violence-with-comedy (*Fargo*) and comedy-with-violence (*Raising Arizona*).

Cleveland native Wes Craven specializes in serious scares and violence. *A Nightmare on Elm Street* (1984) spawned a host of sequels, but Craven cut his teeth with underground cheapies like *Last House on the Left* (1972) and *The Hills Have Eyes* (1977). Craven's trademark is dreamlike imagery combined with shocking gore.

Many well-known novelists have occasionally written screenplays. *Three Comrades* (1938) represents the sole credit for Minnesotan F. Scott Fitzgerald despite years of screenplay work. Most authors leave the adaptation of their work to others, but Indianapolis native Kurt Vonnegut wrote the screenplay for his play *Happy Birthday, Wanda June* (1971). Dan Wakefield, also from Indianapolis, worked his novel *Going All the Way* into a low-budget 1997 film with Ben Affleck.

Further Reading: A. Scott Berg, *Goldwyn: A Biography* (1989).

Eric Grayson
Indianapolis

Mass Media

Mass media in the Midwest developed as America expanded toward the uncharted regions of the West, and its once humble beginnings led to some of the nation's greatest innovations in radio and television and in newspaper and magazine publishing.

Newspaper was the nation's first form of mass media, and as settlers moved farther west, the medium flourished along with the burgeoning country. Among the first midwestern newspapers was the *Indiana Gazette*, founded in 1804 at Vincennes by Elihu Stout. More newspapers thrived in the region, especially as the Great Lakes area, which bordered the outermost regions of the West, became an important transportation and communication thoroughfare to the East. In 1817, Detroit established the *Gazette*, and other communities in the Midwest soon followed. By the 1850s, Cincinnati and St. Louis boasted several daily newspapers and were among the major publishing centers in the Midwest. Chicago and Milwaukee were also industry leaders as the Great Lakes population prospered.

A significant contributor to mass media in the region was Joseph Pulitzer, founder of the *St. Louis Post-Dispatch* and namesake of the illustrious journalism prize, granted annually since 1917. The award recognizes excellence in twenty-one categories, including journalism, photography, poetry, and music. Born in Hungary in 1847, Pulitzer became an American citizen in 1867, three years after volunteering for the Union Army in the Civil War. He endured a series of short-lived jobs, first in New York and eventually in St. Louis. Although he initially struggled with the English language, Pulitzer soon mastered it well enough to become a reporter for the *Westliche Post*, a German-language daily. He gained a reputation among other *Post* reporters as a man whose "chief ambition seemed to be to root out public abuses and expose evildoers." The hard-working Pulitzer became part-owner of the *Post* and began planning for his future.

After a brief time away from St. Louis newspaper work, Pulitzer returned in 1878 and, on December 9, he purchased the *Dispatch*, a bankrupt paper founded in 1864 that was on the block at a sheriff's sale. Within four years, it was the leading evening paper in St. Louis, netting $45,000 annually and challenging reputable morning papers like the *Missouri Republican* and the *Globe-Democrat*, and it would become one of the nation's greatest newspapers.

Together with Managing Editor John A. Cockerill, who joined the staff in 1880, Pulitzer established his contribution to the New Journalism, which combined

Joseph Pulitzer, founder of the *St. Louis Post-Dispatch*. Private Collection of Emily Rauh Pulitzer. Photo by Robert Holt, painted by John Singer Sargent.

sensational and entertaining stories with more traditional, hard-news pieces. The paper emphasized accuracy, lively writing, and the role of the newspaper as a watchdog, investigating crooked politicians, police, and public utilities, as well as wealthy tax evaders. As the *Post-Dispatch* became successful, these New Journalism principles were mimicked by other publications. Editorially, Pulitzer focused on the wealthy St. Louis families who wielded power in the nation's fifth largest city. While he received criticism for emphasizing the concerns of the middle class and small-business owners who associated with him, the community at large benefited from Pulitzer's news coverage.

Pulitzer has often been condemned as the man who "dumbed down" the news in his appeal to the masses. Critics in the nineteenth century complained that his focus on human interest, politics, and crime detracted from more serious news. He flouted the rules of his day by using flashy headlines and photos, and many complained that he oversimplified the news.

The Midwest has been home to many other newspapers of consequence, including the *Chicago Sun-Times, Cleveland Plain Dealer,* and *Minneapolis Star Tribune,* but the most important of them has been the *Chicago Tribune.* Founded in 1847 by James Kelly, John Wheeler, and J.K.C. Forrest, it became the Great

Lakes area's leading newspaper when Joseph Medill and his partners purchased it in 1855. Medill's support for Lincoln was crucial to his 1860 presidential nomination, and the paper became known for its strong pro-Union and antislavery position. The *Tribune* continued its conservative position when, in 1910, Robert Rutherford McCormick and his copublisher and cousin, Joseph Patterson, assumed control. In that year, the *Tribune's* circulation of 241 thousand established the newspaper as the leading Chicago daily. Its conservative stance was what prompted Marshall Field to create a rival morning daily, the *Chicago Sun.* Despite its critics, by the mid-1950s when McCormick's reign ended, the *Tribune* boasted more advertising revenue than its three competitors combined, and its circulation was the largest of any national standard-sized newspaper. Until his death in 1955, McCormick believed the *Tribune* to be "The World's Greatest Newspaper." By the late 1960s, the *Tribune's* ultraconservatism waned, and by the late 1980s, it ranked just behind the *Washington Post* among the nation's largest dailies. Today, the *Chicago Tribune* remains the most important Chicago daily and continues as one of the largest and most influential American newspapers.

As newspaper circulation grew in the Midwest and nationally, so did the black press. In 1905, Robert S. Abbott created the *Chicago Defender,* which would become the cornerstone of America's largest newspaper group. Through both world wars, Abbott attracted a national audience in the black community as an outspoken voice for equal opportunity and an end to segregation. Abbott designed the *Defender* to be similar to other national dailies in its inclusion of sports and women's news, in addition to news and editorial comment. He challenged the Ku Klux Klan and featured stories on lynchings and other threats to black America, while using "race-angling headlines" and sensationalizing crime and scandal stories. By the 1930s, however, he moderated his newspaper content with more personal, social, and cultural news. Abbot died in 1940 and was succeeded by his nephew, John H. Sengstacke.

The *Defender* survived despite the hardships of the Depression era and political turmoil of the 1960s and 1970s. In 1956, Sengstacke added a daily to the weekly *Defender* to increase coverage of Chicago news. Over the next decade, he bought other black dailies and established the nation's largest black-owned network. By 1998, the *Chicago Defender* had become one of only three black dailies still in existence out of some 185, according to the *Editor & Publisher International Year Book.* In 2000, Public Media Works purchased the *Defender* and other sister publications for more than $14 million.

In the early twentieth century, radio became an important aspect of mass media, and the Midwest contributed many pioneering efforts. The University of Wisconsin–Madison is recognized as home to America's first noncommercial radio station, which hit the radio waves in 1914 as 9XM, later WHA. Although the Navy restricted broadcasting in 1917 because of World War I, universities were still able to transmit radio signals under the experimental license agreement. The reputable Wisconsin Public Radio, WPR, is the country's second largest public radio network, after Minnesota Public Radio.

The Midwest region also forged the first radio station to broadcast regularly scheduled news. On August 20, 1920, 8MK began operations from the *Detroit News* building under the newspaper's sponsorship. Some claim that KDKA in Pittsburgh was the first, but it did not broadcast regular news until the November 1920 elections. On August 31 of that year, 8MK broadcast results of a Michigan election and continued daily to integrate talk and news with music programming. The station became WWJ in October 1921, after the *News* obtained full commercial license.

National public radio audiences are transported to the heart of the Midwest each week when they tune in to Garrison Keillor's *A Prairie Home Companion*. It hails from fictitious Lake Wobegon, Minnesota, "where all the women are strong, all the men are good-looking, and all the children are above average," and the show aims to offer a glimpse into the simplicity and charm often associated with the Midwest.

Keillor, who was born in Anoka, Minnesota, in 1942, created the show on KSJN-FM in St. Paul in 1974. He left his show in 1987, and in 1989 started another variety show, *Garrison Keillor's American Radio Company of the Air*. By 1993, the program returned to its original name; it currently broadcasts live from the Fitzgerald Theater in St. Paul, when it's not on the road, and remains a staple of National Public Radio programming.

The Midwest also holds an important place in television history for its many influential talk show personalities, including Phil Donahue and Oprah Winfrey. In 1967 Donahue debuted his phone-in show on WLWD-TV in Dayton, Ohio, and paved the way for many future audience participation talk shows. The program's combination of compassion and controversy, along with audience participation, boosted its success, and in 1969 it became nationally televised. Roving through the audience and encouraging questions and feedback, Donahue appealed to a predominantly female following. He remained on the airwaves for twenty-nine years until retiring in January 1996.

The Midwest spawned another powerful talk show force when Oprah Winfrey debuted in Chicago in 1984. The host appealed to audiences with her close rapport and personally revealing questions, and she soon became the richest woman in talk television. Since debuting nationally in 1986, and in 1995 refocusing her show with a more inspiring, spiritual approach, she continues to be a powerful influence in shaping the many talk shows of today.

Several culturally significant magazines originated in the Midwest, including *Ebony*, *Playboy*, and *Midwest Living*. John H. Johnson challenged the conventional black press when he created *Ebony* in 1945. Instead of focusing on racism and the plight of black America, Johnson concentrated on its successes. The magazine featured sports and entertainment personalities as well as stories of accomplished black men and women, and transformed the way America perceived black culture.

Hugh Hefner tested 1950s mores when *Playboy* magazine hit the newsstands in December 1953. The first issue, complete with legendary starlet Marilyn Monroe as centerfold, sold out its print run of seventy thousand, surpassed the one million mark by 1956, and made Hefner a millionaire before the decade's end. Hefner applied to his magazine the urbane, self-conscious, and timely editorial strategies he had learned while working at *Esquire*, going beyond it in focusing on sex and offering drawings of seductive women and cartoons that were considered racy in their day.

Playboy capitalized on the image of a sophisticated, sexually liberated male, and in both advertising and articles espoused a decidedly middlebrow lifestyle. It published many respectable authors writing on sex, drugs, feminism, travel, war, and professional sports and campaigned against sexual prudishness and the religious right. *Playboy* thrived to a circulation high of 71.2 million in 1972, and established an empire of clubs, books, videos, and television shows. Hefner's magazine invited many imitators and transformed the concept of men's magazines.

Midwest Living is also a significant consumer magazine in the region because it focuses specifically on Midwest travel, lifestyles, home and garden, nutrition, and culture. Meredith Corporation launched the first issue in April of 1987, and the circulation has grown from four hundred thousand to nine hundred thousand in 2003.

Sources and Further Reading: Margaret A. Blanchard, ed., *History of the Mass Media in the United States* (1998); Barbara Ehrenreich, "Playboy Joins the Battle of the Sexes," *Media Journal: Reading and Writing About Popular Culture* (1999); Edwin Emery, Michael Emery, and Nancy L. Roberts, *The Press and America: An Interpretive History of the Mass Media* (1992; 9th ed., 2000); David A. Fryxell, "Garrison Keillor's Twin Cities," *Writer's Digest* (January 2000); Daniel Webster Hollis, *The ABC-CLIO Companion to the Media in America* (1995); Langston Hughes, "55 Ebony's Nativity," *Ebony* (Nov. 2000); Allen Neuharth, "The State of News Standards

Today Compared with Those in the 'Golden Age,'" *Editor & Publisher* (Feb. 26, 1994); Sue Schardt, "Public Radio: A Short History," *The Christian Science Monitor Publishing Company*, http://www.wsvh.org/pubradiohist.htm (1996); Gini Graham Scott, *Can We Talk? The Power and Influence of Talk Shows* (1996); David Segal, "At Wolf Trap, Keillor-Made Comforts of 'Home Companion,'" *The Washington Post* (July 9, 2001).

Heather Mundt
Longmont, Colorado

Agricultural Journalism

Agricultural journalism began in 1819 with the publication of the *American Farmer*, a weekly journal out of Baltimore. Between 1819 and 1860, agricultural publications sprang up as rapidly as crops—numbering over four hundred—but most folded within two years. In 1860, there were about sixty journals that reached a reading public numbering more than 250 thousand. The *Western Farmer and Gardener* of Cincinnati became the first major western journal, while the *Prairie Farmer* of Chicago circulated more widely. The *Michigan Farmer*, *Ohio Cultivator*, and *Ohio Farmer* arose in the 1840s and 1850s. In 1856, the *Cincinnatus*, edited by the Farmer's College near Cincinnati, became the first academic journal of agriculture. The *Wisconsin Farmer* and the *Indiana Farmer* also covered the Midwest. This small sampling suggests the plethora of periodicals devoted to the development of western agriculture.

The rise of the farm press came amidst a more general, national trend toward improvement in practical sciences, manufacturing, and research. The education of the rural mind remained the fundamental goal. The press covered all aspects of agriculture, including stockraising, dairying, horticulture, implements and mechanics, insect pests, chemistry, crop diversity, drainage, fertilization, deep plowing, and crop rotation. Women received training for "useful" work such as sewing, cooking, childcare, and other domestic duties. Keeping women busy at "practical" things was intended to ensure feminine morality. Women bore the responsibility for men's ethical welfare, and journals directed them to instill order, temperance, and moral reform. Agricultural journals and societies worked hand-in-hand to improve the soil and the mind simultaneously.

Agricultural journalists pursued multiple objectives. They urged farmers not to amass more land than properly cultivable and abhorred methods that plundered the soil. They advocated business techniques, teaching the importance of farm records and account books. The periodicals supported the formation of local farmers' clubs for trading agricultural information and creating a communal unity in the isolation of the countryside. Innovation proved key in farming journalism, and the press promoted and popularized new machinery like the steel plow, thresher, mower, and reaper. Editorials battled farmers' unwillingness to change traditional practices, while advertisements worked to accomplish the same goal. Advertising not only informed readers, but proved financially remunerative for the press. Journals heaped praise—or "puffed"—certain products that editors saw as particularly useful or in which they had a monetary interest.

Journals generally avoided politics, but covered important matters related to slavery, elections, and party platforms. The farming press expressed in writing the public indignation at the monopolization by and the high rates of railroads and warehouses. In the 1870s, this crusade fostered support for the Grange movement and later for populism. Periodicals also touched on lighter themes, printing poems and essays that praised the nobility of agriculture. Periodicals warned against crazes over new animal breeds and novelty farm products, but this counsel often only fueled speculative interest. With education as the linchpin, the press endorsed the appointment of state chemists, state funding for geological and agricultural surveys, and the establishment of the federal department of agriculture. The most aggressive campaign was fought for agricultural colleges, and agricultural journalists played an important role in the passage of the Morrill Act that provided funding for land-grant institutions.

By the twentieth century, the farming press was ensconced as educator, promoter, political touchstone, and mentor of the agricultural community. The spread of technology only solidified these roles. Radio proved vital as hundreds of AM stations across the nation became the fastest, and principal, sources of news for the farm family. Frequent crop and market reports kept the farmer updated on financial news, and weather forecasts guided planting and harvesting. The radio was a watershed in agricultural journalism, in many respects finally eradicating the rural isolation of America's farmers.

Sources and Further Reading: Albert L. Demaree, *The American Agricultural Press, 1819–1860* (1941); James F. Evans and Rodolfo N. Salcedo, *Communications in Agriculture* (1974); Donald B. Marti, *To Improve the Soil and the Mind* (1979); William B. Ward, *Reporting Agriculture Through Newspapers, Magazines, Radio, Television* (1952).

Garrit Voggesser
University of Oklahoma

Alternative Journalism

Although the 1950s may have seemed like a paradise to the white upper and middle class, the seeds of dissent and protest of the 1960s were already being planted.

Underground papers like the *Berkeley Barb* and Atlanta's *Great Speckled Bird* began a tradition of opposition publishing and concentrated dissenting thought. In Chicago, the *Seed* and the *Realist* were sounding boards for Yippies like Abbie Hoffman. Other underground papers in the Midwest included the *Kaleidoscope* in Milwaukee, the *Spectator* in Bloomington, Indiana, and *Xanadu* in St. Louis. The antiestablishment message of these papers often led to harassment and arrest by local police.

As the turmoil of the 1960s and early 1970s was winding down, so was the underground press. Changes in political sensibilities of both editors and audiences gave rise to a new kind of publication: the alternative newspaper, an outlet for news and culture that the mainstream dailies avoided. While New York's *Village Voice* was often the inspiration, the most significant historical event in the creation of the modern alt-weekly occurred in Chicago in 1971, when the *Chicago Reader* pioneered the practice of free circulation, a cornerstone of today's alternative papers. The *Reader* also developed a new kind of journalism, ignoring the news and focusing on everyday life and ordinary people. As discussed below, many other Midwest cities also saw alternative journalism emerge in distinct and idiosyncratic ways.

In Cincinnati, several papers, including *Queen's Jester, Exorcist, Rivertown Times, Cincinnati Reporter,* and *Everybody's News,* have appeared over the years, challenged the establishment, and ultimately lost out. Today, the ten-year-old *Cincinnati CityBeat* carries the baton for its predecessors. The history of the alternative press in Cleveland was not unlike that of a lot of other cities until October 2002, when the two largest alternative media companies decided to strike a deal to eliminate competition in Los Angeles and Cleveland. As part of the deal, Village Voice Media gave up the *Cleveland Free Times* and a reported $8 million in cash to Phoenix-based New Times Inc., which ceased publication of *New Times Los Angeles.* That deal left New Times' *Cleveland Scene,* the state's largest alternative newsweekly, founded in 1970 and purchased by New Times in 1998, as the only weekly in town. *Free Times* would remain closed only until April 2003, when an antitrust settlement allowed a group of investors, including former *Free Times* staffers, to reopen under the *Free Times* banner. The *Columbus Free Press* (Ohio) grew out of the same antiwar sentiment that most other alternative weeklies shared in the early 1970s.

The paper ceased weekly publication in 1995, coincident with a glut of weeklies in Columbus, and now exists in a changed format. *Downtown Alive* began publishing in the early 1980s, and the arts-oriented paper now publishes under the banner *Alive.* The same city's *Other Paper* began publishing in 1990 and still remains a news and entertainment weekly. And the *Columbus Guardian* published for several years before closing its doors late in 1996.

In Detroit, the *Metro Times* first rolled off the press in September 1980 and is still publishing today. Sixty miles to the north, Michael Moore, who was later to achieve fame as a best-selling author and Oscar-winning documentary filmmaker, published the alternative monthly *Flint Voice* (later renamed the *Michigan Voice*) from 1977 to 1986.

In July 2002, the future of the alternative press in downstate Illinois was saved in Springfield by a journey to the past. The *Illinois Times* was repurchased by former *Illinois Times* publisher and editor Fletcher Farrar from Yesse Communications, which owned the publication from 1997 to 2002. The *Times* was founded in September 1975 by *Time Magazine* writers Bill Friedman and Alan Anderson in Friedman's hometown. Farrar took over the weekly in July 1977 before selling it to Yesse.

The *Kansas City Pitch Weekly* (Missouri) survived more trouble than befalls most alternative newsweeklies. Started in 1980, the *Pitch* was relatively unchallenged in the marketplace until a group of staffers, fearful the financially strapped paper would fold, walked out and joined its main competitor, *View,* in 1991. The *View* was later renamed the *Kansas City New Times,* not affiliated with the alternative media giant of the same name. *New Times* closed in the late 1990s, and in 1999, the *Pitch* was sold, ironically enough, to alternative media giant New Times Inc. Around the same time, New Times Inc. also acquired the *Riverfront Times,* which has been the dominant alternative weekly in St. Louis since it was founded in 1977 by city native Ray Hartmann.

A downtown entertainment magazine called *Skywalker* was Des Moines's first incarnation of an alternative press. The magazine was purchased by Connie Wimer in 1983, and by the end of the decade, she had renamed the paper *Cityview* and turned it into a full-fledged alternative newsweekly. Competition was nonexistent until a new weekly, *Pointblank,* emerged claiming to be the independent, free-thinking voice of Central Iowa.

In Minneapolis, the *Sweet Potato* started as a music and entertainment magazine and later began covering hard news. In 1981, it changed its name to *City Pages* and found itself in a bitter rivalry with the already established *Twin Cities Reader.* The two would battle until

1997, when Village Voice Media bought both the *City Pages* and the *Reader* and promptly closed the *Reader*.

The three alternative newspapers that began publishing in Milwaukee between 1966 and 1982—the *Kaleidoscope*, the *Bugle American*, and the *Shepherd Express*—all have the distinction of being firebombed during their operation. Only the *Shepherd Express* is still publishing. Madison has had a steady stream of alternative press publications since the underground press boom of the 1960s, but *Isthmus*, which began publishing in 1976, now stands as the city's only alternative newsweekly. Madison is also the home of an alternative magazine, the *Progressive*, which has been in continuous publication since 1909, when it was founded by Wisconsin Senator Robert La Follette as *La Follette's Weekly*.

Sources and Further Reading: Ellen Frankfort, *The Voice: Life at the Village Voice* (1976); Kevin McAuliffe, *The Great American Newspaper* (1978); Richard McCord, *The Chain Gang* (1996); Abe Peck, *Uncovering the Sixties* (1991); Joan Micklin Silver, dir., *Between the Lines* (Midwest Films, 1977).

Richard Karpel
Association of Alternative Newsweeklies
Washington, D.C.

Cartoons and Cartoonists

Although midwestern cities are far from the media centers in New York and Los Angeles, the history of cartooning reveals that cartoonists from the Midwest have shaped their medium more than their colleagues from any other part of the country. The comic that established the daily "strip" format for newspaper comics was *Mutt and Jeff* by Bud Fisher, who was born and raised in Chicago. Minnesota's Charles Schulz

drew *Peanuts*, giving comics a genuine human dimension and setting the fashion in comic strips for at least the last quarter of the twentieth century. Missouri's Chic Young drew *Blondie*, the most enduring of the family situation comedy strips. Ohioan Milton Caniff raised the standard for adventure strips in 1930s and 1940s with *Terry and the Pirates* and, with fellow Ohioan Noel Sickles, deployed a drawing style that created a school of comic strip illustration. Several cartoonists in the Chicago area, most of whom worked for the *Chicago Tribune*, also made their mark: Sidney Smith's *The Gumps* was arguably the first strip to tell a continuing story from day to day, and its popularity spawned the *Chicago Tribune* newspaper syndicate; Frank King's characters in *Gasoline Alley* were the first to age; Harold Gray was the first major syndicated cartoonist to take a political stance, conservative, in *Little Orphan Annie*; Chester Gould virtually created the detective strip genre with *Dick Tracy*. The Chicago Art Institute provided training for a host of artists who turned to cartooning: Roy Crane established the adventure genre with *Wash Tubbs and Captain Easy*; Harold Foster introduced realistic illustration with *Tarzan* and perpetuated it in *Prince Valiant*; and Ken Ernst drew the first soap opera strip, *Mary Worth*, for Cleveland writer Allen Saunders. Two of World War II's soldier cartoonists grew up in Chicago: George Baker, whose *Sad Sack* personified the downtrodden enlisted man, and Dave Breger, whose creation *G.I. Joe* (also published as *Private Breger*), provided the generic term for that war's soldiers.

Two of the medium's early geniuses grew up in the Midwest. Ohioan Richard F. Outcault drew *Yellow Kid* in the mid-1890s, the earliest newspaper comics sensation, and *Buster Brown* (and his dog Tige), which became one of the pioneering merchandising successes with Buster Brown children's shoes. Michigander

Crimefighter Dick Tracy at work. Tribune Media Services and The San Francisco Academy of Comic Art Collection, The Ohio State University Cartoon Research Library.

Winsor McCay demonstrated in *Little Nemo* a mastery of the comic strip form that raised it to fine art. Among the first widely circulated, syndicated editorial cartoonists was J. N. "Ding" Darling, who drew for the *Des Moines Register* from 1917 until his retirement in 1949. Other major editorial cartoonists working in the Midwest included John T. McCutcheon, who introduced the human interest editorial cartoon at the *Chicago Tribune*, Vaughn Shoemaker at the *Chicago Daily News*, Billy Ireland at the *Columbus Dispatch*, and Daniel Fitzpatrick and Bill Mauldin at the *St. Louis Post-Dispatch*. Herb Block ("Herblock"), who coined the term "McCarthyism," was born in Chicago and employed at the Newspaper Enterprise Association in Cleveland, where he won the first of three Pulitzer Prizes before spending the rest of his career and life at the *Washington Post*. The first woman editorial cartoonist at a general circulation newspaper was Edwina Dumm at the *Monitor* in Columbus; she later produced the comic strip *Cap Stubbs and Tippie* for nearly fifty years, a record in itself. And Cathy Guisewite, whose *Cathy* comic strip forged a place in the comics for women's interest strips, grew up in Michigan.

The comic book industry was invigorated (if not actually created) by the superhero genre, which was inaugurated by Superman, a creation of two Cleveland youths, Jerry Siegel and Joe Shuster. Superman's greatest newsstand rival, Captain Marvel, was designed by a Minnesotan, C. C. Beck. Magazine cartoonists from the Midwest include the *New Yorker*'s James Thurber (Ohio) and Helen Hokinson (Illinois); Art Young (Wisconsin), a gentle Socialist; Frederick Burr Opper (Ohio), who also did book illustration, editorial cartoons, and finally, a classic comic strip, *Happy Hooligan*. The cartoonist whose genius set the fashion for theatrical caricatures, Al Hirschfeld, grew to adolescence in St. Louis; another distinctive stylist in the same line of work was Alfred Frueh, who was born in Ohio. This roster is by no means complete, but the foregoing roll call of significant figures in the history of the medium demonstrates beyond question that the sensibilities of the Midwest were well represented by its cartoonists in newspaper comic strips, editorial cartoons, comic books, and magazine cartooning.

Sources and Further Reading: Stephen Becker, *Comic Art in America* (1959); Bill Blackbeard and Dale Crain, *Comic Strip Century* (1995); Ron Goulart, *The Funnies: 100 Years of American Comic Strips* (1995); Jerry Robinson, *The Comics: An Illustrated History of Comic Strip Art* (1974); Brian Walker, *The Comics Since 1945* (2002); Coulton Waugh, *The Comics* (1947).

Robert C. Harvey
Champaign, Illinois

Ebony Magazine

Ebony magazine has the largest circulation of any magazine in the world that produces content about African American life and culture. Founded in Chicago in 1945 by John H. Johnson, who modeled his publication after *Look* and *Life* magazines, *Ebony*'s goal has been to report about success and achievement among African Americans rather than focus on race, civil rights, discrimination, and protest, as does so much of the black press. A typical issue of *Ebony* might include stories about sports and entertainment stars, fashion designers, and high-visibility achievers in education, industry, or other fields. "*Ebony* will try to mirror the happier side of Negro life—the positive everyday achievements from Harlem to Hollywood," promised Johnson in *Ebony*'s inaugural issue. It is a promise the magazine has kept, even during the 1960s and 1970s, when *Ebony* included stories and photos chronicling the black civil rights movement.

Part of the family-owned Johnson Publishing Co. (which includes the weekly *Jet* magazine, the Johnson Book Division, Fashion Fair Cosmetics, and Supreme Beauty Products), *Ebony*'s 2002 monthly circulation was 1.9 million (with a readership estimated at 12 million), placing it fortieth among the top two hundred magazines in the United States, a readership beyond more widely known titles like the *National Enquirer*, *Rolling Stone*, *Star*, *Vogue*, *Vanity Fair*, *New Yorker*, *Forbes*, *Fortune*, *GQ*, *Harper's Bazaar*, and *Esquire*. On the occasion of *Ebony*'s fiftieth birthday in November 1995, founder Johnson observed that "institutions, corporations, magazines, principalities have lived and died since 1945, and *Ebony* is still here, and still number one." He noted that the hopes and dreams of baseball great Jackie Robinson, educator Mary McLeod Bethune, civil rights leader Martin Luther King, Jr., and Supreme Court Justice Earl Warren had not yet been fulfilled, thus calling for "a greater need for a recognition of the *Ebony* idea" to celebrate African American achievement and excellence.

In July 2003, *Ebony* redesigned its graphics, layout, and content, adding more color and white space to give the publication an updated contemporary look, and introducing new features. In an open letter to its readers, the editors reaffirmed and repositioned founder Johnson's vision and promise: "This is a new *Ebony* that gives new color in a new century to a 20th century phenomenon that changed the color and tempo of American journalism."

Sources and Further Reading: Shashank Bengali, "Jetsetter," *Trojan Family Magazine* 34 (Winter 2002); William E. Berry, "The Popular Press as Symbolic Interactionism: A Sociocultural Analysis of Ebony Magazine, 1945–75," PhD diss., University of Illinois at Urbana (1978); John H. Johnson with Lerone Bennett, Jr., *Succeeding against the Odds* (1989).

William Berry
University of Illinois–Urbana-Champaign

Hugh Hefner and *Playboy*

Hugh Marston Hefner, founder of a celebrated media empire headquartered in the Midwest, was born in Chicago on April 9, 1926. After a conventional middle-class upbringing, Hefner graduated from Steinmetz High School and joined the U.S. Army. Returning to Chicago in 1946, he studied briefly at the School of the Art Institute of Chicago before enrolling at the University of Illinois at Urbana-Champaign. Hefner produced cartoons for the student newspaper and edited *Shaft*, an irreverent magazine, to which he added a "Coed of the Month." He graduated in two and a half years.

Hefner gave up a position as a copyright editor at *Esquire* when the magazine moved to New York City. At loose ends, he devised a publication targeted at urban males who had served in World War II. Borrowing eight thousand dollars from a bank, a loan company, and friends, Hefner put together *Playboy* in the kitchen of a Chicago apartment he shared with his wife, Millie. It was an immediate hit. The first issue in December 1953, which featured a now-famous photograph of a nude Marilyn Monroe, sold more than fifty thousand copies.

Hefner was as adept an entrepreneur as he was an editor. By the 1960s, Playboy Enterprises included nightclubs in which women dressed as "bunnies" catered to male "key-holding" customers. Since Hefner's retirement in 1988, his daughter Christie has presided over a corporation that includes a global television enterprise as well as a television pay service designed to be an electronic version of the magazine. The *Playboy* bunny is one of the most recognizable corporate logos in the world.

Men joked that they bought *Playboy* for the articles rather than the photographs of naked women. But in fact the magazine featured interesting fiction and stories as well as a monthly interview with a well-known figure. Permeating everything was the *Playboy* philosophy, which promoted the idea that consensual adult sex is fun and not something to be treated as shameful. *Playboy* became an icon of the sexual revolution sweeping the United States in the 1950s and 1960s. In June 1963, Chicago police arrested Hefner for obscenity. He was acquitted by a hung jury. Hefner has long been a staunch defender of civil liberties and a critic of moral repression.

In the last quarter of the twentieth century, Hefner was a comfortable, if controversial, American institution. His Los Angeles mansion (opened in 1971) became famous for extravagant parties and personal freedom. But his philosophy seemed increasingly tame and naïve. By the 1980s, pornography was widely available to Americans, and the generally discreet nude photographs in *Playboy* were no longer shocking. Conservative religious groups continued to denounce *Playboy* as morally degenerate, but it was no longer a prime target. The same was true of women's rights advocates, who had long lamented *Playboy*'s portrayal of women as sexual toys designed to conform to male stereotypes.

In 1988, Hefner, who had divorced his first wife in 1959, married Playmate Kimberley Conrad, with whom he had two sons. The couple divorced in 1998, and Hefner resumed life as a bachelor.

Sources and Further Reading: Frank Brady, *Hefner* (1974); Gretchen Edgren, *Inside the Playboy Mansion* (1998); Hugh Hefner, *The Playboy Philosophy* (1963); Russell Miller, *Bunny: The Real Story of Playboy* (1986).

Andrew Cayton
Miami University, Oxford, Ohio

Major Mainstream Urban Newspapers

The big city newspapers of the Midwest have not had the impact of their eastern counterparts, but they and their makers have significantly influenced American politics, society, culture, and thought over the past two centuries. In the process, midwestern newspapers also proved the axiom that frontier American development was marked less by the construction of government buildings or cultural institutions than by the establishment of newspapers. That process began with the publication of the *Centinel of the Northwest Territory* in the newly settled "Queen City" of Cincinnati on November 9, 1793, one decade after the last battle of the Revolutionary War. That first issue of the *Centinel* promised that it was "open to all parties; influenced by none," an independent philosophy that has come to characterize much of the region's mainstream urban press as it has attempted to put a uniquely midwestern stamp on American life.

From the Queen City of Cincinnati, newspapers followed the wave of western frontier settlement, spreading up the Mississippi to the "River City" of St. Louis in 1808, across the Great Lakes to Detroit in 1809, to Cleveland in 1818, Chicago in 1833, and Milwaukee in 1836, and on land to Indianapolis in 1822, St. Paul in 1849, Minneapolis and Kansas City (Mis-

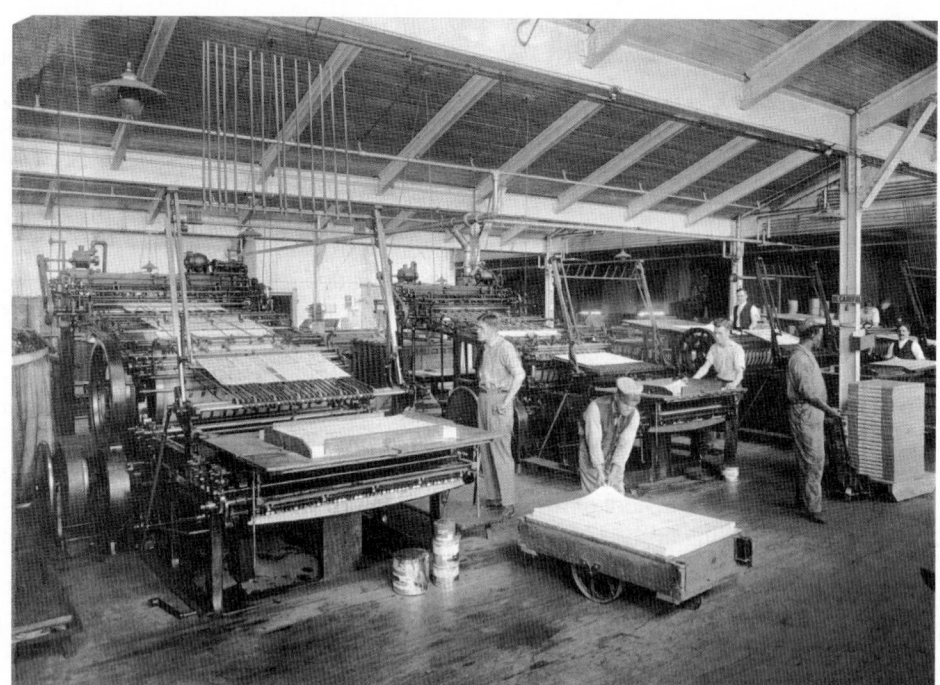

Broadsheet printing presses, Indianapolis, 1916. Bass Photo CD Collection, Indiana Historical Society, neg. no. 49240.

souri) in 1851, Des Moines in 1849, and the Nebraska and Kansas territories in 1854. Many of the earliest midwestern newspapers strove to promote population growth and economic development in their respective settlements. A few advocated political, philosophical, or religious principles such as abolitionism, temperance, or communal living.

As the prospects for their settlements became recognized, better organized and financed daily newspapers began to appear. The *Detroit Free Press* started in 1831 as a Democratic Party–financed organ. The *Cleveland Plain Dealer* began as a weekly in 1842. The *Milwaukee Journal-Sentinel* was first published as the *Sentinel* in 1837, making it one of the oldest extant businesses in Wisconsin. The *Cincinnati Enquirer* appeared in 1841 and in 1848 became one of the first newspapers in the nation to publish a Sunday edition. The *Chicago Tribune* saw the light of day first in 1847, spawned in part from a literary publication known as *Gem of the Prairie*. The *St. Paul Pioneer Press* began as the *Minnesota Pioneer* in 1849. The *Des Moines Register* was founded in 1860 as the first daily in Iowa's capital city. The *Minneapolis Tribune* began in 1867, and the *Star* debuted in 1920; the two merged to form the *Minneapolis Star and Tribune* in 1982, then the *Star-Tribune* in 1987. The *Kansas City Star* was born in 1880. The *Milwaukee Journal* was started in 1882 and remains among the largest employee-owned urban newspapers in the country. The *Omaha World-Herald* began in 1885. The *Chicago Times* first appeared as a

photo tabloid in 1929, and merged with the *Chicago Sun*, established in 1941, to form the *Sun-Times* in 1948.

Some of American journalism's most respected and colorful figures have emerged from the Midwest. Elijah Lovejoy was editor of the *St. Louis Observer*, a strident abolitionist weekly, when he was murdered by a proslavery mob in 1837. *Chicago Tribune* Civil War correspondent Irving Carson was the first American war reporter to be killed in action, in 1862. One of his employers, Joseph Medill, began his newspaper career in Ohio before he purchased a portion of the *Tribune* in 1855. Medill employed his newspaper to influence the nomination of Abraham Lincoln as the 1860 Republican presidential candidate and went on to establish one of the nation's most powerful newspaper families. His grandson, Col. Robert R. McCormick, remade the *Tribune* into what he called the "World's Greatest Newspaper" and used it as a mouthpiece for his ultraconservative political views throughout the first half of the twentieth century. One of print journalism's most famous blunders was the *Chicago Tribune* headline "Dewey Defeats Truman" held aloft by a jubilant, victorious President Harry S Truman on November 3, 1948.

Wilbur F. Storey's fiercely anti-Lincoln *Chicago Times* was the first major urban American newspaper to be suppressed by the government when armed Union troops seized its building and presses briefly in 1863. Storey also developed a unique form of sensationalism between the 1850s and 1870s, first in the *Detroit Free Press* and later in the *Times*, that inspired the rise of literary realism in the Midwest. Two Chicago-based reporters, Ben Hecht and Charles MacArthur, used the techniques of realism to create characters based on real-life Chicago newspapermen in their 1928 Broadway comedy *The Front Page*, which was made into three motion pictures and was honored as one of the twenty-five best twentieth-century American plays.

Immigrant Joseph Pulitzer advanced from a reporter for a German-language newspaper to publisher of the *St. Louis Post-Dispatch* in the decade after the Civil War before he brought his form of sensationalism to New York City in 1883. His *Post-Dispatch* remained in Pulitzer family hands into the twenty-first century. James E. Scripps founded the *Detroit News* in 1873. His half-brother, Edward W. Scripps, introduced the one-cent *Cleveland Penny Press* in 1878 and bought the *Cincinnati Penny Post* in 1883. These two became the parent papers of the first major American newspaper chain. Edward also published the first daily newspaper sustained without advertising, the *Day Book* in Chicago, between 1911 and 1917, where poet Carl Sandburg was a reporter.

Melville E. Stone's *Chicago Daily News* was the first successful one-cent newspaper in Chicago, helping to introduce news as a saleable commodity to the Midwest. Stone moved on to manage the Associated Press, which was reincorporated in Chicago in 1893. Stone's *Daily News*, the *Chicago Inter-Ocean*, and the *Kansas City Star* were three of the nation's leading training grounds for reporters in the twentieth century, even though the University of Missouri began offering the first bachelor's degree in journalism beginning in 1908. William Rockhill Nelson made his *Kansas City Star* famous for his relentless crusades. William Jennings Bryan was an editor for the *Omaha World-Herald* before he became a three-time Democratic presidential candidate.

William Allen White, a reporter for the *Kansas City Star* before he bought the *Emporia Gazette*, wrote a powerful editorial in 1896 titled "What's the Matter with Kansas" that was recopied in almost every other Republican newspaper in the country. Roy W. Howard turned the Cincinnati-based E. W. Scripps newspaper chain toward broadcasting in the early 1920s. The first chapter of the Newspaper Guild, the leading union of newspaper editorial workers, was founded in Cleveland in 1933. The most bitter strike involving the Guild occurred in Chicago and led to the retaliatory closing of William Randolph Hearst's *Chicago Herald & Examiner* in 1939. Eugene Pulliam began a family dynasty when he bought the *Indianapolis Star* and *Indianapolis News* during the 1940s. *Chicago*

Daily News, *Sun-Times*, and *Tribune* columnist Mike Royko wrote daily columns for more than twenty years and won a Pulitzer Prize before his death in 1997. Iowa native Esther (Eppie) Pauline Lederer wrote a nationally syndicated advice column under the pen name Ann Landers after she won a *Chicago Sun-Times* contest in 1955 until her death in 2002. Her twin sister, Pauline Esther Friedman, also wrote a widely syndicated advice column, "Dear Abby."

Several significant newspaper law cases originated in the Midwest. Michigan jurist Thomas M. Cooley wrote a dissenting opinion in an 1881 Michigan Supreme Court case involving the *Detroit Free Press* that served as a precedent for *New York Times v. Sullivan*, a 1964 U.S. Supreme Court decision considered one of the most significant press freedom cases in American history. A since-failed Des Moines daily was responsible for a 1901 Iowa Supreme Court decision, *Cherry v. Des Moines Leader*, which defined fair comment, the right to print one's own thoughts on matters of true opinion. The 1931 U.S. Supreme Court decision *Near v. Minnesota*, involving a Minneapolis-based weekly paper known as the *Saturday Press*, established strict limitations on the government in matters of prior restraint. A case of a different sort involving the *Cincinnati Enquirer* was settled out of court for an estimated $14 million in 1998 after the newspaper retracted stories alleging business wrongdoings at hometown Chiquita Brands.

Although most citizens in Midwest communities have tended to favor multiple local newspapers over a single newspaper outlet for their own community, a number of major afternoon midwestern newspapers disappeared during the later twentieth century due to declining readerships. The *Chicago Daily News* said goodbye to its city in 1978. The *Cleveland Press* ended in 1982. The *St. Louis Globe-Democrat*, founded in 1852, perished in 1986. The *Kansas City Times* all but disappeared in 1990, the same year as the *St. Paul Dispatch*, which had merged with the *St. Paul Pioneer Press* in 1985, had its name removed. The *Indianapolis News* was discontinued in 1999. The Newspaper Preservation Act of 1970 allowed two midwestern cities, Cincinnati and Detroit, to retain their two daily newspapers.

The absorption of newspapers by media conglomerates and the increasing use of alternative distribution methods characterized the midwestern press at the turn of the twenty-first century. All of the major midwestern newspapers introduced Internet editions and online access in the 1990s, and many operate broadcast or cable channels such as E. W. Scripps' HGTV and the *Chicago Tribune*'s CLTV. The Tribune Company merged with the parent of the *Los Angeles Times* in 2000 to make it the third largest media corporation in the country. Newspaper giant Gannett purchased the *Indianapolis Star* in 2000, adding it to its stable of large midwestern newspapers that includes the *Des Moines Register, Detroit News,* and *Cincinnati Enquirer.* In spite of concerns that conglomerates have stifled their uniquely independent voice, however, many mainstream midwestern urban newspapers continue to provide a perspective unavailable in other American newspapers.

Sources and Further Reading: Gerald J. Baldasty, *E. W. Scripps and the Business of Newspapers* (1999); William B. Friedricks, *Covering Iowa* (2000); Fred W. Friendly, *Minnesota Rag* (1981); Rick Kogan, *America's Mom* (2003); John D. McKee, *William Allen White* (1975); Thomas Cruise Palmer, *Bosses of the News Room* (2002); Russell Pulliam, *Publisher Gene Pulliam, Last of the Newspaper Titans* (1984); Richard Norton Smith, *The Colonel* (1997); Lloyd Wendt, *Chicago Tribune* (1979).

Richard Junger
Western Michigan University

Meredith Corporation

Meredith Corporation, headquartered for over a century in Des Moines, Iowa, is one of the nation's leading media and marketing companies. Its businesses include magazine and book publishing, television broadcasting, interactive media, and integrated marketing.

The company was founded in 1902 by Edwin Thomas Meredith. Legend has it that Meredith's grandfather gave him a wedding gift of a fistful of $20 gold pieces. With that money the younger Meredith bought the controlling interest in his grandfather's newspaper, *Farmer's Tribune.* He then started the Meredith Company with the publication of *Successful Farming* magazine in 1902. The magazine grew quickly; by 1914, circulation reached half a million. In 1912, the business moved into corporate headquarters in Des Moines, where it has expanded but still remains. The most recent expansion, a multimillion dollar addition built in 1998, includes *Better Homes and Gardens* test gardens. Meredith Corporation has remained, for all these years, a Des Moines landmark.

Edwin Thomas Meredith was a politician and civic leader as well as publisher. He served as Secretary of Agriculture under President Woodrow Wilson and helped to found the 4-H Clubs. While a contender for the Democratic presidential ticket in 1928, he became ill and did not recover. He died in 1928 at the age of 51.

In 1922, Meredith introduced *Fruit, Garden and Home,* which would later become *Better Homes and Gardens,* still the company's flagship magazine. Soon after, Meredith began to publish special-interest consumer books, including the *Better Homes and Gardens Cook Book.* Meredith Corporation went public in 1946 and began television broadcasting in 1948. Current activities include publication of more than a dozen service magazines for the home and family market, a consumer books branch, a television broadcasting branch reaching nearly 10 percent of all television households, and a diverse list of marketing clients including Iams, Hershey, and Kraft. Meredith purchased *Ladies' Home Journal* magazine in 1986 and began publishing *Midwest Living* in 1987.

Meredith Corporation is a national leader in the home and family market and continues to develop or acquire magazines, books, and Internet sites. Its most recent magazine acquisition is *More,* targeted at women in their forties and fifties. In this venture as in others, Meredith has successfully taken on a challenge in an arena where others have failed. The company's integrated marketing businesses attract new marketing clients with its consumer database, which includes information on seven of ten U.S. households. As of 2002, the company also owned twenty-three branded websites. It is in the forefront of integrating a variety

Midwest Living Magazine, a regional magazine of the Midwest (August 2000). Photo by Layne Kennedy.

of media outlets for the distribution of products and messages. Meredith Corporation currently employs over 2,800 people, with major offices in New York, Chicago, Detroit, San Francisco, and Los Angeles.

Sources and Further Reading: Lisa Granatstein, "Women Want More," *MediaWeek* 10 (Mar. 27, 2000); Jeff Gremillion, "Magazines," *MediaWeek* 8 (Jan. 12, 1998).

Jennifer Scanlon
Bowdoin College, Maine

Small-Town Journalism

Newspapers, the main source for local news in small communities, have a rich history in the Midwest. A glance through a listing of weekly newspapers shows many have their roots in publications established in the mid-1800s, around the same time that many of these states joined the Union. As an indication of the importance and tradition of newspapers in the Midwest, the Wisconsin Newspaper Association proudly boasts of being the world's oldest press association.

At the beginning of the twenty-first century, hundreds of these weekly newspapers served small towns throughout the Midwest, ranging from 432 in Illinois to 162 in Indiana. Many have the familiar names often used for newspapers—Times, News, Herald, Press. Many have names that reflect their beginnings as political tracts—Republican, Democrat, Independent— although by the beginning of the twenty-first century, many of these ties to political viewpoints had weakened considerably. And there are those that reflect the unique aspects of the surrounding environment—the *Northern Light* in Williams, Minnesota; the *Sanborn Pioneer* in Sanborn, Iowa; the *Florence Mining News* in Florence, in the mining area of Wisconsin; and the *Golden Prairie News* in Assumption, Illinois.

The news in these papers was almost entirely generated from within the town. It was for many the only place to find out what decisions were made by the town council and what events were planned by the local churches and civic organizations. A feature that exists today and is unique to these newspapers is the society reports: weddings, births, anniversaries, one hundredth birthdays, and other news from the ordinary folks in town. The news reflects many of the qualities traditionally associated with midwesterners. In the spirit of a traditional barn raising, one can find stories of memorials established to help the family that lost its home in a fire or benefit events to help a local person facing a major operation. Another major source of news for small-town papers is the local school. The athletic and academic exploits of the students are fertile ground for weekly newspapers.

Weekly papers generally serve several thousand readers, so running a weekly newspaper has never been a highly profitable occupation. These papers have small staffs, often just a couple of people, and are supplemented by contributions from the inhabitants of the communities they serve. During the middle to late 1900s, these papers were often part of a larger printing operation. Being dependent on advertising from the local community, publishers would take in other types of print work to supplement their income. It was not unusual for the newspaper to be the least profitable part of the printing operation.

However, with the advent of affordable computer technology, these newspapers start the present century with an interesting paradox: The technology is now available to make it cheaper to produce a newspaper, which may help many communities retain their traditional weekly newspapers despite the pressures of a global economy.

Sources and Further Reading: Editor and Publisher International Yearbook 2000, 80th ed., 3 vols., (2000); Editors of the Harvard Post, *How to Produce a Small Newspaper*, 2nd ed. (1983); Gwen Hamilton Thogmartin and Ardis Hamilton Anderson, *The Gazette Girls of Grundy County* (1994).

Heidi Schwoch
Watertown, Wisconsin

Media Education

Deep-rooted beliefs in the value of education, an agrarian past, a land-grant university system, and urban culture have all been influential factors in shaping media education in the Midwest. As a part of their mission to reach out to as many citizens of their respective states as possible, the major public and land-grant universities of the Midwest have a century's worth of experience in turning to various forms of mass media—film, print, broadcasting, and now the Internet—as vehicles to foster adult and continuing education, as methods to supplement more traditional elementary and secondary school curricula, and as topics worthy of significant study in their own right, partially for research purposes and partially for the training of media professionals.

During the very late nineteenth century and through much of the twentieth century, supporting the agrarian citizens of the Midwest through media education was a common practice for many colleges and universities. Radio programming in particular, but also print media, served as an important adjunct to extension campuses and short-term curricular programs that, on the one hand, did not demand a long-term commitment by agrarian citizens to relocate to a university campus, but on the other hand, did offer easily accessible information and training from university systems. Easily accessible training, in turn, created some of the first demand for full-time expertise in media education to be housed in Midwest universities, spurring the hiring of individual experts in schools and departments of education as well as the formation of entire departments and schools in areas such as agricultural communication, journalism, speech, and broadcasting.

At some universities, like Ohio State or Wisconsin, initial interest in radio began in the late nineteenth century as part of research in physics and the properties of the electromagnetic spectrum. By the 1920s, as radio broadcasting became an everyday reality, new departments emerged with specific interests in the communicative aspects of radio broadcasting, and universities started to become radio education content providers. Even before the 1920s, the University of Wisconsin served as one of several locations for training radiotelegraph operators for U.S. military forces in World War I. At other major midwestern public universities, such as Illinois, Nebraska, and Iowa, the interest in radio education may have come from other areas (agriculture or journalism, for example), but the results were similar: Coincident with the post–World War I rise of media culture as a part of everyday life, many Midwest land-grant universities saw mass media as an opportune vehicle to extend the mandate of their mission in ways that would conceivably reach every citizen of their state, both at home and in the classroom. Many of the various Midwest state public broadcasting systems have their roots in these developments from the 1920s and 1930s.

While the role of land-grant universities in Midwest media education is crucial, the late century rise of urban culture is another significant factor in the region's media education. The rise of the national transportation system, most importantly the railroad, in the latter half of the nineteenth century networked the urban areas of the Midwest and regularly brought everything—including some early examples of what might be considered media education—into midwestern cities. Nationally known public speakers, debaters, Chautauqua lecturers, and others frequented major Midwest cities (and often smaller communities as well) during this period. Many cities became publishing centers, not only for popular and fictional works, but also for educational writings, political works, and materials intended for the education of laborers. The uses of mass media for labor education also had many Midwest examples, including the long-time ownership and programming of radio station WCFL Chicago by organized labor.

Midwest urban universities in the late nineteenth and early twentieth centuries also began to develop particular interests in the intersection of education, media, and performance. Northwestern University began courses in elocution in the 1870s, an enterprise which expanded into its present-day School of Communication, with over 125 faculty. The University of Chicago's early investigations into social issues eventually spurred some of the first studies of the impact of mass media on youth culture. These studies in turn laid the groundwork at many universities, within and beyond the Midwest, for the study of the impact of media consumption and media uses on many different demographic groups—a field of study already taking shape in American higher education before World War II. And higher education's interest in mass media during this period was not confined to social issues: by the late 1920s and throughout the 1930s, professional training in radio acting, announcing, program writing, producing, the skills of debate and public speaking, and professional journalism training became established course offerings at many midwestern colleges and universities.

The period after World War II was marked by a phenomenal growth of media education in the Midwest. In terms of land-grant or major public universities' goals of extending the curriculum to all the citizens of their states, this growth was spurred by two factors: the significant expansion of the various public university systems (both at the main campus as well as in the establishment of more branch campuses and the extension system) and federal government policy regarding the expansion of American radio and television broadcast outlets. A postwar issue that then seemed unrelated to media and higher education—how to increase the number of available TV channels in the U.S.A. to account for the massive postwar interest in television—led to a series of government hearings that, by 1952, significantly expanded the number of potential TV stations by opening the UHF band (channels 14–83). As a part of this expansion, a formula to foster educational TV in every television market—basically, a ratio of one educational TV license for every three commercial TV licenses—had also been put in place in 1952, when it was codified by the Sixth Report and Order of the Federal Communications Commission. This FCC decision opened the UHF band for television, addressed a number of concerns regarding signal interference, expanded the number of potential TV stations in the country, and created this formula for licensing new educational television stations. This support for new educational television licenses had emerged under the leadership of FCC Commissioner Frieda Hennock, a staunch advocate for educational broadcasting.

Many universities in the Midwest and across the country became holders of educational TV licenses as a result of this policy. However, because the FCC provision was not accompanied by federal funding to pay for construction and operation, colleges and universities in smaller and rural markets were among the relatively few with sufficient resources to act on their licenses. And they did. By the end of the 1950s, occasional networking and program-sharing arrangements among these educational stations were already taking hold, and by the 1960s, many of these stations had coalesced into state-level public TV networks.

The formation of the Corporation for Public Broadcasting (CPB) at the federal level in 1967 not only provided some educational TV program funding but also gave a boost to public radio. While many Midwest colleges and universities had been involved in radio broadcasting since the 1920s (and a few even had experimental radio broadcast facilities in the 1910s), the postwar expansion of radio frequencies and the subsequent Public Broadcasting Act of 1967 brought many more Midwest colleges and universities into the radio game. This had a twofold effect on programming: Adult education, assistance to primary and secondary school curricula, and public affairs programming continued as a staple, particularly during daytime hours. In addition, the expansion in the number of colleges and universities with radio stations, along with the social and cultural changes of the 1960s, opened the door to a new kind of college and university broadcasting: the student-programmed college radio station or underground station, featuring college students themselves as on-air hosts and DJs, playing music not ordinarily available on commercial AM formats.

Along with the rise of college and university broadcasting came the expansion of the college and university newspaper, which during the 1960s, significantly expanded beyond the campus news beat into local and occasionally national news coverage. Within the curricular and research structure of the Midwest colleges and universities themselves, areas and departments devoted to media studies also expanded in scale, scope, and complexity. Many of the major Midwest universities expanded these departments and other units into graduate education, and now Midwest universities such as Ohio State, Michigan, Michigan State, Indiana, Minnesota, Illinois, Iowa, Chicago, Northwestern, Wisconsin, and Iowa State are among the many regional universities that produce a large national percentage of Ph.D.s trained in various fields related to media studies and media education.

If radio and journalism in the service of midwestern citizens produced the first wave of Midwest activities in media education, and postwar expansion of Midwest universities and of American educational broadcast licenses produced the second wave of Midwest media education, then it could be said that the computer and the Internet have now produced a third wave of media education. While the Internet wave may seem to be less specific to the Midwest, Midwest universities were among the leaders in the expansion of the Internet beyond the handful of American universities that, working in the late 1960s with the Defense Department, had developed what we now think of as the Internet. Again, federal activities played a role, particularly an initiative by the National Science Foundation (NSF) in the 1970s and 1980s to promote computer interconnectivity throughout American higher education. The NSFNet project from 1987 to 1995, designed to build an Internet backbone to thousands of American universities, colleges, and high schools, involved the National Center for Supercomputing Application (NCSA) at the University of Illinois and a consortium of Michigan universities. Many additional Midwest universities embraced this NSFNet initiative, and their foresight has proven to be an excellent long-term investment. As well as being national leaders in media education, Midwest colleges and universities now provide educational broadcast programming, serve as outlets for alternative radio and journalism, and are among the largest providers of Internet content in the world.

Sources and Further Reading: Robert Blakely, *To Serve the Public Interest* (1979); Susan Brinson, "Frieda Hennock: FCC Activist and the Campaign for Educational Television, 1948–1951," *Historical Journal of Film Radio and Television* 18 (Aug. 1998); James Day, *The Vanishing Vision* (1995); R. Kubey, "Obstacles to the Development of Media Education in the United States," *Journal of Communication* 48 (Mar. 1998); Robert A. Levin and Laurie Moses Hines, "Educational Television, Fred Rogers, and the History of Education," *History of Education Quarterly* 43 (Summer 2003).

James Schwoch
Northwestern University, Illinois

Blacklight Film Festival

The Blacklight Film Festival was held annually in Chicago from 1982 to 1995. It was one of the first major film festivals founded to feature international black cinema, underrepresented filmmakers from Mississippi to Mali and Haiti to Tokyo. Blacklight became a powerful center of black film culture for filmmakers and fans alike. In addition to traditional programming of films, the festival offered workshops and lectures for aspiring filmmakers. Founded by Floyd Webb and Terry Glover, who were greatly influenced by the Commonwealth Institute Film Festival in England, Blacklight screenings were held at a variety of cinema sites in the Chicago area, including the Film Center of the Art Institute of Chicago, DOC films at the University of Chicago, Du Sable Museum, Facets Multimedia, Columbia College, and outdoor screenings through the Chicago Park District. During the festival's thirteen-year run, more than five hundred films from throughout the African Diaspora—not only films from Africa but filmmakers of African heritage from around the world—were exhibited. The festival featured both studio and independent productions and premiered films such as Spike Lee's *Mo' Better Blues* (1990) and Julie Dash's *Daughters of the Dust* (1991).

Sources and Further Reading: Manthia Diawara, *African Cinema: Politics and Culture* (1992); Gen Doy, *Black Visual Culture: Modernity and Postmodernity* (2000); Mark A. Reid, *Redefining Black Film* (1993).

William Grant
Northwestern University, Illinois

Facets Multimedia

Facets Multimedia has historically been one of Chicago's most important nonprofit alternative film venues. It is dedicated to screening difficult-to-see world and independent cinema, documentaries, and experimental film; programming auteur retrospectives; screening children's films in schools, hospitals, and other locations; and offering adult education and media literacy programs.

After programming in the early to mid-1970s in several Chicago locations, including a bookstore and two Lutheran churches, Facets founder Milos Stehlik (born in Czechoslovakia) moved his film screenings into an old printing plant at 1517 W. Fullerton in 1977, where the organization resides to this day. This led to daily programs in two theatres and an expanded educational mission. In 1983 Facets established the International Children's Film Festival and began holding educational workshops on film for children. In the same year, Facets decided—despite some criticism from film purists—to establish what became one of the most influential nonprofit video archives in the United States, with a catalog unparalleled in alternative video. Through this new undertaking, Facets significantly expanded access to alternative film by offering films-on-video to a national viewership, including small-town and rural America. Facets has never shied away from controversial work; it premiered Jean-Luc Godard's *Hail Mary* in Chicago in 1986, for instance,

which was picketed and condemned by conservative Catholics. In the twenty-first century, Facets faces new challenges, including aggressive Internet competition to its video and DVD distribution and changing audience tastes.

Ronald Gregg
University of Chicago

Films, Incorporated

Prior to VCRs, DVDs, video rental stores, pay-per-view, premium cable movie channels, and even specialized basic cable channels, there were two common ways to see motion pictures: attend theatres or drive-ins, or wait two to three years for their broadcast by one of the major broadcast television networks.

Nontheatrical distributors such as Films, Incorporated presented a third way: Not-for-profit organizations such as colleges and universities, high school organizations, community groups, and correctional facilities could rent films and exhibit them as fundraisers or as part of their service missions. They had catalogues of hundreds of titles from which to choose, from blockbusters to B movies, mostly from the 1950s through the 1980s. New titles usually became available about a year or eighteen months after their theatrical release. Some had windows of unavailability, if the major networks had scheduled them for primetime airings. Based in Wilmette, Illinois, Films, Incorporated was one of two major nontheatrical distributors in the Midwest. Swank, in St. Louis, was the other.

As cable, satellite television, and VHS tapes found their way into more and more homes, audiences had more and more opportunities to see major films, and movie nights became less viable as fund-raisers and less attractive as organizational programming. In 1997 Films, Incorporated got out of the nontheatrical distribution business and sold its vast library of titles to Kit Parker Films. Under its new name, Public Media Incorporated, it focused on sale and rental of documentaries and other programs primarily produced for the Public Broadcasting Service (PBS) and public television stations.

Sources and Further Reading: Films, Inc., *Films Incorporated's 1977 Entertainment Catalog* (1977); Linda Moss, "A Classic Case of Sour Notes," *Crain's New York Business* (May 23, 1988); "New Video Series On Quality Control," *Crain's Chicago Business* (Jan. 17, 1994).

Bruce E. Drushel
Miami University, Oxford, Ohio

Garrison Keillor (b. 1942)

Garrison Keillor, whose folksy baritone has become one of the most familiar symbols of the Midwest, was born Gary Keillor in Anoka, Minnesota, on August 7, 1942. He began his radio career as a student at the University of Minnesota. Graduating in 1966, Keillor went to New York City in search of a job at a magazine. He returned home and went to work for Minnesota Public Radio. In 1969, *The New Yorker* published the first of several Keillor stories.

Preparation of an article on the Grand Ole Opry inspired Keillor to launch his own radio variety show. *A Prairie Home Companion* debuted in a theatre at Macalester College in St. Paul on July 6, 1974. There were twelve people in the audience. The mixture of live music and satire soon made the show a Saturday night fixture on National Public Radio. The signature segment was Keillor's weekly report on the news from the fictional town of Lake Wobegon. Like most of Keillor's stories, the monologues affirmed a popular image of the Midwest as a place of earnest, decent, unpretentious, and banal people.

Keillor ended *A Prairie Home Companion* when he moved to New York City in 1987. Two years later he created *Garrison Keillor's American Radio Company of the*

Garrison Keillor, voice of the Midwest. Photo by Ralph Nelson.

Air, which became *A Prairie Home Companion* again when Keillor returned to Minnesota in 1993. Today the program is carried on over four hundred public radio stations. Keillor is the author of many books, including *Lake Wobegon Days* (1985), *Lake Wobegon Boy* (1997), and *Love Me* (2003). Keillor played himself in Robert Altman's film, *A Prairie Home Companion,* in 2006.

Sources and Further Reading: Garrison Keillor, *In Search of Lake Wobegon* (2001); Garrison Keillor, *A Prairie Home Companion: A 25th Anniversary Collection* (1999); Marcia Songer, *Garrison Keillor: A Critical Companion* (2000).

Andrew Cayton
Miami University, Oxford, Ohio

Newton Minow (b. 1926)

Newton Norman Minow, born in Milwaukee in 1926, has achieved a distinguished and varied career in law, public service, and education spanning six decades. He is perhaps best known as the controversial Chair of the Federal Communications Commission who challenged the broadcast networks to produce better quality television programming.

After serving in the U.S. Army and obtaining a law degree from Northwestern University, Minow served as a law clerk to U.S. Chief Justice Fred Vinson and as administrative assistant to Illinois Governor Adlai Stevenson, for whom he campaigned in 1952 and 1956. After working on John F. Kennedy's 1960 presidential campaign, Minow was appointed Chairman of the Federal Communications Commission from 1961 to 1963.

Believing television to be a potentially valuable but as yet unrealized force for public good, in his 1961 speech before the National Convention of Broadcasting Executives, Minow was sharply critical of the excessive violence and commercialization of television, describing commercial TV as a "vast wasteland." His criticisms sparked a national debate over the future of television.

As FCC Chair, he played a key role in the passage of the "All Channel Receiver Act" in 1962, which required all television sets to have UHF as well as VHF capacity, thereby significantly increasing the market for both UHF and VHF stations. Minow was also responsible for the passage of legislation bringing about satellite communication.

Following his tenure as FCC Chair, Minow returned to private law practice. He has served as Chairman of the RAND Corporation, the Carnegie Corporation, the Chicago Educational Television Association, and the Public Broadcasting Service, and he has authored a number of publications.

Sources and Further Reading: Lawrence K. Grossman and Newton N. Minow, *Digital Gift to the Nation* (2001); Newton N. Minow and Craig Lamay, *Abandoned in the Wasteland* (1996).

Barry Donald Mowell
Broward Community College, Florida

The Museum of Broadcast Communications

Founded by Bruce DuMont in 1987 and located in the heart of Chicago, the Museum of Broadcast Communications is a prominent national resource for the study of broadcast history, not only as a repository for a significant collection of radio and television materials that can be accessed in screening carrels but also as a partner in public education. Permanent exhibits, like "The Sports Gallery," highlighting sportscaster Jack Brickhouse, or the display of the camera used in the 1960 Kennedy–Nixon Presidential debate, document Chicago's role as a media hub. Recorded special events featuring midwestern personalities like Bob Wallace, Hugh Downs, and Michael Feldman contribute to the region's oral history, while its "Docufest" program fosters the study of celebrated documentaries in Illinois schools.

In its archives, programs, and services, the MBC also looks beyond the Midwest. On the fortieth anniversary of the JFK assassination, the museum replayed newscasts exactly as they had unfolded on November 22, 1963. Another special event brought together prominent actresses who had played wives and mothers on TV to discuss women's changing roles on television. The MBC acquired the Radio Hall of Fame in 1991, formalizing its national induction process and expanding its programs. Online accessibility further enhances the museum's national and global presence. The MBC website facilitates Internet searches of the museum's archival holdings, provides immediate access to about a thousand entries from *The Encyclopedia of Television* written by more than two hundred fifty contributors, and offers streaming audio and video. The MBC will move to more spacious quarters in Chicago's River North area in 2006.

Sources and Further Reading: Steve Daley, "Broadcasting Hears from Chicago," *Chicago Tribune* (June 15, 1987); Rick Kogan, "Changing Roles," *Chicago Tribune* (Sept. 8, 1993); "The Museum of Broadcast Communications," http://www.museum.tv (Dec. 2002); Horace Newcomb, ed., *The Encyclopedia of Television* (1997).

Marsha F. Cassidy
University of Illinois–Chicago

Public Radio

The Corporation for Public Broadcasting (CPB) provides programming and grants to nearly eight hundred public radio stations in the United States, some of which are affiliates of National Public Radio (NPR). There are about two hundred Midwest NPR member stations, although providing an exact number of noncommercial, public radio stations is difficult given the extensive use of translators for rebroadcasting in rural areas, stations delivered only via Internet or cable television, and the Midwest's over one hundred noncommercial, broadcast, college radio stations unaffiliated with NPR.

A number of popular public radio programs originate in the Midwest. *This American Life*, hosted by Ira Glass and produced by WBEZ in Chicago, reaches more than one and a half million listeners weekly on over two hundred stations. *A Prairie Home Companion*, hosted by Garrison Keillor and produced by Minnesota Public Radio, first aired in 1969 and is heard by nearly three million U.S. listeners weekly on over five hundred public radio stations. Other Midwest-based nationally syndicated programs include *The Savvy Traveler, Marketplace*, and *Sound Money*, all produced by or in association with Minnesota Public Radio, and *Michael Feldman's Whad'Ya Know?* and *Zorba Paster on Your Health*, produced by Wisconsin Public Radio.

With the CPB offering both ready-to-air programming and seed money for locally produced programs, rather than renewable yearly funding, Midwest public radio stations face the challenge of developing and airing innovative local programming while increasingly relying on competitive grants, corporate underwriting, and listener contributions to fund operating and programming expenses.

Sources and Further Reading: Ralph Engelman, *Public Radio and Television in America* (1996); Thomas Looker, *The Sound and the Story* (1995); Tom McCourt, *Conflicting Communication Interests in America* (1999).

Scott A. Webber
Boulder, Colorado

Public Television

The Midwest is home to WKAR in East Lansing, Michigan, the second oldest educational channel in the United States, which began broadcasting in January 1954. (KUHT in Houston first broadcast in May of 1953.) The present-day public television system was born when President Johnson signed the Public

The Frugal Gourmet, an early public television program. "Jacket Cover," from *The Frugal Gourmet* by Jeff Smith, copyright 1984 by Jeff Smith. Illustrations copyright 1984 by Gary Jacobsen. Used by permission of Random House Value Publishing, a division of Random House, Inc.

Broadcasting Act of 1967, creating the Corporation for Public Broadcasting (CPB), which presently funnels money to two programming services, National Public Radio (NPR) and the Public Broadcasting Service (PBS). Ownership and operation of public television in the Midwest is now by a mix of educational institutions (for example, WHA Madison) and nonprofit community groups (WTTW Chicago). Given the significant costs associated with developing and airing television programs, most Midwest public television stations rely heavily on national programming made available from a variety of sources (including other PBS member stations and the CPB-funded National Program Service), and they supplement these shows with locally produced programs covering local politics and environmental issues, regional travel, hobbies and pastimes, and cultural offerings, including art, music, and theatre performances.

As with public television stations across the country, Midwest stations face a number of challenges in the coming years, including continued battles over federal funding for the CPB and the transition to digital broadcasting. KCPT in Kansas City, Missouri, and WMVS in Milwaukee, began offering digital service in 1998 and are recognized by PBS as Digital Pioneer Stations. Public television stations had to build digital facilities by May 1, 2003, and must return their analog licenses to the Federal Communication Commission by January 1, 2007.

Sources and Further Reading: James Day, *The Vanishing Vision* (1995); Ralph Engelman, *Public Radio and Television in America* (1996); David Stewart, *The PBS Companion* (1999).

Scott A. Webber
Boulder, Colorado

Religion and Mass Media

Evangelical seeds cultivated in the Midwest have grown into a national and international broadcasting phenomenon called "televangelism." This term, first used by Jeffrey K. Hadden and Charles E. Swann in 1981, describes a hybrid institution combining urban revivalism and mass broadcasting; the term gained wide usage when scandals turned media attention on televangelists and their multimillion-dollar organizations. In general, it refers to evangelical religious programming dependent on viewers for direct financial support.

Three key revivalists built urban revivalism in the Midwest between the early nineteenth century and 1935. In 1835 Charles Grandison Finney published *Lectures on Revivals of Religion*, still a principal handbook of revivalists in the twentieth century. Finney instructed revivalists to "use any means to stir religious enthusiasms." Whereas Finney profoundly altered the ethos, preaching style, and content, Dwight Lyman Moody rationalized and routinized the organization of revivalism. Moody introduced managerial techniques for improving the effectiveness of revivals. He established Bible schools, which continue today to train evangelical students. Billy Sunday transformed revivals into sophisticated entertainments, glossing much of the broad religious content associated with revival meetings. His emphasis on entertainment gave urban revivalism an ideal organizational infrastructure for entering into the business of broadcast programming at the dawn of the media age.

In 1926, the *Golden Hour of the Little Flower* began weekly broadcasts on WJR radio in Detroit. Father Coughlin's program created an audience for religious broadcasts: At the height of his popularity, he reached one-third of the national audience. However, his free-floating conspiracy theories and blatant anti-Semitism ultimately proved uncomfortable for the Catholic Church, and his last broadcast aired in 1940.

The Moody Bible Institute also began broadcasting in 1926, from Chicago. With a less incendiary and more evangelical focus, it continues today through weekly international radio programs.

The use of television by revivalists started near Akron, Ohio, in 1952, when Rex Humbard built the Cathedral of Tomorrow, a weekly program and a church designed to accommodate television equipment, crew, and chorus, as well as a studio audience. To entertain and retain audiences, Humbard introduced programming that consisted of personalized religious messages, reinforced by inspirational singing and theatricals. Nationally known, Humbard was spiritual advisor to Elvis Presley and officiated at Presley's funeral.

During televangelism's Golden Era in the early 1980s, several major televangelists were influenced by Midwest religious institutions: Billy Graham graduated from Wheaton College, Illinois; Robert Schuller was educated at Western Theological Seminary in Holland, Michigan; Jerry Falwell was educated at Baptist Bible College in Springfield, Missouri; and Jim Bakker attended North Central Bible College in Minneapolis. Bakker and his wife Tammy Faye worked as traveling evangelists in Minnesota and Michigan before affiliating with Pat Robertson and the Christian Broadcast Network.

Today, televangelists reach international audiences. The roots of televangelism are midwestern, and the Midwest has left its mark on thriving evangelical educational facilities as well as on media ministries. Moreover, an expanding Christian marketplace continues to carry the evangelical message into homes across the nation.

Sources and Further Reading: Razelle Frankl, *Televangelism: The Marketing of Popular Religion* (1987); Razelle Frankl, "Televangelism," in William H. Swatos, Jr., ed., *Encyclopedia of Religion and Society* (1998); Jeffrey K. Hadden and Charles E. Swann, *Prime Time Preachers* (1981).

Razelle Frankl
Rowan University, New Jersey

Swank Motion Pictures, Inc.

Anyone who has recently watched a movie anywhere other than at home or a movie theatre, and did so lawfully, likely used the services of Swank Motion Pictures of St. Louis.

Swank is the leading distributor of motion pictures to nontheatrical markets; that is, they are the source for movies on 16-millimeter and 35-millimeter film used by exhibitors beyond the commercial theatre business. Examples of these exhibitors include primary and secondary schools, colleges and universities, hospitals, prisons, cruise ships, passenger trains, and even buses.

As such, Swank fills a gap in the market between traditional cinemas and home video rentals. Although it is legal for private individuals to rent movies on tape or DVD to show to small groups of family and friends in their homes, showings by public entities like schools, airlines, and hospitals constitute a public performance of a copyright work. Swank responds to this legality by establishing standard agreements with nearly every major motion picture company, including Disney, Columbia, Universal, Paramount, MGM, and Warner Brothers. Thousands of titles, from classics to recent box office hits, are available for distribution from Swank's facility in Elmhurst, Illinois. Sales agreements are handled from offices in New York and St. Louis.

Swank is a family-owned company in business since 1938. Its current workforce numbers close to a thousand. In addition to nontheatrical exhibition of entertainment films, it also distributes university-produced educational healthcare videos intended for in-service training of hospital and clinic staffs. A separate division, Swank Audio Visuals, provides media support to hotel conference facilities and leases audiovisual equipment for off-site corporate events.

Source and Further Reading: John D. Zelezny, *Communications Law*, 3rd ed. (2001).

Bruce E. Drushel
Miami University, Oxford, Ohio

The Video Data Bank

What Electronic Arts Intermix is to New York, the Video Data Bank, located at the School of the Art Institute of Chicago, is to the Midwest: the foremost videotape distributor and media archive in the region. Founded in 1976 by Kate Horsfield and the late Lyn Blumenthal, the Video Data Bank houses a collection of fifteen hundred tapes produced over the last thirty-five years, and is known for its advocacy on behalf of artists, dedication to video preservation, and long-standing support of socially committed, alternative work in video and other emerging technologies, including interactive CD-ROMs. Most noteworthy are its special collections, a series of compilation tapes which chart the evolution of video as an art form from the late 1960s to the present day, interview a wide range of video artists, and focus on the work of video-makers of Hispanic or Latin American descent: *Early Video Art* (1968–1980), *Independent Video and Alternative Media* (1980–1999), *On Art and Artists*, and *America Without Borders*. Equally invaluable is the Video Data Bank's role as scholarly and community resource and production facility. It contains a library of rare print resources on the history of video art, equipment for nonlinear editing, an archival storage room for videotapes, and a screening room open to the public. One of the most important ways the Video Data Bank has contributed to the future of new media has been through the Lyn Blumenthal Memorial Fund, which makes annual grants to nominated individual artists and artist collectives working in new electronic media.

Sources and Further Reading: Doug Hall and Sally Jo Fifer, eds., *Illuminating Video* (1991); Michael Renov and Erika Suderburg, eds., *Resolutions: Contemporary Video Practices* (1996).

Melinda Barlow
University of Colorado–Boulder

The WHS Media Collection

Madison, Wisconsin, houses one of the world's largest media history collections. In 1955, news commentator Hans V. Kaltenborn, born and raised in Merrill, Wisconsin, donated the records of his long and influential career to the Wisconsin Historical Society. Other news figures of the era followed his example, and together the Society and the University formed the Mass Communications History Center to develop their holdings.

One of the biggest coups was convincing the National Broadcasting Company (NBC) to deposit its papers in Madison. That collection, the only accessible archive of a major network in the United States, currently holds over six hundred boxes of papers and more than three thousand recordings and scripts, tracing the development of broadcasting from the early 1920s to the late 1960s. Hundreds of other collections in the Archives trace the history of radio and television development in the United States.

In 1960, the University formed the Wisconsin Center for Film and Theater Research (WCRTF) to expand the archives into film, theatre, and television. Its materials include the United Artists collection, containing virtually every film released by Warner Bros., RKO, and Monogram studios between 1930 and 1950. Many individual stars, writers, and producers are represented as well.

In television, the WCRTF acquired, among many others, the archives of MTM Enterprises, producers of *The Mary Tyler Moore Show*. In theatre, significant Wisconsin Historical Society collections include those of Alfred Lunt and Lynn Fontanne. The archive also contains over two million media-related photographs and promotional stills. Finding aids for many of the collections can be explored online.

Sources and Further Reading: Tino Balio, *United Artists: The Company that Changed the Film Industry* (1987); Michele Hilmes, *Radio Voices* (1997); Mass Communications History Center, *Sources for Mass Communications, Film and Theater Research* (1981); http://college.library.wisc.edu/~leeloo/sjmc/.

Michele Hilmes
University of Wisconsin–Madison

Women in the Director's Chair

Women in the Director's Chair (WIDC) is an international media arts and activist organization based in Chicago that distributes, promotes, produces, and exhibits films and videotapes by and about women and girls. Its focus is on media that represent a full breadth of diverse cultural experiences and issues. Its mission is to enhance the visibility of women mediamakers and to support the production of alternative media that challenge demeaning stereotypes perpetuated by mainstream media.

The annual WIDC International Film and Video Festival, which premiered in 1980 and is held annually in Chicago, is the organization's largest event. Since 1990, WIDC also has sponsored a Film and Video Tour that brings media artists to educational and cultural centers around the country. The organization sponsors year-round programming aimed at effecting social change and critical consciousness through examinations of race, class, sexuality, and gender.

WIDC activities include maintaining an educational archive of films and videos produced by women and girls around the world. It programs multimedia installations and media-based performances in its community center, hosts workshops and works-in-progress screenings for emerging media makers, provides fiscal sponsorship of members' projects, and generally works with media artists to curate programs that develop public debate around critical issues affecting women and girls. WIDC also collaborates with health, arts, and community-based advocacy organizations working with girls in detention by bringing video cameras, girl-made tapes, and artist-activists together for media workshops.

Source and Further Reading: More information about Women in the Director's Chair is available at http://www .widc.org.

Laura Vazquez
Northern Illinois University

Media Personalities

The Midwest has produced more than its share of media personalities, especially in the quarter century that followed World War II. A multitude of newscasters, sportscasters, and talk-show hosts were born in the region or learned their craft there. Radio and television stations in Chicago, in particular, nurtured the development of something that might be called a distinctive midwestern style.

The abundance of media figures from the Midwest reflects the ambition and industry of people who came of age at a time when the region was losing its reputation as a dynamic and diverse place. Popular culture increasingly constructed the Midwest as a homogenous Heartland. Midwesterners were nothing if not normal Americans. Indeed, their supposed lack of a distinctive accent and their reputation for civility were advantages in a media world that, from the 1950s through the 1980s, sought to appeal to the widest possible audience by avoiding idiosyncrasy, ideology, and conflict. If the goal was to offer consumers news, sports, and entertainment in a wholesome, nonthreatening, nonconfrontational style, midwesterners seemed tailor-made presenters and hosts.

At a time when dramatic changes in foreign policy, race, gender, sexuality, and music were played out on network television, the apolitical male gravitas of midwesterners was a source of imagined stability. Midwestern-born or -trained men behaved like perfect hosts, keeping things polite, avoiding controversy, and framing their social and political commentary as light-hearted comedy. By the 1970s, the monologues of *Tonight Show* host Johnny Carson, a native of Corning, Iowa, who was raised in Norfolk, Nebraska, had become a relatively reliable barometer of American public opinion. An expert reader of his audience, Carson tended to follow the curve rather than advance new ideas.

Carson's midwestern *modus operandi* was nothing new. Lowell Thomas, perhaps the most well-known voice in mid-twentieth-century America, was born in Woodington, Ohio, and grew up in Colorado. Thomas reported news from all over the world in a voice that was as reassuring as it was authoritative. He made the exotic familiar, a trait in which midwesterners seemed to specialize. Though born in Tulsa, Oklahoma, Paul Harvey perfected his signature delivery of the news in Missouri and Chicago in the 1940s and 1950s. Long-time CBS anchorman Walter Cronkite, a native of St. Joseph, Missouri, grew up in Texas but developed his personal style while working at midwestern radio stations.

As early as the 1930s, radio personalities from the Midwest were successful in part because of their ability to transform local entertainment into mass entertainment. Two cases in point were Benny Kubelsky and Leslie Townes Hope. Born in Chicago, Kubelsky grew up in Waukegan, Illinois, and changed his name to Jack Benny. Hope, a native of London, England, came to Cleveland in 1907 at the age of four. Becoming an entertainer in the area, he adopted the name Bob. These informal names evidenced the desire of the two men to reach the widest possible audience by making themselves broadly appealing. They wanted to

The *Mary Tyler Moore Show*, 1970.
Gunther/MPTV.net.

be American entertainers, not ethnic or immigrant entertainers.

World War II was critical to the emergence of a generation of midwestern media celebrities. Young men who had traveled the globe as soldiers, sailors, and newsmen chose to settle in New York or California when the war ended and seek careers in radio and the infant medium of television. Later, they wrote wistfully about growing up in the Midwest in an era when life seemed simpler and morality, clearer. North Dakota–born CBS reporter and commentator Eric Sevareid's autobiography, *Not So Wild a Dream* (1978), is a model of the genre. The tradition has continued in the published work of NBC anchorman Tom Brokaw of Webster, South Dakota. Other reporters who became prominent television personalities include Chicago-born NBC anchorman John Chancellor and Iowa-born CBS reporter and ABC anchorman Harry Reasoner.

Many notable sportscasters also have midwestern roots, including Hoosier Chris Schenkel and Minnesotan John Madden. Radio announcers for professional and college teams have achieved local or regional cult status, whether or not they were home-grown. Harry Caray became virtually synonymous with the Chicago Cubs. Jack Buck in St. Louis, Ernie Harwell in Detroit, Bob Uecker in Milwaukee, and Marty Brennaman and Joe Nuxhall in Cincinnati inspired similar loyalty.

The dominant broadcast style associated with the Midwest developed most fully in Chicago. Indeed, some observers in the early 1950s referred to a Chicago School of Television. Pioneered by Windy City natives such as puppeteer Burr Tillstrom of *Kukla, Fran, & Ollie* and Studs Terkel of *Studs' Place*, the Chicago School featured a relaxed and apparently intimate atmosphere that recreated an idealized meeting of friends in the comfortable domestic setting of the "coffee klatch." Viewers trusted the genial hosts, and they continued to tune in because no one seemed to know what was going to happen next. The combination of stability and unpredictability proved highly popular.

In July 1951, writer Arch Oboler published a piece in *Theater Arts* locating the origins of the Chicago School in the need to make a virtue out of necessity. In New York City, producers could exploit the theatre for drama, songs, and performers. In Los Angeles, the movie industry dominated the airwaves. But Chicagoans, according to Oboler, had to improvise because they lacked a nearby pool of proven talent. Although some improvisation could, in fact, be found at most American TV stations at this time, the distinctive nature of improvisation on Chicago TV created a unique reputation for certain Chicago programs.

Dave Garroway, a Schenectady, New York, native who graduated from Washington University in St. Louis, became popular in Chicago in the late 1940s as the host of *Garroway at Large*. In 1952, he took the Chicago School to NBC in New York as the first host of the morning program that became the *Today Show*. Garroway's ironic, understated style satisfied viewers who craved low-key humor and information as they ate breakfast and prepared for work.

Although the term "Chicago School" did not last, the format did. Widely emulated both nationally and locally, it has profoundly influenced live television for more than half a century. It is no coincidence that Garroway's immediate successors on the *Today Show* were Hugh Downs, born in Akron, Ohio, South Dakotan Tom Brokaw, and Jane Pauley, an Indianapolis native who got her start at television stations in Indianapolis and Chicago.

The *Tonight Show*, another landmark NBC show, was originally hosted by Steve Allen. At the age of eighteen months, Allen was left by his vaudeville star mother with Irish Catholic relatives in Chicago, where he grew up. Like Garroway, Allen had an improvisational style. Particularly popular were his impromptu interviews with members of the studio audience and the ways in which Allen and his associates laughed at their own skits. Both Garroway and Allen aggressively explored the specificity of the television medium, particularly in on-camera discussions of studio equipment and a willingness to utilize unconventional production techniques in live broadcasts.

Allen was succeeded as host of the *Tonight Show* by Canton, Ohio, native Jack Paar, who proved equally adept at the art of conversation, but who took himself and the program much more seriously. When Paar walked off the program because the NBC censors refused to let him utter the words "water closet," game show host Johnny Carson settled into a decades-long run that made him an icon of American popular culture. Also in the 1960s and 1970s, Chicagoan Mike Douglas (born Michael Dowd) operated a popular syndicated afternoon program out of Philadelphia.

David Letterman, the long-time host of the *Late Show* on CBS, has a style more directly reminiscent of the Chicago School. Understated and ironic, the Indianapolis native invites viewers into a comfortable setting without being truly intimate. He observes and comments more than he participates in the action, both on his show and in the world as a whole.

Letterman has credited his style in part to watching regional hosts such as Paul Dixon, whose morning show flourished in Cincinnati in the 1950s and 1960s. Dixon's program was very much in the Chicago style: nonthreatening and wildly unpredictable, sometimes outrageous. Dixon played second fiddle at WLWT, however, to the extraordinarily popular noontime coffee klatch, the *Fifty-Fifty Club*. Presiding over all was Cincinnatian Ruth Lyons, a formidable figure never afraid to speak her mind. Broadcast throughout Ohio and Indiana, the *Fifty-Fifty Club* claimed to be the most highly rated daytime television show in the United States in the late 1950s. People waited three to five years for tickets to it. Lyons's counterpart in Cleveland was Dorothy Fuldheim, a flinty newscaster with a distinctive, no-nonsense style.

While the midwestern tradition of apolitical congeniality continued in such people as entertainment reporter Mary Hart of Madison, South Dakota, and game show host Pat Sajak of Chicago, American popular culture shifted dramatically in the late 1980s and 1990s. Rather than the cool and comfortable, radio and television shows increasingly featured controversy. Political opinions and dysfunctional families, long taboo, were now front and center. The new form of talk show took shape in Chicago. Cleveland-born Phil Donahue brought his pioneering interactive program from Dayton, Ohio, to the Windy City in the 1970s and met with instant local, then national success. By the 1980s, Donahue had a slew of imitators. The most successful was Mississippi-born newscaster and actress Oprah Winfrey, whose career recapitulated the Great Migration of African Americans to the Midwest.

Winfrey began a show in 1984 on WLS in Chicago that was an overnight success. The *Oprah Winfrey Show* became the most highly rated talk show in the history of television and brought its star endless honors and opportunities. Winfrey emphasized positive messages in her program, ultimately concluding that her show could help transform people into happier human beings. Although not midwestern by birth, Winfrey developed a style that fit well into the midwestern model of domestic intimacy.

Winfrey's competitors tended to target more narrowly focused audiences and presented increasingly salacious content. The most notorious of these shows was hosted by Jerry Springer. Born in London, England, in 1944, Springer grew up in New York City. He graduated from Northwestern University Law School in 1968 and took a job with a Cincinnati law firm. Elected to city council in 1971, Springer went on to serve as the youngest mayor in Cincinnati history before embarking on a decade-long career as a local news anchorman. The *Jerry Springer Show* debuted in 1991 and continues from its Chicago base with a focus on dysfunctional relationships and sexual misadventures.

Radio stations also began to court controversy. Bland, happy hosts were replaced by distinctive personalities with clear-cut political opinions who do not hesitate to opine on the issues of the day in everything from politics to sports. Rush Limbaugh, a native of Cape Girardeau, Missouri, became a hit in the 1990s by offering listeners a political variation on the old Chicago School format. Despite, or perhaps because of, his unrelenting support of conservative causes and his attacks on liberals, Limbaugh was an unpredictable host with a roguish charm many consumers found immensely likeable.

One media personality thematically associated with the Midwest has been Minnesotan Garrison Keillor. By the 1980s his weekly program, *A Prairie Home Companion*, was a national phenomenon on National Public Radio. Keillor is a master of understated humor, although his expert re-creations of imagined small-town life tend to reinforce popular images of the Midwest as bland and banal.

A Prairie Home Companion was popular in part because it was so exceptional. The rise at the end of the twentieth century of programming that deliberately courted controversy by emphasizing the sharp divergence in attitudes more than the convergence of values was a major departure from the Chicago School. The intimate, unpredictable style of the coffee klatch persisted in a multitude of national formats, including *Live with Regis and Kelly* and *The View*. But even these shows tended to thrive on a brassy, opinionated style that was in keeping with contemporary American culture, but still a long way from the understated world of Dave Garroway.

Sources and Further Reading: Bill Carter, *The Late Shift* (1994); Rebecca Goodman, "Ohio Moments," *The Cincinnati Enquirer* (Nov. 7, 2003); Barry M. Horstman, "Paul Baby Paved the Way for Letterman," *The Cincinnati Post* (Feb. 15, 1999); Judy Kessler, *Inside Today* (1992); Arch Oboler, "Windy Kilocycles," *Theatre Arts* (July 1951); Eric Sevareid, *Not So Wild a Dream* (1978); Andrew Tolson, *Television Talk Shows* (2001); Harriet Van Horne, "The Chicago Touch," *Theatre Arts* (July 1951).

Andrew Cayton
Miami University, Oxford, Ohio

Phil Donahue (b. 1935)

Phil Donahue, host of a popular television talk show, was one of the most influential Americans in the last third of the twentieth century. At its peak, the *Phil Donahue Show* was a daily national town hall meeting about issues of particular interest to women.

Born on December 21, 1935, in Cleveland, Phillip John Donahue grew up in a middle-class Catholic family and graduated from the University of Notre Dame in 1957. After working in radio, Donahue joined WLWD television in Dayton in 1967. Unable to attract prominent guests, Donahue experimented with what amounted to interactive television. Focusing each program on one subject and usually one guest, he encouraged his audience in the studio and at home via telephone call-ins to participate in an open-ended discussion.

Success in Dayton led Donahue to national syndication from Chicago in 1974. Eleven years later, he moved again, this time to New York City. By the 1990s, however, his ratings were in decline, in part because of competition from successful imitators, the most important of which was Chicago-based Oprah Winfrey. *Donahue* went off the air in 1996.

A television pioneer in content as well as format, Donahue dealt directly with issues such as divorce, sex, drugs, and religion that were rarely discussed in public when his show debuted. Although not all of his audience shared Donahue's liberal perspective, millions of women appreciated the opportunity to participate in a program specifically designed for "women who think."

Sources and Further Reading: Donal A. Carbaugh, *Talking American: Cultural Discourses on Donahue* (1988); Phil Donahue, *Donahue, My Own Story* (1981); Patricia Joyner Priest, *Public Intimacies: Talk Show participants and Tell-All TV* (1995).

Andrew Cayton
Miami University, Oxford, Ohio

Paul Harvey (b. 1918)

Paul Harvey, a radio broadcaster, became famous for his delivery of news and commercials with unusual rhythms and signature lines such as "Hello, Americans" and "Good day." As important to Harvey's popularity was the extent to which his audience considered him an icon of midwestern common sense.

Born on September 4, 1918, in Tulsa, Oklahoma, Paul Harvey Aurandt started working at local radio stations as a teenager. A graduate of the University of Tulsa, he gained valuable experience at stations in Kansas, Michigan, and Missouri. Service in the Army Air Corps during World War II was followed by success as a newscaster at WENR in Chicago. Lynne "Angel" Cooper, a St. Louis native and graduate of Washington University whom Harvey married in 1940, was his main writer and producer.

In 1951, the ABC Radio Network launched Harvey's *News and Comment* nationally. Based in Chicago, the program flourished for more than half a century, eventually playing on over twelve hundred stations across the country. Equally popular was *The Rest of the Story*, a series created and produced by Paul Harvey

(and written by his son, Paul. Jr.) that began in 1976. In both cases, Harvey moved from information to advertisements so effectively that some listeners—and critics—had trouble telling where one ended and the other began.

The conservative Harvey occasionally adopted liberal positions, most notably support for the Equal Rights Amendment and opposition to the Vietnam War. But it was his unique combination of wit, whimsy, and respect for the values of his listeners that made his voice instantly recognizable.

Sources and Further Reading: Patricia Aufderheide, *The Daily Planet: A Critic on the Capitalist Culture Beat* (2000); Rick Kogan, "Good Days for Paul Harvey," *The Chicago Tribune* (4 Aug. 2000); Dan D. Nimmo and Chevelle Newsome, *Political Commentators in the United States in the 20th Century* (1997).

Andrew Cayton
Miami University, Oxford, Ohio

Irv Kupcinet (1912–2003)

Irv Kupcinet's career in media began in 1935 as a newspaper columnist. Born in Chicago in 1912, he had been a standout college football player at Northwestern University and the University of North Dakota. After an NFL career cut short by injury, Kup also served as an NFL referee, until a protest by the Green Bay Packers of his officiating at a Packers–Bears game put an end to that phase of his career. While continuing his print career throughout the twentieth century, Kupcinet built an equally influential career as a broadcaster, covering 1950s events ranging from Chicago sports to the coronation of Queen Elizabeth. Over the course of his career, Kupcinet developed a distinct style, somewhat reminiscent of Walter Winchell, combining a significant amount of celebrity news with occasional political commentary. He had a well-known habit of "being where the action is," particularly at Chicago nightclubs, to gather news in person rather than relying only on telephone calls. One of his favorite haunts was Booth #1 at Chicago's Ambassador East Pump Room, which he and his wife Essee had replicated in their own dining room. His 1959–1986 TV program *Kup's Show* featured a vast array of guests from Buckminster Fuller to Malcolm X to Henry Kissinger to Judy Garland. It was innovative for its time and explored a very wide range of political and social themes; it is now considered a forerunner to television's current politically themed talk shows. A tireless promoter of charity events and honored with both Emmy and Peabody awards, Kup continued as an active Chicago media personality, with his last *Chicago Sun-Times* column appearing only a few days before his death at age 91 in November 2003.

Source and Further Reading: Irv Kupcinet and Paul Niemark, *Kup: A Man, An Era, A City: Irv Kupcinet's Autobiography* (1988).

James Schwoch
Northwestern University, Illinois

Oprah Winfrey (b. 1954)

Born in 1954 in Kosciusko, Mississippi, Oprah Winfrey moved to Nashville, Tennessee, at age 13. At 19, Winfrey made her TV debut at WTVF-TV in Nashville, where she was the first African American woman news anchor. Following a successful run at Baltimore's WJZ-TV, Winfrey arrived in Chicago in 1984 to host WLS-TV's flagging *A.M. Chicago*. Within weeks she emerged as one of the most popular daytime talk show hosts in the local Chicago market. Within one year, Winfrey's popularity surpassed Phil Donahue's, the then-reigning king of daytime talk television, and *A.M. Chicago* was renamed *The Oprah Winfrey Show*. Signing a national syndication deal with King World Productions, Inc., in 1986, Winfrey then formed Harpo Productions, Inc. Then seen by approximately twenty-three million viewers weekly in the United States, *The Oprah Winfrey Show* expanded to millions more in over a hundred international markets. Receiving thirty-nine Emmy Awards for *The Oprah Winfrey Show*, Winfrey diversified into commercial ventures, capitalizing on her fame and the devotion of her fans. Harpo produced a number of movies, such as the adaptation of Toni Morrison's *Beloved* (1998), the television series *The Women of Brewster Place* (1989), and made-for-television movies like *The Wedding* (1998) and *Their Eyes Were Watching God* (2005). Further, Winfrey launched a lucrative series of personal empowerment seminars, introduced the magazine *O*, and invested in Oxygen Media, Inc., a cable network and Internet venture aimed at women. Based in Chicago, Winfrey built a media empire, became a global celebrity, and in the process, has become one of the most powerful women in the media industries.

Sources and Further Reading: Jessica Madore Fitch, "Oprah Winfrey, 46," *Chicago Sun-Times* (29 Oct. 2000); Bernard M. Timberg and Robert J. Erler, *Television Talk* (2002).

Sherra Schick
Indiana University–Bloomington

Roots of Recorded Music

In 1877, Thomas A. Edison discovered a method of recording and playing back sound on a cylinder wrapped with tinfoil, a contraption he quickly patented as a phonograph. A decade later, Emile Berliner developed a similar device, named the gramaphone, but it used a disc instead of a cylinder. Edison envisioned the phonograph as essentially an office dictating machine with business uses, but it soon developed as an entertainment device, recording both music and the spoken word. Such entertainment caught on with the public, and most of the recording companies were located in New York and New Jersey. But the Midwest was not far behind in launching labels that produced a variety of musical styles, although most specialized in Southern and Midwest roots music—jazz, blues, gospel, country, rhythm-and-blues, and later doo-wop, soul, and rock-and-roll. There were a few large labels and dozens of smaller companies, with the majority located in Chicago.

Henry Gennett and his three sons owned the Starr Piano Company in Richmond, Indiana. In 1915, they branched into phonographs and records, first under the Starr name but later under the name Gennett Records. By the early 1920s, with recording studios in New York City and Richmond, Gennett was issuing thousands of records covering all aspects of popular recorded sound: symphonies, opera, ethnic language, comedy dialogue, black-face vaudeville, marching brass bands, even specialty discs for the Ku Klux Klan. Finding it difficult to compete with the major companies like Victor and Columbia, in 1922 Gennett began recording jazz bands, beginning with the white, Chicago-based New Orleans Rhythm Kings, then King Oliver's Creole Jazz Band with Louis Armstrong, Hoagy Carmichael, Jelly Roll Morton, and Bix Beiderbecke. Branching out from jazz, Gennett soon added country and blues performers: Bradley Kincaid, Gene Autry, Cow Cow Davenport, Thomas A. Dorsey, and Big Bill Broonzy. Gennett fell on hard times in 1929 and ceased to produce music records in the mid-1930s.

Some of the foremost blues musicians of the Deep South were recorded by the Wisconsin Chair Company's Paramount label, located in the small town of Port Washington, with a studio and production plant in nearby Grafton. Founded in the 1880s, Wisconsin Chair began manufacturing phonographs by World War I, and record production followed in 1917. Soon Paramount was issuing gospel, popular song, hillbilly, and ethnic records. But its blues and jazz issues were the most important, numbering more than one thousand different titles between 1922 and 1932, beginning with Alberta Hunter. Initially using recording studios in Chicago (and some in New York), the label issued sides by Ma Rainey, Ida Cox, King Oliver's Creole Jazz Band, Blind Lemon Jefferson, and finally Charley Patton, Son House, and Skip James. The company transferred the bulk of its recording to Grafton in 1929 and collapsed three years later.

The majority of Midwest labels and recording studios were located in Chicago, beginning in the 1920s. For example, Autograph, launched by Orlando Marsh in 1921 and lasting until 1926, released sides by King Oliver and Jelly Roll Morton. The Chicago Record Company, owned by Mayo Williams, started the Black Patti label, which released fifty-five discs of jazz, blues, sermons, spirituals, and vaudeville skits during 1927, then folded. OKeh Records, located in New York City, made significant jazz recordings in Chicago of Louis Armstrong in the mid-1920s. Decca, Victor, Brunswick, the American Record Corporation, and Columbia, all based in New York, also recorded blues, pop, and jazz in Chicago during the 1920s and 1930s.

Most recording companies either collapsed or drastically cut back during the Depression and World War II, but following the war, new labels emerged and the major ones flourished. Irving Green and Berle Adams formed Mercury Records in Chicago in 1945. Initially recording local rhythm-and-blues acts such as Dinah Washington, it quickly moved into pop (Patti Page, Frankie Laine, the Platters), jazz (Sarah Vaughan, Charlie Parker), country (Lester Flatt and Earl Scruggs), and classical markets (the Louisville Orchestra, the Minneapolis Symphony). Mercury lost its local ownership in 1961, but continued to issue a diverse range of performers, including the local Jerry Butler and Gene Chandler, and finally moved to New York in 1980. Vitacoustic, initiated by Universal Recording in 1947, at first succeeded with the very popular Jerry Murad's Harmonicats, a harmonica trio. After issuing a few jazz and country sides, the company folded the following year. Old Swing-Master, headed by DJ Al Benson, began in early 1949, and called it quits the following year after releasing only seventeen singles. James Oden and Joe Brown started their J.O.B. label in 1948, specializing in Southern blues and urban rhythm-and-blues with Sunnyland Slim, Johnny Shines, J. B. Lenoir, John Brim, and Snooky Pryor; it faded away after 1957.

During the 1950s other labels continued to pop up in Chicago. Art Sheridan initiated Chance Records in 1950, and during the next four years cut 360 sides of mostly rhythm-and-blues performers, including the Flamingos. The company also issued jazz, doo-wop, gospel, and pop records. Parrot Records, with its Blue Lake subsidiary, picked up where Chance left off.

Started by Al Benson in 1953 and lasting until 1956, Chance recorded the Flamingos, Coleman Hawkins, and Sunnyland Slim. The United (1951–1957) and States (1952–1957) labels, under the ownership of Leonard Allen and Lew Simpkins, were more successful, with their lineup of jazz (Tab Smith, Gene Ammons), urban blues (Memphis Slim, Roosevelt Sykes), rural blues (Robert Nighthawk, Junior Wells), and gospel (the Caravans). In 1958 Bob Koester moved his Delmark label, begun in 1953, from St. Louis to Chicago. His recording of blues and jazz musicians, including Speckled Red, Big Joe Williams, and Sleepy John Estes, led to a successful career as both a label and record store owner, which has continued into the twenty-first century. Koester inspired the later Chicago blues companies, Alligator (1971) owned by Bruce Iglauer, Earwig (1972) under the guidance of Michael Frank, as well as Check Nessa's jazz label. Flying Fish was started by Bruce Kaplan in Chicago in 1974. Before his death in 1992, Kaplan featured blues, traditional country, and folk, including Tom Paxton, Doc Watson, and Sweet Honey in the Rock.

While most small labels struggled to survive only a few years—for example, Cobra (with Otis Rush), Constellation, and One-derful—Chess Records blossomed into a major indie label. Leonard and Phil Chess launched their recording career in 1949 by purchasing the recently formed Aristocrat label, with records by Muddy Waters and Sunnyland Slim. Chess Records specialized in blues and rhythm-and-blues; the Checker label was created in 1952, followed by Argo in 1956, focusing on jazz. The Chess brothers made their mark with Muddy Waters, Howlin' Wolf, Little Walter, Sonny Boy Williamson, Chuck Berry, the Flamingos, the Moonglows, Bo Diddley, and the Dells. Many of the performers lived in Chicago. The Chess brothers sold the company in 1969.

Another company, Dunwich Records, recorded numerous Midwest rock-and-roll performers in the 1960s, including Shadows of Knight. In 1968 Curtis Mayfield launched his Curtom label, which focused on contemporary black performers. Within a few years Curtom had released records by Mayfield and other Chicago artists such as the Impressions and Gene Chandler, until the then-owner moved the company to Atlanta in 1980.

A spate of new companies also emerged in other Midwest cities. In Cincinnati, for example, Syd Nathan launched King Records, specializing in black and white rural music in 1943: Louis "Grandpa" Jones, Moon Mullican, Cowboy Copas, Homer and Jethro, John Lee Hooker, Big Jay McNeely, and Billy Ward and the Dominos. James Brown's first national hit, "Please, Please, Please," was a King release in 1956 on Nathan's Federal label (1950–1968). Specializing in blues, country, and rhythm-and-blues, the company also branched into polka, comedy, pop, and gospel records. Cincinnati also hosted Louis Epstein's Radio Artists label (1947–1951), and Harry Carlson initiated Fraternity Records in 1954 with four hundred releases over twenty years, including Jimmy Dorsey and Bobby Bare.

Although most companies were white owned, two black-initiated labels made their mark, Vee-Jay in Gary-Chicago and Motown in Detroit. Born in Tunica, Mississippi, Vivian Carter moved to Gary, Indiana, in 1924. Along with her husband, James Bracken, she opened Vivian's Record Shop in 1948, from which they launched Vee-Jay Records in 1953. They first recorded a local group, the Spaniels, whose "Goodnite, Sweetheart, Goodnite" become a popular hit in 1954, as well as bluesman Jimmy Reed; they soon had an eclectic range of doo-wop, gospel, jazz, and blues performers. Chief administrator Ewart Abner, who had launched the subsidiary Abner label in 1957, eventually signed Betty Everett, Jerry Butler, Dee Clark, and the Four Seasons, and even made the Beatles' first U.S. release. In 1954 Vee-Jay moved to Chicago, then briefly to Los Angeles in 1964, and back to Chicago a year later, before declaring bankruptcy in 1966. A few years later the Steeltown label emerged in Gary, the first to feature the local Jackson Five.

Motown was preceded in Detroit by Joe Von Battle's tiny J-V-B label (1945–1968), which focused on rhythm-and-blues, HOB Records, and Fortune, launched in 1947. Berry Gordy ran a jazz record shop and began writing songs in the 1950s. Forming a production company with his wife Raynoma Lilies, Gordy launched Motown in 1959. He was soon using other label names—Tamla, Gordy, and Soul. The company had hits with Mary Wells, Smokey Robinson and the Miracles, the Supremes, Martha and the Vandellas, Marvin Gaye, Gladys Knight and the Pips, the Temptations, and Stevie Wonder throughout the 1960s. Gordy, having drawn heavily upon local black talent, moved the company from Detroit to Los Angeles in 1971.

Numerous smaller labels specializing in soul music appeared in the Motor City, including Karen and Carla, Tri-Phi, Westbound (with the Ohio Players and Funkadelic), D-Town, Revilot, and two labels owned by Ed Wingate, Ric Tic and Golden World. Motown purchased Wingate's labels in 1966, picking up such artists as Edwin Starr and Fantistic Four. In the 1970s, ex-Motown songwriters-producers Eddie Holland, Lamont Dozier, and Brian Holland operated their Hot Wax (Honey Cone) and Invictus (Chairman of the Board) labels out of Detroit.

During the 1960s and until the century's end other labels popped up in scattered Midwest locations. Harry Oster, for example, launched Folk-Lyric Records in Louisiana in 1959, recording traditional blues and Cajun performers such as Jesse Fuller, then moved his label to Iowa when he began teaching at the University of Iowa in 1963. He branched into Scottish, English, and Irish material, including Ewan MacColl and A. L. Lloyd. Folk-Lyric produced almost thirty albums before its sale in 1970. James Kirchstein in Sauk City, Wisconsin, launched the Cuca label in 1959 with numerous pop, rock, rhythm-and-blues, and polka releases through the decade. Lenny LaCour started Magic Touch/Dynamic Sound in nearby Milwaukee in 1966. Even Minneapolis had a few rock-and-roll companies, including Garrett (the Trashmen) and Soma (the Fendermen), while the blues and folk label Red House later emerged in neighboring St. Paul. The Gaither gospel recording empire flourished in east-central Indiana.

Midwestern recording companies ran the gamut from the tiniest, most fleeting, to such successes as Mercury, Chess, Motown, and Vee-Jay. What set most of these companies apart from their national rivals was their focus on local black and white roots performers—country, blues, jazz, rhythm-and-blues, soul, doo-wop, and rock-and-roll—because generally they could not compete in the larger pop market. Most of these companies were founded and dominated by one or two strong personalities who had a musical (and perhaps business) vision. While the major labels were mostly located on the East Coast and then in Los Angeles, Chicago and other midwestern locations could boast numerous companies, large and small.

Sources and Further Reading: Nadine Cohodas, *Spinning Blues Into Gold* (2000); Robert Dixon, John Goodrich, and Howard Rye, *Blues & Gospel Records, 1890–1943* (1997); Nelson George, *Where Did Our Love Go* (1986); Frank Hoffman, ed., *Encyclopedia of Recorded Sound*, 2 vols. (2005); Rick Kennedy and Randy McNutt, *Little Labels—Big Sound* (1999); William H. Kenney, *Recorded Music in American Life* (1999); Randy McNutt, "Fraternity," *Goldmine* (7 Sept. 1990); Andre Millard, *America on Record* (1995); Robert Pruter, *Chicago Soul* (1991); Robert Pruter, *Doowop* (1996); Mike Rowe, *Chicago Blues* (1975); Suzanne E. Smith, *Dancing In the Street* (2000); http://hubcap.clemson.edu/camp-ber/rsrf.html (Sept. 2003); Alex van der Tuuk, *Paramount's Rise and Fall: A History of the Wisconsin Chair Company and its Recording Activities* (2003).

Ronald D. Cohen
Indiana University Northwest

Community and Social Life

Rural Life

SECTION EDITOR
Mary Neth

Section Contents

Overview

When most people think of the Midwest, they envision a rural landscape dotted with farm homes and with fields of corn visible for miles. Indeed, agriculture is central to the concept of the Midwest as a region, and the historical dominance of small family farms is one of its distinctive features. However, while understanding the importance of small groups of kin and neighbors is crucial to understanding rural life, the Midwest's rural landscape can also be described as a middle ground where numerous groups meet and exchange both goods and culture. In addition, rural life has never been separated from larger developments: the history of warfare and conquest, the development of a market economy, the growth of cities, or the consolidation of industry, including the industry of agriculture. Perhaps what best characterizes rural life is this peculiar organization that links agricultural production to a social system of small groups of kin and communities, which remained dominant through the first half of the twentieth century.

The earliest people to practice agriculture lived in villages, participated in extended trading networks, and cultivated plants that would have long-lasting importance. Known only through archeological records, the Adena and Hopewell of the Ohio Valley (c. 1000 B.C. to A.D. 500) cultivated squash, pumpkins, and sunflowers and domesticated other native plants. The Hopewell may also have cultivated corn, a dominant part of Indian and Midwest agriculture. The Mississippian cultures of the Upper Great Lakes and Mississippi River Valley (c. A.D. 900–1600) practiced a more extensive agriculture, switching from garden-size plots to larger fields and introducing what would be the three major crops of Indian agriculture—squash, corn, and beans.

Movement was a crucial part of Native American subsistence patterns, and waterways linked tribes from the eastern tributaries of the Mississippi River to the western tributaries of the Missouri River in the Great Plains. Most lived for a portion of the year in small villages along waterways because the soil was rich and more easily planted than the prairie sod, hardened by the extensive roots of prairie grasses. Communal fields lay outside the village structures and were divided among kinship groups. Women were the agriculturists of Native American societies. Fields first had to be created by girding trees and removing the brush. In the spring and fall, women tended and harvested squash, sunflowers, beans, corn, and melons. In the Great Lakes area, women also harvested and later cultivated wild rice. Villages also claimed larger territories to utilize other resources. Many villages had stands of sugar maples and moved to these in February and March to tap the trees and produce maple mo-

Hoosier farmer. Indiana Historical Society, neg. no. C4595.

lasses that, when mixed with corn, helped to extend the food supply in winter. The borderlands between prairie and forest near waterways were rich with game and migratory birds, fruits, nuts, and other wild plants. Many villages, even those east of the Mississippi, migrated over greater distances in the late fall and winter to hunt larger game, including buffalo. These larger migrations furthered trade among the various tribes. In the period between 1400 and 1600, Algonquian, Siouxan, and Caddoan language speakers increased contact and exchanges, creating cultural syncretism by sharing and adapting cultural practices from each other

Between the mid-1600s and the mid-1700s, the European fur trade, dominated by the French in most of the Midwest, altered both hunting and agricultural practices. As Native American men extended the hunt to bring more furs to trade, women, especially those who lived near trading posts, increased their agricultural production. Europeans were primarily trappers and traders rather than farmers, and the newly formed trading towns provided a ready market for agricultural surplus. By the early nineteenth century, Sauk and Mesquakie (Fox) women cultivated three hundred acres on the eastern shore of the Mississippi River to supply the trade center at Prairie du Chien, Wisconsin. Trade included corn, beans, maple sugar, tallow, wild rice, buffalo meat, squash, and various craft items, as well as furs. Women and older men were the primary labor force, but enslaved Indians and Africans, were also agricultural workers, particularly along the lower Missouri River. The slave and fur trade increased conflict and warfare in the Midwest, but the fur trade also led to alliances, sometimes creating métis communities.

Between the mid-1700s and the mid-1800s, warfare forced Native Americans to the west and the north. Cornfields were an important military target to be destroyed by fire and an important location for resistance. As the Sauk-Mesquakie struggled to keep their land east of the Mississippi River, women demanded access to the fields they planted before removal. When U.S. officials refused, the women secretly crossed the river to harvest the corn after nightfall. By the 1870s, all Native Americans in the region had been forced to cede their territory and move to reservations. U.S. Indian policy demanded that Indians adopt plow agriculture and make men, not women, farmers. Although Native Americans resisted or adapted the new practices, conditions on most reservations did not favor profitable farming.

The earliest European American farmers practiced an agriculture that resembled that of Native Americans. The French origin of the term pioneer, "pionnier," referred to soldiers who opened the way for an army, and those who first entered a territory were not only fighters but farmers. Early settlers built their fields on rivers and lakes, clearing the land much as Indians had, and relying on the same mix of crops and wild game. One family who settled in the "American Bottom," south of the Missouri and Mississippi River confluence, raised a small patch of corn and vegetables, hunted local game, but added to the mix a few hogs, who ran wild in the woods. After the Kickapoo were defeated, this family moved up an Indian trail and squatted on land near a well-known Kickapoo sugar maple grove. The European American settlements of the Midwest depended not only on Native American displacement, but also on their practices and their knowledge of resources.

After Indian removal, European American settlers literally moved into the existing Native American agricultural landscape. Settlers lived along rivers not only to be close to transportation, but also to utilize fields already cleared by Native Americans. Just as Native American agriculture relied on groupings of people based on kinship and village, European American and European migrants to the Midwest practiced agriculture in ways that utilized kinship and communal ties. Although European American farm families lived in scattered nuclear-family dwellings, these homesteads were nevertheless linked. People moved as part of kinship or community groups. As land in these initial communities became scarce, they became the home base for colonies further afield. Norwegians from Balestrand, Norway, first settled in towns in southern Wisconsin and northern Illinois, which then became the base for settlements further west for other migrants from Norway. Similarly, when free African Americans left their homes along the North Carolina–Virginia border, they settled in communities in Ohio and eastern Indiana, which then became base communities for further westward movement.

As immigrants arrived from different regions of the East and Europe with their own agricultural practices, cultural beliefs, and social structures, the Midwest continued as a "middle ground" for cultural exchange and syncretism. Blending probably occurred most quickly in agricultural practices that melded with the natural resources available and existing market conditions. Farmers from the Northeast and mid-Atlantic region who came to the eastern Midwest often grew wheat. Those from the South practiced a corn–livestock agriculture that for some was subsistence-oriented, but for others continued well-developed commercial practices. Over time, a more homogeneous corn–livestock agriculture emerged, as wheat declined and slaughtering and meatpacking plants developed along the riverways throughout the eastern Midwest.

Although adaptation was part of the development

of the Midwest, migrants' cultural practices also persisted. White southern migrants who wanted to maintain slavery moved into Missouri and settled the Little Dixie region along the Missouri River. To make this labor force profitable, they added tobacco and hemp, both labor-intensive crops, to the corn–livestock mix of nearby states that forbid slavery. Norwegians participated in the wheat boom, but utilized barley, oats, and hay more than corn for feeding livestock, continuing Norwegian patterns. German immigrants emphasized passing on their farming traditions of crop rotation and diversification to maintain soil quality.

Gender divisions of labor also reflected ethnic traditions, and farm women's work in the Midwest became a blend of these various traditions. While fieldwork, particularly plowing, defined the core of men's responsibility in most European traditions, women's responsibilities varied. In Missouri's small slaveholding families, the ability of white women to focus on household production and childcare was in part possible because slave women not only cooked and did laundry, but also worked in the fields when needed. German and Norwegian women were more likely to work with livestock, particularly in the dairy, and in the fields than were women from the northeastern United States. Some patterns also crossed ethnic lines. Most women during the frontier years grew and processed food, maintained poultry and eggs, and made butter, soap, candles, and cloth. Most also worked in the fields during planting and harvesting and marketed surplus butter or cloth in nearby towns. As cloth became available for a reasonable price through mass-production, these farm women left cloth-making behind. Within about twenty years of settlement, sales of butter increased among southern and mid-Atlantic migrants in Illinois, Norwegians in Minnesota and Wisconsin, and Yankee migrants in Michigan, and this work was most often done by women.

As rivers gave way to railroads, patterns of agricultural production changed. Wheat production continuously moved westward, and farmers in the eastern areas developed new specializations. Railroads consolidated Chicago as the meatpacking center and further encouraged the growth of the corn-livestock belt in the lower Midwest. Dairying became a specialization of the upper Midwest. Minneapolis serviced the new wheat-growing regions in western Minnesota and the Great Plains, while Kansas City served as the center for southern wheat terminals. Kansas City and a series of cities along the Missouri River—Omaha, St. Joseph, Sioux City—became meatpacking centers for the western Midwest and the Great Plains region. As in the days of Indians and river travel, the Midwest region expanded economic links through the Great Plains, integrating the two regions.

The link between agricultural and industrial growth in the late nineteenth and early twentieth centuries created a rural–urban migratory workforce. From settlement through most of the twentieth century, farm labor was largely unpaid, done by family members or by exchanging work with neighbors. But as farm neighborhoods became more economically stratified, larger farms often hired farm laborers. Labor-intensive crops and seasonal needs also created demand for an expanded labor force. Because agriculture, like extractive industries such as mining and lumbering, utilized workers on a seasonal basis, both rural and urban workers moved to find work when these industries demanded it. Wage labor was an important income-earning option for farm men who sought to supplement hard-scrabble farms with winter seasons in logging, railroad construction, or mining, or with other summer work after the wheat harvest. By the twentieth century, some highly centralized, labor-intensive crop specializations, particularly the sugar beet industry, recruited workers—at first mostly individuals from the region's towns and cities, but by World War I, families from Mexico. During the off-season, these workers moved to cities and sought industrial employment, becoming part of the rural–urban workforce. Midwest agriculture worked in symbiotic relation with other industrial employers to make wage work erratic and exploitive for many laborers.

The growth and consolidation of industry also reshaped the experiences of farm-owning and -operating families. Railroads often charged high rates for the short hauls that dominated farmers' costs, grain elevators often paid farmers much less for their grain than it would ultimately bring, and futures markets determined prices without consideration of the farmers' costs of production. Farmers protested both politically and economically. A series of protest movements, such as the Grange, the Populist Party, and the Non-Partisan League, pushed for government regulation, and sometimes ownership, of the corporations that most affected farmers. Cooperatives, such as the Farmers' Alliance of the late nineteenth century and the Farmers' Union and Farm Bureau of the twentieth, attempted to create marketing alternatives and collectively bargain for better prices. While cooperatives did help farmers, they ultimately had little impact on the structure of an agricultural industry in which farmers had little leverage or control.

In spite of the consolidation of agricultural industries, food production in the Midwest remained decentralized through the first half of the twentieth century, and farming remained rooted in a system of small family-owned farms that relied on kinship and community ties. The primary labor force remained the family, and exchange of labor, services, and products among neighbors was crucial to this system. Exchange was built on social ties of visiting. These social networks served as a security system as well. When a neighbor became ill or died, people from the neighborhood would do the work that needed to be done as well as comfort the surviving family members. Neighborhoods were also linked by important social institutions, especially churches and schools.

While this stage of rural life persisted through the early twentieth century, agriculture was also being transformed by technological innovation and adaptation. A steady stream of new mechanical equipment altered agricultural production. The spread of tractors, replacing horses and mules as the primary power source of field production, encouraged larger farms and increased cash outlays, since fuel had to be purchased, whereas feed for horses could be grown. The tractor made fieldwork physically easier and allowed more work to be done; however, it also changed the rhythm of work and became the basis for further mechanization.

Contrary to popular images of the farm people as backward and resistant to change, they did participate in the consumer society and mass culture revolution of the early twentieth century. The most popular innovations were those that increased farm people's ability to communicate over distances—the radio, the telephone, and the automobile. With automobiles farm people could not only go shopping or to a movie in town more often, but ease their normal rounds of visiting with neighbors. Better transportation also allowed children to move to nearby towns or cities for jobs and still visit family and friends regularly. The automobile both maintained community and neighborhood ties and allowed farm people to move or travel longer distances, reshaping rural neighborhoods.

These changes took place within an increasingly consolidated agricultural industry. Business and government leaders saw a need to modernize agricultural production using an industrial model that replaced labor with technology, consolidation that mirrored economies of scale in factories and required increased costs of production, and a managerial model that emphasized increased production and efficiency over issues of familial persistence on the land or community needs. The economic crisis in agriculture that began in the 1920s and continued through the Great Depression of the 1930s increased pressures to reorganize agriculture. Although many New Deal programs assisted tenants and those who owned smaller farms, its most lasting programs utilized the industrial model and benefited larger landowners. When higher paid wage work opened up in cities during World War II, migrations out of rural areas increased, and labor shortages in the countryside encouraged further mechanization. Although farms often remained family-run in the Midwest, the neighborhoods of small family farms began to decline.

Industrial organization hindered strategies of diversified, low-risk agriculture. Women on small farms earned income by selling eggs and poultry to local groceries or to regional markets. Gradually, state laws regulated production to guarantee a more standardized product, thereby increasing the costs of production and hurting small producers. In addition, larger poultry and egg producers contracted with the increasingly consolidated grocery chains that replaced local stores and regional markets. Similarly, in areas that specialized in fruit and vegetable production, independent growers began to work under contract to corporations who controlled canning factories and recruited seasonal farm workers. By the 1950s, corporations promoted the use of pesticides, herbicides, and mechanization, leading to debt and farm loss for many of their "independent" contract producers and to a declining need for seasonal labor, forcing farm workers to find other work. Industrialized hog and beef cattle production followed similar patterns by the 1980s. Large vertically and horizontally integrated corporations controlled the factories that fed hogs and cattle and the packinghouses that slaughtered the animals and packaged the meat. They then sold the packaged meat to the equally consolidated grocery store chains. Small independent producers rarely found a place within this system.

This reorganization of agriculture that followed World War II has undercut the system of small, family-owned farms and created a new relationship between industry and agriculture that has led to wage labor for most rural midwesterners. Farm women became the first to search for off-farm work, often in the low-paying service sector, to replace the income they had earned from eggs and poultry. Industries also moved to the countryside. The packinghouses that have reshaped the livestock industry also replaced the urban and unionized stockyards that pulled workers into higher-paid jobs after World War II. Rural plants paid lower wages to rural workers. Most farm incomes today need to be supplemented with wage labor. This may be a more geographically stable version of the early twentieth century rural–urban workforce, with commuter travel replacing more wide-ranging migrant labor. While rural communities still exist, the system of small, family-owned farms does not. The reorganization of the last fifty years has transformed the rural Midwest in such profound ways that "rural life" within this new system is leading to new conceptions of and adaptations in both farming and community. The organization of this section is designed to provide information and understanding of the major social, economic, and institutional dimensions of life in the rural Midwest.

Sources and Further Reading: Jane Adams, ed., *Fighting for the Family Farm* (2003); Jane Adams, *The Transformation of Rural Life* (1994); Diane Mutti Burke, "'May We As One Family Live in Peace and Harmony': Relations Between Mistresses and Slave Women in Antebellum Missouri," in LeeAnn Whites, Mary C. Neth, and Gary Kremer, eds., *Women in Missouri History* (2004); Deborah Fink, *Open Country, Iowa* (1986); Jon Gjerde, *From Peasants to Farmers* (1985); Frank Tobias Higbie, *Indispensable Outcasts* (2003); R. Douglas Hurt, *Indian Agriculture in America* (1987); Lucy Eldersveld Murphy, *A Gathering of Rivers* (2000); Mary Neth, *Preserving the Family Farm* (1995); Susan Sessions Rugh, *Our Common Ground* (2001); Tanis C. Thorne, *The Many Hands of My Relations* (1996); Dennis Nodin Valdes, *Al Norte* (1991).

Mary C. Neth
University of Missouri–Columbia

Environment and Rural Life

At the very foundation of rural life in the Midwest is its physical environment. That physical environment, with its minerals, plants, and animals and the wealth their exploitation promised, brought European Americans to the Midwest and sustained them as they established new homes. Midwesterners tend to be apologetic about the appearance of their rural landscape. It lacks the drama of mountains and oceans or the stark beauty of deserts. A casual observer, staring out from a car window on a long drive from Indianapolis to Omaha or Chicago to St. Louis, might conclude that the Midwest is just one vast cornfield. The apparent uniformity is deceptive, however. A remarkable diversity of physical environments has shaped the region's multiple landscapes. Woodlands, prairies, lakes and rivers offer different problems and promises.

The environment that first confronted European American settlers was the oak, hickory, and walnut forests. Newcomers came into wooded areas occupied by Native Americans, who prized the land for its abundant resources, such as game, nuts, and maple sugar. Fur trappers followed the region's rivers and lakes into the interior, seeking the valuable pelts of animals such as the beaver. A vigorous fur trade greatly reduced the numbers of fur-bearing animals. As incoming white farmers followed the trappers, land acquisition generally followed the timber line, leading settlers in states such as Illinois to claim first the southern area of the state, as well as its western border, rather than the vast prairies of the middle portion. The same pattern of settlement was visible in Iowa: Early farmers generally remained in wooded areas and along the courses of streams, and settled in the central prairie only when those areas were filled. There were several reasons for this pattern. Folk knowledge decreed that a farmer could tell the quality of land by examining the types and quantity of trees growing upon it. Land without trees, therefore, was nearly impossi-

The Declining Number of Farms: 1920–1997

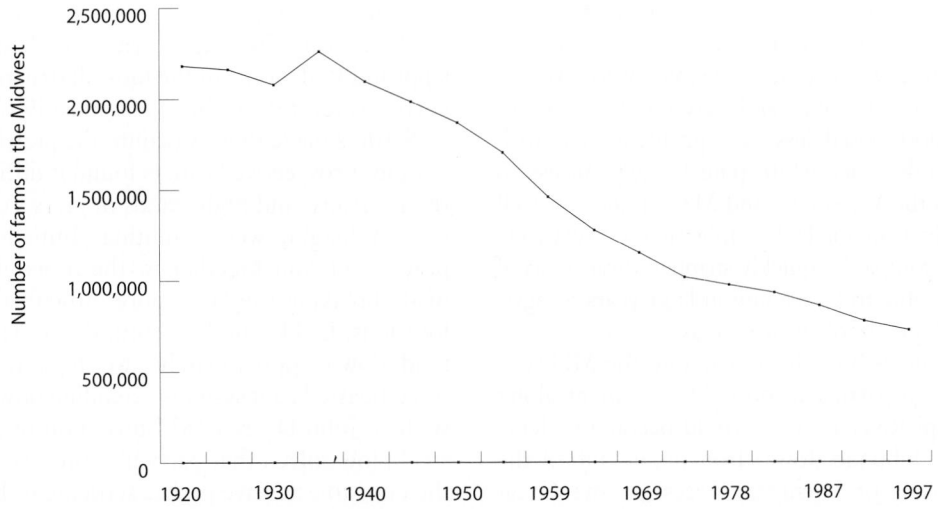

Number of farms by state. Prepared by Sathyan Sundaram. *Source:* Calculated from U.S. Censuses of Agriculture, 1920–1997 by Brad Baltensperger.

University of Wisconsin dairy barns, Madison, Wisconsin, 1931. Melvin E. Diemer Collection, Wisconsin Historical Society.

ble for settlers to judge. Additionally, settlers depended upon trees for many of the essentials of agricultural life, including shelter, heat, and fences. It was far more expensive to develop a farm without trees than a farm with them. Woodlands, too, were familiar territory, since the number of eastern prairies was limited. Although they were popular locations, such wooded lands were low in organic materials, easily eroded, and often did not make the best farms.

Other woodlands drew settlers, as well. To the north in Minnesota and Wisconsin grew heavy stands of white pine, much prized as building material. The trees grew to phenomenal size, as much as six feet in diameter, representing many board feet of lumber. They were among the most preferred woods for building material, since such large white pines generally were free of knots at their broad centers and were relatively easy to work. Transport posed less of a problem than with most hardwoods, since white pine floated. Access to rivers such as the Wisconsin and Menomonee, as well as to Lake Michigan, made the timber harvest relatively easy. Timber companies quickly stripped these areas of the most desirable trees, leading in later years to agricultural development of cutover areas.

Other resources brought miners into the Midwest. Lead mining, in particular, brought settlement along the Mississippi River in what would become Galena, Illinois, and Dubuque, Iowa. Iron mines dotted the Upper Peninsula of Michigan. Access to the Great Lakes and Mississippi River allowed this mineral wealth to be transported to urban areas for processing.

Waterways, in short, were and are important parts of the rural environment. Lakes and rivers served as sources of transportation, taking a host of individuals with different interests into the hinterland. Fur trappers, miners, lumberjacks, and farmers all made their way into the interior. The existence of these lakes and rivers also enabled the land's products to be shipped to manufacturers, processors, and distributors in cities such as Chicago. Unlike the Great Plains, the Midwest did not have to wait for the arrival of the railroad for its economic enterprises to become profitable. But while waterways aided in the development of great wealth, they were also the sources of major disasters. Periodically complacent humans have been shattered by devastating flooding on rivers such as the Mississippi and Red. Some of the most destructive floods occurred as recently as the 1930s and 1990s.

Settlers made their way onto the prairies with trepidation. Prospective farmers found it difficult to assess their fertility, and high stands of grass, sometimes ten feet in height, were daunting. Initially, the tough prairie sod, knit together by the roots of tall grasses, made breaking the land more difficult than in other locations. Unlike modern corn, the roots of which extend down approximately two feet, prairie grasses often boasted root systems extending down as much as six feet. John Deere's 1837 invention of an affordable steel plow solved that particular problem and opened the door to extensive prairie settlement. By the 1850s, large numbers of farmers, hungry for land, were braving the prairie. Some swampy areas in central Illinois and throughout much of the Iowa prairie, however, had to wait for the development of inexpensive drain tile before they could be settled.

Emigrating families had mixed reactions to the prairies. While many saw the land as full of possibilities, others were depressed and frightened by the lack of trees. Settlers also felt isolated, since prairie farms were often farther from neighboring farms than those in eastern communities. Many other physical challenges were inherent in this environment. Mosquitoes carried malaria, a disease that laid low many a pioneer family. Grasshopper infestation periodically destroyed crops. Summer storms often brought hail, tornadoes, or damaging winds. Winter storms brought blinding blizzards. Droughts devastated crops, as did prairie fires, which could burn for miles. The land nevertheless offered much to the hardy. This was, by far, the most fertile agricultural environment in the United States, and farmers replaced nearly three hundred varieties of native prairie plants with fields of wheat, corn, oats, and other crops. Cattle, hogs, and horses quickly outnumbered deer and other native animals. By the late nineteenth century, this area became known as the Corn Belt, with farmers specializing in corn and hog production. In the twentieth century, soybeans also became an important crop. Today, some of the richest farmlands in the United States are found in the prairie states.

While extractive industries and agriculture have defined much of the economic relationship between rural midwesterners and their environment, tourism has been important, too. Although residents of much of the United States define coastal and mountainous environments as more important and aesthetically pleasing environmental resources, midwesterners have found much to enjoy in their natural surroundings. The Great Lakes have been playgrounds as well as important waterways. Resorts have existed on their shores since the middle to late nineteenth century. Smaller lakes, such as Lake Okoboji in northern Iowa, have been vacation destinations for families in Iowa and Nebraska since the closing years of the nineteenth century. The woods of Michigan, Wisconsin, and Minnesota grow in population during the summer, as urbanites escape cities such as Detroit, Milwaukee, and Minneapolis. Minnesota's Boundary Waters draw canoeists from across the nation. Tourism has grown in economic importance as logging, mining, and farming have become less profitable.

While the tourism value of lakes, rivers, and woodlands seems obvious, the aesthetic value of the prairies has been more difficult to grasp. Accustomed to trees, early settlers (as well as many modern-day visitors) often found the view monotonous and intimidating. Some found the waves of grass beautiful and awe inspiring, but others hurried to fill their horizon with trees. Only in recent decades have prairie communities worked to preserve what few pieces of the untouched prairie still exist, or have labored to plant and recreate prairie environments so that modern residents and visitors will be able to experience at least a small portion of what early settlers saw. The Neal Smith National Wildlife Refuge in central Iowa celebrates the area's prairie past, and attempts to recreate the prairie environment, with its distinctive flora and fauna. In addition to more common animals like deer, the refuge is home to reintroduced species like the American bison. On a smaller scale, home and institutional gardeners have discovered the beauty of prairie plants, such as prairie roses, purple coneflower, and tall prairie grasses, and have incorporated them into their landscaping.

In the early twenty-first century, the environment continues to concern rural midwesterners, although in different ways. Whereas the first settlers struggled to make a living from often unyielding land, modern residents are struggling with ways to balance economic needs against their desire to maintain environmental quality. Many questions remain. Can extractive industries, such as logging and mining, be carried out in such a way that the long-term health of the land can be maintained? Can extractive industries exist side-by-side with tourism? To what degree will the last fifty years' use of agricultural chemicals, such as fertilizers and pesticides, impair the health of streams and rivers, not to mention that of the people who consume water from these sources? How can the needs of farmers, making a living from the land, be balanced with the desires of urban and suburban transplants, who have moved to the countryside for its aesthetic qualities? None of these questions has an easy answer, nor will these inherent conflicts be resolved quickly.

While scholars have been quick to acknowledge the impact of environment on history and culture in obviously difficult environments, such as the Great Plains, it must be recognized that the environment has played an important role in areas such as the rural Midwest. The environment shapes the possibilities that individuals see in the land, just as it shapes their ability to live and work on that land. At the same time, human intervention makes its mark on that very same land. With varying degrees of enthusiasm, people have entered into relationships with the woods, waters, and prairies of the Midwest. Each of these environments has provided different economic and aesthetic rewards, and as the United States enters the twenty-first century, each will pose different problems for those living and working within them.

Sources and Further Reading: Allan G. Bogue, *From Prairie to Cornbelt* (1963); Rebecca Burlend and Edward Burlend, *A*

True Picture of Emigration, ed. Milo Milton Quaife (1987); William Cronon, *Nature's Metropolis* (1991); John Mack Faragher, *Sugar Creek: Life on the Illinois Prairie* (1986); Eliza W. Farnham, *Life in Prairie Land* (1988); John Ise, *Sod and Stubble* (1996); James C. Malin, *History and Ecology,* ed. Robert P. Swierenga (1984); Dorothy Schwieder, *Iowa: The Middle Land* (1996).

Pamela Riney-Kehrberg
Iowa State University

The Built Environment of Farming

The earliest midwestern farmhouses often took the form of the I-house with or without wing extensions. Others were gable-roofed boxes. By the mid-nineteenth century, architectural pattern books recommended the independent rural farmstead as America's architectural ideal. The image of groups of simple buildings for dwelling, storing, and working became the standard for farmstead architecture well into the twentieth century. Although pattern book authors intended their designs for a national audience, specific components of the farmstead such as dairy barns and granaries often reflected regional preferences based on local storage demands.

The factors of convenience, appearance, sanitation, and fire protection guided the arrangement of most farmsteads. The cold winter also helped determine the orientation of the buildings on the farmstead so that the dwelling and work areas were protected from the north wind.

The building at the front of most farmsteads is a house large enough for the farm family and, prior to World War II, the hired help. This location provided unobstructed views of the road, yards, and fields. Until the postwar period, most houses were wood-frame, multistoried structures with gabled or hipped roofs and front and rear porches. The bungalow also became popular in the early twentieth century because its compact efficiency offered a more affordable option for smaller farms.

The major difference between farm and urban houses lay in the types of interior spaces. Three areas distinguish the farmhouse from its urban counterpart: the office, the washroom, and the kitchen. Many farmhouses provided a special room for record keeping and accounting, usually overlooking the farmyard, outbuildings, and fields. The washroom could be found immediately inside the rear entrance of the farmhouse. Here, people removed dirty boots and work clothes and washed up before entering the kitchen. The multipurpose farm kitchen was large enough to preserve food and prepare and serve large meals, and sometimes it included space for laundry facilities.

Behind the farmhouse, the variety of buildings depended on the type of crops and livestock raised. The barn was usually the largest building on the farmstead. Although variable in size and form, barns were constructed to accommodate a designated number of animals, their feed, and any equipment associated with their use. Most farms featured a general-purpose barn used to shelter cows and horses and to store hay and other types of feed. However, certain types of farms included specialty barns for dairy cows or sheep.

Other required buildings on the nineteenth- and twentieth-century farmstead included a machine shed for major farming equipment, a poultry house for egg production, and granaries and cribs for long-term storage of livestock feed. Optional structures include a hog house, livestock shelters, silos, a root cellar, and in the twentieth century, a garage.

Sources and Further Reading: Mary Anne Beecher, "Building for 'Mrs. Farmer': Published Farmhouse Designs and the Role of the Rural Female Consumer, 1900–1930," *Agricultural History* 73 (Spring 1999); Deane G. Carter and W. A. Foster, *Farm Buildings* (1941); Sally McMurry, *Families and Farmhouses In Nineteenth-Century America* (1988); Fred W. Peterson, *Homes in the Heartland* (1992); Linda E. Smeins, *Building an American Identity* (1999).

Mary Anne Beecher
University of Oregon

Sustainable Agriculture

Farmers and public interest organizations pioneered "sustainable agriculture" in the Midwest. From the early 1980s, these groups defined the term on three fully integrated dimensions: ecological—sustaining the environment, financial—sustaining farm viability, and social—sustaining farm opportunity and rural communities. Ecologically, "sustainable agriculture" is not defined as set farming practices, but rather expresses an aspiration toward long-term sustainability. Practices can be identified as "more sustainable" or "unsustainable," but "sustainability" implies full ecological balance, regenerative care of the land, and closed loops, including energy self-sufficiency. The integration of social, economic, and ecological goals was reflective of a markedly midwestern collaborative spirit that brought environmental, farmer, and rural development organizations together.

Midwest organizations, such as the Center for Rural Affairs in Nebraska and the Land Stewardship Project in Minnesota, provided national leadership in establishing the first of five regional Sustainable Agriculture Working Groups (SAWGs) in 1988. The Midwestern SAWG (MSAWG) was devoted to influencing federal legislative and institutional policy and to supporting each organization's state or regional projects, such as farmer-to-farmer sharing about more sustainable practices, support for beginning farmers, and initiatives to add value locally to agricultural products, and thereby enhance rural economic vitality.

MSAWG, especially through its lobbying arm, the Sustainable Agriculture Coalition, has focused primarily on federal commodity, conservation, and research and extension policies. Despite periodic setbacks, inevitable in light of powerful opposition from more narrowly focused interest groups, it enjoyed significant successes with the 1990, 1996, and 2002 farm bills and with annual appropriations. By working with key members of Congress, and subsequently with USDA administrators, MSAWG and the Coalition focused greater emphasis on sustainability to research and extension programs, substantially increased funding and improved requirements for resource conservation programs, and helped initiate new programs supporting local value-added initiatives. MSAWG played a critical role in forming the National Campaign for Sustainable Agriculture in the early 1990s.

The sustainable agriculture agenda has continued to expand. A major focus is now local food security; for example, linking food stamps and WIC (the Special Supplemental Nutrition Program for Women, Infants, and Children) coupons with farmers' markets, and critiquing multinational consolidation in the foods industry. The organic foods sector is strong in the Midwest, and Midwest Organic and Sustainable Education Services hosts a large, annual Upper Midwest Organic Farming Conference. The Midwest is host to several of the strongest organic products cooperatives (for example, the Organic Valley label) and enjoys an abundant network of Community Supported Agriculture farms. These market garden farms sell subscriptions or shares to members in the spring, then deliver produce weekly in accord with the changing growing season.

Sources and Further Reading: Elizabeth Ann R. Bird, Gordon L. Bultena, and John C. Gardner, eds., *Planting the Future* (1995); Neva Hassanein, *Changing the Way America Farms* (1999); Wes Jackson, Wendell Berry, and Bruce Colman, eds., *Meeting the Expectations of the Land* (1984); Judith D. Soule and Jon K. Piper, *Farming in Nature's Image* (1992).

Elizabeth Ann R. Bird
University of Wisconsin–Madison

Understanding the Land: Native American and European American Visions

Native American and European American perspectives of land and land use varied by time and place, but were almost always at odds with each other. During the eighteenth century, the future Midwest yielded fur, fish, and game to both indigenous peoples and early European traders. Little more than a hundred years later, the region provided timber, metal ores, and some of the most productive agricultural land on earth to a growing United States. Because of the region's rich natural resources, dozens of Native American tribes and several European nations coveted its bounty. Clashes between groups were inevitable and proliferated on a grand scale in the eighteenth and nineteenth centuries. Much of the conflict revolved around differing of "land."

Initial interactions between Europeans and Native Americans focused on trade, with finished goods and weapons exchanged for skins and pelts. Prior to the arrival of Europeans, the taking of game among indigenous peoples was often highly ritualized, a process filled with symbolism and embedded within the social lives of hunters. Harvests of game were carefully managed, and stripping the grounds of all available animals was usually avoided. The European entrance into this world upset a cultivated balance. Fur trade fever quickly depleted traditional Native American hunting grounds of many animal species and consequently endangered an entire way of life.

Certainly Native Americans altered their landscapes. They used fire to modify grasslands and forests, erected large earthen monuments, and established trails, roads, agricultural settlements, and urban centers. They did not, however, exhaust the landscape, as Europeans did. This single difference is emblematic of deeper worldviews, of contrasting perspectives of land use that have caused considerable conflict between indigenous peoples and European Americans whenever they have encountered one another.

In Native American belief systems, it is often impossible to separate the sacred from the secular in most matters dealing with land. These beliefs tend to emphasize a high degree of interdependence between humans and the land, going so far as to equate land with home, sustenance, and family. The legends and stories of many Indians reveal a great sense of awe and wonder toward providential nature. Land is identified in some Native origin stories as a grandmother figure imbued with a consciousness and from whom all peoples spring and are sustained.

On a less ethereal plain, Native American social and economic manifestations of land could be broadly deemed communalistic. Rarely did individuals or single families possess exclusive rights to particular parcels of land. All tribal members used the land to feed and clothe their families. Boundaries between different tribal territories did exist, and tribes would occasionally go to war over perceived territorial incursions. Still, land was rarely "owned" in the legalistic sense familiar to Western thought.

The ethnically diverse white settlers who entered the Midwest in waves from Europe and the crowded Atlantic seaboard found that it was a short step linguistically from "land" to "landed," from "wilderness" to "property." In spite of their diversity, these groups shared a strategy of land use based on subduing and exploiting the land. The landscape itself was viewed as disorganized, undisciplined nature rich in resources that were ripe for entrepreneurial picking. The principles underlying this mind-set have numerous sources. The chief spiritual wellspring to Europeans, the Judeo-Christian Bible, mandates in the Book of Genesis that humans ought to dominate, not live in harmony with, nature. With the expansion of capitalist markets, land came to be viewed chiefly as a commodity.

The incipient American nationalism, especially as Thomas Jefferson articulated it, celebrated an agrarian society where personal independence was based in large part on the freeholding of land. To this end, U.S. governments surveyed the landscape, supported armed dispossession, removal, or treaty-making with indigenous populations to gain access to their lands, and offered real estate incentives (i.e., sold land cheap) to provide a continuously burgeoning American population with more land. To facilitate American colonization of the region that would become the Midwest, the U.S. Congress passed the Land Ordinance of 1785, under the provision of which huge tracts of territory (considered "public domain" by the ordinance) north of the Ohio River and west of Pennsylvania were sliced into ever smaller rectangular sections to become farms and towns.

Surveying, land enclosure, deeds, and legal definitions of individual ownership all represent American political and economic concepts of "land." To this might be added the mythic notion of land as frontier space, where one might wipe his or her soles clean of civilization or chaos and start anew. Eventually, the combination of American technology, superior numbers, and a belief in the manifest destiny of the United States overwhelmed Native American notions of land. To the extent those notions survive today, they are circumscribed, either literally as peoples relegated to reservations or figuratively as minority opinions clanking in the background.

Today, the landscape of the Midwest has been radically altered by both Native Americans and European Americans from its prehuman state, the latter effecting far more environmental change than the former. White settlers envisioned the landscape as an opportunity to prosper and considered it a duty to convert its resources to productive goods. This vision would eventually reach acute levels, culminating in the clearcutting of the Great Lakes pineries for building materials and the plowing of millions of acres of sod prairie to expose productive agricultural soil. At present, over half the original wetlands of Wisconsin have been drained, and nearly the entire original tallgrass prairie of Illinois has been lost to the plow. And while indigenous peoples are beginning to recover from past invasions and land usurpations, their most visible legacy to present midwestern landscapes are the hundreds of place names denoting their historic interaction with settlers.

Sources and Further Reading: Vine Deloria, Jr., *God is Red*, 2nd ed. (1992); William M. Denevan, "The Pristine Myth: The Landscape of the Americas in 1492," *Annals of the Association of American Geographers* 82 (1992); John Leighly, ed., *Land and Life: A Selection from the Writings of Carl Ortwin Sauer* (1963); Donald W. Meinig, *The Shaping of America* (1993); Gary B. Nash, *Red, White, and Black* (1992); James S. Olson and Raymond Wilson, *Native Americans in the Twentieth Century* (1986); David Ward, ed., *Geographic Perspectives on America's Past* (1979).

Randy James Bertolas
Wayne State College, Nebraska

Tornados, Drought, and Blizzards

Weather provides much of the drama of midwestern rural life because it is highly variable and subject to extremes of heat, cold, and precipitation. Weather is a matter for concern far beyond the simple inconvenience it poses for many Americans.

Over the last one hundred and fifty years, the weather has often caused real distress for rural midwesterners. In the latter half of the nineteenth century, droughts accompanied by grasshopper infestations periodically ruined crops and bankrupted farmers in Minnesota, Kansas, and Nebraska. In the 1880s, severe winter cold and blizzards killed hundreds of thousands of head of livestock and threatened the very existence of farming communities in the eastern Dakotas. During the dust bowl years of the 1930s, the drought and extreme heat that plagued the Great Plains extended several years into midwestern areas, making what were already difficult conditions worse. Tornados, common in most parts of the Midwest, have returned time and again to damage and destroy

Tornado, Pratt County, Kansas, May 7, 2002. Photo by Timothy P. Baker. Courtesy http://www.tornadochaser.net.

homes, barns, crops, and businesses. Hurricanes aside, virtually all of the unpleasant weather phenomena that affect the United States have occurred in the midwest. Discussions of the weather, so common among midwesterners, are not simply small talk; they are an expression of the centrality of this topic to the lives and fortunes of the area's residents.

Sources and Further Reading: Annette Atkins, *Harvest of Grief* (1984); John Ise, *Sod and Stubble* (1996); William B. Meyer, *Americans and Their Weather* (2000); Laura Ingalls Wilder, *The Long Winter* (1940).

Pamela Riney-Kehrberg
Iowa State University

Labor on the Farm

Fertile midwestern lands have been farmed for millennia. While midwestern farming has always had a subsistence component, it has also drawn on larger economic and technological networks and in turn produced surplus, providing for exchange and for complex material development. Over the centuries, the Midwest has supported diverse farming methods and social relations of farm production. Native American farming was largely superseded by European American systems in the nineteenth century, but African Americans and Latin Americans have also been part of the evolving mix of people working the land.

Although cultivated plants appeared in the region as early as 2280 B.C., the Adena culture of Ohio, dating from around 1000 B.C., marked the first known appearance of a cultigen diffused from Mesoamerica. Squash, raised by Adenans, was the first of the later corn-beans-squash triad to spread from its origins in Mexico to dominate all of North American farming before Columbus. By A.D. 1000, the Mississippian culture complex, based on corn cultivation, covered the eastern parts of the future Midwest.

After 1700, westward incursion by both Europeans and Native Americans decimated the elaborate center of Mississippian culture, but its heartland—where the cultural complex seems to have been most elaborate and wealthy—was destroyed before Europeans learned much about it. It is mostly known through archaeological remains. Places like North Dakota did not represent the kind of cultural and material peak in pre-Columbian farming that existed in Ohio and Illinois. North Dakota had a shorter growing season, and the prairie environment was merging into the plains environment. For Native Americans this was a huge difference, because the Great Plains were almost uninhabited until people acquired the horse and began a short-lived and specialized horse and bison adaptation. If we consider the Midwest prairie states as a region, the margins would be the edges of this region.

Native American women raised food crops. Most of the animal protein in the diet was supplied by male hunters. Old men cultivated tobacco, which was used for ceremonies and trade. For Native Americans, farming was a blend of the spiritual and material. Religious rituals having to do with planting, weather, fertility, and harvests were part of the annual cycle. Corn plants had souls that responded to singing and tender care. Indian farming on the more fertile and well-watered lands of the central Midwest may have been collective, but kin-based units of women farmed separately in the regions where they were observed by European Americans.

The most complete account of Native American farming comes from a description recorded in central North Dakota in the early twentieth century. Buffalo Bird Woman, a Hidatsa Indian born about 1839, described her people's cultivations of corn, sunflowers, squash, and beans. Women and men cleared new plots, cutting down small trees and bushes and burning them on successive years. Using wooden digging sticks and hoes made from bison scapulae, women and girls completed the planting, weeding, and harvesting. Young women sang from platforms in the fields in mid-summer to ward off predators. So firmly was gardening associated with women that even when Native American men lost their hunting rights, and hence a major component of the division of labor, women retained their role as cultivators.

European Americans destroyed the food system of Native Americans even as they adopted their cultigens. Bringing iron and steel tools, draft animals, and other domestic livestock, whites appropriated the best land and annihilated the bison and other large mammals that had provided meat, shelter, clothing, and tools for Indians. Although the U.S. government made attempts to train Native American men to farm on marginal lands, very few successfully adapted to farming. When they did, they often abandoned their Indian identity.

When European Americans took over the Midwest, the family farm became the basic unit of production and land came to be individually owned. From the earliest days of settlement, white farmers brought horses and iron tools along with the basic technological, religious, legal, and social elements of European culture. Later farm purchases included steel plows, lumber, nails, cloth, stoves, and furniture. To market grain and livestock, farmers relied on a government-supported transportation system. Thus midwestern farming both undergirded and rested on a far-flung fabric of cultural and economic exchange. Within the larger system, the family farm was a subunit that produced and consumed, hired workers, provided workers for other farm and nonfarm labor, and reproduced itself both on a daily basis and intergenerationally. Although the canonical core of the family farm was the nuclear family, the household was often augmented by other kin and nonkin members. Occasionally a family farm functioned without an intact nuclear family.

The typical farm of the central Midwest in 1920 was a diversified grain and livestock operation. Corn was the most important crop, usually for feed, and it was marketed primarily in the form of hogs and secondarily as cattle or grain. The farm also had fields of wheat and other grains and substantial pastures. Besides the livestock that was marketed in the urban packing yards, the farm kept horses and possibly other draft animals. Dairy cows, poultry, eggs, a garden, and an orchard fed the household and provided another source of income. On the margins of the Midwest or near urban markets for perishable commodities, this pattern gave way to variations. Farmers of Wisconsin and Minnesota specialized in dairy production. Western farms, where rainfall and soil fertility declined, blended into the cattle and sheep production on the Plains. Sugar beets and diverse fruit and vegetable specialties emerged in suitable subclimates throughout the region.

Having appropriated the vast expanse of farmland, European American farmers faced chronic labor shortages. Although there were many exceptions, the usual division of labor assigned the farm man responsibility for field crops and large livestock. The farm woman would often help with fieldwork and barn chores; she was in charge of the poultry and garden as well as housework and childcare. Farm children helped their parents as soon as they were able. Some as young as eight or nine years had long workdays and responsibility for crucial oversight of animals or younger siblings. Many farm youngsters dropped out of school to meet farm labor demands. Live-in hired workers, both male and female, often joined farm households, and day laborers would be added as needed and available. For some production specialties, such as sugar beets, the major part of the labor was hired, Mexican Americans filling out many of the work crews.

In the early twentieth century, the yearly cycle for farm men began in March or April with the birthing of calves and pigs. In April, the ground was prepared; and oats, barley, and spring wheat were seeded. Corn planting started in May. Soon after the corn was in the ground the first crop of hay was cut and stacked. A good farmer interspersed three rounds of corn cultivation in his summer work. In July, grain was harvested and bundled or stacked in preparation for the threshing cycle, in which a ring of farm neighbors shared work and moved from farm to farm. August usually saw another round of haying, especially with alfalfa and clover fields. Winter wheat and rye were sown in September. Beginning in September or October, corn was picked, hauled away, and dried or shelled. Farmers finished the harvested fields with fall plowing to control weeds and prepare for the next year's planting.

Some chores varied by season. The first cold weather meant hog butchering and sausage making together with salting, smoking, and canning pork for the farm household. Snow removal was an ongoing winter challenge. Barns got cleaned and maintained during the winter, and long winter hours were spent repairing and maintaining machinery. Watering and feeding livestock, difficult in frigid weather, was not time-consuming in the summer. Other chores, such as care for sick animals and fence mending, made sporadic demands through heat and cold.

Most farm women managed poultry operations of various kinds, and children did much of the daily labor. Hatching and brooding chicks in the spring required close monitoring, the chicks often being kept in the kitchen close to the stove. By early summer, roosters were ready to be killed, cleaned, and fried; and they frequently made their way to noontime tables of prosperous farmers. As new hens began to lay eggs, older hens were culled, slaughtered, and canned. Supervised by their mothers, farm children gathered and packed eggs. Children often herded and cared for the geese, turkeys, and ducks that were raised yearly for holiday cash and meals.

Farm women had responsibility for the garden, another area for which farm children were recruited. The garden would be tilled and planted in the spring, weeded continuously, and harvested throughout the summer. As garden produce appeared, it had to be immediately cleaned and processed for the table or preservation. Gardening was finished in September.

In doing housework, women were daily reproducing the farm workforce. In 1920, few farmhouses had indoor water supplies, and many buckets of water were needed for laundry, cooking, washing, and cleaning. Although not all women were equally fastidious, all had to struggle to keep the dirt and mud connected with farm work from taking over the interior of the house. Women made bread and other baked goods for the farm table. This table was expanded for hired workers and other helpers, particularly during the July and August threshing season, when crews devoured vast quantities of meat, potatoes, and pie. Women took bushel baskets of sandwiches and cake to field crews for mid-morning and mid-afternoon breaks.

Farm children contributed to virtually every aspect of farm production but they were not without cost. Farm women gave birth to more children than did city women, and they managed the labor-intensive care of these children in their early years. This work was not seasonal, and it circumscribed all other activities.

While men marketed field crops and large livestock, made mortgage payments, paid taxes and major bills, farm women used the income from sales of eggs, butter, cream, poultry, and garden produce to maintain their households and to buy clothing, shoes, school supplies, and other ongoing family necessities.

In general, men worked to maintain and enhance the farm, and women worked to maintain and enhance the farm household. Ultimately these interests coincided, but the daily focus was gendered.

Midwestern farms became increasingly mechanized and less labor intensive. Wars, with their manpower and production demands and population displacement, have been key engines of change. Tractors replaced horses in the wake of World War I. Other mechanization, herbicides, pesticides, and fertilizers were by-products of the heavy equipment and chemical technologies developed during World War II. When these industries were converted to peacetime production, some agricultural labor shifted from farm to factory settings. Factories and other industrial venues took over other food production, further displacing farm-based labor. Since the 1960s, the midwestern farm has specialized in corn and soybean production, with livestock relegated to a smaller number of farm and nonfarm operations. The majority of the 1920s farm population has been pushed and pulled to towns and cities.

By far the majority of midwestern farmers who succeeded the Native Americans on the land were European Americans, but African American farmers also appeared from the mid-nineteenth century onward. The eastern midwestern states that made up the Old Northwest became the home of small numbers of rural enclaves of free African Americans. With diversified family farms, the operations of these black farmers were in many ways similar to those of their white neighbors. However, African American farms tended to be small and inadequately capitalized. Facing ostracism and discrimination from whites, many rural blacks had migrated to cities even before 1900. In the twentieth century, the subsistence component of farming diminished; and greater emphasis on commercial farming made dealings with bankers, livestock dealers, grain merchants, and railroads more critical, placing black farmers at a further disadvantage. Even Missouri, which had the largest post–Civil War African American farming population, saw earlier and more rapid rural-to-urban migration among its rural blacks than its rural whites.

Family farms have predominated in the Midwest since white settlement, but a number of communal farmers have come and mostly gone, Catholic monasteries, Hutterites, Shakers, and the Amana Colonies among them. A few, such as the Amana Colonies, were economically successful and absorbed into the private household–based economic system of the majority culture. Hutterites persist in the Dakotas with thriving and competitive communal enterprises. Secular communes that appeared in the context of 1960s counterculture have almost entirely disappeared.

Sources and Further Reading: William Carter, *Middle West Country* (1975); David Danbom, *Born in the Country* (1995); Deborah Fink, *Open Country, Iowa* (1986); R. Douglas Hurt, *American Agriculture: A Brief History* (1994); R. Douglas Hurt, *Indian Agriculture in America* (1987); Mary Neth, *Preserving the Family Farm* (1995); Stephen A. Vincent, *Southern Seed, Northern Soil* (1999); Gilbert L. Wilson, *Buffalo Bird Woman's Garden* (1987).

Deborah Fink
Ames, Iowa

Field

Corn

Growing corn has been the most common labor of midwestern farmers. Indigenous to the Americas, and the most valuable and extensively grown crop in the United States, corn was particularly significant in the nineteenth century Corn Belt stretching from central Ohio westward through Iowa. Here were the fertile soils, level land, and regular rainfall throughout the growing season that corn needed to thrive.

Corn, a symbol of the Midwest. Library of Congress Prints and Photographs Division, Lloyd Harrison, Harrison-Landauer Inc. Baltimore, LC-USZC4-10124.

The defining characteristics of midwestern corn production have been its adaptability across time, variety in practices, and employment of all family members. Until the mid-twentieth century, farms characteristically grew corn for home consumption in gardens usually tended by women. As a field crop, corn was rotated with oats, wheat, and hay. It could be sold or fed to hogs or cattle. This versatility made corn attractive to midwestern farmers, who increasingly had to hedge against market risks. By the last third of the nineteenth century, corn was the leading crop grown by midwestern farmers of all ethnic backgrounds.

These farmers planted corn in checkerboard rows just inches apart, organizing their fields differently than American Indians, who had characteristically mixed beans, squash, and pumpkins among their maize plants. The introduction in the 1860s of two-row mechanical planters facilitated this regularity. Straddle-row riding cultivators, drawn by two horses, suppressed weeds, replacing the hand-hoeing New England practice often done by children.

Midwestern farmers harvested corn in several ways. Early settlers sometimes let their stock graze in unharvested fields. Especially in dairying regions, green stalks could be cut and chopped for silage. Alternatively, mature stalks might be cut and bound together for drying in shocks. After finishing more pressing fall harvest responsibilities, the farm family could then return to the field and husk the ears. On another farm, the farmer might cut and toss ears into a wagon with a bangboard side, driven by a preadolescent who unloaded the corn into a crib. Community members could strip these ears during an autumn evening "husking frolic." Other farmers preferred to husk corn directly from the stalk in the field. Good harvesters could fill one hundred bushels per day. If necessary, ears could be left on the stalk even over the winter and harvested in the early spring.

Mechanized cutters, which appeared on some midwestern farms during the interwar years, completely transformed the labor of producing corn after 1945. Behemoth combines cut, husked, and shelled. Farmers increasingly specialized in growing corn for sale. The Corn Belt expanded north into Minnesota and Wisconsin, and cattle raising became relatively less important. Farmers could plant narrower rows in fields dependent on herbicides and fertilizers and need no longer practice careful cultivation and crop rotation.

By their various labors, midwestern farmers helped make corn one of the four most important food plants in the world by the beginning of the twentieth century.

Sources and Further Reading: Allan G. Bogue, *From Prairie to Corn Belt* (1963); John C. Hudson, *Making the Corn Belt*

(1994); Mary Neth, *Preserving the Family Farm* (1995); Susan Sessions Rugh, *Our Common Country* (2001).

Robert J. Gough
University of Wisconsin–Eau Claire

Horses and Mules

For most of American history, draft animals provided the primary source of power on American farms. In 1920, there were nearly twenty million horses and colts on American farms and over 5.4 million mules and mule colts. Large draft horses predominated on midwestern farms because of the power needed to pull plows through heavy soils. Some farmers employed mules, but most relied on draft horses.

Horses and mules played a central role in farm life and dictated a certain rhythm. The feeding and care of draft animals demanded significant time and energy from farm families. Horses and mules had to be brushed, harnessed, and hitched before setting out for the field. They required food, water, and rest during the workday. At the end of the day, the animals required care, as well. Horses and mules ate whether they worked or not, and farmers set aside land for growing feed crops for their draft animals. The animals also had to be trained to pull wagons and implements. Farmers gradually shifted to tractors since they were generally found to be more efficient and convenient than draft animals.

Large concentrations of draft horses and mules exist in Amish communities, many of which are in the Midwest, such as Holmes County, Ohio. Breed associations preserve and promote Belgians, Clydesdales, and other breeds. A small number of farmers employ draft horses and mules on their farms today, and publications such as the *Small Farmer's Journal* present an alternative to highly mechanized agricultural production methods.

Sources and Further Reading: Harold B. Barclay, *The Role of the Horse in Man's Culture* (1980); R. Douglas Hurt, *American Agriculture: A Brief History* (1994).

George B. Ellenberg
University of West Florida

Hemp and Tobacco

The use of tobacco and hemp as agricultural commodities can be traced to Native Americans. Southwestern Indians may have been cultivating the tobacco plant *Nicotiana attenuata* by A.D. 630. By the time of Euro-

pean colonization, Indians in North America and the Caribbean cultivated numerous varieties of tobacco. European colonists continued this cultivation and brought tobacco and hemp production to Virginia and Maryland. By the nineteenth century, both crops were found in southern, New England, and Mid-Atlantic states. Population expansion brought tobacco and hemp to midwestern states by the mid-nineteenth century. Warehoused in St. Louis, much of Missouri's tobacco was used in cigar manufacturing. With the popularity of cigarettes and new varieties of tobacco after the Civil War, cultivation continued across the upper South and into Missouri and other midwestern states.

In the United States hemp was grown for fiber and seed. The fiber became rope, and the seed was set aside for the next season. Hemp plants were harvested, dried, and rotted by water or dew to remove the fiber from the stalks. The fiber was manufactured into rope or cloth.

Hemp became a secondary crop in cotton states and a primary crop in Kentucky and Missouri during the era before the Civil War. Dependent on mostly hand labor to cultivate hemp and tobacco, planters rotated their production so that they could benefit from the harvest of corn, hemp, tobacco, and wheat, along with livestock, for commercial sale.

Sources and Further Reading: R. Douglas Hurt, *Agriculture and Slavery in Missouri's Little Dixie* (1992); R. Douglas Hurt, *American Agriculture: A Brief History* (1994); Ann I. Ottesen, "A Reconstruction of the Activities and Outbuildings at Farmington, an Early Nineteenth Century Hemp Farm," *Filson Club History Quarterly* 59 (October 1985).

Stephanie Carpenter
Murray State University, Kentucky

Tractors

Few symbols represent the modern farm more powerfully than the tractor. One of the most revolutionary changes to occur on midwestern farms was the shift from draft animals to tractors. As one component of the larger shift toward technology, including both machinery and such scientific developments as improved seeds and commercial fertilizers, tractors were central to the transformation of farming and farm life during the twentieth century.

Beginning around World War I, the increased use of tractors altered farm life in numerous ways. In comparison with draft animals, power farming increased the efficiency of tasks such as plowing and cultivation. In 1940, a corn farmer driving a two-horse team could plow eight to ten acres daily; a tractor with a four-row

Anders Hultstrand's rig and crew, Fairdale, North Dakota, 1910. Fred Hultstrand History in Pictures Collection, NDIRS-NDSU, Fargo, 2028.143.

cultivator could cover sixty to sixty-five acres in the same time. The machines also provided convenience in the form of a mobile power source for pumping water, grinding grain, or cutting wood. Tractors required less daily care than draft animals, could work in hot weather without rest, and did not require fuel when idle. In addition, farmers could reallocate a significant amount of land away from feed crops. Improved tractors with electric lights, power lifts, pneumatic tires, and power take-offs played an ever increasing role in the daily operation of farms. Another important impact of increased mechanization was that agricultural laborers left the land to seek employment elsewhere. Tractors helped bring about farm consolidation so that ever larger equipment could be used efficiently, but they also made farms more dependent on off-farm fuel and spare parts.

Sources and Further Reading: David B. Danbom, *The Resisted Revolution: Urban America and the Industrialization of Agriculture, 1900–1930* (1979); R. Douglas Hurt, *American Agriculture: A Brief History* (1994); Robert C. Williams, *Fordson, Farmall, and Poppin' Johnny* (1987).

George B. Ellenberg
University of West Florida

Wheat and Other Grains

Early farmers who came to the windswept prairies of the Midwest found a semiarid land of extremes that had to be forced to yield its bounty. Besides the natu-

ral hazards of heat, cold, wind, rain, tornadoes, floods, fires, and grasshoppers, the farm family had to deal with the vicissitudes of a grain market over which they had no control.

Wheat was grown in the early nineteenth century in the well-watered flatlands of northern Ohio, Indiana, Illinois, and southern Michigan. By the 1870s and 1880s, two distinct wheat regions were emerging further west. A Winter Wheat Belt stretched from western Missouri across Kansas and into southern Nebraska, and a Spring Wheat Belt reached from southwestern Minnesota into the Dakotas and Manitoba.

Land west of the Missouri River is made up of the Missouri plateau, the drift plains in the north and East (of the Missouri) River region in the south, and the valley of the Red River of the North. The drift plains are semiarid, but the east-river region has soil similar to its eastern neighbors. All of these regions were originally devoted almost entirely to wheat, with small amounts of barley, oats, flax, rye, and corn. They now yield those crops as well as durum and spring wheat, sunflowers, canola, sorghum, cranby, pinto, navy and other edible dry beans, lentils, field peas, and potatoes. The Red River Valley has some of the richest soil in the world, where farmers raise sugar beets and soybeans, as well as spring wheat, dry beans, corn, and potatoes.

Within a hundred miles west of the Red River in what is now North Dakota, bonanza wheat farms sprang up in the late 1800s on land bought from the bankrupt Northern Pacific Railroad. Many farms consisted of more than twenty thousand acres. One farm had four hundred horses and mules, one hundred broadcast seeders, fifty harrows, one hundred fifteen self-binding harvesters, and four hundred men employed to use them.

Most farming, however, was done by individual farmers on a few hundred acres of land. The routine began in the spring with the plowing and seeding. During the summer, fallow fields were harrowed to provide natural fertilization for next year's crop and haying for the livestock. In the fall, crops were cut and threshed with steam machines and horses. The grain was hauled to the nearest elevator where it was graded for its milling quality, then weighed and docked for impurities, dirt, and other seed. Lower grading and/or reduced weight meant less money for the farmer. Disagreements were frequent between farmers and elevator operators. Farmers blamed the railroads, which charged exorbitant rates to take grain to market because they rarely had competition.

Farmers have attempted to market their grain cooperatively at both the local elevator and through grain terminals in the Twin Cities. The most successful protest movement was the Non-Partisan League in the early 1900s, which attempted to control the marketplace and the railroads by passing laws in each state. But farmers were never able to pass federal legislation that would control corporations beyond state lines because of the diversity of grains and the different needs of those who farm them. Despite increasing government involvement in the process since World War II, grain farming continues to be dependent on decisions made far from farms.

Sources and Further Reading: David B. Danbom, *Born in the Country* (1995); Hiram M. Drache, *The Day of the Bonanza* (1964); Robert L. Morlan, *Political Prairie Fire* (1985).

Kathleen Moum
Bottineau, North Dakota

Yard

Dairying

The development of dairying has shaped the economy and identity of the Midwest since the early settlement of the region. From the early nineteenth through the mid-twentieth century, a large portion of the midwestern population participated in dairy farming. Every farm family member worked, regardless of gender or age. Work on a dairy farm has changed considerably over the years as growing demand for dairy products—milk, butter, and cheese—has led farmers to seek new tools and techniques of production. Dairying continues to be an important source of income and identity, especially in Wisconsin, Minnesota, and the northern parts of Iowa, Illinois, and Ohio.

In the early 1800s, midwestern farm men focused primarily on crop production, leaving the dairy work to women and children. Most farms had fewer than ten cows and used the milk to provide milk, butter, and cheese for the family and to sell for a small income. Even with small herds, milking and caring for cows required a lot of labor. Little mechanization occurred because men did not see a need to improve the efficiency or ease the labor demands. Milking was done by hand, and when commercialization started in the 1850s, women incurred added work in having to clean milk cans used for shipping milk to processing or cheese plants.

Little changed in dairying until the 1870s, when refrigerated railroad cars allowed midwestern farmers to market their products to urban areas in the East. To get more milk from their cows, dairy farmers turned to corn and artificial insemination (AI). Corn provided more nutritional value than wheat, while AI allowed farmers to manipulate cows not only for genetic traits favorable to milk production, but to make dairying a year-round occupation. Both of these changes increased the workload for farm women and children. Feeding cows corn, rather than pasturing them on hay or wheat, required extra work to bring corn from silos to the cows. AI ended the seasonal cycle of breeding and birthing that had given dairy workers time off in the winter months.

Rural electrification in the 1930s and 1940s revolutionized dairy work in the Midwest, driving mechanization and farm growth. Milking machines, invented around 1905, became dependable and popular with a steady source of power. Before World War II, 90 percent of all dairy cows were milked by hand. By 1960, almost all cows were milked by machine, easing the workload for dairy families. With all of these changes, dairy farms quintupled in size from 1950 to 1978.

Many of today's dairy farms still require the labor-intensive effort of farm families. Larger farms however, have mechanized much of the work, from feeding with total mixed-ration machines to milking in automated parlors. Work on large farms is often like factory work. Regardless of farm size, dairying continues to play an important role in the economy, as well as in defining work and life in the Midwest.

Sources and Further Reading: Douglas Harper, *Changing Works: Visions of a Lost Agriculture* (2001); Robert E Jacobson, *Changing Structure of Dairy Farming in the United States: 1940–1979* (1980); Sally McMurry, *Transforming Rural Life: Dairying Families and Agricultural Change, 1820–1885* (1995); Ingolf Vogeler, "Dairying and Dairy Barns in the

Northern Midwest," in Allen G. Noble and Hubert G. H. Wilhelm, *Barns of the Midwest* (1995).

Ryan Stockwell
University of Missouri–Columbia

Chickens and Eggs

Caring for chickens and managing egg production has traditionally been women's work on midwestern farms. Women commonly defined the farm home and adjacent areas, such as the chicken house and gardens, as their special sphere of activity. Under their mothers' direction, older girls and young children of both sexes helped with the chickens.

The process of raising chickens for eggs and meat began either with setting a hen and allowing her to hatch a nest of chicks, or by purchasing chicks, often by mail order. On a daily basis, chickens required food and fresh water, although chickens often scratched in the barnyard during the warmer months. In cold weather, in order to maintain egg production, hens had to be fed more diligently. Eggs were gathered and cleaned on a daily basis and stored for later sale. Feeding and watering chickens, as well as gathering eggs, were often children's chores. Women regularly culled their flocks, keeping the best hens for laying purposes. The culled birds would be killed, plucked, and cleaned either for home use or for sale. Women also inspected their birds for parasites, such as lice, and treated infestations. Cleaning the hen house, one of the least pleasant farm chores, had to be done on a regular basis to

keep the hens healthy. When enough eggs had been accumulated to make a trip to town worthwhile, they would be transported to a general store and exchanged for groceries or credit.

Sources and Further Reading: Deborah Fink, *Open Country, Iowa* (1986); Katherine Jellison, *Entitled to Power* (1993); Pamela Riney-Kehrberg, ed., *Waiting on the Bounty* (1999).

Pamela Riney-Kehrberg
Iowa State University

Gardens and Food Preservation

Visions of what a garden is, or should be, depend on our experiences and expectations. Personally, gardening brings two images to mind. The first is the growing-up me—weeding, watering, and picking. (This was followed by snapping beans, shelling peas, and cleaning corn.) The second image is the look of my grandparents' Illinois farm garden. Peony bushes bordered one side; a strawberry bed filled a corner; and the volume of annual vegetables could have fed half the county. My grandmother, who preferred outside chores to housework, spent a good deal of time in that garden, and her methods combined progressive ideas taken from how-to articles with folk beliefs of uncertain origin. "Plant potatoes on Good Friday"; "Plant seeds during the full moon to get better plants."

Historically, gardens have been essential to family diet. Often, produce sales have also provided an important source of income. Although all family mem-

Chickens in Haskell County, Kansas, 1941. Courtesy National Archives, photo no. RG 83-G, 41934.

bers helped maintain gardens, women and children usually weeded, watered, controlled pests, and harvested. This work was repetitive and tedious. Until the widespread availability and use of insecticides in the mid-1900s, natural substances were only mildly effective, and youngsters often handpicked bugs from plants. Added to these chores was the gathering of wild greens, fruits, and herbs outside the garden plot, as well as seed selection and ground preparation for the next season.

Women and girls were, and are, responsible for preserving garden produce. Working against time at a labor-intensive task, neighbor women often joined together to help one another. They dried some foodstuffs and preserved others in brine. Potatoes, onions, carrots, and parsnips were "put down" in root cellars where they remained edible for months. In the late 1800s, home canning became a viable preservation method for some fruits and vegetables. As technology improved and pressure cookers became common, a larger variety of foods were preserved. After World War II, home freezers offered another option, and many women began to both can and freeze food for out-of-season consumption. Technology altered preservation methods; canning and freezing, for example, diminished the practice of drying fruit.

Technology also changed the traditional mother-to-daughter home instruction. New methods required information provided by the agrarian press, magazines, and promotional literature distributed by the makers of canning jars and household appliances. Comprehensive instruction came from 4-H and home extension/demonstration clubs, which were widespread by the mid-1920s.

During the twentieth century, commercially processed food made gardens less essential—except during times of economic depression or war. Still, the shift from homegrown to store-bought did not spell the end of gardens or homemakers' food preservation efforts. While gardens still dot the landscape and families continue to enjoy the yield, gardening intrinsically evokes the agricultural past of European-American settlers who saw themselves literally and metaphorically carving a garden out of a wilderness. Work in the garden framed rural traditions and values. Whether nostalgically remembered, overlooked as ordinary, or taken for granted, gardens and the work they entail are a microcosm of agriculture—past and present.

Sources and Further Reading: Eleanor Arnold, ed., *Voices of American Homemakers* (1993); Grant Gilmore and Holly Gilmore, *The Homestead Kitchen & Cellar* (1973); Jean Larousse and Bruce E. Brown, eds., *Food Canning Technology* (1997); Patricia M. Tice, *Gardening in America, 1830–1910* (1987).

Marilyn Irvin Holt
Abilene, Kansas

Livestock

Livestock was critical in the development of the Midwest. Cattle and hogs provided meat, and oxen, mules, and horses supplied the power for hauling freight, transporting human beings, plowing, and threshing. Gender division of labor governed livestock on farms. Men managed the feeding and raising of cattle, hogs, and sheep, while women looked after chicken and dairy cattle for family use and sale. Women governed dairy and poultry production—eggs, milk, and cheese —and men supervised animal labor and meat production.

Steam power, railroads, tractors, and other machinery revised the value of livestock. Increasingly, farmers used animals for meat and other marketable products rather than for labor. By the 1870s, Chicago processed more than a million hogs per year, aided by railroad connections to the vast pork hinterland extending across the Corn Belt of Illinois and Iowa. The pork barons drew together the work of grain farmers, stockmen, and butchers, establishing an industrial network for the domination of the meat market. The profit from this mastery of time, work, and space attracted new settlers seeking a piece of the business. Land values rose, necessitating a mixed crop–livestock system that converted open range to cornfields destined for animal rather than human consumption. The feedlot system rationalized meat production and made it more profitable.

Cattle became a cluster of working parts geared toward producing meat and hides that generated dollars. Growing metropolises supplied the demand and lush croplands, the means. Farmers provided the care and labor to make stock ready for market. The highest proceeds lay in butchering beef and shipping it east. Gustavus F. Swift's improved refrigerated railroad car revolutionized profit potential. In the mid-1880s, the major firms of Swift, George Hammond, Nelson Morris, and Philip Armour catapulted beef past pork in the packing industry.

Chicago firms cornered the market with inexpensive beef fed on cheap, western rangeland and corn. Harsh winters, drought, and economic depression in the 1880s and 1890s assaulted the industry and intensified the packer kings' focus on efficiency. In the twentieth century, systematizing the livestock industry meant ignoring the environmental impact of overgrazing, the invasion of exotic plants, soil erosion, the slaughter of predators that might threaten stock, and the industrial pollutants of butchering. It neglected the blood, sweat, and tears of the farmers who raised the stock and of the workers who made the animals into food.

The growing use of electrical power in the twentieth century, particularly after the Great Depression, encouraged mechanization. Farmers had more efficient means to milk cows and increase egg production. Advances in biotechnology after World War II changed the breeding process, provided growth hormones, and offered medicine for ridding livestock of bacteria and disease. As Americans increasingly reinterpreted livestock in terms of meat, animal labor became nearly inconsequential. With the maturing commercialization of chicken, beef, and dairy cattle, domestic animals became more associated with feedlots and agribusiness than with labor on the family farm.

Midwestern livestock management highlights human perceptions of animals and nature. Americans had a disposition for assigning animals—and nature in general—a commercial value. Ultimately, machines replaced animal labor, and Americans assigned livestock greater value as food than as machinery.

Sources and Further Reading: William Cronon, "Annihilating Space: Meat," in *Nature's Metropolis* (1991); David B. Danbom, *Born In the Country* (1995); Margaret Walsh, *The Rise of the Midwestern Meat Packing Industry* (1982); Richard White, "Animals and Enterprise," in Clyde A. Milner II,

Carol A. O'Connor, and Martha A. Sandweiss, eds., *The Oxford History of the American West* (1994).

Garrit Voggesser
University of Oklahoma

Home

Cooking and Cleaning

The farm wife, assisted by children, performed and supervised cooking and cleaning chores. The farm wife cooked three to five meals per day for her family and hired hands. She was often the first awake to prepare meals for the family and labor, and she had to clean up the kitchen after her day's work. Her work assumed daily, weekly, and seasonal routines.

In the early days of settlement, a farm wife battled dirt floors, used wood to fuel the stove, and made simple meals. As the farm became more established, she adopted an electric or gas stove, made more complicated meals, and purchased more foods instead of canning or producing her own, such as butter, cheese, and poultry. Midwestern women of the nineteenth century used lye as their primary cleaning agent for clothing, floors, and the kitchen, making cleaning hard on a woman's hands. Many also had to haul water from streams or pumps.

Indoor plumbing, electricity, and home appliances, especially washing machines, eased the farm wife's cleaning chores. She spent less time feeding laborers as mechanization replaced hired hands. By the middle

Farm woman at work, Shelby County, Iowa, 1941. Courtesy National Archives, photo no. RG 83-G.

to late twentieth century, women produced less food at home, but many women did more fieldwork. Other women spent much of their time driving to town for an off-farm job, to buy food at the store, and to shuttle children to school. Some women welcomed these changes, even though they altered their position on the farm as well as the value of their labor.

Sources and Further Reading: Katherine Jellison, *Entitled to Power* (1993); Mary Neth, *Preserving the Family Farm* (1995); Glenda Riley, *The Female Frontier* (1988).

Alexandra Kindell
Iowa State University

Indoor Plumbing

The foremost symbol of what constituted a "modern" house, a full range of indoor plumbing—including a flush toilet—was slow to be adopted in rural America, especially in the South and the Midwest. The combination of high cost, a limited water supply, and entrenched habits explains the U.S. Census report that only 20 percent of farms in the Midwest had running water in 1930. The figure rose to 64 percent in 1954, still far below the percentage of electrified farms in the Midwest at that time (95 percent). Before widespread electrification, prosperous farmers used hydraulic rams, gasoline engines, windmills, and other innovative means to bring water to the kitchen sink, but most still trod the well-worn path to the outhouse.

Increased electrification after World War II did not change the sanitary practices of farm men and women. Cultural and practical factors included the habit of conserving water. Using an indoor toilet violated the notions of sanitation of many older farm men, who thought these bodily functions should be performed outdoors.

Although reformers thought indoor plumbing would save the overworked farm woman, university studies showed a more complicated picture. Plumbing saved the work of carrying water into the house and carrying out wastewater, and installing a bathroom removed the stigma of having an outhouse. But cleaning a bathroom was much more work than cleaning an outhouse. Ironically, the time saved by indoor plumbing in the kitchen was often used to clean up the most modern part of the house.

Sources and Further Reading: Jane Adams, *The Transformation of Rural Life* (1994); Katherine Jellison, *Entitled to Power* (1993); Ronald R. Kline, *Consumers in the Country* (2000).

Ronald R. Kline
Cornell University, New York

Laundry

Before the widespread adoption of washing machines, washing clothes was one of women's most time-consuming and arduous tasks. Generally, clothes were first boiled in a kettle over a fire, then scrubbed on a clothes board using lye soap, then rinsed, rung out, and hung to dry.

Farm women organized these basic steps in a number of different ways. Poorer women often washed clothes in a spring or stream. Often, they would carry an iron kettle to the water source in which to boil the clothes. Many farm houses had a well with a bucket or pump in the house yard, and some women built fires and washed in kettles and washtubs near the well. More prosperous families built wash houses with a pump, stove, and washtubs or a washing machine.

Most women scrubbed dirt from the clothes on a washboard. Even work-hardened hands were left torn and bleeding by the combination of prolonged immersion in water, harsh lye soaps, and abrasion from rough clothing and the washboard's corrugated surface. Wringing the heavy jeans, sheets, and other clothes was a challenging task, made easier by the mechanical clothes wringer, invented in 1861. Women who could afford it hired a girl to do the laundry. Sometimes men assisted by carrying water.

After World War II, farm families installed running water and purchased electric washing machines. The automatic washers that became widely available in the 1950s often overtaxed cisterns and wells, but town laundromats were a welcome alternative to the arduous chore of the weekly laundry. Customs regarding laundry varied considerably. Some women adhered to a regular weekly schedule, washing on Monday and ironing on Tuesday. Many women believed that frequent washing shortened the fabric's life and rarely, if ever, washed men's work clothes. Nevertheless, laundry remained a strenuous job.

Sources and Further Reading: Jane Adams, *The Transformation of Rural Life* (1994); Katherine Jellison, *Entitled to Power* (1993); Edith Bradley Rendleman, *All Anybody Ever Wanted of Me Was to Work*, ed. Jane Adams (1996).

Jane Adams
Southern Illinois University–Carbondale

Rural Electrification

One of the most successful programs of the New Deal, rural electrification made a major difference in how farm people, especially in the Midwest, worked and lived in the second half of the twentieth century.

❖ **Clotheslines**

Life is a tapestry of lines and patterns woven into a journey. On a map, lines are routes traced by the feet of past explorers. On a face, they are a lifetime of human experiences.

Clotheslines are a part of the midwestern story. They remain much as they have always been, a part of the landscape of rural America. Prairie women harnessed the winds of the Great Plains, which blew relentlessly across the vast spaces that must have seemed like an ocean separating them from the distant worlds they had left behind. Each Monday, wash-day, sheets were transformed into sails, and the landscape was awash with white ships anchored in the backyards of rural farm-houses. A woman's domain was the home, and taking care of it filled most of her waking hours. At the turn of the century, there were still relatively few labor-saving devices in the American home. Women cooked three meals a day, scrubbed the floor, raised the children, did the ironing, and hung out the laundry.

Around the time of my mother's birth in 1919, the exhausting task of standing over a washboard and washtub was being replaced by power-driven washing machines. On farms, gasoline or kerosene engines regularly used for pumping were bor-rowed by the women on wash days. The time spent washing six wash tubs full of clothes, an average wash load for a family of nine or ten people, was reduced from six hours to four. Eventually, the electric storage battery or a direct electric cur-rent from a public service line running through the rural countryside enabled farm women to run the washing machine with an electric motor. Power washing, as it was called, was thought to be such an improvement over handwashing that it might single-handedly banish the chronic fatigue of the housewife, thus leaving her with surplus energy for the piles of ironing that followed.

Although washing clothes by hand would be tiresome and tedious today, there is a quietude and peace connected with the solitary exercise of hanging up the week's laundry. It is an outdoor task, done ideally on a day when there is sun and wind moving through and around the clothes and the woman, warming them both as she stretches and bends between laundry basket and clothesline. As each item of bedding or clothing comes out of the basket, it is given a firm shake before being pinned onto the line. Patterns begin to form, and colors fall between white spaces like a quilt being pieced together. Each washday a new and unique pattern is created and taken apart in the time it takes for the clothes to dry.

Like a quilt, what hangs on the line is, literally, the fabric of our lives. Like the telephone line and rail line, the clothes-line connects us to another time that stretches between our youth and our present age. It is a place where we played in our childhood and stood next to our mothers and sisters. It is an exercise in silence. And it is a connection that I feel to all the women who have ever stood at a clothesline and let warm breezes carry their quiet thoughts and dreams up into the fresh and open air, to be carried . . . who knows where?

Cathy Salter
Hartsburg, Missouri

Originally published in the *Boone County (Missouri) Journal* and the *Columbia (Missouri) Tribune*

When private utility companies were slow to electrify the countryside, the Rural Electrification Administra-tion (REA) was established in 1935. The REA granted low-cost government loans to cooperatives, which dis-tributed power to farms. In 1954, the U.S. Census re-ported that 95 percent of farms in the Midwest were electrified.

The first electrical devices purchased by farmers were overwhelmingly lights and some home appli-ances. The barn was also lit, but only dairy farmers ex-tensively electrified their agricultural operations. Mid-westerners bought mostly irons, radios, washing machines, and refrigerators, despite vigorous attempts by REA home economists to persuade them to buy a full complement of household appliances. Most farm men and women thought electric ranges too expensive and vacuum cleaners foolish luxuries.

Modernizers predicted that electrical appliances would lighten the workload of the farm woman. In-stead, the time spent on housework remained constant at about fifty-four hours per week from the 1920s to the 1960s. Despite the availability of such electrical appliances as the washing machine, women used the time saved to do different types of work such as iron-ing more items. Other women used the time saved to do paid work off the farm. Electricity modernized the house, but the farm family retained many of the pat-terns of rural life.

Sources and Further Reading: D. Clayton Brown, *Electricity for Rural America* (1980); Katherine Jellison, *Entitled to Power* (1993); Ronald R. Kline, *Consumers in the Country* (2000).

Ronald Kline
Cornell University, New York

Sewing

Into the twentieth century, sewing was considered a basic "womanly art"—whether family clothing, house-hold sewing, or fine needlework. Women contributed

❖ **The Geography of America's Most Ubiquitous Dessert**

What is *salad* at a church potluck supper?

What brand name is recognized by 99 percent of the American public and used regularly by 72 percent of American homes?

What product, invented by a young carpenter from rural western New York, made its rather wobbly appearance on the American scene a hundred years ago, was a million-dollar business a decade later, and became the nation's most ubiquitous dessert in the 20th century? Molded, it is synonymous with *salad*. Add whipped cream and it becomes *dessert*. Either way, it is known as Jell-O.

This favorite is ubiquitous in the Midwest. Anyone interested in studying the social impact of this product on American life might be fascinated to learn that its appearance in the Dakotas relates to status and electricity. Poet Kathleen Norris of South Dakota, for example, finds it difficult to talk about Dakota without mentioning Jell-O. In her book, *Dakota: A Spiritual Geography* (1993), she gives the following explanation:

To understand the real meaning of Jell-O in Dakota, one has to think in terms of status. Status and electricity. It wasn't until the advent of electric refrigeration that Jell-O became a staple of the potluck supper or the women's club luncheon, and that meant town women could serve Jell-O long before country women. Jell-O remained elusive for the most remote rural women until well into the 1950s.

Norris' perspective on Jell-O as a marker of status and the reach of electrification into rural Dakota has personal meaning for me. My mother did not discover the magic of Jell-O until she herself was faced with cooking for four little girls and my father. Jell-O was the answer. Quick and simple. Plain or mixed with a can of fruit cocktail. Prepared in fancy mold rings or clear Pyrex custard cups. Unadorned or with sliced bananas and a dollop of peanut butter or mayonnaise. Served as a salad on iceberg lettuce, or as a dessert with a topping of Cool Whip or homemade whipped cream, if time allowed. I now have Mother's old Jell-O recipe book on hand, should a potluck supper pop up on our spring calendar, as it often does.

Cathy Salter
Hartsburg, Missouri

Originally published in the *Boone County (Missouri) Journal* and *the Columbia (Missouri) Tribune*

---

to the family budget by making, rather than buying, clothing and linens; some earned extra money as seamstresses; rural women raffled group-made quilts to support church and school projects; and many found self-expression and creativity through sewing. Traditionally, girls learned from older women, but by the 1920s, homemaker and 4-H clubs, as well as home economics courses in public schools, provided instruction.

Technology greatly influenced the sewing process. The sewing machine, which had its first practical application in the 1840s, was powered by a hand crank and later by a combination crank and foot treadle. In the early 1900s, electric-powered machines appeared, but use among farm women was limited until electricity was widely available. Other innovations included commercially produced patterns for everything from aprons to tailored suits, as well as mass-produced fabrics that made fabric home production (spinning raw materials and weaving them into fabric) an outmoded practice by the late 1800s. By the mid-1900s, artificial fabrics such as rayon were available, and the affordability of ready-made goods increasingly reduced the number of items made at home.

Today, as technology continues to evolve, society no longer expects girls to learn stitching at an early age. Rural women are part of a consumer society. Per-

haps the most dramatic change is in attitude: Sewing is viewed as something women do out of choice rather than necessity.

Sources and Further Reading: Wade Laboissonniere, *Blueprints of Fashion* (1999); Glenna Matthews, *Just a Housewife* (1987); Smithsonian Institution, *Sewing Machines: Historical Trade Literature in Smithsonian Institution Collections* (2001).

Marilyn Irvin Holt
Abilene, Kansas

Off-Farm Labor

One of the fundamental transitions in American agriculture, particularly in the latter half of the twentieth century, has been the steady movement of farmers or their families to off-farm work. The reasons for this change vary with the needs of each family. But there is little doubt that off-farm work represents a modern paradox for many farm families: They work off the farm in order to maintain the possibility of working on the farm.

As farms become fewer, larger, and more dependent on expensive mechanical, chemical, and biological technology, the demands of a farm operation and of a contemporary family wanting to live a comfortable life often are not met by a farm income alone.

This change represents a break from an older American agricultural tradition. Off-farm labor often represented an interim strategy in which people used non-farm wages to purchase the resources necessary for them to start a farm and to derive their living solely from farming. In recent decades, more and more rural people have made off-farm labor a permanent part of their strategy to maintain an agricultural lifestyle. These families do not stop farming when they take off-farm jobs, but instead become dependent on both sources of income.

A 2000 study of farm life found that approximately 60 percent of all farm families in the United States had at least one member working for off-farm wages. This financial source may account for up to 40 percent of total farm income. As early as 1973, perhaps as many as 90 percent of farm families gained some income from off-farm sources. While men and women have long taken off-farm jobs to supplement their income, recent patterns suggest that this income has become more of a necessity. The 2000 study surmises that "Unless family members work at off-farm jobs to supplement the farm's income, there is generally little money to spare for anything but the necessities."

The growing reliance on off-farm labor is especially evident among women. In 1980, a little over one-third of farm women worked off-farm jobs. Much of this work was in clerical or service capacities. Generally, the more a woman could be paid off-farm, the less actual farm work she was likely to perform. These women often began to describe themselves as housewives instead of farmwives.

This changing economic reality almost certainly has a cultural or ideological component, but how farm families categorize themselves and how they express their ambitions and expectations is a bit harder to define. Some scholars find off-farm labor difficult to categorize. A farmer who works off-farm may be "proletarian," yet he or she often maintains many of the economic and cultural attributes of a "single-commodity producer." In a cultural as well as economic sense, is the farm family sacrificing some independence to maintain the illusion of independence? Clearly, many people work off-farm so that they can work on the farm, which suggests something more than an economic attachment to farming.

Sources and Further Reading: John C. Crecink, *Families with Farm Income* (1979); Kathryn Marie Dudley, *Debt and Dispossession* (2000); R. Douglas Hurt, *American Agriculture: A Brief History* (1994); Patrick H. Mooney, "Class Relations and Class Structure in the Midwest," in A. Eugene Havens, ed., *Studies in the Transformation of U.S. Agriculture* (1986).

Robert Faust
University of South Alabama

Variations in Gender Divisions of Labor

Rural midwesterners talk about "men's work" and "women's work" with conviction. The earliest settlers noted that the indigenous people expected men to hunt and women to process, gather, and cultivate. European immigrants and their descendents expected men and boys to work the fields and care for livestock, while women and girls processed foodstuffs and bore children. Class more than culture affected gender divisions, with wealthier women and men freed from the labor, if not the supervision, of their hired or enslaved replacements. Usually labor came from neighboring families, often kin, who exchanged their help for the promise of a return favor at a later date. And the labor invariably followed gender lines. Domestic labor, that is, women's work, provided important resources to sustain the family. Women produced food, clothing, children to replenish the farm labor supply, and eventually income from off-farm jobs. Concomitantly the patriarch or male head of household bore the legal responsibilities for preserving the family as well as the practical demands of keeping the fields tilled and the stock fed. The gender division of labor so permeated farm life that it defined the midwestern rural economy as well as its society.

Gender divisions of labor created dependency among members of the farm family. Women and girls milked the cows and made butter and cheese; they spun wool, flax, and cotton into yarn and wove it into cloth; they maintained gardens and cared for poultry. They prepared meals and cared for children constantly, thus assuming responsibility for family health. And a healthy family generated more labor. Men and boys tended fences, cleared and cultivated the land, cut wood, cared for stock, cleaned the barns, made hay, and harvested crops. While women's work followed daily routines, men's work followed the seasons. Yet women helped men at crucial times, usually with corn planting, cultivating, and harvesting hay and grains.

Family demographics affected the gender division of labor as much as did seasonal demands. Young couples with no families regularly worked together in the fields, and daughters often helped fathers when no other male relatives existed, or the family could not afford hired help. The father, as the legal guardian of the family, controlled production as well as sales. The proceeds generated by the men's and women's work often went back into the farm, increasing the real and personal property of the family and their financial security. Yet women's work had little if any monetary value in this economy when compared to men's work, and that led to the devaluation of women's work in the rural Midwest.

The shift from a subsistence or community economy to a market economy occurred in different places at different times, and it affected the gender division of labor in numerous ways, but not by destroying the gender boundaries. Instead, men and women assumed new responsibilities, but legal authority remained with the male head of household. As agricultural machinery freed farmers from stoop labor and made hired men obsolete, it forced farmers to learn mechanics to keep equipment running. Growing markets increased demands for dairy products and market produce, all traditionally products of women's work. Yet as the demand increased, women's responsibilities tended to be less important to the farm economy, while men assumed more production and marketing tasks. Even mass-produced consumer goods did not reduce the time rural women spent on domestic chores. As opportunities to contribute to the farm economy declined, women focused their energies on poultry production and egg sales to ensure farm solvency.

The increased use of technology on the farm after World War II did not alter the division of labor between men and women; it just created new demands. As egg and poultry income proved increasingly inadequate to meet farm expenses, women began pursuing employment outside the home and off the farm to meet the rising operating costs associated with farming. They taught school, worked as secretaries, or became wage laborers in local factories. Off-farm work no longer seemed a means to earn discretionary income; rather, off-farm work became a necessity to keep farms in operation and meet their families' needs.

Sources and Further Reading: John Mack Faragher, *Sugar Creek: Life on the Illinois Prairie* (1986); Deborah Fink, *Open Country, Iowa* (1986); Katherine Jellison, *Entitled to Power* (1993); Mary Neth, *Preserving the Family Farm* (1995).

Debra A. Reid
Eastern Illinois University

Slavery

Slavery was integral to European and American exploration and colonization of the Midwest. Soon after their introduction around 1720 into the French settlements in the Illinois Country, African (and smaller numbers of Indian) slaves became instrumental in that area's transition from mission centers and fur trading posts to an important grain-producing area. Slave labor was also essential in colonial lead mines (St. Philippe) and salines (Ste. Genevieve). Slaves increased in number from 118 in 1726 to 164 in 1732, and were a quarter to a third of the area's population. In 1752, five years after the French closed the slave trade to the Illinois Country in 1747, the black slave population had increased to 446, and 41 percent of white household heads owned slaves.

Far fewer black slaves were found in the upper Midwest's fur trade, military outposts, and mining communities than in the Illinois Country because French authorities believed that Africans could not survive harsh winters. The French, British, and Canadians instead relied largely on Indian slaves, including war captives acquired from Pawnee tribes of the western plains and, to a lesser extent, slaves obtained through imperial and intertribal conflict.

As the Americans took over the region, Indian slavery declined. Military conquest led to the removal of most Indians to the west. African slavery proved more enduring. The purchase, sale, and hiring of enslaved African Americans has been documented in at least ten of the twelve midwestern states (except the Dakotas), particularly during the territorial era, but in several instances up to 1860.

New slaves were brought into the region by migrating whites as hired workers in states bordering the South and by U.S. Army officers assigned to midwestern military outposts and given a special allowance to purchase or hire slave servants. For military officers, as for Indian agents and territorial elites, enslaved servants were an important indicator of social status.

Slavery therefore continued, as both a *de jure* and *de facto* institution, despite Article Six of the Northwest Ordinance (1787), the Missouri Compromise (1820), several court rulings, and state constitutions that cumulatively but often ineffectively prohibited slavery in every territory and state except Missouri and, for a brief and turbulent period (1854–1861), Kansas. Inhabitants of the original French Illinois settlements and the saline operators at Shawneetown gained protection for their slave property with the interpretation offered by Congress, territorial officials, and local residents that the Northwest Ordinance did not restrict the rights of those slave owners who were living in the Northwest Territory before 1787. With the admission of Ohio (1803) and Indiana (1816) as states with constitutions prohibiting slavery, many slave owners left for southern Illinois, where law and custom protected slave property until the 1848 state constitution finally abolished slavery.

Missouri, which remained a slave state until 1865,

never developed a mature plantation system. Except for a high concentration of slaveholding along the Missouri River, fewer whites owned slaves and they held fewer slaves than in the lower South. Missouri slaves farmed hemp, tobacco, and cotton and worked as artisans and servants, as well as in a host of small industries and the steamboat trade. St. Louis tied the lower South to the upper Midwest through river traffic that included slaves.

Beyond Missouri, support for abolition drew in part on moral arguments, but also on a popular vision of the west as a white republic where the political and economic opportunities of whites were protected by excluding people of African descent as well as any vestige of an elite slave-owning class. Although abolitionists assisted fugitive slaves from south of the Ohio River in their efforts to secure their freedom, slavery persisted, masked by gradual emancipation laws as well as repressive indentures and apprenticeships (legal in Indiana and Illinois, but also practiced extralegally in Iowa, Wisconsin, and Michigan). Restrictions on the migration of free blacks (enacted in Iowa in 1839, Illinois in 1826, and Indiana in 1831) perpetuated the presumption that blacks were slaves, and discriminatory laws restricted African Americans' civil rights and their access to the courts. Some whites migrating out of the slavery-protected areas in Illinois and Indiana brought slaves into Iowa and Wisconsin.

The lax enforcement of antislavery law, the toleration of and even solicitude for visiting slave owners, the inclusion of slave owners among powerful territorial and state officials, and the intense racism of many white settlers placed all midwestern blacks in a very precarious position. The African American population remained quite small, but within that population even free blacks were rarely more than one generation removed from slavery. In 1850, half of Iowa's black population reported a slave state as their birthplace, and another 19 percent had been born in Northern states where slavery persisted. Small communities of free blacks managed to thrive, and a few individuals gained economic security and prestige, but they remained vulnerable to kidnapping and sale, to the threat that their children could be involuntarily apprenticed or seized as slaves, and to their wages being withheld by unscrupulous employers. Black Laws in several states circumscribed their freedom. Although the laws limiting free black migration were unevenly enforced, some blacks diligently registered their free papers and posted the required bonds, hoping to secure a local reputation as a free person and the subsequent protection of local authorities against enslavement.

Several slaves pursued the freedom they believed was constitutionally guaranteed through their permanent or temporary residence in the Midwest. Turning to the courts, some sued for wages, while others sued for their freedom. The most famous of these lawsuits, *Dred Scott v. Sandford* (1857), in which the U.S. Supreme Court ruled that slaveholders could take their property into states that had abolished slavery, was preceded by several successful suits, among them at least three Iowa cases as well as one based on Wisconsin residence.

The Midwest's unreconciled ideas about slavery and freedom were starkly revealed during the Civil War, when thousands of southern slaves claimed their freedom by fleeing to the region or were relocated there by military authorities, civilian relief organizations, or Union soldiers. They were met with vigorous protest and political opposition, and they, as well as the whites who employed them (largely as farm laborers), were threatened and attacked. Some whites tried to curtail the impact of emancipation by proposing new restrictions on black migration.

Black midwesterners, cognizant that a Union victory would secure black freedom in the Midwest as well as in the South, enlisted in black regiments and supported the war effort at home. After the Civil War, black midwesterners were actively involved in efforts to eliminate the vestiges of civil and political inequality in state laws, to gain the male franchise, as well as to challenge segregation in schools and public accommodations.

Sources and Further Reading: Eugene H. Berwanger, *The Frontier Against Slavery* (1967); Carl J. Ekberg, *French Roots in the Illinois Country* (1998); Paul Finkelman, "Evading the Ordinance: The Persistence of Bondage in Indiana and Illinois," *Journal of the Early Republic* 9 (Spring 1989); Lea VanderVelde and Sandhya Subramanian, "Mrs. Dred Scott," *Yale Law Journal* 106 (Dec.–Jan. 1997); Bridgett Williams-Searle, "Resolving the Revolution: Dependency and the Problem of Inequality in Early Indiana, 1795–1835," Ph.D. diss., University of Iowa (2005).

Leslie A. Schwalm
University of Iowa

Wage Work in Midwestern Agriculture

Popular imagination casts the midwestern farm as a self-sufficient family unit, the moral and economic opposite of the southern plantation and the western factory farm. In reality, midwestern farms have always relied on a shifting supply of local workers and long-distance migrants to tend and harvest crops. Wage work has been highly seasonal, contingent on weather and crop conditions, low paying, and largely outside the realm of protective labor legislation. As a result, the region's farm workers have consistently struggled with poverty, inadequate housing, poor health care, irregular education, and political marginalization.

Nineteenth-century farmers hired young men for clearing land and young women for household chores, tasks that were physically demanding and vital to the establishment of rural communities. Often these wage workers were themselves members of struggling farm families. Between the 1880s and 1920s, thousands of migrant harvest hands worked for wages in small grain crops each summer. Most were young men—equally from rural and urban homes—who traveled to the harvest in empty railroad boxcars. Rural communities complained that these workers were a disruptive element, especially when they held out for higher wages. Women also found jobs in the wheat harvest, most often cooking for large harvest crews. Between 1915 and the mid-1920s, harvest hands in the Industrial Workers of the World succeeded in raising wages and improving living conditions for some workers. The wheat harvest migration declined due to farmers' adoption of the combined harvester-thresher, but farmers growing such other crops as sugar beets, fruits, and vegetables continued to rely heavily on migrant labor.

Labor recruiting became more coordinated by the late 1920s as sugar beet processing companies contracted and transported Mexican American families from south Texas to work for beet farmers. Beet worker families subsidized their inadequate income with harvest work in corn, potatoes, and other local crops. Fruit and vegetable growers also drew on the Texas workforce to tend their crops, as well as on the labor of local working-class and poor women and children. Many Texas families returned home during the winter; others settled down and found railroad and factory work, becoming the pioneers of Latino/a communities.

Although they benefited from migrant camps, farm laborers found no place in major New Deal labor and social legislation. Between 1942 and 1964, the federal government's *Bracero* program brought Mexican workers to midwestern farms under contracts with limited rights to protest employer abuses. Smaller numbers of Caribbean workers came to the region through similar programs. By 1970, south Texas migrants once again became the dominant group among farm workers, although former migrants now settled in the Midwest were also a significant part of the labor force. In the 1990s an increasing number of workers came from the agribusiness regions of south Florida. Founded in 1967, the Farm Labor Organizing Committee (FLOC) was recognized as a collective bargaining agent in the mid-1980s. Since then, FLOC has negotiated contracts with corporate growers that eliminate child labor, establish minimum wages, and provide unemployment and workers' compensation insurance, as well as social security payments.

Sources and Further Reading: W. K. Barger and Ernesto M. Reza, *The Farm Labor Movement in the Midwest* (1994); Mary Neth, *Preserving the Family Farm* (1995); David E. Schob, *Hired Hands and Plowboys* (1975); Dennis Nodin Valdés, *Al Norte* (1991).

Tobias Higbie
Newberry Library, Chicago, Illinois

Developing Farms for the Market

The men and women who moved north of the Ohio River in the late eighteenth century sought land for security and independence. Often they squatted on land held by the federal government or speculators who had purchased large tracts of public domain. By the early nineteenth century, farmers increasingly purchased small tracts from the federal government in areas known as Congress Lands or from individual speculators who owned large tracts in the Miami Purchase or Virginia Military District in present-day Ohio. Farm men and women practiced safety-first agriculture, that is, subsistence farming, to provide the essential food needs of their families. Pioneer farmers, however, were never self-sufficient agriculturists because they had to acquire items for daily living, such as shoes, tableware, nails, and other goods, by trading and selling agricultural produce.

Merchants arrived with the earliest settlers and opened shops along the Ohio River. Marietta, Ohio, founded in 1788, became the first major trading center that serviced farmers who settled north of the Ohio River on land acquired from the Ohio Company of Associates. In Cincinnati and other towns, merchants enabled farmers to exchange agricultural commodities for goods that they could not produce on the farm. Merchants thus created a market, and farmers attempted to produce commodities beyond household needs for exchange and sale.

Farmers who settled near the Ohio River in the late eighteenth century and along the Mississippi and Missouri Rivers in the early nineteenth century used these water arteries to reach East Coast and foreign markets. These rivers sped the development of an agricultural market economy and enabled farmers to move beyond subsistence agriculture far more quickly than had they been dependent on land transportation to reach eastern and southern markets for the sale of their produce. During the early nineteenth century, farmers sent but-

Chicago Futures Market, 1970. Series VII.1, photographs, box 7.1/3, file "II. Photographs—Chicago Board of Trade, 1970," USDA History Collection, Special Collections, National Agricultural Library.

ter and cheese, barrels of pork, tobacco, hemp, whiskey, and other products down navigable streams to New Orleans, where merchants purchased them for transshipment to more distant markets.

Farmers who sold surplus produce used the income to improve their operations and increase their standard of living. In all areas of the Midwest except Missouri, family and hired labor enabled farmers to clear trees from forested areas or plow the prairie. In Missouri, particularly after the War of 1812, farmers used slave labor to cultivate tobacco, hemp, and corn and produced these crops in considerable surplus for sale in St. Louis or New Orleans, where merchants, in turn, sent them to other markets. The rich agricultural area along the Missouri River became known as Little Dixie because the early farmers who settled that area primarily emigrated from the South and brought their agricultural practices, including the tobacco and hemp culture and slavery, with them.

Farmers recognized that corn thrived in the hot, humid summer climate and produced the greatest returns for the amount of seed sown. By the early nineteenth century, farmers raised extensive corn crops in the Miami and Scioto River valleys and the Virginia Military District, which they fed to cattle and hogs. The conversion of corn to pork or beef brought farmers the greatest profit. After fattening their livestock on corn, farmers either sold their hogs and cattle to local dealers or hired drovers to trail their livestock overland to eastern markets. Transportation down the Ohio and Mississippi Rivers on flatboats was the cheapest way to send large quantities of packed pork, that is, pork preserved in barrels of salt brine, to market. Packing towns, such as Cincinnati in the early nineteenth century and Chicago in the late nineteenth century, provided large and important markets for farmers who had hogs and cattle to sell. Small packing towns also developed across the Midwest.

By 1840, the Corn Belt was emerging as a clearly recognizable agricultural and geographic region from the Miami Valley to the Mississippi River. A decade later, the Corn Belt had expanded to include the Tipton Till Plain and the Wabash Valley in Indiana, the Sangamon Country, Grand Prairie and Military Tract in Illinois, Little Dixie and the Osage Plain in Missouri, and southeastern Iowa—a distance stretching more than five hundred miles. By 1860, midwestern farmers produced large corn crops that they used to fatten livestock. During the early 1880s, newspaper and magazine writers began using the term "Corn Belt" as a reference for the region.

The sale of corn and livestock contributed the primary source of income to midwestern farm families, and they worked to produce both as efficiently and in the greatest quantity and number as possible to increase their sales and family income. Increasingly, farmers specialized to produce the corn and livestock that brought the greatest earnings at market. Corn also became the most important crop in Michigan, Wisconsin, and Minnesota, where farmers fed it to dairy cattle for the production and sale of butter, cheese, and milk. A century later, farmers in the Corn Belt would lead the nation in the adoption of hybrid corn, created by crossing two or more varieties to create a third variety with special characteristics such as high yield. Hybrid corn further increased production for the market economy.

Women contributed to the household income by raising chickens and selling the eggs to local merchants. They also made butter for local sale and helped their husbands make cheese in quantities beyond household needs. Local merchants either exchanged goods or paid cash for these farm products, which they then shipped down the major rivers to other market towns, including New Orleans. The poultry, dairy, and food processing work of midwestern farm women brought important commercial gain to their farm operations from sale and trade with local merchants.

During the 1870s, farm men and women began to settle the midwestern plains of Kansas and Nebraska, where they acquired land under the Homestead Act of 1862 or purchased acreage from railroad companies, speculators, or the state. Here, the climate proved too dry for corn, but wheat thrived, particularly hard red winter wheat introduced by German Mennonites in the mid-1870s. In Kansas, Nebraska, and the Dakotas, farmers increasingly raised wheat and cattle. St. Paul provided the major market for wheat farmers in the northern Great Plains, while Kansas City became the grain market for the central plains. After completion of the Union Stock Yard in 1865, Chicago served as the major livestock market for the northern Great Plains, while Kansas City, Omaha, Sioux City, and St. Joseph became important livestock markets for cattle and hog producers in Kansas, Nebraska, and South Dakota, as well as Missouri and Iowa. Across the Midwest by the late nineteenth century, then, corn and wheat had become specialty crops, and hogs and cattle the primary emphasis for farmers who produced for the market economy, that is, to make a profit.

Farmers produced for the market as soon as they had sufficient lands improved for production beyond family needs. Markets included local merchants, military posts, emigrants passing through on their way west, southern plantations, cities, famine-plagued Ireland, and British mill towns. They used flatboats and, by the 1820s, steamboats to send agricultural produce down the major rivers. After the opening of the Erie Canal in 1825, farmers in the upper Midwest and the Great Lakes region had greater access to eastern markets, and a host of canals, built in Ohio and Indiana during the early nineteenth century, further expanded their market opportunities. Between 1850 and 1880, railroads revolutionized transportation in the Midwest and gave farmers faster and more convenient access to distant markets. New and improved machinery, such as plows, grain drills, reapers, binders, threshing machines, and steam engines, enabled farmers to plow, plant, and harvest more land with less labor. Production increased, and farmers had greater quantities of grain to sell as livestock feed for pork, beef, or dairy products.

During the twentieth century, midwestern farmers increasingly specialized, rather than practiced diversified production for home use and sale. After World War I, the gasoline-powered tractor became an affordable new implement that further reduced labor needs and helped farmers plow, plant, and harvest with greater speed and efficiency. A special reel that enabled combines to harvest soybeans without shattering the beans from the pods made this crop commercially profitable during the 1920s. Prior to that time, farmers plowed under their soybeans to replenish nitrogen in the soil. With new technology, soybeans could be harvested for markets that processed human and livestock food. High agricultural prices and unlimited production during World War II enabled many farmers to earn sufficient profit to modernize their operations by purchasing tractors, corn pickers, and hybrid seed corn.

By 1945, however, labor-saving technology and the application of new scientific discoveries to agriculture increased expenses and living costs. Midwestern farmers responded to higher costs by adopting more machinery and using more fertilizer to expand production. Large-scale farmers purchased the land of less successful farmers and further expanded their operations to earn greater profits from increased sales volume. Tractors and combines became essential because farmers with large acreage in corn, soybeans, and wheat need work conducted in a timely fashion, particularly during the harvest season. The market economy of the twentieth century mandated an investment in this technology. The days of shared labor and machinery did not let farmers produce extensively within the dictates of the season and earn sufficient profit to remain on the land.

During the mid-twentieth century, midwestern farmers increasingly specialized their operations. Fluid milk production became concentrated in Wisconsin, where it provided the greatest returns for farmers because it brought a higher price from urban consumers in nearby cities than from cheese manufacturers. Michigan farmers also produced more fruit and less corn, while some farmers in Indiana contracted with canners for a guaranteed market and price, and they used mechanical pickers rather than hired workers to harvest their tomato crops.

On the prairies and plains, farmers specialized in grain, corn, and soybean production. Few farmers continued to diversify by raising dairy cows, poultry, and a variety of crops, except for home consumption. Poultry raising soon shifted from outdoor farm production to large-scale, confinement facilities operated by farmers under contract to major feed producers and food processors. As poultry raising became more industrial, it passed from the domain of farm women to male-operated enterprises. During the 1960s, irrigation systems transformed the western Midwest, particularly Kansas and Nebraska, from an area where farmers planted wheat and grain sorghums to a more profitable agriculture based on corn and alfalfa for livestock feed. Surplus production, however, kept earnings low even with federal price supports on many commodities. Many farmers could not afford the investment in land, science, and technology to produce a sufficient surplus to return a profit. During the 1980s many farmers left the land, unable to compete in the market economy. The number of farms declined, therefore, but the size of those that remained increased.

During the last half of the twentieth century, midwestern farmers were increasingly affected by federal price support and production programs, agribusiness, and financial institutions, all of which they needed to participate and succeed in a market economy. At the same time, agriculture became increasingly expensive. Farmers borrowed more from banks and other lending institutions to purchase seed, fertilizer, and equipment to maintain high productivity and profits in the face of falling prices. Price and production programs kept farmers dependent on the federal government, but farmers increasingly left the land for more profitable employment and a higher standard of living elsewhere.

By the early twenty-first century, specialization, high capitalization, and devotion to the market economy characterized midwestern agriculture. Cash grain farming, that is, raising grain crops for sale, dominated agricultural production in the Midwest, while farmers

in the plains used irrigation to produce corn and forage crops, such as sorghum grains, for sale to feedlots, which fattened livestock for sale to nearby meat-packing companies. Food-processing companies and other capital-intensive corporations operated livestock and poultry confinement facilities. Farmers who raised livestock and poultry under contract lost freedom of action in the decision-making process, but they also reduced their financial risk because they received a guaranteed price, and their worry because managers made production decisions for them. Diversified production, which had enabled farmers to spread their financial risk over several crops and forms of livestock production, was rarely practiced.

At the same time, many farmers believed their standard of living would improve if all middlemen were eliminated from the agricultural marketing system, thereby enabling farmers to sell their commodities directly to food processors, grocers, and consumers, while keeping food prices low. Yet despite record productivity, partially due to improvements brought about by new developments in science and technology and good management practices, the old problems remained. Midwestern farmers competed with others across the nation, and surplus production kept prices relatively low. Meat packers often manipulated market prices, particularly regarding the purchase of cattle, while seed and chemical companies merged, thereby reducing competition for products. These mergers caused farmers to fear price increases for seed, herbicides, and pesticides. Midwestern farmers had also learned that a specialized commitment to the market was not an unmitigated good. Surplus production consistently drove down agricultural prices, while dependence on the federal government for price support and either acreage reduction or surplus control programs increased. Operating costs escalated, farm men and women often had great difficulty earning sufficient profits to provide an adequate standard of living for their families, and their children fled the land for better opportunities in the towns and cities. Although most midwestern farmers wanted to remain on their land, the widespread belief that agriculture had become a business rather than a way of life reflected the dominance of the market economy in their lives.

Sources and Further Reading: Jeremy Atack and Fred Bateman, *To Their Own Soil: Agriculture in the Antebellum North* (1987); William Cronon, *Nature's Metropolis: Chicago and the Great West* (1991); Clarence C. Danhof, *Change in Agriculture: The Northern United States, 1820–1870* (1969); Deborah Fitzgerald, *The Business of Breeding: Hybrid Corn in Illinois, 1890–1940* (1990); Mark Friedberger, "The Transformation of the Rural Midwest, 1945–1985," *Old Northwest* 16 (Spring 1992); Paul C. Henlein, *Cattle Kingdom in the Ohio Valley, 1783–1860* (1959); John C. Hudson, *Making the Corn Belt: A*

Geographical History of Middle-Western Agriculture (1994); Mary Neth, *Preserving the Family Farm: Women, Community, and the Foundations of Agribusiness in the Midwest, 1900–1940* (1995); David E. Schob, *Hired Hands and Plow Boys: Farm Labor in the Midwest, 1815–1860* (1975); Margaret Walsh, *The Rise of the Midwestern Meat Packing Industry* (1982).

R. Douglas Hurt
Purdue University, West Lafayette, Indiana

Corn and Livestock Belt

Initially, the southeastern area of the Midwest developed as the focal point for corn and livestock production, but changes in settlement, transportation, and crop genetics have pushed the belt north and west. Crop genetics and mechanization have substantially boosted production throughout the twentieth century, making midwestern farmers major food suppliers to the nation and world.

As settlers migrated through the region, so too did the corn and livestock belt. In 1850, the Corn Belt included one hundred fifty counties, mainly in Ohio, Indiana, and Illinois. By 1880, it consisted of five hundred counties centered in Illinois and Iowa. The draw westward was due in part to the growth of Chicago and the railroads.

In the 1870s and 1880s, farmers began raising Hereford cattle because they grew quickly. The new breed came to dominate the region, pushing out other breeds, such as the longhorn. In the 1920s, farmers started planting soybeans to help fertilize the soil with nitrogen, a nutrient required by corn. Since then, soybeans have gained in popularity for their high yield and multiple uses. Today, around one-third of all midwestern cropland is used for soybean production. The creation of hybrid corn at the beginning of the twentieth century revolutionized farming in the Midwest as new corn varieties not only increased yields, but withstood colder and dryer climates, driving the Corn Belt further north and west into Minnesota and Wisconsin. The new strains aided northern farmers, but provided little help to southern Corn Belt farmers, because the new varieties failed to boost production in hotter and more humid Missouri and southern Illinois. Farmers in these areas eventually turned away from corn and toward wheat or livestock.

To make work easier, farmers adopted tractors and mechanized harvesting. Prevalent by the late 1920s, the mechanical corn picker saved time and human labor, but required considerable capital investment and land to make ownership profitable. With greater production costs and increasing dependency on corn for income, farmers implemented various marketing techniques to get more for their product. Some joined cooperatives to market corn collectively, allowing them to reduce transportation costs. Others built storage facilities so they could hold on to their harvest until the market improved.

Mechanization has led to a cost–price squeeze, pushing out many farmers while increasing the size of surviving farms. From 1889 to 1939, little changed in the average acreage of farms in the corn and livestock belt, but from 1949 to 1982 average acreage nearly doubled, and continues to grow today. This has concentrated production into fewer hands. The sixfold increase in fertilizer use since World War II has created environmental concerns along with corn and soybean surpluses, pushing costs up for farmers while depressing income. Nonetheless, the corn and livestock belt has become a dependable food provider for the world, a fact in which many midwesterners, particularly farmers, take pride.

Sources and Further Reading: Allan G. Bogue, "Changes in Mechanical and Plant Technology: The Corn Belt, 1910–1940," *The Journal of Economic History* 43 (Mar. 1983); John Fraser Hart, "Change in the Corn Belt," *The Geographical Review* 76 (Jan. 1986); John C Hudson, *Making the Corn Belt* (1994); Alan L. Olmstead and Paul Rhode, "The Transformation of Northern Agriculture, 1910–1990," in Stanley Engerman and Robert Gallman, eds., *The Cambridge Economic History of the United States: Volume III, The 20th Century* (2000).

Ryan J. Stockwell
University of Missouri–Columbia

Dairy

Farm families who raised dairy products in the Midwest searched for techniques and markets to meet their families' food needs and to provide income. The first European American settlers grew wheat as a cash crop, but many found that dairying could also be profitable. By 1899, midwestern farmers produced 43 percent of the total value of America's dairy output. At the end of the twentieth century, midwestern dairy production was still significant, but its share of the nation's production had fallen.

Before the Civil War, entrepreneurs in Ohio established cheese factories, contracting with farmers within six or seven miles to provide curd prepared according to the factory manager's instructions. This system guaranteed farmers a return on dairying, but the quality of cheese was uneven and the early factories failed. Similarly, midwestern farm-made butter was inconsistent in quality, which made it difficult to compete with New York and Pennsylvania butter in eastern markets. Fluid milk marketing was also problematic. Farmers competed for urban customers with "swill dairies" located next to distilleries, where cows consumed the by-products of distilling processes. Farm families who lived within four miles of towns and cities transported their milk to market by wagon and returned home within a day. Railroads extended this milkshed as far as thirty miles from major cities, and highways expanded it even farther, making dairying profitable for more farmers.

Farmers used innovations and organization to improve the quantity and quality of their dairy products. Farm journalists promoted "improved" cattle breeds as well as feeding silage and alfalfa to increase milk volume, butterfat content, or both. In 1890, Stephen Babcock of the University of Wisconsin developed a butterfat tester that allowed farmers to assess the quality of their cows and to cull herds accordingly. The centrifugal cream separator allowed farmers to get a higher percentage of cream from their milk, compared to skimming cream from shallow milk pans or cold water separators. Beginning in the 1860s, some dairymen joined associations to promote marketing, while others formed cooperative creameries to cut out the middlemen. Wisconsin dairymen successfully lobbied for regulations limiting the marketing of oleomargarine, a dairy substitute, although consumers liked the lower price of oleomargarine and still continue to purchase large quantities of dairy substitutes.

After World War II, the number of dairy producers declined while total production increased. New sanitary regulations made it more difficult for farm families who kept a few cows to produce grade A milk. Refrigeration and transportation technology meant that local markets gave way to regional markets. Many farmers sold their small dairy herds, while others specialized in dairying with larger, more capital-intensive operations. In 1967, the National Farmers' Organization promoted withholding milk from processors to publicize low prices, dumping milk in many places in the Midwest and across the nation. However, farmers failed to stop the concentration and vertical integration within the dairy and food industry that continues today.

Sources and Further Reading: Robert Leslie Jones, *History of Agriculture in Ohio to 1880* (1983); Steven J. Keillor, *Cooperative Commonwealth* (2000); Eric E. Lampard, *The Rise of the Dairy Industry in Wisconsin* (1963); Mary Neth, *Preserving the Family Farm* (1995); U.S. Bureau of the Census, *Twelfth Census, Agriculture*, vol. 5, part 1: "Farms, Livestock, and Animal Products" (1902).

J. L. Anderson
Iowa State University

Fruits, Vegetables, and Specialty Crops

Though not noted for fruits and vegetables, the Midwest has a proud tradition of horticulture and gardening. Centuries before European American settlement, indigenous inhabitants cultivated a wide variety of berries, fruit trees, and vegetable crops, especially plums, sweet corn, and squash. European immigrants introduced new crops, but the harsh climate characteristic of the Midwest limited their options. Nonetheless, fruits and vegetables were present on almost every farm in the region, grown primarily for home consumption and local markets. Well into the 1950s, they made up a critical part of the region's diversified farm economy.

Specific climatic and soil conditions limited the commercial application of fruit growing to specific locations, particularly to western Michigan and, to a lesser extent, Door County, Wisconsin. A microclimate along the shore of Lake Michigan and its proximity to Chicago provided favorable conditions that persist to this day. Michigan and Wisconsin accounted for 39 percent of all cherries grown in the United States in 1992, and 99 percent of the cherries grown in the Midwest. In 1992, every state in the Midwest produced apples. That year, 1.27 billion pounds of apples, almost a quarter of the nation's output, were grown in the Midwest. Michigan led the way with 77 percent of the regional production, at nearly a billion pounds. In earlier periods, before the advent of refrigerated railroad cars, Wisconsin and Michigan exported fruit crops profitably to all parts of the Midwest and beyond. Migrant labor was long used to harvest commercial fruit crops.

Beginning with the first European American settlers, vegetables were grown on virtually every farm in the region, primarily under the supervision of farm women. Vegetables not consumed on the farm were sold to local markets. Canning companies emerged in many towns and cities, providing ready cash income for farm families and summer employment for city dwellers well into the twentieth century. In 1992, U.S. farmers planted 3,782,358 acres of vegetables and melons, and the Midwest accounted for 25 percent of that total. Wisconsin led the way among midwestern states, followed by Minnesota and Michigan. These three states combined for 77 percent of the region's total.

The emergence of the Minnesota Valley Canning Company, better known as Green Giant, helped make Minnesota and Wisconsin centers of commercial vegetable farming. Initially, Green Giant canned only sweet corn and peas until it added asparagus in 1939 and green beans in 1958. Canning labor employed many midwestern women and children in seasonal jobs at low wages.

Vegetable and fruit farming were encouraged in each midwestern state by land-grant colleges and state horticultural societies. These institutions helped develop varieties of crops and fruits that might survive the winter, grow in shorter seasons, and survive a wide range of pests. Farm families helped themselves on the marketing front by developing cooperatives. Presently, changing dietary patterns in the region are causing more locally grown seasonal produce to be featured in mainstream and organic grocery stores, which, it is hoped, will encourage the region's farmers to experiment once again with diversified agriculture.

Sources and Further Reading: Margaret Beattie Bogue, "The Lake and the Fruit: The Making of Three Farm Types," *Agricultural History* 59 (Oct. 1985); Robert Leslie Jones, *History of Agriculture in Ohio to 1880* (1983); Mary Neth, *Preserving the Family Farm* (1995); William Silag and Rosanne Sizer, "Fruits in Iowa: A Brief History," *The Palimpsest* 62 (1981).

Jeffrey Kolnick
Southwest Minnesota State University

Industrial Agriculture: Pig Prison or Hog Hotel

The industrialization of midwestern agriculture is marked by a system of food production dependent on fossil fuel inputs such as fertilizers and pesticides. It is also characterized by the replacement of family farms with large-scale, capital-intensive production operations and the increasing separation of ownership, management, and labor. Since the 1970s, the rapid industrialization of hog production has dramatically altered the rural social, economic, and cultural landscape in the Midwest.

Midwestern Corn Belt states traditionally provided a natural home for hog production. Considered the mortgage lifters, hogs were part of locally owned, diversified operations in which farmers fed their corn to hogs to add value. In 1965, over a million hog farmers dotted the nation's rural landscape, with most hogs produced outdoors on pasture or open lots. By 2000, less than one hundred thousand hog farms remained, as confined animal feeding operations (CAFOs) took hold.

The shift from pasture-based and open lot production to total animal confinement began in the early 1970s. The ability to control the production environment provided a partial solution to frigid winters that impede animal growth rates and time to market. However, attendant changes in size, ownership structure, markets, and technology engendered deep cultural and social rifts within rural communities faced with hosting CAFOs.

The movement indoors meant a shift from solid manure in outdoor systems to the production of large volumes of liquid manure. The increasing volume of pigs in CAFOs created regional nutrient imbalances between the need to import grain from other areas and the need to find sufficient local land to spread liquid manure. Solid manure was a highly valued fertilizer on diversified farm operations, but liquid manure is a waste by-product. Both farm and nonfarm neighbors of CAFOs frequently expressed their outrage at being

Hog hotel, Waterloo, Iowa. Library of Congress, Prints and Photographs Division, Historical American Engineering Record, HAER, IOWA, 7-WATLO, 4Q.

subjected to the odors and gasses emitted from large volumes of liquid manure. This triggered widespread animosity in rural communities, challenging traditions of neighborliness, reciprocity, trust, and honesty.

Although most hogs continue to be raised in Corn Belt states, a growing number are now raised in concentrated areas of the Atlantic Coast, southern, and western regions. Operations in these areas typify the overarching trend of replacing local with absentee ownership. Contract production, where farmers typically raise hogs for a company, now accounts for the vast majority of pork production. This creates further challenges for rural communities since local social mechanisms traditionally used to ensure responsiveness to community needs are often replaced by absentee owners whose interests and actions are less subject to community wishes. As a result, local rural cultural beliefs embedded in personal relationships are disrupted and displaced. Absentee investors in hog CAFOs are seen by local residents as less receptive to community needs and more responsive to outside financial and legal interests.

When CAFO problems such as odor emerge, community members feel betrayed. This sense of betrayal can lead to disillusionment with notions of democracy and fair play, resulting in apathy toward political participation. However, it also fuels confrontation led by a reinvigorated rural pioneering spirit to maintain communities and traditions.

Sources and Further Reading: Iowa State University and The University of Iowa Study Group, *Iowa Concentrated Animal Feeding Operations Air Quality Study* (2002); Carolyn Johnsen, *Raising a Stink* (2003); Kendall Thu, ed., *Understanding the Impacts of Large-Scale Swine Production* (1996); Kendall Thu and E. Paul Durrenberger, eds., *Pigs, Profits, and Rural Communities* (1998).

Kendall Thu
Northern Illinois University

Poultry and Eggs

The marketing of poultry and eggs has evolved significantly. Traditionally, the care of poultry and marketing of eggs and meat was considered women's work. Women raised poultry to feed their families and to trade with neighbors for other items. Even more important, they could be taken to local general stores and exchanged for groceries.

The profits generated by eggs paid many a family's grocery bills, and in 1940, the Iowa Extension Service—at that time Iowa was the nation's leading producer of eggs—noted that the largest number of flocks in that state were "grocery bill flocks." General stores

then sold eggs to local consumers or shipped them to other areas of the country. Although people might refer to the funds generated from these family farm flocks as "pin money," it often was a significant part of a farm's income and became even more so during hard times.

This began to change in the 1920s, and the pace of change accelerated during World War II. In the 1920s, midwestern states began passing laws standardizing the grading of eggs, which increased the costs of production. Many smaller producers could not afford the increased cost and got out of the poultry business. Later, World War II and military demand vastly increased the markets for eggs. This, combined with various technological and scientific changes, made the development of large-scale, specialized egg and meat factories possible. The size of poultry flocks increased enormously in response to new markets, again pushing out smaller producers. Trading at general stores became a less and less important means of marketing poultry and eggs.

After World War II, legislators in Iowa and other states passed laws making the grading of eggs stricter and more difficult. General stores gave up their egg handling, and larger feed and seed stores took over. These purchasers sent out trucks to pick up eggs, but visited only larger operations. Small operators were restricted to selling in their own neighborhoods, while larger operators sent their chickens and eggs to food processors.

The vertical integration of food processing completely changed the marketing of poultry and eggs. Increasingly, corporations owned the various stages of production, from hatcheries to packing plants, and contracted out egg and poultry production to local farmers, to whom they provided feed and chicks. Only farmers living in close proximity to processing plants were able to participate in egg and poultry production for these processors. This development has seen egg and meat production move out of most of the Midwest (some plants remain in rural Missouri) and into California and the southeastern states, which are home to many of the large food processors. Poultry processing, like so many other industries, has moved into areas where low-wage workers are plentiful. Small-farm flocks have largely disappeared, except among farmers producing poultry and eggs for farmers' markets and specialty stores that cater to consumers desiring organic and free-range eggs and meat.

Sources and Further Reading: Deborah Fink, *Open Country, Iowa* (1986); Katherine Jellison, *Entitled to Power* (1993); Mary Neth, *Preserving the Family Farm* (1995).

Pamela Riney-Kehrberg
Iowa State University

Wheat and Other Grains

Since European Americans and Europeans began farming in the Midwest, they have raised small grains such as wheat, oats, rye, barley, and buckwheat. Cultural traditions, geography and climate, and economic advantages contributed to the development of the Midwest as America's Wheat Belt from 1850 to 1900. Additionally, oats became the primary crop for feeding horses. By the 1930s, a majority of midwestern farmers had abandoned small-grain production, although it is still a cash crop for some. Sowing, reaping, threshing, and winnowing have changed over time as agriculture became mechanized, and producers became removed from the crop.

Wheat and other grains may be sown by either broadcasting the seed or drilling it. Broadcast seeding by hand involves carrying a bag of seed and scattering the grain as evenly as possible across the plowed land. After sowing, small-grain farmers worked the seed into the soil with a harrow pulled by draft animals. A single person usually could plant a crop sizable enough for on-farm use with a modest surplus for market production.

By the late 1850s, mechanical broadcast seeders provided a more even distribution method for planting seeds in the field. Simultaneously, innovators developed effective grain drills. Farmers no longer relied on their sometimes unsteady hand to sow an even crop. By the 1880s, farmers mounted end-gate broadcast seeders on wagons, and ultimately tractor-drawn drills became the norm after 1930. All of these machines expanded the potential acreage of farmers, but harvesting machinery needed to be improved before productivity could be maximized.

Historically, harvesting emphasized the importance of neighborliness and shared work. To harvest the berries, the crop had to be reaped and threshed, and berries separated from the chaff and straw. The prevalent process into the 1930s was to harvest grain while it was still doughy, but not fully ripe, bind it into sheaves that were stacked into shocks, and thresh when possible. Reaping technology moved from sickles and grain cradles to horsedrawn reapers and binders and eventually to combines. Threshing progressed from flails to simple threshing machines to thresher-separators that also winnowed the grain. Steam engines typically powered these threshing machines. Prior to thresher-separators, farmers winnowed the grain in a breeze or with a fanning mill. The crews that shocked grain and threshed the crop often shared work and meals. Farm men spent a few weeks each summer working with each other. By the 1930s, tractor-drawn combines began to replace threshing rings, and today conventional farmers almost exclusively use self-propelled combines.

In many parts of the Midwest, wheat gave way to the more profitable crop of soybeans after World War II. As tractors replaced horses, oat production fell precipitously. However, wheat still plays a role in parts of the Midwest, especially the more arid regions. And by the late twentieth century, most midwestern farmers never touched the small grains they produced.

Sources and Further Reading: Allan Bogue, *From Prairie to Corn Belt* (1994); J. Sanford Rikoon, *Threshing in the Midwest, 1820–1940* (1988).

Leo Landis
Henry Ford Museum and Greenfield Village,
Michigan

Family and Kinship

The family was the fundamental social structure in the economic development of the rural Midwest. The family was the vehicle for migration and settlement, family labor powered farms, shops and industries, and family inheritance was the primary means of transferring property. Social reproduction also centered on the family. It was where children were trained to become citizens, producers, and consumers, and where they acquired the cultural habits and values distinctive to their own heritage.

In the nineteenth century an array of native-born and immigrant peoples coalesced in the Midwest to form a family farm culture that became the bedrock of the heartland values we associate with the region even today, despite the decline in the number of those engaged in an agrarian way of life. The common belief that midwesterners live in white English-speaking traditional families is an idealized notion that belies the more complex patterns of race, ethnicity, and class that characterize kinship in the region.

People tended to migrate to the Midwest in family groups and even extended clans of relatives. Native-born migrants moved overland and via rivers to the Midwest, traveling in extended family groups from their neighborhood of origin. They settled on adjacent parcels of land, and through intermarriage some formed large clans in rural townships. European-born migrants were less likely to be able to afford to travel together, but established migration chains that enabled family members to gather in the Midwest in a sequential fashion. It was not unusual for both the native-born and the immigrant to transplant entire parishes or neighborhoods to the Midwest, where ample land enabled them to form immigrant enclaves in the new country. Such patterns of chain migration resulted in Norwegian farm neighborhoods in Trempealeau County, Wisconsin, and Swedish towns in Isanti County, Minnesota. Practices of endogamy, or marrying within one's own ethnic group, further cemented family bonds and preserved cultural habits from the country of origin.

Household production on the isolated farmstead has always been heavily reliant on family labor and land. Family production fostered a family morality of inherent inequality that subjugated individual desires to family goals. The male household head was most visible as the farmer, but in truth the farming enterprise depended also on the labor of the farmer's wife and their children. As the patriarch, the farmer owned the property and superintended the labor of the other family members in agricultural production. He decided who would milk the cows, muck out the stalls in the barn, or plow the fields. The farm wife generally had responsibility for the labor within the house itself: cooking, sewing, cleaning, and food preparation and preservation. Because gender and age were the primary determinants of work duties, sons in native-born families tended to assist their fathers, and daughters assisted their mothers. Small children were generally sent to school or trained to labor by completing smaller, lighter tasks.

Immigrant families had fewer resources, so they depended more heavily on family labor. As a consequence, age and gender were less salient in assigning tasks, and it was not uncommon for daughters and young children to perform heavy labor that the native-born deemed as inappropriate or even dangerous. In midwestern writer Hamlin Garland's story, "Among the Corn Rows," a young suitor dons his girl's sunbonnet while he hoes to trick her Norwegian father into thinking she was working in the field. Garland deftly exposed the tension between family needs and the aspirations of young immigrants to conform to the prescribed gender roles of the host culture.

Farming entailed not only sustenance and production for market, but also the production of children as laborers and future inheritors of the land to carry on the family enterprise. Because of biological constraints and cultural habits, the labor of reproduction and childcare fell to women, who bore children at an average of two-year intervals. Over time, as land became scarce and machines made human labor less essential, fertility declined. This occurred because women shortened the period of childbearing (starting later and ending sooner), and because families were less likely to take in relatives or elderly parents. Compared to the native-born, immigrants tended to have more children, which enabled them to produce more labor-intensive goods, such as dairy products.

Inheritance, the bequest of property from one generation to the next, was the dominant mechanism for transfer of land in the Midwest. Thus the number of offspring and the quality of family relationships were critical to the perpetuation of the family enterprise. Conversely, the relative abundance or scarcity of family land determined family bonds, with some favored children staying on the homestead, while others were compelled to venture west or to the city to amass the resources needed for the future generation. Children who inherited the family farm were obligated to care for their aging parents, and such obligations reinforced lineal rather than conjugal family bonds.

The timing of the land transfers and decisions about settling the estate varied according to ethnicity, race, and class status. Immigrants tended to regard the land as a patrimony, and through various means managed to keep it in the family, whereas the native-born were more likely to treat land as capital, selling it and transferring the wealth to the next generation in more portable instruments such as cash. For example, tenacity on the land resulted in the eventual dominance of German immigrants in Stearns County, Minnesota, an area that was originally settled by Yankees. For both the native-born and immigrants, sons were favored with land more often than daughters, although by the end of the nineteenth century, fathers attempted to make equal bequests by compensating daughters with cash or valuable furnishings. In the mid-nineteenth century, southern black families formed isolated farm communities where they were able to establish a patrimony to insulate their children somewhat from racial discrimination. Despite ethnic and racial differences, the family remained the primary resource for obtaining land in the Midwest.

Class was likewise an important determinant of family behavior, especially the allocation of work, in the rural Midwest. Poor families were likely to pull children out of school when they reached puberty and could perform farm work, while the wealthier hired laborers so that their children could complete school and in some cases, go to college. Women in families of means were more likely to spend time and money beautifying the home, hanging curtains or laying carpet in the parlor. They could hire servants to do the laundry, iron, clean, and cook, thereby allowing them to contribute to church and community causes. Prosperous farmers bought more elaborate machinery to reduce the time it took to perform farm work, and they could afford to hire servants to assist them. As a consequence, they had more time to devote to civic affairs, self-education, travel, or acquisition of consumer goods.

Family behavior also varied according to location in the region. The Midwest is a large geographic region with wide variations in climate, natural resources, and distance from marketing centers. Environment influenced the means of production, and thus the use of family labor. For example, the large wheat farms of the Dakotas depended more on mechanized production and seasonal farmhands than on family labor. The vast quantities of land required to achieve an economy of scale often meant that families were isolated from neighbors and community rituals such as school socials or church picnics.

The fact that the family was the bedrock of rural society at times led to negative consequences for human rights. Putting family needs above individual desires may have enabled economic progress, but often it occurred at great human cost. Unbridled patriarchal power meant women and children could be physically abused, and the isolated nature of the farmstead meant such abuse could go undetected for long periods of time. Divorce was available but not common, and few women could support themselves and their children alone. Immigrant families in particular were more likely to exploit themselves to keep the farm afloat, depriving themselves and their children of the comforts and even the necessities of life. Because the home was also the place of work, and because children worked in sometimes dangerous environments, accidents that maimed or killed were common. Even today, occupational health and safety standards do not apply to the family enterprise, and accidents can be deadly.

As the basic institution of society, the family adapted to changes in agrarian capitalism and, in turn, enabled new patterns of production and consumption. Families became smaller as rural couples produced fewer children, and the work roles of children diminished as childhood came to be seen as a protected period of education and development. Mechanized machinery such as reapers and mowers eased the demand for male labor, particularly at the critical times of planting and harvesting. Women would continue to sew and put up produce for their own households until after World War II, but they were less likely to depend on selling eggs and cream for significant family income. Wealthier women relinquished domestic production to the home and became involved in community organizations.

The early twentieth century was seen as the golden age of agriculture, and because of frugality and astute inheritance strategies, immigrants were more likely than the native-born to stay on the land. In particular, descendants of German immigrants came to dominate the ranks of midwestern farmers, notably in Illinois and Wisconsin. African Americans from the South tended to migrate to cities and became less visible in the rural Midwest. The Depression brought an end to the era of prosperity, and despite New Deal programs,

the economic downturn dealt a death blow to the dominant ideal of the self-sustaining family farm.

In the mid-twentieth century, trends toward capital-intensive agriculture reduced the need for family labor and led to depopulation of the midwestern countryside after World War II. Farm women, who had been producers of marketable commodities, and whose home production and frugality had been important to sustaining profitability, were encouraged to become consumers. Rural people aspired to urban standards of living unattainable for most families on farms, resulting in discontent among their children, who left the farm for the city. The war tested the limits of family production as young men were called to military duty, but government programs such as the Women's Land Army attempted to fill the shortage of farm labor.

In the last half of the twentieth century, the rural family was transformed. Farm wives contribute to the family economy through off-farm work, and many farmers also work off-farm part-time to sustain the family farm. Today's farm enterprise is more likely to require loans and government subsidies, so it is more vulnerable to downturns in the broader economy. Compared to nineteenth century rural families, who were dependent on their own labor and land, today's family farms are more reliant upon debt. Nevertheless, the romanticized notion of the farm family as the wellspring of national virtues such as hard work, patriotism, piety, and independence persists. Today's rural realities of poor migrant worker families in the fields and meat-packing industries challenge the ideal, but their sacrifices attest to the continuing potency of the American dream for families in the rural Midwest.

Sources and Further Reading: Jane Adams, *The Transformation of Rural Life* (1994); Deborah Fink, *Agrarian Women* (1992); Deborah Fink, *Cutting Into the Meatpacking Line* (1998); Jon Gjerde, *The Minds of the West* (1997); Susan E. Gray, *The Yankee West* (1996); Katherine Jellison, *Entitled to Power* (1993); Mary Neth, *Preserving the Family Farm* (1995); Jane Marie Pederson, *Between Memory and Reality* (1992); Susan S. Rugh, *Our Common Country* (2001); Sonya Salamon, *Prairie Patrimony* (1992).

Susan Sessions Rugh
Brigham Young University, Utah

Childbirth and Childrearing

Childbirth and childrearing were, until recent times, an integral part of rural life, particularly for midwestern women. Traditionally, rural families had more children than urban families since lack of a large labor source could make or break a family farm. In the nineteenth century, rural women gave birth approximately every two years and could expect to lose one or two children through miscarriage, stillbirth, accident, or disease. The danger of death for mother or child added stress to an already physically exhausting nine-month process that might be repeated six to eight times in a woman's life.

As women gained control over their reproductive capacity in the twentieth century, they lost control of the birthing process and the birth room. Midwifery was extensively practiced in the rural Midwest until the early twentieth century, particularly by European immigrants and their descendants. The birthing room was considered the domain of women, and female kin or neighbors often assisted the midwife or doctor with the labor and birthing process—frequently staying on after the birth to care for the family, allowing the new mother a few days to recuperate. The transition from midwives and in-home births to male doctors and eventually hospital births was slow and difficult for many midwestern women. In small rural communities, a midwife could provide prenatal care, be present for labor and birth, and remain with the family assisting with any postnatal complications.

After the birth of the first child, rural women became caregivers for decades; childrearing duties were simply part of each day's activities. Because of the demands of rural life, the family farm functioned as both an economic and social unit. Both parents were involved in childrearing, although men's duties typically began later when children were old enough to provide farm labor. Scholars disagree on the harshness or leniency of rural childrearing practices, which were often determined by ethnic and cultural traditions for first- and second-generation immigrants. Age, gender, and sometimes sibling order determined children's roles and responsibilities. With children of both sexes present in the family, fathers typically trained sons to help with large farm production, and mothers trained daughters in household tasks and responsibilities such as gardening and attending small animals, particularly chickens. Aunts, uncles, grandparents, and sometimes older siblings also served as caregivers and mentors for rural children. However, in a family where there was not a balanced gender mix, young boys might be assigned household duties if older brothers provided the needed outside labor, and young girls might assist with crops if males were absent, particularly during times of planting or harvest when extensive amounts of physical labor were needed in a short period of time.

Although childrearing practices varied from family to family, parents taught children from an early age the importance of work and of duty to the family unit. Children provided important sources of labor for the family farm, and in turn, the family supplied the arena in which crucial lessons in gender expectations and responsibilities were defined and acted out by parents and extended kin.

Sources and Further Reading: Lee L. Bean, Geraldine P. Mineau, and Douglas L. Anderson, *Fertility Change on the American Frontier* (1990); Carol K. Coburn, *Life at Four Corners* (1992); Lucy Eldersveld Murphy and Wendy Hamand Venet, eds., *Midwestern Women* (1997); Elliott West, *Growing Up with the Country* (1989).

Carol K. Coburn
Avila University, Kansas City, Missouri

The Economics of Kinship

The rural Midwest has historically been dominated by family farmers whose kinship practices have shaped local land tenure. While agricultural practices changed as farmers adapted to their new environments, kinship practices, including gender relations, household organization, marriage, and child socialization, remained relatively unchanged well into the twentieth century. Family kinship practices, when aggregated in ethnic group settlements, produced cultural patterns of land use with particular persistence in the rural Midwest.

When workmates are also relatives, enterprise and kinship are entwined. Immigrants to the Midwest selectively appropriated from American inheritance practices those that favored continuity in linking household practices to farming. Rural families tend to have a patrilineal bias because land is passed from fathers to sons. Sons typically take over the family farm, land follows the male line, and couples usually live near the husband's relatives. Families tend to visit, interact, and feel more obligation toward the man's kin. Daughters also inherit family land, but their husbands generally farm it, and a husband's work partnership is usually with his father. Farm families are thus male-centered.

Inheritance customs have varied by ethnicity. Historically, Yankee farmers transferred larger estates and more liquid capital to their sons, thereby reinforcing a concentration of land ownership. Germans socialized all children to cherish farming and divided land among heirs, who each asserted a right to farm it. German farms were smaller and more numerous, thus retarding a concentration of resources in fewer hands.

Lifecourse imperatives require an intergenerational transmission of family land about every thirty years. Kinship priorities determine the transmission of resources. Nineteenth-century ethnic farmers favored males in inheritance, whether they were dividing land (partible) or giving all to the oldest or youngest (impartible). Favoring the farm successor privileged male heirs and perpetuated their advantaged position.

Farm parents today face a dilemma: whether to treat children equally or to favor the successor to the farm. This dilemma pits continuity goals against equity goals, particularly when land and financial resources are limited. Furthermore, dividing family land can effectively destroy a farm because the trend is toward larger operations. Siblings trust that exploitation does not result from parental estate trade-offs between individual rewards and farm continuity. Families today generally split resources equitably among offspring to ensure all equal life chances. Women often work off-farm for fringe benefits such as health insurance, which enhances their status within kinship networks.

Concentration of midwestern land ownership and farm operation among fewer people is fostered by current inheritance laws, which favors heirs to land accumulating greater assets as well as the separation of farming and land ownership.

Sources and Further Reading: Remi Clignet, *Death, Deeds, and Descendants* (1992); Jon Gjerde, *The Minds of the West* (1997); Sonya Salamon, *Prairie Patrimony* (1992); David M. Schneider, *American Kinship*, 2nd ed. (1980); Marty Strange, *Family Farming* (1988).

Sonya Salamon
University of Illinois–Urbana-Champaign

Ethnicity and Kinship

During the nineteenth century, immigrants flooded into the Midwest and created a mosaic of cultures and traditions that continues to mark the rural cultural landscape. By 1880, foreign-born residents accounted for more than half of the farming population in several upper and western midwestern states, and within selected townships, nearly all of the residents were foreign-born. European immigrants settled less frequently in the southern and eastern Midwest, areas that contained larger numbers of settlers from southern states.

Upper midwestern states such as Minnesota and the Dakotas, where nearly sixty percent of the farming population in 1880 was foreign-born, were heavily Scandinavian, whereas states farther south such as Iowa contained settlements of people from Bohemia, Holland, Luxembourg, Switzerland, Wales, and Ireland. German immigrants constituted by far the largest ethnic population in almost every area of the Midwest.

Kinship and family networks guided migration to the Midwest as immigrants frequently moved and settled together. In many areas, immigrant families purchased contiguous farms, although the cadastral system of property demarcation, which marked the land in 160-acre and 80-acre tracts, discouraged the European village and open field system they might have preferred. In spite of this limitation, immigrants often retained familiar social and cultural networks.

At first glance, immigrant farmers seem to have quickly adapted to the midwestern rural environment. In addition to living on widely dispersed farmsteads, they abandoned many traditional farming practices. Unable to change the weather or soil types, immigrants discovered that crops they had raised successfully in Europe, such as potatoes and beets, were not well suited to the midwestern environment. As a result, they turned to traditional midwestern crops such as wheat, corn, oats, hogs, and cattle.

However, immigrants did not abandon all European practices, especially the role of families. By looking carefully at the inner workings of ethnic communities, historians have uncovered kinship patterns that nurtured a complex web of ethnic practices and helped immigrants resist acculturation. These patterns were part of a cultural package that also included religion, attitudes about education and land ownership, and other details of everyday life.

Immigrant families often followed American-born (Yankee) farmers to the midwestern frontier. Immigrants frequently purchased land from these early settlers as the American-born farm families sold their land and moved on. While Yankee farmers used land as a commodity to raise cash that they reinvested or used to explore other nonfarm opportunities, immigrants used land to preserve a way of life centered around family, kinship, and community. Long-term land ownership was critical to the viability and success of an immigrant rural community.

Ethnic farm families clung to traditional family patterns that bound several generations to a piece of land and to a community. They transferred farms from parents to children through closely monitored intrafamilial transactions. The bulk of these transfers were inheritances or subsidized sales, as ethnic farmers seldom sold land outside of the immediate family.

Although the details of these transactions varied from group to group, immigrants used land transfers to forge a link between family members and the land. Ethnic inheritance practices favored sons, but other siblings were not ignored. Within most groups, sons received their inheritance in land, while daughters received cash. However, this practice varied considerably with the number of sons and daughters and among immigrant groups.

Germans who traced their origins to areas west of the Rhine River generally followed partible inheritance practices and divided their farms to ensure that each child received a piece of land. If land and assets were insufficient, as many sons as possible were given land, while daughters received cash or household goods. By contrast, Irish families followed impartible inheritance customs, keeping their farms intact as parents transferred ownership late in life. Typically one son acquired the farm as a gift, a purchase, or a combination of the two. Within each tradition, the primary goal was to ensure a continued presence on the land. Equitable distribution of the assets was a secondary goal.

Immigrant families often relied on bonds of maintenance agreements to link inheriting children to the farm and to their aging parents. These agreements spelled out the obligations between children and parents after farms were transferred to the younger generations. In return for a portion of the farm, children provided living space, food, and other necessities for the remainder of their parent's lives. This arrangement permitted a conditional transfer of ownership so a son or daughter could begin farming if they took responsibility for their parent's well-being. Arrangements that tied land and family also meant immigrant families frequently contained adult children. These older children often lived with their aging parents and married later in life, if at all.

High fertility rates among ethnic farmers offset higher ages at marriage and helped create large families. Parents and community elders discouraged marriages outside of their ethnic group by threatening disinheritance and removal of other financial and social supports. Immigrant communities remained connected with one another, and frequent visits between settlements exposed young people to a wider range of potential marriage partners who shared the same culture. Ideally, marriage allowed parents to step away from the heaviest aspects of farm work as the young husband and wife assumed those responsibilities.

The rural ethnic community survived largely because it was based upon family and kinship. The community buffered families from the corrosive effects of surrounding cultures by channeling the career and marriage choices residents made. These choices, in turn, created the strong families needed to sustain the community.

Even today, ethnic traditions continue to shape rural midwestern communities. Pressures to marry within a particular ethnic group may have eased, but they still remain surprisingly strong. Subsequent generations exhibit many of the behaviors already described—a testament to the strength of traditions and expectations among the various immigrant groups that settled in the Midwest.

Sources and Further Reading: Kathleen Neils Conzen, "Immigrants in Nineteenth-Century Agricultural History," in Lou Ferleger, ed., *Agriculture and National Development* (1990); Kathleen Neils Conzen, "Peasant Pioneers," in Steven Hahn and Jonathan Prude, eds., *The Countryside in an Age of Capitalist Transformation* (1985); Jon Gjerde, *From Peasants to Farmers* (1985); Jon Gjerde, *The Minds of the West* (1997); Robert C. Ostergren, *A Community Transplanted* (1988); Sonya Salamon, *Prairie Patrimony* (1992).

Franklin L. Yoder
University of Iowa

Marriage and Courtship

Historically, rural midwesterners have organized their marriages around husbands' and wives' complementary labor roles and their shared commitment to life on the land.

Most of the indigenous inhabitants of the Midwest were prairie dwellers who subsisted on a diet of meat supplied by hunter-husbands and maize raised by farmer-wives. They organized themselves on a patrilocal model: married couples joined the husband's kinship group and lived with or near his parents. An exception to this arrangement occurred among the Native Americans of northern Ohio, northern Indiana, and southeastern Michigan, where women's farming activities strongly predominated and couples joined the wife's kinship group. Throughout the Midwest, Native American wedding rituals featured gift exchanges that symbolized the mutual dependence of husband and wife and their reliance on family approval and support. A Fox woman's early twentieth-century account of her wedding described a ritual little changed since Europeans first observed it in seventeenth-century Wisconsin: each of her husband's relatives gave her a gift, and she reciprocated with baskets of corn, beans, and pumpkins. Like other Indians, the Fox nation permitted divorce and remarriage and recognized cruelty, sterility, adultery, and laziness as grounds for dissolution.

Citizens of the United States became a strong presence north and west of the Ohio River in the late eighteenth and nineteenth centuries. Most of these settlers were members of nuclear farm families that organized labor according to gender and age. Husbands hunted for game and raised large livestock and grain crops with market value. Wives supplied the farm family with its basic needs by raising vegetables and poultry, processing dairy and meat products, and making clothing, and they worked alongside their husbands in the grain fields during planting and harvest seasons. Wives also assured a growing farm labor force, giving

Ole Myrvik wedding, Milton, North Dakota, 1894. Fred Hultstrand History in Pictures Collection, NDIRS-NDSU, Fargo, Hult.437.

birth to a child approximately every thirty months during their childbearing years. By the age of five or six, children watered and fed animals, collected eggs, milked cows, hauled water, and weeded gardens. Although the labor of both husband and wife was crucial to maintain a successful farm, only the husband held rights to the farm property under the traditions of Anglo-American common law.

Through the first half of the nineteenth century, marriages in the rural midwest remained primarily relationships of economic necessity. While matches based on romantic love and marked by elaborate wedding ceremonies were becoming the urban middle-class norm, rural midwesterners commemorated their marriages with little fanfare. The 1842 wedding of a rural Ohio couple was typical: A Presbyterian pastor conducted a brief ceremony in the bride's home, with only her sisters, the groom's brother, and a few friends in attendance. As farm families settled west of the Mississippi River in the second half of the century, marriages remained economic partnerships, but were sometimes launched with greater flourishes. The Homestead Act of 1862 drew a more diverse population of farmers into the trans-Mississippi Midwest, including German, Scandinavian, and Czech immigrants, who celebrated their marriages with traditional dances and feasts. After the Civil War, recently freed slaves arrived in Kansas to claim farmland under the Homestead Act, bringing with them the African American jumping-the-broom ritual.

In the early twentieth century, reformers affiliated with the Country Life Movement—the rural arm of American Progressivism—encouraged midwestern farmers to adopt an urban middle-class model of marriage and family life. The Department of Agriculture, the nation's agricultural colleges, and periodicals targeting farmers urged families to invest heavily in modern equipment that lessened the need for family labor and freed husbands to become farm managers, wives to become full-time housewives, and children to spend more time at school. Most midwestern farm families lacked both the capital and the desire to follow such prescriptions. Immigrant families particularly resisted the notion that farming was a mere business proposition, preferring instead to view it as a superior way of life to be passed from one generation to the next. Most wives, regardless of their ethnic background, took pride in their accomplishments as farm producers and did not want to relinquish that role to become full-time housewives.

During the agricultural depression of the 1920s and 1930s, farms failed and many midwesterners left the land permanently. Those who remained used new communication and transportation technologies to live lives more closely resembling urban dwellers. Rural courtship, which previously consisted of young men calling on their sweethearts at home or meeting them at church or school functions, evolved into modern dating. Paved roads and automobiles allowed young men to take their dates into town, where couples went to the movies or attended dances where local bands played the popular songs heard on network radio. The influence of the era's mass entertainment industry, particularly motion pictures, prompted romantic love to play a bigger role in rural courtship and marriage partner choices. The poor economy, however, caused most weddings to remain small and celebrated at home.

World War II drafted young men away from the farm and into military service even as the federal government called on the nation's farm families to increase production for the war effort. Wives and daughters consequently extended their participation in grain crop production and became more proficient at running heavy field equipment. When the war ended, many farm women chose to retain their expanded role in field work. Other postwar changes included the in-migration of urban women as marriage partners for rural men. Military service or a college education financed by the GI Bill allowed young men to choose brides from beyond their local neighborhoods. Urban brides often brought with them "city ideas" about weddings and marriage. When Seattle native Elva Allen married a Wisconsin farmer and fellow army veteran in 1946, she did so in big-city style: While the celebration took place in a rural Badger State church, it included an elegant white gown and an elaborate wedding cake. According to an Ohio study, by 1955, one-third of all farm wives in that state were women who had grown up in a town or city.

In the closing years of the twentieth century, midwestern farms resembled those envisioned by Country Life reformers decades earlier. Fewer families remained on the land, but those who were financially able to retain their farms invested extensively in household and field technology that freed them from heavy physical labor. Investment in technology allowed farm wives to join their husbands in field and livestock work that had once required significant upper-body strength. Household modernization relieved wives of some of the most onerous traditional housekeeping activities, and changes in commercial production and retailing practices allowed them to buy many grocery and clothing items more cheaply than they could be made at home. No longer needing children as farm laborers, midwestern farm wives now had small families like their urban counterparts, and they often used the time freed from childcare and home production to work in cash-paying, off-farm jobs that earned capital for future investment in the family farm.

Sources and Further Reading: James Axtell, ed., *The Indian Peoples of Eastern America* (1981); John Mack Faragher, *Women and Men on the Overland Trail* (1979); Deborah Fink, *Open Country, Iowa* (1986); Katherine Jellison, *Entitled to Power* (1993); Katherine Jellison, "From the Farmhouse Parlor to the Pink Barn: The Commercialization of Weddings in the Rural Midwest," *Iowa Heritage Illustrated* 77 (Summer 1996); Mary Neth, *Preserving the Family Farm* (1995); Ellen K. Rothman, *Hands and Hearts* (1984); Sonya Salamon, *Prairie Patrimony* (1992).

Katherine Jellison
Ohio University–Athens

Rural Neighborhoods and Communities

Though perceptions of rural communities are often informed by nostalgia, myth, and stereotypes, in recent years the rich community life of midwestern rural neighborhoods has been studied in meticulous detail, exposing the social relationships and structural realities of rural communities.

In 1959, Merle Curti published the groundbreaking community study of Trempealeau County, Wisconsin, *The Making of an American Community: A Case Study of Democracy in a Frontier County.* Curti argued that early settlers of the American Midwest created the institutions that sustained well-developed communities. He identified the "social creed" of hospitality, mutuality, and neighborliness that informed relationships in the rural Midwest. Motivated by conservative values of land ownership, farming, kinship, religion, and sociability, native-born and European migrants embraced the traditional goals of the yeoman farmer and often found success as farmers. Kinship networks, local churches, country schools, neighborhood organizations, and the family farm system of agriculture assured the persistence of rural cultures well into the twentieth century.

A 1910 immigrant farmer in northern Wisconsin succinctly articulated the importance of community: "We built our schools and churches, and with the passing of years became a church going, law abiding, reasonably prosperous farming community, a good place in which to live and raise our families." Churches, schools, and rural organizations such as the Grange and farmer cooperatives were inclusive institutions that structured a rich network of neighborhood connections. Equally important were informal ties of kinship, ethnicity, visiting, and a tradition of sharing work and resources.

Churches and schools were as hubs of community life. Strong religious traditions facilitated the foundation of rural ethnic cultures. Settlers after 1850 typically came from communities dominated by religion and local churches. Early settlers actively worked to re-create their congregations from clusters of kin and like-minded neighbors. Private homes and itinerant preachers first brought neighbors together, but eventually the steeples of village and country churches dotted the countryside. Rural churches transmitted beliefs, values, languages, and culture in rural neighborhoods. Migrants from the East, both northerners and southerners, transplanted Congregational, Baptist, Methodist, and Presbyterian churches; Germans and Scandinavians brought Lutheran churches; and Irish, German, and Polish Catholics established churches and private schools. This rich diversity inevitably produced conflict, but it also was a tribute to the persistence of faith and tradition in challenging new environments.

Ethnicity often proved to be a foundation for creating communities. Because of ethnic clustering, a homogeneous population frequently sustained vibrant ethnic cultures for three and four generations. Carol K. Coburn in *Life at Four Corners: Religion, Gender, and Education in a German-Lutheran Community, 1868–1945*, traced the interconnections of ethnicity and religion among four generations of German Lutherans in Miami County, Kansas. The church defined the boundaries of community and served as the center of education, ritual, and sociability. Churches bound people together across space and time in social rituals that celebrated important transitions in the life cycle. Although typically men held formal power in many churches, women organized the social dimensions of religious rituals and gatherings related to baptisms, confirmations, marriages, wedding anniversaries, and funerals.

The numerous one-room country schools provided another network of association overlapping that of the churches. For about a century after 1850, country schools educated generations of rural children and served as neighborhood centers. Rural recreation, entertainment, and sociability centered in the schools, including picnics, baseball games, holiday celebrations, community clubs, basket socials, and musical and theatrical productions by local children or adults. School and church activities and those of other rural organizations were open to all. Summer picnics or Christmas celebrations served as moments of homecoming for former members of the community and extended kin networks.

Neighborhood schools and churches supported diverse educational, religious, and social activities. By 1900, rural churches sponsored lay organizations such as Ladies Aid societies for women and organizations for youth. Country schoolhouses welcomed 4-H clubs for children and adolescents, mother's clubs for women, and community clubs for everyone.

Informal social interactions competed with those of the church and the school in significance in binding neighborhoods into communities. In contrast to stereotypes of rural isolation, a daily round of visiting typified rural neighborhoods in the Midwest for much of its history. Visiting was the primary means of rural sociability. Visiting intersected with the needs of seasonal and daily work and reflected gender and age divisions. Men visited to share information and exchange work and equipment; women visited relatives and neighbors and similarly shared work and sociability.

Visiting in many ways intersected with the work of the family farm. American and European farmers depended on neighbors to exchange labor. During settlement, neighbors often relied on each other for survival. Families shared their homes and essentials with newcomers. Social and economic functions were not carefully delineated. Neighborhood women and men joined together in barn raisings and home construction. Women met in quilting bees, shared domestic work, and exchanged products and knowledge. These informal social interactions cemented relationships and created dense networks of interdependence.

The increased mechanization of farming after 1880 intensified traditions of cooperation and interdependence. The steam-powered threshing machine required the labor of large numbers of men. Throughout the Midwest, farmers organized "threshing rings" composed of neighbors. From the introduction of the threshing machine until the 1950s, when combines began to replace threshers, women, men, and children in neighborhoods worked together every year to bring in the harvest. Farmers also shared grain binders, planters, tractors, and horses. Individual farm families depended on their communities to meet their labor needs. Rural neighborhoods often seethed with hostilities, but neighborliness was the foundation of both social ethics and economic survival.

Other forms of sociability helped define rural communities. Barn dances preceded the dance halls that later appeared on the rural midwestern landscape. Homes and barns served as centers of recreation. Within diverse ethnic neighborhoods, distinct cultural traditions shaped social activities. The European tradition of the charivari or "shivaree" celebrated marriage with a noisy nighttime party outside the home of a newly married couple. Revelers demanded treats (which were often alcoholic) and the merriment lasted until dawn. Rural Norwegian Americans brought with them folk traditions including "Julebukking" or "Christmas Fooling." This tradition involved local groups disguising themselves with makeshift costumes and stopping at the homes of their neighbors, where they behaved comically and challenged their hosts to identify them and provide refreshments. These traditions testify to the level of trust in many rural neighborhoods.

Local politics reflected rural values. Neighborhoods identified with specific political parties and voted according to their collective ethnic and religious affiliations. Politicians who ignored local cultures suffered the consequences at the polls. In 1889, Republican Governor William D. Hoard led Wisconsin in the adoption of the Bennett Law, which required teaching exclusively in the English language. Wisconsin's multiethnic voters promptly voted the once-popular governor out of office. Such issues as public schooling, prohibition, and women's rights led to searing political confrontations when cultural expectations and worldviews informed by local cultures clashed.

Rural townships located side by side often voted very differently. High voter turnout depended on the strength of neighborhoods. Particularly before radio and television, state candidates appeared locally. Political success depended on ethnic coalitions and attention to local concerns. Thus neighborhoods profoundly shaped politics in the nineteenth- and early twentieth-century Midwest.

The ethic of mutuality helped rural communities sustain themselves as local enclaves until agribusiness transformed the Midwest, particularly after World War II. Modernity eroded social networks. Modern agribusiness in partnership with activist government policy makers bent on reorganizing the rural economy and social system have steadily drained the vitality of rural neighborhoods by removing local control over education and the economy. Since the early twentieth century, activist policy makers have sought to rationalize agriculture on the model of corporate capitalism. Government programs promoted capital-intensive agriculture over farm family strategies of making do. Neighborhood sharing of labor and resources has steadily been superseded by agriculture dependent on capital and intensive large-scale production. Expensive, high-powered equipment has replaced the numerous neighborhood exchanges of labor that once allowed farmers to survive unpredictable markets and personal crisis.

Every decade since the 1940s has brought a decline in the number of farms in the Midwest. Where once a neighborhood included ten to fifteen farm families, today only one or two large farms remain. They rely on government programs and loans rather than neighbors to negotiate the demands of a market. Poorer and less mature areas were most vulnerable to disruption by public policy and market pressures.

Despite rural midwesterners' commitment to a rural culture, many of the institutions of community life have disappeared. The thousands of one-room country schools that once laced every county of every state have closed as larger consolidated schools have replaced them. In the 1920s, government policy makers and professional educators began a campaign to close the one-room country schools, and they succeeded everywhere by the 1960s, despite extended, bitter opposition by rural people. The closing of the one-room country schools eliminated a cornerstone of rural neighborhood life.

School consolidation, the automobile, the rise of the mass media, and a consumer ethos have shifted the center of sociability away from the local neighborhood. Since World War II, rural families' work and entertainment patterns have progressively paralleled those of urban Americans. Private telephone lines have replaced party lines. High school sports teams and recreation have refocused the lives of the youth. Reasons for regular visits to neighbors diminished dramatically or disappeared entirely. Farms became ever larger, and corporate ownership began to supplant the family farm.

Sources and Further Reading: Jane Adams, *The Transformation of Rural Life: Southern Illinois, 1890–1900* (1994); Hal S. Barron, *Mixed Harvest: The Second Great Transformation in the Rural North, 1870–1930* (1997); David Danbom, *Born in the Country: A History of Rural America* (1995); Wayne Fuller, *The Old Country School: The Story of Rural Education in the Middle West* (1982); Jon Gjerde, *The Minds of the Midwest: Ethnocultural Evolution in the Rural Middle West, 1830–1917* (1997); Robert Gough, *Farming the Cutover: A Social History of Northern Wisconsin, 1900–1940* (1997); Susan Gray, *The Yankee West: Community Life on the Michigan Frontier* (1996); Mary Neth, *Preserving the Family Farm: Women, Community, and the Foundations of Agribusiness in the Midwest, 1900–1940* (1995); Jane Marie Pederson, *Between Memory and Reality: Family and Community in Rural Wisconsin, 1870–1970* (1992); Linda Schelbitzki Pickle, *Contented Among Strangers: Rural German-Speaking Women and Their Families in the Nineteenth-Century Midwest* (1996).

Jane M. Pederson
University of Wisconsin–Eau Claire

African Americans

Like the vast majority of Americans in the nineteenth century, many African Americans in the Midwest were farmers. To be sure, a larger percentage of the midwestern African American population—which constituted one-eighth of the free black population of the United States in the 1850s—tended to settle in urban areas than did their white counterparts. But until the 1880s, the majority of blacks lived in rural communities of fewer than four thousand. Even such famous mixed-race towns as Oberlin, Ohio, were small agrarian communities in the nineteenth century.

The first Great Migration occurred between the

Beech Settlement School, Indiana. Indiana Historical Society, neg. no. C4389.

1820s and the 1840s, and was comprised primarily of free blacks from Virginia, the Carolinas, and Kentucky. While many communities sprang up near white abolitionist towns, exceptions included the community of New Philadelphia, Illinois, which was founded by the black entrepreneur "Free Frank" and settled by both blacks and whites. Some African Americans were runaway slaves and recently freed slaves. Many escaping slaves settled along routes of the Underground Railroad, such as the one that ran from Ohio through Michigan to Canada. These communities were often linked to white Quaker and abolitionist settlements.

The harsh realities of rural life were exacerbated for African Americans by widespread racism and hostility. Legislation was passed in most states to curtail the freedoms of blacks, despite their modest numbers. Despite these Black Codes, African American pioneers were willing to risk multiple moves to find freedom, independence, equality, and success.

After the Civil War, Kansas became a popular destination for African Americans. As early as 1879, four black colonies had been established in Kansas. The most famous was at Nicodemus, founded primarily by migrants from Kentucky and Tennessee. As always, migrants had to deal with white hostility. Still, the movement of blacks to Kansas peaked in the 1880s, with almost fifty thousand African Americans living in the state by 1890.

In general, the rural Midwest offered opportunities for mixed-race communities. They offered interracial interaction and in some cases a degree of equality and integration rarely found in urban areas. Integrated public schools existed in such mixed-race rural communities as Covert, Michigan, and Hamilton County

and Rush County in Indiana. Many of these schools integrated long before mixed-race education was legal in those states. Political freedoms were also gained in rural mixed-race communities in southwestern Michigan, central Indiana, and Ohio, where blacks defeated whites to win such positions as justice of the peace as early as the 1870s.

A unique aspect of black farms in the Midwest was reported by W.E.B. DuBois in his 1906 study of African American farmers. Although by 1899 the U.S. government recorded only 12,255 black-operated farms in the Midwest, those black farmers worked more land that was of higher value than in any other region except the West. (The West was the exception because a handful of black landowners operated large ranches that skewed the results.) When one compares similar types of farms in the Midwest and the South, the differences are truly striking, with midwestern black farmers owning and operating farms that were much larger and more valuable than those in the South. Indeed, the average size of black-operated midwestern farms was 64.2 acres, and 71.9 percent of that land was improved, the highest percentage of improved land for any region in the United States. In Ohio, Indiana, Illinois, Missouri, and Kansas, there were more than a thousand of these large and valuable black-operated farms. In the South, only a quarter of black farmers owned the land that they farmed, whereas over half of the black farmers in the Midwest owned the land they farmed.

Two of the major forces affecting twentieth-century rural African Americans were the growing industrialization of urban America and the slow death of family farms and rural communities. From the 1910s to the 1930s, rural midwestern African Americans were drawn to lucrative wage jobs in cities such as Detroit and Chicago, just as their southern counterparts were. Between 1900 and 1920, the percentage of blacks living in rural communities of fewer than four thousand fell from 34 to 14 percent. There was, however, a small reverse movement in the early and mid-twentieth century with the creation of exclusive camps such as Idlewild in lower Michigan, which catered to middle-class African Americans from Chicago.

Black farmers in the twentieth-century Midwest were adversely affected by the unfair practices of the U.S. Department of Agriculture (USDA), which for decades denied aid to black farmers. In 1999, black farmers won a lawsuit against the USDA, although the damages awarded did little to alleviate the losses incurred.

Many descendants of farm families considered the rural communities they came from to be their homes. To this day, the descendants of rural midwestern black families still meet for family reunions in the communities their families helped to create more than a century ago, and many continue to own the land that has been a part of their lives for generations.

Sources and Further Reading: Anna-Lisa Cox, "A Pocket of Freedom," *The Michigan Historical Review* 21 (Spring 1995); David Gerber, *Black Ohio and the Color Line, 1860–1915* (1976); George Hesslink, *Black Neighbors* (1968); John Squibb, "Roads to Plessy," Ph.D. diss., University of Wisconsin (1992); Roma Jones Stewart "The Migration of a Free People," *Michigan History* 71 (Jan.–Feb. 1987); Emma Lou Thornbrough, *The Negro in Indiana* (1957); Stephen A. Vincent, *Southern Seed, Northern Soil* (2000).

Anna-Lisa Cox
Newberry Library, Chicago, Illinois

Native Americans

Native Americans, of course, were the sole residents of the present day Midwest for thousands of years, and their lifeways have always changed over time.

In the eighteenth and early nineteenth centuries, most Indians adapted to their ecosystem with seasonal migrations that allowed them access to a wide variety of resources. Rivers and lakes were the region's highways, and their shores provided the best land for farming, so summer villages were located near these bodies of water. In the spring, Indian bands returned to these villages, where women planted crops, including corn, beans, melons, and squash.

After spring celebrations, when the crops had a good start, villagers broke into groups. Young men went to fish or hunt buffalo and deer, often far to the west; women with children and elders gathered wild foods and medicines and raw materials for craftwork. Some women dug lead in the upper Mississippi Valley. Late in the summer, the Indians reassembled at their villages to exchange what they had collected. "This is a happy season of the year—having plenty of provisions," the Sauk leader Black Hawk recalled in 1833. "When our corn is getting ripe, our young people watch with anxiety for the signal to pull roasting-ears. . . . When the corn is fit to use, [a] great ceremony takes place, with feasting, and returning thanks to the Great Spirit for giving us corn."

After the harvest, the Indians broke into bands and left for their appointed winter hunting grounds. Early spring was the time to move to the maple groves, where they tapped the trees and spent several weeks making maple syrup and sugar. Before long, it was time to return to the waterside village to start the cycle again. Some tribes varied this routine with harvesting wild rice and intensive fishing.

During the eighteenth- and early-nineteenth centuries, European and Euro-American fur traders ventured into the interior of the Midwest, collecting animal pelts for the European market, giving in exchange guns and ammunition, kettles, blankets, beads, cloth, and tools. These fur traders often married Indian women. During the 1780s, Indians commercialized lead mining near present-day Dubuque. Missionaries preached to many Indian people, attempting to teach them not only a new religion, but also European-style plow agriculture, livestock raising, textile production, and different gender roles. Some Indians resisted these changes, while others adopted them. Native religious leaders, such as the Shawnee Prophet Tenskwatawa (Tecumseh's brother), urged followers to resist acculturation and avoid dependence on European American products such as alcohol.

Between the American Revolution and the mid-1800s, white Americans pushed westward into the Indians' territories, vying for the land. Their livestock ravaged Indians' corn fields; they cut down the forests and competed for game. After violent confrontations, the Indians were forced to sign treaties ceding most of their lands. The majority was removed to reservations on the Plains or in Indian Territory. By 1890, Ohio, Indiana, Illinois, Missouri, Iowa (except Tama), and southern Wisconsin and Minnesota had been officially cleared of Native Americans, although in reality, many refugees hid out in the countryside and lived like other rural people, often with non-Native public identities. The government established reservations for a few tribes in the Dakotas, Nebraska, Kansas, and northern parts of Michigan, Wisconsin, and Minnesota. Most of these lands were in regions too arid or too cold to farm successfully.

From 1854 onward, government policies began to force the allotment of many reservations, that is, to break up the tribes' communally owned lands into family-owned parcels, making unallotted land available to non-Indians. Pressure from speculators, creditors, lumbering companies, and taxes—sometimes abetted by corrupt government officials—caused Indians to lose much of their land and descend into poverty. Increasingly, Native people became tenants or seasonal wage laborers, some of them working in the logging camps of the diminishing north woods.

Schools influenced rural life in several ways. From the 1870s onward, the federal government established boarding schools for Indian children to force acculturation to European-American norms. Thousands of midwestern Indian children, many of them under the age of ten, were compelled to leave their families for months and years at a time to attend these schools. The Flandreau Indian school in South Dakota, the Pipestone boarding school in Minnesota, and the Haskell Institute in Kansas were important institutions where boys were taught Euro-American-style farming and other selected trades such as carpentry. Girls learned the domestic skills officials thought they would need as ideal wives, including cooking, sewing, laundering, and nursing. Most retained ties to their tribal communities and cultures. After their schooling, many applied their training as farmers, clerical workers, plumbers, carpenters, and nurses, while others were chronically unemployed or underemployed due to prejudice and obsolete skills.

In the late twentieth century, Native American organizations in the Midwest struggled with two important challenges. The first was the government policy of Termination from the 1950s through 1970s, which sought to break up some tribes and reservations, and the second was treaty rights violations regarding hunting and fishing. Both of these problems threatened Indian peoples' ability to remain on the land and to make their living from it.

During and after World War II, thousands of Native Americans moved to midwestern cities, particularly after the federal government initiated a relocation program designed to move Indians from reservations to urban areas. According to the 2000 Census, almost 400 thousand Native Americans were living in the twelve states of the Midwest, about half of whom did not live on reservation or tribal trust lands. In Minnesota, Missouri, Nebraska, Ohio, Wisconsin, Kansas, and Indiana, between 20 and 28 percent of Native Americans resided in cities with populations larger than one hundred thousand. In Illinois, where there are no reservations, 39 percent of the Indian population lived in the seven largest cities. The rest of midwestern Indians lived in smaller towns and rural areas, often on farms.

Sources and Further Reading: Emma Helen Blair, ed., *The Indian Tribes of the Upper Mississippi Valley and Region of the Great Lakes* (1911); Brenda J. Child, *Boarding School Seasons* (1998); Gregory Evans Dowd, *A Spirited Resistance* (1992); Donald Jackson, ed., *Black Hawk: An Autobiography* (1990); Rita Kohn and W. Lynwood Montell, eds., *Always a People* (1997); Melissa L. Meyer, *The White Earth Tragedy* (1994); Helen Hornbeck Tanner, ed., *Atlas of Great Lakes Indian History* (1987); Richard White, *The Middle Ground: Indians, Empires, and Republics in the Great Lakes Region, 1650–1815* (1991).

Lucy Eldersveld Murphy
The Ohio State University-Newark

Métis Communities

From the mid-1600s to the mid-1800s, métis communities dotted the waterways of the present-day Midwest. These relatively small transient communities were sustained by the expansive French fur trade. The fur trade encouraged the growth of a biracial and bicultural métis population, because it was based on economic interdependence and promoted constant cultural exchange between the French and Indians. In the seventeenth century, the trappers, traders, and boatmen of New France who ventured into the Ohio Country relied heavily on corn-growing Algonquian Indian bands for pelts, food, women, and security.

Kinship alliances between Frenchmen and Indian women held many advantages for both parties. With a base in his wife's territory, a husband was free to trade and trap. The bilingual and bicultural children of these unions were valuable intermediaries. They also served as a much needed labor force in the fur trade. From the woodlands, the French and their métis kin moved further into the interior of North America, intermarrying with Siouan-speaking, corn-growing people of the prairie and replicating the practices adapted to their survival as a border people.

Wherever places of trade were established at strategic locations along waterways—often adjacent to Indian villages—interrelated French fur traders, Indians, and métis congregated, seeking the comforts and security of community life: social union, a stable place to grow food and rear children, and gainful employment. Roman Catholic missionaries struggled to promote orthodoxy and sedentary habits among these mobile people. Close-knit members of fur-trading families were patrilineal. They embraced the sacraments of the Catholic Church. French was the *lingua franca*. They greatly enjoyed dancing and feasting. Foods, celebrations, and clothing styles in métis communities were a bicultural blend.

The high percentage of French–Indian people was a conspicuous aspect of métis communities. Their heterogenous populations included French nationals, creoles, African Americans, and Indians of different nations. There were lawless and itinerant adventurers, as well as orthodox Catholic farmers and the merchant-entrepreneurs. Corn, wheat, and fruits were grown for local consumption, often with African American slave labor. Most young men in métis communities, however, were engaged in the occupations of the fur trade as hunters, traders, interpreters, or boatmen.

So numerous were the métis that the U.S. government found it "equally politic and humane" after 1812 to make land grants to French "half-breeds." The U.S. recognized that the French–Indians were an "intermediate link" between Americans and Indians. "To secure their permanent attachment to our Government is an important object," wrote Michigan Territory Governor Lewis Cass.

Most métis communities were impermanent, but some trading post communities, such as Michilimackinac in Michigan, and St. Louis and St. Joseph in Missouri, evolved into flourishing outfitting centers for western fur trade expeditions. Others, such as Chicago, ultimately became major urban centers. During the 1830s, Kansas City was briefly a retirement community for Anglo-American fur traders and their Indian families. As long as the fur trade flourished, so did métis communities. The métis communities disappeared as the fur trade economy collapsed.

Sources and Further Reading: John Faragher, "Americans, Mexicans, Metis," in William Cronon, George Miles, and Jay Gitlin, eds., *Under an Open Sky* (1992); Jacqueline Peterson, "The People in Between: Indian-White Marriage and the Genesis of a Metis Society and Culture in the Great Lakes Region, 1680–1830," Ph.D. diss, University of Illinois at Chicago Circle (1981); Jacqueline Peterson and Jennifer S. H. Brown, eds., *The New Peoples: Being and Becoming Metis in North America* (1985); Tanis C. Thorne, *The Many Hands of My Relations: French and Indians on the Lower Missouri* (1996).

Tanis C. Thorne
University of California–Irvine

Class and Farm Neighborhoods

Thomas Jefferson envisioned a mostly rural society of small landholders who would form the foundation of a democratic nation. To that end, he and others devised a system for transferring the public domain into the hands of farmers who would live on and work the land

they owned. In the 1780s and 1790s, the U.S. government implemented the cadastral survey system that in the nineteenth century divided public lands into 80- and 160-acre tracts. This system, along with the relatively low price of public lands, encouraged unusually widespread land ownership throughout the Midwest.

However, speculators, lawyers, and moneylenders, who hoped to make quick profits as land prices rose when government land sales ended, purchased large tracts of land. These "gentlemen farmers" usually lived in or near the growing towns and cities, rented their land to others, and often led the movement for more modern farming techniques and better transportation systems.

Those who actually farmed the land were a mix of landowners, tenants, and farmer–speculators who frequently sold out and moved as land prices rose. The decades immediately following initial settlement were a time of flux and unfettered capitalism as land sold often and people moved frequently. Widespread stability was a myth, and few people remained in one place long enough to get to know their neighbors.

A clear economic and social hierarchy defined local rural neighborhoods. Farmers who owned large tracts of land, were of the proper religious persuasion, and were connected with the elites in local towns and cities occupied the upper echelons of rural society, while itinerant tenant farmers and farm laborers were at the bottom. By the end of the nineteenth century, the change to a family-based agriculture narrowed the gap between the wealthiest and the poorest tenant farmers. The class structure grew more complex as ethnic origins, religion, and education increasingly determined status.

As time passed, speculators sold their holdings and moved on. Often they were replaced by immigrant farmers from northern and western Europe who constructed rural communities based upon family bonds, religion, and Old World traditions and practices.

The class division and strife that characterized urban areas were largely absent in the rural countryside. Those at the bottom of the economic ladder— hired hands and house servants—were usually family members or sons and daughters of neighbors. Likewise, many tenant farmers were sons of local landowners. As part of a family-dominated tenure system, they expected someday to own their own farms with the help of parents who loaned the necessary implements, provided low-cost loans, made outright gifts, or sold land at a reduced cost.

Rural communities occasionally experienced unrest, but the causes of their problems were often ill-defined or uncontrollable. Strikes and riots would not lessen the effects of drought and disease that destroyed crops and livestock. Farmers could not identify the causes of their plight as easily as factory workers or miners. Meat packers, railroads, or banks were blamed for many ills, but farmers' independence and isolation made it difficult for them to confront these organizations. Groups such as the Grange filled a social and intellectual void, but they rarely encouraged farmers to strike or disrupt the economic system.

Financial depressions and weather problems plagued farmers during the latter decades of the nineteenth century, but with the exception of southern midwestern areas where a sharecropping system existed, the idea of a clearly defined class of wealthy or elite farmers was mostly a myth. Farm life was a routine of hard work, low prices, and drudgery.

After 1900, farmers entered a period of prosperity that encouraged speculation. Then, as land and commodity prices dropped after 1920, farmers faced increasingly burdensome debts. The problem grew even worse during the Great Depression of the 1930s as the Midwest became a center of unrest and violent protest. Foreclosures forced farmers from the land, and they began to organize and boycott buyers of farm commodities. Iowa farmers nearly killed a judge who was issuing foreclosure judgments against local farmers. Farmers targeted banks and lenders by intimidating potential bidders at farm auctions, effectively stopping and eventually halting foreclosures altogether.

Tenancy rates increased during the Depression, and the few farmers who had cash bought land at bargain prices. World War II increased the demand for farm products. Farmers who survived the Depression prospered during the 1940s, while those who had lost their land left, usually for work in towns and cities. Landowners increasingly added to their acres by renting additional land. By 1970, a growing number of farmers were both owners and tenants, and the class of tenant farmers who rented all of the land they farmed had largely disappeared.

After 1970, farmers experienced a decade of speculative growth. Just as in the 1920s, they again paid a bitter price for prosperity. Interest rates soared in the 1980s, and farmers could not meet the payments on the loans they had taken out during the previous decade. Farm protests, violence, and even murder proliferated.

Historians dispute the extent to which midwestern rural society is class based. Some view the Midwest as largely egalitarian, while others find evidence that differences have increased during the twentieth century. Compared to urban areas of the late nineteenth and twentieth centuries, rural populations seem homogeneous since almost all residents have been farmers who tend to be practical and invest their wealth in land, livestock, and equipment, not in opulent houses.

Recent trends may signal a new direction. Livestock production has increasingly become concentrated in the hands of a few large operations that contract with farmers who raise, but do not own, chickens, hogs, and cattle. Some vertical integration of production and processing exists, which makes it increasingly difficult for small producers to compete. Yet even here, some farmers are finding niche markets for specialized products such as organic produce and meats. Whether these markets can sustain more than a few farmers remains to be seen.

Sources and Further Reading: John Mack Faragher, *Sugar Creek* (1986); Susan Mann and James M. Dickinson, "Obstacles to the Development of a Capitalist Agriculture," *Journal of Peasant Studies* 5 (July 1978); Patrick H. Mooney, *My Own Boss?* (1988); Susan Rugh, *Our Common Country* (2001); Sonya Salamon, *Prairie Patrimony* (1992); Ingoff Vogeler, *The Myth of the Family Farm* (1981).

Franklin Yoder
University of Iowa

Pioneer Life

Pioneer life in the rural Midwest required significant adjustments. The primary concern was the survival of the family. After building a one-room cabin or sod hut, the most important labor was to clear enough land for the first crop. Every member of the household shared in this labor, according to ability and gender. Men focused on agricultural tasks, including clearing land, plowing fields, and harvesting crops. Women cooked, washed, gave birth, raised vegetables and medicinal herbs, and manufactured homespun clothing, soap, candles, cheese, and butter. However, pioneer life made these traditional domestic tasks more difficult. Open-fire cooking with fewer utensils and ingredients, moreover, resulted in plain, monotonous food.

Settlers confronted illnesses, including typhoid, malaria, and cholera. Death rates were high, especially among children. Home remedies eased symptoms and aided in recovery, despite drafty, damp cabins, lack of trained doctors, and persistent superstitions.

Pioneers created communities and social life through kinship ties. Women exchanged labor, assisted during childbirth, and provided emotional support during sickness and death. Weddings became community affairs, as neighbors, friends, and family from miles around gathered to celebrate the nuptial ceremony, with dances and charivari. Establishing an organized church was important because it served as a spiritual and social center. Church events, including

Pioneer house at Clear Creek, Kansas. Kansas State Historical Society, Gardner Collection, D00000128.

holiday celebrations, brought isolated pioneers together and maintained a sense of community.

Sources and Further Reading: John Mack Faragher, *Sugar Creek* (1986); R. Douglas Hurt, *The Ohio Frontier* (1996); Glenda Riley, *The Female Frontier* (1988).

Petra DeWitt
University of Missouri–Columbia

Automobiles

Initially an object of scorn, the automobile came to be essential to community life in rural America, especially in the Midwest. Often driven recklessly by wealthy city men, the car created havoc by scaring horses and killing livestock. When laws did not stop the "devil wagon," some farmers shot at drivers, others booby-trapped roads and weakened bridges. The anticar crusade ended around 1910, after manufacturers designed cars such as the Model T for rural roads.

Farm men and women saw the automobile differently. Barnyard mechanics turned the car into a small truck, tractor, or a stationary source of power. These uses tended to reinforce male-dominated gender relations because men tinkered with the automobile while women operated a washing machine powered by a belt connected to the rear wheel of a jacked-up car. Driving the family car increased women's freedom, but it also tended to reinforce existing gender relations

when they used the car for such traditional tasks as running an egg route or visiting kin.

The demise of rural institutions such as the country store, church, and trading center is often attributed to the automobile, but farmers actually used the car to make more frequent trips rather than drastically alter their travel patterns. Local transportation still dominated rural life after the advent of the automobile, especially the traditional Saturday trip to town. In these ways, farm men and women were able to tame the devil wagon for their own uses.

Sources and Further Reading: Hal S. Barron, *Mixed Harvest* (1997); Michael Berger, *The Devil Wagon in God's Country* (1979); Ronald R. Kline, *Consumers in the Country* (2000).

Ronald Kline
Cornell University, New York

Telephones

One of the earliest symbols of the attempt by modernizers to urbanize rural America, especially the Midwest, in the twentieth century, the telephone became, instead, a means to re-create rural communication patterns. Farmers especially exercised control over the new technology. When commercial companies proved reluctant to serve scattered farms early in the century, farm men and women created thousands of telephone cooperatives. Typically, they bought their own equip-

The welcome arrival of rural free delivery, Excelsior, Minnesota, 1905. Photo courtesy Minnesota Historical Society. MHS Locator no. HC7.3.r49, neg. no. 10102.

ment, built community lines, operated and maintained the system, and hooked up to the nearest trading center.

Before World War I, farmers as well as folks in town used the telephone in innovative ways. They received news, weather reports, the correct time, and even church services "broadcast" to them over the wire. The habit of playing musical instruments and the phonograph over the phone was common enough in the Midwest for telephone companies and cooperatives to ban the practice because it tied up the lines.

The Rural Electrification Administration greatly increased rural telephone service after World War II. The hallmark of the rural telephone well into the second half of the century was the party line and the inevitable eavesdropping that ensued. Although telephone companies tried to stop what they considered to be a bad-mannered custom, listening in was a popu-

---

❖ Rural Free Delivery: Bringing the Mail to Rural Midwesterners

Rural free delivery (RFD) postal service, as it was known in those days, was established on an experimental basis in 1896 with five routes. It became a permanent service in 1902, and by 1909 there were 40,000 rural routes in the United States.

For many years our mailman was Uncle Tom Blodgett. As I first remember him, he drove a horse and buggy. The buggy was one specially designed for mailmen. It was a box-like affair, with a curtain that would roll down in case of bad weather. It was something like "the surrey with the fringe on top," only different. The curtain was in front and had a transparent window so he could see the horse. There was also a water-proof slot for the reins used to drive the horse. Uncle Tom's old horse was named Buck. I suppose, because he was a buckskin color. He knew the way, and would stop at just the right places for Uncle Tom to push the mail into the roadside mail boxes. Tom would pick up the mail bags at the post office early in the morning and then sort the mail as Buck jogged along the route.

A lot of the merchandise that my grandparents purchased was ordered from the Montgomery Ward or Sears catalogues. One could mail in an order on Monday and expect the merchandise to arrive before the week was out. One of my favorite pastimes was to watch for Uncle Tom and Buck when I was expecting a package or a letter. On one occasion, I ordered a pair of leather high-topped boots. They came on time, but were too small, so I sent them back by return mail. Three days later, I had another pair of boots that fit perfectly. Mail order and RFD service were pretty prompt in those days. Incidentally, the cost of a stamp to mail a letter was raised from two cents to three cents in 1932.

In later years, Uncle Tom purchased a Model T Ford for his rural deliveries. Even later, he bought a Model A Ford and that was another improvement for him. Most of his route was over plain dirt roads that were sometimes impassable in a car. When the weather was nice, he could cover his route in the car in about half the time it took for Buck to make the rounds. But when the weather turned bad, he hitched up Buck and they carried the mail as usual.

Source: George W. Schiller, "Rural Free Delivery," in *Reflections from the Prairie* (1994).

lar pastime. Many farm women in fact viewed it as socially acceptable: Listening in wasn't nosiness, but neighborliness when several people talked on the line at once. The telephone thus allowed people to preserve the venerable rural customs of visiting and providing mutual help.

Sources and Further Reading: Claude S. Fischer, *America Calling* (1992); Ronald R. Kline, *Consumers in the Country* (2000); Lana F. Rakow, *Gender on the Line* (1992).

Ronald R. Kline
Cornell University, New York

Radios

Broadcasting surmounted geographic barriers to inform, entertain, and connect the countryside to town and city life, the nation, and the world. Initially country folk owned fewer radios than city folk, but they listened more, whether at home or at gatherings at general stores and Grange halls. Rural radio addressed the farm family while mediating local, regional, and national differences. Changing work and lifestyle patterns and broadcast industry consolidation combined to divest rural radio of much of its distinctive flavor by the twenty-first century.

In the early 1920s, the United States Department of Agriculture (USDA) and extension divisions of landgrant colleges and universities sponsored weather and market reports, as well as technical and cultural programs. Ohio and Wisconsin produced so-called schools and colleges of the air that reached hundreds of thousands of youths and adult listeners. Locally produced farm-home shows with female hosts catered to rural women. Concerts, comedies and dramas, and sports captured the imaginations of rural families. WLS, an NBC affiliate, produced the "National Farm and Home Hour" and "National Barn Dance." The latter conjoined folksiness, hillbilly music, and mass advertising.

Farm programs remained popular after World War II. Over 83 percent of southern Wisconsin farmers reported listening. The challenge of television spurred innovation in radio, including public affairs and music programs. However, structural shifts transforming the economy of the rural Midwest coupled with broadcast deregulation in the 1980s and 1990s erased the distinctiveness of rural broadcasting. Commercial country music on syndicated radio marked a vestige of a once-distinctive form of rural communication.

Sources and Further Reading: Michele Hilmes, *Radio Voices* (1997); Susan Smulyan, *Selling Radio* (1994); Derek Vaillant, "'Your Voice Came in Last Night but it Sounded a Little Scared': Rural Radio Listening, Progressivism, and 'Talking Back' in Wisconsin, 1920–1932," in Michele Hilmes and Jason Loviglio, eds., *Radio Reader* (2001).

Derek Vaillant
University of Michigan

A family listening to the radio and reading Father Coughlin's *Social Justice*, Royal Oak, Michigan, 1939. Library of Congress, Prints and Photographs Division, LC-USW3-016733-C.

Computers

During the early twentieth century, rural Americans hailed the proliferation of telephone service across the United States. Praised for connecting isolated communities to larger cities, more rural households had telephones by 1920 than urban ones. The Internet, utilizing computers and those same telephone connections pioneered one hundred years before, has been lauded for further shrinking the divide between rural and urban areas at the beginning of the twenty-first century.

The Midwest led the nation in telephone use by 1920. By September 2001, 57 percent of midwesterners used the Internet, compared with 54 percent nationally. Regional computer ownership and Internet use continues to grow quickly. By 2001, Minnesota led the Midwest and ranked third nationally, with over 66 percent of its population online. Rural residents across the nation are adopting computers and the Internet faster than urban and suburban populations. Although urban and suburban midwesterners remain more likely to use computers than their rural counterparts, the gap is rapidly shrinking.

Typically, rural people, like those in rural towns such as Cooperstown, North Dakota, see computer technology as a way to sustain and improve their quality of life. Cooperstown is located within the Griggs-Steele Empowerment Zone, the first of only ten rural federally funded zones in the nation. Other towns have also used computer technology to remain vibrant through applications like telemedicine, videoconferencing, and virtual classrooms. Businesses are attracted by the cheaper, less transient, and more available workforce found in communities across the Midwest.

Like the telephone, electrification, automobile, and radio, computer technology has lessened the gap between rural and urban, the Midwest, and the nation.

Sources and Further Reading: Ronald Kline, *Consumers in the Country* (2000); Minnesota State Historical Records Advisory Board, *Agriculture and Rural Life, Documenting Change* (2001); U.S. Department of Commerce, *A Nation Online* (2002).

Ben Leonard
Minnesota Historical Society,
St. Paul, Minnesota

Rural Institutions and Organizations

Alexis de Tocqueville believed that the *practice* of democracy in America led to exceptional behavior, the most important of which was the recurring formation of independent institutions and organizations. He marveled at both their variety and the social and political powers that they claimed for the common citizen. The representative institutions of rural America, and the Midwest in particular, do, in fact, embody most of the cultural, social, political, and economic values that make the region unique.

The membership, intent, and activities in these collective endeavors is as varied as the weather. Land owners, laborers, tenants, squatters, progressive reformers, "scientific farmers," men, women, and children all lent their time, money, and precious energies to the formation, operation, and survival of thousands of associations. Some, like Tocqueville, saw the purpose of their activity as chiefly political. Others leaned toward the "pecuniary benefits" that could accrue from collective and usually cooperative action. Social, cultural, and religious imperatives led still more to spend their social capital in forming churches, schools, fraternal organizations, unions, and veterans' groups. While a form of *de facto* segregation split many of these groups by ethnicity and kinship, religion, commodity types, class, and partisanship, most rural organizations consciously attempted to break through these barriers. They all relied on the practical experiences of their members and the respectability that participation conveyed.

The genesis of most rural institutions was the numerous agricultural societies and farmers' clubs that emerged in the first half of the nineteenth century. Agricultural societies focused on commercial farming by spreading practical information, testing implements, and promoting county fairs. The experiences in democratic rule, the creation of hierarchies, and the sporadic successes in lobbying elected officials acted as a practical education for many members. Farmers' clubs were more representative of a specific locale, meaning that their imperatives shifted with the men and women who chartered them. Active throughout the region, clubs provided venues where members could discuss the challenges that they faced. These included commercial dependencies, transportation problems, educational needs, and often political representation. In nearly all midwestern rural organizations, the conflict between local members and centralized authority was a constant theme.

Accordingly, the structure and scope of the major rural organizations formed around these broader contours and institutional landmarks. Four general tendencies can be observed in these diverse societies.

Movements. The first are associations that blended economic, social, and political agendas into what historian Lawrence Goodwyn termed a "movement culture." Driven by strong concerns over economic opportunity, rural Americans created organizations, met to discuss their interests, acted to rectify problems, and were changed by their efforts. These groups were animated by protest over "privilege" and a rhetoric that clearly divided citizens between "producers" and "special interests." Although members suffered from nostalgia for a mythic and idyllic past, they had a clear commitment to the present and future.

In the Midwest, the National Grange of the Order of Patrons of Husbandry (the Grange) and the Farmers' Alliance typify this category. The growing awareness of their economic marginalization propelled farmers toward cooperation and third-party politics in an effort to recast the emerging industrial-capitalist order. The Grange, founded in 1867 as a social and fraternal union, quickly transformed itself, following the 1873 depression, into a mass movement of citizens that formed marketing and purchasing cooperatives, promoted state ownership and regulation of railroads, granaries, and currency, and, against the National Grange's own stated charter, advanced political candidates. Although the institution was ultimately incapable of sustaining these goals, members did change their consumer, cooperative, and political behaviors. The evolution of the Northern Farmers' Alliance in the early 1880s conserved the heritage of these experiences. Arguing for the primacy of democratic controls over the marketplace, the Populists proposed not only market reforms but also structural political amendments to the Republic. While saddled with a one-issue political party, fusion with the Democrats, and the shifting economic fortunes of the farm sector, the Alliance established the cooperative as the essential ingredient of the movement culture of the Midwest.

Cooperatives. The first decades of the twentieth century saw a shift in the primary interests of progressive rural organizations. This second phase focused overwhelmingly on the creation and patronage of commodity cooperatives. Here, the central players in the Midwest were the American Society of Equity (ASE), the Farmers' Equity Union (FEU), and the Equity Cooperative Exchange (ECE). Cooperatives generally took two forms: those that forwarded the interest of a particular commodity, such as dairying or wheat in the upper Midwest, and those hoping to bring economic efficiency to individual members through economies of scale. Although it remained strong throughout the first half of the twentieth century, the cooperative movement was particularly popular in the 1920s. By the middle of that decade, the Midwest boasted nearly five thousand cooperative elevators and five hundred thousand active members.

The commercial success of many of these cooperatives points to the central problems of the movement. To thrive in the increasingly capital-intensive marketplace, cooperatives had to maximize their own efficiency. Cooperatives thus discarded what made them so trusted by farm families in the first place: local democratic control. Moreover, by challenging the established, free-market providers, the farmers' cooperatives drew the attention and ire of many well-funded adversaries.

The centrality of the "cooperative question" to rural organizations during this period is seen in the intimate relationship among the ASE, FEU, and ECE. The ASE was founded first in 1902 by James A. Everitt, an Indianapolis farm journalist, to form local chapters in the interest of gathering production data. Market conditions would be studied, outputs tallied, and members advised to maintain specific minimum prices for their commodities. The success of the ASE rested in its ability to interest a large number of commercial farmers to participate, not necessarily with Everitt's leadership or the ASE organization. Accordingly, local tobacco and then wheat farmers easily redirected the mission of their ASE chapters to more aggressive cooperative tactics. The internal split between single-commodity farmers and smaller, more diversified farmers divided the ASE by 1907.

Two new bodies formed by the schism were the FEU and ECE. Founded by C. O. Drayton in 1910, the FEU hoped to curtail the provocative calls made by the wheat faction of the ASE for state-owned utilities and large commodity cooperatives. Drayton proposed a smaller, more localized form of cooperation based on the Rochdale plan, a method employed successfully by the Grange a generation earlier. Members liked that the FEU had little or no central bureaucracy, foreswore the social and fraternal movement culture of the Grange and Alliance, and focused its energies on creating scores of locally owned elevators, creameries, and even some retail outlets. The notion of cooperation contained within the FEU was decidedly local, meeting short-term economic needs, and fully controlled by grass-roots members.

By contrast, George Loftus encouraged the wheat faction of the ASE, concentrated largely in Wisconsin, Minnesota, and the Dakotas, to centralize their cooperative efforts, going toe-to-toe with the big grain market speculators in Minneapolis. Loftus created the ECE in 1908. Essentially a corporation intended to gather, grade, and sell wheat, the ECE retained the key ideological values of a midwestern cooperative: Membership was limited to those who patronized the ECE, one vote per member, and democratic rule throughout. Battling the powerful Minnesota Chamber of Commerce (which controlled the northern wheat markets), the ECE rekindled the protest spirit of earlier agrarian crusades. Still, the rise and fall of the ECE was paced by market conditions for wheat, livestock, and wool between 1914 and 1926, and not by the cooperative ethos of its members.

Transitional. A third distinct phase of rural institution building overlays this cooperative era. Driven by the desire of many midwesterners to find a place in the new economic order, these groups acted as transitional organizations. Dominated by the American Farm Bureau Federation (AFBF), the National Farmers' Union (NFU), and the Non-Partisan League (NPL), the central debate revolved around the question of local versus centralized control and the growing class distinctions within the farm population. The Great Depression and New Deal certainly aided these institutions in drawing stark differences between their methods and their goals.

The purpose of the AFBF was to accommodate centralization. Founded in 1919, the Bureau was originally comprised of local cooperatives, county agents, and representatives from regional colleges and businesses. Coming on the heels of World War I, and in the midst of the Red Scare, the Farm Bureau had a decidedly conservative disposition. They saw as their mission to represent agribusiness and, therefore, opposed all efforts to socialize the marketplace through regulation or state ownership. The Farm Bureau also moved aggressively to lobby federal officials, becoming a key player in what was to be known as the Farm Bloc, a role they continue to play to this day. It was during the New Deal, and as a result of many of that era's redistributive economic policies, that the Bureau emerged as one of the Midwest's most powerful rural organizations. Their claim to represent the farmer as a small businessman (rather than producer) and close connections with the USDA Extension Service gave the Bureau an advantaged position from which it consolidated and centralized this authority.

By contrast, the NFU and NPL saw a very different role for the commodity cooperative. Emerging from the dust of the Populist Revolt, the NFU grew slowly in the Midwest until the 1907 Panic, then steadily into the 1920s. Strongest in Kansas, Illinois, Indiana, and Missouri, the NFU represented farm families that wanted the cooperative to act as a local clearinghouse for produce as well as educational and political ideas. The NPL also retained the strong protest ethos of the People's Party. Emerging in the upper Midwest as the political child of the ASE in 1915, the NPL ran slates of candidates who advocated state ownership of the largest elevators, insurance services, and tax and banking reforms. Both the NFU and NPL saw their members as being unfairly excluded from the market by centralizing forces such as the railroads, the commodity exchange boards, and of course, the banks.

Of these three transitional institutions, the Farm Bureau was better situated to take advantage of the political and economic forces that were transforming American life before 1941. The stated goal of the AFBF was to speak *for* the farm community. Bureau leaders such as Aaron Sapiro were openly contemptuous of established, local cooperatives. Although support for the Bureau was split in the rural Midwest, the lobbying advantages of the Farm Bloc, its closeness to the Extension Service, and the economic staying power of wealthier farmers gave the AFBF a decided advantage during the New Deal. Supporting the controversial Agricultural Adjustment Act, which was opposed by the NFU and the Farm Holiday Association, the Bureau grew while the NFU and NPL languished. The conservative tone of the Bureau persisted after the war, opposing most efforts to aid small producers and agricultural laborers.

Civic. A final characteristic of many midwestern rural organizations was their ability to absorb the diversity of the population. Historian Jon Gjerde refers to this process as the construction of "complementary identit[ies]," and it is here that the flexibility of rural institutions became so useful to local members. Rural midwesterners could celebrate their distinct religious and national heritage and, at the same time, honor the "patriotic" values of individualism, voluntary cooperation, and democracy (legacies that many conserved from the old country).

However, the *civic* action used to form local churches hints at the potential for conflict. Topping the list in numbers and membership, church formation is in many ways the most important institution building in the region. While the process is not unique to the Midwest, the specific configuration of immigrant groups, their high regional concentrations, and the religious denominations involved supports the claim that the Midwest is a distinctive place.

Sources and Further Reading: Peter Argersinger, *The Limits of Agrarian Radicalism* (1995); Hal S. Barron, *Mixed Harvest* (1997); David Blanke, *Sowing the American Dream* (2000); David B. Danbom, *Born in the Country* (1995); Lowell K. Dyson, *Farmers' Organizations* (1986); John Mack Faragher, *Sugar Creek* (1886); Jon Gjerde, *The Minds of the West* (1997); Lawrence Goodwyn, *Democratic Promise* (1976); Steven J. Keillor, *Cooperative Commonwealth* (2000); Ronald R. Kline, *Consumers in the Country* (2000); Susan Sessions Rugh, *Our Common Country* (2001); Thomas A. Woods, *Knights of the Plow* (1991).

David Blanke
Texas A&M University–Corpus Christi

Community Improvement Organizations, Farm Cooperatives, and Economic Organizations

While the rural Midwest has supported a dense farm population, it has also nurtured a rich organizational life of community groups, cooperatives, and other economic organizations. Consequently, its organizations and leaders have often served as national models. From 1950 to the present, as mechanization led to farm consolidation and out-migration, many older organizations folded their tents and departed. A new generation of alliances focuses on economic development, youth, and solving the social problems of an aging population.

Voluntary associations for the specific goal of socioeconomic improvement of rural life affected and were affected by regional identity, politics, class, ethnicity, and religion. Seeking mainly profitability and sustainability for agriculture and related businesses, they often consisted mainly of members from a specific region, class, ethnic group, or church, and thus also indirectly functioned to sustain these other identities. In addition, membership in and leadership of such organizations provided an individual with local status.

A rural desire for consensus often demands that community organizations appear nonpartisan, nonsectarian, and nonprofit. Yet Farm Bureau cooperatives in Corn Belt areas where the consensus was Republican were themselves hardly nonpartisan. Garden clubs in Scandinavian Lutheran areas or Parent-Teacher-Associations in Catholic enclaves were hardly nonsectarian. Farm cooperatives were not nonprofit; they merely divided profits among their members as patronage dividends.

The rural Midwest is not a monolith, and its Corn Belt core fostered different associations than did its periphery. Ethnic enclaves sprinkled throughout the Midwest created their own institutions.

A farmers' club or community club or women's club developed from the grass roots, out of the exchange of labor and goods that characterized rural neighborhoods. After 1910, it was just as likely to be organized at the behest of a county agent or other professional expert from the state university or a government bureau. And yet, even the club that experts helped organize often sponsored programs that went beyond their goals of greater agricultural production and middle-class home management.

Cooperatives were arguably the most numerous economic organizations. Praised as defining parameters of cooperation (but not always or completely obeyed) were the well-known Rochdale rules. Developed in 1844 by members of the Rochdale (England) Society of Equitable Pioneers, they included the idea of one person, one vote; membership open to all regardless of religious or political views; cash sales at market prices; limited returns to investors and a limit to how many shares an investor could own; and profits distributed to members based on their patronage of the cooperative. Cooperatives were nonpartisan, nonsectarian, and not for any one person's profit.

The Rochdale rules were English, but in most cases it is a myth that immigrants modeled their cooperatives after European ones. Yankee migrants brought farmers' mutual fire insurance from New England to Michigan, Ohio, and the rest of the Old Northwest; they patterned their Union stores after New England's; they looked to Orange County, New York, for a model for successful creameries. Immigrants to the Midwest quickly adopted American economic practices over Old World ones, but retained Old World social customs. When Minnesota's Danes heard about Denmark's new cooperative creameries, they waited until they saw a successful one in Iowa before they acted.

Mid-nineteenth-century cooperation as it evolved in Rochdale and other places had a radical, anticapitalist tone. But it was also a plastic concept that was molded into different shapes in Hancock County, Iowa, and Hancock, Michigan. Political, ethnic, and religious movements used cooperation to give members a tangible economic benefit. If they were leftist, as were many Finnish Americans in the Canadian Shield area, then their cooperatives were radical—in this case, the Cooperative Central Exchange and its member stores. In the hands of more conservative dairy farmers or Farm Bureau members, the concept lost its radical connotations. Consumers' cooperation was often seen as more radical than producers' cooperation. A Farmers' Alliance store competing against local merchants indicated political radicalism, whereas the Missouri Farmers Association sold fertilizer without political labels. Cooperation imported from Europe might be seen as more radical than a homegrown variety because it was "alien."

When Old Stock, Republican, prosperous farmers and even Main Street merchants used Rochdale-style cooperation in conservative towns, it supplemented capitalism. From 1900 to 1920, merchants used the Right Relationship League to escape the competition of mail-order retailers; they sold their stores to associations of cooperating customers, who hired the merchant to run the store. In some rural areas, the cooperative did not compete against private business, but brought a needed service (telephones, electricity, a store) that investors and entrepreneurs did not think would be profitable.

Sparks sometimes flew. When merchants in one Minnesota town helped farmers start a cooperative grain elevator, the elevator companies started a store, selling below cost, to punish the merchants. Local organizations fought state or national ones that threatened local autonomy, just as rural school districts fought consolidation. Farmers' elevators resisted the American Farm Bureau Federation's 1921 attempt to set up a national grain marketing pool, the U.S. Grain Growers, Inc.

Women's clubs focused on gendered issues of education, mutual assistance, and community service. They addressed economic issues, but they could not entirely avoid the traditional sexual division of labor. After women gained the vote in 1920, they obtained a greater role in the Farm Bureau and other organizations. They successfully argued for the right to participate in the formerly male sphere of economic decision making and for the formation of Home Bureaus devoted to women's home, garden, and poultry responsibilities.

After World War II, farm consolidation and loss of farm population reduced rural political clout and rendered such interorganizational struggles luxuries that could not be afforded (but were sometimes still fought). In the farm crisis of the mid-1980s, coalition building was stressed in Iowa (the Iowa Farm Unity Coalition), Minnesota (Groundswell), Illinois, and other midwestern states. Women, including Anne Kanten and Lou-Anne Kling, played a greater leadership role than ever before. This 1980s "save the family farm coalition" soldiers on in some areas, but it must share the rural organizational space with general economic development efforts to convince firms to relocate to small towns, whether or not their business relates to agriculture.

Sources and Further Reading: Hal S. Barron, *Mixed Harvest* (1997); Nancy K. Berlage, "Organizing the Farm Bureau: Family, Community, and Professionals, 1914–1928," *Agricultural History* 75 (Fall 2001); Andrew R.L. Cayton and Peter S. Onuf, *The Midwest and the Nation* (1990); Don Doyle, "The Social Functions of Voluntary Associations in a Nineteenth-Century American Town," *Social Science History* 1 (Spring 1977); Mark Friedberger, *Farm Families and Change in Twentieth-Century America* (1988); Steven J. Keillor, *Cooperative Commonwealth: Co-ops in Rural Minnesota, 1859–1939* (2000); Mary Neth, *Preserving the Family Farm* (1995); Jim Schwab, *Raising Less Corn and More Hell* (1988).

Steven J. Keillor
Askov, Minnesota

Country Churches

In the national imagination, sameness and dull monotony characterize the Midwest. This holds true for its religious identity (Christianity) as well as its topography (flat). This assumption, of course, overlooks the diverse geographic, denominational, social, and racial identities that rural churches exhibit. Country churches in the Midwest have served many roles in their communities. Spiritual guidance remains the foremost concern, but social activism—whether as a reform movement or to resist reform—figures prominently, too. Changes in rural life occupy religiously observant midwesterners today just as they did in previous centuries.

Churches in the rural Midwest developed from the work of immigrants from other states as well as Europe. This process took centuries and eventually included the entire denominational gamut. Geography influenced the spread and character of country churches. Lutheran and Catholic settlement, planned or unplanned, characterized the upper Midwest. Catholic settlers to these areas tended to come from Germany and Eastern Europe. Scandinavian immigrants helped Germans extend a broad array of Lutheran churches across the Midwest. Baptists, Methodists, and Presbyterians appeared throughout the region. Great Plains' settlements often reflected colonization attempts by railroad companies. African American churches maintained a small but committed presence; the rural Midwest offered economic as well as religious opportunities unavailable in the East and South.

The Pentecostal movement appeared in the early twentieth century, developing its presence among both rural and urban poor. At the same time many denominations engaged in well-meaning but short-lived agrarian efforts to improve rural life's social and spiritual shortcomings. Some church leaders (including both Catholics and Protestants) saw only inefficiency, social myopia, and denominational bickering. These reform movements hoped to make rural America resemble the efficiency and productivity of the nation's industrial cities. As the center of the nation's farmland, the Midwest figured prominently in these plans. The reformers, though, occasionally denigrated country churches as spiritual and cultural backwaters. Rural reformers also attempted to improve farming methods. This pursuit seemed prescient after the Dust Bowl. Members and pastors of these churches often resisted the religious agenda, preferring their local ways to those of outsiders. So, while agricultural methods improved, churches often offered respite from change.

The rural Midwest remains a bastion of religious diversity. While country churches experience declining memberships, they are often valued as tangible links with the past. Rural reform movements continue to maintain a presence. Some mainstream Protestants today participate in the family farm and ecological movements. The National Catholic Rural Life Conference, founded in 1923 and based in Des Moines, Iowa, pursues many of the same goals. Many evangelical Protestants perceive these movements as too liberal and thus distance themselves. New issues continue to confront country churches: the emergence of Latino/a immigrant communities, the region's shrinking population, and the influence of industrial agribusiness. The rural Midwest's responses reflect the intellectual and spiritual diversity of its churches.

Sources and Further Reading: David Danbom, *The Resisted Revolution* (1979); Jacob Dorn, "The Rural Ideal and Agrarian Realities: Arthur E. Holt and the Vision of a Decentralized America in the Interwar Years," *Church History* 52 (March 1983); James H. Madison, "Reformers and the Rural Church, 1900–1950," *Journal of American History* 73 (Dec. 1986); Jeffrey Marlett, *Saving the Heartland* (2002).

Jeff Marlett
The College of St. Rose, New York

Equity

The American Society of Equity, popularly known as the Equity and occasionally referred to as the American Square Deal Association, was the 1902 brainchild of Indianapolis editor and seedsman James A. Everitt. Reasoning that capital and labor held tremendous bargaining power over the national economy, Everitt determined to organize farmers into a third force. Eschewing railroad regulation, legislative agendas, and cooperative endeavors, Everitt focused his attention upon organizing farmers into a cohesive whole capable of widespread withholding actions. Within a year, some thirty thousand midwestern farmers had joined Everitt's cause, though his failure to hire a corps of professionals left the number well short of his goal of one million. Everitt's next test came in the summer of 1903, when he urged Equity members to hold their wheat until the price rose above one dollar per bushel. When it did, more as a result of a fortuitous accident than Equity's power, membership rose to approximately fifty-nine thousand farmers. Further small successes led to two hundred thousand members in all states and several Canadian provinces. Many new members did not, however, share Everitt's limited vision of what activities a farm organization should undertake, and fissures soon appeared in the Equity.

By 1907, Wisconsin members, guided by national secretary M. Wes Tubbs, wrested control of the Equity from Everitt, broadening the organization's perspective considerably in the process. In an effort to limit profit-robbing middlemen and political machines, Tubbs and his associates encouraged cooperatives and farmer-owned businesses, as well as candidates for political office, and found considerable support in the Spring Wheat Belt of the Dakotas. Rarely meeting with success, the Equity disbanded and merged with the National Farmers' Union in 1934.

These cattle fetched record-breaking prices in a sale negotiated by Equity Cooperative Exchange Salesmen and the Trohms Brothers of Janeway Sale, Union Stockyards, St. Paul (1918). Minnesota Historical Society, Location no. HD7.51 p45, neg. no. 30076.

Sources and Further Reading: Robert H. Bahmer, "The American Society of Equity," *Agricultural History* 14 (Winter 1940); Lowell K. Dyson, *Farmers' Organizations* (1986); James Andrew Everitt, *The Third Power* (1903).

Kimberly K. Porter
University of North Dakota

Sources and Further Reading: Osha Gray Davidson, *Broken Heartland* (1990); Mark Friedberger, *Family Farms and Change in 20th Century America* (1988); Adam Ritscher, "The Ongoing American Farm Crisis," *Socialist Action* (Oct. 1999).

Peter Bratt
The Ohio State University–Columbus

Family Farm Coalitions

Family farm coalitions have long existed as advocacy groups of American farmers. Most agricultural organizations have sprung up during times of crisis in the rural areas of the United States: The crisis of the 1880s and 1890s saw the rise of the Grange and the Populist Party, and the Dust Bowl of the 1930s spurred midwestern farmers to renewed political and social activism. The most recent farm crisis in the Midwest during the 1980s provoked the rise of similar organizations.

The roots of the 1980s farm crisis lay in the previous decade. During the 1970s, farmers were encouraged by the U. S. government to increase the export of agricultural products overseas by purchasing improved machinery and land. Banks lent money freely, and land values rose sharply by the end of the 1970s.

For various reasons, the bubble burst in the early 1980s. The value of the U.S. dollar rose, making American exports more expensive overseas. The demand for agricultural exports declined sharply, as American farmers saw prices fall for their products and their land. Burdened with large mortgages, many farmers were forced off the land. The number of farmers in the United States declined to 2.1 million by 1986, and continues to decline, with only 1.9 million working the land today.

Various agricultural organizations arose to assist midwestern farmers. Most vocal was the American Agriculture Movement (AAM). During the late 1970s and 1980s, this organization led "tractorcades" on various midwestern state capitals. Other militant farm organizations included the Family Farmer Survival Association, the American Agriculture Movement, and Groundswell. Most organizations provided a realm of social services for troubled farmers, ranging from child-care to debt repayment. More traditional farm organizations, like the National Farmers Organization, the Farm Bureaus Federation, and the National Farmers' Union, also began to advocate for governmental relief for small farmers. These organizations, while vocal and supportive of small farmers, failed to prevent the rise of factory farms or to reverse the decline of traditional family farms.

The Farmers' Alliance

Forged amid the economic hardships that struck rural America in the late nineteenth century, the Farmers' Alliance grew quickly into the largest agricultural movement of its time. The Alliance was established in Texas in 1874, but later sank some of its deepest roots in the Midwest, particularly in Kansas and the Dakotas. The movement inherited values, attitudes, and a tradition of participatory democracy from the Granges, Greenbackers, and local agricultural societies that emerged after the Civil War.

Like their agrarian predecessors, Alliance men and women organized out of shared economic and political grievances that accompanied their growing participation in a regional and national market economy. Commercial production had raised farm incomes, but as commodity prices fell throughout the 1880s, farmers struggled to meet the fixed costs levied by railroads and grain elevators. Furthermore, debt and deflation, coupled with a crippling drought, threatened farm families with foreclosure and loss of land. Consequently, the Alliance's St. Louis Platform (1889) articulated a reform agenda that emphasized farmer cooperation and positive government action. These parallel strategies converged most clearly in the movement's innovative subtreasury plan, in which farmers' crops would be used as collateral for low-cost government loans.

While the Alliance agenda resonated with farmers throughout the Midwest, the movement's rise was also made possible by its social organization, which mirrored the everyday structure of rural life. The community-based suballiance, the institutional building block of the Alliance, built upon and reinforced the informal rural neighborhoods that stretched across the countryside. The suballiance also served important political and social functions. While Alliance lectures and reform newspapers facilitated the political self-education of farm families, local meetings provided opportunities for discussion and fellowship that promoted social cohesion and group loyalty within the community of rural reformers. In addition, the cooperation between men and women that was necessary to the survival of family farms also extended to the democratic political culture of the suballiance. Women held equal membership within the Alliance, and their participation included active roles as organizers and lecturers. One notable speaker, Kansas reformer Mary Elizabeth Lease, provided the movement with perhaps its most striking rallying cry when she challenged farmers to "raise less corn and more hell."

From its creation, the Alliance maintained a disciplined strategy of nonpartisan agitation, but as the problems that haunted farmers persisted through the early 1890s, the organization faced a critical decision about its future. Traditionalist members affirmed the need to pursue reform above the partisan fray, but a growing contingent advocated entry into the realm of party politics, whether through the two existing parties or the creation of a new one. The formation of the Populist Party, which endorsed the St. Louis Platform, changed the context of the reform crusade. Denied the right to vote, female insurgents saw their influence diminished, and cooperative local endeavors declined as electing Populist candidates became a central aim of many reformers. Although the weakened and divided Alliance soon collapsed, the democratic vision of its cooperative legacy endured to inspire subsequent generations of agrarian reformers.

Sources and Further Reading: Lawrence Goodwyn, *Democratic Promise* (1976); Robert C. McMath, Jr., *American Populism* (1993); Scott McNall, *The Road to Rebellion* (1988); Jeffrey Ostler, *Prairie Populism* (1993).

Jeremy Neely
University of Missouri–Columbia

The Farm Bureau

The Farm Bureau is the nation's largest general farm organization, comprised of member associations organized at the local, state, and national levels. The Farm Bureau first organized at the local level to help farmers learn about new scientific techniques being developed at the state land-grant colleges and experiment stations. County Farm Bureaus served as a local base for the Cooperative Extension Service, which was established by the Smith-Lever Act of 1914. The Extension Service sent university-trained agricultural and home economics agents into the countryside to demonstrate the new techniques to farm men and women.

While other farmers' groups cooperated with the Extension Service, in the Midwest, the Farm Bureau was by far its strongest supporter, contributing funds and sharing office space with Extension personnel. As the Farm Bureau expanded, however, it began to develop political and economic agendas at odds with the educational mission of the Extension Service. To promote these agendas, state Farm Bureau federations formed in the late 1910s. At the national level, the American Farm Bureau Federation (AFBF) was organized in 1919 and developed into one of the nation's most powerful lobbying groups; it remains so, despite the declining farming population. In the 1950s, the marriage between the Extension Service and Farm Bureau was legally dismantled—a response, in part, to criticism that public Extension funds were being inappropriately used to support the private Farm Bureau.

Part of the continuing appeal of the organization has been the range of services and activities it offers. Farm Bureau projects were at first primarily scientific in scope, but they increasingly focused on social, political, and economic objectives. In the 1920s, the Farm Bureau sought to revive the ailing cooperative movement—which had first gained strength in the late nineteenth century, but then declined—using sophisticated marketing techniques. The Farm Bureau attracted membership through its sponsorship of wool pools, poultry and egg marketing associations, livestock shipping and fertilizer associations, and supply cooperatives. Around the same time, the Farm Bureau began to sell auto, fire, and life insurance, creating affiliated companies that remain a vital part of its program.

Although men dominated the Farm Bureau, women also participated. In Illinois and New York, women formed separate organizations at the county and state levels called the Home Bureau. In Wisconsin and Iowa, members formed auxiliary-type organizations that fostered home economics. While these groups often focused on so-called "women's issues," Bureau women participated in other matters as well. In 1921, the AFBF formed the National Women's Committee, which subsequently became the Home and Community Department and later the Associated Women of the Farm Bureau. The Farm Bureau was also a major supporter of rural youth clubs, helping to organize the boys and girls clubs that later became part of the 4-H Club system.

Traditionally strongest in the Midwest, the Farm Bureau has enjoyed unusual success due to its multifaceted program, strong support at the grassroots level, and political savvy.

Sources and Further Reading: John Mark Hansen, *Gaining Access: Congress and the Farm Lobby, 1919–1981* (1991); John J. Lacey, *Farm Bureau in Illinois* (1965); Julie McDonald, *Ruth Buxton Sayre, First Lady of the Farm* (1980).

Nancy Kay Berlage
History Associates Incorporated,
Rockville, Maryland

Farmers' Markets

As the bell rings to open the farmers' market, the first customers stream in, buying tomatoes, baked goods, green beans, or cut flowers from favorite vendors. A scene much like this occurs throughout the Midwest, in small towns and large cities, from May through October.

As places where producers sell food directly to consumers, farmers' markets are community economic institutions with a long history. They declined with the rise of refrigeration and national supermarket chains, but reemerged during the 1980s Farm Crisis. Producers often see farmers' markets as a profitable alternative to the wholesale commodity markets of an industrial agricultural system. Consumers show growing interest in farm-fresh and regional specialty foods, and municipalities hope to enliven public areas and stimulate local business development.

Farmers' markets in the Midwest are diverse, ranging from busy, upscale urban markets with paid managers and entertainment to informal markets that are little more than a cluster of pickup trucks selling sweet corn on a rural byway. For most vendors, they provide a modest, though welcome income stream. Vendors include specialty and organic producers, immigrant and minority entrepreneurs, artisans and crafters, farm wives developing sidelines to the family's grain or livestock operation, and retirees seeking social interaction and supplemental income. Customers are also diverse. Some farmers' markets draw affluent professionals. Others depend more on low-income residents and senior citizens participating in the USDA's Farmers' Market Nutrition Program. Linking producers and consumers and rural and urban places, farmers' markets are the cultural and economic crossroads for the people and products of the region.

Sources and Further Reading: Lisa M. Hamilton, "The American Farmers Market," *Gastronomica* 2 (Summer 2002); C. Clare Hinrichs, Gilbert W. Gillespie, and Gail W. Feenstra, "Social Learning and Innovation at Retail Farmers' Markets," *Rural Sociology* 69 (Spring 2004). Tim Payne, *U.S. Farmers Markets, 2000: A Study of Emerging Trends* (May 2002).

C. Clare Hinrichs
Pennsylvania State University–University Park

The Farmers' Union

The Farmers' Union, officially known as the Farmers Educational and Cooperative Union of America, celebrated in 2002 a century of struggle and achievement by farmers for political and economic democracy. Although it started as a national organization in Point, Texas, it was the merger with two other midwestern farm movements that allowed the Farmers' Union to achieve its greatest strength. In 1926, the Farmers' Union merged with the Producers' Alliance and the Equity Cooperative Exchange, transforming the Midwest Farmers' Union state affiliates into a new organizational force for education, cooperative economic development, and legislative action.

The Farmers' Union is dedicated to the ideal of a family farming strategy for agriculture. Over time, it favored a graduated land tax, progressive taxes on per-

Farmer's market, Bloomington, Indiana, 2000. Courtesy Folklore Institute, Indiana University.

sonal income, repeal of the sales tax, federal health insurance, and the Missouri Valley Authority. It organized farmers throughout the Midwest to develop cooperatives for marketing, food processing, farm supply, credit unions, and phone service. In 1934, President Franklin Delano Roosevelt requested the National Farmers' Union to lead in electrifying rural America. Farmers' Union locals across the country responded with vigor, resulting in electricity and a profound lifestyle change throughout rural America.

The Farmers' Union educational program is organized through members' active participation in their Farmers' Union locals. Family members learn about and act on policy initiatives and learn the value, structure, and development of cooperatives. The educational process involves all members of a farm family starting at age eight. From the organization's genesis, women participated equally with men. Youth over age sixteen have voting rights, may hold office, and serve as delegates at county, state, and national conventions.

The Farmers' Union established adult and youth educational conferences, institutes, and camping programs. Exploration and critical thinking about Farmers' Union philosophy, policy debate, training in parliamentary procedure, socio-drama, and folk singing and dance continue as primary learning strategies. Group singing is common to nearly all Farmers' Union gatherings. Music from other countries highlights the importance of understanding other cultures and undergirds the organization's stance on civil rights, civil liberties, and cooperative economic development. Ensuring the commitment to global self-determination, the Farmers' Union was a founding member of the International Federation of Agricultural Producers (IFAP) and was a very early supporter of the United Nations.

The Farmers' Union continues to address policy that supports improved quality of life for all Americans, such as education, health care, and civil rights and liberties. The organization has a history of sending busloads of members to Washington, D.C., and statehouses around the nation to bring the voice of family farmers directly to their legislators.

Leadership training, business experience, citizenship involvement, experience, and understanding of national and international policy are experiences that the Farmers' Union has organized for thousands of rural citizens. Spurred on by injustices perpetrated by the powerful grain marketing companies that often ended in bankruptcy for many American farmers, the voice of the Farmers' Union on farm issues continues to support family farms and rural communities. It has generated one hundred years of effective leadership to serve its members' goals.

Sources and Further Reading: Charles Conrad, *50 Years of the North Dakota Farmers Union* (1976); Gladys Talbott Edwards, *The Farmers Union Triangle* (1941); Harold V. Knight, *Grass Roots* (1947); Russell Blaine Nye, *Midwestern Progressive Politics* (1959).

Lorna Miller
University of Wisconsin–Madison

The Grange

The Grange refers to a unit of the Order of Patrons of Husbandry and is the common name for the entire Order. Founded in 1867, the Order started to grow modestly a year later, and soon had forty granges in Minnesota and a handful each in Iowa, Illinois, Ohio, Pennsylvania, and New York. When membership boomed, reaching 858,050 in 1875, the midwestern states with the most granges were Missouri, Indiana, and Iowa. Never again, through its subsequent waves of growth and decline, would the Order be centered in the Midwest. In 2001, its members were most numerous in the northeast, the far west, and Ohio.

The Order's principal founder, Oliver Hudson Kelley, was a Bostonian who moved to Chicago in 1847 and, two years later, worked for the Minnesota Territory's legislature. Kelley claimed some land near Itasca in hope that the territorial capital would move there. When he learned that it would stay in St. Paul, Kelley switched from land speculation to farming and soon helped to organize Minnesota's first agricultural society in Benton County. Then, partly inspired by Masonry's rapid growth, he founded the Patrons of Husbandry as a similar fraternity for rural people.

When the Grange grew, as it did especially in the early 1870s, its great appeals were cooperative distribution of goods including farm equipment, which was pioneered by the Minnesota State Grange's alliance with Montgomery Ward and other retailers, and legislative lobbying for railroad regulations. Grangers, notably in Iowa, took part in such lobbying, but the so-called granger laws were not the work of any one organization, but of farm protesters, often called grangers, although most of them were not members of the Grange.

Membership started to shrink in 1875, dropping to 124,420 in 1880. That decline and subsequent recovery began what D. Sven Nordin, an important historian of the Order, calls the "second Granger Movement." That second movement had a few women leaders, notably though not exclusively in the Midwest. Mary Mayo, Chaplain and Deputy Lecturer of the Michigan State Grange, was an important voice in the Order through most of the nineteenth century's last quarter. Jennie Buell, who succeeded Mayo, wrote a biography of Mayo and contributed articles to many magazines.

Grange membership has since fluctuated enormously, slightly exceeding its 1875 peak in1952 and dropping to around three hundred thousand as of 2004. The Order remains interested in a broad range of issues that concern rural society in particular and the world more generally, and provides services of many kinds to its members.

Sources and Further Reading: Charles M. Gardner, *The Grange, Friend of the Farmer* (1949); David H. Howard, *People, Pride and Progress* (1992); Donald B. Marti, *Women of the Grange* (1991); D. Sven Nordin, *Rich Harvest* (1974); Thomas A. Woods, *Knights of the Plow* (1991).

Donald Marti
Indiana University–South Bend

Homemakers' Clubs

A 1918 U.S. Department of Agriculture publication observed that extension programs for women "will mean better home life on the farm . . . and an ideal rural community life." Although extension/demonstration club work became widespread in the twentieth century, it was by no means the only type of homemaker organization. Since the late 1800s, the Populist movement, the Grange, farmers' institutes, garden clubs, quilting groups, and seed exchanges have engaged women's interest and support, as have local affiliates to national organizations such as the Woman's Christian Temperance Union, General Federation of Women's Clubs, National Farm and Garden Association, and National Congress of Farm Women.

Each offered outlets for socializing, education, and civic involvement. Clubs often formed the nucleus of community activities and improvement projects. Nevertheless, agricultural leaders of the early 1900s worried that no single organization focused on the domestic training that would, they believed, make women more efficient, satisfied, and modern in their approach to rural life. Out of this concern, home extension/demonstration clubs emerged. The agrarian press and the growing medium of radio encouraged women to join. Federal support came with the Smith-Lever Act (1914) and its stipulation that a portion of money received by land-grant colleges had to be used for home extension work.

Throughout the Midwest, extension/demonstration units appeared during World War I when food conservation at home was imperative to winning the war "over there." Many of the first units were organized from preexisting homemaker groups such as canning clubs. Food preparation and preservation were important, but by no means were they the only subjects. Clothing construction, nutrition, first aid, childcare, and learning to use new appliances and to be smart shoppers were among the lessons. Club projects purchased items for schools, funded early hot-lunch programs in some areas, and encouraged local 4-H organization. Club organizers operated on the premise that agrarian women shared common bonds in being both American and rural, but race, ethnicity, and cultural background influenced the degree of women's participation, and acceptance, in these clubs.

During the Great Depression, the organizational structure of extension work was appropriated by a number of New Deal recovery programs to establish canning kitchens, local mattress factories, and lending libraries of books and children's toys. Sewing, gardening, and food preparation methods taught at club meetings also helped many families cope during the hard times of the 1930s. Later, during World War II, clubwomen of both extension and nonextension groups maintained Victory Gardens, directed scrap drives, kept youth clubs operational, and took on additional farm duties while men were in service.

Homemakers' clubs were (and are) integral to rural life. Over the years, social and technological changes have altered the content of club programs and projects. Nevertheless, many basic concerns remain unchanged. Adequate health care, rural school needs, balancing demands of home and family, maintaining and improving the quality of agrarian life, and farm economics are as relevant today as they were a century ago.

Sources and Further Reading: Evelyn Birkby, *Neighboring on the Air* (1991); Anne M. Evans, "Women's Rural Organizations and Their Activities," Bulletin #719, U.S. Department of Agriculture (29 Aug. 1918); Anne Ruggles Gere, *Intimate Practices* (1997); Marilyn Irvin Holt, *Linoleum, Better Babies and The Modern Farm Woman, 1890–1930* (1995); Theodora Martin, *The Sound of Our Own Voices* (1987).

Marilyn Irvin Holt
Abilene, Kansas

The National Farmers Organization

The National Farmers Organization developed out of farmers' frustration with low income as a result of the modernization of agriculture. Due to declining demand for American agricultural products after the Korean War, farm income sagged by 25 percent from 1951 to 1955. In the midst of a drought that covered the Midwest in 1955, farmers in Iowa and Missouri gathered to bring national attention to their situation. Organizers called for a government-enforced floor on farm product prices. Quickly, the NFO gained popularity among midwestern farmers, and by 1957, the new farm group claimed over 180 thousand members.

The NFO sought to raise prices through withholding actions that would force food companies to sign contracts with the NFO before members would sell products. In 1962, the NFO held its first major withholding action across the entire Midwest. Other withholding actions followed in 1963 and 1967. Problems with the withholding actions prevented success. While NFO farmers withheld their products, nonmember farmers continued to sell. This antagonism led to violence between farmers. In frustration, the NFO turned to hog and calf shoots in the late 1960s. NFO farmers shot over fourteen thousand of their own market animals and buried them in pits, which alienated consumers.

In the late 1970s, the NFO turned away from withholding actions to collective marketing, which brought farmers' products together and sold the products to distant markets that paid higher prices. With a current membership of about ten thousand, the NFO continues to provide farmers a chance to get a better return on their production.

Sources and Further Reading: Jon Lauck, "The National Farmers Organization and Farmer Bargaining Power," *Michigan Historical Review* 24 (Fall 1998); Patrick Mooney and Theo Majka, *Farmers' and Farm Workers' Movements* (1995); Don Muhm, *The NFO: A Farm Belt Rebel* (2000).

Ryan Stockwell
University of Missouri–Columbia

The Farm Holiday Association

In 1932, Iowan Milo Reno proposed that farmers, like bankers, have a holiday: a cessation of activity designed to give a shattered rural economy time to recover. By limiting their own production, farmers could, in time, regain control of the production process. Toward that end, the Farm Holiday Association, established in Des Moines, tapped into both older populist, radical ideologies and immediate economic discontent. While some scholars view the Holiday as a failed, last-ditch, antimodern backlash against social and economic change, others argue that New Deal farm programs offered rural activists a means to accept modernity without completely surrendering their rural identity.

The Holiday organized various acts of rural resistance in the early 1930s. Reno and others attempted to organize a farmers' strike throughout the Midwest, although most of this activity was conducted only in some counties of the upper Plains states. The Holiday also broke up foreclosure sales, discouraged nonaffili-

Farm Holiday Association march, St. Paul, Minnesota, 1933. Photo by St. *Paul Daily News*, Minnesota Historical Society, MHS Locator no. SA5.2/p15. Nebr. Courtesy Minnesota Historical Society, SA5.2 p15, 5876.

ated farmers from sending their commodities to market, and of course used public demonstrations to pressure elected officials or intimidate foreclosure judges. Although activities might have varied in different states or counties, the mantra of the Holiday seems to have been "cost of production." Farmers with the Holiday believed that the prices they received for commodities should exceed their investment in production and provide them with a decent standard of living. By limiting production or stopping commodities from reaching markets, the Farmers' Holiday would raise prices and put pressure on legislators to guarantee farmers a living wage. In some parts of the Dakotas, farmers even revived the older populist agendas of further railroad regulation and printing more money.

Although its impact was limited in scope and region, the Holiday certainly gave voice to rural people desperate for action or already inclined to political, even radical, activism. Communists saw an opportunity to organize farmers, but the discontent that gave rise to the Holiday encouraged a variety of populist, socialist, and even fascist plans for redeeming the American farmer. In September of 1932, governors from five states met in Iowa and heard the farmers' complaints, and later that year Communist activists organized the National Farm Emergency Relief Conference. While these events served the critical purpose of bringing attention to the farmers, they did not lead to the implementation of the Holiday's platform.

Holiday activity peaked in 1933 and thereafter steadily declined. One important reason for this was the very culture of independence and individualism that groups like the FHA sought to preserve. It proved difficult for the FHA to direct the activities and loyalties of farmers over such a large area. Some farmers and organizers fought for a way of life, others sought more immediate economic relief. Government aid finally offered by the Agricultural Adjustment Act in 1933 later proved too difficult for many farmers to resist.

Sources and Further Reading: Katherine Marie Dudley, *Debt and Dispossession* (2000); John E. Miller, "Restrained, Respectable Radicals: The South Dakota Farm Holiday," in John R. Wunder, Frances W. Kaye, and Vernon Carstensen, eds., *Americans View Their Dust Bowl Experience* (1999); John L. Shover, *Cornbelt Rebellion* (1965); John L. Shover, "The Farm Holiday Movement in Nebraska," in John R. Wunder, Frances W. Kaye, and Vernon Carstensen, eds., *Americans View Their Dust Bowl Experience* (1999); Catherine McNicol Stock, *Main Street in Crisis* (1992).

Robert Faust
University of South Alabama

The Farmer-Labor Party

Farmer-Laborism, a third-party political movement that spanned several decades, peaked in the 1930s. With roots in Populist and Progressive traditions, the movement espoused a faith in institutional reform, bringing together farmers and laborers who believed that economic improvement could only come about through cooperation rather than a commitment to either Republicans or Democrats. The Minnesota Farmer-Labor Party (1918–1944) was arguably the most impressive, radical state-level third party, winning electoral victories in both rural and urban areas. Farmer-Laborism conspicuously weakened as a result of widespread antiradical, anticommunist sentiment, along with developments in federal agricultural policies and national labor groups in the 1940s.

During the second decade of the twentieth century, a volatile farm economy sparked agricultural discontent in the Wheat Belt of the upper Midwest, leading to the formation of several important political organizations. Specifically, the Non-Partisan League (NPL), from which the Farmer-Labor Party emerged, captured the Republican Party of North Dakota and control of the state's government during World War I. By February 1918, Minnesota had its own Non-Partisan League; however, its success depended on securing organized labor's support. Together, the new Working People's Non-Partisan Political League and the Non-Partisan League sought but failed to win the Republican nomination in that year's primary election. The two groups merged under the Farmer-Labor Party label for the general election and officially formalized the organization in 1923.

By 1930, the party had gained the Minnesota governorship with Floyd Olson, who, after initiating a series of social and economic reforms, used patronage to increase the party's hold on state politics. Although his successor, Elmer Benson, won an overwhelming victory after Olson's death in 1936, he received only about one-third of the vote just two years later, reflecting a shift in attitude and changes ushered in by Franklin Roosevelt's New Deal. The party in effect merged with the Democrats, but managed to maintain a degree of its independence; its longevity, regardless of actual strength, was evidenced by the recurring presence of one of its candidates, Senator Hubert H. Humphrey.

Farmer-Laborism was unique. In 1924, Minnesota's party spawned the Farmer-Labor Association (FLA), a powerful St. Paul entity that would chart the party's course. By 1934, the FLA claimed an active club in each of the state's counties, with a total enrollment that soon exceeded twenty thousand. An educational bureau was established to revitalize these clubs into centers for learning and socializing through home meetings, speakers, and picnics; a Junior Farmer-Labor Association was also created. Following the NPL's lead, the FLA began publishing its own bi-weekly newspaper in 1930 called the *Farmer-Labor Leader*, edited first by Henry G. Teigan, a Socialist with NPL ties. It featured political cartoons, reports on party activities, and legislative voting records, along with socialist doctrine. In 1936, the newspaper, renamed the *Minnesota Leader*, could count forty-four thousand paid subscribers.

During the 1940s, a number of factors contrived to weaken the party permanently: the Roosevelt Administration's support for the Farm Bureau, an agency at odds with the movement; conflict between the American Federation of Labor and the Congress of Industrial Organization that split the labor movement; and rising cold war tensions that cast the party's Communist members as suspect. Farm-Labor candidates have nevertheless persisted in local elections in the upper Midwest.

Sources and Further Reading: Millard L. Gieske, *Minnesota Farmer-Laborism* (1979); Paul S. Holbo, "The Farmer-Labor Association: Minnesota's Party Within a Party," *Minnesota History* 38 (Sept. 1963); Robert L. Morlan, *Political Prairie Fire* (1955); William C. Pratt, "Rural Radicalism on the Northern Plains, 1912–1950," *Montana* 42 (Winter 1992); Edward L. Schapsmeier and Frederick H. Schapsmeier, *Encyclopedia of American Agricultural History* (1975); Richard M. Valelly, *Radicalism in the States* (1989).

Ginette Aley
University of Southern Indiana

The Non-Partisan League

United by low commodity prices, high interest rates, shady practices in the grain trade, and thwarted political goals, North Dakota farmers gathered in 1915 to form the Non-Partisan League (NPL). Coalescing behind A. C. Townley, the NPL was an experiment in socialist agrarian reform.

Failing as a farmer, Townley drifted to Bismarck to observe the 1915 state legislative session. During a heated debate about the need for a state-owned terminal elevator, a legislator told farmers crowding the balcony that running the state was none of their business, and that they should "go home and slop the hogs." Townley met with others to discuss their growing resentment with politics as usual. Declaring that the end had come for politics that left no role for farmers, the assembled men formed the Non-Partisan League.

Rather than form a new party, Townley determined to use existing parties. To gain farmer backing, a candidate needed only to promise support of the NPL's platform, which by 1916 included state ownership of terminal elevators, flour mills, cold storage facilities, and packing plants. The state would develop a hail insurance program, and state-owned banks would offer farmers low-interest loans. Such measures would ensure farmers a fair return, limiting the power of the unscrupulous middlemen who unfairly graded their wheat, speculated on future grain prices, or charged usurious interest rates.

In the November election, the NPL claimed the governorship and state House of Representatives. Its failure to carry the state Senate stalled state socialism, but the organization's forty thousand members still dominated. During the 1917 session, the legislature passed into law a much-improved grain grading system, established a state highway commission, prohibited rate discrimination by railroads, increased aid to education, and proposed a constitutional amendment for woman's suffrage.

In 1918, aided by constitutional amendments sponsored by the League and interpreted by NPL-dominated courts, the organization claimed total victory and began implementing a "New Day for North Dakota." The North Dakota Mill and Elevator Association, the Home Building Association, the Bank of North Dakota, and an Industrial Commission to oversee the development of further state businesses all resulted from the NPL's socialist, agrarian platform.

The party's appeal was not limited to North Dakota, and in 1918 and 1919, the movement expanded into the Midwest and Great Plains. At its height, the NPL claimed over two hundred thousand members in twenty states. Although the NPL held power only in North Dakota, politicians in several states were influenced by the organization.

During the Red Scare that followed World War I and the Russian Revolution, the leadership of the NPL was charged with malfeasance, socialism, and fraud. Prime opposition came from a coalition of disaffected businessmen and Republicans locked out of their own party. Charges from the Independent Voters' Association, as well as the defection of major NPL officeholders, the publication of the salacious *Red Flame*, and the fears of a state enmeshed in the Red Scare ultimately brought the NPL era to a close.

Despite the removal from office of Governor Lynn Frazier on October 28, 1921, North Dakotans voted to uphold the principles of state-sponsored business. Much of the NPL agenda remains in place in North Dakota, and the NPL continues as an offshoot of the present-day Democratic party.

Sources and Further Reading: Patrick K. Coleman and Charles R. Lamb, eds., *The Nonpartisan League, 1915–1922*

(1985); Robert L. Morlan, *Political Prairie Fire* (1955); Kathleen Diane Moum, "Harvest of Discontent," Ph.D. diss., University of California (1986); Elwyn B. Robinson, *History of North Dakota* (1966).

Kimberly K. Porter
University of North Dakota

The Populists

The 1891 formative meeting of the Populist (or People's) Party in Cincinnati, Ohio, and its 1892 founding in Omaha, Nebraska, marked the political culmination of reform agitation that had been spreading across the rural South and trans-Mississippi West since the end of the Civil War. Much of this agitation stemmed from the changes in agrarian life that accompanied the expansion of market capitalism. As farmers struggled against the calamitous droughts and infestations that struck the Midwest in the 1880s, falling prices, tight credit, and a deflated currency shouldered them with seemingly unpayable debts. Meanwhile, farmers also denounced the high costs imposed by railroads, grain elevators, and middlemen that came to represent an exploitative commercial order. Rural discontent was further heightened by the perceived corruption and indifference of a political establishment that seemed to serve only the wealthy corporate interests of the new industrial order, rather than the democratic welfare of the people.

In response, the Grange, the Farmers' Alliance, and other nonpartisan protest groups mobilized hundreds of thousands of rural men and women, who together laid the ideological and institutional foundation upon which Populism developed. These organizations, particularly the Alliance, pursued reforms that promoted economic cooperation and positive government action to address the financial plight of the nation's farmers. Seeking to liberate producers from the high costs imposed by distant middlemen, agrarian insurgents established cooperative agencies where farmers' commodities could be locally marketed and purchased. The cooperative ethic of such grassroots institutions cut against the tide of the expanding commercial system, but reinforced the economic autonomy of rural communities while strengthening the social networks that linked farm people together.

The rapid expansion of Populism can be attributed to the movement's political culture, which encouraged the broad involvement of farm men, women, and children. The participation of entire families was central to the Populist goal of educating rural Americans about the political and economic challenges they faced. The men and women who traveled the country-side lecturing about farming techniques and political issues generated tremendous audiences and enthusiasm. Populist editors like William Peffer of Kansas spread the movement's message and contributed to the political education of midwestern farmers. In addition to the influential reform press, the novels, plays, and songs generated within the movement spoke directly to the values and experiences of farm life.

In spite of its devoted agrarian following, the Populist Party achieved only modest electoral successes in the South and West. Populism's limited regional appeal can be seen within the western Midwest. Though the movement enjoyed strong support from Kansas through the Dakotas, it never attracted a similarly strong following east of the Mississippi River. Historians, however, have demonstrated that Populism amounted to more than a fleeting party of disgruntled farmers. The farm protests of the Populist era represented one element of a larger reform impulse that included suffragists, labor unions, and temperance advocates. Moreover, in an era when rural people still comprised the majority of the American population, Populists mounted the countryside's last, greatest effort to hold the nation to its own democratic ideals.

Sources and Further Reading: Lawrence Goodwyn, *Democratic Promise* (1976); Robert C. McMath, Jr., *American Populism* (1993); Scott McNall, *The Road to Rebellion* (1988); Jeffrey Ostler, *Prairie Populism* (1993).

Jeremy Neely
University of Missouri–Columbia

4-H

4-H, the Extension Service's youth program, celebrated its centennial in 2002 and continues to flourish in the Midwest. Through diverse projects, including genealogy, gardening, entomology, computer science, as well as large and small animals, 4-H retains relevance for rural and nonrural youth in the twenty-first century. Fair week remains the signature summer event in counties across the Midwest.

In 1900, a farmers' institute organizer in Illinois distributed seed corn to five hundred boys, offered prizes, and held a corn show. The experiment was created to reach indifferent farmers and attracted hundreds of farmers and future farmers. In 1902, educators and farmers' institute workers organized boys' clubs focused on corn growing in Illinois and Ohio, and in 1903, they formed the first girls' clubs. Rural youth clubs spread rapidly throughout the Midwest in the decade before 1914. Successfully adapting clubs to local conditions, farmers' institute workers, school of-

Entire Suits made from corn husks by school No. 8, York Co., and exhibited at York and at the National Corn Exhibit at Omaha, 1908.

4-H corn husk suits, Nebraska, 1908. Nebraska State Historical Society Photograph Collections.

ficials, growers' association members, local businessmen, and agricultural college personnel participated in developing a diffuse but energetic club movement. Although the roles of these groups varied, contests at county and state fairs constituted crucial components of youth work in most states. Standardization of youth club work came only with passage of the 1914 Smith-Lever Act, which merged the agricultural colleges and the United States Department of Agriculture (USDA) in a national program of cooperative agricultural extension.

Youth from across the country attended the inaugural National 4-H Club Camp in Washington, D.C., during 1927. At this gathering, state 4-H leaders adopted the motto "To Make the Best Better," and the 4-H pledge, still used with the Pledge of Allegiance to open each meeting: "I pledge my HEAD to clearer thinking; my HEART to greater loyalty; my HANDS to larger service; and my HEALTH to better living for my club, my community, my country, and my world." Projects in the 1920s were suitable only for farm youth; by the 1930s, 4-H had broadened its appeal to include projects in clothing, home management, and food and nutrition for girls, and soil conservation, engineering, and electricity for boys. Many lessons stressed the importance of frugality and conservation during the Depression and World War II.

In succeeding decades, 4-H projects became gender neutral, although far more girls participated in livestock projects than boys in home economics projects. The National 4-H Council and the USDA's Extension Service developed new curriculum categories with disciplines beyond agriculture and home economics in 1990, underscoring its characteristic flexibility. 4-H depends on paid county youth agents, but dedicated volunteer service by older youths and adult leaders has proven to be the most essential ingredient in this enduring program that continues to motivate youths to excel.

Sources and Further Reading: George Farrell, *Boys' and Girls' 4-H Club Work under the Smith-Lever Act, 1914–1924* (1926); Mary Frances Smith and Edward E. Kirkpatrick, *4-H in Indiana, 1904–1990* (1990); Thomas Wessel, *4-H, An American Idea, 1900–1980* (1982).

Barbara Steinson
DePauw University, Indiana

The Extension Service and County Agents

On May 8, 1914, President Woodrow Wilson signed the Smith-Lever Act establishing the Cooperative Extension Service, an educational system for rural people not attending college. The Extension Services sent college-trained "county agents" into the countryside to convince farm men and women to practice the new scientific techniques in agricultural and home economics being developed at the state agricultural colleges and experiment stations. Supporters hoped that this kind of work would improve agriculture and rural life and prevent the degeneration of the countryside that some critics were predicting.

The innovative structure of the Extension Service was quite complex. The program was organized on three levels, federal, state, and local, and was jointly administered by the U.S. Department of Agriculture and the state agricultural colleges. Each state set up its own extension division and appointed a state leader to administer funds and supervise the work. Midwestern states did not develop a formal extension system for African Americans, as occurred in the South: In the Midwest, extension work was carried out by and geared toward whites.

Extension work received additional support at the county level in accordance with Smith-Lever stipulations that federal grants had to be matched by state or local contributions. Smith-Lever specifically allowed for contributions from private individuals, and new groups such as the Farm Bureau organized to help carry out extension work. In some states, including Illinois, Iowa, and Indiana, the Farm Bureau contributed significantly to the extension service, providing financial support, sharing office space and staff, and wielding administrative control over county agents. New rules established in the 1950s, however, mandated a complete separation between extension work and private groups—a response, in part, to criticism that public funds were being used to support the private Farm Bureau.

From the start, most county agents (also known as farm or home advisors) obtained college degrees in agricultural science or home economics, expanding areas of academic research. The state agricultural colleges in Illinois and Iowa were particularly strong in these fields. Drawing from this knowledge base, county agents provided instruction on topics suited to local needs. Popular subjects in midwestern states included raising livestock, soil fertilization, home management, and human nutrition. As agricultural science and home economics became more specialized, so too did extension work. At first, extension agents focused on such simple techniques as pruning trees or culling chickens, but they increasingly drew on more sophisticated biochemical knowledge. The new social sciences encouraged agents to focus on family life and community development. In addition, extension workers also fostered youth activities, which later developed into the 4-H Club system. With the decline in the farm population, the mandate of the extension service has broadened to include new types of programs that accommodate other populations.

Sources and Further Reading: Margaret Esposito, *Places of Pride* (1989); Wayne D. Rasmussen, *Taking the University to the People* (1989); Dorothy Schwieder, *75 Years of Service: Co-operative Extension in Iowa* (1993); Sara Stage and Virginia B. Vincenti, eds., *Rethinking Home Economics* (1997).

Nancy Kay Berlage
History Associates Incorporated,
Rockville, Maryland

Farmers' Institutes

Farmers' institutes offered lectures by successful farmers and land-grant college professors on newer farming methods and scientific principles of agriculture. Establishing bridges between university-trained experts and skeptical farmers, the institutes constituted a transitional phase in the development of agricultural extension. Efforts to develop institutes in the Midwest date from the 1850s, when professors at Oberlin College in Ohio ran a series of programs for farmers. This experiment and others failed. Only with participation in the Grange and other farmers' clubs, and recognition that issues like soil deterioration and competition in expanding markets required expert advice, did farmers welcome the institutes.

Despite structural differences, farmers' institutes had similar purposes and methods. Institutes met in winter months for one to three days, with two or three sessions each day. A typical day featured a series of short lectures followed by questions and answers, meals provided by farm wives, and evening entertainment. An 1890 institute in Illinois held lectures on livestock feeding, wheat, corn, dairy production, rural roads, financial trusts, and the future of small farmers. Although skepticism persisted, institutes decreased distrust of scientific expertise. Increases in appropriations, numbers of institutes, and attendance coincided, after 1900, with farmers' enhanced interest in specialized information. In some states, university extension departments evolved directly from institute work. By 1914, federal support for county agricultural and extension agents eliminated the need for farmers' institutes.

Sources and Further Reading: L. H. Bailey, *Farmers' Institutes* (1900); John Hamilton, *History of Farmers' Institutes in the United States* (1906); Roy V. Scott, *The Reluctant Farmer* (1970).

Barbara Steinson
DePauw University, Indiana

Government Policies and Agencies

The U.S. government has powerfully shaped the development of the rural Midwest by establishing its pattern of landholding, regulating the market for agricultural commodities, and taking measures to stop erosion of the nation's soils.

The national government literally shaped the Midwest before the region had even begun to be settled. The Land Ordinance of 1785 established the region's familiar grid pattern, which begins at the eastern boundary of Ohio. Land was surveyed and divided into townships of thirty-six sections, each measuring one square mile (640 acres). The ordinance provided for orderly land sales and set aside proceeds from these sales to fund public schools. The Northwest Ordinance of 1787 provided for the creation of new territories and states in what was then the Northwest Territory and notably prohibited the institution of slavery in the region.

During the Civil War, the Republican Party sought to enact its vision of a society devoted to the interests of small producers. The Homestead Act of 1862 offered settlers up to one hundred sixty acres of land, provided they occupied and improved their holding. The Morrill Land Grant Act, also passed in 1862, funded the creation of colleges devoted to agriculture and the mechanical arts to accelerate economic growth. The U.S. Department of Agriculture was created in 1862 to oversee the largest sector of America's economy.

Access to railroads integrated the rural Midwest into the national market economy by the 1870s, and the rapid acceleration of industrialization in the 1870s and 1880s challenged agriculture's longstanding preeminence in American society. Farmers met with increasing frustration in marketing their crops profitably and were particularly angered by high railroad freight rates, which cut deeply into their revenues. The Grange, a farmers' organization founded in 1867, challenged railroads' fees, and "Granger laws," which regulated railroad rates, were passed in several midwestern states. The Grangers' activism contributed to the creation of the Interstate Commerce Commission (ICC) in 1887.

In the early twentieth century, many Americans strove to reconcile the interests of farmers with the needs of the nation's booming urban population. Midwesterners fretted about the exodus of young people from the countryside to cities and towns, as well as the dissatisfaction of rural women with the isolation and privations of farm life. President Theodore Roosevelt appointed the Country Life Commission in 1908 to make recommendations concerning the future of American rural life. The commission's report, published in 1911, prescribed several remedies for the discontents of rural residents. "Country Lifers" sought to ensure that American agriculture continued to provide a dependable supply of food for the nation's population, and to maintain the viability of schools, churches, and other institutions of vital importance to rural society.

In response to the commission's recommendations, Congress passed the Smith-Lever Act in 1914, which authorized state universities to undertake Extension work to educate farm people, improve the quality of farm life, and encourage more youth to choose a career in farming. County Extension Agents brought education to the countryside by conducting demonstration sessions for farm residents to teach men and boys to farm more successfully and women and girls to adopt new standards of home economics. In 1916, Congress passed the Farm Loan Act to facilitate farm-

ers' ability to band together to create agricultural cooperatives to purchase supplies and market crops.

The New Deal fundamentally transformed the nation's agricultural economy and rural life. The Agricultural Adjustment Act (AAA) paid farmers to reduce production of many commodities and sought to restore prices to parity with 1909–1914 levels, when farmers were reasonably prosperous. The Act was declared unconstitutional by the U.S. Supreme Court in early 1936. The Roosevelt Administration created the Soil Conservation and Domestic Allotment Act, which paid farmers to conserve soil rather than reduce production. Like the AAA, the Soil Conservation Act was primarily designed to prop up farmers' income, although it did contribute to the growing federal commitment to conserving natural resources. New Dealers initiated the nation's first substantial soil conservation measures, creating the Soil Conservation Service and encouraging farmers to create self-governing Soil Conservation Districts in which they could establish their own land use regulations. Congress passed a second Agricultural Adjustment Act in 1938, and the policy of price supports for many agricultural commodities has endured, despite considerable criticism, to the present.

The New Deal also transformed rural life by creating the Rural Electrification Administration (REA) in 1935, which extended the convenience of electric lights, radios, refrigerators, and other appliances to the countryside. New Dealers addressed the plight of some of the nation's most impoverished farmers by creating the Resettlement Administration (RA) in 1935, which issued "rehabilitation loans" to enable poor farmers to improve their farms and sought to remove farmers from marginal farmland and assist them in resettling elsewhere. Under the Bankhead-Jones Farm Tenant Act of 1937, the RA became the Farm Security Administration (FSA), which issued loans to farmers to purchase land. New Dealers also strove to reduce the incidence of farm tenancy, which skyrocketed during the Great Depression. While the RA and FSA were created specifically to combat the economic troubles of the Great Depression, the New Deal's price supports, soil conservation measures, and rural electrification exerted an enormous and enduring effect on the agricultural economy and on rural life. Price supports, while controversial, remain a fixture of American agriculture.

In 1985 and 1990, the federal government enacted farm bills that strengthened the nation's soil conservation laws by requiring farmers to comply with land use regulations as a precondition for participating in farm price support programs and by taking highly erodible land out of production. In sum, over the past several decades, the number of independent family farms has shrunk, price supports have persisted, and the rate of soil erosion has at last been slowed.

Sources and Further Reading: William Bowers, *The Country Life Movement in America* (1974); Dennis Sven Nordin and Rich Harvest, *A History of the Grange, 1867–1900* (1974); John Opie, *The Law of the Land: Two Hundred Years of American Farmland Policy* (1987); Theodore Saloutos, *The American Farmer and the New Deal* (1982).

Chris Rasmussen
Fairleigh Dickinson University, New Jersey

Leisure and Rural Life

The concept of leisure activities and leisure time has changed drastically over the years. Today, leisure is any endeavor that occurs separate from work or other economic obligations, usually away from the home, and frequently in the company of those other than family. Activities such as movies, exercise, shopping, or travel, share an assumption that each modern citizen has an allotment of "free time" to "spend" as they see fit. Familiar references to 9-to-5 jobs or "living for the weekend" reinforce the idea that, in contemporary society, leisure time is clearly distinct from work time.

By contrast, in an earlier time, this separation was less clear. Personal leisure was closely connected to one's daily life, which in turn, was deeply affected by work patterns as well as family, community, and cultural traditions. Colorful images of barn raisings or quilting bees come to mind. Nineteenth-century farm families would not understand our tendency to regard these events as a mixture of work and pleasure, for no such distinction existed in their world.

The blending of leisure and vocation was most pronounced in the first half of the nineteenth century. No better example exists than the process of harvesting and processing the staple crops at the heart of commercial farming. Although mechanization allowed most individual farmers to get their seeds sown, harvesting the many acres of wheat, corn, or rye required more communal efforts—teams of men, their draft animals, and their implements. To blunt the drudgery, teams competed to see who could work the fastest or most productively, with the victors earning small rewards or simply bragging rights shouted over their collective meals. Female relations often traveled with these teams to assist the farm matron in food preparation, cooking, and cleaning. Men and women later recalled how as children they thrilled to see the teams in action, enjoyed the constant activity in the home, and generally were imbued with a greater sense of community as the demands of work and society merged. Accordingly, the harvest occupied a special place in the "leisure time" of most midwesterners.

Because work-based leisure was so typical, gendered leisure patterns emerged, although these were by no means exclusive. For women, community building and maintenance was an important function. As a result, women often led in promoting church activities, social reforms, education, and the observances of births, marriages, and funerals. Visits between farms and on Sundays at church were both a pleasurable way to stay current with and direct community affairs, as well as a necessary function for communal solidarity. As with the harvest, women worked in groups to perform repetitive labor, such as quilting, preserving perishable goods, or caring for the distressed. While secular and religious holidays were observed by both sexes, women were forceful organizers of picnics and feasts intended to mark, most notably, Easter, the

Boys and girls playing baseball, Shelby, Iowa, 1941. Courtesy National Archives, photo no. RG 83-G.

Fourth of July, Thanksgiving, and Christmas. Their leadership in observing the Sabbath and at periodical camp revivals funneled easily into a concern for social reform, most notably, temperance.

Although men also took an active role in visiting and church functions, pastimes such as hunting, fishing, and meeting at local stores were more typically reserved for them alone. Unlike the saloon, which often served as a family recreation center, and the more elaborate retail shops common after the late nineteenth century, the first rural stores were simple commercial or transportation depots that also served distilled spirits. While useful information about markets, natural pests, and implements was exchanged, the use of alcohol led to more raucous behavior—wrestling, racing, shooting matches, blood sports, and gambling—activities that gave rural women considerable interest in the secular importance of temperance.

The economic rewards of a more informed and sober farmer led many to inaugurate formal agricultural societies or farmers' clubs. These, in turn, underwrote local fairs where livestock was evaluated, agricultural implements displayed, and information about "scientific farming" distributed. Less serious activities, such as horse racing, boxing, and baseball games, provided fairgoers with diversions to while away the last few warm weekends of the year. By the 1850s, midwestern women had staked out an important role in these fairs as participants and, equally important, as paying attendees. Female attendance could determine the financial success of a regional fair. The combination of agricultural societies, fairs, greater interest in the farmers' consumer dollars, and the spreading transportation network provided the necessary foundation for the rise of producer and consumer cooperatives, a movement that further combined work and leisure.

Not all leisure activity of the antebellum years was so public. Increasingly, as prosperity provided many with the means to support more personalized activities, the home was seen as a place of cultural refinement, as economic prosperity provided many with the means for more personalized activities. The phenomenal diversity of published materials such as books, magazines, trade journals, and newspapers suggests that midwesterners both valued and had the time for quiet contemplation of everything from Dickens to chatty advice columns. Children were an integral part of the family economy, but time at home was available for them to explore, learn, and compete with their siblings and peers. The growing sales of musical instruments, mostly violins, brass, and organs, also point to the fact that the home retained an important place in the leisure life of rural America.

From the close of the Civil War to 1920, American culture and society modernized, bringing about significant changes in the nature of leisure pursuits. The merger of farm organizations with "radical" political agendas, intended to deal with the national and global shifts in commercial agriculture, animated participation in a host of new institutions. The earliest, and most vocal in the Midwest was the National Grange of the Order of Patrons of Husbandry, which was founded in 1867 and exerted its greatest influence in the 1870s. Local granges sponsored numerous picnics, lectures, meetings, and publications that had a deep influence on how regional citizens chose to allot their leisure time. Although academics have written volumes intending to separate the political, economic, and social components of farm organizations, the fact remains that citizens placed great value in all three of these goals, often simultaneously. As a result, when the Grange movement faded in the 1880s, it was quickly followed by similar mixed-purpose institutions such as the Farmers' Alliance, the Agricultural Wheel, the Farmers' Union, the Farmers' Equity Union, and the Non-Partisan League. Each varied greatly in its means, membership, and motivation, but they all shared a culture of participation that was part of the leisure pursuits of the rural Midwest.

The Chautauqua was probably the greatest example of the blurred lines that still stood between leisure and work in the modern era. Started in southwestern New York near Lake Chautauqua in 1874, the "assemblies" spread rapidly throughout the country. Combining entertainment, motivational speaking, and social uplift, the events lasted nearly a week and featured prominent speakers and performers, most notably the three-time presidential candidate and rural advocate William Jennings Bryan. Heralded by some as the culmination of rural culture, and scorned by others as hayseed mediocrity and sentimentality, the Chautauqua was a meaningful event in the lives of those who attended, estimated to be more than forty-five million people by the 1920s. Less-celebrated traveling fairs, circuses, novelty performers, and in the twentieth century, aerialists and automobile racers, added shock and amazement to midwesterners' regular diet of the Chautauqua, the farmers' club, or the commemorative picnic.

Ironically, it was at these assemblies that rural Americans often saw their first motion picture or whetted their appetite for star performers in drama, music, Christian revival preaching, and political oratory. This demand, once generated, led many into more modern mass leisure pursuits such as theatergoing or listening to the radio, which supplemented local culture with the national one. The rapid diffusion of electricity, automobility, and urban entertainment from 1900 to 1920 enabled a leisure culture that was truly separate from the workaday world. Most adults simply sampled these new pastimes in the Progressive Era, but their children came to rely on them. In the process, the line between work and play grew more stark, while that between rural and urban was blurred.

Without a doubt, the introduction of a low-cost, simple, and dependable automobile was the single most important change in the leisure patterns of rural midwesterners during this time. Certainly the use of labor-saving devices in the field and the home, and technological innovations like electricity, radio, and the telephone provided the additional time necessary for modern leisure. But these tools often created new and more time-consuming duties within the home, especially for women. By contrast, the automobile made trips of several miles both practical and quick. While it reinforced traditional behavior, such as visiting patterns, family togetherness, and the authority of certain community leaders (such as clergymen, who could now make regular appearances in the home), the automobile transformed such institutions as the local school and, more significantly, the town commercial districts into modern community centers. Teenagers created moving domains through their regular patrols of the main streets, auto camps at key intersections or parking lots, and stops at inexpensive restaurants and ice cream parlors. Window shopping, Sunday drives (often at the expense of church attendance), vacationing, unsupervised dating, weekly moviegoing, and increased consumer borrowing were only a few of the new social activities that flourished in the automobile age.

The growth of radio ownership did much the same for the rural home. Sets were often purchased to provide practical information, such as weather and market conditions, but radio use quickly redefined the expectations and assumptions of leisure time. New activities replaced old, as musicians became listeners, and parishioners and Chautauqua members were transformed into one-way receivers. Nationally-broadcast radio shows of the 1920s, such as *National Barn Dance* and the *Grand Ole Opry*, introduced millions to a popular culture that included music, advertising, humor, and news. While some assumed that bringing modern, urban, and national culture into the countryside could slowly uplift and refine the "backwardness" of traditional, rural, and regional culture, in reality it standardized many farm families' free time and stifled many of the sources of a distinctly rural culture.

While the rural Midwest was, with the rest of America, drawn into a national leisure culture after the 1920s, the farm population continued to seek ways to use their free time to reinforce traditional behaviors rather than simply replace them. A good example was

the rise of spectator sports in the first half of the twentieth century. In rural America, the rise of amateurism and spectator sports followed parallel tracks. As the physical requirements of farm work lessened and free time increased, many turned to such amateur pursuits as skiing, baseball, basketball, golf, tennis, football, rowing, wrestling, lacrosse, and ice hockey. Amateur associations sprang up throughout the country, and from 1900 to 1930, they sought to standardize rules and increase safety.

Larger metropolitan areas were quick to turn to professional spectator sports (aided by mass transit and mass media), but amateurism remained strong throughout the Midwest. Perhaps nowhere is this more evident than in the rise of high school and collegiate athletic programs. Following local football, baseball, and basketball teams, the three most popular sports, lent itself to and reinforced local identities. Early football pioneers such as Knute Rockne and Amos Alonzo Stagg established programs that became traditions in the Midwest. Even more pronounced were local high school programs that retained the best characteristics of amateurism, such as girls basketball and volleyball or boys wrestling programs, without being compromised by commercialism. Rivalries between schools were invested with real cultural pride. Amateurism suggests that, in spite of the homogenizing effects of modern mass culture, leisure activity in the rural Midwest retains a strong sense of regionalism.

Sources and Further Reading: Hal Barron, *Mixed Harvest* (1997); David B. Danbom, *Born in the Country* (1995); John Mack Faragher, *Sugar Creek* (1986); Deborah Fink, *Open Country, Iowa* (1986); Allen Guttmann, *A Whole New Ballgame* (1988); Ronald R. Kline, *Consumers in the Country* (2000); Mary Neth, *Preserving the Family Farm* (1995); Jane Marie Pederson, *Between Memory and Reality* (1992).

David Blanke
Texas A&M University–Corpus Christi

Fishing

In the Midwest, fish and people are intimately linked through diverse historical, social, and cultural relations. Whether subsistence, commercial, recreational, or aquacultured, fishing provides insight into how we understand our environment, others, and ourselves.

Three sociohistorical periods characterize midwestern fishing. First, fish were a food source for Native Americans. Fish were an integral part of subsistence food systems that sustained Native populations for centuries. Second, European colonization and subsequent industrialization irrevocably changed fisheries

Ohio Fish Hatchery, Zoar, Ohio, 1927. Ohio Historical Society, P223 AL02652.

and lake, river, and stream habitats. The Great Black Swamp, an incredibly fecund fish breeding and nursery area in northwestern Ohio, was drained for settler agriculture.

Third, in the twentieth century, highly destructive commercial fisheries, logging, dam building that blocked fish migrations, industrial pollution, and farming practices led to drastically changed fisheries. Partial solutions lay in fish stock enhancement programs, multiuse lake construction, the rise of fishery management, and some lake, river, and stream pollution abatement.

At present, recreational interests dominate fishing in the Midwest. Millions of anglers fish for trout, salmon, bass, walleye, yellow perch, sunfish, catfish, and carp, among other species. In rural communities, small-scale fish farming is also growing as a form of food production. Fishery managers attempt to balance the competing interests of diverse recreational and fisheries groups, to deal with growing demand on fish stocks and aquatic habitats, and to maintain the social role of fisheries in the lives of midwesterners.

Sources and Further Reading: Margaret Beattie Bogue, *Fishing the Great Lakes* (2000); Larry Nesper, *The Walleye War* (2002); Milton Trautmann, *The Fishes of Ohio* (1981); Richard White, *The Middle Ground: Indians, Empires and Republics in the Great Lakes Region, 1650–1815* (1991).

Michael Skladany
Institute for Agriculture and Trade Policy,
Minneapolis, Minnesota

Threshing

Threshing is the culmination of the wheat-growing season. Throughout the Midwest, beginning in July in the southern climates and usually ending in October in the northernmost areas, the labor-intensive process of removing the chaff from the grain has determined a farm family's fortune for the coming year.

The time between harvesting and threshing depended on the weather, machinery, the amount of wheat to thresh, and available labor. In areas outside the Wheat Belt, farmers in more densely settled areas relied on threshing rings. The earliest threshing rings were rooted in cooperative labor agreements among neighboring farmers and a few hired hands. Before the twentieth century, threshing rings seldom owned threshing equipment. Instead, they contracted with a thresherman who brought his machinery to their fields. The vital work of threshing brought farmers (and their families) together, but it was the opportunity for social interaction that many cherished.

Farmers in more isolated regions of the Wheat Belt were more dependent on the labor of strangers to thresh their grain. These harvest hands, called "hoboes" or "bindlestiffs," generally came from areas surrounding the Wheat Belt. Many were in their early twenties, unmarried, and from more populated communities. A vexing problem for wheat farmers was getting enough help at the right time. For decades, reformers and state officials grappled with the problem of allocating harvest labor. Wheat Belt farmers needed transient laborers to work long hours during a short peak season. The uneven supply of laborers gave rise to clashes among farmers over hiring labor, and between farmers and workers about wages and hours. Recovering wages from farmers unwilling or unable to pay their workers was yet another source of conflict.

However, cooperation rather than conflict characterized the nature of threshing. From the earliest forms of threshing, flailing and treading, until the widespread implementation of tractors and especially custom combines, threshing demanded coordinated labor. Before threshing commenced, women prepared to feed and board threshing crews. During threshing, women brought lunches to the men in the fields; they served hearty breakfasts and dinners at the homestead. While men threshed, women often assumed responsibility for many of their daily chores. Children participated by hauling drinking water, passing bundles to the thresher, and keeping a watchful eye on the machinery. As the children aged, their work became gender specific, reflecting the work roles of their parents.

Threshing has a place in the imagination of midwesterners because of the cooperation engendered by the work. A sense of urgency, anticipation, and even carnival marked the days of threshing, and when it was done, farmers held picnics, dances, and dinners to celebrate their labor and rural community. When people "talk threshing," this is what they mean.

Sources and Further Reading: Frank Tobias Higbie, *Indispensable Outcasts* (2003); Thomas D. Isern, *Bull Threshers and Bindlestiffs* (1990); Mary Neth, *Preserving the Family Farm* (1995); J. Sanford Rikoon, *Threshing in the Midwest, 1820–1940* (1988).

Kristine Stilwell
University of Missouri–Columbia

Community Picnics and Suppers

Rural midwesterners socialized, supported institutions, and fostered community through public events focused on eating. Parents and pupils, indeed any resident of a country school district, commonly picnicked on the final day of school. Church suppers often were major fund-raising events, one of the many ways in which women influenced religion.

The participants in a neighborhood threshing ring remembered the supper given by the host farm wife as the most memorable part of threshing. Lutefisk suppers, common among Norwegian groups in the upper Midwest, were the kind of event that helped immigrant communities perpetuate customs. Picnics and suppers also provided opportunities for entire neighborhoods to socialize and brought together country people and village residents. "Everyone went and no one had to be invited or urged" in the 1910s, recalled a resident of Rusk County, Wisconsin.

Nineteenth-century harvest fetes and Fourth of July commemorations evolved into the multiday festivals supported by many communities in the late twentieth century, such as Braham, Minnesota's Pie Day. Seeking to attract tourists by relying on appeals to the "good old days," these events partially reflected emergent commercialization and nostalgic myth-making, but features like service groups' bratwurst stands and free boiled-corn feeds linked them to nineteenth-century eating customs.

Picnics link twentieth-century midwesterners to their past in other ways. After out-migration, regularly scheduled reunion picnics brought together members of dispersed families, churches, and communities. Midwestern migrants to Southern California orga-

A loaded table awaiting the start of a meal, Shelby County, Iowa, 1941. Courtesy National Archives, photo no. RG 83-G.

nized state and other regional associations in which picnics were a major activity. Sharing homemade sandwiches connected people with and through their origins in the rural Midwest.

Sources and Further Reading: Joseph Boskin, "Associations and Picnics as Stabilizing Forces in Southern California," *California Historical Society Quarterly* 44 (Jan. 1965); Linda T. Humphrey, "Small Group Festive Gatherings," *Journal of the Folklore Institute* 16 (Sept. 1979); Robert J. Lavenda, *Corn Fests and Water Carnivals* (1997).

Robert J. Gough
University of Wisconsin–Eau Claire

State and County Fairs

State and county fairs rank among the most significant institutions in the Midwest. Instrumental in the region's development, fairs were among the most eagerly anticipated events on the rural calendar.

Although agricultural fairs originated in New England, they attained their greatest popularity in the Midwest, where counties, territories, and states hosted fairs soon after European American settlement began. State fairs were created as early as 1849 in Michigan and in several other states during the 1850s. Some were state supported, while others were privately organized. Some early fairs were transient, changing location from year to year, while others acquired permanent fairgrounds. By the late nineteenth century, nearly all fairs had constructed permanent fairgrounds, which sometimes covered hundreds of acres and contained substantial buildings.

County and state societies disseminated agricultural information and hosted annual fairs. Farm families competed to win premiums for displaying the finest livestock, crops, inventions, foods, handicrafts, and works of art. Central to any fair's success was its livestock display, in which farmers and breeders vied to win ribbons and cash premiums. Victory could significantly increase the value of the winner's stock. Fairs also included competitions for domestic arts and crafts, manufactured goods, and fine arts, and they were venues for commercial exhibitors to advertise and sell their wares.

In the late nineteenth century, horse races, brass bands, and small traveling shows were the leading entertainments at fairs. The growing prominence of entertainment at fairs provoked debate over whether fairs should focus on agricultural improvement or amusement. Formerly run by proponents of scientific agriculture, fairs were now managed by "fair men," who strove not only to disseminate information regarding scientific agriculture, but also to arrange a popular exhibition. After the Chicago World's Columbian Exhibition of 1893, fairs copied its Midway, a zone devoted to entertainment.

In the twentieth century, fairs simultaneously began to undertake new forms of agricultural education and to book more lavish diversions. Their educational mission was renewed by the creation of 4-H programs and demonstrations of the Extension Service. State fairs, with their larger coffers, also offered more extensive entertainment than county fairs could afford.

The number of county fairs peaked at the outset of the twentieth century, after which they began to dwindle with the advent of the automobile, which facilitated travel to the much larger and more dazzling state fairs. During the first three decades of the century, enormous grandstand spectacles, which typically depicted famous battles or natural disasters, were the main attraction at state fairs. Auto racing supplanted horse racing as swiftly as the Model T supplanted the family mare. When radio and motion pictures challenged fairs' appeal, state fair managers responded by booking leading bands and entertainers. In recent decades, country and rock concerts have become the leading attraction at state fairs.

Today, fairs retain their popular mixture of education, commerce, and entertainment. Their deep roots and their ability to evolve suggest that they will endure well into the twenty-first century.

Sources and Further Reading: Karal Ann Marling, *Blue Ribbon* (1990); John McCarry, *County Fairs* (1997); Wayne C. Neely, *The Agricultural Fair* (1935); Derek Nelson, *The American State Fair* (1999).

Chris Rasmussen
Fairleigh Dickinson University, New Jersey

Farm, Town, and City

The Midwest has always contained both rural and urban areas. The Northwest Ordinance of 1787 said nothing about towns or cities (apart from acknowledging French Canadian fur-trade villages) and, indeed, seemed to disenfranchise them by requiring legislators and voters to own two hundred acres and fifty acres, respectively. It authorized counties and townships, not cities, as political units. Yet settlers and promoters did not doubt that urban places would grace the Northwest Territory, which included the future states of Ohio, Indiana, Illinois, Michigan, Wisconsin, and part of Minnesota. Slavery, primogeniture, and lawlessness, not cities, were seen by the Ordinance's framers as barriers to rural settlement, and the Ordinance created a barrier-free territory in those respects.

In July 1788, the Ohio Company's Associates founded Marietta on an elevated site, bestowed Roman and patriot names on its squares and streets, and mixed urban and rural forms by allocating to each resident a house lot and an eight-acre "out-lot" for farming. Their hopes for an ordered New England town were dashed when back-country settlers created a commercial village in the river bottoms. In the Midwest, urban places and rural–urban relationships would be shaped by topographical, technological, economic, political, and social forces just as unpredictable as the appearance of "Picketed Point" below Marietta.

Different migrants held different notions of rural–urban relations. Yankee settlers placed school and church in town and emphasized that the marketplace rewarded diligent and punished lazy farmers. Dairying and other specialized farming depended on nearby urban customers. Upland Southerners, with their corn and hog farming, needed nothing more than a courthouse and travelers' inn; they drove their hogs to distant river ports and placed church and school in the countryside. Midlanders, too, fattened hogs on corn, but their more commercial approach required urban markets, whose cash nexus was the main force integrating divergent streams of migrants to the Midwest.

All migrants came expecting to develop urban places and rural–urban linkages around the waterborne commerce. The opening of the Erie Canal in 1825 brought midwestern crops to the New York market. Urban places were built along the Ohio and Mississippi steamboat routes. In general, although the topography of the Midwest made road and canal construction relatively straightforward, the challenges of overland transportation were formidable. Peddlers carried goods to farms.

Only with the construction of railroads in the middle of the nineteenth century did urbanization occur in locations away from navigable water. Level topography meant track-laying (and town-platting) proceeded nearly everywhere—a boon to farmers distant from rivers but eager to sell surpluses. This development was highly controversial since improvements were expensive and often brought unanticipated social change. Politically, a Whig coalition of evangelicals, commercial farmers, merchants, and manufacturers favored internal improvements and a market economy. Subsistence-oriented farmers opposed to cities and the market revolution tended to vote Democratic, as did non-evangelicals in ethnic enclaves.

Successors to the Whig coalition, the Republicans who dominated post–Civil War midwestern politics discredited rural localism and anti-urbanism as obstructionist views held by backward southerners and "priest-ridden" ethnic peasants. Free-soil, old-stock American farmers supported a Republican Party led by railroad tycoons, manufacturers, and urban bosses. Meanwhile, railroads raised freight rates, platted and controlled new prairie towns, and favored food-processing monopolies; tariffs raised farmers' living costs; and cities busily added wholesaling, manufacturing, and intracity retailing functions to escape economic dependence on their immediate hinterland.

The meaning of city and town changed. Railroads and telegraph lines made obsolete the close ties between local merchants and farmers: barter and credit resting on personal knowledge and trust; merchants' independence from suppliers (by distance and transport delays) matching farmers' vaunted independence; merchants' long wait between ordering goods and final sale matching farmers' slow seasonal cycle; townspeople helping in the fields at harvest. Now urban business moved at the double-quick: cash sales preferred and no waiting for collection; large volumes; quick ordering by telegraph and quick delivery by rail; Chicago wholesalers sending out traveling salesmen to every nook and cranny of the Midwest; two weeks between the order and the final sale; fish and oysters available at Nebraska stores.

City goods and a consumer ethos came to the country, along with city opinions that rural life was slow and antiquated. True, mechanized farming yielded more bushels more efficiently on larger farms for grain elevators to store, railroads to haul, and millers to process; however, urban capitalists controlled storage, hauling, processing, and (seemingly) prices. Even farmers' machinery was theirs on credit.

Reacting to a loss of status and control, rural midwesterners in Iowa, Missouri, Illinois, Kansas, Minnesota, and other states flocked in the early 1870s to the Patrons of Husbandry, a self-sufficient rural society in whose local Grange Halls men and women could educate each other, socialize, pray, discuss farming, and jointly purchase goods or sell crops—in other words, perform many of Main Street's functions. Women played active roles. Towns with store-bought goods, amenities, and leisure for social life carried the message to rural women (though not all believed it) that urban life was modern and that children would do better by getting educated and pursuing urban careers.

The agrarian answer was to add goods, amenities, and opportunities to rural life. Yankees such as Grange founder Oliver H. Kelley felt the town's pull on farm women and children and acted to counter it. Grangers failed to recruit many immigrant farmers in the Midwest's ethnic enclaves, and their ties to Main Street merchants and editors hampered attempts to bypass town middlemen and deal direct with city wholesalers and food processors. More successful in keeping small-town editors out, the Farmers' Alliance formed crossroads communities of cooperative creameries, elevators, and stores. In the small towns they controlled, rural people partly shaped their interactions with a market economy.

These communities were short-lived, horse-and-buggy exceptions. The main beneficiaries of rural revolt against Main Street merchants were Sears, Roebuck and Mongomery Ward. Rural free delivery and the mail-order catalogue bypassed Main Street merchants; both encouraged a consumer ethos manipulated by urban, corporate advertisers. Midwestern Populists' alliance with southern Democrats and Presidential candidate William Jennings Bryan's defeat in 1896 confirmed urban Progressives' view that farm life was backward and urbanity, the evolutionary future. Sympathetic yet patronizing, the Country Life Commission advocated urbanizing rurality: school and church consolidation, scientific farming, experts at the state universities telling farmers how to plow and what to plant.

These trends prevailed in the core areas dominated by Americans with English-speaking ancestors. But in places where topographical, climatic, linguistic, ethnic, religious, or political barriers inhibited modernization, a defiant rurality persisted. This was true in Democratic Missouri; the lumbering and mining Northern Fringe of Michigan, Wisconsin, and Minnesota; Illinois's Little Egypt; German Catholic and Amish enclaves; and pietistic Norwegian areas of Minnesota and North Dakota.

In these areas, the long agricultural depression of 1921 to 1941 did not lead to devastating out-migration because people were less dependent on major cash crops. Elsewhere, urban prosperity and rural poverty seemed to prove Progressives' case for urban life. The 1930s saw a partial move back to the land whose produce could support an unemployed family, but jobs in urban defense plants during World War II more than reversed that trend. And the tractor revolution greatly reduced farm labor needs.

The agricultural Midwest was incorporated into a dominant urban system as a functional part that exported crops and children to towns and cities on the recipients' terms. Compensating for a loss of autonomy, males embraced a rural image of southern and western stereotypes, including pickup trucks, country-western music, and race cars. A few bought out neighbors and accumulated acres to match a western ranch or southern plantation. Some worked the farm but relied on women's in-town jobs to support the family. Some worked construction or over-the-road trucking

and kept the farm as a winter hobby and net-loss tax shelter.

Mechanized, specialized farming curtailed women's income from egg money as well as poultry and butter sales. In a new rural world apart from agriculture, women found employment in small-town factories, rural tourism, or government offices. Less tied to men's ideal of rural independence, they accepted low-wage work and long hours in retail shops or the nonunion plants that rural areas attracted. During farm crises, they earned more income than the farm's cash crops. Women proved adept at niche marketing and bypassed national markets. They raised sheep for high-quality wool to sell to artisans, operated pick-your-own berry farms, and grew specialty fruits and vegetables for farmers' markets.

The new rural life meant working for city folk who drove to the bed-and-breakfast or the berry farm, owned the shops and factories, or shopped at the farmers' market. Rural truck drivers and construction workers also served urban customers, while driver-owned rigs or a winter off provided an appearance of independence. Rural children's education in consolidated schools gave them skills for urban careers.

The 1970s Back-to-the-Land movement blurred rural-urban distinctions, as did the hobby farmers in exurbia. Did an ex-urbanite with a rural hobby but an urban occupation belong to farm or city? The factors that decoupled midwesterners' place of residence from their source of income included Social Security and other transfer payments, private pensions, computers and high-speed data transmission lines, self-employment, and the ease of commuting on rural interstates.

The northern Midwest, the Ozarks, the Upper Mississippi Bluff Country—areas with scenery or inexpensive land—attracted retirees, the ecologically minded, self-employed professionals, telecommuters, and survivalists. Formerly depressed counties gained population while prime farm counties saw out-migration. Rural areas functioned as playgrounds or museums. Ethnicity was marketed at Pella (Iowa), New Glarus (Wisconsin), Elk Horn (Iowa), and countless other towns. Rural cities trying not to appear urban to tourists sprang up around attractions like Branson (Missouri), Wisconsin Dells (Wisconsin), Mackinac Island (Michigan), and successful casinos.

The Indian Gaming Regulatory Act of 1988 legalized casino gambling on reservations throughout the Midwest. Riverboat gambling on the Mississippi, Missouri, and Ohio Rivers resumed in the 1990s. Such enterprises brought development and jobs to rural areas. So did the wave of new prison construction.

Late-twentieth-century trends cast doubt on old verities. Was farming central to rural life? Did rural people experience more stability and personal connectedness? Was urban life dynamic, unstable, and impersonal, and rural life better suited to raising a family? Still, if the traditional equation of midwestern with rural no longer held, many people persisted in taking pride in their rural heritage. Midwesterners might not live on a farm, but they had some connection to rural life, whether it be grandparents who farmed, a job in food processing, or simply a love of Sunday drives in the country.

Now, what did rural mean? A casino worker living in a trailer in the township—was she urban or rural? Rural folk shopped at Wal-Mart forty miles distant. Exurbia's twenty-acre hobby farms consumed as much seed and fertilizer as former dairying areas hundreds of miles away. Cities came out to meet farms; a small town had the same fast-food franchises as the city; farms grew as large as ranches; lines blurred between rural and urban, farm country and unsettled open spaces.

Sources and Further Reading: David Blanke, *Sowing the American Dream* (2000); Andrew R. L. Cayton and Susan E. Gray, eds., *The American Midwest* (2001); William Cronon, *Nature's Metropolis* (1991); Jon Gjerde, *The Minds of the West* (1997); John C. Hudson, *Plains Country Towns* (1985); R. Douglas Hurt, *The Ohio Frontier: Crucible of the Old Northwest, 1720–1830* (1996); Don S. Kirchner, *City and Country: Rural Responses to Urbanization in the 1920s* (1970); Richard Lingeman, *Small Town America* (1980); Timothy R. Mahoney, *River Towns in the Great West* (1990); Peter J. Schmitt, *Back to Nature: The Arcadian Myth in Urban America* (1969); Thomas A. Woods, *Knights of the Plow* (1991).

Steven J. Keillor
Askov, Minnesota

Gambling and Casinos

Since Florida Seminoles tested the legality of reservation-based high-stakes bingo in 1979, Indian tribes nationwide have embraced gambling as the "new buffalo" of economic development. Tribes in the Dakotas, Minnesota, and Wisconsin quickly followed the Seminoles, and Chippewa bands in Michigan pushed beyond bingo to institute regular casino games. By 1987, when the Supreme Court ruled that states could not extend their gambling laws over reservations, 113 tribal operations were grossing $225 million per year. Congress responded with the Indian Gaming Regulatory Act in 1988, which extended federal supervision over tribal casinos and required tribes to negotiate gaming compacts with state governments. By 2001, 201 of the 526 federally recognized tribes operated 321 casino-type facilities in twenty-nine

states, generating $12.7 billion in annual net revenues, $68 million in charitable contributions, and three hundred thousand jobs.

Midwestern tribes remain prominent players, operating dozens of gaming facilities in Wisconsin, Michigan, Minnesota, South Dakota, North Dakota, Kansas, Nebraska, and Iowa. Most are in nonmetropolitan areas and rural counties. Tribes use profits to fund tribal operations, economic development plans, and social service programs in communities where poverty has been epidemic. Casinos provide employment for Indians and non-Indians, and the economic spillover in tourism, services, and taxes is now driving some rural economies.

Indian gaming as economic development is not without consequences. While some point to the tremendous revitalization of Indian communities and cultures, others fear the loss of tribal sovereignty inherent in negotiating compacts with states.

Sources and Further Reading: Angela Firkus and Donald L. Parman, "Indian Reservation Gaming: Much at Stake," in Organization of American Historians, *Magazine of History* 9 (Summer 1995); Anicca C. Jansen, "American Indian Gaming Operations and Local Development," *Rural Development Perspectives* 10 (Feb. 1995); Nell Jessup Newton and Shawn Frank, "Gaming," in Mary B. Davis, ed., *Native America in the Twentieth Century: An Encyclopedia* (1994).

David Rich Lewis
Utah State University

Living-History Farms

Midwesterners adopted European preservation strategies during the 1920s and began collecting rural buildings and their contents to exhibit on created landscapes. During the 1960s, social historians' emphasis on everyday life reinvigorated the collection of artifacts as big as entire farmsteads. By 1965, the Agricultural History Society and the Smithsonian Institution were encouraging the development of a national network of living-history farms.

In 1970, the Association for Living History, Farm and Agricultural Museums emerged, influenced by William G. Murray, an Iowan who founded Living History Farms in 1967 and served as the first ALH-FAM president. The number of living-history farms increased with the formation of metroparks and conservation districts, which acquired sites and adopted living-history techniques. The Midwest Open Air Museum Coordinating Council was formally organized in 1979 to support staff at the growing number of living-history farms.

These museums preserved corn cribs and chicken houses, root cellars and smokehouses, barns, milk sheds, and silos, as well as historically correct animals and plants. Interpreters shared historic processes, ranging from precontact Indian agricultural techniques to 1930s dairying.

By the 1980s, many living-history farms cooperated with organizations such as the Society for the Preservation of Poultry Antiquities, the American Livestock Breeds Conservancy, and Seed Savers Exchange, to promote the documentation and preservation of endangered domestic species. Not all living-history farms, however, maintain professional standards, and many have been criticized for depicting a simplistic past distorted by nostalgia. Regardless, they provide information and a valuable, though not foolproof, opportunity to explore the rural Midwest.

Sources and Further Reading: American Museum Association, *The Official Museum Directory* (published annually); Jay Anderson, *Time Machines: The World of Living History* (1984); Marion Clawson, "Living Historical Farms: A Proposal For Action," *Agricultural History* 39 (Apr. 1965).

Debra A. Reid
Eastern Illinois University

Mail-Order Catalogs

The golden age of mail-order catalogs in the Midwest extended from the mid- 1800s to the 1920s. Large, general purpose suppliers such as Montgomery Ward, Sears Roebuck, the Boston Store, Seigel Cooper Company of Chicago, R. H. Williams in Milwaukee, and T. M. Roberts of Minneapolis issued "wish books" that listed thousands of products. Specialty catalogs focused on agricultural implements, fabrics, books, patent medicines, bicycles, and sewing machines. Both varieties benefited from an expansion in postal services. Rural Free Delivery provided direct mail service to each home in 1896. In 1912, Parcel Post allowed consumers to receive packages of up to twelve pounds at low rates.

Mail-order catalogs provided two necessary services to midwesterners. First, they extended the consumer marketplace into regions underserved by retail establishments. Proximity to urban suppliers became less important as consumer options expanded. Second, the catalogs shifted the market advantage away from the suppliers of goods and toward consumer demand. Greater options allowed midwesterners to make more individual choices, and prompted a response by local retailers. Coupled with the rise of national advertising

Advertisement for Acme Washer, Sears Catalogue, 1902. Sears, Roebuck Catalogue, 1902.

and chain stores in the 1920s, rural consumers relied less extensively on catalogs to gain access to the marketplace.

Sources and Further Reading: Louis E. Asher and Edith Heal, *Send No Money* (1942); David Blanke, *Sowing the American Dream* (2000); Hal Barron, *Mixed Harvest* (1997).

David Blanke
Texas A&M University–Corpus Christi

Rural Tourism

Rural areas in the Midwest have been attractive tourist destinations for urban Americans since the latter half of the nineteenth century. Forests, lake regions, and resort towns served as temporary havens from crowded, fast-paced industrial cities.

The term rural tourism as it is used today, however, is associated with a more recent phenomenon and specialty niche in the tourism sector. At its core in the Midwest is farm tourism, or agri-tourism, and activities associated with rural and small-town life. This includes visiting working farms, orchards, vineyards, cranberry bogs, cheese factories, bed-and-breakfasts, and historic sites. It involves arts and crafts, wagon rides, horseback riding, cider pressing, and berry picking. In a sense, rural tourism attempts to recapture a romanticized slice of American life that people believe is fading away.

This trend has not gone unnoticed by state and local governments, who see the potential impact rural tourism might have on stagnant rural economies. Most states now highlight rural tourism in their visitor's guides and websites, drawing upon their own unique agricultural and rural past. The 2003 Official Wisconsin Travel Guide asks whether people have picked red raspberries, seen a cow close up, or smelled sweet clover. Since the answer is usually no, the experiences have become marketable commodities.

Timothy Bawden
University of Wisconsin–Eau Claire

Small-Town Life

SECTION EDITOR
Timothy R. Mahoney

Section Contents

Overview

Perhaps no other region in the United States is so closely associated with the image of small-town life as the Midwest. From the first settlement of the region by European American farmers to the present, the small town has played a central role in the region's economic and social development. It has done so, however, within a distinctive economic narrative.

Initially, merchants and entrepreneurs arrived alongside farmers and established a network of countless vibrant small towns that served as central marketplaces where farmers exchanged produce for goods and services from the national market. By the 1840s, however, some towns that enjoyed a better location and access to broader markets than others had expanded and specialized their trade and gradually developed into regional trading centers. A few of these—Cincinnati, St. Louis, Milwaukee, Cleveland, and Chicago—emerged as regional metropolises by the 1850s.

As these metropolises expanded their trading networks and produced more goods for hinterland markets, they undermined the economic functions of many small towns. Although a number of towns were able to tap into metropolitan industrialism or acquire important institutions and thus grow into small cities—for example, state capitals, university or college towns, or specialized industrial or service centers—most small towns had to settle for providing local exchange, service, and transport services along railroad lines or highways that led to the metropolis. Such activity connected them to nearby small cities as well as to the metropolis, but it provided little stimulus for further economic development. Having once dreamed big and imagined themselves a larger place, if not a future metropolis, they had to settle for being "small" and channel their unfulfilled expectations into a new social and cultural identity that valued smallness and took pride in their social and cultural differences from the metropolis.

This section examines the special social and cultural character of the Midwest small town that unfolded within this distinctive slow-growth economic narrative and explores how the small-town ideal has shaped midwestern regional identity. Several essays at the beginning of the section trace the economic history and contemporary economic viability of small towns across the Midwest. John Jakle explores the general economic challenges that the small town has faced throughout its history. He provides a taxonomy of contemporary small towns, based on how they try to maintain economic viability today as a small town "suburb," "themed" town, "covenanted" town, the site of a lucrative institution, a resort, or as a place for retirement, but notes that many Midwest small towns struggle for existence in a kind of "rural ghetto." William Ferraro examines how so many small towns have been compelled to scramble for economic viability in these ways by examining how most small towns emerged in the nineteenth century as central markets serving a local area, only to have their core economic function gradually undermined by regional and national economic forces in the last century. Wilson Warren notes that many small towns responded to the weakening of their central market function by developing manufacturing activity.

From the early nineteenth century to the present

Main Street, Crawfordsville, Indiana. Indiana Historical Society, neg. no. C7608.

this often meant acquiring lumber, mineral, or food processing plants. But such establishments, facing the same competitive forces as merchants on Main Street, arrived and left town according to national economic trends and thus could be a mixed blessing. Sometimes, in lieu of market or manufacturing development, small towns sustained themselves by acquiring a state or county institution, what Jakle calls a kind of "economic prize," and/or developed a tourist industry highlighting a nearby natural attraction, a site associated with a local personality who made good in the national culture, or a distinctive built environment. Jennifer Crets explores the emergence of "Main Street" tourism that markets the small-town experience as a tourist attraction. This developed especially as railroads, then highways, were built across the region and helped sustain many small-town economies. Dorothy Schweider argues that the central marketplace and manufacturing functions at the core of small-town economies fundamentally shaped their social, institutional, and cultural structure. Main Street businesses, booster organizations, civic groups, men's and women's clubs focusing on community betterment, churches, schools, and colleges formed a rich social and institutional bedrock that provided, amid their uncertain economic history, a sense of order and stability.

This insight provides the background for a series of essays that explore the social and cultural history and character of the Midwest small town and help explain how the ideal or ideology of small-town life acquired its almost mythic power in shaping regional identity. Essays by Dwight Hoover and Paula Nelson generally approach this theme by examining the social and cultural structure of the small town. Hoover explores how—whether as a utopian community, a planned social experiment, a religious or ethnic enclave, or a central marketplace centered on Main Street—the small town has always been viewed as a kind of special social model, type, or laboratory of American life. This perspective became especially prominent at the end of the nineteenth century, when writers and social commentators debated the pros and cons of small-town life, reviling its banality, narrowness, and superficiality on the one hand, or praising its social and civic virtues on the other. This debate drew the interest of sociologists and social commentators, who studied the small town as a laboratory representing American society in general. Working at a time when small towns were, in fact, becoming more integrated into American life, it is not surprising that many scholars found that the distinctive features of small towns, such as the viability of their local economies, were gradually eroding.

Paula Nelson digs deeper to explore the characteristics and quality of small-town society and culture

during its nineteenth century heyday. Small towns serving local functions were, according to Nelson, personal places where residents knew each other and interacted intensively on Main Street and in the surrounding neighborhoods to create a rich social and institutional life. In spite of the forces of modernization that have undermined this life, Nelson argues that most small towns are still personal, neighborly places that have a distinctive social milieu.

Several essays follow up on these general insights by examining more closely the social, cultural, and political experiences of different groups in Midwest small towns. John Miller argues that a middle class "power elite" established and ran most small towns and imposed their values on town society, thus giving small-town life its predominantly middle-class character. These town elites, Wilson Warren contends, were challenged by a powerful constituency of farmers and workers, who articulated and acted upon progressive ideas. Andrea Foroughi suggests that women in small towns, though divided by class and limited for most of the period from acquiring much community power, built communities and fostered social cohesion by maintaining households and families, establishing networks of support, working in the economy, forming clubs and organizations, participating in the town's institutional and church life, and acting as citizens.

Jack Blocker examines the experience of ethnic groups and African Americans. In most towns their numbers were small and they lived under considerable pressure to assimilate, so they made little progress in forming their own distinctive communities before they left for the more diverse metropolis after 1900. In those small towns where ethnic groups or African Americans formed a majority, however, they developed rich social, cultural, and institutional frameworks analogous to those formed by the European American elites in most small towns. Native Americans, according to Jerry Stubben, had a similar experience. While Native Americans have been marginalized in most small towns, a number of Native American towns serve as tribal administrative and educational centers near reservations across the region.

Collectively these essays present a portrait of a small-town life dominated by middle-class elites who exerted economic, social, cultural, and political control and marginalized workers, laborers, farmers, women, ethnic groups, and African Americans to the fringes of community life. Their social power was reinforced by distinctive gendered practices and behaviors. When a college or university was located in a small town, as Andrea Radke notes, boosters, often through the local Chamber of Commerce, affirmed their power by supporting educational institutions, establishing businesses and providing services catering to student needs, and enforcing their values if student behavior challenged local laws or values. Kathleen Brosnan explores the emergence of the booster culture and institutions on Main Street through which the elite broadened their social and cultural power. Timothy R. Mahoney takes a closer look at how small-town men, drawing from their collective boyhood experiences, cultivated and employed a male culture of shared values, cooperation, mutuality, and brotherhood within the public and private institutions that formed the booster culture or ethos on Main Street to enhance and consolidate their power and exclude others.

In much the same way, boosters sought to acquire the county seat and build a county courthouse, a state capital, or state institution, as Thomas Wood writes, as a way to secure a town's future. Once a courthouse was established, argues Mark Ellis, middle-class town leaders created a community-based system of courts, institutions, and officers to establish and enforce law and order. The presence of the courts inevitably drew lawyers to town. They invariably established an active local bench and bar culture that intertwined with booster ethos and enhanced the town's middle-class milieu. Gary Crawley reminds us, however, that the complex intertwining of the "individualistic, moralistic, or traditional" political traditions that spread across and intersected in various towns in the Midwest in the nineteenth and early twentieth centuries assured that each town would develop distinct local variations on the generally similar nature of small-scale, personal, community-based political and legal systems that prevailed across the region.

These essays confirm that small-town life in the Midwest has been shaped by a distinctive narrative within a particular small-scale urban place. John Buenker addresses the scale in which the small-town story occurred and suggests that even larger urban places in the Midwest today remain in many ways big small towns. The history of small towns is situated demographically between the village and city and rooted in a notion of community that has eroded in larger urban centers and the metropolis. Buenker explores small-town life indirectly by noting that as the population of larger towns and small cities grew, social interactions became more impersonal, institutional structures more elaborate, land use more differentiated, and society more stratified into diverse groups divided by class, ethnicity, and race. In doing so, he helps us situate the distinctive historical experience of the midwestern small town.

The third part of this section explores this experience in detail in a series of historical, as opposed to thematic, essays. The historical narrative of the Midwest small town began with the settlement of the region, but the history of small towns began only after

the rise of the metropolis relegated many towns to secondary functions, and their residents had to settle for a slower-paced, smaller-scale reality. Kay Carr notes how, before the Civil War, urban boosters organized midwestern economies, societies, and cultures that they hoped would re-create those in the East. Only in time, when they failed to achieve their goals, did boosters retrench and begin to articulate a set of values that historian Robert Wiebe has called the "way of the town." Such boosters imagined an orderly, simple, slower-paced society sustained by a mixture of cooperative and individualistic economic activity. In central place towns from Ohio to Nebraska, a predominantly American-born local elite articulated this local booster vision while building the town economy, establishing law and order, founding civic institutions, and shaping local society.

The shifting patterns of Midwest urban development and the construction of the railroad system across the region from the 1840s through the 1880s transformed the context in which many small-town boosters operated. Overinvestment in local improvements and railroads exposed many boosters across the small-town Midwest to financial reversals that undermined their leadership and threatened the viability of the town. While some left for the metropolis or the urban west to boost other towns, those who stayed behind—and an awareness among some residents that they had chosen to stay behind became a pervasive self-perception in small-town culture—tried to forge a new town ideology. Their efforts would create the core tenets of the small-town myth in the twentieth century.

Edward Agran explores this transition. The midwestern small towns became the places many left behind: metropolitan America's hometowns heralded by boosters as the quintessential middle-class communities. Residents cultivated the old ways and lived more organically connected, personalized, cohesive lives sustained by a strong sense of identity, social responsibility, and morality—even as they balanced limited local economic opportunity with a desire to connect themselves to the national system and modernize somewhat apace with the city, an aspiration made real by the arrival of the railroads.

From the 1870s through the 1910s, small-town life was mostly portrayed in a positive light. Agran discusses the origins and development of this positive image and explores how the small town provided a vehicle for an emerging Progressive reform agenda at the turn of the twentieth century. Americans, in response to the forces of modernism, idealized the simpler middle-class communities that they believed still existed in small towns. Hence the Midwest small town became an idealized model for a modernizing society.

But the "revolt from the village" clearly indicated that many did not share this view. To detractors, small towns were provincial "island communities" out of touch with modern life. They were places in which residents lived parochial lives frustrated by limited social, cultural, and intellectual horizons. Indeed, because they were unable to achieve economies of scale or the specialized expertise of metropolitan institutions, small-town colleges, academies, museums, hospitals, and government services struggled initially to remain competitive, but eventually settled for mere viability. This dichotomy between positive and negative images, rooted in the experiences of residents past and present, framed most people's understanding of small towns in twentieth-century America. These images reflected the contradictory realities of small-town life. During good times, bursts of development and signs of progress seemingly fulfilled positive images. Conversely, when times in the rural Midwest were bad and small towns were particularly hard hit, as they were during the 1890s and again in the 1920s and 1930s, they became the locus of an array of social pathologies and frustrations.

Richard Davies explores the decline of the midwestern small town in the twentieth century in two essays. In the early twentieth century, most small towns ignored the so-called revolt from the village and praised their values of a classless society in an optimistic and self-congratulatory tone. Davies portrays the 1920s as a heyday of small-town civic institutions, churches, lodges, and clubs, intertwined by a vibrant public culture of parades, festivals, and high school and minor league sports, particularly baseball and basketball. Small-town residents were able to maintain traditional community life even as they benefited from some aspects of metropolitan life. The radio, electricity, telephones, movies, and cars broke down traditional isolation and made life more convenient. Many towns embraced modern life and metropolitan influence, but in doing so, opened themselves to the very forces that would, during and after the Great Depression, undermine the balance they had achieved and, in time, their very existence.

But as Davies notes, the dynamics of the national economy increasingly undermined small-town life. Competitive pressures that consolidated farms and enabled larger producers and retailers to penetrate ever broader markets also intensified contact with national life through highways, air travel, television, and recently the Internet. The expansion of the federal government's control over local affairs undermined in stages nearly every aspect of small-town life. Family farms, Main Street merchants, small-scale manufacturing plants, even local government, all gradually went under or lost their local autonomy, leaving small towns as places where people still lived, but had relatively little local control over their lives.

By undermining the economic and political structure of local life, these translocal forces also accelerated social change. The power elites in most towns broke apart. Out migration deprived towns of their youth and vitality. Newcomers had little vested interest in the town and indifferently contributed to the town's erosion into an impersonal bedroom "community of strangers." Even so, Paula Nelson reminds us, the spatial, economic, and social context of small-town life—smaller and still more personalized—remains fundamentally different from metropolitan life. Therefore, while some believe the integration of small-town life into mass culture has eroded any sense of community and local identity, others believe it has allowed small-town people to live fuller lives, thus enabling their towns to maintain population and attract newcomers. This has been true especially of small towns near a metropolis. Gradually subsumed into the metropolis since the 1970s, these exurbs, small-town enclaves beyond the suburbs, have been reconfigured and given new life. For such small towns, wealth and investment have rejuvenated local resources and facilities, intertwining the suburban and small-town ideal into a new American dream.

The small town in the twentieth-century Midwest was simultaneously heralded as a utopian social ideal and pilloried as a dystopian social wasteland. The reality, of course, lay somewhere in between. The Midwest small town remains caught between very real divergent forces. Its increasingly contradictory image reflects the deepening predicament of being small in a mass economy, society, polity, and culture. Two final sections reflect this theme in the experiences of representative towns and individuals. In varying degrees the town biographies, which were selected as particularly notable examples of small towns in each state whose citizens are committed to a small-town ethos, indicate how most Midwest small towns try to balance these pressures. Finally, a series of short biographical essays focuses on a number of individuals born in midwestern small towns who, in varying degrees, drew on their small-town childhoods to shape their public personae. What these town and individual biographies make clear is that, even though most midwesterners live in the metropolis, the small-town life ideal, rooted in the region's rich history, still plays a powerful role in shaping midwestern identity.

Sources and Further Reading: Edward Gale Agran, *Too Good a Town* (1998); Lewis E. Atherton, *Main Street on the Middle Border* (1954); David Contosta, *Lancaster Ohio, 1800–2000* (1999); William Cronon, *Nature's Metropolis* (1991); Richard O. Davies, *Main Street Blues* (1998); Don Harrison

Doyle, *The Social Order of a Frontier Community* (1978); John Hallwas, *The Bootlegger* (1998); John C. Hudson, *Plains Country Towns* (1985); Robert Lynd and Helen Lynd, *Middletown: A Study in American Culture* (1929); Timothy R. Mahoney, *Provincial Lives* (1999); Paula M. Nelson, *The Prairie Winnows Out Its Own* (1996); Catherine McNicol Stock, *Main Street in Crisis* (1992).

Timothy R. Mahoney
University of Nebraska–Lincoln

Economic Structure

The Midwest has been stereotyped as a region of farms and farm towns. It is the Jeffersonian promise of a democratic citizenry owning and working pastoral landscapes that tends to be celebrated, despite the region's large cities. Small towns, the vast majority created with the coming of the railroads, connected family farms to distant markets. Towns in the Midwest were also sustained by mining and lumbering. Some became resorts, and others the seats of colleges and other institutions. Important too were small-town political functions, especially the police, court, welfare, road maintenance and other activities of county government.

In retrospect, too many small towns were created in the Midwest. To control trade, railroad corporations built too many rail lines with too many towns located at regular intervals along them. Automobiles and improved highways shifted commerce, especially retail activity, from small centers to large. Wider ranges of goods and services could be found in cities because economies of scale lowered prices.

Today, most of the region's hamlets and villages—communities with 2,500 people or fewer—have become little more than dormitory places where people live but do not work, and where they shop only to buy common convenience items. Most diminished of all, perhaps, are the mining towns where coal, iron, or other resources played out, forcing mines to close. Some towns have actually disappeared. Forlorn in Michigan's Upper Peninsula, or on the High Plains of North Dakota, is the ghost mining or farming town with its vacated plat of streets containing but a handful of surviving buildings.

The Midwest's small-town heritage is not disappearing. Most towns with more than 2,500 people are sufficiently well established, both as built environments and as legal entities, to preclude abandonment. Unless a disaster—flood, tornado, earthquake—precipitates a move in whole or in part to another location, the region's larger towns represent investments simply too sizable to liquidate. In recent years, moreover, a number of trends have been working in favor of small-town growth.

The Midwest's most viable small towns tend to be those that have become suburbs within easy commuting distance to jobs in nearby cities. They contain a modicum of convenience-oriented retail activity, and even a selection of stores handling specialty merchandise. They may even have a factory- or office-oriented employment base with some reverse-commuting from a nearby city. Residents are often attracted to such towns by low real estate costs and low property taxes. They balance, in the course of everyday living, cheaper housing against higher journey-to-work costs. Residents may also be attracted by a small town's relatively homogeneous population and a perceived lack of social tensions found in diverse neighborhoods and schools. White flight to big city suburbs after World War II was motivated by a quest for stable, manageable communities with enhanced home equity. Farther-out suburbs, exurbs, are often small towns converted to suburban living.

Some small towns are also covenanted communities, that is, places that emphasize a sense of community structured around religion and kinship. Throughout much of Wisconsin and Minnesota and across large sections of other states, farming (both farm ownership and farm operation) is concentrated in the hands of third-, fourth-, and fifth-generation "hyphenated" Americans of German, Swedish, Norwegian, Dutch, and other nineteenth-century immigrant origin. Many families arrived as members of church-oriented colonizing groups: Roman Catholics, Lutherans, Mennonites, Brethren, and Apostolic Christians, among other sects. Valuing the land as a patrimony to be passed from generation to generation, they have vigorously sought to stay on the land, more so than other farm families with historical roots mainly in New England, the Middle Atlantic States, or the Upper South. They remain less inclined to leave farming or to leave their localities for economic opportunities elsewhere. Tightly bound in church-sustained kinship, friendship, and neighboring networks, they focus their energies locally. Because their citizens do their business locally, their main streets tend to contain a larger range of goods and services than those of similarly sized towns.

Indeed, covenanted farm towns tend to grow at the expense of neighboring centers lacking in strong community ties. As the scale of farm operations in the Midwest increases, driven by mechanization and the other technological advances in agriculture geared to reducing costs of production, farm families of covenanted communities, in pursuit of land, increasingly encroach upon the hinterlands of nearby places,

Gano grain elevator, Western Kansas, 1940. Photo by Wright Morris. © 2003 Center for Creative Photography, Arizona Board of Regents.

directing business away from those places. Banking, grain and livestock marketing, implement sales, seed, feed, herbicide, insecticide, and fertilizer sales, and convenience retailing, generally, are reoriented back toward original home precincts.

The themed small town is also common in the Midwest. Small-town traditions intrigue the majority of Americans who live in cities. Many towns in the Midwest have undertaken to market themselves as visitor destinations. Boosters hope to generate tourism and improve their town's appeal to potential employers looking to locate new facilities. A few midwestern towns contain substantial architectural and other historical resources of national import, including Galena, Illinois; Madison, Indiana; and Marshall, Michigan.

Most widespread today is an impulse to refurbish and market Main Street as a specialty shopping district with antiques stores, restaurants, craft shops (featuring country themes), and other nostalgic venues. Main Street and other theme adoptions seek to turn the small-town experience into a saleable commodity. Place commodification works best in towns readily accessible from expressways. Pressure is very strong for towns with interstate highway interchanges to adopt one or another promotional gimmick to attract tourists. On Interstate 80 in Iowa, antiques, a windmill imported from Denmark, the birthplace of an American president (Herbert Hoover), the birthplace of a movie idol (John Wayne), and an elaborate display of American flags, among many other small-town promotions, figure prominently in billboard advertising.

Many small midwestern towns, especially in Michigan, Wisconsin, and Minnesota, thrive as resorts or retirement communities. Situated on one of the Great Lakes, in an area of concentrated inland lakes or along one of the region's great rivers, and/or in rolling terrain (especially reforested hill country), these towns thrive on seasonal, transient tourism, including that of second-home weekending. Many towns in such areas also serve as retirement communities, especially for midwestern urbanites looking to escape big cities and suburbia's rapidly increasing costs of living and hectic lifestyles.

Some towns benefit from having an economic base beyond farming or tourism. Perhaps a town is a county seat. Residents coming to a courthouse to conduct business have the opportunity to patronize nearby stores, a spillover effect favorable to town merchants. Towns with a private or public institution—a college, a hospital, or a prison—similarly benefit. Of course, industrial employment has long held out promise of economic growth. Obtaining a factory has been traditionally the primary goal of most small-town boosters, especially those on a rail line or interstate. However, many, if not most, towns successful at attracting manufacturing, certainly since World War II, have found their successes all too ephemeral. Because firms want cheap, unskilled labor, their operations are notoriously "footloose." After having invested heavily in new public infrastructure (streets, sewers, and water supply, for example) and having committed to financial incentives (such as tax holidays), many towns find themselves abandoned as employers move away to even lower labor or other operating costs elsewhere.

Some Midwest towns have come to embrace what might be called "dirty" economic activity. They have invited companies to locate despite their negative environmental or social implications. In Iowa and Nebraska, packinghouse operations, displaced from Chicago and other metropolitan areas, thrive in selected small towns that have been willing to accept a largely unskilled labor force from outside as well as the challenge of handling the water and air pollutants. Other towns, often desperate for growth, clamor for incinerators, sanitary landfills, and toxic substance recycling centers. Still others tolerate factory farms where hogs and other livestock are fed *en masse* undercover, often with substantial odor.

Clearly, the vast majority of the Midwest's smallest urban places languish today as economic if not social backwaters that have been termed "rural ghettoes." They function primarily as residential places, perhaps most as dormitory communities for low-income families. Commercial activity is minimal. Schools may no longer exist because local students are bused to distant locations as a result of school district consolidation. When a town's schools close, it usually loses its largest payroll and its largest customer for locally provided goods and services. What remains in such towns is very cheap housing: Prices are substantially depressed, and property taxes and rents on leased property are substantially lower than elsewhere. With property taxes deliberately kept low, government expenditures are also minimal. Public facilities receive infrequent maintenance and upgrade. Low maintenance and lack of improvement tend to characterize private property as well, since improvement only inflates property values and, with them, owner tax obligations. Circuits of disinvestment almost guarantee town decline. Many of the Midwest's smallest places, critics charge, function primarily to warehouse the undereducated, the under- and unemployed, and the impoverished, not unlike many inner-city neighborhoods in the region's metropolises. As in the central cities, people in the poorest of these places subsist largely on welfare and other transfer payments.

Just where the line is to be drawn between large towns and small cities is anybody's guess. No population count or tabulation of urban functions suffices. Despite past attempts to identify rank-order hierarchies, today's Midwest is a region of blurred distinctions vis-à-vis categories of urban place. The trauma of post-industrial economic change—characterized by rapid technological advance, highly mobile capital and labor, and a shift of emphasis toward market distribution, service, finance, research, and other white collar activities—occurred because of widespread time–space convergence: selected places made closer by vastly improved electronic communications and air and highway travel. Throughout the nation, many small towns find themselves fully connected in a new electronics-based economy. Increasingly, telemarketing and financial and other services extended over the Internet are being located in small towns.

Substantially energized as part of an expanding metropolitan area, a few midwestern towns have become edge cities or urban villages, with office and research parks, housing estates, and large shopping centers. Naperville, Illinois, near Chicago, has grown into one of the state's largest municipalities, only smaller than Chicago, Rockford, and Aurora in population. And yet through careful land-use planning, including use of historic preservation zoning, Naperville's traditional small-town ambiance survives at its center, a main street business district surrounded by tree-lined residential streets. There, at least, the popular image of the traditional midwestern small town survives.

Sources and Further Reading: Osha Gray Davidson, *Broken Heartland* (1990); Andres Duany, Elizabeth Plater-Zyberk, and Jeff Speck, *Suburban Nation* (2000); Richard Francaviglia, *Main Street Revisited* (1996); Joel Garreau, *Edge City: Life on the New Frontier* (1991); John Hudson, *Plains Country Towns* (1985); Ron Powers, *Far from Home: Life and Loss in Two American Towns* (1991); Ron Powers, *White Town Drowsing* (1986); Sonya Salamon, *Prairie Patrimony* (1992); James R. Shortridge, *The Middle West: Its Meaning in American Culture* (1989).

John A. Jakle
University of Illinois–Urbana-Champaign

Central Market and Mercantile Service Centers

Virtually all people who established settlements in the Midwest envisioned them becoming places of consequence. They wanted the population to increase, the residents to prosper, and the community to support such cultural institutions as churches and schools. Often, these aspirations went unfulfilled, and nascent towns disappeared from the landscape. In other cases, settlements expanded and became central markets and mercantile service centers for nearby farmers.

The earliest towns generally began at transportation junctures. The places where a river emptied into another river or a lake, or was disrupted by a waterfall, provided a natural stopping point for travelers and encouraged a permanent settlement. Attractive places along Indian paths and early roads also became town sites. Some towns grew out of military forts and installations. Political deals or compromises frequently dictated the location of a county seat, and the need for people to conduct government business on a regular basis gave impetus to other economic activity.

Railroads played an increasingly important role in town location during the second half of the nineteenth century. Eager to attract settlers onto the lands granted them by the federal government, railroad companies employed agents to plat towns along their lines as they stretched across the vast prairie west of the Mississippi River. Speculators and promoters who already had sited towns exerted themselves to convince railroad operators to run tracks through their existing plats. Without a railroad, a town could not serve as an effective link between local farmers and distant markets and was fated to languish or die.

Eagerness to establish a viable town economy often led local entrepreneurs to adopt a booster ethos. All sang the praises of their town and strove to minimize differences of opinion concerning tastes, priorities, or policies. The goal of most any small town was to establish a good mix of shops and services. In the early days, a general store, a blacksmith, a barber, a lawyer, and a doctor would be considered desirable, and later, a bank, a hotel, and a restaurant or two. In all events, town merchants sought steady patronage from farmers living within a day's wagon ride—perhaps ten miles—as well as local residents. Ideally, a sense of loyalty would unite the local merchants and customers, as both benefited from their business relationship. Once in balance, the small town and its surrounding area became self-sufficient.

A series of challenges that began in the late nineteenth century, however, made sustaining such a balance difficult. The concentration of wealth and economic power in large cities, especially Chicago, eroded the ability of small-town merchants to make autonomous choices. The credit or merchandise they could procure was often controlled and limited by corporations in the urban centers. Similarly, small-town merchants had little or no recourse against high shipping costs. With the advent of mail-order catalogs and Rural Free Delivery, big city merchants bypassed their small-town counterparts altogether. Town merchants countered by upgrading their store inventories, placing greater emphasis on face-to-face service, and increasing the volume of their paeans to the intrinsic worth of loyalty to the local business community.

The advent of automobiles and highways gave local customers even more freedom to choose where to buy goods or seek services. Small towns designed to accommodate horses and wagons struggled to provide convenient parking for this new mode of transportation and to persuade customers to keep coming, even if a somewhat larger town a bit farther away could offer better goods and services at lower cost. As spending patterns became more dispersed, small towns lost their prominence as central market and mercantile service centers. With startling frequency, small towns that had maintained a measure of prosperity during the railroad era faded away after the trains stopped and highways went elsewhere.

Challenges to small towns intensified in the late twentieth century. Rural areas depopulated as enormous agribusiness operations took over family farms. Without a sufficient customer base, small-town merchants and professionals were forced to close or leave. Suburban malls on the outskirts of large cities reached out into the countryside and attracted shoppers who formerly frequented their nearby small towns. National chains with massive advertising budgets altered tastes and put further pressure on local independent merchants. Besides their mall outlets, many of these chains used seductive catalogs and sophisticated mail-order marketing to grab additional retail business from small-town competitors. Using the Internet to extend this reach has been the logical next step. Without a doubt, the most controversial national chain has been Wal-Mart. The company's expert blend of the rhetoric of small-town business values with relentless price competition has built an immense retailing corporation that has fundamentally changed the economic balance in innumerable small towns.

Despite a dramatically changed economic landscape, the traditional image of the small town as the central market and mercantile service center for people living in its immediate vicinity retains a hold on the popular mind and politicians. Efforts to revive central business districts through Main Street programs, tax incentives, heightened historical awareness, or special downtown celebrations have been numerous and occasionally successful. Particularly successful efforts include Columbus, Indiana; Marshall, Michigan; St. Charles, Missouri; Nebraska City, Nebraska; and Galesburg and Galena, Illinois. More typical are the mixed results in Rock Island, Illinois; Lafayette, Indiana; and Davenport and Dubuque, Iowa. Successes often take the form of boutiques, antiques shops, and trendy eateries filling storefronts once occupied by merchants who provided basic goods such as hardware, home furnishings, and shoes. In most of the Midwest, however, the small town as a self-contained economic entity is a thing of the past. Nostalgia cannot trump radically changed market structures and dynamics.

Sources and Further Reading: Lewis E. Atherton, *Main Street on the Middle Border* (1954); Robert R. Dykstra, *The Cattle Towns* (1968); William Cronon, *Nature's Metropolis* (1991); Richard V. Francaviglia, *Main Street Revisited* (1996); John C. Hudson, *Plains Country Towns* (1985); Richard Lingeman, *Small Town America: A Narrative History, 1620 to the Present* (1980); David Plowden, *Small Town America* (1994).

William M. Ferraro
Southern Illinois University

Manufacturing or Processing Sites

Small towns have been important manufacturing sites in the Midwest since the early 1800s. But the world in which local entrepreneurs initiated this processing activity gave way in the twentieth century, particularly after World War II, to significant manufacturing decentralization from large cities to small towns.

Lumber sawing and planing, flour milling, and meatpacking, among the most important industries in 1900 America in terms of both total value of product and employment, were largely based in the Midwest. Although larger cities accounted for much of this economic activity, many smaller towns were important to the region's manufacturing sector, particularly those industries processing agricultural goods or producing items needed for farming. Peoria, Illinois, with a population of 29,259, was the nation's largest liquor-producing city in 1880. By 1900, Racine, Wisconsin; Springfield, Decatur, and Rockford, Illinois; and South Bend, Indiana, were important centers of agricultural implement production. Saginaw, Muskegon, and Traverse City, Michigan; Winona, Minnesota; Eau Claire and La Crosse, Wisconsin; Clinton and Dubuque, Iowa; Rock Island, Illinois; and Hannibal, Missouri, were all crucial sites for lumber production. In addition to its importance in producing agricultural implements, South Bend, Indiana, became a leading center for carriage and wagon manufacturing after the Civil War.

In the twentieth century, small midwestern towns became even more central to the region's manufacturing economy. During the first half of the century, the town of Battle Creek, Michigan, with a population of just under twenty thousand in 1900, was the nation's leading cereal food production center. Local businessmen, particularly Will Keith Kellogg and Charles W. Post, led this development. More common, especially after World War II, was the shift in midwestern manufacturing from larger cities to smaller towns. In fact, larger midwestern cities became increasingly white-collar trade and service centers, while smaller towns became more predominately blue-collar manufacturing and processing centers.

Although many towns in south-central Iowa experienced declining population with the declining coal-mining industry, small towns across the rest of the state experienced steady population increases between the end of World War II and 1980. Manufacturing employment in large metropolitan counties peaked in 1950, whereas manufacturing employment in the Midwest's small towns, especially those west of the Mississippi River, increased after 1970. Manufacturers found smaller towns attractive because of their cheaper, usually nonunion, labor forces and lower land and tax costs. Employers throughout the rural Midwest could draw upon former and part-time farmers as ready sources of labor. At the same time, smaller rural communities often had access to excellent communication and transportation infrastructure. The establishment of regional airline services and the deregulation of the trucking industry contributed to these infrastructure advantages. In the latter part of the twentieth century, automobile parts, steel, food products, and furniture are some of the important industries that shifted to towns.

The meatpacking industry's development since the end of World War II readily demonstrates this large-city-to-small-town manufacturing transition. Before the 1950s, Chicago, Omaha, and Kansas City were the centers of industry in the Midwest and in the nation as a whole. Although industry began to shift from larger cities to smaller towns long before the 1950s, within two decades following World War II, new meatpacking companies led by Iowa Beef Packers (IBP) established packing plants in small towns across the Midwest and Great Plains. Older plants established next to the larger cities' stockyards began to shut down. Chicago's enormous Cudahy plant closed in 1954, and shortly thereafter, both its Armour and Swift packing plants closed as well.

Between 1956 and 1965, Armour shut down twenty-one plants employing more than fourteen thousand workers, primarily in larger cities with stockyards. IBP built its first plant in Denison, Iowa, in 1961. For the next two decades, IBP established or took over other midwestern plants in Dakota City and West Point, Nebraska; Luverne, Minnesota; and Emporia and Holcomb, Kansas. This shift to rural locations for beef-packing plants accompanied the movement of the cattle industry westward from the Corn Belt to the High Plains.

Most packing companies, particularly IBP and Cargill, now supplement their labor pool with recruits from Latin America and Asia. These recruitment strategies have transformed the populations of many small towns. A 1998 government study of twenty-three counties in Iowa and Nebraska with large meatpacking workforces found that their per capita income and retail sales had improved between 1985 and 1995. During the same period, the level of serious crime rose in most of the same counties. In just over half of the counties, Medicaid costs exceeded statewide averages over the same period. Educational costs associated with English as a second language instruction increased as well.

Many smaller towns rely on one major industrial employer. Of course, this reliance is often disastrous, particularly given many firms' desire to pursue cheaper costs. Workers' pursuit of labor union affiliation has been one major reason why industrial employers have left some small towns for other, often even smaller, locations. More recently, companies often expect communities to provide ongoing financial incentives to retain their business. Albert Lea, Minnesota, a longtime pork-packing center, had been home to a Wilson Foods, then Farmstead Foods' plant from the early twentieth century to the 1980s. In 1990, Albert Lea offered Seaboard Corporation $3 million in incentives to reopen a closed plant. State and federal government incentives to Seaboard totaled another $34 million. But Seaboard was faced with additional costs in upgrading its sewage treatment facilities after it reopened the plant. Despite an additional $12.5 million in assistance from the city and state, Seaboard decided to move its plant to the even smaller and more isolated city of Guymon, Oklahoma, in 1994.

Small-town manufacturing in the Midwest is likely to remain important into the twenty-first century. Yet, as in the case of the meatpacking industry, it is also likely to promise mixed benefits for small towns and their residents.

Sources and Further Reading: Donald L. Barlett and James B. Steele, "The Empire of the Pigs," *Time* 152 (Nov. 30, 1998); John Fraser Hart, "Small Towns and Manufacturing," *Geographical Review* 78 (July 1988); Roger Horowitz, *"Negro and White, Unite and Fight!": A Social History of Industrial Unionism in Meatpacking, 1930–1939* (1997); Brian Page and Richard Walker, "From Settlement to Fordism: The Agro-Industrial Revolution in the American Midwest," *Economic Geography* 67 (Oct. 1991); T. Lynn Smith, "Sociocultural Changes in 12 Midwestern Communities, 1930–1970," *Social Science* 49 (1974); U.S. General Accounting Office, "Community Development: Changes in Nebraska's and Iowa's Counties with Large Meatpacking Plant Workforces," GAO Report RCED-98-62 (Feb. 27, 1998); Wilson J. Warren, *Struggling with "Iowa's Pride"* (2000).

Wilson J. Warren
Western Michigan University

Institutional Centers

Small towns are the heart of the cultural matrix of the Midwest, and within them, social and economic institutions are paramount. Small towns vary according to settlement, size, and location, but almost all have a familiar set of institutions that define society, impose behavioral guidelines, and provide needed services. These institutions provide a stable structure and a sense of order.

The most obvious small-town institutions are religious and educational. Both churches and schools generally appeared shortly after a town's creation. The two institutions operated in both formal and informal ways. Formally, people attended church on Sunday and sometimes mid-week. Women founded ladies' aid societies, and both men and women served on church boards. Informally, the influence of Protestant doctrine and the presence of ministers affected peoples' activities all week long and dominated community notions of morality.

Institutions of education have played a special role in the Midwest. Townspeople quickly created public grammar schools, and by the second half of the nineteenth century, towns were also organizing public high schools. Schools taught the three Rs and emphasized a rote memory learning process. Public school teachers throughout the nineteenth and part of the twentieth centuries also taught morality and social values. Teachers themselves, especially women, were to serve as good moral examples. Students often learned about proper moral behavior from the pages of the McGuffey Readers.

Other institutions were also vital. Economic institutions were best personified by the stores on Main Street, maintained by both men and women. Most towns were retail trade centers, and during the nineteenth and the first half of the twentieth centuries, small towns had a wide array of businesses that provided most of the needs of their citizens. As David J.

St. Joseph, Michigan, 2003. Photo by Sathyan Sundaram.

Russo points out in *American Towns: An Interpretive History*, local businesspeople played "a complex economic role." They sold the goods that local residents could not produce for themselves, as well as farm surpluses. Some early businesspeople performed banking services for their customers. Businesspeople were also expected to be great town boosters, to work to attract new businesses, to bring in more professional people, and to urge local residents to shop at home. Business organizations also promoted town betterment projects. In Presho, South Dakota, during the difficult 1930s, a local business group built a tennis court, started a golf course, and attracted a major business to the community. Small-town merchants sponsored free movies and put up holiday decorations. The vitality of the business community, or the lack of it, often determined whether a town appeared up and coming or was just coasting along.

Main Street also provided a place for socializing. Saturday night was the highlight of the week for small-town residents. Typically, the town band performed, farm families and local residents did their shopping, and everyone mingled together. These gatherings constituted a major social interaction for residents. Many events were open to everyone regardless of age, social class, or religious affiliation.

Present in all small towns were institutions of community improvement. Men and women belonged to groups that worked to create a better business climate or to create organizations that provided moral and cultural uplift. Men's activities tended to deal with concrete issues, such as creating a more attractive Main Street, while women's groups mostly focused on the development of cultural and social organizations. The creation of town libraries, viewed as an essential part of any town, was often carried out by women, especially the local Womens' Clubs. Women also organized study clubs and book clubs, all in an effort to better educate themselves. Thousands of small-town women joined the Women's Christian Temperance Union (WCTU), beginning in 1874. Besides supporting prohibition, members of the WCTU completed other projects designed to improve family and community life.

An important part of community betterment institutions began around 1900 with what Lewis Atheron has termed "the twentieth century cult of joining." In both large and small towns, people joined a plethora of fraternal organizations such as the Masonic Order, Eastern Star, and Modern Woodmen of America. They established chapters of business and professional groups such as Rotary, Lions, and Kiwanis. While viewed as positive additions to the community, the presence of such organizations tended to erode the sense of communalism within small towns by dividing the general community into small groups with restricted membership.

If most small-town institutions were fairly well defined, social class was less so. Small towns have always had class differences. Communal activities notwithstanding, some people always had greater status within the community than others. Educational, religious, and economic institutions all demonstrated that wealth, profession, and/or family prominence meant some town residents were held in higher esteem than others.

By the late twentieth century, small towns had changed dramatically. Developments such as freeways, new technology, and school consolidations greatly altered residents' social and economic habits. Many towns lost population as businesses on Main Street closed or moved away. Still, Americans continued to revere the memories of small towns and the institutions that defined them. As David J. Russo has written, even in the late twentieth century, "the impulse for Americans to live in or to locate their activities and institutions in small local communities was still a vital one."

Sources and Further Reading: Lewis Atherton, *Main Street on the Middle Border* (1954); Richard O. Davies, *Main Street Blues* (1998); Richard Lingeman, *Small Town America: A Narrative History, 1620 to the Present* (1980); Timothy O. Mahoney, *River Towns in the Great West* (1990); Thomas J. Morain, *Prairie Grass Roots* (1988); Christine Pawley, *Reading on the Middle Border* (2001); David J. Russo, *American Towns: An Interpretive History* (2001); Dorothy Hubbard Schwieder, *Growing Up with the Town* (2002).

Dorothy Schwieder
Iowa State University

Resort Centers

Founded mainly for commercial purposes, midwestern small towns in the nineteenth century served as way stations for travelers: They were places to sleep, buy provisions, and pass through as quickly as possible. Only the wealthy could afford to travel for pleasure, and they mostly confined their touring to the Eastern Seaboard and the few high-class hotels and spas accessible by steamboat or early railroads. After the Civil War, leisure spots proliferated in the Midwest. Built with new railroad capital, these resorts and health spas, including Waukesha, Wisconsin, and Battle Creek, Michigan, promised "health, rest and recuperation . . . as elegant and congenial as any offered by similar resorts in the East, that are reached only after a long, tedious and expensive journey." With less wealth and patronage than their eastern counterparts, many of these spas went the way of western mining boom towns: they were abandoned almost as fast as they were founded. Resorts with lasting popularity, such as those in Wisconsin's Door County and Missouri's Ozarks, made entire regions synonymous with leisure and recreation.

Railroads provided access to isolated rural areas for urban outdoorsmen seeking wilderness. Small towns near such areas began to sell associated equipment such as boats, tents, and ammunition. They also provided transportation and guide services to gentlemen sportsmen who sought to establish game preserves for private hunting clubs, state parks for conservation, and small resorts for their families. These towns were unattractive; with their hotels filled with salesmen, cigar smoke, and rough talk, they were unsuitable for women and children.

In the twentieth century, automobile enthusiasts, through the Good Roads movement, encouraged state road building and numbering through highly publicized conventions and cross-country auto tours, such as the 1910s Cross Iowa car races. Printed auto itineraries directed auto tourists through small towns, literally putting some on maps for the first time and rejuvenating local economies. Towns bypassed by railroads demanded roads, and many formed regional road improvement groups. The new automobile tourist economy reversed the traditional farm-to-town-to-city flow of money and culture. Instead of acting as central marketplaces for farmers wanting access to regional and national outlets, small towns became gateways through which tourists from cities passed on their way to rural resorts, summer boarding houses, and natural and historic areas.

As automobile ownership grew in the 1910s and 1920s, urban tourists flocked to the Midwest's biggest attraction, "the simple life." In contrast to cities, midwestern small towns seemed like the "true" America, an agrarian and socially homogeneous paradise. Early hostelries advertised their agrarian credentials with menus that included "their abundance of fresh eggs, good rich milk and butter, delicious fruits and berries and the safest and purest of cold spring water." Overnight, hundreds of small towns became famous as birthplaces of historically significant Americans or sites of historic events. With brochures emphasizing neat homes, tree-lined streets, and white Christian populations, towns successfully enticed families on the road to make small towns their vacation headquarters.

Small towns throughout the Midwest displayed remarkable uniformity, with business and government activities and structures confined mostly to one Main Street. Popularized by postcards and other tourist imagery, Main Street and the small town became a desirable and consumable place in the American landscape.

Businessmen such as Henry Ford and Walt Disney used their wealth to reconstruct from their childhood memories a sentimentalized vision of the midwestern small town. Ford's "Greenfield Village (1929) and Disney's Disneyland (1955) were idealized small towns created specifically for tourist consumption.

With tourism came cultural, even geographical, transformations. Electric companies dammed rivers for hydroelectric power, creating regional vacation-scapes such as the Lake of the Ozarks in Missouri, complete with company-founded towns and resort communities with urban comforts. State park and recreation movements helped small towns market nearby natural attractions. With millions of Americans hitting the roads in their Ford Model Ts, small towns invested in municipal auto-camps to capture weary travelers in mid-journey. Commercial tourist cabins sprouted along routes between small towns and nearby attractions. Later tourist courts and motels mimicked suburban homes, complete with garages and chintz curtains; others took their forms from the regional image itself, emulating log cabins, teepees, stone cottages, and other stereotypical structures. Larger, more successful towns of the railroad era began to coordinate tourism regionally. In these big small towns, commercial tourist associations, such as the Ozark Playgrounds Association, coordinated regional advertising, selling images of area attractions to tourists through postcards, billboards, and other media.

During the Depression of the 1930s, small towns found themselves caught between two worlds, one old and one new. Residents, eager for modern comforts such as electrification remained apprehensive about other, less tangible changes. Generally, however, small-town residents actively supported the building of dams and the establishment of state parks. They knew that artificial lakes and rural parks attracted tourist dollars and state-funded road improvements. New Deal programs, such as the Civilian Conservation Corps and federally administered state planning boards, vastly improved and expanded the tourist landscape of the Midwest. Small towns eagerly proclaimed their gateway function, as entrepreneurial residents sold tourists food, gas, and lodgings. Through its Works Progress Administration state guides, the federal government encouraged auto-touring, a pastime that transformed national roads such as the Lincoln Highway and Route 66 into legendary byways. The small town took its place among many regional and thematic tourist experiences from which families could choose. After World War II, the Midwest became a recognizable vacationscape, and its small towns crucial to an overall regional image.

Today many small towns owe their continued existence to tourism. Large investments in historic preservation have created popular and profitable Main Street shopping districts and bed-and-breakfast accommodations. In both form and function, small towns sell a nostalgia that equates rural settings, historic architecture, antiques shops, and community experience with "the simple life." For contemporary tourists, most of whom come from sprawling urban-suburban areas, the Midwest's many small towns make time travel possible.

Sources and Further Reading: Warren James Belasco, *Americans on the Road* (1979); Rex Buchanan, Robert Sawin, and Wayne Lebsack, "Water of the Most Excellent Kind: Historic Spring in Kansas," *Kansas History* 23 (2000); Jennifer A. Crets, "Conservation or Tourism? The Development of Roaring River State Park," *Gateway Heritage* 18 (Spring 1998); William Cronon, *Nature's Metropolis* (1991); Donovan L. Hofsommer, *Prairie Oasis* (1975); John A. Jakle, *The Tourist: Travel in Twentieth-Century North America* (1985); Lynn Morrow and Linda Myers-Phinney, *Shepherd of the Hills Country* (1999); James W. Ogland, "Picturing Lake Minnetonka," *Minnesota History* 57 (2001).

Jennifer Ann Price
Saint Louis University, Missouri

Social Structure

Midwestern small towns have exhibited a variety of community types and have often acted as social laboratories with utopian communities and social experiments. Most began as trading centers or military strong points. The economic bases for the towns changed as the national transportation network emerged. By the twentieth century, many of the earlier characteristics had faded and commentators looked at the small towns as exemplars of aspects of the larger American society.

Following the Revolutionary War, settlers from the eastern United States spilled into the region north of the Ohio River, although it was still mainly populated by Native Americans. These early settlers founded towns often unlike those that characterized the New England states. Covenanted communities in which citizens states religious and family ties did appear in northeastern Ohio in an area known as the Western Reserve, but in other places communities grew up in an unplanned fashion near rivers, falls, or on Indian traces, and close to military posts or government agencies. In southwest Ohio, a string of towns running north through the Miami Valley marked the path of U.S. military expeditions in the 1790s against American Indians gathered in villages on the Maumee River. Soon, however, these first settlers and town founders were succeeded by promoters who platted communities that they hoped would enrich themselves and grow into large metropolises. Many of these existed only on paper and never had any inhabitants. Others survived by becoming market towns or county seats. Many failed; those residents who left frequently moved on to the next settlement, hoping it would prove to be the next New York or London.

Sprinkled among these towns designed as engines of wealth for their promoters were others with different purposes. The Midwest was home to a number of religious or utopian communities that wished to be models for the world at large. These appeared early in the nineteenth century, and a few persisted into the twentieth. One of the earliest was the Rappite Community of New Harmony in Indiana founded in 1815, but purchased later by Robert Owen. Almost every Midwest state had its own experimental town. Illinois had the Icarians, who moved from Texas to Nauvoo, which had been home to the Mormons. In Iowa, the Amana Colonies retained their communal form until the 1930s.

There were also planned communities that had no religious or utopian origins but reflected instead views of how to improve life by environmental manipulation. One such town was Jeffersonville in southern Indiana, built to a plan suggested by President Thomas Jefferson with alternate blocks of development and trees. This arrangement originated in the belief that diseases were caused by miasmas, bad air, and that trees would act as lungs breathing out good air to counter the bad.

The creation of social order in the utopian communities came from a structure based on a religious creed or other principles usually imposed by the founders. In towns created for economic gain, the process was both more complicated and diverse. John Mack Faragher's *Sugar Creek: Life on the Illinois Prairie* (1986) found leading families to be loci of power. A system of social hierarchy in the community based upon class distinctions empowered the favored families, who set the rules.

A new type of town emerged with the development of a transportation network of canals and, more importantly, of railroads. These towns became connected to larger cities, and their economic structure changed. Towns sprang up along these transit routes or were deliberately planned by developers of the transit facilities. Good examples are the towns built along the route of the Illinois Central Railroad as it moved south, towns with identical street names and similar shapes. The settlements along the routes, whether canals or railroads, also promoted ethnic diversity as Irish canal or railroad workers formed neighborhoods in towns that were predominantly settled by older Protestant Americans. They also contained Germans who had come for greater economic and political freedom.

The Homestead Act of 1862 and the end of the Civil War in 1865 allowed completion of the rail connection between the East and West Coasts and facilitated the settlement of the western Midwest. The railroads in the trans-Mississippi region created towns to serve as centers for the shipment of wheat and other farm products to cities such as Minneapolis or Chicago. Unlike more self-sufficient earlier towns, these did not exist almost entirely to serve local farmers, but became more involved as brokers and transshippers of goods out and into the town. This meant a change in social structure as local elites lost status.

To populate these new towns, the railroads embarked on advertising campaigns that encouraged settlers to obtain free land offered by the Homestead Act or to buy land from the railroad. The advertisements circulated widely in Europe and in the United States. The results seemed to justify the effort. Prior to the 1880s, settlers in the eastern parts of Kansas, Nebraska, and the Dakotas came primarily from eastern midwestern states. After that date, significant numbers of migrants came from Europe—German Mennonites from Russia, as well as Norwegians and Swedes—to farm and to live in their own communities. Unlike other immigrants who settled in large cities, these migrants wanted to farm, and small towns composed of their countrymen sprang up to service them. These new towns, unlike earlier ones, looked to their European origins and instead of emulating towns in the Eastern Seaboard states, carried over an older tradition.

Not all were welcome. African Americans seeking to leave an increasingly segregated and repressive South tried to take up residence in Kansas in the Exodus of 1879. The towns they founded grew despite the efforts of the Kansas Pacific Railroad and the governor of Kansas to prevent them. Of those early towns, only Nicodemus, in western Kansas, still survives.

The ethnic towns were often more homogeneous than their fellow communities, and often tried to replicate the images and values of the land from which they came. Towns bore the names of cities of the Old World, and their citizens celebrated the rituals inherited from their forebears. There was a Holland in Michigan and a Pella in Iowa. Both recall a Dutch origin; both have tulip festivals and sell Dutch letters and wooden shoes. New Glarus in Wisconsin celebrates a Swiss heritage and its Swiss pioneers.

The period from 1900 to 1914 was the golden age of the small town, rooted in the agricultural prosperity of the day. Small towns were still the market centers for surrounding farmers, but increasingly integrated into a national economy.

The spirit of town promotion continued as entrepreneurs tried to find new industries that would move their communities into the ranks of large cities. In the eastern Midwest—Ohio, Indiana, and Michigan—many a small community believed that manufacturing auto parts was the key to rapid growth and economic success. The traffic in goods was only part of the exchange between towns and cities, as entrepreneurs and workers learned their skills in small towns, but migrated to the city in search of better opportunities as time went on.

Despite this close connection, a backward-looking myth of small-town life emerged. This held that small towns were inhabited by sober but friendly nonethnic individuals, virtuous, hard working, and democratic, Protestant and Republican. Best expressed in *The Valley of Democracy* (1918), a collection of essays written by Hoosier author Meredith Nicholson, the myth claimed farmers and small-town residents were the true Americans, the embodiments of national virtue.

This myth of the small town was never truly representative of the complexity of their origins and development. It ignored the commonality of social problems in both cities and towns, the number of towns that were as ethnic as sections of large cities, and the varieties of towns founded by unconventional religions. It consisted of nostalgia for the past and fear of a future of urban domination, a loss of economic and political power to larger cities.

At the same time, a revolt against the small town became evident in American letters. Writers such as Sherwood Anderson in *Winesburg, Ohio* (1919) and Sinclair Lewis in *Main Street* (1920) portrayed the small town as a place bereft of culture and infected with intolerance and boosterism.

This characterization of the Midwest small town as a dismal and provincial place found a counterpart in the pioneering social science study, *Middletown* (1929), Robert S. and Helen M. Lynd's examination of Muncie, Indiana. Their findings appeared to confirm the boosterism and lack of introspection noted by the novelists. A second effort, *Middletown in Transition* (1937), analyzed the impact of the Depression on the town and found that, despite federal aid that had physically changed the fabric of the community, Munsonians held fast to a creed of self-help that was outdated and not reflective of actual circumstances.

The Lynds' work also challenged the idea of the egalitarian small town, finding instead little social mobility and significant class stratification. This conclusion seemed confirmed by Carl Withers's investigation of a Missouri town he called Plainville. An examination of an Illinois town by W. Lloyd Warner, a prominent sociologist, also found limited mobility. In *Jonesville: A Study in Quality and Inequality* (1949),

Warner discovered a well-developed class system that had allowed, however, some integration of Norwegians into the Yankee elite.

A happier view was that of Hervé Varenne, a French-born anthropologist who studied a small town in northern Illinois that he called Appleton. In his book *Americans Together: Structural Diversity in a Midwestern Town* (1977), Varenne was less interested in how Appleton was different from a large city than in how it embodied a larger American culture. The questions for him were how localities modified and presented the values of the society as a whole, not how small towns differed from large cities.

Another more hopeful note was struck by researchers in Middletown III, a rubric used by a team of sociologists led by Theodore Caplow, Howard M. Bahr, and Bruce Chadwick to restudy Muncie. The project, begun in the 1970s, produced two books—*Middletown Families: Fifty Years of Change and Continuity* (1982) and *All Faithful People* (1983)—as well as numerous papers and articles. The changes over time seemed to show that Munsonians' values reflected those of the larger society: more religious tolerance and less boosterism, less difference in class behavior, and less class rigidity. Perhaps this increased sophistication and loss of provincialism resulted from the transition of Muncie from a market town with a strong manufacturing base to a service center providing educational opportunities and medical facilities to the hinterland. Only time will tell; the study continues.

The conception of the midwestern small town as a community with a tradition of tranquility, equality, and the good life was a creation of a particular era, now gone. Perhaps as its economic base changes or withers and local customs fade, it will lose its peculiar self-image, as many areas of the world are doing in this age of globalization.

Sources and Further Reading: Theodore Caplow, Howard M. Bahr, Bruce A. Chadwick, and Dwight W. Hoover, *All Faithful People* (1983); Theodore Caplow and Howard M. Bahr, *Middletown Families* (1982); Kathleen Neils Conzen, "Community Studies, Urban History, and American Local History," in Michael Kammen, ed., *The Past Before Us* (1980); Merle Curti, *The Making of an American Community* (1959); Don Harrison Doyle, *The Social Order of a Frontier Community* (1978); Robert Dykstra, *The Cattle Towns* (1968); John Mack Faragher, *Sugar Creek* (1986); Richard Lingeman, *Small Town America* (1980); William Silag, "Doing Local History: Monographic Approaches to the Smaller Community," in Howard Gillette, Jr., and Zane L. Miller, eds., *American Urbanism* (1987); Hervé Varenne, *Americans Together, Structural Diversity in a Midwestern Town* (1977); Carl Withers, *Plainville USA* (1945).

Dwight Hoover,
Sarasota, Florida

Institutional and Cultural Structure

Small midwestern towns shared several elements in the late nineteenth century. Their success depended on the commitment of citizens to organize churches, schools, associations, and entertainments. Active, committed individuals set the tone and made society work. The story of small midwestern towns in the twentieth century is one of restructuring in the face of technological transformations, economic struggle, and changing definitions of success and "the good life." Small towns remain personal places, however, at least relative to cities, and the role of active, committed individuals is still vital to a town's quality of life.

Neighborhood has always been the foundation of small-town life. People saw each other frequently because they hauled wood, pumped water, tended their chickens, hung out laundry, gardened, and relaxed on the porch or steps, all within sight and earshot of neighbors. They walked everywhere. In summer, windows stayed open and voices rang out across yards.

Many communities built bandstands in local parks or near Main Street. In the political season, speakers promoted their platforms from this location, and temperance rallies or revivals might occupy the space in the warm months.

Because families were relatively large and people rarely lived alone, homes were beehives of activity. Women and children were in and out of the house all day; husbands and employed older children walked home for lunch and dinner. People "visited" with neighbors across the fence, or entertained relatives and friends for long periods.

Because being a good neighbor was important, there were many opportunities to test one's social worth. Women neighbors helped nurse the ill and kept domestic life in order. Men assisted, especially with their extended families and with night watches for neighbors, fellow lodge members, or single male patients without family nearby. Neighbors intervened in cases of spouse, child, elderly, or animal abuse, rushed to aid the injured in time of accident, carried furniture from burning homes, or provided food and clothes for those down on their luck.

Close proximity could breed contempt. A neighbor might shoot a constantly barking dog or impound a roaming pig. In Canton, South Dakota, in the summer of 1899, a father and his two sons were charged with assault after attacking the neighbors on each side of their home. Each neighbor kept pigs and the exceptionally warm, rainy summer made their presence unbearable.

❖ **The Dynamics of a Four-Way Stop**

The most important intersection in the small town of Ashland, Missouri, (population 2,200) is the cardinal-oriented crossing of Broadway and Main Street. This intersection presents on its four corners one of two grocery stores in town, the one video shop, the most distinctive bar and restaurant, and a new antique and flower shop. It also is the closest access to Ashland's three public schools, which span from kindergarten to twelfth grade, in three different locations. This is, as well, the four-way intersection that goes off in three directions to a series of new tract developments marking the community as a residential destination for young families trying to find a place less complex than the nearby university town, Columbia (population 85,000+) or the state capital, Jefferson City (population 40,000+).

More than 3,300 vehicles a day move through this busy, un-stoplighted corner—cars, trucks, vans, SUVs, school buses, motorcycles, farm implements, bicycles—not to mention pedestrian traffic. Over a dozen hours of observation, I counted some 680 vehicles from 7:30 to 9 A.M., 533 from noon until 2 P.M., another 1,736 from 3:30 to 7:00 P.M., and then several hundred others scattered across the dawn, day, and night hours. I also counted a total of 239 pedestrians negotiating this corner. These numbers include some people who crossed two or more times in one day.

At each stopping, all drivers look to see who or what is ready to proceed as the way opens. This sometimes engenders a lifted hand, or several fingers straightened up from the steering wheel, maybe a touch of a hat, and even a flashing of lights. There is an occasional spill as an unexpected greeting evokes an automatic response from a hand holding a cup of hot coffee.

In talking with some locals about the dynamics of the intersection, I was cautioned by one: "Don't be fooled by all of the traffic you see here. Way more than half of these people never come to our streets to spend any money. They mostly think of Columbia or Jeff City as their market town."

Looking west from this four-way stop, the road leads toward pricey new tract developments. Turning south, you see the old highway coming in from the steadily disappearing farm fields that surrounded the town. The four-way stop is a bottleneck and a town meeting for the highly varied backgrounds and futures in this small town. In one way or another, all of Ashland's cultural variety interacts in the dynamics of this intersection.

Kit Salter
Hartsburg, Missouri

In the nineteenth century, many small-town residents made their own entertainments, strove for self-improvement, worked for social reform, and indulged their passion for ritual and pageantry. Churches played a vital role, generally meeting twice on Sunday and, in some denominations, once during the week. Most churches had at least one ladies' aid group, which met for sociability and charitable labor, such as sewing for the poor. Many churches had youth groups, as well.

A community's ethnicity showed most clearly in its churches. Services might be in Norwegian, Danish, Swedish, or German in Lutheran churches. Except in towns where Catholics were a large presence—such as Dubuque, Dyersville, or Holy Cross in Iowa, and Albany, Minnesota, or Kieler in Wisconsin—Catholics tended to remain on the fringes. Of course, many Protestants attended dances, socials, or dinners organized by Catholic groups. Catholic individuals could be thoroughly integrated into the economic, political, and social life of the town. It was through mainstream Protestant churches that the Women's Christian Temperance Union worked to prohibit alcohol consumption and to close saloons. The Anti-Saloon League, a male organization, joined them after 1895. Scandinavian Lutheran churches often participated in anti-alcohol campaigns as well.

Lodges played a vital role in small-town life. All kinds of lodges existed, with many men and women belonging to more than one. The Masons and their various branches were well represented, as was their companion lodge, the Order of the Eastern Star. The Odd Fellows and Rebekahs, the Modern Woodmen and the Royal Neighbors, the Knights of Pythias, the Ancient Order of Pyramids, and others all found homes in small towns.

Lodges shared many important elements that attracted members. They created an automatic brotherhood or sisterhood and provided rituals known only by other members. Lodges created opportunities for sociability. They did good works and provided a social safety net for members. In the 1890s, an ill and partially paralyzed Odd Fellows member traveling from a distant town had to switch trains in Canton, South Dakota. A delegation of Odd Fellows met him, carried him off the train, cared for him during the wait for the next train, then carried him on and got him settled. The man journeyed hundreds of miles with the help of lodge members he had never met. If a member died, lodge members attended the funeral in a body, escorted the casket to the cemetery, and provided rituals of comfort and farewell. When Lutheran ministers or Catholic priests railed against lodges as pseudochurches, their proponents pointed to the numerous acts of charity and fellowship they performed that reinforced churches' roles.

Two particularly important organizations in the post–Civil War small town were the Grand Army of the Republic (GAR) and the Women's Relief Corps (WRC), the Union Army veteran's organization and its companion group. For more than thirty-five years after the end of the Civil War, Union veterans' shaped the rituals, commemorations, and celebrations of their towns. Decoration Day, with its solemn parades, speeches, and adornment of veterans' graves, the remembrances of Washington's Birthday and Lincoln's Birthday, and the 4th of July became the special purview of the GAR and WRC. The veteran's group kept the memory of the Civil War alive with regular "camp fires," where they told war stories, sang songs, and ate beans and hardtack, a hard thin cracker of the type that had made up much of their rations during the war years. When a veteran died, the GAR and WRC marked his passing with special funeral rituals. The war held such importance that the Sons of Veterans organized in the 1880s to keep their fathers' stories alive. After the Spanish–American War (1898), those veterans began their own group, the Marilao Command.

The church youth groups, the WCTU and Anti-Saloon League, the lodges, the GAR and WRC, the Sons of Veterans, and the Marilao Command all shared a governance structure that provided local, state, and national oversight. Locals ran their own affairs, but sent delegates to state meetings, which then sent delegates to national conventions. This ensured consistency of message and activities and allowed local people to move up in the organization and to build links of friendship across the country.

Although many nineteenth-century organizations and institutions persisted, new institutions and organizations developed in the twentieth century. The high school was the most important of these; it helped create popular activities—sports, oratorical, and music contests, and rituals such as proms, Junior–Senior banquets, baccalaureate, and graduation. The growing interest in education beyond the eighth grade kept children in school. Progressive towns had always had an interest in their schools, but until large numbers of teenagers attended, activities at the school were limited to seasonal programs, children's displays of work, and the graduation ceremonies for small classes of young people who had completed high school.

With the growth of organized school sports, townspeople organized caravans of automobiles to transport their young people to neighboring towns to play ball, and ladies' aids from the various churches ensured that visiting teams had a good meal before or after the game. Main Street businesses donated money to buy uniforms and to support travel. The popularity of school sports led to their institutionalization.

Schools organized into conferences and districts and ultimately developed state oversight agencies to manage the system. Today signs inform highway travelers of the local schools' athletic triumphs. School consolidations, which began early in the twentieth century for country schools, struck small-town schools in the last third of the century and continue to be painful as residents face a transformation of identity caused by school closings.

Other changes in the small towns' social world came from the disappearance of the GAR as Civil War veterans died and the rise of the American Legion and its auxiliaries after World War I. The Legion provided opportunities for men with the shared experience of war to socialize together. World War II and the Korean War added large numbers to its membership. Along with the Auxiliary, the Legion built and maintained softball fields and skating rinks, sponsored Santa Claus's Christmas visits, and raised funds to support local hospitals. Other clubs, such as Kiwanis, Rotary, and Optimists, gave businessmen an opportunity for sociability and community service. New technologies such as the movies and the radio provided opportunities for small-town residents to organize parties to attend the show and socialize afterwards.

In the long run, however, the changes of the twentieth century were not kind to small towns. The centralization of economic opportunity in larger towns and cities pulled populations away. The automobile provided a means for shoppers to visit larger towns or cities more easily, which took needed business from Main Street. Chain stores, and in recent years, super stores such as Wal-Mart, forced out small independent businesses. Television offered more glamour and excitement than home talent productions or lodge meetings. Air conditioning pulled people into the comfort of their homes in the summer, leaving porches, yards, and steps empty. The movement of married women into the workforce and the advent of both women and men commuting to larger towns for work drastically reduced the pool of available workers for church groups, lodges, and other voluntary organizations.

Changing values and expectations have also remade the small-town social world. Lodge rituals and young peoples' church picnics no longer hold much appeal for generations raised on action movies, MTV, and the Internet. Relative to big cities, however, small towns continue to be personal places with great potential for an overall sense of community.

Sources and Further Reading: Lewis Atherton, *Main Street on the Middle Border* (1954); Richard Critchfield, *Those Days: An American Album* (1986); Don Harrison Doyle, *The Social Order of a Frontier Community* (1978); Thomas J. Morain,

Prairie Grass Roots (1988); Paula M. Nelson, *After the West Was Won* (1986); Paula M. Nelson, "'Do Everything'—Women in Small Prairie Towns, 1870–1920," *Journal of the West* 36 (Oct. 1997); Paula M. Nelson, *The Prairie Winnows Out Its Own* (1996); Paula M. Nelson, *Real Life in a Gilded Age: The Story of Canton, South Dakota, and Its Chronicler, N. C. Nash, 1877–1905* (forthcoming); William Allen White, *The Autobiography of William Allen White* (1946).

Paula M. Nelson
University of Wisconsin–Platteville

Social Elites and Middle Class Citizens

Small towns in the frontier Midwest relatively quickly engendered rudimentary social elites, and middle-class values predominated. Most country towns became host to an inner circle of families whose middle-class code set the tone for social life. These elites emerged out of a volatile society of considerable geographic and social mobility. Their ability or desire to persist gave them social power quite quickly. People with ability and ambition often progressed rapidly up the social ladder. Change and flux were the norm, and opportunity was abundant.

No single description can possibly encompass the varied experiences of thousands of towns dotting the Midwest, but most followed a common pattern of development. From the beginning, small-town residents attempted to re-create conditions prevailing in the places that spawned them. As three streams of migra-tion pushed westward across the Midwest during the nineteenth century, each was accompanied by its own peculiar set of customs and values. One, deriving largely from Virginia and Kentucky, settled north of the Ohio River in southern Ohio, Indiana, and Illinois. Another, emanating from southern and southwestern Pennsylvania and western and central New York, occupied the central portions of those states. New Englanders moved across the northern sections and beyond.

These broad cultural bands lent themselves to increasing social stratification over time, and a general pattern of class distinction emerged, although the process by which this was achieved varied from place to place and time to time. Early arrivals who committed themselves permanently to a town provided the foundation, which was expanded upon in subsequent years by boosters, proponents of gentility, and champions of culture. Early society was often highly mobile and fragmented, stimulating efforts to engender self-discipline and to impose social order and control by groups associated with the more prestigious Protestant denominations, a proliferation of voluntary associations and temperance groups, and those identified as the better families in the community.

In general, town elites were white, Protestant (especially Episcopalian, Presbyterian, Congregationalist, and Methodist), descended from New Englanders or northern and western Europeans, and well-educated. Wealth, manifested in people's homes, clothing, and possessions, identified elite status. At the

Howell Opera House, Howell, Michigan. Livingston Arts Council.

outset, differences between high and low tended to remain modest and rough equality prevailed, but over time the gap widened and visible wealth became more evident. While transients came and went freely in a community, those who persisted over a period of time generally constituted the elite.

Smaller communities usually displayed less economic stratification than larger ones. By the 1920s, in their classic study of *Middletown* (Muncie, Indiana), Robert and Helen Lynd noted the presence of a power elite that presided over town affairs. Townspeople generally deferred to bankers, lawyers, doctors, and the more prosperous merchants. These groups reinforced their position by joining professional organizations that worked to consolidate their influence.

While men exercised dominant power in public life, women were prominent in church affairs and took the lead in the advancement of culture. Men's fraternal orders, from the Masons and Odd Fellows to the Elks and Woodmen, provided social relaxation and male camaraderie as well as business contacts. Women enjoyed the intimacy of female sociability and an opportunity to expand their horizons, as well as a chance to make an impact on their community through their own social groups, study clubs, ladies aids, and various self-improvement and socially beneficent organizations. These kinds of groups, both male and female, served an integrative function, bringing together people from the range of social status, but they were generally dominated by the economic and social elites of the towns, reinforcing their superior status. A similar dynamic operated in activities that brought both sexes together for the promotion of culture, education, and entertainment through the means of opera houses, Lyceum series, and Chautauquas.

Small-town residents resembled most Americans in claiming to belong to a classless society and in assuming social fluidity, and most of them indeed fell under a broad definition of middle class. This classification could further be broken down into upper middle, middle, and lower middle classes. Criteria for locating families along this spectrum included income and material possessions, occupation of head of household, residence, lifestyle, family background, participation in community affairs, and prestige or reputation. Although egalitarian ideals and rhetoric prevailed, the presence of a social pecking order was widely understood. Class distinctions and social privilege perpetuated themselves across generations through the socialization process, intermarriage, and in some cases, the enrollment of children in prestigious boarding schools and colleges. With the decline of the old fraternal orders, Main Street merchants, and professional booster groups during the early 1900s, new organizations emerged to replace them, such as the Rotary, Lions,

and Kiwanis clubs. The town's professionals and businessmen, who had tended to be Whigs in politics, more often than not joined the Republicans in the 1850s.

As economist Thorstein Veblen noted, small-town elites imposed their views and values upon the general populace in a variety of ways, through the pulpit, the press, and the courts, among others. For some who grew up in them, such as novelist Sinclair Lewis, small-town ways could be pretentious, provincial, and stifling. Many others, however, found the values embodied in McGuffey Readers, Sunday School lessons, and popular songs serviceable. Hard work, perseverance, truthfulness, modesty, and the like were imperatives that might serve the interests of the local elite, but they also represented a social consensus accepted by many people.

Coinciding with the rise of automobiles, radio, movies, and other nationalizing cultural forces during the 1920s and subsequent decades, the cultural hegemony of small-town elites gradually withered. Corporate expansion and consolidation similarly stripped them of their economic dominance. Nevertheless, they remain influential.

Sources and Further Reading: Lewis Atherton, *Main Street on the Middle Border* (1954); Andrew R. L. Cayton and Peter S. Onuf, *The Midwest and the Nation* (1990); Richard O. Davies, *Main Street Blues* (1998); Don Harrison Doyle, *The Social Order of a Frontier Community* (1978); John Mack Faragher, *Sugar Creek* (1986); Richard Lingeman, *Small Town America* (1980); Timothy R. Mahoney, *Provincial Lives* (1999); David J. Russo, *American Towns* (2001).

John E. Miller
South Dakota State University

Farmers and Laborers

Throughout the nineteenth and much of the twentieth centuries, small towns were important economic and political centers for farmers and workers in the rural Midwest. Extractive industries, such as lumber and mining, as well as grain and livestock processing, sustained the economies of many of the region's small towns during this period. The Midwest's small towns were also important service and retail centers for farmers and laborers. The same can be said of politics; arguably the most fundamental political activity for farmers and workers took place in small-town municipal or county government. Indeed, a variety of factors, perhaps most crucially connections to rail transport and county seat status, determined whether small towns attained population stability or slid gradually into demographic stagnation.

Because of the opportunities for interaction given the economic and political nature of the region's small towns, they have also long been centers of farmer–laborer cooperation. Specifically, mutual interests in reform and agreement about their respective fundamental contributions to American society periodically gave rise to alliances and cooperative efforts. Much of the cooperative legacy began during the long economic depression of the 1870s to 1890s and was centered on the creation of the People's or Populist Party in 1891–1892. Primarily through the efforts of the Farmers' Alliances and the Knights of Labor, farmers and laborers developed similar critiques of industrial society. In Iowa, there were several all-farmer assemblies in the Knights of Labor, and at the Knights' 1888 state assembly in Des Moines, nearly half the delegates were farmers. However, the Populist Party of the 1890s was never as successful in the eastern Midwest as it was in the Great Plains and the South. In Iowa and Ohio, unlike Kansas and Nebraska, the Republican Party responded to many of the farmers' demands, thereby reducing potential agrarian support for the Populists.

Arguably the country's most successful populist movement took place after the demise of the People's party in the form of North Dakota's Non-Partisan League. Based primarily on farmers' support, but also involving some workers in small cities such as Fargo and Bismarck, the Non-Partisan League's dominance of North Dakota politics between 1916 and 1921 resulted in the establishment of a state-owned bank, mill, and elevator, a state grain-grading system, a state bank deposit guarantee law, a nine-hour day for women, a land title registration law, reduced rates of tax assessment for farm machinery and improvements, a law forbidding discrimination in rail rates charged on long and short hauls, and major increases in state aid to education.

The other major state-level farmer-labor political party success occurred in Minnesota. From 1918 to 1944, the Minnesota Farmer-Labor Party (FLP) was often the dominant party in the state. With support from both farmers and urban laborers, including radicals from the small towns in the iron-mining Mesabi Range, the FLP enacted progressive legislation, especially during the 1930s. The party supported farmers fighting against foreclosure, workers struggling for union recognition, and unemployed workers' efforts to improve their lives. The progressive stance of both the Non-Partisan League and the FLP influenced politics in North Dakota and Minnesota for many years after their demise.

Nevertheless, independent farmer-laborer political activity waned by the 1930s. With the rise of the New Deal, most reform-minded farmers and laborers affiliated with the Democratic Party. Farmer-laborer cooperation from the mid-twentieth century on focused increasingly on narrower reform efforts directed primarily through progressive farmer or labor movements. During the Congress of Industrial Organization's (CIO) heyday, the two most active proponents of such farmer-laborer cooperation were two affiliated unions, the United Packinghouse Workers of America (UPWA) and United Farm Equipment and Metal Workers Union (FE).

Both unions established full-time farm relations directors in 1946. Lee Simon, a former staff writer for the Des Moines *Register and Tribune*, was the UPWA's farm relations director; Homer Ayres, a former county president of the South Dakota Farmers Union, a member of the Communist-led United Farmers League, and a Farmer-Labor Party candidate for lieutenant governor in South Dakota in 1934, was named the FE's farm relations director. They found the Iowa Farmers Union (IFU), whose president, Fred W. Stover, was particularly receptive to their cooperative efforts. All three organizations espoused programs that resonated with leftist liberals in the late 1940s, including full employment, economic planning, expanded social welfare and civil rights programs, higher farm commodity subsidies, and international cooperation with the Soviet Union. The UPWA, FE, and IFU coordinated several joint farmer-labor efforts in Iowa in 1947, including conferences and Farmer–Labor Day picnics.

After the CIO purged its left-wing elements in 1948, the UPWA shifted its farmer-labor cooperation to educational efforts at county fairs in the Midwest's small cities and towns. In 1949, the UPWA claimed to have set up booths at forty county fairs and mailed its literature to more than a hundred thousand farmers. In the same year, the UPWA sponsored the Union Caravan, a five-member performing troupe modeled on the Progressive Party's Wallace Caravans. In the summer of 1949, the Union Caravan performed at union meetings and county fairs in Iowa and Nebraska. Incorporating the union's message into a forty-five-minute performance of comic skits, folk dances, and topical lyrics set to well-known music, the Union Caravan members talked to audience members before and after their performances about farmer-laborer issues.

The National Farmers Organization (NFO) in the late 1950s and early 1960s pursued farmer-laborer cooperation in the Midwest after communist accusations weakened the Iowa Farmers Union. Formed in 1955 and led by Oren Lee Staley, the NFO focused on aggressive organizing and collective bargaining to help farmers raise commodity prices. After adopting collective bargaining at its 1958 convention, the NFO used holding actions to obtain master contracts with livestock processors and farm commodity buyers. One of its first holding actions occurred in St. Joseph, Missouri, and resulted in the disruption of meatpacking there for an entire week. They conducted successful holding actions in Omaha and Kansas City, among other places, between 1961 and 1964. In Iowa, the NFO worked closely with the Black Hawk Labor Council of the AFL-CIO, in Waterloo, Iowa, on education and political issues. One result was the election of several Democratic officials in that long-time stronghold of the Republican Party.

During the farm crisis of the 1980s, farm groups once again sought support from labor. Across several communities in Iowa, Illinois, and Minnesota, the farm movement and groups such as the Iowa Farm Unity Coalition received assistance from the United Automobile Workers (UAW) through its Community Action Program. Farmers also turned out to back the United Food and Commercial Workers (UFCW) Local P-9 strike, commonly known as the Hormel Strike, in Austin, Minnesota, in 1985.

From the late nineteenth century through the end of the twentieth, farmers' and laborers' cooperative efforts in the rural Midwest formed the backbone of much of the region's progressive political heritage. While episodic and increasingly constrained over time, farmers' and laborers' cooperative efforts consistently rested on shared beliefs in their fundamental contributions to the productive power of the American economy.

Sources and Further Reading: Jon Lauck, *American Agriculture and the Problem of Monopoly* (2000); David Montgomery, "The Farmer-Labor Party," in Paul Buhle and Alan Dawley, eds., *Working for Democracy* (1985); Jeffrey Ostler, *Prairie Populism* (1993); William C. Pratt, "Using History to Make History?: Progressive Farm Organizing During the Farm Revolt of the 1980s," *Annals of Iowa* 55 (Winter 1996); Peter Rachleff, "The Failure of Minnesota Farmer-Laborism," in Kevin Boyle, ed., *Organized Labor and American Politics, 1894–1994* (1998); Larry Remele, "Power to the People" in Thomas W. Howard, ed., *The North Dakota Political Tradition* (1981); Wilson J. Warren, "The 'Peoples' Century' in Iowa: Coalition-Building among Farm and Labor Organizations, 1945–1950," *Annals of Iowa* 49 (Summer 1988); Wilson J. Warren, Bruce Fehn, and Marianne Robinson, "They Met at the Fair: UPWA and Farmer–Labor Cooperation, 1944–1952," *Labor's Heritage* 11 (Fall 2000–Winter 2001).

Wilson J. Warren
Western Michigan University

Women

Since towns were first established in the Midwest in the early nineteenth century, women have participated actively in religious, economic, and social life. With national suffrage in 1920, women became full political members of their communities by voting and holding local office. Over time women have created both informal networks and formal organizations to cope with problems and effect change and to foster a sense of belonging in small-town society.

Before the Civil War, women migrated with their families to small towns in new areas. Eager to replicate familiar eastern social structures and community networks in new towns, women organized fund-raisers to build churches, and then became the majority of members in those congregations. They mobilized for charity work and church socials, which brought community members together and strengthened women's relationships. Inspired by revivals, women were attracted by controversial religious and social movements, including abolitionist settlements in the Kansas Territory. When the Civil War demanded efficient collection and distribution of medical supplies and foodstuffs, women drew on their experience as members of volunteer groups to form local soldiers' aid societies and affiliate with the National Sanitary and Christian Commissions. Women's participation in temperance societies, male clubs' auxiliaries, and other benevolent and suffrage organizations gained momentum in the late nineteenth century. Women also took part in literary societies, public libraries, and lyceums, small-town entertainments that persisted into the twentieth century.

In early towns, men pursued craft, professional, or service trades, sold town lots, and created political and legal institutions; their wives established homes similar to the ones they left and created strong family and community networks through visiting, exchanging goods, and shared labor. Women urged town leaders to establish strong school systems, which then attracted single women as schoolteachers. While many small-town wives aspired to a domestic life based on a husband's income and their own unpaid labor, for many families this was only an illusion, especially during the economic downturns of the late 1830s, the 1850s, the mid-1870s, and the 1890s. Throughout the Midwest women generated income as shopkeepers and innkeepers, newspaper editors and postmistresses, seamstresses and milliners, cooks and domestic servants, prostitutes and dance-hall girls. Although women of all races and ages worked in lower-status jobs, more African American women and young European immigrant women filled these positions than Native American women, who were limited to domestic work in many towns near reservations through the mid-twentieth century. Instead, Native American women and farmwomen traveled to towns to trade items they produced and gathered for cash, credit, or

Street corner conversation, Allegan, Michigan, 1937. Library of Congress, Prints and Photographs Division, LC-USF34-030014-E.

needed goods, thus supplementing their family income. Women from the town and countryside frequented the stores that brought consumer items to rural areas. Attentive to urban and eastern fashions, small-town women relied on magazines, newspapers, pattern books, and later radio and television to stay abreast of trends in home furnishing and dress styles.

The patterns of women's lives in twentieth-century small towns extended trends of the earlier period; women continued to work toward improved economic, social, and religious cohesion in town life. Women filled vital economic roles in small-town communities as beauticians, storekeepers, nurses, schoolteachers and staff, café owners or employees, office workers, and laborers in local businesses and factories. The beauty shop, like a milliner's shop in the nineteenth century, provided women with an exclusively female location to interact both economically and socially. Women continued to spearhead volunteer activities, often under the auspices of local women's clubs; these clubs provided women with educational opportunities as well as leadership experiences in community improvement efforts.

A consistent feature of small-town life has been a core of families who remain in the town over several generations. As rural churches and neighborhoods experienced population loss over the course of the twentieth century, farmwomen turned to towns to reestablish a sense of community; they joined congregations, attended their children's school events, and visited friends in nearby towns. With changes in farm households and in the distribution of farm labor and production, more farmwomen have sought employment in nearby towns to provide a steady income for their families.

Newcomers have changed some small towns into small cities as local industry has flourished and attracted new workers, such as Mexicans who moved in increasing number to most states of the Midwest (except the Dakotas). Mexican wives not only joined their husbands in wage labor or filled more typically female work roles, they also devoted much of their energy to improving their communities through labor organizing, social work, and church and cultural groups. Other newcomers to small towns have been people looking for an ideal small-town life. They work, shop, and spend their leisure hours in a nearby city, converting the small town into a bedroom community. This means either that these new women commute to work in the city, and so are not an integral part of the town's community, or that they are more isolated newcomers who are not fully incorporated into women's activities in the community.

Some scholars suggest that improved transportation—paved roads, personal vehicles, interstates—and technology—telephones, televisions, computers—have not only enhanced small-town women's ability to be in contact with a wider world and with each other, but also have been detrimental to efforts to maintain a vibrant community life. Describing women's position in a small town, Lana F. Rakow argues that these women "live in a community that has undergone slow but dramatic change from an economic and social center to a loosely connected collection of homes and families. Changes in women's economic role have not brought comparable improvements in their family or community power." Other historians, however, stress women's enduring skills as community builders and leaders, even in the face of inequality and disruptive change.

Sources and Further Reading: Lucy Eldersveld Murphy, "Her Own Boss: Businesswomen and Separate Spheres in the Midwest, 1850–1880," *Illinois Historical Journal* 80 (Autumn 1987); Lucy Eldersveld Murphy and Wendy Hamand Venet, eds., *Midwestern Women: Work, Community, and Leadership at the Crossroads* (1997); Paula M. Nelson, " 'Do Everything'—Women in Small Prairie Towns, 1870–1920," *Journal of the West* 36 (Oct. 1997); Lana F. Rakow, *Gender on the Line* (1992); Glenda Riley, *The Female Frontier* (1988); Susan Sessions Rugh, *Our Common Country* (2001); Richard Santillán, "Midwestern Mexican American Women and the Struggle for Gender Equality: A Historical Overview, 1920s–1960s," *Perspectives in Mexican American Studies* 5 (1995).

Andrea R. Foroughi
Union College, New York

Ethnicity and Race

Probably nothing divided midwestern small towns more than ethnicity and race, which also contributed to cleavages in local society rooted in social class, religion, and politics. The exceptions to this rule were towns settled largely or entirely by a single ethnic or racial group. Such places, however, made up a tiny minority of small towns. Ethnic identities may have faded more quickly in small towns than in metropolitan centers because of the greater difficulty residents faced in forming insulated subcommunities, but racial identification persisted as strongly in small towns as elsewhere.

The earliest immigrant groups who moved into the Midwest during the antebellum era, those from England, Ireland, and the German states, generally arrived in small towns following initial settlement by native-born American migrants. Germans, English, and Irish worked as laborers, but Germans and English also included craftsmen, and Irish women filled the ranks of domestic servants. Irish laborers often came to midwestern small towns as builders of canals or railroads, and some stayed behind when the work moved on. Very few all-Irish or all-English small towns are known, but German immigrants sometimes established largely German market centers for their rural settlements, especially in Missouri and Wisconsin. When the major Scandinavian immigration into the upper Midwest began in the 1860s, Norwegians and Swedes, and sometimes the smaller numbers of Danes, established some ethnic-majority communities such as Stoughton and Edgerton in Wisconsin (Norwegian), Lindsborg in Kansas (Swedish), Elk Horn in Iowa, and Tyler and Askov in Minnesota (Danish). Many other Scandinavian immigrants, however, like the Germans, Irish, and English before them, moved into small towns built, and still led, by native-born migrants.

Immigrants who wished to retain their ethnic identity faced special obstacles in the small-town environment. For Germans and Scandinavians, for whom language retention was critical, small numbers made maintaining their own schools and churches a daunting task. German and Irish Catholics, for example, might have to share a single parish.

Despite the erosion of ethnic identities, however, cultural preferences often remained. Drinking alcoholic beverages in particular became politically salient when it clashed with the cultural imperatives of native-born reformers. Yankees drank, but Germans and Irish were generally overrepresented in the ranks of those who dispensed alcohol. In nineteenth-century America, temperance activists tended to blame the seller, rather than the drinker, for drink's ravages. Still, antiliquor campaigns, which were the most durable form of conflict in small towns throughout the late nineteenth and early twentieth centuries, split communities along ethnic lines.

Before the Civil War, the black population of the Midwest was tiny. During the war and for a quarter century afterward, African American migrants from the South—most of whom moved from the upper South into the lower Midwest—settled in rural areas and small towns at least as often as they did in cities. Arriving in communities enmeshed in familiar agricultural cycles, the new residents brought high hopes for acceptance in settings where few if any African Americans had lived before.

Insofar as they were able to do so, African American citizens of small towns adopted the folkways of their new neighbors. Where numbers permitted, they built churches and founded voluntary associations. They supported a network of African American newspapers. Because they came from nearby states, through visiting and correspondence they were better able than European immigrants to sustain connections with family and friends in their places of origin. And as they witnessed the disfranchisement campaigns of the late nineteenth and early twentieth centuries that squeezed black southerners out of the political realm, they petitioned, lobbied, and voted in protest.

By and large, African Americans' aspirations for acceptance in midwestern small towns were disappointed. Few escaped the traditional "Negro jobs" of laboring, barbering, and teamstering for men and domestic service for women. White trade unions generally refused them admittance, and African American strikebreaking contributed to a vicious cycle of mutual hostility between African American and European American workers. Although disciplined African American voting was sometimes able to shift the balance in towns closely divided between white Republicans and Democrats, African American editors constantly complained that their political allegiance went unrewarded by patronage or policy.

Nevertheless, small towns offered some advantages to their African American residents. Evidence from Washington Court House, Ohio, shows that home ownership was more accessible than in cities, and African American residential neighborhoods, while clustered, were not ghettoized. Although average property holdings remained far smaller than those of European Americans, African Americans seem to have narrowed the gap slightly during the late nineteenth century. As struggles over race rioting in Spring Valley, Illinois in 1895, and school segregation in Alton, Illinois during the 1890s and 1900s reveal, communication networks among African American communities facilitated political cooperation beyond the local level.

Beginning in the 1880s and 1890s in Ohio and Indiana, and in the early twentieth century in Illinois, African Americans left small towns and headed for cities, joined by waves of new migrants from the South. A few settled in largely or wholly African American suburbs but most traveled to central cities. Among the factors pushing them from small towns, in addition to stunted occupational opportunities, was an eruption of anti-black violence that generally occurred outside the metropolitan centers. Lynchings in rural areas and small towns and race riots in middle-sized cities made security in greater numbers seem prudent. African Americans were also attracted by the wealth and diversity of burgeoning African American communities in Chicago, Cleveland, Indianapolis, and other metropolitan centers. Although white midwesterners were also moving cityward, African Americans moved proportionately faster. With some exceptions, the new waves of immigrants who flooded into the Midwest from southern and eastern Europe around the turn of the last century also bypassed small towns in favor of the dynamic cities. By the 1920s, for African American and immigrant midwesterners alike, the age of the village was drawing to an end.

Sources and Further Reading: Thomas J. Archdeacon, *Becoming American: An Ethnic History* (1983); Jack S. Blocker,

Jr., "Black Migration to Muncie, 1860–1930," *Indiana Magazine of History* 92 (Dec. 1996); David Noel Doyle, *Irish Americans: Native Rights and National Empires* (1976); Walter D. Kamphoefner, *The Westfalians* (1987); Frederick H. Neuschel, "The Clique vs. the Croakers: Class and Conflict in Small-Town Wisconsin," *Wisconsin Magazine of History* 81 (Winter 1997–1998); Stephan Thernstrom, ed., *Harvard Encyclopedia of American Ethnic Groups* (1980); Caroline A. Waldron, "'Lynch-Law Must Go!'—Race, Citizenship, and the Other in an American Coal Mining Town," *Journal of American Ethnic History* 20 (Fall 2000); Mark Wyman, *Immigrants in the Valley* (1984).

Jack S. Blocker, Jr.
Huron University College, University of
Western Ontario, Canada

Native American Towns and Native Americans in Small Towns

As European settlers spread out across North America, they found the lands dotted with Native American towns, most of them small and temporary, but largely self-sufficient and possessing a variety of private dwellings, public buildings, and common areas. The towns in turn made up chiefdoms, empires, confederations, and alliances of various sizes, durations, and degrees of sophistication. Inhabitants of these towns lived not in the portable wigwams of popular lore, but in functional, more or less fixed houses, some reported to have had as many as five rooms. They enjoyed a standard of living that belies the term "savage" invariably applied to them by the early colonists.

Plains tribes, such as the Mandan, Omaha, Pawnee, and Ponca, lived in round earth lodges, some over one hundred feet across, in towns consisting of one to three clans and roughly two hundred people. These towns often possessed clan, geographic, or more descriptive names, such as the Ponca town called the Fish Smellers Village, whose inhabitants caught and traded fish to other tribal communities in the region. It was located on the banks of the Missouri River near the present town of Verdel, Nebraska. Tribes that dwelt in earth lodges included farmers as well as hunters. The Sioux tended to be more mobile and lived in buffalo skin teepees, which were very protective of the elements and easy to transport to new locations as the bands and tribes followed the buffalo across the Dakotas. Woodlands tribes, such as the Chippewa, Meskwaki, Winnebago, and Oneida in present-day Iowa, Minnesota, and Wisconsin, lived in wooden houses covered with bark.

Some modern towns were established by the first European settlers on Native town sites. Many towns, cities, counties, rivers, and other geographic sites retain Native American names. As most Native American languages were not written, spelling is often a matter of astonishing versatility. Early European settlers and scribes usually mutilated Native names, so the English pronunciation, as well as any notion of original meaning, is frequently impossible to determine. Modern towns with large Native American populations exist mainly on or near reservations; some are old army posts, such as Fort Thompson, South Dakota. The 2000 census reported nearly 2.5 million Native Americans in the United States and over 4.1 million other Americans who claim some Native American blood. Some 40 percent of Native Americans live in urban areas; the remainder live in rural areas, mainly on reservations and in nearby small towns.

Some Native American towns on reservations are the headquarters of tribal governments. A number of political entities serve the citizens in a reservation town, however, including the tribal government, a municipal government, a public and/or tribal school board, the Bureau of Indian Affairs and other federal agencies, state agencies, county agencies, and other local special districts, such as a rural water district.

Native American towns are homes of tribal museums and historical sites. The Northern Ponca Museum and Cultural Offices are in Niobrara, Nebraska; the Mille Lacs Band of Ojibwa Museum is near Onamia, Minnesota; and the Four Bears Museum of the Hidatsa, Arikara, and Mandan is west of New Town, North Dakota. There are also twenty-four active tribal colleges in the United States, eleven of which are located in the Midwest and a majority of which are located in Native American towns. Most Native American adults prefer to attend college in their home community.

Native American towns often display cultural and social aspects, such as tribal powwow grounds or ceremonial sites and neighborhoods inhabited by related families or clans. Tribal casinos have become a major economic and social influence on many Native communities since the passage of the Indian Gaming Regulatory Act in 1988. Casinos have increased employment opportunities, tribal revenues, community infrastructure projects such as new water systems, community and school buildings, businesses and roads, and social services programs and health care. Even with many changes, the key element of a Native American town, as expressed by an elder from Lac du Flambeau, Wisconsin, remains that "we who live in this community are all related."

Sources and Further Reading: American Indian Higher Education Consortium, *Tribal Colleges* (2002); Vine Deloria, Jr., *Spirit & Reason* (1999); James H. Howard, *The Ponca Tribe* (1965); Luther Standing Bear, *The Land of the Spotted Eagle* (1933); U.S. Census Bureau, "Characteristics of American Indians and Alaska Natives by Tribe and Language: 2000" (Dec. 2003); U.S. Census Bureau, *Profile of Selected Economic Characteristics* (2000); Carl Waldman, *Atlas of the North American Indian* (1985); Yerington Paiute Tribe, *Introduction to Tribal Government* (1985).

Jerry Stubben
Iowa State University

Town and Gown

In the nineteenth century, colleges, academies, normal schools, institutes, and universities became an important part of the fabric of midwestern town life. As New Englanders moved west, they brought with them a strong devotion to the Protestant ideals of hard work, education, and community building. As part of the booster ethos of midwestern small towns, businessmen actively supported the establishment of colleges, especially as a means to bring in additional revenue, business, and culture. Some locals served as members of institutional boards and even donated generous endowments for educational support. The first institutions of higher learning were denominational schools, which dotted the midwestern landscape by the late 1840s. The relationship between religious institutions and the communities that housed them laid the foundation for a town and gown dynamic in the Midwest.

The following sampling of early colleges throughout the Midwest portrays their eastern, religious, and reformist roots and illustrates how colleges and communities grew together. In 1833, a group of Baptists chose Kalamazoo, Michigan, as the site for its denominational school. Kalamazoo College grew up along with its home community, displaying the important link between collegiate and town growth. In 1833, revivalist missionaries from New York and New England settled on a spot southwest of Cleveland for their location of Oberlin College—which also gained fame as one of the first coeducational colleges in America. In Illinois in 1837, a group of social reformers established Knox College and named the village of Galesburg after the college's founder, George Washington Gale from New York, who was also associated with the founding of Oberlin College. In 1846, a group of Congregationalist New Englanders established Grinnell College in Davenport, Iowa; the college later moved west to a village that took the college's name. Like many towns, Kalamazoo, Galesburg, Oberlin, and Grinnell grew with their colleges.

The phrase "town and gown" emerged in medieval England to distinguish the often hostile and suspicious relationship between townspeople and the Oxford and

Cambridge university communities. In America by the mid-1800s, town and gown meant the social, political, and economic interchange between collegiate institutions and the communities that housed them. The town and gown relationship in midwestern towns was aptly illustrated with the founding of Beloit College in 1844 in Wisconsin. Lacking needed funds, the college founders asked for and received $7,000 in supplies, labor, and material from the town of Beloit.

Throughout the Midwest, towns have invested their financial and human resources in the support of educational institutions. Joint fund-raising campaigns and municipal and state taxes have further welded the economic and political interests of college and town. Beginning with public state universities in Iowa and Minnesota in the late 1840s and early 1850s, and expanding to land-grant universities founded under the Morrill Act of 1862, public institutions in the Midwest have provided both classical and scientific training, and local communities support research that brings new information for the expansion of agriculture and industry in the region.

In the twentieth century, town and gown relations were plagued by political, economic, and law enforcement conflicts, especially as expanding student populations brought fears of legal and moral unrest. The social activism of some students and professors went against the grain of local conservative politics. Citizens occasionally challenged the influence of the college culture, as in Lincoln, Nebraska, in 1918, when parents and locals demanded the resignation of German professors from the University of Nebraska, fearing that they were teaching anti-American sentiment.

Professors and townspeople have sometimes looked at each other with distrust, the former perceiving locals as backward provincials, and the latter viewing the academic community as superior and condescending. However, some townspeople joined with students and professors in community activism, especially during the temperance and woman's suffrage movements in the nineteenth century and during the 1960s counterculture. In Lawrence, Kansas, in 1968 and 1969, University of Kansas students and professors participated in antiwar demonstrations, causing some backlash by locals who resented the perceived condescension of university intellectuals and feared threats to community stability and security. Beyond student civil disobedience, townspeople worried that student antics and pranks might become destructive or even criminal. In the early years of town and gown relations, community newspapers and university administrations warned students against the evils of saloons and immoral activity. In the twentieth century, students have gained greater freedom through automobiles, reduced

curfews, dancing, and alcoholic consumption. Today, community law enforcement officers use speed traps, undercover bar and club patrols, and raids on fraternities to assist in policing the student populations. In rare cases, students who break laws face arrest or expulsion from the university.

More often, however, town–gown relations have been mutually beneficial. Students live in apartments and rental houses owned or run by local citizens. Students patronize local theatres and restaurants and shop for clothing, shoes, and books at local stores. Town and gown economies have benefited from advertising in campus newspapers, sports sponsorship, and employment for local citizens on campuses.

In the twentieth century, college spectator sports like football and basketball set the stage for a new and even more connected link between town and gown. Local citizens have taken on athletic team loyalty as the most abiding form of town support of their college community. Townspeople also benefit from the availability of college-sponsored cultural events in theatre, music, public forums, and national touring companies.

Today, thousands of students dominate small towns whose citizens remain ambivalent about the presence of their local college or university. Date rapes, alcohol accidents and deaths, and property destruction threaten otherwise beneficial town and gown relations. But colleges and universities now drive the economies of their host communities, especially those under fifteen thousand people, and citizens share a sense of ownership and shared identity with their resident institutions of higher learning.

Sources and Further Reading: Norman P. Auburn, *Akron's Municipal University* (1953); Beth L. Bailey, *From Front Porch to Back Seat: Courtship in Twentieth-Century America* (1988); David Cahan and M. Eugene Rudd, *Science at the American Frontier* (2000); Alexander DeConde, ed., *Student Activism: Town and Gown in Historical Perspective* (1971); Kenneth J. Heineman, *Campus Wars: The Peace Movement at American State Universities in the Vietnam Era* (1993); Robert N. Manley, *Centennial History of the University of Nebraska* (1969); Rusty L. Monhollon, "This is America?" in *The Sixties in Lawrence, Kansas* (2002); Marilyn Yurdan, *Oxford: Town and Gown* (1990).

Andrea G. Radke
Brigham Young University, Utah

Boosterism

In the early 1800s, a land craze swept the United States as European Americans, who had already breached the Appalachians, moved into the region north of the Ohio River. Contemporary images emphasized pioneers erecting cabins on the edge of wilderness, but many settlers first sought the next great metropolis as the place to stake their futures. Rather than claiming farms, they laid out towns. City lots sold for more than agricultural lands, although some towns existed only on paper. Enterprising entrepreneurs, known as boosters, recognized that urban markets controlled transportation, communication, and finances, and thus gave value to surrounding hinterlands. Boosters in Galena, Illinois, greatly profited by "mining" the miners who populated nearby lead fields.

❖ **Boosting Small Towns**

Boosterism has defined midwestern small towns since before they were born. Anxious to make their community a center of commerce, transportation, education, or government, developers sought a distinctive label to attract people and business. Cincinnati's founding fathers led the way by calling their settlement the "Queen City of the West." (Detractors simply called it "Porkopolis.") Soon every crossroads had a catch phrase that summarized its supposed attractions. Today's marketing experts would call the process "branding." In midwestern small towns, branding is all about progress, friendliness, and commerce. Here is a sampling of town mottos from throughout the region.

Adair, Iowa: *It'll Make You Smile*

Battle Creek, Michigan: *Cereal Capital of the World*

Beaman, Iowa: *You're not dreamin', you're in Beaman*

Blue Earth, Minnesota: *Earth so rich the city grows*

Bushnell, South Dakota: *It's not the end of the earth, but you can see it from here*

Byron, Minnesota: *We Are Here to Grow*

Collinsville, Illinois: *Horseradish Capital of the World*

Delphus, Ohio: *America's Friendliest City*

Dodge City, Kansas: *The Wickedest Little City in America*

Fenton, Iowa: *A good town for a home town*

Freeport, Illinois: *Pretzel City, USA*

Harrison, Michigan: *Twenty Lakes in Twenty Minutes*

International Falls, Minnesota: *Cold Spot of the Nation*

La Vista, Nebraska: *The View of Tomorrow . . . Today*

Liberal, Kansas: *The Land of Oz*

Marion, Illinois: *The Hub of the Universe*

Newton, Iowa: *We Saved a Place for You!*

Peculiar, Missouri: *Where the odds are with you*

Prairie du Chien, Wisconsin: *Where the Bald Eagles Soar and the Carp Drop*

Romulus, Michigan: *Gateway to the World*

Springfield, Missouri: *Everybody Should Be Like This*

Zap, North Dakota: *The little town with a big heart*

Andrew Cayton
Miami University, Ohio

As federal surveyors platted the landscape, speculators carefully selected town sites and gambled on the supposed natural advantages of their locations. Geography and even providence, they argued, guaranteed success, but few saw their visions realized. Boosters highlighted regional resources—coal, timber, water power—that enhanced economic potential. Entrepreneurs frequently dominated these early towns. They sold real estate, ran general stores, and guided transportation lines. Successful businessmen invested heavily in the surrounding countryside. Given the extent of their interests, they vigorously promoted their communities in newspapers, broadsides, and books. They commissioned bird's-eye views that publicized natural and economic benefits, and added churches, schools, and other institutions that promoted civility. Such images often represented hopes for the future rather than reality.

In the 1830s and 1840s, almost all new towns were situated along waterways essential to regional economies. Mississippi River towns competed for trade along that natural corridor. When commissioners announced the route of the Illinois & Michigan Canal, the artificial avenue of commerce that secured Chicago's future, communities sprang up along its ninety-some miles. Although some never grew to more than a few buildings, town rivalries sparked the development of a dense, hierarchical urban network. By mid-century, boosters were focused on attracting railroads. Existing towns needed the railroad to secure continued growth; places left off the tracks faded or disappeared. After the Civil War, railroads played an even more central role in urbanization by systematically locating towns according to their own needs across Minnesota, the Dakotas, Nebraska, and Kansas.

The rivalries that drove urban growth were frequently resolved by the 1860s. Speculators tried to claim that each subsequent town represented the next great metropolis, but many boosters recognized the limitations inherent in a central place system. They reordered local economies to supplement and complement other towns, as much or more than to compete with them. In doing so, they accepted their towns' limited horizons and sought community members who valued collective goals. This revised booster ethos asked businessmen to place community concerns ahead of their own, particularly in a town's early years when its population tended to be male, young, and transient.

Local chambers of commerce institutionalized the boosterism of their towns' first generations. These organizations represented the broad range of businesses in a given town, but also spoke for the hinterlands. Members formed committees to investigate issues such as new crops or mining technology and focused on zoning, regulatory schemes, and labor controls. Chambers worked to attract industries that provided jobs and expanded the tax base. In Lemont, Illinois, quarrying initially thrived after the digging of the Illinois & Michigan Canal revealed large pockets of limestone. As the market for building stone collapsed in the 1890s due to economic depression and demands for new building materials, boosters eventually recruited an aluminum factory that filled a similar niche. Throughout such transitions, the preservation of a political and economic order that placed the needs of businessmen ahead of those of other community members remained paramount. In 1912, municipal chambers of commerce merged under the United States Chamber of Commerce to create a national lobbying body for federal policy issues.

The novelist Sinclair Lewis memorably captured the boosters ethos. In *Babbitt* (1922), real estate agent George Babbitt attempts to claim respectability as a land craze sweeps the nation in the 1920s. His bourgeois values represented the good and the bad of small-town, middle-class life. His desire to serve, his optimism, and his faith in his country are transformed into a yearning for acceptance, a disquietude, and jingoism. Lewis denied that his hometown—Sauk Centre, Minnesota—served as the model for the fictional Gopher Prairie in another novel, *Main Street* (1920). Sauk Centre citizens, however, rejected their native son as other readers saw in Gopher Prairie, and by default in Sauk Centre, the compromises that defined the booster ethos and the ordinariness that created a landscape of indistinguishable midwestern towns.

Local chambers of commerce and similar organizations remain centered in midwestern small towns today. As industries have abandoned the region—Lemont's aluminum factory closed in 1977—boosters have sought new ways to promote their communities. The Cedar Rapids (Iowa) Chamber of Commerce and Eau Claire (Wisconsin) Economic Development Corporation lure new businesses by promoting the superior quality of life their towns offer in a gap between urban and rural living. Other communities have attempted to capture a share of the postindustrial tourist trade by highlighting images they once rejected. Sauk Centre's Chamber of Commerce now advertises the town as the "Original Main Street" and embraces its prodigal son with its annual "Sinclair Lewis Days."

Sources and Further Reading: Carl Abbott, *Boosters and Businessmen* (1981); William Cronon, *Nature's Metropolis* (1991); Michael P. Conzen and Carl A. Zimring, eds., *Looking for Lemont* (1994); John C. Hudson, "Settlement of the American Grassland," in Michael P. Conzen, ed., *The Making of the American Landscape* (1990); Hildegard Binder Johnson, "Toward a National Landscape," in Michael P. Conzen,

The Making of the American Landscape (1990); Timothy J. Mahoney, "'A Common Band of Brotherhood': Male Subcultures, the Booster Ethos, and the Origins of Urban Social Order in the Midwest in the 1840s," *Journal of Urban History* 25 (July 1999); Eric Monkkonen, *America Becomes Urban* (1988); Richard C. Wade, *The Urban Frontier,* rev. ed. (1996).

Kathleen A. Brosnan
University of Houston, Texas

Men's Culture

The dominance of men in political and economic institutions has given public life in the midwestern small town a pronounced masculine character.

Since the publication of *Adventures of Tom Sawyer* (1876) and *Adventures of Huckleberry Finn* (1885) by Mark Twain, the midwestern small-town boyhood has acquired almost mythic power. Unlike urban or rural boys, small-town boys supposedly developed strong moral character rooted in the appreciation of hard work and personal autonomy. Most small-town men forged their early identity in gangs. Gang members, or "town boys," held secret meetings, hung out in their favorite places on Main Street, defended their territory, and generally indulged in "boy's amusements." Drug stores, ice cream parlors, harness shops, and livery stables were the precursors of auto garages, barber shops, hotel lobbies, and courthouses as main haunts. Boys went roving in the woods and fields, picking nuts and fruit, swimming in the local swimming hole, fishing in the river, or hiking along a network of trails that led from town across nearby open fields and through local woods to caves and other hideouts in search of adventure. Daily routines were broken by larger events—the circus, the county fair, the 4th of July, street fairs and festivals, and later, auto exhibitions and air shows. Meanwhile, they kept a wary yet curious eye on the strange adult world of fathers, uncles, businessmen, "boomers," traveling salesmen, "loungers," "old soldiers," and "old boys" who drank liquor, chewed tobacco, smoked, and talked about their relationships with women.

The lives of older boys were increasingly structured by work and school-related organized activities and sports. Teenagers found jobs as newsboys, paper boys, shelving clerks, messenger boys, car washers, or doing other kinds of casual labor. More recently, the movie theatre, the hardware store, drug store, or pharmacy, the ice cream drive-in, fast food restaurants by the interstate, and sometimes a nearby factory provided work. From the 1890s through the 1940s, the town gang was the central institution of boy life. Later, Boy Scout troops provided a similar focus.

In the late nineteenth century, dog and horse racing and hunting were the most popular sporting pastimes. By the 1890s, baseball emerged as the focal point of boys' sports. Summer was a time for camp, summer jobs, and gradual entrance into more adult venues of the barber shop, billiard parlor, club, and saloon, where men indulged in chewing and smoking tobacco, drinking alcohol, and talking about women. During the same period, the automobile became an obsession for many young men and transformed their lives. Aside from making the auto repair shop, garage, and drive-in the new centers of socializing, increased mobility, cruising Main Street, drag races, and road trips transformed social relations among men and between men and women.

Among adult men in most small towns across the Midwest, boosters tried to cultivate cohesion by drawing members of different social groups into a public culture of shared values and mutuality. They cultivated camaraderie and male bonding by engaging in a variety of practices such as nicknames, verbal jousts, practical jokes, and mock or spoof events or meetings, as well as by collective behaviors such as gambling, drinking, parties, frolics, and sporting and hunting contests. Such behaviors and activities defused the tensions implicit in the maintenance of order in a society divided by class. In the world of work, the newspaper office, the courthouse or lawyer's office, the town hall, the hotel lobby, the fire and police stations, the sheriff's office, the chamber of commerce office or club, as well as the barber shop, tobacco store, restaurant, or diner have been the main venues of this culture. After hours, the hotel lobby, livery stable, harness shop, or somewhat later, various private men's clubs, supper clubs, restaurants, and above all the bar and saloon were the primary resorts of male sociability.

Men also formed a variety of more formal organizations and clubs. They ranged from the local militia units and volunteer fire companies to a variety of debating, dining, literary, social, fishing, hiking, and hunting clubs. By the mid-nineteenth century, formal fraternal organizations predominated—the Redman, the Masons, the Odd Fellows, followed by the Elks, Moose, Eagles, Lions Clubs, Woodmen of the World, and the Rotary Club. The Chamber of Commerce, the Enterprise Club, Booster Club, Progressive Club, or Commercial Club was often the largest club run by the town boosters. In the 1920s, membership in the Ku Klux Klan increased in small towns across the central Midwest. In addition, between 1870 and 1900, most towns had informal and organized veterans' reunions. Sometimes, the town had a branch of the Grand Army of the Republic, and if large enough, it sent delegates to or held annual regional GAR conventions. Later, the Veterans of Foreign Wars and the

American Legion predominated. Clubs and organizations also ran and contributed to public holiday celebrations, county fairs, and street fairs or festivals. After the 1920s, the country club on the outskirts of town absorbed much of this activity.

Men cultivated and reinforced sociability in the ubiquitous saloon society. At the tavern, gambling hall, or club, middle-class men rubbed shoulders with workers and "undesirable" company. Here tensions among men were vented through a sociability suffused with sarcasm and irony as expressed in nicknames, storytelling, verbal jousting, pranks, practical jokes, and ribaldry. In the nineteenth and early twentieth centuries, more organized events such as the mock trial among lawyers, the "third house"—a mock legislature or town council meeting—among politicians, mock banquets called "roasts" among boosters and professionals, as well as frolics and an occasional charivari—which continued in some towns in the Midwest through the 1920s or 1930s—and mock parades, excursions, and ceremonials involving minstrel shows, elaborate costumes, cross-dressing, and general merriment, interjected this culture into public life. Through the 1870s or 1880s, New Year's Day was a day on which many of the town's men and older boys went calling on the wives and daughters of the middle class. Older men—the "old boys," "croakers," or in the 1880s through 1900s, the "old soldiers"—gathered at the barber shop, the hotel lobby, the mayor's office, or the fraternal club, as unofficial members of each town's "rocking chair club." No matter one's age, the cultivation of brotherhood, civility, and mutuality among males created a cohesive male culture that underlay small-town society.

Sources and Further Reading: Sherwood Anderson, *Tar* (1926); Sherwood Anderson, *Winesburg, Ohio* (1919); Lewis Atherton, *Main Street on the Middle Border* (1954); Ray Bradbury, *Dandelion Wine* (1957); Hamlin Garland, *Boy Life on the Prairie* (1899); John Glenn, *A Memoir* (1999); John E. Hallwas, *The Bootlegger* (1998); Stanley G. Hilton, *Bob Dole: American Political Phoenix* (1988); Edgar Watson Howe, *The Anthology of Another Town* (1920); Edgar Watson Howe, *A Man Story* (1889); Edgar Watson Howe, *Plain People* (1929); Edgar Watson Howe, *Story of a Country Town* (1883); Kent Krause, "From Americanism to Athleticism," M.A. Thesis, University of Nebraska (1998); Timothy R. Mahoney, "'A Common Band of Brotherhood': Male Subcultures, the Booster Ethos, and the Origins of Urban Social Order in the Midwest of the 1840s," *Journal of Urban History* 25 (July 1999); Timothy R. Mahoney, "The Great Sheedy Murder Trial and the Booster Ethos of the Gilded Age in Lincoln," *Nebraska History* 82 (Winter 2001); Edmund Morris, *Dutch: A Memoir of Ronald Reagan* (1999); George H. Nash, *The Life of Herbert Hoover* (1983); Ron Powers, *White Town Drowsing* (1986); W. L. Purcell, *Them Was the Good Old Days* (1922); Mark Twain, *Adventures of Huckleberry Finn* (1885); Mark

Twain, *Adventures of Tom Sawyer* (1876); Reynold Wik, *Henry Ford and Grass-Roots America* (1972).

Timothy R. Mahoney
University of Nebraska–Lincoln

Political Centers

The emblem of a midwestern town's role as a political center is the courthouse square. Courthouses are located in county seats, which are the nuclei of the nearly one thousand counties that are the political cells of the midwestern states. All incorporated towns have a mayor, board or council, and their own local politics. But county seats are the home of the county-wide elected officials (county clerk, recorder, coroner, supervisors), the principal courts, with their attendant judges, clerks and attorneys, as well as the central law enforcement and social service agencies (sheriff, county jail, public health and highways departments, and so forth). County seats are nearly always the commercial and population center of a county, as well, often because of the economic boost accorded by their status as the home of county government. Town founders and proprietors were shrewdly aware of the advantages of playing host to the county government. For this reason, town builders avidly sought the prize of the county seat for their community. In the late nineteenth century particularly, these communities sealed their status by constructing imposing courthouses.

The presence of the county government in a town brought substantial economic benefits: contracts for the construction and maintenance of county buildings; the provision of food, drink and lodging to lawyers, judges, plaintiffs, and defendants attending court; a newspaper to print notices of court actions; the sale of paper and other office supplies for the county offices; and in general the increased traffic a courthouse generated as people came to attend court, record deeds, obtain marriage licenses, and so forth.

As political and judicial centers, county seats attracted crowds for popular functions such as elections, political debates, sensational trials, and public punishments and executions. They also hosted grand occasions of public entertainment, such as fairs, markets, balls, and horse races. George Flower, one of the founders of Albion, the seat of Edwards County, Illinois, described the scene in a Wabash Valley county seat around 1820:

> [A] court or an election would draw the people into the small towns from their most secluded haunts for miles around. . . . The grog-shops (pioneer institu-

tions in all young towns) were in full blast. You could scarcely cross the street . . . without seeing two or three crowds swaying and cheering at some rough-and-tumble fight going on in their midst. . . . The sound of the whip, and the screams of the poor wretch [a thief convicted of stealing a quart of whiskey] sent a nervous thrill through the not over-scrupulous country-people, who came in to see the opening of the court.

These visiting crowds brought money to shopkeepers, innkeepers, and tavern owners and were a significant boost to the economic success and population growth of frontier communities.

The economic advantage of being a county seat was so great that many pioneer towns completely disappeared after they failed to gain that designation. The stakes were so high that the contests between communities were often heated. Sometimes violent "county seat wars" erupted. A disputed election to determine the seat of Gray County, Kansas, resulted in a deadly gunfight in the streets of the town of Ingalls in 1889. A contest in the 1850s between the towns of Marietta and Marshalltown in Marshall County, Iowa, was marked by the mobilization of armed militias who prepared to wage a pitched battle at the steps of the courthouse in Marietta. Violence was narrowly averted, and the county government ultimately located in Marshalltown.

A rivalry between the towns of Naperville and Wheaton for the seat of DuPage County, Illinois, smoldered for decades. The conflict came to a head in 1867 with skirmishes between mobs in the streets of Wheaton. One man was shot through the wrist, and another died after being struck in the head with a stone. After contested elections and years of lawsuits, centrally located Wheaton finally won the courthouse.

In most instances, these wars did not involve actual physical violence. The action took the form of words and legal proceedings. Still, in many instances, mobs, impatient with legal wrangling, simply seized the county records and brought them home in triumph. In other cases, mobs or midnight arsons torched the courthouse in the rival town to force the issue. Sometimes, utilizing a less violent tactic, townspeople would construct a courthouse without legal authorization to make the choice of county seat appear inevitable.

County seat wars were a characteristic political phenomenon of the early Midwest, but they were rare and mild affairs in New England and the South. They began as an occasional occurrence in the early nineteenth century, peaked in number and violence in the Great Plains in the 1880s, and disappeared at the beginning of the twentieth century. These conflicts were fueled by boosterism and fanned by ambitious businessmen, politicians, and partisan newspapers. Typically these battles were finally extinguished only by the intervention of courts or legislatures.

While some state capitals are the principal metropolises of their states, others are smaller cities or overgrown towns. The intimate social scale of these small-town capitals gives a special personal flavor to their political cultures. Even more than in larger cities, legislators, lobbyists, and state officers frequent the same hotels, restaurants, public events, and private parties, making for a particularly intense political society. Small-town attitudes and prejudices also sometimes had a negative effect on visiting legislators. When Corneal Davis, an African American legislator from Chicago, arrived in Springfield in 1942, he and fellow black legislators found to their astonishment that the Abraham Lincoln Hotel refused to accommodate them, as did every other hotel in the city. Davis spent his first night in Springfield sleeping in the train station. He finally discovered that he was sufficiently light-skinned to obtain a suite at a hotel, which he shared with other black legislators.

Sources and Further Reading: Lewis Eldon Atherton, *Main Street on the Middle Border* (1954); Stephen J. Buck, "To Hold the Prize: The County Seat War in Du Page County, 1867–1872," *Illinois Historical Journal* 85 (Winter 1992); Corneal Davis, *Corneal A. Davis Memoir* (1984); George Flower, *History of the English Settlement in Edwards County, Illinois* (1882); James A. Schellenberg, *Conflict Between Communities* (1987); Thomas J. Wood, "'Blood in the Moon': The War for the Seat of Edwards County, 1821–1824," *Illinois Historical Journal* 85 (Autumn 1992).

Thomas J. Wood
University of Illinois–Springfield

Politics

To a large extent, politics in the midwestern small town is a tale of several contrasting styles. Political culture, the nature of elections, and the very structure of government all serve to shape the political setting in this environment. The noted political scientist Daniel Elazar (1966) argued that our national political culture was a "synthesis of three major political subcultures which jointly inhabit the country, existing side by side or even overlapping one another"—moralistic, individualistic, and traditional. D. W. Meinig (1986) described their interaction as the convergence of "settlement streams . . . from distinct seaboard societies." As a result, Andrew Cayton and Peter Onuf (1990) contend that "the Midwest was more like an ethnic and cultural checkerboard than the proverbial melting pot": Indiana, for example, was settled in the south by

Upland Southerners, in the center by mid-Atlantic groups, and in the north by migrants from New England and New York.

Throughout the broader Midwest, Elazar's moralistic culture thrives in northern Kansas, parts of northern Illinois, Iowa, Michigan, Minnesota, North Dakota, South Dakota, and Wisconsin. From this perspective, Elazar contends, politics involves not merely the struggle for power, "but also an effort to exercise power for the betterment of the commonwealth." Government is a positive element to be used for the betterment of the community, and issues have a central place in the political arena. Neighborhood interest groups and "good government" interest groups flourish in small towns. Political participation is higher, people have a low tolerance of corruption, and volunteerism is often strong.

The individualistic culture is most prevalent in Indiana, much of Illinois, and many areas of Ohio. This culture views the role of government as a provider of services. It emphasizes the centrality of private concerns, discourages government intervention into private activities, and asks government to focus its efforts in the economic arena to foster private initiative. Politics in this culture becomes another avenue by which individuals can get ahead either socially or economically. As Elazar notes, "life within the individualistic culture is based on a system of mutual obligations rooted in personal relationships." This system of interrelationships flourishes through political parties as a mechanism for coordinating individual efforts. Given a more businesslike view of politics, citizens look upon government as the province of professionals, amateurism is less likely to play a role, and participation is lower than in the moralistic culture. A classic study of community politics in the Midwest that reflects this orientation is Robert S. Lynd and Helen M. Lynd, *Middletown: A Study in Contemporary American Culture* (1937).

The traditionalistic culture is most prevalent in Missouri, southern Illinois, southern Indiana, and parts of Ohio. Government is accepted as a positive player in the community, but its role is limited to preserving the status quo. Elitism is more prevalent in this culture, and holding political power is confined to those who are born to it or have earned it through their social position. Citizen participation and political parties are deemphasized in the traditionalistic culture, and government leaders fulfill largely conservative and custodial roles.

The nature of elections has also shaped small-town politics. In states such as Kansas and Wisconsin, local elections are nonpartisan. The intent of nonpartisan elections was to loosen the hold parties had over government, and they have served that function well.

However, they also serve to dampen voter turnout, because parties do little to mobilize voters and citizens are left without the party label as a cue to voting. In the small-town setting, voters are faced with candidates running what many term "candidate-centered" campaigns, going door-to-door or meeting voters at the local shopping mall or grocery. Candidates get their message out via telephone calls from a relatively small group of volunteers. Friends and neighbors form the heart of the campaign staff, divisive issues are rare, and the high stakes often associated with big-city politics or state and national office are usually lacking. People are more likely to vote on the basis of personal acquaintanceship.

In states such as Illinois and Indiana, where local elections are partisan, party organization permeates even the smallest towns. Although voter turnout is still quite low, the party helps mobilize the vote, citizens have the cue of the party label on the ballot, and issues are often framed in the context of party politics. In these small-town settings, divisiveness over which party, or which faction of a party, will control government is as vitriolic as it is over more visible offices.

A third factor that helps shape politics in the small towns of the Midwest is the structure of government. Several forms of local government occur in this region. Many Michigan small towns have a council–city manager form of government. Council members are often elected at-large and serve the legislative function of government. City managers are hired to perform the administrative and planning functions of government. Often coupled with nonpartisan elections and lacking a figurehead who provides a focal point for citizens, the political environment is decidedly more low-key. Indiana, on the other hand, requires a strong mayor–city council (or town board) form of government. Typically elected from districts, council members have more incentive to focus on neighborhood interests, foster personal relationships with voters, and work to provide services. Mayors have veto power over council decisions and control over patronage and budget preparation. This environment often leads to heated battles between the major parties or, at times, battles within factions of the same party.

One thing is certain regarding politics within small towns in the Midwest: There is no typical town. While similarities exist, the political culture, nature of elections, and structure of government has led to a wide variety of political environments. As former Speaker of the House Tip O'Neill once stated, "All politics is local." He could have added, and unique to the particular locality.

Sources and Further Reading: David R. Berman, *Local Government and the States* (2003); Ann O'M. Bowman and Rich-

ard C. Kearney, *State and Local Government: The Essentials*, 2nd ed. (2003); Andrew R. L. Cayton and Peter S. Onuf, *The Midwest and the Nation* (1990); Daniel J. Elazar, *American Federalism: A View from the States* (1966); D. W. Meinig, *The Shaping of America, Vol. 1, Atlantic America, 1492–1800* (1986); David C. Saffell and Harry Basehart, *State and Local Government: Politics and Public Policies*, 7th ed. (2001).

Gary L. Crawley
Ball State University, Indiana

Law and Order

Law permeated the nineteenth-century Midwest. Middle-class migrants to nascent towns understood the law and its functions, and strove to re-create the communities from which they had migrated. Well-trained lawyers helped build systems of courts, and the local citizenry elected law enforcement officers in an effort to establish order. Once a community was established, middle-class boosters brought legitimacy by building jails and funding elaborate county courthouses.

The system of courts established in the Midwest resembled a pyramid. At the very top stood the state supreme court, which handled appeals from the lower courts. Although small-town lawyers sometimes found themselves arguing cases before the supreme court, the high court had very little meaning to most small-town residents. A more familiar type of court was the superior, district, or circuit court, which had jurisdiction in felony crimes and heard appeals from the lower courts. Each state was divided into judicial districts that were administered by an elected district court judge who "rode the circuit," holding semiannual court sessions in each county. For small-town midwesterners, particularly in less populated counties, district court sessions, or "court days," were grand entertainment. While citizens served on juries, rural residents made trips to town, politicians "took to the stump," and court watchers followed high-profile criminal trials.

The courts most familiar to the average citizen were the inferior courts, which had limited jurisdiction. These included justice of the peace (JP) courts, police courts, and county or probate courts. Justice of the peace courts usually administered justice in small towns and rural townships far from the county seat. The office of JP was an elected post that did not require legal training. Instead, the JP was usually a respected member of the community who could be counted on to administer community-based justice (that is, to do the right thing) in misdemeanor cases while passing felonies on to the district court. Although JP courts existed in municipalities, the small-

Will County Court House, Joliet, Illinois, 1914. Library of Congress, Prints and Photographs Division, LC-USZ62-73075.

town police court was much more common. As a municipal court of justice, the police court (generally reserved for towns with populations over three thousand) handled a wide array of urban-based crimes such as petty thefts, assaults, public intoxication, gaming violations, and prostitution. Fines collected from such offenses helped finance the city jail and local police force. County or probate courts played a more limited role in enforcing law and order. County courts could be used as an examining court. By the late nineteenth century, these courts began to administer justice in juvenile criminal cases. The lower courts, therefore, were numerous and essentially served as a filtering system, administering community-based justice in misdemeanor cases and passing on felony cases and appeals to the district courts. Lower courts also played an important role in enforcing community moral codes by regulating and fining illicit and immoral acts.

The criminal justice system benefited from the presence of highly trained lawyers. As soon as a community was founded, young and ambitious lawyers appeared, opened law offices, and began building a clientele. These lawyers served the criminal justice system as judges, prosecutors, and defense lawyers. They also were highly visible in local politics and society. Typical was the career of Abraham Lincoln in Springfield, Illinois, in the 1840s and 1850s.

It is popularly assumed that in midwestern communities, particularly those on the Great Plains, law enforcers had to be good with a gun. With a few exceptions, however, midwestern communities had little use for hired gunmen. The office of sheriff was an elected position that usually attracted candidates with little law enforcement experience. The sheriff's primary duties usually involved tax collections and district court and jail administrative duties. Experienced, hired deputy sheriffs handled actual law enforcement. The sheriff's office did little in the way of crime prevention; deputies did not patrol city streets or comb the countryside for stock thieves. Instead, sheriffs and

deputies went to work after the commission of a crime through criminal investigations, jailing, and seeing a defendant through the court system.

Below the sheriff and deputies were law enforcers such as constables, policemen, and railroad detectives who actively tried to prevent crime. Constables were elected by a township and assisted JPs in serving court papers and preserving law and order in areas not served by the sheriff's office. They also assisted the sheriff's office if a crime was committed in their township or if the sheriff needed additional deputies.

Municipal police forces were common by the middle of the nineteenth century. Under the supervision of a police chief or city marshal, paid officers were the front line in fights against crime and immoral behavior. They policed city streets, monitored vice industries, and hauled into the police court violators of municipal ordinances. By the 1880s, corporate law enforcers in the form of railroad policemen joined civil law enforcement. Railroads such as the Union Pacific hired hundreds of lawmen who patrolled rail yards and rail lines.

For small-town midwesterners, the most familiar legal institutions remain their local ones. Citizens continue to elect their sheriffs and judges, serve on juries, and assist in law enforcement through neighborhood watch programs. The small-town lawyer remains a general practitioner who can handle most legal issues. Today Americans generally assume that midwestern small towns are among the safest and most lawful communities in the nation.

Sources and Further Reading: Richard Maxwell Brown, *No Duty to Retreat* (1991); Robert Dykstra, *The Cattle Towns* (1970); William Francis English, "The Pioneer Lawyer and Jurist in Missouri," *The University of Missouri Studies* 21 (1947); Philip D. Jordan, *Frontier Law and Order* (1970); Timothy R. Mahoney, *Provincial Lives* (1999); Patrick Nolan, *Vigilantes on the Middle Border* (1987).

Mark R. Ellis
University of Nebraska–Kearney

Small Cities as "Big Small Towns"

Part of the difficulty inherent in trying to make a distinction between cities and towns lies in a widespread tendency to employ *town* as a generic descriptor of almost all midwestern municipalities. In the vernacular, "going to town" might just as readily describe a visit to the Chicago Field Museum or the Mall of America as a Saturday afternoon trip to the village barbershop. *Downtown* is regularly used to describe the central business district of any municipality, from Chicago's Magnificent Mile to the block-long cluster of shops in a crossroads village. Significantly, *Webster's Dictionary* defines *city* in purely relative terms: "an inhabited place of greater size, population, or importance than a town or village."

No less imprecise and confusing are constitutional and statutory designations. The U.S. Census Bureau has never utilized either term to differentiate urban places from rural places. In more recent years, it has used *city* only to identify municipalities of over fifty thousand people that form the central core of standard metropolitan areas. The designations proffered by the various states resemble nothing so much as a patchwork quilt. In Wisconsin, *towns* are unincorporated rural places of disparate areas and populations. Some of the more populous towns in Wisconsin's southeastern quadrant actually have far more inhabitants than do several cities in the rest of the state. In Illinois, a town is a municipality, an urban place, with a population that generally falls somewhere between that of a village and a city.

Even more daunting is the fact that towns and cities exist not only as physical and social constructs in the material world, but also as images in our minds that tend to distort our perceptions of the very entities we are trying to define. Moreover, both these images are engaged in a dynamic interaction with a third concept, community. For an important segment of the American imagination, the town has long been synonymous with community, while the city has frequently been regarded as its antithesis in both structure and quality. The small town, like the bar in the television series *Cheers*, has long conjured an image of a place where everyone knows your name—and your business. Small-town life presumably focuses upon lifelong high school associations and memories, a highly personalized system of government and law enforcement, a Main Street business mentality, an organic social order, an entrepreneurial, producer's economy, and a variety of localized clubs, churches, and public venues.

Although *community* is an elusive concept, it involves the daily and highly personal interaction and cooperation of people with one or more common ties within a specific locale. At a minimum, these connections include a sense of group solidarity and individual significance, the very qualities so often missing in modern mass society and culture. "For many Americans," historian Richard Lingeman has asserted, the small town is the "lost Atlantis of our youth . . . the archetypal lost home that is nowhere and everywhere, always lost and always there to be found."

Arguably, *community* has the best chance of flowering in a compact locale with a homogeneous population where government can be used to enforce cultural sanctions. Both logic and experience, however, demonstrate that not all small towns are truly communities and that a sense of community can flourish in other environments. There has always been a highly articulate minority that has either bemoaned the oppressive and stultifying nature of small-town life or celebrated a richer sense of community emerging out of the diversity and complexity of city life. The former view was articulated powerfully by such writers as Sinclair Lewis, Thorstein Veblen, and Ole Rolvaag, who stressed the isolation, conformity, cupidity, superficiality, and lack of "heartfelt spontaneous joy" in small-town life. In fact, it would be more accurate to say that most people's impressions of small-town life are ambivalent. The "dichotomy between positive and negative, rooted in the experiences of residents past and present," as Timothy Mahoney has noted, "was the framework in which most people understood small towns in twentieth century America."

The pro-city perspective is best exemplified by the works of twentieth-century intellectuals Frederic Howe, Lewis Mumford, and Richard Sennett. To Howe, the city is "the hope of democracy," where "life is free and eager and countless agencies cooperate to create a warmer sympathy, a broader sense of responsibility, and a more intelligent political sense." To Mumford, the purpose of city life is to convert mechanical power and human energy into social and physical arrangements and meaningful cultural forms, a task facilitated by the diversity and variety of healthy antagonisms and disorder inherent in urban life. To Sennett, densely packed cities are places where people must confront their differences and learn to tolerate ambiguity, uncertainty, diversity, and disorder. For all three, family, neighborhood, voluntary associations, political action, and intelligent intervention provide a strong sense of community to city dwellers.

Imagery and value judgments aside, midwestern small cities are essentially different from the region's small towns in several important ways. Although the difference has a great deal to do with size and scale, those are often as much a matter of perception as of statistics. Whether they acknowledge it or not, most everyone has a notion of the minimum dimensions necessary for a place to qualify as a city, a perception that is inherently relative. *Small town* and *small city* derive their meaning largely in contradistinction to one another, as well as to the metropolis. Equally relative and subjective is our tendency to define cities by the presence of certain functions or structures, such as rows of closely spaced houses, factory districts, multiple commercial areas, a multiplicity of services and shops, and a prevalence of livelihoods not based upon agriculture.

Perhaps the most productive approach is to view towns and cities as evolving stages in the ongoing process of urbanization, rather than as dichotomous categories. No matter how large a midwestern municipality eventually became, it began life as a tiny settlement dwarfed by its agricultural hinterlands. How much and how fast that settlement grew depended primarily on its location and its role in the nation's economic development, although a relative handful thrived through specialization in higher education, state government, transportation, or tourism.

For the most part, midwestern municipalities emerged as agricultural marketplaces and entrepôts for their immediate hinterlands. Some never progressed beyond that stage, while others evolved into centers for processing their products. A somewhat smaller number gradually focused on the manufacture of processing machinery, and a still smaller number eventually became substantial manufacturing centers in their own right. In 1937, William F. Ogburn found that the "average city" in the United States had a population of twenty-five to one hundred thousand and employed roughly 38 percent of its population in manufacturing, 16 percent in trade, 12 percent in personal services, 10 percent in transport, 8 percent in the professions, and 2 percent in public services.

The evolution of municipalities from village to town to city to metropolis correlated closely with the expansion of markets for its products—from local to sectional to regional to national to international. Villages, by definition, never expanded their markets beyond their immediate hinterlands. Whether or not a village grew into a town was in fairly direct proportion to its ability to develop sectional and regional markets for its products. To qualify as a city, a municipality had to have a major impact on the economy of its entire region and to market at least some of its products nationally. Although having significant international markets in a variety of lines is one of the hallmarks of a metropolis, many smaller cities eventually established international outlets for one or two specialized products.

Whatever its eventual size, every municipality's ambition was fueled by two interrelated passions, boosterism and urban rivalry. At some point, nearly every settlement fancied itself a potential New York, a fantasy all but guaranteed to end in failure, frustration, bitterness, and hostility. Nearly all the region's settlements were in fierce competition with their neighbors for settlers, businesses, transportation and communication links, government facilities, tourists, and various forms of services and amenities. They tended to measure themselves in comparative, and frequently invidious, terms, and to rejoice almost as much in their neighbor's setbacks as in their own successes. As the region's economy became progressively more centralized, both small towns and small cities found themselves, as Mahoney describes, caught between aspiration and sense of loss. The more stunted a place's growth, the more likely its residents were to take refuge in nostalgia and alienation.

The tripartite division—albeit imprecise and subjective—of municipalities into small towns, small cities, and metropolises largely occurred between the 1870s and World War I. As the region's population and economy increasingly revolved around metropolitan hubs, thousands of small towns became island communities, serving only secondary or tertiary economic functions and eschewing innovation. Their connections to the mainstream became increasingly tenuous, sometimes nonexistent. However, scores of other midwestern communities—benefited by location, leadership, existing infrastructure, an adaptable labor force, or just plain serendipity—achieved growth patterns that proportionately rivaled those of the region's metropolises. In the process, they took on characteristics that incrementally and relatively separated these small cities from small towns. Although remaining essentially relative and subjective, the hallmarks of these distinctions were scale and diversity, as reflected in the nature of the economy, the ethnic makeup of the citizenry, the social class structure, the degree of residential segregation and stratification, the array and quality of municipal services and amenities, and the pervasiveness of what pioneer sociologist Louis Wirth dubbed the "urban personality."

Cities are far more likely to have a diversified economic base, offering employment in a number of different occupations. The larger the place, the more the specialization and proliferation of economic functions. With a few notable exceptions, cities are also far more likely to have the largest portion of their workforces engaged in manufacturing. They are also generally far more integrated into regional, national, and international economic, transportation, and communication systems. Midwestern small cities—as secondary magnets for both the massive immigration of 1880–1930 and the twentieth-century migrations of Appalachian, African, and Latino/a Americans—are also more ethnically complex, with indexes of diversity rivaling those of the region's metropolises. They also are more likely to have a more articulated hierarchy of social strata: a small but powerful industrial elite, a commercially based upper-middle class, substantial populations of both white- and blue-collar workers, and an observable underclass. As a consequence of their economic and ethnic diversity, small cities tend to be divided into fairly well-defined sections: central business districts, secondary commercial areas, factory districts, and residential areas ranging from affluent to poor. At their very best, small cities are divided into fairly distinct neighborhoods that provide their residents with at least some elements of community.

An equally important barometer of how citified a midwestern municipality has become is its array and quality of services and amenities. To qualify as a city, a municipality has to provide not only the essentials of urban living, such as fire and police protection, water and sewerage, and streets and sidewalks, but at least some of the cultural and emotional enrichment that distinguish the metropolis: museums, theatres and dramatic groups, musical and dance aggregations, philanthropic organizations, parks and recreational facilities, and spectator sports.

Finally, small cities are distinguished from small towns by the degree to which their residents manifest the characteristics of Wirth's urban personality. As municipalities become larger, more densely populated, and heterogeneous, human contacts become more impersonal, superficial, transitory, and segmented, while the number, variety, and velocity of stimuli increase exponentially. People consequently tend toward the extremes of the personality spectrum: increasingly sophisticated, tolerant, and cosmopolitan at one end, and at the other, more prone to every possible form of personal and social breakdown, including addiction, mental illness, suicide, homicide, juvenile delinquency, and economic and political corruption. Either way, the residents of the Midwest's small cities clearly consider themselves every bit as urban as the residents of the metropolis.

Sources and Further Reading: David R. Constasta, *Lancaster, Ohio, 1800–2000* (1999); Otis Dudley Duncan and Albert J. Reiss, *Social Characteristics of Urban and Rural Communities* (1956); Park Dixon Goist, *From Main Street to State Street* (1977); J. Rogers Hollingsworth and Ellen Jane Hollingsworth, *Dimensions in Urban History* (1979); Frederic C. Howe, *The City: The Hope of Democracy* (1905); Richard Lingeman, *Small Town America* (1980); Timothy Mahoney, "The Small City in American History," *Indiana Magazine of History* XCIX (Dec. 2003); Raymond E. Murphy, *The American City: An Urban Geography* (1966); William F. Ogburn, *Social Characteristics of Cities* (1937); Douglas W. Rea, *City: Urbanism and Its End* (2003); Jack L. Tager and Park Dixon

Goist, eds., *The Urban Vision* (1970); Jon C. Teaford, *Cities of the Heartland* (1993).

John D. Buenker
University of Wisconsin–Parkside

Historical Periods

Early Nineteenth Century Origins

Modern American city-dwellers, stressed by the hectic pace of urban life, often envy the inhabitants of midwestern small towns; they idealize the small town as the place where one might experience a traditional and simple lifestyle, free from the chaos of the modern metropolis, with its industrial landscapes, traffic jams, and alienated population. The small town, with its quaint Victorian homes, clean air and water, and friendly neighbors, offers a slower pace. Most Americans want to believe that the contrast between the lives of modern city people and their small-town counterparts is rooted in history, and that midwestern small towns were created as refuges from the increasingly industrial city life of the early nineteenth century. There is some truth to this; the founders of some midwestern towns did intend their communities to be experiments in social engineering and wanted to cure the ills of American society by setting up ideal towns.

Ironically, however, the inhabitants of most midwestern small towns in the early nineteenth century (when many were founded) did not want their communities to differ from those in the East. On the contrary, most wanted to jump right onto the industrial carousel and hoped that their towns would become very much like eastern towns. In Alton, Illinois, the hog-packing industry provided both meat for the tables of local inhabitants and a convenient market for the area's rural corn producers. In Belleville, Illinois, ethnic German and Irish day laborers worked in the local coal mines to produce fuel for the urban residents of nearby St. Louis.

While most community leaders had urban aspirations, their towns differed in their origins and can be categorized according to the circumstances of their founding. A few began as Indian or French settlements—among them Chillicothe, Ohio; Kaskaskia and Cahokia, Illinois; Vincennes, Indiana; and Mackinaw City, Michigan. Others owe their existence to the establishment of early American military or trading posts on their sites—Fort Wayne, Indiana; Copper Harbor, Michigan; Fort Atkinson, Wisconsin; Fort Ripley, Minnesota; and Keokuk, Iowa, are examples. A few communities, such as New Harmony in Indiana and the Amana Colonies in Iowa, were founded by religious separatists.

Most towns trace their histories to the growing commercialization of the early nineteenth century. In fact, the settlement of the Midwest by people from the Eastern Seaboard and by immigrants from northern and western Europe coincided with the takeoff of cotton industrialism in the East and cotton slavery in the South. Most people who moved westward did so to take advantage of the opportunities presented by growing industrialism.

To be sure, most of the settlers did not intend to live in towns, but on farms where they would grow wheat or corn, or raise sheep, cattle, or hogs to be shipped to the burgeoning eastern cities. But towns were necessary if people were to gather and ship their produce. Some towns, such as Belleville, Illinois, and Ashtabula, Ohio, simply grew organically along established trade and travel routes, then incorporated later. The greater number, however, were deliberately founded either by groups or by individuals. Along navigable waterways (at first along rivers and then along the canals), speculators bought and platted whole towns hoping to make their fortunes. Some speculators had already settled in the areas of their towns; others came specifically to speculate in town founding. Such was the case in Burlington, Iowa, and Galena, Illinois.

Whole communities of people, such as those who settled in Princeton and Galesburg, Illinois, bought large plots of land to found towns for immigrants. Federal officials surveyed public land into tracts as small as forty acres. Early town founders (either individuals or groups) simply went to the nearest land office, viewed the plat maps produced by government cartographers, and laid claim to land. They paid with bounties, if they were veterans of the War of 1812, or with loan money from enterprising capitalists, or with hard cash. Prospective town founders then surveyed streets, subdivided plots, and sold or gave land to the newly arriving townspeople, many of whom were also in the business of making money from the processing of goods from the hinterland or by providing services to the townspeople.

To be sure, some towns were founded by people who rejected aspects of the spreading capitalist market economy. Communitarian impulses caused many folk to found settlements such as Robert Owen's New Harmony in Indiana or the socialist colony of Communia in Iowa. European immigrants, such as the English in Albion, Illinois, and the Welsh in Oak Hill, Ohio, traveled *en masse* to the Midwest in attempts to recreate their own homeland communities. But even these group settlers were anxious to take advantage of the opportunities that trade and industrialism had to offer.

In general, small-town midwesterners were on the make. Because their individual fortunes depended upon those of their towns, they argued fiercely about the future of their communities. It was only after the Civil War, when local winners and losers were clearly identifiable, that the simplicity many Americans associate with small-town life actually became possible. That image was a product of failure: It thrived only in towns that did not succeed in becoming central to the regional economy.

Lifestyles in antebellum small towns reflected many of the trends that were important to urban easterners. Inhabitants strove to get as much information as possible from the outside world. Newspapers, in as many languages as there were people who spoke them, were established in almost every town with a population over two thousand. These newspapers, usually published weekly, reflected the political persuasions of their editors and often spurred competitors to establish even more journals. The competing editors, however, did more than express the political views of their constituents; they kept the public record for the towns, recording births and deaths, notifying the public of railroad and shipping schedules, and advertising public lectures, speeches, plays, and meetings. They also provided entertainment, sometimes copying and printing whole chapters from popular novels of the day, usually without the permission of the authors.

Small-town inhabitants enjoyed many forms of entertainment. Private literary societies sponsored poets and authors who came from all over the country, library boards constructed and funded free libraries, fraternal organizations sponsored picnics and baseball tournaments, and churches provided Friday night suppers. The absence of central heating and air conditioning in homes encouraged people to gather in groups to socialize. People relied upon their own institutions to inform and divert them; temperance societies and antislavery groups brought enthusiastic speakers to the towns, and political clubs sponsored local and statewide candidates to debate local and national concerns.

To socialize their children into the rhythms of small-town life, town leaders established common schools, first on a pay-as-you-go basis, then as state-supported, public institutions. Schools were originally conceived as places for the provision of very basic education for youngsters. (The Land Ordinance of 1785 mandated that the sixteenth section of each township be used for the funding of schools.) Later on, schools were seen in part as a mechanism to familiarize immigrant children with middle-class American values. Local newspaper editors often lamented the large numbers of apparently shiftless youth in their towns, seemingly with nothing to do, and called for the establishment of school systems. Small-town leaders advocated urban growth as a means of participating in the larger national society, but were also clearly anxious to curb some of its excesses.

The attachment that the people felt to the national society, however, brought many unavoidable problems. They were concerned with many controversies that were national in origin but local in consequence. The increased consumption of alcohol, Indian claims to local land, the religious fervor and schisms caused by the Second Great Awakening (a new wave of evangelical religious revivals that sought to reenergize Protestantism), and the spread of slavery all caused consternation within small towns. The slavery controversy split many communities down the middle.

Despite the aspirations and energy of small-town midwesterners, only a minority of towns succeeded in becoming bustling urban centers. Circumstances determined whether a particular town would become a regional center or suffer in isolation. A town might survive as a supplier of food and goods to a nearby urban area, as in the case of Belleville, Illinois, and St. Louis, Missouri. More distant communities needed to be on some sort of transportation corridor. The construction of canals in the 1830s and 1840s, followed by the even more important railroads in the 1850s, revived some flagging small towns and created others. Early steam locomotives' dependence on water stops at about twenty-mile intervals spawned many facilities. Established towns vied with one another to attract railroad companies, and aspiring entrepreneurs founded towns along railroad routes.

Some towns were more successful in the race for urban survival because they had a set of founders and leaders who worked together to ensure that they would get the necessary economic breaks. In other towns, the leadership was so fractious, whether along ethnic, political, or social lines, that it was difficult to achieve any sort of consensus on the strategy for dominance or survival. As the losers in the regional scramble for economic dominance became the smaller urban places that many modern Americans idealize, local residents rewrote their histories to show that they had always intended to establish peaceful communities away from the hustle and the bustle of the rat race. But the inhabitants of these smaller places often felt stifled. Populations leveled off or even declined in the twentieth century as children left for big cities, no longer confident that they could find their fortunes in their hometowns.

Sources and Further Reading: Carl Abbott, *Boosters and Businessmen* (1981); Kay J. Carr, *Belleville, Ottawa, and Galesburg* (1996); Andrew R. L. Cayton, *Frontier Indiana* (1996); James E. Davis, *Frontier Illinois* (1998); Don Harrison Doyle,

The Social Order of a Frontier Community (1978); R. Douglas Hurt, *The Ohio Frontier* (1996); Timothy R. Mahoney, *Provincial Lives* (1999); Timothy R. Mahoney, *River Towns in the Great West* (1990); Richard C. Wade, *The Urban Frontier: Pioneer Life in Early Pittsburgh, Cincinnati, Lexington, Louisville, and St. Louis* (1959).

Kay J. Carr
Southern Illinois University

America's Hometown: From the Civil War through World War I

Frederick J. Hoffman, looking back in *The Twenties: American Writing in the Postwar Decade*, observes, "The Middle West had become a metaphor of abuse; it was on the one hand a rural metaphor, of farms, villages, and small towns; on the other, a middle-class metaphor, of conventions, piety and hypocrisy, tastelessness and spiritual poverty."

But the Midwest was not simply "a metaphor of abuse." It was evolving into America's heartland—primarily a twentieth-century construction, but one clearly built from late nineteenth-century materiel. During the early twentieth century, Americans were increasingly consumed with materialism and a commodity-based middle-class identity. A preoccupation by dominant but shaken white Protestants with the region's expansive pioneer–yeoman heritage gave way to the comforting ideal of its hometown past. The Midwest became a synecdoche for American values and norms, and the town became its signature. By the 1920s, regional small towns were a contested symbol of both provincial banality and progressive hope. The idea of the small town embodied a national debate over the meaning of middle-class community that would continue throughout the twentieth century.

James Oliver Robertson, in *American Myth, American Reality*, notes the conflation in the twentieth century of a middling sense of identity: "For Americans, the 'middle'—whether middle class, Middle West, or middle American—is a large, solid, geographical center of almost limitless extent." Within this landscape stands the town, "the American community writ large, a reflection of every real community in America. . . . homogeneous and proximate; therefore, in the logic of the myth, classless, democratic, and equal." Such a construction oversimplifies, but something beyond the metaphorical parameters of small-town life is at work here. In *Community and Social Change in America*, Thomas Bender writes:

Americans seem to have something else in mind when they wistfully recall or assume a past made up of small-town communities. This social memory has a geographic referent, the town, but it is clear from the many layers of emotional meaning attached to the word "community" that the concept means more than a place or local activity. There is an expectation of a special quality of human relationship in a community, and it is this experiential dimension that is crucial to its definition.

Ultimately, for Americans caught up in what sociologists would refer to as the "problem of community"—a late-nineteenth-century migrant from small-town Nebraska to Omaha, a Chicago journalist, a 1910 Greenwich Village bohemian or Lower East Side Jew, a 1920s Iowan transplanted to Los Angeles, Depression-Era architects of "garden cities," mid-century residents of barrios and suburbs, or end-of-the-century denizens of "edge-cities"—Bender's "experiential dimension" was encompassed by the middle-western small town.

The utopian or dystopian concept of middle-class community came to be lodged in a generic, physically wholesome, or psychically repressed hometown. William Allen White, the Emporia (Kansas) journalist and renowned defender of a middle-American cultural ethos, hoisted his town's banner as a standard: "In America most of us are Emporians in one way or another. Some of us live in towns ranging from five thousand to a quarter of a million, others were born in or around these towns, and still others of us cherish golden dreams of going back to some Emporia. People say to us Emporia dwellers: 'Why do you live in Emporia?' and the answer seems simple: 'Everyone does—more or less.'" White made his observation in *Collier's* in 1923 amidst a controversy over rampant urbanism. "But," he prodded, "is that an answer? Does it explain why everyone in reality or in dreams lives in some old home town?"

The answer for White, and for a wide array of commentators, lay in developing a middle-class culture. The nation had become interlocked in a web of far-flung interests, laws, and social institutions designed to ensure equality, justice, and opportunity. The midwestern small town epitomized middle-class life. It had become a symbol of security, for better or worse, within the national community. By 1928, the U.S. presidential election would be waged in large part over where the future of middle-class America most profitably rested: with Herbert Hoover, a midwestern, Protestant icon, or with Al Smith, a New York City, Catholic success story. How had this come to pass?

For Americans who had aspired to do well during the past half century, the answer was clear: Amidst socioeconomic upheaval, cultural bearings had shifted. The small town had arisen either as a beacon of hope or an obstructive stump along America's path to the good life. Decade after decade, politicians, novelists, ministers, and voters took their positions. The coun-

Lawrence, Kansas, 1867. Kansas State Historical Society, Gardner Collection no. 34.

try took on a retooled identity in the twentieth century: The United States manufactured lots of goods
and lots of hopes. It was cross-cut by an energizing
competitive spirit, a variegated commitment to community, and distinctive strains of confidence and fear;
it was characterized by ideals of small-town values, increasingly urban cultural norms, and a tangible claim
of classlessness nestled within an intangible sense of
homogenizing middle-class identity. By the early
1920s, a majority of Americans toasted, albeit illegally,
a New Era, a triumphant American ethos that soon
would be popularly summed up as the American Way
of Life, a huge middle-class success story.

The small town came to embody that story. Richard Slotkin argues in *The Fatal Environment: The Myth
of the Frontier in the Age of Industrialism, 1800–1890*,
that myths are regenerative, current, and ideologically
laden; they are "central to the cultural functioning of
the society that produces them." Warren Susman considers in *Culture as History* what materialized in the
first four decades of the twentieth century: a culture of
abundance mediated by communications and organization revolutions, a new middle class as the recipient of goods, and public opinion shaped, values and
personalities molded. "The concept of the average was
born. The Average American and the Average American Family became central to the new vision of a future culture." According to T. J. Jackson Lears in *No
Place of Grace*, a broad shift "from a Protestant to a
therapeutic orientation within the dominant culture"
was taking place. In *Advertising the American Dream*,
Roland Marchand assesses a critical element in that
therapy:

> Advertisers, then as now, recognized a much larger
> stake in reflecting people's needs and anxieties than in
> depicting their actual circumstances and behavior. It
> was in their efforts to promote the mystique of
> modernity in styles and technology, while simultane-
> ously assuaging the anxieties of consumers about
> losses of community and individual control, that they
> most closely mirrored historical reality—the reality of
> a cultural dilemma.

Middle-class identity was up for grabs. The advertisers, of course, had been around for generations.
Now they were cashing in on a new, amalgamated, nationalizing ethos—and in the process, the frontier had
been transformed into the town, an antidote perfectly
prescribed for a mass market.

The attention of the people had not only been coveted by merchants. No protagonist beyond Madison
Avenue would play a greater role than the politician in
reaching out for the average. Experts at communications and organization, middle-class reformers

courted voters as part of the progressive reform movement. John Whiteclay Chambers II, in *The Tyranny of
Change*, outlines the broad agenda:

> In diverse ways and with divergent goals, the pro-
> gressives sought to modernize American institutions
> while attempting to recapture the ideals and sense of
> community that they believed had existed in the past.
> They battled conservatives, radicals, other reformers,
> and often each other. Progressives played a major role
> in helping Americans to adjust to new conditions and
> create new institutions for coping with the challenges
> of the time. They took the lead in establishing a social
> agenda for modern America.

For hosts of Progressive reformers at the turn of
the twentieth century, the metaphorical town encapsulated the ideal sense of community: prohibitionists
and birth control advocates; women suffragists, southerners disenfranchising blacks, and northerners disenfranchising immigrants; trust-busters and regulators;
City Beautiful and Rural Free Delivery promoters;
machine bosses and reform bosses. The language, the
therapeutic ideal, the amalgamation of community
and identity, the aesthetic, the packaging, have had
staying power—Progressivism has thrived within a
commercial culture. The midwestern small town provided a vehicle through which Americans could idealize their past in the midst of massive change. Triumphant post–Civil War Republicans and later the
Populists turned to it; genteel Victorian novelists fond
of town life faced off against such realist town savagers
as Edgar Watson Howe and Hamlin Garland; in the
early decades of the new century, regionalists such as
Zona Gale and Dorothy Canfield Fisher stood opposed to "modernists" led by the hugely popular Sinclair Lewis. And so, progressive popularizers and
politicians, a huge number of whom hailed from the
Midwest and its small towns, naturally embraced the
town standard, a model for "coping with the challenges of the time," a means "to recapture the ideals
and sense of community" they believed they had lost.

Twentieth-century reformers focused on the small
town as they addressed the larger problem of community. Novelist and native son Sinclair Lewis, generally
viewed as a critic of small towns, in fact wrote about
small-minded communities of all sizes that fell short
of a more expansive middle-class ideal. The town itself
was to be treasured. Lewis was a comrade-in-arms
with William Allen White. The "Sage of Emporia"
saw town life as encapsulating a modern American solution. Somehow a more progressive, urban America
needed to rebuild community based on sound middle-
American values. White editorialized in his *Gazette*, as
controversy swirled about the publication of Lewis'
Babbitt (1922): "Lewis who wrote 'Main Street' two

years ago put a new phrase into the English language. 'Main Street' means something now that it did not mean before. Soon the word 'babbitt' will be coined into a new meaning. Students of our times in other eras must go to Lewis and his fellow protestors to understand what ailed us." It all had started long before: "Our urban life, whether in Toledo or Denver, Minneapolis or Buffalo, Sauk Center or New York, is jammed full of Babbitts. Babbitt is Main Street in tailored clothes. And the story of 'Babbitt' is a story that every American should read—a great philippic against the emptiness of this civilization."

White and Lewis agreed that the small town represented an America endangered by expansive, materialistic rot in the half-century following the Civil War, yet worthy of salvation. Today, the idea of the small town still resonates among those concerned with community.

Sources and Further Reading: Edward Gale Agran, *"Too Good a Town:" William Allen White, Community, and the Emerging Rhetoric of Middle America* (1998); Thomas Bender, *Community and Social Change in America* (1982); Burton S. Bledstein and Robert Johnston, eds., *The Middling Sorts* (2001); John Whiteclay Chambers II, *The Tyranny of Change* (1992); Richard Wightman Fox and T. J. Jackson Lears, eds., *The Culture of Consumption* (1983); Ima Honaker Herron, *The Small Town in American Literature* (1959); Anthony Channell Hilfer, *The Revolt from the Village 1915–1930* (1969); Frederick J. Hoffman, *The Twenties: American Writing in the Postwar Decade* (1955); T. J. Jackson Lears, *No Place of Grace* (1983); Roland Marchand, *Advertising the American Dream* (1985); Jay Martin, *Harvests of Change* (1967); Jean B. Quandt, *From the Small Town to the Great Community* (1970); James Oliver Robertson, *American Myth, American Reality* (1980); David E. Shi, *Facing Facts* (1995); Richard Slotkin, *The Myth of the Frontier in the Age of Industrialism, 1800–1890* (1994); Warren Susman, *Culture as History* (1984); Robert H. Wiebe, *The Search for Order, 1877–1920* (1967).

Edward Gale Agran
Wilmington College, Ohio

Main Street in Transition: 1920–1950

Although some of the four thousand small towns that dotted the Midwest by the early twentieth century were spawned by canal and railroad developments, most took root along natural waterways and at the intersections of country roads. Whatever their origins, all shared the same common function of providing marketplaces for area farmers. These towns went through three distinct phases of development between the end of World War I and 1950. During the 1920s, the approximately four thousand incorporated towns of fewer than five thousand residents enjoyed modest

population growth and generally participated in the nation's prosperity. The economic collapse of the 1930s brought hard times, followed by a revival of economic vitality during and after World War II. Throughout this tumultuous thirty-year period, however, powerful national trends were silently undermining the foundations upon which towns rested. Their dependence on agriculture made them particularly vulnerable.

For a time the future looked reasonably bright along Main Street. Buoyed by the overall booming national economy of the 1920s, a rhetoric of optimism and self-congratulation dominated the conventional wisdom. Reconciled to the reality that their towns were not about to become the next Indianapolis or Des Moines, Main Street boosters focused on a realistic assessment of what constituted the good life. The oft-repeated refrain was that theirs was a friendly town that provided a good place in which to live and raise children. Defenders argued that the homogeneous small midwestern towns offered an attractive range of amenities and personal relationships unavailable in the cities: low crime rates, friendly folk who were helpful to their neighbors in times of distress, progressive local schools, and a vigorous social life built around a myriad of clubs, associations, and churches.

Although their physical appearance and land use patterns suggested a bland sameness, some communities took on a unique image. Hermann, Missouri, and New Ulm, Minnesota, for example, became havens for immigrants from rural Germany in the late nineteenth century, and their architecture and social customs reflected their German heritage. Berne, Indiana; Berlin, Ohio; and Kalona, Iowa, provided havens for Amish residents, where their unique horse-drawn buggies, well-tended and prosperous farms, simple clothing styles, and elegant quilts and other handicraft products contributed to a wholesome community atmosphere.

During the 1920s, a rising crescendo of criticism of the midwestern town emanated from the urban-based intelligentsia. That the harshest critic of all was the product of the prairie town of Sauk Centre, Minnesota, was embarrassing, of course, but Sinclair Lewis's satiric ridicule of life along *Main Street* (1920) ultimately left no permanent scar. Although readers tended to misinterpret Sherwood Anderson's influential novel, *Winesburg, Ohio* (1919), as yet another anti-town attack, his more perceptive readers noted that his was in reality an anguished cry of protest against the external economic forces of modern America that had destroyed the idyllic life he had known as a youth growing up in the northwestern Ohio community of Clyde.

In reality, most residents paid scant attention to the

intellectual's "revolt from the village." Residing in their sturdy frame or brick two-story houses situated well back from the tree-lined streets, they tended to their yards and vegetable gardens, reared their children, complained about the weather, attended an occasional motion picture at the local theatre, engaged in a perpetual whirlwind of gossip that served as an effective means of social control and community policing, went about earning a living, and participated in a complex pattern of economic and social relationships that revolved around work, church, school, and community organizations.

Despite frequent assertions that small town society was classless, well-defined and widely recognized class lines sharply delineated social and economic relationships. An individual's social standing was determined by several factors: income, property holdings, professional standing, and family reputation. It also was defined by membership in important community organizations and churches. The phenomenon of joining secular organizations had become prominent in American life during the 1870s and crested during the 1920s. Rather than unifying a community, as members professed, however, the proliferation of organizations tended to create divisions. At the top of the social scale were the more affluent business and professional men and their wives; the men interacted through such prominent organizations as Rotary, the Masonic Order, and the private country club (if the town was large enough to support a golf course), while their wives participated in literary societies, the Order of the Eastern Star, weekly afternoon bridge clubs, and charitable and service organizations known for their exclusivity. The surefire mark of a lady of high status was whether she had the luxury of part-time help to do the weekly house cleaning and laundry.

Clustered in the middle to lower-middle class were teachers, small merchants, clerks, plumbers, carpenters, electricians, automobile mechanics, day laborers, and handymen who found their social niche in the volunteer fire department, fraternal lodges (Moose, Elks, Odd Fellows, Eagles, Woodmen of the World), and the Lions service club. Their wives socialized through church groups and neighborhood cliques, and their status was often determined by whether or not they took in laundry to supplement a tight family budget.

Every town with an ounce of pride inevitably supported two community institutions, a band and a baseball team. From the late nineteenth century until the mid-1950s, the town band was ubiquitous across the Midwest. Usually an all-male organization of fifteen or so musicians, dressed out in resplendent uniforms, the bands participated in patriotic celebrations, political parades, summer carnivals, fish fries, and ice cream

socials. The band was also prominent on warm summer Saturday nights, when farm families piled into town for shopping and socializing and were joined along Main Street by town residents.

Baseball provided a sense of community-wide identity. Players on the town team carried the pride of the town upon their collective shoulders and provided a focus that superseded class lines. Bitter rivalries with nearby communities that grew out of distant but not forgotten economic and political battles were carried forward from year to year and from decade to decade. Local merchants coughed up an annual donation to help pay for uniforms and equipment, and fans dropped a few coins into a baseball hat passed through the grandstands during the seventh inning stretch. Games were played on Sunday afternoons (night ball would come with postwar affluence and enhanced electrical technology) and attracted large crowds. Town ball died a quick death at the hands of television in the 1950s, but for three quarters of a century, it provided an important source of community.

During the 1920s, high school basketball became firmly entrenched as a major community activity. The season filled an important void during the long, bleak winter months. Football was reserved for the larger towns and urban schools, but even the smallest of high schools could identify at least five youngsters reasonably capable of dribbling and shooting. For several months each winter, the hopes and dreams of small towns were placed upon the shoulders of sixteen- and seventeen-year-olds. Girls' basketball was initially popular, but disappeared by the early 1930s, a victim of the Depression and changing attitudes about the propriety and health risks of vigorous exercise for girls. Only in Iowa, where a unique six-person game captured the public imagination, did girls' basketball survive. The boys' game became an obsession in Indiana, but enjoyed immense popularity all across the Midwest. County school districts held season-ending tournaments, with the winners moving on to district and state competition. Still today, faded signs stand at town limits or peer down from water towers proudly proclaiming a state basketball championship won many decades ago.

Life in small-town America was made increasingly tolerable by the arrival of a myriad assemblage of new appliances and technologies. By the end of the 1920s, towns had availed themselves of the conveniences of electricity that not only powered streetlights, radios, motion pictures, vacuum cleaners, and electric "ice boxes," but also brightly and safely (as opposed to the always dangerous kerosene lamp) illuminated the once gloomy interiors of homes during the short days of winter. Private wells, back porch cisterns, and outdoor privies disappeared as water and sewer systems were installed. The large number of automobiles that chugged around town offered new vistas to their owners for business or pleasure trips. The year and model of automobile a family owned became a new and powerful symbol of social status. To the delight of all, the automobile caused a much-approved disappearance from town streets of the natural residue of the rapidly declining resident horse population. Village governments were placed under intense pressure to pave the muddy (or dusty) streets. In many communities this was accomplished by laying brick in intricate designs, and where they survive, these attractive brick streets remain a sense of community pride.

The universal embrace of the automobile in the 1920s contributed to the sharp decline of Main Street's independence and vitality. The automobile facilitated shopping trips to regional cities, where urban department stores not only offered a much wider variety of goods, but also undercut the prices charged by town merchants. Conversely, delivery trucks from once-distant cities now invaded the towns on a daily basis. Undercapitalized Main Street merchants found themselves increasingly at a serious competitive disadvantage on such essentials as price, variety, volume, and quality. A new form of competition arrived in the form of the national chain store. By 1930, orange and blue Rexall Drug signs swayed in the breezes along Main Street, while the operators of mom-and-pop grocery stores had to contend with the mass merchandizing power of the A&P.

Thus were the seeds of the future economic decline of Main Street America well established by the end of the 1920s. The ensuing Great Depression ruthlessly exposed the vulnerability of small-town merchants. Although historians of the 1930s have focused upon the suffering that occurred in or on farms, small towns took an equally heavy hit. Thousands of small-town banks and savings and loans were forced into receivership due to the collapse of agriculture commodity prices that devastated local economies. Hard-pressed school boards were forced to slash budgets, often resorting to paying teachers with near worthless scrip because residents could not pay their property taxes. Small manufacturing companies, an often unrecognized but important component of small-town economic life, suffered heavy losses. Local charitable organizations were overwhelmed, and town governments, operated largely by part-time officers, lacked the wherewithal to attract much in the way of federal emergency funding from New Deal agencies. Many communities organized self-help groups to assist their community's needy, often ironically called "Progressive Clubs," and joined with churches to do what they could to ameliorate the suffering.

A long decade of economic malaise was reversed in the early 1940s by the war-induced national economic revival. As millions of young men and women from small-town America went off to war, those who remained behind found employment at good wages in nearby cities, and farmers luxuriated in the government-induced high commodity prices. Despite the restrictions of wartime rationing, business once more hummed along Main Street. But the economic revival was centered in the cities, and there ensued a migration to those high-paying defense-related jobs. At war's end, demographers reported that rural and small-town America had lost 17 percent of its population.

The migration to the cities did not end with the war and, in fact, was intensified by postwar conditions. The lure was virtually irresistible—good jobs, enhanced cultural and social opportunities, modern schools, advanced medical services, and a wide range of housing options. Residents who did not abandon their hometowns often commuted to the cities to work and to shop at new shopping centers.

Thus, this bitter irony for the once-proud small towns of the Midwest: Those located very close to larger cities would be swallowed up in the postwar suburban explosion, and although they would become much larger and infinitely more prosperous, they would lose their special identities as independent communities. For the thousands of towns located more distant from the urban centers, postwar prosperity would brush upon their community lives only marginally. The seeds of their impending decline were now beginning to germinate, and would soon produce the all-too-familiar pattern of stagnation, atrophy, and decline that has yet to run its course.

Sources and Further Reading: Joseph Amato, *Rethinking Home: The Case for Writing Local History* (2002); Lewis E. Atherton, *Main Street on the Middle Border* (1954); Richard O. Davies, *Main Street Blues: The Decline of Small-Town America* (1998); Richard O. Davies, Joseph A. Amato, and David R. Pichaske, eds., *A Place Called Home: Writings on the Small Midwestern Town* (2003); Richard V. Francaviglia, *Main Street Revisited: Time, Space, and Image Building in Small-Town America* (1996); Richard Lingeman, *Small Town America* (1980); Robert and Helen Lynd, *Middletown: A Study in Contemporary American Culture* (1929); Robert and Helen Lynd, *Middletown in Transition: A Study in Cultural Conflicts* (1937); Page Smith, *As a City on a Hill: The Town in American History* (1966); Catharine McNicol Stock, *Main Street in Crisis: The Great Depression and the Old Middle Class on the Northern Plains* (1992); Carl Withers, *Plainville, USA* (1945).

Richard O. Davies
University of Nevada–Reno

Main Street in Repose: 1950–2000

Whether one consults hard statistical data or merely takes a day trip off the main roads to visit any small town selected at random, the inescapable conclusion is the same: The proud towns that once formed the backbone of the Midwest have fallen upon hard times. Although there are notable exceptions, the small town has been victimized by the relentless assault upon fragile communities by powerful historical forces located far beyond local control. The smaller the village, the more vulnerable it has been; the further located from a regional city, the more likely that it has fallen upon hard times.

The causes of the decline are many and complex, but they are related to the continued accumulation of population, economic strength, political power, and social dominance by regional cities. Addressing the plight of the communities of the upper Midwest, Joseph Amato concludes that policy makers "must acknowledge that prairie towns since their very beginnings have marched to the beat of the distant drums of the metropolitan centers like Chicago, St. Louis, St. Paul, and Minneapolis."

The primary economic engine powering the midwestern town has been and remains agriculture. But advances in agricultural science and technology have meant a steady decline in the size of the farm population. As the size of farms increased and corporate agriculture found ever more advanced ways to produce more food and fiber on less acreage with ever fewer workers, the viability of the midwestern town was diminished.

In the years immediately following World War II, a handful of observers began reporting on the impending decline of the small town. "Main Street has not only lost population, but also the hope, daring, and originality necessary to fight back," Lewis E. Atherton wrote in 1954, pointing to "vacant store buildings and sagging, unpainted houses, to numerous old people vegetating in village homes, and to boys and girls anxiously looking forward to the time when they can join the rush to the cities." In 1969, the cultural anthropologist Don Martindale described the negative impact upon the western Minnesota town of Benson by what he identified as "translocal forces," powerful economic, political, and social trends of distant origin that swept the small communities along in their wake. The assault upon the small town came in many forms. The inability of the villages to attract health professionals was one of the early warning signals; all across the Midwest, small hospitals and clinics were shut down as the locus of medical care shifted to larger communities.

One of the most pervasive impacts from outside was sparked by the effort of federal and state governments to modernize the nation's highway network. Villages found themselves bypassed by highway planners seeking to speed the flow of interurban traffic. Although travel times were reduced, the economic impact was often devastating. Among the victims were merchants who operated service stations, restaurants, tourist homes, and small motels. The construction of the 42,500-mile Interstate Highway and Defense System left many reasonably prosperous towns cut off from their economic lifeline. For those towns fortunate enough to be located along the new national interstate system, the impact was nonetheless traumatic as downtown business districts were hurt by the corporate chain motels and restaurants constructed at cloverleaf intersections.

Smaller communities also suffered a decline of control over their local affairs. Policies established by distant governments and regulatory bodies increasingly set local political agendas. This process was foreshadowed by the arrival of Department of Agriculture extension agents and various New Deal experts and functionaries. Throughout the Midwest, administrators in state departments of education promulgated minimum standards and new curricular requirements that frequently were beyond the capability of small school districts to meet, resulting in a school consolidation movement that led to the creation of larger regional school districts. Despite improved educational opportunities for students, towns whose local schools had closed felt the loss of the few local institutions that had for decades stimulated community pride and involvement, including the local boys' basketball team.

By the 1970s, town leaders increasingly bemoaned that they no longer controlled their community's destiny. Farmers had long complained that they were forced to spend more time filling out Department of Agriculture forms than they did in the field. Now town and county officials raised the same objections about intrusive state and federal agencies. Rather than setting local priorities and administering those programs, town and rural county governments increasingly found themselves the powerless extensions of distant governing bodies and administrative agencies. State and federal governments imposed their authority in an ever-increasing number of mandates and directives on such matters as environment protection, affirmative action, housing for the aged, Social Security, Medicaid, Medicare, occupational health and safety, school lunches, law enforcement, community action, and public health. Local authorities, often confronted by a shrinking tax base, had to do more with less.

The loss of political control to the state and federal government was only part of the erosion of local autonomy. It also occurred in the private sector. Banking was a classic example, as small locally owned and operated banks, long powerful symbols of local prosperity and autonomy, fell prey to the outward reach of regional and national banking conglomerates.

Even towns with stable economies and growing populations were not immune from translocal forces. The larger the town's population, the greater the likelihood that uninvited heavy hitters would locate new branches in the community. The first wave of this corporate invasion had begun on a small scale during the 1920s with grocery, drug, and variety stores. During the 1950s, the invasion was renewed with the seemingly benign construction of a Dairy Queen, McDonald's, or Bob's Big Boy Restaurant. Owners of Main Street hardware and clothing stores also found themselves in a relentless competition with outlets of such venerable corporations as Sears, Roebuck, J. C. Penney, and Montgomery Ward.

In the 1970s, the corporate invasion of Main Street intensified exponentially with the incredible economic triumph by an aggressive corporation located in the sleepy Arkansas town of Bentonville: Wal-Mart. Initially, founder Sam Walton concentrated upon placing his warehouse-style discount stores in remote smaller cities. Communities with as few as ten thousand residents might have found themselves with a large Wal-Mart mega-store on the edge of town. But these stores were shrewdly designed, located, and marketed as regional facilities; consequently they severely affected the base economies of neighboring towns. Using the most sophisticated of computerized distribution systems to support its high-volume, low-price business strategy, Wal-Mart inevitably overwhelmed local merchants. The firm's executives argued that the big box stores improved life in towns and small cities by providing greater variety at lower prices; Wal-Mart was merely practicing the essentials of American capitalism. They also touted their good citizenship by hiring locals and contributing heavily to local charities and community organizations. Although Wal-Mart was the target of mounting criticism, local customers throughout the Midwest overwhelmingly cast their lot (and their cash) with the Arkansas-based company.

The transformation of towns by powerful translocal political and economic forces, in turn, accelerated social change. In the smaller towns, the outward migration of the young and talented intensified, leaving the elderly behind. Larger and more stable towns confronted a different, but equally perplexing, set of problems—those created by social change and cultural conflict. The changes often surprisingly resulted in communities of strangers. In these towns, various government agencies and corporations rotated their managers through the communities, many of them remaining for a few years before being transferred to another location. They stayed only long enough to enhance their resumes before heading down the road for a career advancement. In those communities fortunate enough to attract new or grow existing enterprises, the influx of new workers often created tension within the community. Many were new immigrants—Hispanic, Vietnamese, Muslim, Tongan—whose customs, language, and values clashed with the long-established Eurocentric values of the natives. Sometimes, as in Iowa and Minnesota, these new residents arrived *en masse* to work in new corporate agricultural settings, where large chicken, turkey, beef, and hog raising and processing plants drastically altered the face of local agriculture.

No matter the size of their census count, the towns of the Midwest reflected a national phenomenon—a declining sense of community and an increasing feeling of social isolation among residents. In towns of fewer than 2,500, the problem was one of finding enough healthy bodies to enable vital community organizations to function effectively. Local elections often took place with a dearth of candidates, and contested elections and meaningful political debate became increasingly rare. Service organizations such as the Lions Club, the ladies' aid societies, and the Progressive Club found themselves struggling to maintain a viable membership. A sharp decline in community-wide activity and involvement was evident everywhere. Changing societal values as well as the much more mobile society also hit hard at the membership levels of such once-powerful social organizations as the Masonic Order, the Elks, the American Legion, and other fraternal organizations. Whereas the residents of small towns had decried life in large cities as impersonal, now familiar patterns of neighborliness and community involvement were in decline even in communities of a few thousand. As ethnic, racial, cultural, class, and economic tensions and conflicts mounted, residents recognized that even in small-town America, once assailed by critics as numbingly conformist, the reality of diversity was challenging the ideal of community.

During the 1920s, it became fashionable to condemn small-town America as an intellectual and cultural wasteland dominated by boobs and frauds. The fictional jeremiads of Sinclair Lewis and other writers faded in the decades following World War II. It seemed that the greater the rate of decline, the kinder and gentler the treatment of the towns became. A wave of syrupy nostalgia wafted over Main Street. Garrison Keillor delighted radio audiences with his whimsical dialogues about the quaint folkways of Lake Wobegon, Minnesota ("where the women are strong, the men are good-looking, and all the children above average"). Television reporter Charles Kuralt entertained urban audiences with his reports of quaint behavior from the back roads of America. William Least Heat-Moon encouraged his readers to abandon the nation's freeways for the secondary "blue highways" that connected travelers to an ever-marginalized small-town America. An idealized version of a typical midwestern town even became the stuff of theme parks. Visitors to Walt Disney's fantasyland had to arrive and depart the Magic Kingdom (ironically located in the megalopolis of Southern California) via "Main Street USA," a colorful replication of the town in which Uncle Walt was raised, Marceline, Missouri.

The midwestern town produced by this rising tide of nostalgia will certainly live on in the collective American memory within a Disneyesque time capsule. So, too, will the thousands of real small towns that have been left far behind in modern America. No doubt they will remain a permanent, although diminished, part of the regional landscape. Some will even flourish, the beneficiaries of unusual circumstances, such as Rising Sun, Indiana; Dubuque, Iowa; Elgin, Illinois; and Booneville, Missouri, which have constructed riverboat casinos to lure gamblers. But most will have to be content with merely hanging on. Eclipsed by regional cities, their fortunes increasingly controlled by distant government and corporate decision-makers, they will fill the small niches left to them.

Sources and Further Reading: Joseph Amato, *Rethinking Home: The Case for Writing Local History* (2002); Joseph Amato with John Meyer, *The Decline of Rural Minnesota* (1993); Joseph Amato with John Meyer, *To Call It Home: The New Immigrants of Southwest Minnesota* (1996); Joseph Amato with John Radzilowski and John Meyer, *A Community of Strangers: Change, Turnover, Turbulence and the Transformation of a Midwestern Country Town* (1999); Lewis E. Atherton, *Main Street on the Middle Border* (1954); William Cronon, *Nature's Metropolis: Chicago and the Great West* (1991); Richard O. Davies, *Main Street Blues: The Decline of Small-Town America* (1998); Richard O. Davies, Joseph A. Amato, and David R. Pichaske, eds., *A Place Called Home: Writings on the Small Midwestern Town* (2003); Art Gallaher, *Plainville Fifteen Years Later* (1961); Don Martindale and R. Galen Hanson, *Small Town and the Nation: The Conflict of Local and Translocal Forces* (1969).

Richard O. Davies
University of Nevada–Reno

Representative Small Towns

Abilene, Kansas

There are band concerts in the park, summer swims at the WPA-built municipal pool, a county fair with a rodeo, and an inordinate number of Victorian homes.

Just off Interstate 70, there is a strip of fast food, motels, and retail stores. With a population of just over 6,500 (roughly double that of 1900), Abilene, Kansas, is typical of small towns that accommodate, even encourage, present-day commercialism against a backdrop of the town's historic past. For Abilene, the past combines conventional stories of town development with sensational events associated with the American West.

In 1867, Abilene was elevated from what one observer called a "small, dead" railroad town to a successful shipping point for longhorn cattle driven up the Chisholm Trail from Texas. Cowboys, cattle buyers, railroad men, and merchants packed the streets; many businesses existed for the sole purpose of separating the cowboy from his hard-earned money. Within five years, Abilene's heady cow-town days ended when the drives moved to railheads farther west. But unlike some cattle towns that dwindled when the drives went elsewhere, Abilene survived by developing a more diverse economy.

In the late 1870s, real estate agents, bankers, and merchants turned their attention to new settlers. Agriculture and the related businesses of milling and shipping became important to the economy, and they remain essential. The fortunes of both farmers and the town's businesses rose and fell with good and bad crop years. As a railroad town and county seat (without the usual courthouse square), the town has been home to what might be expected in retail stores, professional services, and manufacturing. (The more unusual include the early-twentieth-century production of carousel horses and a patent medicine company.) Today, the newest company is the Russell Stover Candies plant. Abilene is no different from other towns that face change. The building of Interstate 70 encouraged commercial development but altered the landscape. A constant, however, is the desire for jobs and stable growth without getting too big and sacrificing a sense of community.

In Abilene, tourism is an industry. The town understood the business long before tourism became a managed business, valued for its economic impact. The saloons, billiard halls, and gambling houses that enticed cowboys were an early form of Abilene tourism. In the 1920s, Brown's Park, developed by a local entrepreneur and philanthropist, attracted thousands each year to an artificial lake, picnic grounds, small zoo, playing fields, and golf course.

Today, the major destination is the Dwight D. Eisenhower Presidential Center. Initially conceived as a memorial to Eisenhower's military accomplishments during World War II, the Center began with private acquisition of the family home in 1946 and the construction of a privately-funded museum in early 1954.

Now a part of the National Archives and Records Administration's presidential library system, the complex consists of a library and archive, museum, Eisenhower's boyhood home, and his gravesite. An average of one hundred thousand visitors per year to the Eisenhower Center and Museum has encouraged development of other museums, shops, and a regional theatre.

Intertwined with the conscious effort to retain the flavor of the small town that Eisenhower knew as a boy is a cultural identification with a frontier past that recalls the days when Wild Bill Hickok was among the citizens of cow-town Abilene. Also remembered, but to a lesser degree, are homesteaders, town builders, and social institutions. Abilene thus highlights the benefits of small-town life while facing the challenge of sustaining progress.

Sources and Further Reading: Robert R. Dykstra, *The Cattle Towns* (1968); David J. Russo, *American Towns* (2001); James R. Shortridge, *The Middle West: Its Meaning in American Culture* (1989); David M. Wrobel and Patrick T. Long, eds., *Seeing and Being Seen* (2001).

Marilyn Irvin Holt
Abilene, Kansas

Baraboo, Wisconsin

Baraboo, Wisconsin, has a unique claim to fame as the birthplace of the Ringling Brothers Circus. This heritage and the association between small-town life and the circus are celebrated today at the Circus World Museum and shared with mass audiences during the Great Circus Parade, which for years was held annually in Milwaukee.

Baraboo owes its existence to the river of the same name that provided power for mills and formed the basis for white settlement in the late 1830s. A drop in elevation of over forty feet in the space of two and a half miles led to the construction of five dams and several mills, which created such items as lumber, shingles, flour, and wool goods. Originally two settlements existed on the river, one platted as Baraboo and one as Adams. The latter became the county seat in 1846. Eventually the two settlements were combined and the village of Baraboo chartered in 1866. The small community served as the center of county government and as a trading center for the agricultural hinterland. Baraboo contributed its share of volunteers to Civil War regiments.

Although the citizens of Baraboo tried several times to lure a railroad to connect it with broader markets, it was not until 1871 that the Chicago and North Western Railroad (C&NW) reached the town. Baraboo's wait was rewarded with the C&NW division headquarters, which included a twenty-eight-stall roundhouse and employed over three hundred and sixty people. The population of the village doubled in the decade after the railroad arrived, and in 1882, it incorporated as a city. The commercial areas were built up with substantial brick buildings after disastrous fires destroyed whole blocks of earlier wood-frame structures.

In 1884, the five Ringling brothers started a traveling circus show that wintered in Baraboo. The enterprise quickly grew and eventually became the largest circus in the nation, often by buying out its competitors. Each winter when the Ringling Brothers would

Al Ringling Theatre, Baraboo, Wisconsin. Sauk County Historical Society, Baraboo, WI and Wisconsin Historical Society, WHi-26100.

return to Baraboo, first by wagon and later by railcar, the local economy would benefit from the demand for animal feed, new costumes, bigger buildings, and new wagons. The wagons were often supplied by the Ringlings' cousins, the Moeller Brothers. Baraboo's claim as a premier circus city was later bolstered when more Ringling cousins, the Gollmar Brothers, started their own circus in 1891.

When the Ringling circus left Baraboo for good in 1918 to winter elsewhere, the local economy suffered, as did the population. But the city, often referred to by its boosters as the Gem City for its setting in the Baraboo Hills, drew on its other assets. These included the creation in the early 1900s of what would become Wisconsin's most popular state park at Devils Lake, just three miles south of the city and a tourist destination since the 1860s.

Though the city's development slowed some during the Great Depression, it was reinvigorated nearly overnight when the federal government decided that a major ammunition powder plant would be built on land just seven miles south of the city. Construction work in 1941 and 1942 employed all available workers, and when the plant became operational, Baraboo was nearly overwhelmed by the influx of thousands of people. The plant continued to dominate the city during the Korean Conflict and the Vietnam War.

Baraboo's history during the latter half of the twentieth century was marked by moderate growth. New schools and county government buildings were built, as were industrial parks and strip shopping malls. The city continues to draw on its heritage with the Circus World Museum at the original Ringling winter quarters, which is now one of the state's top historic sites.

Sources and Further Reading: Harry Ellsworth Cole, ed., *A Standard History of Sauk County, Wisconsin,* 2 vols. (1918); Michael J. Goc, *Many a Fine Harvest* (1990); Michael J. Goc, *Powder, People and Place* (2002); Western Historical Society, *The History of Sauk County, Wisconsin* (1880).

Paul Wolter
Sauk County Historical Society, Wisconsin

Canton, Ohio

The history of Canton, Ohio, epitomizes the transformation of the Midwest from a region of small mill towns in the nineteenth century to the industrial heart of America by the twentieth century, with small cities competing for the interests of regional and national markets. The city made a place for itself in the development of the urban Midwest by its contributions to Ohio's manufacturing history and its centrality to the evolution of professional football. Canton was also home to William McKinley, the twenty-fifth President of the United States.

Bezaleel Wells founded Canton as the first village in Stark County in 1806. In the northeastern part of Ohio, Stark County is noted for arable land, rolling hills, and deposits of shale, clay, limestone, and bituminous coal. From the early nineteenth century to 2000, Canton grew from a small mill town on the Nimishillen River to an industrial city of nearly eighty-one thousand inhabitants, yet it was almost always overshadowed by nearby Youngstown, Akron, and Cleveland.

Prior to the Civil War, Canton's agricultural economy supported a population that grew slowly. It numbered around four thousand in 1860. Sawmills, gristmills, tanneries, and saddle shops accompanied logging and wheat farming, while large Merino sheep plantations provided wool for mills in neighboring Massillon and Steubenville. The earliest settlers in frontier Canton were of German descent from Pennsylvania and English descent from Maryland and Virginia, with a few also from Connecticut and Philadelphia. Like other frontier areas, home manufacturing provided most of the finished goods these settlers required.

When the state laid out the Ohio Canal in 1826, however, it bypassed Canton, and in the subsequent decades the town floundered. In 1851, the Pittsburgh, Fort Wayne, and Chicago Railroad reached Canton, though, and the city began its transition from a frontier community. At the time of Canton's incorporation as a city in 1854, a small industrial base had been established with the production of agricultural equipment. Joshua Gibbs began manufacturing plows in the city in 1836, and in the 1850s the Cornelius Aultman Company began manufacturing reapers.

Canton's development as a small industrial city brought new immigrants and problems of adjustment. In the 1880s, the city's Board of Trade solicited investments to induce the Dueber-Hampden Watch Co. to bring its production to Canton. By the end of the nineteenth century, the city not only produced watches and watchcases, but bricks, stoneware, ceramics, iron and steel, soap, carriages, and engines, as well. Along with new industries came skilled watchmakers from Germany and Switzerland; and both Canton and Stark County recruited thousands more immigrants to fill the city's industrial labor needs. An unfortunate consequence of the new immigration, though, was anti-immigrant and anti-Catholic hostility among Canton's established Anglo-Saxon stock.

Industrial development continued into the 1950s, then began to decline. Between 1900 and 1910, when Canton's population increased from 30,667 to 50,217, the value of products manufactured increased from around $12 million to more than $28 million. By the 1960s, Canton workers produced a variety of metal, rubber, plastic, and paper goods; and in 2000, when African Americans represented 21 percent of Canton, manufacturing establishments in the metropolitan area were producing more than 1,500 different items annually.

After 1950, the city's population began to decline from its peak of 116, 912. Canton, however, has drawn on its heritage as the birthplace of the National Football League, founded in the summer of 1920 when the Canton Bulldogs joined other teams from the industrial Midwest. In 1963, the city opened the Professional Football Hall of Fame, which today attracts thousands of tourists to this NFL mecca.

Sources and Further Reading: Edward Thornton Heald, *History of Stark County* (1963); *The Encyclopedia of Ohio*, 2 Vols. (1999); U.S. Bureau of the Census, *Twelfth Census of the United States Taken in the Year 1900, Vol. VIII* (1902); U.S. Bureau of the Census, *Thirteenth Census of the United States Taken in the Year 1910* (1912); Carl Wittke, ed., *The History of the State of Ohio*, 6 Vols. (1941–1944).

Brian Butler
University of Texas–Pan-American

DeSmet, South Dakota

Resembling countless other small towns in the upper Midwest, DeSmet, South Dakota possesses one distinction setting it apart from the rest. Memorialized in five of Laura Ingalls Wilder's novels as the "Little Town on the Prairie," it came to represent, in many minds, the quintessential small town. Wilder's family arrived a year before the railroad did, in 1879, during the Great Dakota Boom, and she grew up with the town during her teen years as it evolved into a thriving community of several hundred people by the mid-1880s.

Like 80 percent of its counterparts in eastern Dakota Territory established during this period of rapid settlement and growth, DeSmet was a railroad town. Having been located in the center of Kingsbury County by the Chicago and Northwestern Railway, it was platted in March 1880 by a subsidiary, the Western Town Lot Company, which profited from selling lots to eager buyers. The shape of the town followed the regular pattern along that line of traffic, with its main street (Calumet Avenue) running perpendicular to the tracks. Three blocks of businesses extended south from the railroad crossing, and the usual array of stores, shops, hotels, livery stables, and eating places soon appeared. Two newspapers competed for many years. Much of the action in the community during the early days revolved around the two-story train depot. It burned down on Easter Sunday in 1905, and was replaced by a one-story structure, later converted into a historical museum after passenger service ended in the late 1960s.

Wilder's autobiographical children's novels loosely followed the course of events in early DeSmet as she remembered them, rendering her books a source of the social history of small-town life in the Midwest during the late nineteenth century. Church, family, and home operated as anchoring social institutions. Wilder described a variety of cultural activities from literary societies, singing schools, and church programs to horse races, home talent performances, and 4th of July celebrations. Constraints imposed by the format of her books and the limits of her memory (her first book appeared when she was sixty-five) led her to omit roller skating, baseball games, Chautauquas, the

The Ingalls Home, DeSmet, South Dakota. Photo © Laura Ingalls Wilder Memorial Society, DeSmet, S.D.

building of an opera house, and a variety of other activities from her stories.

Populated largely by immigrants from Scandinavia, Germany, and other northern European countries, as well as by a Yankee stream of migration that moved westward across the northern tier of states, DeSmet's residents voted heavily Republican. They joined Catholic, Episcopal, Lutheran, Methodist, Congregational, and other Protestant congregations, and they enrolled in a wide array of largely gender-based social organizations, such as the Grand Army of the Republic, the Women's Relief Corps, the Federated Women's Study Club, the Masonic Lodge and order of Eastern Star, the Knights of Columbus, and a variety of denominational ladies' aids. Begun in 1890, the Old Settlers' Day celebration, held every year on June 10, emerged as DeSmet's signature annual gala day.

Established, like the other towns along the railroad, to provide services to farmers in the surrounding countryside, DeSmet benefited from its central location in the county and its early choice as county seat. With a population of about a thousand—the same as two competing towns—until 1930, it began to outdistance them in later decades. DeSmet's relatively healthy economy has helped maintain the population at around twelve hundred in recent years. An industrial park helped attract several small businesses beginning in the 1960s, and twenty thousand tourists descend on the town annually, mainly to visit the Wilder sites.

Sources and Further Reading: John E. Miller, *Laura Ingalls Wilder's Little Town* (1994); Caryl Poppen, ed., *De Smet: Yesterday and Today* (1976).

John E. Miller
South Dakota State University

Grand Forks, North Dakota

The quest for furs brought the first white people to the confluence of the Red and Red Lake Rivers. In the mid-1740s, French fur traders designated the confluence as a rendezvous point called *Les Grandes Fourches,* which became a mail rider exchange station in the 1850s between Fort Abercrombie, 120 miles to the south, and Fort Garry, 150 miles to the north.

On June 15, 1870, the government established a post office at Les Grandes Fourches, anglicizing the name to Grand Forks. It served ten patrons. The tiny enclave grew rapidly in the 1870s as a river port. James J. Hill, a St. Paul capitalist, and Alexander Griggs, a Mississippi River steamboat captain, formed a company that, by the mid-1870s, had several steamboats carrying people and goods from the railroad eighty

miles south at Fargo to the growing population of Manitoba. Griggs chose Grand Forks because of its location. In 1875, he platted a nine-acre town site, and by 1880, 1,705 people had settled in the village.

The arrival of two railroads, the St. Paul, Minneapolis, and Manitoba (later called the Great Northern) in 1880 and the Northern Pacific in 1882, sparked two decades of economic and population growth. The area's rich farmlands filled with European immigrants, mostly Norwegians, turning Grand Forks into a bustling agricultural and commercial center. A local mill developed a breakfast food called Cream of Wheat.

By 1900, with a population of 7,382, Grand Forks had developed into a city with a full array of governmental and social services and, just west of town, the University of North Dakota, which had graduated its first class in 1889.

Because of unprecedented agricultural prosperity after 1900, the city enjoyed one of its most economically rewarding eras. Between 1900 and 1910, population jumped 63 percent to 12,478. Signs of well-being were everywhere: twenty miles of paved streets, a street-car transit system, four- and five-story banks and hotels, a booming wholesale district, new hospitals and clinics, organized sports teams, two dozen social and fraternal clubs, new city and federal buildings. By the end of World War I, 14,010 people lived in a modern city.

The two decades between the wars were the most difficult in the city's history. The agricultural recession of the 1920s and the Great Depression of the 1930s slowed and then stopped economic development. Population growth tapered off, and there was political instability. The mayor-council form of government gave way to commission government in 1920. During the mid-1920s, the Ku Klux Klan briefly controlled the commission and the school board, waging an anti-Catholic campaign. In 1938, the citizens voted a return to the mayor-council system.

World War II brought prosperity to the farm and Grand Forks. During the post-war years, population continued to grow: 26,836 in 1950, 43,765 in 1970, 49,563 in 1990. The creation in 1954 of the Grand Forks Air Force Base and the expansion of the University of North Dakota to over eleven thousand students contributed to the city's economic security and social diversity.

In 1997, the river that gave Grand Forks its birth rose to unprecedented heights to destroy much of the city and cause millions of dollars in property damage. After a series of ferocious blizzards and ice storms, the Red River broke through its dikes, driving over thirty thousand residents out of the city. A spectacular fire gutted several downtown blocks, including the offices of the Grand Forks *Herald*, which won a Pulitzer Prize for its coverage of the flood. In spite of predictions that the city would lose 20 percent of its population, the 2000 figure stood at 49,321, just slightly less than in 1990.

Sources and Further Reading: W. L. Dudley, *City of Grand Forks, Illustrated* (1897); Grand Forks *Herald, Grand Forks: Proud People, Proud Heritage* (1999); Jan Orvik and Dick Larson, *The Return of Lake Agassiz* (1998); D. Jerome Tweton, *Grand Forks: A Pictorial History* (1986).

D. Jerome Tweton
University of North Dakota

Hannibal, Missouri

Hannibal, Missouri was founded in 1819 as a steamboat stop along the Mississippi River and soon became a regional market and processing center.

A small group of merchants and lawyers ran the city government, boosted the city, and established themselves as a social elite. In 1859, Hannibal became the eastern terminus of the Hannibal and St. Joseph Railroad, transforming the town into a shipping depot for lumber from Minnesota and Wisconsin. Lumber mills and cement and shoe factories joined pork-packing plants, flour mills, and railroad shops to make Hannibal a regional industrial center. A new lumber aristocracy joined the booster elite of City Hall people, who ran the town in a proprietary manner into the 1960s. They built mansions atop the bluffs, as well as hotels, social clubs, and eventually a country club that became the venues of local elite society.

A large working class swelled Hannibal's population to over eighteen thousand by 1910. In the 1860s, 40 percent of Hannibal's workforce were African Americans, both free and slave, but by 1940, their numbers had gradually declined to about 10 percent of the town's population as many left and were replaced by foreign workers. Nevertheless, African Americans maintained their own churches, school, cultural venues, and sports clubs, even as they were segregated and excluded from town affairs until the 1950s and 1960s. The Great Depression, the decline of rail service, and the shift to highways—heralded by the completion of the Mark Twain Bridge in 1936—eroded Hannibal's economic vitality. Since the 1940s, a series of booster efforts organized by the Chamber of Commerce or various Industrial Councils have pursued a variety of strategies to keep or attract industries. Hannibal still struggles to maintain its industrial base and provide adequate infrastructure, educational, health, and lifestyle services for residents.

Unlike so many Midwest small towns, Hannibal's efforts have been helped by a viable tourist industry associated with its preeminent favorite son, Mark Twain. *Adventures of Tom Sawyer, Life on the Mississippi,* and *Adventures of Huckleberry Finn* made Hannibal synonymous with Mark Twain. Born Samuel Clemens in 1835, Mark Twain lived as a boy in Hannibal between 1839 and 1853. Twain afterwards visited Hannibal a number of times and maintained contacts with old friends. In his last visit in 1902, he visited his boyhood home, attended a dinner at the new Mark Twain Hotel, and blessed George Mahan's and other boosters' efforts to cultivate Twain's association with the town.

In 1911, Mahan bought Twain's boyhood home and later donated it to the city. In the 1920s, he formed the Mark Twain Memorial Association, which had a statue of Huck Finn and Tom Sawyer erected above Main Street and placed historical markers at the Twain sites. In 1935, a large centennial celebration took place, and two years later, the Twain boyhood home was opened as a restored historic site. In 1955, boosters launched Tom Sawyer Days. Merged with the town's traditional Fall Festival in 1956, the festivities occur during the week of July 4th.

Over the years the association purchased other structures around the Twain boyhood home. The area was declared a National Historic district in 1978 and listed on the National Register of Historic Places. In 1985, Hannibal celebrated the sesquicentennial of Mark Twain's birth. Meanwhile, restaurants, hotels, institutions, stores, shopping malls, and tourist attractions tirelessly commercialize the Twain angle. In the face of declining economic options, hope springs eternal that tourism will sustain "America's hometown."

Sources and Further Reading: J. Hurley Hagood and Roberta Hagood, *The Story of Hannibal* (1976); J. Hurley Hagood and Roberta Hagood, *Hannibal, Too* (1986); J. Hurley Hagood and Roberta Hagood, *Hannibal Yesterdays* (1992); Ron Powers, *White Town Drowsing* (1986); Writers' Program of the Work Projects Administration, *Missouri, A Guide to the "Show Me" State* (1941).

Timothy R. Mahoney
University of Nebraska–Lincoln

Keokuk, Iowa

A town whose prospects were tied to its location and the fortunes of river traffic, Keokuk originally flourished as the gateway to settlement in Iowa. However, competition from regional industrial centers, other river towns, and alternative transportation routes, as well as changing production markets, have trans-

Main Street, Iowa City, Iowa, 1940. Library of Congress, Prints and Photographs Division, LC-USF33-003503-M2.

formed Keokuk into an aging river town with a notable past.

Keokuk sits at the confluence of the Des Moines and Mississippi Rivers, where treacherous rapids stifled river travel. In 1829, the America Fur Company opened a trading post, naming the place after the Sauk chief Keokuk. The town was platted in 1837.

Steamboats made Keokuk a portage stop. Cargo and passengers were conveyed overland around the rapids to renew river travel on the Mississippi and Des Moines Rivers, while ferries handled travel across the Mississippi. The town's merchants traded with settlers and supplied the boats with fuel and food. Fur traders and river laborers gave Keokuk a reputation as a rough place. Additionally, the land around the town failed to fill with legal settlers until an 1850 court decision determined the ownership of the Half-Breed Tract of 119,000 acres, which surrounded Keokuk.

After the Iowa legislature chartered the town in 1847, officials were elected, a newspaper was established, and Keokuk shared the county seat for Lee County with Fort Madison. In 1850, the College of Physicians and Surgeons opened and became the medical department of the University of Iowa soon after. Public schooling began in Keokuk in 1851. In 1854, the Keokuk *Daily Whig* became the first daily newspaper in Iowa. It was renamed the Keokuk *Gate City* to emphasize the town's role as a gateway. By 1860, Keokuk had a population of over eight thousand, making it the third-largest town in Iowa.

Keokuk was a major military center during the Civil War. Most of the Iowa regiments and some from other states were organized at Keokuk, from where the men were shipped out on steamboats. Because of the medical college, the town also became a center for

the sick and wounded. Keokuk eventually had six hospitals. On July 17, 1862, Keokuk gained a designated national cemetery, the first west of the Mississippi River. It contains the graves of more than four thousand Union and Confederate dead.

Keokuk's role as a commercial nexus for traffic both north–south and east–west grew with the completion of the Keokuk and St. Paul Railroad in the late 1860s, a railroad bridge across the Mississippi in 1871, and a canal around the rapids along the Iowa shore in 1877. In 1913, construction was completed at Keokuk of the biggest dam on the upper Mississippi and the largest electricity generating plant in the world. A mile long, the dam aided navigation and flood control on the river. It also increased shipping facilities, government offices, and dry dock operations, creating many new jobs. A new bridge, completed in 1916, additionally benefited Keokuk.

By 1941, Keokuk's industry included rubber products, rolled oats, corn by-products, steel castings, iron alloys, fiber boxes, black powder (largest manufacturer in the nation), and carbide (second-largest manufacturer in the nation). Keokuk also had a commercial fishing industry and was a center for wholesale distributors. Later, animal and dairy food processing would join the local industries. In 1957, completion of a new river lock, the largest on the Mississippi, further benefited Keokuk.

By the 1970s, Keokuk had turned to history to promote tourism. Preservation of historic homes and buildings began, especially refurbishing and restoring Main Street, for which the town received both funding and awards. Keokuk began to celebrate its Civil War heritage with yearly programs and battle reenactments. In 2000, the town had a population of 11,427.

Despite a slight drop in population and decreased industrial production in recent years, Keokuk continues to work at being a vibrant river town.

Sources and Further Reading: Timothy R. Mahoney, *River Towns in the Great West* (1990); Federal Writers' Project of the Works Progress Administration, *The WPA Guide to 1930s Iowa* (1986); Writers' Program of the Works Progress Administration, *Lee County History* (1942).

Tom Colbert
Marshalltown Community College, Iowa

Marshall, Michigan

Marshall, Michigan, named for U.S. Chief Justice John Marshall, balances its identity as a quintessential small town with its role as a tourist destination, drawing thousands of annual visitors. Its historic commercial district contains a healthy mix of basic businesses that meet local needs and attractive shops to tempt tourists.

Like many midwestern towns, Marshall was founded by entrepreneurial Yankees who seemed seldom to sleep as they fashioned a thriving and stable community. Chief among them was Sidney Ketchum from central New York state. In 1830, he urged his brother George to join him and start a settlement on the land where Rice Creek meets the Kalamazoo River. They platted the town the following year. Mills, inns, shops, and homes soon appeared, first in log structures and then elegant frame or brick buildings, aided by Marshall's prime location on the Territorial Road. The National House Inn was built in 1835, the first brick building in the county and today the oldest operating hostelry in Michigan. Established as the county seat, the town built a fine brick courthouse in 1837, which it replaced in 1874 with a glorious Second Empire confection.

Marshall aspired to become the capital of Michigan when the new state (1837) sought a more central location than Detroit. So confident was Marshall that an area was set aside for the construction of a statehouse, and in 1839, one of the town boosters built a charming Greek Revival house for the governor's mansion. All was for naught; the legislature in 1847 gave the honor to Lansing, forty-five miles to the north. The governor's mansion survives in the part of town still called Capitol Hill.

Its place as a major stagecoach stop, followed by the coming of the railroad in 1844, kept Marshall's population growing, especially with the construction of the roundhouse and railroad machine shops that brought in hundreds of workers. Numerous water-powered industries flourished, and Marshall became a city in 1859. But the loss of the Michigan Central Railroad repair shops in 1874 was a staggering blow. Luckily, Marshall had sufficient resources to survive, including its location at the junction of two roads that in the 1920s became U.S. 27 and U.S. 12.

Largely through the single-minded efforts of Harold C. Brooks (1885–1978), many of Marshall's nineteenth-century buildings were saved well before the concept of historic preservation caught on nationally. As early as the late 1920s, Mayor Brooks promoted the cause of adaptive reuse by hiring Kalamazoo architect Howard F. Young to convert an 1850s stone livery stable on what had once been the courthouse square into Marshall's city hall. Completed in 1930, the building displays the influences of the contemporary restoration of Colonial Williamsburg. In the early 1950s, Brooks purchased what is probably Marshall's most famous attraction, the unusual Honolulu House built in 1860 for Judge Abner Pratt, who had been consul to the Sandwich (Hawaiian) Islands. Unfortunately, the 1874 courthouse was deemed obsolete and demolished in 1953, replaced with the nondescript building that, with additions, houses county offices to the present day.

In 1991, over 850 buildings were designated a National Historic Landmark District. Here, clearly visible, are the commercial and practical values, as well as the aesthetic values, of historic preservation. Year round, Marshall offers events and activities centered on its wealth of historic buildings to lure visitors upon whom the town's economy depends.

Sources and Further Reading: Richard Carver, *A History of Marshall* (1993); Kathryn Bishop Eckert, *Buildings of Michigan* (1993); Mabel Cooper Skjelver, *Nineteenth Century Homes of Marshall, Michigan* (1971).

Glory-June Greiff
Indianapolis, Indiana

Red Cloud, Nebraska

Red Cloud, Nebraska, became a quintessential midwestern hometown when Pulitzer Prize–winning author Willa Cather used it as a prototype in seven of her twelve novels and various short stories. Whether described as the windswept Hanover in *O Pioneers!* or the gray town of Sweet Water in *A Lost Lady*, it was unmistakably Red Cloud. Cather's reading audience, whatever their respective hometowns, believed the town representative of a Midwest where time moved more slowly, provincial values prevailed, and young people craved escape from small-town constraints.

Red Cloud founders had big dreams for the community. Silas Garber, a Civil War veteran looking for land to homestead, settled in the area in 1870 and helped plot the town in 1872. He had visions of families settling the Republican River valley, and hoped Nebraskans would spread across the country. Garber also made certain Red Cloud became the county seat of Webster County. It grew relatively quickly while the Burlington Railroad promised great agricultural opportunities and plentiful land. Webster County grew from sixteen people in 1870 to 7,104 in 1880, and boasted a thriving cheese factory, a busy creamery, and many successful horse and mule breeders. Garber and other boosters claimed Red Cloud would be the main city between Omaha and Denver, and rival any other midwestern community.

The dreams of the boosters, however, were already behind Red Cloud by the 1890s. The Red Cloud *Chief,* the town paper, reported concerns about a failing economy and falling real estate prices. Red Cloud's economy depended on agriculture, and the decline of populism combined with a national recession delivered severe economic blows. As grain and livestock prices plummeted, Red Cloud farmers were forced off their land and into bankruptcy. Willa Cather's family, which had moved to Red Cloud in 1884, left in 1890, returning only for short stays. Because Cather experienced the end of the pioneer era and the beginning of difficult times for the community, her books illustrate the challenges faced by many towns once the boom days of the railroad were over.

Red Cloud has changed very little since the turn of the twentieth century. Struggling family farms, a cattle feed lot, and a small Main Street are the main sources of money for the town. One woman, Mildred Bennett, however, did change Red Cloud in the 1950s. Bennett grew up in Webster County and moved to Red Cloud when her husband became the town's only doctor. She had fallen in love with the works of Cather and wanted to make the town look exactly as it had during the years Willa Cather lived there. Bennett reclaimed and refurbished the Cather childhood home, the bank that Silas Garber had built, and many other structures made famous in Cather's novels. Although Bennett was more a Cather booster than a Red Cloud booster, the town benefited from her efforts.

Today, the Main Street hosts the office of the Willa Cather Pioneer Memorial, an organization dedicated to preserving Cather's Red Cloud, a museum, and the Red Cloud Opera House. Closed for several decades, the recently restored Opera House reopened in May of 2003, and completes the picture of Cather's Main Street.

Sources and Further Reading: Mildred R. Bennett, *The World of Willa Cather* (1961); Willa Cather, *A Lost Lady* (1923); Willa Cather, *O Pioneers!* (1913); James Woodress, *Willa Cather: A Literary Life* (1989).

Ann Tschetter
University of Nebraska–Lincoln

Springfield, Illinois

American poet Vachel Lindsay (1879–1931), Springfield's second-most-famous son, thought his hometown a mystical place. On the surface, this community, with its bland, suburban look of a prosperous, middle-sized everytown, repudiates Lindsay's belief. Springfield, like Albany to New York City and Jacksonville to Miami, would be just another second city and government seat but for one thing: From Milwaukee to Tokyo, it is widely recognized as Abraham Lincoln's home. Tourism centered on Lincoln sites has paid out as steadily as a government bond. Only Arlington National Cemetery has more visitors than Springfield's Oak Ridge Cemetery, where Lincoln's body rests. Despite fervent hopes dashed only a few generations ago to attain the status of a big city, Springfield falls into the comfortable category of middle-size city in everything from its population to the scale of its urban planning and civic vision.

Springfield has the good fortune to be set in the Sangamon River Valley in the midst of some of the richest farmland in the world. Springfield's first settlers were hunters who made temporary camps during the warm season. They were soon followed by an influx of permanent residents, many of whom were boosters and developers. A particularly committed group arrived in the early 1820s—men and women driven by a pragmatic, fundamental belief in material progress and the idea of building a future metropolis. A cluster of log cabins was designated the temporary seat of government for Sangamon County in April of 1821. Townspeople through smooth trickery secured the permanent county seat in 1825. Polished political maneuvering wrested the state capital for Springfield in 1837. When the bubble of hoped-for river town prosperity burst in the 1830s, town leaders backed the newest technology—railroads.

By the 1850s, the town had become the major regional center for the sale and processing of agricultural commodities raised in the surrounding hinterland as well as an important retail and manufacturing place. After the Civil War, the discovery of rich veins of coal fueled new industries that produced watches, steel rails, agricultural implements, and dozens of other items. Mining became a leading industry, and Sangamon County ranks high on pre-1920 industrial census schedules for the amount of coal extracted. Rail lines created a transportation hub in the shadows of St. Louis and Chicago.

The triumvirate of coal, corn, and cattle brought Springfield riches beyond dreaming. But great private wealth contrasted with municipal penury. In the late nineteenth and early twentieth centuries, town civic scandals broke as regularly as new corn shoots, mostly involving aldermen in the public till. A 1908 race riot scandalized the nation, and a regional reputation for gambling, vice, and prostitution drew paying visitors and evangelists, including Billy Sunday. "Politically," said the *Saturday Evening Post* in the 1940s, "The capital is as murky with intrigue as a medieval border state . . . gambling and prostitution blossom like the rose in Springfield . . . machine politics and absence of a vigorous press don't help." Reforms beginning in the early 1950s led to suppression of the most flagrant vice over the next generation.

The shift of the retail trade from the downtown to the outskirts, along with the loss of much of the manufacturing base in the 1960s and 1970s, changed Springfield dramatically. State government, long a presence in the economy, became a bigger player, and "clean" industries such as health care and insurance became prominent employers.

Statistics portray a relentless theme of the twentieth century—decentralization. A 1900 population of 34,000 lived in about five square miles. By 1950, Springfield's 81,000 people occupied over ten square miles, but Springfield's sixty square miles in 2000 had only 111,000 people. Urban sprawl and the growth of national chain restaurants and retail establishments have come to obscure, if not obliterate, what a writer once called Springfield's "abundance of eccentricity."

Sources and Further Reading: Paul M. Angle, *"Here I Have Lived": A History of Lincoln's Springfield, 1821–1865* (1935); Bruce Alexander Campbell, *200 Years: An Illustrated Bicentennial History Of Sangamon County* (1976); James Krohe, Jr., ed., *A Springfield Reader* (1976); Edward J. Russo, *Prairie of Promise* (1983).

Edward J. Russo and Curtis Mann
Springfield, Illinois

Terre Haute, Indiana

French for "high land," Terre Haute was founded on a bluff overlooking the Wabash River in southwestern Indiana in 1816. Before then, the Wea and other Native American groups as well as French men hunted and farmed in the area and are credited with originally clearing the plateau. A permanent settlement was established with the construction of the U.S. Fort Harrison in 1811. Five years later, land speculator Joseph Kitchell organized the Terre Haute Land Company and sold plots to American settlers south of the fort.

Terre Haute's position on the Wabash helped it grow into a hub of flatboat and barge traffic carrying corn, hogs, and other agricultural wares to market in New Orleans. Grist mills and slaughterhouses, as well as other manufacturing companies, harnessed river power. In 1818, state surveyors carved Vigo County from Sullivan County and made Terre Haute the county seat. Transportation remained essential. The National Road reached the city in 1835, followed in 1849 by the Wabash and Erie Canal. The arrival of the Terre Haute and Richmond Railroad in 1852, followed shortly by the Terre Haute and Indianapolis Railroad, interfered with canal profits. Ironically, after the Civil War, the same rails that brought commerce into Terre Haute took it out, as southern pork sales declined and most hog processing and other agricultural industries shifted west to markets in Chicago and Kansas City.

Citizens such as Chauncey Rose embraced Terre Haute and its investments to reinvent the community as an education center following the Civil War. Rose helped found Rose Polytechnic Institute in 1874 (now the Rose-Hulman Institute of Technology), four years after the establishment of the Indiana State Normal School (later Indiana State University). Education and industry dominated Terre Haute into the twentieth century, as its schools expanded and new industries, such as compact disc manufacturing, arrived.

Deeply rooted in its industrial past and present, Terre Haute has always been at the cutting edge of organized labor and workers' rights. It claimed twenty-seven unions in 1900 in its many iron works, breweries, coal mines, and railroads. The city hosted a meeting of multiple unions in 1881 that led to the creation of the American Federation of Labor in 1886, an organization still visible today.

Most notable among those active in Terre Haute's labor community was Eugene Debs, born there in 1855. In 1894, Debs became a Socialist. He wanted to give more direct power to American workers. Debs is remembered most as the American Socialist Party's presidential candidate in virtually all elections from 1900 to 1920. During the 1920 presidential election, Debs received around 913,000 votes even though he was incarcerated in an Atlanta penitentiary.

Terre Haute has nurtured many authors and artists. Paul Dresser published his 1899 novel *On the Banks of the Wabash Far Away*, and poet Max Erhmann wrote "Desiderata" around 1927.

Dogged occasionally by political corruption and industrial excesses, Terre Haute at the beginning of the twenty-first century was a progressive city with an active mayor, Judy Anderson.

Sources and Further Reading: Logan Esarey, *A History of Indiana from 1850 to Present* (1918); Robert E. Taylor, Jr., et al., *Indiana: A New Historical Guide* (1989); Marguerite Young, *Harp Song for a Radical* (1999).

Eugene R. H. Tesdahl
Boulder, Colorado

Winona, Minnesota

When the first European Americans settled on what the indigenous Dakota called Wapashaw's Prairie, they named their settlement Winona, the name given to the first-born daughters of Dakota families. They staked their first claims in October of 1851, just three months after the Dakota Indians signed the treaty ceding twenty million acres of their land. Although the Mdewakanton Dakota continued to hunt and fish along this part of the Upper Mississippi for several years, the new arrivals were quick to make their own mark on the landscape. Very soon, the only remaining trace of indigenous populations was the name of the growing village. By 1867, the growth of lumber mills in Winona as well as wheat fields in the surrounding valleys resulted in a population of about sixty-five hundred.

Like small towns across the Midwest, Winona held great promise for economic development, but a long century of stagnation followed an initial period of rapid growth. In 1873, Winona was the fourth-largest wheat market in the country. Wheat farming soon moved west, however, and the last sawmill closed in 1909. Manufacturing and railroad maintenance provided new jobs, but Winona was on its way to becoming another midwestern small town: The population of around twenty thousand recorded in the 1900 census would remain mostly unchanged for the next century. Unlike many towns, Winona retains a solid manufacturing sector; instead of garments, work gloves, and patent medicines, Winona factories are now producing auto parts, canoes, violin bows, and various industrial products. Winona also continues to build on its nineteenth-century cultural legacy.

Small-town life in turn-of-the-century Winona was quite cosmopolitan. The Winona Normal School, established in 1858, was joined by two more institutions of higher education, St. Mary's College for men and, later, the College of St. Theresa for women. The diverse population of immigrants, who provided the labor for this regional commercial and manufacturing center, published newspapers in German and Polish, and built an Irish church, a Bohemian church, and several Polish churches (all Roman Catholic), in addition to a German Presbyterian church and numerous Scandinavian Lutheran ones. In the first decades of the twentieth century, Winona was home to the Huntley Vaudeville Company, a regional touring vaudeville company that also pioneered in the film industry. So dedicated were Ben and Myrtle Huntley to their Winona home that when their partner and promoter Carl Laemmle, founder of Universal Studios, invited them to join him in Hollywood, they turned him down.

In the early years of the twenty-first century, this cultural heritage remains central to Winona's identity and distinguishes it from many other small towns and river towns across the Midwest. Winona remains known to musicians across the country as the home of Hal Leonard, Inc., the largest print music publisher in the world. Winona State University and St. Mary's University continue to bring to Winona students and staff from around the United States and the world, and to offer the community arts and entertainment opportunities often not available in other small towns. Since the 1970s, the landscape of fertile and scenic valleys has also attracted a substantial population of individuals and families returning to the land. Their legacy includes a food cooperative, several land cooperatives, and numerous artists' studios.

Finally, like many small towns in the Midwest, Winona is turning to tourism for economic development. Winona was a stop on the Grand Excursion 2004, marking the 150th anniversary of a steamboat trip up the Mississippi made by President Millard Fillmore and others eager to develop the resources of the newly acquired lands.

Sources and Further Reading: A. Bailey, *Minnesota Railroad and River Guide* (1867); LaFayette H. Bunnell, *Winona and Its Environs on the Mississippi in Ancient Days and Modern Days* (1897); Willima Crozier, "A Social History of Winona, Minnesota, 1880–1905," Ph.D. diss., University of Nebraska (1975); Herbert T. Hoover and Carol Goss Hoover, *Sioux Country* (2000); Fred. W. Kohlmeyer, *Timber Roots: The Laird, Norton Story, 1855–1905* (1972).

Colette A. Hyman
Winona State University, Minnesota

Representative National Public Figures

William Jennings Bryan (1860–1925)

Born in Salem, Illinois, on March 19, 1860, William Jennings Bryan attended Whipple Academy and Illinois College in Jacksonville, Illinois, and received a law degree from the Union College of Law in Chicago in 1883. He married Mary Baird in 1884, practiced law in Jacksonville until 1887, and then moved to Lincoln, Nebraska, the center of a county that nearly tripled in population between 1880 and 1890.

Although Lincoln was a Republican town, agricultural depression and domination of local politics by railroad interests gave Bryan an opportunity. Promising to solve local problems by securing federal regulation of railroads and an inflationary monetary policy to raise farm incomes, he won election to Congress in 1890 as a Democrat, serving until 1894, when he resigned to run unsuccessfully for the Senate. In 1896, southern and western Democrats rebelled against their leaders and nominated Bryan for the presidency after his electrifying Cross of Gold speech at the party's national convention.

Defeated by William McKinley, Bryan promised to renew the struggle in 1900, but in 1898, the nation fought a brief war with Spain. Bryan served as colonel of the Third Nebraska Regiment of the National Guard, which spent the war in Florida. At the end of the war, he resigned his commission to oppose the annexation of the Philippine Islands. In 1900, he was nominated for a second time on a platform that promised to curb the excesses of big business and end imperialism, but with the country victorious in war and prosperous again at home, he was defeated by a larger margin than in 1896.

In 1901, Bryan founded a weekly newspaper, the *Commoner*. It reflected Bryan's belief that federal authority could be invoked to support small-town values. For a time, he stepped back from active politics, spending much of 1905 and 1906 traveling around the world. Defeated in a third campaign for the presidency against William Howard Taft in 1908, he returned to his small-town roots and focused on moral issues, particularly prohibition and religious fundamentalism.

In 1912, Bryan supported Woodrow Wilson for the presidency. The victorious Wilson appointed him Secretary of State, primarily to secure his influence in support of his domestic program. Bryan was happy to endorse Wilson's program of controlling big business, lowering the tariff, and reforming the banking system, and he welcomed an opportunity to promote his own plan to negotiate treaties requiring the investigation of all international disputes prior to war. Before he resigned in June 1915 in a disagreement with Wilson over American policy on submarine attacks, Bryan completed thirty of his "cooling off" treaties.

Bryan worked hard to prevent American entry into World War I. When he failed, he again loyally volunteered his services. He was too old for the army, but Wilson welcomed his help in strengthening support for the war in the West and South, as well as his support of American membership in the League of Nations. Bryan also worked vigorously during the war for the adoption of Constitutional amendments for prohibition and woman's suffrage.

In 1921, Bryan moved from Nebraska to Florida and became an active lay preacher. He was much in demand both as a Bible teacher and as an outspoken opponent of the teaching of the Darwinian theory of evolution. In July 1925, he went to Dayton, Tennessee, where he assisted the prosecution and testified about his belief in the literal truth of the Bible at the trial of John T. Scopes, who was being prosecuted for teaching evolution in the public schools. Shortly after Scopes was convicted, Bryan died on July 26, 1925.

Sources and Further Reading: LeRoy Ashby, *William Jennings Bryan: Champion of Democracy* (1987); William Jennings Bryan, completed by Mary Baird Bryan, *The Memoirs of William Jennings Bryan* (1925); Robert W. Cherny, *A Righteous Cause* (1985); Paolo E. Coletta, *William Jennings Bryan*, 3 vols. (1964–1969); Lawrence W. Levine, *Defender of the Faith: William Jennings Bryan* (1965).

The orator William Jennings Bryan, Chicago, 1918. Chicago Historical Society, *Chicago Daily News*, DN-0070449.

Kendrick Clements
University of South Carolina–Columbia

Johnny Carson (1925–2005)

John William Carson, born in Corning, Iowa, on October 23, 1925, grew up in several small towns in southwestern Iowa until age eight, when his family moved to Norfolk, Nebraska. Norfolk's ten thousand people made it the major urban center in the northeastern part of the state. Crowned the King of the Night because of his success as a television talk-show host in New York and Los Angeles from 1962 to 1992, the glib master of conversation and repartee never shucked his small-town aura and enjoyed making frequent reference to his origins on the plains of Nebraska. In a sense, viewers who tuned in to his late-night confabs with stars, celebrities, and newsmakers were reliving old-time conversations around the woodstove in small-town stores.

As a student growing up in a comfortable middle-class home during the Great Depression (his father, Homer "Kit" Carson, was local manager of a light and power company), the young man escaped many of the hardships endured by a good portion of his classmates. Never an outstanding athlete or enthusiastic student, Carson developed a passion for magic and performing before audiences after he sent for a mail order magic kit at the age of twelve. Following graduation from Norfolk High School in 1943 and three years of service in the United States Navy, he expanded his interests to include radio broadcasting while studying at the University of Nebraska. Upon completing his degree, Carson landed a job at WOW in Omaha, the most important radio station in Nebraska, which was branching into television. He soon got his own program.

Ambitious and determined, Carson set his eyes on Los Angeles. In 1951, a childhood friend helped him obtain an announcing job at KNXT-TV. Carson was part of a large migration of midwesterners to California after World War II. His big break came when he was selected to host "Who Do You Trust?," a daytime game show in New York that he stayed with from 1957 to 1962. His success led NBC to choose him to replace Jack Paar on "The Tonight Show." During the next three decades, the personable, unflappable stand-up comic, who intuitively understood mid-America's funny bone, set the standard for late-night talk show hosts.

At first an hour and forty-five minutes long, "The Tonight Show" shrank to ninety minutes in 1967, then to one hour in 1980. Meanwhile, Carson's vacation time continually expanded, while his salary climbed from $100,000 in 1962 to $25 million by 1990. Playing the role of a folksy, but savvy, raconteur and interviewer, Carson never upstaged his guests and always maintained tight control over his program. By the 1980s, he had accumulated perhaps as much personal power as any television performer ever had and was referred to in Hollywood as Mr. Television.

Even with all of his power and the cool confidence he projected on screen, Carson never appeared to be comfortable around people. Still, his four wives and opulent life in an $8.9 million house in Malibu did not erode his persona as a down-home, plainspoken refugee from the Heartland. He periodically returned to Norfolk and made several generous contributions to the community, including $650,000 for a new wing of the local hospital, named the Carson Regional Radiation Center in honor of his parents, $600,000 to help pay for a Johnny Carson Theatre in the new high school building, and $100,000 for a local historical society building.

Carson remained reclusive after his retirement in 1992. He played tennis and poker with friends but he rarely talked to the media or made public appearances. Whether shy or diffident, he seemed to many observers to be a product of his midwestern roots. And he agreed: "A guy from the Midwest—that's who I was, that's who I am."

Sources and Further Reading: Paul Corkery, *Carson: The Unauthorized Biography* (1987); Laurence Leamer, *King of the Night* (1989); Craig Tennis, *Johnny Tonight!* (1980).

John E. Miller
South Dakota State University

Henry Ford (1863–1947)

Born in 1863 near present-day Dearborn, Michigan, Henry Ford, a farmer's son and self-taught mechanic and engineer, attended school for only eight years. For him life began in 1903 when, after two false starts as an auto producer, he cofounded the Ford Motor Company. By 1906, he owned a majority of the company's stock and, by 1919, all of it. In 1908, he launched the most influential car ever built, the Model T and, in 1912–1913, introduced mass production to the auto industry. In 1914, Ford more than doubled the pay of most of his employees and, in the 1920s, sold the Model T for around $300. Meanwhile, he had become an international celebrity and American folk hero.

Ford's success was based on several outstanding qualities: native intelligence and common sense, even though the latter occasionally failed him, an intuitive mind that leaped beyond the present, and an engineering talent that combined creativity and practicality.

Ford also had, or made, his share of good luck. His entry into automaking and the introduction of the

Model T were perfectly timed. Moreover, he was teamed with a technical aide, C. Harold Wills, and a business manager, James Couzens, who contributed as much as he did to the Ford Company's early success. Ford also was lucky in love, marrying neighbor Clara Bryant, who understood and complemented him. Three years younger than her husband, Clara was convinced from the time of their marriage in 1888 that Henry would accomplish something notable. Ford called her The Believer.

Henry Ford was an enigmatic paradox. An idealistic innovator in some respects, he was a cynical reactionary in others. He had a selfish, mean, even cruel streak, yet often was generous, kindly, and compassionate. He was ignorant, narrow-minded, and stubborn, yet at times displayed remarkable insight, vision, open-mindedness, and flexibility. He built the world's biggest factory, but found delight in operating small hydroplants. He was sympathetic toward African Americans but anti-Semitic.

Ford idealized the midwestern small town even as his support for high-volume production, low prices, and universal consumption made him a key figure in a far-reaching socioeconomic revolution that undermined the nineteenth-century small town. "History," he proclaimed, "is more or less bunk," as the Chicago *Daily News* reported on May 25, 1916; yet he created a great depository of Americana, the Henry Ford Museum and Greenfield Village. Originally intended to showcase how life was lived in the past, the village became a tribute both to the ingenuity of Ford and others like him and to the individual creativity and can-do pragmatism supposedly nurtured in small towns before the emergence of large-scale, impersonal corporations.

Between 1908 and 1930, the Ford Company sold more than 40 percent of the world's vehicles. In addition to making cars, trucks, and tractors, the firm developed the world's first vertically integrated, yet highly diversified industrial empire. Among its many pursuits were airplane production, coal and iron ore mining, and the operation of a railroad, steel mills, rubber plantations, and lake and ocean fleets.

Ford was much in the public eye because of his crusading and outspokenness. When he was not attacking tobacco manufacturers, distillers, New Dealers, Wall Streeters, or Jews, he was criticizing unionists, accountants, stockholders, and reporters. If not battling auto monopolists or charting a "peace ship," he was saving birds, hiring ex-convicts and the handicapped, or promoting motor camping, old-fashioned music, and soybean consumption.

Ford retired in 1945 and died of a cerebral hemorrhage on April 7, 1947. His wife succumbed to a heart ailment on September 29, 1950. They are buried in Detroit's tiny Ford Cemetery. The irony of Ford's life lay in the juxtaposition of his corporate career with his public image as the epitome of the independent small-town boy who made good.

Sources and Further Reading: Peter Collier and David Horowitz, *The Fords* (1987); Robert Lacey, *Ford: The Men and the Machine* (1986); David L. Lewis, *The Public Image of Henry Ford* (1976); Allan Nevins, *Ford: The Times, the Man, the Company* (1954); Allan Nevins and Frank Ernest Hill, *Ford: Expansion and Challenge, 1915–1933* (1957); Allan Nevins and Frank Ernest Hill, *Ford: Decline and Rebirth, 1933–1962* (1963).

David L. Lewis
University of Michigan

Hamlin Garland (1860–1940)

In his short stories, novels, and autobiographies, Hamlin Garland distilled and enhanced a specific constellation of American images associated with small towns. Initially, he rarefied the healthy, independent, pioneer farmer as the progenitor of Whitmanesque democracy. Subsequently, the attributes of Garland's pioneer farmers became distinctive features ascribed to midwesterners in general, and their characteristics became synonymous with midwestern society. Garland's farmers were white Protestant Americans. With the Midwest as their cultural bastion, Garland's farmers embodied the morals and values Garland imagined as American traits.

The son of Richard Garland, a Civil War veteran, and Isabelle McClintock, he was born in 1860 on a Wisconsin farm. Becoming a worldly author who moved among the literary giants of his time, Garland never wandered far emotionally from the border farms of his youth. His comfortable memories of his extended frontier family and the tiny pioneer enclaves in which they lived, as well as some painful memories of hardship, triggered his long literary career. His regional fiction and autobiographies primarily depicted a romanticized rural pioneer community. In this loose network of farms, Garland created a heroic midwestern culture through his artful manipulation of documentary impressionism. His farmers were strong, righteous, self-sufficient, moral, and imbued with an innate sense of justice, which was continuously refreshed by the exhilarating experience of pioneer farming. Adopting a form of literary realism harvested from such novelists as William Dean Howells, Garland specialized in short stories, which he collected in *Main-Travelled Roads* (1891) and *Prairie Folks* (1893).

Garland believed that the Midwest's unique culture could be traced from the English peasant villages through New England to the Upper Mississippi Valley. Midwestern culture emerged when the spirit of Anglo-Saxon farmers confronted the wilderness and embraced the primitive. This experience could only be maintained within an agrarian community poised between the pristine wilderness and the aristocratic cultural, political, and economic corruption of civilization. Unfortunately, in the last decades of the nineteenth century, the Midwest suffered economic devastation. Enamored of Henry George's *Progress and Poverty* (1879), which espoused the evils of land monopoly, Garland began to campaign for reform to protect his brethren from immigrants, easterners, and monopoly capitalists. In support of the Populist political insurgency, he published three reform novels, *Jason Edwards* (1892), *A Member of the Third House* (1892), and *A Spoil of Office* (1892).

Garland's nostalgia and his compulsion to sanctify his culture even as it ceased to exist dominate his first autobiography, *Boy Life on the Prairie* (1899). After a period of writing romance and adventure novels, Garland returned to the autobiographical form. He retreated into his memories, and wrote a rich series of autobiographies that detailed the growth of the Midwest: *A Son of the Middle Border* (1917) and soon after *A Daughter of the Middle Border* (1921), for which he won the Pulitzer Prize in 1922.

Often praised for his realism, Garland was more emotionally subjective than objective in his prose. He maintained a narrow, romantically tinged view of a bucolic midwestern world and forged images of farmers as tough, infinitely strong, and resourceful individuals who were obstinate, proud, and self-reliant. Garland's passionate prose remains persuasive, and his agrarian portraits have become an indelible part of the American imagination.

Sources and Further Reading: Joseph B. McCullough, *Hamlin Garland* (1978); Donald Pizer, *Hamlin Garland's Early Work and Career* (1960).

Michael Basinski
University at Buffalo,
The State University of New York

Rutherford Birchard Hayes (1822–1893)

Rutherford Birchard Hayes, America's nineteenth President, ended his life as he began it, in a small Ohio town. Elevated to the presidency after the disputed election of 1876, Hayes confronted bitter enemies from both parties who questioned his administration's legitimacy. Nevertheless, the Hayes presidency was marked by steady leadership and sound judgment.

Pledged to serve only a single term, Hayes and his wife Lucy Webb Hayes retired to their Spiegel Grove estate in Fremont, Ohio, in 1881. In retirement, Hayes supported local charities, prison reform, African American education, the Grand Army of the Republic, and his favorite project, The Ohio State University. A model ex-president, Hayes wanted to ensure that the children of small towns would have the same opportunities that he had enjoyed.

Hayes was born to Sophia Birchard Hayes and the late Rutherford Hayes, Jr., on October 4, 1822, in Delaware, Ohio. At the time of his birth, Delaware, according to the national census, boasted a population of approximately four hundred. As an overprotected boy, Hayes enjoyed the friendship of his older sister, Fanny, and treasured such staples of small-town life as maple candy, canoeing on the nearby Olentangy River, and winter sleigh rides. Hayes graduated from Kenyon College in Gambier, Ohio, in 1842, and proceeded to study law at Harvard, where he celebrated his Ohio origins. Despite his Yankee heritage, the young Hayes made a coat of arms with the simple description "R. B. H., Buckeye."

In 1845, Hayes began practicing law in Lower Sandusky (now Fremont), Ohio. Although initially intrigued by life in Lower Sandusky, where his favorite uncle Sardis Birchard lived, Hayes's ambition exceeded the opportunities available to him in the small river town. In 1850, he moved to Cincinnati, where he embarked upon a successful career as a lawyer. When the Civil War began, Hayes helped organize a regiment which became the 23rd Volunteers of Ohio. Wounded in action five different times, Hayes was originally commissioned as a major, but was brevetted a major general.

Hayes's military record and general character led to his election as a Republican Congressman from Cincinnati in 1864. In the 39th and 40th Congresses, the instinctively conservative Hayes found himself siding frequently with the radical wing of the party against President Andrew Johnson, particularly on issues of civil rights.

Hayes went on to become the first governor in Ohio to be elected to three different terms. His strong showing in the 1875 gubernatorial campaign in the key battleground of Ohio augured well for his future. A perfect compromise candidate, Hayes received the Republican nomination for President the following year, when the factions of the party could not agree on other frontrunners. Hayes lost the popular vote but won the presidency when a partisan electoral commission awarded him the disputed electoral votes of Florida, Louisiana, and South Carolina. His margin in the Electoral College was 185 to 184.

Hayes's presidency was tarnished by the circumstances of his election. Nevertheless, his administration provided stability. Hayes advocated civil service reform and a return to the gold standard, and sought to transcend narrow partisan lines. His most memorable phrase came from his letter accepting the Republican nomination: "He serves his party best who serves his country best."

Although his travels took him to many of America's biggest cities, he always enjoyed returning to the simpler pleasures of life at Spiegel Grove and the partnership of his equally talented wife, Lucy Webb Hayes.

Sources and Further Reading: Harry Barnard, *Rutherford B. Hayes and His America* (1954); Ari Hoogenboom, *The Presidency of Rutherford B. Hayes* (1988); Ari Hoogenboom, *Rutherford B. Hayes: Warrior and President* (1995); Charles Richard Williams, ed., *The Diary and Letters of Rutherford B. Hayes,* 5 vols. (1922–1926); C. Vann Woodward, *Reunion and Reaction* (1991).

Edward O. Frantz
University of Indianapolis, Indiana

Sinclair Lewis (1885–1951)

Sinclair Lewis was born on February 7, 1885, in Sauk Centre, Minnesota. His physician father, a stern and practical man, disapproved of his son's dreamy tendencies. The youth's neighbors and schoolmates thought him an odd duck because of his bookishness and idiosyncratic habits. Throughout his life, Lewis considered himself an outsider, a trait that made it difficult for him to communicate and get along with others, but which did much to hone his literary sensibilities. His undergraduate career at Yale, where he had few friends and acquired the nickname of God Forbid, further confirmed his sense of being outside the mainstream. Before becoming a full-time novelist, he was a journalist in Waterloo, Iowa, New York City, San Francisco, and Washington, D.C. In his stories of the medical profession, science, religion, social work, native fascism, marriage, and racial discrimination, among other subjects, Lewis targeted smugness, conformity, provincialism, snobbery, hypocrisy, and prejudice for his barbed appraisals.

The publication of *Main Street* in October of 1920 changed forever the way people thought about their small towns. Although Lewis averred in the introduction that its Main Street was "the continuation of Main Streets everywhere," the fictional Gopher Prairie, Minnesota, clearly was based heavily upon Lewis's memories of growing up in Sauk Centre, a town he removed himself from as quickly as he could. Part of the literary "revolt from the village," the controversial best-selling novel not only of 1921 but of

Small-town icons: Sinclair Lewis, William Lindsay White, Rev. William Stidger, and William Allen White. Courtesy David Walker and Barbara White Walker, from the William Allen White Library, Emporia State University.

the entire period from 1900 to 1925 was passed over by the Pulitzer Prize committee, but along with Lewis's other four novels of the 1920s, it led to his selection in 1930 as the first American to receive the Nobel Prize for Literature.

While the reading public devoured Lewis's constant stream of works, critics and literary historians strongly disagreed about his ultimate achievement. Some dismissed him as a hack who possessed a lively talent for mimicry and reportage, but who was woefully inadequate as a stylist and developer of character. Nobody could deny his impact on American culture, however, especially during the decade and a half after *Main Street*, as one success after another emerged from his typewriter: *Babbitt* (1922), *Arrowsmith* (1925), *Elmer Gantry* (1927), *Dodsworth* (1929), *Ann Vickers* (1933), and *It Can't Happen Here* (1935). Altogether, his twenty-two novels comprised a wide-ranging and generally critical portrait of American life during the first half of the twentieth century.

The man who harbored acerbic—but nevertheless ambivalent—views about American society and culture never discovered a place he could finally call home. After marrying Grace Livingston Hegger (who bore him a son, Wells) in 1914, Lewis divided his time among Long Island, Nantucket, Chicago, Carmel (California), St. Paul, Kansas City, Cape Cod, Minneapolis, Washington, D.C., Maine, New York City, Mankato (Minnesota), England, France, Italy, Germany, and other places until he and Hegger divorced in 1928. His later marriage to the journalist Dorothy Thompson (who bore his second son, Michael) from 1928 to 1942 was stormy. An often violent drunk, Lewis alienated many of his friends and died alone in Rome, on January 10, 1951. His books, however, helped define the mind-set of an entire generation.

Sources and Further Reading: James M. Hutchisson, *The Rise of Sinclair Lewis, 1920–1930* (1996); John J. Koblas, *Sinclair Lewis, Home at Last* (1981); Richard Lingeman, *Sinclair Lewis: Rebel from Main Street* (2002); Mark Schorer, *Sinclair Lewis: An American Life* (1961).

John E. Miller
South Dakota State University

Ronald Wilson Reagan (1911–2004)

Ronald Wilson Reagan was born in Tampico, Illinois, on February 6, 1911, but the family moved frequently to fulfill his father's quest for better employment. In addition to Tampico, the Reagans lived in Chicago, Galesburg, and Dixon, Illinois.

An average student in the Dixon schools, Reagan excelled at both athletics and social activities. In high school, he played three sports, served as student body president, acted in school plays, and wrote for the yearbook. In the summers, he worked as a lifeguard.

Reagan enrolled at Eureka College in the fall of 1928 and majored in economics. As in high school, Reagan was an average student more interested in social activities. He was on the football and swimming teams, performed with the drama club, worked on the school newspaper, was an editor of the college yearbook, and served as president of the student council. To cover his expenses, Reagan washed dishes and worked as a lifeguard and a swimming coach.

After graduation from Eureka, Reagan became a radio sportscaster at WOC in Davenport, Iowa, but soon moved to WHO in Des Moines. By 1936, Reagan had become the primary announcer for major league baseball and Big Ten football in the Midwest. At the urging of a friend, he took a screen test at Warner Brother's studios in California and became a film actor. Reagan never forgot his roots. In his 1990 autobiography *An American Life*, he claimed that the growing up in Dixon allowed him to discover the unique nature of the individual and appreciate common community values.

Reagan made more than fifty films, usually playing the hero or the hero's friend. His best-known role was that of the legendary Notre Dame halfback George Gipp in the 1940 film *Knute Rockne, All American*. Reagan's acting career lasted nearly three decades, from 1937 to 1966.

As Reagan's acting career declined, he became active in politics. Impressing Republican Party activists with both his easy style and stalwart conservatism, he received the Republican nomination for governor of California in 1966. Few pundits thought Reagan had a chance against the incumbent governor, but he won by almost a million votes. The controversial and outspoken Reagan was reelected in 1970.

The secret of Reagan's success was his ability to speak with conviction. He frequently told stories about the values taught to him by his parents as a boy in Illinois. This style appealed to many voters in California who shared Reagan's midwestern origins.

By the end of his second term, Ronald Reagan was the standard-bearer for the right wing of the Republican Party. He narrowly lost the 1976 presidential nomination to Gerald R. Ford, but won it going away in 1980. With the economy in collapse and Americans held hostage in Iran, Reagan defeated incumbent President Jimmy Carter in a landslide.

During his two terms in office, Reagan set out to stimulate economic growth, curb inflation, increase employment, and strengthen national defense. His plan included a tax cut and massive reductions in the nonmilitary functions of the federal government. He did get his tax cut and increases in defense expenditures. Congress would not cut popular programs, however, and the result was a massive federal deficit.

On January 20, 1989, Ronald Reagan left Washington and public life to return to his beloved California. The flight path took him over Illinois and Iowa where he was born, educated, and found his first job. Reagan died on June 5, 2004.

Sources and Further Reading: Lou Cannon, *President Reagan: The Role of a Lifetime*, 2nd ed. (2000); Anne Edwards, *Early Reagan* (1987); Ronald Reagan, *An American Life* (1990); Garry Wills, *Reagan's America: Innocents at Home* (1987).

Timothy Walch
Herbert Hoover Presidential Library,
West Branch, Iowa

Harry S Truman (1884–1972) and Elizabeth Wallace "Bess" Truman (1885–1982)

Harry S Truman was born in Lamar, Missouri, on May 8, 1884, but moved with his parents to Independence when he was six years old. His parents gave him the name Harry, and the S. was added to honor his grandfathers Anderson Shippe Truman and Solomon Young. An average student, he worked for a construction firm and a bank following graduation and turned to farming in 1906. He first met Elizabeth Wallace shortly after he moved to Independence.

Elizabeth Virginia Wallace, known as Bess for most of her life, was born on February 13, 1885, in Independence, Missouri. She was a student at Independence High School in the same class with her future husband. Following graduation, she attended a finishing school, but her life changed when her father committed suicide. Bess returned home to help her mother raise her three brothers.

Starting in 1910, Harry actively courted Bess over her mother's objections. They were engaged shortly before he left with the Army National Guard for France in 1918. They married on June 28, 1919, following his return from the war.

At first, Truman seemed to fail at everything he tried. He opened a haberdashery store in Kansas City in 1919, but it closed for lack of business in 1922. He also lost his family farm and was hounded by creditors. He was something of a desperate man when he stumbled on to his life's work, politics. Setbacks notwithstanding, Truman was an upbeat, outgoing man who was popular in Independence and Jackson County. He was active in the Masons and various civic organizations. It is not surprising, therefore, that he would run for public office.

With the backing of Tom Pendergast's political machine, Truman won election in 1922 as an administrator of Jackson County and served in that position intermittently until 1934. Pendergast backed Truman's successful bid for the U.S. Senate in 1934, and he won a second term in 1940.

During these years, Bess was a homemaker and mother to their only child, Margaret. In an effort to increase their family income, Bess also worked as a paid secretary in her husband's Senate office. Her responsibilities included advising her husband and editing his speeches. In 1940, Truman chaired a committee charged with investigating waste in the military, a position that led to his selection as the Democratic Vice Presidential nominee in 1944.

With the sudden death of Franklin D. Roosevelt in 1945, both Trumans were thrust into new roles. Although Harry focused on the legacy left by FDR, Bess decided not to follow Eleanor Roosevelt. Bess held no press conferences and avoided interviews and speeches during her years as First Lady.

Life in Washington was arduous for both Trumans. They enjoyed Independence and found Washington too large and unfriendly. Bess, in particular, returned home to Missouri frequently.

This did not mean that she was disinterested in her new duties. Bess had a direct role in planning White House receptions, dinners, and teas. Bess also was a close advisor to her husband; he particularly valued her assessment of people and personalities, and she insisted that her views be treated with all due concern.

Harry Truman did not seek reelection in 1952, and he and Bess returned to Independence to live in the family home at 219 North Delaware Street. Although the Trumans had spent almost twenty years in Washington, they never gave any thought to living anywhere other than Independence. In retirement, Mr. Truman devoted himself to writing his memoirs and to the construction of his presidential library. Mrs. Truman returned to the world she had known before Washington. Both Trumans died in their family home, he on December 26, 1972, and she on October 13, 1982.

Sources and Further Reading: Robert H. Ferrell, ed., *Dear Bess: The Letters from Harry to Bess Truman, 1910–1959* (1983); Alonzo Hamby, *Man of the People* (1995); David McCullough, *Truman* (1992); Jhan Robbins, *Bess and Harry: An American Love Story* (1980); Margaret Truman, *Bess W. Truman* (1986).

Timothy Walch
Herbert Hoover Presidential Library,
West Branch, Iowa

John Wayne (1907–1979)

John Wayne still looms large in American popular culture, his visage racing daily across television screens and staring at us from picture frames in bars, barbershops, firehouses, police stations, and truck stops–wherever blue-collar men gather to work and drink.

He was born Marion Robert Morrison on May 25, 1907, in Winterset, Iowa, to Clyde and Mary Morrison. Clyde was a druggist who never stayed more than a step or two ahead of bill collectors. Mary, or Molly, was an odd woman. She had named her first born after her father Robert, but took an immediate dislike to the baby. At first she called him Bobby, but in 1912, when her second son was born, Molly named that child Robert Emmett Morrison and began calling him Bobby. She had her first-born's name legally changed to Marion Mitchell Morrison. No wonder Wayne's recent biographers wrote, "Her chilly disdain was the great mystery of his life—unfathomable, inexplicable, and undeserved."

In 1914, the Morrisons moved to Glendale, California, a suburb of Los Angeles. The oldest boy thrived there. A gifted athlete and student, he graduated second in a high school class of two hundred and won a football scholarship to the University of Southern California. Football players got summer work at the Fox Studio in Hollywood, where director John Ford noticed Morrison and put him to work. A bit part in *Brown of Harvard* soon came his way in 1926, and others followed. Studio heads renamed him John Wayne, although Morrison never used it privately. By the time his big break came in 1930, when director Raoul Walsh cast him as the lead in *The Big Trail*, Wayne had already appeared in eighteen films.

The Big Trail was a box office disaster, and Wayne ended up making "B" films. Between 1931 and 1939, he appeared in sixty-one serials and westerns, most of them the likes of *Texas Cyclone* (1932), *Two-Fisted Law* (1932), and *Haunted Gold* (1932). There, on Saturday afternoons in the darkened theatres of the South and the West, the John Wayne persona emerged and gained a following. Every few weeks or so a new movie was out, framed in western landscapes and featuring a laconic hero who readily employed violence to foil evil. Obscurity ended in 1939 when John Ford cast him as Ringo in the popular and critical success, *Stagecoach*.

World War II proved to be a watershed in Wayne's life. Because he wanted to exploit his recent celebrity, Wayne postponed military service. At thirty-four and the father of four, he was eligible for deferments and took them. During the war, between 1940 and 1945, he made over twenty films, the most famous of which, such as *They Were Expendable* (1945), portrayed him as a soldier battling to save comrades and country.

Wayne felt guilty about being a heroic figure who had never served in the military. That guilt changed his politics. The former Roosevelt Democrat turned to the Republicans and to the flag. As head of the Motion Picture Alliance for the Preservation of American Ideals, Wayne campaigned to root Communists out of the industry. By that time, he had released *Fort Apache* (1948), *The Sands of Iwo Jima* (1949), and *The Quiet Man* (1952). He was the biggest box office draw in Hollywood and the personification of America. In his 1960 film *The Alamo*, he turned early Texas history into a cold war drama, and in *The Green Berets* (1968), he defended the United States war effort in Vietnam.

Wayne mellowed a bit in the 1970s. In his 1969 film *True Grit*, Wayne lampooned his own persona and won an Oscar for Best Actor. In 1976, he appeared in the last of his 177 films, *The Shootist*, the story of an aging gunfighter dying of cancer. Life was imitating art. John Wayne died of cancer on June 11, 1979.

Source: Randy Roberts and James S. Olson, *John Wayne, American* (1995).

James S. Olson
Sam Houston State University, Texas

William Allen White (1868–1944)

William Allen White was born in Emporia, Kansas, established his career in Emporia, and used that base to broadcast his philosophy to Americans for half a century. Reporter, editor, and publisher, social activist, essayist, biographer, and novelist, White associated himself with the ethos of small-town America. It is difficult to find a twentieth-century American whose life better tracked the historical trajectory of the midwestern town and symbolized the transcendence of the small town as an idea. White helped to promulgate a "small-town rhetoric" that encapsulated a homogenized, idealized set of values. As the *Washington Post* said in memorializing him in 1946, "He was a magnificent mirror of mid-America, a perfect facsimile of the best in middle-class culture as it developed toward self-expression and social consciousness." White built himself a career as a spokesman for that ideal.

White preached the "gospel of Emporia." He spoke out on social, political, and moral issues, fashioning himself a progressive and constructing a fairly consistent worldview. While he expressed this outlook in terms of small-town values, he tailored his rhetoric to the needs and values of the growing middle class living in developing urban centers. White selectively used and idealized a set of small-town norms to highlight his own vision of the vast, emerging middling society. The Sage of Emporia published hundreds of articles in magazines and newspapers and over twenty fiction and nonfiction books; his Emporia *Gazette* editorials were widely reprinted. He spoke widely, and he had the ear of opinion makers both behind the scenes and out front, calling shots for Republicans and Progressives. He counted both Roosevelts, Herbert Hoover, and scores of local, state, and national politicians among his friends and close conferees.

White, by all measures, was a "player"—opposing Populism, promoting Progressivism, backing Woodrow Wilson at Versailles, fighting the Klan, propagandizing 1920s small town–urban controversies, supporting the New Deal, and chairing the Committee to Defend America by Aiding the Allies. White's formidable work includes "What's the Matter with Kansas," a stinging 1896 editorial repudiation of Populism; *In Our Town* (1906), a fictional evocation of the small-town ideal; *A Certain Rich Man* (1909), an immensely popular and critically applauded progressive novel; the 1923 Pulitzer Prize-winning editorial "To an Anxious Friend," a plea against the repression of free speech; the 1938 biography of Calvin Coolidge, *A Puritan in Babylon*; and *The Autobiography of William Allen White* (1946).

White had a genuine gusto for life. Commentators admired his mix of small-town provincialism, a democratic vitality reminiscent of the nineteenth-century frontier, and a refined twentieth-century cosmopolitanism. On his seventieth birthday, celebrated by *Life*, *Look*, and Fox Movietone News, White wrote in *Collier's*, "The battle for social and economic justice is not won. It never will be won. The fight gaunts us down, keens our edge, measures our progress." This, for White, was what community was all about. He recalled that he and his town had lived through a magnificent epoch in which individualistic Americans were welded through scientific technology and socialized through political progressivism into a communal, middle-class life: "What a show I have seen, what a grand show!"

White died in his home, a frequent cross-country stop for friends and colleagues. Edna Ferber remembered it as "a mellow blend of roomy red brick house, flagged terrace, lily pond, fried chicken, children, books, ancient elms and the best conversation to be found east (or west) of the Rockies." His wife and lifetime counselor Sallie Lindsay White (1869–1950) survived him, as did his son, journalist and novelist William Lindsay White (1900–1973). Josephus Daniels recalled, "I always thought about him and Will Rogers as typical Uncle Sams of our generation."

Sources and Further Reading: Edward Gale Agran, *"Too Good a Town:" William Allen White, Community, and the Emerging Rhetoric of Middle America* (1998); Sally Foreman Griffith, *Home Town News* (1989); Walter Johnson, *William Allen White's America* (1947); Walter Johnson and Alberta Pantle, "A Bibliography of the Published Works of William Allen White," *Kansas Historical Quarterly* 15 (Feb. 1947); Everett Rich, *William Allen White: The Man from Emporia* (1941).

Edward Gale Agran
Wilmington College, Ohio

John Wooden (b. 1910)

The greatest college basketball coach of all time, Johnny Wooden was also one of the game's great players. He was born on October 14, 1910, the second of four boys of Joshua and Roxie Wooden, who farmed a small acreage near Centerton, twenty miles southwest of Indianapolis. His father, who abandoned farming and moved the family ten miles south to Martinsville in 1924, was a pious man and his son's guiding influence. Blessed with speed and agility, John preferred baseball but was positively brilliant at basketball. A three-time all-state guard at Martinsville High, a three-time All American at Purdue, and national player of the year in 1932, he was proudest of the medal he won as a senior for attaining the best grades of any player in the Big Ten athletic conference. Along with Oscar Robertson and Larry Bird, he remains one of the most outstanding players ever to come out of Indiana, the nation's hotbed of basketball enthusiasm.

While earning adulation as a sports figure, Wooden always considered himself primarily a teacher rather than a coach. A resident of Los Angeles most of his life, he never forgot his rural roots. The values and principles he imbibed as a small-town boy in Indiana shone through brightly in the lessons he imparted on the basketball court. The Pyramid of Success that he made his trademark after formulating it as a high school coach in South Bend, Indiana, emphasized values such as friendship, enthusiasm, and self-control as well as conditioning, skill, and team spirit. A longtime deacon in the Christian church, Wooden remained a moral man as well as a sports figure.

After eleven years of high school coaching and English teaching in Kentucky and Indiana and two more at the college level at Indiana State University at Terre Haute, Wooden gained the attention of big-time basketball powers and took a job at the University of California at Los Angeles in 1948. Immediately turning a mediocre program into a powerhouse on the West Coast, Wooden won accolades for his innovative style of play during his first fifteen years in Los Angeles. But the national title eluded him. In 1964, with no starter taller than 6'5", the hard-driving coach parleyed his fast-breaking, relentlessly pressing attack into an NCAA championship. During his next eleven seasons at UCLA, his teams captured nine more titles, including seven in a row, probably the most remarkable record in the history of college sports. The next winningest coach, Adolph Rupp of the University of Kentucky, won only four national championships.

Detractors attributed the success of the Wizard of Westwood (a term he disliked) to the presence of players such as Kareem Abdul-Jabbar and Bill Walton, but Wooden won with tall teams and short ones, pressing defenses and more standard approaches, and a variety of offensive formations. He considered himself primarily a practice coach, honing his players' skills to such a fine perfection that during games he often had to do little coaching from the bench. His overall record during twenty-seven years at UCLA was 620 victories and 147 defeats, including victory streaks of

88 games during the regular season and 38 in NCAA tournament action. At Pauley Pavilion, opened in 1965, more than a decade after university administrators had promised the coach it would be built, the Bruins compiled a nearly perfect 149 and 2 record. Ironically, Wooden, whose records will probably never be equaled, never emphasized winning to his players, only that they do their absolute best and practice their skills to perfection. In retirement, he continues to do basketball clinics and preach his Pyramid of Success into his nineties.

Sources and Further Reading: Dwight Chapin and Jeff Prugh, *The Wizard of Westwood* (1973); John Wooden with Jack Tobin, *They Call Me Coach* (1988).

John E. Miller
South Dakota State University

Urban and Suburban Life

SECTION EDITOR
Jon C. Teaford

Section Contents

Overview

The Midwest includes a diverse array of cities. From Youngstown and Cleveland in the east to Omaha and Wichita in the west, midwesterners inhabit cities with distinct identities and histories. The Midwest is not a region of cookie-cutter metropolises, each one identical to the next. The Motor City of Detroit, the Windy City of Chicago, the Queen City of Cincinnati, the Gateway to the West of St. Louis, all take pride in their individuality and their unique accomplishments.

Despite the diversity of the region and the prevailing local pride and sense of identity, certain common characteristics distinguish the cities of the metropolitan Midwest from their counterparts elsewhere in the United States. Whereas East Coast cities were founded in the colonial era as hubs of transatlantic trade, the midwestern metropolises all developed in the nineteenth century, for the most part along the region's major navigable rivers or the Great Lakes. Though a few were fur-trading outposts in the eighteenth century, they did not become cities until the nineteenth century when they prospered as centers for marketing and processing the region's resources. They traded and milled the Midwest's grain, butchered the hogs and cattle, fashioned the timber of Michigan, Wisconsin, and Minnesota into furniture, doors, and window frames, and transformed the region's iron ore and coal into steel and machinery. New England's cities profited from a China trade conducted thousands of miles from the region's shores, milled cotton grown in the distant South, and processed shoe leather from hides imported from the equally distant West. New York City was the transshipment center for the continent, the channel through which goods from other regions flowed to Europe and through which foreign products were distributed to the American hinterland. The midwestern cities, in contrast, built their prosperity on the indigenous resources of the rich Mississippi valley and Great Lakes basin.

The heritage of midwestern cities is also distinct from that of southern and western urban areas. Sunbelt cities of the South and West are largely products of the twentieth century and do not owe their prominence to hog butchering or iron and steel fabrication. Sunshine, leisure, social security payments, federal defense spending, oil, and nonunion labor fueled the twentieth-century emergence of the metropolitan Sunbelt. The cold, cloudy, unionized manufacturing hubs of the Midwest stood in sharp contrast to the urban centers that emerged in the twentieth-century South and West. No one could confuse Omaha with Las Vegas, Detroit with Phoenix, or Milwaukee with Orlando. For better or worse, the Midwest's urban byproducts of the nineteenth century were clearly distinguishable from the Sunbelt creations of the twentieth century.

Moreover, a common trajectory of growth unites the metropolitan Midwest. The histories of the heartland cities, though different, follow a similar pattern. During the nineteenth century the leading cities of the Midwest grew rapidly, benefiting from the economic development of their rich hinterlands. No region in the United States was better served by railroads, and during the second half of the nineteenth century, Chicago became the busiest rail center in the world. Chicago's breakneck rate of growth was, in fact, one of the wonders of the world. Over the course of the century, the Illinois metropolis developed from a frontier trading post to a major commercial center, suffered a devastating fire that destroyed its most valu-

The Chicago skyline in daytime. Illinois Department of Commerce and Community Affairs/Mike Gustafson.

able real estate, and then rebuilt and proceeded to increase almost sixfold in population from 1870 to 1900.

On a lesser scale Cleveland, Minneapolis, Omaha, and their fellow midwestern hubs replicated the Chicago success story. Each grew to greatness over the span of a single human lifetime, attracting immigrants from the eastern states and Europe who were eager to share in the profits of the booming American heartland. During the early twentieth century, the development of automobile manufacturing in the eastern half of the Midwest kept the boom alive in such cities as Detroit, Flint, and Akron, with Wichita an important center of airplane manufacture in the western half. But during the second half of the twentieth century, a wave of deindustrialization engulfed the region, earning it the label "Rust Belt." Signature industries abandoned the cities, the steel mills closed in Youngstown, Studebaker went out of business in South Bend, and the fabled stockyards of Chicago passed from the scene. The automobile works in Detroit and Flint downsized, as did Gary's steel plants, Omaha's major meatpacking houses ceased operation, and Minneapolis's flour mills gradually disappeared. Some metropolises advertised themselves as bright spots in the Rust Belt, and others claimed to be comeback cities. But even these supposedly fortunate cities did not deny the region's problems; they simply boasted that they were exceptions to the midwestern rule. The picture was not uniformly dismal, and good economic times in the late 1990s raised hopes that the rust had worn off the region. On the whole, however, the metropolitan Midwest was not deemed a land of opportunity equal to Atlanta, Denver, Las Vegas, or Seattle.

Thus the cities of the Midwest share a common historical foundation. Moreover, they also can take pride in their contributions to urban America as a whole. The midwestern metropolises have not been branch offices of headquarter cities elsewhere in the nation, unthinking followers of the policymakers or trendsetters of New York and Los Angeles. They have often been innovators, leading American urban development and guiding their counterparts in the East, West, and South.

For example, the metropolitan Midwest has at times been a forerunner in the physical development of American cities and suburbs. Chicago architects of the 1880s and 1890s pioneered the construction of skyscrapers, and in nearby Oak Park, Frank Lloyd Wright revolutionized the design of suburban homes. Daniel Burnham of Chicago was one of the founding figures of the American urban planning profession. As construction chief of the Chicago World's Columbian Exposition of 1893, Burnham presided over the creation of a temporary neoclassical wonderland of statuary, reflecting pools, and palatial exhibition halls that

would serve as a model for the city beautiful movement of the early twentieth century. Moreover, in 1903, he designed a trendsetting civic center for Cleveland, and his plan for Chicago published in 1909 is perhaps the most notable single document in the history of American city planning. Meanwhile, Kansas City's George Kessler was designing model park and boulevard plans for his hometown as well as for Cincinnati, Indianapolis, Fort Wayne, and other communities throughout the nation. In the field of urban planning, the Midwest was a leader, not a backwater.

The Midwest could also boast of landmarks in suburban planning. In 1869, Frederick Law Olmsted laid out the suburban community of Riverside outside of Chicago. With curvilinear streets, implying a leisurely lifestyle, and large lots and ample open space, it differed markedly from the straight-line streets and sharp corners of Chicago's grid and the congestion and crowding of the urban hub. Over the next century, other suburban planners would imitate the Riverside model, emphasizing the suburb's role as a sylvan refuge from the hurly-burly existence of the city. In the early twentieth century, the Van Sweringen brothers' Shaker Heights development east of Cleveland and J. C. Nichols's Country Club District in Kansas City won renown as restricted, fashionable suburban tracts that attracted thousands of upper-middle-class urbanites seeking an escape from the dingy central cities. The two midwestern greenbelt communities built by the federal government in the 1930s, one near Cincinnati and the other outside of Milwaukee, experimented with plans for suburban living aimed at the less affluent. And following World War II, Philip Klutznick's Park Forest development south of Chicago was one of the most highly publicized suburban communities built for returning veterans who had joined the growing army of white-collar workers in midwestern cities.

Not only were midwesterners creating highly admired models for urban and suburban development, they were also attempting to fashion ideal schemes of city government. Between 1890 and 1920, the spirit of municipal reform was more prevalent in the Midwest than in any other area of the United States. Mayors Hazen Pingree of Detroit, Tom Johnson of Cleveland, and Samuel Jones of Toledo won national fame for their crusades against the venality of public utility corporations and their initiatives in favor of municipal ownership of streetcar lines and gas and electric works. The idealistic Jones dreamed of transforming Toledo into a cooperative commonwealth, a model of social justice for the working class. Followers of Johnson proclaimed Cleveland to be a city on a hill, a beacon light to the exploited citizens of ill-governed cities elsewhere in the nation. In 1913, Dayton became the first major city in the country to adopt the city manager plan of nonpartisan, expert administration, and during the following decade, reformers throughout the United States studied Dayton as an exemplar of good government. Meanwhile, the Socialists won their greatest electoral successes in a swath of cities running from western Pennsylvania through Wisconsin. In 1910, Socialists captured both the mayor's office and a majority of the city council seats in Milwaukee, and from 1916 to 1940, Daniel W. Hoan was the Socialist mayor of the Wisconsin metropolis and living proof of the viability of left-wing politics in at least one section of the United States. The Midwest was not, then, a bland region of dreary municipal leaders mouthing well-worn platitudes and blindly embracing the policy options pioneered by politicians elsewhere in the country. Instead, many local leaders in the Midwest dared to dream and experiment.

During the second half of the twentieth century, midwestern cities likewise garnered headlines as they confronted the changing racial realities of American politics. In 1967, Gary and Cleveland became the first major American cities to elect black mayors (Richard Hatcher and Carl Stokes, respectively), and in the 1970s, African American Coleman Young secured the executive office in Detroit. In 1983, Harold Washington replicated Young's success, becoming the first African American mayor of Chicago. But none of these victories testified to the racial tolerance of the Midwest. Instead, in Gary, Cleveland, Detroit, and Chicago, the electorate split along racial lines, with blacks overwhelmingly rallying behind the black candidate and whites seeking to retain power by supporting the white contender.

In retailing, the metropolitan Midwest also proved to be a national leader. Hudson's in Detroit, Marshall Field's in Chicago, and Dayton's in Minneapolis were among the nation's most famous department stores. At the beginning of the twenty-first century, the Minneapolis-based Target stores were favorites of discount shoppers, the Kohl's chain founded in Milwaukee was equally successful, the chain of Federated Department Stores centered in Cincinnati became the nation's largest, but K-Mart headquartered in suburban Detroit was faltering. Moreover, in the late nineteenth and early twentieth centuries, Chicago was the unchallenged center of mail-order retailing. The home of the two greatest mail-order giants, Sears Roebuck and Montgomery Ward, Chicago distributed catalogs to rural homes throughout the nation. Sears offered all manner of apparel and home furnishings, and one could even purchase a kit with plans and materials for building a home from the Chicago mail-order firm.

To service the growing number of suburbanites, Midwesterners pioneered the shopping mall. Built in the 1920s, J. C. Nichols's Country Club Plaza on the south side of Kansas City is usually credited as being the first auto-oriented shopping complex. Though some may challenge the claim, the Town and Country Shopping Center built in 1949 in Columbus, Ohio, boasted to be the first suburban-style shopping center in the nation. The more innovative and highly admired layout of Northland Center, which opened in Southfield, Michigan, in 1954, spawned many imitators. No one disputes Southdale Mall's right to the title of first enclosed mall. Opened in 1956 in Edina, Minnesota, west of Minneapolis, Southdale offered two levels of climate-controlled shopping for refugees from the area's frigid winters. During the last decade of the twentieth century, however, Southdale had to yield regional preeminence to the gigantic Mall of America in nearby Bloomington, Minnesota. With 525 stores, a seven-acre theme park complete with a roller coaster, and an eighteen-hole miniature golf course, the Mall of America was the nation's largest shopping center and claimed to draw more visitors than any other attraction in the United States.

Purveyors of fast food thrived, as well, in the metropolitan Midwest. Wichita was the birthplace of the White Castle hamburger chain, and Wendy's began business in Columbus, Ohio. The greatest fast-food chain, however, was McDonald's, headquartered in Oak Brook, Illinois, west of Chicago. Led by Ray Kroc, McDonald's became an icon of the mass production, automobile-borne culture of the second half of the twentieth century. Throughout the world, the chain turned out billions of hamburger patties for hungry consumers lined up at drive-through windows. The leading pizza delivery chain, Dominos, was also a midwestern creation. Though in the popular mind, the Midwest might conjure images of old-fashioned home cooking, in fact, it was the breeding ground of drive-through and home-delivery cuisine.

The mass production of burgers and pizzas was appropriate to a region that pioneered the assembly line and became renowned for its giant manufacturing concerns. During the antebellum era, Cincinnati won a reputation for the breakneck pace of its pork-packing plants, which were slaughtering an average of almost a quarter million hogs annually as early as the mid-1840s. During the late nineteenth century, the lethal efficiency of Chicago's packinghouses was a wonder to visitors from throughout the world, and one British traveler reported watching hogs slaughtered at the rate of eight per minute or approximately five hundred per hour. In the early twentieth century, Henry Ford adapted the assembly line to automobile manufacturing and attempted to turn out automobiles as rapidly as Chicago produced sausage. Meanwhile, giant tire factories were employing thousands of workers in Akron, and the U.S. Steel Corporation was transforming the sand dunes of northwestern Indiana into Gary, one of the world's greatest steel-manufacturing centers. Milwaukee was the nation's renowned brewing hub, Minneapolis was famed for flour milling, and Grand Rapids was synonymous in the public's mind with furniture. In the late nineteenth and early twentieth centuries, the metropolitan Midwest was in the forefront of the industrial world.

While reaping the financial benefits of this productivity, metropolitan midwesterners did not ignore the demands of their consciences. Founded in Cleveland in 1874 and with organizations in many communities in the region, in the 1880s the Women's Christian Temperance Union (WCTU) established its national headquarters in Chicago, and the great WCTU crusader Frances Willard was a resident of suburban Evanston. Though many urban midwesterners frequented saloons and beer gardens, Willard and her organization demonstrated that some heartland residents could not ignore the evils of alcohol. Other women were also battling the social problems of the midwestern metropolis. Chicago's Jane Addams was the most famous American settlement house worker, and her efforts to aid the working-class residents of the Windy City's near west side spawned scores of imitators throughout the nation. Meanwhile in Indiana, Evansville's Albion Fellows Bacon led the crusade for the adoption of housing codes that would improve the living conditions of the urban working class. The University of Chicago boasted the nation's first sociology department. Led by Albion Small, this pioneering department sought to apply social science to the problems of the city and thereby raise the quality of urban life. Chicago sociologists were not dispassionate ivory-tower scholars; they were crusaders who sought to harness scholarship to the real problems of the city and pull the midwestern masses out of the social morass produced by rapid, exploitative industrialization.

The midwestern urban legacy, however, is not uniformly innovative or philanthropic. Cleveland, Detroit, Chicago, and Kansas City have not only made headlines for their achievements in business, government, and planning, but also for their failings. For example, the region has a heritage of urban violence and discord. In the late nineteenth century, Chicago was the scene of both the Haymarket Riots and the Pullman Strike, violent labor uprisings that stirred fears among the nation's business elite and seemed to establish the Illinois metropolis as a center of anarchy and working-class rebellion. The gangster era of the 1920s did little to dispel Chicago's image as a rough, raucous town, a butcher not only of hogs but also of human beings. The city's Al Capone was the nation's

most famous gangster, and the St. Valentine's Day Massacre of 1929, in which the Capone mob murdered seven rival gang members, was America's most notorious example of Prohibition-era violence. In the late twentieth century, the midwestern cities of Gary and Detroit were perennial contenders for the dubious title of murder capital of America. Racial violence erupted throughout the twentieth century. The East St. Louis riot of 1917 resulted in at least forty-seven fatalities, and almost four thousand African Americans left the city in the wake of violence. In 1919, full-scale racial warfare broke out in both Chicago and Omaha, and in 1943, a thirty-six-hour clash between white mobs and black mobs left thirty-four Detroit residents dead. Then in 1967, Detroit secured its reputation for violence with a five-day riot in which arsonists and looters destroyed at least $50 million in property. A minor consolation to the racially divided city was the fact that both blacks and whites participated in the looting.

Racial conflict seemed endemic to the metropolitan Midwest. Late-twentieth-century studies of racial segregation by residence revealed that midwestern cities ranked among the nation's most segregated metropolises. The east side of Cleveland was black, the west side white; the south and west sides of Chicago were black, the north side white; the north side of St. Louis was black, the south side white. Though residential segregation was evident throughout the nation, nowhere was it so pronounced as in the metropolitan Midwest.

In the minds of many Americans, the image of life in the Midwest is as flat as the region's landscape. Yet midwestern metropolises have been anything but bland and featureless. At times they have been tumultuous and strife-torn. They also have been incubators of political and social reform as well as crucibles of commercial and industrial innovation. Over the course of two centuries, they have bred capitalists and socialists, dreamers and mechanics, idealists and hard-headed pragmatists whose collective legacy has not only molded the region but also influenced the life of the nation as a whole. This section examines these matters by beginning with essays on individual localities, then proceeding to entries on general topics regarding midwestern metropolitan life.

Sources and Further Reading: David J. Bodenhamer and Robert G. Barrows, eds., *The Encyclopedia of Indianapolis* (1994); A. Theodore Brown and Lyle W. Dorsett, *K.C.: A History of Kansas City, Missouri* (1978); William Cronon, *Nature's Metropolis* (1991); Lawrence H. Larsen and Barbara J. Cottrell, *The Gate City: A History of Omaha* (1997); Donald L. Miller, *City of the Century: The Epic of Chicago and the Making of America* (1996); James Neal Primm, *Lion of the Valley* (1981); Eric Sandweiss, *St. Louis: The Evolution of an*

American Urban Landscape (2001); Bayrd Still, *Milwaukee: The History of a City* (1948); Thomas J. Sugrue, *The Origins of the Urban Crisis* (1996); Jon C. Teaford, *Cities of the Heartland* (1993); William H. Tishler, ed., *Midwestern Landscape Architecture* (2000); David D. Van Tassel and John J. Grabowski, eds., *The Encyclopedia of Cleveland History* (1987).

Jon C. Teaford
Purdue University, Indiana

Central Cities

Perhaps the best way to approach the Midwest's central cities is by car, preferably from an interstate highway. After mile upon mile of flat farmland, with only an occasional silo or billboard to break the horizon, one sees in the distance a dark mass of buildings stretching to the sky. The particular components of this mass vary according to which city one is approaching—the Gateway Arch of St. Louis, Chicago's Sears Tower, or the more anonymous skylines of Indianapolis, Kansas City, or most other cities of the Midwest. As one drives closer, the roadside environment gradually changes from suburban sprawl to denser urban neighborhoods. Soon it looks as if the highway was cut through the heart of older communities, with residential streets dead-ending against the highway walls. Then the downtown core appears, and that dark mass of buildings comes into focus. Glass and steel skyscrapers stand amidst smaller local landmarks, a baseball stadium here, a local brewery there. And before one can digest this concrete landscape, the highway whisks the car away from the city on the other side, again passing through the concentric rings of urban and suburban neighborhoods and finally on to the open spaces of midwestern farmland.

This brief travelogue portrays the Midwest's central cities as urban centers standing out from an otherwise rural landscape. To be sure, each has its own particular history. Several developed through their geographical proximity to water, whether lakes (Chicago, Milwaukee, Detroit, Cleveland) or rivers (Cincinnati, St. Louis, Kansas City, Omaha, and the Twin Cities). Others were founded as administrative centers or state capitals (Indianapolis, Columbus, Des Moines). Still others, such as Wichita, began as trading outposts on the nineteenth-century western frontier. Despite these varied origins, the Midwest's major cities share their identity, both in relation to the rest of the region and to the larger cities of the East and West Coasts.

When placed against the relief of midwestern farmland, these major urban centers confirm Louis Wirth's definition of the city as a large, dense, and heterogeneous place. On almost any cultural or economic variable, midwestern central cities are different from the rest of the region. The big city "has more of," "is the largest," "has a greater proportion than," and so on—whether ethnic diversity, tall buildings, crime, traffic problems, or medical specialists. Yet, as much as nonurban midwesterners see big cities as something altogether different (perhaps something *non-midwestern*), they also recognize the metropolises as key central places. Whether as centers of commerce, state politics, or culture, the Midwest's central cities offer the most specialized and the widest array of goods and services for the wider rural hinterlands; here are the major medical facilities, universities, shopping centers. These cities are also major centers for recreation and culture; metropolitan symphonies, art museums, and professional sports teams call these central cities home. With the exception of Des Moines, all of the other cities have at least one major league team. Still, although each city acts as a central place for its own hinterland, there is considerable fluidity in catchment areas around these central cities. It is difficult to measure, for example, the dividing line between St. Louis and Kansas City or Indianapolis and Cincinnati. The allegiance to one particular sports team over another is one way to tell, as any baseball fan in Missouri, of course, could explain.

Understanding the major cities of the Midwest within their regional context tells only half the story. At the same time that these cities serve as internal anchors to the region, they are also connected to the broader North American network of metropolitan regions. These connections can be easily overlooked, since a list of the major metropolitan regions in the United States and Canada might show most midwestern cities ranking well down on the list. Still, by examining the central cities of the Midwest in reference to cities in other parts of the continent, a common theme emerges: As befits their geographical location in the middle of the continent, the Midwest's central cities stand as a middle ground between the older, dense metropolises of the East Coast and the younger, sprawling landscapes of the West and South.

Though younger than their eastern neighbors—most of these cities emerged during the first half of the nineteenth century—this collection of urban centers evolved in an era when a city's central business district was truly centralized. Midwestern downtowns contained a dense network of streets lined with tall skyscrapers, major department stores, and likely a civic monument or two. Moreover, the transportation infrastructure in these cities reflected a pre-automobile orientation, with little space given over for parking and few major routes for through traffic.

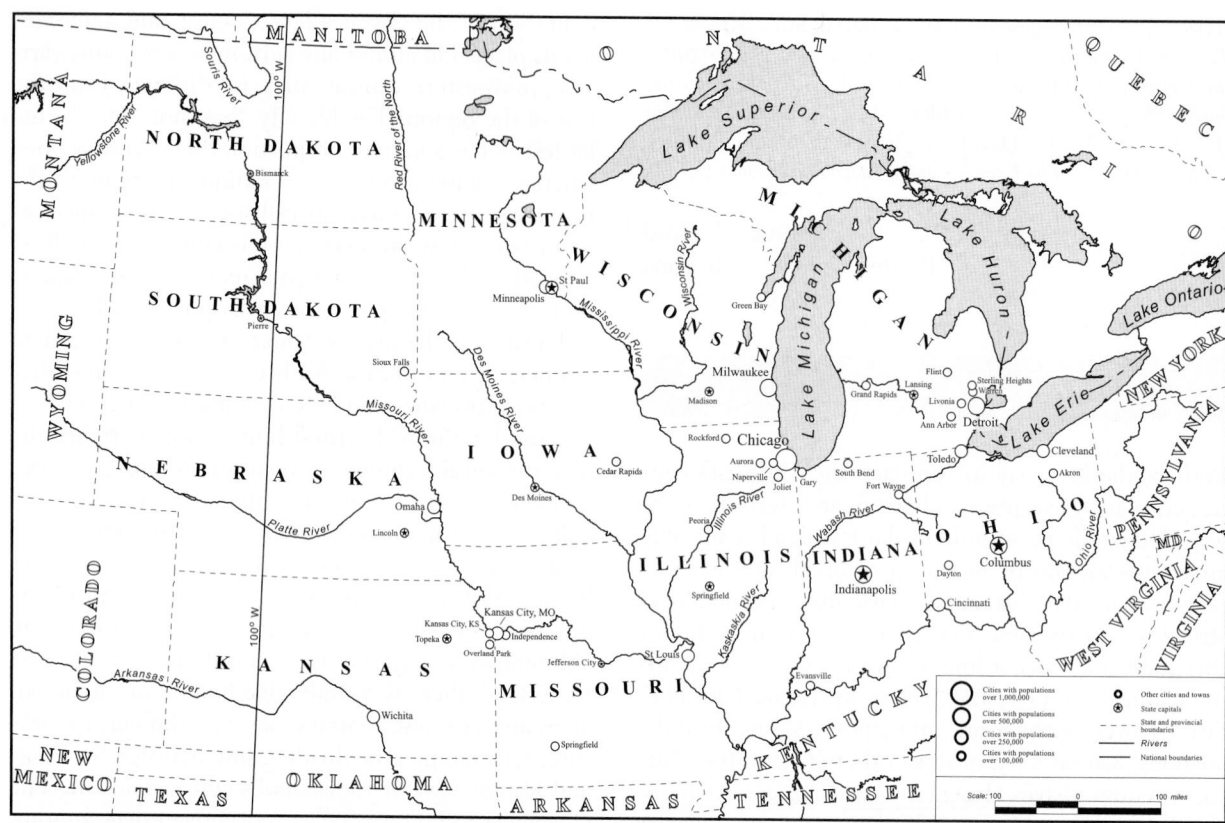

Central cities. Prepared by James DeGrand. *Source: United States Census, 2000;* http://www.nationalatlas.gov/.

Though developed prior to the automobile's ascendance, these cities did not escape the influence of the automobile. Rather, much like their younger western and southern counterparts, the Midwest's central cities have been clearly imprinted by the automobile. Yet unlike those newer metropolises that developed within an automobile culture, the accommodation to the automobile occurred through significant retrofitting and permanent alteration to the region's urban landscape. Road extensions and expansions, the construction of parking facilities, and most notably, expressway construction have permanently reshaped these urban environments. A drive through any midwestern city will pass through dense urban neighborhoods that have been bulldozed in half to accommodate an urban expressway. Such roads were usually built in the name of metropolitan growth, but in reality, they served the suburban population coming into the city and did little for inner city residents living in the path of the concrete ribbon.

If midwestern downtowns resemble those of eastern cities, the residential neighborhoods radiating out from downtown do not. Developed at far lower densities than their eastern counterparts, neighborhoods have few examples of the Philadelphia rowhouse, or even of the New York apartment building. Exceptions occur, such as Chicago's Gold Coast along Lake Shore Boulevard, but the primary residential symbol of the urban neighborhoods is the single-family house. These cities had few of the spatial constraints of their eastern counterparts and could spread out across the landscape with ease. The result of this horizontal development is that central city neighborhoods, though often influenced by the same economic or racial factors as East Coast cities, can appear less troubled because the low density of the housing stock masks the vulnerabilities of the residential population. This pattern of sprawling residential landscapes found fuller expression in the newer cities in the South and West, but it began in earnest in the Midwest.

A look at the cultural landscape of midwestern cities reveals a similar middle ground orientation between the eastern and western metropolises. In this realm, these cities present a unique historical mixture of immigrant and native, Protestant and Catholic, white and black.

During the nineteenth century, the waves of European immigration that flooded eastern cities also came to Cleveland, St. Louis, Chicago, and the other major cities of the region, though with a slightly different ethnic mix. Immigration to the Midwest was heavily German, Nordic, and Slavic, whereas immigration to the Atlantic Seaboard and New England was much more Irish, Italian, and French Canadian. Germans comprised the largest foreign-born group in nineteenth-century midwestern cities (Scandinavians in Minneapolis), while the Irish dominated Atlantic Seaboard cities. The presence of so many newcomers provoked much of the nativist backlash that dominated nineteenth-century politics, and in fact, many of the national nativist movements had midwestern roots. At the close of the nineteenth century, the new migrants to Great Lakes cities were more heavily Slavic and less Jewish than were new migrants to Atlantic Seaboard cities.

When the pace of foreign immigration slowed at the beginning of the twentieth century, these migration patterns had created a cultural mix in the region that was distinctive from that of the Eastern Seaboard. This ethnic distinctiveness continued with the massive movement of southern blacks into midwestern cities during the first half of the century, a migration that added a new complexity to the social and cultural hierarchy. Whereas in previous generations the primary cultural clash occurred along native–foreign fault lines, the issue had now become white versus black. African Americans were segregated into their own neighborhoods, out of sight and mind of the white population, but their growing presence in urban centers made these cities stand out both from their eastern and western counterparts and from their rural hinterlands. Even when the proportion of African Americans was not large, the concentration of blacks in the city and the lack of African Americans in the rural countryside created a perception of midwestern cities as black cities.

The migration of rural whites to midwestern cities during the twentieth century added yet another layer to the cultural mix. Lured by the relative cosmopolitanism of the big city and the opportunity for economic advancement, rural residents left their farmlands and southern Appalachian towns in large numbers. One might have thought that white migrants would have been more welcome than their African American counterparts, but this was not always so. Whereas racial differences allowed whites to all but ignore black in-migrants, racial similarities among whites made the socioeconomic distinctions even stronger. Just as cities had black neighborhoods, most had southern and rural white neighborhoods that were equally segregated from the more economically well-off, native white areas. In fact, it was not uncommon for elite whites to feel greater disdain for rural whites than they did for southern blacks.

Recent immigration from Asia, the Middle East, and Latin America has once again begun to alter the local cultural landscape. This is most evident in places like Chicago and Detroit, home to one of the largest Arab populations outside of the Middle East, as well as in Indianapolis and Cleveland, where Latino immigrants have moved in search of employment opportunities. Still, with the exception of Chicago and Detroit, the region's cities have yet to achieve levels of international migration seen in the major urban centers of the West or East.

The cumulative historical effect of this uniquely midwestern mixture of local urban whites, second-generation immigrant families, African Americans, and migrant rural and southern whites is most obvious in the religious landscapes of the central cities. The Catholic presence, derived from the heavy European immigration, is undeniable. Yet unlike eastern cities, midwestern cities retain a Protestant identity. The social elites hail from historically mainline Protestant denominations: Methodists most commonly, but also Disciples, Baptists, and Presbyterians. The large African American population adds a black Baptist and Pentecostal tradition, while the rural and Appalachian whites add a Holiness dimension. The result is a constellation of cities that contain highly visible mainline Protestant elites, well-established (but separate and mostly nonelite) Catholic communities, and an even stronger (and even more nonelite) conservative Protestant subculture. This contrasts with the Catholic-dominated East Coast cities and the liberal-Protestant-tending-to-secular-and-New-Age cities in the West.

Finally, there is the question of identity. Intangible and probably immeasurable though it is, residents of the Midwest's major cities see their locales as distinct from the larger cities of the East and West. Cities of the region are "friendlier," "less rushed," and "more manageable" than those elsewhere in North America, goes the thinking. Of course, within the region nonurban residents may offer different viewpoints on what their neighboring big cities are like: "too dangerous," "too busy," and "too sprawling" when compared with smaller cities and towns. And visitors from outside the region often view midwestern cities as "boring" and "like big small towns." Contradictory as they are, these competing opinions succeed in capturing the middle ground that the Midwest's central cities occupy in the regional and continental landscape. Neither too big nor too small, neither too dense nor too open, neither too old nor too new, these urban centers are a window through which to look inward to the region's unique character and outward to the rest of the continent.

Sources and Further Reading: Richard M. Bernard, ed., *Snowbelt Cities* (1990); Barry Checkoway and Carl V. Patton, eds., *The Metropolitan Midwest* (1985); William Cronon, *Nature's Metropolis* (1991); Etan Diamond, *Souls of the City: Religion and the Search for Community in Postwar America* (2003); Chauncy D. Harris and Edward L. Ullman, "The Nature of Cities," *Annals of the American Academy of Political and Social Science* 242 (Nov. 1945); Timothy R. Mahoney, *River Towns in the Great West* (1990); Jon Teaford, *Cities of the Heartland* (1993); Louis Wirth, "Urbanism as a Way of Life," *American Journal of Sociology* 44 (July 1938).

Etan Diamond
Toronto, Canada

Chicago, Illinois

Now the major urban center of the Midwest, Chicago rose to preeminence because of its advantages over other cities in the region. First, it was built at the edge of a large body of water that would become a major shipping port for many years; this soon gave it an edge over other nearby sites, like St. Louis and Minneapolis. Second, by the close of the nineteenth century, Chicago had become a major railroad center, the central place in the United States where various lines crossed, creating an in-transit hub for people and goods moving north–south as well as east–west. This made a major difference in the fortunes of the city by furnishing not only a site for the transfer and sale of goods but also an easy destination for people, especially the many immigrants that came to the Midwest late in the nineteenth century. By the mid-twentieth century, that advantage was propelled by the vision of city political officials as air transport displaced rail transport.

The expansion of the city was aided immensely by the rich resources of its hinterlands, forests and grains that stretched as far north as Wisconsin and as far west as Iowa and Nebraska. Its railroads enabled it to become a center for transforming nature into commodities, to use the imagery of William Cronon's *Nature's Metropolis*. Once that occurred, of course, Chicago would become the leading financial center of the Midwest. Finally, unlike a number of other nearby metropolitan areas, Chicago was successful in expanding and incorporating large portions of its surrounding political territory, a *fait accompli* by the end of the nine-

teenth century. Although such proclivity may have appeared insignificant at the time, its accomplishment would later allow Chicago to wield substantial power in disputes with state government and to exercise a competitive advantage over a number of other cities, many of which fell on hard economic times after World War II.

But Chicago is not simply another urban powerhouse. It has taken on a special character: It is a city where newcomers feel comfortable with one another and, as some writers put it, a city of neighborhoods and neighbors. The late-nineteenth-century immigrants settled in different spatial and social niches within the city, creating an array of villages and towns whose origins could be traced to specific parts of Europe. This sense of community became integral to the life of the city.

Unlike most other cities of the Midwest, Chicago has given birth to a catalog of real and fictional images that pervade the national consciousness. It has become the soul of the Midwest in its landscape and its inhabitants—and in its carnage, both of people and animals. Upton Sinclair forever linked Chicago with the stockyards and the slaughter of pigs and cattle, a more horrific example of turning nature into commodity. Frank Lloyd Wright and Louis Sullivan helped to invent a new style of residence, the prairie homes that today can be found scattered throughout the metropolitan area, their simple horizontal lines blending easily into the local environs. Chicago soon became home to many talented architects, including Mies Van Der Rohe, whose skyscrapers of glass and vertical strength recalled the dramatic simplicity of the Wright style.

A populist character to the city emerged in writings about the immigrants and the poor of early-twentieth-century Chicago, including Saul Bellow's Augie March and the seedy characters of Nelson Algren, and continues in the working people whose voices resonate in the writings of Studs Terkel.

Also among the real-life characters are the infamous like Al Capone, a name still identified by many as the essential Chicago even though he died seventy years ago. The St. Valentine's Day Massacre left an indelible mark on the city; parts of the city, such as Cicero, are still known for their various mob connections and gang-related activities.

The city, however, has also been and continues to be home to important forms of social and intellectual creativity and the arts. The organization of the 1893 World's Columbian Exposition announced the arrival of Chicago as one of the world's major cities, the "white city" of neoclassical architecture created for the purpose and visited by some twenty million people serving to introduce the idea of city planning and urban beautification to the nation and the world. Many of the city's major arts and cultural institutions that were created during that time still stand, including the Field Museum, the Chicago Symphony, and the Art Institute of Chicago, home of a distinguished permanent collection, sponsors of significant exhibitions, and whose school has provided advanced education and training to many generations of artists worldwide. The city is home to numerous theatres, the Millenium Park, and the Bears, Blackhawks, Bulls, Cubs, Spartans, and White Sox sports teams. Important generations of writers have at times also called Chicago their home, from Theodore Dreiser and Edgar Lee Masters to Carl Sandburg and Richard Wright, and from Saul Bellow and Studs Terkel to David Mamet.

Chicago has served as an important crucible for the development of American literature, and location to a wide range of higher education institutions, several of which are among America's most distinguished. The most distinguished is the University of Chicago. Founded by John D. Rockefeller in 1890, simultaneously with planning for the 1893 Columbian Exposition, the university rapidly moved to the forefront of American undergraduate and research institutions. Its faculty, staff, and graduates have received numerous awards for scientific achievement, including seventy-eight Nobel Laureates—twenty-two in the field of economics alone.

The underside of Chicago, however, especially in the twentieth century, is also well documented; its social and economic inequalities have come to symbolize those of America itself. Principal among them are the deep racial divisions and inequalities that today mark the United States. Chicago's experience with race began with the great migration from the South, beginning in the 1920s. This movement of people brought many black Americans to Chicago, and within a few short years, a black metropolis grew up on the near south side, and the city became the terminus and showcase of some of the greatest figures in jazz. Once a source of pride and a unique piece of Chicago, however, over the course of the 1960s and 1970s, its residents faced the paralysis of broken families and few jobs.

No sense of the power of Chicago is possible without also acknowledging its rather distinctive political culture and style. By the beginning of the twentieth century, it had become home to many big-time and heavyweight political figures, men who cast a long shadow not only over the city but also over the entire region and the nation. Ultimately the central political icon for the middle part of the twentieth century was Richard J. Daley, a heavyweight by any standard. Daley joined two major political positions, Mayor of the City and Chairman of the Cook County Democratic Party, and managed to wield his power through a close group of neighborhood friends and local ties over the course of two decades. His son, Richard M., evidently learned the lessons well and, beginning in 1989, began a tenure in office that might turn out to be as long as, if not longer than, that of his father.

How, then, to sum up this large, sprawling, friendly den of thieves? Leave it to the poet of the city, Carl Sandburg, in this excerpt from "Chicago":

> They tell me you are wicked and I believe them, for I have seen your painted women under the gas lamps luring the farm boys.
> And they tell me you are crooked and I answer: Yes, it is true I have seen the gunman kill and go free to kill again.
> And they tell me you are brutal and my reply is: On the faces of women and children I have seen the marks of wanton hunger.
> And having answered so I turn once more to those who sneer at this my city, and I give them back the sneer and say to them:
> Come and show me another city with lifted head singing so proud to be alive and coarse and strong and cunning.

Sources and Further Reading: William Cronon, *Nature's Metropolis* (1991); St. Clair Drake and Horace R. Cayton, *Black Metropolis* (1945); James R. Grossman, *Land of Hope* (1991); Harold M. Mayer and Richard C. Wade, *Chicago: Growth of a Metropolis* (1969); Dominic A. Pacyga and Ellen Skerrett, *Chicago, City of Neighborhoods* (1986); Mike Royko, *Boss: Richard J. Daley of Chicago* (1971); Carl Sandburg, *Chicago Poems* (1992); William Julius Wilson, *The Truly Disadvantaged* (1987).

Anthony M. Orum
University of Illinois–Chicago

Cincinnati, Ohio

In 1840, Cincinnati was the largest and most important city in the Midwest, a commercial and manufacturing center of 46,000 people. Ten years later, it was the nation's fastest growing city and second-largest manufacturing center, with a population exceeding 115,000. Cincinnati seemed destined to become the largest city in the westward-expanding nation and a likely future capital. Even as its growth slowed after 1850, Cincinnati defined the American West in the antebellum period. For Easterners as well as Europeans, Cincinnati was an essential stop on the western tour, the urban equivalent of the natural wonder of Niagara Falls. Some saw it as a crude, violent, barbaric settlement, a place overrun with pigs and utterly without culture, "Porkopolis." But for others, it was the "Queen City of the West," the place where the nation's democratic ambitions were most evident and most promising. A "glorious place," the Englishwoman Harriet Martineau described it, "where every man may gratify his virtuous will." Alexis de Tocqueville's analysis of democracy in America crystallized during his stay in Cincinnati. Whether Eastern elites scrambling to build outposts of culture, boosters championing the city's vitality, or artisans trying to square new market opportunities with inherited republican values, Americans believed that the nation's future would be shaped by what happened in Cincinnati.

A rude outpost in the Ohio wilderness founded in 1788, Cincinnati arose upon a 4.5-square-mile natural amphitheater just above the Ohio River flood plain and opposite the Licking River that flowed north through Kentucky. A staging area for federal campaigns against Native Americans, Cincinnati benefited from the military victories that opened the Northwest Territory to settlers. The introduction of the steamboat after 1815 brought two-way traffic between Cincinnati and New Orleans and provided the focus for the city's earliest manufacturing enterprises. The Miami and Erie Canal, connecting the city with Dayton by 1830 and with the Great Lakes by 1845, poured the produce of western Ohio into the city, making it a major processing center, and opened new markets for manufacturers of soap and candles, textiles and leather goods, furniture and hardware. Yet many of the city's key customers (for cotton gins, cheap textiles, furniture) and suppliers (of salt and cotton) remained in the plantation economies of the South.

As the Civil War approached, Cincinnati embodied two key tensions within the nation. An expanding city of economic opportunity, egalitarian democracy and cultural ambition, Cincinnati exemplified free labor values. But the city's prosperity was dependent on markets in the slave South. The Lane Seminary, endowed by eastern capitalists as an outpost of civilizing Christianity, and James Birney's abolitionist newspaper, the *Philanthropist*, illustrated how volatile the mix could be. In 1834, rebellious students at the Lane Seminary, who debated and then endorsed abolitionism, found themselves expelled from school at the behest of local business leaders concerned with southern opinion. Two years later, a mob orchestrated by merchants and manufacturers destroyed Birney's printing press and engaged in three days of rioting.

Filling up with Irish and especially German immigrants, Cincinnati also reflected the tension between immigrant and nativist forces in the expanding nation. In the 1855 city elections, with nativist anger at a peak, mobs invaded German neighborhoods to "protect the polls." As the Republican party articulated an American nationalism that avoided both abolitionism and nativism, Abraham Lincoln's two major speeches in Cincinnati focused on these tensions. In 1859, Lincoln's "Shot Over the Line" addressed Kentucky slaveholders on the distinctions between free soil opposition to the extension of slavery and outright abolitionism. In 1861, the president-elect addressed the city's German citizens on his opposition to immigration restriction and his commitment to equal opportunity.

The decades after the Civil War were difficult for Cincinnati. The rise of Chicago, the elaboration of the east-west railroad network, and the decline of the southern economy undercut the city's position in the urban hierarchy. Simultaneously, the concentration and incorporation of manufacturing led to a period of fierce labor conflict. In the 1880s, strikes, political insurgency, and mounting problems of crime, pollution, and an inadequate and deteriorating infrastructure paralyzed local government. In the 1890s and the first decade of the twentieth century, the political machine of George B. Cox reinvigorated municipal governance, muting some conflicts and resolving others while providing an expanding range of public utilities that addressed the city's problems. In the years before and after World War I, civic reformers toppled the Cox machine but continued his strategy of engaging antagonistic groups in a competition for municipal services that lent itself to compromise. The Charterites, as the reformers became known, secured a city manager charter for the city that streamlined municipal government and facilitated city planning. Geared more to efficiency than popular democracy, the Charterites won for the city the title of the best-governed city in the country.

For the rest of the century, Cincinnati settled into its status as a prosperous, provincial city noted, depending on the observer, for stability and conservatism reflected in the public service of President and Supreme Court Chief Justice William Howard Taft and U. S. Senator Robert A. Taft, or for sterility and backwardness. Less dependent on the automobile industry than other midwestern cities, Cincinnati escaped the fate of the Rust Belt. After World War II, an ambitious program of urban renewal helped it win acclaim as the "blue-chip" city, headquarters of a dozen major corporations. But that same process of urban renewal gutted low-income neighborhoods and left a legacy of distrust. Over-the-Rhine, a nineteenth-century German district transformed into a twentieth-century slum, focused efforts to rethink the function and character of the inner city. Sheltering immigrants from the South, first white then black, the neighborhood also contained a spectacular collection of nineteenth-century buildings and streetscapes that invited visions of urban revitalization. Developers hoped to turn the neighborhood into an upscale residential and entertainment adjunct to downtown. But social welfare activists dug in to defend low-income residents. Once the center of the city's nineteenth-century civic life, the neighborhood had become a symbol of civic paralysis by the late twentieth century. While developers discounted the concerns of impoverished residents, social activists offered little broader vision for solving problems of race and poverty citywide. The riots that erupted in the spring of 2001 again made the neighborhood—and the class and racial tensions it embodies—the focus of civic debate.

Sources and Further Reading: Daniel Aaron, *Cincinnati: Queen City of the West, 1819–1838* (1992); Daniel Hurley, *Cincinnati, The Queen City* (1982); Zane Miller, *Boss Cox's Cincinnati* (1968); Zane L. Miller and Bruce Tucker, *Changing Plans for America's Inner Cities* (1998); Steven J. Ross, *Workers on the Edge* (1985); Jon C. Teaford, *Cities of the Heartland* (1993); Richard C. Wade, *The Urban Frontier: Pioneer Life in Early Pittsburgh, Cincinnati, Lexington, Louisville, and St. Louis* (1959); Robert H. Wiebe, *Self-Rule: A Cultural History of American Democracy* (1995).

John D. Fairfield
Xavier University, Cincinnati, Ohio

Cleveland, Ohio

Situated on the shore of Lake Erie at the mouth of the Cuyahoga River, Cleveland, Ohio, appears to defy characterization as a typical midwestern city. Its rich industrial and multicultural history mirror that of other cities on the Great Lakes, but its Connecticut roots and cultural amenities give it a somewhat eastern persona.

Cleveland was established in 1796 as the capital of the Connecticut Western Reserve. It was named in honor of Moses Cleaveland, who led the first surveying party to the area to plat the land for sale. Cleaveland was an agent and member of the Connecticut Land Company, a consortium of individuals who purchased the Western Reserve lands from Connecticut as a speculative real estate venture.

Cleaveland's surveyors created a typical New England town plan for the new community, complete with a large commons that became known as Public Square. Little emerged from that plan for nearly three decades, however, and the community languished because of poor access, malarial swamps along the riverbed, and uncertainties over title to the land.

Real growth occurred only after construction began on the Ohio and Erie Canal in 1825. Cleveland, the "a" of Cleaveland having been omitted so that the name could fit on the masthead of the local paper, was the northern terminus of the canal that connected Lake Erie with the Ohio River at Portsmouth. The community grew into an important mercantile center on a trade route that stretched from New York City to New Orleans. Between 1830 and 1860, its population jumped from 1,075 to 43,417. A variety of commodities, including grain, lumber, and eventually coal, were shipped through and traded in the city. The commodity business provided the start for John D. Rockefeller's career in Cleveland.

Railroads provided further impetus for growth and further enhanced the value of the city's geographic location. The first were constructed in the early 1850s. By the Civil War, they linked the city to the Eastern Seaboard, Chicago, the Mississippi River valley, and Pennsylvania. This set the stage for the city's evolution into an industrial center in which iron and steel-making and the manufacture of goods from iron and steel would dominate the economy for a century. By 1920, the value of industrial goods produced in Cleveland reached $1.1 billion. With a population of 796,841, the city was the fifth-largest in the United States. During the first two decades of the twentieth century, industrial wealth catalyzed the creation of nationally notable cultural and philanthropic organizations such as the Cleveland Orchestra and the Cleveland Foundation. The city gained a reputation as one of the most progressive in America. During Tom L. Johnson's term as Democratic mayor from 1901 to 1909, Cleveland earned the reputation as the best-governed city in America.

Cleveland's growth coincided with a period of heavy immigration from Europe that provided the majority of its industrial workforce. By 1920, two-thirds of the city's population was of foreign birth or foreign parentage. At least a dozen ethnic groups were represented by significant, self-contained communities within the city, while over fifty groups were represented in the population as a whole. Ethnicity and ethnic neighborhoods became one of the city's hallmarks. Their development differentiated Cleveland from its New England roots.

Also evident by this time was a growing African American population. Cleveland's New England heritage made it a center for antislavery sentiment in the Antebellum period. The 799 free blacks resident in 1860 lived in a relatively tolerant and integrated environment. Those who came during the Great Migration after the 1890s, however, experienced segregation and a hardening of racial attitudes. With the restriction of European immigration in the 1920s, black migrants became the most significant new component of Cleveland's population. By 2000, African Americans constituted the majority of the population.

By the late 1920s, Cleveland was the vibrant center of northeastern Ohio. The new Cleveland Union Terminal complex facing its Public Square provided the actual and visible locus for this center, linking the city to a series of suburbs, including Shaker Heights, that had grown on its immediate corporate borders. With the Depression, however, the city entered a period of change and decline that was still being resolved at the century's end. Depression-era unemployment that reached nearly 31 percent was replaced by a booming World War II economy. However, that boom masked a deeper reality. Industry began to move away from the city during and after the war. Initially attracted by cheaper land in suburbs such as Euclid and Brook Park, industrialists began to look well beyond Cleveland in the 1950s to less expensive, nonunion labor markets. By the 1960s, the decline was visible as the center city lost population, largely to the suburbs, which had by then expanded well beyond the city's immediate boundaries. By the end of the century, Cleveland's population of 478,403 constituted only slightly more than a third of that of surrounding Cuyahoga county.

Racial antipathy, in part, fueled suburban growth. By the 1970s, African Americans constituted 38 percent of the city's population. Cleveland's minority population grew while industrial opportunity declined. This, along with patterns of de facto segregation in schools and housing, resulted in urban riots in the Hough neighborhood in 1966 and the Glenville neighborhood in 1968. These events bracketed the election of Carl B. Stokes, an African American, as mayor in 1967. His election as the first black mayor of a major American city in part typified the city's desire to confront and resolve problems.

The 1970s represented, perhaps, the nadir of Cleveland's history as continuing industrial departures led to a diminished tax base and eventually to financial default in 1978. Default was due, in part, to conflict between the populist mayor, Dennis Kucinich, and the business interests of the city. Those interests in one sense represented a direct tie to Cleveland's New England heritage that dictated that the elite of the community become its stewards. With the advent of industrial fortunes in the nineteenth century, wealth and not necessarily New England background determined the elite. By the early 1900s, the local chamber of commerce was arguably the most powerful body in the city.

At the beginning of the twenty-first century, Cleveland seemed to be resolving the issues that came to the fore in the 1960s and 1970s by creating a new, postindustrial economy based on health care and service industries. The Cleveland Clinic Foundation and University Hospitals of Cleveland were the largest employers in the city and surrounding county. Developments such as the Rock and Roll Hall of Fame and Museum, the Great Lakes Science Center, and new stadiums and arenas for its sports teams refocused attention on its downtown and lakefront. Stewardship of such developments is still effected by the business community, but nongovernmental organizations such as the Cleveland Foundation and the George Gund Foundation increasingly play the central role in such endeavors. The fact that their endowments derive largely from fortunes made in the industrial past provides a tangible reminder of historical continuity in the rapidly changing city.

Sources and Further Reading: Thomas F. Campbell and Edward M. Miggins, eds., *The Birth of Modern Cleveland, 1865–1930* (1988); Edmund Chapman, *Cleveland: Village to Metropolis* (1998); Daniel Hurley, *Cincinnati: The Queen City* (1982); W. Dennis Keating Norman Krumholz, and David C. Perry, eds., *Cleveland: A Metropolitan Reader* (1995); Carol P. Miller and Robert A. Wheeler, *Cleveland: A Concise History, 1796–1996,* 2nd ed. (1997); William Ganson Rose, *Cleveland: The Making of a City* (1950); David D. Van Tassel and John J. Grabowski, eds., *The Encyclopedia of Cleveland History,* 2nd ed. (1996).

John J. Grabowski
Case Western Reserve University, Ohio

Columbus, Ohio

Columbus, the capital of the State of Ohio, is at the eastern edge of the Midwest. An act of the Ohio General Assembly established the site for the capital city in 1812. By 2000, it was the fifteenth largest city in the nation.

The opening of the Old Northwest Territory to settlement in the late 1700s resulted in a complex array of surveys, land grants, and sales by the young federal government in the part of the Territory that was to become Ohio by 1803. Virginians were the first to claim and settle the Territory based on a grant in 1784 and the creation of the Virginia Military District, located between the Scioto River on the east and the Little Miami on the west. By 1797, Virginians had established Franklinton as a settlement on the west bank of the Scioto River near its juncture with the Olentangy River and in the environs that was to eventually become Columbus.

When the Ohio General Assembly sought in 1812 to locate a site for a new capital near the center of the state, Virginians offered land they had acquired on the east bank of the river along with other inducements, such as a capitol building and penitentiary. The Legislature accepted the offer and Columbus was established as Ohio's capital. It was platted on a rectangular grid, and the sale of lots began; it was, in a sense, a planned state capital.

Columbus is located on the central Ohio glacial till plain. The relatively flat plain is cut by the Scioto River and several other north-to-south flowing streams. The glacial boundary and the Appalachian Plateau are to the east and southeast, and relationship with that area has been a factor in the city's development. The new capital grew slowly as a governmental center. The choice of the site was, indeed, based on its perceived central location in the state. Geographic accessibility grew as turnpikes were built, a feeder canal of the Ohio and Erie Canal opened in 1831, and the National Road passed through the area by 1833. Columbus, with 2,435 residents in 1830, was incorporated as a city in 1834 and, by 1850, had a modest population of 17,882, at which time early railroads were in place and a number of small manufacturing firms were in business.

The city remained predominantly a political and commercial center until 1870, but population increased rapidly in the following period of urban industrialization. Columbus was Ohio's third-largest city with 125,560 residents by 1900. Coal, iron ore, and other mineral and timber resources from southeastern counties spurred the growth of a local iron and steel industry and encouraged other manufacturing activities. A mix of home-grown industries, some among the largest of their kind in the world—such as the Columbus Buggy Company, Jeffrey Manufacturing (mining machinery), and Jaeger Machine (cement mixers)—characterized the local economy until World War II.

By 1940, with a population of over 306,000 and an area of approximately forty square miles, Columbus stood alone on the central Ohio till plain. There were relatively few suburbs; most were small rural communities. World War II brought new industry to the city, investment in older local industry, and with the expanding manufacturing base, the in-migration of workers from Appalachia and the south. Following the war, the exodus of business, industry, and residents

from the city to undeveloped suburban areas was commonplace. By 1950, the city had a population of 375,901 and was the central city for the newly designated Columbus Metropolitan Area which, with Franklin County, had a population in excess of 503,000.

At this time, the city embarked on an ambitious annexation program whose purpose was to capture for the city much of the expanding growth in the largely unincorporated surrounding agricultural land. Columbus offered sewer and water services to those areas that chose to be annexed. With rapid suburban growth under way, Delaware and Pickaway Counties to the north and south, respectively, were included in the Columbus Metropolitan Area in 1963. By 1970, twenty years after the start of the annexation program, the city's area had increased to 143 square miles.

By 2000, the Metropolitan Area included six counties and the city's area, over 200 square miles. Columbus, the central city of the area, had a population in excess of 711,470; its metropolitan area has been the fastest growing region in Ohio. Clearly, this region did not share in the Rust Belt experience of many industrial cities in Ohio and the Midwest. Rather, a service economy flowered, reflecting the role of research institutions and related organizations in the area, such as Ohio State University, Battelle Institute, CompuServ, Chemical Abstracts, the Online Computer Library Center, and others engaged in the production, distribution, and use of information. The city has emerged as a major information center. It also became a major center of the insurance industry, represented perhaps most prominently by Nationwide, and more recently of retailing, reflected in the rapid rise of The Limited and associated stores in the last three decades of the twentieth century.

The city and region have been well-served by a network of interstate highways. I-71, the major north-south highway linking Columbus, Cleveland, and Cincinnati, crosses I-70, the major east-west national highway, in downtown Columbus. The 55-mile outerbelt, I-270, around the perimeter of the city, attracted new businesses in warehousing, distribution, and manufacturing. With these systems in place, suburban expansion extended into the adjacent counties within the metropolitan area, and increased residential housing and commuting became facts of life.

Over time, annexations to Columbus occurred in all parts of the region. More dynamic growth to the north was in keeping with the general principle that cities grow upstream. The southern portions of the I-270 Outerbelt have not attracted the business, population, or residential development typical of the northern areas. Across northern Franklin County, several upscale malls have been developed, and upscale housing characterizes much of the area in these fast grow-ing suburbs.

Currently, the metropolitan counties are increasing in size at a faster pace than the central city, and the city-region is confronted, as are other cities of the Midwest, by suburban sprawl and highway congestion. The impact is felt as well in the older urban cores, where a disproportionate share of the region's poor live and where the future of the downtown is uncer-tain. Even so, the Columbus region remains one of the more dynamic areas in the Midwest.

Sources and Further Reading: Ralph H. Brown, *Historical Geography of the United States* (1948); Charles C. Cole, Jr., *A Fragile Capital* (2001); Osman C. Hooper, *History of the City of Columbus, Ohio* (1920); Henry L. Hunker, *Columbus, Ohio: A Personal Geography* (2000); Henry L. Hunker, *Industrial Evolution of Columbus, Ohio* (1958); Roderick Peattie, ed., *Columbus, Ohio: An Analysis of a City's Development* (1930); Alfred J. Wright, *Economic Geography of Ohio* (1953).

Henry L. Hunker
The Ohio State University–Columbus

Des Moines, Iowa

Beginning as a temporary military establishment in 1843, Des Moines incorporated in 1857, and by 1866, had grown to a city of some ten thousand inhabitants. As early as 1850, the city had become a regional trading center with dozens of businesses, two hotels, and sev-eral lawyers and physicians. Des Moines continued to develop following its designation as Iowa's capital in 1857. During the Civil War, telegraph lines reached the city, and in 1866 and 1867, the Des Moines Valley and the Chicago, Rock Island and Pacific railroads linked Des Moines to the country's expanding rail system. A diversified economy featuring light manufacturing, food processing, printing and publishing, wholesaling of durable goods, and a strong financial segment en-abled Des Moines to prosper, and by 1880, it had be-come Iowa's largest city, a position it still holds.

Although Des Moines's population grew during the early twentieth century, the city attracted relatively few immigrants. During the peak immigration from 1890 to 1909, Des Moines's foreign-born population remained around 13 percent, a modest figure com-pared to many of the nation's more industrialized northern cities. Swedes, Norwegians, Danes, English, Irish, and Germans constituted the largest groups of early immigrants, joined later by Russians and Italians. By 1910, the city had grown to over eighty-six thou-sand inhabitants, and institutions established by immi-grants and the city's small African American popula-tion contributed to a municipal culture that included

pastoral and amusement parks, an opera house, several theatres, and the Iowa State Fair. Men and women liv-ing in the city found jobs in a variety of occupations, including trade and manufacturing.

In the first decade of the twentieth century, the people of Des Moines attracted national attention by pioneering a new form of municipal government fea-turing a city council elected on an at-large basis rather than by individual wards. Designed to combat the al-leged corruption and inefficiency in local government that many citizens believed impeded Des Moines's economic growth, the commission government plan won voter approval in 1907, putting Des Moines in the forefront of Progressive era political reform ef-forts.

By 1950, Des Moines's population had grown to 175 thousand, and the city boasted an economy an-chored by retailers like Younkers, insurance organiza-tions like Bankers and Equitable Life, and publishers like the Meredith. The insurance industry began in Des Moines in 1865, and by 1950, forty insurance companies called the city home. Publishing also had a long history in the city, beginning in the mid-nineteenth century. By 1950, one magazine published by Meredith, *Better Homes and Gardens*, claimed a cir-culation of over 3.3 million.

In the 1970s and 1980s, Des Moines's people refur-bished their city's downtown area, constructing a new Civic Center, Convention Center, Botanical Center, and a sometimes controversial system of downtown skyways serving visitors and shoppers. In 2000, Des Moines's population of just over 199 thousand ranked it the ninety-second-largest city in the United States, while the Des Moines's metropolitan area ranked ninetieth with a population exceeding 450 thousand. Des Moines's current residents are part of a 150-year history they share with their pioneering ancestors. Together they built a vibrant city in the nation's heart-land.

Sources and Further Reading: Orin L. Dahl, *Des Moines, Capital City* (1978); Barbara Beving Long, *Des Moines and Polk County* (1988); Howard J. Nelson, "The Economic De-velopment of Des Moines," *Iowa Journal of History* 48 (July 1950); Bradley Robert Rice, *Progressive Cities* (1977).

Robert Bionaz
Chicago State University, Illinois

Detroit, Michigan

Detroit, the largest city in the state of Michigan, is the seat of Wayne County and is known as the Automotive Capital of the World. The city sits at the heart of an official three-county metropolitan region. The city of Ann Arbor is included in its Metropolitan Statistical Area, along with the city of Windsor and Essex County, Ontario, Canada. Detroit is a spatially flat city of single-family homes which encompasses 139 square miles. Five major freeways cut through the area.

Detroit was founded on July 24, 1701, by Antoine de la Mothe Sieur Cadillac, a French military officer and explorer, as a base to block British expansion. The permanent outpost system did not prove successful, however, particularly after the Seven Years War (called the French and Indian War in the United States) resulted in the French losing much of their North American empire to the British. Though the United States gained official control of the region after the American Revolution, the British remained in place until the terms of the Jay Treaty settled the issue in 1796. The first territorial judge, August Woodward, arrived in June 1805 to discover that the primarily French-speaking city had burned to the ground in an accidental fire. He based the design for rebuilding the new city on Pierre L'Enfant's design for Washington, D.C., and used broad avenues radiating fan-like from large, circular centers. The plan never gained favor, and only the downtown still retains the original, limited, Woodward Plan.

The territorial capital, then the state capital resided in Detroit from 1805 to 1847, when it moved to Lansing. Industries including wood product finishing, shipbuilding, metal products, steel-making, and shipping developed before and after the Civil War. Detroit at the time lacked a full-time police force and would not receive one until the 1860s. The Depression of 1893 brought most of Detroit's industries to a halt and placed enormous pressure on the city's charities. Republican mayor Hazen M. Pingree extended public aid to workers and made plots of land available for use as vegetable patches. He also pioneered the expansion of city government into water, sewage, electric, and public transportation services. Immigration also expanded the city's population as waves of Polish, German, Russian, and southern European families arrived in the city to work in the growing industries. African Americans, though still a small part of the population, had established a separate community east of downtown, a segregated ghetto that would remain in place until the 1950s.

Detroit became the financial center of Michigan's natural resource wealth and served as the operational center for lumber barons such as David M. Whitney, Frank Hecker, and Henry B. Joy, who also used it as a base to seek new investment opportunities. Michigan, in general, and specifically Detroit, was home to a variety of entrepreneurs and inventors, including Henry Ford, Horace and John Dodge, and the most successful at the time, Ransom E. Olds, who sought backing

in the city. Detroit quickly developed into the center for the automobile industry through a combination of financial resources, inventiveness, location, and luck. Automobile production expanded rapidly, with concurrent growth in factories and suppliers that would transform Detroit's industrial landscape. The city exploded from being the nation's ninth-largest at 465,766 people in 1910, to fourth-largest at 993,678 in 1920. Detroit managed to avoid most of the large-scale social violence after World War I that plagued other large cities. It instead experienced intense localized incidents, resulting in the Ossian Sweet Trial in 1925 that probed the edges of civil rights in the urban North's housing market.

Violence increased in the Prohibition era, again during the Great Depression, and yet again during the organizing drives of the United Auto Workers (UAW) union and subsequent opposition by the auto companies, primarily the Ford Motor Company. The problems of housing would continue to plague the city, as would its racial tensions, eventually reigniting into violence in June 1943. Poor housing, racial tensions, and a heat wave contributed to the worst rioting the nation had seen thus far, leaving nine whites and twenty-five blacks dead and millions in property damage. The success of the Arsenal of Democracy in World War II would not last long, as the auto industry and white population moved to the suburbs and the open land beyond. Detroit's population hit its high point of 1,849,568 in 1950, then declined rapidly. Deindustrialization left minorities increasingly isolated in the central city areas, and anger at this situation and with the predominantly white police force again sparked violence in July 1967. The increasing economic and social isolation of African Americans in the central city contributed to this outbreak of violence that left forty-three dead and thousands injured. By 1973, Detroit had elected its first African American mayor, Coleman Young, who served until 1993, and who faced the challenge of battling the city's declining economy.

The Motor City would receive a derisive new moniker, the Murder City, as crime and poverty peaked from the mid-1970s to the early 1990s. Instead of a housing shortage, the city now experiences a housing surplus as the city's population dropped to 951,270, down from the controversial figure of 1,027,974 in 1990. Most of the city's problems stemmed from the collapse of the American auto industry and the resulting loss of jobs and tax revenue. At the same time, the postwar trend for whites to move to suburban areas also drew population and funding away from the central city. The election of a new mayor, Dennis W. Archer, in 1993, coincided with the economic boom of the mid- to late-1990s and resulted in some new development within the city. The future of the city's recovery remains uncertain, with casinos and new businesses working to establish themselves and neighborhood development continuing slowly. With the 2001 election of mayor Kwame Kilpatrick, citizens hope for increasing redevelopment.

Sources and Further Reading: Joe T. Darden et al., *Detroit: Race and Uneven Development* (1987); Sidney Glazer, *Detroit: A Study in Urban Development* (1965); David Levine, *Internal Combustion* (1976); Thomas Sugrue, *Origins of the Urban Crisis* (1996); Olivier Zunz, *The Changing Face of Inequality* (1982).

Matthew L. Daley
Bowling Green State University, Ohio

Indianapolis, Indiana

Indianapolis serves as Indiana's state capital and its principle economic center, and was the twelfth largest city in the United States at the time of the 2000 U.S. Census. Since its founding in 1821, the Circle City has mirrored trends in the Midwest. It has been a place of guarded experimentation, middle-class stability, and voluntary service for the public good.

The adherence to middle-class values and the desire for an ordered democratic and capitalist society is reflected in its founding. The Indiana General Assembly wanted the new capital to be centrally located and close to a waterway for political and commercial reasons. The site selection committee, however, believed the White River to be navigable, an error that limited the city's accessibility and growth for more than two decades. Typical of later Indianapolis projects, in which improvements or adjustments were made to successful ideas introduced elsewhere, the first plat borrowed heavily from Pierre L'Enfant's model for Washington, D.C., and provided for a square mile with streets laid out in a grid pattern around a center circle, with orderly sections for religious observance, education, business, and residential space. Although canals and the National Road (U.S. 40) reached Indianapolis by the late 1830s, it would not become a significant commercial center until after 1847, when railroads opened the city to national markets.

Early economic development depended on both public and private support, and public–private partnerships have marked the city's history ever since. The first such venture, launched in 1828, was the Indianapolis Steam Mill Company. One hundred and seventy-five years later, both private and public as well

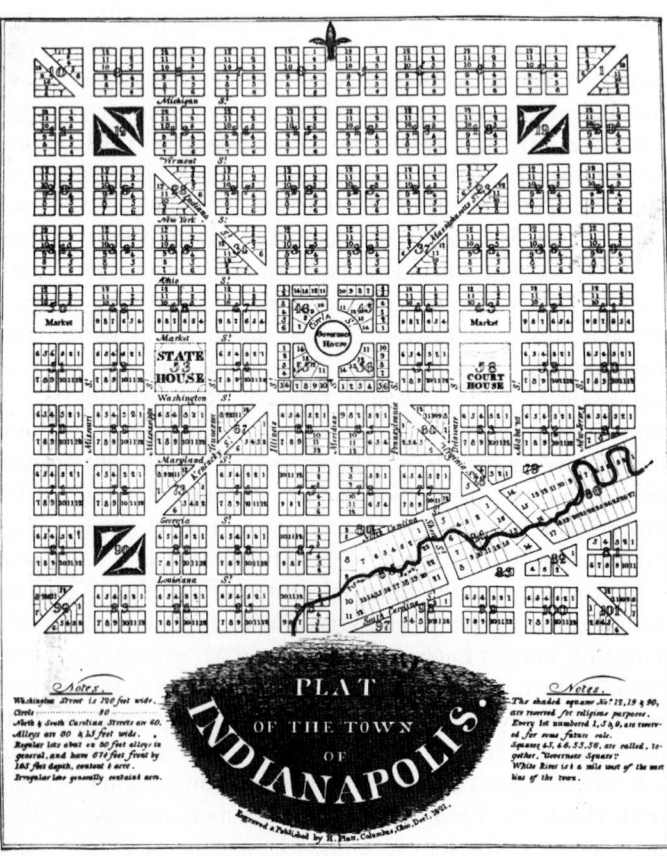

Plat of Indianapolis, 1821. Indiana State Library.

as philanthropic support proved vital to downtown Indianapolis's rebirth.

The city's population and economic trends have mirrored the larger region. With the arrival of the railroads, industry, and agricultural processing to the Midwest, Indianapolis expanded from a village to a city, increasing from 2,600 residents in 1840 to over 75,000 by 1880. Twenty years later, the population stood at 169,000, and in 1970, residents numbered over 744,000. Unlike many midwestern cities, however, most of Indianapolis's growth cannot be attributed to immigration. Irish and German immigrants settled in Indianapolis before 1860 to build canals and railroads or escape war in Europe, but comparatively few immigrants arrived thereafter. In 1850, immigrants made up roughly 35 percent of the city's population, falling to 14 percent in 1880, and to 5 percent in 1920. Only in the 1980s would an immigration surge again reach Indianapolis.

African Americans maintained a continuous presence in the city, with large numbers arriving after 1890. By 1910, Indianapolis had the highest percentage of African Americans in any major city north of the Ohio River. African Americans bolstered the midwestern cultural consensus, planted businesses along Indiana Avenue, and worked in the city's numerous factories. Nativist and racist sentiment ran high during periods of national stress, and the limited cultural diversity contributed to the continuance of legal segregation into the 1950s.

Before World War II, the Indianapolis economy appeared healthy and recession resistant due to the balance among agriculture, food processing, heavy manufacturing, and the wholesale and retail trades. The Great Depression severely affected all cities, but by 1945, Indianapolis had recovered, retaining a large manufacturing base. Between 1940 and the recession of 1979–1982, manufacturing employed roughly 40 percent of Indianapolis workers. Beginning in the 1960s, national economic trends forced many of the largest companies to close or move to the suburbs, accounting for a dip in population between 1970 and 1980 and the flight of residents from the center city. Balance returned to the city's economy after 1980, and in 2002, the three largest employers were government, health-care organizations, and supermarkets; manufacturing employed only 17 percent of city residents. After city leaders focused on sports as an economic vehicle, tourism increased dramatically. The three auto races held at the Indianapolis Motor Speedway alone account for almost one million visitors per year. The population trend also reversed in the 1980s, and the official count in 2000 stood at 860,454 with 71 percent white, non-Hispanic, 24 percent African American, 4 percent Hispanic, 1 percent Asian, and less than 1 percent Native American.

Socially, Indianapolis history can be described as moderately conservative. This is reflected in the 1920s booster literature that touted the city's business atmosphere, the fact that the city refused federal funding until the mid-1960s, and the absence of racial or political riots during the Vietnam Era. It is also significant that the Hudson Institute moved to the city in 1984 because it saw the community as more supportive of its free-market-oriented philosophy than Croton-on-Hudson, New York, where it was originally based.

Traditional midwestern reliance on voluntary associations is clearly visible in Indianapolis cultural history. Most of the city's museums, theatres, and cultural institutions—including the Indianapolis Zoo, the Children's Museum, and the Indianapolis Museum of Art—are principally funded and managed by private organizations. The city is home to over 3,300 philanthropic organizations, with the Lilly Endowment and the Central Indiana Community Foundation the most powerful, well endowed, and well known. The city has a long history of significant leadership in the field of philanthropy and is currently the home of the Center on Philanthropy, located on the campus of Indiana University–Purdue University Indianapolis.

Indianapolis's political history is replete with attempts to administer the city efficiently and to keep taxes low. The most significant change in the capital's political history came in 1969 with the passage of Unigov, which consolidated many county and city government functions. The boundaries of city and county merged, bringing back many suburban taxpayers and voters, enlarging the city's size, and guaranteeing a conservative government for twenty years. A long, and ultimately successful, attempt was made by the Unigov mayors to rebuild the center city to attract visitors, businesses, and residents by using federal funds for slum clearance, using sports to attract tourism and bolster community pride, and working with allies in the private and philanthropic sectors to secure investment in the downtown area.

Sources and Further Reading: David J. Bodenhamer and Robert G. Barrows, eds., *The Encyclopedia of Indianapolis* (1994); David J. Bodenhamer, Lamont Hulse, and Elizabeth B. Monroe, *The Main Stem: The History and Architecture of North Meridian Street* (1992); Jacob P. Dunn, *Greater Indianapolis*, 2 vols. (1910); Edward A. Leary, *Indianapolis: The Story of a City* (1971); Rich Taylor, *Indy: Seventy-Five Years of Racing's Greatest Spectacle* (1991).

Bradford Sample
Indiana Wesleyan University

Kansas City, Missouri

Kansas City is situated in rolling country in northwestern Missouri hard against the Kansas border at the confluence of the Kansas and Missouri Rivers, and it has profited from its centrality. In the mid-nineteenth century, promoter and intellectual William Gilpin drew concentric circles on maps and used mathematical formulas to assert that the Kawsmouth region was at a crucial place on the "axis of intensity" in the "isothermal zodiac," which he said determined the course of high civilization. Gilpin claimed the Kawsmouth was at the center of North America in a concave bowl and the inevitable location of the great world "Centropolis"—the area that would come to harbor Kansas City.

In 1838, a land company had platted the Town of Kansas, its original name, at a landing on the south bank of the Missouri River, a little downstream from the mouth of the Kansas River. The place grew slowly during the border wars of the 1850s in "bleeding Kansas" and during the Civil War from 1861 to 1865. Prospects were bleak until the directors of a railroad running across northern Missouri decided to swing the line to the southwest and bridge the Missouri River at Kansas City. Property given to the railroad directors by the Kansas City business community perhaps influenced the decision. This bridge, the first permanent one over the Missouri River, opened in 1869 and rapid progress followed.

Massive amounts of Boston and Chicago investment capital financed banks, packing plants, stockyards, grain elevators, and warehouses. In 1880, as the frontier in this part of America came to an end, Kansas City already had twelve trunk railroads and, with 55,755 people, was well on the way to becoming a regional metropolis. By 1900, it had tripled in population to 165,752.

Progress continued during the first thirty years of the twentieth century, with the population reaching 394,746 in 1930. The golden age of agriculture and the food demands of World War I brought in a significant expansion of Kansas City's hinterland. A City Beautiful Movement involved the building of a park and boulevard system. Real estate magnate Jesse Clyde Nichols carried the City Beautiful ideal forward in a private sense, developing the south side, upscale residential Country Club District. The city also became a center of jazz and today hosts the Jazz Hall of Fame. Yet by Prohibition and continuing through the Great Depression, the long-standing image of Kansas City was that of a bawdy and corrupt overgrown cow town.

A flourishing vice district that had prevailed from frontier days expanded steadily during the Gilded Age. Visiting cattlemen and railroad transfer passengers provided a ready clientele. In 1878, Kansas City had eighty saloons and as many or more houses of prostitution. Many lowbrow honky-tonks did business in the industrial West Bottoms near the railroad station and packing plants, while higher-brow establishments were downtown in the North End. A political faction, the Goat Democrats, with strong ties to gambling interests, had its greatest strength in these entertainment districts. In 1911, thirty-nine-year-old Thomas J. Pendergast became the Goat leader. A brilliant organizer and ruthless politician, he crushed rival factions and created the all-powerful Pendergast machine.

Except for a brief stint on city council ending in 1915, Pendergast never again held elective office, but he ran Kansas City for nearly two decades. Following a 1925 change in the city charter to a weak mayor–strong city manager plan, Pendergast ran the city government through a handpicked city manager. He established close relations with the local underworld, using criminal enforcers and over sixty thousand illegal "ghost votes" to fix elections. Pendergast dominated the local construction industry and wholesale liquor business. In addition, he forced his way onto numerous corporate boards.

Pendergast personally received over $30 million a year from gambling, prostitution, and narcotics interests. Every legal and illegal business in Kansas City paid at least 5 percent of their annual gross to machine collectors. Pendergast assigned captains in every city block, directed a large welfare system, and publicly boasted that he had twenty thousand informers. In the big leagues of American civic corruption, Pendergast exercised great power at the state level and had a prominent position inside the national Democratic party. He and his family lived lavishly. He treated Kansas City as if it was his own business; a modern version of a medieval city-state.

After Franklin D. Roosevelt became president, the federal government moved against the Pendergast machine. In 1936 and 1937, the federal courts convicted 259 mid-level machine officials of vote fraud. In 1939, Pendergast pleaded guilty to trying to defeat the federal income tax and served a year in Leavenworth penitentiary. His machine collapsed at the municipal level, and he died of a heart attack in 1945. An attempt by local crime boss Charles Binaggio to revive the machine ended with his sensational 1950 murder.

A nonpartisan reform government took hold. The economy, down in the Great Depression, boomed during World War II, as Kansas City added a heavy industrial base that served it well during the rest of the century. In the 1960s and 1970s, the packing plants closed, but agribusiness remained so strong that boosters called Kansas City the agribusiness center of the world. The reformers initially ignored the needs of a growing number of African Americans, and civil disorder swept the inner city in April 1968, after the assassination of Martin Luther King, Jr. Discord over school desegregation led to a 1978 suit in federal court. Developers rebuilt the downtown skyline, but the commercial district lost most if its traditional mercantile functions to suburban shopping centers.

After World War II, Kansas City tried to check suburban growth through an aggressive annexation policy, especially adding territory north of the Missouri River. Even so, municipal Kansas City declined in population from 466,622 in 1950 to 441,545 in 2000. Suburbia grew relentlessly, especially in Johnson County, Kansas. In 1960, the Kansas City metropolitan area reached 1,092,545, moving up to 1,776,062 in 2000. Kansas City entered the new millennium as the thirty-sixth-largest city in the United States; the metropolitan area ranked twenty-sixth. Although Kansas City never reached the heights that Gilpin expected, he did accurately predict the rise of a large metropolis at the Kawsmouth.

Sources and Further Reading: A. Theodore Brown, *Frontier Community: Kansas City* (1963); A. Theodore Brown and Lyle W. Dorsett, *K.C.: A History of Kansas City, Missouri* (1978); Lyle W. Dorsett, *The Pendergast Machine* (1968; reprint, 1980); Charles N. Glaab, *Kansas City and the Railroads* (1962; reprint, 1993); Charles N. Glaab, "Visions of Metropolis," *Wisconsin Magazine of History* 45 (Autumn 1961); Lawrence H. Larsen and Nancy J. Hulston, *Pendergast!* (1997); Rick Montgomery and Shirl Kasper, *Kansas City: An American Story*, ed. Monroe Dodd (1999); William M. Reddig, *Tom's Town* (1947; reprint, 1986); William S. Worley, *J.C. Nichols and the Shaping of Kansas City* (1990).

Lawrence H. Larsen
University of Missouri–Kansas City

Milwaukee, Wisconsin

The city of Milwaukee straddles the banks of the Menominee and Milwaukee Rivers at their outlet into Lake Michigan. Now a city numbering more than half a million residents, at one time in the mid-nineteenth century it actually rivaled its southern neighbor, Chicago, in size. Yet it eventually was eclipsed, as Chicago became a major hub of railroad traffic. Several people played key roles in the early growth of the city, among them Solomon Juneau and Byron Kilbourn, George Walker and Alexander Mitchell. Much like other cities of the Midwest, the Industrial Revolution remade Milwaukee in the 1860s and 1870s. Soon it became a center for the production of heavy machinery, leather goods, and of course, beer.

Milwaukee expanded in large part because of the influx of European immigrants, particularly after about 1860. By this time, it had become home to a very large and active German population and soon became known as a major center of German culture in America. Germans left their mark in many ways, partly through the creation of new industries—the Uihlein brothers built Schlitz Beer, Otto Falk helped to shape the fortunes of Allis-Chalmers—and partly through helping to create various institutions of local culture, from local choral groups to the construction of a local fine arts center, the Pabst Theatre. By the end of the nineteenth century, Polish immigrants also established a large community.

Germans left their mark in other ways as well. It was not simply the affluent Germans who came to Milwaukee, but many political radicals. Among them were Victor and Meta Berger. Victor became a leading figure among the Social Democrats in America, helping to establish the national party and to fuel the growth of a substantial party in Milwaukee. For a period of time, from roughly the 1890s through the 1910s, the Social Democrats were a major force in Milwaukee politics. Indeed, all the mayors were Social Democrats until Henry Maier came to office in 1960.

Milwaukee, like so many other cities, struggled with its growth over the course of the twentieth century. At once a beautiful city, with stately homes on Prospect Avenue overlooking Lake Michigan, it also had far-flung stretches, such as Shorewood and Whitefish Bay, which became home to those residents who preferred to live on the outskirts, away from the heavily industrialized downtown areas. By the 1920s, as Jon Teaford has shown, bitter and divisive struggles grew up between the suburbs and the city. They were fueled, in part, by the fact that Daniel Hoan, a Social Democrat, was Mayor, while many of the newer suburban residents tended to be far more conservative. Over the course of the twentieth century, the division remained; indeed, it became heightened in the years after World War II, when many middle-class residents began to take up residence in Waukesha and other counties lying on the northern and western edges of Milwaukee.

Unlike a number of other cities of the Midwest, for example, Detroit and Chicago, Milwaukee did not have a large minority, especially black, population until the 1970s. By the year 2000, however, the city of Milwaukee contained 37 percent blacks and another 12 percent who were Latino. The rapid growth of the black population over the 1970s and 1980s was responsible, some insist, for the sharp divisions and deeply contentious relations that arose between blacks and whites in the city during the late 1980s and into the 1990s. Partly political divisions, they were demographic, as well. By the early 1990s, Douglas Massey and Nancy Denton could claim that Milwaukee had become one of the most segregated cities in America.

Like so many other industrial cities, Milwaukee was unable to sustain the growth and vitality of its industries over the latter part of the twentieth century. By the 1960s, many of the older and more prominent firms had begun to leave the city for greener pastures in the South, or they simply went out of business, unable to compete with new manufacturing firms abroad. Names that had made Milwaukee famous, like Schlitz, took their business elsewhere; a handful of others, such as Briggs and Stratton, remained in town. The downtown area also suffered decline in the years immediately after World War II, partly because of the tremendous growth of suburban residential and commercial areas and, of course, because of the growth of the expressway system. Milwaukee expressways were intended to bring consumers into the downtown, but unintentionally provided easy entry and exit to work for those who preferred to live in the suburbs. When the Allen-Bradley Company, manufacturer of electronic goods, was bought by Rockwell International, however, the Bradley heirs donated substantially from the proceeds both to new downtown centers and to establishing a leading conservative think tank in the city, the Bradley Foundation.

Though the city has struggled hard to break free from the wraps of its industrial past, Milwaukee has made important progress since the 1990s. In 2001, it became home to a new art museum, hailed as one of the boldest and most novel among new museums in the United States. It also constructed a new baseball park, the Miller Stadium, intended to retain the hometown Brewers and to draw both tourists and local residents. Summerfest, a weeklong event along the shores of Lake Michigan in the downtown area established under Mayor Maier, has clearly become one of the highlights of the year for the city, providing a way for residents to socialize and enjoy some of the good local food, such as bratwursts and kielbasa.

What Milwaukee will become in the twenty-first century is unclear. Problems remain, especially the divisions between minorities and whites in the city. Once an exporter of major equipment to countries across the world, Milwaukee is now simply a small regional center, far overshadowed in the emerging global economy by Chicago. It has yet, in fact, to find its own unique niche and identity in the new century.

Sources and Further Reading: Kathleen Neils Conzen, *Immigrant Milwaukee, 1836–1860* (1976); Douglas Massey and Nancy Denton, *American Apartheid* (1993); Sally M. Miller, "Milwaukee: Of Ethnicity and Labor," in Bruce M. Stave, ed., *Socialism and the Cities* (1975); Sally M. Miller, *Victor Berger and the Promise of Constructive Socialism, 1910–1920* (1973); Frederick I. Olson, "The Milwaukee Socialists, 1897–1941," Ph.D. diss., Harvard University (1952); Anthony M. Orum, *City-Building in America* (1995); Roger D. Simon, *The City-Building Process*, rev. ed. (1996); Jon C. Teaford, *City and Suburb* (1979).

Anthony M. Orum
University of Illinois–Chicago

Omaha, Nebraska

Speculators founded Omaha, Nebraska, on high ground above the Missouri River opposite Council Bluffs, Iowa, on July 4, 1854, after the Kansas–Nebraska Act opened Nebraska Territory to white settlement. Although Omaha was at a ferry crossing at the beginning of the Mormon Trail, it had no special natural advantage over rival Nebraska river cities. Even as the temporary territorial capital, Omaha grew slowly. Then, in 1862, the Union Pacific Railroad established its terminal in Omaha. The railroad stimulated Omaha's economy, negating the impact of losing the capital to Lincoln, fifty miles to the west in 1867, after Nebraska statehood. In 1870, a year after the completion of the Union Pacific–Central Pacific transcontinental system, Omaha boasted a population of 16,083 people. It was the largest city in Nebraska and, according to one promoter, a "signal station at the entrance of a garden."

During the last twenty years of the nineteenth century, Omaha developed at an uneven pace. The Panic of 1873 brought several years of hard times, but was reversed by tremendous progress in the 1880s with rapid agricultural settlement throughout western Nebraska. New packing plants and grain elevators made Omaha an agribusiness center. Warehouses were built for the storage of goods and products distributed over a growing railroad net. Unfortunately, the Panic of 1893, coupled with drought conditions in Nebraska, brought another depression. During the 1890s, by official count, the number of Omaha residents fell from 140,452 to 102,555. Conditions had improved dramatically toward the end of the decade, with the symbol of Omaha's recovery being the Trans-Mississippi and International Exposition of 1898.

During the first forty years of the twentieth century, Omaha experienced considerable social and economic strife, as the population more than doubled to 223,844. In 1909, rioters drove several hundred Greeks out of town. In 1919, sixteen hundred federal troops were brought to Omaha to restore order after a mob of six thousand brutally lynched an African American rape suspect. A conservative business community fought unionization, leading to disruptive packinghouse strikes and transit strikes. A major political boss of the city, Thomas Dennison, promoted Omaha as a wide-open town with laxity in the imposition of law until the state imposed a controversial cleanup in 1929. The Great Depression had a wrenching effect, partially alleviated by New Deal recovery programs.

World War II turned the economy around. One bomber plant employed over twenty thousand war workers. Following hostilities, Omaha gained the headquarters of the Strategic Air Command. Federal money poured into Omaha to finance military activities during the Vietnam War and for the construction of an extensive expressway system. The packing plants closed by the end of the 1970s. Omaha shifted from a blue-collar to white-collar town, with an economy based on insurance, marketing, machinery production, and food processing; many large national corporations have regional headquarters in Omaha. It has a fine art gallery and a large zoo complex. In 2000, the metropolis of 390,007 inhabitants was the central city for a metropolitan statistical area of 716,998 in both Nebraska and Iowa. Transportation, industry, and commerce built up Omaha.

Sources and Further Reading: Harl A. Dalstrom, *A. V. Sorensen and the New Omaha* (1988); Dorothy Devereux Dustin, *Omaha and Douglas County: A Panoramic History* (1980); Lawrence H. Larsen and Barbara J. Cottrell, *The Gate City: A History of Omaha*, enlarged ed. (1997).

Lawrence H. Larsen
University of Missouri–Kansas City

St. Louis, Missouri

Surely other cities can lay equal claim to its perverse combination of "northern charm and southern efficiency," but in few places are the paradoxes and tensions of the Midwest's central position among American regions as deeply or continually felt as they are in St. Louis. Socially and politically diverse and often divided within itself, the St. Louis region mirrors internally the larger divisions that distinguish the region within which it rests.

All cities begin as places of transition, and St. Louis was no exception. The original French village, laid out in 1764 in a manner closely resembling New Orleans, took shape on a bluff rising above the west bank of the Mississippi River. The site was convenient both to the confluence of the Missouri River, leading to the rich fur country of the West, and to existing French agricultural settlements, such as Cahokia and Fort des Chartres, on the opposite bank. Here, too, a dramatic change in the depth of the Mississippi River made for a logical break between deep- and shallow-draft boats.

Atop all of these natural points of convergence were laid the political borders that further established St. Louis as a place of cultural overlap and transition in the eighteenth century. The conclusion of the Seven Years' War had transferred St. Louis, like all of Louisiana, from French to Spanish possession, while the nearby Illinois country to the east passed from French to British hands. With the Mississippi now established as a boundary between empires, St. Louis was transformed from a commercial waystation to a strategic international border post.

With the arrival of American governance in the year following the Louisiana Purchase of 1803, St. Louis became home to a growing number of American-born traders and land speculators. Incorporated as a town in 1809, it drew significant numbers of immigrants from both northern and southern states, as well as a growing number from Ireland and Germany. Together they accounted for the sharp juxtapositions of a city that by the 1850s, would count among its residents Unitarian ministers and French nuns, German radicals and Secessionist planters, Dred Scott and William T. Sherman.

Its population rising steadily, the city jumped its boundaries numerous times in the nineteenth century. The last of these annexations, in 1876, established the city's current boundary line at Skinker Boulevard, just west of the newly created Forest Park. With the change came ratification of the nation's first home-rule charter and the simultaneous separation of the city from its own county—a political peculiarity that subsequently did more to limit the city's ability to annex land and maintain a steady tax base than it did to fulfill supporters' promises of efficient local governance.

This expanded St. Louis, by 1900 the nation's fourth-most populous city, encompassed a vastly more diverse set of land uses, people, and cultural traditions than had the mercantile city of the antebellum era. Its workers quarried clay, forged steel for rails and train cars, brewed beer, made shoes, and refined tobacco and cotton. Its financiers speculated widely across the southwestern trade territories that had opened after the Mexican War. The city boasted three daily German-language newspapers, a growing pool of unionized labor, an active literary scene (centered around William Marion Reedy's widely circulated *Mirror*), and a fertile ground where musicians such as Scott Joplin lay the musical groundwork for ragtime and urban blues.

In 1904, the Louisiana Purchase Exposition drew twenty million visitors to Forest Park, offering them a

The St. Louis Arch. Courtesy Missouri Division of Tourism.

spectacle larger than any previous fair. Fueled by the fair's success in sparking interest in an improved urban landscape, a local volunteer group known as the Civic League of St. Louis produced the nation's first comprehensive city plan in 1907. The plan provided a template onto which was grafted the subsequent work of a number of key American city planners—George Kessler, Henry Wright, and most importantly Harland Bartholomew.

The work of such professional planners would become increasingly important in the twentieth-century city, as residents and businesses alike left the self-contained city for its newer suburbs—a process that diminished the population in St. Louis proper from more than 850 thousand in 1950 to fewer than 350 thousand in 2000. On the waterfront, the Jefferson National Expansion Memorial (popularly known as the Gateway Arch) replaced blocks of aging warehousing and commercial buildings. In the neighborhoods ringing downtown, publicly subsidized, multiunit housing took the place of earlier, densely settled blocks. Interstate highways, masterminded by Bartholomew and his colleagues on the federal highway commission, cut through the north and south sides and sliced the Arch grounds off from the streets of downtown. Politicians and corporate leaders, most notably Civic Progress, a tight-knit conclave of local corporate chiefs, tried to anchor the central city with an economic base of light industry, white-collar employment, and tourism—a task made considerably easier by the enduring popularity of the Cardinals baseball team, who moved downtown from their longtime northside home, the former Sportsman's Park, in 1966. The arrival of the former Los Angeles Rams football team in the 1990s added to the city's sports ca-

chet. At the same time, many of the city's working-class neighborhoods saw little in the way of official support for their imperiled condition.

Racial segregation, enacted briefly by law in 1916 and subsequently enforced through private real estate covenants, had much to do with the fate of the neighborhoods, particularly as the southern black migrations of the twentieth century swelled the city's African American population. By 1970, the north side was largely black and the south side, almost entirely white. With federal support for black neighborhoods largely limited to demolition (as in the case of the city's Mill Creek Valley, bulldozed in 1960) or poorly maintained public housing, deterioration proved a likelier result of public investment than did improvement.

By 2000, the city of St. Louis was a far smaller place, and one less certain of its own destiny, than it had been a century earlier. Nevertheless, it demonstrated a measure of resilience in the face of its challenges. To the city's African American population—now and for the first time, a majority—had been added significant refugee and immigrant populations. Middle-class strongholds remained and in some cases expanded in the city's west side and a handful of other neighborhoods, while a more racially mixed population on the south side suggested a beginning of the end of the city's old lines of segregation. The city's economy had also changed, although the effects of that change remained hard to predict. Health care and service jobs now predominated over the aging industrial base, while corporate takeovers robbed the city of its longstanding claim to the headquarters of such homegrown companies as Monsanto, Ralston-Purina, and McDonnell Douglas. Nevertheless, in its architecture, foodways, and even its enduring social, political, and racial tensions, St. Louis maintained a kernel of the distinctive overlap of regional cultures that had marked its rise to prominence among American cities.

Sources and Further Reading: Jeffrey Adler, *Yankee Merchants and the Making of the Urban West* (1991); Civic League of St. Louis, *A City Plan for St. Louis* (1907); Carl J. Ekberg, *French Roots in the Illinois Country* (1998); Andrew Hurley, ed., *Common Fields: An Environmental History of St. Louis* (1997); James Neal Primm, *Lion of the Valley*, 3rd ed. (1998); Eric Sandweiss, ed., *St. Louis in the Century of Henry Shaw* (2003); Eric Sandweiss, *St. Louis: The Evolution of an American Urban Landscape* (2001); John Wright, *Discovering African American St. Louis*, 2nd ed. (2002).

Eric Sandweiss
Indiana University–Bloomington

Minneapolis and St. Paul, Minnesota

The Twin Cities of Minneapolis and St. Paul form the core of the nation's fifteenth largest metropolitan region. Located in southeastern Minnesota, the Twin Cities encompass 2.9 million people in eleven counties; the functional region extends another nine to eleven counties to the north, west, and south, and east into Wisconsin. Minneapolis is Minnesota's largest city; St. Paul is the state capital. Drained by the Mississippi, Minnesota, and St. Croix Rivers, the region is marked by many smaller streams, creeks, and numerous lakes. With temperatures to −30°F in winter and 100°F in summer, the Twin Cities displays one of the greatest climatic extremes of any major urban area in the United States.

Historically noted for flour milling and progressive politics, these cities grew from an 1820s frontier outpost, Fort Snelling. Founded in the 1830s and 1840s, St. Paul was named after its first church. Founded a decade later, a public contest named Minneapolis from the Sioux *minne,* "water," and the Greek *polis,* "city." Both cities originated in nineteenth century trade and technology: St. Paul became the head of navigation on the Mississippi as steamboats brought settlers and trade goods upriver. The 1870s and 1880s innovations in flour milling made Minneapolis the nation's largest milling center. The region sat on the edge of an expanding trade area in these decades, as railroads and boats moved farm machinery and trade goods to St. Paul, then from Minneapolis to the large western wheat areas.

New Englanders and Canadians were the first migrants to the area, entering a territory that historically divided the Sioux and Chippewa peoples. From 1880 to 1910, newcomers poured in from Germany, Sweden, Norway, Denmark, and Ireland. Minneapolis–St. Paul had nearly one million people by 1900, almost all within the cities. The Twin Cities population continued to grow—and since 1950, primarily in the suburbs—and remained extremely Northern European and Lutheran in ethnic origin and religious preference well into the 1980s. Recent demographic shifts have included a major increase in the size of the traditionally small African American and Native American populations, as well as the establishment of new communities as a result of substantial immigration from Vietnam, Cambodia, Laos, Mexico, Somalia, and Ethiopia. As of the 2000 census, 33 to 34 percent of the core city population is now nonwhite. In the 1990s, the core cities of Minneapolis–St. Paul gained population, 4 to 5 percent, for the first time since 1960. The region anticipates another million people by 2030.

Across the northern tier of the United States, the Twin Cities is the largest commercial center between Chicago and Seattle, serving a regional market of eight states and two Canadian provinces. Minneapolis is the seat of the Ninth Federal Reserve District and has a significant presence of major corporate headquarters. St. Paul remains an important shipping center; with several barge lines still terminating there. As elsewhere in recent decades, the processing of agricultural products and manufacturing have declined, while service industries have dramatically increased. The contemporary Twin Cities economy is reasonably diversified: education; electronic, computer-related, and other "high-tech" industries; graphic arts, film and video production; government, banking, and insurance; product distribution; construction of computers, guidance systems, textiles and apparel, household appliances, and paper; and residual milling functions all thrive. Multinational corporations remain highly visible: 3M, Target, Medtronic, General Mills, and The St. Paul Companies are among the many headquarters firms in the region.

The Twin Cities anchors the upper Midwest transportation network, with the Minneapolis–St. Paul International Airport, one of three Northwest Airlines' hubs, at its core. Two interstate highways pierce the length and breadth of the city, and a major freeway surrounds the first ring of suburbs. Rail service, mainly freight, continues. A light rail transit line is under construction. Minneapolis became the head of navigation on the Mississippi in the 1950s, constructing Lock and Dam #1 adjacent to downtown, however barge traffic is outnumbered by pleasure craft today.

Visitors note the rich educational and cultural life of the region. The University of Minnesota, with more than fifty thousand students, has two campuses spanning the Mississippi River in Minneapolis and a third in St. Paul. While Minneapolis also has several small colleges, St. Paul is the city known for its many four-year institutions: the College of St. Catherine and St. Thomas University, Concordia College, Hamline University, Macalester College, Bethel College and Seminary, the St. Paul Seminary. In addition, fourteen branches of the Minnesota State Colleges and Universities, the state university system, dot the metro region. Nationally regarded as a leading cultural center, the Twin Cities house a range of prominent institutions—from traditional institutions such as the Minneapolis Institute of Arts, Walker Art Center, Minnesota Orchestra, St. Paul Arts and Science Center, and Minnesota History Center (in its 1990 home); to stalwarts from the 1960s and 1970s such as the Guthrie Theater, Science Museum, St. Paul Chamber Orchestra, Children's Theater, Fitzgerald theater, Penumbra Theater, and Ordway Theater; and on to the vibrant alternative theatre scene of recent decades, including Jeune Lune, the Jungle, and the Loring, and two opera companies. Both cities have restored downtown live theatre spaces, and there is a plethora of dance venues in recent years as well. Choral music is another characteristic of the local cultural scene.

The Twin Cities region prides itself on its year-round outdoor activities, largely centered around water, whether liquid or frozen. Minneapolis is known for its excellent park system: 153 parks covering approximately six thousand acres, with twenty-two lakes inside the city limits. St. Paul, with fewer lakes, boasts several state-wide events: the Winter Carnival each January and the annual ten-day Minnesota State Fair, the metropolitan area's yearly opportunity to experience livestock competition, arts and crafts, butter sculpture and midway thrills. The Twin Cities have a variety of professional sports, including the Minnesota Twins baseball team, the Vikings football team, and

the Timberwolves basketball team in Minneapolis. St. Paul is home to Minnesota Wild hockey team and the hugely popular minor league St. Paul Saints baseball team.

The Twin Cities are distinguished by having one of the earliest functioning metropolitan planning and management organizations in the country, the Metropolitan Council, which operates transit and infrastructure and is actively pursuing a "smart growth" agenda. Each of the cities has a different government: St. Paul has a strong mayor system, while Minneapolis has a weak mayor–strong council system.

Sources and Further Reading: John S. Adams and Barbara J. VanDrasek, *Minneapolis-St. Paul: People, Place and Public Life* (1993); Judith A. Martin, "In Fits and Starts," in A. Sancton and D. Rothblatt, eds., *Metropolitan Governance: American/Canadian Intergovernmental Perspectives* (1993); Judith A. Martin and Antony Goddard, *Past Choices, Present Landscapes* (1989); Judith A. Martin and David Lanegran, *Where We Live* (1983).

Judith A. Martin
University of Minnesota

Wichita, Kansas

Since its start as a trading outpost in 1864, Wichita has straddled the border between the Midwest and the Southwest. It has long been a boomtown with a strong entrepreneurial tradition and booster spirit. In the early 1870s, Wichita served as a terminus for the Chisholm cattle trail, as well as the hub for the region's agricultural development. In the 1880s, it boomed briefly into the largest city in the region, but the boom was based largely on real estate speculation, which burst by the 1890s. In the decades that fol-

A modern terminus of the old Chisholm Trail. Wichita-Sedgwick County Historical Museum.

lowed, the city developed into a regional center for western Kansas, Oklahoma, and the Texas Panhandle. Although equidistant from Oklahoma City and Kansas City, Wichita's cultural ties have been stronger with Oklahoma.

In the 1920s, money from local oil development brought new wealth to the region. Financed in part by oil money, Wichita became the home for early leaders in the aviation industry such as Clyde Cessna, Lewis Baird, and the Beech family. As a result, Wichita has been a center for aviation development, enjoying the moniker "the Air Capital" since 1927. Aviation became one of the central supports of the economy during World War II. In the 1950s, Beech, Cessna, Lear, and some of Boeing's operations were headquartered in Wichita.

The aviation industry drew thousands of migrants, both African American and white, from places such as Oklahoma, Missouri, Arkansas, and Texas. Meanwhile, Wichita's boosters dropped the "Southwest" designation and opted instead to identify with the Midwest. However, the most popular image has been that of an all-American city divorced almost entirely from a regional identity.

Wichita has been a pioneer on many fronts. It was the birthplace of such companies as White Castle Hamburgers, Coleman, Mentholatum, Pizza Hut, and Rent-a-Center. Wichita has contributed to a number of social and cultural trends as well. In 1958, one of the first sit-ins challenging segregation took place in Wichita. It was also an important center for the beat movement, home to writer Charles Plymell, and even serving as inspiration for visiting writer Allen Ginsberg, who wrote his *Wichita Vortex Sutra* in 1966.

While Wichita experienced growth as a minor sunbelt center, it quickly lost ground to even more rapidly developing communities such as Oklahoma City and Kansas City, which with their larger population bases, commanded larger airports and better transportation links. Meanwhile, local companies merged with international corporations resulting in lost employment toward the end of the twentieth century.

During this period of transformation, Wichita has struggled with its identity. Some see the community intimately tied to aviation and technology. Others see value in using its "cowtown" past as leaven for tourism. Still others insist that Wichita's benefits lie in its being a livable community and a great place to raise a family. Meanwhile, growing communities of Hispanics, Southeast Asians, and Middle Eastern immigrants continue to make Wichita an ever more diverse place in which to live.

Sources and Further Reading: Richard M. Long, *Wichita Century* (1969); H. Craig Miner, *Wichita: The Early Years,* *1865–1880* (1982); H. Craig Miner, *Wichita: The Magic City* (1988); Joseph Rowe and H. Craig Miner, *Borne on the South Wind* (1994).

Jay Price
Wichita State University, Kansas

Rust Belt Manufacturing Cities

By the 1980s, much of the industrialized Midwest had become synonymous with decline, dereliction, and despair due to the flight of heavy manufacturing, high rates of unemployment, and the decay of urban infrastructure. The term Rust Belt captured the image of a region that had flourished in an age of steel, but now felt the corrosive effects of a high-tech global economy that had passed it by. Although evidence of the Rust Belt phenomenon could be found in both large and small cities throughout the Midwest, it was particularly pronounced in the smaller, single-industry cities situated along the manufacturing corridor stretching from the Appalachian foothills westward to the Mississippi River, bounded by the Great Lakes on the north and the Ohio River on the south. Thus, the late twentieth-century economic crisis highlighted the tight historical connection between heavy manufacturing and urban growth that was distinctive in that portion of the Midwest comprising the Old Northwest Territory.

The origins of the Rust Belt phenomenon lay in the tremendous wave of industrialization that swept into the continental interior on railroad starting in the 1850s. Although industrialization appeared in the Midwest several decades after its arrival in the East, it exerted a far more profound influence on urban development west of the Appalachians. Unlike their eastern counterparts, which had come to maturity in a commercial age, the fledgling cities of the Midwest developed at a historical moment when industrialization was hitting its full stride. Moreover, midwestern urbanization developed in conjunction with the rise of a national market economy that encouraged a rapid shift from broad-based manufacturing for regional consumers to more specialized production for consumers across the country. It was in this context that midwestern entrepreneurs proved particularly adept at developing product lines to take advantage of the region's rich natural resource base. A dynamic agro-industrial complex developed to include livestock and grain processing along with the manufacture of farm machinery. Abundant deposits of coal and iron supported a vast range of metal refining and metal fabricating industries.

Jenny, I'm Sinking Down: The Jeanette
Blast Furnace, Youngstown, Ohio.
Courtesy James Jeffrey Higgins.

While much specialized manufacturing gravitated to the large regional entrepôts like Chicago, Cincinnati, and St. Louis, a great many smaller cities owed their growth to concentrated industrial production. Situated astride central and northern Michigan's expansive hardwood forests, Grand Rapids emerged as a major processor of timber, then as a leading producer of styled furniture. By 1900, this City Built on Wood had developed a national reputation for its fine cabinets, desks, and bedroom sets. Nearly 50 percent of the workforce in this town depended, either directly or indirectly, on the furniture trade for their livelihood. Fort Wayne, Indiana, and Flint, Michigan, also benefited from their proximity to timber sources and emerged as important centers of carriage and wagon production. Closer to the vast midwestern grain belt, cities such as Racine, Wisconsin, and Moline, Illinois, specialized in manufacturing farm machinery. Well before Peoria, Illinois, emerged as a major center of tractor manufacturing, it had established itself as the nation's leading distiller of spirits.

Around the turn of the last century, heavy manufacturing contributed to the rise of dozens of new satellite cities usually located just outside existing metropolitan hubs. These new industrial suburbs arose in conjunction with the second industrial revolution, a series of technological and managerial innovations that enabled giant corporations to maximize economic efficiency by mechanizing production, applying the principles of modern science, and consuming large doses of fossil-fuel energy. Because large-scale mechanized production was incompatible with the dense, mixed-use pattern that characterized existing American cities, metal producers, rubber manufacturers, chemical companies, petroleum refiners, and other enterprises associated with the second industrial revolution showed a distinct preference for peripheral locations at critical junctures of rail and water transport, where land was abundant and cheap. The formation of industrial suburbs was not merely a product of economic and technological forces, however. Factories that emitted heavy smoke, noxious fumes, and toxic chemicals found themselves subject to nuisance laws in many large commercial cities. By transferring operations to outlying sites, large corporations could more easily exploit their economic influence to win concessions from local governments, including lower tax rates and the right to control and mold their surroundings as they wished.

Although satellite cities arose in virtually all sections of the country, they were especially prevalent in the Midwest, which had become by this time the geographical center of the nation's market for finished industrial goods. Some of the densest clusters of satellite cities were located just beyond Chicago and St. Louis. Extending eastward along the Lake Michigan shoreline from the Illinois–Indiana border, Standard Oil, Inland Steel, and U.S. Steel carved out corporate fiefdoms in the towns of Whiting, East Chicago, and Gary, respectively. On the Illinois side of the Mississippi River, across from St. Louis, the new industrial suburbs frequently took the names of their parent corporations: Monsanto (Monsanto Chemical Company), Alorton (Aluminum Ore Company), Granite City (Granite City Steel), and National City (National Stockyards). Crude housing conditions and high pollution levels made life unpleasant for their working-class inhabitants, but these sprawling manufacturing districts became objects of awe and inspiration for the middle-class railroad commuters passing through them and the painters and poets who saw them as emblems of the nation's industrial prowess.

By the 1920s, the automobile emerged as the major engine of midwestern industrial growth, and although Detroit was the primary benefactor of the automotive revolution, much production scattered to the region's secondary urban centers. When General Motors selected Flint, Michigan, as its major production center, it tied that city's fortunes to the motor vehicle, as did the Studebaker Company to South Bend, Indiana, when it located its major production facility there. Many cities also developed or retooled their local industries to supply the major automakers. Sixty miles south of the Motor City along the Lake Erie shoreline, Toledo, Ohio, became the nation's leading supplier of automotive electrical equipment. As early as 1910, the economy of Akron, Ohio, was almost wholly dependent on tire production, with about 50 percent of its workforce directly employed in the city's rubber plants.

Thus, even when not located adjacent to major metropolises, smaller industrial centers were often dependent on them for credit and capital, as well as cultural amenities. Major business deals affecting Peoria and Gary were transacted in Chicago boardrooms and banking offices. Youngstown and Akron residents got most of their news from the major Cleveland newspapers, radio stations, and eventually, television stations. Baseball fans in Toledo and Flint ventured to Detroit's Tiger Stadium when they wanted to see major-league-caliber play.

With an increasing share of the region's industrial enterprise located outside the largest cities, the second-echelon manufacturing cities of the Midwest enjoyed tremendous prosperity during the late nineteenth and early twentieth centuries and drew job seekers from remote regions and countries. Heavy migration from eastern Europe around the turn of the last century supplied the steel mills, auto works, rubber plants, and oil refineries with a steady pool of unskilled labor and propelled the formation of polyglot and ethnically diverse residential districts in the shadows of mammoth factories. When the flow of European migration was cut off during and after World War I, corporations actively recruited workers, both white and black, from nearby southern states. White families from Appalachia were attracted to the much higher wages they could earn in the industrial sector. For African Americans, the benefits of migration included both improved material circumstances and liberation from the oppressive racism of the deep south. The industrial heartland, however, was by no means free from racial tension. In both large and moderately sized cities, conflicts over access to jobs and housing occasionally erupted in violent confrontation. Indeed, the East St. Louis race riot of 1917, which left no less than eight whites and thirty-nine blacks dead, prefigured the more infamous Chicago melee by almost two years.

Despite the obstacles posed by extreme ethnic and racial diversity, midwestern manufacturing cities became hotbeds of union activism in the 1930s, largely inspired by the organizing drives of the Congress of Industrial Organizations. In Flint, Michigan, a sit-down strike launched by the United Auto Workers against General Motors inspired hundreds of similar work stoppages across the region, which ultimately forced the giant industrial firms to recognize workers' right to organize. Labor's continued strength during the wartime and post–World War II booms underwrote widespread prosperity among blue-collar workers, enabling them to purchase single-family suburban homes, fill them with a wide array of consumer possessions, and commute to their jobs by the latest-model cars. It was in midwestern manufacturing cities that the promise of a consumer-oriented American Dream came closest to fulfillment.

Even as blue-collar workers enjoyed the trappings of consumer affluence, economic trends that would eventually undercut the region's prosperity were well under way. Automation, the substitution of machine for human labor, eroded job growth in the 1960s, although its effects went largely unnoticed during the boom years of the 1960s. At the same time, many large corporations began diverting production to lower-wage areas, both within the United States and abroad. Rising levels of international trade and a more thorough integration into the global economy did not bode well for cities that had staked their fortunes on the growth of a national market economy. Steel producers, automakers, and other manufacturers of consumer durables suddenly faced stiff competition from overseas, especially from foreign countries that had thoroughly rebuilt and modernized their industrial infrastructure after the ravages of World War II. Moreover, domestic investment in basic industry lagged as capital flowed toward activities in which the United States enjoyed a comparative advantage in the global marketplace: business and financial services, entertainment, and military armaments.

Due to its historic reliance on capital-intensive, nondefense-related manufacturing, the Midwest was poorly positioned to adapt to these broad structural shifts in the economy. The effects of these transformations became painfully obvious during the economic slowdown of the 1970s and 1980s, especially in those cities that depended most heavily on basic industry. From Gary to Youngstown, plant closings threw thousands of men and women out of work and prompted widespread flight to more prosperous regions of the country. The eight cities included in this section suffered a cumulative population loss of 354 thousand or 22 percent. Residents who remained behind, including large numbers of poor minorities, encountered cities in the throes of dereliction. Lacking customers with disposable income, Main Street shops and downtown department stores went out of business and boarded up their storefronts. Tax revenue shortfalls made it difficult for municipal governments to maintain existing infrastructure. The city of Gary, for instance, was unable to fund regular maintenance in its public parks, while East St. Louis ran out of money for residential garbage collection.

Citizens and local governments developed a variety of strategies designed to reverse or at least halt the decline, although limping into the twenty-first century, they had little to show for their efforts. Initially, union workers exhorted their fellow consumers to "buy American" and boycott cars and appliances manufactured abroad. Public officials, meanwhile, chased a diminishing pool of traditional smokestack industries with tax abatement and subsidy packages. Limited results on both fronts, however, only highlighted the futility of trying to buck powerful international economic forces. Although the Midwest enjoyed a spurt of foreign investment in industrial facilities during the late 1980s and 1990s, much of this activity bypassed the older manufacturing cities in favor of rural locations. Further compounding the problem of redevelopment, potential investors frequently shied away from parcels of land once occupied by manufacturing plants, fearing liability associated with hazardous wastes that may have been left behind. The closure of Toledo's recently built festival marketplace, Portside, in 1990, on the other hand, demonstrated the difficulties of following the model of larger cities in rebuilding their local economies around tourism and high-end consumption. Ultimately, some Rust Belt cities settled for riverboat casino gambling as the most viable means of creating jobs and raising sorely needed tax revenue, although to date this strategy has done little to stimulate economic development on a broader scale.

Sources and Further Reading: John A. Jakle and David Wilson, *Derelict Landscapes* (1992); David R. Meyer, "Emergence of the American Manufacturing Belt," *Journal of Historical Geography* 9 (Apr. 1983); Allan R. Pred, *The Spatial Dynamics of U.S. Urban-Industrial Growth, 1800–1914* (1966); Lloyd Rodwin and Hidehiko Sazanami, eds., *Deindustrialization and Regional Economic Transformation* (1989); Philip Scranton, "Multiple Industrializations," *Journal of Design History* 12 (1999); Graham Romeyn Taylor, *Satellite Cities: A Study of Industrial Suburbs* (1915); Jon C. Teaford, *Cities of the Heartland* (1994).

Andrew Hurley
University of Missouri–St. Louis

Akron, Ohio

As much as any city in the Midwest, Akron embodied dependence on the fate of a single industry. While Gary, Indiana, rose and fell with steel production and Detroit did the same with the automobile industry, the city of Akron worshipped at the altar of the rubber industry.

That Akron became the world leader in rubber production was partially due to geographic factors generally associated with industrial development. Located between the industrial giants of the Great Lakes and the Ohio River Valley—forty miles south of Cleveland, fifty miles west of Youngstown, and a little more than one hundred miles from Pittsburgh—Akron possessed an attractive location. As geography pushed industry toward Akron, city officials maintained an entrepreneurial spirit and pulled in the industry with a series of resolutions set up to make the city more attractive to business interests. Specifically, the Board of Trade advertised for the establishment of manufactories in its town.

In 1870, Benjamin Franklin Goodrich visited Akron, decided to move his New England rubber factory to the city, and with monetary support from the city, built a two-story factory in 1871. After a lean first decade when the company largely produced fire hoses and billiard cushions, the B.F. Goodrich Company was incorporated on May 10, 1880, and Akron commenced its prosperous relationship with the rubber industry. Within the next twenty years, Frank and Charlie Seiberling started Goodyear Tire and Rubber Company, and Harvey Firestone his eponymous Tire and Rubber Company. In 1901, another Akron institution grew, as Ferdinand Schumacher's American Cereal Company was incorporated into the Quaker Oats Company. By the turn of the twentieth century, the Akron economic outlook was bright. The city was the oatmeal capital of America and the Rubber Capital of the World.

With the increase in industry came an increase in population and civic activity. Between 1910 and 1920, Akron's population rose from a little under seventy thousand to more than two hundred thousand residents. During this decade, the trustees of Buchtel College transferred the institution and its assets to the city, creating the University of Akron. Fittingly, the school offered the world's first courses in rubber chemistry and, in 1942, formed the Rubber Technical Institute that aided in wartime innovation and production. It subsequently became an internationally recognized research center in polymer chemistry.

The rubber boom eventually busted. By March of 1982, all of the full-scale tire plants in Akron were closed—although most of the corporations kept their headquarters there—and the city became a full-fledged member of the burgeoning Rust Belt. Akron never completely reinvented itself economically, and the city is still best identified by the icons of its industrial past. Stan Hewitt Hall, Frank Seiberling's multimillion dollar estate, remains one of the nation's great physical testaments to the era, and Quaker Square, built on the remains of Schumacher's factory, now serves as a unique museum and shopping center. Perhaps the greatest memorial to the city's most productive days, exists not on the ground, but in the air. Most Americans are familiar with the sight of the Goodyear Blimp flying above many of America's great sporting events.

Sources and Further Reading: Steve Love and David Giffels, *Wheels of Fortune* (1999); Francis McGovern, *Written on the Hills* (1996); Dale Topping, *When Giants Roamed the Sky,* ed. Eric Brothers (2000).

Ed Krzemienski
Purdue University, Indiana

Dayton, Ohio

Dayton, Ohio, founded in 1796 between the Great Miami and the Mad Rivers, is best known as a city of inventors, manufacturers, and floods. Since 1803, it has served as the county seat for Montgomery County.

Dayton grew slowly but steadily in its first half century. By 1850, it had a population of nearly eleven thousand. Foreign-born residents made up approximately 14 percent of the total, with Germans by far the largest group. Although they would later be joined by Irish, Lithuanian, and Hungarian immigrants, among others, Germans remained the dominant ethnic group in the city. It also had a growing African American community.

As with many cities in the borderlands between the nation's free and slave states, the issue of slavery divided Dayton. It included among its residents both abolitionists and those willing to use violence against the city's African American residents. During the Civil War, it famously served as the home base of Clement Vallandigham, the leader of the Copperheads, northern sympathizers of the South.

Economically, the Civil War proved beneficial, sparking manufacturing activities. In the decades following, Dayton emerged as one of the many medium-sized midwestern cities thriving through its many manufacturers. Though a variety of industrial concerns called Dayton home, a small number emerged as dominant. The first of these was the Barney & Smith Car Company, makers of elegant wooden railroad cars. By the turn of the century, however, Dayton became well known for, and increasingly identified itself as, the home of the National Cash Register Company (NCR).

As the twentieth century dawned, Dayton entered what many consider its golden age. NCR was thriving, residents Wilbur and Orville Wright invented the airplane, Charles Kettering developed the automobile self-starter, and African American poet Paul Lawrence Dunbar achieved widespread acclaim. The defining moment came in 1913, when the city suffered its most destructive flood. To a great extent, Dayton's history is organized before and after this tragic event. Following the flood, the city adopted the city manager form of government, and city leaders pushed for the creation of the Miami Conservancy District (MCD). The city still operates under a city manager, and the MCD's series of dams has effectively ended the periodic flooding that had plagued the city.

Since that so-called golden age, Dayton has struggled to overcome many of the same problems vexing other medium-sized midwestern industrial cities in the twentieth century. Strong opposition to annexation greatly hampered the city's ability to capture the growth on its periphery, and relations between the city and its suburbs often became contentious. Race relations remained tense, periodically resulting in violent outbursts. And the city has suffered under the forces of deindustrialization. On a more positive note, Dayton remains attractive to highly skilled individuals. The presence of nearby Wright-Patterson Air Force Base, which focuses on research and development, serves as a magnet for certain high-technology activities. Local business leaders have helped spark recent revitalization efforts in the downtown area, including construction of a minor league baseball stadium and a riverside park.

Sources and Further Reading: Mark Bernstein, *Grand Eccentrics: Turning the Century* (1996); Virginia Ronald and

Bruce Ronald, *The Lands Between the Miamis* (1996); Judith Sealander, *Grand Plans* (1988).

Janet R. Daly Bednarek
University of Dayton, Ohio

Flint, Michigan

Flint, Michigan, is a classic Rust Belt community whose history reflects the fluctuating fortunes of the midwestern automobile industry. In 1819, Jacob Smith founded a trading post on the site of present-day downtown Flint. During the 1830s, additional white settlers clustered at the frontier outpost, and Flint became the county seat of newly created Genesee County. Over the following few decades, Flint prospered as a lumber milling center, but as late as 1880, it had only 8,409 inhabitants, ranking tenth among Michigan cities.

In the 1880s and 1890s, Flint emerged as a major center for the manufacturing of carts, carriages, and buggies, and by the first decade of the twentieth century, it was known as the Vehicle City. The city's largest manufacturer was the Durant-Dort Carriage Company headed by William C. Durant. A master promoter and salesman, Durant recognized the potential of the horseless carriage and, in 1904, took control of the Buick Motor Company, headquartered in Flint. By 1908, Buick was the nation's largest manufacturer of automobiles, producing more than 8,800 cars that year. To ensure a reliable supply of automobile components, Durant lured other manufacturers to Flint, most notably Charles Stewart Mott's Weston-Mott axle works and Albert Champion's AC Sparkplug factory. Durant sought to consolidate his control over automobile manufacturing by founding the General Motors Corporation, and by 1910, this holding company controlled twenty-seven firms, including Buick, Oldsmobile, and Cadillac. Henceforth, Flint would be a General Motors city.

The rapid expansion of the automobile industry attracted thousands of new residents to Flint, boosting the population from 13,103 in 1900 to 38,550 in 1910, 91,599 in 1920, and 156,492 in 1930. By then, Flint was the third-largest city in Michigan, outranked only by Detroit and Grand Rapids. At the onset of economic depression in 1929, more than half of Genesee County's employed residents worked for General Motors, but as auto sales plummeted in the 1930s, so did employment. In early 1937, Flint acquired a reputation for labor militancy when General Motors workers staged a forty-four-day sit-down strike, occupying the company's plants until management agreed to recognize the United Automobile Workers union as the exclusive bargaining agent for its members. Flint was no longer simply a company town, it was also a union town.

Prosperity returned in the 1940s, and Flint's population peaked in 1960 at 196,940. In the 1960s and 1970s, however, the city lost population as residents migrated to Genesee County's suburban subdivisions. As in many midwestern cities, affluent whites abandoned core neighborhoods, and Flint grew disproportionately poor and black. By 2000, African Americans constituted 55 percent of the 124,943 people remaining in the city.

Exacerbating Flint's decline was the elimination of thousands of General Motors jobs. Between 1978 and 1997, General Motors employment in Genesee County dropped from 76,800 to 33,000, and in 1999, Flint's last Buick plant closed. In 1989, Michael Moore's film *Roger & Me* brought national attention to the plight of Flint's laid-off autoworkers and made the city a symbol of Rust Belt deindustrialization.

Sources and Further Reading: William H. Chafe, "Flint and the Great Depression," *Michigan History* 53 (Fall 1969); Carl Crow, *The City of Flint Grows Up* (1945); Steven P. Dandaneau, *A Town Abandoned* (1996); Ronald Edsforth, *Class Conflict and Cultural Consensus* (1987).

Jon C. Teaford
Purdue University, Indiana

Gary, Indiana

In 1905, Elbert H. Gary, Chairman of the Board of United States Steel Corporation, publicly declared that the company had decided to establish a plant of the most modern standards on the south shore of Lake Michigan in Lake County, Indiana. Contemporaries declared it the beginning of an "industrial utopia." U.S. Steel's Gary Works, and its model company town of Gary, Indiana, were judged to be significant, precedent-setting achievements. The rapid construction and huge scale of both mill and town surprised even the most ardent supporters of the two-pronged project. In February 1909, two open hearths tapped the first heat of steel, and by the end of the year, sixty-eight hundred employees had produced 570 thousand tons of steel.

Though principally committed to building a state-of-the-art integrated steel mill, U.S. Steel officials also sought to create a progressive company town for its skilled workers, foremen, and supervisors. Built simultaneously with the mill, U.S. Steel's First Subdivision, that area of the city on Corporation property, enjoyed paved streets, attractive housing, landscaped neighborhoods, and an economically vibrant downtown

Transporting molten steel, Gary Works, Gary, Indiana. Calumet Regional Archives, Indiana University Northwest.

area. U.S. Steel also donated lots for parks, churches, the public library, YMCA, and other buildings. By 1908, boosters referred to Gary as the Magic City and the City of the Century.

The company paid little attention to the southern end of the city, however, where most of the company's workforce lived, the majority of whom were foreign-born laborers. By 1920, over fifty-two nationalities made their home in Gary, along with a significant number of African American migrants. The newcomers lived in an area known as The Patch, populated by numerous shacks, saloons, and overcrowded boarding-houses, along with a proliferation of real estate specu-lation, gambling, and prostitution. This two-Gary phenomenon divided along economic, ethnic, and racial lines served as a continuous theme in the city's history throughout the twentieth century.

Gary operated as virtually a one-industry town. Its prosperity ebbed and flowed with the cycles of a steel-making economy. The city reached its peak in 1960 with a population of 178,320. During that prosperous time, however, the city began to change, quietly at first, until a number of factors came together to pro-duce Gary's rapid metamorphosis from booming mill town to a shadow of its former self. The rise of subur-ban housing, exodus of downtown businesses, steel in-dustry retrenchment, significant reductions in federal dollars, election of an African American mayor, and white flight combined to propel Gary into a steady economic and social decline. By the year 2000, U.S.

Steel employed less than one-quarter of its 1960 workforce. The 2000 census reported Gary's popula-tion at 102,746.

Realizing that it could no longer depend on the American steel industry, Gary undertook a variety of projects to boost its economy. Construction of a new minor league baseball stadium, development of the Gary–Chicago airport, riverboat gambling revenue, and other endeavors have been pursued in an effort to reverse Gary's decline.

Sources and Further Reading: James B. Lane, *City of the Century* (1978); Raymond A. Mohl and Neil Betten, *Steel City* (1986); Powell A. Moore, *The Calumet Region* (1959).

Stephen McShane
Indiana University-Northwest

Peoria, Illinois

In the late 1600s and throughout the 1700s, Jesuit missionaries and French adventurers established a se-ries of short-lived toeholds along a widening of the Illinois River in the vicinity of present-day Peoria. As a developed community of any permanence, Peoria's origins date back to 1819, when a handful of American settlers planted homesteads in the area. In 1825, the tiny village was incorporated and borrowed its name from the Peoria Indians. About a decade later, it shel-tered almost three hundred souls. By the middle of the 1840s, the enclave had added enough families to be declared a city and a county seat. Peoria's early history was intimately linked to the nearby river; during the 1800s, the town served as an important steamboat port and transportation nexus between the Mississippi and the Great Lakes.

Peoria's population increased slowly throughout the nineteenth and twentieth centuries. It took the small city approximately one hundred years to grow to a population of one hundred thousand. Its biggest pe-riod of expansion occurred in the 1920s, when almost thirty thousand newcomers arrived on the shores of the Illinois. Peoria was never an immigrant metropo-lis. In 1920, foreigners comprised just about 10 per-cent of the river town's citizenry; most arrived before 1900 from northern or western Europe, especially Germany and Ireland.

Although Peoria might not have had the ethnic di-visions that fragmented other American urban land-scapes, class did divide the city's geography. In the late nineteenth and early twentieth centuries, middle-class and elite neighborhoods developed on bluffs over-looking downtown. By the late 1930s, bluff families had annual earnings that were almost twice as much as those who lived closer to the river clustered alongside factories, retail businesses, and rooming houses.

In the 1800s, the city became a major center of alcohol production in the United States. In 1843, the liquor industry's seeds were planted with the founding of Peoria's first distillery. Peoria was ideally located for the rise of distilling interests. Most importantly, the surrounding agricultural hinterland offered massive stores of grain, and the Illinois River (and later railroads) facilitated transport. The production of alcohol fueled the city's development after the Civil War and into the twentieth century. Peoria also earned a regional reputation for having a lively nightlife including vaudeville houses, saloons, and less respectable pursuits like prostitution and gambling.

By the early 1900s, the Peoria region was home to hundreds of manufacturing firms. Much of the area's grain and livestock funneled through the city, as well. The Caterpillar Tractor Company, situated across the Illinois River, employed thousands of Peorians. Like many other northern industrial cities in the late twentieth century, Peoria suffered from deindustrialization and experienced rapid suburban extension. The distillers and brewers left town. While Caterpillar relocated its international headquarters to Peoria proper in 1967, the company faced labor unrest as it downsized in subsequent decades. Economic conditions became more stabilized at the end of the twentieth century, but the prosperity of the city is now almost completely harnessed to the heavy machinery giant.

Sources and Further Reading: Judith A. Franke, *French Peoria and the Illinois Country, 1673–1846* (1995); Jerry Klein, *Peoria!* (1985); George W. May, *Students' History of Peoria County, Illinois* (1968); Bryan J. Ogg, *Peoria Spirits* (1996).

Jerome P. Bjelopera
Bowie State University, Maryland

South Bend, Indiana

South Bend, in north-central Indiana, was named for its location at the most southerly bend of the St. Joseph River. Alexis Coquillard, an agent for the American Fur Company, opened a trading post at the site in 1823 and, together with Lathrop Taylor, platted the town of South Bend in March 1831.

Town government virtually disappeared during the Panic of 1837, but South Bend survived as the county seat and the local commercial center, with the St. Joseph River as its connection with Great Lakes shipping. The Michigan Road, completed in 1832, provided a tenuous link to Indianapolis. Industrial growth began with the completion of a dam in 1844, which supplied water power for a variety of manufactures—grist mills, sawmills, paper making—on the west bank of the St. Joseph River. The coming of the Michigan Southern Railroad in 1851 much improved transportation, and eventually became part of the Chicago–New York trunk line controlled by the New York Central Railroad.

In 1865, South Bend adopted a city form of government for the growing industrial community. Wagon building and plow making were the largest industries, joined in 1868 by a large cabinet-making plant owned

Studebaker truck produced for export to the USSR, World War II. From the collection of Studebaker National Museum, South Bend, Indiana.

by the Singer Sewing Machine Company. By 1890, the Studebaker Brothers Manufacturing Company advertised itself as the world's largest vehicle manufacturer, and the Oliver Chilled Plow Company was a leading producer of farm implements. Immigrants from Poland, beginning in the early 1870s, and from Hungary a decade later, provided ample labor for the city's factories and distinctive ethnic neighborhoods on the west side, symbolized by large Catholic churches and several synagogues. The city's population increased from 3,832 in 1860 to 35,999 at the end of the century, 24 percent of whom were foreign born.

South Bend developed a variety of smaller manufacturing firms—machine tools, toys, clothing, industrial bearings—but horse-drawn wagons and farm implements remained the most important products until 1919. It was then that Albert R. Erskine shifted the Studebaker corporation completely to automobile production and consolidated its manufacturing operations in an expanded South Bend plant. Vincent Bendix moved his automotive parts firm to South Bend in 1923, and it too expanded rapidly. The automobile-centered industry of South Bend was hard hit by the Great Depression, and unemployment exceeded 25 percent by 1933. The United Automobile Workers union became a powerful force, winning recognition at Studebaker in 1935 and at Bendix after a well-publicized sit-down strike in 1936.

World War II brought full employment for South Bend's many factories. The postwar boom continued into the early 1950s, when Studebaker began a disastrous decline in the face of stiff competition and increasing labor disputes. The city's economy recovered with surprising speed from Studebaker's closure in 1963, despite exaggerated Rust Belt reports. Nevertheless, manufacturing did give way to a lower-wage service economy.

Population peaked at 132,445 in 1960, and by 2000 numbered 107,789. Wartime and postwar employment opportunities brought a significant migration of African Americans, a quarter of the city's population by 2000. With most of the area's residential and commercial growth in the neighboring city of Mishawaka and in unincorporated portions of St. Joseph County, South Bend's position as the chief city of the metropolitan region has declined markedly. The University of Notre Dame, established in 1842, is often associated with South Bend, but it remains outside the city limits.

Sources and Further Reading: Donald T. Critchlow, *Studebaker: The Life and Death of an American Corporation* (1996); Dean R. Esslinger, *Immigrants and the City: Ethnicity and Mobility in a Nineteenth-Century Midwestern Community* (1975); Kathleen Ann Smallzried and Dorothy James Roberts, *More*

Than You Promise (1942); Willard H. Smith, *Schuyler Colfax: The Changing Fortunes of a Political Idol* (1952).

Patrick J. Furlong
Indiana University–South Bend

Toledo, Ohio

The early history of Toledo, Ohio, the fifty-seventh-largest American city in 2000, reflects the significance of the urban frontier in midwestern patterns of settlement. The success of the Erie Canal, completed to Buffalo in 1825, led to the projection of interior canals from the Ohio and Wabash Rivers to the western end of Lake Erie. During the subsequent speculative boom, fifteen or more settlements and paper towns planned but unbuilt were to be found along fifteen miles of the Maumee River from its mouth at Lake Erie. Two of these towns united to form the city of Toledo in 1833; other actual village and town settlements eventually became part of the city's metropolitan region.

The Panic of 1837 brought a quick end to the frenzied land speculation; the arrival of the canal did not create the great interior commercial metropolis predicted by its promoters. But the city's chief spokesman, Jesup W. Scott (1799–1874), who became rich from some of his early land purchases, won national attention for his writings on the urban future of the American interior. In a notable short book published in 1868, he continued to proclaim Toledo as *Future Great City of the World*, even though Chicago and other regional cities had surpassed it in importance by then.

In the late nineteenth century, the Toledo economy shifted from a commercial base to manufacturing, particularly in automobiles and glass. Large-scale manufacturing attracted European immigrants—Hungarians, Poles, and Italians. With the highest concentration of home ownership among larger American cities, Toledo's ethnic communities of the late nineteenth and early twentieth centuries remained more cohesive and more permanent than in other similar Midwestern manufacturing cities.

The most notable period in Toledo history occurred at the turn of the twentieth century, when the city became a center of urban progressivism during the mayoral terms of Samuel M. "Golden Rule" Jones, 1897 to 1904, and his dedicated supporter and successor, Brand Whitlock, 1905 to 1913. Building on a local reform tradition represented by Jesup Scott's support of advanced technical education for the children of workers, the free-thinking religious movement, and Jewish intellectuals' advocacy of European socialism,

Jones and Whitlock made Toledo a showplace of the Progressive Movement in the cities.

A radical labor movement acquired considerable support among workers in Toledo manufacturing plants in the late nineteenth century. A number of major strikes occurred in the city during the upheavals of 1877 and 1894, including one against the Pope Automobile Company in 1906, and a near-general strike resulting from union action against the Willys-Overland Automobile plant in 1919. The Electric Auto-Lite strike of 1934, which involved an armed battle between workers and National Guard troops resulting in two deaths, is considered one of the most significant labor–capital confrontations of the Depression decade.

In the late twentieth century, Toledo experienced the loss of several of its leading corporations and manufacturers. In addition to the problem of a declining city population and suburban decentralization of economic activity, the loss of employment in manufacturing and a shift to service industries had caused a significant decline in the city's average family income at the turn of the twenty-first century.

Sources and Further Reading: Charles N. Glaab and Morgan J. Barclay, *Toledo: Gateway to the Great Lakes* (1982); Tana Mosier Porter, *Toledo Profile* (1987).

Charles N. Glaab
University of Toledo, Ohio

Youngstown, Ohio

Youngstown, Ohio typifies the passage of many midwestern cities from frontier settlements to bustling industrial centers to a stagnant part of the Rust Belt. In 1797, John Young founded Youngstown as part of Connecticut's Western Reserve. Growth lagged until Ohio built a canal in the 1830s passing through Youngstown. The discovery of extensive coal deposits attracted Welsh miners and fostered the growth of the iron industry. By 1867, Youngstown had become a city. Many residents of the area participated in the abolitionist movement and the Underground Railroad.

From the end of the Civil War until 1930, Youngstown expanded from eight thousand to 170 thousand residents, dramatic growth reflecting rapid expansion of the iron and steel industry throughout the Great Lakes region. Youngstown's transition to steel production began in the 1890s when Carnegie Steel and Republic Steel bought up locally-owned iron companies. In 1901, local investors established the community-based Youngstown Iron, Sheet and Tube Company. With vertical integration of the companies and linkages with Elbert Gary at his famous steel dinners, the Youngstown area became the fourth-largest steel producer in the country.

The steel industry attracted many Catholic and Jewish workers from southern and eastern Europe, whom older Welsh and German residents viewed with suspicion. Throughout the Midwest, many Presbyterian, Methodist, and Disciples of Christ ministers criticized the new immigrants as violators of the vice laws and a cause of political corruption. In the 1920s, the Ku Klux Klan, supported by these groups, controlled the surrounding Mahoning Valley politically as ministers urged the election of godly 100 percent Americans. Violent reactions, particularly of Irish and Italian residents in nearby Niles, and the exposure of internal corruption in the Klan organization ended its reign by 1926, but not the tensions caused by the rapid melding of cultures.

Steel company managers opposed the Klan, but fought even harder against unions. In 1919, steel companies defeated a strike by labeling the workers as Bolsheviks and importing southern black workers. The New Deal, however, favored the workers. In 1937, the Steel Workers Organizing Committee, part of the newly founded Congress of Industrial Organizations, selected Youngstown as a strike center. Although U.S. Steel settled with workers nationwide, Republic Steel and Youngstown Sheet and Tube refused to recognize the union. Managers won the strike in 1937, but lost eventually when the National Labor Relations Board condemned their tactics and demanded union recognition.

With high transportation costs and a limited water supply, Youngstown plateaued from 1930 to 1970. Steelworker families prospered while passing on jobs to children. Arrival of southern blacks in the 1950s and federal assistance to housing sparked white movement to the suburbs, however, and began Youngstown's population decline to 82,026 residents by 2000. The loss of all major steel companies by the early 1980s pitched Youngstown into a downhill slide. Youngstown's reputation as a center of organized crime and political corruption, first brought to national attention with car bombing episodes in the 1950s, added to its difficulty in recouping. In recent years, Youngstown has begun its transition to a post-industrial city based on service industries.

Sources and Further Reading: Howard C. Aley, *A Heritage to Share* (1975); Frederick J. Blue et al., *Mahoning Memories* (1995); Joseph G. Butler, Jr., *History of Youngstown and the Mahoning Valley, Ohio*, 3 vols. (1921); Thomas G. Fuechtmann, *Steeples and Stacks* (1989).

William D. Jenkins
Youngstown State University, Ohio

Suburbia and Post-Suburbia

The concept of a suburb—a loosely defined settlement peripheral to an existing town or city—has been in use since the Middle Ages. The term, however, has come to have particular legal and social connotations in the United States. Originally implying some type of secondary status with respect to the main or central city, as early as the end of the nineteenth century, suburbanism came to mean not an inferior state, but a chosen political and/or social separation from the central city. While the suburb exists because of the central city—just like in medieval times—suburbs in the Midwest, as throughout the United States, increasingly assumed their own identities and functions during the twentieth century. In metropolitan areas such as Detroit and Chicago, these peripheral settlements became the center of the region. With a majority of Americans both living and working in these so-called suburbs, many American urbanists no longer see the concept of suburbanism as useful in understanding U.S. metropolitan areas in the Midwest or elsewhere.

Although East Coast cities had suburbs as early as 1815, rapid urban growth resulted in midwestern suburbanization by the Civil War. Cincinnati and St. Louis had suburbs by the 1840s. For the most part, these pre–Civil War suburbs were rather marginal communities. Because of central city boosterism and a lack of services in these burgeoning suburbs, the central cities tended to annex these appendages almost as soon as they appeared. Bremen, a suburb north of St. Louis, for example, was surveyed in 1844, incorporated in 1850, and annexed in 1856.

This trend continued for the remainder of the nineteenth century in the Midwest. Midwestern cities such as Chicago, Detroit, Cleveland, and Cincinnati experienced huge increases in both population and physical size in the last quarter of the nineteenth century. St. Louis residents even pushed through the legislature a move to seize a huge chunk of adjacent land while divorcing itself from St. Louis County in the mid-1870s—an action that tripled the size of the city. With the coming of the electric streetcar and the commuter railroad, central cities across the Midwest increasingly gobbled up peripheral towns in their path and made them part of a unified metropolis that had as its hub a clearly defined downtown or central business district.

A counter trend in American suburbanization, however, was developing during the end of the nineteenth century, and it first appeared in the Midwest. This movement involved the creation of suburbs deliberately designed to be independent of the central city. Suburbs like Riverside, near Chicago, had street systems that physically segregated themselves from the central city as well as municipal governments that had the power to protect that separation. As they approached the twentieth century, midwestern suburbanites, like their counterparts in the east, realized that as long as they had a streetcar line or a commuter railroad to take them to the central city and its downtown, separation from the central city gave them more power to shape their own destiny. They could tax, legislate, and eventually zone their community to suit their needs and interests. Moreover, this desire to remain separate was not confined to elite residential communities. Industrialists, too, realized that separation from the central city gave them more power to control their operations as they saw fit. Pullman, near Chicago, was one such industrial suburb.

The proliferation of midwestern suburbs accelerated in the teens and twenties. On one hand, suburbanites had acquired the political power to ward off attempts at annexation by fiscally strapped central cities. On the other, the automobile made it possible to live farther and farther from the central business district. As banks adopted more lax mortgage practices, such as smaller down payments and longer periods of amortization, the automobile enabled suburbanites to take advantage of this distance to build their single-family house on cheaper land. Metropolitan regions in the Midwest, as with their counterparts across the country, ballooned in size as residents stepped off the streetcar and behind the wheel.

While the Great Depression and World War II slowed the wave of suburbanization, it regained momentum from the mid-forties through the late sixties. Stimulated by regional freeways and federal housing policies that favored single-family home ownership, like the income tax deduction and the Federal Housing Administration, the number of suburbs swelled in midwestern metropolitan areas, just as it did across the country. For example, St. Louis County had ninety-eight municipalities by 1959.

This suburban expansion brought about a major structural transformation of the midwestern metropolis during the last third of the twentieth century. Like metropolitan regions across the country, midwestern cities experienced a physical metamorphosis away from the familiar streetcar city design that had dominated the American urban landscape for the previous hundred years. Whereas the automobile initially had merely extended the spokes of the streetcar city away from the downtown core into a ring of bedroom suburbs, by the late 1960s, the automobile had generated a poly-nucleated metropolis in which the distinctions between central city and suburb had become blurred. As freeways stretched the city farther and farther out, the suburbs became the places where the majority of regional residents not only lived, but worked and shopped, as well.

As early as the 1960s, some urban scholars and journalists recognized that suburbs were no longer "sub" to the central city. Clayton, Missouri, near St. Louis, was recognized as one of the first of this new type of metropolitan center as early as 1968 in the *Annals of the Association of American Geographers*. However, the two thinkers who were the most responsible for fully describing this transmutation of the urban form were historian Robert Fishman in *Bourgeois Utopias: The Rise and Fall of Suburbia* and journalist Joel Garreau in *Edge City: Life on the New Frontier*. For Fishman, the new suburbs of the seventies had become technoburbs made possible by the high-tech revolution. Garreau's project, however, was detailing the social, economic, and cultural ramifications of the new office and retail suburban cores. For him, individual Americans living in these edge cities were "inventing a brand-new future." By the mid-1990s, the paradigm shift described by Fishman and Garreau had become so accepted that urbanists spoke of the new city as the post-suburban metropolis.

Midwestern cities were at the forefront of this urban revolution. Detroit, in fact, was used by Garreau as a metaphor for the phenomenon of edge cities. Not only did Detroit epitomize the automobile, which made this new larger urban form possible, it also manifested at a very early stage the ways in which even the character of the city was changed by the automobile. As Garreau points out, Detroit was one of the first cities where the focus of the region was not the downtown, but a beltway surrounding the core and meant to accommodate the automobile. As the automobile became the dominant form of transportation in Detroit and across the country, commerce and employment moved out to the suburbs to find the necessary space to house the ever-growing number of cars. Even in the Motor City, however, there was a need to create a synergy between uses, which necessitated a concentration of activity at certain focal points. As a result, metropolitan regions like Detroit spawned nodes at the intersections of the new beltways with the spoke freeways. Farmington Hills, where I-696 intersects with Grand River Avenue, is a perfect example of this new peripheral center.

Just as these new peripheral cities represented a major physical transformation of the old streetcar cities, they also signified a significant shift in the economic fabric of American cities. The downtown of the streetcar city contained retail and office space, and the core of the metropolitan region contained industrial uses that were positioned to take advantage of the railroad. But when industry became less reliant on the rails and more on truck transport, it too moved to the periphery to take advantage of more abundant land and access to the interstate system. Yet the real force behind the growing economic significance of edge cities was not the exodus of industry away from the core toward the periphery, but the metamorphosis of the American economy away from manufacturing toward a service orientation. As the United States moved into the last quarter of the twentieth century, the office building replaced the factory as the new locus of the American economic system. In fact, Garreau's definition of "edge city" includes five million square feet of office space. Midwestern cities offered perfect examples of this transformation; Schaumburg, for example, became just as much an office center as downtown Chicago. But urban scholars like Robert Fishman and Michael Ebner also saw an entirely new economic function emerging in the edge cities. As America underwent the electronic and biotech revolution at the end of the twentieth century, the places of innovation were located on the periphery to take advantage of the new amenities of the edge cities, as well as their ease of access. In metropolitan Chicago, Naperville was transformed into a cluster of research campuses.

Another way in which post-suburban cities differed from earlier streetcar cities was in their social composition. As famous members of the Chicago School like Ernest Burgess and Harvey Zorbaugh made evident in their germinal studies, the streetcar city had very clear lines of physical demarcation based on class and ethnicity. And as latter scholars such as Allan Spear demonstrated in his study of twentieth-century Chicago, streetcar cities were very racially segregated places, as well. The new post-suburban city, however, became a place that was less physically differentiated along class, ethnicity, and racial lines. For example, Carmel, an edge city north of Indianapolis that had mushroomed in size during the 1980s and 1990s, was still clearly stratified along class lines, but income groups were much more physically integrated there than in the older central city. And although the number of African Americans continued to be relatively small in Carmel, it was not unusual to find African American families living in predominantly white neighborhoods as metropolitan Indianapolis entered the twenty-first century. Moreover, things such as ethnicity and religion increasingly had become nonfactors in urban and suburban social stratification.

Yet another way in which post-suburban cities differed from the mono-nucleated streetcar city of the past was in governance. In the older urban form, a large central city with a unified governing structure dominated surrounding unincorporated areas and small, independent political entities. This system was replaced by a complex, overlapping, conglomeration of political organizations. St. Louis County, for example, included over six hundred different governing bodies by the mid-1980s. Some were traditional suburban governments for towns like tiny Pine Lawn. Some were single-function entities such as the Metropolitan Sewer Districts. Others, like the East-West Gateway Coordinating Council, have a variety of metropolitan-wide duties. Residents of the post-suburban metropolis were represented and served by a multitude of political organizations.

As with metropolitan regions across the United States, the continuing evolution toward post-suburbanism has been a mixed blessing for midwestern urban areas. On one hand, the concentration of retail opportunities in edge city malls and the erection of manicured, office campuses on the periphery of the region represent for many urbanites significant advances in individual choice, convenience, and comfort. Minneapolis's Mall of America, America's largest retail mall, is for many Americans a symbol for everything that is good about post-suburbia. Yet for many urban scholars, post-suburbanism has made the city a sprawling, soul-less, fragmented place. For them, edge cities, such as St. Charles near St. Louis, are models for everything that is bad about post-suburbia. According to these critics of suburbanism, St. Charles and edge cities like it—with their ever-increasing supply of large, mass produced, single-family housing, their abundance of national retail chains, and their lack of cultural outlets—have caused many of the environmental, social, and economic problems that plague early-twenty-first-century America. Nevertheless, it appears that the post-suburban city will remain the dominant urban form in the Midwest and in America for some time to come.

Sources and Further Reading: Howard P. Chudacoff, and Judith E. Smith, *The Evolution of American Urban Society*, 5th ed. (2000); Robert Fishman, *Bourgeois Utopias* (1987); Joel Garreau, *Edge City: Life on the New Frontier* (1991); Kenneth T. Jackson, *The Crabgrass Frontier* (1985); E. Terrence Jones, *Fragmented by Design* (2000); Neil Larry Shumsky, ed., *Encyclopedia of Urban America* (1998); John Stilgoe, *Borderland: Origins of the American Suburb, 1820–1939* (1988); Jon Teaford, *City and Suburb* (1979); Jon Teaford, *Post-Suburbia* (1997); William S. Worley, *J. C. Nichols and the Shaping of Kansas City* (1990).

Mark Abbott
Harris-Stowe State College, Missouri

DuPage County, Illinois

DuPage County is a largely suburban area in the western part of the Chicago metropolitan area. The county's history is inextricably tied to that of Chicago, although its relationship has changed over the past 170 years from an agricultural hinterland and suburban retreat to an employment center for the region. With a 2000 population of 904,161, DuPage County is larger than many midwestern cities. However, it is not a municipality but, instead, contains thirty-six distinct incorporated places including the second- and third-largest cities in Illinois in 2000: Naperville with 128,358 people and Aurora with 142,940.

In 1839, the western part of Cook County became DuPage County. German immigrants were an important part of this settlement. Germans and their English-speaking neighbors built farms and supported the foundations of churches, schools, and other institutions. Agriculture and livestock were principle pursuits on this prairie. In 1848, the Galena and Chicago Railroad began construction across the center of DuPage County. By 1900, five more railroads and an interurban line brought locations along the railroad much closer to the city center, many of which organized as municipalities to provide town residents with water, sewers, and electricity.

DuPage County changed little until after World War II, when the opening of several toll roads, beginning in 1958, brought much of the county into a closer orbit of downtown Chicago. Encouraged by Federal Housing Administration and Veterans Administration insurance programs, residential developers built hundreds of subdivisions across the county after 1958. Jobs also came to the county, especially following the establishment of the Argonne National Laboratory in 1946 and the Fermi National Accelerator in 1966. Dozens of research and development firms drew scientists, researchers, and entrepreneurs to the area, which became known as the Research and Development Corridor along Interstate 88.

The Oak Brook Shopping Center, opened in 1958 along the county's eastern edge, spurred the development of an office and retail agglomeration that continues to expand. By 2000, 277,934 DuPage residents found work within the county, while 152,433 residents commuted to adjacent Cook County. In addition, 256,617 people who lived outside DuPage County held jobs there.

Only thirty-nine farms remained in the county in 1997. Subdivisions, office parks, and shopping centers have replaced the fields and pastures that defined so much of the county a century ago. The suburban governments that once hugged the rail lines have since annexed much of the land in the county in response to the demands of residents and businesses.

DuPage County is the richest and whitest county in the Chicago region. In 1998, under 4 percent of DuPage residents were living in poverty, and the median household income was $67,887. Into 2000, 84 percent of the population identified itself as white, 8 percent as Asian, and 3 percent as African American.

Sources and Further Reading: Stephen J. Buck, "A Vanishing Frontier," *Journal of the Illinois State Historical Society* 93 (Winter 2000–2001); Michael H. Ebner, "Technoburb," *Inland Architect* (Jan. 1, 1993); Richard A. Thompson, *DuPage Roots* (1985).

Ann Durkin Keating
North Central College, Illinois

Johnson County, Kansas

Johnson County, Kansas, has become the most attractive place of residence for middle- to upper-income Kansas City, Missouri, metropolitan inhabitants. As of 2003, it ranked as the most populous and the fastest-growing county in the state of Kansas.

From its origins in the Bleeding Kansas days of the Kansas Territory, Johnson County has been partly defined by its proximity to Missouri in general and Kansas City in particular. From the 1850s until the World War I era, it remained a predominantly rural agricultural county; truck farming, dairies, and livestock dominated. From the 1870s into the early twentieth century, Johnson County was a hotbed of Grange activity that evolved into significant support for the Populists in the 1890s.

The railroads went through the county from the 1860s through the 1880s, and several communities such as Merriam, Lenexa, and Gardner owe their origins to railroad land speculation. These same railroads provided ready access for farm produce to developing Kansas City, Missouri, markets.

In the first decade of the twentieth century, an interurban line crept across the county diagonally from Kansas City, Missouri, to Olathe, the county seat. Known as the Strang Line after its founder, the interurban increased frequency of rail service into the growing city. It also spawned small residential developments in mid-county that came to be known as Overland Park, now the county's largest municipality.

Mere rail access did not result in tremendous suburban growth. County population grew by fewer than fifteen hundred residents between 1880 and 1920. Significant change occurred in the 1920s, however, when the population increased by 50 percent to over twenty-seven thousand. Two major factors effected this change. Kansas City developer J. C. Nichols increased sales in his exclusive Mission Hills area and opened new areas that became Fairway and Westwood Hills. Improved streets and roadways into downtown

Kansas City, Missouri, together with Federal Highway designations late in the decade facilitated commuting. Nichols actually altered the perception of living in Johnson County by placing exclusive country clubs and residential districts in its extreme northeast corner. From the 1920s to the present, some of the most desirable residential sections of the county have developed within one mile of the Missouri state line, continuing Nichols's pattern.

Possibly the most important factor fueling post–World War II growth in the county has been the attractiveness of area school districts. The Shawnee Mission District began as a rural district in the 1920s; similarly, the Blue Valley District in the southeast portion of the county has grown from rural beginnings. Throughout the county, only six major school districts serve more than three times as many municipalities, some as small as a few blocks.

In 1974, a major office park, Corporate Woods, was announced along the corridor formed by circumferential highway I-435. This marked the beginning of Johnson County's acquisition of many regional corporate headquarters formerly found in downtown Kansas City, Missouri. At the turn of the twenty-first century, Johnson County had more jobs than it had residents to fill them. Its days as a bedroom community were in the past. Its role as full partner in the leadership of the metropolitan area was assured.

Sources and Further Reading: Ed Blair, *History of Johnson County, Kansas* (1915); Rick Montgomery and Shirl Kasper, *Kansas City: An American Story* (1999); William S. Worley, *J. C. Nichols and the Shaping of Kansas City* (1990).

William S. Worley
University of Missouri–Kansas City

Oakland County, Michigan

Located immediately north of Detroit, Oakland County in 2000 was the second-most populous county in Michigan (and fourth in the Midwest) with a population of 1,194,156. Organized in 1820 with the county seat at Pontiac, the county developed a prosperous agricultural economy, and by 1870, it led the state in the production of wheat, corn, and hay and in the number of improved farm acres. Moreover, in the late nineteenth century, Pontiac became a leading center of carriage manufacturing. In the early twentieth century, carriage makers shifted to the manufacture of automobiles, and in 1909, William Durant, the founder of General Motors, purchased Pontiac's Oakland Motor Car Company. By 1920, Pontiac was a General Motors company town.

During the following decade, Oakland County's population more than doubled from 90,050 to 211,251, owing not only to increased employment at local auto plants but also to an influx of commuters from Detroit. Bloomfield Hills and Birmingham were winning their reputations as high-class suburban havens, and Royal Oak, Berkley, and Ferndale were attracting thousands of residents employed in Detroit. Suburban migrants followed Woodward Avenue northward, and new municipalities were created to service the needs of these newcomers. Between 1920 and 1930, the number of municipalities in the county increased from fourteen to twenty-four.

After World War II, this suburban influx accelerated so that, by 1960, the county's population was 690,259 and the number of municipalities had risen to thirty-eight. Retailing also moved to Oakland County. In 1954, Northland Center in Southfield became southeastern Michigan's first regional shopping center, with a branch of the J. L. Hudson Department Store and ninety-five smaller retailers. Over the next twenty years, Southfield boomed as both a retailing hub and a center of office employment. Millions of square feet of office space attracted corporate tenants who had been repelled by increasingly shabby and dangerous downtown Detroit. By 1970, 11,352 Detroit residents commuted to work in Southfield, whereas only 8,262 Southfielders were employed in the Motor City.

Southfield was representative of the transformation of Oakland County. By 1990, there was more office space in Southfield than in downtown Detroit, and the Oakland County community called itself the office capital of the Midwest. Meanwhile, in Troy the tax-rich strip of office buildings along Big Beaver Road was dubbed the Golden Corridor. A center of high technology in Rust Belt Michigan, Oakland County boasted 40 percent of the nation's robotics industry and was the site of the Chrysler Technology Center. By the close of the 1980s, Oakland County's population had surpassed that of Detroit, and Oakland ranked first in the state in assessed valuation of property, ahead of Detroit's Wayne County.

Oakland County is a quintessential example of the postsuburban Midwest. In sharp contrast to the midwestern Rust Belt stereotype of sluggish growth and smokestack industries, it is a high-technology hub with wealthy residents, glitzy shopping malls, and high-rise corporate offices. No longer a General Motors company town surrounded by bedroom communities of Detroit commuters, it is an economic powerhouse that overshadows adjacent Detroit.

Sources and Further Reading: Arthur A. Hagman, ed., *Oakland County Book of History* (1970); Trout Pomeroy, *Oakland County: Making It Work in Michigan* (1990); Jon C. Teaford, *Post-Suburbia* (1997).

Jon C. Teaford
Purdue University, Indiana

St. Louis County, Missouri

St. Louis County is a suburban community that surrounds the City of St. Louis. It is located on the eastern periphery of the state of Missouri and abuts both the Mississippi and Missouri Rivers.

St. Louis County assumed its present boundaries in 1876, when the City of St. Louis was made independent of the county. Initial European settlement, however, dates to 1764 when Pierre Laclede founded St. Louis. Although French territories west of the Mississippi had been transferred to Spain shortly before the founding of Laclede's settlement, the area remained predominantly French. Clement Delor established Carondelet in 1767. Florissant was laid out about 1788, and St. Ferdinand and Bridgeton (Marais des Liards) were founded in 1794.

Settlers from Kentucky, Maryland, and Virginia first arrived in the area in the 1790s and concentrated primarily in the Bonhomme Settlement (now Chesterfield) and the Gravois Settlement (now Crestwood). During the decade following the Louisiana Purchase, the pace of American immigration increased markedly, and in 1805, the first U.S. military post west of the Mississippi, Fort Bellefontaine, was constructed on the south bank of the Missouri River. The Missouri Territory was organized in 1812, and St. Louis County was one of the first five counties in the new territory.

After statehood in 1821, the county became a thriving agricultural area with increasing numbers of German immigrants settling after 1840. Although the county remained largely rural throughout the nineteenth century, the advent of the railroad in the 1850s encouraged the development of suburban communities.

By 1900, the City of St. Louis was expanding beyond the sixty-two square miles assigned to it in 1876. The Louisiana Purchase Exposition in 1904 extended from Forest Park, in the western part of the city of St. Louis, into the county, where the Hilltop Campus of Washington University hosted the third modern Olympiad during that same year. New streetcar lines spurred the development of communities abutting the city. These communities boasted of some of the Midwest's finest residential architecture and planning. Some county developers adopted the St. Louis practice of building elite residences along privately owned streets known as private places. However, by the 1920s, early concern about metropolitan fragmentation led to attempts at city–county consolidation in 1926 and a federated metropolitan government in 1930. Suburban desire for local control, though, undermined both of these efforts.

The county's population soared after World War II. Federal Housing Administration financing and the construction of the interstate highway system stimulated out-migration from St. Louis City. During the 1950s, the county's population almost doubled, rising from four hundred to seven hundred thousand. Today St. Louis County has a million people divided among ninety-one cities and villages, as well as large but dwindling unincorporated areas administered directly by the county, making it one of the most politically fragmented counties in the country. Although the county's population has remained stable in recent years, it has begun to experience the consequences of continuing outward expansion in the St. Louis metropolitan region. Inner-ring suburbs have lost population, economic activity, and income as residents move to undeveloped areas of the county and to neighboring counties.

Sources and Further Reading: Robert A. Cohn, *The History and Growth of St. Louis County, Missouri*, 6th ed. (1974); James E. O'Donnell, ed., *St. Louis Currents* (1992); Jon Teaford, *Post-Suburbia* (1997).

Mark Abbott
Harris-Stowe State College, Missouri

Urban and Suburban Planning

The Midwest is a region of planned towns. It hosted experimental models and became the home of people who, through their vision, professional skills, and organizations, were instrumental in shaping America's urban and suburban future.

Following the American Revolution, the eastern portion of the Midwest became the primary site for new communities. Land surveyors, having completed work on the new national capital, flocked to the Old Northwest Territory to subdivide the forests and grasslands beyond Pennsylvania. The Land Ordinance of 1785 had provided that these lands be subdivided into square townships consisting of thirty-six one-mile-square sections, each framed by boundaries oriented to the cardinal points of the compass. This system lent the region a unique and unifying quality characterized by major roads on section lines one mile apart. This macro-organization resulted in further

subdivision into rectangular rural properties and grid-iron urban blocks. As a result, development in the Midwest was more likely to be along north–south and east–west geometric lines than on the Atlantic seaboard, where rural roads followed geographic features producing irregularly shaped properties. Land speculation drove development of this wilderness, resulting in uniform city blocks and lots to facilitate economy in surveying and ease of trading in properties.

Initially, settlements were sited at the intersection of water transportation routes. As such, Marietta, Ohio, the first new town to be built in the Old Northwest Territory, was sited on the Ohio River at the mouth of the Muskingum River. Likewise, Cincinnati was located on the north shore of the Ohio River opposite the mouth of the Licking River in Kentucky. Cleveland was located where the Cuyahoga River enters Lake Erie. Each was a planned town and a service center for provisioning agricultural settlements.

Penetration of settlement from the East was complemented by penetrations from the Northeast and South. Prior to the revolution, French planned settlements dotted the Great Lakes area. The most significant was Detroit, built to assure French control of access to the western Great Lakes. St. Louis, an outpost of New Orleans–based French expansion, was founded during the revolution to become the service center for a network of settlements along the Upper Mississippi and Missouri River systems.

With settlement of the Old Northwest Territory came subdivision into separate territories and ultimately into states. Construction of the first federal highway, connecting Baltimore and Washington to the center of the land between the Great Lakes and the Ohio River, led to creation of planned state capitals along this National Road at Columbus, Ohio, and Indianapolis, Indiana. Many of the new communities of the Midwest were simple, dull, and repetitive speculative grids. In others, the surveyor–planners introduced a touch of class, relieving the monotony of the grid with a large central green space, as at Columbus, or diagonal streets and circles, as at Indianapolis.

Design of the northern-tier settlements of Ohio, Indiana, and Michigan was influenced by the New England Village plan: a central rectangular town common with just a few grid blocks either side of the central green. Settlers from New England brought this pattern with them as they traveled west. Cleveland, metropolitan center of the Connecticut Western Reserve in northern Ohio, was laid out in this way. At Columbus, this concept was combined with the more southern focus on major institutions. Here the town common became the site of the Ohio state capitol, the first state capitol in the United States to be located in a central square, a pattern frequently adopted in future states to the west.

As the frontier moved from east to west, utopian community experiments were sited just ahead of intense settlement. Experiments could be undertaken here free of social constraints, yet they were usually close enough to be accessible to new converts. These included New Harmony, Indiana, the Shaker Union Settlement east of Cleveland, the Amana settlements in Iowa, and Mormon settlements at Kirtland, Ohio, and Nauvoo, Illinois. The Mormons perfected the City of Zion Plan in the Midwest and carried it west to Salt Lake, utilizing it for over four hundred cities in the western United States and Canada. Iowa's Amana settlements remained viable communal societies well into the twentieth century.

The coming of industry and railroads to the region in the mid-nineteenth century created the motivation and the opportunity for the wealthy to leave the city for more amenable surroundings. Railroad satellite suburbs, such as Lake Forest, Illinois (north of Chicago), offered large residential lots and a small commercial district at the railroad station, all well removed from the central city. Frederick Law Olmsted and Calvert Vaux, renowned for their plan of New York's Central Park, designed Riverside, Illinois (west of Chicago), which became the national model for well-to-do suburban America with its curved tree-lined streets, deep residential setbacks, and single-family detached homes.

Future urban and metropolitan planning in America was influenced by the success of park plans realized in the Midwest in the late nineteenth and early twentieth centuries. George Kessler's 1893 Parks Plan for Kansas City, Missouri, introduced the concept of acquiring park lands well beyond the urban fringe and connecting them with wide paseos, future parkways. His plan earned Kansas City national recognition as the City of Parks and Fountains. Park plans for Omaha (Nebraska), Milwaukee (Wisconsin), Minneapolis (Minnesota), and Cincinnati (Ohio) became nationally known and widely imitated.

The Chicago World's Fair of 1893 is credited for giving birth to modern American city planning. There, a distinguished team of architects, landscape architects, sculptors, painters, and engineers, under the direction of Daniel Hudson Burnham, realized the White City. The Chicago fair was a carefully planned organization of all-white buildings, plazas, lakes, and reflecting pools, monumental public sculpture, state-of-the-art utility and transportation systems, and outstanding public services.

The impressive visual and functional coordination of buildings and the public spaces between them at the fair generated a movement to replicate these conditions in other American cities that is commonly referred to as the City Beautiful. The beauty of the fair, in combination with efficient operation and spotless maintenance of the public environment, stood in stark contrast to the visual chaos, inefficiency, and filth of the American city at that time. Visitors to the fair returned to their hometowns inspired to promote planned development.

Pullman, Illinois, an "ideal" new industrial town built in the early 1880s south of Chicago, became the site of a violent strike in 1894. The association of this well-designed new town with such a confrontation between labor and capital stopped cold the paternal industrial town movement in America. Gary, Indiana, exemplified this regression: It had been developed solely for the needs of the industry and residential land speculators.

Inspired by the White City and the 1902 McMillan Plan for Washington, D.C., Cleveland's reform mayor, Tom Johnson, convinced the State of Ohio to fund a plan for downtown Cleveland. This 1903 Group Plan was the first application of the City Beautiful concepts of the Chicago fair to an American city other than the nation's capital. It guided downtown development in Cleveland for the better part of a century and stimulated such civic center plans for major cities throughout the country. Albert Kelsey's ideal small town, experienced by thousands at the 1904 St. Louis World's Fair, spread the civic center concept to communities of lesser means.

In 1909, Wisconsin became the first state to grant its municipalities the right to plan. Daniel Burnham's Plan of Chicago was unveiled that same year; it was America's first metropolitan regional plan. It instituted a permanent commitment to a lakefront park and parkway system, bringing Chicago world renown.

In the Midwest tradition of creating national models, Shaker Heights, one of America's finest trolley car suburbs, was built east of Cleveland shortly before World War I, and early in the 1920s, Mariemont, Ohio, was purposely built to be a national exemplar of a new town totally independent of the automobile.

Historically, the Midwest has been the nurturing ground and home of urban planning organizations and concepts. The American City Planning Institute, the first American professional institute for city planners, was founded at Kansas City, Missouri, in 1917. In the mid-1920s in Cincinnati, Alfred Bettman and Ladislas Segoe combined land-use zoning (initiated in California and New York) with a long-range plan for physical development, resulting in adoption of America's first comprehensive city plan integrating future land use, transportation, and public works. This was followed by adoption of the first municipal capital budget. The comprehensive plan and the capital budget became primary elements of American professional city planning practice. Bettman's *amicus* brief in *Euclid v. Ambler* was instrumental in gaining U.S. Supreme Court approval of the zoning power in 1926.

With Ladislas Segoe in private practice as a planning consultant in Cincinnati, Harland Bartholomew in private consulting practice in St. Louis, and Cincinnati's reputation as an innovator in planning methods, the Midwest became identified as the national leader in community planning. Bartholomew colonized planning offices throughout America, preparing plans under contract and providing staff to implement them, creating ongoing commitments to support local planning.

The American Society of Planning Officials (ASPO) was created in St. Louis, Missouri, in 1934, continuing the Midwest's role as the incubator of planning organizations. Also in the 1930s, the federal government built three new towns to make jobs for the unemployed, to demonstrate the potential of large-scale construction, and to experiment with community design. The Midwest became the site for two of these model towns: Greenhills, Ohio, and Greendale, Wisconsin.

Midwestern leadership in urban planning was further enhanced by the work of Ernest John Bohn, a Republican city councilman in Cleveland, who drafted *A Housing Plan for the United States*. This plan became the basis for the U.S. Housing Act of 1937, the first congressional commitment to public housing. Bohn also initiated construction of Cedar Central, Cleveland, the first federal public housing project.

At the end of World War II, community concern focused on redevelopment of the older portions of central cities. The Midwest established historic precedents for such action: In the early 1800s, Circleville, Ohio, became the first community to be totally redeveloped, and Lake Forest, Illinois, undertook the first commercial area redevelopment shortly before World War I. Redevelopment was a primary thrust of the U.S. Housing Acts of 1949 and 1954, Acts that also included requirements for the preparation of comprehensive plans. This legislation resulted in increased membership of ASPO and its recognition as the primary center for planned development information. Due to their experience and reputation, Segoe in Cincinnati and Bartholomew in St. Louis were often the leading contenders for federally supported comprehensive plan contracts. Sharing in the nation's boom in postwar suburban housing construction, the Midwest became the site of Philip M. Klutznick's new town project, Park Forest, Illinois.

Minneapolis undertook an upper-level, climate-protected pedestrian walk system in its central area in the 1960s that inspired such systems in Cincinnati, Des Moines, and St. Paul, among other cities. In the 1970s, the Metropolitan Council at Minneapolis–St.

Paul became nationally recognized for regional multigovernmental planning and coordination. Also in the 1970s, the Miami Valley Regional Planning Commission (Ohio) adopted America's first regional fair-share housing program, allocating housing for the less-well-to-do to nearby suburban communities. This plan influenced other local fair-share actions and state adoption of its principles in California and elsewhere.

ASPO and the American Institute of Planners, successor to the American City Planning Institute, merged in 1978, creating the American Planning Association (APA) with an internal professional institute, the American Institute of Certified Planners (AICP). In the 1990s, the APA spearheaded a project to evaluate state planning laws and to investigate and promote alternatives. Release of these Smart Growth materials in 2002 further enhanced the position of the APA as the premier American planning organization, with a 2003 membership of thirty-three thousand, including fourteen thousand professionally certified planners.

Sources and Further Reading: Eugenie Ladner Birch, "Advancing the Art and Science of Planning," *APA Journal* 46 (Jan. 1980); Thomas S. Hines, *Burnham of Chicago* (1979); Donald A. Krueckeberg, ed., *The American Planner*, 2nd ed. (1994); John W. Reps, *The Making of Urban America* (1965); John W. Reps, *Town Planning in Frontier America* (1980); David Schuyler, *The New Urban Landscape* (1986); Mel Scott, *American City Planning since 1890* (1969); Jon C. Teaford, *The Twentieth-Century American City* (1986); William H. Wilson, *The City Beautiful Movement* (1989).

Laurence Conway Gerckens
The Ohio State University–Columbus

Harland Bartholomew (1889–1989)

Harland Bartholomew was one of the most consequential planners of the twentieth century. In a career that spanned over fifty years, Harland Bartholomew left an indelible mark on the field of urban planning as Director of St. Louis's Department of City Planning, as Professor of Urban Planning at the University of Illinois, and as the founding partner of Bartholomew and Associates.

Bartholomew's greatest contribution was in developing the concept and use of master plans. A member of the first generation of master planners, no one had more of an impact in defining the components of a comprehensive plan than Bartholomew. Unlike other early master planners such as John Nolen, F.L. Olmsted, Jr., and Daniel Burnham, who viewed the plan as a way of coordinating a number of major projects, Bartholomew conceived the plan as a unified physical design for the whole city that included land use, housing, streets, transit, utilities, transportation, schools, public buildings, and recreation. Because his firm produced 563 master plans for cities around the world, his plans became the model for the construction of comprehensive plans. Bartholomew was also instrumental in establishing the practice that master plans should be the purview of an independent planning commission as opposed to the product of a city assembly.

Another Bartholomew legacy was zoning. Although New York passed the first zoning ordinance in 1916, Bartholomew's 1917 St. Louis ordinance was the first by a major city that was tied to a master plan. Throughout his career, Bartholomew argued for basing any zoning ordinance on a comprehensive plan.

Urban Renewal was a third contribution made by Bartholomew. In the *Existing Conditions Plan* for the Lower East Side of New York City (1932) and in *Urban Land Policy* prepared for St. Louis (1936), Bartholomew was one of the first planners in the United States to discuss the need for rebuilding the older sections of the city. Although Bartholomew's belief that rehabilitation was more important than renewal is often underemphasized, he was influential in shaping postwar urban renewal policy.

A fourth contribution made by Bartholomew was his participation during the forties as a member of the National Interregional Highway Committee, which preceded the development of the interstate highway system. In the Committee report Bartholomew was the architect on the section entitled "Principles of Route Selection in Cities." This chapter created the rationale for extending the proposed national system of freeways into urban cores. Bartholomew argued these new freeways could revive inner cities by making them more accessible, by creating new opportunities for slum clearance, and by relocating excess population. Consequently, Bartholomew is often characterized as the villain behind the "traffic first" philosophy that resulted in the splintering of many communities by the freeways, although the chapter also discussed locating the freeways to be sensitive to the needs of the existing communities.

Sources and Further Reading: Norman J. Johnston, "Harland Bartholomew," *Journal of the American Institute of Planners* 40 (Mar. 1973); Eldridge Lovelace, *Harland Bartholomew* (1993).

Mark Abbott
Harris-Stowe State College, Missouri

Alfred Bettman (1873–1945)

Born in Cincinnati, Ohio, the son of Louis Bettman, a clothing manufacturer, and Rebecca Bloom, Alfred

Bettman was raised in the Reform Jewish community. After receiving his law degree from Harvard in 1898, he returned to Cincinnati, which remained his lifelong base of operations. His marriage to Lillian Wyler was childless.

Bettman's legal career and accomplishments divide into two phases, criminal prosecution and city and regional planning, including the legal groundwork for zoning. Bettman served as the assistant prosecuting attorney for Hamilton County, Ohio, and as Cincinnati city solicitor before being appointed as special assistant to A. Mitchell Palmer, the U.S. Attorney General during World War I. In the latter position, he prosecuted espionage and sedition cases, including one against Eugene Debs, although he left the Justice Department before the infamous Palmer raids and later denounced the excesses of the Red Scare. Imbued with a progressive's commitment to social science, Bettman subsequently pioneered the collection of statistics on Ohio law enforcement.

The quest for rational organization in modern life led Bettman to develop a new expertise in city and regional planning that was to leave an indelible mark on the Ohio landscape and on the nation as a whole. He drafted the first Ohio statute that enabled cities to create planning boards and was instrumental in drafting the national model acts on zoning and city planning. Of even greater importance, he crafted the legal strategy that led to the upholding of zoning against constitutional attacks in the landmark Supreme Court case of *Village of Euclid [Ohio] v. Ambler Realty Company* in 1926.

Sources and Further Reading: Arthur C. Comey, ed., *City and Regional Planning Papers* (1946); Donald A. Krueckeberg, ed., *The American Planner* (1983); "Alfred Bettman, Obituary," *New York Times* (Jan. 23, 1945).

John V. Orth
University of North Carolina-Chapel Hill

George Edward Kessler (1862–1923)

Born in Frankenhausen, Germany, George Kessler moved to the United States with his parents at age three. He attended schools in New York and Dallas, then returned to Germany in 1878 and began private instruction in forestry, botany, and landscape design at Weimar. He later attended the Charlottenburg Polytechnicum and studied civil engineering at the University of Jena.

Kessler returned to the United States in 1882 and a decade later was appointed secretary and engineer of Kansas City's newly created park board. In this capacity he designed the city's integrated system of parks and boulevards. Kessler's successes in Kansas City led to a greatly expanded practice. He designed the site plans for the 1904 Louisiana Purchase Exposition in St. Louis, and subsequently directed the area's restoration into the renowned Forest Park. He opened an office in St. Louis during this work, and in 1910 relocated to that city permanently.

During the first two decades of the twentieth century, at the height of the City Beautiful movement, Kessler was in demand by park boards and planning commissions throughout the country. Although his reputation and practice were national, much of his best-known work was in the Midwest. In addition to Kansas City and St. Louis, he accepted public and private commissions in Cleveland, Cincinnati, Oxford, Toledo, and Springfield, Ohio; Fort Wayne, Indianapolis, South Bend, and Terre Haute, Indiana; East St. Louis and Rock Island, Illinois; Lawrence and Topeka, Kansas; and Omaha, Nebraska. He left an impressive legacy of landscape design and urban planning throughout the region.

Sources and Further Reading: Kurt Culbertson, "George Edward Kessler," in *Midwestern Landscape Architecture*, ed. William H. Tishler (2000); William H. Wilson, *The City Beautiful Movement in Kansas City* (1964).

Robert G. Barrows
Indiana University–Indianapolis

Chicago Plan of 1909

Daniel Burnham and Edward H. Bennett were commissioned by the Merchants' Club of Chicago in 1906 to produce a master plan for the city's growth and development that would provide a rational guide for a modern city and enhance its dramatic lakefront. Called the Plan of Chicago, this project was presented to the public in 1909, and its implementation was made an official policy initiative of the city by Mayor Fred A. Busse. It was both a city and a regional plan, with proposals for developing the downtown Loop, residential districts, and suburban neighborhoods extending sixty miles from the central city. It included recommendations for cultural institutions, monuments, parks, and boulevards and bridges from Milwaukee Avenue and Wacker Drive to North Michigan Avenue and the Michigan Avenue Bridge.

Ideas for the project had begun to appear as early as 1894, just after the close of the Columbian Exposition, when Burnham produced a study for extending the lakefront on the city's south side from Grant Park to Jackson Park. The exposition stimulated an interest in planning and civic development, and it had a strong influence on the growing City Beautiful movement and planning efforts in Chicago.

Daniel Burnham's Plan of Chicago, 1909. Courtesy Chicago Historical Society. Architectural Drawing G1959.217.

During the planning process, Burnham and his assistants collected extensive information about urban development in other American and European cities, especially the boulevard transformations of Georges Haussmann in Paris and the treatment of waterfronts in Paris and dozens of other cities. Burnham also had a great deal of experience with this kind of large-scale urban planning that combined improved transportation with vast civic spaces and monumental buildings. He had completed a master plan for Washington, D.C., in 1902, a plan for the civic center of Cleveland in 1903, and plans for San Francisco, California, and Manila, Philippines, in 1905.

An important reason for the Chicago Plan's success, and for its larger influence beyond Chicago, was the wide-ranging publicity it was given by its backers. The Merchants' Club, which had merged with the larger and more financially sound Commercial Club by 1909, worked extensively with the new Plan Commission and its director, Charles H. Wacker. Together, they developed a promotional campaign to publicize the plan in the press, public lectures, a movie, and printed reports and bulletins. They published several books—*Chicago's Greatest Issue: An Official Plan, Wacker's Manual of the Plan of Chicago*, and *Chicago's World-Wide Influence*—which they distributed to every property owner in the city and gave to grade-school children to use in the civics classes.

In all, it was estimated that in the two decades between the plan's publication in 1909 and the Depression in 1929, $300 million in development occurred in Chicago with the construction of new thoroughfares like North Michigan Avenue, Wacker Drive, and Halsted Street, and civic buildings like the Field Museum and the John Crerar Library, grouped around the newly created Grant Park.

Sources and Further Reading: Carl W. Condit, *Chicago 1910–1929* (1973); Thomas S. Hines, *Burnham of Chicago: Architect and Planner* (1974); Charles Moore, *Daniel H. Burnham*, 2 vols. (1921); John W. Stamper, *Chicago's North Michigan Avenue* (1981).

John Stamper
Notre Dame University, Indiana

The City Beautiful Movement

At its height between 1893 and 1917, the City Beautiful movement promoted the preservation of civic space and virtue in the midst of an industrial revolution that spawned skyscrapers, factories, tenements, and greed in midwestern cities. Soaring crime and disease rates, class conflict, and excessive pollution encouraged philanthropists and politicians to support urban planning proposals that would inspire civic engagement, support democratic values, and mute social conflict. Influenced by Baron Haussmann's design of Paris and the French École des Beaux Arts school of architecture, City Beautiful enthusiasts favored the construction of monumental public buildings such as court houses, museums, symphony centers, and city halls in a neoclassical design reminiscent of ancient Greek and Roman architecture. They endorsed the establishment of parks, handsome boulevards, and other civic areas because, like other Progressives, they believed that a beautiful environment would foster social harmony and decrease urban crime.

Chicago architect Daniel H. Burnham's White City designed for the 1893 World's Columbian Exposition has generally been heralded as the model for the City Beautiful, but the impetus for this preoccupation with urban architecture and space had its roots in a number of nineteenth-century initiatives, including the park, municipal art, housing reform, and sanitation movements. Nevertheless, Burnham's neoclassical White City gave visual expression to the City Beautiful ideal.

Noteworthy for its emphasis on artistic appeal rather than commercial function, the White City encouraged architects and urban planners to press local governments for ordered and aesthetically appealing approaches to urban growth.

Although a national movement, the City Beautiful had strong roots in the Midwest. Senator James McMillan of Michigan headed and Daniel Burnham served on the 1902 commission that realized a good portion of Pierre L'Énfant's original plan for Washington, D.C. Burnham's White City and his subsequent Chicago Plan of 1909 made this city an important center for City Beautiful projects. Similarly, Burnham's plan for the Cleveland Civic Center influenced the design of civic centers throughout the country. In addition, a special effort among midwestern boosters to portray the heartland as the wellspring of American democracy gave the City Beautiful Movement added support in communities such as St. Louis, Kansas City, Detroit, Cleveland, Toledo, and even Springfield, Ohio, the birthplace of the National League of Improvement Associations (later, the American League for Civic Improvement).

In a region that experienced intense industrial growth and a rapid accrual of wealth, it is not surprising that the City Beautiful found devotees. Midwestern architects such as Burnham; his assistant Edward Bennett, who had commissions in Duluth and Minneapolis; Elijah E. Myers of Detroit; and Kansas City–based architects George Edward Kessler, Henry Wright, Sid Hare, and Herbert Hare left their mark on the urban landscape in their home region as well as in the East, West, and South. Whether visiting Chicago's Field Museum, reading in Detroit's Public Library, or relaxing in St. Louis's Bellerive Park, one continues to see evidence throughout the Midwest of this powerful turn-of-the-century movement aimed at creating beauty and fostering civility in America's cities.

Sources and Further Reading: Daniel Bluestone, "Detroit's City Beautiful and the Problem of Commerce," *Journal of the Society of Architectural Historians* 47 (Sept. 1988); William H. Wilson, *The City Beautiful Movement* (1989); William H. Wilson, *The City Beautiful Movement in Kansas City* (1964).

Margaret C. Rung
Roosevelt University, Illinois

Greenbelt Communities

The Greenbelt Communities were planned residential communities constructed by the Resettlement Administration from 1935 to 1938. Planned and administered by Rexford Guy Tugwell, who believed that government should build residential communities modeled on the concepts of Ebenezer Howard's Garden City movement developed in England, these communities were to provide decent housing at affordable rents to workers. No private ownership of the homes was proposed in the original designs.

Originally these communities were to be built across the country. Four were proposed, only three were started, and none were completed as designed. Planning teams were assigned to each of the communities: Jacob L. Crane and Elbert Peets designed Greendale near Milwaukee, Wisconsin; and Justin R. Hartzog and William A. Strong planned Greenhills, near Cincinnati, Ohio.

Greendale was originally planned for 3,511 acres. When halted by the government, only about three hundred acres had been developed. The plan was subdivided into five neighborhoods that surrounded the elementary school and town center. Most units were single-family homes and duplexes. Trails and paths wove through the community and were located away from the primary streets.

Greenhills was located on a 5,930-acre site. The plan placed 676 residential units around the community center and school, while trails and greenbelts connected the residential neighborhoods. Most units were rental apartments and rowhomes; only twenty-four units were detached houses.

These communities were never completed as originally designed because they became too costly to finish. By the 1950s, these three communities would be sold to the existing residents and speculative developers.

Sources and Further Reading: Norman T. Newton, *Design on the Land* (1971); Gregory C. Randall, *America's Original GI Town* (2000); Clarence S. Stein, *Toward New Towns for America*, rev. ed. (1957).

Gregory C. Randall
Walnut Creek, California

Mariemont, Ohio

Mariemont, Ohio, represents an early American interpretation of the English garden city. Planned by John Nolen (1869–1937) in 1921, the community was commissioned by Cincinnati philanthropist Mary Emery (1844–1927). Ten miles east of downtown Cincinnati, it incorporated as a village in 1941. Mariemont achieved National Historic District Status in 1979 as a significant contribution to American planning history and a John Nolen masterpiece.

Nolen based Mariemont on Ebenezer Howard's

(1850–1928) garden city. Two English garden cities, Letchworth (1903) and Welwyn (1920), served as models. Like the English new towns, Nolen gave Mariemont a radial baroque town center, but surrounded it with residential neighborhoods of rectangular or curvilinear design. He located retail activity at the village center, provided for parkland and other amenities, and designated a variety of housing types, including townhouses and free-standing homes of various sizes. A small range of architectural styles including Tudor half-timber, Georgian, and colonial informed building designs. He placed public utilities in an industrial park along the southern border of the community. Like the English models, Mariemont provided residents with some local employment and encouraged light industry. But contrary to English garden cities, Mariemont had no greenbelt of rural land surrounding it. Ebenezer Howard intended the garden city to serve as a boundary to limit the metropolitan growth of London. Nolen rejected the idea that the American metropolis had to be contained and instead used the garden city to foster metropolitan growth by organizing its expansion through careful planning.

Sources and Further Reading: Bradley D. Cross, "Making History," in Robert B. Fairbanks and Patricia Mooney-Melvin, eds., *Making Sense of the City* (2001); Bradley D. Cross, "New Jerusalems for a New World," Ph.D. diss., University of Cincinnati (1997); Millard F. Rogers Jr., *John Nolen and Mariemont* (2001).

Bradley D. Cross
St. Thomas University, Fredericton,
New Brunswick, Canada

Riverside, Illinois

Riverside is the first suburban community designed by Frederick Law Olmsted. The Riverside Improvement Company had acquired sixteen hundred acres along the Des Plaines River about nine miles west of Chicago. Olmsted toured the property in August 1868 and described it as containing "a good deal of rough grove land—very beautiful in contrast with the prairie and attractive." In the midst of the community was the first suburban station of the Chicago, Burlington & Quincy Railroad, which together with a parkway and a proposed street railway, would provide access to downtown.

In his first comprehensive statement about the modern suburb, Olmsted's report portrayed it as a carefully designed space that incorporated both "urban and rural advantages" and as an element in the "counter-tide of migration" from city to periphery. The Riverside report emphasized the importance of developing an infrastructure of well-engineered roads, thoroughly drained walks, and a supply of pure water, as well as the construction of community facilities such as a business block, a hotel, and a nondenominational chapel. Roads were designed to curve gently over the prairie landscape, suggest contemplation and leisure. Provisions for recreation included a series of parks along the Des Plaines River and spaces throughout the community that possessed what Olmsted described as the "character of informal village-greens, commons and playgrounds."

While Olmsted believed communal spaces were important, he also believed that the "essential qualification of a suburb is domesticity" and the privacy of the single-family home on its own property. Families, he insisted, should be able to enjoy privacy both indoors and out with "both public & private outside apartments," the latter defined by a fence, a "sort of outer wall of the house."

Olmsted's Riverside report sketched a community defined by handsome landscapes and public spaces, yet also secluded lots for homes. But the transition from plan to construction proved fraught with difficulties: The development company was undercapitalized; its president, Emery E. Childs, never understood Olmsted's plan and wanted to build his house in the middle of the Long Common, one of the most important park spaces; and the Chicago Fire of October 1871 destroyed the company's records and redirected capital from developing the suburban fringe to rebuilding the city. Over succeeding decades, however, houses were erected along the curving streets of the property east of the Des Plaines River, approximately one thousand acres, and Riverside became the successful suburb Olmsted envisioned.

Olmsted imposed the landscape of the Northeast on the prairie. He was not familiar enough with midwestern climate and topography to develop a design that incorporated regional distinctions, as he had done in plans for California landscapes several years earlier. Nevertheless, the Riverside plan and report were among the most influential documents that promoted a suburban way of life in nineteenth-century America.

Sources and Further Reading: Olmsted, Vaux and Company, *Preliminary Report Upon the Proposed Suburban Village at Riverside, Near Chicago* (1868); David Schuyler and Jane Turner Censer, eds., *The Papers of Frederick Law Olmsted*, vol. 6 (1992).

David Schuyler
Franklin and Marshall College,
Pennsylvania

Shaker Heights, Ohio

A planned residential community near Cleveland, Ohio, Shaker Heights had a population of 29,405 in 2000. It was established in 1905, incorporated in 1912, and incorporated as a city in 1931. The developers of the community were Oris Paxton Van Sweringen and Mantis James Van Sweringen, speculative builders in the Cleveland area who specialized in residential lots and commercial developments.

The original fourteen hundred acres for the community were about eight miles east of Cleveland. Originally owned by the United Society of Believers in the Second Appearing of Christ (the Shakers), it was the center of their largest commune. After the commune declined, the society sold the land for speculative development in 1889. The Van Sweringens purchased the property in 1905 and established Shaker Heights as a village designed for the rich and prosperous.

Highly regarded among planners nationwide, it was an innovative community with preserved parklands, an imaginative street system, and a defined commercial center. Stringent design controls were placed on the community's planning, architectural styles, and landscaping. To facilitate the growth of the community, the builders acquired controlling interest in the New York, Chicago, and St. Louis Railroad and used that right-of-way to connect the village to downtown Cleveland.

Between 1919 and 1929, an average of three hundred expensive custom homes were built each year. The community was expanded by four thousand acres in 1926. Due to financial troubles and the lack of sales, the Van Sweringen's investments in the community were sold in 1933. In the beginning of the twenty-first century, however, Shaker Heights continued to be a successful and influential community on Cleveland's east side.

Sources and Further Reading: Kenneth T. Jackson, *Crabgrass Frontier* (1985); John R. Stilgoe, *Borderland* (1988).

Gregory C. Randall
Walnut Creek, California

Urban Renewal

The Midwest, a region containing many of the country's older industrial cities, was a prime candidate for urban redevelopment in the mid-twentieth century. It became a national leader in creating state and federal redevelopment legislation and was the home of planners, pioneering projects, and events that came to national attention—sometimes positive, sometimes not.

"Urban renewal" means redevelopment of a community to meet contemporary needs and expectations. When the term is capitalized, it refers to a program within the U.S. Housing Act of 1954 that provided support for clearance, rehabilitation, and conservation of subareas of a community. The Urban Renewal program was an outgrowth of the Housing Act of 1949 that provided federal financial support for acquisition, demolition, and redevelopment of deteriorated areas in or around the urban core

Among the leading advocates of renewal legislation was Alfred Bettman, chair of the Cincinnati Planning Commission. During World War II, while preparing a plan to guide postwar development, he identified the need for redeveloping the deteriorated properties surrounding commercial cores. Bettman's draft of a model redevelopment statute became the foundation for legislation passed by Pennsylvania to provide jobs for GIs returning to Pittsburgh, where a postwar recession was expected. The Golden Triangle project was initiated in Pittsburgh at the confluence of the Allegheny and Monongahela Rivers immediately after the war. This dramatic reconstruction of a deteriorated industrial and warehouse area stimulated national support for including a redevelopment program in postwar federal housing legislation.

In the 1940s, Bettman chaired both the Urban Redevelopment Committee of the American Society of Planning Officials and the Legislative Committee of the American Institute of Planners. This put him in the forefront of the redevelopment movement. Politicians concerned about postwar development frequently sought his counsel. The most significant of these was Senator Robert A. Taft (Republican), a fellow resident of Cincinnati. Taft chaired the Subcommittee on Housing and Urban Redevelopment of the Senate Special Committee on Postwar Economic Policy and Planning. In January of 1945, Bettman testified before Taft's committee, citing his credentials as chair of the American Bar Association Committee on Planning Law and Legislation, chair of the American Institute of Planners Committee on Federal Activities, and legal counsel to the National Capitol Park and Planning Commission. Needless to say, Taft's committee reported favorably in support of a federal urban redevelopment program. Senators Allen J. Ellender (Democrat, Louisiana) and Robert Wagner (Democrat, New York) joined Taft in introducing the bill that became the U.S. Housing Act of 1949.

Title I of the Housing Act of 1949 created a program supporting the clearance of deteriorated urban areas. To include redevelopment in a housing act, it was stipulated that more than half of either the deteri-

orated site or the redeveloped site must be housing. Sites occupied by deteriorated housing were most often targeted for clearance.

In 1946, Detroit's city planning director, Charles Blessing, initiated a large-scale, slum-clearance housing project close to downtown Detroit that came to be known as Lafayette Park. Upon passage of the 1949 Housing Act, Lafayette Park became Detroit's first Title I endeavor. With its high- and low-rise residential buildings by world-renowned architect Mies van der Rohe, Lafayette Park brought Detroit, Blessing, and the federal Title I program to national attention.

Lafayette Park and Chicago's Lake Meadow clearance project, a middle-income, racially integrated apartment project, were viewed as the harbingers of success of the 1949 Act. But results elsewhere were disappointing. Nationally, few middle-income families elected center city living, citing a reluctance to live in isolated enclaves bordered by slums.

The U.S. Housing Act of 1954 changed both the nature and extent of redevelopment activities. Under the new designation of "Urban Renewal," clearance programs were no longer inhibited by ties to housing. The focus of redevelopment shifted to commercial revitalization of downtown areas. The 1954 Act included programs not only for total clearance of deteriorated areas, but also for the rehabilitation of areas in the process of decline, for historic preservation, and for conservation of stable areas.

In 1953, a year before passage of the 1954 Housing Act, Blessing initiated a neighborhood conservation program in Detroit, further enhancing the city's national reputation as a leader in planning for renewal. By 1955, Blessing had ten-year programs in place for fifty-five Detroit neighborhoods, establishing the city's position with Chicago in the forefront of the neighborhood conservation movement. In 1949, Chicago's Hyde Park–Kenwood Area Community Conference organized block clubs of homeowners to conserve their middle-class, single-family neighborhood, and from 1956 to 1960, Hyde Park–Kenwood was the neighborhood conservation movement's national poster child. Yet in spite of such successes, the results at Detroit and elsewhere were again disappointing. The inhabitants of most rehabilitation and conservation districts were apathetic.

The Urban Renewal program had its first major national impact in 1958. Demolition began that year for Gateway Center at Minneapolis, a redevelopment that was expected to replace a riverside skid row with high-rise apartments, financial institutions, and a luxury hotel. Many such optimistic projects of the late 1950s and the 1960s featured new downtown hotels, office complexes, civic centers, convention facilities, and luxury apartments.

Prior to or immediately after World War II, many cities in the Midwest had been totally surrounded by autonomous suburbs. With manufacturing facilities moving to the suburbs in the 1950s, the central cities lost much-needed jobs and a tax base. This led to clearance programs to provide sites for new industrial uses inside city limits, within the central city's taxing power. Two of the nation's largest industrial projects were in the Midwest: Cincinnati's Kenyon-Barr Project and the Mill Creek Valley Project in St. Louis. Kenyon-Barr was planned to occupy a four-hundred-acre site close to downtown Cincinnati. The project involved demolition of the homes of twenty-five thousand people, virtually all nonwhite, to provide sites for a large number of light industries and part of a new freeway. The 454-acre Mill Creek Valley Project, begun in 1958, had similar characteristics.

Erieview, in Cleveland, is generally considered the most ambitious Urban Renewal clearance project undertaken in the Midwest. The 1960 plan for Erieview proposed a group of thirty- to forty-story office buildings and six-story structures facing malls and parks to be developed on a 163-acre slum property close to the central business area.

In the mid-twentieth century, Chicago, which had received funding for the Harrison-Halstead Project, the North LaSalle Area, and a number of industrial sites, was the national leader in receipt of financial assistance for Urban Renewal. Chicago with twenty-eight projects, Detroit with twenty-two, and Minneapolis with eleven took the lead in Urban Renewal activity in the Midwest.

But the enthusiasm and optimism of the early 1960s turned sour. In the mid-1960s, the combined effect of Urban Renewal clearance, earlier urban redevelopment programs, and in-town highway construction on the dislocation of the poor, particularly minorities, contributed to widespread riots, such as those in the Hough District of Cleveland (1966) and in Detroit (1967), again bringing the Midwest to national attention.

The time taken in redevelopment processes was so long, and the original estimates of demand for redeveloped sites were so wrong, that years after site acquisition and demolition, little was visible at most clearance project sites except destruction. In the early 1960s, the Mill Creek Project at St. Louis was still primarily 454 acres of nothing. In 1971, 40 percent of the site at Gateway Center in Minneapolis was still being used for parking lots. Likewise, the very first stage of Cleveland's Erieview was not officially declared complete until 1973, eight years behind schedule, thirteen years after initiation of the project, and just a few months before the developers of its 990 upper-middle-income apartment units defaulted on their loans. Most

clearance projects took from ten to fourteen years from land acquisition to build-out, and then usually not for the uses originally intended. The Market-Mohawk project in Columbus, Ohio, took twenty-two years.

The Housing and Community Development Act of 1974 ended the Urban Renewal Program. Visions of shining new alabaster cities were precluded by social and economic errors and administrative delays. Based on its intents—(1) to reverse loss of middle-income families, jobs, and retail trade to the suburbs by rebuilding deteriorated areas of the city; (2) to rehabilitate areas in decline to house middle-income families who will revive central area retail shops; and (3) to provide jobs and taxes through creation of industrial parks inside city limits—the Urban Renewal Program has generally been judged a failure. Funds earmarked for these objectives were inadequate and processes were too slow.

In developing these programs, their drafters assumed that the historic roles of the city center could be restored (they could not), that middle-income families would flood back to the city center if it was rebuilt (they would not), that center city land cleared of deteriorated buildings would be a good investment (given the time lag of these programs, it was not), and that capital would eagerly flow to such investments, supporting demolition and reconstruction, if federally subsidized (it did not).

Sources and Further Reading: Martin Anderson, *The Federal Bulldozer* (1964); Jewel Bellush and Murray Hausknecht, eds., *Urban Renewal: People, Politics, and Planning* (1967); Alexander Garvin, *The American City: What Works, What Doesn't* (1996); Laurence C. Gerckens, "Bettman of Cincinnati" in D. A. Krueckeberg, eds., *The American Planner,* 2nd ed. (1994); Kristine B. Miranne, *Urban Programs of the Federal Government* (1992); Jon C. Teaford, *The Rough Road to Renaissance* (1990); U.S. Department of Housing and Urban Development, *Urban Renewal Directory* (1974); James Q. Wilson, ed., *Urban Renewal: The Record and the Controversy* (1966).

Laurence Conway Gerckens
The Ohio State University–Columbus

Urban Politics and Government

The midwestern states have been at the crossroads of the immigration patterns that have shaped metropolitan development in the United States for more than two centuries. The complex interweaving of the streams of migration account for many of the social and political differences between states and cities. The

Midwest has long been at the forefront of urban reform, and some of its metropolitan regions still produce innovative responses to urban problems. At the same time, some cities and metropolitan regions have been known for their political conservatism and resistance to change. Despite these differences, however, the cities in the Midwest tend to reflect a distinctive regional identity that arises from large-scale population movements.

From the 1790s to the mid-nineteenth century, three streams of internal migration poured into the Midwest from New England, the South, and the Mid-Atlantic states. The Yankee political culture of New England tended to favor strong local government and community responsibility. In cities in the northern Midwest, the Yankee stream shaped local government; later it helped to account for the reform tradition in Michigan, Wisconsin, and Minnesota. Migrants from the South, in contrast, were highly individualistic; they held organized community life and the public sphere suspect. The southern migrants settled especially in smaller towns and cities, where a tradition of limited government tended to prevail. The Mid-Atlantic stream into the southern Midwest took a middle course, viewing government as beneficial as long as it kept to a limited sphere. The clash of these cultures can still be seen in the state politics of the Midwest, which often divides between urban liberal constituencies and small-town conservative ones.

These schisms were reinforced by massive European immigration from the 1840s to the 1920s. Internal migration and foreign immigration precipitated extraordinary growth rates in midwestern cities. For example, St. Louis increased its population tenfold in only twenty years, growing from 16,000 in 1840 to 160,000 by the census of 1860. In the same twenty years, Chicago grew from a frontier village of 4,500 to a city of more than 112,000 and, by 1920, to a staggering 2.7 million people. In the industrial era following the Civil War, cities all over the Midwest grew rapidly, much of the growth fueled by immigration. By 1870, 87 percent of Chicago's population was first- or second-generation immigrants, compared to 36 percent of St. Louis's and 42 percent of Cleveland's residents. The composition of the immigrant population differed significantly from one city to the next, however. In Chicago, Poles and other eastern Europeans were prominent, followed by the Irish and Italians; even today, Poles are the largest ethnic group in Chicago. Milwaukee drew large numbers of Germans, and St. Louis attracted Germans, Italians, eastern Europeans, and even Lebanese. Smaller towns and cities in Wisconsin and Minnesota were settled by large numbers of Swedes and Norwegians; in Illinois, Germans left their imprint on the names of towns such as Schaumburg and Germantown.

African Americans and Hispanics also moved to midwestern cities in large numbers. From 1910 to 1930, African Americans left the South and moved to such cities as Chicago, Detroit, Milwaukee, Indianapolis, St. Louis, East St. Louis, and Cleveland. Another movement streamed North in the three decades after World War II. Chicago at the turn of the century had the second-highest number of African Americans in the country (1,065,009), and Detroit had one of the highest concentrations, 82 percent. Mexicans also moved in large numbers during the same years, so that significant Mexican American communities existed in many midwestern cities by the 1970s. Since the 1970s, large numbers of immigrants have come from Mexico, other countries of Latin America, and the Caribbean, as well as from Asia, the Middle East, and Eastern Europe. Significant Hispanic and Asian populations now reside in all the larger cities of the Midwest and in smaller communities, as well. The 2000 census showed increases in Hispanic population in every state in the Midwest, ranging from 55 percent to 117 percent over the decade.

In the 20th century, the migration of African Americans created racial tensions. In 1917, race riots broke out in East St. Louis, and two years later in Chicago. In many cities African Americans were kept from moving into white areas by restrictive covenants and by intimidation and violence. In the 1960s, racial tensions again boiled over in some midwestern cities, culminating in the nation's worst riots in Detroit in 1967. Older industrial cities in the Midwest still are highly segregated both within cities and between cities and suburbs.

The population movements that made midwestern cities grow defined local political issues and created political conflicts in the Midwest. In the years after the Civil War, party machines came to power in most large and many smaller midwestern cities, including Chicago, East St. Louis, Toledo, Detroit, Cincinnati, Kansas City, and Cleveland. The machines relied on the support of ethnic voters, especially the Irish and Italians. In Kansas City from the 1890s through the 1920s, Jim Pendergast and his more famous brother, Tom, ran powerful organizations. Chicago's machine politics was notoriously corrupt, with vote-buying and stuffed ballots being the norm. In the 1920s, when the machine was infiltrated by organized crime, violence became commonplace, leading to prominent federal investigations in the 1930s. Richard J. Daley, mayor of Chicago from 1955 to 1976, ran the most famous machine organization in the United States. Today his son, Richard M. Daley, is in charge of probably the only classic urban machine still operating in a major U.S. city.

During the Progressive Era from the 1890s to the

1920s, the machines became the target of reform efforts, with some of the nation's most prominent reformers leading the charge: Tom L. Johnson of Cleveland, Samuel "Golden Rule" Jones and Brand Whitlock of Toledo, and Hazen Pingree of Detroit. Reformers claimed that they merely wanted to increase the efficiency of government by attacking the machines, but they also wanted to reduce the influence of ethnic voters. Reformers fought for the adoption of the Australian ballot (which is the printed, secret ballot in common use today), at-large and nonpartisan elections, and commission and council-manager plans.

In 1908, voters in Des Moines, Iowa, approved a charter that became a model for reformers around the country. In addition to a five-member commission, the model included nonpartisan and at-large elections, a civil service system, and provisions for the initiative, referendum, and recall. The commission segment of this reform agenda soon fell out of favor because it combined policy and administrative roles in the elected commissioners. In 1913, Dayton became the first city to adopt a clear alternative when it placed administrative responsibilities in the hands of a city manager. The Dayton Plan soon became the most popular of the reform initiatives of the era.

Over 56 percent of midwestern cities with more than fifty thousand people have adopted city manager government (Dayton Plan) and combined it with reform elements of the Des Moines Plan, compared to 93 percent in the Western states, where most cities were incorporated after reform had been widely accepted throughout the country. In the southern states, 70 percent of cities have adopted reformed governmental structures, compared to only 29 percent of cities in the northeastern states. Five of the midwestern states have seen their larger cities adopt reform government in greater numbers—Kansas at 100 percent, Minnesota at 93 percent, Missouri at 80 percent, Illinois at 77 percent, and Iowa at 78 percent—while others have not adopted reform—Indiana, Nebraska, and South Dakota, all at 0 percent.

The Midwest has witnessed a number of efforts to find regional solutions to metropolitan problems. As in the rest of the United States, urban sprawl is widespread in much of the Midwest. According to an index developed by the Sierra Club of policies to control sprawl—which include open space protection, land use planning, transportation planning, and community revitalization—the twelve Midwest states spread about in the middle of the ranking. Minnesota was found to take the most measures to control sprawl, with an overall ranking of 12, and North Dakota, where sprawl probably does not receive significant attention due to the relative lack of urbanization, was found to take the least, with an overall ranking of 41.

In Illinois, a legislatively appointed Growth Task Force completed a three-year study of growth policies in the state in early 2002. Among their key findings was that many local governments have planning guidelines that are out of date and encourage urban sprawl; the state had limited capacity to coordinate growth and development; state tax policies, especially grossly unequal education funding, has distorted growth and development decisions; and funding has not been adequate to preserve open space despite support for open space preservation. Similar concerns are being heard in states across the increasingly urbanized Midwest, as well as throughout the nation.

Sprawled metropolitan regions tend to be fragmented into a multitude of governments. The Midwest is no exception. Yet, the political cultures in the Midwest have endorsed a regional approach to service delivery in many instances when the case can be made for the improvement of services and where political opposition can be overcome.

The Midwest has examples of almost every type of approach to regional service delivery, from the most difficult to the most simple. An example of consolidation is the governmental structure popularly called Unigov, which was adopted in Indianapolis and Marion County in 1970. The convergence of a popular Republican mayor who advocated consolidation, widespread support in the community, and a Republican-controlled legislature made the consolidation possible. The consolidation unified the county and city under the Mayor and City Council and created an economic development initiative for the entire region. Equally significant, though less well known, is the consolidation of Kansas City and Wyandotte County, Kansas, in 1997.

One of the most discussed urban reform initiatives in the nation is the Twin Cities Metropolitan Council of the Minneapolis–St. Paul region, one of only two examples of this type of governmental structure in the nation (the other being in Portland, Oregon). In this structure of authority, the governor appoints the members of the Metropolitan Council, but each member represents a local district. In the case of the Twin Cities, the Met Council was created in 1967 as a planning body that has since enjoyed an expansion of its authority. The mass transit and wastewater treatment functions of the region, for example, were added to its responsibilities in 1994. In addition to this regional agency, the Minnesota legislature enacted a fiscal disparities law in 1971 that provides communities in the Twin Cities region with shares of 40 percent of the growth in assessed valuation of commercial and industrial property with a consequent narrowing of the previous disparity in the tax-based revenues among municipalities. A similar piece of legislation was adopted for the Iron Range communities in northern Minnesota in 1996.

Besides these ambitious approaches to regional service delivery, there are numerous examples of more easily implemented approaches. A less comprehensive way of dealing with regional service delivery is the use of local special districts, which is more prevalent in Illinois than in many other parts of the United States. Mainly because so many special districts have been created, the state of Illinois has more units of local government than any other state: 6,621 compared to 5,247 in Pennsylvania and 3,884 in Texas, for example.

In an attempt to overcome the negative effects of fragmentation, intergovernmental service contracts are especially common in local governments in the Midwest. Examples such as the joint labor bargaining for a Teamsters contract among more than twenty cities in the Twin Cities region, a police academy for eleven cities along the North Shore of Lake Michigan, and the joint collection of income taxes by municipalities in Ohio reflect different regional approaches. The Midwest is home to just about every imaginable method of regional service delivery mechanism, which shows that the spirit of reform is still alive and well in the region.

Sources and Further Reading: Daniel J. Elazar, *Cities of the Prairie* (1970); Daniel J. Elazar, *The Closing of the Metropolitan Frontier* (2002); Myron Orfield, *Metropolitics* (1997); Dick Simpson, *Rogues, Rebels, and Rubber Stamps* (2001); G. Ross Stephens and Nelson Wikstrom, *Metropolitan Government and Governance* (2000); Jon Teaford, *Post-Suburbia* (1997); Richard C. Wade, *The Urban Frontier* (1959).

Karl Nollenberger and Dennis R. Judd
University of Illinois–Chicago

City Manager Government

During the Progressive Era, many municipal reformers in the United States embraced the notion that a city government ought to operate like a business corporation, which meant that efficiency and technical expertise, not partisan politics, should guide administrative affairs. This effort to apply business principles to city government culminated in the adoption of the city manager plan during the 1910s and 1920s. The city manager plan departed from the traditional council-mayor form of city government by taking executive authority from the mayor, an elected official, and placing it in the hands of an expert manager appointed by the city council. In addition, cities governed by the city manager plan usually abandoned the large city councils elected by ward in favor of small councils elected at-large, a scheme designed to put the interests of the city as a whole above the interests of particular neighborhoods or districts.

Though the adoption of the city manager plan was a national phenomenon, midwestern cities played a leading role in advancing this new form of municipal government. According to one count, of the 425 city-manager cities in the United States by 1931, 116, or 27 percent, were located in the Midwest, more than in any other region of the country. Michigan topped all other states with forty-four city-manager cities, and Ohio ranked eighth with twenty-two, followed by Kansas with sixteen, Iowa with twelve, Wisconsin with eight, Illinois with six, Minnesota with five, and Missouri with three.

Midwestern cities not only embraced the city manager plan in significant numbers, but also did much to alleviate concerns that seemed to limit its appeal. In the first five years of the city manager movement, only a few small cities adopted the plan. This led many to wonder about its viability for larger urban areas. However, such doubts began to subside somewhat in 1913, when Dayton, Ohio, became the first city of over one hundred thousand to adopt the city manager form of government. Thrust into the spotlight, Dayton became more closely identified with the city manager plan than any other city at the time. Although virtually every aspect of city government in Dayton garnered attention, contemporaries showed special interest in the office of the city manager itself.

The experience of Dayton also helped confirm the city manager plan's reputation as a businessman's form of government. Local businesspeople not only dominated the commission that wrote the city manager charter, which provided for a city manager and a small five-member commission elected at-large, but also led an effort to elect a nonpartisan ticket consisting of four businesspeople and one labor representative, in the first election held under the city manager plan. In a stunning victory, they took all five seats on the commission, thus squeezing out other political interests.

What happened in Dayton reinforced the arguments of critics who viewed the city manager plan as undemocratic, and hence unsuitable for American cities, especially large heterogeneous cities. With the hope of democratizing the businessman's government, as some called it, some reformers began advocating the idea of coupling the city manager plan with proportional representation (PR), a voting system designed to guarantee representation for political minorities in proportion to their voting strength. And midwestern cities clearly led this movement, beginning with Ashtabula, Ohio, which in 1915 became the first city in the United States to adopt the city manager plan–PR plan. Kalamazoo, Michigan, was next in 1918. However, the most significant boost for this new reform agenda occurred in 1921, when Cleveland, Ohio, became the first major American city to embrace the city manager–PR concept. With a diverse population of almost eight hundred thousand, Cleveland represented an important test case for reformers. The Cleveland experiment, as they called it, sought to solve one of the most fundamental problems vexing large cities—how to provide for efficiency without losing sight of the ideals of representative government.

Within the next few years, the Cleveland experiment essentially became the Ohio experiment. Inspired by its northern neighbor, Cincinnati, with a population of over four hundred thousand, adopted a city manager–PR charter in 1925. Hamilton and Toledo followed in 1927 and 1935, respectively. Cleveland, however, abandoned both the city manager and proportional representation in 1931, making Cincinnati the new darling of the reformers, a status that city enjoyed through the 1950s.

While reformers praised Cincinnati, they viewed Kansas City, which adopted a city manager charter without proportional representation in 1925, as a tremendous failure. In Kansas City, the local Democratic machine headed by Tom Pendergast won a council majority in the first election held under the city manager plan. This enabled the Democrats to appoint a longtime Pendergast associate as city manager, who proceeded to bestow patronage upon the party faithful. Hence, the adoption of the city manager plan in Kansas City had the unintended effect of giving the machine more control over the city government than it had enjoyed in the past. To some reformers, the Kansas City experience provided further evidence of the need to couple the city manager plan with proportional representation.

By the 1960s, desires for businesslike efficiency and government by experts had given way to a new set of urban concerns that emphasized maximizing citizen participation in the decision-making process. In this context, city managers were often viewed as remote bureaucrats who ignored the desires of various communities of interest and the problems of troubled neighborhoods. Some city-manager cities even began to consider returning to the council-mayor form of city government to secure more responsive executive authority. In the Midwest, this trend manifested in 1999, when Cincinnati opted for direct election of a mayor with enhanced powers, though it retained the office of city manager.

Sources and Further Reading: Kathleen L. Barber, ed., *Proportional Representation and Election Reform in Ohio Cities* (1995); Robert A. Burnham, "The Boss Becomes a Manager" in Robert Fairbanks and Patricia Mooney-Melvin, eds., *Making Sense of the City* (2001); Lyle W. Dorsett, *The Pendergast Machine* (1968); Thomas W. Fletcher, "What Is the Future for Our Cities and the City Manager," *Public Administration Review* 31 (Jan.–Feb. 1971); Rob Gurwitt, "The Lure of the Strong Mayor Plan," *Governing* 6 (July 1993); Chester E. Rightor with Don C. Sowers and Walter Matscheck, *City Manager in Dayton* (1919); W. M. Tugman, "The Cleveland Experiment," *National Municipal Review* 8 (May 1924); Leonard D. White, *The City Manager,* rev. ed. (1931).

Robert Burnham
Macon State College, Georgia

Richard J. Daley (1902–1976)

Born and raised in Chicago, Illinois, Richard J. Daley was the only child of second-generation Irish Catholic immigrants, Michael and Lillian Daley. He was educated at a neighborhood parochial elementary school and a Catholic commercial high school, De La Salle Institute. After attending night school for eleven years, he received a law diploma in 1933 from DePaul University. In 1936, he married Eleanor Guilfoyle; their family ultimately included four sons and three daughters. While nominally practicing law, he increasingly devoted his time to Democratic party politics. Elected to the Illinois House of Representatives in 1936 and the State Senate two years later, he served in the state legislature until 1946. After serving as director of the Illinois Department of Finance for fifteen months, he was elected clerk of Cook County in 1950. Daley was elected mayor of Chicago in 1955 and subsequently won reelection five times over a series of Republican opponents.

A skillful practitioner of machine politics, Daley wielded great power because of his dual role as Chairman of the Cook County Democratic Party and Mayor of Chicago. With control of an estimated thirty-five thousand patronage workers, he made the city workforce an arm of the Democratic machine. Chicago became known as "the city that works," a testament to his meticulous delivery of city services. At a time of fiscal peril when such metropolises as New York City and Cleveland succumbed to bankruptcy, Daley kept Chicago's books balanced and its bond ratings high. Under his supervision, the city underwent a building renaissance that included the completion of a host of architecturally striking skyscrapers downtown (such as the world's then-tallest building, the Sears Tower), an extensive network of expressways, acres of massive high-rise public housing projects, an urban campus of the University of Illinois, and O'Hare International Airport. The plethora of construction projects meant good relations with the building trades and other union locals, and the preservation of a viable downtown pleased real estate and retail interests.

At the same time, Daley's lengthy stay in city hall

produced a large number of critics. Minorities complained that the mayor tolerated insufferable conditions in the city's sprawling ghettos and chafed at his reluctance to admit African Americans into the Democratic party's inner circle. Reformers criticized Daley's heavy-handed treatment of protesters in the summer of 1968, first after the assassination of Martin Luther King, Jr., in April and later at the Democratic National Convention in August. During the latter years of Daley's mayoralty, a federal prosecutor sent several members of his political organization to prison for various offenses, but the mayor remained untouched by scandal. Surviving stormy relations with the press and liberals, who saw him as a symbol of conservatism and repression, Daley continued to enjoy a prolonged love affair with the city's electorate. He was elected to an unprecedented sixth term in 1975, amassing his largest victory margin ever. Daley's dominance of Chicago made him an influential political figure in Illinois and the nation as well.

Sources and Further Reading: Roger Biles, *Richard J. Daley: Politics, Race, and the Governing of Chicago* (1995); Adam Cohen and Elizabeth Taylor, *American Pharaoh* (2000); Mike Royko, *Boss: Richard J. Daley of Chicago* (1971).

Roger Biles
East Carolina University, North Carolina

Daniel Webster Hoan (1881–1961)

Daniel Hoan, Milwaukee's mayor from 1916 to 1940, promoted sewer socialism, a distinctive blend of left-wing policies and political pragmatism. His political career included failed efforts at public ownership of the streetcar and electrical systems, but successful campaigns for low-cost cooperative housing, low per-capita municipal indebtedness, expanded public access to the lakeshore, an end to the use of police as industrial bodyguards, and the promotion of fair wages and hours for municipal workers.

Born in neighboring Waukesha County, Hoan dropped out of high school and worked as a cook before his undergraduate years at the University of Wisconsin; he subsequently attended Chicago's Kent School of Law. Recruited to Milwaukee in the early twentieth century, Hoan was the successful Socialist candidate for city attorney in 1910. He served in that office until his first mayoral victory six years later. He was reelected chief executive in 1918, 1920, and every four years thereafter until a painful defeat in 1940.

Devoted to the well-being of the working class, Hoan continually battled opposition-dominated Common Councils, although during the Great Depression, he garnered support for work relief projects and a baby bond program that kept the city out of bankruptcy. He was an early chair of the U.S. Conference of Mayors and, later, an enthusiastic advocate of a publicly financed St. Lawrence Seaway. Hoan departed the Socialist Party after his 1940 defeat, running unsuccessfully as a Democrat in both gubernatorial and congressional campaigns. He died in 1961, living to see another Socialist serve as Milwaukee mayor from 1948 to 1960.

Sources and Further Reading: Daniel W. Hoan, *City Government* (1936); Melvin Holli, *The American Mayor* (1999); Edward S. Kerstein, *Milwaukee's All-American Mayor* (1966).

Thomas J. Jablonsky
Marquette University, Wisconsin

Tom L. Johnson (1854–1911)

Born in Blue Spring, Kentucky, to Albert and Helen Johnson, Tom Johnson went to work in the streetcar business in Louisville as a fourteen-year-old in 1869. He combined inventive genius with a knack for streetcar operations and behind-the-scenes political maneuvering and, by 1890, had become a millionaire street railroad owner, operating companies in Louisville, Cleveland, St. Louis, Brooklyn, New York, and Johnstown, Pennsylvania.

Young Tom also began to take an interest in party politics during the 1880s, becoming a political supporter and friend of Henry George. Espousing George's single-tax and free trade philosophies, Johnson, a Democrat, served two terms in the United States House of Representatives from 1891 to 1895. Defeated for reelection in 1894, Johnson returned to the street railroad business. In 1901, he won election as mayor of Cleveland on a platform of just taxation, home rule for Ohio cities, and a 3-cent streetcar fare. Eschewing partisan politics in his administrative appointments, Johnson soon achieved a reputation as one of the Progressive Era's most dynamic figures. He fought for equitable taxation, battled the city's privately owned street railroad companies for lower fares, and reformed the city's government, criminal justice system, and parks and public works administrations. Johnson's popularity crested in April 1908, when the city began operating all its street railroad lines. Unfortunately, a bitter street railroad strike soon erupted, creating public disaffection with the mayor. Johnson lost his bid for a fifth term in November 1909, and retired to private life, his reform legacy secure.

Sources and Further Reading: Kenneth Finegold, *Experts and Politicians* (1995); Tom L. Johnson, *My Story*, ed. Elizabeth J. Hauser (1993); Eugene C. Murdock, *Tom Johnson of Cleveland* (1994).

Robert Bionaz
Chicago State University, Illinois

Samuel Milton Jones (1846–1904)

As mayor of Toledo from 1897 until he died in office in 1904, Samuel Milton Jones became a national leader of Urban Progressivism at the time when Ohio was a center of reform causes. Born in Wales, he immigrated with his parents to upstate New York. With little formal education—he said that he attended school for only thirty months—he worked as a youth at various jobs until he found his fortune in the Pennsylvania oil fields. Severely depressed after his wife died in 1885, he moved to the Lima, Ohio, area, then experiencing an oil boom. In 1894, he established in Toledo his highly successful Acme Sucker Rod Company, which manufactured rods used in oil drilling.

Jones's reading during this period of Leo Tolstoy, Walt Whitman, and various social reformers converted him to the general principles of Christian Socialism. Accordingly, he operated his plant on the basis of the Golden Rule, initiated labor practices far ahead of their time, and acquired his public name, "Golden Rule" Jones. Endorsed as a candidate for mayor owing to a bitter division in the state Republican party, he was elected in 1897, soon split with the party, and established an independent movement whose influence spread to the national level. Twice reelected, he publicized the issues and programs of the municipal reform movement. Although his concrete accomplishments were limited, he won a reputation for humane treatment of the unfortunate in society. Toledo, with its Golden Rule Hall and Golden Rule Park, required stops for reformers of the era, became a showplace of Urban Progressivism during his term and that of his successor, Brand Whitlock.

Sources and Further Reading: Charles N. Glaab, *Toledo: Gateway to the Great Lakes* (1982); Marnie Jones, *Holy Toledo: Religion and Politics in the Life of "Golden Rule" Jones* (1998).

Charles Glaab
University of Toledo, Ohio

Thomas Joseph Pendergast (1872–1945)

Thomas J. Pendergast of Kansas City, Missouri, was one of the most powerful city political bosses in American history. He moved from his native St. Joseph, Missouri, to Kansas City in 1890 to work for the Goat Democrats, headed by his brother James Pendergast. The Goats had strong ties with gambling interests in the honky-tonks of the industrial West Bottoms. Tom Pendergast assumed control of the Goats in 1911 and during the next fifteen years transformed the faction into the Pendergast machine. He took over the city government following a 1925 city charter change, using criminal enforcers and sixty thousand illegal votes to stay in power.

He ran Kansas City as if it were his own. He collected 5 percent or more of the annual gross from every business in Kansas City and forced his way on to numerous corporate boards. He received over $30 million a year from gambling, prostitution, and narcotics interests. He lived lavishly and bet extravagantly on the horses. He kept Kansas City a wide-open town with minimal constraints on economic activity, claiming it was good for commerce. He had considerable influence in the Democratic party and started his associate, Harry S. Truman, on the road to the presidency.

During the Great Depression, the federal justice system moved on the machine, convicting 259 middle managers of vote fraud. In 1939, Pendergast pled

Tom Pendergast of Kansas City. Special Collections, Kansas City Public Library, Kansas City, Missouri.

guilty to income tax evasion and went to prison for a year. His machine collapsed at the municipal level, and he lived out his life in poor health.

Sources and Further Reading: Lyle W. Dorsett, *The Pendergast Machine* (1968; reprint, 1980); Lawrence H. Larsen and Nancy J. Hulston, *Pendergast!* (1997); William M. Reddig, *Tom's Town* (1947; reprint, 1986).

Lawrence H. Larsen
University of Missouri–Kansas City

Carl B. Stokes (1927–1996)

On November 7, 1967, Carl Burton Stokes carved his name firmly in the pages of American history by becoming the first person of African American descent to be elected mayor of a major American city, Cleveland, Ohio.

Carl Stokes defeated incumbent Mayor Ralph Locher for the Democratic nomination in 1967 by eighteen thousand votes. Stokes's primary victory was principally a product of high political mobilization in the black community: the black turnout exceeded the white turnout, and Stokes received 96 percent of the black vote. Since Cleveland politics is dominated by the Democratic Party, the outcome of the Democratic primary usually decides the race. In 1967, however, Stokes was confronted by strong opposition from the Republican challenger Seth Taft, a high-profile politician who had to move from his home in the suburb of Pepper Pike to qualify to run for the mayor's office in Cleveland. Capitalizing on white fears that the election of a black mayor would upset hoary social, economic, and political relations in Cleveland, Taft was able to persuade an unprecedented number of white Democrats to cross party lines and cast their votes for him in the mayor's race. But Stokes was able to fight off the Taft challenge by mobilizing the black community. He defeated Taft in the general election by 1,679 votes.

As mayor of Cleveland, Carl Stokes established himself as one of the most talented and progressive public administrators in the history of American local government. He successfully brought in millions of dollars in federal aid, opened the door to minority employment in city jobs, provided city contracts to a significant number of black entrepreneurs, hired General Benjamin Davis as the first black Safety Director of Cleveland, and guided the formation of the Twenty-First District Caucus as a potent instrument of black political power in the Cleveland metropolitan area.

Sources and Further Reading: Leonard N. Moore, *Carl B. Stokes and the Rise of Black Political Power* (2002); William E. Nelson, Jr. and Philip Meranto, *Electing Black Mayors* (1977); Carl B. Stokes, *Promises of Power* (1973).

William Nelson
The Ohio State University–Columbus

William Hale Thompson (1867–1944)

Like other nineteenth century New Englanders, the family of William Hale Thompson ventured west in search of opportunity. By the time their son's political career drew to an end, more than a few Chicagoans wished the Thompsons had stayed in Boston.

Thompson grew up in a wealthy family that tolerated his spending parts of seven years (1886–1891) as an honest-to-goodness cowboy in Wyoming and Nebraska. He also excelled at football and water polo. Size and talent gave him the nickname "Big Bill."

Although a protégé of machine politician William Lorimer in the early 1900s, Thompson never enjoyed organization politics. Ringing doorbells and building coalitions interested him not at all. The election was the thing.

Thompson embraced and discarded issues as need be. In 1915, he promised good government and the Sunday closing of saloons, four years later he introduced 1920s' isolationism, and eight years after that he vowed to ignore Prohibition and make Chicago wetter than "the middle of the Atlantic."

Thompson was a master demagogue who geared his appeal to black, ethnic, and labor voting blocs. Elected mayor of Chicago for three terms (1915–1923 and 1927–1931), he held only one consistent idea—a belief in massive public works as outlined in Daniel Burnham's Chicago Plan of 1909. Projects were purchased at immense cost. Not only was Thompson corrupt, his antiwar views in 1917 and opposition to Prohibition turned Chicago into a metaphor for all that was believed wrong with America.

By the time he lost his bid for a fourth term in 1931, Thompson had given Chicago the reputation as the city that was *in* but no longer *of* the Midwest.

Sources and Further Reading: Douglas Bukowski, *Big Bill Thompson, Chicago, and the Politics of Image* (1998); Herman Kogan and Lloyd Wendt, *Big Bill of Chicago* (1953); Reinhard H. Luthin, *American Demagogues* (1954).

Douglas Bukowski
Berwyn, Illinois

Harold Washington (1922–1987)

Harold Washington, Chicago's first African American mayor and reputed slayer of that city's famed Democratic machine, was born in Cook County Hospital on April 15, 1922. Raised in Chicago's South Side "Black Belt," Washington joined the Army in 1942, and returned from World War II to attend Roosevelt University. Elected class president in 1948, Washington went on to graduate from Northwestern University Law School in 1952.

Chicago's densely packed and segregated black population provided rich opportunities for those who harvested votes in the city's highly competitive and partisan political system. Among them was Washington's father Roy, one of Chicago's earliest black Democrats who served as a precinct captain in the Third Ward and held a political appointment as corporation counsel. Harold subsequently witnessed the rough-and-tumble of Chicago politics first-hand, even to the point of watching his father strap on a gun to settle scores in one bitterly contested election. After Roy's death in 1953, Harold took over his father's precinct and political position.

Washington won election to the Illinois House of Representatives in 1964, even as his loyalties shifted. Breaking with Mayor Richard J. Daley's Cook County Democratic organization over the issue of police brutality, Washington became increasingly independent. He subsequently made an initial run for mayor in 1977, garnering only 11 percent of the vote in a special election following Mayor Daley's death. The still-vital Daley machine then tried—and failed—to purge him in party primaries by entering two other candidates named "Washington" in one election to confuse voters, but he won election to the state Senate later that year, and then to the U.S. House of Representatives in 1980 and 1982. By 1983, both he and a coalition that joined a long-neglected black community, white liberals, and Latinos stood ready to seize control of City Hall.

Most analysts saw Washington as nothing more than a spoiler who would siphon votes from incumbent Jane Byrne and challenger Richard M. Daley, the late mayor's son. When it became apparent that Washington constituted a serious threat, Democratic party chairman Ed Vrdolyak issued his notorious dictum that the election had become a "racial thing." In a succession of racially divisive and narrowly decided contests, Washington edged out his Democratic opposition in the primary and defeated an unknown Republican backed by renegade elements of the old Democratic machine in the general election. Vrdolyak subsequently organized an opposition bloc of twenty-nine of the fifty-member city council and ushered in

an era of political warfare that earned Chicago the sobriquet of "Beirut on the Lake." The court-ordered redrawing of the machine's gerrymandered ward boundaries gave Washington control of the council by the end of his first term, however, and his own political instincts led him to extend an olive branch to white ethnics even as he subordinated the racial chauvinists in his own camp. He had brought the city to the brink of a new political era when a massive coronary struck him down shortly after his reelection in 1987.

Sources and Further Reading: William J. Grimshaw, *Bitter Fruit: Black Politics and the Chicago Machine, 1931–1991* (1992); Paul Kleppner, *Chicago Divided* (1985); Gary Rivlin, *Fire on the Prairie* (1992).

Arnold Hirsch
University of New Orleans, Louisiana

Metropolitan Retailing

Metropolitan retailing moved through two phases in the Midwest. From the 1870s, when the modern city first appeared, through the 1950s, the downtown was the center of urban retailing. In much the same way that cathedrals dominated the spiritual and cultural life in medieval cities, department stores dominated the downtowns and set the style in American cities during this era. In residential areas the most striking characteristic of urban retailing was the number of small neighborhood shops selling more types of goods than most people can easily imagine. Throughout this time personal transportation was uncommon, so each neighborhood was a city within a city where virtually any basic need could be met within walking distance. The second phase of metropolitan retailing began around 1960 when shopping became a motor sport. The suburban shopping centers displaced the downtown department store as the chief shopping destination, and as metropolitan areas oriented to life on wheels, the old neighborhood shopping streets thinned and evolved into strip malls and small commercial centers.

Two institutions dominated the retail trade in the growing cities of the developing Midwest. One, mail order, was an American invention. Aaron Montgomery Ward began the first large mail-order business in Chicago in 1872. Ward was among the first to recognize that the railroad combined with a cheap, efficient postal service (also a product of the railroad) gave retailers in interior cities easy access to farmers throughout the region. Mail order was an immediate success largely because it allowed otherwise isolated rural and small-town consumers access to the low prices and wide selection previously available only to urbanites. Because of the logistics of the business, all the big, general merchandisers were urban, with the largest based in Chicago, the main rail hub of the Midwest. Ultimately the most successful was Sears, Roebuck & Co, which began in 1893 and sold $10 million of goods in 1900. For most of this period, Sears and Ward set the style and served as a main source for consumer goods for much of the rural heartland. In the mid-1920s, Sears began to open retail stores in major cities and, based largely on its ability to tap both urban and rural markets, became the largest retailer in the world, a position it enjoyed until 1991 when it was supplanted by Wal-Mart.

Just as mail order was a child of the railroad, the department store was a child of the streetcar. Cities of the late nineteenth century expanded with the streetcar, and regardless of how far out the lines went, they all ended downtown. This allowed people from all over the city to reach downtown easily, and department stores soon appeared to serve this vast new market. The department store began in Europe when expanding inventories forced owners to organize their goods into departments of similar goods such as women's clothing or household furniture. The first department stores in the Midwest appeared in the mid-nineteenth century, and by 1890, the department store was the undisputed leader in defining urban culture. In every major city, a handful of local stores grew up to satisfy every class of customer. In Chicago, for example, Marshall Field and Company served the high end of the market; Carson, Pirie, Scott served the middle class, while the Boston Store targeted working-class consumers. The top stores were tourist attractions that defined their host cities for tourist and native alike. When Marshall Field opened a new flagship store in the heart of Chicago's Miracle Mile in 1902, the twelve-story building contained more than one million feet of floor space, had twelve entrances, fifty elevators, and seven thousand employees. The store was a lavish but refined place where consumers could shop for goods from around the world, eat a fine meal, send a telegram, reserve theatre tickets, or relax in a well-stocked reading room.

Outside the downtown area, echoes of the old preindustrial walking city remained. People rode downtown for business or pleasure, but they lived in the neighborhood, and in an era without personal transportation, the necessities of life needed to be close. Most neighborhood retailers clustered on shopping streets, although most residential streets also had a few corner stores, and here or there a single shop stood isolated on otherwise residential streets. Street vendors and door-to-door salesmen rounded out the neighborhood retail options. Shopping streets typi-

cally served one or two neighborhoods. The exact retail mix varied by neighborhood and city, but E.B. White's inventory of the businesses located along his neighborhood shopping street in New York City, reported in his *Here is New York*, would serve equally well for a neighborhood retail street in Cleveland, St. Louis, or any other major midwestern city on the eve of the suburban boom:

> . . . a grocery store, a barbershop, a newsstand and shoeshine shack, an ice-coal-and-wood cellar (where you write your order on a pad outside as you walk by), a dry cleaner, a laundry, a delicatessen (beer and sandwiches delivered at any hour to your door), a flower shop, an undertaker's parlor, a movie house, a radio-repair shop, a stationer, a haberdasher, a tailor, a drugstore, a garage, a tearoom, a saloon, a hardware store, a liquor store, a shoe-repair shop.

Of course, any small town in America would have to supply most of these goods and services, but the crowded and compact nature of everyday life in city neighborhoods made shopping there an intimate experience in a way that it could never be in a small town.

Urban consumers also had access to shops in other parts of the city. So, for example, a working-class woman in Chicago or a middle-class woman in Milwaukee might shop daily at her local neighborhood grocer or butcher, visit a favorite bakery or restaurant some blocks away occasionally, and shop downtown to seek bargains or buy clothes for special occasions. Nearly all stores offered free delivery.

American cities were transformed after World War II as nearly universal access to automobiles combined with cheap land and affordable housing to pull people and jobs from the cities to the suburbs. As the city was remade, retailing was remade with it. By the start of the 1960s, the trade of the old retail core became divided among several suburban shopping centers, each of which drew customers from a section of the greater metropolitan area. At best the downtown became just another major retail node, while in the neighborhoods, the number of shopping streets thinned, with the survivors often coalescing into small local shopping centers or strip malls. At the same time much of the regional flavor associated with urban retailing disappeared, and it became difficult to distinguish a suburban mall in Cleveland from one in Atlanta.

The first shopping center in the United States designed to accommodate the automobile was Country Club Plaza in Kansas City, Missouri. Built by J. C. Nichols, the Plaza was a shopping village with one hundred retail shops. The first tenant was a children's photographer in 1923. Built in a Mediterranean style, the plaza featured wide sidewalks, small gardens, fountains, and statuary to create an oasis of upscale shopping on the edge of the city. Nichols integrated free parking into the basic design. The Plaza was an immediate and enduring success. The number of shops doubled over the years and the Plaza remains a major local and regional tourist and shopping destination.

Shopping centers expanded slowly until the 1950s. Once the suburban boom began, however, the Midwest provided fertile ground for new growth. Partly it was a matter of timing. From the 1950s to the 1970s, the prime period of mall construction, the Midwest was the industrial powerhouse of the nation. From the steel centers in Pittsburgh to the belt of auto manufacturing cities that ran from Kenosha, Wisconsin, to Akron, Ohio, the Midwest was a growing region with a large concentration of high-paying union jobs. Midwestern cities like Indianapolis and Omaha were also less hemmed in by established towns and so were better able to expand than their eastern counterparts.

The Midwest is also home to Southdale Mall, the first enclosed shopping center in the United States. Designed by Victor Gruen, who hoped the mall would refocus suburban growth and thereby slow urban sprawl, Southdale opened in suburban Minneapolis, Minnesota, in 1956. Malls did little to slow sprawl but did concentrate retailing; by the 1970s, Americans were spending more time at the mall than any other place except home and work. In 1992, the largest enclosed mall in the world, the Mall of America, opened in another Minneapolis suburb. Containing over five hundred stores, an indoor theme park, and Minnesota's largest aquarium, the Mall of America is the most visited site in the United States, receiving an estimated forty-two million visitors in 2002.

Retailers outside the mall also adapted to the new metropolitan area. A comparison of two fast food pioneers illustrates the difference in the retail environment between the eras. When Wichita-based Walt Anderson and Billy Ingram founded the White Castle Hamburger chain in 1921, the city was the place to be and White Castle was designed for the urban market. Outlets were small, with no tables and only five stools at a single counter. To get customers out quickly, the partners limited their menu to burgers, coke, coffee, and pie. By 1931, there were one hundred twenty Castles, mostly in the cities of the industrial Midwest. By focusing on the high volume urban market, White Castle thrived during the easy years of the 1920s and the harsh times of the 1930s. The company floundered, however, during the suburban boom of the 1950s and 1960s because its management was slow to move to the suburbs and uncertain about how to tap the family and teen oriented market once they did. Castles now had tables, but they were still too small and the atmosphere too old-fashioned. White Castle

developed a nearly cult-like following based on its unique taste and atmosphere but, by the 1960s, was clearly a niche burger rather than an industry leader.

The company that has epitomized fast food since the 1960s is McDonalds. Developed into the first franchise chain by Ray Kroc in 1955, with its corporate headquarters located in the Chicago suburb of Oak Brook, the company has proven remarkably versatile. Originally Kroc preferred to site outlets close to shopping centers in high-traffic areas close to young families with higher-than-average income, but over time the company has invested enormous effort in developing products and outlets flexible enough to flourish in city, suburban, and small-town markets.

The tremendous success of McDonalds, with over ten billion burgers sold in its first seventeen years of operation, highlights two of the major trends in late-twentieth-century retailing. First, the metropolitan area remains the largest and richest retail environment, but its center of gravity has shifted from the city to the suburbs. By 1970, the suburbs had become the crossroads of small-town and urban America and the best location to reach all three markets, as the success of Wal-Mart also illustrates. When Wal-Mart began its efficient distribution complex in Bentonville, Arkansas, it was seen as the savior of small town America because of its ability to bring low prices and wide selection to a market ignored by major retailers. By the 1980s, however, Wal-Mart began to move into metropolitan areas and has found its greatest success in the suburbs.

The final change, which is often blamed on the shopping center but is probably more a result of the growing size of modern retailers, is the decline of a distinctive local character in metropolitan retailing. Chains and franchises like McDonalds and Wal-Mart that dominate contemporary retailing are national or international rather than local or regional. As a result, shopping has become a more homogeneous experience. Local and regional accents still exist and can best be found in the small local businesses in the cities and neighborhoods, away from the major shopping centers.

Sources and Further Reading: Peter Birkeland, *Franchising Dreams* (2002); William Cronon, *Nature's Metropolis* (1991); David Gerard Hogan, *Selling 'em by the Sack* (1997); Michael Johns, *Moment of Grace* (2003); Ann Satterthwaite, *Going Shopping* (2001); Susan Strasser, *Satisfaction Guaranteed* (1989); Jon Teaford, *Cities of the Heartland* (1993); E. B. White, *Here is New York* (1949); William S. Worley, *J. C. Nichols and the Shaping of Kansas City* (1990); James C. Worthy, *Shaping an American Institution* (1984).

Tom Dicke
Southwest Missouri State University

Department Stores

While department stores did not begin in the Midwest, the region produced retailing magnates who influenced the shopping habits of generations of Americans. The rise of department stores came about because of the rapid growth of the United States and the development of a consumer culture in the second half of the nineteenth century. Readily available capital tempted merchants to build palaces filled with every imaginable product, while cheap labor and low taxes offered additional incentives for expansion. A rising standard of living combined with a demand for more and better goods brought a steady stream of customers to the emporiums.

The term "department store" did not enter the lexicon until about 1887. The new name described a store that offered a markedly different experience from that found in small shops or offered by door-to-door peddlers. A customer, generally a woman, could complete all of her shopping with one stop at a central location and without the aggravation of personal price negotiation for each item purchased. Besides offering a fantastic array of goods at a fixed price, department stores typically provided a multitude of new services such as the return of unsatisfactory goods for exchange or refund and sales on credit. Flamboyant promotions, such as spectacular Christmas displays, and heavy advertising made the vast downtown emporiums the fashionable place to be. Customers flocked to the new stores, as much for the goods they offered as for the experience of shopping in such a spectacular setting.

While Ernest Lehmann of Chicago's The Fair is often credited with founding the first department store in 1874, other merchants had a longer-lasting impact. F. & R. Lazarus and Company of Columbus, Ohio, grew slowly after its establishment in 1851. When Fred, Jr., joined the store, he turned the shop into one of the major department stores in the nation. Lazarus shocked the industry by grouping clothing by sizes instead of price, forcing customers to look at more expensive goods that they then often purchased. The store made additional sales by becoming the first in America to sell on the installment plan with no down payment. In 1929, Fred, Jr., joined his family's store with Filene's, Abraham & Straus, and Bloomingdale's to form Federated Department Stores.

Sears, Roebuck and Company began in 1886 as a mail-order seller of watches. The firm soon expanded to sell general merchandise and became the nation's largest retailer as well as its largest advertiser. Sears opened retail outlets to compete with the stores that allowed customers to touch and try on goods. Founded in 1902 in Minneapolis, Dayton's became a retailing giant with nineteen stores. It created a billion-dollar business now known as Target Corporation and pioneered the first indoor shopping mall, Southdale. May Department Stores centered in St. Louis, Missouri, which would become one of the nation's largest department store chains as well as one of the longest-lived, was incorporated in 1910 in New York City. The company claimed that its flagship store, Famous-Barr, a massive white structure overlooking downtown St. Louis's retail district, was the largest office building in the world.

Other department stores also instituted innovations. Marshall Field's of Chicago, with the motto "Give the Lady What She Wants," offered the world's first personal shopping service. Linguists staffed its information desk to answer questions about the store and Chicago in every language known in the city. By 1954, Field's claimed the largest department store restaurant, the largest retail shoe operation, largest china department, largest toy operation, largest book department, while importing the largest amount of linen and ladies' fashions. J. L. Hudson dominated the department store business in Detroit. Hudson's specialized in value, with clearly marked prices, durable products, and fine quality, but paid little attention to style or fashion. Its famous four-acre, sixty-department basement stores sold more bargain merchandise than any other department store.

After World War II, shoppers began patronizing shopping malls, while downtowns died. Following their customers, department stores opened branches in the malls. Unfortunately, the very existence of a mall takes away the convenient shopping and dazzling experience that once only department stores provided. Other merchants now provide more personalized service. Specialty shops in malls, online retailers, and the return of door-to-door peddlers have caused a significant reduction in the profits of department stores, placing the long-term survival of such retailers in considerable doubt.

Sources and Further Reading: John William Ferry, *A History of the Department Store* (1960); Leon Harris, *Merchant Princes* (1979); Robert Hendrickson, *The Grand Emporiums* (1979); William Leach, *Land of Desire* (1993); Ronald D. Michman and Alan J. Greco, *Retailing Triumphs and Blunders* (1995); Jean Maddern Pitrone, *Hudson's: Hub of America's Heartland* (1991).

Caryn E. Neumann
The Ohio State University–Columbus

Restaurant Chains

The Midwest has played an important role in the development of the $420 billion national food service industry. An analysis of location of the top four hundred restaurant company headquarters in America indicates that three of the ten states with the largest number of headquarters are located in the Midwest—Ohio at fourth, Minnesota at seventh, Illinois at ninth, and Michigan at twelfth. The largest food service trade show in the world is held every May in Chicago. The Midwest is the home of the world's second-oldest continuing restaurant chain, White Castle; the world's largest restaurant chain, McDonalds; the nation's largest casual dining restaurant chain, Applebee's; two large family restaurant chains, Big Boy and Bob Evans; the top three pizza chains, Pizza Hut, Domino's, and Little Caesars; the oldest family restaurant, Steak and Shake; and the original soft-serve ice cream restaurant, Dairy Queen. Michigan State University and Ohio State University are two of the top five oldest baccalaureate food service management programs in the country.

The Midwest is also the birthplace of the restaurant franchise systems invented by Ray Kroc in Illinois. According to Robert Emerson, Michigan, Illinois, and Ohio rank among the top ten in number of restaurants per capita. The nation's most popular menu item, the hamburger, was invented in the Midwest and made its debut at the St. Louis World's Fair. Pizza was introduced to America as a chain concept in Wichita,

Kansas, by the Carney brothers as Pizza Hut, and Domino's introduced the concept of the home delivery in Michigan. Dave Thomas perfected the now ubiquitous drive-through concept in Columbus, Ohio. Minnesota is where the soft-serve ice cream concept was first introduced by Dairy Queen. In summary, the Midwest food service industry has made significant contributions in enhancing the quality of American life over the past one hundred years. Since it would be impossible to describe all the food service companies of the Midwest and their contributions, a few selected restaurant pioneers from the Midwest are described here.

Billy Ingram is the acknowledged father of American quick service industry. Prior to the 1920s, Americans considered ground beef unworthy of consumption at home, let alone in restaurants. This belief was based on the Old World practice of grinding together all unwanted beef parts and selling it at reduced prices to the lower classes. In 1916, however, Walter Anderson started selling small hamburger patties cooked with onions and served on a square bun for a nickel on the street corners of Wichita, Kansas. It instantly became popular with the working class. Billy Ingram, an insurance businessman, partnered with Anderson in opening the first White Castle restaurant. So history was made. Billy Ingram expanded the concept from Nebraska to New York City.

McDonald's is a unique American story. Two McDonald brothers, natives of Massachusetts, headed west in search of a better life. They opened their first McDonald's restaurant in San Bernardino, California. It proved revolutionary. They used only convenient foods from frozen meat to frozen fries so that they could offer a whole meal for a few cents. They adapted the assembly line concept and positional specialization to the food service industry, incorporated the display kitchen concept, breaking down the traditional walls between kitchens and dining areas, and emphasized cleanliness as a competitive marketing tool. Ray Kroc, from Illinois, recognized a new business opportunity in McDonald's restaurants and purchased the franchise rights. He expanded the business, ultimately making it the largest restaurant chain in the world, operating some thirty thousand units in over one hundred twenty countries.

The life story of Dave Thomas, founder of Wendy's, is an all-American success story. Adopted by a working-class family that moved to the Midwest in search of work, Dave never finished high school but found a full-time job at a family restaurant. He was the youngest person in charge of an officers' mess hall while on military duty in the Korean War. Upon returning home, he worked in Indiana for a while and later joined a KFC franchise in Columbus, Ohio, as

The original White Castle, Wichita, Kansas, 1921. Photo courtesy White Castle Management Co.

the area manager. He turned the franchise into a highly profitable venture, and became a millionaire at the age of twenty-eight. He then opened the first Wendy's Old Fashioned Hamburger restaurant in Columbus in 1969. Currently, Wendy's International operates over six thousand Wendy's restaurants in twenty-five countries.

In contrast to these three companies, Bob Evans restaurants began as a sausage-making business. By the end of the twentieth century, Bob Evans was one of the largest family-oriented restaurant chains in America. Like White Castle, Bob Evans doesn't offer franchises, but owns and operates 100 percent of its restaurants. In addition to restaurants, Bob Evans also still owns animal farms, six sausage-making facilities, and distribution systems.

Thomas Monaghan started Domino's Pizza in 1960 in Ypsilanti, Michigan. Domino's operates over seven thousand restaurants with nearly $4 billion in annual revenues and over 140 thousand employees in fifty countries. It is the second-largest pizza restaurant company in America and the number one pizza delivery company. The uniqueness of Domino's is *not* its pizza, but its delivery system. Domino's was the first company to guarantee pizza delivery within thirty minutes of placing the order. Many companies have unsuccessfully tried to imitate Domino's delivery system. By guaranteeing a quality product and efficient home delivery, Domino's has changed the food habits of America.

In the late 1940s, according to a U.S. Armed Forces survey, the hamburger was the number one food choice in America, but by the late 1980s, the pizza had replaced it. The Midwest gave America its favorite foods throughout the twentieth century.

Sources and Further Reading: Dave Hogan, *Selling 'Em by the Sack* (1997); John F. Love, *McDonald's: Behind the Arches* (1995); Dave Thomas, *Dave's Way* (1991).

H. G. Parsa
The Ohio State University–Columbus

Shopping Malls

In the second half of the twentieth century, the shopping mall replaced Main Street as the central business district in communities all over the United States. The development of malls began in the Midwest, and the region has continued as a retail pioneer. Malls flourished because the popularity of the automobile, and the growth of the highway system made it possible for Americans to travel with ease. As people moved into the suburbs, malls sprang up to serve the needs of people who preferred to shop where they lived. The visual appeal and comfortable environment of malls contributed to a steady deterioration of the downtown customer base and helped destroy the viability of downtowns.

The shopping mall is a group of buildings, developed and managed as a unit, with a street designated for use by pedestrians only and a special parking area. The first malls were unplanned developments that sprouted alongside Sears or Montgomery Ward outlets in the new suburbs of the early twentieth century.

Southdale Center, Edina, Minnesota, 1956. Minnesota Historical Society MHS Locator no. MH5.9/ED3.1/p3.

Market Square, built in 1916 in the Chicago suburb of Lake Forest, is considered to be the first planned development shopping mall in the nation. Like subsequent malls, Market Square drew shoppers with various entertainments and required its tenants to pay both rent and a percentage of sales to management, as well as a fee for mall maintenance and marketing. The most famous of these early malls, Country Club Plaza, was completed in 1923 on the then-outskirts of Kansas City, Missouri. Created by J. C. Nichols, this Spanish-themed mall on fifty-five acres had streets filled with antique sculptures, columns, tile, murals, wrought iron, and fountains, as well as eight filling stations to serve its many visitors.

During the Great Depression and World War II, the poor retail environment effectively halted mall development, but the great suburban surge of the postwar era renewed it. The postwar malls were regional shopping centers with one or more large department branch stores anchoring the surrounding small specialty shops. The first regional mall, the Town and Country Shopping Center, opened in 1949 in Columbus, Ohio, on a tract of almost forty-six acres. Besides containing the first suburban branches of department stores J.C. Penney and Kresge, it also became the first shopping mall to keep its stores open at night. The sharp extremes of midwestern weather led to the first enclosed mall, the two-level Southdale, in Edina, Minnesota, in 1956. By 1962, the open mall had become obsolete throughout the nation. The new enclosed style would dominate mall construction for the rest of the century.

The perceived safety of malls appealed to customers who continued to flee a downtown that was increasingly viewed as dangerous. This increased demand for malls led to larger buildings, and super-sized regional malls began to appear in the 1960s. With three or more department stores as anchors on more than fifty acres of land, these malls provided both visual spectacle and shopping. Woodfield Mall, just outside Chicago in Schaumburg, Illinois, is the top tourist destination in the state and one of the highest-volume shopping centers in the world, with more than fifty thousand visitors daily. Randall Park in Cleveland had more stores, two hundred fifty, than any other mall until the massive Mall of America opened in the 1970s. Attracting tens of millions of visitors annually from around the world, the 4.2-million-square-foot Mall of America is one of the nation's largest tourist attractions, with over five hundred stores, eighty-three restaurants, fourteen movie theatres, eight nightclubs, an indoor amusement park, and an aquatic park. The designation of tallest mall goes to Chicago's Water Tower Place, which opened in 1975 as a seventy-four-story, mixed-use complex.

The 1980s saw a movement away from suburban malls. Cities attempted to revitalize downtowns by building suburban-style malls, but these efforts had mixed success. Outlet malls, sprawling outdoor complexes selling discounted goods, did well until the end of the century when many closed.

At the start of the twenty-first century, mall development has returned to its beginnings. Open-air malls that mimic old-fashioned downtowns have come into vogue. Easton Town Center, opened in stages beginning in 1999, is a Columbus, Ohio, entertainment and shopping complex that has served as model for similar developments around the country. Reflecting the qualities that made malls popular, it offers visual spectacle, convenient parking, and a safe environment.

Sources and Further Reading: Richard V. Francaviglia, *Main Street Revisited* (1996); Robert Hendrickson, *The Grand Emporiums* (1979); William Severini Kowinski, *The Malling of America* (1985); Eric Nelson, *The Mall of America* (1997).

Caryn E. Neumann
The Ohio State University–Columbus

Metropolitan Financial Institutions

Many features of U.S. financial institutions have Midwest origins. For example, in 1837, Michigan became the first state to enact legislation regulating banking. The Michigan law predates all existing federal legislation and served as a model for banking laws in other states. Wisconsin pioneered the development of a mutual form of insurance in which local communities formed associations for the purpose of providing insurance on farm property and liability. In 1931, twelve Wisconsin towns combined to form the Wisconsin Reinsurance Corporation, which is the earliest recorded effort to help mutual associations diversify the risks of financial loss across multiple communities. Reinsurance is now a common practice throughout the insurance industry. In yet another example of Midwest innovation, Bank One of Columbus, Ohio, is generally regarded as one of the pioneers for automatic teller machines, introduced in Columbus in 1969.

Financial institutions have, in turn, played an important role in the development of the Midwest region. During the century following American independence, as Native Americans were pushed westward, new settlers arrived from the East. The arriving settlers brought new demands for financial services. Young families needed to borrow funds to pur-

❖ Bank One

Bank One originated in 1868 as F.C. Session's bank in Columbus, Ohio. By 1929, through mergers, it had become part of City National Bank and Trust Company. In 1935, the first of three John McCoys who would govern until 2000 became president. Emphasizing consumer banking, in 1950, it was among the first to open a drive-in facility, and in 1966, it introduced the first Visa card outside of California.

In 1967, Bank One formed a bank holding company, First Banc, renamed Banc One in 1979. After deregulation, it expanded into other states, often acquiring smaller banks through stock swaps. Entering Texas in 1989, it bought numerous insolvent bank branches and thrift institutions, and by 1991 was six times larger than it had been seven years earlier. Efficient, disciplined, and avoiding problem loans, it became a national leader in large bank earnings performance. Banc One became the nation's third largest credit card issuer in 1997 by purchasing fourth-ranked First USA.

In 1998, Banc One merged with First Chicago to create Bank One and moved its headquarters to Chicago. It became the Midwest's largest and the nation's fifth largest commercial bank, as well as the nation's sixth largest bank holding company. Nonetheless, disappointing post-merger results led to new management in 2000. In January 2004, Bank One and J.P. Morgan Chase announced a merger, thereby establishing the nation's second largest bank holding company, with $1.1 trillion in assets and twenty-three hundred branches in seventeen states. The new bank will have its headquarters in New York City, but Chicago will serve as the center for its retail financial services and middle market businesses.

Nicholas Lash
Loyola University, Chicago, Illinois

chase essential supplies and to build homes. Established families needed a safe and secure place to keep any savings they might accumulate. Local savings and loan associations, or thrifts, emerged to fill these basic needs.

In addition to a local savings and loan, a town of even modest size required the services of a bank of commerce, or what we now refer to as a commercial bank or even more simply as a bank. One function of the early midwestern banks was to vouch for local merchants who needed to stock their shelves by purchasing goods from suppliers in distant locations, often in eastern states. In exchange for a fee, a bank would affix a special stamp to a merchant's order for goods. The stamp was referred to as a "banker's acceptance" and assured that if the merchant did not pay for the goods on the order, the bank would cover the charge. A seller of goods would not necessarily know, or trust, a bank from a remote region. Hence banks in

the new settlements of the Midwest were typically linked by a correspondent system to a bank in the region of the seller, who would provide a stamp of its own and thereby re-accept the acceptance of the bank of the purchaser.

In many respects, the structure of the early financial institutions was well suited to the development of the Midwest region. As new lands were settled, new savings and loans and new banks were created and linked to an expanding network of correspondent banks. Yet the early structure was not without problems. In particular, none of the federal safeguards that we now take for granted yet existed: there was no federal system for regulating risks taken by banks and savings and loans or for insuring deposits in the event that the financial institutions failed.

The practice of fractional reserving added greatly to the instability of the banking system. Under this practice, a bank or savings and loan that received deposits retained only a small fraction of those deposits as cash on hand at the bank. Most of the funds were reinvested either in the form of loans to other customers or as investments funneled through the correspondent banking system. The theory of fractional reserving was based on the assumption that the cash needs of any given customer are largely unrelated to cash needs of other customers. As a result, on any given day, cash that is deposited covers most, if not all, of the demand for withdrawals. This model worked reasonably well for a large city bank with a diverse customer base; it did not work nearly as well in the early farming communities of the Midwest. Most farmers in a given area needed to borrow at the same time to plant and cultivate crops and would repay at the same time, when they sold their harvest. To complicate this seasonal pattern in cash flow, in years of crop failure by drought or other causes, many farmers in a given community would default on loans and thus undermine the base of assets that a bank or savings and loan could use to repay its depositors.

As a consequence of fractional reserves, no bank or savings and loan had sufficient cash on hand to cover all of its deposits. As a result, even a rumor that an unusual number of depositors intended to withdraw funds at the same time could trigger a "run" that would drain the bank of cash on hand. The bank would thus be required to shut its doors until it could raise enough cash to cover its deposits by selling investments. Local bank runs were common in the early years of Midwest settlement. Large-scale bank runs, or bank panics, led to national economic recessions in 1873, 1884, 1893, and 1907.

Other than two brief and unsuccessful efforts by the U.S. Congress to establish a national banking system in 1791 and 1816, the creation and monitoring of financial institutions was largely a local matter. When Michigan entered the union as the twenty-sixth state in 1837, one of the first acts of the new legislature was to pass a law for chartering and regulating banks within the new state. The Michigan law was the first of its kind. Other states quickly followed suit by passing banking regulations of their own.

Despite the widespread movement for state-level regulation, both the nature of banking laws and the rigor with which those laws were enforced varied widely from state to state during what came to be known as the free banking era. One particularly troublesome problem stemmed from the fact that there was no national currency prior to the Civil War. Various types of gold and silver coins were used, and a substantial amount of coin or "specie" was difficult to transport and safeguard. Early banks filled the need for a lighter-weight medium of exchange by issuing bank notes. These pocket-sized IOUs certified that the issuing bank would make payment of a specified amount, in the form of gold or silver coins, to whomever presented the notes to the bank for payment.

National Banking Acts were passed in 1862 (the Legal Tender Act) and 1863 to help finance the Union's Civil War effort. These new laws had three lasting effects: They created a system for chartering national banks; they created an active market for the sale and trading of bonds issued by the federal government; and they created a uniform national currency. The new national currency was especially successful, and in a matter of years, national greenbacks replaced the hodgepodge of irregular notes that had been issued by individual banks.

Congress extended federal influence on banking by passing the Federal Reserve Act in 1913. The new law created a system of twelve regional Reserve Banks and a Federal Reserve Board to manage the Federal Reserve System. Duties of the Fed included lending money to member banks that were solvent but needed temporary funds to meet unanticipated withdrawals of deposits.

Over the years, concern about undue political influence of large financial institutions led to efforts at both the state and federal levels to limit the scale and scope of financial institutions. Restrictions on scale generally prohibited banks and other financial institutions from operating in more than one state. Some states even prohibited banks from operating out of more than one location or branch. Restrictions on scope limited the variety of financial services that any one institution could offer. For example, for many years savings and loan associations were allowed to pay interest on savings deposits, but were not permitted to offer checking accounts. Banks were allowed to offer checking ac-

counts, but were not allowed to pay interest on savings accounts. Neither savings and loans nor banks were allowed to sell insurance or serve as a broker for the exchange of stocks and bonds. When a large number of banks and savings and loan associations failed in the Great Depression of the 1930s, Congress passed a series of federal laws known collectively as the Glass-Steagall Act, which imposed nationwide restrictions on the scope and scale of financial institutions in the hope of limiting risk to, as well as influence on, the general economy.

By virtue of federal and state restrictions on scale and scope, the structure of financial institutions in the Midwest and throughout the country has been characterized by a large number of highly specialized institutions. In addition to savings and loan associations and banks, credit unions emerged as a competitor in the market for deposit accounts, checking accounts, and retail loans for well-defined groups, such as the employees of a large business or the members of a labor union or fraternal order. Even before the Midwest was settled, private insurance companies had been formed in large eastern cities to offer life, property, and casualty insurance. When private insurance companies failed to keep pace with the spread of new settlements in the Midwest, the mutual form of ownership grew in popularity. In the mutual form of ownership, customers who purchase insurance also serve as the owners of the company. As a result, any profits of the company are returned to policyholders in the form of dividends on their insurance policies.

The mutual form of insurance was well suited for expanding settlements of the Midwest. The original structure, which had been developed for life and fire insurance, was readily adapted for health and automobile coverage, both of which were developed over the first half of the 1900s. But, during the latter half of the 1900s, the insurance industry in the Midwest and throughout the nation had become transformed into a large number of highly specialized institutions.

Despite a general distrust of large financial institutions, the substantial economic efficiencies of large institutions are able to offer a wide array of financial services to customers in dispersed locations. Economic efficiency results in better prices for customers and bigger profits for shareholders. Accordingly, over the last quarter of the twentieth century, large financial institutions lobbied state and federal legislators to reverse restrictions on the scale and scope of individual institutions. As a result of efforts to deregulate financial institutions, large holding companies are now permitted to own a variety of financial institutions, including banks in different states as well as nonbanking financial institutions.

Deregulation greatly increased competition. Financial institutions that were unable to compete either went out of business or merged with other institutions. The effect of increased competition has been especially strong in the Midwest. For example, in 1984, 1,033 out of 1,707 federally insured thrifts in the United States were located in the twelve states comprising the Midwest region. By 2001, only 883 thrifts remained in the nation, and only 481, or less than half, had survived in the Midwest. The pattern is similar, if less dramatic, for commercial banks. In 1984, 6,400 of the 14,496 federally insured banks in the nation were located in the Midwest region. By 2001, the number of U.S. banks had decreased to 8,080, with only 3,585 located in Midwest states.

The insurance industry is also in the midst of change. Large holding companies have been formed to acquire and operate what had been many smaller companies. In addition, whereas many early insurance companies sold policies through a network of independent agents who also sold insurance for other companies, the trend among new large companies is to employ captive agents who only sell insurance for the companies owned by the holding company. Another recent trend is for insurance companies to sell directly to customers through a variety of methods including television and print advertising, mailings, and even the Internet.

The pattern of consolidation in the financial industry is likely to continue, if not accelerate, in response to emergence of the Internet and the growth in e-commerce. The old model of a local bank, a local savings and loan, or a local insurance company that provided specialized service to a single community is rapidly giving way to a new model of financial supermarkets that offer a wide array of competitively priced financial services.

Leading financial institutions in the Midwest appear to be well positioned for future consolidation. For example, State Farm, with headquarters in Bloomington, Illinois, is the largest insurer of property and casualty risks in the country. The Midwest is also home to six of the twenty largest individual banks in the country, and to six of the twenty largest bank holding companies. Joining the Chicago office of Bank One, which is currently fifth on the list of the largest individual banks, are US Bank in Cincinnati at seventh, Keybank in Cleveland at thirteenth, LaSalle Bank in Chicago at eighteenth, the Columbus Office of Bank One at seventeenth, Fifth Third in Cincinnati at twenty-first, and Wells Fargo in Minneapolis at twenty-second.

Sources and Further Reading: Gary A. Dymski, *The Bank Merger Wave* (1999); Edward S. Kaplan, *The Bank of the United States and the American Economy* (1999); Jerry W.

Markham, *A Financial History of the United States*, 3 vols. (2002).

Stephen A. Buser
The Ohio State University–Columbus

African American Financial Institutions

The first African American bank in the Midwest was established in Chicago in 1908 by businessman and former Pullman porter Jesse Binga. The Binga Bank was soon celebrated as a model for black business success. Several other African American banks were soon chartered in Chicago, as was Omnibank in Detroit in 1919. In Chicago in 1922, former slave and former judge Anthony Overton joined P. W. Chavers, another wealthy businessman, to establish the Douglass National Bank, the second nationally chartered African American bank in the nation and the first in the Midwest. The Binga and the Douglass National Banks prospered, and by 1929, they accounted for over one-third of the combined resources of the nation's African American banks. They specialized in real estate loans, which provided the means for Chicago blacks to become property holders.

During the Great Depression, one-third of the nation's banks, including most African American banks, collapsed. In 1930, the Binga Bank became the first Chicago bank to fail. Binga was found guilty of fraud, spent three years in prison, and died penniless in 1950. Two years later, Overton's Douglass National was closed, which along with the demise of the Binga Bank, left a long-term void in Midwest black communities. From 1933 to 1964, only one African American bank was established in the Midwest, Douglass State Bank of Kansas City in 1947.

From 1964 to 1992, however, twenty-two new African American banks were chartered in the Midwest. Nine were established in Chicago and the others were in Cincinnati, Dayton, Detroit, Kansas City, Milwaukee, Minneapolis, Omaha, St. Louis, Springfield (Illinois), Warrensville (Ohio), and Wichita. In Chicago in 1964, black millionaires Alvin Boutte and George Johnson started Independence Bank. One year later a consortium of black businessmen established Chicago's Seaway National Bank. Independence and Seaway grew and competed to be the nation's largest African American bank. In 1979, Independence acquired the deposits of failed African American banks Guaranty Bank and Trust and Gateway National, and in 1980, Independence became part of Indecorp, a bank holding company. When Indecorp bought Drexel National Bank in 1988, it became the nation's first African American bank to acquire a solvent nonminority-owned bank, and the nation's largest African American bank holding company. In the Detroit area in 1988, two black attorneys bought white-owned River Rouge Savings Bank, thereby establishing OmniBanc. In 1994, OmniBanc sought unsuccessfully to acquire Indecorp, which would have created the nation's first African American interstate banking operation. Four years later, OmniBanc failed.

In 1995, nonminority-owned South Shore Bank bought Indecorp. Community groups protested the transfer of Indecorp, then the nation's largest African American bank, to nonminority ownership. Others noted that South Shore enjoyed an outstanding national reputation for community development lending in mostly black Chicago neighborhoods. At the turn of the century, a controversy existed regarding the potential role of African American banks in developing minority communities. Some believe African American banks, handicapped by inadequate size and capitalization, high costs, managerial inexperience, and high loan losses, can contribute little. Others cite evidence suggesting that experience improves African American bank performance. They also suggest that African American banks devote a greater share of their assets to Small Business Administration loans to minorities than do nonminority banks, provide more employment opportunities for minorities in banking, and offer lower loan rates through increased competition.

At the same time, all U.S. banks have come to face new challenges from financial deregulation and increased competition from nonbanking financial institutions. From 1888 to the beginning of the twenty-first century, over one hundred forty African American banks were established nationwide, with thirty in the Midwest. Yet failure has been commonplace; currently, only thirty-one African American banks remain in the country, eight of them in the Midwest. They are First Independence National Bank in Detroit, Douglass National Bank in Kansas City, Gateway National Bank in St. Louis, Legacy Bank and North Milwaukee State Bank in Milwaukee, and in Chicago, Community Bank of Lawndale, Highland Community Bank, and Seaway National Bank, currently the largest African American commercial bank in the nation.

Sources and Further Reading: Lila Ammons, "The Evolution of Black-Owned Banks in the United States between the 1880s and 1990s," *Journal of Black Studies* 26 (Mar. 1996); John A. Cole et al., "Black Banks," *The Review of Black Political Economy* 14 (Summer 1985); Abram L. Harris, *The Negro as Capitalist* (1936).

Nicholas Lash
Loyola University–Chicago, Illinois

Metropolitan Manufacturing

The growth of manufacturing was a defining feature in the rise of the urban Midwest. Industrial production and employment outpaced the rate of population increase in most midwestern cities from the second quarter of the nineteenth century through the second quarter of the twentieth century, giving the region's urban centers a distinctive character and appearance. Moreover, to a greater degree than in other regions, this phenomenon was associated with industrial innovation—the creation of new products and processes. From the mid-nineteenth century, midwestern manufacturers specialized in complex, high-value products. Their success led to opportunities for generations of workers and entrepreneurs, and the formation of an assertive upper class of executives and investors. By the same token, the slowing of industrial innovation during the middle and later decades of the twentieth century reduced the cities' roles as engines of wealth creation and social mobility.

Until the early nineteenth century, urban manufacturers accounted for a comparatively small portion of total industrial production because of the prevalence of household manufacture, water-powered milling, and resource-dependent processing such as forestry and iron smelting. Then the advent of steam power and new forms of transport led to a rapid decline in household production and the rise of factories (facilities that used water or steam power to drive machinery), which made goods that had formerly been produced in the home or handicraft shop. By mid-century, factory production overshadowed other forms of manufacture in the northeastern United States.

This was also the period when the Midwest emerged as a distinctive region with a thriving economy based on continuing contacts with the northeast and the duplication of institutions common to that area. By the 1820s, Cincinnati, the largest western city, could boast most of the crafts common to New York and Philadelphia, as well as industries such as pork packing that relied on local resources. There were meaningful distinctions, however. Midwestern towns and cities would never become centers of textile production. Conversely, because of their locations on navigable rivers and lakes, they quickly developed facilities for steam engine building and repair that rivaled those of larger eastern centers. Expertise in engine building soon led to other forms of machinery manufacture that in turn encouraged the growth of the midwestern iron industry and the adoption of coal-using technologies. By the 1850s, the outline of a new industrial economy based on steam, iron, and ma-

Robot welding cars, Honda of America, Marysville, Ohio. Photo by Doug Martin.

chinery, was apparent. Apart from transport-related machinery, including railroad equipment, the most notable example of this development was the rise of the farm machinery industry.

The McCormick Company, which started operations in Chicago in 1848, symbolized this change. McCormick soon became the largest producer of farm implements in the country and the foundation of the International Harvester Company, the dominant agricultural machinery maker of the first half of the twentieth century. McCormick had an equally profound influence on Chicago. It employed thousands in its factories and steel mills, encouraged the establishment of parts suppliers and other implement manufacturers, and created a community of individuals with knowledge of a variety of metal-working operations.

In the 1870s and 1880s, the development of rich iron ore mines in northern Michigan and especially northern Minnesota reinforced the emerging pattern of urban industrialization. The new ore supplies led to a dramatic shift in iron and steel production to Great Lakes port cities, notably Chicago, Milwaukee, Cleveland, and Detroit. Chicago became the second center (after Pittsburgh) of steel production. Gary, Indiana, a town just east of Chicago that was created by the U.S. Steel Company in 1906, was a testament to the influence of the northern ore mines and the importance of iron and steel manufacture to midwestern urban growth.

Urban manufacturers created numerous employment opportunities in the rapidly growing cities of the region. Two features of this experience stand out. First, they required large numbers of skilled workers who often changed jobs, transferring ideas and techniques between plants and industries—a process that also emphasized the value of locating new factories in existing industrial centers. Second, despite the relatively high wages that industrial workers received,

manufacturers were unable to attract enough local employees to accommodate their growth. European immigrants filled the gap. By the 1870s, midwestern cities had well-developed links with European industrial centers, and the association between industrial work and immigrant communities became stronger. Most skilled workers were veterans of British or German industrial firms, while most laborers had agricultural backgrounds. By 1900, there was a marked contrast between city and countryside, with immigrants and their children dominating the urban population, and northwestern Europeans and their children dominating the more highly skilled, better paid positions.

Midwestern manufacturers were also at the forefront of a movement to improve factory operations. Systematic and scientific management, efforts to increase productivity through centralized management, improved record keeping and communications, and wage incentives originated in northeastern industry in the 1870s and 1880s, but spread rapidly to the new factories of the Midwest. By 1910, the Joseph & Feiss Company of Cleveland was probably the best-known practitioner of scientific management. Midwestern firms were also well known for their pioneering roles in the development of personnel management. Late-nineteenth-century textile firms had introduced welfare programs for women and children to blunt charges that they exploited dependent workers. Midwestern firms that employed large numbers of women and children, such as Chicago and Detroit department stores, also introduced health, education, and savings plans. But manufacturers in the region hired relatively few women or children and were less concerned about outside critics. They were more sensitive to bottlenecks and waste caused by unmotivated or uncooperative employees, male or female.

This was a critical consideration at the National Cash Register (NCR) Company of Dayton, Ohio, the national leader in personnel work after 1900. As production of its new, complex machines increased, NCR introduced systematic management to eliminate production bottlenecks. In the 1890s, it also introduced an extensive welfare program. Yet in 1901, it suffered a long, debilitating strike, suggesting that neither systematic management nor welfare programs had addressed the relationship between the front-line supervisor and the machine worker. After the strike, John Patterson, the company president, introduced major changes in both the management system and the welfare plans. His most significant innovation was a personnel department, which assumed the supervisors' power to hire, fire, and resolve grievances. The welfare program increasingly emphasized insurance, savings, and recreation plans, which had greater appeal to male workers. The new approach became a model for generations of employers who recognized the importance of cooperation and teamwork in the production of complex products.

The emergence of the auto industry in the early twentieth century was an extension of the trends of the previous half-century. The industry located in the Midwest because of the availability of metal-working firms that were able to produce components such as engines, transmissions, and axles. The assemblers located in Detroit, Cleveland, Toledo, Flint, South Bend, and other cities with strong manufacturing infrastructures, while parts suppliers sought out smaller communities where costs were lower.

Detroit symbolized what was happening throughout the region. Its strategic location had long made it an important industrial center, with links to lake shipping, rail car production, and hardware. The rise of the Ford Motor Company during the first decade of the century spurred other assemblers and component manufacturers, and Detroit became the hub of the new industry. Ford's giant Highland Park plant (built in 1910) also became a model for other manufacturers, who quickly adopted innovative techniques such as the moving assembly line. Other firms, such as Dodge and Hudson, contributed major new technologies, and General Motors became the industry leader by combining efficient manufacturing with aggressive marketing. In the meantime, thousands of potential factory workers, mostly eastern European immigrants, were attracted to the industry's high wages.

In the 1930s and 1940s, the Midwest's manufacturers reached a turning point. The severe economic depression of the early 1930s devastated the manufacturing economy, the auto industry in particular. Bankruptcies eliminated the weakest firms. Mass layoffs destroyed the hopes and careers of thousands of industrial workers, creating widespread disillusionment and resentment. The New Deal recovery program, introduced in 1933, at first produced more friction than growth, and the region's industrial cities became the scenes of dramatic industrial conflicts. By the end of the decade, most industrial workers in the largest cities had become union members, and union pressures, institutionalized in elaborate written contracts, had led to higher wages and increasingly ambitious benefit plans. An associated result was a decline in the region's attractiveness to entrepreneurs and investors. To many corporate managers, midwestern cities meant high costs and troubled labor relations.

World War II introduced additional problems. Although war production greatly increased employment and increased profits, government controls also deterred innovation (except in the manufacture of armaments) and weakened internal management. By the mid-1940s, many firms enjoyed a deceptive prosperity. Factories were running overtime, and profits and earnings were higher than at any time in the previous decade. But new product development had slowed or stopped, management controls had weakened, collective bargaining had slowed the introduction of labor-saving processes, and union militancy deterred new investment.

Pent-up consumer demand, continued government spending, and Korean War–related controls extended wartime prosperity for another decade and created the impression that manufacturing would continue to be the foundation of the midwestern economy. High-paying factory jobs sustained many communities and created confidence, even complacency, about the future. By the mid-1950s, however, there were warning signs. The dramatic collapse of the smaller auto companies such as Hudson and Studebaker after the lifting of Korean War production controls was a blow to Detroit and South Bend and to many parts suppliers. The more gradual, less dramatic decline of the steel industry was equally troubling. Only in Ohio's Mahoning Valley, the oldest area of mill concentration, did employment seriously decline before the 1960s, but the industry's lethargic management and persistent labor problems attracted growing concern.

Looking back, economists have discovered a pattern to these developments. Large manufacturing companies continued to operate existing plants, though they made only minimal efforts to modernize or introduce innovative processes or techniques. At the same time, they built new plants in the South and Southwest, where costs were lower and unions had little, if any, power. Thus while employment and wages continued to rise in midwestern cities, the northern plants became increasingly vulnerable. The tire industry provides one of the clearest examples of this pattern. While the industry had been highly concentrated in Ohio before the war, manufacturers built no new Ohio plants after the 1940s, and only four in the Midwest as a whole, while in the early 1960s, they built eight new plants in the South and two in the West. By the end of the 1960s, the tire industry had shifted most of its operations to the upper South.

Thus the Rust Belt phenomena of the 1970s, the waves of plant closings and layoffs that devastated the region's cities, was both a response to the immediate problems of the decade and a consequence of longer-term developments. The severe recessions of 1974–1975 and 1979–1982 led to cutbacks throughout the industrial sector, but the vulnerability of the midwestern plants meant that the reductions were particularly severe there and included plant closings as well as more traditional temporary shut downs and layoffs. The steel mill towns were uniformly devastated, many auto parts plants and every Ohio tire plant closed, and most autoworkers experienced long layoffs. International Harvester, Youngstown Sheet & Tube, and U.S. Rubber, together with hundreds of lesser-known companies, disappeared. Small industrial cities like Gary, Indiana, and Youngstown, Ohio, became severely depressed. Vast areas of Detroit, Chicago, and Cleveland became wastelands.

The economy recovered slowly in the early 1980s, and productivity and employment gradually rose to earlier levels, but there were significant differences. Most of the new activity was in small towns, not cities; in new plants, not established facilities. Wages were lower and most plants were nonunion. By the end of the century, midwestern manufacturing more closely resembled industrial activity in the South and West, had little association with the region's traditional industrial cities, and had ceased to be a source of innovation or an engine of regional growth.

Sources and Further Reading: Donald Finlay Davis, *Conspicuous Production* (1988); Thomas Kochan, Harry C. Katz, and Robert McKersie, *The Transformation of American Industrial Relations* (1986); Daniel Nelson, *Farm and Factory: Workers in the Midwest, 1810–1990* (1995); Jon C. Teaford, *Cities of the Heartland* (1993).

Daniel Nelson
University of Akron, Ohio

Brewing

Brewing, the fermentation of grains into alcoholic beverages, became a significant industry in the Midwest by the end of the nineteenth century. A large market for beer appeared with the migration of central European peoples to the region. This market held fast for much of the history of the Midwest. However, brewers locate production near markets, as distribution costs are significant. So by the twenty-first century, the shift in population growth to the South and West meant that beer production shifted and the Midwest lost its production leadership—although, of course, the Midwest was still the site of large production volumes. Nevertheless, the nation's two largest brewers, Anheuser Busch and Miller, maintained their headquarters in St. Louis and Milwaukee, respectively.

The original European American settlers in the Midwest consumed prodigious amounts of alcoholic beverages produced in small-scale distilleries and cider mills. Although small quantities of beer were produced locally in those years, beer was a less favored beverage until after the arrival of large numbers of immigrants from Germany in the middle of the nineteenth century. The Germans brought with them lager, or stored beer made from bottom-floating yeast. Lager beer required cool temperatures in the brewing process; before the development of pasteurization lager beer had to remain chilled until consumed. Lager beer proved popular in the American market, especially in the heat of the summer. Thus, a modern brewing industry flourished in the Midwest during the second half of the nineteenth century, and by 1895, beer production in the Midwest had surpassed production in other regions. Large populations of thirsty customers in the Midwest were consuming extraordinary quantities of beer by 1900.

❖ Anheuser-Busch

The Anheuser-Busch Companies developed from a small St. Louis Brewery. In 1860, Eberhard Anheuser purchased the local brewery, and in 1864, his son-in-law, Adolphus Busch, went to work for the company. Since 1880, the Busch family has controlled and led the firm, aggressively pushing its products and expanding its operations so that by the end of the twentieth century, it sold more than half of the beer consumed in the United States and was the world's largest brewing firm. The Budweiser brand, established in 1876, eventually became the world's best-selling beer.

The largest American brewer in the twentieth century, Anheuser-Busch became a highly profitable venture, the Busch family ultimately being counted among America's wealthiest. After 1933, the firm expanded beer production while it retained interests in other businesses, including real estate and theme parks. Brewing remained at its heart, however. The firm built or acquired new breweries across the United States to satisfy markets and invested in foreign breweries, producing Budweiser and other brands abroad.

K. Austin Kerr
The Ohio State University–Columbus

By the latter decades of the nineteenth century, three types of brewing companies operated in the Midwest. Wherever there were concentrations of German immigrants, small breweries appeared to satisfy local markets. Some of these small breweries followed expansion policies and shipped beer to regional markets. In addition to the local and regional brewers, a few firms sought national and even international markets for their beer. Known as shipping breweries, they located in Cincinnati, Milwaukee, and St. Louis. In fact, the only breweries distributing beer across the nation at the end of the nineteenth century were in the Midwest, a fact that partly explained the region's dominance in the national brewing industry.

These largest breweries emerged because of the enterprise of their owners and the advantages of location. All three cities had sizable numbers of German immigrants who provided a ready local market for beer, yet neither the Cincinnati nor the Milwaukee nor St. Louis beer markets were large enough to satisfy the ambitions of a few brewers. After the great fire in Chicago in 1871, for example, the Milwaukee brewers found they could sell their beer profitably in that growing metropolis. Milwaukee and St. Louis enjoyed special advantages before the development of efficient mechanical refrigeration toward the end of the nineteenth century. Milwaukee had a ready and reliable supply of natural ice harvested from lakes, and St. Louis brewers used local caves to their advantage. Christian Moerlein, the Cincinnati brewer who developed a shipping business, was at a disadvantage in this respect, and by the 1880s, Cincinnati fell behind both St. Louis and Milwaukee as a center of beer production. The supply of natural ice in Cincinnati was reliable in only one out of three winters, and the costs of shipping ice from the North raised Moerlein's cost of production.

The brewers who expanded successfully into regional and national markets understood the advantages of new technologies and of new systems of business management. The larger brewers learned how to take advantage of the railroad network for distributing their product across long distances, using refrigerated freight cars. They applied the latest science and technology to production. The development of mechanical refrigeration in the last two decades of the nineteenth century was a boon to brewers, and the largest firms made sure that their breweries employed the latest techniques of cooking, cooling, piping, and the like. Brewers promoted pasteurization so that lager beer could be stored at warmer temperatures. This development meant that the size of individual breweries sometimes expanded. The largest of these averaged a production of a few thousand barrels a year (a barrel of beer, a unit developed for taxation purposes, contains

thirty-one gallons) at the time of the Civil War; by the end of the century, the largest plants produced 500 thousand to 800 thousand barrels a year, a volume not that much exceeded a century later. In management, the successful large brewers integrated the acquisition of raw materials, the application of scientific brewing techniques, and modern systems of railroad (and later in the twentieth century, motor truck) distribution. The largest shipping brewers established icing depots along railroad routes to keep refrigerated freight cars cool. The development of the crown cork bottle cap in 1892 enormously facilitated bottling, and bottles of beer produced by large midwestern brewers were appearing in international markets by century's end, though in fairly small volumes.

As the shipping brewers expanded and entered new markets, competition in the midwestern brewing industry grew apace. Competition had two important results. Some brewers lost in the competitive wars and left the business. In fact, the long-term trend in brewing after the Civil War was for business consolidation; there were over time simply fewer and fewer brewers in business. Moreover, competition also greatly increased the number of saloons, the retail outlets for most beer before 1920, in the Midwest. Thus, expanding brewers established thousands of new saloons. Saloons became so prolific that in many communities there was a saloon for just a few customers. For instance, in the early twentieth century the small mining town of Westville, Illinois, with a population of less than one thousand, had sixteen saloons.

With the high level of competition, saloon keepers had great difficulty earning a profit on the sale of beer alone, so they often went into other businesses linked to crime, such as prostitution and gambling. The breweries who supplied them were thus implicated in organized crime. The whole situation was unseemly, and respectable Americans organized to rid their communities of saloons through prohibition. These reformers saw an interconnected complex, which they termed "the liquor traffic," as working evil, encouraging both crime and drinking. Since, by 1890, the brewers had become the main suppliers of liquor, they became a principal object of reform. The Prohibition Movement, in short, targeted both the saloons and the brewers and distillers who supplied the saloons.

The Prohibition Movement was international in scope, but its roots were deeply implanted in the Midwest. In fact, the two main prohibition organizations, the Woman's Christian Temperance Union and the Anti-Saloon League of America, were born in the Midwest (in 1874 and 1893, respectively) where they maintained their headquarters. The prohibitionists succeeded in enacting statewide prohibition in several states, starting with Kansas in 1880, and began a long campaign to eradicate the liquor traffic everywhere. Political support for prohibition grew in the Midwest and elsewhere during the first two decades of the twentieth century. Prohibition laws were so successful that beer consumption began to fall after 1914. The reformers' most important statewide victory occurred in Michigan in 1916. Although they were unable to win state prohibition in any other midwestern state with a large city, the prohibitionists were successful nationally. National prohibition began in 1920 with the Eighteenth Amendment to the United States Constitution.

Prohibition devastated the brewing industry. National policy required brewers to invest their capital in other businesses. Midwestern brewers tried to survive by manufacturing nonalcoholic beverages, ice cream, candy, and other products, none of which was as profitable as beer. Across the nation, about 250 brewers simply went out of business during Prohibition, and all brewers were terribly wounded.

Prohibition ended in 1933 with the belief that the revival of the liquor trades would improve farm markets, increase employment, and augment tax revenues. About 750 breweries, many of them in the Midwest, began producing and selling beer again. Their distribution strategy, however, was to emphasize packaged beer; brewers began packaging beer in cans and bottles in 1934. Packaged beer sales exceeded keg sales after 1940.

The consolidation of the brewing industry into fewer and fewer firms also continued after Prohibition. During the middle third of the twentieth century, the tendency in the industry was for breweries to consolidate on a regional basis, as firms such as Stroh's in Detroit or Heileman in La Crosse, Wisconsin, absorbed small, local breweries. Then in the last third of the century, regional brewing firms disappeared in favor of surviving national producers. In an age of mass consumption, there were advantages to growth in size. Advertising costs were especially important, and larger brewing firms could spread the costs of an advertising campaign—costs that grew enormously with the advent of television—across more barrels of beer. This economic reality meant that gradually even the regional brewers left the business.

By the end of the twentieth century, the two largest brewers were Anheuser Busch, based in St. Louis, which commanded over half of the American beer market, and Miller, based in Milwaukee (but owned by the tobacco and food giant Philip Morris, whose headquarters were in New York). Although both Anheuser Busch and Miller operated substantial breweries in the Midwest, each firm also expanded by purchasing or erecting breweries in other regions. This dispersal meant that the center of beer production had shifted away from the Midwest by 1975. Thereafter, the South led the nation in producing beer.

In the meantime, in a trend that began in California in the 1970s, small local breweries began to appear, microbreweries and brew-pubs. By the start of the twenty-first century, every midwestern city of any size sported such establishments. Brew-pubs produced beer for consumption on the premises and usually included a restaurant. Microbreweries distributed their beer, but usually only in kegs and in local markets. Although these developments greatly added to the variety of beers available to midwestern consumers, these new firms accounted for but a tiny percentage of the beer consumed in the Midwest and elsewhere.

Aside from the emergence of small microbreweries and brew-pubs, few breweries survived the twentieth century in the Midwest, reflecting national trends in the industry of consolidating production into large factories. By this time, per capita consumption in the South exceeded that in the Midwest, as beer production had followed the migration of Americans to the South and West. In 2001, California, Colorado, Texas, and Virginia led the nation in beer-making.

Sources and Further Reading: Thomas Cochran, *The Pabst Brewing Company* (1948); R. G. Wilson and T. R. Gourvish, eds., *The Dynamics of the International Brewing Industry* (1998).

K. Austin Kerr
The Ohio State University–Columbus

Meatpacking

The abundant grain, primarily corn, and pastures of the Midwest make it perfectly suited for meat production. Historically, farmers produced grain and fattened animals in the fall, then drove them to market in December or January. Butchers could process the animals, and the cold of winter aided the preservation process. As the industry matured, the Midwest continued to serve as a primary source of the nation's pork and beef.

Hogs offered midwesterners a source of cash in the early nineteenth century. The fecundity of swine and their ability to reach market weight faster than cattle made them the preferred market animal for farmers. Sometimes a farmer would buy porkers from nearby farmers or cooperate with them to drive livestock to market in larger cities for better prices. Packers preserved the side meat and ham by rubbing it with salt to draw out moisture. The meat could be smoked for additional flavor and then hung in a cellar or packed away for later use.

In the first half of the nineteenth century, no city played a larger role in pork packing than Cincinnati. Elisha Mills is credited with the first meatpacking facility in the town in 1818, and it is recognized as the first such operation in the Ohio Valley. By 1833, Queen City butchers slaughtered eighty-five thousand hogs annually, and by 1844, twenty-six different meatpacking facilities had located there. By the early 1850s, Cincinnati gained the moniker Porkopolis.

The city set the standard with its disassembly line system. Hogs were held in pens, killed or stunned, and then workers cut the hog's jugular vein. After bleeding, workers dunked hogs in scalding water and scraped off their hair. Next a gambrel, a stout wooden pole, was inserted behind the tendon on the back hocks, from which the animal was suspended. As it hung from the gambrel, it was eviscerated, the lard salvaged, and the carcass split in half to cool. Workers moved the carcass to a room for chilling, and it was butchered into cuts. Other river towns mimicked this model, and locales such as Terre Haute, Peoria, and Keokuk became regional hubs for pork processing in the nineteenth century.

The second midwestern meatpacking colossus of the nineteenth century was Chicago. A smallish town on Lake Michigan in the 1840s, it had become the nation's pork and beef center by the 1870s. Railroaders and entrepreneurs created a network of stockyards and packinghouses. In 1864, the Chicago Pork Packers Association and the city's nine railroads issued a prospectus for the creation of the Union Stockyards. Located just south of the city on more than three hundred acres, the stockyards opened in late 1865. The facility served the city for more than a hundred years, and drew meatpackers to Chicago and northern Indiana.

The concentration of the meat industry around Chicago helped foster additional developments in the industry. These firms revolutionized the industry through the use of refrigerated railcars and additional processing. In 1869, George Hammond, a Detroit meatpacker, modified railcars to hold ice and shipped midwestern beef to Boston. Gustavus Swift pioneered the practice of shipping dressed beef. Carcasses shipped cheaper than live animals, and butchers could pick and choose more easily the types of meat they wished to offer to consumers. By the 1880s, the big four meat companies of the Chicago area included Swift & Co., Armour & Co., Nelson Morris & Co., and George H. Hammond Co., which together processed thousands of animals and shipped the meat around the nation. The appalling conditions in the meatpacking industry of Chicago compelled Upton Sinclair's *The Jungle* in 1906. The book outraged the nation and provided impetus for the Pure Food and Drug Act of the same year.

As stockyards and technology for shipping developed, other communities such as St. Louis, Kansas City, and Sioux City became important markets and processors for beef. Through their control or manipulation of transportation networks, packers set prices at these markets, and producers had to accept the prices offered them. These cities packed beef for regional and national markets, and used disassembly methods similar to those employed for pork production. After World War II, refrigerated semitrailer trucks replaced the railroads as primary haulers of meat.

In the last half of the twentieth century, midwestern meatpacking underwent further innovation and disruption. The development of boxed beef in the 1960s further refined the industry. Iowa Beef Packers, later called Iowa Beef Processors, started as a conventional meatpacker in Denison, Iowa. By the 1960s, IBP instituted a practice of shipping vacuum-sealed packages of cuts trimmed of most of the fat boxed to meet the specific demands of retailers. Upstart firms such as IBP and Excel used modern methods and facilities that pressured older firms to keep pace with the change or face elimination.

Additionally, beef processing has shifted further west to states such as Texas, Nebraska, and Kansas. Pork packing has become increasingly important in Missouri and has even shifted to North Carolina. Beef and pork processors began contracting with farmers to raise animals, and consolidation among packers gained momentum. From 1980 to 1997, the four major pork packers increased market share from 34 to 54 percent. Beef packing became more consolidated in the same period, with the top four packers increasing market share from 36 to 78 percent. Farmers reacted by creating their own meatpacking cooperatives such as Pork America, organized in Minnesota in 1999.

Meatpacking offered employment for many immigrants in the Midwest. The danger and filthiness of the work made it among some of the least desirable work. Workers started in messy, low-paying jobs such as pushing cattle blood into gutters on the killing floor, and worked their way up to better-paying jobs on the cutting line. Meatpacking is still an entry-level job for immigrants to the Midwest, as companies recruit workers from across the United States. At the turn of the century, packers such as IBP produce English-Spanish marketing material to entice recent Hispanic immigrants to midwestern towns as laborers. Similarly, Laotian immigrants have moved to a number of midwestern communities to work in meatpacking.

Efforts to unionize meatpacking workers have had varying degrees of success. In the nineteenth century, unions such as the Amalgamated Meat Cutters and Butcher Workmen, founded in 1897, proved profitable for workers. Strikes were frequent beginning in the 1890s, and wages, benefits, and conditions often improved. But after the 1947 Taft-Hartley Act, union power waned. In the 1980s, unions frequently granted concessions at workers' expense. Wages in meatpacking and processing have not kept pace with those for workers in other industries. Simultaneously, union membership decreased from about 50 percent of the workforce to 20 percent.

Meatpacking has an important and ongoing history in the Midwest. By the 1820s, midwestern cities such as St. Louis and Cincinnati were regarded as centers of pork production, and later beef production reached similar proportions in cities such as Chicago, Sioux City, and Kansas City. Though river towns established themselves as meatpacking centers in the nineteenth century, rail networks and roads superseded water transportation in the twentieth century. The industry attracted numerous immigrants to the region. Today, the industry continues to evolve, and midwestern agricultural production nearly guarantees that meatpacking will persist as a major business.

Sources and Further Reading: Deborah Fink, *Cutting into the Meatpacking Line* (1998); James M. MacDonald and Michael E. Ollinger, "Consolidation in Meatpacking," *Agricultural Outlook* (June–July 2000); Jimmy M. Skaggs, *Prime Cut: Livestock Raising and Meatpacking in the United States, 1607–1983* (1986); Louise Carroll Wade, *Chicago's Pride* (1987); Margaret Walsh, *The Rise of the Midwestern Meat Packing Industry* (1982).

Leo E. Landis
Henry Ford Museum and Greenfield Village,
Dearborn, Michigan

Milling

Milling in the Midwest is the story of a transformation from family and local grain processing in rural settings to a capital-intensive and integrated regional, national, and global industry. In the late eighteenth and early nineteenth centuries, Native Americans and European American settlers relied on family members and neighbors to process their grain. But by 1900, that was no longer true as innovators imported improved milling techniques from Europe, while commercial-minded settlers developed transportation systems, improving efficiency and access to markets, which spurred the production of cereal grains as well as the concentration of the milling industry in the cities. In the first years of settlement, European American farmers and the detachments of the U.S. Army constructed small horse- or ox-powered mills.

The lack of markets for grain delayed the construction of water mills in much of the region until the 1830s and 1840s. Beginning in the 1840s, however, many new mills in the Midwest were built with turbines or steam engines rather than water wheels for power, although many established millers continued to use the older water wheels. Community mills enabled farmers to prepare their grain for market, with the millers frequently serving as agents, buying and selling locally grown grain, flour, and meal. Millers retained a portion of the crop as a toll for their service, with tolls varying from state to state and even sometimes by county.

Technological changes of the second half of the nineteenth century made the community mills less economically significant, although they continued to be venues for socializing and local economic activity well into the twentieth century. Railroad connections allowed farmers to get their grain to distant markets at lower per-unit cost, relegating the local mills to secondary functions such as grinding feed for livestock. The New Process milling technique gained popularity in the 1870s because it allowed millers to produce flour with less bran. At the same time, roller mills also became popular; they employed a series of corrugated and smooth rollers that reduced the grain to flour faster and more efficiently than either the old mills or the New Process mills.

The new mills were expensive to build and operate, which meant that it was essential that they be located at major transportation intersections. Thus the new mills were urban rather than rural, marking an important shift in the economics of milling in the region. Furthermore, increasing capitalization brought concentration within the industry. In Minneapolis, for example, a merger between C. A. Pillsbury and Washburn Flour Mills in 1889 compelled six of their competitors to merge in 1891, forming Northwestern Consolidated Milling Company. Three other firms consolidated in 1892, forming the Minneapolis Flour Manufacturing Company. Some of the largest milling operations in the United States have been based in Minneapolis, including General Mills, the International Milling Company, and the Pillsbury Company.

The growing concentration of milling and the importance of the Midwest states, especially Minnesota, Missouri, and Wisconsin, can be seen in the U.S. Census of Manufactures for 1900. While the twelve Midwest states claimed less than a third of the total number of flour and grist mills in the United States, midwestern operations accounted for over one half of the wage earners (19,275) and capital ($110.6 million) of the nation's industry. There was considerable variation within the region, with Kansas showing few milling establishments but a high degree of capitaliza-

Cargill Milling complex, Kenosha, Wisconsin. Cargill Incorporated/Lisa Vickstrom.

tion, and Missouri with many mills but a relatively low degree of capitalization. This contrast illustrates the difference between the development of a newer, more specialized grain-growing area with new and larger mills, on the one hand, and an area with more agricultural diversity, smaller mills, and older technology on the other.

As milling became more concentrated, many commodity producers believed that millers were taking advantage of them. North Dakota's Non-Partisan League invoked the language of producerism, complaining that the middlemen of the Twin Cities preyed upon farmers. In 1919, the League-dominated state legislature enacted a program that included a state-run mill and elevator that would work on behalf of farmers. By the end of the twentieth century, however, many producers cooperated with processors, signing contracts with firms such as Quaker Oats, promising to deliver a specified quantity of grain at a particular time in exchange for a set price. Processors liked these arrangements because they could fix their costs, avoiding seasonal or unanticipated fluctuations in commodity prices. Farmers found that they could also minimize risk by contracting for a guaranteed income against their fixed costs.

At the end of the twentieth century, mergers and consolidations have left much of the grain and soybean processing industry in the hands of a few giants. Cargill (Minneapolis), Archer-Daniels-Midland (Decatur, Illinois), and ConAgra (Omaha) are diversified and integrated concerns, processing almost every kind of seed or grain for consumers around the world, including wet-milling corn for sweeteners and other food products, soybeans for livestock and human consumption, and small grains for food and beverage products.

Sources and Further Reading: Jerry Apps and Allen Strang, *Mills of Wisconsin and the Midwest* (1980); Wayne G. Broehl, Jr., *Cargill: Going Global* (1998); Wayne G. Broehl, Jr., *Cargill: Trading the World's Grain* (1992); John Mack Faragher, *Sugar Creek* (1986); Herman Steen, *Flour Milling in America* (1963); Thomas Vennum, Jr., *Wild Rice and the Ojibway People* (1988).

J. L. Anderson
Iowa State University

Motor Vehicle Manufacturing

The U.S. motor vehicle industry clustered in the Midwest during the first decade of the twentieth century. The focal point was southeastern Michigan, especially within a triangle formed by the cities of Detroit, Flint, and Lansing. Recent changes in production and sales have altered the geography of the U.S. motor vehicle industry, although the Midwest remains an important center.

Several people have been identified as the builder of the first workable gasoline-powered motor vehicle in the United States. Pioneers during the early 1890s—for the most part midwesterners—included John William Lambert in Ohio City, Ohio, in 1891; Gottfried Scholoemer and Frank Toepfer in Milwaukee, Wisconsin, in 1892; Charles H. Black in Indianapolis, Indiana, in 1893; and Elwood P. Haynes in Kokomo, Indiana, in 1894.

The first event that galvanized public interest in motor vehicles was a race sponsored by the *Chicago Times-Herald* newspaper through the streets of Chicago and Evanston, Illinois, on November 25, 1895. Run the day after a paralyzing snowstorm, the race was won by a vehicle built by the Duryea Motor Wagon Company that covered the eighty-six-kilometer (fifty-four-mile) route in ten hours twenty-three minutes.

Because most customers for motor vehicles in 1900 lived in eastern cities, such as New York, Philadelphia, and Boston, many early producers located there. The Duryea Company, based in Springfield, Massachusetts, became the first commercial producer of motor vehicles in the United States, selling four in 1896. The first two vehicles to achieve annual sales of more than one thousand were the Columbia, built in Hartford, Connecticut, and the Locomobile, built in Tarrytown, New York, and Newton, Massachusetts. Northeast manufacturers continued to build low-volume luxury cars and handcrafted car bodies into the 1920s, but by 1903, nearly all motor vehicle production had moved to the Midwest.

Early motor vehicles were produced in many Midwest cities outside of Michigan, including Anderson, Auburn, Connersville, Elkhart, Indianapolis, Kokomo, Muncie, Richmond, and South Bend, Indiana; Chicago, Decatur, Freeport, Moline, Ottawa, and Peoria, Illinois; Cleveland, Dayton, and Toledo, Ohio; and Hartford, Kenosha, Milwaukee, and Racine, Wisconsin. The three highest-volume producers outside of Michigan during the first decade of the twentieth century were Thomas B. Jeffery and Company (later the Nash Motor Company) in Kenosha, Studebaker Brothers Manufacturing Company in South Bend, and Willys-Overland Company in Toledo.

Despite the multiplicity of Midwest production locations, southeastern Michigan quickly emerged in the first few years of the twentieth century as the dominant center. The three best-selling vehicles in 1903—Olds, Ford, and Cadillac—were made in southeastern Michigan, and Michigan was home to 42 percent of U.S. motor vehicle production in 1904. At its peak, producers in southeastern Michigan assembled nearly 80 percent of all vehicles sold in the United States in 1913.

Southeastern Michigan became the center of U.S. motor vehicle production during the first decade of the twentieth century primarily because local manufacturers were able to solve two key technological problems. The first problem was the need for a power source capable of propelling a vehicle. Most nineteenth-century cars were powered by electricity or steam, but gasoline-powered engines dominated after 1900. Gasoline engine experts were already based in southeastern Michigan, including Ransom E. Olds in Lansing, then the nation's leading manufacturer of small stationary gasoline engines, and Henry M. Leland in Detroit, founder of Cadillac and Lincoln and the nation's leading manufacturer of gasoline-powered marine engines.

The other key problem was the need for a body strong enough to hold passengers and the power source. Early motor vehicle bodies, mostly made of wood, were adapted from horse-drawn carriages. The nation's leading manufacturer of horse-drawn carriages in Flint, Michigan was William C. Durant, who founded General Motors in 1908.

Southeastern Michigan also emerged as the center for motor vehicle production because of readily available startup capital. Willing to invest in a high-risk, start-up industry were local entrepreneurs who had recently made fortunes from extracting Michigan's natural resources, especially copper, iron, and lumber. Bankers in New York and elsewhere at the time considered the motor vehicle industry too risky an investment. Michigan's auto industry investors were known as the Princes of Griswold Street, after the street in downtown Detroit where financial institutions were clustered.

Although several hundred companies manufactured motor vehicles in the Midwest during the first decade of the twentieth century, the Ford Motor Company and General Motors became the world's two best-selling vehicle producers in 1910 and remained so without interruption through the twentieth century. Ford's Model T accounted for nearly half of the world's motor vehicle sales during the 1910s. Revolutionary manufacturing methods enabled Ford to produce large quantities of Model Ts and to sell them profitably at a very low price. Workers at Ford's Highland Park, Michigan, factory were assigned specific tasks to be performed repetitively, and they were positioned in a logical sequence through the plant with the tools necessary to do their tasks close at hand. Continuously moving assembly lines installed at Highland Park in 1913 carried materials to the workers at their assigned positions along the line.

Ford made components at Highland Park and shipped them by rail to assembly plants located in major population centers around the country, where they were assembled into finished cars. This arrangement reduced freight costs: The equivalent of twenty-six Model Ts could be jammed into boxcars as parts, compared to seven or eight fully assembled cars. For example, a Ford sold at a Los Angeles dealership had been assembled at a Los Angeles factory from parts made in Michigan, and a Ford sold in New York had been assembled in nearby New Jersey. GM later emulated Ford's strategy. Thus, nearly all parts were made in the Midwest, but most of the final assembly operations were elsewhere.

During the 1920s, Ford moved parts production from Highland Park to the country's largest industrial complex along the banks of the River Rouge in Dearborn, Michigan. At its peak around 1940, the Rouge employed 110,000 workers in 127 structures spread out over 2,000 acres. Iron ore, coal, and other raw materials went in at one end, and finished cars and parts came out at the other end. Ford also established so-called village industries in nineteen then-rural Southeastern Michigan communities such as Milan, Nankin Mills, and Saline.

Billy Durant created General Motors in 1908 by acquiring several struggling Michigan companies, including Buick (based in Flint), Oldsmobile (based in Lansing), Oakland (later renamed Pontiac, based in Pontiac), and Cadillac (based in Detroit). Forced out of GM in 1910 by his investors, Durant established Republic Motors (based in Flint), which made several models including Chevrolet. When Durant regained control of GM in 1916, he merged it with Chevrolet. Forced to relinquish control of GM for a second and final time in 1920, Durant established yet another carmaker in Flint, Durant Motors, which folded during the 1930s. He died in poverty and obscurity in 1947.

Meanwhile, GM came under the control of the DuPont Company, which imposed financial stability. Alfred P. Sloan, President and Chairman of the Board from 1923 to 1956, positioned GM's many products in distinctive price niches, from the best-selling Chevrolet for the masses to the luxury Cadillac for the wealthy few. Sloan also instituted the annual model change, in which improvements—often merely cosmetic—were introduced once a year to encourage people to trade in their still-serviceable older models for new ones.

The geography of motor vehicle production changed sharply during the 1980s. U.S. companies closed nearly all of their East and West Coast assembly plants and consolidated production in the interior of the country. Meanwhile, German and Asian companies built new plants in the interior. Both domestic and foreign companies clustered in a north-south corridor formed by I-65 and I-75, now known as auto alley or *kanban* alley after the Japanese word for just-in-time delivery.

Some of these auto alley plants were in Midwest states—including Ohio, Illinois, Indiana, and Michigan—but most were in states at the southern end of the corridor—such as Alabama, Kentucky, Mississippi, and Tennessee. Even new plants in the Midwest were for the most part located in communities not traditionally associated with motor vehicle production, such as Lafayette, Indiana; Marysville, Ohio; and Normal, Illinois. These nontraditional communities offered good access to the national market via the interstate highway system and a local labor force with little incentive to join the United Auto Workers union.

Into the twenty-first century, only one-half of the nation's parts plants and one-half of final assembly operations are in the Midwest, and only one-fourth of the parts and assembly plants are in Michigan. Motor vehicle employment in Flint, for example, declined from seventy-seven thousand in 1978 to twenty-seven thousand in 2000, primarily because GM closed many of its assembly and parts plants there. While declining as a manufacturing center, southeastern Michigan has taken on a new role as the location of corporate headquarters and research facilities for the hundreds of independent parts suppliers who now play a much greater role in the development and production of motor vehicles.

Sources and Further Reading: Ed Cray, *Chrome Colossus* (1980); Ralph C. Epstein, *The Automobile Industry: Its Economic and Commercial Development* (1928); James M. Flink, *The Automobile Age* (1988); David Gelsanliter, *Jump Start* (1990); George S. May, *A Most Unique Machine* (1975); Allan Nevins and Frank Ernest Hill, *Ford*, 3 vols. (1954–1963); James M. Rubenstein, *The Changing U.S. Auto Industry* (1992); James M. Rubenstein, *Making and Selling Cars* (2001); James P. Womack, Daniel T. Jones, and Daniel Roos, *The Machine That Changed the World* (1990).

James M. Rubenstein
Miami University, Oxford, Ohio

The Rubber Industry

The story of Akron, Ohio, can't be told without the story of rubber, nor can the story of the American tire industry be told without Akron. The two were intertwined for all of the twentieth century, as rubber defined Akron and Akron defined rubber, and together they demonstrated how a midwestern city could gain its personality from its industry.

It began in 1870, when Benjamin Franklin Goodrich was looking to relocate his Hudson Rubber Company from Melrose, New York. During a visit to Akron, he convinced a group of local businessmen to put up a $13,600 loan, allowing him to set up shop near the Ohio and Erie Canal in Akron's downtown. Goodrich thrived, becoming the cornerstone of a new industry.

Others sensed the possibilities, especially as rubber tires became more popular. In 1898, F. A. and Charles Seiberling founded the Goodyear Tire and Rubber Company, purchasing an abandoned strawboard factory on the Little Cuyahoga River in East Akron. Goodyear struggled at first, making bicycle and carriage tires. But the advent of the automobile provided new promise. In 1900, Harvey Samuel Firestone founded the Firestone Tire and Rubber Company. After a stint selling rubber buggy tires in Chicago,

Firestone, a farm boy from Columbiana, Ohio, relocated to Akron to move into manufacturing.

The pieces were in place and would stay there for most of the century; the only major American tire company outside Akron was U.S. Rubber (later Uniroyal), based in New York. With the automobile age, tire makers flourished. World War I provided a boom; by 1920, three hundred American companies were making tires, more than twenty of which were in Akron. In 1915, William Francis O'Neil, the son of a prominent Akron department store owner, founded General Tire with a small partnership, part of a second wave of entrants of which only a few would survive.

Together, Akron's Big Four became a national force, supplying Detroit's booming automobile industry and having an indelible influence on Akron. With increasing numbers of factory jobs, European immigrants and Appalachian migrants flocked to the city. The large number of southern arrivals gave Akron its nickname, the capital of West Virginia. Between 1910 and 1920, Akron was one of the fastest growing cities in the nation, with the population surging from 69,067 to 208,435.

The Seiberlings and Firestone became millionaires and founded company neighborhoods, Goodyear Heights and Firestone Park, respectively. The rubber barons built mansions that became local landmarks. The names of the men and their companies eventually became attached to streets, banks, parks, and schools, and Akron became known as the Rubber Capital of the World.

The United Rubber Workers formed in 1935, an industrial union that would establish a powerful headquarters in Akron. The union staged a bitter and historic strike in 1936, and in its aftermath, union membership increased tenfold from the previous year, to forty thousand.

World War II provided another boom. The factories employed large numbers of women, and converted some operations to the manufacture of warplanes, machine guns, life vests, barrage balloons, and observation blimps. By 1950, Akron was a thriving industrial city, with the major headquarters accompanying a landscape of manufacturing plants and research laboratories. The industry's influence was tangible and personal. People defined Akron by its smell, the pungent tang of burning rubber carried from the factory smokestacks. Although jobs began trickling to non-unionized southern states, few Akron families didn't define themselves in some way by rubber.

Goodyear and Firestone had established dominance on the world tire market. Goodrich and General were right behind, but those companies also diversified. Goodrich produced an array of products that included golf balls, rubber bands, hoses, and spacesuits. General branched out into aerospace.

By the 1960s, there was a hint of change in the industry. While Akron cranked along, foreign tire makers such as France's Michelin and Japan's Bridgestone began eyeing the American market. Both of those companies were investing heavily in new radial tire technology, which the Americans had resisted. And in the 1970s, Akron's tire industry began to decline, then crumble. The powerful URW led a series of strikes that built to a historic four-month standoff in 1976. During that strike, Michelin established its first American radial tire plant. Meanwhile, Akron's outdated tire factories began to close. The number of Akron-area jobs in the tire industry dropped from 37,100 in 1964 to 15,400 in 1984.

The major companies had not kept up with radial technology, and when consumers began to gravitate toward the longer-lasting tires, foreign competitors were poised to strike. Continental A.G. of Germany bought General Tire in 1987. Firestone, weakened by a massive recall of its Firestone 500 tire in 1978, was sold to Bridgestone in 1988. Goodrich, which had merged with Uniroyal, was bought by Michelin in 1990. Akron also suffered from the decentralization of tire production by American companies within the United States, and Ohio's share of all tire industry employees in the country dropped from 43 percent in 1947 to 25 percent in 1972, while the South's share increased from just under 14 percent to over 33 percent during the same period. In Akron only Goodyear maintained American ownership. Akron's downtown, once a bustling center, was shuttered and desolate by the late 1980s.

One by one, the new owners moved headquarters out of Akron. "Changing the culture" became the buzz phrase in a city that had defined the culture. With all the commercial tire plants closed by the end of 1982, the local identity was diluted, a trend that continued in 1995, when the URW merged with the United Steelworkers of America.

By the twenty-first century, the Rubber City is an outdated nickname. Akron remains an important force in rubber and polymer research. Bridgestone Firestone maintains a research and development facility at the old headquarters, but most of the massive complex stands vacant. Meanwhile, downtown has been reinvigorated with a minor league baseball stadium—notable for its brick architecture and clock tower that mirrored the old tire plants—that opened in 1997. Abandoned storefronts became restaurants, and the old B.F. Goodrich complex was successfully converted into a network of offices and small manufacturing operations.

Goodyear remains, but Akron is a different place.

The population had declined from 290,000 in mid-century to 217,000 in 2000. Akron has recovered, but it is no longer the Rubber Capital of the World.

Sources and Further Reading: Hugh Allen, *The House of Goodyear* (1949); Hugh Allen, *Rubber's Home Town* (1949); Mansel G. Blackford and K. Austin Kerr, *BF Goodrich* (1996); George W. Knepper, *Akron: City at the Summit* (1994); Alfred Lief, *The Firestone Story* (1951); Steve Love and David Giffels, *Wheels of Fortune* (1999); Dennis O'Neill, *A Whale of a Territory* (1966); Jon C. Teaford, *Cities of the Heartland* (1993).

David Giffels
Akron Beacon Journal, Ohio

The Iron and Steel Industry

Iron is an element found in many locations, but almost never in its pure form. Ironmaking, thus, consists of manufacturing processes that smelt ores rich in iron, heating them in combination with carbon and crushed limestone to produce a liquid iron. Iron can be malleable and wrought into various useful items, or it can be brittle and cast as a liquid into products. Steel is a refined iron produced by introducing oxygen in the smelting process to drive off almost all carbon or other impurities. Steel is harder and tougher than iron and is widely used in manufactured products. Although Europeans have made steel since the fifteenth century, it was very expensive until the commercial introduction of the Bessemer process in 1867. Thanks to the opportunities provided by this technology, in the last third of the nineteenth century, steel was at the heart of the industrial economy, and the Midwest was becoming the heart of steel making in the United States.

Iron making began in the Midwest almost as soon as Europeans settled there. They found small deposits of high-grade iron ore in the Ohio Valley, along with limestone for processing and hardwood for fuel. In 1860, Ohio was second among the states in producing pig iron, the basic product. Steelmaking, a more sophisticated process, became the most common process, and steel manufacture was central to the midwestern economy for more than a century thereafter. Several factors contributed to this. The region had plentiful supplies of coal and limestone, rich (and huge) deposits of iron ore (especially in Michigan and Minnesota), and by 1890, the transportation systems to bring these ingredients together. Steel mills were located along banks of the upper Ohio River, and especially in Cleveland, Chicago, and Gary, Indiana, with their access to

The Hull-Rust-Mahoning Mine, Hibbing, Minnesota. Minnesota Historical Society MHS Locator no. HD3.112/p22.

low-cost lake shipping. Those mills in turn made rails, beams, girders, and wire. They supplied shipyards, railroad equipment manufacturers, automobile manufacturers, bridge and building trades, and countless other fabricators of industrial goods. This period, which ended in the 1970s, was the heyday of iron and steel in the Midwest and the United States.

Two types of firms characterized the steel industry. The integrated firms combined in one business the acquisition of raw materials, the blast furnaces for smelting ore and converting iron to steel, and mills that made finished products such as rails and pipes. The leader of the integrated firms was the United States Steel Corporation, founded in 1901 and based in Pittsburgh, but with far-flung operations that included significant investments in the Midwest. U.S. Steel had interests in iron-ore mines in Michigan and Minnesota; it owned fleets of ships to carry ore and railroad lines to bring raw materials to its furnaces. U.S. Steel had investments in bridge building, pipe making, rolling mills, and the like. In 1905, the firm announced an enormous expansion of capacity with the construction of a huge new plant and the creation of a new city, Gary, Indiana, on the south shore of Lake Michigan. There the firm had acquired seventy-five hundred acres of land for its urban-industrial development. Completed in 1911, for years thereafter the Gary mill was the largest in the world.

The structure of this industry resembled a pyramid. U.S. Steel stood at the apex. Thanks to its investments in Gary and elsewhere, U.S. Steel was, for a time, the world's largest corporation of any kind and for decades led the world's steel industry, as well. Its integrated operations produced high-quality steel at low cost. The firm was so large that for decades it was known as "Big Steel," while the seven other integrated firms, each of which was a very large business, were collectively known as "Little Steel." They occupied the middle of the structure. Six of these seven firms—Bethlehem Steel, Republic Steel, National Steel, Inland Steel, Armco Steel, and Youngstown Sheet and Tube—had important operations and headquarters in the Midwest. At the base were thousands of other firms engaged in specialized operations, some very sizable but dwarfed nevertheless by the eight integrated firms. For example, in Columbus, Ohio, Buckeye Steel Castings produced couplers and other parts for railroads, and later, near his River Rouge factory in Dearborn, Michigan, Henry Ford operated a steel mill to supply his automotive assembly lines.

Collectively, these steel companies provided the sinew for the expansion of the midwestern industrial economy during the twentieth century. Thousands of miners dug iron ore from huge pit mines in Michigan and Minnesota, while others excavated coal in Ohio,

Indiana, Illinois, and Iowa. Seamen operated ships carrying ore to the plants, as railroads, themselves major consumers of steel, hauled long trains of coal, ore, and steel goods. Automobile manufacturers located their industry in Detroit, initially in part because of its proximity to sources of steel. In any given year, tens of thousands of midwesterners worked in steel and its supporting industries, while hundreds of thousands of other people worked in the factories supplied by the mills.

While the steel industry generated great industrial prosperity, problems accompanied its growth. Foremost among them was bitter labor–management strife. The men who managed the steel companies (there were historically no women in the highest posts) sought constantly to control and reduce costs. Their drive to do so included the introduction of technologies that reduced the need for skilled workers, and ultimately reduced the numbers of workers required to make a ton of steel or steel products. Management also sought to hold down wages, an important component of costs. Most brutal was the requirement in many mills of the twelve-hour workday with a seven-day work week. Workers sometimes resisted management policies, and the midwestern steel industry was the scene of periodic outbreaks of labor–management conflict and bitter, sometimes violent, strikes. Most noteworthy were the 1919 strike, which centered in Gary, and the strike against the Little Steel companies in 1937.

In response to the privations of the Great Depression in the 1930s, workers across the Midwest joined unions and sought to introduce collective bargaining into steel and other basic industries in which management had retained control over the terms of employment. Their union movement, led now by the Congress of Industrial Organizations (CIO), enjoyed mixed success in the steel industry. In 1937, after automobile workers organized by the CIO held a successful sit-down strike against General Motors, steelworkers threatened action against U.S. Steel. That spring, wishing to avoid the disruption and bad publicity suffered by General Motors, U.S. Steel agreed to accept the steelworkers' union and signed a collective bargaining agreement. Averting an organizing strike against the industry's leading firm, the new union, called the United Steel Workers of America, became a powerful voice. Management of Little Steel, on the other hand, continued to reject collective bargaining as a matter of principle, believing that management should have exclusive authority over the terms of employment. Several bitter strikes ensued.

Tensions between labor and management did not ease until the mobilization for World War II, when the federal government in effect required management to recognize unions and engage in collective bargaining in the interests of full production. After the war, there were strikes from time to time in the midwestern steel industry, but the issues were over wages, working conditions, and economic security, not the principle of union recognition and collective bargaining. All of the major steel firms in the Midwest accepted the United Steel Workers, however grudgingly. During the thirty years following the war, the midwestern and American steel industry led the world, producing enormous volumes of steel at low cost, while paying the highest steelmaking wages in the world.

That situation came to an end in the 1970s when the American steel industry faced two basic hardships, both of which meant that it would forever after be less important in the economy than it had been. First, the market for steel changed and, relatively, diminished, while American and foreign steel producers had expanded capacity in anticipation of larger sales. Automobile manufacturers, for example, reduced their use of steel by using thinner sheets and substituting plastic and other metals in an effort to lighten weight, improve fuel economy, and increase durability. The construction industry, although still a major consumer of steel, also learned to replace steel with reinforced concrete. To worsen the situation, the second hardship appeared at the same time: foreign competition. Around the world were new investments in steel mills, sometimes government investments, and always investments that threatened American and midwestern steel producers. Simply expressed, by 1975, the Midwest no longer enjoyed the advantages of location for steel. The nearby sources of high-grade iron ore were consumed, and foreign producers could bring high-grade ores from Australia, Brazil, and elsewhere to new steel mills located on seacoasts for cheap shipping costs. And those new mills proved more efficient than many midwestern mills. The result was the slow decay of the integrated midwestern steel mill, a decay that was at the heart of the deindustrialization of the region and its transformation into the Rust Belt during the last decades of the twentieth century.

In the meantime, technological opportunities changed, leading to the rise of the so-called mini-mill. By the 1970s, entrepreneurs were learning that new electric furnaces could efficiently melt steel scrap. This recycled steel could be reused and sold at competitive prices. The mini-mills, which initially arose outside of the traditional pyramid structure of the industry, could be located near markets and new population centers in the South and West, thereby avoiding transportation costs. The growth of mini-mills meant that the American steel industry dispersed outside of its traditional locations, although mini-mills remained

a very important part of the midwestern economy. Ohio, for instance, led the nation in 2000 in value-added iron and steel processing. Still, the midwestern steel industry struggled to remain viable in a changing economic environment. At the start of the new century, Cleveland lost its last steel mill. They were also gone from nearby Youngstown, while Gary and Chicago operations were a shadow of what they had been. Those mills that remained had adapted new technologies and successfully reduced the size of the workforce to a small fraction of what it once was. The iron and steel industry had simply become relatively less important to the region's economy than any observer could have imagined, even as recently as 1975.

Sources and Further Reading: William T. Hogan, *Economic History of the Iron and Steel Industry in the United States*, 5 vols. (1971); Paul Tiffany, *The Decline of American Steel* (1988).

K. Austin Kerr
The Ohio State University–Columbus

Urban Philanthropy

Philanthropy has been an important element in the development of urban life and institutions in Midwest cities. Fostered by religious and ethical concerns at a personal level, promoted by community authorities, and reinforced by legal protections and encouragements, philanthropy has done much to mollify and improve urban life.

Philanthropy includes a spectrum of giving of time and money that extends from specific acts of charity to a range of nonpartisan, nongovernmental civic commitments. Large donations by individuals or corporations often capture newspaper headlines and may be important in certain areas of the public weal, but the majority of philanthropic activity is comprised of small contributions by individuals, often directed to or through religious institutions.

Over the two centuries since the founding of the earliest of the midwestern cities, philanthropic activity has passed through five overlapping phases. In the earliest years (1800–1860), religious and communitarian ideals fostered the establishment of churches and civic associations that included in their purposes caring for the poor, sick, and elderly. With growing populations came increased need, and specific institutions were created to focus the philanthropic impulse (1850–1890). Reacting to a proliferation of institutions and organizations, there followed a wave of attempts to coordinate giving and make most efficient use of resources (1880–1920). Then the rapid growth of urban populations, including both foreign and domestic immigrants, accompanied by increasing disparities of wealth and class, created a sense of division and chaos that engendered an urge toward reorganization and reform (1910–1950). Most recently, urban philanthropy has attempted comprehensive and long-term strategies for the amelioration of urban ills, often through community-wide institutions that attempt to adjust to new needs and to distribute philanthropic resources flexibly (1940–present). In each of these phases, philanthropic initiatives have occurred within the overarching strictures of government, and increasingly have had to take account of the power of profit-making corporations.

Within two or three decades of their founding, midwestern cities created community institutions to provide care for needy citizens. Usually these were inspired by churches, because in all faiths care of the poor, ill, elderly, and the incarcerated is regarded as a moral obligation. Moreover, church members regularly aided those suffering from natural or human disasters such as fire, flood, or death of family members. In the center of growing midwestern cities, the most visible public buildings were churches, not government offices. Yet the rapid growth of midwestern cities resulted in accumulations of wealth that could be diverted to philanthropic purposes at surprisingly early dates: On his death in 1818, for example, Cincinnatian John Kidd bequeathed a permanent endowment for the education of poor children in his city.

Midwestern urbanites early showed a talent for creating nonprofit associations. Drawing on New England traditions but adapting them to the needs of a new region, associations in midwestern cities were the epitome of what the French commentator Alexis de Tocqueville thought of as the particular genius of America. Many were fundamentally philanthropic in intent and provided direct aid to the needy. For example, the Martha Washington and Dorcas Society was formed in Cleveland in 1843 to deal with family poverty caused by alcohol abuse. Even social associations often included philanthropic functions in their agendas: immigrant mutual aid associations combined self-help with distinct philanthropic functions, such as paying the cost of burial for indigent people.

The next step in the development of urban philanthropy was the creation of institutions, usually with permanent quarters and staff. The earliest were oriented toward the needy, but fifty years after their founding, most Midwest cities also began to establish cultural institutions that depended on donations for support.

Women played an important role in creating institutions. Often they developed leadership skills in or-

ganizations derived from church-related activities, such as antislavery and temperance groups that flourished from the 1830s. During the Civil War, many women devoted themselves to soldiers' aid groups, particularly the Sanitary Fairs that raised money for medical supplies and other needs.

As ethnic and racial groups began to establish significant footholds in the cities, they extended their philanthropic activities to founding athletic associations, choral and theatrical groups, and literary societies. Some drew together sufficient funds to erect or purchase neighborhood buildings that then became gathering places for other groups with philanthropic impulses.

Typical institutions founded in the mid-nineteenth century were homes for orphans and the elderly, alcohol-free inns, residential schools for indigent children and unwed mothers, hospitals, and insane asylums. Such institutions were intended to attract the unwanted and undesirable, insulating them from the temptations and problems of urban life and at the same time protecting the general citizenry from the perceived lawlessness and immorality of these marginalized populations.

Parks and recreation were thought by many to be critical contributions to the improvement of cities. In Cleveland, where temperance forces were strong, Friendly Inns were established in 1874 to provide alcohol-free sites for men to gather for reading and lodging. The most significant philanthropic act of John D. Rockefeller, Sr., in Cleveland was the donation of land for a park (1896) that included recreational facilities. Stipulating that alcoholic beverages could never be sold within the park boundaries, Rockefeller believed that the park's natural surroundings and fresh air would be an antidote to the increasingly crowded and polluted city.

Many charities depended in part on government funding, which was furnished in the belief that if their residents were not cared for by private institutions they would eventually become public charges in jails or poorhouses. However, philanthropy sustained the institutions, and as they multiplied, potential donors experienced increasing calls for support. Beginning in the late 1880s, civic leaders created charity societies in the larger cities that consolidated the raising and distribution of money, although most solicitations continued to be aimed at the wealthy. These organizations also evaluated the worthiness of institutions and denied funding to those that were badly managed, duplicated services, or espoused causes that offended upper-class values.

An important agency for the philanthropically minded was the settlement house movement, which brought mostly middle-class men and women to communal residences in immigrant and poor districts of the larger cities. Settlements provided educational and recreational opportunities for neighborhoods; the most progressive, such as Hull House in Chicago, also put community needs on the political agenda.

Two women, Louise de Koven Bowen of Chicago and Annie Laws of Cincinnati, typified the philanthropic possibilities that the burgeoning needs of cities offered in the late nineteenth and early twentieth centuries. Bowen's autobiography, *Growing Up with a City*, described an upbringing that instilled in her a belief that with wealth came social responsibility. As an adult she engaged in a wide variety of service activities, including teaching Sunday school and serving on boards of hospitals, the Visiting Nurse Association, a settlement house, and an auxiliary of the city's juvenile court. Annie Laws promoted visiting nursing organizations and kindergartens, serving as an officer not only of Cincinnati organizations, but also of the International Kindergarten Union. Although Bowen was wealthy and made substantial monetary gifts, she also visited the homes of recent immigrants and lobbied city and state governments to provide adequate playgrounds and factory inspections. Laws was specifically concerned with protecting child workers and supporting their education.

The brief but unifying war chest campaigns resulting from the United States's entry into World War I, in 1917–1918, created new possibilities for urban philanthropy by demonstrating the potential of mass appeals for the support of urban charities. In virtually every Midwest city, the interrelationships and fund-raising techniques of its war chest organization were transformed into a community chest: In Indianapolis and Toledo this happened in 1920 as soon as war-related efforts were terminated. Other cities such as Champaign-Urbana, Des Moines, Jefferson City, and Omaha followed soon after, and by the 1930s, cities throughout the Midwest had followed their leads.

At the same time that nonprofits attempted to raise funds from a broader spectrum of urbanites, their elite supporters were beginning to move out of cities to outlying suburbs, such as Shaker Heights (Ohio), Grosse Pointe (Michigan), or Oak Park (Illinois). Often the former inner-city mansions of the wealthy became the first homes of the charitable institutions they founded or favored. However, the generosity of the new arrivals in Midwest cities, such as the benefactions of entrepreneur Madame C. J. Walker in Indianapolis, did little to reverse the elite's lessened interest in the needs of poor and working-class citizens. Increasingly the philanthropic impulses of the wealthy focused on creating the great libraries, symphony halls, museums, historical societies, and other institutions that still dominate the cultural cityscapes of the Midwest.

The urban upper class also turned to a new institutional form, the perpetual foundation, as an outlet for their philanthropy. Beginning in Cleveland (1914), but followed closely by Chicago, Detroit, Milwaukee, and Minneapolis (1915), Indianapolis (1916) and then others, community foundations were created to draw in portions of the fortunes created in the Midwest's rapid industrial and commercial growth, and benefited from tax laws favoring charitable bequests. Usually managed by leading banks in each city, these foundations grew gradually, but eventually their annual distributions for community purposes were substantial. The Cleveland Foundation became one of the largest foundations in the United States, and in the Midwest community foundations became more important to urban life than in any other region in the nation.

In spite of successes in philanthropic organization, as the twentieth century wore on, many cities experienced a decline in reform spirit. Cities seemed to spin out of control because of the failures of Prohibition that encouraged crime, racist and nativist policies that confined new immigrants to substandard housing, and the Great Depression of the 1930s that intensified poverty. By the 1930s, many charitable organizations, particularly in immigrant communities, were unable to cope with the enormous needs of the cities.

At mid-twentieth century, many Americans regarded urban cores as decaying and dangerous, even while cities remained critical to the industrial, commercial, and governmental life of America. Philanthropy provided responses to this dilemma at both metropolitan and neighborhood levels. In 1950, Omaha's Community Chest created a unified fund-raising, budgeting, and planning structure, and others began to adopt more aggressive strategies that extended their reach beyond city limits into adjacent areas, even across state lines. New names adopted in the 1970s reflected these broader visions: Sioux Empire United Way (Sioux Falls, South Dakota); United Way of Central Missouri (Jefferson City); and United Way of Greater St. Louis (Missouri). Moreover, in the 1990s, United Ways began to emulate the success of community foundations, creating their own foundations to attract large gifts and to provide an underpinning for their annual campaigns. In general, the generosity of citizens of the urban Midwest made their region's United Ways among the most effective fund-raisers in the nation.

In urban neighborhoods religious congregations, new and old, sometimes took on functions formerly the province of business or government. Using their members' resources and mobilizing government and foundation grants, they founded nonprofit corporations to rehabilitate or build housing, established medical services, created child care institutions, and supported senior citizens. Some churches pursued other opportunities: In 1993, St. Andrew–Redeemer Lutheran Church in Detroit established a profit-making corporation to provide jobs in its economically devastated area.

Throughout the Midwest, community foundations played a significant role in attempts to revitalize urban areas by funding long-term planning, providing seed money for initiatives that were expected to be followed by government action, and responding more flexibly than government to perceived crises. The Cleveland Foundation supported downtown renewal by funding the creation of a new theatre complex. In the 1980s, the Dayton (Ohio) Foundation supported classroom innovations in the local schools. Substantial resources were available for such initiatives: By 2002, among the hundred largest American foundations were the community foundations of Cleveland, Chicago, Kansas City (Missouri), Columbus (Ohio), St. Paul, and Minneapolis. Those of southeastern Michigan, Omaha, Cincinnati, and Milwaukee were not far behind. Local leadership, sometimes with the encouragement of the Ford, Gannett, Lilly, MacArthur, or Mott foundations, created new foundations for smaller cities throughout the region. Overall, philanthropic activity in urban areas had a significant effect on the fiscal health of midwestern cities.

Sources and Further Reading: Louis de Koven Bowen, *Growing Up with a City* (2002); Robert T. Grimm, Jr., ed., *Notable American Philanthropists* (2002); Nile Harper, *Urban Churches, Vital Signs* (1999); Richard Magat, ed., *An Agile Servant* (1989); Lester Salamon, ed., *The State of Nonprofit America* (2002); Jon C. Teaford, *Cities of the Heartland* (1993); David D. Van Tassel and John J. Grabowski, eds., *Cleveland: A Tradition of Reform* (1986).

Darwin H. Stapleton
Rockefeller Archive Center,
Sleepy Hollow, New York

Jane Addams and the Settlement House Movement

As the best-known settlement house leader in the United States and perhaps the world, Jane Addams (1860–1935) did a lot to put the Midwest in the forefront of Progressive Era social reform. Addams adapted the settlement house, originally a place where well-to-do people could live and/or volunteer their services to help their impoverished urban neighbors, usually with educational and recreational programs, to Chicago and quickly became the settlement movement's leading spokesperson. Addams also put the settlement house movement and the Midwest into the

Jane Addams, social worker and Nobel laureate. Courtesy North Wind Picture Archives.

vanguard of numerous reforms in the areas of social welfare, labor, civil rights, feminism, and peace.

Jane Addams spent most of her life in Illinois. She was born and grew up in Cedarville, the daughter of a successful businessman and member of the Illinois State Senate, John Huy Addams. Part of the first generation of women to graduate from college in significant numbers, she attended Rockford Female Seminary. In 1889, she brought the settlement house movement to the Midwest by founding Hull-House in a heavily immigrant neighborhood near downtown Chicago. Hull-House would be her home for the rest of her life.

Addams's ability to draw on Chicago's social and cultural resources contributed to the success of Hull House. Chicago's wealthy elite funded her efforts. Numerous well-educated individuals drawn to an innovative social experiment donated their services, most typically as club leaders and class teachers. More so than any other settlement house leader, Jane Addams made her settlement a base for other reformers and encouraged them in their reform projects. These people included Florence Kelley, who campaigned for better working conditions; Julia Lathrop, who went on to become the first head of the federal government's Children's Bureau; and Alice Hamilton, a physician who pioneered the study of industrial medicine. Hull-House also sponsored demonstration projects. It established Chicago's first playground, then convinced the city government to construct a network of playgrounds around the city. Hull-House also offered the first citizenship classes for immigrants in the United States, a service that other settlement houses and school boards around the United States adopted.

Addams was effective in part because she had developed a strong public reputation. She risked that reputation when she became a vocal pacifist during World War I, but in 1931, she won the Nobel Peace Prize. A prolific writer and moving speaker, she published eleven books, including the classic *Twenty Years at Hull-House* (1910).

Addams's greatest impact was probably in her role as a promoter of the settlement house movement. When she established Hull-House, it was only the third settlement house in the United States, but by the time of World War I, the United States had at least two hundred settlement houses—or four hundred, including religion-sponsored houses. Other outstanding Chicago settlements included Chicago Commons, which Graham Taylor, another prolific writer on social issues, founded. Mary McDowell, a social welfare and labor activist, led the University of Chicago Settlement. After George Bellamy heard Graham Taylor speak, Bellamy decided to establish the first settlement house in Cleveland, Hiram House. Hiram House ran a model summer playground program and, like Hull-House, campaigned successfully for the establishment of public playgrounds throughout Cleveland.

Originally, most settlement workers sought to serve immigrants, but a few, particularly in the Midwest, established houses for African Americans. Although Jane Addams was a founding member of the National Association for the Advancement of Colored People, Hull-House under her leadership actually served only a token number of blacks. Both Cleveland and Minneapolis had Phyllis Wheatley Houses that served the black community, with that in Minneapolis more strongly identifying with the settlement house movement. Following World War II, however, settlement house work with racial minorities surpassed work with disadvantaged whites.

A number of other changes occurred after World War II. The practice of living in the settlement house disappeared. Holders of the Master of Social Work degree took over the leadership, many being people of color; and men for the first time outnumbered women as heads of settlements. Hull-House lost its historic building to Circle Campus of the University of Illinois and transformed to a multisite operation. Other settle-ments, often in the Midwest, also developed simultaneous operations in different neighborhoods. Meanwhile, reform efforts faded as settlements experienced funding pressures from organizations such as the United Way, plus a growing reliance on private and government grants. Following Jane Addams's death, leadership of the national movement left the Midwest, but settlements have been versatile enough to survive throughout the country.

Sources and Further Reading: Allen F. Davis, *American Heroine: The Life and Legend of Jane Addams* (1973); Allen F. Davis, *Spearheads for Reform* (1967); James Weber Linn, *Jane Addams: A Biography* (1935; reprint, 2000); Robyn Muncy, *Creating a Female Dominion in American Reform, 1890–1935* (1991); Judith Ann Trolander, *Professionalism and Social Change* (1987); Judith Ann Trolander, *Settlement Houses and the Great Depression* (1975).

Judith Ann Trolander
University of Minnesota–Duluth

The Community Chest

Community chests began when the Cleveland Chamber of Commerce created the Federation of Charities and Philanthropy in 1913, and the model quickly proliferated to hundreds of cities after World War I. The first chests were forged in the midst of a revolution in productive and social relations that imbued Americans with a sense that new community organizations premised on reinvigorated citizenship were necessary to gain control of a volatile social order. Urban institutions that functioned like private governments, chests evinced a Progressive belief that social problems like poverty and urban squalor were similar in type to other industrial problems, and thus required efficient, systematic, and coordinated approaches to their fundamental tasks. Although systematized charity antedated Community chests, having roots in the Scientific Charity movement of the late nineteenth century, chests were nevertheless pioneers of organized philanthropy.

The way chests conceived of their missions, conducted mass fund-raising, and were administered, bore a distinctively midwestern stamp. Whereas approaches to giving in the Northeast were often influenced by civic privatism, a sense that community leaders would assume social responsibility on their own accord and in their own terms, midwestern community leaders, who tended to be businessmen as opposed to the scions of established families, sought to rally and guide the energies and resources of a given locale. The community groups, businessmen, and attorneys who ran the chests proved capable fund-raisers, their close local ties helping to secure resources from corporations, the wealthy, and the electorate alike. As avowedly secular institutions, chests could fulfill their self-appointed role as umbrella associations under which religious and nonreligious local charities could work toward common goals without sectarian strife. Pursuing an enduring American desire, chests sought to utilize modern organizational, cooperative strategies for private giving to reestablish community in ever more complex urban environments and social stratification.

Community chests had limitations. Since they depended on industry for the bulk of their resources, funding was susceptible to economic downturns, which made them less able to cope with need when times pressed harder. Associated with welfare capitalism, an approach to social service that relied on and legitimized market-based approaches to social problems, chests placed themselves above politics and were biased against socioeconomic reform. Their political and social philosophies often brought chests into conflict with those who worked in the nation's many settlement houses, reformers who had intimate familiarity with the problems that beset the immigrant and working poor, to the detriment of potentially useful coalitions. Yet the community chests' innovative efforts to rationally manage the charitable resources of the nation's urban areas have proved durable. Their legacy survives in such charitable organizations as the United Way and community foundations, both of which enjoy strong public support in the Midwest.

Sources and Further Reading: David C. Hammack, "Community Foundations," in Richard Magat, ed., *An Agile Servant* (1989); Peter Dobkin Hall, *Inventing the Nonprofit Sector and other Essays on Philanthropy, Voluntarism and Nonprofit Organizations* (1992); Michael B. Katz, *In the Shadow of the Poorhouse* (1986).

Scott Lien
University of Chicago, Illinois

Philanthropic Foundations

Philanthropy is not only alive and well in the Midwest, it is an inherent characteristic of midwestern people. Each state has its own unique personality, its own approach to philanthropy. The independence and entrepreneurial nature of midwesterners is reflected in the way philanthropy has developed in the region. The philanthropy of the Midwest has shaped philanthropy across the United States.

Cleveland, Ohio, was the birthplace of the United Way movement early in the twentieth century and was the site of the nation's first community foundation, the Cleveland Foundation, created in 1914. Today, more than one fourth of the nation's community foundations are found in three midwestern states, Ohio, Indiana, and Michigan. In 2002, twenty-nine of the top one hundred community foundations in the United States in terms of asset size were located in the Midwest, ranging from $1.3 billion in Cleveland to $53.8 million in Hamilton, Ohio.

Corporations with giving programs in the region bear many familiar names: the Ford Motor Company Fund, General Motors, Inc., Foundation, and Daimler Chrysler Corporation Fund in Michigan; the Proctor and Gamble Fund in Ohio; the Eli Lilly and Company Foundation in Indiana; the General Mills and 3M Foundations in Minnesota; the Bank One and BP Foundations in Illinois—the list could go on and on.

Large private independent foundations in several midwestern states dominate the scene: the John D. and Catherine T. MacArthur Foundation in Illinois; the Lilly Endowment in Indianapolis; the W. K. Kellogg, Charles Stewart Mott, and Kresge Foundations in Michigan; the McKnight Foundation in Minnesota; the Ewing Marion Kauffman, Hall Family, and Danforth Foundations in Missouri. Successful midwesterners have been generous and have contributed substantially to the philanthropic assets of the nation. Many of the large independent foundations in the Midwest are international grant-makers, and nonprofit organizations on many continents have been touched and assisted from the heartland of America.

United Way organizations throughout the region have a long history of successful annual fund-raising and have enhanced life in the Midwest for generations through their funding of health and human services organizations.

The following paragraphs highlight the development of philanthropy in the twelve midwestern states.

Illinois—Number of foundations: 3,602; total assets: $22.6 billion. Illinois is a state characterized by its major players. A significant concentration of the population and philanthropy in Illinois resides in Chicago. The John D. and Catherine T. MacArthur Foundation, established in the 1970s, a relative newcomer to the scene, is the largest independent foundation in Illinois. Real estate tycoon John D. MacArthur did not create this foundation during his lifetime, but its innovative grant-making and Genius Awards have made the MacArthur name renowned throughout the country. The Robert R. McCormick Tribune Foundation and the Joyce Foundation trail closely on MacArthur's heels in terms of asset size, and the Chicago Community Trust, appropriately for the nation's third-largest city, is its third-largest community foundation with assets of more than $1 billion.

Ohio—Number of foundations: 2,967; total assets: $13.2 billion. The philanthropic character of Ohio is that of community foundations. For whatever reason, even though significant industrial wealth existed in Ohio in the late nineteenth and early twentieth centuries, few large private foundations were created. The community foundation concept originated in Ohio in 1914, and those organizations have dominated the state's philanthropy ever since.

The Cleveland Foundation is second only to the New York Community Trust in asset size and is the country's oldest community foundation. The Columbus Foundation led the nation for a decade in terms of per capita giving and in demonstrating creative approaches to community foundation development, including staffing and the acquisition of major gifts. Today, the community foundations in Columbus, Greater Cincinnati, Dayton, Akron, Toledo, Youngstown, and Hamilton all rank in the top one hundred in terms of assets. Private foundations include the Kettering Foundation (Kettering), George Gund Foundation (Cleveland), and the Timken Foundation (Canton).

Michigan—Number of foundations: 1,851; total assets: $20.8 billion. The philanthropic personality of Michigan has been shaped by the generosity of its sons and daughters who acquired enormous personal wealth and created private foundations in their hometowns. Henry Ford and his son, Edsel, founded the Ford Foundation in Detroit in 1936. Battle Creek, the site of the Kellogg Sanitarium and Kellogg Cereals, has its W. K. Kellogg Foundation. Flint was the home of Charles Stewart Mott and is the headquarters of the foundation he created. Troy (a suburb of Detroit) is the home of the Kresge Foundation. Midland is home to a significant foundation created by members of the Dow family. The Upjohn family has led philanthropy in Kalamazoo. More recently, the DeVos and Van Andel families have created foundations in Grand Rapids.

The development of community foundations—philanthropic organizations that are based on the gifts of many donors for the benefit of specific geographic locations—lagged behind, but in the early 1990s, the Kellogg Foundation mounted a program to initiate and/or grow community foundations throughout Michigan, with the result that all residents of the state have access to one of these foundations. The Mott Foundation has a long history of encouraging the development and growth of community foundations, both in the United States and in selected locations abroad. The Kresge Foundation has played an impor-

tant role in assisting the recent growth of the Community Foundation for Southeastern Michigan (the Detroit Metropolitan area). The community foundations in Southeastern Michigan—Kalamazoo, Fremont, Grand Rapids, Flint, Muskegon, and Battle Creek—are included among the nation's top one hundred community foundations in terms of assets.

Wisconsin—Number of foundations: 1,787; total assets: $5.8 billion. Wisconsin, the home of progressive politics and populism, has a philanthropic tradition in keeping with its personality. The Lynde and Harry Bradley Foundation, Wisconsin's largest independent foundation, was established in 1942 to support projects that cultivate a renewed, healthier, and vigorous sense of citizenship, both nationally and internationally.

The director of the second-ranking grant-maker in the state, the Milwaukee Foundation, has long provided significant leadership in the community foundation field. Racine is home of Wingspread, the Frank Lloyd Wright facility operated by the Johnson Foundation and the site of many important national and international meetings. Community foundations dot the landscape in Wisconsin and provide donors with significant opportunities for giving.

Missouri—Number of foundations: 1,239; total assets: $8.2 billion. The philanthropic personality of Missouri reflects its position as the only midwestern state with two clearly defined population centers: St. Louis on the east and Kansas City on the west. The Danforth Foundation and the Emerson Charitable Trust led independent grant-makers in the St. Louis area, and the Ewing Marion Kauffman, Hall Family, and William T. Kemper Foundations led in the west. The community foundation in St. Louis, the second community foundation created in the United States, which slept for many years and only started an aggressive pattern of growth in the 1990s, is also ranked in the top one hundred nationally.

Minnesota—Number of foundations: 1,235; total assets: $10 billion. Corporate giving has been an outstanding hallmark of philanthropy in Minnesota. The Minneapolis–St. Paul area has led the nation in the generosity of its business community. The Twin Cities of Minneapolis and St. Paul are the homes of two of the nation's largest community foundations, which, if their assets were aggregated, would become the nation's third-largest community foundation. Independent foundations that dominate the scene include the McKnight Foundation in Minneapolis and the Northwest Area Foundation in St. Paul, an organization that supports programs throughout the upper Midwest. Corporate giving in Minnesota has been outstanding, with philanthropic programs operated by such diverse business interests as Kohler, Target, General Mills and Pillsbury, 3M, and Best Buy.

Indiana—Number of foundations: 1,097; total assets: $18.5 billion. The Lilly Endowment, Inc., with assets in excess of $5 billion, has shaped philanthropy in Indiana since being founded in 1937 and has been the primary force in shaping the state's philanthropic personality. In addition to its significant support for religion, education, and community development, the Lilly Endowment undertook support for the development of community foundations throughout Indiana in the early 1990s. As in Michigan, this has resulted in all Hoosiers having access to community-based philanthropic organizations. The Central Indiana Community Foundation (Indianapolis), Fort Wayne and St. Joseph County Community Foundations, and the Community Foundation Alliance, Inc. (Evansville) all rank in the top one hundred.

Iowa, Nebraska, North and South Dakota, and Kansas—Number of foundations: 2,106; total assets: $6.7 billion. The philanthropic character of these states is a work in progress. As the population thins in the west, so do the numbers of philanthropic organizations. The largest independent foundation in Iowa, the Iowa West Foundation in Council Bluffs, supports programs and projects in both its home state and its neighbor, Nebraska. Only the Omaha Community Foundation ranks in the top one hundred, but there are active community foundations in all of the states, some of them experiencing rapid growth.

As illustrated above, the midwestern philanthropic profile varies from state to state. In each state, organized philanthropy has played an important role. Organized philanthropy enhances the lives of the people of the Midwest, and in many respects, the generosity of midwestern people has set a pace for the rest of the nation. Corporate giving has been strong in this section of the country. Community foundations, which now exist on every continent except Antarctica, were born here. The region's numerous private independent foundations have proved to be innovative grant-makers and have made significant contributions to the lives of Americans and millions of others abroad who have benefited from their generosity. Philanthropy is a basic midwestern value.

Sources and Further Reading: Foundation Center, *The Foundation Directory*, pts. 1 and 2, 25th ed. (2003); Maggie Jaruzel, *Sowing the Seeds of Local Philanthropy* (2001).

Dorothy M. Reynolds
Albuquerque, New Mexico

James I. Luck
Global 3E, Columbus, Ohio

Housing

The Midwest has come closer to realizing the American housing dream than any other section of the country. Historically it has been the land of the owner-occupied, single-family, detached dwellings. New York–style tenements, New England triple-deckers, and Philadelphia- and Baltimore-style row houses were alien to midwestern cities, and the rented shanties typical of the South were not the midwestern norm. In 1890, 31 to 34 percent of the families in the eleven midwestern cities with more than one hundred thousand inhabitants lived in owner-occupied dwellings, as compared to the average of just under 23 percent for all twenty-eight American cities in this population category. Nine of the eleven midwestern cities exceeded the national average. Fifty years later the situation was much the same. Of the eighteen midwestern cities with more than one hundred thousand inhabitants, fourteen showed over 45 percent owner occupancy. The 2000 census likewise reported that the owner occupancy rate of each of the midwestern states surpassed the national average of 66.2 percent. Though variation exists within the Midwest, it is generally a region of homes, yards, and mortgages.

Throughout the nineteenth century, the most common form of working-class housing in midwestern cities was the one- or one-and-a-half-story frame cottage. Because of their simple design and the abundance of lumber from the upper Midwest, such cottages could be constructed cheaply and quickly. Moreover, owing to the broad, flat terrain and the absence of topographic barriers to urban expansion, lots were relatively inexpensive in midwestern cities. Many newcomers from Europe purchased small lots and with the help of friends and neighbors built their own cottages. By the early twentieth century, Poles on Milwaukee's south side had constructed block after block of these houses, as had their compatriots in Detroit. In their great conflagration of 1871, Chicagoans discovered that the vast acreage of frame dwellings posed a serious fire hazard. But in one city after another, the working class continued to live and invest in modest wooden structures.

As midwestern cities grew in population, a pattern of social segregation developed, with some neighborhoods reserved for the wealthy. In the late nineteenth century, showplace mansions lined Euclid Avenue in Cleveland, Woodward Avenue in Detroit, Prairie Avenue in Chicago, and clustered along Vandeventer Place in St. Louis and on Quality Hill in Kansas City. These massive Victorian manses of brick and stone situated on manicured lawns along tree-lined thor-

❖ **Lustron Corporation**

The Lustron Corporation of Columbus, Ohio, was an innovative builder of prefabricated houses constructed with porcelain-enameled steel panels that were supported by steel framing secured to a poured concrete foundation. It produced 2,680 houses from April 1948 to May 1950. The federal government's Reconstruction Finance Corporation (RFC) foreclosed on the company in 1951 and forced its remaining assets to be liquidated.

The concept was developed by Carl G. Strandlund (1888–1974), an innovative engineer and manager who, in 1942, joined Chicago Vitreous Enamel Products Company in Cicero, Illinois. In 1932, the thirteen-year-old company formed the Porcelain Products Company to develop and market porcelain-enamel steel panels for use in decorative storefronts for theatres, gas stations, and other areas subject to wear and damage. The trade name "Lustron" was applied to this process in 1937. Strandlund proposed using these enameled panels for house construction in 1945 and applied the name of the product to the company. The company moved from Chicago to Columbus, Ohio, where the majority of the homes were manufactured.

The homes were two- and three-bedroom structures that ranged from 713 to 1,209 square feet. They were priced from $7,000 to $10,000 in 1948. Most houses were assembled in midwestern and eastern states.

The company's failure was a result of its inability to meet the payments for the short-term government financing, an unmanageable scale of manufacturing, a bad financial structure, an unsympathetic press, and the association with controversial political and government officials.

Gregory C. Randall
Walnut Creek, California

oughfares were symbols of success, but they also symbolized the emerging social mosaic of the midwestern city. The rich and poor would not share residential space; instead, residence in some neighborhoods would connote economic success, whereas other areas of the city became known as lower-class slums.

Some well-to-do midwesterners were not oblivious to the purported plight of the slum dwellers, and by the beginning of the twentieth century reformers were exposing the housing problems of the city. Though few midwestern families lived in five- or six-story brick tenements comparable to those in New York City, there was crowding in working-class neighborhoods. To earn rental income and thereby help pay for their homes, many working-class families built an additional rental house at the rear of their lot facing the alley or rented a part of their house, often the basement, to newcomers to the city. Though low-rise structures prevailed, the squeezing of more than one house on each lot and more than one family in each house produced population densities that shocked more affluent urbanites and seemed to endanger the public health. Moreover, the cheap frame structures often lacked plumbing facilities, and thus the outdoor privy was more common in midwestern cities than in New York or Boston.

Responding to such conditions, reformers conducted a number of housing surveys and drafted a series of state laws and local ordinances. For example, in 1901 the reform-minded City Homes Association published a report on tenement house conditions in Chicago, and the following year the city adopted an ordinance that restricted the percentage of each lot that could be occupied by a structure, specified the minimum size of rooms, required a window in each room, imposed certain fire protection measures, and mandated a separate toilet for each apartment except for one- or two-room apartments, which could share facilities.

Such provisions, modeled after those adopted earlier in New York City, were proposed in housing surveys and incorporated in laws and ordinances throughout the Midwest. In 1902, the Cleveland Chamber of Commerce created a committee on housing, a series of reports and surveys followed, and in 1915, the city adopted a housing ordinance known as the Sunlight Code, because it calculated the angle of sunlight at Cleveland's latitude and used that calculation to compute the amount of open space to be reserved around future dwellings. In 1906, the mayor of Kansas City, Missouri, appointed a tenement house commission, and a housing survey in 1912 revealed the overcrowding, dilapidation, and lack of sanitary facilities in that city's poor districts. Wisconsin adopted a restrictive housing law in 1907, and in 1913, Indiana's housing reformer Albion Fellows Bacon secured a state code regulating the construction of multifamily structures. A housing survey of Minneapolis published in 1914 resulted in a restrictive code for that city, and in 1917, Michigan enacted a housing law to guarantee minimum standards in Detroit. That same year, a housing survey in Des Moines found no tenement problem, but proposed a state code to ensure that the Iowa capital did not in the future follow the example of less fortunate urban centers.

Meanwhile, those innovative midwestern architects

dubbed the Prairie School were experimenting with new designs for housing. Distinguished architects had traditionally deemed residential projects, other than the most lavish mansions, as unworthy of their talents. The Prairie School, however, devoted much of its energy to residential commissions, and throughout his life the school's greatest practitioner, Frank Lloyd Wright, strove to create moderately priced housing that conformed to his high aesthetic standards. In 1895, he designed a moderate-rent apartment building, the Francisco Terrace, in Chicago, and twelve years later, he published his famous plan for a $5,000 fireproof house in *Ladies Home Journal*. From 1911 to 1916, he designed prefabricated dwellings for American System Built Homes, and four of his prefab duplexes and two prefab bungalows were built in Milwaukee. From the late 1930s through the 1950s, he experimented with the construction of reasonably priced dwellings that he called Usonian houses, and in the last years of his life he returned to the design of mass-produced, prefabricated dwellings. Wright also built many innovative structures for the more affluent, though the Midwest's plutocratic elite generally turned to more traditional architects for their mansions.

Other Prairie School architects, such as Walter Burley Griffin of Chicago and George Elmslie and William Purcell of Minneapolis, accepted numerous residential commissions, building homes for the middle and upper-middle classes as well as public and commercial buildings. The flat, wide-open spaces of the Midwest inspired the horizontal lines, stark geometry, and low, overhanging roofs of Prairie School houses, whose designers defiantly rejected the ornament and architectural vocabulary inherited from Europe. With their disdain for the aristocratic aesthetic pretensions of Europe and the eastern United States, the Prairie School architects believed they were creating a new democratic architecture, a physical embodiment of the progressive political revolt sweeping the Midwest. Though they never succeeded in placing many moderate-income midwesterners in Prairie School structures, their architecture reflected the midwestern mythology of Lincolnian democracy, the linear, spare midwestern topography, and the midwestern devotion to the low-rise, detached dwelling.

Most midwesterners, however, found shelter in less innovative residences. Some of the wealthy opted for the high-rise, luxury apartments that sprouted up along Chicago's Lake Shore Drive in the first three decades of the twentieth century. Other less affluent midwesterners moved into the thousands of modest bungalows constructed during these same years. Lining the streets of Chicago's bungalow belt were rows of one- and one-and-a-half-story detached dwellings,

each with a living room, dining room, kitchen, two or three bedrooms, and one bath. The south side of Minneapolis was also bungalow territory where thousands of Minnesotans fulfilled their dream of a home and yard.

Yet some midwesterners sought a more restricted residential environment, and during the first four decades of the twentieth century, subdivision developers catered to their wishes. In Kansas City, J. C. Nichols won a reputation as one of the nation's leading residential community builders. He developed much of Kansas City's south side as a refuge for the affluent, imposing restrictions on the purchasers of lots in his subdivisions. Besides prohibiting the sale or lease of property to blacks, he required that his company approve floor and lot plans of houses prior to construction. In their Shaker Heights development, the Van Sweringen brothers of Cleveland also endeavored to create a restricted residential community for the wealthy. Meanwhile, E. H. Close was laying out Ottawa Hills, Toledo's version of Shaker Heights, and outside of Columbus, King Thompson was selling lots in his exclusive community of Upper Arlington.

With the onset of economic depression after 1929, residential construction came to a virtual halt. To create jobs for unemployed workers and to provide decent housing for the poor, the federal government embarked on a public housing program. In the early 1920s, the City and County of Milwaukee pioneered the public subsidy of housing when they financed the Garden Homes project, 105 single- and double-family buildings intended to combat the housing shortage after World War I. In the 1930s, however, the federal government helped finance the development of projects throughout the Midwest. Cleveland's Ernest Bohn was a key figure in the public housing movement and lobbied for passage of the Wagner-Steagall Housing Act of 1937, which authorized federal subsidies to local housing authorities for the construction of low-rent dwellings. During the late 1930s, public housing units were predominantly low-rise and housing officials were selective about project tenants, preferring families with an employed male breadwinner.

After World War II, however, giant high-rise projects were constructed in the Midwest's major cities, and they became symbols for all that was wrong with public housing. On Chicago's south side, a wall of bleak, look-alike high-rises lined the Dan Ryan Expressway. With a virtually all-black population, these projects were publicly subsidized ghettoes, poorly maintained and notorious for violence and crime. St. Louis's Pruitt-Igoe project was a massive high-rise development constructed in the 1950s. Within two decades, it was a widely publicized failure and slated for demolition. In such conservative cities as Omaha and Indianapolis, public housing offended many voters as "socialistic," and local authorities faced an uphill battle in securing approval for the construction of projects. Moreover, many midwesterners opposed the location of public housing projects in their neighborhoods and the consequent influx of poor people. Often there was a racial component to this opposition, as whites sought to keep black residents out of their neighborhoods. But in the late 1960s, middle-class black residents of Cleveland's Lee-Seville district fought plans for public housing for African Americans, presenting the same arguments used by whites. In the end, class counted more than color.

More significant than the construction of public housing were the massive private housing tracts built during the post–World War II era. South of Chicago, Philip Klutznick's American Community Builders created the new community of Park Forest during the late 1940s and early 1950s, with three thousand apartment units and fifty-five hundred single-family houses. Meanwhile, west of Chicago in DuPage County, Jay Stream built Carol Stream, a planned community for middle-class midwesterners, and nearby Albert and Jack Kaufman were laying out the new town of Woodridge. In every midwestern metropolitan area, developers were clearing cornfields and erecting rows of single-family dwellings.

During the last decades of the twentieth century, some midwesterners were moving back to central city neighborhoods on the north side of Chicago, on the east side of Milwaukee, and in the West End of St. Louis and rehabilitating older houses. But the prevailing trend was sprawl, as the penchant for the single-family, owner-occupied home consumed thousands of additional acres of countryside each year.

Sources and Further Reading: Edith Abbott, *The Tenements of Chicago, 1908–1935* (1936); Robert G. Barrows, *Albion Fellows Bacon* (2000); Devereux Bowly, Jr., *The Poorhouse* (1978); Jan Cigliano and Sarah Bradford Landau, eds., *The Grand American Avenue 1850–1920* (1994); Robert B. Fairbanks, *Making Better Citizens* (1988); Thomas Lee Philpott, *The Slum and the Ghetto* (1978); Gregory C. Randall, *America's Original GI Town* (2000); Roger D. Simon, *The City-Building Process*, rev. ed. (1996); William S. Worley, *J. C. Nichols and the Shaping of Kansas City* (1990); Olivier Zunz, *The Changing Face of Inequality* (1982).

Jon C. Teaford
Purdue University, Indiana

Albion Fellows Bacon (1865–1933)

Albion Fellows was born in Evansville, Indiana, the daughter of Reverend Albion Fellows and Mary Erskine Fellows. Reared in a nearby hamlet, she later credited nostalgia for the pastoral environment of her youth with motivating her urban-oriented reform efforts. Following graduation (as salutatorian) from Evansville High School, she worked as a legal secretary, toured Europe, married local merchant Hilary Bacon in 1888, and settled into a comfortable routine of middle-class domesticity.

She eventually found outlets for her intelligence and creativity in voluntary associations and social welfare campaigns. These activities included "friendly visiting" in homes of the city's poor and founding a Working Girls' Association to aid rural migrants to the city. Bacon became best known, regionally and even nationally, for her work on behalf of tenement reform and was instrumental in the passage of several state laws to improve housing conditions. She was also involved in child welfare work, city planning and zoning, and public health efforts. She lectured often, especially in the Midwest, regarding housing reform and other social welfare issues. In addition, she found time to write articles, pamphlets, and a book related to her reform efforts, as well as poetry, pageants, and several pieces that proclaimed her strong Methodist faith. Edith Elmer Wood, a leading housing economist, writing in 1919, identified Bacon as one of the "three magnetic personalities" (the others were Jacob Riis and Lawrence Veiller) produced by the era's housing reform movement.

Sources and Further Reading: Albion Fellows Bacon, *Beauty for Ashes* (1914); Robert G. Barrows, *Albion Fellows Bacon* (2000); Roy Lubove, "Albion Fellows Bacon and the Awakening of a State," *Midwest Review* (1962); Edith Elmer Wood, *The Housing of the Unskilled Wage Earner* (1919).

Robert G. Barrows
Purdue University–Indianapolis, Indiana

Ernest J. Bohn (1901–1975)

Ernest J. Bohn achieved national recognition for his work in city planning and public housing. An émigré to Cleveland, Ohio, from Rumania in 1911, Bohn graduated from Western Reserve University in 1924 and its law school in 1926. He entered politics as a progressive Republican serving on the Cleveland City Council from 1930 to 1940.

To deal with Cleveland's slum problem, Bohn began an intensive study of city planning and public housing. He latched upon the Garden City ideals of Sir Ebenezer Howard and created a local adjunct of Lewis Mumford's Regional Planning Association of America. Because of his efforts, Cleveland created a strong City Planning Commission in 1942 and appointed him as chairman, a position he held until 1966.

Bohn took advantage of the New Deal to establish Cleveland and Ohio as leaders in the public housing movement. In 1933, Bohn secured passage of the nation's first state law authorizing municipal housing authorities. As the Director of the Cleveland Metropolitan Housing Authority (1933–1968), Bohn also founded the National Association for Housing and Redevelopment Officials and was an effective lobbyist for the passage of the Wagner Housing Act of 1937. Throughout his career he served as an advisor to many housing officials throughout the nation.

In the 1950s, his efforts at urban renewal fell afoul of the racial and class attitudes of ethnic Clevelanders. By the 1960s, he was also under attack from civil rights advocates who wanted immediate integration throughout the city and county. Deeply disappointed, Bohn retired in 1968.

Sources and Further Reading: William D. Jenkins, "Beyond Downtown," *Journal of Urban History* 27 (May 2001); William D. Jenkins, "Ernest J. Bohn and the Configuration of Housing and Planning in Cleveland, Ohio, 1932–1945," *Proceedings of the Fifth National Planning History Conference* (1995).

William D. Jenkins
Youngstown State University, Ohio

Philip M. Klutznick (1907–1999)

Philip M. Klutznick was a statesman and community developer born in Kansas City, Missouri, to eastern European Orthodox Jewish parents. Educated at the University of Kansas and Creighton Law School in Omaha, Nebraska, he became an activist and leader in the American Jewish community, an author, and served as president of the World Jewish Congress, as president of B'nai B'rith, as commissioner of the Federal Public Housing Authority, and as administrator of the U.S. Housing Authority from 1944 to 1946.

With Nathan Manilow, he formed American Community Builders in 1946 to build one of the first postwar planned communities in the United States in Park Forest, Illinois. This community was an important housing innovation and influenced the postwar housing boom as well as the development of the American suburb. He was also an early developer of the modern American shopping center, building the Old Orchard Shopping Center, Oak Brook Shopping Center, and the first high-rise shopping center and mixed-use development in the United States, Water Tower Place, all in or near Chicago.

Klutznick developed the port city of Ashdod in Israel and assisted in developing the Nahum Goldmann Museum of the Jewish Diaspora. Due in large measure to his friendships with Anwar Sadat and Menachem Begin, he became an important advisor to the Carter Administration. His involvement with Jewish organizations placed him in a unique role as advisor to Israel's various prime ministers from 1955 to the mid-1980s. He served as a member of the permanent mission to the United Nations from 1961 to 1962, and was Secretary of Commerce in the Carter Administration in 1980. With the end of Carter's term, Klutznick returned to Chicago and spent much of the rest of his life supporting education and other philanthropic causes.

Sources and Further Reading: Philip M. Klutznick, *Angles of Vision* (1991); Gregory C. Randall, *America's Original GI Town* (2000).

Gregory C. Randall
Walnut Creek, California

J. C. Nichols (1880–1950)

Jesse Clyde [J.C.] Nichols became the premier innovative land developer of the Kansas City region by creating neighborhoods and shopping districts that met the needs of his middle- to upper-income residents. Nichols obtained two bachelor's degrees, one from the University of Kansas in 1902 and another from Harvard College in 1903. He gained admission to Phi Beta Kappa while a student at the University of Kansas.

Nichols began his land development career in 1903 in Kansas City, Kansas, with a working-class neighborhood. He moved to land south of the Kansas City, Missouri, city limits in 1905. By 1908, with financial backing from wealthy Kansas Citians, he solidified ownership or sales contracts for over one thousand acres of potential residential land on both sides of the Missouri–Kansas state line.

By acquiring rights to land surrounding the Kansas City Country Club, Nichols began using the term "Country Club District" to describe his holdings. Later, he established two additional country clubs in that development, along with several private golf clubs. Nichols thus pioneered the concept of residential–recreational living environments.

Because his Country Club District was located over five miles south of Kansas City, Nichols recognized the need both for transportation improvements and of shops for residents. He organized streetcar service and, with his investors, donated land to the city for streets and boulevards that connected with and extended Kansas City's growing Park and Boulevard system, originally designed by George Kessler.

By 1921, Nichols had three small shopping districts operating along the eastern edges of his residential development. The following year he announced plans for a very large shopping area to be located at the north end of his Missouri development along the Brush Creek valley. This plan evolved into the internationally known Country Club Plaza. Planned to serve both the growing apartment and single-family home populations, the Plaza was located with one of the city's boulevards leading downtown forming its eastern border and within one block of a streetcar stop. By the late 1920s, Nichols gained routing of U.S. 50 directly through the Plaza. From its inception, parking has always been free and abundant.

Nichols also innovated the use of homeowners' associations and developed extensive deed restrictions to require homeowners to build attractively and maintain their properties well. The deed restrictions included racial exclusions against blacks, as did most middle- to upper-income subdivisions across the country at the time.

Ultimately, J.C. Nichols's ideas for residential and shopping developments have greatly influenced such activity across the nation, in part through his leadership in the National Association of Real Estate Boards and in the founding of the Urban Land Institute. His Brookside development has been recognized as a model for New Urban design throughout the 1990s. Kansas City and the nation have something of a different face in their most attractive residential areas through the contributions of this creative businessman.

Sources and Further Reading: Robert Pearson and Brad Pearson, *The J. C. Nichols Chronicle* (1994); William S. Worley, *J. C. Nichols and the Shaping of Kansas City* (1990); William S. Worley, *The Plaza, First and Always* (1997).

William S. Worley
University of Missouri–Kansas City

Pruitt-Igoe

The Pruitt-Igoe residential complex in St. Louis, Missouri, was a large high-rise public housing project that became beset by crime and vandalism and gained national notoriety as the first public housing project in the United States to be demolished.

Completed in 1956, the development of the adjacent Wendell Oliver Pruitt Homes and William L. Igoe Apartments were one of several large physical improvement projects, such as the Jefferson Memorial Arch, carried out in St. Louis during the postwar period. The original design for Pruitt-Igoe was ambitious. The principal architect, Minoru Yamasaki, proposed a combination of eight-story elevator apartment buildings, row houses, and a winding park of trees and grassy lawns. Yamasaki designed the apartment buildings in a straight line or slab design and, employing a device that was both economic and fashionable at the time, placed elevator stops on every third floor. Along one outer wall of each high-rise building were deep hallways or galleries, which were intended to function as "vertical neighborhoods," including playgrounds, open-air porches, and entries to adjoining laundry and storage rooms.

The actual project, however, never realized its architect's vision. Under pressure from the federal government that provided the funding, the St. Louis Housing Authority trimmed the plans to reconcile sky-high construction costs and the cost ceilings set by the federal government. The number of apartment buildings grew to thirty-three identical buildings, their height grew to eleven stories, the row houses were omitted, and the total number of dwelling units increased to 2,870. As cost-saving measures, the authority did away with insulation on the steam pipes, screens on the gallery windows, and public toilets on the ground floors. The green spaces became expanses of pavement. Although at one time the St. Louis Housing Authority had planned for some whites to live in Pruitt-Igoe, the project became entirely African American.

Soon after it was built, Pruitt-Igoe became known as an unpleasant and dangerous place to live. Children used the elevators as toilets, the washing machines broke down, and the locks on the storage rooms in the galleries were often jimmied. There were numerous robberies, and gangs roamed Yamasaki's galleries, which the tenants renamed "gauntlets." The project's tenant body grew increasingly poor and the number of vacancies climbed, decreasing the rental income from which maintenance costs were to be paid. Without sufficient revenue, the housing authority cut back on maintenance, and conditions at the project grew worse.

So bad was the situation that in 1965, the federal government gave the St. Louis Housing Authority funds to rehabilitate Pruitt-Igoe, the first time government expenditures were employed to rescue a public housing project. The government eventually spent more than $5 million to redesign and repair Pruitt-Igoe, but the housing project continued to be plagued by crime, disrepair, and vacancies.

In 1972 as a last ditch effort, the St. Louis Housing

Authority gained approval from the federal government to raze three of Pruitt-Igoe's high-rise buildings. The national news media gave extensive coverage to the demolition. The following year the housing authority and the federal government concluded the project's problems were irreversible and flattened the remaining buildings. Again the press reproduced dramatic images of the unprecedented destruction of a public housing project. The demise of Pruitt-Igoe became a major national event, interpreted variously as a symbol of the failure of public housing, American social policy, and even modernist-style architecture.

Sources and Further Reading: Katharine G. Bristol, "The Pruitt-Igoe Myth," *Journal of Architecture Education* (May 1991); Eugene J. Meehan, *The Quality of Federal Policymaking* (1979); Roger Montgomery, "Pruitt-Igoe," in Barry Checkoway and Carl V. Patton, eds., *The Metropolitan Midwest* (1985); Alexander von Hoffman, "Why They Built Pruitt-Igoe," in John F. Bauman, Roger Biles, and Kristin M. Szylvian, eds., *From Tenements to the Taylor Homes* (2000).

Alexander von Hoffman
Harvard University, Massachusetts

Crime, Violence, and Law Enforcement

Many early-twenty-first-century Americans associate the great urban centers of the Midwest with crime, violence, and police corruption. Chicago, after all, is the city of the Haymarket Bombing of 1886, the Race Riot of 1919, the St. Valentine Day's Massacre of 1929, and the baton-wielding policemen who battled with protesters outside the 1968 Democratic Party Convention. It was also the home of Nathan Leopold and Richard Loeb and, of course, Al Capone. Likewise, Detroit evokes images of labor racketeering and bloody race riots in 1943 and 1967, while Cleveland, Gary, St. Louis, and East St. Louis often bring to mind media reports of grinding poverty and spiraling street crime. These images are particularly powerful and enduring because they are implicitly cast against the perception of a peaceful, wholesome region of crime-free small towns and safe, close-knit farming communities. Not surprisingly, both sets of images represent caricatures.

The major cities of the Midwest are not the most violent, crime-infested urban centers in the United States. This distinction belongs to southern cities, which have typically suffered from far higher rates of violence than heartland metropolises. Nor is there evidence that midwestern law enforcers have been less capable or more corrupt than their counterparts in other regions. Although highly publicized episodes of brutality and corruption have tainted the reputations of Chicago and Detroit police departments, law enforcers in Los Angeles, New York, and New Orleans have been dogged by serious scandals, as well.

If the cities of the Midwest have not been uniquely lawless, their histories of crime, violence, and law enforcement have been distinctive nonetheless. During the nineteenth century, midwestern cities grew and industrialized faster than urban centers elsewhere in the nation. St. Louis, for example, was the fastest growing major city during the antebellum era, when American cities expanded at their quickest pace. Likewise, in the Industrial Age, Chicago emerged as a manufacturing giant, and Detroit's automobile industry and Gary's steel industry became symbols of America's industrial might. As a result of the explosive rates of urbanization and industrialization in the Midwest, patterns of crime, violence, and law enforcement became exaggerated. The developments and trends of Boston, New York, and Philadelphia, for example, appeared in accelerated, distorted forms in the mushrooming cities of the Midwest. A comparable process unfolded during the late twentieth century, as the crushing effects of economic change transformed the industrial belt into the Rust Belt. The problems that plagued the nation's manufacturing centers hit the Midwest's industrial cities particularly hard, and the poverty and social turmoil of the era were especially acute in Detroit, Gary, Cleveland, St. Louis, Cincinnati, and Kansas City. In short, during good times and bad, the cities of the heartland have experienced exaggerated versions of national trends in crime, violence, and law enforcement.

This pattern is apparent in the history of law enforcement in the Midwest. During the early stages in the development of modern policing, midwestern policy makers were seldom innovators. By the time Chicago and Milwaukee received town charters, Bostonians had been struggling to maintain law and order for two centuries. Thus, long before the great cities of the heartland confronted urban problems, the older cities of the northeast had experimented with sheriffs and constables, day guards and night watches, magistrates and marshals. During the 1830s and 1840s, a wave of riots, an influx of immigrants, and accompanying concerns about social stability led policy makers in Boston and New York to establish full-time, preventive police forces. Borrowing from London's law enforcers, New York officials created a modern-style police department in 1844. Within a decade, New York law enforcers donned uniforms and became increasingly professional. During the same period, settlers poured into the Midwest, and within decades Cincinnati, St. Louis, Chicago, and other small towns became major urban centers and grappled with big-city problems. Municipal officials in these entrepôts rapidly established New York–style police forces. By the end of the Civil War, Cincinnati, St. Louis, Chicago, and Indianapolis had full-time, uniformed, preventive law enforcers, and by 1870, Detroit, Cleveland, Columbus, Omaha, and Toledo had followed suit. A process of institutional innovation that spanned centuries on the Atlantic coast was compressed into a few decades in the Midwest.

By the late nineteenth century, midwestern law enforcers were similar to their northeastern counterparts. Nor is this surprising; according to a leading historian of the American criminal justice system, innovations in policing moved from one big city to the next. In 1857, for example, state legislators imposed control over New York City's police department. Similar power struggles produced state takeovers of municipal policing in Detroit in 1865, Cleveland in 1866, and Cincinnati in 1877. Often such battles reflected conflicts between immigrant-dominated political machines and native-born reformers from rural parts of large states. Just as half of New York policemen in 1890 were foreign born, comparable proportions of law enforcers in Chicago, Minneapolis, Cleveland, and Milwaukee were likewise immigrants from foreign lands. In short, the pressures that buffeted law enforcers in New York and Boston were reproduced, often in more extreme fashion, in the cities of the heartland.

Having caught up with their counterparts on the Atlantic Seaboard, during the late nineteenth and early twentieth centuries, policy makers in the Midwest often became the innovators. In 1872, for example, Chicago officials appointed the first African American policeman outside the South, and in 1880, the Lake Michigan metropolis became the first city in the nation to establish a system of call boxes. Like their counterparts elsewhere, midwestern policemen during the late nineteenth century performed a broad range of social welfare and social control functions, devoting much of their time to finding lost children and to managing street life, rather than to directly preventing or solving crime. Because migrants poured into these burgeoning cities, midwestern policemen arrested enormous numbers of vagrants, tramps, and drunkards during the late nineteenth century. Waves of reform changed law enforcement after the turn of the century, and police departments in midwestern cities became more centralized and more specialized. As a result, law enforcers focused increasing attention on solving crime rather than on trawling the streets for beggars, rowdies, and hoboes.

Over the course of the twentieth century, cycles of urban growth and innovation on the one hand and decline and retrenchment on the other hand made midwestern police departments paragons of progressive reform on some occasions and backwaters of corruption on others. Cleveland's police department, for example, became a pioneer in crime prevention strategies during the opening decade of the twentieth century and a hotbed for corruption and brutality during the 1960s. Similarly, the Chicago police department was infected by political corruption during the 1960s and 1970s, but it was heralded as an innovator in community-oriented policing at the end of the twentieth century.

The history of urban violence in the region has followed a similar pattern, revealing an exaggerated version of national trends. Like northeastern urban centers, midwestern cities experienced low levels of violence during the late nineteenth century, as the demands of industrial society inculcated discipline and self-control. Around the turn of the century, however, violent crime spiked, and the increase was particularly sharp in midwestern urban centers. During the early twentieth century, rates of violence were highest—by a wide margin—in southern cities, but homicide rates in St. Louis, Cincinnati, Chicago, and Cleveland soared above those of Atlantic coast cities. In terms of the number (as opposed to the rate) of homicides, Chicago led the nation and St. Louis ranked third.

The jarring pace of population growth and the resulting social and cultural stresses contributed to this surge. Midwestern industrial giants attracted huge streams of immigrants; of the ten urban centers with the highest proportion of foreign-born residents in 1890, six were located in the Midwest. Moreover, the 1911 report of the U.S. Congress's Dillingham Commission on the role of immigrants in American society concluded that levels of violence rose among recently arrived newcomers, and fell thereafter. In Chicago, where immigrants comprised over one-third of the population, the homicide rate doubled during the first decades of the twentieth century, as it did in Omaha, where more than one-fifth of the residents were foreign born.

A second demographic change also contributed to the rising tide of violence. Hundreds of thousands of African Americans migrated from the South during the early twentieth century, and midwestern cities received especially large numbers of these migrants. The newcomers, however, confronted intense racial hostility, and competition over work and neighborhoods triggered bloody race riots in East St. Louis, Springfield, and Chicago during the early twentieth century. Racism and poverty also fueled violence within the bursting ghettos of the Midwest, and homicide rates among African Americans were more than ten times those of whites in Chicago, Cleveland,

Omaha, East St. Louis, and Cincinnati. The pressures that increased violence throughout urban America during the early twentieth century produced especially high levels of homicide in the industrial centers of the heartland.

This pattern, in which national trends were exaggerated in the Midwest, was repeated during the 1920s. With large immigrant populations that were at best ambivalent about Prohibition, and with easy access to alcohol smuggled from Canada, midwestern cities such as Detroit, Cleveland, and Chicago became major bootlegging centers during the 1920s. According to one estimate, Al Capone's bootlegging network generated $60 million per year during this period. Although such illegal enterprises lacked the level of organization portrayed in Mafia movies, the sudden, explosive growth of underground markets for alcohol produced instability and resulted in pitched, often violent battles over suppliers and turf—in much the same way that the crack epidemic of the late 1980s generated violence. During Chicago's Beer Wars of the mid-1920s, local gangsters, for example, murdered more than two hundred people, and policemen killed an additional 160 gangsters. The confluence of demographic, geographic, and economic factors made Prohibition particularly violent in Chicago, Detroit, and other cities in the region.

During the 1930s, 1940s, and 1950s, violence in the urban Midwest, as in cities throughout the nation, fell. Chicago's homicide rate, for instance, plunged by nearly 50 percent between 1930 and 1950. Halcyon days for the nation's manufacturing centers, the 1940s and the 1950s was a peaceful era for midwestern cities.

Urban violence exploded during the 1960s, 1970s, and 1980s, and the surge was unusually pronounced in midwestern cities. Racial conflict, including waves of riots during the "long, hot summers" of the 1960s, soaring levels of poverty as America's manufacturing sector crumbled, a rise in gang warfare, and the crack epidemic combined to ravage the industrial centers of the region. Chicago's homicide rate more than quadrupled between 1950 and 1990, and rates of violence skyrocketed throughout the urban Midwest. Though still typically trailing the cities of the South, Detroit, St. Louis, and East St. Louis ranked among the nation's most violent metropolises. In 1986, Detroit—briefly—became America's murder capital, and in 1993, St. Louis had the third-highest homicide rate, the fourth-highest robbery rate, and the fifth-highest aggravated assault rate in the nation.

The cities of the heartland have also followed the most recent trend in violent crime. Rates of violence plummeted during the late 1990s, and levels of murder and assault plunged throughout the urban Midwest. This pattern reflected the shift to a post-industrial, information-based economy, the decline in the use of crack, the implementation of new policing strategies, and the aging of the population of midwestern cities.

The urban centers of the region have become so thoroughly integrated into the national economy that future shifts in both law enforcement and crime will likely continue to reveal themselves on the streets of midwestern cities. Just as the urban centers of the heartland grew and industrialized faster than their northeastern counterparts during the nineteenth and early twentieth centuries, and contracted and deindustrialized faster during the late twentieth century, economic and structural transformations will continue to produce exaggerated patterns well into the twenty-first century, making Chicago, Detroit, St. Louis, and Cleveland bellwethers for national trends in crime and punishment.

Sources and Further Reading: Alfred Blumstein and Joel Wallman, eds., *The Crime Drop in America* (2000); H. C. Brearley, *Homicide in the United States* (1932); John Landesco, *Organized Crime in Chicago* (1929; reprint, 1968); Roger Lane, *Murder in America: A History* (1997); Richard C. Lindberg, *To Serve and Collect* (1991); Eric H. Monkkonen, *Police in Urban America, 1860–1920* (1981); Elliott M. Rudwick, *Race Riot at East St. Louis, July 2, 1917* (1964); John C. Schneider, *Detroit and the Problem of Order, 1830–1880* (1980); William M. Tuttle Jr., *Race Riot* (1970); Samuel Walker, *A Critical History of Police Reform* (1977).

Jeffrey S. Adler
University of Florida

Al Capone (1899–1947)

Al Capone was born on January 17, 1899, in Brooklyn, New York, to law-abiding Italian immigrant parents. As a youth, he worked for the local boss of Italian gangland, Frank Ioele (better known as Frankie Yale). Soon wanted by the law and the rival mobsters, Capone was sent off to Chicago in about 1919, where he joined the gang led by James "Big Jim" Colosimo and John Torrio. He started in Chicago as a bouncer in the brothel known as the Four Deuces at 2222 South Wabash Avenue.

After Colosimo's murder in 1920, Torrio led the group into bootlegging and Capone quickly rose through the ranks, becoming Torrio's underboss by 1923. When Torrio left Chicago in 1925 after being shot by North Side gangsters, Capone took over the city's strongest gang. By the late 1920s, the Capone mob was heavily involved in gambling, labor and business racketeering, and to a lesser extent prostitution, along with the crown jewel, bootlegging.

Al Capone with attorney, Chicago, Ill., 1929. Chicago Historical Society, ICHi-14414. Photo by Jun Fujita.

During the Prohibition Era gang wars in Chicago, Capone often sought to compromise with foes. But repeated problems with the North Side Weiss-Drucci-Moran gang led to continual conflict. The defeat of the North Siders by the Capone forces by 1931 put him at the top of Chicago gangland at the age of thirty-two.

However, the violence in Chicago during Prohibition and Capone's own flamboyant style made him a visible target for the law, causing the federal government to move against him. Eliot Ness and other Prohibition agents raided his breweries, damaging the Capone gang financially. Simultaneously, the IRS investigated his income taxes, resulting in Capone's conviction for income tax evasion in October 1931. After serving in the federal penitentiary in Atlanta, Capone was transferred to Alcatraz Island. However, syphilis incapacitated him to such a degree that he was paroled in 1939. Capone joined his family in a house on Miami's Palm Island and lived there until his death in January 1947.

All in all, Al Capone's criminal career was an incredible roller-coaster ride. Not surprisingly, a number of myths have arisen about his intelligence, his behavior, and his fortune. In reality, Capone was about as violent as the average Prohibition Era gangster and quite a bit smarter, as evidenced by the fact that he

built a formidable criminal empire. There is also no lost fortune to be discovered by treasure hunters, Capone having spent his personal wealth during his pre-prison years.

Al Capone did, however, lay an excellent foundation for his successor, Frank Nitti, who along with other Capone protégés, such as Paul Ricca, Tony Accardo, Jake Guzik, and Murray Humphreys, built the criminal organization known as the Outfit. The Outfit became the most successful of the Cosa Nostra families, controlling, since the end of Prohibition, organized crime in the Chicago area and various parts of Illinois and Indiana, as well as operating in other parts of the country, such as Milwaukee, Kansas City, Los Angeles, and especially Las Vegas through the rest of the century.

Sources and Further Reading: John J. Binder, *The Chicago Outfit* (2003); Robert J. Schoenberg, *Mr. Capone* (1992).

John J. Binder
University of Illinois–Chicago

Eliot Ness (1902–1957)

Born in Chicago in 1902, Eliot Ness earned a Ph.B. (similar to a bachelor's) degree in political economy from the University of Chicago in 1925 and worked in the business world before becoming a Prohibition agent in 1926. Through his brother-in-law Alexander Jamie's political connections, Ness was made the head of a special squad, later dubbed "The Untouchables," in late 1929. Over the next two years, they raided Al Capone's stills and breweries and occasionally arrested lower-level Capone hoodlums. Ness and company did not, however, "dry up" Chicago or "get" Capone, who was convicted of income tax evasion resulting from a separate IRS investigation.

Eliot Ness left Chicago in 1933 and worked in liquor enforcement in Cincinnati and Cleveland. In 1935, he was appointed Cleveland's Director of Public Safety. In this role Ness made his greatest contributions to the public good, reforming a corrupt and scandal-ridden police department.

After resigning his position in Cleveland in 1942 due to a minor incident, Ness worked to suppress venereal disease in the military during World War II. Following the war he was involved in several business ventures, none of which were financially rewarding, as well as an unsuccessful campaign for mayor of Cleveland in 1947. Ness died in 1957, before his account of his Chicago days, *The Untouchables* (coauthored by Oscar Fraley) was released, with the wealth and fame he probably deserved, given his excellent record of public service in the Midwest, eluding him during his lifetime.

Sources and Further Reading: John J. Binder, *The Chicago Outfit* (2003); Paul W. Heimel, *Eliot Ness: The Real Story* (1997).

John J. Binder
University of Illinois–Chicago

Gangs

Media accounts of gangs tend to use the term rather indiscriminately to refer to a disparate array of groups—youth gangs, biker gangs, hate groups, neo-Nazi skinheads, Jamaican posses, prison gangs, and organized crime groups, among others. While each of these groups is worthy of comment, the use of the term "gang" in this discussion refers exclusively to youth gangs. Some prefer the term "street gang," since the average age of gang members has increased over the past decade, with more than half now eighteen years of age or older. Although there is no universally accepted definition of youth gangs, they are defined here as a collectivity or group consisting primarily of adolescents and young adults who (a) interact frequently with each other; (b) are frequently and deliberately involved in illegal activities; (c) share a common collective identity that is usually expressed through a gang name; and (d) typically express that identity by adopting certain symbols and/or claiming control over certain turf, including persons, places, things, and/or economic markets.

The original and classic study of gangs in urban America focused on the Midwest, Frederic Thrasher's *The Gang: A Study of 1,313 Gangs in Chicago* in 1927. Thrasher observed that other midwestern cities, such as Minneapolis, Cleveland, and St. Louis, also had gangs in the 1920s. However, Chicago and New York commanded most of the nation's attention with respect to gangs until the 1960s, when the emergence of the Crips and the Bloods began to shift much of the media's gang focus to Los Angeles, just as the nation's media center was also shifting from New York to Southern California. Today, however, gangs are no longer limited to mega-cities such as Chicago or Los Angeles. Midwestern cities other than Chicago have seen the emergence or, in some cases, reemergence of gangs on their streets. Gang presence has become a more commonplace phenomenon in American society, including many suburban and rural areas, as well.

In 1960, only fifty-eight cities officially acknowledged the presence of gangs, and those cities were primarily located in California and the southwest, the Chicago region, and the East Coast. By 1970, the number of cities with gangs had nearly doubled (to 101), but the geographic distribution was generally similar to 1960. By 1980, the number of cities reporting gangs had grown to 179, with the same geographic distribution. This changed dramatically in the 1980s, however, and by 1992, the number of cities reporting gangs more than quadrupled to 769, and the midwestern region was saturated with gang-involved cities stretching from Omaha and Wichita to Cleveland and Columbus.

One of Thrasher's most enduring observations was that no two gangs are exactly alike. It might be added that no two gang cities are exactly alike, either. In the past two decades, studies of midwestern gangs have demonstrated that gang presence has expanded far beyond Chicago and that there are both similarities and significant diversity among gangs as among cities. For example, while both Los Angeles and Chicago have long and sustained histories of gangs in their communities, midwestern cities other than Chicago have not had the same experience. Even those midwestern cities that had gangs as early as the 1920s—such as St. Louis, Minneapolis, and Cleveland—have not experienced the institutionalization of gang cultures that occurred in Los Angeles and Chicago. Instead, the midwestern gang experience (with the exception of Chicago) involves newly emerging or reemergence of gangs. One of the main implications of this is that (again, with the exception of Chicago) midwestern cities have not had to confront the intergenerational transmission of gang cultures that have existed for a century or so. As a result of this difference, gangs in most of the Midwest are more loosely organized, and gang culture is a hybrid of symbols and sentiments from different generations and places.

The social organization of gangs in Chicago involves two "gang nations," or "supergangs," under which there are many smaller gang "sets." The two gang nations are known as the Folks and the People. These gang nations in Chicago have had much better-developed organizational structures and behavioral norms than has generally been the case in other parts of the nation. Some of the major Chicago gangs in the past have included the Gangster Disciples, the Latin Kings, the Vicelords, and the Blackstone Rangers (later known as the Black P. Stone Nation and, subsequently, as the El Ruk'ns).

Gangs that developed in the Midwest during the last two decades of the twentieth century have frequently adopted names that are based on those in Chicago or Los Angeles. Many local citizens, seeing the names of these gangs in graffiti, assumed that their areas were being invaded by gangs from either Chicago or Los Angeles. However, research has consistently established that the adoption of gang names from Chicago or Los Angeles has not usually reflected substantial gang migration. Instead, it generally reflected the diffusion of the cultural symbols represented by gangs and the fact that local youth wanted to emulate those symbols of gang life, including the adoption of gang names, clothing styles, language, and graffiti.

By the early 1990s, however, more than seven hundred U.S. cities, including many in the Midwest, reported some in-migration of gang members from elsewhere, although the *number* of gang migrants was small. Local gangs still consisted overwhelmingly of local youth. In some cases, gangs have reemerged from earlier eras. In others, the development of gangs is a new phenomenon. In both cases, the antecedent conditions associated with gangs are often similar.

The history of gangs in St. Louis and Milwaukee is illustrative of the midwestern experience outside of Chicago. The first presence in St. Louis of groups that we would now define as gangs was documented as early as 1878. The earliest gangs were largely located in areas of the city such as the river district north of downtown that experienced more severe socioeconomic problems, partly related to the patterns of immigration and industrialization that were taking place in St. Louis at that time. Most of the gang members were recent Irish and German immigrants. Gangs reemerged in St. Louis in the 1950s, again due to rapid changes in the demographic and socioeconomic structure of the city. Most of these gang members were white, but for the first time, African American gangs began to appear in the western and northwestern neighborhoods, with which they strongly identified. Contemporary gangs of St. Louis continue to reflect some of the same underlying factors that can be found in the genesis of the earliest known gangs in the city.

Gangs emerged in Milwaukee in the 1950s, when the children of minority immigrant factory workers formed gangs that then faded out of existence as their members matured. Contemporary gangs in Milwaukee, mostly African American and Hispanic, emerged in the early 1980s from competition and conflict between break-dancing groups and between informal corner groups. Although Milwaukee can be considered a city with emergent rather than reemergent gangs, some of the factors contributing to gang formation are similar to those in St. Louis, Cleveland, and elsewhere—severe economic decline associated with deindustrialization and rapid sociodemographic change.

Sources and Further Reading: Scott H. Decker and Barrik Van Winkle, *Life in the Gang* (1996); Arnold Goldstein and C. Ronald Huff, *The Gang Intervention Handbook* (1993); John M. Hagedorn, *People and Folks* (1988); C. Ronald Huff, *Gangs in America III* (2002); Malcolm W. Klein, *The American Street Gang* (1995); Jody Miller, *One of the Guys: Girls, Gangs, and Gender* (2001); Irving A. Spergel, *The Youth Gang Problem* (1995); Frederic Thrasher, *The Gang: A Study of 1,313 Gangs in Chicago* (1927).

C. Ronald Huff
University of California–Irvine

Police

Midwestern police departments do not differ radically from other police departments around the nation, but the police officers that work in this region of the country do serve within a unique and dynamic setting. According to the Federal Bureau of Investigation, the Midwest has the lowest regional violent crime rate in the country and the second-lowest rate of property crime. These relatively low crime levels do not mean that crime is an unimportant issue in the Midwest or that police officers are less essential there. While the Midwest as a whole can boast comparatively low crime rates, the urban areas of the Midwest exhibit a differentiated patchwork of criminal activity. Communities like Troy, Michigan, and Fargo, North Dakota, exhibit very low levels of crime, but other cities like St. Louis, Missouri, Detroit, Michigan, and Topeka, Kansas, have some of the highest crime rates in the country.

To reduce crime rates, midwestern cities have recruited and trained thousands of men and women to maintain order and enforce the law. Historically, the midwestern pattern of policing was influenced by the London Metropolitan System, as well as other American police departments such as those of New York City and Philadelphia.

The Midwest has also distinctly contributed to the advancement and professionalization of policing in the United States. As early as 1866, the Detroit Police Department systematically located and graphically mapped out areas of their city that were thought to be vulnerable to crime. This was an important precursor to the more sophisticated statistical crime-mapping programs that many large city police departments use today. In the late nineteenth century, Chicago was the first city to install call boxes along police beats. This innovation allowed police officers to respond to community problems more quickly and with the proper personnel. Subsequently many police departments around the country implemented this midwestern invention. Although police cruisers are a common sight today, the practice of utilizing automobiles in police work did not occur until 1899, when police officers in

Akron, Ohio, used them for the first time. Other policing innovations of the Midwest include road-blocks, radio patrol cars, and the nation's first crime detection laboratory. With so many important advancements, the Midwest was a major pioneer in developing new police technologies and procedures.

The Midwest continues to play an important leadership role in American law enforcement. At the turn of the century, over 120,000 full-time law enforcement officers were employed in the region. Chicago has the second-largest metropolitan police force in the United States, with approximately 13,500 sworn officers on its payroll. Like most U.S. police departments, the Chicago Police Department is styled after a military command hierarchy. The individual at the top of the command structure is the Superintendent of Police, who is personally selected by the mayor from a list of three nominees provided by the Chicago Police Commission. Other ranks in the department include Commander, Captain, Lieutenant, Sergeant, and Police Officer. As with most urban police departments, new recruits in Chicago begin their service as patrol officers, then after a designated period of time, have the option of applying for a transfer to a specialized unit. Some popular specialized units in the Chicago Police Department include homicide detectives, canine officers, mounted police, gang taskforce, marine patrol, and rapid response officers.

Police work involves a wide variety of duties and service functions. A great deal of an officer's time is spent providing assistance to people seeking help with particular problems. Midwestern police departments have generally performed these services well, but there have been times when police brutality and police corruption have damaged the relationship between the police and the communities they serve. Perhaps one of the most famous instances of police brutality occurred in Chicago during the 1968 Democratic Presidential Convention. While Democrats were in the process of nominating Hubert Humphrey as their candidate for President, demonstrators protesting the Vietnam War were clashing with police personnel on the streets of Chicago. Many of the protestors were interested only in carrying out peaceful demonstrations, but some fully intended to create as much chaos as possible. Overreacting to the vociferous and disruptive crowds, many Chicago police officers beat and assaulted demonstrators. Many of these beatings were captured on film by the national media and subsequently broadcast around the world. By the end of the convention, over one hundred demonstrators had been hospitalized and several hundred more had been injured. The incident tarnished the reputation of the Chicago Police Department as it drew national attention to the topic of police brutality.

As with police departments in other regions of the country, those in the Midwest have had to deal with corruption and the misuse of authority for personal benefit. In 1991, for example, nine Detroit police officers were arrested on drug corruption charges. In 1998, forty-four members of five law enforcement agencies in Ohio were charged with protecting drug trafficking operations in Cleveland and northern Ohio. While professional probity has been violated in a number of instances, most officers serve their communities with high standards of professional service.

Ultimately urban and suburban police officers in the Midwest have the responsibility to enforce the law and maintain order. While the typical situations an officer encounters will vary considerably depending on the size of the community and his or her assignment, all midwestern officers work within a region that has a long history of supporting and advancing law enforcement. While the Midwest sometimes experiences problems related to improper policing, the region has benefited considerably from a long tradition of technological advancements and community service.

Sources and Further Reading: Egon Bittner, *Aspects of Police Work* (1990); Larry K. Gaines and Victor E. Kappeler, *Policing in America*, 4th ed. (2003); Richard C. Lindberg, *To Serve and Collect* (1998); Ann L. Pastore and Kathleen Maguire, eds., *Sourcebook of Criminal Justice Statistics, 2001* (2002); Louis A. Radelet and David L. Carter, *The Police and the Community*, 5th ed. (1994); James F. Richardson, *Urban Police in the United States* (1974); John C. Schneider, *Detroit and the Problem of Order, 1830–1880* (1980); Daniel Walker, *Rights in Conflict: Chicago's 7 Brutal Days* (1968).

Richard Featherstone
University of Northern Iowa

Race Riots

Race riots in the United States have deep and powerful roots. Social convulsions of this kind have, in fact, become integral components of the American political landscape, and function as pivotal points of the social and political history of the Midwest.

The syndrome of racial violence in the Midwest was initiated in Evansville, Indiana, in 1903 by a white mob intent on lynching a black prisoner accused of murdering a white man. Blacks armed with guns attempted to clear the white mob out, but were chased from the downtown area after a white man was shot. Mob violence erupted in Springfield, Ohio, in 1904, from the shooting of a white policeman by a black man involved in a domestic dispute. The black defendant was dragged from jail by an angry white mob,

Commencement of the race riot at 29th Street Beach. The Chicago Commission on Race Relations, *The Negro in Chicago* (Chicago: University of Chicago Press, 1922).

shot, and hoisted by his neck from a telephone pole. In subsequent days, groups of white citizens organized raids on the black business district called the Levee and burned it to the ground. Racial violence returned to Springfield in 1906. The precipitating event on this occasion was the arrest of two black men on suspicion of cutting two white men during a fight and killing a white railroad brakeman. Before the violence subsided, a number of black businesses and homes were burned. Eight whites who were arrested and found guilty of rioting were sentenced to one dollar plus court costs, which would be suspended if the defendants demonstrated good behavior.

Another major riot took place in Springfield, Illinois, in 1908. The white community of Springfield was whipped into a frenzy by the alleged murder of a white engineer by a black drifter and allegations of the rape of a white woman by a local black man. Pressure on the black community was so intense that many blacks left Springfield to live temporarily in other Illinois cities. Black fears were confirmed when a black man seeking to protect his property was lynched by a white mob. Whites also destroyed a number of black homes and businesses in black areas called the Levee and the Badlands.

Racial violence in the Midwest escalated to a fever pitch during the years surrounding World War I. One of the most serious riot outbreaks took place in 1917 in East St. Louis, Illinois. City Democrats fanned the flames of racial resentment by accusing the Republicans of importing blacks into the city and rigging elections by "colonizing" the black vote. White trade unionists stirred resentment against blacks by accusing them of being brought in as strike breakers. These sentiments became the seedbed for racial violence when white trade union members left a meeting and began beating unmercifully every black person they encountered. The situation was transformed into mob violence that penetrated the black community and destroyed black property, including homes, churches, and schools. Blacks fought back valiantly. When the smoke cleared, nine whites and thirty-nine blacks were dead, making the East St. Louis riots the deadliest race riots in American history. Two years later, the proliferation of race riots reached such an unprecedented level that the summer of 1919 would be known as the Red Summer.

Clashes between blacks and whites at Chicago beaches led to an incredible series of violent racial confrontations across the city. The attack on black communities was led by Chicago's "athletic clubs," gangs of white youth that attacked blacks to "keep them in their place." Experiencing hostility and violence from their white coworkers in the stockyards, black workers stayed away from their jobs by the thousands during the height of the 1919 Chicago riots.

Racial violence continued to flare up periodically in the Midwest in the 1920s, 1930s, 1940s, and 1950s. Riots in Tulsa, Oklahoma, in 1921 resulted in the death of numerous black citizens. On August 7, 1930, three blacks accused of killing a white youth and attacking his girlfriend were lynched by a mob of over a thousand in Marion, Indiana. Smoldering racial conflict centering on black movement into the automobile industry led to a major riot in Detroit in 1943. Pulsating for thirty hours without letup, the Detroit riot left twenty-five black people and nine white people dead.

These events would be surpassed by the racial clashes transpiring in American cities in the 1960s. Fueled by rising black political and racial consciousness, the riots of the 1960s would push cities in the Midwest toward unparalleled plateaus of violence. Civil disorder erupted in Cleveland when blacks gathered to protest at a white bar that displayed a racially offensive sign. Violence raged in Cleveland's black community for a full week. When it finally ended, four blacks had been killed, hundreds of people injured, and blocks of buildings gutted. Cincinnati experienced civil disorder during the turbulent summer of 1967. Black youngsters who attended a community meeting at a local junior high school began to set small fires on the street and throw Molotov cocktails. Police were called in after firemen were blocked from putting out fires. These events led to several days of rioting that came to a halt only with the imposition of National Guard troops. The race riots in Detroit in 1967 were the product of long years of conflict between the black community and the police. A police raid on a black after-hours club escalated into a major riot that left thirty-three blacks and ten whites dead. Much of the death and destruction came at the hands of National Guard personnel untrained in handling a major urban uprising. The outbreak of rioting in Cincinnati again, in 2001, clearly demonstrates that the issue of black community–police relations remains a continuing source of social and political conflict for cities in the Midwest.

Sources and Further Reading: Kerner Commission, *Report of the National Advisory Commission on Civil Disorders* (1968); Anthony M. Landis, "They Refused to Stay in Their Place," M.A. thesis, Southern Illinois University, Edwardsville (2002); Alfred McClung Lee and Norman D. Humphrey, *Race Riot, Detroit 1943* (1968); J. Paul Mitchell, ed., *Race Riots in Black and White* (1970); Elliot Rudwick, *Race Riot at East Saint Louis, July 2, 1917* (1964); Carl Sandburg, *The Chicago Race Riots, July, 1919* (1969); David O. Sears and John B. McConahay, *Los Angeles Riot Study: Riot Participation* (1967).

William Nelson
The Ohio State University

Economy and Technology

Labor Movements and Working-Class Culture

SECTION EDITOR
Richard Schneirov

Section Contents

Overview

From the Civil War era until the mid-twentieth century, the Midwest was the storm center of the American labor movement. From the Haymarket Affair in 1886 and the Pullman Strike in 1894, to the General Motors Sit-Down Strike of 1936–1937 and the defeats of the Staley, Caterpillar, and newspaper workers' strikes in the mid-1990s, midwestern workers were central to the unfolding of American labor history.

The Midwest's first wageworkers serviced the region's agricultural economy as harvest hands, timber cutters, skilled plowers, and teamsters. However, the first large group of wageworkers who had a consciousness of themselves as a distinct social class were the German and Irish immigrants, who in the 1830s, 1840s, and 1850s, dug the region's canals—among them, the Wabash and Erie canal and the Illinois and Michigan canal in Indiana and Illinois. These men were unique because they were attracted from the East by the premium wages. They worked in gangs, faced extremely hazardous working conditions—notably, the ever-present threat of epidemic disease and accidents from gunpowder blasting and hard labor with pick and shovel—and were utterly dependent on wages. Beginning in the 1850s, a second group of migrants known as "boomers" built, operated, and repaired the region's first railroads.

The transportation revolution made possible by the labor of these men paved the way for the midwestern industrialization boom in the mid-nineteenth century. By 1870, cities including Detroit, Chicago, St. Louis, and Milwaukee were major manufacturing centers and sites for agricultural processing, banking, insurance, and other mercantile activities. Steelmaking and manufacturing, coal and iron ore mining, slaughtering and meatpacking, lumbering and furniture making, along with rail transportation were the most dynamic sectors of the Midwest economy and provided employment for its workforce, generally first- and second-generation immigrants.

Railroad workers became the first large group of workers to organize unions in the Midwest. At first, these men enjoyed high wages and excellent working conditions because of the Midwest's labor scarcity. But recurrent financial panics beginning in the 1870s, largely due to railroad overbuilding, and the new managerial strategies devised by the railroad corporations combined to threaten workers' existing standards and created the framework for extended labor conflict. Three great national labor upheavals marked the last quarter of the nineteenth century, and in all of them Midwest railroaders and urban industrial workers played major roles.

In 1877, a spontaneous national railroad strike against depression wage-cutting spread from West Virginia into the cities and railroad junctions of Pennsylvania, Indiana, Illinois, and Missouri. The railroad strike precipitated strikes involving other industrial workers, and police and militia efforts to escort strikebreakers or to attack crowds of strikers resulted in violent confrontations and riots. By the end of the great 1877 upheaval, tens of thousands had participated, and over a hundred lay dead.

As chief railroad and industrial center of the Midwest, Chicago became the staging point for the second great labor upheaval of this period. By the mid-1880s, the deepening crisis of overproduction that beset national industry in this period found its flash point in that city, with its well-organized workforce and strong socialist influence. As one labor leader boasted, Chicago "makes labor history and makes it fast. The exceptional is always apt to happen here. . . . Chicago is the workers' paradise."

Foreman, Lykes-Youngstown Corporation, Youngstown, Ohio, 1920. Ohio Historical Society, N 59 S.

In 1885, following victories by the Knights of Labor, a labor organization with aspirations to enroll all the nation's workers, over railroad tycoon Jay Gould's Midwest-based railroad system, thousands of workers streamed into the Knights and other unions. In 1886, almost ninety thousand organized Chicago workers struck to establish the eight-hour day. At a protest meeting sponsored by anarchists on May 4 in Chicago's Haymarket Square, a bomb exploded that eventually martyred seven police officers. In the ensuing Red Scare, police arrested seven anarchist leaders, and four were convicted on insubstantial evidence and eventually hanged. The Haymarket Affair and the martyred anarchists became labor's first great *cause célèbre*, both nationally and internationally.

In response to the 1886 labor upheaval, railroad managers united to form the General Manager's Association (GMA) to coordinate antiunion efforts. The GMA gave the railroad corporations the upper hand in labor relations and led directly to the defeat of the skilled workers "brotherhoods" in the 1888 Burlington Strike. At least one man realized the need to create a new type of labor organization that would not only federate the brotherhoods, but draw in less skilled railroad workers. Eugene V. Debs of Terre Haute, Indiana, founded the American Railway Union (ARU) in 1893, the nation's first large industrial union. The ARU-led Pullman Strike, the third great upheaval of this period, the following year shut down the nation's rail arteries from the Midwest to the Pacific Coast for two weeks before it was crushed by a federal court injunction and federal troops.

Using its experience of success as well as defeat, the labor movement consolidated and moved in new directions. In 1886, the same year as Haymarket, the craft unions, soon joined by remnants of the Knights, came together in the new American Federation of Labor (AFL) under the leadership of Samuel Gompers. The craft unions believed that autonomous national craft unions with centralized strike funds and benefits under the direction of paid, full-time leaders would enable members to permanently improve their pay and working conditions. They were right. After a slow start, the AFL grew to 1.7 million members in 1904, about 18 percent of them in Chicago.

The Midwest's high level of labor organization, its large number of immigrant workers with radical traditions, and the region's bitter class conflict made it fertile ground for labor, radical, and socialist parties. Between 1885 and 1888, labor parties could be counted in seventy-eight midwestern towns and cities. The Socialist Labor Party (founded in 1876), the anarchist International Working People's Association (1883), the Labor-Populist alliance within the People's Party (1894), the forerunners of Debs's Socialist Party of

America (1901), and the Communist movement (1919) were all centered, at least initially, in Chicago. According to one survey, 70 percent of Socialist office-holders elected in 1911 came from ten midwestern states, and generally small- to medium-sized cities such as Dayton and Marysville in Ohio; Flint, Michigan; Marion, Indiana; and a few large cities, notably Minneapolis and Milwaukee. Indeed, a Socialist mayor ran the Milwaukee municipal government from 1910 to 1940 with one four-year exception. The party's largest newspaper, the *Appeal to Reason*, was published in Girard, Kansas. Two of the party's three national leaders were based in Terre Haute and Milwaukee, Debs and Victor Berger. Other Socialist leaders also hailed from the Midwest: Algie Simons from Chicago, Max Hayes from Cleveland, William English Walling from Indianapolis, and later Norman Thomas from Marion, Ohio.

No mention of Midwest labor's political leanings and political influence would be complete without a discussion of Progressivism, which had its origins in the Midwest. The labor movement and ethnic working people were major elements in the diverse constituencies, campaign appeals, and administration policies of Hazen Pingree in Detroit, Sam "Golden Rule" Jones and Brand Whitlock in Toledo, Robert La Follette in Wisconsin, and John Peter Altgeld and Edward F. Dunne in Chicago. The Progressivism of the Midwest during the turn of the last century laid the groundwork for strong state-level movements and then the national Progressivism of Theodore Roosevelt, William Howard Taft, Woodrow Wilson, and the Farmer-Labor Party.

Socially conscious women comprised another key progressive group with midwestern origins. Most notably, Jane Addams and Florence Kelley emerged from Chicago's social settlement house, Hull House, to national prominence. Addams became a leading women's suffrage and peace advocate, ultimately awarded the Nobel Peace Prize, while Kelley inaugurated the movement against sweatshop labor and, in 1899, formed the National Consumers League, the most important Progressive lobbying group for statewide legislation addressing the concerns of working women and, indeed, consumers generally.

The most distinctive contribution of midwestern labor progressives was the idea of "industrial democracy," a term coined by Chicagoan Henry Demarest Lloyd in 1893, which became a focus of public debate during the period of World War I. Frank Walsh, a lawyer and Kansas City newspaper editor and a pro-labor Irish nationalist, became the key figure linking the labor movement, progressive reform causes, and electoral politics. In 1916, Walsh wrote the majority report for a major federal commission investigating labor relations, which became a precursor of New Deal policies on social welfare and collective bargaining. When the war broke out, Walsh and the so-called Indianapolis group of trade unions based in the Midwest worked to parlay labor's support of the war effort into federal support for collective bargaining for America's working people.

The mainstay of Midwest labor's strength in the period between 1900 and the advent of 1930s industrial unionism were "craft-industrial" unions, which comprised the large majority of AFL unions. Originally craft in nature, they realized the need to organize other crafts and lesser skilled workers to survive. By organizing metropolitan and sometimes regional markets, these unions were able to set minimum wages and mitigate the intense competition faced by small- to medium-sized employers. The most important AFL industrial union, the United Mine Workers Union, used the same strategy to organize the Midwest's Central Competitive Field. But, except during World War I, AFL unions were unable to organize the bastions of large-scale corporate-run industry, whose markets were national and international in scope.

American industry experienced a second industrial revolution around the beginning of the twentieth century. As industrial growth slowed in clothing manufacture, mining, and the railroads, a new group of industries emerged as the leading sector of the nation's economic growth. They were operated by corporate bureaucracies, which set up welfare programs to manage employee discontent. These new industries relied primarily on technologies, such as electricity, synthetics, and automobiles; employed mass production technologies, such as Henry Ford's new assembly line, that marginalized skilled craft workers; and stabilized competition without union help through advertising, consumer lending, and oligopolistic market practices. These new industries were concentrated in the Midwest. Detroit became the center of the auto industry; Youngstown, Cleveland, Pittsburgh, Gary, and East Chicago became major sites for steelmaking; Akron was the core of the rubber industry; Chicago, Kansas City, and Omaha served as the location of the meatpacking industry; and the electrical industry dispersed throughout the Midwest and the rest of the country.

The common steel, electrical, and autoworker was an immigrant. But the Irish and Germans, who flooded the labor market in the middle to late nineteenth century had, by the early twentieth century, moved up to skilled, supervisory, and white-collar positions within the job hierarchy. Southern and eastern European immigrants and, to a lesser extent, African Americans and Mexicans, took their place at the bottom. One estimate is that 60 percent of the workforce in basic industry was composed of new European immigrants and their children. By the 1910s, the ethnic identification of these workers fused into a strong class awareness for the first time. America's working people in this period built a deeply rooted, working-class culture based in industrial communities and networks of churches, union halls, leisure institutions, and benevolent societies. Its prime characteristic was an intense sociability and defensive solidarity, which allowed workers and their families to cope with the ever-present threat of economic insecurity. No less important, however, was the immense pride working people felt in having built the country they loved with their own hard labor and sacrificed disproportionately for it in virtually every war.

Beginning in the mid-1930s, John L. Lewis, who was raised in an Iowa coal town, helped create and then led the Congress of Industrial Organizations (CIO) in mobilizing unprecedented numbers of workers in a fight for workplace dignity. CIO workers, largely in the Midwest, staged a series of epic contests whose effect on America's working class was every bit as significant as the great railroad struggles of the late nineteenth century. In 1934, violent strikes and confrontations mobilized thousands of supporters in Minneapolis and Toledo and helped push Franklin D. Roosevelt's administration to support the National Labor Relations Act (also called the Wagner Act), labor's charter for collective bargaining. Then in 1936–1937, the autoworkers in Flint, Michigan, sat down in buildings of the big General Motors plant and achieved the first great breakthrough in unionizing corporate-run industry. A sit-down wave spread to downtown Detroit and then to other Midwest industrial centers; altogether about 500 thousand workers participated. Within the year, U.S. Steel capitulated, but the smaller "Little Steel" companies held on, precipitating a 1937 strike still remembered because of a Memorial Day Massacre of strikers by police in Chicago. Meanwhile, the Teamsters Union led a comeback of AFL-sponsored unionism resulting from a series of bitter strikes in Midwest cities, including Detroit and Minneapolis. By the end of World War II, when labor solidified its gains with a union security agreement with the federal government, more than fifteen million workers had become union members, as compared with three million in 1933.

During this period, large numbers of African Americans moved north and became members of industrial unions such as the United Auto Workers (UAW) and United Steel Workers. African Americans, however, still faced harsh and systematic discrimination, although of a qualitatively different kind than that faced even by the most downtrodden white ethnics. The CIO and UAW supported the struggle for equal rights, led at the time by A. Philip Randolph of the Brotherhood of Sleeping Car Porters and the National Association for the Advancement of Colored People (NAACP), resulting in the establishment of Fair Employment Practices Commissions in many midwestern states. Still, many of the newly organized ethnic workers, as well as other urban whites, balked at full racial equality.

In the postwar era, the Midwest working class was reconstituted in another way. Housewives left the kitchen for the factory and office, first during the war and more dramatically during the 1950s and 1960s. At first, many unions resisted opening up skilled trades positions to blacks and women, and as a result many became objects of court orders following the 1964 Civil Rights Act. Not only did blacks benefit from the new law, but women, for the first time, could successfully challenge in court sex-segregated job categories and seniority lists and lower wages for the same work.

Many unions took advantage of the new workforce composition, resulting in a surge of unionization by public employees on the federal, state, and local levels following President John F. Kennedy's executive order granting collective bargaining to federal employees. Taking the lead in the nation, all the states comprising the Old Northwest Territory (except Indiana) had comprehensive collective bargaining statutes for public workers by the mid-1980s. The American Federation of State, County, and Municipal Employees (AFSCME) and the Service Employees International Union (SEIU) were among the fastest-growing Midwest unions. By the 1980s, the combined membership of the two teachers unions—whose origin can be traced to Chicago's Margaret Haley, founder of the American Federation of Teachers—exceeded that of any industrial union. Nonetheless, unlike the ethnic workers of the 1930s, the new female and minority workers looked as much to civil rights groups beyond the workplace as to unions for support. The racial and gender struggles unleashed by the 1960s continued into the following decades, giving rise to an array of new social rights, for example, the rights to privacy, a safe workplace, freedom from sexual harassment and age discrimination, and family and medical leave, as well as affirmative action hiring.

The spread of a consumer culture that was in part the fruit of hard-won struggles for higher wages and job security in the 1930s and 1940s was widely seen by the 1960s as having bought off urban ethnic workers, as evidenced by their lack of support for those currently struggling. Indeed, scholars and journalists debated whether a distinct working-class way of life still existed in the wake of the doubling of take-home pay

and the large rise in home ownership between 1948 and 1973. This analysis was rendered moot by the 1980s as midwestern workers endured the brunt of intensifying global competition (especially from Japan), deindustrialization, corporate outsourcing, and the shift to service employment. In addition, the anti-union animus of Ronald Reagan's administration emboldened organized labor's enemies. Altogether, unionized industrial employment in the Midwest sustained a devastating blow. The region took on the appellation Rust Belt as jobs shifted to the "green fields" of the Sun Belt, Mexico, and overseas. In the first half of the 1980s, employment declined in the Midwest, while it rose by 7 percent in the rest of the nation. Once-prosperous working-class communities in the East and Great Lakes region became "brown fields" as $15-an-hour steel workers were forced to take $5-an-hour jobs at McDonald's and Wal-Mart, and urban tax bases required to meet the costs of essential public services eroded.

After a series of major defeats during extended strikes, the packinghouse workers at Hormel in Austin, Minnesota, in 1985–1986, the Caterpillar workers in Peoria in 1994–1995, the Staley workers in Decatur in 1993–1995, and newspaper workers in Detroit in 1995–1997 were forced to accept concessionary contracts. Union prestige and membership plummeted in the Midwest's industrial centers. Though starting at a higher percentage, the decline in unionization in the industrial areas of the Midwest, from 39 percent in 1964 to 19 percent in 2000, closely tracked that of the nation, from 29.3 percent in 1964 to 13.6 percent in 2000.

It would be a mistake to exaggerate the significance of the decline of a working-class way of life and labor organization. As it was a century ago, midwestern labor is in a period of major readjustment. A third industrial revolution is taking shape, characterized by rising investment in new Information Age technologies in the workplace, corporate reengineering, and a continuing racial, ethnic, and sexual recomposition of the labor force. Virtually all new growth in union organizing has occurred among new groups of workers, particularly those in the public and service sectors. For example, by 2002, 42.5 percent of public workers in the twelve Midwest states belonged to unions. Amid this structural change in the economy, the Midwest continues to be more unionized than the nation as a whole, and Midwest labor remains a major, albeit weakened, cultural and political force.

The following section on labor movements and working-class culture in the Midwest is organized both chronologically, to allow readers to grasp the sweep and impact of historical developments, and topically, to facilitate special treatment of such subjects as women and African Americans along with aspects of everyday working-class life.

Sources and Further Reading: James R. Barrett, *Work and Community in the Jungle: Chicago's Packinghouse Workers, 1894–1922* (1987); Kevin Boyle, *The UAW and the Heyday of American Liberalism, 1945–1968* (1995); Lizabeth Cohen, *Making a New Deal: Industrial Workers in Chicago, 1919–1939* (1990); Charles Craypo and Bruce Nissen, eds., *Grand Designs: The Impact of Corporate Strategies on Workers, Unions, and Communities* (1993); Lisa M. Fine, *The Souls of the Skyscraper: Female Clerical Workers in Chicago, 1870–1930* (1990); Sidney Fine, *Sit-Down: The General Motors Strike of 1936–1937* (1969); Stephen Franklin, *Three Strikes: Labor's Heartland Losses and What They Mean for Working Americans* (2001); Nelson Lichtenstein, *State of the Union: A Century of American Labor—Politics and Society in Twentieth-Century* (2002); Daniel Nelson, *Farm and Factory: Workers in the Midwest, 1880–1990* (1995); Cheri Register, *Packinghouse Daughter: A Memoir* (2001); Nick Salvatore, *Eugene V. Debs: Citizen and Socialist* (1982); Richard Schneirov, *Labor and Urban Politics: Class Conflict and the Origins of Modern Liberalism in Chicago, 1864–97* (1998); Richard Schneirov, *Pride and Solidarity: A History of the Plumbers and Pipefitters of Columbus, Ohio, 1889–1989* (1992); Shelton Stromquist, *A Generation of Boomers: The Pattern of Railroad Labor Conflict in Nineteenth-Century America* (1987).

Richard Schneirov
Indiana State University

Antebellum Labor

The region that became known as the Midwest was conquered and absorbed into the American republic at a unique juncture in history. Created by the Northwest Ordinance at a time when the Spirit of '76 momentarily weakened the grip of slavery, the region was the nation's first frontier free of slavery. Land hunger in older sections of the nation had grown acute due to the steady growth of farm families and by impediments to western settlement, first by English edict, then by Revolutionary War, and later by Native American resistance. Finally in 1794, with the defeat of the stronghold of native resistance in the Battle of Fallen Timbers, the floodgates of westward migration opened, and farmers began to stream over the Appalachians. In a fairly short time, an extensive crescent of settlement arced along the northern shore of the Ohio River from Steubenville to St. Louis. Opened to American settlement in the youth of its national unity, the Midwest's early population was a fairly equal mix of Yankees and southerners, and its commercial ties with the East just as equally stretched along both the Erie Canal to New York and the National Road through Virginia to Baltimore.

At the base of the economic pyramid was farming. To the south of this crescent were Virginians and Kentuckians who raised corn and hogs in plots carved out of woodlands, while to the north were New Englanders and New Yorkers who built dairy farms. After the introduction of heavy steel plows that could turn the dauntingly thick sod of the prairies, an empire in wheat set in motion the nation's transformation to an industrial economy.

Though much of the work of day-to-day farming was confined to the family, and therefore outside the realm of wages, even the most isolated and self-sufficient farms could not escape the pull of market relations. Early settlers had no choice but to carve their homesteads out of forested areas, and the initial labor of clearing the land was performed by countless numbers of itinerant workers whom they hired to chop down trees, dig out stumps, and build fences. In the prairies farmer-owners employed skilled plowers to break the virgin sod. Farmers who needed to get their goods to the nearest river port or market town often had to hire teamsters. Across the region, late summer and early fall set in motion the slow migration of harvest hands, workers who reaped wheat and wages, following the line of ripening grain north from the Ohio River to the Great Lakes. But because these workers labored in a place and time of rapid growth and change, and because many of them were young and viewed their work as either a phase of life, a stepping stone to something better, or a season in a year filled with other struggles, they did not identify themselves with their work or even view themselves as part of a larger group of workers.

Many of the products of these workers were consumed in subsistence, but an increasing volume moved down rivers and crude roads to market towns where they were processed, packed, and shipped to points around the globe. Flour mills spread westward with the expanding cultivation of wheat and constituted the first industries in a crescent of cities from Akron to Milwaukee to Minneapolis. Steubenville, Ohio, became a center for wool processing and, by 1830, had a steam-powered woolen mill that employed 158 laborers. Towns such as Marietta and Portsmouth became early centers of shipbuilding for the booming river trade, but were soon eclipsed by Cincinnati, which emerged as the Queen City of the West by funneling Ohio's bounty down the Ohio River. Likewise, Indiana's largest town in 1850 was New Albany, its best port on the Ohio.

In order to capture a larger share of the wealth generated by trade in farm products, in the two decades between the 1820s and 1840s, states competed to extend canals to integrate their waterways. The work of digging these deep ditches brought to the Midwest thousands of Irish immigrants for whom such rude and cruel labor was all America offered. Unlike the seasonal or temporary farmworkers, canalers did view themselves as a distinct group, even a class with common interests. Ethnicity bound them together, certainly, but so did the gang labor they performed, the isolated bunkhouses they shared, and their dependence on their boss who subcontracted the work they subsisted on. Though they often fought among themselves, when pushed by their bosses or surrounding communities, they could act with violent unity. Before the canal era ended, midwestern canal workers banded together in at least eight riots and four strikes.

Other pockets of wageworkers who worked together in gangs were located throughout the Midwest. A lead-mining boom brought thousands of treasure-seekers to the Fever River basin around Galena, Illinois, by 1828. When the surface nuggets were all dug out, the boomtown mining camps were succeeded by an influx of ten thousand, mostly Cornish, miners who cut the deep shafts and eventually supplied the union army with shot. Further north, stands of valuable white pine sent thousands of young men to the Wisconsin woods and to the sawmills at Green Bay, Oshkosh, and Eau Claire. By the 1850s, when the sawmills converted from water to steam power, their workers managed to cut an average of 200 million board feet each season. North yet from the pineries was the Keweenaw district of the Upper Peninsula of Michigan where the discovery of copper bodies, some weighing hundreds of tons, created the beginnings of a massive copper mining industry in the 1850s.

But most people who did not work the land and lived by their labor gravitated to the region's growing towns. In these places, labor was in great demand to move and process agricultural goods, to supply manufactured goods to farmers, and to build the towns themselves. Throughout the antebellum period, much of this work remained small in scale and personal. Milwaukee's Best family brewery, like the twenty-five other breweries in the city, operated with four employees in the 1850s, some of whom boarded with the Bests in their small clapboard house. Indiana's hardwood groves attracted skilled woodworkers and furniture makers who set up small shops with only a few employees in virtually every town. In many areas the artisan system of apprenticeship, graduating to journeymen's independence, leading in some cases to self-employed master's status, still prevailed.

The greatest concentration of workers in the Midwest was in the city of Cincinnati, the region's largest city. By 1840, nearly one-third of Cincinnati's population was composed of workers of some variety (mostly in manufacturing), a proportion higher than any other city in the United States. Cincinnati had large steamboat yards employing scores of men, its slaughterhouse workers disassembled nearly a quarter million hogs each year, and its iron workers supplied a large proportion of the Midwest's farmers with hardware. It was in Cincinnati and a handful of other growing cities—Detroit, Cleveland, Milwaukee, Columbus, and Chicago—that the region's first labor unions arose.

Skilled workers were the first to form unions and proved the most politically ambitious segment of workers throughout the period. The first unions were organized by printers, building trades workers, cabinetmakers, and tailors in the 1830s. Most of them viewed their role as essentially conservative: defending the traditions and customs of their crafts against the changes wrought by a modernizing economy. Early unions protested against employers' attempts to cut wages and rallied around the demand for a ten-hour day, but much of their interest was political. Still, by the end of the 1840s, the economic gravity of the region began to pull the center of labor activism westward. In 1849, a national congress of labor unions and labor reformers was held in Cincinnati. The following year it convened in Chicago, and in 1855 it held one of its last annual gatherings in Cleveland.

Politically, organized workers pointed blame at those forces that seemed to impede fair competition, such as land speculators, bankers, and corrupt politicians. Because of its distance from eastern financial centers, weak local banks, and chronic shortage of hard currency, the Midwest felt the effects of the nation's periodic financial panics and depressions with particular fury. Workers suffered not only from inflation in the price of their necessities, but from the variability in the value of the bank notes ("shinplasters," they called them) they were often paid with. These problems pushed many to think broadly about their problems. In 1836, Cincinnati's unions sent two delegates to the National Trades Union Convention (both of whom would later serve as Cincinnati mayors). One of these men, David S. Snellbaker, moved that the convention "enquire into the sources of the great system of speculation, by which they who produce nothing receive nearly all the products of the labor of those that produce. . . ."

Likewise in several midwestern towns in the 1840s, labor activists organized Working Man's Parties, which briefly challenged the political monopoly of Whigs and Democrats, but just as quickly fell apart as Andrew Jackson Democrats co-opted their agenda. Still, the independent political energy left after the demise of the workingmen's parties went in many directions. Some, however, was concentrated in a more focused political movement, the National Reformers, who demanded an end to the engrossment of land and a homestead program whereby landless workers could gain farms. Their slogan, "Vote Yourself a Farm," had wide appeal to artisans who felt increasingly trapped in the status of wage earners. The movement narrowly failed to pass a land limitation law in Wisconsin in 1851. Other workers turned inward and attempted to control the conditions in their trades by forming producer cooperatives. In Steubenville, Ohio, a group of ironworkers established a successful but short-lived cooperative foundry. Those even more radical attempted to establish utopian communes; the Midwest had a history of these, all of them failures, stretching back to 1825 when Robert Owen established the cooperative community of New Harmony, Indiana.

Like workers elsewhere in the United States, political independence and unity proved elusive as a new development affecting both economic and social issues appeared—immigration. Beginning in the 1840s, the composition of the urban working class in the Midwest began to change dramatically. Increasing numbers of German and Irish immigrants sought opportunities and refuge in midwestern cities. By 1850, nearly one-quarter of the overall population of the Old Northwest were foreign-born, with many counties containing double that proportion. Ethnic tensions and rivalries divided neighborhoods and workshops. In 1848, a Milwaukee employer ended a strike of German shoemakers by threatening to hire American-born workers if they didn't return to work. In 1855, a Protestant mob of American-born citizens rampaged through the German Over-the-Rhine neighborhood in Cincinnati. For a time the anti-Catholic Know-Nothing political movement found a foothold in the Midwest, though deeper issues of economic inequality and the political question of the still-further western territories quickly eclipsed it. Subsequently, the Midwest's unique mixture of agriculture, industry, and ethnicity served as the cradle of the Republican Party.

In the 1850s, the great expansion of the railroad through midwestern states altered forever the social and economic geography of the region. Relatively flat and agriculturally rich, the Midwest became the center of railroad growth in America. Small towns such as Indianapolis, Toledo, and Peoria grew quickly as railroad centers, while Chicago emerged as the industrial capital of the region. The iron horse not only allowed for more efficient shipment of goods from farm to city, it also facilitated the movement of manufactured goods back to farmers. Greatest of these were the new farm machines, especially Chicagoan Cyrus McCormick's mechanical harvester that replaced armies of seasonal workers. These were the seeds of another stage in the region's industrialization, one that would fundamentally alter society and the region's working-class communities after the Civil War.

Sources and Further Reading: Raymond Boryczka and Lorin Cary, *No Strength Without Union* (1982); Lawrence Lipin, *Producers, Proletarians, and Politicians* (1994); Doris McLaughlin, *Michigan Labor* (1970); Robert W. Ozanne, *The Labor Movement in Wisconsin* (1984); Steven J. Ross, *Workers on the Edge* (1985); Peter Way, *Common Labor* (1993).

Timothy Messer-Kruse
University of Toledo, Ohio

From the Knights of Labor through the American Federation of Labor, 1877–1935

The half century from the 1870s to the onset of the Great Depression in the 1930s saw dramatic changes in the character of work, in the relations between employers and employees, and in the labor force itself. Some of these changes, such as the advent of new production technologies and second wave of European immigration are well known; others are more obscure. Three broad innovations of this period are of special importance for understanding the transformation of working-class life in the Midwest: the emergence of large-scale industry, the growing heterogeneity of the labor force, and the emergence of a durable, bureaucratic labor movement, symbolized by the decline of the Knights of Labor and the growth of the American Federation of Labor.

In the middle decades of the nineteenth century, midwestern workers were concentrated in extractive industry: farming, forestry, and mining, especially coal mining. Though employment in these industries continued to grow after the 1870s, the limits to the mid-century economy were increasingly apparent. The best agricultural land had been occupied, farming in many areas was becoming highly mechanized, the great forests of the upper Midwest had been decimated, and the mines of Ohio, Indiana, and some Illinois fields faced increased competition. Local and regional manufacturing firms were also losing ground to manufacturers who produced for national markets.

By the time of the Civil War, the outlines of a new economy and a new labor force were already evident. The dramatic growth of railroading between the 1850s and 1870s marked the beginning of the era of big business. Employees were now spread over regions and states, answerable to supervisors who might be hundreds of miles away and beyond the control of local individuals, communities, and even states. The Burlington Railroad strike of 1888, in which Burlington management crushed the powerful Brotherhood of Locomotive Engineers, showed that even highly-skilled workers were no match for large corporations. The bitter Pullman Strike of 1894 reemphasized that lesson. To many midwestern workers, exemplified by Terre Haute's Eugene V. Debs, the antidote to such concentrated power was the creation of an even more powerful, worker-controlled state.

It was the great factory, however, that soon became the Midwest's most distinctive feature. By the 1870s, the Midwest had developed substantial iron smelting, processing, and fabricating industries that produced hardware, stoves, farm machinery, steam engines, rail-road track, and railroad cars. Midwestern entrepreneurs hired British immigrants for the skilled positions; and since the unskilled jobs in such plants were unattractive to local workers, they employed Irish and central European immigrants in those positions. By the Civil War, this process had created important urban centers in areas like Ohio's Mahoning Valley.

New technologies in the post–Civil War years made steel competitive with iron and stimulated the industry. By the turn of the century, they had helped make Chicago the region's industrial center and had spurred activity in many other Great Lakes cities, where mills were supplied by the great iron ore mines of northern Michigan and Minnesota. Despite the industry's dynamism, the social pattern of a half-century earlier persisted: Northern European workers filled the skilled positions, while southern and eastern European immigrants filled the less-skilled jobs.

Iron and steel fabricating were equally important in shaping the new labor force. By 1900, each of the largest cities in the region had hundreds of firms that made iron or steel objects. They, too, employed a combination of skilled and unskilled employees, drawing from the same sources. It was the expertise and experience of these firms that became the foundation for the single most famous example of industrial growth, the rise of the auto industry.

It is no surprise that auto manufacturing developed in existing centers of machinery production. Early automakers were principally assemblers who subcontracted work to machinery makers. Yet within a few years, a handful of midwestern auto firms built factories that overshadowed all but the largest steel mills. Led by Ford and General Motors, these firms produced more and more of their components, driving down costs through mass production in larger and larger plants. Ford's Highland Park plant employed thirty thousand by the 1910s, and the new River Rouge plant, the world's largest factory, employed sixty thousand in the mid-1920s.

Still, no auto firm ever produced all of its parts, and there were abundant opportunities for manufacturers of auto bodies, tires, electrical components, and a host of other parts. The most successful of them embraced the strategies of Ford and General Motors, creating giant plants in Toledo, Akron, Milwaukee, and other communities.

By the 1920s, iron and steel, autos, and auto parts dominated the region's manufacturing. Though farming continued to prosper, and mining, railroading, and other forms of manufacturing were locally important, the Midwest had become closely identified with large-scale manufacturing. That link was a critical factor in the evolution of the Midwest's labor force.

By the 1880s, most new jobs were in urban areas and in industrial activities. The decline of farming and other extractive industries around the periphery of the Midwest—the northern cut-over regions and the arid regions of the Dakotas and western Iowa, for example—created a reservoir of underemployed people who might have been attracted to these jobs. But in fact there was little migration from the countryside to the cities before World War I. Instead, employers hired immigrants, who were available, cheap, often tractable, and in many cases equipped with industry-specific skills. Most firms preferred northern Europeans, but by 1900, most job seekers came from Italy, southeastern Europe, and the Russian empire. The entrance of these new immigrants into midwestern industry, at first overwhelmingly in low-skill positions, was the first and most important of the demographic and cultural changes that ultimately transformed the urban working class of the late nineteenth century.

Together, the "old" and "new" immigrants dominated urban society. By the turn of the century, three quarters of Milwaukee, Chicago, Detroit, and Cleveland residents or their children were immigrants. In smaller cities such as Minneapolis and Cincinnati, the total was lower, but still over 60 percent. Virtually every community of twenty-five thousand or more was at least half immigrant. These proportions were a measure of the appeal of industrial employment, but also of the gulf that had developed between country and city. By the early twentieth century, the Midwest consisted of two societies, one rural, agricultural, and native-born for at least several generations, the other urban, industrial, and immigrant.

Outside the workplace ethnic identities were all-important. Workers who spoke the same languages and shared a similar heritage tended to live in the same areas. Informal contacts provided employment information, mutual assistance, and other informal services vital to success in a new and unfamiliar environment.

World War I brought this distinctive era to an end by introducing even greater diversity to working-class life. By ending international immigration, the war struck at one of the foundations of industrial growth. Desperate for labor, employers sought to attract workers from the backwaters of the Midwest and from the upper South, and a new pattern soon emerged. Rural and southern white workers generally favored small industrial cities, while black workers overwhelmingly chose Chicago and Detroit. The newcomers introduced a new and often volatile element to urban life. The postwar years featured intensified ethnic and racial conflict.

Worker protests were an important and persistent theme of midwestern life and were closely associated with the emergence of formal organizations that gave workers a voice in industry. The brief but dramatic spread of union activity in the 1880s, associated with the rise of the loosely organized, all-inclusive Knights of Labor, suggested the potential of organized labor. Prosperity, near-full employment, and agitation for labor reforms such as the eight-hour day led to an upsurge in union membership together with the creation of corollary institutions, such as cooperatives and independent political parties. This activity culminated in 1886, when the challenges of translating worker enthusiasm into an effective institutional presence became inescapable. The Knights of Labor failed this test, and many other unions fared almost as badly. The infamous Haymarket Affair in Chicago symbolized their vulnerability. By 1890, the Knights of Labor was virtually moribund, and most trade unions had suffered substantial losses.

Yet there were at least two lasting results: the formation of the American Federation of Labor (AFL) in 1886 and the United Mine Workers (UMW) in 1890. The AFL brought together most unions—largely organizations of highly-skilled workers that eschewed broad political goals for pure and simple economic gains—in a confederation that set overall policies, mediated disputes, and lobbied Congress and the legislatures. The UMW was a combination of state organizations and Knights of Labor assemblies. Its central figure, John McBride of the Ohio Miners Association, served as president before successfully challenging Samuel Gompers for the presidency of the AFL in 1894. Under his successors, the UMW became the largest American union; its core remained the Central Competitive Field, the midwestern mines.

Many other unions revived or emerged at the turn of the last century. They were overwhelmingly organizations of autonomous workers, such as carpenters, plumbers, and molders, who had considerable power in the workplace. They organized by occupation and skill, affiliated with the AFL, and opposed associations with less skilled workers. Some, like the construction trades, printers, and potters, developed power-sharing arrangements with employers; others played more confrontational roles. In many small cities, they also worked with socialist politicians to gain a larger voice in municipal affairs. In large cities, they were more likely to align with reform mayors such as Samuel "Golden Rule" Jones in Toledo and Tom Johnson in Cleveland. Milwaukee, with a powerful but politically moderate socialist party, based on union voters, was the exception to this large-city trend.

The most distinctive feature of these unions, however, was their durability. Following the examples of the AFL, the UMW, and some of the older craft organizations, they established bureaucratic organizations with full-time officers and staffs, elaborate procedures and rules, and substantial treasuries. With such resources, they were able to withstand economic fluctuations, strike losses, and other setbacks. Still, they were no match for the most aggressive industrialists. Apart from the elite railroad brotherhoods, which were well-established by 1910, they seldom were able to make inroads in large-scale industry. Temporary successes (as in the Chicago meatpacking industry at the turn of the century) were followed by total defeat.

The boom years of the World War I era, 1915–1920, re-created the atmosphere of the 1880s. Labor shortages and a large government role in labor relations created new opportunities. Union membership in midwestern cities rose rapidly and included many steel and machinery workers. The most famous organizing campaign of the war period, a 1919 effort by AFL unions to organize the steel industry, briefly resulted in substantial inroads in Ohio, Illinois, and Wisconsin mills. The retreat of government after the war, the failure of the great steel strike of 1919–1920, and the postwar recession of 1920 had devastating effects. By 1922, the labor movement was again largely confined to small industrial firms and customary strongholds such as construction and coal mining.

This pattern remained largely unchanged through the 1920s. Union membership declined modestly, as gains in construction and urban trades only partly offset the precipitous decline of the UMW, which was decimated by mine closings and internal dissension. An affluent economy and the growth of personnel management in the largest firms were added deterrents to organization. While the labor movement remained an established feature of midwestern society, it was excluded from the fastest-growing, most dynamic firms.

The Depression was a devastating blow to industry in the region and the majority of its employees. The collapse of the early 1930s forced a reexamination of virtually every aspect of midwestern society, not least the roles of industrialists and workers, and of the state in the operation of the economy. Out of that process emerged a new group of institutions and institutional relationships, symbolized by a new generation of unions that successfully organized workers in the Midwest's biggest businesses, the steel, auto, and auto parts makers.

Sources and Further Reading: James R. Barrett, *Work and Community in the Jungle: Chicago's Packinghouse Workers, 1894–1922* (1987); Lizabeth Cohen, *Making a New Deal: Industrial Workers in Chicago, 1919–1939* (1990); Daniel Nelson, *Farm and Factory: Workers in the Midwest, 1880–1990* (1995); Richard J. Oestreicher, *Solidarity and Fragmentation: Working People and Class Consciousness in Detroit, 1875–1900* (1986); Steven J. Ross, *Workers on the Edge: Work, Leisure, and Politics in Industrializing Cincinnati, 1788–1890* (1985); Richard Schneirov and Thomas J. Suhrbur, *Union Brotherhood, Union Town* (1988); Olivier Zunz, *The Changing Face of Inequality: Urbanization, Industrial Development, and Immigrants in Detroit, 1880–1920* (1982).

Daniel Nelson
University of Akron, Ohio

The Midwestern Labor Market and Its Integration into the National Market

By the term "labor market," economists mean the variety of mechanisms that link employers and job seekers by providing information about employment opportunities and facilitating the interactions necessary to form employment relationships. Historically, the expansion of market boundaries through the reduction of transportation and communication costs and the increasing efficiency of market institutions has been an important contributor to American economic growth.

During the early nineteenth century, the geographic scope of markets was relatively constrained. In this sense, there was not a single midwestern labor market, but a number of imperfectly integrated labor markets distinguished by geography and industry. During the course of the nineteenth century, improvements in transportation and communication and concurrent institutional changes caused these markets to become increasingly integrated with each other and with labor markets in other parts of the United States and Western Europe, a fact reflected in declining geographic wage differentials. By the 1870s or 1880s, we might speak not of a purely midwestern labor market, but of a northern labor market encompassing both the midwestern states and most of the New England and Middle Atlantic regions. In the twentieth century, connections with regions of the South and West continued to strengthen, producing what might today be viewed as essentially a national labor market.

In the nineteenth century, the expansion of water and rail transportation networks into the Midwest, combined with the discovery and exploitation of a variety of natural resources, created a rapidly expanding demand for labor in the region. This demand raised wages above prevailing eastern levels—real common labor wages were 33 percent higher than eastern wages in the 1820s, while artisans could earn a 75 percent premium. These differences helped to stimulate an influx of labor, which in turn steadily reduced regional wage differences. By the 1880s, wages in the East North Central census division (Ohio, Indiana, Illinois, Michigan, and Wisconsin) were essentially equal to those in the Northeast, and a similar convergence was apparent by the 1890s for wages in the West North Central region (Missouri, Iowa Minnesota, Kansas, Nebraska, and the Dakotas). In the twentieth century, wage levels in the Midwest have closely tracked national trends, clearly indicating the region's integration within a national labor market.

After 1870, net migration into the Midwest was dominated by European immigrants. By 1890, foreign-born workers made up more than half the labor force in Chicago and St. Paul, and close to a third in St. Louis and Cincinnati. Meanwhile, there was a net outflow of native-born workers. As immigrants filled urban and industrial jobs, native-born midwesterners moved west, seeking agricultural opportunities. When World War I cut off European immigration, employers in the Midwest turned to the South. Their recruiting helped create networks of information that facilitated the Great Migration of Southern Blacks.

During the last half of the twentieth century this pattern of migration accelerated given the employment opportunities in northern cities during World War II. Black migration was paralleled by that of southern whites during this time as well. Midwestern growth slowed, reflecting the decline of heavy industry in the region. While short-run shocks have produced episodes of intense unemployment, integration into a national labor market has encouraged outmigration and helped to equalize wages with other regions, thus reducing the negative effects of declining industries.

Sources and Further Reading: Olivier Jean Blanchard and Lawrence F. Katz, "Regional Evolutions," *Brookings Papers on Economic Activity* 1 (1992); Simon S. Kuznets and Dorothy Swaine Thomas, *Population Redistribution and Economic Growth, 1870–1950*, 3 vols. (1957–1964); Robert A. Margo, *Wages and Labor Markets in the United States, 1820–1860* (2000); Joshua L. Rosenbloom, *Looking for Work, Searching for Workers* (2002).

Joshua Rosenbloom
The University of Kansas

Canal Workers

Canal workers brought the Transportation Revolution to the Midwest, opening the region to mass settlement, economic exchange, and urban development by digging such canals as the Ohio and Erie, Wabash and Erie, Illinois and Michigan, and St. Mary's.

First drawn from among local farmers, Germans and, especially, Irish immigrants soon dominated canal construction. Wage rates on midwestern canals, higher than those back east due to labor shortages, attracted workers. Canal construction was very laborious work, aided only by beasts of burden and gunpowder. Sunup to sundown the day ran, with breaks for meals and regular dispensing of alcohol. Workers faced injury and death from rock slides, drowning, and blasting, and illness from annual seasons of malaria, typhoid, and smallpox outbreaks, and deadly cholera epidemics.

Pay often came late, and occasionally in devalued company scrip or as "truck pay," that is, credit at a company store. Contractors (builders who were responsible for labor recruitment and management) regularly experienced financial trouble and some absconded, leaving workers unpaid.

Canalers lived in temporary shantytowns along the canals or on town fringes. Poorly constructed shanties housed families, including male boarders; in other cases, barracks accommodated gangs of men. Shantytowns fostered excessive drinking, interpersonal strife, battles with local citizens, and ethnic violence.

Rival factions of canalers, organized on the basis of county of origin in Ireland, rioted regularly over control of employment, seeking to raise wages by creating labor scarcity. Canalers also waged strikes: for example, to shorten the workday and raise pay on the

Illinois and Michigan in 1847 and for a ten-hour day on the St. Mary's in 1853.

A depression beginning in 1837 led to the shutdown of public works throughout the Midwest. Canal construction revitalized in the late 1840s, only to be overtaken by railroads, often built by the same workers.

Sources and Further Reading: Harry N. Scheiber, *Ohio Canal Era* (1969); Catherine Teresa Tobin, "The Lowly Muscular Digger: Irish Canal Workers in the Nineteenth Century," Ph.D. diss., University of Notre Dame (1987); Peter Way, *Common Labour: Workers and the Digging of North American Canals, 1780–1860* (1993).

Peter Way
Bowling Green State University, Ohio

Railroad Workers

Although nineteenth- and early twentieth-century railroaders moved frequently, they developed a strong presence in the Midwest. During the early 1860s, locomotive engineers working on the Michigan Central objected to their fluctuating wages and dangerous working conditions. In 1863, they met in Detroit to organize the Brotherhood of Locomotive Engineers (BLE). The BLE's conservative leaders hoped that by focusing on self-improvement, the Brotherhood would gain the respect of railroad managers. The 1877 national railroad strike that hit Chicago from July 24 to 27 dispelled this idea among many midwestern railroaders.

In 1888, engineers and firemen on the Chicago, Burlington & Quincy went on strike. The Burlington Strike unraveled when engineers refused to acknowledge firemen and switchmen as equals. The Indiana-based

Canal boat entering locks. Ohio Historical Society, AV9 AL00890.

Atchison, Topeka & Santa Fe Railroad workers. Kansas State Historical Society, HE.10, ATSF. DOCPro 1875.

Brotherhood of Locomotive Firemen (BLF), led by Eugene V. Debs, introduced a federation plan in 1889 to address this problem, but the BLE refused to endorse it. At a December 1892, meeting in Cedar Rapids, Iowa, the brotherhoods finally adopted a plan of federation.

Unwilling, however, to cooperate fully to solve labor grievances, the brotherhoods—led by midwestern railroaders—did address issues of safety and occupational disability. Inspired by Iowa's Safety Appliance Act (1890), they lobbied for the passage of the Federal Safety Appliance Act (1893).

In June 1893, Debs established the American Railway Union (ARU) in Chicago. The ARU's powers peaked after winning the Great Northern Strike during the spring of 1894. Defeat soon followed, however, when a federal injunction ended the Pullman boycott that summer.

The ARU demonstrated the organizing potential of industrial unionism. It limited membership, however, to whites. African Americans established their own organizations during the beginning of the twentieth century. The Chicago-based Railway Men's International Benevolent Industrial Association used a model that rejected craft-based organizing, in which each skill had its own union, in favor of industry-wide organizing. Other organizations included the influential Brotherhood of Sleeping Car Porters (BSCP), which battled the paternalistic Pullman Company in Chicago at the end of the 1920s and used its organizing of African American porters to launch a national black civil rights movement.

Before World War I, rising fuel and labor costs resulted in economic crisis. The government tried to alleviate this crisis by mediating between railroads and their workers. The Erdman Act (1898), for example, established federal arbitration of railroad labor disputes.

When traffic increased in 1916, the brotherhoods demanded an eight-hour day. Woodrow Wilson moderated negotiations, but an agreement could not be reached. To avoid a nationwide strike, Congress passed the Adamson Act (1916), which provided an eight-hour day for railroaders.

Cooperation between the BLE and the American Federation of Labor (AFL) during World War I convinced some BLE members that affiliation would be a good idea. Fearing domination by the building trades that controlled the AFL executive council, however, the BLE turned away at the last moment.

Ultimately, craft elitism and prejudice governed the history of the midwestern railroad worker during the late nineteenth and early twentieth centuries. This resulted in gains for some privileged workers, but at the cost of sacrificing the ideal of solidarity among all midwestern railroaders.

Sources and Further Reading: Eric Arnesen, *Brotherhoods of Color* (2001); Donald L. McMurry, *The Great Burlington Strike of 1888* (1956); Shelton Stromquist, *A Generation of Boomers* (1987); John Williams-Searle, "Courting Risk: Disability, Masculinity, and Liability on Iowa's Railroads, 1868–1900," *Annals of Iowa* 58 (Winter 1999).

John Williams-Searle
University of Iowa

Labor's Great Upheaval and the Struggle for the Eight-Hour Day

The movement for the eight-hour day peaked in 1886, immediately following a period of depression between 1883 and 1885. Wage reductions plagued the indus-

❖ **Steel Mills**

The mills
That grind and grind,
That grind out new steel
And grind away the lives
Of men,—
In the sunset
Their stacks
Are great black silhouettes
Against the sky.
In the dawn
They belch red fire.
The mills,—
Grinding out new steel,
Old men.

Langston Hughes

Source: Langston Hughes, "Steel Mills," in *The Collected Works of Langston Hughes: The Poems, 1921–1940* (2001).

trial centers of the Midwest, uniting both skilled and unskilled labor in opposition. With the rising popularity of the Knights of Labor, workers turned toward boycotts and collective bargaining in the attempt to attain the eight-hour workday and an increase in wages.

The philosophy behind the eight-hour movement emerged from the overproduction crisis that was consuming many industries. Markets were being flooded with both industrial and agricultural commodities. As a solution, workers championed the eight-hour day. Labor leaders contended that a reduction in hours would compel employers to add more jobs. The resulting increase in leisure time and decline in labor market competition would encourage workers to pursue a higher standard of living and wage increases. Higher wages would also stimulate workers' consumer purchasing power, which would absorb excess capital and end overproduction.

The Federation of Organized Trades and Labor Unions ultimately called for a general strike for the eight-hour day on May 1, 1886. Statistics compiled by the U.S Bureau of Labor's 1887 and 1894 reports on strikes and lockouts reveal that the Midwest was the center of the labor movement. In Illinois alone, approximately 68 percent of strikes during 1886, most in Chicago, occurred in conjunction with the eight-hour movement. Strike totals peaked in all of the midwestern states except Iowa in 1886, with Illinois and Ohio at the forefront of the eight-hour movement. Forty percent of strikes in Illinois and 52 percent in Ohio at this time gained either partial or complete victory. The overall success rate in the Midwest was approximately 44 percent, which included both partial and

full victories. The high success rate compared to earlier strike attempts owed largely to the reliance of workers on unions.

However, the tide would soon turn. The Haymarket Affair in Chicago sparked the initial decline of labor in 1886, followed by the Packinghouse Strike failure a few months later. Even though the labor movement was not directly linked to the events at Haymarket Square, there was a great backlash against socialists and labor unions. Picketing became impossible, and unions were frequently raided. Corporations employed a variety of methods to restrict the power of labor, ranging from the blacklist to the use of Pinkerton detectives to break strikes.

The counteroffensive took its toll on the Knights of Labor, and by July 1887, national membership had dropped by approximately 30 percent from the previous year. Despite the significant success rate in the Midwest, the number of strikes gradually tapered off in 1887. Labor's Great Upheaval of 1886–1887 signified a shift toward the eight-hour day and a higher level of commitment to labor organization.

Sources and Further Reading: John R. Commons, Daniel Saposs, Helen L. Sumner, H. E. Mittleman, John B. Andrews, Selig Perlman, and Don D. Lescohier, *History of Labour in the United States*, vol. 2 (1918); Lemuel Danryid, *History and Philosophy of the Eight-Hour Movement* (1889); Melvyn Dubofsky and Foster Rhea Dulles, *Labor in America*, 6th ed. (1999); Richard Schneirov, *Labor and Urban Politics* (1998).

Laura E. C. Bergstrom
Indiana State University

The Pullman Strike of 1894

On May 11, 1894, almost 80 percent of the thirty-three hundred employees of the Pullman Palace Car Company walked off their jobs to protest the declining wages and high living costs they faced in the "model" company town of Pullman, fourteen miles south of Chicago. Within seven weeks, that local labor conflict had grown into a national railway strike that placed the Midwest at the center of the industrial tensions that characterized late-nineteenth-century America.

Workers in Pullman town built the popular railway cars whose brand name was synonymous with passenger travel. Amid the depression of 1893–1894, these native-born and western European workers were laid off, then rehired if they were willing to work at drastically reduced wages and live in company-owned housing, where rent was not reduced. Bitterness at these

Troops, Trains and the Pullman Strike.
Reprinted from *The Illustrated American*, vol. XVI (1894): 80.

conditions was compounded by workers' anger that management salaries did not decline and that stockholders' dividends were maintained at the annual 8 percent return rate that George Pullman guaranteed to his investors.

For these reasons, workers in Pullman town joined the American Railway Union (ARU) in the spring of 1894 and voted to strike when the Pullman Company refused to negotiate with the union. The local strike escalated into a national boycott after the Pullman Company rebuffed all pleas for arbitration from workers, social reformers, business leaders, and civic officials. The ARU's 150 thousand members, led by Eugene V. Debs, then voted to strike in sympathy by refusing to handle any Pullman cars on the nation's rail lines. In response, the General Managers' Association (GMA), representing the twenty-four railroads that converged in Chicago, agreed to fire any employee who boycotted Pullman cars and to hire strikebreakers in their place. Over the subsequent six weeks, heated conflict erupted on rail lines from Chicago to Los Angeles.

The trade and transport chaos caused by the Pullman Strike demonstrated that the industrial Midwest lay at the hub of the modern national economy. The strike also crystallized public debate over the rights of management and labor in an industrializing society where individual freedom, freedom of association, economic stability, and social harmony were all valued. President Grover Cleveland's government sought to resolve that debate in the Pullman Strike by defending the railroads, issuing a sweeping injunction that rendered all ARU activity illegal, and then dispatching fourteen thousand armed federal agents to Chicago to enforce it. The response in the summer streets of Chicago and other cities was violence and arson, which the ARU did not support and could not contain.

The Pullman workers lost their strike; those not blacklisted had to work under contracts that forbade unionization. Debs, as ARU president, was charged with violating the federal injunction. Supreme Court affirmation of the guilty verdict in Debs's case seemed to vindicate government use of the injunction to stop labor action. But, at the same time, the presidentially appointed Pullman Strike Commission unanimously called for a U.S. policy of labor arbitration, thereby using this Chicago-based crisis to point toward a new direction in American labor relations.

Sources and Further Reading: Stanley Buder, *Pullman: An Experiment in Industrial Order and Community Planning, 1880–1930* (1967); James Gilbert, *Perfect Cities* (1991); David Ray Papke, *The Pullman Case* (1999); Richard Schneirov, Shelton Stromquist, and Nick Salvatore, eds., *The Pullman Strike and the Crisis of the 1890s* (1999).

Victoria Bissell Brown
Grinnell College, Iowa

The Carpenters Union

The Brotherhood of Carpenters and Joiners, one of the most important unions in the American Federation of Labor, has its roots in the Midwest. The union was founded in 1881 in Chicago owing largely to the efforts of Peter J. McGuire and the St. Louis and Chicago locals.

The rapid growth of cities in the late-nineteenth-century Midwest created an enormous construction boom and demand for carpenters, the largest of the building trades. Meanwhile, factory-made woodwork undermined the craft of carpenters. The result was the rise of "piecework," the subdivision of carpentry into specialized tasks that were performed by cheaply paid immigrants employed by subcontractors. To combat this trend carpenters formed unions.

By 1886–1887, the eight-hour day had become the unifying issue for carpenters, especially those in Chicago, who were among the major participants in the strikes of that year. During the Columbian Exposition, the union organized a series of walkouts that persuaded the Fair's business leaders to sign the city's first large-scale collective bargaining agreement. Led by the carpenters in the 1890s, Chicago became a union town, with the most militant labor movement in the country.

The dominance of the union in the city's construction industry was initially marked by numerous strikes, most of them jurisdictional in nature. In 1900, contractors counterattacked with a thirteen-month lockout and forced the union to limit its freedom of action. In 1921, corporate leaders intervened in the industry and tried to outlaw the carpenters' and allied construction unions. The union responded by organizing nonunion journeymen, and by 1924, the union shop returned. A labor peace of forty-seven years followed, lasting until a strike in 1972. In the 1990s, the union established an organizing program in response to a growing threat from nonunion, residential contractors. At the turn of the twenty-first century, Chicago was among the few cities to retain a large membership in residential building trades unions, the District Council in the Chicago-Indiana region having over thirty-six thousand members in 2002.

Sources and Further Reading: Robert Christie, *Empire in Wood* (1956); Richard Schneirov and Thomas Suhrbur, *Union Brotherhood, Union Town* (1988).

Tom Suhrbur
Illinois Education Association,
Springfield, Illinois

The Knights of Labor

The Noble and Holy Order of the Knights of Labor (KOL) was the largest labor federation of the nineteenth century. Its broad platform included land reform, ending the wage system, and substituting boycotts and arbitration for strikes. Members included wage earners, farmers, shopkeepers, small manufacturers, and social reformers.

The KOL was founded in Pennsylvania in 1869, from whence it organized coal miners, iron molders, shoemakers, and other industrial workers in the contiguous Midwest. In 1878, three Ohioans served on its first national executive board. When Terence Powderly became KOL head in 1879, his efforts to expand the KOL were aided by midwesterners like William Bailey of Shawnee, Ohio, Thomas Barry of Bay City, Michigan, and Richard Griffiths of Chicago.

By 1885, the KOL contained hundreds of midwestern assemblies, including packinghouse workers, miners, and railroad workers. The Knights even owned a coal mine in Cannelburg, Indiana, from 1884 to 1897. After winning a strike against Jay Gould's Southwestern railway conglomerate in 1885, there was scarcely a region of the Midwest that did not contain KOL assemblies. In the immediate aftermath of the 1886 Haymarket Affair, Knights stood for political office in at least ninety-one midwestern locales, with twenty-eight reporting victory.

Powderly sought to distance the Knights from anarchists after Haymarket, but his refusal to endorse clemency for the eight men convicted of the Haymarket bombing caused many midwesterners to quit the organization. Knights were concentrated heavily in companies controlled by Gilded Age industrialists who offered little quarter, and most strikes were lost, including the disastrous 1886 Chicago stockyards strike that caused ill will with trade unions. Both William Bailey and Thomas Barry denounced the Knights, the latter founding a rival organization. Many workers left the KOL and joined national trade unions, with whom the KOL battled for members. Especially troublesome was the Brotherhood of Locomotive Engineers, which frequently scabbed on the Knights. When the KOL retaliated during the 1888 Chicago, Burlington & Quincy strike, it further tarred the organization as anti–trade union.

More midwestern assemblies folded in 1890 when the KOL lost a strike against the New York Central Railroad, a system with branch lines across the Midwest. After 1891, the KOL took on an agrarian cast. Knights were early supporters of the People's Party, and eventually fused with rural Populism. In late 1893, a coalition of eastern socialists and midwestern agrarian radicals ousted Powderly and chose James Sovereign, an Iowa editor, to head the KOL.

Sovereign held that post through 1897, but was unable to staunch the decline. Despite its uneven record, the KOL was important for the future of midwestern labor. It was the first labor organization to recruit heavily among women, African Americans, and unskilled workers. Several future leaders—including Mary "Mother" Jones and Mary Lease—honed their talents in the KOL, as did organizers of the Brotherhood of Sleeping Car Porters. Collapsed KOL assemblies also provided the structural basis for new organizations like the American Railway Union, the United Mine Workers, and the United Packinghouse Workers. The KOL also pioneered industrial unionism tactics that were used successfully by the Congress of Industrial Organizations in the 1930s.

Sources and Further Reading: Leon Fink, *Workingmen's Democracy* (1983); Richard Jules Oestreicher, *Solidarity and Fragmentation: Working People and Class Consciousness in Detroit, 1875–1900* (1986); Norman Ware, *The Labor Movement in the United States, 1860–1895* (1929; reprint 1959); Robert E. Weir, *Knights Unhorsed* (2000).

Robert E. Weir
Bay Path College, Massachusetts

The Rise of Building Trade Unions

Midwestern construction workers have formed some of America's most successful unions. Construction requires large investments in land and materials; relatively little is spent on wages, but good labor relations are essential. Capitalizing on their position, construction workers first unionized in larger urban areas where commercial construction projects were especially vulnerable to disruptions. In the Midwest, the first construction unions were formed in Chicago and St. Louis, and by 1880, there were twenty-six local unions of construction workers in Illinois and twenty-three in Missouri.

From there, unions grew quickly. In 1881, P. J. McGuire of St. Louis helped to found the Brotherhood of Carpenters and Joiners; the first Carpenter's local was in Chicago, the second in Cincinnati, with eleven of the first twenty in the Midwest. By 1904, one-third of construction workers were unionized, triple the rate in other industries. The unionization rate was even higher among midwestern construction workers, especially in large cities like Chicago and St. Louis where nearly all belonged to unions.

Construction unions significantly reduced the hours of work and raised wages for their members, especially in highly organized large cities like Chicago. Socialists, including P. J. McGuire, hoped that unions would improve working conditions and wages for all workers, and competition with unionized workplaces may have raised wages for nonunion workers, especially in highly unionized large cities. But craft orga-

nization also focused union gains on skilled tradesmen. Disappointing McGuire, some construction tradesmen, once entrenched in their craft organizations, have shown little concern for the unorganized and the unskilled.

Sources and Further Reading: Gerald Friedman, *State-Making and Labor Movements* (1998); Robert Max Jackson, *The Formation of Craft Labor Markets* (1984); Royal Montgomery, *Industrial Relations in the Chicago Building Trades* (1927); Richard Schneirov and Thomas J. Suhrbur, *Union Brotherhood, Union Town* (1988).

Gerald Friedman
University of Massachusetts–Amherst

The United Mine Workers of America and the Central Competitive Field

By the winter of 1885–1886, coal operators in the midwestern coal trade were ready for a comprehensive solution to the industry's problems. After decades of ongoing crisis, they had had enough of prices that all too often dipped below the cost of production, disruptive strikes, and railroad freight rate wars. They had waited in vain for competition to settle the industry. They had experimented with massive capitalization, mergers, and unrelenting antiunionism. They had tried trade associations and politics. Nothing worked. At this point, after all else failed, union leaders offered them a new option, and some operators became more willing to talk to them.

In September 1885, coal miners pushed for interstate contract negotiations through the National Federation of Miners and Mine Laborers, which in 1890 merged with the Knights of Labor miners to become the United Mine Workers of America (UMW). In the winter of 1886, coal miners and operators negotiated a contract covering Ohio, Illinois, Indiana, and western Pennsylvania. Collectively, these states made up the nation's main coal-mining region, what became known as the Central Competitive Field (CCF).

Only in 1897, however, after the UMW won a national strike (focused in the Midwest), did negotiations based in the CCF become a successful, stable strategy for ordering the industry. Both operators and miners liked to say that the negotiations of the 1880s and 1890s had been a school. It was an education that paid off. Many coal operators actually *supported* the UMW in the 1897 strike.

Between 1897 and 1915, CCF negotiators achieved a semblance of industrial peace. It became a model for industry-wide collective bargaining and made the modern UMW a major force in America's industrializing economy. CCF negotiations addressed every aspect of production. Instead of uniform wages, negotiators set rates in each of the CCF states, then negotiated "differentials" based on the costs of production and transportation. Operators with higher expenses paid slightly lower wages. Operators with lower expenses paid slightly higher wages. The result fell somewhere between unbridled competition and centralized administration. This rough system of so-called competitive equality encouraged even the marginal coal operators to join in annual negotiations with the union.

Still, if the CCF system remained relatively stable between 1897 and 1915, it did so despite constant erosion from the mostly nonunion coal operators in West Virginia and other southern coalfields. In World War I, CCF negotiations collapsed in nasty spasms of wartime profiteering. When postwar strikes idled midwestern coal mines, southern mines proved able to supply the market. By 1927, the UMW had nearly disappeared; the CCF had become irrelevant.

In 1933, aided by the New Deal's support for the right to organize, American coal miners rebuilt their organization, this time including the South. Acknowledging the now dominant role of these fields, the UMW negotiated the Appalachian Agreement. As conceived by UMW president John L. Lewis, the new agreement rewarded large-scale capitalization, centralized production, and mechanization. In doing so, it reinforced the growth of coal mining corporations in the South and the decline of smaller-scale coal operations in the midwestern CCF region.

Sources and Further Reading: John R. Bowman, "When Workers Organize Capitalists: The Case of the Bituminous Coal Industry," *Politics & Society* 14 (1985); David Brody, *In Labor's Cause: Main Themes on History of the American Worker* (1993); David Montgomery, *Fall of the House of Labor* (1989).

Andrew B. Arnold
Kutztown University of Pennsylvania

Company Welfare Programs and Company Unions

Midwestern employers figured prominently in the introduction of privately financed benefit plans for nonexecutive employees. Their motives included a desire to attract capable workers, foster loyalty to the firm, increase productivity, thwart outside unions, and quiet social critics. Religious and philanthropic concerns were influential in some cases, but John H. Patterson—president of National Cash Register in Dayton, Ohio, the firm that had the best-known U.S.

corporate welfare program—summarized the dominant theme of the movement: "It pays!"

Twentieth-century welfare capitalism grew out of welfare work, which gained momentum in the late nineteenth century, especially among employers who operated in remote locations or had many female employees. Calumet & Hecla, the northern Michigan copper mining company, and Marshall Field, the Chicago department store, were pioneers. Depending on the setting, welfare work could include in-plant services such as lunchrooms and medical departments, savings and insurance plans, and community services.

It was the intangible benefits of these activities, together with the turn-of-the (last)-century upsurge in union organizing that transformed welfare work into the systematic activity that flourished for the next quarter century. National Cash Register provided the best example of this transition. A 1901 strike in the NCR foundry soon spread to the rest of the factory, halting production for more than a month. Analyzing this debacle, Patterson concluded that his welfare programs (including health and accident assistance, savings plans, and recreational and educational programs) were largely unrelated to the operation of the factory. In response, he created a new Labor Department to run them, to hire and fire (typically the supervisor's responsibility), and to resolve grievances. The welfare program thus became part of a broader effort to manage the labor force. In the following years, many large midwestern manufacturing companies adopted the NCR formula. By 1915, they accounted for at least a quarter of the nation's leading advocates of welfare capitalism, and a Cleveland suit manufacturer, Joseph & Feiss, rivaled NCR as the best-known practitioner.

A handful of firms went beyond financial incentives, insurance plans, and recreational programs to give employees a voice in company operations through employee representation or company union plans. Some, led by Goodyear Tire & Rubber of Akron and International Harvester of Chicago, sought to enlist employees more fully in their work. Others installed company unions primarily to preempt AFL organizations. Neither type of organization emphasized wages or engaged in actual bargaining. Those that survived the 1920 recession successfully involved employees in the solution of shop floor problems. For that reason, and because they were often promoted as features of union avoidance plans, company unions remained highly controversial. When the Depression led to new cutbacks in employee benefits, and New Deal legislation enhanced the power of organized labor, they became targets. The Wagner Act of 1935, which outlawed employer assistance to labor organizations, led to the dissolution of most company unions.

As the economy revived, welfare capitalism made a

comeback. Yet there were fundamental changes. Social Security and other government programs created nationwide pension, relief, and unemployment insurance systems. A more powerful labor movement increasingly included nonwage benefits in collective bargaining contracts. One result of the new environment was the emergence of a complex, interrelated system of public and private benefit programs. Another was the eclipse of midwestern leadership. By mid-century, the Midwest's large manufacturing companies were approaching maturity. While still among the leaders in terms of coverage and expenditures, they increasingly looked to other institutions for ideas and initiatives.

Sources and Further Reading: Stuart D. Brandes, *American Welfare Capitalism, 1880–1940* (1976); David J. Goldberg, "Richard A Feiss, Mary Barnett Gilson, and Scientific Management at Joseph & Feiss, 1909–1925," in Daniel Nelson, ed., *A Mental Revolution* (1992); Daniel Nelson, *Managers and Workers*, 2nd ed. (1995); Robert Ozanne, *A Century of Labor-Management Relations at McCormick and International Harvester* (1967).

Daniel Nelson
University of Akron, Ohio

The 1919 Steel Strike

Stretching from Chicago to Pittsburgh, the 1919 steel strike ranks among the most important strikes of U.S. history. More than 250 thousand workers struck in the fall of 1919 in a bitter and often violent confrontation against U.S. Steel and allied concerns.

Organized under the National Committee for the Organization of Iron and Steel Workers, an umbrella organization of twenty-four American Federation of Labor (AFL) unions, and led by the future leader of the Communist Party, William Z. Foster, the strike faced major obstacles, including jurisdictional rivalries among participating AFL unions, fierce resistance from steel interests, a public atmosphere of antiforeigner and anticommunist hysteria, and antiunion intervention from local, state, and national authorities. The strike also cast into stark relief major fissures within the U.S. working class. Recent immigrants from eastern and southern Europe, largely confined to unskilled jobs, seized the initiative during the strike, while among the skilled "American" element (primarily older immigrant groups such as Irish, British, German, and Scandinavian workers), the strike attracted less support. Meanwhile, African American workers, present in the North in large numbers following World War I's Great Migration, were occasionally employed as strikebreakers.

Coming at the apex of the largest strike wave in American history (1916–1922), the strike's failure signified a temporary ebb of intense industrial conflict, ushering in a period of open-shop dominance during the 1920s. Yet the industry-wide strike demonstrated the potential for organizing masses of unskilled industrial workers and provided both a prototype and inspiration for the later industrial unionism of the Congress of Industrial Organizations in the 1930s.

Sources and Further Reading: David Brody, *Labor in Crisis* (1965); Lizabeth Cohen, *Making a New Deal* (1990); Bruce Nelson, *Divided We Stand: American Workers and the Struggle for Black Equality* (2001).

Tom Mackaman
University of Illinois–Urbana-Champaign

Mine Disasters

The rapid expansion of the midwestern mining industry in the years between the Civil War and World War I increased both employment opportunities and workplace dangers for underground toilers. Threats to miners' safety included gas explosions, fires, flooding, rock falls, mechanical failures, and human errors. Although injury or death came most often to miners individually, disasters involving mass fatalities were far from rare. Disasters in close-knit communities often killed relatives, friends, and neighbors.

Mine disasters typically involved shock, valiant rescue efforts, monetary relief for widows and orphans, and the passage of new legislation. Funding for widows and orphans typically was distributed according to family size and arose from a variety of sources, including the public at large, coal companies, and state governments.

The disaster at Cherry, Illinois, which began on November 13, 1909, and took 259 lives, is illustrative. Hay lowered into the mine for mules caught fire and set the mine ablaze. Meager efforts to squelch the blaze failed, and much of the mine was soon engulfed in flames. Several community members who attempted to rescue miners perished. Twenty-one men who ventured to a far tunnel in the mine were rescued after eight days. Many of the victims were immigrants from Italy, Lithuania, and other European countries. The disaster resulted in the passage of Illinois' Workmen's Compensation Act.

Other notable disasters included those at St. Clairsville, Ohio, in 1940—72 victims; Diamond, Illinois in 1883—74 victims; Millfield, Ohio in 1930—82 victims; Centralia, Illinois in 1947—111 victims; and West Frankfort, Illinois in 1951—119 victims.

Sources and Further Reading: Philip A. Kalisch, "Death Down Below: Coal Mine Disasters in Three Illinois Counties, 1904–1962," *Journal of the Illinois State Historical Society* 65 (Spring 1972); Steve Stout, "The Cherry Mine Disaster," *Journal of the Illinois State Historical Society* 72 (Feb. 1979); Karen Tintori, *Trapped: the 1909 Cherry Mine Disaster* (2002).

Richard P. Joyce
Coal City, Illinois

Strikebreaking and the Open Shop

Before the New Deal and the mass unionization of the 1930s, many Midwest workers experienced the despotic rule of employers and the widespread denial of basic labor and civil rights. For employers, on the other hand, it was the era of the open shop, a golden age of untrammeled managerial authority. Despite numerous confrontations with employers, labor organizations generally found themselves confined to local craft labor markets.

For employers, the key to defeating unions was a large repertoire of battle-tested methods for combating strikes. Practically all the methods were in place by 1900. Subsequent years saw a further refinement of these techniques, together with an added emphasis on preventing unionization and collective bargaining by means of corporate-sponsored employee welfare pro-

Battle of the Overpass: Ford Servicemen Breaking Strike, May 27, 1937. Walter P. Reuther Library, Wayne State University.

grams and company unions. Over time, strikebreaking also became more systematic and less ad hoc.

Strikes tested the will and endurance of employers and workers. Employers went into conflicts hoping to force strikers back to work on management's terms. Seeking to break the morale of strikers, employers frequently attempted to replace them with strikebreakers, even at the risk of escalating conflicts. Obtained from near and far, on their own, and through labor recruiters, employers' use of scabs usually outraged strikers. This was particularly the case if strikebreakers were imported from outside a locality, if they came to fight strikers, or if employers replaced white strikers with African Americans, as happened in Chicago during several packinghouse strikes, the teamster's strike of 1905, and the steel strike of 1919. Sometimes, employers had to quarter and feed strikebreakers. Always they had to protect them from the moral appeals of workers to desert, as well as from the intimidation and assaults of strikers and their supporters.

Violence brought government repression down on strikers. Although strikers could and often did battle police and deputized armed guards, they were no match for state militia or federal troops.

Court-issued labor injunctions accompanied the repression of strikers. Used on a massive scale for the first time during the Pullman boycott of 1894, the labor injunction quickly became the primary legal weapon in the arsenal of employers.

In attempting to isolate and put pressure on strikers, employers tried to prevent them from working elsewhere. The railroads excelled in the use of the blacklist, though by the early 1900s, the so-called reference check more subtly accomplished the same end. Those workers fortunate to be rehired after the loss of a strike sometimes had to sign special "yellow dog" contracts, whereby as a condition of employment, they agreed not to join a labor organization. During the Progressive Era, the U.S. Supreme Court repeatedly struck down federal and state laws that barred these devices.

In the Norris-LaGuardia Act of 1932, Congress once again outlawed yellow dog contracts, proclaimed the right of workers to strike, assemble, and peacefully picket, and restricted the authority of federal courts to issue injunctions in labor disputes. Similar provisions appeared in statutes enacted by many states. Matters turned worse for employers when Congressional endorsement of independent trade unions and collective bargaining in 1933, and again with the Wagner Act of 1935, spurred workers to take action. Employers met workers with their customary strikebreaking methods. Workers responded with mass picketing, their own paramilitary formations knows as "flying squadrons," and the sit-down strike, an ingenious tactic that enabled a relatively small number of strikers to hold an industrial facility hostage while avoiding police truncheons on a picket line.

In the face of determined workers and the reluctance of President Franklin Roosevelt and Democratic governors like Frank Murphy of Michigan to send troops to shoot strikers, major corporations recognized and signed agreements with new industrial unions.

Sources and Further Reading: Howell John Harris, *Bloodless Victories* (2000); Darryl Holter, "Labor Spies and Union-Busting in Wisconsin, 1890–1940," *Wisconsin Magazine of History* (Summer 1985); William Millikan, *A Union Against Unions* (2001); Stephen Norwood, *Strikebreaking and Intimidation* (2002); Joshua L. Rosenbloom, "Strikebreaking and the Labor Market in the United States, 1881–1894," *The Journal of Economic History* 58 (Mar. 1998).

Tom Klug
Marygrove College, Michigan

Early Midwestern Labor Reformers

John R. Commons (1862–1945)

Born in Hollansburg, Ohio, John R. Commons was the son of abolitionists John and Clarissa Rogers Commons. Commons attended Oberlin College (A.B., 1888), then began graduate study with Richard T. Ely at Johns Hopkins University. Commons departed in 1890 without finishing his doctorate, taught college economics, but was dismissed from two instructorships for his radical views. In 1890, he married Oberlin classmate Ella B. Downey.

Commons's contributions to policymaking began with research on immigration and labor for the U.S. Industrial Commission (1898–1902). He then assisted the National Civic Federation (1902–1904) with investigations of industrial disputes. In 1904, Commons joined Ely at the University of Wisconsin, where he taught until 1932. He became principal editor of the ten-volume *A Documentary History of American Industrial Society* (1910–1911) and editor of two of the four volumes of *History of Labor in the United States* (1918–1935), key works of the Wisconsin School of labor history. Commons's theoretical writings, which focused on the importance of law, custom, and ethics in collective action, included *The Industrial Goodwill* (1919), *Legal Foundations of Capitalism* (1924), and *Institutional Economics* (1934).

To administer state labor laws, Commons helped establish and served on the Wisconsin Industrial Commission in 1911. Appointed to the U.S. Commission of Industrial Relations (1913–1915), he helped organize its Research Division and advocated the creation of permanent federal and state industrial commissions. Commons and his students profoundly

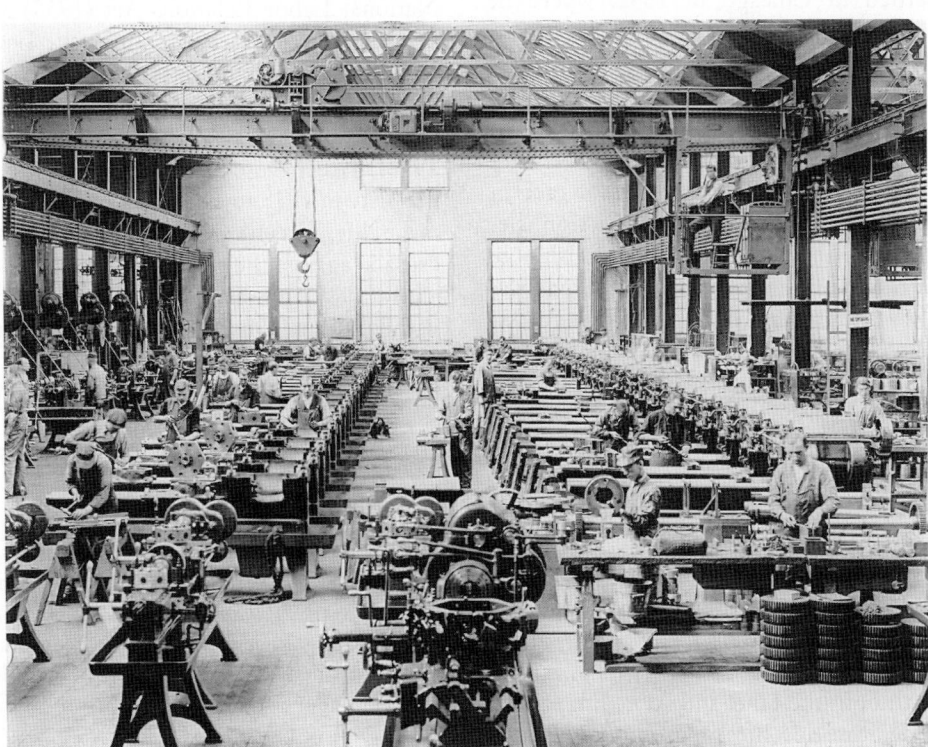

Turret Lathe Assembly Department, Warner & Swasey, Cleveland, 1912. The Cleveland Press Collection, Cleveland State University Library.

shaped the modern, multidisciplinary field of industrial relations and exercised a major influence over the New Deal bureaucracy's administration of U.S. labor relations policy. The legitimacy of a uniquely American system of collective bargaining and grievance arbitration in both law and policy in the twentieth century owes much to the contributions of Commons and his students.

Sources and Further Reading: John R. Commons, *Myself, the Autobiography of John R. Commons* (1963); Lafayette G. Harter, *John R. Commons, His Assault on Laissez-Faire* (1962); Bruce E. Kaufman, *The Origins & Evolution of Industrial Relations in the United States* (1993).

Clarence E. Wunderlin, Jr.
Kent State University, Ohio

John Fitzpatrick (1871–1946)

John Fitzpatrick was an important Chicago labor leader during the first half of the twentieth century, known mostly as president of the Chicago Federation of Labor (CFL) from 1905 to his death in 1946 (with the exception of one brief term in which he voluntarily did not serve). Fitzpatrick believed in industrial unionism, whereby all workers, regardless of skill, were eligible for union membership. The Irish-born Fitzpatrick settled in Chicago in 1882, where he worked in the stockyards as a blacksmith and a horseshoer.

In 1905, Fitzpatrick was elected president of the CFL as a way to combat the corruption within the organization. Upon his election, Fitzpatrick worked for the betterment of all workers, regardless of race or gender. Moreover, he supported political action. Besides promoting prolabor politicians and legislation, he agitated for the creation of a labor party, which was founded in 1919 and under which he ran unsuccessfully for several offices. The CFL abandoned the labor party in 1924. In 1926, under Fitzpatrick's leadership, the CFL established the nation's first labor-owned radio station, WCFL. The labor newspaper created in conjunction with the labor party in 1919, *The New Majority*, would become *Federation News* in 1924, a publication that still exists at the beginning of the twenty-first century. Initially both papers attempted to reach out to the public as a whole, although *Federation News* is now available only to affiliated unions.

Working with both the CFL and AFL, Fitzpatrick continued to dedicate his life to promoting labor's cause, both in Chicago and across the nation. Fitzpatrick is remembered for his dedication, honesty, and

desire to better the cause of all workers. He continued to live in Chicago until his death in 1946.

Sources and Further Reading: Nathan Godfried, *WCFL, Chicago's Voice of Labor, 1926–1978* (1997); Barbara Newell, *Chicago and the Labor Movement* (1961); Mitchell Newton-Matza, "Intelligent and Honest Radicals," Ph.D. diss., The Catholic University of America (1999).

Mitchell Newton-Matza
University of St. Francis, Illinois

William Green (1870–1952)

The son of immigrants from Great Britain, Green was born in the mining town of Coshocton, Ohio. Ambition and intelligence led to his steady rise in the United Mine Workers (UMW). In 1913, he was elected UMW secretary-treasurer and was placed on the American Federation of Labor (AFL) executive council. Upon the death of Samuel Gompers in December 1924, AFL council members elected Green to succeed him.

Throughout his twenty-eight years as AFL president, Green tried to sell unionism to industry and the public through moral appeals. During the Great Depression he served as labor's leading lobbyist, playing a significant role in many New Deal reforms such as the National Labor Relations Act (1935) and the Social Security Act (1935). After John L. Lewis and other heads of industrial unions created the rival Committee for Industrial Organization (CIO) in 1936 (which became the Congress of Industrial Organizations in 1938), Green voted with the AFL executive council majority in 1938 to expel the CIO unions. For the rest of his life, Green's energies would be consumed by a crusade against the rebel movement.

By 1939, however, Green's power and influence within the AFL began to decline with the rise of an ambitious George Meany in the post of secretary-treasurer. Green did spearhead a vigorous but unsuccessful campaign to repeal the Taft-Hartley Act of 1947, yet by the time of his death in 1952, he had become a largely forgotten figure.

Sources and Further Reading: Irving Bernstein, *The Lean Years: A History of the American Worker, 1920–1933* (1960); Craig Phelan, *William Green: Biography of a Labor Leader* (1989); Craig Phelan, "William Green and the Ideal of Christian Cooperation," in Melvyn Dubofsky and Warren Van Tine, eds., *Labor Leaders in America* (1987).

Craig Phelan
University of Wales, Swansea, United Kingdom

John Mitchell (1870–1919)

Born in the mining town of Braidwood, Illinois, John Mitchell endured an unhappy, fatherless childhood. He began mining at age twelve, and at seventeen settled at Spring Valley, Illinois.

Keen intelligence led to his rapid rise in the United Mine Workers (UMW). By 1897, he was a UMW vice president, and the following year was appointed acting UMW president. Mitchell gained a reputation as a responsible leader who worked feverishly to extend and uphold collective bargaining agreements in soft coal regions. He was also hailed for his conduct of two monumental northeast Pennsylvania anthracite strikes, in 1900 and 1902, which helped to establish the union in the hard coal industry. Mitchell's towering reputation as a moderate leader earned him praise from luminaries such as Mark Hanna and President Theodore Roosevelt.

Praise, said some, turned Mitchell's head. Mitchell pursued financial investments that were clear conflicts of interest, and he took a leading role in the National Civic Federation (NCF), an organization founded by industrialists and politicians seeking peaceful labor relations. By 1908, Mitchell's alcoholism forced him to resign as UMW president, and in 1911, insurgents in the UMW forced him to resign from the NCF. In 1915, he was named chairman of the New York State Industrial Commission, and in 1919, he died of pneumonia complicated by alcoholism. Mitchell's legacy is an impressive one. During his tenure, UMW membership rose from thirty thousand to 300 thousand, making the UMW the largest American labor union of its day.

Sources and Further Reading: Elsie Glück, *John Mitchell, Miner* (1929); Craig Phelan, *Divided Loyalties: The Public and Private Life of Labor Leader John Mitchell* (1994).

Craig Phelan
University of Wales, Swansea, United Kingdom

John H. Patterson (1844–1922)

Dayton industrialist John H. Patterson attained international fame for his innovative business methods and his progressive worker welfare and civic reform programs.

In 1884, he and his brother, Frank, purchased a failing cash register firm and renamed it the National Cash Register Company. Patterson immediately set out to create a market for his machine by teaching reluctant buyers how cash registers could increase profitability. He also introduced the now common practice of systematically training employees when he established the first sales school in 1894. Patterson quickly evolved the cash register from a simple adding machine into a sophisticated data gathering device, which revolutionized the retail trade and made his company a pioneer in information technology.

Perhaps his most important contributions were his extensive worker welfare and civic reform programs, by 1900 the country's most highly developed. Believing that employees were most productive when healthy and well fed, he introduced an extensive series of worker welfare programs into the factory. The spotlessly clean buildings with 80 percent glass walls, employees' dining rooms, medical services, and a multitude of educational and recreational opportunities gave NCR a reputation as the model factory of the world and reflected Patterson's faith in the power of efficient business methods to correct societal ills. He further applied his philosophy to the city of Dayton, where he pushed a myriad of civic reforms.

An idealist who believed that the twentieth century would see the end of war, poverty, and disease, Patterson proselytized his ideas across the nation and the world, ultimately impacting the lives of millions.

Sources and Further Reading: Samuel Crowther, Samuel H. Patterson, *Pioneer in Industrial Welfare* (2003); Judith Sealander, *Grand Plans: Business Progressivism and Social Change in Ohio's Miami Valley, 1890–1929* (1988).

Claudia L. Watson
Montgomery County Historical Society,
Dayton, Ohio

Labor and Midwest Politics

Workers, particularly organized workers, have played a large and controversial role in the political life of the Midwest over the last century and a half. They have attracted more hostility and organized opposition than most interest groups, in part because of their numbers and potential power and in part because of several factors that alienated politicians and supporters of the major parties. First, midwestern union leaders repeatedly attempted to form worker-based third parties. Second, they were among the most persistent and determined opponents of the region's strong Republican orientation. And third, as members of national and international unions, they have often embraced broad reform agendas and rejected the parochialism of state and local politics.

As large numbers of midwestern workers became union members in the post–Civil War years, the issue of political action inevitably arose. Unions, notably miners unions and the United Mine Workers, mounted effective lobbying efforts in state capitals based on a strategy of rewarding friends and punishing enemies. Yet the close and compromising associations of both major parties with business interests left a persistent impression that workers were unrepresented and that unions ought to operate as political as well as economic organizations. Simple mathematics suggested that industrial workers, voting as a group, could match or exceed the totals of Republicans or Democrats in most communities. The result was a series of third-party efforts, beginning in the 1870s and continuing through the 1930s, usually coinciding with periods of substantial membership growth. Though these efforts did not lead to permanent organizations or (with several notable exceptions) undermine the major parties, they were an effective if indirect force for social and political reform.

The dramatic rise of the Knights of Labor in the 1880s produced more than a dozen successful local labor party campaigns in 1886 and 1887. Knights-backed candidates took control of the Milwaukee city government and formed substantial minorities in the city councils of Chicago and Cincinnati. In smaller communities, the Knights were even more successful. Yet in what would become a familiar pattern, labor successes produced an antilabor backlash. Republicans and Democrats joined ranks to oppose the labor parties and had defeated and eliminated them by the end of the decade.

Although the severe depression of the mid-1890s produced one of the great protest movements in American history—the emergence of the People's Party from the Farmers' Alliance movement—relatively few midwestern farmers and even fewer urban workers became involved. Most midwestern unions merely struggled to survive, and industrial workers who did remain active often turned to more immediate tasks, such as agitating for unemployment relief—Coxey's famous 1894 march on Washington, for example. The People's Party did enjoy a brief vogue in mining towns, probably the most depressed of all midwestern communities, but the effects were negligible. Populism had little immediate impact except to suggest the potential power of a mobilized working class.

As the economy revived and the labor movement began a period of dramatic growth, political activism increased. The political environment also became more complicated as the American Federation of Labor (AFL), which claimed the allegiance of most unions, informally allied itself with the Democratic Party, and the progressive movement within both major parties made them more receptive to labor influence.

Still, third-party activism continued to have broad appeal among midwestern workers, especially miners and skilled industrial employees. Many of them turned to the new Socialist Party of America, which had emerged at the turn of the last century under Indiana union leader Eugene V. Debs and other activists. In Milwaukee, newspaper publisher Victor Berger and other German intellectuals, working with local labor leaders, created a movement that dominated local government for a quarter century. In other communities, socialist strength peaked in the early 1920s as workers elected dozens of mayors and hundreds of city council members.

The socialists' victories resulted from their critiques of the economic and political status quo, together with promises to expand public services. They called for municipally owned utilities and other public service firms, regulation of industrial activity, investment in public schools and community parks, and state health and pension programs. Republican and Democratic politicians were uniformly hostile (while often embracing the socialists' more moderate demands) and succeeded in limiting socialist inroads to cities with large numbers of industrial workers.

During and after World War I, when union membership grew rapidly, many leftist leaders believed that labor parties could take the place of socialist organizations. A few local parties emerged in 1918 and 1919, but the Red Scare, the interwar open-shop campaign, and the onset of the recession undercut their appeal and eliminated many of their leaders. The one major exception, however, was the rise of the Farmer-Labor Party of Minnesota, which grew during the interwar years and replaced the Democrats as the state's second major party. By joining a militant farmers' organization, the Non-Partisan League, the state labor movement was able to broaden its base and insulate itself against the forces that undercut labor activism in other states. Nevertheless, this approach made the unions dependent on an ally whose principal grievance was the post–World War I contraction in international commodity prices.

One other legacy of the war years resulted in the most important third-party initiative of the 1920s. Railroad workers had been among the most important beneficiaries of the wartime government takeover of the railway system, and the railroad unions agitated for a continuation of government ownership after the war. Led by the generally conservative operating brotherhoods, this effort, which had its base in the Midwest, resulted in the formation of the Progressive Party of 1924 and the formidable but unsuccessful presidential campaign of Sen. Robert M. La Follette of Wisconsin.

The revival of the labor movement in 1933 and

1934 led to another wave of political activism and more third-party efforts, but such initiatives soon gave way to an alliance with the progressive wing of the Democratic party. Union leaders and especially leaders of the new Committee on Industrial Organization (CIO, renamed the Congress of Industrial Organizations in 1938), which drew most of its strength from the industrial organizations that were just emerging in the Midwest, led the way. By the presidential election of 1936, the process was complete. In later years, the Roosevelt Administration faced challenges from a variety of populist critics such as Charles Coughlin, the "radio priest" of Royal Oak, Michigan, but union groups remained staunch supporters of the New Deal. In 1940, when John L. Lewis, president of the UMW and the CIO, broke with Roosevelt and endorsed his opponent, midwestern workers, like most of those in other regions, disavowed Lewis and voted overwhelmingly for Roosevelt. Organized workers had become closely identified with the Democratic party.

Despite the Democratic Party's links to various business interests, most union members were first- or second-generation immigrants and, like most Americans of immigrant stock, identified with it. The AFL's increasingly close association with the Democrats reflected this preference. Yet after the mid-1890s, the Democrats were the minority party in Washington as well as in most midwestern states, and the rise of a progressive faction in the Republican party reinforced the argument against a Democratic alliance.

As a consequence the preferred choice of most industrial workers (apart from a labor-oriented third party) was an alliance with progressives, regardless of party. Unions and working-class voters were an important component of the La Follette movement in Wisconsin. They aided individual progressive candidates such as James Cox, Ohio's Democratic governor in the 1910s. At the municipal level they were critical to the success of Samuel "Golden Rule" Jones (a nominal Republican) in Toledo and Tom Johnson (a Democrat) in Cleveland. The payoff was substantial. The midwestern states were leaders in devising workers compensation systems, regulating the labor of women and children in the workplace, and expanding state and municipal services. By the 1910s, midwestern workers were closely identified with progressive reform. Most workers preferred Democrats to Republicans, but were more concerned about legislative and administrative initiatives than party identity.

The collapse of progressive reform activity after World War I and the growing influence of antiunion employers in both parties left organized labor on the defensive and politically adrift in the 1920s. Their plight helped explain the appeal of La Follette's candidacy in 1924 and their enthusiastic reaction to

Franklin D. Roosevelt's election in 1932. By that time most union leaders had concluded that an activist pro-labor Democrat was preferable to either a third party or a Republican progressive.

The celebrated alliance between the AFL and CIO and the New Deal became the single most significant feature of midwestern political life in the 1930s. It was not synonymous with a union-Democratic alliance; in Wisconsin and Minnesota, for example, the La Follette Progressives and Farmer-Laborites retained their holds on union voters and became those states' de facto New Deal affiliates. There were also anomalies, such as Ohio's Democratic governor Martin Davey, who achieved notoriety as an anti–New Deal, anti-CIO zealot, and Indiana's Democratic governor Paul McNutt, who was often hostile to organized labor. Regardless of local peculiarities, the New Deal and its labor allies were the central element in the new political alignment, and Republicans increasingly identified with antiunion employer groups. In 1938, when the New Deal suffered numerous electoral setbacks, the victorious Republican gubernatorial candidates ranged from the moderate Harold Stassen in Minnesota to the reactionary John W. Bricker in Ohio, but they were uniformly hostile to organized labor. Whenever Republicans took control of state government, antiunion legislation was a virtual certainty.

The dramatic growth of union membership during World War II materially reduced this threat. In Michigan, for example, the United Automobile Workers emerged as the state's most important political force, a landmark change in union influence. In Wisconsin, the La Follette Republicans merged with the Democrats to create a competitive Democratic party. And in Minnesota, the Farmer-Labor party merged with the Democrats to create a new majority party. National political developments were factors in each case, but it was the promise of union votes that transformed these traditionally Republican states into two-party battlegrounds.

For the next thirty years, organized labor remained the single most influential Democratic interest group and a critical element in state politics. It accounted for the Democrats' ascendancy in Illinois and Michigan through the 1950s and for many of their victories in other states. In Ohio, union-backed campaigns nearly defeated the prominent antiunion senator, Robert Taft, in 1950, and defeated the entire Republican ticket, including Senator John Bricker, in 1956.

The problem for unions and Democrats alike was that union membership growth stalled in the 1950s, then gradually declined. Fewer union votes soon translated into fewer Democratic votes, which in turn often meant less political support for union-related causes. The change was not dramatic and may not have been decisive in any single election. By the 1990s, however, it was clear that a cycle had been completed: Worker and union influence and Democratic power were on the wane, as they had been before the New Deal.

Do workers have political influence except as union members? As members of other special interest groups they often do. But few of those groups systematically address issues of wages, hours, working conditions, and economic security. The decline of union power has also meant that employer groups have become more influential. The result has been a gradual reversal of the pattern of improved working conditions and benefits that many mid-twentieth-century workers took for granted.

Over a century and a half, then, dramatic changes have characterized the relationships among workers, politics, and government. For most of that period, workers had considerable influence, though the mechanisms for exerting that influence constantly changed. At some times, third parties seemed to be the best approach; at others, informal or formal alliances with the Democratic party or progressive factions of both major parties seemed more appropriate. The common theme of this complex history has been a search for ways to ensure that government represents its worker constituency and acts upon issues related to employment, working conditions, and economic security that, in the absence of formal organization, would likely be disregarded.

Sources and Further Reading: Milton Derber, *Labor in Illinois* (1989); Thomas W. Gavett, *Development of the Labor Movement in Milwaukee* (1965); Doris B. McLaughlin, *Michigan Labor* (1970); Daniel Nelson, *Farm and Factory* (1995); William F. Thompson, *The History of Wisconsin, Volume VI* (1988).

Daniel Nelson
University of Akron, Ohio

Labor Parties

By awarding election to the candidate with the most votes, American election law discourages third-party voting because voters fear voting for their absolute preference may enable the election of the less desirable of the major party candidates. But despite the obstacles raised by election law, there has been significant third-party voting in most national elections since 1876, especially among voters on ideological extremes and from regions neglected by national party managers. Because major party rivalry has usually involved competition for the votes and financial contributions of the affluent, many independent campaigns, especially before the New Deal, have had an explicitly

working-class orientation. These include the world's first independent working-class political party, Philadelphia's Workingmen's Party of the 1830s, as well as the Greenback and Union Labor Parties of the 1870s and 1880s, the Populists of the 1890s, and Socialist, Communist, and Progressive Parties in the twentieth century.

Labor parties were most prominent after 1876. The end of Reconstruction left the United States evenly divided politically. National elections were decided in a few Mid-Atlantic states, where the two major parties competed for the votes of affluent urban voters opposed to currency inflation or other schemes to redistribute income toward workers and farmers. Some local Republicans and more Democrats favored social reform, but they had little influence in national parties focused on winning the votes of conservative middle-class, eastern voters.

Dismissed by the major parties, midwestern farmer and labor activists nominated General James B. Weaver of Iowa for President on the Greenback–Labor Party ticket in 1880. The first modern third-party candidate, Weaver attracted enthusiastic crowds but only 300 thousand votes because sympathetic farmers, workers, and small businessmen abandoned him to choose the lesser of evils between the Republican and Democratic candidates. Nearly two-thirds of Weaver's votes came from the Midwest, where he drew 6 percent of the vote, compared with 2 percent elsewhere. His strongest showings, 10 percent in heavily Republican Michigan and Iowa, came in states where the Republican majority was strong enough that Greenback voters had no concern that their votes were needed to prevent the election of the Democratic candidate.

Weaver's disappointing showing set a pattern for farmer-labor politics, including the Greenbacks (1884), the Union-Labor Party (1888), and the Populist Party (which ran Weaver again in 1892). All received their strongest support among small farmers and wage earners in regions like the Midwest with little political competition. They were supported by some labor unions, notably the Knights of Labor in the mid-1880s, the Mineworkers, and some urban craft unions. Union-labor parties were especially active in the mid-1880s, when they entered candidates in 189 town and city elections, winning in a third. Nearly half of these parties and electoral victories were in the Midwest, including strong campaigns in Chicago, Detroit, Milwaukee, and Minneapolis. Midwestern unions would support insurgent political movements in the mid-1890s and after World War I, but the unions themselves were too weak to make an insurgent political party competitive in a two-party system. Labor parties were shooting stars, occasionally brilliant but rarely surviving more than two elections.

The Populists of the 1890s were succeeded by the Socialist Party of America. In addition to support among industrial wage earners and union members, the Socialists were supported by immigrants with ties to Socialist parties in their native lands, notably Germans (especially in Wisconsin), Russian Jews, and Michigan's Finnish miners. After World War I, the Socialists formed Farmer-Labor alliances in the upper Midwest to protest depressed farm prices. Running for President as a Farmer-Labor Progressive in 1924, Senator Robert La Follette of Wisconsin received 17 percent of the vote nationwide, including over 45 percent in the upper Midwest.

La Follette's campaign was the strongest showing by a labor candidate in American history. It was also the last strong showing. In the 1930s, the New Deal undermined independent labor politics by drawing farmer and labor activists into the Democratic Party and by making the Democrats competitive in previously Republican-dominated regions like the upper Midwest. Socialists and Communists provided important support to labor organizers and Civil Rights activists in the 1930s and 1940s. But since the New Deal, third-party electoral activity has dwindled on the labor left. Strong midwestern third-party movements either merged with the Democrats, as in North Dakota and Minnesota, or withered, as in Wisconsin and Michigan. Since the New Deal, most labor activists have confined their electoral activity to work within the Democratic Party.

Sources and Further Reading: Kevin Boyle, ed., *Organized Labor and American Politics, 1894–1994* (1998); Leon Fink, *Workingmen's Democracy* (1983); Mark A. Lause, *The Civil War's Last Campaign* (2001); Steven J. Rosenstone, Roy L. Behr, and Edward H. Lazarus, *Third Parties in America*, 2nd ed. (1996); Richard Schneirov, *Labor and Urban Politics* (1998); James L. Sundquist, *Dynamics of the Party System*, rev. ed. (1983).

Gerald Friedman
University of Massachusetts–Amherst

The Minnesota Democratic-Farmer-Labor Party

Organized in 1918 by the Non-Partisan League and the Minnesota State Federation of Labor (AFL), the Farmer-Labor Party (FLP) became Minnesota's second-strongest party in the 1920s, behind the Republicans, and dominated state politics in the mid-1930s. Labor unions paid dues and had direct voting representation in Farmer-Labor conventions that endorsed candidates for the party primary. The FLP de-

clined after 1938, and in 1944, it put aside its earlier social democratic "cooperative commonwealth" radicalism for New Deal liberalism and merged with the Democratic Party. The merged party adopted the name Democratic-Farmer-Labor Party (DFL). Labor unions were major supporters of the new DFL, but did not have direct representation as in the FLP.

The new DFL won two congressional seats in 1944. In 1946, DFL control passed to a Popular Front faction headed by former Farmer-Labor Governor and U.S. Senator Elmer Benson. In early 1948, Benson announced he would disaffiliate the DFL from the Democratic Party and shift it to Henry Wallace's new Progressive Party. Anti-Communist liberals led by Minneapolis Mayor Hubert Humphrey regained control at the 1948 DFL convention, and Humphrey's election as U.S. Senator consolidated anti-Communist supremacy. The election of Orville Freeman as governor in 1954 signaled the DFL's emergence as a formidable rival to the long-dominant Republicans. By the 1960s, the DFL and Republican parties were closely balanced, with state control passing back and forth through the rest of the century. Throughout this period the DFL maintained a reputation as one of the most liberal state parties.

Sources and Further Reading: Jennifer A. Delton, *Making Minnesota Liberal* (2002); John Earl Haynes, *Dubious Alliance: The Making of Minnesota's DFL Party* (1984); Richard M. Valelly, *Radicalism in the States: The Minnesota Farmer-Labor Party and the American Political Economy* (1989).

John Earl Haynes
Library of Congress, Washington, D.C.

Frank Walsh (1864–1939)

Frank Walsh built his reputation as a successful litigator and entered politics in opposition to Kansas City's dominant Democratic party boss, Thomas Pendergast. Walsh also supported Progressive governor Joseph W. Folk in his quest to reform state government. He remained active in Kansas City reform circles and public administration, serving on the city tenement commission (1906–1908), creating the city's Board of Public Welfare (1908), and acting as president of the Board of Civil Service (1911–1913). The election of Woodrow Wilson as president in 1912 brought Walsh onto a larger stage.

President Wilson appointed the Missourian as chair of the U.S. Commission on Industrial Relations (CIR, 1913–1915). Created originally by the Taft administration to probe the causes of industrial violence, the CIR conducted nationwide public hearings, financed the research of young social scientists, and issued three separate sets of recommendations for eliminating the causes of industrial conflict. The plurality report endorsed by Walsh and the union representatives condemned the maldistribution of wealth and income in the United States, autocratic management, and the absence of industrial democracy; it called for progressive taxation, worker organization, and collective bargaining, foreshadowing the reforms of the New Deal. The final report, Walsh's harsh questioning of John D. Rockefeller, Jr., and his warm embrace of such labor radicals as William D. "Big Bill" Haywood and Vincent St. John won him a reputation as a radical Democrat.

During World War I, President Wilson appointed Walsh as cochair of the National War Labor Board (NWLB, 1918–1919). The NWLB encouraged the growth of unionism and collective bargaining (trade unions nearly doubled their membership under the aegis of the board), mandated the eight-hour day, and instituted equal pay for equal work, among a slew of other labor reforms. Behind the scenes, Walsh assisted such labor radicals as William Z. Foster and John Fitzpatrick in unionizing the meatpacking and steel industries.

In the 1920s Walsh remained a reformer and a radical. He supported Irish independence from Britain and defended leaders of the Irish Republican Army. He befriended political prisoners and the communist William Z. Foster, and he pleaded the cause of the condemned Italian American anarchists, Nicola Sacco and Bartolomeo Vanzetti. He also moved to New York City and served as Governor Franklin D. Roosevelt's chair of the State Power Authority (1931). In 1936, Walsh became the first president of the National Lawyers Guild, a left-wing alternative to the American Bar Association. He also grew increasingly active in Catholic affairs and became a trustee of St. Patrick's Cathedral. Walsh's Catholicism led him to resign from the National Lawyers Guild in 1939, owing to the latter's support for the Republican side in the Spanish Civil War and its insufficient anti-Communist stance. Walsh died of a heart attack in New York and was buried in Kansas City.

Sources and Further Reading: Graham Adams, Jr., *Age of Industrial Violence, 1910–1915* (1966); Julie Greene, *Pure and Simple Politics* (1998); Joseph A. McCartin, *Labor's Great War* (1997); Shelton Stromquist, "Class Wars: Frank Walsh, the Reformers, and the Crisis of Progressivism," in Eric Arnesen, Julie Greene, and Bruce Laurie, eds., *Labor Histories* (1998).

Melvyn Dubofsky
State University of New York–Binghamton

Industrial Democracy and World War I

The entry of the United States into World War I in April 1917 created a labor crisis that brought into question the autocratic management styles that predominated in prewar workplaces. The wartime labor crisis opened the door to a limited, yet important, period of reform, as government officials, unionists, workers, and employers struggled to replace the old model of labor management with competing versions of industrial democracy. This period of experimentation, which saw unions nearly overturn the open-shop practices of many midwestern industries, held lasting consequences both for American unions and industrial management.

U.S. entry into World War I exacerbated labor relations in already conflict-ridden prewar workplaces. During the first six months of the war, some three thousand strikes afflicted U.S. war industries, affecting industrial states such as Illinois and Ohio with special ferocity. The chaos created by these walkouts prompted the administration of President Woodrow Wilson to respond with both repression and reform. On the one hand, the administration ruthlessly destroyed the radical Industrial Workers of the World, jailing more than a hundred of its top leaders on conspiracy charges. On the other hand, the administration created several agencies to promote labor peace and reform.

The most important of these was the National War Labor Board (NWLB), cochaired by former President William H. Taft and progressive labor lawyer Frank P. Walsh of St. Louis, Missouri. The NWLB promulgated rules of wartime labor relations that forbade the discriminatory firing of union members and called upon employers to bargain collectively with workers. Without specifically requiring that employers recognize unions, the NWLB did provide for the election of shop committees in open-shop industries to carry out collective bargaining. With tacit federal support, membership in the American Federation of Labor grew by roughly one million during the brief period of U.S. participation in the war, soaring past the 3.2 million mark. Union growth was especially marked in midwestern meatpacking, coal, and steel industries in states such as Ohio and Illinois.

Following World War I, politically powerful opponents of federal regulation successfully terminated reform-oriented agencies such as the NWLB. Employers organized a potent open-shop campaign, and unions were defeated in a wave of postwar strikes. Yet a number of large-scale employers did not roll back wartime reforms in their entirety. Rather, these employers—including some influential midwestern firms such as Wisconsin Steel—implemented limited welfare programs for their employees, restricted the powers of autocratic foremen, and created company unions through which workers could air grievances. Although such reforms were but a pale imitation of what many workers had hoped to win during the war, they did elevate the expectations that postwar workers pinned on their employers. When the welfare capitalism of those employers collapsed during the Great Depression of the 1930s, thousands of labor activists who had first gained organizing experience during World War I revived American unionism, and scores of government officials who had participated in the industrial democracy experiments of the World War I era took a hand in crafting New Deal labor policies.

Sources and Further Reading: Jeffrey Haydu, *Making American Industry Safe for Democracy* (1997); Nelson Lichtenstein and Howell John Harris, *Industrial Democracy in America* (1993); Joseph A. McCartin, *Labor's Great War* (1997).

Joseph A. McCartin
Georgetown University, Washington, D.C.

Labor and the Left

Between the 1870s and 1960s, the Midwest was the nation's industrial heartland. No region had a greater concentration of basic mass-production industries—steel, automobiles, meatpacking, farm machinery—or more varied extractive industries—coal, iron and copper ore, timber. Concentrated in such industrial metropolises as Chicago, Detroit, Minneapolis–St. Paul, St. Louis, and Cincinnati, and in scores of smaller industrial cities, wageworkers formed the masses among whom labor activists and political radicals recruited their followers. Thus midwestern metropolises became nodes of labor activism, militancy, and leftist politics.

Leftist politics grew in the late-nineteenth-century Midwest along with the rise of primary and secondary industries. The United Brewery Workers of America, a union whose German American founders and leaders were linked firmly to socialism, organized the brewing industry with its German immigrant labor force and became a substantial presence in Cincinnati, Milwaukee, and St. Louis. Coal miners in Ohio, Indiana, Illinois, Iowa, and Kansas supported farmer-labor parties, Populism, and socialism. Nowhere, however, was the labor activism and political ferment of the late nineteenth century more abundant than in Chicago. Chicago's workers built diverse unions, joined them in substantial numbers, and created a vibrant leftist cul-

ture. During the great labor upheaval of 1885–1886, Chicago workers led the movement for the eight-hour day through strikes and political action. The militancy of Chicago's workers combined with the influence of anarchists culminated in the Haymarket riot of 1886 and the nation's first red scare. In the aftermath of Haymarket, police repression and antiradicalism, independent labor action peaked in the Midwest, especially in Cook and Milwaukee counties, only to subside when the forces of repression proved more powerful than the advocates of labor solidarity and radical politics.

The next wave of midwestern radical labor politics crested with the rise of Populism and the creation of the American Railway Union by Eugene V. Debs, the region's preeminent advocate of a marriage between militant unionism and the political left. Originating among staple-crop farmers (cotton and wheat) in the South and the Plains states, who were plagued by low prices and high indebtedness, Populism challenged the two major parties. The deep depression of the 1890s fed the fires of political protest. In the Midwest, however, farmers proved reluctant Populists. Coal miners, railroad workers, and brewery workers by contrast cast votes for Populism in Ohio, Indiana, Illinois, Wisconsin, Iowa, and Minnesota. Indeed, union members and workers in the Midwest served as the primary recruits to the politics of protest during the depression years.

Workers also resorted to industrial action, bituminous coal miners engaging in region-wide strikes in 1894 and 1898, and railroad employees associated with Debs's American Railway Union initiating the Pullman boycott and strike of 1894. The crushing of the Pullman strike drove Debs and his allies further to the left. In the aftermath of Pullman, the imprisoned Debs drifted from Democratic party politics to Populism and then socialism, as did many other midwestern unionists and workers. In coal-mining districts, railroad centers, and smaller industrial cities, workers often turned to socialism. Debs, a quintessential midwesterner, became the acknowledged leader of the Socialist Party of America (SPA) and its four-time candidate for president.

Chicago and Milwaukee, each in its own way, became centers of socialism. The SPA established its national headquarters in Chicago and published its major journal of opinion there, the *International Socialist Review*. In Milwaukee, local socialists built the most successful left-wing political organization in the nation under the leadership of Victor Berger and other German and Austrian immigrants. Socialists allied to trade unionists also gained municipal power in a number of smaller industrial cities in Ohio, Indiana, and Illinois, where they implemented their own versions of Milwaukee's "gas, water, and sewer" socialism. And on the eve of World War I, socialists won the mayor's office in Minneapolis, electing a former member of the Machinists' union.

Many midwestern socialists belonged to unions affiliated with the American Federation of Labor (AFL) and preferred policies in which immediate reforms and quotidian human needs preceded revolution and a utopian future. To a militant minority among workers and trade unionists, however, the AFL and reform socialism exemplified opportunism and the betrayal of working-class interests. These militants offered workers an alternative to the business unionism practiced by affiliates of the AFL and the gas, water, and sewer socialism implemented by Milwaukee's socialists and their smaller-city brethren. In place of craft unionism and reform socialism, they espoused industrial unionism and revolutionary syndicalism. Meeting together in Chicago in 1904, the militants released an "Industrial Union Manifesto" that asked sympathizers to convene in Chicago to create a new revolutionary labor organization.

In June 1905, such famous radicals as Debs, Daniel DeLeon, William D. "Big Bill" Haywood, Mary "Mother" Jones, and Lucy Parsons, the widow of Haymarket martyr Albert Parsons, joined together at Brand's Hall to found the Industrial Workers of the World (IWW), called the Wobblies. The IWW's founders promised to organize all workers, regardless of craft, nationality, race, and gender, into "One Big Union" that would form the embryo of the new society in the womb of the old.

If not primarily a midwestern organization, the IWW's history became intimately associated with the region. The organization maintained its national headquarters on North Halstead in Chicago; it led organizing initiatives among rubber workers in Akron, automobile workers in Detroit, especially at Henry Ford's new sites of mass production, iron ore miners on Minnesota's Mesabi Range, and harvesters in the wheat fields of Kansas, Nebraska, and the Dakotas. Chicago, moreover, was the site for the most dramatic episode in IWW history, the September 1917 federal raid on its national headquarters and the subsequent (spring 1918) federal trial of its leaders (more than a hundred in all) for violations of the World War I sedition and espionage acts. Perhaps the most infamous single political show trial in U.S. history prior to that of U.S. Communist Party leaders in 1950, the 1918 Chicago trial resulted in the conviction of all defendants on all charges. A similar but less notable trial of minor IWW officials occurred in Wichita the following year with similar results. The conviction and imprisonment of an entire generation of IWW leaders spelled disaster for the organization, but it did not at first shatter the links between labor and the left in the Midwest.

During World War I and immediately afterward, Chicago became the epicenter of a revitalized labor left. Although wartime repression and the rise of Communist parties after the Bolshevik Revolution debilitated the SPA, the Chicago Federation of Labor under the leadership of John Fitzpatrick promoted its own version of leftist politics. Initially creating a local labor party that evolved into a national organization, Fitzpatrick sought to build a labor-farmer political coalition. His efforts to create such a coalition foundered on internecine conflicts between socialists and Communists, more conservative business unionists and radical laborites, and the divergent interests of farmers and workers. A coalition of sorts did materialize in 1924 during the presidential candidacy of Robert La Follette of Wisconsin, who in the Midwest drew the votes of many farmers and workers.

The Great Depression and the coming of the New Deal saw the Midwest once again become a center of independent, leftist labor actions. With probably the greatest proportion of blue-collar industrial workers in the nation, the region played a prominent part in the development of the Congress of Industrial Organizations (CIO). Several of the depression decade's most notable industrial conflicts occurred in the Midwest, including the 1934 citywide strikes in Minneapolis–St. Paul and Toledo; the 1936 Goodyear sitdown strike in Akron and its subsequent spread to other rubber workers in the city; the 1936–1937 Flint sit-down strike by General Motors' workers; and the Little Steel strike of 1937 that affected mills in Ohio, Indiana, and Illinois and culminated in the Chicago Memorial Day massacre.

The bulk of the left wing and Communist-influenced unions in the CIO, especially the United Automobile Workers, the Steelworkers' Organizing Committee, the Packinghouse Workers' Organizing Committee, and the Farm Equipment workers, had their primary membership and influence in the Midwest. After 1936 when Communist party policy endorsed a popular front, the CIO acted as the key constituency among New Deal Democrats who came to dominate the party in Ohio, Michigan, Indiana, and Illinois. In the upper Midwest, including Wisconsin, Minnesota, and the Dakotas, workers and farmers allied in farmer-labor, Democratic politics (in the Dakotas, Republicans were included) that came to dominate those states through the World War II years and after.

The CIO's packinghouse worker organizing campaign brought progressive politics and a concern for civil rights to smaller cities in Iowa, Minnesota, Nebraska, and the Dakotas. Its Farm Equipment workers spread leftist politics in Milwaukee and its suburbs, in

Peoria, Illinois, and in the Davenport metropolitan area on the Illinois–Iowa border. In Michigan and Detroit, the United Automobile Workers became synonymous with the Democratic party and formed an alliance with the NAACP to unionize African American workers and to promote civil rights. In Minneapolis–St. Paul, where the violent Teamsters' strike of 1934 coincided with the rise of farmer-labor political dominance in the state, the unionists who led the conflict were schismatic Communists (Trotskyists) who repudiated Josef Stalin's version of Communism in favor of Leon Trotsky's. Overall, however, midwestern union officials from the most left wing to the most conventional supported the Roosevelt New Deal Democratic party, as did the vast majority of working people. For most midwestern industrial unionists the New Deal exemplified a U.S. version of European social democracy, one in which government (the state) tamed capitalism's excesses in the interest of the common person and the common welfare.

During the World War II years, the popular front encompassed nearly all the midwestern labor unionists. In return for their support of wartime national policies and commitment to high productivity, unions flourished and members gained job security, rising annual incomes, and a plethora of fringe benefits. Between 1945 and 1953, trade unions achieved their peak historical density. CIO unions became so integrated into the Democratic party that they made loyalty to Harry S Truman a litmus test for affiliates during the election of 1948. The CIO's left-wing unions, which supported the independent candidacy of Henry Wallace, were expelled in 1949–1950 on charges of placing the interests of the Soviet Union above those of CIO. Afterward, with the leftist Farm Equipment workers having been absorbed by the United Auto Workers (UAW), the Communist-influenced Mine, Mill, and Smelter Workers picked apart by the steelworkers, and the Communist-led United Electrical Workers challenged by the International Union of Electrical Workers, the labor left declined in the Midwest.

During the heyday of postwar prosperity and the age of affluence (1949–1973), what remained of a labor left in the Midwest expressed itself within CIO unions or the Democratic party and its farmer-labor variation in Minnesota. Unionists supported Adlai Stevenson's candidacies for the presidency, John F. Kennedy's New Frontier, and Lyndon B. Johnson's Great Society. The United Automobile Workers and the United Packinghouse Workers of America (UPWA), headquartered in Detroit and Chicago, respectively, and with the bulk of their members in the Midwest, lobbied assiduously for expansion of the welfare state (especially Medicare), higher minimum wages, state-financed jobs for the unemployed, and full civil rights for African Americans. Indeed, the UAW and UPWA devoted more resources to the cause of civil rights than other unions. The labor movement, especially the UAW, claimed the greater part of the credit for the expansion of social security, the adoption of Medicare, and the passage of the Civil Rights Acts of 1964 and 1965. The mid-1960s and the Great Society represented the high point of achievement for what remained of a midwestern labor left.

After 1973, however, the entire midwestern labor movement began to decline. Even during the height of the Great Society, cracks appeared in the trade unions. The Vietnam War divided trade unionists, so much so that Walter Reuther, president of the UAW, dissented from the AFL-CIO's ardent support of President Johnson's war and marched his union out of the AFL-CIO. Even within the UAW, dissenters condemned the conservatism and opportunism of Reuther and his fellow officers. In Michigan, especially Detroit, African American automobile workers challenged union leadership. These African American militants formed their own schismatic revolutionary organizations such as DRUM, the Dodge Revolutionary Union Movement. Meanwhile, the packinghouse workers saw their membership collapse as the meatpacking companies closed their big-city plants and moved operations into the countryside. The fate suffered by the UPWA soon befell other midwestern industrial unions after 1973, as rising global competition for market share, technological change, two oil crises, and a series of economic recessions turned the Midwest into a Rust Belt. With fewer members and smaller treasuries, the unions lost political influence. Like the remainder of the nation, the Midwest after 1973 drifted away from its affinity for Democratic party–style social democracy, moved closer to the Republicans and their preference for market-based policies, and bred a new generation of working-class voters characterized as Reagan Democrats.

Although the Rust Belt removed some of its tarnish and revived some of its industrial plants during the 1990s, neither the trade unions nor the labor left recovered. The industrial unions continued to bleed members, proved unable to recruit new ones, and saw their political influence further diminished. Even the election of a new AFL-CIO leadership in 1995, one which promised to revitalize the unions and to act more aggressively and progressively in politics, had few echoes in the Midwest. What passed for a labor left as the new millennium opened was a group of so-called progressives in Detroit clustered around the monthly newsletter *Labor Notes* and active in such union caucuses as Teamsters for a Democratic Union and New Directions in the UAW.

Sources and Further Reading: Paul Avrich, *The Haymarket Tragedy* (1984); Donald T. Critchlow, ed., *Socialism in the Heartland* (1986); Rick Halpern, *Down on the Killing Floor* (1997); Elizabeth McKillen, *Chicago Labor and the Quest for a Democratic Diplomacy, 1914–1924* (1995); Stephen Meyer, *"Stalin over Wisconsin": The Making and Unmaking of Militant Unionism, 1900–1950* (1992); Sally Miller, *Victor Berger and the Promise of Constructive Socialism, 1910–1920* (1973); Bruce C. Nelson, *Beyond the Martyrs* (1988); Daniel Nelson, *Farm and Factory: Workers in the Midwest, 1880–1990* (1995); Nick Salvatore, *Eugene V. Debs: Citizen and Socialist* (1982); Richard Schneirov, *Labor and Urban Politics* (1998); Richard A. Valelly, *Radicalism in the States* (1989).

Melvyn Dubofsky
State University of New York—Binghamton

The Haymarket Affair

"In the name of the people of the state of Illinois, I command this meeting immediately and peaceably to disperse." Soon after Captain Ward of the Chicago police uttered these words on May 4, 1886, to the crowd (estimated at six hundred to three thousand) attending an anarchist-organized rally in support of McCormick Harvester strikers, a bomb exploded. Eight policemen and at least that many protesters lost their lives in the blast and the ensuing hail of bullets from police weapons. The identity of the bomb thrower remains a mystery. Yet there is little doubt about the chain of events leading up to the bombing and the repression that followed.

The Haymarket Affair occurred during the Great Upheaval (1885–1886), one of the most powerful working-class upsurges in American history. Hundreds of thousands of working people from across the nation, most of them without previous labor movement experience, joined strikes, local labor parties, trade unions, and the Knights of Labor. In 1886, there was a dramatic upsurge in the number of strikes compared to the years immediately preceding, and membership of the Knights swelled sixfold. Most of the excitement centered on the Federation of Organized Trades and Labor Unions' (FOTLU) call for a general strike on May 1 to secure the eight-hour day. Chicago was in the forefront of this national movement. Tens of thousands of Chicago workers responded enthusiastically to the strike call.

The resulting tragedy in Chicago stemmed from two sources: the ferocity of city officials intent on quashing labor militancy and the public fear caused by the anarchist element in the city's labor movement. Mayor Carter Harrison had appointed John Bonfield police captain in part because of the latter's belief that "the club today saves the bullet tomorrow." When the strikes began on May 1, Chicago's police under Bonfield's direction were quick to resort to force. The anarchists were actually a small minority within the city's labor movement, but the International Working People's Association (IWPA), which blended anarchism, socialism, and syndicalism, had strong support among German-speaking immigrants. For two years before Haymarket, IWPA members published articles under provocative headings such as "Dynamite," "Assassination," and "Bombs." Whether or not the IWPA was prepared to carry out propaganda by deed, their extremist rhetoric helps to explain the panic that erupted with the eight-hour strikes and that engulfed the city after the Haymarket explosion.

Trouble began on May 3, when strikers harassed

The bomb exploding at the Chicago Haymarket: A perspective from *Harper's Weekly.* Courtesy Chicago Historical Society/Harper's Weekly.

strikebreakers at the McCormick Harvester plant. The police arrived and fired indiscriminately into the crowd. Two strikers lay dead and several others were wounded. IWPA leader August Spies thereupon issued the call for the May 4 meeting at Haymarket Square to honor the dead and protest police violence. "Revenge! Workingmen, to arms!!" emblazoned one of the IWPA's leaflets. Rain kept attendance at the May 4 meeting low. Spies took the platform first, followed by Albert Parsons, his wife Lucy Parsons, and finally Samuel Fielden. The meeting was about to disperse when Captain Bonfield arrived with 180 police. Once the bomb exploded, a police riot ensued that was bloodier than the bomb itself.

Repression was swift in Chicago. As the city's newspapers blasted immigrant labor activists, especially anarchists, and warned of red revolution, police raided the headquarters of anarchist-affiliated labor organizations. Amid this red scare atmosphere, the state tried eight IWPA members for conspiracy to murder. Although no hard evidence was offered to connect these men to the bomb, all eight were convicted in August 1886. On November 11, 1887, despite a nationwide campaign for clemency, four of the convicted men were executed. One of the convicted committed suicide while in prison, and the other three remained incarcerated until 1893, when they were pardoned by Illinois Governor John Peter Altgeld.

The Haymarket Affair dealt a harsh blow to the labor movement and radicalism. It set back the labor movement in Chicago, helped to stimulate employer hostility toward the Knights of Labor across the nation, and tarred all labor activity with the brush of radical un-Americanism. The Haymarket anarchists themselves, however, became martyrs to many, folk heroes of the crusade for social justice.

Sources and Further Reading: Paul Avrich, *The Haymarket Tragedy* (1984); Henry David, *The History of the Haymarket Affair,* 2nd ed. (1958); Bruce C. Nelson, *Beyond the Martyrs* (1988); Craig Phelan, *Grand Master Workman* (2000).

Craig Phelan
University of Wales, Swansea, United Kingdom

Anarchists

Anarchism was a radical international labor movement that emerged in Europe in the 1840s and took root in the United States about twenty-five years later. Here it was concentrated in—but not limited to—large midwestern industrial cities, and Chicago was its American nerve center. Prominent anarchists in the United States included Albert Parsons, Dyer D. Lum, Benjamin R. Tucker, Joseph Labadie, August Spies,

and Johann Most. Anarchists rejected the state, perceiving it to be a source of injustice and oppression, and foresaw a new order rooted in voluntary self-governing associations. The anarchists' priority on eliminating the state put them at odds with both socialists and Communists.

German-speaking craft workers constituted the largest group among anarchists in America, and the movement naturally spread along the paths of labor and ethnic migration, linking cities such as Cincinnati, Pittsburgh, Chicago, St. Louis, and Milwaukee. By the 1880s, anarchists had built an extensive set of cultural and political organizations appealing to a multiethnic constituency of workers. In 1886, the Chicago anarchists' main organization had about twenty-eight hundred members and counted four times that many sympathizers.

Anarchism peaked in the United States with the Haymarket Affair of 1886, when a bomb explosion in Chicago killed several policemen and numerous others. Police raids, along with a notorious political trial, ended anarchism's place as a dynamic movement in America. Nonetheless, anarchist groups remained, and an anarchist assassinated President William McKinley in 1901. Anarchism had an influence well beyond its relatively small number of adherents, shaping, for example, the syndicalism evident in both the American Federation of Labor and the radical Industrial Workers of the World. Syndicalists distrusted, or completely rejected, the ability of the state to solve labor's problems, advocating the self-mobilization of workers and their direct action.

Sources and Further Reading: Paul Avrich, *The Haymarket Tragedy* (1984); Frank H. Brooks, "Ideology, Strategy, and Organization: Dyer Lum and the American Anarchist Movement," *Labor History* 34 (Winter 1993); Bruce C. Nelson, *Beyond the Martyrs* (1988).

John B. Jentz
Marquette University, Wisconsin

The Socialist Party

Midwesterners were a strong component of the pre–World War I international socialist movement. The Socialist Party of America was the most electorally successful Marxist party in U.S. history, and its perennial candidate for the Presidency was Eugene V. Debs of Terre Haute, Indiana. His strongest race, in 1912, drew more than one-third of its nearly 900 thousand votes from the Midwest. Milwaukee, Wisconsin, elected Socialists to office from 1904 to 1940, and into the 1950s, including a member of the House of Representatives, while dozens of midwestern towns elected

Socialists in 1910 and 1911, and five midwestern states chose Socialist state legislators in that peak year of electoral success. Socialist newspapers were published across the Midwest: Chicago, the party's national headquarters, produced the first Socialist daily in the country, and the most widely sold Socialist paper in the world, the *Appeal to Reason*, was published in rural Kansas. Every state of the Midwest demonstrated some degree of support for the Socialist Party.

The party was organized in 1901 when social democratic groups united behind the Marxist goal of the collective ownership of the means of production and distribution. That goal was encased in a practical program seeking to appeal to trade unionists and promoting social legislation. Accordingly, political electioneering and immediate demands, rather than revolutionary rhetoric, dominated platforms. Workers formed the bulk of the party's following, buttressed by some intellectuals and middle-class supporters. From factory districts, mill towns, mining camps, and port cities, some workers were attracted to the party's message of economic and political egalitarianism and social justice.

Strong support also came from specific ethnic groups such as some segments of German communities in the region and especially the Finns of the upper Midwest, many of whom had been social democrats prior to their immigration. On the local level, party branches provided a congenial environment that offered members cultural programming, musical and literary events, women's groups, children's activities, summer carnivals, and holiday bazaars. By World War I, Socialist centers had emerged in metropolitan areas including Milwaukee, Chicago, Cleveland, Minneapolis, and St. Louis, as well as in smaller cities such as Dayton, Ohio, and Flint, Michigan, throughout the Midwest.

The crisis of World War I disrupted the party, and the subsequent red scare and the postwar schism between Socialists and the emerging Communist movement led to the decline of the Socialist Party throughout the United States.

Sources and Further Reading: Donald T. Critchlow, ed., *Socialism in the Heartland* (1986); Richard W. Judd, *Socialist Cities* (1989); David A. Shannon, *The Socialist Party of America* (1967); James Weinstein, *The Decline of Socialism in America, 1912–1925* (1967).

Sally M. Miller
University of the Pacific, California

The Communist Party and Labor

From the U.S. Communist party's founding in 1919 until its demise in the late 1950s, Communist trade unionists focused on the Midwest. Because the region was home to the largest concentration of industrial workers in the country in the basic and heavy industries of coal, steel, auto, railroad, and meatpacking, Communist activists believed Midwest workers would understand the need for socialism in America.

From 1921 until 1935, Communists created their own labor organizations, the Trade Union Educational League (TUEL), which existed from 1921 until 1929, and the Trade Union Unity League (TUUL), which lasted from 1929 through 1935. At the TUEL's height in late 1923 and early 1924, Communists claimed five hundred members in about forty-five cities around the country. Its main center of activity was Chicago, where its members worked within established unions; they had the most success in the International Ladies/Garment Workers Union, the Amalgamated Clothing Workers Union, the Cap Makers' Union, the Fur Workers Union, and the Carpenters' Union. Other prominent TUEL opposition groups existed in the southern Illinois coalfields, in Detroit's Carpenters' Union, and in railroad unions through the region.

AFL purges of Communists, state and employer repression, and Soviet directives pushed Communists in 1929 to abandon the TUEL for the TUUL, a separate federation of Communist-led labor unions for workers, like themselves, who were excluded from the mainstream labor movement. TUUL organizers led strikes and organized workers in industries such as coal, electric, auto, metal, steel, railroad, meatpacking, and garment throughout the Midwest. Using party resources, they wrote and distributed leaflets, set up worker schools, and rallied support from Communist Party auxiliary organizations. In March of 1935, Communist leaders dissolved the TUUL and encouraged its members to enter AFL locals once again. Once there, Communists pushed for major organizing drives in the meatpacking and steel industries, a move soon accomplished by the Congress of Industrial Organizations (CIO).

Communist Party members' drive, persistence, and experience convinced John L. Lewis to hire many of them as union organizers. They welcomed the opportunity and experienced their greatest influence among working people organizing for various midwestern CIO unions. Party organizers worked closely with picket captains in the 1936 Akron strikes, were attacked with other workers in Chicago's Memorial Day Massacre at Republic Steel of 1937, participated in Toledo's Chevrolet strike of 1935, and coordinated and supported General Motors workers' 1937 sit-down strike in Flint, as well as Detroit's 1936 sit-down strikes at Bendix, Midland Steel, and Kelsey-Hayes. By the end of World War II, the CIO had firmly established itself as a strong labor federation throughout the Midwest, and Communists had served as some of its best organizers.

The post–World War II years proved difficult for Communist trade unionists. Cold war tensions eroded relations between Communists and the CIO. Differences between Communist and CIO positions on Henry Wallace's presidential campaign and the Marshall Plan created rifts in the CIO. The Taft-Hartley Act's provision that union officers sign affidavits stating that they were not Communists allowed CIO leaders to purge eleven of their left-led unions, after which Communist influence among labor never regained its lost ground.

Sources and Further Reading: James R. Barrett, *William Z. Foster and the Tragedy of American Radicalism* (1999); Bert Cochran, *Labor and Communism* (1977); Harvey Levenstein, *Communism, Anti-Communism, and the CIO* (1981); Steve Meyer, *"Stalin Over Wisconsin": The Making and Unmaking of Militant Unionism, 1900–1950* (1992).

Randi Storch
State University of New York–Cortland

Victor L. Berger (1860–1929)

Victor L. Berger was the leading figure of the socialist movement that dominated Milwaukee city politics in the early twentieth century. Berger served on the city council and represented Wisconsin's Fifth Congressional District in Congress (1910–1912, 1922–1928), the first of three socialists ever elected to Congress. Berger was born in the Austro-Hungarian Empire and immigrated to the United States in 1878. Settling in Milwaukee, he became a teacher and soon was quite active in third-party politics. He edited socialist and unionist newspapers, especially the *Milwaukee Leader,* and was a founder of the Socialist Party of America in 1901.

Berger's revisionist socialist views shaped the Milwaukee Socialist Party so that it worked closely with organized labor, campaigned for public office, and endorsed social legislation and a collectivist economy. In Congress, he introduced legislation to improve working conditions and sponsored hearings that highlighted the exploitation of working people. Defeated by a fusion ticket in 1912, he was reelected in 1918 but unconstitutionally denied his seat by the House because of his opposition to World War I and conviction under the Espionage Act, which was later overturned by the Supreme Court. The turmoil nearly destroyed his newspaper, and the emergence of the rival Communist Party decimated the Socialist Party. Berger

continued to lead the remnants of the Socialist Party, spending three more terms in Congress where he collaborated with other reformers. He died in Milwaukee on August 7, 1929, as a result of a streetcar accident.

Sources and Further Reading: Sally M. Miller, *Victor Berger and the Promise of Constructive Socialism, 1910–1920* (1973); Michael E. Stevens, ed., *The Family Letters of Victor and Meta Berger, 1894–1929* (1995).

Sally M. Miller
University of the Pacific, California

Eugene V. Debs (1855–1926)

Eugene Victor Debs was born in Terre Haute, Indiana, where his French immigrant parents operated a small grocery store. He joined the Brotherhood of Locomotive Firemen's Vigo County local in 1875, serving as organizer and recording secretary. His commitment and skill impressed national leaders, and by 1880, he had become editor of the *Brotherhood of Locomotive Firemen's Magazine,* which under his tenure, became one of the nation's most highly respected labor periodicals.

During the 1880s, Debs increasingly turned away from craft unionism toward industrial unionism. In 1893, he founded the American Railway Union (ARU) and in spring 1894, won a decisive strike against the Great Northern Railroad. By June's convention, the ARU's membership stood at 150 thousand, larger than the railroad brotherhoods' combined total. Convention delegates, over Debs's caution, endorsed a boycott of Pullman sleeping cars to aid a strike of the workers who lived and labored in George Pullman's company town of Pullman, Illinois.

The Pullman boycott, or Debs Rebellion, tied up trains around Chicago and throughout the Midwest and West. Attorney General Richard Olney, at the railroad magnates' behest, issued an injunction against the boycott. Debs defied it, leading to his arrest. By the end of July, the rebellion was over. The ARU never recovered. For defying the injunction, Debs was sentenced to six months in prison. He left prison a celebrity—for some, the embodiment of demagoguery, for others, a hero of mythic proportions.

The Pullman Strike had wearied Debs of economic action. After campaigning vigorously for the People's Party, Debs concluded that socialism, which he had studied in prison, was the workers' only salvation. His socialism grew out of the American democratic tradition, which had strong midwestern roots. In his speeches and writings he articulated a vision that

Eugene Debs speaks in Canton, Ohio, 1918.
Debs Foundation, Terre Haute, Indiana.

scholars have come to call "labor republicanism," which rested on the belief that active citizenship would protect the nation against competitive capitalism's ruthlessness.

In 1897, he joined forces with Milwaukee socialist Victor L. Berger to form what became the Social Democratic Party in 1898. In 1900, he made his first run for president, receiving almost ninety-seven thousand votes. After the creation of the Socialist Party of America in 1901, he ran under its auspices in 1904, 1908, and 1912, the latter marking the high tide of socialism in the United States. In that election, Debs received almost 900 thousand votes, 6 percent of the total cast.

Socialists' opposition to World War I attracted government repression. In June 1918, Debs was arrested for an antiwar speech he gave in Canton, Ohio. He was tried, found guilty, and sentenced to a ten-year prison sentence, of which he served three. At his sentencing hearing, Debs proudly identified with those whom his accusers held in contempt: "While there is a lower class, I am in it; while there is a criminal element, I am of it; while there is a soul in prison, I am not free." In 1920, prisoner #9653 received the Socialist Party's presidential nomination and ran the campaign from his cell. More Americans voted for him in 1920 than 1912, but his percentage of the total vote cast had declined from six to three. Prison broke Debs's health. He spent his few remaining years trying to rebuild the Socialist movement that he had ably served for almost thirty years, but to no avail.

Sources and Further Reading: Eugene V. Debs, *Letters of Eugene V. Debs*, J. Robert Constantine, ed. (1990); Ray Gin-ger, *The Bending Cross* (1949); Nick Salvatore, *Eugene V. Debs: Citizen and Socialist* (1982).

Jason D. Martinek
Carnegie Mellon University, Pennsylvania

William Z. Foster (1881–1961)

Born in Taunton, Massachusetts, and raised in the slums of Philadelphia, William Z. Foster traveled around the country and the world, working at a variety of jobs and passing through a series of radical movements, including the Socialist Party, the Industrial Workers of the World, a succession of his own syndicalist organizations, and finally the Communist Party of the USA, which he joined in late 1921.

Settling in Chicago around 1912, he made it the center for his project to "bore from within" the mainstream labor movement and turn it toward a program of class struggle. After several years as a delegate to the Chicago Federation of Labor, Foster convinced the federation's leader, John Fitzpatrick, and other progressives to support his 1917 drive to organize the Chicago stockyards. Foster and his organizers scored a brilliant success, winning a series of important concessions and drawing the government into a wartime system of arbitration.

In the summer of 1918, Foster launched an even more ambitious project, to organize the steel industry centered around the mill towns along the southern shore of Lake Michigan. On September 22, 1919, Foster's organizers initiated the Great Steel Strike, the largest industrial conflict in U.S. history to date. Both the steelworkers' and the meatpackers' organizations were destroyed in the open-shop campaigns of 1919–1922. In the meantime, using Chicago as his base, Foster established the Trade Union Educational League (TUEL), which functioned throughout the 1920s as the Communist movement's labor arm, and built strong organizations in several key industries. Marginalized by party General Secretary Earl Browder throughout the late 1930s and during World War II, Foster reemerged as leader of the party in 1945, and he remained in its leadership through its repression and decline in the 1950s.

Foster died in Moscow in September 1961, but was buried with other American radicals near the memorial to the Haymarket Martyrs in Forest Lawn Cemetery, Chicago.

Sources and Further Reading: James R. Barrett, *William Z. Foster and the Tragedy of American Radicalism* (1999); Edward P. Johanningsmeier, *Forging American Communism* (1994).

James R. Barrett
University of Illinois–Urbana-Champaign

The Garland Fund

Founded by philanthropist Charles Garland and radical acquaintances in 1922, the Garland Fund (officially the American Fund for Public Service) supported labor, farmer, civil rights, and radical causes in the Midwest until 1941. Among recipients of the Fund's limited resources were various workers' publications and labor schools, including those in Chicago and Detroit, as well as those in Minnesota, Ohio, and Arkansas, which sought to encourage workers to challenge their employers and capitalism itself.

In support of racial justice, the Fund paid for the initial research that eventually led to the landmark legal decision in *Brown v. Board of Education.* The Fund also lent significant backing to the nascent Chicago-based Brotherhood of Sleeping Car Porters, which became not only a labor union, but an incubator of black civil rights activists. Although Garland usually chose to be a nonparticipant in the Fund's activities, he did request in 1934 that money be directed to assist struggling American farmers. The Communists' Farm Research Inc. yearly received money for its general budget. The socialists' Southern Tenant Farmers Union received assistance, as did the Communist-led United Cannery, Agricultural, Packing, and Allied Workers, including support for a convention of sugar beet workers. The Garland Fund dissolved in 1941, a victim of the depression and left-wing political battles. Garland suffered a nervous breakdown and retired from philanthropy and public life. Born in 1899, he died in 1974.

Sources and Further Reading: Merle Curti, "Subsidizing Red Radicalism: The American Fund for Public Service 1921–1941," *Social Science Review* 33 (Sept. 1959); Gloria Garrett Samson, *The American Fund for Public Service: Charles Garland and Radical Philanthropy 1922–1941* (1996).

Gloria Samson
Cranston, Rhode Island

Joseph A. Labadie (1850–1933)

Joseph A. Labadie was one of labor's earliest and most influential activists as the Midwest underwent rapid industrialization at the end of the nineteenth century. After growing up among Pottawatomi tribes in southern Michigan, at age seventeen he began five years of "tramp" (itinerant) printing and eventually settled in Detroit.

That same year he joined the newly formed Socialist Labor Party. "Jo," as he was always called, organized Detroit's first assembly of the Knights of Labor in 1878. In 1880, he served as first president of the Detroit Trades Council and continued issuing a succession of labor papers and columns for the national labor press. Disenchanted with socialism, Labadie embraced individualist anarchism in 1883, a nonviolent and evolutionary doctrine. Although he did not support the militant anarchism of the Haymarket anarchists, he fought for their clemency and broke with the Knights of Labor because its leader, Terence Powderly, repudiated them.

In 1889, Labadie organized the Michigan Federation of Labor, became its first president, and forged an alliance with Samuel Gompers. In 1908, the city postal inspector banned his mail because it bore stickers with anarchist quotations. A month later the Detroit water board, where he was a clerk, dismissed him for expressing anarchist sentiments. In both cases, the officials were forced to back down in the face of massive public protest for Detroit's "Gentle Anarchist."

Beginning in the early 1900s, Labadie's extensive collection of labor literature was sought by several universities. Labadie chose the University of Michigan, where it formed the nucleus of the renowned Labadie Collection, the most comprehensive repository of labor and radical literature in the United States. His son, Laurance, followed in his footsteps as an anarchist essayist.

Sources and Further Reading: Carlotta R. Anderson, *All-American Anarchist: Joseph A. Labadie and the Labor Movement*

(1998); Labadie Collection, Special Collections Library, University of Michigan, Ann Arbor; James J. Martin, *Men Against the State* (1970); William O. Reichert, *Partisans of Freedom* (1976).

Carlotta Anderson
Glen Echo, Maryland

Thomas J. Morgan (1847–1912)

Thomas J. Morgan ranks as Chicago's foremost socialist in the last quarter of the nineteenth century. Born into a poor working-class family in Birmingham, England, Morgan immigrated to the United States in 1869 and settled in Chicago. He embraced socialism during the panic of 1873, and subsequently found employment as a machinist for the Illinois Central Railroad.

A consistent and combative political socialist, Morgan became the leading figure in the Socialist Labor Party and ran for a variety of public offices on that ticket, including his unsuccessful bid for mayor in 1891. Hoping to broaden the field of socialist agitation, he cooperated with progressive labor and farmer elements and unsuccessfully pushed Marxism and independent labor politics at the 1894 American Federation of Labor convention. He played a crucial role in the formation of the United Labor Party in 1886 and the Labor–People's Party alliance in 1894. After the Socialist Labor Party split in 1899, he helped with the reorganization that led to the formation of the Socialist Party.

A militant trade unionist, Morgan's affiliations included the Machinists' and Blacksmiths' Union, the Knights of Labor, and the Socialist Trade and Labor Alliance. He helped organize the Chicago Trade and Labor Assembly and the International Machinists' Union. He authored Chicago's first factory inspection statute and spearheaded the movement that resulted in the creation of the Illinois Bureau of Labor Statistics.

Morgan became a lawyer in 1895 and maintained a practice dedicated to protecting the interests of wage earners and socialists. Primarily an activist and organizer rather than a theoretician, he remained an indefatigable exponent of socialism and trade unionism.

Sources and Further Reading: Ralph William Scharnau, "Thomas J. Morgan and the Chicago Socialist Movement, 1876–1901," Ph.D. diss., Northern Illinois University, 1970; Ralph William Scharnau, "Thomas J. Morgan and the United Labor Party of Chicago," *Journal of the Illinois State Historical Society* 66 (Spring 1973).

Ralph Scharnau
Northeast Iowa Community College–Peosta

Immigration, Ethnicity, and Employment

The configuration of workers in the Midwest resulted from successive waves of immigration of peoples from different ethnic groups who assumed different and changing roles in the workforce over time.

Among the earliest settlers were Scots-Irish and English frontiersmen who settled the region from the South. On the whole they were farmers. The lands they settled were less fertile than the Corn Belt, and they were never pushed out by competing ethnic groups. Yankees, of English descent, started arriving by the 1830s via New England or New York. Many started farms in the corn and dairy regions but soon moved to town. They created great new cities. Cleveland and Cincinnati were important magnets. The Yankees practically invented Chicago and infused it with a peculiar dynamism. For a century they dominated banking, insurance, law, education, medicine, railroads, shipping, manufacturing, architecture, journalism, philanthropy, high society, and progressive reform in cities throughout the region, and continue to maintain a powerful presence. Their strengths included skill at fashioning complex organizations of cooperating strangers that involved identifying talent, trusting expertise, and winning the confidence of investors back East, especially those from Boston.

The German Jewish immigration of the middle nineteenth century brought innovative retail merchandizing to a thousand Main Streets. Among nineteenth century immigrants, particularly the Scots, Scots-Irish, and English included numerous entrepreneurs and engineers, of whom electricity czar Samuel Insull was the most prominent.

The rich farmlands of the Corn Belt and dairy regions attracted hundreds of thousands of German, Scandinavian, and Dutch farmers. We can include in this grouping the Pennsylvania "Dutch" (Germans) who moved to Ohio. They worked hard, saved money, and bought out other ethnic farmers, especially Yankees who preferred urban lifestyles and white collar jobs. The representative Yankee farmer was an innovator, who operated most effectively via agricultural colleges and experiment stations. The agrarian Germans displayed a deep attachment to rural life that caused them to postpone as long as possible the inevitable exodus to the cities. Urban Germans came in large numbers as well, and settled in every medium and large city on the river and lakes systems. By 1890, Cincinnati, Milwaukee, Davenport, Dubuque, and St. Louis formed German strongholds, as did the northern third of Chicago and large tracts in Detroit, Cleveland, Indianapolis, Columbus, and other large cities. Urban Germans avoided both the middle range, as craftsmen, butchers, bakers, musicians, carpenters, saloonkeepers, mechanics, and brewers, and were more attracted to careers in unskilled manual labor and white collar or managerial careers.

Other western European immigrants brought special skills. Walloon Belgian glass makers flocked to factories in Muncie and the Indiana gas district, and Flemish Belgians went to Mishawaka's rubber works. Dutch bench carpenters opened furniture factories in Grand Rapids. Over a third of the buildings in Chicago and Minneapolis were constructed by Swedes. Englishmen from Staffordshire created the pottery industry of East Liverpool, Ohio. Throughout the region, foremen, toolmakers, and engineers were disproportionately English and Scottish. The lumber regions attracted Finns and Canadians. Indeed, Detroit and all the border districts had large numbers of British Canadians (few French Canadians came to the Midwest.)

Irish Catholics represented a unique labor experience from the 1830s to the 1880s. The Irish Potato Famine drove many to North American shores as extremely poor immigrants in poor physical shape with limited industrial or agricultural skills. However, they demonstrated a genius for organization. They formed labor gangs, contracted to build canals and railroads, and soon were represented in every transportation center. Few entered agriculture. The Irish strongly promoted group solidarity and deemphasized individual achievement; "all for one" was the motto, and some were not averse to violence or strikes to enhance the bargaining position of their work gang or labor union. They soon discovered that their remarkable political solidarity could be translated into jobs via the patronage system. By the late nineteenth century, the Irish were heavily represented among municipal jobs, including policemen, firemen, transit workers, utility workers, and teachers. As civil service reform took hold, the Irish sent their youth to Catholic schools and colleges. Many became lawyers, politicians, and priests; the few attracted to business were primarily saloonkeepers or construction contractors. By 1900, half or more trade union leaders in the American Federation of Labor were Irishmen, preaching the gospel of labor solidarity.

The Irish believed that they were discriminated against by Protestants in the job market. They were not confronted by "No Irish Need Apply" signs; rather they created and repeated this urban myth to help maintain solidarity and discourage individualism. Irish women dominated the market for domestic servants in many cities. Some thought Irish domestic servants had a reputation for mediocre quality work, but they offered some advantages over other immigrant groups. They spoke English. Along with African Americans and Swedes, they had a strong commitment to service jobs and were available in large numbers. Because of late marriage and spinsterhood, they spent years in service, accumulating experience and maturity that made them more useful than inexperienced teenagers. Off the job they built a cohesive support network that provided friendship, entertainment, and advice. The network set informal job standards regarding working hours, housing, food, perquisites, and pay scales. Enforcement came by the maid immediately quitting if the employer violated the standards; she could be confident her friends would help her find a new position.

By World War II, Irish solidarity faltered. The maids traded their aprons for jobs in war factories and never returned. The urban political machines crumbled one by one; even the last survivor, Daley's Chicago machine, lost most of its patronage. High levels of education opened up corporate and management jobs that promoted individualism and made ethnic solidarity irrelevant. By the 1950s, the Irish ranked well above average in terms of job status and income.

After 1850, few southerners migrated north of the Ohio River until the 1920s, when numbers of Appalachians took factory jobs in Cincinnati, Dayton, Muncie, Evansville, Detroit, Akron, and other cities that were within driving radius of their relatives back in the hills. Although black ghettoes could be found in Chicago, St. Louis, Cincinnati, and a few other midwestern cities before 1917, they contained few good jobs. George Pullman, Henry Ford, and a few other industrialists made it a policy to hire blacks, but most African American workers were relegated to unskilled labor, service jobs, and activity at the margins of the law. Some were hired as strikebreakers in coal, steel, and meatpacking, which led to racial tensions, including major riots in Chicago in 1919. The large influx of black workers in World War II, at a time of severe housing shortages, led to fears of another round of riots. However, except for an outbreak in Detroit in 1943, there was no major violence over jobs. The blacks were the only major group to suffer significant and systematic job discrimination.

As industrialization gained momentum after 1880, the majority of new hires in the new factories and mines were recent immigrants. After 1890, the source shifted away from Britain, Germany, and Scandinavia to Italy, Russia, and southeastern Europe. The immigrants of this era typically had very little money and, apart from the Jews, had scant education and few skills. The Jews concentrated in the clothing trades in New York, and to a lesser extent in Chicago. The Italians, Poles, Hungarians, Greeks, Serbs, Slovaks, and others headed to the mill towns, mines, and industrial districts of the Northeast and Midwest. Burgeoning industry needed energy, so the coalfields expanded enormously. The workforce at first comprised relatively skilled English, Welsh, Irish, and German immigrants. But after 1890, Slavic and Italian miners came in large numbers, bringing much less experience and a lower wage rate. In the peculiar economics of coal, labor strikes benefited both labor (by raising wages) and the owners (by creating shortages and higher prices.) However the ethnic clashes between established ethnic communities and new immigrant groups tended to escalate strike tensions, leading in 1894 to the Pullman Strike that wrought serious damage on the national economy. In the early twentieth century, the United Mine Workers union took control of labor relations and ended the interethnic violence.

Restriction on the overall flow of immigration was a high priority of the American Federation of Labor. It warned that large inflows of unskilled workers lowered wage rates overall, and encouraged employers to rely on large numbers of unskilled workers rather than train a smaller pool for more skilled, higher paying jobs. With no influx during World War I, the pool of new immigrant workers increased in age and experience and managed to save large sums of money that otherwise would have been remitted to the old country. Military training and extensive Americanization programs made permanent Americans out of many young men who originally planned a temporary sojourn. As a result, in the 1920s, a national consensus formed behind the AFL program of restricting the inflow of job seekers. Industrialists who sought unlimited pools of unskilled labor, typified by giant U.S. Steel, were defeated in Congress, as were nativists who wanted to exclude what they considered to be "inferior" Europeans. Numerical quotas were established to exactly replicate the current population, so that future immigration would not upset the ethnic balance that had been achieved. After the Immigration Act of 1924, immigration slowed to a trickle, often below the quotas. The new demography, combined with the rapid growth of high schools, helped move all ethnic groups out of the unskilled pool into semiskilled and skilled labor categories. Business discovered it could profit more by reliance on complex machinery and procedures that assumed a level of skill well beyond what was available early in the century.

During the Great Depression, the process of upskilling accelerated as employment offices systematically discriminated in favor of better educated, more skilled workers. The result was severe long-term unemployment for the unskilled, most of whom were recent immigrants and blacks. World War II saw the immediate end of long-term unemployment. Skill levels rose again in the 1940s thanks to massive crafts training by the armed services, the continued expansion of high schools, the GI Bill, and the increased use of in-house training programs by corporations. By 1950, the occupational distinctiveness of European ethnic groups had practically disappeared.

In 1965, the federal government radically changed the immigration laws, for the first time putting a premium on job skills. The result was an unprecedented influx of well-educated professionals from India, China, Korea, and other Asian countries. Many attended American graduate schools and became well-paid computer scientists, physicians, engineers, and college professors. Indians maintained strong ties to their homeland and established a flourishing software industry there. The same 1965 legislation for the first time restricted immigration from Mexico and Latin America.

Regardless, the North American job machine was irresistible—the United States created over a million new jobs a year, year in and year out. The supply of workers was reduced by expanding higher education and early retirement. Much of the vacuum was filled by undocumented unskilled workers from Latin America. Half the new arrivals went to California and Texas, but Chicago was also a magnet, and practically all midwestern metropolitan areas saw rapid growth in their Hispanic populations. Thus census data indicated half the new growth in Illinois and Missouri from 1990 to 2000 was attributed to the influx of approximately 700 thousand Hispanics. Small towns in rural areas that had not seen new immigrants in eighty years suddenly had their own *colonias*. By the mid 1990s, Hispanics and Asians dominated the labor force in meatpacking plants in the Midwest. Most of the Hispanics were young workers, willing to take low-paying nonunion jobs in restaurants, hospitals, factories, construction sites, and farms. They had relatively high birth rates and high school dropout rates, which tended to lock them at the bottom of the job ladder.

Demographers and economists continue to debate the economic impact of the recent migrants. The consensus seems to be that on the whole the economy is helped, but that less-educated native-born groups risk slippage in competition with the new migrants for low-skilled jobs.

Sources and Further Reading: June D. Holmquist, ed., *They Chose Minnesota* (1988); David Levinson and Melvin Ember, eds., *American Immigrant Cultures* (1997); Robert M. Taylor, Jr., and Connie A. McBirney, eds., *Peopling Indiana* (1996); Stephan Thernstrom, ed., *Harvard Encyclopedia of American Ethnic Groups* (1980).

Richard Jensen
University of Illinois–Chicago

German American Workers

Although German immigrants to the Midwest came from diverse backgrounds and classes, the majority were working-class people. Emerging midwestern urban centers offered opportunities for both unskilled and skilled German workers, although the latter were more important in both numbers and impact on industrial development and the organization of labor. Given the significant proportions of Germans in the populations of all midwestern towns, German workers could be found in various employments. However, their presence was particularly felt in some areas like the food industry (bakers, butchers, brewers), woodworking (furniture workers), and cigar making, as well as in building and construction (brick masons, carpenters, and joiners), where they contributed the overwhelming majority of workers or a significant minority among several ethnic groups. They were able to utilize skills acquired in Germany as apprentices and journeymen, but had been unable to translate into independent artisan status. Early immigrants to the Midwest often realized such goals, but toward the turn of the twentieth century, skilled workers increasingly lost out to industrial concentration and often became trapped in dead-end careers.

German workers also introduced European liberal, even radical, democratic traditions into both midwestern urban politics and the emerging American labor movement. The failure of the mid-nineteenth-century revolutionary movement in Germany and Europe swept thousands of German workers to the United States who had participated in, or at least shared the goals of, those uprisings. The consensus of middle-class and artisan political visions before the Civil War often encouraged more liberal policies advanced by associations like the gymnastic societies. From the mid-1860s, the rise of the German Social Democracy—at a time when many more immigrant workers continued to arrive in the Midwest—nourished radical working-class traditions of a German, often Marxian, bent.

German ideological thought and organizational traditions helped shape the midwestern labor movement in several ways. The importance of craft as the common ground for lasting solidarity and effective organization carried the day over fierce ideological infighting between Lasalleans, Marxists, and anarchists. German labor leaders also used organizational traditions to build an intricate network of initially ethnic, working-class institutions. In several midwestern towns, the German-language labor press often was the recognized center of working-class organization and leisure-time activities. Labor editors, like Conrad Conzett, Paul Grottkau, August Spies, and Julius

Vahlteich at the *Chicagoer Arbeiter-Zeitung* and the *Vorbote*, were also in the forefront of union organization. They helped build a rich working-class cultural tradition.

The major challenge for German immigrant workers and the institutions they created was to overcome ethnic barriers and ethnic isolation. This process involved discarding feelings of ideological and cultural superiority, engaging in common forms of organization with other ethnic labor unions, like local and state central bodies, and especially accepting English as the common language. Thus, such labor papers as the *Deutsch-Amerikanische Buchdruckerzeitung* around the turn of the twentieth century began publishing articles in both English and German before turning completely to English. As ethnic identity waned—a development also welcomed by German Americans in the Socialist party after 1901, when leadership was increasingly assumed by Americans—German-American labor organizations still tried to cling to egalitarian concepts of social justice. During the Progressive Era, they helped implement these on the municipal level, especially in Milwaukee, where Emil Seidel was elected mayor in 1910 on the Social Democratic party ticket.

It is this social justice tradition—which resurfaced once again during the New Deal in industrial unionism, for example, when the Reuther brothers helped organize the automobile workers—that is the most significant contribution of German American workers to the mainstream of the American labor movement.

Sources and Further Reading: Bruce Levine, *The Spirit of 1848: German Immigrants, Labor Conflict, and the Coming of the Civil War* (1992); Hartmut Keil, ed., *German Workers' Culture in the United States, 1850 to 1920* (1988); Hartmut Keil, "German Working-Class Radicalism after the Civil War" in Frank Trommler and Elliott Shore, eds., *The German-American Encounter: Conflict and Cooperation between Two Cultures, 1800–2000* (2001); Hartmut Keil and John B. Jentz, eds., *German Workers in Industrial Chicago, 1850–1910* (1983).

Hartmut Keil
University of Leipzig, Germany

Irish American Workers

Irish American workers have traditionally experienced both industrial exploitation and discrimination, struggling not just over wages and conditions, but against perceived ethnic stereotypes of drunkenness and violence that initially consigned the Irish to a low occupational strata in America. In the wake of the Great Famine (1845–1850), Irish immigrants flocked to the American Midwest armed with a keen insight into the nature of injustice. As general laborers, organizers, and politicians, Irish Americans have been active and influential participants in the development of the infrastructure and labor organizations of the region.

As unskilled laborers, Irish American workers played an important role in building the canals and railways of the Midwest that became the lifelines of American industry. Irish rural migration patterns in the nineteenth century often followed the routes of canals and railways, since payment in land was a cheap alternative for state governments when budgets were tight. In areas like Michigan's Keweenaw Peninsula, Irish workers followed migration networks that employed their traditional skills in the copper mines. Throughout the coalfields of Ohio, Indiana, and Illinois, Irish miners extracted the raw materials necessary for industrial growth. Irish lumberjacks also played a major role in logging the forests of Northern Michigan, supplying the building materials necessary for Midwest urban and rural development.

As Lawrence McCaffrey has observed, the Irish American experience was primarily an urban one. In expanding cities, the Irish played a vital role in the building trades, domestic services, unskilled factory labor, and public construction projects. In massive urban centers like Chicago, politicized concentrations of Irish immigrants helped to advance Midwest labor organization and politics. Chicago became a storm center of labor radicalism with events like the Haymarket Affair (1886), the founding of the Industrial Workers of the World (1905), and the short-lived Progressivism of the Farmer-Labor Party (1920) led by John Fitzpatrick's Chicago Federation of Labor. Irish cultural and nationalist activities in urban centers helped bridge the gap between skilled and unskilled workers, using their common ethnic identity to advance a common class identity.

Irish America produced both radical agitators like Mary Harris ("Mother") Jones and conservative labor leaders like John Mitchell of the American Federation of Labor. Through the Knights of Labor and the Irish Land League, Irish Americans gave expression to maturing working-class economic and political grievances through trade organization and employing Irish boycott tactics. The anarcho-syndicalist Association of Catholic Trade Unionists helped to mature the notions of industrial unionism that were vital to widespread Midwest organizing efforts. While Irish leaders in the United Mine Workers sought a program of industrial peace, Irish leaders in the Congress of Industrial Organizations pressed for a militant strategy in labor disputes.

Since Irish identity centered on a rejection of perceived English tyranny, the anti-Catholic and anti-union perceptions of the Republican Party led the Irish to a parallel political rejection. Common bonds between Fenians, the Democratic Party, and trade unions enabled Irish Americans to forge a progressive agenda that facilitated Irish social, cultural, economic, and political influence in the Midwest into the twentieth century.

Sources and Further Reading: Michael Glazier ed., *The Encyclopedia of the Irish in America* (1999); Lawrence J. McCaffrey, *The Irish Catholic Diaspora in America* (1997); David Montgomery, "The Irish and the American Labor Movement," in David Noel Doyle and Owen Dudley Edwards, eds., *America and Ireland, 1776–1976* (1980); Timothy M. O'Neil, "Miners in Migration: The Case of Nineteenth-Century Irish and Irish-American Copper Miners," *Éire-Ireland* 36 (Spring–Summer 2001).

Joel A. Lewis
Central Michigan University

Polish American Workers

Polish immigrants began to arrive in the Midwest during the mid-nineteenth century, often fleeing war, political repression, religious persecution, or economic hardships at home. Poles came in ever-increasing numbers, especially after the 1870s, and by 1920, well over 2.5 million had settled in the United States, mainly in the Midwest. Poles saw hard work as the means of achieving a better life, no matter how difficult or dangerous it might be. Drawn to the largest Midwest industrial cities such as Chicago, Cleveland, Detroit, and Milwaukee by the high demand for laborers, Poles could be found performing some of the most difficult and dangerous occupations in America such as meatpacking, steel production, automotive work, and coal mining.

By settling into close-knit ethnic communities, Poles maintained many traditions and values from their homeland. Among these was their willingness to protest. Just as people in Poland rose up in revolt against their foreign occupiers, so too did Polish American workers organize, rise up, and strike to ensure their rights were not denied. They participated heavily in the labor movements of the early twentieth century, which established better working conditions for all Americans, immigrant and native-born alike. Polish American labor leaders such as Leo Krzycki and Stanley Nowak helped bring about the rise of labor unions, including the Congress of Industrial Organizations, the Amalgamated Clothing Workers of America, and the United Auto Workers during the mid 1930s. Nowak, well known for labor activism, went on to serve in the Michigan state senate from 1939 to 1948.

Sources and Further Reading: William G. Falkowski, "Labor, Radicalism, and the Polish-American Worker," in John J. Bukowczyk, ed., *Polish Americans and their History* (1996); Eugene Miller, "Leo Krzycki—Polish American Labor Leader," *Polish American Studies* 33 (Fall 1976); Margaret Collingwood Nowak, *Two Who Were There* (1989).

Roman A. Nitze
The Ohio State University–Columbus

Mexican American Workers

Mexican American workers, many of them Mexican immigrants and Texans, first entered the Midwest in large numbers after 1900, recruited by specific employers. By the late 1930s, Mexican Americans were employed in rail work, migratory agricultural labor, steel manufacturing, meatpacking, tanneries, and sugar refineries.

Primarily speaking Spanish and living in small enclaves, these workers began to establish Mexican neighborhoods in Detroit, Chicago, Milwaukee, Minneapolis–St. Paul, Kansas City, and other smaller towns. These primarily working-class neighborhoods expanded for most of the century, as immigrants and Mexican Americans founded churches, small businesses, and newspapers. After World War II, these communities continued to grow as immigrant and Tejano workers entered the Midwest as factory workers and service workers. After 1960, residents of Chicago, Detroit, and Milwaukee, pushed for labor and civil rights, establishing in the process many community organizations. By 2000, many Mexican American workers had entered the mainstream of American society as their children, in some cases, have moved out of factory and service work and into jobs that required a college education. The 2000 census reported that Chicago, Illinois, had one of the largest populations of ethnic Mexican residents in the nation, and many smaller cities and towns saw rapid growth as migrants settled outside the larger cities.

Despite their permanence and success, the Mexican American and immigrant population continues to suffer from low wages, poor working conditions, and a lack of social and civil rights, as many work in conditions similar to those experienced by settlers in the early twentieth century.

Sources and Further Reading: Manuel Gamio, *Mexican Immigration to the United States* (1971); Dennis N. Valdes, *Barrios Nortenos* (2000).

Marc S. Rodriguez
Princeton University, New Jersey

Mexican American workers in the beet fields, Finney County, Kansas. Kansas State Historical Society, Sue Rodriguez Collection, FK2.F1.5.

Native American Workers

Midwestern Native Americans entered the wage labor market during the mid-1800s. The United States emptied the states of Ohio, Indiana, Illinois, and Missouri of their Native American populations during the 1830s. Native Americans in Michigan, Minnesota, Wisconsin, Kansas, and the Dakotas have lived on and around federal reservations at the fringe of American settlement throughout the nineteenth and twentieth centuries. People in reservation communities harvested indigenous crops for subsistence and sale and worked as day laborers in commercial fishing, lumbering, and farming. They maintained a dual economic strategy throughout the early twentieth century, hunting, fishing, and gathering when the market economy could not provide cash and working for cash when labor presented better opportunities.

Federal policies favored assimilation of indigenous populations into mainstream American society throughout most of the 1800s and 1900s. Between 1880 and 1930, government-funded day schools and boarding schools taught native children the English language, basic math and reading skills, trained them as unskilled laborers for domestic and factory work, and often sent them off-reservation for employment. Girls cooked, sewed, and learned to labor as domestics. Boys learned farming, carpentry, masonry, sign painting, and similar vocational skills.

Upon graduation, students often became wage laborers working in towns and cities within or adjacent to their reservations. For example, the Oneidas of Wisconsin enjoyed easy access to Green Bay and surrounding towns; the Saginaw Chippewas of Michigan worked at occupations in the city of Mt. Pleasant, which was built within their reservation boundaries; the Pokagon Potawatomis of Michigan often found work in the city of Berrien Springs, which was adjacent to their rural community; and the Grand River Ottawas of Michigan worked at Hart or Ludington, which were adjacent to their reservations. By 1900, midwestern Native Americans regularly traveled from reservations to large urban areas at Grand Rapids, Detroit, or Muskegon, Michigan, to Chicago, Illinois, to Milwaukee, Wisconsin, and to Minneapolis, Minnesota, for seasonal or short-term employment that helped their families to survive the economic poverty of reservation life.

Whole families moved from rural reservation communities into urban centers to support themselves by wage labor after the Great Depression, and their populations in Detroit, Chicago, Milwaukee, and Minneapolis–St. Paul grew large while reservation populations dwindled. The participation of Native American soldiers in the armed services during World War II and the entry of returning soldiers into the U.S. industrial workplace further increased their participation in wage labor in urban areas.

During the 1950s and 1960s, the urban populations organized "Indian Clubs" or associations in large cities. These organizations served as centers for the dissemination of history, culture, and social services and became the organizing vehicles for political mobilization during the late 1960s and 1970s. The trend of workers urbanizing began to reverse only late in the twentieth century, when federal programs fostered on-reservation employment opportunities. Native Americans who served as leaders and officers in urban organizations often served on tribal councils, as well, when local wage labor opportunities allowed them to return to their nineteenth century reservations during the 1980s.

Modern Native American tribes offer their members employment in many economic endeavors within and outside of their traditionally used territories and reservations. New generations of tribe members educated in urban schools during the postwar years and living in communities throughout the United States now participate in almost all occupations available in the American economy. A growing number of tribes now operate gaming facilities, which have generated substantial capital. For the first time in two hundred years, tribes now generate wage labor positions that allow their scattered members to return to traditional tribal territories. The ability of tribes to hire their own members has helped to restore communities damaged by a century of out-migration.

Sources and Further Reading: Rolf Knight, *Indians At Work* (1978); Alice Littlefield and Martha C. Knack, eds., *Native Americans and Wage Labor* (1996); Francis Paul Prucha, *Atlas of American Indian Affairs* (1990).

James M. McClurken
Lansing, Michigan

Finnish American Workers

Finns had a significant impact on the labor movement and radical politics of the upper Midwest, where approximately half of the 300 thousand Finnish immigrants settled between 1870 and 1920. Immigrants found employment among the ranks of unskilled laborers in copper and iron mines, in the logging industry, and on the docks of the Great Lakes.

The harsh conditions of extractive industries proved fertile ground for labor militancy. A sizable segment of the Finnish community responded by affiliating with various left-wing political parties and labor unions, constituting perhaps the most radical ethnic group in the nation. Scholars estimate that between one-fourth and one-third of Finnish Americans participated in the institutional network forged by radicals. Between 1906 and 1914, the Finnish Socialist Federation was the largest of the Socialist Party's foreign language federations.

After 1914 Finns converted in droves to industrial unionism, becoming the dominant ethnic group in the Industrial Workers of the World (IWW). Founded by democratic socialists, the Work People's College, located outside of Duluth, affiliated with the IWW. During the Red Decade of the 1920s and through the 1930s, Finns shifted toward Communism, coming to constitute nearly 45 percent of the Workers Party. Several thousand leftists departed for Soviet Karelia in the early 1930s to help build the Labor Republic. At the same time, many Finns began to shift away from the far-left, finding a home in the growing industrial union movement and the Democratic Party. Though Finnish American radicalism eroded considerably after World War II, the Communist remnant persisted for several decades more.

Sources and Further Reading: A. William Hoglund, *Finnish Immigrants in America* (1960); Peter Kivisto, *Immigrant Socialists in the United States* (1984); Carl Ross, *The Finn Factor in American Labor, Culture, and Society* (1977).

Peter Kivisto
Augustana College, Illinois

Jewish American Workers

Jewish workers have not generally been associated with the American Midwest, but have nonetheless played a significant role in its history. The Midwest was promoted among immigrant Jews as an alternative to the New York working-class ghetto, but proved not to be the egalitarian haven for all who immigrated there. Although Chicago has been the primary location of a Jewish working class, other cities of the region such as Cleveland and St. Louis have also had sizable working-class Jewish communities.

Although the early Jewish immigrants to the Midwest experienced a relatively egalitarian working environment, with the first massive arrival of Russian and eastern European Jewish immigrants in the 1880s, industrial employment and the class stratification it engendered became facts of life in major cities of the region. Immigrant Jews played an important role in the garment trades and became a driving force in the garment trades union movement. Many notable events in American Jewish labor history occurred in midwestern cities, such as the 1911 and 1915 Chicago garment workers strikes and the Cleveland Strike of 1911, the latter being part of an effort to equalize labor conditions in the industry.

Also, the Chicago Cloakmakers Union, with primarily Jewish membership in its early years, played a significant role in founding the Amalgamated Clothing Workers of America in 1915. However, Jewish workers in the Midwest moved up to the middle class within a generation or two, resulting in the marked decline of a Jewish labor movement by the late 1920s.

Sources and Further Reading: Hyman H. Bookbinder and Associates, *To Promote the General Welfare* (1950); Irving Cutler, *The Jews of Chicago* (1996); Lewis L. Lorwin, *The Women's Garment Workers* (1924).

Susan Breitzer
University of Iowa

The Great Migration of African Americans

During and after World War I and again between 1940 and 1970, African Americans migrated from the southern United States to the North and West in unprecedented numbers, laying the foundation for conditions that forever transformed America. Estimates vary, but between 1915 and 1918, approximately 500 to 700 thousand black southerners moved to the North and West, followed by at least another 700 thousand blacks who relocated to northern and western cities during the 1920s. Migration slowed during the Great Depression, but picked up again between 1940 and 1970, when net migration out of the South reached nearly 4.5 million, more than a third of whom moved to the Midwest.

Economic factors "pulled" African Americans

Perspective from the Great Migration. Library of Congress, Prints and Photographs Division, LC-USZ62-130701 DLC. FSA-OWI Collection, 1935–1945, LC-USF33-016151-M5 DLC.

north and westward. While American industrial production increased during World War I, the flow of European immigrants dropped sharply, creating a critical labor shortage. To meet the demand for labor, employers began hiring southern black laborers, a previously untapped source of industrial workers. For the majority of African Americans, this was the first opportunity to work in the most dynamic sectors of the industrial economy—iron, steel, meatpacking, autos (by the twenties), and rubber (by the forties). Although the packinghouses of Chicago employed thousands of black men and women, industrial jobs were limited for African American women, who worked largely in the domestic service sector of the economy. Nevertheless, black women earned much more in the North than in the South. Migration patterns during World War II closely resembled those of World War I. African Americans left the South for work in large industrial centers. Roughly 65 thousand and 60 thousand black Americans had settled in Chicago and Detroit, respectively, by 1944, a migration that was slightly larger than that during World War I.

Socioeconomic and political factors in the South helped "push" the issue of migration to the fore. The economic exploitation common in the sharecropping system that typified southern agricultural labor relations for black workers, combined with political disenfranchisement and white violence, compelled black men and women to head to the Promised Land. The *Chicago Defender*, widely distributed in the South and a promoter of black migration, advocated heading North, and many heeded its advice. However, the majority of migrants out of the rural South between World War I and 1930 moved not to northern and western cities but to those in the urban South. And between 1940 and 1950, although African Americans continued to migrate to the urban South, where the population increased by 35 percent, the black urban population in northern and western states increased by 70 percent.

For many, migration Northward was a two-step process, similar to that of Richard Wright, author of *Native Son* and *Black Boy*, who moved from Alabama to Memphis, Tennessee, in the 1920s. After a few years in the urban South, he migrated to Chicago in 1927. He left the South for the promise of freedom that lay in the mythic land north of the Ohio River, where he imagined he would be free from the suffocation of the southern caste system. A. Philip Randolph, head of the Brotherhood of Sleeping Car Porters, who went North to free himself from second-class citizenship, thought all African Americans needed to create as much distance as possible between themselves and the social relations of slavery—those customs, beliefs, and

practices in the Jim Crow South that continued to shape daily life decades after the end of slavery. Although the second phase of the Great Migration, the period from 1940 to 1970, was inspired more by "push" than "pull" factors, it was a two-stage push out of agriculture. The 1940s represented a mix of push and pull factors, but during the 1950s, when complete mechanization pushed black laborers from the cotton harvest, African American migration to northern and western cities grew by 2.7 million.

Migrants like Randolph, who did not find the equality they sought in the North, became part of the New Negro Movement, in which a new group of African Americans rose to the fore in northern black communities to claim their rights as citizens. The process of migrating from rural to urban areas, from agricultural to industrial employment, and from the southern to the northern and western climates transformed the perspective and politics of black America, which found restrictive the "places" defined in the North for black Americans to work, live, and play. The transformation led to the rise of an aggressive protest politics, pioneered by the New Negro, that galvanized the black community and challenged the old-style negotiations with established authorities, and planted the seeds for the civil rights movement that followed.

Black Americans during the first phase of migration from the South and the post–World War II years of the second phase realized new economic opportunities in the job market and in the organized labor movement. However, those who migrated during the 1950s often faced a choice between migrating or starving, as agricultural work disappeared along with assistance from government relief agencies in the South.

Sources and Further Reading: Eric Arnesen, *Black Protest and the Great Migration* (2003); James R. Grossman, *Land of Hope: Chicago, Black Southerners, and the Great Migration* (1989); Carole Marks, *Farewell—We're Good and Gone* (1989); Joe William Trotter, Jr., ed., *The Great Migration in Historical Perspective* (1991).

Beth Tompkins Bates
Wayne State University, Michigan

The Southern White Migration

Southern white migrants in the Midwest (or elsewhere) have not been the source of much scholarly attention. Nevertheless, they significantly affected the region, shaping not only its political economy but its culture, as well. Southern whites began to move to midwestern states, specifically Illinois, Indiana, Michigan, Ohio, and Wisconsin, during World War I. By 1920, they accounted for 4 percent of the area's white population.

The migrants came largely for factory jobs in cities, although many settled on farms where they frequently engaged in sharecropping or in seasonal work. Despite the return of some migrants "down home" in the 1930s and 1940s, the Great Depression and particularly World War II intensified the movement of southern white workers into the Midwest. By 1950, they were 7 percent of the region's white population. Within a decade (at the zenith of what historian Chad Berry has called the "great white migration"), they constituted 8 percent, a proportion that has not been surpassed. In fact, since the 1960s, the southern white population of the Midwest has been decreasing. This trend coincided with the deindustrialization of the region.

Although the experiences of southern whites in the region varied considerably, there were some commonalities. One was overcoming the prejudice of native midwesterners, who viewed the migrants as racist, nativist, clannish, antiunion, poor, proud, disorderly, uneducated, and unsophisticated. There is no denying that some white migrants had these attributes, but in many cases these were ill-fitting stereotypes. For example, many southern white migrants in fact joined both industrial and agricultural unions. Most achieved economic success. Furthermore, blaming only southern white migrants for strained race relations in the Midwest masks the significant problems before their arrival. The stereotypes also minimize the cultural influences of the region. The traditions of southern white migrants resonated with and reinforced midwestern folkways. The migrants' independent and individualistic spirit often mirrored that of the people whom they met.

Southern white migrants also helped to transform midwestern politics. Some historians have argued that the postwar growth in working-class conservatism can be traced to the presence of white southerners in the North. In 1964 and in 1968, presidential candidate George Wallace did quite well in the Midwest, particularly in Wisconsin, Indiana, and Michigan. White migrants not only voted for Henry Wallace (and Barry Goldwater), but they also worked on those campaigns at the local level. Something in the racist, populist rhetoric also hit home for many native midwesterners, however. And if southern racial politics found fertile ground in the Midwest, so did southern music. In fact, country music was literally the soundtrack for the segregationist political campaigns of the 1960s.

Aside from politics, there are other examples of the "southernization" of the Midwest. In food and especially in religion, southern migrants left their mark.

The Baptist and other Protestant congregations that southern whites formed drew members from outside migrant communities. Although for many decades southern migrants, like other midwesterners, have been leaving the Rust Belt, their social and culture legacies remain.

Sources and Further Reading: Harriette Arnow, *The Dollmaker* (1954); Chad Berry, *Southern Migrants, Northern Exiles* (2000); James N. Gregory, "Southernizing the American Working Class: Post-War Episodes of Regional and Class Transformation," *Labor History* 39 (May 1998); James N. Gregory, Grace Elizabeth Hale, Alex Lichtenstein, and Thomas J. Sugrue, "Commentary and Response to James N. Gregory: Southernizing the American Working Class," *Labor History* 39 (1998).

Andrew E. Kersten
University of Wisconsin–Green Bay

The Brotherhood of Sleeping Car Porters

On August 25, 1925, the Brotherhood of Sleeping Car Porters (BSCP) was founded secretly in New York City by A. Philip Randolph, a major figure in the American labor and civil rights movements. The Chicago Division, under the leadership of the dynamic Milton P. Webster, however, became the most important local. The St. Louis Division was headed by E. J. Bradley, and Chicagoan Halena Wilson was president of the Women's Auxiliary. These three Midwest leaders played an influential role in the BSCP becoming the nation's first successful black labor union. The BSCP trained its members in collective bargaining and taught them to make demands rather than to beg for favors from the white power structure. After twelve years of struggle, the Pullman Company finally signed a contract with the BSCP on August 25, 1937, bringing improved working conditions and income to the porters.

Meanwhile, the BSCP provided support for civil rights activity by lobbying the American Federation of Labor and contributing people and funds for Randolph's various equality movements. The porters were active in Randolph's threatened March on Washington in 1941, which resulted in the wartime Fair Employment Practices Committee, and they backed his threat of a boycott of Universal Military Training in 1948, which resulted in President Truman's Executive Order integrating the military. The BSCP supported the Montgomery Bus Boycott in 1955, Randolph's Prayer Pilgrimage in 1957, his Marches on Washington for Integrated Schools in 1958 and 1959, and the March on Washington for Jobs and Freedom in 1963. With the postwar decline of the railroad industry and the aging of the porters, in 1978 the BSCP merged with the Brotherhood of Railway and Airline Clerks.

Sources and Further Reading: William H. Harris, *Keeping the Faith: A. Philip Randolph, Milton P. Webster, and the Brotherhood of Sleeping Car Porters, 1925–1937* (1977); Paula F. Pfeffer, *A. Philip Randolph, Pioneer of the Civil Rights Movement* (1990); Joseph F. Wilson, *Tearing Down the Color Bar* (1989).

Paula F. Pfeffer
Loyola University–Chicago, Illinois

The Fair Employment Practices Committee

The advent of the Second World War reversed the economic misfortunes of the Midwest caused by the Great Depression. Infused with federal dollars, defense contractors reopened industrial gates from Chicago to Cincinnati, allowing thousands who lacked jobs to obtain well-paying war work. There were, however, definite limits to these opportunities. African Americans and other minorities were frequently denied the chance to work in midwestern defense factories.

Spurred to action by civil rights leader and President of the Brotherhood of Sleeping Car Porters, A. Philip Randolph, on June 25, 1941, President Franklin D. Roosevelt issued Executive Order 8802, which banned discrimination in wartime employment nationwide and created the Fair Employment Practices Committee (FEPC) to enforce the edict. Though the FEPC failed to eradicate job bias, it was quite successful in opening previously closed job opportunities in cities such as Chicago, Cleveland, Detroit, and Milwaukee. It was largely unsuccessful in cities close to the South such as Cincinnati, East Alton (Illinois), and Evansville (Indiana), owing to the lack of commitment of local labor organizations to interracial unionism, unsympathetic government officials, and the weakness of local civil rights movements.

Although the FEPC's efforts had uneven results, they did constitute an important industrial precedent. When the federal FEPC was disbanded, midwestern city and state governments created their own fair employment agencies to continue the fight against job discrimination. These bodies were not very effective, but they provided a critical transition between the wartime FEPC and the federal Equal Employment Opportunity Commission established by the 1964 Civil Rights Act.

Sources and Further Reading: Andrew E. Kersten, *Race, Jobs, and the War* (2000); Merl E. Reed, *Seedtime for the Modern Civil Rights Movement* (1991).

Andrew E. Kersten
University of Wisconsin–Green Bay

The 1919 Race Riot

At the end of World War I, African Americans in Chicago clashed with whites over housing and jobs. As black migrants jockeyed to keep the jobs that became available to them during the labor shortage of World War I, bitterness set in when the doors of economic opportunity began closing. By early May 1919, black unemployment was at approximately ten thousand.

While the black population increased by 65,491 between 1910 and 1920 in Chicago, fifty thousand of the new residents arrived during an eighteen-month period in 1917–1918. Housing covenants restricted where blacks could live, and other racial codes limited their physical mobility. The huge increase in the black population was confined to the "black belt," which had an acute shortage of housing. When black residents tried to expand their area of settlement on the South Side, they faced bombs, bullets, and collective efforts designed to keep them in a space narrowly circumscribed by the wishes of associations of white property owners.

The presence of fifty thousand additional black people increased the tension in the conflict over private space—and increasingly structured the relationship between black and white Chicagoans whenever they met in public places. In addition, competition for jobs increased dramatically after World War I, as thousands of veterans added to the already overcrowded labor market. Irish street gangs, located just east of the stockyards, led the attack on the black community by targeting black workers as they left the stockyards on the 27th.

On Sunday, July 27, 1919, issues of space, race, and work erupted into the Chicago race riot. That day was one of several during July when the temperature rose into the nineties. Both black and white citizens had taken to the streets and beaches for relief. When a raft of young black boys floated across an imaginary line dividing Twenty-ninth Street and Lake Michigan beach into "white" and "black" sections, Eugene Williams, one of the boys, was pelted with a rock by a white man, fell unconscious into the water and drowned, sparking the riot. White street gangs were major contributors to the violence and mayhem that continued through August 2. By the time the disaster was over, thirty-eight were dead and 537 were wounded.

In the aftermath of the riot, black Chicago learned to loathe invisible Jim Crow boundaries, and white Chicago learned that the city's black citizens were, as W.E.B. DuBois had observed, a different people than before World War I. Not only did white rioters kill twenty-three black citizens, but black people fought back, killing fifteen white citizens. The five-day riot shattered the African American illusion that the war would make America safe for democracy, and reinforced the efforts of New Negroes (African Americans who aggressively worked to claim citizenship rights) to demand an equal share in the democracy that black soldiers had fought for during World War I.

Sources and Further Reading: Chicago Commission on Race Relations, *The Negro in Chicago* (1922); William M. Tuttle, Jr., *Race Riot: Chicago in the Red Summer of 1919* (1970); Arthur I. Waskow, *From Race Riot to Sit-In: 1919 and the 1960s* (1966).

Beth Tompkins Bates
Wayne State University, Michigan

Metropolitan Unionism

Metropolitan unionism refers to distinctive behavior by labor unions whose members and industries were deeply rooted in particular cities. When successful, these unions controlled the labor supply and put a floor under wages through metropolitan-wide contracts. Such contracts stabilized their industries by moderating competition: Employers could not compete with each other by lowering wages below the minimum in the contract. Though not limited to the Midwest, metropolitan unionism had strong roots there, with Chicago providing a noteworthy example. Although strongest in the first third of the twentieth century, metropolitan unionism has been seen as a possible model for a revived labor movement today.

Unlike industrial unions, which organized all occupations in nationwide industries, metropolitan labor organizations concentrated on workers of a particular trade in one geographic area, such as janitors, construction workers, waitresses, and teamsters. They also organized in metropolitan markets instead of regional or national ones, and their industries typically had numerous small- to medium-sized businesses, not a few large corporations. Just as important, labor constituted a high proportion of total costs in the sectors of urban economies where metropolitan unionism took hold. Businesses in these industries were especially dependent on a reliable supply of labor; and because their markets were local, they could not simply move out of town to get away from labor organizations: apartment building owners could not move their properties to get away from unionized janitors. The strongest metropolitan unions both controlled the labor market and provided a reliable supply of workers in industries unusually dependent on labor, functions that also stabilized their sectors of the local economy.

Because their industries had so many small businesses, metropolitan unions were often organizationally more advanced than their business counterparts. Employers' associations frequently pulled themselves together in response to a challenge from labor. Such trade associations and labor unions sometimes cooperated to control prices and access to their local markets, particularly if the unions were strong enough to protect themselves from nonunion competition. This cooperation could also lead to charges of price fixing and corruption, especially if the unions and business associations used the local government to help them achieve their goals.

Unions organizing in such industries had distinctive problems. Since they were unable to rely on shared experience in a few large factories, metropolitan unions struggled to create a common culture to hold their organizations together. To do so, they frequently drew on the traditions of craft unions, even when their members held unskilled jobs of low status, such as janitors or waitresses. Unions of waitresses, for example, used work rules to define the kinds of work their members would and would not do, as they tried to turn an unskilled job into a higher status occupation. They also defined and enforced new levels of performance expected of members.

Metropolitan unionism was most prevalent in the construction trades, some service occupations, and branches of manufacturing with deep local roots. In the early twentieth century, baking and brewing had local markets because their perishable products were difficult to ship over long distances. They also had ethnic clienteles with specialized tastes that were best satisfied by local producers. In some respects, job printing and the garment industry had similar characteristics. Janitors and teamsters had to accommodate the diverse needs of large and small customers scattered over the entire city. Waitresses labored in restaurants practically too numerous to count, but all had local clienteles and owners faced with competition nearby. Yet the most important industry where metropolitan unionism took hold was construction. Every city had its building industry, and everywhere it was primarily local in both its ownership and its market. The construction industry was also a substantial component of any local economy, making the unions who organized it key players in the city's labor movement and politics.

Metropolitan unionism in the Midwest could not have existed without aid from the region's substantial urban labor movements, strong working-class communities, and energetic progressives. Organizing numerous small firms was costly: unions gained only a few workers in confrontations with any one employer; and the battle had to be fought over and over again.

Moreover, many of the occupations organized by metropolitan unions had unskilled and often demoralized workers who lacked the cultural and financial resources to build institutions. Unions organizing such workers needed help, and they had to get it from other unions. This meant that metropolitan unions developed most frequently in cities with strong local union movements, usually institutionalized in central labor bodies. These organizations could coordinate the aid needed by metropolitan unions, as well as mediate the inevitable jurisdictional disputes that arose. Commonly at the core of these central labor bodies were the building trades unions and the teamsters, although other unions, such as the United Auto Workers in Detroit, could perform the same function.

Ethnic factors also sustained metropolitan unionism. While the members of metropolitan unions came from all ethnic groups and both races, their leaders tended to be of Old Immigrant stock, that is, from Great Britain and Ireland, central Europe, and Scandinavia. Midwestern cities had unusually large representations of central European and Scandinavian craftsmen whose traditions helped them organize unions, and their political values made them more favorably disposed to using their unions and the local government to manage metropolitan markets.

The region's substantial ethnic working-class communities, of whatever national origin, supported local unions primarily through boycotting the products and services of offending employers, a common tactic that ranked with strikes among labor's weapons in the United States. By engaging in boycotts, members of these communities were not only showing solidarity with unions, many of whose members they knew personally, but also managing local markets. They had to do this indirectly because they could not control prices or access to the market—the tools available to organized business and labor. Thus local ethnic communities supported or opposed market players to achieve their ends. One can view metropolitan unionism as part of the effort by America's urban working class to control the economic environment in which it lived and worked. The ferocity of employers' attacks on boycotts indicates the considerable success of these local efforts at managing markets.

Also contributing to metropolitan unionism in the Midwest was a strong progressive reform movement that opposed the laissez-faire policies of the Gilded Age and sought to use government positively to address the ills of urban industrial society. Although not a working-class movement, progressivism created a political climate in which unions could more easily achieve their objectives, particularly in cities such as Chicago, Detroit, Toledo, and Cleveland, where it was especially strong. Progressives could be mobilized to support union boycotts of nonunion employers, and they formed alliances with labor to promote common goals such as a shorter working day and municipal ownership of utilities and streetcar lines. Progressive organizations of women were particularly strong in the Midwest. The Chicago chapter of the Women's Trade Union League was notably effective in supporting union label campaigns and organizing drives of female workers.

An overview of metropolitan unions in the Midwest should begin with Chicago, since the city was a nerve center in labor affairs, not just in the region but also in the nation. A substantial union movement in the city's building trades emerged out of the mass strikes of the 1880s. By the 1890s, the city had a Building Trades Council and a new central labor association, the Chicago Federation of Labor. Despite relying heavily on unions of skilled workers, these two bodies actively promoted the unionization of the unskilled in an aggressive organizing drive beginning in the late 1890s. Although a business counterattack stymied this movement, labor organizing revived in the World War I era. Strikes in Chicago's needle trades resulted in an agreement covering most of the local garment industry and including an arbitration mechanism for managing disputes. In 1915, the Chicago building trades achieved a comprehensive agreement that covered over a thousand employers and nearly eighty thousand workers. Again, an arbitration mechanism was central to the agreement. In 1917, the janitors in residential buildings achieved their first industry-wide contract, and it contained arbitration mechanisms copied from the building trades.

Typical of metropolitan unionism, these three agreements, including their arbitration features, witnessed labor unions forming uneasy alliances with associations of modest-sized businesses in an effort to manage recurring disputes in their local industries. In some of the building trades, the alliances became so close that they constituted collusion, in which unions, construction contractors, and manufacturers of building materials conspired to raise prices and mutually profit from the gain. Such practices provided an opening for a concerted drive by employers against the building trades unions after World War I. Despite these cycles of advance and retreat, Chicago's metropolitan unions among the building trades workers, teamsters, and building service workers gained a strong foothold and remained at the core of the local labor movement.

Both political and economic developments reduced the significance of metropolitan unionism after the 1930s. The weakening of both supportive ethnic constituencies and progressivism made the political environments for local labor movements less hospitable for metropolitan unionism. Progressivism declined nationally after World War I, and so did immigration, as the immigration quota laws of the early twenties, then the Depression constricted the flow. For a combination of reasons, the ethnic working-class constituencies more favorable to unions in midwestern cities receded in influence. Employers promoted this reduction of local working-class power by challenging boycotts in politics and the courts; their ultimate victory came in 1947, when the Taft-Hartley Act banned secondary boycotts, which prevened a nonunion manufacturer from selling products to those who did business with a union manufacturer. Labor's New Deal alliance with the Democratic Party also weakened the urban political base for metropolitan unionism by making it harder for local unions to engage in the independent political initiatives and alliances that had been conducive to metropolitan organizing in the past. Finally, the suburban expansion after World War II reduced the political significance of cities while contracting their economic base, thus weakening urban interests, including unions based in cities.

Yet the emergence of new economic forces was the most critical reason for the decline of metropolitan unionism. Expansion of firms acting in national markets reduced or destroyed the local and regional markets that defined the industries in which metropolitan unions had prospered. National firms entered local markets for beer and baked goods and changed the dynamics of competition in construction and janitorial services. This Second Industrial Revolution culminated in the 1920s as large corporations, such as General Electric and Ford, harnessed electricity to power mass production facilities that used assembly lines to make an unheard-of variety and volume of inexpensive consumer goods. These national corporations acted in markets beyond the influence of local boycotts that were rooted in urban working-class neighborhoods.

During the New Deal, the unions in the Congress of Industrial Organizations not only organized workers in these corporations of the Second Industrial Revolution, but also helped create a system of collective bargaining inhospitable to metropolitan unionism. Among the primary goals of the New Deal's collective bargaining system was to stimulate economic recovery by stabilizing competition among employers and containing conflict between capital and labor. The New Dealers saw national labor agreements in whole branches of industry as conducive to this larger aim. The critical labor contracts were now negotiated in sectors of the economy—such as auto, rubber, and oil—among parties with national constituencies and responsibilities. The nature and needs of local unions were seen as low priorities or even obstacles. These sectoral labor contracts also had political reverbera-tions because they undermined the rationale for labor's independent metropolitan political initiatives: Since the critical labor agreements were not made locally, local political power carried little weight in collective bargaining.

Metropolitan unionism is more than a significant chapter in labor history. It also provides an alternative model for how labor relations might be conducted today. In its organization of janitors and nursing home workers, the Service Employees International Union has pursued strategies reminiscent of the metropolitan unions prevalent in the first third of the twentieth century, particularly in its Union Cities campaigns. Those strategies are also seen in the work of living wage advocates across the country.

Sources and Further Reading: C. Lawrence Christenson, *Collective Bargaining in Chicago, 1929–1930: A Study of the Economic Significance of the Industrial Location of Trade-Unionism* (1933); Dorothy Sue Cobble, *Dishing It Out: Waitresses and Their Unions in the Twentieth Century* (1991); J. R. Commons, "Types of American Labor Organization—The Teamsters of Chicago," *The Quarterly Journal of Economics* 19 (May 1905); Colin Gordon, "The Lost City of Solidarity: Metropolitan Unionism in Historical Perspective," *Politics & Society* 27 (Dec. 1999); William Haber, *Industrial Relations in the Building Industry* (1930); Colette A. Hyman, "Labor Organizing and Female Institution Building: The Chicago Women's Trade Union League, 1904–1924" in Ruth Milkman, ed., *Women, Work and Protest: A Century of U.S. Women's Labor History* (1985); John B. Jentz, "Unions, Cartels, and the Political Economy of American Cities: The Chicago Flat Janitors' Union in the Progressive Era and 1920s," *Studies in American Political Development* 14 (Spring 2000); Barbara Newell, *Chicago and the Labor Movement: Metropolitan Unionism in the 1930s* (1961); Richard Schneirov, *Labor and Urban Politics* (1998).

John B. Jentz
Marquette University, Wisconsin

The Cleveland Labor Movement

Cleveland has had a long history as an industrial center due to its location on the shore of Lake Erie and at the mouth of the Cuyahoga River in northeast Ohio. As the city became a manufacturing center, its unions gained strength, and relations between workers and employers were stable. As a result, Cleveland did not witness as much violence or the number of strikes as other large industrial centers.

The construction of the Ohio and Erie Canal in 1825 lured workers to Cleveland. Beginning in the 1830s, skilled workers in printing, carpentry, and mechanics began unionization efforts to improve wages and limit work hours. Poor national economic conditions hampered these attempts. Sporadic efforts in the 1840s revealed the increasing strength of unions, but none endured.

In the next two decades, workers organized in larger numbers, but employers vigorously fought these efforts. In the late 1860s, strikes occurred in the coopers', railroad shop workers', and telegraphers' trades. As individual unions gained momentum, general associations sprang up to represent workers. In 1877, a strike against Standard Oil led to violence in the streets, which intensified antiunion feelings among the city's elite. Wealthy citizens countered by organizing private militias and built an armory.

In the last two decades of the nineteenth century, conditions improved for Cleveland workers as unemployment rates fell and wages increased. Unions staged successful strikes, despite tactics to thwart these efforts. Backed by the unions, labor leader Martin A. Foran was elected to Congress in 1886. Max S. Hayes and Henry C. Long founded a union newspaper, the *Cleveland Citizen*, in 1891.

In 1900, Cleveland had one hundred unions, most affiliated with the Cleveland Federation of Labor, a part of the American Federation of Labor. The continuing waves of immigrants into the region further weakened unionization attempts. Most unions worked to consolidate power, rather than expand to include unskilled and semiskilled workers. During World War I, many African Americans immigrated to the city from the South, but few were admitted to unions.

In the 1930s, Cleveland experienced labor unrest on par with other large cities. A December 1936 sit-down strike in the Fisher Body Division of General Motors led to a similar strike in Flint, Michigan. The Little Steel Strike of 1937 was the most violent and bloody strike in city history. In both, armed strike-breakers and company police assaulted steelworkers and their families. During and after World War II, unions expanded to include women, unskilled workers, and minorities and broadened their reform efforts. The prosperity of the region led to generally good relations between labor and employers.

From the 1970s through the turn of the century, Cleveland's unions lost power as the economy soured, then moved from an industrial to service base, thus weakening labor's attempts to enact greater reform. The growth of the suburbs also contributed to labor's declining influence, as the city center became more racially polarized and manufacturing jobs were filled with unskilled workers. In recent times, Cleveland has transformed into a technology-, medical-, and service-based economy even less reliant on manufacturing. As a result, most existing union strength resides among white-collar workers, such as teachers and service workers.

Sources and Further Reading: Carol Poh Miller and Robert A. Wheeler, *Cleveland: A Concise History, 1796–1990* (1990); William Ganson Rose, *Cleveland: The Making of a City* (1990).

Bob Batchelor
Cleveland, Ohio

The Detroit Labor Movement

Until the 1920s, Detroit's unions followed national patterns; by the 1930s, however, they had become leaders. The Knights of Labor (KOL), formed its first Detroit local in 1878. As the national KOL declined after 1886, so went the Knights of Detroit. The American Federation of Labor (AFL) also initiated Detroit locals, which prospered, especially after 1901. But the success of early AFL unions in Detroit evoked the ire of employers and inspired their creation of the Employers' Association of Detroit, which severely repressed Detroit's unions. The radical Industrial Workers of the World led Detroit's first major autoworkers' strike in 1913, but failed to create a long-term presence. Through the late 1920s, Detroit was an open-shop town.

With strong industrial growth beginning at the turn of the last century, Detroit came to be primarily a one-industry town. The de-skilling of auto work was a key component of this growth and led to a loss of skilled workers' power. Employers embarked upon extensive recruiting campaigns, which brought foreign-born and southern workers to perform the expanding semiskilled and unskilled jobs. In response to these dynamics, the Carriage, Wagon and Automobile Workers Union tended to ignore craft distinctions. It was expelled from the AFL in 1918 and collapsed in 1921. Communist trade unionists, however, revived it as the Auto Workers Union (AWU) in the mid-1920s and affiliated it with the Trade Union Unity League in 1929, though without much success.

By the 1930s, Detroit's unions set the pace for the nation's labor movement. The Depression hit Detroit harder than most cities, and the unemployed organized under the banner of the Communist-run Unemployed Councils, which were regarded as among the most effective in the country. It and the AWU led the 1932 Ford Hunger March, which resulted in the deaths of four young Communists and, a few days later, a funeral procession of tens of thousands of workers who marched in their memory.

Following its founding in 1935, the United Auto Workers (UAW) grew quickly in Detroit by launching extensive organizing drives and supporting sit-down strikers. By 1937, it secured contracts with General Motors and Chrysler, and by 1941, with Ford. The UAW became one of the largest American unions, and its power was heightened by its centralization in Detroit. In no other metropolitan area was there such a concentration of union members, and of Congress of Industrial Organizations members in particular. By mid-century, 60 percent of Detroit's adult population belonged to a union family (compared to 31 percent nationwide), and the majority of these belonged to the UAW.

During the postwar period, the UAW was a formidable power both inside the workplace and in the community. Inside, it sought more favorable work rules and worker control and led groundbreaking fights for better benefits and job security. In the community, it lent support and resources to struggles of economic and social justice, including the black Civil Rights Movement and legislation preventing discrimination against women. Beginning in the 1950s, employers in Detroit's auto and related industries responded by severely reducing the size of the workforce. They introduced automation and a major decentralization of the industry, leading to the drastic decline of Detroit's production jobs, citywide economic crises, and a decline and industrial diversification of UAW membership.

Sources and Further Reading: Steve Babson, *Working Detroit* (1984); R. Dodge, "Some Aspects of the Political Behavior of Labor Union Members in the Detroit Metropolitan Area," Ph.D. diss., University of Michigan (1953); Christopher Johnson, *Maurice Sugar* (1988); Thomas Sugrue, *The Origins of the Urban Crisis: Race and Inequality in Postwar Detroit* (1996).

Judith Stepan-Norris
University of California–Irvine

The Milwaukee Labor Movement

Milwaukee emerged as an important manufacturing center in the years following the Civil War. The city became a magnet for struggling farmers in the Midwest and immigrants from Europe, especially from Germany, Britain, Scandinavia, and later, Poland. Strikes were recorded in the 1840s, and several local unions were chartered as early as the 1850s. In 1886, the Knights of Labor, which championed the eight-hour day, led a series of mass demonstrations in Milwaukee that prompted Governor Jeremiah Rusk to deploy the state militia to quell riots, and nine people were killed or wounded by militia gunfire. This episode became known as the Bay View Massacre.

By 1900, Milwaukee labor leaders had aligned themselves with the Socialist movement. Frank J. Weber, an experienced organizer who was born in Wisconsin, helped found the State Federation of Labor and led the Milwaukee Federated Trades Council in organizing and political action. In 1911, Socialist Party leader Victor Berger created a daily newspaper, *The Leader,* which survived until 1939. Labor in Milwaukee helped enact landmark state legislation on workers compensation, jobless benefits, limits on employers' use of injunctions, and collective bargaining rights for public employees.

The Great Depression saw a steep decline in union power, but the passage of the National Industrial Recovery Act in 1933 sparked a remarkable revival. Unions in Milwaukee moved quickly to capture the enthusiasm created by these national events and enroll workers into existing or newly created unions, especially federal labor unions. In 1936, the Committee on Industrial Organization (CIO, renamed the Congress of Industrial Organizations in 1938) broke with the American Federation of Labor (AFL) and began to organize electrical, automotive, agricultural equipment, and communications mass production workers who had been left out of the older craft unions. Unions gained stability and new members when the United States entered World War II, and a more cooperative attitude between business and labor emerged. The arrival of black workers during and following the war occasionally sparked controversy in white-dominated local unions, but several CIO unions were active in supporting racial equality. War's end ushered in the cold war and a divisive controversy over the role of Communists and radicals in the Milwaukee labor movement. When a radical faction led union members into militant strikes at the Allis Chalmers plant in 1946 and 1947, virtually the entire Milwaukee establishment backed the drive to oust Communist elements from the labor movement.

In the 1950s and 1960s, the labor movement in Milwaukee continued to represent a large majority of the wage-working population, although the percentage of union density began to decline after 1970. The Wisconsin state AFL and CIO reunited in 1958, and did so in Milwaukee in 1959 to form the Milwaukee County Labor Council. As a consequence their organizations became better integrated into the city's civic and political activities. Local unionists were active in political campaigns, school boards, community groups that later became the United Way, and the local vocational school system. Since the 1930s, a long list of Milwaukee labor leaders have filled important positions at the national level, among them Catherine Conroy, a leader of the communications workers

Members of the Brotherhood of Railway and Airline Clerks strike against Northwest Airlines, Milwaukee, 1970. Wisconsin Historical Society, MJS-6171.

union, who was a founding member of the National Organization of Women.

Because of the relative vitality of its organizations, Milwaukee remains a union town in the twenty-first century.

Sources and Further Reading: Thomas W. Gavett, *Development of the Labor Movement in Milwaukee* (1965); Darryl Holter, *Workers and Unions in Wisconsin* (1999); Stephen Meyer, *"Stalin over Wisconsin": The Making and Unmaking of Militant Unionism, 1900–1950* (1992); Robert W. Ozanne, *The Labor Movement in Wisconsin* (1984).

Darryl Holter
University of Southern California

The Minneapolis Labor Movement

In the first three years of the twentieth century, Minneapolis machinists, teamsters, and flour mill workers struck for better wages and working conditions. Recognizing a threat to their industrial empire, the city's major employers organized the Minneapolis Citizens Alliance (CA) and declared war on organized Minneapolis workers. Proclaiming a devotion to property rights and individual freedom, the CA refused to negotiate with any union. Backed by flour milling giants Washburn-Crosby and Pillsbury, the CA used special police, out-of-town strikebreakers, and labor injunctions to crush every strike.

The suppression of unions, however, gradually radicalized the workforce. In 1916, Minneapolis workers had elected a Socialist Mayor, and twelve hundred striking teamsters had shut down the city. The CA responded with an extensive expansion of their operations. From 1920 to 1933, the CA unleashed a massive propaganda campaign against socialism, operated a network of intelligence agencies, gained control over the National Guard, trained open-shop workers, and financed the election of conservative judges and legislators to assure the passage and enforcement of antilabor laws.

By 1934, widespread unemployment had forced many Minneapolis workers to the edge of rebellion. Organized by members of the Socialist Worker's Party, the Teamsters union shut down the city. Local 574 sent roving pickets across the city to detect and stop all nonunion trucks, with force if necessary. On May 22, hundreds of club-wielding Teamsters routed the employers' "citizen army." The iron grip of the CA had been broken. Within two years, mass picketing and sit-down strikes supported by the Teamsters had forced union recognition in many open-shop companies.

Out-fought in the streets, the CA wrote and promoted the passage of the 1939 Minnesota Labor Relations Act, which outlawed sit-down strikes, the obstruction of plant entrances, mass picketing, and any interference with vehicles or roads. The Taft-Hartley Act, modeled on the CA plan, outlawed the same direct-action tactics on the national level in 1947. Four years later, a new Minnesota statute outlawed strikes by public employees.

Despite this extensive antilabor legislation, union representation gradually increased across the state under the leadership of the Minnesota AFL-CIO. In 1970, the Minneapolis Federation of Teachers defied the state's no-strike law, demanding better wages and working conditions. Three years later, a legislature controlled by the liberal Democratic-Farmer-Labor Party passed a minimum wage law, an occupational safety and health act, and a public employee labor relations act. With 30 percent of the workforce unionized, the future of Minnesota's unions appeared bright.

Encouraged by President Ronald Reagan's firing of the country's air traffic controllers in 1981, however, the CA (now Employers Association, Inc.) led Minnesota employers on a campaign to replace union strikers and intimidate union organization drives. Despite valiant union efforts, the dramatic union defeat at Hormel in Austin brought the employers' assault to national attention. By 2002, Minnesota union membership in private industry had dropped to below 11 percent. Only the state's public employee unions had managed to maintain their strength, winning the largest strike in Minnesota history in 2001.

Sources and Further Reading: Farrell Dobbs, *Teamster Rebellion* (1972); Elizabeth Faue, *Community of Suffering & Struggle* (1991); William Millikan, *A Union Against Unions* (2001); Peter Rachleff, *Hard-Pressed in the Heartland* (1993).

William Millikan
Minneapolis, Minnesota

Industrial Workers in the Era of the CIO, 1935–1965

By 1934, the Midwest was a profoundly troubled place. The region's industrial base had collapsed under the weight of the Great Depression. Poverty haunted its cities and towns. Its factories and working-class neighborhoods seethed with the frustration of dashed hopes. "The depression began," a Detroit worker wrote Franklin Roosevelt, "and they went down and down until now they are about as bad as things could be. I used to have money in the bank, a car and some decent clothes to wear and now I have nothing."

The cataclysm had its roots in the region's dizzying economic growth. The Midwest had become a major industrial center in the late nineteenth century. Its slaughterhouses and furniture factories transformed the bounty of the countryside into the commodities the city craved, while its metal works shaped Pennsylvania iron and steel into the machines, farm implements, and railroad cars that propelled industrialization forward. In the first three decades of the twentieth century, a cadre of visionary businessmen built upon the region's strengths to make the Midwest one of the world's great industrial areas. Henry Leland, Ransom Olds, John and Horace Dodge, and Henry Ford used the skills of the metal workers to create a new industry, automobile manufacturing. Drawing on the complex production process of Chicago's meatpacking plants, Ford and his advisors organized the fledgling auto industry into a marvel of mass production. As demand for the shiny new—and suddenly affordable—product skyrocketed, businesses across the Midwest integrated with the auto industry. Detroit became the auto capital.

But automobile manufacturing spread across the Midwest, into smaller Michigan cities like Flint and Lansing, outward to Toledo and Cleveland, and on to

❖ The Memorial Day Massacre: A Reminiscence

In 1937, the newly formed CIO made organizing the steel industry its primary focus. Although U.S. Steel had signed a collective bargaining contract in June of that year, most of the "Little Steel" companies—Bethlehem, Youngstown, Inland, American, and Republic—remained intransigent in their opposition to unionism. When the CIO called a strike for union recognition in the spring of 1937, these companies had the support of local governments and police in Chicago, Cleveland, Youngstown, and Massillon.

In Chicago, the union called a peaceful march on Sunday, May 30, to protest a ban on picketing. Approximately two thousand people were in attendance, including many women and children. As the demonstrators came closer to the plant, they were met by tear gas. I was eighteen years old, and was in the fifth line from the front. The tear gas affected my vision, and I was knocked down. There were shots; many of us fell to the ground. Five or six people were on top of me. When I was finally helped to my feet, I felt something in my back. It was a policeman pointing a pistol in my back, and he said, "Get off the field or I'll put a bullet in your back!" I looked around, and for the first time in my life I saw a MASSACRE. Bodies were strewn all over. Ten demonstrators lay dead, seven killed by bullets in the back and three in the side. Thirty more were shot, and dozens more were wounded, all without the slightest provocation. This experience changed my life. It made me understand who starts and provokes violence in strikes.

Mollie West
Illinois Labor History Society, Chicago, Illinois

South Bend, Indianapolis, and Kenosha, Wisconsin. Manufacturers in other midwestern towns established operations that provided the auto industry with the many parts it needed. Akron's B.F. Goodrich, Goodyear, and Firestone produced tires. Canton's Timken Company supplied axles. In Gary, Indiana, Youngstown, Ohio, and south Chicago, the massive plants of Republic, Jones and Laughlin, Youngstown Sheet and Tube, and U.S. Steel rolled out the metal for car bodies. It is impossible to exaggerate the extent of the economic boom. By 1929, the Midwest accounted for almost 40 percent of the value added to the nation's manufactured goods.

The Midwest's economic growth made it a magnet for workers from around the globe. Metalworkers from the British shipyards joined with displaced peasants from eastern and southern Europe and laborers from Mexico in a massive wave of immigration. Poor whites from the hollows of Appalachia and poor blacks from the farmlands of Alabama made their way north. And the sons and daughters of farmers left the country for the burgeoning factory towns. They brought with them a host of often clashing cultural practices, religious traditions, and political commitments. They were Communists and Klansmen, socialists and Catholic traditionalists, Trotskyites and Irish nationalists—all brought together by the power of the Midwest's booming economy.

Those newcomers who secured factory work in the 1910s and 1920s often earned some of the highest wages paid to industrial workers. An Akron tire builder earned $3.50 to $4.50 a day in 1912, for example, and the typical autoworker in 1925 earned almost $6.00 a day. But the work was extraordinarily insecure. The slightest downturn in the economy triggered large cuts in factory workforces, and even in good years, many workers faced weeks of layoffs as their employers cleared inventory. Midwestern factory work was also extremely dangerous and demanding. Employers maintained only minimal safety standards, while supervisors relentlessly pushed their workers to increase the pace at which they worked. Laborers often returned home discouraged and exhausted. Almost without exception, manufacturers were virulently opposed to unionization. Factory hands had few ways of improving their situation. Those workers who dared to question the burdens placed on them, moreover, ran the risk of being summarily fired.

The frustrations of industrial work multiplied when the nation plunged into depression in 1929. Car sales plummeted by 75 percent over the next three years. As they did so, the region's economy bottomed out. Unemployment crept to 50 percent in Toledo, Cleveland, and Detroit, higher still in some smaller towns. Desperate to squeeze out whatever profit they could, em-ployers pushed those workers they kept on payroll harder and harder and paid them less and less. A St. Louis autoworker reported working twelve-hour shifts for thirty straight days in 1933. "I would get home at ten o'clock," he said, "and I would be so tired I could not eat my supper. I would drop in a chair and cry myself to sleep."

Throughout the early 1930s, labor activists, many of them Communists, tried to convince workers that unionization offered them the best hope of improved conditions. Those efforts received a dramatic boost in 1933, when the newly elected president, Franklin Roosevelt, endorsed workers' right to organize unions without employer interference. A series of dramatic strikes rolled across the Midwest in the next year and a half, as workers tried to put the administration's promise into practice. The outbursts were too sporadic to constitute a sustained assault on industrialists' power, but they dramatized the depth of midwestern workers' anger. And they convinced at least some mainstream union leaders that the time had come to unionize the heartland of industrial America.

John L. Lewis, the Iowa-born president of the United Mine Workers, took the lead. For years, Lewis had been urging his fellow unionists inside the American Federation of Labor (AFL) to launch a sustained campaign to organize the mass of workers in the nation's major industries, but most of the AFL leaders resisted the idea. So in 1935, Lewis and seven other union presidents left the AFL to organize a rival federation, the Committee on Industrial Organization (CIO, reformed as the Congress of Industrial Organizations in 1938), committed to bringing unionization to the industrial core.

The CIO was not solely a midwestern undertaking. Some of its most important figures, such as Sidney Hillman and Philip Murray, were based in the Northeast. Because the Midwest had such a concentration of industrial might, however, the CIO's formative campaign was inevitably a midwestern affair. Lewis had planned to devote 1936 to quietly organizing the CIO's first challenges to corporate power, but the workers forced his hand. In February and March 1936, rubber workers at Akron's Goodyear plant staged another of the epic strikes that had hit the Midwest since 1933. CIO leaders rushed to the strikers' aid, helping to forge a settlement that won the workers valuable gains. That autumn, autoworkers in Kansas City, Cleveland, and Detroit staged sit-down strikes, occupying the factories and refusing to leave until their demands were met. Again, the CIO endorsed the strikes. Then, on December 30, 1936, workers sat down at two Fisher Body plants in Flint. In form, the Flint strike was not different than the sit-downs that had preceded it, but the Flint strikers had taken on a much bigger target. Fisher Body made auto bodies for its parent company, General Motors (GM), the largest industrial corporation in the world. If the strikers could force such a powerful company to recognize their right to unionize, they would have a victory of unprecedented dimension.

The strikers held the plant for six weeks. Finally, on February 11, 1937, GM agreed to recognize a CIO union, the United Automobile Workers (UAW), as the autoworkers' representative. That victory opened the floodgates for the CIO. Across the Midwest in 1937, steelworkers, rubber workers, glass workers, electrical workers, autoworkers, and meatpackers rushed to join CIO unions. They were not always successful in forcing their employers to grant them union rights. Most major steel companies, for instance, refused to recognize workers' demands for union representation, as did the Ford Motor Company. But the CIO nevertheless made extraordinary progress. By the end of 1937, it had three million members, the vast majority in the major industries that dominated the region.

The spectacular growth of the CIO slowed over the next few years, as union activists turned to the slow work of transforming a mass movement into a permanent and stable labor organization. The CIO used legal challenges and the occasional strike to force some of the most virulently antiunion companies, such as Ford, to concede their workers' right to representation. Once representation was secured, union members set about establishing the seniority and grievance procedures, the wage scales and work rules that met workers' immediate needs.

Many of the CIO's activists hoped that the labor movement could do more. Some unionists believed that the CIO could use its new power to make the nation's economy more just. They envisioned sweeping changes: the nationalization of some industries, the regulation of basic business decisions such as product pricing, the creation of factory work councils that would give laborers a say in the running of their plants. Some CIO members also hoped that the labor movement could remake the working class. With the CIO to lead them, they said, working people could set aside the racial, religious, and political differences that divided them.

It was not to be. Almost as soon as the CIO began its mass organizing, conservative politicians launched a massive counterattack. The CIO was a radical threat to the American way of life, they charged, dedicated to destroying free enterprise. The labor federation was also wracked by internal tensions, and the CIO's varied political groups battled for control. Catholic unionists condemned the CIO's radicals; Communists and Socialists assailed each other; Trotskyites attacked Stalinists; Republicans like John L. Lewis turned

against Democrats. The rank-and-file also divided. Racial conflict broke out in many plants during World War II, for example, as African American workers moved into jobs that had long been considered the reserve of whites.

These conflicts took their toll. Conservatives' charges of CIO radicalism took on greater and greater force in the late 1940s, as the United States slid into the cold war. The fear of Communism forced many CIO leaders to downplay their commitment to reshaping the nation's economy, an idea that sounded subversive in the age of McCarthyism. At the same time, the CIO's anti-Communists—many of them former socialists—used the cold war hysteria to drive their political opponents from the movement. In 1949, the CIO's leaders purged eleven Communist-led unions from the organization, at a cost of 900 thousand members. Under such circumstances, the CIO simply could not sustain the momentum it had built in the late 1930s.

Even as its great hopes faded, however, the labor movement changed the face of the Midwest. Union protections gave working people the ability to challenge the worst abuses of management. No longer did workers have to silently endure the brutal pace of work and the dangers of unsafe plants. Union leaders also used their power to raise workers' standards of living to unprecedented heights. The working people of the region became some of the highest paid laborers in the country in the years after World War II. They also won a host of benefits unimaginable before the union era. By the 1960s, union members had health care and retirement plans, paid vacations, and profit-sharing programs. These gains did not push union members into the middle class, but they did wipe out the scourge of insecurity that had stalked working-class families for generations.

Organized labor also anchored the progressive politics of the postwar era. A generation of midwestern liberals—Hubert Humphrey of Minnesota, Paul Douglas of Illinois, G. Mennen Williams and Philip Hart of Michigan—rose to power in large part because of labor's support. CIO unions also championed a wide array of liberal policies, including national health care, the expansion of the welfare state, aid to education, public housing, and urban renewal. Unions also played a pivotal role in the great social movements of the postwar era, particularly the struggles for African American and women's rights. Some CIO unions, such as the Packinghouse Workers and the United Automobile Workers, offered the black civil rights movement substantial financial and political support. More importantly, unions served as training grounds for many African American and feminist activists in the postwar era.

But labor's efforts also hit very real limits. In the 1950s and 1960s, a new generation of African American migrants came north to seek their share of the postwar bounty. In city after city, they pushed the boundaries of the black ghetto outward. As they did so, many white workers abandoned the city for the new blue-collar suburbs. Other whites tried to maintain the color line, both in their neighborhoods and on the factory floor. Racial conflict thus flared throughout the period. At the same time, there were disturbing signs that workers' hard-fought gains were eroding. In the late 1940s, corporations began experimenting with new technologies—early versions of robotics—designed to replace workers with machines. A postwar merger movement shut some of the businesses that had served as the bedrock of some midwestern towns. When Studebaker closed its doors in 1963, for example, South Bend lost most of its economic base. "Everybody was bawling and crying," a worker said, "especially old-timers, because they couldn't get jobs anywhere else." Perhaps worst of all, to reduce labor costs and union power, some corporations began to move production out of the Midwest entirely. In 1947, Ohio was home to 43 percent of the nation's tire workers. By 1967, the state had only 33 percent.

It is important not to overstate the rate of change. In the mid-1960s, the Midwest was still the center of American manufacturing, and the region's working people still enjoyed a level of affluence and security unimaginable in the dark days of 1934. But the Midwest was also beset by racial and economic tensions that raised genuine fears for the region's future. Midwestern workers had gained so much in the previous three decades. They had much to lose.

Sources and Further Reading: Irving Bernstein, *Turbulent Years: A History of the American Worker, 1933–1941* (1971); Kevin Boyle, *The UAW and the Heyday of American Liberalism, 1945–1968* (1995); Lizabeth Cohen, *Making a New Deal: Industrial Workers in Chicago, 1919–1939* (1990); Melyvn Dubosky and Warren Van Tine, *John L. Lewis: A Biography* (1977); Sidney Fine, *Sit-Down: The General Motors Strike of 1936–1937* (1969); Nancy Gabin, *Feminism in the Labor Movement Women and the United Auto Workers, 1935–1975* (1990); Rick Halpern, *Down on the Killing Floor* (1997); Roger Horowitz, *Negro and White, Unite and Fight!* (1997); Nelson Lichtenstein, *The Most Dangerous Man in Detroit* (1995); Daniel Nelson, *American Rubber Workers and Organized Labor, 1900–1941* (1988); Thomas Sugrue, *The Origins of the Urban Crisis: Race and Inequality in Postwar Detroit* (1996); Jon Teaford, *Cities of the Heartland* (1993); Robert Zieger, *The CIO, 1935–1955* (1995).

Kevin Boyle
The Ohio State University–Columbus

Mass Production and Ford's Five-Dollar Day

In 1908, the Detroit automobile manufacturer Henry Ford declared, "I will build a motor car for the great multitude." His new automobile would be "small," made of the "best materials," and have "the simplest designs that modern engineering can devise." That automobile for everyman, the Model T Ford, inaugurated a system of mass production, transformed industry on a global scale, and had enormous implications for how people worked in factories.

To satisfy a steadily and rapidly growing demand for the immensely popular Model T, Ford and his industrial engineers constructed the Highland Park, Michigan, plant from 1910 to 1914. They utilized and amalgamated the best and most recent ideas and practices for factory production, including standard design of the product, standardization of work processes and machines, and the integration and synchronization of all production operations. The latter entailed the now famous assembly line, or as Ford and his associates labeled it, "progressive production" and "progressive assembly."

This new industrial technology had an enormous social impact on how workers performed their tasks, the social structure of work, and the control of the workforce. Work became de-skilled, routinized, repetitive, and monotonous. The cycles of machines, the sequential organization of tasks, or the speed of assembly lines, all rigidly controlled their pace of production.

The new Highland Park factory experienced serious labor problems. The gains in productivity fell far short of anticipated levels. Absenteeism rose dramatically to an average 10 percent of the workforce each day. Labor turnover, or the quit rate, soared to an astounding 370 percent for the year.

Recognizing these severe labor problems, Ford and his associates announced the now-famous Five-Dollar Day in January 1914. The proposal to double the average Ford workman's daily wage was much more than benevolent corporate paternalism. The Five-Dollar Day was a sophisticated scheme to adapt unskilled immigrant workers to the rigors of mass production and transform them into efficient, Americanized workers. Labeled a profit-sharing plan and not a wage increase, a Ford worker's wage was divided into two parts, original wages and profits.

A worker received wages for work performed in the factory and their profits for "right living." Believing in the Progressive Era's notion that a good environment produced good (and productive) people, Ford officials created a Sociological Department to investigate how Ford workers lived and whether or not their marital status, home conditions, habits, and thrift were good. If the investigator approved of the worker's lifestyle, he received the Ford profits. If not, and if the Ford worker did not improve within six months, he was dismissed.

Over the short run, the Five-Dollar Day was immensely successful, prompting thousands of workers to flock to Detroit. Though repetitive and monotonous work continued, absenteeism and labor turnover declined spectacularly. Other automobile firms adopted Ford's innovations in production. A post–World War I strike wave resulted in a new managerial toughness. Gradually, the Ford Sociological Department devolved into the Ford Service Department, which under the notorious Harry Bennett, established a brutal regime of thuggery and corruption to discipline recalcitrant workers.

Sources and Further Reading: Martha May, "The Historical Problem of the Family Wage: The Ford Motor Company and the Five Dollar Day," *Feminist Studies* 8 (Summer 1982); Stephen Meyer, *The Five Dollar Day* (1981); Joyce Shaw Peterson, *American Automobile Workers, 1900–1933* (1987).

Steve Meyer
University of Wisconsin–Milwaukee

The 1937 Flint Sit-Down Strike

The Flint Sit-Down Strike established the right of union representation for the common factory worker. On December 30, 1936, the workers of the Fisher Body Plant stopped work and sat down, thereby stopping production of the automobile bodies for much of General Motors (GM). Flint, Michigan, was the heart of General Motors, the world's largest corporation. At the time, GM employed over forty-seven thousand people in Flint, with a large proportion employed at the Fisher Body Plant. The strike soon spread across the country. GM had sixty-nine automotive plants in fourteen states and a total employment of 230,572 at the end of 1936 with assets that exceeded $1.5 billion.

The Flint strike was organized by the United Auto Workers (UAW) and led by Robert Travis, whose daughter is the author of these words, and his main assistant was Roy Reuther, later joined by Victor Reuther. Walter Reuther, their brother, who was leading a strike in Detroit, would become the most famous of the United Auto Workers union presidents.

Worker complaints centered on the cruel and relentless intensity of the work in which they were employed. Workers often went home dizzy and nauseated with swollen and pained limbs. There were no bathroom breaks; workers would urinate on the dirt floor where they stood or in a corner or risk being fired if they ran to the toilet. When they ran out of parts and had to stop work, GM required that workers stay and sit at the line without pay.

The tactic of seizing the plant, instead of picketing outside, was being used with great success in France and experimented with in Atlanta, Detroit, and St. Louis. GM Chairman Alfred P. Sloan was antiunion to the core. The corporation employed fourteen detective agencies and spent over a million dollars on antiunion espionage between January 1, 1934, and July 1, 1936. On January 11 1937, a bloody attack by company police failed to get the men out. The Governor of Michigan, Frank Murphy, sent in the National Guard to preserve peace, not to remove the strikers. U.S. Secretary of Labor Francis Perkins attempted but failed to settle the strike. On February 1, 1937, the

United Automobile Workers sit-down strikers at Fisher Body Number 1 in Flint, Michigan, celebrate the end of their strike, February 11, 1937. At left, holding the newspaper, is strike leader Bud Simons. Walter P. Reuther Library, Wayne State University.

beleaguered strikers took the offensive once again and seized the Chevrolet plant. On February 11, 1937, after forty-four days and nights, the company settled. The agreement recognized the United Auto Workers as the union for workers of seventeen General Motors plants across the country and declared a truce to negotiate the terms and conditions of employment. No workers who participated in the strike lost their jobs.

The Flint Sit-Down Strike, perhaps the most important union victory in American history, set off a wave of sit-down strikes across the nation involving some 400 thousand workers. It was also the turning point in the establishment of industrial unionism in the nation's mass production industries. Three weeks after the Flint victory, U.S. Steel recognized the United Steel Workers.

Sources and Further Reading: Sidney Fine, *Sit-Down: The General Motors Strike of 1936–1937* (1969); Henry Kraus, *The Many and the Few: The Chronicle of the Dynamic Auto Workers* (1947); Robert H. Zieger, *The CIO, 1935–1955* (1995).

Carole Travis
Service Employees International Union (SEIU),
Washington, D.C.

Packinghouse Workers

From the Civil War's end through the mid-twentieth century, the Midwest supplied virtually all the nation's beef and pork. Cattle butchers at the Big Four (Armour, Swift, Cudahy, and Wilson) stockyard plants in Chicago, Kansas City, and Omaha formed the backbone of the Amalgamated Meat Cutters and Butcher Workmen (AMCBW), the American Federation of Labor's (AFL) packinghouse and retail butchers' union. This union experienced some success in the major midwestern stockyard plants between 1900 and the end of World War I, but the union's incomplete organizing strategy resulted in two major failed strikes, those of 1904 and 1921–1922.

Union-organizing strategies changed considerably during the New Deal era, especially because pork production shifted increasingly to small-town midwestern plants away from the former hubs. Union leaders realized that successful organization required not only gaining adherents at the Big Four's stockyards plants, but also among the large independent firms, including George A. Hormel based in Austin, Minnesota, and John Morrell based in Ottumwa, Iowa. The AMCBW, after its failed nationwide strike in 1921–1922, attempted to gain members again following passage in 1933 of the New Deal's National Industrial Recovery

Act (NIRA) with its Section 7a provision for collective bargaining. Although the Amalgamated recruited new members in many midwestern packing plants, the Congress of Industrial Organizations' (CIO) packinghouse unions found greater success. Helped by independent union movements based in Austin and Cedar Rapids, Iowa, the Packinghouse Workers Organizing Committee (PWOC) of the CIO grew rapidly by 1937.

In contrast to the Amalgamated's strategy through the 1920s, the PWOC, followed by its successor union, the United Packinghouse Workers of America (UPWA) in 1943, not only recruited butchers, but also earned followings among the masses of unskilled laborers in the packinghouses. The PWOC and UPWA were especially successful in recruiting African American workers, who dominated Chicago's and Kansas City's packinghouses, and rural whites in cities like Austin and Ottumwa. By the end of World War II, the UPWA had organized the largest packing plants in the Midwest, except the Oscar Mayer plant in Madison, Wisconsin, which was organized by the Amalgamated. The CIO and AFL packinghouse unions not only brought workers better pay and working conditions, they also helped to transform politics at the local and state levels, especially in Iowa.

Union success in meatpacking was relatively short lived. A new Big Three—IBP, ConAgra, and Cargill—led by IBP, originally Iowa Beef Packers founded in 1960, transformed the industry. By establishing plants in locations closer to animal populations, such as Garden City, Kansas, for beef packing, and by introducing new technologies that required less skill, the new Big Three drove many older firms out of business. The unionized stockyards plants in Chicago and elsewhere closed. The new Big Three also hired large numbers of transient immigrants, primarily Hispanics and Asians, which further undermined unionism in the industry. Partly in an attempt to more effectively organize the new packers' plants, the UPWA and Amalgamated joined forces in 1968 to form the Amalgamated Meat Cutters and Butcher Workmen.

Sources and Further Reading: Rick Halpern, *Down on the Killing Floor* (1997); Roger Horowitz, *Negro and White, Unite and Fight!* (1997); Wilson J. Warren, *Struggling with "Iowa's Pride"* (2000).

Wilson J. Warren
Western Michigan University

Steelworkers

From the 1930s to the 1960s, the American steel industry was as midwestern as a cornfield. About three-

A steel mill at work. © Larry Hamill Photography, TKI-049-04.

quarters of the industry was located along a relatively narrow band traced by the mainline of the old Pennsylvania Railroad (later Amtrak's Broadway Limited) from Pittsburgh to Chicago. Steubenville, Youngstown, Cleveland, and Lorain in Ohio and Gary, East Chicago, and Whiting in Indiana were part of the backbone of the American economy then.

Though both production and productivity more than doubled during these decades, the basics of the steelmaking process did not change much. But the lives of steelworkers—about 400 thousand wageworkers at the beginning and end of the period, with 544 thousand at the industry's peak in 1953—changed dramatically and much for the better.

In 1936, when the Committee for Industrial Organization (CIO, renamed the Congress of Industrial Organizations in 1938) formed what would become the United Steelworkers of America (USWA), steelworkers worked from forty-eight to sixty hours a week for poverty-level wages. There was no such thing as weekends or retirement then, for steel or any other workers. There was no health insurance, no job security, no paid vacations, holidays or sick days, no unemployment compensation, and no possibility of discussing your grievances with management.

All this had completely changed by the 1960s, when steelworkers had what was considered a middle-class income. They also had considerable job security, and while they still experienced extended layoffs, after 1956, they typically received 80 percent of their wages while laid off. The five-day, forty-hour week became standard for American workers after World War II,

though steelworkers still worked swing shifts, including lots of weekends. Paid vacations, holidays, and sick days increased steadily during this period, and by the 1960s, steelworkers were beginning to retire after thirty years of what was still brutally hard and dangerous work.

Aided by New Deal legislation in the 1930s, most of this dramatic change was achieved by the USWA through a series of hard-fought strikes from 1937 through 1959. The Little Steel Strike of 1937 was a bitter defeat, with police clubbing and shooting strikers and breaking up picket lines across the Steel Belt. Ten were killed in Chicago in the Memorial Day Massacre, three more in Massillon, Ohio, and others in Cleveland and Youngstown; scores more were crippled and injured. But by 1941, the USWA had forced the Little Steel companies to join U.S. Steel in recognizing the union. The postwar steel strikes—in 1946, 1949, 1952, 1955, 1956, and 1959—were massive, nationwide, nonviolent affairs, typically involving a half million workers who shut down more than 90 percent of the industry. All were decisive victories for the union. Each, like the forty-two-day strike in 1949 when both health insurance and pensions were first established, won some new improvements, many of which were subsequently gained in other workplaces.

Though steelworkers and steel towns in the Midwest would later face defeat and decline, during this period, they were at the heart of the struggle to achieve what became known worldwide as an American standard of living.

Sources and Further Reading: Irving Bernstein, "Breakthrough in Steel" in *Turbulent Years: A History of the American Worker, 1933–1941* (1969); E. Robert Livernash, *Collective Bargaining in the Basic Steel Industry: A Study of the Public Interest and the Role of Government* (1961); Jack Metzgar, *Striking Steel: Solidarity Remembered* (2000); Ruth Needleman, *Black Freedom Fighters in Steel* (2003).

Jack Metzgar
Roosevelt University, Illinois

Farm Implement Workers

Midwestern farm implement workers produced the machines that mechanized farming in the Midwest and around the globe. When they organized in the mid-twentieth century, these workers became part of a battle against corporate control of the workplace. Their struggle took place in the context of old and new midwestern radicalism and the politics of the cold war.

The Farm Equipment Workers Union (FEW, part of the Congress of Industrial Organizations, CIO) developed a concerted organizational and ideological challenge to the powerful International Harvester Corporation (IH), a global agricultural machine producer, by the mid-twentieth century. Events at IH's McCormick works in 1886 had led to the Haymarket affair and a bitter backlash against unionism. In the post–World War I era, IH led another effort to avert unionism through careful selection of workers and company-controlled employee representation plans (ERPs)—cynically dubbed "industrial democracy." When an aggressive organizing drive took root under the aegis of the CIO in the late 1930s, and finally resulted in union victory even at the McCormick stronghold, it seemed to herald a new era of industrial democracy for farm implement workers. At the height of its power, the FEW was a feisty defender of workers and a vehicle for a serious challenge to management rights and the hated incentive pay schemes. By the late 1940s, farm implement workers in the FEW had gained a dramatic increase in living standards.

The FEW was constantly under siege during this period, from management, from the rival American Federation of Labor, and from a fellow CIO union, the United Automobile Workers (UAW), which had organized a number of John Deere plants and began raids on the FEW as early as 1945. When the CIO, engulfed by the rising anti-Communist tide, expelled the FEW in 1949 (along with eleven other CIO unions), the UAW argued that the FEW was outside the house of labor. The raids depleted the union's re-

sources and forced it to concentrate on a rearguard action. When it lost a 1952 strike during which IH used the "Red issue" to reestablish managerial prerogatives and control of the incentive wage system, the little union was devastated. By 1955, the FEW merged into the UAW, and the era of union insurgency was over. Still, workers remained well-paid compared to the earlier era.

By the late 1970s, farm implement companies were global operators committed to weakening workers' rights through a labor–management cooperation agenda and expansion of nonunion operations. Workers were urged to grant wage and benefit concessions so the company could be more competitive in the global market. In 1992, Caterpillar refused to sign a pattern agreement already agreed to by John Deere. When the UAW struck, the company used replacement workers, and though some UAW locals sought to deploy more militant means of fighting back, the UAW lost the strike. As the twentieth century drew to a close, unionized agricultural implement workers were granting management most of their demands in negotiations, and all but a small percentage of workers in the industry were nonunion, as they had been in the early part of the twentieth century.

Sources and Further Reading: Lizabeth Cohen, *Making A New Deal: Industrial Workers in Chicago, 1919–1939* (1990); Toni Gilpin, "Left by Themselves: A History of the United Farm Equipment and Metal Workers Union, 1938–1955," Ph.D. diss., Yale University (1992).

Rosemary Feurer
Northern Illinois University

Walter Reuther (1907–1970)

Walter Reuther, who served as president of the United Automobile Workers from 1946 to 1970, was born into a German, working-class family on September 1, 1907, in Wheeling, West Virginia. A skilled tool and die worker, Reuther worked for five years at Ford's great Rouge complex in Dearborn, Michigan, before taking a two-year sojourn with brother Victor to Europe and the Soviet Union during 1933–1935.

He returned to Detroit in time to play an important role in organizing workers in the motor city's West Side factories. Though initially close to UAW Communists, Reuther soon emerged as the leader of a Socialist-Catholic "right-wing" caucus that sought to advance UAW power through an alliance with the Rooseveltian warfare state. During World War II, he won a large following, within the union movement and without, as a proponent of labor's participation in the governance of the war production industries. His leadership of a 113-day General Motors strike in 1945–1946 sought to defend price controls, politicize the level of corporate profits, and dramatically boost working-class wages. General Motors rebuffed Reuther's ambitions, but his articulate leadership of the strike helped elect him UAW president in 1946.

A year later, the Reuther faction consolidated its control of America's most important union in an election which resulted in the evisceration of Communist influence from the UAW. By 1948, Reuther was America's most influential trade unionist, which may have helped account for a bloody, but unsuccessful, assassination attempt that spring. He served as president of the Congress of Industrial Organizations from 1952 until 1955, when he helped merge the CIO with the American Federation of Labor.

Reuther tempered his socialist ambitions in the years thereafter. In 1950, he signed a five-year contract, dubbed by Fortune Magazine the "Treaty of Detroit," that assured autoworkers cost of living adjustments and real wage gains, but only in return for industrial discipline within the factories. Reuther failed to secure a guaranteed annual wage for his membership during the 1950s, but he did win important pension and health insurance benefits for unionized autoworkers.

Reuther was a liberal Democrat in the 1950s and 1960s: he wanted to temper the cold war, boost social spending, advance national civil rights legislation, and rebuild the cities. But Reuther's UAW became increasingly estranged from the New Left and the more militant elements of the black civil rights movement in the 1960s. He backed President Lyndon Johnson's Vietnam policies well into 1968 and saw the black power insurgency as a threat to UAW solidarity.

Reuther and his wife May died in an airplane crash in Northern Michigan on May 9, 1970.

Sources and Further Reading: Kevin Boyle, *The UAW and the Heyday of American Liberalism* (1995); Martin Halpern, *UAW Politics in the Cold War Era* (1988); Nelson Lichtenstein, *Walter Reuther: The Most Dangerous Man in Detroit* (1995); Victor Reuther, *The Brothers Reuther and the Story of the UAW* (1976).

Nelson Lichtenstein
University of California–Santa Barbara

Jimmy Hoffa (1913–1982)

Born in Brazil, Indiana, on Valentine's Day of 1913, James "Jimmy" Hoffa referred to himself as "the meanest bastard God ever created." Hoffa took pride in his toughness as he battled his employers as a worker, owners as a union organizer, and the federal government as a union officer.

After his father, John, died in 1920, Hoffa's mother Viola moved her family to Detroit to be closer to relatives. Wanting to help his mother, Hoffa quit school in the seventh grade to work full-time. In 1931, he took a job unloading food shipments. Later that year, poor pay and an overbearing supervisor prompted the eighteen-year-old to lead his fellow workers in a spontaneous strike. Demonstrating shrewdness, Hoffa negotiated raises and union recognition for all 175 laborers.

Hoffa's abilities as a hard-headed negotiator created a new model for labor relations in the Midwest. In 1935, Detroit Teamsters Local 299 hired him as an organizer. He immediately increased membership by adding over-the-road drivers and warehouse workers to the already organized delivery drivers. In expanding the membership, Hoffa had to battle employer resistance and jurisdictional issues. When owners blocked Hoffa's organizing efforts, he informed them that if they did not want their trucks blown up, they would recognize the Teamsters.

Jurisdictional problems proved more complex. For example, a Local 299 long-hauler was no longer considered a union worker after leaving Detroit. In 1937, Minneapolis Teamsters created the Central States Drivers Council (CSDC) to end this problem. At first the organization did little, but when Hoffa became bargaining committee chair in 1940, it succeeded. Drivers in twelve midwestern states gained cross-state recognition, a unified pay scale, and benefits. By 1947, the CSDC represented 125 thousand drivers. Hoffa's successes culminated in his much heralded 1957 election as Teamster President. Under Hoffa's leadership, the Teamsters Union claimed two million members, and they were among the highest paid unionists in the country in the 1960s.

Hoffa's organizing methods, however, brought him under legal scrutiny. When the U.S. Senate's McClellan Committee formed to investigate racketeering, committee member Robert Kennedy made Hoffa his prime target. Kennedy's investigation found that Hoffa had business dealings with Mafia-run companies and discovered money missing from the union's pension fund. Through the McClellan Committee and later as Attorney General, Kennedy brought Hoffa to trial twice for racketeering-related offenses. Both ended in acquittal. A third trial, for jury tampering in 1962, sent Hoffa to jail. After he had spent four and a half years in prison, President Richard Nixon granted Hoffa clemency in 1971.

During his incarceration, mobsters had consolidated their power within the Teamsters. Seeking to come to an agreement and hoping to regain his office,

Hoffa agreed to meet Detroit Mafia leaders on July 30, 1975. The Mafia men never arrived, and since walking out of the Red Fox restaurant that day Hoffa has not been seen. He was legally declared dead in 1982.

Sources and Further Reading: Steven Brill, *The Teamsters* (1978); Thaddeus Russell, *Out of the Jungle* (2001); Walter Sheridan, *The Fall and Rise of Jimmy Hoffa* (1972); Arthur A. Sloane, *Hoffa* (1991).

John Enyeart
Stanford University, California

Company Towns

From the mid-nineteenth through the early twentieth century, entrepreneurs in extractive and transportation industries such as mining, lumber, and railroads established many company towns throughout the Midwest that were much like those created for similar reasons in other parts of the country.

Perhaps the most famous midwestern company town was Pullman, Illinois, founded by George M. Pullman in 1880 for the employees of his railroad sleeping car factory. He envisioned his town as an ideal community; its planned development would benefit workers and keep them from turning to unions. Built outside Chicago, Pullman included paved streets, attractive parks and playgrounds, retail stores, a library, and homes with indoor plumbing. However, the American Railway Union's national railroad strike in 1894, centered on Pullman, ended disastrously for workers. The company had divested itself of its nonfactory holdings in Pullman by the early years of the century.

Company towns were established throughout the Midwest. Some of the more important included Pequaming, Michigan, a large-scale lumbering and milling center; Calumet, Michigan, an enormous copper-mining site; Gwinn, Michigan, an iron-mining center; Wells, Michigan, site of the state's largest lumber operation; Ilasco, Missouri, a cement town; Leclaire, Illinois, a plumbing goods manufacturing center; and Kohler, Wisconsin, home to an agricultural implement, kitchen wares, and plumbing fixtures manufacturer. Interestingly, Buxton, Iowa, a coal-mining town made up of nearly equal numbers of whites and blacks from 1900 to 1928, was notable for its racial harmony. Employers founded 175 company towns in Minnesota's Mesabi iron range, as well as many small coal-mining centers in southern Kansas and several lumber company towns in Wisconsin. Nearly all such towns shared many characteristics of Pullman's paternalistic and rather short-lived experiment.

Sources and Further Reading: Margaret Crawford, *Building the Workingman's Paradise* (1995); Richard Schneirov, Shelton Stromquist, and Nick Salvatore, eds., *The Pullman Strike and the Crisis of the 1890s* (1999).

Wilson J. Warren
Western Michigan University

Working-Class Americanism in the Midwest

The workers of the United States have long drawn heavily upon the traditional rhetoric and imagery of American democracy, republicanism, liberty, and equality in their battle with employers and their allies.

Pullman Industrial Complex workers' housing, 1933. Library of Congress, Prints and Photographs Division, Historic American Buildings Survey, HABS, ILL, 16-CHIG, 102A-2.

Embraced by diverse leaders such as Eugene Debs, Samuel Gompers, John L. Lewis, and Walter Reuther, this working-class Americanism claimed the worker deserved, as a right merely for being American, a voice in the workplace, termed "industrial democracy," and an "American standard of living" at home, born of higher wages, job security, and fewer hours.

Dominated by the American Federation of Labor in the late nineteenth and early twentieth centuries, labor rarely extended its definition of "American" to women, African Americans, and immigrants. However, beginning in the late 1930s, the Congress of Industrial Organizations organized among the heavily ethnic workforces in the basic industries such as auto, steel, and various manufacturing concerns, mostly located in the heavily ethnic industrial centers of the Midwest. As a result, a new pluralistic vision of America came into being that included all workers, native-born and immigrant alike. This Americanism from above was mirrored by an Americanism from below, as ethnic workers increasingly expressed their discontent through the language of America. Thus, workers from across the social and ideological spectrum found common cause in a multiethnic unionism and the New Deal.

This working-class unity was an essential source of the successes of labor during the 1930s, 1940s, and 1950s, yet lost its power as the hyper-nationalism of the cold war dominated any discussion of who was "American" and why.

Sources and Further Reading: James R. Barrett, *Work and Community in the Jungle: Chicago's Packinghouse Workers, 1894–1922* (1987); Lizabeth Cohen, *Making a New Deal* (1990); Gary Gerstle, *Working-Class Americanism* (1989).

Mark Marianek
University of Missouri–Columbia

Retail, Wholesale, and Department Store Union Members on strike. Ohio Historical Society, P264 AL00049.

Labor since the Sixties

In 1960, blue-collar workers in the Midwest prospered more than their counterparts in most other areas of the country, except the Northeast. This was true for two reasons: Blue-collar workers had higher unionization rates, bringing higher compensation levels, and the mix of jobs in the Midwest was tilted toward manufacturing, in particular heavy manufacturing where compensation levels were higher.

In the 1960s, the Midwest was the most unionized region in the country. By 1964, the overall U.S. unionization rate (the percentage of nonagricultural employees in unions) was 29 percent, with six of the eight full states in the region having rates well in ex-

cess of 30 percent: Michigan (highest of the fifty states at 45 percent), Indiana (3rd highest at 41 percent), Ohio (8th at 38 percent), Minnesota (10th at 37 percent), Illinois (12th at 36 percent), and Wisconsin (14th at 34 percent). However, the states on the western edge of the region departed from this unionized pattern: South Dakota, North Dakota, Kansas, and Nebraska were well below national norms, and Iowa too fell somewhat below the national average.

High unionization rates stemmed from the heavily industrialized nature of the economy in most midwestern states. The Midwest was the heartland of production of automobiles (Michigan), steel (Indiana and Ohio), agricultural and earthmoving equipment (Illinois and surrounding states), heavy and light home appliances (many states, especially Ohio and Iowa), meat processing (Minnesota, Iowa, Nebraska, Kansas, Missouri, Illinois, Wisconsin), beer (Wisconsin and Missouri), aerospace (Missouri), and numerous other products that were often directly or indirectly related to the primary manufacturing industries just listed. All of these industries were heavily unionized as a result of the Congress of Industrial Organizations (CIO) upsurge in the 1930s. Combined with the building trades' craft unions in the urban areas, telephone workers, and transportation and diversified unions such as the Teamsters, the labor movement thus represented a substantial portion of the blue-collar workforce in the Midwest by the 1960s.

Midwestern unions faced a series of challenges in the decades between 1960 and 2000, however. First, the civil rights and subsequent black power movements challenged many unions. As was their custom, white craft unions in the building trades initially resisted integration, causing considerable ill will in minority communities. Among these the building trades unions were later to reverse their resistance, however, and by 2001, unionized construction workers were *more* likely to be African American than their nonunion counterparts. Even a progressive union that had played a role in passage of the 1964 Civil Rights Act, the United Auto Workers (UAW), faced a major rebellion in the Detroit auto plants. From 1967 to 1974, the UAW fought against black factory-based organizations, protesting racism, and intolerable working conditions in the plants. In the steel mills of the Gary–Chicago area, both the steel companies and the United Steel Workers (USWA) were forced to sign a consent decree opening jobs in formerly segregated areas to African Americans. The unions' adjustment to the revolution in race relations was rocky and problematic, although in time, unions became among the most integrated institutions in the region and country, as well as defenders of the civil rights of their new minority members.

Similarly, many unions initially had either indifferent or troubled relations with the modern women's movement, stemming from the 1960s and 1970s. Unions in traditionally male occupations, such as the building trades or the skilled trades, in manufacturing plants sometimes resisted the entrance of women or (more often) did nothing to ally with or welcome them. The student and antiwar movements of the 1960s and 1970s had even more strained relations with organized labor. Differences over "youth culture" and the war in Vietnam created a chasm between the labor movement and a broad swath of university-educated people who considered themselves liberals or progressives. The environmental movement likewise clashed at times with unions when there was a perceived conflict between job creation and environmental preservation. And later movements, such as the gay and lesbian movement, likewise initially were at best disconnected from, or at worst at odds with, the mainstream of organized labor.

Thus, from the 1960s through the 1980s, the New Deal Coalition that had sustained the Democratic Party and generally liberal policies since the 1930s broke up. Differences over the cold war, the Vietnam War, racial issues, gender and "lifestyle" issues, and the like tore apart the coalition of labor, minorities, urban residents, Catholics, and progressive intellectuals, with the labor movement usually taking the less liberal side of disputes. The labor movement thus entered the 1980s divorced from the supportive environment it had somewhat enjoyed in previous decades. Suburbanization and the destruction of older (usually ethnic) working-class communities were having the same effect.

By the 1980s, European and Japanese competitors became major rivals to U.S. corporations. Imports competing with midwestern-produced products like automobiles and steel took ever-growing shares of the U.S. market. In response, midwestern manufacturers demanded massive concessions from unionized workers, closed plants at a breathtaking speed, downsized other facilities, reinvested in southern U.S. states or abroad, engaged in union busting in situations where relocation was impractical, and diverted capital from productive facilities to financial and speculative forms of profit making.

Such developments devastated midwestern towns and industries, giving rise to the Rust Belt image prominent in the mainstream media during the 1980s. Manufacturing unions were ravaged; the UAW, the USWA, and the International Association of Machinists (IAM) lost between 20 and 65 percent of their memberships in the course of the decade. In addition, the political system turned decisively to the right in that decade, with Republican Presidents Ronald Reagan and George H.W. Bush tilting in an antilabor direction.

Unions initially failed to respond effectively. Public opinion often blamed unions for many of the economic ills facing the nation, with public approval of unions dropping to 55 percent in the Gallup polls in the early 1980s, the lowest it had ever been. Cut off from natural allies as the New Deal Coalition continued to unravel, they initially undertook only defensive strategies of the most conventional sort: bargaining concessions, severance pay, and calling for legislative protection of their industrial employers.

In time, however, unions began to develop more innovative responses. One response was to reach out to potential allies in the local industrial communities. In northwest Indiana a labor-community coalition, The Calumet Project for Industrial Jobs, engaged in battles to save jobs and maintain living standards. Though most were unsuccessful in keeping facilities open, in 1991, this group succeeded in passing a Gary city ordinance that prefigured the many living wage ordinances later passed throughout the country. These ordinances require corporate public aid recipients or public contractors to pay a living wage above the poverty level for a family of four.

In Chicago, the Midwest Center for Labor Research played a similar role in building coalitions to stabilize the manufacturing base and to create local industrial policies that encouraged ownership and zoning arrangements aimed at keeping well-paying jobs in the city. In Milwaukee, the Campaign for a Sustainable Milwaukee, initiated by the local Central Labor Council, developed a sophisticated labor–community coalition to steer economic development policies in a procommunity, proworker direction. Coalition efforts included encouragement of unionization, alliances between building trades unions and minority communities, and worker training and light rail transportation programs geared toward working-class communities. In other cities like Cleveland, activists established strong chapters of Jobs with Justice, a labor-led coalition of unions and community forces.

Other responses to the massive assault on living standards and unions arose in some heavily industrialized midsized towns in the Midwest. Union locals and community and political allies brought court suits to force companies closing or relocating plants to live up to previous commitments made in exchange for public subsidies or union contract terms. Examples include the Amhoist Corporation in St. Paul, Minnesota (1985–1987), Diamond Tool Corporation in Duluth, Minnesota (1987), the Chrysler Corporation in Kenosha, Wisconsin (1988), and General Motors in Ypsilanti, Michigan (1993). Results were mixed, ranging from out-of-court settlements to defeat, as the courts reverted to their historic stance favoring capital over labor. But these community battles and corporate responsibility lawsuits also helped stimulate a growing nationwide movement against corporate welfare and efforts to require public gains (jobs, incomes, and so forth) in exchange for public corporate subsidies.

In some industrial communities, plant closings or demands on unions for massive concessions sparked outbursts of union militancy. The best-known included a strike and boycott at the Hormel meat packing plant in Austin, Minnesota (1985–1986), a series of strikes at the Caterpillar earthmoving equipment plants in Peoria and Decatur, Illinois (1991–1998), a lockout at the Staley corn processing plant in Decatur (1993–1995), and a strike followed by a massive corporate campaign at the Bridgestone-Firestone tire plant in Decatur (1994–1996). In the mid-1990s, Decatur became known as a war zone because of its struggles between absentee corporate owners and labor–community forces. The Hormel and Staley struggles ended in major defeats for the unions, while the Caterpillar struggle ended on terms mostly unfavorable to the union. The Bridgestone-Firestone struggle was a qualified success for the union due to innovative use of corporate campaign tactics.

Despite the defeats, these struggles led to a more innovative and less complacent labor movement. They also created stronger ties between unions and communities and turned the public's attention to workers' concerns. National movements enduring into the twenty-first century, including the living wage movement and the corporate accountability movement had their first seeds in these midwestern struggles.

Nevertheless, the center of gravity of the U.S. economy, workforce, and the labor movement shifted in this period away from industrial workers and unions. Public sector and service sector employment took up the slack. Following President John Kennedy's executive order granting unionization rights to federal workers in the early 1960s, public sector unionism spread rapidly at all levels of government. From a rate around 10 percent in 1960, the public sector unionization rate exploded to 35 to 40 percent by the turn of the century. Meanwhile the private sector unionization rate plummeted from around 30 percent to approximately 9 percent by the year 2000.

The future of the labor movement in the Midwest and elsewhere appears to lie with public sector and service workers. The prevalence of heavy industry in the Midwest economy and workforce, despite deindustrialization, helps maintain Midwest unionization rates well above the national average. In 1964, the Midwest region had four of the top ten most unionized states, and seven of the top twenty. By 2000, it still had four of the top ten, and had slipped only slightly to six of the top twenty.

Established private sector industrial unions in midwestern states adapted by organizing outside their traditional jurisdictions. Thus in 2001, one can find public sector workers who are members of the United Auto Workers and hospital workers who are members of the United Steel Workers. As memberships dropped, unions have used their remaining long-standing presence and resources to penetrate new segments of the workforce.

Nevertheless, union presence is greatly diminished in midwestern states, as elsewhere. The highest midwestern unionization rate, Michigan at 21 percent, in 2000 was well below the 30+ percent rate in seven midwestern states in 1964. But comparatively, the Midwest labor movement has done no worse in the 1960–2000 period than the overall U.S. labor movement.

Vastly increased immigration is another challenge facing the Midwest labor movement as it enters the twenty-first century. Communities and unions now have to integrate increasing numbers of Mexican, Central American, Vietnamese, Bosnian, and other immigrants into their ranks. In this respect, the Midwest is catching up with those areas near the eastern, western, or southern borders of the country. Adjustments will be required, but resilient working-class communities and unions are likely to remain a force in the Midwest.

Sources and Further Reading: Barry Bluestone and Bennett Harrison, *The Deindustrialization of America: Plant Closings, Community Abandonment, and the Dismantling of Basic Industry* (1982); Charles Craypo and Bruce Nissen, eds., *Grand Designs: The Impact of Corporate Strategies on Workers, Unions, and Communities* (1993); Kathryn Marie Dudley, *The End of the Line: Lost Jobs, New Lives in Postindustrial America* (1994); Suzan Erem, *Labor Pains: Inside America's New Union Movement* (2001); Stephen Franklin, *Three Strikes: Labor's Heartland Losses and What They Mean for Working Americans* (2001); Dan Georgakas and Marvin Surkin, *Detroit, I Do Mind Dying: A Study in Urban Revolution* (1975); Hardy Green, *On Strike at Hormel: The Struggle for a Democratic Labor Movement* (1990); Barry T. Hirsch, David A. Macpherson, and Wayne G. Vroman, "Estimates of Union Density, by State", *Monthly Labor Review* 124 (July 2001); Bruce Nissen, *Fighting for Jobs: Case Studies of Labor-Community Coalitions Confronting Plant Closings* (1995); Peter Rachleff, *Hard-Pressed in the Heartland: The Hormel Strike and the Future of the Labor Movement* (1993).

Bruce Nissen
Florida International University

Working-Class Communities and Deindustrialization

While the common cliché defines the Midwest as the breadbasket of America, we often forget that it was also the nation's industrial Heartland. Large cities such as Cleveland and Chicago, smaller urban areas such as Gary and Youngstown, and small rural towns such as Canton, Illinois, or Austin, Minnesota, housed factories making everything from raw steel to farm equipment. These factories drew waves of immigrants from Europe and migrants from the South, who formed strong working-class industrial communities throughout the Midwest.

During the first half of the twentieth century, working-class communities developed networks centered around neighborhoods and churches, with social clubs, union halls, parochial schools, bars, and shops within walking distance. People who grew up in such neighborhoods talk fondly about the sense of togetherness and commonality that saw them through difficult times. The solidarity of working-class communities enabled workers to band together in successful union organizing drives, although the process was marked by conflict and even violence. At the same time, the working class was often divided along lines of race, ethnicity, and gender, fighting over ownership of jobs and union representation. As unionized workers gained economic ground, white working-class communities spread into the suburbs surrounding the cities. As whites moved out, African Americans and other people of color established strong urban communities.

The industrial working class gained reliable employment with good wages and benefits. Many became homeowners, sent their children to college, and enjoyed a middle-class standard of living. In mid-century, the working class of the industrial Midwest seemed to embody the American dream. But when economic conditions began to change in the 1970s, working-class people and their communities faced severe challenges. As factories closed and industries reorganized, hundreds of thousands of midwestern industrial workers lost their jobs, and their communities lost their solid tax bases and community pride. Yet deindustrialization affected working-class communities differently, and different communities responded in different ways.

For large cities, deindustrialization exacerbated a process of economic decline that had begun as early as the 1940s, with white flight to the suburbs and the development of new factories on the edges of cities. Urban working-class communities in the 1960s and 1970s were struggling, despite gains made by African American workers in some industries, such as steel and auto. While employment opportunities had increased marginally, urban working-class communities had been undermined by urban renewal and transportation projects that displaced families, disrupted small business operations, and directed commercial traffic to the suburbs. As factories closed in the 1970s and 1980s and the Rust Belt spread from Chicago to Buffalo, urban working-class communities were especially hard hit. Poverty, crime, and a variety of social problems all increased, while access to jobs, health care, education, and other services all decreased. In the early twenty-first century, many midwestern cities continue to struggle with the long-term effects of deindustrialization.

But most large cities were not dependent solely on a single industry, but rather sat amid the diversified economies of sprawling metropolitan areas. This provided some measure of economic stability, which masked the effects of major job losses. Thus, large cities could boast of economic revitalization on the margins of the city and in some downtown areas, where targeted demolition and renovation created small areas of prosperity. Detroit's Renaissance Center and Cleveland's downtown stadiums, museums, and shopping centers exemplify the kind of central city renewal that invites visitors to ignore the continued economic struggle in the rest of the city.

Smaller cities, such as Youngstown, Gary, and Flint, each depended on a single industry. Thus, they were harder hit by deindustrialization, which tended to affect several companies of a single industry at approximately the same time, and less able to mask the effects of economic loss. As in the large cities, workers lost homes, health care, and economic stability, but smaller deindustrialized cities suffered more significantly from such losses. For example, Youngstown lost approximately fifty thousand steel-related jobs in a decade, and both the local economy and local government depended on the purchasing power and taxes of steelworkers. With fewer other industries to turn to than in Cleveland or Pittsburgh, individual workers were more likely to have to leave to find work. The proportion of houses lost to foreclosure, abandonment, and even arson was higher. The loss of homes undermined social and community networks as families, churches, and social clubs lost members. Further, because the community's identity was so closely tied to its dominant industry, communities struggled to redefine themselves. With smaller populations and tax bases, smaller cities faced greater challenges in attracting either federal aid or new business. While such communities drew on the coherence of their working-class communities to organize campaigns to try to save local factories and develop new businesses, their continued economic struggles have led residents, politicians, and journalists to view the problems as the communities' own fault. Decades after the factories shut down, succeeding generations are moving away from such cities, continuing the process of population decline that undermines community identity and coherence.

During the same period, the rural Midwest saw a major economic restructuring in agriculture-related and heavy equipment industries. Companies began to outsource some of their production, downsized their workforces, moved corporate offices, and in some cases shut down entire plants. This caused significant job loss, leading many rural residents to move to cities and other regions. At the same time, agriculture and related industries restructured their operations, opening new, smaller factories. Some of these new factories were built in towns that had recently seen major job losses with the closing of large plants. Although new factories seemed to promise economic hope, in many cases companies turned to cheaper immigrant labor. As increasing numbers of Mexican and southeast Asian immigrants moved into communities where white workers had recently lost jobs, many communities developed racial and economic tensions similar to those that had occurred in urban areas earlier in the century. The landscape of the rural Midwest changed, not only in terms of the scale of industry but also in terms of population and community identity.

Sources and Further Reading: David Bensman and Roberta Lynch, *Rusted Dreams* (1987); Barry Bluestone and Bennett Harrison, *The Deindustrialization of America: Plant Closings, Community Abandonment, and the Dismantling of Basic Industry* (1982); Jefferson Cowie and Joseph Heathcott, eds., *Beyond the Ruins: Deindustrialization and the Meanings of Modern America* (2004); Steven P. Dandaneau, *A Town Abandoned* (1996); Kathryn Marie Dudley, *The End of the Line: Lost Jobs, New Lives in Postindustrial America* (1994); Steven High, *Industrial Sunset* (2003); Sherry Lee Linkon and John Russo, *Steeltown U.S.A.* (2002).

John Russo and Sherry Lee Linkon
Youngstown State University, Ohio

The Decline of Building Trade Unions

Construction workers in the Midwest account for approximately 5 percent of the overall labor force. Compared to labor in other industrial sectors in the region as well as to construction workers in other parts of the country, midwestern construction workers are heavily unionized. With an average construction unionization rate of 58 percent from 1977 to 2000, Illinois had the highest unionization rate of any state in the country. Overall the Midwest accounts for seven of the top eleven states in construction unionization rates. At the other extreme, South Dakota with 8 percent ranked sixth from the bottom. Iowa, Kansas, and North Dakota are in the middle of the pack with average unionization rates over the same period between 20 and 25 percent, and Nebraska is in the bottom half at 15 percent.

The unionization rate among construction workers in the Midwest, like unionization rates elsewhere, declined as a proportion of the workforce during the last decades of the twentieth century. While the construction labor force grew from 930 thousand in 1973 to 1.46 million in 2000, the number of union members increased disproportionately from 520 thousand to 567 thousand.

Union and nonunion construction work in the Midwest historically has been disproportionately male (98 percent) and disproportionately non-Hispanic white (92 percent). In recent years, however, Hispanic males have grown from less than 2 percent in the 1980s to 6 percent at the turn of the century. They are currently "over-represented" in construction, when compared to 4 percent of the overall midwestern labor force. Black workers had the highest level of union membership in the industry in the latter part of the twentieth century, followed by non-Hispanic whites, and then Hispanics.

Historically, formal training in construction has relied upon provisions in collective bargaining agreements to create and finance most apprenticeship programs. For instance, between 1989 and 1995 in Ohio, collectively bargained, union–management cooperative apprenticeship programs accounted for 75 percent of all graduating apprentices. The decline in unionization, however, has led to a decline in apprenticeship training. In 1973, 18,300 new apprentices entered registered construction apprentice programs in the Midwest, whereas by 1995, only 10,900 new apprentices entered the programs. Thus, whereas the construction labor force expanded substantially in the region during the last three decades of the twentieth century, union membership essentially held constant in terms of numbers and registered apprenticeship trainees declined almost by half.

The decline in unions and apprenticeship training corresponds to the real decline in construction worker income during this period. On average, in 1972, midwestern construction workers earned $44,282 per year in 2001 dollars. Average income, however, had declined by more than a quarter to $33,111 in 1997, again in 2001 dollars. Despite this substantial decline in real income, construction unions in the Midwest have been able to secure modest improvement in worker health insurance and pension benefits. Between 1977 and 1997, employer contributions to health and pension benefits, not including social security or workers compensation payments, increased from $3,543 to $4,147 in 2001 dollars. Outside the Midwest, where collective bargaining is less common, construction workers in 1997 earned $29,659 in 2001 dollars (12 percent less than in the Midwest) and their contractors paid $2,474 (52 percent less) into health and pension benefits.

Thus, even though construction worker income has slipped substantially, midwestern construction unions continue to play an important role in preserving health insurance and pension benefits within this industry, and they remain the primary providers of training.

Sources and Further Reading: Steven G. Allen, "Developments in Collective Bargaining in Construction in the 1980s and 1990s" in Paula Voos, ed., *Contemporary Collective Bargaining in the Private Sector* (1994); Herbert Applebaum, *Construction Workers, U.S.A.* (1999); Gerald Finkel, *The Economics of the Construction Industry* (1997); Richard B. Freeman and James L. Medoff, *What Do Unions Do?* (1984).

Peter Philips and Mark A. Price
University of Utah

Ed Sadlowski and Steelworkers Fight Back, 1973–1977

Ed Sadlowski, of Steelworkers Fight Back, ran for President of the United Steelworkers of America In-

ternational Union (USWA) in 1977. Steelworkers Fight Back began in the Calumet region of northwest Indiana and northeast Illinois. It had roots in the militant unionism that had simmered there since the 1930s, but was fueled by steelworkers' desire to have a greater voice in factories and in unions.

In 1973, Sadlowski challenged the leadership for the position of District 31 Director. His defeat was overturned by the Justice Department on the grounds of election irregularities; Fight Back prevailed by a 2-to-1 margin in the revote. Thereafter, Sadlowski emerged as a spokesman for workers' grievances, articulating a class-conscious anger at management, corporate decision makers, and labor officials.

In 1977, when the Steelworkers' leadership named Lloyd McBride to run for President, Fight Back nominated Sadlowski. He argued that steelworkers ought to be allowed to vote on the Experimental Negotiating Agreement (ENA), which had governed labor relations and banned strikes since 1972. Although wages had climbed under the ENA, steelworkers complained that their grievances were not being taken seriously.

The insurgency enlisted support at integrated mills but in smaller workplaces and outside the basic steel industry, where workers were dependent on the International, McBride forces were stronger. Although Fight Back charged election fraud in its 57-to-43 percent defeat, the Justice Department declined to intervene.

Within two years, a depression closed many mills. McBride could not unify the steelworkers to reach agreement with the steel companies on stabilizing the industry and preserving jobs and incomes. His successor, Lynn Williams, was more successful at uniting steelworkers, especially after the economic recovery of 1985.

While the Fight Back insurgency lost its steam during the mill closings of 1980–1985, many of those mobilized by the campaign participated in revitalizing the labor movement under the leadership of John Sweeney in the decade that followed.

Sources and Further Reading: David Bensman and Roberta Lynch, *Rusted Dreams* (1987); James B. Lane and Mike Olszanski, eds., *Steelworkers Fight Back* (2000); Philip Nyden, *Steelworkers Rank-and-File* (1984).

David Bensman
Rutgers University, New Jersey

Labor and Politics at the State Level

The political influence of organized labor varies dramatically across the Midwest because of the varying economies of each state and the percentage of its workforce that is unionized. Labor's presence is less significant in rural and agrarian North and South Dakota, but more consequential in urban and industrialized Illinois, Michigan, and Ohio. A large union presence with its associated financial and manpower resources gives unions more clout in state politics.

Labor's role also depends on its traditional relationships with the major political parties. In states such as Minnesota and Michigan, the creation of a programmatic, progressive Democratic Party entailed a coalition between labor, liberal activists, agrarian interests, and others. Thus, Minnesota has the Democratic-Farmer-Labor Party. In Michigan, the United Auto Workers union was a key player in the establishment of the modern Democratic Party during the Great Depression. In other midwestern states, labor had no tradition as an integral component of the Democratic Party, even though unions typically supported Democratic candidates and initiatives.

The changing size and composition of union membership also affects labor's political clout. Union members have declined as a percentage of the workforce, particularly in the Midwest with the decline of heavy industries. Moreover, the union movement has become more diverse demographically and politically, and more heterogeneous with respect to the kinds of unions to which members belong. In the past, the typical union member was white and male; today there is a much higher proportion of women and racial and ethnic minorities. Likewise, unions themselves have changed. In the past, major unions represented workers in sectors of the economy such as steel, automobiles, automotive parts, coal, and durable goods. Today, for example, steel and coal have witnessed sharp declines in membership. The growth areas for unions have been public employees such as state government workers and public schoolteachers. But white-collar government workers and teachers have different economic interests and partisan leanings than industrial workers, making political cohesion more difficult to achieve.

Organized labor has also had to accommodate the political realities of the Midwest. Democratic Party sympathies notwithstanding, many unions throughout the 1990s and well into the twenty-first century faced heavily Republican political environments. For example, in Ohio the GOP won the governorship in 1990, 1994, 1998, and 2002, controlled the Ohio Senate, and held the Ohio House from 1995 on. This has resulted in some Ohio unions endorsing some statewide GOP candidates even as the major labor federation—the Ohio AFL-CIO—remains strongly Democratic.

In summary, organized labor has lost clout in the Midwest, yet it remains a very powerful membership organization, able to mobilize voters and lobby legislators on issues central to the organization. A Democratic resurgence in the Midwest would enhance labor's role. But Republican dominance in some states has forced accommodations between the Republican Party and certain unions, and encouraged the GOP to cultivate particular unions such as the Teamsters. Some labor leaders and some Republican officeholders have recognized that unbridled hostility between them may not serve either party's interest.

Sources and Further Reading: Herbert B. Asher et al., *American Labor Unions in the Electoral Arena* (2001); Taylor E. Dark, *The Unions and the Democrats* (1999); William Form, *Segmented Labor, Fractured Politics* (1995); Mark J. Rozell and Clyde Wilcox, *Interest Groups in American Campaigns* (1999).

Herbert B. Asher
The Ohio State University–Columbus

Organized Labor and Organized Philanthropy

Foundations in the Midwest have made grants with or related to organized labor in an array of fields, economic revitalization, school reform, research, and religion among them. Typical of Rust Belt economic revival programs, in the 1980s the Cleveland and Gund foundations teamed up with the United Labor Agency, the human-services arm of area unions, to create the Regional Industry Center. The center operated an early warning system to enable workers to recognize signals that their plants were in trouble. It helped retain many jobs, though it did not persuade the Cleveland *Plain Dealer* to remain in the city.

A Wisconsin Modernization Institute, a labor–business–community collaboration in Milwaukee, received substantial foundation funding. With foundation grants, the Federation for Industrial Retention and Renewal, Chicago, promotes and provides backup for local retention projects. The foundation-supported 9 to 5, the National Association of Working Women, and builds coalitions among low-wage women workers' organizations. Several foundations have assisted such labor insurgent groups as the Detroit-based Teamster Rank and File Education and Legal Defense Foundation, and Steelworkers Fight Back, which promotes democratic procedures in union management.

Foundations and labor found common ground in the run-up to the Chicago School Reform Act of 1988, which mandated a decentralized school system. Civic groups concerned with education received some

$15 million, and unprecedented grants of more than $1 million were made by the John D. and Catherine T. MacArthur Foundation and others to the Chicago Teachers Union. The foundation-financed Youth Project helped the Bailly Alliance in Gary, Indiana, rally unions against construction of a nuclear power plant.

Among the few foundations that have attempted to strengthen unions is the New World Foundation, which arose in 1954 from roots in Chicago through the International Harvester Company and the McCormick family. A half century later, the foundation established the Phoenix Fund for Workers and Communities, to which several other foundations have contributed, that assists with projects that empower the poor to address denial of benefits to contingent workers, the exploitation of immigrants in sweatshops, and health hazards in unregulated industries.

Research has been one of the strongest and continuing avenues of connection between foundations and the labor movement. The pioneering research center for labor-oriented intellectuals was the University of Wisconsin. There, labor economist Richard T. Ely, with funds from reform-minded philanthropists, established the American Bureau of Industrial Research, which he placed in the charge of a former student, John R. Commons. The Carnegie Institution of Washington financed a pathbreaking product of the Bureau, the magisterial eleven-volume *Documentary History of the American Industrial Society 1910–11*.

Foundation-supported research on labor figures prominently in new social science centers that flourished in the 1920s—the Brookings Institution, the Social Science Research Council, the National Bureau of Economic Research, and the Laura Spelman Rockefeller Memorial. The latter's funding for the University of Chicago's Social Science Group underwrote empirical research focused on labor, such as *Industrial Relations in the Chicago Building Trades* (1927) and *The Railroad Labor Board* (1927).

Some foundation-supported research aroused union opposition, such as the research by Elton Mayo on the psychological and social habits of industrial workers, especially at the Hawthorne Works of Western Electric near Chicago. In the early 1970s, the American Federation of State, County, and Municipal Employees resented a Ford Foundation grant for the training of government officials in collective bargaining and labor relations.

Stronger connections between organized labor and foundations were stimulated by the reform-slate election of John Sweeney to the presidency of the AFL-CIO in 1995. That event energized labor to reconnect with the intellectual and academic community, with which many foundation staff members have ties. The

strong bonds liberals and intellectuals had forged with labor in the 1930s and 1940s frayed after World War II. The reasons included disclosures of union corruption and racketeering, jurisdictional disputes, featherbedding (hiring more workers than required), denial of democratic rights of union members, AFL-CIO support of the cold war, Vietnam in particular, and continued union discrimination against minorities. Soon after Sweeney's election, forty-three liberals and intellectuals issued a statement celebrating "the rebirth of a strong and progressive labor movement." Labor teach-ins were held at several universities, and Sweeney created a full-time position of liaison with foundations within the AFL-CIO and staffed it with a former foundation official.

A consortium of private and community foundations, the Neighborhood Funders Group (NFG), established a Working Group on Organized Labor and Community in 1997, declaring, "Organized labor . . . represents a potential ally of enormous significance for low-income and working-class communities." Its conferences have examined problems of jobs and income, rural America, and asset building. By 2002, it had grown to 250 members from such foundations as New Prospect in Wilmette, Illinois; Hudson-Webber in Detroit; Northwest Area and Amherst H. Wilder in St. Paul; McKnight in Minneapolis; MacArthur, Woods Fund, Polk Brothers, and Wieboldt, in Chicago; W.K. Kellogg in Battle Creek; and the Lilly Endowment in Indianapolis. Also drawing closer to organized labor is the religious community. A National Interfaith Committee for Workers Justice was established in 1996 in Chicago with support from unions and foundations.

Reflecting the AFL-CIO's change in position on immigrant workers, contact between unions and foundations on this issue grew. Thus NFG members visited with Haitian nursing home workers in Florida, meatpacking workers in Omaha, and Latino janitors in Los Angeles.

Foundations became more sensitive to organized labor as more white-collar and professional workers—from doctors to engineers—began unionizing toward the end of the twentieth century. Labor also made inroads in universities and other nonprofit organizations that draw foundation support. For example, graduate students have struck at Yale and the Universities of Iowa, Kansas, and Illinois.

Organized labor itself also began stepping up its work in areas of foundation interest. The AFL-CIO in 1999 created a Union Community Fund, which raises funds to meet human service needs identified by working families. Like foundations that include "social benefit" in their criteria for investing their assets, it also established a Center for Working Capital, which helps union pension funds, some of which run into the billions, challenge questionable corporate behavior.

Sources and Further Reading: Daniel Bell, "Labor's New Men of Power," *Fortune* 47 (June 1953); Thomas J. Billitteri, "Organizing Better Links to Labor: Foundations Begin to See Unions as Allies on Social-Policy Fronts," *Chronicle of Philanthropy* (Mar. 25, 1999); Kenneth C. Crowe, *Collision: How the Rank and File Took Back the Teamsters* (1993); Howard M. Gitelman, *Legacy of the Ludlow Massacre* (1988); Steven Greenhouse, "Labor and the Left: Getting Cozy Again," *New York Times* (Sept. 5, 1998); Robert Kanigel, *The One Best Way* (1997); Richard Magat, *Unlikely Partners: Philanthropic Foundations and the Labor Movement* (1999); Gloria Garrett Samson and Richard Magat, "Grants for Labor: The Record of the Garland Fund and the Ford Foundation," *Labor's Heritage* 8 (Spring 1997).

Richard Magat
Community Resource Exchange,
New York City

The Rise of Teacher Unionism

The history of teacher unionism in the Midwest dates back to the turn of the last century. In Chicago, a group of teachers formed the Chicago Teachers Federation in 1897 and aligned themselves with the city's trade union council in late 1902. This was the first Midwest teachers' union to affiliate with labor; the first in the nation was in San Antonio, Texas, which affiliated with the American Federation of Labor.

Although teachers joined the local union affiliates of the National Education Association (NEA) and the American Federation of Teachers (AFT), they could not bargain for a contract under state or city laws, which limited membership and the rights that teachers could claim in their work environment. Teachers in St. Paul, tired of noncompliance from the school board, struck for five weeks in 1946. These teachers, with the threat of being fired, won the strike for needed building repairs and the guarantee that salaries would not be cut. By the late 1950s, bargaining laws for public employees were gaining strength, which led to the representation elections between the AFT and the NEA; the first was in St. Louis, Missouri, in which the AFT affiliate won.

In 1960, the United Federation of Teachers of New York City struck for one day. The following year, the union won bargaining rights to represent all of the teachers, roughly 45 thousand, and negotiated a contract, which ignited the teacher union movement. By 1964, the Detroit Federation of Teachers, Chicago Teachers Union, and Cleveland Teachers Union won the rights to represent teachers in their cities, all being

AFT affiliates. In Milwaukee, the NEA affiliate had won the rights for those city teachers. With these elections, negotiation laws were changing to include teachers. These laws varied from state to state. In Michigan and Wisconsin, they were considered labor laws in which defined groups of teachers fell under the term "labor organizations"; other states designed new laws for teachers rather then group them in municipal union labor laws. By 1974, twenty-six states, eight of them in the Midwest, had enacted laws pertaining to the rights of teachers to bargain collectively, and over 1.4 million teachers were represented by negotiated contracts.

With teacher unionism came strikes as well. In Hamtramck, Michigan, teachers conducted a sit-down strike that lasted three days in 1965. By the end of the 1960s, there had been over three hundred teacher strikes. Striking teachers' demands ranged from better pay to smaller class size.

College teachers also started mass organizing with the AFT, NEA, and with the American Association of University Professors. In 1969, an NEA affiliate at Central Michigan University negotiated the first collective bargaining agreement in a four-year institution in the Midwest. Once faculty began organizing, graduate teaching assistants did, as well, the first being the Teaching Assistants' Association at the University of Wisconsin–Madison in 1969. Today, teacher unionism is a part of the fabric of the day-to-day operation of the education systems in the Midwest and the entire country.

Sources and Further Reading: Samuel Blumenfeld, *NEA, Trojan Horse in American Education* (1984); William Edward Eaton, *The American Federation of Teachers, 1916–1961* (1975); Marjorie Murphy, *Blackboard Unions* (1990); Wayne J. Urban, *Why Teachers Organized* (1982).

Daniel Golodner
Wayne State University, Michigan

The Rise of Public Employees' Unionism

Arguably, the Midwest was the midwife of the public sector labor movement. The American Federation of State, County, and Municipal Employees (AFSCME, 1.3 million members) and the American Federation of Teachers (AFT, 900,000 members) were founded in Wisconsin and Illinois, respectively. Interestingly, both unions were organized by professional employees, personnel administrators (AFSCME), and teachers (AFT). Additionally, the Service Employees International Union (SEIU) began life in Chicago as the private sector flat janitors union. Today, about

700,000 of SEIU's 1.4 million members are public workers.

All public employees—federal, state, and local—are excluded from coverage under the 1935 National Labor Relations Act. Therefore, nonfederal public employees had to win collective bargaining rights on a state-by-state or local government basis through either de jure, de facto, or ad hoc arrangements.

In 1959, Wisconsin adopted the nation's first public sector collective bargaining statute, covering only local government workers. In 1966, a law covering state employees was enacted. Michigan is the only state where collective bargaining for state employees is embedded in the state constitution (since 1980), rather than by statute, and is implemented by Civil Service Commission regulations. Local government workers were covered by statute in 1978. In Nebraska, state employee bargaining rights are uniquely guaranteed by both the state constitution and statute. Illinois was the first state to provide broad collective bargaining rights for state employees: In the absence of bargaining legislation, Governor Ogilvie issued an Executive Order in 1972, which was subsequently replaced by comprehensive legislation in 1984. Minnesota adopted a comprehensive statute in 1971; Ohio followed in 1983.

By the mid-1980s, Indiana was the only state of the Old Northwest Territory that had not adopted comprehensive collective bargaining legislation. Indiana operates under a Governor's Executive Order (1990) that provides for state employee collective bargaining, including wages, and a state statute covering teachers (1973). Many other local government public workers have achieved bargaining rights either through enactment of an ordinance or simply a de facto arrangement.

Iowa (1974) and Nebraska (1969) are the only other midwestern states that have adopted comprehensive bargaining laws. These laws cover a substantial majority of public employees; provide procedures for unit and representation determination and exclusivity; establish the duty to bargain on wages, hours and conditions of employment; and define unfair labor practices. The laws also provide for a neutral independent administrative agency, as well as procedures both for resolving grievances and for negotiating impasses.

Meet-and-confer statutes in Kansas (1971), Missouri (1967), and South Dakota (1969) vary widely in breadth of coverage, scope of bargaining rights, and thoroughness. Although these laws cover almost all employees, the scope of meet-and-confer rights differs. One common thread is that local government employees are extended broader rights than state employees. Local government workers may negotiate wages, but state employees lack that right. In Kansas, however, local governments must opt in to be covered. Kansas also has a separate statute for teachers (1970).

Missouri state employees are now permitted to bargain for wages under a Governor's Executive Order issued in 2001. North Dakota's statute (1975) covers teachers only. Most Midwest states have amended their original statutes; none, however, has revoked statutory bargaining rights.

Professors Barry T. Hirsch and David A. Macpherson, using Current Population Survey data, compiled the most reliable information about union membership. For purposes of the following comparisons, "public employees" also include both federal and postal workers. However, aggregated data for the United States reveals that state and local government employment constitutes more than 83 percent of public employment. Whereas just under 38 percent of all public workers in the nation are union members, 43 percent of public workers are union members in the twelve midwestern states. The total number of public employee union members in the United States is 7.3 million, of whom more than 1.7 million are in the twelve midwestern states.

The breakdown within the twelve Midwest states is more pertinent and perhaps even more revealing. Aggregating data for the seven states with comprehensive collecting bargaining statutes shows that of their 2.95 million public workers, 1.47 million or 49.7 percent are union members. Conversely, in the five states with less than comprehensive statutes, there are almost 1.13 million employees, of whom slightly fewer than 267 thousand or only 23.6 percent are union members. It could be argued that these latter states are essentially more rural, and therefore, the workers less receptive to union organization. An equally or more persuasive case could be made that where the substantial majority of workers are covered by comprehensive legislation providing for bargaining on wages and other economic matters, the workers are much more likely to want a union to represent their interests.

Sources and Further Reading: Kate Bronfenbrenner and Tom Juravich, *The Impact of Employer Opposition on Union Certification Win Rates* (1995); Barry T. Hirsch and David A. Macpherson, *Union Membership and Earnings Data Book* (2003).

Donald S. Wasserman
Washington, D.C.

Temporary Faculty in Higher Education

By 2000, full and part-time temporary college teachers constituted the majority of college faculty in the Midwest, although proportions vary substantially between types of institutions. Often generically called adjuncts or part-timers, along with graduate student employees, they taught most college classes without job security or tenure, mostly without benefits, academic freedom, or the salary of regular faculty.

Administrators began hiring temporary faculty in the mid-1970s when faced with greater enrollment of part-time working students, whose numbers were more difficult to predict than new high school graduates. As stagflation reduced budget growth in both public and private institutions, contingent faculty represented a much cheaper and more flexible teaching force. In response, contingent faculty, starting on the coasts and spreading to the Midwest, built a movement for more equitable treatment, using especially unions, but also professional associations and the local academic senates, with graduate employees a leading part of this effort.

Among other contingent faculty, community college part-timers have been the most active and are the most organized in public-sector institutions, where most full-timers were already unionized. In the late 1990s, adjuncts unionized by themselves in two Chicago private institutions, Columbia College and Roosevelt University. This national breakthrough, along with U.S.–Canada Campus Equity Week's coordinated activity in fall 2001, sparked renewed organizing in the Chicago area. During this period, two of the largest community college districts in the nation, College of DuPage (Illinois) and City Colleges of Chicago, also saw active organizing, potentially affecting five thousand part-timers, which promised to continue and spread. Other recent campaigns have included University of Cincinnati and Columbus State in Ohio, and the University of Michigan and Michigan State. Organizing activity has also surfaced in states without collective bargaining laws, such as Missouri, with University of Missouri–Kansas City, a particular center of activity. The selection of Chicago as the site for the Sixth Coalition of Contingent Academic Labor (North American) conference suggests that the leadership of the movement sees the Midwest as an important area for immediate growth.

Sources and Further Reading: Tom Johnson, "A Proposal to Organize Non-Tenured Faculty: Our Time Has Come," *Against the Current*, vol. 6 (Jan.–Feb. 1992); Barbara Wolf, *Degrees of Shame* (video, 1997).

Joe T. Berry
Chicago Coalition of Contingent Academic
Labor, Illinois

Women and Unions

Millions of women became wage-earners in the decades during and following World War II; surpris-

ing numbers joined unions, as well. In fact, women accounted for 60 percent of all new union members between 1960 and 1980. Union organizing after midcentury developed primarily in traditionally female occupations: teaching, health care, and public and other service work. A broad base of women activists came into the unions through these drives, especially in urban centers such as Chicago, Detroit, Cleveland, and Milwaukee.

Encouraged by Title VII of the 1964 Civil Rights Act, women overcame employment barriers in steel and auto plants and coal mines. The lack of basic on-the-job protection forced women to form organizations within unions to demand representation. The United Auto Workers Union's Women's Department pioneered the formation of local union women's committees and played a leading role, first in Michigan and then nationally, in bringing the issue of sexual harassment before the public. In the Chicago–Northwest Indiana district of the United Steelworkers of America, a multiracial group of women organized the District 31 Women's Caucus to battle discrimination, sexual harassment, and inequality. Union women marched for the Equal Rights Amendment in Illinois. A Cincinnati women's group produced a film on pregnancy leave discrimination as part of the campaign to pass the 1978 Pregnancy Disability Act. Women scored victories that forced employers to provide such benefits as bathroom and shower facilities, equal health coverage, and pay equity. By 2000, skillful pressure from women brought forward demands for accessible child care, paid family leave, and promotional opportunities to union bargaining and legislative agendas.

In 1974, activists from almost every union gathered in Chicago to form the Coalition of Labor Union Women (CLUW). This network provided training and mentoring for thousands more women. Spurred by black civil rights struggles, women activists sustained the labor movement through the decades after 1954, the year of highest union density; 34 percent of the workforce was union, but only 8 percent of union membership was female. By 1990, 15 percent of women belonged to unions. With declining union density, only 11 percent of women belonged to unions by 1998, but they accounted for 39 percent of union membership.

Women's increasing union participation initiated a long-overdue transformation in union priorities and challenged a culture of unionism long dominated by white men. But efforts to gain leadership positions, even in female-dominated unions, faced persistent barriers. Entrenched leaders refused to slate women for elected positions and dismissed demands for child-care and family leave as "not real union issues." Women advanced first at the grass roots. Supported by local CLUW chapters and by annual Midwest Summer Schools for union women, female activists moved from shop-floor steward positions to local presidents, to city and statewide positions, and increasingly onto union staff and executive boards.

In a 2002 study of women in retail service, union women earned 31 percent more than their nonunion counterparts, and 68 percent of women in unions had health-care benefits, compared to only 36 percent of those not in unions. In highly unionized states like Michigan, Illinois, and Minnesota, women's median annual earnings are among the highest in the country.

Sources and Further Reading: Dorothy Sue Cobble, *Women and Unions* (1993); Mary Margaret Fonow, *Union Women* (2003); Nancy F. Gabin, *Feminism in the Labor Movement* (1990); Institute for Women's Policy Research, *The Status of Women in the States* (2003).

Ruth Needleman
Indiana University–Bloomington

The Caterpillar Strikes and the Staley Lock-Out

In the 1990s, two major labor conflicts erupted at Caterpillar and A.E. Staley, both in Illinois. Over 12,400 United Automobile Workers union members struck twice, in 1991–1992 and 1994–1995, against the multinational earthmoving equipment company. Both strikes ended in defeat, and a concessionary contract was negotiated in 1998. In 1992, 760 Allied Industrial Workers Local 837 members employed at the Decatur, Illinois, Staley corn-processing plant rejected a contract, but continued working in the plant. In 1993, the unionists were locked out and, after a thirty-month battle, signed a deeply concessionary contract in 1995.

Both managements joined the growing corporate trend in arguing that massive concessions were required from their workforces to compete in the global marketplace. The companies brought in replacement workers or "scabs"—in Caterpillar's case, the largest such use of scabs by a U.S. industrial employer since the Great Depression.

Both unions initiated innovative "work-to-rule" campaigns whereby workers strictly followed supervisors' orders and took no initiatives of their own, with the goal of slowing production. The Staley workers, through a small local union, galvanized tremendous national support and media attention for their fight, and ultimately merged with the Industrial Paperworkers International Union and secured professional expertise to initiate a national corporate campaign to mobilize popular pressure on the corporation. Dozens of solidarity committees were set up across the coun-

try. In Decatur, both unions participated in several large demonstrations involving nonviolent civil disobedience, and sent rank-and-file Road Warriors across the country to garner support for their cause.

Sources and Further Reading: Jeremy Brecher, *Strike!* (1997); Isaac Cohen, "The Caterpillar Labor Dispute and the UAW, 1991–1998," *Labor Studies Journal* 27 (Winter 2003); Stephen Franklin, *Three Strikes* (2001).

Steven Ashby
Indiana University–Bloomington

Firefighter Strikes

In 1968, the International Association of Fire Fighters (AFL-CIO) lifted its 1920s ban on firefighter strikes. The union launched a series of controversial strikes in states without public employee collective bargaining laws, including Ohio, Indiana, Missouri, and Illinois. The union hoped to win local contracts and pressure state governments for collective bargaining laws.

In 1977 and 1978, firefighters struck in twenty-four different midwestern communities. In 1977, in University City, Missouri, and other towns, firefighters picketed burning buildings. Illinois firefighters developed a unique tactic, which they christened the Silver Spanner strike. A spanner is a large wrench used to open hydrants. In these job actions firefighters picketed their station, responding in their own vehicles to alarms, returning to the picket line after suppressing the fire.

In the longest strike, in Normal, Illinois, in 1978, the entire fire union, Local 2442, was sentenced to forty-two days in jail, and the fire station reopened as a police-sanctioned work release center. They won a contract after a fifty-six-day job action, including jail time. The strike wave ended in Chicago in 1980, following a twenty-three-day strike with over twenty fire-related deaths. Chicago refused the strikers' offer of a silver spanner volunteer response system.

These strikes built momentum for firefighter collective bargaining laws, which passed in Ohio in 1982, Minnesota in 1984, and Illinois in 1985. Indiana public employees organized under a 1990 Governor's executive order, and Missouri still lacks a law.

Sources and Further Reading: David Lewin, Raymond D. Horton, and James W. Kuhn, *Collective Bargaining and Manpower Utilization in Big City Governments* (1979); Michael G. Matejka, *Fiery Struggle* (2002).

Michael G. Matejka
Laborers–Employers Cooperation & Education
Trust, Bloomington, Illinois

The Hormel Strike

In 1985–1986 1,529 workers organized in United Food and Commercial Workers (UFCW) Local P-9 struck the Hormel company's Austin, Minnesota, plant. One small local union became a national symbol of labor resistance in the 1980s to corporate demands for wage and benefit cuts. The strike was captured in Barbara Kopple's Academy Award–winning film *American Dream.*

The union sent rank-and-file workers across the country to build support for their strike and for a boycott of Hormel's meat products. Local P-9 solidarity committees were formed across the Midwest to publicize the strike. Following the example of President Ronald Reagan, who fired 11,300 striking air traffic controllers in 1981, Hormel brought in replacement workers, or scabs. In response, Hormel workers and supporters repeatedly engaged *en masse* in nonviolent civil disobedience, resulting in scores of arrests. Local P-9 hired maverick labor consultant Ray Rogers to launch a national corporate campaign against Hormel, with the goal of winning broad popular support to pressure the company to negotiate a fair contract.

The Hormel strike revealed the schism within the labor movement between labor leaders who saw no alternative to accepting concessions and those workers who wanted to fight back militantly and revitalize a weakened labor movement. The UFCW opposed the local union's corporate campaign and civil disobedience tactics, and urged the workers to accept the drastic wage cuts. Finally, in May 1986, the UFCW took over control of Local P-9, ordered the Hormel workers to return to work, and eventually signed a concessionary contract.

Sources and Further Reading: Hardy Green, *On Strike at Hormel* (1990); Dave Hage and Paul Klauda, *No Retreat, No Surrender* (1989); Peter Rachleff, *Hard-Pressed in the Heartland* (1993).

Steven K. Ashby
Indiana University–Bloomington

Women Workers and the Labor Movement

The shift from agriculture to industry, which began in the Midwest in the antebellum period, diversified the location and character of women's work. The home continued to be the site of women's paid work—more women were employed as domestic servants than any other occupation throughout the nineteenth century, and many women, especially married women, worked for wages in their homes, by taking in piecework, laundry, or boarders. But jobs outside the home increased greatly in number after the Civil War. Until the mid-twentieth century, the typical female jobholder was a young, unmarried woman. Although many lived at home and contributed their wages to the family economy, others left their homes in search of employment. Indeed in the late nineteenth century, single young women migrated at a greater rate and earlier age than single men to seek work in midwestern cities.

The jobs held by women depended on a number of factors, including ethnicity, race, class, and location, as well as sex. Women factory workers clustered in a few industries, particularly garments, food processing, and electrical goods; within those industries, women held a status separate and unequal to men. White-collar work emerged as industry and commerce grew. In offices and shops, women worked as secretaries and salesclerks, often earning less than factory workers, but preferring the aura of feminine respectability that surrounded work considered clean and appropriate for native-born, English-speaking, white women. Generally barred from the "men's" professions—law, medicine, and the ministry—college-educated women created their own place in the occupational hierarchy. The so-called women's professions offered unmarried women salaried employment as librarians, nurses, teachers, and social workers. All these groups of workers eventually joined the labor movement. But the first to organize successfully and build long-lasting institutions were factory workers. Later in the twentieth century, women who worked in offices and shops organized or sought to organize, as well.

In the 1880s, the Knights of Labor consolidated midwestern workers' discontent into a national movement. This relatively new labor federation organized workers regardless of race, nationality, occupation, skill level, or sex and embraced the idea of equal pay for women and men, equal rights for women within all organizations, and respect for women's work, whether unpaid in the home or for wages in the factory or mill. Women in all the Midwest states took advantage of this unique vehicle for organization and collective protest. At the height of their success, about 10 percent of all Knights—some fifty thousand members—were women. Women were organized in all-female and in mixed assemblies, or local unions. The second female assembly in the nation was chartered in Chicago, with Elizabeth Rodgers as Master Workman. Many all-female assemblies were organized throughout the Midwest, including the Our Girls Co-op garment workers assembly in Chicago, the Martha Washington Assembly and underwear workers cooperative

Indiana Bell employees, Indianapolis, 1947. Bass Photo CD Collection, Indiana Historical Society, neg. no. 268629-5.

in Indianapolis, the Good Will Assembly of domestic workers in Shawnee, Ohio, the Joan of Arc mixed assembly in Toledo, and the Zanesville Ladies of Labor in Ohio.

Women served as local leaders, and some gained regional reputations. Rodgers, for example, served for a period as Master Workman of the Chicago District Assembly, presiding over its six hundred delegates, who represented forty thousand male and female Knights. The Knights, however, collapsed in the late 1880s. The unions that replaced the Knights represented skilled, craft workers, who were predominantly male. These unions, many of which affiliated with the fledgling American Federation of Labor (AFL), at best ignored and at worst were hostile toward women workers, whom they regarded as unstable, unreliable, unworthy, and a threat to job standards.

The hostility of working men and the AFL prompted some working women to organize somewhat independent, single-sex, labor organizations and to seek leaders from among their own ranks. In the Midwest at the turn of the twentieth century, these efforts had some success under such leaders as Elizabeth Morgan, Lizzie Swank Holmes, and Mary Kenney O'Sullivan. Morgan, for example, was a Knights leader in Chicago who reorganized her following as the all-female Federal Local 2703 of the AFL in 1888. With clerks, typists, candymakers, bookbinders, and dressmakers as early recruits, Morgan organized twenty-three different AFL unions of women in four years and won substantial gains for them. By 1903, thirty-five thousand Chicago women workers in twenty-six different trades belonged to unions.

The Progressive era offered other opportunities for women workers' collective action. As they participated in the era's great "woman movement" to humanize an urban, industrial society, working women encountered and sometimes allied with middle-class women. In the Midwest (as elsewhere), working-class women were assisted by middle-class women in groups like the Women's Trade Union League (WTUL), settlement houses like Hull House in Chicago, and residential institutions like the Young Women's Christian Association (YWCA). Reformers shared working women's concerns about job conditions, and together they pursued two paths: protective labor laws for women and union organization to improve working conditions through collective bargaining. The WTUL was a particularly effective group and of inestimable help during the great garment workers' strikes that took place between 1910 and 1920 in Chicago, Cleveland, and smaller cities in the Midwest. The garment workers' organizations that emerged in this period were industrial unions that sought women and men as members. They were an important exception to the gender-specific organizations prevalent at the time.

The Great Depression and the New Deal's collective bargaining policy dramatically altered women's relationship to the labor movement. Mass-production workers, ignored and mistreated by the AFL for decades, formed their own industrial unions that recruited members on the basis not of skill or job assignment, but of their employment in production. This more democratic form of organization meant that women were invited to join, regardless of job assignment or wage status. And join they did. As the industrial heartland, the Midwest was the nerve center for this dramatic decade in American labor history. Autoworkers, steelworkers, electrical goods workers, rubber workers, and meatpacking workers, many of them women, all created new, durable unions in their industries. Retail workers, clerical workers, food service workers, laundry workers, and even domestic servants—a majority of whom were female—also sought unionization. And workers in trades that had unionized before the 1930s—garment workers, for example—extended collective bargaining in their fields. Women actively participated in all the organizing drives and strikes and sought leadership positions in their locals.

What they tended not to do was challenge employment discrimination. The new contracts that covered labor practices and relations codified job segregation by sex. Thus, sex-differentiated wage rates, occupational categories, and seniority lists were standard features of the new collective bargaining agreements ratified beginning in the 1930s. Industrial unionism introduced a language of fair and equal treatment and incorporated women into the labor movement to an unprecedented extent, but it did not *ipso facto* eliminate women's unequal status at work and in unions.

Several trends altered women's relationship to work and the labor movement after 1940. Women's share of union membership rose along with their share of the labor force during World War II. Their increased presence as well as fresh perspective on gender hierarchy and inequality prompted changes in the administration of unions. Many of these changes evaporated in the aftermath of the war, but some survived, particularly networks of female union activists and at least verbal commitments by many unions to pursue gender equality. In the postwar period, midwestern union women continued to challenge sex discrimination, first to secure their jobs when decentralization and automation began to threaten the prominence of mass-production in the heartland, and later to test the promise of federal equal employment legislation to secure gender-neutral treatment. Women in a host of unions made the Midwest a central site for the reevaluation of gender segregation and hierarchy in the workplace.

The expansion of the service sector after World War II also increased the size of the female labor force by increasing the number of jobs typically held by women. The fastest-growing occupations in the Midwest between 1950 and 1970, for example, were in education and in hospitals and health-related fields where women predominated. Beginning in the 1960s, service workers, male and female, turned to formal collective action to a degree not evident earlier, helping to transform the midwestern labor movement.

Public employees led the way, and because women comprised a large proportion of public sector union membership, they often acquired new prominence as leaders. The American Federation of State, County, and Municipal Employees (AFSCME) was founded in Madison, Wisconsin, and Wisconsin passed the nation's first comprehensive public employee bargaining law. Most other midwestern states followed suit, and AFSCME became one of the largest and most influential midwestern labor organizations. Teachers, most of whom were female, unionized, too. The American Federation of Teachers (AFT) organized the Chicago, Detroit, and Cleveland public school systems by the 1950s; in the 1960s, the National Education Association (NEA) embraced collective bargaining and competed with the AFT to extend unionism in teaching. After 1962, the NEA made rapid gains in suburban school systems and became, by some accounts, the most formidable new force in the midwestern labor movement. Public-sector clerical workers organized, along with teachers and maintenance workers in the 1960s. In the 1970s, the focus shifted to office workers in the private sector. Women Employed was a successful all-female union of clerical workers in Chicago. Clerical workers in Madison, Wisconsin, won collective bargaining rights for women in insurance agencies and banks in that state. Hospital workers, food service and hotel workers, and retail workers joined unions in the late twentieth century, as well. The expansion of the labor movement in the service sector helped compensate for its contraction in the manufacturing sector as the industrial heartland lost jobs in the 1970s and 1980s.

By 1970, a large group of female union leaders were recognized inside their own unions, in the midwestern labor movement, and on the national stage as influential pacesetters and advocates of midwestern women workers. These included Addie Wyatt of the United Packinghouse Workers; Catherine Conroy, who was a Communications Workers of America officer and the first women on the governing board of the Wisconsin State Federation of Labor; Olga Madar, who was the first woman to sit on the executive board of the United Auto Workers (UAW); and Myra Wolfgang of the Hotel Employees and Restaurant Employees. These women secured their own place in labor and women's history when they convened the founding meeting of the Coalition of Labor Union Women (CLUW) in Chicago in 1974. CLUW vowed to organize women workers, to demand sex-blind treatment in the workplace, and to encourage women to become more active and to gain a larger share of power and influence in the unions.

As they had since the 1890s, midwestern women labor leaders relied on legislatures and the courts as well as workplace-based organizing to advance gender equality in the late twentieth century. Reflecting the post–World War II shift from a female labor force of working girls to one of working mothers, the UAW, for example, led the campaign for the Pregnancy Discrimination Act that requires employers to provide the same fringe benefits for pregnancy-related disabilities as for other disabilities. The union then cited the act when it successfully charged midwestern battery-maker Johnson Controls with sex discrimination for restricting women from certain jobs on the basis that lead exposure could harm a fetus. In another effort to challenge gender hierarchy, Iowa, Minnesota, and Wisconsin public employees tested the promise of comparable worth to achieve pay equity by legislation in the 1980s and 1990s.

Women workers have not always had an easy relationship with the labor movement. Male disinterest, resistance, and hostility have prompted women to use gender-specific organizations when integrated unions threaten to obstruct or silence the female rank and file. Women also have turned to cross-class alliances with other women outside the labor movement as well as to legislation and court decisions to advance their interests. But women have always worked and always been part of the Midwest's vibrant, dynamic, and powerful labor movement.

Sources and Further Reading: Raymond Boryczka and Lorin Lee Cary, *No Strength Without Union* (1982); Dennis Deslippe, *Rights, not Roses* (2000); Elizabeth Faue, *Community of Suffering and Struggle* (1991); Lisa M. Fine, *The Souls of the Skyscraper* (1990); Nancy Gabin, *Feminism in the Labor Movement* (1990); Darryl Holter, *Workers and Unions in Wisconsin* (2000); Ruth Milkman, ed., *Women, Work and Protest* (1985); Lucy Eldersveld Murphy and Wendy Hamand Venet, eds., *Midwestern Women* (1997); Daniel Nelson, *Farm and Factory* (1995); Shelton Stromquist, *Solidarity and Survival* (1993).

Nancy Gabin
Purdue University, Indiana

Clerical Workers

In the late nineteenth century, demand for clerical workers expanded dramatically to meet the record-keeping needs of larger, more complex businesses. Greater availability of high school and business school education and introduction of typewriters, comptometers (early adding machines), and dictaphones—made by midwestern firms such as Felt and Tarrant of Chicago, National Cash Register of Dayton, and Burroughs of St. Louis—encouraged women's entrance into clerical jobs. By World War I, almost all typists, stenographers, and secretaries were women, while bookkeeping and accounting were feminized more slowly. By 1930, the majority of clerical workers were women.

Women office workers earned more than women in manufacturing but less than male office workers. Thus, clerical work represented some upward mobility for working-class and middle-class women who were unable or unwilling to enter the few professions open to them. Clerical workers ranged from stenographers in small-town hardware stores to clerks in Chicago's giant mail-order houses. Despite low wages, clerical jobs in midwestern cities offered young women from rural areas new opportunities for independence. Clerical jobs incorporated gender, race, and class stereotypes; employers favored pretty, young, white, single women. Employers lifted the so-called marriage ban as office work expanded during World War II and the cold war, allowing women to continue working after marriage. Although black women employed in clerical work were generally better educated than whites, few were hired before the Civil Rights Act of 1964. Prohibition of overt gender discrimination has not, however, eroded feminization: In 2001, 98 percent of secretaries and 95 percent of typists were women.

Sources and Further Reading: Lisa M. Fine, *The Souls of the Skyscraper* (1990); Angel Kwolek-Folland, *Engendering Business* (1994); Sharon Hartman Strom, *Beyond the Typewriter* (1992).

M. Christine Anderson
Xavier University, Ohio

Garment Workers

By 1905, men's clothing production in Chicago ranked second only to New York, while Cleveland ranked fourth in the production of women's clothing. The Chicago men's garment industry employed over ten thousand women workers, the majority of whom were the daughters of southern and eastern European immigrants. These women performed semiskilled tasks in an increasingly mechanized industry. Although they sporadically protested against the long hours and low piece rates, the United Garment Workers Union (the only union in the industry) refused to organize immigrant women workers.

In 1910, piece rates dropped, and a young Russian, Bessie Abramowitz, responded by walking off her job at Hart, Schaffner, and Marx, the largest factory in Chicago. The walkout evolved into a general strike that affected over forty thousand workers and halted men's garment production. Settlement residents at

Hull-House, members of the Women's Trade Union League, and the Chicago Federation of Labor provided immense financial aid and moral support. The *Chicago Daily Socialist* provided coverage of the strike throughout the bitter winter of 1910–1911. Two strikers were killed in clashes with police, and hundreds were arrested. Five months after the strike began, a coalition of Chicago reformers, along with Jane Addams and Margaret Dreier Robins, helped to negotiate an end to the violent conflict.

Some strikers lost their jobs, but Hart, Schaffner, and Marx employees returned to work with the guarantee of an arbitration board to hear their complaints. The settlement laid the foundation for the resolution of future grievances and paved the way for the creation of the Amalgamated Clothing Workers of America, the largest men's clothing workers union in the nation.

Sources and Further Reading: Illinois Bureau of Labor Statistics, *Fourteenth Biennial Report, 1906* (1908); Karen Pastorello and N. Sue Weiler, "Bessie Abramowitz Hillman," in Rima Lunin Schultz and Adele Hast, eds., *Women Building Chicago, 1790–1990* (2001); U.S. Senate, *Report on Conditions of Women and Child Wage Earners in The United States, 1911–1915* (1919).

Karen Pastorello
Tompkins Cortland Community College,
New York

Household Workers

Household work, including the occupations of housekeeper, maid, cook, laundress, and nursemaid, provided an important source of employment for immigrant women, their native-born daughters, and African American women in the nineteenth- and early twentieth-century Midwest. In the cities of the upper Midwest, including the Dakotas, Minnesota, Wisconsin, and Michigan's Upper Peninsula, domestics were primarily Scandinavian immigrants, their daughters, or white rural migrants. In other cities, the field was dominated by Irish and German immigrants, their daughters, and white rural migrants, until large numbers of African Americans migrated north in the World War I era.

In the early twentieth century, as all other groups became increasingly less likely to work as household employees, black servants increased in numbers, and by 1930, they dominated the field numerically in most cities of the Midwest. Because married African American women insisted on living with their own families, the occupation shifted from live-in service to day work during the first half of the twentieth century.

With most households employing only one or two servants, attempts to organize domestics into labor unions met with little success throughout the nineteenth and twentieth centuries. Household employees were also among those explicitly exempted from federal labor laws, including the minimum wage and Social Security legislation passed in the 1930s. Most employed African American women continued to work in household employment until World War II. In the later twentieth century, as the number of domestics dropped dramatically, increasing numbers of Hispanic, Asian, and Pacific Islander immigrants moved into household service in the Midwest.

Sources and Further Reading: Faye E. Dudden, *Serving Women* (1983); David M. Katzman, *Seven Days a Week* (1978); Phyllis Palmer, *Domesticity and Dirt* (1989).

Virginia R. Boynton
Western Illinois University

Elizabeth C. Morgan (1850–1944)

Elizabeth C. Morgan established a reputation as Chicago's leading champion of wage-earning women and children in the late nineteenth century. Brought up in a Birmingham, England home headed by unskilled factory operatives, the youthful Morgan became a Chicago resident in 1869. She and her husband, Thomas J. Morgan, converted to socialism during the Panic of 1873 and launched a spirited defense of workers' rights. Elizabeth Morgan became a charter member of the Sovereigns of Industry, a cooperative society, in 1874. She helped organize a Knights of Labor local assembly for female workers in 1881. Seven years later, she founded the Ladies' Federal Labor Union No. 2703, affiliated with the American Federation of Labor (AFL).

In the fall of 1888, she forged a coalition of female socialists, settlement house workers, and trade unionists under an umbrella organization, the Illinois Women's Alliance. Guided by Morgan, the Alliance documented the horrendous working conditions for women and children employed by Chicago's clothing manufacturers. Responding to Alliance pressure, both the city of Chicago and the state of Illinois enacted child labor laws and created standards for healthier and safer workplaces. Morgan became the first woman nominated as an AFL first vice-president candidate in 1894, though she was not elected.

Elizabeth Morgan used her extraordinary advocacy and organizational talents to build the Chicago labor movement. The years from 1888 to 1895 marked the zenith of her influence as she combined trade unionism and political action to improve the lives of working-class women and children.

Sources and Further Reading: Ellen M. Ritter, "Elizabeth Morgan: Pioneer Female Labor Agitator," *Central States Speech Journal* (Fall 1971); Ralph Scharnau, "Elizabeth Morgan, Crusader for Labor Reform," *Labor History* 14 (Summer 1973); Ralph William Scharnau, "Thomas J. Morgan and the Chicago Socialist Movement, 1876–1901," Ph.D. diss., Northern Illinois University (1970).

Ralph Scharnau
Northeast Iowa Community College–Peosta

Margaret Haley (1861–1939)

Margaret Haley was known in the antilabor press as the Princess of Petitions and the Lady Labor Slugger. These public nicknames describe a woman who became the voice of teachers in the national scene of education politics.

Margaret Haley was born in Joliet, Illinois, on November 15, 1861, to Irish immigrant parents. She left Joliet to teach the sixth grade in the stockyard district of Chicago. Her classroom had sixty children, and she faced brutal working conditions.

Haley soon joined the newly formed Chicago Teachers' Federation (CTF) in 1897. In three years, she had become a full-time organizer and vicepresident of the CTF. The union fought for higher salaries, pensions, and tenure, as well as better working conditions. In 1901, she became the first woman to speak from the floor of the National Education Association's general meeting.

In 1902, the CTF aligned itself with the Chicago Federation of Labor (CFL). Haley saw that organized labor and teachers had common interests in the protection of workers' rights. The CTF and eight other teacher unions formed the American Federation of Teachers (AFT) in Chicago in 1916, and Margaret Haley was named the organizer for this new union. However, the next year under political pressure from the Chicago Board of Education, Haley had to disaffiliate with the AFT and the CFL, but she continued her fight for the rights of teachers. Haley died in Chicago on January 5, 1939.

Sources and Further Reading: Margaret Haley, *Battleground: The Autobiography of Margaret A. Haley,* ed. Robert L. Reid (1982); M. J. Herrick, *The Chicago Schools: A Social and Political History* (1971); Paula O'Connor, "Grade-School Teachers Become Labor Leaders," *Labor's Heritage* 7 (Fall 1995).

Daniel Golodner
Wayne State University, Michigan

Cultural Patterns in Working-Class Communities

Workers are never merely economic tools. It is true that they labor for most of their lives, but their lives are not governed entirely by economic necessity. Work, however, determines a great deal about the social relationships they adopt and how they define themselves when they are not on the boss's time. From front porches to mill gates, working-class people constructed vibrant cultural patterns of life that not only enriched the quality of their social relationships but provided a defense against the bottom-line ethic of work for hire.

To write of working-class cultural patterns requires making clear what "class culture" means. Simply put, class culture represents the kind of relationships that working people develop with each other and the larger culture over time. The focus of culture is how people live, work, spend leisure time, identify socially, and the symbols and images they create that portray those relationships and experiences. Workers from Topeka, Kansas, to Flint, Michigan, have constructed complex interrelationships between their workplaces and neighborhoods, political and social lives, ethnic and mainstream cultures. At all times, however, their cultural identity was built upon long-standing formative experiences growing out of intense social relationships that link the workplace to the community.

These relationships are predicated on common conditions. From at least the early 1940s until the devastating deindustrialization era beginning in the late 1970s, the primary unifying quality was the work people performed. Often workers were employed in the same industry, even by the same employer. For example, for most of the late nineteenth and twentieth centuries, Chicago, northwest Indiana, and Youngstown, Ohio, were massive steelmaking centers. Akron, Ohio, featured rubber workers, and large parts of southern Illinois had thousands of souls digging coal out of the earth. In rural Illinois and Iowa, the manufacturing of farm equipment and agricultural labor dominated economic production. In Detroit, Milwaukee, central Indiana, and northern Ohio, the automobile industry provided employment to additional thousands. South Chicago was the meatpacking and slaughterhouse capital of the world, while in southern Indiana generations of families made electrical appliances. In the northern region of Minnesota, thousands of miners toiled on the iron ore range, and dockworkers moved cargo around the land of many lakes. Horse-drawn teamsters and later truck drivers created economic unity out of this social labor by moving goods within and between metropolitan areas.

❖ Blue Collar Ethic: A Testimony

I am a child of union labor's heyday, raised in Albert Lea, Minnesota, a meatpacking town of about fifteen thousand, where the working class included pioneer stock who had lost their farms, the children of Northern European immigrants, and Mexican Americans who had settled out of the farm labor migration. Forty years beyond childhood, one hundred miles from home, and privileged to work with my mind, I still feel working class.

I distrust rich people, having learned that there is no honest way to get rich. I hoard money, fearing that it will run out at any time. I wear old clothes so my good clothes will stay nice. I buy only sale items, knowing that prices are inflated far above the wages of the people who make these things. I avoid companies with questionable labor policies, meaning my choices are severely limited. I look for the union label, but rarely find it.

I eat supper at six o'clock. "Dinner" is too exalted a word for the hotdish I am likely to serve. "Father" means God, not my dad. Though I never say "pret'near," it is standard English where I come from.

When someone tells me, "We're building a new house out in Woodbury," I imagine her in a carpenter's apron, straddling a rafter, the way I remember my dad building ours. Before I buy clothes, I inspect the seams, which rarely match the quality of my mom's sewing. I delay household repairs while I struggle with the shameful notion of hiring help. I clean my house myself and apologize for the mess.

Upton Sinclair's *The Jungle* was the only novel my dad took time to read in his adulthood. I justify my reading by telling myself that my work would suffer without it. Calling writing "work" is hard, because I do it at home, sitting down, on my own schedule, and there is no steady paycheck. My leisure time is seldom guilt-free.

I don't ask easily for what I want, because I don't expect to get it. The entitlement displayed by my wealthier friends baffles me. Money is power, but there is strength in numbers. I believe that collective bargaining is a fundamental human right. Without it, "the little guys," "the ordinary working people" count for nothing. I have learned to speak up about this, because I know I speak for others.

I don't cross picket lines. I don't need to hear both sides of the argument. I know first-hand that a strike is a great hardship, never undertaken lightly. I assume that people willing to risk their jobs to improve them have a legitimate grievance.

I mourn the state of the world since manufacturers moved "off-shore." I mourn the decline of industrial towns like Albert Lea. I will not buy rugs woven by people who sleep on dirt floors. My best wish for the workers behind the "Made in" labels is the globalization of union organizing. Justice is a matter of common decency I learned in childhood: When fairness prevails over greed, all will be well.

Cheri Register
Minneapolis, Minnesota

Sources and Further Reading: C. L. Barney Dews and Carolyn Leste Law, eds., *This Fine Place So Far From Home* (1995); Rick Halpern and Roger Horowitz, *Meatpackers* (1996); Cheri Register, *Packinghouse Daughter* (2000); Mary Lethert Wingerd, *Claiming the City* (2001).

Working in the same industry made it possible for people to share a common economic reality. Whether Italian or Croatian or African American or Hispanic, if one worked in the mines or on the docks or in the mills, workers knew they were dependent on their labor for survival and that to the company they were merely "check numbers." Being working-class did not mean that race and gender were not important ways that working people defined themselves. Economic reality did not prevent ugly and violent racism, but it did give impetus to the construction of recognizably working-class communities and relationships.

Often, a working-class community defined itself by the kind of work its members performed. In Struthers, Ohio, for example, a week-long citywide pageant known as the Cradle of Steel portrayed the community's generational reliance on steel production. The depth out of which a collective class identity was forged can be found in the following poem, anonymously written on the occasion of the pageant:

> Oh give me a job where the smelters roar,
> Where the fiery monsters gulp the ore,
> Where the thundering furnaces rock the earth
> And labor hard to bring the birth
> Of steel, America's natural cream
> That sputters and flows in a white-hot stream,
> There, where the base of our wealth is laid
> There let me work at my job and my trade.

Workers typically lived within short walking distance from their workplaces; consequently, even with a degree of housing segregated by ethnicity, they had many opportunities to deepen their work relationships at home. Beaten footpaths, bus routes, bars, bowling allies, churches, dance halls, and other meeting places connected work and community life. Houses were small and located close to one another. Long porches, perfect for visiting, were set neatly alongside gravel and cement driveways. It was normal for entire streets or blocks of streets to be occupied by Italian or black steelworkers, Polish meatpackers, German beer makers and butchers, Mexican autoworkers, or Jewish garment workers. In densely populated steel towns like Gary, Indiana, and Youngstown, Ohio, some streets were so heavily populated with steelworkers that they could have been renamed Steelworker Alley. Many streets in Struthers, Ohio, had a steelworker density of nearly 20 percent, and if one included every home with a manual laborer, the proportion would climb to 95 percent.

Lacking the personal resources and ability to withdraw into self-indulgent spaces, neighbors had little choice but to open their lives to one another. That did not mean that workers devalued their privacy, but it did mean that there was plenty of opportunity for casual and local common interaction. Front porches, streets, and backyards were invitations to chat, visit, pontificate, wonder, and play. In numerous cultural depictions, workers proclaim that their closest friends were other similarly situated workers. Workers were "all from the mason department," "lived all over the street," or the people "I worked with I also grew up with." They were coworkers and often either elementary or high school friends or transplants from some other less inviting places. Meager means often required working-class families to double up their residences, and sometimes two or three relatives lived in the same house or on the same block.

Though originating as company towns, working-class communities often evolved into autonomous spaces for workers. Within each community the music, food, dress, language, and religious observances may have been different, but the cultural symbols and practices shared one remarkable common characteristic: Working-class people lived within the company of one another in order to protect themselves from a property-owning nonworking-class of business owners. These relations of class helped to forge a form of social interaction that at times united work and community into a unified ethno-class outlook. To take the example of musical tastes: It might have been Benny Goodman swing, dance polkas, gospel songs, Mississippi blues, or St. Louis jazz emanating from neighborhood windows and social clubs, but the musical expressions of working-class families were usually about struggle, hard work, and perseverance.

When not singing and dancing, workers were often praying. Working-class Poles prayed at St. Michael's, the Croatians at Sacred Heart; the Mexicans at Our Lady of Guadalupe, and the Irish at St. Patrick's, while the Jews honored their synagogues. There were indeed many different ways of worshipping, but often each congregation's working-class patrons shared the sacraments together in the same way. Workers baptized other workers, and workers stood as lifetime witnesses for one another during religious rites of passage.

They also organized to offer help to those in need. Workers established charitable associations and mutual benefit societies to provide members with opportunities for sociability and a supporting hand when times were tough. Usually formed within their particular ethnic group, institutions like the Sons of Italy, Polish Falcons, Jewish National Workers Alliance, and Bohemian Charitable Association offered workers an additional means to navigate through America's often unforgiving economic and social structure. Hard times were common and families adjusted in every way they could imagine. Within the family, even daily responses to economic insecurity contributed to a shared cultural identity. "Poor man's pizza," baked bread and grated cheese, and "beans and baloney," red kidney beans, bologna, and onions mixed into a stew, were cheap and filling delicacies for Italian and Slovak working families. Every nationality had its ethnic dishes. Each initially served to fill a hungry stomach and to spread the family resources a little further, but over time the meals became identified with a particular working-class place. As a result, workers' lives in the Midwest became deeply embedded in local behavior and custom. Workers identified less with the Midwest or a particular state or even a town, and more with a self-named neighborhood or small geographic area.

A working-class life was constituted by hard work and economic insecurity, as well as community identity and a powerful sense of inevitability. A person was expected to work with their hands and to build something that lasted. Tomorrow was to be made by the sweat of a worker's brow, then carefully handed down to others. Obligation, not freedom, was the defining principle to live by. In truth, workers were workers because they had few options to be otherwise. People made choices, but class was something one inherited, and only a select few could escape through education or personal savings. While workers' culture encouraged personal achievement, it was not to be achieved at the expense of the group, or at least not without acknowledging the family and community that had nurtured one's life. The work ethic had burrowed deeply, and people were not ashamed of being working class, but the culture prioritized that the children of immigrant workers do better. While proud of their status as workers, mothers and fathers wanted their children to do something better with their lives. To have the things that signaled success and respect in America, it was necessary not to work in the steel mills of Gary, Indiana. However, the desire for generational mobility did not signify a loss of dignity for those friends, neighbors, and co-workers who had proudly performed manual labor. It was that working-class adults knew that they had less material freedom, fewer work options, and less chance of an education; consequently, their self-respect came from the way they interacted with one another. In this respect, working-class people never quite fully melted into middle-class society or mainstream culture.

For most of the past one hundred years, cultural life in midwestern working-class communities has been characterized by collective need, individual accountability, and extensive sociability. However, in the last thirty years, much has changed. Industrial work has sometimes moved elsewhere. People have been forced to live farther from their workplaces. Since the late 1970s, thousands of manufacturing jobs have migrated away from the region. By the end of the twentieth century, economic growth has practically disappeared in old urban auto and steel towns. With job loss has come a significant depopulation of these once great Midwest industrial centers.

In working-class neighborhoods, fences have sprouted up where none existed before. Newer non-European nationalities have replaced older European groups. South American, Asian American, and Caribbean immigrants now construct communities where Italians, Slovaks, Russians, and Germans had once lived. Chicago's Polish-majority Packingtown no longer exists, but its Hispanic Pilsen does. Youngstown's Italian Briar Hill section has lost its steel mills, but people still work and raise families in the area. In some respects, the Midwest's new working-class entrants are not much different from their white, ethnic working-class brothers and sisters. They too value work, individual rights, ethnic traditions, and collective destinies.

Nonetheless, there are examples, as in the mid-1990s in Decatur, Illinois, of ethnic and racial differences inflamed by a painful series of labor–management disputes, which created tensions within working-class communities. Hard times today, as in most periods of limited economic opportunities, have challenged people's sense of class identity. However, except for moments of extreme crisis, these usually remain communities not of strangers with similar street addresses, but of people known as neighbors and co-workers. It would seem that some things have not changed. Working-class culture continues to inhabit and give special meaning to the places where working people work and the spaces where working people congregate.

Sources and Further Reading: John Bodnar, *Workers' World: Kinship, Community and Protest in an Industrial Society, 1900–1940* (1982); John Bodnar, Roger Simon, and Michael Weber, *Lives of Their Own: Blacks, Italians and Poles in Pittsburgh, 1900–1960* (1982); Robert Bruno, *Steelworker Alley: How Class Works in Youngstown* (1999); Lizabeth Cohen, *Making A New Deal: Industrial Workers in Chicago, 1919–1939* (1990); David Halle, *America's Working Man: Work, Home and Politics Among Blue-Collar Property Owners* (1984); William Kornblum, *Blue Collar Community* (1974); John Legget, *Class, Race and Labor: Working-Class Consciousness in Detroit* (1968); Sar Levitan, *Blue-Collar Workers: A Symposium on Middle America* (1971); Cheri Register, *Packinghouse Daughter* (2000); Joe W. Trotter, *Black Milwaukee: The Making of An Industrial Proletariat, 1915–1945* (1985).

Robert Bruno
University of Illinois-Chicago

Religion and the Working Class

The ties between organized religion and the working class emerged across the Midwest in the decades after the Civil War. Workers saw great value in having the clergy on their side in any struggle against their employers, and many clergymen were sympathetic to the plight of the workers and articulated the grievances of the working class.

The relationship varied by denomination. As members of the upper middle class, mainstream Protestants were suspicious of organized labor. Their clergymen preached free-market capitalism and posited that wealth was a sign of virtue, not greed. In the Protestant mind, poverty among the working class was a sign of idleness, not injustice. Even evangelical clergymen were antithetical to the working class. For example, the famed Chicago evangelist Dwight L. Moody railed against unions as organizations that protected the weak and lazy. Moody and his followers were individualists who argued that laborers deserved their fate and that they would never emerge from poverty until they had accepted Jesus Christ as their personal savior.

One strong expression of unity between Protestantism and the working class in the Midwest was the Social Gospel Movement. Founded in Columbus, Ohio, by Washington Gladden and others, the movement grew into a national effort by clergy to infuse religious values into the workplace. Ministers sought to convince industry leaders, as well as workingmen, to use Jesus as their model. Most Social Gospel ministers stressed the need for better working conditions for the American laborer.

In stark contrast to the mainstream Protestant indifference to the plight of the worker, Catholic priests and bishops defended organized labor. Archbishop James Gibbons of Baltimore traveled to Rome to convince Vatican officials to remain neutral on the matter of labor unions. Gibbons argued that by opposing unions, the hearts of the people would be lost, for which the support of a few rich would offer no compensation. Gibbons's statement was written largely by Archbishop John Ireland of St. Paul.

The new century brought new ties between religion and labor in the Midwest. In the early 1900s, a select number of Protestant denominations focused on the problems of child labor, women's rights in the workplace, and the quest for an eight-hour day and a just wage. Both Catholic and Protestant clergymen across the Midwest began working with the American Federation of Labor to reach these goals.

The onset of the Great Depression in the 1930s and the rise of anti-Semitism led to the establishment of the Jewish Labor Committee (JLC). Founded in New York in 1934, the JLC quickly spread to Chicago, whose chapter has worked tirelessly for three quarters of a century to strengthen bonds between Jewish moral and social principles and the labor and civil rights movements.

Another response to the Great Depression was the Catholic Worker movement founded by Dorothy Day and Peter Maurin. This radical religious organization established "houses of hospitality" for distressed workers in cities across the country including St. Louis, Chicago, and Cleveland. An important extension of the Catholic Worker movement was the Association of Catholic Trade Unionists (ACTU), a national organization that was particularly active in Chicago in the 1930s. ACTU members rallied Catholic activists, including a number of bishops, to support the cause of workers in industrial strikes across the Midwest.

The ties between religion and labor in the Midwest in the decades from the 1930s to the 1950s were nurtured by the National Religion and Labor Foundation. Established in 1932, the Foundation's goal was to build stronger ties and find common goals between the religions and labor movements. There were active chapters in Columbus, Cincinnati, Detroit, Fargo, and Minneapolis.

The industrial crisis in the 1970s led to a major partnership between religion and labor in Youngstown, Ohio. The closure of Youngstown Steel and Tube with the loss of thousands of jobs led Catholic and Protestant leaders to take action and attempt to partner with the United Steelworkers to purchase the plant. Although the effort failed, it drew attention to the ties between religion and labor.

In the last years of the twentieth century, church and labor leaders in Chicago and other midwestern cities established interfaith committees that focused on worker issues. To date, clergymen and laborers in dozens of cities across the region have such committees. Yet the relationship between religion and labor remains troubled, with liberal congregations supporting organized labor and conservative evangelical churches vigorously opposed to unions.

Sources and Further Reading: Clark D. Halker, *For Democracy, Workers, and God* (1991); Mel Piehl, *Breaking Bread: The Catholic Worker and the Origin of Catholic Radicalism in America* (1982).

Timothy Walch
Hoover Presidential Library,
West Branch, Iowa

Studs Terkel on Midwest Labor

Louis "Studs" Terkel became known throughout the Midwest on WCFL, Chicago's "Voice of Labor." Terkel came of age during the hard times he later wrote about, learning the tools of his trade on the WPA Illinois Writers' Project, Radio Division, from 1935 to 1941. In his early career as an actor with the famed Chicago Repertory Group, his job was to dramatize labor's struggles by using the technique of agitprop in which audiences were encouraged to take on such perceived social iniquities as capitalism.

As recalled by Terkel in his *Talking to Myself* (1977), the thirties was a tumultuous decade of strikes: "Hearst, the Chicago Newspaper Guild, Memorial Day Massacre, union suits, and the Old Chicago Red Squad." Also known as the Industrial Squad, their job was to break strikes.

In 1939, Studs Terkel was engaged by the U.S. Department of Labor (DOL) to write a radio drama with Sam Ross telling the story about the passage of the Fair Labor Standards Act of 1935. A slide film was produced along with the radio drama for the DOL's Wage and Hour Division. The script and resulting broadcast, called "Forty-Forty," showed remarkable restraint in that it completely ignored the violence of labor agitation and glossed over unionism. Even so, the DOL apparently thought the script too strongly biased and engaged another writer to sanitize it, and it was turned into a traditional, dull, and detached slide film common to the period. Terkel would go on to collaborate with Louis Scofield on another labor program depicting the historical development of the labor movement in America entitled "The Progress of Labor," produced for the Chicago Federation of Labor and broadcast on WCFL in September 1944.

While labor activism was not a profession in itself for Terkel, he became a prolabor political activist, inspired by his high school teacher Lillian Herstein, a delegate to the Chicago Federation of Labor, as well as by Midwest populists like "Fighting" Bob La Fol-

Studs Terkel and Michael Moore. Photo courtesy Alan Harris Stein. © 2004 All Rights Reserved.

lette and Henry Wallace. Terkel was a founding member of the American Radio Actors Union (AFRA) in the 1930s; that union subsequently became the American Federation of Radio and Television Actors–Screen Actors Guild (AFTRA-SAG). Terkel was the Master of Ceremonies at the Haymarket Workers' Memorial Committee in 1969, leading to the formation of the Illinois Labor History Society later that year. He was inducted into the Union Hall of Honor of the Illinois Labor History Society in the year 2000. The Communications Workers of America thanked him "for being the microphone of America's workforce."

As evidenced by his most popular book and subsequent musical, *Working*, Terkel has been the advocate of working-class America and greatly influenced and inspired Midwest labor organizers, labor leaders, activists, academics, and historians. When Youngstown State University in northeast Ohio instituted the first-ever Center for Working Class Studies in 1996, conference cofounder Bill Mullen recognized Terkel's contribution to the understanding of work and the working class: "Your work as a scholar, writer and activist seems to embody many of the ideas and ideals for which the Center stands. Your own cataloguing of the history of work also provides a profound foundation for work's future."

Labor historians Staughton Lynd and James B.

Lane have both been influenced by Terkel's use of oral history to document the lives of rank-and-file workers of the Midwest, especially in the Calumet Region during the 1970s. In *Steel Shavings*, Lane acknowledged "a considerable intellectual debt" to Terkel, calling him "the father of oral history."

In May of 1975, a free speech rally was held in Chicago's Bug House Square, and Studs Terkel mounted a soapbox and spoke on the historical importance of that square where the likes of Lucy Parsons, Eugene V. Debs, and Emma Goldman had once spoken. Terkel would become the prominent "Mayor of Bughouse Square" for many years. On Labor Day 2003, Studs sat down in front of the Congress Hotel with strikers, prominent labor leaders, and other union members, to highlight the struggle of the Congress strikers for justice. Speaking through an amplified bullhorn, Terkel asserted that not since the late 1930s "has organized labor in Chicago staged a civil disobedience action on behalf of striking union members."

That same year, *Hope Dies Last* was published, the final book of an oral history trilogy with a strong emphasis on labor. Sixty-five years after interviewing Bob Travis for *Hard Times* (1970), Studs interviewed his daughter, Carole Travis, an official in the Service Employees International Union (SEIU). Also included in the book are Victor Reuther of the UAW, who is also featured in *Coming of Age* (1995), Ken Paff, the founder of Teamsters for a Democratic Union in Detroit, Roberta Lynch, the deputy director for the Illinois Council of AFSCME, and Eliseo Medina, Executive Vice President of the SEIU, whom Terkel had met in 1972 when Medina was an organizer for Cesar Chavez and the United Farm Workers in the Midwest Region.

When the UAW launched its union history website on Labor Day 1996, it used audio excerpts from Terkel's interview with retired Flint autoworker Bob Stinson. The original interview was conducted in November of 1967, and was incorporated onto the web with text, photographs, and audio to document the history of the Flint Sit-Down strike of 1936–1937.

Terkel's library of voices includes notable labor historians, activists, and organizers including Ed Sadlowski, Victor Reuther, Joe Glazer, and Michael Moore. All of these interviews are contained in Studs Terkel's archives at the Chicago Historical Society, where Terkel has been Scholar-in-Residence since 1998. His entire body of work, centrally located for researchers, includes the taped interviews of working men and women, as well as the core of leaders and organizers, and many of the accompanying transcripts to his oral history books. It is safe to say that there is no comparable collection on Midwest labor and oral history.

Sources and Further Reading: Rick Ayers, *Studs Terkel's Working: A Teaching Guide* (2001); Nathan Godfried, *WCFL: Chicago's Voice of Labor, 1926–1978* (1997); James B. Lane and Mike Olszanski, "Steelworkers Fight Back: Rank and File Insurgency in the Calumet Region during the 1970s," *Steel Shavings* 30 (2000); Leslie F. Orear, "Chicago Labor Greets the New Plaque in Haymarket Square," *Illinois Labor History Reporter*, no. 52 (June 1996); Studs Terkel, *Talking To Myself: A Memoir of My Times* (1973).

Alan Harris Stein
Consortium of Oral History Educators,
Wheeling, Illinois

Working-Class Musical Tastes in the Twentieth Century

After 1900, urbanization and industrialization decisively shaped midwestern working-class musical tastes. In the depopulating rural areas, farm folk struggled to maintain traditional ensembles such as brass bands, string bands, and vocal quartets that performed at many social events. These types of groups, mostly originating in the British Isles and Scandinavia, adapted to city leisure venues. Appalachian immigrants brought traditional Celtic ballads, fiddle music, and dances into the industrial Midwest and helped to develop bluegrass music after 1940. More traditionally

urban German American bands and vocal groups made similar adjustments to industrialization, but proved less influential nationally. Cities also increasingly welcomed new immigrants from southern and eastern Europe, who introduced polka bands and similar ensembles with accordion-type lead instruments. Churches and social clubs played host to vocal and instrumental musical activity and provided space for dances and other functions. Also, during periods of intense labor organizing, such unions as the Industrial Workers of the World and the United Mine Workers used songs to enlist and to inspire midwestern members. The prevalence of mining and automobile manufacturing, as well as a mixing of diverse new migrants from the American South and from western and eastern Europe, made the Midwest a unique crucible for popular music.

Above all, the growing nationwide popular music and phonograph industries increasingly brought Tin Pan Alley, ragtime, and other nonindigenous music into leisure and home settings in the Midwest. By the 1930s, motion pictures and radio were dramatically reshaping working-class musical tastes, even in rural areas. These mass media helped to create a national working-class consciousness during the New Deal era, but also endangered ethnic identities. African American jazz, rhythm and blues, and soul also became prominent in large new urban enclaves and on city radio stations. Generational splits engendered by the rise of swing, urban blues, and rock and roll music also increased the tensions and contrasts in working-class midwestern musical tastes.

Sources and Further Reading: Lizabeth Cohen, *Making a New Deal* (1990); Victor Greene, *A Passion For Polka* (1992); Kip Lornell and Anne K. Rasmussen eds., *Musics of Multicultural America* (1997).

Burton W. Peretti
Western Connecticut State University

Working-Class Sports and Recreation

Opportunities for participation in sports among working-class people depended largely on the amount of leisure time available. Large urban communities in the Midwest influenced the character of ethnic and religious sports programs, while industrial programs complemented family and neighborhood activities.

The long working hours of laborers left little time for sports and leisure. At the beginning of the twentieth century, it was common to spend sixty hours a week on the job. Urban congestion limited the areas allocated for outdoor recreation. Young boys played street games such as stickball, football, and handball. Throughout the early part of the twentieth century, billiard parlors and bowling alleys were plentiful and provided relatively inexpensive entertainment within access of working-class neighborhoods. In 1910, Chicago recorded 230 bowling alleys and 1,179 poolrooms. Continuous influx of immigrants into the Midwest provided diversity to working-class sports programs. The majority of new immigrants preferred to spend leisure time relaxing with family members. One early exception was gymnastics in the Bohemian *sokol* movement, which began in St. Louis in 1865 and soon spread to other Czech neighborhoods.

Various religious and social organizations provided a means for physical development for the children of working-class families. The Catholic Youth Organization (CYO) began in Chicago in 1930. It was popular and created an alternative influence to the public school system. Best known for boxing, it also offered baseball and basketball leagues that ultimately expanded throughout the country. Settlement houses provided a social progressive approach in an urban setting. First- and second-generation immigrants enjoyed basketball, gymnastics, and boxing. Hull House in Chicago sponsored gymnastics and team sports for both boys and girls. Settlement house workers advocated improved public recreation facilities within reach of the working-class neighborhoods. Unlike the YMCA and Boy Scouts, which were mainly middle-class associations, the settlement houses provided local support for working-class families.

The Pullman Company on the southern edge of Chicago was the first major American company to establish athletic programs for its workers. The company encouraged recreational and competitive sports including rowing, baseball, cycling, and soccer. Beginning in 1881 at the Pullman Company, welfare capitalism spread to other industrial firms, reaching its height in the 1920s. Large firms made available indoor gymnasiums, swimming pools, and game rooms. Companies heavily promoted baseball, believing it would help instill teamwork. Company programs started many NFL football teams, such as the Decatur Staleys, which evolved into the Chicago Bears. The Great Depression reduced the number of programs, but a 1937 report in Chicago showed that nearly half the industrial plants surveyed by the Recreation Commission retained some athletic programs, usually bowling and softball.

During WWII, the Federal Security Agency encouraged industry to work with labor unions and develop sports and recreation in plants. Experts believed that physical fitness would reduce fatigue and allow for greater production efficiency. The government also encouraged the team sports of softball, volleyball, basketball, and bowling. Relationships between industry and government continued to develop during the cold war with the Presidents Council on Physical Fitness and Sports, and continued through the remainder of the century.

Sources and Further Reading: Jane Addams, Victoria Bissell Brown, ed., *Twenty Years at Hull-House* (1999); Martin Henry Blatt and Martha K. Norkunas, eds., *Work, Recreation, and Culture* (1996); Floyd Dotson, "Patterns of Voluntary Association Among Urban Working-Class Families," *American Sociological Review* 16 (Oct. 1951); Steven A. Reiss, *City Game* (1989).

Ken Kasperski
Loyola University–Chicago, Illinois

Back of the Yards

Back of the Yards is one of Chicago's—and America's—most famous communities, being formed around the city's Union Stockyards. In the late nineteenth century, the majority of its residents came from Ireland and Germany, but the demographic trend shifted toward newcomers from eastern Europe. Of these, the most prominent were the Poles who were joined, in turn, by immigrants from Lithuania, Bohemia, Slovakia, Russia, and the Ukraine. By the 1920s, a sizable Mexican community also had taken root.

The most important institution in the community was always the Roman Catholic Church; the neighborhood was often referred to as one of "smokestacks and steeples." Churches gave more than just succor; they provided the main social services of the neighborhood, ranging from a comprehensive system of schools to the Guardian Angel Day Nursery and Home for Girls, which provided a free clinic as well.

These churches, however, were separated, as was the neighborhood, by rigid lines of ethnicity. In 1939, Saul Alinsky and Joseph Meegan founded the Back of the Yards Neighborhood Council, the oldest community organization in America still in existence. The council became a vehicle to overcome these local rivalries and to deal with community-wide problems. Originally it helped support the budding CIO labor movement, then turned to social services, especially in the area of youth and child care. Later, as the neighborhood matured, the Council led a campaign to fight urban blight, and after the Stockyards closed, turned to economic development and job creation.

Sources and Further Reading: James Barrett, *Work and Community in the Jungle* (1987); Dominic Pacyga, *Polish Im-*

migrants and Industrial Chicago (1991); Robert Slayton, *Back of the Yards* (1986).

Robert A. Slayton
Chapman University, California

The Labor Education Movement in Chicago

In the late nineteenth century, Chicago became the center of an education movement supporting labor organizing and collective bargaining. The University of Chicago, Hull House, and the University of Chicago Settlement provided the setting for an exceptional community of learning. Labor education in Chicago helped build popular support leading to pro worker legislation in industrialized states and eventually to the policies of the New Deal.

The University of Chicago encouraged the study of labor problems in its social science curriculum, offering courses and campus lectures on trade unionism, social legislation, sweatshops, child labor, and related topics. The University's Extension Division held off-campus labor courses that frequently attracted hundreds of participants. Lecture study courses were available throughout Chicago as well as in dozens of cities across the Midwest.

Besides their own classes aimed at workers, the settlements comprised a broad social network of labor educators. There was considerable union activity in the garment industry and packinghouses, with settlements providing strike support and even office and meeting space for union organizing. Faculty and students often lived in the settlements and, rather than merely studying neighborhood workers, were directly engaged with their struggles. The Women's Trade Union League, itself closely involved with settlement work, established the Training School for Women Organizers in Chicago. Forty-four union activists took courses at area schools between 1914 and 1926, most at the University of Chicago.

Today, fourteen midwestern universities, and forty nationwide, offer labor education programs. They owe much to the initial efforts in Chicago.

Sources and Further Reading: Jane Addams, *On Education* (1994); Robin Miller Jacoby, "The Women's Trade Union League Training School for Women Organizers, 1914–1926" in Joyce L. Kornbluh and Mary Frederickson, eds., *Sisterhood and Solidarity* (1984); Florence Kelly, *The Autobiography of Florence Kelley* (1986); Julie Reuben, *The Making of the Modern University* (1996).

Jeff Vincent
Indiana University–Bloomington

Labor Newspapers

Some of the country's most important working-class newspapers were published out of the Midwest, including the *Chicagoer Arbeiter-Zeitung, Cleveland Citizen, Dziennik Ludowy* (published in Chicago and Detroit), *Milwaukee Leader,* and *The New Majority.* This labor press was as diverse as the movement it served, ranging from union bulletins devoted to internal business to foreign-language dailies such as the Duluth-based *Industrialisti,* which offered Finnish-speaking syndicalists a vibrant mix of community-oriented news and an expansive social vision. In Chicago, for example, labor dailies were published in the Czech, English, German, Lithuanian, Polish, Slovene, and Yiddish languages; weekly papers were published to serve nearly every significant immigrant community in the region.

Unions published journals for their own members, but also endorsed as official organs publications that sought to bring working-class perspectives into broader social discourse. Many of these papers developed a close rapport with their readers, who often doubled as circulation agents and local correspondents and might have a voice in newspaper policy through cooperative publishing structures.

Even the smallest towns often supported labor weeklies, many of which sought to fuse agrarian and labor constituencies. Most successful at this synthesis was the Girard, Kansas–based *Appeal to Reason,* which reached hundreds of thousands of subscribers. But scores of weeklies continued to identify themselves as farmer-labor publications into the 1940s, giving voice to an alliance that helped transform the region.

The labor press was thus part of a vital alternative public sphere, in which immigrant and other workers could ensure coverage of their activities and concerns, develop an awareness of their own interests, and engage the larger society.

Sources and Further Reading: Jon Bekken, "The Working-Class Press at the Turn of the Century," in William S. Solomon and Robert W. McChesney, eds., *Ruthless Criticism* (1993); Dirk Hoerder, ed., *The Immigrant Labor Press in North America, 1840s–1970s* (1987); Elliott Shore, *Talkin' Socialism* (1988).

Jon Bekken
Albright College, Pennsylvania

Labor Songs

In 1865, Charles Haynes, a blind Chicago musician, penned his "Eight Hour Song," urging listeners to fight for the eight-hour day: "We must rally for the fight, / stand for justice and for right, / Till the law for work be made 8 hours a day." Haynes and other midwesterners wrote thousands of labor songs from 1865 to 1920; more came out of the Midwest than from any other region of the country.

Labor songs expressed social criticism and prolabor sentiments while addressing specific issues such as unionism, working conditions, immigration, strikes, child labor, and socialism. Composers of music and lyrics sometimes treated matters as personal as love, nature, and death. Works appeared in songbooks, papers, and broadsides and at strikes, meetings, and socials. Influences informing labor songs included folksongs, popular poetry, hymns, minstrelsy, Civil War music, ethnic traditions, and antebellum reform songs. After 1900, vaudeville, early country, and Tin Pan Alley exerted influence.

Writers of these songs typically came from working-class backgrounds. Coal miners and iron molders proved especially skilled. Machinists, stonecutters, coopers, female operatives, and railroad workers contributed, too. Some shopkeepers and activists joined them. German workers produced numerous songsters. Chicago yielded many writers, but Detroit, St. Louis, Omaha, Cleveland, Scranton (Kansas), Corning (Ohio), Eau Claire (Wisconsin), and Saginaw (Michigan) also counted bards. Such geographic diversity was uniquely midwestern.

The Industrial Workers of the World (IWW), CIO affiliates, and radical organizations diligently promoted music from 1910 to 1945, even as the tradition generally declined in midwestern ranks. The Chicago-based IWW published the popular *Little Red Songbook* (1909) and Lombard, Illinois, resident and IWW songwriter Ralph Chaplin wrote "Solidarity Forever" in 1915, which became the anthem of the American labor movement by the 1930s.

Sources and Further Reading: Philip Foner, *American Labor Songs of the Nineteenth Century* (1975); Clark "Bucky" Halker, *For Democracy, Workers and God* (1991); Industrial Workers of the World, *Little Red Songbook* (1909).

Clark Halker
Illinois Humanities Council, Chicago, Illinois

Transportation

SECTION EDITOR
R. Douglas Hurt

Section Contents

Overview

The history of transportation in the Midwest is varied and complex. It is the story of men and women dealing with time and space across a broad and varied geographical landscape. The Midwest is a vast region that includes forests, prairies, lakes, and rivers, all of which have influenced the location of towns and cities, trails, roads, railways, and canals, as well as the use of wagons, trains, automobiles, subways, trucks, buses, and airplanes that serve both the cities and countryside. The Midwest was the geographical depot for the settlement of the continental United States and the integration of its western regions within the larger national economy. In this section, the major features of transportation are organized chronologically and topically. Because many developments overlapped, clearly delineated time frames for various changes in transportation are impossible to determine. The developments presented here, however, will provide the reader with a general overview of the region's transportation history.

The transportation history of the Midwest begins with the early Indian peoples who carried packs laden with goods from one location to another via trails, rivers, and lakes. After the commencement of European settlement, footpaths and natural waterways were traced by wagon roads and canals that, in turn, were replaced by paved roads, railroads, and airports. Ships, boats, automobiles, trucks, and aircraft ultimately foreshortened time and space and reduced the obstacles of geography. As a result, transportation systems not only played a fundamental role in the development of the region's economy and served to connect the nation's regions with one another, but also determined immigration and settlement patterns. Simply put, transportation systems have touched the lives of everyone who has lived in the region, and they have helped shape the history of the Midwest. The history of transportation in the American heartland is an ongoing story of change within the context of place.

In many respects, the transportation history of the Midwest is the story of building programs supported by the federal government. The development of a transportation system, often called "internal improvements" in the early nineteenth century, required the aid of the federal government, because the scale of the projects required financial assistance that individuals or local and state governments were unable to provide. Dredging rivers, digging canals, and laying railroad track required expertise, as well. Insufficient funds and politics prevented the magnitude and pace of development that advocates of internal improvements sought, but roads, canals, and railroads were built with government support. During the twentieth century, the federal government subsidized highway construction and by so doing determined that automobiles and trucks would replace railroads as the primary means of transportation in the region. The federal government's subsidy of airports also helped relegate bus transportation to a minor role in the Midwest. Creating a transportation system connecting the Midwest and radiating from it was deemed essential to economic growth, national integration, and the development of the American state.

The history of midwestern transportation, however, is also the story of individual entrepreneurs who both met and created a demand for their services by forging cattle trails, laying railroads, establishing freighting companies over land and water, or founding airlines. This history also includes the stories of the men and women who have traveled through the region on every form of conveyance. As men, women, and children moved into the Midwest by land, water,

Five modes of transportation near Dayton, Ohio. Ohio Historical Society, SC 1270.

and later air, their transportation networks fostered the growth and development of agriculture, mining, timbering, and both light and heavy industry that, in turn, required increasingly efficient, convenient, and reliable transportation.

By the time of European contact, a host of Indian trails led to and from the major rivers, distant villages, and along the Great Lakes. Indian traders in prehistoric times were part of a network that brought precious materials from the southern Appalachians, Isle Royale, the Gulf of Mexico, and the Rocky Mountains to satisfy consumer demand. They also carried corn, furs, and other goods to exchange with cultural groups within and beyond the region. After the arrival of the French fur traders in the late seventeenth century, the rivers and trails used by the Indians became more heavily traveled, because European trade goods—such as knives, axes, firearms, cooking ware, clothing, and items of adornment—became necessities rather than luxuries. As a result, the fur trade expanded rapidly, with Indians and whites transporting pelts out of the region in bundles over the trails, down the streams and rivers, and across the lakes. The Indians also used the trails and rivers to further the movement of fighting men in time of war. The Warrior Path that bisected Ohio from north to south, the Great Trail that linked the Illinois and Ohio Country, or the South Bend Trail that ultimately linked the St. Joseph with the Mississippi River later became the passageways for others who traveled through the same area and in some cases over the same routes, but on asphalt and concrete roads in trucks and automobiles.

During the nineteenth century, the western fringe of the Midwest provided points of embarkation for settlers and traders who traveled west over the Santa Fe and Oregon Trails, as well as the terminus of the Chisholm Trail, along which Texas cowboys drove cattle to markets in Kansas. Wagon makers in St. Louis and Independence, Missouri, capitalized on the Santa Fe trade; small boat builders flourished on the rivers, as did builders of larger vessels on the lakes; and ultimately other firms, such as Studebaker Brothers of South Bend, Indiana, and John Deere of Moline, Illinois, sought sales to farmers. During the twentieth century, trucks powered by internal combustion engines replaced horse-drawn wagons on the farms and in the cities because of the increased speed and volume for hauling. Improved highways further promoted truck transport for freight.

The Ohio River became the first major artery for the transport of settlers and goods into the region by water. The Ohio River carried flat-bottomed boats or barges, commonly called Kentucky boats, and later keelboats from Pittsburgh to its junction with the Mississippi River near Cairo, Illinois. In time, the Ohio, Wabash, Illinois, Mississippi, and Missouri Rivers provided access to eastern and foreign markets through New Orleans. Farmers sent grain, butter, cheese, pork, and during the early nineteenth century, slaves from the Little Dixie area of central Missouri downriver to market on flatboats, keelboats, and steamboats. In 1811, steamboats became sufficiently powerful to carry people and goods up the Mississippi and Ohio Rivers, and the rivers of the Midwest became important commercial networks that affected the economic life of the nation.

Steamboat transportation flourished on midwestern rivers after 1820. By 1830, steamboats provided the preferred method for river transportation, and Cincinnati and St. Louis had become major ports. During the nineteenth century, steamboats churned the waters of the major rivers, hauling freight and fashionable people who ate in opulent dining rooms and slept in well-tended cabins. During the twentieth century, diesel-powered towboats, which actually pushed rather than pulled barges of cargo, helped create major inland ports along the Ohio, Mississippi, and Missouri Rivers. The Red River of the North, which links Minnesota and North Dakota to Lake Winnipeg, gave some midwestern settlers access to markets in Canada.

The Great Lakes—Superior, Michigan, Huron, and Erie, which border the Midwest, and Ontario to the East—stretch nearly one thousand air miles from Duluth to Montreal and provide a waterway of approximately 95 thousand square miles. Over the centuries, travel and transport on the Great Lakes has transformed from birch bark canoes to thousand-foot freighters. The Great Lakes provided access to Montreal where Indian and French traders sold their pelts for needed goods. In 1763, Great Britain gained control of the Great Lakes at the conclusion of the French and Indian War, and private merchant ships did not sail the Great Lakes until 1788 because of British restrictions. England lost sole control of shipping on the Great Lakes with the conclusion of the War of 1812. Completion of the Erie Canal in 1825 opened the Midwest via Lake Erie to the Hudson River and New York City. Thirty years later, transportation from Lake Superior to the lower Great Lakes became possible with the completion of locks at Sault Ste. Marie, Michigan. Travel and shipping the two thousand miles from Minnesota to the Atlantic Ocean ultimately became possible with the completion of the St. Lawrence Seaway locks in 1959.

Thousands of immigrants also entered the Midwest after transport by ship became available across the Great Lakes. Usually sail, steam, and petrol-fueled ships of the Great Lakes carried passengers and freight west and raw materials east. Transport over the

Great Lakes, however, often proved dangerous, and storms have wrecked or sunk many ships with the loss of considerable property and a number of lives. During the nineteenth century, the Great Lakes ranked among the most dangerous waters in the world for ships. By the late twentieth century, however, improved technology and safety regulations, together with a general decline in shipping, significantly helped reduce the accidents on the Great Lakes that resulted from weather and human error.

Canals connecting major natural waterways were constructed in the second quarter of the nineteenth century to facilitate transportation of both people and goods both within the region and with other regions. During the 1820s, Ohio became the first state in the Midwest to begin the long, difficult, and expensive process of developing a canal system to transport freight and people, particularly between Lake Erie and the Ohio River. The Illinois and Michigan Canal linked Lake Michigan with the Mississippi River and New Orleans, while the Des Moines Rapids Canal enabled shippers to bypass dangerous waters on the Mississippi. Other midwestern states followed with less grandiose canal projects, but all were intended to facilitate the trade of midwestern commodities, usually agricultural, for eastern manufactured products far more cheaply and quickly than by transport via the Ohio and Mississippi Rivers alone.

Before the canal networks reached their full potential, and before entrepreneurs and states recovered their investments, a new form of transportation—railroads—began to crisscross the region. Railroads gave travelers and shippers greater flexibility, because track could be laid away from the river networks and because railroad cars carried more freight at greater speed than flatboats, steamboats, and canal boats. Railroads also provided a transportation bridge between interior and river towns. By 1850, railroads provided the most important form of transportation in the Midwest and continued to do so for more than a century. The steel rails and steam-powered locomotives easily carried freight and passengers where the rivers and canals could not go. Railroads imparted a vibrant economic life to the towns far removed from the rivers. Often the railroads followed or paralleled the old trails or roads. The Union Pacific, for example, followed the Oregon Trail west from Council Bluffs and Omaha, which, in turn, had followed the Platte River upstream.

By the late nineteenth century, railroads linked Chicago with St. Louis and a host of midwestern towns with New York and Boston. Midwestern passengers and freight increasingly moved east and west rather than north and south on the Ohio, Missouri, and Mississippi Rivers. Towns bypassed by a railroad or unable to lure the construction of a branch line soon experienced economic hardship and population decline. The towns and cities that attracted railroads thrived economically, and railroads, in turn, shaped the use of public and urban spaces. City governments supported the construction of large, handsome railroad stations to serve thousands of travelers daily and to signify the importance of railroad transportation to the area.

At the turn of the twentieth century, railroads linked the major cities, and branch lines reached many villages, which helped lessen isolation and improved local economies. Railroads enabled all-weather transportation. Rain, snow, ice, and mud seldom created travel or shipment problems, and railroads went where people wanted to go and shippers wanted to reach. Indeed, they were built for those purposes. Early railroad travel, however, was not comfortable. Travelers endured wooden benches, wood and coal soot, and an absence of restrooms. By the late nineteenth century, travelers could sleep on bunks in Pullman cars, named after their manufacturer, and eat in dining cars with white linen tablecloths and fine china. Flush toilets, air conditioning, and diesel engines improved the comfort and speed of railroad travel during the twentieth century. By the twenty-first century, the vestiges of several stations remained, such as the Union Stations in Kansas City, Cincinnati, and Chicago, and the Terminal Tower in Cleveland, although each served different commercial purposes than during the railroad years.

Increasing construction, labor, and operating costs combined with the Great Depression of the 1930s to end the boom years for the railroads. Improved highways, trucks, and automobiles gave shippers and travelers greater flexibility and comfort. Federal and state government spending was stimulated in part by the National Defense Highway Act of 1956, known as the Federal Highway Act, which authorized the interstate highway system, and railroad transportation further declined until ultimately local passenger and freight traffic came to an end. By the 1950s, midwesterners preferred the freedom gained by owning an automobile, and shippers usually sought truck transportation because of cheaper cost, improved delivery speed, and greater access to markets than possible with railroad service.

Although railroad travel became the preferred form of transportation in the Midwest after the Civil War, electric railways called "interurbans" linked many small towns and villages. Interurban transportation was distinctive to the Midwest because of the region's relatively high population density, numerous small towns, and the availability of cheap electric power. Interurbans provided convenient, inexpensive, and efficient travel to the larger towns and cities for rural residents who did not have steam locomotive railway service. In contrast to railroads, interurbans stopped whenever a passenger wanted on or off the car. The age of interurbans lasted only about twenty years, from the 1890s to the beginning of World War I. Truck and automobile transportation replaced the last of the interurbans during the Great Depression, just as railroads and interurbans had driven the stage and freight lines from the transportation business in the late nineteenth century.

Improved roads made from planks, crushed rock (macadam), or later asphalt and concrete stimulated wagon, buggy, truck, and automobile manufacturing. By the mid-twentieth century, the midwestern automobile industry, centered in Detroit, had become essential to the economic prosperity of the region. During the 1920s, automobile transportation began to change the work, recreational, and industrial patterns of the Midwest and, even more than railroads, helped break down rural isolation. At the same time, midwestern consumers increasingly used the automobile to travel to urban areas where they had more shopping choices and cheaper prices, all to the detriment of small-town merchants.

Automobiles and trucks provided the major form of transportation in the Midwest after 1920. Henry Ford, Eddie Rickenbacker, and others drew on the geography of the Midwest to operate profitable automobile manufacturing companies. Iron ore came from the ranges near Lake Superior, coal from Appalachia, fresh water from nearly everywhere, and an abundant reliable labor force from across the region. By the twenty-first century, automobile manufacturing plants had dispersed beyond the Detroit area into Ohio, Illinois, Indiana, and Missouri. Automobiles dramatically changed social patterns across the Midwest and nation. The population became highly mobile, and automobiles gave independence and freedom to drivers as well as revolutionized courting practices and altered living and work patterns.

Automobiles needed hard-surface, all-weather roads to perform efficiently. The Lincoln Highway, or U.S. Highway 30, and the National Road, now essentially U.S. Highway 40 or Interstate 70 across most of the region, were among the first to support automobile and truck transportation which, in turn, has changed the midwestern landscape by fostering restaurants, fuel stations, and repair shops across the region. Highways determined building, business, and residence patterns. Federal legislation also encouraged transport and travel by providing funding for highway construction. Towns bypassed by major highways and interstate systems soon declined, much like the towns missed by railroads during the nineteenth century. If

possible, businesses relocated near the highway, thereby retaining economic life for the town. Businesses also located in areas where highways linked to ensure better access to markets and provided access to areas where tourism could develop. Highways also made businesses independent of rivers and railroads. During the twentieth century, midwestern cities became automobile cities. Cars, trucks, and buses brought people, goods, and resources together at optimal locations that fostered economic growth and population change.

Air transportation also became important to the Midwest during the twentieth century, particularly for the manufacturing of small or light planes and for business and leisure travel. Regular airmail delivery began between Chicago and Cleveland in May 1919, and service between Chicago and other cities such as St. Louis, Omaha, and Minneapolis, as well as between Detroit and Cleveland soon followed. Airmail contracts with the federal government provided the funds necessary to keep many small companies flying, but local governments, supported by chambers of commerce, established the airports. By the late twentieth century, air service had become the primary method to transport first-class mail. Private delivery companies, such as Airborne Express, Federal Express, and United Parcel Service, also used airplanes to transport packages between the major cities in the region.

During the late twentieth century, Chicago became the major airport hub for passenger and freight service. O'Hare Field opened for domestic service in 1955 and became known as Chicago–O'Hare International Airport three years later. O'Hare provides access to the Midwest for the largest and heaviest jets that carry passengers and freight. Lambert–St. Louis International, Kansas City, Minneapolis–St. Paul, and Omaha airports also indicate the political and economic necessity for large midwestern cities to have air transport services.

Regional transportation networks have altered the landscape and the environment. Bridge builders cut vast numbers of trees for timber, while miners gouged the hillsides to provide iron ore for the steel mills that made rails for the railroads. Although a host of structural designs permitted builders to bridge rivers and valleys, some, such as Eads Bridge across the Mississippi River at St. Louis, are important works of art. In turn, the Great Lakes remain beautiful waterways for the transport of people and goods, but their waters have been dangerously polluted by industry. The U.S. Army Corps of Engineers has also altered the course of many rivers to aid transportation, although critics have challenged that practice because of damage to the environment.

The Midwest is the crossroads of the nation for transportation. The rivers transported early settlers who used the riverine system to send agricultural and manufactured goods to market. At the same time, the Great Lakes remain important waterways for shippers, and the St. Lawrence Seaway gives them access to the world. Only nineteenth-century technology keeps shippers prisoners of the past, because the locks of the Great Lakes and St. Lawrence Seaway limit the size of the ships that can negotiate those waters.

Throughout its history, the Midwest has been the center of the development of modern transportation. Its automotive industries put the nation and the world on wheels, its waterways became the fulcrum for trade and industrialization, and its airports serve as major links with the world. Since Indian peoples first inhabited the region, the transportation systems that developed have indelibly shaped the economic and social history of the region and nation. As a result of its diverse transportation systems, the Midwest is not insular but rather a region that thrives on commerce and communication with the world.

Sources and Further Reading: Darrel E. Bigham, *Towns and Villages of the Lower Ohio* (1998); R. Carlyle Buley, *The Old Northwest*, vol. 1 (1978); George Cantor, *Old Roads of the Midwest* (1997); William Cronon, *Nature's Metropolis* (1991); David Dary, *The Santa Fe Trail* (2000); H. Roger Grant, ed., *We Took the Train* (1990); Drake Hokanson, *The Lincoln Highway* (1988); John Lauritz Larson, *Internal Improvement* (2001); William E. Lass, *A History of Steamboating on the Upper Missouri River* (1962); William Middleton, *South Shore*, rev. 2nd ed. (1999); Craig Sanders, *Limiteds, Locals, and Expresses in Indiana, 1838–1871* (2003); Harry N. Scheiber, *Ohio Canal Era* (1987); John F. Stover, *American Railroads*, 2nd ed. (1997); Mark L. Thompson, *Steamboats and Sailors of the Great Lakes* (1991); John D. Unruh, Jr., *The Plains Across* (1979).

R. Douglas Hurt
Purdue University, Indiana

Riverine Systems

The rivers of the Midwest provided a natural highway system that facilitated the movement of the indigenous peoples and the incoming Europeans and Americans. They flowed to the sea in three directions.

All of the streams feeding into the Mississippi follow it southward to the Gulf of Mexico. The Mississippi, rising from Lake Itasca in Minnesota, was the nation's main natural north-south route. Its two principal tributaries, the Ohio and the Missouri, with an approximately two-hundred-mile stretch of the Mis-

sissippi, provided a heavily used east-west route connecting the East and Midwest. Other significant tributaries that flowed directly into the Mississippi and were used as trade routes were the Illinois, Fever, Wisconsin, Chippewa, St. Croix, and Minnesota Rivers. The Wabash River was the Midwest's most significant tributary of the Ohio, and the Lower Missouri's principal navigable tributaries were the Gasconade, Osage, and Kansas Rivers.

Rivers leading into the Great Lakes are part of the Gulf of St. Lawrence drainage area. Important streams in this eastward-flowing system are the Fox, Chicago, and St. Joseph that flow into Lake Michigan, the St. Louis and Pigeon that drain into Lake Superior, and the Maumee and Cuyahoga whose mouths are on Lake Erie.

The third drainage system runs northward to Hudson Bay, a great gulf of the Arctic Ocean. Streams north of the continental divide that lay east-west across central and northern Minnesota lead to Lake Winnipeg and its outlet on Hudson Bay. The most important of these is the Red River. It starts at the junction of the *Bois des Sioux* and Otter Tail Rivers at present-day Breckenridge, Minnesota, and empties into Lake Winnipeg about forty miles north of present-day Winnipeg, Manitoba. The Rainy is the other principal river affecting northwestern Minnesota. Connecting Rainy Lake and Lake of the Woods, it leads to the Winnipeg River, which, in turn, is the route from Lake of the Woods to Lake Winnipeg.

These three drainage systems figured prominently in European American exploration and settlement of the Midwest. They provided relatively easy access to the interior country and, because they were discrete systems, spurred exploration for connecting passages, the development of depots that served more than one river system, and the construction of connecting canals to assure through-navigation across divides.

Rivers and large lakes were the easiest trade and travel routes for Native Americans. Consequently, they tended to locate their villages on or near navigable water. Throughout the Midwest, Native Americans relied on various types of canoes—bark, dugout, and hide. Generally, bark canoes were used in the waters of the northern Midwest where some water passages were clear, whereas dugout canoes were used on murky streams with hidden obstructions such as the Missouri. Nonetheless, there was some overlapping of the ranges depending on the local availability of suitable building materials.

Bark canoes were usually made of birch bark placed on a cedar frame. Most were twenty to twenty-five feet long and about three feet wide. Even when loaded to their capacity of about a ton, they drew only several

The Jolly Flatboatmen in Port, by George Caleb Bingham, 1857. St. Louis Art Museum. Museum Purchase.

inches. When empty they could be easily portaged by two men. Carefully caulked with pitch, these graceful, decorated craft afforded relatively rapid transportation.

Native Americans carved dugout canoes, which had about the same dimensions as bark vessels, from large logs. Builders preferred soft wood such as cypress or cottonwood, but would sometimes use black walnut, a very hard wood. Dugouts, much heavier than bark canoes, were sturdy enough to withstand glancing blows from submerged snags.

Hide canoes were sometimes employed by Native Americans instead of dugouts. Their wooden frames were covered with sections of bison hides. Since bull hides were customarily used because of their greater size and toughness, such craft are sometimes called bullboats.

However, hide canoes should not be confused with the tub-like bullboats used on the Missouri and some of its shallow tributaries. The small circular bullboat consisted of a single bull bison hide stretched over an interwoven bough frame. While unsuitable for long trips because the hides would become waterlogged, bullboats were often used for stream crossings.

French explorers, the first Europeans to reach the Midwest, depended on Native American guides and their canoes. While seeking a direct water route to the fabled Western Sea in 1673, Jacques Marquette and Louis Jolliet canoed from Lake Michigan to the Lower Mississippi by way of the Fox–Wisconsin portage in Wisconsin. Seven years later, René-Robert Cavalier, known as Sieur de La Salle, followed the canoe routes of the Chicago and St. Joseph Rivers from southern Lake Michigan to reach the Illinois and its parent stream, the Mississippi.

Subsequent explorer-traders throughout the French period, which lasted until 1763, developed a system of canoe routes connecting the Midwest's three drainage systems. These pathways typically required much portaging. For example, the trade route from Lake Superior to Rainy Lake in the present-day Minnesota–Ontario border country included thirty-six places where canoes had to be carried overland. In this area especially the *canot du nord,* as the birch bark canoe came to be called, was vital to conducting the fur trade.

For trade on the Ohio, Mississippi, and Missouri Rivers, the French developed the *pirogue,* which was of two types. Some *pirogues* were dugouts up to three times as long as the typical dugout canoe, but the name was also used to describe a two-hulled vessel of paralleled dugouts connected by a storage platform.

The limited capacity of *pirogues* caused the French to develop the *bateau,* which they introduced on the upper reaches of the Ohio slightly before the French and Indian War. *Bateaux* were flat-bottomed and keelless, with pointed bows and sterns. Often forty to fifty feet long, about ten feet wide, and made of planks, they were ordinarily somewhat lighter than platformed *pirogues.* Propelled by rowing, poling, or sailing, they could transport as much as forty tons of cargo, a crew of twenty rowers, and some passengers. *Bateaux* were heavily used by the British after they seized Fort Duquesne (and renamed it Fort Pitt) in 1758. Likewise, American settlers, whose population west of the Allegheny Mountains was estimated at thirty thousand in 1775, used *bateaux.*

The British, who legally claimed the Midwest east of Spanish Louisiana from 1763 to 1783, treated the western and northern portions of the area as a wilderness. They continued the French goals of engaging in the fur trade and searching for a water passage to the Pacific Ocean. Thus, like the French, they depended on the *canot du nord* in the western Great Lakes region.

The newly independent United States, which achieved a western boundary of the Mississippi in 1783 at the end of the Revolutionary War, encouraged aggressive expansion. Its liberal land sales and plans to add states north of the Ohio River as stipulated in the ordinances of 1785 and 1787 spurred settlement, which in turn caused rapid changes in river transportation. By about 1790, flatboats and keelboats, which were first used during the Revolutionary War, had generally replaced the *bateaux*, which did not have as much capacity as flatboats and did not hold a course as well as keelboats.

Flatboats were rectangular craft made of plank with a length of anywhere from twenty to one hundred feet and a width of from twelve to twenty feet. With one- to two-foot gunwales, their decks were partially or sometimes wholly covered with cabin-like structures. Since they floated downstream with the current, they were used only for one-way trips. Navigators kept them in the current with a long stern oar and at least two sweeps on each side. At their destinations, they were usually sold for their lumber, which was often used for constructing homes and buildings in New Orleans and other places. Although some were homemade, most were manufactured by professional boat builders in or near Pittsburgh or in Ohio River communities such as Marietta, Gallipolis, and Cincinnati.

In their heyday, flatboats were often identified by such names as New Orleans or Kentucky boats for their destinations, as "broadhorns" because of their projecting sweep pivots, or as "arks" for their supposed resemblance to Noah's fabled vessel. In the late 1820s, an estimated four thousand flatboats descended the Ohio annually.

Prior to steamboats, keelboats were the only practical two-way craft. Featuring a longitudinal keel, they were made sturdily of lumber. Their normal length was forty to eighty feet and their width about seven to ten feet. Cargo storage and sometimes passenger cabins were in a six-foot-high box covering most of the deck. The boats were usually towed, or cordelled, by anywhere from twenty to forty men onshore, who pulled on a heavy rope as much as a thousand feet long. Cordelling was supplemented by poling and sailing.

Since flatboats and keelboats were cheaper to build and operate than steamboats and more suitable for shallow tributaries, they persisted long into the steamboat age. As late as 1846, an estimated four thousand flatboats and keelboats were being navigated in the Mississippi River system.

After the War of 1812, midwesterners readily turned to steamboats, which promised unprecedented speed and reliable upstream navigation. In their first generation, steamboats were small (usually less than 150 feet long), heavily constructed like oceangoing vessels, and cumbersome. But by about 1840, the boating fraternity had developed large, light-draft, highly maneuverable boats designed to cope with shallow streams. With a length of at least one hundred yards and as many as three tiered decks, some of these ornately decorated craft gained reputations as "floating palaces."

By the mid-1840s, steamboating on the Mississippi River system was a massive business. In 1846, 1,190 steamboats with an aggregate value of almost $16.2 million were being operated on the Mississippi and its tributaries. The boats had annual operating costs of nearly $33 million and employed an estimated 41,650 people.

Despite their popularity, steamboats were vigorously criticized by the public because of their seasonality, high operating costs, and excessive accident rates. Heavy newspaper publicity of catastrophic boiler explosions stimulated calls for federal regulation, which resulted in the creation of an effective Steamboat Inspection Service in 1852. The hazards of steamboating also caused businesses and travelers to turn to railroads.

By the late 1850s, railroad extensions detrimentally affected steamboating on the Ohio, Upper Mississippi, and Lower Missouri. Within another score of years, railroad extensions tapped into the remote Upper Missouri region, as well. Although steamboating persisted after railroad construction, it was reduced to local hauls from railheads to river towns that had been bypassed by railroads.

With the sharp decline in steamboating came renewed public interest in river commerce. Farm groups, especially, saw river trade as an effective means of forcing lower railroad rates. To make river transportation more efficient, they called for radical river improvement by the federal government and the use of large-capacity steel barges.

Unlike antebellum river improvements that emphasized removal of channel obstructions, late-nineteenth-century projects aimed to reroute river portions and establish permanent navigable channels. Alteration of the Ohio to achieve a six-foot channel was approved by Congress in 1875. Creating the channel involved constructing a system of locks and dams, rerouting the stream across meanders, and dredging. The development of larger barges with deeper draft caused the government, through its Army Corps of Engineers, to deepen the channel to nine feet in the first three decades of the twentieth century.

Ohio River channelization became the model for the Upper Mississippi and Illinois. The original plan for the Upper Mississippi called for a four-foot channel, but that was subsequently changed to six feet, and after World War I to nine feet. Public and congressional support for these massive projects was stimulated by the desire for flood control and the nation's World War I transportation crisis.

During the 1930s, the government also started channelizing the Missouri River as far upstream as Sioux City, Iowa. As provided in the World War II Pick-Sloan Plan, the nine-foot channel on this portion of the river was to be maintained partially by the release of upstream waters harnessed by five earthen dams.

Today, strings of barges annually move great quantities of grain, coal, petroleum, and other products on the Mississippi River system. For the period 1996–2000 inclusive, the average annual commerce of the Mississippi, Ohio, Illinois, and Missouri Rivers was, respectively, 398.0, 239.5, 43.8, and 8.5 millions of tons. As they have historically, the Midwest's main rivers serve as vital commercial links.

Sources and Further Reading: Charles Henry Ambler, *A History of Transportation in the Ohio Valley* (1931); Leland D. Baldwin, *The Keelboat Age on Western Waters* (1941); Hiram Martin Chittenden, *History of Early Steamboat Navigation on the Missouri River* (1903); Mildred L. Hartsough, *From Canoe to Steel Barge on the Upper Mississippi* (1934); Leland R. Johnson, *The Ohio River Division, U.S. Army Corps of Engineers* (1992); Grace Lee Nute, *The Voyageur's Highway* (1941); Robert L. Reid, ed., *Always a River: The Ohio River and the American Experience* (1991); Robert Kelley Schneiders, *Unruly River* (1999); Christine Whitacre, ed., *Gateways to Commerce* (1992).

William E. Lass
Minnesota State University–Mankato

Ohio River

Few American rivers can rival the Ohio. Formed in Pittsburgh at the confluence of the Allegheny and Monongahela Rivers, it flows westward 981 miles and enters the Mississippi at Cairo, Illinois, descending from 710 to 290 feet above sea level. The Ohio and its eighteen major tributaries drain 203,910 square miles. The river links six states—Pennsylvania, West Virginia, Ohio, Kentucky, Indiana, and Illinois; its watershed encompasses fourteen. Although smaller in land area than its sister Mississippi tributary, the Missouri, the Ohio supplies the largest volume of water to the "Father of Waters." Mineral and natural resources and agricultural products abound.

Length, direction, and navigable tributaries have long made the Ohio an "interstate highway." Settlement patterns, though, have been uneven. Its valleys and those of its tributaries were home to successive civilizations before European settlement. Thoroughfare for Indian hunters and European trappers, the Ohio carried countless settlers westward. Most initially resided in the Upper Valley. But Kentucky was the first new state (1792) downriver from Pennsylvania and Virginia. The largest three cities—Cincinnati, Louisville, and Pittsburgh—emerged before 1790. Clarksville, Indiana, the first American town in the Old Northwest, was established in 1784 for Revolutionary War veterans.

Most settlers were Upland Southerners of Scots-Irish and English extraction. New Yorkers, Pennsylvanians, and New Englanders tended to cluster in the Upper Valley. German and Irish immigrants began arriving in the 1830s. Because they were slave states, immigrants generally avoided Kentucky and what is now West Virginia. Differences between cultures, observed by visitors like Alexis de Tocqueville in the 1830s, persisted. The river divided two visions of land development—the natural feature surveying of metes and bounds to the south, and the rectangular survey to the north—as well as, until 1865, two labor systems. This prompted Abraham Lincoln's father, Thomas, for example, to move his family to Indiana in 1816. With the exception of the steel mill corridor below Pittsburgh, "new immigrants" from southern and eastern Europe bypassed the Ohio.

Topography also made a difference. In the upper reaches, steep ridges define both banks, but floodplain is dominant in the last 250 miles. The elevation of the land drops sharply before Cincinnati, and tributaries below it are much larger, making periodic flooding a greater problem there. The worst flooding occurred in January 1937, exceeding that of 1884 and 1913.

Towns created to make money were spearheads of settlement. Many names reflect optimism—America, Aurora, Rising Sun, and Metropolis. Most did not turn out as intended; many disappeared. Elevation and location did not guarantee success. Incredible variety continues. Among external factors were the Land Ordinance of 1785 and the Northwest Ordinance of 1787. These shaped land development, state-making, public education, and labor on the north shore. Others included the distinctive political cultures of the six states that rise from its banks. Railroad companies, with distant headquarters, made decisions on bridge locations. Vehicular bridges, introduced in the late 1920s, depended on state government support. Today, many choices are made in corporate boardrooms in Germany and Japan.

Internal factors such as culture also mattered. The

orderly Swiss Germans at Tell City, for instance, needed no jail for the first twenty-five years. Yankees tended to settle in places like Cincinnati, where economic opportunity was substantial and a Whig vision was appreciated in public funding for internal improvements, as well as in the Western Reserve in the northern part of the state. Yankees also advocated public education. Southern German customs were abundant in southwestern Ohio and southeastern Indiana. Local decision-making counted, and sometimes it erred. Leavenworth, Indiana, and Shawneetown, Illinois, for example, were relocated after the flood of 1937.

The Ohio River has also stimulated economic growth. The river was the "Oyo" to the Iroquois and *La Belle Rivière* ("river of beauty") to a series of French explorers, commencing with LaSalle. Most, like Christopher Gist, a land agent for the Ohio Company of Virginia in the 1750s, envisioned the Ohio as a river of opportunity. The wilderness was to be transformed, not preserved. Conflicting claims between English and French traders led to the commencement of the French and Indian War in the 1750s. New England speculators in the 1780s used virgin lands of southeast Ohio to commence white settlement of the Old Northwest.

The chief phases of the Ohio's economic history were the early national phase, the age of the steamboat, and the post-steamboat era. In the first, after 1815, the magnet for national progress was the Ohio, and accessing it from the East was critical. This accounted, for instance, for the creation of the Chesapeake and Ohio Canal and the Baltimore and Ohio Railroad. In the steamboat's golden age, 1840–1880, passengers and freight were carried with unprecedented speed and low cost, connecting settlements via long distance and local packets. Paradoxically, these improvements, the building of bridges, and the application of steam to rails opened up the interior of the Midwest, and after 1880 many towns stagnated. Notable exceptions were Cincinnati, Evansville, Louisville, and Pittsburgh, all of which had ample rail and industrial assets.

However, diesel tows, steel barges, and locks and dams—completed in 1929—enhanced the importance of the Ohio. The minimum level, referred to as the "year-round 9-foot pool," raised after the 1960s with fewer and larger locks and dams, facilitated year-round transport. Many Ohio River cities became integral to the industrial heartland, a process advanced during World War II. Cheap energy from water, wood, and coal resources fueled economic expansion, like the construction of the nation's first atomic plant during World War II and the building of hundreds of coal- or nuclear-powered electrical generators after it.

With state government aid, the nation's largest inland ports were created at Huntington, West Virginia; Jeffersonville, Indiana; and Mount Vernon, Indiana. Through them pass vast quantities of coal, grain, chemicals, petroleum, and automotive and metal products, linking the Midwest to world markets. In the late 1990s, Illinois, Indiana, and Ohio created a national scenic byway, another tool for economic progress—in this case, tourism.

Natural and environmental challenges continue. Flooding persists. Water quality, nuclear waste, and air pollution are problematic, as is the preservation of wetlands. Yet the Ohio River is, as it has been, a stimulus for creativity and innovation. Although many cities and towns have blocked off the river by levees, their Main Street remains the Ohio.

Sources and Further Reading: R. E. Banta, *The Ohio* (1949); Darrel E. Bigham, *Towns and Villages of the Lower Ohio* (1998); Walter Havighurst, *River to the West: Three Centuries of the Ohio* (1970); John A. Jakle, *Images of the Ohio Valley* (1977); Benjamin F. Klein, ed., *The Ohio River: Handbook and Picture Album*, rev. ed. (1969); Robert L. Reid, ed., *Always a River: The Ohio River and the American Experience* (1991); Michael C. Robinson, *History of Navigation in the Ohio River Basin* (1983).

Darrel E. Bigham
University of Southern Indiana

Mississippi River

The Mississippi River has played a major role in the history of American transportation and economic development. The Mississippi drains the North American continent from its Lake Itasca (Minnesota) headwaters to the Gulf of Mexico. It is home to diverse and distinctive species of flora and fauna and was populated between A.D. 500 and 1500 by mound-building Mississippian Indians. Beginning in 1541, Spanish and French explorers traversed the Mississippi Valley; they were soon followed by British and, later, American explorers, adventurers, and entrepreneurs.

The economic history of the Mississippi River is one of technological innovation, beginning with Indian canoes and frontier keelboats and flatboats, moving onto the Steamboat Age, and culminating in the twentieth-century development of diesel-powered towboat and barge commerce along this mighty river's banks.

The first Mississippi rivermen were Indians, paddling their sleek, wooden canoes up and down its waters. Cruder Indian bullboats, constructed from branches, mud, and buffalo hide formed into a bowl shape, forded goods and people across the river and

Confluence of the Mississippi and Missouri
Rivers. Missouri Department of Natural
Resources.

downstream. A river-born commerce emerged and adapted to the seventeenth-century arrival of French, Spanish, and English fur traders and entrepreneurs.

In the late eighteenth century, immediately following the American Revolution, the Keelboat Age began in the Ohio and Mississippi valleys. The keelboat was a sleek, upstream-craft, averaging sixty feet in length and eight feet in width. Keelboatmen steered these vessels swiftly downstream, but the job of moving them upriver was extremely difficult. Using oars, sails, and reeled lines, boatmen inched cargoes of coffee, sugar, and other trade goods upstream. The 1811 introduction of steamboats on the western rivers, however, quickly ran the keelboats out of business.

Interestingly, the cruder nonsteam flatboat craft introduced in the late 1700s endured well past the Civil War and the advent of steam power. The flatboats' longevity can be attributed to the fact that they were very cheap to build and easily resold for scrap lumber or, during the Steamboat Age, as tow barges. The flatboat was thus perfectly suited to the freewheeling, entrepreneurial economy of antebellum America.

Flatboats were flat-bottomed (hence the name), box-shaped craft averaging fifty feet in length and twelve feet in width. Rivermen navigated flatboats by means of a huge stern oar and three smaller oars, one each on the bow, port, and starboard sides. Flatboats carried pork, corn, furs, nonperishable fruit and vegetables, and whiskey downstream only. Many of the wooden sidewalks and outbuildings of early Natchez, Baton Rouge, and New Orleans were built from scrap flatboat lumber. Having sold their loads and boats, flatboatmen walked home, braving Indians, outlaws, and wild forces of nature along the Natchez Trace route. After 1811, flatboatmen purchased deck passage aboard northbound steamers.

The average keelboat and flatboat worker did not always conform to the rough and tough image portrayed in folktales and printed stories about Mississippi River heroes like Big Mike Fink, the "King of the River." Fink was a reputed "rip snorter" and a "ring-tailed roarer" who could out-shoot any man in the territories. Many early boatmen were coarse and violent frontiersmen. As time progressed, however, a boating workforce developed that was characterized by more civilized family men and young farm boys. The average nonsteam (that is, flatboat and keelboat) riverman was a white Ohio or Mississippi Valley male of English or Celtic ancestry, averaging twenty-eight years of age. Blacks, Indians, and French rivermen also plied this trade, but in smaller numbers. There were no women on commercial flatboat or keelboat crews, though some rode and worked on frontier emigrant flatboats. Most early rivermen were single, but after 1811, the steamboat made a faster commute—and family life—possible. At any given time, the body of rivermen included a number of young bachelors getting a start in life, out for their first real adventure away from home.

Lumber raft crews before and after the Civil War, navigating large log assemblages down the Ohio and Mississippi, fit most of the above descriptions. But like steamboat crews, they reflected the greater ethnic diversity of increasing northern European (Irish, German, and Scandinavian) immigration and the growing economic role of blacks freed after the Civil War.

The workaday Mississippi steamboat, from 1811 until 1903, was a small craft of 150 to 250 tons that exhibited very little gilt or fancy trappings. The average steamboat's lifespan was five years. Like flat and keel commerce, peak steamboat shipping time was during high water—the high waters of late fall and early spring greatly reduced the chances of running aground.

During high water, the Mississippi was dotted with steamers carrying pork, whiskey, lead, tobacco, cotton, and other goods. They carried human cargo too, as European immigrants, frontier farmers, northbound flatboatmen, businessmen, and even a few riverboat gamblers bought tickets and flocked on board.

Ultimately, the railroads proved the steamboat's economic undoing. First introduced in 1829, railroads served all of the major Mississippi River ports by the 1850s and a vast inland trade that boatmen could never reach. To compete with railroads, rivermen needed a new, faster kind of boat and government-subsidized locks and dams to provide a year-round navigation depth, especially on the Mississippi above St. Louis, as well as the Ohio. By the early twentieth century, the screw-propellered towboat and the growth of the Army Corps of Engineers filled both of these needs. The snub-nosed, twin-screw, diesel-powered *Herbert Hoover* set the standard for western river towboats in 1931, and World War II brought increased commercial traffic on the Mississippi River, supervised by the Army Corps of Engineers.

Though it has endured, Mississippi River commerce never again dominated the American economic landscape as it did during the keelboat, flatboat, and steamboat eras prior to the advent of the railroad, truck, and airplane. However, today's Mississippi River towboats continue to play an important role in the shipment of agricultural produce, fertilizer, petroleum, and many other goods on America's western rivers. A boom in tourism via cruise ship–type "steamers" like the *Delta Queen* and *Mississippi Queen* has added a new dimension to river commerce. Each year tens of thousands of tourists retrace America's history along the course of this great river.

Indeed, reflecting on both the economic and cultural role of the Mississippi River in American civilization, a quote from Mark Twain's *Life on the Mississippi* still rings true: "the basin of the Mississippi is the Body of the Nation. All the other parts are but members, important in themselves, yet more important in their relation to this."

Sources and Further Reading: Michael Allen, "Life on the Mississippi—Towboat Style," *The Lookout* 74 (June–July 1982); Michael Allen, *Western Rivermen, 1763–1861* (1990); Leland D. Baldwin, *The Keelboat Age on Western Waters* (1941); Erik F. Haites, James Mak, and Gary Walton, *Western River Transportation* (1975); Louis C. Hunter, *Steamboats on the Western Rivers* (1949; reprint, 1993); Mark Twain, *Life on the Mississippi* (1883; reprint, 1996).

Michael Allen
University of Washington–Tacoma

Missouri River

The Missouri stretches 2,341 miles from the Three Forks of the Gallatin, Madison, and Jefferson Rivers in southwestern Montana to its mouth near St. Louis, Missouri. In the early nineteenth century, prior to European American settlement of the Missouri Valley, the river flowed approximately two hundred miles further than it does today. The river's sinuous channel contributed to its greater length. In the mid-nineteenth century, a wetter precipitation cycle and subsequent higher flows forced the river through a shorter, straighter, braided channel. The Mighty Missouri shrank in the twentieth century when the U.S. Army Corps of Engineers channelized the stream to create a barge navigation channel from Sioux City, Iowa, to the river's mouth.

Before the colossal engineering projects of the twentieth century, the Missouri River experienced two annual flood events, known as the spring or April fresh (for freshet) and the summer or June rise. The spring fresh resulted from the melting of the snow lying atop the prairies and plains and the commencement of the rainy season. The June rise emerged from the thawing Rocky Mountain snowpack. The Missouri's largest tributary, the Yellowstone, which drains the Bighorn, Absaroka, Gallatin, and Crazy mountain ranges, supplied the bulk of the water for the Missouri's June rise. The April fresh and June rise, which occurred every year since the Wisconsin glaciations, reshaped the

Hide bullboats used in early river transportation. Museum of the South Dakota Historical Society, Pierre S.D.

Missouri's channel form, turning islands to scoured sandbars, sinking trees into snags, cutting off bends to carve oxbow lakes, and digging a new channel through alluvium.

The floods also maintained habitat diversity within the Missouri Valley. High flows and the river's propensity to shift course prevented any single habitat type from dominating the valley's ecosystem. As a result, the greatest concentration of species within the Midwest converged in the Missouri Valley. A whole host of creatures thrived in the Missouri's dark waters or in its adjacent valley bottoms—birds like the piping plover, least tern, Canadian goose, wood duck, and bald eagle; mammals such as the grizzly bear, black bear, elk, white-tailed deer, mule deer, and bison; fish like the pallid sturgeon, paddlefish, channel catfish, blue catfish, and buffalo fish; and reptiles such as turtles, frogs, and snakes. The Missouri River Valley was the great heart center of the entire Missouri Basin.

Much of the Missouri Basin's species entourage, including bison, migrated to and from the Missouri River trench in a discernible pattern. The migration of bison and other species mimicked the Missouri River's flow regime. In the winter months of December, January, and February, when the Missouri dipped to its lowest, species huddled in the Missouri River Valley, seeking succor from the cold and wind that made the uplands uninhabitable. In the months of April, May, and June, when the Missouri achieved its peak water volume, species abandoned the soggy Missouri River trench and moved up the river's tributary valleys toward the highlands. In late July, August, and September, when the Missouri fell back behind its banks for lack of water, species retreated to the Missouri to find refuge in the valley's moist high grasses during the dry season. At the start of the fall rainy season, species once more traveled outward as the plains and prairies greened and the Missouri rose. Species returned to the Missouri with the onset of winter, beginning anew the annual cycle.

What the migration patterns of mammals, birds, fish, and reptiles indicate is that the Missouri Basin—including the Missouri main stem, its tributaries, and drainage area—functioned as a living system, with the Missouri proper serving as the heart center and the tributaries acting as watery arteries. The Missouri's feeder streams carried life back and forth from the core ecological zone to the basin's most distant districts. The pulse of the Missouri River revealed itself in the river's predam hydrograph. The erratic lines of the hydrograph, similar to the vital signs displayed in an electrocardiogram, reflected the system's ecological health. The greatest energy flows moved through the system in April and June and fell off substantially in December and January.

Indigenous peoples, recognizing the Missouri River trench as a prime resource area, occupied the valley bottoms. They established temporary hunting camps or more permanent village sites at key ecological chokepoints in the valley, most notably where large mammalian roads intersected the big river. The roads traced the Missouri's tributaries. The most significant trails lay adjacent to the largest tributaries. Consequently, Indian village sites rested on the valley's terraces at the mouths of such streams as the Grand, Kaw, Platte, White, Cheyenne, and Heart Rivers. At the time of the Lewis and Clark expedition, 1803–1806, a number of tribes either visited or lived on the banks of the magnificent Missouri. Members of the Missouri, Osage, Kansa, Iowa, Oto, Pawnee, Omaha, Ponca, Sioux, Arikara, Mandan, Hidatsa, Assiniboine, Crow, Blackfeet, and Shoshone exploited the Missouri Valley and its biological diversity to sustain their lifeways.

European American settlers advanced up the Missouri Valley in ever-increasing numbers in the years after the return of the Lewis and Clark expedition. The Missouri River drew European Americans to its sides for the same reasons it attracted Indians. European Americans found a plethora of game animals for food, rich bluestem grasses for their cattle, cottonwood timber for cabin construction, fuel, and fences, and cool drinking water. European Americans also employed the Missouri River as a thru-navigation route between the more heavily populated Mississippi Valley and sparsely settled American perimeter. The Missouri played a crucial role in the penetration, conquest, and integration of the entire Missouri Basin into the United States.

Sources and Further Reading: Maria R. Audubon, "The Missouri River Journals, 1843," in Elliot Coues, ed., *Audubon and His Journals*, vols. 1–2 (1897; reprint, 1960); Paul Russell Cutright, *Lewis and Clark: Pioneering Naturalists* (1969); John C. Ewers, *Indian Life on the Upper Missouri* (1968); Jean Baptiste Trudeau, "Trudeau's Description of the Upper Missouri," *Mississippi Valley Historical Review* 8 (June–Sept. 1921); Stanley Vestal, *The Missouri* (1945; reprint, 1964).

Robert K. Schneiders
Minneapolis, Minnesota

Red River of the North

The Red River of the North is a small, winding, watercourse that marks the border between North Dakota, northeastern South Dakota, and Minnesota as it makes its way northward into Manitoba and its final destination in Lake Winnipeg. Formed by the Bois de Sioux and Ottertail Rivers near Breckenridge, Minnesota, the Red is part of the Hudson Bay watershed. Minuscule compared to the Mississippi, Missouri, and other major American rivers, an early-twentieth-century writer disparagingly called it "a sort of overgrown ditch carrying a flow of muddy water." The Red plays no role in the region's transportation history today. Yet because of its position south of Hudson Bay and northwest of the metropolitan areas in southern Minnesota, the Red once provided a crucial link between fur trade and agricultural settlements in present-day Manitoba and the frontier community of St. Paul along the upper Mississippi River.

For decades fur traders and their native partners in middle and western Canada were furnished with supplies by means of a far-flung transportation network centered on Hudson Bay. The Hudson Bay Company (HBC), from its inception in 1670, maintained a post on the bay, York Factory, from which it shipped goods down the Hayes River in heavy York boats. Requiring numerous and burdensome portages, laborious rowing, and towing of boats along the river bank, this seven-hundred-mile route terminated at Fort Garry, the HBC outpost near the confluence of the Assiniboine and Red Rivers in present-day Manitoba.

By the early nineteenth century, fur traders operating south of Fort Garry established a trade route in the opposite direction, toward posts and early settlements in Minnesota. Buffalo became increasingly important both as a source of food as well as a commodity of trade. Métis hunters who lived in and around Fort Pembina began using two-wheeled carts drawn by a horse or ox to haul buffalo robes and other trade goods to newly established Fort Snelling in 1819, and later to a wharf on the Mississippi in what would become St. Paul. A lively trade developed between Fort Snelling and the métis buffalo hunters in the northern Red River Valley. The heyday of this traffic occurred in the 1850s and 1860s, when as many as five hundred carts made the annual trek via three major rutted thoroughfares along the Red River Valley corridor. These carts carried thousands of pounds of robes, pemmican, and grease, as well as beaded and quilled moccasins and jackets for the tourist trade. Northbound, the carts carried dry food staples, tobacco, calicos, woolens, nails, guns, and ammunition.

In the late 1850s, gold strikes in British Columbia, coupled with the success of steamboats on the upper Mississippi and Minnesota Rivers, led to declining use of the carts and the placement of steamboats on the Red. Merchants in St. Paul, interested in boosting their business to traders and settlers on both sides of the border, offered $2,000 to someone who would put a vessel on the Red. In June 1859, Anson Northrup did

so and ferried the first steamboat to Fort Garry. Less than three years later, the Hudson Bay Company launched its own vessel, the *International*, and the scramble to monopolize the steamboat trade was on. Steamboat traffic diminished, however, following the 1862 Dakota conflict along the Minnesota River. Then subjugation of the Sioux by 1865, establishment of Manitoba in 1870, and arrival of the Northern Pacific Railroad at Moorhead in 1871 all combined to set the stage for a revived steamboat industry and its greatest decade along the Red.

James J. Hill, a Canadian in the shipping and freight business in St. Paul, understood how the arrival of the railroad on the Red provided a golden opportunity for a vigorous steamboat trade with Winnipeg, since more goods could be ferried to the river from the railhead at Duluth. Hill and his partners launched the *Selkirk* in 1871, and took 115 passengers and 125 tons of freight to Fort Garry in May of that year. At first, Hill competed against the *International*, but the steamboat trade proved so profitable that Hill and the HBC's Norman Kittson joined forces in the Red River Transportation Line in 1872.

In the middle 1870s, the company operated several steamboats and numerous flatboats between Moorhead, Grand Forks, and Winnipeg. Steamboats carried emigrants from the United States into Canada, particularly Mennonites destined for Manitoba. They also ferried livestock, stoves, machinery, grain, and numerous household goods.

Steamboating on the Red River was rarely hazardous, although a few crashes occurred among the competing boats. A bigger problem was navigating this small river of numerous twists and turns. Goose Rapids north of Moorhead offered a challenge at certain water levels and prompted calls for the Canadian and United States governments to appropriate funds to remove snags and make other improvements.

Throughout the 1870s, the Red River Transportation Line monopolized the steamboat business, while James J. Hill laid plans to cash in on the coming age of railroads. By the middle 1870s, Hill was planning a takeover of the St. Paul and Pacific Railroad, which reached the Red River at Breckenridge and eventually formed the foundation of the Great Northern. Meanwhile, his steamboats transported steel rails and construction materials for the Canadian Pacific. Completion of a railroad between the upper Red River and Winnipeg in the early 1880s put the Red River steamboat trade into rapid decline. Some traffic continued in the late nineteenth and early twentieth centuries, primarily shipment of grain to elevators in Grand Forks and Fargo.

With the end of steamboats in 1912, the Red took on its dominant role throughout the twentieth century as a source of domestic water as well as anxiety among valley residents who endured its flooding. The latter was especially pronounced after the record flood of 1997, when the river topped its banks and devastated Grand Forks and portions of other communities.

Sources and Further Reading: Aubrey Fullerton, "St. Paul, Red River, and York Factory," *The Bellman* (June 23, 1917); Rhoda R. Gilman, Carolyn Gilman, and Deborah M. Stultz, *The Red River Trails* (1979); Donald S. Lilleboe, "Steam Navigation on the Red River of the North, 1859–1881," M.A. thesis, University of North Dakota (1977); Michael P. Malone, *James J. Hill: Empire Builder of the Northwest* (1996); Elwyn B. Robinson, *History of North Dakota* (1966).

Mark Harvey
North Dakota State University–Fargo

Kentucky Boats

Kentucky boats are flat-bottom boats that were employed to bring people from the East down the Ohio River to Kentucky. These boats were rectangular in shape, from fifteen to twenty-five feet wide and fifty to one hundred feet long, and carried as much as eighty tons. They should not be confused with rafts, as these boats had sides that came up a few feet above the water line. Additionally, Kentucky boats had a roof or cabin at the stern, providing some protection and sleeping space. A rear and several side oars were used for steering; a forty-foot boat required at least three men to navigate. Once on the river, these boats might travel fifty to one hundred miles a day if conditions were good; otherwise the boats became caught on sandbars or immobilized by low water. Emigrants might build their own boat, then make use of the lumber when they reached their destination. Or they purchased a manufactured boat that sold for about $1 per running foot.

This boat became important due to its ability to travel in shallow rivers without getting caught on the bottom. Beginning in Pittsburgh, travelers depended on a Kentucky boat to carry them to Ohio and points west of the Midwest, as well as to places south of the Ohio River. In the early nineteenth century, the Ohio River was the "interstate" of western transportation, as people jumped off at Wheeling, Cincinnati, Louisville, and other points along the river.

Sources and Further Reading: Lowell H. Harrison and James C. Klotter, *A New History of Kentucky* (1997); R. Douglas Hurt, *The Ohio Frontier* (1996).

Stephanie Carpenter
Murray State University, Kentucky

Steamboats

Steamboats dominated midwestern river transportation for much of the nineteenth century. In 1811, only four years after Robert Fulton successfully ran the *Clermont* on the Hudson River, his company had the *New Orleans* built at Pittsburgh. That fall it was navigated down the Ohio and Mississippi Rivers to New Orleans.

Steamboating spread rapidly during the economic boom following the War of 1812. The first steamboat to reach St. Louis arrived in 1817, and six years later the *Virginia* was navigated up the Mississippi to Fort Snelling, several miles above present-day St. Paul. Steamboating spread westward up the Missouri with the advance of the farming frontier. By 1829, Independence, near Missouri's western boundary, was connected to St. Louis by a regular steam packet service. St. Louis–based fur traders extended steamboating to the distant Upper Missouri in 1831.

Despite their seasonality, high costs, and short life spans, steamboats were the preferred river transportation of the rapidly growing Midwest. By 1830, Cincinnati and Louisville were the great ports on the Ohio River, and St. Louis was the base for the Upper Mississippi, including such significant tributaries as the Illinois and Fever Rivers. From its beginning in 1838, St. Paul was the practical head of navigation on the Upper Mississippi. During the 1850s, St. Paul–based lines began operating on the Minnesota River and on a portion of the Mississippi above the Falls of St. Anthony (present-day Minneapolis), which blocked through-navigation.

Outside the Mississippi River system, steamboats were used on short rivers feeding into the Great Lakes, such as the Fox and Maumee. In the northwestern portion of the Midwest, steamboating was introduced on the northward-flowing Red River in 1859. Until the completion of a Minnesota-based railroad to near Winnipeg in 1878, it was a key link in supplying valley settlers.

The golden age of steamboats was short. On its main Mississippi River system routes, steamboating peaked for about a decade starting in the mid-1840s. In 1848, Cincinnati had about four thousand arrivals and St. Louis, the home port for 122 steamboats, had approximately three thousand.

The increasing population and trade that caused a boom in steamboating also created a mania for railroads, which promised faster and cheaper year-round service. Although disastrous to steamboating in the long run, railroads often created temporary economic advantages for certain river railheads. The completion of a railroad from Chicago to Rock Island in 1854 sharply increased Mississippi River steamboating from there to St. Paul. But conversely, it helped diminish the much longer St. Louis route. Key railroad extensions that forced steamboats to adjust to a new economy included the completion of lines from Pittsburgh to Cincinnati in 1853, Hannibal to St. Joseph in 1859, and St. Louis to Kansas City in 1865.

Steamboat operators initially adjusted by relying more on local hauls between rail lines and shifting to the Upper Missouri—that portion above Sioux City, Iowa. But by 1887, even that trade was reduced to short routes. Nonetheless, some steamboating persisted on the Midwest's main rivers into the twentieth century, only to be superseded by barge lines that benefited from massive federal government river improvement projects. At the beginning of the twenty-first century, restored steamboats plied the Ohio and Mississippi Rivers and selected tributaries as cruise vessels recalling the elegance and leisurely travel of days past.

Sources and Further Reading: Louis C. Hunter, *Steamboats on the Western Rivers* (1949); William E. Lass, *A History of Steamboating on the Upper Missouri River* (1962); William J. Petersen, *Steamboating on the Upper Mississippi* (1937).

William E. Lass
Minnesota State University–Mankato

Towboats

River transportation has long been a part of the United States. Although the use of railways became dominant during the last half of the nineteenth century, in the Midwest rivers and canals continued to be a preferred method to transport goods. Goods transported on rivers were carried on barges. The barges were initially powered by steam or pushed by steamboats and traveled up and down the rivers. The service provided, however, was slow and at times irregular. Thus, even with low freight rates and better boats, steamboats vanished from the nation's rivers, to be replaced by towboats. For large, bulky cargoes such as coal, salt, and grain, the most cost-effective means of moving them was still on the river, and river commerce shifted toward the towing industry.

Towboats pushed or towed freight-laden barges up and down rivers. Initially powered by steam, these small boats experienced many technological advances in the twentieth century. Common on midwestern rivers, towboats locked onto barges to push them down the river. Because of the technology used, tow boats are capable of pushing multiple barges down river at one time. The use of towboats in the United States became important during the nineteenth cen-

tury and expanded into the twentieth century, during which time they started to operate with diesel engines. Towboats and barges remain a common sight on the rivers of the Midwest as they seem to lazily, though quite effectively, move their cargoes on the region's waters.

Source and Further Reading: Leona S. Morris, "A Pictorial Glimpse of Life Aboard the Brownville, 1960s," *Missouri Historical Review* 81 (Apr. 1987).

Stephanie Carpenter
Murray State University, Kentucky

Delta Queen

The mid-nineteenth century saw the proliferation of steam-powered riverboats that came to dominate the rivers. But as the railroad moved west, steamboats lost their importance for carrying freight and passengers. Trains were more reliable and had taken over by the end of the nineteenth century. Steamboats did not lose their appeal, however, and in the twentieth century were brought back to revive the luxury excursion business. Constructed for $875 thousand in the 1920s for the California Transportation Company, the *Delta Queen* and its twin, the *Delta King*, ran on the Sacramento River. Reaching a top speed of twelve miles per hour, the *Delta Queen* enjoyed a good business from 1927 to 1940.

In 1939, the Isbrandsten Steamship Company, out of Denmark, purchased both boats and prepared to transport them to the East. World War II intervened, and the two boats found themselves in the Navy. The *Delta Queen* served the war as a ferry boat in San Francisco Bay and was released from service in 1946, only a few months after the *Delta King*, which after many changes in ownership came to rest in 1985 on the Sacramento, California Waterfront hotel, theatre, and restaurant. Purchased by Green Line Steamers of Cincinnati, the *Delta Queen* was towed from the West Coast to the Ohio River via the Panama Canal in 1947. After significant refurbishing, the *Delta Queen* began service on the Mississippi and Ohio Rivers in 1948. Since that time, the boat has changed hands many times, but remains active on the river. In 1970, the *Delta Queen* was named to the National Register of Historic Places.

Source and Further Reading: Sonie Liebler, "The Legendary Delta Queen," *Journal of the West* 31 (Apr. 1992).

Stephanie Carpenter
Murray State University, Kentucky

The *Delta Queen* on the Ohio River. Courtesy Delta Queen Steamboat Company.

Ferries

Ferry boats were found in most locations across the country where rivers or lakes needed to be crossed. In contrast to steamboats, barges, or flat boats that traveled up and down the nation's rivers, ferry boats provided transportation across rivers and lakes. In the eighteenth and nineteenth centuries, ferries connected roads or traces where no bridge existed. Operating on a fixed schedule, these boats carried passengers and property. In many locales, ownership and control of the boats were given to private citizens after a grant or contract with the colonial, local, or state government. In some instances in the Midwest, however, state or local governments controlled the river crossings.

During periods of initial settlement, these boats were simple craft, no more than rafts, that moved across the rivers with a guideline or poles. In most cases owned by individuals, these simple ferries provided owners with supplemental income. Fares were inexpensive and graduated depending on the number of people, livestock, and supplies to be carried and the width of the river. These early ferries could be found up and down the Ohio and Mississippi Rivers as well as on their tributaries and were generally located in commercial areas. The advancement of steam power in the early nineteenth century brought faster and larger ships to the rivers and lakes. Along with steam power came standardization. Technological advancements of the nineteenth century included improved ship design, reversible engines, paddle wheels, and broad decks. The paddle wheel ferry led the way for some gunboats in the American Civil War.

In the post–Civil War era, however, ferry boats did not bear the same importance as in the antebellum period. Railroads in the late nineteenth century and toll-free highways and bridges in the twentieth century have removed the necessity for ferries in the United States. They still exist in some locations where no bridge is available for people to get to desired destinations. On Lake Superior, for example, a popular site and destination is Madeline Island; on Lake Erie, passengers travel from Marblehead, Ohio, to Kelleys Island; and on Lake Michigan, ferry travel runs from Manitowoc, Wisconsin, to Ludington, Michigan. Although the age of the ferry boat ended in the United States by the end of the twentieth century, in other parts of the world, ferry boats remain a primary mode of transportation.

Source and Further Reading: Balthasar Henry Meyer et al., *History of Transportation in the United States before 1860* (1948).

Stephanie Carpenter
Murray State University, Kentucky

The Corps of Engineers

In 1779, Congress first established a separate Corps of Engineers within the United States Army. Originally charged with the design and construction of military fortifications, the Corps of Engineers received from Congress an increasing list of national responsibilities in the nineteenth and twentieth centuries. The Corps of Engineers eventually engaged in not only building battlements, but also surveyed and mapped western lands, built roads, modified natural harbors to facilitate oceanic commerce, and engineered inland waters for keelboat, steamboat, and barge navigation.

By the middle of the twentieth century, Congress

authorized the Corps to engage in the multiple-purpose development of entire river basins. In the post–World War II era, Army engineers tackled the gargantuan task of remaking the Missouri River to serve the multiple purposes of navigation, flood control, hydroelectric generation, and irrigation agriculture. The Corps contributed to the transformation of the midwestern region from perceived wilderness to an agricultural and industrial land and waterscape. Arguably, it established and maintained a greater presence in the Midwest, especially along the Mississippi River, than elsewhere in the United States.

To make the Mississippi, Ohio, and Missouri Rivers routes of commerce and conquest, Congress directed the Corps of Engineers to remove impediments to navigation such as sandbars, snags, rocks, and rapids. The Corps initiated similar work along the Missouri River in the 1830s. These efforts along the Ohio, Mississippi, and Missouri rose in tandem with the increase in steamboat traffic. More boats on the water meant more Corps projects to eliminate obstructions to their passage.

After the demise of steamboat traffic in the 1870s and 1880s and the rise of railroad transportation, the Corps of Engineers received support from Congress and farmers throughout the Midwest to build deeper, channelized inland waterway systems capable of floating barges. The Corps of Engineers sought to create a hydraulic transportation system that would carry cargo at lower cost than the railroads. By the middle of the twentieth century, the Corps of Engineers, employing dams and locks, created a nine-foot-deep slack water navigation channel along the Ohio River from Pittsburgh, Pennsylvania, to Cairo, Illinois, and another channel along the Mississippi River from Alton, Illinois, to St. Paul, Minnesota. Unable to dam the Lower Missouri Valley because of geographical and hydromorphic barriers, the Corps of Engineers opted to construct an open water channel from Sioux City, Iowa, to the Missouri's mouth using jetties to divert, narrow, and deepen that silt-laden stream.

The dams and locks astride the Ohio contributed to commerce but at a high cost in aesthetic, historical, cultural, and ecological values. The Missouri River hydraulic system failed in all respects. The engineering projects along the Mississippi led to the heavy use of that stream by commodity shippers. The Corps of Engineers maintains a strong presence in the Midwest, and its legal and physical hold on the waters of the Mississippi, Ohio, and Missouri grants the Army engineers a tremendous influence on the midwestern economy and environment.

Sources and Further Reading: John R. Ferrell, *Big Dam Era* (1993); John R. Ferrell, *Soundings: One Hundred Years of the*

Navigation Project (1996); U.S. Army Corps of Engineers, *Annual Report of the Chief of Engineers* (1876–1979); U.S. Army Corps of Engineers, *Missouri River,* 73rd Cong., 2nd sess., H. Doc. 238 (1935).

Robert K. Schneiders
Minneapolis, Minnesota

The Great Lakes

The Great Lakes form what is perhaps the greatest inland transportation network on Earth. With a total surface area of approximately 95,000 square miles, they constitute a part of a body of water that stretches nearly 1,000 miles across the heart of the North American continent, extending from the St. Lawrence River and the Atlantic Ocean to northern Minnesota. For thousands of years, the Great Lakes have carried travelers and their goods, from the bark canoes of Native Americans to the thousand-foot freighters of today.

In their first commercial application, the upper Great Lakes—Erie, Huron, Michigan, and Superior—stood at the center of the Native and European fur trade. The richest fur country was northwest of Lake Superior, and the main import–export center for the trade was in Montreal on the St. Lawrence River. Each summer, canoe brigades loaded with trade goods would travel from Montreal up the Ottawa River and across Lake Nipissing, then down the French River into Lake Huron. As they continued west, they met eastbound brigades coming from Lake Superior, loaded with furs. The furs and goods were exchanged, and the brigades returned to their respective starting points until the next year.

Large-scale commercial exploitation of the upper Great Lakes began in 1679 when the French explorer Sieur de La Salle (born René-Robert Cavelier) constructed the sixty-foot ship *Griffon* above Niagara Falls. She was intended to ferry furs from the forests surrounding Lakes Huron and Michigan to French posts on eastern Lake Erie, but the enterprise was a false start for Great Lakes shipping. The *Griffon* sailed to Green Bay on her maiden voyage, took on a load of furs, and set off for Niagara, never to be seen again. The ship's fate remains a mystery.

The next large ships would not sail the upper lakes until the mid-1700s when the British patrolled Lake Erie with two naval vessels. It was policy until well after the American Revolution that only British government vessels could sail on the lakes. Not until 1788 were privately owned merchant ships permitted. The first of those carried furs, like the *Griffon* more than a century before.

The first vessel to sail the upper lakes under the American flag, the *Detroit*, was launched at her namesake city in 1793. She was a military craft and helped U.S. forces secure a firm hold on Great Lakes country still dominated by the British, who lost claim to much of it after the Revolution.

The upper Great Lakes saw dramatic military action during the War of 1812. Both American and British forces built squadrons of ships with the intent of controlling the waterways. The navies met in 1814 at the Battle of Lake Erie, where U.S. Commodore Oliver Hazard Perry secured victory and control of the upper lakes.

With the end of war, shipbuilding increased. Among the new vessels was the *Walk-in-the-Water*, launched near Buffalo in 1818. She was the first steam-powered ship on the upper lakes, and carried passengers between Buffalo and Detroit. Her groundbreaking career ended in a storm off Buffalo in 1821.

The opening of the Erie Canal in 1825 joined the upper Great Lakes with the Atlantic Ocean via the Hudson River. Four years later the Welland Canal, built around Niagara Falls, connected Lake Ontario to the upper Lakes. Further improvements, going into the 1840s, bypassed the rapids of the St. Lawrence River and tied the lakes with the Atlantic via that route. Other canals connected Lake Erie with the Ohio River, and the Illinois and Michigan Canal tied Lake Michigan with the Mississippi River and the Gulf of Mexico.

When the Soo Locks opened at Sault Ste. Marie, Michigan, in 1855, Lake Superior was connected to the lower four lakes, and uninterrupted navigation from northern Minnesota to the Atlantic was possible. The easy transportation provided by these canals and by the Great Lakes themselves encouraged settlement, and the population of the American upper lakes soared from 800,000 in 1820 to 9 million in 1860.

Other improvements took place. In 1818, two U.S. lighthouses went into service on Lake Erie. The first light on Lake Huron came in 1825, on Lake Michigan in 1832, and on Lake Superior in 1849. The growing population and navigational enhancements made Great Lakes shipping serious business. The combined capacity of lakes ships in 1860 was 463,000 gross tons, almost a tenth of the total for all U.S. ships that year.

The discovery of iron ore in Michigan's Upper Peninsula in the 1840s and the subsequent opening of the Soo Locks brought a new boom. Some 1,400 tons of ore were carried in 1855, the figure increasing to 124,000 tons in 1860. By 1888, ore was the lakes' most important cargo, topping a list that included wheat, copper, lumber, and coal. The elemental traffic pattern was set: Freighters loaded ore in the western Lake Superior iron ranges and delivered it to industries on the southern shores of Lakes Michigan and Erie.

Long after passengers first moved over the Great

The Great Lakes from above.
Provided by SeaWiFS Project,
NASA/Goddard Space Flight Center,
and ORBIMAGE.

Lakes by steam, freight still moved by sail. With spacious cargo holds uninterrupted by machinery and open decks easy to load and unload, sailing vessels enjoyed particular advantages for the movement of freight. Unlike steamboats, however, they were entirely dependent on the weather, and could not keep reliable schedules. In the years before the Civil War, shippers sought to have the best of both worlds by towing sailing vessels with steam tugs. The practice began in confined harbors and rivers where winds were sporadic, but soon spread to open water. Tugs moved across the upper lakes with up to five sailing vessels in tow.

The keel for the first steam-powered freighter was laid in 1869. The *R.J. Hackett* was designed specifically to address the problems of handling bulk cargoes. Her steam works were all the way aft, and her pilothouse all the way forward. In between was a boxy hull free from superstructures, boasting the room of a sailing vessel. The 211-foot craft was unlike anything seen before, but it was a brilliant design that became the prototype for almost every Great Lakes freighter built over the next century. The *Hackett* and the steamers that followed her design brought the end of sail. The last new full-rigged schooner built on the lakes was launched in 1889.

In 1892, Lake Michigan became involved in rail transportation when the first freight train was moved over water from Michigan to Wisconsin. The lake crossing provided more direct access to northwestern markets and avoided delays in crowded Chicago yards, and soon three different lines were operating car ferries between various Lake Michigan ports. Improved rail traffic patterns in Chicago ultimately conspired with longer trains to bring an end to this unique service, and the last rail car was ferried across the lake in 1990.

Through the twentieth century, ships continued to follow the *R.J. Hackett*'s design, but grew longer. By 1906, the benchmark was 600 feet; twenty years later it was 633 feet. By the 1950s, ships were nearing 700 feet. The infrastructure of upper lakes shipping continued to improve as well. Loading ships was done by means of tall docks and gravity, but unloading was more difficult. The use of crews to shovel ore out of ships' holds was expensive and inefficient, and the first automated unloading cranes debuted in 1880. In 1899, came the Hulett unloader, a crane nimble enough to drop into a ship's hold and large enough to remove fifteen tons at a time. In 1902, the freighter *Hennepin* was fitted with a conveyor device that allowed the ship to discharge its own cargo. Self-unloading vessels were slow to catch on, but by the 1920s their numbers grew. They would dominate the U.S. Great Lakes fleet by the close of the twentieth century.

The single greatest tragedy on the Great Lakes occurred in 1915 when the overcrowded passenger steamer *Eastland* capsized and drowned 835 people only feet from her Chicago dock. Despite the disaster, passenger business boomed. The Detroit and Cleveland Navigation Company, the largest line on the lakes, built ships with fifteen hundred beds in 1924, and even toyed with the idea of operating large seaplanes before the Great Depression intervened. The aging lakes passenger fleet survived the Depression and did well through World War II, only to fall victim to improved roads and stricter safety standards in the 1950s.

In 1959, the Great Lakes saw the most important improvement since the Erie Canal. The St. Lawrence Seaway opened, which together with an enlarged Welland Canal, allowed large ships uninhibited navigation from the Atlantic to all points on the lakes. The joint venture between the U.S. and Canada was supposed to make the lakes North America's "fourth seacoast," but the promise was never fulfilled. Just as the seaway opened, oceanic shippers turned toward containerization and super ships too big for the seaway's 766-foot-long locks. Discussion about enlarging the seaway continued through the turn of the century, but nothing materialized.

For a time, seaway-sized freighters, built to the maximum dimensions allowed by the St. Lawrence locks, ruled the lakes. Respect for that size limit was not to last, however. In 1972, the *Stewart J. Cort* became the first thousand-footer to enter the taconite trade. She carried twice the load of a seaway-sized boat, and her success led to a fleet of thousand-footers. Too big for the Welland and St. Lawrence Canals, these ships are true creatures of the upper lakes, confined to those waters. The thousand-footers barely fit through the Soo Locks—the only reason even larger ships have not been built.

The thousand-footers broke with typical freighter design in other ways, as well. All were equipped as self-unloaders, and most had aft pilothouses instead of the forward structures used since the *R.J. Hackett*. Surprisingly, the thousand-footers are among the most maneuverable vessels on the lakes, equipped with thrusters that allow them to turn in tight spaces.

Lock sizes are not the only impediment to Great Lakes transportation. For three months of the year, ice chokes the system. Icebreaking vessels can extend the season a few weeks, but year-round navigation is another matter. With cooperation between lakes shippers and the Coast Guard, the shipping season grew progressively longer through the late 1960s and early 1970s until, in 1974–1975, transport on the Great Lakes continued year-round for the first time in history. Except for a severe freeze in February 1977, lake shipping continued uninterrupted until the winter of 1979–1980, when an economic recession made year-round shipping impractical. There were other problems, however, including safety and environmental concerns.

When the *Edmund Fitzgerald* went down with her crew of twenty-nine in a November 1975 gale on Lake Superior, she was the latest victim of what is traditionally the lakes' most dangerous month. The worst storm occurred on Lake Huron on November 9, 1913. The squall blew for sixteen hours, wrecked at least twenty ships, and claimed approximately 240 lives. Eight freighters were lost with all hands. The 1940 Armistice Day storm took seventy lives on Lake Michigan. In November 1958, the *Carl D. Bradley* and thirty-three of her crew were lost on Lake Michigan. Eight years later the *Daniel J. Morrell* took twenty-eight lives in a Lake Huron storm. Lake Erie's worst blow came on October 20, 1916, when fifty-five lives were lost.

At the beginning of the twenty-first century, maritime commerce on the Great Lakes was more efficient than ever, with ships that can carry up to four times the loads of their counterparts from a generation earlier. Iron ore continues to be the most important cargo, followed distantly by wheat, coal, limestone, and oil. The Duluth–Superior complex is among the busiest ports in the world, and the Soo Locks see more traffic each year than the Panama Canal. Ships of all nations call at lake ports, primarily to load grain and coal for delivery back to their countries. The most noteworthy foreign visitors of late have been cruise liners, which have brought the first regular overnight passenger service to the upper lakes since the 1960s.

Despite occasional slowdowns due to economic recession, Great Lakes shipping is alive and well. All indications are that it is here to stay, continuing a tradition of waterborne commerce that stretches back three hundred years to European settlement, and many more still among Native Americans.

Sources and Further Reading: William Ashworth, *The Late, Great Lakes* (1987); James P. Barry, *Ships of the Great Lakes* (1973); Dana Thomas Bowen, *Memories of the Lakes* (1946); Victoria Brehm, ed., *A Fully Accredited Ocean* (1998); Harlan Hatcher and Erich A. Walter, *A Pictorial History of the Great Lakes* (1963); Charles K. Hyde, *The Northern Lights* (1995); Jacques Lesstrang, *Seaway* (1976); William Ratigan, *Great Lakes Shipwrecks and Survivals* (1977); Mark L. Thompson, *Steamboats and Sailors of the Great Lakes* (1991); Karl Zimmerman, *Lake Michigan's Railroad Car Ferries* (1993).

Matthew G. Anderson
Fort Miami Heritage Society,
St. Joseph, Michigan

Lake Erie

Lake Erie is distinguished from the other Great Lakes by virtue of its geography. It is the smallest of the upper lakes, measuring 240 miles long by fifty-seven miles wide, with a surface area of 9,932 square miles. It is the shallowest, with a maximum depth of 210 feet and an average depth of fifty-eight feet. It is also the southernmost of the Great Lakes. Lake Erie's unique position—at the eastern end of the upper lakes and halfway between the Chicago industrial complex and the cities of the Northeast—has given the lake an importance disproportionate to its size.

Lake Erie was the last of the Great Lakes to be seen by Europeans, who bypassed it by following other routes directly into Lake Huron. In 1679, the French explorer Sieur de La Salle (born René-Robert Cavelier) built the *Griffon*, the first ship on the Great Lakes, near Lake Erie's eastern shore. About two decades later, the French founded Detroit just upstream from the western shore, securing Lake Erie's strategic importance. When the British took control of French claims on the Great Lakes, they quickly built a pair of naval vessels to patrol Lake Erie. When the United States fought Britain for control of the upper lakes in the War of 1812, the decisive battle was on Lake Erie.

The first steamship on the upper lakes, *Walk-on-the-Water*, debuted on Lake Erie in 1818, making runs between Buffalo and Detroit. The opening of the Erie Canal in 1825 connected Lake Erie with the Atlantic Ocean by way of the Hudson River and New York City. The Welland Canal, which bypassed Niagara Falls and connected Lake Erie with Lake Ontario, opened in 1829. Together with other improvements along the St. Lawrence River, the Welland gave Lake Erie another link with the Atlantic, and other canals were built to connect the lake with the Ohio River. With the canals came lighthouses; Lake Erie boasted seventeen by 1840. Through the nineteenth century, Lake Erie fostered a number of cities that would become major urban centers of the Midwest: Buffalo, Erie, Toledo, and Cleveland, among others. Each city had its own particular advantages.

Buffalo was the Erie Canal's terminus on the lake, and in the years after the canal opened, the city became an important center of the grain trade. Erie became home to a large shipbuilding industry and, as Pennsylvania's only lake port, served as a funnel through which materials were moved to and from industries at Pittsburgh. Toledo was located on the Maumee River, the largest river flowing into any of the Great Lakes. This exceptional natural waterway facilitated the city's becoming a major coal port and industrial center. It was Cleveland, however, that would become Lake Erie's hub and, arguably, the heart of the Great Lakes shipping industry itself.

Cleveland was the site of many important developments in shipping technology. The *R.J. Hackett*, which was the prototype for the modern Great Lakes bulk carrier with its forward pilothouse, aft engine house, and long deck in between, was launched in Cleveland in 1869. The *Spokane*, the first steel-hulled bulk carrier on the lakes, was launched there in 1886. In 1892, the Lake Carriers Association, the largest support organization for Great Lakes shippers, established its headquarters in the city. Cleveland engineer George Hulett developed the Hulett unloader, the nimble crane that finally eliminated manual shoveling of ore from ship's holds, in the 1890s.

Ore became the most significant cargo moved on Lake Erie. Some of it was shipped directly to plants on the lake's shore. Much of it was transferred from ship to railcar and sent to plants at Youngstown and Pittsburgh. The Ohio ports of Ashtabula and Conneaut developed as major points for this lake–rail transfer. Ore was not the only major commodity on Lake Erie. The lake's proximity to the coalfields of Appalachia provided a convenient and profitable backhaul cargo for unloaded ore ships. By the early 1900s, the tonnages of coal going out of and ore coming in to Lake Erie ports were nearly equal.

Passenger service on Lake Erie continued well into the twentieth century. The Detroit and Cleveland Navigation Company, the largest passenger operator on the Great Lakes, continued runs between its namesake cities until the mid-twentieth century, when the company ended all service.

The opening of the St. Lawrence Seaway in 1959, which improved navigation between the Great Lakes and the Atlantic Ocean, promised to increase Lake Erie commerce until its ports rivaled Atlantic Seaboard terminals. Though the seaway did bring an increase in foreign trade, it was less than hoped for, and ocean vessels soon outgrew the seaway's 766-foot locks, preventing them from reaching the lakes.

The size of Lake Erie freighters was growing as well. The *Stewart J. Cort* was assembled at Erie in 1971. At a thousand feet in length, the *Cort* was over 250 feet longer than the largest lake vessels of its time. The *Cort*'s capacity of over fifty thousand tons was more than twice that of any other freighter on the lakes.

Lake Erie's prominence in upper lakes shipping came at a cost. For more than a century and a half, industrial pollutants, fertilizers, and sewage ran into the lake. By the 1960s, algae was the lake's most abundant form of plant life, literally squeezing out other native species, and Lake Erie stood on the brink of ecological disaster. National attention was brought to the problem when an oil slick on Cleveland's Cuyahoga River caught fire in 1969, creating the illusion that the river itself was burning. Limits on chemical discharge were imposed, and by the 1990s, Lake Erie had rebounded.

Lake Erie's role in Great Lakes shipping is as vital today as ever. The Coast Guard's Ninth District, which covers all of the Great Lakes, is headquartered in Cleveland. Shipyards at Lorain and Erie remain active and have together produced seven of the thirteen thousand-footers now on the upper lakes. No doubt Lake Erie will continue in its prominent role well into the future.

Sources and Further Reading: William Ashworth, *The Late, Great Lakes* (1987); Harlan Hatcher, *Lake Erie* (1945); Harlan Hatcher and Erich A. Walter, *A Pictorial History of the Great Lakes* (1963); Charles K. Hyde, *The Northern Lights* (1995); Jacques Lesstrang, *Seaway* (1976); Mark L. Thompson, *Steamboats and Sailors of the Great Lakes* (1991).

Matthew G. Anderson
Fort Miami Heritage Society,
St. Joseph, Michigan

Lake Huron

The first travel on Lake Huron was by Native Americans with small dugouts and birch-bark canoes. With European expansion into the Midwest, transportation on the lake had become particularly important by 1700, when French settlers established on its shores the first center of French civilization west of the St. Lawrence Valley. By the 1780s, French traders on Lake Huron had devised a new craft in the form of multiperson canoes, called *bateaux*, which were normally forty feet long and about six feet wide at the middle and could carry up to five tons of cargo. Travelers in *bateaux* often navigated waterways in brigades of four to ten vessels.

In 1788, British military engineer Gother Mann completed the first survey of Lake Huron and gathered geographical intelligence to aid British military movement. The lake became important for military transportation during the War of 1812. The exploration of the lake by Lewis Cass in 1820 and the opening of the Erie Canal in 1825 linking Lakes Erie, Huron, and Michigan to the Hudson River and the Eastern Seaboard encouraged the expansion of settlement and trade.

The Great Lakes region experienced enormous population and commercial growth in the years between 1825 and 1860. Many settlers to the upper Midwest passed through the village of Collingwood at the southern tip of Lake Huron's Georgian Bay. Railways came to Georgian Bay during the 1850s as the Northern Railway connected to lake transportation at the Collingwood port, thereby linking Lake Huron grain shipment directly to New England. The number of steamboats and barges harbored at Collingwood increased yearly, as did construction of grain elevators along the shoreline. Railway companies chartered fleets of sidewheelers (wooden boats propelled by side-mounted paddlewheels) on occasional runs between Collingwood and Chicago beginning in 1855.

Lighthouses occupy an esteemed place in Great Lakes lore. Lake Huron's first lighthouse was built at Fort Gratiot in 1825. The most famous Lake Huron lighthouses, however, are probably a pair of floating lightships. The first lightship on any of the Great Lakes was stationed in 1832 at Waugoshance Point where ships turn northeast to enter Lake Huron from Lake Michigan. The last of the Great Lakes lightships was *Lightship Huron*, stationed at Corsica Shoals (six miles north of Port Huron) from 1935 to 1970, the last thirty years of which she was the only American lightship on the Great Lakes. Today the *Huron* rests on shore at Port Huron and is open year-round to visitors.

As with other of the Great Lakes, boating accidents frequented transportation on Lake Huron, in many cases due to bottoming out in shallow waters. Concern about transport safety and efficiency prompted the U.S. Congress in 1841 to mandate the Great Lakes Survey, completed in 1882. The survey charted the lakes to a depth of eighteen feet, which was six feet deeper than the draft of the largest vessels at the time. A subsequent need for still deeper channels called for additional appropriations, made in 1900, for a project to chart the lakes to a depth of thirty feet.

Lake Huron has witnessed a series of transportation eras on its waters. The steamboat era began in the 1840s. Entire fleets of wooden vessels were built in the Georgian Bay shipyards, where steel soon supplanted wood as the preferred construction material for steamers. By the 1870s, shipping vessels for grain, lumber, and ore usually were barges tied together in small clusters, pulled behind powerful steamers.

During the early 1870s, service was initiated by the Georgian Bay Navigation Company, later renamed the Great Northern Transit Company, to pursue commercial shipping on Lake Huron. The company built a fleet of white-coated steamers, popularly known as the White Line. When the North Shore Navigation Company entered competition on Lake Huron in 1890, its vessels, painted black, were dubbed the Black Line. Rivalry for a Lake Huron shipping monopoly grew so intense between the two lines that passengers could travel at extremely low fares. The two companies amalgamated in 1899 as the Northern Navigation Company of Ontario.

Steel-bulk carriers were the next vessels to bear commodities on Lake Huron. The carriers transported loads of ore heavy enough that some channels were not deep enough, the channel into Lake Huron from the Detroit River across Lake St. Clair requiring particular attention in this regard. A famous steel-bulk carrier on the lake was the whaleback, or so-called pig. Designed in the Georgian Bay district, the first whaleback was launched in 1888, and by 1906, the whaleback reached a length of 600 feet. The best-known whaleback probably was the 362-foot, five-deck *Christopher Columbus*, used to carry fair crowds at the 1893 Chicago World's Fair.

Tanker ships appeared on the lakes in 1910. The following year, shippers established the general practice of using separate lanes seven miles apart for upbound and downbound traffic on Lake Huron. The size of Great Lakes ships reached its maximum allowable limit, 730 feet, by the 1930s. Such vessels were referred to as "Seaway length," the maximum length that the system of Great Lakes locks could handle.

The last major evolution in Great Lakes freighters was during the 1960s when international companies integrated transportation by truck, railroad, and ship with the aid of standardized metal-box containers. Because many oceangoing container ships were too large to pass through the Great Lakes locks system, some companies built fleets of smaller freighters of about 270 feet and designed to carry stacked containers on the Great Lakes. Ports along the Georgian Bay entered a period of renewal as rail-to-ship connections again became an economically competitive means of transportation.

Present-day transportation on Lake Huron is highly diversified. In addition to the transport of raw materials and manufactured goods, commercial fishing is important on the lake. Popular recreational activities include power-boating and sailing, and campgrounds and park areas along the shore of Lake Huron are connected by a series of roadways and ferry systems that closely encircle the lake in nearly all places.

Sources and Further Reading: James P. Barry, *Ships of the Great Lakes* (1973); Charles E. Feltner and Jeri Baron Feltner, *Great Lakes Maritime History* (1982); Charles K. Hyde, *The Northern Lights: Lighthouses of the Upper Great Lakes* (1986); Fred Landon, *Lake Huron* (1944); W. Neil Thornton, *Trails, Sails and High Iron Along the Huron Shore* (1982); Arthur M. Woodford, *Charting the Inland Seas* (1991).

David L. Seim
Iowa State University

Lake Michigan

Michigan, Indiana, Illinois, and Wisconsin border Lake Michigan, and its waters have supported many peoples. Lake Michigan formed after the Ice Age about

A western view on Lake Michigan. Photo by Sathyan Sundaram, 2002.

10,000 years ago. It is the second-largest Great Lake by volume with 1,180 cubic miles of water, and is the only Great Lake entirely within the United States. Approximately 118 miles wide and 307 miles long, Lake Michigan has more than 1,600 miles of shoreline. The lake averages 279 feet in depth, and is 925 feet at its deepest point. Lake Michigan is joined by the Straits of Mackinac to Lake Huron.

Lake Michigan has had a history of names. Samuel de Champlain called it *Grand Lac.* Jean Nicolet, the first European in Wisconsin, landed in Green Bay and interacted with the Winnebagos, whom the French called *Puans*; consequently it was referred to as *Lac des Puans* on an incomplete 1670 map of the region that depicted only the northern shores of the lake. But it is only Green Bay that is labeled as *Baye de Puans* on maps from 1688 and 1708. At times, the French referred to it as *Lac des Illinois* after other native people of the region. Louis Jolliet and Jacques Marquette provided its final name of Michigan from the Ashinabe words *michi gami* meaning "great water."

Lake Michigan contains a colder northern tier but also a more temperate southern basin that includes Milwaukee, Chicago, part of northwest Indiana, and southwest Michigan. Sand dunes border the eastern and southern shores of the lake. Indiana Dunes National Lakeshore is found along the Lake Michigan coast in Indiana, and Sleeping Bear Dunes National Lakeshore is located along the Lake Michigan coast in the northern portion of Michigan's lower peninsula. The dunes along Lake Michigan are among the most significant freshwater dunes in the world, and Sleeping Bear Dunes are believed to be the largest active freshwater dunes in the United States.

In the nineteenth century, Lake Michigan supported a thriving lumber industry and grain trade. By the 1840s, entrepreneurs had constructed sawmills along the lake, many of which continued as part of a major industry into the 1900s. Logging crews cut the timber from late fall until spring, when the rivers to the lake reopened after the winter's freeze. Logs floated down rivers to sawmills, and the sawn lumber was loaded on ships and taken to Chicago. The port of Chicago served as America's great lumber center for nearly forty years.

Farmers and farm laborers spent their winters harvesting trees to float to sawmills along the lake. The white pine forests of Michigan and Wisconsin became homes and buildings across the nation. While trees from the northern Midwest traveled the rivers to Lake Michigan, grain came overland. Milwaukee and Chicago established important grain markets, and the Chicago Board of Trade, established in 1848, became the arbiter of the nation's farm commodity prices. Lake Michigan served as the route to and from these cities.

In the late twentieth century, the primary harbors in Lake Michigan were Calumet, Burns Harbor, Milwaukee, Green Bay, and Sturgeon Bay. The Calumet River and Lake Calumet Harbor of Illinois handled nearly 900 thousand tons of cargo in 2002. The inbound cargo was primarily steel, liquid bulk, stone, cement, and sugar, while ships hauled out steel and scrap, grain, and liquid bulk. The port of Burns Harbor in Indiana handled about six million tons in 2001. Inbound materials included steel, fertilizer, potash, and salt, and freighters hauled away coal, containers, fertilizer, grain, and steel.

The Wisconsin ports of Milwaukee, Green Bay, and Sturgeon Bay serve the northwestern shore of the lake. Milwaukee remains a grain-shipping hub, while it receives shipments of salt, coal, and cement; in 1999 it handled total shipments of nearly three million tons. In the late twentieth century, Green Bay received diverse cargos of coal, limestone, cement, salt, pig iron, and liquid bulk, the primary outgoing commodity being tallow. In 1999, the port of Green Bay handled nearly two million tons of goods. Sturgeon Bay is unique among Lake Michigan ports, as it continues to be a shipbuilding center in the twenty-first century. The Manitowoc Shipbuilding Company, for example, constructed ships in the early 1900s, built submarines during World War II, and in the postwar era, returned to commercial production. In the late 1990s, the company constructed cutters, tugs, and freighters, among other vessels that plied both Lake Michigan and other international waters. Ships can dry-dock for storage and repair in Sturgeon Bay; other ports have repair facilities, as well.

Lake Michigan supported a commercial fishing industry in the nineteenth and early twentieth centuries. It is believed the lake supports nearly one hundred species of fish; whitefish, lake trout, lake herring, and perch are among the most commercially significant. Invasive species and pollution, however, have competed with the native species; the sea lamprey decimated the lake trout, and alewives out-competed the lake herring. Dead alewives washed up on beaches as populations crashed due to a lack of predation from the dwindling numbers of lake trout. In 1965, fishery managers stocked Coho salmon, a Pacific Ocean native, in Lake Michigan, and in 1966, they planted Chinook salmon smelts, also from the Pacific. These populations are now self-sustaining, and in addition to brown trout, called steelhead, have reduced the alewife population. Chemical treatments in Lake Michigan tributaries that are lethal to lamprey, but not other species, have disrupted these populations. The salmon and trout supported a resurgence in the sport fishery, but not the commercial fishery. Exotic species such as zebra mussels and gobies continue to concern fisheries managers.

Pollution, especially on the lake's southern tier where development is greatest, endangers life in and around Lake Michigan. Sources such as soil and chemical runoff from agriculture, municipal waste, and industrial areas discharge contaminate the lake. Chemicals affecting the lake include pesticides, Atrazine, DDT, bacteria, heavy metals, mercury, and PCBs. These pollutants cloud the lake's future, and how the resources and life the lake supports will endure is uncertain.

Sources and Further Reading: Margaret Beattie Bogue, *Around the Shores of Lake Michigan* (1985); William Cronon, *Nature's Metropolis* (1991); U.S. Department of Commerce, "National Oceanic and Atmospheric Administration," *United States Coast Pilot 6* (2000); U.S. Environmental Protection Agency and Environment Canada, *The Great Lakes: An Environmental Atlas and Resource Book* (1995).

Leo E. Landis
Henry Ford Museum and Greenfield Village,
Dearborn, Michigan

Lake Superior

In describing Lake Superior in the summer of 1849, Harvard scientist Louis Agassiz remarked, "Lake Superior is to be figured to the mind as a vast basin with a high rocky rim." Vast it is—Superior is the largest of the Great Lakes. With a surface area of 31,700 square miles, it is the largest freshwater lake in the world. It stretches 350 miles in length and 160 miles in width. Its deepest part is over 1,300 feet. Geologically, the lake is youthful, having been formed less than ten thousand years ago.

Hardwood and coniferous trees grew along the shore, as glaciers finally retreated fully from the region eight thousand years ago. At least twenty times over a five-hundred-year span about nine thousand years ago, an ice dam between Lake Agassiz and Lake Nipigon gave way and floods surged into the lake. The cataclysm raised lake levels as much as 160 feet. Its clear cold water has satisfied generations of midwesterners for their existence or pleasure.

Native peoples settled around Lake Superior more than nine thousand years ago. Hunting and gathering indigenes witnessed the formation of the lake as it is largely known today. Eventually the descendants of these peoples referred to themselves as the Ashinabeg and included the Chippewa, Ottawa, and Potawatomi tribes.

They settled along the shore and on islands; on Madeline Island off the Wisconsin coast, the Chippewa settlement at times totaled over two thousand inhabitants. They fashioned homes of timber and tools from copper, stone, and animal bone, and relied on fish such as sturgeon, suckers, whitefish, and lake trout. They produced maple sugar and hunted game. The people ate a variety of plants for subsistence, especially the fall harvest of wild rice. The Chippewa gave the lake the name *kitchi gami* meaning "great ocean" or "grand ocean." French explorers called it *le lac superieur,* meaning "the uppermost lake."

Around the year 1620, Etienne Brulé explored Lake

Superior, perhaps as far west as Isle Royale. He is credited with the first European expedition onto the lake. It wasn't until 1654 that Pierre-Esprit Radisson and Médard Chouart des Groseilliers contacted the native peoples at the "Head of the Lakes" near present-day Duluth, Minnesota. They returned in 1660, and theirs were the first known European excursions across the lake. On their return trip, they filled canoes with furs. Unfortunately, French officials tried and jailed the pair for failure to acquire a license to engage in the fur trade.

The French did not conduct a formal trade on western Lake Superior until the 1670s. Explorer Daniel Greysolon, also known as Sieur du Lhut, began to establish communications with indigenes on a westward mission in the 1670s. In 1679, du Lhut engaged in a peacemaking voyage, as he tried to negotiate a truce among the warring native peoples of the western Great Lakes region. Du Lhut convinced the Chippewa and Sioux to recognize the authority of King Louis XIV and cease their battles. This opened western Lake Superior to the fur trade.

The United States secured control of Lake Superior with the Treaty of Paris in 1783. The new nation allowed the native peoples to remain until the early nineteenth century. Over time, the U.S. government negotiated treaties with the native peoples to cede their land rights. Settlers squatted before legal settlement, and American citizens could not legally settle the Duluth area until the Treaty of La Pointe in 1854.

The earliest commercial enterprises on Lake Superior included mining, lumbering, and fishing. Copper and iron mines enticed entrepreneurs with opportunities. Native people dug pits to mine copper, but Europeans mined much deeper into the earth. A rush began in 1842, and through the nineteenth century, Cornish, Irish, and Finnish miners came to the copper country. By the mid-twentieth century, copper mining and shipping faded. Iron mining and later taconite proved another source of wealth. In 1844, a government surveying party discovered iron, and by 1846 iron bloomeries, one-or-two-man iron furnaces, operated near what became Negaunee. The Marquette Iron Range offered one of the richest supplies in the nation. Towns and cities such as Houghton, Michigan, and Ashland, Wisconsin, became important to the iron industry. As better ore was exhausted, processes for pelletizing taconite were developed in the 1950s. This rejuvenated the industry, and as of the turn of the century iron shipping on Superior is expected to continue for decades.

Fishing, lumbering, and grain shipping employed residents of Lake Superior towns. Herring, whitefish, sturgeon, and lake trout provided bountiful harvests. Sportsmen fished for brook trout and other species.

Eventually over-fishing and exotic species, especially sea lampreys, caused a collapse of the commercial fishery, and sport fishing became the most economically significant fishery on the lake. In the nineteenth century, vast forests bordered the lake. These trees provided quality lumber, but today the industry is based on faster-growing, lower-quality pulpwood. Grain shipping gained increasing prominence in the early twentieth century. Rail connections allowed Minnesota farmers and entrepreneurs to establish a major port at Duluth. In 2003, it included six grain elevators with a storage capacity of fifty-five million bushels of wheat.

Today Duluth–Superior is the busiest inland port in the United States with taconite and coal being the major domestic cargoes. In addition to Duluth–Superior, the Minnesota ports of Two Harbors, Silver Bay, Taconite Harbor, and Marquette, Michigan, play important shipping functions. Unfortunately, most of these industries contribute pollution to the lake. Pollutants such as mercury and PCBs are stored by fish and pose a health threat to human consumption. Because of remoteness and a lesser degree of development, however, Lake Superior is less polluted than the other Great Lakes.

The vastness of Lake Superior connects it to a hinterland beyond the Midwest. Ships from around the world ply the lake's waters. Logging, pollution, and nonnative species have altered its appearance, but its size and beauty add complexity to the Midwest stereotype as the nation's Farm Belt. The natural splendor of Lake Superior attracts recreational users who fish, camp, and hike the shore and islands. Lake Superior provides unforgettable experiences to all who see her waters.

Sources and Further Reading: Louis Agassiz, *Lake Superior* (1850; reprint, 1974); Margaret Beattie Bogue, *Around the Shores of Lake Superior* (1979); Edmund Jefferson Danziger, Jr., *The Chippewas of Lake Superior* (1990); John Mahan and Ann Mahan, *Lake Superior: Story and Spirit* (1998); Thomas F. Waters, *The Superior North Shore* (1987); U.S. Environmental Protection Agency and Government of Canada, *The Great Lakes: An Environmental Atlas and Resource Book* (1995).

Leo E. Landis
Henry Ford Museum and Greenfield Village,
Dearborn, Michigan

Fishing Vessels of the Great Lakes

Commercial and subsistence fishing has been conducted on the Great Lakes through a variety of fishing vessels and small watercraft. This tradition was in place

Chippewa dip-net fisherman. Clarke Historical Library.

before the arrival of Europeans, as Native American groups—particularly the Ojibway, Ottawa, Menominee, and Potawatomi—plied the region's inshore waters for whitefish and lake trout in bark canoes. The first European explorers, traders, and settlers marveled at Native skills in maneuvering their boats, which ranged between ten and twenty-four feet in length. They were made of cedar frames covered with birch bark, bound with spruce root, and seams sealed with spruce pitch. Their lightweight construction allowed easy portaging between lakes and rivers, and ready transporting to Great Lakes fishing camps when Native American groups migrated to these sites at appointed times of the year. For centuries, until the early twentieth century, Great Lakes Indians speared, gill-netted, and dip-netted fish from birch-bark canoes. After contact with Europeans, Native Americans built these canoes using plank-on-frame construction.

While longtime French immigration to the Upper Midwest influenced boat types and boat-building technologies used in the emergent commercial fisheries of the Great Lakes region, it was the arrival of Northern European immigrants in the second half of the nineteenth century that significantly expanded the range of boats and vessels used. Most noticeable were a variety of small schooner and sloop-rigged boats used in the pound net and gill net fisheries. Among these lesser-known watercraft were the ketch and schooner-rigged Huron boat and the sloop-rigged Norwegian boat, both measuring thirty to forty feet in length. Also in use were the twenty-two- to thirty-foot schooner-rigged pound net boat and the sixteen- to eighteen-foot pound net dinghy or skiff, which evolved into the more well-known oar-powered and motorized pound net boat used during the first half of the twentieth century. Pound nets, at one time a signature element of the region's maritime landscape, were staked perpendicular to the shoreline, where fishers tended the main entrapment area.

Among the sailing craft used in the Great Lakes fisheries, the Mackinaw boat was arguably the most regionally distinctive. Not surprisingly, this was not lost on U.S. Fish Commission officials James Milner and Joseph Collins, who commented on the boat's sharp stern (for a double-ended appearance) and full bow. Although Mackinaw boats are usually associated with their double-ended appearance, some were built with transom sterns. These characteristics, along with a bulging midsection, combined to give the boat remarkably strong sheer—a graceful design that seemingly belied the arduous conditions under which it worked. Ranging in length from twenty-two to twenty-six feet, with some as long as thirty-two feet, Mackinaw boats launched the modern-day gill net fishery on Lake Michigan in the mid-nineteenth century. Along with their conspicuous standing areas and storage facilities, Mackinaw boats sported double masts that were either schooner or ketch rigged to ensure maneuverability. As gill net fishermen ventured further distances on the Great Lakes, the Mackinaw boat developed more deadrise—a deeper keel—to enhance stability in rougher water. Although this feature made beaching less practical, the rise of permanent fishing stations provided needed dock space.

Great Lakes maritime commerce increased dramatically at the midpoint of the nineteenth century, and in this context, it took little time for the region's commercial fishers to adopt the steam-powered tugboat. This boat enabled fishers to venture further from shore, to change ports of operation more frequently, and to harvest greater numbers of whitefish, lake trout, and minor whitefish such as lake herring and chubs.

Early vessels of this boat class, known initially as fishing tugs, fishing steamers, and gill net steamers, ranged in size from sixty-one to seventy-five feet in length and bore the same features as standard steam-powered towing tugs—a plumb stem, round stern, and deep draft. Notable adaptations included net bars or rollers on the bow, powered net lifters, and a greater storage area below deck in the vessel's aft section. But in the early twentieth century, Great Lakes fishers began covering the fishing tug's open deck space to mitigate the difficulty of working in harsh weather conditions. This decked-over space, sometimes known as turtlebacking, began to consume the tug's open deck space incrementally, with particular emphasis placed on the highly exposed bow section. Gradually, the entire topside of the boat was enclosed, giving it the distinctive appearance that led to its regionally derived label, the Great Lakes fish tug. The enclosed deck space of tugs used in the Great Lakes fishery became so occupationally associated with the region that smaller gill net skiffs—boats with no structural connections to conventional tugs—were decked-over and also called Great Lakes fish tugs. After 1930, the size of fish tugs ranged from approximately twenty-five to fifty-feet in length, and in the 1940s, welded, all-steel construction was preferable to wood. During the 1940s and 1950s, fishers began moving the pilothouse further toward the stern to create a more efficient work environment and more versatile space below deck.

In the 1890s, the modern trap net was introduced to the Great Lakes, and it gained gradual acceptance over the next thirty to thirty-five years. A submerged version of the pound net, it is used in water from sixty to 125 feet deep. To retrieve the trap net's pot (the principal entrapment section) more efficiently, fishers of the Great Lakes needed a motorized boat with an open midship and aft section. Boats specifically designed for trap net use were thus readily distinguished by the far-forward placement of their pilothouses. Similar to other regional watercraft, the Great Lakes trap net boat came in a variety of sizes but generally averaged forty feet in length. Starting in the 1970s, fishers worked from the earlier trap net boat designs of the early and middle twentieth century to devise the variety of steel and aluminum trap net boats that are conspicuous on the Great Lakes today.

Sources and Further Reading: Edwin Tappan Adney and Howard I. Chapelle, *The Bark and Skin Boats of North America* (1983); Margaret Beattie Bogue, *Fishing the Great Lakes: An Environmental History, 1783–1933* (2000); Charles E. Cleland, *Rites of Conquest: The History and Culture of Michigan's Native Americans* (1992); Walter Koelz, *Fishing Industry of the Great Lakes* (1926); Timothy C. Lloyd and Patrick B. Mullen, *Lake Erie Fishermen* (1990).

Michael J. Chiarappa
Western Michigan University

Shipping on the Great Lakes

The Great Lakes comprise Lakes Superior, Michigan, Huron, Erie, and Ontario, and the first four serve as the northern border of the Midwest. These inland seas make an impressive network that reaches approximately one thousand miles east to west—with the St. Lawrence Seaway adding more than another thousand miles–and have long served as a network for water transportation. Native peoples plied these waters for travel and trade.

Ships taking on ore, Port Calcite, Michigan. Environmental Protection Agency.

In the colonial era, the French and English built their fur-trading economies across the Great Lakes and demonstrated the potential of this resource as a transportation network. Initially, the French claimed the region based on the exploration of Jean Nicolet and others. Their dominance covered most of the region until the cessation of the Seven Years War in 1763, when the English gained control of the lakes and held it until the War of 1812.

In the early nineteenth century, grain, lumber, and humans constituted the bulk of cargo on the Great Lakes. Schooners and steamers hauled goods and passengers from the East to the Midwest. As settlers located along the northern Ohio border, Cleveland and Toledo became important wheat markets. Later, Michigan, Indiana, Wisconsin, and Minnesota developed cities reliant on the grain trade. The ports served as grain hubs, and Chicago became the center of the nation's grain trade. Steamers proved doubly valuable in their ability to handle cargo and hundreds of passengers. Ships brought tens of thousands of immigrants and contributed to the exchange of grain, furs, and other goods from the midwestern interior and the East. Passengers and freight went west, and typically raw material returned east.

By the 1850s, iron became a significant cargo. The principal harbors included Minnesota's Duluth and Two Harbors, Ashland in Wisconsin, and the Michigan cities of Marquette and Escanaba. Shipments began with a few barrels of ore from Marquette in 1852. When the Soo Locks opened in 1855, the first ore ship hauled 120 tons of iron for the Cleveland Iron Mining Company; in total, 1,447 tons of ore passed through the locks that year. By the end of the twentieth century, over 75 percent of the iron ore produced in the United States passed through the Soo Locks.

One characteristic of shipping on the Great Lakes has been the adaptability and innovation of shipbuilders. Steamboats and schooners established the Great Lakes ports of the Midwest. Schooners remained popular ships for hauling lumber, minerals, and grain after the American Civil War. These ships relied first on sail power, later on steam.

Schooners grew in size as navigation improved on the Great Lakes. By the 1850s, schooners approached 160 feet and could haul close to a thousand tons. By the early 1870s, after the St. Clair Flats north of Detroit was dredged, schooners topped two hundred feet in length and could haul over fifteen hundred tons of cargo.

In contrast to large schooners, smaller ships were used for short runs. In the 1870s, these vessels hauled lumber from ports such as Green Bay or Muskegon to Milwaukee. On the return trip, coastal schooners hauled general merchandise, grain, and meat. By the late nineteenth century, larger, more efficient steamships had largely replaced schooners.

A new era commenced when the bulk freighter debuted in 1869 with the 210-foot *Robert J. Hackett*. Most bulk freighters had masts and carried sails until the 1890s, and all had their pilothouses mounted forward to maximize visibility. By 1900, 500-foot freighters appeared, and most were built of steel. The innovation of the self-unloading freighter in 1908 with the launch of the *Wyandotte* foreshadowed the predominance of this technology.

Self-unloading freighters came into common use in the 1950s. Prior to that, ships were unloaded with a system called the Hulett Unloader. The steam-powered machine that Hulett perfected in 1899 employed a clamshell bucket, suspended from an oscillating beam, that could grab and unload 618 tons in an hour. By 1900, Hulett incorporated a ten-ton bucket, and in 1960, the capacity of a Hulett's bucket increased to twenty-three tons. The machines stood 92 feet tall and weighed 1,500 tons.

Today, self-unloaders have made Huletts obsolete. The ships can transport and unload almost any dry bulk commodity, including iron ore, limestone, and grain. A system of conveyors is built into the hull. Self-unloading freighters range in size from 500 to over 1,000 feet and can transport more than 70,000 tons per trip. The first 1,000-foot freighter was the *Stewart J. Cort* built in 1972. The *Cort* can carry 58,000 tons and is able to unload her cargo at a rate of 20,000 tons per hour.

Shipping on the Great Lakes occasionally proved dangerous. Perhaps the best known wreck, the *Edmund Fitzgerald*, overshadows the other ships that did not make it to port. The *Edmund Fitzgerald* went down in Lake Superior in over five hundred feet of water on November 10, 1975. Twenty-nine lives were lost, and though the Coast Guard investigation blamed the sinking on leaking hatches that allowed excessive amounts of water into the hold, no conclusive evidence explains what caused the ship to sink in extreme conditions. Sixty-four years previous, the Big Blow of November 1913 destroyed twenty Great Lakes vessels, damaged seventy-two more, and officially drowned 248 sailors, though more may have perished. In total, almost 5,000 ships are documented as total losses in the Great Lakes, with a human expense of almost 30,000 lives.

Shipping on the Midwest's four Great Lakes continues to play an important role in economic development and culture. Water levels have fluctuated over time, and when the lakes are low, ships must reduce their cargo by as much as 8 percent. The size of the individual lakes effects navigation, too. Lake Superior seldom freezes solid. Conversely, Lake Erie is the shallowest and smallest lake, and it freezes earlier but also warms quickly, allowing a return to navigation earlier in the spring. The ships that navigate the midwestern Great Lakes supply resources for the steel, iron, and automobile industries, haul stone, grain, and cement, and will sustain the midwestern shipping industry for generations.

Sources and Further Reading: Frederick Clever Bald, *The Sault Canal through 100 Years* (1954); James P. Barry, *Ships of the Great Lakes*, rev. ed. (1996); David G. Brown, *White Hurricane* (2002); Mary Dempsey, "The Witch of November," *Michigan History Magazine* 83 (Nov.–Dec. 1999); Christine Rohn Hilston, "Hulett's Mechanical Marvel," *Timeline* (Sept.–Oct. 1994; Theodore J. Karamanski, *Schooner Passage* (2000); Frank E. Kirby and A.P. Rankin, "The Bulk Freighter of the Great Lakes," *Inland Seas* 34 (Fall 1978); T.A. Sykora, "A New Era in Great Lakes Transportation" *Inland Seas* 28 (Summer 1972).

Leo E. Landis
Henry Ford Museum and Greenfield Village,
Dearborn, Michigan

Shipwrecks on the Great Lakes

With the possible exception of the coast of Great Britain, no body of water has been more hazardous to ships and seamen than the Great Lakes. While the exact number of wrecks and thousands of sailors who have died are unknown because careful records were not kept before 1936, an examination of the data suggests that the number of accidents on the Great Lakes could exceed 25,000 in the 350 years of shipping, with 3,500 to 5,000 of them being considered major enough to result in shipwrecks. At times in its history, travel on the Great Lakes to the Midwest was exceedingly risky. In 1871, of the 2,475 vessels navigating the waters, for example, 25 percent were involved in accidents.

Yet what is most interesting about the history of shipwrecks is how Great Lakes officials learned from the calamities and took steps to avert them in the future until, at present, there has not been a shipwreck on the Great Lakes since 1990, when the tanker *Jupiter* burned in a gas explosion. The last ship to sink was the *Edmund Fitzgerald*, made famous by folk singer Gordon Lightfoot, which disappeared in 1975 with its twenty-nine-member crew. The last ship lost in a collision was the *Sidney E. Smith Jr.* in 1972, and not a single ship has run aground since the *Frontenac* in 1979. This record is outstanding considering that only 260 bulk freighters sunk in the oceans of the world during the last two decades of the twentieth century.

The first ship known to have sunk on the Great Lakes was the *Griffon* in 1679. The sixty-foot craft was loaded with fur pelts when it struck a sandbar in a violent storm in the Straits of Mackinac on Lake Huron. The first report of a shipwreck on Lake Superior was in 1816 when the schooner *Invincible* ran ashore near Whitefish Point in a storm; in fact, this region of Lake Superior has become known as the Graveyard of the Lakes for its treacherous waters. The *Hercules* and all its hands was the first victim of Lake Michigan in 1818.

In an era before sonar and radio, ships faced an incredible number of hazards from thick fogs, heavy rains, and the smoke from forest fires, which caused ships to run aground or collide with each other. The hazards of travel led to the establishment of lifesaving stations. Between 1876 and 1914, these stations assisted 9,763 ships and 55,639 people from ships that ran ashore. Since 1840, there have been over 200 major ship collisions and more than 9,000 minor accidents between vessels.

It was also not uncommon for fires to break out or boilers to explode. Roughly 14 percent of steamships in the United States experienced boiler explosions before Congress passed a number of safety regulations in 1838. Even after that, ships like the *Alaska* (1879), *E.M. Peck* (1913), and *Omar D. Conger* (1922) experienced accidents with their boilers. It was not until the 1960s, that technology improved enough to eliminate such incidents. Furthermore, fires often started from hot ash, sparks, cigarettes, kerosene lamps, and even arson. Of the ninety-six wooden ships built by two major shipyards on the Great Lakes between 1871 and 1907, 20 percent were destroyed by fire. Of the sixty-nine ships that experienced fires between 1920 and 1949, 64 percent had wooden hulls. Mandatory drills, governmental regulations, and iron and steel hulls have reduced fires on ships on the lakes.

Between 1846 and 1930, at least one ship foundered in a storm each year. A total of 1,077 ships are known to have been destroyed in storms on the lakes, with the loss of sailors and passengers estimated in the tens of thousands. In 1905 alone, fifty-nine ships went down. The month of November is particularly harsh. Sailors refer to the gales as "the curse of the eleventh month," and it has been estimated that one-third of all ships wrecked in storms occurred within those thirty days of the year.

The most famous shipwreck on the Great Lakes was the 729-foot steamer *Edmund Fitzgerald*, which disappeared on November 10, 1975, after encountering thirty-five-foot waves and gusts of one hundred miles an hour on Lake Superior. Shortly after 7 P.M., the *Fitzgerald* took her twenty-nine-member crew to the bottom in more than five hundred feet of water. The loss of the "Queen of the Lakes" has inspired numerous books and has become a cultural icon for maritime tragedy.

Although shipwrecks are exceedingly rare on the modern lakes, the legacy of these wrecks remains important to the Midwest. Because of its fresh water environment, shipwrecks on the Great Lakes are incredibly well preserved. With the location of more than two thousand of these ships known, a tourist diving industry has developed around these wrecks. Tales of ghost ships have delighted thousands of readers, and places like Great Lakes Shipwreck Museum at Whitefish Point, Michigan, and the Mariners' Church in Detroit draw tourists from all over the United States.

Sources and Further Reading: James Donahue, *Steaming Through Smoke and Fire* (1997); Karl E. Heden, *The Great Lakes Guide to Sunken Ships* (1993); Wes Olezewski, *Ghost Ships, Gales and Forgotten Tales* (1996); Wes Olezewski, *Sounds of Disaster* (1993); William Ratigan, *Great Lakes Shipwrecks and Survivals* (1960); Mark L. Thompson, *Graveyard of the Lakes* (2000).

T. Jason Soderstrum
Iowa State University

S.S. Edmund Fitzgerald

Sometime after 7:00 P.M. on November 10, 1975, the *S.S. Edmund Fitzgerald* mysteriously sank in the icy waters of Lake Superior. Although only one of approximately 6,000 shipwrecks on the Great Lakes, the disappearance of the boat known as the *Fitz* captured the attention of the nation because of the mysterious circumstances under which it went down.

At the time it was built in 1958, the *Edmund Fitzgerald* was the biggest ship to sail fresh water and remained the largest vessel to sail the Great Lakes until 1971. The 729-foot freighter weighed 13,632 tons, and its engines generated 7,000 horsepower. Named after the president of Northwestern Mutual Insurance, the company built the freighter to ship processed iron ore. The company spent $8 million to build the *Fitz*, which in turn brought pride and financial rewards to the company. It broke a variety of shipping records for the amount of ore it carried.

Prior to leaving dock in Superior, Wisconsin, the *Edmund Fitzgerald* had been inspected and loaded with 26,000 tons of ore in the form of taconite pellets destined for Detroit, Michigan. It also carried lifeboats and preservers for more than the twenty-nine crew members and was equipped with the necessary communication and radar systems, including backup systems.

Deemed seaworthy by the inspector, the ship departed on November 9 with clear weather, although a storm was moving northeast from the Oklahoma Panhandle. Sailors experienced many severe storms on Lake Superior, yet in November cold arctic winds could collide with warm southern winds to create even more dangerous conditions. The *Edmund Fitzgerald* was not alone on the lake. The *Arthur M. Anderson* followed the *Fitz* during much of the storm. At the height of the storm, winds reached an estimated seventy miles per hour, and ten- to thirty-foot waves battered the ships. Unlike the *Anderson*, however, the *Edmund Fitzgerald* began taking on water soon after the storm hit the lake on November 10. Later the *Fitz* lost both main and backup radar systems. Visibility was low due to the storm, so the crew of the *Anderson* followed to aid the *Fitz*'s crew. Ernest McSorley, the captain of the *Fitz*, radioed that his ship was taking on more water, but he did not seem panicked. Yet within a few hours, McSorley's ship dropped off the *Anderson*'s radar.

Despite the storm, the Coast Guard initiated a search effort immediately, turning up no sign of the ship. A series of investigations starting that November and continuing until 1995 led investigators to a site near Whitefish Bay, Michigan. The Coast Guard and the National Transportation Safety Board both postulated that the *Fitz* took on water through the hatches. Advocates of another theory argue that a wave phenomenon called the Three Sisters, or three big seas, pummeled the freighter in three successive waves with ten million pounds of water; considering that the ship already had fifty-two million pounds of cargo and had been taking on water, the *Fitz* could not withstand the weight of the Three Sisters. Although research dives have provided more data about the condition of the ship, the cause of the wreck has not been definitively determined.

Investigators have determined, however, that the freighter probably went down too fast for the crew to escape, and they may have remained trapped alive in a pocket of air. Even if they had been able to access rescue boats, their survival was unlikely since Lake Superior is the coldest of the Great Lakes. The water rarely gets above 40 degrees Fahrenheit, even in the summer. The combination of storms and cold water make surviving a shipwreck on the lake nearly impossible. The families of the twenty-nine crew members requested that the 1995 effort to recover the bell of the ship be the last trip to the *Edmund Fitzgerald* and that the area be considered a cemetery.

The sinking of the *Fitz* fascinated people at the time and for the next two decades. The manner of its disappearance, the reasons for its sinking, and the lack of witnesses and survivors have shrouded the event with mystery. In 1976, singer Gordon Lightfoot memorialized the ship in a ballad, "The Wreck of the Edmund Fitzgerald," and since then numerous books and documentaries have been produced. The sustained interest in the causes led to the use of the latest underwater technology as it came available.

Sources and Further Reading: Hugh E. Bishop, *The Night the Fitz Went Down* (2000); Andrew Kantar, *29 Missing* (1998); Joseph MacInnis, *Fitzgerald's Storm* (1998); Frederick Stonehouse, *The Wreck of the Edmund Fitzgerald* (1977).

Alexandra Kindell
Iowa State University

St. Lawrence Seaway

Extending from the Atlantic Ocean to Duluth, Minnesota, on Lake Superior, a distance of 2,342 miles, this waterway provides large oceangoing vessels access to important markets in and exports from the Midwest. Known as "the fourth coast," it includes approximately 95 thousand square miles of navigable water,

approximately sixty miles of canals, fifteen locks, and three dams. Almost 50 percent of the traffic using the seaway travels to and from overseas ports, particularly Europe, the Middle East, and Africa, providing the heartland with opportunities previously unknown. On average, fifty million tons of cargo a year is shipped through the seaway, and since 1959, more than two billion tons of freight valued at $300 billion have made ports such as Cleveland, Toledo, Detroit, Chicago, Milwaukee, Buffalo, and Duluth invaluable to the economy of the region. It is the cheapest means of transporting grains, minerals, coal, and other manufactured products such as automobiles and steel.

This complex system of locks and canals linking the Great Lakes to the Atlantic officially opened in 1959, but its inception dates back to the fur trade of the seventeenth century. Yet it wasn't until 1932 that Canada and the United States signed the St. Lawrence Deep Waterway Treaty (the Hoover-Bennett Treaty), in which construction of the seaway was agreed to.

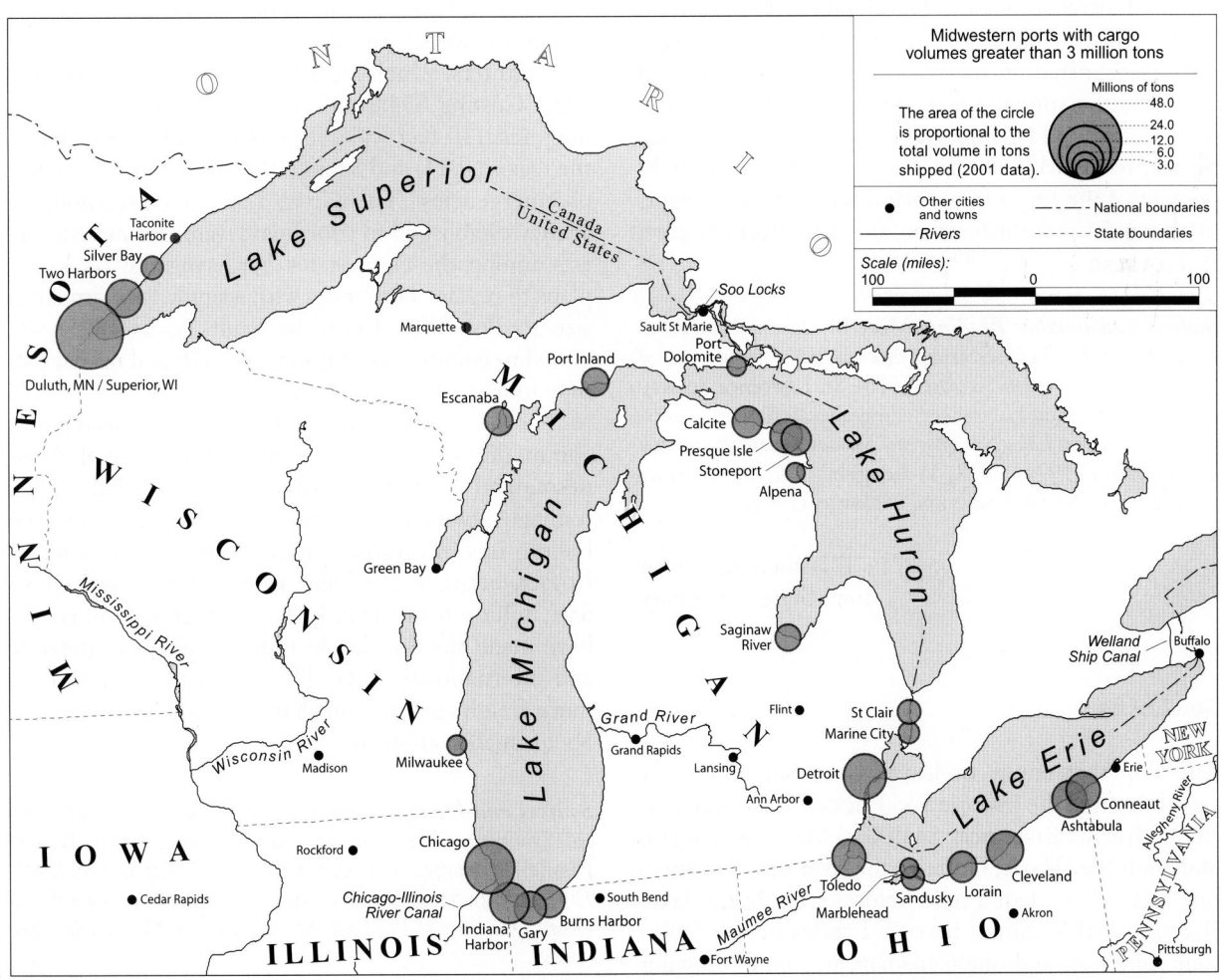

St. Lawrence Seaway system in the Great Lakes. Prepared by James DeGrand. *Source:* Army Corps of Engineers—Institute for Water Resources, *Waterborne Commerce of the United States, Calendar Year 2001: Part 3 Waterways and Harbors, Great Lakes,* Document no. IWR-WCUS-01-3.

World War II and the influences of rail and private industry delayed the project until 1954, when the demand for transport of steel and coal and a new Eisenhower administration led to the signing of the Wiley-Donderro Act, which authorized construction to begin. Over the next five years, to increase the depth of the channel to twenty-seven feet with fifteen locks, more than 252 million cubic yards of earth was moved, and more than 7.4 million cubic yards of concrete poured. Each lock had to be at least 765 feet in length and 80 feet in width. Along with this mammoth building effort, 6,500 people and 550 homes had to be moved from the 40,000 acres of farmland that were flooded. On April 25, 1959, at a cost of $470 million dollars (of which the United States paid $133.8 million and Canada the remainder), the St. Lawrence Seaway opened. President Eisenhower and Queen Elizabeth II dedicated the seaway in a ceremony on June 26, 1959.

The canals and locks are operated and maintained by the St. Lawrence Seaway Authority in Canada and the St. Lawrence Seaway Development Corporation in the United States. Twenty million tons of freight were transported on the seaway in the first year, and by 1973, the tonnage had increased to fifty million tons annually. The importance of the St. Lawrence Seaway to the Midwest can be seen in the fact that 40 percent of the cargo transported is agricultural crops, of which 50 percent is wheat and 30 percent is corn and soybeans.

Sources and Further Reading: Mary Blocksma, *The Fourth Coast* (1995); Jacques LesStrang, *Seaway: The Untold Story of North America's Fourth Seacoast* (1976); St. Lawrence Seaway Authority and Saint Lawrence Seaway Development Corporation, *The Great Lakes St. Lawrence Seaway System: Handbook and Directory* (1997); W. R. Willoughby, *The St. Lawrence Waterway: A Study in Politics and Diplomacy* (1961).

T. Jason Soderstrum
Iowa State University

Soo Locks

Any ship that enters or leaves Lake Superior must travel through the historic Soo Locks. Constructed on the St. Mary's River near Sault Ste. Marie, Michigan, and Sault Ste. Marie, Ontario, the river drops twenty-one feet in less than a mile before entering the lake. Because of this natural barrier, a series of five locks, four American and one Canadian, was built allowing ships to avoid St. Mary's Falls. They are the busiest locks in the world.

With early European trade in the Northwest Terri-

tory increasing, traders found themselves constricted by the expense and time involved in loading and unloading boats at the rapids to get to Lake Superior. In 1852, Congress granted 750,000 acres of public land to the State of Michigan to compensate any company that the state could find willing to take up the project of designing and constructing a system of locks. Because of its extensive mining interests in the Upper Peninsula, the Fairbanks Scale Company undertook construction in 1853. On May 31, 1855, Fairbanks turned over the two locks to the state. The steamer *Illinois* passed through the locks on June 22, the first ship to have an unobstructed path between Lakes Superior and Huron. In 1881, because increased traffic required new locks to be built, Michigan turned the locks over to the United States government, which placed them under the jurisdiction of the U.S. Army Corps of Engineers.

Presently, the canal system includes four locks. The MacArthur Lock was completed on July 11, 1943, at a cost of $12.7 million and updated in 2000; it is 800 feet long and 80 feet wide. The Poe Lock, the longest lock in the world, was designed to handle the large superfreighters, which are 1,000 feet long and 100 feet wide. Costing $34.8 million in 1969, it is 1,200 feet long and 110 feet wide. Two older and smaller locks, the Davis (1914) and Sabin (1919), are available in case of emergencies. The Great Lakes Commission, an agency established to coordinate water resource interests among the eight states bordering the lakes, has plans to replace both locks with a single lock similar in size to Poe. The Canadian Sault Lock (1895) was closed to commercial shipping in 1978 and now serves only tourist and recreational interests.

The Soo Locks play a vital role in the movement of commodities through the upper Midwest, with Minnesota and Michigan accounting for over half of the tonnage moving through the locks. Through 1997, 8.4 billion tons of cargo has moved through these locks. In fact, between 1987 and 1996, a yearly average of 85.5 million tons—mainly iron ore, grain, and coal—have made the Soo Locks indispensable to interstate and international trade. This series of locks handles more freight per annum than the Panama, Suez, and Kiel Canals combined.

Sources and Further Reading: Brian S. Osborne and Donald Swainson, *The Sault Ste. Marie Canal* (1986); Robert Passfiel, *Technology in Transition: The 'Soo' Ship Canal, 1889–1985* (1989); U.S. Army Corps of Engineers, *General and Detail Drawings of Poe Lock, St. Mary's Falls Canal, Michigan* (1909).

T. Jason Soderstrum
Iowa State University

Canals

Throughout the Midwest, in varying stages of decay and abandonment, are the landscape constructions that once formed the heart of a mid-nineteenth-century canal system. Unlike the nostalgic rundown barns and mills that are recognizable symbols of the region's past and vanishing present, midwestern canals often appear as crumbling masonry and grown-over ditches, representing a bygone era whose importance is less known. The Midwest's canal era is usually overshadowed by New York's illustrious Erie Canal or by the rise of railroads to dominance by the 1850s. Yet efforts to preserve and interpret canals have revealed an interconnected history of water, people, and place that included vigorous politics, mixed economic results, impressive technology, social adaptations, and regional development. Locks, aqueducts, Irish laborers, expectant farmers and merchants, and canal boats were once familiar midwestern features.

As of 1815, the state of transportation was abysmal in the territory northwest of the Ohio River, from which would emerge the Midwest states of Ohio, Indiana, Michigan, Illinois, and Wisconsin. Both the potential and the problem of western inland waterways occupied statesmen like George Washington. If, as Washington believed, the key to America's future greatness lay in the ability of the West's prospective farmers to engage in commerce and to move their products to market, then canals and other internal improvements had to be constructed. But the politics of economic development, especially concerning federal funding, became a hotly debated constitutional issue. President James Madison's veto of the 1817 Bonus Bill essentially shifted the burden of funding to the states.

While New York's Erie Canal promoters moved ahead, state-level initiatives for canals in the Midwest were continually frustrated. Self-interested biases stymied state assemblies with ambitious designs, fierce localism, political and personal greed, railroad proponents, and miscalculations in time and money. Meanwhile the Erie Canal's immediate success and the sight of steamboats on western rivers intensified the Midwest's canal mania and led to fiscally and conceptually reckless decisions. Ohio did well in following New York's lead. Funded by general bonds sales and backed by state taxes and exceptional credit, Ohio launched the West's first major public works program in 1825.

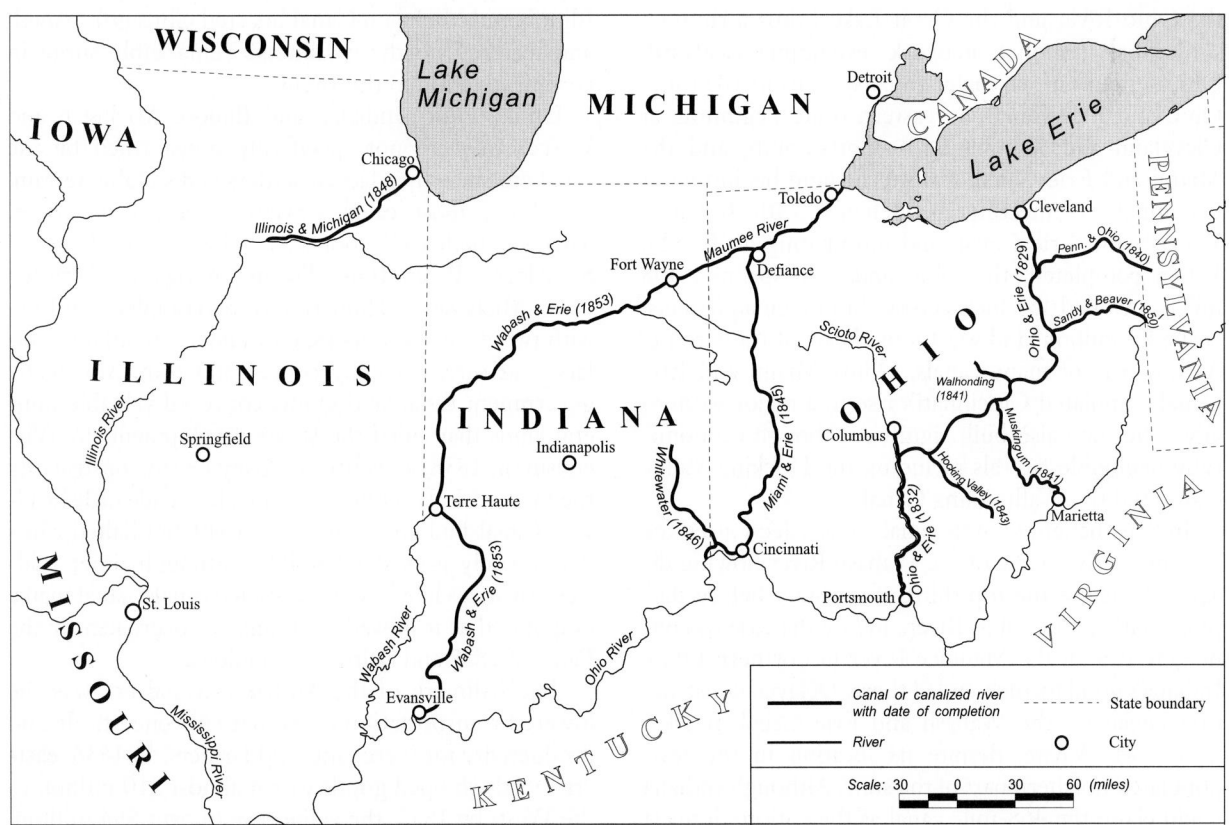

Midwestern canal network, c. 1850. Prepared by James DeGrand. *Source:* Ronald E. Shaw, *Canals for a Nation: The Canal Era in the United States, 1790–1860* (Lexington: University Press of Kentucky, 1990).

Ohio's 1837 Loan Law allowed public funds to be loaned to private investors interested in public works, and other states adopted this form of mixed enterprise, particularly after that year's Panic.

Conversely, Indiana's canal financing wavered disastrously. Following poor proceeds from early canal land sales in 1830, the state approved loans and bond sales beginning in 1832, culminating in a $10 million loan to finance its "Mammoth System" in 1836. This incredibly ambitious program called for the simultaneous construction of major canals, a railroad, a state road, and additional surveys, but afforded no fiscal protection from the Panic of 1837. Several years later, Indiana became insolvent, and the state debt approached $15 million. Illinois initially followed Indiana's lead in canal funding and planning, with similarly ruinous results. More sparsely settled Michigan and Wisconsin were less affected by the region's canal mania, yet all these states benefited from the 4.5 million acres in state and federal canal land grants, one of which paid for most of the Illinois and Michigan Canal.

Keenly aware of the advantages, canal promoters pushed for a route through their own locales. Location was central to midwesterners and was, as the Cincinnati *Gazette* reported in 1824, "a question of greatly more importance to us . . . than who shall be President." Most midwestern canals connected with the Ohio River and the Great Lakes, thus forming a substantial regional network extending eastward. Ohio settled on two major canal systems in 1825: the Ohio and Erie Canal, an eastern route beginning at Cleveland and terminating at Portsmouth, and the Miami and Erie Canal, a western route beginning at Cincinnati, connecting at Defiance with Indiana's Wabash and Erie Canal, and terminating at Toledo. When completed, the Ohio and Erie spanned 308 miles, included 151 locks, crossed fourteen aqueducts, cost $4.3 million, and was Ohio's heaviest trade route. As was true of many canals, Ohio's Miami and Erie Canal stimulated Cincinnati's rise to a major western city. The state also built significant though economically negligible laterals including the Hocking Valley Canal and the Walhonding Canal.

Indiana benefited in its canal route selection by the southwesterly course of the Wabash River flowing diagonally across the top third of the state before dipping south to the Ohio River, and by the ease of connecting it with the Maumee River in northern Ohio. Indiana's good fortune ended there. Delayed construction began on the Wabash and Erie Canal in 1832 near Fort Wayne, despite its location in the less-populated northern part of the state. Although Indiana could claim the 468-mile canal as the nation's longest when completed in 1853, it had been forced to surmount labor problems, acute financial distress after the Panic of 1837, inconsistent forward progress, and low toll receipts. Nonetheless, Evansville became a major river port, receiving millions of pounds of bacon, pork, lard, and tobacco, and over 250 thousand bushels of wheat between 1853 and 1859. The state's Whitewater Canal, with its fifty-six locks and seven feeder dams, served the more populous southeastern part of the state, and the Central Canal was routed through Indianapolis but saw little construction.

Canal building in Illinois, Wisconsin, and Michigan represented the potential and the limits of the Midwest's canal era. Illinois's experience resembled Indiana's. The major Illinois River route ran diagonally from Lake Michigan in the north to the Mississippi River at the western edge of the state. The vital ninety-six-mile Illinois and Michigan Canal, beginning at Chicago and terminating at LaSalle, commenced construction in 1836. As was typical of the Midwest's canal era, the Panic of 1837 hit state canal projects hard, wrecking plans, halting construction, collapsing the state bank in 1842, and nearly bankrupting Illinois. Finally, Congressman Abraham Lincoln announced the completion of the Illinois and Michigan, the state's only major canal, to the House of Representatives in 1848. The canal comprised fifteen locks and four aqueducts, for a cost of $6.4 million. Especially consequential to regional development, the Illinois and Michigan Canal boosted Chicago's growth and fostered northern Illinois's remarkable surge in corn production in the 1850s.

Unlike Ohio, Indiana, and Illinois, Michigan and Wisconsin were not specifically transformed by the canal era since they lacked settlers and suitable terrain. For both, most canal surveys remained on paper. Michigan built a 350-foot canal to bypass the falls of the St. Mary's River, thus allowing navigation between Lakes Michigan and Superior. It was completed in 1855 with two deep-water locks, cost under one million dollars, and carried chiefly copper and iron. Michigan's government canal land grants conveyed valuable mineral lands that aided the state's development. In Wisconsin, in 1838, a private company began constructing the Wisconsin River portage canal but made little headway. Canal-building resumed in 1849, but halted when it ultimately proved unfeasible. Although other midwestern states like Iowa constructed canals, canal mania evaporated as it moved west and was overtaken by the Panic of 1837 and railroad technology.

The hallmark of the Midwest's canal era was the lowered transportation costs that enlivened trade and productivity for merchants and farmers. In 1836, eastern canals shipped goods worth almost $10 million to the West; by 1853, the value rose to over $94 million. For farmers the changes wrought by the canal era were even more profound. Traveling on Indiana's

Wabash and Erie Canal in 1843, it struck Charles H. Titus that "A new day has now dawned upon the agriculturist of this region." Canals served as ready markets with good prices. Titus noted that corn sold locally for ten cents a bushel, but went fast on the canal for thirty-seven and a half cents a bushel. In linking to eastern markets, Midwest canals formed the arteries of trade in the market revolution.

Ronald E. Shaw compares canals to mechanical structures of both simple and complex design. Basic canal dimensions included a twenty-six-foot-wide bed that was forty feet wide at the waterline, with a depth of four feet. Brush was grubbed twenty feet on both sides at surface level to reduce canal hazards. On the river side, a ten-foot-wide towpath was cut for the mule driver. Because canal boats had to haul the maximum amount of tonnage or passengers with the least amount of tractive resistance, they had flat bottoms, curved hulls, and ranged from seventy to eighty feet long and fourteen feet wide. The cabins housed the captain and his family, the crew, and the spare mule team. Line boats were modified freight boats, with a covered cargo hold and built-up sides with shuttered windows, that could transport bulk grain or immigrant passengers. Passenger packets carried from fifty to seventy-five passengers, traveled around the clock, and were characterized by a long, low cabin with an upper, open deck that required travelers to beware low bridges. A typical fare of two cents a mile included meals and modest lodging.

Much of the complex technology in expertise and labor originated in the East and was adapted to the Midwest. Many former Erie Canal engineers came west, including Benjamin Wright, the Erie's original chief engineer who advised the Illinois and Michigan Canal, and James Geddes, who was taught by Wright and then worked on the Ohio and Erie Canal. Others like Jesse L. Williams began as a surveyor on the Ohio and Erie Canal and by age twenty-four was chief engineer on Indiana's Wabash and Erie Canal. Engineers encountered numerous environmental, financial, and labor challenges. The crucial requirement that canals be grade-free led to the construction of several remarkable locks and aqueducts. A lock functions like a water elevator. The watertight chamber was cut out parallel to the canal and was built at intervals for the purpose of raising or lowering boats to meet the next water level. Locks and other engineering marvels adeptly maneuvered boats to Ohio's Akron, Licking, and Loramie summits, and facilitated Indiana's Whitewater Canal's five-hundred-foot climb in fifty miles. Similarly impressive stone arched aqueducts, such as the Whitewater's Duck Creek aqueduct, were constructed to maintain a steady water level as canals crossed rivers and streams.

A labor force of mainly Irish and German migrants from the East and local farmers achieved engineers' designs. Wages varied by skill, and most laborers received room and board, although poor living and dangerous working conditions were standard. Simple shanties housed about twenty men, and those with families lived in huts. Endless digging and grubbing consumed the men, as did mosquitoes and whiskey allotments. Many labored deep in mud since large portions of these canals ran through marshes. During the 1830s, sporadic armed conflict erupted, often linked to rival Irish factions. Perhaps most insidious was the laborers' susceptibility to malaria and cholera outbreaks. In 1838, malaria claimed as many as one thousand men on the Illinois and Michigan, and an 1852 cholera epidemic devastated Wabash and Erie laborers.

Laboring conditions were deadly, but canals nonetheless brought life to many midwestern communities. Canal traffic created busy ports and infused urban centers like Cincinnati and Cleveland. Wharves and warehouses formed part of a new canal culture, as did canal activities, innovations, and customs. For example, people organized canal celebrations, usually on the Fourth of July. Communities used the new waterways for swimming, ice skating, and wedding party boats. Canals also diminished remoteness by serving as novel mediums for popular culture. Floating libraries, museums, bookstores, even circus boats stopped at canal towns. A protocol in boat customs emerged as well. Boat speed was not to exceed four to ten miles per hour (but often did) to control bank erosion, and right-of-way was bestowed upon downward traffic.

By the 1850s, railroads were becoming the most efficient transportation. Canals, however, had done much to shape the Midwest's economic and social activities, serving as conduits for migration, agricultural expansion, shipping, travel, and especially, regional development.

Sources and Further Reading: R. Carlyle Buley, *The Old Northwest Pioneer Period, 1815–1840*, 2 vols. (1950); George P. Clark, "Through Indiana by Stagecoach and Canal Boat," *Indiana Magazine of History* 85 (Sept. 1989); Jack Gieck, *A Photo Album of Ohio's Canal Era, 1825–1913* (1992); John Lauritz Larson, *Internal Improvement: National Public Works and the Promise of Popular Government in the Early United States* (2001); Alan I. Marcus and Howard P. Segal, *Technology in America: A Brief History*, 2nd ed. (1999); Peter S. Onuf, "Liberty, Development, and Union," *William and Mary Quarterly*, 3rd ser., 43 (Apr. 1986); Harry N. Scheiber, *Ohio Canal Era* (1969); Ronald E. Shaw, *Canals for a Nation* (1990); George Rogers Taylor, *The Transportation Revolution, 1815–1860* (1951); Peter Way, *Common Labour* (1993).

Ginette Aley
Iowa State University

Ohio Canals

After the defeat of the Shawnee and their British allies in the War of 1812, the most pressing problem facing Ohioans was the state's isolation. Farmers had to ship their goods either down the Ohio and Mississippi Rivers on flatboats to New Orleans, where they could be loaded onto oceangoing ships, or across the Appalachian Mountains over primitive roads and trails. Both routes were long, arduous, dangerous, and expensive. Ohioans were also isolated from each other. Many early Ohio leaders feared that the isolation of individual communities prevented the cohesion necessary for republican government. They warned that each section of the state would work for its own interest rather than the common good.

To remedy this isolation, many early Ohio leaders urged the state to embark on a program of internal improvements, especially a canal linking the Ohio River to Lake Erie. By allowing Ohio producers to ship goods inexpensively to the east via New York's recently started Erie Canal and linking sparsely populated northern Ohio with the more populous Miami, Scioto, and Muskingum Valleys, such a canal would, according to Governor Ethan Allen Brown, become the "veins and arteries to the body politic" providing "supplies, health, vigor and animation" to the state.

Brown's 1818 proposal that the state study building a Ohio-to-Erie canal met with hostility. Some argued that Ohio lacked the financial resources for such an undertaking. Others felt that the national government should bear responsibility for internal improvements. The proposal also aroused sectional jealousies as legislators sought to ensure that any canal would pass through their communities. In 1820, the legislature authorized the survey of possible routes, but only if Congress gave Ohio land to pay for construction. When Congress did not act, the survey was canceled.

Realizing that toll revenue would be enough to repay construction loans, the legislature in 1822 created a commission to study possible routes. Commission members included some of Ohio's most experienced political leaders: Brown, now a U.S. Senator, Thomas Worthington, Alfred Kelly, Ebenezer Buckingham, Benjamin Tappan, Isaac Minor, and Jeremiah Morrow. Route selection proved to be difficult; each section of the state wanted the canal routed through its area and threatened to withhold support if it did not. Commissioners believed that they could build the political support for a route that followed the Scioto and Sandusky Rivers through the center of the state, but the route did not have enough water. This presented political problems. Bypassing the politically powerful Scioto Valley could threaten legislative approval. Running the canal through the Muskingum–Cuyahoga corridor would anger those along the Miami–Maumee corridor and vice versa. The commission solved these dilemmas by proposing not one but two canals at a cost of $3 million. The 308-mile long Ohio and Erie Canal would follow the Cuyahoga to the Tuscarawas and Muskingum; north of Zanesville the route would turn west, meeting up with the Scioto just south of Columbus. Lower Muskingum residents were promised that the river would be canalized. The plan also called for the creation of Buckeye and Summit Lakes to ensure adequate water. The 66-mile-long Miami Canal would follow the Miami Valley from Cincinnati to Dayton with assurances that it would be extended north to Lake Erie via the Auglaize and Maumee Valleys.

On February 4, 1825, the General Assembly passed the bill authorizing construction. To secure passage, legislators made several deals: improvement of the Sandusky–Columbus road, internal improvements for eastern Ohio, and increased aid for public education. With the success of New York's Erie Canal and Ohio's small debt, the state easily sold construction bonds at advantageous rates. Construction of the canal project began on July 4, 1825, with a ceremony near Newark. Contractors, many of whom had worked on the Erie Canal, followed the same specifications here: The depth would be four feet and the width would be forty feet at the waterline and twenty-six feet at the base. Work began at Lake Erie and moved southward, opening up the lake to the interior and allowing the collection of tolls. Construction fueled Ohio's economy. Payment to contractors, laborers, and for land injected much-needed currency into the economy. Construction proceeded smoothly with both canals completed on schedule, the Miami in 1829 and the Ohio and Erie in 1832. At $4.3 million, the final cost was far more than expected.

The canals proved to be a boon for the state. Canal boats—sixty feet long, fifteen feet wide, and capable of carrying sixty tons—provided cheap transportation for the state's producers and consumers. Along the canals new towns sprang up, the price of agricultural goods increased, and the cost of land rose. The canals also helped end Ohio's isolation and convince its residents that they were an integral part of the nation. Calls for additional canals began before completion of the Ohio and Erie and Miami Canals. The federal government even granted the state 500,000 acres in northwest Ohio to pay for the extension of the Miami Canal to Lake Erie, which was completed in 1845. The late 1830s witnessed the start of over a dozen new canals, extensions, and feeders connecting more remote locations to established canals. The state financed some of these, while local governments or private concerns funded others. By 1850, Ohio had more than a thousand miles of canals.

Ohio's canal boom came to an end in the 1850s as enthusiasm for railroad building reached a fever pitch. In 1850, the state had 323 miles of track and by the end of the decade, 2,635 miles. Unable to compete with the faster and less-water-bound railroads, many canals went bankrupt in the 1850s, leaving the state saddled with debt. Portions of the Ohio and Erie continued to operate profitably, shipping bulky goods like corn, coal, and iron ore, until the flood of 1913 destroyed the locks.

Sources and Further Reading: Andrew R.L. Cayton, *The Frontier Republic* (1986); H. Roger Grant, *Ohio on the Move* (2000); Harry N. Scheiber, *Ohio Canal Era* (1969); John S. Still, "Ethan Allen Brown and Ohio's Canal System" *Ohio History* 66 (Jan. 1957).

Michael Pierce
University of Arkansas

Indiana Canals

Although largely overlooked in the contemporary landscape, Indiana's canals provide a useful index to the state's political economy during the first half of the nineteenth century. Following the War of 1812, as European American settlers began to move inland from those few towns that had been established along the northern bank of the Ohio River, the dearth of navigable streams in the state's interior became apparent. Roads were few and often impassible during inclement weather. One of the first remedies that members of the pioneering generation seized upon was inspired by New York's prosperous Erie Canal, which demonstrated what could be accomplished through the right combination of visionary political leadership, popular will, and prudent capitalization. That winning formula, however, proved elusive in Indiana, especially following the Panics of 1837 and 1839. Because the General Assembly had borrowed heavily to finance an ambitious internal improvements program ($10 million at 5 percent interest during a time when annual revenue averaged $75,000), the state faced insolvency by the end of its third decade and its projected system of canals, roads, and rail lines was left largely uncompleted.

The first enterprise to complete and operate an engineered waterway in Indiana was the Whitewater Canal Company, which was incorporated in 1826 to provide a more efficient artery of transportation for the southeast, then the state's most populous district. Although it would take ten years and the backing of the General Assembly before construction commenced, in that same span of time, the Whitewater

Canal had connected Lawrenceburg on the Ohio with Hagerstown on the National Road, seventy-six miles distant; an extension financed by Cincinnati investors added their city as a terminus by 1843. At 468 miles, the longest canal to be constructed in the nation during this period was the Wabash and Erie (1832–1853), which connected Toledo on Lake Erie with the Ohio River port of Evansville. The canal was completed to Peru on the Wabash by 1837. Progress on the Wabash and Erie Canal encouraged the General Assembly to authorize a survey of the Whitewater Canal in 1834, which in turn led legislators to finance its construction through the Internal Improvements Act of 1836.

This would prove to be the most important and far-reaching state legislation of the century, proposing as it did the construction of basic transportation infrastructure to every part of Indiana. Canals came first: $3.5 million for a proposed Central Canal to link the Wabash and Erie Canal near Peru with the capital at Indianapolis and from there to Evansville; $1.4 million for the Whitewater Canal, enabling its construction to begin; and $1.3 million for the Wabash and Erie to extend it from Lafayette to Terre Haute, with another $50 thousand to remove obstructions from the Wabash River. Finally, a survey was authorized for either a canal or a railroad between Fort Wayne and Michigan City, although no funds were appropriated for this purpose. A total of $10 million in bonds were sold by a Board of Fund Commissioners to finance the canal and road system, to be supervised by a six-member Board of Improvements.

What came to be called the Mammoth Internal Improvements Act was immediately beset by intractable problems, chief among them the financial panics and ensuing depression of the late 1830s. The state defaulted on its loan payments, and work ground to a halt on all of the construction projects by 1839. The projects themselves were as poorly executed as they were broadly conceived. Contracts had been let on segments of the canals, roads, and railroad, and construction commenced in a piecemeal fashion with the intent of guaranteeing a more expedient and widespread distribution of expenditures throughout the state. Five years into this undertaking, a total of ninety miles had been added to the Wabash and Erie Canal, while thirty miles of the Whitewater Canal and nine miles of the Central Canal had been dug. Another three hundred miles of canal or roadwork had been started but remained unfinished.

By 1841, state officials were forced to concede that they could pay neither interest nor principal on the debt. New York and London creditors hired attorney Charles Butler to negotiate a repayment plan. The resulting Butler Bill of 1847 held the state responsible for paying half of its debt, then calculated at over $11 million. The remaining debt was to be assumed by the bondholders, who were in turn issued stock in the Wabash and Erie Canal. This settlement also obligated the bondholders to complete the canal to Evansville, a commitment that was secured only through the receipt of a sizable land grant by the federal government. Ultimately, the state made good on its portion of the debt, even as its former creditors suffered sizable losses on their Wabash and Erie Canal investment. By this time, Indiana's canal fever had subsided. Privately financed rail lines and public roads built during the second half of the century fulfilled the earlier dream of a reliable transportation network that crisscrossed the state.

Despite the failure of the system of 1836, Indiana canals for a time helped expand the state's economy while decreasing its isolation. At its peak during the 1850s, the Wabash and Erie Canal contributed to Evansville's growth as a river port and carried an enormous quantity of commodities, livestock, raw materials, and manufactured items. The eastern terminus of that same canal saw equally voluminous quantities of corn, wheat, and flour carried from the state's northern interior to the Great Lakes port of Toledo. Employment opportunities attracted thousands of canal workers from elsewhere in the nation and the world, notable among them the Irish. They began arriving in significant numbers in 1832, when construction commenced on the Wabash and Erie Canal at Fort Wayne. By the time that canal was completed in 1853, Irish immigrants represented the second-largest group of foreign-born citizens in the state.

Sources and Further Reading: "Canal Construction in Indiana," *The Indiana Historian* (Sept. 1997); "Canal Mania in Indiana," *The Indiana Historian* (June 1997); Logan Esarey, *Internal Improvements in Early Indiana* (1912); Paul Fatout, *Indiana Canals* (1972); Ralph D. Gray, "The Canal Era in Indiana," in Indiana Historical Society, *Transportation and the Early Nation* (1982); Ronald E. Shaw, "The Canals of the Old Northwest," in *Canals for a Nation* (1990); Peter Way, *Common Labour: Workers and the Digging of North American Canals 1780–1860* (1993).

Michael William Doyle
Ball State University, Indiana

Illinois Canals

As early as 1673, French explorer Louis Joliet envisioned a prosperous trade waterway that would connect Lake Michigan and the Illinois River to the Mississippi River. Certainly American Fur Company traders in 1818 demonstrated the hardships associated with travel and commerce without one, as they spent three weeks heaving their goods and slogging through deep mud, tall grass, bloodsuckers, and mosquitoes. Thirty years later with the opening of Illinois's only major canal, the Illinois and Michigan, the once treacherous journey between Chicago, LaSalle, and Peru was now done in about twenty hours on a horse-drawn boat moving at five miles per hour. Some public officials, such as Secretary of War John C. Calhoun in 1819, argued that the canal was militarily necessary. Yet, the Illinois and Michigan Canal's great achievement lay in inaugurating the state's transportation, agricultural, and industrial revolutions, while boosting Chicago's development into the region's leading commercial center.

After several false starts, Illinois, a state since 1818, settled on a canal commission in 1835 and embarked upon its troubled though ultimately successful canal-building program. Generous proceeds from the speculative land sales in Chicago and those generated by the sale of government canal land grants, along with loans from New York investors, enabled the Illinois and Michigan's groundbreaking in Bridgeport on July 4, 1836. As in other midwestern states, however, Illinois's internal improvement projects were overly ambitious and were hit hard the next year by the financial Panic of 1837. Canal work ceased in 1840 when workers could not be paid, and two years later, the state bank's failure nearly bankrupted Illinois. The state resolved its financial reversals, adding a state tax, and completed the canal in 1848. In its first year, the Illinois and Michigan collected $88 thousand in tolls, licensed 162 boats, and began transporting more than two million bushels of grain through Chicago. By 1871, tolls and canal land sales had paid off the canal debt.

The Illinois and Michigan transformed a portion of the prairie landscape into water-connected communities dotted with wharves, tollhouses, tow paths, lock-tenders' houses, and canal-side grain elevators and industrial enterprises. As was typical of midwestern canal building, expertise, technology, and labor were transferred from the East. Former Erie Canal Chief Engineer Benjamin Wright evaluated and backed the plans of Chief Engineer William Gooding, who himself came by way of canal work in New York, Ohio, and Indiana. The ninety-six-mile canal would begin at Chicago, terminate at LaSalle, and comprise fifteen locks, four aqueducts, several feeders, and an enlarged channel sixty feet wide and six feet deep.

Irish laborers were also recruited from the East—as many as two thousand in 1838—and brought those plans to fruition under harsh living and working conditions. Housed in shanties and often paid with badly depreciated canal scrip valued at sixty-five cents on the dollar in 1840 and only thirty cents in 1842, laborers used little more than shovels and wheelbarrows to dig and grub the channel. They were prone to violence and epidemics, with malaria claiming between seven hundred and one thousand laborers in 1838.

Local farmers had eagerly anticipated what this new accessible transportation would mean for prices and markets. One Lewiston, Illinois, farmer reported to New York *Tribune* readers in 1842 that "we are pinched beyond all example for money. Even wheat does not bring it now. When the Illinois and Michigan Canal is completed, we shall have a market, but not till then." So, amid great fanfare on April 23, 1848, the *General Thorton* arrived at Chicago, the first boat laden with New Orleans produce bound ultimately for Buffalo, New York. One of the few midwestern canals to fulfill the hopes of its promoters, the Illinois and Michigan initially carried nearly equal volumes of wheat and corn. Corn production and trade skyrocketed in the early 1850s, however, and corn soon became Chicago's most valuable commodity. The canal influenced a number of related changes. Produce that had previously moved south to St. Louis and New Orleans markets now flowed to Chicago, part of a larger shift in trade away from the South and to the North and East. A new group of eastern migrants and European immigrants began populating the state when the Illinois and Michigan opened, outnumbering the former prevalence of southerners; this demographic trend would influence a host of areas in Illinois, including politics. Overall, though, canal passenger travel declined early with the relative ease and speed of railroad travel.

In accelerating Chicago's growth, the Illinois and Michigan revealed a deadly consequence of prosperity as well as a means of rescue through technological innovation. With Chicago's rise as a leading meatpacking center came the problem of sanitation and water supply, a situation made dire because of the routine dumping of sewage into the Chicago River, which ran into Lake Michigan, from which the city took its water. In 1854, 5 percent of Chicagoans died of cholera. Through an 1865 enabling act, city officials and canal commissioners opted to deepen the channel, making a "deep cut" that would pull water from the lake into the river, actually reversing the water flow with a canal pumping station. The sanitation project was completed in 1871, but periodic heavy rains reduced the canal's efficiency and led to even deadlier outbreaks of cholera and typhoid. In 1892, construction began on a new Drainage (later the Sanitary and Ship) Canal that would achieve a permanent reversal of the flow of the Chicago River and dramatically improve Chicago's water sanitation and health. Partly opening in 1900, the twenty-eight-mile canal was a remarkable twenty-five feet deep and one hundred sixty

feet wide, and built by a workforce of mainly black migrants and Polish immigrants. In 1911, work began on yet another sanitary canal, the Cal-Sag Channel, which opened in 1922. By 1933, the Cal-Sag was a vital shipping lane, which coupled with the more efficient railroad transportation, made the Illinois and Michigan obsolete. Although long-since closed, parts of the Illinois and Michigan Canal are preserved and maintained as scenic, historic, and recreation sites.

Sources and Further Reading: John G. Clark, *The Grain Trade in the Old Northwest* (1966); William Cronon, *Nature's Metropolis* (1991); John M. Lamb, "Early Days on the Illinois & Michigan Canal," *Chicago History* 3 (Fall–Winter 1974–1975); Edward Ranney, *Prairie Passage* (1998); William H. Shank, *Towpaths to Tugboats* (1982); Ronald E. Shaw, *Canals For a Nation* (1990); Leslie C. Swanson, *Canals of MidAmerica* (1964); Catherine T. Tobin, "Irish Labor on American Canals," *Canal History and Technology Proceedings* 9 (Mar. 1990); Peter Way, *Common Labour* (1993).

Ginette Aley
Iowa State University

Iowa: The Des Moines Rapids Canal

Constructed by the Army Corps of Engineers between 1867 and 1877, the Des Moines Rapids Canal (sometimes known as the Iowa Canal) provided a solution to the longstanding problems experienced by steamboat traffic on the upper Mississippi River caused by a series of rapids between Nashville and Keokuk, Iowa.

Lieutenant (later Confederate General) Robert E. Lee and Second Lieutenant Montgomery C. Meigs conducted the first survey of the Des Moines rapids in 1837 (during which their own boat ran aground), mapping the rapids and suggesting that, "one of the natural channels" of the river could be artificially widened and deepened to accommodate loaded craft. The federal government did not pursue these recommendations.

As steam traffic began to ply the waters of the upper Mississippi after the 1830s, the difficulties imposed by the rapids became apparent. Boats were required to unload cargo and transport it overland in an attempt to raise their keels in the water. Specialized pilots were often hired by boat captains to guide their vessels through the rapids.

Advocates promoted several proposals, including constructing a series of locks and dams on the river itself, but the impracticality of such measures prevented their execution. In 1866, Major General J. H. Wilson surveyed the rapids and proposed a canal and locks to run parallel to the river on the Iowa side. This canal plan received congressional approval in March of

1867, and construction began that October under the direction of Colonel J. N. Macomb, with most work contracted to the firms of James J. Dull of Pittsburgh and George Williams of Keokuk.

The canal was created by building a guard bank three to four hundred feet from the shore, and excavating the channel in the enclosed area so that it would be five feet deep even in times of low water. Black powder set in hand-drilled holes was used by the construction crews to break through the rocky bottom of the channel, along with three chisel boats equipped with chisel heads attached to pile drivers on their bows. Between one and two thousand men, primarily Swedish and Irish immigrant laborers, worked on the construction. At least two workmen were killed in the decade-long project, and many more were injured. The finished canal was opened for boat traffic on August 22, 1877.

The canal was 7.6 miles in length, running from the town of Nashville, Iowa, south to Keokuk. The 8-foot-deep channel varied from 250 to 300 feet wide along its course, which had a fall of 18.75 feet. Two lift locks, each 350 feet long by 80 feet wide with stonewalls 23 feet high and steam-powered wooden gates, raised and lowered vessels to accommodate the fall in water level.

The canal operated until 1913, when a second government project, the construction of a hydroelectric dam at Keokuk, permanently raised the level of the river, creating Lake Cooper and obscuring both the rapids and the canal that had been used for a mere thirty-five years to circumvent them.

Sources and Further Reading: Ron W. Deiss, "'Shortening the River,'" *Iowa Heritage Illustrated* 78 (Fall 1997); Ben H. Wilson, "The Des Moines Rapids Canal," *Palimpsest* 5 (Apr. 1924).

Peter Hoehnle
Iowa State University

Michigan Canals

Canal building in Michigan, at times as hysterical as in its midwestern neighbors, proved more bluster than action until the 1850s. Settlement began in the southeastern corner of the state, and eastern markets enticed settlers and politicians to look for natural and artificial waterways to ship their goods. As the population increased, a canal fever captured the progressivist bent of Michigan politicians.

The state government promoted internal improvements shortly after statehood. In 1837, the state appropriated funds to build a canal or a canal and rail-road from the town of Mt. Clemens on the Clinton River, which flowed into Lake Huron, to the mouth of the Kalamazoo, which flowed into Lake Michigan. It also provided funds to begin a canal from the eastern Saginaw River to the western Grand River. An additional piece of legislation provided funds for a canal around the falls on the St. Marys River in the Upper Peninsula.

Only sixteen miles of the Mt. Clemens–Kalamazoo Canal, a stretch near Mt. Clemens, was completed, and the canal work proved costly as the state expended over $93 thousand before 1840. The state legislature had authorized Governor Stevens T. Mason to expend $5 million, but the canal would never be allowed to consume the state's funds. Nor would it ever be a financial success. The one canal boat on the waterway generated a total revenue of $90.23 in its first two years. By 1846, the state looked to reduce its responsibilities for the once-anticipated canal, and no additional work was completed.

The other canals proposed in the project met similar fates. In 1840, work on the Saginaw Canal and the St. Marys Canal was suspended after economic hardships of the late 1830s, and the Saginaw effort was abandoned. Later, a canal devised in the early 1930s from Grand Rapids to Lake Michigan also faltered. Other canals would be proposed throughout the nineteenth century, and the St. Marys Falls Canal was completed.

The canals at the St. Marys Falls are the most enduring and famous canals in Michigan. Located at Sault Ste. Marie, the locks are commonly referred to as the Soo Canal. This canal connects Lake Superior to the St. Marys River and eventually Lake Huron. The canal bypasses the St. Marys Rapids, where the water falls about twenty-one feet from the level of Lake Superior to the level of the lower Great Lakes. The Northwest Fur Company constructed a navigation lock on the Canadian side of the river in 1797, but it was destroyed in the War of 1812. The state of Michigan began construction of the canal on the St. Marys in 1853, and it opened in 1855.

By the year 2000, a typical season allowed about eight thousand ships and boats to pass through the Soo Canal, about double what moves through the Panama Canal. The U.S. canal consists of the Davis Lock, opened in 1914, the Macarthur Lock, completed in 1943, and the Poe Lock, completed by 1969. The Macarthur and Poe handle the bulk of the commercial traffic, while recreational users and empty ships typically move through the Davis Lock. Eventually the U.S. Army Corps of Engineers administered the locks, and usage fees were reduced.

Other successful canals include the Portage Lake Ship Canal, which connected the Keweenaw Bay of

Lake Superior, on the eastern side of the Keweenaw Peninsula, with Portage Lake. The canal opened in June 1860, and it provided water access to Lake Superior from the copper-mining region around Hancock, Michigan. The path was completed across the peninsula in 1874, and today it is known as the Keweenaw Waterway. The canal served as an important bypass for the copper country. Also, a canal was dug between St. Joseph and what would become Benton Harbor. Completed in 1862, the canal proved so popular that it needed to be enlarged from its original fifty-foot width to a hundred feet wide and fifteen feet deep in 1875.

A similar "canal," though without locks, was the dredging of the St. Clair River north of Detroit. In 1855, the federal government commenced dredging, and after almost $1 million, it was completed in 1865. The government continued to widen and deepen the channel through the nineteenth century, considering the effort complete in 1896. The channel is twenty feet deep and 260 feet wide. This work insured that the waterway could handle the most massive ships, such as those that began hauling ore for the automobile industry.

As the Midwest's only peninsula, Michigan continues to view canals as an important tool for economic improvement. Unlike most midwestern states, canals remain important to the transportation infrastructure, and continue to be so into the twenty-first century.

Sources and Further Reading: William John Armstrong, "The Bung Town Canal," *Michigan History* 76 (Jan.–Feb. 1992); LeRoy Barnett, "Lac La Belle: Keweenaw's First Ship Canal," *Michigan History* 69 (Jan.–Feb. 1985); Christian J. Buys, "Grand Rapids International Seaport of the Midwest," *Michigan History* 81 (Jan.–Feb. 1997); Willis Frederick Dunbar, *Michigan: A History of the Wolverine State*, 2nd ed. (1970); Susan Crissman Gower, "Canal Dreams," *Michigan History* 81 (July–Aug. 1997); John A. Sturm, "The Clinton and Kalamazoo Canal—The Glory That Was," *Northwest Ohio Quarterly* 55 (Summer 1983); L. H. Wood, *Geography of Michigan* (1922).

Leo E. Landis
Henry Ford Museum and Greenfield Village,
Dearborn, Michigan

Canal Boats

Midwestern canal boats may be divided into two classes, freight barges and passenger packets. On the Ohio and Erie Canal, boats averaged seventy-five feet long and fourteen feet wide. Their hulls were flat-bottomed and squared off, looking much like bathtubs afloat on the water. The captain occupied a cabin near the bow of the vessel and the rest of his crew toward the stern. A long salon and retiring room of some thirty-six feet occupied the middle of the boat. No private rooms existed on the packets, and at night tiers of bunks were rigged up in the salon. Barges each carried fifty to eighty tons of bulk freight.

Canal boats were drawn by horses or mules that followed alongside the canals on towpaths. A trip across Ohio from Cleveland to Portsmouth, a distance of 309 miles, took eighty hours. Upstream vessels had the right-of-way. Downstream vessels slackened their towropes, allowing the other to pass over it on the port side.

The best of the passenger packets had carpets, chandeliers, and filigree. Despite this, trips could be uncomfortable. One traveler noted that it seemed as if "all of the heat spent by the sun during the day had settled down into that hot and stuffy little room, and that all the mosquitoes ever hatched in the mud puddles of Indiana were condensed into one humming, ravenous swarm right around my hard little bed." Still, canal rides were preferable to jarring rides by stagecoach, despite the complaints of such notables as Charles Dickens and Frances Trollope.

Sources and Further Reading: Paul Fatout, *Indiana Canals* (1972); Alvin Fay Harlow, *Old Towpaths* (1926); Maurice Thompson, *Stories of Indiana* (1898); Frank Wilcox, *The Ohio Canals* (1969).

Philip L. Frana
University of Central Arkansas

Locks

Locks were literally a gateway to the Midwest. Some of the earliest locks built in the hinterlands of America facilitated navigation on canals. The Erie Canal joining the Hudson River to Lake Erie, with its eighty-four locks and a total lift of 689 feet, opened up Ohio and the Great Lakes to water travel and transport in 1825. The canal boom that followed brought immigrants and commerce to many midwestern towns and cities. Constructed between 1825 and 1845, the Miami and Erie Canal, for example, running nearly 250 miles from Cincinnati on the Ohio River to Toledo on Lake Erie, required three guard locks to control the natural flow of water into the canal and a flight of 103 lift locks to raise and lower the boats, each with an average lift of eight feet.

Locks were created by walling off boat-sized chambers alongside the main channel where falls or rapids might otherwise exist. Boats brought through watertight gates into the chamber could then be lowered or raised by pumping in or releasing water. Locks joined together different parts of a canal located at different altitudes with a series of pools. Navigation on the rivers of the Midwest has also been greatly facilitated by locks on the Ohio and Mississippi Rivers built by the U.S. Army Corps of Engineers. Attempts to create systems of navigable locks and dams on other natural waterways largely failed because of fluctuating river levels and siltation.

Sources and Further Reading: Carl M. Becker and Leland R. Johnson, "History at the Bar," *Journal of Transport History* 12 (Sept. 1991); Harry G. Black et al., eds. *The Miami, Wabash, and Erie Canal Country* (1991); R. Douglas Hurt, *The Ohio Frontier* (1996).

Philip L. Frana
University of Central Arkansas

Roads, Routes, and Trails

One of the central problems that shaped the early history of the Midwest was simply getting there. The Great Lakes watershed—that vast fertile basin at the center of eastern North America—lay hundreds of miles from anywhere. What became the Midwest was approached best by water, using three great rivers and their tributaries: the St. Lawrence, Mississippi, and Ohio. Even so, any trip from the coasts into the heart of the region required paddling in excess of a thousand miles, upstream all the way. It was a land designed for easy getting out but not getting in.

The oldest approach used by Europeans was up the St. Lawrence River and through the chain of the Great Lakes themselves. Starting from Quebec (itself accessible by sailing ship), canoeists labored upstream to Montreal on a huge river that sometimes spilled out into lakes five miles across. From there the right fork followed the Ottawa River into Upper Canada and (via portages) to the north shore of Lake Huron. The southern route stayed on the St. Lawrence, hugged either shore of Lake Ontario, surmounted the cataract at Niagara, and traversed the length of Lake Erie to arrive at Detroit or continue (also via portages) into Lake Huron from the south. Lesser streams running into Lake Erie gave access to Lake Michigan (for example, the Grand, Kalamazoo, or St. Joseph Rivers), and the near-junction of the Maumee and the Eel near Ft. Wayne, Indiana, forged an important (if grueling) waterway down the Wabash to the Ohio. A similar portage linked Lake Erie with the Great Miami in Ohio, leading to the Ohio River near Cincinnati, and another connected the South Bend of the St. Joseph with the Kankakee, the Illinois, and finally the Mississippi.

The alternative approach simply reversed the final legs of these northern journeys, starting at New Orleans and struggling up the winding Mississippi and Ohio systems into the Illinois and Wabash until the canoes had to be dragged into the waters descending to the lakes. The Mississippi route also approached the vast forests of Wisconsin and well north into central Minnesota, where another portage gave passage down the St. Louis River to Duluth and the icy waters of Lake Superior. Distances in this undeveloped land staggered the European imagination: New Orleans to Duluth (as the crow flies) is about as far as Paris to Kiev, but the twisting courses of the rivers added significantly to the mileage. Factor in the difficulties of securing food and shelter, punishing weather, and a questionable welcome by native people, and these months-long journeys begin to acquire the daunting character so vividly portrayed in the accounts of the voyageurs.

As the French developed their interest in the interior of North America, they planted forts at key spots along these trade routes, gathering points and landmarks that anchored the map in European minds: Michilimackinac, Detroit, Miami (Fort Wayne), Vincennes, Kaskaskia, Peoria, St. Louis, Prairie du Chien, Green Bay. As traders gradually gave way to permanent settlers, these outposts—along with new ones planted by Americans in the 1790s at Sandusky, Fort Wayne, and Chicago—grew into towns and became destinations for the first generation of pioneers from the new United States. However, for most Americans in 1783, when they won their independence and claimed the entire region south of the lakes and east of the Mississippi River, the map of the Midwest was a blank sheet on which they believed they could inscribe desired features at will. First among those features would be roads or traces linking the coastal Atlantic communities with this trans-Appalachian frontier.

Before the American Revolution, the most important routes going west were military tracks: Braddock's Trace (1755) from Cumberland on the Potomac and Forbes's Road (1758) from Philadelphia, both touching the Ohio River near Pittsburgh. Crudely blazed trails barely wide enough for a gun carriage, these relics of the mid-eighteenth century wars for empire would be widened for civilian use after the Revolution. Meanwhile, in 1774 and 1775, Daniel Boone blazed a trace (later called the Wilderness Road) through the Cumberland Gap to Boonesborough (southeast of Lexington), a western fork of which soon extended through Crab Orchard to the Falls of the Ohio

(Louisville) and on to Vincennes (on the Wabash). Like its northern counterparts, this Wilderness Road remained a foot and bridle path well into the nineteenth century.

Thus at the beginning of their national history, Americans knew two reliable (if arduous) ways to get into the western country, one from either end of the Great Valley of Virginia. Additional routes followed—the Genesee Road from Albany to Buffalo, its extension around Lake Erie to Detroit, sometimes called the Old Lakeshore Road, and Ebenezer Zane's trace between Wheeling and Maysville, Kentucky—each pointing the way, if not much improving the topography itself, for the westward flood of people that would populate the midwestern states in the first five decades of the nineteenth century. Astonishingly, many tens of thousands already had made the trip before any sort of wagon traffic was practicable on either route.

The process of settling the Old Northwest did more than anything to stimulate road building and improvements. The first thousands of immigrants who walked to Kentucky alongside their carts and livestock or floated down the Ohio after hiking through Pennsylvania would not long be content with such primitive thoroughfares. Settlements sprang up at the mouths of rivers, at the sites of old Shawnee and Delaware villages, at junctions, falls, and other impediments in the natural network of waterways. Once settled, these American pioneers demanded markets for their produce, coffee, nails, and window glass for their comforts, and regular mail to keep them informed of life back home. Steamboat navigation on western rivers, beginning in 1811 and flourishing after 1816, simply hastened the spread of settlers up and down the Ohio, up the tributary rivers (Scioto, Miami, Whitewater, Wabash, Kaskaskia, Illinois), and on up the Mississippi into the Iowa, Wisconsin, and Minnesota territories. Therefore, cutting roads became a first-generation priority for private parties and governments local, territorial, state, and even national.

Zane's Trace (1796) was the first western road authorized (although not directly funded) by Congress. Under auspices of the post office, Congress also started designating post roads that followed settlers by only a very few years. In 1802, Ohio's enabling act set aside revenue from public land sales to facilitate road work inside the new state. The same legislation created the first federal highway, the Cumberland Road, to be built by the national government through the punishing country west of Frederick, Maryland, that separated Ohio from its eastern neighbors. Started in 1806, this "National Road" immediately attracted the bulk of the transmontane commerce, which kept the highway in chronic disrepair, a perpetual drain on the purse of Congress, and eventually a magnet for the political controversies that swirled around the topic of internal improvements.

The maintenance of local roads typically fell to the owners of land such thoroughfares crossed—a traditional arrangement that kept taxes low, governments small, and roads notoriously bad. Territorial governments could do little more than beg for rights-of-way and money from an unsympathetic Congress. After statehood, Ohio (1803), Indiana (1816), and Illinois (1818) almost immediately scattered roads (or at least lines on their maps) in all directions, connecting the isolated dots of waterborne settlements and probing the fertile lands that lay between the waters. By their central locations, state capital cities—Columbus, Indianapolis, and Springfield—bore witness to the confidence pioneer lawmakers placed in their capacity to make roads appear in the wilderness, a confidence not entirely warranted in the first generation.

The War of 1812 brought home to a fledgling nation the fragility of political control where government could neither mobilize an army nor move it from place to place. Correspondingly, in 1819, Secretary of War John C. Calhoun drew up an ambitious plan for frontier military roads to be built by soldiers on fatigue duty as part of a national defense program. Upstate New York and the Upper Great Lakes felt some early benefit from this initiative, as well as from the opening in 1825 of New York's Erie Canal, which redirected immigrants along the northern approach to the Midwest. Army road building soon sank into the quagmire of politics surrounding congressional internal improvements; nevertheless important precedents were set, and federal aid to territorial roads played a much larger role than before in opening Wisconsin, Iowa, and Minnesota.

The desire to maneuver Indians off their lands also stimulated frontier road building. Beginning in 1795, treaties ceding land to the federal government invariably left native people in legal possession of the balance of their holdings as long as they chose to remain. Soon pioneers were looking for ways to discourage their native neighbors from the peaceful enjoyment of their traditional lands, and driving roads deep into Indian country proved a useful device. Ostensibly to facilitate trade, to deliver Indian annuities and treaty payments, or to join Anglo-American settlements separated by Indian lands, these routes through Indian country required federal permission, special treaty concessions, and sometimes grants of land to finance road building itself. The darker motives often showed through: Speaking of his state's planned road from Indianapolis to the virtually uninhabited shore of Lake Michigan, Indiana Governor James Brown Ray enthused that "it will weaken the attachment of the Potawattamie to his country."

A final word is in order about the nature of these routes and roads and the experience of travel upon them. The hardships of very early travel by canoe scarcely need elaboration. Exposure to wind, contrary currents, bad weather, fourteen-hour days kneeling and paddling, interrupted by furious efforts to lug craft and cargo around falls and across portages—nothing in the voyageurs' mode of travel encouraged wholesale immigration by families. Overland routes before 1815 rarely admitted travel by coach or wagon; rather, horses and oxen carried packs while people walked beside, sometimes pushing handcarts as well. After 1815, as "improvements" proliferated, roadways grew wider (maybe forty feet or more) and acquired the occasional bridge or drainage ditch. But large tree stumps remained in most roads into the 1830s (trimmed to twelve inches or less), and were in fact a blessing, in that when they were grubbed out, the resulting mudholes rendered good roads impassable after even moderate rain. Few midwestern pioneers ever saw "macadamized" pavements (broken stone layered for drainage) or any other carpet of select material on their roads, save the occasional "corduroy" of logs laid at right angles to the route, creating a bone-jarring firmament to span swamps, bogs, and potholes.

Conveyances evolved little more than the roads themselves during the prerailroad pioneer period. Wagons with high axles, long rigid boxes, and narrow, iron-tired wheels cut deep ruts in dirt roads that, once wet and churned into slurry by the hooves of animals, forced traffic into forest turnouts until the quagmire extended many yards in all directions. Stagecoaches stood even higher off the ground, egg-shaped, top-heavy, suspended on leather straps (instead of springs), drawn by four or more horses, with the single virtue of sometimes sporting wider tires that did less damage to the surface of the road. The famed Pennsylvania or Conestoga wagon—broad-tired, heavy, sloping outward, ship-like, to center the load—clearly deserved its reputation as the best vehicle for heavy cargo, but the fleet of midwestern carriers probably never boasted a majority of these "Cadillacs." All travelers had to contend with herds of cattle and hogs being driven to market along the roads, leaving predictable waste and wreckage in their wake.

In all, poor transportation plagued the Midwest throughout the prerailroad era. That immigrants made it to Ohio, Indiana, Illinois, and to the Michigan, Iowa, and Wisconsin territories at all testifies to their determination, endurance, and obsessive motivation. Not surprisingly, transportation improvement preoccupied their minds once there, and the political agenda of an entire generation never failed to include internal improvements as a top priority and a key to future growth, prosperity, and comfort.

Sources and Further Reading: R. Carlyle Buley, *The Old Northwest*, 2 vols. (1951); Seymour Dunbar, *History of Travel in America* (1915); Caroline E. MacGill et al., *History of Transportation in the United States before 1860* (1917); Laurence J. Malone, *Opening the West* (1998).

John Lauritz Larson
Purdue University, Indiana

Native American Trails

While the majority of early settlers viewed the Midwest region as an untouched frontier, Native Americans had lived upon and explored the land for centuries. In so doing they created settlements, both large and small, and trails and footpaths in the process. These trails indicate their life cycles, the places they went to meet their needs, their food supply, their sources of lithic and marine material, and where they conducted important ceremonies. For example, along the trails in Michigan, archeologists have identified a thousand mounds, eighty enclosures and embankments, thirty garden beds, 750 village sites, and 260 burial grounds. Near these paths is also evidence of such artifacts as drills, hoes, spades, pipes, knives, arrowheads, hammers, pottery, stone effigies, shells, and minerals from outside the region, as well as evidence of copper mining.

These roads, "buffalo traces" as early settlers called them, led to important sources of livelihood such as salt springs, fresh water, edible plants, and game, as well as much-needed resources such as flint, rock, and metals. Bison found the best locations to cross streams and to negotiate through hills and mountains. Several Indian tribes called these paths *alanantonamiowee*, a term some linguists believe Native Americans took from the sounds of wildcats in nearby woods. Early pioneers and explorers of the region utilized, followed, and exploited many of these paths for transit and transportation. Newcomers to the region widened these trails, early settlers and travelers having described them as merely wide enough for an individual to walk on or pass through on horseback. The United States Army broadened many of these traces to give supply wagons access to interior forts. Other newcomers to the region also expanded the width of the paths to accommodate their wagons and herds. Many midwestern cities like Detroit, as well as forts and trading posts, were established on these thoroughfares.

One of the most important Indian trails in the Midwest was the Warrior's Path, which originated in the Cumberland Gap as a branch of the Old Wilderness Road, proceeded through Limestone (Maysville, Kentucky), to Fort Washington (present-day Cincinnati, Ohio), ending at Lake Erie. The main throughway of

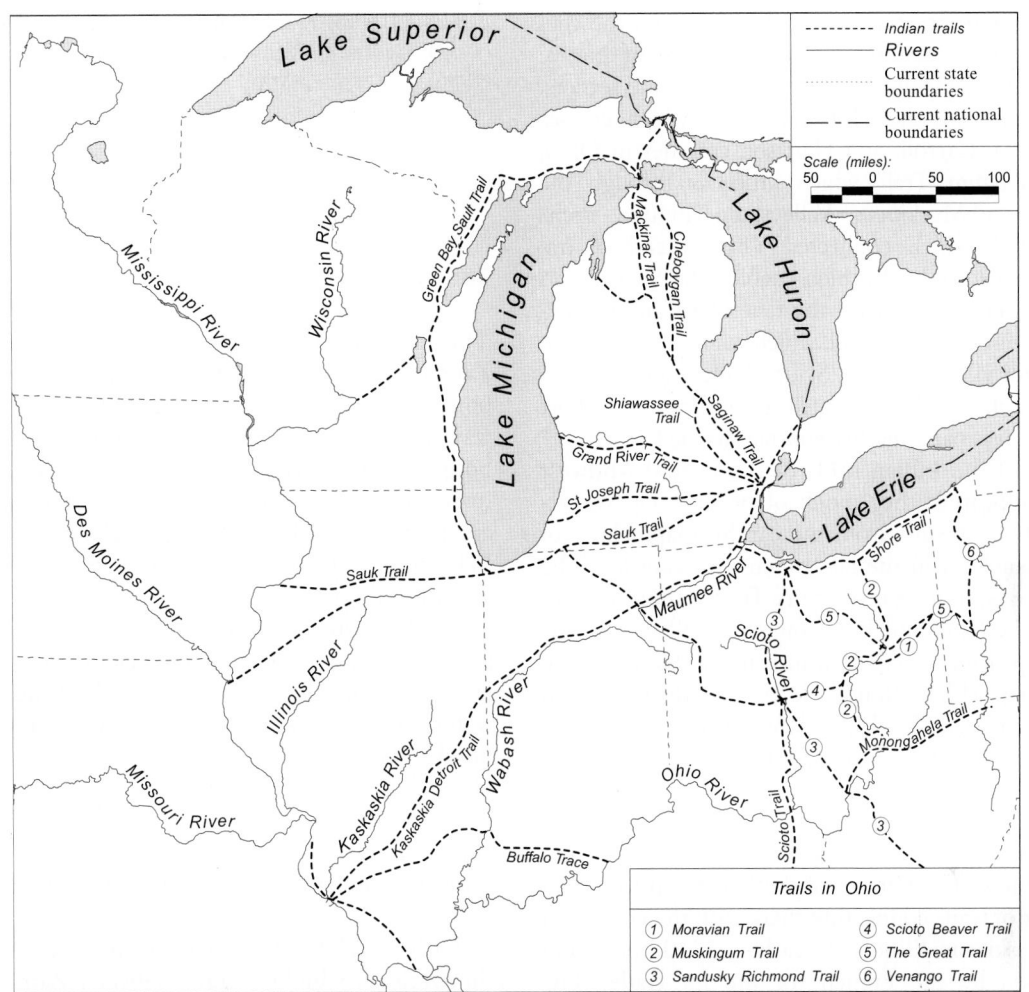

Important trails in the area of the Northwest Territory, c. 1760. Prepared by James DeGrand. *Source: Archer Butler Hulbert Historic Highways of America, vol. 2: Indian Thoroughfares* (1971 [reprinted from 1902 ed.]), 105; George Wilson and Gayle Thornbrough, *The Buffalo Trace* (Indianapolis: Indiana Historical Society, 1946); http://www.geo.msu.edu/geo333/indian_trails.html; C. M. Davis, *Readings in the Geography of Michigan* (Ann Arbor, MI: Ann Arbor Publishers, 1964); http://www.iltrails.org; Randall Parrish, *Historic Illinois* (1907), ch. 8.

Native American tribes in this region, it became the road that many early settlers used to come into the Ohio Territory. Another Indian trail of equivalent importance in the history of the region is the Great Trail, also called the Big Trail. This major buffalo trace was the most important trail in expansion to the west, and connected with Nemacolin's Path and Braddock's Trace, or the National Road. This road system connected Baltimore with Cumberland, Maryland, continuing westward across the Allegheny Mountains to Wheeling, Virginia, from there into the Ohio country, and eventually traversing Indiana and Illinois. This trail was followed and widened by General Edward Braddock and fourteen hundred British regulars and five hundred colonial troops in 1755, as they marched to attack the French at Fort Duquesne, on the site of the present city of Pittsburgh, Pennsylvania.

In 1827, this Great Trail, now known as the National Road, was completed into Columbus, Ohio, and three years later extended through Indianapolis, Indiana.

Other Indian trails of note in the Ohio territory include the Fort Miami Trail, the principal route from southern and southwestern Ohio to Detroit. It is best known as the route General Anthony "Mad Anthony" Wayne and his troops followed in 1794 to the fateful Battle of Fallen Timbers. The Mahoning Trail was an early trade route between Pittsburgh and Detroit, and is described in great detail by Colonel James Hilman, one of the early white travelers in this region. The Monongahela Trail was an important Shawnee thoroughfare that connected villages in the Scioto and Monongahela Valleys. It is best known as the warpath taken by indigenous peoples in Ohio to the southwestern Pennsylvania frontier settlements of the Long Knives, an Indian appellation for frontiersmen from Virginia, and the trail that Tecumseh used to forge his alliance of Native American tribes against the encroaching white settlers. Also of note are the Moravian Trail, which crosses Columbiana, Carroll, and Harrison counties in Ohio; the Muskingum Trail, which proceeds through the Cuyahoga and Muskingum Valleys; the Sandusky–Richmond Trail, which connected Virginia and central Ohio; the Scioto Trail, which enabled the Shawnee to move southward to engage the Cherokees and Catawbas; the Scioto–Beaver Trail, which connected Shawnee and Miami villages in the Scioto Valley; and the Venango Trail, which connected Lake Erie with Fort Boeuf and was particularly important to the French.

Many of the Indian trails of the central Midwest have disappeared, thus much of present-day knowledge of them results from the careful mapmaking of Rufus Blanchard in the late nineteenth century. The most famous of these is the Sauk Trail, a thoroughfare used by the Sauk and Fox from their villages on the Mississippi River to Malden in Canada. Beginning in present-day Milan, Illinois, it crossed through both Potawattomie and Kickapoo land. Other parts of this trail system in the central Midwest stretched from French villages on the Mississippi to Detroit and from St. Louis to Vincennes, a branch of which extended from the mouth of the Des Moines River to Peoria Lake, Illinois. The villages of the Peorias in Iowa had a number of trails connecting them with the villages of the Kaskaskias in Illinois. As early as 1720, they were being used by the French for the fur trade. The French also exploited the trail between Kaskaskia and Detroit for trading and military purposes, and the trail from Fort Massac on the Ohio River to Kaskaskia, Illinois, was utilized by George Rogers Clark and his military in their successful foray against the French at Kaskaskia and Vincennes in 1778.

Traces of most of the Native American trails west of the Mississippi River, especially the small ones, disappeared upon arrival of early settlers, and much archeological work will be needed to rediscover them. These trails, which generally ran east to west given the terrain, were used by the pioneer schooners or returned to the prairie vegetation as Native Americans retreated west. One of the most famous of these was the Mormon Trail, which was used by many settlers to cross southern Iowa. Hernando de Soto used Indian trails to enter Missouri in 1541, and the Panane (Pawnee) Trail brought the Spanish into Nebraska in 1720. Other trails such as the Santa Fe Trail and the Smoky Hill Trail in Kansas linked the Native Americans in the region with tribes in the west.

Sources and Further Reading: Archer Butler Hulbert, *Red-Men's Roads* (1900); William H. Shank, *Indian Trails to Super-highways* (1996); Frank Nelson Wilcox, *Ohio Indian Trails* (1933); George R. Wilson, *Early Indiana Trails and Surveys* (1986).

T. Jason Soderstrum
Iowa State University

Zane's Trace

The first inland highway to cross present-day Ohio, Zane's Trace was the brainchild of Ebenezer Zane, born in the Potomac Valley in 1747. Zane made his way to the Ohio River in 1770 and claimed land on both sides of the river in the Wheeling vicinity, eventually amassing nearly thirteen thousand acres. Sufficient settlers arrived by 1793 that Zane filed a plat for Wheeling, and land and lot sales began, bringing him a comfortable income.

As the primary land developer in the Wheeling area, Zane had an obvious financial stake in an overland route into the Ohio country. He recognized that water transport on the Ohio River was subject to both flood and drought and was impossible during ice jams. He and his brother Jonathan had gained a familiarity with what is now southeastern Ohio while hunting and with various military expeditions. In addition, Zane already had experience building two other area roads.

Early in 1796, Zane petitioned Congress for authorization to build a trace between Zanesville and Limestone (now Maysville), Kentucky. Passed on May 17, 1796, the bill granted, as requested, three separate mile-square sections of land where the proposed road crossed the Muskingum, Hocking, and Scioto Rivers. All three rivers were already important water trade routes into the interior, and a road crossing had attractive development potential. In return, Zane agreed to operate ferries on these three rivers and was responsible for surveying the tracts.

Zane enlisted the aid of his knowledgeable brother Jonathan, son-in-law John McIntire, and an Indian guide named Tomepomehala to blaze the trace that summer. Congress's allocation of less than seven months for the job indicates the basic bridle trail expected. Much of the eastern portion followed two long-established Indian trails, and large segments of the southern portion between the Scioto and Ohio Rivers aligned with a military road established in 1787 by Kentucky militia. The seven-man crew, headed by Jonathan Zane, did not complete its work until the summer of 1797. Following Ohio statehood, public funds became available for improvements, and by 1804, a twenty-foot wagon road existed along its entire length. Despite efforts to improve marshy stretches,

English traveler Fortescue Cuming claimed in 1810 that Zane's Trace was "the most wretched road imaginable" due to "the frequency of sloughs of stiff mud and clay."

Its condition notwithstanding, Zane's Trace was an important factor in the interior settlement of Ohio. The cities of Zanesville, Lancaster, and Chillicothe grew up around Zane's three tracts and ferries. Connections with Pennsylvania on the east brought early German settlements to Somerset and Lancaster, Guernsey Islanders to Cambridge, and Welsh to central Licking County. Significant cattle and hog herds moved from the Bluegrass region of Kentucky and the Scioto Valley to eastern markets.

In the late 1820s, the eastern portion of the trace became the foundation for the new National Road. The following decade, the western section was incorporated in a toll route known as the Zanesville and Maysville Road. Today, segments of the trace are still identified as Wheeling Street in Zanesville, Cambridge, and Lancaster.

Sources and Further Reading: Fortescue Cuming, *Sketches of a Tour to the Western Country* (1810); Clement L. Martzolff, "Zane's Trace," *Ohio Archaeological and Historical Publications* 13 (1904); John Gerald Patterson, "Ebenezer Zane, Frontiersman," *West Virginia History* 12 (Oct. 1950); John Bernard Ray, "Zane's Trace, 1796–1812," Ph.D. diss., Indiana University (1968).

David Simmons
Ohio Historical Society, Columbus, Ohio

Internal Improvements

Among the leading problems facing new states in the Midwest was the demand for transportation—what they called "internal improvements." Both interregional and local transportation had been limited in the pioneer period by the natural flow of navigable streams and a few land routes carved out of mountain or forested landscapes. As settlers made the thousand-mile trek into the Old Northwest from the eastern states and Virginia, they soon demanded improvements in those routes as well as a network of local avenues on which to gain access to new lands and markets. The continental scale of the problem called for attention from the federal government. By the 1810s, however, regional jealousies, fear of taxes, and suspicions about consolidated power made internal improvements the most important national problem that Congress could not solve. Therefore, it was the states—including the new states of the Midwest—that pioneered public works of internal improvement before the triumph of railroad corporations.

State-level internal improvements commenced with New York's successful opening of the Erie Canal. In 1817, New York authorized loans up to $7 million and began work on the water route from the Hudson to Lake Erie. By the time the canal was completed in 1825, revenues were already retiring the debt, financing additional New York waterways, and relieving New Yorkers of the ordinary burdens of taxation. Other states scurried to build their own "golden" waterways.

Ohio took up the challenge of the Erie Canal almost immediately, mounting projects designed to open the interior and link the Ohio River with Lake Erie. Legislation in 1825 launched a long canal from Cleveland through Columbus and down the Scioto River, as well as a short one up the Great Miami from Cincinnati to Dayton. Cost overruns and technical difficulties consumed the money borrowed for these projects, but jealousy and enthusiasm elsewhere in the state quickly buried the public works commission with unceasing demands for extra canals and roads. By 1837, when overstrained capital markets collapsed, Ohio was overextended, and only refinancing and retrenchment prevented default. Chastened, Ohio lawmakers scaled back their programs and adopted, in 1851, a new constitution prohibiting state borrowing for public works.

Indiana confronted divergent opportunities because its waterways flowed out of state in all directions. The most promising route—the upper Wabash between Lafayette and Fort Wayne—remained in the 1820s inhabited entirely by Indians, and in 1825 the new state capital of Indianapolis sat landlocked in the center of a virtual wilderness. In 1827, Congress offered land grants to Illinois, Indiana, and Ohio if they would build canals to open (respectively) the Lake Michigan–Illinois and the Lake Erie–Miami–Wabash portages, completing major interregional circuits between the eastern and western waterways. To garner local support for this project, Indiana pieced together by 1836 a mammoth system of roads and canals (and one experimental railway) that centered commerce on Indianapolis and scattered benefits to all inhabited corners of the state. Borrowed money—$10 million at first—was supposed to build the system, while tolls and economic growth would eventually retire the debt. Unfortunately, the Panic of 1837 hit just as Indiana issued its bonds, and in a spiraling combination of bad luck and bad judgment, the money disappeared before any facilities were completed. Indiana sank into bankruptcy in 1841 and, in 1850, like Ohio, swore off public debt forever.

The Illinois experience closely paralleled that of Indiana. The first capital assistance for internal improvements came from Congress to open the portage between Lake Michigan and the Illinois River. This Illinois and Michigan Canal clearly was the hobby of Chicago boomers, but the 1827 land grant made it hard to ignore. In 1837, just weeks before the panic, they adopted a statewide system embracing the Illinois and Michigan Canal and numerous railroads linking all parts of the state. As in Indiana, the money ran out by 1839, and Illinois defaulted on its debt.

Farther north in Michigan, internal improvements first took the form of wilderness roads laid out and paid for by Congress. United States Army personnel cut the first roads across Michigan—from Detroit to St. Joseph in 1820, and on to Chicago in 1825. Similar military roads crossed the Black Swamp southward from Detroit to the Rapids of the Maumee (near Toledo) and north toward present-day Saginaw. In 1837, the new state of Michigan immediately plunged itself $5 million into debt for three cross-state railroads, two canals, and a dozen other internal improvement projects. Required by law to spend equally on all installations, the state quickly squandered its cash and went broke, eventually salvaging what it could in the middle 1840s by selling its partly built railways to eastern investors and defaulting on the balance of the debt.

Wisconsin, Iowa, and Minnesota escaped the canal mania and public works bankruptcies of the internal improvement movement because they still lay beyond the frontiers of earliest and most intense settlement. Except for federal military roads, this northwestern fringe of the Midwest saw no significant infrastructure improvement until the long depression of 1837–1845 had discredited public canals and identified private railroads as preferred instruments for developmental investment. But following the negative example of their closest neighbors, these states avoided public works programs and turned to the newest instrument of internal development, the railroad corporation, for the improvement of transportation.

The internal improvement movement of the late 1820s and 1830s marked a turning point in the history of the Midwest. Prior to 1845, many people expected government to support and regulate internal transportation systems. During the 1850s, the maturation of railroad technology combined with the evolution of the business corporation to enable the building and operating of railways across many states without the benefit of governmental authority. Midwestern states embraced railroads as virtual lifelines to the national and world economies, only to find themselves locked in new struggles to regulate those railroads and reestablish some semblance of the economic independence they had dreamed of in antebellum days.

Sources and Further Reading: John Lauritz Larson, *Internal Improvement* (2001); Ronald E. Shaw, *Canals for a Nation*

(1990); John F. Stover, *Iron Road to the West* (1978); Leslie C. Swanson, *Canals of MidAmerica* (1984).

John Lauritz Larson
Purdue University, Indiana

The National Road

The demand for roads in America brought together men like George Washington and Thomas Jefferson, who saw the benefits of roads on a large scale, and Ebenezer Zane, who knew that his trace in Ohio and Kentucky provided residents with the only road in the region. With statehood, Ohio citizens called for improved roads as migrants traveled west over wilderness trails.

Albert Gallatin, U.S. Secretary of the Treasury, answered that call. He suggested that proceeds from land sales be used to construct roads. In 1803, Ohio's constitutional convention determined that 3 percent of the 5 percent set-aside from land sales would be used to fund roads within the state, and the remaining 2 percent for roads to and through the state. In 1805, Uriah Tracy filed a report with the U.S. Senate that discussed proposed routes for a National Road. Tracy recommended Cumberland, Maryland, as the eastern terminus and the Mississippi River in the west. The Senate approved the Road in December 1805, but the House of Representatives delayed. Pennsylvania, Virginia, and South Carolina opposed the route for reasons that included its not passing through their state and the loss of population as people migrated west.

States that did not have a location along the route petitioned Congress for inclusion. Although Pittsburgh did not find itself along the proposed route, Pennsylvania was appeased with other stops along the road. The choice of Wheeling, Virginia, as the Ohio River crossing was determined by Wheeling's importance as a regional crossroad, its location across the river from Zane's Trace, and the political maneuverings of Henry Clay. Due to the largess of this job, construction would take several years and several million dollars to complete. As the National Road covered several states, numerous contractors were involved in construction, which placed further delay and a haphazardness to the overall project. Construction began in 1811 from Cumberland, Maryland, along the Braddock Trace, continued to Brownsville, Pennsylvania, and reached Wheeling in 1818.

In Ohio, the National Road followed a mail route known as Zane's Trace. By 1830, construction had reached Zanesville and continued toward Columbus. The road could not be built fast enough, however,

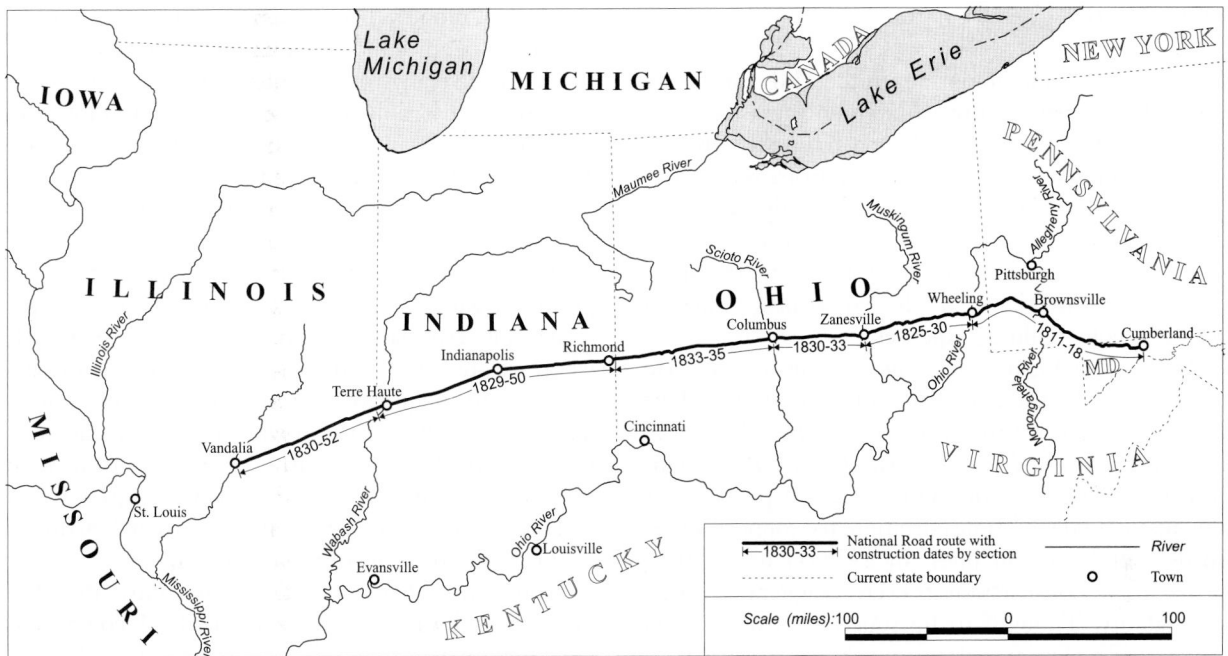

National Road. Prepared by James DeGrand. *Source:* Karl Raitz, ed., *The National Road* (Baltimore: Johns Hopkins University Press, 1996).

for people moving west; Indiana and Illinois became states while the completed road remained in Ohio. The route, although marked and cut, was not completed through Indiana until the 1850s. Eventually the National Road reached Vandalia, Illinois. The construction of canals, then railroads by midcentury, made major road construction almost obsolete. It became cheaper and more cost-effective to ship goods and travel along canal and rail lines. From the 1830s, the federal government placed a lower priority on internal improvements and passed that responsibility to states. Not until the arrival of the automobile did the federal government return to building roads, and the National Road was incorporated into U.S. 40 in 1926.

Sources and Further Reading: Philip D. Jordan, *The National Road* (1948); Norris F. Schneider, "The National Road," *Ohio History* 83 (Spring 1974).

Stephanie Carpenter
Murray State University, Kentucky

Frank Lloyd Wright service station. Library of Congress, Prints and Photographs Division, Historic American Buildings Survey, HABS, MINN, 9-CLO.

Plank Roads

Plank roads became important in the Midwest during the mid-nineteenth century. Extending across the nation from New York and Canada by the 1840s, the idea of plank roads quickly caught on in areas not serviced by canal or rail lines. Financed mostly by private companies and less expensive to construct than railways, plank roads gave farmers a way to transport commodities overland, as the companies collected tolls to recoup building expenses.

Illinois, Michigan, and Ohio led the way in road construction by the late 1840s. Influenced by Robert Dale Owen and his work, *A Brief Practical Treatise on the Construction and Management of Plank Roads* published in 1850, local promoters deemed plank roads the main mode of transportation to connect other roads, canals, or rail lines. In addition to detailing plank road construction, Owen exaggerated their profitability. Thought to be superior to other road surfaces like dirt and stone, plank roads were constructed of wooden slabs that would provide an all-weather surface and were stated to last from seven to twelve years. Owen assured promoters that the tolls collected from high traffic volume would be sufficient to replace worn planks as well as show a profit. In actuality, however, plank roads lasted less than five years, due to rot and a variety of other destructive elements, and without available funds to replank, many road companies went bankrupt during the nineteenth century. With the companies bankrupt, little effort was made to resurface these roads until the arrival of the automobile.

Sources and Further Reading: Carl Abbott, "The Plank Road Enthusiasm in the Antebellum Middle West." *Indiana Magazine of History* 67 (June 1971); Daniel Klein and John Majewski, *Promoters and Investors in Antebellum America* (1991).

Stephanie Carpenter
Murray State University, Kentucky

Good Roads Movement

The good roads movement began as an attempt by middle-class reformers to modernize the countryside by improving the quality of rural roads. Bicyclists, organized as the League of American Wheelmen, wanted to bicycle through pastoral settings on hard, level surfaces. Beginning in the 1880s, wheelmen attempted to convince urban and rural people that farmers would also benefit from all-weather roads.

Rural residents contended that improved roads cost too much money, benefited urban travelers rather than rural people, and that local authorities were best suited to solve any road problems. Other farmers denied that road problems existed. Farmers traditionally paid road taxes in kind with their labor, dragging roads, repairing culverts, and maintaining drainage ditches. Improved roads, however, necessitated new techniques, which required cash rather than labor, pinching farmers during years of low prices for farm products. Rural opposition to the good roads movement was especially pronounced in the Midwest, where relatively few farmers would shoulder the increased and inequitable tax burden. Road promoters launched a campaign to convince farmers of the need for good roads. In the early 1900s, the Iowa State Highway Commission organized demonstration trains and road schools and participated in farmers' institutes to spread the message of improvement.

Opponents of good roads relaxed only after the Federal Highway Acts of 1916 and 1921 committed federal money for highway construction, and states began to appropriate funds for road improvement, spreading the tax burden between rural and urban areas. For example, in 1939, the Iowa legislature passed a farm-to-market bill, appropriating funds for rural secondary road improvement to offset the previous emphasis on primary highways.

Sources and Further Reading: Hal S. Barron, *Mixed Harvest: The Second Great Transformation in the Rural North, 1870–1930* (1997); Leo Landis, *Building Better Roads* (1997).

J. L. Anderson
Iowa State University

The Lincoln Highway

In 1912, Carl G. Fisher, Indiana businessman and promoter, conceived a transcontinental highway through the Midwest known as the Coast-to-Coast Rock Highway. In 1913, Packard Automobile President and auto enthusiast Henry B. Joy suggested the name Lincoln Highway, noting that a toll-free, hard-surface road could serve as a fitting monument to the former president. The Lincoln Highway Association, organized in 1913, announced the proposed route that year and began marking the 3,389-mile road from New York to San Francisco with distinctive red, white, and blue posts bearing the letter "L."

The Lincoln Highway, known today as U. S. Highway 30, crosses the Midwest states of Ohio, Indiana, Illinois, Iowa, and Nebraska. The road enters Ohio at East Liverpool, proceeds through Fort Wayne, Indiana, bypasses Chicago via Joliet, crosses the Missis-

Marker on the Lincoln Highway, Illinois. Rick Bunton/Lincoln Highway Association of Illinois.

situation improved in the 1920s, in large part due to federal funds authorized by Congress in the 1916 and 1921 Federal Highway Acts. Better road conditions encouraged travel. Community leaders representing towns that were not selected to be on the highway protested their exclusion, even erecting competing and misleading markers to lure travelers and their cash. Engineers made wider and deeper cuts through the land to even the grade, and workers drained the roadbeds to help ensure a stable, paved surface. Hotels and restaurants flourished in town centers, but as the volume of traffic increased, savvy businesspeople established new and improved motels and diners adjacent to the highway on the outskirts of town to accommodate travelers who did not wish to get off the main road or stop in town.

Historians, community boosters, auto enthusiasts, and preservationists have sparked renewed interest in the Lincoln Highway, even reviving the Lincoln Highway Association. Some sections of the original surface and landscape exist, albeit altered by use or neglect.

Sources and Further Reading: Gregory M. Franzwa, *The Lincoln Highway* (1995); Effie Price Gladdin, *Across the Continent by the Lincoln Highway* (1915); Drake Hokanson, *The Lincoln Highway: Main Street Across America* (1999).

J. L. Anderson
Iowa State University

sippi River at Clinton, Iowa, crosses the Missouri River near Omaha, and follows the Platte River through central Nebraska. The rural landscape of the route attracted the attention of travelers. Effie Price Gladding, who published an account of her eastward journey on the highway in 1915, provided a colorful image from a vantage point in western Iowa that suggests the importance of agriculture to the region. "As we approached Carroll," Gladding observed, "we came to a hill top from which we looked down on a valley of tasseled corn fields. It was exactly like looking down on an immense, shining green rug, with yellow tufts thrown up over its green surface."

Road building and the associated economic activity of travel brought changes to the Midwest landscape. Restaurants, hotels, fuel stations, and repair shops in communities along the highway experienced an economic boom as traffic increased on the road, a result of newly published guidebooks and maps as well as a growing number of automobile owners. Early travelers reported on the miserable road conditions, but the

Interstate Highways

In 1956 President Eisenhower signed legislation authorizing the survey, construction, and financing of a national highway system to facilitate travel and commerce as well as connect defense installations with areas of supply and major population centers. The new interstates would help bind the nation together, handling increased traffic volume at higher speeds and with limited access points. Much of the present interstate system lies within the Old Northwest states of Illinois, Indiana, Michigan, Ohio, and Wisconsin, reflecting the high population density and industrial development of the region relative to other regions at the time planning and construction commenced.

Planning for interstate highway routes was contentious. While some community leaders feared the loss of taxable property, others saw the advantages to commerce and the promised relief from traffic congestion. In Indianapolis, business leaders generally supported the plan for their city's interstate, although they were concerned that a proposal for building the road below grade would require them to pay for relocating underground utilities. Many people saw commercial advantages to the new roads, but others saw threats to their homes and communities. The engineers who planned the routes frequently selected the most inexpensive land for the interstates, motivated by cost concerns; African Americans frequently occupied that inexpensive real estate and protested the route selection. Religious and community representatives in Indianapolis argued that the low payments for their existing housing would not be enough for them to afford new housing, forcing homeowners to become renters. The Indianapolis Taxpayers Association opposed certain routes in the inner city because of ethnic considerations. This group, as well as people in Minneapolis and Des Moines, feared that dislocation from interstate construction would force people of different classes and races to seek housing elsewhere, including middle-class neighborhoods.

In 1966, Congress passed the National Historic Preservation Act, requiring federal agencies to determine if their activities would affect significant cultural resources. As a result of Section 106, highway construction in the Midwest was researched, and archaeologists and historians have enhanced our understanding of prehistoric and historic cultural development in the region.

The interstates facilitated commuter traffic and the abandonment of central cities by the middle class in favor of the suburbs. Midwesterners embraced the automobile and automobile culture with zeal, choosing to drive to work on the interstates. Many businesses attempted to cut costs by purchasing inexpensive land along the interstate on the edges of the region's cities, avoiding the congestion of the central business districts. Public funding for mass transit alternatives to the automobile declined significantly after the passage of the Interstate Highway Act, reinforcing the importance of automobiles and trucking in national and regional life.

Sources and Further Reading: Kenneth T. Jackson, *Crabgrass Frontier* (1985); David A. Ripple, *History of the Interstate Highway System in Indiana* (1975); Mark H. Rose, *Interstate: Express Highway Politics, 1939–1989* (1990).

J. L. Anderson
Iowa State University

Bridges

As public structures requiring engineering, material utilization, and financing, bridges are useful gauges of their era and the society that created them. Starting about 1800, bridge builders in the Midwest re-created wooden truss systems first developed in central Eu-

rope, based on empirical concepts and experience. In the 1830s, military engineers introduced scientifically derived designs.

During the 1850s, railroad expansion dramatically altered the bridge-building business. Midwestern track laid during this decade exceeded the railroad construction in either the South or Northeast, and by 1860, Ohio and Illinois mileage led the nation. The lines created an unprecedented demand for bridges and fostered both standardization as well as creative designs. An 1873 index of American bridge patent holders indicated the importance of Cincinnati, Cleveland, Chicago, and St. Louis. Finally, railroads expanded bridge builders' territory and stimulated the growth of fabrication companies. With ready access to iron production centers in the upper Ohio Valley and southern shore of Lake Erie, many of these firms operated in Ohio, but practically every state in the Midwest was home to major metal bridge builders.

It was also in the Midwest, over the Ohio and upper Mississippi Rivers, that the federal government first accepted responsibility for mediating conflicts between navigation and railroad interests over river crossings. The opening salvo came as the 1,010-foot Wheeling Suspension Bridge was being constructed over the Ohio River in 1849. Authorized by Virginia, an injunction filed by Pennsylvania claiming it was a hazard for steamboats came before the U.S. Supreme Court. Its ruling in favor of the steamboat was negated when Congress declared the bridge part of a federal "post road." While the outcome was inconclusive for the government, the project prompted a twenty-five-year spate of highway suspension bridges throughout the mid-Ohio Valley. The completion of the record-setting 1,057-foot suspension bridge at Cincinnati, which avoided interference with river navigation, further encouraged the trend. But suspension bridge technology was little used in the upper Mississippi Valley where east-west routes were initially for rail traffic rather than highways, and railroad builders questioned the rigidity of suspension bridges.

Topography also explains the westward technology transfer failure. Elevated bridges that avoided steamboat chimneys were practical in the Ohio Valley where prominent hilltop banks were common. Steamboat navigators also needed elevated pilothouses to see a vessel's sides and to read signs of deep or shoal water. Achieving adequate bridge elevation over the wide flood plain of the Mississippi Valley below Red Wing, Minnesota, required long gradient approaches unattractive to railroads. Additionally, most population centers, upon which railroads were dependent, lay in the valley itself, so there low-level bridges with drawbridges were preferred.

The first bridge over the Mississippi River also involved questions of jurisdiction. Shortly after a bridge at Rock Island, Illinois, opened in 1856, the steamboat *Effie Afton* struck and partially destroyed it. Navigation interests celebrated the demise of the bridge, and the steamboat owner sued for damages. The defense attorney for the railroad, Abraham Lincoln, asserted that expanding east-to-west travel was no less important than river traffic. The legal wrangling ended in 1862 when the Supreme Court ruled for the bridge. The Rock Island Bridge set a precedent for low-level bridges with pivoting draw spans but had serious design flaws. Subsequent Congressional legislation required that bridge piers be parallel to a river's current.

The Civil War forced Congress to acknowledge its responsibility for regulating bridges across navigable rivers. Completed in 1864, the Steubenville, Ohio, railway bridge, built on tall piers, had an unprecedented channel span of 320 feet and represented the best in American truss design and fabrication. It proved the practicality of such long spans.

The last important Mississippi Valley crossing built with only state authorization was completed in 1865 at Clinton, Iowa. This low-level structure was the first in the valley to use an iron draw span, but its positioning was problematic and led to court cases. Ultimately, the U.S. Supreme Court ruled that the bridge could operate as constructed.

Congress passed legislation in 1866 authorizing a series of seven elevated bridges in the Mississippi Valley between Winona, Minnesota, and St. Louis, Missouri. Completed between 1868 and 1871, all followed the Rock Island and Clinton precedents. Also included in the legislation was a requirement for a five-hundred-foot span at St. Louis, assuming that this length would be impossible to construct. They had not, of course, figured on James Eads and his world record–setting arch structure, completed in 1874.

After 1870, the U.S. Army Corps of Engineers examined both old and new Ohio River bridges. Navigation interests on the Ohio lobbied for wider channels beneath bridge piers. Railroad engineers obliged by steadily designing and building ever-longer trusses. Guided by conservative army engineers, the St. Louis arch precedent was ignored in favor of conventional horizontal trusses, culminating in 1917 with the 720-foot simple truss of the Metropolis, Illinois, Bridge. That same year the Chesapeake and Ohio Railroad completed a record 1,550-foot continuous truss over the Ohio at Portsmouth. To accommodate a shifting channel, the army demanded two equal, 775-foot openings on either side of a central pier. Nearly 130 feet tall over this pier, it is still one of the heaviest trusses ever built.

One St. Louis precedent was utilized in both river valleys: cantilever designs that avoided placing temporary staging in an active waterway. The characteristic cantilever form in both valleys—large, soaring, anchor trusses flanking a suspended span—was established in 1888 with Cincinnati's Chesapeake and Ohio Railway Bridge.

For similar reasons, suspension bridges proved popular among some bridge designers during the early twentieth century. Only the towers created navigation hazards, and the superstructure could be fabricated without waterway interference. But generally, designers found it difficult to compete with the economy of cantilever designs.

The arch finally returned to the Mississippi with the 1940 multiple tied-arch bridge near Rock Island, Illinois. Once established, economic considerations and the enthusiasm of river interests made the tied arch popular in both valleys for nearly thirty years, especially on the interstate system.

In the 1980s, a variation on the suspension bridge, the cable-stayed design, gained acceptance because it permitted cantilever construction without waterway interference and, in moderate lengths, was more economical than suspension bridges. It was aesthetically appealing to designers, since it allowed roadways that were visually "thin" from a side perspective.

At the end of the twentieth century, designs have returned to the precedents set when the Mississippi was first bridged 150 years ago. Although cable-stayed designs remain popular, truss bridges are again being erected. But as long as waterways remain major bulk-goods avenues in the Midwest, the conflict between navigation interests and bridging will continue.

Sources and Further Reading: Carl W. Condit, *American Building Art* (1961); Mary Charlotte Aubry Costello, *Climbing the Mississippi River Bridge by Bridge* (1995); F. B. Maltby, "The Mississippi River Bridges," *Journal of the Western Society of Engineers* 8 (Aug. 1903); Mansfield Merriman and Henry S. Jacoby, *A Text-Book on Roofs and Bridges*, vol. 4, 3rd ed. (1907); David Plowden, *Bridges: The Spans of North America* (1974); David A. Simmons, "Light, Aerial Structures of Modern Engineering," *Proceedings of the International Conference on Historic Bridges to Celebrate the 150th Anniversary of the Wheeling Suspension Bridge* (1999); G. K. Warren, "Report on Bridging the Mississippi River Between Saint Paul and St. Louis," *Annual Report of the Chief of Engineers* (1878).

David Simmons
Ohio Historical Society, Columbus, Ohio

Eads Bridge

Labeled for its designer but formally called the Illinois and St. Louis Bridge, the Eads Bridge designed to

Eads Bridge, built in 1874. Library of Congress, Prints and Photographs Division, Historic American Buildings Survey, HABS, MO, 96-SALU, 77-1.

spur railway transport is among the nineteenth-century's most remarkable engineering achievements. Through it St. Louis hoped to challenge Chicago's control of east-west railroad traffic. Alliances were built with Eastern capitalists seeking a transcontinental rail empire. As originally conceived, branch railroads to Iowa and Kansas would funnel grain-laden traffic to St. Louis, where a new bridge across the Mississippi would avoid the Great Lakes.

Congress authorized the Eads Bridge in 1866, but with stipulations concocted by steamboat interests for a span thought impossibly long. James Buchanan Eads, who ironically had become famous aiding river commerce by salvaging steamboats, determined to accept the challenge despite his lack of formal engineering training or experience in bridge construction. Eads was accepted because he was a major stockholder and because of his past successes supplying Civil War gunboats. He was also widely recognized as a financier and had an uncanny ability to manipulate people through a forceful personality.

The most basic design innovation was the 1867 proposal to use, instead of traditional trusses, unprecedented arches of 520 and 502 feet. Because some civil engineers condemned the proposal and were reluctant to follow this daring precedent, the record would stand for two decades. Eads wisely hired two experienced German engineers as assistants and a mathematician to verify their computations. A second major departure from previous practice was using tubes for the arches rather than built-up members. Even more unusual was fabricating the tubes like barrel staves. This probably stemmed from his third, and most daring, proposal: making the arches of higher-strength

steel. This caused great difficulty for Eads and the contractor, Keystone Bridge Company. With steel production in its infancy, Eads eventually was forced to use cast and wrought iron for many of the bridge elements. Nonetheless, the Eads Bridge is noteworthy as the first large-scale use of structural steel in America. Finally the artistic merit of Eads's design, graceful arches springing from simple, solid-looking piers, was immediately recognized. Both poet Walt Whitman and architect Louis Sullivan found inspiration in its "perfection and beauty unsurpassable."

The actual construction established numerous American standards. The two river piers were completed using the plenum pneumatic process in which workmen sank open-bottomed caissons, kept free of water by compressed air, into the river bed while masonry was built on top. Common by this time in Europe, it had no American parallel in size, strength, or depth. Unfortunately some workmen were sacrificed to the negative and, at that time, little understood health effects of compressed air. Eads's material specifications required unprecedented precision and necessitated creating the world's largest yet most exacting testing machine. The unique superstructure erection method also became common; temporary towers and cables held the arches as they were cantilevered out from each pier to the center.

Opening to great fanfare and celebration on July 4, 1874, the Eads Bridge was a dismal business failure. The heavy railroad use required for solvency never developed because of problems in building connecting lines and terminal facilities. Vital leadership was lost with a prime stockholder fatally ill and Eads preoccupied by another river project. Tolls from the highway alone were inadequate, and the company was forced into receivership less than a year after the opening. Now jointly owned by the city and a regional transportation authority, both highway and rail decks have been restored and are operating as originally intended.

Sources and Further Reading: Carl W. Condit, *American Building Art,* 2 vols. (1960); Robert W. Jackson, *Rails Across the Mississippi* (2001); John A. Kouwenhoven, "The Designing of the Eads Bridge," *Technology and Culture* 32 (Oct. 1982); Howard S. Miller and Quinta Scott, *The Eads Bridge* (1979).

David Simmons
Ohio Historical Society, Columbus, Ohio

Mackinac Bridge

Also known as Big Mac and Mighty Mac, the Mackinac Bridge is the longest suspension bridge in North America. Five miles long, located at the straits between Lake Michigan and Lake Huron, it unites Michigan's lower and upper peninsulas. Proponents for the bridge date back to Cornelius Vanderbilt in the nineteenth century, yet it was not until the 1920s that advocates began to push for the bridge in earnest. Given the distance, it was believed that a bridge between Mackinaw City and St. Ignace was impossible because the ground would not support the structure's weight and the harsh weather would destroy anything erected. The State Highway Department's $30 million cost estimate in 1928 proved an additional hindrance.

The project was not pursued until the Great Depression. In 1934, the Mackinac Straits Bridge Authority was created to pursue New Deal funds for development and construction, but World War II intervened. After the War, however, proponents formed the Inter-Peninsula Communication Council to build public support, and the Authority created more than a decade before was reorganized under Senator Prentiss M. Brown in 1950. Armed with favorable reports on the feasibility of the project, Brown and colleagues were able to get the project signed into law on April 30, 1952. In January of 1953, D. B. Steinman was selected as chief engineer.

After a series of legal problems and three rounds of bond sales to secure necessary funding, construction on the project began on May 7, 1954. Employing 3,500 men and the second-largest armada of marine construction equipment ever assembled, the bridge had thirty-four support foundations, with a main span length of 3,800 feet and towers that rose 552 feet in the air. This main span was the second longest in the world, and in overall suspended deck length, it was the longest in the world until 1998. Even with all the challenges of construction, the bridge opened on schedule to traffic on November 1, 1957. Michigan Governor G. Mennen Williams declared at the formal dedication, "The North and South of the state have long been engaged. They now have a wedding ring!"

Up to 6,000 cars per hour can use the bridge, compared to the 462 cars per hour that could be ferried across the Straits prior to the 1957 opening, eliminating waiting times as long as nineteen hours. On September 25, 1984, the fifty millionth vehicle crossed the bridge, and more than 100 million had used the bridge by the turn of the century. Architects of the bridge estimate that it will last for a thousand years, although an $80 million painting project and $189 million resurfacing project was launched in 2000. Even after forty-five years, it still stands as a monument to human ingenuity and construction prowess.

Sources and Further Reading: Prentiss M. Brown, *The Mackinac Bridge Story* (1956); Willliam Ratigan, *The Long Crossing* (1959); William Ratigan, *Straits of Mackinac! Crossroads of the Great Lakes* (1957); Lawrence A. Rubin, *Bridging the Straits* (1985); David B. Steinman, *Miracle Bridge at Mackinac* (1957).

T. Jason Soderstrum
Iowa State University

Cattle Trails

The cattle industry played a vital role in the economic life of the Midwest in the late nineteenth century. Shipping and packing centers such as Chicago, St. Louis, and Kansas City thrived as they sought to satisfy a seemingly insatiable eastern appetite for beef. For about two decades following the Civil War, the stockyards were filled and the packing houses were kept busy because cattlemen in Texas and entrepreneurs in Kansas devised a unique transportation and marketing system called "the long drive." Moved up the cattle trails from Texas to railheads or shipping points in Kansas, livestock was fattened on the rich prairie grasses before finishing their long journey north and east by rail.

Cattle drives and trails were not invented in the 1860s, but this was the time when they developed on a massive scale and became an integral part of the cattle transportation system. At the end of the Civil War, beef was in short supply in northeastern states. At the same time, several million longhorns grazed on Texas ranches. Yankees were hungry for beef and were willing to pay high prices. Texans had the beef but no readily accessible market. With war's end, railroad construction resumed in earnest in Kansas, and enterprising southerners and midwesterners envisioned a solution. Long drives to railheads in Kansas could ultimately deliver Texas beef to northern appetites. Although cattle had been driven to Kansas and Missouri, and even to Iowa, Illinois, and beyond before 1865, the long drives conducted after 1867 were carried out on a scale never before seen. Abilene shipped about thirty-five thousand head of Texas cattle that first year

and some 150 thousand in 1869; but this was just the beginning. Over the next two decades, hundreds of thousands of longhorns made their way north on the cattle trails.

Several Kansas towns vied for the prestige and profits that would accrue to a major cattle-shipping center. Promoters such as Joseph G. McCoy, an Illinois cattle trader who settled in Abilene, went to great lengths to convince Texas cattlemen to make this town the trail's end. Towns were packaged and marketed in the same way a merchant would attempt to sell his wares.

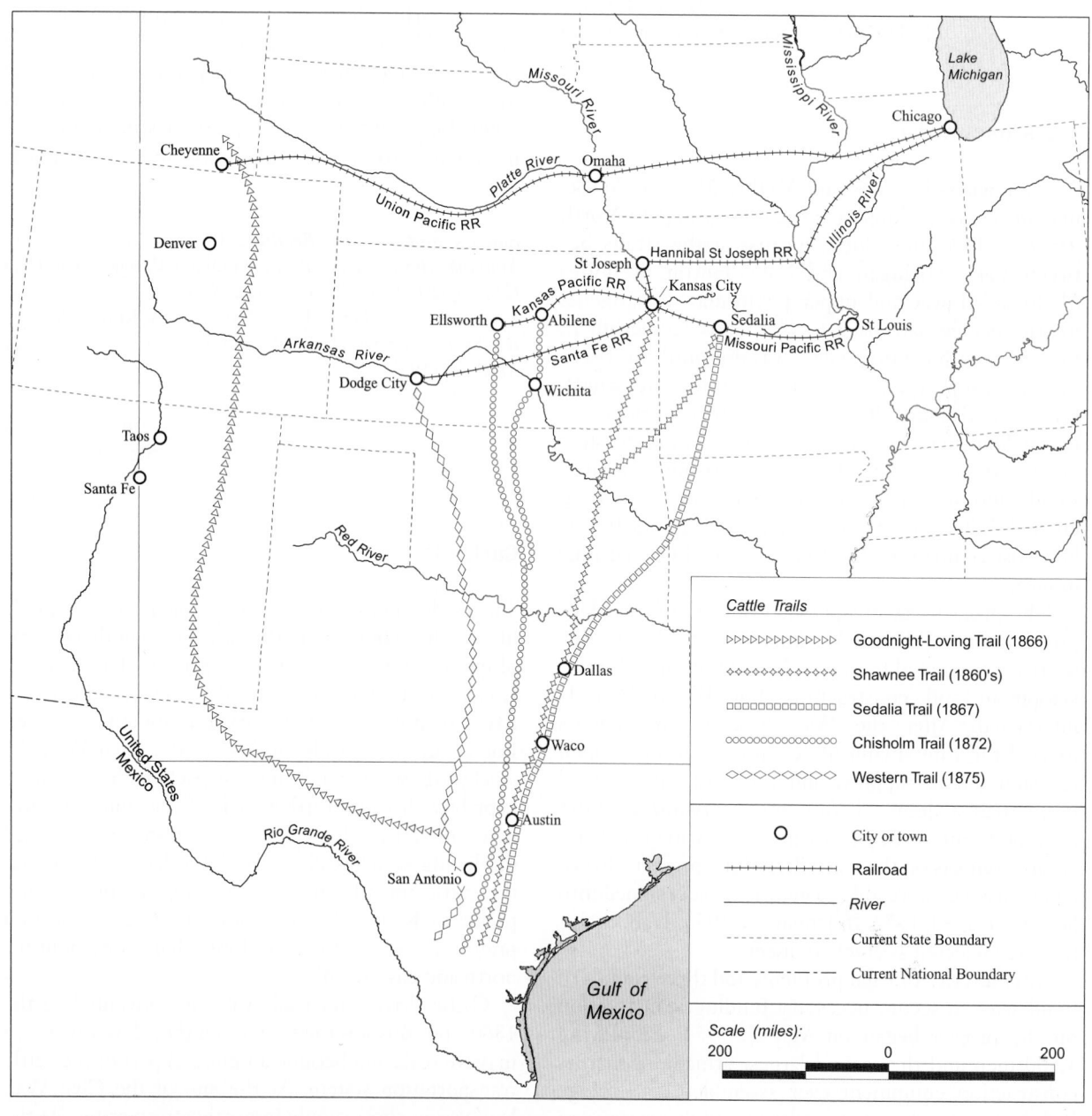

Cattle trails leading to midwestern railheads. Prepared by James DeGrand. *Source:* Carl Waldman, *Atlas of the North American Indian* (New York: Facts on File, 2000); Ray Allen Billington and Martin Ridge, *Westward Expansion* (New York: Macmillan, 1982); http://www.rra.dst.tx.us/c_t/Transportation/SHAWNEE%20TRAIL.cfm.

On the trail, the typical cowboy worked with about a dozen other men to drive a herd of two thousand to twenty-five hundred cattle. Contrary to their romanticized image, cowhands worked hard, long hours on both the ranch and the trail. They had little time or opportunity to live the glamorous, exciting life portrayed in the western movie. Although some excitement came with an occasional stampede or Indian threat, their routine was quite different from the life depicted in myth.

Several cattle trails—the Shawnee, Sedalia, Goodnight-Loving, and Western Trails—carried herds from Texas to Colorado, ranches on the Northern Plains, and Kansas railheads, but the Chisholm Trail holds the most romance and was certainly the most significant arterial route for the Midwest. Named for Jesse Chisholm (1805–1868), a government interpreter, guide, and Indian trader before the Civil War, this famous trail began as a wagon road south from Chisholm's trading post near present-day Wichita, Kansas, through Indian Territory, to the Red River on the Texas border. After the war, this legendary trail extended south to San Antonio, Texas, and north to the Kansas Pacific Railway in north-central Kansas, and included many feeder trails and alternate routes.

Western cattle trails and the merchandise they carried were business ventures for numerous nineteenth-century capitalists. Among the first were the famous Jesse Chisholm himself and Joseph McCoy, who opened Chisholm's trail to Texas cattlemen and gained prominence by making Abilene, Kansas, the Midwest's principal shipping point for Texas cattle. Other Chisholm Trail entrepreneurs included the relatively small-time drover–ranchers who trailed their own cattle from Texas to meatpacking barons such as Armour and Swift of the East Coast, Chicago, and later Kansas City.

In less than twenty years, the trail driving era had come to a close. Quarantine laws and the homesteaders' barbed wire fence spelled death for the cattle drives. In addition, cattle could be shipped by rail directly from their Texas ranches. The bluestem pastures of the central and northern plains still fattened livestock from Texas and elsewhere and helped supply midwestern and eastern markets, but the cattle trailing industry was no more. During their relatively short life span, however, the cattle trails were a vital link in the nation's transportation system.

Sources and Further Reading: Everett Dick, "The Long Drive," *Kansas History: A Journal of the Central Plains* 17 (1928); Stan Hoig, *Jesse Chisholm: Ambassador of the Plains* (1991); Joseph G. McCoy, *Historic Sketches of the Cattle Trade of the West and Southwest* (1874); Jimmy M. Skaggs, *The Cattle-Trailing Industry* (1973); Don Worcester, *The Chisholm Trail: High Road of the Cattle Kingdom* (1980).

Virgil W. Dean
Kansas State Historical Society, Topeka, Kansas

The Oregon Trail

Starting in the early 1840s, the migration of settlers moving west of the Missouri River began in earnest. As they traveled through Nebraska, these pioneers followed the Platte River. It was not by chance that the migrants chose to follow this river basin. Early exploration indicated the land on either side of the Platte formed a natural corridor well suited for travel. The first wagon train trip occurred in 1830 and was followed in 1832 and 1833 by two more. The first large migration of settlers bound for Oregon left Independence, Missouri, in 1843. From this time on, traffic along the Platte River route increased substantially as pioneers set out primarily for Utah, Oregon, and California.

Although the name Oregon Trail implies there was only one route, it had various starting points on the Missouri River. The major ones were at Independence and St. Joseph, Missouri; Weston-Leavenworth, Kansas; and Omaha and Table Creek, Nebraska. These five travel routes eventually came together into one main trunkline at Fort Kearney (near present-day Kearney, Nebraska) to form the Oregon Trail.

The entire trail system from the jumping-off points along the Missouri River to Fort Kearney provided a variety of travel experiences as a result of, among other factors, topography, vegetation, and water availability. Heading west from the Missouri River, the emigrants initially encountered relatively treeless, grassy plains. Despite the scarcity of heavy vegetation, progress was slowed by the necessity of following winding contours to avoid as many stream crossings as possible. When the inevitable crossing was necessary, the oxen or mule teams were often unhitched, stream banks cut down, and wagons pulled across by hand. All of this, of course, further impeded the emigrants' daily progress.

As travelers journeyed further west, the topography began to flatten and wagon trains, once confined to a single file, could break into two or more columns that allowed for increased speed. This became more possible as the wagons reached the Platte River Valley en route to Fort Kearney (est. 1848) and on to Fort Laramie (est. 1834). Continuing the trek beyond the Midwest region of the country, the wagon trains would encounter the difficulties of mountains and deserts, bringing the accompanying problems of slow travel, lack of water, and lack of fuel for fire.

In the Midwest, encounters with Native American tribes, primarily the Pawnee, Cheyenne, and Sioux, could also cause problems. Most of the interaction between the emigrants and Native Americans was friendly and centered around trade. Still, violence did occur. As the number of settlers on the trail increased, Native Americans realized the potential threat the overland caravans represented to their traditional lifestyle. Attempts to prevent further incursions were sometimes violent and often resulted in an aggressive reaction by the emigrants and/or the military. These confrontations endured as long as the Oregon Trail was used.

The Midwest portion of the Oregon Trail, from the Missouri River to approximately Fort Laramie (Wyoming), was used by both emigrants and overland freighters. Between 1841 and 1866, an estimated 350 thousand settlers used this trail. For both the emigrant and the freighter, the main means of transportation was the wagon. Ideally, the wagon was constructed of hardwood, weighed between sixteen hundred and twenty-five hundred pounds, and was pulled by four to eight oxen or mules. More animals were generally required for the heavier freight wagons. Popular imagery often portrays horse-drawn wagons. However, oxen and mules were used most often because they could survive on prairie grass, whereas horses could not.

For many the Oregon Trail was a means to an end. It provided an opportunity to leave an old lifestyle and begin anew. The overland trip was never easy, and most travelers were well aware of the dangers and difficulties. Still, a somewhat romantic vision of life on the trail and hope of a better life at the end drew many people to cross the untamed plains on the Oregon Trail.

Sources and Further Reading: John Faragher, *Women and Men on the Overland Trail* (1979); William E. Lass, *From the Missouri to the Great Salt Lake* (1972); Merrill J. Mattes, *The Great Platte River Road* (1969); John D. Unruh, *The Plains Across* (1979).

Gregory A. Miller
Nebraska State Historical Society,
Lincoln, Nebraska

The Santa Fe Trail

The development of the Santa Fe Trail actually moved from west to east. The Spanish established the town of Santa Fe in 1609, but eastward exploration did not begin for a number of years. There is some evidence that Spanish explorers may have reached the Arkansas River in present-day southwestern Kansas by about 1634. Although solid documentation is lacking, it is certainly probable that missionaries, traders, and explorers had traveled the route into Kansas. Certainly by the 1700s, the road from Santa Fe to Kansas was known to the Spaniards.

The opening of the Santa Fe Trail in 1821 is credited to William Becknell. Setting out from Franklin, Missouri, his mule string passed through what became known as Council Grove in Kansas, then on to Santa Fe. The next year, Becknell led a train of freight wagons. He followed the same route until he reached a point near present-day Dodge City, Kansas. Here he guided the wagons in a more southwesterly direction. This new road, later called the Cimarron Cutoff (because it crossed the Cimarron River), shortened the travel time and distance, but went through more desolate country. Eventually, however, the Cimarron Cutoff became the preferred route.

Unlike emigrant routes, the Santa Fe Trail was used mainly for commercial purposes. Goods such as clothing, cutlery, hardware, and other consumer items were taken to Santa Fe and traded primarily for furs and silver. By 1825, the profits made by American traders and the route they used was of such commercial value that Congress authorized an official survey of the trail. Additionally, the federal government appropriated money to purchase the right-of-way from various Native American tribes where the trail traversed their land.

Over the years the route of the Santa Fe Trail remained the same, but circumstances contributed to its colorful history. With the beginning of the Mexican War in 1846, Colonel Stephen W. Kearney led troops down the trail, eventually occupying Santa Fe the same year. At the conclusion of the war, both the beginning and ending points of the Santa Fe Trail were in U.S. possession.

While commercial activity continued to increase, other events affected the amount of traffic on the trail. In 1843, the westward migration to Oregon began, followed by the gold rushes to California in 1849 and to Colorado in 1859. In addition, the stagecoach began using this route during the 1850s. All of these brought new activity to the Santa Fe Trail.

With increased usage came new military forts to protect travelers and relay stations to provide for the stagecoaches. Some Native Americans tolerated the ever-expanding European American presence along the Santa Fe Trail; others did not. Dissatisfied with this continual expansion, some tribes fought back—especially the Pawnee, Cheyenne, and Comanche—and this escalating violence plagued the Santa Fe Trail throughout much of its history.

Travelers on the Santa Fe Trail encountered other

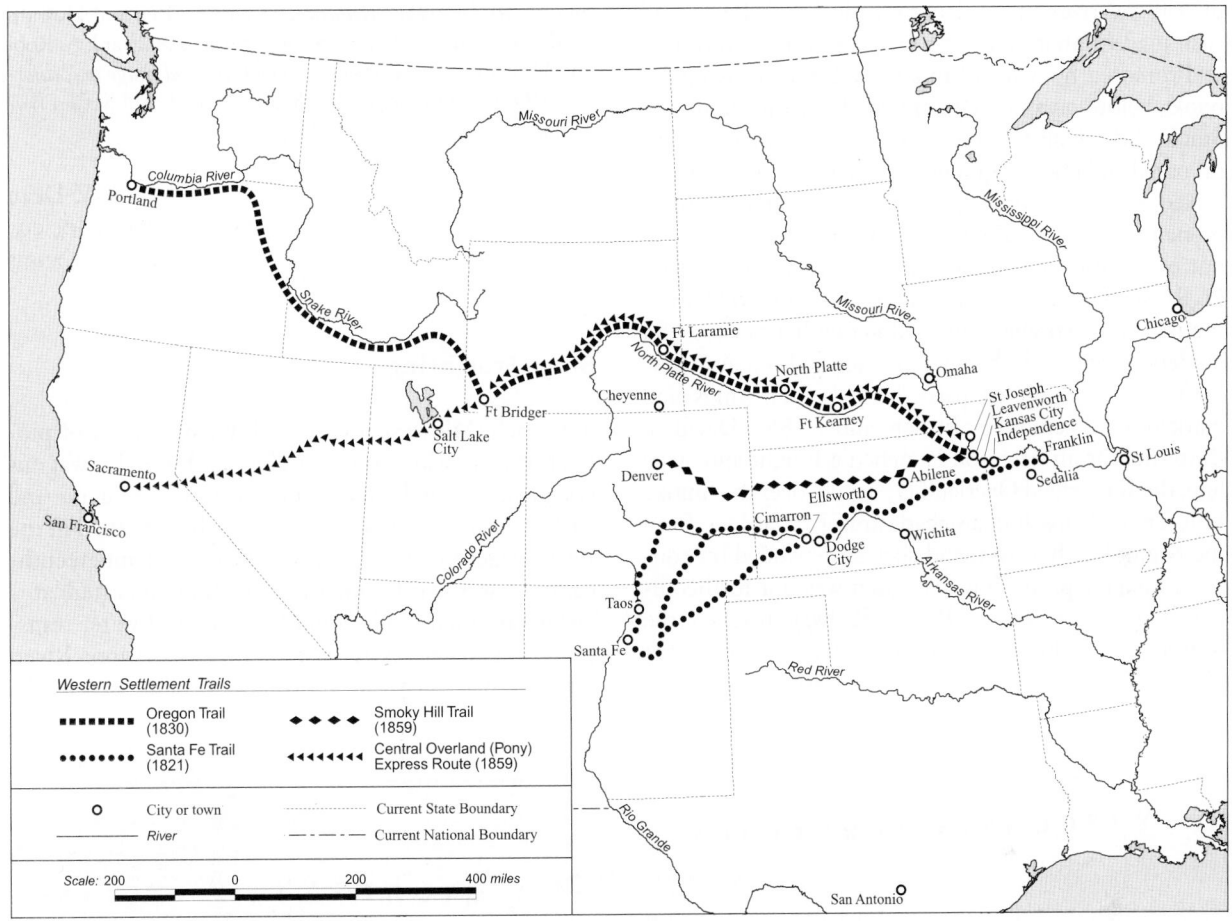

Overland routes for settlement of the West. Prepared by James DeGrand. *Source:* Carl Waldman, *Atlas of the North American Indian* (New York: Facts on File, 2000); Ray Allen Billington and Martin Ridge, *Westward Expansion* (New York: Macmillan, 1982).

hardships as well. Diseases such as typhoid, malaria, and especially cholera were a constant threat. Lack of water and provisions posed additional problems. Also, even though the route was well established, the trip itself was long and arduous. Despite all this, the Santa Fe Trail was used continually from 1821 to 1880. The nearly sixty-year expanse is far longer than that of many other famous trails. It was not until the railroad reached Santa Fe in 1880 that the trail's usefulness finally ended.

What explains the Santa Fe Trail's longevity? Certainly the commercial rewards were substantial. In 1822, trade on the trail was valued at $15 thousand. By 1860, the amount had increased to $3.5 million. Individual accounts detail various reasons for making the journey. For some, it was the adventure of traveling to what at the time was a foreign land. Many enjoyed the excitement of crossing an untamed land. For still others it was the lure of the mysterious and magical destination, Santa Fe. Combined, these reasons have made the Santa Fe Trail one of the most storied in the country.

Sources and Further Reading: David Dary, *The Santa Fe Trail: Its History, Legends, and Lore* (2002); Mark Gardner, *Wagons for the Santa Fe Trade* (2000); Marc Simmons, *The Old Trail to Santa Fe* (1996); Marc Simmons, ed., *On the Santa Fe Trail* (1986).

Gregory A. Miller
Nebraska State Historical Society,
Lincoln, Nebraska

The Smoky Hill Trail

Opened in 1859 to provide a relatively short route across Kansas Territory to the gold mines in the front range of the Rocky Mountains, the Smoky Hill Trail followed the river of the same name through much of Kansas and was about one hundred miles shorter than its alternatives—the Santa Fe Trail and the Platte River Road. Indians had traveled this Smoky Hill valley route for many years, and John C. Fremont explored the river in 1844 before the Pike's Peak gold rush made it an important European American trail.

Promoted by word of mouth and numerous guidebooks before anyone knew much about the route, the Smoky Hill Trail was the literal death of many an ill-prepared and poorly equipped traveler and for a time received a woeful moniker, the "starvation trail." Entrepreneurs in eastern Kansas and western Missouri were not easily discouraged, however, and in 1859, William G. Russell led a survey party along the route to Denver. He issued a favorable report, along with a more useful guidebook and map than had previously been available. Soon a second survey party improved crossings and marked good campsites. In September 1865, David A. Butterfield from Atchison launched a freight and stage line, the Butterfield Overland Despatch, over the Smoky Hill Trail. Plains Indians made travel hazardous from the beginning, however, and success depended on constant military protection that often was not forthcoming. When the Kansas Pacific Railway reached the Kansas–Colorado line in 1870, the trail's significant place in the nation's transportation infrastructure ended.

Sources and Further Reading: Wayne C. Lee and Howard C. Raynesford, *Trails of the Smoky Hill* (1980); Frank A. Root and William Elsey Connelley, *The Overland Stage to California* (1901); Raymond W. Settle and Mary Lund Settle, *War Drums and Wagon Wheels* (1966).

Virgil W. Dean
Kansas State Historical Society,
Topeka, Kansas

Stage Freighting

The early Midwest was settled during an era of pioneer travel, when stagecoaches and freight wagons constituted rapid land transportation. A stage and freight system developed more slowly here than in the East, largely because of two realities of nineteenth-century westward expansion: People migrated at a faster rate than roads could be built; and water transportation, particularly east of the Mississippi River, was cheaper, relatively more comfortable, accessible,

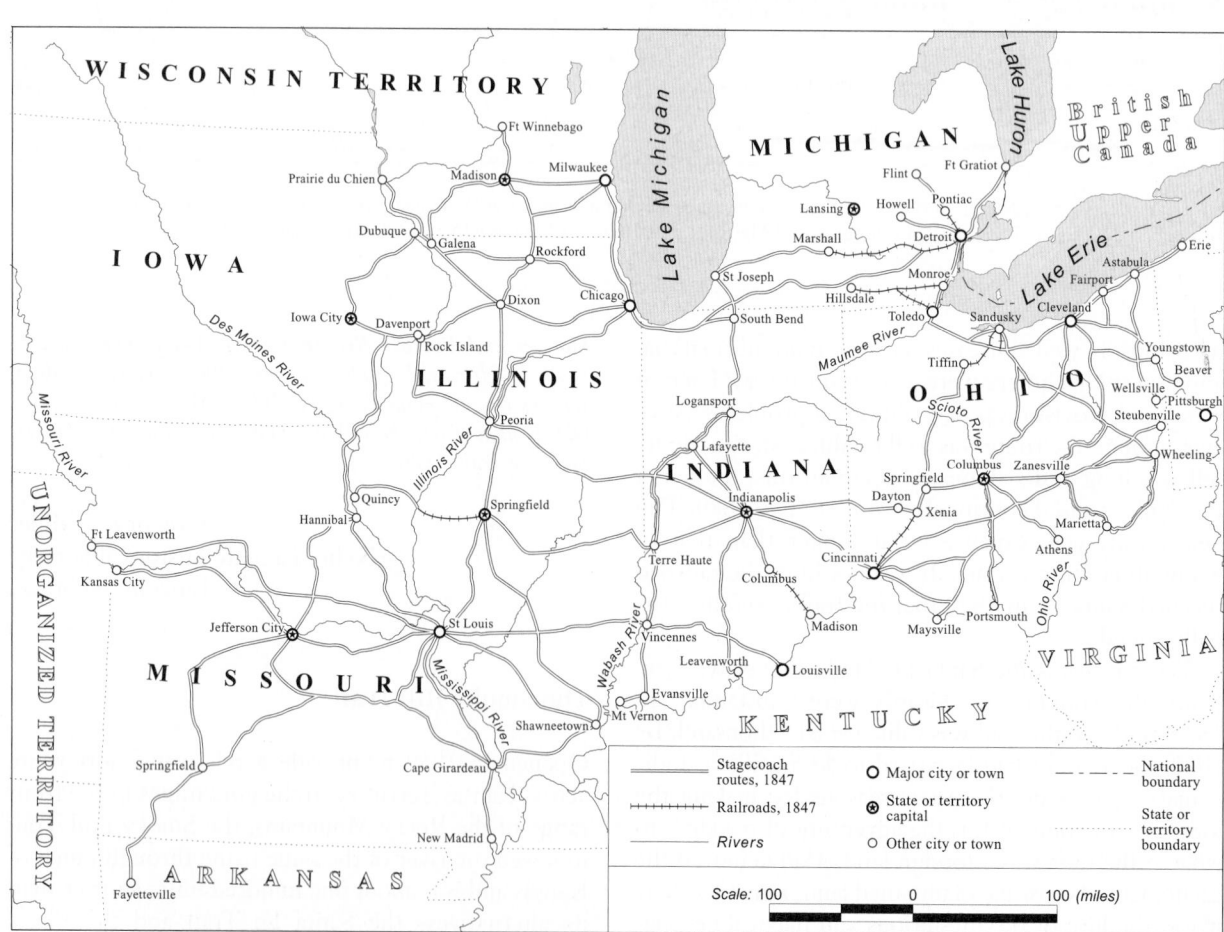

Stagecoach routes and railroads, 1847. Prepared by James DeGrand. *Source:* S. Augustus Mitchell, *A Route Book Adapted to Mitchell's National Map of the American Republic; Comprising Tables of the Principal Railroad, Steamboat and Stage Routes throughout the United States* (1847).

and dependable than stage travel. Decent roads were essential to the ability of stage and freight companies (and offshoot express companies) to operate with any efficiency and with passenger and client confidence; midwestern roads were frequently labeled "dreadful." Dubuque's *Iowa News* advised its readers who were considering stage travel from Galena, Illinois, to St. Louis, Missouri, in 1837, to brace themselves to walk half the way and carry a fence rail the remainder, indicating both the impassable quality of the roads and the probability of having to pry the wheels out of mudholes as part of their travel.

Before the War of 1812, the major road in the Old Northwest over which stagecoaches operated was Zane's Trace, the primary land route to the West and the most important road in Ohio until 1832. Columbus became a major staging area, with the first stagecoach service arriving from Chillicothe in 1816. As early as 1820, efforts were made to create stage lines from Louisville to Vincennes, Indiana, across southern Illinois, and on to St. Louis. Obtaining a contract to move the U.S. Mail was a lucrative endeavor, and both the U.S. Postal Service and westward migration figure prominently in the history of stage and freight. After the 1830s, stagecoaches carried mail west from Zanesville, Ohio, over the National Road, to Indiana, Illinois, and Missouri pioneers. In Iowa, stages ran on irregular schedules in 1837 and continued for about thirty years.

What stagecoaching was to passenger and mail conveyance, wagon-freighting was to moving a host of bulky goods. Despite the nineteenth-century eastern communities' preference for water transportation, followed by the railroad, four-horse wagon freight companies managed a steady business on Ohio turnpikes. West of the Mississippi, however, the freighting business was important to the local and regional economies in areas such as the Missouri Valley. Council Bluffs, Iowa, and Omaha, Nebraska, were the northernmost entrepôts until the 1876 gold rush into the Black Hills created a brief burst of wagon-freighting in Sioux City. Freighting spawned a large number of supporting businesses such as the raising and pasturing of draft animals and the building of warehouses, taverns and inns, and wagons. It was of even more consequence to commerce in general; it has been estimated that from about 1840 until after the Civil War, freighters transported half of the business of Missouri River towns. Some freighting operations were immense. Jones and Cartwright freighted out of Leavenworth, Kansas, and in October of 1860, the company sent out twenty-one wagon train caravans, nineteen of which comprised twenty-seven wagons each pulled by 324 oxen and driven by thirty men.

The role of stage freighting in the pioneering and development of the Midwest has been understated, being overshadowed by the railroads as early as 1870. That year, the last stage left Des Moines, Iowa, and coaches that once fetched one thousand dollars were soon sold for ten dollars as scrap.

Sources and Further Reading: Harry Ellsworth Cole, *Stagecoach and Tavern Tales of the Old Northwest* (1972); Kenneth E. Colton, "Stagecoach Travel in Iowa," *Annals of Iowa* 22 (Jan. 1940); Joseph R. Frese and Jacob Judd, eds., *An Emerging Independent American Economy, 1815–1875* (1980); LeRoy Pratt, "Ten Cents a Mile and a Fence Rail," *Annals of Iowa* 39 (Spring 1969); George Rogers Taylor, *The Transportation Revolution, 1815–1860* (1951); Henry Pickering Walker, *The Wagonmasters* (1966).

Ginette Aley
Iowa State University

The Pony Express

Established during the winter of 1859–1860 as a fast overland route to deliver news and mail to and from the West Coast, the Pony Express route extended from Sacramento, California, to St. Joseph, Missouri. Pony Express riders could relay information and letters over nearly two thousand miles in less than ten days—half the time needed to travel around Cape Horn. The Pony Express also provided a national symbol for opening the West to immigration and settlement.

Cutting through the midwestern state of Missouri and territories of Kansas and Nebraska, the headquarters and starting point for the Pony Express was the Patee House in St. Joseph, Missouri. Under a government contract, William H. Russell of the freighting firm of Russell, Majors and Waddell established the Central Overland California and Pikes Peak Express (Pony Express) to carry mail once a week out of St. Joseph, west into northeastern Kansas. Proceeding through the towns of Hollenberg, Marysville, and Seneca, often riding near the Little Blue River, riders entered the Nebraska territory at Fort Mitchell station and proceeded up the Northern Platte River Valley to Fort Kearney, exiting the state at the Rock Creek station and from there through Colorado, Wyoming, Utah, and Nevada and into California. Stations for fresh horses were spaced anywhere from ten to fifteen miles apart, while riders were relieved every seventy-five to one hundred miles.

Although it lasted for less than two years and did not pay for itself financially, it reinforced for eastern leaders the belief that the Central Route could be used by railroads to bind the country together. It is estimated that it had cost Russell $200,000 by the time it ceased operations, but provided much-needed monetary compensation for riders, station keepers, stock tenders, and route superintendents. In the end, the telegraph spelled the ultimate demise of the Pony Express system and any further attempts to develop similar systems.

Sources and Further Reading: Roy S. Bloss, *Pony Express: The Great Gamble* (1959); Arthur Chapman, *The Pony Express: The Record of a Romantic Adventure in Business* (1932); Le Roy R. Hafen, *The Overland Mail 1849–1869* (1969).

T. Jason Soderstrum
Iowa State University

Rural Free Delivery

Prior to the development of rural free delivery by the United States Postal Service, rural midwesterners depended on contract carriers who brought mail over "star routes" to fourth-class post offices located in rural stores and homes, to which farm families often had to walk as far as five miles.

Agitation for a system of rural mail delivery began through the efforts of Illinois newspaperman John Stahl and Georgia Congressman Thomas Watson. By the 1890s, the populist movement adopted the issue and lent it support. Although the public began to demand the service, its cost led government officials to oppose it. Congress, however, responded to public opinion and launched a rural delivery system, and trial delivery began in rural West Virginia on October 1, 1896. Two weeks later, another trial began in Ohio. Mail carriers followed country roads, placing the mail in the crude mailboxes erected by grateful farmers. Additional pioneer routes in states like Illinois proved that although rural delivery could not pay for itself, it was feasible, so long as the government was willing to fund it.

Although opponents attempted to kill the young and expanding system, it found friends in the McKinley administration and among the millions of rural Americans that it could potentially serve. The program became a permanent part of the U.S. Postal Service in 1902. Within only three years, twenty-four thousand routes were established, in part because farmers petitioned their representatives for the service, particularly in the Midwest, and the representatives realized the political expediency of satisfying their constituents' demands for the service.

The new rural free delivery system, or RFD, meant the end of the old fourth-class post offices and star routes. Many storekeepers depended on the presence of a post office in their establishment to draw cus-tomers, and they protested, but to little avail. Conversely, the system helped to destroy the little communities that had formed around the old rural post offices, and the magazines, newspapers, and catalogs brought to the farms encouraged young people in their flight to the cities. By 1926, when the system reached its all-time high, 45,315 mail routes served rural residents nationwide.

Rural free delivery played an enormously beneficial role in the lives of midwestern rural residents. It helped to end rural isolation by bringing farmers daily newspapers, mail, catalogs, and the daily visit of the mail carrier. Mail-order companies, such as Sears Roebuck and Montgomery Ward, thrived on the business generated through their catalogs by rural patrons. Rural delivery was the first appearance of the government in the lives of rural midwesterners, but it was a presence that they welcomed. One rural woman, writing in 1947, echoed the sentiments of other midwesterners in proclaiming, "Thank God and Government for rural free delivery."

Sources and Further Reading: Wayne Fuller, "RFD," *Timeline* 4 (Apr.–May 1987); Wayne Fuller, *RFD: The Changing Face of Rural America* (1964); Carl Scheele, *A Short History of the Mail Service* (1970).

Peter Hoehnle
Iowa State University

Ben Holladay (1819–1887)

Born in Carlisle County, Kentucky, Holladay spent much of his youth in western Missouri. He married Notley Ann Calvert of Weston, Missouri, and had seven children. An early entrepreneur in the settlement of the West, Holladay pursued numerous business ventures including a hotel, general store, and saloon, as well as postmaster, and engaged in trade with the American Indians who had been relocated in eastern Kansas.

Holladay captured a government contract to supply General Stephen Watts Kearny's Army of the West during the Mexican War, and through this, built up his freighting business and commercial trade with settlers moving west after the war. Holladay also entered into a business relationship with the firm of Russell, Majors and Waddell and helped finance the partners' Pony Express. When the Express's parent company, the Central Overland California and Pike's Peak Express Company, failed in 1862, Holladay took over some of its assets and established the Overland Stage Line, which captured mail contracts and provided passenger service to San Francisco. Indian attacks caused financial problems for the business in the mid-1860s, and Holladay sold out to Wells, Fargo and Company. He then entered the steamship business on the West Coast and became primary owner of the Oregon Central Railroad Company.

A second marriage in 1873 to Esther Campbell produced two more children, but Holladay's economic fortunes never recovered from the panic of that year. He died in Portland, Oregon, on July 8, 1887.

Sources and Further Reading: J. V. Frederick and Ben Holladay, *The Stagecoach King* (1940); Frank A. Root and William Elsey Connelley, *The Overland Stage to California* (1901).

Virgil W. Dean
Kansas State Historical Society, Topeka, Kansas

Alexander Majors (1814–1900)

Born in Franklin, Simpson County, Kentucky, Majors spent much of his youth with his family in Lafayette and then Jackson County, Missouri. His father, Benjamin Majors, managed a large farm, as well as a flour and saw mill, in Missouri from 1825 to 1858. Majors married Katherine Stallcup in 1834 and operated his own farm in Jackson County to support his family and finance his initial entry into the freighting business from Independence to Santa Fe in August 1848.

Majors transported government supplies to outposts in New Mexico, Colorado, and Utah for several years, then entered into a partnership with William H. Russell and William B. Waddell—Russell, Majors and Waddell—in 1855 with Russell as the entrepreneur pursuing contracts. Majors managed the firm's extensive on-road activities—over four thousand men, forty thousand oxen, and a thousand mules. The business operated a stagecoach line from Leavenworth to Denver after 1859, and on April 3, 1860, it launched the Pony Express, which briefly (before the completion of the telegraph) provided vital communication for a nation rapidly moving toward civil war.

Russell, Majors and Waddell folded in 1862, but Majors was able to continue in the freighting business for several more years; subsequently he worked on the Union Pacific and as a Utah silver prospector, living in Salt Lake City for a decade before returning to the Kansas City area. Majors published a reminiscence of his long, eventful career as a Western entrepreneur, *Seventy Years on the Frontier*, in 1893, and he died in Chicago on January 12, 1900.

Sources and Further Reading: Alexander Majors, *Seventy Years on the Frontier* (1893); Frank A. Root and William

Elsey Connelley, *The Overland Stage to California* (1901); Raymond W. Settle and Mary Lund Settle, *War Drums and Wagon Wheels* (1966).

Virgil W. Dean
Kansas State Historical Society, Topeka, Kansas

Joseph G. McCoy (1837–1915)

In 1867, Joseph McCoy, a young cattle dealer from Sangamon County, Illinois, decided Abilene, Kansas, would make a profitable shipping point for the thousands of head of Texas cattle in need of a market. For the next four years, his town reigned as the primary railhead at the end of the long drive.

McCoy faced many obstacles when he first arrived in the tiny settlement, and the railroad was skeptical about his plan. This quickly changed, however, when McCoy built chutes and pens for the anticipated cattle herds and convinced the Kansas Pacific Railroad to construct a spur to accommodate cattle cars. McCoy then sent agents to Texas to convince cattlemen that taking the Chisholm Trail to Abilene was the best way to get their cattle to market. The persistent midwesterner's entrepreneurial efforts were successful: The cattle came, to the tune of 1.5 million head between 1867 and 1871; the first shipment left Abilene on September 5, 1867; the little town boomed; and McCoy prospered.

Although Abilene lost most of its cattle trade to newer cow towns in Kansas within five years, McCoy continued his business activities in the state of Kansas, moving to the new cow town of Wichita in 1872. He also wrote a popular book about the industry he had done so much to promote, *Historic Sketches of the Cattle Trade of the West and Southwest* (1874). Joseph McCoy died in Kansas City, Missouri, on October 19, 1915.

Sources and Further Reading: George L. Cushman, "Abilene, First of the Kansas Cow Towns," *Kansas Historical Quarterly* 9 (Aug. 1940); Joseph G. McCoy, *Historic Sketches of the Cattle Trade of the West and Southwest* (1874); John E. Wickman, "A Visionary on the Prairie," *Journal of the West* 25 (Jan. 1986).

Virgil W. Dean
Kansas State Historical Society, Topeka, Kansas

William B. Waddell (1807–1872)

The first-born child of Catherine Bradford and John Waddell II, William Bradford Waddell was born on October 14, 1807, in Fauquier County, Virginia. The family moved to Mason County, Kentucky, in 1815, and in 1824, the young Waddell joined the westward migration, moving first to Galena, Illinois, where he worked in the lead mines, and then to St. Louis, Missouri. In the latter city Waddell clerked in a general store, before returning to Kentucky, marrying Susan Byram in 1829, and starting his own dry goods business.

Waddell moved back to Missouri in 1936, this time to Lexington where he ran a store and commission business and was a town builder and promoter. Soon he made the acquaintance of one William H. Russell, with whom he would have numerous business dealings for the next fifteen years. In 1853, the two midwestern entrepreneurs purchased an established Lexington mercantile firm and renamed it Waddell and Russell. Late the following year, they established a copartnership with Alexander Majors, and thus was born the firm of Russell, Majors and Waddell. In 1855, the partners chose Leavenworth in the Kansas Territory for their headquarters.

Among their expansive mercantile and freighting enterprises, the firm established the Central Overland California and Pike's Peak Express Company which, at William Russell's urging, launched the legendary Pony Express in 1860. This colossal financial failure and the onset of the Civil War contributed to the firm's 1862 collapse, from which Waddell never recovered nor did Russell. He died on his daughter's farm near Lexington, Missouri, on April 1, 1872.

Sources and Further Reading: Frank A. Root and William Elsey Connelley, *The Overland Stage to California* (1901); Raymond W. Settle and Mary Lund Settle, *War Drums and Wagon Wheels* (1966).

Virgil W. Dean
Kansas State Historical Society, Topeka, Kansas

Ground Transportation

Transportation played an especially decisive role in the historical development of the Midwest. Situated in the center of the nation, the region became a crossroads for travel and commerce. Its extensive system of rivers and lakes, utilized first by its aboriginal inhabitants, provided ready-made transportation routes for European explorers and waves of fur traders, agriculturalists, and business entrepreneurs as they entered the region. Its relatively flat terrain allowed for easy movement across country on foot, on horseback, or by other means. In the long run, more important than geographic endowment in determining the region's

growth and development were the myriad human decisions that were made in constructing a ground transportation system that efficiently moved people and goods from place to place, from wagons and stage vehicles to trains, trucks, and planes.

Midwestern railroad expansion lagged somewhat behind that of New England and the Middle Atlantic states for a couple of decades after the appearance of the new technology, but during the decade before the Civil War, the region came into its own. States like Ohio and Indiana underwent tenfold increases in their transportation systems during the 1850s, and the former maintained its primacy among all states in miles of track per square mile of area throughout the twentieth century. The earliest rail lines linked parts of the interior that were not served by water routes to the Ohio River and the Great Lakes and primarily served small local areas, backed by aspiring towns and cities. By the 1850s, many of these small lines were being absorbed by larger companies, and after the Civil War several large trunk lines connected Chicago and St. Louis to eastern metropolises. The rise of the railroad coincided with the demise of canals and steamboats and delayed efforts to improve roads for wagon transport.

The railroads completed what the Erie Canal had earlier begun in shifting the direction of movement in the interior from a counterclockwise path, leading down the Ohio and Mississippi Rivers to New Orleans and back around to Atlantic seaports, to primarily east-west, cross-country routes. Also, like their waterborne predecessors, railroads significantly reduced transportation costs, increased economic activity along their routes, stimulated real estate prices, and influenced the location of towns and cities along their routes. Beyond that, either through the process of actually platting out the original towns or through their influence on the location of track facilities, factories, and warehouses, railroads were a crucial factor in determining the shape and texture of nineteenth-century urban places.

Between 1848, when its first rail link was established, and 1860, when nearly a dozen railroads radiated out from the city, Chicago emerged as the dominant commercial, industrial, and agricultural processing center in the heartland. In little more than half a decade, it also became the largest rail center in the world. Railroads enabled the lakeshore city to wrest economic supremacy from St. Louis, whose original identity was as a river town. They likewise facilitated the rise of Detroit, Cleveland, and Minneapolis, which began to overshadow Ohio River towns like Cincinnati and Louisville, and in general, railroads were highly influential in establishing the midwestern hierarchy of urban places. The first sub-

Expansion of highways. Prepared by James DeGrand. *Source: Atlas of Historical Geography of the United States* (1932), plate 140 A; Phillip John Davies et al., *The History Atlas of North America* (New York: Macmillan, 1998), 88–89.

stantial federal land grant for building railroads, in 1850 to the Illinois Central linking Chicago and the Gulf Coast, presaged larger ones after the Civil War connecting the Midwest with the Pacific Coast. With the completion of the first railway bridge across the Mississippi River in 1856 at Rock Island, Illinois, producers in the surrounding region gained access to Chicago and eastern markets, and during the next thirty years, fifteen more bridges spanned the Upper Mississippi.

The extensive rail system constructed in the Midwest contributed to Union victories during the Civil War. During the late nineteenth century, as the nation underwent a second industrial revolution and as the pace of urbanization accelerated, railroads continued to expand in spectacular fashion, providing a foundation for agricultural as well as industrial and commercial growth. As America's first big business, the railroad industry provided a model for others to emulate, as they, too, sought to expand their operations and increase their profits. In turn, it became a target for criticism and opposition by client groups and by a public that frequently perceived it as monopolistic, unfair, and exploitative. Granger laws passed by agrarian-influenced midwestern legislatures during the 1870s established precedents for further state and federal regulation in subsequent decades.

Technologies akin to those revolutionizing interurban traffic began to transform intraurban mobility during the 1880s. Cable cars were the first to replace horsepower with mechanical power in moving cars on fixed tracks on city streets. Kansas City, Cincinnati, St. Louis, Omaha, St. Paul, Grand Rapids, and Sioux City all experimented with cable systems, but Chicago built the most extensive one, its eighty-two miles of track making it the main center of cable traction in the country. During the 1890s, electric trolleys, which were faster than cable cars, proved capable of navigating grades of 8 to 10 percent or steeper and quickly put cable cars out of business. The new device rapidly spread all over the Midwest during the decade. Electric streetcars speeded movement, stimulated commercial activity, elevated property values, and encouraged expanded use of leisure time. Although it is an exaggeration to say that streetcars created the suburbs, they did much to facilitate their growth as their lines extended out miles beyond the boundaries of the city. Around the turn of the century, Chicago became one of the few cities in the United States to build a subway system.

By 1900, ground transportation in urban areas had exceeded that in rural areas, despite the impressive accomplishments of the railroad. Country roads, which serviced the needs of the vast majority of the population, were hardly better than they had been a century earlier. Most were still dirt and became muddy morasses in rainy weather, dusty and rutted in dry, and virtually impassible under winter snows. What first directed people's attention to the problem of rural transportation and the need to improve it was the cycling craze that developed during the years after safety bicycles were introduced in the late 1880s. Reduced in weight and cost and much easier to ride than earlier high-wheelers, the new safety bicycle encouraged women as well as men to participate. By 1896, there were four million bicycles in the United States, and their riders emerged as the prime force in pushing a good roads movement, which began achieving significant results by the early years of the new century.

In pushing for smooth-surfaced roads for their vehicles, bicyclists' interests coincided with those of the new automobilists. The best roads in America were in New England and the Mid-Atlantic region, the worst in the South and the rural Midwest. It was no coincidence that early production centers of automobiles concentrated in places enjoying smoother pavements. New England took the early lead in car manufacturing, concentrating its attention on electric and steam vehicles. In quick order, however, the Midwest emerged to a dominant position, gaining an advantage developing the gasoline-fueled internal combustion engine. Some early manufacturers, such as the Studebakers of South Bend, were wagon makers who entered the car business as a hedge against the possibility of consumers shifting their preference from horse-drawn to mechanical transportation. While hundreds of midwestern towns and cities from Ohio to South Dakota entered the business at one time or another, by the early 1900s, the American automobile industry centered in a dozen or so cities in northern Ohio, northern Indiana, and southern Michigan within a two-hundred-mile radius of Fort Wayne, Indiana.

Automobile manufacturing became the backbone of a new consumer goods–oriented economy and a mainstay of economic prosperity and development in the region during the first half of the twentieth century. Detroit emerged as the actual and symbolic center of the business, but scores of other towns and cities benefited from the boom. More than a mode of locomotion, the new technology brought about sweeping changes in residential patterns, work habits, the use of leisure time, courtship practices, the socialization of the young, and the breakdown of rural isolation, especially for housewives. Like the railroad before it, automobile manufacturing evolved into America's biggest business, and practices initiated by the industry established the norm for firms in a variety of other fields. Automobiles became the prime shaper of urban space, a key factor in the business cycle, a major item in family budgets, and an underlying reason for the strong sense of freedom and individualism that most Americans exhibited. No area of the country felt the impact of the auto more than the Midwest. After some initial resistance by rural dwellers, its residents were among the most enthusiastic purchasers of automobiles in the country. By the late 1920s, midwesterners were more likely to own automobiles than people in most other sections of the country.

While bringing many benefits to their owners, automobiles also carried some negative side effects. Accident rates were high, and traffic fatalities were numerous. Small-town storeowners benefited from the ability of shoppers to drive into town more easily and frequently. Saturday nights became big shopping nights in towns all over the Midwest from the 1920s through the 1950s. But the same automobiles that carried people into town could also take them farther down the road to larger retail centers. It is no coincidence that smaller towns began losing customers to larger places at the same time that car ownership became common. In recent decades, small towns have found it difficult to survive when potential customers do most of their big-ticket buying in shopping centers and malls accessible by automobile.

While emerging during the early 1900s and gaining prominence during the interwar period, bus and truck transportation also enhanced people's lives even as they exacerbated certain problems. Buses began as local operations; long-distance bus lines emerged during the latter decade. The Greyhound Company, a creation of the 1930s, had its origins in Hibbing, Minnesota, before World War I. The growth of bus ridership during the decade after World War I coincided with the beginning of the decline of railroad passenger service. In like manner, increasing truck ownership contributed to reduced freight shipments on railroads. Ironically, problems experienced by the railroads during the wartime emergency had encouraged truck transportation. With the building of the interstate highway system after 1956, over-the-road trucks increasingly replaced railroads for the transportation of many goods.

Like railroad passenger trains, electric interurban railways found themselves unable to compete with the rise of the automobile after World War I. Interurbans lasted for only two decades as an important phenomenon. Some lines went into operation during the 1890s, but the great investment boom occurred during the first decade of the new century. The industry enjoyed its greatest popularity in the Midwest, with Ohio far ahead of every other state in mileage, and Indiana and Illinois ranking second and fourth, respectively. Indianapolis, with thirteen lines, had the largest network in the country. During the 1920s, the rise of the automobile killed the viability of interurban trains. Mean-

while, motorcycle riding became primarily a recreational activity for the adventuresome, who remained a tiny fraction of road passengers.

Ground transportation, in general, was one of the most important factors in the development of the Midwest over the course of more than two centuries, playing a major role in the economic, political, social, and cultural conditions of its citizens. Beyond its tremendous impact on every aspect of midwestern life was its constant tendency to evolve as new technologies emerged and as economic and political conditions altered over time.

Sources and Further Reading: Jean-Pierre Bardou et al., *The Automobile Revolution: The Impact of an Industry* (1982); Burton B. Crandall, *The Growth of the Intercity Bus Industry* (1954); James J. Flink, *America Adopts the Automobile, 1895–1910* (1970); George W. Hilton, *The Cable Car in America* (1971); George W. Hilton and John F. Due, *The Electric Interurban Railways in America* (1960); Richard Hough and L.J.K. Setright, *A History of the World's Motorcycles* (1973); David L. Lewis and Laurence Goldstein, eds., *The Automobile and American Culture* (1983); Albro Martin, *Railroads Triumphant* (1992); Clay McShane, *Down the Asphalt Path* (1994); Robert A. Smith, *A Social History of the Bicycle* (1972).

John E. Miller
South Dakota State University

Wagons

Wagons played a central role in the development of the Midwest. While families and businesspeople came to the region by water, rail, or over land, it was almost impossible to relocate or establish a business without using a wagon to transport furnishings, supplies, tools, or inventory. Settlers who arrived at river towns, lakeside cities, canal ports, or railroad towns frequently hired farmers with wagons to deliver their goods across town or to farms. Some settlers came to the region with massive Conestoga wagons that were well suited for long-distance travel because of their size, but required too many horses to be useful on farms. Wagons were most useful for transporting agricultural products on the farm and to market. Farmers moved bulky items such as corn, oats, and hay from the field to the crib or barn for livestock. Wagons and teams carried cash crops, notably wheat and butter in the nineteenth century and corn, wheat, and soybeans in the twentieth century, to market for distribution to processors and consumers.

Wagons varied in use, size, and construction. Wagon makers in St. Louis and Independence, Missouri, constructed freight wagons of the Santa Fe and Conestoga types for the Santa Fe trade from the 1820s through the

1870s. Commercial vehicles such as express, grocery, beer, ice, and oil wagons were common in towns and cities, while hayracks became important after farmers adopted mechanical hay mowers and hay carriers for putting hay in barns. Throughout the late 1800s and early 1900s, farm wagon capacity ranged from fifteen hundred to six thousand pounds, with the weight of running gear and box ranging from eight hundred to fifteen hundred pounds. Wagon boxes with flared sides became popular in the twentieth century, especially after farmers began to use mechanical corn pickers, replacing the side-mounted bangboards used for hand harvesting. In the mid 1900s, pneumatic tires that decreased rolling resistance gained popularity, especially as communities built more hard-surfaced roads.

Wagon making was an established industry in the Midwest by 1900, with leading firms including the Troy Wagon Works Company of Troy, Ohio, Studebaker Brothers of South Bend, Indiana, and the Weber Wagon Company of Chicago. Census data indicate that by 1905, the Midwest accounted for six of the top ten states in number of vehicle manufacturing establishments, value of products and repairs, and number of employees. Wagon making became more centralized during the early twentieth century as corporations acquired competing companies to obtain distribution networks, production facilities, and increased market share. For example, between 1910 and 1912, John Deere purchased the Moline Wagon Company of Moline, Illinois, the Davenport Wagon Company of Davenport, Iowa, and the Fort Smith Wagon Company of Fort Smith, Arkansas. Wagon making declined after World War II as farmers began to use more trucks for hauling, although wagon making is still important in the region. Kinze Manufacturing, Inc., of Williamsburg, Iowa, builds wagons with a capacity of almost a thousand bushels that can be unloaded in less than three minutes, reflecting the increased scale and productivity of modern agriculture.

Sources and Further Reading: Mark L. Gardner, *Wagons for the Santa Fe Trade* (2000); Ralph C. Hughes, *John Deere Buggies and Wagons* (1995); Marvin McKinley, *Wheels of Farm Progress* (1980).

J. L. Anderson
Iowa State University

Stage Vehicles

Stage vehicles take their name from their use for travel in successive lengths between stops. Each portion of the journey, generally ten to twelve miles, was known as a stage. The driver stopped at designated locations to exchange the teams of four or six fatigued animals for fresh ones, covering up to sixty miles per day in several stages. Stage lines were a vital part of transportation in the Midwest, carrying passengers and mail throughout the region.

Stage lines conducted business with a variety of vehicles, including stage wagons (also known as "mud wagons") and the more recognizable Concord or Troy coaches, manufactured from 1826 by, respectively, Abbot and Downing of Concord, New Hampshire, and various makers in Troy, New York. Stage wagons had a cover and up to four fixed benches to accommodate as many as twelve passengers and a driver. Stagecoaches rested on leather braces suspended on a running gear and could carry up to sixteen passengers. Stage companies used both wagons and coaches, depending on location and length of route.

Fares and service varied across the region and throughout the nineteenth century. Stage service developed quickly on the Chicago Road from Detroit to Chicago. In 1830, only two stages per week ventured from Detroit. In 1832, three stages per week made the trip, and in 1835, travelers could count on daily service. By the 1850s, some stage companies consolidated, offering through service at a set price. Fares on most routes varied from five to ten cents per mile, although in a few instances, observers reported lower or higher rates. Demand for service, length of route, economic conditions, and availability of feed and forage for the animals could influence fare schedules. A traveler from Rock Island to Chicago paid $9 in 1850, and a traveler from Iowa City to Council Bluffs paid $21 in 1857, both approximately nine cents per mile. In newly opened areas, stage operators ventured greater risks, while developed areas supported more regular service and operators enjoyed the potential for greater profit.

Few and bad roads, lack of passenger comfort, limited luggage capacity, and dispersed population plagued stage lines of the Midwest. Travelers from the United States and abroad complained about the bone-jarring ride in dry weather and the excruciatingly slow pace during bad weather. Proprietors of roadside inns known as stage stands offered food and rest of mixed quality for travelers.

Although stages were scarce in the eastern Midwest by the late 1860s, stage service continued through the mid-1870s in the western parts of the region. Competition from railroad and interurban lines forced most stage lines out of business. Still, some companies coexisted with rail service during the early years of railroad development, serving as feeder lines for passengers to get to distant rail stations throughout the 1860s. Passengers, however, readily abandoned stage vehicles for the more regular schedule, improved comfort, and greater speed of railroad travel, relegating stage service to the sparsely populated Great Plains, Mountain West, and Pacific Coast.

Sources and Further Reading: Donald H. Berkebile, *Carriage Terminology: An Historical Dictionary* (1978); Kenneth E. Colton, "Bringing the Stage Coach to Iowa," *Annals of Iowa* 22 (July 1939); Kenneth E. Colton, "Stagecoach Travel in Iowa" *Annals of Iowa* 22 (Jan. 1940).

J. L. Anderson
Iowa State University

The Development of Railroads

During the formative years of railroad development, the Midwest region contributed substantially to this evolving form of intercity transportation. Although early in the 1830s, the first prototype railroads appeared in Maryland, New York, and South Carolina, several made their debut in the Midwest.

One of these historic pikes was the Erie and Kalamazoo Railroad (E&K), chartered in 1833 by the Territory of Michigan. Backers planned to construct a rail line between the Maumee and Kalamazoo Rivers. This locational strategy, linking two bodies of navigable water, was typical of infant railroad schemes. A few years later the building process began, and soon a thirty-three-mile section opened between Adrian, Michigan, and Toledo, Ohio. (In 1837, boundary adjustments placed the Maumee terminal in Ohio.) But largely because of hard times sparked by the Panic of 1837, this "Pioneer Railway of the West" never reached its northwestern destination, 180 miles away. Like similar emerging midwestern roads, including the Northern Cross Railroad of Illinois, the E&K initially used horses for its motive power, although it soon employed steam. Since the all-iron trail had yet to be perfected, laborers on the E&K fastened iron strap rail onto oak rails.

The E&K was privately financed, although some midwestern states underwrote early railroad construction. The Northern Cross, for one, was a project of the State of Illinois. This venture into public ownership was mainly a response to the scarcity of local capital. Eastern investors, as well as those from abroad, more likely found railroad projects in New England and the Middle Atlantic more attractive. But when private development became practical, those states that had constructed lines sold them, sometimes at a financial loss. Politicians were anxious to reduce public debt and fully embraced the spirit of free enterprise.

Because of the enormous economic potential of the Midwest, railroad expansion proceeded rapidly. By 1848, approximately seven hundred miles had been built, and by 1860, mileage exceeded ten thousand, or roughly one-third of the nation's total rail mileage. Yet the great wave of line construction would not occur until the post-Civil War period, particularly between 1879 and 1893. It was during these halcyon years that Chicago, Cleveland, Indianapolis, Minneapolis–St. Paul, and St. Louis became national rail centers, with Chicago boasting that it was "America's Rail Mecca." The railroad maps of several midwestern states, most notably Illinois, Iowa, Minnesota, and Ohio, resembled plates of wet spaghetti. Illinois claimed approximately twelve thousand miles, Iowa ten thousand, and Minnesota and Ohio about eighty-five hundred each. Although mileage expanded during the latter part of the nineteenth century, the number of principal carriers declined. "System building" produced monster corporations, and by 1900, such giants owned or controlled a majority of the trackage in the Midwest: the Chicago and North Western; Chicago, Burlington and Quincy; Chicago, Milwaukee and St. Paul; Chicago, Rock Island and Pacific; Great Northern, Illinois Central; New York Central; and Pennsylvania. Even the smaller trunk lines, including the Chicago Great Western, Monon and Wabash, were the result of frequent corporate unions.

Stability in the midwestern rail network continued until the 1930s. It was during the Great Depression that railroads began to make major efforts to reduce mileage, abandoning those branches that regulatory authorities would permit. Not only did retrenchment include trackage, but because of keen modal competition, largely from the automobile, service declined, especially branch-line and local passenger service.

Just as midwestern carriers had played a vital role during earlier national conflicts, their contributions between 1941 and 1945 were enormous. They handled all varieties of war materials and dispatched thousands of troop trains. Although the extra wear on physical plant and personnel was high, companies that had entered bankruptcy in the 1930s, including the Chicago and North Western and the Chicago Great Western and Wabash, commonly experienced successful corporate reorganizations, and all roads set aside wartime profits for postwar improvements.

Soon after peace returned, midwestern roads made major capital improvements that gained public attention, most of all introduction of lightweight "streamliners" between major cities. About the same time, they enthusiastically embraced a major replacement technology, the diesel-electric locomotive. One of the final carriers to dieselize fully in the Midwest, the Nickel Plate Road, retired its last steamers in the late 1950s. Although expenditures were great, savings from dieselization led to enhanced balance sheets.

By the late 1950s, however, the railroad picture in the Midwest dimmed considerably. The savings of retiring steam locomotives had largely run its course, and competition from highways increased immensely, in part triggered by the opening of strategic toll roads in Indiana and Ohio and the construction of thousands of miles of freeways authorized by the National Defense Highway Act of 1956. Railroads responded by additional cutbacks, especially unwanted trackage (a process made easier by the Transportation Act of 1958), and by proposing corporate mergers. One of the earliest mergers occurred in 1960 when the ten-thousand-mile Chicago and North Western absorbed a fifteen-hundred-mile competitor, the Minneapolis and St. Louis. By 1970, virtually every major carrier in the Midwest had participated in the merger process. A decade or so later, "super" mergers helped to redefine midwestern railroading, with the appearance of such giants as CSX and Norfolk Southern. Ironically, as rail super-roads appeared, the phenomenon of "new" railroads developed: Scores of short lines and regional carriers emerged, consisting of trackage that the major freight roads considered to be uneconomical. One example is Wisconsin Central Ltd., which was launched in 1987 and assumed control over a network of former Soo Line mileage in Wisconsin, upper Michigan, eastern Minnesota, and northern Illinois.

In a sense, railroads in the Midwest have come nearly full circle: Pioneer shortlines became part of larger corporations, and then new shortlines emerged in recent years when the giants discarded trackage. Just as governmental bodies initially aided railroads, state and municipal authorities have more recently acquired endangered lines and have entered the passenger business. Amtrak, the National Railroad Passenger Corporation, which began in May 1971, frequently works with public units to maintain passenger service in several midwestern corridors. As with freight railroads nationally, midwestern roads are mostly prospering at the turn of the twenty-first century, in part because of need, reduced labor costs, and regulatory freedoms.

Sources and Further Reading: Albro Martin, *Railroads Triumphant* (1992); Frederick C. Gamst, ed., *Early American Railroads* (1997); H. Roger Grant, *The North Western* (1996); John Lauritz Larson, *Bonds of Enterprise* (1984); Albro Martin, *Railroads Triumphant* (1992); Richard C. Overton, *Burlington Route: A History of the Burlington Lines* (1965); Richard Saunders, Jr., *Merging Lines* (2001).

H. Roger Grant
Clemson University, South Carolina

Travel on Railroads

When the first railroads appeared in the Midwest, the public found them to be exceptional conveniences. Unlike travel by water, a railroad could be expected to operate year-round. Moreover, lines directly connected important places, something that navigable waterways and even canals did not always do. Speeds, too, were markedly greater, fifteen to thirty miles per hour or more, as compared to about five miles per hour with water transport.

Initially, passengers did not enjoy posh accommodations. The small wooden coaches featured low ceilings, closely spaced bench seating, primitive heating and ventilation, and flickering candles for illumination. These early pieces of rolling stock lacked such amenities as water closets and vestibules that later became standard.

Even before passenger equipment grew in comfort, trains changed lifestyles. Only a few months after service began on the initial section of Chicago's first railroad, the Galena and Chicago Union, the weekly Chicago *Democrat*, in its December 1, 1849, edition related that "Persons . . . often ride into the city by the evening train, visit their friends, . . . go to the theatre or some other place or public amusement, and return on the morning train to their homes." Passenger trains also brought express packages, newspapers, and the U.S. Mail.

With dramatic expansion of the midwestern rail network following the Civil War, citizens became almost totally dependent on intercity passenger trains for their personal travel needs. Canal packets had disappeared, and so had most passenger-carrying steamboats; only Great Lakes vessels, mostly on Lake Erie and Lake Michigan, continued to transport sizable numbers of passengers. Still steam-power trains varied in quality. Riders on branch lines and shortlines encountered vintage equipment, while those who took mainline "varnish" might experience luxury. By the late 1870s, the Pullman Hotel Car, a combination sleeper and drawing room car, had become a fixture on first-class trains throughout the Midwest.

Early in the twentieth century, accommodations on the best trains remained very high in quality. The principal changes that travelers encountered were all-steel equipment, flush toilets, and improved heating and ventilation. By the 1930s, air-conditioning became common on the crack "name-trains," like the Burlington's Exposition Flyer or the Wabash's Banner Blue.

Quality rail travel in the Midwest continued after World War II. Chicago-based Burlington had introduced America's first diesel-powered streamlined train in 1934, and within a few years, other midwestern carriers inaugurated similar service, ranging from North

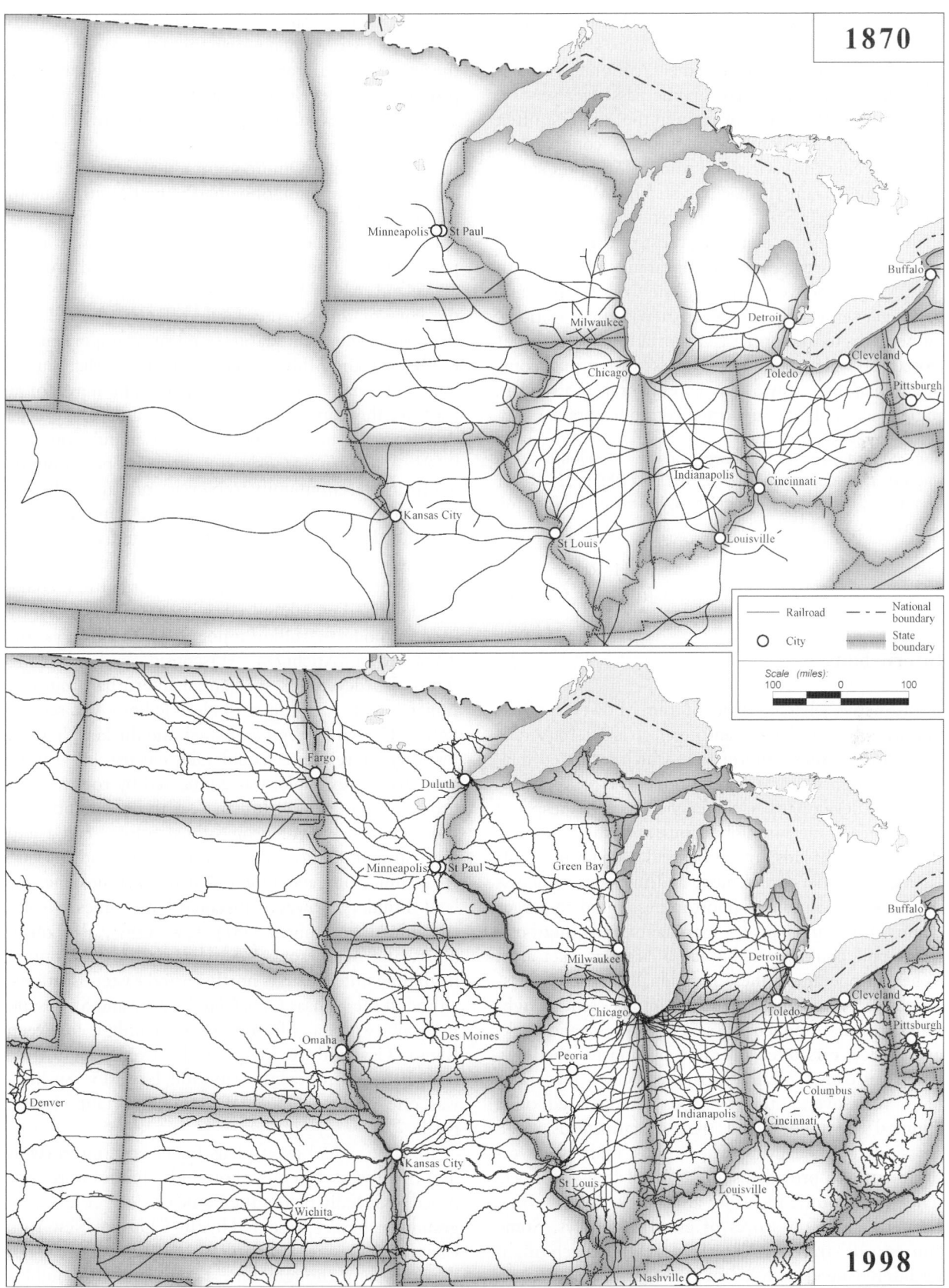

Expansion of railways. Prepared by James DeGrand. *Source: Atlas of Historical Geography of the United States* (1932), plate 140 A; Phillip John Davies et al., *The History Atlas of North America* (New York: Macmillan, 1998), 88–89.

Western's 400s to Rock Island's Rockets. Following World War II, nearly every important carrier had its fleet of streamliners; management continued to believe that a market existed for fine passenger service. But by the 1960s, travel by train in the Midwest often had become less convenient and less comfortable. Carriers reduced service, and some allowed their former premier trains to become shabby. When in the late 1960s the U.S. Post Office ended practically all Railway Post Office contracts, most of the remaining trains disappeared. Only the appearance of Amtrak in May 1971 preserved a skeletal network of regional passenger service. The great urban passenger stations, monuments to the former transportation boom, either closed forever or became much less glamorous, commonly handling only a few daily Amtrak runs and in some places publicly supported commuter trains.

Sources and Further Reading: George H. Douglas, *All Aboard! The Railroad in American Life* (1992); H. Roger Grant, ed., *We Took the Train* (1990); Freeman H. Hubbard, *Railroad Avenue* (1945).

H. Roger Grant
Clemson University, South Carolina

Interurbans

A distinctive characteristic of the Midwest's transportation heritage has been the electric intercity railway. Most of these interurbans, which appeared during the twenty-year period prior to World War I, helped to develop urban centers before the widespread appearance of the automobile, bus, and truck. More so than steam railroads, interurbans allowed farmers, villagers, and others convenient and inexpensive access to the socioeconomic opportunities found in larger communities, and bankers, merchants, and other businesspeople could profitably tap a larger market area. When in operation, these individually powered, passenger carrying cars that moved on a system of light rails, provided frequent passenger, express, and package service; cars often operated on hourly schedules, while railroads typically dispatched only a few trains daily. Moreover, interurbans, unless operated on a "limited" fashion, would stop at farmsteads, road crossings, or virtually anywhere. Most midwestern interurbans also provided some form of freight service. The "box motor," in reality an electric boxcar, was a common sight on scores of electric railways. Some "juice roads" transported carload freight, which might be interchanged with steam railroads, depending on physical conditions of the interurban's track and equipment and the steam railroad's willingness to accept such traffic.

Since Ohio became the interurban heartland, with a network that reached nearly three thousand miles by the eve of World War I, development here became the prototype for development nationally. On December 28, 1889, the seven-mile Newark and Granville Street Railway, in reality a rural trolley, opened between these two central Ohio communities. Later this firm gained the distinction of being the first electric line to become part of a general network of interurbans. Perhaps the first true interurban in the nation also appeared in the Buckeye State, the Akron, Bedford and Cleveland, which began service in 1895 and became the core of the Northern Ohio Traction and Light Company, one of the largest and most important interurbans in the Midwest. When the interurban building spree finally ended, every Ohio community of at least five thousand boasted an electric line. The exception was Coshocton, whose 1910 population was 9,603: At least four Coshocton firms proposed building from this community to Newark or Zanesville, but no project ever progressed beyond the planning stage.

Ohio developed into the banner interurban state largely because of numerous large and medium-sized cities, a prosperous, well-populated agricultural countryside dotted with hundreds of villages, and generally level to modestly rolling topography. But Illinois, Indiana, Iowa, Michigan, Wisconsin, and adjoining states also developed substantial interurban mileage. Indiana, with 1,825 miles of electric lines, was second only to Ohio in coverage. As with the Buckeye State, a majority of residents could take electric cars. Indianapolis, for example, was connected by routes to all urban areas in central Indiana—with the exception of Bloomington, where promotional efforts failed and railroad competition proved too strong. Indiana laid 1,422 miles of track, much of it blanketing Chicagoland. Builders, however, installed fewer miles of electric lines in Michigan (981), Iowa (489), Wisconsin (383), and Minnesota (77). Missouri claimed only a negligible mileage in its northern and eastern sections, although the Kansas City, Clay County and St. Joseph Railway, with a fifty-one-mile mainline between Kansas City and St. Joseph and a twenty-eight-mile branch between Kansas City and Excelsior Springs, was one of the Midwest's more important electric roads.

Promoters had great plans for electric interurbans in the Midwest. Literally thousands of miles were proposed, especially before the Panic of 1907. A few were grandiose, best represented by the Chicago–New York Electric Air Line Railroad (CNYEAL). Officers of this company thought big: They sought to build a largely level, double-track electric railroad between Chicago and New York. Speeds of electric trains along this "arrow route" would exceed one hundred miles per hour. Although the company raised some money, generated largely through local investment clubs in the Midwest (stockholders received their slick monthly publication, *Air Line News*), the craziness of this scheme, coupled with the Panic of 1907, doomed completion. Yet, the CNYEAL eventually opened a short section between South La Porte and Goodrum, Indiana, and in time this modest trackage became part of the Gary Street Railway.

By World War I, excitement for electric interurbans in the Midwest and elsewhere had flagged. For the most part, the interurban had served its brief role as a transition between steam passenger railroads and the automobile and bus. In the 1920s, scores of weaker railroads faltered; some were reorganized or fused into larger systems, and others were abandoned in whole or in part. Stronger interurbans continued, but a majority closed during the Great Depression. Even creativity—which might include intermodal road-rail freight and express service, lightweight, high-speed cars, and even joint air-rail passenger connections— failed to save what some thought to be viable operations.

The major exception to the rapid demise of midwestern interurbans involved roads that developed a substantial carload freight business with steam railroads. Some carriers survived into the 1950s—the Cedar Rapids and Iowa City; Chicago, Aurora and Elgin; Chicago, North Shore and Milwaukee; Chicago, South Shore and South Bend; Fort Dodge, Des Moines and Southern; Illinois Terminal (nee Illinois Traction); and Youngstown and Southern—some even continuing into the twenty-first century as independent diesel-powered shortlines or part of larger freight railroads. But the vast majority of midwestern interurbans never had the option of carrying carload freight. Extensive street running, sharp curves, and building obstructions hampered such prospects. Companies simply lacked financial resources to rebuild their lines and to acquire better freight equipment.

As with the old canals, not much remains of the infrastructure of most midwestern interurbans. A few continue to handle freight, only the South Shore continues as a passenger carrier, but most have vanished. Yet an observant person might detect portions of former rights-of-way, especially those marked by utility pole lines. A few stretches have become biking, hiking, or nature trails, and scattered depots, electrical substations, and concrete bridge abutments remain.

Sources and Further Reading: Thomas R. Bullard, *Faster than the Limiteds* (1991); H. Roger Grant, *Ohio on the Move* (2000); Herbert H. Harwood, Jr., and Robert S. Korach, *The Lake Shore Electric Story* (2000); George W. Hilton and John F. Due, *The Electric Interurban Railways in America* (1960);

Jack Keenan, *Cincinnati and Lake Erie Railroad* (1974); William D. Middleton, *The Interurban Era* (1961).

H. Roger Grant
Clemson University, South Carolina

Subways

Although subway mass transit is not associated with the Midwest, the cities of Cleveland, Chicago, Detroit, and St. Louis all have some kind of light rail system with an underground component. The subterranean aspects of rail transport is Detroit, St. Louis, and Cleveland are minor in scale, but the largest and most famous of these systems in the Chicago "L," which first opened in 1943. Digging began on December 17, 1938, on North State Street near Chicago Avenue. On June 22, 1958, the West Side Subway was opened, attracting worldwide attention for being the first rapid rail transit built in the grade-separated right-of-way of a multilane automobile expressway.

The earliest effort to build a subway system in the region was in Cincinnati. It was conceived as early as 1905 as the best utilization of the obsolete Miami-Erie canal, which ran through the city. Construction began in 1920 and was discontinued in 1925 when the $6 million bond raised in 1916 for the project ran out. Proposals to use the tunnels were seriously considered into the 1980s. For the most part, midwestern cities have not engaged in massive subway projects due to the federal government's focus on the Interstate Highway System after World War II. The federal government offered up to 90 percent of funding for road-building efforts, but no funds for subway mass transit systems. In the 1970s, the federal government under the Carter administration offered to provide between 50 and 75 percent of funding for rail projects, but several midwestern cities rejected modern subway systems as not economically viable and undesirable.

Sources and Further Reading: Chicago Department of Subways and Superhighways, *The Chicago Subways* (1943); Oswald Stevens Nock, *Underground Railways of the World* (1973); Edward Emelin White and Muriel White, *Famous Subways and Tunnels of the World* (1953).

T. Jason Soderstrum
Iowa State University

Trolley Cars

Just as the Midwest was the cradle of the electric interurban, it enjoys a similar claim on the electric trolley. Although most large and medium-sized midwestern cities after the Civil War had animal-powered car lines, some, including Chicago, Cincinnati, and St. Paul, experimented with cable cars, "steam dummies," and incline planes. Perfection of the electric streetcar in the late 1880s prompted midwestern municipalities to embrace this technology.

Within a year after inventor-promoter Frank Sprague demonstrated the practicality of the trolley, new or existing transit firms bought electric cars, strung a cobweb of overhead wires, and introduced their service. With its advent, midwesterners gained more than a convenient way to get to work, for now they could "take the car" to a variety of pleasure spots, including amusement parks, dance halls, and fairgrounds.

Despite the practical and even romantic nature of the trolley, midwesterners repeatedly had expressed their unhappiness with traction companies. During the crippling depression of the 1890s, concerned citizens from Cleveland to Detroit to Omaha lashed out against various acts of "corporate arrogance," charging that these privately owned concerns dodged their tax bills and often provided poor service and excessive fares. These attitudes led to stiff regulation and occasionally municipal ownership. But as automobile use increased, streetcar firms experienced financial difficulties. Their responses to these difficulties varied: acquiring one-person trolleys, adding bus service, and abandoning some or all of their electric lines. By the 1950s, few trolleys could be found in the Midwest. The period since 1980 has witnessed a national resurgence of the streetcar, now called "light rail," and cities like St. Louis and Minneapolis sported the latest generation of the trolley.

Sources and Further Reading: Debra Brill, *History of the J.G. Brill Company* (2001); Alan R. Lind, *From Horsecars to Streamliners* (1978); James A. Toman and Blaine S. Hays, *Cleveland's Transit Vehicles* (1996).

H. Roger Grant
Clemson University, South Carolina

Bicycles

Bicycles have been an important part of the midwestern scene for over a century. First developed in the early nineteenth century, the bicycle gained in popularity in 1878 when Colonel Albert Pope began to manufacture high-wheeled "Ordinaries" in Hartford, Connecticut. The introduction of the safety bicycle in the late 1800s led to a surge in the popularity, as staid Victorians had the opportunity to speed along road-

Ordinary and cyclist, c. 1870. Kentucky Library, Western Kentucky University.

ways. The safety bike, with two identically sized wheels, solid triangular frame, and reliable chain drive, quickly gained popularity, and manufacturers across the Midwest rushed to meet the demand. Among these entrepreneurs were future airplane inventors Orville and Wilbur Wright, who opened their first bicycle repair shop in Dayton, Ohio, in 1892. The Wrights not only repaired bicycles and sold bicycle accessories, but also marketed their own lines of bicycles.

The bicycle craze reached its apex in the 1890s, then declined. During its high point, enthusiasts formed organizations, including the League of American Wheelmen, to promote this sport and to encourage construction of good roads, particularly in the Midwest. The cycling craze also initiated changes in women's clothing, as female cyclists began to wear less restrictive garments when riding.

Following the end of the 1890s bicycle craze, manufacturers such as Schwinn (founded as Arnold, Schwinn and Company in Chicago in 1895), shifted attention away from the adult market and, instead, developed and marketed bicycles geared toward children. Bicycling remains a popular hobby among young and old in the Midwest. Bicycle races and events such as the GOBA, Great Ohio Bicycle Adventure, and the annual RAGBRAI, *Register*'s Annual Great Bicycle Ride Across Iowa, draw thousands of spectators and participants.

Sources and Further Reading: Annie Curtis Chittenden, "League of American Wheelmen," *Timeline* 12 (July–Aug. 1995); Saralee R. Howard-Filler, "Women A Wheel," *Michigan History* 64 (Sept.–Oct. 1980); Ron Spreng, "The 1890s Bicycling Craze in the Red River Valley," *Minnesota History* 54 (Summer 1995).

Peter Hoehnle
Iowa State University

Automobiles

Images of automobile manufacture and automobiling are inextricably intertwined with the American Midwest. The Model T, after all, fitted well the needs of a respectable working people. The region and its open roads, made famous by Beat generation writer Jack Kerouac, was adored by the thousands who experienced its green and golden prairies from the shoulder of old Route 66 and the Lincoln Highway. It is home to the raucous Indianapolis Motor Speedway and to scores of abandoned roadside motor inns, tourist cabins, drive-in restaurants, garages, gas stations, and Main Streets.

At the time that the American automobile industry reached its golden age in the mid-1950s, it intersected with the regionalism of the Lynds's *Middletown* (1929) and the dazzling sameness of William Whyte's *The Organization Man* (1956). Today the people of the region still revel in their abundant supply of auto—now RV—campgrounds and the endless rural grid of good roads, while lamenting the loss of splendid isolation to long commutes and senseless highway tragedies. The Midwest as transformed by the automobile is understood best by one of its best regional artists, Grant Wood. Despite his affinity for painting rolling geometric hills zigzagged by perfectly parabolic roads, only once did Wood depict motor vehicles, and then only in grim prelude to a crash: *Death on the Ridge Road* (1935).

The trend toward regionalism is concretely evoked in the decentralized network of auto manufacturing and parts supply. The brainchild of Henry Ford, "village industries," established first in southern Michigan and then everywhere, merged farm and factory into one package. Set in the pastoral landscape, Ford's factories brought culture, opportunity, and cutting-edge automotive technology to small communities while preserving the most salubrious aspects of rural life as well as traditional values. "Rule 1 at all the small plants," marveled one commentator, "is that any man may leave at any time to work on the farm, [and] may have his job back—barring shutdowns—when he gets through farming." Even Ford's largest plants at Highland Park and River Rouge, built away from the city center in the distant suburbs, began as experiments in decentralization. Ford also pioneered in the on-site processing of agricultural products like soybeans,

Blossom queens meet at a Model T, Benton Harbor, Michigan, 1926. Chicago Historical Society, *Chicago Daily News*, DN-0080885.

corn, cattle, and wool, into car parts, solvents, and fluids, calling this "greenfield" transplant the Industrialized American Barn.

Henry Ford set the standard for automobile production in the Midwest and, for decades, mass production of all kinds in the rest of the world. Despite the nickname "Motor City," the first gasoline-powered American car was not manufactured in Detroit, but rather in Springfield, Massachusetts. As late as 1900, Detroit was one of dozens in the country with aspirations as the national center of automotive production. But those vying metropolises were without a doubt thickest in its midsection: Cleveland, Toledo, and Elyria, Ohio; Indianapolis and Kokoma, Indiana; St. Louis, Missouri; Kenosha, Wisconsin; and Moline, Illinois. The reason for this concentration was due in part to access to raw materials: iron ore from the ranges surrounding Lake Superior, coal from Appalachia, hardwood from the Upper Peninsula of Michigan, and nearly everywhere plentiful fresh water for production and distribution of finished product. But that would not have been enough without a catalyzing congregation of aspiring captains of industry in the Midwest: David Buick, John and Horace Dodge, Ransom Olds, Frederick Fish (Studebaker), Charles Nash, and of course, Henry Ford.

Other less fortunate inventors shadowed their footsteps. Around the turn of the twentieth century, Illinois farmboys-turned-bicycle mechanics, Charles and Frank Duryea, marketed a one-cylinder horseless vehicle—described by the Peoria *Evening Times* as "the most practical carriage of the kind yet manufactured"—that could reach the tremendous speed of five miles per hour. Monroe Seiberling in Indiana, a competitor of another former farmboy, Harvey Firestone, who had gone from his home in Columbiana County, Ohio, to Akron, made the Duryea's tires. In Grinnell, Iowa, Henry W. Spaulding turned out as many as a thousand self-propelled vehicles between 1909 and 1916 as head of the Spaulding Manufacturing Company. And in the Dakotas and Minnesota, dozens of tinkerers turned out all manner of homemade runabouts, ramblers, and roadsters. Midwestern factories for auto parts and supplies—as well as significant research laboratories—were founded by Dr. Benjamin Franklin Goodrich (rubber and vinyl), Charles Goodyear (rubber), and Henry Timken (roller bearings).

Not everyone was impressed by the ingenuity of these native sons. Worried about their roaming livestock, farmers sought new protections from these "devil wagons." Police officers set up special speed traps to net offenders breaking the ten-mile-per-hour speed limit. Many complained that these noisy, self-propelled carriages terrified horses sharing the road, and some saw fit to pelt their owners with rotten tomatoes and worse. Others deprecated the impracticality of these machines that were such "poor hill climbers" and so unsafe. Such features prompted North Dakota poet James W. Foley to write of the automobilist:

Through many streets my way I jog,
Too fast for safety, maybe.
And here and there I kill a dog,
And here and there a baby.

I chug and blow and toot and puff,
And wheeze and groan and rattle,
I sound like seven thousand men
All riding off to battle.

Though automobiling's village industries and industrialized barns have withered away, their legacy on the midwestern landscape endures. Even today as the Japanese "just-in-time" model for auto manufacturing with highly nimble throughput with little overhead supplants Ford and GM's lumbering historic "just-in-case" system of parts warehouses, the Heartland of North America remains, contrary to popular wisdom, at the center of the automobile's industrial ecology. And it is no longer an ossified enterprise as foreign capital and ideas have flowed into the region. Despite the dispersal of new "Toyota cities" in the nonunionized South, Honda built its first auto assembly plant in Marysville, Ohio, and a second in nearby East Liberty; Mazda in Flat Rock, Michigan; Mitsubishi in Normal, Illinois; Subaru-Isuzu in Lafayette, Indiana; and Nissan in Avon Lake, Ohio. Into the early 1990s, 1.2 million of the 1.9 million cars manufactured each year in wholly or partly owned Japanese factories in America emerged from midwestern plants.

The automobile—along with popular magazines, motion pictures, and the revival movement—facilitated and magnified certain types of expression in the Midwest. It satisfied a pent-up demand for geographic, economic, and social mobility to an extent never before seen in modern times. Backseats, rumble seats, and running boards also proved effective places for illicit liaisons, as did the drive-in restaurants, roadside motels, and later, the drive-in theatres that sprouted up along the roadsides. In Robert S. and Helen Merrell Lynd's 1929 sociological account of *Middletown* (actually Muncie, Indiana), a juvenile court judge went so far as to cite the automobile as a "house of prostitution on wheels."

Sunday drives to remote locales also threatened church attendance, prompting one Middletown pastor to denounce the disease "automobilitis." Yet the automobile also worked as an agent for family solidarity in the same way, encouraging touring the midwestern countryside, reducing the need for overnight stays in distant cities, and making possible regular holiday visits to kin living far away.

Sources and Further Reading: Donald T. Critchlow, *Studebaker: The Life and Death of an American Corporation* (1996); Charles E. Dickson, "Prosperity Rides on Rubber Tires," *North Dakota History* 53 (Summer 1986); Romeo B. Garrett, "The Role of the Duryea Brothers in the Development of the Gasoline Automobile," *Journal of the Illinois State Historical Society* 68 (Apr. 1975); Carl W. Larson, "A History of the Automobile in North Dakota to 1911," *North Dakota History* 54 (Fall 1987); Andrew Mair et al., "The New Geography of Automobile Production," *Economic Geography* 64 (Oct. 1988); Curt McConnell, *Great Cars of the Great Plains* (1995); Anedith Nash, "Death on the Ridge Road," *Prospects* 8 (1983); John B. Rae, "Why Michigan?" *Michigan History* 80 (Mar.–Apr. 1996); Howard P. Segal, "Little Plants in the Country," *Prospects* 13 (1988).

Philip Frana
University of Central Arkansas

The Eddie Rickenbacker Motor Company

Advertised as "a car worthy of its name," the Rickenbacker automobile was manufactured in Detroit between 1921 and 1927. Named after Captain Eddie Rickenbacker, America's "ace of aces" during World War I and the commanding officer of the "Hat in the Ring" Squadron, the Rickenbacker was constructed to former automobile racer Captain Eddie's own specifications. In 1919, Rickenbacker decided that he would build a passenger vehicle that incorporated such advanced race-proven engineering features as a rigid frame, four-wheel brakes, and a high standard of quality construction. This automobile was also to be affordable to white-collar workers, prosperous farmers, and "women of taste," thus fitting in the market somewhere between the low-end Ford Model T and the far-higher-priced Cadillac and Packard.

Rickenbacker sold his idea to Maxwell executive Harry L. Cunningham, who subsequently recruited an impressive management team. Coach builder Barney F. Everitt agreed to serve as President and General Manager and legendary Ford Motor Car Company production manager Walter E. Flanders was appointed as a Director of the fledgling firm. With Cunningham as Secretary and Treasurer and Rickenbacker as Vice President and Sales Manager, the Rickenbacker Motor Company initially was well positioned.

During the early 1920s, a six-cylinder prototype was built and tested, $5 million dollars worth of stock was sold, and a plant with a capacity of twelve thousand units was acquired. Three Rickenbacker models debuted in 1922—a Tourer, Opera Coupe, and Closed Sedan—and more than thirty-seven hundred vehicles were sold, resulting in a 5 percent stock dividend.

From its beginnings, Rickenbacker six-cylinder models, and later a more expensive eight-cylinder version with bright two-tone color schemes, were characterized by innovative technology and enhanced safety features. While not the first American automobile to offer four-wheel brakes, it was the first moderately-priced car to do so. Other advances not found in moderately-priced cars included a vibration-free two-flywheel engine, ignition and transmission locks, an ingenious system to purify engine oil and avoid crankcase dilution, a carburetor air cleaner, and automatic windshield cleaner. Minor but significant improvements were subsequently introduced, and the Rickenbacker owner could sing along to a popular tune "Merrily I roll along... and there's nothing wrong... in my cracker jacker, Rickenbacker."

Despite its promising start, the company never took off and began to experience production and financial difficulties in 1925. By then, Walter Flanders had died, the result of an unfortunate accident. Handicapped with small profit margins, Everitt cut prices without consulting dealers and stockholders. Marginal dealers went bankrupt, stockholders and management began to squabble, and in 1926, the turmoil caused Captain Eddie to resign. With Everitt on his own, the company ceased operation in February 1927, its machinery and engines sold to German industrialist J. A. Rassmussen, who used Rickenbacker engines in his Audi Dresden Sixes and Zwickau Eights between 1928 and 1932. Like the Richelieu, Saxon, Dort, Flint, Winton, King, Jewett, Wills Ste. Clair, and numerous other midwestern automobile companies, the Rickenbacker could not survive competition from more-highly-capitalized and cost-efficient firms, even during the 1920s, America's prosperity decade.

Sources and Further Reading: Finis Farr, *Rickenbacker's Luck* (1979); Ken Gross, "The Car Worthy of Its Name," *Special Interest Autos* (May–June 1975); Stephen G. Ostrander, "A Car Worthy of Its Name," *Michigan History Magazine* 76 (Jan.–Feb. 1992); Edward V. Rickenbacker, *Rickenbacker* (1967).

John A. Heitmann
University of Dayton

Buses

The employment of buses as a means of transportation commenced in the early twentieth century when numerous local entrepreneurs started carrying fare-paying passengers over public highways. One of the earliest was in the Iron Range of northern Minnesota in 1914, where operators such as Eric Wickman of Hibbing drove miners to various locations for fixed fares. By 1915, he formed the Mesabi Transportation Company (later Greyhound), which was soon operating eighteen buses. Within the next five years, every state in the Midwest had some type of bus service and had enacted legislation to protect the consumer and regulate the industry. Improvements in bus design and operating practices in the early 1920s ushered in a number of bus builders, including the White Company of Cleveland, Ohio, and General Motors of Pontiac, Michigan.

The 1930s proved to be a painful decade for bus companies in the Midwest with the Great Depression and new federal regulations. Though the decline in business was not as severe as in other sectors of the economy, many firms collapsed. Those that survived faced the extra expense of compliance with the Motor Carrier Act (1935), which required certain safety devices, regulated accounting and business practices in the industry, protected consumers through the publication and regulation of fares, and governed mergers and competition in the industry.

World War II had a great impact of the bus industry. Because of limited wartime production and rationing, many Americans were forced to rely on buses for transportation. By 1944, buses accounted for over 41 percent of the passenger miles in America, compared with 11 percent in 1939. In 1942, municipal buses hauled 134 percent more passengers than the previous year and had become a realistic means of getting around a city. The next year, due to wartime production ceilings and personnel lost to higher-paying war-related jobs, companies converted tractor trailers into service, calling them "victory buses."

In the postwar years, the industry's share of the transportation industry fell as the American consumer embraced the automobile. The number of cars on American roads increased by 65 percent between 1946 and 1953. While trying to update their equipment and provide a more comfortable ride and more attractive facilities, midwestern carriers found it very difficult to persuade Americans to ride buses.

While Trailways and Greyhound dominate bus travel in the Midwest, with Greyhound accounting for over 50 percent of bus traffic since the late 1960s and 19 million passengers in 2000, smaller companies have maintained scheduled routes offering special services within the region. The most famous of these is Jefferson Lines, Inc., which became the eighth largest busing firm after purchasing the Crown Coach Company in 1966, and operates mostly within Minnesota, Iowa, and Missouri.

Sources and Further Reading: Susan Meikle Mandell et al., *A Historical Survey of Transit Buses in the United States* (1990); A. E. Meier and J. P. Hoschek, *Over the Road* (1975); Margaret Walsh, *Making Connections: The Long-Distance Bus Industry in the USA* (2000).

T. Jason Soderstrum
Iowa State University

School Buses

Public education in the United States began early in the 1800s, but for most of the century, schoolchildren walked to their one-room schoolhouses. By the 1870s, some children were transported to school in wagons called hacks or barges. These open horse-drawn vehicles were often converted mail wagons or hand-constructed specifically for student transportation. These early school buses were about twelve feet long and could carry up to fifteen students. By 1909, farm families began to demand more comfort and convenience, so wagons were mounted on automobile chassis and were made to carry about twice as many children. Wooden buses were standard from 1915 until 1935. Light in weight, these wooden buses were dangerous and were often destroyed by fire and accident. By the early 1930s, steel replaced wood and buses were painted a more visible yellow or orange, instead of the previously preferred black or green.

In the late 1800s, America's growing public school system prompted states to legislate funds for transportation to and from schoolhouses. By 1900, eighteen states had some sort of school transportation law, and by 1919, all forty-eight states provided funds for transportation. Midwestern states were right in the middle of this trend, beginning with Ohio in 1894 and ending with Illinois in 1911.

School desegregation changed the school bus from a convenience for rural families to an intruder into urban neighborhoods. By the 1970s, many midwestern cities like Chicago, Kansas City, and St. Paul began busing and greatly expanded the role of their school transportation services. The courts have since discontinued forced desegregation in most areas, but school buses remain a main fixture on country roads, highways, and city streets across the Midwest today.

Sources and Further Reading: Wayne E. Fuller, *One-Room Schools of the Middle West* (1994); Andrew Gulliford, *America's Country Schools* (1984).

Leah F. Tookey
Iowa State University

Trucks

The first trucks appeared in the Midwest in 1896 when Charles Wood's American Electric Vehicle Company of Chicago built two electric delivery wagons for Charles A. Stevens Brothers, a silk house in Chicago. The same year, C. S. Fairfield of Portland, Missouri, adapted a ten-horsepower kerosene motor to a buckboard to carry passengers in the surrounding resorts. By 1898, the Winton Motor Carriage Company of Cleveland introduced the first gasoline-powered trucks to the Midwest. By the end of the nineteenth century, the U.S. Post Office was experimenting with the use of trucks in mail delivery around Cleveland, the U.S. Signal Corps had ordered two electric wagons from the Fischer Equipment Company of Chicago, and a patrol wagon had been designed for the Akron, Ohio, Police Department by Frank Fowler Loomis.

The twentieth century opened with the motor truck perceived as a luxury of city life. Merchants, farmers, and others began attaching wagon beds to car skeletons to create light delivery wagons. Small motor truck factories began to appear throughout the region, including the People's Automobile Company of Cleveland, Milwaukee Automobile Company, St. Louis Motor Carriage, Three-Hub-Motor of Chicago, and Henry Ford's Detroit Automobile Company. A growing truck-building industry began to cluster in Michigan and Indiana led by Ford, the Studebakers, and Max Grabowsky's Rapid Motor Company (later General Motors).

The truck industry grew so fast during the years before World War I that most states adopted regulations regarding trucks and operators. Yet, it was World War I and the U.S. Army's need for trucks that dramatically increased truck production by more than 500 percent in the Midwest over prewar levels. The army's need for specialized trucks such as ambulances, searchlight trucks, and kitchen trucks further expanded truck technology. The federal government furthered the demand for and use of trucks by building roads under the Federal Road Act of 1916 and the Federal Highway Act of 1921. In 1919, the Department of Agriculture spent $300 million on road construction in rural areas of America.

The 1920s and 1930s saw the diversity of truck usage in the Midwest increase. Even though truck sales decreased with the Great Depression, the diesel engine, improved aerodynamics, and refrigerated trucks were introduced to consumers. The Midwest trucking industry saw another boom with World War II and Interstate highway construction in the 1950s. By 1944, Dodge was producing 300 thousand trucks annually for the war effort. By 1947, 18 million trucks had been built on assembly lines, a majority of which were now centrally located in the Midwest. The post-war years saw diversification and expansion of the type of trucks on the road as wealth and the highway system had increased the use of trucks. The 1970s witnessed truck sales topping $4 million a year, with light trucks accounting for more than 90 percent of the truck market. Trucks provided the Midwest with an economically strong industry and stimulated incalculable growth.

Sources and Further Reading: James H. Thomas, *The Long Haul: Truckers, Truck Stops and Trucking* (1979); James A. Wren and Genevieve Wren, *Motor Trucks of America* (1979); D. Daryl Wyckoff, *Truck Drivers in America* (1979).

T. Jason Soderstrum
Iowa State University

Pickup Trucks

One of the most overlooked innovations that changed midwestern rural life is the pickup truck. This invention transformed daily activities and came to symbolize the agrarian life for most Americans. Pickup trucks had the carrying capacity of wagons and the horsepower to perform many of the vital daily tasks of farm life. They provided a way to convey supplies, visit neighbors, and accomplish daily tasks.

The first pickup trucks began to appear in the Midwest at the turn of the twentieth century when the Winton Motor Carriage Company of Cleveland, Ohio, introduced a delivery wagon in 1898. Other trucks were being developed across the nation around the same time. Ford produced the Model C Delivery Car in 1905, of which only ten were made and sold for $950 each. Until the Dodge and Chevrolet trucks began to offer trucks to consumers, individuals converted Ford Model Ts for hauling purposes or had light trucks specially built.

Although various companies purduced light trucks over the next decade, it was not until 1918 that pickup trucks became mass-marketed across the region. William Durant and Louis Chevrolet, using Ford's mass production of the Model T, produced the first Chevrolet trucks in 1918. The Chevrolet 490 Light Delivery, a four-cylinder light pickup, could carry a payload of a thousand pounds and sold for $595. Customers were expected to provide their own cab and body for the truck or purchase these parts from independent body companies. The Dodge Brothers began to mass-produce pickup trucks in World War I when the federal government asked them to supply twenty thousand half-ton chassis cowls, cargo trucks, light repair trucks, and ambulances. When the war ended, the Dodge brothers introduced the Screenside as its 1918 Model to the American consumer. In 1921, after an agreement with the Graham brothers, Dodge expanded production of their trucks. The Ford company did not begin the mass production of trucks until they introduced the Ford Model T Runabout with Pickup Body on April 25, 1925. This Detroit-made truck cost $281 and had a roadster-style body and all-steel bed. Ford sold almost thirty-four thousand of them that year alone, and sold more trucks than any other manufacturer for the rest of the century. These three manufacturers, with their factories all located in the Midwest, offered the consumer a reasonably priced light truck, with modifications such as diesel and four-wheel drive being introduced in later years. More pickup trucks are assembled in Michigan than in any other state in the nation.

Pickup ownership in the Midwest increased dramatically after World War II, with the truck and tractor replacing the horse as source of power and transportation in rural areas. In 1994, it was estimated that 30 percent of vehicles on the road in the Midwest were light pickup trucks. With annual sales in cars and trucks of $392.9 billion dollars, pickup trucks will remain an economically important industry in the Midwest.

Sources and Further Reading: James Koons, *Pickup Trucks* (1996); Justin Lukach, *Pickup Trucks: A History of the Great American Vehicle* (1998); Mike Mueller, *The American Pickup Truck* (1999).

T. Jason Soderstrum
Iowa State University

Motorcycles

Gottlieb Daimler in Germany first developed the motorcycle in 1885. By the 1890s, American mechanics and blacksmiths worked to perfect their own versions of the motorcycle, leading to the formation of several small manufacturing companies across the United States, many centered in the Midwest. Many different brands of motorcycles were manufactured in the midwestern states of Ohio, Michigan, Indiana, Illinois, Wisconsin, and Minnesota between 1900 and 1930.

Most companies produced only a small number of machines during their limited existence, although two, Excelsior and Harley Davidson, became nationally known brands that survived for many years. Ignanz Schwinn, founder of the Schwinn Bicycle Company, bought and expanded the Excelsior Company in 1911. Headquartered in Chicago, Excelsior produced mo-

torcycles until 1931 when, due to the Great Depression, Schwinn abandoned motorcycle production. Harley Davidson, by contrast, remains the most noted brand of American motorcycle. Founded in Milwaukee, Wisconsin, by brothers Arthur and Walter Davidson and their friend, William Harley, the firm produced its first motorcycle in 1903. Production increased to meet the growing demand through the early 1900s until the automobile captured people's imaginations after the 1920s.

Motorcycles remain an integral feature on midwestern roadways, and numerous events cater to the hobbyists who continue to succumb to the lure of the open road.

Sources and Further Reading: Dario Agrati et al., *One Hundred Years of Motorcycles* (1988); Hugo Wilson, *The Encyclopedia of the Motorcycle* (1995).

Peter Hoehnle
Iowa State University

Chicago's Union Station

Chicago's Union Station is one of the few remaining original train stations in the city. Chicago's first Union Station opened in 1881 at the corner of Madison and Canal Streets, just west of the Chicago River, and was in use until the new structure was completed in 1925.

This building, constructed for the Pennsylvania Company by architect W. W. Boyington, was used jointly by four tenant railroads. This red brick structure served the Pennsylvania Railroad and its affiliates until the new and current terminal was erected between Jackson Boulevard and Clinton, Adams, and Canal Streets. During the tenure of the first Union Station, rail service in Chicago blossomed, changing the city from a remote western outpost to the nexus of the rail system in the United States. By the early 1900s, Union Station was congested, crowded, dilapidated, and overshadowed by the newer downtown stations like La Salle (1903), Grand Central (1890), and the critically acclaimed Chicago and Northwestern Terminal (1911). For the Pennsylvania Railroad to continue to attract customers to its most important transfer point, it needed to create for itself and its tenant railroads adequate and modern accommodations.

The Chicago architectural firm of Graham, Anderson, Probst and White, overseen by the Pennsylvania Railroad's engineers, designed the new terminal, and by the time it opened it served four railways—the Pennsylvania, the Chicago, Burlington and Quincy, the Chicago, Milwaukee and St. Paul, and the Chicago and Alton. Construction of this monumental structure

Roosevelt Roads Railyard and skyscape of downtown Chicago. Courtesy Bill Gustason.

began in 1914, but was not completed until 1925; it had been derailed by World War I, government regulation of railroads, labor strikes, City of Chicago building ordinances and regulations, and changes in plans for the station itself. When the new Union Station was being planned, conventional wisdom encouraged extravagant buildings that spoke not only of the power of the railroad but also of the message the sponsoring city wished to project. Chicago, as the transportation hub for the Midwest and the nation, needed an appropriate edifice that would welcome visitors in the appropriate style. To that end, the 1925 Union Station was full of marble-clad columns (larger than the ones on the Chicago and Northwestern Station down the block), expansive waiting rooms, and convenient services like barbershops, shoe shines, restaurants, meeting rooms, and even a jail. At its busiest, it served almost one hundred thousand passengers and three hundred trains daily.

By 1969, Union Station again needed renovation for the early-twentieth-century architecture no longer served the aesthetic or practical needs of commuter travelers. A thirty-three-story office building was erected on the site, making better economic use of the valuable property at a time when passenger rail service greatly decreased because of convenient expressways and air travel. Though this renovation offered some modern conveniences, it lacked the grandeur that the Pennsylvania exuded at the height of its power. Civic leaders and railroad fans intervened, however, and the glory of the original waiting room was reopened to the public in 1991 after a $32 million renovation. No longer the nexus of cross-country rail service, the Union Station today services suburban commuters.

Sources and Further Reading: Carl Condit, *The Chicago School of Architecture: A History of Commercial and Public Building in the Chicago Area 1875–1925* (1964); William Cronon, *Nature's Metropolis* (1991); Carroll L.V. Meeks, *The Railroad Station: An Architectural History* (1956).

Laura E. Milsk
Loyola University–Chicago, Illinois

Cincinnati's Union Terminal

Universally know as "Cinci," the Cincinnati Union Station is the largest art deco–style railroad terminal building in the world and now the home of the Cincinnati Museum Center. Construction of the grand terminal was a cooperative project between the seven railroad companies that served the city from five different terminals and civic leaders led by George Dent Crabbs as a way to reduce chaos, congestion, and needless delays in rail service.

Located on the site of the old Lincoln Park, one mile northwest of the center of the city, construction work on the station started in August 1929, and was completed on March 31, 1933, at a cost of $41 million, including the purchase of ground and readjustment of railroad facilities. The huge project included twenty-two buildings, 8.25 million bricks, 5.66 million cubic yards of fill material, and 45,421 tons of steel. New York architects Alfred Fellheimer, Stewart Wagner, and Paul Phillipe Cret designed the structure. The passenger station itself cost $8.6 million and was jointly owned by the Norfolk and Western, Baltimore and Ohio, Louisville and Nashville, Southern, New York Central, Chesapeake

Cincinnati Union Terminal, opened 1933. Ohio
Historical Society, P191 AL00352.

and Ohio, and Pennsylvania Railroads. The rotunda
rises 120 feet with a span of 190 feet. Soft leather covered the settees and chairs; aluminum, Verona marble,
terrazzo, and exotic South American woods increased
the grandeur. Union Station is most famous for its murals designed by German artist Winold Reiss. After sub-
mitting the drawing in 1931, Reiss created a huge mosaic on the upper walls that expressed symbolically the
development of the nation from early colonial days to
the industrial era, with special attention to the development of the Ohio River Valley and Cincinnati.

This massive ten-story limestone and glass structure served up to seventeen thousand passengers daily
and during World War II was a major transfer point
for soldiers. Capable of serving 216 trains a day, it
contained specialty shops, newsstands, barbershops,
restaurants, and a one-hundred-seat theatre that
showed the latest newsreels.

After the war, railroad traffic declined due to expansion of airlines and the interstate highway system.
By 1970, only two trains a day passed through the station, and on October 28, 1972, service was completely
halted. Three years later, the city of Cincinnati bought
the terminal. In 1980, a Columbus developer converted the structure into a shopping mall that failed in
the recession that soon followed. The Cincinnati Museum of Natural History and The Cincinnati Historical Society then decided to develop the structure into
a giant museum. In 1986, Hamilton county residents
approved a $33 million bond issue to restore the sta-
tion; the state of Ohio and the city also contributed
$11 million toward the project. Cincinnati Union Sta-
tion reopened in November 1990 as a Museum Center, with an educational and cultural complex including the Museum and Library and the Robert D.
Lindner Family Omnimax Theater. On July 29, 1991,

train service was restored to the famous structure. At
the turn of the twenty-first century, over one million
people visited the station annually.

Sources and Further Reading: Cincinnati Historical Society, *The Cincinnati Union Terminal: Pictorial History* (1987);
Linda C. Rose et al., eds., *Cincinnati Union Terminal* (1999).

T. Jason Soderstrum
Iowa State University

Cleveland's Union Terminal

Cleveland's Union Terminal, more commonly referred to as the Terminal Tower, remains the dominant architectural symbol of Cleveland, Ohio. When
completed in 1927, the fifty-two-story, 708-foot-tall
building designed by the Chicago firm of Graham,
Anderson, Probst and White was the tallest structure
outside of New York City.

The structure's significance rests neither in its
height nor style, but rather in the fact that it was
planned as an inter- and intraurban rail transportation
center. Its proponents and builders, the brothers Oris
Paxton and Mantis James Van Sweringen, initially
needed a central downtown terminal for the electric
railroad that served their Shaker Heights suburban
development. Their increasing involvement in and
ownership of steam railroads in the 1910s and 1920s
gave the project its broader purpose. However, their
desire for a central terminal was antithetical to long-
standing plans for a lakefront railroad station that was
to be part of a Progressive-era complex of civic buildings known as the Group Plan. This necessitated a
special referendum in 1919, in which the Van Sweringen proposal was approved.

Construction of the terminal, a series of three associated office buildings, a major department store, track approaches, and bridges constituted one of the largest such projects in the United States and took over seven years to complete. Over a thousand buildings were razed to clear the seventeen acres of land needed for the buildings and their associated air rights. The tower's position at the southwest corner of Cleveland's central Public Square served to revitalize that area and, for the period from the 1930s to the 1960s, make it the center of the city's downtown, thereby drawing attention away from the lakefront.

Intercity rail service through the structure began in 1929. For three decades, the terminal bustled with railroad-related activity. It served the Van Sweringen–owned New York, Chicago, and St. Louis; the New York Central; the Erie; and the Baltimore and Ohio. Of the railroads serving the city, only the Pennsylvania chose not to use the structure. The tower itself housed the local offices of many national railroads as well as those of prominent law firms.

The decline in intercity rail transport after World War II, and particularly after 1960, stripped the structure of its primary purpose. The last intercity train used the terminal in 1977. Its main concourse was largely abandoned and, at one time, was given over to a series of indoor tennis courts. However, the terminal remained the central stop for light rail intracity service, including a line to the city's airport.

In the late 1980s the disused steam railroad concourse became the focal point of a major, $400 million renewal project that reconfigured much of the lower portion of the structure into a modern, three-level shopping mall known as Tower City Center, while the tower section remained a prestigious location for offices. The construction of a new luxury hotel and office tower adjacent to the site, completed in 1991, made the endeavor a pivotal factor in the city's late-twentieth-century downtown revitalization.

Sources and Further Reading: John J. Grabowski and Walter Leedy, *The Terminal Tower, Tower City Center* (1990); Ian Haberman, *The Van Sweringens of Cleveland* (1979); Herbert H. Harwood, Jr., *Invisible Giants: The Empires of Cleveland's Van Sweringen Brothers* (2003); Jim Toman and Dan Cook, *The Terminal Tower Complex* (1980).

John J. Grabowski
Case Western Reserve University, Ohio

Kansas City's Union Station

From its opening in 1914 until after World War II, Kansas City's Union Station was one of the busiest railway depots in the nation. Situated in the southwestern portion of the Midwest, Kansas City served as a regional rail center, with travelers and cargo passing through in all directions. When the 1878 West Bottoms depot proved inadequate and subject to flooding, the railroad companies serving the city determined to build a new station. Following a lengthy disagreement, a site south of the downtown area was finally selected in 1906. Twelve rail lines ultimately formed the Kansas City Terminal Railway Company to oversee the construction and management of the station.

Chicago architect Janis Hunt designed the Beaux Art station. Influenced by the works architect Daniel Burnham built for the 1893 Chicago World's Fair and his Washington, D.C., railroad terminal, Hunt's 1909 design was, by his own description, "monumental." The building featured an exterior of Indiana-quarried Bedford limestone, interior finish materials of marble and terra cotta, and an ornately plastered ceiling. When completed, Union Station ranked third in square footage among American railroad stations. Its facilities could handle the railway transportation needs of a city of two million people; Kansas City's population was not quite 250 thousand. The station reflected the city leaders' optimism about the future of their metropolis.

Train traffic peaked at Union Station just three years after it opened. Ticket sales reached their maximum in 1920. Despite the gradual decline in passenger traffic, Union Station remained a popular fixture. Its retail shops and dining establishments drew local residents. Thousands celebrated New Year's Eve in the station beginning in 1920, a tradition that continued through the early 1950s.

The station gained national notoriety on June 17, 1933, when men tried to free murderer and prison escapee Frank Nash, who was being returned to the federal prison at Leavenworth, Kansas. Four lawmen and Nash died from gunshot wounds. Recent scholarship suggests that Nash and three of the law officers killed during the Union Station Massacre may have been unintentionally shot by one of the federal agents.

Following World War II and a nationwide reduction in rail passenger traffic, Union Station declined in importance. By the late 1960s, despite earlier attempts to modernize the shops and the building, the station was largely abandoned. Portions of the structure were rented to enterprises unrelated to railroads.

When a plan to demolish Union Station surfaced in 1971, local citizens opposed the move, and the city's Landmarks Commission succeeded in having the building placed on the National Register of Historic Places. Reuse and renovation plans for the building languished throughout the 1970s and 1980s. A lawsuit filed by the city in 1988 and settled in 1994 resulted in

Union Station being sold to a nonprofit group. Earlier plans to use the facility as a science museum resurfaced, and the passage of a bistate tax involving the metropolitan area on both sides of the Missouri–Kansas state line allowed restoration to begin in the late 1990s. In 1999, a meticulously restored Kansas City landmark reopened as Science City–Union Station.

Sources and Further Reading: George Ehrlich, *Kansas City, Missouri: An Architectural History, 1826–1990*, rev. ed. (1992); Jeffrey Spivak, *Union Station, Kansas City* (1999); Robert Unger, *The Union Station Massacre: The Original Sin of J. Edgar Hoover's FBI* (1997).

Lynn Wolf Gentzler
State Historical Society of Missouri,
Columbia, Missouri

St. Louis's Union Station

St. Louis's Union Station opened in 1894 in a city that ranked second only to Chicago as a railroad center. Strategically located, St. Louis had emerged as a commercial and transportation hub following the development of steamboat travel on the Mississippi and Missouri Rivers. By the mid-1850s, city leaders realized that railroads would surpass the rivers as carriers of freight and passengers.

In 1889, six railroads organized the Terminal Railroad Association of St. Louis and determined to replace the outdated 1875 Union Depot. The association acquired land to the west of the city center and organized a national competition to select an architect. Theodore C. Link, a German-born St. Louisan, won the competition with a Romanesque design. A notable feature of Link's plan was a four-faced clock tower, which rose 230 feet above track level atop the headhouse on the northeast corner of the station

Well arranged to meet travelers' needs, the complex included the headhouse, a train shed that covered thirty-two tracks, and the concourse between them called the Midway. The train shed was the largest such structure built up to that time. Union Station functioned as a true terminal—there were no through trains—and was built with a stub-end track system in which all trains backed into the yard, with passenger cars at the end. The station featured a barrel-vaulted great hall on the first floor, waiting rooms designated for men and women, and a dining room. The ground floor included waiting rooms, a coffee shop, ticket and information booths, and shops. Offices were housed on the third and fourth floors. Bedford limestone covered the exterior on the north and east sides; all the in-

terior finishes were of top quality. On the west side of the station was the Terminal Hotel, used by railroad workers and travelers wanting inexpensive, clean rooms.

As railroad traffic increased during the early decades of the twentieth century, the Terminal Railroad Association expanded Union Station. Preparations for the 1904 St. Louis World's Fair included adding gates and reshuffling services. Further enlargements and renovations occurred in the late 1920s and early 1940s.

In 1912, three hundred trains passed through Union Station each day. Passenger traffic, however, began to decline following World War I and, except for a significant increase during World War II, decreased until the last passenger train left the station in 1978. By the mid-1950s, city leaders and railroad executives had begun searching for a new use for the once-grand building. The station's architectural significance was recognized in the 1970s by its designation as a National Historic Landmark. An investment group purchased the building in 1974, but their multipurpose redevelopment plan never materialized.

Purchased by a New York firm in 1979, Union Station underwent a high-quality restoration beginning in 1983. Two years later it reopened as a luxury retail, entertainment, and hotel complex. Originally built as a grand portal for railway passengers and city highlight for St. Louisans, Union Station once again draws travelers and residents charmed by its distinctive architecture, central location, and varied attractions.

Sources and Further Reading: H. Roger Grant, Don L. Hofsommer, and Osmund Overby, *St. Louis Union Station: A Place for People, A Place for Trains* (1994); Mary Patricia Holmes, "St. Louis Union Station," *Bulletin of the Missouri Historical Society* 27 (July 1971); Norbury Wayman, *St. Louis Union Station and Its Railroads* (1986).

Lynn Wolf Gentzler
State Historical Society of Missouri,
Columbia, Missouri

Air Transportation

Almost from the beginning of scheduled air transportation in the United States, Midwest cities served as important centers of activity. Chicago, Cleveland, Minneapolis, St. Louis, and Detroit became key terminal points for a number of early airlines. Even smaller cities such as Columbus, Ohio, and Omaha and Wichita, Kansas, witnessed significant air activity. From the days of the intrepid airmail pilots to the jet age, the Midwest remains a key region in the national system of air transportation.

The U.S. Post Office blazed the trail, creating a transcontinental airmail route by the mid-1920s. Pursuant to the Air Mail Act of 1925, however, the Post Office had turned operation of its routes over to private contractors by 1927. Ambitious would-be airline executives across the country rushed to take advantage of the opportunities presented by this action. In transferring its operations to the private sector, the Post Office created thirty-four contract airmail routes. Nearly half had terminal points in the Midwest; ten began or ended in Chicago. Just as Chicago served as a major rail center, it emerged as a major air transportation center. The most important of the many routes radiating from Chicago were the Chicago–Dallas and New York–Chicago routes operated by National Air Transport (NAT) and the San Francisco–Chicago route held by Boeing. Through a series of complicated mergers, these airlines would provide much of the foundation for what became United Airlines.

Detroit also emerged as an important early aviation center through the efforts of Henry Ford, who became interested in commercial aviation in 1924. Even before the Post Office began awarding airmail contracts, he built an airport and established a private express airline between Detroit and Chicago and between Detroit and Cleveland. He then successfully bid for the airmail contracts for those routes. Ford's interest in aviation, though, proved short-lived. He left the airline business in 1931 and closed his airport in 1933.

Cleveland was another pioneer air terminal city, with its four airmail routes beginning or ending in Detroit, Pittsburgh, Albany, and Louisville. St. Louis was the fourth Midwest city acting as a terminal point on more than one airmail route, boasting service to Chicago and to Omaha. Both routes were operated by Robertson, a company made famous by an early employee, Charles Lindbergh. The route between St. Louis and Chicago is considered one of the foundations of what became American Airlines. Other Midwest cities with ties to the early airmail routes were Minneapolis, later home of Northwest Airlines, and Cincinnati, later home of Embry-Riddle, another company that through a series of mergers formed a foundation for American Airlines.

Although the Post Office initially established only thirty-four contract airmail routes, thus limiting the number of companies that could benefit from such contracts, many other airline companies emerged. Many of these fledgling companies hoped to capture some future route created by the Post Office. Some, while still holding that hope, jumped into the airline business simply for the love of aviation. Americans generally had responded quite positively to the intro-

duction of the airplane. Dreams of a future in which Americans would take to the skies in vast numbers were not uncommon. That air-mindedness was further sparked by Charles Lindbergh's solo flight across the Atlantic. Aviation enthusiasm was widespread in the late 1920s.

The Midwest was crisscrossed, if only briefly, by dozens of small airline companies. They flew from Minneapolis to Rochester, Wichita to Omaha, Kansas City to Minneapolis, Kansas City to Springfield, Sioux City to St. Paul, and Watertown to Rapid City. Most were founded in a flush of excitement in 1929; many were gone within a year of their first flights, and most of the remainder were out of business by 1933. A few survived, but only because they were absorbed by the larger airlines with the airmail contracts.

Whether large or small, airlines depended not only on airmail contracts and willing investors, but also on air-minded citizens in their home cities. Airlines need airports. With few exceptions, the nation's fledgling airlines could not afford the outlays of capital necessary to establish the ground-based infrastructure they needed. Instead, they first built upon the foundation laid by the Post Office, and further encouraged local interests, public and private, to provide them with the necessary landing fields.

As the Post Office worked to create a transcontinental airmail route, it did so with a somewhat limited budget. Planes, pilots, and air navigation aids consumed most of the available funds. Post Office officials, therefore, traveled to cities on existing and projected routes. In these cities, the officials appealed to boosterism, strongly encouraging local interests to provide the landing fields: No landing field, no airmail. Throughout the Midwest, local interests responded with a good deal of enthusiasm. While the task of establishing the first airports often fell to local private interests like Chambers of Commerce or local chapters of the Aero Club of America, in many cities, the local government took the lead. To do so, however, they needed legislation empowering them to establish municipal landing fields or airports. Indiana passed the first enabling legislation in 1920; Kansas, Nebraska, and Wisconsin followed suit the next year. Minnesota enacted its first airport legislation in 1923, and Ohio in 1926. The record of action by Midwest states is remarkable since only two others, Washington and Kentucky, had enacted airport enabling legislation by 1926. Most other states passed no airport legislation until after 1927.

With early state action and positioned at the center of aviation activity, the Midwest became home to a number of early, important airports. Most dated from the mid to late 1920s, and many are still major hubs today. Airmail flights into Chicago at first utilized three small fields: Grant Park, Checkerboard Field, and Maywood Field. Finally, in 1925, the city leased property from the Board of Education. The following year it approved $25 thousand for improvements to what became Chicago's first major airport, Chicago Municipal Airport (now Midway Airport). Cleveland acted to establish its municipal airport as soon as Ohio passed the enabling legislation in 1926. Cincinnati accepted a gift of land from an early flight school operator in 1925. Two years later, the city purchased an additional 870 acres, expanding the airport area to approximately a thousand acres, and in 1930, the city dedicated Lunken Field, at the time the world's largest (in terms of land area) municipal airport. (Lunken now serves as a reliever airport for Cincinnati.) In 1928, St. Louis purchased a private airport that had been functioning as its municipal airport since the early 1920s. Lambert–St. Louis Municipal was dedicated in 1930. Wayne County established what would become the major airport in the Detroit area in the late 1920s. What is now the main airport in Minneapolis dates to 1920 when the local Aero Club rented a former auto racetrack. Northwest Airways (now Northwest Airlines) began operations there in 1926. In 1928, the Minneapolis Park Board assumed responsibility for the field and renamed it the Minneapolis Municipal Airport.

After a scandal involving charges of bid fixing on the part of the Postmaster General, the Post Office once again awarded airmail contracts in 1934. Improvements in aircraft technology allowed longer and fewer routes, thirty-two instead of thirty-four. However, the Midwest, especially Chicago, remained an important center of activity. Seven of the new routes radiated from Chicago; others radiated from Detroit and Cleveland. Another route serving the Midwest was flown by Handford's Tri-State Airlines between St. Paul and Omaha. Three of the four major airlines of the time—United, American, and TWA—provided service to Midwest cities. Several smaller airlines also operated in the region. In addition to Handford's Tri-State, these included Braniff, Pacific Seaboard, Central, and Pennsylvania. The last two merged in 1936 to form Pennsylvania-Central.

In the 1930s and 1940s a number of local service airlines also appeared in the Midwest. Minneapolis–St. Paul, Indianapolis, St. Louis, and Kansas City all housed airlines focused on the Midwest market. A number of these airlines remained independent for some years before disappearing during one of the periodic waves of mergers in the airline industry. Minneapolis–St. Paul became home to what began as Wisconsin Central Airlines and became North Central Airlines when it moved to the Twin Cities in 1952. It served communities throughout Wisconsin and linked

the Twin Cities to Chicago. North Central merged in 1979 with Southern Airways to form Republic Airlines. Republic and Northwest merged in 1986.

Purdue Aeronautics Corporation, based in Lafayette, Indiana, briefly operated an airline route between Lafayette and Chicago in the 1940s. In 1950, however, its temporary certificate expired and local airline service in Indiana moved to the Indianapolis Airport and Turner Airlines (originally named after the air racer Roscoe Turner). Turner changed its name to Lake Central Airlines in 1950 and continued to offer a number of flights out of Indianapolis until its merger with Allegheny Airlines in 1968.

East St. Louis played host to Parks Air Transport, another local service dating to the 1940s. When its certificate was canceled in 1950, its routes were awarded to two other local service airlines. The first was Ozark Airlines, based in St. Louis, and the second was Mid-Continent Airlines, based in Kansas City, which had grown out of Handford's Tri-State Airlines. Ozark provided service throughout the Midwest and eventually into the South and Southwest, until it merged with TWA in 1986.

A number of cities benefited from federal spending for military flying facilities during World War II. Chicago and Cincinnati, for example, transformed former Army Air fields into new airports. Other cities, such as Dayton and Omaha, came out of the war with improved airports. Major new airport construction was quite rare after the war; only Kansas City, Missouri, built an entirely new airport.

The 1940s, 1950s, and particularly the 1960s saw an explosion in what the FAA came to call third level airlines. In 1964, twelve of these small scheduled air taxi services were operating nationwide, and by the end of 1968, there were more than two hundred, twenty-nine of them in the Midwest. They served cities both large and small, from Chicago, Indianapolis, and Cleveland to Morris, Illinois; Terre Haute, Indiana; and Port Clinton, Ohio. Although many operations were and remained relatively small, they were busy: Carl R. Keller Field in Port Clinton, Ohio, made the U.S. Census's recent list of primary airports, with at least ten thousand individuals enplaned per year.

Deregulation of the airline industry in the early 1980s completed the transformation of air travel from a service for the elite to a form of nearly mass transportation. The hub-and-spoke system worked to concentrate the growing passenger traffic at a relatively few large airports. Deregulation ended much of the subsidies for airline service to the nation's smaller communities. All of this reshaped air transportation in the Midwest and across the nation. Many of the smallest cities lost access to scheduled airline service.

Medium-sized cities often lost the jet service they had enjoyed. Instead, new regional airlines (many eventually came to be affiliated with the remaining major airlines) introduced new, smaller turbo-prop airplanes. Regional jets, though, did make an appearance by the 1990s.

Despite all the changes, a number of Midwest airports, important from the late 1920s, remained among the most active not only in the nation, but also in the world. At the dawn of the twenty-first century, the top thirty airports in terms of passengers enplaned included Chicago, Minneapolis–St. Paul, Detroit, and St. Louis. Chicago and Indianapolis both ranked among the top twenty in terms of cargo. And when measured by the total number of takeoffs and landings, Chicago, Minneapolis–St. Paul, Detroit, Cincinnati, and St. Louis all ranked in the top twenty.

Sources and Further Reading: Robert E. Adwers, *Rudder, Stick, and Throttle* (1994); Noel E. Allard and Gerald N. Sandvick, *Minnesota Aviation History, 1857–1945* (1993); Janet R. Daly Bednarek, *America's Airports* (2001); R.E.G. Davies, *Airlines of the United States Since 1914* (1972); Michael J. Goc, *Forward in Flight* (1998); Ann Holtgren Pellegreno, *Iowa Takes to the Air* (1980); Frank Joseph Rowe and Craig Miner, *Borne on the South Wind* (1994); Howard L. Scamehorn, *Balloons to Jets* (2000).

Janet R. Daly Bednarek
University of Dayton, Ohio

Dirigibles

Dirigibles are lighter-than-air craft, often with a rigid frame, that can be maneuvered through the use of a motor and propeller. They were first effectively developed in France in the 1880s and first flown in the Midwest in the 1890s.

Missouri-born Thomas Baldwin, a noted early balloonist, was among the first people in the United States to experiment with the new form of craft, constructing his first version in 1892. In 1904, Baldwin constructed the *California Arrow*, which his assistant, Roy Knabenshue, successfully piloted at the St. Louis World's Fair that year. Knabenshue returned to his hometown of Lancaster, Ohio, and constructed a craft that he exhibited at midwestern events.

During World War I, dirigibles were used for spying and bombing raids but were soon abandoned because they were unwieldy and made easy targets. Following the war, Count Zeppelin and his associates in Germany began to experiment with the construction of rigid-framed lighter-than-air craft. Gigantic airships, such as the *Graf Zeppelin* and the *Hindenburg*,

provided transatlantic passenger service. In the Midwest, the Goodyear Tire and Rubber Company became involved in commercially licensed airship construction and, after 1925, produced large airships for the United States government in a huge hangar at Akron, Ohio.

Following the *Hindenburg* disaster of 1936, airships quickly declined in favor and were abandoned as a practical means of transportation. Blimps, filled with helium rather than hydrogen gas, particularly those flown for exhibition and advertising purposes by the Goodyear Company, continue to remind onlookers of the now-long-past day of the dirigible.

Sources and Further Reading: Ann Holtgren Pellegreno, *Iowa Takes to the Air* (1980); John Toland, *The Great Dirigibles* (1972); Bob Waligunda and Larry Sheehan, *The Great American Balloon Book* (1981).

Peter Hoehnle
Iowa State University

Airplanes

The airplane was born in the Midwest. Though the first flight happened on the Atlantic Coast, Orville and Wilbur Wright conducted the important experimental work behind that first flight in Dayton, Ohio. After perfecting their craft, the Wrights demonstrated it to the world in 1908. Almost immediately the nation was swept up in a wave of enthusiasm for this new technology. The Midwest in particular became an early hotbed of activity, as mechanically-minded individuals sought to join the Wrights in the sky. Although most military and commercial aviation manufacturing would move to the coasts, seeking either year-round flying weather or access to politicians or investment capital, the Midwest emerged as the important center for the construction of light aircraft. Wichita, Kansas, and southern Ohio proved especially important locations for light aircraft manufacturing, although every state in the Midwest had some activity, especially before World War II.

In the earliest years of powered flight, any number of ambitious individuals with imagination and some mechanical aptitude sought to design and construct their own aircraft. All Midwest states witnessed efforts by individuals to take to the skies in their homemade flying machines. Most built one or two aircraft, made a few attempts at flight, and then moved on to safer, more secure occupations. A very few, though, persevered and pioneered the light plane industry in the United States.

Wichita, Kansas, emerged as an early center of activity by some of the more stubborn and gifted individuals determined to earn a living in aviation. Clyde Cessna made plans to build an affordable aircraft of his own design even before the U.S. entry into World War I. The war put a hold on his ambitions, but during the 1920s, he and several others, helped by an enthusiastic business community, established Wichita as an early and enduring center of light plane manufacturing. In the 1920s, Wichita became home to aircraft manufacturing companies founded jointly or singly by Clyde Cessna, Walter Beech, and Lloyd Stearman. By the 1930s, Stearman had left for California, but Beech and Cessna (whose company was now controlled by his nephews) remained in Wichita. Airplanes designed and built there became some of the most popular aircraft of the 1930s. Cessna's Airmaster and Beech's famous Staggerwing in many ways set the standards for the decade.

After World War II, a precipitous drop in demand for light aircraft forced a major restructuring of the industry. Many companies simply went out of business. Cessna and Beechcraft, still based in Wichita, were among the few to weather the storm. They emerged in the 1950s as two of the three major producers of light aircraft in the United States. Again, Cessna's 172 and Beechcraft's Bonanza were among the most popular light planes in the world. Both companies are still based in Wichita, and they still build a range of general aviation aircraft.

Southern Ohio can also stake a claim to early leadership in the light aircraft industry. The same city that gave birth to the airplane was also the home of the designers behind the nation's first truly affordable personal aircraft. Jean Roche and a number of his fellow employees at McCook Army Air Field in Dayton developed the design for a small, one-seat aircraft powered by a 26-hp engine. A group of Cincinnati businessmen bought his design for their new company, the Aeronautical Corporation of America, better known as Aeronca. Cincinnati's Lunken Airport housed the company's factory. After a flood in the 1930s, Aeronca moved its operation to Middletown, Ohio, where it continued to build light aircraft until the early 1950s. Even after ceasing production of aircraft, Aeronca remained in the aviation industry. Now a component of Magellan Aerospace Corporation, it produces aircraft substructures.

Troy, Ohio, just a few miles north of Dayton, was the home of one of the most successful manufacturers of light aircraft in the late 1920s and early 1930s. Founded in the 1920s as the Weaver Aircraft Company, the manufacturer and its planes soon became best known by the acronym WACO. WACO was the first aircraft manufacturer in the United States to use tubular steel construction. In 1929, it sold more aircraft than any other company. Its powerful sport biplanes remained popular throughout the 1930s. The company switched to the production of combat gliders during World War II. Unable to make a successful transition back to powered nonmilitary aircraft manufacturing after World War II, WACO exited the aviation business in 1946.

Kansas and Ohio became key centers of activity, but light aircraft companies operated in many states of the Midwest at one time or another. Most appeared in the 1920s and 1930s. Most disappeared by the 1950s. Giuseppe Bellanca briefly built aircraft in Omaha, Nebraska, and Lincoln was home to an aircraft factory as well as the flight school attended by Charles Lindbergh. Don Luscombe founded his first aircraft company, Monocoupe, in Moline, Iowa, before briefly moving operations to St. Louis, Missouri. The Funk brothers got their start in Ohio before moving to Kansas. Davis sport biplanes were built in Indiana.

In addition to Cessna and Beechcraft in Wichita, a number of other aircraft companies contribute to the Midwest's continuing role as a center of light aircraft manufacturing. Bellanca aircraft models have been built in Alexandria, Minnesota. Citabrias are built in Rochester, Wisconsin. The latest company to join the ranks of Midwest light aircraft manufacturers is the Cirrus Design Corporation based in Duluth, Minnesota. Cirrus began as a kit plane manufacturer in the 1980s. By the late 1990s, however, the company had gained FAA certification for their aircraft. Cirrus aircraft are built using state-of-the-art composite construction techniques. They are best known, however, for one unusual feature: Seeking to build an extremely safe aircraft, all Cirrus models are designed to hold a parachute the pilot can deploy in the case of an emergency.

Though the light airplane industry has been in a prolonged slump, those who believe it may make a comeback have pinned many of their hopes on Midwest companies still pursuing the dream of personal aviation.

Sources and Further Reading: Bruce Bissonette, *The Wichita 4* (1999); James Fallows, *Free Flight: From Airline Hell to a New Age of Travel* (2001); Bob Hollenbaugh and John Houser, *Aeronca: A Photo History* (1993); Fred O. Kobernuss, *WACO, Symbol of Courage and Excellence*, vols. 1, 2 (1992, 1999); Edward H. Phillips, *Beechcraft: Pursuit of Perfection*, 2nd ed. (1992); Edward H. Phillips, *Cessna: A Master's Expression* (1985); Jay P. Spenser, *Bellanca C.F.* (1982); James B. Zazas, *Visions of Luscombe* (1993).

Janet R. Daly Bednarek
University of Dayton, Ohio

Air Mail

Aerial mail service did not begin in the Midwest until September 1918 when experimental flights were made to link New York and Chicago as part of the establishment of a New York–to–San Francisco aerial route. The first part of this transcontinental route was from Cleveland to Chicago, with a stop in Bryan, Ohio. The second major leg of the circuit was New York to Cleveland in 1919.

With a transcontinental route established across the Midwest, early pilots began flying on a regular basis across the region. These early pilots, the most famous of whom were James "Jack" Knight and Charles Lindbergh, faced hostile weather to ensure that the mail got through. During the nine years the Post Office Department operated the Airmail Service, there were over sixty-five hundred forced landings. The average flying life span of these pilots was relatively short—about nine hundred flying hours. By 1924, seventy-four planes were flying the route. During 1923 and 1924, aviators flew 1,853,251 miles and delivered 60,001,360 pieces of first-class mail.

In 1925, Congress authorized twelve new routes, a majority of which were in the Midwest, the two most important being Detroit-to-Cleveland and Detroit-to-Chicago. Public confidence was boosted when Lindbergh became a national hero in 1927. Post Master General Harry New convinced Lindbergh to make a special flight over his old route between Springfield, Illinois, and St. Louis in February of 1927, and aerial mail increased by 20 percent between May and June of that year. By 1928, well over a million pounds of air mail was being transported annually. On the eve of the Great Depression, airmail service exploded, with 8,845,968 pounds being carried in 1932.

Although the Depression saw a decrease by almost two million pounds a year, it was the 1933 hearings of Senator Hugo Black's Special Committee on Investigation of Airmail and Ocean Mail Contracts that received the most public attention. It was charged that many of the air contracts to deliver mail, particularly in the Midwest because of its key location and size, had been given to favored clients with no competitive bidding. All existing contracts were declared illegal, and on February 19, 1934, the Army Air Corps began

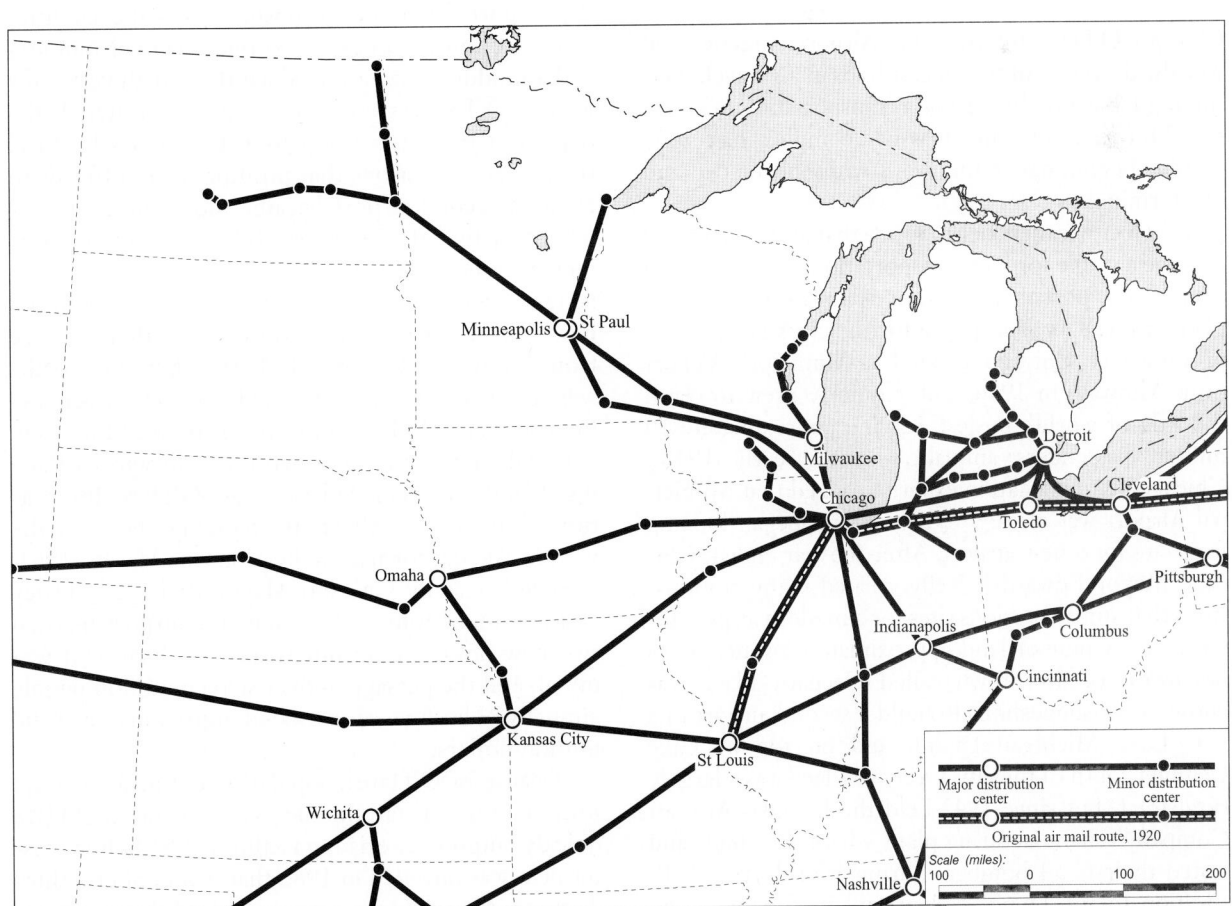

Airmail routes, 1931. Prepared by James DeGrand. *Source: Atlas of Historical Geography of the United States* (1932), plate 141 J.

flying the mail. The excessive amount of mail carried and limitations in equipment led to several aerial disasters. Finally in 1941, Commissioner Richard Akers of the U.S. Court of Claims absolved postal officials and airline operators of any fraud.

By the late 1940s, advances in mail processing and a decline in rail services spurred the U.S. Post Office's use of the airways. By 1954, the Post Office attempted to deliver mail anywhere in the country within a day by using jets. Air service became the dominant form of mail transportation over the next two decades. Federal Express, United Postal Service, and other private carriers have intensified this trend.

Sources and Further Reading: Bob Hollenbaugh and John Houser, *Aeronca: A Photo History* (1993); William M. Leary, *Aerial Pioneers* (1985); Carl H. Scheele, *A Short History of the Mail Service* (1970); Francis A. Spencer, *Air Mail Payment and the Government* (1941).

T. Jason Soderstrum
Iowa State University

Chicago–O'Hare International Airport

Chicago–O'Hare International Airport is recognized worldwide as one of the busiest hubs in air travel, continuing Chicago's history of a transportation nexus in the Midwest. Yet this massive complex had very humble beginnings in the 1940s with one airstrip and one terminal.

When city leaders began to see that air travel would become a viable form of transportation, they sought to create an airport that would be adequate for the new planes as well as appropriate for the city's growth and prominence. Chicago created a Municipal Airport (now Midway) in 1926, and it quickly grew to claim the title of world's busiest, serving approximately 10 million passengers annually. By the early 1940s, Chicagoans and aviation experts realized that Municipal Airport was already too small and began looking for a site for a new airport. After the war ended, Chicago Mayor Edward J. Kelly created many commissions that studied various sites for a modern airport for Chicago. A plot of land approximately twenty miles northwest of downtown called Orchard Place was chosen over suggestions to build a second airport in a new Lake Michigan landfill and on top of Lake Calumet south of the city. Orchard Place was a largely rural tract, but since 1942 held the Douglas Aircraft Company's manufacturing plant where they built and tested their C-54 bombers during World War II. In addition to the Douglas plant and its four concrete runways, the area was also amenable for growth be-

cause it was located near prime railroad lines—important for transporting passengers as well as constructing the facilities—and in a relatively undeveloped area of greater Chicago, suitable for future commercial development.

The city and many agencies drafted many proposals—some of which called for as many as twelve runways. In 1946, the city acquired 1,080 acres of land through the War Surplus Act and continued to annex and purchase surrounding property until over seven thousand acres were amassed. It would be another nine years before O'Hare would open for commercial traffic, but since it was one of the few in the area capable of handling large, four-engine planes, it still conducted some business for the military and small aircraft. During those nine years, Chicago's second airport, Midway, continued to serve about two million passengers and handled approximately 900 thousand takeoffs and landings. In 1949, the airport's name changed from Orchard Place (Douglas) Airport, to O'Hare Field to honor the memory of WWII naval flying hero, Lieutenant Commander Edward H. (Butch) O'Hare, Jr. The legacy of the orchard remains in the airport's call letters, ORD, still used on baggage today.

In October 1955, a TWA propeller plane opened the airport for domestic business, yet the facilities were still quite modest—just one terminal building and a muddy parking lot. Since the Northwest (now Kennedy) Expressway was not yet constructed, the trip from the city's Loop took two hours by local roads. Yet the reasons that prompted city officials to create a second airport became more and more apparent by the late 1950s, as Midway Airport became increasingly crowded and congested, and its 1926 runways could not handle the weight and size of the newer jets. Airlines soon transferred their service from Midway to O'Hare. By 1959, when the Northwest Expressway was completed, over seventeen airlines serviced O'Hare. The airport opened for international travel in 1958 with a Chicago-to-Paris flight and was renamed Chicago–O'Hare International Airport to reflect its changing status in the world. At its formal dedication in March 1963, presided over by Chicago Mayor Richard J. Daley and President John F. Kennedy, the airport boasted two new domestic terminals, one international terminal, and the passage of over sixteen million people annually. The final cost totaled approximately $200 million dollars.

Because of O'Hare's popularity, the general trend toward jet travel, and the success of air travel, O'Hare quickly outgrew its existing facilities. A $1 billion master plan was unveiled in 1982 that would offer a third domestic terminal, new restaurant facilities, new runways, people movers, better transportation to and within the airport, a new control tower, and a new international terminal with better customs facilities by 1990. Architect Helmut Jahn designed the local transportation station in the airport and was responsible for the United Airlines Terminal (Terminal 1), which brought passengers to their gates through a futuristic journey of steel, colored, dancing lights, and moving sidewalks. The United Terminal opened for business in 1987.

As use of the airport increased, it also had a prominent effect on the surrounding landscape. With the Kennedy Expressway and more than fifteen million people using the airport annually, suburbs developed in the shadow of the runways, spurring some staggering long-range residential and commercial development. As the airport grew and the surrounding communities' populations increased, noise reduction and traffic became contested issues.

Chicago–O'Hare International Airport is a major point of both domestic and international arrivals and departures, thus congestion and delays at O'Hare affect airports throughout the country and around the world. Though the 1982 master plan sought to foresee all regional travel needs into the twenty-first century, it has proven insufficient. By 2001, Chicago–O'Hare served 911,861 flights and reclaimed its title as world's busiest airport from Atlanta's Hartsfield International Airport. Late that year, Chicago Mayor Richard M. Daley, Jr., and Illinois Governor George Ryan reached an agreement to create an eighth runway, relocate the seven existing runways to include southern access, build a new entrance on the western side of O'Hare, offer an additional $450 million to soundproof schools and homes in the flight paths, create a third airport in Peotone, Illinois, south of Chicago, and eventually close Meigs Field, a small private airstrip on the Lake Michigan shore. From its modest beginnings, Chicago–O'Hare International Airport continues to keep Chicago's place as a premier transportation hub.

Sources and Further Reading: Janet Daly Bednarek, *America's Airports: Airfield Development, 1918–1947* (2001); Richard P. Doherty, "The Origin and Development of Chicago-O'Hare International Airport," Ph.D. diss., Ball State University (1970); David Young and Neil Callahan, *Fill the Heavens with Commerce* (1981).

Laura E. Milsk
Loyola University–Chicago, Illinois

Kansas City International Airport

The location and design of Kansas City International Airport (KCI), dedicated in October 1972, under-

scored the rural nature of the region. Built almost twenty miles north of the downtown area on over four thousand acres of Platte County farmland, the airport featured a decentralized design that diffused passenger services among three well-spaced terminals. Thirty years later, the airport comprised over ten thousand acres, and the land not used for airport operations continued to support cattle grazing and row crops.

The construction of KCI continued a heritage of support for air travel in the area. Kansas City Municipal Airport, built immediately north across the Missouri River from the city's business and retail center, had opened in 1927. Transcontinental Air Transport chose the airport as its headquarters in 1929. A year later, the merger of Transcontinental Air Transport, Maddux Airlines, and Western Air Express brought into existence Transcontinental and Western Air (TWA), which under various names, played a major role in the aviation history of Kansas City throughout the remainder of the twentieth century.

A devastating flood in 1951 damaged substantial portions of Kansas City's industrial area, including the TWA facilities. Shortly thereafter, city officials began to search for land suitable for another airport. In the early 1950s, the city purchased acreage in Platte County to lease to TWA for its maintenance base. Hangars for maintenance and overhaul and two runways were in use there by 1957. Steep bluffs and high-rise buildings to the south coupled with increased air traffic and larger planes requiring longer runways made the downtown airport increasingly dangerous for commercial use by the 1960s. In 1966, Kansas City residents passed revenue bonds to finance construction of a municipal airport adjacent to the TWA base in Platte County.

Originally designated as Mid-Continent International Airport, the facility opened in 1972 as Kansas City International Airport. Three C-shaped terminals, each twenty-three-hundred feet long and sixty-five feet wide, were designed by the Kansas City architectural firm of Kivett and Myers. They housed ticketing, waiting, and passenger-loading areas on the first floor; the ground floor, on level with the runways and aprons, contained baggage-handling facilities. Short-term parking lots occupied the open center of each structure. This decentralized configuration, often referred to as a Drive-to-your-gate design, minimized the distance between automobile and boarding gate and reduced traffic and passenger congestion within the airport. A control tower and administrative offices completed the initial building phase at KCI. The rural location and the dependence on private automobile transportation necessitated the construction of easily accessible long-term parking lots on the airport's perimeter.

Kansas City International Airport continued to expand. Major renovations to the terminals were begun in 2001 with a view to updating their appearance; however, the Drive-to-your-gate design remained a hallmark of the airport. With the beginning of the twenty-first century, KCI was served by fifteen passenger airlines and eight cargo lines. With an annual passenger traffic of nearly twelve million, the airport bills itself as "middle America's link to the world."

Source and Further Reading: George Ehrlich, *Kansas City, Missouri: An Architectural History, 1826–1990*, rev. ed. (1992).

Lynn Wolf Gentzler
State Historical Society of Missouri,
Columbia, Missouri

Lambert–St. Louis International Airport

The first municipally owned airport in the nation, Lambert–St. Louis International Airport symbolizes St. Louis's prominence in aviation history. Founded in 1920, it was purchased by the city in 1928. The leadership provided by aeronautics enthusiasts and other St. Louisans interested in flight led the city to assume an important role in the aviation industry.

Albert Bond Lambert, a wealthy pharmaceutical company president, was an early leader in St. Louis aviation. In 1920, he leased 160 acres located eleven miles northwest of downtown St. Louis to develop as an airfield. Lambert paid for improving the grounds and erecting hangars while allowing free use of the field by anyone interested in flying. By 1923, the facility was known as the Lambert–St. Louis Flying Field. Lambert bought the property in 1925 and offered it to the city in 1927 at the price he had paid for the land. Within a year, city residents overwhelmingly approved a bond issue to purchase it and to make improvements. Two years later, the busy facility was dedicated as Lambert–St. Louis Municipal Airport. Passenger and cargo airlines, aviation service companies, flight schools, two military units, flying clubs, and an aircraft manufacturing firm shared the field.

Continued heavy demand for flights in the St. Louis area throughout the 1930s compelled the expansion of Lambert–St. Louis and stimulated the call for a secondary airport. In 1942, over 80 percent of the voters approved a bond issue aimed at maintaining the city's stature as an aviation center. Development at Lambert–St. Louis continued. World War II and opposition by the airlines, however, quashed the construction of another airport.

In 1956, the airport dedicated a new terminal building whose distinctive domed design served as a model for terminals later built in New York City and Paris. Passenger jets began to use the airport in 1959, and in 1964, the first flight to Europe left the field. Continuing St. Louis's tradition as an aeronautical center, McDonnell Aircraft Corporation, situated on the airport's northwest side, produced the Mercury and Gemini spacecraft and used the field to test aircraft developed for the American military.

Almost continual expansion marked Lambert–St. Louis throughout the last half of the twentieth century. Land purchases increased the size of the facility. Additional runways, passenger concourses, and terminals were built to try to keep pace with increased traffic. Plans to build a secondary airport to relieve the burden on Lambert–St. Louis were developed and discarded.

By the turn of the twenty-first century, the airport was in the midst of a major expansion program that necessitated the purchase of over one thousand private dwellings, businesses, places of worship, and schools and the relocation of roads and highways. Planned improvements include the construction of a parallel runway to reduce flight delays during inclement weather, the relocation of some airport services, and expansion of the terminal. St. Louis officials struggled to enhance Lambert–St. Louis International Airport's image as a major gateway to the Midwest in the face of a loss in the city's population and a decline in manufacturing.

Source and Further Reading: James J. Horgan, *City of Flight: The History of Aviation in St. Louis* (1984).

Lynn Wolf Gentzler
State Historical Society of Missouri,
Columbia, Missouri

Midway Airport, Chicago

Named in 1949 to commemorate the World War II Battle of the Midway, Chicago's Midway Airport is today the smaller of Chicago's two airports, though it once held a very prominent place in the city, the region, and the world.

Chicago was one of the many American cities to feel the need to create an airport that would serve the needs of the burgeoning air traffic industry, and Midway was originally named Municipal Airport in 1926. At 63rd Street and Cicero Avenue about nine miles southwest of the city center, the site had been a practice airfield for the Chicago Aero Club since 1922. Many municipalities at the time created airports to service either the Post Office or the cause of national defense, but city leaders and boosters also realized that if Chicago were to remain a transportation center, as it was for cross-country rail travel in the United States, it would need an active and appropriate airport. A National Air Transport (later United Airlines) plane departed from Municipal Airport with mail in 1926, but the first commercial flights did not take off for another year.

In the late 1920s, Chicago Municipal Airport was a state-of-the-art facility. It had one modern, concrete terminal, nineteen hangars, a control tower, and complete lights for night activity. It quickly became a tourist attraction and was often referred to as the "Union Station of the Sky." By the 1940s, it was declared the world's busiest airport, handling over ten million people annually by the end of that decade. At the same time, Chicago civic and aviation leaders soon realized that Municipal's congestion was a hazard and began to look for a site to accommodate a new airfield, for the city of Chicago had grown around the Municipal Airport so that further expansion was impossible. In 1946, land northwest of the city was acquired for what would become Chicago–O'Hare International Airport, though it did not open for full commercial service until 1955. Midway remained an active and congested airport well throughout the 1950s, but by 1959, seventeen major airlines had transferred their service to the new and better-equipped O'Hare. While cutting-edge in 1926, Municipal's runways were not capable of accommodating the new jets that dominated the air. In 1962, the last commercial flight for the foreseeable future took off from a virtual ghost town.

Yet planners realized that Chicago still needed two airports, and a 1967 renovation program brought modern facilities back to the southwest side. Commercial flights resumed in 1968, easing some of the congestion at O'Hare. Midway continued to struggle however, and in the early 1980s began offering shorter, low-cost flights to smaller markets, creating a home for carriers like Southwest Airlines and the original Midway Airlines. Midway Airport again underwent an extensive renovation and reopened passenger terminals and parking facilities in late 2001. Although O'Hare is often considered Chicago's airport, Midway continues to serve as a critical spoke in the nation's air transportation network.

Sources and Further Reading: Janet Daly Bednarek, *America's Airports: Airfield Development, 1918–1947* (2001); David Young and Neil Callahan, *Fill the Heavens with Commerce* (1981).

Laura E. Milsk
Loyola University–Chicago, Illinois

Minneapolis–St. Paul International Airport

The Minneapolis–St. Paul Airport began at a site near the confluence of the Mississippi and Minnesota Rivers where a local auto-racing club had prepared a concrete track similar in size to the Brickyard in Indianapolis. When the Twin Cities Motor Speedway scheme came to nothing, the land partially reverted to cornfields and hog pens. In 1920, the Minneapolis Aero Club leased the site as a feeder link to the transcontinental air trunk line used to shuttle mail across the country. First called Speedway Field, the dirt landing strip in the middle of the still visible concrete oval was rechristened Wold-Chamberlain Field in honor of two Minnesota pilots lost in action over France during the First World War. The first aircraft carrying Post Office mail arrived from Chicago on August 10, 1920. A festival of aerobatic feats and parachuting capped the event, witnessed by many. Regular mail service by Post Office aviators, however, ended on June 30, 1921, when it was determined that mail delivered on overnight trains could adequately replace feeder lines.

Regular commercial service returned to the Twin Cities on June 7, 1926, after Congress passed the Kelly Act. This act authorized the Postmaster General to pay a direct subsidy to commercial air operations carrying the mail. The first Minneapolis company to contract for the mail under the new law was Dickinson Airlines. Dickinson, however, quit the business several months later after a number of spectacular near misses and one pilot's death.

In September 1926, Louis Hotchkiss Brittin snatched up the route for his recently formed company, Northwest Airways of Michigan. The first three Northwest biplane pilots to fly the airmail route between Chicago and Minneapolis (by way of Milwaukee and La Crosse, Wisconsin) were David L. Behncke, Charles "Speed" Holman, and Robert W. Radall. Passenger service was inaugurated by the airline on July 5, 1927. By 1929, over nine thousand passengers had been landed by the company without mishap.

In 1927, the Park Board of the city of Minneapolis took over operation of airport facilities, which by 1928, included eight aircraft hangars, a main terminal, a control tower, and 325 acres of land. In 1943, the Park Board turned over management of the field to the Metropolitan Airports Commission. Several other airlines joined Northwest at Wold-Chamberlain, including Hanford Airlines (1933), North Central Airlines (1952), Republic Airlines (1979), and KLM Royal Dutch Airlines (1991). Today the Minneapolis–St. Paul International Airport is the seventh busiest hub in the United States, handling almost seven hundred takeoffs and landings each day. Because the airport is less than ten miles from the centers of two major cities, noise abatement has been a contentious issue since the 1940s.

In 1933, Northwest Airlines pioneered the Northern Transcontinental route from the Twin Cities to Seattle and Tacoma, Washington. The airline introduced service to Asia via Anchorage and Shemya, Alaska, in 1947. At the beginning of the twenty-first century, Northwest passengers boarding at Minneapolis–St. Paul could take regular nonstop flights to Tokyo, Osaka, Hong Kong, Honolulu, London, and Amsterdam, as well as many destinations in continental North America.

Sources and Further Reading: Noel E. Allard, *Speed: The Biography of Charles W. Holman* (1976); Gerald N. Sandvick, "The Birth of Powered Flight in Minnesota," *Minnesota History* 48 (Summer 1982); Gerald N. Sandvick, "Enterprise in the Skies," *Minnesota History* 50 (Fall 1986).

Philip L. Frana
University of Central Arkansas

Omaha Airport

With the commencement of the age of flight, many business and political leaders in Omaha believed if the city were to become a major commercial center in the Midwest, it would have to establish itself as a major hub of air activity. The city got a big boost in 1920 when the U.S. Government selected it as a station along the transcontinental airmail route. These initial flights originated from the Omaha Chamber of Commerce's hangar at Ak-Sar-Ben Field. The Chamber of Commerce created the Aerial Transportation Committee to oversee this service.

Although operations seemed to be going smoothly, unanticipated changes occurred in 1924. The federal postal authorities determined the Ak-Sar-Ben Field too small for night flying, which was becoming a common occurrence. To alleviate this problem, the airmail planes were moved to Fort Crook, a military installation south of Omaha. The facility was larger and equipped with lights.

This event concerned the Aerial Transportation Committee, which feared the move would permanently remove Omaha as a mail station. Consequently, they looked for vacant land closer to the city where a new airport, under their jurisdiction, could be built and the Chamber of Commerce hangar relocated. The dreams were smashed, literally, on June 22, 1924, when a tornado destroyed the hangar at Ak-Sar-Ben. This did not have much of an impact on the mail service, as the federal postal service had nearly completed a new hangar at Fort Crook where the operations were transferred.

Despite the setback, the Aerial Transportation Committee pursued its attempt to make Omaha a hub of Midwest air activity by continuing the search for land to build a new airport. These efforts paid off when on May 5, 1925, the Omaha City Council adopted an ordinance to acquire a tract of land just east of the city that eventually became the Omaha Municipal Airfield.

Although some basic improvements were made at the location, development was stymied by the lack of public funding. This began to change in October of 1926, when the City Council turned over complete responsibility for field improvements to the city's Street Cleaning and Maintenance Department. Using part of their budget, numerous improvements were made in the first months of 1927. The next big boost came in 1928, when the city voted to issue general obligation bonds for five years to improve the airfield. As a result, by 1930, Omaha boasted an airfield that compared favorably with any in the Midwest, and as improvements continued, airlines began regular operations from the Omaha Municipal Airfield.

On March 3, 1959, the Omaha Airport Authority was created. During the same year, the Eugene C. Eppley Foundation provided a grant of $1 million to be matched with Federal funds for airport development. In recognition of the grant, the Airport Authority renamed the airport Eppley Airfield. Centrally located, it is an important airline hub in the Midwest that caters to both a regional and national clientele.

Sources and Further Reading: Harl Adams Dalstrom, *Eugene C. Eppley: His Life and Legacy* (1969); Leslie R. Valentine, "The Development of the Omaha Municipal Airfield, 1924–1930," *Nebraska History* 61 (Winter 1980).

Gregory A. Miller
Nebraska State Historical Society,
Lincoln, Nebraska

Orville Wright (1871–1948)

Orville Wright, sixth child of Milton and Susan Wright of Dayton, Ohio, piloted the first sustained, controlled flight of a powered machine in the world, carrying him aloft for twelve seconds near Kitty Hawk, North Carolina, on December 17, 1903.

Unlike his brother and business partner Wilbur, Orville was shy and reticent, refusing for much of his life to speak in public. In his personal writings, however, Orville described the moment he fell in love with flight as a child while living briefly in Cedar Rapids, Iowa: "Father brought home to us a small toy [heli-

The Wright brothers at Kitty Hawk, North Carolina, 1903. Wright State University.

copter] actuated by a rubber spring which would lift itself into the air."

Orville as a boy was also interested in the printing trade, and drew his brother Wilbur into the business for three years beginning in 1889. During the bicycle craze of the 1890s, Orville and Wilbur opened a repair shop and renewed their interest in the technology of flight. Together the brothers discovered that the real problem with flight had been one of control, and so invented wing warping to make turns and forward elevators for ascent and descent.

Following the successful first flight near Kitty Hawk, Orville began testing the brothers' Wright Military Flyer for the War Department. He suffered a serious accident during one of these tests in 1908, killing his passenger. It was the first death of the powered aircraft age. In 1910, Orville started flying schools in Alabama and at Huffman Prairie outside Dayton, and continued his intellectual interest in aeronautics, but sold his financial interest in the Wright Company in 1916, four years after his brother's death. He was extended many awards for his scientific accomplishments, including election to the National Academy of Sciences in 1936. He died in 1948 in his hometown of Dayton, Ohio.

Sources and Further Reading: Roger E. Bilstein, *Flight in America* (1994); Tom D. Crouch, *The Bishop's Boys* (1989); Peter L. Jakab and Rick Young, eds., *The Published Writings of Wilbur and Orville Wright* (2000).

Philip L. Frana
University of Central Arkansas

Wilbur Wright (1867–1912)

Wilbur Wright, third son of Milton and Susan Wright, was born near Millville, Indiana, and grew up

in Dayton, Ohio. He is best known as coinventor of the Wright Flyer, which on December 17, 1903, made the first sustained, powered flight carrying and controlled by a pilot. Wilbur did not pilot the first flight himself—that honor was reserved for his brother and business partner Orville Wright—but he is generally acknowledged as the first to explore the idea of powered flight, which led to construction of the aircraft that leapt into the air at Kill Devil Hill, near Kitty Hawk, North Carolina. In particular, Wilbur discovered a critical design problem in the models of earlier flight attempts by others, namely, an inability of pilot control of the aircraft in every dimension—a lesson derived from his years as a bicycle mechanic in Dayton.

Wilbur became a hero in France and elsewhere in Europe during public exhibitions of flight between 1908 and 1909. Wilbur hoped that his flights, which were witnessed by kings and generals, would stimulate interest in military applications of the machines. Though dogged by depression and invalidism following a tragic childhood accident, Wilbur became a fine public speaker and well read in not only science and engineering, but also philosophy, history, and literature. After 1910, Wilbur left the piloting of aircraft in shows largely to Orville, dedicating himself instead to fighting a series of patent infringement cases against competitors including Glenn Curtiss, the father of naval aviation. Typhoid fever claimed Wilbur's life on May 30, 1912.

Sources and Further Reading: Roger E. Bilstein, *Flight in America*, rev. ed. (1994); Tom D. Crouch, *The Bishop's Boys* (1989); Peter L. Jakab, *Visions of a Flying Machine* (1990).

Philip L. Frana
University of Central Arkansas

Travel Literature

Travel literature has played a vital role in the perception and understanding of the Midwest. Over the years, travelers have written about the Midwest in diaries, letters, journals, newspaper articles, poems, and short stories, in addition to lengthy travel narratives and novels.

At its most optimistic, the travel literature traces the emergence and persistence of midwestern towns and cities as signs of American progress and stability, and reveals the diversity of the region's geography and its inhabitants. At its most critical, it reduces the Midwest to a flat, monotonous waste, a place of stifling regularity and cultural homogeneity that should be passed through rather than lingered in, a blank space between the more dramatic topography of the West and the urbanized East.

The mesmerizing flatness and seeming endlessness of the midwestern prairie is perhaps the one constant among the disparate groups of travelers who have traversed the region over the years. This impression was pervasive enough to prompt Charles Dickens in his *American Notes* (1842) to describe the Illinois landscape some thirty miles east of St. Louis as "oppressive in its barren monotony," and it was apparently characteristic enough to Iowa native Bill Bryson, who drove from Quincy, Illinois, into Missouri nearly 150 years later to prompt this remark in *The Lost Continent: Travels in Small-Town America* (1989): "Missouri looked precisely the same as Illinois, which had looked precisely the same as Iowa. The only difference was that the car license plates were a different color."

Far fewer travelers remained in one place long enough to tease out the subtleties of the midwestern landscape or ranged wide enough to encounter its geographical variety. The more northern and topographically diverse states of Michigan, Wisconsin, and Minnesota, for example, often required special trips away from the main routes of travel, and fewer travelers were willing to make them. However, those who did often left accounts that described a more heterogeneous region.

Along the principal travel routes, midwestern cities marked the most striking contrast from the prairie flatness. Travelers considered St. Louis and Cincinnati bustling yet "civilized" antebellum cities. In the latter half of the nineteenth century, few travelers missed the opportunity to visit Chicago and revel in its urban energy. Even the small midwestern cities—places like Dayton, Ohio; Terre Haute, Indiana; and Alton, Illinois—signaled "progress" to many travelers.

The earliest years of written documentation about the region featured narratives on discovery and exploration. In the seventeenth century, French explorers and missionaries like Louis Joliet, Jacques Marquette, Louis Hennepin, and René-Robert Cavelier (known as Sieur de LaSalle) explored the region by canoe and horseback, noting in their diaries and journals landscape features and impressions of Native Americans. In the eighteenth century, English-language accounts accompanied French ones. British travelers, many of whom were military personnel or surveyors for land development companies, commonly explored the region to assess its potential for settlement and commercial expansion.

Travel narratives about the Midwest increased considerably in the nineteenth century, as did travel itself, particularly between 1830 and 1850. The growth in travel was spurred by improved routes (such as canals and macadamized roads) and the emergence of faster, more convenient, and luxurious modes of transportation, including steamboats and railroads. The new forms of transport permitted travelers to direct their attention to the surroundings without worrying about their modes of conveyance, their next meal, or encounters with Native Americans. Entrepreneurs also built luxury hotels in the major cities to cater to those travelers. The newly paved, westward-moving National Road—which had reached Zanesville, Ohio, by 1832, and St. Louis, Missouri, and Alton, Illinois, by the 1850s—prompted English essayist James Silk Buckingham in 1842 to write: "To us, indeed, who had been jolted and shaken, plunged and precipitated, over the rough roads and deep pits of other states . . . it was no ordinary luxury to travel on this smooth and equable National Road."

Yet many travelers still found the Midwest disappointing because it did not satisfy their desire for dramatic mountain ranges, pastoral vistas, varied topography, surprise, delight, or sheer natural force—aspects of the picturesque and the sublime. The picturesque and sublime dominated the literary and visual discourse of the antebellum years, and travelers were conditioned to seek them out. The railroad decreased the amount of time travelers were subjected to this landscape, but speed had little effect on their interpretations. Scottish tourist John Francis Campbell, riding the rails in 1864 near Joliet, Illinois, noted that the "iron horse gallops over a sea of green grass, which has no apparent limit but the horizon."

Midwestern towns and cities were more compelling to travelers. They interpreted the gradual transformation of this once sparsely inhabited landscape—considered part of the American West in the antebellum years—as suggestive of "western" progress. In the antebellum years, this progress was best exemplified by larger cities like St. Louis and Cincinnati, and both could be reached by steamboat. While St. Louis, its Eads Bridge, and the busy shipping activity along its levee drew considerable traveler interest, Cincinnati remained the pre–Civil War "western" urban tourist attraction par excellence. Cincinnati featured a mix of industry and domesticity against a hilly backdrop, signaling a prosperous town whose landscape defied prevailing impressions of flatness. Swedish traveler Karl Arfwedson, arriving in Cincinnati in the early 1830s, noted "handsome brick houses, wide streets, and magnificent public buildings." Given that antebellum Cincinnati was far from the nation's population centers along the Eastern Seaboard, Arfwedson noted that the "first glance leaves an impression of splendour, which the traveller is far from anticipating in these remote western regions."

Though steamboats continued to ply the region's waterways, by the 1870s, most visitors traveled into or through the Midwest via the railroad. Nevertheless, Baedeker's first American guidebook, *The United States, with an Excursion into Mexico*, indicated that it was still possible to travel by steamboat via two different transportation companies through the Great Lakes from Buffalo, New York, to Chicago or Milwaukee—provided one made stops in either Cleveland, Detroit, Port Huron, or Sault Ste. Marie. To urge travelers to consider this option, the guidebook explained that "Cleveland, one of the most beautiful cities on the great lakes, is seen to advantage from the steamer." Few travelers, however, wrote about Cleveland, Detroit, or other medium-sized nineteenth-century midwestern cities.

If travelers focused on the urban Midwest in the late nineteenth century, they mostly turned to Chicago. That city caught the traveler's attention especially in 1893, when over twenty million people paid admission to visit the World's Columbian Exposition. But Chicago was also a marquee attraction because of its extraordinary industrial, commercial, and population growth distinguished by frenetic street activity and the world's first collection of steel-frame skyscrapers. To East Coast–based journalist Julian Ralph in 1893, Chicago was the most crowded, loud, and energetic city on earth. "To those who are in the crowds," he wrote, "even Chicago seems small and cramped; even her street cars, running in brakeneck trains, prove far too few; even her streets that connect horizon with horizon seem each night to roar at the city officials for further annexation in the morning." At the same time, travelers were also impressed with Chicago's "civilized" side: its exquisite skyscraper lobbies, its grand hotels and theatres, and its many parks.

But some travelers were as frightened by Chicago as they were fascinated by it. Midwestern novelist Hamlin Garland, recalling his first trip there in the 1880s, wrote in *A Son of the Middle Border* (1917) that he would "never forget the feeling of dismay" upon seeing "a huge smoke-cloud which embraced the whole eastern horizon." Novelist Theodore Dreiser set his novel *Sister Carrie* (1900) in Chicago to highlight the conflicting messages of exhilaration and alienation that the nineteenth-century industrial metropolis could inflict upon its subjects. The novel opens with eighteen-year-old Carrie, who had never left her small Wisconsin hometown, gazing from the train window as the green landscape familiar to her slowly transforms into the telegraph poles, signs, and smokestacks marking outer Chicago. Finally, Carrie arrives in Chicago under a "great shadowy train shed" that is "alive with the clatter and clang of life."

Aside from the verticality of Chicago and a few other midwestern cities, however, most travelers encountered the Midwest as essentially flat. By the 1920s, most travel literature was generated by those who moved around and through this landscape via automobile, which quickly became the most popular form of twentieth-century transportation. The automobile offered a significant speed advance over the stagecoach and, unlike the bus, did not follow prescribed routes or require prescheduling. Travelers also noted that the roadside landscape had changed to meet the new automobile craze, but they were not always thrilled with the changes. Poet Michael J. Rosen, remembering his family trips across U.S. 40 (the old National Road) in the late 1950s, recalled the deadening sameness of commercial signage flanking the road. To Rosen, U.S. 40 was "a familiar procession of wacky neon and vernacular architecture—the Bambi Lodge, the Robert E. Lee, the Clean Rooms with Free TV and Telephone."

For those who wished to pass through the Midwest as quickly as possible, the automobile—if one was willing to risk it—also permitted frightening speeds. Few travelers, however, passed through at quite the same rate as Sal Paradise and Dean Moriarty in Jack Kerouac's novel *On the Road* (1957). With the exception of Chicago, Moriarty and Paradise found the Midwest most appropriately encountered at more than a hundred miles per hour.

The creation of the national interstate highway system in the 1950s greatly facilitated automobile travel through the Midwest, but as critics and scholars have almost universally declared, it also reduced local variety into interchangeable motels, gas stations, and fast-food restaurants. To cultural geographer Richard H. Schein, as observed in his "The Interstate 70 Landscape," the interstates represent the efforts of federal authorities to "rationally order and control American space." Along the midwestern stretches of Interstate 70—an interstate that both bypassed and encompassed U.S. 40 within its fold—the driver sees little save for exit interchanges and billboards. "Small-town America," Schein laments, "is now out of sight, and can be conveniently 'out of mind.'"

The freedom from prescribed routes of travel offered by the automobile did not, however, necessarily mean that travelers found the midwestern landscape strikingly different than they found it more than a hundred years earlier. Though parts of Michigan featured thick forests instead of prairie, travel writer Bill Bryson was unmoved during the late 1980s drive across America reported in his *The Lost Continent* (1989): "Michigan is shaped like an oven mitt and is often about as exciting, he wrote. . . . .The Manistee forest was dense and dull—endless groves of uniform pine trees—and the highway through it was straight and flat."

Traveling by airplane, meanwhile, offered perspectives that could only be imagined from the ground. As early as 1925, the Ford Air Transport Company combined regular mail routes with passenger service between Detroit, Chicago, and Cleveland; by 1929, the Transcontinental Air Transport Company was promising a forty-eight-hour coast-to-coast journey from New York to Los Angeles—a combination of air and rail travel that included stops in the midwestern cities of Columbus, Indianapolis, St. Louis, Kansas City, and Wichita. By the mid-twentieth century, travelers could fly into or over the Midwest with some frequency. Although to some travelers, the Midwest from the air seems little more than an "empty space that holds the two coasts apart," to writer Michael Mar-

tone, it also reveals the regularity of the township grid that marks the National Land Ordinance of 1785. Viewed through the window of a 737, Martone spotted "the signature of the township grid, the rumpled patchwork quilt of the land."

Such a view was interesting to some, less so to others. For historian Bernard DeVoto, the township grid, oriented to the cardinal points, offered the only clues to the direction of plane travel. From an elevation of eleven thousand feet somewhere south of Wisconsin in 1952, DeVoto's Midwest was a "monotonous landscape" that provided little food for thought: "There is little for the mind to focus on and it sinks into reverie." He was, of course, in the air, and not on the ground.

Sources and Further Reading: Karl Arfwedson, *The United States and Canada* (1834); Karl Baedeker, ed., *The United States with an Excursion into Mexico* (1893; reprint, 1971); Bernard DeVoto, "The Easy Chair: Transcontinental Flight," *Harper's* (July 1952); M. H. Dunlop, *Sixty Miles from Contentment* (1995); Walter Havighurst, ed., *Land of the Long Horizons* (1960); Robert R. Hubach, *Early Midwestern Travel Narratives* (1961); John Jakle, *Images of the Ohio Valley* (1977); Michael Martone, *The Flatness and Other Landscapes* (2000); Michael Martone, ed., *A Place of Sense* (1988); Karl Raitz, ed., *The National Road* (1996); Julian Ralph, *Our Great West* (1893; reprint, 1970).

J. Philip Gruen
University of California–Berkeley

Science and Technology, Health and Medicine

SECTION EDITOR
George W. Paulson, M.D.

Section Contents

Overview

Although they caused difficulty for the early settlers, the geology, climate, and topography of the Midwest also offered opportunity, and the numerous streams, rivers, and great lakes encouraged as well as blocked movement. Early means of transportation were through these bodies of water, facilitated by canals, and then by advances in shipping, rail, and aviation technology. Some of the most innovative bridges in history were built in the Midwest, including an early suspension bridge in Cincinnati and formidably long ones that spanned the Mississippi. Draining the swamps (notably the famous Black Swamp in northwest Ohio) and eliminating standing water from agricultural fields by the use of tile channels was crucial for the settlement of the Midwest; it made possible its agriculture and sustained the soil that was destined to produce food for much of the world.

Water was not the only natural element that had to be managed. To conquer the land, trees were eliminated by "girdling" the trunk (that is, removing a band of bark), as well as by ax work and sawmills. Trees were so effectively stripped from the landscape that the entire state of Wisconsin could have been covered by two feet of the plank lumber prepared from the trees that were removed from its surface. Much of the deforestation occurred to supply fuel to make iron or to generate warmth in a cold land, but wood was also the primary building material for shelter. Scattered log cabins are still one of the symbols of the Midwest

and of its pioneer settlements. The shelters in the Midwest reflected the evolution of settlements nationwide, as housing evolved from lean-tos to log cabins to framed houses. With the advent of the railroad, it became possible to move heavy beams and finished products for construction. With the development of steel, skyscrapers became possible; some of the construction facilitated by steel was aesthetically unique as well as solidly functional.

Power, after it was no longer produced by burning wood, depended on the abundant coal supplies or on electricity from sources such as waterfalls. In addition, much of the nation's nuclear and windmill power developed in the Midwest. Oil was once a major industry in the Midwest, and many of the earliest developed pockets of oil and natural gas were beneath the midwestern states. Some of the intensive agricultural cultivation and rapid settlement led ultimately to a need for pollution control and thereby encouraged conservation. The formerly vigorous clearing of the trees and elimination of the prairie has led to a push for the reconstruction of nature and preservation or restoration of the once widespread prairie life.

Transportation technology initially reflected advances in shipping and packing and other areas that supported the railroad network. More recently, however, transportation has come to mean the automobile and the airplane. Starting with the Wright brothers, the preeminence of the Midwest in the development of the airplane is clear. The automobile industry is likewise identified with the Midwest, and particularly with Detroit, because of such developers as Henry Ford and a legion of other local entrepreneurs and in-

Henry Ford, Thomas Edison, Warren G. Harding, and Harvey Firestone camping, 1921. Ohio Historical Society, AL01138.

ventors who possessed both vision and determination. Automobiles that in retrospect seem ephemeral (the Cord, for instance) and inventors that would be remarkable in any age (Kettering and his self-starter, as one example) were nurtured in the Midwest. Exchange, competition, and the response to needs can be documented over and over. The Ford Motor Company developed one of the most reliable, and surely one of the most noisy, airplanes of all time with the Ford Trimotor. Henry Timken went from carriage making, to devising a better spring to cushion the ride, then to a ball bearing to reduce friction, and he thereby built a giant of an industry. Among the obvious reasons that steel, automobiles, and airplanes developed in this region was the ready availability of iron ore from the states that border the Great Lakes, labor that could be trained, and the inventive spirit.

Technology to feed the United States now depends a great deal on plant genetics, but much earlier, food production had been increased by the development of a new style of plow, with John Deere one of its chief innovators. The tractor became possible first with steam and then gasoline engines, and tractors and earthmoving equipment of all types are still identified with Peoria, Illinois. Rubber industries, vulcanization, and embedded steel for radial tires may not have originated in the Midwest, but soon rubber products became identified with midwestern companies like Goodyear and Goodrich, as well as with the city of Akron and other newly urban centers that were near the wagon, then the bicycle, then the automobile manufacturing giants of the Midwest. Creativity was not limited to the farm or factory, however: State universities throughout the Midwest, largely land-grant products of the Morrill Act, led in developing extension services in agriculture for both education and research. The first half dozen Nobel Prize winners in physics came from the Midwest, and individual schools such as Washington University of St. Louis and the University of Chicago each claim over a dozen Nobel Prize winners among their faculty. The first woman physician in the country came from the Midwest, as did six of the first seven, and women in science and in medicine had more opportunity in the Midwest than in much of the rest of the country.

The Midwest is home to internationally known general medical clinics like the Mayo, as well as to more specialized ones like the Kinsey Institute. It is home, as well, to numerous large and small specialized scientific research centers. Some, like the Battelle Institute based in Columbus, Ohio, are identified with research for new products and claim hundreds of new patents yearly. Others also have been historically significant; the atomic bomb and nuclear energy will forever be linked to the Fermi Laboratories in Chicago.

Every field of technology and science is represented in the Midwest. There is even a technology of merchandizing; after all, who was better at catalog production and selling than Sears and Roebuck? As is often the case, a single person, like Walgreen for drug stores, or a family, like the Balls for glass jars, takes a basic technology and extends it into a business that evolves, merges with others, and then sponsors new products. Not uncommonly, the next step for the corporation or family is philanthropy and community service. There is a technology, as well as a museum, for outer space in the seemingly limitless space of the Midwest, but the region can also claim important innovations in nanotechnology, the study of molecular-sized particles for communication and production. Perhaps as much as in any section of the United States, local resources, individual inventiveness, and entrepreneurship have led to procedures and corporations that built and still sustain all of the nation. In some areas the Midwest truly leads the world.

Medicine and health are not isolated from science and technology, and the major advances in medical care have come from science and technology. Indians coped with fractures, wounds, infectious diseases, death, and despair, as well as with the persistent impact of weather and nutrition on health. The medical experts in Indian culture, shamans and chiefs, were honored, of course, and magical potions and herbal therapy were common. Sweating and purging were employed both by the Indians and then extensively by the early European settlers. The Euroamericans, in addition to bringing new and devastating diseases to the natives, often utilized Indian lore to treat their own diseases. Both contended with malaria, since swampland and mosquitoes were both plentiful. Some have even suggested that the once pervasive malaria was originally brought with the Europeans. With the draining of the swamps and the reduction in mosquitoes, malaria has almost disappeared from the Midwest. The European Americans did introduce smallpox, and it decimated entire Indian tribes. A few diseases came from plants growing in the Midwest; milk sickness, for example, was said to have killed Abraham Lincoln's mother. More common were epidemic diseases that arose from human contact or contaminated water. Cholera and typhoid swept through communities all over the Midwest until public health measures purified the water in the early part of the twentieth century. Almost universally safe drinking water, fluoridation, sewage disposal, and public health measures—even the concept of public health itself—were slow to evolve.

For the pioneers, most medical care was delivered in the home or field, and less often by conventional physicians than by lay practitioners. There was a tendency for every man to be his own doctor. This was certainly necessary in the absence of ready access to trained physicians; it was also desirable when only a few truly useful medications and pernicious practices were regularly employed. These included so-called heroic measures (the medical term for extreme measures), such as bleeding, intense purging, and toxic medications including calomel (mercury). There continues to be in the Midwest—in fact, in all of the United States—a reliance on natural products, largely herbal, as mainstays of treatment. Side by side with scientific advances, medical care has gone from root, to potion, to pill, to antibiotic, and now can be seen circling back to include natural products again.

There were always, however, gradual moves in the Midwest toward a more scientific and more rational approach to illness, and two of the leading practitioners of the day remain the best known of the time. Daniel Drake of Cincinnati, an expert in the geology and fauna of his area, established several medical schools and led in the effort to house and treat the mentally ill. William Beaumont of St. Louis was another local leader in the practice of medicine. Before it was fashionable, he studied the physiology of a unique patient; by observing a wound opening into the stomach of one of his patients, Beaumont carefully defined the physiology of gastric secretion. Scattered physicians who had learned medicine through didactic lectures, and through an apprenticeship whenever they could obtain one, began to appear throughout the Midwest. Soon medical schools and teaching hospitals were founded; hospitals built primarily to teach medical students, rather than to house the poor, actually began in the Midwest.

In the early 1900s an influential report by Abraham Flexner, who reviewed medical education all over the United States, flayed the inadequate medical teaching that was characteristic of the entire Midwest. Indeed, teaching was poor across the entire country. As a result, many medical schools that functioned largely for profit were closed, and more adequate ones were opened. National trends, including bedside teaching and scientific medicine, were spread to the Midwest by visitors such as Sir William Osler. Professional organizations, first the American Medical Association and then separate organizations for virtually all of the specialties, began to benefit practice and teaching throughout the Midwest. Many of these professional organizations started or were housed in the Midwest. Possibly the great distance between centers, or a feeling of neglect by eastern authorities, but probably most of all the midwestern traits of neighborliness, cooperation, and innovation led to these cooperative organizations. As there were the granges and 4-H in agriculture, groups for mutual support and education in health flowered in the Midwest.

Undoubtedly, at times, the entrepreneurial spirit stood side by side with idealism as experts in all health fields moved to enhance as well as limit practice. Most specialty groups began when a single individual recruited others with like interest and began to establish an organizational structure. Both specialty and freestanding general clinics—including large and internationally successful ones like the Mayo, Marshfield, and Cleveland Clinics—were really invented in the Midwest. An institution like Mayo might be placed in a seemingly unlikely area like Rochester, Minnesota, because of the vision of its founders and not because it was necessarily logical to have a large medical center located in a near wilderness. Nobel Prize winners have come from these clinics, and patients from all over the world have enjoyed their scientific and medical expertise. The Cleveland Clinic has led the world in vascular surgery and cardiac intervention, and clinical research has been a feature at all the major centers in the region.

The effort to enhance medical education has taken many forms in the Midwest. States approached the problem in different ways, although every midwestern state established programs for related or allied medical specialties, including physical therapy and hospital administration. Medical education was organized in varied fashion throughout the Midwest. Ohio, for example, chose to have eight medical schools of various types, whereas Iowa supported only one allopathic school and developed a statewide ambulance service to transport patients to the center. Illinois built a series of campuses around the state and now claims the largest medical school in the United States. South Dakota, on the other hand, only recently expanded its single two-year school to a four-year school. The dental schools were, at first, linked with the medical colleges, but most soon became independent, although they still were often part of the larger university. Nursing has similarly achieved greater autonomy in the last few decades, along with advanced degrees and professionalism. The Midwest was the major place of origin for both chiropractic and osteopathic medicine, and osteopathic medicine has now joined conventional medicine in the mainstream of patient care while it continues to emphasize care for the entire family.

The traditional self-help and community cooperation noted so often in the Midwest has by no means disappeared. Support groups for patients, a phenomenon of the last half of the twentieth century, developed all over the Midwest with groups for heart, epilepsy, dyslexia, and Parkinson's disease. Some of these support organizations, including AA (Alcoholics Anonymous), soon became worldwide in scope. Others such as WCTU (the Women's Christian Temperance Union) may no longer have major influence in society, but they once spoke courageously for temperate alcohol use, for women's rights, and for female suffrage. Rehabilitation and sports medicine was not peculiar to the Midwest, but the importance of football and other outdoor activities in the region has probably enhanced midwestern development of sports medicine. Rapid evacuation by medicopter, which began largely after World War II, first appeared in the Midwest, and as related phenomena trauma centers and emergency room medicine flowered in the region.

Another development in health and medicine, and a major one which in large degree began in the Midwest, was the American pharmaceutical industry. Companies such as Pfizer, Upjohn, and Lilly often began when a single individual, or a family, developed new techniques to deliver medications, then formed a company with mergers and expansion. Ultimately, most of the midwestern pharmaceutical companies developed both research and philanthropic divisions as well as national and international sales branches. Several firms in the Midwest collaborated during World War II to make early antibiotics, and they continue to cooperate in developing vaccines to ward off epidemics.

In addition to innovations such as medicopters and electric stimulators for heart and brain, work in genetics, both for plants and humans, has been significant in the Midwest. Health maintenance organizations, a major effort to control costs, began in this region. Occasionally an innovation actually changes an entire town, such as joint implants did in DeKalb, Illinois, where three companies lead the world in production of artificial joints.

This section accounts for some, by no means all, of the at times seamless interactions of science, technology, health, and medicine that midwesterners contributed to or originated. The section as a whole is divided into two parts—science and technology, and health and medicine. Subsections within those major categories are ordered mainly chronologically, and the entries within them are presented alphabetically. Brief subsection overviews, written by the senior consulting editor of the section, introduce the major themes in each group of related topics.

George Paulson
The Ohio State University–Columbus

Taming the Wilderness

The story of America includes the Indians, the explorers, the pioneers, and the merchants, as well as wonderful tales of their isolation, interaction, dreams, successes, and failures. Taming, conquering, using, even exploiting the land they entered seems at times to have been more the pattern than conserving or protecting. Tools and ideas were needed for it all. Before the white settlers, the Indians practiced sophisticated agriculture as well as hunting and warfare, and had to occupy the land and develop their own tools, shelters, and social structure. The European immigrants to the Indian lands brought the tools of Europe along with its cultures. Occasionally a major social decision, how long forgotten but crucial at the time, such as the decision to ban slavery from the Northwest Territory, established the pattern of settlement and work for generations.

Shelters changed from lean-tos, to log cabins, to frame houses for the new settlements, often built at the very place Indian villages once stood. In addition to specific tools for warfare and protection, metal instruments to cut and shape wood accompanied the settlers, and soon plows, saws, adzes, and knives were being produced in the Old Northwest. If we marked history by a single tool, we could compare the Indian stone knife-edge with a university microtome, or Indian baskets to transport dirt to the tons of dirt moved by Big Muskie to expose precious veins of coal. One of the major reasons for the success of midwesterners, native and settler alike, is the presence of water—ample rain, the largest freshwater lakes in the world, and rivers to fish, travel on, and even redirect.

Building Shelter

The western frontier of the newly formed United States was extended following the Revolutionary War by the acquisition of the Northwest Territory in 1787. The territory was then opened for settlement, but squatters had been living along its major inland waterways and in the Indian villages of the region since the mid-eighteenth century. Housing varied according to the ethnicity of the settlers, the availability of timber, the labor pool, and whether they were older colonialists or newly arrived immigrants, but life and architecture on the ever-expanding western frontier was relatively consistent, as travel journals, immigrants' guides, diaries, and letters testify. First came the backwoodsmen, who explored but made no permanent homes; then the squatters, often families living on land they did not own and moving with the frontier; and then the pioneers, who purchased land and made improvements. All often moved farther west with the frontier, selling their homesteads and clearings to the true settlers who soon established governments and socioeconomic systems within townships and counties. Finally, there were the entrepreneurs in the settled communities. The use of log cabin symbolism in the Harrison presidential campaign of 1840 indicated a frontier romanticism already in place in the Midwest.

The backwoodsmen and squatters built lean-tos and cabins made of poles, but pioneers needed the solid shelter of the log cabin, which was to remain the symbol of the frontier into the twenty-first century. In a standard pattern the log cabin would be followed by a log house, then a frame or brick house—from a rude but industrious beginning to stolid Victorian propriety. The log cabin was not necessarily the first habitation constructed—even a cabin required skill, time, and material. A tent, wagon bed, or rough lean-to of poles and bark served for shelter until the cabin could be raised. These first shelters were generally referred to as "camps." The early prosperous landowner John Cleves Symmes constructed at North Bend (west of Cincinnati) near the Ohio River in 1789 "a camp, by settling two forks of saplins [sic] in the ground, a ridge-pole across, and leaning boat-boards . . . against the ridge-pole." One end was closed, the other left open to a fire; Symmes lived in this camp for six weeks during winter before he could erect a house for his family. The lean-to was simply three walls and a sloping roof. Several of these lean-tos roughly grouped together in a square with connecting palisades acquired the name "Kentucky Station" and were common along the Ohio River Valley through the Indian wars of the 1790s.

The log cabin dominated the frontier clearings from the 1790s well into the 1820s and was a product of the Northern European Forest Culture, particularly Scandinavia. The cabin was quickly and roughly constructed, but efficient and livable. The walls were made of small, round timbers approximately eight inches in diameter. Floors were often compacted earth with a fire pit and its chimney in the center. The framing technique of the entire cabin evolved without the need for iron. The roof was composed of ribs that ran the length of the log pen and supported the trapping, the log gable ends of the house. The roof covering could be as simple as bark (slippery elm was common) or hand-riven clapboards three to four feet in length. The bark or clapboards were held in place by weight poles, which were small saplings placed above the ribs; these poles were separated by knees, short blocks of wood. The weighted roof was notorious for leaking, and the cabin was drafty even though the spaces between the logs were chinked and daubed with wood chips and clay. A firebox and chimney could be constructed entirely of wood and clay, but such cattled chimneys were prone to catching fire. The doorway was closed with a board door or simply a blanket. There could be a window, covered with oiled paper or animal skin. More ambitious was a puncheon floor made of small split saplings laid on timbers placed directly on the earth. Log cabin construction evolved its own descriptive jargon, understood on the frontier but

seldom recorded in print because the cabin was not considered formal architecture.

Once the cabin was built, energy was devoted to clearing the land for farm fields by barking, or girdling, the trees to kill them. When the standing timber was dead and dry, it could be burned, and crops could be grown among the leafless trees. Finally, a barn would be needed, either log or frame. Hewed log barns are still not rare; they usually consist of two log pens separated by the length of one pen, all under the same roof.

Although a simple log cabin could be constructed with only an ax and one or two people to lift, more sophisticated hewed log homes required a labor force working in unison at the raising, a term implying the beginning of social organization on the frontier. A work party felled and hewed the tree trunks to proper size before the raising. Typical house timbers could be fifteen to twenty-four feet long, twelve to eighteen inches in diameter; these would be hewed on both sides to approximately eight inches in width. On the day of the raising, four axmen were appointed to hew the corner notches, the rest of the party to slide the timbers up to these corner men. The log pen, with no openings, constituted the traditional one-day raising. Doors, windows, and fireplace openings were then sawed and framed, the jamb boards held in place with wooden pins or large iron spikes. Often the raising party added the roof rafters and floor joists. The log house could then be finished by a carpenter, a mason, or the owner. Most owners did not physically construct their log houses; they supplied the food and whiskey and exchanged labor. The roof was shingled; flooring, doors, and windows were installed; partition walls were made of vertical boards; a staircase constructed; and a brick or stone firebox and chimney was laid. A cellar was usually dug after the house was done. The log house could be a solid, well-finished home of one or two stories, no different from one constructed of brick or stone. It could also be trimmed with decorative moldings, doors, and mantles in the current fashion, such as Federal or Greek Revival, and with exterior siding.

Braced framing is as old as log construction, though it apparently originated in the Mediterranean region rather than in Northern Europe. The skeleton of a braced-frame structure is composed of hewed or sawed eight-inch-square timbers connected by mortise-and-tenon joints stiffened by diagonal bracing, sometimes called barn framing. These rigid frames were covered on the exterior with long, sawed or split clapboards, and were usually lathed and plastered on the interior (as were many log houses). Today, the braced-frame house is as rare as the log house and can be as old or older; it is often overlooked as an early settlement home. The older wood construction techniques gave way to the balloon frame in the 1840s, largely as a result of the newly efficient steam-driven planing mills that turned out dimensioned lumber as well as paneled doors, window mullions, and a wide variety of molding patterns for baseboards, chair and coat rails, fireplace mantels, staircase banisters, balusters, and other items once shaped by hand.

Despite these technical advances, log and braced-frame construction continued in the Midwest into the twentieth century as alternate building techniques and into the twenty-first century as nostalgic revivals. If the settler could afford the cost, and the craftsmen and material were available, any type of construction and luxury was possible on the frontier.

Sources and Further Reading: Beverly W. Bond, Jr., ed., *The Correspondence of John Cleves Symmes* (1926); E. Dana, *Geographical Sketches of the Western Country* (1819); Joseph Doddridge, *Notes on the Settlement and Indian Wars, of the Western Parts of Virginia and Pennsylvania* (1824); Donald A. Hutslar, *The Architecture of Migration* (1986); Terry G. Jordan, *American Log Buildings* (1985); Joseph Moxon, *Mechanick Exercises, or the Doctrine of Handy-Works* (1703; reprint, 1970); Harold L. Peterson, *Americans at Home* (1971); Reuben Gold Thwaites, ed., *Early Western Travels, 1748–1846*, 32 vols. (1904–1907); Marcus Whiffen, *American Architecture since 1780* (1969).

Donald A. Hutslar
Columbus, Ohio

Claiming the Land, the Forest, and the Waters

People settled the Midwest not by adapting to local environments but by actively transforming the landscape. Many left the East to escape land shortages or arrived from other countries with fresh memories of poverty, famine, and disease. They knew that those who owned land had a better chance to survive, but they also realized that through persistence and industry on the land it was possible to build a family fortune. However, this required that vast and highly diverse wilderness environments first be domesticated. An eagerness to invent and adopt new technologies, combined with the fortitude of individual settlers, community-level cooperation, and federal policy reshaped the landscapes of the Midwest. Variation in the environment required different technologies to claim the land. This is most evident when examining farming, the one activity that, in its quest for maximum yield, most alters nature. While much land required little more than removal of trees to become productive, other areas were impossible to farm until developments in agricultural and transportation technology enabled their conversion.

The first European American settlers did not always encounter a pristine wilderness, previously unaltered by humanity. The Indian presence in the Midwest is twelve thousand years long, yet we know little of its imprint upon the land in prehistory. Foods and raw materials obtained directly from nature were always important to Native Americans, but other pre-European developments had distinct impacts on the land, including the domestication of native plants and widespread maize farming, the redistribution of goods between settlements, and regional trade in various raw materials. Archaeological sites are common in resource-rich areas such as floodplains, backwater ponds, and lakeshores. Early European American settlers, recognizing the advantages of the Native American sites, often occupied the locations of older Indian villages.

Federal actions and policies facilitated the entry of the settlers. Such policies included the purchase of lands from France and Spain, and the removal or pacification of the Indians. Once this was accomplished, most lands were acquired by settlers or speculators under the terms of the Northwest Ordinance of 1787 and its Public Lands Survey System, the legal framework for the now familiar arrangement of rectangular properties across most of the Midwest. This scientific survey system regulated the subdivision and sale of federal lands, established standardized lot sizes, and set aside lands for the financing of free public schools. Abraham Lincoln's father, twice the victim of faulty land sales under the older irregular survey system in Kentucky, migrated to Indiana in part because of the accuracy of land titles in the Midwest. This revolutionary method of converting wilderness to property was rooted in the Enlightenment ideal of reason and science in the service of a liberalizing democracy, and greatly facilitated the rapid peopling of the Midwest.

The majority of settlers began their lives in the new territories hewing a home from the wilderness by hand, with ax and fire, making what they could from natural materials, and when it was economically possible, purchasing tools and devices. Some could afford to buy the newest farming technologies from the East, but midwesterners soon proved themselves prolific inventors and early adopters of technology. Commercial agriculture became the principal economic pursuit in the Midwest by 1800, and spurred the development of new technologies to ease the backbreaking task of turning a profit on new land. John Deere's polished steel plow (1837), invented in Illinois, Cyrus McCormick's reaper (1834), popularized in Chicago, and the Moore-Hascall sixteen-horse combine (1836), designed in Michigan, revolutionized agriculture and speeded the conversion of prairies and forests to farmland.

North Dakota settlers with tools, c. 1900. Fred Hultstrand History in Pictures Collection, NDIRS-NDSU, Fargo, 2028.257a.

Vast low-lying wetlands near the Great Lakes and other waterways could not be profitably farmed until the adoption of a technology using drain tiles under the soil. Farmers combined their efforts in local drainage cooperatives, forming efficient networks of drainage ditches and levees. Entire lakes and swamps were drained and streams were channelized, yielding immensely productive land. By 1900, nearly all land south of the Great Lakes was in some form of cultivation, and the great forests of the upper Midwest were largely gone.

Regional differences in the rate of settlement can be explained in part by the relationship between transportation routes, which facilitated economic integration, and settlement. For those with easy access to markets, the transition from wilderness to large, profitable farms happened in only a few years, whereas remote areas remained relatively sparsely settled until routes such as the National Road were constructed. This federal road project aided farmers in getting their goods to market and spurred further settlement.

Demands for lumber and fuel were huge drivers of deforestation, especially as the cities of the Midwest expanded. Mechanization made logging profitable and hastened the deforestation of vast areas. As early as the mid-nineteenth century, concern was growing over soil depletion caused by deforestation and straight-line plowing of hilly areas, a problem familiar to settlers from back East. This concern was addressed by promoters of the agronomic sciences. Information on new technologies for soil conservation, wire fencing, animal husbandry, and crop varieties was transmitted through land-grant colleges, soil societies, and agricultural journals, and was closely followed by the more heavily capitalized, large-scale farmers on the prime lands. Free-range pasturage of animals and shifting cultivation of smaller plots in forest openings persisted for decades among the less successful or smaller-scale farmers.

As new farms were being created at the population frontier, other areas were bypassed, not to be farmed until later. Federal policy changes after the Civil War greatly reduced the cost of a homestead, resulting in millions of acres of new farms. The markets made possible by improvements in rail, canal, and road-based transportation made farming more profitable. Lands characterized by unfavorable terrain and soils unable to support crops or pasture continued to be farmed unsustainably if at all. The interaction of settler attitudes, environment, government policy, market forces, and the growth of technology is key to understanding the relationship between populations and the claiming of the lands of the Midwest.

Sources and Further Reading: Willard W. Cochrane, *The Development of American Agriculture*, 2nd ed. (1993); R. Douglas Hurt, *American Agriculture: A Brief History*, rev. ed. (2002); Richard K. Olson and Thomas A. Lyson, eds., *Under the Blade* (1999); John R. Stilgoe, *Common Landscape of America, 1580 to 1845* (1982); U.S. Department of Agriculture, *Our American Land* (1987); Michael Williams, *Americans and Their Forests* (1989).

Staffan Peterson
Indiana University–Bloomington

Indians' Weapons, Tools, and Products

Indian craftsmanship is characterized by great diversity and innovation in the production of tools, foods, medicines, clothing, architecture, and ritual items over the twelve-thousand-year span of midwestern prehistory. The Midwest had a mosaic of differing Indian cultures occupying different ecological zones, each with distinctive adaptive strategies and tool kits. Most of what we know of prehistoric technology and lifeways is based on stone or ceramic artifacts found at archaeological sites, because most prehistoric technology, including implements of wood, fiber, bone, or leather, is nondurable. Generally, locally available materials were used, but special-purpose raw materials were traded both into and out of the Midwest.

Little is known about the tools of the earliest Paleo-indian people (10,000 to 8000 B.C.), who used spears with finely made flint points mounted on long wooden shafts to hunt large mammals such as the wooly mammoth, mastodon, and bison at the end of the Ice Age. The Archaic period (8000 to 1000 B.C.) saw increasing social and material complexity, with larger populations creating new tool kits, including the spear thrower (or *atlatl*), grooved stone axes, and adzes for woodworking, fish nets, hooks, harpoons, and weirs, and stone mortars and pestles for grinding food, making it possible to hunt and gather in increasingly diverse landscapes arising from the warming climate.

The lifestyles developed during the Archaic period continued into the Woodland period (500 B.C. to A.D. 1500), but with important technical, social, and economic developments. Ceramics first appeared during the Early Woodland period, eventually becoming an important adaptation that allowed new ways of cooking and storing food. Indian ceramics were made of local clays, with sand, grit, or crushed mussel shell added for strength, and fired in open hearths. Middle Woodland groups such as the Adena and Hopewell participated in broad exchange networks of exotic raw materials such as Great Lakes copper, Illinois galena, and Rocky Mountain obsidian, and Gulf of Mexico marine shell and shark teeth. These were used to create striking artifacts for elite and ritual purposes. Accompanying this huge increase in contact between diverse groups in the Midwest were the first attempts at agriculture, following earlier success at cultivation of such native seed crops as gourds and sunflowers. Bow-and-arrow hunting began around A.D. 500, using much smaller stone points than before. Very large and distinctive burial mounds and earthworks dating to this period appear from Ohio to Minnesota. The first known houses were made of logs or branches and covered with hides, or were plastered with earth and topped with thatch roofs; they were used for individual families or as larger community structures.

By the Late Woodland period (A.D. 500 to 1000), corn or maize agriculture was perfected, eventually becoming the dominant crop for many groups. The Mississippian people grew maize, beans, and squash and lived in isolated farmsteads, hamlets, or towns, the latter surrounded by large defensive palisades. Prehistoric agricultural technology allowed increases in population as well as increasing differences in social status.

In the historic period, settlers adopted some Indian innovations such as certain crops and herbal medicines, while Indians began to utilize European American weapons, tools, and materials.

Sources and Further Reading: Sally A. K. Chappell, *Cahokia: Mirror of the Cosmos* (2002); Jesse D. Jennings, *Prehistory of North America*, 3rd ed. (1989); Paul E. Minnis, ed., *People and Plants in Ancient Eastern North America* (2003); Bruce G. Trigger, ed., *Handbook of North American Indians*, vol. 15, *Northeast* (1978).

Staffan Peterson
Indiana University–Bloomington

Moving Dirt

Amerindians created elaborate mounds and dirt breastworks. These had ritual, social, and protective purposes and required transporting many cubic yards of dirt. Although the work was done without horses, and with the use of only simple containers, early European settlers were amazed at the structures made by people carrying hundreds of baskets of dirt. For several generations, the Europeans were reluctant to credit the thousands of mounds in the region to the work of Indians alone. With their arrival, European Midwest settlers began moving dirt systematically. Agriculture and the construction of canals, mines, roads, railroads, dams, and cities contributed to a significantly altered landscape. As a result of this passion for moving dirt, the Midwest became home to several leading manufacturers of agricultural and earthmoving equipment, companies whose products have been utilized worldwide.

The name John Deere is almost synonymous with moving dirt. His personal fame rested on his production of steel plows that turned the sticky soils of the Midwest more efficiently than had their wooden and cast-iron predecessors. By 1849, he was mass-producing plows at Moline, Illinois, still the world headquarters of his company. The plow business became the foundation for a full line of agricultural machinery and tractors after 1918, including machines designed for earthmoving.

Because of their technical expertise, it was natural for Deere and other well-known midwestern agricultural machinery manufacturers, including International Harvester and Case, to develop construction equipment lines. Although none of these companies except Deere survives independently today (for example, various International Harvester lines were sold to Caterpillar, Dresser, and Tenneco–J.I. Case beginning in the 1970s), they made significant contributions to earthmoving technology in their heyday. It was, however, left to companies such as Caterpillar, Bucyrus-Erie, and Marion Power Shovel to build the largest earthmovers.

Caterpillar was created by the merger in 1925 of the Holt and Best tractor companies, pioneers in crawlers for use in soft soils. With headquarters and primary manufacturing facilities in East Peoria, Illinois, Caterpillar became the world's leading manufacturer of bulldozers, scrapers, hydraulic loaders, off-road trucks, and other large earthmoving equipment. With its commitment to engineering excellence and quality manufacturing, Caterpillar has continued as a leader in its traditional equipment lines and has entered the fields of large agricultural tractors and giant mining machinery as well.

Bucyrus-Erie began in 1882, when its first steam shovel was produced at Bucyrus, Ohio. The company soon moved to South Milwaukee, Wisconsin. Marion Power Shovel, the brainchild of designer Henry M. Barnhart and industrialist Edward Huber, began in 1884 at Marion, Ohio. With their superior designs, Bucyrus and Marion became the industry leaders in power shovels, draglines, excavators, and other huge machines, providing most of the equipment for digging the Panama Canal and for such domestic projects as the Hoover Dam. The Marion 6360 (The Captain) was the largest shovel ever built, and the Bucyrus-Erie 4250-W walking dragline (Big Muskie) was the largest mobile earthmoving machine ever constructed. In the 1940s, Pawling and Harnischfeger (P&H) of West Milwaukee joined them, forming the big three of excavating. Beginning in the 1970s, however, financial conditions dictated a consolidation of the industry. Today, Bucyrus International continues the Bucyrus-Erie and Marion businesses, and P&H is part of Joy Global Inc.

These and other midwestern firms have manufactured agricultural, construction, and mining equipment that has moved literally mountains of dirt over the past two centuries, remaking the landscape of not only the Midwest but of much of the world.

Sources and Further Reading: Rod Beemer and Chester Peterson, Jr., *Inside John Deere* (1999); Randy Leffingwell, *Illustrated History of the American Farm Tractor* (1999); Eric C. Orlemann, *Caterpillar Chronicle* (2000); Eric C. Orlemann, *Giant Earth-Moving Equipment* (1995).

Donald L. Huber
Trinity Lutheran Seminary, Columbus, Ohio

Removing the Trees

In the nineteenth- and twentieth-century Midwest, trees were both burden and blessing. Removing the trees was a requirement for survival and an intellectual reaction to wilderness. Midwesterners simultaneously saw forests as obstacles to progress, revered nature's beauty, and envisioned clearing as a new dawning of civilization. "Tree hatred" figured into pioneer visions, but clearing also involved the more basic component of economics, of reaping revenue from the harvested trees and the crops to be planted in their place.

An intimate connection existed between woods and wheat, between farming and the felling of trees. For the common settler, needing an immediately prosperous farm, trees represented not an asset but an impediment. From the mid-nineteenth century on, midwesterners utilized girdling—encircling the bark to kill the tree—and cut-and-burn techniques to remove the trees at an unprecedented rate. Women certainly shared the masculine hostility to wilderness, but many women's vision of progress had the different aim of creating homes and building familial communities out of the forest. Women's values often dictated accommodation, requiring houses and farms wrested from, but not wholly destructive to, the landscape. Still, midwestern farmers cleared over fifty-seven million acres between 1850 and 1910.

While agriculture made simultaneous inroads, lumbering had the most drastic effect. Lumber and other wood products linked directly into the goals of westward expansion and the burgeoning industrial economy of the United States. With depleted reserves in the East, the timber industry moved to the Midwest, where it was essential for building railroads and cities. Large, broad stands of white pine in Michigan, Wisconsin, and Minnesota fueled the industry. The endeavor was fraught with optimism and exploitation, overproduction and cutthroat competition, and economic boom and bust. Eastern financiers sent the labor, capital, and technology westward to reap the harvest of timber. Between 1869 and 1899, Michigan lumber reigned supreme as thousands of men cut swaths from the Lower to Upper Peninsulas. When those supplies dwindled, the men and money that backed them moved on to Wisconsin and Minnesota. In the three states, loggers sawed almost nine billion board feet in 1900; in the next thirty years, production from the Great Lakes states plummeted to 1.5 billion. Ambition for lumber laid bare close to sixty million acres in the Midwest.

Exploitation of midwestern forests rested on three pillars. Technology—steam-driven mills, water power, and more durable band saws—ratcheted up the use and the abuse of native forests. Transportation improvements—canals, dams, steam locomotive tractors, steamboats, and railroads—contributed to the growth of the timber industry. Organization and industrial capitalism—mergers, consolidations, trusts, big-money investment, speculative buying, horizontal and vertical integration—made lumbering a big business.

While midwesterners confronted the forest from the 1840s onward, trees had shaped the culture of Great Lakes Indians for close to twelve thousand years. Indians utilized timber in myriad ways, but with a fundamental difference from their European American successors—Indians' use of and adaptation to forests did not focus on short-term economic gain. While they made use of timber, they also sacralized forests. The lumbering of the Menominee tribe in the twentieth century, for example, coupled economic subsistence with a plan for sustained yield.

The clearing and lumbering of the Midwest reaped enormous profit and extraordinary waste. Capital, technology, organization, and simple diligence depleted the forests. The deleterious effects of removing the trees did not go unchecked, as figures like George Perkins Marsh forced Americans to confront the non-monetary value of the woods and the folly of unquestioningly felling the forests. To understand the removal of trees, we must grasp the ideology of the time. Put simply, trees meant profit, and the land beneath those trees promised a prosperous future for a society with unrelenting agrarian roots.

Sources and Further Reading: Thomas R. Cox et al., *This Well-Wooded Land* (1985); Susan L. Flader, ed., *The Great Lakes Forest* (1983); Annette Kolodny, *The Land Before Her* (1984); Michael Williams, *Americans and Their Forests* (1989).

Garrit Voggesser
University of Oklahoma

Settlers' Weapons, Tools, and Products

The hand tools required for the various trades and crafts were legion and found their way to the American frontier; but every settler needed shelter, and tools for that purpose were common to all. The American felling ax, the prime tool of settlement in the Northwest Territory, evolved during the eighteenth century. The European ax had an iron blade with a round eye to slide onto a straight round wooden haft. It required an abrupt chopping motion to keep the unbalanced blade from glancing. The American ax had a counter-balanced head, achieved by adding weight, called the "poll," opposite the cutting edge. Further improving

the striking power of the ax, the haft became oval in cross section rather than round and was given a sinuous S-curve to allow the hands to slide during the stroke: it was an ax to cut deep rather than chop. To quote William Blane:

> Every individual is brought up from his youth to the use of this tool, which is of a peculiar construction, and differs essentially from the European Broad Axe. To see the short space of time in which a Backwoodsman can cut down the largest tree, and the power he has of making it fall in whatever direction he pleases, astonishes a foreigner, who must labour for years in order to attain the same skill.

The broadax, with its large cutting edge for hewing round timber into squared balks, was used in building a wide variety of structures from log to braced-frame houses and barns, shops and warehouses. The broadax was sharpened on one side of the blade, like a chisel, so it would cut flat to a line, and its haft was offset at an

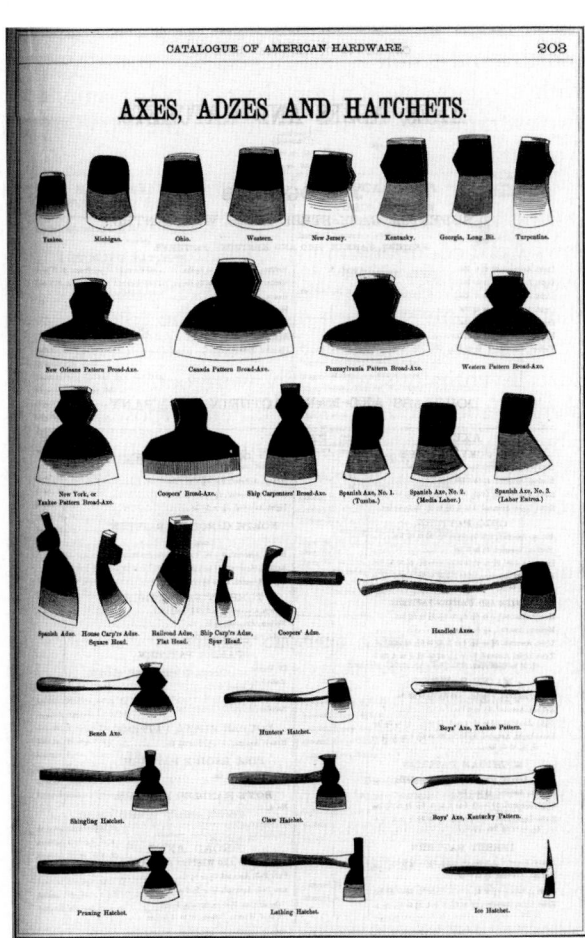

Midwestern settlers' tools from an 1865 catalog. Russell & Erwin Manufacturing Co. *Illustrated Catalogue of American Hardware* (1865).

angle so the hewer's hands wouldn't scrape the timber. The broadax was not designed to fell trees. The long-handled foot-adze was sharpened with a chisel edge like the broadax so it would cut flat and even on a surface. It was used to level such surfaces as floor puncheons, rafters, and joists, and to remove hewing marks to square small timber. This adze was used in a standing position; there was also a short-handled hand-adze. The adze could have a concave cutting edge for hollowing troughs and bowls.

The frow (or froe) was a common but important carpenter's tool. It was used to cleave or split shakes, shingles, and clapboards from blocks of wood. Usually the iron frow was about twelve inches long and two inches wide; like the broadax and adze, the frow had a chisel edge. The handle was at a right angle to the blade. The frow was driven into the end of a block of wood with a mallet, called a "beetle." By rocking the haft back and forth and driving the frow downward, thin, flat pieces of wood could be split away.

The hand-auger was a necessary carpenter's tool of the past three centuries but devoid of the romance of the felling ax or broadax today. The augur made a hole for wooden pins to fasten jamb boards, rafters, and mortise-and-tenon joints. Augers were usually made with a removable horizontal wooden bar ample for two workmen to twist the bit into the wood—hard work at best.

Rounding out the more important hand tools used during the settlement period is the handsaw. Handsaws were common among carpenters, if not among average settlers. Saws had to be sharpened often, but there was only so much metal and the edge couldn't be replaced (steeled) as could the edge of an ax or adze. Eventually saws simply wore out, and the thin metal blades were used for other purposes. That is why early examples are not common today and many have the wrong impression that saws were rare on the frontier.

Finally, the most important tool for obtaining meat and animal hides, the firearm. To the settler, the rifle was a tool for sustenance. Private eastern arms makers, particularly in Pennsylvania, provided plain rifles for the western migrants as well as highly inlaid and carved rifles for the well-established settlers east of the Ohio River. These rifles were small-caliber flintlocks designed for hunting and target shooting rather than military conflict, though many were used for that purpose. Another firearm ubiquitous to the frontier was the large-caliber, smoothbore military musket, loaned, borrowed, or scavenged during wars from the Revolution to the War of 1812. Muskets were adaptable to frontier conditions because they could be loaded with small bird shot or a solid lead ball and used for hunting a wide variety of game. The old flintlock musket was commonplace during the first half of the nineteenth century. As frontier settlements progressed into stable communities after the War of 1812, independent gunsmiths produced hunting and target rifles, plain and fancy, as the trade demanded. The backwoodsman and pioneer and their trusty rifles became romanticized in nineteenth century literature and art: the rugged individual defying man, beast, and the elements. The settler might worry about the weather, but was not much concerned about man or beast because he had firearms for protection.

Sources and Further Reading: William Blane, *Excursion Through the United States and Canada* (1824); Cecil Alec Hewett, *The Development of Carpentry, 1200–1700* (1969); Joe Kindig, *Thoughts on the Kentucky Rifle in Its Golden Age* (1960); Kenneth D. Roberts, *Tools for the Trades and Crafts* (1976); R. A. Salaman, *Dictionary of Tools Used in the Woodworking and Allied Trades, c. 1700–1970* (1975).

Donald A. Hutslar
Columbus, Ohio

Water Technology

The development of water technologies has changed the face of the United States. From humble beginnings, with ditches and trenches serving as outhouses and gutters, engineers have developed elaborate sewer systems and water treatment plants. Growth in water technology and engineering have helped the United States to become the powerful nation it is today. During the nation's development, engineers reversed the flow of rivers, drained swamps, constrained rivers, and constructed locks to ease waterway travel, forever changing and modifying the waterways and the landscapes of this country. All of these changes have been made in Midwest waterways, sometimes for the first time anywhere.

In 1900 the Chicago River was permanently reversed in direction, made to flow away from Lake Michigan instead of toward it, in order to save the city. Years of use as a dump for sewage and waste had made the river toxic, and it directly connected to the water source for Chicago, Lake Michigan. During heavy rains, the river overflowed into Lake Michigan, spreading pollution as well as typhoid and cholera, which killed 5 percent or more of the population during rainy years. Consequently, the U.S. Congress gave permission for the construction of the Illinois and Michigan Canal. Begun in 1822, the canal project was not finished until 1848, and it did not solve all the sanitation problems. A new plan was devised to deepen the original canal and construct a shallower one, using pumps to fill it, rather than constructing a totally new large canal. This failed within a year, and the Sanitary District of Chicago, now called the Metropolitan Water Reclamation District of Greater Chicago, was created in 1889 and developed a new plan. Following construction in 1900 of the Sanitary and Ship Canal, the Chicago River ran in the opposite direction, and the river mouth was turned into a port that served thousands of ships annually and opened up several new waterways across America's landscape.

The draining of the Great Black Swamp in Ohio is an equally astonishing feat of human engineering and water technology, one that is also largely forgotten. When driving through northwest Ohio today, one sees mile upon mile of flat farmland. This abundance of agriculture was not the reality in the 1800s, when that farmland was actually a massive swamp forty miles long north to south and 120 miles northeast to southwest. The swamp was nearly impassable and proved to be so daunting that the area was the last place in Ohio to be settled. To begin draining this massive swamp, downed tree limbs and branches clogging natural streams had to be removed. Then, following a series of state ditch laws in 1859, timber crews began removing the trees, clearing about an acre of land a month. Engineers marked out and dug canals and ditches with the help of plow teams and timber crews. These actions cleared the water from the surface, but the ground remained swampy. Since the muddy land would bubble up with every step and the water would kill agricultural crops, the settlers devised a complex system of under-drainage. This system of underground piping, tiling, and tunnels, using enough material to reach the moon, successfully drained the land. The area is now some of Ohio's most fertile farmland.

Built to pass between Lake Superior and Lake Huron, the Soo Locks are another demonstration of mankind's ingenuity when faced with environmental problems. The locks were constructed at an area of the St. Mary's River between Canada and the United States where the steep rapids drop twenty-one feet in less than a mile as they leave Lake Superior. This drop forced early traders to unload their cargo and carry it around the rapids, then reload onto another boat. In 1797, the Northwest Fur Company constructed a small lock, but it was destroyed in the War of 1812. In 1852, Congress granted 750 thousand acres of public land to Michigan to contract with a company to build a lock. This was finished by 1855. The U.S. Army Corps of Engineers took control of the locks in 1881, and as freighters got bigger, they oversaw the construction of two more locks, the MacArthur Lock in 1943 and the Poe Lock in 1969. Together, these locks smoothly lifted the ships up and down the twenty-one feet of rapids. There are plans for a new lock, but the

project has not yet received funding. The four current locks serve as a major tourist attraction for U.S. and Canadian citizens, as well as being the stars of the Soo Locks Festival.

The Mississippi River is another place where engineers changed the face of the nation; in fact, the river is one of the most heavily engineered natural resources in the country. Wetlands around the river have been drained to accommodate urbanization and agriculture, leading at times to problems, but most of the engineering has involved the construction and maintenance of levees. Levees are raised barriers of earth used to contain rising levels of water, and they are a key defense against flooding. Constructed as early as 1717 to protect towns on the banks of the Mississippi, the levees are now regularly monitored by the modern U.S. Army Corp of Engineers. The levees became standardized in 1917 with the Flood Control Act, and since 1926, the improved system has held back several (though not all) major floods. Over the years, the levees have been built higher to reflect new floodwater predictions and still continue to save hundreds of houses annually, at the same time reshaping the Mississippi River and its surrounding countryside.

Through perseverance, ingenuity, and determination, engineers and workers have contributed to the advancement of water technology, changing this country's waterways from hindrances into advantages.

Sources and Further Reading: Chicago Municipal Reference Library, "1900 Flow of Chicago River Reversed" (Aug. 1997); Harold M. Mayer and Richard C. Wade, *Chicago: Growth of a Metropolis* (1969); Donald L. Miller, *City of the Century: The Epic of Chicago and the Making of America* (1997); Jim Mollenkopf, *The Great Black Swamp: Historical Tales of 19th-Century Northwest Ohio* (1999); Jim Mollenkopf, *The Great Black Swamp II: More Historical Tales of Northwestern Ohio* (2000); David Solzman, *The Chicago River: An Illustrated History and Guide to the River and Its Waterways* (1998).

Arthur Holst
Philadelphia Water Department, Pennsylvania

Wetlands

Wetlands are places were water saturates the soil much of the time so that only plants specially adapted to wetness can thrive. Today, we seldom think of the Midwest as being swampy, but wetlands once comprised seventy-five million acres—nearly 16 percent—of the landscape. When glaciers left the region flat and poorly drained, several different types of wetlands formed. Forested swamps grew in the bottomlands along rivers and around lakes. Bogs and peatlands developed in the north. Wet prairies spread across broad expanses of Indiana, Illinois, and Iowa. Distinctive prairie potholes pocked a wide swath of the Dakotas and Minnesota, serving as breeding grounds for much of the nation's waterfowl. Many of these wetlands provided Native North Americans with a rich subsistence.

The numerous swamps and marshes presented challenges to European settlers. Thick wetland muck made travel difficult. Malaria, which may have arrived with the earliest Europeans, soon became endemic in the swampy, mosquito-filled Midwest. Most important, wetlands made poor farms. Settlers seeking homesteads often arrived on wet prairies after summer heat had dried them and found what looked to be fertile and level lands. Only after winter rains did they realize their new farms were nonarable wetlands.

This combination of disease and difficulties, together with increasing demand for fresh farmland, provided strong incentives for draining wetlands. In 1850 the Swamplands Act granted fifteen million swampy acres to seven Midwest states to promote "improvement," but drying out wetlands proved to be difficult and costly. Not until the end of the nineteenth century, when mass-produced drainage tiles and ditch diggers became available, did drainage proceed apace. Between 1906 and 1922 nine million acres of wetlands in seven Midwest states were drained. New farm technologies and growing urban markets increased pressure to drain through the twentieth century.

As more and more wetlands were converted to farms, troubling changes in the Midwest environment sparked concern and interest in conservation. The marked decline of the region's once abundant waterfowl populations inspired influential Iowa cartoonist Jay Norwood "Ding" Darling to criticize national policies promoting drainage of duck habitats. Appointed to head the Bureau of Biological Survey in the 1930s, Darling established the federal Duck Stamp program to raise funds to acquire wetland refuges critical for waterfowl habitat.

As scientists learned more about the public value of wetlands for wildlife habitat, water quality, and floodwater retention, concern for protecting wetlands grew. However, even as state and federal wildlife agencies began to conserve wetlands, the U.S. Department of Agriculture continued to push for their drainage well into the 1980s, when the landmark federal policy known as Swampbuster finally stopped subsidizing farmers who drained wetlands.

By then, however, more than 85 percent of the wetlands in Ohio, Indiana, Illinois, Iowa, and Missouri had been converted to farmland, and the Midwest had lost more of its wetlands than any other region of the country. Though growing consensus about the public value of wetlands makes conservation and restoration increasingly possible, a powerful cultural heritage that favors drainage continues to challenge the protection of these landscapes in the Midwest.

Sources and Further Reading: Thomas. E. Dahl, *Wetland Losses in the United States, 1780s to 1980s* (1990); Hugh Prince, *Wetlands of the American Midwest* (1997); Ann Vileisis, *Discovering the Unknown Landscape* (1997).

Ann Vileisis
Port Orford, Oregon

Harvesting Natural Resources

Blessed with climate, soil, and water that encouraged settlement, the Midwest has sustained intense harvesting of its natural resources. Trees, the "giant butts" of Conrad Richter's Pulitzer Prize–winning novels, were both an initial barrier for farmers and their primary resource for shelter and fuel. The forests were stripped by logging, the logs were burned to make iron from ore, and family sawmills were soon swallowed up by giant lumber companies.

Vast beds of coal were discovered and intensively mined both below the surface and by stripping away miles and miles of topsoil to uncover the black treasure. Coal continues to be the major source of fuel for generating electricity for the interlocking network of power lines across the Midwest and adjacent regions. Petroleum is now identified with Texas and Oklahoma, but in the early 1900s the wildcatters and entrepreneurs such as Rockefeller were located in the eastern part of the Midwest. Ready sources of petroleum and giant iron ore deposits in the upper Midwest, in the hands of such entrepreneurs as Henry Ford, helped make Detroit the automobile capital of the world.

Salt and minerals are still mined in the Midwest. The first gold rush of the westward expansion brought prospectors to South Dakota. Zinc was discovered in Kansas before 1800, and from 1850 to 1950 half of all the zinc mined in America came from that location. Aluminum, the lightweight but strong material that made flight possible and one of the most common elements in the earth's surface, became readily available through the efforts of one determined scientist in a small laboratory in rural Ohio.

Although the technology has changed, the purposes of hunting and fishing and of harvesting and gathering have not changed with time. The modern Midwest's increased awareness of finite resources and of the need

Harvesting corn, Iowa, 1939. Library of Congress, Prints and Photographs Division, LC-USF34-028185-D.

for renewable energy sources and for conservation has intensified its focus on wind power, prairie restoration, and wetlands preservation.

Electricity

Electricity in the Midwest is largely defined by two interconnected legacies, manufacturing and coal. As a manufacturing-intensive region, the Midwest has relied on cheap and plentiful electricity to power its factories. Even by 2000, the industrial sector in the Midwest states consumed nearly 40 percent of total electricity in the region. This contrasts sharply with the nation as a whole, where residential consumption makes the greatest claim on electricity production, and the industrial sector's share is 29 percent. In order to generate electricity, the region has exploited its abundant supply of coal. In 2000, coal constituted 74 percent of the energy input for electricity generated in the twelve-state region. In contrast, for the rest of the United States, coal comprised only 49 percent of the input for electricity.

This interconnected legacy has come at a cost. Coal is not as clean as natural gas, nuclear, or even fuel oil in terms of air emissions. The tension between coal as a cheap fuel and its environmental effects has become strained, and there is increased concern about global warming. This has led to an increasing preference for natural gas as fuel for new utility plants. For coal-fired utilities, the higher sulfur content of native midwestern coal makes it less desirable than higher quality western coal as a fuel source. Higher quality implies anthracite coal, which is cleaner when burned; bituminous coal is softer and produces more pollutants. Clean coal technology may improve the environmental performance of utilities, while the search for alternative fuels and renewable electricity continues.

A final issue facing the region is the need for improvements in the electricity transmission system. Transmission congestion impairs the ability of the region to import power across the upper Midwest and from Canada. In the late 1990s several midwestern states moved aggressively to restructure electricity regulation in order to encourage competition among electricity generators. The goal was improved efficiency in electricity production and better choices for industrial, commercial, and residential consumers. To accomplish this, more efficient movement of electricity across the transmission grid is required. In the wake of the California energy crisis of the 1990s, blamed in part on that state's restructuring efforts, interest in electricity restructuring in the Midwest has waned. Nevertheless, there are continued efforts to improve the operation of a multistate regional grid for an easier flow of electricity.

The region's electricity challenge is to continue to provide relatively cheap and reliable power while shifting to more environmentally friendly electricity generation. This requires developing renewable energy sources such as wind power, biomass, photovoltaic, and other technologies to reduce the traditional dependence on fossil fuels.

Sources and Further Reading: Richard H. Mattoon, "Electricity and the Midwest: A Survey of Conditions and Issues," *Chicago Fed Letter* No. 170 (Oct. 2001); U.S. Department of Energy, Energy Information Administration, "State Profiles" at http://www.eia.doe.gov/emeu/states/_states.html (Mar. 2004).

Richard H. Mattoon
Federal Reserve Bank of Chicago

Extracting Aluminum—Charles M. Hall (1863–1914)

Prior to Charles Hall's late-nineteenth-century discovery of the process for extracting aluminum from ore, aluminum was seen as a semiprecious metal with a cost similar to silver. In those days lustrous metals were available only for jewelry and other high-cost items. With the development of the aluminum industry, an inexpensive shiny metal became available for everyday uses. Aluminum metal, its production dependent on electricity, became essential as the metal for carrying electricity over the long-distance, high-tension lines that crisscross the country and make an electricity-based civilization possible. With aluminum, designers produced shiny, durable appliances to brighten kitchens and other workplaces. Trains and other vehicles were streamlined and lightened. The aircraft industry took flight. A shining, early example of the ornamental use of aluminum metal in buildings is Severance Hall, the home of the Cleveland Orchestra, built in 1930.

Hall's discovery of the electrochemical process for extracting aluminum metal from its refractory oxide ore occurred in his Oberlin, Ohio, laboratory on February 23, 1886, and in 1888 the process became the technical foundation for the Pittsburgh Reduction Company, renamed Alcoa in 1907. It remains the basis for the aluminum industry worldwide.

As a youth, Hall developed an interest in chemistry and in invention and experimented in a woodshed with processes for extracting pure aluminum from its ore. When he entered Oberlin College in 1880, he met Professor Frank F. Jewett, who possessed a sample of aluminum metal acquired during his studies in Professor Friedrich Wöhler's world-renowned laboratory in Göttingen, Germany. Jewett was well-educated and well-experienced in chemistry, with two degrees from

Yale, studies in Germany, experience as a research assistant at Harvard, and four years as teacher at the Imperial University in Japan. Supported by Jewett's extensive knowledge of chemistry, his laboratory resources at the college, and his library, Hall soon began a series of experiments to extract aluminum from its bauxite ore. These experiments culminated in the production of aluminum pellets in February 1886, seven months after his graduation from college. Hall had to overcome many chemical and equipment challenges before his successful experiment of electrolyzing aluminum oxide dissolved in molten cryolite in a graphite crucible near 1000°C (1832°F).

Oberlin's proximity to industrially robust Cleveland was another important contributor to Hall's success. From Cleveland Hall obtained gasoline (from Standard Oil) for firing his homebuilt furnace, graphite rods (from Brush Electric) for electrodes and for fashioning the graphite crucible, and chemical supplies.

Although Hall conducted his successful electrolysis experiments with electric energy drawn from a large array of homebuilt batteries, he knew that dynamos for producing electricity were being developed rapidly. Using electricity generated from water power, Hall worked to develop his new process with the Cleveland-based Cowles Electric Smelting and Aluminum Company, but the owners did not stay the course. Finally, in 1888, Captain Alfred Hunt in Pittsburgh organized adequate financial support for Hall's successful industrialization of his discovery.

Unknown to Hall until he applied for a U.S. patent was the parallel discovery in France by Paul Héroult, who worked with a dynamo. The electrolysis process for extracting aluminum metal is now known as the Hall-Héroult process, in recognition of the simultaneity of the invention. The Hall-Héroult process was an early entrant in the large electrochemical industry that emerged in the latter part of the nineteenth century, an industry that married newly available, large-scale electric energy with chemical processing. A center of this development and the location of Pittsburgh Reduction's first large plant was Niagara Falls, New York, where water power from the falls was the source of electric energy and where Charles Hall lived for the last twenty years of his life.

In addition to his engagement with science and industry, Hall had enduring interests in music, art, education, and conservation. These interests were strongly linked to Oberlin College, and he made a number of gifts to the college from the fortune he made in the aluminum industry. Hall was a member of Oberlin's Board of Trustees from 1905 until his death in 1914. In 1911, he was awarded the prestigious Perkins medal for his contributions to science and commerce.

Sources and Further Reading: Norman C. Craig, "Charles Martin Hall—The Young Man, His Mentor, and His Metal," *Journal of Chemical Education* 63 (July 1986); Junius Edwards, *The Immortal Woodshed* (1955); Oberlin College Archives, Charles M. Hall letters, will, and other holdings; Rosamond McPherson Young, *Made of Aluminum* (1965).

Norman C. Craig
Oberlin College, Ohio

Fishing Technology

Home to the largest freshwater lakes in the world, and crisscrossed east to west and north to south by majestic rivers, it is no surprise that the Midwest has had abundant commercial and, more recently, enthusiastic sport fishing.

The story of lures is a midwestern one that reflects the popularity of fishing in the region and typifies the inventiveness and entrepreneurship of the Midwest. Lures—artificial bait—were developed before recorded time, and in the United States in the early 1800s, J. T. Buel developed a metal fishing "spoon." The first patent for the now classic wooden lure was granted to two Americans, David Huard and Charles Dunbar of Wisconsin in 1874, although James Heddon of Michigan is often credited with manufacturing the first wooden fishing lure. By 1883, a patent was granted to Ernest Pflueger for artificial lures coated with a luminous paint that permitted fishing at night. Soon numerous types of jointed wooden plugs were in the marketplace and bait shops, and by 1940 American spinning reels were becoming readily available. The race for a better way to attract fish was on, and it continues to this day.

The Pflueger Company was begun in 1864 in Akron, Ohio, by Ernest Pflueger. He established the Enterprise Manufacturing Company, which offered several new lures, including the Flying Hellgrammite and the Luminous Crystal Minnow. In the late 1800s, William Shakespeare, Jr., invented a wheel that wound the line evenly on the spool, and in 1897 he launched the Shakespeare Company, which acquired the patent rights of Jay Rhodes of Kalamazoo, Michigan. Eventually there developed a patent dispute between the Pflueger Company and the Shakespeare Company; Shakespeare won and proceeded to acquire the Pflueger Company.

In 1894 F. G. Worden in South Bend, Indiana, also began making lures and invented the Buck tail bait. His bait company changed its name to South Bend Tackle Company in 1955 and continued to be successful, although it in turn was sold to the B. F. Gladding Company. In 1902 James Heddon and his two sons,

William and Charles, began making their lures in their mother's kitchen at Dowagiac, Michigan. Soon they had been granted a patent, and by 1950 Heddon and Sons Rod Company was producing many commercial lures and was famous for its elegant fishing rods. By 1959 that company was also sold, to the Daisy Manufacturing Company.

The legendary Creek Chub Bait Company of Garrett, Indiana, was formed in 1910 by three fishing buddies who worked on all the new concepts. Henry Dills developed their first new bait, called the "wiggler." The Creek Chub Company grew into an internationally famous bait company and, in 1978, was sold to the Lazy Ike Corporation.

This emphasis on lures is not meant to obscure other midwestern techniques, such as spear fishing by the Indians and their use of nets or traps, techniques more relevant earlier than now. One of the reasons the Indians established settlements along the shores in the first place was for access to fish. The romance, development, and evolution of lures is but one of the scenes common along riversides, lakeshores, and waters. Varied usage and needs of the midwestern waters continue today: Ice fishing has now become a culture, even a cult, of its own; boats for sport fishing proliferate and pollute; hatcheries try to keep up with the needs and obviate disputes related to conservation; and fishing camps come and go.

Any discussion of fishing technology, however, must acknowledge the related importance of commercial fishing and toxic invaders. The annual catch of fish for potential sale from the Great Lakes is over two hundred million pounds, and more than half of it is caught from the side of a sport boat. More money is now made from recreational fishing than from the large trawlers that once dragged the lakes. Michigan with over eight hundred registered fishing boats is but one of many busy recreational areas in the Midwest, and no one can match Minnesota's myriad of lakes or the fact that the most fishing licenses in the Midwest are sold in that state.

Commercial fishing has led to overfishing and even to the extinction of a few species, such as the blue pike from Lake Erie. Hatcheries helped supply Chinook and Coho salmon as partial replacement for depleted species, but now only pockets of lucrative commercial fishing remain. In the effort to protect the fish, gill fishing is being phased out, although native Americans still retain special fishing rights. Federal regulations now clearly prohibit the sale of fish that contain toxic levels of heavy metals or other potential hazards. The federal government is also involved in sustained battles against invasive creatures like grass carp, zebra mussels, and sea lamprey. The balance between environmental pressures, human recreation, and governmental control is one of the continuing stories worked out in the fishing lands of the Midwest.

Sources and Further Reading: Ed Koch, *Fishing the Midge* (1988); Carl F. Luckey, *Old Fishing Lures and Tackle*, 2nd ed. (1986).

George Paulson
The Ohio State University–Columbus

Indian Harvesting Practices

Hunting, fishing, and the gathering of plants continues to play a critical role in the economic and cultural life of Indian communities in the Midwest. The harvesting depends on what is available in an area at the time. Native people may interrupt their work schedules to hunt, fish, and gather as opportunities to augment their income and household consumption are offered by the change of season. Harvesting technologies integrate traditional as well as European American ways of fishing, hunting, and gathering. Native American harvesters develop, experiment with, and implement the most efficient harvesting techniques, and harvesting continues to be an important cultural activity. Harvesting activities have symbolic value and are a key aspect of indigenous identity. Today, native harvesting occurs both on and off reservations. Off reservation harvesting occurs primarily in Michigan, Wisconsin, and Minnesota where Ojibwe and Ottawa tribes reserved a treaty right to hunt, fish, and gather on public lands, the Great Lakes, and inland lakes.

Three indigenous harvesting regimes were evident when European Americans first established trade relations with midwestern native communities in the seventeenth century and then occupied the region in the nineteenth century. The first harvesting regime was found in the mixed coniferous–deciduous forests of northern Wisconsin, Michigan, and Minnesota. In this forested and lake-studded region of long winters and short summers, native groups such as the Ojibwe developed a seasonal nomadic hunting and collecting pattern. In winter, the Ojibwe traveled in small family groups, hunting large game such as deer, moose, and bear, trapping small animals, hunting waterfowl, and ice fishing with spears. In early spring, they collected maple sap and processed it into maple sugar. In April, they traveled to nearby lakes and streams to net, hook, and spear spawning fish. Summer villages were established beside inland lakes where they planted small gardens of corn, beans, and squash. They continued to fish using hooks, spears, and nets and to gather wild berries and other plant materials such as birch bark, which was used for constructing canoes and contain-

ers. In late August and early September, they traveled to shallow lakes and streams to harvest wild rice. Using birch-bark canoes, they collected the rice, actually a cereal grass, and brought it ashore, where it was dried and parched for use as a staple over the winter months.

The second harvesting regime was found along the shores of Lake Michigan, Lake Huron, and eastern Lake Superior. In this lake-centered environment, Ojibwe and Ottawa Indians developed an economy centered on fishing. From lakeside villages in late fall and early winter they used scoop nets and gill nets to capture spawning whitefish and lake trout along the shoreline. Fishing was complemented by hunting, collecting wild plants, occasional gardening, and gathering maple sap.

The third harvesting regime was a mixed hunting and farming economy. Seasonal hunting, fishing, and gathering and the production of corn, beans, and squash occurred in the oak–hickory forest and open prairie of the southern Great Lakes—in what is now southern Michigan and Wisconsin and southeastern Minnesota. In these areas, the southern Ojibwe, Ho-Chunk (Winnebago), and Dakota (Santee) integrated a wide range of hunting, fishing, and collecting activities with garden agriculture. In spring they hunted small mammals and used spears and arrows to catch spawning fish in streams near villages. In summer they cultivated gardens of corn, beans, and squash. The surplus production and storage of corn distinguished this economy from the hunting and collecting economy found to the north and west. In early summer, the community left the village and traveled west of the Mississippi River for a communal bison hunt. Early fall was spent harvesting and storing crops and harvesting wild rice. Late fall and early winter was spent away from the village hunting for deer and bear before returning to the established village for most of the winter months.

In the eastern Great Plains, using what is called a riverine horticulture pattern, Indians lived in permanent villages in fertile river bottoms and valleys. Crop production centered on corn, beans, and squash, but also included tobacco and sunflowers. Indian communities such as the Omaha, Ponca, Iowa, and Pawnee supplemented crop production with one or two bison hunts annually on nearby grasslands. They also hunted deer, elk, bear, rabbit, beaver, and otter, fished in the rivers, and collected wild plants such as fruits, berries, and nuts near their villages.

Despite the loss of tribal homelands and the degradation of ecosystems caused by non-Indian settlement, many Indians still hunt, fish, and gather. In the upper Midwest, Ojibwe, Ottawa, Potawatomi, and other Indians practice their seasonal harvest rotation on their reservations, and Ojibwe tribes with off-reservation treaty rights also harvest on public lands and waters outside their reservations. Activities still include spring spearfishing and gillnetting, fall wild ricing, winter deer hunting, trapping furbearing animals, and gathering a variety of food and nonfood plants. Ojibwe and Ottawa Indians also engage in commercial gillnet fishing of whitefish and lake trout along the shores of Lake Superior, Lake Huron, and Lake Michigan. The Menominee Indians of northeastern Wisconsin practice sustained yield forestry. Over the last one hundred years, they have maintained the productivity and biodiversity of the forest that covers most of their reservation. Many Menominee continue to practice their seasonal harvest sequence in the forest. Although they no longer hunt for wild bison, the Ho-Chunk of southern Wisconsin recently established a 639-acre bison farm where they raise a herd of more than 150 bison for tribal members' consumption. As part of their Winnebago Bison Project, the Winnebago in Nebraska (related to the Ho-Chunk of Wisconsin) maintain a refuge where they are raising approximately eighty bison.

Today, native peoples in the Midwest participate in the management and enhancement of natural resources located on and off their reservations. Most tribes practice conservation programs to enhance fish, game, and plant populations on reservations. Tribally-operated fish hatcheries are found on many reservations in the western Great Lakes. The Ojibwe and Ottawa tribes that have off-reservation hunting, fishing, and gathering treaty rights have formed intertribal conservation organizations such as the Great Lakes

Indian Fish and Wildlife Commission and the Chippewa Ottawa Resource Authority. They conduct scientific studies and survey fish, plant, and animal populations. They cooperate closely with state and federal conservation agencies to protect and manage fish, game, and critical habitats.

Sources and Further Reading: Robert E. Bieder, *Native American Communities in Wisconsin, 1600–1960* (1995); Thomas Davis, *Sustaining the Forest, the People, and the Spirit* (2000); Raymond J. DeMaillie, ed., *Handbook of North American Indians, Plains,* vol. 13, parts 1 and 2 (2001); Loretta Fowler, *The Columbia Guide to American Indians of the Great Plains* (2003); Larry Nesper, *The Walleye War* (2002); Helen Hornbeck Tanner, ed., *Atlas of Great Lakes Indian History* (1987); Bruce G. Trigger, ed., *Handbook of North American Indians, Northeast,* vol. 15 (1978); Thomas Vennum, Jr., *Wild Rice and the Ojibway People* (1988).

Steven E. Silvern
Salem State College, Massachusetts

Mining Technology

Mining in the Midwest began with Native Americans using rock and mineral resources such as chert, flint, clay, colored rocks, and catlinite (a red clay) to fashion tools, pottery, and art objects, and evolved into the present-day mining of barite, clay, cobalt, coal, copper, gold, gypsum, iron, lead, limestone, nickel, salt, sand, silver, slate, stone, tripoli, and zinc. These minerals have been used for everything from generating electricity, creating utilitarian and ornamental work,

Big Muskie, built 1969. Ohio Historical Society, SC1539/Tom Root.

forming pottery, and building highways, to manufacturing a wide variety of products for agricultural applications.

Mining lead for utilitarian uses and ornamental objects began in northeast Iowa near Dubuque in prehistoric times and continued well into the nineteenth century. Native American tribes such as the Sauk, Meskwaki, and Winnebago mined lead into the eighteenth century. Prior to 1700, the Ioway, Oto, Omaha, and Ponca tribes mined clay and pipestone. In the mid-nineteenth century, mining was expanded to include coal and stone quarrying. In 1859, three million pounds of lead were shipped from the Upper Mississippi Valley region.

The first discovery of coal in North America was in Illinois by Jacques Marquette and Louis Joliet. In 1673, they observed and recorded coal outcrops along the Illinois River. However, it was not until the 1800s that the settlers first mined outcropped coal for blacksmithing and other domestic uses. Underground mining began in about 1848 at Belleville, Illinois. The real boom began about 1864 near the town of Braidwood, Illinois, when a farmer struck coal while drilling a well for water. Will, Grundy, and Kankakee counties became the center of the industry until 1914. Coal has been mined in seventy-three counties in Illinois, and more than forty-five hundred coal mines have operated since commercial mining began in 1810. Famed president of the United Mine Workers of America, John L. Lewis, spent several years mining coal in Panama, Illinois.

Some of the earliest strip mines in the United States were operated during the 1870s in Bourbon, Cherokee, and Osage Counties in Kansas. In 1889, Osage County had 118 mines, employed twenty-two hundred miners, and produced over 400 thousand tons of coal. Today, the only active strip mines in Kansas are located in southern Linn County.

The northern part of the upper Midwest region, close to Lake Superior, contained huge deposits of copper near the Keweenaw Peninsula and of iron ore in the Mesabi Range in Minnesota and in several locations on the Upper Peninsula. After the depletion of timber with which to smelt iron ore, the ore had to be shipped east to Chicago, Cleveland, and Pittsburgh, resulting in the building of the Sault Ste. Marie canal in 1855 connecting Lake Superior to the other Great Lakes. Michigan's mining history includes extracting copper, iron, gold, silver, gypsum, slate, salt, coal, and limestone. The discovery of gold in northern Minnesota led to the Vermillion Lake gold rush of 1865–1866. Minnesota also contains granite, limestone, marble, and sandstone quarries.

One of the first mining booms in the United States occurred in the lead region of southwestern Wisconsin from 1825 to 1850. Lead was used to manufacture shot, bullets, paint, plates, candlesticks, and roof and window waterproofing. In addition, zinc was mined in Wisconsin in Lafayette County. At the onset of World War I, five thousand miners were at work in the region. In 1917, when the United States entered the war, they produced sixty-four thousand tons of zinc. Zinc also became very important in the production of tanks, aircraft, warships, and die-cast precision parts during World War II. Iron ore was also important in Minnesota's history after its discovery in the Vermilion Range in 1884, the Mesabi Range in 1892, and the Cuyuna Range in 1911.

Just prior to and continuing into the twentieth century, the southeastern Ohio counties of Athens, Hocking, and Perry became dotted with "patch towns" built by various coal companies. Ohio's worst underground tragedy occurred at Millfield on November 5, 1930, when the Sunday Creek Coal Company Mine #6 exploded, killing eighty-two men.

Vast deposits of lignite coal in western North Dakota brought the mining industry there in the fall of 1873, when Dennis Hannifin and John S. Warn claimed some soft coal veins near Bismarck and, because of hostile Sioux Indians, were escorted to their claim by Lieutenant Colonel George A. Custer. By the turn of the twentieth century, newspapers and railroad companies claimed that coal deposits were present in inexhaustible supplies, enough to warm the population of the United States for ten thousand years. In response to the need for electrical generation, the lignite coal industry grew at a tremendous rate in the 1970s. By the 1980s, more than eight generating facilities dotted the landscape in western North Dakota

Bituminous coal was first discovered in Indiana along the Wabash River in 1804. Before 1850, it was used principally as fuel for steamboats on the Ohio River, for heating, or for blacksmiths' forges. The first Indiana coal company to be incorporated and granted a charter was the American Cannel Coal Company of Cannelton in Perry County in 1837. The first underground mine shaft in Indiana was developed in 1850 at Newburgh, Indiana. Most of the coal deposits in Indiana are located in eighteen counties in the southwestern part of the state.

Missouri contains extensive mineable deposits of lead, zinc, copper, nickel, cobalt, tripoli, stone, clay, industrial sand, lime, barite, and coal. Mining has been an important part of the economic and social fabric of the state since 1728. One of the oldest mine schools in the nation was The Missouri School of Mines and Metallurgy, chartered at Rolla in 1865.

Despite the fact that Nebraska ranks forty-fourth nationally in total nonfuel mineral production—which includes cement, clay, gemstones, lime, sand, and gravel—the direct and indirect economic gain from the mining industry is over $2 billion.

The ethnicities in the Midwest mining areas are more varied than the Scots-Irish patterns farther south. Miners from England, Wales, Scotland, France, Germany, Italy, Sweden, Finland, Croatia, and a variety of other eastern European Slavic countries were attracted to work in the mines of the Midwest.

Public and private entities in the Midwest are conducting a variety of mine-related research projects in the early twenty-first century. For example, the Department of Geologic and Mining Engineering and Sciences at Michigan Technological University is researching such topics as mine health, environmental impacts of mining, and rock mechanics. The Chemical Reaction Laboratory of Washington University in St. Louis is among those partnering with researchers in Ohio to produce alternative fuels from coal. This research will allow clean use of coal-derived carbon monoxide and hydrogen gases. Researchers at Southern Illinois University at Carbondale (SIUC) are combining fly ash, waste material from coal mines, human or animal hair, and a foaming agent to produce a lightweight, cheaper material to replace the traditional wood supports in coal mines. Another team at SIUC has a grant to transform acidic ponds into environmentally safe fields through a multistep process that involves treating slurry in a reverse-action washing machine that separates usable particles from pollutants, which are then rendered benign and returned as a backfill.

Sources and Further Reading: Milton Derber, *Labor in Illinois* (1989); Scott Frickel and William R. Freudenburg, "Mining the Past," *Social Problems* 43 (Nov. 1996); William S. Greever, *The Bonanza West* (1963); Charles H. Harris, *The Harris History: A Collection of Tales of Long Ago of Southeastern Ohio and Adjoining Territories* (1957); Larry Lankton, *Cradle to Grave: Life, Work, and Death at the Lake Superior Copper Mines* (1991); Peter M. Molloy, *The History of Metal Mining and Metallurgy* (1986); Clark Spence, *Mining Engineers and the American West* (1970); William Joseph Trimble, *The Mining Advance into the Inland Empire* (1909; reprint, 1986).

James B. Goode
The University of Kentucky and
Lexington Community College

Nuclear Energy and Power

In 1960 commercial nuclear power was introduced to the Midwest when the Dresden-1 Nuclear Power Station began operation in Illinois. During the next fifteen years, ten more nuclear power plants were built in the Midwest. By 2003, twenty of the sixty-six commercial nuclear power plants operating in the United States were located in ten of the twelve Midwest states (not in North and South Dakota).

Although scientists had been experimenting with nuclear energy since the early twentieth century, it was physicist Enrico Fermi's work with uranium during the 1930s and 1940s that accelerated research into the applications of nuclear energy. While working at the University of Chicago, Fermi and his team built a crude nuclear reactor, the Chicago Pile-1, in a gymnasium under the University's athletic stadium. On December 2, 1942, the Chicago Pile-1 became the site of the world's first self-sustaining nuclear reaction. World War II generally limited nuclear research to military and scientific applications, and it was not until after 1945 that the development of commercial nuclear energy became an important national objective.

In 1953, President Dwight Eisenhower initiated the Atoms for Peace program, which encouraged civilian use of nuclear energy. It was during this early initiative for the investment in the peaceful applications of nuclear energy that the Dresden-1 Nuclear Power Station became the first privately-funded nuclear power plant in the United States. The Dresden-I unit operated for eighteen years before it was taken off-line in 1978. It has since been designated by the American Nuclear Society as a Nuclear Historic Landmark.

Early proponents of nuclear energy were encouraged by its potential as an inexpensive source of electricity for the United States. Nuclear energy also appeared to cause less air pollution than did such traditional sources of energy as coal and natural gas. These reasons, along with future energy consumption forecasts, help account for the initial popularity of nuclear power as a viable source of commercial energy. This popularity peaked between 1966 and 1972 when electric utility companies applied for the construction of 213 nuclear plants nationwide. Although most of these proposed plants were never built, numerous commercial nuclear reactors were constructed in the Midwest. In 1974, the Commonwealth Edison Zion Nuclear Power Station I, located in Illinois, was the first thousand-megawatt electric nuclear power plant to go into service. In 1986, the Perry Power Plant in Ohio became the one hundredth nuclear power plant in the country. As of 2003, Illinois had six operating commercial nuclear plants—more than any other state.

However, nuclear power is a controversial source of energy due to concerns about power plant safety and the storage of nuclear waste. For example, the residents of Mdewakanton Dakota Prairie Island in Minnesota contested nearby Prairie Island nuclear plant's proposal to store nuclear waste in close proximity to a child-care center. Although it may not have been able to fulfill its early promise as a primary source of energy in the United States, nuclear power accounts for 20 percent of the electricity utilized in the nation. Research into nuclear uses and waste storage and disposal continues.

Sources and Further Reading: Jack Holl, Roger Anders, and Alice Buck, *United States Civilian Nuclear Power Policy, 1954–1984* (1986); Winona LaDuke, *All Our Relations* (1999); Richard Rhodes, *Nuclear Renewal* (1993); U.S. Department of Energy, *The History of Nuclear Energy,* DOE/NE-0088 (Aug. 2003).

Julia Chenot GoodFox
University of Kansas

Oil Technology

In terms of petroleum resources, geology has been kind to the Midwest. New wells in search of crude oil and natural gas have been drilled in all twelve Midwest states, and commercial quantities have been found in all but three—Minnesota, Wisconsin, and Iowa. With varying amounts, oil and gas are still produced in nine of these states, and each of those has benefited from improving technology developed during the past 140 years.

Just a few months after Colonel Edwin Drake drilled his famous oil well in August 1859 in Titusville, Pennsylvania, oil was struck about sixty miles to the west in Mecca Township, Trumbull County, Ohio. So right from the start, the Midwest played a major role in the advances of oil technology that originated on the American continent and later spread around the world.

The Drake well was drilled near a known oil seep, where oil percolated to the surface. Other early oil wells were drilled close to former salt water wells where the "nuisance" of oil was encountered. In the Midwest, this search spread westward from Ohio into Indiana, Illinois, Missouri, and Kansas.

Between 1884 and 1910 more than a hundred thousand wells were drilled in northwest Ohio and eastern Indiana. The production from the Lima-Indiana fields helped John D. Rockefeller become a wealthier man and strengthened the position of the Standard Oil Trust. Their dubious business practices in production, refining, and pipelining were later addressed by politicians and the U.S. Supreme Court, and the trust was broken up in 1911. A number of major oil companies, like Exxon-Mobil and Chevron-Texaco, trace their roots to this breakup. According to statistics from the American Petroleum Institute (API), Ohio led the nation in oil production from 1895 to 1902. Large

amounts of natural gas were also discovered near Findlay and Tiffin, Ohio, but the lack of major pipelines kept this resource close to the producing fields until later in the 1900s.

By 1900, the United States had produced its first eight thousand automobiles, and the Age of Gasoline was inaugurated. Petroleum production, and consequently consumption, grew exponentially. API numbers indicate American oil production rose from about 209 million barrels in 1910, to 443 million in 1920, to 898 million in 1930. Production from Midwest states like Indiana, Illinois, Kansas, and Ohio contributed to this total.

Research and development continued in the Midwest and elsewhere after World War I. Better rigs and drilling bits were manufactured. Aerial black-and-white photographs were used in search of surface clues to oil-bearing geology. Gravity meters (or gravimeters, instruments for measuring the force of gravity or, for geological purposes, the density of rocks) made the first geophysical oilfield discovery over a salt dome in east Texas in 1924. That same year the Atlantic Refining Company made the first seismically staked find. Using dynamite to generate underground waves, it became possible to interpret underground features when sound waves were reflected off differing rock formation interfaces. Today, giant vibrators mounted on trucks or electrical discharges provide similar sound waves for seismic evaluation, a must for any wildcat or isolated well.

Defense-related research during World War II resulted in improvements in oilfield instrumentation and aerial surveillance and the demand for new sources of energy continued after World War II. Developed by Gulf Research, magnetic instruments flown to detect submarines were used after the war to map underground igneous rock structures. Geochemical analysis also improved; it can measure minute amounts of hydrocarbons or other elements that may have seeped upward from an oil or gas reservoir.

Remote sensing became possible as Landsat images were used to interpret direct and indirect evidence of hydrocarbons and other natural resources from more than four hundred miles above the earth's surface. The most important technological advances in the search for liquid energy involved computerization. Improved downhole tools lowered into wells after drilling measure the radioactive, electrical, or other properties of subsurface rock formations, analyzed by computer techniques to provide indications of rock type, porosity, fluid content, and other characteristics.

Oil production in the Midwest occurred first in Ohio, Indiana, Illinois, Missouri, and Kansas, and after World War II, finds were made in Michigan, Nebraska, North Dakota, and South Dakota. Most of the production in Nebraska, North Dakota, and South Dakota was made in the western parts of these states, west of the 100th meridian. A few thousand wells are still drilled in the Midwest each year, mostly by smaller independent operators. Ohio, which produces 0.03 percent of U.S. oil, and Michigan are two of the busier states: The Ohio Department of Natural Resources estimated 677 wells were drilled in the Buckeye State in 2001, and the Michigan Department of Environmental Quality, Geological and Land Management Division, reported 449 well completions for the same year.

Natural gas has become the hydrocarbon of choice for both producers and energy consumers alike. Thousands of miles of pipelines move natural gas around the nation, connecting producing wellheads to homes and schools, businesses and factories. Up to 40 percent of the power used by industry in the United States is supplied by natural gas, and the Midwest, particularly Michigan and Ohio, has substantial reserves.

Sources and Further Reading: American Petroleum Institute, *Petroleum Facts and Figures* (1971); Robert O. Anderson, *Fundamentals of the Petroleum Industry* (1984); Ohio Department of Natural Resources, Division of Mineral Resources Management, *2001 Annual Report* (2001).

Andy Maslowski
Columbus, Ohio

Prairie Restoration

In the mid-1930s, a team of University of Wisconsin academics, assisted by Civilian Conservation Corps members, set out to rebuild one of North America's most diverse and complex natural communities, the tallgrass prairie. These lush grasslands of big bluestem, Indian grass, switchgrass, and dozens of other native grasses and sedges, mingled with hundreds of species of forbs (legumes, sunflowers, and others), had dominated much of the rolling midwestern landscape for at least five thousand years. Driving to nearby prairie remnants, the team collected hay, seeds, and clumps of sod to spread on an abandoned horse pasture near the university campus. With that simple act, these midwesterners unknowingly initiated a new scientific discipline, Restoration Ecology, which is today applied to ecosystems around the world.

Tallgrass prairies had met their demise through another midwestern creation, John Deere's self-scouring moldboard plow, introduced in the mid-1800s. This tool eased the plowing of the prairie's deep, tough roots so dramatically that North America's richest grasslands were destroyed more rapidly and completely than any of the world's previous natural communities. Most tallgrass prairie land became cropland; relatively few plots survived as pastures, hayfields, or obscure "wastelands" (for example, railroad corridors, cemeteries, or inaccessible hinterlands). Today, only a few percent of the once vast prairies remain.

As the Wisconsin prairie planting matured, ecologists became increasingly aware that future generations would come to know tallgrass prairies only if many more of these dynamic grasslands were returned to life. Thus, the second half of the twentieth century was marked by numerous attempts to nurture prairie plantings and to locate, preserve, and manage remaining prairie remnants. Today the techniques of prairie restoration are well established, and local-ecotype seeds and plants (those adapted to a specific regional climate) are widely commercially available. Professionals and amateurs across the Midwest have planted small prairies in lawns and schoolyards, along roadsides, and on the grounds of corporate headquarters. Landscape-scale restorations are starting to cover government lands such as Iowa's Neal Smith National Wildlife Refuge and the Midewin National Tallgrass Prairie near Chicago, as well as private rural holdings (for instance, parts of Minnesota's Bluestem Prairie).

Many prairies have been established on bare ground. Increasingly, restorationists are realizing that prairie seed sowed into old fields or established sods will slowly but steadily take control of nonprairie grasslands. The key is to apply fire, a force with which prairies evolved, which had for eons maintained the Midwest's extensive grassy coverage. Fire not only sets back trees, shrubs, and other competitors that are attempting to invade prairies; it also stimulates the growth of fire-adapted prairie plants, which store most of their reserves (as well as their growing tips) safely underneath the ground. Fire (along with manual clearing of woody invaders) is thus also used regularly on native prairie remnants.

Prescribed burns have revealed some unexpected surprises: The firing of unplowed pastures and "weedy" farmlands inaccessible to the plow has, in some places, stimulated the proliferation of dozens of prairie grasses and forbs that had survived as struggling, tiny relicts of past ages. Fire is also a major tool in recent attempts to restore the savannas and open oak-dominated woodlands that once dissected our tallgrass prairies on their eastern edges. By adopting fire as a tool that heals rather than harms, midwesterners have demonstrated that native communities (and nature more generally) cannot always heal itself in today's highly altered landscape. Humans need to take an active role in reintroducing natural processes and protecting nature preserves from further disruption, such as the destructive invasion of leafy spurge and other aggressive plants brought here from other continents.

No one asserts that the several to dozens of plant species typically found in prairie plantings replicate our native prairie remnants, which contain as many as three hundred plant species. Even the best native remnants are a far cry from the Midwest's original vast grassland seas, with their thundering herds of bison and elk, clouds of passenger pigeons and waterfowl, and billions of buzzing and whirling insects. Today's restorations are in a sense dismemberments of a once-whole body, clumsy attempts to reassemble the parts of an incomprehensible puzzle. Yet land managers are finding that these restorations can return health to our beleaguered landscape: Prairie plantings and native remnants build (rather than erode) soil, infiltrate (rather than shed) rain, capture and detoxify (rather than release) agricultural pollutants, fight weeds, house diverse wildlife, and provide numerous other free "ecological services" that equate with a healthy, sustainable environment. These functional benefits combine with the joy of working in, and with, natural systems to make prairie restoration a boon to the spirit, community, and environment.

Sources and Further Reading: Thomas J. Blewett and Grant Cottam, "History of the University of Wisconsin Arboretum Prairies," *Transactions of the Wisconsin Academy of Sciences, Arts and Letters* 72 (1984); Carl Kurtz, *A Practical Guide to Prairie Reconstruction* (2001); John Madson, *Where the Sky Began* (1982); Stephen Packard and Cornelia F. Mutel, eds., *The Tallgrass Restoration Handbook* (1997).

Cornelia F. Mutel
University of Iowa

Salt Mining Technology

Sodium chloride is a necessary nutrient, a flavor enhancer, important for winter highway safety, the building block for a vast array of chemicals, and it has many industrial and commercial uses. Salt production was a driving force throughout world history and was equally important to the midwestern United States. Native Americans and early settlers made salt by boiling brine at numerous sites in Illinois, Michigan, Missouri, Ohio, and elsewhere. Early settlers became aware of animal trails leading to salt springs or licks, and a number of cities and towns contain references to salt licks or salt springs in their names.

Well drillers found brine in Kansas in the 1860s and began conventional mining of pure rock salt by 1887. Commercial salt production in Michigan began when the state geologist recommended drilling for salt in 1838. Salt boiling required large amounts of energy. Thus, suitable brine sources near lumber operations were valuable because salt makers could burn waste wood as fuel to boil salt brine. Midwest salt production contributed to a rapid drop in salt imports from England after 1883. By 1896, Michigan was the largest U.S. producer of common fine salt, followed by Ohio and Kansas. All three states remained among the top four U.S. salt-producing states during the late 1890s and early 1900s.

During the mid-1800s, salt makers found reliable sources of concentrated brine by drilling wells and injecting water into underground rock salt deposits. Water injected into the salt formation returned concentrated brine. Salt makers boiled the brine in open pans to make crystalline salt. Next, they applied steam in submerged pipes to heat the open-pan brine. Then salt makers found they could produce salt from solution-mined brine more efficiently in enclosed, reduced-pressure vacuum pans. Multiple-stage evaporators produced pure, white salt very efficiently. Chemical producers made chlorine and caustic soda and other salt-based chemicals from solution-mined brine.

Shaft-sinking for the first conventional rock salt mines in Kansas and Michigan began during the 1890s. Today, salt producers make solution-mined evaporated salt or conventionally mined rock salt in Kansas, Michigan, and Ohio.

Research by David Marine and O. P. Kimball in 1916 showed that dietary iodine could eliminate iodine-deficiency disorders. Goiter was one such common ailment in the Midwest and elsewhere. Table salt is an ideal carrier of iodine because virtually everyone consumes it in cooking and at the table. During 1924, Michigan salt makers cooperating with the Michigan State Medical Society began producing iodized table salt at no additional cost to consumers. This cooperative effort soon eliminated iodine deficiency throughout the United States.

The Midwest is home to important salt distribution centers in states such as Illinois, Indiana, Iowa, Kansas, Michigan, Minnesota, Ohio, and Wisconsin. Salt is a vital part of the region's economy. Today, Midwest salt producers are a major source of the nation's salt supplies and contribute substantially to the U.S. position as the world's largest salt producer.

Sources and Further Reading: Bruce M. Bertram, "Sodium Halides, Sodium Chloride," in Jacqueline I. Kroschwitz, ed., *Kirk-Othmer Encyclopedia of Chemical Technology*, vol. 22, 4th ed. (1997); Dale W. Kaufmann, ed., *Sodium Chloride: The Production and Properties of Salt and Brine* (1960); O. P. Kimball, "Twenty Years in the Prevention of Goiter (1916–1936)," *The Ohio State Medical Journal* 35 (July 1939); Robert P. Multhauf, *Neptune's Gift* (1978).

Bruce M. Bertram
Alexandria, Virginia

Wind turbines generating energy in Minnesota. National Renewable Energy Laboratory NREL/PIX, Pix no. 06331.

Wind-Turbine Power

Since the beginning of civilization, wind power has helped move people across water in sailboats, grind grains for food, and pump water for irrigation and consumption. Exploitation of wind by land-based machines began in Persia, China, and eastern Europe, moved to western Europe, and since the late 1800s, has been used in the United States. From the late 1800s through the mid 1900s, water-pumping wind machines were used extensively in the developing American West, where the primary source of water was groundwater. In the late nineteenth century, the first wind power system for generating electricity was operating in Cleveland.

By the 1920s, fossil fuel plants eliminated the need for small wind generators in the eastern United States. However, throughout the 1920s and 1930s, these machines were widely used across the Great Plains to power lights and charge batteries on rural American farms. In the 1930s and 1940s, small wind turbines were replaced by traditional electrical generation as the U.S. government intervened to electrify rural America.

Wind does not blow all the time, nor is it consistently strong enough for wind turbines to generate full power all the time. The power output of a wind-turbine generator depends on the area of the rotor, the density of the air, and most importantly, the speed of the wind. Power output is proportional to the cube of the wind speed, and small changes in wind speed result in big differences in power production. Hence, measuring the wind is important for characterizing the wind resource prior to the installation of any wind turbines. Wind resource assessments usually take a year and require the installation of anemometers and direction vanes on tall towers.

Wind resource maps categorize wind power into seven classes. Each class represents a range of mean wind power density or equivalent mean wind speed at a designated height above the ground. Wind power Class 3 or greater is considered suitable for wind energy development based on current technology. Wind resource mapping is now quite sophisticated, using modern computing power to develop detailed wind resource maps. Although the ranking is occasionally debated, work by the Pacific Northwest Laboratory has ranked the top ten states for wind energy potential, and they include six from the Midwest: North Dakota in first place, Kansas in third, South Dakota in fourth, Nebraska in sixth, Minnesota in ninth, and Iowa in tenth.

Today's wind turbines are highly sophisticated machines. The wind turbines that are being mass-produced and installed throughout the United States are three-bladed, upwind, horizontal-axis machines: The axis of rotation is horizontal, the rotor is made up of three blades, and the rotor is upwind of the tower. The main components of a wind turbine are the tower, nacelle (or enclosure for the power plant), and the rotor. The rotor comprises the blades and a hub. The nacelle houses a gearbox, generator, and braking system. Most commonly used wind turbines have blades that are either fixed-pitch or variable-pitch; the most important difference is that fixed-pitch blades are bolted to the hub at a fixed angle, whereas variable-pitch wind turbines can change depending on the wind.

Regardless of the type of wind turbine, the power curves of the generators that produce the electricity are comparable. The generator will typically start producing electricity at around 8 or 9 miles per hour (mph), or 4 meters per second (m/s). This is known as the cut-in speed. The generator output will increase with wind speed up to the generator's rated speed, which is typically around 35 mph, or 15 m/s. At this point, the generator will be producing its maximum output, also known as rated output. As wind speeds increase, maximum output will continue to increase to the cut-out speed—approximately 55 mph, or 25 m/s—at which time the wind turbine will apply the brakes, shutting down rotation of the blades and "parking" itself.

Wind turbine performance and, ultimately, economic performance are based on how much time the wind turbine generator spends at different parts of the generator power curve. The relationship is called the capacity factor, which is defined as the actual production of the generator over a set time period divided by the theoretical 100 percent production over the same time period. Generally speaking, average wind generation sites will have an annual capacity factor of 30 to 35 percent, with some of the best sites achieving annual capacity factors greater than 40 percent.

Sources and Further Reading: D. L. Elliott et al., *Wind Energy Resource Atlas of the United States* (1987); D. L. Elliott, L. L. Wendell, and G. L. Gower, *An Assessment of the Available Windy Land Area and Wind Energy Potential in the Contiguous United States* (1991); Vaughn Nelson, *Wind Energy and Wind Turbines* (CD, 2004); Robert W. Righter, *Wind Energy in America* (1996).

Bradley G. Stevens and Troy Simonsen
University of North Dakota

Producing the Food

If there is a single thing for which the Midwest is famous, it is serving as the breadbasket for the world. Once the Ukraine could claim that title, but with scientific agriculture, a free society, favorable soil, and supportive climate, the Midwest now leads the world in the efficiency and productivity of its farms. Large farms using new genetic strains of corn or maize, which was once called Indian corn (for indeed, it was a staple in the midwestern Indian diet), have made it possible to feed the people of this nation, their animals, and the hungry populations overseas.

Cheese processing in Wisconsin and breakfast cereals manufacturing from grain in Michigan expanded markets and preserved food value. Seed varieties are produced close to the farms where they are used, and

agricultural experiment stations are studded across all the states. Nearly all the midwestern states have a university, state, or federal agricultural agent available in every county. The Morrill Act, that most remarkable of all federal programs in education, assured the linkage of the new universities, usually called "State," with successful animal husbandry and fruitful agriculture. The tie to the university scientific community made it possible to attack pests, discover new products, and encourage those who develop mechanical equipment and new plants for the farmer who works the soil. Not all is work, however; some consider the production of wine both an art and a pleasure. On the shores of the giant freshwater Great Lakes, vineyards abound, and even a variety of American champagne has been claimed for the Midwest.

Agricultural Experiment Stations

Each state or territory has at least one agricultural experiment station (AES) identified formally as part of the State Agricultural Experiment Station System (SAES). An AES ordinarily administers research conducted at several research stations and research farms, as well as in campus-based laboratories, workrooms, offices, and other facilities.

The Midwest—or the North Central Region of the SAES—includes AESs in all twelve states. Regional organizational structure includes regional associations of AES directors and regional research committees of university scientists, and these all interact with national groups. AESs were preceded historically by research farms and research stations. Of research stations still in existence, the Rothamsted Experimental Station, established near Harpenden, England, in 1843, is the oldest. Active agricultural research programs in Germany inspired agriculturalists to establish agricultural research stations in the United States. The oldest continuously operated research plots and the oldest continuous experiment in the Western Hemisphere are at the Morrow Plots, maintained as a National Historic Landmark on the campus of the University of Illinois. The experiment, a study of crop rotation and fertilization practices, was established in 1876, twelve years before the establishment of the Illinois AES. The second-oldest continuously operated research station in the United States is Sanborn Field, established in 1888 and still maintained as an active research site on the campus of the University of Missouri at Columbia.

The Hatch Act (1887), sponsored by representative William H. Hatch of Missouri, authorized the use of federal funds for the creation of state AESs within each of the land-grant institutions created earlier by the Morrill Act (1862). Hatch saw this as a way to make the U.S. agricultural products more competitive in world markets. Through other grants and federal acts, the land-grant institutions of the 1890s (historically African American) have now been integrated into the federally supported agricultural research system. Lincoln University in Jefferson City, Missouri, is the only one of the land grant colleges founded in the 1890s that is located in the Midwest.

Research, teaching, and extension were not new concepts when the land-grant institutions were created, but integrating them into universities that were open to all was a unique approach in higher education and one that has yielded tremendous benefits for the nation. The Hatch appropriation, now distributed to the states by formula, grew from $15 thousand in 1887 to more than $165 million in 2002. Nevertheless, the Hatch appropriation makes up only about 8 percent of the funds expended by AESs; the rest comes from state appropriations, other federal appropriations, grants, contracts, and gifts. The Midwest state AESs expended over $750 million in 2002 and employed thousands of scientists, other professionals, and technicians.

The Hatch Act assigned to the land-grant institutions responsibility, in the language of the Act, "to conduct original and other researches, investigations, and experiments bearing directly on and contributing to the establishment and maintenance of a permanent and effective agricultural industry of the United States, including researches basic to the problems of agriculture in its broadest aspects, and such investigations as have for their purpose the development and improvement of the rural home and rural life and the maximum contribution by agriculture to the welfare of the consumer, as may be deemed advisable, having due regard to the varying conditions and needs of the respective states." The AESs still respond to this overall charge, but the scope and depth of the research required to fulfill it has increased tremendously.

Early AESs conducted research in support of farmers, who comprised most of the population. Now, AES research ranges from narrowly focused basic research in molecular biology to the broad but complex issues of agricultural policy. AES research also includes disciplines historically associated with the field of home economics, now conducted under many different names. For example, the Illinois AES has an entire building devoted to child development research, administered within a unit called Human and Community Development. This arrangement reflects the continuity that exists across the subject matter of agricultural research, from the planting of seed to the manifestations of agricultural products and services in the health and welfare of consumers.

Sources and Further Reading: Donald A. Holt, "Agricultural Experiment Stations," in Charles J. Arntzen and Ellen M. Ritter, eds., *Encyclopedia of Agricultural Science* (1994); Norwood Allen Kerr, *The Legacy: A Centennial History of the State Agricultural Experiment Stations, 1887–1987* (1987); H. C. Knoblauch, E. M. Law, and W. P. Meyer, *State Agricultural Experiment Stations: A History of Research Policy and Procedure* (1962); Alfred Charles True, *A History of Agricultural Experimentation and Research in the United States, 1607–1925* (1937); Rothamsted Research, http://www.rothamsted.bbsrc.ac.uk/iacr/tiacrhome.html (June 10, 2005).

Donald A. Holt
University of Illinois–Urbana-Champaign

Food Processing

The production and processing of food employs one out of seven workers in the Midwest. As a tribute to their efficiency, in 1950 around 20 percent of personal income was spent for food; today it is about ten cents of the earned dollar. The industry is huge, with the yearly average per capita consumption of food at over nineteen hundred pounds, split about evenly between animal and plant products.

Food processing is usually heat treatment of the product after the container is permanently sealed. The temperature and time must be sufficient to destroy any organisms with resistance to heat. As a generality, "processing" refers to canned or glass-packed food, but it also includes food that is frozen, dehydrated, fermented, or concentrated, as well as food manufactured into preserves, jams, jellies, or spreads.

In 1809 Nicholas Appert, a French chef, preserved food when he placed it in a wide-mouth glass container, sealed it with cotton, and applied heat. Appert did not know why the food kept; Louis Pasteur, in 1864, clarified the concept of heating and sealing and thereby began the canning industry. In the early 1800s, a canister with a hole in the top was invented, and these cans could be heated in boiling water with a cap placed loosely over the hole and later hand-soldered over the hole. A sanitary can was developed in the early 1890s, and later machines were developed to crimp the lid. According to the Ohio Canners Association, the sanitary can and the new crimping machine were unveiled at the Southern Hotel in Columbus, Ohio, in 1912.

Wm. Underwood and Company of Boston was one of the first food processors to pack pickles, ketchup, sauces, and jellies. Thomas Kensett preserved foods in New York. Both men followed Appert's earlier methods. Kensett and Ezra Dagget received a patent in 1825 for making cans in the United States. This cre-

Cheese processed in Wisconsin. Photo courtesy
Wisconsin Milk Marketing Board, Inc.

ated a whole new industry. Canning moved rapidly to the Midwest, but the industry was still having trouble with cans of processed food simply exploding. Harry Russell in Wisconsin and Samuel K. Prescott and Underwood in Massachusetts showed that insufficient heat was being applied to the canned food to destroy the microorganisms. After the correct process of time and temperature was established, the industry started to develop.

There was another major stumbling block: Sometimes the crops did not mature properly and yields were low. This time it was horticulturists who stepped to the forefront and improved yields, developing new, more reliable varieties. Agricultural engineers next invented efficient machines to harvest and thus eliminated hand-harvesting. With these innovations between 1940 and 1960, industrial capacity grew from fifty to more than three hundred cans per minute. Factories became larger, handling from ten to well over a hundred tons per hour. Quality was also superior to what it once had been because of new practices introduced for quality assurance. Among the improved methods of manufacture was chemical peeling for tomatoes. Researchers at Ohio State devised a system of water-handling tomatoes and improved chemical peeling methods to eliminate what was once hand work.

New varieties of tomatoes changed the industry from a strictly peeling industry to one offering many styles and types of products, including tomato juice, developed in 1923, and stewed tomatoes, developed in 1947. Pulp and paste production expanded in the early 1940s, and manufacturing of salsa developed as recently as 1980. Ketchup was a product of the 1800s,

and Ohio can boast of having the largest ketchup plant in the world. Soups and tomato beverages, including V-8 and Bloody Mary mixes, dominate the market today. The tomato industry now manufactures tomato paste for year-round remanufacture into various products.

Peas, corn, and other vegetables dominate canning in Wisconsin and Minnesota. Cherries, peaches, and apples are the main crops from Michigan. Potatoes are grown and processed as French fries and potato chips in North Dakota, Minnesota, Wisconsin, and Michigan, with Ohio leading the nation in potato chip manufacture. Illinois remains a leader in meat and poultry processing, and Wisconsin is a leading state for milk processing and cheese production.

Sources and Further Reading: Wilbur A. Gould, *Tomato Production, Processing and Technology* (1992); Earl Chapin May, *The Canning Clan* (1937).

Wilbur A. Gould
Cape Coral, Florida

Food Production

The rural landscape of the Midwest is characterized by food production on large farms with modern agricultural methods. Current agro-ecosystem managers are highly efficient in use of land and labor to produce food, feed, and raw materials for other industrial processes.

Agriculture is dominated by a relatively small number of crop and animal species. Corn and soybeans in rotation occupy the majority of cultivated acres in the Midwest. For example, in Iowa in 2002, there were over twelve million acres in corn and ten million acres in soybeans, and this two-year rotation represented over two-thirds of all farmed acres in the state.

This specialized sector is adopting increasingly industrialized production methods. Admired by people around the world as a model of production efficiency, the Midwest helps to feed a rapidly growing human population. Yet this agricultural system is based on large investments of technology and fossil fuels, and carries the potential long-term limitations inherent in a system highly dependent on nonrenewable resources. Concentration of livestock in confined feeding operations is becoming the norm in poultry, swine, milk, and beef production. Although this has increased productivity, it has also enhanced concern about animal rights.

There are dynamic social changes in Midwest agriculture, including ownership of land involving fewer people and thus larger farms and a skewed distribution of benefits. Consolidated ownership of land and resources is contributing to loss of family farms. In Nebraska there were almost fifty-five thousand farms in 1997, but this number dwindled to just over forty-nine thousand farms according to the 2002 census—a loss of nearly six thousand family farms in only five years.

Native prairies grazed by bison and other large mammals and small cropping areas along riverine lowlands that were already cultivated by Native Americans were transformed by the European immigrants who brought in new crop and livestock species. Introduced species quickly replaced many native plants and animals. Early food production systems in the Midwest were based on family farming, and most people lived on farms or in rural communities. The interdependent mixture of crops and animals provided families with most of their food needs. With the industrial revolution came the steel plow, the planter and thresher, and finally the self-propelled grain combine. Industry brought people to cities, and farms were consolidated for production of one or two crops grown in monocultures (large fields of single species) and the arrival of the commodity-based agriculture we know today. This midwestern farming style has been highly successful in producing a small range of economically important species: corn, wheat, soybean, alfalfa, grain sorghum, beef, dairy cattle, hogs, and poultry. To a lesser extent, commercial vegetables and fruits are grown near cities where the climate is favorable, markets are close, and labor is available.

Large farms plus consolidation and specialization have created today's industrial agriculture. The system is quite productive per unit of land and is especially productive per day of labor. Cheap food is supplied to consumers, but the farmers and ranchers who produce this food receive only 10 to 15 percent of what is spent in the supermarket by consumers. At least 25 percent of what consumers pay goes for fertilizers, pesticides, field equipment, and fossil fuels for irrigation and other mechanized activities on the farm. The rest of the food dollar goes into processing, packaging, marketing, and transportation. More energy is spent from the time food leaves the farm until it reaches consumers' tables than is required in the entire farm production process.

In the Midwest, a small number of companies are increasingly linked through marketing agreements or by outright ownership; in the late 1970s, 80 percent of the commercial grain trade, for example, was controlled by five major corporations, and this concentration is becoming more prevalent across the industry. Vertical integration, control of multiple aspects from production to final sale of production, gives even greater efficiency to the large food corporations. This industrial system provides a food supply that costs U.S. consumers only 11 percent of their income, but several social and political changes have occurred. To continue to produce these commodities, the system is highly dependent on federal farm subsidies. Consolidation of farms has resulted in fewer owners of farmland; at the opening of the twenty-first century in the United States, about one percent of the population was engaged in production agriculture, a number so low that it will soon not be reported in the national census. Land resources are concentrated in the hands of a small fraction of the rural population, the number of minimum-wage jobs is increasing, and many rural communities have become almost ghost towns.

Current concerns about decreasing supplies of nonrenewable fossil fuels, the environmental impacts of chemical pesticide and fertilizer use, and narrow ownership patterns in the food system are leading thoughtful citizens all over the Midwest to explore alternatives. The majority experiences the advantages of a cheap food policy, but interest is growing among some consumers about where and how food is grown and who is benefiting from the system. Interest is growing about producing foods without use of chemical pesticides or fertilizers, and a national set of standards that regulate organic farming was developed in 2002. Farmers are exploring methods of direct marketing such as subscription farming (often called consumer- or community-supported agriculture, CSA), farmers' markets, and sales directly from the farm to the consumer. There are now more than fifty CSAs operating in the state of Iowa, up from only a handful a decade ago.

Following the purchase of several of the large organic processing and distributing companies by multinationals, some consumers and farmers are beginning to focus on local foods rather than a global system. This requires the consumption of more fruits and vegetables produced in season, and it requires the consumer to become reacquainted with local food producers. In other words, concern about the environmental impacts of industrial farming has led to support for farmers who use alternative production methods. It is this mixture of production methods and markets that today represents the food system throughout the U.S. Midwest, a system that continues to evolve in response to new information and technology as well as to changing consumer demand.

Sources and Further Reading: Gretchen C. Daily, ed., *Nature's Services* (1997); Charles A. Francis, Cornelia Butler Flora, and Larry D. King, eds., *Sustainable Agriculture in Temperate Zones* (1990); Stephen R. Gliessman, ed., *Agroecology* (1998); Dana L. Jackson and Laura L. Jackson, eds., *The Farm as Natural Habitat* (2002); Wes Jackson, *New Roots for Agriculture* (1980); Donald Lotter, "Organic Agriculture," *Journal of Sustainable Agriculture* 21 (2002); Marion Nestle, *Food Politics* (2002); Richard C. Olson, Charles Francis, and Stephen Kaffka, eds., *Exploring the Role of Diversity in Sustainable Agriculture* (1995).

Charles A. Francis
University of Nebraska–Lincoln

Organic Farming

Agricultural production without the application of chemical pesticides or fertilizers, along with adherence to a number of other rules, is called organic farming. These systems became popular in the mid-twentieth century and over the past decade have become economically important for a small number of farmers in the Midwest. In 2001 the U.S. food system was about 2 percent organic production, and the use of organic principles is growing steadily at more than 20 percent per year. Organic farming methods use crop rotation, resistant varieties, and diverse planting patterns to achieve pest management, rather than employing chemical pesticides. The goal is preservation of soil fertility through legumes and grass cover, prevention of soil erosion, rotation of crops and pastures, application of animal manure or composts, and diversity of crops. Since even before the days of Louis Bromfield, the Ohio novelist, and his grass-based sustainable farming of 1938, cultures such as the Amish of Ohio and Iowa and the Hutterites of South Dakota have used similar methods.

Most modern organic farmers insist that this type of production is not possible without including animal manure in the system, and thus organic farms often

have mixed crops and animal enterprises. Rules forbid use of transgenic (genetically modified organism, GMO) crops, antibiotics or growth stimulants in livestock, and all nonorganic feeds. A national set of standards for organic farming was written in 2002 that must be met for products to be labeled with this designation. To be certified as an organic farmer, it is essential to keep careful records of production practices and products used in farming and to submit to inspections by the certifying group. One of the largest certifying groups in the world is the Organic Crop Improvement Association (OCIA) with headquarters in Lincoln, Nebraska, and another in the Midwest is Farm Verified Organics whose offices are in North Dakota. In 2001 six of the top ten states in number of certified organic acres were in the Midwest: North Dakota (#2, 145 thousand acres), Minnesota (#3, 98 thousand acres), Wisconsin (#4, 79 thousand acres), Iowa (#5, 72 thousand acres), South Dakota (#9, 50 thousand acres), and Michigan (#10, 45 thousand acres).

Debate continues about the degree to which organic farming is safer for people and better for the environment than conventional agriculture. Organic food is safer, since less pesticide residue is present on organic foods than on those produced in conventional farming, but traces of pesticide can be present in all categories of food. Organic farming leads to less pesticide loss and enhanced water quality in nearby streams and lakes. Whether more or less soil is lost from organic farms depends on the methods used. There is no conclusive evidence for a higher nutritional quality of food produced in organic systems than in conventional systems. Reported differences are often due to different crop varieties, cultural practices, nitrogen application levels, or crop yields that are difficult to control. Organic produce is often fresher since it tends to be sold locally, often at farmers markets, rather than shipped greater distances. Locally grown organic food may even promote a personal connection between those who farm and those who consume the products, an important step in educating the public about where and how food is produced.

One current concern is the rapid growth and industrialization of organic farming. Most organic farmers are concerned about working conditions on the farm, size and scale of the operation, fair treatment of farm labor, and the equity of distribution of benefits that accrue from the system. Such economic and social goals are difficult to achieve in an industrial food system, and therefore most farmers are promoting both organic certification as well as local production wherever possible. Continued growth of the organic farming sector is likely as consumers become concerned about where and how their food is produced and about the effects of the production system on farm families, rural communities, and the environment.

Sources and Further Reading: Louis Bromfield, *Malabar Farm* (1948); D. Lotter, "Organic Agriculture," *Journal of Sustainable Agriculture* 21 (4) (2003); J. I. Rodale, *Pay Dirt* (1945); Jane Sooby, *State of the States: Organic Farming Systems Research at Land Grant Institutions 2001–2003,* 2nd ed. (2003).

Charles A. Francis
University of Nebraska–Lincoln

Plant Genetics

Plant genetics in the Midwest is largely synonymous with crop improvement. Genetics is studied to increase understanding of plants as a legitimate goal in its own right, but its primary goal is to develop improved varieties of economically important plant species. Implicit in this activity is the midwestern belief in progressivism, the expectation that improvement is attainable and worthy of effort. Beginning in the late nineteenth century, great effort was dedicated to crop genetics in land-grant universities, in the U.S. Department of Agriculture, and in the private sector seed industry. Although not the only place where crop improvement has been practiced, the Midwest features a unique confluence of climate, soils, and human factors that has resulted in a rapidly evolving plant genetics industry.

Appropriately for the area known as the Corn Belt, the most spectacular accomplishment in twentieth-century plant breeding was hybrid corn. The Midwest's corn-growing areas provided the laboratory for this first experiment in the economic exploitation of hybrid vigor, or heterosis, the increased yield produced when two different genetic strains are crossed. Eventually, hybrid corn spread to other regions. In addition, principles and techniques learned while creating the hybrid corn industry were applied to other crops, including sorghum, tomato, and sunflower, leading to the worldwide use of hybrids in those species.

Corn yields in the United States showed little increase from the Civil War to about 1930, when the hybrids were introduced. Since 1930, yields have increased dramatically and at an accelerating pace. Comparisons of open-pollinated varieties and hybrids of early and recent eras indicate a steady genetic gain exceeding one percent annually.

Hybrid vigor depends on genetic diversity. Midwestern corn growers, beginning in pre-Columbian times and continuing through the nineteenth century,

laid the foundation for the hybrid corn industry when they brought diverse open-pollinated corn varieties into the Midwest. Growers and researchers noted the favorable result of crossing strains having hard flint kernels with dent strains, which feature softer starch and a dent at the kernel tip, leading initially to the development of improved open-pollinated varieties. An example was "Reid Yellow Dent," which became popular after winning a prize at the World's Fair in Chicago in 1893. Patterns of hybrid vigor among varieties were exploited by corn breeders, who projected the changes into hybrids of inbred lines derived from the same varieties.

Corn growers adopted hybrid corn because of its superior yield and other attributes. In doing so they abandoned their role as producers of their own seed corn and relegated that specialized task to seed companies, which in turn employed researchers to develop and produce a continuous supply of improved hybrids. Specialization of seed production eventually extended to crops where hybrids could not be produced economically, such as wheat and soybeans, and where it was impossible for crop producers to save their own seed for replanting. Companies worked to persuade producers that their product was superior to the farmer-saved seed. They released newer, better varieties annually, which resulted in short life spans for individual varieties but continuous improvement to attract the customer's attention.

Most recently, an understanding of genetics at the molecular level has led to the development of a biotechnology industry. Currently more than a third of the Midwest's corn fields and three quarters of soybean fields are planted with transgenic crops, sometimes called genetically modified organisms (GMOs), which carry genes deliberately inserted from other species. For the most part, these crops have been accepted by farmers and consumers in the United States, but rejected as hazardous or "unnatural" by many Europeans and some Asians. A less controversial but potentially powerful tool of biotechnology is molecular mapping, which allows breeders to examine the DNA of a potential new variety as an aid to selection.

Additional ramifications of private investment in crop genetics include patent protection on crop varieties, which legally prohibits farmers from saving seed, consolidation of the seed industry into fewer, larger companies, and the neglect of minor crops for which research is not economically rewarding.

Genetic change in midwestern crops has brought with it changes in economic and social structures. For the crops, at least, there are objective criteria for identifying any specified change as "improvement," such as increased yield, pest resistance, or nutritional quality. The associated social changes are more difficult to evaluate. Nevertheless, in more than one sense, the Midwest continues its role as an experimental laboratory for the area that has fed so much of the world.

Sources and Further Reading: John C. Hudson, *Making the Corn Belt* (1994); C. Wayne Smith, *Crop Production* (1995); A. Forrest Troyer, "Background of U.S. Hybrid Corn," *Crop Science* 39 (May–June 1999); Henry A. Wallace and William L. Brown, *Corn and Its Early Fathers* (1956).

Steven K. St. Martin
The Ohio State University–Columbus

Seed Production

Grass and legume seed production has a long history in the development of midwestern agriculture. The first major accomplishment in the development of forage crops and seed production was Grimm alfalfa (*Medicago sativa* L.), named for a German immigrant, Wendelin Grimm, who brought a small quantity of alfalfa seed with him to Minnesota in 1857. For thirty years, he selected seed from the surviving plants and, by 1895, had established a strain of alfalfa that tolerated winter and allowed utilization of this forage in the upper Midwest and Canada. Grimm alfalfa was not only winter-hardy, it also offered good yield and was excellent animal feed. During the 1930s and 1940s, ten to twelve million pounds of Grimm alfalfa seed were produced annually in Minnesota.

As land was opened for settlers, it was routine for them to grow alfalfa or clover on the newly broken land. These legume crops enhanced the quality of the soil through their symbiotic relationship with nitrogen-fixing bacteria, while producing useful and economically important seed and forage crops. In addition, if the land was not well suited to traditional row crops, perennial seed crops such as alfalfa, red clover, sweet clover, and alsike clover could be produced instead. With the outbreak of World War II, flax and other annual row crops became desirable and prices were high, so Midwest farmers replaced their traditional legume seed crops with annual row crops that diminished the acreage used for seed production.

Seed production of cool-season grasses and legumes is environmentally sensitive, and it is now seldom efficient to produce seed in the area of the Midwest where the crop is best utilized. Most of these cool-season grasses and legumes were never native to the United States and arrived in the Midwest with immigrants who planted them as feed for their livestock. Previously, seed production was necessary as forage to sustain the livestock. Now, cool-season grass and legume seed production has been localized to the northern regions of the upper Midwest reserved for areas where annual row crops are less productive. These northern areas remain suited to seed production since cool-season grasses need to be vernalized, that is, subjected to cool temperatures for eight or more weeks. The regime of cool nights followed by long days favors reproductive growth over vegetative growth and results in high seed yields.

More recently, seed production of plant species that are native to the upper Midwest has gained in popularity. Native perennial grasses, legumes, and forbs (plants other than grasses) found in meadows were

Seeding corn, North Dakota, 1913. F.A. Pazandak Photograph Collection, NDIRS-NDSU, Fargo, 2026.079.

once basic components of the prairie ecosystems of the upper Midwest. Recently, there has been a resurgence in their popularity for use in prairie restoration, revegetation along roadsides, riparian areas, landscapes, and agricultural biomass systems. Such native species also confer numerous ecological benefits, including increased resilience because of their adaptation to local climatic conditions and pests and because their extensive root systems decrease soil erosion and nutrient leaching. These plants may decrease dependence on fertilizer and pesticides.

Plant breeding or selection has been limited so far, and seed production tends to be localized to a relatively narrow geographic area near the initial collection sites. Seed production of these native species is spreading throughout the upper Midwest in an effort to preserve the diversity and adaptability of these native plant populations to specific ecoregions. Often, because of the complexity of handling native plants in cultivated production systems, and because of the specialized farming equipment needed, native seed producers specialize in this type of agriculture and are not at the same time involved in traditional agricultural cropping systems.

The seed production of both the native and cool-season grass and legume species offers many rewards for the producer, both environmentally and financially. The perennial nature of these seed crops is environmentally advantageous, and they protect the soil from wind and water erosion by maintaining cover on the soil surface and by limiting tillage. Seed production fields also provide habitat to wildlife and contribute to the diversification of midwestern agricultural systems. Finally, the economic return on these crops can be quite high to the producer, and may exceed the economic returns from annual cropping systems.

Sources and Further Reading: R. F. Barnes, D. A. Miller, and C. J. Nelson, eds., *Forages*, vol. 1, *An Introduction to Grassland Agriculture*, 5th ed. (1995); A. A. Hanson, D. K. Barnes, and R. R. Hill, eds., *Alfalfa and Alfalfa Improvement* (1988); M. B. McDonald and L. O. Copeland, *Seed Production: Principles and Practices* (1997); L. E. Moser, D. R. Buxton, and M. D. Casler, eds., *Cool-Season Forage Grasses* (1996).

Nancy Jo Ehlke
University of Minnesota

Winemaking Technology

The Midwest has a rich history of grape growing and wine production. Swiss settlers led by John James Dufour settled along the Ohio River near Vevay, Indiana, in the early 1800s, planted vines, and established what would become the first successful commercial winery in the nation. Similar successes occurred throughout the 1800s as German and French settlers arrived in places such as Hermann, Missouri; Harmony, Indiana; and Nauvoo, Illinois. By the late 1820s, the Cincinnati area was known as the Rhineland of America for the production of the Catawba grape introduced to the region by Nicholas Longworth. Sparkling wines, "American champagne," made from this grape were considered among the best in the world. By the 1880s there were thousands of acres of grapes grown across the region, with over a million gallons of wine produced.

A combination of harsh weather, new diseases, and aggressive insects led to a decline in grape production in many areas of the Midwest, and Prohibition ended the Midwest's widespread production of wine. It took many years for the industry to rebound.

The Midwest is characterized by a Continental climate, with frequent temperature swings and often bitterly cold winters. Unlike the Mediterranean climate of California, weather extremes are common in the Midwest. Cold northern air masses meet with warm southwestern air to create extreme conditions during spring and fall. Hot, humid summers with torrential rainfall can wreak havoc on crops. Only grape varieties well adapted to the climate survive and flourish, and there is a diverse pool of grape varieties to choose from in the Midwest. In the early years, growers learned to grow grapes by trial and error. Today's industry is supported by research and education from the state Agricultural Experiment Stations, land-grant universities, and local wine associations. Educational programs exist in every state in the Midwest, and such research-based support has led to a rebirth of the industry in the region. State and federal programs to provide assistance in growing grapes, producing wines, and promoting and marketing those wines have had a significant impact on the industry.

The efficiency of grape production has also increased. Development of new varieties by programs in New York, Minnesota, and Arkansas led to greatly improved grape and wine quality. Improved pest management practices and modern reduced-risk pesticides have increased fruit quality and reduced environmental impact. Standard practices now include modern trellising systems, advanced canopy management techniques, and careful crop control to increase fruit quality. Growers now use global positioning and geographic information systems to match varieties to the soils and climates of specific sites. Careful attention to fruit quality and optimum harvest dates is necessary for premium wines.

Nevertheless, the wine industry still relies on the artisan skills of the winemaker. Age-old practices of carefully tending and skillfully blending the wines have changed very little, but new grape crushers, destemmers, and presses have improved efficiency. Better pumps, filtering systems, and automated bottling lines lessen oxidation and maintain quality, and temperature-controlled tanks let winemakers closely manage fermentation. Better quality corks or cork substitutes and screw cap closures have reduced the age-old problem of cork failure. New yeast strains enhance flavor and aroma and improve mouth feel. New enzymes and other products and processes to improve wine quality have been designed specifically to meet the needs of the industry. Increased knowledge of modern microbiological principles and improvement in winery sanitation has reduced wine spoilage problems.

The improved quality follows through to the marketing of Midwest wines, too. As a tourism-based industry, the marketing of wines has been closely associated with agro-tourism, resulting in millions of dollars of economic impact. As the industry continues to grow, market research is increasingly used to target audiences and improve overall profitability.

Today, over three hundred wineries across the region produce more than three million gallons of wine from almost eighteen thousand acres of grapes. Operations range from small boutique wineries to major corporations. The Midwest wine industry has regained the prominence it once had and maintains a reputation for premium wine production.

Sources and Further Reading: John J. Baxevanis, *The Wine Regions of America* (1992); James L. Butler and John J. Butler, *Indiana Wine* (2001).

Bruce P. Bordelon
Purdue University, Indiana

Moving the People

In this most mobile of all societies, the citizens of the Midwest, specifically Indiana, developed what was for a time the most extensive railway system in America. Even earlier, and later supplying a path for the railroads, canals crossed from east to west and north to south, utilizing the numerous rivers and creating large reservoir lakes that still remain as recreational centers. The development of steel and elaboration of the suspension bridge following the successful early attempt in Cincinnati made it possible to cross even the widest of rivers. James Eads organized the construction of the longest bridge of its day, a steel one that spanned the mighty Mississippi at St. Louis.

Automobiles have been, quite properly, identified with Detroit, but it is less apparent that dozens of related industries also rose up to supply axles, batteries, tires, and other products needed for the automobile age. Although vulcanization, the treatment of rubber that made air usable for tires, was not discovered in the Midwest, it was Akron, Ohio, that became the center of the rubber industry. Tires were needed for bicycles and automobiles, and even rubber for a blimp, a lighter-than-air vehicle that can carry a few passengers and televise football games. Both North Carolina, where they flew, and Ohio, where their shop was once located, claim the Wright brothers. Ohio is where the Wright brothers did their original work, designed the first wind tunnels, and made airplanes that could actually fly. As inconceivable as it still seems, within several decades after the invention of airplanes, a man walked on the moon, and a museum for Neil Armstrong and space exploration is now located in his hometown of Wapakoneta, Ohio.

Electric streetcars for mass transit were present in the large cities on the Great Lakes as early as they appeared anywhere in the United States. On this same shore one can see not only merchant ships and yachts, but successful ship and boat construction. "We move" could be the motto for the Midwest.

Automobile Technology

When America entered World War II in 1941, the job of gearing up domestic production fell to Lt. General Brekon Somervell, commander of the all-important U.S. Army Services and Supply. Somervell had a secret weapon to meet Hitler's industrial challenge: a midwestern Arsenal of Democracy forged from the complex host of materials suppliers, parts manufacturers, and assemblers already engaged in the mass production of automobiles. "For, when Hitler put his war on wheels," Somervell remarked at the time, "he ran it straight down our alley."

That Somervell could pin the hopes of the Free World on such a production miracle in the industrial Midwest remains nothing short of astounding. It was only fifty years before that two bicycle mechanics from rural Illinois, Charles and Frank Duryea, began planning a revolutionary gasoline-powered auto, the Duryea Motor Wagon. The success of the Duryea car in an 1895 Chicago *Times-Herald* race paved the way for the sale of twelve Duryea cars the following year and spurred further tinkering with internal combustion engines by experimenters throughout the Midwest: Elwood Haynes and the Apperson brothers in Kokomo, Indiana; Ransom Olds in Lansing, Michigan; and Henry Ford in Detroit. Such gasoline-powered vehicles were favored over the electric-powered carriages of New England in part because of the poor state of the midwestern roads and the unavailability of rural electricity. A concentration of talent and abundant resources also made the region a natural base for auto industry concentration.

The Duryeas painstakingly crafted their first cars out of hand-tooled and fitted parts. Duryea cars were put together without the benefit of special-purpose machine tools, systematic jigs and fixtures, or interchangeable parts. High-volume production of automobiles demanded a new emphasis on such technologies. As early as 1906 Henry Ford began preparing for more systematic car building in developing techniques for producing the Model T. The price of the Model T, manufactured in Highland Park, Michigan, fell throughout the 1910s and 1920s to less than $300 and became emblematic of the spirit of mass production, interchangeability, and scientific management styles that reinvigorated American industry generally.

By 1929 the United States boasted more than twenty-three million registered automobiles. Ford, however, had not fared well against the decentralized General Motors Corporation (GM) under the direction of Alfred P. Sloan, Jr. GM in the 1920s secured by accretion divisions, subsidiaries, and suppliers in such places as Dayton, Ohio, and Flint, Pontiac, and Detroit in Michigan. Under Sloan the company ushered in so-called flexible mass production with general-purpose tools, movable plant machinery, and the annual model change. One model, all black, might have been enough once, but not after GM.

By the time Lt. General Somervell uttered his prophetic line about Hitler's chances against the American automobile industry, the industry was already well on its way to converting to wartime production. By midsummer 1941 thirteen thousand GM workers were already engaged in defense production. After Pearl Harbor, the industry suspended altogether domestic production of cars.

The Big Three automakers—Ford, GM, and Chrysler (which had built a large M-3 tank factory in Warren, Michigan)—rapidly dismantled their wartime facilities in 1945 and resumed civilian auto production, dominating the industry as a tightly controlled oligopoly. But despite current nostalgia about a presumed 1950s Golden Age of auto manufacturing, the automakers struggled against customer dissatisfaction brought on by high-pressure dealers and increasingly bloated offerings. By the mid-1960s, suffering from malaise that would become exacerbated by aging midwestern Rust Belt plants and Arab oil shocks, the industry began introducing more fuel-efficient compacts. But with an uneven safety record and foreign competitors like Volkswagen and the Japanese Ministry of International Trade and Industry (MITI), the American auto industry went into a steep 1970s decline.

The nadir of the midwestern auto industry may have been reached in 1982, when the Honda Motor Company moved its first car off the assembly line in a state-of-the-art plant in Marysville, Ohio. The Japanese dominance of the auto industry precipitated great soul-searching on the part of American corporations and resulted in more than a little Japan-bashing. But a quiet revolution in American automaking was also taking place, despite a flurry of devastating post mortems, the most famous of which is Michael Moore's eye-opening documentary *Roger and Me* (1989), about the closure of the GM plant in Flint. In many ways the globalization of Japanese research and development ideas—particularly total quality management, just-in-time parts delivery, and lean production—revitalized the midwestern domestic auto industry and presaged new growth into the new millennium.

Sources and Further Reading: James J. Flink, *The Automobile Age* (1988); Richard Florida and Martin Kenney, "The Globalization of Japanese R&D: The Economic Geography of Japanese R&D Investment in the United States," *Economic Geography* 70 (Oct. 1994); Paul Ingrassia and Joseph B. White, *Comeback: The Fall and Rise of the American Automobile Industry* (1994); Larry Lankton, "Autos to Armaments: Detroit Becomes the Arsenal of Democracy," *Michigan History* 75 (Nov.–Dec. 1991); Taiichi Ono, *Toyota Production System* (1988); Richard P. Scharchburg, *Carriages Without Horses* (1993).

Philip L. Frana
University of Central Arkansas

Aviation Technology

At first glance, the Midwest seems significant in the history of aviation mostly as a place to fly over. The first transcontinental flight (1911), the first nonstop transcontinental flight (1923), and the first round-the-world flight (1924) all passed over it. Chicago and St. Louis were key stops on the air mail routes established in the 1920s and on the airline routes that evolved from them. The airlines' shift to a hub-and-spoke route system in the late 1970s ensured that millions of travelers each year pass through airports in Chicago (United), St. Louis (TWA, bought out by American in 2001), Cincinnati (Delta), Minneapolis (Northwest), and Detroit (Northwest) on their way to and from destinations far beyond the Midwest.

The Midwest's role in aviation dates to the beginning of flight. The region has been, since the 1890s, a center of innovation in aeronautics and aviation technology. It has also been, since the 1910s, a key setting for the democratization of aviation. The two roles are intimately entwined with each other, and with the broader midwestern traditions of populism, technological innovation, and industrial growth.

The history of the Midwest as a center of American aviation begins with Octave Chanute, who came to the United States as a teenager, established himself as a civil engineer, and settled in Chicago. Chanute was, by 1890, America's leading authority on flying machines, building and flying gliders as well as writing and lecturing on them. His most crucial contribution to aviation, however, was his role as a central figure in the growing community of aviators. He kept up a voluminous correspondence with American and foreign colleagues, helped to finance some promising ventures, and offered encouragement to many more. When the Wright brothers became interested in aviation, they wrote to the Smithsonian Institution for information, but turned to Chanute for personal guidance.

Orville and Wilbur Wright went on, of course, to surpass their famous mentor. They made the first controlled, powered flight on the beaches of North Carolina in December 1903, but Dayton, Ohio, remained their base of operations. The wind tunnel they built in their Dayton workshop allowed them, between 1901 and 1903, to conduct the first systematic tests of different airfoil and propeller shapes. Huffman Prairie, on the outskirts of the city, served as the flight test center for every machine they built from 1904 through 1915. Huffman Prairie also became a school for aspiring pilots. Orville Wright later estimated that he had personally taught 115 students there in the decade preceding World War I. Many went on to become leading exhibition pilots or officers in the fledgling Army Air Service—ambassadors from the nascent aviation community to the American public.

Demobilized military pilots flying war surplus planes like the Curtiss JN-4D (the famous "Jenny") served as a different kind of aviation ambassador in the 1920s. Some—called gypsies or, later, barnstormers—flew from town to town selling rides and doing stunts, acrobatics or (with the help of an assistant) parachute jumping and wing walking. Others—eventually known as fixed-base operators—settled down at small airfields where they sold rides, instruction, and charter services. Neither the barnstormers nor the fixed-base operators were a purely midwestern phenomenon, but the region's combination of extensive flat terrain and abundant small towns enabled both to flourish there. Collectively, the two groups gave thousands of Americans their first experience with flight, promoting what contemporaries called "air-mindedness." The comfortable familiarity with airplanes that they fostered created a customer base for the airlines and the emerging small plane industry.

American airplanes began to take on their modern form in the early 1930s. Boxy wood-and-fabric biplanes gave way to streamlined metal monoplanes, fixed wheels to retractable ones, and open cockpits to enclosed cabins. The changes took place, more or less simultaneously, across the entire spectrum of airplane types. The first modern airliners took shape in the engineering departments of West Coast aircraft manufacturers. The first modern warplanes and private planes, on the other hand, were products of the Midwest.

McCook Field, on the outskirts of Dayton, served as the flight test center for the Army Air Corps (later the Army Air Force) from 1917 until 1927. Wright Field, which replaced it, functioned both as a flight test center and as the headquarters of the Materiel Command—the branch of the Corps charged with developing new technology. Colonel Oliver Echols, who directed the Materiel Command's technical section in the 1930s, spearheaded the creation of what became the B-17 Flying Fortress—America's first long-range bomber. He also orchestrated the collaboration between the Curtiss-Wright Corporation, North American Aviation, and the National Advisory Committee for Aeronautics (NACA), which produced the legendary P-51 Mustang fighter in 1941. Wright Field personnel also tested a wide range of experimental components and systems: an automatic landing system in 1937, aircraft-mounted 75mm cannon in 1939, and rocket-assisted takeoff in 1941. During World War II, they were instrumental in the early development of the XP-59, America's first jet airplane.

Small planes designed expressly for private ownership began to appear in the mid-1920s. They were, overwhelmingly, the products of small companies drawn to the Midwest by the same combination of weather and topography that had attracted the barnstormers. Wichita, where an oil boom created investment capital and a pool of wealthy buyers, was the acknowledged center of the new small-plane industry. Lloyd Stearman, Clyde Cessna, and Walter Beech formed the Travel Air Manufacturing Company there in the mid-1920s. All three men had, by the early 1930s, gone their separate ways and founded aircraft companies under their own names—companies that prospered as the effects of the Depression eased.

Small-plane design and manufacturing was not, however, confined to Wichita or to small entrepreneurial firms. Curtiss-Robbins, a branch of the enormous Curtiss-Wright corporation, turned out its popular entry-level Robin monoplane in St. Louis. Detroit's Stinson Aircraft, which had merged with the E.L. Cord Corporation in 1929, began in 1933 to produce the luxurious six-seat Reliant, whose leather-

and-walnut interior matched the luxury of Cord's automobiles. Aeronautical Corporation of America, founded in Cincinnati and later headquartered in Middletown, Ohio, gave aviation its first approximation of the Ford Model T in its 1929 Aeronca C-2. Simple, robust, and cheap, the C-2 was the first small airplane mass-produced for sale to "ordinary" Americans. It anticipated, both in design and purpose, the true Model T of the air: William Piper's J-3 Cub of 1938.

The end of World War II also marked the end of military flight test operations at Wright Field. By the time it achieved independence from the Army in 1947, the U.S. Air Force had already shifted flight testing to Muroc Field—later Edwards Air Force Base—in California. Cutting-edge flight research continued in the Midwest, however, at the Lewis Research Center that NACA had established on the outskirts of Cleveland during the war. Research at Lewis focused not on whole aircraft but on components: de-icing mechanisms, high-energy fuels, engine troubleshooting procedures, and advanced propulsion systems including ramjets. Neil Armstrong, whose "one small step" onto the Moon in 1969 made him world-famous, spent time at Lewis in the mid-1950s before transferring to Edwards.

Many small-plane makers disappeared after World War II, but the industry as a whole prospered. Beechcraft and Cessna produced improved versions of their popular prewar machines and introduced new ones with longer ranges, more powerful engines, and tricycle-style landing gear that improved stability. Cessna's two- and four-seat airplanes, along with the new Cubs emerging from the Piper factory in Lock Haven, Pennsylvania, provided the impetus for a postwar boom in private flying that lasted through the 1950s. Beechcraft tapped the same market with its V-tailed Bonanza and continued to dominate the market for luxurious twin-engine planes. In the early 1960s, however, a serious competitor emerged in Wichita: William Lear, whose six-passenger Learjet ushered in the age of the private jet transport. Airport congestion, rising fuel costs, and costly lawsuits generated by crashes posed a more serious, long-term threat. They sent small-plane manufacturing into a decline so long and steep that, by the mid-1980s, development of new single-engine models and production of old ones had virtually ceased.

Midwestern aviation remains, however, as strong and diverse an enterprise in the first years of the twenty-first century as it was in the first years of the twentieth. Lewis Research Center—now renamed for Ohio-born astronaut John Glenn and run by NACA's successor agency, the National Aeronautics and Space Administration—is still in operation. The economic boom of the 1990s, combined with a 1994 law limiting manufacturers' liability in crashes, has revived the small-plane industry. Most impressive perhaps, the Experimental Aircraft Association of Oshkosh, Wisconsin, remains the country's leading promoter of recreational and sport flying. Over ten thousand planes and more than three-quarters of a million people came together for its fifty-first annual AirVenture summer gathering in August 2003. Huffman Prairie has long since disappeared beneath the asphalt of Wright-Patterson Air Force Base, but its spirit is alive and well.

Sources and Further Reading: Roger Bilstein, *The Enterprise of Flight* (2001); Roger Bilstein, *Flight in America: From the Wrights to the Astronauts*, 3rd ed. (2001); Tom Crouch, *The Bishop's Boys* (1989); R.E.G. Davies, *Airlines of the United States since 1914* (1982); Frank J. Rowe and H. Craig Miner, *Borne on the South Wind: A Century of Aviation in Kansas* (1994).

A. Bowdoin Van Riper
Southern Polytechnic State University, Georgia

Bridge Technology

The Midwest is defined by its bodies of water—the Ohio, Mississippi, and Missouri Rivers and the Great Lakes. These bodies of water helped determine pathways of commerce through the region. However, for all of the commercial advantages of riverside and lakeside locations, water also presented obstacles to transportation, especially as water-based transportation was supplanted first by railroads, then by trucks.

The first bridges in the Midwest were made from wood. Bridges supported by wooden trusses could support spans of one hundred to two hundred feet, and they could cross only modest waterways, leaving the major rivers of the Midwest traversable only by boat until after the Civil War. Nevertheless, in their heyday of 1830 to 1870, thousands of covered bridges facilitated modest transportation, even early railway crossings. Although covered bridges are still found all over the country, the greatest number (approximately two thousand) were originally built in Ohio, and a significant proportion of the existing bridges are in the Midwest. Covered bridges continue to be a tourist attraction, and many are still in use.

The era of covered bridges came to an end with the development of inexpensive structural steel in the 1860s. Railroad traffic demanded longer, sturdier, fireproof bridges, and the development of structural steel

View of the Turnpike Bridge in Lawrence, Kansas, 1867. Kansas State Historical Society, Gardner Collection, D00000024.

fit these requirements. Building bridges from steel required more than simply adapting old designs to use a new material, and new designs and construction techniques were developed to take advantage of steel's unique properties. One of the most important developments in bridge design was the cable suspension bridge. The first of these to be built in the Midwest was Charles Ellet's 1,010-foot crossing of the Ohio River at Wheeling in 1849. In 1867, John A. Roebling surpassed Ellet's effort with the Cincinnati Bridge, begun in 1856. Roebling's bridge was also the longest suspension bridge in the world at the time, spanning 1,057 feet. This opened the era of great bridges in America, built to accommodate the growth of railroads and increasing transcontinental traffic.

The Transcontinental Railroad, opened in 1869, accelerated bridge building, especially in the Midwest, with two of America's most important commercial centers in Chicago and St. Louis. Chicago's lakeside location did not lend itself to major bridge projects, but St. Louis's position on the Mississippi provided a site for one of the most important bridges of the nineteenth century—James Eads's St. Louis Bridge. Eads's interest in the bridge stemmed from his concerns that a bridge across the Mississippi might impede ship traffic, despite the boost it might provide to rail transport. Eads's design for the bridge reflected this concern, and his cantilever design allowed for an open span of five

hundred feet for river traffic. The St. Louis Bridge, which opened in 1874 and was soon renamed the Eads Bridge, represents the transition from east to west, as does the St. Louis Arch in a more modern era. Eads's spanning of the Mississippi for the first time remains a symbol of the importance of the Midwest in the commercial development of the nation.

In the twentieth century, the most important aesthetic development in bridge design was the cable-stayed bridge. Originating in Germany in the late 1950s, cable-stayed bridges are very light structures that span considerable distance and many have clear spans well over a thousand feet. The first cable-stayed bridge in the United States was the Sitka Harbor Bridge in Alaska in the 1970s, but several cable-stayed bridges were subsequently built in the Midwest, including the East Huntington Bridge across the Ohio in 1985, and a year later the Quincy Bridge across the Mississippi.

Sources and Further Reading: David P. Billington, *The Tower and the Bridge* (1985); James Marston Fitch, *American Building: The Historical Forces That Shaped It*, 2nd ed. (1973); Eda Kranakis, *Constructing a Bridge* (1997); Brian J. McKee, *Historic American Covered Bridges* (1997); Henry Petroski, *Engineers of Dreams* (1996).

Ann Johnson
University of South Carolina

Railroad Technology

Railroads built the Midwest, but the Midwest did its part to build railroads as well. Many innovations developed in the region made rail transportation of passengers and freight safe, fast, and economical throughout North America. Some of the largest locomotive and car builders were located there, along with railroad and engineering companies that pioneered railroad technologies.

George M. Pullman's Pioneer sleeping car of 1865 cost five times the amount of a typical passenger car of its day, but it established a new standard in luxurious travel. First used in Abraham Lincoln's funeral train, the Pioneer entered regular service shortly thereafter. By 1910, Pullman cars built at the company's Chicago plant featured electric lights, steam heat, enclosed vestibules between cars, and all-steel construction. Pullman also built the nation's first streamlined train, Union Pacific's M-10000, in 1934 to usher in a new era of speed and style. Besides Pullman (called Pullman-Standard after 1947), other major passenger and freight car builders included Barney and Smith in Dayton, Ohio, American Car and Foundry in St. Charles, Missouri, St. Louis Car in St. Louis, Ortner Freight Car in Cincinnati, and Thrall in Chicago. Individual railroads also contributed innovations. The Chicago, Burlington and Quincy's shop in Aurora, Illinois, rebuilt a streamlined coach into the first dome car with a glass-enclosed upper floor for panoramic viewing in 1945, and the Illinois Central put the first dining car with an all-electric galley into service between Chicago and St. Louis in 1949.

Important freight car developments came from the Midwest, as well. Two types of cars enabled the rise of stockyards and packinghouses throughout much of the region after 1865. Stock cars with slatted sides carried millions of live animals to huge stockyards in Chicago, Kansas City (Missouri), Cincinnati, and Omaha. Though they remained much the same for decades, there were innovations, such as Northern Pacific's double-decked Pig Palace in 1958. Experimental refrigerator cars appeared as early as 1842, but the first reasonably successful shipments of chilled food occurred in 1866, when Parker Earle, a fruit grower in Cobden, Illinois, shipped strawberries to Chicago in dual-compartment, insulated chests packed with berries in one side and ice in the other, which were loaded into boxcars. The next year, J. B. Sutherland of Detroit patented a true refrigerator car, and the Michigan Car Company began producing an improved design in 1868. It used three tons of ice in bunkers at the car's ends, replenished periodically on long trips, to chill 120 beef quarters. By 1900, several companies operated over sixty-eight thousand refrigerator cars. Mechanical refrigeration systems began to replace ice after 1945, and many modern cars have such good insulation that only precooling the car and cargo before the trip is necessary.

Piggyback, or intermodal, service originated before 1900 with the occasional carriage of farmers' wagons on Long Island, New York, but the Chicago, North Shore and Milwaukee introduced scheduled ferry truck service in 1926, and the Chicago Great Western began Chicago–Minneapolis service a decade later. Trailer Train, headquartered in Chicago, has furnished most of the flat cars for modern intermodal service since its founding in 1955.

The railroad roller bearing, required on cars and locomotives built after 1963, was developed primarily by Timken of Canton, Ohio. Timken's AP tapered roller bearing, introduced in 1954, was the first roller bearing widely used on freight car axles, and it offered substantial safety and cost improvements over the older journal bearings.

The Midwest has long been home to locomotive builders. At least five builders manufactured steam locomotives in Cincinnati before 1868. The Lima Locomotive Works produced approximately seventy-five hundred steam and diesel locomotives in Lima, Ohio, between 1878 and 1951; Lima was also responsible for developing the modern, Super-Power steam locomotive in 1927. New York Central had the Case School of Science in Cleveland design the first cowling to streamline a steam locomotive in 1934. The Electro-Motive Division (EMD) of General Motors in La Grange, Illinois, did not invent the diesel-electric locomotive, but EMD developed the first mass-produced designs that largely replaced steam power by 1955. By 2004, EMD had produced over fifty-eight thousand locomotives. Fairbanks-Morse of Beloit, Wisconsin, built over fifteen hundred diesel locomotives between 1944 and 1963, including the first single-engine, high-horsepower locomotives in 1953.

Another midwestern innovation improved train control. The first installation of centralized traffic control (CTC) began operation in 1927, controlling a forty-mile section of the Toledo and Ohio Central between Toledo and Berwick, Ohio. Now widely used, CTC allows the dispatcher to control all switches, signals, and train movements directly from a single console.

Sources and Further Reading: Mary Brignano and Hax McCullough, *The Search for Safety* (1981); Eric Hirsimaki, *Lima: The History* (1986); Franklin Reck, *On Time: The History of the Electro-Motive Division of General Motors Corporation* (1948); John H. White, Jr., *The American Railroad Freight Car* (1993); John H. White, Jr., *The American Railroad Passenger Car* (1978); John H. White, Jr., *The Great Yellow Fleet* (1986).

J. Lawrence Lee
National Park Service, Washington, D.C.

Shipping and Packaging Technologies

The movement of raw materials and goods has required continual revision of packaging and shipping methods. The development of technologies for packaging and shipping raw materials and finished goods has centered on three major areas: the amount of materials moved, devices to move and transport the materials, and the transfer of information about the materials being delivered. Integration of these into new technologies has provided significant competitive advantages for midwestern products.

Until the mid-nineteenth century, human and animal power moved most goods, and this limited amounts and distances. Small finished goods could travel great distances, but raw materials and agricultural commodities remained essentially local industries, and production and consumption took place in the same location. Movement by water, when possible, allowed greater amounts of cargo to move greater distances. Nevertheless, the loading and unloading of sizable amounts remained difficult, and coordination and distribution were often primitive.

The introduction of steam-powered machinery and the telegraph presented an opportunity for increased specialization in the transportation and movement of goods. Railroads permitted the movement of materials deep into the continental hinterlands, and ships could take cargoes around the globe. Sophisticated telegraph and telephone systems led to schedules and large-scale distribution networks. The Chicago mail-order firms of Montgomery Ward and Sears, Roebuck, and Company used all of these connections through their catalogs to reach consumers in the Midwest and Plains states.

Goods were increasingly packed in standard containers, wooden or metal, and freezer cars extended the range for meat and other perishable goods. The meatpacking empire of Philip Armour in Chicago sent frozen meat to the East and West Coasts and ended the great cattle drives from Texas. By the mid-nineteenth century, the industrialized world was utilizing cranes, and the skyscrapers of the prairie, grain elevators, began to appear. The Panama and Suez Canals as well as the locks at Sault Ste. Marie, Michigan, facilitated the movement of large shipments of raw materials with greater ease. Andrew Carnegie and John D. Rockefeller mined Minnesota iron ore, used mechanical equipment for handling, tied into rail networks, and produced the nation's steel.

Once in place, railway, roadway, and water networks began to specialize in particular areas, such as the iron ore transportation system on the Great Lakes that used single-purpose vessels and enormous Hulett ore-unloading systems to link the Minnesota iron mines with lower lakes railroads and steel mills. Standard packing and labeling systems made national brands possible. Bureaucracies were established to trace the movement of finished goods across the rail, sea, and (later) air and highway systems, further integrating distribution networks. The introduction of standardized shipping containers for moving finished goods via ship and trucks allowed greater connectivity for global shipments from the Midwest. This new network utilized the St. Lawrence Seaway's access to the major ports on the Great Lakes to provide close access to international markets. The use of computers, satellites, and global positioning systems has now made the shipping of midwestern goods a nearly seamless web of movement and information around the world.

Sources and Further Reading: William Cronon, *Nature's Metropolis: Chicago and the Great West* (1991); Richard Wright, *Freshwater Whales: A History of the American Shipbuilding Company and Its Predecessors* (1969).

Matthew L. Daley
Bowling Green State University, Ohio

Space Exploration Technology

Without the contributions of the Midwest, the United States would not have been able to send people or machines into space. From the opening of the Space Age in 1957, the highly skilled labor force, scientific and research capabilities, and precision manufacturing resources of the nation's industrial heartland were mobilized to land a man on the Moon and send robotic explorers throughout the solar system. This should not be a surprise, since the Midwest gave birth to the Age of Flight, and the mobilization of industry during World War II depended on the Midwest, where the production of planes, such as B-24 bombers in Ford Motor Company's Willow Run factory, helped win that war.

In 1941 the National Advisory Committee for Aeronautics established a research laboratory in Cleveland to develop innovations in aircraft engine technology. George Lewis, for whom the laboratory was later named, remarked that this was appropriate, because it was only an hour's flight from where the Wright brothers had built the first airplane, in Dayton, Ohio. By the end of World War II, the Lewis Laboratory (renamed in 1999 for John Glenn) was developing rocket engines for guided missiles and high-energy liquid propellants. When President Eisenhower announced that the United States would send astronauts into Earth orbit, the Lewis Laboratory began applying its knowledge of aviation to space

The Space Power Facility, used for the study of space propulsion, at the NASA Lewis Research Center (now Glenn Research Center), Ohio. Photo by Paul Riedel/Martin Brown, NASA GRIN Image Database, GPN-2000-001462.

flight. The Laboratory designed the instrumentation for the Mercury capsule and retrorockets to allow the spacecraft to reenter the atmosphere. The automatic control systems, to stabilize the Mercury capsule after it separated from its booster rocket, were designed at Lewis, with the help of the Minneapolis-Honeywell Regulator Company. Each of the seven Mercury astronauts came to Cleveland for training to practice stabilizing a tumbling spacecraft. And astronauts trained at Wright-Patterson Air Force Base, near Dayton, in a simulated zero-gravity chamber produced by the Guardite Company of Chicago.

Meanwhile, the Mercury spacecraft itself was being built in St. Louis by the McDonnell Aircraft Corporation, which later also built the ten Gemini spacecraft used for missions with pairs of astronauts. Every corner of the Midwest was involved in manned space flight throughout the 1960s. In 1934 Russ Colley, an engineer at the B.F. Goodrich Company in Akron, Ohio, developed the first pressure suit, which allowed pilots to fly above thirty thousand feet. In 1961, he helped design the Mercury spacesuit to protect the astronauts. The Cincinnati Testing and Research Laboratory built the heat shield for the Mercury capsule to protect the crew during reentry. And Motorola, Incor-

porated, in Franklin Park, Illinois, provided components for the onboard communications system that allowed contact between the astronauts and Mission Control.

At the same time that industry was focused on solving the technical problems of manned space flight, the Lewis Research Center, now part of the National Aeronautics and Space Administration (NASA), was preparing the technology to take explorers throughout the solar system. Scientists at NASA Lewis had been studying how to make use of advanced propulsion techniques, such as liquid hydrogen and nuclear energy, to launch spacecraft for long-distance flight. The Apollo astronauts would not have reached the Moon were it not for the liquid hydrogen Centaur rocket engines developed at Lewis, which were used for the two upper stages of the massive Saturn V Moon rocket.

The rocket engine and propulsion research conducted at Lewis was also the foundation for the unmanned spacecraft the United States would launch to explore nearby planets. Before astronauts could venture to the Moon, robotic explorers had to be sent to make sure it would be safe and to scout potential landing sites. Agena upper-stage rockets, managed at NASA Lewis, sent the unmanned Ranger, Surveyor, and Lunar Orbiter spacecraft to the Moon to prepare the way for astronauts. In 1964, a Mariner spacecraft was launched to Mars aboard an Atlas rocket, using an Agena upper stage, and in 1967, an Atlas-Agena sent Mariner V on its way to Venus. The solar system was open for exploration.

From the earliest history of the space program, the universities and educational institutions of the Midwest have contributed scientific expertise and conducted studies for the new aerospace endeavor. In 2003, several Midwest research and educational institutions—the Universities of Wisconsin–Madison, Minnesota, and Michigan, Case Western Reserve University, and Battelle Memorial Institute— each received grants of over $5 million from NASA for space-related studies. They are providing the talented people who will create the space programs of the future.

The Midwest has continued to contribute to manned space flight. Each Space Shuttle orbiter lands back on Earth on the tires, brake assemblies, wheels, and landing gear produced by the Goodrich Corporation's plants in Cleveland and Troy, Ohio. The 3M Company in St. Paul produces the fibers for the critical thermal protection tiles, which protect the orbiter on its fiery reentry through the Earth's atmosphere. McDonnell Douglas (now part of the Boeing Company) in St. Louis produces the orbital engines that allow the Space Shuttle crews to maneuver the spaceplane in orbit, and Honeywell South Bend (formerly the Bendix Corporation) in Indiana contributes components to distribute electrical power aboard the orbiters. Today's most exciting planetary exploration programs also benefit from the contributions of the Midwest. In its 245-thousand-square-foot research facility in Canton, Ohio, the Timken Company designed the precision ball bearings that have allowed the Mars Exploration Rovers, *Spirit* and *Opportunity*, to wander about the surface of Mars since the beginning of 2004, rewriting the textbooks on planetary science.

Sources and Further Reading: Roger E. Bilstein, *Stages to Saturn* (1980); Joan Lisa Bromberg, *NASA and the Space Industry* (1999); Virginia P. Dawson, *Engines and Innovation* (1991); Lloyd Swenson, Jr., James Grimwood, and Charles Alexander, *This New Ocean* (1966).

Marsha Freeman
21st Century Science & Technology,
Washington, D.C.

Creating for Progress

It was not by chance that ceramic and glass manufacturing flowered a hundred years ago in the Midwest. The soil was ideal, it was expensive to ship heavy pottery and more practical to make it nearby, and the first university professorship for ceramics in America was established in the Midwest. Convenience, need, and natural resources aren't enough to assure beauty, but the workmanship also managed to do just that at Rookwood, Astoria, and elsewhere. Research centers such as Battelle and Fermi produced concepts that now are communicated by computers and other advances of the electronic age. Working in university or public research laboratories, the first six Nobel prize-winners in physics were midwesterners, and other scientists from the region have received international recognition. Someone had to select, list, and record all the work done; and in one narrow area, Chemical Abstracts has done just that. Nanotechnology may be the major advance of the time, and Midwest firms research uses for the extremely small molecules of this technology. Women of the Midwest have been active contributors in the creation of objects for utility, for science, and for beauty.

Ceramics

Shaping and heating clay for function and beauty did not originate in the Midwest, but the move from bricks to ceramics has been led by the region. The fact that the Midwest contained large deposits of exceptional indigenous clay facilitated the process. Midwestern inventions, education, research, and natural resources have had great impact on ceramics in the United States.

Prior to the Philadelphia Centennial Exhibition of 1876, American commercial potteries, many located in the Midwest, produced utilitarian tableware using European methods. The Exhibition inspired innovations in art pottery and ceramics designed to be artistic. Fascinated by French Haviland pottery decorated under the surface glaze, Cincinnati's Mary Louise McLaughlin successfully developed an underglaze painting technique in 1878, which revolutionized the worldwide pottery industry. Rookwood Pottery in Cincinnati, founded in 1880 by Maria Longworth Nichols, received numerous national and international awards, and although the pottery ceased production in 1960, Rookwood is still considered the finest American art pottery. The Rookwood Approach, the development of ceramic advances using modern industrial techniques, was adapted by many other U.S. art potteries. An example was the invention of an airbrush technique in 1883 by decorator Laura Fry. This first use of the spray gun to create softly blended underglaze colors soon became an almost universal application.

Achievements were made possible through scientific knowledge and education. Karl Langenbeck, hired by Rookwood in 1884, became the first glaze chemist in the nation. Education and scientific advances enhanced the development of cooperative efforts. The Ohio State University (OSU) founded the first school of ceramics in the country, followed by other midwestern universities like Iowa State, Illinois, and North Dakota.

Midwest ceramists have used scientific ingenuity to develop ceramic materials in hundreds of different industries. Their contributions have had a tremendous impact in areas such as electronics, medical devices, and space technology. The transformation of clay into objects of utility and beauty is memorialized in local ceramic and glass museums found in most of the midwestern states. Several of these museums reflect local history and the impact of leading associations; the American Ceramic Society museum in Westerville, Ohio, for instance, is located near the place of origin (OSU) of the first course in ceramics offered in any American university. That museum displays industrial products made of clay, the most famous of which are heat-resistant devices such as the tiles that protect spacecraft. Plastics and glass may be added to clay, as is done by the Akron Porcelain and Plastics Company, which serves the electrical and foundry industries.

Sources and Further Reading: Paul Evans, *Art Pottery of the United States,* 2nd. ed. (1987); Marion John Nelson, *Art Pottery of the Midwest* (1988); Nancy E. Owen, *Rookwood and the Industry of Art* (2001).

Darlene Hurst Dommel
Golden Valley, Minnesota

Chemical Abstracts Service

When *Chemical Abstracts* (CA) began, the yearly issues contained about twelve thousand abstracts of scientific papers, patents, and books. By 2002, Chemical Abstracts Service (CAS) covered more than 750 thousand abstracts annually, bringing the total over the years to more than twenty-one million documents coming from 150 nations, published in fifty-six languages. Today, CAS is the only comprehensive digital information service for access to the literature of chemical science and technology.

CAS moved to The Ohio State University (OSU) campus in Columbus in 1909, where it remained until 1965, when it moved to its own building on sixty acres bordering OSU to the north. Two-thirds of its thirteen hundred international staff members are professional scientists who analyze, summarize, and index in English all newly published results of research and development from around the world.

CAS experimented in the late 1950s with new electronic and graphic communication methods, leading in 1961 to the world's first computer-produced periodical, *Chemical Titles.* Between 1965 and 1975, CAS built an automated information-handling system, which became the world's first efficient and economical model of an electronic publishing system.

In addition to abstracts of articles, CAS identifies unambiguously the molecular structures of *every* new compound. This Registry, as of September 2002, includes 20.5 million chemical substances and 22.5 million nucleotide and protein sequence records. As of 2002, CASREACT, its chemical reaction database, contains over 6.3 million single and multiple reactions with CAS Registry Numbers, reactants, solvents, yields, catalysts, and products, as well as bibliographic and textual information.

In 1965 CAS established cooperative agreements with the United Kingdom, the Federal Republic of (West) Germany, France, and Japan for electronic input and output search services, resulting in the international online searching of CAS computer tapes. By 1983, West Germany's FIZ Karlsruhe and CAS established a global online computer database network, thus creating STN International, now covering more than two hundred databases of scientific and technical information. In 1986, Japan established a fully operational STN node. All STN files can be searched from any computer with a Web browser. CAS's educational efforts for academicians and service for the world of chemistry and science at large began small, but now it occupies its own substantial campus from which it serves the world.

Sources and Further Reading: American Chemical Society, *CAS Today* (1980); American Chemical Society, "Celebrating 125 Years of the American Chemical Society," *Chemical and Engineering News* (Mar. 26, 2001); Charles Albert Browne and Mary Elvira Weeks, *A History of the American Chemical Society* (1952).

Dale Baker
Chemical Abstracts Service, Columbus, Ohio

Computer Technology

Academic institutions, national laboratories, and industries located in the Midwest have made substantial contributions to the development of computer technologies, in particular to the fields of computer engineering, networking, and software development.

Beginning shortly after World War II, several midwestern universities initiated programs dedicated to the development of large-scale electronic digital computers. Between 1949 and 1952 engineers and scientists at the University of Illinois built two general-purpose computers modeled after the computer in Princeton's Institute for Advanced Study. The ORD-VAC (Ordnance Variable Automatic Computer), built for the Army's Ballistic Research Laboratory, and the ILLIAC I (Illinois Automatic Computer), designed for use in scientific and engineering research, incorporated university-designed circuits that set new standards for speed and reliability. When completed, the five-ton ILLIAC I was one of the most powerful computers in existence—and it had only 5K of memory. These two early machines established the University of Illinois as world leader in computer system development.

In 1965, this tradition continued as University of Illinois researchers designed the ILLIAC IV, the world's first large-scale-array computer, representing a new development in parallel-processing architecture. Computers were used in the design of ILLIAC IV's intricate circuit cards, marking the first time this had been accomplished by someplace other than IBM. Over its life span, the ILLIAC IV was applied to complex problems in meteorology, cryptanalysis, economics, and the simulation of fluid flows.

Computer scientists at the University of Illinois

❖ Robert Noyce, Inventor (1927–1990)

Robert Noyce was born in 1927 and grew up in Grinnell, Iowa, a small town in the middle of the state's Midland Corn Belt. Noyce began his study of transistors at Grinnell College, and he obtained a Ph.D. in physics from Massachusetts Institute of Technology. The transistor was a new device—only invented in 1948 by Wisconsin's John Bardeen and Walter Brattain—which like the vacuum tube (invented by Iowan Lee De Forest) isolated and amplified an electric signal. But it was smaller, cheaper, and more efficient. Noyce had an explanation for the midwestern dominance in engineering: "In a small town, when something breaks down, you don't wait around for a new part, because it's not coming. You make it yourself."

After working for Philco and for Shockley Labs, he and seven other former Shockley engineers founded Fairchild Semiconductor. He was determined to create a new business culture, and he realized that human capital was the key and that with the right people he could obtain financial capital. The year was 1957, Sputnik had just been launched, and the current clumsy vacuum tubes were not sufficient for the American space and missile programs. With this national security impetus, miniaturization became a major goal. Hewlett Packard and IBM were developing electronic computers, but the transistors used had to be wired by hand, and this raised costs and increased errors.

Noyce offered a solution. While at Fairchild Semiconductor, he had co-invented with Missourian Jack Kilby the integrated circuit—a silicon chip with numerous transistors etched onto it—that forms the basis for modern microprocessors. Realizing the significance of this development, Fairchild Camera bought out Fairchild Semiconductor for $250 thousand in stock (in 1959 dollars, or more than $1.5 million today). When NASA chose Noyce's integrated circuit for its Gemini program computers, Fairchild Semiconductor expanded with sales of over $100 million.

Fairchild Semiconductor, under Noyce's leadership, developed the Silicon Valley business culture of a casual but creative atmosphere. Perhaps reflecting the midwestern informality he had learned at Grinnell, the company offered no reserved parking, no dress code, and no offices per se, only cubicles. And while he provided overall guidelines, Noyce gave employees wide latitude to explore and innovate what and how they wished. Eastern capital could still direct major investments, and profits continued to be sought.for employees in established fields, but the company awarded stock options for employees who developed big breakthroughs.

Corporate changes continued, and in 1968, Shockley and Fairchild alums Bob Noyce and Gordon Moore cofounded Intel Corporation. Capitalizing on the less glamorous field of memory chips, Noyce oversaw Ted Hoff's development of the microprocessor, which offered the functionality of a computer on a small chip. For Noyce, Hoff's innovation confirmed once again the creative value of the business culture he had invented.

Noyce was awarded the National Medal of Science in 1980, inducted into the National Inventors Hall of Fame in 1983, and honored by the U.S. Business Hall of Fame in 1989. Iowa roots were deep, and he served on Grinnell College's board of trustees until his death in 1990.

Sathyan Sundaram
The Ohio State University

Source and Further Reading: Tom Wolfe, "The Tinkerings of Robert Noyce," *Esquire* 100 (Dec. 1983).

were also integral to the development of the software and hardware that powered the ARPANET, the direct precursor to today's Internet, and the University was one of the original fifteen nodes connected to the network in 1971.

The University of Michigan also had a strong program in computer development and built two experimental machines in the early 1950s, the MIDAC (Michigan Digital Automatic Computer) and the MIDSAC (Michigan Digital Special Automatic Computer). In addition, by the mid-1950s, University of Michigan researchers had produced an early standardized language called MAD (Michigan Algorithm Decoder) that was used extensively to train computer scientists in the design of complex software programs. Over the next decade, University of Michigan computer scientists led the development of time-sharing systems, which enabled many people to access a computer simultaneously and allowed for its more efficient use.

Argonne National Laboratory (ANL), located fifteen miles outside of Chicago, made significant contributions to the development of computer technologies. ANL built some of the first general-purpose digital computers in the early 1950s, but its work in applying computer technology to image processing, data collection and analysis, and developing mathematical software has been more significant. Computer experts at this Atomic Energy Commission laboratory applied computers in novel ways to help scientists conduct experiments, analyze data, and create increasingly sophisticated computational models of physical phenomena related to basic research in the nuclear sciences.

In the 1960s, ANL researchers introduced the CHLOE system, one of the first computer-controlled machines designed to digitize photographic information and perform calculations on the data obtained. Applied primarily to the analysis of photographic images produced by the passage of charged subatomic particles through spark chambers, CHLOE was so versatile that it was also used to analyze chromosome pairs for biologists studying genetic mutations.

Computers at Argonne were also linked to a Van de Graaff particle accelerator and used to help scientists acquire and process data in real time, thereby allowing them to adjust experiments while they were being performed.

Finally, computer scientists within the Applied Mathematics Division of ANL were at the forefront of efforts to produce robust, reliable mathematical software that was also portable—meaning the code could be run on any computer system. Portability of mathematical routines allowed scientists to share their work easily, even if it was produced on otherwise incompatible computer systems.

The integration of computers into scientific experiments and the development of quality mathematical software were key steps in the creation of computational science, a new methodological approach to scientific research in which entire experiments are conducted by computer. In each of these examples, ANL garnered international recognition as a pioneer in the application of computers to scientific research.

Beyond academe and the national laboratory system, the Midwest has been home to several companies whose products have changed the face of computing. Engineering Research Associates, Inc. (ERA), incorporated in 1946 in St. Paul, was one of the first companies to build electronic digital computers for the commercial market. ERA was also the first computer manufacturer to offer magnetic core memory in its machines, a fast random-access memory unit that increased the speed at which computers could retrieve information. Remington Rand's purchase of ERA in 1952 motivated several of its founding members to form Control Data Corporation (CDC), and throughout the 1960s and 1970s, CDC produced some of the world's fastest supercomputers. Their flagship product, the CDC 6600, introduced in 1965, is generally considered the first commercially available supercomputer, and it routinely outperformed its competitors by a factor of ten. Designed by Seymour Cray, a gifted engineering graduate from the University of Minnesota, the CDC line of supercomputers became the standard for high-energy physicists at universities and national labs such as Los Alamos, where they were used to design atomic weapons.

In 1972 Seymour Cray left CDC to form his own company, Cray Research, where he continued his cutting-edge design of supercomputers. With headquarters in Minneapolis and research and development facilities in Chippewa Falls, Wisconsin, Cray introduced the Cray 1 in 1976. Installed at Los Alamos, it was the fastest supercomputer in the world and included many innovations that have since become standard, such as a design that made the physical connections between the integrated circuits as short as possible through the use of refrigerants like Freon that cooled the machine. In the ensuing years, Cray Research has continued to push the supercomputing field by offering successively more powerful units, including the first multiprocessor supercomputer in 1982 and the first massively parallel processing system in 1993.

The Midwest also has served as an important player in the development of popular software, often noncommercial and university-based. The core applications that have opened the Internet to nontechnical users came from the University of Illinois's National Center for Supercomputing Applications (NCSA) in the form of HTTP daemon Apache and graphical browser Mosaic, the second of which produced a commercial venture, Netscape. When Microsoft entered this market with Internet Explorer, it relied heavily upon Mosaic code. The leading text browser, Lynx, also emanates from the Midwest, developed at the University of Kansas.

The popular e-mail client Eudora began its life as UIUCMail. Even before Berners-Lee's hypertext initiative, the Midwest was a leader in making electronic information hosted on remote servers easier to use. The University of Minnesota developed the gopher protocol—named after the school's mascot—which allowed content creators to provide text and downloadable files in a standardized, visual format with a simple, hierarchical navigation scheme. The Midwest has been home to two popular commercial image-editing applications: Photoshop, written for the Apple Macintosh operating system by Thomas Knoll in Ann Arbor, Michigan, and Jasc's Paint Shop Pro, which continues to reside in Eden Prairie, Minnesota. The leading data mining and statistics application SPSS saw much of its development at the University of Chicago.

In hardware, software, and networks, the Midwest has continued its role as a key innovator of information technology.

Sources and Further Reading: Janet Abbate, *Inventing the Internet* (1999); Paul E. Ceruzzi, *A History of Modern Computing* (1998); Herman H. Goldstine, *The Computer from Pascal to Von Neumann* (1972); Nicolas Metropolis, J. Howlett, and Gian-Carlo Rota, eds., *A History of Computing in the Twentieth Century* (1980); Charles J. Murray, *The Supermen* (1997); Arthur L. Norberg and Judy E. O'Neill,

Transforming Computer Technology (1996); James C. Worthy, *William C. Norris* (1987); Charles N. Yood, "Building Big Iron: Computers and the Rise of Computational Science in America's Atomic Labs," Ph.D. diss., The Pennsylvania State University (2004).

Charles N. Yood
The Pennsylvania State University

Sathyan Sundaram
The Ohio State University–Columbus

Merchandizing Technology

The Midwest, with its wide open spaces linked by foot, horses, canals, and railroads, has always been an area that required innovation, entrepreneurship, salesmanship, and original merchandizing. Sales often created empires of industry as well as focal points for community service.

The technology depended, of course, on what was available; it also reflected the ingenuity of the salesperson, for often the salesperson was also the inventor, and the inventor became the entrepreneur. John Deere did not just devise a new plow; he went into farmers' fields to demonstrate it. As electronic appliances proliferated, Richard Schulze opened what he called an "audio hobby" store in St. Paul in 1966, and when a tornado destroyed his primary store he declared a "grab and go" sale in the parking lot.

Management changes do often reflect imagination and can enhance sales, and the same Schulze discovered that his sales force was more successful, and more courteous, on a salary than when they were working for a commission on each sale. By 2002 his company, Best Buy, had become North America's largest consumer electronics retailer, with over eighteen hundred retail outlets. There are many such midwestern stories. Sometimes a change in management policy makes for a great advertisement, as was true of Henry Ford's widely promoted five-dollar, eight-hour day. The same Ford, however, got left behind when he was said to insist that the customer could have any color for his car so long as it was black.

Several legendary retail chains began in the Midwest. Charles Walgreen, whose Swedish family in the prior generation was called Olofsson, was a self-taught pharmacist in Chicago who increased sales by adding window displays and offering civic leaders free flights when airplane barnstorming was new. He proved he could sell a thick rich ice cream, full of butterfat, even in the coldest winter, from lunch counters installed in neighborhood drugstores. The company is still based in Illinois.

Owners of the fledgling company now called Sears,

Roebuck and Company of Illinois were creative as they sought to bypass the middleman. It was they who established the largest mail-order merchandizing service in the world. The customers in the most remote hamlets of the Midwest could order the most chic fashions, unique tools, even a new home, right from their kitchen table. The five Ball brothers came to Muncie, Indiana, and used the expired patent of John Mason to produce glass jars suitable for housewives to use in canning their garden vegetables. The Balls next developed their own patent to produce millions of glass jars automatically; they advertised widely and later spent much of their fortune endowing Ball State University as well as parks and statues in Muncie.

If merchandizing means to promote sales, to trade, and to display, then the innovations of George Brown qualify as good examples. In 1878, he felt that American consumers were ready for a change from black and genderless shoes to shoes with style and comfort. At the St. Louis Fair, he discovered the cartoon characters invented by Richard Outcault, Buster Brown and his dog Tige. The cartoon figures were adopted as the company logo, and little Buster Brown sold lots of shoes to little boys and girls—so many, in fact, that Brown's widow could endow the George Warren Brown School of Social Work at Washington University in St. Louis.

Not infrequently, the style and technique of merchandizing a product becomes possible because the product is a new invention. Earl Bakken repaired medical equipment in his garage in Minneapolis, near the center of new medical advances in heart pacing and electronic stimulation of the nervous system. When he was told of the need for user-friendly monitors, Bakken fashioned the world's first wearable, battery-powered, external cardiac monitor. Medtronic soon became a billion-dollar business and is still based in Minneapolis.

If there is any single group of products in which science, sales, and the Midwest have combined for the benefit of all, it is the pharmaceutical industry. Two American-born men of Welsh decent, the Upjohn brothers, settled near Kalamazoo, Michigan, in the 1830s. Patent medicines were popular then, and the Upjohns developed a pill-making machine to produce a standardized product that would dissolve in the stomach. At the time, Kalamazoo called itself the "windmill capital of the world" and was a major producer of buggies in 1887, but soon the Upjohn Company was the largest company in town. Members of the Upjohn family sought additional medical education and expanded their research, and eventually the company was bought by another pharmaceutical firm. Both Eli Lilly and Company (headquartered in Indianapolis) and Parke-Davis (Detroit) created new drugs for heart and brain diseases. Several Midwest companies cooperated in World War II to produce penicillin.

As with Graeter's ice cream in Cincinnati and Proctor and Gamble's white soap in the same town, there is no midwestern community in which some fledgling company with ideas and salesmanship has not begun, expanded, and merchandized its wares. The techniques and technology of sales have differed from word-of-mouth to press to electronics, but the stories are similar and the goals are familiar to all.

Sources and Further Reading: Russ Banham, *The Ford Century* (2002); Robert D. B. Carlisle, *A Century of Caring* (1987); David L. Cohn, *The Good Old Days* (1976); Kirk Jeffrey, *Machines in Our Hearts* (2001); Herman Kogan and Rick Kogan, *Pharmacist to the Nation* (1989).

George Paulson
The Ohio State University–Columbus

Nanotechnology

The original nanotechnology challenge was put forward by the great physicist, Richard P. Feynman, on December 29, 1959, at the annual meeting of the American Physical Society in a talk entitled "There's Plenty of Room at the Bottom." The term *nanotechnology* was originally applied to the fabrication of devices and machines on the scale of nanometers (a billionth of a meter). In most cases, they represent a top-down approach to manufacturing, that is, the structures are formed by large machines, which in turn produce smaller structures. A bottom-up approach involves assembling nanodevices from smaller building blocks, such as individual atoms or molecules, and putting them together in a precise and defined manner. Currently, biotechnology provides the most successful and practical applications of nanotechnology. Important progress also is being made in micro-electromechanical systems (MEMS), which combine the mechanical elements, sensors, actuators, and electronics through microfabrication technology. Nanomaterials such as coatings, composites, and nanoparticles are currently used in many areas, including in electronics.

Today, nanotechnology activities are present in the Midwest in academia, state technology initiatives, government laboratories, and industry. State technology initiatives typically support universities, existing technology-based companies and the relocation of existing nanotechnology companies and encourage creation of regional nanotechnology start-up companies. The work at most regional national laboratories stimulates activity in academia and industry. The new, na-

tionally praised Birck Nanotechnology Center at Purdue University is a classic midwestern shared resource facility. Existing technology and production industries often support in-house nanotechnology activities and fund external research; however, technology development is most often an internal company activity. Industrial nano-applications include nanomaterials, biological and chemical sensors, nanotubes, thin-layer technologies, coatings, fuel cells, electro-optical modulators, and motion controls.

Within ten years, commercially available fuel cells and solar cells as well as other functional nanomaterials will be not only better but also much cheaper than what is available now. The medical applications of nanotechnology—"smart drugs" with nanoparticles selectively dispersing the drugs where they are needed—may need a little more time because of FDA approval and clinical studies requirements. The use of functional nanoparticles in diagnostics and life sciences is already a common practice within the genomics field. It is expected that true nanomachines, produced cheaply and efficiently by nanomachines themselves or through spontaneous (though obviously staged) aggregation (self-assembly), will enter the mainstream of daily life.

Sources and Further Reading: http://nanodot.org/article.pl?sid=02/07/14/0759209; http://www.purdue.edu/Research/vpr/publications/docs/resrev/rr-Dec03Jan04.pdf.

Charlie Bender
The Plains, Ohio

Pollution Control

The Clean Water Act became federal law more than thirty years ago, revolutionizing the collection, treatment, and discharge of wastes into the receiving waters of the United States. The state of Midwest waters in the 1970s influenced public opinion across the whole country, thus playing an important role in the passage of the Clean Water Act. Ohio's Cuyahoga River showed up in flames on national television. "Lake Erie is dead" became a household remark. A hundred years earlier, Chicago suffered major outbreaks of frequently fatal waterborne illnesses as a direct result of dumping city wastes into Lake Michigan via the Chicago River. The nineteenth-century solution to this problem was to reverse the flow of the Chicago River and to construct a sanitary canal to carry the wastes away from Lake Michigan, dumping them instead into the Illinois River, merely moving the problem rather than resolving it.

The Detroit Water and Sewerage Department

(DWSD) treatment plant, providing only primary treatment, first went into service in 1940. In 1961, Governor John B. Swainson of Michigan requested that the Public Health Service of the U.S. Department of Health, Education, and Welfare undertake a detailed study and then report on the pollution of the Detroit River, its tributaries, and the Michigan waters of Lake Erie. Primary treatment allows raw sewage to settle out into a sludge, but secondary treatment by means of oxidation beds is required to remove most organic and toxic material. In 1965 the completed report concluded that the Detroit sewage treatment plant discharged major domestic sources of wastes into these waters. In June of that year a public hearing focused upon the results of the Public Health Service Report and the subsequent federal recommendation to upgrade the Detroit sewage treatment plant to full secondary treatment. According to Gladwin Hill,

> The City of Detroit, which daily pours 540 million gallons of partly treated sewage into Lake Erie's main tributary, expressed flat opposition to a Federal proposal to institute "secondary" treatment of the sort employed by upward of 50% of the nation's municipalities. The reasons given were the relevant "data" were lacking and that "nobody could tell" how much the additional processing would reduce the severe pollution in the Detroit River. . . .

Passage of the Clean Water Act, followed by enforcement of its regulations, was required to alter such historical, unsustainable national practices, which were designed to minimize the cost to communities by maximizing the flow of wastewater to the receiving waters. Not surprisingly, one of the first, largest, and longest-running enforcement actions under the Clean Water Act began in 1977, when the federal government sued the City of Detroit for failure to comply. While the Detroit sewage plant was being expanded at that time to provide full secondary treatment to over six hundred million gallons per day of wastewater, the plant simply did not have the treatment capacity in place on schedule—by July 1, 1977—to meet the requirements of the Act. In December 1978, the secondary treatment capacity for the treatment plant was only 150 million gallons per day; the remaining 450 million gallons of wastewater received only two-stage settling as primary treatment.

The process of bringing the DWSD treatment plant into full compliance with the Clean Water Act required precedent-setting scientific, technological, and administrative innovation. And because the plant incinerates sewage sludge on site, air pollution prevention was soon integrated into the technological challenge to comply with the Clean Air Act. Regulatory and judicial precedents also arose through this massive undertaking, as federal district judge John Feikens adjudicated all matters related to achieving and maintaining compliance by the City of Detroit with both Acts.

Today, the DWSD treatment plant complies fully with both the Clean Water Act and the Clean Air Act, resulting in massive pollution prevention downstream and downwind of this critical facility. Public health and aquatic and terrestrial ecosystems are protected, and Lake Erie's water quality continues to improve. To counteract Chicago's deliverance of wastes to the Illinois River for eventual discharge into the Gulf of Mexico, and to protect downstream users, appropriate treatment plants have been added to the Chicago system. Both of these major cities offer important examples of innovation and evolution to protect and ensure protection of both human and ecological health in the Midwest.

Water pollution has been presented as one example, but pollution—contamination of the environment by humans—is much broader. Industrial pollutants in the Midwest, a major manufacturing region, include thousands of chemicals as well as more generally recognized threats such as asbestos, mercury, and lead. Clean up and waste disposal is a major industry and includes policies for hazardous and medical wastes, radioactive material, land dumps, pesticides, and compost heaps. Waste is not limited to water and air, but with regard to the latter the disappearance of brown smog from over Chicago and Gary, Indiana was a notable success of the hast half of the twentieth century. Support and neighborhood groups often wage local battles over noise pollution, and even discuss measures to keep the night sky dark. Every Midwest state and most of its municipalities have developed laws, policies, and agencies dedicated to improving the environment.

Sources and Further Reading: Jonathan W. Bulkley, "The State of Michigan's General Storm Water Discharge Permit: An Innovative Approach Contributing to Watershed Planning and Management," in *Living Downstream in the Next Millennium* (2000); Gladwin Hill, "Detroit Opposes U.S. Sewage Plan," *New York Times* (June 18, 1965); Jon Naar, *Design for a Livable Planet* (1990).

Jonathan W. Bulkley
University of Michigan–Ann Arbor

The Pharmaceutical Industry

The roots of the modern Midwest pharmaceutical industry can be found in businesses established in the nineteenth century, some of which, like Eli Lilly and

Abbott, have retained their original names, while others, such as Parke-Davis and Upjohn have become part of larger global companies. These are companies that weathered the change from a traditional world of botanical products and animal extracts marketed with little, if any, research, to the modern world of potent synthetic medicines and recombinant proteins marketed after many years of research and development.

The Michigan cities of Detroit, Ann Arbor (Parke-Davis/Pfizer), and Kalamazoo (Upjohn/Pharmacia), Indianapolis (Eli Lilly), St. Louis (Monsanto), and Chicago (Searle, Baxter, and Abbott) are home to great companies that have been highly successful in developing new products in the twentieth century. In addition, two large Japanese companies, Fujisawa and Takeda, have established their U.S. headquarters in Chicago.

Midwest companies developed five of the top-selling medicines—Lipitor, Neurontin, Prozac, Zyprexa, and Celebrex; three other medicines—Gemzar, Reo-Pro, and Depo-Provera—are the leaders in their therapeutic category. Parke-Davis developed Lipitor and Neurontin. Lipitor, a medicine to lower cholesterol in the blood, is the world's number-one selling medicine, with annual sales now greater than $10 billion. Neurontin is used to treat epilepsy and certain forms of neuropathic pain. Eli Lilly has led the development of new medicines for the treatment of psychiatric disorders. Prozac was a major advance for the treatment of depression, as was Zyprexa for the treatment of schizophrenia. GD Searle developed Celebrex, the first in a new class of medicines for the treatment of arthritis.

Midwest companies have pioneered some critical pharmaceutical breakthroughs. Eli Lilly developed the first commercially available insulin in 1923, followed by the first available recombinant human insulin. Some medicines discovered many years ago remain mainstays of treatment. Dilantin, discovered by Parke-Davis in 1937, is still in wide use today for the treatment of epilepsy. Midwest companies discovered three powerful antibiotics. Parke-Davis discovered the first broad-spectrum antibiotic, chloromycetin, and Eli Lilly discovered vancomycin; they are still two of the most effective medicines for serious infections. Eli Lilly isolated the first cephalosporin antibiotic from a fungus taken from a compost heap sample and developed it into the first of a new class of antibiotics in use in every family practice. There was remarkable cooperation between several of these competitors to develop antibiotics during World War II. Other firsts include medicines to treat Alzheimer's Disease (Cognex from Parke-Davis) and hair loss (Rogaine from Upjohn) as well as the first antihistamine, Benadryl from Parke-Davis.

The large pharmaceutical companies in the Mid-

west are now complemented by a growing biotechnology industry, which was traditionally seen as predominantly a phenomenon of the Northeast or the West Coast. Michigan, currently ranked tenth in the nation for the number of biotech companies, is leading the Midwest with the creation of the Life Sciences Corridor Initiative, backed by a long-term financial commitment from the state. Following closely behind is the Chicago area, which is home to more than 130 biotech companies.

Sources and Further Reading: Robert D. B. Carlisle, *A Century of Caring: The Upjohn Story* (1987); James Madison, *Eli Lilly: A Life, 1885–1977* (1989).

David Canter
Ann Arbor, Michigan

Research Centers

Research centers are common in the Midwest. Some are affiliated with colleges and universities, such as the Swedish Immigration Research Center at Augustana College in Illinois or the National Primate Research Center at the University of Wisconsin, but many are independent. Dozens of research groups deal with health, the production of medications, or clinical trials. The midwestern characteristics of cooperative competition, philanthropy, and entrepreneurship have encouraged numerous research facilities linked with industry, pharmaceuticals, and state governments. The Midwest also has been a leading area for contract research, investigations undertaken on behalf of a client, for a price, to solve a specific problem.

One of the best known is Battelle Memorial Institute. The fortune amassed by John Battelle helped him establish a steel company in Columbus, and his son Gordon studied metallurgy and foresaw what research could accomplish in industry. General Electric Company had already established an industrial research laboratory in the early 1900s, but this and most of the industrial laboratories of the time performed only repetitive testing. Gordon Battelle died at age forty, before he realized his dream of an industrial research laboratory, but his will left the funds for Battelle Memorial Institute, which was established in 1929. The Columbus *Evening Dispatch* in 1930 predicted that, although Battelle had but fifty names on its payroll, its importance to the development of Columbus would surpass even the city's largest industries. By 2000, the Institute had grown to include over seventy-five hundred people in thirty countries, and during that year Battelle was named on sixty-five patents.

Initially the Institute concentrated on iron and steel

❖ **Selected Midwest Inventions and Improvements**

Midwesterners have been ingenious in solving problems and creative in developing products. Here is a list of some of their inventions and their improvements on earlier ones.

Invention	Inventor, Developer	Associated State
Airplane	Orville and Wilbur Wright	Ohio
Airplane radio-compass, Autopilot	William Lear	Missouri
Aluminum extraction	Charles Hall	Ohio
Audion radio tube	Lee De Forest	Iowa
Automobile assembly line	Henry Ford	Michigan
Automobile ignition, Self-starter	Charles Kettering	Ohio
Barbed wire	Joseph Glidden	Illinois
Breakfast cereals	John and William Kellogg (Corn Flakes)	Michigan
	George Cormack (Wheaties)	Michigan
	Charles William Post (Grape Nuts)	Michigan
Cash register	James Ritty, John Patterson	Ohio
Cast steel plow	John Deere	Illinois
Cracker Jack	Frederick and Louis Rueckheim	Illinois
Cyclotron	Ernest Lawrence	South Dakota
Dial telephone	A. B. Stronger	Missouri
Disposable diapers	Marion Donovan	Indiana
Fast food franchises	Ray Kroc (McDonald's)	Illinois
	Dave Thomas (Wendy's)	Ohio
	Edgar Ingram, J. Walter Anderson (White Castle)	Kansas
Ferris wheel	George Ferris	Illinois
Fishing lure	Ernest Pflueger	Ohio
Foot plasters	William Scholl	Illinois
Formica	Herbert Faber, Daniel O'Conor	Ohio
Fountain pen	George Parker	Wisconsin
Free home delivery of mail	Joseph Briggs	Ohio
Glass canning jars	Edmund, Frank, George, Lucius, and William Ball	Indiana
Gatling gun	Richard Gatling	Ohio
Greeting card	Joyce, Rollie, and William Hall	Missouri
Kitty litter	Edward Lowe	Michigan
Kleenex	Kimberly Clark Co.	Wisconsin
Kool-Aid	Edwin Perkins	Nebraska
Lincoln Logs	John Lloyd Wright	Wisconsin
Mail order catalog	Richard Sears	Minnesota
Mechanical reaper	Cyrus McCormick	Illinois
Microchip for computers	Jack Kilby	Wisconsin
	Robert Noyce	Iowa
Milk carton	John Van Wormer	Ohio
Modern golf ball	Coburn Haskell, Bertram Work	Ohio
New variety of wheat	Norman Borlaug	Iowa
Nuclear reactor	Enrico Fermi	Illinois
Peanut products	George Carver	Missouri
Post-it Notes	Art Fry	Minnesota
Processed cheese	James Lewis Kraft	Illinois
Phonograph, Electric light	Thomas Edison	Ohio
Qwerty keyboard typewriter	Christopher Scholes	Wisconsin

❖ **Selected Midwest Inventions and Improvements (*continued*)**

Invention	Inventor, Developer	Associated State
Railroad sleeping car	George Pullman	Illinois
"Scotch" tape	Richard Drew	Minnesota
Shopping bag	Walter Deubner	Minnesota
Stainless steel	Elwood Hayes	Indiana
Strobe light	Harold Edgerton	Nebraska
Supercomputer	Seymour Cray	Minnesota
Stabilizing gyroscope	Charles Draper	Missouri
Skyscraper	William Le Baron Jenney	Illinois
Suction vacuum cleaner	Ives McGaggey	Ohio
Tinker Toys	Charles Pajeau	Illinois
Traffic signal	Garrett Morgan	Ohio
Two-wheel grass mower	Lewis Miller	Illinois
Weather service	Cleveland Abbe	Ohio
White bar soap	William Procter	Ohio
Wire coat hangers	Albert Parkhouse	Michigan
Zipper	Whitcomb Judson	Illinois

research and worked closely with the Worthington Pump Company to build a pump that could withstand high temperatures. Success was achieved by adding molybdenum to the steel. Other triumphs followed, among them better alloys for watch springs for Elgin Watch Company. Battelle never guaranteed success to its client companies, but would try to solve any industrial problem. In 1939 Battelle signed a contract to improve armor plate for military purposes, and soon new alloys were developed to withstand intense temperatures and great pressure, particularly for jet turbine blades. Battelle developed fuels for the compact nuclear reactor placed in the first atomic submarine in the United States. Each scientist was urged to consider himself an entrepreneur. The company's first major financial success was with xerography. The inventor, Chester Carlson, had been born to parents of Swedish extraction and had worked out his ideas over the kitchen sink. Carlson obtained very broad patent protection because the copying process was entirely new, and the name for the machine was changed to Xerox.

At any one time, Battelle is engaged in as many as five thousand projects for as many as fifteen hundred commercial and government clients, and up to a hundred new patents are expected in a year. Battelle discovered how to make sandwich coins, now routinely used for dimes, quarters, and silver dollars, and Battelle led with the bar code symbol. The original Battelle motto is still used: "Putting technology to work."

The Stowers Institute for Medical Research is one of the largest research institutes ever established for primarily biomedical investigation. Jim and Virginia Stowers, both of whom survived cancer, dedicated their fortune to supporting basic research and, in 2000, funded a new $200 million research facility. Their interest is the neural crest and stem cell growth mechanisms. Stem cell research is expected to be helpful for diseases such as Parkinson's and Alzheimer's. Other scientists study ubiquitin for its role in regulating cell function as well as for its potential participation in destruction from within the cells themselves. The new Stowers Institute is situated on a ten-acre campus in the heart of Kansas City, Missouri.

The concept of a freestanding (not university-affiliated and not governmental) research institute is relatively new, as is seen in the history of Battelle and Stowers. The Midwest Research Institute (MRI), also headquartered in Kansas City, Missouri, was established in 1944, and currently conducts programs in health, pharmaceutical product development, and agriculture and food safety, as well as in national security and defense. Research in food safety is intended to help ensure a safe and abundant food supply for the world. This is a typical midwestern, even a typical American, dream. The National Renewable Energy Laboratory in Colorado, still owned by the Department of Energy, is now managed by MRI. Its efforts include research on genetics, immunology, and toxicology, and the thrust of all of its laboratories is to offer research facilities for the needs of others. The concept of biological threats and the awareness of the necessity for chemical defense has linked MRI tightly with the Centers for Disease Control and with the U.S. Department of Defense. Because of its connection with the federal government, MRI has opened a new laboratory in Rockville, Maryland, primarily to assist government labs and meet the recently increased necessity for quick analysis of various samples.

Through only these three examples the Midwest's heritage of independent research can be seen to complement the more standard university, industry, and governmental research laboratories.

Sources and Further Reading: George A. W. Boehm and Alex Groner, *Science in the Service of Mankind* (1986); Steve Bunk, "Big Plans for Kansas City: Stowers Institute Inspires Drive for Biomedical Leadership," *The Scientist* 14 (27 Nov. 2000), available at http://www.zurichmednet.org/features/BigPlansforKansasCity.htm; Charles N. Kimball, *Midwest Research Institute: Some Recollections of the First 30 years, 1945–1975* (1985).

George Paulson
The Ohio State University–Columbus

Women in Science

It takes great ambition, courage, and intelligence for women to select and survive the difficult path of a scientific journey through life. The United States was not ready to accept women in careers like mathematics, physics, chemistry, biology, medicine, engineering, botany, and space sciences until recently. Women in science from the Midwest fit into a unique category because they evolved in an environment of vast land and endless skies and had deep roots in the value and ethic of hard work. Dreaming of big cities and big universities and wanting to see the world they had read about helped motivate them to learn. Women scientists have been prominent in every midwestern state, and many have contributed in various areas of scholarship and service.

Ohioan Rachel Littler Bodley classified numerous botanical specimens from around the country and, in 1865, became the first woman professor of chemistry in the country. Iowan Ida Henrietta Hyde, who taught at the University of Kansas from 1898 to 1920, became a noted physiologist and early emphasized the importance of public health with regard to communicable diseases. In 1889 Nebraskan Susan LaFlesche Picotte became the first Native American woman to earn a medical degree. Indianan Alice Hamilton raised the standards for industrial safety and pointed the way for occupational safety practices. Her comments on her own upbringing in *Exploring the Dangerous Trades* (1943) sum up many of the attributes of women scientists from the Midwest:

We never questioned the rightfulness of truth-telling, honorable dealing, unselfishness, self-control. To base them on practical advantage to oneself or even to society would have been to shake the foundations of our moral world. Actions were right or they were wrong, and when they were wrong we knew that the eyes of the Lord are in every place beholding the evil and the good. This unquestioning acceptance of a moral code, together with a strong family background, made us more "rooted and grounded."

Nebraskan Gladys Rowena Dick worked as a physician and with her husband isolated the toxin for scarlet fever in 1924. Michigander Elizabeth Caroline Crosby became an established expert in brain morphology with her 1936 publication of *The Comparative Anatomy of the Nervous System of Vertebrates, Including Man* and, in 1962, furthered the knowledge of neuroanatomy with her *Correlative Anatomy of the Nervous System*. Missourian chemist Icie Hoobler made great strides in the field of nutrition, winning the American Chemical Society's Garvan Medal in 1946. Wisconsinite Elda Emma Anderson was the only woman involved in the development of the atomic bomb and raised awareness of radiation safety. Ohioan Judith Resnik earned a Ph.D. in electrical engineering before she became an astronaut for NASA in 1978.

Sources and Further Reading: Alice Hamilton, *Exploring the Dangerous Trades* (1943); Benjamin F. Shearer and Barbara S. Shearer, eds., *Notable Women in the Life Sciences* (1996); Benjamin F. Shearer and Barbara S. Shearer, eds., *Notable Women in the Physical Sciences* (1997); Laura Windsor, *Women in Medicine: An Encyclopedia* (2002).

Laura Windsor
Ohio University

Beginning to Fight Disease

The triumph over diseases in the Midwest has been so astounding that one almost takes for granted the absence of cholera, smallpox, typhoid, and malaria. Such confidence was not warranted in the 1800s, when cholera and typhoid, before clean water, and malaria, before the swamps were drained, were major impediments to settlement of all the Midwest. Early doctors such as Drake and Beaumont were among the first medical scientists in the region, and both studied, wrote, delivered care, and helped establish medical schools or medical societies in their areas. The first hospital in America primarily for medical education was built in Ohio, but others soon followed. The tradition of pioneer medicine was strong in the Midwest, and herbal and what now would be called alternative therapies were used by both the Indians and the pioneers. As this section will make clear, many of the country's professional organizations and associations of specialists, even subspecialists, began or were nurtured in the Midwest.

Pathfinders in Medicine: William Beaumont (1785–1853) and Daniel Drake (1785–1852)

The Midwest has had more than one legendary physician. Some, including the Mayos in Minnesota and George Crile in Cleveland, were founders of world-famous clinics. William Beaumont and Daniel Drake are representative of the many pioneer physicians who deserve particular note, both for their personal accomplishments and for their early efforts to improve medical care and medical scholarship in the Midwest.

William Beaumont was one of the first Americans to achieve an international reputation in medical science. He accomplished this with his book *Experiments and Observations on the Gastric Juice and the Physiology of Digestion* (1833), which contributed significantly to the study of human digestion. In the early nineteenth century, physiologists in major medical centers in the United States and Europe were engaged in a prolonged controversy concerning the existence and function of gastric fluid in the digestive process of human beings, and Beaumont's data was decisive in resolving this dispute.

Two aspects of Beaumont's work made it remarkable. First, his scientific experiments were conducted on the American frontier from 1822 to 1833. An Army surgeon, he was stationed during this period at Fort Mackinac, Fort Niagara, Fort Crawford, and finally at Jefferson Barracks near St. Louis. He performed his research in the crude facilities of army hospitals; his equipment was primitive and homemade.

Second, his experiments were performed on a human being, Alexis St. Martin, a nineteen-year-old French Canadian fur trapper who was accidentally shot in the stomach. Beaumont treated the patient at Fort Mackinac, and after months of care, it was apparent that St. Martin's wound had healed improperly, not closing the aperture but healing around the margins of the wound, producing a fistula or opening into the stomach. With the guidance of the Surgeon General of the Army, Beaumont began to make experimental use of St. Martin's peculiar wound. He was aware that his opportunity to observe the process of human digestion in a healthy human being was important to medical science. He collected gastric fluid, and by introducing various foods into the wound and with-

drawing them at intervals, Beaumont calculated the rate at which foods were digested.

With the publication of his book in 1833, Beaumont became a well-known physiologist, but he brought to this project only the modest training of a medical apprenticeship rather than a university education. He was self-taught, largely using borrowed books, and he was forced to remain in the army to make a living. His book was translated and circulated among scientists in Great Britain and Europe because it offered a meticulous report of human digestion and proved definitively the existence and solvent properties of gastric fluid.

Beaumont spent the final twenty years of his life in St. Louis where, in addition to his military duties, he developed a large private practice. He was involved in early efforts to establish a medical society and in efforts to raise the standard of medical practice in the city. His life reflected the beginnings of both scientific medicine and of the American Republic. Born in Lebanon, Connecticut, at the end of the American Revolution, he served in both the War of 1812 and the Black Hawk War, but he refused duty in the war against the Seminoles in Florida. He died in St. Louis in 1853, just before the nation was transiently split by the Civil War.

Daniel Drake had already begun the study of medicine by age fifteen. He started it at a time when separate disease entities were not recognized, and medicine was still dominated by concepts of bodily fluids and humoralism. Losantiville, soon to be called Cincinnati, had been in existence for twelve years when Drake arrived in 1800 as its first official medical apprentice. In 1805, Drake received the first diploma awarded west of the Allegheny Mountains, one signed by a surgeon of the Ohio Militia. After five months of additional study in Philadelphia, he returned to practice in Cincinnati. Drake's early professional advertisements suggested he would accept whiskey, tallow, beeswax, lard, snake root, or sugar in lieu of payment.

It was quickly apparent that he was a gifted speaker and an active political force in his community, and he began to publish extensively. He was perhaps the most persistent publicity agent for Cincinnati, authoring botanic and geographic articles on natural and statistical views of Cincinnati and nearby areas. He attended and then taught classes at Transylvania Medical College in Kentucky and studied again in Philadelphia, where he joined the faculty of Jefferson Medical College. By 1820 Drake had become accepted as the most successful and most well known physician in what was often still called the Northwest. He was also controversial, and he often criticized his colleagues. After helping to establish the Medical College of Ohio, and while still serving as its president, he was dismissed by his colleagues, but the public outcry led to his reinstatement. He was consulted by the famous, including Abraham Lincoln, and Drake's skill in percussion (tapping) and auscultation (listening), both used to detect disorders of the lung, was widely recognized. Drake was equally well known as an educator, and he established several competing medical schools in Cincinnati. He began an infirmary for those with diseases of the eye, and launched an asylum for the mentally ill. He emphasized the need for teaching in hospitals, and reflecting his backwoods background, he felt that the physician should use his own judgment whenever his observations questioned conventional wisdom. As he said, "Medicine is a physical science, but a social art." It was his awareness of social issues that led him to champion medical care in all areas of the Ohio Valley. His scientific traits helped him produce many books, and his desire to teach prompted him to accept the last in a series of distinguished professorships back at the school he had established, the Medical College of Ohio, only days before he died.

Sources and Further Reading: Emmet F. Horine, *Daniel Drake, 1785–1852* (1961); Reginald Horsman, *Frontier Doctor: William Beaumont, America's First Great Medical Scientist* (1996); Jesse S. Myer, *Life and Letters of Dr. William Beaumont* (1912); Cynthia DeHaven Pitcock, "William Beaumont and Malpractice: The Mary Dugan Case, 1844," *Journal of the History of Medicine and Allied Science* 47 (Apr. 1992); Cynthia DeHaven Pitcock, "The Involvement of William Beaumont, M.D., in a Medical-Legal Controversy: The Darnes-Davis Case, 1840," *Missouri Historical Review* 59 (Oct. 1964); David A. Tucker, "Daniel Drake and the Origin of Medicine in the Ohio Valley," *Ohio Archeological and Historical Quarterly* 44 (Oct. 1935).

Cynthia DeHaven Pitcock
University of Arkansas for Medical Sciences

George Paulson
The Ohio State University–Columbus

Common Diseases

Pre-Columbian Native American civilization in the Midwest was characterized by widely dispersed settlements of small groups that were in balance with nature and lowered susceptibility to illnesses associated with crowding and poor sanitation. Native Americans were also completely isolated from many of the worst human diseases that had evolved in the Old World, so they lacked immunity to the diseases introduced by settlers, notably measles, chicken pox, typhoid, and smallpox. The rapid European settlement of the Midwest was facilitated by the high mortality rate among Native Americans, who contracted the diseases to which white people had grown accustomed.

European settlers lacked access to physicians and relied on their wits and folk remedies when they became ill. Early reports mention the very high prevalence of numerous fevers, often termed the *ague*. Infectious diseases were common, mortality was high, and whole families were sometimes affected. The difficulty in maintaining sufficient health to work the land plus the harshness of the climate led some to question whether the Midwest could ever be settled. The settlers astutely connected illness with wet conditions of swamps, blaming the heavy and damp (miasmatic) air for sickness. It was true that the Midwest included much land needing artificial drainage, especially in Michigan and Minnesota, but it was not the atmosphere, the miasma, that killed. The standing water was an ideal breeding ground for the various mosquitoes associated with vector-borne diseases. As farmers drained more and more agricultural land for cultivation, they eliminated breeding places of mosquitoes. So the expansion in food production indirectly helped control some of the fevers the early settlers experienced.

Malaria was perhaps the most prevalent of all the diseases during the nineteenth century, and was likely introduced to the United States by infected Europeans and African slaves. By the mid-1800s, it had spread to most of the Midwest and was well-established along the Mississippi River. Wide fluctuations in fevers and epidemics occurred seasonally, probably due to climatic conditions and variable infestations with anopheles mosquitoes. The founders of the Mayo Clinic moved from their malarial environment in Indiana to Minnesota, a place that at the time was free of malaria. In the late 1800s, the prevalence of malaria was diminished by changes in the human population and changes in the environment on which mosquitoes depended. There were now cattle as well as humans to feed upon; the number of infected new immigrants declined; the population became more concentrated in cities and towns removed from standing water problems; and living conditions improved within settlements as screens began to appear in windows and quinine became available for treatment.

Numerous other diseases plagued the early settlers in addition to malaria, including typhoid, dysentery, cholera, meningitis, tuberculosis, and influenza. Over the course of the 1800s, diseases such as typhoid, cholera, and dysentery caused by contaminated water became a bigger threat than those caused by mosquitoes. Drinking water for growing cities was compromised by upstream fouling and well water contamination with human feces and urine. This led to many large-scale epidemics (sudden and widespread) as well

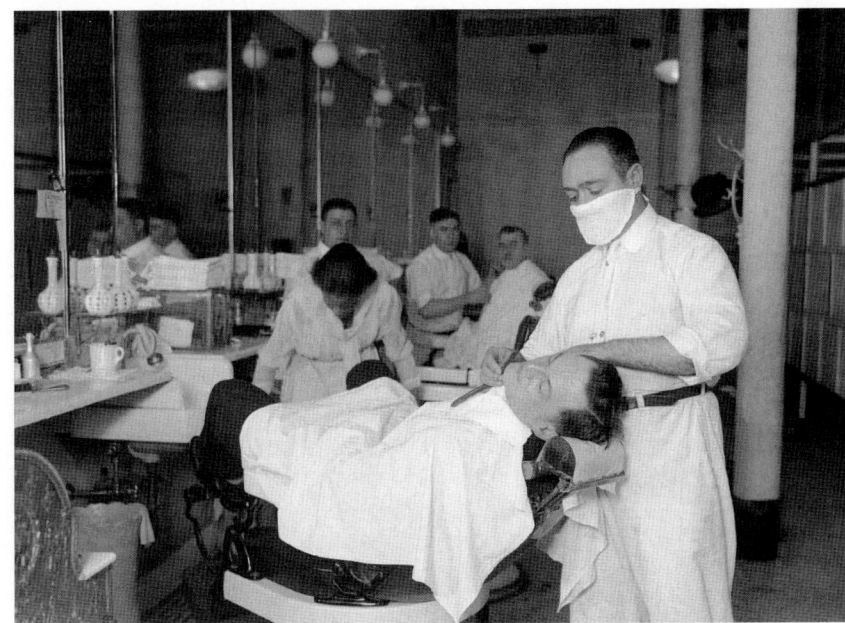

Protecting against the flu epidemic of 1918. Chicago Historical Society, *Chicago Daily News*, DN-0070554.

as continuing endemic (local) infections. Important epidemiological and medical work around the world was revealing the bacteriological origins of many diseases, and this knowledge also reached the Midwest. Walter Reed, of later yellow fever fame, was stationed in midwestern military camps during the 1880s and studied typhoid fever infection among soldiers. He later contributed to the understanding of the etiology and epidemiology of typhoid and yellow fever. The diseases linked to contaminated water declined during the late 1800s and early 1900s. For example, typhoid fever mortality declined in the United States from 31.3 per hundred thousand people in 1900 to 3.6 by 1933, primarily because of filtration and chlorination of drinking water, milk pasteurization, and better public health administration.

The declining rate of infant and maternal mortality during the 1900s is evidence of improving sanitary, social, and medical conditions in the Midwest during this time. The 1800s had been a period of very high birth rates and very high infant and maternal death rates. The infant mortality rate in the Midwest declined from 125 per thousand births in 1900, to 88 in 1920, to 44 in 1940. By 2000, the infant mortality rate had declined to 7 per thousand, representing an eighteenfold decrease since 1900.

One particular triumph of Midwest medicine has been the control of goiter, an enlargement of the thyroid gland. Cleveland's high goiter rate was obvious by the middle of the nineteenth century, and for decades the Midwest was referred to as the Goiter Belt. Goiter has now become relatively rare in the Midwest, simply because of the use of iodized salt.

David Marine at Western Reserve University linked endemic goiter and iodine deficiency. Salt prepared away from the seashore, salt mined in the Midwest, was low in iodine. More serious than goiter was linkage of the hypothyroid (low thyroid activity) hormone state with mental retardation, the classic cretin. In the early 1920s the Michigan State Department of Health examined sixty-six thousand schoolchildren up to eighth grade, and 39 percent of these had enlarged thyroid glands. Subsequently, the Michigan State Medical Society launched a goiter prevention program using salt with added iodine. Techniques for adding iodine were easily applied and became well known internationally, and the program essentially erased iodine deficiency, mental retardation due to hypothyroidism, and goiter from the Midwest. Another example of dietary supplementation has been the addition of fluoride to drinking water, a measure largely responsible for the almost uniformly good teeth now seen in the Midwest as compared to a hundred years ago.

It is not possible to separate the beneficial effects of clean water and air, public health, medicine, and adequate food, but it is possible, and certainly it is fortunate, to be able to state that life in the Midwest is now among the healthiest in the entire world.

Sources and Further Reading: Erwin H. Ackerknecht, "Diseases in the Middle West," in *Essays in the History of Medicine: In Honor of David J. Davis, M.D., Ph.D.* (1965).

John Paulson
Ohio Department of Health

Establishment of Teaching Hospitals

In 1800 only five medical colleges in the United States existed that claimed a connection to colleges of arts and science, but none was directly affiliated with a hospital. Shelters or asylums for the ill and poor were available in several major cities, but such facilities were separate from medical education.

Changes came fast. By 1876, sixty-four of the eighty medical colleges that had been previously established were still functioning. Nevertheless, few students had access to a hospital, and lecture-style medical education was the rule. Lucky students had an apprenticeship in a local doctor's office. In 1849 the infant American Medical Association's Committee on Education reported that only nine of the leading thirty-five American medical schools required any hospital experience at all to achieve a diploma. Until the early twentieth century, one could graduate from a medical school and never set foot in a hospital.

One of the early midwestern schools, Willoughby Medical College in Ohio, was incorporated in 1834, but dissension and rumors of grave robbing soon split the faculty, and the school moved 150 miles south to Columbus in 1847. At the time there were already successful medical schools in Lexington, Kentucky, and in Cincinnati. In Columbus, an early settler and successful entrepreneur, Lyne Starling, who had become wealthy during the War of 1812, offered $30 thousand to "sustain an infirmary or hospital, or some other benevolent institution, under the supervision and control of said medical college, and in said city of Columbus." The resultant St. Francis Hospital was staffed by German-speaking nuns and was the first hospital built in America primarily to teach medical students. In 1869 the Department of Medicine of the University of Michigan also began a university hospital in a remodeled guest house that accommodated twenty patients.

Other hospitals, some of which had been originally established to deliver medical care to the poor, were linked formally with medical colleges for instruction. Leading medical educators, including Sir William Osler, encouraged bedside teaching. Can we truly claim the development of teaching hospitals for the Midwest? Probably yes. The Pennsylvania Hospital was founded in 1751, New York Hospital was founded in 1770, and Charity Hospital in New Orleans was already established in 1736, long before New Orleans became a part of the United States. Teaching was occasionally carried on in these hospitals, but any affiliated medical schools were totally separate entities. The Midwest led in hospitals that were constructed primarily to teach medicine. Except for tuberculosis sanatoria, which were often designed to protect and treat the middle class, hospitals were not common until the early twentieth century.

The University of Michigan Medical School, founded in 1850, built its own hospital in 1880, and was also one of the first to require a full three-year medical curriculum. This medical school now has over 650 medical students and has graduated eighteen thousand since the first six students, all males and all white, graduated in 1851. The University of Wisconsin only later achieved its full development, although Wisconsin Governor Nelson Dewey had proposed a medical school as early as 1848. Several Midwest cities proudly claim more than one medical school—Chicago, St. Louis, and Omaha. One of the schools in St. Louis, the Washington University School of Medicine, was established in 1891 to meet the national need for more adequately trained scientific physicians. This eminent school claims seventeen Nobel Prize winners.

Source and Further Reading: George W. Paulson, "To Teach and to Heal: St. Francis Hospital," *Timeline* 16 (Jan.–Feb. 1999).

George Paulson
The Ohio State University–Columbus

Native American and Herbal Medicine

Prior to the European conquest of the Midwest and the epidemic diseases that preceded and accompanied the invaders, the people of the many tribal nations of the region enjoyed good health and were generally free of chronic diseases. Underlying their healing practices was their understanding that illness arises out of a disharmony among the sick person, the community, and the natural and supernatural realms. Using herbs, sweat lodges, rituals, and ceremony, indigenous healers created an environment in which healing could take place.

Although early European settlers relied upon the native healers' knowledge of medicinal plants, forced removal of many indigenous nations, combined with Christian attacks on traditional religions, disrupted or suppressed native medical practice, since many healers were also spiritual leaders. For example, the Ojibwe, whose territory extended along the top third of today's Midwest, practiced the Grand Medicine or Midewiwin society, whose senior leaders underwent twenty-year apprenticeships.

The extensive herbal knowledge of indigenous healers is acknowledged by the fact that the modern scientific community lists over two hundred medicines, which had been used prior to the European invasion in the *Pharmacopoeia of the United States*. Some widely used medicines from the Midwest are goldenseal, ginseng, and slippery elm bark. While Western medicine is used by most American Indians today, there has been a resurgence in traditional interventions that address the social and cultural causes of chronic diseases. Some contemporary tribal nations, such as the Menominee, have established their own health-care facilities that incorporate modern and traditional methods.

Source and Further Reading: Virgil J. Vogel, *American Indian Medicine* (1970).

Kathleen Tigerman
University of Wisconsin–Platteville

Pioneer Medicine

Close on the heels of the earliest frontiersmen who tramped the Ohio Valley were bands of pioneers who cleared forests, built homes among the stumps, and raised families among remnants of the Native American population. Learned doctors were a rare occurrence in colonial America and equally scarce among families migrating into the Midwest. Not surprisingly, many of these frontier men and women attained the status of doctor simply by assuming the responsibility of healer. Lack of formal medical education was no barrier for people outside the reach of educational institutions and professional societies. Those gifted with native abilities, including the capacity to inspire confidence, assumed the title without the formal distinctions that existed in the Old World. Farmers, women, indentured servants, and even slaves acquired reputa-

tions as competent healers. Along with numerous itinerant pretenders, they plied their trade, irrespective of education, degrees, or licensing. The term "doctor" was bestowed out of respect for accomplishment rather than any claim to education.

There was no one source from which pioneers of the Midwest learned how to heal. Transmission of European medical theories and practices by academically trained physicians was surprisingly limited. At the time of the American Revolution, not more than four hundred of the estimated thirty-five hundred doctors practicing in the colonies had received any formal training, and of that number, less than half had earned a degree. This allowed for alternate routes of medical information to spring up, including the contributions of Native American healers, experienced midwives who learned through apprenticeship and oral healing traditions, young men apprenticed to practicing doctors, and a myriad of self-proclaimed quacks and empirics who stumped between towns and villages and tested on themselves and others their newest concoctions. Despite theoretical differences between medieval Galenic humoral and solidist theories, or the belief that disease resulted from an imbalance of basic humors or from a single cause, both systems migrated into learned and lay practices whose healers relied heavily on the use of emetics, cathartics, narcotics, tonics, diuretics, emollients, plasters, astringents, and bleedings—all treatments intended to adjust the patient's equilibrium.

Much has been made of the knowledge gleaned from Native American healers. No doubt this source of herbal lore existed in many regions of the Midwest, as is evident in the lives of pioneers and naturalists who learned the use of indigenous roots and herbs and in the practices of numerous midwives who claimed

The medicine wagon driving into Black River Falls, Wisconsin, 1890s. Wisconsin Historical Society, WHi-1931.

some degree of Native ancestry. However, the temptation to attribute the American pioneer's plant-based *materia medica* to Native Americans must be tempered by the fact that the pioneers were longtime users of folk and domestic medicines and were also used to searching among New World plants for likely substitutes for familiar Old World medicines. Most early plant remedies were simply Old World transplants. This explains the heavy reliance of healers, midwives, and individual families on Gervase Markham's *The English Housewife* (1615), the herbals of John Parkinson and John Gerard, and Nicholas Culpeper's astrological herbal, *The English Physician* (1708).

In this self-help environment, which demanded less specialization and more general knowledge, individuals, families, and communities had available to them a wide assortment of folk and domestic recipes, oral traditions, Shaker medicines, imported patent medicines and pharmaceuticals, astrological advice, almanacs, and do-it-yourself books. Among the more popular eighteenth-century texts to be found in the home were Cotton Mather's *The Angel of Bethesda* (1722), John Tennent's *Every Man His Own Doctor: or, The Poor Planter's Physician* (1734), John Wesley's *Primitive Physick* (1747), which went through twenty-four American editions and included the virtues of many plants,

and William Buchan's *Domestic Medicine* (1769), which in 142 editions mixed folk medicines, empiricism, and common sense with more rationalistic therapies.

By the 1820s and 1830s academically trained physicians lost what few privileges they had garnered from colonial times as legislatures began disassembling licensing practices that had given state medical societies the power to pass on the qualifications of physicians entering practice. As popular democracy gained in strength and confidence, the power and wisdom of the Common Man flowered into a militant sectarianism that boldly condemned medical orthodoxy. Faced with waves of medical reformers and irregular practitioners—herbalists, American Indian and root doctors, botanics, hydropaths, homeopaths, eclectics, the various adherents to the teachings of Samuel Thomson— all demanding access to the public and equal rights before the law, and unable to distinguish legitimate from illegitimate medicine, legislators chose to allow the marketplace to determine the success or failure of a given healer. It was a phenomenon short on intellectual proposition but strong on emotion, antimonopoly, antielitism, and democracy, encouraging people to trust in free choice. It represented a reaction to the overly aggressive regimens of regular physicians, whose mineral and vegetable remedies and anti-inflammatory techniques intended to counteract fevers and inflammation had reached lethal proportions. It also reflected the response of citizens and town fathers as they traced the course of cholera and yellow fever epidemics that decimated whole communities while orthodox physicians wrung their hands in helpless frustration.

There is a tendency to remember the self-help medicine of the early nineteenth century more for its faults than for its benefits. It should not be imagined, however, that these books produced only a narrow or misguided view of medicine, or that the advice was wrongheaded. Noteworthy self-help treatises included Samuel Henry's *A New and Complete American Family Herbal* (1814), Samuel Thomson's *New Guide to Health* (1822), Samuel Robinson's *A Course of Fifteen Lectures on Medical Botany* (1829), Elisha Smith's *The Botanic Physician* (1830), John Gunn's *Gunn's Domestic Medicine* (1830), Wooster Beach's *The American Practice of Medicine* (1833), Horton Howard's *An Improved System of Botanic Medicine* (1832), and numerous hydropathic, homeopathic, and eclectic domestic texts. The literature is remarkable for its enlightenment as well as its confusion, its science as well as its pseudoscience. Several million individuals and their families depended on these self-help texts. They provided a modicum of health care to a population beyond the reach of academically-educated doctors. They also served indirectly as a catalyst to medical orthodoxy's introspection and eventual reform.

Rennebohm Drug Store, Madison, Wisconsin, 1944. Wisconsin Historical Society, WHi-13275.

Sources and Further Reading: Alex Berman and Michael Flannery, *America's Botanico-Medical Movements* (2001); John Duffy, *The Healers: A History of American Medicine* (1979); John S. Haller, Jr., *Medical Protestants* (1994); John S. Haller, Jr., *The People's Doctors* (2000); Madge E. Pickard and R. Carlyle Buley, *The Midwest Pioneer* (1946); Guenter B. Risse, Ronald L. Numbers, and Judith Walzer Leavitt, eds., *Medicine Without Doctors* (1977).

John S. Haller, Jr.
Southern Illinois University–Carbondale

Professional Organizations in American Medicine

Organizations and politics have probably been present whenever people were gathered, and certainly professional organizations are centuries old. Nevertheless, the Midwest can properly claim to be the home, and often the founding location, of many current medical specialty groups. Perhaps great distance, perhaps the tendency to reshape and cooperate, perhaps mistrust of the eastern establishment contributed to the flowering and later splintering of many specialty groups. Only a few such groups will be mentioned, for the story is similar. A physician encourages other physicians to join for the benefit of both patients and themselves, and education, fellowship, and more recently research and lobbying have become a reason for meetings, publications, and planning. The American Medical Association is the largest, but for many physicians, the relationship with their own specialty group has become paramount.

The American Medical Society (AMA) was conceived in the 1840s by Nathan Smith Davis, a physician who tried unsuccessfully to introduce resolutions on medical education to the New York State Medical Society. Davis felt a national effort was required to update the education of physicians. In 1849 Davis accepted the Chair of Physiology and Pathology at Rush Medical College in Chicago, a city which then boasted thirty thousand inhabitants. During the Civil War, regular meetings of physicians began to occur, particularly in Chicago, and Davis was the primary organizer. He became the first editor of the Journal of the AMA (JAMA) in 1882 when he was already sixty-five years old, and he solidified the AMA's home in Chicago. Efforts of the AMA to limit "quackery" during much of the nineteenth and early twentieth centuries consumed the energy of the membership and of its rapidly developing boards and committees. Increasing attention to medical education included heightened efforts by the AMA to supervise residency programs, supervision which still continues with the recent suggestion of limited work hours and insistence on lifetime educational efforts.

At first, the majority of the leaders in the AMA were academicians, often deans, and invariably men with impeccable scientific credentials. More recently the leadership of the AMA has a higher percentage of active practitioners, and it is uncommon for a medical school dean to lead the modern AMA. There have been recent efforts to incorporate specialty groups into the AMA and to preserve the often tenuous relationships of the AMA with state and county medical associations. Allopathic physicians, osteopathic physicians, nonmembers, and groups such as libraries and foreign and local news services all tap the AMA for medical information and advice. The resources include highly successful peer-reviewed journals, pamphlets, and television and web services.

The rise of specialization and the organizational impulses so typical of the Midwest were reflected in the establishment of formal associations of medical specialists. Each group is unique and often narrow in interest, and groups have merged, fragmented, or spun off additional subspecialty groups. Administrative headquarters may move from the East to the Midwest or vice versa. Among the many local groups are the Neurologists of St. Louis and the Internists of Ohio. At least a dozen large national groups have a special midwestern history. Ninety percent of American physicians now classify themselves as specialist in some field, and many also achieve further subspecialization within the field. The internist becomes also a cardiologist, or the cardiologist becomes an interventionalist who does catheterization of the heart, and so on. Most of the specialty areas have selected their own criteria for existence, established examinations, and offered educational efforts, but they are usually not part of a federal oversight program.

The American College of Physicians (ACP) has now combined with the American Society of Internal Medicine (ASIM). ACP was started in 1915 in New York by Heinrich Stern, but after his death in 1919, the offices moved to Chicago. The move reflected the enthusiasm of one of the founders, Frank Smithies of Chicago, who served as Secretary General and who established the *Annals of Internal Medicine*. The college was so successful that a paid secretary was soon necessary. In 1926 the ACP moved back east to Philadelphia. It is one of the first six Masters, or major medical organizations, that were variously located in Chicago, Ann Arbor, Michigan, or Detroit.

The American Academy of Family Physicians was founded in 1947 in Kansas City, Missouri, and is one of the largest of the national medical organizations, with 93,500 family physicians, residents, or students as members. The stated goals are to help provide high-quality and cost-effective care and to offer guidelines for continuity of care for all people of all ages. As has become standard for all specialty groups, continuing medical education is offered to meet requirements for state medical licensure. Peer-reviewed publications and instruction in specific medical technologies and therapy are offered. Other than the large size and the extensive political lobbying for educational funds, the group representing Family Medicine is now no different from many similar ones. It is more recent in origin than most, however, and is unusual in maintaining its headquarters where it began, in Kansas.

The American College of Radiology (ACR) now claims over forty thousand members and offers one of the most extensive of educational offerings of any specialty group. One feature of the college is the large number of splinter groups; as of 2002, there were at least forty-five groups as varied as the Society of Gastrointestinal Radiologists, the Institute of Ultrasound, and the Brachytherapy Society. All these, plus varied boards, rest reasonably comfortably under the ACR's umbrella. The ACR began its umbrella policy in 1923 and now includes radiologists, physicists, radiation oncologists, and other related subspecialties. The organization is based in Virginia and Pennsylvania, but its major annual meeting is still in Chicago.

The history of the professional organizations in radiology is actually older than the American College of Radiology. The American Roentgen Society was formed in 1900 on the East Coast, but within a decade radiologists in St. Louis, Chicago, Detroit, and Cleveland felt left out and far away. Thus in 1915 five physicians from St. Louis and Springfield, Illinois, established a new group, which met in downtown Chicago and soon garnered sixty five members from seventeen states. Within two years a journal was organized, and by 1919 membership exceeded five hundred. After extensive discussion, the name was changed from Western Roentgen Society to the Radiologic Society of North America. It is currently headquartered in Oak Brook, Illinois.

American neurologists organized the American Neurological Association (ANA) over 125 years ago in New York City, and for decades the group met exclusively in Atlantic City, New Jersey, with presentations by the few members. While claiming to speak for all of America's neurologists, a thesis and fifteen published articles were required for membership. Disturbed by the dominance of neurology by professors on the East and West Coasts, a group of midwestern neurologists led by A. B. Baker of Minneapolis established the American Academy of Neurology (AAN), which is now the dominant organization for neurologic education, with over fifty courses offered at the annual meeting. These meetings include as many as eight thousand of the eighteen thousand senior, active, and junior members. The offices of both the ANA and AAN are now located together in Minneapolis.

The American College of Obstetricians and Gynecologists represents forty-five thousand members. It was founded in 1951 in Chicago, and represents the group of professionals who provide health care for women. The college promotes education for members as well as for their patients, and it has become a major advocate for optimal patient care for women. As with all the major specialty groups, the ACOG offers annual educational meetings and a quality journal.

Source and Further Reading: Morris Fishbein, *A History of the American Medical Association, 1847 to 1947* (1947).

Philip Cass
Columbus Medical Foundation, Ohio

Developing Specialties

One example of a person who shaped a single specialty—Ralph Waters in anesthesia or Harvey Cushing in neurosurgery—serves as a reminder that a single individual can redirect or initiate a specialty in medicine. The Cleveland Clinic's innovative programs to treat cardiac and vascular disease illustrate the fact that the culture of an entire institution can lead change as well as follow a new idea in medical science. Sometimes a single town, like Warsaw, Indiana, seems to have developed or captured a specialty: The three major companies that produce joint replacements are present in this "orthopedic capital of the world."

The Midwest has been home for several world-famous clinics, such as Minnesota's Mayo Clinic and Wisconsin's Marshfield Clinic, and it was in the Midwest that various specialists joined together for the benefit of both patients and themselves. Mayo Clinic and the Cleveland Clinic have also established major teaching programs that complement their superb efforts in patient care and research. As psychiatric care evolved from incarceration or home care, to state asylums, to a few patients housed in a doctor's home, private psychiatric institutions arose. The Menningers in Kansas and Harding in Ohio flowered, served, and then merged with nearby university programs. The Kinsey Institute is a midwestern example of a research program in a very focused area, sexuality, and this Institute helped establish standards for responsible reporting and creative research. Sleep research, begun in the Midwest, has led to the proliferation of sleep centers all over America. Populism, social awareness, and concern for clean water and fresh air have been embodied in the Wisconsin Public Health initiatives and are visible daily in the cleaner atmosphere over our larger cities.

The Kinsey Institute

In 1938, Indiana University (IU) asked professor of zoology Alfred C. Kinsey to teach a course tailored for students either recently married or considering matrimony. In preparing his lectures, Kinsey found little scientific research on human sexual behavior. His attempt to address this scarcity led to the creation of the Institute for Sex Research, which grew to become one of the world's leading scientific organizations dedicated to the study of human sexuality.

Born in Hoboken, New Jersey, in 1894, Alfred Kinsey graduated magna cum laude from Bowdoin College in 1916 with a B.S. in biology and psychology. He received his Sc.D. in biology from Harvard in 1919.

Kinsey applied a taxonomic approach—the classification of species and the study of individual variations—to his research on human sexual behavior. Believing that face-to-face discussions generate greater honesty and confidentiality than do questionnaires, Kinsey hired IU-trained psychologist Wardell Pomeroy, among others, to assist with countless interviews. The National Research Council began thirteen years of financial support in 1941. The not-for-profit institute affiliated with IU in 1947, incorporated, and resolved to research human sexual behavior and to accept, hold, use, and administer research materials, a library, case histories, and other materials.

Data from the institute's initial study was published in 1948 as *Sexual Behavior in the Human Male. Sexual Behavior in the Human Female* followed in 1953. Although highly technical, both works became bestsellers and were translated into many languages, evidence of the vast desire for knowledge about the nature of human sexuality.

Controversial from the outset, the Institute for Sex Research was the target of repeated challenges. In 1957, after a long-fought legal battle with the U.S. Customs Department, the institute was allowed to import sexually explicit art and books for the purpose of making them available for research. In recent years, challenges to the institute's methodology and conclusions have appeared in both the Indiana Legislature and the U.S. Congress. The unwavering support of longtime IU president Herman B Wells (1938–1962) is credited with keeping Kinsey's work afloat in the face of such criticism.

Although Dr. Kinsey passed away in 1956, the institute's original study continued until 1963, by which time staff had conducted over eighteen thousand interviews. The institute continues today, renamed the Kinsey institute for Research in Sex, Gender and Reproduction, Inc. Housed on the IU campus in Bloomington, Indiana, the institute employs fifteen full-time staffers along with many student interns, and serves over fifteen hundred scholars annually. Since 1981 the institute has offered a minor in human sexuality to doctoral students enrolled in counseling, education, psychology, and sociology programs at IU. The institute also sponsors international symposia, lectures, workshops, exhibits, and conferences, as well as two sexual health clinics.

The Kinsey staff continues its history of prolific publishing, and the institute's archive and collection provide an invaluable resource for educators and students. Its holdings include more than seventy-five thousand images, twelve thousand films and videos, eight thousand artifacts and art objects, a voluminous collection of monographs, journals, reports, unpublished papers, manuscripts, recordings, CD-ROMs, books, magazines, newspapers, and pulp fiction.

Sources and Further Reading: John Bancroft, "Alfred Kinsey's Work 50 Years Later," in Alfred Kinsey et al., eds., *Sexual Behavior in the Human Male* (1998); Jonathan Gathorne-Hardy, *Sex, The Measure of All Things* (2000); Kinsey Institute, http://www.kinseyinstitute.org.

R. Dale Ogden
Indiana State Museum & Historic Sites, Indiana

Major Clinics: Marshfield, Mayo, and Cleveland

Group medical practice is now the norm in all of the United States, but it was not always so. World-class medical clinics began in the Midwest because of its culture of cooperation and the fact that its people were uninhibited by prior opinions or negative predictions. Three such clinics are representative. Two of them were established to serve rural areas, but all three evolved sophisticated management techniques and developed unique areas of expertise. The clinics' ability to retrieve prior records and maintain a supportive referral base has been the envy of more conventional medical schools. The clinics helped facilitate the development of HMOs, and although two of these three (the Mayo and Cleveland Clinics) are involved heavily in conventional medical education, and all participate in research, it has been through exemplary clinical service to ill citizens that they have prospered and enriched not only their own local areas but all medical practices throughout the nation.

The Marshfield Clinic, with more than seven hundred physicians and five thousand other staff, serves 144 thousand patients each year at forty-one sites in central, northern, and western Wisconsin. Six physicians formed Marshfield Clinic, based in Marshfield, Wisconsin, in 1916. Their choice to form a group

William James Mayo, William Worrall Mayo, and Charles Horace Mayo, founders of the Mayo Clinic. Photo courtesy Mayo Foundation Archives.

medical practice, pooling their practice interests to provide better care for patients, was unique. Each physician developed a special area of practice, allowing in-depth study and improved patient care. Marshfield Clinic is still governed by its physicians, each having a vote in the clinic's future. In the late nineteenth century, Marshfield was a hub of rural railroad connections and a city poised to grow. Trains still pass through daily, but the city is now more widely known as home to Marshfield Clinic, and patients arrive there from every state and from all counties in Wisconsin.

An electronic medical record developed at Marshfield Clinic captures patient data, including X-rays, magnetic resonance images, computed tomography, lab work, and results of other diagnostics, and makes records immediately available at any of the Marshfield Clinic locations.

In 1981, the clinic became not-for-profit, and all revenue supports the clinic's mission and is funneled back into patient care, education, and research. The Medical Research Foundation was formed in 1959 with a first federal grant to study Farmer's Lung Disease, a common debilitating illness affecting farmers. Marshfield Clinic researchers performed groundbreaking studies on this and other lung diseases, including Maple Bark Disease. Researchers were involved in the Human Genome Project and continue research on genes responsible for Huntington's disease, prostate cancer, and obesity. Marshfield Clinic launched a Personalized Medicine Research Project in 2002, an effort to combine medical record data and DNA from forty thousand volunteer participants to search for causes of disease and to learn how people metabolize medications.

Marshfield Laboratories, a division of the clinic, serves as a reference laboratory for the region and provides clinical and anatomical testing of human specimens. In addition, it has food safety, veterinary, and forensic toxicology laboratories. More than twenty million tests per year are conducted for about two thousand clients or medical groups in Wisconsin, Minnesota, Illinois, Ohio, and Pennsylvania. A courier service logs about five thousand miles per day delivering specimens for fast turnaround of lab tests.

Security Health Plan of Wisconsin, Inc., a health maintenance organization (HMO) sponsored by Marshfield Clinic, was established in 1986 as an outgrowth of the Greater Marshfield Community Health Plan and is one of the nation's first rural HMOs. Careful recordkeeping, compassionate care, volunteers, state encouragement, and a merger of scholarly medical practice, research, and sound business practices has made this clinic a model for both academic and private groups in and beyond the Midwest.

The Mayo Clinic has its roots in the Civil War. President Abraham Lincoln appointed William Worrall Mayo as examining surgeon for the Union enrollment board for the First Minnesota District on April 24, 1863. The board's headquarters were in Rochester, Minnesota, and in January 1864, Mayo purchased two plots of land and moved his family to Rochester. Two of his sons also became surgeons—William James Mayo, born June 29, 1861, and Charles Horace Mayo, born July 19, 1865. William graduated from the University of Michigan Medical School in 1883, and Charles graduated in 1888 from the medical school at Northwestern University.

When a tornado struck Rochester on August 21, 1883, W. W. Mayo responded to the disaster. Some of the injured were carried to the convent of the Sisters of St. Francis. Mayo sought assistance from the Mother Superior and thereby began a relationship among the Mayos, Mother Alfred, and the Sisters of St. Francis. From this association came the opening of the twenty-seven-bed Saint Mary's Hospital in 1889.

W. W. Mayo often said, "No one is big enough to be independent of others." The Mayo brothers joined their father's medical practice as surgeons, and soon they hired medical men and women with expertise in cardiology, renal disease, radiology, and other specialties. Several of these individuals became nationally recognized. Henry S. Plummer, for instance, recruited in 1901, made contributions to hematology, roentgenology, bronchoscopy, esophagoscopy, electrocardiography, and the physiology and pathology of the thyroid gland. Recognition of the era of specialties led to the opening of the first Mayo Clinic Building. By 1915, the Mayo Clinic had evolved from a relatively small clinic primarily interested in surgical treatment to one that provided all types of medical care. The Mayo Clinic became established as an institution with a three-fold purpose: practice, education, and research.

In 1915, the Mayo brothers provided an endowment for one of the world's first formal graduate medical training programs for physicians. Initially known as the Mayo Foundation for Medical Education and Research, the program became the Mayo Graduate School of Medicine and has grown to include the Mayo Clinic College of Medicine, the Mayo School of Graduate Medical Education, the Mayo Graduate School, the Mayo School of Continuing Medical Education, and the Mayo School of Health Sciences.

The Mayo brothers in 1919 dissolved their partnership and donated the Mayo Clinic name, assets, and the bulk of their life savings to consolidate the Mayo Foundation as a private, charitable, not-for-profit organization. Physicians were to be employees and receive a salary but otherwise not benefit personally from the proceeds of the practice. The Mayo Clinic still operates in the same manner, and proceeds beyond operating expenses are disbursed for patient care, education, and research.

More than six million people have been treated at the Mayo Clinic. The clinic has grown through the years, and in 1984 announced its decision to expand outside of Minnesota. A new Mayo Clinic opened in Jacksonville, Florida, in 1986, followed by another in Scottsdale, Arizona, in 1987. The integration of Mayo Clinic, St. Mary's Hospital, and Rochester Methodist Hospital also occurred in 1986. In the 1990s, the Mayo Health System was developed. This network of clinics and hospitals serves sixty-two communities in Minnesota, Iowa, and Wisconsin.

Research is an integral part of the Mayo Clinic. William J. Mayo stated, "The glory of medicine is that it is constantly moving forward, that there is always more to learn." Research is essential to move medicine forward. Initially under the direction of Dr. Isabella Herb, laboratories date back to 1900 at the Mayo Clinic, and important advances originated at Mayo, such as those in aldosterone and in the modern use of steroids. In October 2001, the Gonda Building opened, which is a twenty-story integrated practice building.

The Cleveland Clinic Foundation, founded in 1921, has become a major economic driver of northeastern Ohio, a respected national academic center, and a major location for international referrals. The Cleveland Clinic's success rests on good leadership and careful adherence to its four underlying principles: academic mission, employed physician group, nonprofit structure, and physician management but not physician ownership.

George Washington Crile formulated the basic concepts underlying the Cleveland Clinic's structure on a World War I battlefield in France. Crile and his former medical school classmate, Frank Bunts (1861–1928), had become partners in medical practice in Cleveland in 1890. Along with Crile's cousin, William E. Lower, they served together in several wars and came to recognize the value of cooperation and teamwork that characterized battlefield medicine. In his journal, Crile summed this up by coining the phrase "to act as a unit," an informal motto of the Cleveland Clinic to this day.

Crile, Bunts, and Lower, all surgeons, had already made their marks in medicine. Each had an academic appointment at one of Cleveland's many hospitals. Each had been president of the Academy of Medicine of Cleveland. Crile had gained a national reputation as one of the founders of the American College of Surgeons. All were well known and extensively published.

During the long nights in France in 1918 Crile and Bunts made their plans to establish a medical group practice, an unusual concept for the time, which would emphasize this spirit of cooperation. The organization would also encourage the development of great expertise in various areas of medicine through another concept that was new at the time, specialization. After returning from France, Crile, Bunts, and Lower recruited a highly regarded internist, John Phillips (1879–1929), to join the project. Phillips was at that time president of the Academy of Medicine of Cleveland, a professor at Western Reserve University's School of Medicine, and was well known to Crile from Phillips's house-staff days at Western Reserve.

On a somewhat dreary day in late February 1921 the four founders opened the Cleveland Clinic's doors for the first time in a new building at the corner of East 93rd and Euclid Avenue, with thirteen employed doctors. The organization was chartered as a non-profit foundation with all physicians employed and salaried, including the founders. A prominent Cleveland attorney, Edward Daoust, who also happened to be Bunts's son-in-law, was responsible for crafting the Cleveland Clinic's charter, which stands to this day as the main document defining the organization. Although Daoust is not officially one of the founders, he is often regarded within the institution as the fifth founder.

It would be an understatement to say that the Cleveland Clinic's reception by the local medical community was chilly. Fear of competition by an organized medical group was probably the major issue. The original vision of the founders did not include a hospital; they had felt that with all the good hospitals in the area, there was no need for another. They had not, however, counted on the harsh reaction of their colleagues outside the clinic, men who made sure that they lost not only their leadership posts at the university and on the hospital staffs on which they served but also their very privileges to practice at these hospitals. The founders responded to this by building the Cleveland Clinic Hospital, which opened in 1924 and is now the busiest and largest hospital in the state.

During its early years, the Cleveland Clinic weathered additional challenging times and events. Three such events occurred over the space of two years: the unexpected death of Bunts in 1928; a disastrous fire in the clinic's X-ray film storage facility that killed 123 people, including Phillips, in 1929; and the onset of the Great Depression later that same year. While this would have closed many organizations, the remaining founders, Crile and Lower, the full medical staff, and the institution's trustees led by John Sherwin mustered sufficient resources to ensure the Cleveland Clinic's survival.

After the deaths of Crile, Lower, and Daoust in the 1940s, the Cleveland Clinic in 1955 adopted a more democratic form of governance, deliberately led by a physician-CEO. This structure assured that the collegial, mutually supportive, medically appropriate mode of operation envisioned by the founders has continued to drive the organization. The resulting atmosphere, almost unique in American medicine, made it possible to recruit and develop some of twentieth-century medicine's brightest lights.

During its eighty-five years of existence, the Cleveland Clinic has grown from its beginnings in a single small building to a main campus of about 155 acres with more than thirty buildings, fourteen satellite clinics, ambulatory surgery units in all parts of the greater Cleveland area, as well as ten hospitals. The employed medical staff has grown from the original thirteen to more than a thousand, including physicians and research scientists. Just over twelve hundred private practice physicians in Greater Cleveland admit patients to the clinic's hospitals and belong to its Physicians' Organization. In 1988, Cleveland Clinic Florida began operations in Fort Lauderdale, and in 2002 new facilities opened in Weston and Naples, Florida. A new medical school, in partnership with Case Western Reserve University's School of Medicine, enrolled its first class in 2004. This school will feature a five-year curriculum intended to graduate physician-investigators rather than clinicians.

Sources and Further Reading: Helen Clapesattle, *The Doctors Mayo* (1941); John D. Clough, ed., *To Act as a Unit*, 3rd ed. (1996); George W. Crile, *George Crile, an Autobiography* (1947); Philip K. Strand, *A Century of Caring 1889–1989* (1988).

Rebecca Normington and Sarah Fuelleman
Marshfield Clinic, Wisconsin

Thomas M. Habermann and Renee E. Ziemer
Mayo Clinic, Minnesota

John D. Clough
Cleveland Clinic Foundation, Ohio

Orthopedic Implants

Warsaw, Indiana, calls itself the Orthopedic Capital of the World, and with good reason. Today, three of the world's top five orthopedic companies are headquartered in this north-central Indiana town of approximately twelve thousand. While orthopedics is defined broadly to include all kinds of bone and joint treatments, the largest modern segment is artificial joint replacements, and that's where Warsaw dominates the market. In 2002 Warsaw-based companies held more than 55 percent of the worldwide market for hip replacement products and more than 60 percent of the worldwide knee replacement market. When Stryker Corporation, located in Kalamazoo, Michigan, is added to complete the Midwest orthopedics roster, the market shares are even higher—a total of nearly 80 percent in both the hip and knee replacement. What caused such a concentration of high-tech, medical device firms? Much like the concentration of computer businesses in Silicon Valley, the answer seems to be mostly serendipity—that's where the founders of the industry happened to live when they got their start.

The first modern company in orthopedics was

DePuy, founded in 1895 by Italian immigrant Revra DePuy. A traveling pharmaceutical salesperson who also invented a formula for sugar-coated pills, DePuy located his splint business in Warsaw. In 1905 DePuy hired Justin O. Zimmer, a Warsaw native, as the company's first salesperson. Zimmer had no medical training or experience but was able to increase DePuy's business significantly. When Revra DePuy died in 1921, Zimmer approached DePuy's widow about assuming an ownership position in the company and a more active role in its management. Mrs. DePuy, who remarried in 1924, repeatedly rebuffed Zimmer, at one point telling him that he'd always be "small potatoes." So, Zimmer, on his own, in 1927 started the Zimmer Manufacturing Company in Warsaw, which specialized in a perforated aluminum splint. Such perforations allowed physicians to see on X-rays how a patient's fracture was healing. Zimmer's company was an immediate success, and Zimmer Manufacturing displaced DePuy as the world's largest orthopedic company.

Much like Silicon Valley, Warsaw has spawned other concentrations of related activity. In 1934 a DePuy sales representative, Don Richards, left the company to start his own business in Memphis, Tennessee. Richards Manufacturing then formed the basis of the orthopedic business of Smith and Nephew, a British-based health-care manufacturer. Tennessee is also home to the headquarters of Medtronic Sofamor Danek, the world's largest maker of implants designed for treatment of spinal disease. Medtronic Sofamor Danek, product of a company that began in Minnesota, also maintains its principal manufacturing facilities in Warsaw.

During the 1940s Homer Stryker, a physician from Kalamazoo, began selling his inventions, and in 1946, formed the Orthopedic Frame Company, the predecessor to the company that now bears his name.

In the 1950s the Warsaw orthopedic industry began developing the products that form the core of the modern industry, artificial joint replacements. Not until the 1950s had designs and materials become sophisticated enough to form the basis for mainstream research and development of artificial joints. By the 1970s joint replacements were more common, although materials and designs were still being improved in search of implants that would maintain their strength and function for years, while not reacting negatively within the body. In 1977 Dane Miller, a former Zimmer engineer, helped put together Biomet, a new orthopedic company to capitalize on the growth of the joint replacement business. In the 1980s joint replacement became common. Implants could be counted on to last a decade or more, and surgeons had become sufficiently skilled in the required surgical

procedures that the treatment became widely available around the world. The result has been an explosive growth in the orthopedics industry.

Demographics favor continued growth of the orthopedics industry as the Baby Boomer generation enters the time of life most closely associated with arthritic diseases and the need for joint replacement. That's good news for the Midwest's big four orthopedic companies and the dozen or so local suppliers in and around Warsaw and Kalamazoo. In the town of Warsaw, they say it's a "hip" place to be, and it's likely to stay that way for years to come.

Source and Further Reading: Michelle Bormet, *A History of the City of Warsaw, Indiana* (2001).

Bradley Bishop
Warsaw, Indiana

Populism

Lawrence Goodwin described populism as "the largest democratic mass movement in American history." As it applies to medicine, the concept of populism cannot be separated from this source. In its most widely disseminated form, political populism found expression in the People's party, led most notably by presidential hopeful and radical thinker William Jennings Bryan. Its germinal roots, founded on a strong rural culture, lay in the Grange movement and the Northern and Southern Farmers' Alliances that developed through the 1880s and early 1890s. These organizations were the most successful of a host of institutions that gave farmers a sense of their social and economic place in the emerging system of capitalist modernization growing up around them. While rural residents of the Midwest helped lay the foundation for a very different view of the country's political life in the late nineteenth century, the region also proved a fertile milieu for fostering alternatives in the understanding of health and well being.

As urban medical practitioners, particularly in Chicago, lauded the theoretical principles of scientific medicine and the structural principles of the business world applied to medical practice, they faced stiff competition in the open-ended American medical marketplace. The persistence, even growth, of unorthodox practices in medicine owes much to the midwestern experience. Osteopathy and chiropractic both have their origins in this region. Osteopathy was developed by a Missouri physician, Andrew Taylor Still, while chiropractic was the brainchild of Daniel David Palmer, an Iowa grocer. Both systems incorporated the idea that health was based on the regulation of "nervous fluids," a notion that can be traced back to unorthodox medical theorists in Europe like Franz Anton Mesmer. In the late nineteenth century, alternative medical practitioners—osteopaths and chiropractors, along with others who looked to homeopathy, hydropathy (water-cure), Christian Science, Thomsonian botanical medicine, and eclectics—were a powerful force, challenging the emerging therapeutic consensus based on scientific medicine that reflected the economic and social goals of elite urban physicians. This was a battle fought at the crossroads of the modern and the traditional, the urban and the rural, even the scientific and the superstitious. Medical populism can be seen in the persistence of alternative or unorthodox medical ideas into the twentieth century.

Populism, or its echoes, can also be seen in the new Progressive Era. Robert La Follette, for example, grew up in the Grange era and, when he became governor of Wisconsin, championed reform and regulation (particularly of public utilities) that became the Wisconsin Idea. It emphasized experts as advisors to the state and encouraged close contact between university academics and government officials. Widespread emphasis on efficiency, regulation, and public control helped midwestern medicine evolve from frontier heroics to applied science. This synthesis was a boon in the realm of public health, where university and government cooperated. In Wisconsin, for example, the 1918–1919 influenza epidemic was limited in its impact through strict measures that prevented all public gatherings and closed schools, churches, and theatres. In addition, record keeping was more standardized than in most states, and lives were saved.

Across the midwestern landscape, medicine was altered dramatically by the growth of hospitals, which tended to centralize and standardize practice. The automobile, a major force of social change, allowed doctors the opportunity to reach patients farther afield than ever before. This undermined the influence of traditional rural approaches and reinforced the power of allopaths (practitioners who emphasized scientific medicine). The end of the horse-and-buggy era also marked the extinction of the old archetype of the country doctor. Professionalization and specialization further contributed to the ultimate dominance of mainstream medicine. American Medical Association (AMA) membership, for example, grew from about eight thousand in 1900 to over seventy thousand in 1910.

After the controversial Flexner Report in 1910, changes in medical education further marginalized unorthodox practitioners, though in the case of chiropractic and osteopathy their ability to attract patients and practice unheeded by stringent and restrictive regulation continues to this day. Educational reform, licensing, economic status and social prestige, a strong

national organization (the AMA), and a positive public image characterize the modern profession. Rapid economic growth and the transformation of an agrarian and mercantile society into an urban industrial complex created the markets for modern medicine and supplied the capital to build medical schools, research centers, clinics, and hospitals. Scientific medicine was enhanced by modernization, and unorthodox practitioners diminished in numbers and prestige.

Political populism is one clue to medical populism. At its heart, it was agrarian. Agrarian revolt and its ultimate demise provide insight into the rise and fall of medical populism. When pressed by modernization and an economic and financial structure that made them feel abandoned to the cause of progress, rural residents of the Midwest developed broad-based strategies to challenge the new and all-encompassing capitalist order. Nevertheless, urban reform movements triumphed in the twentieth century, and whether for good or ill, became embedded within institutions that persist to this day. The decline of populism in the political arena (except insofar as it remains a valuable rhetorical device in the hands of the political elite) was almost complete by the mid-twentieth century, but populism remains influential in the medical realm.

Sources and Further Reading: Lawrence Goodwyn, *The Populist Moment*, abridged ed. (1978); Michael Kazin, *The Populist Persuasion*, rev. ed. (1998); Robert C. McMath, Jr., *Populist Vanguard* (1975); Ronald L. Numbers, "The Fall and Rise of the American Medical Profession," in Nathan O. Hatch, ed., *The Professions in American History* (1988); Ronald L. Numbers and Judith Walzer Leavitt, eds., *Wisconsin Medicine* (1981); Paul Starr, *The Social Transformation of American Medicine* (1982); Rosemary Stevens, *American Medicine and the Public Interest*, rev. ed. (1998).

Sebastian Normandin
McGill University, Montreal, Quebec

Psychiatric Centers

By 2002 the Substance Abuse and Mental Health Services Administration (SAMHSA) estimated that 8.3 percent of the U.S. adult population experienced a serious mental illness during the past year. Prevalence in the Midwest was similar to nationwide estimates. Social stereotypes about the Midwest and rural settings bring to mind notions of hard work, stoicism, hardiness, and mental sturdiness. The idyllic image of rural places has played an important role in mental health care in the Midwest.

By the nineteenth century, care for those with a mental disorder began to change, and humane prac-

The Minnesota State Psychiatric Hospital at Fergus Falls, which was built on the Kirkbride plan, c. 1915. Minnesota Historical Society, Location, M08.9 FF7.2 rp.

tices were beginning to emerge. In October 1844 thirteen superintendents of asylums and hospitals, called alienists, met to develop practices for change in institutionalized psychiatric care. The American Psychiatric Association, first known as the Association of Medical Superintendents of the American Institutions for the Insane, emerged out of this meeting, as did new standards of practice, issued in 1851. Dr. William McClay Awl, Superintendent of the Central Ohio Lunatic Asylum in Columbus, became the second president of the group. During this time asylums developed to serve a primarily custodial function for mental patients. These facilities were often built in rural places and stressed pastoral, peaceful, and healthful lifestyle as the proper treatment for patients.

Thomas Story Kirkbride devised an architectural design with a central administration building flanked by two wings that allowed for the segregation of patients by sex and symptoms. The plan emphasized fresh air, natural light, and beautiful grounds to calm and stimulate patients. Patients were encouraged to work in the surrounding farms and communities. During the 1800s every state in the Midwest (except Nebraska and South Dakota) had an asylum built on the Kirkbride plan. As the medical model began to permeate mental health care in the early twentieth century, psychoanalysis, drug therapy, and other treatments rendered this plan and conventional asylums obsolete.

The Menninger Clinic, founded in Topeka, Kansas, in 1925 by Will, Karl, and C. F. Menninger, sought to revolutionize the field of psychiatry. They originated the concept of milieu therapy, using the total environment to benefit the patient. This innovation moved the care of those with mental disorders from asylum warehousing to treatment and a return

home. Murray Bowen, a Menninger psychiatrist, developed the Family Systems Theory approach that emphasized the family unit as an important facet of treatment. The Menninger Clinic also explored the relationships between religion and mental health.

Many events have contributed to changes in mental health care treatment in the Midwest, such as the establishment of the Juvenile Psychopathic Institute in Chicago in 1909 and the passage of federal legislation, including the 1946 Mental Health Act that provided for grants to establish mental health clinics and treatment facilities. A 1950s report entitled *Action for Mental Health* made recommendations for better research into mental illness and improved treatment of those with mental disorders, and this led to rebuilding the mental health system. In the 1970s began the modern movement in mental health care, which continues the deinstitutionalization and emphasis on scientific and clinical efforts to expand neuroscience and an understanding of brain chemistry.

Sources and Further Reading: William C. Cockerham, *Sociology of Mental Disorder,* 5th ed. (2000); Hugh Freeman, ed., *A Century for Psychiatry* (1999); Edward Shorter, *A History of Psychiatry* (1997); Douglas Wright, *State Estimates of Substance Use from the 2001 National Household Survey on Drug Abuse,* vol. 1, *Findings* (2003).

Sharon L. Larson
Substance Abuse and Mental Health
Services Administration
Rockville, Maryland

Note: The views expressed in this publication do not necessarily reflect the views of the United States Department of Health and Human Services.

Ralph Waters [1883–1979] and Anesthesia

No one person builds a specialty in medicine, but a single individual such as Ralph Waters can make unique contributions. Ralph Waters received his medical degree from Case Western Reserve and immediately went into private practice in Sioux City, Iowa. From there, he relocated to Kansas City, where he established an ambulatory anesthesia clinic within an early outpatient surgical center.

Even though his private practice was very busy, he was able to improve the field of anesthesiology through his research efforts. Waters wrote extensively on carbon dioxide absorption, a major problem at the time, and developed a cuffed endotracheal tube with Dr. Arthur Guedel. This tube was destined to save many lives. It protected a patient's airway in coma or during surgery and provided a better method to deliver inhaled anesthetics to keep the patient unconscious.

In 1927 Waters moved to Madison, Wisconsin, where he started the first university-based residency training program in anesthesia. After establishing his program, Waters hoped to export his model to other parts of the country. His first chance to do this arrived in 1935, when Dr. Emery Rovenstine, a resident under Waters, accepted the position of Director of Anesthesia at Bellevue Hospital in New York. Many of Waters's other residents went on to head anesthesia departments throughout the United States.

Waters did many things well and was often among the first to do them, including establishing residency training in a form still utilized today, one that integrates basic science and clinical research. He was also skilled in administrating both his department and national organizations and helped to establish specialty certification for anesthesia.

Sources and Further Reading: Douglas R. Bacon and Richard Ament, "Ralph Waters and the Beginning of Academic Anesthesiology in the United States: The Wisconsin Template," *Journal of Clinical Anesthesia* 7 (Sept. 1995); Douglas R. Bacon, "Why Celebrate Ralph Milton Waters?" *ASA Newsletter* 65 (Sept. 2001).

Robert Sands
Roswell Park Cancer Institute, New York

Sleep Research to Sleep Medicine

Nathaniel Kleitman, a pioneer in sleep research and famous for his Mammoth Caves experiments, discovered with Eugene Aserinsky rapid eye movement (REM) sleep in 1953 at the University of Chicago Medical School (UCMS). William Dement, a student of Kleitman, described REM sleep cyclicity and the duality of REM versus non-REM sleep that changed the scientific community's view of the sleeping brain from one of rest and dormancy to one also experiencing complex activities. Allen Rechtschaffen, at UCMS, proved that REM sleep is essential for life, and that REM sleep deprivation can result in death. He identified muscle paralysis, normal in REM sleep, as the underlying cause of cataplexy or the sudden weakness characteristic of narcolepsy. Contributions from University of Michigan neurologist Michael Aldrich helped demonstrate that the neurotransmitter orexin (hypocretin) can be deficient, even absent, in brains of narcoleptics.

In 1961 Dement pioneered what is now the Sleep Research Society. Fourteen years later in Chicago, the Association of Sleep Disorders Centers (ASDC), now the American Academy of Sleep Medicine, came into existence. Accreditation of sleep disorders centers (1976), the first examination of sleep specialists (1978), publication of the journal *Sleep* (1978), and the new nosology of sleep disorders (1979) rapidly followed, all with major contributions from midwesterners. REM behavior disorder was described in 1985 by neurologists in Minneapolis, though the first case description occurred in 1969 at The Ohio State University.

In the 1990s the proliferation of sleep disorder centers became exponential with entry into the sleep field by clinicians from many disciplines. The growing awareness of sleep-disordered breathing (SDB) as a major public health problem was facilitated by the prolific research of several Midwest groups, such as Henry Ford Hospital staff who pioneered surgical approaches to SDB and emphasized pharmacological approaches to all sleep-related disorders. Researchers at the University of Wisconsin, Madison have confirmed sleep apnea as a major cause of hypertension, independent of other known risk factors. Numerous other cardiovascular and neurological consequences of SDB are becoming evident, including documented erectile dysfunction as a consequence of chronic intermittent hypoxemia.

The Ohio State Sleep Disorders Center was the first in the Midwest to be accredited and, in 1986, hosted the first annual meeting of the newly created Association of Professional Sleep Societies. The ASDC examination committee initiated the process to establish an independent American Board of Sleep Medicine, which was unanimously approved by the ASDC board in November 1990, appointing a midwesterner as its first president. Another midwesterner, Meir Kryger (from Winnipeg), coauthored with Roth and Dement the first textbook on sleep medicine (1989) and created a task force that led to official

American Medical Association recognition of sleep medicine on January 1, 1995. This process, culminating in clear educational and examination requirements, scientific meetings, publications, and formal recognition, is a modern example of the development of a medical specialty.

Sources and Further Reading: American Sleep Disorders Association, *The International Classification of Sleep Disorders: Diagnostic and Coding Manual* (1990); Nathaniel Kleitman, *Sleep and Wakefulness*, rev. and enlarged ed. (1963); Meir H. Kryger, Thomas Roth, and William C. Dement, eds., *Principles and Practice of Sleep Medicine*, 3rd ed. (2000).

Helmut S. Schmidt
Ohio Sleep Medicine Institute, Dublin, Ohio

Helping People Help Themselves

One of the major, if unheralded, medical advances of the past fifty years has been the change in education and self-help for patients. This change is evidenced in health classes in schools, medical newsletters, the Internet, and the proliferation of support groups. The Midwest was particularly strong in alternative medicine, in nontraditional schools, and in self-help and utilization of doctor books for the home; it was also the area that spawned several of the major self-help organizations. The Battle Creek Sanitarium espoused a high-fiber diet decades before it was accepted as healthy, and linked religion to healing. Religion was also a feature of Alcoholics Anonymous, and religious zeal characterized the women of the Women's Christian Temperance Union.

Many of the programs of patient support tied to specific diseases have come out of the Midwest, and throughout the region there is no disease, minor or major, that is not represented by a local support group. Some, such as Alzheimer's or epilepsy societies, concentrate heavily on counseling for family members. Most of the larger groups have developed a lobbying presence, and many have established funds for research. At the same time societal changes have influenced care, public health, and governmental regulations to enhance health for citizens throughout the region.

The Battle Creek Sanitarium

The Battle Creek (Michigan) Sanitarium was dedicated to making and keeping people healthy through a plan that substituted exercise, a vegetarian diet, fresh air, nonrestrictive clothing, and the use of pure water in the form of baths, wraps, and sprays for conventional medicine and drugs. It flourished from 1876 until 1930.

The sanitarium treatment had its origin in a health reform movement of the mid-nineteenth century. In 1867 Ellen G. White, a leader of Seventh-Day Adventists who settled in Battle Creek, inspired the founding of the Western Health Reform Institute, combining health reform and religion for healing. In 1876 John Harvey Kellogg, a Seventh-Day Adventist and physician at the institute, was put in charge. Under him, the institute became known as the Battle Creek Sanitarium, and both the health program and the facility were enlarged, popularized, and secularized. The institution grew from a small, failing facility known only to Adventists to an elegant one caring for well over a thousand people a day from all over the world.

Retrospectively, the most successful parts of the sanitarium program were diet and exercise. Diet stressed nuts, soy, cereal products, fruits, and vegetables. Kellogg himself developed many of the foods used in the diet, and he marketed them outside the sanitarium through several food companies. He and his brother, William K. Kellogg, developed a process of flaking grain to make it digestible. One of the early products was cornflakes, which became a staple of the

John Harvey Kellogg, superintendent of the Battle Creek Sanitarium, Michigan. E. E. Doty, 1914, Library of Congress Prints and Photographs Division, LC-USZ62-87210.

company that bears the Kellogg name. A gymnasium with running track, rooms filled with mechanical exercise devices, and swimming pools provided cardiovascular fitness, muscle strength, and flexibility. While the diet and exercise programs would meet many of today's requirements, they had limited scientific and medical support at the time. Nevertheless, Kellogg convinced thousands that they were the only key to health.

The extensive use of laxatives and enemas was a less pleasant part of the treatment. Kellogg believed that most illness was the result of a "lazy" colon, causing constipation and the build up of poisons in the body. It was necessary to rid the body of the poisons, Kellogg thought, while diet, exercise, and other aspects of the sanitarium program restored colon health and therefore general health.

Several schools were associated with the sanitarium, including schools of nursing, education, and nutrition. Instruction was provided for Adventist medical students. The sanitarium treatment was made available in several locations throughout the country at branch sanitaria.

An illness and ongoing rift with the Adventists finally cost Kellogg some of his power over the sanitarium in the 1920s. In 1928, against his advice, a huge addition was added to an already large facility opened in 1903. Debt coupled with the Great Depression drove the sanitarium into bankruptcy. Although Kellogg tried to restructure the sanitarium in the 1930s, it never fully recovered. The buildings, which still exist, were sold to the federal government in 1942. The sanitarium continued in smaller facilities for many years after Kellogg's death in 1943, but began moving toward more conventional hospital status in the 1950s.

Sources and Further Reading: Patsy Gerstner, *The Temple of Health* (1996); Richard W. Schwarz, *John Harvey Kellogg* (1970; reprinted 1981).

Patsy Gerstner
Cleveland

Increased Social Control

Social control refers to any and all coercive, manipulative, or conditioning techniques promoting acceptance of the social order. French philosopher Michel Foucault defined a relationship between knowledge and power, showing how social control, also called social engineering, has advanced with science and "medicalization." The introduction of increasingly rigid norms of behavior, the crusading impulses of reform,

and the expert's important role in promoting social hygiene and purity can also be characterized as forms of social engineering.

The first major wave of social control through medicine was linked to growing concern regarding public health in the nineteenth century, as epidemics became identified with infectious agents and contaminated water. The development of public health initiatives evolved from spotty and haphazard local programs in the middle and late nineteenth century to a national Public Health Service in 1912. Public health reforms were spurred by a fear among the elite that degeneration and decay—often associated with immigrant-filled urban slums—were undermining traditional rural and small-town American values. These values were considered typical for rural areas of the Midwest, though public health reform achieved significant gains in the urban centers of Chicago and Milwaukee. Minnesota was one of the earliest states to introduce a Board of Health, in 1872. In contrast to broad-based public health reforms advocated by physicians and engineers from the East Coast, the Minnesota approach reflected the work of Hibbert Winslow Hall, whose book *The New Public Health* (1916) advocated modern scientific reform in lieu of broad social reform. The findings and application of bacteriology in the 1880s and 1890s changed the face of public health, but these changes were slower to spread to other more crusading elements of social reform, except in efforts to prevent epidemics.

In the early decades of the twentieth century social hygiene became a major concern among reformers, and though rooted in the late-nineteenth-century quest for social purity, the movement was also scientific. Alcoholism, venereal disease, and feeblemindedness were the three most readily perceived faces of social decay, and prohibition, blood tests for marriage licenses, and eugenics, respectively, became the proposed solutions. Eugenics, an idea of human improvement based on the reproductive restriction of the unfit (negative eugenics) or the encouragement of the fit (positive eugenics), was the most invasive element of this wing of social control. The term was coined in 1883 by Sir Francis Galton, cousin of Charles Darwin, to describe what he called "the study of the agencies under social control that may improve or impair the racial qualities of future generations, either physically or mentally."

Eugenics achieved significant popularity in some midwestern states. In 1906 breakfast cereal magnate J.H. Kellogg created the Race Betterment Foundation in Battle Creek, Michigan, which sponsored a series of lectures on the topic in 1914 and 1915 and again in 1928. Indiana was the first state in the country to introduce eugenic sterilization laws in 1907, and the

American Eugenics Society sponsored "fitter families" contests at state fairs across the Midwest in the 1920s. The popularity of eugenics in the Midwest may also be associated with improvements in the realm of animal breeding and husbandry, and the American Breeders Association was a proponent of many eugenic ideas. That human stock and livestock were considered similarly may have been unsettling to some, but seemed like common sense to others.

The motivation to develop an increasingly sophisticated system of social engineering was brought about by a series of shared assumptions about the state of society. Some leaders perceived industrialization, mechanization, urban growth, and rampant competitive individualism as destabilizing influences on accepted class, religious, and family relations, and a source of tension in society. In response, psychologists and medical practitioners articulated a new model of social control that moved away from conventional adjustments through state authority and proposed a "science" of society. Sociologist Edward A. Ross's *Social Control* (1901) was the movement's foremost text. Social engineering attempted to facilitate adjustment to modern urban industrial society by methods based on psychology and sociology that included public opinion, advertising, leadership, suggestion, and group discussion. Jane Addams's Chicago-based settlement house movement, the quest to Americanize the new immigrant, and the applied sociology of the Chicago School are representative midwestern examples of this trend. The central importance of professionals and experts in this social change cannot be overstated, and in many cases their prestige depended on their role as social advisors.

Medical professionals also played a major role in the social control drama. They advised mothers on proper childcare techniques, spread the gospel of cleanliness as a means to control endemic and epidemic disease, and denounced the "bad habits" of the rural and urban poor. They thereby helped medicalize many aspects of daily life. As the Progressive Era gave way to the New Deal and the rise of the liberal managerial state, the impact of medical experts became increasingly tied to bureaucratic power and the benefits of the welfare state.

The post–World War II social milieu witnessed a rapid decline in certain elements of social control— eugenics, for one, because of its association with Nazi Germany—and the rise of others. Psychiatry and the pharmaceutical industry took on a larger role, and the medicalization of depression, anxiety, and other psychological problems followed as a matter of course. The widespread introduction of modern birth control methods in the early 1960s dramatically affected society and sexuality. Contemporary issues surrounding the new realm of genetic testing and gene therapy, the AIDS crisis, and cloning seem to raise the specter of outdated ideas like eugenics and the crusade against venereal disease.

Because the Midwest grew and developed at the same time as modernization changed the American social landscape, aspects of social control were heavily influential in the lives of many midwesterners. Tensions surrounding the issue of social control persist, and as midwestern culture continues to celebrate ethnicity, independence, and even eccentricity, there are elements of resistance to what Foucault describes in *Birth of the Clinic* (1973) as the power of the medical "gaze." Social engineering continues to reflect scientific principles, but fortunately law, tradition, and idealism continue to modify psychological or medical intrusion into the lives of midwesterners.

Sources and Further Reading: John C. Burnham, *Bad Habits* (1993); Dolan DNA Learning Center, www.eugenics archive.org; Daniel J. Kevles, *In the Name of Eugenics* (1985); Elizabeth Lunbeck, *The Psychiatric Persuasion* (1994); Nancy Tomes, *The Gospel of Germs* (1998); Robert H. Wiebe, *The Search for Order, 1877–1920* (1967).

Sebastian Normandin
McGill University, Montreal, Quebec

Patient Support Organizations

In the twentieth century, developments in medical care, politics, and education included not only proliferation of specialty groups among physicians, but also the dramatic emergence of patient support groups. Almost every disease, no matter how uncommon, found a local and then a national champion for social and educational support. Some groups remained amorphous or competitive despite representing the same disease, as was the case with several competitive Parkinson's Disease groups. Other groups, including those interested in epilepsy or in heart disease, successfully merged to present a common national front for fundraising, political lobbying, publications, and educational seminars. The Midwest, with its tradition of cooperation, often led the way in creating such groups, several of which seem representative.

Physicians and social workers formed an informal association for the prevention and relief of heart disease in New York City in 1915, and as cardiology formed as a discipline, six physicians representing various medical groups formed the American Heart Association (AHA) in 1924. The six included Robert B. Prabel and James B. Harrick of Chicago and Hugh D. McCulloch of St. Louis. In the 1930s and 1940s the

AHA deliberately spread its efforts to the public, moving beyond physicians and scientists. The AHA reorganized in 1948 into a voluntary health agency to further efforts in public education, fund-raising, and community service.

The Research Milestone awards supported by the AHA have included many innovations from the Midwest, each accompanied by financial support from the AHA and its affiliates. In 1956 Ancel Keys, utilizing funds from AHA and the University of Minnesota, linked dietary fat with cholesterol and began the move toward a lower-fat diet for all Americans. The Minnesota group, including William Wierich, Vincent Gott, and Walter Lillehei, developed the first externally powered pacemaker. The 1958 Milestone Award from AHA went to Louis Sapirstein of Minnesota, who led in the use of radioactive potassium and rubidium to measure blood flow.

None of these individuals worked alone. Keys worked with Minnesota colleagues Joseph Anderson and Franciso Grande to define the relationships between fat composition in the diet and serum cholesterol. This pioneer work led to awareness of risk factors based on cholesterol levels. Research at the University of Minnesota and the work of Earl E. Bakken, who collaborated with Lillehei on pacemakers, eventually resulted in what is now the Medtronic Corporation, still based in Minneapolis, with customers at the Mayo Clinic, the National Institutes of Health, and the Walter Reed Medical Center. Worldwide, according to Value Line, Medtronic employs more than thirty thousand people, has annual earnings of over $9 billion, and continues to lead the world in the production of cardiac pacemakers. Recently, Medtronic has begun innovative programs in deep-brain stimulation for relief of pain and tremor, and continued to lead its field, illustrative of the complex relationship of organization, individuals, and business.

An example of the impact of lay organizations on education and public policy is the story of the Alzheimer's Association. In the 1970s several areas in the Midwest, from central Ohio to northern Wisconsin, developed a local cluster of caregivers for Alzheimer's patients. By 1980 a group of such caregivers merged efforts to establish the Alzheimer's Association. Within only a few years the organization solidified and grew to claim over two hundred chapters. Thousands of volunteers assure continued attention and help encourage millions to donate time and money. Services, public awareness, training programs, and above all efforts to increase national funding and influence national policy have been paramount. The association reports that its first grant for research, $78 thousand, was awarded in 1982, but millions more have been given to support programs selected by ex-

perts in the field in an open and competitive fashion. The awarding of grants by a peer review system involves many in the nationwide organization, which remains based in Chicago.

The International Dyslexia Foundation is actually the direct descendant of the pioneering work of physician Samuel T. Orton of the University of Iowa, who identified dyslexia (though not by that word) as a specific neurologic disorder. He and psychologist and educator Anna Gillingham devoted a lifetime of research to language and reading problems. Orton's suggestion that the lesions in dyslexia might be similar to those produced by traumatic brain injury has not been fully supported by modern imaging, but there is now wide acceptance that dyslexia is an organic neurologic disorder. Orton's concepts became crystallized into several alternative methods of teaching, and educational approaches for individuals who have major problems with reading differ widely across the nation. Nevertheless, the acceptance that learning disabilities, most specifically dyslexia, do not imply laziness or stupidity and are physical disorders has made it possible for many children to lead more productive and happier lives. For a time, the Orton Society was the official name of the largest group involved with dyslexia, but the name has now been changed to the International Dyslexia Association, which claims thirteen thousand members and forty branches. Although financial support remains modest, educational programs, conferences, and international linkages have dramatically expanded during the past twenty years, and many public school systems have benefited from the association's work.

Sources and Further Reading: Neal R. Cutler and John J. Sramek, *Understanding Alzheimer's Disease* (1996); T. R. Miles and Elaine Miles, *Dyslexia: A Hundred Years On* (1999); William Moore, *Fighting For Life* (1983); David Shenk, *The Forgetting: Alzheimer's, Portrait of an Epidemic* (2001).

George Paulson
The Ohio State University–Columbus

Rehabilitation and Sports Medicine

Drawing its ethos from sources as varied as the American Orthopedic Association and the nineteenth-century fringe practice of electrotherapy, the rehabilitation professions began to define themselves around the time of World War I. Originally spearheaded by developments in Massachusetts General Hospital and the use of physical reconstructionists by the U.S. Army (largely orthopedic surgeons and physical therapy physicians), the practice of physical medicine did not formally acquire medical specialty status until 1947.

Several midwestern individuals and institutions played prominent roles in the maturation of physical medicine. Indeed, in 1926 World War I veteran John Stanley Coulter joined the faculty of the Northwestern University Medical School to become the first full-time academic physical medicine physician. Coulter served as a leader in the development of education and training for physical medicine for the next two decades. His initial programs consisted of short three- to six-month courses. Later, these were extended to include a one-year training period for physicians in practice.

The 1930s continued the resolute organization of the field of rehabilitation. Frank Krusen instituted the Physical Medicine Program and the first three-year residency in Physical Medicine at the Mayo Clinic in 1936. Both Coulter and Krusen were leaders for the American Academy of Physical Medicine, now called the American Academy of Physical Medicine and Rehabilitation (AAPM&R). In 1938 the Academy began to popularize a word coined by Krusen, "physiatrist," which was meant to designate the physician who employed both physical and medical therapeutics in the treatment of neurological and musculoskeletal disorders. In 1941 Krusen wrote the first widely used textbook for physical medicine study.

One of the seminal influences on the practice of physical medicine arose from the inquisitiveness of an internist from Missouri, Howard A. Rusk. Stationed with the Army Air Corps Convalescent and Rehabilitation Services during World War II, Rusk noted that a passive or inactive convalescence resulted in the physical and emotional deterioration of the recovering soldiers. He set up an experiment in which one barracks carried out active rehabilitation, while another barracks carried on with its passive convalescence. There was a dramatic recovery of strength and return to active duty in those soldiers who were aggressively rehabilitated. The value of this approach was obvious, and it remains a basic tenet of rehabilitation practice today.

Because the search continued for additional empiric clarification in physical medicine and rehabilitation, in 1967 the Association of Academic Physiatrists (AAP) was formed. The group of educators who organized the AAP was led by Ernest W. Johnson of The Ohio State University. The AAP continues to promote methods of teaching and scholarship in physical medicine.

The specialty field of physiatry has grown to include seventy-nine accredited residency training programs, with many of the recognized premier sites located in the Midwest.

Sports medicine is an equally rich and diverse area. A nebulous umbrella term that originally referred to the diagnosis and treatment of athletic injuries, sports medicine has evolved to encompass a number of related subdisciplines, including clinical medicine, orthopedics, exercise physiology, biomechanics, physical therapy, athletic training, sports nutrition, and sports psychology. In the early nineteenth century hot topics in sports medicine were strikingly similar to today's interests—dieting, general information about exercise, training for sport, and the dangers of alcohol and tobacco. One difference, however, has been the relatively recent emphasis on prevention: reducing the incidence of disease and injury by modifying environmental or behavioral factors that are causally related to it. Several institutions in the Midwest have been at the forefront of this evolution, particularly with regard to the inextricable links between medicine, health, and exercise.

By the middle of the nineteenth century, medical schools began providing graduating physicians with the opportunity to teach and research in medical school or become affiliated with departments of physical education. In 1925, the University of Illinois started one of the first programs in the nation emphasizing research in exercise physiology. Over the next eight decades, a vast anthology of epidemiologic evidence, much of it from the Midwest, has helped bolster the connection between exercise and disease, particularly the close association between physical inactivity and heart disease, high blood pressure, diabetes, and osteoporosis.

Since the 1950s the American College of Sports Medicine (ACSM) has been the leading authority in sports medicine. Originally conceived as the convergence of medicine, physical education, and physiology, ACSM now exists to enhance the health, performance, fitness, health care, and well-being of all people. Several scientists from the Midwest played prominent leadership roles in its development, helping it to become both a scholarly and service-oriented institution. For example, Bruno Balke was the president of ACSM from 1965 to 1966 while on faculty at the University of Wisconsin at Madison. During his tenure, Balke helped move ACSM's central office from Ann Arbor, Michigan, to Madison, where it remained until 1983, when it was placed permanently in Indianapolis.

Examples of other prominent Midwest scientists who helped define and refine the sports medicine field are Ancel Keys, who formulated meals for combat soldiers that became known as "K rations" and who founded the Laboratory of Physiological Hygiene at the University of Minnesota; Elsworth R. Buskirk at The Pennsylvania State University, who is known for his work in body fluid balance during exercise and environmental stress;

Thomas K. Cureton, who developed the YMCA's National Aquatic Program for youth during his tenure at the University of Illinois, Urbana-Champaign; Sid Robinson, who examined the physiology of exercise and temperature regulation in collaboration with Harvard physiologists while at Indiana University in Bloomington; David L. Costill, who directed the world-renowned Human Performance Laboratory at Ball State University; Harwood S. Belding, who started the Environmental Physiology Laboratory at the University of Pittsburgh; and Victor L. Katch, who performed extensive research in the area of body composition, nutrition, exercise, and weight control at the University of Michigan.

Without question, technological advances in the future will help the fields of rehabilitation and sports medicine flourish. The contributions of these physicians and scientists have helped permanently root these exciting fields in the Midwest region.

Sources and Further Reading: J. W. Berryman, "ACSM: 50 years of progress and service," *Advances in Sports Medicine and Exercise Science: 50 Years of ACSM* 1 (2004); T. M. Cole, "The Greening of Physiatry in a Golden Era of Rehabilitation,"*Archives of Physical Medicine and Rehabilitation* 74 (1993); Glenn Gritzer, *The Making of Rehabilitation: A Political Economy of Medicine Specialization 1890-1980* (1985); W. D. McArdle, F. I. Katch, and V. L. Katch, *Exercise Physiology: Energy, Nutrition, and Human Performance*, 4th ed. (1996); E. E. Vogel, "The Beginnings of Modern Physiotherapy," *Phsyicas Therapy* 56 (1976).

Tim N. Ziegenfuss
Perry, Ohio

James A. Landis
Lakeland Community College, Ohio

The Woman's Christian Temperance Union and Alcoholics Anonymous

Following the Civil War, vast societal change began to occur throughout the United States. Immigration from all parts of the world, construction of railroads, and the increasing urbanization of the United States all contributed to a new social order. Along with this societal change came the ills often associated with such change. Increasingly, crime and immoral behavior were attributed, justly or not, to the use of alcohol and narcotics. Over time, various organizations arose that sought to promote temperance and abstinence from alcohol; two in particular have had important Midwest roots, the Woman's Christian Temperance Union and Alcoholics Anonymous.

Temperance movements developed in the 1870s. The women of Fredonia, New York, were among the

An Ohio Anti-Saloon League message. Courtesy The Westerville Public Library.

first to organize and visit local saloons to press their cause, and on December 22, 1873, they adopted the name Woman's Christian Temperance Union (WCTU). The movement quickly gained popularity and increasing influence. On December 23, 1873, Dio Lewis made a presentation on temperance in Hillsboro, Ohio, and in response, the women of the town took to the streets on the following day to begin the Woman's Temperance Crusade. Eliza Thompson, daughter of a former governor, led a group of seventy women from the local Presbyterian church to the saloons while singing "Give to the Winds Thy Fears," which later became known as the Crusade Hymn. Every day they visited saloons, drugstores, and anywhere else alcohol was sold, praying on the floors of the establishments or, if they were not allowed in, outside on their knees in the snow. They continued until almost all of the businesses capitulated. The success of these women ignited the growth of the temperance movement throughout the Midwest, and Mother Thompson, as she became known, inspired many women to face fearlessly the rebuke of those who opposed the temperance cause. It is estimated that during the Crusade of 1873–1874, liquor was eliminated in over 250 settlements, and there was a great surge in church attendance and a substantial decline in crime.

Following a planning session at Chautauqua, New York, in 1874, the women decided to hold a national convention in Cleveland. The national WCTU, now intending to be more than a local effort, chose Annie Wittenmyer as its first president. During her tenure, the organization spread to twenty-three states and claimed over twenty-six thousand members. Her successor, Frances Willard, further extended the influence of the WCTU by expanding the organization internationally and began to utilize political means as well as moral persuasion to effect change. Willard had previously served as the first Dean of Women at Northwestern University. During her presidency, the scope of the WCTU broadened to address all social issues of importance to women, including voting rights and participation in church administration. She is one of the few women represented in Statuary Hall in the United States Capitol Building.

In many ways, the impact that the Woman's Christian Temperance Crusade had on the sale and consumption of liquor was a watershed in the nation's history. It spoke for the power that an organized group of women could have, even without the right to vote, and most certainly contributed to the development of the suffrage movement and subsequent passage of the Nineteenth Amendment. Since its founding, the WCTU has influenced not only substance abuse policy but also numerous other social policies that affect the lives of the population as a whole. It continues to be an active organization, headquartered in Evanston, Illinois, not far from the former residence of Frances Willard.

One of the world's largest support organizations, Alcoholics Anonymous (AA) was created in Akron, Ohio, following a meeting in 1935 of William Wilson and Robert Smith. Wilson had been a successful New York stockbroker until he became unemployable and debt-ridden as a result of chronic alcoholism. He had once been admired for his notion of individual stock analysis, which he had partly devised so that employment would not block his alcohol use. A "spiritual awakening" led to Wilson's first meaningful period of abstinence in late 1934 and early 1935. He became associated with Smith, an Akron physician whose medical career had been destroyed by his own alcoholism, and these two established AA.

The concept of alcoholism as a disease was gaining acceptance at the time, and this contributed to the two men's thinking. The program they established was based on absolute abstinence as a fundamental core of therapy, plus a series of specific steps to be practiced to create a new life for the alcoholic. There was to be complete avoidance of any hierarchy based on class, race, gender, or religious differences. Nevertheless, the AA program is laced with religious concepts, many of which Wilson had embraced as a result of his exposure to the Oxford Group of scholarly students of the Christian Bible.

AA demonstrated that one alcoholic could influence and lead another alcoholic to recovery better than anyone else. After the establishment of the first AA fellowship in Akron, subsequent groups appeared in New York and Cleveland. There are now hundreds of such groups throughout the world, and millions of individuals call themselves members. Spousal support groups, groups for children, groups for drug addicts, and similar initiatives have followed the lead of AA. The central features of AA are largely unchanged from those originally espoused by its founders in the 1930s.

Sources and Further Reading: Jack S. Blocker, Jr., *"Give to the Winds Thy Fears": The Women's Temperance Crusade, 1873–1874* (1985); Jed Dannenbaum, *Drink and Disorder: Temperance Reform in Cincinnati from the Washingtonian Revival to the WCTU* (1984); Vince Fox, *Addiction, Change and Choice* (1993); Ernest Kurtz, *A.A.: The Story* (1988).

Mark Hurst
Twin Valley Psychiatric Center,
Columbus, Ohio

Educating the Healers

Education for the healing arts in the Midwest has been occasionally innovative and may at times seem locally inspired, but more usually it reflects national trends in enhanced requirements and response to social pressures. Admission policies at medical schools serve as a microcosm of educational trends in science, dentistry, and even law. There has been an astounding change in the percentage of women in admitted classes; the last generation witnessed a shift from 5 percent women in the medical class to essentially gender parity. Minority groups have fared less well, except for those of Asian and Indian descent. Nursing schools have begun to include more men and have raised educational standards. The aptitude of the average student seems as high as ever, as the educational curriculum has shifted more toward a hands-on approach. The unique nature of each state is illustrated by their different approaches to and forms of medical education, ranging from a single school to multiple branches or to several individual and state-supported but competing units. From the early example of William Osler, a practical "bedside" educational model has dominated in the Midwest. Science has been emphasized in several programs, but so have innovative curricula like the one at

Case Western Reserve in Cleveland. The Midwest has been the home not only for alternative medical approaches since pioneer days but also for the development of chiropractic and osteopathic medicine.

Admissions Policies

The selection process for determining student admission to American medical schools is highly complex and is governed by strict national codes, recommendations, and formal standards. The Admissions Committee at every school pays close attention to academic accomplishments, performance on standardized tests, apparent motivation and character, history of research experience and community service, and potential for leadership. Extraordinary care is taken to ensure that the student has an understanding of medicine as a profession and has demonstrated the necessary academic rigor.

This has not always been the case, however. Over the past century, admission to medical schools, both in the midwestern states and throughout the nation, has changed markedly. Examination of admissions requirements in the Midwest in the early 1900s reveals minimal criteria; often little college course work or formal education was required. Student admission to medical school was often based on family connection, personal relationships, or simply on the ability to pay tuition. Medical schools often had no affiliation with universities, and many early universities viewed instruction in medicine as more trade-based than professional or science-based.

Dramatic changes took place at the start of the twentieth century, beginning with the Flexner Report (1910), an indictment of the status of medical education in the United States. The Midwest paralleled the nation with the evolution of its medical schools and medical education, but there are regional differences as well as great variety within the Midwest. Schools in the Midwest range from among the nation's smallest in student enrollment to some of the nation's largest, and from schools with an emphasis on primary care to those emphasizing comprehensive research. Although the broad range in size and scope of midwestern medical centers is not unique, they are widely recognized as being at the cutting edge in maintaining the delicate balance of education, research, and patient care. There are currently thirty-two accredited M.D.-granting medical schools in the Midwest: seven in Illinois, six in Ohio, four in Missouri, three in Michigan, three in Minnesota, two in Wisconsin, two in Nebraska and one each in Indiana, Iowa, Kansas, North Dakota, and South Dakota.

National statistics reflect fluctuations in the num-

ber of applicants for medical school. In the earliest years of records (1926–1927), 10,250 students applied to American medical schools; 6,099 of them enrolled in the first year. In 1949–1950, 24,434 applied. Fluctuations were seen over the years, and 1996–1997 saw an all-time record number of applicants, 46,965 with 16,201 enrolled in the first year. Applications again have declined, with 34,859 applicants to medical schools in the 2001–2002 cycle and 16,365 students in first-year enrollment. Such fluctuations in applicants to medical school also applied in the Midwest and reflect the national economy and periods of war or national conflict, but recently they have been influenced by unprecedented debt levels of recent graduates, uncertainty about the future of practice, the length of medical education, and possibly even widely publicized concerns about litigation from patients.

Even more interesting changes have taken place since the early years of medical education, when applicants were almost exclusively males from the majority population. We can now document a significant nationwide increase in both applicants and matriculants who are women, as well as an increase in students from underrepresented minority populations. In the 1965–1966 applicant cycle, of 18,703 total applicants, only 1,676 (9 percent) were women, and of 8,554 matriculants, 799 (9.3 percent) were women. In the 2001–2002 entering class, of the 34,859 applicants, 16,717 (47.9 percent) were women, and of the 16,365 matriculants, 7,784 (47.5 percent) were women. Similar changes have occurred throughout the Midwest. The Midwest was among the leaders early in encouraging women. The first woman medical student in America, Elizabeth Blackwell, was from Cincinnati, and six of the first seven women trained in the United States were from the Midwest.

Underrepresented minority groups, defined as African American, Native American, Mexican American, and Mainland Puerto Rican, have also increased significantly. In the 1970–1971 entering class, of the 1,250 underrepresented applicants, 808 students (7.1 percent) enrolled in first-year classes. Applications from minority students peaked during the 1996–1997 cycle, when of 5,157 applicants to medical school, 2,223 students (13.1 percent) enrolled in first-year classes. More recently, both applicants and matriculants have declined, probably reflecting increased opportunities in other fields. Even if admissions are similar throughout the Midwest (and echo national trends) and curricula are standard in all schools, the midwestern states differ markedly in their educational facilities.

Sources and Further Reading: Association of American Medical Colleges, *AAMC Data Book: Statistical Information*

Related to Medical Schools and Teaching Hospitals (2002); Janet Bickel, *Women in Medicine* (2000).

Mark Notestine
The Ohio State University–Columbus

Chiropractic Medicine

Although founder Daniel David Palmer was actually born near Port Perry, Ontario, in 1845, Davenport, Iowa, where he did his work, is the birthplace of chiropractic. Three generations of Palmers, male and female, developed the current discipline of chiropractic.

Palmer, reflecting some of the earlier midwestern ideas of therapy, suggested that the body itself had ample natural healing power that it transmitted through the nervous system. If an organ failed to function properly, it must be because it was deprived of its normal nerve supply. Misalignment or subluxation of the vertebrae might be the cause, and by 1895 Palmer became convinced that his use of spinal adjustments had relieved one man of deafness and another of heart trouble. Two years later, he started teaching his methods, and today chiropractic is the third-largest healthcare profession in the United States, after medicine and dentistry. Success of the discipline required battle on many fronts; not only financial challenges, but legislative obstacles resisted the licensing of chiropractors. Organized medicine was particularly resistant.

The grandson of the founder, David Palmer, became president of the Palmer School in 1961 and changed its name to the Palmer College of Chiropractic. Branches of the college have since been established in San Jose, California, and Port Orange, Florida. In Davenport, there remains a chiropractic museum with a collection of more than twenty-two hundred human skeletal specimens as well as many chiropractic artifacts. The Palmer family is also honored by preservation of the Palmer mansion, and in Port Perry, Ontario, they are remembered in a Memorial Park with a bust of the native son. The best remembrance of the Palmer family, however, is the increased acceptance of chiropractic and even cooperative efforts of chiropractic and allopathic, or conventional, physicians in the effort to assist patients.

Two professional associations, both with roots in Iowa, represent chiropractic at the national level. The American Chiropractic Association moved from Webster City, Iowa, and the International Chiropractors Association relocated from Davenport, Iowa, to headquarters in Virginia near the nation's capital, which is also the location for some of the associations' numerous conferences on such problems as whiplash, spinal trauma, muscle, and bone diseases. Preventative health care, posture, sports injuries, and foot diseases are also frequent topics. Although many chiropractors employ heat, massage, and therapeutic stimulation as adjunctive therapies, chiropractic remains focused on the removal of subluxations and misalignments through adjustments of the spine and extremities. Advanced studies in pediatrics, neurology, orthopedics, radiology, and the treatment of athletes are offered through diplomate programs of the professional associations. Every state has a presence of chiropractic expertise, and in all states, health boards establish and enforce standards of care.

Sources and Further Reading: Hans A. Baer, "Chiropractic as the Foremost Professionalized Heterodox Medical System," in Hans A. Baer, ed. *Biomedicine and Alternative Healing Systems in America* (2001); Scott Haldeman. *Principles and Practice of Chiropractic*, 3rd ed. (2004); Dennis Peterson and Glenda Wiese, *Chiropractic: An Illustrated History* (1995); Walter I. Wardwell, *Chiropractic: History and Evolution of a New Profession* (1992).

Alana K. Callender
Palmer Foundation for Chiropractic History,
Davenport, Iowa

Dentistry

The first dentists in America were British barber-surgeons in the Plymouth colony. A century later, French and English dentists immigrated to Boston, New York, and Philadelphia. Following the War of 1812, westward expansion brought dentists into the Ohio Valley. They were constantly on the move and growing in number. In 1830, there were four dentists in Cincinnati; a decade later, there were forty-two.

The first national dental organization, the American Society of Dental Surgeons, founded in New York City in 1840 by Atlantic Seaboard dentists, lasted only sixteen years. Dentists west of the Allegheny Mountains founded the Mississippi Valley Association of Dental Surgeons in Cincinnati in 1844. It published the *Dental Register*, a scientific journal with a successful national circulation. Jonathan Taft, an Ohio dentist and the first dean of the University of Michigan School of Dentistry, edited the journal for nearly forty years. As populations and numbers of dentists grew in the Midwest, state dental societies were formed: Michigan in 1855, Indiana in 1858, Iowa in 1863, Illinois in 1865, Missouri in 1865, Ohio in 1866, Nebraska in 1868, Kansas in 1871, Wisconsin in 1871, Minnesota in 1872, South Dakota in 1883, and North Dakota in 1906. In 1859, reflecting the need for a new national society, the American Dental Association was founded. Of the first

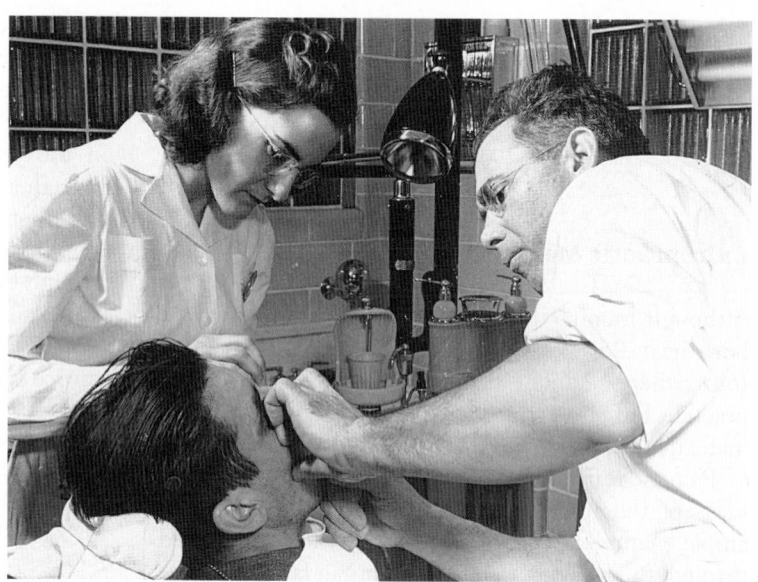

A worker receiving free company dental care, 1942. Library of Congress, Prints and Photographs Division, LC-USE6-D-004331.

twenty presidents of the Association, twelve were from the Midwest. The Association established its first permanent headquarters in Chicago in 1931.

The first dental school, the Baltimore (Maryland) College of Dental Surgery, was founded in 1840, partly by Chapin Harris, physician and dentist. Chapin Harris learned the practice of dentistry in Bainbridge, Ohio, from his brother and mentor, John Harris, a physician, dentist, and teacher. Another of John's students, James Taylor, established the world's second dental school, the Ohio College of Dental Surgery, in 1845 in Cincinnati. John Harris's office and home in Bainbridge has been designated "The Cradle of Dental Education" by the American Dental Association.

Presently, thirteen dental schools are operating in the Midwest, and they annually produce about 25 percent of American dental graduates: the University of Illinois at Chicago, Southern Illinois University in Alton, Indiana University School of Dentistry in Indianapolis, University of Iowa in Iowa City, University of Detroit Mercy, University of Michigan in Ann Arbor, University of Minnesota in Minneapolis, University of Missouri at Kansas City, Creighton University in Omaha, University of Nebraska Medical Center in Omaha, Case Western Reserve University in Cleveland, The Ohio State University in Columbus, and Marquette University in Milwaukee.

The Midwest has a rich tradition in dental research. Greene V. Black, the late-nineteenth-century Illinois educator and researcher, is considered the father of American dental research. Ohioan Weston A. Price founded the American Dental Association's Research Institute, and George C. Paffenbarger of Ohio established the Dental Research Section of the U.S. Bureau

of Standards. H. Trendley Dean (Missouri), Francis Arnold (Ohio), Francis Bull (Wisconsin), and Don Galagan (Iowa) were early researchers in communal water fluoridation. Indiana's Charles Gish, Charles Howell, and Joseph Muhler developed topical fluoride agents and fluoride toothpastes.

Sources and Further Reading: Milton B. Asbell, *Dentistry: A Historical Perspective* (1988); M.D.K. Bremner, *The Story of Dentistry*, 3rd ed. (1954); Van B. Dalton, *The Genesis of Dental Education in the United States* (1946); Charles R. E. Koch, ed., *History of Dental Surgery* (1909).

Donald F. Bowers
The Ohio State University–Columbus

Medical Education: Different Approaches in Illinois, Iowa, and Ohio

Each state in the Midwest developed its system of medical education differently, and "allied" medical specialties such as physical medicine, rehabilitation, laboratory technology, nursing, and graduate programs are present in each state. The programs for medical education in Illinois, Iowa, and Ohio illustrate the variety. Illinois solved its concern for the regional needs of rural areas as well as for the major metropolis at Chicago by developing multiple, scattered programs. Iowa has a single allopathic (conventional) medical school and a single osteopathic school. Ohio has funded seven medical schools, one of which is osteopathic, and recently the Cleveland Clinic partnered with Case Western Reserve University to establish

Ohio's eighth medical education program. To some degree, all these states responded to the work of Abraham Flexner, whose assessment of medical programs at the beginning of the twentieth century identified the then woefully inadequate proprietary schools organized more for profit than for education. The states responded with a move toward full-time faculties and a scientific basis for the curriculum.

Medical education in Illinois has a complex history, reflecting the tension between excellence and regional access in a state divided between Chicago and downstate. Chicago has been an important center for medical education in the Midwest since the nineteenth century. Rush Medical College was chartered in 1837, before Chicago became a city, and by 1900 Chicago had over fifteen for-profit medical schools. When Carnegie Foundation investigator Flexner evaluated the schools in 1909, he proclaimed Chicago "the plague spot of the country" and suggested preserving only Rush, which was affiliated with the University of Chicago; Northwestern; and the College of Physicians and Surgeons, which was affiliated with the University of Illinois.

The University of Illinois's College of Medicine (UICOM) grew out of the College of Physicians and Surgeons, which opened in 1882 on Chicago's near west side, across from Cook County Hospital. It affiliated with the University of Illinois in 1897, becoming its College of Medicine in 1913. UICOM is now the largest medical school in the country, with roughly four thousand faculty members. Over a quarter of

each entering class are minorities, and almost 40 percent of those admitted are women.

In 1941 the state created the Illinois Medical District to coordinate the largest single concentration of medical education and research facilities in the Midwest, including UICOM, Rush University, Cook County Hospital, and West Side Veterans' Administration, along with several state health facilities. In the 1940s UICOM was a leader in medical research and education. It installed one of the first betatrons for cancer research, and its vice president, Andrew Ivy, MD, helped draft the Nuremberg codes for human subject research. Ivy soon plunged the college into its most severe crisis, however, when he announced, before clinical trials, the useless drug Krebiozen as a cancer "cure." The resultant public embarrassment led trustees to fire University president George Stoddard in 1953, and numerous department heads resigned in protest. Research suffered severely as UICOM shifted priorities toward education rather than research, an approach that persisted until the 1980s.

The passage of Medicare in 1965 led to a nationwide doctor shortage, and Congress authorized funds for the expansion of medical education. Downstate Illinois complained that the concentration of schools in Chicago limited medical care in the rest of the state, so the legislature mandated regionalization. In 1970 Southern Illinois University broke what some considered the University of Illinois's monopoly on public medical education by creating a new medical school in Springfield. In response, UICOM established three

Dissecting a cadaver at the Chicago College of Physicians and Surgeons. Wisconsin Historical Society, WHi-8535.

downstate branches, in Rockford, Peoria, and Urbana. This unique experiment in community-based medical education led to accreditation difficulties in the 1970s, but has survived and sponsored both research and community-based education.

In 1982 UICOM consolidated with the University of Illinois's Chicago Circle campus to become the University of Illinois at Chicago (UIC). This merger created Illinois's second public research university, making Illinois the only state in the Midwest to have four Carnegie Research One Universities: Northwestern, University of Chicago, University of Illinois at Urbana-Champaign, and UIC.

The University of Iowa Hospitals and Clinics, despite its rural roots and modest beginnings, has flourished to become one of the largest and most distinguished teaching hospitals in the country. When the Department of Medicine began in 1870, the need for an adequate clinical teaching facility was recognized immediately. Tentative attempts to provide such facilities from the area proved largely unsatisfactory, and in 1898, a solely owned university teaching hospital was constructed, the first such hospital west of the Mississippi.

Despite the new facilities, Flexner, after visiting the school as part of his influential nationwide survey, was unsparing in his criticism, and he noted in particular the already inadequate hospital facilities. He also doubted the college could survive in a community with a population base as small as Iowa City's was then. In response, the college recruited and hired faculty members whose stature and talent raised the profile of the college and the hospital to national prominence. With the passage of the first of Iowa's indigent care laws in 1915, the Hospital began to receive and care for a greater number and variety of patients, and in 1932 organized the nation's first and only statewide hospital ambulance service for patients unable to pay for their own transportation. This program continues to the present day.

In 1928, with matching funding from the Rockefeller Foundation, a new hospital of seven-hundred-plus beds was completed on the west side of the campus; its gothic tower remains the symbol of health care at the university. After weathering difficult financial storms during the Depression and World War II, University Hospitals (renamed as such in 1919) was able to take advantage of a booming postwar economy and refocused its efforts toward more specialized medicine, redefining its role as the state provider of tertiary care.

With the passage of Medicare and Medicaid legislation in the 1960s, the College of Medicine and University Hospitals used burgeoning federal dollars to position the university's health-care enterprise in the forefront of medical research and advanced patient care. In keeping with its expanding mission, Univer-

sity Hospitals was renamed the University of Iowa Hospitals and Clinics in 1972.

In 1974 the UIHC began an extraordinary half-billion-dollar capital improvement project, using self-generated revenue and generous private donations. The new medical complex now accommodates a wide array of specialized services and clinics as well as nationally recognized centers of excellence in a variety of fields. For several decades, the University of Iowa has been at or near the top of the Big Ten universities for federal research support. With the pervasive influence of managed care, the UIHC and the College of Medicine have also worked together to strengthen their alliance with other Iowa community-based hospitals. This partnership has spawned clinical outreach services and a comprehensive primary care network, in keeping with its century-old covenant with the people of Iowa, while enhancing its vitality in the new health-care marketplace.

In Flexner's 1910 epic report on medical education, eight schools were reported for Ohio. Only three of these remain: those at Case Western Reserve University, the University of Cincinnati, and The Ohio State University. Although the inadequate for-profit schools are gone, replacements make a total of eight schools in Ohio, including the above three. The established ones will be discussed in order of their founding and as an example of one midwestern state's approach to medical education.

In 1819 Daniel Drake founded the Cincinnati College and Medical College of Ohio. He also established the first in a succession of hospitals that evolved into the University Hospital of today. In 1977 the municipal University of Cincinnati and its College of Medicine became one of the public universities of the state of Ohio. The Medical Center includes the College of Medicine, six hospitals in Cincinnati and northern Kentucky, and the Colleges of Nursing, Pharmacy, and Allied Health Services.

Western Reserve College, founded in Hudson in 1826, but moved to Cleveland and renamed Western Reserve University in 1882, established a medical school in 1843. In 1967 a federation between Western Reserve University and the Case Institute of Technology formed Case Western Reserve University (CWRU). Its medical school was among the first to integrate basic and clinical services, early exposure of students to patients, and a focus on organ systems. The CWRU Medical Center includes the schools of medicine, nursing, and dentistry, in addition to University Hospitals, with which the University has just established a fifty-year partnership. Relationships with Cleveland Clinic suggest that additional partnerships will follow.

The Ohio State University (OSU) College of Medicine claims an origin in 1834 with the founding of the Willoughby Medical University in Willoughby, Ohio. Willoughby moved to Columbus, Ohio, in 1846, and soon a prominent Columbus resident, Lyne Starling, donated $30 thousand to purchase land and construct a medical school and hospital. The name became Starling Medical College. The hospital was the first in the United States constructed specifically to serve as a teaching hospital. In 1914 the trustees of what was by then the Starling-Ohio Medical College transferred all of the properties to the state of Ohio, and the Ohio General Assembly formally established the College of Medicine as part of OSU. The academic medical center includes colleges of dentistry, medicine and public health, nursing, optometry, pharmacy, and veterinary medicine, as well as University Hospitals and the James Cancer Hospital and Solove Research Institute. This constellation of colleges and hospitals constitutes the most comprehensive medical center in the United States located on a single university campus.

In response to efforts by the mayor and citizens of Toledo, in 1964 the Medical College of Ohio (MCO) was established by the Ohio General Assembly. Since its first graduating class, MCO has graduated more than three thousand MDs, more than 260 PhDs, and more than eight hundred master's degrees in biomedical services, nursing, occupational health, occupational therapy, and public health assistance.

Northeastern Ohio Universities College of Medicine (NEOUCOM) is unique in its affiliations and in its curriculum. In cooperation with the University of Akron, Kent State University, and Youngstown State University, NEOUCOM offers students an opportunity to obtain a combined BS-MD in as few as six years. For clinical and basic training, NEUOCOM utilizes the three universities and seventeen associated hospitals in the Akron, Canton, and Youngstown areas. The General Assembly established NEOUCOM in 1973, and the college now graduates approximately one hundred physicians each year.

The desire for a community-based medical school at Wright State University (WSU) that would emphasize family practice led physicians and community leaders of Dayton to propose existing hospitals as a cost-effective model for medical education. It was argued that a new medical school in Dayton would strengthen the health-care system of the entire Miami Valley region. In response, the Ohio General Assembly established the WSU School of Medicine in 1973. Since the first class graduated in 1980, over nineteen hundred physicians have received their degrees. The sixteen basic science departments are located on the WSU main campus, and, as planned, the clinical departments are based in teaching hospitals throughout the community.

The preceding six institutions are allopathic medical schools that provide the MD (Medical Doctorate) degree. Ohio University houses an osteopathic medical school offering the DO (Doctor of Osteopathy) degree. The principles of osteopathy were established over 125 years ago by the founder of osteopathic medicine, Andrew Still, and osteopathy provides the foundation for medical education at Ohio University. Created in 1975, the Ohio University College of Osteopathic Medicine (OU-COM) is one of nineteen osteopathic medical schools nationwide.

By contrast, the University of South Dakota School of Medicine is an example of a two-year medical school that became a four-year school. The Dakota Territorial Legislature established the University of South Dakota in 1862 and a School of Medicine in 1907. The original curriculum consisted of two years of premedical study and two years of medicine. The South Dakota legislature, in 1974, after years of deliberation, authorized the development of a complete four-year, degree-granting and family practice–oriented program of medical education. After sixty-eight years as a two-year medical school, the School of Medicine began its full clinical program and graduated its first Doctors of Medicine on May 14, 1977. The clinical aspects of the third year are provided in hospitals at Sioux Falls, Rapid City, and Yankton, but for the fourth year hospitals and ambulatory clinics across the entire state are used. More than in any other midwestern state, the South Dakota effort is a statewide cooperative endeavor. Additional and more recent programs include medical technology, physical therapy, and a certificate program for physician assistants.

As is apparent, other midwestern states have had a long, varied, and rich tradition in medical education.

Sources and Further Reading: Thomas Neville Bonner, *Medicine in Chicago, 1850–1950,* 2nd ed. (1991); Dennis Connaughton, *Warren Cole, MD, and the Ascent of Scientific Surgery* (1991); Abraham Flexner, *Medical Education in the United States and Canada* (1910); John C. Gerber, *A Pictorial History of the University of Iowa* (1988); Samuel Levey, *The Rise of a University Teaching Hospital* (1997); George D. Stoddard, "*Krebiozen*": *The Great Cancer Mystery* (1955); Patricia Spain Ward, "100 Years: A History," '*Scope* 8, Centennial Special Edition (1981–1982).

Fred W. Beuttler
University of Illinois–Chicago

Edwin A. Holtum
University of Iowa

Ronald L. St. Pierre
The Ohio State University–Columbus

Nursing

Innovation in nursing in the Midwest is not new. In 1922 Sigma Theta Tau, now international nursing's honor society, was founded at Indiana University by six student nurses committed to university education at a time when that was a rarity for nurses. That nursing organization is now the second-largest in the world, with chapters at over five hundred universities around the globe, and it recently became the first large nursing organization to elect a male nurse as president.

The latest listing of research funding by the National Institutes of Health (2002) reveals that more nursing schools in the top thirty are based in the Midwest than in any other region. Contributing to this investment in innovation is the Midwest Nursing Research Society, now the largest regional organization devoted exclusively to nursing research. Another reason that the Midwest has been a powerhouse for Nursing is the Michigan-based Kellogg Foundation. Dr. John Harvey Kellogg set in motion the courses that led to a training school for nurses opening in Battle Creek in 1883. Since the establishment of the Kellogg Foundation in 1930, that organization has done much to encourage community-based care and to influence national public health policy, particularly health care for the underserved.

In the 1970s the Michigan Nurses Association undertook the first major nursing research project, "Using Research to Improve Nursing Practice." More recently, the University of Wisconsin at Milwaukee has taken the lead in linking twenty-one community nursing centers representing twelve universities to establish the Midwest Nursing Centers Consortium Research Network.

Nursing in the Midwest has been innovative in many respects, from the development of multicampus nursing schools at several of the large public universities to the recent formation of a Clinical Nursing and Health Informatics Consortium linking several Big Ten nursing schools—Indiana, Iowa, Michigan, and Wisconsin at Madison—through the Consortium on Inter-institutional Collaboration (CIC). The latter is continuing the region's tradition of cooperation as well as leadership in learning at a distance by offering web-based courses in this growing specialty.

The Midwest has been innovative in facilitating entry into the practice of nursing as well as seamless transitions from one level of education to another. To address the nursing shortage, several schools have developed accelerated programs for students who already hold college degrees in other fields. The University of Wisconsin campuses have collaborated to use their collective resources to enable registered nurses around the state to obtain a bachelor's degree, thereby enhancing the educational level of those in the field.

Opportunities for evidence-based practice and for academic excellence have been characteristic of modern nursing, and nowhere more so than in the Midwest. Recognizing the leadership that nurses in the Midwest have exerted historically, the University of Minnesota established the Katharine J. Densford International Center for Nursing Leadership. Named for a midwestern inductee into the American Nurses Association's Hall of Fame, this center is but one way that Midwest nurses seek to maintain the innovative edge in changing times.

Sources and Further Reading: Helen K. Grace and Gloria R. Smith, "Nursing's Role in Mobilizing Public Response: Yesterday, Today and Tomorrow," in Angela Barron McBride, comp., *Nursing and Philanthropy* (2000); Nell J. Watts, *The Adventurous Years* (1997).

Angela Barron McBride
Indiana University School of
Nursing–Indianapolis

Oslerian Medicine

The peripatetic career of William Osler (1849–1919) as physician, medical educator, and leadership figure began in Montreal (McGill University), continued in Philadelphia (University of Pennsylvania), moved to Baltimore (Johns Hopkins University), and ended at Oxford University in England. He was Professor of Clinical Medicine at the University of Pennsylvania (1884–1889), then Physician-in-Chief at Johns Hopkins Hospital and Professor of Medicine at Johns Hopkins Medical School, Baltimore (1889–1905). These were his most productive years, and his example influenced medicine throughout the Midwest.

Osler's persona and his abilities as a teacher, clinician, author, and historian formed the basis for the Oslerian tradition that remains a lively inspiration to the medical profession a century later. As teacher and clinician at Hopkins, he created the upper resident staff with an extended training period, introduced the British system of interns and residents, taught students at the bedside, and introduced students to laboratory diagnosis—prototypes for every developing medical clinic in North America. As author, his 1892 textbook *The Principles and Practice of Medicine* became the most influential book in American medicine, every medical student's bible for decades, with sixteen editions in fifty-five years and sales greater than half a million. The Eli Lilly Company of Indianapolis awarded *Aequanimitas*, his collected essays, lay ser-

Portrait of William Osler by Thomas C. Corner, 1905. Photo by Aaron Levin. The Alan Mason Chesney Medical Archives of the Johns Hopkins Medical Institutions.

mons, and addresses to 150,000 graduating U.S. medical students (1932–1953). Osler's writings enhanced his reputation as the foremost physician and medical educator of his era.

One of his most effective addresses, "Teacher and Student," was delivered at the University of Minnesota in 1892, at the time when medical education in the Midwest was chaotic, and at the very beginnings of the association of medical colleges with state universities. He discussed the contentious matter of state or university control of medical schools, concluding that an institution's fate lies in the men who work in its halls and in the ideals they cherish and teach rather than in the location of their work. He spoke of the need for effective medical licensure in his talk to the Minnesota Academy of Medicine in St. Paul the next day. His 1899 visit to Columbus involved a patient consultation, a clinic, and lecture, with memorable remarks addressed to the medical students.

Osler's encounters with generations of Canadian and U.S. students and trainees in Montreal, Philadelphia, and Baltimore left lasting impressions; many assumed leadership positions in North American medicine. In the Midwest, George Dock was Osler's pupil

in Philadelphia, and his students went on to important positions at Michigan and Cincinnati. Dock was Professor of Medicine at the University of Michigan (1891–1908), and later was chair of medicine and dean at Washington University. Campbell Howard, Osler's resident at Hopkins, son of Osler's teacher Palmer Howard, became Chairman of Medicine at the University of Iowa with Osler's support. Other Osler protégés at Hopkins included Edward Perkins Carter, a major figure in Cleveland academic medicine, and Charles Phillips Emerson, Professor of Medicine, Indiana University. W. J. Mayo and Osler shared a long friendship; the Osler Medical Historical Society at the Mayo Foundation (1920–1925) preceded the Mayo Foundation History of Medicine Society.

Within the legacy of the Oslerian tradition, it is possible to discern Osler's significant influence during the formative years of Midwest medicine.

Sources and Further Reading: Michael Bliss, *William Osler: A Life in Medicine* (1999); Harvey Cushing, *The Life of Sir William Osler* (1925); James Russel Eckman, *Osler in Minnesota* (1948); William Osler, "Teacher and Student" in *Aequanimitas*, 3rd ed. (1932).

Charles F. Wooley
The Ohio State University–Columbus

Innovating for Health

If we can emphasize scientific and technological inventiveness that springs out of the Midwest, we can also point at innovations in the area of health. Out of the "every man his own doctor" philosophy prevalent in the nineteenth century, a half dozen men, often amateur physicians, established pharmaceutical empires. The Upjohns in Michigan and Eli Lilly in Indiana are important examples, and from early production of patent medicines, at a time when there were less than a dozen truly effective drugs, research and science soon produced antibiotics and vaccines. Major Midwest pharmaceutical firms, normally fiercely competitive, cooperated during World War II to produce large quantities of the revolutionary new antibiotic, penicillin. Several leaders in research or in clinical observations in the now rapidly expanding area of genetics are midwestern.

Just as inventiveness and cooperation are features of the Midwest from the earliest barn raising days, people in communities in the Midwest have helped one another in health and sickness. One of the major social changes after World War II began in Minnesota with the appearance of HMOs and PPOs, programs intended to offer better service at less cost. These programs had and continue to have a national impact. Medicopters, drawing on the lessons of Vietnam medical care, are now available for essentially every large hospital in the Midwest. As techniques have become available, whether laser surgery or in vitro fertilization, institutions in the Midwest have led the way.

Antibiotics and Vaccines

For more than a hundred years, the Midwest has been a focus for the discovery, development, and production of vaccines and antibiotics. This activity accelerated during the 1940s and 1950s, with midwestern companies banding together to produce penicillin during World War II, and with polio vaccine discoverers Jonas Salk and Albert Sabin relying on midwestern universities and companies to test and commercialize their developments.

Vaccine production began after 1903 when Parke-Davis and Company—formed in 1866 in Detroit as the first pharmaceutical company in the Midwest, and now part of New York–based Pfizer—gained the nation's first license to produce biological vaccines. By 1907, Parke-Davis introduced a line of important vaccines protecting against tetanus, diphtheria, influenza, and pertussis.

But the golden age of vaccines began in 1952, with Salk's discovery of an injectable polio vaccine at the University of Pittsburgh. Massive field trials for his breakthrough were executed at the University of Michigan, which declared the Salk vaccine safe and effective in 1955. In the mid-1950s, at the University of Cincinnati, virologist Sabin developed a poliovirus strain that was attenuated and live, unlike Salk's inactivated virus, and the Sabin oral vaccine was approved in 1960. The two breakthroughs ended the threat of polio in the United States and have nearly wiped out polio worldwide.

British scientist Sir Alexander Fleming discovered the first overwhelmingly effective antibiotic, penicillin, in 1928. However, it wasn't until the 1940s that penicillin became readily available, largely through technologies invented by Pfizer and Eli Lilly, based in Indianapolis. Parke-Davis, Eli Lilly, Abbott Laboratories in Chicago, and Upjohn in Kalamazoo, Michigan, were among the first in the world to produce penicillin, helping to save thousands of lives during World War II. The cooperation of these companies was a remarkable accomplishment in itself and perhaps symbolic of midwestern values.

These companies learned a great deal about the chemistry of antibiotics during the war, and several set out to produce new antibiotics to rival penicillin. In the 1950s Lilly created a new class of antibiotics, the mycins, including vancomycin, which remains the last line of defense against many deadly diseases. In the mid 1950s midwestern companies produced a string of second-generation antibiotics, including Upjohn's albamycin and Panalba, Parke-Davis's chloromycetin, and Abbott's erythromycin. Abbott introduced the first third-generation antibiotic, the macrolide Biaxin, and in 2000, Pharmacia, which merged with Upjohn,

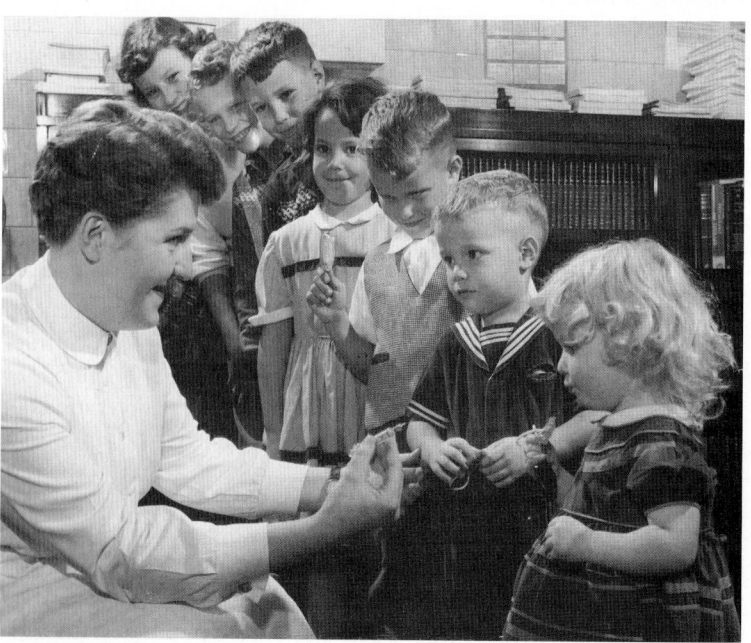

Polio shot time, Milwaukee, Wisconsin, 1955.
Wisconsin Historical Society, WHi-8530.

developed a totally new class of antibiotic, an oxazolidine known as Zyvox, in its Kalamazoo labs.

With mergers and acquisitions in the pharmaceutical industry, some of these pioneer companies have new names and headquarters, but they continue to make medical breakthroughs. In addition, a number of midwestern universities, notably The Ohio State University, Washington University in St. Louis, the University of Wisconsin, and the University of Michigan, sustain world-class programs in virology and pathology. Undoubtedly, the partnership of private and public research, which worked so well in making polio vaccines and penicillin, will lead to new breakthroughs against humanity's most devastating diseases.

Sources and Further Reading: Robert D. B. Carlisle, *A Century of Caring, the Upjohn Story* (1987); Larry B. Massie and Peter J. Schmitt, *Kalamazoo, the Place Behind the Product* (1998); Jeffrey L. Rodengen, *The Legend of Pfizer* (1999).

Leslie Gross Klaff and John Santoro
New York, New York.

Endocrinology and Infertility Management

Midwest educational and therapy programs for endocrinology and metabolism usually do not depend on the work of single individuals, and in fact cooperation among medical school departments is the rule. Several remarkable midwestern contributors to progress in these areas deserve particular mention.

David Marine, Sr., considered the father of thyroidology, is generally credited with eliminating thyroid goiter from the Goiter Belt on the south shores of the Great Lakes by the simple expedient of introducing iodine into table salt. E. V. McCullom is internationally famous as the discoverer of Vitamin A, found during his studies of nutrition. While this Kansan was on the staff of the College of Agriculture of the University of Wisconsin at Madison, he also alerted the world to the possibility that malnutrition could occur despite adequate caloric intake. As recently as June of 2004, the Copenhagen Conference of Nobel Prize–winning economists listed malnutrition resulting from the absence of vitamins and key minerals as the second-most pressing economic problem for the world. (AIDS was the first.)

J. W. Conn, an endocrinologist who spent his entire career at the University of Wisconsin, discovered aldosterone, a major mineralocorticoid hormone secreted by the adrenal gland, and he described a disease caused by excess secretion of the hormone now called Conn's syndrome. P. S. Hench of the Mayo Clinic won the Nobel Prize for Medicine in 1950 for his systematic studies of the amazing effect of cortisone on arthritis. Harry Goldblatt, of Cleveland, defined one of the major causes of hypertension, particularly through studies of the enzyme rennin, which is produced in the kidney. The so-called Goldblatt Kidney is one in which the blood supply has been limited experimentally by a clamp, as in human disease the vessels are narrowed by arterial obstruction.

One of the busiest areas of endocrinology and hormonal effects on the human body is human reproduction. No aspect of infertility treatment has developed more rapidly than that of artificial fertilization, an area in which the Midwest has been among the leaders. Several medical advances in human fertility and reproduction became well known in the Midwest in the last quarter of the twentieth century. The new surgical technique of laparoscopy allowed surgeries to be shortened and less invasive. New medications for treatment of infertility were introduced, the most exciting of which was in vitro fertilization (IVF). The first birth from IVF occurred in England in 1978. IVF procedures were being performed in most of the Midwest before 1985, with a birth in 1982 at The Ohio State University and in 1983 at the Cleveland Clinic. Protocols for performing IVF have steadily improved, and live birth occurs in an average of 35 percent of cycles in women under age thirty-five. The government requires all clinics to report their success rates on a yearly basis, and success rates vary considerably. For example, in 2001, the twenty-three reporting clinics in Illinois had success rates ranging from 12 percent to over 50 percent per retrieval for women under age thirty-five.

Advancing age makes fertility treatment less successful due to the loss of oocytes with age. The introduction of oocyte donation now gives older women a chance to have successful pregnancies. Donor oocyte pregnancy success rates range between 40 and 50 percent. IVF originally required a surgery to retrieve the oocytes, but the procedure is now done in an outpatient setting with transvaginal ultrasound-guided retrieval.

IVF has also facilitated improvements in the treatment of male infertility. A sperm from ejaculate or harvested from the testicles or epididymis can be directly inserted into a harvested oocyte through an intracytoplasmic sperm injection (ICSI) procedure. This has dramatically improved success rates and allowed insemination by the chosen father in cases where donor sperm would previously have been recommended. Access to the embryo prior to implantation also allows for the possibility of genetic testing to rule out the presence of disease when the parents carry a recessive gene. This is currently offered in several Midwest centers.

Several institutions in the Midwest have contributed to the rapid development and spread of innovations and procedures in this area. This is above all a tribute to the ability to share information quickly and the drive to produce successful pregnancies in patients.

Sources and Further Reading: American Society for Reproductive Medicine Committee Opinion, *Aging and Infertility in Women* (Jan. 2002); American Society for Reproductive Medicine Committee Opinion, *Optimal Evaluation of the Infertile Female* (May 2003); U.S. Department of Health and Human Services, *Assisted Reproductive Technology Success Rates* (2003).

Elizabeth Kennard
The Ohio State University–Columbus

Thomas O'Dorisio
University of Iowa

Genetics

Midwesterners have contributed to the field of genetics since at least the time when George Huntington described the best-known, dominantly inherited neurological disorder, now called Huntington's disease, in Pomeroy, Ohio, in 1872. In fact, several eminent geneticists emerged from the Midwest or spent productive years in midwestern institutes. As a summary of what is in fact a very remarkable story, we can mention several of the Nobel Prize winners from this region.

George W. Beadle was born at Wahoo, Nebraska, in 1903, the son of a farmer. In 1926 he graduated from the University of Nebraska, and over the next several decades studied the genetics of wheat, corn, fruit flies, and most important of all, the fungus neurospora. Through their studies of neurospora, Beadle and Edward Tatum discovered that genes act by regulating chemical events, a finding for which they shared the Nobel Prize with Josh Lederberg. After many years at the California Institute of Technology, Beadle returned to the Midwest as Chancellor, and later President, of the University of Chicago.

Joshua Lederberg, the son of a rabbi immigrant, was born in 1925 in New Jersey and attended Columbia University. While a student at Columbia Medical School, he had an idea for demonstrating sex in bacteria. He went to Yale and carried out the experiments in collaboration with Edward Tatum, another midwesterner who was educated at the Universities of Chicago and Wisconsin. The experiment was successful and opened the way for genetic study of bacteria. After about ten years on the faculty of the University of Wisconsin, in 1947 he moved to Stanford, and then to the presidency of Rockefeller University.

Har Gobind Khorana was awarded the 1968 Nobel Prize for Physiology and Medicine, together with Marshall Niremberg and Robert Holley, for his studies interpreting the genetic code and its function in protein synthesis. Born in what is now Pakistan, Khorana trained in England and Canada before moving to the Institute for Enzyme Research at the University of Wisconsin in 1960. It was in Madison that he carried out his seminal studies of nucleotide synthesis that helped solve a fundamental puzzle in genetics—how genes encode proteins.

Howard Temin graduated from Swarthmore College and did graduate work at California Institute of Technology. He joined the faculty of the University of Wisconsin and, in 1975, was awarded the Nobel Prize for the discovery of reverse transcriptase, the enzyme that makes DNA from RNA.

Ed Lewis, recipient of the Nobel Prize in 1995 for his work in the genetics of development, grew up in Minnesota, where he trained at the University of Minnesota before moving to Cal Tech as a graduate student and remaining as a faculty member.

America's greatest population geneticist, Sewall Wright (1889–1988), grew up in Illinois, worked for the United States Department of Agriculture in Washington, taught at the University of Chicago, and retired to the University of Wisconsin. His best-known work is his inbreeding coefficient, which he devised in 1921 as an algorithm for measuring the decrease in heterozygosity for any pedigree, however complex. He also played a central role in developing a mathematical theory of evolution.

Some geneticists' names have become household words and helped educate an entire generation. One of these is James D. Watson (1928–), who discovered the DNA double helix with Francis Crick (1916–2004). Watson was born and raised in Chicago, then received a fellowship for graduate studies at Indiana University in Bloomington, where he received his PhD in 1950. At Indiana, the influence of his advisor, Salvador Luria (1912–1991), and the geneticists H. J. Muller (1890–1967) and T. M. Sonnenborn (1905–1981) led him to pursue studies in England on the fundamental basis of heredity. Together with Crick, Watson discovered the double helix structure of DNA, beginning the era of molecular genetics that continues today.

Aside from the Universities of Indiana and Wisconsin, which continue to educate and innovate, many other midwestern universities remain influential in genetic research. While on the faculty at the University of Michigan, Francis Collins helped identify the genetic basis of several important inherited human diseases, including cystic fibrosis, neurofibromatosis, and Huntington's disease. He was later picked to head the Human Genome Project, which mapped the entire human genome. James

Neel pioneered the study of human genetics and was among the first to foresee its importance in the diagnosis and treatment of medical conditions. During his career at the University of Michigan Medical School, Neel established one of the first clinics to evaluate and counsel people with hereditary diseases as well as the first academic department of human genetics in the country. He directed the genetic study of children whose parents were exposed to the atom bomb in Japan.

Leaders in the field, as is typical for the Midwest, reached out to incorporate others. While at Indiana University, Herman J. Muller became the first president of the American Society of Human Genetics, which remains the major professional organization for human geneticists. Miller was an early authority on gene mutation, and his discovery in 1927 that X-rays can cause genes to mutate led to new investigations into the biochemical nature of gene action. He won the Nobel Prize in 1946.

Throughout much of the twentieth century, the University of Wisconsin has been a major center for genetics, and even earlier the University of Missouri contributed to the field. The remarkable Barbara McClintock, also one of the midwestern Nobel Prize winners and perhaps appropriately using corn, was there. Also at Missouri was L.J. Stadler who, along with Muller, discovered the induction of mutations by radiation. On a more practical level, Orville Redenbacher (1907–1995), an agronomist from Purdue University, experimented with thousands of varieties of corn to obtain the "perfect gourmet popcorn." Many other centers can claim contributions—Indiana in fruit fly research, or Ohio State with the first formal course in human genetics offered by Laurance Snyder before World War II. At present, every major university in the Midwest offers formal education in genetics and sponsors research and counseling for patients, families, and the community.

Sources and Further Reading: John C. Avise, *Molecular Markers, Natural History, and Evolution* (2004); James D. Watson, *The Double Helix* (1968).

Henry Paulson
University of Iowa

HMOs and PPOs

Health maintenance organizations (HMOs) and preferred provider organizations (PPOs) are products of the evolutionary changes that occurred following enactment of the HMO Act of 1973. This legislation was championed by Dr. Paul Ellwood, then of Minneapolis. Elwood and others convinced the Nixon Administration that promoting wellness through insurance coverage was superior to providing simply coverage for those who are sick. Preventing illness or identifying it in early stages was the primary objective. Both kinds of organizations represent an effort to provide services more efficiently and with reduced cost. HMO has become a broad category encompassing a variety of health-care delivery systems that provide alternatives to fee-for-service private practice. PPOs are organizations of physicians and other providers who agree to offer their services on a discounted-fee basis to employer groups and others through third-party administrators.

Prior to 1973 closed-panel group practice programs were really HMOs without the name. The best example was the Kaiser program, initiated in California and Oregon by shipbuilder Henry Kaiser during World War II. Following that war, other prepaid group practice programs evolved, including the well-known Group Health in Minnesota.

The HMO Act of 1973 provided grants for feasibility studies and development of HMOs as well as formation of independent practice associations (IPAs). IPAs gave individual physicians and other health-care providers an alternative to the closed-panel system exemplified by the Permanente group practices of the Kaiser programs.

Soon, various states passed legislation similar to the Federal Act of 1973 but without some of the requirements that made the Federal Act more restrictive. From the mid-1970s on many of these HMOs and HMO-IPAs flourished, particularly in the states of the Midwest. Unfortunately, there were early failures, mostly the result of insufficient capital or mismanagement.

HMO-IPAs developed successfully in Minnesota, Wisconsin, Michigan, and Ohio during the 1970s and in other states in the next decade. Many HMO-IPAs started as not-for-profit structures, and some converted to for-profit companies to raise capital for expansion. One example was the Physicians Health Plan of Central Ohio, founded in 1979 by the Franklin County (Ohio) Medical Society. This company converted to a for-profit entity in 1985 by selling stock to physicians and became known as PHP of Ohio. In 1992 it became a statewide organization when it was purchased by United Health Care. The Foundation of the Franklin County Medical Society benefited from the sale, becoming a well-funded organization that was required by statute to use those funds to support health-related programs in the community.

The HMO and HMO-IPA concept of wellness care forced traditional health insurance companies to develop competing programs, including PPOs, which are free of many of the HMO and HMO-IPA restrictions, because the latter are risk-taking entities operating under state insurance regulations.

Today, HMOs and PPOs are sponsored by for-profit companies, hospitals, insurance companies, Blue Cross/Blue Shield, physician organizations, and entrepreneurs. This has resulted in a wide spectrum of choice for employer groups and individuals in the delivery and financing of their health-care needs. Additionally, HMOs are offered as an option to individuals eligible for Medicaid and Medicare.

H. William Porterfield
The Ohio State University–Columbus

Imaging and the Revitalization of Anatomy

Until the close of the nineteenth century, dissection of the human body provided the only means, except surgery, of seeing structures hidden by the skin. Then, in 1895, the German physicist Wilhelm Roentgen used X-rays to see the bones in his wife's hand, and the acquisition of anatomical knowledge was changed forever. Today, conventional radiology, computed tomography (CT), and magnetic resonance imaging (MRI) form the core of any hospital's imaging facility.

Though technical improvements have produced remarkable enhancements in resolution, conventional radiology uses the same components that Roentgen used in 1895—a stationary source of X-rays and a photographic means of detecting an image. In the 1920s Hollis E. Potter in Chicago developed a reciprocating grid that eliminated the scattering of X-ray beams that contributed to poor resolution. Potter's grids also allowed examination of larger areas of the body, and because large glass photographic plates were cumbersome, his work stimulated the replacement of glass with photographic film.

CT became available in the 1970s and combined X-rays with the ability of the computer to create an image. In CT, the source of X-rays moves around the body in a circle, as do detectors that are positioned opposite the X-ray source. A computer receives the signal generated during this scan to create an image that appears as a slice through the body. Subsequently, the computer can take a series of consecutive slices and re-

---

❖ **Selected Midwestern Medical Inventions and Advances**

Advances in health and medicine reflect the work of many investigators, but midwestern contributions are easily demonstrated by this list.

Advances	Developer	Associated State
Aldosterone (Hormone)	Jerome Conn	Michigan
Angioplasty	Mason Sones	Ohio
Artificial Kidney	William J. Kolff	Ohio
Bacteria as a Cause of Rheumatic Fever	Charles Rammelkamp	Illinois
Cortisone Therapy	Phillip Showalter Hench	Minnesota
Improved Production of Penicillin	John Sheehan	Indiana
	Andrew Moyer	Michigan
Physiology of Sleep	William Dement	Illinois
Role of Kidney in Hypertension	Harry Goldblatt	Ohio
Early Schools for the Blind	James Ray	Indiana
Erythromycin Antibiotic	Lilly, Abbott, and Upjohn Pharmaceutical	Ohio
Dental Education	John Harris	Ohio
Free Treatment for Indigent Children	The 1915 Iowa State Legislature	Iowa
Vitamin D Addition to Milk	Harry Steenblock	Wisconsin
Whooping Cough Vaccine	J. Norton	Michigan
Heimlich Maneuver	Henry Heimlich	Ohio
Open Heart Surgery	Claude Beck	Ohio
Oral Polio Vaccine	Albert Sabin	Ohio
Radiopaque Dye for Imaging	Graham and Cole	Missouri
Vagotomy for Sympathetic Disorders	Lester Dragstedt	Illinois
Radioisotopes	John Lawrence	South Dakota
	William Myers	Ohio

construct the body in three dimensions. One of the first commercial CT scanners went into service at the Mayo Clinic (Rochester, Minnesota) in June 1973, and the Mayo Clinic became a leader in the clinical use of CT. The initial CT scanners were only large enough to accommodate the head of the patient. The Delta Scanner, developed at the Cleveland Clinic in 1975, was the first CT scanner capable of imaging the entire body.

Unlike conventional radiology and CT, which both use ionizing radiation to generate a signal, MRI uses a magnetic field and specific radio frequencies to manipulate the hydrogen nuclei in body tissues. Changes in the energy states of hydrogen nuclei are detected and delivered to a computer. The computer then uses algorithms similar to those used in CT to generate two-dimensional slices through the body and three-dimensional reconstructions.

One might assume that the rise in imaging technology and the ability of the computer to display anatomy would signal a decline in the need for anatomical dissection. On the contrary, the development of imaging technology relies on dissection to validate the images that are produced. One might also assume that the study of images produced by the computer, particularly three-dimensional and virtual images, could replace dissection as a means to learn anatomical structure. In fact, dissection continues to provide the context for the anatomical information that physicians need to interpret the complex images that they routinely consult. An additional benefit to society is that dissection—as an interaction between medical student and "first patient"—is used to nurture humanistic values and to narrow the separation between doctor and patient that technology often introduces.

Sources and Further Reading: Bettyann Holtzmann Keveles, *Naked to the Bone* (1997); Kenneth M. Ludmerer, *Time to Heal: American Medical Education from the Turn of the Century to the Era of Managed Care* (1999).

Robert M. DePhilip
The Ohio State University–Columbus

Medical Education Reform and Case Western Reserve

Case Western Reserve University School of Medicine (CWRUSM), founded in 1843, was one of the first medical schools in the country to employ instructors devoted to full-time teaching and research. Six of the first seven women to receive medical degrees from recognized allopathic medical schools in the United States graduated from the Medical Department of Western Reserve College, CWRUSM's predecessor.

Emily Blackwell, who graduated in 1854, was the younger sister of Elizabeth Blackwell, the first woman to earn a medical degree in the United States. Emily Blackwell succeeded her sister as dean of the Women's Medical College of New York. Marie E. Zakrzewska, an 1856 graduate, founded New England Hospital for Women and Children and the first training school for nurses in the country.

The school is still committed to diversity. One study found that CWRUSM had the highest percentage of black students among the twenty-five most highly ranked U.S. medical schools. Another ranked CWRUSM third in the ratio of its African American first-year students to the African Americans in the population from which the school draws students. CWRUSM was the only private medical school to make the top ten.

A consistent stress on research may account for the presence of eleven Nobel Prize winners among former students and faculty members. Graduates also have included two U.S. Surgeons General and two directors of the Centers for Disease Control and Prevention.

CWRUSM is perhaps best known, however, for the revolutionary curriculum it introduced in 1952. This curriculum integrated the basic and clinical sciences, focused on organ systems rather than individual body parts, and featured team teaching. The innovative curriculum introduced a pass-fail grading system for first- and second-year students; exposed students to clinical work almost as soon as they arrived on campus at a time when students at other medical schools did not have contact with patients until the third year of school; and provided unscheduled time so that students could study, conduct research, and pursue additional interests. This curriculum reflected a philosophy that medical students were to be thought of as junior colleagues of the faculty members. Many other medical schools later adopted these concepts, which remain at the core of CWRUSM's curriculum today.

Faculty of CWRUSM have received four prestigious Abraham Flexner Awards for Distinguished Service to Medical Education from the Association of American Medical Colleges, and more recent developments offer evidence of the continued leadership role the school continues to play in the area of medical education. In the 1990s the medical school became the first in the United States to provide all students with laptop computers. In 2002 the school became only the third institution in history to receive the best review possible from the authority that grants accreditation to U.S. and Canadian medical degree programs, the Liaison Committee on Medical Education. In 2004 the Cleveland Clinic Lerner College of Medicine of Case Western Reserve University enrolled its first class of future physician-scientists in a program within CWRUSM.

Sources and Further Reading: C. H. Cramer, *Case Western Reserve* (1976); Thomas Hale Ham, *The Student as Colleague* (1976); Frederick Clayton Waite, *Western Reserve University Centennial History of the School of Medicine* (1946); Greer Williams, *Western Reserve's Experiment in Medical Education and Its Outcome* (1980).

Lindsey C. Henson
Case Western Reserve University
School of Medicine, Cleveland

Medicopters

The Midwest has led the country both in academic courses in aviation medicine and in air evacuation of the injured. The first civilian course in Aviation Medicine began at The Ohio State University in 1956. Neither emergency squads nor air evacuation then existed, and paramedics were not yet available. Civilian rescue squad personnel were restricted from administering lifesaving treatment at the scene of a highway accident; they could not even provide intravenous fluids and drugs. Subsequent ground transportation to the nearest hospital frequently delayed medical care past the currently recognized "golden hour" after injury, the time during which the initiation of medical care dramatically reduces loss of life.

At the same time, with the use of transport helicopters, soldiers in Vietnam had a better chance of survival than did motorists in the United States. Lessons learned in Vietnam were soon transferred to civilian emergency medicine, and helicopter transportation of injured or ill patients became commonplace.

The U.S. Surgeon General, even before 1930, had urged use of air transportation to reduce loss of life. Hospital-based medicopters began service in earnest on November 7, 1967, when the Ohio Highway Patrol coordinated communications and security for an Army National Guard helicopter to transport a critically ill man to nearby Ohio State University Hospital. A Sikorsky helicopter was used initially, followed by a Huey helicopter similar to those used in Vietnam, and by 1970 over forty people had been transported by helicopter in Ohio. Within less than a decade, most large hospitals, both community and university, had prepared a helipad and arranged linkage with helicopter services. For many hospitals in the Midwest and in the rest of the country, this entailed complex negotiations with highway patrol and political authorities.

Following rapid evacuation, better resuscitation and life support appeared, then a specialty in emergency medicine began to develop. Cooperative efforts, assisted by legislation, have led to the designation of fully qualified trauma units and hospitals. Modern communication nationwide allows helicopter crews to alert the receiving hospital of incoming patients and prepare for lifesaving care. The generally good community relationships, wide open spaces, and effective highway patrols facilitated the development of air evac, medicopters, and the rapid response teams that appeared first in the Midwest and are now standard nationally.

Source and Further Reading: S. Roberts et al., "Medicopter: An Airborne Intensive Care Unit," *Annals of Surgery* 172 (Sept. 1970).

Cynthia Roberts
The Ohio State University–Columbus

Osteopathic Medicine

Osteopathic medicine was founded in Kirksville, Missouri, by the frontier physician Andrew Taylor Still (1828–1917). The discipline has evolved from an emphasis on hands-on manipulations into full participation in mainstream medicine. Still probably studied medicine through course work at the Kansas City Medical School, which no longer exists, and through apprenticeship to his father, a physician and traveling Protestant minister.

As a Union physician in the Civil War, Still was exposed to much of the most gruesome medicine of his time. That experience, along with the loss of members of his own family to spinal meningitis in 1864, convinced him of the useless and often harmful nature of many of the medicines of his day. After a decade of much introspection and study of anatomy, Still "flung to the breeze the banner of Osteopathy" in 1874. As was later defined, this new approach to healing centered on four key principles:

1. The body is a unit; the person is a unit of body, mind, and spirit.
2. The body is capable of self-regulation, self-healing, and health maintenance.
3. Structure and function are reciprocally interrelated.
4. Rational treatment is based upon an understanding of the basic principles of body unity, self-regulation, and the interrelationship of structure and function.

Still's perspective, with an emphasis on hands-on manipulation for the treatment of many musculoskeletal and medical conditions, and his successes soon gained him widespread fame. In 1892 he established the American School of Osteopathy in Kirksville, now called the Kirksville College of Osteopathic Medicine, and in 1894 he established a clinic for osteopathic treatment there. The mission statement of the school, as stated in its 1894 revised charter, was "to improve our present system of surgery, obstetrics, and treatment of diseases generally, and place the same on a more rational and scientific basis." So great were his successes that the number of scheduled trains to Kirksville had to be increased to accommodate his patients.

In what was a rare move for medical schools of the time, women were enrolled in the first class at the American School of Osteopathy. Although the school's charter allowed the granting of an MD degree, Still chose to grant a DO (Diplomate in Osteopathy, now Doctor of Osteopathic Medicine) to distinguish physicians who ascribed to the osteopathic approach.

While at first shunned by MDs, over the decades DOs have slowly gained recognition as physicians of equal standing. Today's DOs attend four years of medical school at an accredited college of osteopathic medicine, followed by internship and residency training. DOs enjoy recognition in all fifty states as fully licensed physicians, participating in the full range of medical practice and specialization. More than fourteen thousand of the some forty-nine thousand osteopathic physicians in the nation practice in the Midwest. Six of the nation's nineteen osteopathic medical schools are located in the Midwest: Kirksville College of Osteopathic Medicine (Kirksville, Missouri), Midwestern University's Chicago College of Osteopathic Medicine (Downers Grove, Illinois), Osteopathic Medical Center College of Osteopathic Medicine and Surgery (Des Moines), University of Health Sciences College of Osteopathic Medicine (Kansas City, Missouri), Michigan State University College of Osteopathic Medicine (East Lansing, Michigan), and Ohio University College of Osteopathic Medicine (Athens, Ohio).

Although osteopathic medicine has provided for all aspects of the medical needs of midwesterners, it has had its greatest impact in the primary care specialties—family practice, general internal medicine, general pediatrics, and obstetrics and gynecology—with 64 percent of all DOs practicing in these areas. DOs account for only 6 percent of the nation's physicians, but they account for 18 percent of all family physicians and 15 percent of all physicians practicing in communities of ten thousand or fewer.

Osteopathic medicine is a uniquely midwestern invention. From its inception in 1874 to today, osteopathic physicians have been helping to care for, and have been cared for by, the midwestern communities they serve.

Sources and Further Reading: Norman Gevitz, *The D.O.'s* (1982); A. T. Still, *Autobiography of Andrew T. Still* (1897); Robert C. Ward, ed., *Foundations for Osteopathic Medicine* (1997).

E. Simcha Shapiro
Doctors Hospital, Columbus, Ohio

Timothy Duffey
Westerville, Ohio

Public Life

Constitutional and Legal Culture

SECTION EDITOR
Kermit L. Hall

Section Contents

Overview

The great prairie lawyer Abraham Lincoln once said of an opposing legal counsel's argument: "He caught on to something, but only by the hind leg." Lincoln's observation applies to our current understanding of the legal culture of the Midwest. Because the body of scholarship devoted to it is not large, we should not conclude that the region's legal history is unimportant. For the national community of jurists, the Midwest has been anything but a legal backwater. Judges and treatise writers in the nation's other regions have increasingly paid attention. The high courts of Illinois, Ohio, Michigan, Minnesota, and Wisconsin have been cited not only by other courts in the region, but by courts throughout the nation. While not commanding, at least in terms of citation power, the reputation of either New York or Massachusetts, these courts have nevertheless been important, especially in selected areas of private law, notably property, torts,

Old St. Louis, Missouri, Court House: Site of the commencement of the *Dred Scott* case. Jefferson National Expansion Memorial/National Park Service.

and contracts. On surveys of judicial reputation, the high courts of the Midwest consistently rank above their counterparts in the South and the Great Plains.

The status of these courts reflects the simple fact that states with the most complex economic, social, and cultural settings also produce the richest legal environments. The movement of the Midwest from rural to urban, from a subsistence to a market economy, from ethnic and racial homogeneity to diversity, have all generated significant legal developments. Moreover, the Midwest, especially since the beginning of the twentieth century, has been a machine producing legal talent for not only the region but the entire nation. By the early twentieth century, a majority of midwestern state judges received their legal education in the region. The University of Michigan, the University of Chicago, and Northwestern University, for example, are among the nation's most distinguished institutions of legal learning, and they have been complemented by several other strong public and private law schools, whose graduates have filled the region's benches and bars. Today, the Midwest exports legal talent across the nation and throughout the world.

Innovation has been a central feature of the law and legal institutions in the region, and those innovations have had national consequences. John Henry Wigmore, of Northwestern Law School, for example, was the architect of modern criminal law. Chicago pioneered the development of juvenile justice and courts; Cleveland established a model by which to administer urban courts. These advances were driven by growing populations, industrialization, and the movement from rural to urban. The famous sit-down strikes in the automobile industry during the Great Depression contributed to a wholesale rewriting of labor law, a subject that eastern lawmakers had dominated for the previous century. In the late nineteenth century, Illinois led the nation in attempting to bring order to the rapid development of the railroad for both inter- and intrastate commerce.

And the contributions of the region have come in other ways and at different times. As that great midwestern legal thinker Roscoe Pound once observed: "The law must be stable, but it must not stand still." For example, a rich harvest of Supreme Court cases has mirrored the social changes that have swept over the Midwest. These range from issues of racial segregation (*Brown v. Board of Education*, 1954, 1955) and affirmative action (*Grutter v. University of Michigan*, 2003), to First Amendment matters of speech (*Brandenburg v. Ohio*, 1969), press (*Near v. Minnesota*, 1933), and religion (*Wisconsin v. Yoder*, 1972), to the rights of the accused (*Mapp v. Ohio*, 1961). The region has also sent more justices to the high court than any other. At the same time, the Midwest has taken a leading, if sometimes contradictory, role in questioning the use of capital punishment.

There is little doubt that the Midwest has played a distinctive role in the nation's legal development, but has the region had and does it now have a unique, as opposed to merely distinctive, legal culture? The Midwest, like other regions, has certainly generated particular demands—industrialization, immigration, and such—that have, in turn, produced laws and legal institutions whose contributions have been distinctive, although not necessarily original. How different these changes really have been, both as a matter of inter- and intraregional comparison, are important. Still, distinctiveness and adaptation of older legal forms to newer circumstances does not necessarily herald a new legal culture, especially in the American legal system that places a high value on predictability. We should also remember that in a region as expansive as the Midwest, there have been and will continue to be variations, and important ones, within the broader themes of legal development.

Take the way in which the availability of the most basic resources—water, land, and animals—shaped the region's laws. Remember that a significant portion of what we term the Midwest—North and South Dakota, Nebraska, and Kansas—is also part of the Great Plains. That section, in contrast to the eastern portion of the Midwest, is characterized by its flatness, lack of trees, and semiaridity. Once easterners crossed the 100th meridian, the availability of water changed dramatically, and so too did the laws.

The scarcity of fencing materials in the treeless plain prompted cattlemen to urge the abrogation of the English common-law requirement to fence livestock, placing the burden of fencing on crop farmers. In other parts of the Midwest, however, where fencing materials were abundant, the law placed the burden on the cattle owner rather than the farmer. In both sections, however, ranchers and farmers borrowed legal doctrine from the East, although the ways in which that borrowing occurred differed markedly.

What gave visibility to these differing approaches to fencing statutes in the Midwest was not their novelty, but the fact that they sought to resolve conflicts among farmers, free-grass cattlemen, and barbed-wire ranchers. Hence, the legal culture of the nineteenth-century Midwest resonated to economic pressures to develop successful modes of agricultural production.

The law of property rights was equally instrumental. Initially, land in the Midwest was not a scarce resource, although it eventually became so. For much of the nineteenth century, "squatter sovereignty" was sufficient for settling land ownership questions in the Great Plains sections of the region, while more formalized schemes prevailed in that portion organized by the famous Northwest Ordinance. Cattlemen in the plains initially persuaded their state legislators to enact laws that punished those who drove their stock from the accustomed range, but by the 1880s, stock growers' associations influenced several state legislatures to adopt statutes patterned on practices in Illinois, Ohio, and Indiana. Those states restricted entry onto the range through control of access to limited water supplies. The entire movement in land law in the Midwest by the end of the nineteenth century was from communal to exclusive ownership. That development had long been under way in the East, and it has continued unabated as more and more of the Midwest's productive agricultural capacity has been placed in fewer and fewer hands. This consolidation of landholding mocks the myth of the small, self-reliant, midwestern farmer.

Much the same has happened with water law. As with land and livestock, however, innovation informed distinctiveness with a good deal of borrowing from practices in the East. Water was a particularly crucial resource in the semiarid Great Plains states of the Midwest. Access to it and control of it shaped economic fortunes. Most of the Midwest adopted the riparian system of water rights, which meant that the right to the use of water accrued to the one who owned the bank of the stream and who had access to it by virtue of position. The Great Lakes states have abundant water resources, and in these areas riparian rights made sense, just as they did in the humid East. With population growth in the plains states of the Midwest, however, the legal rules evolved in a different way. Law on the plains granted the first appropriator of water an exclusive right to use it. Later appropriators' rights were conditioned upon the rights of those who had gone before them. The new rules also permitted the diversion of waters to nonriparian lands, the extinguishment of rights to water if not used, and the transfer of water rights from one person to another.

Yet even in the seemingly unique plains areas, borrowing from established legal traditions elsewhere was a central feature of the law. The states of the Midwest did not build their own system of water law *de novo;* instead they borrowed lavishly, water-abundant states often from the humid East, more arid plains states often from California's legislature and Supreme Court. The law of water flowed from West to East as well as East to West. In the rest of the region, a common-law riparian model was adopted almost fully. Furthermore, the long-term pattern throughout the Midwest was to reward the heavily capitalized businesses that make modern agribusiness work.

Interregional differences in legal culture and the

habit of borrowing were evident in another area: the legal status of women. Here as elsewhere, midwestern lawmakers seemed sensitive to economic necessity, crafting the law as it related especially to single women in instrumental ways, while treating married women in a way that protected the integrity and earning power of the family. Take, for example, Nebraska. Its divorce law included grounds of desertion, adultery, extreme cruelty, intemperance, and an omnibus provision of other but less utilized causes, including impotency and conviction for a felony. In this regard, Nebraska divorce law mimicked developments elsewhere in the country. But in the nineteenth-century Midwest, with large numbers of farms, a "dower" clause was attached to most divorce statutes. It entitled a wronged wife to her dower right (one-third of the property) should her spouse be blamed for the dissolution of the marriage. The dower clause, in short, complicated divorce in late-nineteenth-century Nebraska and demonstrated the influence of homestead-based land ownership on divorce in much of the Midwest.

The dower clause certainly influenced husbands. We know, for example, that more men than women filed for divorce in Nebraska and probably in most of the rest of the region, employing a preemptive strike strategy to shift blame to their wives and protect their farms from execution. For a short period in the 1870s and 1880s, the lenient divorce and residency laws in North and South Dakota made them havens for migratory divorces, often from states further east in the region.

There were also differences in the legal provisions governing property rights of married women. The Midwest almost uniformly adopted the common rather than the civil law system. Several midwestern states also wrote some degree of protection for married women's property rights into their constitutions, with Ohio, Illinois, and Michigan leading the way. At the same time, married women were effectively blocked from joining the legal profession in several late-nineteenth-century midwestern states, a position affirmed by the U.S. Supreme Court in *Bradwell v. Illinois* (1873).

For all of its seeming democratic and individualistic tendencies, the Midwest's legal culture also rested on a strong belief in the power of the state to regulate the creation of wealth. The region led the nation in the nineteenth century in developing regulation of railroads. For example, Michigan, in an action mimicked by other states, amended its constitution to prevent the merging of railroads with parallel tracks in an effort to maintain competition. Illinois established a railroad regulation commission that attempted to fix rates. That pattern diverged from other regulatory practices in the East, especially where such commissions were merely advisory. This difference in approach is largely explained by the fact that the Midwest was not only a vital market but also the neck through which east–west traffic passed, with Chicago and St. Louis emerging as the nation's greatest railroad cities.

Inevitably tied to local interests, state regulation of intrastate charges in the Midwest exacerbated the national controversy over rate regulation during railroad's Gilded Age. Midwest states had every incentive to impose low rates on railroads for local traffic, and in effect shift the economic burden of railroading to interstate shippers. Among other things such efforts undermined effective national regulation through the Interstate Commerce Commission. As a result, states of the Midwest regularly appeared in the U.S. Supreme Court to defend their positions. First Illinois in 1890, then Nebraska in 1898, found a hostile Supreme Court rejecting their efforts to regulate, through local control, the national railroad market.

These developments remind us of another important point about law in the Midwest. It often has been shaped by distant eastern and world markets. As the Midwest emerged in the late nineteenth century as an industrial powerhouse, its law had to change as well. Again water played a critical role, with traffic in raw materials and finished goods moving across the Great Lakes. Chicago, Milwaukee, Detroit, and Cleveland became national centers of admiralty and maritime law. Parts of the Midwest, especially in the plains and northern part of the region, have been exploited by eastern manufacturers and railroads, so much so that in the late nineteenth and early twentieth centuries, some of these states were something like third-world nations. Their economies depended on the export of agricultural commodities and raw materials to attain eastern credit and technology. These developments gave birth to first the Grange, then the Populist, and finally the Progressive political movements.

Many midwestern farmers believed that they were cheated by elevator owners, robbed by railroad barons, and overcharged by eastern manufacturers. The Grange movement of the 1870s was especially strong in Kansas and Nebraska, where small-town merchants and businessmen, who also suffered from predatory pricing policies, joined with farmers. These states were joined in the early twentieth century by the four upper–Mississippi Valley states of the region—Illinois, Iowa, Wisconsin, and Minnesota—as models of regulation, in large measure because the Republican and Democratic parties were evenly balanced there and hence susceptible to efforts by the Grange.

Midwest Populism was as much a quasilegal revival

as a political movement in which farmers rallied to seek legal solutions to the crushing debt and the burdensome taxes that they faced. The agrarian revolt in the 1890s produced startling legal results that endure even today: the creation of a flexible currency through the Federal Reserve; railroad regulation; honesty, economy, and greater openness in government; the direct election of U.S. Senators; postal savings banks; and a graduated income tax. The initiative and referendum the Populists desired, and the recall they considered too radical, were in general use not only in the Midwest but throughout the nation after 1912.

These developments were abetted by another wave of politically driven legal reform, the Progressive movement of the early twentieth century, that sought to redress the growing inequities in the burgeoning cities and towns of the Midwest. The Seventeenth Amendment, describing the composition of the U.S. Senate, came shortly after, as did gubernatorial term limits, stepped-up regulation of politics and elections, local nonpartisan elections, adoption of zoning and land use codes to bring order to the mayhem of cities such as Cleveland and Chicago, and efforts to turn previously private utilities, such as electricity and gas, into publicly owned entities. Eventually, the moral force of the Progressive movement brought about sharp limitations in the states on the production and consumption of alcohol, making the Midwest fertile ground for passage of the Eighteenth Amendment and for organized crime in its major cities.

While the general drift in twentieth-century legal culture has been to secure individual rights, often lawmakers tended to moral absolutism and fear of those from afar. Powerful nativist, anti-immigration tendencies, Protestant evangelical religion, and the power of a free labor ideology sometimes combined to form a cocktail of cultural intolerance. The Midwest developed legal strategies that maintained the Underground Railroad of the 1840s and 1850s, but permitted the Ku Klux Klan to maintain an ugly presence, particularly in Indiana and Ohio. In the 1960s, many of the large industrial cities of the Midwest, including Cleveland and Detroit, erupted in racial violence abetted by predominately white police forces and decades of de facto residential and economic discrimination. And in the Great Plains states of the Midwest, the Native American population struggled to maintain not only its cultural identity, but its legal identity.

At least on first impression, those qualities that seem to set the Midwest apart—individualism, innovation, and democracy—appear on closer inspection to be muffled by a legal culture susceptible to nativism, parochialism, and racism. The Midwest states have been, throughout their history, strongholds of political conservatism, ambivalence toward issues of gender, sexual preference, and even racial equality, and a preference for the maintenance of an agrarian social order in an increasingly industrialized and interdependent world economy.

Taken together, these developments caution against any effort to describe the Midwest as a unique legal culture. There is, of course, no such thing as *the* legal culture of the Midwest. In such a diverse area, there are all sorts of attitudes and opinions about law. That is not to say, however, that we should ignore the distinctive contributions and evolution of law and legal institutions in the Midwest. Thus, Lincoln's words remind us that, when it comes to the legal culture of the Midwest, we have caught something, but only by the hind leg.

The subsections here are organized thematically and chronologically, and the articles within each subsection are ordered alphabetically.

Sources and Further Reading: Andrew R. L. Cayton and Peter Onuf, *The Midwest and the Nation* (1990); James W. Ely, Jr., *Railroads and American Law* (2001); Lawrence M. Friedman, *Total Justice* (1985); Kermit L. Hall, *The Magic Mirror: Law in American History* (1989); Kermit L. Hall, ed., *The Oxford Companion to American Law* (2002); Kermit L. Hall and James W. Ely, Jr., *Constitutionalism in the History of the South* (1989); Peter Harris, "Ecology and Culture in the Communication of Precedent Among State Supreme Courts," *Law & Society Review* 19 (1985); John P. Heinz and Edward O. Laumann, *Chicago Lawyers: The Social Structure of the Bar* (1994); J. Willard Hurst, *The Growth of American Law: The Law Makers* (1965); Robert A. Kagan, Bobby D. Infelise, and Robert R. Detlefsen, "American State Supreme Court Justices, 1900–1970," *American Bar Foundation Research Journal* (1984); Walter Prescott Webb, *The Great Plains* (1931).

Kermit L. Hall
State University of New York–Albany

The Constitutional and Legal Culture of the Midwest

Midwestern legal and constitutional culture is a historical web of choices about boundaries, land use, and ownership; regulation of commerce; response to urbanization and industrialization; and the legal rights of its inhabitants, with special attention to women and ethnic minorities. Informal social values are an integral element of this web. Midwestern legal culture is a blend of progressivism and conservatism that attempts to balance the interests of farmers, industrial workers, corporations and banks, small-town business entrepreneurs, and urbanites. The same progressive mid-

Corson County Courthouse, McIntosh, South Dakota. Photo by Calvin L. Beale, Economic Research Service, United States Department of Agriculture.

westerners who created the cooperative farm movement have also been strong proponents of individual responsibility and have thus fought often for their civil liberties in the courts. The Midwest has influenced the entire United States constitutional culture through the many landmark cases that originated in this region.

Midwestern soil is, acre for acre, among the most fertile in the world. Although much of the land has therefore been used for agriculture, some has been given to lumbering, mining and other heavy industry, transportation, and cities. The conflicts and balances struck for this land have determined its legal and constitutional culture. Jane Smiley's Pulitzer Prize–winning novel, *A Thousand Acres*, portrays legal culture on an Iowa farm. One of its inhabitants muses:

> . . . the soil yielded a treasure of schemes and plots as well. Each acre was something to covet, something hard to get that enough of could not be gotten. Any field or farm was the emblem of some historic passion. On the way to Cabot or Pike or Henry Grove, my father would tell us who owned what indistinguishable flat black acreage, how he had gotten it, what he had done, and should have done with it, who got it after him and by what tricks or betrayals.

Unlike earlier American colonies, the midwestern states were not formed by royal charters, but by the United States government through purchases from foreign countries and through armed conflict, treaty, or outright occupation of land inhabited by indigenous peoples, explorers, and trappers. The American Indian and common law definitions of land ownership clashed from the beginning. Indians viewed the land as collectively held by its inhabitants. Europeans believed that nomads had no land rights; this outlook made it all the easier for them to force Indians off their ancestral lands.

Article I of the U.S. Constitution defined Indians as a separate nation, not as citizens, slaves, or dependents of the United States. On the early frontier, however, there was often no enforceable legal structure to deal with the conflicts between Indians and the European settlers.

The large, nineteenth-century settler incursion initially caused Indians to flee westward into other tribes' lands, which sparked intertribal conflict. When Indians decided to stand their ground, the settlers often retaliated with vigilante law. Squatters tried to settle before public land policies were in place. In 1785, Congress raised troops to evict them, to no avail. By 1815, Indians had virtually been driven out of the Illinois Territory through wars and government purchase of their land. A similar chain of events occurred in each territory, until the reservation system was formulated in the 1840s. Since 1871, the United States has not used treaties to negotiate with Indians; instead, relations are governed by federal legislation or executive order.

The late twentieth century witnessed continuing conflict regarding the return of Indian lands obtained illegally in the nineteenth century, fishing and hunting rights, the establishment of casinos for economic development on reservations, and the return of Indian remains from museums for proper burial.

At the same time as the Indian–settler difficulties, federal land policies and ordinances played a profound role in defining the future legal culture of the region with regard to education, civil liberties, and constitutional governance. These land policies were aimed at making small, inexpensive parcels of land available as incentive to farmers of modest means to move west.

Concurrently, deeds and inheritance laws were rewritten and simplified from the common law traditions.

The Land Ordinance of 1785 and the Northwest Ordinance of 1787 provided a process for the federal government to establish Western territories with a governor and three judges to ride circuit. A population of five thousand free male inhabitants enabled the territory to elect a general assembly and write a constitution. At sixty thousand inhabitants, the Congress could admit a new state with the same rights as the thirteen original ones.

In the Northwest Ordinance, slavery was expressly forbidden. This policy coincided with the national struggles over the issue of slavery. There was a tacit agreement in Congress that states entering the union had to be balanced between slave and free. The 1820 Missouri Compromise, for example, rendered Missouri a slave state to balance with Maine; the Kansas-Nebraska Act of 1854 created those two states and opened Kansas to slave settlement.

The Midwest joined the rest of the North in the growing abolitionist sentiments of the early nineteenth century. While some of this feeling was no doubt moral outrage, much was based on economic considerations. Abraham Lincoln framed the issue as an effort to protect the value of free farmers' labor, not to encourage racial intermingling. In fact, midwestern states had a series of complex laws and unwritten customs for dealing with African Americans. Illinois had an 1829 statute requiring African Americans to post $1,000 bond for good behavior surety. Some states prohibited freed slaves or free blacks from living in them, and none provided high-quality public education on a par with that for whites.

The states of the region resented having to enforce the Fugitive Slave Law of 1850, initiated by Southern interests, which denied captured slaves any legal rights or habeas corpus. In the Racine, Wisconsin, case, *Ableman v. Booth* (1859), the Wisconsin Supreme Court declared the Fugitive Slave Law unconstitutional, though later the U.S. Supreme Court upheld the supremacy of the federal courts in this and all cases. The Wisconsin Supreme Court particularly resented that the federal government would support such policies and, in *Dred Scott v. Sandford* (1857), would declare the Missouri Compromise to be unconstitutional.

Midwestern states entered the union at a time of great territorial expansion, with jockeying among local, state, and federal authorities about how much this expansion should be regulated. From the beginning, it was clear that the public land sale laws and policies were creating a legal culture promoting middle-class ownership of property. At the same time, these farmers wanted to expand their markets, which encouraged governments to build canals and railroads and, eventually, to establish corporations. Courts began to uphold the rights of railroads or canals over those of individual property owners. Eventually farmers came to feel at the mercy of the railroads setting shipping rates and of faraway banks and markets determining credit and crop prices. Some legal decisions did favor the farmers. *Munn v. Illinois* (1877), for example, upheld the legality of states setting maximum rates for storing grain, stating that private property devoted to public use is subject to regulation. But in most cases, the courts supported individual rights over privilege conferred by the state.

Collaboration of states with private interests to promote transportation and commerce caused problems like those in Indiana, which in the 1830s passed legislation to build a network of roads, canals, and railroads to be financed by bonds. This overly ambitious project rendered Indiana virtually bankrupt by 1840 and gave Hoosiers an abiding distrust of big government projects.

The legal culture of business expansion eventually prompted a public backlash, leading to a redress of balance and a distinctively midwestern agrarian revolt and progressive era. By the 1860s, farmers and workers had begun to organize the Grange and other populist movements to confront the power of railroads and banks. Such organizations as the Northern Farmers' Alliance and the Non-Partisan League had a crucial balance of power in the state legislatures of Nebraska, Minnesota, and the Dakotas by the 1890s. In Minnesota, the Farmer-Labor Party was established in 1918 to build state-owned cooperatives for meatpacking, flour milling, and grain storage in an attempt to cut out the middleman and to ensure fair prices.

At the same time that farmers were gaining power, the legal culture was responding to additional factors—urbanization and the resultant labor movement. The progressive agenda had a distinguished midwestern heritage, with Robert La Follette and his state of Wisconsin playing a major role. In 1901, Wisconsin established the first Legislative Reference Bureau, to teach and model good written law. The state passed the first workmen's compensation law in 1911. The land-grant University of Wisconsin at Madison was the intellectual center for this agenda, called The Wisconsin Idea. It is no accident that many progressive politicians of the late twentieth century came from this part of the Midwest: Eugene McCarthy, Paul Wellstone, Hubert Humphrey, and Walter Mondale of Minnesota; Harold Hughes from Iowa; and George McGovern from South Dakota. However, Wisconsin also produced the ultra-conservative Senator Joseph McCarthy, who in the 1950s exploited anti-Communist sentiments to launch investigations in the

Senate of political leaders, government officials, artists, and others he believed to be affiliated with the Communist Party.

By the 1830s, unions had emerged in such cities as Chicago. In 1894, the American Railway Union struck against the Pullman Palace Car Company over a proposed wage cut, and President Cleveland sent in federal troops to break the strike. Indiana native and union activist Eugene V. Debs was held in contempt. He appealed to the U.S. Supreme Court for a writ of habeas corpus, which was denied. *In re Debs* 158 U.S. 564 (1895) claimed supremacy of the federal courts over state courts and defended the use of the injunction as a legitimate means to prevent damage to private property and commerce.

The union movement grew rapidly in Detroit after the National Labor Relations Act of 1935 guaranteed the right of workers to join unions and enter into collective bargaining with their employers. The Flint, Michigan autoworkers, suffering from the Great Depression, accepted the United Auto Workers as their bargaining unit in the 1930s. The 1936–1937 sit-down strikes at General Motors auto plants set a model that would have a lasting impact on labor–management relations in the twentieth century.

Progressivism and World War I fostered an era of public concern over civil liberties and other rights. The country had become increasingly diverse, with a significant African American population and women demanding equal rights. Such states as Minnesota, Wisconsin, and Iowa actually advertised in European newspapers for immigrant settlers.

When the states of the Midwest were established, the only group with full access to, and the right to determine, the legal culture was the upper class, property-owning white male. In *Bradwell v. Illinois* (1873), a woman who had passed the bar was nonetheless prohibited from practicing law in Illinois. But in that same year, a woman was admitted to the Iowa bar. Women in the Midwest did not get the right to vote until the Nineteenth Amendment, with limited exceptions in Illinois and Kansas. Women began to run for public office, but even in such progressive states as Minnesota, there were not more than a handful of women in the state legislature until 1962. By 1990, however, Minnesota was the first state whose high court was composed of a female majority.

One of the most important civil rights cases in the twentieth century was *Brown v. Board of Education of Topeka, Kansas* (1954), which ordered an end to segregated schools and was the major impetus for African American civil rights legislations in the 1960s and beyond. The Midwest was the source for several other landmark civil liberties and constitutional rights cases in the twentieth century. *Near v. Minnesota* (1931) prohibited prior restraint against a publication exposing

corruption in the Minneapolis city government that was, in addition, peppered with anti-Semitism. In a five-to-four decision, the U.S. Supreme Court, including Oliver Wendell Holmes and Louis Brandeis, judged a Minnesota statute to be illegal because its prior restraint chilled political speech and was "the essence of censorship."

Illinois ex rel. McCollum v. Board of Education (1948) prohibited the Champaign, Illinois, school district from holding voluntary religion classes on public school premises. A six-to-one U.S. Supreme Court ruled that the program violated the Establishment Clause of the U.S. Constitution.

Tinker v. Des Moines Independent Community School District (1969) upheld the right of high school students to wear anti–Vietnam War armbands on school property. In what legal theorists call a "symbolic speech" case, the U.S. Supreme Court overturned the expulsion of three students, whose armbands had been deemed to be disruptive and mocking of school discipline. *Wisconsin v. Yoder* (1972) confronted the religious rights of the Amish defendants who refused to obey the Wisconsin state law requiring their children to attend school until the age of sixteen. The U.S. Supreme Court decided that the state could not impose its authority on this sect's religious life.

The U.S. District Court for the Northern District of Illinois heard the famous 1969–1970 trial of the "Conspiracy Eight" (which became the "Chicago Seven" after Bobby Seale was severed from the case). *United States of America v. David T. Dellinger et al.* grew out of the anti–Vietnam War demonstrations surrounding the 1968 Democratic National Convention in Chicago. Eight demonstrators were charged with crossing state lines to incite riots—a violation of a 1968 federal law—and conspiracy. Judge Julius J. Hoffman, a liberal but old-school judge who demanded absolute decorum in his court, was pitted against the wild clothing and dramatics of the defendants. Judge Hoffman found all defendants and their lawyers in contempt of court and sentenced them to jail terms. The jury found all defendants not guilty of the conspiracy charges, but some guilty of violating the anti-riot act. Legal battles continued until 1973, when a judge decided that no further jail sentences were warranted.

The nineteenth-century penal reform movement attempted to restrict the application of the death penalty to only the most heinous crimes. Though the Midwest was not the only region seeking penal reform, in 1845, Michigan was the first state to abolish the death penalty, followed by Wisconsin. Individual state practice and public opinion fluctuated and varied widely until 1972, when *Furman v. Georgia* vacated the death sentences of around six hundred inmates nationwide after determining that the existing Georgia death

penalty procedures were a violation of "the ban on cruel and unusual punishment in the Eighth Amendment." As a result, thirty-seven states had to rewrite their statutes. Most had reinstated the death penalty by 2000, when Illinois Governor George Ryan announced his plan to block further executions in Illinois until an inquiry was conducted to determine the reason for so many erroneous convictions. His final act of office on January 11, 2003, was to empty Illinois's death row, causing a sharply divided and passionate public reaction.

In *Grutter v. Bollinger* (2003), University of Michigan's affirmative action policies were upheld, and this case is likely to have ramifications for higher education well into the twenty-first century.

Sources and Further Reading: Richard Cahan, *A Court That Shaped America* (2002); A.R.L. Clayton and S.E. Gray, eds., *The American Midwest* (2001); Lawrence M. Friedman, *A History of American Law*, 2nd ed. (1985); Kermit Hall, *The Magic Mirror* (1989); S.B. Presser and J.S. Zainaldin, eds., *Law and Jurisprudence in American History* (2000); Malcolm Rohrbough, *The Trans-Appalachian Frontier* (1978); Jane Smiley, *A Thousand Acres* (1991); Melvin Urofsky and Paul Finkelman, *A March of Liberty*, 2nd ed. (2002); Charles F. Wilkinson, *American Indians, Time, and the Law* (1987).

Barbara Jones
Wesleyan University, Connecticut

Admiralty and Maritime Law

Since the early nineteenth century, the navigable rivers and Great Lakes, because they have been so essential to the commercial development of the Midwest, have provided a source of legal conflicts over admiralty and maritime matters. Admiralty and maritime law is the distinct body of law governing navigation and shipping and includes such matters as cargo damage, collision, personal injury, and even piracy. In 1845, Congress extended the admiralty jurisdiction to most commercial shipping on the Great Lakes and the navigable rivers, such as the Mississippi and the Ohio. The Supreme Court subsequently held that the statute was unnecessary, as the Constitutional grant of admiralty jurisdiction applied to these waters. The Supreme Court has held that most admiralty disputes can be heard in either state or federal court and that the same law must be applied wherever the case is tried. In the nineteenth century, a number of midwestern states (notably Michigan, Illinois, and Iowa) tried to aid businesses that supplied materials to vessels by conferring *in rem* or concurrent jurisdiction on their state courts. The Supreme Court struck down these statutes.

State law has been applied in admiralty cases, particularly when the state has a strong interest in doing so. In 1960, the Supreme Court upheld the City of Detroit's right to regulate the smoke emissions from vessels. More recently the Court suggested that Illinois law might govern some aspects of a major dispute that arose when a construction crane sitting on a barge in the Chicago River created a flood of the Chicago Loop.

Sources and Further Reading: Grant Gilmore and Charles L. Black, Jr., *The Law of Admiralty*, 2nd ed. (1975); David W. Robertson, *Admiralty and Federalism* (1970); Thomas J. Schoenbaum, *Admiralty and Maritime Law*, 2nd ed. (1994).

Steven F. Friedell
Rutgers University–Camden, New Jersey

Education, Religion, and Social Control

The 1890 Census of Wisconsin reported 249,164 Catholics and 160,919 Lutherans in the state, which comprised about 75 percent of the communicants of the state's religious bodies. Wisconsin ranked first among the relatively heterogeneous states of the Midwest in nonpublic school enrollment, with 66,065 students, of which 37,855 were in Catholic schools and 26,359 in Lutheran schools.

These demographics led to two conflicts in the state, which existed in several other midwestern states as well. The first of these was over the devotional reading of the King James Version of the Bible, with attendant religious devotions. This practice, widespread in the nation's public schools, had played an important part in public schooling. Wisconsin's mainstream Protestants (Baptists, Congregationalists, Methodists, and Presbyterians) generally supported the practice. They deemed it nonsectarian Christian, sufficient to make the schools morally acceptable to all children.

Challenges to the practice grew as the state became more religiously heterogeneous. In the 1880s, in Edgerton, Wisconsin, a group of Catholics brought suit on behalf of their children, who were pupils in the public schools of that city. They charged that the practice violated their children's rights of conscience because it constituted sectarian instruction, which was forbidden by the Wisconsin constitution. Their cause was taken up by the *Catholic Citizen*, the English-language newspaper published in Milwaukee.

In 1888, Circuit Court Judge John R. Bennett upheld the practice. The Wisconsin Supreme Court, however, ruled in 1890 that the practice violated the Wisconsin constitution because: (1) it constituted sectarian instruction and hence violated the rights of conscience of the plaintiffs, and (2) it made the public school a place of worship. The state's Protestants were generally disappointed, even outraged, at the decision, regarding it as a triumph of sectarianism. Catholics, Unitarians, and liberals rejoiced. The decision was the first of its kind in the nation.

The second issue involved the attempt by the state to gain some measure of control over nonpublic schools, ostensibly to ensure that they put sufficient emphasis on "good citizenship" through use of the English language. In 1889, the Wisconsin legislature passed the Bennett Law, similar to the Edwards Law in Illinois, in response to Republican Governor William Dempster Hoard's request for legislation that would empower local superintendents of schools to inspect all schools in their districts to see that certain courses were being taught in English. The law's two most objectionable features to Catholic and Lutheran leaders were: (1) the requirement that a child attend school in the "town or school district in which he resides," and (2) the mandate that certain subjects must be taught in the English language for the institution to qualify as a school, thereby satisfying the compulsory attendance laws of the state.

Collectively, Catholic and Lutheran leaders termed the law a usurpation of the rights of parent and church. The Catholic bishops of the state called it "unnecessary, offensive, and unjust." Governor Hoard and his allies hailed the law as necessary to enable the youth of the state to obtain full citizenship.

Governor Hoard was defeated in a bitter gubernatorial campaign in the fall of 1890. The Bennett Law was the salient issue in the contest. The Wisconsin legislature made the repeal of the law and the passage of its replacement, which met with the approval of Catholic and Lutheran leaders, its first order of business in 1891.

Sources and Further Reading: Thomas C. Hunt, "The Bennett Law of 1890: Focus of Conflict between Church and State," *Journal of Church and State* 23 (Winter 1981); Thomas C. Hunt, "The Edgerton Bible Decision: The End of an Era," *The Catholic Historical Review* 67 (Oct. 1981); *The State of Wisconsin ex rel. Weiss and others, Appellant v. The District Board of School District No. Eight of the City of Edgerton, Respondent,* 76 Wis. 177 (1890); William F. Whyte, "The Bennett Law Campaign," *Wisconsin Magazine of History* 4 (June 1927).

Thomas C. Hunt
The University of Dayton, Ohio

Family Law

Family law encompasses state laws regarding adoption; assisted reproduction; child custody, access and support; entry into and rights during marriage; divorce; parentage; pre- and postmarital agreements; rights of cohabitants; and family torts. State laws cannot impinge on the fundamental right to privacy, to marry, or to choose to bear and rear children. Federal laws cover some aspects of family law including tax, bankruptcy, child support enforcement, domestic violence, family leave, and allocation of federal benefits. International family law includes the Hague Convention on the Civil Aspects of International Child Abduction and the Hague Convention on Cooperation in Respect to Intercountry Adoption.

Midwest states are similar to the rest of the country in their procedural and substantive requirements for marriage—a license, witnesses, and solemnization. Parties must be eighteen years of age or have parental consent, be one man and one woman, and not be related too closely by blood. Of the nine states that permit couples to enter into a common law marriage, two are in the Midwest, Iowa and Kansas. Twenty-eight states, including Illinois, Indiana, Iowa, Kansas, Nebraska, and Wisconsin, use the Uniform Premarital Agreement Act, which allows parties to change some of the consequences of marriage and divorce. Midwest states, except Illinois, allow cohabitants to seek property division based on contract or equitable theories, but none allows death benefits.

Spouses in the Midwest can own separate property, enter contracts, and keep earnings. All fifty states have at least one no-fault ground for divorce. Iowa, Michigan, Minnesota, Nebraska, and Wisconsin have only a no-fault ground. The trend is toward shorter alimony based on the need of the dependent spouse and on the ability of the other to pay, ages, length of marriage, standard of living, earning capacities, and economic fault. Marital fault is not a factor in most midwestern states.

States provide for equitable division of property upon divorce. Wisconsin, a marital property state, divides only the marital property. While several other states classify property as "marital" and "nonmarital" according to when it was acquired and in whose name it is titled, Indiana, Iowa, Kansas, Michigan, Nebraska, North Dakota, and South Dakota classify *all* property, whenever acquired and however titled, as "marital" upon divorce. A few states presume a fifty-fifty division of property, but in most states, the judge has discretion to award more property to one spouse if equitable, such as in the case of a long-term marriage and homemaker spouse.

Mothers and fathers, married or not, have equal rights to custody unless found unfit. If separated, custody is awarded according to the best interest of the child. All states authorize joint or shared custody. Third parties can be granted visitation over the objec-

tion of a fit parent if they can show a substantial relationship with the child and that it would harm the child to discontinue the relationship. Child support guidelines in all states determine the amount separated parents must pay at least until the child reaches the age of eighteen.

Family law is in a transformative period. Changes in family form and function have altered the laws governing families. What constitutes family law fifty years from today is likely to be different as society and the law continue to expand and develop.

Sources and Further Reading: Homer Clark, *The Law of Domestic Relations*, 2nd ed. (1988); Linda Henry Elrod, *Child Custody Practice and Procedure* (1993; Supp., 2002); Ann M. Haralambie, *Handling Child Custody, Abuse and Adoption Cases* (1993); Harry D. Krause, *Family Law*, 2nd ed. (1996).

Linda D. Elrod
Washburn University, Kansas

Labor Law

The Civil War and its aftermath created unprecedented demands for industrial production. With westward migration, midwestern cities became industrial powerhouses. Growing industries led to conflicts between company owners and workers, leading to the development of law regulating labor relations and the workplace.

Labor law began with the railroads. Conflicts often resulted in strikes, such as the Railroad Strike of 1877, which started in West Virginia and rippled across the Midwest to cities such as Chicago, St. Louis, Peoria, and Columbus, fueling the anxieties of business owners. In the wake of the strike, labor leaders started to work within the political system to affect labor relations to try and combat a legal system that regularly charged and convicted workers of illegal conspiracies of organizing, incitement to riot, and other crimes in an effort to combat unionization. Following a series of railroad strikes, the federal government passed the first labor relations law (1888) mandating arbitration of disputes. Partially in response to the Pullman Strike (1894), Congress passed the Erdman Act (1898), amending the earlier law.

Passage of the 1890 Sherman Antitrust Act and the 1914 Clayton Act initially gave workers hope that business combinations would benefit workers, but the optimism proved short-lived when courts, using these laws, began finding union action tantamount to illegal combinations in restraint of trade. However, by the 1930s, the federal government expressed support for workers with the passage of New Deal legislation.

Workers in places such as South Bend, Detroit, and Akron took advantage of the changing legal landscape and used sit-down strikes to organize the automobile and rubber industries.

Today's labor law encompasses such traditional union actions like collective bargaining, handling of workers compensation claims, and managing union pension and welfare funds. Modern labor law also governs matters relating to the industries throughout the Midwest as heavy industrial production moves overseas.

Sources and Further Reading: Bruce Feldacker, *Labor Guide to Labor Law*, 4th ed. (2000); Ronald L. Filippelli, *Labor in the USA: A History* (1984); Walter E. Oberer, Kurt L. Hanslowe, and Timothy J. Heinsz, *Cases and Materials on Labor Law: Collective Bargaining in a Free Society*, 5th ed. (2002). Numerous excellent websites exist, including the Illinois Labor History Society site at www.kentlaw.edu/ilhs/ and the Walter P. Reuther Library site at www.reuther.wayne.edu/.

Janice Lynne Durbin
Anderson, Missouri

Law in Literature

Beginning with Mark Twain, midwestern authors have frequently employed law and legal themes in their work. Twain's *The Gilded Age* (1873) pillories the federal lawmaking process as well as the criminal justice process. In *The Adventures of Huckleberry Finn* (1885), Huck's decision to break the law and help Jim escape slavery is one of the most powerful moments in American literature. *Pudd'nhead Wilson* (1894) features Attorney Wilson and assures the reader that all the trial scenes have been scrupulously checked by a feed store clerk in Italy who had studied the law in Missouri thirty-five years earlier.

In the Populist–Progressive Era, midwestern literature often cast law as an agent of injustice. Hamlin Garland's "Under the Lion's Paw" (1889) tells the story of an Iowa farmer who rents and improves the land only to see his manipulative landlord profit. Confronted by the outraged renter wielding a pitchfork, the landlord explains, "It's the law. The regular thing. Everybody does it." Upton Sinclair set *The Jungle* (1906) in the stockyards and slums of Chicago, where those in power use law to exploit the immigrant working class. When the novel supposedly led to Congressional investigations of the meatpacking industry and to pure food legislation, Sinclair felt readers had missed his socialist point. Journalist and proto-feminist Susan Glaspell crafted the play *Trifles* (1916) and then rewrote it as a short story, "A Jury of Her

Peers" (1917). The plot derives from an actual case of spousal abuse, but Glaspell refashions it to suggest that country women might substitute their own judgment for that of the masculinist legal system.

Theodore Dreiser, the son of German immigrants who had settled in Terre Haute and later Warsaw, Indiana, began his literary career with *Sister Carrie* (1900). But it was his *American Tragedy* (1925) that most extensively addressed legal concerns. Clyde Griffiths, the novel's protagonist, kills or allows to die the pregnant working-class girl who stands in the way of his marriage to a wealthy girl. The second half of the novel then wrestles with the issue of whether a man who is the product of his conditions can be convicted of a crime into which he stumbles.

Richard Wright set his powerful *Native Son* (1940) in the Windy City. Wright's Bigger Thomas kills a white woman and his African American girlfriend. Thomas's uneven trial suggests that even though law and legal institutions might dictate verdicts and judgments on the surface of American life, the same law and legal institutions contribute on a deeper level to American racial oppression.

In the present, Chicagoan Scott Turow has authored a half-dozen best-selling novels about lawyers and legal proceedings. *Presumed Innocent* (1987), the first of these works, involves the prosecution of a prosecutor for murder. All of Turow's works are set in the Midwest's fictional Kindle County, and he provocatively criticizes law firms, government offices, and power-mad judges.

The exact nature of the midwestern writers' critique of the law has changed with the times. Yet the various writers' distrust of the law contrasts with the Midwest's workaday assumptions that law facilitates the market economy and, more generally, contributes to stability and justice.

Sources and Further Reading: Barry R. Schaller, *A Vision of American Law* (1997); Richard Clark Sterne, *Dark Mirror: The Sense of Injustice in Modern European and American Literature* (1994).

David Ray Papke
Marquette University, Wisconsin

Militia (Common Law) Movements

Radical militia movements, which are most prevalent in the rural Midwest, include the Common Law Movement and the Posse Comitatus organization, a blending of antitax and ultra-right-wing, pseudo-Christian beliefs. The fundamental cause for their emergence was the farming crisis of the 1980s, which led many farmers to join the Posse Comitatus.

Legal justifications for their positions vary from the Magna Carta, Declaration of Independence, Constitution, Uniform Commercial Code, and the U.S. Supreme Court case *Erie Railroad Co. v. Tompkins* (1938), in which they claim the government illegally abolished common law, but which actually held only that there is no general federal common law. Coupled with their assertion that President Franklin D. Roosevelt suspended the Constitution in 1933, this rejection proves to members that the country has been in a state of lawlessness since 1938.

Members reject Social Security numbers and drivers licenses, disobey gun laws, refuse to pay taxes, and file frivolous liens against public officials. "Common Law Courts" issue their own divorce decrees, absolve members of traffic violations, and issue edicts to public officials calling for their deaths by hanging.

Adherence to principles of the rule of law by most citizens in midwestern states, and counteractions by legislators, law enforcement, and judges have diminished the appeal of the common law court movement. For example, legislatures have criminalized the simulation of legal processes, and courts have increasingly issued sanctions and injunctions for frivolous lawsuits.

Sources and Further Reading: Thomas Halpern and Brian Levin, *The Limits of Dissent* (1996); Susan P. Koniak, "The Chosen People in Our Wilderness," *Michigan Law Review* 95 (May 1997); Francis X. Sullivan, "The 'Usurping Octopus of Jurisdictional Authority': The Legal Theories of the Sovereign Citizen Movement," *Wisconsin Law Review* (1999).

Thomas J. Moyer
Chief Justice, Supreme Court of Ohio

State Bills of Rights

Illinois, Indiana, Michigan, Ohio, and Wisconsin—the original midwestern states—were created in the first half of the nineteenth century, with the specter of slavery haunting the nation, from the territory governed by the 1787 Northwest Ordinance. Accordingly, each constitution specifically prohibited slavery.

Their constitutions devoted a separate article to an itemization of approximately twenty widely recognized civil, criminal, and natural rights that were included in East Coast declarations and in the first nine amendments to the U.S. Constitution. By incorporating rights into the constitutions, rather than attaching them as prefatory or amended declarations, the midwesterners departed from the founding tradition and set the example for subsequent regions including California and the upper Midwest.

Iowa, Minnesota, Missouri, Kansas, and Nebraska

were created from the 1803 Louisiana Purchase, and each devoted an article in their constitution to standard rights. They differed from each other, and the original five midwestern states, with respect to the prohibition of slavery. Iowa was antislavery, but the 1820 Missouri Compromise and the 1854 Kansas-Nebraska Acts, which diluted the solid midwestern opposition, were vital in the creation of state bills of rights and the nationwide discussion on human rights, property rights, and states rights.

North Dakota and South Dakota entered the union in 1889 free of the quarrels over slavery and race. They also incorporated a bill of rights into their constitutions, and progressive South Dakota entertained the possibility of enfranchising women.

Source and Further Reading: F. N. Thorpe, *The Federal and State Constitutions* (1909).

Gordon Lloyd
Pepperdine University, California

States' Rights

The South is correctly seen as the center of states' rights sentiment. Antebellum midwesterners, however, also included states' rights advocates. Some involved economic issues; for example, in *Osborn v. Bank of the United States* (1824), the U.S. Supreme Court struck down an Ohio law that undermined the Bank of the United States. However, most midwestern states' rights arguments were over slavery.

With southerners and their northern allies dominating Congress, the courts, and presidency, opponents of slavery often challenged the federal government. In the 1840s and 1850s, most midwestern states passed strong personal liberty laws, withdrawing state support for the enforcement of federal fugitive slave laws. In 1854 and 1855, the Wisconsin Supreme Court issued writs of habeas corpus to release Sherman Booth, a runaway slave, from federal custody after he was arrested, and then later convicted, of violating the Fugitive Slave Law of 1850. The Supreme Court rejected this challenge to federal authority in *Ableman v. Booth* (1859). In *Ex parte Bushnell* and *Ex parte Langston* (1859), the Ohio Supreme Court failed, by one vote, to challenge the federal government's prosecution of abolitionists after the Oberlin-Wellington Rescue. Had the state court not issued a writ of habeas corpus for Bushnell and Langston, Governor Salmon P. Chase indicated he was prepared to use the state militia to force the federal government to release the prisoners.

Both Chase and his successor, Governor William Dennison, made states' rights arguments in their refusal to deliver for extradition Willis Lago, a free black wanted in Kentucky for helping a slave escape into Ohio. The Ohio governors argued that because Ohio did not recognize slavery, it could not recognize the "crime" of slave-stealing with which Lago was charged. In *Kentucky v. Dennison* (1861), the Supreme Court upheld the right of Ohio to refuse to honor the extradition requisition, while at the same time chastising Ohio for failing to live up to its constitutional obligation to deliver Lago. Once the Civil War broke out, however, opponents of slavery no longer needed states' rights doctrines, and easily abandoned them for a more nationalistic outlook.

Sources and Further Reading: Paul Finkelman, *An Imperfect Union: Slavery, Federalism, and Comity* (1981); Paul Finkelman, "States' Rights North and South in Antebellum America," in Kermit Hall and James W. Ely, Jr., eds., *An Uncertain Tradition: Constitutionalism and the History of the South* (1989); Thomas D. Morris, *Free Men All: The Personal Liberty Laws of the North, 1780–1861* (1974).

Paul Finkelman
University of Tulsa, Oklahoma

Women and the Law

The unique environment of the Midwest—prairie, rich farmland, Great Lakes waterways, prime industrial sites—and its location at the crossroads of America and in the path of the pioneer migration westward provided opportunities for women to participate in developments that affected the entire country. Throughout history women have advocated for many legal reforms including voting (suffrage), civil rights, and the labor movement. Women in midwestern states initiated and supported many legal milestones. The issues, and those who support them today, continue to influence legal thought and legislation.

Women sought the right to practice law fifty years before they won the right to vote. Admission to the bar often was not required to practice at the local level. In 1869, Arabella "Belle" Babb Mansfield became the first woman admitted to a state bar (Iowa). In Illinois, Myra Colby Bradwell, editor of the *Chicago Legal News*, passed the bar, but the U.S. Supreme Court held in *Bradwell v. Illinois* (1873) that the denial of her right to practice law did not violate the Fourteenth Amendment guaranteeing the rights of citizenship. Ada H. Kepler, the first woman law school graduate (1870, Union College, now Northwestern University), also was denied admission in Illinois. However, during the *Bradwell* case, Alta M. Hulett became Illinois's first woman lawyer at age nineteen after legislation was enacted that stated no person could be excluded from any employment because of sex.

Lemma Barkaloo of Missouri, the first woman law student in the nation, was admitted to the Missouri bar after one year of study. Phoebe Wilson Couzins of Missouri was admitted to the Missouri, Arkansas, Utah, and Kansas bars and the Dakota Territory federal courts. Other firsts include Rhoda Lavinia Goodell in Wisconsin, Nettie Cronise Lutes in Ohio, and Ada Bittenbender in Nebraska. By 1905, each of these midwestern states had admitted its first woman to practice; North Dakota was last, nine years after South Dakota.

In 1886, Lettie Burlingame founded the Equity Club, the first professional organization for women law students and lawyers, at the University of Michigan. The first nationwide meeting of women lawyers was held at the 1893 World's Fair in Chicago. During the nineteenth and twentieth centuries, midwestern women lawyers and activists were involved in establishing the National Association for the Advancement of Colored People, the League of Women Voters, and other national organizations.

Among the midwestern states, Illinois was first to appoint a woman judge: Catharine McCulloch, Justice of the Peace, 1907. Other early appointments include Frances Hopkins (Missouri, 1915); Florence Ellinwood Allen, first woman on a state supreme court (Ohio, 1922) and first woman federal appeals judge (1934); and Genevieve Rose Cline, first woman to become a federal judge (Ohio, 1928, U.S. Customs Court). In the 1920s, many women entered office to fulfill the terms of their deceased husbands; in 1927, two women were governors, and five served in Congress. During the 1980s, three women became governor including Kay Orr (Nebraska). From 1993 through 1995, women in Congress held 11 percent of the seats in the House and 7 percent in the Senate, and a decade later these proportions had increased to 14 percent and 11 percent, respectively.

Women legislators from midwestern states have been instrumental in the passage of important legislation. Minnesotan Coya Knutson helped create the federal student loan fund, in Title II of the National Defense Education Act of 1958. Women benefited from the Civil Rights Act of 1964, especially Title VII and the addition Martha W. Griffiths (Michigan) proposed prohibiting discrimination based on sex. Griffiths also sponsored the unsuccessful Equal Rights Amendment in 1972. In 1970, Harriette Vesta Bailey Conn (Indiana) became the first woman and first African American to be appointed State Public Defender. In 1972, Title IX of the Education Amend-

ments Act was passed, guaranteeing equal access to academic and athletic resources.

Elected in 1973, Cardiss Robertson Collins of Missouri spent twenty-three years in the U.S. House as a representative from a congressional district in Illinois, the longest tenure of any African American woman. She introduced the first mammogram bill securing Medicare coverage. Connie Binsfield, Michigan's Lieutenant Governor (1991–1998), as a legislator in 1978, introduced the state's first domestic violence legislation. Virginia C. Blomer Nordby helped draft the Michigan Sexual Conduct Code, adopted by twenty-eight states. Katie Beatrice Green Hall sponsored the Martin Luther King, Jr., holiday legislation and was the first African American elected to Congress from Indiana. Patricia J. Boyle left the federal bench to sit on the Michigan State Supreme Court in 1983 and helped reform Michigan's rape law. Carol Moseley-Braun (Illinois) was the first African American woman elected to the Senate (1992) and one of the first women to be named to the Senate Judiciary Committee.

Nebraskan Margaret Jane Carns is reported to be the first woman member of the American Bar Association. Five women lawyers were counted in the 1870 census. In 1980, 8 percent of all lawyers were women; the figure reached 25 percent in 1995. Women now represent about 30 percent of all lawyers; women of color, 3 percent. At the turn of the century, women represented 15 percent of all partners in law firms and federal judges and 10 percent of general counsels and law school deans, while the percentage of women law students in ABA-accredited law schools in the Midwest averaged nearly 50 percent. The statistics for women law professors are less consistent, with a range of 20 to 48 percent in ABA-accredited law schools in the Midwest in 2004.

The dual roles of women as lawyers and as primary caretakers have led to advocacy for maternity leave, innovative workplace structures, and flexible criteria for partnership. The activism of women in the law has contributed to the coining of the phrases "mommy track" and "glass ceiling" and the creation of "feminine jurisprudence" legal theory. The presence of women in the profession thus highlights concerns about gender stereotypes, bias, sexual harassment, job dissatisfaction, and the retention of women lawyers.

Sources and Further Reading: American Bar Association, Commission on Women. *A Snapshot of Women in the Law in the Year* (2000); Maria Braden, *Women Politicians and the Media* (1996); Virginia G. Drachman, *Sisters in Law* (1998); La-Verne McCain Gill, *African American Women in Congress* (1997); Law School Admission Council and the American

Bar Association, *ABA-LSAC Official Guide to ABA-Approved Law Schools, 2003* (2002); Deborah L. Rhode, *The Unfinished Agenda: A Report on the Status of Women in the Legal Profession* (2001); Robert Crown Library, Stanford Law School, *Women's Legal History Biography Project* (Feb.–Apr. 2003).

Debra Lynn Denslaw
Indiana University–Indianapolis

The Legal Status of Free Blacks in the Antebellum Midwest

The antebellum Midwest provided opportunity, danger, and frustration for free blacks and fugitive slaves. Missouri, which for some purposes is midwestern, was clearly a southern state in this period, maintaining slavery until the end of the Civil War. Thus, this discussion of the rights of free blacks in the antebellum Midwest focuses on the free states north of the Ohio River, or north of Missouri.

The conditions of free blacks in this region changed dramatically over time and varied tremendously within the region. The antebellum Midwest has long had a reputation of extreme hostility to free blacks, but this history is actually quite mixed. Some midwestern free blacks lived in dire poverty with limited economic opportunities. Some of their children were able to attend school, but they were usually separate from and inferior to white schools. Free blacks throughout the region were shut out of the voting booth and the jury box.

On the other hand, by 1860, some free blacks in the region were landowners, sending their children to integrated public schools, and participating in public life. More than a third of all school-age black children attended school in Ohio, Michigan, and Iowa by 1860, and a greater percent of black children attended school in Ohio than in Pennsylvania, New Jersey, and New York. This was also a greater percentage of children in school than for white children in Virginia, Tennessee, Florida, Louisiana, and Arkansas. In 1860, 5,671 black children from six to twenty years of age (out of a total of 14,202) attended school in Ohio. This was more than attended school in all fifteen southern states combined, where more than ninety thousand free black children lived. In Michigan, a greater percentage of black children attended school than did white children in ten southern slave states.

Perhaps emblematic of the region was the largest city, Cincinnati. In the 1850s, Cincinnati would resist state requirements to provide education for blacks, but despite its racism, the city ranked third in the nation both in the number of free blacks owning property and in the total and average value of that property.

Although seen as "free soil," the Midwest began with slavery. In 1787, the Northwest Ordinance provided that there would be "neither slavery nor involuntary servitude" in the northwest territories. Well before the Revolution, however, slaveowners of French origin settled in present-day Illinois and Indiana. Thus, while the Ordinance banned slavery, it did nothing to end it. Blacks were held in bondage in Indiana and Illinois throughout the territorial period. In 1820, Indiana still had 190 slaves, and Illinois, a state for only two years at this point, had 917 slaves. Court decisions in Indiana quickly ended slavery, and by 1830, the census found only three slaves. Illinois, on the other hand, had 747 slaves in 1830 and 331 in 1840. Illinois finally abolished slavery completely in its 1847 constitution. During this period many masters in Indiana and Illinois held blacks as indentured servants for periods of time of up to 99 years, in essence converting their slaves into lifetime servants. The territorial laws allowed these indentures, and especially in Illinois, the courts ignored them for decades after statehood.

The Northwest Ordinance also allowed masters to recover their fugitive slaves in the Territory. The Constitution of 1787 provided a similar right, which Congress enforced with statutes in 1793 and 1850. The states of the lower Midwest initially provided good-faith enforcement of the federal fugitive slave law, while at the same time trying to prevent the kidnapping of free blacks. The rise of the antislavery movement, combined with more aggressive southern demands for the return of fugitive slaves, led to a breakdown of what was once a moderate cooperation between the states of the lower Midwest and the upper South. Although some fugitive slaves were successfully taken out of the region and returned to slavery, for the most part, especially after about 1840, resistance to the enforcement of the fugitive slave laws led to the growth of the black population in the Midwest. In parts of Ohio, like Oberlin and Wilberforce, as well as in Cass County, Michigan, fugitive slaves lived openly.

Antikidnapping laws provided some protection for free blacks, although some were kidnapped. In 1850, kidnappers seized eight children and grandchildren of a black Ohioan named Peyton Polly, taking them to Virginia and Kentucky where they were sold as slaves. Ohio authorities intervened and were able to bring four of the blacks back to their home with the intervention of Kentucky's attorney general, James Harlan (father of future Supreme Court Justice John Marshall Harlan). But Virginia stonewalled on the matter, and these free blacks were held as slaves until the Civil War led to their liberty.

As early as 1817, the Ohio Supreme Court liberated a slave whose master voluntarily brought him into the state. This was not a reported decision, and did not set a precedent. Throughout the 1830s and 1840s, some courts in the lower Midwest upheld the slave status of slaves in transit, while other courts did not. By the 1850s, however, every midwestern state except Indiana and Illinois had taken the position that slaves became free if masters voluntarily brought them into a free state. The Ohio Supreme Court confirmed this position in *Anderson v. Poindexter* (1856). These decisions led to a small growth in the free black population. More importantly, such decisions reaffirmed that the Midwest, with the exception of Indiana and Illinois, favored freedom and would be a safe haven, as much as possible, for all African Americans.

One measure of the condition of free blacks in the region is the growth of the black population. In the early part of the century Ohio, Indiana, and Illinois discouraged black migration with a variety of statutes. Ohio's laws of 1804 and 1807 required blacks coming into the state to register with county officials, and within two years after moving provide proof of their freedom. The registration fees were modest—twelve and a half cents—but still could have been onerous for the poorest black migrants. The 1807 law required that the blacks find two or more sureties to offer a bond of $500 to guarantee their good behavior and that they would not require public assistance. The law did not require, as some historians have incorrectly asserted, that anyone actually post a cash bond. The law provided fines for people who hired unregistered blacks. Under the 1807 law, blacks who failed to register could be expelled from the county by the overseers of the poor. These laws also provided heavy penalties for kidnappers of free blacks.

Indiana and Illinois adopted similar laws when they became states, and Michigan maintained such a law during part of its territorial period. Iowa passed such a law in the 1850s, but it is not clear if the law was ever in effect. While on the books, these laws were rarely enforced. There are few cases involving them and scant records of blacks actually registering. Those who did register were bona fide free people with papers to prove it. By registering, they in effect were able to confirm their free status and perhaps use that registration to protect their liberty. Those blacks whose status was doubtful—or who clearly were fugitive slaves— simply did not register and, with a few exceptions, were left alone.

Ohio repealed its registration laws in 1849, and except in Indiana, in the 1850s these laws had little effect on the growth of the free black population of the region. In its 1851 Constitution, Indiana prohibited black immigration, and between 1850 and 1860, the black population growth in that state virtually stopped. But before that decade, Indiana, like the rest of the lower Midwest, had an impressive growth in its black population. In 1800, Ohio had only 337 free blacks. Despite the registration laws, the free black population grew by over 500 percent between 1800 and 1810 and continued to grow in every decade, reaching 9,568 by 1830, over 25,000 by 1850, and over 36,000 by 1860. Illinois went from about 450 free blacks and slightly over 900 slaves in 1820 to more than 3,500 free blacks in 1840 and over 7,600 in 1860. In 1851, an Iowa law provided a $2-a-day fine for any black entering the state. Nevertheless, the free black population grew by more than 300 percent in the 1850s, reaching over 1,000 by 1860. Michigan's black population went from just over 700 in 1840 to about 6,800 in 1860. In 1840, the states and territories of the Midwest had about 29,000 free blacks; by 1869, this figure had more than doubled, to about 69,000.

The growth of the free black population in this region was far more rapid than in the rest of the North. In 1810, Ohio ranked seventh among Northern states in its free black population; by 1850, it had the third-largest black population in the North. Similarly, Indiana had the ninth largest black population in the North in 1820, and the fifth by 1860. In 1850, more than half the free blacks in the Midwest had been born outside of the state in which they lived.

No midwestern state gave free blacks full political rights. The Ohio Supreme Court ruled that people of mixed race could vote if they were more than half white, but this decision affected few people. In 1859, the legislature decreed that no one with a "visible admixture of African blood" could vote in the state, but the state supreme court held in *Anderson v. Milliken* (1859) that this law could not affect people who were more than half white. Local officials in parts of Ohio, such as Greene and Lorain County, and perhaps Cleveland, allowed free blacks to vote, as did officials in Detroit in some elections. In Cass County, Michigan, there were so many black property owners that, after 1855, the state allowed all property owners, even blacks, to vote in school board and bond elections. Ohio allowed blacks to vote for school board officials where there were separate schools. Although blacks were generally unable to vote, at least one, John Mercer Langston, was elected to public office in the abolitionist hotbed of Lorain County, Ohio. Because jury service was typically tied to the franchise, blacks were not allowed to serve on juries anywhere in the Midwest. Langston was also admitted to the bar, however, and practiced law in the region.

At statehood or immediately thereafter, Ohio, Indiana, and Illinois denied blacks the right to testify against whites. These laws undermined the ability of blacks to use the legal system to protect themselves from either criminal or civil assaults. This was unquestionably the most onerous assault on black rights in the Midwest; no one else was isolated as second-class citizens in this way. By comparison, other midwesterners faced various disabilities. Although citizens, white women and white children could not vote or serve on juries; immigrant white males could not vote; poor white settlers might be expelled from the community by the overseers of the poor. But all of these classes of people could defend their rights in court, could testify against their assailants, and could witness on behalf of others. Blacks, whatever their age, gender, or economic status, however, were denied the right to testify in court against whites.

In 1849 in a dramatic shift in its politics, Ohio repealed most of its black laws and gave free blacks the right to testify against whites. The states of the upper Midwest had never denied this right to them. Thus, while still denied the vote or equal schooling in much of the Midwest, on the eve of the Civil War, free blacks in all but Indiana and Illinois were far better off than they had been in the past and were witnessing huge changes in law that brought them closer to legal equality.

Sources and Further Reading: Paul Finkelman, *An Imperfect Union* (1981); Paul Finkelman, *Slavery and the Founders*, 2nd ed. (2001); Leon W. Litwack, *North of Slavery* (1961); Stephen Middleton, *The Black Laws in the Old Northwest: A Documentary History* (1993); James Simeone, *Democracy and Slavery in Frontier Illinois* (2000).

Paul Finkelman
University of Tulsa, Oklahoma

Slavery, Pre-1787 to 1848

Struggles over slavery played a significant role in the emergence of the Midwest as a region defined in the mid-nineteenth century by its staunch support for free labor ideals. Ostensibly, slavery was prohibited in the Northwest Territory by Article VI of the Northwest Ordinance of 1787. Over the sixty years thereafter, this exclusion was ultimately given force through legislation opposed to slavery. Nonetheless, the path toward exclusion of slavery was neither easy nor straightforward. Throughout the late eighteenth and early nineteenth centuries, slavery was widely accepted in many areas, especially in the first-settled portions of the lower Midwest. Consequently the institution's prohibition took effect only after rancorous debate.

Controversy developed initially over the precise scope and effect of the Northwest Ordinance's prohibition of slavery. As Paul Finkelman has shown, the sections of the Ordinance related to slavery were ambiguous and internally inconsistent. While Article VI declared that "[t]here shall be neither slavery nor involuntary servitude in the said territory," the document was silent on the means through which the prohibition would take effect and in other sections occasionally seemed to implicitly accept the presence of slavery. Especially problematic was a passage granting French and Canadian settlers—the region's principle slaveholders before 1787—the right to retain their "laws and customs" concerning property. Questions also quickly emerged about the authority of the Northwest Ordinance and whether its provisions might be repealed or revised by the U.S. Congress or the people of the Northwest.

In the first decades following 1787, the settlers of the Old Northwest were deeply divided over slavery's fate. In southern sections of Ohio, Indiana, and Illinois, many of the first post-1787 immigrants were southerners whose views toward slavery were either favorable or ambivalent; in the western half of this area, the presence of colonial-era slaveholders gave proslavery advocates a clear majority. Early territorial leaders, including Governors Arthur St. Clair, William Henry Harrison, and Ninian Edwards, opposed immediate emancipation and were hostile to prohibiting slavery entirely. Antislavery advocates, in contrast, were initially strongest in eastern and southern Ohio. At the beginning of the nineteenth century, opponents of slavery held the balance of power only in the area that would become Ohio, and even there, their dominance was limited at best.

Proponents of slavery adopted a number of strategies to delay or prevent Article VI's implementation. From 1787 to 1807, petitions were sent to Congress requesting that it either modify or repeal the provision. Most sought permission to bring slaves into the Old Northwest while indicating a willingness to accept gradual emancipation at a later date. Congress consistently refused to act on these petitions, thus signaling support for slavery's exclusion. Proslavery advocates next turned to subterfuge. Beginning in 1803, the territorial and state governments of Indiana and Illinois implemented de facto systems of slavery through laws that introduced long-term indentures, rental contracts, enforcement statutes, and recognition of the status of slaves present in 1787. Indiana's system was dismantled through subsequent legislation and court decisions between 1810 and 1820. In Illinois, slavery was effectively abolished only in 1848,

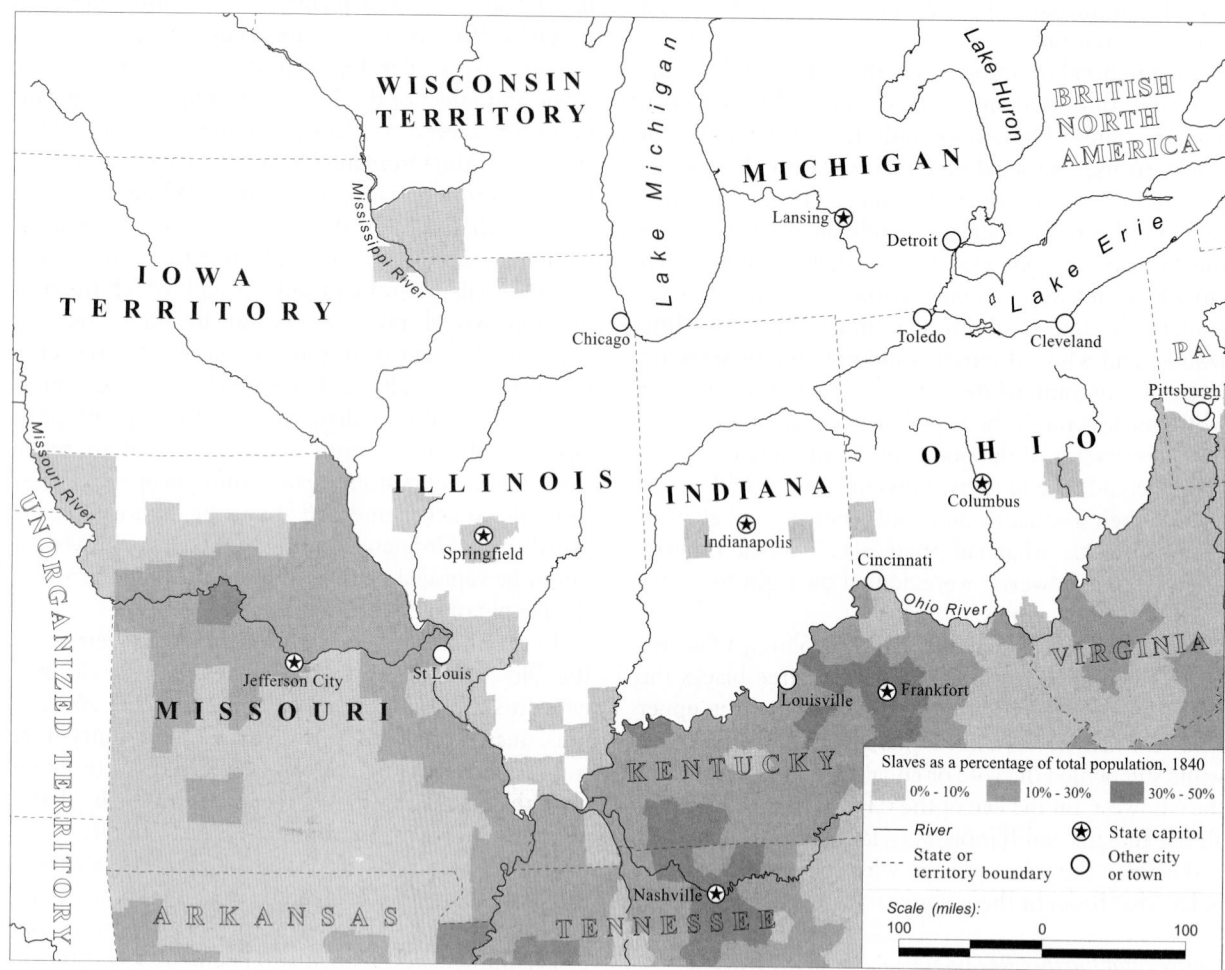

Distribution of slaves as proportion of population, 1840. Prepared by James DeGrand. *Source:* Charles Oscar Paullin, *Atlas of Historical Geography of the United States* (1932), plate 67 G.

more than six decades after the passage of the Northwest Ordinance.

While slavery in the Midwest was always limited—fewer than three thousand individuals were apparently enslaved in the principle slaveholding states of Illinois and Indiana between 1787 and 1848—the accompanying furor over slavery's place in the emerging region was intense, a reflection of the fact that the debate was intertwined with broader concerns about the region's development and future character. Frustrated by the slow pace of the Northwest's settlement in the early nineteenth century, proslavery advocates argued that the region's population would grow more quickly and its economy would develop most rapidly if slavery was legalized. Excluding slavery was thus an impediment to the region's progress. Antislavery advocates initially countered that slavery was contrary to the nation's republican ideals and a factor that would retard white immigration among those opposed to the institution.

By the early 1820s, as opponents of slavery came to dominate the region, this position was extended and refined, emphasizing the superiority of free labor as a system of production, the more rapid accumulation of wealth under free institutions, and the basic incompatibility of slavery and free labor.

The growing acceptance of these ideals was subsequently seen in the region's close identification with the free-labor Republican Party from 1854 and (excluding Missouri) in the absence of debate over slavery in later-settled areas of the Midwest.

Sources and Further Reading: Eugene H. Berwanger, *The Frontier Against Slavery: Western Anti-Negro Prejudice* (1967); Paul Finkelman, "Evading the Ordinance: The Persistence of Bondage in Indiana and Illinois," *Journal of the Early Republic* 9 (Spring 1989); Paul Finkelman, "Slavery and the Northwest Ordinance: A Study in Ambiguity," *Journal of the Early Republic* 6 (Winter 1986); Stephen Middleton, *The Black Laws in the Old Northwest* (1993); Peter S. Onuf, *State-*

hood and Union: A History of the Northwest Ordinance (1987); James Simeone, *Democracy and Slavery in Frontier Illinois: The Bottomland Republic* (2000).

Stephen A. Vincent
University of Wisconsin–Whitewater

Fugitive Slaves

The free states of the Midwest shared more than a thousand miles of borders with the slave states of Virginia, Kentucky, and Missouri. This long connection between slavery and freedom led to thousands of slaves crossing the Ohio and Mississippi Rivers into Ohio, Indiana, and Illinois, and the northern border of Missouri into Iowa. Despite discrimination and racism in much of the lower Midwest, the region was a powerful beacon of freedom for slaves. Moreover, in the upper Midwest along the Great Lakes, freedom had concrete reality as blacks gained substantial legal rights and economic success there.

The first national fugitive slave legislation appeared in Article VI of the Northwest Ordinance, which provided "That any person escaping into the same, from whom labor or service is lawfully claimed in any one of

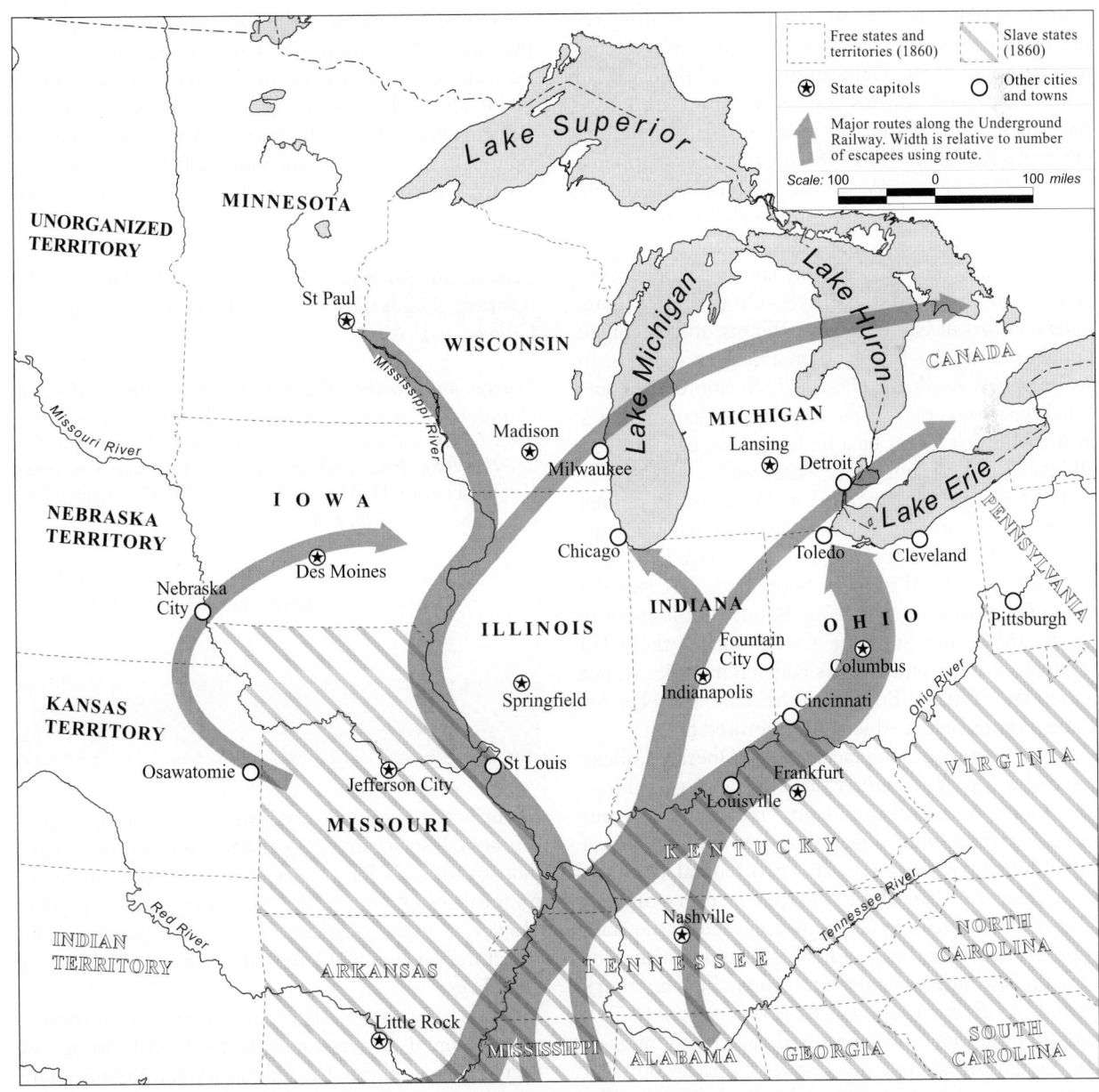

Principal routes of the Underground Railroad. Prepared by James DeGrand. *Source:* Charles Oscar Paullin, *Atlas of Historical Geography of the United States* (1932), plate 67 G.

the original States, such fugitive may be lawfully re-claimed and conveyed to the person claiming his or her labor or service as aforesaid." The provision was never tested in court, mostly because during the terri-torial period, the governments in the lower Midwest were notoriously sympathetic to slavery and hostile to free blacks. However, by the second decade of the nineteenth century, the issue of fugitive slaves cap-tured the imagination of many midwesterners. Harriet Beecher Stowe relied on her experiences growing up in Ohio when writing *Uncle Tom's Cabin* (1851). She modeled Tom after the famous fugitive slave Josiah Henson and one of her white characters after John Van Zandt, a Quaker abolitionist who was successfully sued for aiding runaway slaves.

In the 1840s and 1850s, midwesterners often re-sisted enforcement of the federal Fugitive Slave Laws of 1793 and 1850. Gatherings of abolitionists and other concerned citizens rescued recaptured fugitive slaves from their masters or police officials in, among other places, Salem, Iowa (1848), South Bend, Indiana (1849), Milwaukee, Wisconsin (1854), Wellington, Ohio (1858), and Ottawa, Illinois (1859), and Iberia, Ohio (1860). In the 1840s and 1850s, most midwest-ern states passed personal liberty laws, designed to im-pede the return of fugitive slaves. On the other hand, federal courts in Ohio, Indiana, Illinois, and Michigan upheld the fugitive slave laws in a number of cases. In *Jones v. Van Zandt* (1847), the U.S. Supreme Court ruled that it was reasonable to presume that any black in the Midwest might be a fugitive slave, even though all blacks legally living there were free.

In 1854, the U.S. marshal in Wisconsin, Stephen Ableman, arrested the abolitionist newspaper editor Sherman Booth for rescuing a fugitive slave from fed-eral custody. The Wisconsin Supreme Court issued a writ of habeas corpus freeing Booth. In *Ableman v. Booth* (1859), the Supreme Court upheld the 1850 fugitive slave law and Booth's conviction under it, but a mob later rescued Booth, and he made speeches for some months before Ableman recaptured him.

In 1858, students and faculty from Oberlin College rescued a captured fugitive slave in nearby Welling-ton, Ohio. A federal grand jury indicted numerous rescuers, while Ohio officials secured indictments of the Kentucky slaveowners and two federal marshals for kidnapping. Two of the convicted rescuers, Simeon Bushnell and Charles Langston, appealed to the state supreme court for a writ of habeas corpus, which con-tests the lawfulness of a person being held in another's custody. In *Ex parte Bushnell, Ex parte Langston* (1859), the Ohio Supreme Court refused to issue the writ of habeas corpus to free the rescuers, thus avoiding a confrontation between state and federal officials. The state then dropped charges against the Kentucky slaveowners, and the federal government released all the rescuers after imposing token fines. Had the Ohio Supreme Court issued the writ, Governor Salmon P. Chase of Ohio was prepared to call out the state mili-tia to enforce the court's order and keep Bushnell and Langston in custody.

Located on the border between slavery and free-dom, the free states of the Midwest became the desti-nation of tens of thousands of fugitive slaves. The very presence of so many people seeking freedom altered the nature of politics in the region, as white midwest-erners were confronted by the reality of slavery and the brutality of masters trying to recapture their human property. In 1856, Margaret Garner, a fugitive from Kentucky, killed her own child rather than al-lowing her to be returned to bondage. This act of des-peration, while unique and horrifying, underscored how the emotional issue of fugitives seeking liberty could affect the politics and feelings of the region. Perhaps symbolic of the power of this issue was the political success of Ohio's Salmon P. Chase, who was involved in so many fugitive slave cases that he earned the nickname "the Attorney General for Fugitive Slaves." This reputation helped him rise to the U.S. Senate, the governor's mansion, and ultimately to the position of Chief Justice of the United States Supreme Court.

Sources and Further Reading: Frederick Blue, *Salmon P. Chase: A Life in Politics* (1987); Stanley W. Campbell, *The Slave Catchers: Enforcement of the Fugitive Slave Law, 1850–1860* (1968); Paul Finkelman, *Slavery in the Courtroom* (1985); Thomas D. Morris, *Free Men All: The Personal Lib-erty Laws of the North, 1780–1860* (1974).

Paul Finkelman
University of Tulsa, Oklahoma

Constitutional History and Contemporary Patterns of Governance

When we think about a constitution creating a gov-ernmental structure, it is usually the United States Constitution. It has a special place in the American political system and in the American political psyche. However, state constitutions and the governmental structures they create have the greatest effect on our daily lives.

State governments share the tripartite separation of governmental powers found in the Constitution, but they do not duplicate the federal system. Because state constitutions reflect the varied social, economic, geo-graphic, and political environments of their respective states, governmental institutions created under their aegis represent a rich set of variations on the constitutional theme of self-government. The constitutional history of midwestern governance reflects a continuing struggle among groups to find a balance between governmental power and popular sovereignty as those environments changed.

The twelve midwestern states have had a total of twenty-five constitutions, with hundreds of proposed and ratified amendments to those constitutions. In the Midwest, the nineteenth century was the time of constitution-making as states came into the Union and tried to devise workable governmental structures. Only four constitutions are products of the twentieth century, Illinois's 1970 constitution being the most recent. The twentieth century, especially the latter half, was the time of constitutional amendment and revision as states sought to modernize their nineteenth-century governmental structures to deal with the needs of a new time.

The earliest state constitutions—Ohio in 1802, Indiana in 1816, Illinois in 1818, and Missouri in 1820—established governments for sparsely populated states and vested extensive power in the legislature. The governor was extremely weak, as were the courts. Local governments existed, but they too had little real authority. These early governmental arrangements quickly proved inadequate in responding to the needs of developing states. Especially problematic were expensive and questionable internal improvement schemes that saddled the new states with substantial debt.

In part these problems resulted from the local politics surrounding the hasty framing of the first constitutions and from the limitations of their authors. The problems were also an artifact of the nature of state power and the lack of any significant limitations on that power. Unlike the federal government, states possess plenary power. This means a legislature can do anything that is not prohibited by either the state constitution or the U.S. Constitution. The Tenth Amendment to the U.S. Constitution recognizes the broad power of the states: "The powers not delegated to the United States by the Constitution, nor prohibited by it to the states, are reserved to the State respectively, or to the people."

In contrast, the federal government is one of limited, delegated powers. Consequently, it can act only if there is a grant of power, explicitly or implicitly, in the U.S. Constitution. Whole areas of governmental power are not granted to the federal government, but are left to the states. Most important are the police powers, the broad power to protect the health, safety, morals, and welfare of the people.

The first-line limitations on plenary power, especially as exercised by the legislature, are found in the state bills of rights. This is reflected in the organization of the state constitutions themselves. These statements of rights appear at the very beginning of every midwestern constitution except South Dakota's (in which it is Article VI), before the power of the state government is outlined. However, these limitations alone proved inadequate for dealing with the abuses of powers experienced in the earliest governments.

Dissatisfaction with the original constitutions led to their replacement during the middle third of the nineteenth century. These replacement constitutions sought additional ways of limiting state power, especially the power of the legislature. So did the constitutions of the five states that entered the Union during this period (Iowa, Kansas, Minnesota, Nebraska, and Wisconsin) and the constitutions of North Dakota and South Dakota when they became states in 1889. Reflecting the influence of Jacksonian democracy and the idea of popular sovereignty, these subsequent midwestern constitutions established both structural and substantive limitations on plenary power—limitations that continue to shape midwestern government today.

The structural changes designated by these second-generation state constitutions of the mid-1800s emphasized popular control. More officials at both the state and local levels were elected directly by the people, and Indiana even imposed term limits on many officials. The franchise was extended to a wider set of people (at least a wider set of white males), and the number and authority of elected local governments were increased significantly. Structural limitations were also placed directly on legislative power, including limiting the amount of time the legislature is in session and increasing the power of the governor, particularly with regard to the veto.

The substantive limitations on power came in the form of specific prohibitions included in state constitutions. These were things legislatures could not do, and prime among them were limits on the amount of state debt and direct involvement of the state in internal improvement projects. There were others. For example, both the 1848 and 1870 Illinois constitutions forbade the state from chartering a bank, and the 1875 Nebraska constitution (still in effect) forbids the legislature from donating any lands under the state's control to railroads, private corporations, or individuals. The Missouri constitution has a section listing fifteen specific limitations on legislative power. Additionally, all constitutions since the middle third of the nineteenth century have required that any bill passed by the legislature must encompass only one subject, which is to be stated in the title (the Single Subject rule).

Another set of limitations first appeared at the end

of the nineteenth century. A continuing legacy of the Populist and Progressive movements, they are found in constitutional provisions for various forms of direct democracy. Today, six constitutions—Michigan, Missouri, Nebraska, North Dakota, Ohio, and South Dakota—allow for the initiative and referendum with regard to statewide legislation. All six added these provisions to their constitutions between 1898 and 1918. At the same time, five of these states, except for Nebraska, added constitutional provisions allowing the initiative in proposing constitutional amendments. The 1970 Illinois constitution also allows for proposing amendments by initiative.

Perhaps the ultimate popular check on the exercise of power can be found in the constitutions of five states. These constitutions require that at some set interval of years, there must be placed on the ballot a binding referendum asking the question of whether a constitutional convention should be called: Iowa every ten years, Michigan every sixteen years, and Illinois, Missouri, and Ohio every twenty years.

Structural changes came mostly in the latter part of the twentieth century, which was the era of constitutional revision commissions. In the years since 1960, every state had a review commission looking at all or part of its constitution and suggesting changes. By the 1970s, the states were making changes, and the most important dealt with matters such as strengthening the governor, streamlining the executive branch, streamlining the courts, and enhancing the authority of state supreme courts. Although there were also changes affecting legislatures (such as allowing longer or more frequent sessions), many of the older limitations on legislative power, such as the Single Subject rule, remained unchanged.

With the exception of Nebraska with its unicameral legislature, midwestern states today (as all other states) have bicameral legislatures. Membership in lower houses varies from seventy in South Dakota to 163 in Missouri, and in senates from thirty-three in Ohio and Wisconsin to sixty-seven in Minnesota. All members of lower houses are elected for two-year terms, and members of senates are elected for four-year terms, with two exceptions. Senators in South Dakota are elected for two years. In Illinois, the terms for each senate district are set by the legislature after every decennial redistricting as a combination of two and four year terms with the combinations equaling ten years. The senators of Nebraska's unicameral legislature are elected for four-year terms.

Midwestern governors today are more powerful than in the past. They have broader appointing power. All are now elected for four-year terms. All have veto power, and in nine states, this power has been expanded to include a line-item veto for appropriations bills (the exceptions are Indiana, Michigan, and Missouri). Three governors even have an amendatory veto, which allows the governor to actually make changes in some legislation.

Despite such changes, the way the executive branch is structured still imposes substantial limitations on the governor. Midwestern constitutions create a number of constitutional officers who are heads of executive branch offices—for example, attorney general, secretary of state, treasurer—and who are elected. This gives these officers substantial independence from the governor, and it means that the executive branch of a state may not have a single, consistent approach to certain issues.

The latter part of the twentieth century also saw constitutional change to modernization of court systems. This included giving administrative authority for the running of a state's court system to the state supreme court. Supreme courts were also granted more discretionary control over their dockets to allow them to focus on the most important policy issues. Additionally, states moved away from a cumbersome system of multiple levels of trial courts toward a unified court system that consisted of a supreme court, an intermediate level of appellate courts, and a single level of trial courts. For Kansas, this meant the creation of intermediate appellate courts. For Illinois, it meant abolishing an older three-tiered system of trial courts. Still, some midwestern states continue to have multiple types of trial courts, and North Dakota and South Dakota do not have a permanent intermediate appellate court.

The constitutional changes also included some movement away from the partisan election of judges toward some aspects of a merit-based system. Five states still rely exclusively on contested elections for choosing and retaining judges (Michigan, Minnesota, North Dakota, Ohio, and Wisconsin). Two states rely exclusively on a merit system (Iowa and Nebraska). The remaining states have some hybrid of election and merit (Indiana, Illinois, Kansas, South Dakota, and Missouri). Midwestern states are especially reluctant to completely remove the people from the process of selecting trial judges, the judges closest to the voters.

Beneath state-level institutions are the many units of local government. Consistent with the nineteenth century idea of popular sovereignty, the states of the region have a plethora of county-level and local governmental bodies, most elected. Eight of the constitutions have an entire article devoted to substate governments, and they mandate the election of key county officials. Seven constitutions specifically deal with home rule for county and/or local government; home rule gives a government substantial power to make its own rules and policies independent of the state legislature. Whether by constitutional provision or by statute, midwestern states tend to have more units of substate government than states in other parts of the country. On average, midwestern states have 3,304 units of county and/or local government, compared to a national average of 1,757 units.

Despite the efforts to modernize, governmental structures today are still a mixture of the old and the new. While the changes of the late twentieth century allow states to respond more effectively to new issues and problems, many older constitutional provisions that limit state power still remain. Starting in the 1990s, older ideas on popular control reemerged with constitutional amendments imposing term limits on many elected state officials. Since 1992, five states have amended their constitutions to impose term limits on members of the legislature (Michigan, Missouri, Nebraska, Ohio, and South Dakota). Indiana amended its constitution to impose term limits on governors in 1972. In short, the political struggle to find a balance between governmental power and popular sovereignty continues.

Sources and Further Reading: The Council of State Governments, *The Book of the States*, vol. 34 (2002); Susan P. Fino, *The Michigan State Constitution* (1996); Francis H. Heller, *The Kansas State Constitution* (1992); William P. McLauchlan, *The Indiana State Constitution* (1996); Robert Miewald and Peter Longo, *The Nebraska State Constitution* (1993); Mary Jane Morrison, *The Minnesota State Constitution* (2002); Jack Stark, *The Iowa State Constitution* (1998); Jack Stark, *The Wisconsin State Constitution: A Reference Guide* (1997); G. Alan Tarr, *Understanding State Constitutions* (1998); U.S. Census Bureau, *2002 Census of Governments*, vol. 1. *Government Organization* (2002).

Stephen Daniels
American Bar Foundation, Chicago, Illinois

The Federal Government

The Midwest has always had a close relationship with the federal government. This relationship over time has changed from one of midwestern dependency on the federal government for political organization and security, to one of controversy and regional division, and then to one of economic and social regulation and protection. The federal government has been intimately involved with the peoples of the Midwest throughout the region's existence, and during the nation's second century, the federal government was powerfully affected by midwesterners and midwestern interests.

Two early laws directly shaped the Midwest as a region. The first was the Land Ordinance of 1785, which divided the landscape into six-mile squares and sections of one square mile. Once the land was surveyed, the federal government publicly auctioned all of the land except one section in each township (this was later amended to two sections), which was reserved for the benefit of public schools. Settlement and education walked hand-in-hand in the building of the new nation. The first surveying was accomplished in Ohio, and the grid system was applied throughout the Midwest and other parts of the nation as the United States expanded.

The second important statute was the Northwest Ordinance of 1787. This federal law established the means by which new lands obtained by the original United States would be organized and incorporated into the nation. The Northwest Ordinance created the Northwest Territory with rudimentary forms of representative government and a process whereby new states created from the territory would be equal to the original states. Once a territory achieved a population of sixty thousand, its residents applied for formal admission to the federal union. The Northwest Territory eventually was divided into Ohio, Indiana, Illinois, Michigan, Wisconsin, and a part of Minnesota. The Northwest Ordinance today remains an active model for territorial governance.

The Midwest is the homeland of many indigenous peoples, and federal leadership assumed control over Indian diplomatic relations. In order for settlement to occur, the Land Ordinance to function, and the Northwest Territory to be organized, government felt that Indian land titles had to be quieted. Although numerous treaties were negotiated, many tribes continued to exercise sovereignty over their homelands and resisted incursions by settlers. To establish control and assist settlement, the federal government built a network of forts and prepared troops, and General Anthony Wayne accomplished this along with a watershed victory in 1794 at the Battle of Fallen Timbers against Little Turtle and the Miamis. The resulting Treaty of Greenville in June 1795 forced cessions of much of the present state of Ohio and parts of Indiana, and began the movement of indigenous peoples out of the region.

The federal government by the 1820s implemented Indian Removal, a policy forcing many tribes from their lands in Ohio, Indiana, Wisconsin, and Illinois and moving them to Iowa, Nebraska, and Kansas, and subsequently to Oklahoma. William Henry Harrison, governor of the Indiana Territory from 1800 to 1812, concluded fifteen treaties with most of the Indian nations of the Midwest. Using questionable ethics and scruples, often paying just over one cent per acre,

Harrison acquired tribal title to most of Indiana and Illinois. His last purchase, in the Treaty of Fort Wayne in 1809, provided the incentive for Shawnee leaders Tecumseh and his brother The Prophet to build a coalition and attempt to defeat the United States during the War of 1812. The Indian coalition was defeated at the Battle of Tippecanoe Creek by Harrison and federal troops.

The policy of Indian Removal in practice was backed up by a series of federal Indian trade acts and the creation of a separate bureaucracy in the federal government to handle Indian issues in the Midwest. In 1832, Congress created the office of the Commissioner of Indian Affairs, and two years later ratified the establishment of what would become the Bureau of Indian Affairs. This federal agency established the permanent policy of dependency on the federal government for the Midwest's indigenous peoples. That same year the most important law governing Indian trade, the Indian Trade and Intercourse Act, redefined how the federal government was to conduct trade with Native Americans, with regulatory powers over all dealings with indigenous peoples and annual annuity payments to tribal representatives.

The Midwest, by 1850, was America's middle ground. The establishment of the Corps of Topographical Engineers (1838) to survey vast areas of unsettled midwestern territory promoted early settlement in the Midwest. In 1849, Congress established the Department of the Interior, a federal agency that supervised management of the public lands and the distribution of land to new settlers. As the nation careened toward civil war, it was in the Midwest where the flash points evolved, where solutions to resolve the volatile issues were tried and failed. Slavery had never been a successful transplant in the Midwest. In the original Northwest Territory, slavery was prohibited, although slaves could be transported through parts of the region. Missouri had closer connections to the South, and when advocates pushed for Missouri statehood, a compromise was struck in 1820 admitting Missouri as a slave state and Maine, separated from Massachusetts, as a free state.

When the time came to create new territories on the Midwest's western borderlands, the issue of the extension of slavery came to the fore. What emerged from a paralyzed Congress seeking to avoid the splintering of the nation was the Kansas-Nebraska Act of 1854. This law authored by Illinois Senator Stephen Douglas chartered the organization of two new territories, but it allowed each of them to decide on the extension of slavery within their boundaries, effectively unraveling the Missouri Compromise. The application of popular sovereignty propelled a few thousand voters into Kansas to decide the issue of slavery expan-

sion. Many in the North viewed the law as provocative and unfair, and agitation against it evolved into the Republican Party and guerrilla warfare in Kansas.

Meanwhile, the issue of slavery and congressional authority over its territorial expansion was litigated in the Midwest's courtrooms. In Missouri, a case was brought on behalf of Dred Scott, a slave who sued to receive his freedom after he had been moved from the slave state of Missouri to the free state of Illinois and the free territory of Wisconsin. In the U.S. Supreme Court, slave-holding Chief Justice Roger Taney ruled for a divided court in *Dred Scott v. Sandford* (1857) that slaves could not possibly be citizens possessing substantive rights, and that Congress had exceeded its constitutional authority when it forbade or abolished slavery in the territories. The decision increased sectional tension. The South viewed the election of Illinois Republican Abraham Lincoln as President as a signal to secede, and the nation plunged into Civil War for four years.

The existence of pro-Southern conspiracies in the Midwest constituted a serious problem for the Union. President Lincoln curtailed the use of habeas corpus and certain civil liberties and authorized the use of military courts to prevent those with southern sympathies from acting to assist the Confederacy. In Indiana, attorney Lambdin Milligan and two others were arrested and charged with treason and conspiracy to aid the Confederates; a military commission quickly found them guilty in October 1864, and sentenced them to death in May 1865. In the interim, President Lincoln had been assassinated. At first President Andrew Johnson agreed with the sentence, but then he commuted Milligan's sentence to life imprisonment. Milligan, who had several distinguished legal defenders, including the future President and Ohioan James Garfield, appealed to the U.S. Supreme Court. The justices in the aftermath of the Civil War decided in *Ex parte Milligan* (1866) to overturn Milligan's conviction because military courts could not have jurisdiction over civilians during a time of war when civilian courts were also functioning. This controversial decision seemed like a potential threat to the federal government's Reconstruction programs, but subsequently the case has been considered a landmark decision for civil liberties.

While the war was proceeding, the federal government solidified its relationships with the Midwest through a series of national laws. In 1862, the Republican "free soil" proponents revolutionized federal land programs with the passage of three bills: the Homestead Act, the Pacific Railroad Act, and the Morrill Act. Under the Homestead Act, 160-acre parcels of public domain were made available to citizens and noncitizens who agreed to live on and farm their claims. The sponsors of the bill wanted to encourage unemployed northern workers to resettle on federal lands and begin lives as independent landowners in the Midwest and West. The Pacific Railroad Act provided a means of financing the massive capital cost of a transcontinental railroad by deeding millions of acres of federal land along the right of way to railroad companies, who could sell the land to finance rail construction. The Morrill Act provided grants of federal land to the states to finance a system of higher education intended to serve farmers and skilled urban laborers with specific instruction in agriculture and engineering. These efforts led to the eventual creation of land-grant universities, which came to include some of the major centers of research, service, and learning in the country. Had the nation not been at war and southern congressmen unrepresented in Congress, it is unlikely these far-reaching federal experiments that have had such a major influence on the Midwest would have been approved.

Clearly the Civil War had a significant impact on the relationship of the Midwest to the federal government. Midwesterners even in the slave state of Missouri chose to remain with the Union, but the toll was heavy. Although the Midwest was free of the most bitter fighting during the war, the internal division, death, and destruction was severely felt by the Midwest's families and communities. The war's end brought a profound sense of urgency to rebuild and to move ahead economically, and the region turned to the federal government for assistance.

When midwestern state legislators responding to constituent cries of economic unfairness began to use their police powers to regulate the increasing power of private business, the U.S. Supreme Court in *Munn v. Illinois* (1877) upheld those powers. The Illinois Granger laws, which set the rates that Illinois grain elevators operating in Chicago could charge rural customers, were found to be valid exercises of state police authority, and *Munn* became the classic statement of judicial restraint and deference to legislative authority. Justice Stephen Field's strong dissent, which less than twenty years later became the majority position of the Court, articulated the basis for the legal argument of "substantive due process." By 1897, in *Chicago, Burlington & Quincy Railroad Company v. Chicago*, the Supreme Court ruled that the Fourteenth Amendment's due process clause compelled the states to award just compensation when it took private property for public use (in this case a public street across a railroad track). The economic dimensions of the change from *Munn* to *C, B & Q* created an economic system that encouraged the rapid growth of national corporations operating out of major transportation hubs in the Midwest, often at the expense of farmers, small businessmen, women, and laborers.

When the Great Depression hit the Midwest in the 1930s, the federal government reacted with a host of rural initiatives that slowly transformed the economy and culture of the region. Rural electrification established electrical service for the first time for millions of midwesterners. The Civil Works Administration, the Civilian Conservation Corps, and the Public Works Administration undertook public projects that employed tens of thousands of unemployed workers in the Midwest. Farmers, bent under the burdens of debt and drought, benefited from the Agricultural Adjustment Act (1933) that mitigated the vagaries of the market but did not challenge the market logic of farming. Federal involvement in Midwest agriculture grew to unprecedented proportions during the New Deal and created a lasting dependency relationship between midwestern farmers and the federal government.

Civil rights and constitutional liberties have been keenly affected by federal involvement, and many of the crucial issues have been tested in the Midwest. Midwestern religious and ethnic populations have proven resistant to the diminishment of fundamental freedoms, albeit often the target of federal regulation. While most Americans today recognize the Mormon community of Utah, before the great migration west, Mormon communities were centered first in Ohio, and then in Missouri and Illinois. Forced out of those areas by violent opposition, Mormons moved westward and had settled in Utah by the 1850s.

German immigrants in the Midwest faced a different repression as America plunged into war against Germany in 1917. Nebraska imposed a restriction on the teaching and speaking of German to grade school children. The U.S. Supreme Court, in *Meyer v. Nebraska* (1923), concluded that the Nebraska state statute was a violation of the due process clause of the Fourteenth Amendment. The case later resurfaced as an important precedent for the constitutional right to privacy and for the protection of Amish religious beliefs in Wisconsin when confronted with state educational regulations.

First Amendment rights of free expression came under attack with the burgeoning of yellow journalism. In 1925, Minnesota passed the Minnesota Gag Law permitting a judge to enjoin the publication of a newspaper if the judge found it obscene and scandalous. Designed to remedy the evils of irresponsible journalism, First Amendment advocates reacted when it was applied against the Minnesota *Saturday Press*. In *Near v. Minnesota* (1931), the U.S. Supreme Court struck down the law and held that press freedoms were within the due process protections of the Fourteenth Amendment. Thirty years later in *Tinker v. Des Moines Independent Community School District* (1969), the court ruled that the symbolic wearing of black armbands by

Iowa public school students to protest the Vietnam War was also protected free speech.

Federal judicial involvement altered fundamental midwestern state interpretations of national constitutional rights and established boundaries for the protection of those individual rights. The most significant of these judgments occurred nearly one hundred years after the infamous case of *Dred Scott v. Sandford*. In 1954, the U.S. Supreme Court reconsidered the destructive racial doctrine of "separate but equal" established by *Plessy v. Ferguson* (1896), which permitted racial segregation of public facilities if the facilities were equal. In *Brown v. Board of Education of Topeka* (1954), the Supreme Court held that separate school facilities were inherently unequal and therefore unconstitutional. Future cases arose in Missouri and a dozen other states and the District of Columbia, as the Court set off a violent reaction when it overturned the separate-but-equal policy, and a year later ordered that school districts desegregate their schools promptly. *Brown v. Board of Education*, this midwestern watershed legal opinion, and subsequent Supreme Court orders emboldened civil rights activists to move toward greater action that broke down the walls of discrimination throughout much of American society.

In the area of criminal jurisprudence, midwestern landmark cases from Ohio, *Mapp v. Ohio* (1961), and Illinois, *Escobedo v. Illinois* (1964), guaranteed the exercise of fundamental constitutional rights. In *Mapp*, the U.S. Supreme Court developed the exclusionary rule, which prevents the introduction of illegally obtained evidence at trial. *Escobedo* placed the accused's right to counsel at the beginning stages of a criminal investigation. Both of these rights, while controversial, remain a part of the fundamental protections accorded all Americans.

The Midwest also was an important region in the fight for women's rights. Although women did not obtain the right to vote in the Midwest before other states and territories, women did gain the ability to participate as jurors and school board members early in the drive for full citizenship. Illinois became the first state challenged to allow the practice of law by women, and its state supreme court in *Bradwell v. Illinois* (1873) ruled against women. It would fall to Iowa to let women practice law. Illinois also hindered the drive of women for equal rights when in the 1970s its legislature refused to ratify the Equal Rights Amendment, the only midwestern state to refuse to do so, ending the possibility of the ERA being added to the U.S. Constitution. Some states in the Midwest have attempted to tamper with a woman's right to an abortion. The latest state efforts, those of Nebraska to restrict an abortion by intact dilation and extraction (or IDX, which is also known as "partial birth abortion"),

were found to be unconstitutional by the U.S. Supreme Court in *Stenberg v. Carhart* (2000).

Thus, federal involvement in the Midwest began with the region's very creation as a distinct area. From the time of the first immigrants to the present, the federal government has been active in midwestern economic, social, and political life. Congressional involvement in federal land administration and with the first indigenous peoples of the region continues to affect the Midwest. Federal farm policy remains a significant economic consideration for a region still heavily dependent on agriculture. From security to guarantees of civil rights and liberties, midwesterners have depended on federal policies and institutional authority.

Sources and Further Reading: Andrew R. L. Cayton and Peter S. Onuf, *The Midwest and the Nation: Rethinking the History of an American Region* (1990); James H. Madison, ed., *Heartland: Comparative Histories of the Midwestern States* (1988); Richard Rhodes, *The Inland Ground: An Evocation of the American Middle West*, rev. ed. (1991); Harry N. Scheiber, ed., *The Old Northwest: Studies in Regional History, 1787–1910* (1969); James R. Shortridge, *The Middle West: Its Meaning in American Culture* (1989).

John R. Wunder
University of Nebraska–Lincoln

Kurt Hohenstein
University of Virginia

Abortion

Midwestern states were sites of controversy over the regulation of abortion as the nation confronted conflicts between pro-choice and pro-life forces in the second half of the twentieth century, and the Midwest was representative of the nation as a whole. For example, the United States Supreme Court used a case from Ohio to consider, and hold unconstitutional, a regulation requiring a woman seeking abortion to wait twenty-four hours after her initial consultation before obtaining the abortion (*City of Akron v. Akron Center for Reproductive Health, Inc.*, 1983, overruled in 1992). A case from Nebraska invalidated a ban on so-called partial birth abortions (*Stenberg v. Carhart*, 2000). States throughout the nation had adopted similar regulations, and it was essentially a matter of chance that the Supreme Court used cases from the Midwest as vehicles for its actions.

Two important episodes in the history of abortion as a public policy question in the late 1960s occurred in the Midwest. Pro-choice activists developed the legal theory that abortion regulations violated a constitutionally protected right of privacy after the

Supreme Court's decision in *Griswold v. Connecticut* (1965), which struck down a ban on contraceptive use by married couples. In 1969, a Milwaukee doctor, indicted for performing an abortion without going through Wisconsin's procedures for determining that an abortion was necessary to save the woman's life, filed an action in federal court to block his prosecution. A small local abortion reform organization supported his claim with an extensive legal brief relying on *Griswold* and the arguments developed in litigation elsewhere. The federal court's decision upholding the doctor's position was one of the first rulings holding a ban on abortions unconstitutional (*Babbitz v. McCann*, 1970), and was cited throughout the litigation that ended with the Supreme Court's abortion decision in 1973.

Critics of the Supreme Court's decisions sometimes suggest that the Court's intervention unnecessarily provoked a controversy that might have been resolved through ordinary politics, citing the adoption of liberalized abortion statutes in New York and California, and the liberalization of the position taken on abortion by the American Law Institute, a lawyers' organization that presented itself as concerned solely with technical aspects of law. A Michigan referendum in 1972 indicates that this suggestion may be mistaken. Pro-choice activists worked in the state legislature for several years, finally obtaining a favorable vote from the state senate on a relatively mild modification of the state's abortion law. Finding themselves unable to get the state house of representatives to act, the activists organized a referendum for a law that would allow unregulated abortions in the first twenty weeks of a woman's pregnancy. Surveys conducted in the months before the referendum indicated that a substantial majority supported the pro-choice proposal. Anti-abortion activists mobilized in the three weeks preceding the November election, broadcasting a large number of anti-referendum advertisements. On election day, the referendum was defeated by a margin of 61 to 39 percent. Coupled with antiabortion mobilizations in New York and Pennsylvania, the Michigan referendum's results confirmed the view of pro-choice activists that they could succeed only if the courts upheld their constitutional claims.

After pro-choice litigation succeeded in the Supreme Court, antiabortion activists sought to overturn the Court's decisions by generating public opposition to unregulated abortions. They used a variety of techniques, including direct action against abortion providers. By the late 1980s, the most widely known group was Operation Rescue, officially founded in 1988 in New York by Randall Terry. Operation Rescue's primary tactic was to block the entrances to clinics where abortions were performed. After the

Supreme Court hinted in 1989 that it might overrule its 1973 decisions, Operation Rescue's efforts expanded. After a year of planning, Operation Rescue organized a substantial direct-action campaign in Wichita, Kansas. Starting on July 15, 1991, and lasting for several weeks, the protests capitalized on support from the local police chief, mayor, and city manager, and substantially interfered with clinic operations. Courtroom confrontations with federal district judge Patrick Kelly broke the back of the protests. Judge Kelly issued orders banning the clinic blockades, and then ordered federal marshals to arrest the protestors who ignored his orders. Ultimately over twenty-five hundred demonstrators were arrested, and the clinics resumed operations.

Supporters and opponents of abortion rights in the Midwest were elements of national networks. They drew upon arguments and tactics developed all over the country, and their actions in turn reinforced the positions taken by their allies elsewhere. Both in its largest contours and in many of its details, the abortion issue in the Midwest reflected the issue in the nation as a whole.

Sources and Further Reading: David J. Garrow, *Liberty and Sexuality: The Right to Privacy and the Making of* Roe v. Wade (1994); Faye Ginsburg, "Rescuing the Nation: Operation Rescue and the Rise of Anti-Abortion Militance," in Rickie Solinger, ed., *Abortion Wars: A Half Century of Struggle, 1950–2000* (1998).

Mark Tushnet
Georgetown University, Washington, D.C.

Civil Liberties

Nurtured by the region's progressive political tradition, civil liberties have long flourished in the Midwest. Throughout the region's history, these personal, natural rights—which include the freedoms of press, speech, assembly, and religion, as well as protections for the rights of criminal defendants—have remained largely free from government-imposed restraints. The relatively rare encroachments upon them by state authorities have been resisted by midwesterners who believe that the preservation of such core democratic freedoms is essential to the smooth functioning of a free and open society. By turning to the courts to oppose infringements on civil liberties, these citizens have helped to create an influential body of law that has benefited Americans living in all regions of the country.

The earliest protections for civil liberties in the region were codified in the Northwest Ordinance, en-

❖ The Northwest Ordinance of 1787

The following Articles from the Northwest Ordinance (1787) set forth the "fundamental principles of civil and religious liberty" that would provide "the basis of all laws, constitutions, and governments" for the states there to be created and admitted to "a share in the federal councils on an equal footing with the original States."

Article 1. No person, demeaning himself in a peaceable and orderly manner, shall ever be molested on account of his mode of worship or religious sentiments, in the said territory.

Article 2. The inhabitants of the said territory shall always be entitled to the benefits of the writ of *habeas corpus*, and of the trial by jury; of a proportionate representation of the people in the legislature; and of judicial proceedings according to the course of the common law. All persons shall be bailable, unless for capital offenses, where the proof shall be evident or the presumption great. All fines shall be moderate; and no cruel or unusual punishments shall be inflicted. No man shall be deprived of his liberty or property, but by the judgment of his peers or the law of the land.

Article 3. Religion, morality, and knowledge, being necessary to good government and the happiness of mankind, schools and the means of education shall forever be encouraged. The utmost good faith shall always be observed towards the Indians; their lands and property shall never be taken from them without their consent; and, in their property, rights, and liberty, they shall never be invaded or disturbed, unless in just and lawful wars authorized by Congress; but laws founded in justice and humanity, shall from time to time be made for preventing wrongs being done to them, and for preserving peace and friendship with them.

Article 6. There shall be neither slavery nor involuntary servitude in the said territory, otherwise than in the punishment of crimes whereof the party shall have been duly convicted: *Provided, always,* That any person escaping into the same, from whom labor or service is lawfully claimed in any one of the original States, such fugitive may be lawfully reclaimed and conveyed to the person claiming his or her labor or service as aforesaid.

acted by Congress in 1787. Perhaps the most important piece of legislation passed by that body under the Articles of Confederation, the Ordinance spelled out the process by which midwestern land was to be organized as territories and then full-fledged states. Among its most significant provisions were specific safeguards for civil liberties—something the Articles notably lacked. Anticipating the protections that would be afforded by the federal Constitution's Bill of Rights, the Northwest Ordinance provided guarantees for such basic liberties as religious freedom and the right to trial by jury.

The constitutions enacted by midwestern states as they entered the union throughout the nineteenth century echoed the federal constitution and reinforced safeguards for civil liberties. All of these state charters contained language aimed at shielding individual rights. Iowa's constitution, for instance, began with an extensive Bill of Rights designed to safeguard the free exercise of religion, press, and speech freedoms, and the "rights of persons accused" of crimes. A similar section of the Indiana Constitution contained no fewer than six separate provisions regarding the free exercise and establishment of religion. Minnesota's constitution contained similar stipulations. Moreover, it shielded press freedoms and guaranteed individuals the right to express their opinions through speaking, writing, or publishing (although it also cautioned that citizens would be held accountable if they abused those freedoms).

Despite the clear safeguards for civil liberties furnished by the federal Bill of Rights and the various Midwest state constitutions, state authorities have periodically encroached on individuals' core personal freedoms. When state and federal courts have been called upon by aggrieved citizens to stop these infringements, they often have chosen to curb the power of the state and fortify protections for individual liberties. Thanks in part to the "rights revolution" spearheaded by the U.S. Supreme Court during the tenure of Chief Justice Earl Warren, the courts have been particularly sensitive to shielding civil liberties in the Midwest in the past half-century. This period has seen a notable expansion of the rights afforded to defendants in criminal proceedings, with the courts moving to protect individuals from improper police tactics (such as unreasonable searches) and to ensure that they are represented by counsel and thus are cognizant of their rights. An important case in this area arose in the Midwest: in *Escobedo v. Illinois* (1964), the U.S. Supreme Court threw out the confession of a murder suspect because he was denied access to an attorney.

Perhaps the most noteworthy clash over religious liberty in the Midwest involved a group of Old Order Amish farmers who settled in tiny New Glarus, Wisconsin, in the late 1960s. These deeply religious people clashed with state authorities over the enforcement of Wisconsin's compulsory school attendance law, which the Amish resisted on religious grounds. (Similar conflicts involving the Amish also had cropped up in Ohio and Indiana.) The U.S. Supreme Court eventually resolved this conflict in favor of the Amish in its landmark opinion in *Wisconsin v. Yoder* (1972), which bolstered judicial protections for freedom of worship.

Midwestern litigation involving press freedoms also has yielded judicial precedent shielding civil liberties. The landmark case *Near v. Minnesota* (1931) involved Jay Near, a muckraking publisher who was targeted by a state gag law designed to bar the publication of any newspaper found to be "malicious, scandalous or defamatory." The U.S. Supreme Court struck down the state statute as unconstitutional and established an important safeguard for press freedoms.

Civil liberties in the region have faced some of their greatest challenges in times of great social and political upheaval. War eras have been particularly turbulent. The patriotic fervor that swept across the country during World War II had a devastating impact on Jehovah's Witnesses in the Midwest. Mistakenly believing that the Witnesses' refusal to salute the American flag signaled their disloyalty, state and local authorities throughout the region suppressed their civil liberties. The Witnesses repeatedly went to court to fight this oppression, and their efforts yielded numerous decisions safeguarding the freedoms of worship, speech, and assembly. A generation later, American military involvement in Vietnam prompted spirited protests from thousands of midwesterners who mounted an unprecedented effort to use their speech and assembly rights to help shape public policy. Public authorities did not always welcome their efforts. In Des Moines, Iowa, authorities suspended a group of students after they wore black armbands—symbols of their opposition to the war's carnage—to school. In its landmark opinion in *Tinker v. Des Moines* (1969), the U.S. Supreme Court ruled in favor of the students, holding that their symbolic protest involved "primary First Amendment rights" and thus merited protection.

Midwesterners involved in many such disputes have been aided by state civil liberties unions. In their quest to preserve those rights, the American Civil Liberties Union (ACLU) and its affiliates have taken up some unpopular causes over the years. Perhaps most famously, in the late 1970s, the ACLU defended the right of Nazi sympathizers to stage a public march in Skokie, Illinois, a town with a large Jewish population that included several Holocaust survivors. For civil liberties in the Midwest, however, the acrimony of the Skokie dispute has been the exception rather than the rule.

Sources and Further Reading: Lee Epstein and Thomas G. Walker, *Constitutional Law for a Changing America: Rights, Liberties, and Justice*, 4th ed. (2000); Kermit Hall, ed., *The Oxford Companion to the Supreme Court of the United States* (1992); John W. Johnson, *The Struggle for Student Rights* (1997); Leonard Williams Levy, *Origins of the Bill of Rights* (2001); Shawn Francis Peters, *Judging Jehovah's Witnesses* (2000); Philippa Strum, *When the Nazis Came to Skokie* (1999).

Shawn Francis Peters
University of Wisconsin–Madison,
Odyssey Project

Civil Rights

The function of civil rights laws is to prevent discrimination against disfavored groups in important areas of American life, such as access to public accommodations, employment, and housing. Civil rights laws were first enacted in response to widespread discrimination against African Americans and other minorities, and prohibited discrimination on the basis of race, color, national origin, and religion. Over the years their coverage has expanded to include sex, age, and disability. However, many civil rights laws today do not include discrimination on the basis of sexual orientation.

In the American constitutional system, both the federal government and the states (which include local governments) have the power to enact civil rights laws. This means that the states can move ahead of the federal government by prohibiting discrimination that is not prohibited by federal law. This phenomenon has been evident in the Midwest with respect to prohibitions against racial discrimination. In 1883, the U.S. Supreme Court held that Congress could not prohibit racial discrimination in places of public accommodation. In 1885, Illinois, Indiana, Michigan, and Minnesota responded by enacting laws providing that all persons in these states enjoyed the right of full and equal access to places of public accommodation in the state. Ohio enacted an access to public accommodations law in 1890, with Wisconsin doing so in 1895, and Iowa, where the courts had earlier required equal treatment for steamship passengers, following in 1897.

A number of Midwest states were also ahead of the federal government in prohibiting racial discrimination in employment. During World War II, President Franklin Roosevelt issued Executive Order 9346 in 1943, prohibiting racial discrimination in employment by the federal government and governmental contractors. This sparked a drive to lobby Congress and the states to enact fair employment laws. The drive had an early success in Wisconsin, which enacted a law in 1945 prohibiting employment discrimination on the basis of "race, creed, color, national origin and ancestry." In 1953, Kansas established a fair employment practices commission and gave it enforcement powers in 1961. Michigan and Minnesota enacted fair employment laws in 1955, and Illinois and Indiana did so in 1961.

Congress was finally able to overcome very strong opposition to enact a federal civil rights law, the Civil Rights Act of 1964. The act prohibits discrimination on the basis of race, color, religion, and national origin in public accommodations and employment. The act's opponents tried to secure its defeat by adding a prohibition against employment discrimination on the basis of sex, thinking that this would cause a number of supporters to vote against the bill. The strategy failed and the act passed with the prohibition, so for the first time in the nation's history, discrimination on the basis of sex was covered by a civil rights law. In 1967, Congress enacted the Age Discrimination in Employment Act, which prohibits employment discrimination against persons forty years of age and older and which has brought an almost complete end to mandatory retirement in the United States.

In 1968, following the assassination of civil rights leader Martin Luther King, Jr., the Civil Rights Act was extended to prohibit discrimination in housing, and with subsequent amendments, the act prohibits discrimination in housing on the basis of race, color, religion, national origin, sex, handicap, and familial status (families with children).

By the end of the 1960s, then, Congress had enacted laws prohibiting discrimination in public accommodations, employment, and housing, and the prohibitions included sex and age in employment and sex, handicap, and familial status in housing. Now it was the turn of the states to follow the lead of Congress, and states in the Midwest, as elsewhere, did so. By the early 1970s, virtually all of the Midwest states had enacted laws prohibiting discrimination in public accommodations, employment, and housing and had expanded the scope of the laws' coverage to accord with that provided by federal law.

Congress first acted to prevent discrimination against people with disabilities in the 1970s, and this culminated in the Americans with Disabilities Act of 1990. The act is designed to prevent discrimination against people with disabilities by requiring a reasonable accommodation for disability with respect to access to places of public accommodations, entitlement to public services, and employment. All of the Midwest states have enacted similar laws providing protection to people with disabilities.

It had become evident by the end of the twentieth century that federal civil rights laws and the civil rights laws of the Midwest states operated together to provide expansive protection against discrimination in important areas of American life. The one notable exception to this expansive protection is discrimination on the basis of sexual orientation. Congress has not included discrimination on the basis of sexual orientation in the protection of federal civil rights laws, and is not likely to do so in the near future. This is an area, therefore, where it is possible for the states again to move ahead of the federal government in the protection of civil rights. By the turn of the century two Midwest states, Minnesota and Wisconsin, prohibited discrimination on the basis of sexual orientation in their civil rights laws. In addition, many important cities in the Midwest have prohibited such discrimination in their local civil rights laws. These include Chicago, Illinois; Des Moines and Cedar Rapids, Iowa; Detroit and Grand Rapids, Michigan; Minneapolis and St. Paul, Minnesota; St. Louis and Kansas City, Missouri; Cleveland, Columbus, and Toledo, Ohio; and Milwaukee and Madison, Wisconsin.

Civil rights laws play a significant role in preventing discrimination against disfavored groups in important areas of American life. History has witnessed the Midwest states at times forging ahead of the federal government in the protection of civil rights and at other times following the federal government's lead. By the turn of the twenty-first century, history had also witnessed some states and cities in the Midwest stepping ahead of the federal government by prohibiting discrimination on the basis of sexual orientation when Congress has failed to do so.

Sources and Further Reading: Arthur Earl Bonfield, "The Origin and Development of American Fair Employment Legislation," *Iowa Law Review* 52 (June 1967); Sidney Fine, *Expanding the Frontiers of Civil Rights* (2000); Owen M. Fiss, "A Theory of Fair Employment Laws," *University of Chicago Law Review* 38 (Winter 1971); Harold S. Lewis, Jr., and Elizabeth J. Norman, *Civil Rights Law and Practice* (2001); Harold S. Lewis, Jr., and Elizabeth J. Norman, *Employment Discrimination Law and Practice* (2001); Robert D. Levy, ed., *The Civil Rights Act of 1964* (1997). Information about the civil rights laws of each state will be found on the official state website, see e.g., the website of the Illinois Department of Human Rights at http://www.state.il.us/dhr/.

Robert A. Sedler
Wayne State University, Michigan

Equal Rights Amendment

The campaign for an Equal Rights Amendment (ERA) has been waged at both the national and state levels, rendering the Midwest an important battleground. Discussion of an ERA began after ratification of the Nineteenth Amendment in 1920, as part of broader national and state efforts to clarify women's new status. In 1921, Wisconsin passed an Equal Rights bill granting women equal rights under the law, but exempting laws establishing special protections for women.

The proposed national ERA did not share these exemptions, compelling many female activists to oppose it. Drafted by Alice Paul, a suffragist and founder of the National Woman's Party, it was first introduced in Congress in 1923, and then reintroduced annually.

In 1972, in a climate of renewed activism, Congress passed the ERA on to the states for ratification. All but two midwestern states ratified; indeed Nebraska,

Iowa, Kansas, Wisconsin, and Michigan ratified before year's end. Nebraska, however, rescinded its ratification in 1973. The effectiveness of statewide ERA coalitions was particularly noteworthy in Indiana, which in 1977, became the last state to ratify, in the context of much organized opposition.

Of the nonratifying states nationwide, all were southern or heavily Mormon except Missouri, which is often grouped with the South, and Illinois, which required a three-fifths legislative majority for ratification. ERA opponents in both states were particularly aided by Alton, Illinois's, famed anti-ERA campaigner, Phyllis Schlafly. Although the ERA did not become law, Illinois later passed its own ERA, and Iowa recently added "women" to state constitutional language about equality.

Sources and Further Reading: Susan D. Becker, *The Origins of the Equal Rights Amendment* (1981); Jane J. Mansbridge, *Why We Lost the ERA* (1986); Joseph A. Ranney, "Wisconsin Women and the Law since 1920," *Wisconsin Lawyer* 69 (Feb. 1996).

Catherine Rymph
University of Missouri–Columbia

Suffrage and Voting

From its territorial beginnings to the present, the Midwest has been strongly committed to republican ideals of citizenship, including the duty of qualified citizens to vote and play a democratic role in their communities. In the nineteenth century, manhood and voting were linked. At twenty-one years, a young white man came of age and was entitled to vote. Frederick Jackson Turner often stressed the democratic nature of midwestern society and politics, in contrast to the East and South. Historian John Barnhart's detailed examination of the constitution-making process showed how the midwestern states systematically aimed toward a universal suffrage.

Still, universal suffrage remained a point of contention. For example, racial qualifications were bitterly debated during the 1860s, but with passage of the Fifteenth Amendment in 1870, midwestern states dropped legal efforts to restrict black voting. Fast-growing rural states, eager to attract immigrant farmers, allowed noncitizens to vote in Wisconsin (1848–1908), Michigan (1850–1894), Indiana (1851–1921), Kansas (1859–1917), Nebraska (1867–1918), Missouri (1870–1924), North Dakota (1889–1913), and South Dakota (1889–1918).

Woman suffrage came eastward into America, starting from the more democratic far west. Traditional family structures, especially among Germans, slowed acceptance of the idea that women could be independent decision makers. The linkage of women with child rearing and educational matters led to suffrage in school board elections in Michigan, Kansas, the Dakota Territory, Nebraska, Wisconsin, Illinois, Ohio, and Iowa. The tremendous support women provided the World War I effort in 1917 and 1918 convinced midwesterners that women's hour had come.

An Ohio meeting of suffragists, Columbus, Ohio, July 30, 1914. Ohio Historical Society, AL00707.

The region never imposed literacy tests on ethnic voters. Unlike neighboring Canada in World War I, it did not strip suffrage from naturalized citizens who came from Germany or Austria.

The style of voting until 1890 was open and celebratory. A man's partisanship was a public matter and a point of pride. Politics was more than a spectator sport; it demanded participation through parades, picnics, schoolhouse meetings, and reading party newspapers. By the 1880s, however, voters in the rural Midwest, especially the areas bypassed by modernization, began to demand that candidates buy their vote. In Adams County, in southern Ohio, over a fourth of the voters pleaded guilty to charges they had sold their votes. Most men would only sell their votes to their own party, but enough "floaters" were available to swing a very close election, such as in 1888. That year William Dudley, a national Republican Party official, told Indiana's county chairmen to "Divide the floaters into blocs of five, and put a trusted man with the necessary funds in charge of these five, and make them responsible that none get away and that all vote our ticket." His preemptive strike backfired when Democrats filched the letter and distributed hundreds of thousands of copies in the last days of the campaign, proving the "holier than thou" Republicans were just as guilty as the presumably less moral Democrats. The issue stimulated the movement to replace ballots printed and distributed by the parties with the secret Australian-style ballot controlled by local government. The politicians never liked vote buying—it was too expensive and was always matched by the other side—so they gladly abolished the practice as a Progressive reform.

Other Progressive reforms, such as registration laws in the cities, weakened the ability of urban machines to control blocs of votes. Wisconsin popularized the primary system as a way to defeat entrenched machines, but when Robert La Follette himself built a machine, the reform lost its allure. The region used a mix of primaries and party conventions to select state and local candidates. In the aftermath of Chicago's bloody Democratic National Convention in 1968, the primary finally replaced the convention system.

The various Progressive reforms were seen as a way of purifying democracy by eliminating ignorant voters, dishonest politicians, and corrupt parties. Midwestern elections were basically honest, especially major statewide contests. Tricks like repeat voting were not common. The statistics that show over 95 percent turnout statewide in 1896 were legitimate for Illinois, Indiana, Iowa, Michigan, and Ohio. The proportion passed 100 percent in some counties because the canvassers discovered some men the census had overlooked, and made sure they voted. The Progres-

sive reforms also weakened parties and made voting voluntary. Turnout began slipping, yet remained 10 to 20 points higher in the Midwest than in the rest of the nation.

At the end of the twentieth century, the West and Midwest continued to lead the nation in registration turnout. More than two-thirds of midwesterners in 1998 were registered to vote. North Dakota and Minnesota boasted the highest registration rates, with 91 and 83 percent, respectively. In 1998, Minnesota recorded the nation's highest voter turnout, at 66 percent, with Virginia at the bottom at 31 percent.

Sources and Further Reading: John Barnhart, *Valley of Democracy* (1953); Daniel J. Elazar, *Cities of the Prairie* (1970); Richard Jensen, *The Winning of the Midwest: Political and Social Conflict, 1888–1896* (1971); Alexander Keyssar, *The Right to Vote* (2000); Paul Kleppner, *Continuity and Change in Electoral Politics, 1893–1928* (1987); Paul Kleppner, *The Third Electoral System, 1853–1892* (1979).

Richard Jensen
University of Illinois–Chicago

Governance

Underlying the history of midwestern governance is a faith in popular self-government. From the earliest period of territorial rule to the close of the twentieth century, midwesterners have sought to determine their own destiny through the creation of new state governments as well as through the formation and preservation of a myriad municipalities, townships, and special districts.

Reflecting the region's devotion to grassroots rule, the Midwest has perennially led the nation in the number of local governments. In 1942, the twelve midwestern states constituted only one quarter of the nation's states, but they claimed 62 percent of the country's governmental units. The number of units declined in the ensuing half century. Yet at the end of the twentieth century, Illinois had more governments than any other state, and eleven of the fifteen states with the largest number of local units were in the Midwest.

Moreover, midwesterners have periodically expressed great faith in the wonder-working potential of their governments. In the nineteenth and early twentieth centuries, they believed that the public sector could create expansive transportation networks, transform morals, and fulfill the dream of urban democracy. The midwestern tradition was not antigovernment. Residents of the heartland states believed in the great potential of government, but they sought to

keep close control over public authority and ensure a local voice in the governance of the region.

The seminal document for midwestern government was the Northwest Ordinance. Adopted by the Confederation Congress in 1787, the ordinance provided that the territory north and west of the Ohio River and east of the Mississippi River would be divided into three to five states to be admitted to the Union on an equal basis with the existing thirteen states. Prior to statehood, a governor appointed by the national government would preside over the territory, though when the territory's free adult male population reached five thousand, a legislature was to be elected. Intended only for the Northwest Territory, the ordinance provided a blueprint for the evolution of government in the trans-Mississippi Midwest as well. Each of the territories in the Midwest would pass through a period of federal tutelage, but the eventual goal, unquestioned throughout the region, was statehood and local self-determination subject only to the limited constraints of the federal union.

The territorial experience varied. Ohioans rebelled against the purported tyranny of their federally appointed governor Arthur St. Clair and ironically celebrated their entry into the federal union as liberation from federal authority. Many territorial governors were more adroit politically than St. Clair and stirred less resentment. But everywhere statehood was the goal, and from Ohio in 1803 to South and North Dakota in 1889, the midwestern territories eventually achieved this end.

Territorial and early state legislatures devoted much of their time to the creation of local governments. Local boosters lobbied vigorously for the formation of new counties, and competition was fierce among frontier settlements for designation as county seat. Most counties were subdivided into townships. These small units were generally responsible for rural roads, poor relief, and weed control. In Michigan, Wisconsin, and Illinois, the chief township officer was the supervisor who also served on the principal governing body of the county, the board of supervisors. In most other areas, a three- to seven-member board or commission elected at large or by district oversaw county government, exercising both executive and legislative functions.

Besides counties and townships, nineteenth-century midwesterners created tens of thousands of miniscule school districts. Basically, there was a district and elected school board for each one-room schoolhouse, thus ensuring parents a strong voice in the education of their children. Though state and county superintendents enforced educational standards, schooling in the nineteenth-century Midwest was not the responsibility of a central bureaucracy, but was subject to grassroots governance.

At the state level, nineteenth-century lawmakers fought over the limits of governmental power, with some backing extraordinary public initiatives and others doubting the efficacy of any but the most minimal government. During the 1820s and 1830s, lawmakers in Ohio, Indiana, Illinois, and Michigan expressed great faith in the ability of state government to build massive systems of canals, roads, and railroads. Some of these projects were completed, others remained paper dreams. But everywhere the public works schemes strained the financial resources of the young states and generated fiscal crises. The result was a series of state constitutional provisions that restricted additional public borrowing or spending for internal improvements.

In the 1870s, legislators in Illinois, Iowa, Wisconsin, and Minnesota further tested the capacity of state government when they pioneered railroad regulatory legislation. By outlawing certain malpractices and authorizing state determination of maximum rail rates, lawmakers used the power of state government to protect small shippers. Midwesterners also tested the ability of their states to cleanse the moral environment. In the 1880s, voters in Kansas, Iowa, North Dakota, and South Dakota all approved state constitutional provisions that prohibited the sale and manufacture of alcoholic beverages. In no other area, except northern New England, was the commitment to state suppression of alcohol so strong as in the Midwest. Enforcement of state prohibition laws, however, proved difficult, demonstrating government's limited ability to police morals.

Meanwhile, permissive municipal incorporation procedures were spawning thousands of additional units of local government. By 1910, Illinois led the nation with 1,066 incorporated cities and villages, Ohio could boast of 784, and Minnesota 645. To halt demands for legislation individually tailored to each city, framers of midwestern state constitutions, beginning with Ohio's document of 1851, forbade special legislation for cities and mandated general laws defining the structure and powers of municipalities. To evade this requirement, lawmakers soon developed classification schemes and enacted legislation that applied only to cities of a certain population class. In many cases only one city was in a population class, so the legislation was in fact, if not in law, special legislation.

To limit such special measures, some states took further action and adopted home rule constitutional provisions for their cities. These permitted home rule cities to formulate their own structures of government and legislate on all local questions without having to win prior authorization from the state legislature. Statewide concerns remained exclusively the responsibility of state lawmakers. In 1875, Missouri was the first state in the nation to adopt a home rule provision; Minnesota did so in 1896, Michigan in 1908, and Ohio and Nebraska in 1912. Though hailed by some as vital to the liberation of city government, home rule provisions generated considerable litigation over which matters were local and which were of statewide concern. Moreover, they did not free cities from their subservience to the states.

Home rule was only one of the planks in a broader urban reform platform. Between 1890 and 1920, such midwestern mayors as Detroit's Hazen Pingree, Cleveland's Tom Johnson, Toledo's Samuel Jones, and Chicago's Edward F. Dunne battled for municipal ownership of the supposedly venal public utility companies and campaigned for lower streetcar fares for transit-dependent city dwellers. Johnson, Jones, and their followers dreamed of the city as a cooperative commonwealth with a government dedicated to securing lower utility rates and better and more equitable municipal services for the downtrodden working class. Dayton, Ohio, won nationwide recognition as a model of city manager government. A professional manager hired by the city council administered the municipality and reportedly achieved a level of governmental efficiency unknown in cities guided by partisan politicians.

Midwestern reformers at the state level expressed a similar faith in the capacity of government to right the wrongs of the world. Under Governor Robert La Follette, Wisconsin became a model for state-level reformers throughout the nation. La Follette and his followers introduced primary elections, thereby eliminating the caucus and convention method of selecting candidates, which had been controlled by purportedly corrupt party bosses. They also pioneered state public utility regulation and adopted the first effective graduated state income tax, thus relieving some of the tax burden on cash-poor farmers and shifting it to those who could better afford it. Missouri's Governor Joseph Folk likewise sought to provide honest government and battled the corrupting influence of business interests. To the north, Iowa's Governor Albert Cummins earned a similar reputation for progressive reform.

No state, however, was as daring in its experiments as North Dakota. In 1916, the Non-Partisan League, a farmer protest group, captured control of the state government and embarked on a scheme of state socialism. To loosen the grip of Minneapolis and St. Paul entrepreneurs on North Dakota's struggling wheat farmers, the legislature authorized the establishment of state-owned grain elevators and flour mills, as well as a state-owned bank and a state-controlled building and loan society to provide public funding for home construction. In the early 1920s, the Non-Partisan League lost control of the state's government, but for a few years North Dakotans embraced government

enterprise as a means of liberating themselves from Minnesota capitalists.

During the late nineteenth and early twentieth centuries, midwestern states also introduced reforms intended to ensure responsive and informed lawmaking. In 1898, South Dakota became the first state in the nation to adopt initiative and referendum procedures. They allowed voters to bypass the legislature and through petition place measures directly on the ballot for approval by the general electorate. Voters could also petition for a referendum to invalidate legislative acts. During the following two decades, North Dakota, Nebraska, Missouri, Michigan, and Ohio would follow South Dakota's example and embrace this form of direct democracy.

Meanwhile, Wisconsin's Charles McCarthy created a model legislative reference bureau that aided lawmakers by providing research and bill-drafting services. In the 1930s, Kansas established the nation's first legislative council, a body intended to study issues and formulate a program of legislation during the interim between legislative sessions. As in the case of the legislative reference bureau, the goal was to enhance lawmaking expertise. In 1937, Nebraska took the daring step of instituting a one-house, nonpartisan legislature. Bicameralism was a long-established feature of American lawmaking, but Nebraskans opted to abolish the traditional second house. In 1940, Missouri moved into the forefront of judicial reform when it adopted the so-called merit plan for selecting judges. Rejecting the election of judges in partisan, adversarial contests, the Missouri plan provided for the governor to appoint jurists from a list submitted by a nominating commission. After the governor's appointee had served a year on the bench, the electorate would vote whether to retain or dismiss the new judge. Though unicameralism remained unique to Nebraska, the legislative reference bureau, legislative council, and Missouri plan of judicial selection became features of state government throughout the nation.

Midwesterners also reformed their local structures of government. Most notably during the mid-twentieth century, they eliminated thousands of school district governments. State centralization was the watchword of the era. State treasuries contributed an increasing share of educational funding, and lawmakers pressured localities to close one-room schools and create larger districts capable of supporting modern school systems. In the late 1930s, Illinois had about twelve thousand school districts, the largest number of any state in the nation. By 1954, this number had fallen to 2,349. Throughout the Midwest similar statistics testified to a marked reorganization of school government.

Other local units adapted to changing demands.

Though twentieth-century political scientists predicted the imminent demise of the township, these small units survived in most midwestern states. In fact, many townships, especially in urbanizing areas, assumed a broader range of responsibilities. A number of counties opted for a mayoral figure to supervise their growing list of functions and created the office of county executive. Meanwhile, special district governments proliferated. Metropolitan-wide special districts enabled central city and suburban residents to cooperate in the governance of such functions as parks or sewage disposal. The Midwest thus remained a crazy quilt of multitudinous cities, counties, townships, park districts, sewerage districts, and school districts, each of the many units adding to the complexity of the region's government.

Sources and Further Reading: Lord Richard Acton and Patricia Nassif Acton, *To Go Free* (1995); Ballard C. Campbell, *Representative Democracy* (1980); Thomas Howard, ed., *The North Dakota Political Tradition* (1981); James F. Keane and Gary Koch, eds., *Illinois Local Government* (1990); Howard Lee McBain, *The Law and the Practice of Municipal Home Rule* (1916); Robert D. Miewald, ed., *Nebraska Government and Politics* (1984); Peter S. Onuf, *Statehood and Union* (1987); Jon C. Teaford, *The Rise of the States* (2002); Paul W. Wager, ed., *County Government Across the Nation* (1950); Justin E. Walsh, *The Centennial History of the Indiana General Assembly, 1816–1978* (1987).

Jon C. Teaford
Purdue University, Indiana

City Councils

In the Midwest, as in the United States as a whole, city councils are the principal legislative bodies of municipal corporations. There is no distinctive midwestern pattern of city council development; the Midwest has conformed to national trends. During the nineteenth century, American city councils gradually yielded authority to mayors and independent boards charged with such specific responsibilities as the government of parks or libraries. This erosion of power was in part owing to the poor reputation of councils. Elected by wards, city councils were assemblies of plebeian neighborhood representatives, many of whom were deemed unqualified and corrupt by the social and economic elite.

During the late nineteenth and early twentieth centuries, reformers sought to rehabilitate councils. In the 1890s, Chicago's Municipal Voters' League battled the members of a corrupt council coalition known as the Gray Wolves. Other cities eliminated their large, ward-based councils, rejecting the principle of neigh-

borhood representation, and replaced them with smaller bodies whose members would be elected at large and command a citywide following. Detroit did so in 1918, and Cincinnati followed suit in 1924. Chicago, Cleveland, and Milwaukee retained large councils elected by wards, thus preserving representation for working-class and ethnic neighborhoods. Between 1908 and 1914, Des Moines, Wichita, and St. Paul abolished their councils, opting instead for a small body of commissioners who exercised both executive and legislative authority. By the late twentieth century, few cities retained the commission plan. Most were governed by either a mayor and council or a city manager and council.

Sources and Further Reading: Dick W. Simpson, *Rogues, Rebels, and Rubber Stamps* (2001); Jon C. Teaford, *The Unheralded Triumph* (1984).

Jon C. Teaford
Purdue University, Indiana

Mayors

In the Midwest, as in the nation as a whole, mayors are the chief executives of city government. Over the course of the nineteenth and twentieth centuries, the powers and duties of mayors have varied greatly. During the nineteenth century, the trend in the Midwest, and in the United States generally, was to enhance the authority of the mayor and replicate in municipal government the separation of legislative and executive powers characteristic of the state and federal governments. Whereas before 1820, mayors were usually appointed by city councils, by 1850 popular election was the norm. Moreover, by 1900, mayors had acquired the power to veto council measures and to appoint executive officers. In most of the largest cities, mayors no longer presided over council meetings, though in Chicago and many smaller municipalities they remained the presiding officer of the municipal legislature.

In 1887, the citizens of Argonia, Kansas, deviated sharply from tradition when they elected the nation's first woman mayor, and by 1900, at least fifteen other small Kansas municipalities had also chosen female executives. Small-town Kansas voters hoped that election of teetotaling females would cleanse their communities of sin and win their towns free publicity in eastern newspapers, which reported these deviations from traditional gender roles.

In the 1890s and early twentieth century, a number of progressive midwestern mayors also attracted national attention. Samuel Jones and Brand Whitlock in

Milwaukee, Wisconsin, mayor Daniel Hoan. Photo courtesy Milwaukee County Historical Society.

Toledo, Tom Johnson and Newton Baker in Cleveland, Hazen Pingree in Detroit, and Edward Dunne in Chicago all battled for municipal ownership of public utilities and sought to use the mayor's office to correct some of the social and economic inequities of urban life. Jones and Johnson especially gained fame for their idealistic vision of the city as a cooperative commonwealth dedicated to ensuring a good life for all of its citizens. During the 1910s, Socialist Daniel W. Hoan won the Milwaukee mayor's office and sought to advance his party's agenda. In no other section of the nation were mayors so bold in their dreams or so willing to challenge the capitalist status quo. Midwestern mayors were in the forefront of municipal progressivism in the nation.

During the early twentieth century, however, two new plans for municipal governance proposed a reduced role for mayors. Originating in Galveston, Texas, in 1901, the commission plan of government gained its first foothold in the Midwest in 1908 in Des Moines, Iowa. Under the commission plan, a board of commissioners shared all executive and legislative authority. Though one of the commissioners might be designated mayor, this title simply meant the official presided over commission meetings and acted as ceremonial head of the municipality. Similarly, under the city manager plan of government, the mayor was largely a ceremonial figure who cut ribbons and welcomed important visitors. In manager municipalities, mayors served on the city council and presided over its meetings but had no greater power than the other council members. The administration of the city rested in the hands of the city manager who was chosen by the council and ideally would be a nonpartisan, expert administrator.

In 1913, Dayton, Ohio, became the first midwestern city to adopt city manager government, and it soon supplanted commission rule as the preferred plan of municipal reformers. Support for city manager government varied in the Midwest. By 1940, Michigan had forty-seven city manager municipalities, more than any other state. With twenty-three manager cities, Ohio ranked eighth in the nation, but only six of the many cities in Illinois had opted for the scheme, only five in Minnesota, and only one each in Nebraska and North Dakota. Indiana permitted neither the commission nor the manager plan, ensuring the continued prevalence of strong-mayor government.

After World War II, a growing number of midwestern municipalities adopted the manager plan, though in some of the largest cities powerful executives proved the efficacy of mayoral rule. Hubert Humphrey began his political career as the successful mayor of Minneapolis, Henry Maier was the outspoken chief executive of Milwaukee from 1960 to 1988, and Mayor Richard J. Daley ruled Chicago from 1955 to 1976, earning the Illinois metropolis a reputation as the city that worked.

Some midwestern cities also made national headlines by electing African American mayors. In 1967, Gary, Indiana, and Cleveland, Ohio, became the first major cities in the nation to elect black executives; in 1974, Coleman Young became Detroit's first black mayor; and in 1983, African American Harold Washington won the mayor's office in Chicago.

Sources and Further Reading: John A. Fairlie, *Municipal Administration* (1901); Paul M. Green and Melvin G. Holli, eds., *The Mayors: The Chicago Political Tradition* (1987); William E. Nelson, Jr., and Philip J. Meranto, *Electing Black Mayors* (1977); Russell McCulloch Story, *The American Municipal Executive* (1918); Jon C. Teaford, *The Unheralded Triumph* (1984).

Jon C. Teaford
Purdue University, Indiana

State Constitutions

The original midwestern state constitutions were adopted over a period beginning with Ohio in 1803 and ending with the Dakotas in 1889. All the constitutions written before Wisconsin's in 1848 have been revised, however, so that Wisconsin's is now the oldest, Ohio's and Indiana's present constitutions having been adopted in 1851.

Many of the first constitutions reflected a sort of class tension between rugged settlers and the interests of the wealthy growers. Five of the earliest constitutions were from states created from the Northwest Territory and bring into constitutional law the distinct ideas of the Northwest Ordinance. Following the requirements of that ordinance, the early constitutions banned slavery and provided for religious liberty in an era when established churches existed in some of the original thirteen states. The abolition of slavery was ideologically linked to a broader conception of human equality, and the resulting population of the region by nonslaveowners may partly explain the characteristic pattern of popular democracy.

It is in the constitutions written and revised after 1848, however, that one can more clearly see a pattern that exists throughout the region. This regional pattern has three main parts: (1) concern for public debt, connected with the dangers of direct subsidy for private corporations; (2) constitutional recognition of social rights, rather than the limited statement of negative political rights characteristic of the seaboard state constitutions; and (3) early expressions of a populist, bottom-up, model of political legitimacy.

In 1836 in Indiana, for example, the legislature had authorized vast public borrowing for internal improvements—mainly canals on the eve of railroad supremacy—that left the state near bankruptcy. Thus the new Indiana Constitution of 1851, like the Wisconsin Constitution of 1848, essentially prohibited long-term borrowing except in cases of rebellion or invasion. Similar but somewhat less draconian provisions were common in other states in the period, although by the twentieth century, creative lawyering had found a number of devices that, in reality, allowed the issuance of long-term state bonds. Partly reflecting the related concern with special privileges for corporate beneficiaries, nineteenth century midwestern constitutions typically prohibited "special privileges or immunities" (in the language of the Kansas Constitution of 1861). These clauses, which predate the Fourteenth Amendment to the U.S. Constitution, are notable because, unlike the Fourteenth Amendment, they focus on not benefiting the powerful rather than on lifting burdens from the weak.

Following the lead of the Northwest Ordinance, the nineteenth-century constitutions, as in the case of Illinois's preamble, state as a purpose to "eliminate poverty and inequality; assure legal, social and economic justice; provide opportunity for the fullest development of the individual." Throughout the region, a similar goal was implemented by provisions guaranteeing public education, often also creating a state university and sometimes, as in Michigan, guaranteeing some academic freedom from direct legislative control. Many of the midwestern constitutions also articulate specific responsibilities for the care of the poor and of prisoners.

In both the writing and amending of constitutions, the region shows a strong commitment to a populist spirit. Indiana, for example, provided that the electorate, in voting on the adoption of the 1851 constitution, should vote separately on the status of African Americans—one of the first uses of a popular referendum in American government. South Dakota, in 1898, was the first state to adopt the general popular right of referendum. An amendment to the Wisconsin Constitution, in 1908, established the first income tax. In 1920, the Nebraska Constitution extended the state legislature unambiguous powers to regulate labor disputes and to restrict child labor. These twentieth-century examples, although connected directly to the Progressive movement, are also linked to the founding ideologies of the earlier constitutions, a modern manifestation of the egalitarianism beginning with the abolition of slavery and anti-aristocratic sentiment, developed through the commitment to education and popular sovereignty.

These patterns illustrate a larger conception of constitutional government. The eastern constitutions sketched a general framework, constrained by some specified individual rights. They relied on the legislature to provide direction, growth, and change within a framework of countervailing powers, harmonized by a republican tradition that political leaders would provide vision and reflection to support the energy of private and commercial life. These elegant mechanisms were substantially modified in the rugged political climate of the Midwest. Following Iowa's example in its 1846 constitution, the election (rather than appointment) of judges became standard. Calling for election of a great many minor officials also became a standard way to limit the power of government leaders. The midwestern constitutions prescribed details with respect to what would have seemed to eastern constitution-makers as minutia. The Illinois Constitution of 1870 is typical: In addition to a standard list of political and civil rights, the document has articles on street railroads, freight and passenger rates, grain warehouse receipts, bank stocks, justices of the peace in Chicago, the ventilation of mines, and numerous other subjects that a more trusting electorate might have left to elected legislatures to consider. The overall effect of this mistrustful perspective was to limit the ability and flexibility of ordinary legislation to drive the public commitments of the states.

Sources and Further Reading: Susan P. Fino, *The Michigan State Constitution* (1996); Francis H. Heller, *The Kansas State Constitution* (1992); William P. McLauchlan, *The Indiana State Constitution* (1996); Robert D. Miewald and Peter J. Longo, *The Nebraska State Constitution* (1993); Jack Stark, *The Iowa State Constitution* (1998); Jack Stark, *The Wisconsin State Constitution* (1997).

Patrick Baude
Indiana University–Bloomington

Territorial Governance and Government

Several of the original thirteen states ceded their claims to land north and west of the Ohio River, and from it the Confederation Congress created the Northwest Territory in the 1780s. The new national domain was supposed to be surveyed and sold for the benefit of the union as a whole; the Virginia cession (March 1, 1784) also stipulated "that the territory so ceded shall be laid out and formed into States." Congress's Land Ordinance of May 20, 1785, set up a federal land office, and its Northwest Ordinance of July 13, 1787 (reenacted by the first federal Congress on August 7, 1789), established a system of government for the region bounded by the western border of Pennsylvania, the Ohio River, the Mississippi River, and the Canadian border. Under the terms of the ordinance and with the approval of Congress, all of this area would eventually be organized into states.

In the first stage of territorial government prescribed by the ordinance, Congress governed through an appointed governor, Arthur St. Clair of Pennsylvania, a secretary, and three judges. Settlers would gain legislative representation in the second stage, when the population had grown to five thousand free adult males in the territory, and admission to the union was guaranteed when "any of the said States shall have sixty thousand free inhabitants." After the creation of Ohio (1803), Congress exercised its authority to establish new territories (within new boundaries) in the remainder of the Northwest Territory and across the Mississippi River in the region annexed by the Louisiana Purchase (1803). Congress exercised a preponderant role in territorial governance through control over patronage, Indian policy, land sales, internal improvements, and other public expenditures. Despite the ordinance's promise, Congress also insisted on its

absolute control over its own membership, delaying statehood in Michigan until 1837, when its population exceeded 140 thousand, and in Wisconsin until 1846, when its population exceeded 223 thousand.

Sources and Further Reading: Andrew R.L. Cayton, *The Frontier Republic* (1986); Peter S. Onuf, *The Origins of the Federal Republic* (1983); Peter S. Onuf, *Statehood and Union* (1987).

Peter Onuf
University of Virginia

Zoning

Zoning is the systematic regulation of the use of privately owned land by local governmental bodies. Public land use controls found their origin in the common law of nuisance and the practice of prohibiting certain activities by restrictive covenants in deeds. In the early twentieth century, proponents of zoning hoped to divide communities into districts or zones, and to keep business, industry, and multidwelling units out of single-family residential areas.

Zoning adherents were motivated by a cluster of beliefs, including the preservation of property values and the desire to exclude undesirable uses and people from residential districts. Although some cities had previously limited building heights, New York City enacted the first modern zoning law in 1916. Zoning proved very popular and spread rapidly in the 1920s, not just in the Midwest but in the nation. State courts, however, were divided as to whether zoning constituted an unconstitutional deprivation of the right to use property without due process of law.

The Village of Euclid, a town near Cleveland, Ohio, created a comprehensive zoning scheme that banned industrial facilities in residential areas. In the leading case of *Village of Euclid v. Ambler Realty Company* (1926), the U.S. Supreme Court sustained the constitutionality of such arrangements. Writing for the Court, Justice George Sutherland ruled that zoning regulations promoted the health, safety, and morals of the public. He analogized zoning to the doctrine of nuisance, and held that state police power encompassed the authority to classify land uses and protect residential neighborhoods. Zoning, however, was gradually employed to accomplish other objects, such as historical preservation and aesthetic harmony.

Sources and Further Reading: Martha A. Lees, "Preserving Property Values? Preserving Proper Homes? Preserving Privilege? The Pre-Euclid Debate over Zoning for Exclusively Private Residential Areas, 1916–1926," *University of*

Pittsburgh Law Review 56 (Winter 1994); Daniel R. Mandelker, *Land Use Law* (1997); Seymour I. Toll, *Zoned American* (1969).

James W. Ely, Jr.
Vanderbilt University, Tennessee

Legal and Judicial Institutions

Like the original American colonies, the Midwest based its legal and judicial institutions on the English common law tradition, adapted to the developing legal culture of the region. The Midwest's legal institutions reflect the nineteenth-century transition from frontier to territories to states, with increased urbanization and diversification of inhabitants, land use, and commerce. The historical development of its legal institutions reveals what is arguably a unique midwestern blend of conservatism and progressivism—a dedication to maintaining basic judicial structures, but reforming them when they appear to be mired in special interests or elitism.

The first midwestern legal structures were found among Indian tribes and in scattered French villages fiercely loyal to their legal traditions. In Illinois, French inhabitants resisted English common law even after the 1763 Treaty of Paris ceded Illinois to the English. Each town retained a board of arbitrators to try civil cases and a judge for all other matters.

Eighteenth- and early-nineteenth-century Indian legal institutions were based on the tribe as the legal unit, with its own laws and means of conflict resolution. Article I of the U.S. Constitution authorizes Congress to regulate commerce with Indian tribes and establishes federal primacy over state authority in Indian affairs. Indian tribes are treated as sovereign entities, so that the relationship between the United States and an Indian tribe is that of one government to another. Indians therefore began to create their own system of tribal courts under the strong influence of the U.S. Bureau of Indian Affairs. In 1934, the Indian Reorganization Act allowed Indians to establish their own law codes and court systems to enforce tribal laws. Many tribes now have written constitutions.

The tribal legal structure often parallels, and sometimes conflicts with, that of the state in which the reservation is located. Before the 1870s, reservations were occupied almost exclusively by Indians; but as white settlers moved in, the territories became a patchwork of settler lands intermingled with reservations so that state or federal laws applied in some cases. To this day, some unresolved sovereignty and jurisdictional disputes remain over issues of taxation authority, natural resource rights, and the reach of state regulatory powers on reservations. Where there is no congressional legislation, the courts piece together information from treaties, historical understandings, and legislative history.

The midwestern territories were carved from these western lands when the relatively new federal government had not yet penetrated this frontier area. The lack of a legal and judicial structure prompted some settlers to form their own local associations as needed. "Claim clubs," especially popular in Wisconsin and Iowa, were organized in the absence of federal public laws and policies. Settlers selected their property, and these clubs recorded and adjudicated their land claims. When the federal government eventually tried to enforce public land laws, these squatters often refused to vacate their land, especially if the land had been formerly inhabited by Indians. Settler and Indian relations were precariously tense in this unstructured situation, and there are documented cases of lynchings and other illegal and violent actions on both sides.

Formal legal codes and institutions, however, made their way into what is now the Midwest. The Land Ordinance of 1785 and the Northwest Ordinance of 1787 were created by the Congress of the Confederation and are among the most important legal documents of the United States. The goal of these documents was to provide an orderly process for breaking up the territory into smaller geographical units, which would eventually become states on an equal footing with the original ones. It was also crucial to provide governmental and legal structures for the political and economic security of settlers—even if it meant they were not granted full U.S. citizenship rights until their territories became states.

Early planning for the settlement of the northwest lands assumed that individual state boundaries should be fixed in advance to prohibit squatting, to control settlement patterns, and to prevent later political haggling. In fact, a 1784 Congressional ordinance specified boundaries for sixteen new states, on a grid pattern, in addition to a rudimentary governmental and legal system. The Land Ordinance of 1785 provided a complementary document for selling land, surveying and laying out townships, and preserving mines and other natural resources. However, Congress and settlers became increasingly uncomfortable with the policy of laying out territories in advance because of their lack of knowledge of natural boundaries and the uncertainty of settlement patterns.

Thus the Northwest Ordinance of 1787 specified the boundaries for the first three states and left the rest to Congressional discretion. Nonetheless, boundary disputes ensued, one of the most problematic being between Ohio and Michigan. The 1787 ordinance also provided legal and judicial institutions. Five appointed administrators ran the territorial government. The governor held executive and legislative powers, including the appointment of other territorial officers. Once the territory had five thousand free adult males, a legislature could be elected. In addition to the governor, a general court of three judges comprised the judicial system and helped the governor write the territorial laws. The judicial institutions were also based on the common law tradition, tempered by local conditions. Territorial judges served as the court of appeals and as the court of original jurisdiction in criminal cases. They also rode circuit to help build up a legal culture in the remote areas. During his first six months in office, Governor Arthur St. Clair drew up the legal code and a rudimentary court system that has provided a lasting influence on midwestern judicial institutions. A secretary rounded out the five officers of the Northwest Territory.

Illinois provides one example of the organization and history of judicial institutions in the Northwest Territory. The first elected judiciary in Illinois was established in 1778 by George Rogers Clark, who took possession of "Illinois County" for the Republic of Virginia. The term "county" was then used to describe the entire land of Illinois as distinct from, but part of, Virginia. Seven judges served in each "settlement"—the term used to describe an area before it had achieved statehood—with Clark himself as the court of appeal. In 1779, John Todd reorganized the courts into three districts, each with six elected judges. The courts met monthly, and the English common law began to be more visible with such traditions as the jury trial. In 1784, Virginia relinquished its claim of Illinois County to the United States of America, but there was no official government until the Northwest Ordinance in 1787. Because St. Clair did not arrive until 1790, the new Illinois Territory spent six years with no government except whatever local citizens decided to establish in the interim.

Once the Northwest Territory established a judicial system, the Illinois Territory had grown so large that it needed to be divided up into counties, and district courts were established to ease the burden for the circuit riders. Jails were built for each county seat. The district courts included courts of common pleas for civil suits, courts of general quarter sessions for minor criminal cases, justices of the peace, and probate courts. In 1809, strong antislavery sentiment in the western reaches of the Illinois Territory led the Indiana Territory to break away, with the remaining Illinois Territory including the present states of Wisconsin and Illinois. The Indiana Territory established a similar judicial system. When the Supreme Court of the Illinois Territory was established in 1814, the general court and court of common pleas were abolished. In Nebraska, distances were extremely difficult before the railroad; some circuit judges traveled ten thousand miles a year by horseback or stagecoach.

The judicial structure for the western territories continued to grow because of the extraordinary number of land, commerce, and debt cases. Judicial histories from Indiana to Kansas document the inadequate number of judges and courts to meet the needs of the population explosion during this time. This new bureaucracy provided jobs for attorneys moving west, many of whom were amateurs. People used the courts as entertainment, and would travel for miles to watch a trial.

In the nineteenth century, all the midwestern territories became states and all wrote constitutions. In the Northwest Territory, the constitution could be written once the territory had sixty thousand inhabitants, and Congress could then admit the territory as a state.

Some states were more successful at constitution writing than others. Drafters often copied from earlier states' documents, sometimes unsuccessfully. The Wisconsin constitution of 1848 borrowed passages from the New York state constitution about long-term land leases, even though the New York document was focused on problems unique to the Hudson River Valley. State constitutions from all regions tended to be very lengthy, and the Midwest was no exception. Nineteenth-century drafters distrusted and were unwilling to rely on state legislatures, so there was a preference of constitutional over legislative law. Citizens were increasingly concerned about the economic power and influence wielded by big business and banks. North Dakota's 1889 constitution had a long list of issues that could not be legislated by a special law—for example, granting rights to lay railroad tracks or rates of interest on money. The 1870 Illinois constitution specified the regulation of grain elevators, and limited the General Assembly's control over the judiciary. This specificity in these written constitutions led to frequent revisions and often created barriers. Early constitutions of Wisconsin, Indiana, and Michigan prohibited the state from taking on debt, which became a problem when dealing with twentieth-century public finance practices.

The state constitutions from this period are important legal documents reflecting conditions in the Midwest at that time. These constitutions set up the judicial systems at the state level. Each midwestern state created a somewhat different structure that changed as constitutions were revised, but the Illinois model contains the basic structures common to most states. The Illinois General Assembly appointed judges and set up the judicial structure in its first state constitution in 1818. The judicial system was described as a Supreme Court of four judges, appointed by the General Assembly, with primarily appellate jurisdiction. In the early days the judges rode circuit, with circuits added as the population grew.

At statehood, Illinois and other states added more appellate layers to the judicial system. County-level courts to settle small claims and minor crimes became a major influence on midwestern legal culture. In Illinois and many other states, justice-of-the-peace courts had jurisdiction at the county level for small civil suits, including issues about African Americans, whether slave or free.

In states like Indiana and Illinois, some courts were subject to their state's legislative branch for appointments, a policy that left some courts in disarray and confusion, and dependent on the whims of the legislators. The 1848 Illinois constitution created a more independent judiciary, and additional judges and courts were added to meet the population increase. Cities and towns added police magistrates and courts of common pleas. But even with improvements, the 1848 judicial structure was still geared to a rural state. Thus in 1870, a new constitution was established to incorporate industrialization and urbanization. An appellate layer of courts was established with geographical divisions throughout the state. Cook County (Chicago) was given its own circuit with five judges, plus additional judges, branches, and other bureaucratic staffing. At the end of the twentieth century, the Circuit Court of Cook County was one of the largest unified court systems in the world.

Urbanization also brought the need for new types of courts to address such issues as juvenile crime and probate. Juvenile justice reform had strong roots in Chicago, where such social activists as Jane Addams and civic and professional groups like the Chicago Bar Association lobbied the 1898 state legislation for a juvenile court system, which took control from politicians and police and gave it to judicial authorities.

The Illinois Judicial Article of 1964 established the familiar three-tier system of most state court systems—Supreme Court, Appellate Court, and Circuit Courts. On the trial level, all courts except for the circuit courts were abolished. In 1970, the Illinois constitution was rewritten to favor an appointed judiciary, but this proposed change was rejected by the voters. Some changes were made in regard to death penalty and other serious cases. One major addition was a judicial disciplinary system for monitoring the professional conduct and competency of judges.

The twentieth century saw shorter state constitutions, but the same tug of war between legislatures and the courts remained. Judicial review became a frequently used means for the courts to control the legislative process. Between 1885 and 1899, the Minnesota Supreme Court struck down dozens of state

statutes. Often the wordiness of these early state constitutions so muddled the meaning that a court could declare a law unconstitutional on a technicality. In 1901, as part of their lively progressive movement, Wisconsin established the country's first Legislative Reference Bureau to model well-written legislation.

The trend to elect rather than appoint judges continued into the twentieth century. In 1940, the Missouri Plan was adopted as an amendment to the Missouri constitution. It stipulated that judicial candidates be screened by a committee of lawyers, judges, and ordinary citizens, with three appointed by the governor of the state for set terms, then eligible for retention through election by the voters. Hybrids of this system have been adopted nationwide. However, the American Bar Association and other groups continued to fight for the professionalization of the law as a preventive measure to corruption and unethical behavior among lawyers and judges.

After the Judiciary Act of 1789, the judicial clause of the U.S. Constitution was activated and a federal court system established. Strong proponents of the new federal government supported this new court system as a way to coordinate state activities in commerce, transportation, Indian affairs, and the mail. The act also established federal judicial review of state legislation. It was fortunate, though, that local legal structures were kept in place, because it took the federal judicial system some time to penetrate the western territories. In 1837, federal legislation established circuits west of the Appalachians to make travel easier and to meet the growing caseload.

Four midwesterners became Chief Justices of the U.S. Supreme Court: Salmon P. Chase, Ohio, 1864–1873; Morrison R. Waite, Ohio, 1874–1888; Melville W. Fuller, Illinois, 1888–1910; and Warren Burger, appointed from Virginia but born in St. Paul, Minnesota, 1969–1986. Among the nineteen U.S. Supreme Court justices are Sherman Minton, Indiana; Potter Stewart, Ohio; Arthur Goldberg, Illinois; Harry Blackmun, Minnesota; and John Paul Stevens, Illinois, who has served since 1975.

The current Appellate Courts of Appeal for the Midwest states and the dates they were established are: the Sixth Circuit Court of Appeals, 1866, Kentucky, Michigan, Ohio, and Tennessee; the Seventh, 1866, Illinois, Indiana, and Wisconsin; the Eighth, 1929, Iowa, Minnesota, Missouri, Nebraska, the Dakotas, and Arkansas; and the Tenth, 1929, Kansas, Colorado, New Mexico, Oklahoma, Utah, and Wyoming.

Like many midwestern district trial courts, the U.S. District Court for the Northern District of Illinois has been the scene for some of the most important—as well as sensational—trials in U.S. history. This court was founded in 1855, at a critical time for the growth of industry, cities, and the labor movement in the Midwest. Abraham Lincoln tried several cases there. This court oversaw such cases as a patent suit filed by Cyrus McCormick to protect his reaper, the Great Railway Strike of 1877, the Pullman Strike of 1894, the antitrust trials of the meatpacking industry "Beef Kings," the breaking up of the Rockefeller Standard Oil monopoly, the conviction of Al Capone, and the trial of the Chicago Seven during the Vietnam War era.

Midwestern jurisprudence distinguished itself in the area of codification of the law when, in 1849, New York state adopted the Field Code as a major codification and reform of court procedure to adapt to the particular legal issues of the United States. Although many eastern states resisted, viewing the code as an affront to common law proceedings, Missouri, Iowa, Minnesota, Indiana, Ohio, Nebraska, Wisconsin, and Kansas adopted it before the Civil War, and the Dakotas followed by the end of the century. Their enthusiasm for this reform resulted from the history of land dispute cases in the Midwest: The common law definitions and procedures were cumbersome in litigation over land.

Professionalization of the law developed in the late nineteenth and early twentieth centuries, as progressivism and other reform movements influenced midwestern legal and judicial institutions. Legal education and literature became more standardized on a national basis. The American Bar Association was founded in 1878 and is currently headquartered in Chicago. West Publishing was founded in 1872 in St. Paul, Minnesota, with a weekly record of excerpts from Minnesota courts, soon expanded to the now essential National Reporter System. West now offers computer-assisted legal research services and numerous other products, and is still considered a leading law publisher. *The Northwest Reporter* (1879) was the first regional reporter of court decisions. All the major public universities of the Midwest, including most land-grant institutions, established law schools. In 1913, William Harley incorporated the American Judicature Society under Illinois law. Harley was a leader in the movement for bar integration, calling for mandatory membership in the state bar association to ensure quality control over admission to the bar and to legal education. By 1940, many states had passed integration statutes.

Though Illinois prohibited a woman from practicing law in 1873 (*Bradwell v. Illinois*), another woman was admitted to the Iowa bar the same year. The University of Michigan Law School was the first to admit women, in 1870. The Women's Bar Association of Illinois was founded in 1914, and the Portia Club of Milwaukee in 1920.

In 1854, Ohioan John Mercer Langston became the first documented African American man to practice law. He entered Oberlin College in 1849, received his law license in 1854, and became the first Dean of Howard University Law School in 1868 and then the University President. In 1992, the Minnesota American Indian Bar Association, one of the first such organizations in the United States, was formally incorporated.

Sources and Further Reading: Richard Cahan, *A Court That Shaped America* (2002); Lawrence M. Friedman, *A History of American Law*, 2nd ed. (1985); Gerard W. Gawalt, ed., *The New High Priests: Lawyers in Post–Civil War America* (1984); Joanne L. Goodwin, *Gender and the Politics of Welfare Reform* (1997); Kermit Hall, *The Magic Mirror: Law in American History* (1989); Terence C. Halliday, *Beyond Monopoly: Lawyers, State Crises, and Professional Empowerment* (1987); Peter Onuf, *Statehood and Union* (1987).

Barbara Jones
Wesleyan University, Connecticut

Lawyers

The cities of the Midwest, particularly Chicago, Illinois, have been the site of much research about the social structure of the legal profession and the work of lawyers. Indeed, much of what is known about lawyers in the United States comes from studies of attorneys in this region.

The practice of law has changed since the 1950s in that fewer attorneys practice alone, and law firms have grown to encompass hundreds of lawyers. In the large cities of the Midwest, such as Chicago, Cleveland, Detroit, and St. Louis, the growth in the size of law firms has been particularly acute. For example, Baker and McKenzie had four lawyers when it was formed in Chicago in 1949. By 2004, the firm had 3,213 attorneys in sixty-eight offices spread across thirty-eight countries. Similarly, Kirkland and Ellis employs about five hundred lawyers in its main Chicago office and the remainder of their nearly one thousand attorneys in offices in Los Angeles, New York, San Francisco, Washington, D.C., and London, England. Other areas of the Midwest have also experienced significant growth in the size of law firms. In St. Louis, the Bryan Cave firm employs eight hundred lawyers. Kansas City, Missouri–based Shook, Hardy and Bacon employs 601 lawyers, Cleveland's Thompson Hine firm has 365 attorneys, and Detroit-based firm Dykema Gossett employs 275 attorneys.

As law firms have grown, the number of urban lawyers working in large firms has increased, while the prevalence of individual and small-firm practice has declined. According to the *National Law Journal*, between 1987 and 2002, the largest 250 law firms in the United States grew from 58,533 to 108,361 attorneys. In Chicago, approximately 14 percent of attorneys worked in large business-oriented law firms in 1975, but by 1995, that figure had more than doubled, to 32 percent. Medium-size firms accounted for nearly 13 percent of Chicago's legal practices in 1995, up from 8 percent in 1975, and small-firm practice declined from 30 percent of all lawyers to about 17 percent over the same period. The growth of urban law firms is the result of strong demand from businesses for legal services relating to mergers, acquisitions, government regulations, and lawsuits between large businesses.

The social and demographic characteristics of attorneys working at large law firms have also changed during the last fifty years. Law firms were once dominated by white, male, Protestant lawyers who attended elite top-ranked law schools. In 1975, for example, 31 percent of Chicago lawyers with law degrees from elite law schools and 22 percent of lawyers with degrees from prestigious and highly regarded schools worked in large law firms, whereas only 17 percent with law degrees from regional schools and 2 percent with degrees from local schools worked for large law firms.

By the turn of the last century, law firms had become increasingly diverse, with more representation of women, African Americans, Hispanics, Asians, and religions other than Protestant denominations than in the past. The diversity found in many large law firms is the direct result of court decisions that have made law school more accessible to women and minorities, as well as affirmative action programs instituted by law firms seeking to expand their clientele. This has also led an increasing number of lawyers with law degrees from local and regional schools to enter large law firms. For example, by 1995, large law firms in Chicago included 17 percent of attorneys with law degrees from local schools and 37 percent from regional schools.

The diversity of large law firms, however, has been based mainly on the recruitment of new law school graduates and is not necessarily reflected in the partnership decisions and management structure of the firms. Women and minority lawyers face a number of obstacles to advancement in large law firms. Fewer women and minorities than white men are promoted to partner, and both are more likely to leave partnership tracks and work in lower status nonpartnership-oriented positions as temporary or part-time employees, or leave the practice of law altogether. Women often find that law firm culture is male dominated, and childbirth and domestic needs are not well accommodated.

Whereas urban law practices are dominated by large law firms that serve business interests, rural and suburban practices are often based in smaller law practices (less than twenty attorneys) that are oriented toward serving a more general clientele. For example, in Indiana only plaintiffs' personal injury lawyers in metropolitan areas, such as Indianapolis, are able to specialize mainly in tort (injury) claims. In the rural and suburban areas of the state, attorneys representing individuals in injury cases tend to be general practitioners.

The trend among suburban legal practitioners appears to be moving toward entrepreneurial practices. The lawyers engaged in these practices use a variety of advertising and referral techniques to attract clients. The movement toward entrepreneurial practices began in the 1970s, when the U.S. Supreme Court legalized advertising by lawyers. The early use of advertising by lawyers was championed by Joel Hyatt and his firm, Hyatt Legal Services. Based in Ohio, Hyatt set up a network of storefront law offices that offered standardized personal legal services, such as wills, divorces, name changes, and routine personal injury cases, at standardized prices. Hyatt and similar firms used television and radio advertising to reach potential customers and computerized forms to deliver the services at a low cost. These firms were based on the franchise model and had much in common with McDonalds and other franchised businesses. Attorneys at these storefront offices were often paid modest annual salaries and were given bonuses for selling services to a large number of clients. Lawyers tended to become disgruntled by the low income and lack of workplace autonomy, and turnover was high.

For the most part, the large franchise law firms did not survive into the twenty-first century. However, the entrepreneurial practices of advertising for clients and using technology to de-skill and routinize the practice of law have remained. Although these practices are most often associated with plaintiffs' personal injury lawyers, they are also used by practitioners seeking clients in divorce, personal bankruptcy, wills and estates, residential real estate, and immigration.

In rural settings, attorneys are overwhelmingly general practitioners who deal with local businesses as well as the problems of the local populations, including (but not limited to) real estate transactions, divorce and child custody, estate and probate, and workplace or personal injury. These attorneys often cannot afford to serve any one population exclusively. For example, while it is common for personal injury lawyers in metropolitan areas to represent either plaintiffs or defendants, in rural settings attorneys handling personal injuries may sometimes represent defendants and at other times represent plaintiffs. Indeed, having a smaller population to serve, rural lawyers may struggle to make their law practices a full-time vocation. It is not uncommon for rural attorneys to have means of support beyond the practice of law. These extralegal occupations include (but are not limited to) selling real estate, selling insurance, banking, tax preparation, and owning other businesses, such as auto dealerships and restaurants.

The Midwest has been at the forefront of law firm growth and innovation in legal practices. The innovations in large law firm practices and in the delivery of personal legal services that began in the Midwest have spread throughout the nation and much of the industrialized world. However, although legal practices in metropolitan areas are well understood, research about the practice of law in rural areas is limited and more work is needed.

Sources and Further Reading: Jerome E. Carlin, *Lawyers on Their Own*, rev. ed. (1994); Joel F. Handler, *The Lawyer and His Community* (1967); David Hechler, "The NLJ 250 Survey Shows the Pace has Slowed by Half, to 3.7%," *National Law Journal* 25 (Nov. 2002); John P. Heinz and Edward O. Laumann, *Chicago Lawyers*, rev. ed. (1994); John P. Heinz, Kathleen Hull, and Ava Harter, "Lawyers and Their Discontents," *Indiana Law Journal* 74 (Summer 1999); Harris H. Kim, "The Changing Patterns of Career Mobility in the Legal Profession," in Jerry Van Hoy, ed., *Legal Professions* (2001); Donald D. Landon, *Country Lawyers* (1990); Jerry Van Hoy, *Franchise Law Firms and the Transformation of Personal Legal Services* (1997); Jerry Van Hoy, "Markets and Contingency," *International Journal of the Legal Profession* 6 (Nov. 1999).

Jerry Van Hoy
University of Toledo, Ohio

African American Lawyers

Between 1854 and 1942, twenty-two black men and women were the first black lawyers admitted to the bar in the states of the Midwest. They included graduates of law schools in the Midwest. Some studied under the tutelage of local lawyers. Others were educated at established law schools or were self-taught. Other black lawyers remained in the Midwest for only brief periods, likely because of the dearth of African Americans who could afford their services and the dearth of white clients. In spite of daunting challenges, both black women and men who remained or returned to the Midwest broke ground in politics and other areas of public service. What follows is a list of the first black men and women lawyers admitted to practice in Midwest states for the period stated. Particularly impressive is the number of black women who pursued careers as lawyers.

In Ohio, John Mercer Langston, who was born in Virginia, was admitted to the bar in 1854 and became the first black lawyer to practice in the state. Langston became the first black dean of an American law school, Howard University School of Law, in 1869. In 1919, Daisy D. Perkins became the first black woman admitted to the Ohio bar. She studied law in Columbus, Ohio, under Judge M. B. Earnhart, a white judge. She practiced law and served as a prosecutor in the Office of the Columbus Prosecutor.

The Indiana state bar admitted Hiram R. Revels to practice in the 1860s, after which he relocated to Mississippi, from where he was elected to the U.S. Senate in 1870. Helen Elsie Austin was admitted to the Indiana bar in 1930. She is the first black female graduate of the University of Cincinnati School of Law. Upon graduation she joined the law firm of Henry J. Richardson, Jr., a prominent lawyer and member of the Indiana State Assembly; she subsequently relocated to Washington, D.C.

Lloyd G. Wheeler was admitted to the Illinois bar in 1869, though he subsequently relocated to Arkansas, where he became a dominant player in Republican Party politics. Ida G. Platt, a former legal stenographer, was admitted to the Illinois bar in 1894. She earned her law degree from the Chicago College

Early African American lawyer John Mercer Langston. John Mercer Langston, *From the Virginia Plantation to the National Capital* (1894).

of Law and was the third black woman to graduate from an American law school.

In Michigan, John C. McLeod was admitted to the state bar in 1870. He practiced in Detroit, where with little training he became a leading criminal defense lawyer. Grace G. Costavas was admitted in 1923, the same year that she earned a law degree from the Detroit College of Law. Little, however, is known about her career.

In 1871, John H. Johnson was admitted to the bar in Missouri, having been sponsored by A. J. Garesche, a white Democrat and secessionist. Johnson used his talent to help former slaves emigrate to the North. More than half a century later, in 1942, Dorothy L. Freeman was admitted to the Missouri bar, though little is known about her or who sponsored her admission.

Also in 1871, notice of the admission of John H. Morris, a barber, to the bar in Kansas reached a newspaper in Louisiana. Little is known about his success as a lawyer. Lutie A. Lytle is the third black woman lawyer admitted to the bar in the United States. She was admitted to the Kansas bar in 1897, and upon her admission to the bar in Tennessee, she became the first black woman admitted to the bar in the South. In 1897, she joined the faculty of Central Tennessee Law School, becoming the first woman to teach law in the United States.

Judge Drayer of Keokut admitted A. H. Watkins, a schoolteacher, to the bar in Iowa in 1874. Little more is known. Gertrude Elzora Durden Rush studied law under the instruction of her husband, James B. Rush, and via the correspondence law course offered by LaSalle Extension at the University of Chicago. She was admitted to the Iowa bar in 1918. Rush holds the distinction of being the first black woman to cofound a bar association, the National Bar Association, founded in Des Moines, Iowa, in 1925.

Everett E. Simpson, an 1888 law graduate of Wisconsin Law School, was admitted to the Wisconsin state bar in the same year, although he soon left the state. William T. Green, an 1892 graduate of the University of Wisconsin, was admitted to the bar and became a prominent civil rights lawyer in the state. Mabel Watson Raimey was admitted to the Wisconsin bar in 1927 after self-study and enrolling in the evening law program at Marquette University. She practiced law in Milwaukee for several years, and by 1941 she was listed as one of approximately fifty black women lawyers in the United States.

In Minnesota, Frederick L. McGhee was admitted to the bar in 1889, and had the distinction of being one of the first black lawyers in the Midwest to graduate from a law school, Union Law School, which ultimately became the Law School of Northwestern University. McGhee was one of the early lawyers in the Midwest to organize a civil rights organization, the National Afro-American Council, around 1900. He was also cofounder of the National Association for the Advancement of Colored People (NAACP) in 1909 in Buffalo, New York. Booker T. Washington, the president of Tuskegee Institute, was among the national figures who lauded McGhee's civil rights advocacy in the Midwest.

Lena Olive Smith was admitted to the Minnesota bar in 1921. She became an active and dominate member of the NAACP and the Urban League. She is the first woman elected as president of the Minneapolis branch of the NAACP. She received a law degree from Northwestern College of Law (later renamed William Mitchell Law School). She dedicated her legal training to the field of civil rights.

Silas Robbins was admitted to the Nebraska state bar in 1889 and practiced law in Omaha. He was the second black person to run for a seat in the Nebraska unicameral legislature and was elected in 1898. Zanzye H. A. Hill, a graduate of the Nebraska University School of Law, was admitted to the bar in 1929. She became the legal counsel to the Woodman of Union Insurance Company in Hot Springs, Arkansas.

In the case of North Dakota, there is sparse information concerning early African American participation in the legal profession. Notably, in South Dakota Will F. Reden was admitted to the bar in 1908, after graduating from the University of Iowa School of Law. He practiced law in Sioux Falls, and in 1936 became a regional director of the National Bar Association, a black bar group.

Sources and Further Reading: Ann Juergens, "Lena Olive Smith," *William Mitchell Law Review* 28 (2001); John Mercer Langston, *From the Virginia Plantation to the National Capitol* (1894); J. Clay Smith, Jr., *Emancipation: The Making of the Black Lawyer: 1844–1944* (1993); J. Clay Smith, Jr., ed., *Rebels in Law* (1998); Phoebe Weaver Williams, "A Black Woman's Voice: The Story of Mabel Raimey, 'Shero,'" *Marquette Law Review* 74 (Spring–Summer 1991).

J. Clay Smith, Jr.
Howard University, Washington, D.C.

Common Law

The term *common law* has two distinct meanings. First, it refers to the English legal tradition that passed with much of its doctrine, structure, and culture to most of the United States, including all of the Midwest. Books provided the transmission medium. Common law in this meaning contrasts with the civil law tradition, which spread from continental Europe to colonial empires in America and remains important today in Louisiana, Puerto Rico, and to a lesser extent the southwestern United States.

American jurists such as James Kent (1763–1847) and Joseph Story (1779–1845) wrote commentaries that blended American, English, Roman, and civil law sources and cite an increasing number of midwestern court cases. Roscoe Pound (1870–1964), a Nebraska native son and dean of its law school, drew from these eclectic sources to develop his influential theory of sociological jurisprudence and to push for court reform. His later position as dean of Harvard Law School illustrates the fluidity that exists between the Midwest and other parts of the United States as an aspect of America's pragmatic legal culture.

Second, *common law* refers to judicial decisions as a source of law distinct from rules created by the other two branches of government, that is, statutes (legislative) and regulations (executive).

The Midwest's common law cohesion is primarily a historical accident. The West Publishing Company created its regional reporter system for state courts in the late nineteenth century, and the *North Eastern Reporter* and *North Western Reporter* included all but two of the Midwest's twelve states, tracking the geographic division of Midwest states in the federal Seventh and Eighth Circuits. Lawyers and judges predominantly cited cases from their own geographic region or circuit, which led to mutual communication among some of the Midwest's twelve states.

Sources and Further Reading: David S. Clark and Tugrul Ansay, eds., *Introduction to the Law of the United States*, 2nd ed. (2002); Lawrence M. Friedman, *A History of American Law*, 2nd ed. (1985); Kermit L. Hall, *The Magic Mirror: Law in American History* (1989).

David S. Clark
Willamette University, Oregon

Courthouse Architecture

Midwestern courthouses dotted the oldest settled areas at roughly thirty-mile intervals, first along the navigable waterways, then along the improved roads. Farther west and north, later sparser settlement expanded county borders to forty- and fifty-mile intervals. Within the county seats, commissioners placed courthouses along river bluffs, in central town squares, or where major roads or railroads converged. And prominence of site was complemented by dominance of form. Once the initial settlement period was over, courthouses, whether county, state, or federal, assumed grand proportions, classical or symbolic designs, and expensive materials. They embodied the prosperity of their communities and were points of pride to local citizens.

With rare exceptions courthouses were built for the purpose. Initial temporary structures of logs often served as courthouse, jail, and jailor's residence. After only a few years, however, these buildings were replaced by differentiated permanent buildings. The earliest permanent courthouses contained on the first level well-lit offices for clerks and brick or stone vaults for securing records—land conveyance, probate, governance. The second story was devoted to the court-

Dallas County Courthouse, Adel, Iowa. Photo by Calvin L. Beale, Economic Research Service, United States Department of Agriculture.

room. No matter what the architectural style—from the simple, brick Meigs County, Ohio, courthouse of 1823 to the large, stone Marshall County, Kansas, courthouse of 1891—the two-story plans were functionally the same. Occasionally county courthouses also served as city halls as in the City-County Building for Minneapolis and Hennepin County built between 1887 and 1906. Another variation comprised the federal district court buildings, which also accommodated local post offices, customs houses, and other federal administrative functions, like the U.S. Court House at Indianapolis, Indiana, built in 1905.

Increasing bureaucracy and court functions at the county level, especially in metropolitan areas in the late twentieth and early twenty-first centuries, has led to abandonment of old courthouses for newer county administration buildings. Often the historic courthouse in the square has been converted to museum use, although many of these symbols of nineteenth-century Midwest heritage have been destroyed. At the federal level, office space for modern programs—Internal Revenue Service, Health and Human Services, and the like—and expanded older functions has led to the construction of separate federal buildings and post offices. Thus, county courts and their ancillary functions no longer have pride of place in distinctive courthouse buildings, but are subsumed in modern all-purpose office buildings, while federal courts and their support personnel, including U.S. Marshals and attorneys, have expanded to fill many historic downtown federal court buildings of distinction and grandeur.

Sources and Further Reading: Richard Pare, ed., *Court House: A Photographic Document* (1978). Most midwestern states have one-volume illustrated histories of their courthouses. A recent example of this type of publication is Susan W. Thrane, *County Courthouses of Ohio* (2000).

Elizabeth Brand Monroe
Indiana University-Purdue University,
Indianapolis

Major Constitutional and Legal Cases Associated with the Midwest

Ableman v. Booth, 62 U.S. (21 How.) 506 (1859): Fugitive Slavery in Wisconsin

On March 10, 1854, acting with the aid of U.S. Marshal Stephen Ableman, Bennami S. Garland, a Missourian, seized his runaway slave, Joshua Glover, just outside of Racine, Wisconsin, and brought him to Milwaukee. On March 11, a mob led by Sherman Booth and John Rycraft rescued Glover, who was soon taken to Canada. Shortly after this, the sheriff of Racine County arrested Garland for kidnapping, but the U.S. District Judge ordered his release. On March 15, U.S. Marshal Ableman arrested Booth and Rycraft, who were convicted in November 1854 and January 1855, respectively. In *In re Booth and Rycraft* (1855), the Wisconsin Supreme Court issued a writ of habeas corpus, declaring that the federal fugitive slave law of 1850 was unconstitutional. Threatened with arrest and contempt of court, Ableman released the two men.

Marshal Ableman appealed the case to the U.S. Supreme Court, but the Wisconsin Supreme Court refused to forward the record of the case. Finally, in 1859, the U.S. Supreme Court decided the case, using the Wisconsin Supreme Court Reports as the record. In a powerful decision, which still remains vital, Chief Justice Roger B. Taney, speaking for a unanimous Court, rejected the idea that state courts could overturn the decisions of federal courts. Booth was subsequently jailed, freed by mobs, and rearrested. President James Buchanan, at the end of his term of office, pardoned Booth. Rycraft was imprisoned for ten days and fined $200.

Sources and Further Reading: Stanley W. Campbell, *The Slave Catchers* (1968); Thomas D. Morris, *Free Men All* (1974).

Paul Finkelman
University of Tulsa, Oklahoma

Bradwell v. Illinois, 83 U.S. 130 (1873): Women Barred from Practicing Law

Myra Bradwell, a Chicago lawyer and probably the most prominent female lawyer in the United States in the nineteenth century, appealed an 1869 Illinois Supreme Court decision that barred her from practicing law on the grounds that, as a married woman, she was not a free agent. In their case before the U.S. Supreme Court, Bradwell's lawyer argued that, under the Privileges and Immunities clause of the Fourteenth Amendment, Bradwell had the right to pursue her profession. The high court disagreed, ruling that the guarantees of citizenship under the Fourteenth Amendment did not extend to compelling a state to accept women to the bar if it did not choose to. Disinclined to beg, Bradwell refused to pursue admittance to the Illinois Bar, even though a new 1872 state law granted to women and men freedom of occupational choice.

Bradwell's importance lies not only in its explicit exclusion of women from professions, which it did, but also in its ringing reinforcement of conventional gen-

❖ The Supreme Court Upholds Sexual Difference

In *Bradwell v. Illinois*, the U.S. Supreme Court upheld the Illinois Supreme Court's decision to reject Myra Bradwell's application to practice law because she was a married woman and therefore not a free agent. In a separate concurrent opinion, U.S. Supreme Court justice Joseph P. Bradley insisted upon inherent differences between women and men and tied an ideology of separate spheres to constitutional law. He wrote:

Man is, or should be, woman's protector and defender. The natural and proper timidity and delicacy which belongs to the female sex evidently unfits it for many of the occupations of civil life. The constitution of the family organization, which is founded in the divine ordinance, as well as in the nature of things, indicates the domestic sphere as that which properly belongs to the domain and functions of womanhood. The harmony . . . of interests and views which belong . . . to the family institution is repugnant to the idea of a woman adopting a distinct and independent career from that of her husband.

So firmly fixed was this sentiment in the founders of the common law that it became a maxim of that system of jurisprudence that a woman had no legal existence separate from her husband, who was regarded as her head and representative in the social state; and, notwithstanding some recent modifications of this civil status, many of the special rules of law flowing from and dependent upon this cardinal principle still exist in full force in most States. One of these is, that a married woman is incapable, without her husband's consent, of making contracts which shall be binding on her or him. This very incapacity was one circumstance that the Supreme Court of Illinois deemed important in rendering a married woman incompetent to perform fully the duties and trusts that belong to the office of an attorney and counselor.

Source: Bradwell v. State of Illinois, 83 U.S. Reports 130 (1873).

der boundaries at a time when Americans were exploring the implications of the Reconstruction Amendments, especially the Fourteenth Amendment's Privileges and Immunities clause. In a concurring opinion, Justice Joseph P. Bradley wrote, "Man is, or should be, woman's protector and defender. The natural and proper timidity and delicacy which belongs to the female sex evidently unfits it for many of the occupations of civil life." Not until 1971, when Ruth Bader Ginsburg argued *Reed v. Reed*, would the U.S. Supreme Court overturn its assumption and accept arguments that sex discrimination was unconstitutional.

Sources and Further Reading: Jane M. Friedman, *America's First Woman Lawyer* (1993); Linda K. Kerber, *No Constitutional Right to Be Ladies* (1998); Sandra F. VanBurkleo, *Belonging to the World: Women's Rights and American Constitutional Culture* (2001).

Rachel E. Bohlmann
The Newberry Library, Chicago, Illinois

Brown v. Board of Education of Topeka, Kansas, 347 U.S. 483 (1954), 349 U.S. 294 (1955): The End of the Separate-but-Equal Doctrine in Schools

Brown v. Board of Education is widely viewed as among the most important Supreme Court decisions of the twentieth century, indeed of all time.

Brown involved constitutional challenges to racial segregation in public elementary and secondary schools. In 1952, when the case was brought, seventeen Southern and Border states, including Missouri and the District of Columbia, required public school segregation by law, while four other states, including Kansas, allowed local segregation. The plaintiffs were represented by the National Association for the Advancement of Colored People and its lead lawyer, Thurgood Marshall, later the first African American Supreme Court Justice.

On May 17, 1954, Chief Justice Earl Warren delivered the unanimous opinion of the Supreme Court, finding that racial segregation of public schools violated the Equal Protection clause of the Fourteenth Amendment. In the second *Brown* decision (1955), the Court held that because the challenge of ending segregation varied, the lower federal courts were in the best position to assure compliance. They were ordered to act "with all deliberate speed."

Brown was furiously criticized and openly defied. In 1956, 101 members of the U.S. Congress signed the Southern Manifesto pledging resistance to the decision. Southern states enacted hundreds of new laws strengthening school segregation. By the 1963–1964 school year, barely one in a hundred African American school children in the states of the old Confederacy was in a school with whites. Despite *Brown*, desegregation did not occur until the late 1960s and early 1970s, a full fifteen years after the decision, as a result of congressional action.

Brown did not directly apply in most of the Midwest because school segregation, although prevalent, was not required by law. Rather, school segregation was the de facto result of housing segregation, racial prejudice, and unequal economic opportunities, especially in the suburbs. Efforts to provide school busing across city-suburban lines were rejected by the Supreme Court in a case from Michigan, *Milliken v. Bradley* (1974).

Some proponents of racial equality also criticize the decisions for only addressing de jure segregation—that is, segregation resulting from law—and not de facto segregation. They point out that throughout the cities of the Midwest, as well as the rest of the country, many public schools remain racially segregated. Others maintain that what African American children need most is not white classmates but sufficient resources to hire well-trained teachers and provide adequate facilities.

Despite these criticisms, *Brown v. Board of Education* remains a constitutional landmark, a symbol of America's commitment to racial equality.

Sources and Further Reading: Jack Balkin, *What "Brown v Board of Education" Should Have Said: The Nation's Top Legal Experts Rewrite America's Landmark Civil Rights Decision* (2001); Richard Kluger, *Simple Justice: The History of Brown v Board of Education and Black America's Struggle for Equality* (1976); Gerald N. Rosenberg, *The Hollow Hope: Can Courts Bring About Social Change* (1991); Mark Tushnet, *The NAACP's Legal Strategy Against Segregated Education, 1925–1950* (1987).

Gerald N. Rosenberg
University of Chicago, Illinois

Chicago, Burlington & Quincy Railroad Company v. Chicago, 166 U.S. 226 (1897): Railroad Regulation and Substantive Due Process of Law

This landmark case arose when the city of Chicago utilized eminent domain to open a street across part of a railroad right-of-way. The jury in the condemnation proceeding fixed the amount of $1 as the compensation due to the railroad for the land taken. After this judgment was affirmed by the Illinois Supreme Court, the railroad appealed to the U.S. Supreme Court, arguing that the Illinois proceeding had deprived it of property without due process of law in violation of the Fourteenth Amendment. The city responded that the amount of compensation to be awarded for land taken was a matter of local law and posed no federal constitutional question. The Bill of Rights, including the Takings clause, was originally understood as restraining the federal government, not the states.

Speaking for the Court, Justice John Marshall Harlan rejected the city's argument and ruled that payment of just compensation when private property was taken for public use was an essential element of due process. He observed that the mere form of a proceeding did not satisfy due process if the owner was deprived of property without compensation. In this path-breaking decision, the Court read the due process clause as imposing a substantive restraint on state exercise of eminent domain. Consequently, the just compensation norm became in effect the first provision of the Bill of Rights to be applied to the states. Moreover, the decision was a harbinger of later cases, which found that other provisions of the Bill of Rights were incorporated into the Fourteenth Amendment and protected against abridgement by the states.

Sources and Further Reading: James W. Ely, Jr., "The Fuller Court and Takings Jurisprudence," *1996 Journal of Supreme Court History 2* (1996); John E. Semonche, *Charting the Future: The Supreme Court Responds to a Changing Society, 1890–1920* (1978).

James W. Ely, Jr.
Vanderbilt University, Tennessee

Dred Scott v. Sandford, 60 U.S. (19 How.) 393 (1857): Fugitive Slavery and Race, Missouri, Minnesota, and Illinois

In the 1830s, Dr. John Emerson, a U.S. Army surgeon from Missouri, brought his slave Dred Scott to military posts in Illinois and that part of the Wisconsin territory that later became Minnesota. In 1846, Scott sued Emerson's widow, Irene, for freedom based on his residence in those two free jurisdictions. Scott argued that under Illinois's 1818 constitution, he became free the moment Emerson took him to that state, and that he also gained his freedom in Minnesota under the Missouri Compromise, which banned slavery north and west of the state of Missouri.

In 1850, a jury in St. Louis declared Scott free, but in *Scott v. Emerson* (1852), the Missouri Supreme Court, reversing state precedents dating from 1824, held that residence in free jurisdictions did not change Scott's legal status. Irene Emerson soon remarried and transferred ownership of Scott to her brother, John Sanford (the Supreme Court misspelled his name in the case), who lived in New York City. Scott then sued in federal court for his freedom, asserting that the Court had diversity jurisdiction because this suit was between citizens of different states. Relying on state law, the federal court in Missouri held Scott was still a slave.

The U.S. Supreme Court, by a vote of seven to two, upheld this result, holding that the Illinois constitution could not affect his status once he left Illinois, and that the Missouri Compromise's ban on slavery in the territories was unconstitutional. Chief Justice Roger B. Taney further ruled that no black, whether slave or free, could ever be considered a citizen of the United States. Opposition to this decision launched the career of Abraham Lincoln, who campaigned against the decision in the 1858 senatorial race and later in his successful bid to be the Republican nominee for president in 1860.

Sources and Further Reading: Don E. Fehrenbacher, *The Dred Scott Case: Its Significance in American Law and Politics* (1978); Paul Finkelman, *Dred Scott v Sandford: A Brief History* (1997).

Paul Finkelman
University of Tulsa, Oklahoma

Escobedo v. Illinois, 378 U.S. 478 (1964): Right to Counsel in a Criminal Investigation

The U.S. Supreme Court decision in *Escobedo v. Illinois* (1964) had an impact on politics and popular culture as well as on constitutional law. It raised the issue of when a person in police custody can claim the constitutional right to an attorney.

While being aggressively interrogated by Chicago police about the murder of his brother-in-law, Danny Escobedo repeatedly asked to consult his attorney, who was simultaneously demanding to see him. Denied a lawyer, Escobedo finally confessed and was subsequently convicted. The Supreme Court, in a five-to-four decision, threw out this confession and reversed Escobedo's conviction.

Justice Arthur Goldberg's majority opinion held that a person in custody needed an attorney whenever he or she became the prime suspect or the focus of an investigation that had shifted to an accusatory mode. This decision enraged police officials, and prominent Republicans cited it during the 1964 campaign as proof of the Supreme Court's disregard for law and order. Attorneys quickly flooded the courts with "Escobedo cases," appeals involving the denial of a lawyer. Facing intense political and legal pressure, the Supreme Court in 1966 abandoned the Escobedo rationale in favor of the famous, and easier to administer, Miranda warning.

Meanwhile, Danny Escobedo remained a notorious though minor celebrity in Chicago. He became an amateur artist, even selling several paintings to the curious. But continual run-ins with the law on charges ranging from weapons violations to child molestation continued for nearly forty years and eventually earned Escobedo the label of career criminal.

Sources and Further Reading: Lucas A. Powe, Jr., *The Warren Court and American Politics* (2000); Melvin I. Urofsky, *The Warren Court: Justices, Rulings, and Legacy* (2001).

Norman L. Rosenberg
Macalester College, Minnesota

Euclid v. Ambler Realty Co., 272 U.S. 365 (1926): Zoning in Cleveland, Ohio

Efforts by the Village of Euclid, a suburb of Cleveland, to preserve its rural and residential character gave rise to a landmark decision upholding comprehensive zoning. Although still largely rural in 1900, Euclid was in the path of industrial growth emanating from Cleveland. In the 1910s, Ambler Realty purchased farmland in the village in anticipation of future industrial growth. However, in November 1922, the village adopted a zoning ordinance that restricted much of the land owned by Ambler Realty to residential purposes. Fueled in part by the desire to maintain residential property values and to exclude undesirable uses from residential districts, zoning controls were widely adopted in the United States during the 1920s. Ambler Realty challenged the ordinance as a deprivation of property without due process in violation of the Fourteenth Amendment. The federal district judge invalidated the Euclid zoning ordinance, and observed that the village could only achieve its goal by acquiring the land through eminent domain. He added that the result of this ordinance would be to straitjacket undeveloped land and to foster economic segregation.

By a vote of six to three, the Supreme Court reversed the district judge and sustained the constitutionality of zoning. The Court embraced the view that urban congestion required increased restrictions on the use of privately-owned land, and that the establishment of an environment favorable for single-family dwellings was within the state police power to safeguard public health and safety. The decision gave impetus to restrictive zoning in suburbs, which in turn made housing more expensive. Ironically, the land involved in the *Euclid* case later was developed for manufacturing.

Sources and Further Reading: Charles M. Haar and Jerold S. Kayden, eds. *Zoning and the American Dream* (1989); Seymour I. Toll, *Zoned American* (1969).

James W. Ely, Jr.
Vanderbilt University, Tennessee

Ex Parte Milligan, 71 U.S. 2 (1866): Authority of Military Courts over Civilians during the Civil War, Indiana

Ex parte Milligan is a ringing affirmation of American civil liberties in wartime as well as in times of peace. The case began in the deeply partisan politics surrounding the 1864 presidential election in Indiana. Lambdin P. Milligan, a prominent antiwar Democrat, was arrested along with several other members of a secret society, the Sons of Liberty, and charged with numerous offenses including conspiracy against the government of the United States and giving aid and comfort to the enemy. Milligan was tried by a military commission, convicted, and sentenced to hang. After the South's surrender at Appomattox, ending the Civil War, he petitioned the federal courts for a writ of habeas corpus, insisting that military trials were unconstitutional where the civil courts were functioning.

Milligan provided the opportunity for the U.S. Supreme Court to examine the extent of governmental authority during wartime. Lincoln had suspended habeas corpus throughout the nation in 1862, and kept dissent in check thereafter with thousands of arrests and trials of civilians in the North and Midwest. The Court unanimously agreed with Milligan that military courts had no jurisdiction to try civilians outside the theater of war in areas that had remained loyal to the United States. Justice David Davis acknowledged the government's right to suspend habeas corpus, which was necessary during times of crisis, but insisted that the founders intended the rights of trial by jury and due process to "remain forever inviolable." Martial law was a "gross usurpation of power" where civilian courts were open and functioning. Significantly, *Milligan* was decided after the war, when danger was past. The case came to be considered a bulwark of American civil liberties.

Sources and Further Reading: Frank L. Klement, "The Indianapolis Treason Trials and *ex parte Milligan*," in Michael R. Belknap, ed., *American Political Trials*, rev. ed. (1994); Mark E. Neeley, Jr., *The Fate of Liberty* (1991).

Lou Williams
Kansas State University

The Genesee Chief v. The Fitzhugh, 484 U.S. 469, 470 (1852): Admiralty Regulation on the Great Lakes

A collision between two ships on Lake Ontario set the stage for the Supreme Court to enlarge the scope of federal admiralty jurisdiction. The Constitution states that federal judicial power extends "to all cases of admiralty or maritime jurisdiction." In 1845, Congress expanded the jurisdiction of the federal courts to certain cases arising on the Great Lakes because of rapid growth of commerce in the region. The traditional English rule confined admiralty jurisdiction to tidal waters, and this view had previously been adopted by the Supreme Court. In *Genesee Chief*, however, the Court ruled that congressional authority encompassed navigable waters and was not dependent on the ebb and flow of the tide. Speaking for the Court, Chief Justice Roger B. Taney stressed that the English rule was impractical in the United States, with its major rivers and large inland lakes. It followed that the 1845 act was a valid exercise of congressional authority over admiralty matters. Justice Peter V. Daniel dissented, arguing that federal admiralty jurisdiction was fixed by the English practice at the time the Constitution was adopted.

The outcome in *Genesee Chief* meant that uniform federal admiralty principles would govern shipping on the Great Lakes and interior river arteries. This development facilitated the growth of navigation and commerce on inland waters. Further, the decision demonstrated the Supreme Court's willingness to modify legal doctrine to take account of new technology. The emergence of the steamboat cast travel on inland waterways in a new light and compelled a reconsideration of prior doctrine.

Sources and Further Reading: Milton Conover, "The Abandonment of the 'Tidewater' Concept of Admiralty Jurisdiction in the United States," *Oregon Law Review* 38 (Dec. 1958); Carl B. Swisher, *The Taney Period, 1836–64* (1974); Charles Warren, *The Supreme Court in United States History* (1926).

James W. Ely, Jr.
Vanderbilt University, Tennessee

Home Building and Loan Association v. Blaisdell, 290 U.S. 398 (1934): Mortgage Moratorium and the Great Depression, Minnesota

In 1933, Minnesota passed a Mortgage Moratorium Act authorizing its state courts to consider exempting mortgaged property from bank foreclosures. Such legislation was common among midwestern states seeking to provide relief to debtors in the throes of the Great Depression of the 1930s. A test of the law's constitutionality took place when a mortgagor, the Home Building and Loan Association, refused to allow Mr. and Mrs. John H. Blaisdell, mortgagees, to extend their mortgage redemption period for a house and lot in Minneapolis and attempted to foreclose on the Blaisdell's property.

In a five-to-four decision, the U.S. Supreme Court upheld the constitutionality of the Minnesota legislation. Chief Justice Charles Evans Hughes, writing for the majority, held that the law did not run afoul of language in the U.S. Constitution that forbids states from passing legislation "impairing the Obligation for Contracts." Hughes maintained that a state always possesses the authority to safeguard the vital interests of its citizens. In his words, "[w]hile emergency does not create power, emergency may furnish the occasion for the exercise of power."

The four justices in dissent refused to acknowledge that an economic emergency, even one on the scale of the Great Depression, could justify state modification of contracts. While this literalist interpretation was in the minority on the Supreme Court in this instance, it captured another vote or two in many other economic regulation cases coming before the Court in the 1930s. In fact, it was not until 1937 that a majority of the Supreme Court could be counted upon to affirm consistently state or federal regulatory legislation attempting to address the ills of the Great Depression.

Sources and Further Reading: Charles A. Bieneman, "Legal Interpretation and a Constitutional Case: *Home Building & Loan Association* v *Blaisdell*," *Michigan Law Review* 90 (Aug. 1992); William Prosser, "The Minnesota Mortgage Moratorium," *Southern California Law Review* 7 (May 1934); G. Edward White, *The Constitution and the New Deal* (2000).

John W. Johnson
University of Northern Iowa

Illinois ex rel. McCollum v. Board of Education, 333 U.S. 203 (1948): The First Amendment and Religion in Schools

Beginning in 1940, the Champaign, Illinois, school system, like many across the country, put aside one hour a week when clergymen from all denominations could come into the schools and provide religious instruction to adherents of their sects. The clergy received no public funds, but were subject to approval by the school superintendent. Students whose parents did not request religious instruction went elsewhere in the building; those enrolled were required to attend the religious classes. The case was brought by Vashti McCollum, who became a leading humanist and an honorary officer of the Freedom from Religion Foundation.

Of the nine justices, only Stanley Reed thought the plan constitutional. Justice Hugo L. Black, writing for the majority, declared it an unacceptable public benefit to religion. Justice Felix Frankfurter agreed with Black that the plan violated the First Amendment, but Frankfurter wanted the Court's decision to include all forms of public support for religious schools. The key to Frankfurter's decision in *McCollum* is his view of the public school as an Americanizing and unifying force, a place where children from all backgrounds developed a common American outlook.

The *McCollum* decision stirred up a nationwide furor among religious groups, nearly all of whom operated some form of released time program in the public schools. Enforcement of the opinion varied. In northern states where religious instruction actually took place in public school classrooms, there seems to have been general compliance. But in most southern states and in areas where local school boards could differentiate between the Illinois model and theirs, religious instruction continued.

Sources and Further Reading: Leonard W. Levy, *The Establishment Clause: Religion and the First Amendment* (1986); Frank J. Sorauf, *The Wall of Separation: The Constitutional Politics of Church and State* (1976).

Melvin I. Urofsky
Virginia Commonwealth University

Mapp v. Ohio, 367 U.S. 643 (1961): The Exclusionary Rule

Mapp v. Ohio (1961) is a landmark Supreme Court case establishing that any evidence obtained in violation of the search-and-seizure protection of the Fourth Amendment is not admissible in a state court proceeding. This exclusion of evidence is referred to as the exclusionary rule.

The case involved Dollree Mapp, who resided in Cleveland, Ohio. The police came to her home looking for a bombing suspect. Mapp refused to admit the officers without a search warrant. The police forced entry into the home and presented a piece of paper as a search warrant. The police searched the home without Mapp's permission or allowing her to see the warrant. During the search, "lewd and lascivious" books were found. Mapp was arrested and charged with possession of obscene materials.

Although no search warrant was produced at the trial, Mapp was found guilty. Mapp appealed her case to the Ohio Supreme Court but was denied. Mapp then appealed to the U.S. Supreme Court, which held that the search was illegal and that the evidence should be excluded from the trial.

❖ **The Exclusionary Rule**

The majority opinion of Justice Tom C. Clark in *Mapp v. Ohio*, which established the landmark Exclusionary Rule, is excerpted below:

Since the Fourth Amendment's right of privacy has been declared enforceable against the States through the Due Process Clause of the Fourteenth, it is enforceable against them by the same sanction of exclusion as is used against the Federal Government. Were it otherwise, then . . . the assurance against unreasonable federal searches and seizures would be "a form of words," valueless and undeserving of mention in a perpetual charter of inestimable human liberties, so too, without that rule the freedom from state invasions of privacy would be so ephemeral and so neatly severed from its conceptual nexus with the freedom from all brutish means of coercing evidence as not to merit this Court's high regard as a freedom "implicit in the concept of ordered liberty". . . . Therefore, in extending the substantive protections of due process to all constitutionally unreasonable searches—state or federal—it was logically and constitutionally necessary that the exclusion doctrine—an essential part of the right to privacy—be also insisted upon as an essential ingredient of the right newly recognized by the Wolf case. [*Wolf v. Colorado*, 338 U.S. 25 (1949)]

. . . Having once recognized that the right to privacy embodied in the Fourth Amendment is enforceable against the state, and that the right to be secure against rude invasions of privacy by state officers is, therefore, constitutional in origin, we can no longer permit that right to remain an empty promise. Because it is enforceable in the same manner and to the like effect as other basic rights secured by the Due Process Clause, we can no longer permit it to be revocable at the whim of any police officer who, in the name of law enforcement itself, chooses to suspend its enjoyment.

Our decision, founded on reason and truth, gives to the individual no more than that which the Constitution guarantees him, to the police officer no less than that to which honest law enforcement is entitled, and, to the courts, that judicial integrity so necessary in the true administration of justice.

Source: Mapp v. Ohio, 367 U.S. Reports 643 (1961).

In prior Supreme Court cases, *Weeks v. United States* (1914) and *Wolf v. Colorado* (1949), the court applied the exclusionary rule to federal proceedings and held that the Fourth Amendment was binding on the states. However, the Wolf ruling did not make the Fourteenth Amendment binding in state proceedings. Not until *Mapp v. Ohio* did the Supreme Court reconsider the Wolf ruling and determine that the Fourteenth Amendment applied to the states and thus also did the exclusionary rule.

Sources and Further Reading: *Mapp* v *Ohio*, 367 U.S. 643 (1961); *Weeks* v *United States*, 232 U.S. 383 (1914); *Wolf* v *Colorado*, 338 U.S. 25 (1949).

N. Y. Parsons-Pollard
Virginia Commonwealth University

Minor v. Happersett, 88 U.S. (21 Wall.) 162 (1875): Missouri Constitutionally Forbade Women the Vote

Minor v. Happersett was a landmark case that denied women the right to vote, affecting the strategy of the women's suffrage movement. In 1869, Missouri suffrage activists Virginia and Francis Minor argued that women's rights were protected by the U.S. Constitution because voting was an element of popular sovereignty. Although the Reconstruction Amendments did not mention women's rights, the Minors argued that the Fourteenth Amendment protected women's voting rights because it protected the "privileges and immunities" of U.S. citizens, and women were citizens. Based on such arguments, many women sought to exercise the right to vote. Virginia Minor tried to register to vote in St. Louis, Missouri, on October 15, 1872. Following state law, Registrar Reese Happersett refused to register her. This gave the Minors grounds for a case testing the constitutionality of voting restrictions.

A St. Louis trial court and the Missouri Supreme Court upheld Happersett's actions, and the Minors appealed to the U.S. Supreme Court. The State of Missouri was so confident about the outcome that it did not send an attorney to argue its case. On March 29, 1875, a unanimous Supreme Court ruled that states did not violate the Constitution when they denied women the right to vote. Women were citizens of the United States, the Court found, but voting was not a right of citizenship.

Minor foreclosed the argument that women's right to vote was protected by existing constitutional provisions. Some suffragists therefore sought a federal constitutional amendment, while others worked to reform state voting laws. The Nineteenth Amendment to the U.S. Constitution, guaranteeing women's right to vote, was ratified in 1920.

Sources and Further Reading: Norma Basch, "Reconstructing Female Citizenship: *Minor* v *Happersett*," in Donald G. Nieman, ed., *The Constitution, Law, and American Life* (1992); Ellen Carol DuBois, *Woman Suffrage and Women's Rights* (1998); Eleanor Flexner and Ellen Fitzpatrick, *Century of Struggle*, enlarged ed. (1996).

Mary L. Dudziak
University of Southern California

Missouri v. Holland, 252 U.S. 416 (1920): Migratory Bird Treaty and Its Impact on the Midwest

In 1913, conservationists were successful in gaining a federal law protecting all migratory birds. This was seen as a way of sidestepping state legislatures that provided little or no regulations on hunting. The legislation was buried as a rider to the Agriculture Appropriations Bill. President William H. Taft signed the bill in the closing hours of his administration in March 1913 without reading it, and later stated he would not have signed it if he had known of the rider. The broad sweep of the rider, known as the Weeks-McLean Act, challenged many of the constitutional scruples of the day. States immediately questioned the validity of the act, and several lower courts ruled that the law was unconstitutional because it violated the Tenth Amendment, which reserves for the states all powers not specifically delegated to the federal government by the Constitution.

Fearful that the U.S. Supreme Court would declare the law unconstitutional, conservationists scurried to find a way to bolster their case. Acting on the advice of Senator Elihu Root of New York, conservationists lobbied the new administration of President Woodrow Wilson to enter negotiations with Great Britain and Canada to form a treaty that would extend protection of migratory birds to the Arctic. This tactic was intended to provide a sound legal foundation to the conservationists' goals, since under the constitution, treaties become binding law in the United States. The treaties were signed and ratified in December 1916. Congress passed the Migratory Bird Treaty Act as enabling legislation in July 1918.

States' rights proponents in Missouri denounced the law as an unconstitutional restraint on hunting on the major migratory flyway through the state. Mis-

souri went to court to enjoin a federal game warden, Ray Holland, from enforcing the regulations of the 1918 act, claiming that it violated the Tenth Amendment to the Constitution.

On April 19, 1920, the U.S. Supreme Court affirmed that the treaty-making powers of the federal government represent the law of the land and cannot be restrained by the Tenth Amendment, even if the treaty enacted a law that had been previously declared unconstitutional in a lower court. *Missouri vs. Holland* was a landmark in the march of federal power during the twentieth century and a significant enhancement of environmental policy designed to protect millions of migratory birds.

Sources and Further Reading: Alexander M. Bickel and Benno C. Schmidt, Jr., *History of the Supreme Court of the United States*, vol. 9 (1984); Kurkpatrick Dorsey, *The Dawn of Conservation Diplomacy* (1998); Thomas Healy, "Is *Missouri* v *Holland* Still Good Law? Federalism and the Treaty Power," *Columbia Law Review* 98 (Nov. 1998).

Gregory Dehler
Front Range Community College, Colorado

Missouri ex rel. Gaines v. Canada, 305 U.S. 337 (1938): Admission of an African American to an All-White Law School

Prior to the Supreme Court's landmark 1954 decision in *Brown v. Board of Education*, outlawing all state-imposed segregation, the separate-but-equal doctrine allowed southern and border states, such as Missouri, to operate racially segregated public schools and universities. In the 1930s, lawyers for the National Association for the Advancement of Colored People (NAACP) developed a strategy that ultimately resulted in the *Brown* decision. The strategy began with challenges to the most discriminatory features of segregated higher education.

Missouri was the target state. Like many of the states with segregated universities, Missouri did not provide graduate or professional schools for African Americans within the state, but instead arranged to pay their tuition in neighboring states. In 1935, the NAACP challenged this practice on behalf of Lloyd Gaines, an African American who would have been admitted to the University of Missouri law school but for his race. The case was litigated within the analytical framework of the separate-but-equal doctrine, and the NAACP argued that if Missouri provided a law school for whites within the state, it had to provide one for African Americans within the state as well.

In 1938, the Supreme Court agreed. It held that whatever benefit the state provided for one race within the state had to be provided equally for the other race. The Supreme Court had now cut sharply into the separate-but-equal doctrine and was on its way to burying it in the landmark *Brown* decision.

Sources and Further Reading: Richard Kluger, *Simple Justice* (1976); Loren Miller, *The Petitioners* (1966); Mark V. Tushnet, *The NAACP's Legal Strategy Against Segregated Education, 1925–1950* (1987).

Robert A. Sedler
Wayne State University, Michigan

Near v. Minnesota, 283 U.S. 697 (1931): The First Amendment and Yellow Journalism

In the late 1920s, the *Saturday Press* was one of hundreds of scandal-mongering newspapers published in the United States. Publishers Howard Guilford and Jay M. Near, however, focused their energies on attacking corrupt government in the Twin Cities of Minneapolis and St. Paul, Minnesota. Their weekly attacks were aimed not only at government leaders, but also at Jews, nonwhites, labor unions, and other minorities. Earlier, at the turn of the twentieth century, Joseph Pulitzer (*New York World*) and William Randolph Hearst (*New York Journal American*) had introduced sensationalism and wildly biased reporting in their papers that came to be known as yellow journalism, derived from a comic strip "The Yellow Kid" that appeared in their papers.

Eventually, local government officials had enough. Invoking a public nuisance law, they succeeded in having the newspaper closed. Under the law, an offending publication was required to prove not only the truth of its publication but also its good motives. Near, who was abandoned by Guilford, had little money with which to fight the charges. He received some support from the fledgling American Civil Liberties Union, but most of his help came from Weymouth Kirkland, the attorney for the *Chicago Tribune*. Kirkland convinced *Tribune* publisher Colonel Robert R. McCormick that it would be in the best interests of the *Tribune* to help the *Saturday Press* fight the prior restraint.

The Minnesota Supreme Court upheld Near's conviction. Kirkland appealed to the Supreme Court but was not optimistic, in part because of one of the Court's newest Justices, Louis Brandeis. Brandeis was Jewish, and the *Saturday Press* had often attacked Jews.

Brandeis voted with the majority, however, holding that the Minnesota law was a violation of the First Amendment. Writing for five members of the Court, Chief Justice Charles Evans Hughes found the law to be a prior restraint, which the Court said for the first time, was unconstitutional.

Sources and Further Reading: Fred W. Friendly, *Minnesota Rag* (1981); *Near v Minnesota*, 283 U.S. 697 (1931).

W. Wat Hopkins
Virginia Polytechnic Institute
and State University

Northern Securities Co. v. United States, 193 U.S. 197 (1904): Sherman Antitrust Act and the Regulation of Business, Minnesota

Northern involves the merger of the Great Northern and Northern Pacific Railway into a holding company, in which JP Morgan held interests. The railroads operated parallel trunk lines connecting the Great Lakes region to the Pacific Northwest. *Northern* was found by the U.S. Circuit Court in Minnesota to reduce competition in freight and passenger commerce under the Sherman Antitrust Act of 1890. On appeal, the case intrigued "trust-busting" president Theodore Roosevelt, who favored the act as a means to bring big business under closer executive administrative control and the scrutiny of a public leery of corporate combinations. In 1903, Congress passed legislation to expedite antitrust cases. Legislation, complemented by Roosevelt appointee and friend Justice Oliver Wendell Holmes, Jr., made the act a potential swift threat to trusts.

The U.S. Supreme Court upheld the *Northern* decision, following a literal interpretation of Section One of the act: "Every contract, combination in the form of trust or otherwise, or conspiracy, in restraint of trade or commerce among the several States, or with foreign nations, is hereby declared to be illegal." Much to the disappointment of Roosevelt, however, Holmes produced an eloquent dissent. Holmes favored common law, which condemned combinations that harm strangers (such as price-fixing). Furthermore, both parties were trading ownership of stocks, which is neither interstate commerce nor a direct violation of the act. Inherent in the decision is the juxtaposed legacy of the act: Populist, agrarian anger, tempered by Progressive "reasonable" restraints of trade. *Northern* affirmed governmental ability to regulate trusts and ruined the friendship between Roosevelt and Holmes.

❖ **Great cases make bad law**

The dissenting opinion of Justice Oliver Wendell Holmes in the case of *Northern Securities Co. v. United States* (1904) is excerpted below:

> I am unable to agree with the judgment of the majority of the court, and although I think it useless and undesirable, as a rule, to express dissent, I feel bound to do so in this case, and to give my reasons for it.
>
> Great cases, like hard cases, make bad law. For great cases are called great, not by reason of their real importance in shaping the law of the future, but because of some accident of immediate overwhelming interest which appeals to the feelings and distorts the judgment. These immediate interests exercise a kind of hydraulic pressure which makes what previously was clear seem doubtful, and before which even well settled principles of law will bend. What we have to do in this case is to find the meaning of some not very difficult words. We must try, I have tried, to do it with the same freedom of natural and spontaneous interpretation that one would be sure of if the same question arose upon an indictment for a similar act which excited no public attention, and was of importance only to a prisoner before the court. . . .
>
> I am happy to know that only a minority of my brethren adopt an interpretation of the law which in my opinion would make eternal the *bellum omnium contra omnes* [a war of all against all] and disintegrate society so far as it could into individual atoms. If that were its intent, I should regard calling such a law a regulation of commerce as a mere pretense. It would be an attempt to reconstruct society. I am not concerned with the wisdom of such an attempt, but I believe that Congress was not entrusted by the Constitution with the power to make it, and I am deeply persuaded that it has not tried.

Source: Northern Securities Co. v. United States, 193 U.S. Report 197 (1904).

Sources and Further Reading: Balthasar Henry Meyer, *A History of the Northern Securities Case* (1906); *Northern Securities Co. v United States*, 193 U.S. 197 (1904); Richard H. Wagner, "A Falling Out: The Relationship Between Oliver Wendell Holmes and Theodore Roosevelt," *Journal of Supreme Court History* (July 2002); Albert H. Walker, *History of the Sherman Law of the United States of America* (1980).

Timothy L. Miller
Art Institute of California–Orange County

Presser v. Illinois, 116 U.S. 252 (1886): Right to Bear Arms and Parade with Them

In *Presser*, the U.S. Supreme Court upheld a state statute that prohibited armed parading by groups other than the organized militia. The case began in 1879, when Herman Presser was convicted of unlawfully leading a private company of four hundred armed men in a parade in Chicago. He appealed, arguing that an Illinois statute violated the Second Amendment's right to bear arms and the Fourteenth Amendment. The Supreme Court's opinion, written by Justice William Burnham Woods, rejected Presser's claims, holding that the Second Amendment only applied to the federal government and that the Fourteenth Amendment, reserving for the states all powers not specifically assigned to the federal government by the Constitution, did not make the Second Amendment applicable to the states.

Justice Woods noted that the statute did not interfere with the right to keep and bear arms. The opinion also noted that states could not disarm their populations because that would interfere with the federal government's ability to raise a militia from the population at large. Despite this, the opinion stressed that the Second Amendment only limited action by the federal government.

The modern validity of *Presser* is unclear. It is still relied on by lower federal courts, but its reasoning contradicts much of modern constitutional jurisprudence. In the twentieth century, the Supreme Court used the Fourteenth Amendment to apply most of the provisions of the Bill of Rights to the states. It has not done so with the Second Amendment, but the Supreme Court heard only one Second Amendment case in the twentieth century.

Source and Further Reading: David B. Kopel, "The Second Amendment in the Nineteenth Century," *Brigham Young University Law Review* 116 (1998).

Robert J. Cottrol
George Washington University,
Washington, D.C.

Shelley v. Kraemer and *McGhee v. Sipes*, 334 U.S. 1 (1948): Racially Restricted Home Ownership

Prior to the Supreme Court's 1948 decision in cases coming from Missouri and Michigan, it was possible for white residents to use racially restrictive covenants to keep African Americans and other racial minorities from buying homes in the neighborhood.

The covenant would provide that no minority person could own a home in the neighborhood, and if a minority person did manage to buy a home there, the other homeowners could secure a court order requiring the minority person to leave. In these cases, the Supreme Court held that state court enforcement of racially restrictive covenants violated the constitutional rights of the minority homeowner.

Since the Constitution applies only to governmental or state action, and not to the actions of private persons, the covenants themselves were not illegal. But the Supreme Court held that the Constitution prohibited the state courts from enforcing them. The enforcement of the covenants constituted state action, and it violated the Constitution, because the courts would be using their power to prevent people from buying a home solely because of their race.

The decision was very important. It stopped enforcement of racially restrictive covenants, which were not only widespread among homeowners, but were actually required by the Federal Housing Authority (FHA) as a condition for an FHA-backed loan. It also resulted in an expansive interpretation of "state action" in later cases where the state was found to be involved in the racial discrimination practiced by private individuals, so that there was a constitutional violation.

Sources and Further Reading: Louis Henkin, "*Shelley* v. *Kraemer:* Notes for a Revised Opinion," *University of Pennsylvania Law Review* 110 (Feb. 1962); Richard Kluger, *Simple Justice* (1976); Loren Miller, *The Petitioners* (1966).

Robert A. Sedler
Wayne State University, Michigan

Swift & Company v. United States, 196 U.S. 375 (1905): Antitrust and Meatpacking, Illinois

Gustavus F. Swift built a huge meatpacking business during the last quarter of the nineteenth century. Based in Chicago, Swift & Company became one of the five largest meatpacking firms in the United States. It was part of the Beef Trust, which by the beginning of the twentieth century, collectively dominated the business of bringing meat products to consumers throughout the country.

In 1902, the U.S. Attorney General charged the Beef Trust with violation of the Sherman Antitrust Act by conspiring and combining to control livestock, fix meat prices, suppress competition, and restrain interstate trade. Swift countered that the company had not participated in interstate commerce because its livestock was bought and sold locally.

In 1905, the U.S. Supreme Court unanimously rejected Swift's argument. Justice Oliver Wendell Holmes, Jr., wrote that the federal government has authority to regulate commerce within a state if it is part of a "current of commerce among the states, and the purchase of the cattle is a part and incident of such commerce."

The Court concluded that local economic activities could be tied intentionally and inseparably by a "stream of commerce" whereby particular intrastate transactions, such as the buying and selling of livestock, could be connected subsequently to the national distribution of meat products. If so, then the business was subject to federal regulation in the public interest. The Court's stream of commerce doctrine expanded the federal government's commerce power far beyond the narrow conception proclaimed in *United States v. E. C. Knight Company* (1895).

Source and Further Reading: David Gordon, "*Swift & Company* v. *United States:* The Beef Trust and the Stream of Commerce Doctrine," *American Journal of Legal History* 28 (July 1984).

John J. Patrick
Indiana University–Bloomington

Tinker v. Des Moines Independent Community School District, 393 U.S. 503 (1969): Symbolic Speech and the First Amendment, Vietnam War

In December 1965, a handful of teenagers in Des Moines, Iowa, decided to wear black armbands to school to express sorrow for casualties in the Vietnam War and to encourage a truce in hostilities. The city school district suspended some of the offending students for violating a rule prohibiting the classroom display of protest materials. Represented by the Iowa Civil Liberties Union, three of the armband-wearing students—Christopher Eckhardt, John Tinker, and Mary Beth Tinker—challenged the school district's position in federal court.

Although not as newsworthy or as unruly as antiwar demonstrations elsewhere, the peaceful armband protest in America's Heartland led to the U.S. Supreme Court's most significant decision on student rights. In the 1969 opinion of Associate Justice Abe Fortas in *Tinker v. Des Moines,* and joined by all but two of its members, the Court held that "[i]t can hardly be

❖ **Education and the First Amendment**

The majority and dissenting opinions of the U. S. Supreme Court in the case of *Tinker v. Des Moines* (1969) are excerpted below:

First Amendment rights, applied in light of the special characteristics of the school environment, are available to teachers and students. It can hardly be argued that either students or teachers shed their constitutional rights to freedom of speech or expression at the schoolhouse gate. . . . In our system, state-operated schools may not be enclaves of totalitarianism. School officials do not possess absolute authority over their students. Students in school as well as out of school are 'persons' under our Constitution. They are possessed of fundamental rights which the State must respect, just as they themselves must respect their obligations to the State. Associate Justice Abe Fortas, majority opinion

One does not need to be a prophet or the son of a prophet to know that after the Court's holding today some students in Iowa schools . . . will be ready, able, and willing to defy their teachers on practically all orders. This is the more unfortunate for the schools since groups of students all over the land are already running loose, conducting break-ins, sit-ins, lie-ins, and smash-ins. . . . This case . . . , wholly without constitutional reasons in my judgment, subjects all the public schools in the country to the whims and caprices of their loudest-mouthed, but maybe not their brightest, students. Associate Justice Hugo Black, dissenting opinion

Source: Tinker v. Des Moines, 393 U.S. Report 503 (1969).

argued that . . . students . . . shed their constitutional rights to freedom of . . . expression at the schoolhouse gate," and since the conduct of the armband-wearing students did not constitute "substantial disruption of or material interference with school activities," their demonstration of conviction was protected under the First Amendment to the U.S. Constitution.

Over the last three decades, the *Tinker* precedent has been greatly qualified. For example, in another case from the Midwest, *Hazelwood School District v. Kuhlmeier* (1988), the U.S. Supreme Court upheld censorship of a Missouri high school newspaper, concluding that a school principal's decision to excise some material because it might be disturbing to readers was reasonably grounded in the law. *Hazelwood* notwithstanding, *Tinker v. Des Moines* remains the starting point for discussions of student rights.

Source and Further Reading: John W. Johnson, *The Struggle for Student Rights* (1997).

John W. Johnson
University of Northern Iowa

Wisconsin v. Yoder, 406 U.S. 205 (1972): Application of Mandatory School Attendance Law to the Amish Mennonite Church

In a case decided by the Supreme Court on May 15, 1972, by vote of six to one, Chief Justice Warren Burger ruled that states may not force the Amish to send their children to public high school because compulsory attendance violated the free exercise of religion under the First Amendment. The case arose in New Glarus, in Green County, Wisconsin, where a new Amish settlement was being formed. Three Conservative Amish Mennonite fathers were arrested in 1968 because they failed to enroll their children in high school, in violation of Wisconsin's compulsory school attendance law.

The majority agreed with the Amish that enforcement of this law would gravely endanger their religious beliefs and the survival of the sect, in light of their long history as a self-sufficient, unique religious community. The Amish also argued that high school attendance emphasizes intellectual and scientific accomplishments, self-distinction, and competitiveness, values that conflicted with the Amish values of learning through doing, community welfare, and separation from worldly society. The Amish met the difficult burden of demonstrating that their alternative mode of informal vocational education did not violate the objectives upon which the Wisconsin compulsory school law was based.

The Court emphasized that without such a long history of uniqueness and self-sufficiency, courts should not grant religious exemptions from compulsory school attendance. Scholars question the Court's reasoning in favoring students with prescribed religious beliefs and long-standing membership in religious communities while withholding such opportunities from others whose moral choices are based on secular grounds.

Sources and Further Reading: John A. Hostetler, *Amish Society,* 4th ed. (1993); James Davison Hunter and Os Guiness, eds., *Articles of Faith, Articles of Peace* (1990); Donald B. Kraybill, *The Riddle of Amish Culture,* rev. ed. (2001).

Ronald Kahn
Oberlin College, Ohio

The Haymarket Trials, Illinois

The Haymarket Trials are remembered as among the most unjust in American history. On May 1, 1886, forty thousand workers in Chicago went out on strike in an attempt to establish an eight-hour working day. A protest rally began on the evening of May 4 near the Haymarket in response to the killing of a striker by the police at the McCormick Reaper Works plant. As the protest was drawing to a close, 180 Chicago police arrived, led by Inspector John Bonfield and Captain William Ward, and demanded that the rally disperse. A protester threw a bomb at the police, who responded by opening fire. In all, eight police were killed and approximately sixty more were injured. The exact number of casualties among the protesters is unknown, though the number is thought to have equaled the police losses. Although the police never identified the bomb thrower, eight protesters faced trial.

Prosecutors secured a favorable jury, and Judge Joseph E. Gary was openly biased against the defendants. The jury found the defendants guilty on the ground that they had given inflammatory speeches that had incited the protesters. The defendants unsuccessfully appealed their convictions to the Illinois Supreme Court, and the U.S. Supreme Court refused to review their case. On November 11, 1887, four of those convicted were hanged: Albert R. Parsons, August Spies, George Engel, and Adolph Fischer. A fifth, Louis Ling, committed suicide the day before his execution. Illinois Governor Richard Oglesby refused to grant pardons to the remaining prisoners, but after his election as governor in 1893, John P. Altgeld issued full pardons to Oscar W. Neebe, Samuel Fielden, and Michael Schwab on the grounds that the jury had been packed and that Judge Gary had been biased.

Sources and Further Reading: Paul Avrich, *The Haymarket Tragedy* (1984); Henry David, *The History of the Haymarket Affair,* 2nd ed. (1958).

R. Blake Brown
Dalhousie University, Nova Scotia, Canada

The Sam Sheppard Trial, Ohio

The trial of Dr. Sam Sheppard led to an important U.S. Supreme Court ruling on the constitutional protections of defendants in criminal actions against prejudicial publicity.

Dr. Sheppard's pregnant wife was beaten to death on July 4, 1954, inside her home in suburban Cleveland. Dr. Sheppard, who was having an affair with another woman, was immediately suspected. The ensuing murder trial became one of the most notorious trials of the century. As the Supreme Court later found, "bedlam reigned at the courthouse," and reporters "took over practically the entire courtroom." A holiday atmosphere infused the proceedings.

Following his conviction, Sheppard appealed to the U.S. Supreme Court, headed by Chief Justice Earl Warren, which then reversed that conviction on the ground that Sheppard had not received a fair trial. In breaking with the judicial custom of placing few constraints on the press' reporting of criminal trials, the Court held that publicity could become so sensational and prejudicial as to deprive the defendant of a fair trial. The Court also outlined various actions the trial judge should have taken to prevent such pervasive and prejudicial publicity or to minimize the effects of it.

The *Sheppard* case was one of the landmark cases of the Warren Court's expansion of Sixth Amendment rights—to trial by an impartial jury—during the 1960s, and it sought to accommodate the news media's First Amendment rights with the defendant's right to trial by an impartial jury.

Source and Further Reading: Lawrence M. Friedman, *Crime and Punishment in American History* (1993).

Patrick M. Garry
Minneapolis, Minnesota

The Chicago Seven, Illinois

The trial began in September 1969, based on the so-called Rap Brown law that made it illegal to cross state lines and make speeches with the intent to "incite, organize, promote, and encourage, participate in, and carry on a riot...." A several-thousand-strong protest against the Vietnam War at the August 1968 Democratic National Convention in Chicago boiled into a full riot. Originally, eight defendants were arrested and prosecuted for a conspiracy to incite riots. Seven of the eight stood trial together: Abbie Hoffman and Jerry Rubin of the Youth International Party, known as "Yippies"; David Dellinger, chair of the National Mobilization against the War; Rennie Davis and Tom Hayden of the Students for a Democratic Society; and John Froines and Lee Weiner, local organizers. All were convicted. Bobby Seale, cofounder of the Black Panther Party, was convicted in a separate trial for contempt.

Lasting five months, the proceedings consolidated national support against the Vietnam War. William Kunstler and Leonard Weinglass, representing the defendants, castigated American culture and politics. They claimed that, as the Walker Report that resulted from the work of the Chicago Study Team established by the National Commission on the Causes and Prevention of Violence found, the brutal response from police forces, inspired by Democratic Mayor Richard Daley, provoked much of the violence. Kunstler used celebrities and advocates to amplify resistance to the military–industrial complex and to advance a progressive social and economic agenda. Prosecutor Thomas Foran and Judge Julius Hoffman clashed continually with the defendants, causing the reversal of their convictions in 1972.

Sources and Further Reading: James Tracy, *Direct Action* (1996); *United States v. Dellinger*, 472 F.2d 340 (7th Cir. 1972), cert. denied, 410 U.S. 970, 93 S. Ct. 1443, 35 L. Ed. 2d 706 (1973); Daniel Walker, *Rights in Conflict* (1968).

Itai Sneh
City University of New York

Major Legal and Judicial Figures Associated with the Midwest

John Armor Bingham (1815–1900)

The son of Hugh Bingham and Ester Bailey Bingham, John Bingham spent his childhood in Pennsylvania and was educated at antislavery Franklin College in New Athens, Ohio. After studying law with two prominent Pennsylvania lawyers, he was admitted to the Pennsylvania and Ohio bars in 1840.

A skilled trial lawyer, Bingham was prosecutor of Tuscarawas County, Ohio, from 1846 to 1850. He called for "No more slave states; No more slave territories . . ." at the 1848 Whig National Convention. Elected to Congress in 1854 as a Republican, he served until 1863, and then again from 1865 to 1872. In 1862, he prosecuted the impeachment and removal of U.S. District Judge West Humphreys for becoming a Confederate Judge.

In 1863, Lincoln appointed Bingham Court of Claims Solicitor and Major in the Judge Advocate General's Corps. Bingham was one of the prosecutors in the trial of the Lincoln assassins. He gave the closing argument in the Andrew Johnson impeachment

John Armor Bingham. Photo by Alexander Gardener (1821–1882). Courtesy James Wadsworth Family Papers, Library of Congress Manuscript Division, LC-MSS-44297-33-107.

trial. A member of the Joint Committee on Reconstruction, he authored the portions of the Fourteenth Amendment guaranteeing privileges or immunities, equal protection, and due process. Bingham believed that the amendment would enforce the Bill of Rights against the states.

President Grant appointed Bingham Minister Plenipotentiary to Japan. He served from 1873 until 1885 and was viewed as a friend of the Japanese. Upon his return from Japan, he continued to support the Republican Party, campaigning for Benjamin Harrison and William McKinley.

Sources and Further Reading: Richard L. Aynes, *The Antislavery and Abolitionist Background of John A. Bingham* (1988); Donald C. Swift, *John A. Bingham and Reconstruction* (1968).

Richard L. Aynes
University of Akron, Ohio

Harry Andrew Blackmun (1908–1999)

Harry Andrew Blackmun served on the U.S. Supreme Court from 1970 to 1994. He was born in Nashville, Illinois, but raised in Minneapolis and St. Paul, Min-

Associate Supreme Court Justice Harry Blackmun. Photo by Joseph D. Lavenburg, National Geographic Society. The Supreme Court Historical Society.

nesota. Blackmun completed a major in mathematics at Harvard, graduating with highest honors in 1929. Dropping initial plans to become a physician, he next enrolled at Harvard Law School, where he graduated in 1932. Following a clerkship with a judge of the U.S. Court of Appeals for the Eighth Circuit, he joined a Minneapolis firm, eventually becoming a partner. In 1950, Blackmun became resident counsel at the Mayo Clinic in Rochester, Minnesota, a position he held until his appointment by President Eisenhower in 1959 to the Eighth Circuit federal appeals court.

In 1970, President Nixon named Blackmun to the Supreme Court with the strong support of his boyhood friend, Warren E. Burger, whom Nixon had appointed Chief Justice the previous year. During his early years as a justice, Blackmun voted so regularly and conservatively with Chief Justice Burger in civil liberties cases that the two were dubbed the Minnesota Twins. Beginning with the Court's 1975–1976 term, however, their agreement rate declined precipitously. Best known as the author of *Roe v. Wade* (1973), the landmark case establishing a woman's right to terminate pregnancy, Blackmun developed a liberal stance in many other

civil liberties fields, as well. In his last term, for example, he reversed himself on the death penalty, concluding that there was no way to eliminate the arbitrariness inherent in the imposition of capital punishment, which he had always personally abhorred but long considered constitutionally acceptable.

Sources and Further Reading: Tinsley E. Yarbrough, *The Burger Court: Justices, Rulings, and Legacy* (2000); Tinsley E. Yarbrough, *The Rehnquist Court and the Constitution* (2000).

Tinsley E. Yarbrough
East Carolina University

David Josiah Brewer (1837–1910)

The son of Congregational missionaries, Brewer attended Wesleyan and Yale universities and Albany Law School before moving to Kansas shortly before the Civil War. From 1870 to 1884, he served on the state's Supreme Court, and in *Kansas v. Mugler* (1883), he initially expressed the conservative values that typified his judicial career. The following year, President Chester A. Arthur appointed him to the Eighth Circuit Court of Appeals. Brewer asserted that judges had a duty to inquire into the reasonableness of rates regulating railroads, to overturn legislation that failed to yield a fair return on invested capital, and to require compensation to owners of property taken for a public purpose.

These views prompted President Benjamin Harrison in 1890 to appoint Brewer an associate justice of the U.S. Supreme Court, a position he held until his death. Brewer unabashedly relied on judicial power to assert the doctrines of freedom to contract and substantive due process of law to protect property owners from the incursions of state and federal legislatures. The lone exception was his opinion for a unanimous court in *Muller v. Oregon* (1908). Brewer held that because of the supposed physical disabilities of women, the Oregon legislature acted within its powers to impose a ten-hour work limit on them. In every other instance, however, Brewer's jurisprudence, which included more than two hundred dissents, forcefully proclaimed that material wealth and human progress, values closely associated with the emerging corporate elite of the Midwest, went hand-in-hand.

Sources and Further Reading: Michael J. Brodhead, *David J. Brewer: The Life of a Supreme Court Justice, 1837–1910* (1994); Kermit L. Hall, "David J. Brewer," in Leonard W. Levy, ed., *Encyclopedia of the American Constitution*, vol. 1 (1986).

Kermit L. Hall
State University of New York, Albany

Warren Earl Burger (1907–1995)

Warren Burger was born in St. Paul, Minnesota, to a working-class family. His night school education, while selling insurance by day, earned him an undergraduate degree from the University of Minnesota and a law degree from the St. Paul College of Law. Burger pursued private practice for twenty years, was active in Republican politics, and as Harold Stassen's protégé, managed his 1939 gubernatorial campaign and was Floor Manager for his 1948 and 1952 presidential bids. In 1953, Dwight Eisenhower named Burger Assistant U.S. Attorney, advancing him in 1955 to the Washington, D.C. Circuit Court of Appeals. In 1969, Richard Nixon elevated Burger to the Supreme Court, replacing Earl Warren as Chief Justice.

Perceived as a conservative "strict constructionist" in Nixon's image, Burger authored more than 250 opinions, but did not lead the Court in a counter-revolution against the Warren Court's liberalism. Indeed, Burger's Court endorsed affirmative action and legalized abortion, while he himself authored the first opinion sanctioning school busing, as well as the opinion ordering the release of secret White House tapes in *U.S. v. Nixon* 418 U.S. 683 (1974). Known more for championing administrative efficiency and for advocating ongoing legal education than for juristic talents, Burger fostered many institutional initiatives including the Supreme Court Historical Society, the Judicial Fellows Program, the National Center for State Courts, and the Institute for Court Management.

Burger left the Court in 1986 to head the Constitution's Bicentennial Commission. With his full white mane and patrician manner, and his service as Chancellor of William and Mary (1986–1993), Burger seemed more the consummate Virginian than a son of the Midwest upon his death in 1995.

Sources and Further Reading: Herman Schwartz, ed., *The Burger Years* (1987); Tinsley E. Yarbrough, *The Burger Court: Justices, Rulings and Legacy* (2000).

Elliot Slotnick
The Ohio State University–Columbus

Salmon P. Chase (1808–1873)

New Hampshire born and Dartmouth educated, Salmon P. Chase studied law under U.S. Attorney General Willard Wirt. Following admission to the Washington, D.C., bar in 1829, Chase relocated to Cincinnati, Ohio, and was admitted to the Ohio bar in 1830.

Though initially a business lawyer, Chase became

Salmon P. Chase. Photo by Mathew B. Brady (1823–1896). Courtesy Brady National Photographic Art Gallery, Library of Congress.

involved in free speech issues raised by James G. Birney's attempt to publish an abolitionist newspaper in Cincinnati. The defense of free speech led to the defense of fugitive slaves, and eventually Chase became the key strategist in national antislavery litigation. Unlike those who considered the constitution a covenant with hell, Chase advanced the midwestern idea of "Freedom National, Slavery Local," declaring that slavery was a local matter and thus separating it from national politics and jurisdiction.

An advocate of free male suffrage from as early as the 1830s, Chase was twice elected Governor of Ohio and appointed by the legislature as U.S. Senator. He was a serious Presidential contender in every election from 1860 to 1872. During the first part of the Civil War, Chase excelled as Secretary of Treasury and is generally given credit for laying the foundation for the modern national banking system.

Upon the death of Chief Justice Roger B. Taney, Lincoln named Chase as Chief Justice of the Supreme Court because of his soundness on the legal issues that would likely arise from the Civil War. Chase presided over a fractionalized Court, a majority of whom probably did not follow his lead in supporting the Fourteenth Amendment. His most enduring opinion was *Texas v. White* 74 U.S. 700 (1869), for which Chase wrote of the indestructible states in an indestructible Union.

Sources and Further Reading: Michael Les Benedict, "Salmon P. Chase and Constitutional Politics," *Law & Social Inquiry* 22 (Spring 1997); Harold M. Hyman, *Reconstruction Justice Salmon P. Chase* (1997); John Niven, *Salmon P. Chase* (1995).

Richard L. Aynes
University of Akron, Ohio

Thomas McIntyre Cooley (1824–1898)

Born into a farm family in upstate New York, Cooley moved to Michigan in 1843 and completed his legal education there. Although Cooley became a Republican in the mid-1850s, he was strongly influenced by the tenets of Jacksonian Democracy that he absorbed in his youth. Cooley was elected to the Michigan Supreme Court in 1864 and remained on the bench until 1885 after being defeated for reelection.

Much of Cooley's historical reputation is based upon his landmark treatise, *The Constitutional Limitations Which Rest Upon the Legislative Power of the States of the American Union* (1868). Cooley's primary goal was to devise limits on arbitrary legislative action. He fused the Jacksonian principles of equal rights and hostility to special economic privilege with due process protection of property rights. Cooley championed a broad reading of the due process norm as a substantive restraint on legislative power. He defined liberty as encompassing the right to make contracts and hold property. Cooley's work provided much of the intellectual support for judicial moves to fashion the due process clause of the Fourteenth Amendment into a formidable protection for economic rights in the late nineteenth century.

Cooley was equally concerned about the growth of monopoly and concentration of economic power. He opposed the use of public resources to subsidize private enterprise, insisting that taxation could only be imposed for a public purpose. Nor was Cooley's defense of individual rights limited to economic matters. He was supportive of freedom of expression and religious liberty.

In 1887, President Grover Cleveland named Cooley chairman of the newly formed Interstate Commerce Commission. Cooley received praise for his efforts to make the agency effective in eliminating railroad abuses while respecting the interests of all parties.

Sources and Further Reading: Clyde Edward Jacobs, *Law Writers and the Courts* (1954); Alan R. Jones, *The Constitu-*

tional Conservatism of Thomas McIntyre Cooley (1987); Alan R. Jones, "Thomas M. Cooley and the Michigan Supreme Court: 1865–1885," *American Journal of Legal History* 10 (Apr. 1966).

James W. Ely, Jr.
Vanderbilt University, Tennessee

Clarence Steward Darrow (1857–1938)

Born into a working-class family in tiny Kinsman, Ohio, Clarence Darrow grew up in the traditions of midwestern nineteenth-century rationalism as propounded by his father, Amirus Darrow, a college-educated craftsman. Joining the Ohio bar in 1878, Darrow practiced in Ashtabula County for nine years until he was inspired by reading a scathing critique of the criminal justice system by Chicago lawyer and reformer, John Peter Altgeld. Bored by small-town practice, Darrow moved to Chicago in 1887 to work with Altgeld.

Darrow threw himself into the life of the city and, with Altgeld's support, flourished there. He held a succession of public and private posts that left him free to promote radical political and social causes. He found his voice as a public speaker and his identity in opposing governmental and religious limits on individual

Clarence Darrow during the Leopold and Loeb case, 1924.
Chicago Historical Society, *Chicago Daily News*, DN-0077499.

freedom. During the period from 1894 to 1911, Darrow built a national reputation defending labor union organizers against criminal charges arising from the violent clashes that then marked labor relations. This phase of Darrow's career ended with his defense in a strike-related bombing. Labor lionized the defendants until Darrow plead them guilty, then labor turned on both Darrow and the defendants.

Darrow rebuilt his legal practice with high-paying criminal cases and high-visibility cause lawyering. He was again America's most famous criminal lawyer by the 1920s, when in a succession of sensational trials he defended the wealthy teenage murderers Nathan Leopold and Richard Loeb, John Scopes for teaching evolution in Tennessee, and the Sweet brothers for murder in the protection of their home from a racist Detroit mob. Lawyers particularly admired his innovative techniques of selecting jurors, interrogating hostile witnesses, and making closing arguments. He also mastered a vivid style of public speaking and writing that was quite popular. Although Darrow became a nationally known voice of Midwest urban radicalism, he always retained the manners and style of his small-town Ohio roots.

Sources and Further Reading: Irving Stone, *Clarence Darrow for the Defense* (1941); Kevin Tierney, *Darrow: A Biography* (1979); Arthur Weinberg and Lila Weinberg, *Clarence Darrow, A Sentimental Rebel* (1980).

Edward Larson
University of Georgia

Melville Weston Fuller (1833–1910)

Melville W. Fuller was the first midwesterner to become Chief Justice of the United States. Born in Maine in 1833 and educated at Bowdoin College and Harvard Law School, Fuller moved at age twenty-three to Chicago, where he established a successful law practice. During three decades in Chicago, Fuller also was active in Democratic politics and prospered through real estate investments.

Fuller's midwestern connection was critical to his Supreme Court appointment in 1888 because President Grover Cleveland hoped that Fuller's nomination would help him to win reelection by increasing his midwestern support, particularly in populous Illinois. At a time when geography heavily influenced Supreme Court appointments, Cleveland also sought a midwesterner because no members of the Court were from the federal judiciary's Seventh Circuit, which comprised Illinois, Wisconsin, and Indiana. Since

Fuller was little known beyond Chicago, his nomination provoked widespread surprise.

Although Fuller distinguished himself as an excellent administrator and was popular with his judicial brethren during his twenty-two years as Chief Justice, he did not make a mark as an innovative thinker. A lifelong political conservative, Fuller consistently supported restraint of governmental power in judicial decisions that often contravened the strong populist and progressive political impulses of the Midwest. During Fuller's Chief Justiceship, the Court increasingly invalidated federal and state regulatory legislation that was intended to ameliorate the abuses of the Industrial Revolution. Fuller was the author of landmark opinions striking down federal income tax laws, limiting the scope of the federal antitrust laws, and restricting labor union activities.

Sources and Further Reading: James W. Ely, Jr., *The Chief Justiceship of Melville W. Fuller, 1888–1910* (1995); Willard L. King, *Melville Weston Fuller* (1950).

William Ross
Stamford University, Alabama

Arthur J. Goldberg (1908–1990)

Arthur Goldberg was born in Chicago, the youngest son of poor eastern European immigrants. At twenty-one, he graduated from Northwestern University School of Law. He then practiced law in Chicago, working initially for commercial clients and then increasingly representing labor unions. His first prominent work for unions was on behalf of the Chicago Newspaper Guild in a bitter strike in 1938. During World War II he served with the Office of Strategic Services in intelligence work often involving overseas labor groups. As general counsel to the United Steelworkers of America and the Congress of Industrial Organizations (CIO), he moved to Washington, D.C. in 1949. In 1955, he played a pivotal role in negotiating the merger of the CIO and the American Federation of Labor. Active in Democratic politics, he was named by President John F. Kennedy as Secretary of Labor in 1961.

In 1962, the President elevated him to the Supreme Court, where he articulated liberal and often creative constitutional positions. In July 1965, President Johnson persuaded him to leave the Court and become the nation's United Nations ambassador. Goldberg ascribed this shocking career change—which eventually he regretted—to a patriotic desire to apply his negotiating experience to ending the Vietnam War. Unable to accomplish this task, he left the U.N. position in 1968, returned to law practice in New York, unsuccessfully ran for governor there in 1970, then practiced law in Washington, and continued his lifelong involvement in social causes.

Sources and Further Reading: Arthur J. Goldberg, *Equal Justice: The Warren Era of the Supreme Court* (1971); David L. Stebenne, *Arthur J. Goldberg* (1996).

Kenneth Manaster
Santa Clara University, California

Abraham Lincoln (1809–1865)

Abraham Lincoln's quarter-century legal career in antebellum Illinois reflected the larger patterns of the practice of law in the Midwest. Lincoln learned the law by reading William Blackstone's *Commentaries* and various legal treatises before he was admitted to the bar in September 1836. His legal education continued when he became the junior partner of John Todd Stuart, his future wife's cousin, in April 1837. Four years later, he became the junior partner of Stephen T. Logan, who had a more extensive appellate and federal

President Abraham Lincoln. Chicago Historical Society, *Chicago Daily News*, DN-00007070.

❖ A House Divided

In his speech to the Illinois Republican Party State Convention, June 16, 1858, Abraham Lincoln made his famous "A House Divided" statement that set forth his views on slavery.

> In my opinion, [the current slavery agitation] will not cease, until a crisis shall have been reached, and passed—"A house divided against itself cannot stand."
>
> I believe this government cannot endure, permanently half *slave* and half *free*. I do not expect the Union to be dissolved—I do not expect the house to fall—but I do expect it will cease to be divided. It will become all one thing, or all the other. Either the opponents of slavery, will arrest the further spread of it, and place it where the public mind shall rest in the belief that it is in the course of ultimate extinction; or its advocates will push it forward, till it shall become alike lawful in all the States, old as well as new—North as well as South.
>
> Have we no tendency to the latter condition?

Source: William H. Townsend, ed., *Famous Speeches of Abraham Lincoln* (1935).

practice. In December 1844, Lincoln made William H. Herndon his junior partner, a relationship that continued until Lincoln's death in April 1865.

Lincoln handled more than five thousand cases with his three successive partners. Most were in county circuit courts throughout central Illinois, but they also argued more than four hundred cases before the Illinois Supreme Court and several hundred cases in the federal courts in Illinois. A few of their cases even reached the United States Supreme Court. Approximately 60 percent of Lincoln's cases involved the collection of debts, but he also handled litigation concerning contracts, land titles and transfers, inheritance, family law, and a small number of criminal cases.

Like other attorneys, Lincoln blended his legal career with his political ambitions. During several terms in the Illinois state legislature and one term in Congress (1847–1849), he gained experience creating the laws that the courts enforced. His law practice reenforced his political career by sharpening his analytical and oratorical skills, by introducing him to numerous other lawyer-politicians, and by placing him in regular contact with a wide array of voters. His political career enhanced his legal career by spreading his reputation among other Illinois attorneys and to out-of-state clients. The habits of mind and expression he crafted during his legal career prepared him as President to face the great constitutional crises of the Civil War.

Sources and Further Reading: Martha Benner, Cullom Davis, et al., eds., *The Law Practice of Abraham Lincoln: Complete Documentary Edition* (DVD-ROM, 2000); John P. Frank, *Lincoln as a Lawyer* (1961; reprint, 1991); Daniel W. Stowell, ed., *In Tender Consideration: Women, Families, and the Law in Abraham Lincoln's Illinois* (2002).

Daniel W. Stowell
Lincoln Legal Papers Project,
Springfield, Illinois

Harry Olson (1867–1935)

Standing six feet tall with an imposing bald dome, Harry Olson cut a prominent figure in Republican politics, law enforcement, and judicial reform in Progressive Era Chicago. The son of Swedish immigrants, Olson grew up in Kansas, where he taught primary school and attended Washburn College. In 1891, he received an L.L.B. from the Union College of Law in Chicago. From 1896 to 1906, Olson worked as an assistant state's attorney in Cook County, serving eight years under State's Attorney Charles S. Deneen, the future governor. In 1906, Olson was elected the first chief justice of the Municipal Court of Chicago, a position he occupied until 1930.

In public lectures and as chairman of the Chicago-based American Judicature Society, Olson promoted the municipal court as a national model for judicial efficiency, procedural reform, adult probation, and other "scientific" techniques for "treating" criminals. He worked with social activists, including Jane Addams, to create specialized criminal courts for desertion and nonsupport cases, prostitution, and youth offenses. In 1914, he established the Psychopathic Laboratory, a clinic within the Municipal Court, and became a leading national propagandist for the sterilization of criminals. Olson sought the Republican nomination for mayor in 1915 and 1919, losing both bids to William Hale "Big Bill" Thompson. Highly respected by the professional bar and the progressive reform community, Olson remained in office until the citywide Democratic sweep in 1930. At the time of Olson's death, some forty American cities had reorganized their court systems on the Chicago model, though his eugenic theories of criminality had been largely discredited.

Sources and Further Reading: Michal R. Belknap, *To Improve the Administration of Justice* (1992); Michael Willrich, *City of Courts: Socializing Justice in Progressive-Era Chicago* (2003).

Michael Willrich
Brandeis University, Massachusetts

Richard Allen Posner (b. 1939)

Richard Posner, federal judge for the U.S. Seventh Circuit Court of Appeals based in Chicago, is one of the leading jurists and scholars of contemporary American law. Born in New York City, Posner graduated from Harvard Law School in 1962. He served as a law clerk for Supreme Court Justice William Brennan, then worked as an attorney for the federal government. Posner briefly taught at Stanford Law School before joining the faculty at the University of Chicago Law School in 1969, where he still teaches as a Senior Lecturer.

Between 1969 and 1981, Posner rose to prominence for his scholarly works applying economic analysis and theory to many areas of the law, particularly antitrust. During this period, Posner wrote numerous books and articles, including the landmark *Economic Analysis of the Law*, emerged as a leader of the Chicago school of antitrust theory, and founded the *Journal of Legal Studies*. In 1981, President Ronald Reagan appointed Posner to his current position as judge for the Seventh Circuit, where he also served as chief judge from 1993 to 2000.

Posner is one of the most prolific opinion writers on the federal bench, and certain opinions suggest a pragmatic approach, at times showing his interest in economic theory. He has authored over thirty books and three hundred articles and reviews, as well as numerous appellate opinions. The volume of his works combined with his writing style provokes discussion among the general public as well as in the legal and academic communities.

Sources and Further Reading: Larissa MacFarquhar, "The Bench Burner," *The New Yorker* (Dec. 10, 2001); "Richard A. Posner," in Megan Chase, Andrea Houlihan, Virginia Stanley, and Lori Tripoli, eds., *Almanac of the Federal Judiciary*, 2 vols. (2003-1 Supplement); Richard A. Posner, *Economic Analysis of Law*, 6th ed. (2003).

Jonathan W. Singer
St. Louis, Missouri

Roscoe Pound (1870–1964)

Roscoe Pound was for over thirty years a chaired professor and twenty years dean of Harvard Law School (1916–1936). He was one of the most prolific American legal scholars who ever lived, with over three hundred books and major articles.

A pioneer of modern American jurisprudence, Roscoe Pound came by his iconoclasm naturally. His great-grandfather's Quaker family home near Farmington, New York, had served as a stop on the Underground Railroad. His father, Judge Stephen Pound, had abandoned an established practice of law in his forebears' long-settled home in Ontario, New York, to seek his fortune in frontier Lincoln, Nebraska. Young Nathan Roscoe (he dropped his first name early in life) was educated at home before entering the Latin School of the University of Nebraska for two years, and then entered the University of Nebraska at age thirteen. After graduating with Bachelors and Masters degrees in botany, Pound decided to follow his father into the law. He studied for a year at Harvard Law School and then returned to Nebraska to work in his father's firm. Pound never received a nonhonorific law degree.

Even though he did not complete the three-year program at Harvard, Pound successfully sat for the bar upon his return to Nebraska and began practicing law, completing at the same time his doctorate in botany and serving as the director of the Nebraska Botanical Survey. In 1901, he was appointed a commissioner (an assistant judge) of the Supreme Court of Nebraska and was subsequently offered the deanship of the law department of the University of Nebraska, where he introduced Harvard methods of legal education.

In his writings, Pound called for a "sociological jurisprudence" in which legislators and judges were to take into account currents of opinion and the need for legal reform. This flew in the face of the prevailing classical or formalist jurisprudence in which judges were to decide cases according to objectively discovered principles of law as if they existed independently of social and economic conditions. Pound's sociological view argues that rules should be adapted to social, economic, and political reality. Pound's bold assault on the established view inspired younger "legal realist" scholars to open jurisprudential rebellion against formalist canon.

Pound's scholarship led to his appointment as Story Professor of Law at Harvard in 1910, and six years later to the deanship of Harvard Law School. There he defended free speech during the first Red Scare after World War I and supported unpopular liberal legal causes. He grew circumspect of rapid constitutional changes during the 1930s and condemned President Franklin Roosevelt's New Deal initiatives, particularly the president's plan to pack the Supreme Court with justices supportive of his initiatives. In an era in which Mussolini, Hitler, and Stalin exercised increasing executive powers, Pound became wary of all positivist legal maneuvers that circumvented traditional constitutional constraints on executive power.

Sources and Further Reading: N.E.H. Hull, *Roscoe Pound and Karl Llewellyn* (1997); Paul Sayre, *The Life of Roscoe Pound* (1948); David Wigdor, *Roscoe Pound: Philosopher of Law* (1974).

N.E.H. Hull
Rutgers University–Camden, New Jersey

John Paul Stevens (b. 1920)

John Paul Stevens was born in Chicago, the city to which his paternal grandfather had moved in the 1890s from southern Illinois. His mother was from northern Indiana. The Stevens family had achieved some prominence in business and real estate in Chicago. Stevens graduated from the University of Chicago in 1941, served in the Navy until 1945, and then achieved outstanding academic success as a law student at Northwestern University.

Following a clerkship at the Supreme Court, Stevens entered private law practice in Chicago, returning to Washington in 1951 for one year as counsel to a congressional antitrust committee. In the small law firm he cofounded in 1952, Stevens developed further antitrust expertise and became a skilled litigator. In 1969, he served as chief counsel for a special commission investigating a bribery scandal in the Illinois Supreme Court. His widely praised performance in that role led to his appointment in 1970 to the U.S. Court of Appeals covering Illinois, Wisconsin, and Indiana.

In 1975, President Gerald Ford named him to the U.S. Supreme Court, having identified him as a highly skilled judge whose nomination would not invite political controversy. Seen at first as moderate on many issues, over the decades of his tenure on the Court, Stevens emerged as a consistently independent thinker. He gradually became identified with the liberal wing of an increasingly conservative Court. Among his best known opinions is his eloquent and stinging dissent in *Bush v. Gore*, the case that resolved the 2000 presidential election.

Sources and Further Reading: Kenneth A. Manaster, *Illinois Justice* (2001); Robert Judd Sickels, *John Paul Stevens and the Constitution* (1988).

Kenneth Manaster
Santa Clara University, California

Potter Stewart (1915–1985)

Potter Stewart was born in Jackson, Michigan, and was raised in Cincinnati, Ohio. He graduated at the top of his class at Yale Law School in 1941, where he served as an editor of the Yale *Law Journal*. In 1943, he married Mary Ann Bertles with whom he had three children. He practiced law in New York and Cincinnati and served with distinction in the navy during World War II. President Dwight Eisenhower appointed him to the Sixth Circuit Court of Appeals in 1954.

Four years later, Eisenhower elevated him to the United States Supreme Court. It has been said that Stewart was both a conservative on a liberal court and a liberal on a conservative court. Stewart's concise opinions expanded First Amendment rights, particularly in obscenity cases. In *Jacobellis v. Ohio* (378 U.S. 184, 1964), he famously wrote of obscenity, "I know it when I see it." Stewart also wrote several important civil rights opinions, especially concerning housing discrimination.

Arguably Stewart's most important opinions helped define search and seizure. In *Katz v. United States* (389 U.S. 347, 1967), he signaled a fundamental change by holding that the Fourth Amendment "protects people and not simply 'areas'" and was based on the defendant's reasonable expectation of privacy. Stewart's later opinions further delineated the constitutional protection by clarifying the circumstances in which the police need a search warrant.

Stewart retired in 1981. Throughout his retirement he served on international panels and the President's Commission on Organized Crime, and made recordings of textbooks for the blind. Stewart died of complications from a stroke in 1985.

Sources and Further Reading: Daniel M. Berman, "Mr. Justice Stewart: A Preliminary Appraisal," *University of Cincinnati Law Review* 28 (1959); Leon Friedman and Fred L. Israel, eds., *The Justices of the United States Supreme Court: Their Lives and Major Opinions*, vol. 4, rev. ed. (1997); Tinsley E. Yarbrough, "Justice Potter Stewart: Decisional Patterns in Search of Doctrinal Moorings" in Charles M. Lamb and Stephen C. Halpern, eds., *The Burger Court: Political and Judicial Profiles* (1991).

Samuel H. Porter
Columbus, Ohio

William Howard Taft (1857–1930)

On September 15, 1857, Taft was born in Cincinnati, the son and grandson of Ohio judges. He graduated second in his class from Yale University in 1878. Two years later, he received his law degree from the Cincinnati Law School and was admitted to the Ohio bar. In 1887, he filled a vacant judgeship on the Ohio Superior Court. In February of 1890, he became the

solicitor general in the administration of President Benjamin Harrison, another Ohioan. This position required Taft to argue before the Supreme Court, a task at which he excelled. In 1892, he became a federal circuit court judge.

In 1900, at the insistence of President William McKinley, Taft became the president of the Philippine Commission and later Civil Governor of the Philippines. Taft stayed on until February 1904, despite twice being offered an appointment to the U.S. Supreme Court by President Theodore Roosevelt. After a successful stint as Roosevelt's Secretary of War, he became the twenty-seventh president of the United States. He did not win reelection.

Taft was happy to leave politics and retired to Yale University to teach constitutional law. In 1921, President Warren G. Harding, another Ohioan, appointed him chief justice of the United States Supreme Court, a role he coveted. Having been both a judge and a constitutional law professor, Taft was well versed in the philosophical and practical aspects of the Court; having been a successful cabinet-level secretary, he also knew how to make complicated institutions run well. The Court was badly divided when Taft was appointed, so he needed both skills.

One of his main goals was making the Court more efficient. As president, Taft took every opportunity in his public addresses to encourage reform in the procedure of the federal judiciary. As chief justice, he continued this quest. The changes he sought were made across the board. This included more than just clearing a clogged docket. He took a special interest in improving legal aid to the poor, raising standards of legal education, and making sure judicial ethics were taken seriously.

As a jurist, Taft was also quite distinguished and somewhat controversial. He was a moderate conservative and strong believer in property rights on a Court that would hear some of the most important cases in American jurisprudence, many of which are still taught in law schools today. Opinions dealing with labor, commerce, free speech, federalism, and the authority of the executive branch of government—in short, the essential questions of the United States Constitution—often brought the Taft Court criticism in a time of popular progressivism. It was the Taft Court that recognized that the stockyard industry was national in scope and therefore open to federal regulation; this Court also upheld the President's right to remove executive appointees without the concurrence of the Senate.

Taft retired from the bench in February of 1930 because of health problems. He died a month later on March 8, 1930, in Washington, D.C.

Sources and Further Reading: Donald F. Anderson, *William Howard Taft: A Conservative's Conception of the Presidency* (1973); Alpheus Thomas Mason, *William Howard Taft: Chief Justice* (1965); Henry F. Pringle, *The Life and Times of William Howard Taft* (1964); Allen E. Ragan, *Chief Justice Taft* (1938).

Travis McDade
The Ohio State University–Columbus

Morrison Remick Waite (1816–1888)

Born in Lyme, Connecticut, Morrison R. Waite graduated from Yale College and studied law by the time-honored apprenticeship system. He practiced law in Toledo, Ohio, and became active in the newly organized Republican Party. Waite gained national attention when he was named one of the American Counselors to the Geneva Arbitration Tribunal to settle U.S. damage claims against Great Britain for allowing the Confederacy to purchase the *Alabama* and other warships during the Civil War. Thereafter, he was elected president of the Ohio constitutional convention. Early in 1874, after failed efforts to advance other candidates, President Ulysses S. Grant nominated Waite to be chief justice.

Despite initial doubts from some of the other justices, Waite established himself as a skillful manager of the Supreme Court. A man of high integrity, Waite had a judicial philosophy marked by respect for precedent and deference to legislative decision-making. He generally supported state autonomy regarding civil rights and economic regulations. During his tenure, the Supreme Court narrowly construed the protection afforded newly freed slaves, and ruled in the *Civil Rights Cases* (1883) that the Fourteenth Amendment banned only state interference with individual rights, not discriminatory private conduct. Likewise, Waite upheld the power of the states to regulate businesses "affected with a public interest" in *Munn v. Illinois* (94 U.S. 113, 130, 1877). The Waite Court also held that the contract clause safeguarded the holders of municipal bonds from repudiation. Waite further declared that corporations were persons for the purpose of Fourteenth Amendment guarantees, and cautioned that the power to regulate would not justify confiscation of private property.

Sources and Further Reading: Charles Fairman, *Reconstruction and Reunion, 1864–88*, Part Two (1987); C. Peter Magrath, *Morrison R. Waite* (1963).

James W. Ely, Jr.
Vanderbilt University, Tennessee

John Henry Wigmore (1863–1943)

John Henry Wigmore played a crucial role in developing sophisticated legal education in Chicago and the Midwest. He graduated from Harvard College in 1883 and the Harvard Law School in 1887. After several years practicing in Boston, he served for three years as Professor of Anglo-American Law at Keio University in Tokyo, where he developed a lifelong interest in Japanese law. In 1893, he accepted a faculty appointment at the Northwestern University Law School in downtown Chicago. The school was small, lacked prestige, and had come under Northwestern's exclusive management only two years earlier. President Eliot of Harvard commended Wigmore for accepting a position in a "missionary diocese."

Wigmore was a professor at Northwestern University Law School for thirteen years and served as its Dean from 1901 to 1929. A provocative teacher, he required students to memorize Shakespeare and asked them to shuffle their feet when a classmate was speaking in order to simulate the distractions in municipal court. As a scholar, Wigmore was prolific, publishing forty-six original books, thirty-six edited volumes, and sixteen short studies of Japan. His multivolume *Treatise on Evidence* remains influential. As Dean, he prompted adoption of the case method, greatly expanded the law library, developed a critically-minded rather than practice-oriented law review, and founded the Order of the Coif, a national legal honor society. Although Wigmore was disappointed when others rejected his proposals for a four-year course of legal study, he deserves primary credit for making Northwestern a leader in the modernization of legal education.

Sources and Further Reading: James A. Rahl and Kurt Schwerin, *Northwestern University School of Law: A Short History* (1960); William R. Roalfe, *John Henry Wigmore* (1977).

David Ray Papke
Marquette University, Wisconsin

Politics

SECTION EDITOR
Peverill Squire

Section Contents

Overview

The existence of the Midwest as a political region in American politics is widely assumed. A Lexis-Nexis search of major newspapers for the six months from October 2003 through March 2004, for example, reveals almost three hundred news stories explicitly linking the region with the 2004 presidential election. But to what extent is the Midwest truly a cohesive geographic unit in its politics?

Many Americans stereotype midwesterners and their politics. Members of the Nixon administration, for example, would justify many of their policy decisions with the observation that "it will play in Peoria." According to William Safire, America's leading political lexicographer, the reference to Peoria, and by extension to the whole Midwest, was a way for White House aides to "excuse cornball gestures" made by the president. Indeed, John Ehrlichman, the Nixon advisor who was credited with twisting the old vaudeville question for political purposes, said Peoria, "personified—exemplified—a place removed from the media centers on the coasts, where the national verdict is cast. . . ." Underlying this claim is an assumption that a consensus about politics exists in the American hinterlands. That assumption merits examination.

The first question to ask is whether there is something distinctive or cohesive about the political culture in the Midwest. Impressionistically, we can easily raise doubts about any cohesiveness. Even people with only a passing knowledge of politics in the region would recognize that the political culture in Illinois differs fundamentally from the political culture just across the border in Iowa. But the concept of political culture is notoriously hazy; it can mean different things to different people. Daniel Elazar, a social scientist, developed the most rigorous assessment of political culture in the American states. In developing this assessment, he examined population migrations and how different groups of people evolved different notions about how their governments were supposed to operate. Elazar identified three political cultures: individualistic, moralistic, and traditionalistic. The individualistic culture emphasizes the role of government as a referee, acting to regulate the marketplace and to promote economic development. Social policies are initiated only when demanded by the public. Politics is left to professional politicians, and political parties compete to win office and thereby control the distribution of government resources. In contrast, the moralistic culture emphasizes the role of government to promote the common good. Policies are initiated when those elected to run the government determine that they are in the larger public interest. The citizenry is encouraged to participate in politics, and issues drive competition among political parties. The final culture, the traditionalistic, is focused on maintaining the status quo. Control of government is left in the hands of the social and economic elite, and political participation by the general public is discouraged. The interests of the elite are expected to dominate.

Elazar recognized that his political cultures were ideal types not to be found in the real world, but models that could nonetheless indicate concentrations and

Stump Speaking by George Caleb Bingham: Electioneering in the nineteenth century. The St. Louis Art Museum. Gift of Bank of America.

strong tendencies of practice and belief. He further realized that particular states would contain strains of two or more cultures, that regions within states might differ significantly in their cultures, and that state cultures might change over time as populations change. In spite of the limitations, Elazar's cultures have proven to capture the essence of different orientations to politics across the states.

Does Elazar report anything distinctive about political culture in the Midwest? A cursory examination of table 1 would suggest that little distinguishes the states in the Midwest from those in much of the rest of the country. The various combinations of political cultures that appear in the Midwest appear in other parts of the country as well. But this should not come as a surprise. After all, cultures arrive with the people who settle an area and are carried with them when they leave. Migratory patterns brought the political cultures found in the Midwest from the East, from the South, and from abroad, and midwesterners transplanted them in places further west. It is important to observe, however, that a larger percentage of states in the Midwest have a stronger component of the moralistic culture than is found in the rest of the country. States with streaks of individualistic culture are found in slightly greater numbers in the Midwest, and traditionalistic cultures do not surface at all in the Midwest, although Elazar does note that the southern regions of both Illinois and Ohio exhibit some characteristics of that culture. Overall, while the political cultures found in the Midwest are also found in other states, the region has a stronger flavor of the moralistic culture, with its concerns about promotion of the common good.

This leads us to the second question: Does the Midwest evidence any differences from the rest of the country in its political behavior? It seems clear from examining the history of the region that political ideology of every stripe has found a home within it. Although the traditional Main Street conservatism associated a generation ago with Senator Robert Taft of Ohio or more recently with Senator Robert Dole of Kansas may be what many Americans think will play in Peoria, it is clear that competing perspectives have also struck a chord. After all, the Midwest spawned the ardent liberalism of Minnesota senators Hubert Humphrey, Eugene McCarthy, Walter Mondale, and a host of others of national note. Third-party movements and independent candidacies have been launched in the region, as well. In just the last century, they have ranged from the Progressive Movement of Wisconsin's Robert La Follette to the reform governorship of Minnesota's Jesse Ventura.

Over time the Midwest has also been a hotbed of social agitation of all sorts. On the right, the Ku Klux Klan became a major power in Indiana state politics in the 1920s, while the anti-Communist crusade of Wisconsin's Senator Joe McCarthy and the appeals of the conservative John Birch Society attracted interest and support. On the left, student radicalism in the 1960s fostered the creation of the Students for a Democratic Society and the issuance of the Port Huron Statement, both in Michigan, and earlier the region was crucible to the socialist advocacy of Eugene V. Debs, the internationalist appeals of Henry Wallace, and the aggressive unionization and labor activity in the urbanizing and industrializing years. So the Midwest has been fertile ground for many different views on politics and public policy.

Not surprisingly, the ideology of the Midwest states ranges from more conservative than the average of the nonmidwestern states to more liberal than the average. The state rankings presented in table 2 are from 1999 data and are based on updated public opinion surveys used by political scientists Robert Erikson, Gerald Wright, and John McIver to gauge public opinion across the fifty states. Comparing the findings on citizen ideology in the midwestern states to the other

Table 1. Political Cultures in the Midwest and the Rest of the Nation

	Moralistic	Moralistic Individualistic	Individualistic Moralistic	Individualistic	Individualistic Traditionalistic	Traditionalistic Individualistic	Traditionalistic	Traditionalistic Moralistic
Midwest (12 States)	4 (MI, MN, ND, WI) 33%	3 (IA, KS, SD) 25%	1 (NE) 8%	3 (IL, IN, OH) 25%	1 (MO) 8%	0	0	0
Rest of Nation (38 States)	5 13%	5 13%	5 13%	6 16%	1 3%	6 16%	8 21%	2 5%

Source: Adapted from Daniel Elazar, *American Federalism: A View from the States*, 3rd ed., New York: Harper & Row, 1984, p. 135.

Table 2. Ideological Orientation of Midwest States, 1999

More Conservative	South Dakota
	North Dakota
	Kansas
	Missouri
	Nebraska
	Iowa
	Indiana
	Wisconsin
	Michigan
	Median of other 38 states
	Ohio
	Illinois
More Liberal	Minnesota

Source: Adapted from data gathered by Professor Gerald C. Wright that can be found on his webpage, http://mypage.iu.edu/~wright1/. The data are from CBS/New York Times surveys.

thirty-eight states is particularly revealing. Clearly, the Midwest is tilted more to the conservative end of the spectrum than the rest of the country, with nine of the region's twelve states being more conservative than the median of the other thirty-eight states in the union. Indeed, South Dakota, North Dakota, and Kansas are among the most conservative states in the land. And the most liberal states in the Midwest—Ohio, Illinois, and Minnesota—are not among the most liberal states

nationally. But, again, when looking at only the states in the Midwest, it is important to note the considerable variation across them. Politics in South Dakota, to take the most extreme example, is far more conservative than politics in neighboring Minnesota.

Are these differences manifest in the polling booth? It is true that from the last half of the nineteenth century until only the last two decades the Midwest was solidly Republican. The GOP, which was born in the region—the exact places is a point of considerable contention—enjoyed a near-stranglehold on voting at nearly every level. The party's grip on the region was so tight that in 1885, Jonathan P. Dolliver, a Republican U.S. Senator from Iowa, forecast with confidence that "Iowa will go Democratic when Hell goes Methodist." As shown in table 3, as recently as the 1950s, Republicans routinely received the electoral votes in presidential elections from virtually every midwestern state. This was true even though the Democratic nominee in both 1952 and 1956 was Illinois governor Adlai Stevenson, who lost his home state and most others to Dwight Eisenhower, another midwesterner. With the exception of 1964, when every state in the North went to the Democrats, only a few cracks appeared in the GOP's control of the region in the 1960s, 1970s, and early 1980s. But starting in the late 1980s and continuing through the 1990s, the Midwest became considerably more competitive between the two parties at the presidential level.

The Midwest became competitive at other electoral levels as well. In Iowa, for example, the Democrats held only 10 percent of the seats in the state legislature as recently as the late 1940s. Their numbers slowly began to rise over the next two decades, briefly taking control of both chambers in the 1960s, and then alter-

Table 3. Presidential Vote by Major Political Party in the Midwest and the Nation, 1952–2000

State	1952	1956	1960	1964	1968	1972	1976	1980	1984	1988	1992	1996	2000
Ohio	R	R	R	D	R	R	D	R	R	R	D	D	R
Michigan	R	R	D	D	D	R	R	R	R	R	D	D	D
Indiana	R	R	R	D	R	R	R	R	R	R	R	R	R
Illinois	R	R	D	D	R	R	R	R	R	R	D	D	D
Wisconsin	R	R	R	D	R	R	D	R	R	D	D	D	D
Minnesota	R	R	D	D	D	R	D	D	D	D	D	D	D
Iowa	R	R	R	D	R	R	R	R	R	D	D	D	D
Missouri	R	D	D	D	R	R	D	R	R	R	D	D	R
North Dakota	R	R	R	D	R	R	R	R	R	R	R	R	R
South Dakota	R	R	R	D	R	R	R	R	R	R	R	R	R
Nebraska	R	R	R	D	R	R	R	R	R	R	R	R	R
Kansas	R	R	R	D	R	R	R	R	R	R	R	R	R
Entire nation	R	R	D	D	R	R	D	R	R	R	D	D	R

Source: Compiled by author from various editions of the *Statistical Abstract of the United States.*

Table 4. Willingness to Engage the Political System in the Midwest and the Rest of the Nation

Region	Eligible citizens registered to vote in 2000	Eligible citizens who voted in 2000	Residents who responded to 2000 U.S. Census
Midwest	73%	63%	72%
Rest of the nation	69%	59%	65%
United States total	70%	59%	67%

Sources: Voting and registration figures were calculated from data in U.S. Census Bureau, "Voting and Registration in the Election of November 2000," Feb. 2002. Census response rates were calculated from U.S. Census Bureau, "Census 2000 Response Rates—Detailed Tables," Sept. 18, 2000.

nating control with the Republicans starting in the 1970s. Similar trends played out in other midwestern states; where Republicans once dominated, Democrats now are competitive. In 2004, Republicans controlled both houses of the state legislatures in Iowa, Kansas, Michigan, Missouri, North Dakota, Ohio, South Dakota, and Wisconsin. Control of the state legislatures was split between the two parties in Indiana and Minnesota, while the Democrats were in undisputed charge in Illinois. (Nebraska elects its legislators on a nonpartisan ballot.) But again, it is critical to remember that, while the GOP in the early twenty-first century enjoys a strong position in the region's statehouses, its fortunes have ebbed and flowed over the last twenty years. In 1990, for example, the Democrats controlled four of the Midwest's state legislatures, and power was divided in another six legislatures. At that time the Republicans had majorities in both houses only in South Dakota.

It appears, then, that the Midwest has become competitive between the two major parties. Republicans enjoy their traditional dominance only in the Dakotas and Kansas. Does this make the Midwest distinctive as a region? The answer is probably not. Some states in the rest of the nation are clearly in the hands of one party or the other, but a majority of states outside the region are also reasonably competitive between the two parties. So, whereas the lack of party competition might have made the Midwest a distinct, cohesive geographic political entity several generations ago, such a characterization does not seem to be apt at the beginning of the new century.

In one area of political behavior, however, the Midwest may distinguish itself from the other regions in the country. Midwesterners seem to be more willing to engage with the political system than their counterparts elsewhere. The evidence for this claim is a bit thin, but what data there are support the claim. The percentage of midwesterners who were registered to vote in 2000 was higher than in the other thirty-eight states, as shown in table 4. Similarly, the percentage of midwesterners who cast a ballot in that year's presidential election was higher than elsewhere in the nation. And more midwesterners were willing to complete the Census forms sent out by the government in 2000 than were residents of other states. Indeed, nine of the top ten states in responding to the Census were in the Midwest. The differences between these engagement rates may be only a few percentage points, but those percentage points translate into millions of people more willing to perform their citizen duties.

These findings are consistent with those generated by social scientists examining the notion of social capital, or the level of citizen engagement in community affairs. In the most important study of social capital in the states, Harvard political scientist Robert Putnam found that several midwestern states—Iowa, Minnesota, South Dakota, and North Dakota—were among the handful of states enjoying the highest levels of citizen engagement. Overall, social capital was found to a greater degree in the Midwest than in other regions. Higher levels of social capital are important. Putnam found, for example, that support for racial and gender equality increases with social capital. And similarly to the findings reported in table 4, Putnam found fewer Internal Revenue Service criminal referrals and convictions in higher social capital states than in lower social capital states.

Can we conclude that the Midwest is a distinct political region? On the one hand, the region enjoys considerable political diversity. A single political culture does not bind it together. Various ideological orientations have been born and promoted in the regions. And in the last two decades, the region has become very competitive between the two major political parties. Consequently, it is easy to argue that the Midwest does not exhibit political cohesion. On the other hand, there is evidence to suggest that people in the Midwest are considerably more engaged with their political system than people in other regions of the country. Thus, the Midwest's political distinctiveness is not rooted in some stereotypical notion of traditional conservatism, but rather in the region's successful promotion of the norm of civic duty in pursuit of the common good among its citizenry.

Each aspect of politics in the Midwest merits attention, both those in which the region is distinctive and those in which it may be like the rest of the country. But critical to the examination is a historical dimension. The role of the Midwest in national politics has evolved in significant ways over time, and that evolution demands consideration. This involves looking at, among other things, midwesterners who have played important roles on the national political stage as well as at such structural factors as the political implications of the changing Midwest economy and the demographic composition of the populace.

Sources and Further Reading: Daniel Elazar, *American Federalism: A View from the States*, 3rd ed. (1984); Robert S. Erikson, Gerald C. Wright, and John P. McIver, *Statehouse Democracy* (1993); Jack Frymier and Arliss Roaden, *Cultures of the States* (2003); James Gimpel, *National Elections and the Autonomy of American State Party Systems* (1996); Virginia Gray and Russell L. Hanson, eds., *Politics in the American States*, 8th ed. (2004); Kendra A. Hovey and Harold A. Hovey, *CQ's State Fact Finder 2003* (2003); Maureen Moakley, *Party Realignment and State Politics* (1992); Robert D. Putnam, *Bowling Alone* (2000); William Safire, *Safire's New Political Dictionary* (1993); Frederick Jackson Turner, *The Significance of Sections in American History* (1932).

Peverill Squire
University of Iowa

The Agrarian Roots of Midwestern Politics

If American politics is the voice of diversity, the politics of the Midwest speaks with a peculiar farm drawl. Compared to the rest of the nation, Midwest farmers generally have been more moderate and less bombastic, bringing a conservative label to Heartland politics.

Even if the influence of the Northeast and South were felt earlier in national politics, the idealism of America's hope for the future was reflected in settling the Midwest. Rousseau and Jefferson elevated the virtues of pastoralism as the hope for democratic well-being. During the early part of American history, farmers who owned and farmed their lands were portrayed as hardworking and vigorous, possessing the will and the moral capacity to govern best. By the Civil War, the South was divided between plantation agriculture and rural poverty. Beyond eastern Nebraska and Kansas, settlement was erratic and unstable, with the farmers' place on the frontier uncertain. Pastoralism, to whatever extent it was real, was left to the Midwest, especially to employ as an image in furthering farm interests.

After the Civil War, Midwest farmers had ample opportunity to prosper and win influence. Homestead laws provided incentive for populating its sparsely settled regions, providing lands at low cost. Land-grant colleges offered inexpensive education; federal experiment stations were added in the states to research local crops and production; a federal Department of Agriculture began as an agency to identify and distribute better seeds and plants; state governments also established agriculture departments; extension workers advised farmers locally.

In a laissez-faire or largely unregulated economy, U.S. farmers were provided an unparalleled set of such public institutions for their benefit. With large farm populations, the desire of the states to advance farming, and low prices motivating farmers to seek to promote their economic security, these institutions were most developed and most used in the Midwest. The tendency of farmers to vote frequently and to lean Republican gave those who wished to enhance service institutions considerable leverage in political battles between a victorious Republican North and a reconstructed Democratic South. Stronger institutions, in turn, gave farmers who used the services economic advantages. Those who employed the most advanced technology were becoming larger and more commercial. The Midwest led the way.

The result of these emerging trends was that Midwest farmers were slow to rile. Instead, they pressed advantages through the use of government services, more efficient production practices, and neighborhood farmers clubs. Each grew wheat, hay, and corn; most raised beef, hogs, chickens, and dairy cows. Other crops and vegetable and fruit gardens were common. Climate and soil advantages helped produce multiple commercial goods plus family self-sufficiency. Midwest farmers were rarely at the mercy of encroaching industry, a company store, recurring drought, or a plague of grasshoppers.

Few farmers, as a result, joined nineteenth-century farm protest movements such as the National Farmers' Alliance. Supporters of that group were more likely from the impoverished South and the Great Plains. The Alliance and groups like it spun off radical support to insurrectionist partisan efforts on behalf of free silver or the Greenbacks, groups promoting inflated currency as a way of reducing the burden on debtors such as farmers. By century's end, economically disaffected farmers from beyond the Republican Midwest helped capture the Democratic Party for Nebraskan William Jennings Bryan. The Great Plains also gave rise to agrarian economic schemes, such as the Non-Partisan League's plan to shift debt burdens from borrowers to lenders after taking control of state governments. Less favorable growing conditions, little

Farm protest in Wisconsin. Wisconsin Historical Society, WHi-2038.

self-sufficiency, dependency on wheat as a single crop, and huge losses in the persistent depression of the 1880s made League plans seem like an empowering idea for struggling Plains farmers.

Although scattered support for the Alliance and the League were found in the Midwest, quite different types of farmer interest groups emerged in the region. The first of note was the Patrons of Husbandry, the Grange. The Grange was initially not a political group, but rather a fraternal organization in which farmers could gain self-awareness and learn to succeed. It was, in complementing farm service institutions, dedicated to better farming and the recognition of those who increased their productivity.

As crop prices fell dramatically after the Civil War, and after a decade of establishing Grange locals in the East, West, and South, the membership began to promote political activism. The National Grange encouraged only low-profile politics: A single committee lobbied government when members complained; lobbying of public officials was by formal letters; personal contacts were discouraged until officials approached Grangers; member protest actions were banned.

It would be incorrect, though, to portray all early Midwest farmer politics as conservative and proestablishment. The region's farm population was too diverse and the circumstances they faced too varied for such a blanket statement. Midwesterners who immigrated to the region had been Northeastern Yankees, Middle Atlantic fishermen, and Southern sharecroppers and soldiers. There were Germans, Irish, Scandi-navians, and eastern Europeans. All brought their own perspectives, cultures, and values; most settled within their own areas. For example, Scandinavians dominated the upper Midwest, often settling late into the least favorable climates and soils. Mining and forestry dominated these locations, and farmers lacked political influence. Michigan, Wisconsin, and Minnesota were settled first by lumberers and miners. Wisconsin, Michigan, and Illinois were states where early urban interests competed with farmers. Agrarian politics in such states were confrontational, with farmers likely to support economic protests, schemes, and cooperatives. Some supported alliances with labor in large cities in the Midwest. They gravitated toward Bryan and to the Democratic Party. Southern Indiana, Ohio, and Illinois farmers reflected the political attitudes of their Democratic and less commercial farming peers in the South.

Midwest farmers in places where agriculture was not the dominant interest were especially active in support of the radical Populist Party, with its 1880s theme of antielitism. However, Populist sentiment was greatest in Eastern Kansas and Northern Missouri: areas adjacent to the Great Plains with less favorable growing conditions and closer to the movement's West Kansas home.

More than geography created farmer support for the new century's reformist Progressives. This Wisconsin party attracted moralistic German and Yankee farm settlers because of perspective and culture. Yet the open-door government proposals of the Progressives aligned downstate Wisconsin farmers with business interests against wealthy lumber and mine owners of the North. Progressives vowed to halt government secrecy, break the trusts, and further regulate the economy. Progressivism, in support of belittled commoners, spread to Yankee and German neighbors in Michigan and Minnesota.

The spread of the Midwest's second major farm interest group, the American Farm Bureau Federation (AFBF), shows differences with the Progressives. After the United States Department of Agriculture (USDA) organized the first Farm Bureau, the model expanded nationally. The Farm Bureau idea was simple: With farmers still seen as not doing all they could to follow service institution advice in adopting scientific advances in agricultural technology, it was hoped that local farmers' groups could promote farm modernization among peers. The Agricultural Extension Service and USDA were to organize nonpolitical Farm Bureaus in each county government, locating them within Extension offices. This plan caught on most completely in the Midwest, where a larger percentage of farmers were already increasing their farm sizes and the use of science and technology.

As a deep depression hit American agriculture in 1930, local Farm Bureaus took readily to politics, eventually helping swing most farmers to voting Democratic in 1932. The Farm Bureau's partisan shifts were in large measure induced by its participation in the Corn Belt Committee of Farm Organizations (CBC), where moderates were influenced by radical farm peers and by anti-Hoover institutional professionals. The newly created AFBF also took to Washington lobbying. Farmer organizations from the West and South were more economically radical, rejecting the New Deal Agricultural Adjustment Administration plan of providing direct price supports and guaranteed loans to the largest crop producers. The most prominent of the opposition was the National Farmers' Union (NFU), another member of CBC, a traditional Democratic ally, descendant of the National Farmers' Alliance, and the lobby for the Progressive National Milk Producers Federation. The 1930s began a bitter rivalry between AFBF and NFU.

After the Depression and World War II, Midwest Farm Bureaus returned to their Republican roots. The Republican AFBF's major effort in the postwar years was to maintain and adjust federal price support and loan programs. The Farm Bureau also helped turn federal policymakers to favor international trade as the means of raising chronically low farm commodity prices. Midwest members of Congress, thus, fought hardest for price and trade programs for corn and soybeans, crops dominant in the Midwest; other legislators attended to wheat, cotton, tobacco, and peanut interests. Democrats and the NFU most influenced

non-Midwest federal support policies, creating fragmentation in the U.S. government's treatment of farmers.

It was at the state and local political levels where Midwest Farm Bureaus were most powerful on more issues. Counties set tax rates for assessing farmland property. Midwest farmers, Farm Bureau or not, wanted low property taxes and excellent rural services. The conservative farmer label stuck firmly in local politics. The same happened in state government. Rural state legislators tended to be Republicans in most of the Midwest and in almost all of the states in the legislative majority. As with counties, the number of rural legislative districts far outnumbered urban ones. The principle of similarly sized electoral districts was not mandated by the U.S. Supreme Court until the early 1960s. Each elected official did not have to represent the same number of citizens for each of the same offices. Each township in the county generally elected a county commissioner, and each county in the state usually had its own member of the lower state house. State senates were similarly malapportioned, as was Nebraska's unicameral legislature. For most Midwest states prior to 1964, legislatures reflected the biases of the region's farmers: socially conservative, economically austere, neglectful of education and human services, and unresponsive to urban and racial demands.

There were exceptions to this conservative character. Minnesota, Wisconsin, and Michigan farmers were often Democrats and NFU members. All three states were resplendent with small-scale dairy farmers. The Farmer-Labor Party then merged with urban Democrats to bring a liberal tenor to state politics, particularly in Minnesota with its Democratic-Farmer-Labor Party. Bumps in the economic road also brought about radical political forays after 1930.

Times, though, changed Midwest agrarian politics. More recent radical farm groups, such as the Farmers' Holiday Association, National Farmers Organization, and the American Agriculture Movement all lost their zeal soon after their founding because public support and critical media coverage were limited. The USDA separated Farm Bureaus from the Extension Service. The biggest change, however, has been in the decline of farm family numbers and farmer votes, and the rise of large agribusinesses that replace family farms. Modern Midwest farmers exert their political influence fiscally as one of the major sectors in each state's fragile economy. Thus, farm interest groups still rank among the most effective lobbies in all of the Midwest states.

Sources and Further Reading: William P. Browne, *Cultivating Congress* (1995); William P. Browne, *Private Interests, Public Policy, and American Agriculture* (1988); Christiana

McFayden Campbell, *The Farm Bureau and the New Deal* (1962); Willard W. Cochrane, *The Development of American Agriculture* (1979); John C. Culver and John Hyde, *American Dreamer: A Life of Henry A. Wallace* (2000); John Mark Hansen, *Gaining Access: Congress and the Farm Lobby 1919–1981* (1991); Ronald J. Hrebenar and Clive S. Thomas, eds., *Interest Group Politics in the Midwestern States* (1993); Theodore Saloutos and John D. Hicks, *Agricultural Discontent in the Middle West, 1900–1939* (1951); Elizabeth Sanders, *Roots of Reform: Farmers, Workers, and the American State* (1999); James R. Shortridge, *The Middle West: Its Meaning in American Culture* (1989).

William P. Browne
Central Michigan University

Center Ring or Sideshow? The Role of the Midwest in National Politics

As the 2000 election approached, pundits, politicos, and professors all looked to the Midwest as the pivotal region in American electoral politics. States like Missouri, Minnesota, Wisconsin, Iowa, Illinois, and Ohio became the constant targets of presidential candidates' visits and extensive television advertising. After all, these hotly contested states would likely provide the margin of victory for the next president of the United States. In the end, of course, Florida's twenty-five electoral votes would prove decisive in tilting the election to George W. Bush.

But the experts were not wrong: The election was decided in the Midwest, far more than any other region. For example, even though Democrats narrowly won the governorship and a U.S. Senate seat in Missouri, Al Gore lost the state's eleven electoral votes by a slender margin. Unlike the Pacific Coast and the Northeast, which gave Gore solid support, or those in the South and the Mountain West, which Bush came close to sweeping, the Midwest proved a battleground where both parties vigorously contested the election.

Ironically, the political import of the Midwest at the beginning of the twenty-first century—as a pivotal region in a country that is closely divided—has increased at a time when its strength should be waning. After all, throughout the twentieth century, the region's population steadily declined as a proportion of the entire nation's. Moreover, the country as a whole has become more homogeneous in an age of mass media, Microsoft, McDonald's, and Wal-Mart. Regardless, the very competitiveness of midwestern politics, both for congressional seats and for electoral votes, places many of its states in the center ring of American politics, even as its core economic interests of agriculture and manufacturing have grown less significant in the information age. Taking a closer look at

the Midwest in terms of electoral politics, national leadership, and interest-based influence will offer a more nuanced picture of the region's role in national politics.

Since the Eisenhower administration of the 1950s, divided government between the legislative and executive branches has been much more the rule than the exception in American politics. And since 1994, the margin of partisan power in Congress has become extremely narrow. With the "perfect tie" of the 2000 election and the steep decline in the number of competitive congressional seats, midwestern electoral politics ordinarily exerts a disproportionate influence on who controls the presidency and both the House and Senate. Indeed, partisan balance has been the rule for the region as a whole. Between 1966 and 2000, voters in midwestern states elected a total of 1,040 Republicans and 1,032 Democrats to the U.S. House. And although the states in the region have supported Republican presidential candidates at nearly a 70 percent clip over this period, the more populous states have been highly competitive. Thus, in 2000, Bush won seven of twelve midwestern states, but Gore's victories in the remaining five gave him more than half the region's electoral votes (68 of 129). Strangely enough, the overall partisan competitiveness is not well reflected in Senate elections, in that Democrats have won considerably more Senate seats over the 1966–2000 period, capturing 63 percent of the seats at stake.

Over the past century, at least in terms of raw numbers, the Midwest's electoral base has dwindled significantly (see table 5). After the 1900 census, midwestern states held more than a third of the seats in the House of Representatives, and almost exactly a third of the nation's electoral votes. No other region equaled the Midwest's numerical advantage; the East, for example, had 118 Representatives (30 percent) as opposed to the 136 from the Midwest. The midwestern percentages slide steadily through the twentieth century, to the point where less than one representative in four hails from the region in the post-2000 Census reapportionment of seats.

The Electoral College figures illustrate a similar trend and may infer that the Midwest has lost—and might well lose more—clout in national elections. But such an inference would be unwarranted, given the national composition of electoral competition at both presidential and congressional levels. Even as its percentage of the nation's population has declined, followed by losses in Representatives and Electoral College votes, the Midwest has grown increasingly important as the battleground upon which national elections are decided. For example, of the ten states with the most even party competition in the 1968–1998 period, four—Iowa, Illinois, Michigan, and

Table 5. Midwest Representation: The U.S. House and Electoral College, 1900–2000, Percent of Total Representatives and Electors from Midwestern States

	Decade									
	1900s[a]	*1910s*	*1930s*[b]	*1940s*	*1950s*	*1960s*	*1970s*	*1980s*	*1990s*	*2000s*
House	34.7	32.9	31.5	32.0	29.7	28.7	28.2	25.7	24.2	23.0
Electoral College	33.3	31.5	30.3	30.7	28.8	27.9	27.5	25.3	24.0	23.0

[a]The House had 391 representatives after 1900, 435 from 1910 on.
[b]No reapportionment was conducted in 1920.

Sources: Harold W. Stanley and Richard G. Niemi, *Vital Statistics on American Politics, 1999–2000* (2000), pp. 197-98.

Ohio—were in the Midwest. With a total of sixty-five electoral votes in the wake of the 2000 census, these states could easily swing a close presidential election.

In short, even as the Midwest loses population relative to the South and the West, its competitive politics—especially in Missouri, the upper Midwest, and the populous Great Lakes States—make the region exceptionally important in both presidential and congressional elections. Indeed, more intense campaigning occurs in the Midwest than in any other region of the country.

If national elections have placed the Midwest at the center of the action, the conclusion might be drawn that midwesterners would be attractive candidates for the presidency. But the last elected presidents to have even modest midwestern connections were Dwight Eisenhower, who grew up in Abilene, Kansas, and Ronald Reagan, who was born and raised in Illinois, but both lived the bulk of their adult lives in other parts of the country. A convincing argument can be made that the last true midwesterner to win the presidency was Missouri's Harry S Truman in 1948. Gerald Ford of Michigan, an appointed vice president who rose to the presidency with Richard Nixon's resignation, lost in his 1976 attempt to capture the White House, as did Minnesotans Hubert Humphrey in 1968 and Walter Mondale in 1984, and Kansan Bob Dole in 1996. The Electoral College math has led parties to nominate from their political base (Republican George W. Bush from Texas) or from their opponent's base (Southern Democrats Jimmy Carter and Bill Clinton, respectively). Moreover, midwestern governors have proven unable to convert their state office to a national candidacy, in contrast to governors Jimmy Carter, Ronald Reagan, Bill Clinton, and George W. Bush.

At the other end of Pennsylvania Avenue, however, midwesterners have become major players within the congressional leadership in the last fifty years, especially in the post-1980 period. After Senate Majority Leader Robert Taft's death in 1953, several midwestern legislators held top leadership positions in Con-

gress, including Illinois Republican Everett Dirksen as the Senate minority leader, and Indiana's Charles Halleck, Michigan's Gerald Ford, and Illinois's Bob Michel as House minority leaders. From the 99th Congress (1985–1986) through the 107th Congress (2001–2002), midwesterners have been prominent in the ranks of top congressional leaders. Senator Bob Dole (Republican, Kansas) served as GOP leader in the Senate from 1985 until 1996, and was Majority Leader in the 99th and 104th Congress. Michel continued to serve as House Minority Leader until 1995, and Representative Dennis Hastert (Republican, Illinois) began his tenure as Speaker in 1999.

In the Senate, Tom Daschle of South Dakota became Democratic floor leader in 1995, and moved into the majority leader position in 2001 (only to be defeated in his bid for re-election in 2004). And in the House, Representative Richard Gephardt (Democrat, Missouri) assumed the minority leader position in 1995, and held it through the 107th Congress. Thus, at the turn of the century, three of the four top party leaders in Congress hailed from the Midwest. Geography was an especially important element of Hastert's unexpected rise to lead House Republicans. Despite a conservative voting record, the well-liked Hastert had demonstrated an ability to get along with all GOP factions in the House. His openness and common sense has served him well in dealing with a highly ideological, intensely partisan House.

Although the political geography of the Electoral College has dictated a Southern–Western domination of presidential politicking, congressional leadership has demonstrated an opposing trend, in which midwesterners like Bob Dole and Dennis Hastert have played roles as brokers among partisan factions. Winning the presidency seems to require a calculus that plays to partisan bases, whereas congressional leadership has required a combination of skills that combines partisanship with the capacity to strike bargains—a set of traits that may well be fostered by the pragmatic politics of the Midwest.

The relative decline of the Midwest as a population

center has not meant that the region has declined in political influence; its overall electoral competitiveness continues to make it extremely important to national campaigns. And its status as the home of many top congressional party leaders means that the region will remain influential on Capitol Hill for the foreseeable future. Still, the national import of the Midwest cannot rely solely on elections or congressional clout. Rather, influence flows from power of organized interests to shape policy debates and win legislative battles in Washington. Over the course of the twentieth century, considerable power shifted from the states to the national government, especially as the federal government programs and spending exploded since the 1960s.

Reacting to the growth of federal spending programs, complexities in taxation, and the reach of regulation, organized interests have placed a growing emphasis on national policy making in the Congress and the executive bureaucracy. Even as the number of trade associations in the United States grew steadily from the 1950s to the 1990s, more tended to locate their headquarters in Washington. Thus, between 1971 and 1990, the percentage of associations with their main offices in metropolitan Washington rose from 19 percent to 32 percent. Moreover, midwestern interests have declined in importance in this power shift. Among *Fortune* magazine's twenty-five most influential lobbies in 2001, for example, only the American Farm Bureau Federation might be thought to have a midwestern power base. Most of the top lobbies were truly national in scope, as with the National Rifle Association and the American Association for Retired People. Still, lobbies representing the motion picture industry, health insurers, broadcasters, and the pharmaceutical industry drew their strength disproportionately from other regions.

In a similar vein, no midwestern newspapers or other media outlets offer voices beyond the region, although the Tribune Company of Chicago, Illinois, owns the *Los Angeles Times* among other newspapers. Conversely, New York, California, and Washington, D.C., provide numerous national voices, whether through newspapers, network television, or cable.

At the same time, state capitals have become more and more important in both making policy and funneling federal funds, and organized interests have responded by directing more attention to these venues for decision making. Thus, between 1975 and 1990, the number of interest groups registered to lobby in midwestern state capitals more than tripled, from an average of 190 groups in 1975 to 630 in 1990. And in the region's most populous states—Illinois, Michigan, and Ohio—the average growth approaches a sevenfold increase, from 473 groups in 1975 to more than three

thousand in 1990. Ironically, the growth of federal programs has meant that all states—especially the industrialized Midwest—have experienced marked growth in their interest group communities. Interests cannot afford to neglect Capitol Hill, but neither can they ignore the politics of Madison, Springfield, or Columbus, where hundreds of important decisions, on everything from reimbursement of drug costs to telecommunications regulations to educational funding, are decided every year.

In sum, the Midwest remains central within a narrowly divided American political system. Several large swing states within the region may well provide the margin of victory in closely contested presidential elections for the foreseeable future. Likewise, the results of midwestern congressional elections may well determine which party controls the House and Senate. And midwestern state capitals have become hotbeds of political struggle among rapidly growing numbers of interest groups. Still, in an information age, the region has lost some clout, as organized interests and the media—knowingly or not—seek to affect, even control, a national policy agenda that often has little room for distinctive midwestern issues.

Sources and Further Reading: Michael Barone and Richard E. Cohen, *The Almanac of American Politics, 1999–2000* (2001); William Browne, *Private Interests, Public Policy, and American Agriculture* (1988); John Fenton, *Midwest Politics* (1966); Virginia Gray and David Lowery, *The Population Ecology of Interest Representation* (1996); Ronald J. Hrebenar and Clive S. Thomas, eds., *Interest Group Politics in the Midwestern States* (1993); Neil R. Peirce, *The Great Plains States of America* (1973); Neil Peirce and John Keefe, *The Great Lakes States of America* (1980); Kevin Phillips, *Arrogant Capital* (1994).

Burdett A. Loomis
University of Kansas

William Henry Harrison (1773–1841) and Benjamin Harrison (1833–1901): The Rise of the Midwest in Nineteenth-Century Politics

The lives of William Henry Harrison and Benjamin Harrison, the only grandfather and grandson to serve as presidents of the United States, are inseparable from the history of the Midwest and its emergence as a distinct region in the nineteenth century. William Henry Harrison is closely identified with the early history of the Old Northwest, that part of the Midwest north of the Ohio River and east of the Mississippi River. Eventually the area would be carved into five states and, with a significant proportion of the electoral vote, produce president after president in the late nineteenth century, including Benjamin Harrison.

President William Henry Harrison. Library of Congress, Prints and Photographs Division, LC-USZ62-7567 DLC.

President Benjamin Harrison. Library of Congress, Prints and Photographs Division, LC-USZ61-480 DLC.

Born in 1773, William Henry Harrison entered the army in 1791 and was assigned to the Old Northwest. He resigned from the army in 1798 to become Secretary of the Old Northwest, then served as the area's first representative to Congress in 1799. Harrison led the movement to have the Old Northwest split into two territories, Indiana and Ohio. When Congress approved his initiative, Harrison became Governor of the Indiana Territory in 1800 and held that office for twelve years.

Harrison, acting on presidential orders, obtained millions of acres of land from the Native Americans. When the charismatic Native American leader Tecumseh threatened to use any means necessary to stop the cession of land, Harrison led approximately a thousand men against the Native Americans in what became known as the Battle of Tippecanoe, near Ft. Wayne, Indiana, in November 1811. He achieved a dubious victory, suffering very high casualties, but Americans chose to declare Harrison a military hero, thereby establishing a reputation that led to the White House thirty years later.

At the outbreak of the War of 1812, Harrison became a Brigadier General and Commander of the Army of the Northwest. When the tide of war turned against Great Britain in 1813, Harrison, now a Major General, recaptured Detroit in late September and pursued the British into Canada. At the Battle of the Thames in early October, Harrison decisively defeated the British and, with the death of Tecumseh in the battle, effectively eliminated the Native American presence in the Old Northwest.

After the war, Harrison established residence in North Bend, Ohio. He served one term in the U.S. House of Representatives and three years in the U.S. Senate. He then faded into obscurity until the Whig Party rediscovered him in the mid 1830s.

In the presidential election of 1836, the Whigs fielded three candidates to try to prevent Democrat Martin Van Buren from winning a majority of the electoral vote. The strategy failed, but Harrison made the most impressive showing of the Whig candidates, carrying seven states, including Indiana and Ohio. Whigs surmised that Harrison, with the Midwest as his base, could win the next presidential election. In the aftermath of the economic depression that started in 1837, Harrison defeated incumbent President Van Buren in a landslide in 1840, carrying Indiana, Ohio, and the new state of Michigan. Harrison died in office just thirty days after his inauguration, but his victory had revealed the political potential of the Midwest.

Benjamin Harrison, born in 1833 on his grandfather's estate in North Bend, Ohio, graduated from Miami University in Oxford, Ohio, in 1852, then moved west to Indianapolis in 1854 to launch a legal practice. Harrison commanded the 70th Indiana Regiment in the Civil War, rising to the rank of Brigadier General. He became leader of the Republican Party in Indiana in the late 1870s and served one term in the United States Senate (1881–1887).

Harrison's name recognition, his Civil War record, and the importance of Indiana in presidential elections of the late nineteenth century made him a serious candidate for the Republican Party nomination in 1888. Eight of the ten states that then constituted the Midwest could be counted on to vote Republican in post–Civil War presidential elections, with Missouri firmly Democratic and Indiana the only swing state.

The 1888 and 1892 elections demonstrated the growing political clout of the Midwest. Harrison won the Republican nomination in 1888 and defeated the incumbent Democrat, Grover Cleveland, by an electoral vote count of 233 to 168. Harrison carried every state in the Midwest except Missouri. The Midwest gave Harrison a total of 118 electoral votes, more than half of the electoral votes that put him in office.

Over the next two years, many Republican leaders realized that the party had lost ground with Catholic voters in the Midwest as Republicans promoted their nineteenth-century version of a social agenda. When both Iowa and Ohio elected Democratic governors in 1889, Harrison responded in 1890 with a three-thousand-mile tour through six states of the Midwest: Illinois, Indiana, Iowa, Kansas, Missouri, and Ohio. Nevertheless, the Democrats captured control of the House of Representatives in a landslide, with Republican seats in the House nearly halved, from 166 to a mere 88.

The presidential election of 1892 featured a rematch between Harrison and Cleveland. The Midwest loomed as the key battleground, with a total of 152 electoral votes, or more than one third of the total of 444. An increase of eighteen electoral votes since 1888 reflected reapportionment based on the Census of 1890 and the addition of two new states to the Midwest in 1889, North Dakota and South Dakota.

Cleveland won the election with a comfortable margin in the Electoral College, 277 to 145. Much of the Midwest turned against the Republican Party. In addition to losing Missouri, Harrison lost one elec-

toral vote in Ohio, five in Michigan, two of three in North Dakota, his own state of Indiana, plus Illinois, Kansas, and Wisconsin. The Midwest proved decisive, but Republicans learned an important political lesson: They would concentrate on the nation's economy rather than on a social agenda, and they would retake the Midwest beginning with the Congressional election of 1894, in the midst of the worst depression to date in the nation's history.

Sources and Further Reading: Robert W. Cherny, *American Politics in the Gilded Age, 1868–1900* (1997); John A. Garraty and Mark C. Carnes, eds., *American National Biography*, vol. 10 (1999); Michael F. Holt, *The Rise and Fall of the American Whig Party* (1999); Richard Jensen, *The Winning of the Midwest* (1971); John L. Moore, ed., *Congressional Quarterly's Guide to U.S. Elections*, 3rd ed. (1994); Norma Lois Peterson, *The Presidencies of William Henry Harrison and John Tyler* (1989); Harry J. Sievers, S.J., *Benjamin Harrison, Hoosier President* (1968); Homer E. Socolofsky and Allan B. Spetter, *The Presidency of Benjamin Harrison* (1987).

Allan B. Spetter
Wright State University, Ohio

Presidential Ticket-Balancing

The Midwest has proved an important source of presidential and vice-presidential candidates in American history. The region achieved its greatest influence in this regard during the late nineteenth century. Although it continues to provide national candidates, the Midwest has recently declined as such a source.

The Northeast and South provided early presidential candidates during the time they constituted the union. Even at the middle of the nineteenth century, midwestern candidates were still rare—William Henry Harrison of Ohio, the Whig presidential candidate in 1836 and 1840, and Lewis Cass of Michigan, the Democratic standard-bearer in 1848. Beginning in 1860, however, the Midwest emerged as the leading source of Republican presidential candidates and Democratic vice-presidential candidates. For the ten elections from 1860 to 1896 inclusive, the Republicans nominated nine presidential candidates from the region—Abraham Lincoln (1860, 1864) and Ulysses S. Grant (1868, 1872) of Illinois; Rutherford B. Hayes (1876), James Garfield (1880), and William McKinley (1896) of Ohio; and Benjamin Harrison (1888, 1892) of Indiana. Although the Democrats rarely chose a midwestern presidential candidate during this period—only Stephen A. Douglas of Illinois in 1860 and William Jennings Bryan of Nebraska in 1896—they balanced the ticket with midwesterners as vice presidential candidates on the other eight occasions: George Pendleton and Allen Thurman of Ohio, Frank P. Blair, Jr., and Benjamin G. Brown of Missouri, Thomas Hendricks (twice) and William English of Indiana, and Adlai Stevenson of Illinois.

This regional pattern of influence continued during the early twentieth century when fifteen of twenty-eight major party candidates came from the Midwest. In the seven elections from 1900 to 1924, seven presidential candidates from the two major parties came from the region—William McKinley (1896, 1900), William Howard Taft (1908, 1912), James Cox (1920), and Warren Harding (1920) of Ohio, and William Jennings Bryan (1900, 1908) of Nebraska. Indiana provided five vice-presidential candidates of the major parties defining that period—Charles Warren Fairbanks (1904, 1916), John W. Kern (1908), and Thomas Riley Marshall (1912, 1916).

Two developments soon occurred that limited the midwestern candidates on national tickets. First, the South returned as a force within the Democratic Party. From 1928 to 1960, it claimed the second spot on the Democratic ticket except in 1940 and 1944. Second, California emerged as a new source of Republican presidential and vice-presidential candidates—Herbert Hoover, Earl Warren, Richard M. Nixon, and Ronald Reagan, although both Hoover and Reagan were Midwest natives. Accordingly, as national candidates came from four regions rather than two, the Midwest's share predictably declined; from 1928 to 2000, midwesterners accounted for twenty-three of the seventy-seven major party candidates.

During the twentieth century, the region has claimed more than a one-quarter share of national candidates. Indeed, in the twenty-six elections from 1900 to 2000, midwestern residents claimed 36 percent of the presidential or vice-presidential positions. The percentage exceeds 40 if midwestern natives Hoover, Eisenhower, Ford, and Reagan are counted. The thirty-nine candidates were divided roughly evenly between Democrats (twenty) and Republicans (nineteen) and presidential (eighteen) and vice-presidential (twenty-one) candidates.

Yet the tide is moving away from the Midwest. In 1900, three of the four candidates (Bryan, Stevenson, and McKinley) came from the Midwest; a hundred years later, none did. Of course, no single election year can accurately portray pertinent trends. After all, the 1976 campaign included three midwesterners—Gerald Ford, Bob Dole, and Walter Mondale. Yet the decline of the Midwest seems clear. In the six elections after 1976, Democrats and Republicans have each nominated only one midwestern presidential candidate (Mondale and Dole) and together three vice-presidential candidates (Mondale and Quayle, twice). In essence, in recent elections, midwesterners account for about 25 percent of the major party candidates.

There is little evidence to suggest that geography explains the nomination of midwestern presidential candidates. With few exceptions, they were chosen owing to their standing in the party or their success in primaries, not due to their regional characteristics. Once nominated, presidential candidates do consider geography in broad terms in choosing running mates. Generally speaking, candidates look outside their own region for a running mate to balance the ticket; on rare occasions they seek to reinforce their identity by seeking a running mate from their region (for example, Bill Clinton and Al Gore). Yet few, if any, recent vice-presidential candidates were chosen because they were from the Midwest. George McGovern chose Missouri's Thomas Eagleton but only after others, including several Easterners, declined. Carter's list of prospective running mates included three midwesterners, but also two from the East and one from the West. Lacking background in national government, Carter emphasized beltway experience and ties to important Democratic constituencies, not geography, in choosing Mondale. Ford chose Dole largely because he was more acceptable to the Reagan wing of the party; Quayle's youth and conservative credentials, not geography, explained his selection.

Choosing a midwestern running mate does not guarantee electoral success in the region. The Republicans ran Kansas Governor Alf Landon and Illinois publisher Frank Knox in 1936 but failed to carry a single midwestern state in Franklin Roosevelt's landslide. Mondale helped Carter carry only Minnesota in 1980; they did better in the region four years earlier running against two midwesterners. Most midwestern electoral votes went to Clinton and Gore in 1992 against midwesterner Quayle.

The nationalization of politics has reduced the significance of the Midwest as a source of national party candidates. One factor is suggested above: with four, rather than two, regions providing candidates, the Midwest's share has understandably declined. As technology facilitates travel and disseminates information, candidates must be plausible nationally, not just attractive to a single region.

Even in this new environment, the Midwest may be relatively well placed to provide vice-presidential candidates. Vice-presidential candidates sometimes are chosen to help in their home states. The Midwest includes three large states—Illinois, Michigan, and Ohio—and several modest prizes—Missouri, Minnesota, Indiana, and Wisconsin; candidates from these states may prove attractive. Presidential candidates from other regions look to the Midwest as one source of running mates. Midwestern presidential candidates may, on occasion, choose a midwestern running mate as did Bryan (twice), Landon, McGovern, and Ford. It seems unlikely that eastern or western candidates will choose from their own region; they did not do so in the twentieth century. Accordingly, the system may contain a slight bias to the advantage of the Midwest.

Sources and Further Reading: Congressional Quarterly, Inc., *Presidential Elections, 1789–1992* (1995); Joel K. Goldstein, *The Modern American Vice Presidency* (1982); James T. Havel, *U.S. Presidential Candidates and the Elections,* 2 vols. (1996); Joseph Nathan Kane, *Facts About the Presidents,* 6th ed. (1993); Nelson Polsby and Aaron Wildavsky, *Presidential Elections: Strategies and Structures of American Politics,* 10th ed. (2000); Arthur M. Schlesinger, Jr., ed., *History of American Presidential Elections, 1789–1968* (1971); Leslie H. Southwick, *Presidential Also-Rans and Running Mates, 1788–1996,* 2nd ed. (1998).

Joel K. Goldstein
Saint Louis University, Missouri

The Iowa Precinct Caucuses

Previously obscure, the Iowa precinct caucuses took a modest step toward national prominence in 1972, when the state's Democratic Party moved its caucus date forward to January 24, which positioned the caucuses ahead of the New Hampshire primary election, the traditional first event in a presidential election year. The earlier date resulted from reforms in the caucus and convention system that the Iowa Democrats adopted between 1968 and 1972 to comply with national party rule changes.

Two Democratic presidential candidates, George McGovern and Jimmy Carter, were the first to use the caucuses successfully to gain attention for their campaigns, and in so doing contributed to their growth as a national event. McGovern's 1972 Iowa campaign got limited national coverage, but even that limited attention was more than the caucuses had ever received. In 1975, Carter launched an all-out effort in Iowa. He became the Democratic front-runner after a strong showing, which generated considerable attention from the national media, and when he gained the party nomination and was elected president, the Iowa caucuses became a fixture in the presidential nominating process.

From 1984 to 1996, the winners in Iowa did not go on to win their party's nomination. In 2000, however, Iowa winners Al Gore and George W. Bush both became their party's candidates. But the front-loading of the primary season and importance of paid TV have altered the dynamics of the presidential race. George

H. W. Bush and Michael Dukakis in 1988 and Bob Dole in 1996 showed that well-financed candidates could rebound after setbacks in the caucuses. The tightened nominating schedule and the huge funding required to successfully compete for office may have reduced the ability of Iowa (and New Hampshire) to offer sufficient momentum for a dark-horse candidate to win a presidential nomination. It has been more than twenty-five years since the last obscure candidate, Jimmy Carter, rode the momentum from Iowa to the White House.

Although the Iowa caucuses may not make presidential candidacies, they do break them. Many candidates may enter the presidential race, but fewer are viable after Iowa and New Hampshire. In 1984, only three of the eight Democratic candidates were still in the race a month after the Iowa caucuses. In 1988, three of the six Republican and three of the seven Democratic candidates were effectively eliminated by the two states; five of the nine Republican candidates in 1996, and three of the six Republicans in 2000 met the same fate. In 2004, the two states effectively eliminated five of the nine Democrats and put two others— Howard Dean and Wesley Clark—on life support.

The 1972 and 1976 caucuses marked the beginning

Cartoon by Brian Duffy. © 1983, *Des Moines Register,* reprinted by permission

The larger states are unhappy that Iowa and New Hampshire have emerged as kingmakers in the presidential nominating process. Although many states have moved their primary events closer to the beginning of the nominating season, Iowa and New Hampshire continue to deliver knockout blows in the bout for the presidency.

A perspective on the Iowa caucuses. Courtesy Brian Duffy.

of a dramatic change in American electoral politics. As the Iowa caucuses grew in importance, other states moved their primary events forward. What had been a traditional four-month primary season—starting in New Hampshire in March and ending in California in June—was significantly altered. The schedule of primary events was compressed, and a new front-loaded season emphasizing the nominating processes in Iowa and New Hampshire developed.

Sources and Further Reading: Emmett H. Buell, Jr., "The Invisible Primary," in William G. Mayer, ed., *In Pursuit of the White House* (1996); William G. Mayer, "Caucuses: How They Work, What Difference They Make," in William G. Mayer, ed., *In Pursuit of the White House* (1996); Peverill Squire, ed., *The Iowa Caucuses and the Presidential Nominating Process* (1989); Hugh Winebrenner, *The Iowa Precinct Caucuses*, 2nd ed. (1998).

Hugh Winebrenner
Drake University, Iowa

Joseph Gurney Cannon (1836–1926)

Joe Cannon, a longtime U.S. Representative from Illinois, was arguably the most powerful Speaker in the history of the chamber.

Cannon was born in North Carolina on May 7, 1836. As a small child, he moved with his family to Indiana. After studying at the Cincinnati Law School, he first practiced law in Indiana before moving to Illinois, where he established a practice in 1859.

Cannon began his political career as a district attorney in Coles County, Illinois. He lost his first campaign for the U.S. House in 1870, but won in his next try two years later. He represented the Danville, Illinois, area from 1873 to 1891, again from 1893 to 1913, and finally from 1915 to 1923.

During his congressional career, Cannon's earthy language, energetic oratory, and hayseed persona earned him the nickname "Uncle Joe." A staunch Republican, Cannon authored no important legislation during his career; instead he was a "stand-patter." As chair of the House Appropriations Committee, he once remarked, "You think my business is to make appropriations, but it is not. It is to prevent their being made." Cannon's opposition to conservation spending was similarly blunt: "not one cent for scenery." Protecting high tariffs was his main legislative passion.

Cannon served as Speaker from 1903 to 1911. He dominated House proceedings, making all committee appointments and controlling which bills would be considered and who would get to speak on them. His opposition to legislation pushed by Republican progressives led them to join with Democrats to signifi-

cantly reduce the speaker's powers in 1910. No speaker has ever again been as powerful as Cannon.

Cannon retired from the House voluntarily in 1923 and died in Danville, Illinois, on November 12, 1926.

Sources and Further Reading: Blair Bolles, *Tyrant from Illinois* (1951); L. White Busbey, *Uncle Joe Cannon* (1927); Richard B. Cheney and Lynne V. Cheney, *Kings of the Hill* (1996).

Peverill Squire
University of Iowa

Everett McKinley Dirksen (1896–1969)

Born in Pekin, Illinois, on January 4, 1896, Everett McKinley Dirksen was one of three sons of Johann and Antje Dirksen, recent immigrants from Germany. Dirksen attended the University of Minnesota before serving in the Army Balloon Corps during World War I. He returned home in 1919, eventually joined his brothers' bakery business, and won election to Pekin's City Council in 1926. He married Louella Carver that year; their daughter, Danice Joy, was born in 1929.

Dirksen won a seat in the U.S. House of Representatives in 1932, and served until deciding against seeking reelection in 1948, given his suffering from an eye ailment. Two years later, however, he campaigned for one of Illinois's U.S. Senate seats, the first of his four successful Senate races. Elected as a midwestern conservative, Dirksen moderated his views during his years in the Senate. "I am just a garden variety Republican who, like Lincoln, believes in the Constitution and in the Bill of Rights and in our free-enterprise system," he often explained. His Republican colleagues elected him Minority Leader of the Senate in 1959, a post he retained until his death ten years later.

Dirksen was instrumental in crafting much of the Great Society legislation in the 1960s. He is most remembered for his pivotal role in passing the Civil Rights Act of 1964, when he delivered enough Republican votes to break a filibuster led by Southern Democrats and give President Lyndon Johnson, also a Democrat, one of his greatest legislative victories. This effort exemplified Dirksen's legislative prowess, political skill, oratorical ability, and personal conviction.

Sources and Further Reading: Everett M. Dirksen, *The Education of a Senator* (1998); Byron Hulsey, *Everett Dirksen and His Presidents* (2000); Neil MacNeil, *Dirksen: Portrait of a Public Man* (1970).

Frank H. Mackaman
The Dirksen Congressional Center,
Pekin, Illinois

Robert Joseph Dole (b. 1923)

Born and raised in depression-era Russell, Kansas, Bob Dole gained prominence as one of the most powerful and enduring figures of late-twentieth-century American politics. Wounded by a mortar explosion in the hills of Italy in 1945, Dole persevered through years of hospitalization and rehabilitation and was left without the use of one arm. After serving eight years as Russell County Attorney, Dole was elected to the United States House of Representatives in 1960. After four terms in the House, he was elected to the U.S. Senate in 1968. Kansas voters reelected him to the Senate in 1974, 1980, 1986, and 1992.

In 1976, President Gerald Ford selected Dole as his vice-presidential running mate on the Republican ticket. Ford and Dole lost narrowly to Democrats Jimmy Carter and Walter Mondale. Dole served as Republican leader of the Senate from 1985 to 1996. He earned a reputation as a masterful legislative tactician with an ability to reach bipartisan consensus. Dole resigned from the Senate in June 1996, after securing enough delegates to become the Republican Party nominee for president. A strong American economy helped to ensure the reelection of President Bill Clinton and Vice President Al Gore and the defeat of Dole and his running mate, former New York Congressman Jack Kemp. In 1974, Dole married Elizabeth Hanford, who went on to serve in the cabinets of Presidents Ronald Reagan and George Bush and in the U.S. Senate. He and his former wife, Phyllis Holden, have a daughter, Robin, born in 1954. Well known for his keen wit, Dole has authored two books on political humor.

Sources and Further Reading: Robert Dole, *Great Political Wit* (1998); Robert and Elizabeth Dole, *Unlimited Partners* (1996); Jake Thompson, *Bob Dole: The Republican's Man for All Seasons* (1994).

Kerry Tymchuk
Beaverton, Oregon

Stephen Arnold Douglas (1813–1861)

Born in Brandon, Vermont, Stephen Arnold Douglas became a powerful Illinois senator and played a leading role in the conflict over slavery during the 1850s. Douglas went to Illinois in 1833 and quickly organized Illinois's Democratic Party. Party leaders and voters rewarded him by placing him on the state Supreme Court in 1841 and by electing him to the U.S. House of Representatives in 1843 and to the Senate in 1846. A strong proponent of western states like Illinois, Douglas advocated a homestead policy to spur

settlement, the construction of railroads to develop western commerce, and territorial laws that speeded the development of new western states.

His expansionistic tendencies, however, ultimately helped draw the Union into civil war. In 1854, Douglas sponsored the Kansas-Nebraska Act, which permitted slaveholders to settle in the newly-created Kansas and Nebraska territories. Although Douglas expected the territories to become free states, angry antislavery Northerners established the Republican Party that year to combat slavery's expansion. Believing that the triumph of the Republican Party would destroy the Union, Douglas spent the next six years attempting to quell the antislavery uprising by promoting a territorial policy called "popular sovereignty," which empowered territorial settlers to legalize or outlaw slavery. However, a majority of both Northerners and southerners rejected popular sovereignty, and the triumph of the Republican Party in the 1860 Presidential election over Democratic Party candidate Douglas catalyzed southern secession and Civil War. Douglas died in 1861 while attempting to rally northern Democrats to the cause of the Union.

Sources and Further Reading: Harry V. Jaffa, *Crisis of the House Divided* (1959); Robert W. Johannsen, ed., *The Letters of Stephen A. Douglas* (1961); Robert W. Johannsen, *Stephen A. Douglas* (1973).

Graham A. Peck
Saint Xavier University, Chicago and
Orlando Park, Illinois

Dwight David Eisenhower (1890–1969)

Dwight Eisenhower, thirty-fourth president of the United States, was born the son of David and Ida Stover Eisenhower on October 14, 1890, in Denison, Texas. In 1892, his family returned to Kansas, where they settled in Abilene. In 1911, Eisenhower enrolled at the U.S. Military Academy at West Point, graduating in the upper half of the class of 1915. He was assigned to Fort Sam Houston in Texas, where he met Mamie Geneva Doud, a native of Boone, Iowa. They were married in Denver on July 1, 1916.

Although Eisenhower did not receive a combat command during World War I, he served with distinction as commanding officer of a tank brigade at Camp Colt, Gettysburg, Pennsylvania. In 1926, Eisenhower distinguished himself by graduating first in his class at the Army's Command and General Staff College at Ft. Leavenworth, Kansas. Thereafter, he served on the staffs of Generals Douglas MacArthur in the Philippines (1935–1939) and George C. Marshall in Wash-

Dwight D. Eisenhower. Photo by Fabian Bachrach, c. 1952, Library of Congress, Prints and Photographs Division, LC-USZ62-84331 DLC.

ington, D.C., (1941–1942) prior to becoming Commanding General of the European Theater of Operations in the spring of 1942.

As president, Eisenhower wanted to end the Korean War, fought for a balanced federal budget, and sought to stop the proliferation of nuclear weapons. The 1950s during his administration was characterized by "peace and prosperity" and known for the beginning of the black civil rights movement. President Eisenhower died on March 28, 1969, at Walter Reed Army Hospital and was buried at the Place of Meditation on the grounds of the Eisenhower Center in Abilene, Kansas.

Sources and Further Reading: Stephen E. Ambrose, *Eisenhower: Soldier and President* (1990); Carlo D'Este, *Eisenhower: A Soldier's Life* (2002); Dwight D. Eisenhower, *At Ease: Stories I Tell My Friends* (1967).

Jack M. Holl
Kansas State University

Gerald Rudolph Ford (b. 1913)

Gerald Ford, born July 14, 1913, in Omaha, Nebraska, served as thirty-eighth president of the United States.

Originally named Leslie King, Jr., Ford informally took his stepfather's name at age three following his parents' divorce and his mother's subsequent remarriage to Grand Rapids, Michigan, businessman Gerald R. Ford. (His name was not legally changed until 1935.) In 1948, he married Elizabeth (Betty) Bloomer. They share four children.

Ford graduated from the University of Michigan in 1935 and Yale University Law School in 1941. He served in the U.S. Navy from 1942 to 1946. After being discharged, Ford returned to Grand Rapids and joined a Republican reform group that counted Senator Arthur Vandenberg among its members. In 1948, Vandenberg urged Ford to challenge incumbent Republican U.S. Representative Bartel Jonkman in the primary election because of Jonkman's isolationist views on foreign policy. Ford won the primary and general elections that year. He was reelected to the House twelve times. In 1965, Ford was selected House Minority Leader, a post he held for the rest of his House career. He also served on the Warren Commission, the government panel appointed to investigate the Kennedy assassination.

In October 1973, Vice President Spiro Agnew resigned amidst allegations of criminal conduct. President Nixon appointed Ford as his replacement. By 1974, the Nixon presidency was mired in the scandal commonly known as Watergate, precipitated by a 1972 break-in at Democratic National Headquarters. On August 9, 1974, Nixon resigned from office, making Ford the nation's first president never elected to the presidency or vice-presidency. He moved quickly to offer a conditional amnesty program for Vietnam draft evaders, address economic problems, and more controversially, pardon former president Nixon for any and all federal crimes that he may have committed in office. The pardon negatively affected Ford's prestige with the public and Congress, hampering his ability to govern. In 1976, he lost a closely contested reelection bid to Jimmy Carter.

Sources and Further Reading: James Cannon, *Time and Chance: Gerald Ford's Appointment with History* (1994); Michael A. Genovese, *The Power of the American Presidency, 1789–2000* (2001); Yanek Mieczkowski, *The Routledge Historical Atlas of Presidential Elections* (2001).

Rhonda Kinney
Eastern Michigan University

Ulysses S. Grant (1822–1885)

Hiram Ulysses Grant, as he was first named, was born on April 27, 1822, at Point Pleasant, Ohio, the son of

Jesse Grant, a tanner, and Hannah Simpson. His father wangled him an appointment to West Point, which Ulysses attended reluctantly, but he graduated respectably in the middle of his class thanks to an aptitude for mathematics. As a young officer at Jefferson Barracks south of St. Louis, he fell in love with Julia Dent, daughter of a nearby planter. The Mexican War interrupted the courtship, but marriage followed in 1848. Tensions between Grant's antislavery father and slaveholding father-in-law shadowed the young couple.

Grant resigned from the army in 1854, intending to become a Missouri farmer. Unsuccessful in farming and business, Grant was clerking in his father's leather goods store in Galena, Illinois, when the Civil War began. Within four years, he captured three Confederate armies and won the war.

Although content to remain a postwar officer with comfortable lifetime employment and pay, he believed that duty required him to accept the Republican nomination for president. In office from 1869 to 1877, he protected freedmen and crushed the Ku Klux Klan, presided over negotiations with Britain that averted conflict, began a peace policy with Native Americans, and supported civil service reform. He also pursued stubbornly but unsuccessfully an effort to annex Santo Domingo and received blame for corruption of public officials in his administration. Contemporaries admired his reticence, modesty, resilience, and determination. Late in life, dying of cancer, he wrote an autobiography that became a classic.

Sources and Further Reading: Ulysses S. Grant, *Personal Memoirs of U. S. Grant*, 2 vols. (1885); John Y. Simon, ed., *The Papers of Ulysses S. Grant*, 24 vols. (1966–2000); Jean Edward Smith, *Grant* (2001).

John Y. Simon
Southern Illinois University–Carbondale

Marcus Alonzo Hanna (1837–1904)

Hanna was born on September 24, 1837, in New Lisbon, Ohio, the son of Leonard and Samantha Converse Hanna. He spent a brief period at Western Reserve College and then worked in his family's grocery business. When he married Charlotte Augusta Rhodes in 1865, he became involved in his father-in-law's interests in coal and iron. For the next two decades, Hanna ran one of the leading industrial firms in the Midwest.

During the 1870s, Hanna met Congressman William McKinley of Ohio, but their political partnership did not begin until the end of the 1880s. Hanna decided to push McKinley's political fortunes,

first for the Ohio governorship in the early 1890s and then for the Republican nomination for president in 1896. Though he was not the dominant force in their alliance, Hanna displayed organizing skill and fundraising abilities that facilitated McKinley's successful run for the presidency. In the process, Democratic newspapers depicted Hanna as "Dollar Mark" and the embodiment of avaricious capitalism.

Appointed to the Senate in 1897, Hanna won a full term in 1898. In Washington, he was identified with subsidies for American shipping and the construction of a canal across Central America. Following McKinley's assassination in 1901, Hanna cooperated with president Theodore Roosevelt, who still feared the Ohio senator as a possible rival for the Republican nomination in 1904. Hanna died in early 1904 after a brief illness. Despite his depiction as a ruthless capitalist, Hanna believed in the harmony of business and labor, and was the most important representative of the role of the Midwest in Republican politics at the end of the nineteenth century.

Sources and Further Reading: Thomas Beer, *Hanna* (1929); Herbert Croly, *Marcus Alonzo Hanna: His Life and Work* (1912); Fred C. Shoemaker, *Mark Hanna and the Transformation of the Republican Party* (1992).

Lewis L. Gould
University of Texas–Austin

Warren G. Harding (1865–1923)

Born on a farm near the village of Blooming Grove, Ohio, Warren Gamaliel Harding grew up in Caledonia, near Marion, and attended what was virtually a high school, Ohio Central College in Iberia. In Marion he soon purchased a newspaper, the *Star*, which after his marriage to Florence Kling De Wolfe (1891), flourished under her business management and Harding's flair for editorials. Elected on the Republican ticket to the state senate in 1899 and to the lieutenant governorship in 1903, he retired from state politics at the end of his term in the latter office. He subsequently contested successfully for election to the U.S. Senate and was elected to the presidency in 1920.

President Harding was enormously popular, and accomplished some notable achievements in the two and one-half years in office before his death in 1923: formally ending the war with Germany in the Treaty of Berlin of 1921 (the Senate had refused to consent to the Treaty of Versailles), creating the Bureau of the Budget (1921), and arranging the Washington Naval Conference (1921–1922).

It was only after Harding's death that accusations against him and his administration emerged. His personal reputation and administrative actions were perhaps the most maligned in the history of the presidency. It was claimed that he tolerated the selling of naval oil reserves to private oilmen in what became known as the Teapot Dome Scandal, a scandal in the Veterans' Bureau, and management of an unsavory bank account by his attorney general, Harry M. Daugherty. A salacious book published in 1927 claimed an affair resulting in a daughter. In 1930, a book by a convicted felon accused Harding's wife of poisoning him. He died, however, of a heart attack in San Francisco on August 2, 1923.

Sources and Further Reading: John W. Dean, *Warren G. Harding* (2004); Robert H. Ferrell, *The Strange Deaths of President Harding* (1996); Eugene P. Trani and David L. Wilson, *The Presidency of Warren G. Harding* (1977).

Robert H. Ferrell
Ann Arbor, Michigan

Herbert Hoover (1874–1964)

Herbert Clark Hoover was born on August 10, 1874, to Quaker parents, in West Branch, Iowa. Orphaned at the age of ten, he left Iowa in 1885 for Oregon where he lived with an uncle for six years and worked in his Oregon Land Company. In 1891 he entered the Leland Stanford Junior University in Palo Alto, California. There he was active in student affairs, studied geology, and went on to make a fortune as a mining engineer. He and his college sweetheart were married in 1899 and had two sons, Herbert and Allan.

Having tired of his lucrative career as an international mining engineer, Hoover turned his energies to humanitarian relief work during World War I. He became U.S. Food Administrator in 1917, oversaw food shipments to Europe during World War I, and fought the widespread famine there after the war. Hoover became secretary of commerce in 1921 and was the single most important member of the executive branch during the 1920s. When Calvin Coolidge declined to run for reelection in 1928, Hoover won both the Republican nomination and the presidency.

As president, Hoover promoted social action through a series of conferences and commissions and, following the stock market crash of 1929, established new agencies to stimulate the economy. These efforts were largely ineffective, and he lost the presidency to Franklin D. Roosevelt in the election of 1932. He devoted the next dozen years to the Republican fight against the New Deal. In March 1946, he worked with President Harry S Truman to assess world food needs and led a commission to reorganize the executive branch of the federal government.

Hoover also supported social causes such as the Boys Clubs of America and wrote more than forty books of political philosophy and a memoir. He died on October 20, 1964, after having served the longest tenure of any man as a former president of the United States. He chose to be buried in his boyhood hometown.

Sources and Further Reading: Kendrick Clements, *Hoover, Conservation, and Consumerism* (2000); Timothy Walch, ed., *Uncommon Americans: The Lives and Legacies of Herbert and*

The Birthplace of Herbert Hoover, West Branch, Iowa. Grant Wood's depiction of Herbert Hoover's birthplace. Purchased jointly by The Minneapolis Institute of Arts and the Des Moines Art Center with funds from the John R. Van Derlip Fund, Mrs. Howard H. Frank, and the Edmundson Art Foundation, Inc.; Art © Estate of Grant Wood/Licensed by VAGA, New York, NY.

Lou Henry Hoover (2003); Joan Hoff Wilson, *Herbert Hoover: Forgotten Progressive* (1975).

Timothy Walch
Hoover Presidential Library,
West Branch, Iowa

Nancy Landon Kassebaum (b. 1932)

In the midst of her father's first gubernatorial campaign, on July 29, 1932, Nancy Josephine Landon literally was born into Kansas politics, and before her fourth birthday, she took the national stage as the daughter of Governor Alfred M. Landon, Republican candidate for president. But the GOP's quintessential midwestern family did not become the nation's first family, and Nancy Landon grew up in a big white house in Topeka, Kansas. She attended the capital city's public schools, graduated from the University of Kansas, and earned a master's degree in diplomatic history at the University of Michigan.

In 1956, Nancy Landon married Philip Kassebaum and moved to the Wichita suburb of Maize, Kansas, where they raised four children. Nancy Kassebaum served as vice-president of the family business, accepted appointment to the state's Governmental Ethics Commission and Committee on the Humanities, and won a position on the local school board. Kassebaum served in Washington as an aide to Kansas senator James B. Pearson in 1975 and, three years later, won the right to succeed her former boss. In the progressive Republican tradition of her father, Senator Kassebaum remained hard to label during her three full terms in the U.S. Senate (reelected in 1984 and 1990), being conservative on most issues, but relatively moderate to liberal on others. She championed welfare and healthcare reform and chaired the Committee on Labor and Human Resources. Just before her official departure from the U.S. Senate, Nancy Kassebaum married former Tennessee senator Howard H. Baker.

Sources and Further Reading: Anne Commire, ed., *Women in World History: A Biographical Encyclopedia* (2000); Eleanor Marshall-White, *Women: Catalysts for Change* (1991); Charles Moritz, ed., *Current Biography Yearbook, 1982* (1983).

Virgil W. Dean
Kansas State Historical Society, Topeka, Kansas

Alfred Mossman Landon (1887–1987)

From the Progressive Era through the cold war, Alf Landon was actively involved in the major economic and political issues facing not only Kansas and the Midwest, but also the nation and the world. Landon was born in Pennsylvania, grew up in Ohio, and moved with his parents to Independence, Kansas, in 1904. He graduated from the University of Kansas and soon went into business for himself, first in oil, later in radio.

Politically, Landon was a fiscal conservative, but otherwise a liberal Republican, a follower of Theodore Roosevelt, in support of whom he bolted the party in 1912. After bolting again in 1924, he returned to the Republican fold with his progressive ideals intact, though pragmatic compromise and party unity now became the hallmarks of his political activities. Elected governor in 1932, his reelection in 1934 brought him national prominence and the Republican nomination for president in 1936. He lost in a landslide, but continued to oppose the New Deal's spending and economic planning programs.

Over the years he championed freedom of speech and desegregation and opposed right-to-work laws. In foreign affairs, Landon was never an isolationist; he supported free trade, the United Nations, the Truman Doctrine, the Marshall Plan, American military intervention in Korea, and the admission of Communist China to the United Nations. Landon was a political maverick and often at odds with his own party and with midwestern public opinion, but when he died in 1987, he was hailed as the party's Grand Old Man.

Sources and Further Reading: Richard B. Fowler, ed., *America at the Crossroads* (1936); Donald R. McCoy, *Landon of Kansas* (1966); Arthur M. Schlesinger, Jr., *The Age of Roosevelt*, vol. 3, *The Politics of Upheaval* (1960).

Loren E. Pennington
Emporia State University, Kansas

Abraham Lincoln (1809–1865)

Abraham Lincoln was born in Kentucky on February 12, 1809, and raised in Indiana from the age of seven. His childhood and youth thus rode the Ohio River, the boundary between North and South, slavery and freedom. When of age in 1831, Lincoln left his father's house in Macon County, Illinois, and for the next thirty years made his home elsewhere in that state. In its formative years, Illinois was under conflicting cultural influences, with Southern or Hoosier mores dominating in the region south of St. Louis, and those of New England and the Middle Atlantic states prevailing north of the mouth of Rock River. The central region of the state was one of shifting political and cultural majorities, where statewide elections had to be won. Lincoln rode to political success from central Illinois, in this volatile environment.

From his youth Lincoln had strong political ambitions, which he vented as a Whig in four terms in the Illinois General Assembly and one in the U.S. Congress. He was basically a political operator in these early offices, working for the success of his party and his constituency. But he also affirmed his opposition to slavery, placing himself on record to that effect both in the Illinois legislature and Congress. He essentially retired from politics upon returning from Congress in 1849, seeing no further political prospects for himself in a state where Whigs were clearly a permanent minority.

Lincoln reentered politics in 1854, galvanized as many citizens of the state were by the Kansas-Nebraska Act, which allowed the inhabitants of new western territories to determine if slavery should be permitted. Thereafter mere partisan success was no longer Lincoln's main goal. Though he partook of the anti-Negro prejudices of most Illinoisians, and though willing to tolerate slavery in states where it existed, he acknowledged that the Declaration of Independence applied to blacks as well as whites, and he was appalled at the prospect of an institution that so profoundly violated basic human rights being allowed to enter new American territories. His position coincided with that of enough other citizens of the state to ensure the possibility of victory in the new antislavery Republican Party, and Lincoln made close if unsuccessful runs for the U.S. Senate in 1855 and 1858, the latter year garnering recognition as Illinois's Republican leader and national notice from his debates with Stephen A. Douglas.

In 1860, it was fairly clear that whomever the Republicans nominated would win the presidency. Lincoln was an attractive potential nominee because he was considered not as radical as Salmon P. Chase or William H. Seward; had he been, political success would have eluded him in Illinois. Nor was he as conservative on the slavery issue or anti-immigration as was Edward Bates of Missouri. Finally it seemed that a midwesterner would be necessary to defeat fellow Illinoisian Stephen A. Douglas. Lincoln's nomination and victory followed, and on March 4, 1861, he was the first midwesterner, by virtue of nurture and long residence, to be inaugurated President of the United States.

He would successfully preside over arguably the most dangerous crisis in American history. He proved a decisive and politically astute commander-in-chief, with a quick sense of the differing abilities and characters of his generals. No less decisive and astute in political leadership, his first term in office witnessed the adoption of legislation that would have a lasting impact on American society and on the westward movement and settlement from the Midwest to the shores of the Pacific. This legislation included the Home-

stead Act of 1862 that provided private ownership of up to 160 acres of public land at minimal cost to citizens who would stake a claim and work the land for five years. The Morrill Act of 1862 granted substantial acreage of federal lands for each state to utilize or sell for the purpose of establishing public colleges and universities for the education of students from families of modest means in the mechanical and agricultural sciences. Many of these land-grant colleges and universities were to develop into some of the leading institutions of higher education in the United States.

Further encouraging the creation of national development, the Pacific Railway Act of 1862 spurred the building of the transcontinental railroad facilitating migration and settlement and the integration of a national market. The National Bank Act of 1864 established a new system of national banks and encouraged the creation of a national currency. Lincoln's Emancipation Proclamation of 1863 freed slaves in all territories of the Confederacy still in rebellion, and set the course for the complete abolition of slavery in the United States. Two of his public statements—the Gettysburg Address and his Second Inaugural Address—articulated fundamental principles of American democracy. His suspension of *habeas corpus*—the right of prisoners to be brought before a court in a timely manner—in 1863, however, was denounced by many as an unconstitutional abridgement of a fundamental right, a claim that was ultimately confirmed by the United States Supreme Court in *Ex Parte Milligan* 71 U.S. 2 (1866).

Lincoln was assassinated on April 14, 1865, by John Wilkes Booth while attending a performance of the play "Our American Cousin" with his wife, Mary, at Ford's Theater in the nation's capital. He died the following morning, six days after General Robert E. Lee surrendered his Confederate Army of Northern Virginia to Union General Ulysses S. Grant at Appomattox Court House, Virginia.

Sources and Further Reading: Roy P. Basler et al., eds., *The Collected Works of Abraham Lincoln*, 8 vols. (1953–1955); David Herbert Donald, *Lincoln* (1995); William Lee Miller, *Lincoln's Virtues: An Ethical Biography* (2002); Kenneth Winkle, *The Young Eagle* (2001).

Rodney O. Davis
Knox College, Illinois

George Stanley McGovern (b. 1922)

George McGovern was born July 19, 1922, to Rev. Joseph and Frances McGovern at Avon, South Dakota, and he grew up in Mitchell, South Dakota. During World War II, he was an Army Air Force

Inauguration of President William McKinley, 1897. Photo by J. C. Hemment, c. 1897. Library of Congress, Prints and Photographs Division, LC-USZ62-237 DLC.

bomber pilot, earning the Distinguished Flying Cross. He married Eleanor Stegeberg in 1943, and they had five children. He graduated from Dakota Wesleyan University in 1946 and taught there from 1950 to 1955. In 1953, he earned a PhD in history from Northwestern University and became executive secretary of the South Dakota Democratic Party.

He reorganized and revitalized the party at the grassroots level, earning the farmers' support. He was elected to a seat in the U.S. House in 1956 and served two terms. In 1960, President John F. Kennedy appointed him director of the Food for Peace Program, which supplied developing countries with surplus farm commodities. In 1962, McGovern was elected to the U.S. Senate, where he served three terms. He advocated nutrition programs for children, opposed the Vietnam War, and helped reform the Democratic Party. He was the 1972 Democratic candidate for president but lost the election.

After losing the 1980 Senate election, he continued a life of public service as author, lecturer, and visiting professor. He served as president of the Middle East Policy Council from 1991 to 1998, when he was appointed ambassador to the United Nations Food and Agriculture Organization. In 2000, he received the Presidential Medal of Freedom, and in 2001, he was appointed the first United Nations global ambassador on hunger.

Sources and Further Reading: Robert Sam Anson, *McGovern: A Biography* (1972); David Kranz, "U.N. Taps McGovern for New Post," *Sioux Falls Argus Leader* (Nov. 28, 2001); George McGovern, *Grassroots: The Autobiography of George McGovern* (1977).

Laurie Hall Langland
Dakota Wesleyan University,
South Dakota

William McKinley, Jr. (1843–1901)

Born on January 29, 1843, in Niles, Ohio, William McKinley, Jr., was the son of William and Nancy McKinley, both longtime residents in northern Ohio. McKinley attended Allegheny College and then fought in the Civil War as one of the volunteers from the Midwest that made up the backbone of the Union Army. Leaving the army with the rank of major, McKinley studied at the Albany Law School. He settled in Canton, Ohio, in 1867 and married Ida Saxton.

After a term as county prosecutor, McKinley was elected to Congress in 1876 as a Republican and became identified with the protective tariff during his seven terms. He ran successfully for governor of Ohio in 1891 and was reelected in 1893 in the midst of the hard economic times of the mid-1890s. His assumed ability to carry Ohio—a key midwestern state—and his popularity with Republicans won him the party's presidential nomination in 1896. He waged a front-porch campaign from his home in Canton that emphasized his regional roots. Elected over William Jennings Bryan, McKinley led the nation through the Spanish-American War and the overseas expansion that followed. He was reelected in 1900 and then assassinated in 1901.

Tolerant and inclusive in his approach to politics, McKinley stressed the virtues of the small-town Ohio he knew as a boy. Throughout his political career, he was seen as the embodiment of the economic and cultural values of the Midwest.

Sources and Further Reading: Lewis L. Gould, *The Presidency of William McKinley* (1980); H. Wayne Morgan, *William McKinley and His America* (1963).

Lewis L. Gould
University of Texas–Austin

Walter Frederick Mondale (b. 1928)

Born shortly before the Depression, the second son of Reverend Theodore and Claribel Mondale, "Fritz" spent his childhood in small rural Minnesota towns. He attended Macalaster College and the University of Minnesota, where he received his law degree. During college, he became involved with the Democratic-Farmer-Labor Party and its captivating leader, Minneapolis Mayor Hubert H. Humphrey.

One of the party's bright lights, Mondale was appointed, then elected, Minnesota's Attorney General in 1960. He attracted national attention when he helped engineer a compromise at the 1964 Democratic convention regarding a challenge to Mississippi's segregated delegation. When Humphrey was elected vice president, Mondale was appointed in 1964, then elected in 1966 and 1972, to Humphrey's Senate seat. Mondale was a respected liberal senator able to collaborate across the aisle. After deciding against a presidential bid in 1976, Mondale became Jimmy Carter's running mate, and his impressive campaign helped secure the ticket's success.

Mondale was the first influential modern vice president, as an important advisor with easy access to Carter, and his tenure became the model for his successors. Carter and Mondale lost their reelection campaign in 1980, but Mondale became the Democratic nominee four years later. He selected Geraldine Ferraro as his running mate, the first woman on a national ticket. He lost in Ronald Reagan's landslide reelection. Mondale served as President Clinton's Ambassador to Japan from 1993 to 1996. Following the death of Senator Paul Wellstone in an airplane accident just days before the 2002 elections, Mondale became the Minnesota Democratic Party's substitute candidate for U.S. Senate. His reentry into public life proved brief as he lost the election.

Sources and Further Reading: Steven M. Gillon, *The Democrat's Dilemma* (1992); Finlay Lewis, *Mondale*, rev. ed. (1984).

Joel K. Goldstein
Saint Louis University, Missouri

John Sherman (1823–1900)

Born in Lancaster, Ohio, on May 10, 1823, John Sherman represented Ohio and the Midwest on the national scene for more than forty years in the U.S. Senate and in two presidential cabinets. Sherman had limited formal schooling, but he moved to Mansfield, Ohio, in 1840 to read law and launched a legal practice in 1844.

The antislavery coalition that revolutionized the politics of the Midwest in the 1850s supported Sherman's successful campaign for a seat in Congress in 1854. Sherman then helped found the Republican Party in Ohio. He remained in the House of Representatives until the Ohio legislature elected him to the U.S. Senate in 1861. (Senators were indirectly elected until the adoption of the Seventeenth Amendment in 1913, which provided for direct election by the voters of a state.) Sherman's first tour of duty in the Senate ended when President Rutherford B. Hayes chose him to serve as Secretary of the Treasury in 1877.

While five Ohio Republicans served as President between 1869 and 1900, an indication of the importance of the Midwest and particularly of Ohio in national politics, the prize always eluded Sherman, who sought the nomination at every Republican National Convention between 1880 and 1888. It may have been a matter of his personality. He has been described as the "Ohio Icicle," who "carried the political cross of dullness."

Sherman returned to the Senate between 1881 and 1897 and served briefly as Secretary of State in 1897 and 1898. Sherman had set a record for longevity in the Senate. His legacy included the Sherman Anti-Trust Act and the Sherman Silver Purchase Act, both passed by a Republican-controlled Congress in 1890.

Sources and Further Reading: Robert D. Marcus, *Grand Old Party: Political Structure in the Gilded Age, 1880–1896* (1971); George H. Mayer, *The Republican Party, 1854–1964* (1964); H. Wayne Morgan, *From Hayes to McKinley* (1969).

Allan B. Spetter
Wright State University, Ohio

Paul Simon (1928–2003)

Paul Simon became a decorated soldier for good government before he was old enough to vote. As the nation's youngest newspaper publisher, the future U.S. Senator battled corrupt public officials and organized crime on the Illinois side of the St. Louis metropolitan area. His exposés thrust him into the national spotlight and helped Simon, at 25, to buck a formidable political machine as he captured an Illinois House seat in 1954. The Democrat quickly gained—and maintained throughout a public service career that spanned five decades—a reputation as an icon for integrity, a fighter for racial equality, and a persistent advocate for the disadvantaged.

Simon was born November 29, 1928, in Eugene, Oregon, and attended the University of Oregon and Dana College before taking over the struggling Troy (Illinois) *Tribune* at age nineteen. Simon married fellow state lawmaker Jeanne Hurley in 1960. She died in

February 2000. He married Patricia Derge, widow of a university president, in May 2001.

Simon was elected lieutenant governor in 1968, while voters chose a Republican for governor, a singular event in Illinois history. After being upset in a 1972 gubernatorial bid, he rebounded in 1974 to launch a twenty-two-year career in the U.S. House (1975–1984) and Senate (1985–1996), where he played a substantial role in education, foreign affairs, and disability policy initiatives, including passage of the National Literacy Act of 1991. In 1988, Simon ran unsuccessfully for the Democratic presidential nomination.

Simon, author of more than twenty books, founded and directed the Public Policy Institute at Southern Illinois University, where he taught political science, journalism, and history until his untimely death due to complications from heart surgery on December 9, 2003.

Sources and Further Reading: Paul Simon, *P.S.: The Autobiography of Paul Simon* (1999); Paul Simon, *Tapped Out* (1998).

Mike Lawrence
Southern Illinois University

Adlai Ewing Stevenson (1900–1965)

Governor of Illinois from 1948 to 1952, Adlai Stevenson was the Democratic nominee for the presidency in 1952 and 1956. Throughout his life he presented himself to national audiences as a spokesperson for midwestern values of steadiness, good sense, and civility. In 1961, he became Ambassador to the United Nations.

Born on February 5, 1900, in Los Angeles into a well-known Illinois family—his grandfather, Adlai E. Stevenson, served as vice president in Grover Cleveland's second administration. The family returned to Illinois in 1906. Stevenson was educated in public schools in Bloomington, Illinois, and at Choate, a boarding school in Connecticut. Later he graduated from Princeton University and Northwestern Law School. In 1928, he married Ellen Borden. Before their divorce the couple had three sons, the eldest of whom, Adlai Stevenson III, served as a U.S. Senator from 1971 to 1982.

In 1948, after appointive jobs in Washington, Stevenson was elected governor of Illinois on a reform platform. His contributions included modernizing the

---

❖ **Adlai Stevenson's Cat Bill Veto**

In 1949, the Illinois state legislature passed a bill to protect birds by forcing cat owners to limit the ability of their pets to roam. Governor Adlai Stevenson vetoed the measure. Unlike most veto messages, which are dry and full of legalese, Stevenson's statement is witty and persuasive.

SPRINGFIELD, April 23, 1949.

To the Honorable, the Members of the Senate of the Sixty-Sixth General Assembly:

I herewith return, without my approval, Senate Bill No. 93, entitled, "An Act to Provide Protection to Insectivorous Birds by Restraining Cats." This is the so-called "Cat Bill."

. . . I cannot believe there is a widespread public demand for this law or that it could, as a practical matter, be enforced.

Furthermore, I cannot agree that it should be the declared public policy of Illinois that a cat visiting a neighbor's yard or crossing the highway is a public nuisance. It is in the nature of cats to do a certain amount of unescorted roaming. Many live with their owners in apartments or other restricted premises, and I doubt if we want to make their every brief foray an opportunity for a small game hunt by zealous citizens—with traps or otherwise. I am afraid this Bill could only create discord, recrimination and enmity. Also consider the owner's dilemma: To escort a cat abroad on a leash is against the nature of the cat, and to permit it to venture forth for exercise unattended into a night of new dangers is against the nature of the owner. Moreover, cats perform useful service, particularly in rural areas, in combating rodents—work they necessarily perform alone and without regard for property lines.

We are all interested in protecting certain varieties of birds. That cats destroy some birds, I well know, but I believe this legislation would further but little the worthy cause to which its proponents give such unselfish effort. The problem of cat versus bird is as old as time. If we attempt to resolve it by legislation who knows but what we may be called upon to take sides as well in the age old problems of dog versus cat, bird versus bird, or even bird versus worm. In my opinion, the State of Illinois and its local governing bodies already have enough to do without trying to control feline delinquency.

For these reasons, and not because I love birds the less or cats the more, I veto and withhold my approval from Senate Bill No. 93.

Respectfully,
ADLAI E. STEVENSON, Governor

Source: State of Illinois, *Veto Messages of Adlai E. Stevenson, Governor of Illinois, on Senate and House Bills Passed by the 66th General Assembly of Illinois* (1949).

state government and removing the state police from the patronage system, which gave people jobs based on their political connections rather than on merit. Twice defeated for the presidency by Republican Dwight Eisenhower, he remained an important spokesman for the Democratic Party. His campaign oratory found an audience among many Americans. Incisive, clever, and urbane, Stevenson was known for his impromptu and witty comments on the stump. In the 1956 campaign, he promised that "If the Republican Party will stop telling lies about us, we'll stop telling the truth about them." On another occasion he declared, "Eggheads of the world unite. I was even going to add that you have nothing to lose but your yolks." Although he hoped to be Secretary of State, in 1961, President John Kennedy appointed him Ambassador to the United Nations, where he served until his death in 1965.

Sources and Further Reading: Jean H. Baker, *The Stevensons: Biography of an American Family* (1996); Walter Johnson, ed., *The Papers of Adlai Stevenson* (1972); John Bartlow Martin, *Adlai Stevenson of Illinois* (1977).

Jean H. Baker
Goucher College, Maryland

William Howard Taft (1857–1930)

William Howard Taft enjoys a unique place in the history of the Republic. He alone served as president *and* chief justice of the United States. Born in Cincinnati to Louisa Torrey and Alphonso Taft, an Ohio judge and a member of President Grant's cabinet, Taft took his father as a model of public service. Schooled in his hometown and then at Yale, he returned to Cincinnati to study law.

Successively an Ohio judge, solicitor general of the United States, and a federal appeals judge, his career took a sharp turn away from the law when President McKinley appointed him civil governor of the Philippines. He held this position until 1904, when Theodore Roosevelt named him secretary of war. In this post he was the senior administrator in charge of the construction of the Panama Canal, and laid the foundation of Japanese–American friendship by negotiating the Taft-Katsura Agreement.

Elected president in 1908, he broke with Roosevelt mainly over his handling of conservation policy; Taft's Dollar Diplomacy was markedly different from Roosevelt's Big Stick. Defeated for reelection, Taft joined the Yale faculty as professor of law. During World War I, he became cochairman of the National War Labor and was the chief spokesman for the League to Enforce Peace. He supported President Wilson's peace initia-

tives in broad terms but differed with him in significant detail. Named chief justice in 1921, Taft passed on a legacy of reform of Court procedure. Before he died, he successfully lobbied Congress for funds to construct the Supreme Court building.

Sources and Further Reading: David H. Burton, *William Howard Taft in the Public Service* (1986); Paolo E. Coletta, *The Presidency of William Howard Taft* (1973); Alpheus T. Mason, *William Howard Taft, Chief Justice* (1965).

David Burton
St. Joseph's University,
Pennsylvania

Harry S Truman (1884–1972)

The future president was born in Lamar, Missouri, a farm village south of Kansas City, and grew up on farms and in the farming town of Independence adjacent to Kansas City. Graduating from high school in 1901, he worked in Kansas City banks and farmed until 1917, when America entered World War I, during which he served in France as a captain of field artillery. Upon his return, he married Elizabeth Virginia "Bess" Wallace to whom he was engaged before he departed for Europe. Their only child, Mary Margaret, was born in 1924.

From 1919 to 1922 he helped manage a haberdashery, and was elected to his initial public office, county judge (county commissioner) of Jackson County in 1922 but was defeated for reelection. In 1924 he was elected presiding judge of a three-person court. Elected to the U.S. Senate in 1934, he served until after his election to the vice presidency in 1944, and became president upon the death of President Franklin D. Roosevelt on April 12, 1945.

In the presidency, he was responsible for bringing the United States into world affairs on a permanent basis. The Roosevelt administration did not anticipate America's emergence as a superpower and the responsibilities that came with it. Truman sponsored the Truman Doctrine (1947), Marshall Plan (1947), Berlin airlift (1948–1949), North Atlantic Treaty (1949), and entrance into the Korean War (1950). He took responsibility for dropping nuclear weapons on Japan in 1945, an act that later brought much criticism.

In domestic affairs, his administration sought to continue the New Deal under a program known as the Fair Deal, but few of its reform measures passed Congress. By executive act, the president sought valiantly to better the lot of African Americans in the military and in government employ.

Retiring in 1953, he returned to Independence where for nearly twenty years he was active in Demo-

President Harry S Truman on election night, 1948. Missouri State Archives.

cratic politics and then died in 1972. His wife, Bess, continued to live in their family home until her death in 1982.

Sources and Further Reading: Robert H. Ferrell, *Harry S. Truman: A Life* (1994); Alonzo L. Hamby, *Man of the People: A Life of Harry S. Truman* (1995); David McCullough, *Truman* (1992).

Robert H. Ferrell
Ann Arbor, Michigan

Arthur Hendrick Vandenberg (1884–1951)

Born in Grand Rapids, Michigan, on March 22, 1884, Arthur Vandenberg studied law at the University of Michigan and became editor of the *Grand Rapids Herald* in 1906. His appointment to the U.S. Senate in 1928 began a twenty-three-year tenure in that body. Until the 1940s, Vandenberg was a well-known isolationist, opposing U.S. membership in the League of Nations and Franklin Roosevelt's Lend-Lease policy, while advocating for strict U.S. neutrality laws.

World War II and the new position in the world it foisted on the United States caused Vandenberg to embrace an internationalist position. During the war, he supported the creation of a postwar international organization and spoke out against what he considered the errors of isolationism. As a delegate to the San Francisco conference in 1945, he was essential to both the creation of the United Nations and the Senate's ratification of the U.N. Charter. After World War II, Vandenberg insisted on consultation between the

president and Congress to facilitate bipartisan cooperation and mutual responsibility.

As chairman of the Senate Foreign Relations Committee (1947–1949), he was central to the bipartisan development of the containment strategy, the formulation of the Truman Doctrine, and a tougher approach toward the Soviet Union. Additionally, Vandenberg cooperated with the State Department to create the Marshall Plan, eventually cosponsoring the Economic Cooperation Act (1948) in the Senate. Later, the 1948 Vandenberg Resolution paved the way for the Senate's support for the creation of the North Atlantic Treaty Organization. Vandenberg's death in 1951 deprived the Republican Party of its leading internationalist foreign policy advocate in the U.S. Senate.

Sources and Further Reading: James A. Gazell, "Arthur H. Vandenberg, Internationalism, and the United Nations," *Political Science Quarterly* 88 (Sept. 1973); C. David Tompkins, *Senator Arthur H. Vandenberg: The Evolution of a Modern Republican, 1884–1945* (1970); Arthur H. Vandenberg, Jr., and J. A. Morris, eds., *The Private Papers of Senator Vandenberg* (1952).

James M. Scott and Carie A. Steele
University of Nebraska–Kearney

Wendell Lewis Willkie (1892–1944)

One of the Midwest's most interesting politicians, Wendell Willkie grew up in Elwood, Indiana, and earned a law degree at Indiana University in 1916. His law practice took him to Akron, Ohio, and then to

New York, where in 1933, he became president of Commonwealth & Southern Corporation, a public utility holding company. New Deal regulation of utilities pulled him into politics.

With little political experience, Willkie emerged as the Republican candidate for president in 1940, one of the great dark horses in American history. Though a corporate executive, Willkie campaigned with an easy banter, tousled hair, and Hoosier accent that played on his midwestern origins. After a grand kickoff in Elwood, his disorganized campaign fell to Franklin D. Roosevelt's masterly skills.

Willkie's major contributions came later, when his midwestern progressive side emerged. Reporting on his trip around the world in 1942, his 1943 book *One World* (which sold some two million copies) offered a strong case for internationalism. *One World* portrayed the people of Russia, China, and Africa much like his midwestern neighbors. Willkie also became one of the nation's most visible advocates of racial equality as he wrote and spoke about racial discrimination in the military and Hollywood films.

His global vision and advocacy of racial equality were too advanced for many Republicans. The party rejected his presidential bid in 1944. His death later that year removed a progressive voice from cold war politics.

Sources and Further Reading: Ellsworth Barnard, *Wendell Willkie, Fighter for Freedom* (1966); James H. Madison, ed., *Wendell Willkie: Hoosier Internationalist* (1992); Steve Neal, *Dark Horse: A Biography of Wendell Willkie* (1984).

James H. Madison
Indiana University–Bloomington

Coleman Alexander Young (1918–1997)

Born in 1918, in Tuscaloosa, Alabama, Coleman Young's family moved to Detroit in 1923. The future mayor of Detroit graduated from Eastern High School and went to work in the Ford automobile plant. While a factory worker, he became an organizer in the fledgling labor movement. During World War II, Coleman entered the Army Air Force and received training as a bombardier but never saw action. After the war, Young took a job as a labor organizer for the Congress of Industrial Organizations.

His political career started as a campaign manager for unsuccessful city council candidates. In 1948, he was the Michigan campaign director for Henry Wallace, the Progressive Party presidential candidate. Young was also active in the National Negro Labor Council, which was branded as a Communist front or-

ganization. In 1952, Young gained his first fame as a defiant witness before the House Un-American Activities Committee.

In 1961, Coleman Young was elected as a delegate to the Michigan Constitutional Convention (Con Con). Although he lost a state representative race in 1962, he won a state senate seat in 1964, and in 1973, Young was elected mayor of Detroit. This commenced a twenty-year career that paralleled the social and economic transformation of the city. Detroit lost its dominance in the automobile industry, and the city continues its economic downturn and population losses. Mayor Young was popular with his constituency, but also gained a reputation as a confrontational personality and a strong defender of Detroit home rule. After retiring from office, he remained active in public affairs and served as a member of the faculty of Wayne State University. While his two marriages produced no children, he had a son, Coleman Young Jr., at age 60. His legacy includes changing the function of downtown and promoting the city as an entertainment center. He died on November 29, 1997.

Sources and Further Reading: Joe Darden, June Thomas, and Richard Hill, *Detroit: Race and Uneven Development* (1987); Wilbur Rich, *Coleman Young and Detroit Politics* (1989); Coleman Young and Lonnie Wheeler, *Hard Stuff: The Autobiography of Coleman Young* (1994).

Wilbur C. Rich
Wellesley College, Massachusetts

Social Agitation

This essay looks at frameworks that historians have employed to explain politicized agitation—frontier, sectionalism, ethnoculturalism, and republicanism.

In the 1890s, Frederick Jackson Turner proposed that social and economic forces shaped midwestern politics. The frontier was of central importance in his model of social and economic evolution, which in turn caused the political evolution of the region. Scholars would later call the process "modernization."

Starting from the Atlantic Coast, each successive generation of pioneers moved further and further west, until the frontier finally ended in 1890. Each generation began with certain ways of thought and behavior that had originated in Europe, but were no longer suited to the new environment, and hence had to be abandoned or refitted. As each generation moved another couple hundred miles westward, more and more old traditions disappeared and more and more new adaptations appeared. The Europeans were becoming Americans; the further west one went, the more "American" the people. Europeans soon depicted Americans as cowboys. While the first settlers in any one location were primitive, their successors in the same locale developed more sophisticated solutions to such problems as the optimum use of land, the development of transportation systems, and the building of political parties and governmental institutions.

Established elite families seldom moved west; they kept their hold on class-bound eastern cities, whereas new men could rise much more easily in the more egalitarian west. Turner felt that Easterners remained more conservative because they had not evolved as much as the Westerners, who were more innovative, individualistic, and democratic. On the other hand, the Easterners showed a much better grasp of the high culture—the best of European art, science, education, and literature. The frontier promoted freedom and a liberal society that emphasized individualism, social equality, upward social mobility, independence, efficiency, innovation, opposition to taxation, and a preference for locally controlled democratic government. Turner's frontier model thus could be used to explain why the entire Midwest became, compared to the East, a hotbed of social agitation.

In addition to the frontier, Turner developed a model of sectionalism. Every subregion of the Midwest had peculiar characteristics, such as natural transportation routes and varied types of soil conditions. The different landscapes attracted different social groups, which in turn displayed distinctive political styles. The Yankees from New England settled the upper Midwest, and were noted for their organizational and entrepreneurial skills in business, banking, and railroading. They showed a strong moralistic streak; they became leaders of reform causes such as antislavery, temperance, woman suffrage, good-government crusades, and the Progressive Movement. Apart from Stephen Douglas, they produced few first-line politicians, but many experts and professionals. The southerners who moved up from below the Ohio River showed far less organizational skill and seemed content to engage in subsistence farming. They celebrated physical strength and charisma more than brainpower, which helped them produce many outstanding politicians. Southerners favored county-wide government, which could be controlled by relatively small courthouse cliques of professional politicians. Settlers from Pennsylvania and New York tended to locate somewhere in the middle, both politically and geographically.

Immigration complicated the social forces at work in shaping the frontier. The largest group, the Germans, came directly from a fairly traditional society and had missed the transforming experience of the frontier. Most were quite conservative economically and politically, and resisted abolitionism, temperance, woman suffrage, Populism, and the Progressive Movement. Surprisingly few became politicians. Not all Germans were conservatives. The German 48ers brought their version of republicanism, typified by Carl Schurz in Wisconsin and Missouri. German socialists provided the core of anticapitalist political activism in midwestern cities, especially in their stronghold of Milwaukee where Victor Berger was their outstanding spokesperson. Like the Germans, Scandinavians enjoyed a reputation as solid farmers and reliable tradesmen. Politically they were much more liberal in their outlook and often were active in social agitation opposed by the Germans, especially prohibition and progressivism.

Irish Catholic immigrants, on the other hand, were city folk with no frontier experience. They displayed very high levels of group solidarity (nearly all were Democrats) and steered their youth toward conformity rather than individualism. Few were businessmen, but many were priests or politicians; they controlled their party in most large cities for more than a century after the Civil War. The Irish rarely supported antislavery or prohibition movements, but they did support Progressive measures that directly helped their relatively poor constituencies. Their religiosity and organizational skills gave them control of the Catholic Church in most of the country, while their collective spirit made them leaders in the labor union movement. Their conservatism guaranteed that few American labor unions would endorse socialism.

The Turnerian model of sectional development helps explain many political phenomena. The constitutions of all the new western states were significantly more democratic than those back east. It was easier to vote, with fewer property restrictions. Voters displayed less deference and demanded more equality. Turner himself argued that Jacksonian democracy as it emerged in the 1820s was a distinctly western phenomenon rooted in the frontier experience. A strong distrust of big business, monopolies, and especially banks characterized the Jacksonians. Although abolitionism was weak in the Midwest, antislavery was a powerful force in politics, as exemplified by Abraham Lincoln. The Turnerian model sought out economic reasons. Midwestern individualists felt threatened by the plantation system—they demanded a free labor system without slavery, and promoted the Homestead plan to maximize the number of small family-owned farms.

Historians Charles and Mary Beard developed a variant of the Turnerian sectionalism model in their explanation of the Civil War as a sectional rivalry over the direction of national economic development. The rural Midwest had to choose an alliance either with the urban, industrial Northeast or with the plantation South, whose economy was based on slave labor. The emergence of an east–west railroad network in the 1850s allowed closer links to the Northeast to replace the previously critical Mississippi River links to the deep South, while the new Republican party promised homesteads and free land for farmers who moved west. Alliance of the Midwest and Northeast guaranteed the victory of the Union in the war. The Beards emphasized that it also led to the postwar dominance of railroads, banks, and the whole industrial system.

Dissenters who opposed the Civil War—especially the Copperheads led by Clement Vallandigham of Ohio—hated every aspect of the alliance with New York and Boston. Dissenters opposed modernization. They denounced Wall Street, banks, railroads, and industrialization, glorified the small self-sufficient farm, distrusted all cities, and ridiculed their Yankified elites. They bewailed the victorious alliance and maintained considerable strength, especially in the southern half of the Midwest, which modernized much less rapidly than the northern half. Their antimodernizing, egalitarian rhetoric echoed in the Greenback movement, which demanded cheap paper-based money that would favor midwestern farmers. This was picked up by the Populists of the early 1890s and the silverites of the mid-1890s. William Jennings Bryan of Nebraska was their greatest Populist spokesperson, as he championed free silver to destroy the power of the goldbugs over the farmers and workers. Bryan was met and defeated on the electoral battlefield of the Midwest by William McKinley of Ohio, who saw even more rapid modernization as the solution to economic ills and a formula that would bring Americans together in harmony and prosperity for all.

Midwestern women who had been politicized by the antislavery movement, and learned organizational skills in the U.S. Sanitary Commission and other volunteer efforts during the Civil War, turned to temperance reform in the 1870s. They created the Woman's Christian Temperance Union with a strong base in the Midwest under Frances Willard of Illinois. In turn the political skills learned in that crusade energized the movement for woman suffrage, as led by Carrie Chapman Catt of Iowa and Jane Addams of Illinois. The western states were far more equalitarian toward women; therefore woman's suffrage itself spread from west to east. The Turnerian model thus could explain why popular democracy generally was stronger in the west and much weaker back east and why Populism would be strongest in the western states that most recently experienced the frontier, especially Kansas and Nebraska. Furthermore, the Turnerians could celebrate the remarkable strength of the Progressive movement in Wisconsin and California, while predicting the East would continue to be a stronghold of conservatism because it was politically underdeveloped.

Turner's frontier and sectionalism models emphasized hard, objective factors such as economics and downplayed subjective values, which it usually dismissed as mere rhetoric. The ethnocultural historians of the 1960s brought values back into history by examining the religion and moral culture of different ethnic groups. The great revivals of the 1830s made the Midwest quite religious, but there were two distinct moral cultures. The "pietists" were evangelical Christians whose theology disposed them toward social and political activism. They believed Christ had commanded them individually to actively purge sin, including such social sins as liquor and slavery. They put a high value on introspection, self-improvement, education, change, and future orientation. They were predisposed toward modernization and worked easily in large complex organizations.

The "liturgicals," by contrast, had a different moral logic. They were loyal to their church and its priests and bishops; heresy was wicked. They believed God wanted them to obey their ordained leaders, not go off on crusades against miscellaneous evils. They saw the pietists as Puritans and fanatics. In response, the pietists focused on the priest-dominated Catholic church as an abomination—it was the Reformation all over again. Socially they stuck with the group and discouraged experimentation. Training was all right, but not education that encouraged youth to think for themselves and question the values of the community.

The pietists dominated most Protestant denominations including the Methodists, Congregationalists, Quakers, and Christians (Church of Christ). The Baptists and Presbyterians in the Midwest were mostly pietistic, with a vocal liturgical minority. The Episcopalians were split, with frequent bitter debates between the two wings. The Lutherans split mostly along ethnic lines. The Scandinavian Lutherans were predominantly pietistic, with liturgicals dominant among the German Lutheran synods, especially the large Missouri Synod. Catholics were overwhelmingly liturgical. The Democratic Party of the mid-1800s accommodated liturgicals, while the Republican Party attracted mostly pietists, apart from the more fervent agitators. The ethnocultural model can explain the paradox of why people with similar economic status could be on opposite sides of the political fence. That is, people joined political parties because of their personal moral beliefs, and church membership was both a good indicator of what those beliefs were and a social mechanism that brought like-minded people together every week and reinforced their values.

In the 1960s, historians started explaining the American Revolution in terms of the ideology of "republicanism," and the framework has been extended to the Midwest. It sharply rejected the older notion that political rhetoric was so much claptrap. On the contrary, rhetoric expressed deeply meaningful political values and should be studied closely. Republicanism focused on a few themes, all of them strongly emphasized in midwestern political discourse. The republicanism model holds that all Americans since 1776 have been deeply committed to a common core of "republican" values. The most important are a commitment to civic virtue, the duty of every citizen to support the community (especially in time of war), support for the Bill of Rights, and hostility to all forms of special privilege, aristocracy, and selfish corruption.

Lincoln now reappears not so much as a self-made man or transplanted southerner, but rather as the most articulate spokesperson for republican values since Jefferson. He and the other founders of the Republican Party very deliberately chose that name. Students of economic liberalism, like Turner, emphasize social and economic causes of political activism, whereas students of republicanism emphasize ideas and values. The advantage of the Turnerian model is that it specifies geographically where political innovation will occur, and which economic issues will be pivotal. Republicanism explains the intensity of social agitation as caused by the fervent belief of the crusaders that the opposition has betrayed republican values and should be exposed and rooted out.

Sources and Further Reading: John D. Barnhart, *Valley of Democracy* (1953); Ray Billington, *America's Frontier Heritage* (1974); Allan G. Bogue, *Frederick Jackson Turner* (1998); Daniel Judah Elazar, *Cities of the Prairie* (1970); Nicole Etcheson, *The Emerging Midwest* (1996); Jon Gjerde, *The Minds of the West* (1997); Richard Jensen, "Historiography of American Political History," in Jack Greene, ed., *Encyclopedia of American Political History*, vol. 1 (1984); Richard Jensen, *Illinois: A History* (2001); Richard Jensen, *The Winning of the Midwest* (1971); Paul Kleppner, *The Third Electoral System 1853–1892* (1979).

Richard Jensen
University of Illinois–Chicago

Utopians and Radical Reformers

The nineteenth-century Midwest provided a hospitable environment for agriculturally based communal experimentation and radical reform movements because it offered affordable land and a relatively tolerant populace. Inspired by charismatic leaders and united by shared beliefs, communal experiments proliferated in the Midwest in the aftermath of the economic Panic of 1837 and during a boom from the mid-1840s to the late-1850s. This economic, political, and social context encouraged the spread of numerous reform movements, including those seeking to perfect the individual as well as society.

A number of early communal experiments in the Midwest were pietistic in origin. In 1814, German pietists led by George Rapp moved from Pennsylvania to present-day New Harmony, Indiana. The area offered the Harmonists several advantages, among them access to the Wabash River and acreage suitable for fruit and vine culture. Earning a reputation for industry, the Harmonists eventually purchased thirty thousand acres, established industries, and erected permanent buildings, some of which are still standing. Desire for improved access to markets led Rapp to sell the land to British Social Reformer Robert Owen and to relocate to the village of Economy, near Pittsburgh, Pennsylvania, in 1825. A second group of German pietists followed Joseph Michael Bimeler to northern Ohio in 1817, purchased land, and became known as the Separatists of Zoar. Viewing Zoar as a refuge from an evil world, they adopted Communism and celibacy (later discontinued) for a pragmatic reason—economic survival. Peaking by the early 1840s, the experiment declined after Bimeler's death in 1853, but did not completely dissolve until 1898.

A third German pietistic sect, the Amana Society, or the Community of True Inspiration, originally settled in New York. In the 1850s, however, Christian Metz and community elders looked to the Midwest for a more isolated, yet fertile location. Purchasing twenty-six thousand acres in the Iowa River valley, the Inspirationists established seven villages, incorporated under state law, and prospered as an agricultural and manufacturing community for decades. Devastating financial setbacks during the 1920s led members to adopt the "Great Change" in 1932, shifting from a communal system to a joint-stock business corporation. The reorganized Amana Society gained national repute for its manufacture of household appliances, and the Amana Church Society endures today as a separate entity. More recently, the Amana Colonies have become a major tourist attraction. In contrast, the Swedish pietists who followed a temperamental Eric Jansson to Bishop Hill, Illinois, in 1846, had a more tumultuous experience. Enduring initial hardships on the Illinois frontier, the industrious communitarians flourished during an era of high agricultural prices and extensive land speculation. Chartered in 1853, the Janssonists struggled with such issues as celibacy, risky investments, and consequent factionalism before dissolving in 1861.

Other religious communal experiments established

in the nineteenth-century Midwest included the Shakers, who established communities in Sullivan County, Indiana (1810–1827), and Cuyahoga County (1822–1889), Warren County (1805–1912), Montgomery County (1806–1910), and Hamilton County (1824–1907), Ohio. Envisioning God as both male and female, the Shakers are known for celibacy and a unique religious service that featured spiritually inspired dancing. Practicing division of labor and diversified agriculture, they also earned a reputation for the production of medicinal herbs, seeds, and finely crafted furniture. Peaking in 1850, Shakers nationwide declined until today only one community in Sabbathday Lake, Maine, remains.

Secular communal experiments tended to have a shorter life expectancy than did religiously based communities. As a youth, Robert Owen abandoned religious belief and became interested in the scientific reorganization of society. Purchasing New Harmony in 1825, he established a socialistic society that he believed would become a model for the rest of the world. Owens's community, which appealed to radical intellectuals, developed progressive schools, inspired the creation of Workingmen's libraries, professed belief in equality of the sexes, and maintained an active social and cultural life. In 1827, however, dissension prompted by internal factionalism and economic problems triumphed, and New Harmony collapsed.

The ideas of French social theorist Charles Fourier inspired the establishment of fourteen Fourieristic phalanxes (scientifically organized cooperative communities) in six midwestern states between 1843 and 1858. Ohio claimed the most, with four. Established in the aftermath of the Panic of 1837, most were of relatively short duration and lost their appeal as better times returned to the region. Another French-inspired communal group, the Icarians, settled in Nauvoo, Illinois, in 1849. The Panic of 1857 and depressed agricultural prices prompted their move to southern Iowa, where they prospered until converts from France spurred internal dissension that led the Icarians to dissolve in 1898. Other short-lived secular communities dotted the landscape, among them the Kansas Vegetarian Company (1850s), the Union Home (1844–1846) in Randolph County, Indiana, and Ohio's Marlboro Association (1843–1845), Memnonia Institute (1856–1857), Berlin Heights Free Lovers (mid- to late-1850s), and Spirit Fruit Society (1899–c. 1920). Antislavery advocates established black emancipation communities in Illinois, Indiana, Michigan, and Ohio between 1819 and the onset of the Civil War.

Migration patterns, developments in transportation, and a proliferation of reform newspapers and periodicals enabled a number of radical reform movements to flourish in the nineteenth-century Midwest. The reform-minded men and women who moved from New York State's Burned-Over district to Ohio's Western Reserve and the Firelands region devoted themselves to such causes as abolitionism, spiritualism, temperance, and women's rights. Revivalists and itinerant lecturers swept across the region, offering hope to people who felt unsettled by the spread of slavery and unmoored by periodic economic downturns. Those who believed that the solution to the world's problems lie in reforming the body adopted a Graham diet, donned the reform dress (a knee-length dress worn with trousers), embraced hydropathy (water treatments) in place of orthodox medicine, and foreswore the use of alcohol. Others fought to ensure that women as well as slaves lived in freedom. The Western Reserve Women's Emancipation Society declared its commitment to women's equality at its first meeting, held in Ravenna, Ohio, in 1873.

Midwestern reformers who yearned to read publications expressing their viewpoints became a receptive audience for the numerous periodicals issued from the region. Abolitionists turned to the *Anti-Slavery Bugle*, published in Salem, Ohio; temperance advocates read *The Lily*, which moved from New York to Richmond, Indiana; women's rights activists turned to the *Agitator* (Cleveland and Chicago); free-lovers and freethinkers devoured *Foundation Principles* (Clinton, Iowa) and *Nichols' Monthly*, *Social Revolutionist*, *Age of Freedom*, and *The Good Time Coming*, all published in Ohio, and reform-minded Spiritualists digested such titles as *The American Spiritualist* (Chicago and Cleveland) and *The Universe* (Chicago).

The Midwest's history of radical reform activism and the presence of utopian communities to this day (for instance, the City of David near Benton Harbor, Michigan) illustrate the region's role as a social laboratory for people struggling with the problems that face American society. Although most of these ventures are fading memories, their legacies are preserved in archival documents, historic sites, and the idealism that inspires today's humanitarian causes.

Sources and Further Reading: Arthur Bestor, *Backwoods Utopias* (1950); Ann Braude, *Radical Spirits*, 2nd ed. (2001); Carl J. Guarneri, *The Utopian Alternative* (1991); Thomas D. Hamm, *God's Government Begun* (1995); John Humphrey Noyes, *History of American Socialism* (1870); Donald E. Pitzer, ed., *America's Communal Utopias* (1997); Catherine M. Rokicky, *Creating a Perfect World* (2002).

Joanne E. Passet
Indiana University East

The Lincoln–Douglas Debates

On June 16, 1858, the Illinois state convention of the Republican Party, meeting in Springfield, resolved that Abraham Lincoln was their "first, last, and only" candidate for the United States Senate seat, then occupied by Stephen A. Douglas, whose term was expiring. The aforesaid resolution was remarkable for two reasons. First, under the Constitution of 1787 (and prior to the Seventeenth Amendment), U.S. senators were chosen by joint meetings of state legislatures. Electioneering began among state legislators after the general election. This was the first time that the question of who would be the next senator was presented to the voters at the general election. Second, the resolution reflected an internal difference within the Republican Party, an act of defiance by Illinois Republicans of eastern leaders of the party, who wanted the Illinois Republicans to support Douglas for reelection. One must understand the circumstances surrounding this nomination of Lincoln to understand his response to it—the House Divided speech—and the campaign which followed, including the seven joint debates.

The crisis in which the nation was immersed in 1858 began with the passage of Senator Douglas's Kansas–Nebraska Act in the spring of 1854. In opening these lands to settlement and eventual statehood, the act provided that it was "the true intent and meaning of this act not to legislate slavery into any Territory or State, nor to exclude it therefrom, but to leave the people thereof perfectly free to form and regulate their domestic institutions in their own way, subject only to the Constitution of the United States." This expressed Douglas's doctrine of popular sovereignty. To implement it he had to secure repeal of that portion of the Missouri legislation of 1820 that mandated the exclusion of slavery from all the remaining Louisiana Territory north of 36 degrees 30 minutes, the southern boundary of Missouri. Douglas's bill thus opened to slavery a vast area from which it had previously been excluded by law. It created the greatest firestorm seen in American political history. Its immediate effect was a mini–civil war in Kansas, as proslavery and antislavery immigrants battled for supremacy. Its broader effect was to catapult the question of slavery in the territories into the foreground of national politics, where it finally brought on the Civil War.

When the Kansas–Nebraska bill passed in the spring of 1854, the Republican Party did not exist. As a result of the elections in the fall of 1854, the newly formed party elected one hundred members to the House of Representatives. To the free soil movement and its embodiment in the Republican Party, Douglas was then anathema. Yet four years later, he came to be regarded as their Savior. This amazing transformation happened when President Buchanan backed a bill admitting Kansas to the Union under the Lecompton constitution, which had been drafted by proslavery settlers before the large influx of free-state settlers had occurred, and before they had had time to organize and express themselves at the ballot box. Lecompton did not therefore meet Douglas's requirement that the settlers in the territory be "perfectly free" to decide the slavery question for themselves. He thereupon led the opposition to the President's bill, and led the Republicans in Congress to victory over it.

In 1857, the Supreme Court, in the case of *Dred Scott* declared that the Missouri Compromise was unconstitutional and that Congress had no power to outlaw slavery in the Territories. The only power of Congress over slavery in the Territories, the Chief Justice declared, was the power, coupled with the duty, of protecting the slaveowner in his rights. This decision undercut the positions of both Lincoln and Douglas: Lincoln because it declared that Congress had no power to exclude slavery from the Territories, and Douglas because it denied the right of the settlers to exclude slavery if they wished to do so. Lincoln, however, refused to accept the ruling of the Court as binding upon the political branches of the government. Douglas endorsed the decision, however, but denied that it prevented the settlers in the Territories from excluding slavery if they wished. The right of a slaveowner to take his slaves into a Territory, Douglas said, was merely an "abstract right," unless the local inhabitants wished to provide the slaveowners with police protection. Lincoln countered that if Douglas endorsed *Dred Scott*, he was logically and morally committed to protecting slave property in the Territories, whether the settlers there wanted it or not. To accept *Dred Scott* and then deny that protection would put him, Lincoln said, with the abolitionists, who would deny the constitutional obligation to return fugitive slaves.

In the fall elections of 1858, the Republicans, under Lincoln's leadership, carried the statewide offices by approximately 125 thousand votes to one hundred thousand. This established Lincoln's ability to carry the state in a presidential contest and did much to influence the Republican national convention to nominate him in 1860. In 1858, however, the Republicans did not elect enough members of the state legislature to counter the holdover Democrats in the state senate, and Douglas was reelected U.S. senator.

Lincoln's demonstration of Douglas's inconsistency in accepting *Dred Scott* while insisting that the local inhabitants in the Territories could still exclude slavery bore fruit in the Democratic national convention in

Charleston in April of 1860. A majority of that convention wished to nominate Douglas as their presidential candidate, but could not reach the required two-thirds without some votes from the seven states of the Deep South. These states would not give their votes for Douglas unless he promised them federal protection of slavery in the territories. No politician could make such a promise without losing every vote in a free state. When these states seceded accordingly from the Charleston convention, they split the Democratic Party and assured the election of the Republican candidate. Their secession from the Union in 1860 and 1861 was the direct result of their earlier secession from the Democratic convention. All this resulted from the tactics Lincoln had pursued in the joint debates in 1858.

Sources and Further Reading: Don E. Fehrenbacher, *Prelude to Greatness* (1962); Harry V. Jaffa, *Crisis of the House Divided* (1959); Harry V. Jaffa and Robert W. Johannsen, *In the Name of the People: Speeches and Writings of Lincoln and Douglas in the Ohio Campaign of 1859* (1959); Robert Johannsen, ed., *The Lincoln–Douglas Debates of 1858* (1965).

Harry V. Jaffa
Claremont, California

The Copperheads and Clement Vallandigham

Civil War Republicans first used "Copperheads" to discredit their Northern Democratic foes who questioned Union war objectives. Named after the venomous snake, many Peace Democrats embraced this intended epithet while denying that they were traitors. Copperheads were concentrated in the lower Midwest and Pennsylvania. Many had Southern origins and were adversely affected by the end of Southern trade following the war's outbreak. Adopting the slogan "The Constitution as it is, the Union as it was," Copperheads resisted emancipation. Many opposed coercing the South's return to the Union, and some sympathized with Southern war objectives. Following the 1862 elections, Copperheads controlled the lower houses of the Illinois and Indiana legislatures, where they denounced emancipation and favored limiting their governors' military powers. A few called for an armistice, which would have effectively recognized Confederate independence. Some Copperheads formed secret societies, and a few conspired with Confederate agents. Nevertheless, Republican charges of Copperhead conspiracies were generally overblown.

The best-known and principal leader of the Copperheads was Clement Vallandigham, Congressman from Ohio and the state's Democratic Party's unsuccessful gubernatorial nominee in 1863. To President Lincoln's opponents, Vallandigham's imprisonment and subsequent exile to the Confederacy for what were deemed as traitorous speeches and activities symbolized the administration's suppression of civil liberties. Modern scholarship has shown, however, that the Lincoln administration's civilian arrests were more likely to be of draft evaders, blockade runners, guerrillas, and Confederate citizens than political opponents. Copperhead sentiment appeared to be strong during the summer of 1864, when Union military victories seemed illusive. This soon changed, however, as wartime prosperity, the Confederate surrender of Atlanta in September 1864, and Lincoln's reelection two months later undermined the Copperhead movement.

Sources and Further Reading: Frank L. Klement, *The Copperheads in the Middle West* (1960); Mark E. Neely, Jr., *The Fate of Liberty* (1991); Hubert H. Wubben, *Civil War Iowa and the Copperhead Movement* (1980).

John W. Quist
Shippensburg University, Pennsylvania

William Jennings Bryan (1860–1925) and the Rise and Fall of Populism

William Jennings Bryan, a Democratic Party leader who brought Populist proposals into the political mainstream, lived in Lincoln, Nebraska, for nearly all his political career. Born in Salem, Illinois, on March 19, 1860, he graduated from Illinois College and from Union College of Law in Chicago. He married Mary Baird, who played an important role in his long career. In 1887, the Bryans moved to Lincoln, arriving at a crucial juncture in the political history of the western Midwest.

During the late 1880s, membership in the Farmers' Alliance boomed where farmers were most hard-pressed economically. Formed in Chicago in 1880, the Alliance resembled similarly named groups in the South. Local Alliance meetings became forums for debating economics and politics, and weekly newspapers across the western Midwest trumpeted Alliance views. In 1890, low crop prices and high railroad rates spurred Alliance members to independent political action. In Kansas, Nebraska, the Dakotas, Minnesota, and elsewhere, they formed new, state political parties to contest state and local elections. Women sometimes took a prominent part in the new parties' campaigning, especially in Kansas and Nebraska. Mary Elizabeth Lease of Kansas acquired lasting fame when newspapers quoted her as urging farmers to "Raise less corn and more hell!" The new parties' greatest successes in 1890 came in Kansas, Nebraska, and

❖ When Bryan Speaks

When Bryan speaks, the town's a hive.
From miles around, the autos drive.
The sparrow chirps. The rooster crows.
The place is kicking and alive.

When Bryan speaks, the bunting glows.
The raw procession onward flows.
The small dogs bark. The children laugh.
A wind of springtime fancy blows.

When Bryan speaks, the wigwam shakes.
The corporation magnate quakes.
The pre-convention plot is smashed.
The valiant pleb full-armed awakes.

When Bryan speaks, the sky is ours,
The wheat, the forests, and the flowers.
And who is here to say us nay?
Fled are the ancient tyrant powers.

When Bryan speaks, then I rejoice.
His is the strange composite voice
Of many million singing souls
Who make world-brotherhood their choice.

Vachel Lindsay

Source: Vachel Lindsay, "When Bryan Speaks," in *The Chinese Nightingale and Other Poems* (1917).

South Dakota, where their members won election as local officials, members of state legislatures, and members of the federal Congress. In 1891, they gained two members of the U.S. Senate, from South Dakota and Kansas. Elsewhere in the region, where the agricultural economy was less desperate, the new parties did poorly. In some places, ethnic conflict over prohibition or school laws received more attention than economic issues.

The new parties soon joined groups from the South and West to form the People's Party, or Populists. Their national nominating convention in 1892 was held in Omaha. The Omaha Platform called for governmental action to restrict powerful corporations that, the Populists argued, restricted the economic opportunities and political rights of ordinary citizens. They sought sweeping changes in federal monetary and banking policies, especially expansion of the currency to counteract the prevalent deflation, government ownership of the railroads and the telegraph and telephone systems, structural reforms to make government more responsive to voters (including the secret ballot and the initiative and referendum), the eight-hour day for wage earners, a graduated income tax, and other reforms. For president, they nominated James B. Weaver of Iowa, who had been the Greenback Party candidate in 1880.

In the western Midwest, Populists drew their greatest support from farmers on marginally productive land who often carried large mortgages at high interest rates. There, too, railroads charged much more to transport produce to market. Throughout the western Midwest, Democrats were reduced to a tiny third party and sometimes threw their support behind Populist candidates. Such fusion brought gubernatorial victories in 1892 in Kansas and North Dakota.

Bryan entered politics as a Democrat in the same year that the Populists first organized. He won election to the U.S. House of Representatives in 1890 due to his effective campaigning and to the disruption of politics caused by the Populists, and narrowly won re-election in 1892. Gaining national attention by his speeches in Congress, he emerged as a leading advocate for currency stabilization through silver coinage. In Nebraska, Bryan consistently favored cooperation between Democrats and Populists, notably in the election of one Populist to the U.S. Senate in 1893 and another as governor in 1894.

During 1895 and early 1896, Bryan traveled the country advocating changing U.S. currency from the gold to the silver standard. He well understood the effect of the prevailing currency deflation on debtors, especially debtor farmers, and used telling rural metaphors to argue for silver. Bryan's "Cross of Gold" speech to the 1896 Democratic national convention has become the standard example for capturing a convention through oratory. Though not a declared candidate when he began to speak, he won the Democrats' presidential nomination on the fifth ballot. The Populists and the Silver Republicans, a splinter group, also nominated him.

The Republican candidate was William McKinley of Ohio, who promoted the gold standard and the protective tariff as the best means to restore prosperity. Bryan emphasized silver but did not ignore the tariff, income tax, and other reforms.

Bryan took his case to the people, traveling eighteen thousand miles and delivering six hundred speeches, mostly in the crucial Midwest. Voters turned out in extraordinary numbers—turnout rates of up to 95 percent in some midwestern states and nearly 80 percent for the nation as a whole. Bryan carried the South and much of the West, including the western Midwest. Populists with Democratic support won the governorship in Kansas, Nebraska, and South Dakota. Elsewhere, however, Republican tariff arguments and fears of inflation gave McKinley the edge among the urban middle class, many workers, and the more prosperous farmers. Bryan supporters pointed to fraud and intimidation, especially in parts of the Midwest, but McKinley's victory marked a significant, long-term shift in voter loyalties.

In 1900, Bryan again sought the presidency, basing his campaign on opposition to imperialism and monopolies and on support for silver coinage. He easily secured the Democratic and Silver Republican presidential nominations. What remained of the Populists divided, with one faction supporting Bryan and the other running their own candidate. McKinley won by a larger margin than before, and the Populist and Silver Republican Parties soon faded away.

Bryan remained the Democratic Party's most significant leader until 1912, speaking frequently throughout the country and editing a weekly newspaper, *The Commoner*. As party leader, Bryan led many Democrats to reject the commitment to minimal government, characteristic of their party since Andrew Jackson. Instead, like the Populists, Bryan fused Jacksonian antimonopolism to a commitment to governmental intervention on behalf of the citizenry and against powerful economic interests. He sought the presidency again, unsuccessfully, in 1908. In 1912, he supported Woodrow Wilson for the Democratic nomination; as president, Wilson appointed Bryan as secretary of state. During his final decade, Bryan promoted woman suffrage and prohibition and opposed the teaching of evolution, which he believed, undermined the religious faith that he considered the necessary basis for a moral society. He died on July 26, 1925.

Sources and Further Reading: Peter Argersinger, *The Limits of Agrarian Radicalism* (1995); Robert W. Cherny, *Populism, Progressivism, and the Transformation of Nebraska Politics, 1885–1915* (1981); Robert W. Cherny, *A Righteous Cause* (1985); O. Gene Clanton, *Kansas Populism* (1969); John D. Hicks, *The Populist Revolt* (1959); Richard J. Jensen, *The Winning of the Midwest: Social and Political Conflict, 1888–1896* (1971); Robert C. McMath, Jr., *American Populism* (1993); Jeffrey Ostler, *Prairie Populism* (1993).

Robert W. Cherny
San Francisco State University, California

Temperance and Prohibition

American efforts to suppress the use of alcoholic beverages, while not originating in the Midwest, grew strong in the region. There the temperance and prohibition movement acquired the organizational strength to place an alcohol ban in the U.S. Constitution. There, too, were the cultural contradictions and conflicts that led ultimately to the demise of national prohibition.

The American antialcohol movement arose in the East as midwestern settlement was beginning. Rooted in revolutionary fervor, religious revivalism, and the

A perspective on the 18th Amendment. Temperance Collection, Westerville Public Library.

shift from agriculture to industrial labor, the quest for sobriety moved gradually from voluntary temperance to abstinence and legal prohibition. In the 1850s, a dozen states restricted alcohol to save those thought too addicted to save themselves.

A second, more persistent wave of temperance agitation sprang from the Midwest after the Civil War. Women unhappy with the impact of male drinking on spousal relations, family economies, and child neglect held public demonstrations in 1873 to close saloons in Hillsboro and Washington Court House, Ohio. The crusade led to the creation of the Woman's Christian Temperance Movement (WCTU) in Cleveland in November 1874. Under the leadership of Frances Willard of Evanston, Illinois, the WCTU expanded its feminist and family agenda while keeping its focus on alcohol. The WCTU's most famous member, Carry Nation of Kansas, moved from involvement in the long, only partially successful legislative campaign to ban liquor from her state to a series of highly publicized attacks on saloons. Her hatchet became a national symbol of temperance rage against alcohol.

Ohio also spawned the Anti-Saloon League of America. Founded in Oberlin in 1893, this organization worked primarily through Protestant clergy and congregations to pressure political candidates to support its demand for alcohol prohibition. Single-minded in purpose and skillfully led, the Anti-Saloon League had become a powerful force by the 1910s.

Both the WCTU and the Anti-Saloon League enlisted a large midwestern membership, particularly in small towns and rural areas. In contrast, the region's major urban centers as well as some smaller communities developed, as did cities in other parts of the country, a culture accepting of alcohol. The very saloons against which the Anti-Saloon League railed were neighborhood social centers from Cleveland to Kansas City. Saloons were places where job seekers located work, transients received mail, immigrants read a homeland newspaper, the overwhelmingly young and male urban population found entertainment at the pool or poker table, politicians interacted with constituents, all for the price of a drink. And most served simple meals, too.

Alcohol production as well as consumption characterized the urban Midwest. Cincinnati, St. Louis, and Milwaukee, cities with large concentrations of German Americans, became centers of the brewing industry. Agricultural hinterlands produced the raw materials for brewing and distilling, but this reality did not create cultural or political bonds. Distrust of the cities, particularly their large clusters of recent immigrants from unfamiliar cultures in which alcohol use played a noticeable role, dominated rural attitudes.

The Anti-Saloon League's success by 1916 in winning congressional pledges of support, together with soon-to-follow wartime hostility to all things German, propelled to success the campaign for a constitutional amendment imposing national prohibition. Congress approved the measure by more than the required two-thirds in 1917, while the war's outcome remained in doubt. State ratification took only thirteen months. Of the twelve midwestern state legislatures, only Illinois and Indiana failed to endorse the Eighteenth Amendment. Enthusiasm for prohibition may not have been as great as it appeared, however. A 1919 Ohio referendum found voters almost evenly divided on prohibition. Congress, nevertheless, adopted a strict enforcement law designed by the Anti-Saloon League and Minnesota Representative Andrew Volstead that banned all beverages with more than one-half percent alcohol, though loopholes remained.

National prohibition was widely accepted throughout the Midwest after January 1920. Farmers fermenting hard cider and immigrants making wine for personal use correctly believed that they were not violating the law. Likewise, patients could legally drink a daily dose of physician-prescribed "medicinal spirits." Wealthy elites with well-stocked liquor cabi-

nets were allowed to consume anything purchased before the Volstead Act. Finally, like other Americans, many midwesterners stopped drinking alcohol when the law took effect, joining an estimated forty percent of the nation's population that did not drink before prohibition.

A significant minority of midwesterners, however, did not regard imbibing as improper. This included members of various ethnic communities and a rapidly growing urban upper-middle class. An illicit network of smugglers, manufacturers, and distributors arose to supply "bootleg" alcohol. Because they conducted business without police protection, indeed in the face of police opposition, competing bootleggers were often violent toward one another, though rarely toward customers upon whom they depended. The best-known bootlegger, Chicago's Al Capone, headed an organization that brutally suppressed competition. Cleveland's Mayfield Road Mob, Detroit's Purple Gang, and organizations in other cities operated in similar fashion. Smaller communities had their bootleggers, as well.

Those who sought to end prohibition were not the bootleggers who profited from it. Ethnic community leaders such as Anton Cermak of Chicago formed cross-cultural political alliances to agitate for repeal. By the late 1920s, groups of middle- and upper-class men and women expressed concern with eroding law and order. The onset of the Great Depression brought calls to reduce expenditure on enforcement and restore legitimate jobs. The Democratic Party embraced all of these arguments in its 1932 campaign against a Republican Party that had enforced prohibition for twelve years.

Following the sweeping 1932 Democratic victory, a repeal amendment was approved by Congress and sent to state ratifying conventions. Delegate elections showed how sharply the Midwest had turned against prohibition. Kansas, Nebraska, and the Dakotas took no action. The region's more populous states, however, all overwhelmingly rejected prohibition in 1933. Over three of four voters in Illinois, Michigan, Missouri, and Wisconsin chose repeal, while roughly two-thirds of those in Indiana, Iowa, Minnesota, and Ohio did likewise. Ohio's ratifying convention on December 5, 1933, along with simultaneous proceedings in Pennsylvania and Utah, completed adoption of the Twenty-First Amendment and ended national prohibition in the United States, although alcohol consumption did not regain pre-prohibition levels until the 1970s.

Sources and Further Reading: Robert S. Bader, *Prohibition in Kansas* (1986); Jack S. Blocker, Jr., *American Temperance Movements: Cycles of Reform* (1989); Perry Duis, *The Saloon:*

Public Drinking in Chicago and Boston, 1880–1920 (1983); John E. Hallwas, *The Bootlegger: A Story of Small-Town America* (1998); Richard F. Hamm, *Shaping the Eighteenth Amendment: Temperance Reform, Legal Culture, and the Polity, 1880–1920* (1995); K. Austin Kerr, *Organized for Prohibition: A New History of the Anti-Saloon League* (1985); David E. Kyvig, *Repealing National Prohibition*, 2nd ed. (2000); Catherine G. Murdock, *Domesticating Drink: Women, Men, and Alcohol in America, 1870–1940* (1998).

David E. Kyvig
Northern Illinois University

The Woman's Christian Temperance Union

The Woman's Christian Temperance Union (WCTU) is a national, nonsectarian, women's organization promoting complete abstinence from alcohol, tobacco, illegal drugs, gambling, and pornography. The WCTU was founded in November 1874 in Cleveland, Ohio. Hillsboro and Washington Court House, Ohio, witnessed numerous marches by women to protest saloons and liquor-selling drugstores in late 1873 and early 1874. The success of these marches in discouraging proprietors from sale and patrons from consumption of alcohol spurred efforts in neighboring communities. The Woman's Temperance Crusade eliminated liquor in 250 towns by the summer of 1874, including Cleveland, Columbus, and Dayton, Ohio; Indianapolis, Indiana; Chicago and Rockford, Illinois; Lansing, Grand Rapids, and Flint, Michigan; Ripon, Wisconsin; Clinton, Iowa; and Carthage, Missouri. The WCTU was formed to institutionalize this social movement.

The WCTU expanded its issue concerns from alcohol to other social ills under the leadership of its second president, Frances Willard of Evanston, Illinois, who led the WCTU from 1879 until her death in 1898. Willard viewed women as a moral compass on issues such as the consumption of alcohol, and she argued that women could best promote moral standards in American society through political means. To protect their homes and families, women needed to be able to vote, control their property, and seek custody of their children after divorce.

Although abstinence from alcohol, tobacco, and other drugs was the cause that launched the WCTU, it viewed social ills as linked and advocated sweeping social reform. Its goal was the creation of a morally upright and wholesome society. To accomplish this goal, the WCTU agitated for political rights for women, lobbied for legislative remedies, particularly Prohibition, exhorted individuals to moral living, and also sought to shape cultural media to ensure its purity. The WCTU supported censorship of cultural products that were not morally sound, and it produced its own children's magazine, motion pictures, and inexpensive copies of famous paintings in order to provide the morally pure culture that it deemed lacking.

In linking culture and morals, the WCTU sought to institute a "middlebrow" culture. It explicitly rejected the elitism of high art such as nude sculptures, ballet, and literary realism. It also rejected lowbrow culture such as boxing and dime novels. Pure, or middlebrow, culture promoted piety, gentility, and social responsibility.

Today, the WCTU, with headquarters in Evanston, Illinois, primarily provides public education on the harmful effects of alcohol, tobacco, illegal drugs, gambling, and pornography, as well as their opinions on other social ills. It encourages candidates for public office to sign pledges not to take campaign contributions from alcohol, tobacco, or gambling interests, and citizens to petition candidates to sign the pledge. The national WCTU has five thousand members. Its forty state unions have organizations for elementary-aged children and teens that require them to sign a pledge committing to total abstinence from alcohol, tobacco, and other drugs.

Sources and Further Reading: Ruth Birgitta Bordin, *Woman and Temperance: The Quest for Power and Liberty, 1873–1900* (1981); Elizabeth Putnam Gordon, *Women Torch-Bearers: The Story of the Woman's Christian Temperance Union* (1924); Alison M. Parker, "Hearts Uplifted and Minds Refreshed": The Woman's Christian Temperance Union and the Production of Pure Culture in the United States, 1880–1930," *Journal of Women's History* 11 (Summer 1999).

Joan M. Blauwkamp
University of Nebraska–Kearney

Pacifism and Opposition to Particular Conflicts

Although a majority of midwesterners have always rallied around the flag during wartime, others marched to a different drummer. Members of the historic "peace churches"—Quaker, Mennonite, Amish, and Church of the Brethren—hold that war is incompatible with Christianity. Seventh-Day Adventists agree to serve in the military only as medics and even trained their young men for such service. Jehovah's Witnesses would fight only in the final battle of Armageddon. Members of these groups, as well as some from other denominations, refused military service. Moreover, an American antiwar tradition has included nonpacifists whose political and economic views led them to reject particular wars. Some wars have divided the population, provoking public response and political opposition. The complex history of this antiwar strain is an important but often-forgotten aspect of American and Midwest history.

One of the most divisive of American military adventures was the Mexican-American War of 1846–1848. Mexican attacks in disputed territory led President James K. Polk to charge that American blood had been shed on American soil, justifying a declaration of war. Some Whig congressmen, including a young Abraham Lincoln, challenged Polk's assertion. A faction of northern Whigs and abolitionists charged that the war was fought only to expand slave territory. Thomas Corwin, Ohio's Whig senator, told the Senate that if he were a Mexican, he would greet the Americans "with bloody hands, and welcome [them] to hospitable graves."

Political opposition to particular wars may wax and wane, but opposition to war itself has been a constant in United States history. In the Midwest, philosophical, ethical, and religious pacifists have opposed each war in turn. The American Civil War was especially challenging for those pacifists who opposed both slavery and war. When the Union and Confederate governments instituted military conscription, pacifist young men faced hard decisions. Inducted involuntarily into the Union Army, a few midwestern pacifists endured physical torture when they refused orders. After reviewing individual complaints, the Lincoln administration usually granted relief to such objectors. In the Midwest, as elsewhere in the nation, Shaker societies and other communitarian groups including the Amish were steadfastly pacifist, encouraging their young men to refuse military service. Opposition to the 1863 draft, which some thought unfairly targeted poor whites, resulted in antidraft protests in Holmes and Morrow counties, Ohio, and in several Wisconsin communities, though none was as serious as the three-day riots in New York City.

Republicans supported efforts to crush the southern rebellion, but northern Democrats were sharply divided. Peace Democrats blamed abolitionist agitation for the conflict and advocated a negotiated settlement. The Lincoln administration regarded Peace Democrats as traitors and labeled them Copperheads, to suggest poisonous snakes ready to strike. Their best-known standard-bearer was Congressman Clement L. Vallandigham of Dayton, Ohio, whose determination to speak out against the war led to his arrest and conviction by a military court. A sentence of imprisonment for the duration of the rebellion led to outraged protests, forcing Lincoln to exile Vallandigham to the Confederate states. Widespread rumors of a Midwest-based Confederate conspiracy involving such organizations as the Knights of the Golden Circle proved to be vastly exaggerated or fictitious.

The Spanish-American War was too brief to provoke much opposition, but the imperialism it spawned did. United States acquisition of the Philippines stirred armed resistance and led to several years of brutal warfare against native peoples. Some midwesterners, like Missouri's Carl Schurz and members of the Anti-Imperialist League, opposed annexing the Philippines.

When World War I broke out in Europe, most Americans opposed United States entry. An American movement to promote a negotiated peace included Chicago's Jane Addams, who presided at the International Congress of Women at The Hague in 1915. A cofounder of the Women's International League for Peace and Freedom, Addams worked tirelessly against war and, in 1931, was corecipient of the Nobel Peace Prize. In 1917, six senators, including Robert M. La Follette of Wisconsin, as well as fifty members of the House of Representatives, voted against the resolution to enter World War I. While some German Americans sympathized with their homeland, most overt opposition came from progressives, socialists, anarchists, and members of the Industrial Workers of the World, and in the Midwest several were jailed with little regard for their constitutional rights. Most famous was Eugene V. Debs of Terre Haute, Indiana, whose antiwar speech in Canton, Ohio, brought him a ten-year prison sentence. In 1920, while still in prison, Debs polled 919,799 votes for president.

When World War I hysteria provoked the burning of German books and even banning the music of German composers, pacifists, too, met persecution. A conscription act provided noncombatant military service only for conscientious objectors who were members of the historic peace churches. Those who refused all military service were sometimes inducted involuntarily and held in military prisons, at times suffering solitary confinement or being chained in an upright position to the bars of a cell.

Disillusionment with World War I, accompanied by a strong strain of isolationism, contributed to antiwar sentiment in the 1920s and 1930s. Such views were especially strong in the Midwest. In 1928, Secretary of State Frank B. Kellogg from Minnesota cosponsored an international pact renouncing war as an instrument of national policy. In 1935, Congressman Louis Ludlow of Indiana introduced resolutions calling for popular votes on declarations of war. North Dakota's Senator Gerald P. Nye conducted an investigation into the role of the munitions industry in U.S. entry into World War I. Senators Arthur Capper of Kansas, Arthur Vandenberg of Michigan, and Robert Taft of Ohio were part of a faction supporting a series of neutrality acts and opposing United States entry into World War II. Also influential as isolationists were Charles Lindbergh of Minnesota and the anti-Semitic Father Charles Coughlin of Detroit.

In 1932, college students held an antiwar conference in Chicago that planned student strikes and circulated the Oxford Pledge to refuse to go to war. In 1940, a few students from Antioch College in Ohio established Ahimsa Farm, a pacifist community near Cleveland, where they studied and practiced Gandhian nonviolence.

The Japanese attack on Pearl Harbor largely eliminated political opposition to World War II, though most pacifists continued their lonely witness. Midwestern peace church colleges declined to host military units on their campuses, putting themselves at financial risk. To avoid the brutal treatment accorded conscientious objectors during World War I, government officials and peace church leaders devised alternative civilian service for objectors motivated by religious training or belief, and in 1940, Congress wrote the program into the new conscription law. Civilian Public Service or CPS camps, funded by the churches, remained under Selective Service control. Camps were located across the country and in most midwestern states. After the Selective Service permitted some objectors to serve outside the camps, numerous hospitals acquired much-needed workers.

Objectors who refused or were denied alternative service were convicted and sentenced to federal prisons, including those at Milan, Michigan; Sandstone, Minnesota; and Chillicothe, Ohio. Some participated in work and hunger strikes against racially segregated dining halls and dormitories, mistreatment of other prisoners, or mail censorship. A majority of the six thousand objectors receiving punishment ranging from imprisonment to fines were Jehovah's Witnesses, whose claims for ministerial exemption were denied by Selective Service. Federal judges in the Midwest were especially harsh, often sentencing objectors to five years, the maximum penalty under the law.

World War II also had a profound effect on pacifist women. Some followed their husbands to live and work near CPS camps, served in the camps as cooks, or took jobs in hospitals where male objectors were assigned. Wives and girlfriends supported imprisoned resisters with correspondence and visits. When the war ended, women picketed the White House demanding release and amnesty for imprisoned resisters.

Coming so soon after World War II and at the start of the cold war, the Korean conflict had little overt opposition, though it was not a popular war. Once again, some pacifist resisters were jailed. A decade later, however, as the United States became deeply involved in the civil war in Vietnam, protests broke out on midwestern campuses, as elsewhere throughout the nation.

As American involvement in Vietnam escalated, so did opposition. Small, local antiwar actions became part of a national movement, with marches and demonstrations in Washington and other major cities. At the University of Michigan, site of the first antiwar teach-in, radical members of Students for a Democratic Society (SDS) produced an influential statement of purpose known as the Port Huron Statement. Ad hoc committees representing virtually all segments of the population organized demonstrations. Although for pacifists the Vietnamese conflict was just another war, the majority opposed it for more specific reasons. Some believed the United States was supporting the wrong side, while others, having concluded that it could not be won, thought it foolish and wrong to continue the fighting. Chartered buses carried thousands of midwesterners to the demonstrations in Washington.

Protest became resistance when young men refused to be drafted or citizens refused to pay a portion of their taxes for war. The Cincinnati-based Peacemakers' call for nonpayment of war taxes blossomed into a national movement. A weekly protest vigil outside the gates of Wright-Patterson Air Force Base near Dayton, Ohio, continued for more than a year and supported Dr. Bruce Ashley, an Air Force officer whose antiwar stand led to his court martial. The May 4, 1970, killing of four Kent State University students and the wounding of nine others by Ohio National Guardsmen stunned the world and shocked those working and studying in midwestern institutions.

While the overwhelming majority of antiwar activities were intentionally nonviolent, news reports highlighted a few acts of vandalism and violence. The Weatherman faction of the SDS attempted guerrilla warfare and organized the Chicago Days of Rage in 1969. The burning of the Kent State Reserve Officer Training Corps building, at the urging of an unknown provocateur, set the stage for the tragedy on that campus. In Madison, Wisconsin, a few radical activists unintentionally caused the death of a researcher when they detonated a bomb in a university building.

Gradually, antiwar activism became political. Antiwar Senator Eugene McCarthy of Minnesota had the support of a peace faction in the Democratic Party in his 1968 bid for the presidency. Massive demonstrations at the 1968 Democratic convention in Chicago brought police overreaction, brutal beatings, and hundreds of arrests, poisoning public discourse during the subsequent campaign. The subsequent trial in federal court of the Chicago Seven made headlines around the world.

The brief Persian Gulf War also produced a growing popular opposition. Demonstrations occurred in Dayton, Ohio, and other midwestern communities. In

Milwaukee, Professor Alex Molnar wrote and published a powerful letter of protest to President George H. W. Bush entitled "If My Marine Son Is Killed." Although Bush had declared the peace movement dead, Molnar's letter got national attention and proved the president wrong. Again, there were teach-ins and vigils in midwestern colleges and universities, as elsewhere in the country. After the Persian Gulf War, activists in Dayton, Ohio, led a multifaceted campaign with rallies, vigils, even billboards, to influence public sentiment for ending economic sanctions against Iraq, sanctions they held responsible for the deaths of millions of children.

Insulation by distance from both coasts, a prevailing provincialism, and the presence of many peace churches have contributed to antiwar and isolationist traditions in the Midwest. In 1973, suspension of an active draft lifted the threat of enforced military service from the region's young men. Since Vietnam, relatively brief wars have seemed remote, yet each of them, including an ongoing war against terrorism, has sparked a nascent peace movement in the Midwest, as in the rest of the nation. During every war in which the United States was involved, some midwesterners, for religious or other reasons, have opposed American participation. Moreover, a smaller number has worked to abolish all war, believing the institution itself is a threat to human survival in the nuclear age.

Sources and Further Reading: Peter Brock, *Pacifism in the United States from the Colonial Era to the First World War* (1968); Charles Chatfield, *For Peace and Justice: Pacifism in America, 1914–1941* (1971); Heather T. Frazer and John O'Sullivan, eds., *"We Have Just Begun To Not Fight": An Oral History of Conscientious Objectors During World War II* (1996); Larry Gara and Lenna Mae Gara, eds., *A Few Small Candles: War Resisters of World War II Tell Their Stories* (1999); Rachel Walter Goosen, *Women Against the Good War: Conscientious Objection and Gender on the American Home Front, 1941–1947* (1997); Staughton Lynd and Alice Lynd, eds., *Nonviolence in America: A Documentary History* (1995); H. C. Peterson and Gilbert C. Fite, *Opponents of War 1917–1918* (1957); Mulford Q. Sibley and Philip Jacob, *Conscription of Conscience* (1952); Lawrence Wittner, *Rebels Against War: The American Peace Movement, 1941–1960* (1969); Edward Needles Wright, *Conscientious Objectors in the Civil War* (1961).

Larry Gara
Wilmington College of Ohio

Students for a Democratic Society

Students for a Democratic Society, known commonly as SDS, was founded by Robert Alan Haber, its first president. He planned to rejuvenate the dormant Student League for Industrial Democracy (SLID), an arm of the International Ladies Garment Workers Association and the oldest student political organization in the United States, into an active national student movement committed to liberal causes. After four black students staged a sit-in at a segregated lunch counter in Greensboro, North Carolina, in February 1960, Haber, with University of Michigan students Sharon Jeffrey and Bob Ross, took up the emerging cause of civil rights in the North. On April 28, 1960, SDS debuted with a civil rights conference and gained a $10,000 organizational grant from the United Auto Workers, allowing Haber to work full time at developing a national student organization.

By 1962, according to Tom Hayden, the second president of SDS, the organization consisted of "Al Haber using a phone and mimeograph in New York; a few functioning chapters in such places as Ann Arbor,

Student protesters in Chicago, 1968. Chicago Historical Society, Oscar & Associates, ICHi-26289.

Oberlin, and Swarthmore; 800 dues paying members (at one dollar per year); and 2,000 scattered activists on mailing lists." The event that converted this diffuse beginning to an effective national movement was the Port Huron Convention, held June 11–15, 1962, in an AFL-CIO retreat facility at Port Huron, a town about ninety miles north of Detroit. Sixty people attended this conference from which emerged the Port Huron Statement, a self-proclaimed "manifesto of hope" offering "an agenda for a generation."

SDS began as a university-based movement for civil rights, but when antiwar sentiment increased dramatically on college campuses, the focus shifted to antiwar activism. SDS organized a national March on Washington in April 1965, that about 25,000 people attended. Nonviolence, cited as a fundamental SDS value in the Port Huron Statement, eroded as a control, and the organization grew increasingly radical, spawning in 1969 the Weather Underground, a paramilitary terrorist organization. As Paris peace negotiations slowly led to a ceasefire, SDS lost relevance and adherents. By the mid 1970s, Students for a Democratic Society faded from the political scene.

Sources and Further Reading: Alan Adelson, *SDS* (1972); Philip G. Altbach, ed., *Student Political Activism* (1989); Tom Hayden, *Reunion: A Memoir* (1988).

Thomas Minnick
The Ohio State University–Columbus

Robert M. La Follette (1855–1925) and the Reform Element in Midwestern Politics

Robert Marion La Follette was a major figure in Progressive politics in the early twentieth century. Born in Primrose, Wisconsin, in 1855, he graduated from the University of Wisconsin in 1879. He served as district attorney for Dane County from 1880 to 1884, was elected to the U.S. House of Representatives in 1884 and served from 1885 to 1891, was elected governor of Wisconsin for three terms (1901–1906), and then served in the U.S. Senate from 1906 until his death in 1925. Known for his idealism and commitment to political reform, "Fighting Bob" La Follette was very influential in Wisconsin and national politics in the first quarter of the twentieth century. While he remained a member of the Republican Party for his entire career, he ran for president as a Progressive in 1924.

A turning point in La Follette's career came after his initial and unsuccessful gubernatorial campaign in 1896, when he learned that twenty delegates to the Republican state convention had accepted bribes in

exchange for their support of the machine's candidate. Fueled by his outrage over the corruption within his party, La Follette ran two more times for governor, winning in a landslide in 1900. Much of La Follette's early political thinking was presented in the speech that kicked off his second gubernatorial campaign on July 4, 1897. In that speech, entitled "The Danger Threatening Representative Government," La Follette issued a scathing critique of corporate influence over American economic and political life. Arguing that corporations controlled the political machines and that machines dictated every move of politicians, La Follette rallied his supporters to resist this corrupting influence:

> Let us here today under this flag we love, hallowed by the memory of all that has been sacrificed for it and for us, dedicate ourselves to winning back the independence of this country, to emancipating this generation and throwing off from the neck of the freemen of America, the yoke of the political machine.

La Follette made important contributions in three areas: political reform, social policy, and foreign policy. As governor he fulfilled his promise to fight the power of political machines when Wisconsin became the first state to establish a direct primary system in 1903, thus giving voters control over party nominations. La Follette also implemented other Progressive reforms, such as replacing party patronage (the lifeblood of party machines) with civil service, implementing popular referenda and recall, and placing major administrative agencies under the control of citizen boards.

He was a vigorous advocate of social reform and fought for programs for unemployment compensation, social security, progressive income taxation, and the regulation of the railroad and banking industries. Under his leadership, Wisconsin became one of the first states to adopt child labor laws and to pass the woman's suffrage amendment. La Follette's efforts on social policy were also influenced by his Progressive ideals. Rejecting the cronyism and corruption of machine politics, La Follette championed the scientific ideals of independence and expertise and cultivated a strong relationship with the University of Wisconsin. Historian Richard Hofstadter notes the "intimate union between the La Follette regime and the state university at Madison that foreshadowed all later brain trusts." The regular meetings between La Follette and scholars such as Edward A. Ross, John R. Commons, and Charles Van Hise were motivated by a concept known as the Wisconsin Idea, which maintained that the University would be committed to serving the state through policy making and that the incorporation of academic expertise improved the performance of government.

On foreign policy, La Follette was one of the most articulate and outspoken isolationists in the period leading up to World War I. As a senator from a state with a large German American population, his views were popular with many of his constituents. However, he came under intense criticism and was subjected to many death threats for being one of the six senators to vote against the Congressional declaration of war. The death threats included one from a federal judge in Texas who volunteered to convene a grand jury that would bring charges of treason against La Follette; this judge went so far as to volunteer to serve on the firing squad. Speaking on the floor of the Senate, La Follette presented an eloquent reminder of the importance of protecting civil liberties and freedom of speech during wartime:

> Remember in time of war the citizen must be more alert to the preservation of his right to control his Government. He must be most watchful of the encroachment of the military upon the civil power. He must beware of those precedents in support of arbitrary action by administrative officials, which excused on the plea of necessity in war time, become the fixed rule when the necessity has passed and normal conditions have been restored. More than all, the citizen and his representative in Congress in time of war must maintain his right of free speech . . . More than in times of peace it is necessary that the channels for free public discussion of governmental policies shall be open and unclogged.

La Follette's impact on political reform was focused on Wisconsin and Midwest politics but also had a national dimension. La Follette's national exposure peaked in 1924 when he received 17 percent of the national vote and carried Wisconsin as a Progressive candidate for President. His campaign platform advocated public ownership of natural resources and railroads, farm relief measures, lower taxes for people with moderate incomes, and greater regulation of large corporations. For Wisconsin politics, in addition to the central contributions outlined above, his legacy was carried on by his sons, Robert M. La Follette, Jr., and Phillip La Follette, who established the Progressive Party of Wisconsin in 1934. The party was quite successful until it faded away in 1946, after Robert La Follette, Jr., made a futile run for the Republican nomination for U.S. senator.

La Follette, Sr.'s, reform lives on today in Wisconsin in many ways, with the state's strong commitment to clean government, exceptionally high voter turnout and citizen involvement, and innovative policies in areas such as welfare reform and health care for the working poor that have been emulated around the nation.

Sources and Further Reading: Albert Barton, *La Follette's Winning of Wisconsin* (1922); Thomas Dreier, *Heroes of Insurgency* (1910); Richard Hofstadter, *The Age of Reform* (1955); Robert M. La Follette, *The Papers of Robert M. La Follette, Sr., at the State Historical Society of Wisconsin, 1879–1910, 1922, 1924;* David P. Thelen, *The Early Life of Robert M. La Follette, 1855–1884* (1966); David P. Thelen, *Robert M. La Follette and the Insurgent Spirit* (1985); William Allen White, *Politics: the Citizen's Business* (1924); Donald Young, ed., *Adventure in Politics* (1970).

David T. Canon
University of Wisconsin–Madison

The Ku Klux Klan

Most Americans associate the Ku Klux Klan with the South, but during the 1920s and 1930s, it thrived in many parts of the Midwest. The reason for its growth was the influx of millions of immigrants from southern and eastern Europe into rapidly expanding industrial cities like Chicago, Cleveland, Detroit, Gary, St. Louis, and Youngstown. These immigrants brought cultures and religions—Catholicism and Judaism—that prompted suspicions among the old settlers in the region about their loyalty to American ideals. Their participation in the violation of Protestant vice laws and their occasional association with corrupt political machines fostered resistance to permitting continued migration into the country. The dramatic size of the influx increased cultural and ethnic conflict and resulted in a political reaction, just as the migrations from Germany and Ireland in the 1830s and 1840s had prompted the Know Nothing Movement.

As these immigrants arrived in the 1880s, some old stock Americans began restrictive movements led by the American Protective Association and the Immigrant Restriction League. Concurrently, mainline Protestant denominations, such as the Baptist, Methodist, Presbyterian, and Disciples of Christ, launched a moral crusade for the passage of vice laws. Their work culminated in the formation of the Anti-Saloon League with its national headquarters in Westerville, Ohio. Literature generated by these groups blamed political corruption and social problems on the immigrants.

Meanwhile, the Ku Klux Klan, which the federal government had suppressed in the 1870s for its violent, night-riding tactics against black citizens, reappeared in 1915 after the premier of D. W. Griffith's *Birth of a Nation,* which justified the Klan's actions after the Civil War. Resurrected by Colonel William J.

A Ku Klux Klan march. Wisconsin
Historical Society, WHi-1902.

Simmons in Atlanta, Georgia, it languished there and in Alabama until 1920, when Simmons hired the Southern Publicity Association to advertise the formation of a fraternal organization for 100 percent Americans—white, Anglo-Saxon, Protestants. Although the Klan retained its racist attitudes toward blacks, it was its dedication to saving America from the onslaught of alien hordes that prompted its spread throughout the nation. The Southern Publicity Association sent over eleven hundred kleagles (salesmen) into communities in every state, gathering by the mid-1920s an estimated three million members nationally. Ohio, Indiana, and Illinois constituted three of the five top states in membership nationally. Comparatively, Michigan, Missouri, Iowa, Kansas, and Nebraska attracted together only 40 percent as many members as those three states, while the Dakotas, Wisconsin, and Minnesota lagged far behind.

Kleagles contacted Baptist, Presbyterian, Methodist, and Disciple of Christ ministers, as well as evangelical Lutheran churches for support. These ministers often spoke from the pulpit on behalf of the Klan and accepted donations from hooded Klan members who paraded into their churches. As a secret society, the Klan brought families into a social organization that held picnics and parades, founded country clubs, burned crosses, and organized politically. It was also concerned with enforcement of the vice laws, sometimes as vigilantes. The passage of the Eighteenth Amendment after World War I led directly to the rise of the Klan in many areas. As enforcement of prohibition became a major issue, politicians and the political parties were under extreme pressure to crack down. When corruption persisted, local Protestants

readied themselves to cleanse local politics and eliminate vice. In many areas of the Midwest, the Klan appealed to those wanting to nominate or endorse political candidates who agreed with Protestant moral principles; it provided a vehicle to campaign for their values.

Klan success varied from state to state in the Midwest. Klan chapters appeared in both rural and urban areas. The state of Kansas received *New York Times* coverage when the editor of the *Emporia Gazette*, William Allen White, entered the gubernatorial race in 1924 as an independent. His attacks on the Klan as moral cowards garnered him 150,000 votes, only half as many as the Klan candidate.

Indiana was by far the strongest Klan state nationally. It elected a Klan governor and senator, and led the charge against the anti-Klan plank of the Democratic party in 1924. Ohio had the second largest Klan, but it failed to elect its candidate for governor in 1924, Joseph Sieber. The Klan attracted many members in the seven largest Ohio cities, as well as in the smaller cities and villages characteristic of Ohio. In the Mahoning Valley surrounding Youngstown, it elected mayors and the majorities in city councils and school boards in 1923.

As Klan political successes multiplied in 1923 and 1924, immigrant reactions posed limits to their continuance. Irish Americans in Chicago formed the American Unity League, led by Patrick O'Donnell, and a subsidiary, the Tolerance Publishing Company. O'Donnell encouraged stealing Klan membership rosters and publishing the lists, oftentimes as a pamphlet entitled "Is Your Neighbor a Kluxer?" As such tactics spread throughout the Midwest, Klan members experienced embarrassing encounters with immigrant neighbors and boycotts of their businesses. They also faced violence when they attempted to march in immigrant-dominated cities, such as Niles and Steubenville in Ohio and Herrin in Illinois. Italians and Irish, some of them local bootleggers and gamblers, led these confrontations marked by throwing bricks, stones, and pipes and by blockades enforced with guns, knives, and physical intimidation.

Internal problems, however, were the cause of further decline. Questions arose about the large amounts of money that flowed into Klan coffers, much of it to Atlanta or into kleagle pockets. Worse yet were the revelations of the moral corruption of Klan leaders. The most devastating case was that of D. C. Stephenson, former Grand Goblin of the Great Lakes region, who was convicted of raping and murdering a young woman in 1925. Finally, factionalism among Klan leaders, marked by the formation of rival organizations, fostered doubts among existing members, many of whom resigned.

The Klan declined rapidly after 1926 throughout the entire nation, though widely publicized Klan marches continued episodically through the remainder of the twentieth century. Nationally, however, the presidential election of 1928 between Al Smith, a wet Roman Catholic, and Herbert Hoover, a dry Protestant with Iowa roots, reverberated with the Klan. The Klan had been symptomatic of the conflicts generated by rapid cultural and ethnic mixing, but its demise marked more the faults and failure of its leaders than the arrival of tolerance.

Sources and Further Reading: David M. Chalmers, *Hooded Americanism*, 3rd ed. (1981); Kenneth Jackson, *The Ku Klux Klan in the City, 1915–1930* (1967); William D. Jenkins, *Steel Valley Klan* (1990); M. William Lutholtz, *Grand Dragon* (1991); Leonard J. Moore, *Citizen Klansmen* (1991); Norman F. Weaver, "The Knights of the Ku Klux Klan in Wisconsin, Indiana, Ohio, and Michigan," Ph.D. diss., University of Wisconsin (1954).

William Jenkins
Youngstown State University, Ohio

The Midwest and the American Indian Movement

The contemporary geographic and political concept of the Midwest is an artifact of the colonizers boundaries; however, the Midwest as place, roughly dovetailing with the Great Plains and the last of the Indian territories, is critical to an understanding of the Amer-

---

❖ **Excerpts from the Declaration of Indian Purpose**

American Indian Chicago Conference, June 13–20, 1961

WE BELIEVE in the inherent right of all people to retain spiritual and cultural values, and that the free exercise of these values is necessary to the normal development of any people. Indians exercised this inherent right to live their own lives for thousands of years before the white man came and took their lands. It is a more complex world in which the Indians live today, but the Indian people who first settled the New World and built the great civilizations which only now are being dug out of the past, long ago demonstrated that they could master complexity.

WE BELIEVE that the history and development of America show that the Indian has been subjected to duress, undue influence, unwarranted pressures, and policies which have produced uncertainty, frustration, and despair. Only when the public understands these conditions and is moved to take action toward the formulation and adoption of sound and consistent policies and programs will these destroying factors be removed and the Indian resume his normal growth and make his maximum contribution to modern society.

WE BELIEVE in the future of a greater America, an America which we were the first to love, where life, liberty, and the pursuit of happiness will be a reality. In such future, with Indians and all other Americans cooperating, a cultural climate will be created in which the Indian people will grow and develop as members of a free society. . . .

WE BELIEVE that where programs have failed in the past, the reasons were lack of Indian understanding, planning, participation, and approval.

. . . A plan of development should be prepared by each Indian group, whose land or other assets are held in trust, whether such lands or assets are fully defined or not; such plans to be designed to bring about maximum utilization of physical resources by the dependent population and the development of that population to its full potential; such plans to be prepared by the Indians of the respective groups, with authority to call upon the agencies of the federal government for technical assistance, and the ultimate purpose of such planning to be the growth and development of the resources and the people. . . .

Source: Alvin M. Josephy, Jr., Joane Nagel, and Troy Johnson, eds., *Red Power: The American Indians' Fight for Freedom* (1999).

ican Indian Movement (AIM) in that it describes a distinct region that has produced key actors, living memories of the American Indian holocaust, and ideas that have had significant influence in the formation and ongoing actions of the movement.

Emerging out of the Heartland in the 1960s, AIM's political agenda and the consequent renaissance of indigenous cultures was a politically and spiritually organized reaction to colonization and the extremism of the invaders, settlers, and their economic greed, including the theft of land and resources. Initially AIM protested the corruption in tribal and federal government, including law enforcement; violations of treaties; and federal controls over First Peoples. Contemporary AIM efforts include the ongoing insistence that the U.S. government acknowledge its treaty obligations and respect civil rights, honor its financial trust responsibilities, revoke federal termination and relocation policies, support tribal self-determination, and respect the spiritual rebirth of the First Peoples' nations. In other words, the primary agenda is the move toward decolonization.

The Missouri River and other socially significant sites, both sacred and secular, to American Indians are part of the Midwest landscape. Historically, as recently as the nineteenth century, Indian tribes throughout the United States were pushed into the last "Indian territories" in what is now Kansas and Oklahoma before being forced into even smaller tracts of land called "reservations." By 2000, First Peoples retained only 5 percent of their original land throughout the United States; an important part of that land base and its resources can still be found in the Dakotas and other parts of Midwest Indian Country.

Place for most American Indians is multilocal; most urban Indians maintain various types of connection to their homeland reservations, as well as to various spiritual sites not located on reservations. Urban Indians in Omaha or Sioux Falls, for example, are not unaware of their cultural and political legacies, although they may not know all of the specific details. For instance, most know that the United States violated the 1868 Fort Laramie Treaty, which formally recognized Sioux sovereignty; many do not know that the sovereignty covered much of what is now the Dakotas, Montana, Wyoming, and Nebraska.

Boarding and mission schools and state and federal prisons have been primary institutions for socializing to the majority culture since the late 1800s. Haskell University in Lawrence, Kansas, was originally a boarding school that a number of the parents and grandparents of AIM leaders and active members were forced to attend. During the 1960s, throughout the U.S. correctional system, American Indians, who were and still are disproportionately incarcerated, began in-

dividual and cultural group explorations of indigenous heritages. Three founders of AIM, brothers Clyde and Vernon Bellecourt and Dennis Banks, incarcerated at Stillwater Correctional Facility in Stillwater, Minnesota, began to study their roots as a source of personal and potentially collective strength. Today, AIM activist Leonard Peltier, considered a political prisoner by many, remains imprisoned at Leavenworth Federal Prison in Kansas.

Throughout the 1960s, War on Poverty representatives pressured the U.S. government and non-Indians to do right by American Indians. The Chicago and Cleveland urban Indian centers were instrumental in human rights activities. In 1961, 420 Indians from sixty-seven tribes wrote the Declaration of Indian Purpose while attending the National Indian Youth Council held during the American Indian Chicago Conference at the University of Chicago. On July 28, 1968, AIM was founded in Minneapolis, Minnesota. Much of its early political activity occurred in the Midwest. Examples include federal property occupations in Minneapolis, Lake Michigan near Chicago, Milwaukee, Missoula and Billings (Montana), Cleveland, and Denver, and in 1968, the formation of the Minneapolis AIM patrol to address extensive police brutality and the creation of the Minneapolis Legal Rights Center. In 1971, the first Native Peoples survival school, serving grades K through 12, began to address the extremely high drop-out rates among Minneapolis American Indian students. That same year during the First Nations Conference, eighteen chapters of AIM convened to develop long-range strategies for the future directions of the movement. In the fall of 1972, participants in the Trail of Broken Treaties spent almost a week at the Fairgrounds in Minneapolis.

Some eighty-two years after the December 28, 1890, massacre at Wounded Knee Creek—in which 250 women, children, and elderly and almost a hundred warriors were killed—AIM was contacted by Oglala Lakota Elders from Pine Ridge Reservation, South Dakota, to deal with corruption within the U.S. Bureau of Indian Affairs and the Tribal Council. On February 27, 1973, AIM and its allies began seventy-one days' occupation of Wounded Knee, gaining international attention. The Wounded Knee trials, which lasted for eight months, were held in Minneapolis in 1974. That same year, AIM women formed Women of All Red Nations (WARN) in Minneapolis, and the International Indian Treaty Council (IITC) was founded at an AIM gathering at Standing Rock, South Dakota, to represent indigenous peoples through the western hemisphere at the United Nations. Over four thousand Indians representing ninety-eight Indian Nations were present. In 1977, the Treaty Council was recognized by the United Nations Commission on Human Rights.

By the late 1980s and 1990s, Midwest AIM activists were still setting the model for other human rights advocates throughout Indian Country. The Elaine Stately Indian Youth Services (ESIYS) was created in 1989 as an alternative for Indian youth to gang involvement in Minneapolis. In 1991, the Peacemaker Center in Minneapolis was founded to house the AIM Patrol and ESIYS. The Center also promotes cultural activities such as the sugar bush camp, purification ceremonies (sweat lodges), the Gathering of the Sacred Pipes Sundance, and the On the Red Road Celebration, an alcohol- and drug-free New Year's Eve dance.

AIM has had and continues to have significant Midwest representation. Midwest intellectual and political leaders and activists, human rights advocates, and spiritual leaders—not necessarily mutually exclusive categories—were key actors during the occupation of Alcatraz Island by Indians of All Tribes in 1969–1971, the Trail of Broken Treaties in 1972, the Trail of Self-Determination in 1976, the Longest Walk in 1978, the Walk for Justice in 1994, and the annual Sacred Run.

Twenty-two of the forty-two members of the American Indian Task Force (including AIM leaders) were from the Midwest and/or had Midwest cultural and homeland roots. The Task Force presented statements to Vice President Spiro Agnew, the White House Staff, and the U.S. Congress during November 1969.

The following partial list of Midwest AIM leaders and activists further illustrates the influence of Midwest roots: Crow Dog (Rosebud Sioux), Vine Deloria, Jr. (Lakota), Ward Churchill (Keetoowah Cherokee), Woody Kipp (Blackfoot) Montana, Floyd Red Crow Westerman (Dakota, Sisseton Sioux), Clyde and Vernon Bellcourt (Anishinabe-Ojibwe, Minnesota), Dennis Banks (Anishinabe-Ojibwe), Russell Means (Oglala Lakota), William Means (Oglala Lakota), Ted Means (Oglala Lakota), Mryna Boyd (Nakota, Lakota), Hank Adams (Nakota), Curly Bear (Blackfoot), Lorelei DeCora Means (Minneconjou Lakota), Madonna Thunderhawk (Hunkapapa Lakota), Phyllis Young (Hunkapapa Lakota), Birgil Kills Straight (Oglala Lakota), Edward Benton Banai (Lac Court Orielles Band, Ojibway Nation), and Michael Haney (Seminole–Sioux).

Of the twenty-six speakers currently endorsed by the AIM speakers bureau, the International Indigenous Peoples Program Bureau, in Minneapolis, eleven—almost half—have Great Plains and Midwest roots.

The American Indian Movement, initially rooted in the Great Plains and upper Midwest, continues to promote American Indian culture, welfare, and civil rights. Its ongoing mission includes the political rebirth of almost six hundred American Indian nations (including those with federal recognition); the organizational growth of a broad spectrum of American Indian social institutions and groups; a growing sophistication about land claims and resource rights; a dramatic cultural and spiritual renewal; and an important First People's population resurgence.

Sources and Further Reading: Ward Churchill and Jim Vander Wall, *Agents of Repression* (2002); Stephen Cornell, *The Return of the Native: American Indian Political Resurgence* (1988); Vine Deloria, Jr., *Behind the Trail of Broken Treaties* (1974); Vine Deloria, Jr., and Clifford Lytle, *The Nations Within* (1984); Troy Johnson, Joane Nagel, and Duane Champagne, eds., *American Indian Activism* (1997); Alvin Josephy, Jr., Joane Nagel, and Troy Johnson, *The American Indians' Fight for Freedom*, 2nd ed. (1999); Russell Means, *Where White Men Fear to Tread* (1995); Leonard Peltier, *Prison Writings: My Life Is My Sundance* (1999); Stephen L. Pevar, *The Rights of Indians and Tribes*, 2nd ed. (1992).

Karren Baird-Olson
California State University–Northridge

The Black Civil Rights Movement

Although public and scholarly attention to the civil rights movement of the 1950s and 1960s has focused on the South, the Midwest was a fertile area for both Jim Crow segregation practices and organized opposition to them.

President Franklin D. Roosevelt's 1941 Executive Order No. 8802 that outlawed racial discrimination in hiring by corporations receiving defense contracts came at a time when defense industries were growing rapidly in the Midwest, producing technology for Britain and, after Pearl Harbor, for the U.S. war effort. African Americans who had been confined to cleaning and food service suddenly had access to industrial jobs, thanks to No. 8802 and the shortage of manpower caused by expanded production for the defense sector and the military draft. The Great Migration of blacks out of the South to the cities of the North, Midwest, and West increased momentum in the 1940s and 1950s, altering the demographics of midwestern cities. As World War II ended, black veterans returned from fighting Hitler's racism to find racism at home increasingly intolerable. They and college-educated black women homemakers formed a vanguard of protest against segregated schools and workplace discrimination in the late 1940s and 1950s.

The most extensive study of civil rights protest in the Midwest during this time focused on Wichita, the largest city in Kansas, where employment in the aircraft industry swelled from 1,478 in 1940, to 40,563 by the end of 1942, and per capita revenue from aircraft contracts exceeded that of any other city during the war. The black population grew from 5 percent before the War to 8 percent after, and the Korean War continued to stimulate the defense industry production with military bases (such as Wichita's McConnell Air Force Base), bringing servicemen "home" to the Midwest.

In Kansas, state laws banned racial and religious discrimination by places of amusement and public entertainment (1874) and by city and state agencies in hiring for public projects (1930). Those laws, however, were not enforced. From 1906, state law allowed towns and cities to decide whether or not to maintain racially segregated schools. Cities with small black populations did not segregate their schools, but larger cities like Wichita and Topeka built separate schools for black children to attend from kindergarten through the eighth grade. This policy met repeated protests from black parents and the local National Association for the Advancement of Colored People (NAACP).

The NAACP, formed in 1909, maintained branches across the Midwest from its first decade of operation. Its focus was court cases that chipped away at the separate-but-equal doctrine the Supreme Court had upheld since 1896. The NAACP won a major victory May 17, 1954, when a unanimous Supreme Court ruled that segregated schools were "inherently unequal." *Brown v. Topeka Board of Education* took its name from the only Midwest school district among the five districts sued by the black plaintiffs, supported by the NAACP, and was to become one of the most momentous decisions in the history of the Court.

In July 1958, inspired by stories of sit-ins attempted in the 1940s by the Congress of Racial Equality (CORE), NAACP youth in Wichita conducted their own sustained sit-in, doing so against the instructions of the national NAACP. Backed by their local branch, the students sat-in for three weeks at the lunch counter at a Dockums Drug Store in Wichita. When they decided to escalate their sit-ins from two to six days a week, the Dockums management agreed to serve them and, pressed by local NAACP president Chester I. Lewis, Jr., agreed to change its policy throughout the state. The Rexall chain, the largest drugstore chain in Kansas, agreed to desegregate its lunch counters in response to a student-led sit-in two years before sit-ins by students swept across the South. Within two weeks, Oklahoma NAACP youth were also staging sit-ins, followed by youth in St. Louis, Chicago, and other Midwest cities. Eventually the NAACP conceded that the students' tactic was effec-

tive and commended them, but only after learning that the sit-ins in Oklahoma City had added two thousand young members to the NAACP!

The Midwest produced other civil rights victories and firsts. In 1957, in Wichita, Chester Lewis filed complaints with President Eisenhower's Committee on Government Contracts and successfully challenged the employment practices of the largest employer in Wichita, Boeing Aircraft. For five years, a dozen black organizations in the city had sustained protests and sit-ins over hiring discrimination and public accommodations. The Young Women's Christian Association and church and temple women's groups formed a biracial coalition, the Community Committee on Social Action that visited restaurants to seek full public accommodation, lobbied the state legislature for low-cost and fair housing legislation, and formed the Panel of American Women that brought Jewish, Catholic, Protestant (black and white) women into towns across Kansas to speak about their lives to generate intergroup understanding. In 1961, Lewis filed complaints against the Kansas State Employment Service, which accepted racially specific job listings and practiced race discrimination in identifying workers for government training programs. Lewis got a federal injunction that the courts upheld against the state agency. By 1963, Kansas passed a law making discriminating in public accommodations a misdemeanor punishable with a fine or jail sentence.

In 1966, when NAACP's Lewis filed a complaint with the federal government against Wichita's de facto segregated schools, the federal government turned its attention to de facto school segregation, investigating the Wichita schools beginning in 1967—the first federal investigation of segregation in a midwestern school district and the second investigation of a school district outside the South. By 1971, that investigation found the Wichita schools to be in violation of the 1964 Civil Rights Act and federal funds were ordered withheld from the city until the school board altered the racial composition of the public schools in a way that mixed children and teachers interracially.

Although the most extensive study of a midwestern city to date has been of Wichita, anecdotal evidence suggests that civil rights activism rooted in the local NAACP and Urban League during the 1950s and 1960s was characteristic of midwestern cities at this time. By the mid-1960s, federal laws were in place to enforce the Fourteenth Amendment's guarantees of equal protection and due process for all citizens—the Civil Rights Act of 1964 and the Voting Rights Act of 1965. Individuals from Kansas had lobbied for their passage, traveling to Washington, D.C., to lobby congress and to Selma, Alabama, to join Dr. Martin Luther King, Jr.'s, Selma-to-Montgomery Voting

Rights March in 1965. During this march, Kansas native Rev. James Reeb became the movement's first white American martyr. Another Kansan, Arthur Fletcher, would later push the federal government to enforce Affirmative Action policies under Nixon.

Dozens of cities in the Midwest and around the nation experienced urban rebellions from 1964 to 1969 as shifts in government policy raised expectations of improved conditions for African Americans, the Vietnam War drained tax dollars that had been promised to President Johnson's War on Poverty, and white backlash set in. Polarization within black communities pitted Black Nationalists against Integrationists. The intensity of their polarization became manifest when midwesterner Chester Lewis led a movement against the chief executive of the NAACP, midwesterner Roy Wilkins, but in 1968 Wilkins defeated that challenge and the movement dissipated. The civil rights movement in the Midwest subsequently focused on taking advantage of both public and private programs devoted to assisting the advancement of people of color.

Sources and Further Reading: Gretchen Cassel Eick, *Dissent in Wichita: The Civil Rights Movement in the Midwest, 1954–1972* (2001); Johanna L. Hall, "The African-American Community in Topeka, Kansas, 1940–1951," M.A. thesis, University of Kansas (1993); Clara Luper, *Behold the Walls* (1979); Rusty L. Monhollan, *This Is America?* (2002); Christopher R. Reed, *The Chicago NAACP and the Rise of Black Professional Leadership, 1910–1966* (1997); Jeanne Theoharis and Komozi Woodard, eds., *Freedom North* (2003); Wichita School District, *School and Society in One City, Summary Report* (1969).

Gretchen Cassel Eick
Friends University, Kansas

Jesse Jackson (b. 1941) and PUSH

Born Jesse Louis Burns in Greenville, South Carolina, Jesse L. Jackson became one of the world's most noted civil rights leaders. Although Jackson is recognized worldwide, the Midwest (Chicago) is the headquarters of the Rainbow/PUSH Coalition (RPC) and the Citizenship Education Fund, and a launching point for his global and national advocacy. Jackson attended the University of Illinois at Urbana-Champaign from 1959 to 1960 and, in 1961, transferred to North Carolina Agricultural and Technical State University in Greensboro, from which he graduated in May 1964. In 1962, he married Jacqueline Lavinia Brown. As a student, Jackson led civil rights demonstrations in Greensboro and was arrested for "inciting a riot and disturbing the peace and dignity of the state."

In 1964, Jackson entered the Chicago Theological Seminary; however, after viewing news coverage of Bloody Sunday, depicting the Selma-to-Montgomery civil rights march of March 7, 1965, on television, he left his studies to travel to Selma, Alabama, where he met Dr. Martin Luther King, Jr. In 1966, Dr. King appointed him to head the Chicago chapter of the Southern Christian Leadership Conference's (SCLC) Operation Breadbasket, where he launched economic boycotts against local stores for discriminatory practices. The following year, Jackson became the national director of Operation Breadbasket. After Dr. King's assassination in 1968, Jackson became an ordained minister and resigned from SCLC to establish Operation PUSH, People United to Serve Humanity.

In 1975, Jackson founded PUSH for Excellence (PUSH-Excel), a scholarship fund and program to encourage inner-city youth and their parents to strive toward academic excellence. In 1984, Jackson entered the Democratic presidential race and garnered over 3.3 million votes in the primaries, which represented 18.3 percent of the total primary vote. Although an impressive showing, he received only 10 percent of the delegates at the Democratic Party convention. In 1988, he made a second bid for the presidency, coming in second for the Democratic nomination with 6.7 million votes, for 29 percent of the total primary vote. In contrast to 1984, however, he received 27 percent of the delegates.

In 1984, Jackson founded the National Rainbow Coalition, and the Christian Education Fund (CEF). A key component of the CEF is the Wall Street Project, which promotes economic opportunity for African Americans and other minorities.

In 1989, Jackson moved to Washington, D.C., and was elected "shadow" senator—a largely ceremonial lobbying position without the qualifications required to vote on legislation—of the District of Columbia, serving from 1990 to 1996. In 1996, Jackson returned to Operation PUSH in Chicago, where he soon merged the National Rainbow Coalition and Operation PUSH to form the Rainbow/PUSH Coalition.

In the international arena, Jackson made a controversial visit to the Middle East in 1979, traveled to Syria and secured the freedom of downed U.S. pilot Robert Goodman in 1984, won the release of hundreds of foreign nationals being held in Kuwait by Saddam Hussein in 1991, became President Clinton's "special envoy for democracy" in Africa in 1997, and negotiated the release of three U.S. POWs during the Kosovo War in 1999. He continues his involvement in public affairs nationally and internationally in the first decade of the new century. In 1995, his son, Jesse Jackson, Jr., was elected to a seat in the U.S. House of Representatives from Chicago where he continues to serve.

Sources and Further Reading: Lucius J. Barker, Mack H. Jones, and Katherine Tate, *African Americans and the American Political System*, 3rd ed. (1999); Marshall Frady, *Jesse: The Life and Pilgrimage of Jesse Jackson* (1996).

Valerie C. Johnson
DePaul University, Illinois

The Women's Movement before 1950

After the Civil War, midwestern women led the country in creating and joining mass single-sex organizations to promote programs to protect women, children, and public health. Begun in the Northeast in the 1840s, the "woman movement" was prompted by several factors: the growing awareness of women's legal disabilities, the widely held belief in women's moral superiority, migration from farms into villages and cities, the expansion of the middle class and women's education, the fall of the birth rate, and challenges to women posed by male drinking.

Women's rights groups met in Ohio, Indiana, Michigan, and Iowa in the 1850s, and some Ohio women gathered to destroy liquor holdings before 1860. But the Civil War brought women into public work for the first time, as members of soldiers' aid groups, and the U.S. Sanitary Commission appointed women as nurses, agents, and office managers. Mary Livermore and Jane Hoge of Chicago ran the Northwest Sanitary Commission that oversaw societies in several states and became famous for inventing the mammoth fund-raising fair. Livermore became a suffragist and lectured nationwide to paying audiences.

But for decades, few midwesterners supported women's suffrage. Instead, women's political activism was prompted by the fear of male drinking. In the winter of 1874, a spontaneous uprising of middle-class, small-town Ohio churchwomen against saloons inspired a mass movement: Forty-seven thousand midwestern women, 86 percent of all demonstrators, took part in "crusades," demonstrations unprecedented both in size and duration, in 333 places. Women formed "praying bands," exhorting saloon owners and customers to shut down the business. Some were successful, but the women's action in male spaces against male drinking was revolutionary.

Crusaders created the Women's Christian Temperance Union (WCTU), the first mass organization of women, with 150 thousand members by 1890. Its principal strength was in the Midwest; in 1879, over 60 percent of the "auxiliaries" in the nation were there. Its leaders included Iowa's Civil War heroine, Annie Wittenmyer, the first president, followed in 1879 by Evanston's charismatic Frances Willard, former dean of women at Northwestern University. Willard served for twenty years, arguing that women needed suffrage to protect their homes and urging them to "make the whole world homelike." WCTU worked to raise the age of consent (from ten to sixteen), appoint police matrons, teach children the dangers of alcohol, and establish the eight-hour day. Members learned to conduct meetings and projects without male oversight. They were overwhelmingly native-born white Protestants—although there were national departments for work among the Germans and among African Americans (in Indianapolis in 1884, there were four black local auxiliaries). Their Protestant style alienated Catholics and Jews, while their rejection of immigrants' bier gartens and the "continental Sunday," which involved spending the day in recreation and not just in church, limited the WCTU's appeal.

Women's clubs sprang up throughout the late 1870s and 1880s, as well, for "study and self-culture." Ambitious clubs such as the Chicago Woman's Club (CWC), founded in 1876, undertook public projects and even lobbied to get a woman on the school board. In 1890, a group of club leaders organized the General Federation of Women's Clubs (GFWC), the second large women's organization, with midwestern states quick to form state federations. When CWC's Ellen Martin Henrotin became president of the GFWC in 1894, she urged the clubs into social action. Henrotin and fellow CWC member Bertha Honore Palmer had planned the women's exhibits and congresses at the Chicago World's Fair, which prompted the formation of the National Council of Jewish Women (NCJW) and the National Association of Colored Women. NCJW founder Pauline Steinem of Toledo, a German immigrant, later became president of the Toledo federation of clubs and was elected to the school board. The Illinois Federation of Colored Women's Clubs represented eighty clubs by 1922 and provided social services to the state's burgeoning black population.

Midwestern women shaped the policies the national women's movement supported. Rockford College (Illinois) graduate Jane Addams (1860–1935) of Hull House, Chicago's pioneer settlement house, was a national heroine who spoke for social justice and democracy. Julia Lathrop of Illinois was the first head of the U.S. Children's Bureau; Grace Abbott of Nebraska (Lathrop's successor) and her sister Edith helped found the social work profession; Alice Hamilton of Indiana (M.D., University of Michigan) invented industrial medicine. These leaders worked with women's organizations to create social policies often tested in midwestern state and local programs: mother's pensions, juvenile courts, visiting nurses, public playgrounds, safe milk and water supplies, garbage collection, kindergartens, housing reform, restricted hours for children and women workers, factory inspectors, and woman suffrage.

By 1900, suffrage was a popular reform among midwestern women; GFWC endorsed it in 1914. Several states permitted women to vote on school issues in the 1870s, and Kansas women acquired municipal suffrage in 1887 for their efforts in passing and enforcing prohibition. Illinois in 1913 became the first industrialized state to give women the vote, though only in presidential and municipal elections; Nebraska, Minnesota, Iowa, Missouri, Wisconsin, Michigan, Indiana, and Ohio followed within a few years. Iowan Carrie Chapman Catt, president of National American Woman Suffrage Association (NAWSA) after 1915, organized the remarkable campaigns that led to the suffrage with the passage of the Nineteenth Amendment in 1919 and its ratification in 1920.

After 1920, midwestern women's organizations became divided. Leaders argued bitterly over a national Equal Rights Amendment, which threatened protective legislation for women and children; Wisconsin's passage of an equal rights law that preserved those protections satisfied neither side. GFWC supported the Shepherd-Towner Act to provide care to mothers and infants in rural areas, but opponents, such as the Illinois Medical Association, attacked as Communists the Children's Bureau and the visiting nurses who ran the program, and the program ended in 1927.

During the New Deal, women-supported social programs became federal law, but they were negotiated behind the scenes where women had little power. Women's organizations aged during the 1930s and 1940s; younger women joined PTAs and religiously-based groups. More women attended colleges and worked outside the home, but most people denigrated career women and urged domesticity for women.

Sources and Further Reading: Jack S. Blocker, *"Give to the Winds Thy Fears": The Women's Temperance Crusade, 1873–1874* (1985); Ruth Bordin, *Frances Willard: A Biography* (1986); Lynne Curry, *Modern Mothers in the Heartland* (1999); Maureen A. Flanagan, *Seeing with Their Hearts* (2002); Michael Lewis Goldberg, *An Army of Women* (1997); Anne Meis Knupfer, *Toward a Tenderer Humanity and a Nobler Womanhood* (1996); Lucy Eldersveld Murphy and Wendy Hamand Venet, eds., *Midwestern Women* (1997).

Lana Ruegamer
Indiana University

Feminism

Second-wave feminism has often been construed as a movement emerging from the urban centers such as New York, Boston, Washington, D.C., and Chicago.

However, the post-1960s women's movement owed its origins, ideas, events, and personnel as much to the Midwest as to any other geographic region of the United States.

As Judith Ezekiel demonstrates in *Feminism in the Heartland* (2002), midwestern or heartland feminism was as radical, vibrant, and challenging as that which emerged in the large urban centers. Betty Friedan, founding mother of second-wave feminism, was born in Peoria, Illinois; Gloria Steinem, unifying persona for feminism, in Toledo, Ohio. A disproportionate number of national leaders in the women's movement were from the Midwest, such as Dorothy Haener, organizer of the United Automobile Workers; Addie Wyatt, leader of Chicago's United Packinghouse Workers' Union and member of the NAACP; and Kay Clarenbach, chair of the Wisconsin State Commission on the status of women, who also served on President Kennedy's Commission on the Status of Women, which was pivotal in the rebirth of the women's movement. The Midwest, with its progressive traditions of strong trade unionism and consumer and political activism, provided women with greater opportunities to become organizers and leaders. In 1964, two years after the formation of the Commission on the Status of Women, Michigan Republican representative Martha Griffiths, supporter of women's rights, helped forge a coalition that successfully included the word "sex" in Title VII, the section of the Civil Rights bill that prohibited discrimination in employment based upon race, color, religion, or national origin.

The formation of the National Organization for Women (NOW) marked the emergence of organized liberal feminism. Founded in October 1966, 126 of the three hundred founding members came from the Midwest. NOW has chapters in every midwestern state.

The other strand within the women's movement was radical feminism, and its roots are as much in the heartland as anywhere. In the 1960s, younger women, with experience in the civil rights, antiwar, and student movements, began to challenge the gendered status quo. At the 1965 conference of the radical Students for a Democratic Society (SDS) in Illinois, a resolution supporting the idea of women's liberation was first raised. In August 1967, at the Chicago National Conference on New Politics (NCNP), a women's caucus demanded that their grievances be taken seriously. The refusal by the male new left to take women and women's issues seriously contributed to the rise of radical feminism.

The Chicago Women's Liberation Union (CWLU) was a pioneering organization; a number of leading feminist theorists and activists such as Jo Freeman, author of "The Tyranny of Structurelessness," Naomi Weisstein of the Women's Liberation Rock Band and author of "Psychology Constructs the Female," and historians and political activists such as Ellen Dubois, Amy Kesselman, Heather Booth, and Vivian Rothstein came out of the CWLU. Jane, an underground abortion service, was affiliated with the Union. Women's liberation groups sprung up spontaneously throughout the Midwest including in Columbus, Pittsburgh, Detroit, Minneapolis, and St. Paul. One of the first demonstrations against *Playboy* magazine took place at Grinnell, Iowa. Fort Wayne, Indiana feminists organized Take Back the Night marches, rape crisis hotlines, battered women's shelters, feminist bookstores, and coffee houses. In 1969, feminists organized consciousness-raising groups in the archetypical heartland city of Dayton, Ohio. In the mid 1970s, Dayton Women's Liberation organized a phone bank, speakers bureau, a woman's center, a lending library, and extensive child-care and educational programs. In 1969, Julia Reichert, Antioch college graduate, pioneered the first feminist and women's radio program at YWSO in Yellow Springs, Ohio. Women's Studies, the academic manifestation of feminism, proliferates at almost every college and university throughout the Midwest.

By the early 1970s, the women's movement began to focus on issues facing women in the paid labor force. The Cleveland Council of Union Women, founded in 1972, was organized to address problems facing women in trade unions; Cleveland Women Working was established to improve the status of women office workers; Hard Hatted Women focused on women in traditional male trades. Three thousand trade union women met in Chicago in 1974 and founded the Coalition of Labor Union Women (CLUW), whose stated goals were organizing unorganized women, political action and legislation, affirmative action in the workplace, and participation of women within their unions. Its feminist agenda expanded to include support for reproductive rights, on-the-job child-care, and an end to sexual harassment. In Ohio alone, CLUW chapters were organized in Youngstown, Cleveland, Akron, Toledo, Dayton, Columbus, and Cincinnati.

In the 1970s, much of the movement for reproductive rights was centered in the Midwest, particularly in Ohio. The rising "New Right" focused on attacking feminists' key issues: the Equal Rights Amendment, child care, homosexual rights, sex education, battered women's shelters, but most of all a woman's right to abortion. Clinics in major cities in the region were firebombed throughout the seventies.

In 1974, in response to the attacks, the National Abortion Rights Action League (NARAL) was founded in Chicago. In 1978, Faye Wattleton was the first African American and the first woman since Margaret Sanger to be elected president of national Planned Parenthood. A graduate of The Ohio State

University, she began her career as an effective coalition builder for reproductive rights in Dayton, Ohio. Radical feminists organized the Reproductive Rights National Network (R2N2), an organization that connected abortion rights, opposition to coercive sterilization, racism, and homophobia into a comprehensive vision regarding reproductive rights and feminist health care. At the founding meeting in Yellow Springs, Ohio, women from reproductive rights groups in Chicago, Minneapolis, Pittsburgh, Detroit, Cincinnati, Dayton, and Cleveland organized the first-ever demonstration against the antiabortion Right-to-Life organization in Cincinnati in 1979. Subsequent conferences were held in Cleveland and Chicago.

Women of color participated in some feminist organizations, most notably in the Coalition of Labor Union Women and other workingwomen's groups. The National Black Feminist Organization, founded in 1973, had chapters in Chicago and Detroit. The Chicago branch changed its name to the National Black Feminist Alliance and, under the leadership of Brenda Eichelberger, continued until 1981.

The women's movement declined in the 1980s. NOW chapters, women's bookstores, women's studies programs in colleges and universities, reproductive rights and other political organizations, workingwomen's organizations, lesbian and women-of-color feminist organizations have endured the conservative backlash of the past twenty years.

Sources and Further Reading: Rosalyn Baxandall and Linda Gordon, eds., *Dear Sisters* (2000); Susan Brownmiller, *In Our Time: Memoir of a Revolution* (1999); Rachel DuPlessis and Ann Snitow, eds., *The Feminist Memoir Project* (1998); Alice Echols, *Daring to Be Bad* (1989); Judith Ezekiel, *Feminism in the Heartland* (2002); Jo Freeman, *The Politics of Women's Liberation* (1975); Ruth Rosen, *The World Split Open* (2000); Deborah Gray White, *Too Heavy a Load* (1999).

Barbara Winslow
Brooklyn College, City University of New York

Kent State

The May 4, 1970, tragedy at Kent State University sparked campus demonstrations across the country and highlighted divisions in American society. On April 30, 1970, President Richard Nixon announced a military invasion into Cambodia. In response, protestors rioted in Kent, a small, northeastern Ohio town. Students and nonstudents alike destroyed private property, threw bottles at the police, and burned the ROTC building.

Ohio Governor James Rhodes sent the Ohio National Guard to quell the unrest. He enflamed matters

Kent State, 1970. News Service
Photographs. May 4 Collection.
Department of Special Collections
and Archives. Kent State University
Libraries and Media Services.

with his brutal rhetoric, promising "to eradicate the problem." On May 4, several hundred protestors taunted the guardsmen. A few threw rocks. The Guard responded at first with tear gas. Then, without a clear order, several Guardsmen fired on protestors and innocent bystanders, killing four and wounding nine. In his *Grand Expectations*, James Patterson notes that Kent State triggered a wave of confrontations that hit over three hundred campuses and included an estimated two million students.

The turbulence of May 1970 betrayed a divided America. The sides were often described starkly, if too simplistically: university radicals against the patriotic working class. At a New York City memorial rally shortly after Kent State, approximately two hundred construction workers descended on the group and beat them, using hardhats as weapons. Days later, the local union chief presented Nixon with a hardhat. He accepted the gift as symbolic of American "freedom and patriotism."

Sources and Further Reading: Todd Gitlin, *The Sixties: Years of Hope, Days of Rage* (1987); James Patterson, *Grand Expectations: The United States, 1945–1974* (1996); President's Commission on Campus Unrest, *The Report of the President's Commission on Campus Unrest* (1970).

William Russell Coil
The Ohio State University–Columbus

The Port Huron Statement

The Port Huron Statement was a declaration of principles and intentions published by the organizing group of Students for a Democratic Society (SDS), developed at a convention in Port Huron, Michigan, from June 11 to 15, 1962. This document was intended as a "manifesto of hope" and the "agenda for a generation." The statement was drafted by Tom Hayden, 1960–1961 editor of the University of Michigan *Daily*, the campus newspaper, second president of SDS, and later a member of both the Chicago Eight and the California state legislature. Delegates to the Port Huron Convention hotly debated the language of Hayden's draft, approved it as the official policy of SDS, then published twenty thousand copies. Reprinted many times, it became the most widely read pamphlet of the 1960s.

In his autobiography, *Reunion: A Memoir*, Hayden identifies the central theme of the Port Huron Statement as the assertion that "democracy, real *participative democracy*, rests on the independence of the ordinary people." The intellectual sources of the statement were varied, including many leftist thinkers and Pope John XXIII's encyclical *Pacem in Terris*.

The statement opens: "We are people of this generation, bred in at least modest comfort, housed now in universities, looking uncomfortably to the world we inherit." The introduction asserts that because of the "Southern struggle against racial bigotry" and the "Cold War, symbolized by the presence of the [atomic] Bomb," the students in this generation began to see "complicated and disturbing paradoxes in our surrounding America. The declaration 'all men are created equal . . .' rang hollow before the facts of Negro life in the South and the big cities of the North." Thus motivated, the statement declares the ideals and values of "this generation," sets forth political and economic goals, and focuses on universities as the likeliest means to resolve the paradoxes between idealized American rhetoric and the realities of power in an era that included McCarthyism.

Sources and Further Reading: Tom Hayden, *Reunion: A Memoir* (1988); Peter B. Levy, ed., *America in the Sixties—Right, Left, and Center* (1998).

Thomas Minnick
The Ohio State University–Columbus

Abortion and Politics

By virtue of the 1973 U.S. Supreme Court decision *Roe v. Wade* (410 U.S. 113), abortion is legal in the Midwest as it is throughout the United States. This ruling prohibited states from interfering with abortion during the first trimester of pregnancy. During the second trimester, the state had the power to regulate abortion only in ways designed to preserve and protect the woman's health. In the third trimester, the protection of fetal life became a compelling reason sufficient under *Roe* to justify interference with the exercise of the right to choose abortion. By permitting state discretion, *Roe v. Wade* federalized, rather than nationalized, abortion policy. As a result, state abortion politics intensified, and states became key players in developing abortion policies.

Although the fifty states have enacted over twenty different abortion restrictions, four major types of state abortion restrictions are: (1) mandating parental consent or notification for abortions to minors, (2) prohibiting the use of state funds for abortions for low-income women, (3) requiring a waiting period and the dissemination of specific information before a woman can obtain an abortion, and (4) targeted regulation of abortion providers.

As a group, midwestern states are more restrictive than the rest of the nation in requiring and enforcing parental consent laws. All twelve states mandate parental consent or notification, and all but one (Illinois) actually enforce those laws. Enforcement rates for the country as a whole are considerably lower: Of the forty-three states that have laws requiring minors to obtain the consent of or to notify a parent or another adult prior to obtaining an abortion, only thirty-three states actually enforce those laws.

States may fund abortions for low-income women who are eligible for Medicaid, and they may pay for medical insurance for public employees that covers abortion. As a group, midwestern states are less likely to pay for these procedures for low-income women than are other states. Of the sixteen state medical assistance programs that covered abortion in most or all circumstances in 2001, only two were in midwestern states, In-diana and Minnesota. Midwestern states are more likely to prohibit public funds from paying for health insurance that includes abortion. Of the twelve states that prohibited this coverage in 2001, four were in the Midwest—Illinois, Michigan, Nebraska, and Ohio.

Midwestern states are more likely to require a waiting period and/or a state-mandated lecture or written materials intended to dissuade a woman ("informed consent") before an abortion can be performed. As of 2001, twenty-one of the fifty states had mandatory waiting periods and/or informed consent requirements, whereas two-thirds of states in the Midwest had codified this practice—Indiana, Kansas, Michigan, Nebraska, North Dakota, Ohio, South Dakota, and Wisconsin. This type of restriction, which includes a waiting period, is particularly difficult for rural women since almost all abortion providers are located in urban areas.

Midwestern states have a disproportionately higher number of regulations for abortion clinics than do other parts of the country. The purpose of these laws is generally to discourage abortion providers from locating or staying in an area, and they are often redundant of other codes governing clinics and private medical practices. While twenty-eight states in the nation have enforceable targeted regulations, ten of the twelve midwestern states have this type of regulation.

In a ranking of states on overall abortion accessibility, only two midwestern states were in the upper half of the rankings: Minnesota at eighteenth most accessible and Iowa at twenty-first most accessible. The remainder were in the lower half of the accessibility rankings. Among them, Missouri was rated forty-seventh and North Dakota was fiftieth, the state with the least access to abortion.

The intensity of midwestern abortion politics is made evident by the number and importance of the judicial cases that have reached the U.S. Supreme Court. At least a third of the Court's twenty-six rulings on abortion since *Roe* have emanated from the Midwest. These include *Webster v. Reproductive Health Services* (1989), which permitted far more state restrictions than the Court had allowed since *Roe*; *Hodgson v. Minnesota* (1990) and *Ohio v. Akron Center for Reproductive Health* (1990), which clarified parental notification, and *Stenberg v. Carhart* (2000), which addressed second-trimester abortion.

Although the level of political activity on the abortion issue in the region is disproportionately high relative to the rest of the nation, the incidence of abortion is relatively low in these states. Eleven of the twelve states have the same or lower abortion rates than the national average; only Illinois has a higher rate. Among teens, who account for a disproportionate number of abortions nationally, the midwestern rates are also low. Only Illinois has a higher teenage abortion rate than the national average, Michigan has the same rate as the national average, and the other Midwest states have considerably lower rates. Research has shown that these lower abortion rates are largely the result of lower pregnancy rates among teens and older women, and not of state abortion restrictions. This finding suggests that midwesterners use contraception more effectively than do many other Americans.

Given the fact that the incidence of abortion is lower in the Midwest than in other parts of the country, why are abortion politics so volatile in this region of the country? Simply put, Midwest politics combines both elements that would restrict abortion—such as conservative strength, religious fundamentalism, Catholicism—along with other factors that favor accessibility to abortion—such as progressive ideology, large numbers of employed women, and grass roots advocacy.

Sources and Further Reading: Glen A. Halva-Neubauer, "The States After Roe: No 'Paper Tigers,'" in Malcolm L. Goggin, ed., *Understanding the New Politics of Abortion* (1993); Deborah R. McFarlane and Kenneth J. Meier, *The Politics of Fertility Control: Family Planning and Abortion Policies in the American States* (2001); NARAL and NARAL Foundation, *Who Decides? A State by State Review of Abortion and Reproductive Rights*, 11th ed. (2002); Lawrence H. Tribe, *Abortion: The Clash of Absolutes* (1992).

Deborah R. McFarlane
University of New Mexico

The Politics of Gay Rights

The term "gay rights" refers to the political and social struggle over the status of people with a homosexual orientation. Gays and lesbians argue that they should not face discrimination or oppression because of their sexual orientation, and thus ask for government policies to protect their civil rights and liberties. Opponents argue that gays are already provided legal protection and that government should not provide additional or "special" rights on the basis of behavior, especially if that behavior is seen as chosen and immoral. This pattern of debate is relatively consistent throughout the country, including the Midwest.

The rise of a political movement to ensure the civil rights and liberties of gays and lesbians is frequently viewed as a phenomenon relegated to the East and West Coasts of the United States. Although this was more often the case when the movement started in the late 1960s, by the late 1970s, the political battle over gay rights had become widespread in the Midwest. Indeed, many urban areas and college towns in the Midwest provided the gay movement with some of its most significant early victories.

As the gay movement grew on the coasts during the early 1970s, gay communities in the Midwest began mobilizing as well, especially in urban centers such as Chicago, Minneapolis, St. Louis, Detroit, and Des Moines. Further, college towns like Ann Arbor, Michigan, Madison, Wisconsin, and Columbus saw gays and lesbians mobilize to form interest groups, hold annual gay pride marches, and become involved in party politics for the first time. By the 1980s, in Chicago and Minneapolis, gays were a significant voting bloc courted by winning candidates for mayor and city council seats. In Iowa and Ohio, the number of gays and lesbians serving as delegates to the 2000 National Democratic Party Convention had grown significantly. Further, gay Republicans in the Midwest found a voice in chapters of the Log Cabin Republicans, with the leader of a Wisconsin chapter eventually being appointed to a federal government position by George W. Bush.

Although midwestern states have lagged behind other parts of the country in protecting the civil rights and liberties of lesbians and gays, some localities and states in the region have been quite innovative. Indeed, two cities in Michigan, Ann Arbor and East Lansing, and St. Louis, Missouri, were the first localities to adopt antidiscrimination protections for gays in 1972, and Wisconsin was the first state in the country to pass a law banning discrimination based on sexual orientation in 1982. At the same time, St. Paul, Minnesota, and Wichita, Kansas, adopted antidiscrimination policies in the 1970s, only to have them repealed by voters at the ballot box in 1978. By the end of the 1990s, only Minnesota had adopted gay rights law through statute, but several other midwestern states, including Illinois, Ohio, and Michigan, adopted similar policies through temporary executive orders issued by governors.

Further, some of the first openly gay or lesbian elected officials in the country held offices in the Midwest, including Kathy Kozachenko, who became the first openly gay or lesbian person elected to any office in the country when she won a seat on the Ann Arbor, Michigan, city council in April 1974, and Alan Spear, who became the second openly gay state legislator in the country when he revealed his sexual orientation to the Minnesota Senate in late 1974. Spear went on to serve in the Minnesota Senate as president in 1993 and retired in 2000. And although other states have elected far more gay officials than most midwestern states, in 1998, Wisconsin became the first state to elect a lesbian and nonincumbent gay or lesbian to Congress with the election of Democratic representative Tammy Baldwin.

Midwestern states have also adopted or maintained a considerable number of policies that infringe on gay rights, and most states have few openly gay officials or policies to protect gay civil rights. For example, Minnesota maintained its law banning homosexual sexual relations until 2001, when it was repealed through a court challenge to its constitutionality. Kansas and Michigan had antisodomy laws until 2003, when the U.S. Supreme Court struck down all state antisodomy laws in its ruling on *Lawrence v. Texas*. Missouri, Kansas, Illinois, and South Dakota were some of the first states to pass bans on same-sex marriage in 1996.

In sum, although the pattern of politics surrounding gay rights in the Midwest tends to be more favorable in some states than in others, and urban areas in the Midwest generally appear supportive of gay civil rights, most of the populace in the region is relatively unsupportive of gay civil rights and state policies tend to reflect those preferences. Despite considerable variation across the states, with a few exceptions, midwestern states tend to have fewer gay interest group resources, fewer policies that protect gay civil rights and more antigay policies, lower public support for gay rights, and a lower gay population than other regions or than the national average. In a sense, the Midwest appears to maintain competing views of gay rights, and unlike other regions of the country, such as the South, there is evidence of both strong support and strong opposition. The Midwest does not speak with a single voice on gay rights, and this suggests that midwestern states may be developing dissimilar patterns of politics, especially on issues that inflame religious and moral concerns.

Sources and Further Reading: Robert W. Bailey, *Gay Politics, Urban Politics* (1999); James W. Button, Barbara A. Rienzo, and Kenneth D. Wald, *Private Lives, Public Conflicts* (1997); Donald P. Haider-Markel, "Lesbian and Gay Politics in the States," in Craig A. Rimmerman, Kenneth D. Wald, and Clyde Wilcox, eds., *The Politics of Gay Rights* (2000); Lisa Keen, "By the Books: D.C. Ranks Second in Survey of States Treatment of Gays," *The Washington Blade* (Nov. 9, 2001); Gregory B. Lewis and Jonathan L. Edelson, "DOMA and ENDA," in Craig A. Rimmerman, Kenneth D. Wald, and Clyde Wilcox, eds., *The Politics of Gay Rights* (2000); Raymond A. Smith and Donald P. Haider-Markel, *Gay and Lesbian Americans and Political Participation* (2002).

Donald P. Haider-Markel
University of Kansas

Father Charles Edward Coughlin (1891–1979)

When radio reigned across the Midwest during the 1930s, Father Charles E. Coughlin's voice was promi-

nent. Born and educated for Roman Catholic priesthood in Canada, he moved to Detroit, Michigan, and established a parish in suburban Royal Oak. To raise funds for his new church, Coughlin began broadcasting on WJR in 1926. His subsequent weekly programs increasingly addressed dire economic conditions during the Great Depression and vehemently denounced those ostensibly causing the calamity.

Receiving overwhelmingly positive responses, Coughlin's broadcasts were aired by a chain of twenty-seven stations by 1932, with audiences that often reached from fifteen to thirty million Americans, who responded by sending him hundreds of thousands of laudatory letters. Coughlin actively supported Franklin D. Roosevelt's first presidential bid with the slogan "Roosevelt *or* Ruin"; but shunned by FDR, the priest's programs soon proclaimed "Roosevelt *and* Ruin." With his weekly newspaper, *Social Justice*, Coughlin in 1934 formed the National Union for Social Justice (NUSJ), an incipient political party, and to test its power in 1935, he denounced American entry into the World Court. He successfully urged his listeners to deluge the Senate with telegrams and helped defeat the bill. The NUSJ then ran William Lemke for president in 1936. Lemke's dismal showing caused Coughlin briefly to stop broadcasting. Upon resuming programs, he lapsed into anti-Semitic content. With World War II approaching, he finally was pressured to cease broadcasting, and *Social Justice* was banned from the mails. For virtually a decade, however, Coughlin voiced the hopes and fears of many disaffected Americans.

Sources and Further Reading: Ronald H. Carpenter, *Father Charles E. Coughlin* (1998); Alfred McClung Lee and Elizabeth Briant Lee, eds., *The Fine Art of Propaganda* (1939); Charles J. Tull, *Father Coughlin and the New Deal* (1965).

Ronald H. Carpenter
University of Florida

Betty Friedan (1921–2006)

Bettye Naomi Goldstein was born in Peoria, Illinois, the daughter of a freethinking Jewish jeweler named Harry Goldstein and Miriam Horowitz Goldstein, who gave up a career in journalism to marry. The eldest of three, she observed her mother's suppressed ambition and experienced Peoria's narrowness. She excelled academically despite being ostracized socially, and discovered a talent for leadership. Fulfilling her mother's aspirations for her, she matriculated at Smith College, edited the college newspaper, studied psychology and sociology, and graduated Phi

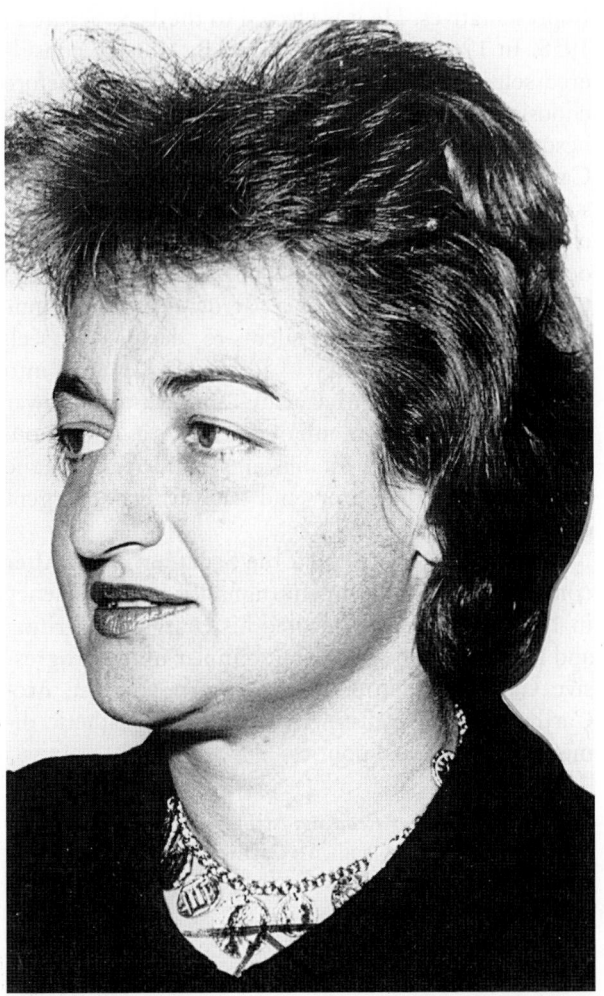

Author and feminist leader Betty Friedan. Library of Congress, New York World-Telegram and Sun Newspaper Photograph Collection, LC-USZ62-114907.

Beta Kappa in 1942. She went on to do graduate work at the University of California at Berkeley. Married to theatrical producer Carl Friedan in 1947, the couple moved to suburban New York City, where she worked as a journalist while raising the first of three children. Fired after requesting a second maternity leave, she described the frustrations experienced by suburban women like herself in *The Feminine Mystique* (1963), a book that earned Friedan instant fame.

A leader in the women's movement, she helped organize the National Organization for Women in 1966, serving as its first president until 1970. Divorced in 1969, she taught, lectured, wrote, and helped found the National Women's Political Caucus in 1971. She also convened the International Feminist Congress (1973) and established the First Women's Bank (1973) and the Economic Think Tank for Women (1974). Increasingly radicalized, she edited a feminist anthology,

It Changed My Life (1976), campaigned actively for the Equal Rights Amendment, and published *The Second Stage* (1981), *The Fountain of Age* (1993), and *Life So Far* (2000). In Friedan's youthful struggles, we see the midwestern origins of the twentieth-century women's movement.

Sources and Further Reading: Judith Adler Hennessee, *Betty Friedan: Her Life* (1999); Daniel Horowitz, *Betty Friedan and the Making of the Feminine Mystique* (1998).

Joanne Passet
Indiana University–East

Richard G. Hatcher (b. 1933)

When Richard G. Hatcher was elected mayor of Gary, Indiana, in November 1967, he became the first African American elected to lead a major American city. His election came at the apex of America's civil rights struggle and heralded a renaissance in black communities nationwide. Hatcher had to overcome Democratic machine politics so corrupt his election required the presence of federal troops. At the time Gary was the largest city in the world that had been built in the twentieth century.

Hatcher's election accelerated white flight to the suburbs. He became a national figure and spent much of his time at events around the country as the city wasted away. By his third four-year term, U.S. Steel, which was at one time the largest single steel-producing mill in the country and the city's primary employer, became a victim of the severe recession that led to dramatic layoffs.

Lacking a vibrant middle class and with skyrocketing unemployment, many businesses boarded up, and with a school system called the worst in Indiana, Gary continued to stagnate. Hatcher, who lured the 1972 Black National Political Convention to his city, remained in demand on the national circuit. But after steel's collapse, and despite more than $300 million in federal aid, Hatcher could no longer hide the fact he had few solutions for the city's mounting problems, and ultimately he was identified with its failure. In 1987, after twenty years as mayor, he was voted out of office.

Born July 10, 1933, in Michigan City, Indiana, to Carleton and Katherine Hatcher, both factory workers, Hatcher grew up in a politically aware family and one concerned with the conditions and rights of factory workers. He received his B.S. degree from Indiana University in 1956 and his LLB and JD degrees from Valparaiso University in 1959. After his lengthy mayoral career, he devoted time to various civic organizations and public causes and has served as an adjunct professor of Afro-American Studies at Indiana University–Northwest.

Sources and Further Reading: Robert A. Catlin, Racial Politics and Urban Planning: Gary Indiana 1980–1989 (1993); Peter Jennings and Todd Brewster, *In Search of America* (2002); James B. Lane, *City of the Century: A History of Gary, Indiana* (1978); Alex Poinsett, *Black Power, Gary Style: The Making of Mayor Richard Gordon Hatcher* (1970); The Trustees of Indiana University, "Richard Gordon Hatcher," Indiana University Northwest Department of Minority Studies, http://www.iun.edu/hatcher/index.htm (December 12, 1999).

Richard Grey
Post-Tribune, Gary, Indiana

Eugene Joseph McCarthy (1916–2005)

Born in Watkins, Minnesota, a farming village in Meeker County, Eugene McCarthy was the son of Michael and Anna Baden McCarthy. He graduated from St. John's University in Collegeville, Minnesota, and married Abigail Quigley in 1945. Inspired by the Catholic rural life movement, they lived briefly on a farm near Watkins before moving to St. Paul, where McCarthy taught economics and sociology at the College of St. Thomas.

McCarthy entered politics in 1947 as an organizer for the Democratic-Farmer-Labor Party. The following year, he handily won election to the U.S. House of Representatives. He was elected to the U.S. Senate in 1958. In 1964, President Lyndon B. Johnson considered selecting McCarthy as his running mate before choosing instead his Senate colleague from Minnesota, Hubert H. Humphrey. By 1967, however, McCarthy had grown disenchanted with Johnson's pursuit of military victory in Vietnam, and he agreed to challenge the president in the New Hampshire Democratic primary in March 1968. McCarthy shocked the nation when he lost by a narrow margin to Johnson, prompting the president to decline to seek renomination. The entry of Robert F. Kennedy into the race undermined McCarthy's appeal as the antiwar candidate. In the aftermath of Kennedy's assassination, the Democratic Party establishment rallied around the candidacy of Humphrey, and McCarthy's insurgent campaign quickly faded.

Eugene J. McCarthy left the Senate in 1970. After conducting short-lived campaigns for the presidency in 1972 and 1976, he devoted his energies to writing and lecturing. A poet and an exemplar of the progressive Catholic tradition of the upper Midwest, McCarthy brought a distinctive moral and esthetic dimension to national politics.

Sources and Further Reading: Arthur Herzog, *McCarthy for President* (1969); Abigail McCarthy, *Private Faces/Public Places* (1972); Eugene J. McCarthy, *Up 'til Now: A Memoir* (1987).

James T. Fisher
Fordham University, New York

Senator Eugene McCarthy in the 1968 presidential campaign. Courtesy Minnesota Historical Society. MHS Locator no. por/5860/p26, neg. no. 83661.

Senator Joseph McCarthy and Roy Cohn. Wisconsin Historical Society, WHi-8004.

Joseph McCarthy (1908–1957)

Joseph McCarthy was born on November 14, 1908, in Grand Chute Township, Wisconsin. In 1930, McCarthy enrolled at Marquette University in Milwaukee, where he studied engineering before pursuing a law degree. He was also active in boxing and debate. Upon earning his law degree in 1935, McCarthy established a solo practice in Waupaca, Wisconsin—but he had higher ambitions.

In 1946, he demonstrated his penchant for identifying the pulse of Wisconsin voters as he focused his successful campaign for the U.S. Senate on repealing New Deal farm legislation. In 1950, in search of a reelection theme, McCarthy seized on his constituents' growing fear of Communism. In a speech in Wheeling, West Virginia, McCarthy accused the U.S. State Department of harboring Communists. These charges, which McCarthy continued to make on the Senate floor, were well received in Wisconsin. Whatever political gain McCarthy realized from his anti-Communist speeches, however, his professional and personal losses were greater. His detractors referred to his antics as "McCarthyism," implying that McCarthy invented his charges for political gain. In 1954, after his controver-

sial hearings into Communist activities in the U.S. Army, the Senate voted to censure McCarthy.

It was a rebuke from which McCarthy never recovered. With his political career in shambles, McCarthy turned to alcohol. He died of complications from alcoholism in 1957. Even after his death, McCarthy's contention that the United States was "soft on communism" continued to preoccupy and dominate American foreign policy makers for the next forty years.

Sources and Further Reading: Arthur Herman, *Joseph McCarthy* (2000); Michael O'Brien, *McCarthy and McCarthyism in Wisconsin* (1980); Thomas C. Reeves, *The Life and Times of Joe McCarthy* (1997).

Geoffrey Larson
University of Iowa

George William Norris (1861–1944)

George William Norris represented Nebraska in the U.S. House of Representatives (1902–1912) and U.S. Senate (1912–1942) for forty years. Known as the "fighting liberal," Norris battled throughout his career to make government more accountable to the needs of the ordinary citizen. Norris was born on July 11, 1861, near Clyde, Ohio, graduated from Northern Indiana Normal School in 1880, and was admitted to the bar in 1883. In 1885, he headed to Nebraska, where he established a law practice in Beaver City.

Inclined toward politics, Norris was elected Furnas County attorney in 1892, and three years later, became a district court judge, where he gained a reputation for protecting farmers and businessmen from foreclosures. Elected to the U.S. House of Representatives in 1902, he avidly supported progressive reforms such as the initiative, referendum, recall, and the direct election of senators. Elevated to the Senate in 1912, he strongly opposed Woodrow Wilson's foreign policy, refusing to declare war on Germany and later voting against ratification of the Treaty of Versailles. During the Great Depression, Norris spearheaded the Norris–La Guardia Act, drafted the Twentieth Amendment to the U.S. Constitution, and shaped legislation that created the Tennessee Valley Authority and the Rural Electrification Administration. Among other accomplishments, he helped create Nebraska's unicameral legislature.

Although nominally a Republican, Norris followed his conscience and regularly crossed party lines. In 1936, he abandoned the party and won reelection as an Independent. Defeated for a sixth term in 1942, Norris returned to McCook, Nebraska, where he spent his final years writing his memoirs. Published after his death in 1944, *Fighting Liberal* is a fitting title for the biography of a political maverick who spent his career fighting to protect the rights of the common citizen.

Sources and Further Reading: Richard Lowitt, *The Making of a Progressive, 1861–1912* (1963); Richard Lowitt, *The Persistence of a Progressive, 1913–1933* (1971); Richard Lowitt, *The Triumph of a Progressive, 1933–1944* (1978); George W. Norris, *Fighting Liberal* (1945).

Mark R. Ellis
University of Nebraska–Kearney

Gloria Steinem (b. 1934)

Gloria Steinem, symbol of the American women's movement, was born March 25, 1934, in Toledo, Ohio. Her paternal grandmother, Pauline Perlmutter Steinem, was an Ohio suffragist. Graduating magna cum laude from Smith College in 1956, she left the Midwest permanently in 1960 and moved to New York City to become a journalist.

In the early 1960s, she marched with Women's Strike for Peace against the war in Vietnam and worked closely with Dolores Huerta of the United Farm Workers Union. In 1969, she attended a meeting on abortion organized by Redstockings, a New York–based radical women's liberation organization, which motivated her full activism in the women's movement. A founder of the National Women's Political Caucus and the Women's Action Alliance, she was also the founder of *Ms.*, the first mass-market feminist magazine, which took up every feminist issue from abortion rights, sexuality, economic justice, marriage, the family, and feminist culture. The word "Ms.," an appellation that signified neither married nor unmarried status, became part of the national lexicon. She lobbied state legislators for the Equal Rights Amendment, and in 1977, she served as a commissioner to the National Committee of the Observance of International Women's Year. Her publications include *Outrageous Acts and Everyday Rebellions* (1983), a collection of essays and articles; *Marilyn* with George Barris (1986), a biography of Marilyn Monroe; the semi-autobiographical *Revolution from Within: A Book of Self Esteem* (1992), *Moving Beyond Words* (1994) another volume of essays and one short story, and her soon-to-be published *Doing Sixty*.

Sources and Further Reading: Carolyn Heilbrun, *The Education of a Woman* (1995); Sondra Henry and Emily Taitz, *One Woman's Power* (1987).

Barbara Winslow
Brooklyn College, City University of New York

The Interest Group Universe

Looking at interest groups in the midwestern states in 1900, an observer would find broad similarities across the region, both in the domination of agriculture and railroad interests, and in the emergence of populist agrarian movements that challenged the power of the major economic organizations. Over the course of the twentieth century, politics throughout the Midwest became more pluralistic as the economic base of most states diversified, sometimes in unexpected ways. For example, years ago who would have suspected that major banking interests would find South Dakota an excellent place to conduct their national credit card business, and thus come to have a great interest in that state's politics? Or that railroads would decline dramatically in influence at both state and national levels?

Although the politics of organized interests has experienced many changes over the past century, most have fallen within two broad categories. First is the growing number and heterogeneity of interests that are represented in all state capitals; this means that a few key groups are unlikely to dominate the policy-making process the way they might have a century ago. Second, in general, organized interests from the region have lost influence at the national level; trade unions, agricultural groups, and railroads, for example, have all declined in relative importance over the last fifty years, while financial institutions, the communications industry, and high-technology firms—best represented on the coasts—have grown increasingly important, especially over the past twenty years.

There are many reasons why interest group influence in Midwest states changed over time. In the early 1960s, for example, the 125-seat Kansas House of Representatives consisted of one representative from each of the state's 105 counties, with the remaining twenty legislators being apportioned on a population basis. In the wake of the mid-1960s' "one person, one vote" Supreme Court rulings, Kansas's legislative districts shifted dramatically toward urban and suburban areas in the wake of a court-mandated redistricting. Although agricultural interests were already beginning to decline, the redistricting revolution accelerated their loss of power, especially in Kansas, but generally across the Midwest. Moreover, the public sectors in most states began to grow substantially in the 1960s. Interests came to depend more on governmental programs, and these programs spawned both more and larger interest groups. For example, the growth of federal highway programs meant that states would spend increasing amounts on road construction and maintenance. Increased economic diversity and growing urbanization have also worked to reduce the impact of agricultural interests.

Throughout the Midwest, the number and variety of organized interests increased markedly between 1975 and 1990 and continues to increase. And nowhere were these changes more profound than in the industrial states of Michigan, Ohio, and Illinois. In 1975, these states reported a total of 473 groups registered with their legislatures; a mere fifteen years later that number stood at 3,011, an overall increase of more than sixfold. Michigan alone went from 145 to 1,160 groups, for an eightfold increase, magnified somewhat due to a change in registration requirements. The state could scarcely be dominated by the auto industry and its unions; too many other interests had entered the fray, from environmentalists to tobacco firms to pro-life groups.

An increase in the number of organized interests has brought a commensurate increase in the number of lobbyists. This is not a one-to-one relationship, but the linkage is clear. Of particular note is the growing importance of contract lobbyists, those who are hired to work for many clients, in the statehouses throughout the region; lobbying has become more expensive and more professionalized as the stakes have grown higher. Gambling interests, telecommunications firms, tobacco companies, among others, have invested increasing attention and money in affecting state policies throughout the Midwest. Top lobbyists can earn well into six figures in most states, and many former legislators discover that working as a lobbyist offers them considerably more compensation and much better hours. Combined with term-limit laws adopted in Michigan, Missouri, Nebraska, Ohio, and South Dakota, the growing professionalism of the lobbying corps means that organized interests may often bring greater expertise to the policy-making process than do either legislators or executives. Overall, a visit to Springfield, Illinois, or Jefferson City, Missouri, or any other capital city would demonstrate that the context of lobbying has changed from the wide-open days of booze and occasional bribes in the midcentury to more professional lobbyists who represent their interests to more professional legislators.

Although groups and lobbyists in midwestern state capitols have often borrowed techniques from their Washington, D.C., counterparts, organized interests in the region have been leaders in successfully exploiting grassroots tactics. Indeed, lobbyists in Des Moines or Indianapolis or Madison typically rely on constituents to make the appeals that will resonate with particular legislators. And many, if not most, groups can mount effective grassroots efforts, given the limited travel required to bring either a large contingent or a few key leaders to the state capital.

Although the Michigan experience reflects an extreme instance of interest group proliferation, similar trends have emerged in all midwestern states (and in the nation as a whole). The proliferation of groups meant that state policies and politics became much more contested, and traditional groups lost some of their clout. For much of the region, the foremost state loser has been the agriculture sector, both because of more competing interests and because the most important farm policy decisions have migrated to the federal government. As opposed to education, where states continue to dominate policy making, farm issues came to be resolved in complex deals within the agricultural policy community, which included all commodity groups, general farm organizations, and many environmental and consumer organizations. In this mix, the particular policy preferences of midwestern farm interests, although they continued to be heard, were only a part of a much larger collection of groups.

Within the region, studies in Hrebenar and Thomas (1993) report that the most effective organized interests in contemporary politics include teachers' organizations, banking groups, broad labor associations (such as the AFL-CIO), and state chambers of commerce; in a majority of midwestern states, these interests were all ranked among the "most effective" groups. In contrast, general farm organizations, while significant, received the "most effective" label in only three states. But farm organizations have generally retained some real clout, in contrast to the railroads, which often dominated state politics early in the twentieth century. In no midwestern state is a railroad interest seen as a major player, and in only two are they regarded as even secondary actors.

Although group power continues to have an economic basis, the strongest organizations are those who enjoy well-developed support across the state. Teachers' unions, banks, and labor all rely on extensive local contacts, widely distributed. Indeed, the education and banking interests comprise the core of most small cities within a state; it's no wonder that legislators regard them as powerful actors in a region that continues to have a strong rural makeup (and mythology), even as it becomes more urbanized. The clout wielded by small-town teachers and the bankers may offset the declining power of the agriculture groups, and as a result rural interests remain better represented throughout the Midwest than mere population figures might suggest.

Beyond the particular patterns of influence that have evolved, group politics within the region is distinct from the politics of other parts of the United States. For example, in the South and West, organized interests play important, even dominant, roles in shaping the nature of state politics. In the East, where political parties are stronger, groups are less significant independent forces. The Midwest, according to the most detailed regional study of organized interests by Hrebenar and Thomas, provides a context in which groups tend to play complementary roles to the parties and other major elements of state politics. In some states, such as Michigan, relatively strong parties continue to shape state politics, whereas in others, especially in the upper Midwest, the moralistic climate of politics may limit the power of organized interests. Nebraska, with its nonpartisan unicameral legislature, represents an exception, in that groups do not have to vie with the contending parties in their bid to frame issues that face the state.

All in all, the activities of organized interests in the Midwest state capitols have come to resemble the mix of message politics, electoral support, well-prepared information, and social lobbying that characterizes group behavior in Washington, D.C. There may not be the twenty thousand lobbyists or the fifteen thousand groups that populate the nation's capital, but the continuing presence of a professional interest group community means that most interests are capably represented most of the time.

If organized interests in the midwestern states have grown more professional and more broadly representational of all interests within the states, this same set of patterns, writ large in Washington, D.C., may work to reduce the region's influence. The most important secular trend is the declining influence of agricultural interests, especially broadly representative organizations like the American Farm Bureau Federation. On the surface, agricultural interests appear relatively strong, as the federal government continues to provide substantial payments to farmers large and small. But the dominance of the venerable cotton–corn alliance between the South and Midwest, once a hallmark of congressional decision making, has long since fragmented into dozens of smaller crop-based groups. Even more important has been the entry of major environmental—and more recently, animal rights—groups into the lobbying mix. The agricultural policy community in Washington, even more so than in the states, has become home to a diverse set of interests that are rarely on the same policy page.

In addition, core midwestern industrial interests, such as the automobile and steel industries, have lost much of their Washington clout, given their reduced role in the American economy. Likewise, labor unions, although they have stemmed their membership losses of the 1960–1990 period, enjoyed considerably less influence by the 1990s than they had held thirty years earlier. With sharp declines in the membership of many industrial unions, the Midwest was especially hard hit by the labor movement's lessened ability to affect policy. Moreover, interest groups from other regions—with either fast-growing populations (South, Southwest) or strong economic growth (West, parts of the East)—have become more powerful than interests centered in the Midwest. In particular, the information industry (broadly defined) and the financial services industry have become increasingly important in shaping the national policy agenda.

In many ways, the midwestern states typify the nationwide growth of advocacy groups that represent more and different organized interests in state capitals. Although some groups, like the state teachers' organizations, are consistently strong, single interests can rarely dominate state politics in various midwestern states, as agriculture or milling or the auto industry or the railroads once could. Within the region, interest group populations have grown in size and sophistication, with substantial numbers of contract-lobbying firms to represent any interest that can pay for their services. At the same time, the array of social service agencies and programs has led to the organization of more interests to represent social workers, children, and the disabled. Still, economic interests remain better and more completely represented in the statehouses, in part because national corporations have begun to participate actively in the states, especially on issues such as gambling, insurance, and telecommunications.

In sum, Midwest states have grown increasingly pluralistic with the growth of interest groups. Rarely can a single organized interest, whether membership group, trade association, or corporation, dominate whole segments of state politics. Moreover, both government and its agencies (including universities) have begun to represent interests, such as the mentally ill or migrant workers, who have traditionally gone unrepresented. At the same time, in looking to Washington, D.C., the region's organized interests have almost certainly lost some of their clout over the past century as railroads, agriculture, and industrial unions have declined in their ability to influence national policy decisions.

Sources and Further Reading: Farrell Dobbs, *Teamster Politics* (1975); Virginia Gray and David Lowery, *The Population Ecology of Interest Representation* (1996); Harold D. Guither, *The Food Lobbyists* (1980); Ronald J. Hrebenar and Clive S. Thomas, eds., *Interest Group Politics in the Midwestern States* (1993); Burdett Loomis, *Time, Politics and Policies* (1994); Robert Morlan and Larry Remele, *Political Prairie Fire* (1985); Anthony Nownes, *Pressure and Power* (2001); Alan Rosenthal, *The Third House: Lobbyists and Lobbying in the States*, 2nd ed. (2001); Laura Woliver, *From Outrage to Action* (1993); L. Harmon Ziegler, "Interest Groups in the States," in Virginia Gray, Herbert Jacob, and Kenneth Vines, eds., *Interest Group Politics in the American States*, 4th ed. (1993).

Burdett Loomis
University of Kansas

Isolationism and Globalism

Over the past several decades, political analysts have disagreed over the effect of regional variation on popular attitudes toward isolationism and globalism in American foreign policy. Some have argued that residents of coastal regions of the country are more likely to favor global involvement, since they are more likely to have contact with individuals from other nations, while residents of the interior states are more likely to favor isolationism, since they are less likely to have many international contacts. Others contend that isolationist or globalist attitudes are not solely, or even importantly, a function of regional ties; instead, such attitudes are a function of party affiliation, personal ideology, and the nature of the issue, among other factors.

Within this context we will here examine whether those living in the Midwest possess particular foreign policy attitudes, the extent to which they tend to be isolationist or globalist, and the extent to which the distribution of these sentiments and preferences has changed during the twentieth century

It is important to note at the outset that Midwest states share common social, economic, and political histories. All of these states were formed during the 1800s, with Ohio on the eastern edge of the region the oldest state, joining the Union in 1803, Iowa in the heart of the region a somewhat younger state, joining in 1846, and North Dakota and South Dakota on the western edge the youngest states, joining in 1889. The states were carved out of the Northwest Territory and the Louisiana Purchase, some in turn having been carved out of others. For instance, before Wisconsin achieved statehood, it was part of the Indiana, Illinois, and Michigan territories. All of these states, too, share an agrarian, frontier, and homesteading tradition. Importantly, the traditions in these states contrasted with those in the Northeast and the South at the time of their founding—and those differences continue to this day. Seemingly, then, the Midwest region with its distinct historical traditions and political and economic cultures would also exhibit distinct views on foreign policy issues as compared with other regions of the country.

Historically, the simplistic explanation has been that the Midwest is considered the traditional home of isolationism because of its geographical separateness from the outside world. This characterization has been especially used to describe midwestern attitudes during the first half of the twentieth century. Both the direct evidence from congressional voting on foreign policy issues and the indirect evidence of public sentiment gleaned from presidential voting patterns over the first six decades of the twentieth century provide some support for the concept of Midwest isolationism. In addition, several prominent national political leaders from the Midwest promoted isolationist views on key foreign policy issues. Despite this evidence, important qualifications operate against any easy conclusion regarding midwestern isolation in the first half of the twentieth century.

In their examination of voting in the House of Representatives from the early 1930s to the late 1950s, two prominent analysts, Smuckler and Rieselbach, found some limited evidence for isolationism in the region. More importantly, however, they found that the extent of isolationist voting during these periods was as much a function of the Representative's party (Republicans were more isolationist than Democrats), the type of the district (rural districts and districts with low ethnic composition were usually more isolationist than urban districts and districts with Irish or German ethnic composition), and the type of issue (foreign aid may elicit more isolationist sentiment than foreign trade) as it was a function of the region itself. Indeed, isolationism existed across several areas of the country and was not solely defined by a single region, such as the Midwest. In addition, the degree of isolationist voting changed over time and actually diminished by the middle of the century, indicating again the limited effect of the region itself as the source of an individual's worldviews.

Analysis of voting in presidential elections during the first half of the twentieth century tells much the same story. Midwesterners usually supported the more isolationist, usually Republican, candidates for president, but they also deviated from this pattern and significantly abandoned it at various times. With the exception of the elections of Woodrow Wilson in 1912 and Franklin Delano Roosevelt in 1932, most Midwest voters gave their electoral support to the Republican presidential candidate, at least up to the 1960 election. These Republican candidates were generally more isolationist in foreign policy outlook than were their Democratic rivals. That is, Republican Presidents Warren Harding, a native of Ohio, and Calvin Coolidge advocated a "return to normalcy"—isolationism—in foreign policy after Wilson's internationalism, and Iowan Herbert Hoover governed at a time when isolationist political and economic measures were enacted into law. Yet, other Republican presidents, Ohioan William McKinley and Theodore Roosevelt, set in motion American globalism and imperialism at the turn of the twentieth century. Later, of course, Dwight D. Eisenhower, who grew up in Kansas, firmly entrenched a globalist cold war posture on American foreign policy, but he still captured virtually all of the Midwest (and other regions) in the 1952 and 1956 elections. In short, Midwest voters did not necessarily choose or reject a candidate simply because he advocated an isolationist or globalist stance in foreign policy.

In other leadership domains, several prominent Midwest politicians led the charge for isolationist foreign policy actions from 1900 to 1950, lending further credence to this regional portrayal. After World War I, for instance, Senator Gerald Nye of North Dakota held a series of hearings seeking to illustrate that bankers and munitions makers were responsible for American involvement in World War I, thus propelling the adoption of the neutrality acts during the 1930s. After World War II, Senator Robert Taft, a Republican from Ohio, was skeptical of the Truman Doctrine and its implications for the American economy. Similarly, another senator from Ohio, John Bricker, introduced legislation to curb international commitments via treaty or executive agreement that would curtail any domestic rights and that would allow more global impact on domestic affairs.

In contrast, other prominent Midwest politicians endorsed globalism. Secretary of Commerce (and earlier Vice President) Henry A. Wallace, a native of Iowa, was a staunch advocate of America's global involvement after World War II, including continuing cooperative relations with the Soviet Union. Vice President and later President Harry S Truman, a native of Missouri, initiated the containment policy, a sweeping globalism in concept and execution. Most importantly, perhaps, Senator Arthur Vandenberg, Republican of Michigan and chairman of the Senate Foreign Relations Committee, changed his views from being a staunch advocate of isolationism to a symbol of bipartisan internationalism by endorsing the key elements of Truman's foreign policy. On balance, then, Midwest political leaders came to represent an admixture of those espousing isolationism and globalism.

As the demographic composition of the Midwest began to change and the region became more urban and less rural by the middle of the twentieth century, and as the country as a whole became more involved globally, Midwest politicians and Midwest voters followed suit. The composition of U.S. House and Senate membership from the Midwest moved in the direction of the Democratic Party, especially in the 1970s, 1980s, and early 1990s, and with it, generally more support for globalist policy. Indeed, the leading foreign policy committees of the House and the Senate, the House Foreign Affairs (now, International Relations) Committee, and the Senate Foreign Relations Committee, were dominated by members from the East and the Midwest. These members largely endorsed the activist, globalist policy of succeeding Re-

publican and Democratic presidents. Only in recent Congresses have we begun to witness sharper divisions among these committees. Still, the policy divisions rarely reflect a sharp split along a globalist–isolationist dimension; instead, they involve shades of selective internationalism on the part of most members.

For congressional voting over the last half century, regional divisions have not proved to be an important explanation. Instead, party division and ideological beliefs seemed to be more powerful predictors of congressional voting on foreign policy than home region. Whether examining specific foreign policy issues, such as the approval of the Panama Canal Treaties or the disapproval of the nuclear freeze resolutions, or assessing all foreign policy votes over the past fifty years, the effects of party affiliation, personal ideology, and presidential leadership were usually the critical factors in accounting for congressional decisions.

Over the past three decades, the Chicago Council on Foreign Relations has conducted surveys on foreign policy attitudes among the public and found that roughly two-thirds of Americans endorse an active part for the United States in world affairs. In a detailed analysis of these quadrennial surveys, Eugene R. Wittkopf demonstrated that up to three quarters of the American public expressed support for varying degrees of globalism—what he labels the internationalists, hardliners, and accommodationists—and slightly less than one-quarter were labeled isolationists. Significantly, the Midwest as a region tended to correlate with the three globalist categories, and no region correlated with the isolationist one. Importantly, personal ideology was the best predictor of foreign policy beliefs across the country.

Midwest politicians of virtually every political persuasion also supported American globalism over the past several decades. Internationalists ranged from such key figures as Hubert Humphrey, longtime senator, vice president, and Democratic presidential candidate from Minnesota, and George McGovern, a senator from South Dakota and Democratic presidential candidate in 1972 on the left, to Everett McKinley Dirksen, a senator from Illinois and longtime minority leader in the Senate, and Richard Lugar, a senator from Indiana and former chair of the Senate Foreign Relations Committee on the right. To be sure, these political leaders differed on the nature of American internationalism, but none embraced isolationism. In this sense, they are largely in line with the globalist attitudes of the public within the region.

Are these attitudes likely to change as we move into the twenty-first century? The short answer is no, since globalist attitudes are so firmly entrenched and the region is increasingly involved with the rest of the world through the forces of trade and technology. Still, the Midwest is one region that could be increasingly buffeted by the positive and negative effects of globalization—the political, economic, and social forces that are driving peoples together without regard to boundaries. The Midwest may become fragmented across the array of security, economic, and environmental issues that continue to dominate America's foreign policy agenda.

Sources and Further Reading: Robert H. Ferrell, *American Diplomacy: A History* (1959); Ralph B. Levering, *The Public and American Foreign Policy, 1918–1978* (1978); James M. McCormick, "Congressional Voting on the Nuclear Freeze Resolutions," *American Politics Quarterly* 13 (Jan. 1985); James M. McCormick, "Decision Making in the Foreign Affairs and Foreign Relations Committees," in Randall B. Ripley and James M. Lindsay, eds., *Congress Resurgent: Foreign and Defense Policy on Capitol Hill* (1993); James M. McCormick and Eugene R. Wittkopf, "At the Water's Edge: The Effects of Party, Ideology, and Issues on Congressional Foreign Policy Voting, 1947–1988," *American Politics Quarterly* 20 (Jan. 1992); James M. McCormick and Eugene R. Wittkopf, "Bipartisanship, Partisanship, and Ideology in Congressional-Executive Foreign Policy Relations, 1947–1988," *The Journal of Politics* 52 (Nov. 1990); Norman J. Ornstein, Thomas E. Mann, and Michael J. Malbin with Amy Schenkenberg, *Vital Statistics on Congress 1995–1996* (1996); John E. Rielly, ed., *American Public Opinion and U.S. Foreign Policy 1999* (1999); Leroy N. Rieselbach, *The Roots of Isolationism* (1966); Ralph H. Smuckler, "The Region of Isolationism," *The American Political Science Review* 47 (June 1953); Peter Trubowitz, *Defining the National Interest* (1998); Eugene R. Wittkopf, *Faces of Internationalism: Public Opinion and American Foreign Policy* (1990).

James M. McCormick
Iowa State University

The Evolution of the Political Party System

Each midwestern state has its own peculiar blend of history, economy, and demographic composition, which has resulted in two dominant political subcultures. Ohio, Indiana, Illinois, and Missouri have been characterized by Daniel Elazar in *American Federalism: A View from the States* (1984) as having an individualist political subculture that emphasizes government's role in promoting individual economic interests, while the moralist culture of the upper Great Lakes and Plains states stresses the government's role as a positive force in advancing the public interest. Although none of the states are pure examples of these subcultures, the predominant political cultures interacting with the states' economic and social conditions, national forces, and public opinion have caused the national political alignment to extend itself in different ways among the states. As the Midwest enters the twenty-first century, these differences have created patterns of Republican–Democratic electoral competition that in some states is quite evenly balanced, while in others one of the two major parties is favored. None of the region's states, however, can be considered a one-party state.

Reflecting the national reach of the Democratic and Whig Parties, the midwestern states that had entered the Union by the 1850s had active interparty competition from the 1830s through the early 1850s. However, in the midst of the controversy over slavery immediately prior to the Civil War, the Whig Party collapsed as a political force in the Midwest and was replaced first by the Free Soil Party and then by the Republicans.

A claimed birthplace of the Republican Party, Fond du Lac County, Wisconsin. Library of Congress, Prints and Photographs Division, Historic American Buildings Survey, HABS, WIS, 20-RIPO, 1-1.

Competitive party politics has not been a consistent feature of the Midwest. It was the birthplace of the Republican Party in 1854. Ripon, Wisconsin, and Jackson, Michigan, both claim to be the locale of the party's founding amid the antislavery forces' dissatisfaction with the Kansas-Nebraska Act. The GOP was the dominant party in the region from the Civil War until the Great Depression of the 1930s. The Republican electoral hegemony was reflected in gubernatorial elections. For example, from the Civil War until 1932, no Democrat was elected governor of Iowa; Illinois and Michigan had but two Democratic governors; and Wisconsin only three. Similarly, from statehood (1889) to 1932, South Dakota elected no Democratic governors and North Dakota but one. Eight of the eleven Republican presidents elected between 1860 and 1928 were from the Midwest region, including five from Ohio.

Even after the 1930s New Deal Democratic electoral realignment that made the Democrats the national majority party, it was the Midwest that provided a base, albeit a much weakened one, for the GOP's survival during the party's bleak Depression and World War II–era performance. Two-party competitive politics first developed in the region during the post–World War II era in the more urban and industrial states of Illinois, Michigan, and Ohio, where organized labor, concentrations of ethnic minority groups, and big-city party organizations provided the Democrats with a growing base of support to compete with Republican majorities in rural areas, small and medium-sized cities, and suburbs. Competitive two-party politics moved more slowly into the less urbanized areas of the upper Midwest and Plains. It is noteworthy that the bulk of postwar Republican congressional leaders emerged from the Midwest, among them House GOP leaders Charles Halleck from Indiana, Gerald Ford from Michigan, and Robert Michel and Dennis Hastert from Illinois; and Senate leaders Robert A. Taft of Ohio, Kenneth Wherry of Nebraska, Everett Dirksen of Illinois, and Robert Dole of Kansas.

A unique aspect in the party system's evolution was the presence of the twentieth century's only third parties that were sufficiently successful to win governorships, control both legislative chambers, and elect U.S. senators and representatives. Minnesota's Farmer-Labor Party and Wisconsin's Progressives in the 1930s effectively displaced the Democrats as one of the two major parties in state politics and constituted the principal opposition to the Republicans. However, neither of these third parties survived beyond the mid-1940s. Each succumbed to the influence of national electoral forces that overwhelmed these states' political cultures, which had been hospitable to third-party politics. After sustaining losses, the Farmer-Labor

party in 1944 merged into the Democratic Party to form the Minnesota Democratic-Farmer-Labor Party; and the Wisconsin Progressives, who also fared badly after 1936, were led back into the Republican Party in 1946 by Senator Robert M. La Follette, Jr., although many below the leadership level joined the Democratic ranks and helped create a competitive two-party environment. In both Minnesota and Wisconsin, the demise of homegrown third parties and their incorporation largely into the Democratic Party created a competitive two-party system similar to the national party alignment.

Another movement that contributed to the creation of competitive two-party politics was the Non-Partisan League (NPL), an organization of radical agrarian reform centered in North Dakota. It reached the zenith of its influence between 1916 and 1919 when its members controlled the state legislature and statewide offices. Although the NPL declined as a regional force after 1921, it continued to function in North Dakota as a disciplined faction within the dominant GOP until the 1950s. Liberal NPL activists then became restive operating within the Republican Party and joined with the Farmers' Union to merge the League with the Democratic Party, thereby creating a competitive two-party system in the state.

It should also be noted that, amid renewed national interest in third parties engendered by Ross Perot's Reform Party in the 1990s, only in Minnesota did the party win a statewide electoral victory when its nominee, Jesse Ventura, was elected governor in 1998. Ventura, however, abandoned the Reform Party in 2000 and had little success in creating a viable new third party. When Ventura chose not to seek reelection, his Independence Party was able to gain only 16 percent of the popular vote for governor in 2002.

The current competitiveness of the region's statewide elections is demonstrated by the fact that every state elected both Republican and Democratic governors between 1970 and 2002, and every state but Kansas elected U.S. senators from both parties during this time period. The relatively homogeneous socioeconomic character of a substantial number of congressional districts, along with the advantages of incumbency, has meant that most midwestern districts have not been competitive between the parties since the 1980s. However, the overall distribution of Republican versus Democratic seats reflects the existence of strong bases for support within each of the states for both parties and the overall competitiveness of the region. Thus, in 1991, the Democrats held 59 percent of the U.S. House seats to the Republicans' 41 percent, but in 2003, the proportions were reversed, with the Republicans controlling 61 percent and the Democrats 39 percent. These changes in the percentage of seats held by the two parties reflect the existence of a limited number of competitive swing districts, open seats created by incumbent retirements, redistricting, and episodic victories by candidates of the minority party in districts normally controlled by the majority party.

The two parties also compete for control of state legislative chambers, as demonstrated by the fact that Democrats controlled 68 percent of the twenty-two partisan chambers (Nebraska has a nonpartisan unicameral legislature) in 1991, but by 2003, the Republicans held 82 percent. The ability of candidates of either party to win federal and state offices reflects a nationwide trend away from party-centered politics toward a more candidate-centered electoral system.

The competitive nature of the region's politics should not obscure the fact that some of the states lean toward the Democrats and others toward the Republicans. According to the index of competitiveness reported by Jewell and Morehouse in *Political Parties and Elections in the American States* (2001), Missouri and Minnesota tilt strongly toward the Democrats, with Kansas, North Dakota, and South Dakota tending most heavily to the Republicans. The remainder fall in the two-party competitive category.

In terms of the political culture and party organizational ethos, there is substantial diversity particularly between the southern tier of states, which entered the Union early in the nineteenth century, and the states of the upper Midwest and Plains. In *Placing Parties in American Politics* (1986), David Mayhew describes Ohio, Indiana, Illinois, and Missouri as fostering traditional party structures that tend toward material rewards (such as patronage), hierarchy, and attempts to control party nominations. Since the 1960s, party organizations in these states have been weakened and their politics has become more issue oriented, but the style and type of party organization in this southern tier remains distinctly different from that of the other midwestern states.

States of the upper Midwest and Plains were heavily influenced by the Progressive Movement of the early twentieth century and its antiparty ethos. In this part of the region, the political culture has been described as moralist and issue-oriented. It was in Wisconsin, led by progressive governor Robert M. La Follette, Jr., that the nation's first party-weakening direct primary law was enacted in 1903. By contrast, to the south in Indiana, it was not until the 1960s that primaries became an accepted part of state politics. Party organizations in the Midwest's northern and western reaches tend to be nonhierarchical, devoid of significant patronage, and unable to control party nominations. These party organizations operate in a highly candidate-centered environment and tend to be

organizations in service to their candidates. This is also a part of the country with high voter turnout rates. Thus, Minnesota led the nation in 2000 with 68.8 percent of its voting age population going to the polls, and Iowa, Wisconsin, and North Dakota also had rates over 60 percent.

The features of the Midwest's party system that stand out most clearly are its competitive two-party character, the contrast between the southern and northern tiers of states in terms of political culture and party organizational structure, and the heritage of progressive and third-party movements that have shaped the politics in several of the states.

The competitiveness of the region makes it a critical battleground in the interparty struggle for control of Congress, the presidency, and the nation's governors. However, the Midwest has declined in its share of the nation's population relative to other regions, particularly the South and West. With its share of seats in the U.S. House of Representatives having fallen from 30 percent (134) in 1950 to 25 percent (109) after the 2000 census, and its total electoral votes down from 162 to 137 in 2004, the region has lost influence in Congress and presidential politics.

Sources and Further Reading: Daniel J. Elazar, *American Federalism: A View from the States,* 3rd ed. (1984); Leon D. Epstein, *Political Parties in the American Mold* (1986); John Fenton, *Midwest Politics* (1966); Virginia Gray, Russell L. Hanson, and Herbert Jacob, eds., *Politics in the American States,* 7th ed. (1999); Malcolm E. Jewell and Sarah M. Morehouse, *Political Parties and Elections in American States,* 4th ed. (2001); V. O. Key, Jr., *American State Politics* (1956); David R. Mayhew, *Placing Parties in American Politics* (1986); Maureen Moakley, ed., *Party Realignment and State Politics* (1992); Mildred A. Schwartz, *The Party Network* (1990).

John F. Bibby
University of Wisconsin–Milwaukee

John Bayard Anderson (b. 1922)

John Bayard Anderson was born in Rockford, Illinois, on February 15, 1922, to Albin and Mabel Anderson. Anderson's parents, first- and second-generation immigrants, raised Anderson to be a devout Christian. After serving in the Field Artillery during World War II, Anderson received law degrees from the University of Illinois in 1946 and Harvard University in 1949. Anderson served as an advisor on the staff of the U.S. High Commissioner for Germany from 1952 to 1955. He was elected State's Attorney of Winnebago County, Illinois, in 1956. In 1960, the moderate Republican was elected to the U.S. House of Representatives, where he served until 1981.

In 1980, Anderson launched a bid for the presidency. After he failed to get the Republican Party nomination, he ran unsuccessfully as an Independent. His progressive platform reflected his midwestern roots and the Christian ethics of his Rockford upbringing, promoting greater inclusion of the underrepresented. During his campaign, Anderson castigated both Democrats and Republicans for perpetuating the two-party system to the neglect of serious social problems, and he attempted to build a political base with a broad economic cross section.

Anderson continues to promote a vision of politics tied to the puritan religious values of his midwestern upbringing, advocating political meritocracy over the politics of influence. His influence on contemporary politics is evidenced by the Democratic and Republican Parties' increasing efforts to depict themselves as the more inclusive party, as well as by continuing efforts in some quarters to change campaign finance laws.

Sources and Further Reading: John Bayard Anderson, *The American Economy We Need* (1984); John Bayard Anderson, *Between Two Worlds: A Congressman's Choice* (1970); Seymour Martin Lipset, ed., *Party Coalitions in the 1980s* (1981).

Geoffrey Larson
University of Iowa

Raymond Charles Bliss (1907–1981)

Between 1931 and 1969, Akron, Ohio–native Ray Bliss was the quintessential Republican manager. The son of German immigrants, the short, stocky Bliss was a chain-smoking, popcorn-loving perfectionist. In 1959, three years after his mother's death, Bliss married his college sweetheart. They had no children; he had no hobbies.

Nominally an insurance executive, Bliss was actually a full-time political organizer. He was known as a "nuts-and-bolts" technician who valued victory over ideology. In 1931, he entered local politics, the protégé of Akron's Republican boss James Corey. From 1949 to 1965, Bliss ran the Ohio Republican Party. From 1965 to 1969, he commanded the national party, an organization that had become divided and demoralized by Barry Goldwater's disastrous 1964 presidential campaign. Bliss rebuilt the party through pragmatic, expert management. His reward was the election of President Richard Nixon, who promptly fired him.

National events more than regional factors shaped Bliss's career. As early as 1935, he explored political uses of opinion surveys. In 1937, the Akron mayoral

election was not merely a local contest; it tested the organizational power of the emerging Congress of Industrial Organizations against the money of anti-union big businesses. Republicans won, earning Bliss a national reputation. In 1950, he discovered television's potential as he traveled by train between Washington and Philadelphia, noticing many antennas along the way. He then talked with bartenders in Akron, learning that people crowded in bars to watch TV. In 1965, he gained national power precisely because his managerial approach transcended the regionalism of conservative Western insurgents and liberal Northeastern elites. After his tenure as chair of the Republican National Committee, he continued to be active in public affairs. He was a long-term member of the Board of Trustees of the University of Akron at the time of his death in 1981. The university established the Ray C. Bliss Institute of Applied Politics in 1986 to honor the political career of this 1935 alumnus.

Sources and Further Reading: David S. Broder, "Bliss Rides the Elephant," *The New York Times Magazine* (Mar. 21, 1965); John C. Green, ed., *Politics, Professionalism, and Power* (1994); William Hershey, "The Party's Not Over," *The Beacon Magazine* (June 7, 1981).

William Russell Coil
The Ohio State University–Columbus

Jesse Ventura (b. 1951)

Electing former professional wrestler Jesse Ventura their governor-in 1998 is a manifestation of the fact that Minnesotans are a people of two hearts. First is an egalitarian communitarianism, a mainstay of Minnesotan culture, appearing in their politics as a long history of progressive projects pursued to improve the common lot—schools, hospitals, colleges, libraries, and conservation have always been priorities. This has helped contribute to one of the highest rates of high school and college graduation, the second-longest life expectancy, and one of the best qualities of life in the nation. Minnesota's sense of fair play allowed Ventura to run an authentic campaign: As a candidate of a "major party" (because the Reform Party took at least 5 percent in the previous election), he was given $300 thousand of public money, and his opponents' spending was capped at approximately $2 million. Granted automatic entry to televised debates, he dominated with unrehearsed common sense, admitting when he did not know things. And the 16 percent of the electorate who voted for the first time were allowed by state law to register on Election Day.

But the other side of the Minnesota heart appears

Former Minnesota governor Jesse Ventura. Office of the Minnesota Secretary of State.

in *why* people voted for him: Minnesota has a long history of populism. These quiet people have an irascible streak, a penchant for experimentation with the political order. Historically suspicious of people who put on airs, Minnesotans saw in Ventura the common man running against two career politicians, and they took the chance to shake things up, once again. Jesse Ventura was born in Minneapolis on July 15, 1951, and served as governor of Minnesota from 1999 to 2003.

Sources and Further Reading: Webb Garrison, *A Treasury of Minnesota Tales* (1998); William E. Lass, *Minnesota: A History,* 2nd ed. (1998); Jacob Lentz, *Electing Jesse Ventura* (2002).

Jacob Lentz
Los Angeles, California

Henry Agard Wallace (1888–1965)

Born on a farm in Iowa, Henry A. Wallace was the scion of a prominent family. When his father, Henry C. Wallace, became secretary of agriculture in the Harding administration, Henry A. Wallace succeeded him as editor of *Wallaces' Farmer,* the family's influential farm journal. During the 1920s, he also founded the world's first hybrid seed company, Pioneer Hi-Bred, which over time helped produce vast increases in agricultural productivity around the world. Increasingly critical of Republican farm policies, Wallace split with the GOP in 1928, and in 1932, publicly supported the candidacy of Democrat Franklin D. Roosevelt. Wallace served as secretary of agriculture from 1933 to 1940, ushering in sweeping changes in federal farm policy.

In 1940, Roosevelt insisted on Wallace as his running mate, in part because of his midwestern roots and internationalist views. As vice president, Wallace championed the cause of democracy over fascism, and as chief of the Board of Economic Warfare, he was the first vice president to head an executive branch agency. In 1944, Wallace was replaced on the ticket by Missouri senator Harry S Truman, who was more acceptable to the party's urban bosses and southern conservatives.

Wallace served as secretary of commerce in the Truman administration until the president fired him over their foreign policy differences. In 1948, Wallace ran for president as the candidate of the left-wing Progressive Party to challenge Truman's cold war and civil rights policies. Wallace received only about 2 percent of the popular vote and no electoral votes. Thereafter, Wallace retired to his farm in Westchester County, New York, and resumed his highly successful experiments on corn, chickens, strawberries, and gladioli.

Sources and Further Reading: John Morton Blum, ed., *The Price of Vision* (1973); John C. Culver and John Hyde, *American Dreamer: The Life and Times of Henry A. Wallace* (2000); Henry A. Wallace, *New Frontiers* (1934).

John C. Hyde
Fund for Investigative Journalism,
Washington, D.C.

James Baird Weaver (1833–1912)

An energetic politician and powerful orator, James Baird Weaver was a leading agrarian reformer in the latter nineteenth century noted as an advocate of soft money and free silver, as well as regulation of monopolies and other concerns of farmers and laborers. Born June 12, 1833, in Ohio, Weaver moved to Iowa in 1842. He began practicing law in 1856. In 1861, he enlisted in the Union forces as a private, rose to colonel, and ultimately received the rank of brevetted brigadier general.

After the Civil War, Weaver sought office as a Republican. However, his views on prohibition and the economy coupled with party factionalism led to unexpected defeats. In 1877, Weaver joined the Greenback Party. With help from Democratic voters, he was elected to the U.S. House of Representatives in 1878. In 1880, he was the Greenback candidate for president. Campaigning on currency reform, temperance, and opening public land to settlement, Weaver received over three hundred thousand votes.

Weaver experienced further defeats when he ran again for Congress in 1882 and for governor of Iowa in 1883. In 1884, however, he was again elected to Congress with Democratic help, serving two terms before losing in 1888. He joined the Populist Party and became their presidential nominee in 1892. He received twenty-two electoral votes.

In 1896, Weaver promoted an alliance between Populists and Democrats to elect William Jennings Bryan president, one of Bryan's three unsuccessful bids for the presidency. During his last years, as Populism declined, Weaver worked with the Democratic Party while many friends and old foes publicly commended his political life.

Sources and Further Reading: Thomas Burnell Colbert, "Disgruntled 'Chronic Office Seeker' or Man of Political Integrity: James Baird Weaver and the Republican Party in Iowa, 1857–1877," *Annals of Iowa* 49 (1988); Thomas Burnell Colbert, "Political Fusion in Iowa: The Election of James Baird Weaver to Congress in 1878," *Arizona and the West* 20 (1978); Fred Emory Haynes, *James Baird Weaver* (1919).

Thomas Burnell Colbert
Marshalltown Community College, Iowa

The Political Cultures

The Midwest is the most American of America's regions, according to Frederick Jackson Turner, famous historian of the frontier. Turner's fellow midwesterners would certainly agree, and they would spin the characterization positively: To them, the heartland is home to all that is right with America and most of what is distinctive about it. After all, the economic might of the nation is centered in the region, which is not only the nation's breadbasket, but also America's foundry. The immense output of these vital goods and services is held to be the work of resourceful and industrious people whose aspirations are thoroughly middle class and family oriented. Religious, fraternal, and civic organizations abound, and patriotism runs

deep. Furthermore, the region's politics are reliably middle-of-the-road, generally avoiding the extremes of class war, although there have been lapses into progressivism and nativism.

To outsiders, these middling features of midwestern life seem bland, and the invocation of heartland imagery to describe them seems downright corny. Dyed-in-the-wool midwesterners feel slighted by such judgments, holding that centrism is a primary virtue, one that is essential for economic progress, social stability, and good government. In fact, a sizable number of midwesterners believe the rest of the country would benefit by embracing heartland values, and they frequently dispatch politicians to the nation's capital to conduct missionary work.

Differences among midwesterners run deeper than their stereotypical similarities, however, and the differences infuse the region's politics. The Midwest is where America comes together. It is the western province of the East, eastern territory of the West, and northern neighbor of the border South. Midwestern culture is correspondingly diverse. In some places, the local culture is heavily influenced by eastern ways; in others, the culture is more southern or western. To some extent, this is a border phenomenon reflecting proximity to other regions, but eastern, western, and southern streams of migration also flow to urban centers deep in the interior of the Midwest. Hence, cities like St. Louis, Chicago, and Detroit are true microcosms of American society.

Cultural differences arose because early migrants did not leave their heritage behind or set it aside when they arrived in the Midwest. To the contrary, most of them gravitated toward ethnic enclaves where familiar ways of life flourished in new surroundings. This included political customs from other places, with different cultural assumptions about the nature of government, its function in social and economic life, and the role of citizens in political decision making. As these customs brought from elsewhere took root in the heartland's rich soil, the principal varieties of the nation's political culture spread across the center of the country.

Daniel J. Elazar has identified three of the most important political subcultures in the United States, each of which has influenced Midwest politics. The moralistic political subculture is the domain of politics in the "public interest," variously defined. It is a communal affair, and citizens are encouraged to promote the general welfare by private means whenever possible, and through their support for government action if necessary. In this context, political leadership is considered a form of public service, and elected officeholders are expected to place the common good above party agendas or personal interests when they conflict.

So are public administrators, whose professional dedication, competence, and impartiality are dictated by civil service requirements meant to ensure "clean government."

Politics is conceived as a marketplace in the individualistic political subculture. Goods and services are dispensed by governments, which are controlled by political parties advancing the interests of their supporters, not some overarching public purpose. At the center of this process of partisan logrolling are people who make a career of politics and expect to profit from it in material ways, so long as they satisfy their constituents. In this environment, ordinary citizens' only responsibility is to reward their champions at the polls on Election Day. The urban political machine is the ultimate expression of this political subculture.

An organic community is central to the traditionalistic political subculture, but the preferred community is one where power is concentrated in the hands of the few rather than spread around to the hands of the many (as it is in moralistic subculture). In this idealized community, a ruling class exercises power by virtue of its social and economic standing. The object is to preserve the status quo against external threats or internal challenges. People in the lower ranks are expected to know their place, deferring to their betters and abstaining from voting and other forms of political action. The one-party states of the Old South typify this subculture.

Each of these three political subcultures was deposited at various times and locations by streams of migration originating outside the Midwest. The streams are charted in Figure 1, which shows how the Midwest has been shaped by successive waves of domestic migration. These cultural deposits are mapped in Figure 2, which displays the diversity of political subcultures across and within the states comprising the Midwest.

Figure 2 shows that some states have relatively homogeneous political subcultures, probably because of their location on the margins of a great westward movement of people. Minnesota has a purely moralistic political subculture, which is also the predominant orientation in the eastern Dakotas, Iowa, and Wisconsin. The individualistic political subculture prevails in Ohio, Indiana, and Illinois, where the diversity of eth-

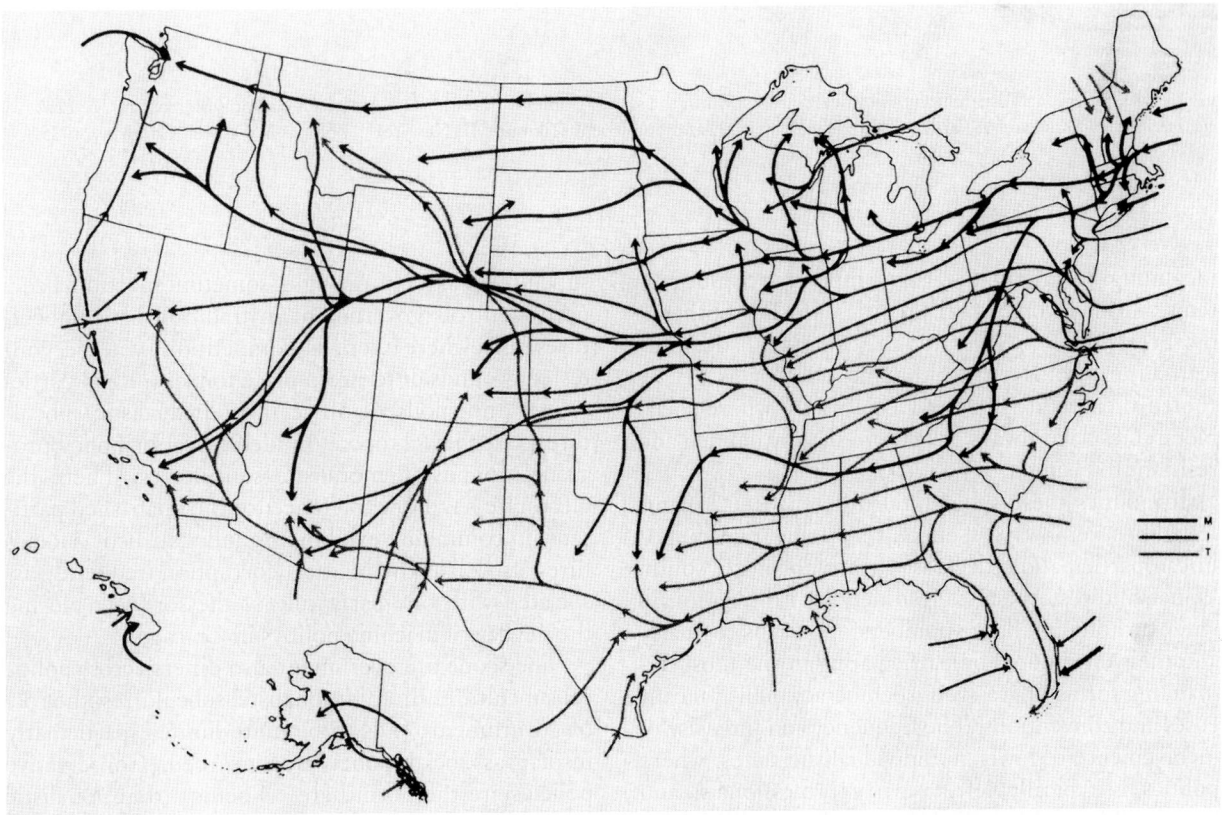

Figure 1. Generalized map of migration of cultural streams across the United States. Daniel J. Elazar, "The American Cultural Matrix," in *The Ecology of American Political Culture: Readings*, edited by Daniel J. Elazar and Joseph Zikmund II. New York: Thomas Y. Crowell Company, 1975.

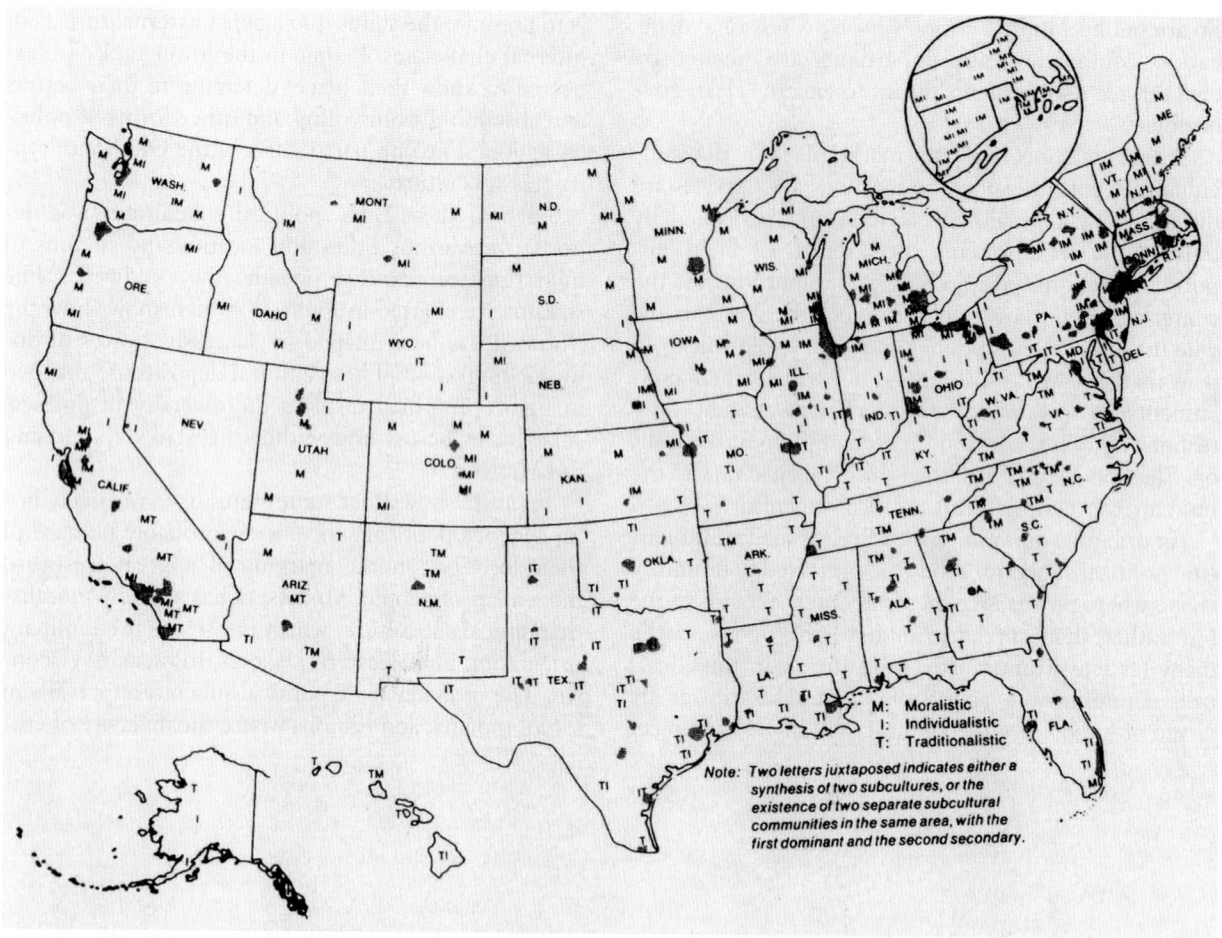

Figure 2. The regional distribution of political cultures within the states. Daniel J. Elazar, "The American Cultural Matrix," in *The Ecology of American Political Culture: Readings*, edited by Daniel J. Elazar and Joseph Zikmund II. New York: Thomas Y. Crowell Company, 1975.

nic immigrants mitigates against monolithic value systems and in favor of party politics. In the southernmost reaches of the Midwest, the traditionalistic political culture holds sway, although it is not as deeply rooted there as it is in the Deep South, where social hierarchies have always been more sharply defined and resistant to change.

In politics these subcultural differences are manifested in several ways. Generally speaking, rates of political participation decrease from north to south. Upper midwestern states routinely lead the nation in voter turnout, and large numbers of citizens regularly "do their civic duty" by participating in the most demanding forms of grassroots democracy, political caucuses and conventions. The frequency and intensity of involvement are lower in individualistic states, where politics is typically left to party professionals, and lower still in traditionalistic areas, where politics is an elite preserve.

The nature of political competition differs across

subcultures as well. A single, sometimes factionalized, party controls government in traditionalistic subcultures. Elsewhere there is competition, yet the contested grounds differ from place to place: Rival parties vie for the spoils of office in individualistic subcultures, but they compete on ideological or policy program grounds in moralistic subcultures. There the electorate has a low tolerance for the unabashed partisanship commonly exhibited in individualistic subcultures, as well as the political corruption frequently associated with one-party rule of the sort seen during the heyday of machine politics in Chicago.

The scope of government also differs across political subcultures. In traditionalistic subcultures, the role of government tends to be quite limited, particularly insofar as social policy is concerned. Conservative policies are the norm here, as befits a traditionalistic value system. The social responsibilities of government are much more broadly defined in moralistic subcultures, where "good government" is presumed to be active and progressive in orientation. Since this is part of the ethos of the moralistic subculture, it matters less which party is in control of policy-making institutions; in fact, Republicans from states with moralistic subcultures often seem more liberal than Democrats from states with individualistic subcultures. There the size and ideological direction of government goes back and forth as one party displaces the other and pursues policies favored by its constituents.

Finally, each political subculture has a unique style of governance. The style is quite personal in traditionalistic subcultures, and often exclusive and secretive. The style is openly brawling and combative in individualistic subcultures, where rural courthouse gangs and city bosses like Kansas City's Thomas Pendergast, Cincinnati's George Cox, and Chicago's Richard Daley, Sr., long tried to outmaneuver their rivals. The style is more formal and consensual in moralistic subcultures, but politicians with a cause also thrive in this political milieu of right and rectitude. Progressive governors like Wisconsin's "Fighting Bob" La Follette come to mind, as well as reform mayors like Hubert Humphrey of Minneapolis.

If political differences across states can be at least partially explained in cultural terms, so can political conflicts within diverse states. Some midwestern states have enclaves with customs different from those of the dominant political subculture. The industrial states of Ohio, Indiana, and Illinois are predominantly individualistic in political orientation, but each has areas colonized by the moralistic or traditionalistic political subcultures. Conversely, individualistic values are prominent in the industrial centers of lower Michigan, while the moralistic political subculture pervades the Upper Peninsula.

In states such as Illinois and Indiana, conflicts between urban and rural areas in the legislative arena and statewide elections draw energy from underlying cultural differences. This is particularly true in states with regionally dominant political parties. Rural Republican parties often oppose urban Democratic organizations in the Midwest, and when this line of cleavage has a cultural edge to it, the contests become quite rancorous. Chicago and Cairo are both in Illinois, but the political distance between them is measured in light-years!

Long-standing cultural conflicts in midwestern states may subside over time, however. Rural communities are shrinking because young people are moving to metropolitan areas in search of better economic opportunities. As rural populations decline, so does the political potency of these subcultural communities, especially now that state legislatures must be apportioned on the basis of "one person, one vote." There has been a corresponding growth in the population of urban centers. In Minnesota and Illinois, more than half the population now resides in a single metropolitan area; so do a third or more of the people in Michigan, Wisconsin, and Nebraska. The associated increase in political influence is likely to extend the cultural hegemony of these metropolitan areas.

Meanwhile, streams of migration continue to wash over the heartland, eroding cultural deposits from the past and leaving new ones in their place. The cities of the prairie are beginning to attract large numbers of Asian, Hispanic, and African immigrants, as well as native citizens from rural areas. As a result, new forms of conflict are beginning to surface in some urban areas. For the first time in many areas, white citizens of European ancestry are being challenged by immigrants from very different racial, social, religious, and political backgrounds. Not surprisingly, the reaction to new immigrants varies by political subculture.

Broadly speaking, the moralistic subculture works to assimilate new cultures into its broader public perspective; citizens are expected to set aside their differences in favor of the common good. Often this is constructive, but it can become oppressive when the common good proves elusive and blame is laid on newcomers seen as refusing to adapt or overly demanding. The individualistic subculture works to accommodate new cultures; differences are acknowledged and even celebrated, with the result that politics becomes an exercise in strategic coalition building. Groups without strategic importance are left out of this process. The traditionalistic subculture emphasizes conformity, reflecting its status quo orientation. Historically, challengers have been sanctioned or even suppressed, although the federal government has preempted the latter option.

Given these tendencies, we can expect different resolutions of the tensions arising from recent immigration, with the greatest potential for heightened conflict in moralistic and traditionalistic subcultures. Yet we should also note the operation of certain unifying forces. Increasingly, Americans of all sorts are being drawn into a common culture of consumer goods, entertainment options, and mass communications that saturate city and countryside alike. The distinctiveness of different ways of life is diminishing in the face of these homogenizing tendencies, and the corresponding differences between political subcultures are shrinking.

Tied as it is to economic integration and technological development, the progress of homogenization seems irreversible. On that basis, we might predict cultural convergence in the not-too-distant future if it were only a matter of peoples' values and behavior. But patterns of participation, the nature of political competition, and the scope and functions of government change very slowly. They also exert a reciprocal effect on what Alexis de Tocqueville called our "habits of the heart," so we should expect the Midwest's political subcultures to survive into the foreseeable future.

Sources and Further Reading: Daniel J. Elazar, *American Mosaic: the Impact of Space, Time and Culture on American Politics* (1994); Daniel J. Elazar, *Cities of the Prairie* (1970); Daniel J. Elazar et al., *Cities of the Prairie Revisited* (1986); Richard Ellis, *American Political Subcultures* (1993); Robert Erikson, Gerald C. Wright, and John McIver, *Statehouse Democracy* (1993); Joel Garreau, *The Nine Nations of North America* (1981); Neal Peirce, *The Great Plains States of America* (1973); Neal Peirce and John Keefe, *The Great Lakes States of America* (1980); Alexis de Tocqueville, *Democracy in America*, ed. J.P. Mayer, trans. George Lawrence (1969); Frederick Jackson Turner, *The Frontier in American History* (1920); Frederick Jackson Turner, *The Significance of Sections in American History* (1932).

Russell L. Hanson
Indiana University–Bloomington

Why Some Midwestern Governors Serve for So Long

Governors fulfill the same role in midwestern states that they do elsewhere: They are generally the state's leading political figure, they initiate new policies, they get blamed when things go poorly in their state, and they reap the benefits when things go well. After the President, a state's governor is typically the most recognized politician by citizens, and voters generally have more information, particularly policy information, about their governors than they do about any other statewide official. However, the careers of five Republican governors from the Midwest provide some interesting insights into executive office politics as well as the politics of the region. These five are: Bob Ray, Iowa's governor from 1969 to 1983; Terry Branstad, Iowa's governor from 1983 to 1999; Jim Thompson, Illinois's governor from 1977 to 1991; Tommy Thompson, Wisconsin's governor from 1987 to 2001; and John Engler, Michigan's governor from 1991 to 2003. Although differences among them surely exist, the lengthy careers of these governors point to some common lessons about politics in the Midwest.

Governor Ray, first elected in 1968, followed the widely popular governorship of liberal Democrat Harold Hughes. Given this, it may seem peculiar that the Republican Ray was able to win election and re-election by comfortably wide margins. What made Ray popular, however, was his moderate to liberal stands on many issues, which kept him in line with Iowa voters, as did his reputation for honesty and his ability to compromise with Democrats when they controlled the state legislature.

Political tides in Iowa shifted in 1978–1980 with the defeat of two liberal Democrats in the U.S. Senate by conservative Republicans and a GOP takeover of the state legislature. Furthermore, the two GOP senators had defeated moderate candidates connected to Governor Ray in their primaries. However, Ray's hold on the governorship remained firm. By this time, he had established a strong personal following while also maintaining his moderate policy stands.

Ray did not run for reelection in 1982 and was succeeded in office by his then lieutenant governor, Terry Branstad. Ray governed as a moderate, but Branstad was clearly a conservative. He narrowly won his first race, and most of his reelection margins were much narrower than Ray's. Branstad, however, continued to hold office because he moderated many of his policy views, and he focused his attention on farm policy and tax cuts. Like Ray, Branstad proved to be quite adept at dealing with a state legislature controlled by the Democratic Party until his last few years in office. Though never as moderate as Ray, Branstad was nevertheless seriously challenged from the right by U.S. Representative Fred Grandy in the GOP gubernatorial primary in 1994.

Jim Thompson became governor of Illinois in 1976 in the wake of conflict within the state's Democratic Party. Viewed as a moderate, Thompson gained prominence as a federal prosecutor pursuing political corruption cases in the Chicago area. As governor, Thompson often dealt with a state legislature controlled by the opposition party. His success in reaching compromises helped sustain his electoral support. Like Ray of Iowa, Thompson's name was occasionally mentioned as a potential candidate for president or vice president. However, again like Ray, his views and his record were generally considered to be too moderate for the national Republican Party. Indeed, he was endorsed by the AFL-CIO during his tight reelection run in 1986.

Tommy Thompson came to office in 1987 in Wisconsin with a bolder agenda of reform than Ray, Branstad, or Jim Thompson. He called for welfare reform and tax cuts during his first campaign, an agenda he continued to pursue during most of his fourteen years in office. However, like Branstad, Thompson proved to be much more adept at working with a Democratically-controlled state legislature than his conservative credentials and campaign rhetoric might have predicted. Thompson took moderate to liberal positions on abortion, the environment, and state spending for education and child-care programs. Thompson strongly supported school choice and voucher programs for education, and he became famous for his aggressive use of Wisconsin's line item veto provision to cut hundreds of spending and tax proposals.

John Engler came to office in 1991. He followed

Tommy Thompson's agenda of tax cuts, welfare reform, school choice, and increased spending for education. He avoided social issues like abortion, focusing instead on economic development. Although Democrats controlled the state legislature when he took office, Republicans soon won the majority. Thus, Engler had less pressure to compromise with leaders from the opposing party than did any of the other four governors discussed here. Engler took another page from Tommy Thompson's book by proposing a number of pro-environment programs, which helped him appear more moderate.

Though all five governors were Republicans, one should not conclude that all four of these states are consistently GOP havens. Wisconsin and Iowa tend, if anything, to be counter-cyclical compared to national partisan trends, and all four have elected Democrats and Republicans for statewide office in recent years. Each of these governors succeeded by being able to compromise with leaders from the opposing party and by cultivating an image as a moderate on some important issues. While each attracted some attention at the national level, certainly all but Branstad were viewed as too moderate to compete seriously for the GOP presidential nomination. Personally, each governor cultivated a reputation as honest and hardworking. Each avoided personal controversy and managed to navigate changing political waters by staying in touch with their citizens. They adapted to changing social, political, and economic trends, yet each took great care to attend to the issues that united their states—such as farm policy in Iowa, dairy farming in Wisconsin, and the auto industry in Michigan. The lessons learned from these five with respect to governing a midwestern state, then, seem centered on policy moderation and compromise, personal integrity, and an ability to adapt to changing circumstances while never straying too far away from dominant economic interests in the state.

Sources and Further Reading: William P. Brown and Kenneth VerBerg, *Michigan Politics and Government* (1995); Congressional Quarterly, Inc., *Congressional Quarterly's Politics in America* (1990–1998); Samuel K. Gove and James D. Nowlan, *Illinois Politics and Government* (1996); Lee A. Osbun and Steffen W. Schmidt, eds., *Issues in Iowa Politics* (1990); Neil Staebler, *Out of the Smoke-Filled Room* (1991).

Thomas M. Carsey
Florida State University

Harold Royce Gross (1899–1987) and the Curmudgeonly Side of Midwestern Politics

Harold Royce Gross represented Iowa's third district as a Republican member of Congress from 1949 to 1974. His Congressional career spanned five presidencies, but he never initiated any significant legislation, and despite his lengthy tenure, Gross never chaired a House committee. He served on the Post Office and Civil Service Committee, becoming the second-ranking Republican on the committee, and served on the Foreign Affairs Committee and the Manpower Utilization subcommittee. Devoted to the concept of limited government, Gross never pushed for pork barrel projects in his district. Yet his constituents kept returning H. R. Gross to Capitol Hill until he retired.

Born near Arispe, Iowa, on June 30, 1899, Gross left the family farm in 1916 to join the United States Army for the Mexican border campaign and served in France during World War I. Upon his return, he attended journalism school, then worked as a newspaper reporter and radio news commentator in Iowa between the wars. He wrote for the *Iowa Farmers Union* during the Great Depression, establishing a reputation as a populist advocate for farmers. In 1940, Gross resigned from his position as newscaster in Des Moines to enter the Republican gubernatorial primary against the incumbent George Wilson. He lost a hotly contested election, but carried a majority of Iowa's rural counties.

When Gross reentered Iowa politics in the 1948 campaign, he once again ran against an incumbent, John W. Gwynne, Iowa's longest-serving member of Congress. This time he won. In each election that followed, Gross piled up large majorities, consistently outpolling the rest of the Republican ticket. His only close election occurred in 1964, when he retained his seat by only 419 votes in the wake of Lyndon Johnson's landslide victory over Barry Goldwater. Gross was the only Iowa Republican returned to Congress that year. Until 1970, Gross never spent more than $1,500 on his campaigns. He won handily despite limited legislative accomplishments, less-than-imposing physical presence, and minimalist campaigns.

Throughout his congressional career, Gross was noted for his steadfast fiscal conservatism, conscientious study of issues, and near-perfect attendance. He was a staunch advocate of limited government and earned a reputation as a tight-fisted conservative. He fought against what he viewed as needless expansion of federal spending, especially when this spending was in the form of foreign aid, Great Society programs, or pay raises for federal employees. Gross reportedly read every line of every bill that came before the House, pointing out items that proved embarrassing to sponsors of the bill (and costly to the taxpayers). Gross's vigilance won him the nicknames Watchdog of the Treasury and Conscience of the House. But his abrasive style and sarcastic comments on legislation sought by his colleagues led many to regard Gross as a curmudgeon.

Gross's stubborn stands on the floor of the House rarely stopped legislation. He did little to endear himself to colleagues on either side of the aisle, voting against spending bills no matter which party proposed them. Each session, he proposed legislation (always numbered H.R. 144) that called for balancing the budget and the gradual reduction of the national debt. Each session this bill was referred to the Ways and Means Committee, never to be discussed on the floor of the House. Gross was a stickler for parliamentary procedure, calling for quorums and roll call votes in situations where other representatives preferred the quiet passage of legislation.

Gross reveled in his status as an irascible obstructionist. His reflexive opposition to discretionary spending, "fact-finding" junkets, and expansion of federal bureaucracy won him nationwide support among conservatives. Gross played up his role as a curmudgeon. He took pains to ensure that press coverage mentioned the framed quotation that sat on his desk: "Nothing is easier than the expenditure of public money. It does not appear to belong to anybody. The temptation is overwhelming to bestow it on somebody." He never voted for foreign aid, questioned the value of the Marshall Plan, and opposed United States military action in Korea and Vietnam. He voted against all Great Society measures, including Medicare, arguing that the federal government should not take on debt to pay for social welfare.

Gross's political career raised the obvious question: Why did his constituents continue to elect him? The benefits of an incumbent running in a rural Republican district cannot be dismissed, but Gross's appeal was substantive. His cantankerous approach appealed to his constituents, many of whom longed to give a thumb to the eye of the establishment. They saw Gross as representing their interests, standing up to the power elite of the East. This was evident by the popularity of Gross's opposition to raising Congressional salaries, which moved from $12,500 in 1950 to $42,500 by 1974. At each step, Gross worked to force Congressmen to make public their stands on raising their own pay. While he failed to stop these salary increases, Gross won enormous public support for his efforts. He was hailed as a principled loner.

In following this path as an independent Republican, Gross was well within an Iowan and midwestern tradition of cranky iconoclasm. In the 1920s, Smith Brookhart often broke ranks with Iowa's old guard Republicans, yet he continued to win elections. When Gross was identified by *Redbook* in 1952 as one of Our Worst Congressmen, many other midwesterners were also listed: Representative Clare Hoffman (Michigan), Senator William Jenner (Indiana), and Senator Joe McCarthy (Wisconsin.) Curmudgeons all, and each took perverse pride in this distinction.

After retiring from Congress in 1974, H. R. Gross lived with his wife in the Washington, D.C., area so that they could be close to their two sons. He died in September 1987 at the age of eighty-eight.

Sources and Further Reading: Robert E. Bauman, "H. R. Gross: The Taxpayers' Favorite Mr. No" *Human Events* 29 (Feb. 1969); *Biographical Directory of the United States Congress, 1774–1989,* s.v. "Harold Royce Gross, 1899–1987" (1989); James L. Butler, "A Study of H. R. Gross and How He Gets Elected to Congress," Ph.D. diss., State University of Iowa (1956); Jacques Leslie, "H. R. Gross: Conscience of the House," *Reader's Digest* (Aug. 1972); Vernon Louviere, "The House is Losing Its 'Conscience,'" *Nation's Business* 62 (June 1974); Bert Mills, "The Remarkable Mr. Gross of Iowa," *National Publishers* 41 (July 1961); Clark Mollenhoff, "H. R. Gross is Retiring: A Symbol of Incorruptible Integrity and Independence," *Des Moines Register* (Jan. 6, 1974); Howard Whitman, "Our Worst Congressmen," *Redbook* (Oct. 1952).

Matthew T. Schaefer
Herbert Hoover Presidential Library-Museum,
West Branch, Iowa

Immigrants and the Shaping of Midwestern Politics

Midwestern immigration started with the migration of settlers from New England and other nearby states, creating what Cayton and Onuf describe as "a patchwork quilt of transplanted communities," giving the region more of "an ethnic and cultural checkerboard than the proverbial melting pot." Early settlement created many isolated ethnic communities, producing a politics of self-interest and preservation.

Immigrants created a new life largely devoid of comfort or familiarity, but their ability to adapt and assimilate defined the region and beyond. Historian Frederick Jackson Turner believed the frontier played a crucial role in defining American democracy. It demanded hard work and self-sufficiency, encouraged cooperative efforts but respected diversity, and promoted egalitarian attitudes along with moral integrity. The settlement of the Midwest—fueled by immigrants—anchored Turner's influential theory.

Germans, Irish, and Scandinavians dominated the formative years of midwestern immigration. Germans provided the backbone for many of the region's family farms and rural communities, having perhaps their greatest influence in Wisconsin. German political development was the product of several factors. Internal turmoil at home sent a large wave of Germans to the region in 1848. These so-called Forty-Eighters became active in the antislavery movement, creating a wedge that would drive many from their Democratic roots into the newly emergent Republican Party by 1860. In that year, Germans played a key role in the nomination and election of Abraham Lincoln, including Carl Schurz, the most prominent German American politician at that time. Schurz would later serve in the U.S. Senate from Missouri and edit the *Saturday Evening Post*.

Germans were also mobilized by nativist politics, best represented by the Know-Nothing Party and the Temperance crusade. Many were not about to give up their love of beer and frivolity, nor cower from attacks on their ancestry. Prominent German brewers in Cincinnati, Milwaukee, and St. Louis financed many anti-Temperance efforts and encouraged German municipal candidacies. German numerical strength quickly translated into greater political power, but politics never became a consuming interest for most. Germans excelled at organizing, ranging from social clubs to labor unions—along with *turnvereine* societies for athletic activities—but did little political organizing for longer-term purposes. Size, dispersion, and variety complicated German political influence. There were sizable numbers of Germans in urban and rural areas, in both major political parties, and they held divergent ideological views. All of this meant any notion of a unified German vote diminished rather quickly.

The greatest concentration of Irish immigrants was in Illinois and Ohio. Low economic status generally limited their mobility westward from Chicago, one of many cities where the Irish were primarily engaged in low-wage occupations. Unable to afford land, the Irish clustered in larger cities, living in extended families held together by Catholicism and outside persecution. Urban concentration and ethnic solidarity, combined with social and economic needs, contributed to the rise of prominent Irish political machines in the region. Irish politicians—tough yet compassionate—were able to use bloc voting and quid pro quo politics to establish significant bases of urban power. Their entry into politics was also assisted by the fact that they did not need to learn English, a linguistic facility that proved central to their leading citizenship and voting rates among all immigrants. Although Irish machines had elements of corruption, they also engaged in reformist activity, mobilizing public opinion and voting, both internally and among other immigrants.

As Irish politicians gained control of many local governments in the Midwest, they were in a position to secure public sector jobs for Irish loyalists and to reward Irish tradesmen with lucrative city contracts. Enhanced job security and generous benefits through union contracts dramatically expanded the size of the Irish middle class and other immigrant groups, as well. Irish legislators from midwestern cities also gained power and seniority in their respective state governments.

In contrast to other groups, Scandinavians came from more than one country in Europe. Largely an upper Midwest population, their greatest concentration extended from northeastern Iowa and nearby Wisconsin, into Minnesota and eastern North Dakota. Scandinavian immigrants were literate, owned land, and possessed many advantageous skills, all making their assimilation much easier. By the early twentieth century, they were players in politics and government, but not always within the traditional two parties. A prominent Swede elected governor of Minnesota in the 1930s was the legendary Floyd B. Olson, who presided during the heyday of the Farmer-Labor Party and was, in the words of one critical observer, "the most successful case of a radical state-level third party that American politics has seen." Some of Olson's "radical" ideas enacted into law include a moratorium on mortgage foreclosures, a state income tax, and labor rights legislation. Even though many Scandinavian voters supported progressive ideas, in the nineteenth century, a majority in the region voted consistently Republican, drawn to the party by antislavery politics and an aversion to nativist elements in the Democratic Party.

Dutch settlement in the upper Midwest is also worth noting, as an immigrant population widely known for their strong work ethic and conservative politics. Western Michigan is both strongly Dutch and Republican, a pattern also found in Northwest Iowa.

Black migration from the rural South into many midwestern cities in the twentieth century had an impact on the increasingly competitive politics of the region. The growth of suburbs and white flight gradually transformed cities like Chicago, St. Louis, Cleveland, and Detroit into significant African American enclaves, providing a crucial component to Democratic strength across the region.

The political influence of immigrants, in the Midwest and elsewhere, cuts two ways. The impressive volume of immigration into the region made migration the key variable to settlement and population growth, guaranteeing through their votes and activities that these new Americans would be very important indeed. Diversity is an important element in the culture of accommodation that has made the Midwest distinctive, even though the region collectively is much less heterogeneous than other parts of the country. Despite their differences, settlers in the region were ambitious optimists who found much in common with each other, even as they maintained cultural differences and kept some distance between each other. Although conflicts did arise, the durable presence of religion in the lives of many offered inducements toward compromise and moderation. This social history is a central part of the political moderation that has always characterized the region.

Immigrants themselves have also been an occasional political issue in the region. The presence of newcomers and their "foreign ways" have aroused suspicion and periodic backlashes. This happened to many Germans in the region during both World Wars and can be seen today in the mixed reaction to the influx of many Hispanic workers in the region's meatpacking industry and agricultural labor force. Refugees from Indochina started making the Midwest their home in the mid-1970s, with sizable communities in Minnesota and other states in the region. A large Arab immigrant population is today an important dimension to the politics of metropolitan Detroit. These recent arrivals have not always faced a tolerant and welcoming reception, but in the main, have become part of the social and political fabric of the region much as their predecessors did.

Sources and Further Reading: Andrew R.L. Cayton and Peter S. Onuf, *The Midwest and the Nation: Rethinking the History of an American Region* (1990); Dennis Clark, "Irish-Americans," in John D. Buenker and Lorman A. Ratner, eds., *Multiculturalism in the United States* (1992); R. Douglas Hurt, "Midwestern Distinctiveness," in Andrew R.L. Cayton and Susan E. Gray, eds., *The American Midwest* (2001); Peter McClelland and Richard J. Zeckhauser, *Demographic Dimensions of the New Republic* (1982); Thomas Sowell, *Ethnic America: A History* (1981); Ronald Takaki, *A Different Mirror: A History of Multicultural America* (1993); Frederick Jackson Turner, *The Frontier in American History* (1920); Richard M. Valelly, *Radicalism in the States: The Farmer-Labor Party and the American Political Economy* (1989).

Jonathan P. Euchner
Missouri Western State College

The Missouri Plan, or the Merit System

The method of selecting judges known as the Missouri Plan, or the merit system, was an outgrowth of the Progressive movement. Initial efforts to democratize judicial selection by using partisan elections often gave party bosses control of the judiciary. Attempts to reduce the influence of political parties through nonpartisan judicial elections were largely unsuccessful, and reformers eventually developed a merit system for selecting judges. Although versions were in existence since the early 1900s, in 1940, Missouri was the first state to formally adopt a merit system. To date, approximately half of the states in the country have adopted variants of the merit system, including Indiana, Iowa, Kansas, Nebraska, and South Dakota in addition to Missouri.

In a merit system, the process of filling a judicial vacancy begins with a judicial nominating commission. Commission members examine the qualifications of those being considered and submit a list of three choices to the governor. The governor must then choose one of the three to fill the vacancy. Typically, one year after taking office, the new judge must face the voters in an election using what is known as a "retention ballot." On this ballot the voter is simply asked, for example, "Should Judge Smith be retained in office?" If a majority of the voters answer yes, the judge then serves a full term in office (usually between four and eight years). At the end of the full term, the judge must again face the voters using a retention ballot. If a judge is not retained, the process starts over with the judicial nominating commission.

The composition of the judicial nominating commission tends to follow a pattern: two to five members who are lawyers selected by the state bar association, an equal number of members appointed by the governor (who may be nonlawyers), and one member who is a senior judge (and a member of the state bar). States may have more than one commission, dividing the duties by court level or district. Iowa, for example, has one judicial nominating commission to fill vacancies to the appellate courts and separate commissions for each of the districts into which the trial courts are administratively divided.

One result of the merit system is that very few judges fail to be retained. Proponents of the system argue the high retention rate demonstrates the high quality of the judges selected. Skeptics argue the retention ballot makes defeat unlikely in that it is difficult to beat someone with no one. There is also debate over whether the plan removes politics from the process. Even to the extent that the role of party politics is reduced, a majority of commission members will be members of the state bar association, which often has a political agenda of its own. Thus, some argue, the merit plan merely substitutes one set of interests for another. Nevertheless, even if the advantages of the merit system are largely symbolic, the combination of expert examination, gubernatorial appointment, and voter retention seems to satisfy the public's desire for a highly qualified, independent judiciary.

Sources and Further Reading: Robert A. Carp and Ronald Stidham, *Judicial Process in America*, 4th ed. (1998); Walter F. Murphy, C. Herman Pritchett, and Lee Epstein, eds., *Courts, Judges, & Politics*, 5th ed. (2002); Harry P. Stumpf and John H. Culver, *The Politics of State Courts* (1992).

Timothy M. Hagle
University of Iowa

The Northwest Ordinance

In 1787, the Continental Congress defined the process by which three to five new states would be created in the region north and west of the Ohio River. Heavily contested during the American Revolution, this area had been formally gained from Great Britain only four years before in the Peace of Paris. Now Congress was making plans for what some described as an American empire in the new west. But remembering recent experiences of the American Revolution, the Congressmen also desired solutions that would avoid the colonial errors and abuses that they associated with royalist Britain. The result was a fundamental law at once imperial, revolutionary, and republican.

The Ordinance incorporated both a plan for self-government and a guarantee of citizens' rights. Permanent subordinate status for a colonial dependency was rejected. Instead, the new territories—which eventually became Ohio, Indiana, Illinois, Michigan, and Wisconsin—were to undergo a process that allowed each to enter the union on an equal footing with the original thirteen states. The process allowed much more public participation in its final stages than in its initial arrangements. At the start, a governor and three judges named by Congress would adopt the early laws of each territory. Only later would popularly elected assemblies begin to exercise checks and balances. When the population of each territory equaled that of an existing state, the voters could select a constitutional convention and apply for equal statehood. The first territory, Ohio, went through the entire process in only sixteen years.

The Ordinance guaranteed fundamental republican liberties and civic norms to all who settled in the new region. Assurances of religious toleration and habeas corpus, the elimination of primogeniture in land title, and the rights to secure an education and serve in a militia all made the Ordinance an early bill of rights. The rights enumerated were a mixture of the practical and the idealistic. Traders were thus guaranteed free use of the region's rivers at the same time that Indians were promised good faith in negotiations. Perhaps most revolutionary, Congress banned slavery everywhere in the territory.

This antislavery provision also reflected regional considerations in Congress. Northern land speculators and developers, such as the members of the Ohio Company of Massachusetts, had lobbied for the Ordinance in the hope it would encourage emigration from the New England and Middle Atlantic states. Modern interpreters are quick to remind us that existing residents of the Old Northwest often followed alternative lifestyles, whether in French-speaking towns such as Detroit and Vincennes, in Indian towns and villages, or in frontier hunting communities peopled by early southern migrants. In describing ideals and aspirations of the East and the North, the members of Congress were choosing among alternatives. They made such choices, moreover, at the exact time the Constitutional Convention was in session, seeking to balance northern and southern interests. In all these ways, the distinctive regional choices of the Northwest Ordinance produced enduring national consequences.

Sources and Further Reading: Andrew R. L. Cayton, *The Frontier Republic* (1986); Richard P. McCormick, "Ambiguous Authority: The Ordinances of the Confederation Congress, 1781–1789," *American Journal of Legal History* 41 (Oct. 1997); Peter Onuf, *Statehood and Union* (1987); Robert M. Taylor, Jr., ed., *The Northwest Ordinance, 1787* (1987).

George W. Geib
Butler University, Indiana

Civic Life and Political Participation

Political activity in the Midwest can be dramatic and vigorous. Major movements for social change have taken root there. Advocates of populism, prohibition, and progressivism rallied large numbers. Farm protesters earlier, civil rights protesters later, were much in the news. Extremism has come in waves, such as the power of the Ku Klux Klan in the 1920s and the John Birch Society in the 1960s. At times, the Midwest displays a politics of deep contradiction. The virulent anti-Communism born in the 1950s did not prevent the widespread anti–Vietnam War demonstrations of the 1970s. Senator Joseph McCarthy of Wisconsin stood for one faction of Midwest militants, while Senator Eugene McCarthy of Minnesota came to stand for another. Of course, not everyone was caught up in these political causes. Both McCarthys faded away rather quickly, and midwesterners returned to the politics of everyday life, with its routines, conventions, and demands. In what follows we describe the characteristic political participation of the common men and women of the Midwest. Do they vote? How often? How else do they engage in the political process? How are they different from other Americans? Finally, we consider the features of the midwestern political and social system that account for these differences.

Democracy means the people govern. But that does not mean that every citizen is involved in every public decision. Political participation is, of necessity, selective. Some individuals choose to vote, give money, campaign, contact government officials, write letters, organize, and even run for office. For these people, democratic politics consumes much time and energy. For others, politics is at the margin of their lives, and they may not even vote. Especially since the 1950s, political scientists have systematically investigated the type and extent of citizen participation in America. Through large scientific public opinion surveys, much has been discovered about political behavior. Important insights can be gleaned from such surveys, most especially the American National Election Study (NES) conducted from the University of Michigan and the General Social Survey (GSS) conducted from the University of Chicago.

To begin, it is helpful to think of conventional political participation as a continuum of activity, ranging from relatively easy, low-cost actions at one end (such as voting), to rather difficult, even costly actions at the other end (such as running for office). Actions in between include trying to influence the political opinions of others and giving money to candidates. What do midwesterners look like, as political participants? Let us take a recent (1998) NES survey, which polled a representative sample of Americans, and break out the midwesterners—those respondents in Illinois, Indiana, Iowa, Kansas, Michigan, Minnesota, Missouri, Nebraska, North Dakota, Ohio, South Dakota, and Wisconsin. When asked if they voted in the 1998 congressional race, 63 percent said yes. Asked if they tried to influence the politics of others, fully 22 percent said yes. About giving money to a candidate or party, 8 percent indicated they had. Only 5 percent said they actu-

ally went to a political meeting, and a mere one percent worked for a candidate. These numbers provide a typical contemporary profile of conventional political participation in the Midwest. There is a broad base of participation in politics at the lower levels, of voting and talking, but when it comes to the more demanding tasks of doing and paying, involvement narrows considerably.

Although one could always hope for more participation at all levels, this profile in itself is not cause for much comment. More than a few are engaged in most things, and part of democracy is deciding to participate—or not. What's interesting is comparing the Midwest with other regions. Relevant data for the last half of the twentieth century are presented in Figure 3. Take the voting question in the 1998 NES survey, for example. Only 50 percent of the non-midwesterners said yes, they had voted, which is 13 percentage points less than midwesterners. Across the entire post–World War II period, in fact, midwesterners consistently report that they are more likely to vote. Examining the twenty-one surveys the NES conducted in presidential and congressional elections, 1952–1998, midwesterners always report greater voting turnout than voters from other regions, with the exceptions of 1980 and 1982, when it was about even. On average for the forty-six-year period, the difference in favor of the Midwest is a substantial 7 percentage points.

Clearly, midwesterners are much more likely to

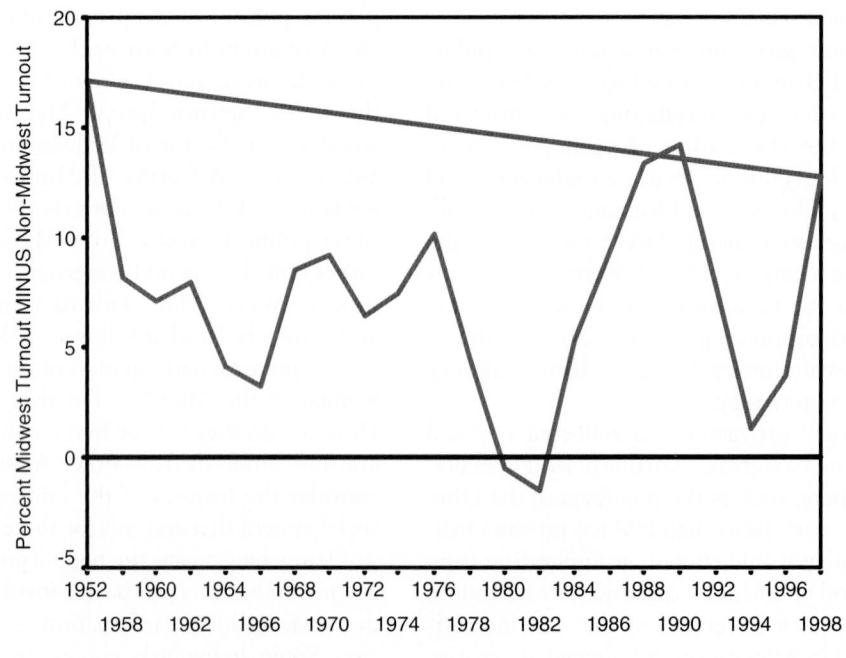

Figure 3. Difference in voting rates in the Midwest and non-Midwest regions, 1952–1998.

vote than their fellow Americans. They are also more participative in other ways. In fourteen of these twenty-one surveys, the evidence indicates that midwesterners more often donated money to campaigns than their fellow citizens in other regions. They were also more likely to display a political button or sticker (in fifteen of these twenty-one surveys). Further, they are more willing to contact public officials. In eight different national polls conducted by the NES from 1964 to 1990, respondents were asked if they had ever written a letter to a public official or contacted a member of Congress; midwestern "yes" responses exceeded nonmidwestern ones in all but one of the surveys.

Does this higher rate of participation extend to other dimensions? No. In the twenty-one surveys mentioned above, respondents were also asked about trying to influence the politics of others, going to political meetings, working for candidates, strongly identifying with political parties, and supporting third parties. For none of these characteristics did a consistent Midwest–non-Midwest difference emerge. Rather, for these important kinds of political participation, midwesterners look like everyone else. Take, for example, going to political meetings. About half of the time, the Midwest shows a slightly higher percentage, the other half of the time, a slightly lower percentage; the average percentage difference across the series is less than two-tenths of a point, showing the regions are effectively equal.

With respect to conventional forms of political participation, then, the Midwest distinguishes itself from the rest of the country by its greater reliance on the individual gesture—the vote, the donation, the button. But this does not exhaust its difference, as data on unconventional forms of participation make plain. Various national surveys have asked representative samples of American adults how they felt about protest meetings, civil disobedience, or demonstrations. For example, in 1970, in the midst of the Vietnam War, respondents were asked whether they approved of protest meetings. Among midwesterners, fully 56 percent disapproved, in contrast to 43 percent of the non-midwesterners. Overall, in twelve of the fifteen surveys (1968–1996) asking similar questions, midwesterners' disapproval exceeded that of other regions. It is evident that midwesterners are less tolerant of unconventional political action.

For the post–World War II period, the pattern of popular midwestern political participation is straightforward. Compared to people from other parts of the nation, midwesterners are more engaged in accepted individual political actions, such as voting; less engaged in controversial political actions, such as protesting; and neither more nor less engaged in group politics, such as going to meetings. It is not dif-

ficult to explain these features. Midwesterners are politically individualist because they believe those individual acts count for something. In seven NES surveys (1952–1980), midwesterners were always more likely to say their vote mattered. Indeed, on average, 92 percent said so. This sense of political efficacy comes from a larger sense of trust in government. Across America, confidence in public officials has been eroding, but it is still greater in the Midwest than elsewhere. Over the course of the NES surveys, 52 percent of the midwesterners, on average, agreed that public officials cared about what they thought. And the midwestern percentage exceeded the non-midwestern percentage in seventeen of the twenty-one surveys. The greater trust midwesterners give government may be seen as a part of a broader belief in the kindness of others. Most midwesterners think folks will give them a hand. For example, when a 1992 national survey asked whether people were generally helpful, 62 percent of those in the Midwest said yes. In the six such surveys from 1966 to 1992, Midwest belief in the helpfulness of others always exceeded the scores of other regions by an average of over 5 percent.

In other words, midwesterners evince a high level of mutual trust, which they draw on to support their particular politics. Individual political acts are the most highly valued because they are most likely to work. They are believed to work because they are carried out in a cooperative community. Because the political community, and the larger society, is to be trusted, group political action is less necessary. Good, public-spirited citizens and politicians working at their selected and elected tasks will bring things out right. This ethos of individual efficacy and social trust accounts for the relative intolerance of organized dissent. The individual actions of community-minded leaders can best solve political problems. In that light, street demonstrations violate the social contract the midwesterner makes between self and neighbor.

The uniquely individualist, traditional political participation found in the region flows from the structure of the region's society and politics. The Midwest political style owes much to its rural heritage, with farms tied to small towns, cooperating to grow and prosper. The Jeffersonian ideal of a yeoman democracy of freeholders still resonates, as do Iowa native Herbert Hoover's ideas of individualism and public service. That the ideas may be antiquated need not make them less powerful, especially as they still have some geographic basis. In particular, the Midwest is still comparatively rural. Even by the 1990 census, about 28 percent of the population lived in places defined by the Census Bureau as "rural," just behind the South's 31 percent (a difference expected to shrink with Southern urbanization). Most tellingly, the Midwest had the highest proportion of its population living in small towns (of less than 2,500 inhabitants) of any region, the South included. The friend and neighbor qualities of the rural Midwest affects the politics of these small communities, and the politics of those who emigrate from them to the midwestern cities. Anecdotal evidence on the latter can come from a visit to Chicago, a friendly big "small town."

Besides society, the region's political organization shapes the individual politics. Political scientists commonly examine state governments in terms of interest group and political party influence. A study by Cotter and his colleagues ranked state parties in terms of organizational strength, showing that 75 percent of the state Democrat and Republican party organizations in the Midwest were "moderately strong" or "strong." Further, party competition in the Midwest was healthy. A study measuring electoral competition found that the Midwest claimed ten of the top eighteen most electorally competitive states, far more than any other region, and included the most electorally competitive state in the nation, North Dakota. The Midwest system of strong, competitive party politics on a statewide basis helps generate its high level of voting, as well as campaign contributions and button wearing. In addition to parties, interest groups—business lobbies, local government, colleges, labor unions, farm organizations, teachers—shape state politics. In a study by Gray and colleagues, more midwestern states were found to have dominant interest groups than in other regions. Interest group pressure, all things being equal, should produce more individual participation. These groups either "get out the vote," or the citizens themselves, in reaction to the interest groups, actually engage more politically as a counterweight.

Political participation in the Midwest differs in some ways from that in other parts of the country. midwesterners are individual activists. They are not especially political joiners. A sense of self-efficacy and community responsibility leads them to support their candidate with dollars, words, and votes. They believe the system works, easily and well enough. What is needed is to stay with the basics. In these ways, the typical midwesterner remains true to an age-old liberal individualism that is unabashedly American— these real regional political differences rendering them, with irony, stereotypically American.

Sources and Further Reading: Cornelius P. Cotter et al., *Party Organizations in American Politics* (1984); Virginia Gray, Russell L. Hanson, and Herbert Jacob, *Politics in the American States: A Comparative Analysis*, 7th ed. (1999); Thomas M. Holbrook and Emily Van Dunk, "Electoral Competition in the American States," *American Political Science Review* 87 (1993); Thomas Jefferson, *Notes on the State of Virginia*, ed. William Peden (1995); University of Chicago, Inter-University Consortium for Political and Social Research, *General Social Survey, 1972–1998* (1998).

Andrew A. Bargen and Michael S. Lewis-Beck
University of Iowa

Electoral Rules and Procedures

Home to noted industrial centers and rural landscapes, midwestern states offer great potential for electoral variety. More than 64 million people live in the Midwest—23 percent of the U.S. population and 124 electoral votes—a diversity that guarantees active interest in the region's electoral rules and processes.

North Dakota is the only state in the country with no voter registration, while Minnesota and Wisconsin pioneered same-day registration in the 1970s. Four other states—Iowa, Kansas, Nebraska, and South Dakota—have registration closing deadlines more lenient than the national average of twenty-five days. The states of the region also rank high in registration successes. In 2000, 88 percent of all eligible voters were registered, compared to the national average of 80 percent. Easier registration procedures are one element explaining the region's above-average turnout. Midwesterners also have longer hours to vote than most, with thirteen-hour election days the norm. Iowa and Kansas are among a handful of states extending voting to fourteen hours in an effort to encourage greater turnout.

Collectively, midwestern states rank high on other measures of voter accommodation, including generous absentee ballot provisions and improvements in registration systems. However, current reforms like early voting, mail and electronic systems, and on-line technologies are viewed cautiously in the region. For example, currently only five of the twelve states permit early voting, none have come close to elections by mail. Midwestern states have joined others in lining up for federal financing of new and more accurate vote-counting technologies, along with the uniform registration procedures provided in the Help America Vote Act of 2002.

Two counterbalancing forces in the region likely complicate greater reforms: vigorous party competition and a cautious attitude found in the region's rural states and areas. Partisans can be expected to evaluate suggested reforms for their potential impact on party fortunes first, with less commitment to more balanced, open, and effective voting systems. Many rural residents—already independent and suspicious of urban interests—will not be easy converts to reforms they may feel are unnecessary, costly, and not in their best interest.

Several states in the region are perennial turnout leaders, most notably Iowa, Minnesota, North Dakota, South Dakota, and Wisconsin. A healthy civic culture, party competition, and other socioeconomic factors are all important regional determinants of this impressive record. In the background, however, are many institutional factors that also play a role.

Wisconsin was the first state to enact a primary law in 1903, an idea that quickly spread to all other states. Midwestern states are balanced in the design of their primary laws. Seven states have open or semi-open primaries (Illinois, Indiana, Michigan, Minnesota, Missouri, North Dakota, and Wisconsin), while the remaining five contest closed or semi-closed events. Semi-closed primaries allow voters to register with a party (or change their existing registration) on Election Day; semi-open do not require party membership, only that a voter request a party ballot.

A majority of states contest their primaries in early May or June, while the others opt for early August or September. Competitive primaries for statewide offices are the norm. Even though there is generally lower turnout than in the fall general elections, primary turnout is typically higher than in other regions. A few states permit pre-primary party endorsements, notably Michigan, Minnesota, and Ohio. Midwestern voters have a history of dividing prominent offices between the two major parties, and they spring an occasional surprise like the election of independent Jesse Ventura as governor of Minnesota in 1998.

The midwestern role in presidential selection is most prominent with Iowa's first-in-the-nation caucuses in January, but the larger-state primaries in Illinois, Indiana, Michigan, and Ohio also draw extensive candidate and voter interest. Wisconsin's "wide open" presidential primary permits any registered voter to choose to vote in a primary other than that of the party in which they are registered. Independents also have the right to vote in party primaries.

Continuing vestiges of the Progressive Era are found in other electoral rules. Voters in North Dakota still elect twelve statewide officials (the most in the country), while it is not unusual to see several states retain election to such offices as agricultural and insurance commissioner. In Michigan, voters still select statewide regents to administer their public universities and colleges. The Missouri Plan to select judges is the most common selection system across the region.

Even though western states have the greatest reputation for electoral populism, South Dakota was the first state to enact an initiative law in 1898. Great variety exists in how initiative and referendum laws work. They can be direct (by voters) or indirect (via the legislature first), with the subject matter either constitutional or statutory. Seven midwestern states permit direct initiatives on constitutional amendments (none use the indirect process); six authorize legislative initiatives (ballot statutes), and five permit petition initiatives, where voters can approve or reject laws passed by their legislature. There is overlap with respect to these three initiative options, and some states permit all three while others permit one or two of the three. Significantly, midwestern states steeped in the history of the Progressive movement—Iowa, Minnesota, and Wisconsin—do not permit any kind of initiatives. There is not widespread use of initiative powers in the region, with the exception of North Dakota, a state typically one of the most active nationally in its use of ballot initiatives.

All states permit constitutional referenda whereby voters are given the final say on any legislatively proposed amendments. Recall of officials, although not widely available in the Midwest, does have a historical connection. North Dakota voters in 1921 were the first to recall a governor, the only state to do so until California in 2003. Kansas, Michigan, and Minnesota also allow recall, but only Minnesota permits the recall of judges.

A handful of cultural and political expectations combine to make midwestern electoral institutions and processes hospitable to healthy political competition and civic participation. The social compact between the region's people and their governments is sustained by wide support for an engaged citizenry, faith in government to do good, along with a healthy degree of skepticism and rectitude toward politics. Midwestern electoral rules and procedures are at the intersection of these values.

Sources and Further Reading: John F. Bibby, *Politics, Parties, and Elections in America,* 5th ed. (2002); Council of State Governments, *The Book of the States* (2003); Fenton S. Martin and Robert U. Goehlert, *How to Research Elections* (2000); Michael P. McDonald and Samuel L. Popkin, "The Myth of the Vanishing Voter," *American Political Science Review* 95 (Dec. 2001); Bruce Wetterau, ed., *Congressional Quarterly's Desk Reference on the States* (1999).

Jonathan P. Euchner
Missouri Western State College

The Emergence of African Americans as a Political Force

Before the mid-1960s, the politics of Cleveland, Detroit, and Chicago were dominated by white politicians. Black elected officials played only supporting roles when white Democratic politicians controlled these cities. Black voters were not taken seriously by

Cleveland mayor Carl B. Stokes, 1967. The Cleveland Press Collection, Cleveland State University Library.

the Democratic political machines because of their low turnout and, from the 1930s on, overwhelming support of Democratic candidates. Therefore, the black vote was considered predictable and controllable.

That changed as black voters grew increasingly dissatisfied with machine politics and white politicians, and became more antimachine and independent. Because of these sentiments and a rise in political efficacy, political sophistication, mobilization, and group consciousness, black voter registration and turnout would increase substantially in subsequent elections. Simultaneously, parties declined in strength, and viable black candidates sought the position of mayor. Blacks then developed political ties based on race, not class, and were able to use those ties to exercise their political influence. In time, black voters in Cleveland, Detroit, and Chicago secured the election of mayors they preferred.

Carl Stokes became Cleveland's, and America's (along with Richard Hatcher of Gary, Indiana), first black mayor in 1967. Coleman Young became Detroit's first black mayor in 1973, and Chicago elected its first black mayor in 1983 with Harold Washington. Several forces propelled these men to the helm of their respective cities. Stokes, Young, and Washington shared the same paths to power regarding their city's

population shift, black political mobilization, political independence, race consciousness, and racial voting.

Foremost was the change in the demographic makeup of each city's population. The black population in these cities grew enormously from the second quarter through the mid-twentieth century. In fact, there was greater migration to the industrial Midwest than to other parts of the country. The population of blacks in the central cities grew rapidly partly from black in-migration and partly from white flight to the suburbs. Such demographic change resulted in blacks becoming a majority or sizable minority in Cleveland, Detroit, and Chicago. The departure of working-class and middle-class whites began during the 1960s with the growing tide of racial tension and became more pronounced during the 1970s. The shift in these cities' demographics would have significant political implications, primarily in allowing blacks to command greater political influence and paving the way for black leadership.

Second, the black mayors were the beneficiaries of intense grassroots movements to energize the black electorate. The result of these efforts was an increase in the number of black Cleveland, Detroit, and Chicago citizens who registered to vote and who voted. Stokes, Young, and Washington appealed to many black voters, for they emphasized the redistribution of power so blacks could shape their futures and enjoy the benefits of descriptive representation. They were able to provide incentives for black political participation by running on economic revitalization, law and order, and government reform platforms.

Independence is a third factor that paved the way for each to dominate their city's politics. These massive mobilization drives allowed the black community to become an independent political force in local government and politics, particularly important since the Democratic Party and the city political machines withheld support and resources from the black mayors when running for office. The base of Stokes's political strength was the Twenty-First District Caucus. The Caucus was an independent entity that severed ties with the Democratic Party in an attempt to become a permanent political force and enact a broad set of social, political, and economic policies geared toward enhancing the quality of life of Cleveland's black population. Coleman Young and Harold Washington were also able to develop strong political bases of black voters independent of the Democratic Party in Detroit and the Daley machine in Chicago, respectively.

A fourth common element was the widespread sense in these black communities of black nationalism and self-determination moored in their belief that their lives would be better if a black mayor was elected. They no longer felt white politicians would execute necessary reforms to redress the varied economic and social problems suffered by the black community. They wanted to elect a black mayor to have influence over public policy and other tangible benefits. Ironically, in order to win, these black mayors could not make overt racial statements. Common in their strategies were attempts to deracialize their positions, campaigns, and images, especially when interacting with white citizens. They ran nonracial campaigns that focused generally on six broad issue areas: economic and business development, crime, education, urban renewal, housing, and transportation.

A final parallel among these victors is how they won their elections. The increases in black registration and turnout were not enough to win. Stokes, Young, and Washington had to win near-unanimous support, close to 90 percent of the vote, in the black districts or wards. The black mayors would then have to capture approximately 10 to 20 percent of the nonblack vote. In several precincts or wards, white, longtime Democrats voted for the white Republican candidate, thus pointing to race as a greater influence than party affiliation. In essence, these candidates' ascendance to the office of the mayor largely resulted from overwhelming support garnered in black wards, indeed gaining near unanimous support in most of them, and performing well in Hispanic and liberal white wards. Even though race was not an explicit factor in these campaigns, the percentage of voters voting for the candidate of their own race certainly suggests that race was important, together with racial appeals made by aides of white Republican candidates. The victories of these three leaders enhanced the importance of the black community in the electorates of these and other cities of the region.

Sources and Further Reading: David R. Colburn and Jeffrey S. Adler, eds., *African-American Mayors* (2001); Paul Kleppner, *Chicago Divided* (1985); Michael B. Preston, Lenneal J. Henderson, Jr., and Paul L. Puryear, eds., *The New Black Politics*, 2nd ed. (1987); Wilbur Rich, *Coleman Young and Detroit Politics* (1989).

Maurice Mangum
Southern Illinois University–Edwardsville

Political Campaigning

Campaign politics in the Midwest has been marked by substantial variation, both across and within states. Yet it can be characterized throughout the region by a general movement from a more personalized politics to one shaped by the mass media. In other words, the front porch has been displaced by the TV room as the venue for political campaigning. But this movement follows a path marked by twists and turns. Indeed, the new campaign politics in many cases builds on the traditions of the old and respects the urban-rural dichotomy that marks internally many of the states in the Midwest.

In the late nineteenth and early twentieth centuries, the political diversity of the region was borne out in campaigns. In states such as Ohio, Indiana, and Illinois, strong political parties prevailed and affected the ways in which electoral politics was run. Political machines, especially in the local areas, provided for a face-to-face campaign experience, with the political party organization as the middleman between the candidates and the voter. Given the persuasive appeal of patronage and strong party ties among the electorate, politics was in large part an elaborate get-out-the-vote operation in which bosses like Republican George B. Cox of Cincinnati orchestrated the exchange of votes for jobs, contracts, or protection. The model did extend to the west, with a notable example being Kansas City's Pendergast machine.

States in the Plains and the upper Midwest, however, tended to be more rural in nature with a strong populist and agrarian orientation; they experienced a

Harding's Front Porch campaign, 1920. Ohio Historical Society, AL00774.

brand of campaign politics built on these qualities. Rousing oratory by the region's political notables was common. The likes of Minnesotan Ignatious Donnelly, Nebraskan William Jennings Bryan, and Wisconsinite Robert M. La Follette ignited the crowds, both in their own states and beyond. Rallies and protests, especially from ranks of farmers, marked the policy-making and electoral arenas.

This early campaign politics, though not always literally front porch, was marked across the region by a retail quality, often with parties or party leaders making the sale. The task, however, was quite different in the rural and urban areas. In all of the states, an urban-rural divide has been evident. Ranging from states with multiple urban centers like Ohio, to states with one or even no real urban centers like Minnesota and Iowa, respectively, the Midwest has presented campaigns suited to these varied environments. The more densely populated areas of all of these states have tended to be the targets for statewide and presidential campaigns, contributing to a more vibrant and professional campaign politics. In contrast, politics in rural areas has tended to be more amateur and low-key in nature.

By the second half of the twentieth century, politics throughout the Midwest had changed. Like the entire nation, midwestern campaigns had taken on a more candidate-centered focus. Candidates on the statewide ballot in the urban states of the Midwest—Ohio, Michigan, Illinois—exploited, early on, the broadcast media as the vehicle to reach the voters. And these states, typically highly competitive in the presidential contests, were among the targeted states in the fall; presidential candidates themselves, and their images on television advertisements, marked campaign seasons. At the same time, the legacy of strong and traditional party organizations, and even patronage organizations, prevailed in states like Indiana and localities like Cook County, Illinois.

The upper Midwest in general entered into the broadcast era later than those midwestern states to the east. The rural setting lends itself to a more intimate campaigning. But institutions and practices unique to particular states also contribute to a lingering front porch atmosphere, even for the presidential nomination contest, which is reliant elsewhere on mass media–driven politics. Since the 1970s, the Iowa caucuses, for example, have brought into that state presidential nomination candidates who use a retail approach. During competitive nomination seasons, presidential hopefuls blanket the state, even attending events and gatherings in the homes of political activists. This pattern applies to other contests in other states across the region, as well. Still today, candidates for state legislative seats "door-knock" their districts in the upper Midwest. And even congressional and statewide candidates, as well as those for lower-level offices, are mainstays on the parade, county fair, and state fair circuits—a tradition that continues uninterrupted from the days before electronic media. Notably now, however, the candidate can travel from one traditional venue to another by airplane, or some other comfortable and modern means of transportation, making calls on his cell phone along the way. In other words, modern technology helps the candidate exploit the potential of the face-to-face politics.

But the personal has also given way to "wholesale" politics. Beginning in the 1990s, presidential nomination hopefuls campaigned for the Iowa caucuses by blanketing the airwaves of the state. Certainly throughout even the rural states in the Midwest, the occasional state legislative candidate reaches the voter through the paid media. And in some presidential contests, the traditional front-porch states are targeted, indeed blitzed, by the candidates' and the parties' television appeals. During the election of 2000, for example, the presidential candidates of both major parties, as well as the political parties through issue advocacy ads that were thinly disguised candidate appeals and attacks, bombarded the airwaves of Wisconsin and Minnesota, which were particularly competitive that year.

At the same time, wholesale methods, as delivered through the broadcast media, have been used to foster a return to a new brand of the old machine model. Conjuring up images of the machine-like efforts, the coordinated campaigns—that is, those party-generated entities that pool campaigns in the interest of efficiency—engage in voter registration, absentee voting, and get-out-the-vote efforts. Mobilizing people through traditional door-to-door as well as more modern direct mail and "voice broadcast" telephone technology, the coordinated campaigns emulate a more traditional and face-to-face mobilization effort. These efforts are undertaken across the nation, though the states of the Midwest—especially Michigan, Ohio, and Iowa—have been marked by particularly vibrant efforts at the turn of the twenty-first century. This modern-day mixture of old and new underscores the twists and turns, even *returns*, that campaign politics has taken over time in the Midwest.

Sources and Further Reading: John H. Fenton, *Midwest Politics* (1966); Malcolm E. Jewell and Sarah M. Morehouse, *Political Parties and Elections in American States*, 4th ed. (2001); Milton L. Rakove, *Don't Make No Waves—Don't Back No Losers* (1975); James A. Thurber, Candice J. Nelson, and David A. Dulio, eds., *Crowded Airwaves* (2000); Hugh Winebrenner, *The Iowa Precinct Caucuses: The Making of a Media Event*, 2nd ed. (1998).

Barbara Trish
Grinnell College, Iowa

Labor and Politics in the Sweeney Era

John J. Sweeney was elected president of the American Federation of Labor–Council of Industrial Organizations (AFL-CIO) in 1995 on a platform of reenergizing the labor movement. His election followed the Republican Party's gain of majority control in Congress and many state legislatures in the 1994 elections. Labor could no longer rely on Democratic Party leaders for protection. Sweeney's program has been to mobilize labor's membership base in order to affect the outcomes of elections and make politicians more responsive to labor's agenda.

Part of the mobilization strategy includes increasing union membership, judged necessary for union organizations to survive. Union membership declined from one-third of the workforce to 13 percent of the workforce, and unions' spending on organizing fell from nearly 40 percent to only 3 percent of their budgets over the latter half of the twentieth century. Sweeney urged unions to devote 30 percent of their budgets to organizing and offered financial and logistical assistance from the AFL-CIO. Unions increasingly have sought the support of local politicians and leaders of community organizations to broaden support for union organizing.

The success of the new organizing efforts has been mixed. By 2001, only twelve of the sixty-six internationals in the AFL-CIO have met the goal of spending 30 percent of their budgets on organizing. Unions, however, have tripled their recruitment of new members to three hundred thousand members per year under Sweeney, but this has not kept pace with the growth of the workforce or replaced membership losses in declining industries. In 2001, 13.5 percent of the workforce was organized, compared to 14.9 percent at the beginning of Sweeney's presidency. Despite declines in membership, the Midwest in 2000 remained the most unionized region of the country with 17.4 percent of its workforce organized in unions.

Sweeney has also sought to mobilize union members more effectively politically. In the 1996 midterm elections, the AFL-CIO spent $35 million on issue advertising designed to link Republican candidates in competitive districts to unpopular issue positions. The AFL-CIO sent staff to targeted congressional races to assist state and local labor federations and union locals to work on behalf of congressional candidates, in addition to state and local candidates. It turned union organizers into political recruiters to help local union officers engage in more face-to-face political education and get-out-the-vote efforts for union members. Political education has increasingly consisted of contrasting candidates' positions on salient issues, rather than merely disseminating an endorsement.

The AFL-CIO's electoral mobilization has worked. In the 1998 midterm election, the percentage of union members voting and participating in election activities increased. In the 2000 presidential election, union households' share of the electorate increased to 26 percent from 23 percent in the 1996 presidential election. The AFL-CIO's efforts helped the Democrats pick up seats in Congress in the 1996, 1998, and 2000 elections, as well as helping Al Gore win a number of contested states in the Midwest in the 2000 presidential contest.

Under Sweeney, labor has not reversed its long-term decline in membership, but it has become more innovative and aggressive in organizing and political mobilization.

Sources and Further Reading: Herbert B. Asher et al., *American Labor Unions in the Electoral Arena* (2001); Taylor Dark, *The Unions and the Democrats* (1999); John J. Sweeney, *America Needs a Raise* (1996).

Eric S. Heberlig
University of North Carolina–Charlotte

The Regional Political Economy

The economic development of the Midwest has centered on two interrelated factors, agricultural expansion and urbanization. The westward expansion that started in the mid-1850s produced substantial population growth in both the rural and urban sectors of the region. By 1860, much of the Midwest was connected to the eastern United States by rail, more easily facilitating the movement of people and goods. The result was tremendous urban and rural population growth. For instance, in 1860, the Midwest boasted three of America's ten most populous cities: Cincinnati at seventh, St. Louis at eighth, and Chicago at ninth. Much of their growth can be attributed to the fact that they were important transportation hubs, with Chicago emerging as a prominent rail center, and growing industrial sectors.

From 1860 to 1920, lands dedicated to farming increased by 548.2 million acres, 192.3 million acres of which were homesteads. Population expansion in the region was not limited to cities; the agricultural sector produced tremendous growth, as well. A number of factors contributed to the Midwest's agricultural expansion. First, transportation advances facilitated settlement in the region. The railroads received large land grants from the government, which they sold to prospective farmers at attractive prices to ensure that there would be a market for rail freight service. The passage of the Homestead Act in 1862 facilitated the agricultural expansion in the Midwest by providing free land to those willing to settle it.

This combination of an expanded transportation system coupled with growing cities and an expanding agricultural sector wrote an important success story for the region. Numerous technological advances in farm machinery coupled with large expanses of farmable land garnered the region the title of the Farm Belt. The improvements in transportation allowed farmers to easily ship their crops to market, leading to the continued growth and development of important urban areas in the region based largely on agricultural industries: futures markets in Chicago, milling in Minneapolis and St. Paul, and stockyards in Omaha, Kansas City, and Chicago. The industrial centers of the Midwest had their roots as transportation hubs for the farms and rural parts of the region.

Much of the political reputation of the midwestern region stems directly from consequences of its economic development. Unlike the overwhelmingly Democratic Solid South, the Midwest has a more subtle political identity. For much of the post–Civil War era, the majority of the midwestern states were solidly Republican. Many midwesterners still viewed the Democrats as the party of Rum, Romanism, and Rebellion, or, according to Sundquist (1983), "the party of the Catholics, the 'wets,' and the immigrants." Despite the Republican leanings of the region in the late 1800s and early 1900s, the region was far from politically homogeneous. As agricultural production increased, commodity prices dropped, transportation costs (rail freight rates) increased, and midwestern farmers became increasingly upset with what they perceived to be

hostile treatment from the entrenched political interests of the time. The result was increased political activity by midwestern agrarian interests.

This unrest manifested itself in different ways with pushes for reform from within the two major parties, to the creation of myriad third parties. Insurgent Republicans in Congress wrested power away from a staunch conservative, Joe Cannon. A populist faction within the Democratic Party succeeded in nominating William Jennings Bryan in 1896, 1900, and 1908. Progressive third parties fared extremely well in some states. Robert La Follette left the Republican Party and established his Progressive Party as a political powerhouse in Wisconsin. The Farmer-Labor Party in Minnesota won statewide elections and emerged as one of the two major parties in that state.

If midwestern politics in the late nineteenth and early twentieth centuries was marked by great unrest and third-party proliferation, the post–World War II era is one of closely fought battles between the two major parties. A number of indicators show a relatively stable system of partisan competition. State and federal electoral data highlight the closely fought partisan battles in the region. The Ranney Index of party competition classifies six of the twelve midwestern states as competitive two-party systems, four as modified one-party Republican Party systems, and one as modified one-party Democratic Party system. (Nebraska is not included since it elects state legislators on a nonpartisan ballot.)

Figure 4 displays the number of midwestern Democratic and Republican House members from the 80th to 106th Congresses.

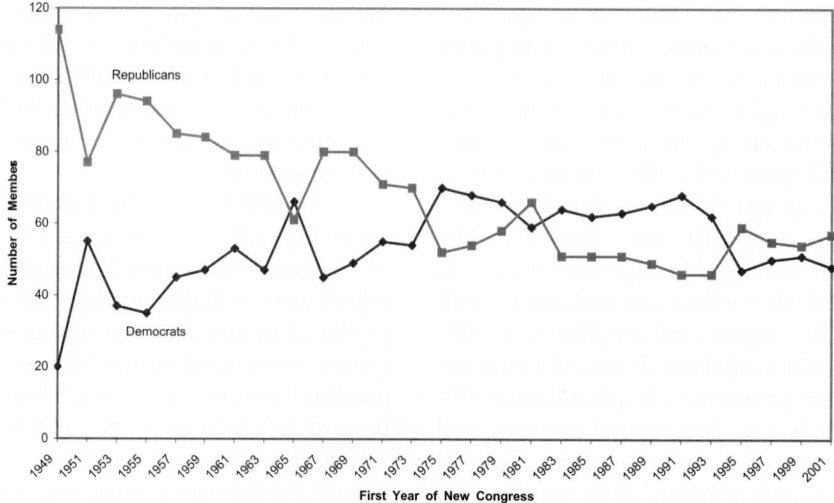

Figure 4. Party composition of midwestern House delegations. Keith T. Poole's DW NOMINATE Data, http://voteview.uh.edu/dwnomin.htm.

A period of large Republican majorities from the Midwest in the 1950s gave way to roughly equal numbers in recent congresses. From 1980 to 2000, five states—Indiana, Kansas, Nebraska, North Dakota, and South Dakota—cast their electoral votes only for Republicans, while Minnesota went Democratic in all the elections. Two states, Missouri and Ohio, cast their electoral votes for the winning candidate in each of the six elections. Comparing roll call behavior in Congress, midwestern House members closely resemble their non-midwestern colleagues. Early in the post–World War II era, midwestern Democrats tended to comprise the liberal wing of the party, forming an ideological counter to the conservative Southern delegations. In recent Congresses, however, the ideological composition of both the Democratic and Republican Parties show virtually no regional factions.

One could well argue that the increasingly competitive political environment is a sign of larger changes in the political economy of the region. The economic and demographic composition of the region is becoming increasingly diverse. In the past, differences such as an urban-versus-rural divide might not have led to important political divisions. With economic issues driving increasing political polarization, it should come as no surprise that increasingly stark economic and demographic differences should lead to notable shifts in the political landscape of the Midwest.

Sources and Further Reading: Paul Allen Beck and Marjorie Randon Hershey, *Party Politics in America*, 9th ed. (2000); Richard F. Bensel, *The Political Economy of American Industrialization, 1877–1900* (2000); John F. Bibby and L. Sandy Maisel, *Two Parties—Or More?* (1998); Joseph Cooper and David W. Brady, "Institutional Context and Leadership Style: The House from Cannon to Rayburn," *American Political Science Review* 75 (June 1981); Jonathan Hughes and Louis P. Cain, *American Economic History*, 4th ed. (1994); Nolan M. McCarty, Keith T. Poole, and Howard Rosenthal, *Income Redistribution and the Realignment of American Politics* (1997); Keith T. Poole and Howard Rosenthal, *Congress: A Political-Economic History of Roll Call Voting* (1997); James L. Sundquist, *Dynamics of the Party System*, rev. ed. (1983); Richard M. Valelly, *Radicalism in the States* (1989).

Timothy P. Nokken
University of Houston, Texas

The Politician and Political Machines

At the beginning of the twentieth century, a new era of urban politics in the United States began to take shape. Characterized by steep increases in urban population and growth, the result was a dramatic exacerbation of social problems. The days were filled with labor problems, ethnic unrest, excessive crime, and poverty. Disorder spread into the political system as election violence increased, while hungry and unemployed workers struggled to get their candidates into power. Three major political machines and political bosses emerged in the cities of the urban Midwest: George B. Cox in Cincinnati, Thomas J. Pendergast in Kansas City, and Richard Daley in Chicago.

To grasp the amount of power and authority that these men controlled in their individual cities, it is essential to understand the operation of early-twentieth-century political machines. Rapid urbanization had led to an increase in the gap between rich and poor, from which political machines emerged. Designed to get a particular candidate into power or to keep one in power, political machines expanded their influence into all realms of government. Often, the leader of the political machine, typically known as the Boss, held office, but in most cases he handpicked those who would run for the various offices and positions and helped them to get elected.

When political machines were highly developed, they controlled all government jobs. Corruption was rampant, as bosses often demanded payment for their services. Political machines began to offer social services to the masses of poor immigrants and unemployed urban residents, further enhancing their base of power.

George B. Cox from Cincinnati was a leader of what many viewed as a positive and benevolent Republican political machine. Cox, born in Cincinnati in 1853, was from an industrious and active family and soon rose to the status of self-made man. His first political move came as a member of the Cincinnati Council in 1879, and when he later took an active role in the frenzied elections of 1884 and 1885, he was quickly recognized as one who fought for the masses, and his fame spread citywide.

He clamped down on all instruments of public authority in Cincinnati, holding complete control of the city. As his power spread to the state and national levels, Cox used his political machine to help national candidates like fellow Cincinnatian Nicholas Longworth to get elected to the U.S. House of Representatives, to build marvelous civic buildings throughout Cincinnati, and to establish a type of welfare system for the impoverished citizens of the city. By the end of his political career, Cox had held almost absolute control from 1886 to 1916.

Cox never liked to write things down and kept paperwork to an absolute minimum, believing that without a paper trail, he could never be convicted. Indeed in 1906, Cox was indicted on corruption charges, but was never found guilty because of a lack of evidence and witnesses. To many of his contemporaries, Cox was a savior and an honest man, but to many others, he was a tyrant.

Thomas J. Pendergast successfully controlled Kansas City during the early twentieth century. Born in St. Joseph, Missouri, in 1873, Pendergast was one of nine children, and moved to Kansas City in the mid-1890s to work in his brother Jim's saloon. There, Pendergast learned about the political system in the city and the advantages offered by controlling positions of authority in the city government. Pendergast's older brother, Jim, was active in Democratic Party politics and passed control of his political organization to Tom upon his death.

Pendergast accumulated power by posing as a simple businessman who merely managed his brother's saloon, but in actuality he was single-handedly providing all the vices in Kansas City. He supplied alcohol during prohibition and set up gambling establishments. Under his direction, Pendergast arranged for the casting of large numbers of ballots in elections to keep political friends in power. In return for his help, the companies he controlled were awarded prime government contracts.

Pendergast had many well-known achievements, including the passage of a $40 million federal bond issue, which kept Kansas City afloat during the Great Depression. Notably, he substantially aided Harry S Truman's rise in politics. In the end, Pendergast was arraigned for tax evasion in 1939, found guilty, and sentenced to a fifteen-month prison term, effectively ending his political career.

Richard J. Daley is perhaps the most famous of the political bosses, controlling and exercising authority over the largest city of the Midwest, Chicago. Born in 1902 in a Chicago neighborhood near Comiskey Park, Daley was first elected at a relatively young age to the Illinois legislature as a Republican, which he joined out of political convenience. After finishing an unexpired term, he rejoined the Democratic Party, where he made his mark.

Daley organized an effective political machine, getting himself elected mayor of Chicago first in 1955, after which he would serve six straight terms until his death in office in 1976. Known nationwide as an icon for party politics and political machines, Daley accumulated so much power that many political analysts attributed John F. Kennedy's 1960 election as president in part to his political maneuvers.

Using his political machine, Daley controlled the majority of seats on the Chicago City Council. "Vote early and often" was the phrase most often associated with Daley's political machine, since many accused him of using precinct captains to "deliver" votes for his handpicked candidates.

Daley was known for bringing many projects to the city of Chicago, including the construction of O'Hare International Airport, the Sears Tower, and Mc-Cormick Place. He was notorious for his orders for police to shoot at rioters who protested after the assassination of Martin Luther King, Jr., and his actions and those of the police in the civil disorder at the 1968 Democratic National Convention. Like Cox and Pendergast, Daley had his share of supporters and dissenters. Scholars and citizens alike debate the successes and failures of "bossism" in the urban Midwest to this day.

Sources and Further Reading: Roger Biles, *Richard J. Daley: Politics, Race, and the Governing of Chicago* (1995); Adam Cohen and Elizabeth Taylor, *American Pharaoh* (2000); Lyle W. Dorsett, *The Pendergast Machine* (1980); Robert H. Ferrell, *Truman and Pendergast* (1999); Rudolph H. Hartmann and Robert H. Ferrell, eds., *The Kansas City Investigation* (1999); Lawrence H. Larsen, Nancy J. Hulston, and William E. Foley, eds., *Pendergast* (1997); Zane L. Miller, *Boss Cox's Cincinnati* (1968; reprint, 1980); Mike Royko, *Boss: Richard J. Daley of Chicago* (1971; reprint, 1988).

Arthur Holst
Philadelphia, Pennsylvania

Unicameralism in Nebraska

The Nebraska Legislature is unique in American politics in two ways: It is the only unicameral or one-house state legislature, and the only state legislature that elects its members on a nonpartisan ballot. These two characteristics, enacted as a constitutional amendment in 1934 through the initiative process, were products of their times and of Nebraska's political culture, labeled Individualist–Moralist by political scientist Daniel Elazar.

Individualism in Nebraska leads to fiscal conservatism and an inventive spirit that accepts unique solutions. At the height of the Great Depression, the thought of eliminating more than one-half of the state legislators struck a responsive chord with Nebraskans.

Moralism played an even greater role. U.S. Senator George Norris, a principal proponent of these reforms, argued that unicameralism would eliminate two great "sins" of bicameralism: buck passing, or voting opportunistically while knowing the other house would defeat a measure, and the conference committee in which deals could be struck out of public view. He expected a unicameral legislature to be more open and understandable, leading to responsible, efficient, and businesslike government and to a stronger legislature to balance the governor's office. Certainly the process is simpler, there are no conference committees, and the legislature has a reputation for being rel-

Nebraska state capitol building. Nebraska Unicameral Information Office.

and although in 2002, registered Republicans held thirty-two of the forty-nine seats, Democrats chaired five of the fourteen legislative committees. Few bills reflect partisan voting blocs.

Unicameralism and nonpartisanship may make it easier to override vetoes, and the budget that emerges from the legislature often is less conservative than the governor's proposal. Yet, nonpartisanship seems to allow easier cooperation between the legislature and governor.

Could a nonpartisan unicameral legislature have been created elsewhere than in the Midwest? Certainly, there has been no serious movement to parrot Nebraska anywhere in the United States, even within the Midwest. Its enactment resulted from a confluence of culture, timing (the Depression), and personality (the leadership of George Norris) such that even in Nebraska, its passage was, perhaps, a fluke.

Sources and Further Reading: John Comer, "Almost Heaven," in Ronald J. Hrebenar and Clive S. Thomas, eds., *Interest Group Politics in the Midwestern States* (1993); John Comer and James B. Johnson, eds., *Nonpartisanship in the Legislative Process* (1978); James B. Johnson, "The Nebraska Legislative System," Ph.D. diss., Northwestern University (1972); Robert Miewald, ed., *Nebraska Government and Politics* (1984).

James B. Johnson
University of Nebraska–Omaha

atively independent of the governor (this latter perhaps due more to nonpartisanship than to unicameralism). The unicameral structure has now lasted over sixty years, and the legislature has come to be known as "the Unicameral."

Moralism was also apparent in Norris's promotion of a nonpartisan Nebraska Legislature. Nonpartisanship, a movement of the early twentieth century, has strong midwestern roots, especially in the moralistic centers of North Dakota, which spawned the Non-Partisan League, and Minnesota, which enacted a nonpartisan ballot for its legislature in 1913 (and kept it until 1973). Norris's arguments displayed a distrust of political parties as corrupt and a belief that they detract from the electoral process—obstacles that separate the people from their elected representatives.

The spirit of nonpartisanship quickly took hold within the Unicameral. Although registered Democrats outnumbered Republicans in the first Unicameral (1936), the speakership and one-third of the committee chairs went to Republicans. This spirit remains to the present. More recently, Republican majorities have elected a relatively liberal Democrat as speaker,

The Evolving Role of Women in Midwestern Politics

From the woman suffrage movement of the nineteenth century to their leadership as elected officials in the twenty-first century, women have played an important role in the political life of the Midwest. Several midwestern states were among the first to approve laws granting women the right to vote, five of the twelve states in the region have above-average records in electing women legislators, and two elected women governors in 2002.

Kansas was the first state in the Midwest—and among the first in the nation—to grant women full suffrage rights. When Kansas entered the Union in 1861, women could vote in local school elections. In 1886, the women's vote was extended to municipal elections. The nation's first woman mayor, Susanna Madora Salter, was elected the following year in Argonia, and an all-woman city council with a woman mayor took office in Oskaloosa in 1888. The women of Kansas were granted tax and bond suffrage in 1903, and won full suffrage through a constitutional amendment in 1912. At that time, only eight other states—all in the West—granted full suffrage to women.

Two other midwestern states granted women full suffrage before the ratification of the Nineteenth Amendment to the U.S. Constitution giving women the right to vote in 1920. The women of Michigan won school suffrage in 1875, the right to vote on tax and bond issues in 1908, presidential suffrage in 1917, and full suffrage through a state constitutional amendment in 1918. The women of South Dakota gained school suffrage in 1887, and full suffrage via a state constitutional amendment in 1918.

All other midwestern states approved limited suffrage prior to ratification of the Nineteenth Amendment. The women of Wisconsin could run for school boards and other elective school offices in 1869, vote on issues related to schools in 1900, and vote in presidential elections in 1919. The women of Minnesota first voted in school elections in 1875 and presidential elections in 1919. The women of Nebraska voted in school elections in 1883 and presidential elections in 1917. The women of North Dakota gained school suffrage in 1889, and in 1893, Superintendent of Education Laura Eisenhuth (Democrat) became the first woman in the nation to hold statewide elective office. The women of Ohio voted in school elections in 1891 and presidential elections in 1919. In 1913, Illinois women won the right to vote in municipal and presidential elections. Women in North Dakota and Indiana had presidential suffrage in 1917. Women in Iowa were granted presidential suffrage in 1919.

Once the Nineteenth Amendment was proposed to the state legislatures on June 4, 1919, by the 66th Congress, midwestern states were among the first to ratify—Illinois, Michigan, and Wisconsin on June 10, Kansas and Ohio on June 16, Iowa on July 2, Missouri on July 3, Nebraska on August 2, Minnesota on September 8, North Dakota on December 1, and South Dakota on December 4, 1919. Indiana ratified on January 16, 1920. Ratification was completed, with the vote of the Tennessee legislature, on August 18, 1920.

During the seventy-two-year campaign for woman suffrage, several midwestern women led the way. Carrie Chapman Catt, who was born in Ripon, Wisconsin, in 1859, and raised on a farm near Charles City, Iowa, dedicated most of her life to the cause. After attending her first state suffrage convention in 1885 and national convention in 1890, she rose quickly through the ranks of the movement, becoming Susan B. Anthony's chosen successor as president of the National American Woman Suffrage Association in 1900. Catt again became president of the NAWSA in 1915, and led the woman suffrage cause to victory in 1920.

Other midwestern women with prominent roles in the suffrage movement include former slave Sojourner Truth, who became a speaker on women's rights in 1850 and lived in Battle Creek, Michigan, from 1867 to her death in 1883; Amelia Bloomer, who moved from Seneca Falls, New York, where she was editor of the nation's first women's rights newspaper, *The Lily*, to Council Bluffs, Iowa, in 1855, and campaigned for woman suffrage in Iowa and Nebraska; Dr. Mary Thomas of Indiana, who edited *The Lily* when it moved to Richmond in 1855; Virginia Minor of Missouri, whose suit against the state for denying her the vote in 1872 was heard by the U.S. Supreme Court; Frances Willard of Illinois, who, as president of the Woman's Christian Temperance Union from 1879 to 1897, helped link suffrage to temperance and contributed vast resources to the cause; and Ida Wells-Barnett, who formed the first black female suffrage club in Illinois and marched in the NAWSA parade with her white colleagues in 1913, thus helping integrate the movement.

Since the suffrage movement, most midwestern states have continued to make progress in women's political participation. In 2003, when the national average of women in state legislatures stood at 22 percent, more than 25 percent of the members of four midwestern state legislatures were women—Kansas, Illinois, Minnesota, and Wisconsin. Michigan also ranked above the national average in 2003 with a legislature that was 24 percent women.

Kansas boasts several firsts in terms of electing women to federal and state office. In 1978, Nancy Landon Kassebaum (Republican) became the first woman elected to serve in the U.S. Senate without having previously filled an unexpired term. She was the only woman in the Senate at the time of her election. Kassebaum was reelected twice and, in 1995, became the first woman to head a major Senate committee when she became chair of Labor and Human Resources. In 1991, Joan Finney (Democrat) became the first woman to serve as governor by defeating the incumbent. In 2002, Kansas voters elected Kathleen Sebelius (Democrat) as their second woman governor.

Illinois has a strong record of electing women to political office, dating back to 1922 when Winnifred S. M. Huck (Republican) won a special election to the U.S. House of Representatives to fill a vacancy caused by the death of her father. In 1928, Ruth Hanna McCormick (Republican) was elected to the U.S. House. In every subsequent decade, Illinois elected a woman to the U.S. Congress. Eleven different women have represented the state in the U.S. House, and in 1992, Carol Moseley-Braun was elected to the U.S. Senate from Illinois, becoming the first African American woman to so serve. Over a decade earlier, Jane Byrne (Democrat) was elected mayor of Chicago and served from 1979 to 1983.

Minnesota also has provided a receptive environment for women in politics. Women from the state have served in the U.S. Senate, U.S. House of Representatives, and in a variety of statewide elected executive offices including lieutenant governor, secretary of state, state treasurer, and state auditor.

Although Wisconsin has elected only one woman to Congress, in 1998, U.S. Representative Tammy Baldwin (Democrat) became the first openly gay woman to be elected to Congress. In 1978, Secretary of State Vel R. Phillips (Democrat) became the first African American woman in the country elected statewide to an executive post.

In 2002, Michigan voters elected Jennifer Granholm (Democrat) governor as well as their second woman secretary of state. Patricia Birkholz (Republican) was elected president pro tempore of the Michigan Senate; and three women represented the state in Congress. Michigan boasts being one of the nation's leaders in the campaign for women's equality. Martha Wright Griffiths (Democrat), who served as a member of the House of Representatives from 1955 to 1974, played an instrumental role in ensuring that women were included within the purview of the Civil Rights Act of 1964. In 1970, she successfully filed a discharge petition to get the Equal Rights Amendment—which had been buried in congressional committees for forty-seven years—out of the House Judiciary Committee.

In Missouri, women were barred from running for office until an amendment to the state constitution passed on August 2, 1921. In 1922, Mellcene Smith (Democrat) and Sarah Lucille Turner (Democrat) were the first women elected to the Missouri legislature. In 2003, Catherine Hanaway (Republican) was elected speaker of the Missouri House of Representatives. Five women have represented Missouri in the U.S. House, beginning with Leonor Kretzer Sullivan (Democrat) in 1953. U.S. Senator Jean Carnahan (Democrat) was appointed to a seat won posthumously by her husband in 2000, but was defeated in her election bid in 2002. Former Lt. Gov. Harriett Woods (Democrat) subsequently pursued her political career at the national level, where she served as president of the National Women's Political Caucus and head of the Coalition for Women's Appointments.

Until the state constitution was amended in 1926, women were not allowed to serve in the state legislature of Iowa. However, within two years, Carolyn Campbell Pendray (Democrat) became the first woman elected to the House of Representatives of the state, and in 1933, she became the first woman elected to the state Senate. At the turn of the century, Iowa became one of two states with a woman elected to serve as secretary of agriculture. Three women have

served consecutively as lieutenant governor from 1987 to 2006, and the Iowa state Senate has been led by a woman president since 1997. Iowa is one of only five states, however, that has never elected a woman to national public office.

The other states of the Midwest have less progressive records in electing women to office, but with some highlights. For example, in 1986, Nebraska's Kay Orr became the first Republican woman to be elected governor in any state and the first woman to run against another woman for a gubernatorial post. In 2003, three women represented Ohio in the U.S. House of Representatives, and two served in statewide executive office as lieutenant governor and attorney general. Just prior to that, another served as Speaker of the House in the state legislature. One Indiana woman served in the U.S. House of Representatives, and two held statewide executive office in 2003.

In the case of North Dakota, only one woman, Jocelyn Birch Burdick (Democrat) has represented the state in Congress, having been appointed in 1992 to fill the vacancy created by the death of her husband. In 1993, Janet Wentz (Republican) was elected speaker of the North Dakota House of Representatives, joining two other North Dakota women who are among the fifteen women who have previously served as speakers of their state houses.

Two women have represented South Dakota in the U.S. Senate, both filling the unexpired terms of men who died in office. South Dakota does have a long history of electing women to statewide executive office, particularly secretary of state. Fifteen women have served in this capacity from 1927 to 2002.

A 1998 study comparing the number of women in state legislatures from 1964 to 1995 found that women were most numerous in legislatures in the Northeast and West, and least numerous in the South and Mid-Atlantic regions, though in recent years the West and Midwest—principally in Kansas and Minnesota—the election of women to state legislatures has expanded most noticeably. Primarily, there is a higher proportion of women in the legislatures of those states with a large pool of potential women candidates, interest group strength, moralistic political cultures, multi-member districts, and high levels of turnover.

Sources and Further Reading: Louise Bernikow, *The American Women's Almanac* (1997); Clara Bingham, *Women on the Hill* (1997); R. Darcy, Susan Welch, and Janet Clark, *Women, Elections, and Representation*, 2nd ed. (1994); Lynn E. Ford, *Women and Politics: The Pursuit of Equality* (2002); Barbara Norrander and Clyde Wilcox, "The Geography of Gender Power," in Sue Thomas and Clyde Wilcox, eds., *Women and Elective Office: Past, Present, and Future* (1998); Louise R. Noun, *Strong-Minded Women* (1969); Lynn Sherr, *Failure Is*

Impossible (1995); Linda Witt, Karen M. Paget, and Glenna Matthews, *Running as a Woman* (1994).

Dianne G. Bystrom
Iowa State University

Jane Byrne (b. 1934)

Jane Byrne made political history when she became the first woman mayor of Chicago. Margaret Jane Burke was born on May 24, 1934, in Chicago, Illinois. She received her Bachelor's degree from Barat College in 1955, and her teacher's certification from the University of Illinois in 1961. Byrne's start in politics came not long after the accidental death of her Marine pilot husband, Bill Byrne, in 1959. Married in 1956, they had a daughter, Katherine, born a year later.

In 1960, the prospect of an Irish Catholic president mobilized people in Byrne's social circle, and she volunteered for John Kennedy's presidential campaign of that year. Byrne managed to catch the attention of Chicago's powerful mayor, Richard Daley, who appointed Byrne to the Committee on Urban Opportunity in 1965, and later as Commissioner of the Department of Consumer Sales, Weights and Measures. In 1975, Daley made Byrne the cochairperson of the Democratic Central Committee.

In 1979, Byrne ran for mayor against Daley's machine-picked successor, Michael Bilandic. Serendipity intervened when the machine couldn't handle snow removal after a harsh storm, and Bilandic was blamed. Byrne's surprising primary win virtually guaranteed her the mayoralty in heavily Democratic Chicago. She received 82 percent of the vote against her Republican opponent.

During her four years as mayor (1979–1983), Lady Jane, as she was called, earned the reputation of being feisty and confrontational. Though she helped put the Windy City on the entertainment map by promoting ChicagoFest and the Chicago Jazz Festival and by welcoming the film industry, a survey of historians, social scientists, and journalists rated Byrne one of America's all-time, ten worst mayors. Her administration was plagued by high turnover, policy flip-flops, economic woes, and conflict with the black community.

Byrne's disregard for the black community came back to haunt her as she sought reelection in 1983. A coalition of black civic groups called POWER (People Organized for Welfare and Black Politics) helped register over 127 thousand voters during Byrne's term. POWER's candidate, Harold Washington, beat Byrne in the primary, 37 to 33 percent. In 1987 and 1991, Byrne tried unsuccessfully to reenter mayoral politics.

Since publication of her memoir, *My Chicago*, in 1992, she has devoted her time to family, friends, and her quarterly quotes on political affairs.

Sources and Further Reading: Jane Byrne, *My Chicago* (1992); Bill Granger and Lori Granger, *Fighting Jane* (1980); Melvin G. Holli, *The American Mayor* (1999).

Michelle Brophy-Baermann
University of Wisconsin–Stevens Point

Carrie Lane Chapman Catt (1859–1947)

Born in Ripon, Wisconsin, and raised in Charles City, Iowa, Carrie Lane Chapman Catt unceasingly manifested her family's progressive pioneer attitudes and their commitment to organization and self-reliance. Carrie Lane worked her way through Iowa State Agricultural College, graduating in 1880 with a B.S. in the General Science Course for Women. She served as principal and superintendent of schools in Mason City, Iowa, until her 1885 marriage to Leo Chapman.

Widowed in 1886, she supported herself primarily as a woman suffrage lecturer and columnist. She represented Iowa at the 1890 National American Woman Suffrage Association (NAWSA) convention. Later that year, she married George Catt, whose wealth gave Catt the lifelong financial independence necessary to pursue full-time political activism. The premier organizer of the later suffrage movement, Catt succeeded Susan B. Anthony as NAWSA president from 1900 to 1904, serving again from 1915 to 1920; she also organized the International Woman Suffrage Alliance in 1902. Catt's "Winning Plan," a campaign for both state and federal suffrage, was instrumental in achieving victory as she explained in *Woman Suffrage and Politics* (1923).

Catt founded the League of Women Voters in 1920, but spent most of the rest of her life devoted to peace activism such as aiding Jewish refugees, establishing the Conference on the Cause and Cure of War in 1925, and near the end of her life, supporting the creation of the United Nations. Catt moved from regional to national and international leadership in progressive causes through both articulate advocacy and strategic organizational planning.

Sources and Further Reading: Robert Booth Fowler, *Carrie Catt: Feminist Politician* (1986); Mary Gray Peck, *Carrie Chapman Catt: A Biography* (1944); Jacqueline VanVoris, *Carrie Chapman Catt: A Public Life* (1987).

E. Claire Jerry
MacMurray College, Illinois

Carrie Chapman Catt in her home. Wisconsin Historical Society, WHi-3359.

"Will It Play in Peoria?" Public Opinion in Regional and National Politics

The phrase "Will it play in Peoria" comes from the early vaudeville days when new shows often debuted in Peoria. Now it is used to ask "Will something be acceptable in middle America." Thus, behind the title of this essay is the implicit question: Does the political orientation of the Midwest differ from that of the nation as a whole?

The American public appears to have an image of the Midwest as a unitary political and cultural entity. Thoughts of rolling hills, flat plains, and family farms dominate that public image. Fostered by Grant Wood's somber portraits in his classic, *American Gothic*, midwestern farmers are thought of as people devoted to honest, hard toil, guardians of the land. In this image rural life is marked by simple virtues and egalitarian democratic ways. Farm life reflects the maintenance of tradition connecting the past with the future. The passing of the family farm from generation to generation adds a sense of continuity not found in the hectic, discontinuous life of the urban centers. Presumably from this timeless continuity arises a politics of prudence and deep-seated wisdom. Such sentiments breed a political outlook more conservative and isolationist than the nation as a whole.

Although some elements of this popular image of the Midwest have a basis in reality, much is fictitious or no longer true. Farmers certainly were more pre-

dominant in the region during the 1800s and early 1900s, but this is no longer the case. Farmers and farming may be more prominent in the Midwest than elsewhere in the United States, but they comprise only 5 percent of the workforce, only slightly more than in the country as a whole. In short, the reality is that the image of the Midwest as a monolithic agricultural society is one held mainly by those who live in regions other than the Midwest.

To understand the broader variation in public opinion and political attitudes of the region compared to the nation, one first needs to realize what the people who live in the Midwest are like demographically. Over the past two decades, population surveys of the nation and the Midwest reveal that the region had a slightly lower unemployment rate than the nation, and a somewhat larger percentage of both students and retired people. The Midwest also has fewer poor people and a larger number who can be considered middle class, and relative to the rest of the nation, it has a higher proportion of people with at least some college education. It is also more racially uniform than the rest of the nation with fewer African American, Asian, and Native American residents.

Contrary to the idea of the Midwest as a place of cultural traditionalism, the degree to which women remain home in the traditional housewife role is no greater in the Midwest than it is nationally. Similarly, the percentage of working women is virtually the same in the region and the nation. Also, whereas the Midwest is popularly considered to be more Protestant and less Catholic than the entire country, the difference is very minor and in the opposite direction. The Midwest, in fact, has a slightly lower proportion of Protestants than the nation and a higher proportion of Catholics, but the differences are negligible.

In short, midwesterners are similar to the rest of the nation in some regards, yet with respect to other characteristics, they are different. It is these similarities and differences that help us to understand the political orientation expressed by the people of the Midwest. For example, political participation, defined as the percentage of people voting in elections at all levels of government (local, state, and national) during the past three decades tends to be somewhat higher (usually by 5 to 10 percentage points) in the Midwest than in the rest of the country. This higher level of participation is understandable given that more of the population of the region has at least some higher education and is slightly older on average than in the rest of the country. Both education level and age are factors strongly related with higher rates of participation.

The Midwest is often thought to be a bastion of conservative political thought. Again this is a public image that grows out of the popular stereotype of the Midwest as a traditional agrarian society. Historically the region has witnessed some examples of visible political leaders who represent a conservative political ideology. The Taft family of Ohio is perhaps the best example of conservative political leaders from the Midwest. William Howard Taft from Cincinnati, Ohio, served as the twenty-seventh president of the United States from 1909 to 1913 and subsequently as chief justice of the Supreme Court. Taft's administration, however, alienated liberal Republicans by favoring high tariffs and by failing to carry out many of Theodore Roosevelt's conservation policies. In reaction, liberal Republicans formed the Progressive Party. In 1912, when the Republicans renominated Taft to run for President, Theodore Roosevelt joined the Progressives and ran in the election as a third-party candidate, thereby guaranteeing Woodrow Wilson's victory.

Three of Taft's descendants also had long and distinguished political careers. Robert A. Taft, son of William Howard Taft, served as the senator from Ohio from 1939 to 1953. Robert Taft was probably best known for his sponsorship of the Taft-Hartley Act, which was designed to create equity in the collective bargaining between labor and management, thereby curbing somewhat the importance and power of labor unions. William Howard Taft's grandson, Robert Taft, Jr., served in both the U.S. House and Senate, and his great-grandson, Bob Taft, was elected governor of Ohio in 1998. All reflected a conservative strain in American politics.

The Taft family provides a good example of Main Street conservative thinking in the Midwest, but conservative is not the only strain of political ideology evident in the region. Notable liberals can also be found in the Midwest, perhaps the most visible spokesperson for the liberal persuasion in recent history having been Hubert H. Humphrey, Jr., from Minnesota. Although he was born in South Dakota, Hubert Humphrey made Minnesota his adult home state. He was mayor of Minneapolis from 1945 to 1948, when he was elected to the U.S. Senate and served there until December 29, 1964, when he became vice president of the United States under President Lyndon Johnson. He was nominated in 1968 to run as the Democratic candidate against Republican Richard Nixon. The Democratic convention in Chicago was disrupted by anti–Vietnam War demonstrations, and Humphrey went on to be defeated by Nixon. After his unsuccessful presidential bid, his role in government continued when he was returned to the U.S. Senate by the people of Minnesota, where he served until his death in 1978.

Humphrey was very much a Franklin D. Roosevelt–style New Deal Democrat who believed in using the resources and power of the federal government to promote the welfare and well-being of the people. He was a champion of civil rights and the politics of equality of opportunity for minorities in the United States. He was, in many ways, the archetypical liberal Democrat. Clearly the Midwest reflects some variation in political orientations, as does the entire country.

Over the past three decades, however, trends in the political ideology among midwesterners reveal a rise in the percentage of conservatives and a decline in moderates and liberals. In the early 1970s, the percentages of liberals and conservatives were quite similar (33 percent conservative, 30 percent liberal, 37 percent moderate). By the end of the 1970s, however, the percentage of conservatives started to increase, while the percent of liberals declined. By 2000, conservatives represented the largest group with 37 percent, while moderates were at 34 percent, and liberals formed 29 percent of the Midwest population.

The trend in political orientation seen for the region during the past three decades mirrors changes taking place in the country as a whole. For the nation, however, liberals were slightly more prevalent than conservatives in the early 1970s, at 32 percent to conservatives' 29 percent. By 2000, conservatives had increased all across the country and constituted 35 percent of the public, while liberals constituted 28 percent. Moderates, on the other hand, continued to be the largest group for the country as a whole, at 37 percent in the early 1970s as well as in 2000. In general, the Midwest remains slightly more conservative than the nation as a whole, but with variations. Illinois, Minnesota, Michigan, and Wisconsin are among the more liberal states of the region, while the Dakotas, Indiana, Kansas, and Nebraska are among the most conservative, judged by how the people classify their personal political beliefs.

These broader ideological divisions, as well as the socioeconomic characteristics of the region, are also reflected in the policy preferences exhibited and voting choices of the region. When it comes to social issues, the conservative Republicans of the Midwest generally give great emphasis to moral and social issues such as abortion, gay rights, and women's rights. Since the 1970s, the United States has witnessed a slow evolution toward more acceptance of a woman's right to have an abortion. There has also been an increase in the acceptance of women's and gay rights in the country as a whole. This trend is also evident for the Midwest, but the Midwest has lagged slightly behind the rest of the country and remains a bit more traditional in its views of women's and gay rights. The Christian Coalition and other conservative religious groups have been fairly strong in parts of the Midwest. The strength of these groups helps account for the strong showings of presidential candidates Evangelical minister Pat Robertson in the 1988 Iowa Republican caucuses and Patrick Buchanan in the 1992 caucuses. Both stressed family values, antiabortion, and antigay themes in their campaigns.

When the issue focus shifts to domestic and foreign policy, the Midwest is again similar to the rest of the nation in some respects, yet different in others. Like the rest of the country, midwesterners were aware of the growth in economic prosperity for the country as a whole under both Presidents Ronald Reagan and Bill Clinton. Yet at the same time, they were less likely to feel that they were personally benefiting from that increased economic prosperity. The Midwest was also among the first regions of the country to be concerned about the federal budget deficit that occurred under President Ronald Reagan. This concern, expressed particularly among the more rural states of the region, helps account for the slightly higher vote that Ross Perot, the Reform Party candidate, received in the Midwest relative to the rest of the country in the 1992 presidential election.

When it comes to foreign policy, the Midwest is often considered more isolationist and less international in its orientation. Landlocked in the middle of the country, it is reasonable to assume that midwesterners are less interested in other countries than are those who live on the coasts or along the borders of the United States. Yet public opinion evidence over the years has demonstrated that, in fact, midwesterners are slightly less likely than the rest of the country to say that "the U.S. would have fewer problems if we just stayed home and did not concern ourselves with problems in other parts of the world."

The Midwest does not fit the old stereotype of a traditional agrarian society. On the contrary, at the start of the twenty-first century, the region was diverse and varied just like the rest of the country. Nonetheless, the Midwest is distinctive politically in certain regards. While the region has become more Democratic than in the 1950s, it remains almost evenly divided between Democrats and Republicans and is marked by a slightly higher percentage of conservatives than the rest of the country. In short, the region reflects both liberal and conservative elements as exemplified by the lives of the Tafts from Ohio and Hubert Humphrey from Minnesota.

Sources and Further Reading: Douglas Madsen, Arthur H. Miller, and James A. Stimson, eds., *American Politics in the Heartland* (1990); Ishbel Ross, *An American Family: The Tafts, 1678–1964* (1964); Timothy N. Thurber, *The Politics of Equality: Hubert H. Humphrey and the African American Freedom Struggle* (1999).

Arthur H. Miller
University of Iowa

Hubert Horatio Humphrey (1911–1978) and Liberalism in the Midwest

It would be difficult to find a more ardent apostle of post–World War II liberalism than Democratic Senator and Vice President Hubert H. Humphrey of Minnesota. An active proponent of civil rights, labor, and the Great Society, Humphrey dedicated his life to fostering a responsive welfare state and a liberal, issues-based Democratic Party. Later castigated as "big government" by Ronald Reagan, postwar liberalism promoted the idea of a benevolent, reformist state. Eventually housed in the Democratic Party, it held that politics were, or ought to be, national in scope and programmatic in ends. Thus, postwar liberalism rejected the historic regionalism of American politics. And yet, it is also true that midwesterners like Hubert Humphrey, Walter Mondale, and Eugene McCarthy were unusually involved in developing the national politics on which postwar liberalism rested.

Born in a South Dakota farming community where his father was the local druggist, Hubert Humphrey was reared in the shadow of midwestern populism. His father's heroes were Ignatius Donnelly and William Jennings Bryan. Humphrey saw himself as heir to the great agrarian movements: the Grange, the Greenbackers, the Non-Partisan League, and the Farmer-Labor Party. Most observers saw him as rooted in

Senator Hubert Humphrey at the 1948 Democratic National Convention. Photo by International News Photo. Courtesy Minnesota Historical Society. MHS Locator no. por/4185/p66, neg. no. 83939.

Minnesota's Farmer-Labor Party. As Humphrey knew, however, such third-party movements were regional phenomena, whereas the New Deal progressivism he espoused was necessarily national.

If Humphrey's populist sympathies came from the South Dakota plains, his political knowledge came from the University of Minnesota, which he attended in the 1930s. His political science professors were advocates of the New Deal's pragmatic, programmatic approach. They taught the young Humphrey that populist concerns about economic justice could be addressed through a strong federal government. While they admired the old agrarian movements, they also believed such movements were the result of decentralized, laissez-faire government, which was, hopefully, a thing of the past. In the future, they believed, two centralized, issues-based parties would organize the demands of various interest groups.

Their ideas made sense to Humphrey, who took the New Deal crusade into politics. In 1943, he ran for

mayor of Minneapolis. His surprising second-place finish, energetic style, and support for labor got him noticed by Farmer-Laborites, Democrats, and Republicans alike. Humphrey's burgeoning career was jeopardized, however, by Minnesota's Farmer-Labor Party. Although riven by factionalism and Communists, the Farmer-Labor Party was still the main rival to the Republican party. Minnesota Democrats were ineffectual and marginal.

Humphrey believed that the Democratic Party was the only viable political vehicle for maintaining the New Deal. This assumption was belied by the national Democratic Party, a loose coalition of white southerners and urban machine bosses. Its ends were not a set of issues, but rather patronage and power. New Dealers hoped that organized labor's entrance into the Democratic Party after 1933 would make the party more liberal and responsive to working peoples' concerns. In Minnesota, however, organized labor supported the Farmer-Labor Party, and thus had no liberalizing impact on Minnesota's Democratic Party. The Farmer-Labor Party's continued existence kept state Democrats marginalized and split the non-Republican vote. In 1944, with Roosevelt seeking an unprecedented fourth term, New Dealers in Minnesota sought a merger.

Humphrey helped negotiate the merger between the Farmer-Labor Party and the Democrats, which created the Democratic-Farmer-Labor (DFL) Party in April 1944. With his homegrown sympathy for the old third parties, he understood the sacrifice he was asking Farmer-Laborites to make. But he also knew that their aspirations would come to naught unless they conformed to the realities of America's two-party political system. Humphrey promised that a liberal, centralized Democratic Party could fulfill old Farmer-Labor ideals for more Americans more efficiently than the old region-specific Farmer-Labor Party. He spent his career trying to keep that promise.

Humphrey's dedication to civil rights and economic opportunity for all Americans should be seen as part of his attempt to liberalize the national Democratic Party. As Minneapolis mayor (1945–1948), he set up a municipal Fair Employment Practices Committee (FEPC), prohibiting racial and religious employment discrimination. As U.S. Senator (1949–1965, 1971–1978), he worked for antidiscrimination and full employment legislation. He maneuvered the 1964 Civil Rights Act through the Senate. Humphrey sincerely believed in civil rights, but the issue was also central in his battle to create a liberal, centralized Democratic Party. This aim was impeded by the preferences of white southerners, many of whom believed in white supremacy and states' rights, and obstructed efforts to strengthen the federal government. Southern voting restrictions gave white southerners disproportionate power in Congress, as well as in the Democratic Party.

After World War II, liberals such as Humphrey finally confronted southern Democrats, mainly to prevent Wallace progressives from splitting the party. In 1948, Henry Wallace's Progressive Party challenged Truman's cold war policies and laxness on civil rights. To thwart this challenge, Humphrey led liberal Democrats in securing a civil rights platform plank at the 1948 convention, thus proving that Democrats were not hostage to southerners. His speech electrified the convention. Southern Democrats bolted the party, while erstwhile Wallace supporters and black voters stayed. To solidify the ascendance of liberalism in the Democratic Party, Humphrey proposed a series of political reforms. Although unsuccessful in the 1950s, his proposals laid the groundwork for reforms that finally occurred between 1968 and 1972, in part with the guidance of another Minnesota liberal, Donald Fraser.

Humphrey achieved his greatest successes in the Senate. As Lyndon Johnson's vice president, he was politically marginalized. Domestic unrest and his support for the Vietnam War marred his 1968 presidential campaign. When he returned to the Senate in 1971, he continued his work for economic and racial justice.

Postwar liberalism was later criticized for its top-down, administrative view of politics and its purported neglect of the white working class. These shortcomings, critics claimed, alienated the so-called heartland voters. Hubert Humphrey, however, was one "egghead" liberal who appealed to rural, small-town voters as well as urbane city dwellers, to white workers as well as to African Americans. Born in Wallace, South Dakota on May 27, 1911, he married Muriel Fay Buck on September 3, 1936. Their son, Hubert Horatio "Skip" Humphrey III, has carried on his family tradition of involvement in public life.

Sources and Further Reading: American Political Science Association, *Toward a More Responsible Two-Party System* (1950); Jennifer Delton, *Making Minnesota Liberal* (2002); John Earl Haynes, *Dubious Alliance* (1984); Sidney Milkis, *The President and the Parties* (1993); Timothy Thurber, *The Politics of Equality* (1999).

Jennifer A. Delton
Skidmore College, New York

Robert Alphonso Taft (1889–1953) and Main Street Conservatism

It is standard fare for scholars writing about the political career of Robert A. Taft to emphasize that his staunch conservatism was intricately related to his

Robert Taft. Ohio Historical Society, SC4262 AL01078.

midwestern roots. Detailed analysis of his three hard-fought but successful elections for the United States Senate indicates that the core of his support rested along the Main Streets of small-town Ohio, and that his always strong opposition relied upon strength in the industrial cities. Further, the devastating defeats that Taft suffered during his three quests for the Republican presidential nomination were attributed by his supporters, and himself, as resulting from an inherent conflict between Taft and the forces of the urban "Eastern establishment."

Taft's political instincts, of course, were deeply rooted in his native Ohio, and his political life was often explained as such by journalists and scholars. Yet the same Midwest of his time also produced many a fiery labor union leader, New Deal liberal, and staunch internationalist. Just as the Midwest spawned such conservatives and isolationists as Taft, John Bricker, Robert McCormick, William Jenner, and Everett Dirksen, it also was home to Robert La Follette, Eugene Debs, John L. Lewis, Walter Reuther, Clarence Darrow, and Harry S Truman.

Thus to equate Taft's conservatism with his midwestern origins and his embrace of the values of the small towns of Ohio oversimplifies a much more complex story. Such a stereotype also ignores other influences that helped shape his political views. The substantial body of Taft historiography points to his family's lofty social position, the great influence his father had upon his thinking, his reserved and sometimes aloof nature, his lack of intellectual curiosity, and a pervasive unwillingness to embrace—or even consider—new ideas. Although he graduated from preparatory school, college, and law school at the head of his classes, he was not an innovative thinker. "Very bright but . . . too practical a mind," a disappointed Harvard philosophy professor once perceptively concluded.

Taft was born to lead. His grandfather Alphonzo served in the cabinet of Ulysses S. Grant, and his father William Howard lived an exemplary life of public service that was capped by a term as president and nine years as chief justice of the U.S. Supreme Court. Biographer James Patterson convincingly demonstrates that Taft, "Mr. Republican," was fundamentally influenced in his political thinking by his father. By the time he had graduated from Yale University (Class of 1910) and Harvard Law School (1913), Taft's political outlook had coalesced, and it would not change in any fundamental way throughout his lifetime. His education apparently did little to influence innovative thinking; he was aptly described by a fellow law student as "so firm in his convictions that it made him somewhat adamant and autocratic."

Those essential views he held in 1913 did not change over the next forty years. Like his father, he viewed labor unions as threats to the nation's economic health, was fearful of the powers of monopolies, and viewed Wall Street with deep skepticism. Although he was open to modest government programs to advance the needs of society's less fortunate (witness his support for a modest public housing program in the late 1940s), he remained deeply fearful of the tyranny that could result from an overly zealous government, and saw only threats to individual freedom from large government bureaucracies. A champion of individual rights, he took solace in the Constitution's separation of powers and enthusiastically championed states' rights as a means of protecting citizens from a potentially oppressive federal government.

The views he expressed in the United States Senate from 1939 until 1953, of course, were widely popular along the Main Streets of the Midwest; not surprisingly, they seldom gained traction in the industrial cities of the same region. It was in the towns and villages, along with the white collar suburbs, that Taft's views most clearly resonated. His unrelenting hostility to the New Deal, his deep fear of the implications of aiding Great Britain in its fight for survival against Adolph Hitler's forces, his sponsorship of far-reaching legislation to curb the powers of organized labor in 1947, and his deep reservations about the internationalist thrust of the foreign policy of Harry S Truman (he grudgingly supported the Truman Doctrine and the Marshall Plan, but voted against membership in NATO) were logical extensions of the view of the world he formed in his college days. At times his fierce partisanship led him onto questionable grounds, as when he joined forces with the China Lobby to flail the Truman Administration over the fall of Nationalist China, sought partisan advantage when the war in Korea turned sour in 1951, or when he cavalierly advised Joseph McCarthy that if one charge of communist influence did not stick, "bring up another."

In 1953, Taft found that he had much in common with the new Republican president, Dwight D. Eisenhower, himself the product of a small Kansas town. But this relationship, which was fast producing a new friendship and commonality of goals, ended with Taft's sudden death of cancer on July 31 of that year. Although Taft has frequently been dismissed as being hopelessly out of touch with his tumultuous times that were dominated by the great depression, the New Deal, a World War, and the standoff with the Soviet Union, he steadfastly remained true to his beliefs. Denounced by his many contemporaries as having "the best mind in the Senate—until he makes it up," more recently scholars have taken a more tolerant view of his career, noting that his domestic policies anticipated the resurgence of Republican conservatism under Barry Goldwater and Ronald Reagan, and that his fears about international buccaneering anticipated the disaster of Vietnam.

This serious and driven man from Cincinnati served his country well by holding fast to his principles even when doing so contributed significantly to defeat at three presidential nominating conventions. Although himself the resident of the upscale Cincinnati suburb of Indian Hills, Taft gave expression to the heartfelt sentiments that were widely shared along the Main Streets of his beloved Midwest. Born in Cincinnati on September 8, 1889, he married the former Martha Wheating Bamars in 1914. They had two sons, Robert Taft, Jr., who served as a U.S. senator, and William H. Taft III, who served as U.S. ambassador to Ireland. His grandson, Bob Taft, was elected to his second term as governor of Ohio in 2002.

Sources and Further Reading: Richard O. Davies, *Defender of the Old Guard* (1993); Lee Edwards, *The Conservative Revolution* (1999); Norman Graebner, *The New Isolationism* (1956); Alonzo Hamby, *Liberalism and Its Challengers*, 2nd ed. (1992); Russell Kirk and James McClellan, *The Political Principles of Robert A. Taft* (1967); James Patterson, *Mr. Republican* (1972); David Reinhard, *The Republican Right Since 1945* (1983); William S. White, *The Taft Story* (1954).

Richard O. Davies
University of Nevada–Reno

Phyllis Schlafly (b. 1924) and the Basis of Family Values

Phyllis Schlafly, "sweetheart of the silent majority," as biographer Carol Felsenthal aptly described her, is an interesting if not ironic representative of the important role of women in midwestern politics. Best known for almost single-handedly defeating ratification of the Equal Rights Amendment (ERA) in the 1970s, Schlafly served at the forefront of what became the pro-family movement. That her family values message found fertile soil throughout the Midwest is not surprising given the region's moralistic political subculture. Nonetheless, Schlafly remains for many a contradiction.

Born Phyllis McAlpin Stewart in 1924—a year after an ERA was first introduced in Congress—Schlafly grew up in Depression-era St. Louis. This setting clearly colored her outlook and instilled in Schlafly a sense of survival as well as a strong work ethic. Her primary and secondary education at City House, an all-girls Sacred Heart school, where the values of an old-line Catholic family were taught and reinforced, also influenced Schlafly's development. In 1944, she received her B.A. after three years at Washington University; a year later she obtained a Masters degree in Political Science from Radcliffe College. Slightly more than three decades later, Schlafly tackled law school, receiving her JD from Washington University. She married attorney Fred Schlafly, fifteen years her senior, in 1949. They had six children.

In 1964, Schlafly self-published a succinct treatise entitled *A Choice Not An Echo*. This history of GOP presidential conventions served a twofold purpose: to show how eastern establishment internationalists—so-called Rockefeller Republicans or, according to Schlafly, "kingmakers"—manipulated the nominating process of the Republican Party and, as importantly, to promote the candidacy of Barry Goldwater. In the wake of its astounding reception, her book sold over three million copies, Schlafly gained instant national name recognition. Taking full advantage of her celebrity status, she began publishing a monthly newsletter in 1967, *The Phyllis Schlafly Report*.

A column Schlafly penned in 1972 on "What's Wrong with the ERA?" drew an unprecedented response from readers and proved the impetus behind launching the National Committee to Stop ERA. By this time, the ERA had already easily passed both houses of Congress, gained the unqualified support of President Richard Nixon, and had been integrated into the platforms of both the Republican and Democratic Parties. In order to become part of the Constitution, however, the ERA required ratification by three-fourths of state legislatures. In other words,

within seven years thirty-eight states needed to approve this proposed amendment. After only one year, thirty had done so. Over the next six years, though five additional states endorsed the ERA, an equal number rescinded their earlier consent.

What happened? Simply put, Schlafly derailed lobbying efforts spearheaded by the National Organization for Women and other advocacy organizations. While the amendment appeared simple and straightforward—"Section 1. Equality of rights under the law shall not be denied or abridged by the United States or by any state on account of sex. Section 2. The Congress shall have the power to enforce, by appropriate legislation, the provisions of this article,"—Schlafly thought it deceptive. Among other things, she argued men and women are not equal in all ways. Claiming the ERA would paper over traditional differences between the sexes, Schlafly feared it would drive homemakers out of the home (that radical feminists scarcely hid their disdain for housewives only assisted her efforts). Moreover, she maintained the ERA would open a Pandora's box of unisex restrooms, female combat soldiers, and gay marriages, to name but a few concerns. These allegations appeared questionable, but they drove home Schlafly's chief charge: the ERA meant things were going to change in possibly radical and unpredictable ways.

Having achieved its goal by the early 1980s, Schlafly's Stop ERA organization gave way to Eagle Forum, with a national membership in excess of eighty thousand and its more broadly based agenda. A conservative, pro-family group that remains active at the beginning of the twenty-first century, the forum defines family values to include issues other than the customary opposition to abortion or homosexual rights or federal funding of the arts. The group has diversified its focus to the extent that recent legislative efforts have targeted patent reform, computer encryption, as well as fast-track trade authority. This unusual mix directly reflects Schlafly's own interests as well as her belief that these issues affect the family. It also underscores the fact that, for many political and religious leaders alike, family values, however delineated, are a defining issue in American politics. Much of this results from the fact that, as James Hunter argues, the family occupies important symbolic territory. It serves in many ways as "the most conspicuous field of conflict in the contemporary culture war."

Phyllis Schlafly, as Felsenthal contends, stands as both a heroine of the right and a traitor to her gender. While insistent that she is, and always has been, first and foremost a wife and mother, this symbol of the traditional woman is in the estimation of her feminist opponents ironically liberated. For them, Schlafly's vehement opposition to the ERA and her general aversion to the women's liberation movement seems strangely juxtaposed to a remarkable lifetime of achievement outside the home. In response, Schlafly sees no such contradiction in these accomplishments, only conviction and commitment.

Sources and Further Reading: Daniel J. Elazar, *American Federalism: A View from the States*, 3rd ed. (1984); Daniel J. Elazar, *The American Mosaic* (1994); Carol Felsenthal, *The Sweetheart of the Silent Majority* (1981); James Davison Hunter, *Culture Wars: The Struggle to Define America* (1991); Louis Jacobson, "Squawk! The Eagle Forum, Most Noted for Sinking Its Talons into 'Pro-Family' Issues, Is Swooping Down on a Variety of Fronts," *National Journal* 29 (Oct. 1997); Phyllis Schlafly, *A Choice Not an Echo*, 3rd ed. (1964); Phyllis Schlafly, *The Power of the Positive Woman* (1977).

Jeffrey A. VanDerWerff
Northwestern College, Iowa

George Horace Gallup (1901–1984)

Born in Jefferson, Iowa, in 1901, George H. Gallup earned a PhD in 1928 from the University of Iowa. As student newspaper editor, he became interested in how readers responded to newspaper stories. This led to his first survey of readers of the Des Moines *Register* to learn what they liked to read. He found that comics, pictures, and feature stories were preferred over the front page stories generally believed most popular. Following college, Gallup taught at several universities while running reader surveys for newspapers and magazines. His work caught the attention of the advertising agency Young & Rubicam, which in 1932, invited Gallup to New York.

In 1935, Gallup founded the American Institute of Public Opinion, which focused on studying American's social and political attitudes. His first election poll, conducted in 1936, correctly predicted an easy reelection for Roosevelt, despite a *Literary Digest* survey of over 2.3 million predicting a Landon victory. Gallup attributed his accuracy to interviewing the "man on the street" to learn what the "average voter" thought, although he actually employed scientifically-based random sampling procedures, something the *Literary Digest* failed to do. Gallup's reputation grew, and the Gallup Poll began investigating nearly every aspect of American life. His famous failure in 1948 was the prediction that the Republican candidate Thomas Dewey would defeat President Harry S Truman. Truman won; Gallup said the embarrassment taught him to keep polling up until Election Day, something he did not do in 1948. Over time, Gallup's name became synonymous around the world with public opinion polling. Gallup married Ophelia Smith Miller of Washington, Iowa, in 1925 and they had three children. The family moved to Princeton, New Jersey, in 1935 where Gallup lived until his death of a heart attack in 1984.

Sources and Further Reading: Steven H. Chaffee, "George Gallup and Ralph Nafziger: Pioneers of Audience Research," *Mass Communication and Society* 3 (Spring/Summer 2000); "Dr. Gallup's Finger on America's Pulse," *The Economist* (Sept. 27, 1997); George H. Gallup and Saul Forbes Rae, *The Pulse of Democracy* (1940).

David Redlawsk
University of Iowa

Robert Rutherford McCormick (1880–1955)

Born in Chicago, Robert Rutherford McCormick was the son of Robert and Katherine McCormick, whose marriage was a confluence of the industrial fortune derived from the McCormick reaper, which mechanized agriculture, and the Medill newspaper line that was long associated with the *Chicago Tribune*. He graduated from Yale University in 1903, and earned a law degree from Northwestern University in 1908. In 1911, McCormick was elected president of the Tribune Company, and he and cousin Joseph Medill Patterson rebuilt the *Tribune* into the city's leading newspaper. He took breaks for National Guard service on the Mexican border in 1916 and in France in 1917 and 1918, and was subsequently promoted to colonel in 1919. Around the *Tribune* he thereafter enjoyed being known as "the Colonel."

McCormick's stamp was clear on the *Tribune's* editorial page, which was nationalistic and isolationist. McCormick had a particular dislike of the British, as reflected in the newspaper's fervent opposition to U.S. assistance to Britain against Germany, which continued almost up to U.S. entry into World War II. In politics the *Tribune* editorial page was firmly Republican under McCormick. In the 1930s, it was a leading critic of President Franklin Roosevelt, a Democrat, and his New Deal reforms. In 1952, however, the *Tribune* declined to endorse war hero Dwight Eisenhower, the Republican presidential candidate, given the editorial judgment that he was not conservative enough.

McCormick was firm that the press should be free of government restraint. In this libertarian spirit, he bankrolled the appeal of *Near v. Minnesota*, which led to the 1931 U.S. Supreme Court landmark opinion against prior restraint. In 1947, when the Hutchins Commission on a Free and Responsible Press cited press excesses and called for social responsibility, Mc-

Cormick perceived a threat to freedom of the press. He crusaded to discredit the commission and assigned a *Tribune* reporter to write a book to counter the Hutchins recommendations.

McCormick's strong views were sometimes quirky. In 1934, he launched a Page One crusade for spelling reform. Henceforth, the *Tribune* used such phonetic oddities as *thru, thoro, frate, burocrat, jaz,* and *iland.* Although reform spellings never caught on beyond the *Tribune,* the newspaper didn't abandon them until 1975. Under McCormick, the *Tribune* grew into the leading Midwest newspaper with home delivery in several adjoining states. The Tribune Company included radio station WGN, whose signal reached the entire Midwest and which carried McCormick commentaries.

Sources and Further Reading: Joseph Gies, *The Colonel of Chicago* (1979); Philip Kinsley, *The Chicago Tribune,* 5 vols. (1943–1946); Richard Norton Smith, *The Colonel: The Life and Legend of Robert R. McCormick, 1880–1955* (1997); Frank C. Waldrop, *McCormick of Chicago* (1966).

John Vivian
Winona State University, Minnesota

William Allen White (1868–1944)

Born in Emporia, Kansas, William Allen White was the son of Dr. Allen and Mary Ann Hatton White. White's editorials and short stories reflected his midwestern values, and many outside the region looked to his work as a reflection of what the Midwest was thinking.

In 1869, his parents moved to El Dorado, Kansas, and his father eventually served as its mayor. In 1890, White left college to become the assistant editor of the *El Dorado Republican.* He married Kansas City schoolteacher Sallie Lindsay in 1893. After stints with newspapers in Kansas City, he returned to Emporia in 1895, purchased the *Emporia Gazette,* and served as its editor until his death in 1944. His 1896 article "What's the Matter with Kansas?" brought him to national prominence, and many of his editorials and short stories were redistributed by other newspapers and national magazines including *McClure's, Collier's,* and the *Saturday Evening Post.*

Following in his father's footsteps, White was also active in local, state, and national politics. The editor first met his lifelong hero, Theodore Roosevelt, in 1897, and helped him found the Progressive Party in 1912. In 1924, White ran against party gubernatorial candidates representing the Ku Klux Klan. As World War I approached, White chaired the Committee to Defend America by Aiding the Allies. White wrote a Pulitzer Prize–winning editorial in 1922 in defense of freedom of speech and won another Pulitzer Prize for his posthumously published autobiography in 1947.

Sources and Further Reading: Sally Foreman Griffith, *The Autobiography of William Allen White,* 2nd ed. (1990); Sally Foreman Griffith, *Home Town News* (1989); E. Jay Jernigan, *William Allen White* (1983).

Kelly A. Woestman
Pittsburg State University, Kansas

Political Thought and Action

Political thought in the Midwest comprises a dialogue between republicanism and classic liberalism. In practice this has been a debate between the claims of civic virtue and fears of corruption on the one hand and, on the other, a search for ways in which the free enterprise system could be made more efficient and generate faster economic growth.

The pioneers from 1800 to the 1850s debated civic virtue and strongly opposed aristocracy. Midwesterners were proud of their republicanism, which they expressed in terms of expansion of the right to vote and to hold office. As restrictions loosened and parties became efficiently organized, turnout soared; men expressed their devotion to republicanism through voting, discussions, and eager expression of party loyalty. Democratic Party leaders Stephen Douglas of Illinois and Lewis Cass of Michigan projected the midwestern ethic to the territories further west, calling for a popular sovereignty that would trump all other issues (including slavery). Philosophically, the Democrats were classical and rules-oriented: They believed moral standards were eternal and that the Bible endorsed slavery. Abolitionists in the Yankee and Quaker communities, energized by the Romantic spirit, retorted that the force of Progress meant that new moral standards could and should emerge. They argued that slavery was a corruption of republican values and could never be validated by the old rules (the Constitution). Many voters bought the free soil argument that slavery in the Midwest would lead to an aristocracy of rich landlords who would dominate politics and squeeze the little man off the best lands.

On the whole the Democratic Party was most vigorous in promoting equalitarian civic virtue and widespread sharing of offices, whereas the Whigs argued it was more efficient to place the most talented men in office—such as judgeships—by appointment rather than popular elections. With widespread property ownership, the Midwest supported an ethos of civic virtue grounded in equal rights for all who were citizens. Midwestern historians, especially Frederick Jackson Turner, not only took pride in the region's democracy, but argued that the midwestern frontier had been a powerful force for social evolution because it sloughed off outmoded European aristocratic forms and molded something new, the true American character.

Economic liberalism took the shape of federal and state promotion of internal improvements (ports, canals, roads, and railroads) and banks. Whigs enthusiastically supported it and gained the support of most entrepreneurs. The Democrats, appealing to subsistence farmers least involved in the market economy, repeatedly warned against the dangers of an aristocracy of wealth. Being practical, middle-of-the-roaders, midwesterners elected Democrats and adopted Whig economic policies.

The Midwest was fertile soil for the new Republican Party from its founding in the mid-1850s, providing a leader who not only saved the Union and abolished slavery, but redefined the American credo of republicanism. "Free Soil, Free Labor, and Free Speech" was the credo of the new party, with "free labor" soon to be expanded into "free enterprise." The "slave power" was so corrupt it could never permanently coexist with republicanism, Abraham Lincoln argued: "A house divided against itself can not stand." The attack on Fort Sumter led to a rally behind the flag in 1861 and a permanent commitment to patriotism. A significant minority of Democrats, however, strongest in the lower Midwest and led by Rep. Clement Vallandigham of Ohio, took up the Copperhead refrain that Lincoln was an unrepublican dictator whose corrupt administration was a greater evil than secession. They were bested by superior political organization in a series of hard-fought elections, augmented by some federal arrests and prosecution of potential subversives. Upon his martyrdom, Republicans enshrined Lincoln, who came to replace Washington as the model of the true republican citizen, the man of common sense and enduring vision who sprang from humble roots with no aristocratic pretenses.

During Reconstruction the midwestern Republicans developed a middle-of-the-road policy somewhat softer than the radicalism in fashion back East. They promoted the Fourteenth Amendment to encapsulate their new sense of federal responsibility for the protection of liberty. Democrats warned that "liberty" too often meant undeserved political and economic power for banks, railroads, and (after 1880) trusts and monopolies. The region's Republican leaders responded to the free enterprise credo by promoting a strong finan-

cial system and high tariffs for manufacturing, and at the same time creating a federal antitrust policy designed to prevent the corruption of the economic system. Democrats argued monopoly was inherently corrupt; Republicans just said it was inefficient by limiting entrepreneurial opportunity. When public opinion turned against big business around 1906, Theodore Roosevelt and William Howard Taft (of Ohio) responded with a vigorous antitrust program that kept the GOP united. The labor strife of the late nineteenth century led to another compromise, featuring a system of cooperation between management and labor through the National Civic Federation sponsored by Ohio senator Mark Hanna and coal miners' union leader John Mitchell of Illinois. After 1910, it was replaced by the unilateral creation of welfare capitalism by the railroads and industrial corporations.

The money issue pitted Democrats who warned against rich bankers against Republicans who argued that a fast-growing economy needed an efficient money supply run by expert bankers. The crisis came in 1896, when Nebraska's William Jennings Bryan promised that free silver would destroy the evil money-changers, purge the economic system, and restore pristine republicanism. He was on the verge of sweeping the region until the McKinley-Hanna counter-crusade succeeded in identifying Bryan with anarchism and fanaticism, and promised that the combination of gold ("Sound Money") and high tariffs would guarantee prosperity for everyone. The Midwest decisively voted for McKinley and gold.

The fears of corrupt urban machines that agitated the Eastern Mugwumps and Southern Redeemers did not greatly trouble the midwesterners, save in Wisconsin. There Robert La Follette built a Republican faction—almost a machine—on the corruption issue. On the tariff, the Democrats rallied to President Grover Cleveland's warning that unnecessary taxation is inherently corrupt and that high tariffs were thus morally wrong. Republicans in the industrial Midwest strongly supported McKinley's counter-argument that tariffs promoted economic growth and efficiency, and were not corrupt because they were essential to protect the American standards of high wages and high profits. Once the realignment of 1896 guaranteed GOP dominance, disagreements about political philosophy surfaced. Republicans from farm states, led by Albert Cummins of Iowa, argued that high tariffs caused monopolies to flourish and raised prices unjustly.

An unexpected crisis struck the GOP in 1910, when Theodore Roosevelt started attacking the judiciary as corrupt because judges catered to corporations; he demanded popular referenda that would overturn state supreme court decisions. President Taft rallied the conservatives with the argument that the judicial system was a highly efficient process in which experts in fairness made the final decisions, not politicians who could bamboozle the public over abstruse legal issues. Taft lost reelection in 1912 but won the issue by permanently discrediting referenda on judicial decisions, and indeed by promoting the notion that the Supreme Court should be the final arbiter of all issues of fairness and efficiency.

The Progressive Era was characterized by a widespread faith that any social, economic, and political problem could be solved if experts analyzed it dispassionately; they would always find the one best solution. After 1900, therefore, the distinctive midwestern contribution to political thought came primarily from its intellectuals. Each state built strong public universities, designed to promote civic virtue and enhance efficiency. In Wisconsin, the La Follette progressives found leadership in Charles McCarthy at the Legislative Reference Bureau and among experts at the University of Wisconsin. The combination created the Wisconsin Idea, an intellectual base for new models of governmental service and regulation, but in 1914, the reaction set in, in the form of tax revolts that claimed that taxation and bureaucracy were both forms of corruption and needed to be strenuously resisted. In Chicago and later Michigan, schools of political science emerged that largely dominated all academic political science for a period from 1920 until after mid-century. Chicago echoed the realism of the streets, as exemplified by Jane Addams, John Dewey, Arthur Bentley, and Charles Merriam, who called the city "the jungle of human nature." They emphasized the use of the public school system as a tool to educate all citizens, helping them reach a higher stage of self-realization. Schools equaled efficiency, and ignorance became the worst form of corruption. Merriam created a powerful school of political science that stressed empirical research at the grass roots, with special attention to the psychological dimensions of politics and federal planning as the most efficient solution to all problems. He himself was active in Chicago. Chicago's public administration program, led by Leonard White, sent numerous students to Washington.

Bentley, who spent fourteen years as a Chicago newspaper reporter before retiring to a farm in Indiana, argued in *The Process of Government* (1908) that moral issues (of the republican variety) were irrelevant "mind stuff" because politics was really just an amoral jungle in which the savage players were groups, not individuals. But individualism was not dead. Starting in the mid-1940s, an interdisciplinary team of behavioral scientists, Angus Campbell, Philip Converse, Donald Stokes, and Warren Miller, made the University of Michigan and its Inter-University Consortium for Po-

litical and Social Research the center for quantitative behavioral political science. In *The American Voter* (1960), they downplayed the role of groups and showed how to use sophisticated public opinion polls to provide a psychological explanation of the behavior of individual voters. The postmodern inward-looking ethos that downplayed groups and stressed individualism made their gospel attractive.

The "Chicago School" emerged in the postwar years from intense discussions among University of Chicago economists Milton Friedman, George Stigler, Aaron Director, Ronald Coase, and Gary Becker and their many students, with a bit of input from Friedrich Hayek. The school explicitly rooted itself in neoclassical economic theory, assuming that identical economic laws apply to all people at all points in history (leaving no room for evolving norms). With the fervor of biblical prophets, proponents of the Chicago School proclaimed that efficiency consists in comporting with these eternal laws; corruption consists in trying to circumvent them. They denied the Marxian and Keynesian arguments that capitalism was inherently unstable and rejected the Progressive notion that the government could efficiently regulate the economy. Government was inherently inefficient because unintended consequences always sabotaged the best intentions. Regulation of industry failed, Stigler argued, because the regulatees sooner or later took control of the process for their own special interest, rather than the common good.

The Chicago School of political economy inspired the Law and Economics movement in jurisprudence led by Coase and Richard Posner. Antitrust policies, Posner argued, were generally inefficient and unnecessary. By redefining "free enterprise" in terms of maximizing benefits to the consumer, by denying that ruthless competition was itself corrupt, and by showing monopolies often lowered prices to the consumer, Chicago repudiated the antitrust consensus that had emerged in political thought a century before. Friedman showed that the Federal Reserve was guilty of turning a minor recession into the Great Depression. He concluded that the competitive economy generated "natural" rates of unemployment and output that could not be improved upon by government action. Across the country conservatives listened closely to his argument that government bureaucracies, including public schools, were inherently self-centered and thus corrupt. Once government became active, private interests would lobby to obtain favors—a form of rent seeking the Chicago School proponents damned as both inefficient and corrupt. The Law and Economics movement argued that well-defined property rights, supervised by judges following traditional rules of common law, produced the fairest and most efficient economic system. Posner and Becker, making the basic assumption that everyone is a rational maximizer of goals, extended the reach of economic theory into wholly unexpected legal and social domains.

The Chicago School could claim major credit for undercutting what as recently as 1970 had been a national consensus behind liberal Keynesianism. Their ideas led directly to ending the military draft in 1973 and to deregulation of banking, transportation, and communications in the 1970s and 1980s, and they provided intellectual underpinning for conservative demands after 1994 that welfare be replaced and taxes and spending be reduced sharply.

Sources and Further Reading: Ray Billington, *America's Frontier Heritage* (1966); Jean Converse, *Survey Research in the U.S.: Roots & Emergence, 1890–1960* (1987); Clyde H. Coombs, "Angus Campbell," *National Academy of Sciences, Biographical Memoirs* 56 (1987); Milton Friedman and Rose Friedman, *Two Lucky People* (1998); Richard Jensen, *Illinois: A History* (2001); Barry Karl, *Charles E. Merriam and the Study of Politics* (1974); J. Merrill Shanks, "Warren E. Miller," *PS: Political Science and Politics* 32 (June 1999); Mark C. Smith, *Social Science in the Crucible* (1994).

Richard Jensen
University of Illinois–Chicago

Arthur Bentley and the Birth of Group Theory in American Politics

Arthur Fisher Bentley (1870–1957) is one of the most enigmatic figures in American social science. Born in Illinois in 1870, he grew up in a small Nebraska town, and except for his years pursuing academic degrees at Johns Hopkins and in Germany, he spent his entire life in the Midwest. After a brief and unsatisfactory stint at the University of Chicago, he turned to journalism, reporting on local affairs and writing editorials for Chicago dailies. Following the publication of his best-known book, *The Process of Government* (1908), he moved to a farm in Indiana where he remained until his death in 1957, writing steadily but receiving only occasional response from mainstream academia. *The Process of Government* itself, characterized by slashing criticisms of contemporary social theorists and often obscure formulations of its own point of view, was largely ignored when it came out, and it had little impact until after it was reprinted, first in 1935 and again in 1949. Thereafter, it came to be regarded as the foundation statement of interest group analysis in political science.

Bentley's primary concern, however, was linguistic, not political analysis. He sought to create a language that would enable the investigator of any social phenomena to avoid segmenting observations into separate compartments of individual or group action, stating them instead in terms of masses of activity. "Interest" and "group" were rough linguistic approximations for the flows of pressures that, for Bentley, constituted the observable world. His later work, some of it written in collaboration with John Dewey, explored these issues in still more abstract linguistic forms with little overt connection to politics. Nevertheless, in spite of his very special uses of the words, Bentley was widely understood to have argued that everything of importance in the political process could be stated in terms of interest groups. He contended that every observable action—every speech, every statute, every decision—should be understood as representing some interest, some group that gave it political meaning. Even the loftiest claims of justice or the public interest could be deconstructed to discover the groups employing or opposing the language. Nothing could be observed except "interested" activity tending in one direction or another.

Prior to World War II, several studies of interest groups in American politics had been conducted, but in the late 1940s a virtual flood of case studies documented the impact of private interests on the making of public policy, and these were given historical dimension by the revival of interest in James Madison's contributions to the *Federalist Papers* (specifically the number ten) and Alexis de Tocqueville's *Democracy in America*. The intellectual influence of this work was greatly enhanced by *The Governmental Process* (1951), in which David Truman, while claiming a major debt to Bentley, went on not only to summarize and consolidate a vast research literature, but also to develop his own theoretical statement.

Both Bentley and Truman saw interest groups as a tool enabling a more realistic analysis of the political process. For Bentley, however, groups were a concept with which to organize all the observable behavioral data of political life. Truman focused on the nongovernmental organizations seeking to influence the policy decisions of governmental officials. He did not claim that group activity constituted the only phenomena in the political world, but he and others, such as Robert Dahl, building on Madison more than on Bentley, contended that interest group pressures were of enormous importance in shaping what government did. Moreover, because of the great diversity of organized interests and the fragmentation of governmental authority, many groups could gain access and achieve some degree of policy influence. Thus, they argued, although groups rather than individual citizens were the primary actors, and interests rather than ideals were the motivating forces, the resulting system—interest group pluralism—was relatively benign.

Critics vigorously attacked pluralist theory. They said that the importance of interest groups had been overstated; they were far from the dominant factor in American policy making and of even less significance in other democracies. More importantly, pluralist theory, it was claimed, treated only the surfaces of politics, ignoring the more subtle but fundamental power of class and race. Further, the apparent equilibrium of pluralism was purchased at an excessive price of logrolling and compromise that made it impossible to achieve important common purposes. Perhaps the most deeply felt criticism was the profound dismay over the core of Bentley's position; namely, that not only a legislative enactment or a stump speech, but even an abstract principle or a philosophical discourse "represented" some interest, and that it was the clash of interests that gave the political process its meaning.

A considerable number of the early-twentieth-century writers who contributed to the literary and philosophical "Revolt Against Formalism" were, like Bentley, born and raised in the Midwest and did much of their early work there. In the next generation, the University of Chicago nurtured behavioral political scientists including Truman, and after World War II, the University of Illinois became a major breeding ground for Bentleyan political science. Perhaps this was happenstance. But that so much antiformalism originated in the heartland may not have been accidental. Bentley and his cohort were the second generation of small-town midwesterners. Their experience was marked by an incredible pace of change; new technologies, the rapid growth of corporate and financial structures of great power, cities suddenly grown huge with new immigration, and a politics that was filled with social protest and rife with corruption. American society was too dynamic, too complex for concepts like class or region to describe adequately the patterns of conflict, but unifying myths of common purpose like the "state" or the "public interest" were not persuasive either. What they saw was Interests! Everywhere! Nothing else! Group pressures of every conceivable variety pushing and pulling in quests for advantage. To describe this phantasmagoria in all its richness might enable the construction of a realistic social science. This was the Bentleyan vision, and arguably, it had distinctively midwestern roots.

Sources and Further Reading: Frank R. Baumgartner and Beth Leech, *Basic Interests* (1998); Arthur F. Bentley, *The Process of Government* (1908); Paul F. Kress, *Social Science and the Idea of Process* (1970); Daniel T. Rodgers, *Contested Truths* (1987); Robert H. Salisbury, "Interest Groups," in Fred I. Greenstein and Nelson W. Polsby, eds., *Handbook of Political Science*, vol. 4 (1975); Robert H. Salisbury, *Interests and In-* *stitutions* (1992); Richard W. Taylor, ed., *Life, Language, Law* (1957); David B. Truman, *The Governmental Process* (1951).

Robert H. Salisbury
Washington University, Missouri

Milton Friedman and the Chicago School of Economics

Milton Friedman (born 1912), who joined the faculty of the University of Chicago in 1946, is one of the most important figures in the history of economics. He is best known for his contributions to monetary theory, the quantity theory of money, and the natural rate of unemployment, and his research on consumption, which showed that an individual's consumption was determined by his expected permanent income or expected lifetime wealth. However his work on microeconomic issues, such as the incomes of physicians and other professionals, his analysis of risk preferences done with L. J. Savage, and his criticism of the theories of monopolistic and imperfect competition of Edward H. Chamberlin and Joan Robinson have also had an enormous influence.

Friedman is unique among economists in that his popular fame is matched by his professional stature, and he has been continuously engaged in public policy debates. He has advocated tax cuts to reduce the size of government, elimination of trade barriers, a flat income tax, a tax on consumption rather than income, revenue sharing between federal and state governments, and a system of vouchers for education. Some of the proposals he advocated were adopted in part because of his support, including an all-volunteer army and free-floating currency exchange rates. His vehement opposition to certain types of regulation was a factor in either bringing about their abolition or severely stunting their growth: Regulations in this category include wage and price controls, rent control, the minimum wage, tax breaks or overt government subsidies for industries, and bailouts for failing corporations.

The major themes of Friedman's contributions to economics and public policy can be summarized as follows: (1) his contention that the value of theories or economic models is to be determined solely by their predictive ability; (2) an abiding conviction that free markets are ideally suited to foster productivity, innovation, and economic growth; and (3) an utter disregard for disciplinary boundaries, either within economics or between economics and other fields.

Although there have been other economists of great prominence at the University of Chicago—to date twenty-two Nobel Laureates since the prize in Economics was first awarded in 1969, and six winners of the John Bates Clark Medal, awarded biannually to an economics scholar of exceptional accomplishment and promise under the age of forty—none has had a greater influence either on economics or on public policy than Friedman. It is therefore useful to identify the salient characteristics of neoclassical economics or, as journalists call it, the Chicago School, and compare them to Friedman's legacy. In research by neoclassical economists, incentives are at center stage, and government regulations are subjected to an independent cost–benefit analysis; there is no presumption that the principal effect of regulations will be what is claimed in the legislative committee reports. In addition, business practices that were previously assumed to be anti-competitive are reevaluated to see if they might represent the efficient solution of a competitive market.

In many studies, neoclassical economists develop and then test the implications of individuals maximizing utility in response to some form of government intervention, actual or proposed. The best way to illustrate how economics has been transformed by Chicago School economists is through some specific examples. Consider a study by Samuel Peltzman on automobile safety regulation (mandatory seat belts and other vehicle design standards). Peltzman developed a model implying that, since drivers were better protected against accidents, they would be inclined to drive faster and take more risks; the consequence could be an increase in injuries to pedestrians and property damage. Peltzman's analysis found that because of these offsetting effects, auto safety regulation did not affect the highway death rate, and there was a shift of the burden of accidents from drivers to pedestrians and an increase in property damage.

Consider another example, this one from economic analysis of law, a field in which Chicago School economists have had an enormous impact. The problem of court congestion and delay has prompted many proposals for court reform. Most studies of court congestion have assumed that the time to trial or to settlement of cases can be substantially reduced if the court would only take certain specified measures to expedite the processing of cases. However, a very different perspective is provided by the neoclassical economists Richard Posner and George Priest. Posner compared the problem of court congestion to traffic congestion on an expressway. Traffic engineers have learned that adding lanes to an existing expressway may not do much to relieve traffic congestion in the long run, because the volume of traffic on the expressway does not remain the same after the improvement. Drivers who were previously traveling on other routes will switch to the expressway; this process will continue until

there is enough additional traffic so that travel time for commuters on the expanded expressway is about the same as it is on alternative routes. According to Posner and Priest, the same principle applies to changes in court administration that reduce the time to trial. If cases can be resolved much more quickly in Court A because, for example, the number of judges in that court is doubled, litigants who previously would have filed cases in other courts will be attracted to Court A, and this process will continue until a new equilibrium is reached in which the time to trial in Court A is about the same as it is in other forums.

These examples both suggest the continuing influence of Milton Friedman on the study of economics and illustrate how modern economic research and public policy analysis have been thoroughly transformed by Chicago economists.

Sources and Further Reading: Milton Friedman, *Essays in Positive Economics* (1953); Milton Friedman, *A Theory of the Consumption Function* (1957); Milton Friedman and Rose D. Friedman, *Two Lucky People* (1998); Milton Friedman and L.J. Savage, "The Utility Analysis of Choices Involving Risk," *Journal of Political Economy* 56 (Aug. 1948); Milton Friedman and Anna J. Schwartz, *A Monetary History of the United States, 1867–1960* (1963); Sam Peltzman, "The Effects of Automobile Safety Regulation," *Journal of Political Economy* 83 (Aug. 1975); Richard A. Posner, "An Economic Approach to Legal Procedure and Judicial Administration," *Journal of Legal Studies* 2 (June 1973); George L. Priest, "Private Litigants and the Court Congestion Problem," *Boston University Law Review* 69 (May 1989).

Stephen J. Spurr
Wayne State University, Michigan

The Midwest and Understanding American Politics

Some of the most important and original documents written on democracy and republican government were composed as a result of the American system of governance. These include the writings of John Jay, James Madison, and Alexander Hamilton in the Federalist Papers, the various writings of John Adams and Thomas Jefferson among others, and Alexis de Tocqueville's classic, *Democracy in America*. The United States has a long history of political experimentation and debate. America had college courses on politics and ethics as early as 1642. In 1880, a Department of Political Science was established at Columbia University, and universities had much earlier encompassed the study of constitutional history and law. Development continued to progress rapidly in the United States, and many new advances in the study of politics and social change and development had as their crucible universities in the Midwest.

As much of the most original thought about democratic governance came from the minds and experience of the founders of the American republic, so much of the most fundamental thought on twentieth-century American and international politics originated at the University of Chicago in the minds and experiences of its teachers and its students—the Chicago School—as well as other intellectual leaders and institutions. Among the most influential figures in the development of the modern study of American politics were Charles E. Merriam and Harold D. Lasswell. In his formative *A History of American Political Theories* (1903), Merriam examined how the theories leading to the founding of the United States—natural law and the natural rights of man—were being augmented by the work of new generations of European social scientists, just as the founders had been influenced by earlier reformist thinkers from England and the Continent. Merriam, a positivist, expressed his belief that industrialization and rapid advances in the experimental sciences, unknown to the earlier generations of observers, would serve to enhance the strength of the citizen, instead of destroying the citizenry's power as some envisioned and feared. In the 1920s, he called for a change from armchair theorizing and prescribing to the study of the actual social and political behavior of citizens as activists, holders of opinions, and voters, and to thereby develop an understanding of public life in the realities of everyday experience. Thus originated what came to be called "behavioralism" in the study of politics and society. To this end, Merriam himself was active in public life throughout his academic career, once running for the office of mayor of Chicago, though unsuccessfully.

Lasswell, who archives great advances in the fields of communications, psychology, and the social bases of the law, consulted with Merriam while writing one of his most influential works, *Politics: Who Gets What, When and How* (1958). With Merriam's practical experience in Chicago politics and Lasswell's influential advances in behavioral social science, the University of Chicago faculty was at the forefront of the study of political life in both the United States and abroad. Their students continued this tradition of inquiry and thought in many of the major universities in the country.

Harold F. Gosnell, also at the University of Chicago, was the first to use statistical and experimental methods in the study of politics, especially of public opinion and voting behavior. His work *Non-Voting: Causes and Methods of Control* (1924) and *Getting Out the Vote: An Experiment in the Simulation of Voting* (1927) revolutionized the study and understanding of politics in America. Gosnell gathered statistical data on voter age, sex, citizenship, and length of residence. He interviewed party officials, officeholders, and election activists. Gosnell's *Machine Politics: Chicago Model* (1937) applied correlation, regression, and factor analysis for the first time in a systematic way to study political behavior. The use of political opinion polls and surveys of attitude originated at the University of Chicago.

A graduate of the Chicago School, Alfred de Grazia advanced the behavioralism movement as the founder and editor of the American Behavioral Scientist. De Grazia also developed the Universal Reference System, a computerized social science bibliographic service. While the political science department made significant contributions to the field, other University of Chicago departments also made their unique marks. Perhaps most influential among these was its Department of Economics, which became internationally renowned through the monetarist and free market theories developed and espoused by Milton Friedman, George Stigler, and Gary Becker, all awarded the Nobel Prize in Economics, in addition to some nineteen other members of the economics faculty at Chicago.

Many other scientists have roots in the Midwest or did their work there. At the University of Iowa, Kurt Lewin made great advances in the field of psychology and is considered one of the founders of the fields of social and organizational psychology. He also made seminal contributions to field theory, which explains social outcomes in groups as a result of a complex interaction of personal factors and variously structured situations.

The scholars and educational institutions in the Midwest have made fundamental contributions to the study of social history and political behavior. Charles A. Beard from Indiana developed important theories concerning the relationships between politics and economics, historically and contemporarily, and spent a great deal of his life promoting the teaching of history. Frederick Jackson Turner from Wisconsin, one of the premier scholars of American history in the twentieth century, developed theories of regionalism and the American frontier and was awarded a posthumous Pulitzer Prize for *The Significance of Sections in American History* (1932), a work debated through the turn of the twenty-first century. Herbert A. Simon was a pioneer in the field of artificial intelligence. Born in Wisconsin in 1916, he pioneered the quantitative modeling of human behavior and was awarded the Nobel Prize in Economics in 1978. Carl Becker, born in Iowa in 1873 and known for his work on American intellectual and social history, taught at the University of

Kansas from 1902 to 1916. Arthur S. Schlesinger, Sr., born in Xenia, Ohio, taught at The Ohio State University and the University of Iowa before moving to Harvard, and was a central figure in the field of American social and political history, a tradition nobly carried on by his son, Arthur S. Schlesinger, Jr., born in Columbus, Ohio.

For the past six decades, the understanding of American public opinion and political behavior has been elevated by the Survey Research Center, founded in 1946, at the University of Michigan and by the National Opinion Research Center, founded at the University of Chicago in 1941. The work developed within these institutions fundamentally advanced the study and understanding of public opinion and political behavior in democracies around the globe.

Sources and Further Reading: Martin Gold, ed., *The Complete Social Scientist* (1999); Barry Dean Karl, *Charles E. Merriam and the Study of Politics* (1974); Harold D. Lasswell, *Politics: Who Gets What, When and How* (1950); Harold D. Lasswell, *Psychopathology and Politics* (1930; reprint, 1986); Charles E. Merriam, *Chicago: A More Intimate View of Urban Politics (The Rise of Urban America)* (1929); Arthur Meier Schlesinger, Sr., and Andrea Tuttle Kornbluh, *The Rise of the City, 1878–1898* (1999).

Arthur Holst
Philadelphia, Pennsylvania

Posner, Easterbrook, and Economic Approaches to the Law

Richard A. Posner is a judge of the U.S. Court of Appeals for the Seventh Circuit and a Senior Lecturer at the University of Chicago Law School. Before his appointment to the Court in 1981, he was the Lee and Brena Freeman Professor of Law at the University of Chicago.

Posner is widely regarded as the world's foremost authority in the area of law and economics, or economic analysis of law. The author of more than thirty books and over three hundred articles or book reviews, Posner's influence on the literatures of both law and economics is, by any measure, staggering. In virtually every area of law—property law, torts, contracts, constitutional law, taxation, corporations, public utility regulation, labor law, civil procedure, antitrust, family law, court administration—Posner has written several articles or book chapters that are among the most-cited in the area; and once the profession has digested his contributions, the issues in that area are essentially defined by his analysis. A recent comparative study of citations of leading legal scholars in the Social Sciences Citation Index found that Posner was the most cited, with 7,981 citations, and 78 percent more citations than the scholar in second place, Ronald Dworkin.

Posner's textbook, *Economic Analysis of Law*, first published in 1973 and now in its fifth edition, has probably done more to advance law and economics than any other publication. In 1972, Posner founded the *Journal of Legal Studies* primarily to encourage economic analysis of law. It is now one of the most prestigious journals in this field.

Frank Easterbrook is, like Posner, a judge on the Seventh Circuit Court of Appeals, and also a former Lee and Brena Freeman Professor of Law at the University of Chicago. He has published widely on antitrust law, corporations, and criminal law and procedure. One of his best-known publications is the *Economic Structure of Corporate Law* (1991), written with Daniel R. Fischel. He is also extensively cited in law journals, and ranked twenty-first in a list that includes not only living scholars but also such eminent figures from the past as Jerome Frank, Oliver Wendell Holmes, Jr., and Karl Llewellyn.

Under the economic approach, legal rules are measured against the standard of efficiency. Individuals are assumed to be rational and to respond to incentives. In accordance with the work of Gary Becker, an economist who has greatly influenced both Easterbrook and Posner, economics is assumed to apply to the full panoply of human behavior, including crime, sexual behavior, marriage, and interaction among family members. Many of the most important contributors to law and economics—Posner, Becker, Ronald Coase, Easterbrook, Richard Epstein, and William Landes (an economist who is Posner's most frequent collaborator)—have spent most or all of their careers at the University of Chicago, which has been the epicenter of this intellectual revolution.

This has been a revolution from the top. Economic analysis was first introduced into the classroom at the elite law schools, most notably Chicago and Yale, and subsequently percolated down to the others. Now in virtually any classroom in the major law schools, the discussion may be laced with terms like *risk aversion, efficiency, opportunity cost, moral hazard, rent-seeking behavior, economies of scale*, and the like. Almost any recent issue of a major law journal will include articles employing economic analysis, often including diagrams and a formal mathematical model. A recent study measured the influence of the economic approach by the frequency of use of economic terms in law review articles and found that the influence of economics has continued to grow steadily. In 1991, the American Law and Economics Association was founded to coordinate research efforts in the economic analysis of law. This association now has more than six hundred members including law professors, practicing lawyers, judges, and economists.

During earlier years, law students may have considered economic analysis to be something like a parlor game—a fascinating exercise, but something they would leave behind once they had graduated and entered into practice. Today, they will quite likely encounter applications of economics in law practice. The Supreme Court has increasingly relied on publications that apply the rigorous analytical methods of the social sciences. Another important development has been the appointment to the executive branch and the federal bench of individuals whose decisions are frequently based on applications of economics. With respect to the federal judiciary, this group includes, in addition to Posner and Easterbrook of the Seventh Circuit, Guido Calabresi and Ralph Winter of the Second Circuit, Alex Kozinski of the Ninth Circuit, Douglas Ginsburg and Stephen Williams of the D.C. Circuit, and Supreme Court Justices Stephen Breyer and Antonin Scalia.

All indications are that the role of economic analysis in the study of law and the formation of public policy will continue to grow in the future.

Sources and Further Reading: Robert C. Ellickson, "Trends in Legal Scholarship: A Statistical Study," *Journal of Legal Studies* 29 (Jan. 2000); Fred R. Shapiro, "The Most-Cited Legal Scholars," *Journal of Legal Studies* 29 (Jan. 2000).

Stephen J. Spurr
Wayne State University, Michigan

The Midwest and the Rise of Survey Research

Modern public opinion polling originated in the 1930s when George H. Gallup (an Iowa native and graduate of the University of Iowa), Elmo Roper, and Archibald M. Crossley all founded national firms to conduct market and opinion research. Their firms were located in New Jersey and New York, an area that remains the center of market and commercial public opinion research.

Academic survey research emerged a few years later with the founding of the Bureau of Applied Social Research (BASR) in 1939 in New York City (subsequently affiliated with Columbia University), the National Opinion Research Center (NORC) in 1941 at the University of Denver, and the Survey Research Center in 1946 (merged with the Institute for Social Research, ISR, in 1949) at the University of Michigan. BASR was founded by the Austrian social scientist

Paul Lazarsfeld. While the research home of the pioneering work of Lazarsfeld, Bernard Bereleson, Robert Merton, and others at Columbia, BASR never became fully institutionalized. It never developed its own national field staff and, with the passing of its founders, declined and eventually closed.

NORC was founded by Englishman Harry Field, who had worked for Gallup in Britain and came to the United States to found an organization to measure public opinion in the public interest. Because of ties Field had with its president, Field originally located NORC at the University of Denver. After Field's death in 1946, NORC relocated to the University of Chicago, desiring affiliation with a university very strong in empirical social science and a location much closer to NORC's main clients, eastern foundations and government agencies in Washington, D.C.

ISR also moved to the Midwest, but the move came before it was even founded. In 1946, the U.S. government closed down one of its major units for monitoring public opinion during World War II, Program Surveys at the Agriculture Department. Rather than individually dispersing to find new positions, the staff of Program Surveys—Rensis Likert, Angus Campbell, Charles Cannell, George Katona, Leslie Kish, and others—sought a home at a university and ultimately chose the University of Michigan.

NORC and ISR would become the two leading academic survey research institutes in the United States. Their relocation in the Midwest cannot be seen as merely resulting from happenstance and coincidence. In part it occurred because the great eastern universities appeared less open to the new discipline of survey research. For example, while Harvard and Princeton had leading scholars of the new field of public opinion research (respectively, Samuel Stouffer and Hadley Cantril), they never established survey research centers. Even Columbia's association with BASR was only a partial exception since BASR never matured into a full-fledged, survey research institute. Chicago and Michigan were more willing to fully embrace the new field. Chicago, of course, had since the 1910s been a leader in empirical data collection (especially their departments of Sociology and Political Science), and national surveys merely constituted a new tool to facilitate their inquiries. Michigan and ISR teamed up in part because the university was persuaded by Likert's argument that "universities had new responsibilities to undertake research of social and scientific importance."

Having arrived in Chicago and Ann Arbor in 1946–1947, NORC and the Survey Research Center had university homes, but not much else. Except for modest office space, the universities provided little more to the institutes. To survive and thrive they had to attract both business and scientific respect for the quality of their research. In part they met this challenge by establishing long-term data collection projects. The Survey Research Center started its Survey of Consumer Attitudes in 1946 (while still part of the government), the National Election Studies (NES) in 1948, the Detroit Area Studies in 1951, and the Panel Survey of Income Dynamics (PSID) in 1968. These have all continued into the twenty-first century.

NORC, which had conducted a series of surveys for the Office of War Information during World War II, continued to collect data for the Department of State from 1944 to 1957. NORC also conducted a series of studies on intergroup relations starting in 1942 with the first race relations survey ever conducted and continuing into the early 1970s. This theme was taken up by the General Social Survey (GSS) in 1972, which has continued to monitor this and many other topics.

Such studies not only sustained the institutes financially, but also established their outstanding intellectual reputations. NES and PSID at ISR and the GSS at NORC are supported by the National Science Foundation and have become part of the core infrastructure of labor economics, political science, social psychology, sociology, and other fields devoted to the understanding of human behavior. NORC and ISR have also taken the leading role in cross-national, comparative research with respectively the International Social Survey Program and the World Values Study Group.

NORC and ISR also established themselves by becoming leaders in survey and quantitative, social science methodology. At NORC Herbert Hyman and colleagues "wrote the book" on interviewers and interviewing, and at ISR Kish did the same for sampling. In 1947, NORC conducted the first national study to measure occupational prestige, and ISR developed the Likert scale for measuring attitudes. NORC and ISR have continued to make major methodological contributions to the present day.

In addition to NORC and ISR, the Midwest is home to major, survey methods programs at the Survey Research Laboratory at the University of Illinois at Urbana-Champaign, The Ohio State University, the University of Akron, and the University of Cincinnati.

NORC and ISR helped secure their prominent positions by actively building the discipline of survey research. Both the American Association for Public Opinion Research (AAPOR) and the World Association for Public Opinion Research originated from the Central City Conference organized by Field in 1946, and NORC and ISR researchers have won approximately a third of AAPOR's life achievement awards. ISR has also helped to build the field through its edu-

cational programs, the summer courses by the Summer Institute, its Inter-University Consortium for Political and Social Research, and more recently its Joint Program in Survey Methodology with the University of Maryland.

In sum, the Midwest became the home of the two oldest and largest university-based, survey research institutes in part because the University of Chicago and the University of Michigan aligned with the new discipline of public opinion and survey research. Since their founding more than half a century ago, NORC and ISR have become central pillars in the study of human behavior in the United States and around the world.

Sources and Further Reading: Jean M. Converse, *Survey Research in the United States* (1987); Archibald M. Crossley, "Early Days of Public Opinion Research," *Public Opinion Quarterly* 21 (Spring 1957); Jeff Hackett, *America by Number: NORC Report 1991* (1992); Herbert H. Hyman et al., *Interviewing in Social Research* (1954); Leslie Kish, *Survey Sampling* (1965).

Tom W. Smith
National Opinion Research Center,
Chicago, Illinois

Are Midwesterners Bowling Alone? Social Capital and Midwestern Life

The term *social capital* has been popularized recently through the writings of political scientist Robert Putnam, a native midwesterner from Port Clinton, Ohio. He and other scholars consider social capital to be the interpersonal trust and human networks that facilitate collective problem solving. Any time people come together to accomplish shared objectives, it is both the product of social capital and a contributor to it. In this sense, social capital has much in common with other concepts such as fraternity, civic culture, civil society, and even neighborliness.

Many social analysts are concerned that social capital has been declining in America in recent decades and that this may have dire consequences for our society. In his book *Bowling Alone: The Collapse and Revival of American Community*, Putnam assembles a rich array of evidence primarily from the second half of the twentieth century that indicates people are withdrawing from group activities and withholding interpersonal trust. Church attendance and charitable giving are down, voluntary service organizations are having difficulty replacing older members, and even informal social activities, such as playing cards and entertaining at home, are in decline. Putnam also cites the catchy and title-inspiring statistic that league bowling is down even though more people than ever are bowling. America, he fears, is becoming a society where people are bowling alone. This is troubling because researchers have shown that societies high in social capital tend to have healthier economies, healthier and happier citizens, better performing governments, and less crime.

The Midwest has long enjoyed high levels of social capital. Early records, largely anecdotal, reveal a world where settlers, often scattered miles apart, came together to help each other through the hardships of pioneer farming. For instance, in the beloved *Little House* series, author Laura Ingalls Wilder recounts many examples of trust and cooperation that are certainly the product of social capital. She describes a time when Pa borrowed much-needed nails from a man he had just met chopping down trees in the woods. "That's what I call a good neighbor!" Pa exclaimed and he vowed to "pay him back every nail." Other passages tell of farmers coming together to harvest crops and dig wells, and there are many examples of neighbors sharing food and tools and examples throughout the region of joint labor in threshing and barn raisings.

As the population density increased in the late nineteenth century, midwesterners, according to historian Kenneth Walker, became joiners, forming many social and service associations. Chautauquas and lectures were common, as were local chapters of organizations such as the Grange and Odd Fellows. Although the purpose of these events and clubs was often recreational, they helped build the interpersonal cohesion that makes social capital possible.

This Midwest spirit of assistance and responsibility was also evident during the Progressive Era of the early 1900s. Many of the contemporary national service clubs were founded in the Midwest. Chicago insurance man Melvin Jones, who felt that business organizations should serve their community, started the Lions Club in 1917, and Henry Giessenbier founded the Jaycees in St. Louis in 1915 to help young men develop civic leadership skills. The first Rotary Club was formed in Chicago in 1905 to bring small-town neighborly values to the burgeoning business community, and the Kiwanis Club, a society of businesspeople to serve the needs of children, was started in Detroit in 1914. People continued to come together for purely recreational purposes, too. The number of community drama clubs per capita in 1930 was higher in the Midwest than in any other region, and many towns initiated annual festivals and celebrations.

In a comprehensive study of the history of social capital in the American states, Tom Rice and Marshall Arnett combine data from the U.S. Census Bureau and other sources to develop social capital scores, called civic culture scores, by state for the 1880s, 1930s, and 1990s. Their results indicate that the states in the Midwest and Northeast have long had average or above-average levels of social capital. Michigan, Iowa, and Minnesota had especially high social capital in the 1880s, and by the 1990s, ten of the twelve Midwest states ranked in the top twenty-five in terms of social capital.

Putnam's state index of contemporary social capital finds much the same. He reports that the primary social capital high-pressure area is centered right over the Midwest and "extends east and west along the Canadian border." His extensive data analyses reveal that North Dakota and South Dakota have the highest social capital in the country, and that Minnesota, Nebraska, and Iowa also rank near the top. Midwesterners are especially likely to be involved in clubs and community organizations, as well as to trust other people. They also tend to entertain at home more regularly than people in other regions, and they report visiting with friends more often.

While midwesterners may not be bowling alone as often as people from other regions, social capital in the Midwest is declining just as it is elsewhere. For example, data from the widely respected General Social Surveys indicate the percentage of midwesterners who say that "people can be trusted" has fallen from 51 percent in 1972 to 40 percent in 2000 (compared to a decline from 45 percent to 34 percent for the rest of the nation). Other data reveal that the percentage of midwesterners who participate in service clubs has declined since 1960, as has the percentage who vote, attend church, and give to charity.

The reasons for the decline in social capital in the Midwest and across the nation are complex and not fully understood, but three factors seem to play major roles. The proliferation of television and other similar entertainment isolates people, taking them away from the face-to-face interaction with others that helps create social capital. Studies have shown, for instance, that heavy TV watchers are less likely to participate in voluntary associations. Urban sprawl has also served to isolate people from each other. Suburban residents often have homes on large lots that physically separate them from their neighbors, and they often spend a great deal of time each day commuting to and from work alone in their automobiles. The pressures of time and money on contemporary families have taken a toll on social capital as well. With the increase in dual-career and single-parent families, there is less time for parents to engage formally and informally with others outside the family.

It is important to note that not all scholars agree

that social capital has declined in recent years. Everett Carl Ladd, for instance, reports that people are simply changing the types of groups they belong to, from traditional service and professional clubs to new groups, such as environmental organizations and neighborhood improvement associations. It is also possible that the Internet serves to build social capital in ways that are not yet recognized.

Social capital in the Midwest varies from state to state and even from town to town. According to Putnam, rural Midwest states tend to have slightly higher social capital than urban states. As for communities, a study by Iowa State University shows that social capital tends to be higher in smaller Iowa towns and in towns that are more ethnically homogeneous. The results also reveal that communities high in social capital tend to have older and better-educated populations. Moreover, social capital appears to help make towns more livable. For example, high social capital is associated with more effective local government, better-maintained private and public property, and stronger community attachment.

The task of rejuvenating social capital in the Midwest and across the nation has attracted a great deal of attention in the late twentieth and early twenty-first centuries. Although the job is daunting, midwesterners, like many Americans, seem to be taking up the challenge. Numerous Midwest schools, for example, have developed classes on civic responsibility, and many others now encourage community service as part of existing courses. Some schools have even challenged stu-

dents to forgo TV in favor of face-to-face social interaction with family, friends, and neighbors. While efforts like these are a start, the contemporary trends that have eroded social capital, such as the increased reliance on screen-based technology and increased suburbanization, will prove difficult to reverse. Healthy social capital in the future may depend on finding ways to use these trends to build social capital today.

The rapid growth in social capital during the Progressive Era in the early decades of the twentieth century came partly in response to the vast economic and social upheaval of the late nineteenth century, so perhaps the current economic and social changes will eventually spur renewed social interaction. Until then, though, midwesterners—and other Americans—may be bowling alone in large numbers.

Sources and Further Reading: Stephen Baron, John Field, and Tom Schuller, eds., *Social Capital: Critical Perspectives* (2001); Everett Carll Ladd, *The Ladd Report* (1999); Nan Lin, Karen Cook, and Ronald S. Burt, eds., *Social Capital* (2001); Robert D. Putnam, *Bowling Alone* (2000); Robert D. Putnam, *Making Democracy Work* (1993); Tom W. Rice, "Social Capital and Government Performance in Iowa Communities," *Journal of Urban Affairs* 23 (July 2001); Tom W. Rice and Marshall Arnett, "Civic Culture and Socioeconomic Development in the United States: A View from the States, 1880s–1990s," *Social Science Journal* 38 (Spring 2001); Kenneth R. Walker, *A History of the Middle West from the Beginning to 1970* (1972).

Tom W. Rice
University of Iowa

Military Affairs

SECTION EDITOR
David Curtis Skaggs

Section Contents

Throughout its history the Midwest has been at the fringe of conflicts fought elsewhere. Military operations on its soil have been minor compared to those at the centers of combat. Nonetheless, important actions have been joined here, especially during Native American prehistory, the European quests for empire in the region, and wars between Indians and European Americans. From the region have come some important leaders of military affairs who won fame in other parts of the nation and globe—Ulysses S. Grant, William Tecumseh Sherman, John J. Pershing, Billy Mitchell, Ernest J. King, Dwight D. Eisenhower, Omar Bradley, Curtis LeMay, and Bernard Rogers, for instance. At times midwestern battles have produced their own heroes—Pontiac, George Rogers Clark, Little Turtle, Blue Jacket, Anthony Wayne, Tecumseh, William Henry Harrison, and Oliver Hazard Perry being prominent among them. But not since the War of 1812 has significant combat occurred on midwestern soil. Instead the region has been the granary, industrial base, and arsenal of the nation, the furnisher and trainer of airmen, soldiers, and sailors for combat elsewhere, and the launching pad for cold war intercontinental bombers and missiles. The articles in this section are organized in a chronological sequence to convey and elucidate this historical change.

Indian Warfare before European Contact. Although no written evidence remains, warfare played an important role in pre-Columbian Native American societies. Armed with bow and arrow, flint and obsidian knives, and wooden war clubs, warriors engaged in combat for a variety of motives. Organized into loose political alliances with weak executive authority, the native peoples engaged in limited wars over matters of territorial jurisdiction or hunting lands, personal antagonisms, or ritualized "mourning" expeditions. The latter involved the taking of prisoners who were supposed to replace a deceased tribal member. Upon returning home from such a raid, group leaders apportioned prisoners among grieving families whose women elders determined whether to adopt or execute them.

Such warfare placed a premium on individual over group valor and sought to avoid casualties in societies always short on population. The true test of a warrior's bravery and combat skill resulted more from the number of prisoners he seized than from the number of scalps taken from fallen foes. Fear of severe losses in combat often caused native warriors to break off engagements, even when on the verge of victory, because casualties were deemed to be excessive. Tactically the

George Rogers Clark and the surprise at Vincennes. Courtesy Indiana Historical Bureau, State of Indiana.

ambush and surprise attack were the most common forms of engagement. To provide some security against such attacks, woodland Indians often palisaded their villages.

What little knowledge survives indicates that native peoples seldom, if ever, engaged in wars of annihilation. There was lots of space in the midwestern world, and contests for territory, influence, and prisoners were limited in scope. Tribal rivalries that contributed to warfare in the pre-European era continued long after the arrival of the Europeans.

Wars with and against the Europeans.

The European contact with the Midwest began with Francisco Vásquez de Coronado's military expedition from modern Mexico into what is now central Kansas in the 1540s. It had little lasting impact on Native Americans, but it marked the first of many military-led explorations into and through the region over the next three hundred years. Shortly after Coronado traveled into the Great Plains, Frenchmen began venturing into the Great Lakes and the Mississippi Valley. In 1681–1682, Sieur de La Salle, born René-Robert Cavalier, led an expedition from the lakes down that great river valley to the Gulf of Mexico and claimed the entire watershed it drained in the name of King Louis XIV of France. From a European standpoint, most of what would eventually become the Midwest belonged to the French Crown, an assertion and perspective that was vigorously contested by native peoples.

From the outset the contest for the Midwest contained distinctive features that differed significantly from the contacts between Europeans and Indians along the coasts. First and foremost, the European advantage of mobility that came from their control of the Atlantic was lost in the midwestern world. Midwestern tribes did not suffer the substantial numbers of deaths from European-borne disease as did the Atlantic tribes, and they received some reinforcement from tribes like the Delaware and a group of Iroquois peoples known as the Mingos, who had migrated westward by the mid-eighteenth century. Finally, midwestern tribes had critical trading materials at their disposal in the form of furs, buffalo hides, and deerskins that found an eager market among the European traders who rushed into the region. Such traders quite willingly turned over the Europeans' technological advantage of guns and gunpowder to the natives in exchange for these precious commodities.

But they did face considerable disadvantages. The tactical practice of taking prisoners and of emphasis on individual over group valor gave an advantage to the corporate ethic of European military tradition. The individualism of native warriors hurt efforts to provide coherent, long-term leadership during military struggles. The linguistic, cultural, and political diversity among the rival tribes of the region enabled the Europeans and the European Americans to utilize traditional native enmities to exploit one group against the other. Whereas three European nations and one North American state faced the natives, literally dozens of Indian tribal and intratribal rivalries could be utilized to the advantage of those seeking to move into the region. Efforts to find Indian unity failed to secure it, but it reached an important acme in the late eighteenth century. The Native Americans never developed the logistical capability to sustain long-term expeditions deep into enemy territory.

The Sixty Years' Struggle for the Midwest, 1754–1814.

French dominance, however, would not last for long. Beginning in the mid-eighteenth century, the Anglo-Europeans began their first treks into the region. The British claim rested on the supposed Iroquois suzerainty over the western Algonquian peoples and the even more dubious sea-to-sea charters of such colonies as Virginia. Since the Iroquois Confederacy of New York was bound to the British by the Covenant Chain of Friendship, this provided the subterfuge for colonists' efforts to trade with the interior tribes.

Under the leadership of Ange de Menneville, marquis de Duquesne, the French moved to counter British encroachments into the Midwest. Duquesne directed the construction of a series of outposts in the upper Ohio Valley to curtail British encroachments. Thus opened what became known in America as the French and Indian War and in Europe as the Seven Years' War. Midwestern Native Americans furnished important numbers of warriors that participated in several significant engagements—the battle of the Monongahela in 1755, the siege of Fort William Henry in 1757, and the defense of Fort Ticonderoga in 1758. On the other hand, it was the distaste of General Louis-Joseph, marquis de Montcalm, of the "savages'" tactics that contributed to the limited presence of Native American fighters during the French losses in campaigns of 1759 and 1760. The French cession of Quebec to the British and of Louisiana to the Spanish in 1763 changed dramatically the political-military balance in the Midwest.

Another antagonism arose, however, affecting the security of the Midwest—the encroachment of British colonists from Virginia and Pennsylvania into the Ohio Valley. British efforts to stop the intrusion failed despite the Proclamation of 1763, the stationing of troops at various outposts, and the Treaty of Fort Stanwix of 1768, each of which limited western migration to areas below the Ohio River line. This latter treaty made by the Iroquois, but without Shawnee consent, opened traditional Shawnee hunting grounds in Kentucky to settlement. Consequently the Shawnee came in conflict with the Virginians and thereby induced that colony's governor, Lord Dunmore, to send an expedition into eastern Ohio in 1774. Though brief, Lord Dunmore's War forced the Shawnee to concede the Ohio River line, known as the Fort Stanwix line. For the next forty years, midwestern Indians sought to keep the Fort Stanwix line as the boundary between European Americans and Native Americans.

In hindsight, Midwest Natives' efforts to contain European American encroachment were clearly doomed, but from the perspective of the mid-1770s, it must have seemed possible. For the most part, the natives of the Midwest were loyal to the British during the American Revolution (1775–1783), but their enthusiasm came at a cost—the alienation of white settlers and prospective settlers in the Midwest. Virginia supported Kentucky attacks into modern Illinois and Indiana under the leadership of George Rogers Clark. Meanwhile, the Continental Congress established a small garrison at Fort Pitt, Pennsylvania, and from there sought to assert authority in the upper Ohio Valley. Assisting the natives in the region were Pennsylvania Loyalists Alexander McKee, Matthew Elliott, and Simon Girty. American attempts to maintain Indian neutrality collapsed with the murder of Shawnee chief Cornstalk in 1777. Shortly thereafter the British at Detroit supported a series of Indian raids from central Kentucky to western Pennsylvania that lasted for the rest of the war. The Americans responded with a series of counterraids, but by the end of 1782, not a single American garrison existed north of the Ohio River.

At the negotiation table, the Americans fared far better than their military efforts merited. Desperate to disengage from the American War and to focus their military efforts against the French and Spanish, His Majesty's Government negotiated the line-of-lakes boundary as the northern border of the newly independent United States. This Peace of Paris of 1783 placed the natives who had fought so long and well at the not-so-tender mercies of the Americans. For the next dozen years they fought a long, bitter, bloody struggle with the United States that would end in defeat, disillusionment, and disunity. Betrayed for their support by the whim of British power politics, the Indians found themselves with few options but to continue their relations with His Majesty's forces or to fall prey to the land-grabbing pioneers of the New Republic.

In the 1780s, there emerged the closest thing to a unified Indian coalition against American intrusion that would ever exist. Miami and Shawnee chiefs Little Turtle and Blue Jacket led an important effort to create a multitribal coalition as whites crossed the Ohio and settled in the fertile Muskingum, Scioto, Miami, and Wabash Valleys. American negotiations with the Iroquois, Wyandots, and Delawares ceded lands claimed by other tribes, and hostilities broke out between the Kentuckians and the Miamis and Shawnees in 1786. Two years later, the Ohio Company began its settlement at Marietta and thereby breached the Fort Stanwix line. General Arthur St. Clair became governor of the Northwest Territory, created in 1787, which encompassed the entire region between the Ohio and the Great Lakes. For the new federal administration, opening this region to gradual settlement was a prime policy. Soon the various Ohio and Indiana tribes moved to the upper Wabash and Maumee River valleys, where they could raise corn in relative security and coordinate with British officials out of Detroit. Unable to entice them to the negotiating table, Governor St. Clair sent Brigadier General Josiah Harmar to "pacify" the Indians by force. The result was total American failure in two engagements at the forks of the Maumee (Fort Wayne, Indiana) in October 1790. Little Turtle, leader of the Miamis, proved to be a most capable opponent at the battle of Kekionga, and the victory enhanced his reputation. Consequently, the size of the confederacy opposed to American advancement grew.

Governor General St. Clair brought a second expedition northward; it met defeat at the battle of the Wabash (Fort Recovery, Ohio) on November 4, 1791. This encounter constitutes the most disastrous rout of the U.S. Army by Native Americans in the entire history of the country. It would take three years before a reconstituted Legion of the United States commanded by Major General Anthony Wayne could advance into the Maumee Valley and defeat the disintegrating Indian coalition at the battle of Fallen Timbers (Maumee, Ohio) on August 20, 1794. Not only did this engagement terminate the most comprehensive and cohesive Native American coalition in American history, but Wayne's victory with an army of professional soldiers justified the continuation of a regular army by a nation inclined to rely on the militia. Once again, the British deserted their erstwhile allies at the moment of crisis. Several months later at the Treaty of Greenville, the Shawnees and Miamis joined other tribes in agreeing to concede the Ohio River line to American advancement. After Jay's Treaty in 1795, the British withdrew from Detroit and Mackinac, and American control to the line-of-lakes was for the first time effectively asserted.

Various accommodationist natives began to adapt to American control of the Midwest during the fifteen-year peace following the Greenville Treaty. But around the shores of Lake Michigan, growing hostility to the encroachment of settlers into traditional Indian hunting grounds and farmlands fostered a faction that followed the teachings of the Shawnee prophet Tenskwatawa and the political-military leadership of his brother Tecumseh. Although they controlled a minority of the Shawnees, their resistance movement attracted allies among the Wyandots, Potawatomis, and Ottawas. In the upper Mississippi Valley, the British flag still flew in many villages, and the intrigues of Irish fur trader Robert Dickson of Green Bay allied the Sioux and Chippewas to His Majesty's side. These advocates of Native culture and religion sought a military solution to their difficulties, but they learned to their detriment that without British assistance, they could no longer withstand the Americans.

The natives' opportunity came with the outbreak of the War of 1812. In a series of tactical victories supported by British forces led by Governor General Isaac Brock of upper Canada (modern Ontario), the garrisons at Forts Mackinac, Detroit, and Dearborn surrendered. The Americans withstood attacks on Forts Wayne, Harrison, and Madison, and from the former staged a counterattack that eventually retook the Lower Peninsula of Michigan and secured southwestern upper Canada with the victory at the Thames River on October 5, 1813. This victory would have been impossible had not Oliver Hazard Perry led a U.S. Navy squadron to a victory over a Royal Navy flotilla at the Battle of Lake Erie on September 10, 1813. The next year American efforts to retake Fort Mackinac and to secure the Wisconsin River region resulted in failure. On the Missouri frontier, the Osages staged raids on outlying settlements, but never threatened American penetration into the trans-Mississippi West. The Treaty of Ghent in December 1814 restored the political boundaries to the prewar status quo. For the third time, His Majesty's Government deserted its Native American allies, and never again would the British support Indian uprisings against the United States.

The Midwest and Manifest Destiny. The half century following the War of 1812 found the military engaged in fortifying the frontiers, mapping the lakes and plains, guarding the trails to Santa Fe and the Pacific, constructing roads and facilitating river navigation to ease transportation difficulties, and moving the natives out of the Great Lakes basin and onto reservations on the edge of the Great Plains. At critical junctures along the Canadian–American border, the United States also maintained a series of token outposts—Fort Wayne at Detroit and Forts Gratiot, Mackinac, and Brady in Michigan were vital symbols of national sovereignty along the long-contested boundary. The pacification of the interior natives re-

sulted in transporting them across the Mississippi into what is now eastern Kansas. Thereafter, the American military establishment abandoned formerly important interior posts such as Forts Wayne and Harrison in Indiana and moved to a series of new installations in the upper Midwest—Forts Crawford, Snelling, Leavenworth, and Riley. This was the vanguard of what was referred to from the 1840s on as Manifest Destiny—a sense of popular mission in the United States to extend its culture and control from the Atlantic to the Pacific.

Of lasting importance were the military-led scientific explorations under the direction of the Corps of Topographical Engineers. Military-led expeditions explored and mapped the upper Great Lakes and Mississippi Valley. The activities of such officers as John C. Frémont expanded the knowledge of the trans-Mississippi West for a nation eager for a better understanding of the Louisiana Purchase and the routes to the Pacific. The most detailed effort was the Pacific railroad surveys ordered by Congress in 1853. These expeditions did not result in a conclusive, scientific-based route westward, but the final thirteen-volume report collated important data on the intricacies of western geography, geology, ethnology, and biology. The meteorological data gathered by post surgeons constituted the first widespread, systematic gathering of such data in history. At Forts Mackinac and Crawford, surgeon Dr. William Beaumont's investigations of digestive juices won him world renown.

The Corps of Engineers began their efforts, that continue into the twenty-first century, to improve the navigation of the rivers and lakes of the region. Based upon supposed military transportation needs, the construction of roads in the states of Michigan, Minnesota, Kansas, and Nebraska under U.S. Army direction became a harbinger of pork barrel projects that would follow. Waterway improvements on the Great Lakes and the Ohio, Mississippi, and Missouri Rivers assisted not only military mobility, but also that of civilian steamboats. Often forgotten is the army's role in the social development of the region. Military balls, regimental bands, post libraries, garrison schools, military chaplains, and surgeons brought touches of civilization to wilderness life. In these ways, the military contributed mightily to stimulating development of the new nation.

Wars of Expansion and Union. The Mexican–American War and the Civil War witnessed the Midwest becoming more a source of troops, supplies, and transportation than a zone of combat. In both conflicts the Midwest was a major source of personnel for wartime units that fought on fronts far from their homes. During the Mexican War, Fort Leavenworth became a point of embarkation for the war zone in what was then northern Mexico. Brigadier General Stephen W. Kearny led an expedition from that post that resulted in the capture of both Santa Fe and San Diego. The Mormon Battalion, led by Regular Army Lieutenant Colonel Philip St. George Cooke, seized Tucson before marching to California. Perhaps the most famous volunteer unit of the war was the First Missouri Mounted Volunteers, commanded by Colonel Alexander Doniphan, which rode to Santa Fe and then marched south to El Paso and Chihuahua in an epic 2,100-mile campaign.

Midwesterners played a prominent role in raising regiments for this conflict. At the same time, a large antiwar sentiment existed in the region, reflecting a growing feeling of the unjustness of the war and of its being part of a slaveholder conspiracy to expand the South's peculiar institution. Such sentiment increased rapidly with the passage of the Kansas-Nebraska Act and the subsequent struggle over popular sovereignty in the Kansas Territory. For the Army, "Bleeding Kansas" demanded neutrality as units from Forts Leavenworth and Riley tried to quell fighting between free state and slave state partisans. Participation in such domestic peace actions would become a frequent Regular Army duty until the passage of the Posse Comitatus Act in 1878.

The outbreak of the Civil War in 1861 found the Midwest at the center of military efforts to quash Southern secession from the Union. With the exception of Missouri, little actual combat occurred in the region, but the Midwest was the source of much manpower, agriculture, industrial, transportation, and leadership support of the Union effort. Midwesterners—most importantly, Abraham Lincoln of Illinois as president, and Salmon P. Chase and Edwin M. Stanton, both of Ohio, as secretaries of the treasury and war, respectively—held important civilian leadership positions in the United States Government.

Certainly one of the more important strategic surprises of the war was the nationalistic sentiment of the Midwest that brought so many soldiers to the Union cause. The region produced several of the most senior combat leaders of the Union effort—Ulysses S. Grant, William T. Sherman, Philip H. Sheridan, Don Carlos Buell, William S. Rosecrans, Ambrose E. Burnside, James H. Wilson, Irvin McDowell, and James B. McPherson, among others. Hundreds of thousands of midwesterners in hundreds of regiments fought in significant actions in the eastern, western, and trans-Mississippi theaters. Grant's famous victories at Vicksburg and Chattanooga and Sherman's notable march through Georgia to the sea were largely supported by midwestern troops.

One must never conclude that there was no opposi-tion to the war in the Midwest. Instead pacifism, ne-grophobia, southern sympathy, war weariness, draft opposition, and political ambition created a strong antiwar movement. Although its importance faded after Union victories in the summer of 1863, this Copperhead movement (along with other, less organized movements) was an important counterpoint to the war effort.

In the five states of the Old Northwest—Ohio, Indiana, Illinois, Michigan, and Wisconsin—an estimated 680 thousand men left farms to join Union regiments, constituting approximately 47 percent of the eighteen- to forty-five-year-old workforce. At the same time agricultural production in the region increased. Women expanded their usual household and farmyard duties to tend the fields. Immigrants filled many farm jobs. Wages for farmhands nearly doubled between 1860 and 1865. Farm machinery increased productivity. The demand for cattle, hogs, horses, and mules outstripped production. Ohio's cattle population dropped by over six hundred thousand, its hog production by 1.3 million. In the midst of all this loss of farm labor and increased military demand, midwestern farm sales overseas rose. The Civil War accelerated prewar agricultural trends, growing mechanization, increased integration with the market system, and greater specialization. It was an era of immense farm prosperity.

Industrial expansion in the war increased opportunities for the unemployed and underemployed, but there was a constant conflict between increased wages and rising inflation. The factory system expanded greatly, especially in cities like Cincinnati, Chicago, and St. Louis. The Missouri metropolis became the center of a shipyard that invented, designed, and built ironclads for riverine warfare. Cincinnati prospered by introducing the factory method to the production of uniforms. One amazed British visitor found industrial and agricultural output increasing; railroads, businesses, factories, and houses being built; agricultural land use expanding; and trade increasing. His astonishment increased when he recognized that the small state of Indiana could contribute 125 thousand men to the war effort and still expand its economy.

For most of the postwar years, the military became increasingly irrelevant to the region's economy and protection. With the termination of the final Great Plains Indian battles in the 1890s, the need for military presence became less necessary and economically significant. The army school system peaked at what became the Command and General Staff College at Fort Leavenworth. Increasingly, education was more important than military experience.

Although the region provided its share of soldiers and sailors for the Spanish–American War, most notable was the closing of many regional battalion and regimental posts in the late nineteenth and early twentieth centuries. A growing midwestern isolationist sentiment symbolized by William Jennings Bryan of Nebraska opposed the internationalist and interventionist attitudes of many leaders from the coastal areas of the country. From the 1890s until the American entry in World War II, the region dominated the isolationist wings of both political parties.

Rise of a Superpower. World War I saw several high command positions dominated by midwesterners—John J. Pershing of Missouri commanded the American Expeditionary Force in France, and James G. Harbord of Illinois was his able commander of the AEF Services of Supply. Brigadier General William "Billy" Mitchell of Wisconsin emerged from the war as a champion of airpower. Former Cleveland mayor Newton D. Baker served as secretary of war throughout the conflict. The region supplied its share of troops and productive capacity for the war effort, but a decided shift in training programs took the Army's major new posts outside the Midwest to land that was less expensive and less intensely cultivated and to a climate more suited to year-round operations. The only new permanent Army post established in the era was Fort Leonard Wood, Missouri; other existing bases were expanded to support the war effort.

By far the Midwest's major contribution was again its agricultural productivity and its industrial output. Demand for American agricultural products by the armed forces and Europe brought unparalleled prosperity to the region's farmers. The war accentuated the growing urbanization of the region. Demand for the revolution in warfare and transportation brought by the internal combustion engine made the midwestern automotive and airplane factories and their suppliers centers of productive output. Besides the core cities of Chicago and St. Louis, midwestern communities like Cleveland, Columbus, Cincinnati, Dayton, Toledo, Detroit, Grand Rapids, Milwaukee, and Minneapolis–St. Paul received considerable emigration from the farms and small towns of the Midwest. Jobs for women expanded exponentially. Of particular importance was the dramatic movement of African Americans out of the South into jobs at the steel mills, mines, factories, and packinghouses of the Midwest. All of this sparked racial discrimination and race riots, most notably in East St. Louis, Illinois. People in European ethnic communities, especially German Americans, faced considerable discrimination in many midwestern locales, particularly if they opposed the war.

The Great War, as contemporaries called World War I, contributed to the growing nationalization of the economy, centralization of authority, ideological

conformity, and social change. It marks the beginning of the loss of regional identity and a decline in the Midwest's importance in military affairs. The new military would be more focused on the South and coastal regions, which had the capacity to train soldiers most of the year and the ability to move American forces more easily to international trouble spots. Still the region's manpower, agricultural, and industrial resources represented an important element in the nation's military potential.

The Midwest was a leading factor in postwar disillusionment that swept the nation following the failure of the war to make the world safe for democracy. Writers like Ernest Hemingway and John Dos Passos, both born in Illinois though influenced by other experiences, wrote antiwar novels that received wide circulation. Senator Gerald Nye of North Dakota headed a senatorial committee that blamed New York financiers for American entry into the war. Aviation hero Charles A. Lindbergh of Missouri and publisher Robert McCormick of the Chicago *Tribune* led the interwar isolationist effort, arguing that defense of the Western Hemisphere was the only American obligation. Midwestern politicians were stalwarts behind the Neutrality acts of 1935, 1936, and 1937. Not until the fall of Poland and France to German forces in 1939 and 1940, respectively, did sentiment begin to change.

With the bombing of Pearl Harbor, the Midwest became an enthusiastic supporter of the war effort. Again its people, farms, mines, factories, and transportation network labored for victory. The industrial states of the Old Northwest again devoted their vast capacity to the war effort. The expansion of communities was explosive. The Ford Motor Company built B-24 bombers in its new Willow Run plant in Michigan, and soon the once tiny community found itself housing ninety thousand defense industry workers and thirty-five thousand military personnel in barns, garages, rented rooms, and trailers. St. Louis and Wichita became important aircraft manufacturing communities. Almost overnight Seneca, Illinois, became a significant shipbuilding center for LSTs, specialized large landing craft. The electronics industry from Cincinnati to Des Moines grew dramatically. The Midwest's largely mechanized agriculture proved capable of expanding production while reducing the labor force. Women, African Americans, and Appalachian whites vied with one another for the new jobs and necessary housing facilities in overcrowded cities. The resulting social tensions brought race riots in various communities, most conspicuously Detroit.

World War II represents the acme of Midwest influence in military affairs. It provided more than its share of the leadership, personnel, industrial output, and agricultural produce necessary for victory. Despite the large percentage of wartime industrial contracts that went to the region, the real shift in military affairs was to the South, Southwest, and Pacific Coast. Moreover, the war and its immediate aftermath saw many of the Midwest's sons and daughters migrate to the newly discovered enticements of the Far West. Industrial production rose dramatically in the Pacific states, and never again would the Heartland's dominance of the national productive output be as great as it was during World War II.

The war also changed the isolationist tendencies of the region's political figures. Senator Arthur Vandenberg of Michigan went from being an America First leader to an internationalist. Major cold war political figures such as Harry S Truman of Missouri, Dwight D. Eisenhower and Robert J. Dole of Kansas, and Hubert Humphrey of Minnesota were at the forefront of the nation's involvement in world affairs. Midwestern professional military personnel continued in leadership positions in the armed services. Among the more conspicuous, Nathan F. Twining of Wisconsin was the first Air Force officer to chair the Joint Chiefs of Staff, Curtis LeMay of Ohio developed the Strategic Air Command, and Army General Bernard Rogers of Kansas became the longest-serving commander of the North Atlantic Treaty Organization.

The Air Force saw the Midwest as a logical location for many of its intercontinental bombers and missile bases. Offutt Air Force Base outside Omaha became the headquarters of the Strategic Air Command, later known as the Strategic Command. Missile and bomber bases proliferated throughout the Midwest, especially in the trans-Mississippi states.

Midwestern opposition to the Vietnam War was instrumental in driving national sentiment against that conflict and the military in general. Students for a Democratic Society organized in Michigan, radical activists bombed a defense research facility at the University of Wisconsin, war protestors and the police clashed at the 1968 Democratic Convention in Chicago, and the National Guard killing of four war protestors at Kent State University in Ohio in 1970 marked a milestone in domestic discontent over the war. Senator George S. McGovern of South Dakota led much of the opposition to Vietnam involvement. In many Midwest states, recruitment for the armed forces was below the national average, and with the end of the cold war and the reduction in the size of the armed forces, the Midwest faced a serious decline in the number of military installations located on its soil. Yet, the Midwest probably remained more supportive of this conflict and later ones than any other region of the country except the South.

Despite its remaining bases and military procurement from its industrial concerns, most midwestern states had a net outflow of tax dollars for military expenditures to other regions of the nation. Even so, missile bases remain throughout the Great Plains; B-2 bombers fly intercontinental missions from midwestern bases; Forts Leonard Wood, Riley, and Leavenworth continue as important Army posts; the Great Lakes Naval Training Center is the focus of most naval education; and Wright-Patterson Air Force Base has a larger number of Air Force and civilian employees than any Air Force installation. In keeping with a long tradition of midwestern leadership in the professional military, at the dawn of the twenty-first century, the chairman of the Joint Chiefs of Staff, Air Force General Richard B. Myers, was a Kansan, and the Chief of Naval Operations, Admiral Vern Clark, was born in Iowa and raised in Nebraska, Missouri, and Illinois. Though military installations and expenditures in the Midwest have been reduced since the end of the cold war, a major military presence remains.

Sources and Further Reading: Robert S. Allen, *His Majesty's Indian Allies* (1992); Stephen E. Ambrose, *Undaunted Courage* (1997); John M. Blum, *V Was for Victory* (1976); Edward M. Coffman, *The War to End All Wars* (1968); Gregory Evans Dowd, *A Spirited Resistance* (1992); William H. Goetzmann, *Army Exploration in the American West, 1803–1863* (1959); Michael N. McConnell, *A Country Between* (1997); Francis Paul Prucha, *Broadax and Bayonet* (1953); Francis Paul Prucha, *The Sword of the Republic* (1969); William B. Skelton, *An American Profession of Arms* (1992); Roger J. Spiller, ed., *Dictionary of American Military Biography*, 3 vols. (1984); Robert M. Utley, *Frontiersmen in Blue* (1967); Robert M. Utley, *Frontier Regulars* (1973); Richard White, *The Middle Ground* (1991).

David Curtis Skaggs
Bowling Green State University, Ohio

Indian Warfare

Whether fought for personal motives of vengeance or advancement, or for group motives of competition for hunting grounds or access to other resources, wars were a fact of daily life for the native peoples of the Midwest prior to the arrival of Europeans. After 1650, the scope and intensity of native warfare in the Midwest increased with the influx of firearms, the fur trade economy, and demographic crises stemming from the influx of European epidemic diseases. Conflicts between the Midwest's indigenous peoples and the European settler population exerted great influence over the course of the region's history between 1760 and 1890; these conflicts also shaped enduring stereotypes of native peoples as wild, bloodthirsty "savages." Since

1890, many Native Americans from the Midwest have preserved long-standing military traditions in their cultures through service in the United States military.

Although precontact native weaponry consisted of only bows and arrows, knives and spears of bone or stone, and wooden clubs, warfare before the arrival of Europeans, while limited in its objectives, could be quite violent. Archaeological evidence of palisaded villages, mass graves, and skeletal remains with embedded projectile points indicates that war was more than a sport. Small-scale, ambush-style raiding for captives represented the most frequent type of warfare, but

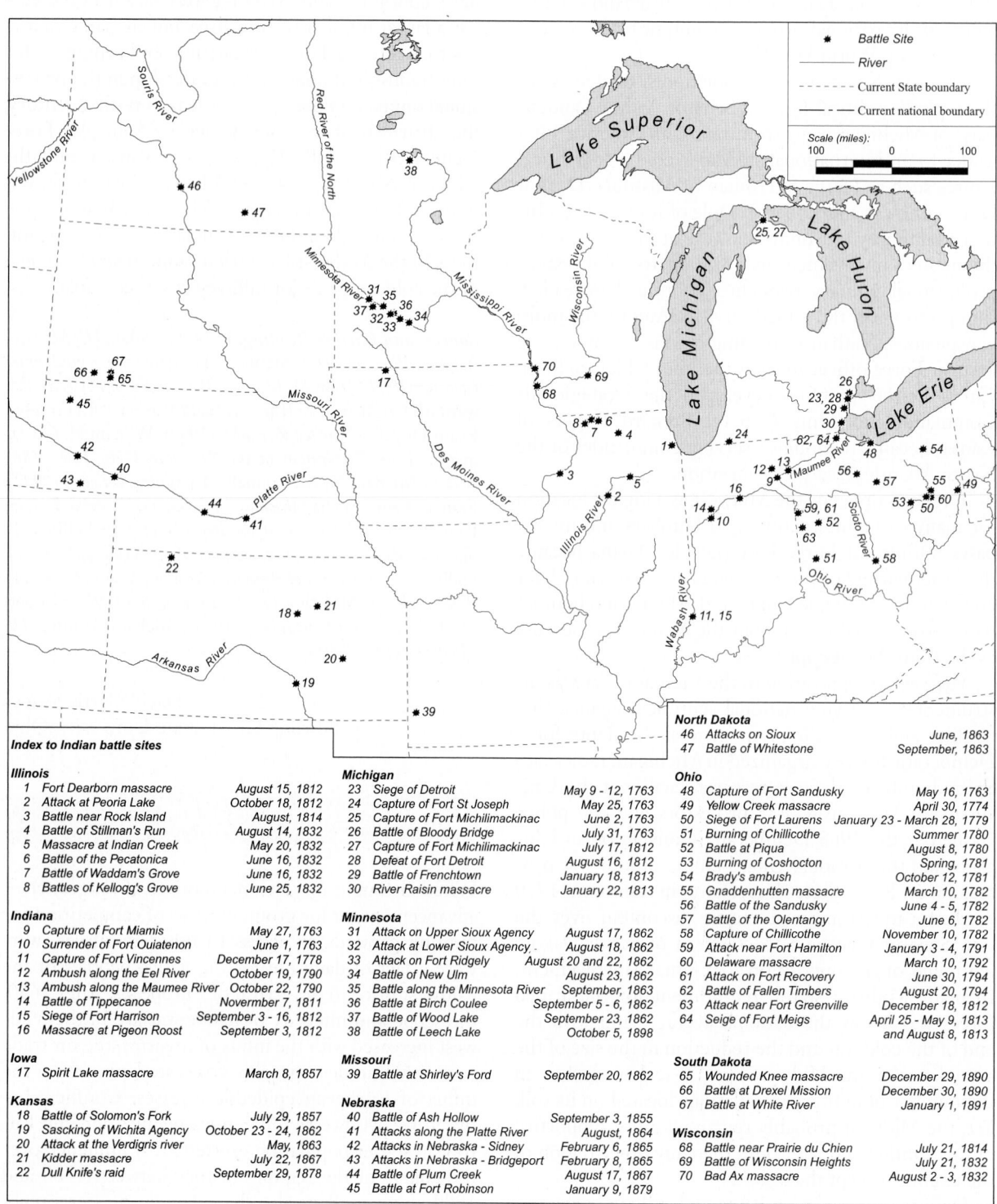

Index to Indian battle sites

Illinois
1	Fort Dearborn massacre	August 15, 1812
2	Attack at Peoria Lake	October 18, 1812
3	Battle near Rock Island	August, 1814
4	Battle of Stillman's Run	August 14, 1832
5	Massacre at Indian Creek	May 20, 1832
6	Battle of the Pecatonica	June 16, 1832
7	Battle of Waddam's Grove	June 16, 1832
8	Battles of Kellogg's Grove	June 25, 1832

Indiana
9	Capture of Fort Miamis	May 27, 1763
10	Surrender of Fort Ouiatenon	June 1, 1763
11	Capture of Fort Vincennes	December 17, 1778
12	Ambush along the Eel River	October 19, 1790
13	Ambush along the Maumee River	October 22, 1790
14	Battle of Tippecanoe	Novermber 7, 1811
15	Siege of Fort Harrison	September 3 - 16, 1812
16	Massacre at Pigeon Roost	September 3, 1812

Iowa
| 17 | Spirit Lake massacre | March 8, 1857 |

Kansas
18	Battle of Solomon's Fork	July 29, 1857
19	Sascking of Wichita Agency	October 23 - 24, 1862
20	Attack at the Verdigris river	May, 1863
21	Kidder massacre	July 22, 1867
22	Dull Knife's raid	September 29, 1878

Michigan
23	Siege of Detroit	May 9 - 12, 1763
24	Capture of Fort St Joseph	May 25, 1763
25	Capture of Fort Michilimackinac	June 2, 1763
26	Battle of Bloody Bridge	July 31, 1763
27	Capture of Fort Michilimackinac	July 17, 1812
28	Defeat of Fort Detroit	August 16, 1812
29	Battle of Frenchtown	January 18, 1813
30	River Raisin massacre	January 22, 1813

Minnesota
31	Attack on Upper Sioux Agency	August 17, 1862
32	Attack at Lower Sioux Agency	August 18, 1862
33	Attack on Fort Ridgely	August 20 and 22, 1862
34	Battle of New Ulm	August 23, 1862
35	Battle along the Minnesota River	September, 1863
36	Battle at Birch Coulee	September 5 - 6, 1862
37	Battle of Wood Lake	September 23, 1862
38	Battle of Leech Lake	October 5, 1898

Missouri
| 39 | Battle at Shirley's Ford | September 20, 1862 |

Nebraska
40	Battle of Ash Hollow	September 3, 1855
41	Attacks along the Platte River	August, 1864
42	Attacks in Nebraska - Sidney	February 6, 1865
43	Attacks in Nebraska - Bridgeport	February 8, 1865
44	Battle of Plum Creek	August 17, 1867
45	Battle at Fort Robinson	January 9, 1879

North Dakota
| 46 | Attacks on Sioux | June, 1863 |
| 47 | Battle of Whitestone | September, 1863 |

Ohio
48	Capture of Fort Sandusky	May 16, 1763
49	Yellow Creek massacre	April 30, 1774
50	Siege of Fort Laurens	January 23 - March 28, 1779
51	Burning of Chillicothe	Summer 1780
52	Battle at Piqua	August 8, 1780
53	Burning of Coshocton	Spring, 1781
54	Brady's ambush	October 12, 1781
55	Gnaddenhutten massacre	March 10, 1782
56	Battle of the Sandusky	June 4 - 5, 1782
57	Battle of the Olentangy	June 6, 1782
58	Capture of Chillicothe	November 10, 1782
59	Attack on Fort Hamilton	January 3 - 4, 1791
60	Delaware massacre	March 10, 1792
61	Attack on Fort Recovery	June 30, 1794
62	Battle of Fallen Timbers	August 20, 1794
63	Attack near Fort Greenville	December 18, 1812
64	Seige of Fort Meigs	April 25 - May 9, 1813 and August 8, 1813

South Dakota
65	Wounded Knee massacre	December 29, 1890
66	Battle at Drexel Mission	December 30, 1890
67	Battle at White River	January 1, 1891

Wisconsin
68	Battle near Prairie du Chien	July 21, 1814
69	Battle of Wisconsin Heights	July 21, 1832
70	Bad Ax massacre	August 2 - 3, 1832

Indian battles. Prepared by James DeGrand. *Source:* Brian Leigh Dunnigan, *Atlas of Great Lakes Native Americans* (2001).

large groups of Native warriors occasionally engaged in massed battlefield tactics.

Native military leaders' status derived from their ability to achieve victories while minimizing casualties. They lacked coercive authority over their warriors, especially younger men seeking enhanced social standing through military exploits. Native youths first accompanied war parties around the age of fifteen, often after an appropriate vision, and many nations required the attainment of some war honors ("coups") before recognizing a young man as an adult member of the community. Native women frequently played roles in encouraging attacks on enemies, participated in the defense of their home villages, and accompanied large expeditionary forces in support roles, sometimes as warriors.

The era of hostile European contact in the Midwest began in the early summer of 1541, when Francisco Vásquez de Coronado and his men, frustrated over their failure to locate the mythical kingdom of Quivira, executed their native guide near modern Lyons, Kansas. Prolonged, intense warfare with outsiders did not begin for the native people of the Midwest until after 1649, when firearms-bearing Iroquois warriors from modern New York routed the Hurons and dispersed the remaining Huron population from the Bruce Peninsula in modern Ontario into the upper Great Lakes region.

The westward expansion of the Iroquois after 1650, in search of furs and captives, caused significant political and economic upheaval in the Midwest. Retreating from a wave of Iroquois assaults that began in 1653, Sauk, Fox, Miami, Ojibwe, and Potawatomi populations trespassed on the territory of Siouan peoples, inaugurating a new series of intertribal conflicts. The Ojibway–Dakota war, which originated in competition for hunting territory northeast of the Mississippi River during the 1670s, persisted for nearly two centuries.

French explorer Nicolas Perrot reached Green Bay in 1665, adding new economic motivation (via the fur trade) and access to firearms to an already volatile military situation. Iroquois warriors continued to launch expeditions into the Midwest until 1680, when they attacked the Illinois. However, French support enabled the region's peoples to retaliate, and warriors from a variety of nations joined French invasions of Iroquois territory in the 1680s and 1690s. Similarly, French allies assisted the Pawnees in repelling Navajo attackers in 1697, but the Navajos returned the next year and destroyed three Pawnee villages.

By about 1700, native warriors had largely converted from bows and arrows to flintlock muskets, which entered the Midwest from the northeast. The western Sioux employed firearms to launch a series of

❖ Logan's Lament

On April 30, 1774 family members and relatives of a Cayuga Indian known as John Logan were massacred along the Ohio River, opposite the mouth of Yellow Creek near present day Wellsville, Ohio. Logan spent the next months avenging these deaths by attacking white settlers, taking both scalps and prisoners. During this time a larger war, Lord Dunmore's War, between tribes living in the Ohio Country and troops of the Colony of Virginia ensued, culminating in the defeat of Indian forces at the Battle of Point Pleasant on October 10, 1774. Logan's war party returned from their final raid after that battle had ended and peace negotiations had begun. Logan did not participate in the peace process, but in his famous Lament, privately justified his actions to trader and interpreter John Gibson, who recited Logan's words to Lord Dunmore, Governor of Virginia, at Camp Charlotte, near present day Chillicothe, Ohio. Logan's statement was widely published and was unquestioned as to its authenticity for nearly a quarter of a century after it was first delivered, though it became embroiled in controversy after Thomas Jefferson included it as set forth below, in his *Notes on the State of Virginia* (1787) as an example of Indian eloquence.

I appeal to any white man to say, if ever he entered Logan's cabin hungry, and he gave him not meat; if ever he came cold and naked, and he clothed him not. During the course of the last long and bloody war [the French and Indian War, 1755–1763], Logan remained idle in his cabin, an advocate for peace. Such was my love for the whites, that my countrymen pointed as they passed, and said, "Logan is the friend of white men." I had even thought to have lived with you, but for the injuries of one man. Col. Cresap, the last spring, in cold blood, and unprovoked, murdered all the relations of Logan, not sparing even my women and children. There runs not a drop of my blood in the veins of any living creature. This called on me for revenge. I have sought it: I have killed many: I have fully glutted my vengeance. For my country, I rejoice at the beams of peace. But do not harbour a thought that mine is the joy of fear. Logan never felt fear. He will not turn on his heel to save his life. Who is there to mourn for Logan?—Not one.

Source: Alan D. Gutchess, West Salem, Ohio.

attacks on the Illinois, Fox, and Miamis during the 1690s. The introduction of horses from the Spanish colonies in the southwest also had a transforming effect on warfare in the Midwest. Horse-propelled Osage warriors raided the Pawnees for slaves to trade to the French colony of Louisiana after 1700, but the Pawnees quickly adapted. In August 1720, they used a stampede on horseback and French firearms to evict a Spanish expeditionary force from their village on the Platte River (near modern Columbus, Nebraska).

Further to the east, French efforts to control the diverse native population began to involve military force. French troops, with the assistance of Huron and Ottawa allies, slaughtered several hundred Fox at Detroit in 1711. The French then spent two decades pursuing the Fox in an unsuccessful attempt to exterminate that nation. They also protected their network of trade and alliances by attacking native groups who entertained English traders. French officers at Detroit quelled an uprising by the Wyandots of Sandusky in 1747, and employed a large contingent of Ottawa warriors to destroy the upstart British-allied Miami village at Pickawillany (near modern Piqua, Ohio) in 1752.

Many allied native warriors assisted the French in the French and Indian War (1754–1760). Nearly a thousand fought in the November 1755 defeat of British General Edward Braddock, and many returned yearly to Fort Duquesne (modern Pittsburgh) to harass the Pennsylvania and New York frontiers. Their effectiveness as fighters was noted by one contemporary observer, who exclaimed that they "approach like foxes, fight like lions, and disappear like birds." In addition to these military honors, Odawa, Potawatomi, and Menominee warriors returned to their Great Lakes villages with horses and, after the 1757 massacre at Fort William Henry, with a devastating epidemic of smallpox.

Despite consistent assistance from allied native warriors the French were defeated by the British in 1760, a state of affairs recognized by treaty in 1763. The British reoccupied former French posts, but their inability to meet native expectations and tacit obligations as alliance partners initiated six decades of hostilities with European American soldiers and settlers.

Although British officials tried to enforce boundaries to protect native villages and hunting territories, the relentless expansion of settler population into the Midwest after 1760 encouraged the rise of militant nativism among the region's Indian nations. Urged by a series of prophets to abandon accommodation with the newcomers and to return to traditional lifestyles, many former tribal enemies set aside long-standing disputes to achieve unprecedented unity of purpose in resisting white encroachment. The Great Lakes Algonquian nations commenced this effort with fifteen consecutive months of hostilities against British military installations and European American settlers after May 1763. Before peace terms ending Pontiac's War were negotiated in 1766, Algonquian warriors had killed an estimated two thousand settlers and four hundred soldiers, and they had captured, destroyed, or forced the abandonment of nine interior forts. The extent of native military success influenced the establishment of the Ohio River as a settlement boundary line in the 1768 Treaty of Fort Stanwix. Yet ongoing settler trespass into native territory continued to fuel an escalating cycle of murders and retaliatory attacks between native and European American communities.

The outbreak of the American Revolutionary War in 1775 found most of the native peoples of modern Ohio and Michigan supporting the British. Utilizing Crown-supplied arms and ammunition, they continued their own war on American settlers and soldiers, concentrating on the Kentucky frontier between 1777 and 1779. Meanwhile, native peoples in Illinois country, influenced by their former ties with the French and by their recent Spanish alliance, supported American military efforts in the region between 1778 and 1781.

After the United States achieved independence from Great Britain in 1783, midwestern native peoples faced constant aggression from an expansion-oriented population convinced of its right to appropriate, occupy, and improve land that "savages" merely roamed. Between 1782 and 1791, confederated native armies under Miami and Shawnee leadership proved superior to American regular forces, but internal disagreements about the viability of ongoing resistance contributed to General "Mad" Anthony Wayne's crucial victory at the August 20, 1794, Battle of Fallen Timbers (near modern Maumee, Ohio). The resulting Treaty of Greenville, in 1795, required extensive cessions of native territory in the Midwest.

The revived nativist message of the Shawnee Prophet Tenskwatawa after 1805 inspired his brother Tecumseh and others to reconstitute a pan-tribal military force at Prophet's Town (near modern Lafayette, Indiana). Attacked by American troops in the November 1811 Battle of Tippecanoe, Tecumseh and his allied warriors joined with the British in the War of 1812. Despite several early battlefield victories, their success proved fleeting. Tecumseh's death at the October 1813 Battle of the Thames and the devolution of the conflict into military stalemate ended any prospect of Midwest natives halting American settler expansion after 1815.

The acquisition of Louisiana by the United States in 1803 brought native peoples living west of the Mississippi River into sustained conflict with Americans for the first time. Many of these groups had only recently taken advantage of imported horses and firearms to move onto the Plains and to establish a new cultural complex founded on equestrian buffalo hunting. The western Sioux, for example, employed horses and firearms over the course of the eighteenth century to displace the sedentary Mandans, Hidatsas, Arikaras, and Omahas from the Missouri River valley. During that time, the Sioux and other groups developed highly skilled cavalries with an intense warrior ethos.

Resistance to American expansion by Midwest Nations without horses was sporadic and easily put down by American forces after 1816. Winnebago leader Red Bird's brief 1827 uprising in Wisconsin ended with the threat of federal retaliation; Sauk leader Black Hawk's effort to reoccupy tribal territory in Illinois in 1832 was crushed by fire from American gunships and the assistance of Sioux warriors. Sioux aggression also targeted American settlers and armies. In August 1862, attacks by the Mdewakanton and Wahpekute bands of the Santee Sioux on settlers in Minnesota elicited retaliatory attacks by American troops on all Santee Sioux. Six years later, Sioux warriors joined the Cheyennes and Arapahoes in an intense besiegement of American forces under George A. Forsyth at Beecher's Island on the Republican River in Kansas. Intertribal conflicts continued, however, complicating the situation. The Sioux, for example, subjected the Pawnees—who had surrendered their weapons and renounced warfare in 1833 to live as agrarians ostensibly under American protection—to four decades of unremitting attacks.

American officials responded to the military crisis on the Plains with a program of total war after 1865. With waves of settlers entering their territory by wagon and by rail, the decimation of vast numbers of buffalo, and with a determined and experienced American cavalry assisted by native scouts, the tide of hostilities increasingly swung against the Midwest Indian nations. The so-called Indian Wars ended on December 29, 1890, at Wounded Knee on the Pine Ridge Sioux Reservation in South Dakota. Here, American troops employed artillery and repeating rifles to kill at least one hundred and fifty Sioux men, women, and children affiliated with Chief Big Foot, who were considered part of the messianic Ghost Dance movement that had prophesied the return of traditional lifestyles and the disappearance of the American settler population.

By 1890, nearly two hundred and fifty years of warfare had exacted a heavy toll on the native people of the Midwest. Confined to reservations, often at great distances from their traditional homelands, and militarily defeated, their communities struggled to cope with the collapse of traditional values and institutions that attended their loss of independence. Ironically, since the turn of the twentieth century, one way in which Native American men and women have restored both traditional tribal customs and a sense of personal empowerment has been through service in all branches of the United States armed forces.

Sources and Further Reading: Colin G. Calloway, *New Worlds for All* (1997); Gregory E. Dowd, *A Spirited Resistance* (1992); R. David Edmunds and Joseph L. Peyser, *The Fox Wars* (1993); Howard H. Peckham, *Pontiac and the Indian Uprising* (1947); Francis Paul Prucha, *The Sword of the Republic* (1977); Frank R. Secoy, *Changing Military Patterns of the Great Plains Indians* (1992); David C. Skaggs and Larry L. Nelson, eds. *The Sixty Years' War for the Great Lakes, 1754–1814* (2001); Armstrong Starkey, *European and Native American Warfare, 1675–1815* (1998); Wiley Sword, *President Washington's Indian War* (1985); Richard White, *The Middle Ground* (1991); Robert M. Utley, *The Indian Frontier of the American West, 1846–1890* (1984).

Jon Parmenter
Cornell University, New York

Black Hawk (Makataimeshekiakiak, c. 1767–1838)

Born at Saukenuk (modern Rock Island, Illinois), into the Thunder clan of the Sauk nation, Black Hawk witnessed the dramatic transformation of his people's independent lifestyle brought about by the westward expansion of the United States after 1783. Although often characterized as a vengeful and violent resistance leader because of his colorful and defiant oratory, Black Hawk actually expressed his commitment to traditional Sauk values in a largely nonviolent manner. Black Hawk's struggle involved not only conflict with American settlers and soldiers; he also opposed fellow Sauk leaders who supported accommodation with the United States.

Black Hawk supported Tecumseh's vision of united native resistance to American expansion and fought with the Shawnee leader's confederacy in the War of 1812. Increasingly alienated after 1816 from the United States and from fellow Sauk leader Keokuk, whose willingness to trade his people's land for peace antagonized many Sauks, Black Hawk and his followers sought diplomatic ties with the British at Fort Malden (modern Amherstburg, Ontario). In 1829, Keokuk formally ceded to the United States all Sauk lands in Illinois in exchange for lands in Iowa and an annuity payment. Black Hawk returned from spring hunting in 1829 to discover American settlers occupying Saukenuk. He and his followers coexisted peacefully with the Americans at Saukenuk, in defiance of Keokuk's cession, until forced out by American troops in June 1831.

Retreating across the Mississippi, Black Hawk sought guidance from his uncle, the Winnebago-Sauk spiritual leader Wabokieshiek, prior to assembling a group of nearly two thousand Sauk, Mesquakie, and Kickapoo men, women, and children to return to traditional Illinois homelands in April 1832. However, Black Hawk's search for support among other Algonquian nations in Illinois and Wisconsin proved fruitless, and he prepared to surrender peacefully. On May 14, 1832, under a white flag of truce, his party was fired on by Illinois militiamen. Black Hawk routed the state troops in a battle known as Stillman's Run, and this event triggered the summer-long Black Hawk War of 1832, which consisted primarily of American search-and-destroy missions against the retreating Sauks. Black Hawk formally surrendered at Fort Crawford (modern Prairie du Chien, Wisconsin), on August 27, 1832. Incarcerated at Jefferson Barracks in St. Louis until April 1833, Black Hawk and a number of his warriors were then sent to Washington, D.C., where they met President Andrew Jackson. American officials then escorted Black Hawk's party on a tour of eastern cities and military installations, intending to impress upon the Indians the futility of future resistance to the United States.

Black Hawk dictated his *Autobiography* in 1833. This text, avidly read by the American public as the final speech of a defeated native leader, actually reaffirmed the traditional Sauk practice of coup tales related by warriors. Through his *Autobiography*, Black Hawk validated his native identity, expressed bitter contempt toward his rival Keokuk, and ensured that his rationale for resistance to the American expansionism would be remembered.

Black Hawk died on October 3, 1838, at Iowaville on the Des Moines River. His remains were later disinterred and placed on display in the Iowa Territorial governor's office. His wife, Asshewagua, survived him.

Sources and Further Reading: Donald Jackson, ed., *Black Hawk: An Autobiography* (1990); Roger L. Nichols, *Black Hawk and the Warrior's Path* (1992).

Jon Parmenter
Cornell University, New York

Charles-Michel Mouet de Langlade (c. 1729–1802)

Baptized at Michilimackinac in 1729, Charles Langlade was the son of Augustin Mouet de Langlade, a French trader, and Domitilde, sister of Nissowaquet, a prominent Ottawa chief. Langlade played a prominent and influential role in the colonial history of the United States and the early Midwest. His importance stemmed mainly from his ability to mediate between various Native American communities of the *pays d'en haut*, and British, French, and American officials. Along with his Native American kin and allies, Langlade played a prominent role in the Seven Years' War in America—most significantly, leading a raid against the Miami village of Pickawillany, in present-

day Ohio, which helped precipitate the start of the war. After the Seven Years' War, Langlade played a significant role in Pontiac's Rebellion and the American Revolution, during which he and his Indian allies served against George Rogers Clark at Vincennes (now in Indiana) and organized an unsuccessful expedition into Illinois country in 1780 to assist in an attack on Spanish St. Louis (now in Missouri).

Langlade not only helped shape and maintain a balance of power between Native Americans and various imperial intrusions in the Midwest during the latter half of the eighteenth century, but he also ultimately helped pave the way for future European American expansion in the area. Langlade developed and maintained extensive and lasting trading networks throughout Michigan and Wisconsin, finally making a more permanent home at La Baye (Green Bay), where he also served as a militia captain. He is considered by some the Father of Wisconsin, with at least one county and one town in that state named after him. He married Charlote Ambroisine Bourassa on August 12, 1754, at Fort Mechillimackinac, located in what is now Michigan. They had two daughters.

Source and Further Reading: Michael A. McDonnell, "Charles-Michel Mouet de Langlade," in David C. Skaggs and Larry L. Nelson, eds., *The Sixty Years' War for the Great Lakes, 1754–1814* (2001).

Michael A. McDonnell
University of Wales, Swansea, United Kingdom

Pontiac (Obwandiyag, c. 1720–1769)

Known primarily for his role in the war that bears his name, Pontiac remains the subject of much historical debate. While some scholars credit him with masterminding a succession of military attacks against European American forts and settlements throughout the Great Lakes region during the summer of 1763, others dispute the extent of his political influence and military activity beyond his home settlement near Detroit. Whether or not Pontiac organized a far-reaching conspiracy, he served as the catalyst for a native resistance movement unprecedented in both its geographic scope and its ultimate diplomatic success.

Little is known of Pontiac's life before 1757, when he delivered a speech to French authorities at Fort Duquesne (modern Pittsburgh). An active partisan on behalf of the French during the Seven Years' War (1756–1763), Pontiac remained loyal to his allies after the conquest of Canada by Great Britain on September 8, 1760. Many of his subsequent activities were devoted to effecting the return of conditions his

Portrayal of Pontiac, chief of the Odawa. Ohio Historical Society, SC1663.

people experienced in relations with French civil and military officials.

Following the takeover of former French forts by British Army troops (1760–1761), numerous Algonquian nations grew aggrieved by the parsimony of British officials in diplomatic negotiations, as well as by the failure of the British to fulfill an earlier promise to ban settlement west of the Appalachian Mountains. Pontiac worked to meld this growing anti-English sentiment among the region's native peoples with nativist messages of spiritual revival emanating from Delaware villages in the Ohio country. By April 27, 1763, Pontiac had prepared his plans for an assault on the key British fort at Detroit.

Pontiac commenced his siege of Detroit on May 9, 1763. Within a month, he had nearly nine hundred Odawa, Ojibway, Potawatomi, and Huron warriors fighting with him. Other nations followed Pontiac's lead, and by the end of June 1763, nine British-occupied forts between western Pennsylvania and Wisconsin had been either destroyed by native attacks or abandoned. The troops at Detroit held out until reinforcements arrived on October 3, 1763. On October 30, 1763, Pontiac learned that assistance from French

soldiers posted in Illinois would not be forthcoming, and he raised his siege.

Hostilities in Pontiac's War continued intermittently for the next two years, and during that time, Pontiac visited native communities throughout modern Ohio, Michigan, Indiana, and Illinois, urging continued resistance to the British regime. As his notoriety grew, Pontiac came to be seen by the British authorities as crucial to ending the wasting conflict. In talks with British negotiators at Fort Ouiatanon (near modern Lafayette, Indiana) in July 1765, Pontiac agreed to preliminary terms of peace. Pontiac's demand that the British purchase land in the Great Lakes region before settling the region was endorsed in the July 1766 Treaty of Oswego, which ended Pontiac's War.

After fighting the British to a military stalemate and securing a key diplomatic victory for his native allies, Pontiac attempted to follow a peaceful life of hunting. Yet his reputation attracted attention and fear, and he was murdered by a Peoria Indian in the Illinois village of Cahokia on April 20, 1769. He reportedly had several wives, the last being Kan-tucke-qun (the Woman Canoe Paddler), sister of a former wife, with whom he had one son. He had at least two older sons.

Sources and Further Reading: Gregory Evans Dowd, *War Under Heaven* (2002); Howard H. Peckham, *Pontiac and the Indian Uprising* (1947); Richard White, *The Middle Ground* (1991).

Jon Parmenter
Cornell University, New York

The American Revolution, 1775–1783

At the outbreak of the American Revolution in 1775, that part of the Midwest comprising the future states of Ohio, Indiana, Illinois, and Michigan was populated by Indian tribes: Shawnee, Miami, Wyandot, Delaware, Ottawa, Mingo, and others. They were part of British North America and relied upon the British at Fort Detroit to help them resist encroachments by Americans pressing against their territory from Pennsylvania, Virginia, and Kentucky.

In the years of the Revolution, however, the American pioneers, far from endangering the Indians, were exposed to attack. Their settlements were few in number, and the Continental Congress, hard put to repel British assaults in the east, could offer little protection. Until 1777, Indian activity along the borders of white settlement was initiated by the natives themselves,

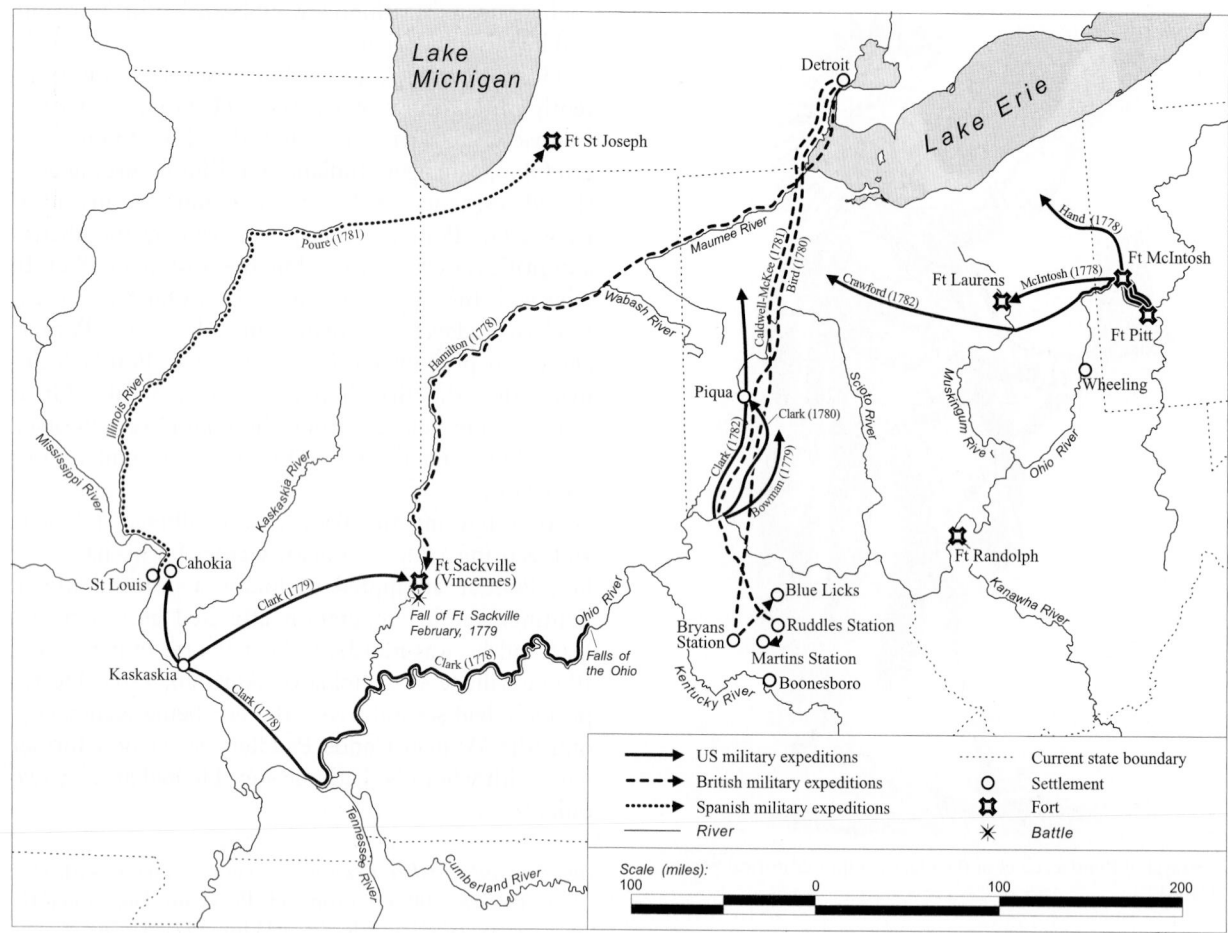

The Midwest in the American Revolution. Prepared by James DeGrand. *Source:* David Curtis Skaggs, ed., *The Old Northwest in the American Revolution* (1977), maps 2–5.

with whatever small logistical support they could procure from the British. Henry Hamilton, British lieutenant governor at Detroit, had been admonished by his superior, Governor Guy Carleton at Quebec, to keep the Indians friendly to the king and neutral toward the Americans, while holding expenditures to a minimum. In any case, the American occupation of the St. Lawrence River valley during their invasion of Canada in 1775–1776 made it impossible for the British to provide the Indians north of the Ohio River with adequate provisions for sustained offensive warfare.

The new settlers in Kentucky and all along the southern bank of the Ohio to Pittsburgh were terrified by the potential threat of Indian attack. In the summer of 1775, many temporarily fled eastward. The Virginia Revolutionary government, relying on its own resources, bestirred itself to defend the frontier. On September 11, it dispatched Colonel John Neville and a small body of militia to occupy Fort Pitt in western Pennsylvania. In two Indian conferences held at Pitts-

burgh in 1775 and 1776, the Virginians secured a truce along the Ohio frontier, with participating Indians pledging neutrality in the war and the Americans promising not to settle north of the Ohio River. But this arrangement was violated by both sides, and the frontiersmen lived in constant dread of Indian war parties, while Indian tribes lived in fear of unrelenting expansion of white settlement.

In the spring of 1776, the Mingos launched raids into Kentucky, and by October, they had compelled the abandonment of all but three stations in what came to be called "the dark and bloody ground." Hamilton in Detroit deplored these raids and attempted to stop them, but with little success. Soon the Kentuckians, however, were calling him "Hair-Buyer," an inaccurate but politically effective sobriquet coined by the Kentucky Indian fighter George Rogers Clark, in the belief that Hamilton paid the Indians for white scalps. The Virginia government responded by putting small garrisons of militiamen into Fort Henry at Wheeling and Fort Randolph at the mouth of the

Kanawha River. Thus did it gain strategic control of the Ohio River line that had been established in the Treaty of Fort Stanwix of 1768.

Nevertheless, Indian attacks intensified, and in late February 1777, a mixed band of Shawnee, Delaware, and Wyandot warriors joined the Mingos in attacking Wheeling, Boonesborough, and other stations in hopes of compelling the settlers to abandon the country. Patrick Henry, governor of Virginia, contemplated a retaliatory expedition against the Mingos, but was persuaded against it by his military chiefs for fear it would only drive more Indians into hostility. The shaky frontier truce was ending in any case. The American invasion of Canada had collapsed in 1776, and it was now possible for the British to support offensive Indian warfare in the West. On June 16, 1777, Hamilton received orders from the British government to employ Indians to create a diversion by exciting alarm on the Virginia and Pennsylvania frontiers. These orders, in diametrical opposition to the policy that Carleton had pursued since the inception of the rebellion, opened the British phase of frontier warfare in the West. This new phase was accelerated by two spectacular injustices committed by Americans against Indians. In July, settlers at Pittsburgh fired upon a party of Senecas arriving for a conference, killing several. Shortly thereafter, Cornstalk, leader of a pro-American group of Shawnees, was seized as a hostage and murdered by frontiersmen.

In immediate response to his orders, Hamilton organized his military forces in the summer of 1777, and unleashed attacks by more-than-willing Indians against the Americans. His long-term plans were more grandiose: to seize all Spanish territory in the Mississippi River basin for the British Empire. Fort Statler on Dunkard Creek, a branch of the Monongahela River, was attacked, and other hostile acts were perpetrated. For the patriots, the obvious remedy was to capture Detroit, seize Hamilton, and thus end the western war. On April 10, 1777, George Washington dispatched General Edward Hand to Fort Pitt with orders to take the offensive against the Indians and, if possible, march against Detroit. During the summer and fall, Hand attempted to organize an expedition, but could not get surrounding counties to provide him with the necessary troops. Finally, in February 1778, he led five hundred men toward Sandusky in an operation that was thwarted by foul weather. Ridiculed by the western Pennsylvanians for what they dubbed a "squaw campaign," Hand was relieved of command later in the year and replaced by General Lachlan McIntosh, who conducted another abortive campaign against Detroit.

In early 1778, both Hamilton in Detroit and the Americans along the upper Ohio were forced to re-assess their strategic goals. Hamilton's scheme to overthrow Spanish power in the Mississippi Valley had received no support whatsoever from Carleton or anyone else. In fact, Francisco Cruzat, Spanish lieutenant governor at St. Louis, later reversed the tables by dispatching militiamen to capture St. Joseph in present-day Michigan. In the spring, because of the efforts of the peace negotiators, Hamilton declared a temporary cessation of military activity against the Americans. His only major military effort for the summer of 1778 was to support attacks by the Shawnee chieftain, Blackfish, against the Kentucky stations.

While this was happening, American attempts to capture Detroit by launching attacks from Fort Pitt had been taken over from Washington and the local militias by the Continental Congress, because previous attempts had proven totally inadequate to the task. In mid-1778, Congress approved the stationing of two regiments of Continental troops in the West and the construction of a permanent fort in Indian country, preparatory to a conquest of Detroit. General McIntosh, charged by Congress with the execution of this grand scheme, launched an ill-prepared expedition from Fort Pitt down the Ohio River in early October. After founding Fort McIntosh at the mouth of Beaver Creek, he marched northward into the Ohio country toward Detroit, reaching Coshocton in late November. There he erected Fort Laurens and installed a tiny garrison, but ignominiously withdrew to Fort Pitt with the rest of his army after exhausting his food supplies. On March 5, 1779, he was relieved of command by Colonel Daniel Brodhead, who quickly discovered that Fort Laurens was not a dagger pointed toward the enemy's heart but an albatross around his own neck. In May 1779, the post was saved from serious Indian threat only because Colonel John Bowman of Kentucky diverted the natives' attention by attacking the Shawnee towns. In July, Brodhead was compelled to abandon Fort Laurens, and the Continental strategy for capturing Detroit was in utter shambles.

Meanwhile, George Rogers Clark was conducting his own operations from Kentucky against British power in the Illinois country. Appointed a major of the Virginia militia in March 1777, he exerted himself in fending off Indian attacks during the summer and fall. Like his compatriots, he was convinced that Americans must take the war to the British and Indians north of the Ohio, and if possible capture Detroit and Henry Hamilton. Persuading Governor Patrick Henry that he was the man for the job, he was promoted to lieutenant colonel and, in early 1778, with an army of 175 Kentuckians, launched an expedition from the Falls of the Ohio against Kaskaskia. He and his men, though half-starved after a six-day march through the wilderness, surprised the garrison at that post and forced its surrender on July 4. Placating Indians that might have destroyed his army, Clark dispatched detachments to Cahokia and Vincennes and cast covetous eyes toward Detroit.

Hamilton, caught completely off guard by Clark's audacious offensive, reacted quickly with the approval of Governor Frederick Haldimand, who had replaced Carleton. Organizing an army of five hundred men consisting of British regulars, militiamen, and Indians, Hamilton marched on October 7 to recapture the lost posts. He arrived at Vincennes on December 17 and forced the surrender of Captain Leonard Helm and his small garrison. Thereupon he suspended operations because of midwinter floods and set to repairing the defenses of Vincennes.

At Kaskaskia, Clark learned of Hamilton's triumph in late January 1779 and immediately determined to reverse the decision. With a force of 170 men, he marched almost two hundred miles in an epic of hardship and endurance to Vincennes. On February 25, he compelled Hamilton and his garrison of seventy-nine regulars and militiamen to surrender. Clark sent Hamilton under escort to Williamsburg, where Governor Thomas Jefferson kept him in close confinement until he was paroled on October 10, 1780. Exhilarated by his success, Clark prepared for the conquest of Detroit; but he had neither troops nor supplies to effect his purpose. He made similar unsuccessful attempts in 1780 and 1781. Although the conquered villages in the Illinois country continued to acknowledge American political sway, Clark could not stop Indian and Tory raids in the Ohio Valley and, in fact, had to withdraw troops from garrisons there.

In October 1779, loyalist Simon Girty ambushed Colonel David Rogers and seventy men in a flotilla carrying supplies from New Orleans to Fort Pitt on the Ohio River. Rogers and most of his men were killed, and strategic control of the river was lost. In 1780, Colonel Henry Bird led 150 Tories and a 1,000 Indians into the Licking River Valley. He captured two forts and one hundred prisoners; many of the latter were slaughtered. Clark retaliated in August by leading one thousand men on a highly successful expedition into the Shawnee country, destroying Chillicothe, the Shawnee "mother town." He also defeated Simon Girty and the Shawnees in a savage battle at Piqua.

Unremitting warfare continued in the Ohio Valley during the next two years, and in fact became more intense. Indians attacked Kentucky settlements in 1781, and Chief Joseph Brant's Iroquois warriors annihilated a force of one hundred Pennsylvania militia moving down the Ohio River. News of the British surrender at Yorktown on October 19, 1781, did not abate warfare in the Ohio Valley. In the spring of 1782, Colonel William Crawford led an American force of three hundred men from Pittsburgh to the upper Sandusky River Valley, hoping to surprise the Shawnees and Wyandots. On June 4 and 5, his force was defeated by Captain William Caldwell's British force of Tories and Indians. Crawford was captured, tortured, and killed.

In August, Caldwell, Simon Girty, and Alexander McKee at the head of three hundred Indian warriors invaded Kentucky and attacked Bryan's Station, only five miles from Lexington. Unable to force the surrender of that post, they withdrew toward the Ohio River, pursued by 182 militiamen under John Todd, Stephen Trigg, and Daniel Boone. On August 19, the raiders ambushed the frontiersmen at Blue Licks. As the Kentuckians recklessly attacked, they were assaulted by the Indians. Over a third were killed, and the rest were routed in terror. In November, Clark, now a brigadier general, retaliated by leading 1,050 Kentucky militiamen in an invasion of the Shawnee country. Against slight resistance, he rampaged for eighteen days, burning six villages and killing ten Indians, though not much impairing the Shawnees' fighting power. The warfare along the Ohio abated only after Britain and America made peace in 1783.

Although neither side had won a decisive or dramatic victory in the west, the Americans reaped the fruits of victory, securing the old Northwest Territory in the peace settlement. For more than a decade thereafter, the British occupied Detroit and encouraged Indians north of the Ohio to harass Americans. But in the next generation, the new republic eliminated Indian and British power in the future midwestern states of Ohio, Indiana, and Illinois, and European settlement pushed inexorably westward.

Sources and Further Reading: John Bakeless, *Background to Glory* (1957); John D. Barnhart, *Henry Hamilton and George Rogers Clark in the American Revolution* (1951); Colin G. Calloway, *The American Revolution in Indian Country* (1995); Randolph C. Downes, *Council Fires on the Upper Ohio* (1940); Lowell H. Harrison, *George Rogers Clark and the War in the West* (1976); Paul David Nelson, *General Sir Guy Carleton, Lord Dorchester* (2000); Louise Phelps Kellogg, ed., *Frontier Advance on the Upper Ohio* (1916); Jack M. Sosin, *The Revolutionary Frontier, 1763–1783* (1967); Reuben G. Thwaites and Louise Phelps Kellogg, eds., *Frontier Defense on the Upper Ohio, 1777–1778* (1912); Dale Van Every, *A Company of Heroes* (1962).

Paul David Nelson
Berea College, Kentucky

The Gnadenhutten Massacre

On March 8, 1782, the Moravian Indian village of Gnadenhutten, in present-day Tuscarawas County,

Ohio, was destroyed. Following the Clark expeditions of 1778–1779, the Ohio Country ceased to be the scene of large-scale warfare as the British garrison at Detroit and the Continental garrison at Fort Pitt primarily utilized Native American allies to strike at one another.

Among Native Americans, several Delaware communities, who had converted to Christianity, remained neutral. These communities had embraced the pietist faith of the German Moravian church and were known as the Moravian Indians. During the 1770s, the Moravians established three villages on the Tuscarawas River in the disputed territory between Detroit and southwestern Pennsylvania. Both sides accused the Moravians of aiding their enemy. Additionally, many in southwestern Pennsylvania disapproved of the Continental commanders' alliances with local Native Americans.

Following several raids during the winter of 1781–1782, farmers in Washington County, Pennsylvania, organized a militia company and marched to the Moravian villages. They captured almost a hundred Moravian men, women, and children at Gnadenhutten. The next day, the militia systematically killed every villager, then burned all of Gnadenhutten to the ground. Two of the young survived. The militia returned to the Pittsburgh region, where some attacked a Delaware camp and threatened the acting commander of Fort Pitt, a longtime Indian trader. The new commander, William Irvine, restored order in southwestern Pennsylvania, although additional raids by both the British and Americans continued through spring 1782.

Aside from Moravian missionaries, few contemporaries recorded details of the Gnadenhutten Massacre; historians have generally regarded it as one of the most notorious incidents of frontier violence.

Sources and Further Reading: Leonard Sadosky, "Rethinking the Gnadenhutten Massacre," in David Skaggs and Larry L. Nelson, eds., *The Sixty Years' War for the Great Lakes, 1754–1814* (2001); Thomas P. Slaughter, *The Whiskey Rebellion: Frontier Epilogue to the American Revolution* (1986); Richard White, *The Middle Ground: Indians, Empires, and Republics in the Great Lakes Region, 1650–1815* (1991).

Leonard J. Sadosky
University of Virginia

George Rogers Clark (1752–1818)

George Rogers Clark was born November 19, 1752, in Albemarle County, Virginia. As a surveyor, captain in Dunmore's War, captor of Kaskaskia and Vin-

cennes, and Indian commissioner, he greatly influenced the course of history for the old Northwest Territories. In 1772, Clark traveled west of the Appalachian Mountains, surveyed for the Ohio Land Company, and served as a militia captain in Lord Dunmore's War in 1774.

Once the American Revolutionary War began, Clark helped convince the Virginia Assembly to admit Kentucky as a county and, in March 1777, led the Kentucky defenses against Shawnee raids. He persuaded the Virginia government to launch an offensive north of the Ohio River against the British-held French settlements in the Indiana and Illinois territories. Promoted to lieutenant colonel, Clark led 175 men down the Ohio River and surprised the town of Kaskaskia, near the Mississippi River, on July 4, 1778, then sent troops to occupy Cahokia, across from St. Louis, and Vincennes by the end of July. The French residents accepted American control, and Clark convinced the western Indian nations to remain neutral.

Lieutenant Governor Henry Hamilton, the British commander in Detroit, led British soldiers, militia, and a few hundred Indian warriors, and recaptured Vincennes in December. While Hamilton waited for spring, Clark countered by leading 170 men across the flooded plains to capture Hamilton and Vincennes in February 1779. His successes thwarted several planned expeditions in 1779 aimed at American posts north and south of the Ohio River, and weakened British influence with the Indian nations between the Wabash and Mississippi Rivers. Thousands of settlers flooded into Kentucky after his victories.

Clark remained commander of Virginia's western lands against intensified attacks in 1780 and 1781. He led a retaliatory raid of a thousand men into Ohio in August 1780. Appointed a brigadier general in 1781, he launched one last raid into Ohio in 1782, ultimately abandoned the posts north of the Ohio, and remained in command in Kentucky through the end of the war.

In the peace treaty of 1783, the United States kept Kentucky and received the territories north of the Ohio and east of the Mississippi. This acquisition was due partly to deals between the warring nations and Britain's desire to ease relations with the United States. However, increased settlement of Kentucky due to Clark's victories, his success at thwarting British plans to eliminate Kentucky settlements, and the fact that the French militia who held Kaskaskia, Cahokia, and Vincennes were formally in the pay of Virginia, all strengthened U.S. claims to the land.

After the war, Clark helped establish Clarksville, Indiana, the first authorized settlement in the Northwest Territories. As an Indian Commissioner in 1786, he convinced several Indian nations to accept U.S. settlement in Ohio, but the Shawnees resisted. Reinstated a general, he led eighteen hundred men up the Wabash. While Clark negotiated, he sent a second raid to destroy several Shawnee villages in Ohio. In the spring of 1787, he concluded treaties with the Shawnees and other nations, who accepted U.S. settlement in southern Ohio. He then retired and lived several years in Clarksville. Never married and with no children, he died on February 13, 1818, after a series of strokes in the home of his sister, Lucy Croghan, in Locust Grove, near Louisville, Kentucky.

Sources and Further Reading: Robert C. Alberts, *George Rogers Clark and the Winning of the Old Northwest* (1975); Allan W. Eckert, *That Dark and Bloody River* (1995); Dale Van Every, *A Company of Heroes: The American Frontier 1775–1783* (1962); George M. Waller, *The American Revolution in the West* (1976).

Mark V. Kwasny
The Ohio State University–Newark

The Old Northwest Indian War, 1786–1795

In conjunction with diplomatic and demographic pressures, American military might in the early 1790s established American hegemony over the Native American peoples of the Ohio Valley north of the Ohio River. Several long-term trends had already weakened Native American military power, but only an offensive war marked by several bloody battles enabled the Americans to overcome these politically autonomous groups. Despite the paucity of soldiers involved and their middling military success, American soldiers helped bring about a significant victory that sealed later Native American subjugation elsewhere.

Following the unexpected 1783 Treaty of Paris concessions to the United States of Indian lands west of the Appalachians to the Mississippi River, both the Americans and the native peoples prepared for war. After this gratuitous grant by the English of land they neither owned nor controlled, the most urgent priority of the new American government was to dominate the area so that settlement could begin. With the ever-increasing settlements threatened from north and south, Washington's government avoided potentially disastrous two-front warfare by buying temporary peace in the area south of Kentucky through the 1790 Treaty of New York with the Creek Nation of present-day Georgia. North of the Ohio River, the Americans faced an unusually united confederation of diverse Native American peoples insistent on the Ohio River as a boundary between Native America and the United States. At Grand Councils held in 1783, 1786, and 1792, Indian spokesmen clearly laid out their principle: Americans must not move north of the Ohio River. The American governments, federal and territorial, remained equally unmovable from their overall imperialistic goal, but President Washington changed the Articles of Confederation's rhetoric and mode of conduct from that of a harsh conqueror to that of a rich businessman ready to buy land. Even this latter, more benign posture, would require military force.

Most of the opposition would come from the Shawnee, Miami, and Delaware Indian nations who formed in the 1790s the southern tier of the Ohio Valley. The Delaware had traditionally not been a fighting people until external events forced them into that role in the second half of the eighteenth century. Despite some notable military successes and heroic leaders, the Delaware (or Lenni Lenape) had been forcibly exiled farther and farther west from their original lands in Pennsylvania and the Eastern Seaboard. The Delaware were now badly divided between angry nativists desiring all-out war against the Americans and those seeking accommodation with the new juggernaut. In contrast, the Shawnee were a noted military people, but they had been deeply wounded in the 1770s when several large segments of the tribe—including most of the traditional warrior clan—moved beyond the Mississippi River. The Miami assumed some precedence among the lower tier of tribes because they were both noted soldiers and had so far escaped decimation by conflict with the Europeans and Americans.

North of these tribes were the Council of the Three Fires—Ottawa, Chippewa–Ojibway, and Potawatomi— and the Wyandots who were the remnants of the Huron Nation of the seventeenth century. Their soldiers performed exceptionally well because only the able and willing traveled south to fight. However, distance dictated the timing of their military presence. Distance also determined some political decisions divisive of pan-Indian unity at crucial meetings with the American representatives. Finally, the Iroquois Confederacy of New York sought to exert diplomatic and military leadership over the Algonquian-speaking tribes of the Midwest. For historical and cultural reasons, the midwestern tribes always viewed Iroquoian leaders with deep suspicion.

In short, Indian confederate unity was rather fragile. Besides this tenuous political front, a number of other nonmilitary realities circumscribed the political and military world of the Ohio Valley Natives. Most importantly, white Kentuckians outnumbered all the Indians in the greater Ohio Valley. A similarly decisive disproportion of military arms and supplies was mitigated, however, by aid from Great Britain, which had

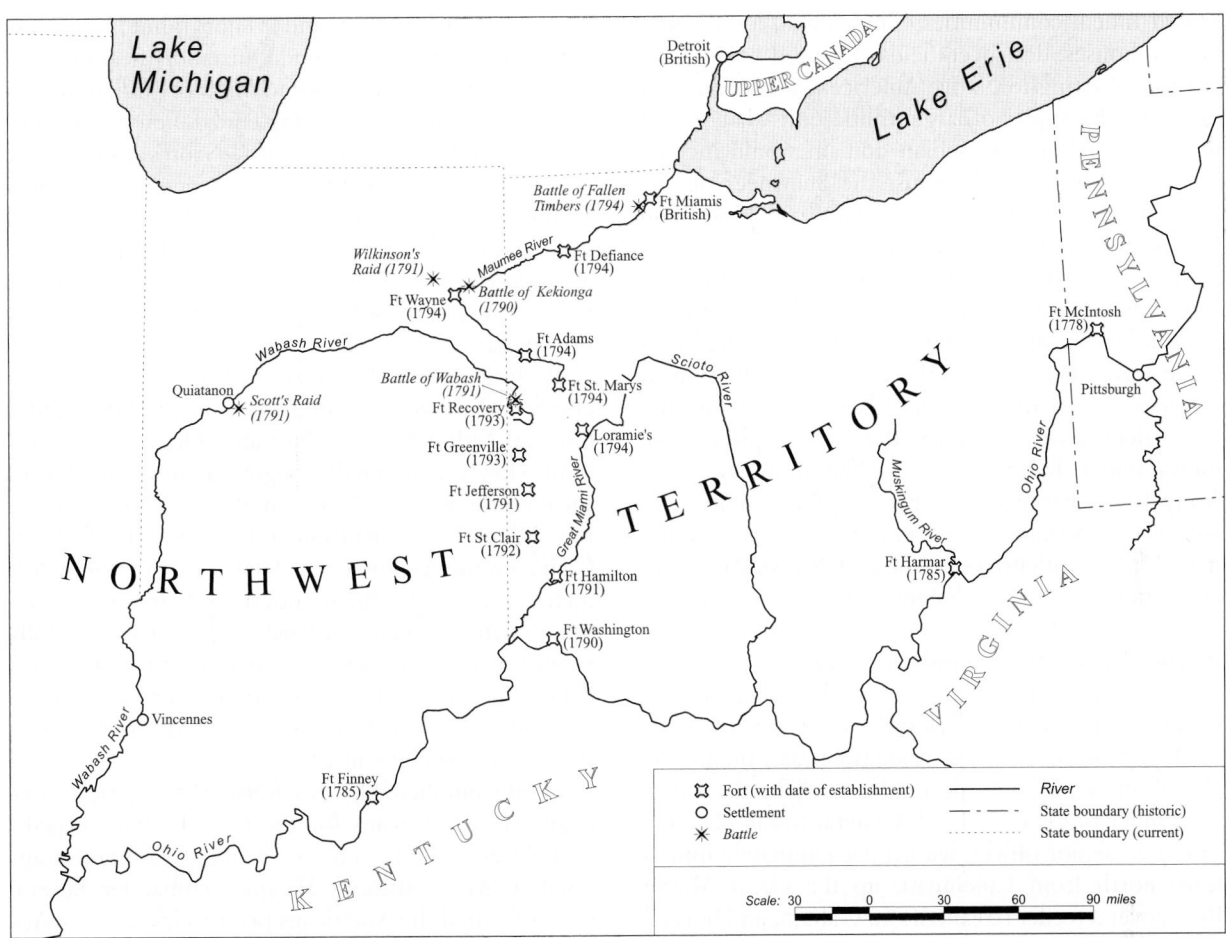

The Old Northwest Indian War, 1786–95. Prepared by James DeGrand. *Source:* David Skaggs and Larry Nelson, eds., *The Sixty Years' War for the Great Lakes* (East Lansing: Michigan State University Press, 2001), map 3; Carl Waldman, *Atlas of the North American Indian* (New York: Facts on File, 2000), p. 138.

quickly realized the practical and diplomatic absurdity of the terms of the 1783 peace treaty. Ultimately, British support proved uncertain at best and disappeared entirely at the crucial 1794 military moment.

Also undercutting the apparent Native American diplomatic consensus was the activity of American agents. Assiduous, if not always astute, activity by American agents cleaved Native American unity by playing off the large—perhaps larger—peace factions against the heroic factions attempting to defend their traditional homelands against the American onslaught. Early dealings with the agents of the U.S. government intensified the beliefs of both Indian factions. At meetings at Ft. Stanwix (New York, 1784), Ft. McIntosh (Pennsylvania, 1785), and Ft. Finney (Ohio, 1786), the commissioners browbeat dumbfounded Indians by hammering home the suspect thesis that America had conquered the Native Americans. The insensitive belaboring either caused Indians to opt for peace at all costs or insist on American capitulation. The 1789 Treaty at Ft. Harmar (present-day

Marietta, Ohio), at a place illustrating American indifference to the central geographic Indian position, further divided Native Americans because the representatives of the new Republic replaced their original bargaining position—that the Native Americans had actually been conquered during the American Revolution—with the more attractive admission of Indian ownership of the land and the duty of the federal government to pay for land acquired. Greed now joined war fatigue to divide Indian councils.

By 1790, official U.S. military activities began to augment the earlier and rather effective settler violence. Individuals and small groups had regularly and for personal reasons invaded the territory north of Ohio. Certainly, the Kentuckians had already pushed native villages north first toward central Ohio, and then by 1790, to northern Ohio and Indiana.

The Kentucky state militia represented an organized and larger version of these individualistic anti-Indian activities. When mounted on horses, the state militia on a number of occasions wreaked havoc on settled Indian communities. They killed, looted, and burned houses, destroyed fields, captured horses, and most debilitating to Native American resistance, took prisoners. Examples of large militia units that spread terror throughout the Indian domain would include Benjamin Logan's raid against the Shawnees on the Mad River (Logan County, Ohio) in 1786, and George Rogers Clark's raid against Vincennes in the same year. Even when the individual and militia violence hurt friendly Indians, as in Logan's 1786 raid, or as John Hardin did in 1789 on the Wabash, the long-range reaction reinforced the usual tribal division of accommodation or resistance. Not surprisingly, the new federal government saw that it must place these forays under federal control. The miniscule U.S. Army took charge of the major military initiatives during the Washington administration. None of the Army's major offensives eliminated Native American opposition, but the persistence of the U.S. military (with its eager militia components) slowly destroyed Indian military and political opposition.

On three important occasions, the militia joined with the official Federal Army. Regulars formed only a small part of the first two expeditions, and the militia played an important role in the third battle. From September to October 1790, General Josiah Harmar, America's senior officer, led his predominately militia force north from Cincinnati, up the Great Miami River, over a feeder stream of the Wabash, and burned the seven Indian villages forming the principal Miami center of Kekionga (present-day Fort Wayne, Indiana). Two defeats marred this achievement, however. On October 19, around 150 militia and thirty regulars rushed headlong into an ambush orchestrated by Little Turtle. The pell-mell flight of the militia sacrificed most of the regulars, who held their ground and died. The next day, the army started its return to its home base. About 340 militia and sixty soldiers returned to Kekionga that night to surprise any Indians who might have returned. To herd the presumably scattered natives into the trap, and not realizing that a large number of Northern warriors had just arrived to augment the locals, the soldiers subdivided into a complex three-pronged attack at daybreak. Again, almost all of the regulars died. Many historians blame the debacle on ill-disciplined militia. In contrast, contemporary militia accounts vividly describe a bitterly contested tree-to-tree battle between determined combatants. In any case, Kentucky observers did not for a moment accept the official position that Harmar had triumphed.

In 1791, the Americans tried a second time to overawe the Indians. While a large army was assembling near Cincinnati, two militia raids attacked Indian settlements on the Wabash River. In June, Brigadier General Charles Scott and Major John Hardin attacked several villages around Quiatanon (near present-day Lafayette, Indiana). Some thirty-six Indian bodies were found after the shooting ended, houses were destroyed, and most importantly, Scott's forces took about fifty prisoners. In August, Lieutenant Colonel James Wilkinson led approximately five hundred mounted militia into the same area and, on August 7, attacked the Miami village of Little Turtle. His forces killed few Indian soldiers but captured over thirty prisoners.

Both Scott and Wilkinson had been helped by the absence of warriors waiting for the main army under General Arthur St. Clair. Not until October 4 did this army slowly and blindly begin to move northward through the woods. On the morning of November 4, the Native confederation effectively attacked St. Clair's encamped force. St. Clair's loss of about 630 men easily doubles the number lost in the more celebrated defeat of General Custer. Historians generally claim Little Turtle as the architect of this victory. Indian traditions also assigned important roles to the Shawnee Blue Jacket and to an anonymous leader of the Great Lakes Indians.

While humiliated by this defeat, the Americans immediately made plans for the third military expedition. After some hesitation, George Washington appointed "Mad" Anthony Wayne commander. Several events favored the Americans prior to the decisive August 20, 1794, Battle of Fallen Timbers (near present-day Toledo, Ohio). While Wayne's methodical training of the bungling army to mold it into a disciplined fighting force annoyed more impatient American observers, it increasingly worried Indian opponents. In particular, Little Turtle began to argue for a negotiated peace. When overturned, he allowed Blue Jacket to take military precedence. This officer shift may account for inept Indian activity at the Battle of Fallen Timbers, which showed none of the genius of the 1791 battlefield plan and performance against the forces of St. Clair. Most assuredly, the Indian warriors who assembled at Fallen Timbers suffered from grievous losses sustained during an uncharacteristic Native American frontal attack on Fort Recovery (Ohio) on June 30. There, a successful ambush of an American supply team preceded a foolhardy attack on the fort.

Mutual recriminations among the mauled Indian participants followed, and in the aftermath, nearly half of the entire assembly of Indians waiting for Wayne packed and left. Furthermore, Native Americans increasingly realized that British orders were to foment Indian opposition to America without involving British troops. The Ohio Valley and Great Lakes Indians quickly came to understand that they had built plans with an imaginary wartime ally. Finally, and for the first time in the 1790s, the Americans found dependable spies whose heroic fact-gathering presented Wayne with accurate and detailed information. Curiously, William Wells, a former white captive and now son-in-law of Little Turtle, joined Wayne's spies.

The final battle of Fallen Timbers on August 20, 1794, turned out to be relatively bloodless but decisive. Wayne's corps at one point wavered after his advance guard was ambushed, but a disciplined charge easily swept the field of the essentially disorganized Native American soldiers. Besides the oncoming bayonets, the Native Americans were quite aware of a large mounted militia riding to envelop the initial Indian position. Fleeing five miles to Fort Miami, the Indian soldiers found that the British commander had closed the doors to them. Neither the American military superiority nor the British political betrayal was lost on the Native Americans. The next year representatives of the defeated Ohio Valley tribes signed the Treaty of Greenville that surrendered three-quarters of Ohio and the southeastern corner of Indiana to the federal government and established the foundation for expanded white settlement of the Old Northwest Territory.

Sources and Further Reading: Colin Calloway, *The American Revolution in Indian Country* (1995); James Smith, *Scoouwa* (1799); Wiley Sword, *President Washington's Indian War* (1985); Richard White, *The Middle Ground* (1991).

L. V. Eid
University of Dayton, Ohio

Little Turtle (Michikinakoua, c. 1752–1812)

Little Turtle, whose documented military career spanned fifteen years (1780–1794), participated in two of the most significant battles in the history of Native American warfare with the United States. On November 3, 1791, he and 1,400 Miami, Shawnee, and Delaware warriors engaged American General Arthur St. Clair's expeditionary force at Kekionga (near modern Fort Wayne, Indiana); the Americans suffered 630 men killed and 264 wounded, the worst defeat to that time for American forces in any engagement with native peoples, in terms of the numbers engaged. On August 20, 1794, Little Turtle was present (although not in command) at the Battle of Fallen Timbers, where, after being denied both assistance and refuge by the British at nearby Fort Miamis (modern Maumee, Ohio), his confederated warriors were defeated by American General "Mad" Anthony Wayne.

The son of Aquenochqua, a Miami war leader, and a Mohican woman, Little Turtle's first recorded military activity occurred on November 5, 1780, when he attacked and defeated a French and American force that had occupied and plundered his village. After the American Revolution, British military officers remaining in the Great Lakes region sponsored Native American attacks on frontier settlers in an effort to discourage American westward expansion. A veteran of many such raids by 1790, Little Turtle emerged as a highly respected leader of large, multinational Native war parties organized to confront United States Army invasions of their territory.

Although most often remembered as a great military leader, Little Turtle eschewed Tecumseh's pan-Native military resistance movement, and instead spent the final eighteen years of his life seeking accommodation with the new American republic. He protested American terms offered in the 1795 Treaty of Greenville negotiations, but ultimately signed the peace agreement and abided by it for the rest of his life. In a January 7, 1802, speech to American officials in Washington, D.C., Little Turtle requested agricultural training and the prohibition of alcohol trading among his nation. Characterizing American society as "spread[ing] like oil on a blanket," while Native people "melt like snow in the spring sunshine," Little Turtle believed that "if we do not alter course, the race of red men cannot possibly survive."

Little Turtle's vision of the Miamis' future was not universally accepted by his people, since not all Miami men were eager to exchange lives of hunting and warfare for farming, which was traditionally women's domain. Yet Little Turtle's ability to lead through influence and example enabled him to frustrate Tecumseh's recruiting efforts among Miami warriors from 1806 to Little Turtle's death at Fort Wayne on July 14, 1812. Two months later, American troops burned Little Turtle's then-deserted home village on the Eel River, northwest of Fort Wayne, but left the deceased leader's home standing out of respect for his memory. He reportedly was married twice and had five children.

Sources and Further Reading: Harvey L. Carter, *The Life and Times of Little Turtle* (1987); *Dictionary of Canadian Biography*, s.v. "Michikinakoua," vol. 5 (1983); Richard White, *The Middle Ground* (1991).

Jon Parmenter
Cornell University, New York

Anthony Wayne (1745–1796)

While growing up in Chester County, Pennsylvania, Wayne dreamed of becoming a swashbuckling soldier. He was educated as a surveyor and worked in that profession before serving in the Pennsylvania legislature. His political career was abbreviated when in 1776, he received his chance to pursue his dream of becoming a soldier by being commissioned a colonel in the Continental Army. He fought bravely at Trois-Rivières in Canada and commanded Fort Ticonderoga the following winter. Promoted brigadier general in 1777, he served with George Washington at Brandywine, Germantown, and Monmouth, and was defeated at Paoli in late September of that year. He led an elite light infantry corps on July 15, 1779, in a brilliant assault on Stony Point, New York. He helped thwart Benedict Arnold's treasonous plans in 1780, and a year later suppressed two mutinies. He served with the Marquis de Lafayette and Nathanael Greene in the South, resigning in 1783 as a brevet major general.

Unsuccessful as a politician and farmer, Wayne accepted Washington's offer in 1792 to command the Legion of the United States and suppress Indian power in the future midwestern states of Ohio and Indiana. He spent the next two years training a formidable army, while resisting secret attempts by his second in command, James Wilkinson, to ruin his reputation. On August 20, 1794, at Fallen Timbers, he decisively routed a force of Delawares, Shawnees, Miamis, and others. He imposed his will upon the natives by constructing forts, including at Fort Wayne, Indiana, in the newly conquered territory, then concluded the Treaty of Greenville in 1795, which opened up Ohio and Indiana to white settlement. He married Mary Penrose in 1766 with whom he had two children. Estranged after a decade of marriage, he developed a relationship with Mary Vining in the 1780s. He died on duty at Presque Isle, Pennsylvania, in 1796. Vain, brave, and impetuous, he was popularly called "Mad Anthony" because of his demanding regimen of training and his audacity in battle.

Sources and Further Reading: Paul David Nelson, *Anthony Wayne: Soldier of the Early Republic* (1985); Wiley Sword, *President Washington's Indian War* (1985).

Paul David Nelson
Berea College, Kentucky

The War of 1812

In June 1812, the United States declared war on Great Britain, touching off a struggle that would continue for the next two and a half years. Of all America's wars, this conflict most directly involved the Midwest, with fighting taking place in almost every part of the sparsely populated region, on land and on the waters of the Great Lakes. The contest involved regular military forces on both sides, supplemented by the militias of several states and territories and the province of upper Canada. It was also an Indian war, complete with frontier skirmishes and raids of the type that had marked the struggle for the Ohio Valley during the American Revolution and the decade following.

The War of 1812 in the Midwest entailed two parallel conflicts. On the one hand, it was part of a national contest between the United States and Great Britain that had its origins in the economic and maritime competition created by the Napoleonic Wars. On the other, the conflict was the last major organized military resistance by the Native American nations of the Great Lakes region against relentless United States pressure on their lands. American residents of Kentucky and the Midwest blamed the British in Canada for inciting and supporting the hostility of the Indian nations. When war came in 1812, most of the region's Native Americans allied themselves with the British.

Fighting commenced in the Midwest more than six months before the United States declared war on Great Britain. Native American resistance to American land pressure in Indiana and Michigan had coalesced around the Shawnee leader Tecumseh and his brother, Tenskwatawa, "the Prophet." United States troops were sent to Indiana in 1811, and territorial Governor William Henry Harrison led a preemptive expedition from Vincennes that autumn against Tecumseh's towns on the upper Wabash River. Tenskwatawa, in Tecumseh's absence, attacked Harrison's army, but his warriors were repulsed in the hard-fought Battle of Tippecanoe on November 7. The Indian towns were destroyed the following day, but a frontier war had begun.

The United States prepared for war with Britain during the winter and spring of 1812 by substantially enlarging its army. Canada was the only practical target for American land forces, and there was much confidence that the thinly populated and lightly garrisoned British colony would fall quickly. Three separate thrusts were planned against Canada at the outbreak of the war. The most westerly of these originated in Ohio and Michigan and was aimed at upper Canada (today's Ontario). Michigan governor William Hull was persuaded to lead this army, should war come. Late in the spring, he took command of a mixed force of Ohio militia and U.S. troops and marched toward Detroit, arriving on July 5, much to the relief of the residents and garrison of the town, who had been anticipating an Indian attack.

Hull found that war had been declared while his army was on the march, but he did not learn this in time to prevent the British from seizing an unwary vessel carrying the official papers of his army. The invasion of Canada commenced, nonetheless, on July 12. The American commander's caution, dissension within his army, and British naval control of Lake Erie and the Detroit River contributed to a lackluster and timid advance on the British post at Fort Malden. Hull's vulnerable supply line to Ohio was exposed to British and Indian raids across the Detroit River. Small actions at Brownstown (August 5) and Monguagon (August 9) on the Michigan shore convinced the American general that he was in danger of being cut off and that he could not support his offensive. On August 11, Hull withdrew to Detroit where British forces, by this time commanded by General Isaac Brock, were able to concentrate against him. Brock's aggressive tactics and Hull's fears for the fate of the civilian population caused him to surrender Fort Detroit and his army on August 16. The fiasco sent shock waves through the Midwest. The fall of Detroit and the loss of Hull's army exposed Ohio to attack and put the Michigan Territory in British hands.

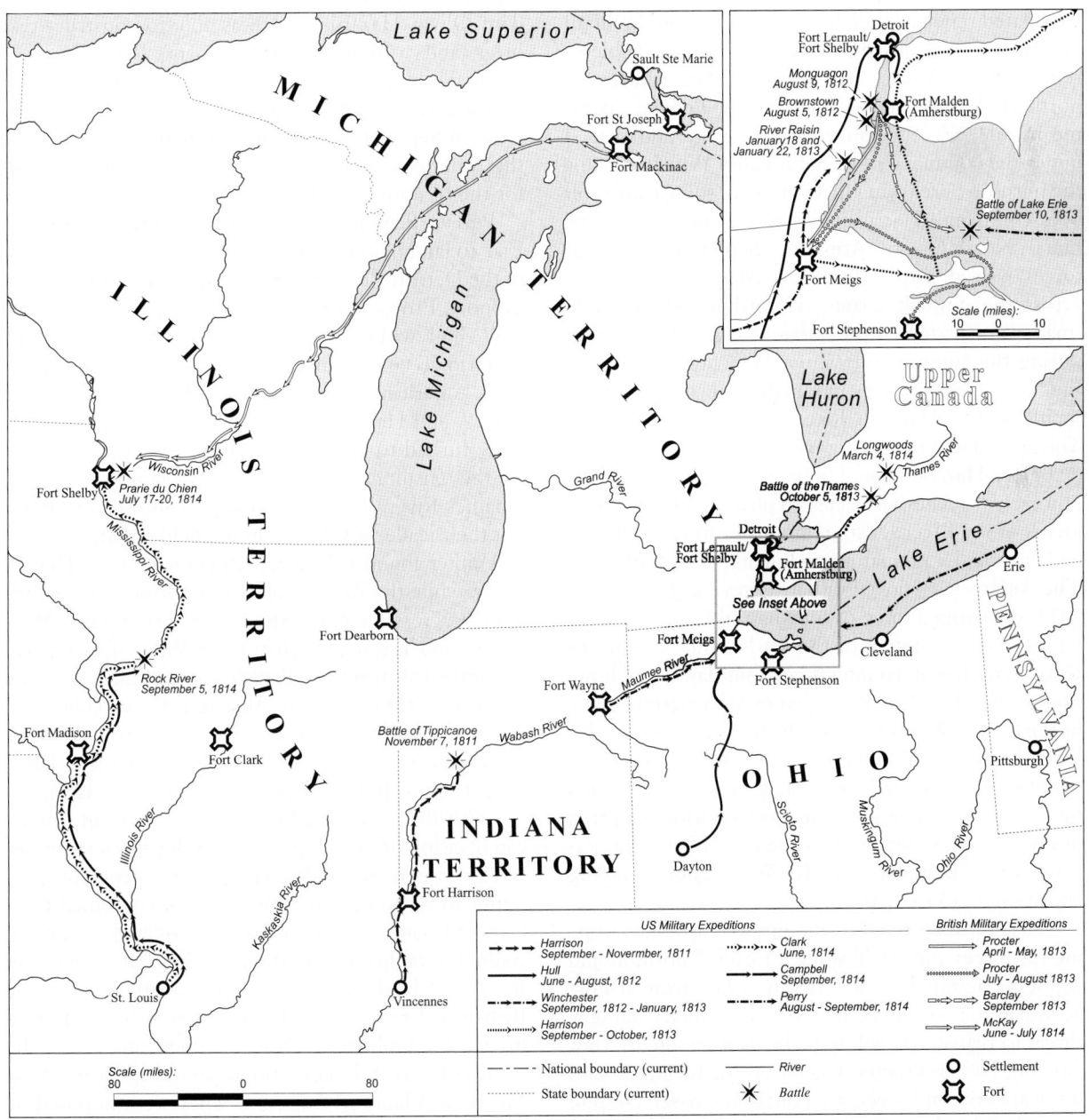

The Midwest in the War of 1812. Prepared by James DeGrand. *Source:* David Skaggs and Larry Nelson, eds., *The Sixty Years' War for the Great Lakes* (East Lansing: Michigan State University Press, 2001), map 4; Alec Gilpin, *The War of 1812 in the Old Northwest* (East Lansing: Michigan State University Press, 1958).

The entire Midwest frontier was under attack by that time. On July 17, British soldiers, Indians, and Canadian militia had surprised Fort Mackinac and forced its tiny garrison to surrender. An all Native American force scored another victory against the garrison of isolated Fort Dearborn (Chicago) on August 15, after they had evacuated their defenses. The month of September found American posts at Fort Wayne, Fort Harrison (both in Indiana), and Fort Madison (Iowa) besieged by local Native American groups.

These setbacks placed the settlements of Ohio and Indiana Territory in jeopardy. Hull's predicament had stimulated renewed military efforts, however. William Henry Harrison raised a militia army and was able to relieve Fort Wayne and attack Indian villages in northern Indiana and Ohio. A new Federal Army, meanwhile, was assembled in Kentucky and placed under the command of General James Winchester for the purpose of relieving Detroit. After some confusion over command, Harrison was named to lead a combined Northwestern Army on September 17. His forces moved slowly down the Maumee River and across the difficult terrain of northern Ohio, while smaller units attacked the Indian villages of the region during the autumn and winter. Winchester's wing of the Northwestern Army gradually concentrated at the rapids of the Maumee River, not far from modern Toledo and within striking range of Detroit.

Before Harrison could fully organize his campaign, however, Winchester reacted to pleas for aid from residents of the River Raisin region (Monroe, Michigan) and launched a premature and unauthorized advance. The Americans enjoyed initial success on January 18, 1813, defeating a force of Indians and Canadian militia and taking control of the settlement. A vigorous British and Indian counterattack four days later, however, resulted in the total defeat of Winchester's army in the Battle of River Raisin. In the aftermath of this second American military disaster in the Midwest, many of the wounded were attacked and many killed by the Indians. The incident received wide attention in the United States and provided an effective propaganda tool. "Remember the Raisin" became a rallying cry of the 1813 campaign.

Harrison responded to the disaster by concentrating his forces and establishing a fortified position and depot at the rapids of the Maumee. His army at Fort Meigs, as the post was called, was the primary military threat to British control of the Detroit region. In May, Colonel Henry Procter, supported by Tecumseh and his warriors, laid siege to Harrison's base. Despite heavy bombardment and a serious defeat inflicted on an American relief force, Fort Meigs held out. Procter made another attempt on the position late in July, but his forces were weaker, and the siege was of brief duration. After withdrawing from Fort Meigs, the British made an attempt on Fort Stephenson, a small post on the Sandusky River. Overconfident, their assault was bloodily repulsed on August 2, ending serious British offensive operations in northern Ohio.

The outcome of the campaign would be resolved on Lake Erie. The waterway was critical to British logistics, but their control of the lake was about to be challenged. An American squadron had been under construction since the winter at Erie, Pennsylvania. Laboring under similar shortages of manpower and supplies as his British opponents, Master Commandant Oliver Hazard Perry was able to construct two brigs and a number of gunboats. Perry's vessels avoided a blockade by the British squadron, and then encountered the enemy near the western end of Lake Erie on September 10. With the Battle of Lake Erie, the American victory was complete, clearing the way for the recapture of Detroit.

Perry's fleet ferried Harrison's army across Lake Erie to land below Amherstburg on the Canadian side of the Detroit River. Short of supplies and cut off from support, Procter burned Fort Malden, evacuated Detroit, and withdrew toward British forces on Lake Ontario. Tecumseh and his warriors joined in their retreat. American forces reoccupied Detroit on September 29, and Harrison commenced a pursuit. Procter's force turned to fight on October 5, but was scattered in the ensuing battle near Moraviantown on the Thames River. Tecumseh's troops continued to fight, but their leader was killed on the field of battle.

Winter found U.S. forces in control of the Detroit River, while the British held Mackinac and exerted influence across the northern Great Lakes and into Wisconsin and the upper Mississippi Valley. Detroit was strengthened against a British counterattack, but the threat never materialized. American forces conducted foraging expeditions and raids deep into western upper Canada that winter, one of which resulted in a hard-fought action at the Longwoods on March 4, 1814.

With British troops heavily engaged by an American invasion of the Niagara region during the summer of 1814, the reduced U.S. garrison at Detroit could attempt to recapture Fort Mackinac. A combined military and naval operation commenced in July. British trading establishments at Sault Ste. Marie and St. Joseph's Island (Ontario) were destroyed, but the British had reinforced Mackinac and were supported by large numbers of Native Americans from the northern Great Lakes. American troops landed on Mackinac Island on August 4. They were opposed by the greater part of the British garrison, and their Indian allies and were forced to retreat. Two schooners that remained to blockade Mackinac were surprised and captured by British soldiers and sailors early in September. Fort Mackinac and the northern lakes would remain under British control until after the end of hostilities.

The summer of 1814 also saw an intensification of the conflict in the Mississippi Valley. That region and its Native American population were particularly important to British fur-trading interests. United States troops began establishing posts up the Mississippi from St. Louis in the fall of 1813. In June 1814, a detachment began to construct Fort Shelby at Prairie du Chien near the mouth of the Wisconsin River. Local traders and Indians notified the commandant of Fort Mackinac, who quickly assembled a force of Indians, volunteers, and a few soldiers to reassert British authority. Armed with a small cannon, the force bombarded Fort Shelby. The American garrison surrendered on July 20, and the post was renamed Fort McKay. The British–Indian victory was confirmed when they repulsed another American force at the Rock River in Illinois on September 5. These small actions were of great significance in that they allowed the British to retain control of the upper Mississippi Valley for the rest of the war.

Although a peace settlement was signed at Ghent in Belgium on Christmas Eve of 1814, news was slow to reach the Midwest. The British were preparing for another campaign to wrest naval control of the upper Great Lakes from the Americans. For their part, U.S. forces planned a renewed effort to recover Fort Mackinac. However, news of the peace settlement reached the region during March. The provisions of the treaty called for the return of captured territory by both sides. Local commanders worked out the arrangements of the transfer. Fort McKay at Prairie du Chien was abandoned in May, and its British garrison returned to Mackinac. American troops evacuated Amherstburg at the beginning of July, and the British gave up Fort Mackinac on the 18th of the same month.

The War of 1812 did nothing to alter British and American territory along the boundaries of the Midwest, other than to emphasize the need for a better survey of the international boundary along the Great Lakes. This was specified in the treaty, and the work was conducted in the early 1820s. The postwar years saw increasing American military and commercial activity in the northern part of the Midwest. New forts would be established at Green Bay, Sault Ste. Marie, and Chicago on the Great Lakes and along the upper Mississippi at Rock Island, Prairie du Chien, and the later site of St. Paul, Minnesota. New restrictions on British and Canadian traders placed the fur trade within U.S. territory firmly in the hands of American merchants.

The Native American residents of the Midwest bore the brunt of the peace. Their military power was broken by the war, and some withdrew to Canada to become wards of the British. The postwar years witnessed increasing settlement throughout the region, particularly once the fears of another Indian war had been allayed. The end of the War of 1812 paved the way for the increasingly rapid settlement of Ohio, Indiana, Illinois, and Michigan.

Sources and Further Reading: Robert S. Allen, *His Majesty's Indian Allies* (1992); Brian Leigh Dunnigan, *The British Army at Mackinac, 1812–1815* (1980); Alec R. Gilpin, *The War of 1812 in the Old Northwest* (1958); J. Mackay Hitsman, *The Incredible War of 1812* (1965); Larry L. Nelson, *Men of Patriotism, Courage, and Enterprise* (1985); David Curtis Skaggs and Gerard T. Altoff, *A Signal Victory: The Lake Erie Campaign, 1812–1813* (1997); George F. G. Stanley, *The War of 1812: Land Operations* (1983).

Brian Leigh Dunnigan
University of Michigan–Ann Arbor

Fort Dearborn

At the time of the Louisiana Purchase, Fort Dearborn, named in honor of Secretary of War Henry Dearborn, was America's most extreme western military outpost. Built in 1803 on a small rise of land near the mouth of the Chicago River, the fort established a strategic foothold for American efforts to secure free access to the Mississippi River and an opportunity to dislodge the British stronghold on trade with the Native Americans in the region. The plan of the fort was a quadrangle of wooden structures with two prominent blockhouses and a double palisade. Under the command of Captain John Whistler, American trade expanded and peace prevailed; the promise of business and security drew new settlers to Chicago, forming the nascent outlines of a city.

By 1812, the growing influence of Tecumseh in the Northwest and the war between Great Britain and America rekindled latent tensions in the region. Ordered by General William Hull to evacuate and proceed to the safety of Detroit, Captain Nathan Heald, his garrison, and a small group of citizens abandoned Fort Dearborn on August 15. Less than a mile and a half south of the fort, between four and five hundred Potawatomis attacked them, killing fifty-two soldiers, men, women, and children. The following day, the Indians burned the fort to the ground. Four years later, a second Fort Dearborn was built and garrisoned. As Chicago grew in scale and population, however, the importance of the fort as a military outpost and as a social center diminished. In 1835, the fort was converted to government offices. Most of the fort was dismantled in 1857, and any remaining buildings were destroyed in the Chicago Fire of 1871.

Sources and Further Reading: Arthur H. Frazier, "Military Frontier," *Chicago History* 9 (Summer 1980); Joseph Kirkland, *The Chicago Massacre of 1812* (1893); Helen Hornbeck Tanner, ed., *Atlas of Great Lakes Indian History* (1987).

Russell Lewis
Chicago Historical Society, Illinois

The Battle of Lake Erie

The Battle of Lake Erie ended in a crushing victory for the Americans over the British naval forces in the War of 1812. The control of Lake Erie and neighboring Lake Ontario assumed paramount importance in the war, as the British outposts in upper Canada (present-day Ontario) depended on the two waterways for logistical support.

The engagement itself took place on September 10, 1813, near South Bass Island and close to Put-in-Bay at the western end of the lake. The American commander, Oliver Hazard Perry, outnumbered his opponent nine ships to six, and his force was more heavily armed and better manned, as well. Yet, Perry nearly squandered his advantages by forging ahead in his flagship, the twenty-gun brig *Lawrence*, prematurely engaging the British line before the rest of his squadron was in a supporting position. At the height of the battle, though, he clambered into a small cutter and had himself rowed over to *Lawrence*'s sister ship, the *Niagara*. Taking personal command of the brig, he steered her into the thick of the fray. The addition of the *Nia-*

gara's undamaged gun batteries turned the tide and led to the surrender of the entire British squadron.

The Battle of Lake Erie stands out as one of the few decisive encounters in a war otherwise known for its inconclusiveness. Perry's triumph restored the Michigan Territory to American hands and secured Ohio's exposed frontier from attack for the rest of the war. The battle also contributed to the collapse of Tecumseh's confederacy in the Old Northwest, a process that was largely completed by the rout of a British–Indian army at the River Thames in October 1813.

Sources and Further Reading: David Curtis Skaggs and Gerard T. Altoff, *A Signal Victory: The Lake Erie Campaign, 1812–1813* (1997); William Jeffrey Welsh and David Curtis Skaggs, eds., *War on the Great Lakes: Essays Commemorating the 175th Anniversary of the Battle of Lake Erie* (1991).

Jeff Seiken
The Ohio State University

The Battle of the River Raisin

The Battle of the River Raisin, fought January 22, 1813, was a substantial American defeat during the early months of the War of 1812.

In August 1812, Major General William Hull surrendered Detroit to the British. Later that year, a second U.S. Army led by Brigadier General James Winchester attempted to repatriate the American outpost. Winchester began his offensive in late fall 1812. His army, numbering nearly twelve hundred men, suffered terribly because of inadequate provisions. By December, the Americans were destitute and reduced to grubbing roots and stripping bark from trees for food.

Commodore Oliver Hazard Perry and the Battle of Lake Erie. Courtesy U.S. Senate Collection.

On January 18, 1813, Winchester deployed 667 men against Frenchtown (modern Monroe, Michigan) on the River Raisin where grain and other provisions were rumored to be abundant. A small detachment of British and Indians guarding the village offered only slight resistance. By nightfall, the village was in American hands.

Winchester brought the remainder of his army forward and established his camp on the outskirts of town. At dawn on January 22, thirteen hundred British troops and native allies commanded by Colonel Henry Procter attacked the American position. Although some American companies continued to resist for some time, by midafternoon Procter had captured Winchester and destroyed the invading army. Compounding the defeat, Indians executed upwards of sixty wounded Americans left on the field after the British and their prisoners returned to Canada.

The execution of these prisoners made "Remember the Raisin!" an emotional rallying cry for revengeful American troops serving on the Detroit frontier throughout the remainder of the war.

Sources and Further Reading: Dennis M. Au, *War on the Raisin* (1981); G. Glenn Clift, *Remember the Raisin* (1961); Alec R. Gilpin, *The War of 1812 in the Old Northwest* (1958).

Larry L. Nelson
Firelands College, Huron, Ohio

The Battle of the Thames

The American victory at the Battle of the Thames marked the end of British military influence along the Detroit frontier during the War of 1812 and the collapse of nearly three generations of Indian resistance to European settlement in the Old Northwest.

Commandant Oliver Hazard Perry's victory over the British naval squadron near Put-In-Bay on Lake Erie on September 10, 1813, cut off British forces at Fort Malden from reinforcements and provisions and paved the way for the repatriation of Detroit and a long-anticipated invasion of Canada by American forces. On September 24, the British commander, Major General Henry Procter, abandoned Malden with more than 560 regulars and over a thousand native allies led by Tecumseh, and began a slow retreat up the Thames River. Within days, the British force was being pursued closely by nearly thirty-five hundred American troops commanded by William Henry Harrison.

Harrison caught his prey on October 5 near Moraviantown (in modern Ontario), a small Indian mission on the Thames River. Procter deployed his men in two lines, two hundred and fifty yards from the Thames.

Tecumseh placed his warriors throughout a thick bog on the British right. As the battle began, the British infantry, outnumbered and demoralized, fired only two volleys before fleeing. The Indians continued to fight tenaciously, but the death of Tecumseh brought an end to the battle. With the British Army defeated, the Indian confederacy leaderless, and the American Navy firmly in control of Lake Erie, the American victory was the last significant military action along the Detroit frontier for the remainder of the war.

Sources and Further Reading: Robert S. Allen, *His Majesty's Indian Allies* (1992); Sandy Antal, *A Wampum Denied* (1997); John Sugden, *Tecumseh's Last Stand* (1985).

Larry L. Nelson
Firelands College, Huron, Ohio

Sir Isaac Brock (1769–1812)

Born on the island of Guernsey, October 6, 1769, Isaac Brock entered the British Army in 1785, and by age twenty-eight, was lieutenant colonel of the Forty-Ninth Regiment. He saw service in Holland and at Copenhagen from 1799 to 1801, and in 1802, he was sent with his regiment to Canada, then a British colony. He had various postings at Quebec, Niagara, and York (Toronto) until the outbreak of the War of 1812. He was promoted colonel in 1805, major general in 1811, and just before the outbreak of hostilities, president and administrator of upper Canada (present-day Ontario).

General Brock set in place the system of defense for upper Canada, and developed a system of forward advance for the capture of American posts—Michilimackinac, Detroit, and other posts in Ohio and Michigan—at or shortly after the outbreak of war. He was the leader, civilian as well as military, in the defense of upper Canada in the early days of the war. He was a close ally of Tecumseh, who greatly admired and trusted him. He captured Detroit on August 15, 1812, and on October 13, his troops defeated the American invaders at Queenston on the Niagara frontier. During the battle, however, Brock fell, mortally wounded, and died the same day.

Tall and resolute, courageous and determined, he is regarded as the military savior of upper Canada. For services in connection with the capture of Detroit, he was given a knighthood, a Knight Commander of the Order of Bath. He was not married. To his memory a magnificent column was erected not far from the battlefield. It has been said many times of Brock that he was worth several regiments in the war against the Americans.

Sources and Further Reading: W. Kaye Lamb, *The Hero of Upper Canada* (1962); Welsey B. Turner, *British Generals in the War of 1812* (1999); Keith Walden, *Isaac Brock: Man and Myth* (1972).

Barry M. Gough
Wilfrid Laurier University, Ontario, Canada

Henry Adolphus Procter (1787–1859)

Born in Wales, Henry Adolphus Procter entered the British Army and was sent to Canada before the outbreak of the War of 1812. He commanded the Forty-First Regiment, otherwise known as the Welsh Regiment. In the campaigns of 1812 and 1813, enjoying the rank of major general, he commanded the Amherstburg sector based at Fort Malden, opposite Detroit, and in concert with Tecumseh and his Indian allies, inflicted severe reverses on the American forces in southern Michigan and western Ohio. Americans blamed his lack of supervision of prisoners taken at the River Raisin battle for the Indians' killing many of them. In 1813 his sieges of Forts Meigs and Stephenson in Ohio failed. The American naval victory at the Battle of Lake Erie, September 10, 1813, obliged him to retreat from Amherstburg (which he burned) and up the Thames River of upper Canada to Moraviantown. Tecumseh, fearing abandonment, urged him to take a stand against American forces. Procter made a feeble defense and then fled the field of battle, leaving his troops and Indian allies to their fate.

Procter has been charged with self-interested cowardice, but good evidence exists that being cut off from supply lines to York (Toronto) placed him and his army in an imperiled situation. Procter was court-martialed for his behavior at the Battle of the Thames. He was suspended for six months from rank and pay. He resumed his service in the Army at a later date, but the stain of cowardice stayed with him.

Sources and Further Reading: Sandy Antal, *A Wampum Denied: Procter's War of 1812* (1997); John Sugden, *Tecumseh: A Life* (1997).

Barry M. Gough
Wilfrid Laurier University, Ontario, Canada

Tecumseh (c. 1768–1813)

Tecumseh was one of the most influential Native American leaders to emerge following the end of the Old Northwest Indian Wars (1786–1795). Shawnee warrior and diplomat, he worked zealously during the first years of the nineteenth century to form a pan-Indian military and political alliance capable of resisting European expansion into the Old Northwest.

Tecumseh was born around 1768 into the Kispoko division of the Shawnee nation. Little is known of his early years. His father, Pukeshinwau, was killed on October 10, 1774, at the Battle of Point Pleasant. Tradition holds that Tecumseh acted as a scout for the Shawnees during Arthur St. Clair's invasion of western Ohio in the fall of 1791, and participated in the Battle of Fallen Timbers on August 15, 1794. His personal life is equally obscure. He married twice. He and his second wife, Mamate, had one son, Pachetha, who was raised by Tecumseh's sister, Tecumpease, following Tecumseh's death in 1813.

Tecumseh's activities are poorly documented until about 1805, when his brother, the charismatic mystic Lalawethika, received a series of visions in which he claimed to have visited Heaven. During these visions, he spoke to the "Master of Life" who instructed him to abandon white ways, Christianity, and alcohol and to urge other Indians to do likewise. In addition, Indians were to return to traditional customs and rituals to further distance themselves from the corrupting influence of European culture. Following his spiritual ordination, Lalawethika changed his name to Tenskwatawa (Prophet, or Open Door) and devoted all of his efforts to creating and directing a new religious

Portrayal of Tecumseh, Shawnee warrior, leader, and diplomat. Ohio Historical Society, AL00198.

movement based upon these revelations. In this, he was eminently successful, and the new faith attracted numerous adherents from throughout the Old Northwest and beyond.

Tecumseh distinguished himself in his brother's service. Traveling widely among the eastern Indian nations, he began to combine his own political insights with his brother's faith, eventually creating a plan for a pan-Indian confederacy based upon mutual respect among native peoples, political, economic, and military solidarity, and the concept that Indian lands were owned in common and that no nation or individual had the right to cede land belonging to all.

Tecumseh used his considerable talents as an orator to further the new ideology. He was a powerful and eloquent public speaker seemingly never "at a loss for an appropriate answer to all questions and enquiries." His ability to persuade, claimed those who heard him, compared favorably with that of Henry Clay's.

The actions of British agents enhanced Tecumseh's political aspirations for the confederacy. Tensions between the United States and Great Britain escalated in the aftermath of the Orders in Council of January and November 1807, which resulted in the interdiction of trade between France and the United States and the Chesapeake-Leopard Affair on June 22, 1807, in which the crew of the British warship HMS Leopard attacked and boarded the American frigate USS Chesapeake off the coast of Norfolk, Virginia, killing and wounding many and taking several alleged British deserters captive. The British Indian Department began to parlay with the Old Northwest Indian nations in an attempt to reestablish the military and economic alliance that had existed between the Crown and the region's native peoples throughout the colonial era, but which had fallen into neglect after the 1795 Treaty of Greenville.

By 1807, the Prophet's religion had attracted so many followers that he and Tecumseh relocated their village from Ohio to Prophetstown, located near the confluence of the Wabash and Tippecanoe Rivers in northeastern Indiana.

Congress appointed William Henry Harrison governor of the Indiana Territory in May 1800. Assuming office in January 1801, Harrison began to negotiate aggressively with the territory's Indian nations, seeking to acquire land that would attract settlers and thus propel the territory toward statehood. In this, Harrison was successful, eventually concluding a series of treaties in which he obtained title to much of present-day Illinois and southern Indiana.

In August 1810 and July 1811, Tecumseh confronted Harrison personally in Vincennes about these land cessions. The meetings were angry and at the second, he and Harrison nearly came to blows. The confrontations did not end Tecumseh's opposition, but Harrison left these encounters with a high opinion of his adversary, calling the Shawnee leader "one of those uncommon geniuses which spring up occasionally to produce revolutions and overturn the established order of things.... No difficulties deter him ... [W]herever he goes he makes an impression favorable to his purpose." Following his meetings with Harrison, Tecumseh began to travel extensively throughout the south, seeking to expand his confederacy to include the Chickasaws, Choctaws, and Creeks.

Tecumseh rose to prominence following the Battle of Tippecanoe. Concerned over increasing native resistance as settlers streamed into the region, Harrison gathered a thousand troops made up of U.S. regulars and militia from Kentucky and Indiana, and effected a preemptive strike against Tenskwatawa and his followers living at Prophetstown on November 7, 1811. The attack came as Tecumseh was away from the village recruiting in the south. The battle successfully destroyed the village, inflicted casualties, dispersed the survivors, and diminished the Prophet's prestige. This action and the subsequent opening of the War of 1812 on June 18 changed the Indian revival from a spiritual movement to a military one. Thus, as the Prophet's influence declined, Tecumseh's considerable political and martial abilities enabled him to assume leadership of the Indian effort at a critical juncture.

As a field commander, Tecumseh was energetic and courageous throughout the war, leading the Crown's native allies at the Battles of Brownstown, Monguagon (in which he was wounded), and the Thames, and in the sieges of Detroit and Fort Meigs. Known for his bravery and skill in combat, Tecumseh also acquired a reputation for dealing with captives and noncombatants in a humane and dignified manner. He frequently interceded on the behalf of prisoners and was responsible for halting a general massacre during the first siege of Fort Meigs.

Tecumseh's influence declined following British defeats at Fort Stephenson on August 2, 1813, and in the Battle of Lake Erie on September 10, 1813. The Indian confederacy, which only a year earlier could field over fifteen hundred combatants, suffered from massive desertions. When Harrison began his pursuit, Shawnee leaders loyal to the United States, including Black Hoof, Captain Lewis, and Black Snake, along with more than two hundred warriors advanced with the American Army. At the same time, Tecumseh's command had dwindled to fewer than five hundred.

The two armies engaged one another near Moraviantown close to the Thames River on October 5, 1813. British forces capitulated rapidly, but Tecumseh's troops continued to fight until Tecumseh was killed in a skirmish with Kentucky mounted militia led by Colonel Richard M. Johnson.

No other Native leader of Tecumseh's stature emerged during the conflict. Therefore, when Tecumseh was killed, the rudderless Indian confederacy quickly collapsed. Today, Tecumseh is remembered for his remarkable vision, iron integrity, and unswerving loyalty to the Indian cause.

Sources and Further Reading: Robert S. Allen, *His Majesty's Indian Allies* (1992); Colin G. Calloway, *Crown and Calumet* (1987); R. David Edmunds, *The Shawnee Prophet* (1983); R. David Edmunds, "'A Watchful Safeguard to Our Habitations': Black Hoof and the Loyal Shawnees," in Frederick E. Hoxie, Ronald Hoffman, and Peter J. Albert, eds., *Native Americans and the Early Republic* (1999); Bil Gilbert, *God Gave Us This Country* (1989); Alec R. Gilpen, *The War of 1812 in the Old Northwest* (1958); John Sugden, *Tecumseh: A Life* (1997).

Larry L. Nelson
Firelands College, Huron, Ohio

Military Exploration of the Midwest

The Peace of Paris of 1783 ending the American War for Independence secured the vast territory of the Old Northwest (today's Ohio, Indiana, Illinois, Michigan, Wisconsin, and Minnesota east of the Mississippi), and the acquisition of the Louisiana Territory in 1803 added even more territory (Minnesota west of the Mississippi, Iowa, Missouri, Kansas, Nebraska, and the Dakotas) to the young Republic. The early missions for the U.S. Army required it to establish a minimal national presence in the Midwest, to determine the national boundaries, and to explore and map this region whose geography was largely unknown to the European Americans.

While the Army protected civilian surveyors in the Ohio River Valley as early as 1786, its initial efforts included building a string of forts from Ft. Washington (Cincinnati), west and north into Michigan. From these it sent out expeditions in the early nineteenth century to map and explore the new territories.

The first was Lewis and Clark's Corps of Discovery, which gained its impetus and secured most of its men during the voyage down the Ohio River and up the Mississippi River to St. Louis. Meriwether Lewis recruited men as he rowed down the Ohio in 1803, where he joined William Clark in Clarksville, near the Falls of the Ohio, adding most of the expedition's forces at Forts Massac and Kaskaskia in modern Illinois. Wintering at Camp Wood outside St. Louis,

Statue of Lewis and Clark with Sacagawea in Kansas City, Missouri. Sculpture by Eugene Daub. Photo courtesy Michael Mihalevich (© 2003 Michael Mihalevich).

they prepared for their western expedition. One of the highlights of that winter and spring was the formal transfer of the Louisiana Territory (the northern section of the Louisiana Purchase) from French to American hands on March 10, 1804, at St. Louis.

Departing Camp Wood in May 1804, the Corps struggled up the Missouri River, as Lewis and Clark mapped the river and sent small expeditions to explore the surrounding area. While local trappers knew much of the river, the expedition was the first systematic exploration of the Missouri and its tributaries. By July, the Corps completed its nearly due-west trek across Missouri and turned north, mapping and meeting with local Indians. Present-day Council Bluffs, Iowa, was the site of the first great meeting on August 2 and 3, 1804, when the Corps exchanged gifts with Missouri and Otoe tribesmen. Crossing the Dakotas, Lewis and Clark wintered at Fort Mandan near modern Bismarck. Before departing westward into the unknown on April 7, 1805, Lewis sent part of the Corps back to St. Louis with maps and descriptions of the river and its environs, the first such data on the northern Missouri.

As the Corps of Discovery moved west, the Army was busy exploring other sections of the Midwest. President Thomas Jefferson, driven by scientific curiosity, directed the exploration of the unknown Northwest. Further, Jefferson ordered General James Wilkinson, governor of the Louisiana Territory, to prevent Canadian trade on the western side of the Mississippi, and Wilkinson needed to locate the river's source to fulfill his orders. In 1805, he sent Lieutenant Zebulon Pike up the Mississippi River to discover its headwaters.

Departing St. Louis in August 1805, Pike rowed up the Mississippi, arriving in Little Falls, Minnesota, by winter. Building a stockade there, he proceeded by dogsled and foot farther north, discovering Leech Lake, which he believed was the headwaters, then returned to St. Louis in April 1806. His exploration provided the first accurate information on the river along Iowa's eastern border and in Minnesota, and piqued interest in the Minnesota–Wisconsin frontier. On his second and by far his most famous expedition, Pike explored western Missouri, Kansas, and Colorado before becoming lost and then captured by Spanish forces in New Mexico. His expedition, really a military recon-

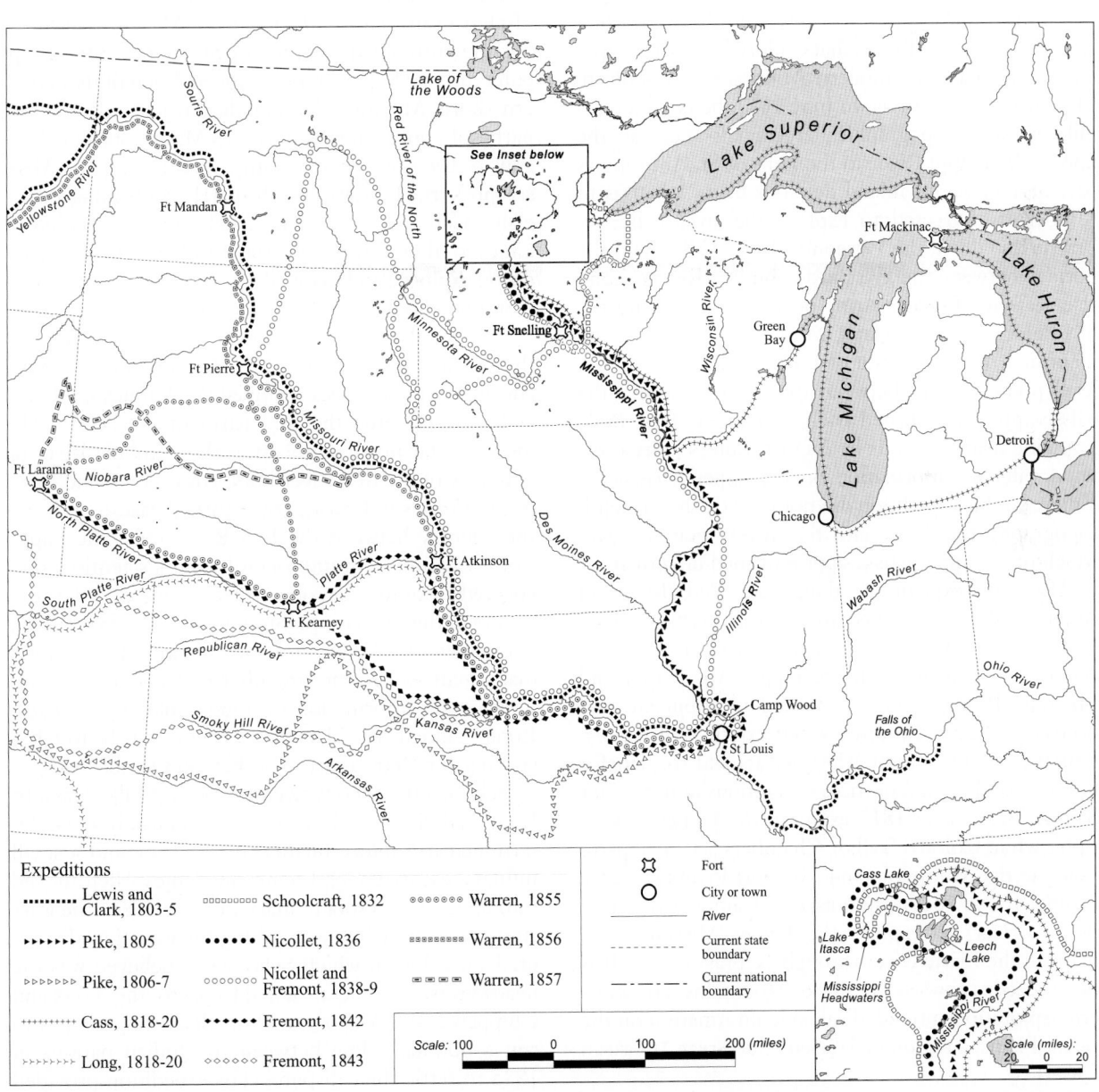

Military exploration. Prepared by James DeGrand. *Source:* Ray Allen Billington, *Westward Expansion* (New York: Macmillan, 1982); William H. Goetzman, *Army Exploration in the American West* (New Haven: Yale University Press, 1959); http://www.lib.utexas.edu/maps/united_states.html.

naissance, touched on the Republican, Kansas, and Smoky Hill Rivers in modern Kansas before moving west, further filling in the Midwest map.

Military exploration assumed lesser importance as the United States engaged in a series of confrontations with Great Britain, culminating in the War of 1812. With the Old Northwest an active theater of operations in that conflict, the Army spent little time on exploration. When the war ended, President James Monroe and Secretary of War John C. Calhoun initiated a new era of exploration that unlocked most of the remaining mysteries in the Old Northwest's uncharted regions.

Major Stephen Long was the most active of these military explorers. As the only experienced topographical engineer on the northwestern frontier, Long led a series of expeditions that explored the Mississippi Valley and parts of modern Minnesota, Wisconsin, Missouri, and Arkansas. In June 1817, he conducted a military and topographical reconnaissance of the upper Mississippi River to the Falls of St. Anthony as part of a survey of inland defenses from Arkansas to Minnesota. Directed to explore the river valley to Prairie du Chien, the Wisconsin River Valley, and the portage between the Wisconsin and Fox Rivers, Long also searched for new Army post sites. Exploring the St. Peter's River (today's Minnesota River), Long identified the future site of Fort Snelling on a high, level point of land between the Minnesota and the Mississippi, then turned back, arriving at Fort Belle Fontaine near St. Louis by August. Long's journal offered valuable information on the upper Mississippi Valley, but his expedition did not provide the in-depth topography the Army and the government needed. Much of the upper Mississippi remained unknown.

After an expedition along the Red River in Arkansas, Long returned to the Midwest in 1818–1819 as part of Secretary Calhoun's effort to assert American dominance on the Upper Mississippi and Missouri Rivers. Calhoun wanted to subjugate and pacify the Native Americans, but exploration was essential to identify their whereabouts and to plan for more forts. The first of these expeditions under Major Samuel Storrow in 1817 explored the Upper Mississippi, while Colonel Talbot Chambers sent troops to examine the Minnesota and Missouri Rivers in 1818. From 1818 to 1819, Long used a steamboat (the first on the river) to explore the Upper Missouri, and mapped the Platte River through Nebraska in 1820 as he proceeded toward the Rocky Mountains. His western explorations provided valuable information on the Great Plains, a region he labeled "the Great American Desert."

With the pace of military exploration accelerating in 1819, Colonel Henry Leavenworth traversed the upper Mississippi and used Long's maps to establish a cantonment at the site of what eventually became Fort Snelling. In 1820, an overland force tramped from Fort Missouri to Snelling, completing the first transit across modern Iowa and surveying a military road connecting the two posts. That same year, a military survey laid a road between Council Bluffs and Chariton, Missouri, while another party explored the Michigan territory around Mackinac, Green Bay, and Sault Ste. Marie. An 1820 infantry march from Council Bluffs to Fort Snelling provided information on northern Iowa and southern Minnesota.

Michigan Territorial Governor Lewis Cass led the last of the 1818–1820 expeditions. Accompanied by troops under Major Robert Forsyth, Cass canoed out of Detroit in May 1820, arriving at Mackinac in June. Passing through the Straits of St. Mary's, the group entered Lake Superior and mapped much of its southern shore. Moving inland at the St. Louis River, the party split up, exploring northern Minnesota and Wisconsin. Cass proceeded south, searching for the Mississippi's true headwaters, ultimately confirming Pike's claim. Canoeing down Lake Michigan, Cass landed at Chicago, then traveled overland to Detroit. His expedition explored and mapped a vast area, covering more than four thousand miles in four months.

Stephen Long's final expedition returned him to the northern regions. In 1823, he explored the Wisconsin–Minnesota area, mapped the Minnesota River, and reconnoitered the Red River of the North. He moved as far north and west as the Pembina River (a tributary of the Red River in North Dakota) and Lake of the Woods in Canada, then turned east, examining the country between the Red River and Lake Superior. Giacomo Beltrami, one of Long's scientists, discovered Lake Julia, erroneously claiming it as the true source of the Mississippi. Stopping at Sault Ste. Marie, Long met with Henry Schoolcraft, the Michigan Indian agent and former member of Cass's expedition. Exchanging information on topography and Indians, Long canoed to Mackinac, where he boarded a steamer for Detroit, arriving there in October 1823.

Schoolcraft, unconvinced that either Pike, Cass, or Long had discovered the Mississippi's headwaters, determined to explore further. In 1832, he and a small military escort under Lieutenant James Allen moved into upper Minnesota to make peace between the warring Sioux and Chippewa. Along the way, they discovered Lake Itasca, which Schoolcraft believed was the headwaters. Schoolcraft failed to pacify the Sioux and Chippewa, and Major Jonathon Bean was ordered to run a boundary line between the Indian nations in 1835 to settle their disputes. His expedition provided additional information on the Minnesota frontier.

In 1836, Frenchman Joseph Nicollet explored the

region with military assistance and discovered a large creek flowing into Lake Itasca, which he identified as the headwaters of the Mississippi, since then commonly accepted as the great river's source and Nicollet the discoverer. His findings led to a second expedition in 1838 with Lieutenant John Charles Frémont of the Topographical Engineers. Frémont's experiences on the Minnesota frontier proved invaluable when he moved into western exploration in the next decade.

Two factors changed the Army's role in exploration in the 1830s. The official formation of the Corps of Topographical Engineers in 1838 and the settlement of the Old Northwest and civilian movement into the trans-Mississippi regions meant that the Army placed more emphasis on opening the land for civilian use. The Corps used geologists, artists, and naturalists to prepare reports that both met military needs and fired the public's imagination, promoting the emerging idea of Manifest Destiny that supposed the United States was destined to expand from the Atlantic to the Pacific.

Military exploration in the Midwest slowed in the 1830s and 1840s as the nation expanded to the Pacific Ocean. Army dragoons from Iowa forts conducted campaigns and surveys between the Missouri and the Mississippi, laying out the northern section of the western military road. In 1849, dragoons under Major Samuel Woods surveyed along the Red River valley and the northern international border. As exploration abated, soldiers provided other important services: surveying the coasts of the Great Lakes, laying out canal routes in Ohio and Illinois, surveying lead mines in Minnesota, demarcating a boundary between the Sac and Fox and Sioux Indians, and building military roads.

While military exploration shifted its focus westward, there remained unfinished projects in the Midwest. Frémont's 1842 expedition charted the eastern portion of the Oregon Trail along the Platte River Valley in Nebraska, laying the foundation for the Pony Express route, the Overland Stage, the telegraph lines, and the Union Pacific Railroad. As railroads assumed national importance, the Army explored potential routes. In 1850, Captain Howard Stansbury surveyed the central route through Nebraska, following Frémont's maps. In 1853, future general Grenville Dodge completed a trans-Iowa survey to Council Bluffs, and Lieutenant E. G. Beckwith surveyed the central route from Council Bluffs to San Francisco, the basis for the Central Pacific line. The same year, Governor Isaac Stevens and his military escort surveyed the northern route, the future line for much of the Northern Pacific.

Lieutenant Gouverneur Warren conducted a series of explorations in Nebraska and South Dakota between 1855 and 1857, mapping much of the overlooked trans-Mississippi West. After surveying a military reservation for the Sioux near Ft. Pierre (modern Pierre, South Dakota), Warren explored Nebraska's Niobrara River and the Sand Hills region. His maps outlined a new road from Ft. Kearney on the Platte to Ft. Pierre on the Missouri. In 1857, he completed his explorations after examining the Loup River, the Niobrara to its confluence with the Missouri, the Sand Hills, and potential railroad routes to Ft. Laramie in Wyoming. Published in 1858, his maps filled in many blank areas of the Great Plains and were an important contribution to opening the trans-Mississippi Midwest.

The last significant Army exploration of the Midwest occurred in the early 1870s, as military engineers surveyed railroad lines and Army troops escorted civilian survey parties. The majority of these expeditions were treks across North Dakota and Montana to survey and plat the Northern Pacific Railroad. Culminating in 1874, when Northern Pacific engineer Thomas Rosser was accompanied by General David Stanley and Lieutenant Colonel George Armstrong Custer, these surveys mapped the route from the Minnesota border, across North Dakota, and into eastern Montana. As the rails moved across the Missouri River at Bismarck, the Army's role in exploration of the Midwest ended.

Sources and Further Reading: Stephen Ambrose, *Undaunted Courage* (1996); John Charles Frémont, *Narratives of Exploration and Adventure*, ed. Allan Nevins (1956); William H. Goetzmann, *Army Exploration in the American West, 1803–1863* (1959); Donald Jackson, *Thomas Jefferson and the Stony Mountains* (1981); Donald Jackson, ed., *The Journals and Letters of Zebulon Montgomery Pike* (1966); Ted Morgan, *A Shovel of Stars* (1995); Francis Paul Prucha, *Broadax and Bayonet* (1953); Francis Paul Prucha, *The Sword of the Republic* (1969); John Hoyt Williams, *A Great and Shining Road* (1988); Mentor L. Williams, ed., *Schoolcraft's Narrative Journal of Travels* (1992).

Mark Van Rhyn
University of Nebraska–Lincoln

The Indian Removal Policy

Removal of the Native American population of the Midwest, a prevalent component of federal treaties with the region's tribes after 1817, was a prolonged, complex, and ultimately incomplete process. Unlike the southern Indians, who experienced tragedy on forced marches to unfamiliar territory west of the Mississippi River after 1830, native people of the Midwest often succeeded in deferring or avoiding removal

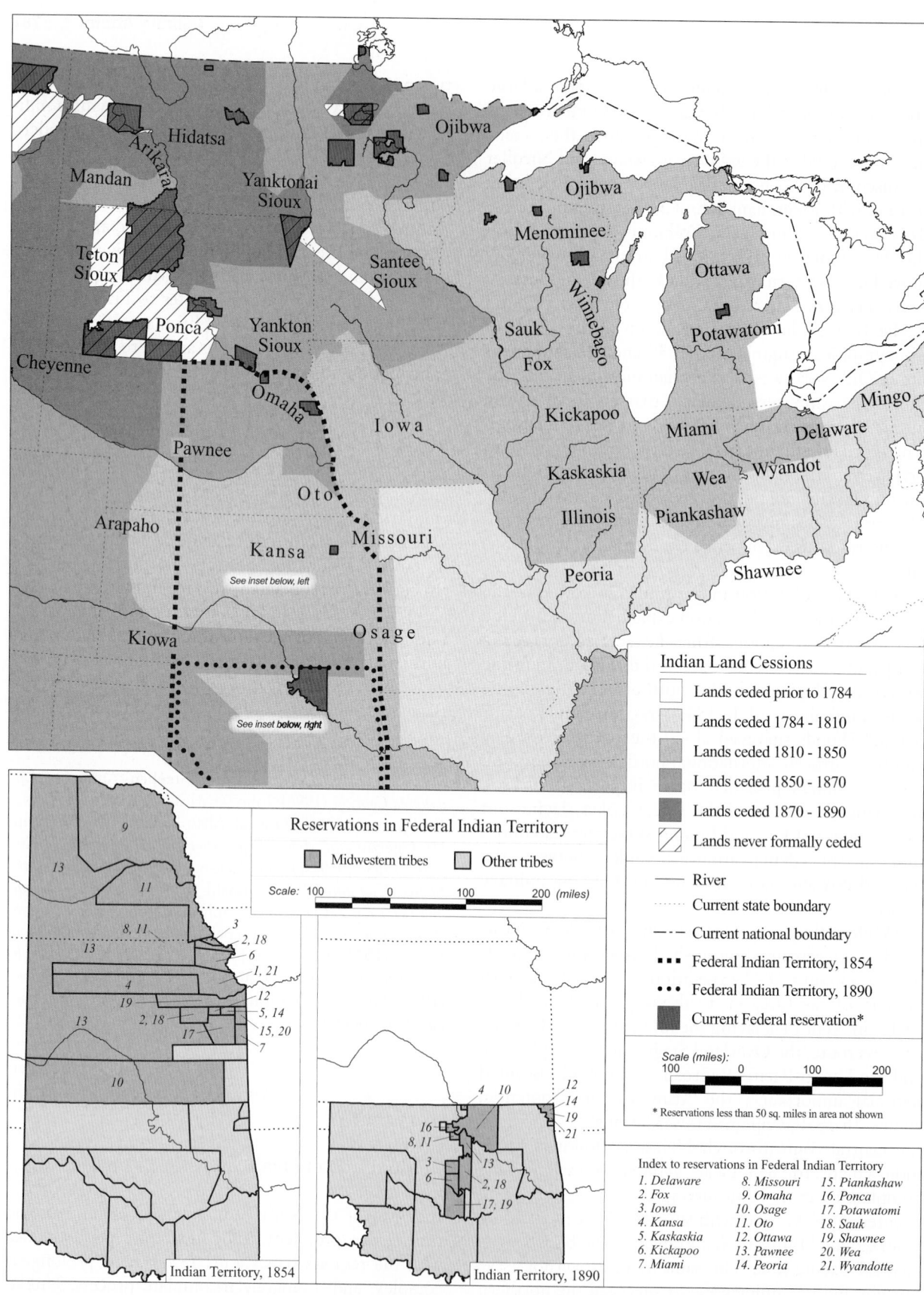

Indian land cessions and reservations. Prepared by James DeGrand. *Source:* Charles Royce, *Indian Land Cessions in the United States* (1900); United States Geological Survey, *Federal lands and Indian Reservations of the United States* (2000); Carl Waldman, *Atlas of the North American Indian* (New York: Facts on File, 2000).

with land cessions. Because of the proximity of British officials offering native communities refuge in Canada, and because of the uneven advancement of white settlers into the region, many Midwest native tribes secured permanent reservations in their traditional homelands through treaty negotiations. In other cases, the Midwest was the center of a chain of removals, with one removal spawning another. Some groups, like the Oneidas and Stockbridges, agreed to removal from eastern states into Wisconsin after 1818, which displaced the local Winnebagos and Menominees. Similarly, "emigrant Indians" removed from the northern Midwest after 1830 intruded on the territory of tribes resident in eastern Kansas. Removal of both the emigrant and indigenous native populations from Kansas did not occur until after 1870.

Almost from the nation's inception, the U.S. federal government looked to the west as a potential receptacle for native peoples. President Thomas Jefferson envisioned the vast extent of territory obtained in the 1803 Louisiana Purchase as a means of solving ongoing warfare between native peoples and settlers east of the Mississippi River. Relocated to the trans-Mississippi west, Indians could be isolated, subjected to a program of "civilization" (which involved education, Christian missionaries, and instruction in mainstream agricultural methods), and thus prepared for eventual assimilation into American society. President James Monroe first proposed a comprehensive program of federally funded transfers of the native population east of the Mississippi to western territory in 1824. After plans to create a distinct Indian Territory in the upper Midwest failed in Congress during the late 1820s, the Indian Removal Act of 1830 mandated the principle of encouraging eastern Indian tribes to exchange their lands for reserved tracts west of the Mississippi River.

Pressure on native populations to accept removal was initially most intense for those groups resident in Ohio, Indiana, and Illinois. In the northern Great Lakes region, minimal interest by white settlers left local Indians' residency largely intact, and native communities in Michigan and Wisconsin often provided refuge for Indians displaced from elsewhere. Throughout the Midwest, however, coerced removals were the exception to the rule. More commonly, individual native nations negotiated progressive surrenders of portions of their territory to the United States, concentrated their population in smaller areas, but also reserved rights to hunt, fish, and gather foods on ceded lands until these were surveyed and sold.

The Potawatomis, for example, signed thirty-nine treaties with the United States between 1789 and 1837, which left them with only small tracts of land in Indiana, Michigan, Illinois, and Wisconsin. Despite the diminution of their homelands, individual Potawatomi bands continued to exercise agency over their choice of residency, investigating alternative possibilities in Iowa, Kansas, and Canada before deciding where to remove. Similarly, the Wyandots of Ohio spent a dozen years investigating alternative locations proposed to them before agreeing to removal in 1843. The Mdewakonton Dakotas were generously remunerated by federal authorities for agreeing to removal in September 1837 from lands in western Wisconsin that they had not occupied for decades, owing to conflict with the Ojibway as well as ecological pressures. Lake Superior Ojibway from northern Wisconsin and Michigan's Upper Peninsula resisted deceptive efforts by federal and state officials to relocate them to the Sandy Lake region of northern Minnesota over the winter of 1850–1851. Their 1854 treaty with the United States enabled them to remain on reservations in Michigan, Wisconsin, and Minnesota.

An 1842 Congressional report on the progress of the federal removal policy estimated that 82,118 Indians from nearly thirty different eastern nations had been moved into lands west of the Mississippi River. The relocation of eastern Indians into the trans-Mississippi West necessarily forced indigenous nations to surrender portions of their territory and to accept geographically bounded homelands. Plans to resettle Algonquians into the eastern Plains cited prior adaptations by the Siouan Osage, Kansa, and Oto peoples to seasonal buffalo hunting, and the territories of "emigrant Indians" in Kansas were laid out to provide roughly equal access to buffalo ranges.

Yet pressure on the trans-Missouri Plains by settlers, town site speculators, railroad entrepreneurs, and political advocates of continentalism after 1840 eroded the notion of that region as a permanent sanctuary for the Indians. Reservations of both emigrant and indigenous Indians in Kansas and Nebraska sat astride major routes west to Oregon and California, and calls for removal of these populations, as well as those in the Wisconsin and Iowa territories, increased during the 1840s. The Kansas-Nebraska Act of 1854 created an anarchical struggle for much of the remaining Indian-held land in the Midwest.

The latter half of the nineteenth century witnessed a decided shift toward federally legislated rather than negotiated removals. Beginning in 1853, Bureau of Indian Affairs Commissioner George Manypenny initiated a process that anticipated the federal termination policy of the 1950s. In these treaties, emigrant Delaware, Shawnee, Miami, Wyandot, and Ottawa communities in Kansas had their status as recognized tribes revoked, ceded a portion of their reserved territory, and had the remainder allotted separately to individual tribal members. An 1867 treaty with the Indians of Kansas led to their final removal to Indian Territory in modern northeastern Oklahoma, where they received new reservations and had their tribal status restored. By 1880, Kansas had been largely cleared of its Native population. The process of removal and concentration of the Native population of the Midwest on reservations concluded in 1889, when the Great Sioux Reservation spanning the Dakotas was broken up into six smaller reservations, and eleven million acres of tribal lands were appropriated by the federal government.

Sources and Further Reading: James A. Clifton, *A Place of Refuge for All Time* (1975); Laurence M. Hauptman and L. Gordon McLester III, eds., *The Oneida Indian Journey* (1999); Francis P. Prucha, *The Great Father* (1984); Ronald N. Satz, *American Indian Policy in the Jacksonian Era* (1975); Helen H. Tanner, ed., *Atlas of Great Lakes Indian History* (1987); David J. Wishart, *An Unspeakable Sadness* (1994).

Jon Parmenter
Cornell University, New York

Weapons of Exploration and the Westward Movement

Through the remarkable American Revolution and the end of the eighteenth century, the American colonies and the new American government endured substantial dependence on their English adversaries for firearms. President George Washington recognized early the need for standardized weapons both for his new military forces as well as for gifts to present and items to trade with the native Indians, who had become accustomed to such favors from the British.

Thus in 1795, the first United States Armory located in Springfield, Massachusetts, began production of this nation's first standard military musket patterned after the French Charleville. Not surprisingly, it was named the Springfield Model 1795. This pattern was the backbone of the U.S. military forces for the next two decades, during which time 80,000 such muskets were produced.

Though thorough in their observations of fauna, flora, native inhabitants, geographical terrain, and the everyday conditions of the Corps of Discovery, Lewis and Clark did an inadequate job of recording the specific types of weapons upon which they relied during their adventure to the Pacific. It was indeed, however, a military mission of exploration upon which President Jefferson had sent them, and as such, it is logical that they would have been provided with the latest U.S. military weapons available. Certainly they carried the Model 1795, and it is known that they also had at least one airgun in addition to a variety of Kentucky rifles of the type commonly produced by makers around Lancaster, Pennsylvania.

By the time of the departure of the Corps of Discovery (1803), a second U.S. Armory had been established at Harpers Ferry, Virginia, and it was there that a rather notable new weapon was first produced. Until this time, substantially all military and hunting weapons were smoothbore muskets such as the French Charleville and the British Brown Bess. But with the development of the Kentucky rifles, American frontiersmen had acquired an appreciation for such heavy-barreled rifles that provided greater accuracy and at greater distance. This new military weapon was designated the Harpers Ferry Model 1803 and was designed to accommodate the needs for exploration, hunting, and defense on the American frontier.

The development of the Harpers Ferry Model 1803 was a response to market demand in those areas that were to become the Midwest. Those who had first ventured west of the Mississippi were adamant about the need for firearms adequate to down a moose, buffalo, or grizzly. The early muskets or small-bore Kentucky rifles were sufficient for the small game of the East, but they were relatively useless for the challenges faced in the exploration and settlement of the West. And the long barrels were a hindrance when on horseback. The solution was the .54 caliber, short-barreled, half-stocked Model 1803, which Lewis and Clark had wished they had, but which they had not. It was Lieutenant Zebulon Pike who first was issued such advanced weapons for his important military expedition in 1805 to explore the upper reaches of the Mississippi and subsequently in his important expedition into the Rocky Mountains in 1806. The same weapons were carried in the military expeditions led by Major Stephen Long in his explorations from Arkansas to the upper Mississippi Valley and the northern regions of the Old Northwest Territory in the second decade of the century.

The new American government also felt it essential to produce a weapon that would appeal specifically to its Native American allies and to compete with the "Northwest Indian Trade Gun," with its brass serpent sideplate, which had been so effectively gifted and traded by the British to their Indian allies in return for their military support against the insurgent colonists. Thus came about the Springfield Model 1807, commonly called the Indian Carbine. This little musket, however, failed to satisfy the Indian market and was soon terminated in favor of more economical, attractive, and effective privately made weapons.

With the rise of commercial enthusiasm and the spirit of adventure as the new country spread westward, an expanded market was created in rifle-making since firearms were considered fundamentally essential to all heading into the wilderness, whether the purpose was military exploration, participation in the fur trade, or pushing forward the frontiers of settlement. To meet this demand, a number of private gunmakers in Philadelphia created major enterprises for selling guns to the new government as well as to traders and explorers. These included such makers as Henry Deringer and George Tyron, while elsewhere in Pennsylvania, John Joseph Henry and Henry Leman took advantage of the growing demand for weaponry, as well.

Weapons and ultimately the weapon makers themselves began to move to the Midwest, following the Ohio down to the Mississippi, close to the frontier and to launching points for military exploration and the western movement. An important example was the Hawken family whose patron, Christian, began making guns in the late eighteenth century in Hagerstown, Maryland. He soon had some family members working at Harpers Ferry, with others venturing into the Ohio country, some settling in Springfield, Ohio. His most notable offspring, however, Jake and Sam, continued on down the Ohio River to St. Louis, where by the 1830s they were making the famous Plains Rifles for various explorers, guides, and mountain men, including the likes of Jim Bridger, Kit Carson, and Mariano Medina.

While various gunmakers had begun operating in Cincinnati and Louisville early in the nineteenth century, it was St. Louis that dominated the firearms trade in the Midwest from the 1820s to the Civil War. This was the jumping-off point for explorers, traders, trappers, and other adventurers heading west. All wanted a rifle made by Hawken or perhaps Dimick, Child and Pratt, Beauvais, Albright, or Gemmer. Lives often depended on the quality of weapons.

Toward midcentury, however, explorers and those moving west desired access to firearms that employed the new percussion system of ignition (rather than the old flintlocks), a technology employed by a variety of quality gunsmiths then in the Midwest. The percussion cap was more reliable and quicker to ignite than the old flintlocks. But still, the large preponderance of weapons in use through the Civil War were muzzle-loaders.

By the late 1860s, however, substantial improvements had been made in firearms technology, particularly in ammunition and the self-contained cartridge. Inventors and entrepreneurs combined to form companies like Smith & Wesson, Colt, and Winchester, and soon the trusted and time-honored muzzle-loading rifle was a thing of the past. Within a decade of the Civil War, breech-loading repeating weapons had become dominant in the firearms industry, the new technology constituting a veritable revolution in weaponry.

Only the military failed to seize the opportunity to put this new technology to advantage. As the Indian Wars consumed the West in the 1870s, U.S. troops including the cavalry under George Custer were primarily armed with the latest offering from the Springfield Armory—the Model 1873 Springfield Carbine, not a repeater, but a simple single-shot weapon. Many in the military hierarchy contended that were they given repeaters, the troops would simply waste ammunition. Custer and his men would pay a price for this in 1876 at the Battle of the Little Bighorn. It was near the end of the century before the U.S. military set aside its old single-shot weapons. By then, however, the West had been "won," or at least substantially settled, the frontier had all but vanished, and an extraordinary era of exploration and settlement and the weaponry that assisted it faded into history.

Sources and Further Reading: Louis Garavaglia and Charles G. Worman, *Firearms of the American West, 1803–1865* (1998); S. James Gooding, *Trade Guns of the Hudson's Bay Company, 1670–1970* (2003); Charles Hanson, Jr., *The Plains Rifle* (1960); Henry J. Kauffman, *Early American Gunsmiths, 1650–1850* (1952); George D. Moeller, *American Military Shoulder Arms* (1993).

James D. Gordon
Santa Fe, New Mexico

The Mexican War, 1846–1848

When the United States and Mexico declared war in 1846, the U.S. Congress voted for war overwhelmingly, forty to two in the Senate and 174 to fourteen in the House. Of those senators recording negative votes, none came from the Midwest states in the Union at that time—Ohio, Michigan, Indiana, Illinois, Iowa, and Missouri. In the House, five of fourteen negative votes came from the Midwest, all from Ohio Whigs. Revealing an undercurrent against the war in their state, the Ohioans expressed one or a combination of reasons for their votes. Some objected to the use of military power against Mexico, a friendly neighbor. Others stood against American expansion into the West out of fear of starting wars with either Mexico or Britain (over Oregon). They also opposed the possibility or likelihood that slavery would expand into any lands captured in a war with Mexico.

Congress authorized President James K. Polk to issue a call for fifty thousand volunteers to supplement the Regular Army. Closest to the theaters of war, states in the Midwest and South raised and sent soldiers expeditiously into service. Thousands of midwesterners quickly demonstrated their nationalism, support for the war, and adherence to Manifest Destiny, the popular concept advocating that the United States was destined to expand from the Atlantic to the Pacific.

During the course of the war, the states raised sixty volunteer regiments, each enrolling around eight hundred men, along with numerous smaller battalions (of two to three hundred men) and companies (of one hundred men or less). Many soldiers enlisted for one year, though some signed on for six months. The Midwest recruited twenty-one regiments, six from Illinois, five each from Indiana and Ohio, four from Missouri, and one from Michigan. Missouri also contributed six separate battalions, and Iowa raised three independent companies. The South produced thirty-one regiments and more than twenty separate battalions or companies. From the East came only five regiments, limited to Massachusetts, Pennsylvania, and New York. Recruitment, public rallies favoring the war, and editorial support from midwestern newspapers was strongest in the war's first year. Thus, the Midwest's contribution to the U.S. war effort compared favorably to the South and overshadowed the East.

President Polk, a Democrat, rallied members of his party, but support for the war was not monolithic; both Democrats and Whigs in the Midwest responded to Polk's call for troops. The war's ardent opponents were Whigs, but a minority of Whigs favored expansion, recruited volunteers, and became leaders in military units. Although some Whigs supported the war, Polk commissioned only Democrats as volunteer generals. Four of thirteen volunteer generals came from the Midwest. They included former Ohio congressman Thomas Hamer, Illinois politician James Shields, Indiana state senator Joseph Lane, and Missouri congressman Sterling Price. Hamer, Shields, and Price all established creditable records. Of the twenty-one midwesterners elected or appointed as regimental colonels, twelve were Democrats or likely Democrats, five were Whigs or likely Whigs, and four affiliations remain unidentified. Of the midwestern colonels, all civilians in 1846, only five were West Point alumni: Michigan's Thomas Stockton, a probable Democrat, and from Ohio, George Morgan, a Democrat, Samuel Curtis and Alexander Mitchell, both likely Whigs, and William Irvin of unconfirmed party.

Some officers and regiments from the Midwest rendered stalwart service, but others were disappointing. Achieving national renown was Alexander Doniphan, a prominent Whig legislator from Missouri. Doniphan led a regiment as part of an expedition that captured Santa Fe, New Mexico, and Chihuahua City, Chihuahua, Mexico. Illinois contributed Colonel John Hardin, a former Whig congressman, killed at the Battle of Buena Vista; Colonel William

Bissell, a Democrat, who fought well at Buena Vista (Coahuila, Mexico); and another Whig, Colonel Edward Baker, who led a successful assault in the Battle of Cerro Gordo (Veracruz, Mexico). Notable officers from Indiana included William Bowles, leading the Second Indiana Regiment, and General Joseph Lane and Colonel James Lane (no relation) of the Third Indiana; all three were Democrats. General Zachary Taylor criticized Joseph Lane's leadership, finding fault with his inability to work well with other volunteers and failing to cooperate with Regular Army officers. In contrast, James Lane won recognition for bravery at Buena Vista (Coahuila, Mexico), while Bowles's regiment fled the field. Sterling Price, another Democrat, commanded a Missouri regiment at Santa Fe and a second campaign into Chihuahua, Mexico. Ohio's Alexander Mitchell, a likely Whig, was wounded at the Battle of Monterrey (Nuevo Leon, Mexico) and then acted as military governor there. Colonel Samuel Curtis, a Whig lawyer and engineer, served on military occupation duty in Camargo, Mexico. Some volunteer officers drew upon their military service to continue political careers after the war.

Although most midwesterners supported the war, some journalists, abolitionists, religious leaders, and politicians voiced their opposition. For example, in December 1847, Abraham Lincoln, an Illinois Whig congressman, delivered a partisan speech in the House demanding to know the exact spot where the war began. In his controversial "spot resolution," Lincoln questioned President Polk's assertion that Mexico began the conflict by "shed[ding] American blood upon the American soil." Thomas Corwin, a U.S. senator from Ohio, broke along with most fellow Whigs by actually voting against funds for conducting the war. Employing stinging rhetoric, Corwin asserted: "If I were a Mexican, I would tell you [Americans], 'Have you not room in your own country to bury your dead men?'"

As the war concluded, many midwestern representatives and newspapers sustained the controversial Wilmot Proviso. Introduced several times in the House by Pennsylvania Democrat David Wilmot, it stated that no slavery would be allowed in any land taken from Mexico. The proviso passed the House, but failed in the Senate. The war that had added so much land to the United States also resulted in a bitter controversy over expansion of slavery into the territories.

Sources and Further Reading: Hal Bochin, "Tom Corwin's Speech Against the Mexican War," *Ohio History* 90 (Winter 1981); Joseph Chance, ed., *Mexico Under Fire: Being the Diary of Samuel Ryan Curtis, Third Ohio Volunteer Regiment* (1994); G. W. Cullum, *Biographical Register of the Officers and Graduates of the United States Military Academy*, 2 vols. (1868); Joseph G. Dawson III, *Doniphan's Epic March* (1999);

Donald Frazier, ed., *The United States and Mexico at War* (1998); Clayton Charles Kohl, *Claims as a Cause of the Mexican War* (1914); John H. Schroeder, *Mr. Polk's War: American Opposition and Dissent* (1973); Ezra Warner, *Generals in Blue* (1964); Richard Winders, *Mr. Polk's Army* (1997).

Joseph G. Dawson III
Texas A & M University

Alexander W. Doniphan (1808–1887)

Born near Maysville, Mason County, Kentucky, on July 9, 1808, Doniphan graduated from Augusta College, at Augusta, Kentucky, in 1826. He read law and moved to Missouri in 1830, opening an office near Kansas City. When war began with Mexico in 1846, Doniphan, an advocate of Manifest Destiny, helped recruit eight hundred men for the First Missouri Regiment of Mounted Volunteers; two hundred other Missourians served with regimental support units. Drawing upon his legal renown, he was elected colonel after enlisting as a private. He became one of the war's most notable volunteer officers.

Under Brigadier General Stephen W. Kearny, Doniphan and his regiment marched from Fort Leavenworth to capture Santa Fe, New Mexico, on August 18, 1846. There Doniphan acted as one of America's first military governors, negotiating a treaty with the Navajo Indians and drafting a constitution for New Mexico.

Campaigning deeper into Mexico, Doniphan led his regiment to victory in two battles. The first came against twelve hundred Mexicans at Brazito on December 25, 1846, enabling him to capture El Paso del Norte (Juárez, Mexico). The second was fought against three thousand Mexicans on February 28, 1847, at the Sacramento River, near Chihuahua City, leading to the fall of Chihuahua on March 2. A few weeks later Doniphan and his men marched to Matamoros and took steamboats home to Missouri. Doniphan's March of fifty-five hundred miles prompted American journalists to compare him favorably with Xenophon, a Greek military commander of ancient times.

Doniphan resumed his law practice and was re-elected to the Missouri legislature. While many of his veterans served the Confederacy during the Civil War, Doniphan refused to support secession, even though he was a slaveowner.

Sources and Further Reading: Joseph G. Dawson III, *Doniphan's Epic March* (1999); Roger D. Launius, *Alexander William Doniphan, Portrait of a Missouri Moderate* (1997).

Joseph G. Dawson III
Texas A & M University

The Civil War, 1861–1865

The region identified as the Midwest played a major role—politically, militarily, and economically—in Union victory in the Civil War. From states of the Old Northwest (Ohio, Michigan, Indiana, Illinois, Wisconsin, and Minnesota east of the Mississippi) to those carved from the Louisiana Purchase (Iowa, Missouri, Minnesota west of the Mississippi, and the eastern portions of Kansas, Nebraska Territory and Dakota Territory), this area symbolized the fruits of Manifest Destiny. By midcentury, however, the region's economic growth, increased political power, and proximity to the western frontier had entangled it in the sectional debates over the expansion of slavery into the territories. When war erupted in 1861, the manpower, material resources, and political muscle of the midwestern states would prove vital to the survival of the Union and the elimination of slavery.

The Midwest supplied volunteers, draftees, and substitutes to the Union armies, and these men fought in most of the critical battles in all theaters during the war. Ohio provided the most manpower with over three hundred thousand men donning blue uniforms, including over 5,000 blacks recruited after 1863. By war's end, 35,000 black and white Ohioans had fallen in combat or to disease. Many Ohio regiments proved their worth in battle, especially the Eighth Ohio of the Gibraltar Brigade, which helped repel Pickett's Charge at Gettysburg. To the north, Michigan furnished 87,000 troops (1,387 of them black), and over 14,000 gave their lives to the Union cause. The Twenty-Fourth Michigan Infantry perhaps best represents both the fighting ability and sacrifice of the Michigan troops: The regiment fought in many of the key Eastern campaigns and at Gettysburg suffered horrendous casualties, losing 80 percent of its men on the first day.

In Illinois, 259,000 whites flocked to the colors, and over 1,800 blacks answered the call, many serving in the 29th U.S. Colored Troops (USCT). At war's end, Illinoisans mourned the loss of nearly 35,000 fellow citizens, including Abraham Lincoln, who was felled by an assassin's bullet in 1865. Illinois's geographic location also enhanced the state's strategic importance. Situated at the confluence of the Mississippi and Ohio Rivers, the tiny hamlet of Cairo became a staging area for Union operations against Confederate-occupied Kentucky and played a key role in an early battle for control of the Mississippi Valley.

The remaining states of the Old Northwest, Wisconsin and Indiana, sent 91,379 and 196,363 men, respectively. Nearly 200 Wisconsin blacks and another 1,500 from Indiana also joined the fray. Wisconsin's death toll neared 12,000, while the Hoosier State lost over 7,000 in combat and another 18,000 to various diseases. Both states also boasted famous regiments. Along with the Twenty-Fourth Michigan, three Wisconsin regiments (Second, Sixth, and Seventh) and the Nineteenth Indiana formed the famous Iron Brigade in the Army of the Potomac. These units earned their reputation in many key battles in the East, but also paid a terrible price. On the first day of the Battle of Gettysburg, the Second Wisconsin suffered casualties of 77 percent, while the Nineteenth Indiana lost nearly 72 percent of its strength. In addition, the Seventy-Second Indiana of the famed Lightning Brigade proved the worth of mounted infantry in the western theater.

The four states of the Louisiana Purchase also contributed to the Union cause. Iowa sent over 76,000 troops, and over half of its military-age males served in uniform, approximately 13,000 of whom never returned to the Hawkeye State, the highest percentage loss of all midwestern states. Though possessing some of the most restrictive anti-black immigration laws in the Union, more than 440 Iowa blacks served in the Union Army. Even older Iowans did their part by joining the Thirty-Seventh Iowa Infantry, better known as the Greybeards.

Minnesota also played a significant role, committing nearly 25,000—including over one hundred blacks—for service in the East. Though many Minnesota regiments served with distinction, one stands out. The First Minnesota earned special honors at Gettysburg when the regiment charged a superior force on July 2. This heroic action staved off potential disaster to Union forces, but at a cost of 215 casualties out of 262 engaged, the highest percentage loss (82 percent) of any regiment during the war.

Though the youngest state in the Midwest, Kansas was already a household word by 1861. The passage of the Kansas-Nebraska Act in 1854 polarized factions in the slavery debate and led to violence in Kansas between pro- and antislave factions. This internecine conflict spawned the likes of John Brown, who made Potawatomie Creek run red with blood rather than permit slave owners to reside in the state. Armed groups from both camps—Jayhawkers, Red Legs, Border Ruffians—only fueled the conflagration. After achieving statehood in 1861, over 20,000 Kansans fought in blue, including the First Kansas Colored Volunteers, which became the first black regiment from a northern state to fight in battle.

The territories of the Midwest also supported the Union. Despite fears that the withdrawal of U.S. Army garrisons would encourage Indian uprisings, Nebraskans answered Lincoln's appeal for volunteers and sent the second largest number of recruits of all the territories. The First Nebraska Infantry fought at Fort Donelson and Shiloh, and cavalry units campaigned in Tennessee and Alabama. After the 1862 Sioux Uprising in Minnesota, Nebraska units returned home to protect white settlers and launch raids against the Sioux, Cheyenne, and Arapaho.

Inhabitants of the Dakota Territory also feared Indian attacks on its small white population. When the garrisons at Forts Abercrombie and Randall headed east, local volunteers assumed their duties. The governor raised one company of Dakotans for the Union Army, but the fear of Indian troubles kept it close to home. Volunteers formed other units like the Vermillion Rangers and the Yankton Home Guard, but all remained in the territory to protect white settlers. Those Dakotans wishing to fight Confederates joined units from Nebraska and Iowa.

The final state considered part of the Midwest followed a far different path before and during the war. As part of the Compromise of 1820, Missouri entered the Union as a slave state, the only one in the Midwest. When southern states seceded in 1860 and 1861, the loyalties of this border state were divided, resulting in two separate state governments and polarization of the state militia into pro-secession and pro-Union camps. As a result, Missourians fought each other, both in organized armies of the Union or Confederacy and as guerrillas and bushwhackers. As a result, the state lapsed into an long cycle of violence at the hands of "Bloody Bill" Anderson, James Lane, Charles Jennison, William Quantrill, and others of that stripe.

Missouri was also one of the few midwestern states to be both a battlefront and a homefront. The state was the site of 1,162 battles and skirmishes, placing it behind only Virginia and Tennessee in this category. The struggle for control of the Mississippi and Missouri Rivers, as well as for the key city of St. Louis, led to significant fighting within the state. Early battles at Wilson's Creek (August 10, 1861), a Union defeat that opened the state to invasion by Confederates, and Belmont (November 7, 1861), where Ulysses S. Grant first commanded troops in battle, were but the beginning of the bloodletting in this border state. Other actions at Fredericktown, Lexington, and Island Mound (the first time black troops from a northern state saw combat) transformed the state into a no-man's-land.

Undoubtedly, Missourians felt the hard hand of war far more than any other state in the Midwest, but there was fighting elsewhere in the region. In Kansas, William Quantrill's infamous Sack of Lawrence (August 21, 1863) and the massacre of both black and white Union troops at Baxter Springs in October 1863 struck fear in the hearts of locals. The nightmare of Minnesotans came true in 1862, when Santee Sioux Indians raided settlements along the Minnesota River and killed hundreds of whites. In retaliation, authorities hanged thirty-eight Sioux participants, which became the largest mass execution in American history.

The Old Northwest also experienced the war firsthand when John Hunt Morgan's Confederate cavalry slashed its way across the southern portions of Indiana and Ohio in 1863. During a wild ride of more than a thousand miles, Morgan's troopers terrorized civilians and galloped through the suburbs of Cincinnati. Union troops finally cornered the raiders at Buffington Island on July 19. Incarcerated at the Ohio Penitentiary, Morgan managed to escape and fight another day.

Not all midwesterners felt threatened by the enemy at the gates, but many civilians had to live with the enemy *behind* the gates. Prisoner-of-war camps established at Camp Chase and Johnson's Island in Ohio, at Rock Island, Alton, and Camp Douglas in Illinois, and at Camp Morton, Indiana, brought southerners into communities far removed from the battlefield and gave many citizens their first glimpse of rebels. Besides the thousands of Confederates behind the stockades, there were also many enemies of the Union roaming freely in the Midwest. Clement L. Vallandigham, a Democratic congressman from Ohio, vehemently opposed the Lincoln administration's prosecution of the war and was branded a Copperhead, a term indiscriminately applied to others, mostly Democrats, who opposed the war. Arrested in 1863, Lincoln banished him to the Confederacy.

More enterprising southern sympathizers attempted to aid the Confederacy by launching an insurrection in the Midwest in 1864. Hatched by Confederate agents in Canada and supported by Copperheads in the Midwest, the so-called Northwest Conspiracy was a plot to overthrow the state governments of Ohio, Indiana, and Illinois using liberated Confederate prisoners. The conspirators then hoped to establish a proSouthern Northwest Confederacy and force Lincoln to negotiate for peace. However, Union officials uncovered the plot in time to squelch it.

The Midwest was home to many prominent Union officers. Illinois produced Ulysses S. Grant (though Ohio also lays claim to him as their own), John Logan, James H. Wilson, Wesley Merritt, W.H.L. Wallace, and Benjamin Grierson. William T. Sherman, Philip Sheridan, Jacob D. Cox, Don Carlos Buell, and future presidents Rutherford B. Hayes and James Garfield hailed from Ohio, while Indiana claimed Lew Wallace (future author of *Ben Hur*). Michigan boasted of George Armstrong Custer, and Iowa proudly claimed Grenville M. Dodge. Missouri produced officers for

both sides during the war, including Frederick Dent, Sterling Price, and M. Jeff Thompson.

The region also supplied the sinews of war. Midwesterners mined tons of lead (Wisconsin alone produced seventeen million pounds), grew millions of acres of food, sheared thousands of sheep, and manufactured an abundance of military and civilian goods. Financially, Ohio native Jay Cooke helped the government pay for the war by persuading average citizens—not just wealthy financiers—to purchase government bonds in support of the war, selling $853 million worth in 1865 alone. Besides contributing material and financial resources, midwesterners also championed humanitarian relief efforts. In 1861, Ohioans formed the nation's first soldier's aid association and later founded the U.S. Sanitary Commission in Cincinnati.

The region that gave birth to the Republican Party in 1854 became a tremendous political asset for the Lincoln administration. War governors Oliver P. Morton (Indiana), Richard Yates (Illinois), and Samuel Kirkwood (Iowa) maintained steadfast support for the war and ensured an uninterrupted flow of men and materiel from their states. Other midwesterners like Salmon P. Chase, Edwin M. Stanton, and Benjamin Wade, not to mention Abraham Lincoln, helped shape both wartime and postwar policies.

In the final analysis, the Midwest proved vital to Union victory, but at a high cost. More than 156,000 midwesterners gave their lives, and thousands more returned home wounded—both physically and psychologically—and would live out their days scarred by the war. For those veterans unable to care for themselves, two of the three branches of the National Asylum for Disabled Volunteer Soldiers (later called the National Military Home) were located in the Midwest—in Milwaukee, Wisconsin, and Dayton, Ohio. Whether fighting, farming, manufacturing, or caring for the grizzled old veterans of Shiloh and Gettysburg, the citizens of the Midwest made tremendous sacrifices that not only helped save the Union and abolish slavery, but also transformed the region into a powerful economic, political, and moral center for the nation as it entered the twentieth century.

Sources and Further Reading: Albert Castel, *A Frontier State at War* (1958); Michael Fellman, *Inside War: The Guerrilla Conflict in Missouri During the American Civil War* (1989); Hondon B. Hargrove, *Black Union Soldiers in the Civil War* (1988); Frank L. Klement, *The Limits of Dissent: Clement L. Vallandigham and the Civil War* (1970); Frank L. Klement, *Wisconsin and the Civil War* (1963); Benton McAdams, *Rebels at Rock Island* (2000); Richard Moe, *The Last Full Measure: The Life and Death of the First Minnesota Volunteers* (1993); Alan Nolan, *The Iron Brigade* (1961); Ellis Paxson Oberholtzer, *Jay Cooke: Financier of the Civil War*, 2 vols. (1907); Carl Wittke, ed., *A History of the State of Ohio*, vol. 4, Eugene H. Roseboom, ed., *The Civil War Era* (1944).

William B. Feis
Buena Vista University, Iowa

Wilson's Creek, Missouri

Although Missouri remained in the Union, during the spring of 1861, fighting erupted between the pro-secessionist Missouri State Guard led by Major General Sterling Price and Union forces under Brigadier General Nathaniel Lyon. Lyon and his subordinates fought several skirmishes against the State Guard before concentrating in Springfield in late July. Lyon named his command the Army of the West.

To assist Price, Brigadier General Ben McCulloch entered Missouri with a brigade of Confederates from northwest Arkansas. They joined with the State Guard to form the Western Army, 10,125 strong, under McCulloch's command. On August 6, they camped along Wilson's Creek, nine miles from Springfield. McCulloch ordered an advance during the evening of August 9, but cancelled it when rain threatened.

Lyon had fewer than 7,000 men in Springfield, but he was determined to uphold the prestige of the Union cause. Leaving a guard in Springfield, Lyon divided 5,431 men into two columns and advanced on the unsuspecting southerners during the night of August 9. He achieved complete surprise, striking the northern and southern ends of McCulloch's camps simultaneously at dawn on August 10. McCulloch and Price responded skillfully to the crisis, however, and five hours of desperate fighting ensued. Lyon was killed and the Union retreated. On August 11, they withdrew from Springfield to Rolla, in south central Missouri. Price advanced to the Missouri River in September, but Union countermoves in the winter of 1861–1862 kept the state firmly in Union hands.

Sources and Further Reading: Edwin C. Bearss, *The Battle of Wilson's Creek* (1975); William Garrett Piston and Richard W. Hatcher III, *Wilson's Creek: The Second Battle of the Civil War and the Men Who Fought It* (2000).

William Garrett Piston
Southwest Missouri State University

Sterling Price (1809–1867)

Born in Prince Edward County, Virginia, in September 1809, Sterling Price graduated from Hampden-Sidney College and studied law, but moved to Missouri where he became a slaveholding tobacco planter and businessman. He married Martha Head in 1833; the couple had six children.

A Democrat, Price was elected to the Missouri House of Representatives and to the U.S. Congress. During the Mexican War, he was a brevet brigadier general of volunteers, winning minor victories in northern Mexico. He was governor of Missouri from 1853 to 1857.

Price chaired the March 1861 state convention that rejected secession, but his sympathies were with the South. Appointed field commander of the Missouri State Guard, his opposition to Union authority culminated in victories at the battles of Wilson's Creek and Lexington in August and September 1861. After Missouri was admitted to the Confederacy in December, Price was commissioned a major general. He fought at Pea Ridge, Iuka, Corinth, and in the defense of Little Rock. In September 1864, Price returned to Missouri with twelve thousand men, most of whom were mounted, in a daring maneuver that threatened both St. Louis and Jefferson City, but captured neither. He was defeated at Westport (near Kansas City) on October 23, 1864, in the largest battle west of the Mississippi. He returned to Arkansas, having covered over fourteen hundred miles—the longest such raid in American military history. When the Confederacy fell, Price chose exile in Mexico, but he returned to Missouri in 1867. He died on September 29, 1867, and is buried in St. Louis.

Price was a formidable political figure in the 1850s and a charismatic leader in wartime. He was beloved by his soldiers, who called him Old Pap, but he neglected discipline and his generalship was not distinguished.

Sources and Further Reading: Albert Castel, *General Sterling Price and the Civil War in the West* (1968); Thomas L. Snead, *The Fight for Missouri* (1886).

William Garrett Piston
Southwest Missouri State University

Philip Henry Sheridan (1831–1888)

Born in Albany, New York—or possibly Ireland—Sheridan grew up in Somerset, Ohio. Appointed to West Point's Class of 1852, he was suspended for fighting and did not graduate until 1853. Still a second lieutenant in 1861, his meteoric rise through the ranks began with an appointment as colonel of the Second Michigan Cavalry. Promoted brigadier general in September 1862, he won high praise for his aggressiveness at Perryville (Kentucky) in October and Murfreesboro (Tennessee) in December. Promoted to major general in March 1863, he fought hard at Chickamauga (Georgia) in September, and his division of midwestern troops stormed Missionary Ridge at Chattanooga (Tennessee) in November.

When the Army of the Potomac marched against Lee in the spring of 1864, Sheridan served as its chief of cavalry during General U. S. Grant's Overland campaign. Commanding all Union forces in the Shenandoah Valley in the fall of 1864, he crushed the Confederate defenders and stripped bare that key southern breadbasket. Sheridan's men stormed the southern lines at Five Forks in April 1865, breaking the siege of Petersburg and pursuing General Robert E. Lee's men to Appomattox. While commanding the Fifth Military District (Texas and Louisiana) during Reconstruction, Sheridan was relieved of duty because of his harsh governance. Nonetheless, promoted to lieutenant general in 1869, he took an active role in the Indian Wars. In 1883, he was named commanding general of the U.S. Army and won promotion to full general in June 1888, two months before his death.

Sources and Further Reading: Roy Morris, Jr., *Sheridan: The Life and Wars of General Phil Sheridan* (1992); Philip H. Sheridan, *Personal Memoirs of P. H. Sheridan* (1888).

Carol Reardon
Pennsylvania State University

General William Tecumseh Sherman. Library of Congress, Prints and Photographs Division, LC-B813-6454A.

William Tecumseh Sherman (1820–1891)

Born in Lancaster, Ohio, William T. Sherman was appointed to West Point by Senator Thomas Ewing, his guardian and future father-in-law. Graduating sixth in the Class of 1840, Sherman remained in the U.S. Army until 1853, including a stint in California during the Mexican War.

In May 1861, Sherman reentered military service as a colonel and fought at the first Battle of Bull Run in July 1861. Promoted to brigadier general in August, he soon became inextricably linked with the Civil War's western theater. Sherman's green division of Midwest troops was overrun at Shiloh in April 1862, but he rallied them and became a major general in May. His good service in the Vicksburg and Chattanooga campaigns in 1863 impressed General Ulysses S. Grant, who considered Sherman his most reliable subordinate. When Grant took command of all Union armies in March 1864, Sherman assumed command of the western theater, which included much of the South, and launched a successful campaign to capture Atlanta. In November, he conducted his famous March to the Sea, cutting a path of destruction from Atlanta to Savannah and taking the war to the people of Georgia. In April 1865, he accepted the surrender of General Joseph E. Johnston's army in North Carolina.

Sherman was promoted to lieutenant general in 1866, and in 1868 to full general, succeeding Grant as commanding general of the U.S. Army. He retired in 1884, after laying the foundation for the professional military education system, including what eventually became the Army Command and General Staff College at Fort Leavenworth, Kansas.

Sherman married Ellen Boyle Ewing. Their wedding, held in Washington, D.C., in the home of the bride's father and groom's guardian, was attended by notable political figures including Daniel Webster, Henry Clay, and President Zachary Taylor and his cabinet. Sherman and his wife had eight children. Sherman died in New York City. One of his pallbearers was General John E. Johnston, the officer who commanded Confederate forces that provided resistance to Sherman's troops as they marched through Georgia.

Sources and Further Reading: Basil Henry Liddell-Hart, *Sherman: Soldier, Realist, American* (1958); John F. Marszalek, *Sherman: A Soldier's Passion for Order* (1993); William T. Sherman, *Memoirs of General William T. Sherman by Himself* (1875).

Carol Reardon
Pennsylvania State University

The United States–Dakota War of 1862

The United States–Dakota War of 1862 (referred to by white settlers as the Sioux War) marked the first in a series of conflicts on the northern plains that would not end until the massacre at Wounded Knee in 1890. The war erupted on August 17 when, following mounting tensions, four Dakota men from the Mdewakantunwan Rice Creek Village killed five white settlers over an incident concerning the taking of eggs. By the end of 1862, approximately 450 whites had died. The death toll for the Eastern Dakota remains unknown, but for them, 1862 marked the beginning of a policy of extermination and forced removal from their homelands.

Since the beginning of the nineteenth century, the Dakota Nation had been faced with increasing intrusions into the place they referred to as *Minisota Makoce*, or "Land Where the Waters Reflect the Skies." The construction in 1819 of what would later become Fort Snelling created a portal into the lands of the Dakota, as well as a haven for soldiers, traders, missionaries, and white settlers. After having had most of their lands wrested away in the fraudulently negotiated treaties of 1851 and 1858, the Dakota were confined to two small reservation tracts (each approximately ten miles wide and seventy miles long) bordering the Minnesota River in southwestern Minnesota. The Dakota faced the difficult adaptation to reservation life, rapidly depleting populations of game, constant encroachments on reservation lands, the U.S. government's repeated violations of their treaties, and unrelenting attacks on their traditional way of life. Ceaseless pressure to conform to Western notions of civilization led to growing factionalism among the Dakota, between "farmer Indians" or "cut-hairs" who were acquiescing to white pressures and "blanket Indians" who were resisting assimilation and clinging to Dakota traditions.

The winter of 1861–1862 was one of near starvation, not only for those who were struggling to find game for subsistence but also for those who had faced a crop failure the previous fall. The government's delay in providing the treaty-required monetary subsidies in the summer of 1862 only worsened the sense of despair among the Dakota. Food and supplies had arrived and were sitting in agency warehouses, but Indian agent Thomas Galbraith refused to distribute them before the gold arrived, and traders also refused

The hanging of Dakota warriors after the United States–Dakota conflict, 1862. Painting by J. Thullen. Courtesy the Minnesota Historical Society.

to issue credit to the starving Dakota. When identifying the causes of the war, many Dakota blamed trader Andrew Myrick, for his brutal declaration, "If they are hungry, let them eat grass or their own dung!" By mid-August, the Dakota were in a state of desperation and held the U.S. government and its citizens responsible.

After the August 1862 killings, the four men responsible consulted with the leaders among the Dakota of the lower bands, as well as their warriors. While most agreed that war with the whites was futile and were reluctant to join, Little Crow agreed to lead the fight after jeers of cowardice arose from the younger warriors. Their declaration of war made, on August 18 they attacked the Lower Sioux Agency. Myrick, one of the first casualties, was found later with his mouth stuffed with grass.

With the element of surprise in their favor, the Dakota killed many of the whites they encountered, and took many others, primarily women and children, prisoner. Upon hearing of the attacks, many white settlers fled to the only military post in the southwestern region of Minnesota, Fort Ridgely, while others headed for the safety of nearby towns.

When news of the war reached Governor Alexander Ramsey in St. Paul on August 19, he commissioned Henry H. Sibley, a longtime Indian trader, as a colonel. Sibley was sent to lead an expedition against the Dakota with fourteen hundred men, forming the Sixth Minnesota Regiment.

Unable to capture Fort Ridgely and New Ulm, Minnesota, the key strongholds necessary for victory, and with white reinforcements arriving from the capital, the Dakota moved to a defensive position. Factionalism among the Dakota also continued and, after approximately six weeks of fighting, the Battle of Wood Lake on September 23 and the release of 269 white and mixed-blood captives on September 26 ended the war. Whites in Minnesota used that opportunity to rid themselves of the "Indian problem" and seized Dakota lands. Having declared that "the Sioux Indians of Minnesota must be exterminated or driven forever beyond the borders of the state," Governor Ramsey set into motion plans to implement those goals.

Many Dakota fled Minnesota after the Battle of Wood Lake, but 1,200 who believed they would be treated fairly as prisoners of war surrendered to Sibley and were taken into custody. This number quickly grew to 2,000. On September 28, Sibley appointed a five-man military tribunal to try Dakota men for war crimes. On November 5, with the completion of 392 trials, some lasting as little as five minutes, 307 Dakota men were sentenced to death and sixteen were given prison terms. On December 26, 1862, at the order of President Lincoln, thirty-eight Dakota men were hanged in what remains the largest mass execution in United States history. Those with commuted death sentences were imprisoned in Davenport, Iowa, where they remained for three years. By 1866, 120 had died during their incarceration.

Meanwhile, in November of 1862, 1,700 Dakota were forcibly marched to and imprisoned at Fort Snelling, the Midwest's first prison camp. In May of 1863, the 1,300 who survived were sent to a new reservation beyond Minnesota's borders, in Crow Creek, South Dakota. Bounties were placed on the scalps of Dakota people, while the treaty money that had arrived too late the previous summer was sent back to Washington for redistribution to white settlers. The treaties were abrogated, the Dakota were exiled from their homeland, and their lands were opened to white settlement. It would be twenty-five years before small numbers of Dakota people began trickling back into their homeland, where they now occupy four scant reservations in southern Minnesota.

Sources and Further Reading: Gary Clayton Anderson, *Little Crow: Spokesman for the Sioux* (1986); Gary Clayton Anderson and Alan R. Woolworth, eds., *Through Dakota Eyes* (1988); James H. Baker, *The Lives of the Governors of Minnesota*, vol. 12 (1908); Kenneth Carley, *The Sioux Uprising of 1862*, 2nd ed. (1976); William Watts Folwell, *A History of Minnesota*, vol. 2, rev. ed. (1961); Roy W. Meyer, *History of the Santee Sioux* (1967).

Angela Cavender Wilson
Arizona State University

Military Installations before 1900

The French established the first European military installations at small outposts such as Detroit, Michilimackinac (Mackinaw City, Michigan), and La Baye (Green Bay, Wisconsin), sited at vital junctions in the Great Lakes region, and at garrisons like Forts Sandusky (Sandusky, Ohio), Miamis (Fort Wayne, Indiana), St. Joseph (Niles, Michigan), Ouiatenon (West Lafayette, Indiana), St. Louis (Utica, Illinois), and De Chartres (near present-day Prairie du Rocher, Illinois) that commanded critical locations along the river systems connecting the lakes with the Mississippi Valley. These posts were often established near small villages for *habitants* and Native Americans, and served as centers for mission work and the fur trade.

Following their abandonment by the French after the conclusion of the French and Indian Wars in 1763,

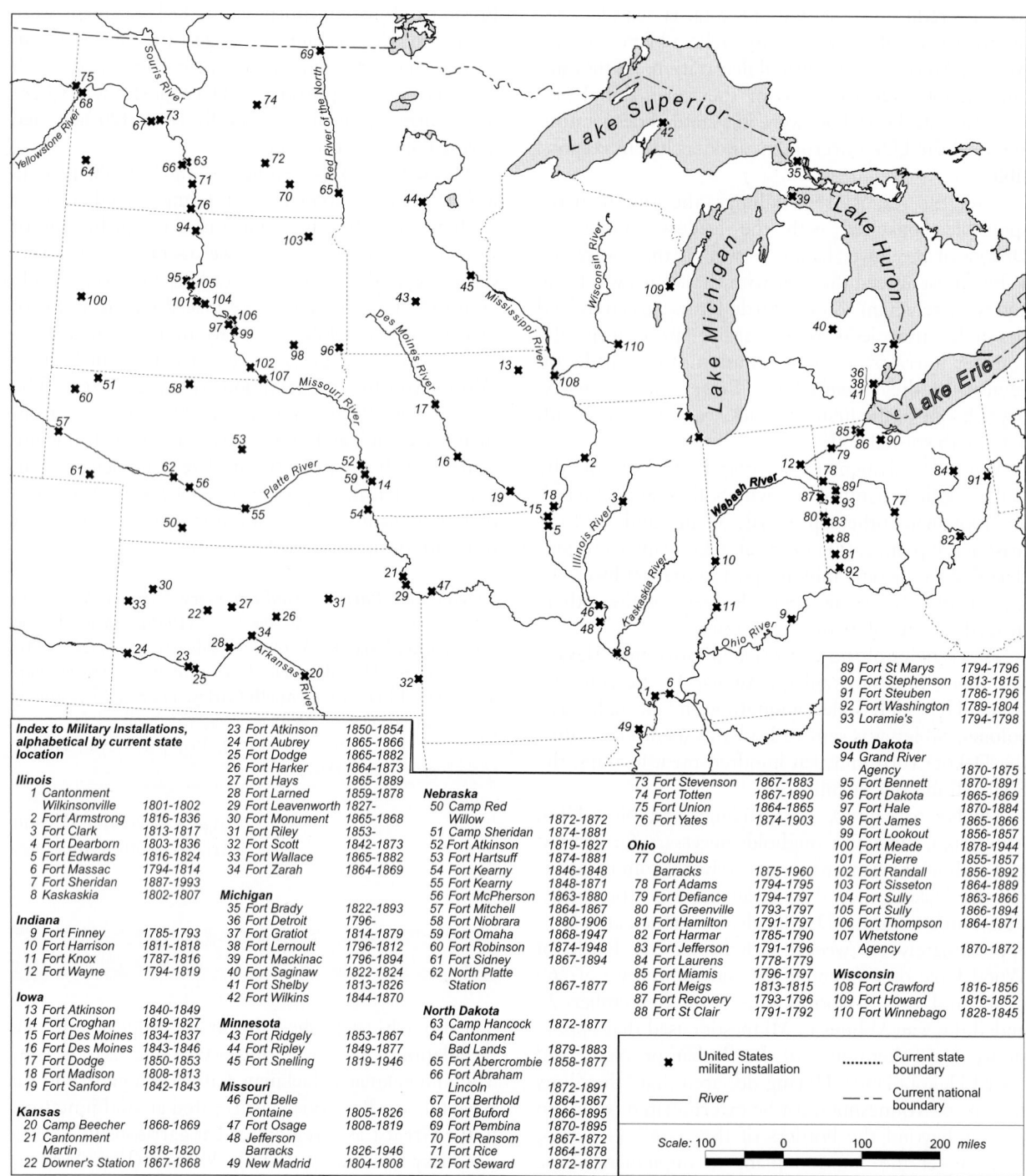

Military installations prior to 1900. Prepared by James DeGrand. *Source:* Francis Prucha, *A Guide to Military Posts of the United States* (Madison: State Historical Society of Wisconsin, 1964), plates 14, 16, 17. Note: This map depicts only American military installations.

British troops occupied many of these posts including those at Detroit, St. Joseph, Michilimackinac, La Baye, Sandusky, and Ouiatenon.

Many American military posts throughout the Midwest during the late eighteenth and early nineteenth centuries were built during active military cam-

paigns waged against the British and their Native allies. Others were established to provide protection and other services to settlers as part of the generally peaceful expansion into recently acquired territories occurring in the wake of the Old Northwest Indian War (1786–1795) and the War of 1812.

The first American military post erected in the Old Northwest was Fort Laurens, constructed in 1778 on the Tuscarawas River near present-day Bolivar, Ohio. The post, along with Fort McIntosh on Beaver Creek north of Pittsburgh, were the first in a series of American garrisons that were intended to stretch across the Ohio country from Pittsburgh to Detroit. Poor logistical support and a season of harassment by British agents and their Native allies caused the post to be abandoned in early 1779.

Following the Revolution, the United States established a series of posts along the Ohio River Valley, including Forts Harmar and Finney (1785) and Fort Knox at Vincennes on the Wabash River (1732). These early posts acted as a fence and were built to prevent squatters from illegally entering federal lands north of the Ohio, to serve as a check against Indian raids into Kentucky, western Pennsylvania, and Virginia, and to act as centers for diplomatic contact with the Indian nations still living in the Ohio country.

Indian hostility flared into open warfare in 1790. American generals Josiah Harmar (1790), Arthur St. Clair (1791), and Anthony Wayne (1792–1794) constructed a line of forts extending from Fort Washington (present-day Cincinnati) up the Miami Valley to the Maumee River in northwest Ohio. These posts, positioned approximately one day's journey apart, included Forts Washington (1790), Hamilton (1791), Jefferson (1791), St. Clair (1792), Recovery (1793), Greenville (1793), Adams (1794), Loramie (1794), St. Marys (1794), Defiance (1794), and Wayne (1794). Unlike the American forts constructed along the Ohio River in the immediate post-Revolutionary era, these posts acted like a dagger pointed at an enemy's heart. They served as a line of attack, reinforcement, supply, and communication during the military's campaigns against the Ohio tribes.

Whereas Indian forces achieved notable victories during the American Revolution and thereafter culminating in victories over the forces of both Generals Harmar (1790) and St. Clair (1791), the Indian confederacy opposing the United States received a major setback at an engagement fought at Fort Recovery in July 1794. The campaigns culminated with the American victory at Fallen Timbers on August 20, 1794, that led to the Treaty of Greenville in 1795, the provisions of which included the ceding of a substantial proportion of Indian land in Ohio on the part of selected representatives of the tribes to the new American government.

Throughout the Indian Wars era, settlers living in the Ohio, Muskinghum, and Miami River Valleys constructed temporary blockhouses and stockaded settlements when Indian violence seemed likely, and then abandoned these posts when the danger had passed.

Among these was the seat of government for the Northwest Territory, Campus Martius, built at Marietta in 1788. Manned by militia companies or groups of frontier irregulars, these station sites provided an important measure of defense along the frontier until the conflict ended in 1795.

Britain also erected a strong fortification, Fort Miamis, at the foot of the Maumee River Rapids (present-day Maumee, Ohio) in the spring of 1794. This post served as a forward base for the defense of Detroit, some forty miles to its north, and was occupied by British forces until 1796, when the conclusion of the Old Northwest Indian Wars and the provisions of Jay's Treaty compelled the British to withdraw into Canada. American troops commanded by Anthony Wayne approached, but did not attack, Fort Miamis in the aftermath of Fallen Timbers.

American military posts were constructed as far west as the Mississippi River Valley after the outbreak of the War of 1812. Major engagements were fought at Fort Meigs (near present-day Toledo, Ohio) in April–May and July 1813, Fort Stephenson (present-day Fremont, Ohio) in July 1813, and Fort Mackinac in August 1813. Likewise, American Army garrisons, including those found at Jefferson Barracks in St. Louis and Fort Snelling (near present-day Minneapolis–St. Paul, Minnesota), were used to quell the region's last major Indian uprising, the Blackhawk War, in 1832.

Beginning with the 1795 Treaty of Greenville, the United States gradually acquired uncontested title to lands lying north of the Ohio and east of the Mississippi River. This process concluded in the 1850s when treaties with the Sioux in 1851 and the Ojibway in 1854 and 1855 resulted in the eviction of the last significant populations of native peoples from the region. Negotiations for these treaties were nearly always conducted either at U.S. military installations or within their immediate vicinity. These forts served as the basis for either tacit or voiced threats that warned of violence if negotiations broke down.

From 1796 to 1822, military posts were also the site of government "factories," or Indian trading posts. Military personnel assisted traders and attempted to use their influence to bring a sense of fairness and legitimacy to a business recognized widely as dominated by unscrupulous agents.

During the first and second quarters of the nineteenth century, military posts served as centers where scientific information about the West was accumulated. This information was then used to facilitate the settlement and economic exploitation of the region. Military personnel used forts as bases from which they scouted, surveyed, and mapped new territories. In the course of these expeditions, soldiers amassed information about area resources and the disposition of Indians who lived within the region. In 1820, Lewis Cass led a force throughout much of the as-yet-unexplored Michigan Territory. Later surveys commanded by Stephen Long in 1823 and Henry Schoolcraft in 1832 added greatly to the nation's store of knowledge of the Old Northwest. The information compiled by these surveys was the most reliable then available. It aided professionals like cartographers and assisted settlers who were interested in evaluating the region's uninhabited areas.

Once explored and surveyed, the Army also used forts as stations from which to construct roads. These byways facilitated military operations and, as new lands were opened to settlement, assisted emigrants as they moved into the area. Following the War of 1812, many settlers moving to the Northwest did so over military roads constructed from Fort Meigs in northwestern Ohio to Detroit, and from Detroit to Fort Dearborn (Chicago). In addition, civilians supervised by military engineers constructed other roads within the region. Federal authorities understood that these roads benefited pioneer communities by easing the difficulties of transportation into the region, made the defense of outlying settlements more practical, and stimulated the region's economy. Lastly, military scientists conducted the first systematic meteorological observations in the nation's history, as well as a host of other scientific studies, adding to the country's store of scientific studies.

Following the Civil War and the end of the Western Indian Wars in the late nineteenth century, military posts were no longer built for use during regional military campaigns (such as Fort Meigs) or for extended periods of frontier defense (such as Fort Wayne, Indiana, and Fort Larned, Kansas). Because construction of rail lines and the rapid increase in settlement on western lands made the speedy deployment and logistical support of the Army possible in times of emergency, the Army quartered its soldiers at large, permanent posts throughout the Midwest, such as Fort Leavenworth, Kansas, and Fort Mackinac, Michigan, until the end of the century.

Sources and Further Reading: Francis Paul Prucha, *Broadax and Bayonet* (1953); Francis Paul Prucha, *A Guide to the Military Posts of the United States, 1789–1895* (1964); Francis Paul Prucha, *The Sword of the Republic* (1968); Richard Scamyhorn and John Steinle, *Stockades in the Wilderness* (1986); David A. Simmons, *The Forts of Anthony Wayne* (1977); Robert M. Utley, *Frontier Regulars: The United States Army and the Indian, 1866–1891* (1973); Robert M. Utley, *Frontiersmen in Blue* (1981); Edgar B. Wesley, *Guarding the Frontier* (1935).

Larry L. Nelson
Firelands College, Huron, Ohio

Fort Detroit and Fort Wayne, Michigan

In July 1701, the French established a settlement on the Detroit River, making Detroit the oldest major city of the Midwest. The fortified village was called Fort Pontchartrain, although the post was known as Detroit. It dominated the water route between Lakes Erie and Huron. The settlement and fort passed to British control in November 1760.

The British had held Detroit for less than three years when it was attacked by Pontiac's coalition of Native American warriors in 1763. The garrison was besieged for five months. Following the conclusion of hostilities, the troops established fortified barracks— the Citadel—in the western end of the town. This remained the center of military activities until 1778, when construction of Fort Lernoult began on a commanding hill north of the village. Detroit was a base for British and Indian raids throughout the American Revolution, and it sheltered a British garrison during the Ohio Indian wars in the 1780s and 90s. The post was turned over to the United States in July 1796.

Fort Lernoult was officially renamed Fort Detroit in 1805. It fell to the British on August 16, 1812, but was reoccupied by U.S. forces in September 1813. Renamed Fort Shelby in 1814, the post was abandoned in 1826.

Detroit was without a garrison until the Canadian Rebellion of 1837–1838. The ensuing border tensions prompted the construction of Fort Wayne at Spring Wells, about three miles below the city, between 1844 and 1847. Fort Wayne was never armed, but it served as the nucleus of a military post until 1971.

Sources and Further Reading: F. Clever Bald, *Detroit's First American Decade, 1796 to 1805* (1948); Brian Leigh Dunnigan, *Frontier Metropolis: Picturing Early Detroit, 1701–1838* (2001); Philip P. Mason, *Detroit, Fort Lernoult, and the American Revolution* (1964); Howard H. Peckham, *Pontiac and the Indian Uprising* (1994).

Brian Leigh Dunnigan
University of Michigan–Ann Arbor

Fort Leavenworth, Kansas

Fort Leavenworth, Kansas, is located near the site of a Kansa Indian village dating to between 1724 and 1744 and of Fort de Cavagnial, a fortified trading post and outpost of imperial France from 1744 to 1764. Meriwether Lewis and William Clark's expedition of exploration in 1804 camped on an island in the river nearly opposite present-day Fort Leavenworth. Colonel Henry Leavenworth, as ordered by the Adjutant General's Office of the U.S. Army, led an expedition up the Missouri River in the spring of 1827 to establish a permanent camp past the mouth of the Little Platte River. He selected a location on the bluffs of the west bank, high above the Missouri River, and established the post on May 8, 1827. In September, the site was officially approved and called Cantonment Leavenworth.

The post's name became Fort Leavenworth in 1832, and the fort provided protection for settlers and merchandise moving west on the Oregon and Santa Fe Trails. Branches of both trails pass near the fort. Traders, wagon trains, settlers, Indian agents, and soldiers all used the fort in the 1830s. By 1838, dredging operations had improved the navigability of the Missouri River, and steamboats traveled between St. Louis and the fort. During the Mexican War in 1846–1848, Fort Leavenworth was the point of departure for three major expeditions led by Stephen Watts Kearney, Alexander W. Doniphan, and Sterling Price.

As the edge of the frontier moved farther west from Fort Leavenworth, the fort still had an important role as a starting point for major military expeditions to the west, as a depot for supplies, and as a headquarters for troops trying to keep the peace between pro- and anti-slavery factions in the 1850s. During the Civil War, Fort Leavenworth served as an arsenal and supply base, as well as an enrollment center and training camp for Kansas Union volunteer units. Following the Civil War, it was the headquarters for the Department of the Missouri from 1870 to 1890, an important supply depot and location of the military prison, which opened in 1875. The famous Tenth Cavalry originated at Fort Leavenworth in 1867.

Fort Leavenworth is well known as the location of the U.S. Army Command and General Staff College, which is a center of education and training for U.S. Army officers. The beginnings of officer education at Fort Leavenworth date to 1881 when the Commanding General of the Army, William T. Sherman, created the School of Application for Infantry and Cavalry. Renamed the U.S. Infantry and Cavalry School in 1886, the school taught basic subjects until 1888 when practical, problem-solving work began. In the following years, Leavenworth developed into a learning center for junior officers. In 1904, Grant Hall, with its distinctive bell tower, was constructed to house the school. The Army Service Schools emerged between 1902 and 1910, including the School of the Line and the Army Staff College.

The schools at Fort Leavenworth closed during World War I, reopening in 1919 as the U.S. Army Command and General Staff School (later College). Major Dwight D. Eisenhower attended the 1926 class and graduated first in his class of 245 students. Professional study at Fort Leavenworth was vital preparation

for most U.S. Army leaders in World War II: thirty-three of the thirty-four combat corps commanders were Leavenworth graduates. Special General Staff Courses established during World War II at Fort Leavenworth graduated more than nineteen thousand officers.

Fort Leavenworth is headquarters of the Combined Arms Center and is a center for Army officer education, leader development, training, and doctrine writing. It also features the Buffalo Soldiers Museum that portrays the role of black soldiers in the settlement of the West, along with a beautiful Buffalo Soldier monument to memorialize the service of the Ninth and Tenth U.S. Cavalry and their African American troopers.

The U.S. Army Command and General Staff College includes the principal field grade officer course, a course for captains, the School of Advanced Military Studies (SAMS) for military planners, and the School of Command Preparation for senior commanders. In 2002, Fort Leavenworth replaced the old prison with a state-of-the-art, maximum-security facility.

Sources and Further Reading: Elvid Hunt, *History of Fort Leavenworth, 1827–1927* (1979); Timothy K. Nenninger, *The Leavenworth Schools and the Old Army* (1978); John W. Partin, ed., *A Brief History of Fort Leavenworth 1827–1983* (1983).

Robert H. Berlin
U.S. Army Command and General Staff College
Fort Leavenworth, Kansas

Fort Michilimackinac and Fort Mackinac, Michigan

The passage between Lakes Huron and Erie was a primary transportation link of the early Midwest. Critical to the fur trade, the Straits of Mackinac attracted traders and soldiers for more than two centuries. The first French military post, called Michilimackinac, was established on Michigan's Upper Peninsula mainland (St. Ignace) in 1680, but abandoned in 1697.

The French returned in 1715, during a prolonged war against the Fox Indians of Wisconsin, and established a new post on the Lower Peninsula shore (Mackinaw City). Also called Michilimackinac, it developed into a fortified village with a small garrison. Michilimackinac was ceded to Britain in 1760, and occupied by British troops in 1761. It was the largest post captured by the Indians during Pontiac's War of 1763. Reoccupied in 1764, Michilimackinac remained a British base through the first five years of the American Revolution.

The post was relocated to nearby Mackinac Island for greater security in 1779–1780, and the fort was separated from the town. The name "Fort Mackinac" gradually replaced "Michilimackinac" in common usage after 1800. Britain ceded the post to the United States in 1796, but retook it on July 17, 1812. It was returned to permanent U.S. control in 1815.

Although its military usefulness waned following the War of 1812, Fort Mackinac remained an active U.S. post until 1895. The fort became the centerpiece of a national park in 1875. It was transferred to the State of Michigan twenty years later when the last soldiers were withdrawn.

Sources and Further Reading: David A. Armour, *Colonial Michilimackinac* (2000); David A. Armour and Keith R. Widder, *At the Crossroads: Michilimackinac During the American Revolution* (1986); Phil Porter, *Mackinac: An Island Famous in These Regions* (1998); Keith R. Widder, *Reveille Till Taps* (1972).

Brian Leigh Dunnigan
University of Michigan–Ann Arbor

Fort St. Joseph, Michigan

Fort St. Joseph, originally known as the St. Joseph River Post, was built in 1691 during the Iroquois wars by order of New France's Governor General Louis de Buade de Frontenac to help protect the western fur trade from Iroquois and English incursions. The fort was strategically situated approximately twenty miles south of Lake Michigan (at present-day Niles, Michigan) on the east bank of the St. Joseph River, a few miles downstream from the important portage to the Kankakee, Illinois, and Mississippi Rivers. The fort's wooden palisade enclosed the commandant's house, soldiers' barracks, warehouse, trading post, and a blacksmith's shop. It was erected near the Jesuit mission, built around 1684, and the French-allied Miami Indian village.

In 1695, the fort was attacked by three hundred Iroquois who were repulsed with heavy losses. By 1723, the Miamis had largely been replaced there by Potawatomis, who provided several hundred warriors in support of the eighteen-man French garrison. The fort was a staging area and supply base for campaigns being waged as far away as Illinois (1730), Wisconsin (1731), Mississippi (1739–1740), and New York (1746–1747). In addition to missionary efforts among the Indians, the settlement's Jesuits played an active, if somewhat sporadic, role in French and métis life at the post until 1761.

The fort was ceded to and garrisoned by the British in 1761, but fell to the Potawatomis during Pontiac's War in 1763. In 1781, a raiding party from St. Louis under the Spanish flag briefly captured and looted the ungarrisoned fort after which it fell into disuse. In 1998, an archaeological survey team located artifacts and architectural remains associated with the colonial occupation of Fort St. Joseph.

Sources and Further Reading: Dunning Idle, "The Post of the St. Joseph River during the French Régime 1679–1761," Ph.D. diss., University of Illinois (1946); Robert C. Myers and Joseph L. Peyser, "Four Flags over Fort St. Joseph," *Michigan History Magazine* 75 (Sept.–Oct. 1991); Michael S. Nassaney, ed., *An Archaeological Reconnaissance Survey to Locate the Remains of Fort St. Joseph*, Niles, Michigan, Archaeological Report No. 22 (1999); Joseph L. Peyser, *Letters from New France* (1992).

Joseph L. Peyser
Indiana University–South Bend

Fort Snelling, Minnesota

Fort Snelling has mirrored the changes of the Twin Cities metropolitan area that surrounds it. Conceived as the anchor military post of a vast northwest wilderness, the massive 1820s stone fortress was constructed by Army labor on a high bluff above the Mississippi and Minnesota Rivers. The fort kept peace among the American Indian tribes of the region, but it also promoted and protected the lucrative fur trade. Treaties signed in 1837 and 1851 opened the area to a land rush, and in 1858, Minnesota became a state.

Although a destination for settlers and a jumping-off point for exploration, Fort Snelling was deemed unnecessary for defense. The Civil War, however, renewed it as a training ground for Minnesota's 24,000 Union volunteers. The Regular Army returned after the war and continually expanded the fort. Known as the Country Club of the Army during the twentieth century, Fort Snelling was like a beautiful tree-shaded campus, with the best sports facilities of any Army post. Fort Snelling soldiers were recruited in the Midwest and enjoyed a supportive local community. After performing its final function as a center for training World War II soldiers to speak Japanese, the fort was closed.

Minnesota's centennial celebration focused public interest on preserving the oldest portions of Fort Snelling. Some eighteen buildings were meticulously restored or reconstructed by the Minnesota Historical Society. Historic Fort Snelling today features dynamic living history programs, tours, and exhibits. Fort Snelling State Park surrounds the fort, and a popular

Fort Snelling, Minnesota, 1848.
Minnesota Historical Society Art
Collection, AV1991.85.35.

youth sports complex now occupies portions of the twentieth-century military post.

Sources and Further Reading: Stephen Hall, *Fort Snelling: Colossus of the Wilderness* (1987); Marcus L. Hansen, *Old Fort Snelling, 1819–1858* (1918; reprint, 1958); Evan Jones, *Citadel in the Wilderness* (2001).

Stephen E. Osman
Minnesota Historical Society, St. Paul

Jefferson Barracks, Missouri

Established just south of St. Louis in 1826 and named for Thomas Jefferson, Jefferson Barracks played an important role in U.S. Army operations for the remainder of the nineteenth century. The post answered the Army's need for a convenient river supply base and a training area west of the Mississippi River. In the antebellum period, it was also the site of the formation of three famous regiments: the First Dragoons (1833), the Regiment of Mounted Riflemen (1846), and the Second Cavalry (1855).

During the Civil War, the Barracks was used for training Union troops, but in early 1862, a hospital was established and an elaborate medical complex was constructed and used by Union forces for the remainder of the war. Following the Civil War, Jefferson Barracks was maintained as an engineer and ordnance depot, but in 1878, the area was designated a cavalry recruiting depot. In 1891, the Army began building new structures, and three years later, the site was gar-risoned as a regular military post. During the Spanish–American War and both world wars, the barracks continued in its role as an induction and training center. During World War II, it was used as an Army Air Force technical training center and as a prisoner-of-war compound. The Army finally left the post in 1946.

A number of famous figures served at Jefferson Barracks, including Ulysses S. Grant and Robert E. Lee. Part of the pre–Civil War post has been preserved as a county park, and the Jefferson Barracks National Cemetery is open to visitors.

Sources and Further Reading: Robert G. Ferris, ed., *Soldier and Brave: Historic Places Associated with Indian Affairs and the Indian Wars in the Trans-Mississippi West*, vol. 12 (new ed., 1971); J. Thomas Scharf, *History of St. Louis City and County*, 2 vols. (1883).

Jeffrey L. Patrick
National Park Service, Republic, Missouri

World War I, 1914–1918

The war that engulfed most of the nations of Europe, as well as others around the world, from 1914 to 1918, was called "the World War" or simply "the Great War." The U.S. Army and Navy mobilized about 4 million soldiers and 800,000 sailors, mostly men. Half of the army was sent to France, beginning in the summer of 1917. The eight eastern Midwest states—Ohio, Indiana, Illinois, Michigan, Wisconsin,

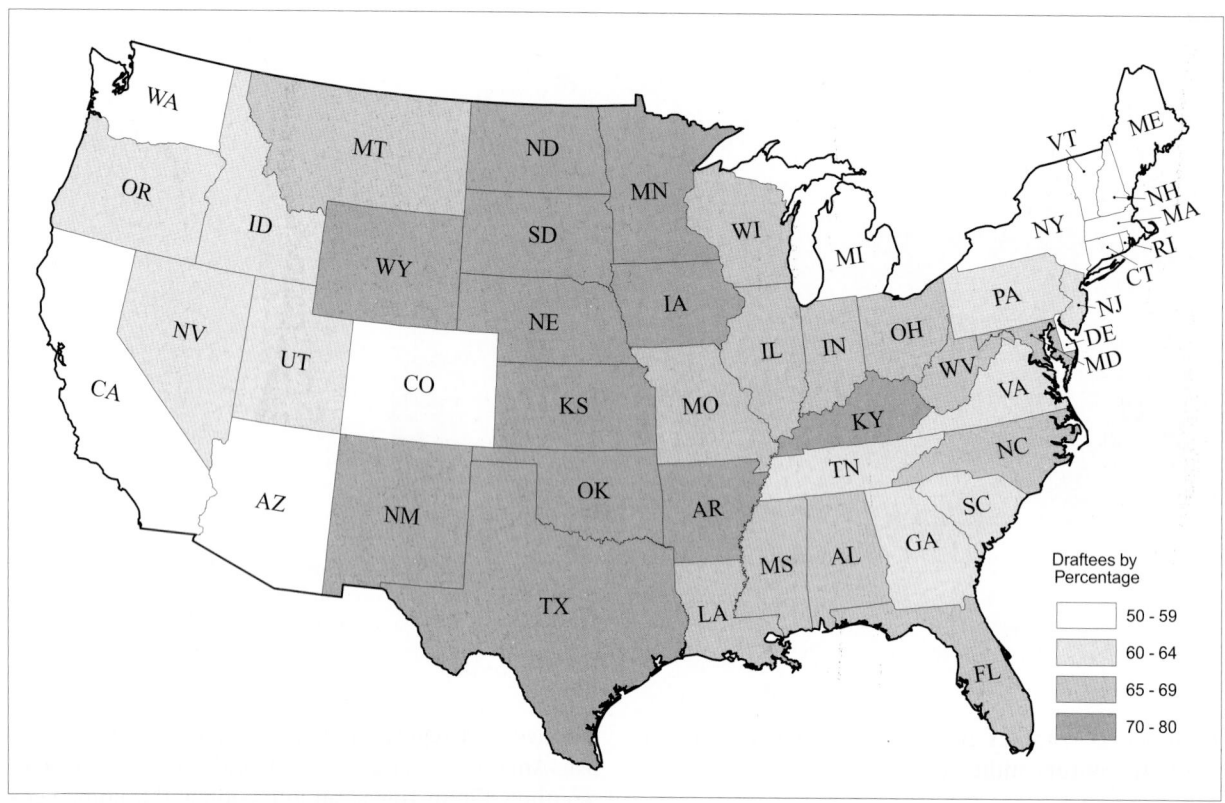

Percentage of drafted men passing World War I physical examination, by state. Prepared by James DeGrand. *Source:* Leonard Ayres, *The War with Germany: A Statistical Summary* (Washington, DC: GPO, 1919), p. 21, map 1.

Minnesota, Iowa, and Missouri—provided 34.4 percent of the total fighting force. The four western Midwest states—North and South Dakota, Nebraska, and Kansas—contributed another 4.2 percent, for a total Midwest manpower contribution of nearly 40 percent.

Midwesterners were qualified for service 65 to 80 percent of the time, the best group record in the nation. All twelve states showed growth in total population and total male population in the same decade. Individual volunteer enlistments for the Army, Navy, and Marine Corps in 1917 and 1918 were affected by the action of the Selective Service System lottery in each of the midwestern states. With the possibility of the draft lottery snaring them, some men chose to volunteer to gain some choice in the matter of service, and even unit assignment.

In World War I, there were three categories of Army divisions, which were ground combat organizations of about 28,000 men each: The Regular divisions (numbered One through Twenty) were made up of Regular Army units plus some volunteers and inductees; the National Guard divisions (numbered Twenty-Six through Forty-Two) were formed from the various state militia organizations; and the National Army divisions (numbered Seventy-Six through

Ninety-Three) consisted almost entirely of men inducted via the draft. About 60 percent of all inductees were drafted.

The National Guard divisions recruited from midwestern states included: the Thirty-Second (Michigan, Wisconsin), the Thirty-Third (Illinois), the Thirty-Fourth (Nebraska, Iowa, South and North Dakota, Minnesota), the Thirty-Fifth (Missouri, Kansas), the Thirty-Seventh (Ohio), and the Thirty-Eighth (Indiana, Kentucky, West Virginia). The Forty-First and Forty-Second (Rainbow) divisions that trained at Fremont, California, and Mills, New York, respectively, drew their soldiers from a number of different states.

The National Army divisions recruited from midwestern states included: the Eighty-Third (Ohio, western Pennsylvania), the Eighty-Fourth (Kentucky, Indiana, southern Illinois), the Eighty-Fifth (Michigan, eastern Wisconsin), the Eighty-Sixth (Chicago, northern Illinois), the Eighty-Eighth (North Dakota, Minnesota, Iowa, western Illinois), and the Eighty-Ninth (Kansas, Missouri, South Dakota, Nebraska). The Ninety-Second and Ninety-Third divisions were "Colored" units made up of African American soldiers and mostly Caucasian officers. Only the Ninety-Second served as a division with the American Expeditionary Forces (AEF). The four infantry regiments assigned to the Ninety-Third division (369th, 370th, 371st, and 372nd) served as separate units attached to the French Army. The Eighth Illinois Infantry, which received federal designation as the 370th Infantry, had lost its black colonel, but retained most of its black officers. These four regiments gained many citations and accolades and were generally well treated and respected by their French comrades-in-arms, but the units of the Ninety-Second were subjected to discrimination mostly on the strength of the unsatisfactory combat performance of the 368th Infantry Regiment in the Argonne Forest fighting in October 1918.

Midwesterners made good, sturdy soldiers. As a rule, they were as amenable to discipline and the tasks of soldiering as were soldiers from other sections of the country. The gregarious midwestern Doughboy (the nickname of the American infantry soldier) made friends easily, which facilitated the formation of cohesive fighting units. All American ground combat divisions were infantry organizations. Aerial combat units were formed late in the war and were organized into squadrons of eighteen to twenty-five aircraft each. Captain Edward Vernon Rickenbacker of Columbus, Ohio, was one of the thousands of pilots who served in France; he was an "ace" with more than five aerial combat victories and a recipient of the Medal of Honor. Both ground and air units were controlled by the AEF staff. The role of the infantry in ground combat was to seize and hold ground by close fighting with rifles, bayonets, grenades, and the supporting fire of mortars, artillery, flame throwers, tanks, machine guns, and occasionally aircraft.

Many support organizations tended to the details of supply, transportation, commissary and medical activities. Midwesterners served in ambulance units (some of which were auxiliary rather than assigned to front-line military units), hospitals, and many kinds of troop morale organizations, such as the Red Cross and Young Men's Christian Association. The World War I army of the United States required many draft animals, and midwestern men were ideal candidates for blacksmiths, farriers, and all the associated animal husbandry skills.

Ben H. Bernheisel, Max Ottenfeld, Daniel J. Birmingham, and Robert R. McCormick were Great War Doughboys with a midwestern identity who served in the First Division, a Regular Army unit. Bernheisel and his cousin Bob attempted to enlist in the Navy at Cincinnati shortly after the United States declared war on the Central Powers in April 1917. Faced with a four-year enlistment, the pair marched over to the Army recruiting station and signed up "for the duration" in the infantry. After the usual rounds of being fitted for uniforms and indoctrinated in the barest es-

sentials of drill and discipline, Ben and his fellow recruits entrained for El Paso, Texas, where he and cousin Bob both were assigned to F Company, Sixteenth Infantry Regiment. Later, in France, it was F Company, Sixteenth Infantry, First Division that suffered the first of the AEF combat casualties during a German raid on the regiment's trench warfare training positions near Bathelémont. In the fall of 1917, in northeastern France near Toul, the First Division was gaining the necessary battle experience to go into the line. Ben Bernheisel remembered that "the duties of a soldier were carried on. Our rifles were kept clean and we tried to brush ourselves up a bit . . . now that we looked ourselves over, what a sight we were. Mud clung to our overcoats in big lumps. Our appearance was that of men dug out of graves without the protection of caskets." En route home on the *Pocahontas*, a German ship seized during the war, Ben celebrated his twenty-third birthday on October 19, 1919. The rations aboard ship were miserable—corn meal, soggy bread, and meat that was often rotten. After a stormy crossing, Bernheisel was mustered out at Camp Dix (now a fort), New Jersey, on November 5 in his olive drab uniform and overcoat with an extra $60 and a railroad ticket in his pocket.

Max Ottenfeld, the son of a baker, enlisted in the Army in Chicago in November 1917, right after his eighteenth birthday. Max, who weighed about 120 pounds soaking wet, was an inspirational, gritty man who was very proud of his country and of his service in the Great War. Private Ottenfeld (he never was promoted to private first class, something he was quite proud of) was a signal wireman in the Eighteenth Infantry Regiment. A recipient of the Silver Star for valor in battle, Max was responsible for keeping the wire communications between his headquarters company and the rest of the regiment intact. He had to trace the wire by hand to find any breaks, then repair them, often under fire. He spoke often about the gamesmanship with the German gunners who tried to pick him off as he dashed across a clearing or crossed a road. On one occasion, he thought he had been wounded because he felt a warm stream of fluid running down his back. As it turned out, it was the juice from a punctured can of beans in his knapsack! Max wrote to his parents at home in Madison, Wisconsin, on October 15, 1918, from a hospital bed where he was recovering from gas received on October 9 in the Meuse-Argonne fighting. After the war, the twenty-year-old veteran returned to study law at the University of Wisconsin.

Daniel Birmingham was born in Ireland and immigrated to the United States in 1904. He found work first in New York, then in Cleveland, Ohio. After April 1917, Birmingham, a thirty-one-year-old member of the New York National Guard's "Fighting Sixty-Ninth" Infantry Regiment, volunteered for active service. He trained at Plattsburg, New York, was commissioned a lieutenant and, in January 1918, shipped out for England, ultimately destined for France. His cousin Bill Cleary, also an Irish immigrant, had signed up for service on the Mexican border in 1916 and was in France as a corporal in I Company, Sixteenth Infantry Regiment when Dan arrived from England. Dan was assigned to M Company, Twenty-Eighth Infantry Regiment, thereby joining his cousin Bill in the First Division. During the battle at the small rural farming village of Cantigny in May 1918, Lieutenant Birmingham behaved gallantly under fire and was cited with what later was the Silver Star and the French Croix de Guerre. Later in July, during the Second Marne campaign, he was decorated with the Distinguished Service Cross, America's second-highest decoration for valor. Just before the action, Dan wrote to his brother Bill, "How some of the machine gun bullets missed me and the shells from the Boche artillery didn't crack me in two, is a mystery. Men shot down and blown to pieces right at your side does nothing more than make you repeat a prayer and crack a joke about Fritz to your men."

Robert R. McCormick was a citizen-soldier from Wheaton, Illinois. Forever after his World War service, McCormick was known as "the Colonel." He was fiercely proud of his service, but later in life became skeptical about American participation in the Second World War. An isolationist in the 1930s and a tenacious opponent of the New Deal policies of Franklin Roosevelt's administration, McCormick in his own way remained faithful to the hard-won independence of mind that he attributed to his World War experiences. McCormick was assigned to the Illinois National Guard's First Cavalry Regiment during the Punitive Expedition led by Brigadier General John J. Pershing. When Pershing was named to lead the AEF, McCormick petitioned him for a place on his staff. Major McCormick, the citizen-soldier, was also the future publisher and editor of the Chicago *Tribune*. During the World War, the Chicago *Tribune Army Edition* had its offices in Paris near the Place de la Concorde and employed a group of able war correspondents, including Floyd Gibbons and Peggy Hull, one of the Great War's first female war correspondents.

These four soldiers, and many others like them, served bravely and with distinction throughout the Great War. Hundreds of thousands of men served in the National Army or National Guard divisions, and both men and women served in the Navy. One of the National Army divisions, the Eighty-Eighth, was or-ganized on September 4, 1917, at Camp Dodge, Iowa. Officers from the reserve training camps at Forts Snelling, Sheridan, and Benjamin Harrison provided the leadership. After arriving in France in July 1918, the division was assigned to the U.S. First Army. Although not serving directly in combat, the division suffered nearly eight thousand cases of influenza or pneumonia, with 444 deaths. After a short tour in the trenches, the division was withdrawn on November 1 and assigned to the U.S. Second Army.

The Illinois National Guard division is representative of those from the Midwest. The Thirty-Third published a full set of histories after the war. In addition to three volumes detailing the military operations in France by Lieutenant Colonel Frederic Louis Huidekoper, several volumes explained the wartime organization of the state and collected the various documents and speeches relating to war service by the Illinois guardsmen. Huidekoper, a well-known and respected military historian, crafted a competent and readable account of the men of Major General George Bell, Jr.'s, "Prairie" division. The Illinois division had the distinction of fighting with the British, the French, and the Americans in France, the only division in our history to do so. The soldiers of the Thirty-Third proudly recalled that they fulfilled every combat order issued and took every objective assigned.

Although the United States entered the fighting in France later than the other belligerent powers, the AEF still suffered 50,280 battle deaths and 205,690 men wounded. The Midwest National Guard and National Army divisions that served in active sectors sustained 9,584 battle deaths (19 percent) and 52,859 soldiers wounded (26 percent) of AEF total casualties. Approximately 33 percent of the total casualties (killed, wounded, died of wounds, captured, missing) of the AEF were midwesterners.

As the veterans returned home after the war, issues of health care, jobs, and homes were at the forefront of the political agendas in Washington and in the midwestern state capitals. Midwestern values paid substantial rewards for the nation during the ordeal of World War I. As soldiers those men served ably and valiantly; as veterans they continued to serve their communities with the same dedication. The United States was fortunate to be able to call on them.

Sources and Further Reading: Leonard P. Ayres, *The War with Germany: A Statistical Summary* (1919); Arthur E. Barbeau and Florette Henri, *The Unknown Soldiers* (1996); Edward M. Coffman, *The War to End All Wars: The American Military Experience in World War I* (1968); Frederic Louis Huidekoper, *The History of the 33rd Division, A.E.F.*, 3 vols.

(1921); Papers of Ben H. Bernheisel, Daniel J. Birmingham, Robert R. McCormick, and Max Otterfield, McCormick Research Center, Wheaton, Illinois; Richard Norton Smith, *The Colonel: The Life and Legend of Robert R. McCormick 1880–1955* (1997); Society of the First [Infantry] Division, *History of the First Division during the World War 1917–1919* (1922).

John F. Votaw
First Division Museum, Wheaton, Illinois

Newton D. Baker (1871–1937)

Newton D. Baker made his reputation in Cleveland, Ohio, as Mayor Tom Johnson's city solicitor, and later as mayor in his own right. In March 1916, he became Secretary of War in the cabinet of President Woodrow Wilson, whom he had met while an undergraduate student at Johns Hopkins University and from which he graduated in 1892. He received his law degree from Washington and Lee University in 1894. He married Elizabeth Leopold in 1902 with whom he had three children.

A compassionate man, Baker balanced concern for justice with commitment to order. A man of peace, he became an accomplished war maker. A social reformer, he did not do as much to combat wartime racial and political prejudice in the Army as his prewar associates believed possible. A man with no experience in foreign affairs, he protected the independence of the American Expeditionary Forces against the French and British, and secured President Wilson a strong hand at the peace table.

Baker was of the school that believed most problems went away if you left them alone. During the mobilization crisis of 1917–1918, he refused to act hastily, and it was April 1918 before authority was concentrated in the General Staff. Baker also refused to resolve command issues between the War Department and the AEF. In the difficulties between General John J. Pershing and Chief of Staff Peyton C. March, he did not decide in March's favor until the war was nearly over.

Baker retired from public office in March 1921. Success gave him freedom to pursue philanthropic, educational, and political activities. Adlai Stevenson called his plea for the League of Nations at the Democratic convention of 1924 the greatest speech he had ever heard. During the 1930s, Baker served on various Army commissions including the Baker Board on the reorganization of the Army Air Corps.

Sources and Further Reading: Daniel R. Beaver, *Newton D. Baker and the American War Effort 1917–1919* (1966);

Clarence H. Cramer, *Newton D. Baker: A Biography* (1961); Frederick Palmer, *Newton D. Baker: America at War*, 2 vols. (1931).

Daniel R. Beaver
University of Cincinnati, Ohio

James G. Harbord (1866–1947)

The son of farm parents, James Harbord was born near Bloomington, Illinois. He grew up in Missouri and Kansas and earned a bachelor's degree and a master's degree at Kansas State Agricultural College. In 1889, Harbord enlisted as a private in the U.S. Army, and two years later he was commissioned a second lieutenant. He served in Cuba during the Spanish–American War, and from 1903 to 1914, he was assistant chief of the Philippine Constabulary. In this period, Harbord developed a close friendship with Brigadier General John J. Pershing, which commenced during the Spanish–American War and was cemented during their overlapping tours in the Philippines.

After the United States entered World War I, Pershing, commander of the American Expeditionary Forces (AEF), appointed Harbord his chief of staff, and from 1917 to 1918, Harbord played a major role in the formation of the AEF. In June 1918, he commanded the Fourth Brigade in the battle for Belleau Wood, and in July led the Second Division in the Allied counterattack at Soissons. At the end of July, Pershing named Harbord head of the Services of Supply (SOS), then struggling to keep the expanding AEF fully supplied. Traveling extensively throughout his vast command, Harbord reinvigorated the SOS so that, by the end of the war, it had dramatically improved the efficiency of the Army's logistical system.

Harbord retired from the Army in 1922 following a tour as War Department deputy chief of staff. Afterward he served as president and later chairman of the board of the Radio Corporation of America. An able administrator and a forceful commander, Harbord stands out as Pershing's closest and most trusted subordinate and for his contributions to the success of the AEF.

Sources and Further Reading: James G. Harbord, *The American Army in France, 1917–1919* (1936); James G. Harbord, *Leaves from a War Diary* (1925); Frank E. Vandiver, *Black Jack: The Life and Times of John J. Pershing*, 2 vols. (1977).

John Kennedy Ohl
Mesa Community College, Arizona

William "Billy" Mitchell (1879–1936)

William Mitchell was born in France and spent his boyhood in Milwaukee, Wisconsin. The son of a U.S. senator, Mitchell enjoyed a privileged youth; a boyhood friend of his, Douglas MacArthur, later gained fame as a general during World War II. In 1898, Mitchell enlisted in the Army during the Spanish–American War and rose rapidly into the officer corps. A brilliant, suave, and aggressive man, Mitchell became the youngest member of the Army General Staff in 1912. Using family money, he learned to fly in 1916 and served in the American Expeditionary Force during World War I, becoming assistant chief of the U.S. Air Service in 1919.

In fighting along the Western Front during the summer of 1918, Mitchell commanded the largest air armada assembled to date. After the war, he returned to the United States determined to remake the American military in the age of aviation. Conservative Army officers opposed his plans, however, and Mitchell's ambitions led him into a deepening struggle between air and ground officers. He took his case for airpower to the public in a series of speeches and articles. In 1921, pilots under his command sank the old German battleship *Ostfriesland*, although careful analysis of the demonstration rendered the feat inconclusive. In 1925, Mitchell was court-martialed for insubordination after publicly charging the nation's military leadership with negligence following a crash of a Navy dirigible. He resigned his commission and devoted time to championing aviation. Twice married, with five children, he died in New York City in 1936. The Japanese attack on Pearl Harbor in 1941 seemed to vindicate some of his ideas, and Congress awarded him a posthumous Medal of Honor in 1948.

Sources and Further Reading: Alfred Hurley, *Billy Mitchell: Crusader for Air Power* (1964); Anthony Summer "Billy Mitchell: Aviation's Prophet," *American History Illustrated 9* (Dec. 1974).

Thomas Hughes
Maxwell Air Force Base, Montgomery, Alabama

John J. Pershing (1860–1948)

In May 1917, John J. Pershing sailed for France to command the American Expeditionary Force (AEF). Steel-willed and ambitious, he was destined to become the only General of the Armies of the United States since George Washington.

Pershing grew up near Laclede, Missouri, and taught high school for several years. In 1882, an opportunity arose to take the qualifying examination for West Point, from which he graduated in 1886. Pershing saw service with the Sixth and Tenth Cavalries during the last days of the Indian Fighting Army (1886–1890). In 1891, in a move which proved among the best he ever made, he accepted the post of commander of the officer training battalion at the University of Nebraska at Lincoln. There he earned a law degree and met a young attorney, Charles G. Dawes, who would play an important role in his later career as a brigadier general in charge of organizing logistics for the American Expeditionary Force in World War I. He then taught at West Point and served as Commanding General Nelson Miles's aide in Washington.

Pershing's career was catalyzed by the war with Spain (1898) and in 1906, after service in Cuba and the Philippines, he was promoted to brigadier general. The same year he married Frances Warren, the daughter of Senator Francis Warren of Wyoming. They had four children. During the next ten years, Pershing held important posts in Washington and in the Philippines. In 1916, he commanded the punitive expedition into northern Mexico. He impressed Secretary of War

General John J. Pershing. Courtesy National Archives, photo no. 111-SC-22902.

Newton D. Baker and President Woodrow Wilson, and in May 1917, they chose him to command the AEF. During the next eighteen months, Pershing built an independent American army and committed it to battle, gaining President Wilson a strong negotiating position at the Versailles Conference. Pershing later served as Army Chief of Staff and undertook several important diplomatic missions for the United States. He died at Walter Reed Hospital in 1948.

Sources and Further Reading: John J. Pershing, *My Experiences in the World War,* 2 vols. (1931); Donald Smythe, *Guerrilla Warrior: The Early Life of John J. Pershing* (1973); Donald Smythe, *Pershing: General of the Armies* (1986).

Daniel R. Beaver
University of Cincinnati, Ohio

Wilbur Wright (1867–1912) and Orville Wright (1871–1948)

Wilbur Wright and Orville Wright were born near Millville, Indiana, and Dayton, Ohio, respectively. Sons of a bishop of the Church of the United Brethren, both attended Dayton public schools, but only Wilbur graduated from high school; neither held college degrees. Their early collaboration in a modest Dayton printing business and bicycle shop established a close working partnership that carried them into and through their experiments with airplanes around the turn of the century.

Relying on systematic reading, natural engineering intuition, and craft skills honed in the bike shop, the Wright brothers made great strides in developing a working aircraft in the 1890s. They traveled to Kitty Hawk, North Carolina, in the summer of 1900 to test a glider and returned there each year to experiment with progressively more complicated machines. They made history on December 17, 1903, when Orville Wright piloted the first successful flight in a heavier-than-air machine, covering 120 feet in twelve seconds. The brothers concentrated on improving their invention in 1904 and 1905 with different models flown from a field near Dayton, and Wilbur made their first public flights in France in 1908. Fame and some fortune quickly followed, but the brothers were dogged by patent infringements on their invention. After Wilbur died of typhoid fever in 1912, Orville, the quieter and shier of the two, avoided public appearances and spent his time in a private workshop in Dayton. He was elected to the National Academy of Sciences in 1936. By the time Orville died, the Wright brothers were the acknowledged inventors of the airplane. Neither married.

Sources and Further Reading: Tom Crouch, *The Bishop's Boys* (1990); Peter Jakab, *Visions of A Flying Machine* (1990).

Thomas Hughes
Maxwell Air Force Base, Montgomery, Alabama

The National Guard and Reserves

Midwestern National Guard and reserve forces have played a vital role in regional security and national defense. The militia system first came to the Midwest with the westward migration that followed the American Revolution. Militiamen in the Northwest Territory provided local defense, enforced laws, conducted reprisal raids against Native Americans, and operated alongside regulars against the British and their Native American allies. As midwestern states joined the Union, military legislation stipulated the specifics of each state's militia system.

Following the War of 1812, the mandatory militia system entered a period of neglect and decline. The second victory over Great Britain and the receding threat to settlers from Native American populations prompted most citizens to question the value of mandatory militia service. An expanded network of volunteer militia companies soon emerged that infused midwestern citizen-soldiers with a new sense of purpose. As much social as military organizations, militia outfits conducted regular training musters and hosted frequent entertainment and philanthropic events. One of the most prominent units in the nation was the Detroit Light Guards.

Militia units of the 1850s also reflected the movement of immigrants to the Midwest. Milwaukee, for example, hosted two Irish companies, five German units, and one native-born American outfit, the Milwaukee Light Guards. On the eve of the Civil War, Colonel Elmer Ellsworth of Chicago was the nation's most celebrated militiaman because he had introduced to America the flamboyant uniforms and intricate drill maneuvers of the French Zouaves. Colonel Ellsworth formed the U.S. Zouave Cadets of Chicago and led them on a national tour that inspired the creation of Zouave militia companies in both the North and South. At the beginning of the Civil War, Ellsworth gained national recognition as the first northern regimental commander killed in the conflict.

Midwestern militiamen performed several important functions during the Civil War. Militia companies formed the basis for large numbers of volunteer regiments, units raised by the states for federal service. For example, four militia companies from Minnesota helped to form the First Minnesota Volunteer In-

❖ **National Guard and Flood Relief**

As a military institution with both federal and state responsibilities, the National Guard responds to the needs of the nation at large and to the citizens of the individual states. A key function of the National Guard in its state role is to preserve life and protect property, especially during natural disasters.

A notable example of the National Guard's ability to provide aid and comfort to state residents occurred during the historic Midwestern Flood of 1993. Unusual weather conditions that summer produced some of the most severe flooding ever experienced along the upper Mississippi River. A huge, inland lake formed that inundated farmlands and swept away or threatened hundreds of communities.

National Guard men and women performed several important duties throughout the crisis. They labored alongside local residents to build and maintain sandbag levees against the rising tide of water. In areas the flood had already inundated, state soldiers rescued and evacuated residents and livestock. The flooding contaminated normal sources of fresh drinking water, and the National Guard deployed to the upper Midwest special water purification units that generated potable water. Guard units established temporary medical treatment facilities and assisted at evacuation centers filled with citizens driven from their homes. The floodwaters hit Des Moines, Iowa, especially hard, and nearly twenty-three hundred National Guard members from six states—Iowa, North Dakota, Ohio, Alabama, Arkansas, and Texas—arrived to provide flood relief and potable water to the city's nearly 200,000 residents.

Before the waters subsided, nearly eighty-four hundred Guard troops from the midwestern states affected by the flooding had seen duty. Guard members provided important materiel and psychological succor to flood victims and gave them hope for the future.

Michael D. Doubler
Alexandria, Virginia

fantry, the first regiment of northern soldiers offered to the federal government to preserve the Union. Many militia officers received commissions in the Union Army, and several, like Lew Wallace of Indianapolis, rose to prominent rank. Midwestern citizen-soldiers manned forts, protected coastlines and the Canadian border, garrisoned the Indian frontier, and guarded Confederate prisoners. The states often raised militia regiments for ninety days of service for specific, short-term missions. At other times, the states mobilized large numbers of militiamen on short notice in response to unexpected emergencies. In July 1863, both Ohio and Indiana turned out militiamen in large numbers to repel a raid north of the Ohio River by southern marauders under John Hunt Morgan.

In the decades following the Civil War, militiamen in the Midwest mobilized against labor unrest and helped to transform the militia into the National Guard. The Great Railroad Strike of 1877 thrust state militias back onto the national scene when those of Illinois, Indiana, and Missouri were employed to put down the strikers. Repeated calls to strike duty and support of local law enforcement, however, prompted a move to seek a new mission as a federal reserve force to the U.S. Army. In October 1879, prominent militia leaders held the first national conference of the National Guard Association in St. Louis. For the next two decades, these midwestern citizen-soldiers were part of a national movement that sought federal funding and reform legislation.

Prior to America's entry into World War I, reserve forces became part of the national military establishment. Unlike the National Guard, members of the reserve components are federal assets with no responsibility for state service. Midwesterners played an important role in the early development of reserve organizations. Drs. Charles H. and William J. Mayo, for example, were prominent surgeons who achieved the rank of brigadier general in the Army's Officers' Reserve Corps and founded the prestigious Mayo Clinic in Rochester, Minnesota. Colonel Ralph D. Mershon, a distinguished Ohio State University alumnus, helped to lead the public effort to create the legislation that was the forerunner of the Reserve Officer Training Corps on college campuses nationwide. The Mershon Center at Ohio State University, which advances the scholarly study and intellectual understanding of national security matters, is named in honor of Colonel Mershon's public service achievements and his substantial contribution to the university for the purpose.

One of the most significant contributions of Guardsmen and reservists in the twentieth century was to form the basis of the American Expeditionary Forces sent to France in World War I. Of the eighteen National Guard divisions sent to the Western Front, seven included Guardsmen from the twelve midwestern states. One of the Guard's most illustrious members in World War I was Captain Harry S Truman of Independence, Missouri, who commanded Battery D, 129th Field Artillery of the Thirty-Fifth Division and went on to become the thirty-third president of the United States. The National Guard's service in World War I solidified its place in the defense establishment as a federal reserve force in addition to its state responsibilities. Seven divisions of midwestern reservists and draftees also served during World War I. One such command was the Eighty-Fourth "Railsplitter" Division that provided replacements in France during the war and still serves as a Wisconsin-based training division in the U.S. Army Reserve.

During the interwar years, Guard units made important advances. In the early 1920s, Minnesota's Thirty-Fourth Division activated the Guard's first-ever observation squadron and tank company. Lieutenant Colonel Charles B. Winder of Ohio became the first Guard officer to achieve a flight rating as a reserve military aviator. The most dramatic accomplishment of any Guard aviator came on May 20, 1927, when Captain Charles A. Lindbergh of Missouri's 110th Observation Squadron completed his daring solo flight across the Atlantic.

Midwestern Guard units and reservists were at the forefront of Allied offensives during World War II. Following the attack on Pearl Harbor, the Guard's Thirty-Fourth Infantry Division—from Minnesota, Iowa, South Dakota, and North Dakota—was the first American combat division to deploy overseas. The Thirty-Fifth Infantry Division, with Guard units from Kansas, Missouri, and Nebraska, received its baptism by fire in Normandy in July 1944, and ended the war in the heart of Germany. The Thirty-Second Infantry Division from Michigan and Wisconsin arrived in Australia in May 1942, and before the end of the summer, it was in combat on New Guinea. In one of the most grueling campaigns of the entire war, the Thirty-Second wrested the Japanese bastion at Buna from enemy hands. Illinois's Thirty-Third Infantry Division saw repeated action in the atolls of the South Pacific and helped to force the final Japanese surrender in the Philippines. Ohio's Thirty-Seventh Infantry Division accrued an outstanding combat record in the Solomon Islands and played a key role in the capture of Manila. Three National Guard regiments from Illinois, North Dakota, and Massachusetts were combined early in the war to form the American Division that saw heavy combat on Guadalcanal, the Solomon Islands, and Leyte. The Eighty-Fifth Infantry Division with midwestern reservist roots received high commendation in the Mediterranean and remains in the U.S. Army Reserve, with units in six midwestern states.

Midwestern National Guard and reserve units also made valuable contributions to national defense in the early decades of the cold war. With the establishment of a new and independent U.S. Air Force, the National Guard organized the Air National Guard to serve alongside the Army Guard. During the Korean War, nearly 185,000 Guard members served on active duty. Ohio's Thirty-Seventh Division, Illinois's Forty-Fourth Division, and the Forty-Seventh Division

from Minnesota and North Dakota mobilized and constituted a ready reserve that remained stateside. A manpower crisis early in the Korean conflict prompted a massive call-up of Army and Marine Corps reservists, including those from the Midwest.

Problems stemming from the Korean War mobilization resulted in the Armed Forces Reserve Act of 1952 that reorganized and strengthened reserve component forces. The legislation formally recognized seven reserve components—the Army National Guard; the Air National Guard; and the Army, Air Force, Navy, Marine Corps, and Coast Guard Reserves—and organized them into categories of ready, standby, and retired reserves. Because of the Midwest's location away from the nation's major coastlines, reservists in the region have favored membership in the National Guard and the Army and Air Force Reserves rather than the other reserve components. Nevertheless, the Navy, Marine Corps, and Coast Guard Reserves maintain a presence in the Midwest.

Midwestern citizen-soldiers have also participated in important homeland defense missions. Following the Korean War, Soviet strategic bombers constituted a viable threat against the United States. The Air Force implemented a thorough air defense plan, with the Air National Guard participating in the Runway Alert Program. Air Guard fighter-interceptors stationed at selected military airfields across the Midwest stood at strip alert to respond to possible incursions of American airspace. Meanwhile, the U.S. Army implemented the Nike Missile Program, a series of air defense missile zones across the nation designed to protect centers of population and industry from aerial attack. By the 1960s, the Army Guard was heavily involved in the Nike Missile Program, with units from Illinois and Michigan manning missile sites that defended the Chicago and Detroit metropolitan areas.

The Johnson Administration's decision to not mobilize the reserve components for the Vietnam War resulted in the popular view that the National Guard was a haven for young men seeking to avoid military service. During the conflict, however, National Guard units were ordered to help contain domestic unrest prompted by the war and racial discord in major cities. The heaviest commitment of midwesterners to put down urban rioting occurred in Detroit in July 1967, with the deployment of 10,000 Michigan Guardsmen, backed by 5,000 federal troops. One of the most unfortunate moments in National Guard history occurred during a confrontation with antiwar protesters at Kent State University in Ohio. On May 4, 1970, elements of the Ohio National Guard that were sent to quell violent antiwar protests on the campus opened fire on student protesters, killing four and wounding nine others.

The Tet Offensive by North Vietnamese forces and the seizure of the USS *Pueblo* by North Korea in early 1968 precipitated a national crisis that finally prompted Guard and reserve mobilization, but midwestern citizen-soldiers served in Vietnam in only limited numbers. Company D (Ranger), 151st Infantry from the Indiana National Guard was the only ground maneuver sent to Vietnam. The Sixty-Ninth Infantry Brigade of the Kansas National Guard, reinforced by an Iowa infantry battalion, was ordered to active duty, and nearly half of its members volunteered for Vietnam service.

National Guard and reserve units were involved in military maneuvers during the remainder of the cold war. Midwestern Guard units often deployed to Europe to train for a possible war there against the Warsaw Pact. In 1972, the Minnesota Guard started an overseas exchange program with Norway that became a model for training programs with other European powers. A decade later, Indiana was the first state to deploy major units to Europe for annual training. In 1986, the entire Thirty-Second Brigade from Wisconsin deployed to Europe with all of its personnel and equipment for maneuvers.

After the end of the cold war, midwestern Guard and reserve units were assigned to serve in various conflicts abroad. During the Persian Gulf War in 1991, Guard and reserve units from across the region deployed quickly and participated fully in the war effort. In a similar fashion, midwestern units made significant contributions to peacekeeping efforts in the Balkans in the late 1990s. Events at home also challenged the National Guard. Unusual weather conditions during 1993 resulted in a historic flood along the upper Mississippi River. Flood relief efforts resulted in the mobilization of nearly 10,000 Guard members from the midwestern states most affected by the disaster.

Following the attacks on the World Trade Center and the Pentagon on September 11, 2001, midwestern units performed homeland defense missions and supported overseas campaigns. National Guard units, for example, maintained combat air patrols over the region's largest cities, protecting critical infrastructure, and enhancing security at commercial airports, border crossing points, and major port facilities, as well as serving in the conflicts in Afghanistan and Iraq. As the twenty-first century progresses, National Guard and reserve units will no doubt continue to make key contributions to America's defense while preserving life and protecting property in all of the midwestern states.

Sources and Further Reading: Michael D. Doubler, *Civilian in Peace, Soldier in War* (2003); Jim Dan Hill, *The Minute Man in Peace and War* (1964); Bennie J. Wilson III, ed., *The Guard and Reserve in the Total Force* (1985).

Michael D. Doubler
Alexandria, Virginia

Charles W. F. Dick (1858–1945)

Born in Akron, Ohio, Charles Dick enjoyed a long life of public service as an elected representative and National Guard officer. His military career began in 1876 when he volunteered for militia service in Company B, Eighth Regiment, Ohio Infantry. Dick eventually rose to the rank of lieutenant colonel, and served with the Eighth Ohio Infantry in Cuba during the Spanish–American War.

In November 1898, he was elected to the U.S. House of Representatives. Six years later, he entered the U.S. Senate and served until losing a reelection bid in 1911. During this time, Dick championed the Militia Act of 1903, replacing the Military Act of 1792 and its 1908 amendments. Commonly referred to as the Dick Act, it began the transformation of the state militias into a better trained and equipped National Guard that functioned as a federal reserve force. While in Congress, his military career flourished. In 1900, Dick became the commander of the Ohio Division, National Guard, with the rank of major general. In 1902, he was elected president of the National Guard Association and held that position for seven years.

After leaving the Senate in 1911, Dick resumed his law practice, begun in Akron in 1894, at which time he was admitted to the Ohio bar. He ran again for the Senate in 1922 but lost the election. He died in Akron on March 13, 1945, and is buried in Glendale Cemetery. Since 1988, the National Guard Association's Charles Dick Medal of Merit recognizes support rendered to the National Guard by state and national elected representatives.

Sources and Further Reading: Michael D. Doubler, *Civilian in Peace, Soldier in War* (2003); Jim Dan Hill, *The Minute Man in Peace and War* (1964).

Michael D. Doubler
Alexandria, Virginia

Ellard A. Walsh (1887–1975)

Ellard Walsh enjoyed a long and distinguished career as a citizen-soldier while serving as adjutant general of Minnesota and influential leader of the National Guard Association of the United States. Born in Canada, his family moved to Minnesota while he was a child. His military career began in 1905 when he enlisted in the First Minnesota Infantry, and served with the regiment during the Mexican Border Crisis of 1916. Walsh received an officer's commission in World War I and served with the National Guard's Thirty-Fourth Division in France. In 1927, he was appointed Minnesota's adjutant general, a post he held for forty-two years. The following year, Walsh served a two-year term as president of the National Guard Association. Promoted to major general in July 1940, he became commander of the Thirty-Fourth Division, and entered active duty with the division in February 1941. Chronic ulcers, however, forced him to return to Minnesota where he continued in his post as adjutant general. In 1943, he was reelected president of the National Guard Association, a position he held for fourteen years.

Walsh provided the leadership that transformed the National Guard Association into a premier lobbying organization in Washington, D.C., with a full-time staff, an imposing headquarters, and a monthly magazine. An articulate, tireless advocate, he worked to ensure that the National Guard retained a prominent role in the nation's defenses following World War II. The Walsh-Reckord Hall of States in the National Guard Memorial in Washington, D.C., stands as a permanent monument to his tireless efforts.

Sources and Further Reading: Martha Derthick, *The National Guard in Politics* (1965); Michael D. Doubler, *Civilian in Peace, Soldier in War* (2003).

Michael D. Doubler
Alexandria, Virginia

World War II, 1939–1945

In 1940 and 1941 the Midwest was a bastion of isolationism as war engulfed Europe and the Soviet Union as well as East Asia. From Robert Taft of Ohio and Arthur Vandenburg of Michigan to Arthur Capper of Kansas and Gerald Nye of North Dakota, the Midwest's contingent in the United States Senate was sharply critical of any move by the Roosevelt administration to involve the nation in war. The region's leading newspaper, the Chicago *Tribune*, was the chief mouthpiece of isolationism, and Chicago was the headquarters of the noninterventionist America First Committee. Seemingly secure in the heart of the continent and far removed from Asia and Europe, midwesterners sought to avoid entry into another world war and viewed suspiciously East Coast internationalists.

Yet ten-year-old Juanita Wagner in rural Iowa felt the consequences of the war when, in the spring of 1940, she became a pen pal of Anne Frank of Amsterdam. After one exchange of letters, the Germans marched into the Netherlands and Juanita never again heard from Anne Frank. On December 7, 1941, the Japanese bombed Pearl Harbor, Hawaii, and Midwesterners came to realize that their region could not escape the tragedy of world conflict. The Netherlands's war was also the Midwest's war.

Responding to the crisis, millions of midwesterners volunteered for military service or awaited their draft notice. Moreover, midwesterners took pride in the military leadership of Kansas-raised Dwight Eisenhower, Missourian Omar Bradley, and Ohioan Ernest King. Yet the American armed forces in World War II were not organized along regional lines. Unlike in the nineteenth century, when state militia companies shouldered much of the burden of warfare, in World War II, a central army command eschewed geographically defined units and generally viewed National Guard commanders with disdain. Thus midwestern soldiers served with easterners, westerners, and southerners in regionally heterogeneous units, and Illinois or Ohio could not claim that their infantry companies liberated Europe while Virginians or Californians lagged behind. America's armed forces were national, and the Midwest did not play an identifiably distinctive role in combat.

Yet the war effort was not confined to Europe and the Pacific, and World War II did have a profound impact on the midwestern home front. For example, midwesterners came in direct contact with the enemy through the numerous prisoner-of-war camps in the heartland states. From Camp Perry in Ohio to Camp Concordia in Kansas, major internment facilities dotted the Midwest landscape. But the prisoners of war did not remain confined to the camps. Responding to demands for help with planting and harvesting, the federal government sent thousands of prisoners to midwestern farms. In 1945, almost 5,000 prisoners labored on Missouri farms, and in 1944 and 1945, Michigan farmers and agricultural processors put between 4 and 5,000 of the Axis captives to work. In Minnesota prisoners not only harvested peas and corn but also worked in logging camps.

Meanwhile, American recruits trained at military facilities across the region. Missouri's Camp Crowder was the nation's largest signal corps training center, and Kansas's Fort Riley was a major source of mechanized troops. Giant military reservations sprawled across the fields of the Heartland; Fort Leonard Wood in Missouri encompassed 86,000 acres, with barracks for 30,000 troops and 425 miles of paved thoroughfares. Very quickly the military transformed midwest-

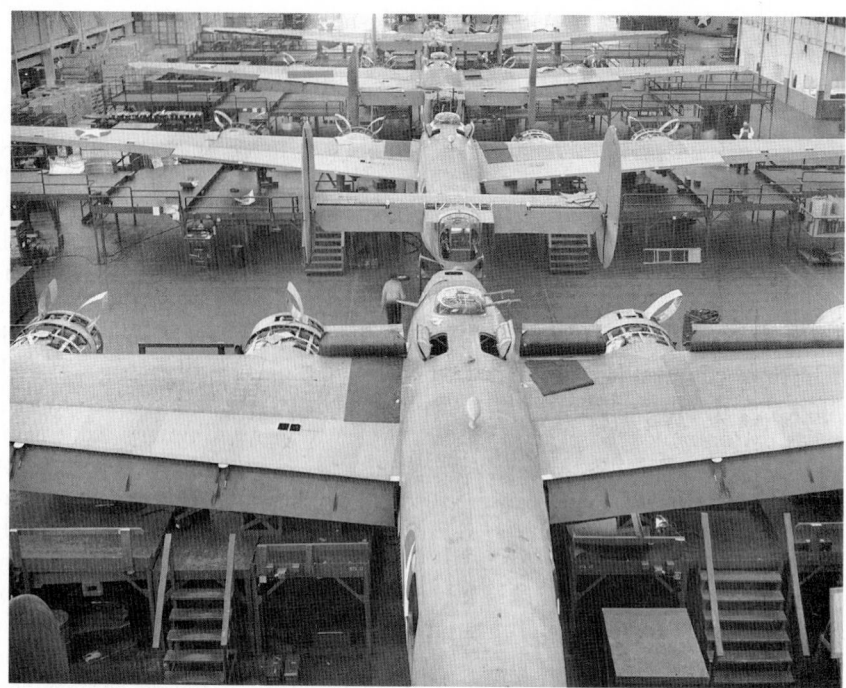

B-24 bomber assembly plant, Willow Run, Michigan. Library of Congress, Prints and Photographs Division, LC-USE6-D008795.

ern pastures and woodlands into training bases. During the first half of 1942, the federal government evicted 700 families from 40,000 acres in south-central Indiana to create Camp Atterbury. More than 14,000 workers were employed to construct the base's 1,700 buildings as well as its roads, water supply and sewerage systems, and a 125-car railroad siding. Even the dead had to yield to the war effort, as hundreds of bodies in area cemeteries were removed for reburial outside the camp.

Military installations and prisoner-of-war camps, however, were not unique to the Midwest. What set the region apart from the East, West, or South was its vital contribution as a supplier of both military equipment and foodstuffs. As the nation's breadbasket and the world's great center of motor vehicle manufacturing, the Midwest proved an invaluable asset to the allied cause. President Roosevelt declared the United States "the great arsenal of democracy," but the heart of that arsenal was the heavily industrialized eastern half of the Midwest. Moreover, rich farmlands throughout the region were to feed allied soldiers and civilians. If an army marches on its stomach, then the Midwest was vital to the locomotion of allied forces.

The midwestern centers of automobile production proved especially significant as suppliers of war materiel. Michigan ranked first among the states in major war supply contracts. With only 4 percent of the nation's population, it was responsible for 11 percent of the contracts for war supplies. Chrysler produced more than 25,000 tanks at its arsenal in Warren, Michigan, General Motors also turned out tanks at a plant south of Flint, and Packard built Rolls Royce aircraft engines in Detroit. Other states in the eastern Midwest joined Michigan in producing an inordinate share of armaments and weaponry. Ohio ranked fourth in major war contracts, Illinois seventh, and Indiana eighth. Toledo turned out Jeeps, and DuPont operated the largest powder plant in the world at Charlestown, Indiana. More than 5,000 workers at the Weldon Spring Ordnance Plant west of St. Louis produced TNT, and the Lake City plant outside of Kansas City, Missouri, employed 21,800 at peak production to manufacture ammunition.

On a per capita basis, no American city produced more than South Bend, Indiana. With a metropolitan population of only 162,000, it accounted for $1.9 billion in war supplies; thirty-three of the forty-eight states produced less war materiel than this Indiana city. During the war, Studebaker, South Bend's best-known manufacturer, turned out almost 200,000 trucks for the military as well as 64,000 aircraft engines. Altogether the five states of the Old Northwest Territory manufactured 36 percent of the nation's combat equipment.

The Midwest also contributed significantly to the nation's naval effort. Employing 19,600 workers at its peak, a giant shipyard in Evansville, Indiana, produced essential landing craft known as LSTs (landing ship, tank); Milwaukee's Falk Company was primary contractor for the gear drives in the LSTs. Meanwhile, the Hudson Motor Car Company operated a navy gun arsenal outside of Detroit. Land, air, and naval forces all relied on midwestern manufacturing for the implements of warfare.

Symbolic of the might of the midwestern war machine was Ford's Willow Run plant west of Detroit. The largest bomber plant in the world, its main building covered sixty-seven acres with a mile-long assembly line. At its peak in 1943, the gargantuan airplane factory employed 42,000 people, and during the last years of the war, B-24 Liberators rolled off the assembly line at the rate of one every sixty-three minutes.

To remedy the labor shortage resulting from the military draft and the massive escalation of defense production, midwestern women took manufacturing jobs formerly reserved for men. "Rosie the Riveter" signed up to work in midwestern factories, abandoning her former place in the kitchen, behind the typewriter, or at the retail counter. Moreover, thousands of southern blacks and whites migrated to Michigan, Indiana, Ohio, and Illinois to find employment in the defense plants. Willow Run's crowded temporary structures housed the army of workers needed to fulfill Henry Ford's dream of mass-produced aircraft. In other industrial centers, housing was also in short supply, and newcomers had to adjust to the sometimes hostile or suspicious local population. Racial tension divided Detroit and culminated in a full-scale race riot in June 1943. White mobs battled blacks, resulting in more than 600 casualties and 1,832 arrests. The military had to be called in to suppress the unrest, patrolling the streets in armed personnel carriers and camping on the lawn of the public library.

The picture was different in most of the trans-Mississippi Midwest. Devoid of much heavy industry before the war, the agricultural heartland attracted fewer military contracts or defense production facilities. Whereas Michigan ranked first in major war contracts, South and North Dakota ranked dead last, in forty-eighth and forty-seventh position, respectively. Though local boosters attempted to attract defense dollars, the military preferred to rely on the existing industrial infrastructure of the automobile giants in Michigan, Ohio, and Indiana rather than subsidize a program of industrialization in the Great Plains.

The most notable exception to this Great Plains pattern of limited defense production was Wichita, Kansas. In early 1940, only 1,600 Kansans were employed in aircraft manufacturing, primarily at the Boeing, Beech, and Cessna plants in Wichita. But as the United States stepped up its defense preparedness, these relatively small existing plants expanded rapidly.

Between August 1940 and August 1941, manufacturing employment in Wichita soared 168 percent, the sharpest increase of any city in the nation. Between 1940 and 1943, the estimated civilian population rose 36 percent, a figure surpassed only by the naval centers of Norfolk (Virginia), San Diego (California), Mobile (Alabama), and Charleston (South Carolina). By the close of the war, the number of aircraft workers in Wichita alone was half again as many as the number employed in aircraft manufacturing in the entire United States in 1940. In other words, Wichita was one of the war's preeminent boomtowns, and an exception to the rather dismal defense industry records of many communities in the trans-Mississippi Midwest.

Iowa, the Dakotas, and neighboring states, however, could take pride in, and enjoy the profits from, a massive agricultural initiative to feed the war effort. After a decade of low prices and drought, the war years proved the economic salvation of many hard-pressed farmers. Improved weather combined with wartime demand to bring much-needed cash into the pockets of rural midwesterners. North Dakota enjoyed above-average precipitation every year from 1940 to 1944, and 1941 was the wettest year on record. Meanwhile, wheat prices jumped from 67 cents a bushel in 1940 to $1.53 a bushel in 1945. The same factors enriched Kansans; between 1939 and 1945, the annual net income for wheat growers in the southern Great Plains soared 2,000 percent. In the Corn Belt the change was less dramatic, but even there net farm income rose 300 percent during the war years. Pressed by the federal government to produce as much as possible, midwestern farmers enlarged their acreage of cropland. The amount of Kansas land in cultivation increased 22 percent during the war, and even industrial Michigan saw a 9 percent rise in acres harvested between 1939 and 1944.

Just as Detroit and Wichita seemed to work industrial miracles for the war effort, midwestern farmers produced bumper crops and marketed record numbers of cattle and hogs. In 1943, the midwestern states accounted for 46 percent of the nation's cash farm receipts. Iowa ranked first among the forty-eight states in cash receipts, and eight of the top ten states were in the Midwest. On the farm and in the factory, the Midwest proved to be a productive dynamo that provided invaluable support to the allied cause.

Whereas industrial prosperity attracted thousands of new residents to Detroit and Wichita, a marked decline in the farm population accompanied the agricultural boom. Farm wages could not match those in the aircraft factories, and the economic and social advantages of the city lured many rural dwellers. Though Iowa farmers never had it so good, in twenty-seven of the state's rural counties, the civilian population dropped 15 percent or more between 1940 and 1943. The military draft accounted for part of the loss, but equally significant was the rush of rural midwesterners to defense jobs in the cities.

Thus the war had marked demographic and economic consequences for the Midwest. It drew thousands of black and white southerners and rural midwesterners to the region's manufacturing centers. And it boosted both industry and agriculture after a decade of economic depression. Midwestern-manufactured armaments changed the face of Europe and Asia, but at the same time, the war transformed the Heartland, bringing jobs and prosperity to Depression-weary factory workers and farmers and stepping up the pace of urban migration.

Sources and Further Reading: Max Parvin Cavnes, *The Hoosier Community at War* (1961); Alan Clive, *State of War: Michigan in World War II* (1979); Peter Fearon, "Ploughshares into Airplanes," *Kansas History* 22 (Winter 1999–2000); Michael J. Grant, "Food Will Win the War and Write the Peace," *Kansas History* 20 (Winter 1997–1998); John Gurda, "Profits and Patriotism," *Wisconsin Magazine of History* 78 (Autumn 1994); Larry Lankton, "Autos to Armaments," *Michigan History* 75 (Nov.–Dec. 1991); Patrick G. O'Brien, Thomas D. Isern, and R. Daniel Lumley, "Stalag Sunflower," *Kansas History* 7 (Autumn 1984); Edward J. Pluth, "Prisoner of War Employment in Minnesota During World War II," *Minnesota History* 44 (Winter 1975); Dorothy Riker, comp., *The Hoosier Training Ground* (1952); Marion F. Wilson, *The Story of Willow Run* (1956).

Jon C. Teaford
Purdue University, Indiana

Robert S. Beightler (1892–1978)

Born in Marysville, Ohio, Robert Beightler was the son of William P. and Joana Sprague Beightler. After attending The Ohio State University, Beightler was appointed an engineer for Union County, Ohio, in 1911. That same year he enlisted as a private in the Fourth Infantry Regiment of the Ohio National Guard. Commissioned a second lieutenant in the Guard in 1914, Beightler was a staff officer with the 166th U.S. Infantry Regiment in France during World War I.

Between the world wars, Beightler worked with the Ohio highway department, was a private contractor, and from 1939 to 1940 served as Ohio's director of highways. He also pursued his career as a Guardsman, and when the Thirty-Seventh Division (the Ohio National Guard) was federalized in October 1940, he was named commander with the rank of major general. During World War II, Beightler was the only Guard

general to command his division for the duration of the war, as well as the Army's longest-serving division commander. Overcoming the hostility that many Regular Army officers felt for Guardsmen, he successfully led his division against the Japanese in the New Georgia, Bougainville, and Luzon campaigns.

Following the war, Beightler accepted a commission in the Regular Army and finished his military career in 1953 as the head of the Ryukyus Command and the senior major general in the U.S. Army. Thereafter he was executive director of the Ohio Turnpike Commission until 1955. A strong proponent of the organized state militia with its responsibilities for disaster relief, civil disturbances, and national defense, and a highly regarded combat commander, Beightler was one of the most prominent Guardsmen of the twentieth century. Twice married, he had two children. He died in Columbus, Ohio, in 1978.

Source and Further Reading: John Kennedy Ohl, *Minuteman: The Military Career of General Robert S. Beightler* (2001).

John Kennedy Ohl
Mesa Community College, Arizona

Omar Bradley (1893–1981)

Omar Bradley was born in Clark, Missouri, to a schoolteacher father and a seamstress mother. Lacking family money for an education beyond high school, Bradley successfully competed for an appointment to the U.S. Military Academy at West Point. He graduated in 1915, a part of the class that produced fifty-nine generals during World War II.

Bradley spent World War I in training jobs in the United States, and passed the bulk of the 1920s and 1930s in teaching positions, serving on the faculties of West Point, the Infantry Training School, and the Army's Command and General Staff School. He married Mary Elizabeth Quayle in 1916 and had one child. In 1941, as a brigadier general, he became Commandant of the Infantry School. Early in World War II, Bradley commanded an Army division in North Africa and the II Corps during the invasion of Sicily. Bradley led the First American Army during the invasion of Normandy in June 1944, became the commander of the U.S. Twelfth Army Group in August, and thereafter commanded the entire American force in Western Europe that fought into Germany until the European war ended in May 1945.

After the war, Bradley headed the Veterans Affairs Administration before being appointed the Army Chief of Staff in 1947 and the Chairman of the Joint Chiefs of Staff in 1949. In the latter capacity, Bradley became the last of the five-star generals of the U.S. Army and was the senior military advisor to President Truman during the Korean War. Bradley retired in August 1953, a month after the Korean Armistice, and spent his remaining years serving on corporate boards and writing his memoirs.

Sources and Further Reading: Omar Bradley with Clay Blair, *A General's Life* (1983); Omar Bradley with Chester Hansen, *A Soldier's Story* (1951); Russell Weigley, *Eisenhower's Lieutenants* (1981).

Thomas Hughes
Maxwell Air Force Base, Montgomery, Alabama

Ernest J. King (1878–1956)

From a working-class family in Lorain, Ohio, King won admission to the U.S. Naval Academy by competitive examination. Seeing action in the Spanish–American War and graduating fourth in his class of 1901, King revealed a remarkable versatility during his career by serving in surface, submarine, support, and aviation units as well as in staff, shore, and educational billets.

Abrasive, a womanizer, and drinker, King was detailed to a dead-end assignment in 1939. World War II revivified his career, and he soon took command of the Atlantic Squadron. Following Pearl Harbor, he was named commander-in-chief of the fleet and then chief of naval operations, ultimately combining both positions.

As the navy's representative on the Joint Chiefs of Staff, King fought successfully to keep pressure on the Japanese despite the Allied policy that prioritized Germany. He shaped many key decisions, such as the use of carriers to strike the Japanese homeland and the Guadalcanal landings, both in 1942. He was notably successful in pushing for a cross-Pacific offensive and in winning resources to build the greatest navy in history.

On the debit side, King was initially slow to react to German submarine attacks off American shores, and he quarreled so frequently with the British that he was denounced as an Anglophobe. Nonetheless, he retained the confidence of President Roosevelt, who prized King's strategic acumen. King was promoted to the five-star rank of admiral of the fleet in December 1944. He never formally retired, although he relinquished the post of chief of naval operations in December 1945. He died in the Naval Hospital, Portsmouth, New Hampshire, on June 25, 1956.

Sources and Further Reading: Thomas B. Buell, *Master of Sea Power* (1980); Ernest J. King and Walter Muir White- hill, *Fleet Admiral King* (1952); Robert William Love, Jr., ed., *The Chiefs of Naval Operations* (1980).

Malcolm Muir, Jr.
Austin Peay State University, Tennessee

African Americans and the Military

An African American military presence in the Midwest has existed for some time. When Jean Du Sable arrived to start the trading post that would become Chicago, he did so as part of a military expedition. As Americans pushed toward the West, the relevance of the African American contributions grew.

Although it can be assumed that African Americans contributed to westward movement from the colonial period through the antebellum period, it was during the Civil War that these contributions grew in number and are best documented. At the start of the Civil War, President Abraham Lincoln refused to allow the enlistment of African Americans into the Union forces, and he maintained this position until after 1863. Despite his stand, African Americans found the opportu-

Buffalo soldier monument, Ft. Leavenworth, Kansas. Photo courtesy Nathan Thomas and Dennis Behling, photographers, of Conceive, Believe, Achieve. Sculptor, Eddie Dixon.

nity to support the Union cause as early as 1862 in Kansas under the leadership of James Lane. Indeed, in order to accept a commission as a brigadier general in the Union Army, Lane resigned his seat in the United States Senate. Returning to Kansas, he began to enlist African Americans, ignoring repeated notifications from the War Department that he did not have the necessary authorization to organize black troops. Lane's men were among the first African American troops to see combat when they clashed with a large number of Missouri Confederate guerrillas.

In Cincinnati that same year, black Ohioans came to the aid of the city when the mayor requested volunteers in response to fears of invasion by Confederate forces and guerrillas. The African American citizens of the city responded with a determination underlining the importance of the war. It was shortly thereafter that President Lincoln approved the use of black troops.

This new effort to draw on untapped manpower gave rise to the best known of African American forces during the Civil War. Early in 1863, John Andrew, the governor of Massachusetts, received word from Washington that his state could recruit African Americans for service in its state units. Massachusetts pursued the opportunity aggressively, recruiting heavily from the Midwest. The state filled the ranks of one company of the Fifty-Fourth Massachusetts Infantry Regiment with men from Ohio and attracted at least twenty-three African Americans from Ohio for the Fifty-Fifth.

A number of the midwestern states changed their recruitment policies, since many black men from their states were leaving to join the Massachusetts units, causing them to lose these recruits in the count toward their enlistment quotas. Upon receiving word that Massachusetts would not be able to accept the twenty-three men because the Fifty-Fifth had already filled its ranks, Ohio governor David Tod authorized the recruitment of African American men across the state to serve in the 127th Ohio Volunteer Infantry (OVI). The men of the 127th OVI were mustered into service in November 1863 as the Fifth United States Colored Troops, also known as the United States Colored Infantry, at Camp Delaware, Ohio.

With the end of the Civil War, Congress passed legislation reorganizing the Army, which allowed for the permanent establishment of four African American units. These four units, the Ninth and Tenth Cavalry and the Twenty-Fourth and Twenty-Fifth Infantry, were stationed throughout the West, including service in the Dakotas, Nebraska, and Kansas. During much of this period, the Army's attention was focused on fighting the Indians, and these units played a major role in these engagements. The activities of these Buffalo soldiers are chronicled at the Buffalo Soldiers Museum at Fort Leavenworth, Kansas, including a listing of their Medal of Honor winners.

These combat-hardened units were not to see action in the nation's war to save democracy. When the United States entered the First World War, it did so with two newly formed African American units, the Ninety-Second and Ninety-Third Infantry Divisions, which were trained at Camp Funston, Kansas, now part of Fort Riley. While African Americans were demanding the chance to fight, they were also demanding the right to lead. By the spring of 1917, the U.S. Army had commissioned only three black officers: Colonel Charles Young and Lieutenants Benjamin O. Davis, Sr., and John Green.

To increase the number of black officers, the War Department established an officer training school in Des Moines, Iowa, and on October 15, 1917, 639 black officers received commissions from that program. African Americans expected that Colonel Young would be promoted to general and placed in command of one of the new units, but he was forced into an early medical retirement. Young fought this forced retirement by riding horseback from Wilberforce, Ohio, where he ran the school's program for training Black National Guard officers for the state, to Washington, D.C., and back. He was returned to service just before the war's end, but was never promoted to general. The demands of black Americans during World War I in many ways foreshadowed actions taken later. While in Kansas, members of the Ninety-Second spoke out against, and at times refused to follow, illegal Jim Crow practices.

Change came slowly. The nation entered World War II as it had World War I. After World War I, the nation downsized the Army, much of that accomplished by allowing the four black units to go undermanned. The limited number of officers remained an issue as well. The first black to graduate from West Point since 1889 was Benjamin O. Davis, Jr., in 1936. The Navy had no black officers until March 1944, when it graduated its first African American officers from training at the Great Lakes Naval Training Center in Illinois.

During the Second World War, African American U.S. Air Corps personnel occupied a number of different bases throughout the Midwest. Most noteworthy were their actions at Selfridge Field, Michigan, and Freeman Field, Indiana. At both of these bases, conflicts started as African American combat pilots refused to obey illegal orders intended to enact Jim Crow practices. The desegregation of the armed services after World War II ended the distinctive role the Midwest played in the organization and training of African American troops that commenced during the Civil War.

Sources and Further Reading: Richard M. Dalfiume, *Desegregation of the U.S. Armed Forces* (1969); Willard B. Gatewood, *"Smoked Yankees" and the Struggle for Empire* (1971); Joseph Glatthar, *Forged in Battle* (1990); Bernard Nalty, *Strength for the Fight* (1986); Benjamin Quarles, *The Negro in the Civil War* (1989); Stanley Sandler, *Segregated Skies* (1992); Paul Stillwell, ed., *The Golden Thirteen* (1993); Versalle Washington, *Eagles on Their Buttons* (1999).

Anthony Milburn
Central State University, Ohio

Patriotism and Patriotic Organizations

Love of country and the organizations that promote that love defines and embraces the long, complex history of patriotism in the United States and the role of the Midwest in its varied expressions. Patriotism is the emotional bond holding together the "imagined communities" that Benedict Anderson discusses, which move consciousness of a shared nationalism beyond intellectual and ideological commonalities to a connection of the heart. Whether it is employed in vernacular use or to serve official interests, patriotism is always both affective and rhetorical in its expressions:

It is not enough merely to love, but action is demanded in the service of that love. Organizations from the Boy Scouts to the Ku Klux Klan use patriotic language, symbols, and ritual to enhance the importance and legitimacy of their claims upon the service of their supporters.

Patriotic expressions pervade the landscape and customs of the Midwest. These include calendar events such as the parades and fireworks displays of the Fourth of July, the wreath-laying ceremonies at war memorials and cemeteries for Memorial Day and Veterans Day, museums at Wright-Patterson Air Force Base in Ohio or the First Infantry Museum in Illinois, as well as preserved military posts such as Fort Mackinac (Michigan), Fort Snelling (Minnesota), and Fort Larned (Kansas). They include military reenactment groups for battles on American soil, such as the 1813 siege at Fort Meigs in Perrysburg, Ohio; formal memorials of all kinds, from simple carved stones in a town square with the names of local men and women who served in a particular war, to large-scale war memorials in Indianapolis and Kansas City; or memorial stadia, such as those at Indiana University or the University of Wisconsin.

The symbol of the veteran is a vital part of all of these patriotic expressions. John Bodnar has identified

Grand Army of the Republic parade, Indianapolis, 1920. Bass Photo CD Collection, Indiana Historical Society, neg. no. 71801.

the veteran as a prominent symbol of patriotic veneration and commemoration. Veterans come from all walks of life, providing an egalitarian symbol of patriotism. They participate in war, that most nationalistic of national pursuits, which can require their death as the price of their service to the nation. Alongside their symbolic veneration, the very real issue of the treatment of veterans is ever present in the national discussion of reciprocity for patriotic service. Two kinds of patriotic organizations are centrally concerned with controlling the meaning of veterans in the United States: organizations formed by veterans themselves, and those formed by descendants of veterans of particular wars, the hereditary patriotic organizations.

The Midwest has proven to be fertile ground for patriotic organizations. The three largest veterans' organizations in the United States have their roots in the Midwest: the Grand Army of the Republic, the Veterans of Foreign Wars of the United States, and the American Legion. A number of patriotic hereditary organizations such as the Daughters of Union Veterans of the Civil War and the Daughters of the American Revolution maintain an active but often overlooked presence in the Midwest. Part of the reason for this concentration of activity is pragmatic: The Midwest is centrally located, which is a good reason to establish national headquarters there. These organizations have ready constituencies in the region's many veterans. The Midwest's many small towns offer amicable locations to establish local units, providing a social outlet where there may not be many other leisure opportunities competing for members' time. The Midwest's identity as what James Madison calls "the most representative part of the American nation" symbolically places these organizations in the midst of Heartland values.

The Grand Army of the Republic (GAR) was founded in 1866 as a fraternal and service organization for Union veterans of the Civil War, and made its first national encampment in Indianapolis that same year. The GAR's official founder was Dr. Benjamin Franklin Stephenson, an Illinois veteran who saw in the organization an opportunity both to serve veterans and to shape political careers and policies concerning veterans, such as pension benefits. It also shaped the symbolic representation of veterans and the Civil War, transforming patriotic commemoration and public space by promoting Memorial Day and erecting memorials throughout the Midwest and the nation.

By positioning their organization as representing the men who were the saviors, and then the guardians, of a particular vision of the nation, the GAR provided a successful model for the Veterans of Foreign Wars and American Legion to follow. And in claiming the position of guardians of American values, their engagement with issues of gender and race relations brought an added intensity to their debates on the nature of national service, loyalty, and reciprocity. The GAR's relegation of women and blacks to marginal status within its organizational structure—women serving in the auxiliary Woman's Relief Corps but never accorded full membership in the GAR, and blacks informally segregated into all-black units, if they were admitted to membership at all—was also a legacy that later veterans' organizations would have to confront.

The GAR had a limited life as an organization because it would not admit veterans of later conflicts into its ranks; the last member of the GAR died in 1956. However, the GAR spawned several Allied Orders to ensure its perpetuity, among them the Sons of Union Veterans of the Civil War (SUVCW) founded in 1881 and the Daughters of Union Veterans of the Civil War (DUVCW) founded in 1885, transmuting from veterans' organization to hereditary patriotic organizations. The memberships of these organizations are only a few thousand each, and the members' influence is felt largely at the local level. They continue to support the symbology of the Civil War veteran created by the GAR. They mark the graves of Civil War soldiers, conduct genealogical projects, help preserve historic sites, support local historical societies and veterans' hospitals, and participate in patriotic observances. The DUVCW has its national headquarters in Springfield, Illinois, where it maintains a Civil War museum and lays a wreath at Lincoln's tomb each year on the anniversary of his death.

Through these activities, the SUVCW and DUVCW, as well as other hereditary patriotic organizations such as the Daughters of the American Revolution founded in 1890 and the Sons of the American Revolution founded in 1899, inscribe the landscape of the Midwest with physical and ritual markers that use the symbol of the veteran to connect the region's history to the history of the nation. Wallace Davies notes that the hereditary patriotic organizations differed from the veterans' organizations in their size and influence, and in the nature of their membership. Both kinds of organizations provide members with opportunities for patriotic service and sociability, but the hereditary organizations have a cachet of status and class consciousness, while the wider membership base of veterans organizations provides the potential for more egalitarian comradeship. Both kinds of organizations find common ground in their approach to and uses of the nation's martial past to address issues in the present.

The Veterans of Foreign Wars (VFW) was founded by veterans of the Spanish–American War and the Philippines conflict. One of the earliest chapters of the

VFW formed in Ohio, and the organization chose Kansas City, Missouri, for its national headquarters. Unlike the GAR, the VFW opened its membership to male veterans of all later conflicts who earned an overseas campaign or expeditionary medal. Working with its Ladies Auxiliary—the wives or female relatives of men eligible for membership—the VFW forms teams with organizations such as the Red Cross in local community service. A part of its mission is the promotion of "Americanism" through education. To this end, the VFW hosts student essay contests for seventh and eighth graders, sponsors Boy Scout units, offers college scholarships and awards to students, and extends an annual National Citizenship Education Teachers' Award. One of its most visible fund-raising efforts is the Buddy Poppy program, selling poppies, a powerful symbol of soldiers' sacrifice from World War I. The funds support veteran service programs and the VFW National Home for Children in Eaton Rapids, Michigan, a home for orphaned or single-parent children of VFW members.

The American Legion was founded in 1919 by the American Expeditionary Force in Paris. Its first annual convention that same year was in Minneapolis, where the membership voted to locate their headquarters in Indianapolis rather than in Washington, D.C., to be closer to the "center of the flag." The state of Indiana built the new organization its headquarters in the city center as part of a five-block World War Memorial Plaza, not far from the Soldiers and Sailors Monument erected in 1902 at the urging of the GAR. The American Legion's political successes include lobbying for the creation of the U.S. Veterans Bureau, which later became the Department of Veterans Affairs, and spearheading the GI Bill of Rights, guaranteeing the rights and benefits due GIs returning from World War II. In 1923, the Legion drafted the first Flag Code, defining proper treatment of an American flag, which was adopted by the U.S. Congress in 1942, and the Legion campaigns today for a constitutional amendment to forbid flag desecration.

Through its local posts and in concert with its Auxiliary, the Legion sponsors Scout troops and youth baseball teams. The Auxiliary, which identifies itself as the world's largest women's patriotic service organization, sells crepe poppies to raise funds for service to veterans and maintains a number of scholarships. The Legion and Auxiliary run Boys State and Girls State conventions to teach students about the organization and functions of American government as part of its commitment to patriotic education. The Legion's commitment to promoting "Americanism" made it a center of conservative ideology during the cold war, a role it continues today in its political activism. In keeping with its self-appointed role as protector of the symbolic representation of American veterans, the Legion polices how American history—particularly American military history—is interpreted for public display. Most recently this commitment played out in the Legion's criticism of the exhibit plans for the bomber Enola Gay by the Smithsonian Institution.

After the Gulf War and prior to the September 11, 2001 terrorist attacks on the World Trade Center and the Pentagon, public patriotic expressions in the Midwest largely clustered around Memorial Day, Veterans Day, and the Fourth of July. Members of veterans' and hereditary patriotic organizations complained that patriotism was on the wane in the United States and worried about dwindling membership in their ranks. Outside of these organizations that made patriotic expression part of their group identity and service, rites of national loyalty were conducted by citizens in familial and communal settings, freely intermingled with the pursuit of leisure and sociability.

Following the September 11, 2001 attacks, which media coverage made an event the entire country and the entire world watched together, patriotic expression was everywhere. Flags flew on houses and cars. Businesses displayed signs that read "God Bless America" and "United We Stand." All the outlets of popular media—decals, bumper stickers, lawn signs, commemorative coins, websites, memorial funds—mobilized to meet the demand for symbolic expression of American nationhood united in the face of an enemy. Even traditional public displays were transformed by September 11th. Regional newspapers reported people mingling patriotic symbols and colors with the usual lights and trimmings of their outdoor Christmas decorations.

Veterans' and hereditary patriotic organizations across the country have found their services in greater demand, their political agendas more attended to, and the meanings of their symbolic terrain renegotiated as Americans grapple with the unfolding events of this new era. The nature of military service is changing with the shifting definition of who or what is the enemy. The nature of patriotism is also in debate as citizens publicly and privately discuss the values of the nation, the demands of service to those values, and the limits of that service. In the Midwest, as in the rest of the country, that debate is carried forward not only in the media, but in the symbols of patriotic expression: the sites, objects, rituals, events, and historical narratives invested with layers of meaning about our collective past that give shape to our imagined future.

Sources and Further Reading: Benedict Anderson, *Imagined Communities: Reflections on the Origin and Spread of Nationalism* (1983); John Bodnar, ed., *Bonds of Affection: Americans Define Their Patriotism* (1996); John Bodnar, *Remaking Amer-*

ica: Public Memory, Commemoration, and Patriotism in the Twentieth Century (1992); Andrew R. L. Cayton and Peter S. Onuf, *The Midwest and the Nation* (1990); Wallace Evan Davies, *Patriotism on Parade: The Story of Veterans' and Hereditary Organizations in America, 1783–1900* (1955); James H. Madison, ed., *Heartland: Comparative Histories of the Midwestern States* (1988); Stuart McConnell, *Glorious Contentment* (1992); William Pencak, *For God and Country: The American Legion, 1919–1941* (1989); Thomas A. Rumer, *The American Legion: An Official History, 1919–1989* (1990); Kent C. Ryden, "Writing the Midwest," *Geographical Review* 89 (Oct. 1999).

Barbara Truesdell
Indiana University–Bloomington

Military Installations, 1900–2000

In the twentieth century, Midwest military installations changed considerably from their nineteenth-century counterparts in type, mission, size, and organization. After the Spanish–American War in 1898, Congress became more willing to support defense. Increases in War and Navy Department appropriations allowed for maintenance and expansion of military posts.

Some of the Midwest military installations retained their nineteenth-century mission. Columbus Barracks (Ohio) and Jefferson Barracks (Missouri) continued as recruit depots; Rock Island Arsenal (Illinois) and Jeffersonville Quartermaster Depot (Indiana) also continued their missions. Others were in the process of change, like Fort Leavenworth (Kansas), formerly a frontier post, which was becoming a center for various Army schools. The Army established new posts like Fort Benjamin Harrison (Indianapolis), which opened as an infantry post in 1903. The Navy reestablished its presence in the region with the opening of the Great Lakes Naval Training Center near Chicago in 1911.

Entry into World War I spurred the establishment of additional posts for the care and training of men before their deployment and upon their return, as well as for the production and storage of materiel. War construction and expansion occurred at permanent posts such as Fort Crook (Nebraska), Jefferson Barracks (Missouri), Fort Omaha (Nebraska), Rock Island Arsenal (Illinois), and Fort Snelling (Minnesota). The Army also retained some installations originally intended as temporary posts at Camp Custer and Selfridge Field (Michigan), Camp Dodge (Iowa), Savanna Proving Ground (Illinois), and Wright Field (Ohio) after the war ended.

The onset of World War II in 1939 expanded the military presence in the Midwest. Some of the training posts like Camp McCoy (Wisconsin) underwent substantial construction and expansion. The Army also created new posts such as Camp Atterbury and Jefferson Proving Ground (Indiana), Fort Leonard Wood and Camp Crowder (Missouri), Camp Ellis and Joliet Arsenal (Illinois), Camp Phillips (Kansas), Camp Savage (Minnesota), and Camp Williams (Wisconsin). The new Army Air Force established numerous bases across the region and expanded older posts like Wright Field and Selfridge Field into major installations.

The U.S. Navy had numerous installations in the region during World War II. In the 1930s, the Navy established four reserve air bases in the Midwest at Grosse Ile (Michigan), Glenview (Illinois), Minneapolis, and St. Louis; these installations became naval air stations during World War II. In 1942, the Navy established additional naval air stations at Olathe and Hutchinson (Kansas), Bunker Hill (Indiana), and Ottumwa (Iowa). The Navy opened its Central Spare Parts Warehouse at Joliet, Illinois, in 1943.

Following World War II, the military cut back considerably, and most of the wartime installations disappeared from the active list. Numerous small historic posts ceased active-duty service in the war's aftermath. Among those decommissioned were Fort Snelling, Forts Custer and Brady (Michigan), Jefferson Barracks, and Fort Hayes (formerly Columbus Barracks).

Congress created the U.S. Air Force as a separate military service in 1947, which meant that most of the Army Air Bases and related facilities became a part of the new service, with at least partial name changes. Fort Crook, for example, became Offutt Air Force Base, and the airfields in the Dayton, Ohio, area consolidated as Wright-Patterson Air Force Base. As Army installations became more permanent, their names often changed from camp to fort, such as Fort McCoy. Summertime National Guard training centered on Camp Ripley (Minnesota) and Camp Graying (Michigan). Except for the Glenview Naval Air Station and Great Lakes Naval Training Center, the sea service's active duty presence in the region after World War II virtually disappeared.

The cold war brought construction of new installations as the region became the center of the intercontinental bomber and missile fleets. The Air Force established new bases such as McConnell in Kansas and K. I. Sawyer in Michigan, and dozens of intercontinental ballistic missile sites dotted the Plains. Air defense missile sites were built around major cities, numerous fighter bases appeared to counteract potential Soviet bomber fleets, and Offutt AFB became the home of the Strategic Air Command.

With the end of the cold war and the signing of the

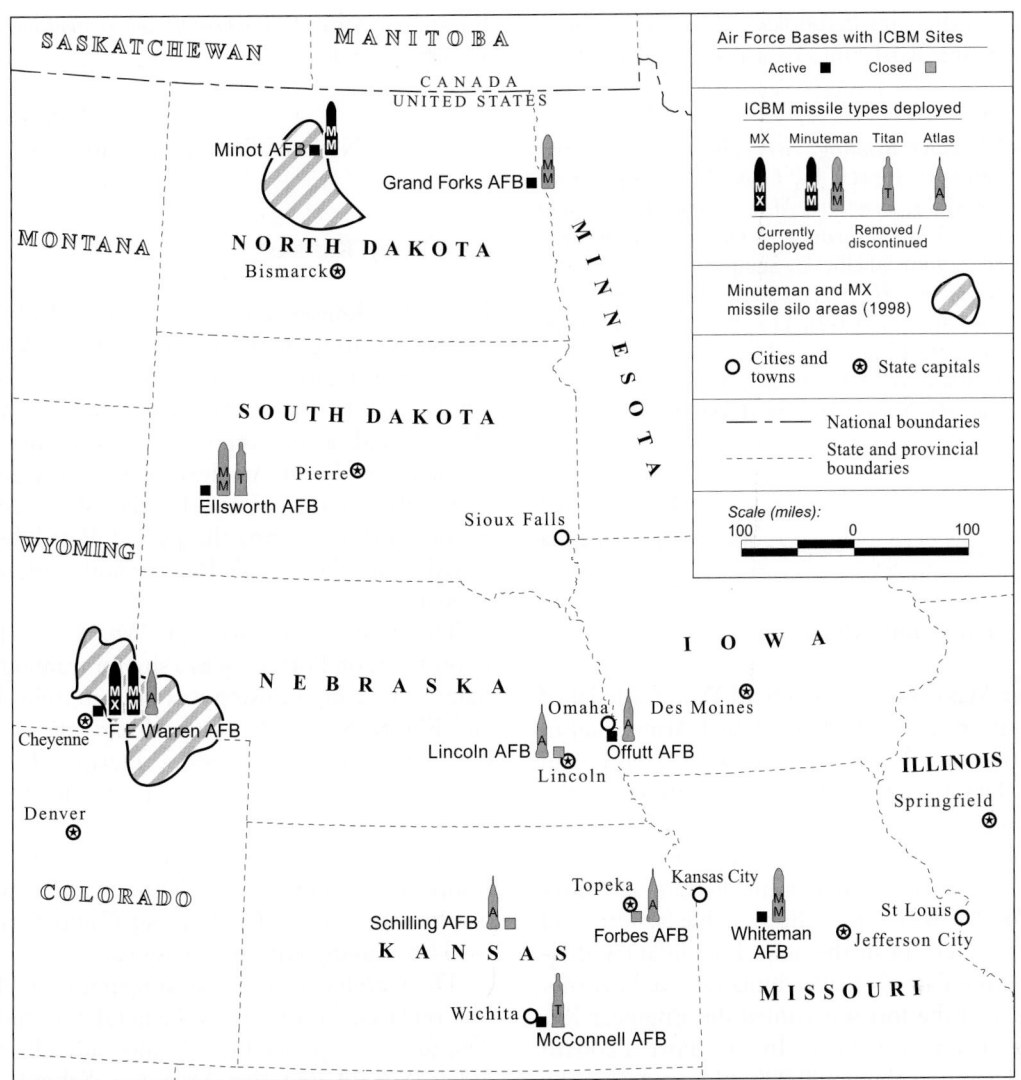

Missile sites in the Upper Midwest. Prepared by James DeGrand. *Source:* William Arkin, Robert Norris, and Joshua Handler, *Taking Stock: Worldwide Nuclear Deployments* (1998); http://www.fas.org; http://www.ceip.org/files /nonprolif/numbers/us.asp.

Strategic Arms Reduction Treaties, the need for many of these installations became less apparent. However, Congressmen and Senators feared electoral reprisal if they gave up installations in their district or state. Eventually Congress enacted legislation requiring all-or-nothing votes on lists of military installation recommended for closure. The Defense Authorization Amendments and Base Closure and Realignment Act of 1988 and the Defense Base Closure and Realignment Act of 1990 led to the closing of numerous Midwest military installations in 1988, 1991, 1993, and 1995. The Midwest base closings, which were significantly higher than in most regions of the country, included Fort Sheridan, Glenview Naval Air Station, and Chanute AFB in Illinois; Jefferson Proving Ground, Fort Benjamin Harrison, and Grissom AFB

in Indiana; Fort Des Moines in Iowa; Wurtsmith and K. I. Sawyer AFB in Michigan; Richards-Gebaur AFB in Missouri; and Rickenbacker and Newark AFB in Ohio. Iowa, Michigan, Minnesota, and Wisconsin now have no major active-duty military presence.

However, reorganization brought the enlargement of bases and responsibilities to several midwestern installations. Fort Leonard Wood, for instance, became the Corps of Engineers Headquarters Post by the early 1990s when the various Army engineer schools were concentrated there. Offutt AFB became the headquarters of the new joint U.S. Strategic Command, and Scott AFB of the joint U.S. Transportation Command.

Thus, Midwest communities have witnessed numerous changes at military installations that affected their lives and their pocketbooks. Some communities are still suffering hard times as a result of local base closures.

Sources and Further Reading: Army Almanac (1950; 2nd ed., 1959); James E. Hewes, Jr., *From Root to McNamara* (1975); Walter Millis, *Arms and Men: A Study of American Military* (1956); Tom Scanlan, ed., *Guide to Army Posts* (1963; 2nd ed., 1966); Shelby L. Stanton, *Order of Battle, U.S. Army, World War II* (1984); Charles J. Sullivan, *Army Posts and Towns*, 4th ed. (1942); U.S. Army War College, *Order of Battle of the United States Land Forces in the World War*, vol. 3, *Zone of Interior* (1949); U.S. Bureau of Yards and Docks, *Building the Navy's Bases in World War II*, 2 vols. (1947).

Dale E. Floyd
Springfield, Virginia

Fort Leonard Wood, Missouri

Named for Major General Leonard Wood, Medal of Honor recipient and pre–World War I Army chief of staff, this post near Rolla, Missouri, was established in late 1940. Despite numerous logistical problems, the fort was completed in June 1941, having been carved in less than six months out of a wilderness of forests and hills. The post served as a major training center during World War II, due to the available facilities and the variety of terrain in the area. Five infantry divisions and a number of smaller units received instruction there, and the fort was named the Engineer Replacement Training Center. In all, Fort Leonard Wood was home to about 300,000 soldiers during the war. Thousands of German and Italian prisoners of war were interned there, as well.

Following World War II, the post was declared inactive, but was reopened for training after the start of the Korean War. The fort was made a permanent installation and designated as an engineer training center in the 1950s, but provided various forms of military training during the Vietnam War. In 1985, the U.S. Army Engineer School moved from Fort Belvoir, Virginia, to Fort Leonard Wood. Units from the post were sent to participate in Operation Desert Shield and Desert Storm in the early 1990s. With the closure of Fort McClellan, Alabama, in 1995, Fort Leonard Wood also became the home of the Army's Chemical and Military Police Schools. At the turn of the twenty-first century, approximately 11,200 active-duty personnel and 4,400 civilian employees were assigned to or employed by the post.

Sources and Further Reading: Wilson Bell, ed., *State of Missouri Official Manual for Years 1945–1946* (1946); Dwight H. Brown, ed., *State of Missouri Official Manual for Years 1941 and 1942* (1942).

Jeffrey L. Patrick
National Park Service, Republic, Missouri

Fort Riley, Kansas

Fort Riley, Kansas, was established in 1853 as a frontier post. During the 1850s and the Civil War, the fort served as a staging area to protect overland trails and advancing settlements. Following the Civil War, Fort Riley served as an outpost for troops. In 1892, the Cavalry and Light Artillery School was established there, then was replaced by the Mounted Service School in 1907. During this period, Fort Riley was selected to host large-scale Regular and National Guard maneuvers.

The nation's entrance into World War I focused importance on Fort Riley as a site for training and mobilization. Camp Funston was built to train the Tenth and Eighty-Ninth Divisions, along with elements of the Ninety-Second Division. During the interwar years of the 1920s and 1930s, Fort Riley was again a center for instruction, training, and summer camps. During World War II, the post trained and deployed troops. Camp Forsyth was home to the Cavalry Replacement Training Center, and Camp Funston was used for training armored divisions.

The Cavalry School ceased operation in 1946 and was replaced by the Army General Ground School. The fort also operated the Army's only Officers Candidate School and the Aggressor School. Between 1948 and 1954, the Tenth Infantry Division conducted basic training for new recruits. The service of the Tenth was especially important during the Korean Conflict. In 1955, the First Infantry Division was ordered to Fort Riley. They were deployed to Southeast Asia in the mid-1960s and to Southwest Asia in 1990–1991. In 1999, Fort Riley became headquarters for the Twenty-Fourth Infantry Division.

Sources and Further Reading: William Dobak, *Fort Riley and Its Neighbors* (1998); William McKale and William D. Young, *Fort Riley: Citadel of the Frontier West* (2000).

William McKale
Fort Riley, Kansas

Intercontinental Missile Sites

The midwestern states played an important role in the basing of intercontinental ballistic missiles (ICBM), from the inception of the concept to the Strategic Arms Reduction Talks treaties of the 1980s and 1990s. The Midwest location was selected because of its remoteness, allowing missiles to fly over sparsely populated areas; readily available Strategic Air Command bases; and the maximum distance from an enemy attack by submarine-launched missiles off either coast. As the cold war ended, the need for massive retaliation waned and only the most easily maintained system, Minuteman, was retained.

Every ICBM program was represented in the Midwest: the first-generation, liquid-fuel Atlas missiles, Titan I and Titan II, as well as the solid-fuel Minuteman system. With the introduction of the solid-fuel Minuteman in the 1960s, missiles could be widely dispersed due to lower maintenance requirements. Minuteman I, II, and III missiles were deployed at various times at Minot and Grand Forks Air Force Bases (North Dakota), Ellsworth AFB (South Dakota), Whitman AFB (Missouri), and the missile sites extending into Nebraska from F. E. Warren AFB (Wyoming).

By the year 2000, all of the Minuteman II missiles were gone, leaving only 200 Minuteman IIIs deployed at Malmstrom AFB (Montana), 150 at Minot, and one hundred fifty at F. E. Warren. Fifty Peacekeeper missiles at F. E. Warren are scheduled to be deactivated by 2007.

Source and Further Reading: William Arkin, Robert Norris, and Joshua Handler, *Taking Stock: Worldwide Nuclear Deployments 1998* (1998).

David K. Stumpf
Tucson, Arizona

Minot Air Force Base, North Dakota

Established in 1955 near Minot, North Dakota, this Air Force base was named for the town after local citizens and businesses donated approximately $50,000 to buy land for the base. The base activated in 1957 as home to interceptors poised to repel an attack from over the North Pole by Soviet bombers. Air-to-air refueling aircraft soon joined the fighters, followed by intercontinental bombers. By 1964, Minot AFB added intercontinental ballistic missiles to its arsenal.

In 1975, a series of racial incidents came to a climax when twenty-five African American airmen barricaded themselves in the base dining hall. The protesters believed that a tour at Minot AFB was intolerable for young blacks due to perceived racist attitudes on base and the failure of the local community to provide support and black-oriented recreation. The national media initially reported that up to 300 airmen were involved, a considerable exaggeration. The dissidents ended their occupation after being permitted to talk with Congresswoman Shirley Chisholm. The Air Force concluded that, although the airmen had legitimate concerns about a tour in the largely white community of Minot, leadership and discipline failures at the base were the most important factors prompting the rebellion.

Since 1975, Minot AFB has rarely made national headlines, but has become a key link in the Air Force's post–cold war strategy. In 1988, the base lost its fighter mission but retained its other functions. Minot AFB employed approximately twelve thousand military and civilian personnel in 2002, and is home base to B-52 bombers, KC-135 air refueling aircraft, and Minuteman III intercontinental ballistic missiles.

Boeing B-52 Stratofortress on patrol. Photo courtesy the United States Air Force Museum.

Sources and Further Reading: Robert R. Gifford, *Travis, Laredo, and Minot* (1976); Keith Strom, *A Fortieth Anniversary History of the Minot Air Force Base*, Minot, North Dakota (1995).

Grant Thomas Weller
United States Air Force Academy,
Colorado Springs, Colorado

Naval Training Center, Great Lakes, Illinois

Located approximately forty-five miles north of downtown Chicago, the Naval Training Center (NTC), Great Lakes, is today the United States Navy's largest training center. Consisting of more than fourteen hundred acres, NTC offers 175 courses within fifteen technical schools and is home to the Navy's first and, since 1993, only Recruit Training Command or boot camp.

NTC has from its very beginning had a deep commitment and partnership with the local community and Midwest leaders. In 1904, the federal government received the original 172 acres for its establishment, and over the next six years it allocated almost $3.5 million for base construction. Many of these original buildings still stand and are part of its historical preservation programs. At the turn of the century, nearly $250 million in construction projects were under way; future construction includes an $800 million project at Recruit Training Command. The base had a regional economic impact of over $1.7 billion in 1999.

The center has had many notable milestones. The first recruit reported for duty on July 13, 1911; in 1917, John Philip Sousa became bandmaster; the first "Negro" recruit reported June 5, 1942, for segregated training; and in 1944, the Navy implemented integrated training at Great Lakes. Later in 1944, thirteen black sailors graduated as the service's first African American commissioned officers. During World War II, NTC Great Lakes trained over one million officers and enlisted personnel. Today, more than 73,000 officers, enlisted, and foreign students receive training each year.

At the beginning of the twenty-first century, NTC's staff of more than 2,300 military and 1,600 civilian personnel are actively involved in the base and civilian communities.

Sources and Further Reading: Committee of Friends of the Navy, *Gates to Glory* (1996); Great Lakes Naval Museum Foundation, *The Navy in The Heartland* (1991).

Donald "J" Gunter
Naval Training Center, Great Lakes, Illinois

Offutt Air Force Base and Strategic Air Command, Nebraska

Located ten miles south of Omaha, Nebraska, Offutt Air Force Base earned fame as the headquarters of the U.S. Air Force's Strategic Air Command during the Cold War. Before its days as the nerve center for America's nuclear arsenal, Offutt was known as Fort Crook, an Army post founded in 1890 and named after Major General George Crook, renowned for his actions in the Indian Wars and in the Civil War. As Fort Crook, the post hosted a number of infantry garrisons, including the Twenty-Second, Sixteenth, Tenth, and Sixth U.S. Infantry Regiments from 1896 to 1922. During World War I, the Sixty-First Balloon Company became the first air unit assigned to the installation.

On May 10, 1924, the Army designated Fort Crook's airfield as Offutt Field in honor of First Lieutenant Jarvis J. Offutt, Omaha's first air casualty of World War I. In 1940, the Glenn L. Martin-Nebraska Company leased over five hundred acres of Offutt Field to build a bomber assembly plant. In full operation by June 1942, the Martin bomber factory produced over fifteen hundred twin-engine Martin B-26 "Marauders" and 531 massive Boeing B-29 "Superfortresses," including both planes that dropped atomic bombs on Japan.

Renamed Offutt Air Force Base on January 13, 1948, the base's large runway, abundant office space, and central geographic location made it attractive as the new headquarters of the Strategic Air Command (SAC). Under the leadership of General Curtis E. LeMay, SAC provided the foundation of the nation's nuclear deterrent force. A symbol of readiness and resolve, the SAC underground command post located in Building 500 coordinated alert missile and bomber forces beginning in 1957. In 1960, Secretary of Defense Thomas S. Gates, Jr., established the Joint Strategic Target Planning Staff at Offutt, which was responsible for preparing the National Strategic Target List and a Single Integrated Operational Plan.

Offutt's role as the nuclear planning hub was enhanced in July 1960 when Boeing KC-135 (later named EC-135, "Looking Glass") Airborne Command Post aircraft began operating from the base. Additionally, beginning in January 1965, the Fifty-Fifth Strategic Reconnaissance Wing (SRW) provided a little-known, but vital, component of cold war intelligence for national command authorities. Flying Boeing RC-135 aircraft, the unit conducted electronic surveillance missions along the borders of Soviet-controlled territory. In the 1980s and 1990s, Fifty-Fifth SRW aircraft supported U.S. contingency operations in Grenada, Libya, Panama, and Iraq, and assisted peacekeeping efforts in Haiti, Bosnia, and Kosovo.

With the end of the cold war and collapse of the Soviet Union, a joint-service U.S. Strategic Command (STRATCOM) replaced the Air Force's SAC on June 1, 1992. The new STRATCOM continued SAC's nuclear deterrence mission, but further integrated Army, Navy, Marine, and Air Force personnel to face current global challenges. On October 1, 2002, the Department of Defense merged U.S. Space Command and U.S. Strategic Command, with the combined headquarters at Offutt responsible for land-based intercontinental ballistic missiles, submarine-launched ballistic missiles, strategic bombers, and a wide variety of U.S. military satellites and other space assets.

On September 11, 2001, the base provided a place of security for President Bush after the terrorist attacks of that day. With a workforce of more than 9,000 military and civilian personnel, and approximately 21,000 military dependents and 40,000 military retirees in the local area, Offutt AFB plays a major economic role, contributing $395 million dollars in expenditures and $534 million dollars in military, civilian, and retiree payrolls to the Omaha economy.

Sources and Further Reading: J. C. Hopkins and Sheldon A. Goldbery, *Development of Strategic Air Command, 1946–1986* (1986); Norman Polmar and Timothy M. Laur, eds., *Strategic Air Command: People, Aircraft, and Missiles,* 2nd ed. (1990).

John T. Farquhar
United States Air Force Academy,
Colorado Springs, Colorado

Scott Air Force Base, Illinois

Established in 1917 and named after Corporal Frank S. Scott, who died in a military plane crash, the base has four distinct historical periods. Scott Field trained over five hundred pilots and hundreds of mechanics and ground crews during World War I. Throughout the 1920s and 1930s, Scott Field was *the* center for lighter-than-air activities in the Army. From World War II through the 1950s, over 150 thousand received communications and technical training at Scott. From the late 1950s forward, Scott Air Force Base has served as the headquarters for several major defense organizations, including the U.S. Transportation Command, the Air Mobility Command, and the Air Force Communications Agency.

The U.S. Transportation Command, established at Scott in April 1987, is a unified command with world-wide responsibilities as the single manager of the Defense Transportation System. It is comprised of the Air Force's Air Mobility Command, the Navy's Sealift Command, and the Army's Traffic Management Command. The Air Mobility Command has worldwide responsibilities for airlift and air refueling resources.

The Air Force Communications Agency ensures the integration and interoperability of communications and information systems throughout the Air Force. The agency manages commercial communications services for the Air Force that total more than $240 million annually.

At the beginning of the century, Scott Air Force Base employed approximately 8,300 military and 4,600 civilian personnel, and was assigned C-9A aeromedical and KC-135 air refueling aircraft. Considering salaries, local and vendor contracts, and construction projects, the base's economic impact exceeds $1 billion annually.

Sources and Further Reading: Betty R. Kennedy, *An Illustrated History of Scott Air Force Base, 1917–1987* (1987). Patricia K. Warner, *A Brief History of Scott Air Force Base, 1917–1992* (1992).

Betty Raab Kennedy
United States Air Force, Belleville, Illinois

Wright-Patterson Air Force Base, Ohio

Located approximately six miles northeast of Dayton, Ohio, Wright-Patterson Air Force Base encompasses approximately 8,357 acres, including Wright Field, named for aviation pioneers Orville and Wilbur Wright, and Patterson Field, named for First Lieutenant Frank S. Patterson, an Army Air Service pilot and prominent Dayton family scion killed in a 1918 test flight crash.

Military aviation research and development began to flourish at Wright-Patterson during World War I. In 1917, a pilot training school was established at then Wilbur Wright Field (now part of the base's Area C). That fall, McCook Field opened nearby as an Air Service engineering center. In 1927, both operations were combined into new research facilities at Wright Field, an aerodrome built about two miles to the east (on base land now called Area B).

Wright-Patterson AFB's aerospace acquisition and logistics heritage also dates from 1917, when the Fairfield Air Depot was activated adjacent to Wilbur Wright Field (on base property now called Area A). In 1931, the Fairfield Air Depot, Wilbur Wright Field, and Huffman Prairie (site of Wright brothers' flight trials, 1904–1908) were consolidated and renamed

Patterson Field. Wright and Patterson Fields merged to become Wright-Patterson AFB in 1948.

Wright-Patterson AFB houses one of the largest military aerospace research and development complexes in the world. In fiscal year 1999, its combined annual payroll of over $871 million for 20,000 military and civilian personnel made it Ohio's biggest single-site employer. Operated by the Aeronautical Systems Center, the base hosts more than sixty Air Force and Department of Defense organizations, including the headquarters of the Air Force Materiel Command, the Air Force Research Laboratory, the Air Force Institute of Technology, and the National Air Intelligence Center. The Air Force Museum is a major Midwest tourist destination, receiving over 1.2 million visitors annually.

Sources and Further Reading: Diana Good Cornelisse, *Remarkable Journey: The Wright Field Heritage in Photographs* (1991); Bernard J. Termena, Layne B. Peiffer, and H. P. Carlin, *Logistics: An Illustrated History of AFLC and Its Antecedents, 1921–1981* (1981); Lois E. Walker and Shelby E. Wickam, *From Huffman Prairie to the Moon* (1986).

George W. Cully
Wright-Patterson Air Force Base,
Dayton, Ohio

Cold Warriors and Astronauts

Curtis LeMay (1906–1990)

Curtis LeMay was born in Columbus, Ohio, the son of an ironworker and housewife. He attended Ohio State University but quit in 1928 to accept a commission in the Army. LeMay became a pilot, and throughout the 1930s he held a variety of flying billets in the Army Air Corps, including a tour of duty at Selfridge Field, Michigan. He returned to Ohio State and graduated in 1932, and by World War II, he had developed a reputation as a hard worker and an excellent pilot and navigator.

During World War II, LeMay commanded a bombardment group in England and flew bombing raids over Germany. Transferred to the Pacific theater in early 1945, he directed the massive firebombing raids against Tokyo. In August 1945, these raids culminated in the atomic bombings of Hiroshima and Nagasaki that helped end World War II.

After the war, LeMay became the commander of the newly independent Air Force's Strategic Air Command (SAC), with headquarters at Offutt Air Force Base in Nebraska. During the early cold war, LeMay used his blunt command style as well as first-rate analytical and administrative abilities to mold SAC into the nation's primary nuclear deterrent. He became the Air Force Chief of Staff in 1961, although his aggressive military posture put him at odds with President John F. Kennedy. LeMay retired in 1965 and was George Wallace's running mate in the presidential election of 1968. In retirement, LeMay continued to exercise wide and powerful influence over the Air Force's strategic bombing forces. He married Helen E. Maitland in 1934 and had one child. He died on October 1, 1990, at March Air Force Base, Riverside, California.

Sources and Further Reading: Thomas Coffey, *Iron Eagle: The Turbulent Life of General Curtis LeMay* (1986); Curtis LeMay with MacKinlay Kantor, *Mission with LeMay* (1965).

Thomas Hughes
Maxwell Air Force Base, Montgomery, Alabama

Bernard W. Rogers (b. 1921)

General Bernard William Rogers was born on July 16, 1921, in Fairview, Kansas. After attending Kansas State College from 1939 to 1940, Rogers received an appointment to West Point, from which he graduated in 1943. After several stateside assignments, he became aide to General Mark Clark, commander of American forces in Austria, in 1946.

Rogers attended Oxford University as a Rhodes Scholar from 1947 to 1950, and subsequently commanded an infantry battalion during the Korean Conflict. After attending the U.S. Army Command and General Staff College, he served in the Office of the Army Chief of Staff between 1958 and 1960. He subsequently attended the Army War College and was assigned to the Nineteenth and Twenty-Fourth Infantry Divisions in Germany. From 1962 to 1966, he served on the Joint Staff as General Maxwell Taylor's executive officer.

From 1966 to 1967, Brigadier General Rogers served in Vietnam as an assistant division commander, after which he became West Point's Commandant of Cadets. In 1970, he took command of the Fifth Infantry Division at Fort Carson, Colorado. After achieving four-star rank in 1974, he served as commander of U.S. Army Forces Command and subsequently as Army Chief of Staff. There he defended the volunteer army concept, strove to ensure the proper treatment of black soldiers, and worked to develop the twenty-four-division, all-component force.

In 1979, President Jimmy Carter appointed Rogers to be the supreme commander of the North Atlantic

Treaty Organization (NATO). During his tenure, Rogers played a key role in enticing Greece back into the alliance and in ensuring NATO's flexibility regarding potential arms control agreements with the Soviet Union. General Rogers retired from the Army in 1987.

Source and Further Reading: "Bernard W. Rogers," aog.usma.edu/AOG/AWARDS/DGA/95-ROGER.TXT.

David J. Fitzpatrick
Washtenaw Community College,
Michigan

John W. Vessey, Jr. (b. 1922)

General John William Vessey, Jr., was born in Minneapolis, Minnesota, on June 29, 1922. While still a high school student, Vessey joined the Minnesota National Guard and entered active service in 1940. During World War II, he served as an artilleryman in North Africa and Italy, rising through the ranks to first sergeant and receiving a battlefield commission on the Anzio beachhead in May 1944.

After the war, Vessey served with the Fourth Infantry and Third Armored Divisions in Germany, and attended the U.S. Army Command and General Staff College, among other military schools. In Vietnam, he commanded an artillery battalion and was awarded the Distinguished Service Cross for gallantry. He subsequently coordinated military operations in Thailand and Laos after being promoted to brigadier general in 1971.

Promoted to major general in 1974, he assumed command of the Fourth Infantry Division at Fort Carson, Colorado. Upon promotion to lieutenant general, he became the Army's Deputy Chief of Staff for Operations. Vessey moved to Korea in 1976 where, as a four-star general, he assumed command of the U.S. Eighth Army, the United Nations Command, and the United States–Republic of Korea Combined Forces Command.

In 1979, General Vessey became the Army's Vice Chief of Staff, and in 1982, was appointed Chairman of the Joint Chiefs of Staff, the only person to achieve that position from the ranks of the National Guard. General Vessey retired in 1985. In 1988 he became President Reagan's presidential emissary to Vietnam regarding prisoner-of-war and missing-in-action affairs, and he served Presidents George H. W. Bush and Bill Clinton in that capacity. He married Avis Funk in July 1945. They have two sons and two daughters.

Sources and Further Reading: "John W. Vessey, Jr.," http://www.aog.usma.edu/AOG/AWARDS/TA/96Citation.htm.

David J. Fitzpatrick
Washtenaw Community College,
Michigan

Neil Armstrong (b. 1930)

Born in his grandmother's farmhouse on August 5, 1930, near Wapakoneta, Ohio, Neil Armstrong developed a love of airplanes and flight in his early years. After earning his diploma from Blume High School— and still intrigued by the sky—Armstrong joined the U.S. Navy, eventually earning his pilot wings. He flew seventy-eight combat missions over Korea and was forced to eject on one sortie after taking heavy anti-aircraft fire. The Armistice brought Armstrong home. He finished his bachelor's degree in Aeronautical Engineering at Purdue University, where he fell in love

Neil Armstrong: "One small step for (a) man, one giant leap for mankind." Photo courtesy NASA.

with Janet Shearon. The two were wed in 1956 and have two sons.

Armstrong moved to the Flight Test Center and Edwards AFB in California, where he flew experimental aircraft including the X-5 and X-15. His work there served as a springboard to the National Aeronautics and Space Administration. While at NASA, Armstrong was involved with the Gemini and Apollo projects, including the famous Apollo Eleven mission. On that mission, Armstrong and Edwin "Buzz" Aldrin landed the lunar module *Eagle* in the Sea of Tranquility and set foot onto the surface of the moon. As Armstrong put it, "That's one small step for (a) man, one giant leap for mankind." Armstrong has since worked for various NASA agencies and continues to further efforts to explore space. A midwesterner and American hero, Armstrong lives with his second wife Carol in Ohio.

Sources and Further Reading: Douglas MacKinnon and Joseph Baldanza, *Footprints: The 12 Men Who Walked on the Moon Reflect on Their Flights, Their Lives, and the Future* (1989).

James Wright
Lacey, Washington

Senator John Glenn prepared for space flight, 1998. Photo courtesy NASA.

John Glenn (b. 1921)

John Glenn was born in Cambridge, Ohio, and grew up in nearby New Concord. He was a stand-out athlete in high school and attended local Muskingum College. In 1943, Glenn left school to become a pilot in the Marine Corps. He flew fifty-nine combat missions during World War II and shot down three North Korean MiG fighters during the Korean Conflict.

After returning from Korea, Glenn became a military test pilot, and at one point held a transcontinental flight record of three hours and twenty-three minutes. In April 1959, as a lieutenant colonel in the Marine Corps, Glenn became one of the seven original Mercury astronauts. On February 20, 1962, he became the first American to orbit Earth, circling the planet three times in his capsule *Friendship Seven*. He was the second of three Ohio contributions critical to the age of flight, the Wright brothers and Neil Armstrong completing the frame.

Glenn retired from the Marine Corps in 1965 with six Distinguished Flying Crosses and eighteen Air Medals. After successful stints in business, he was elected to the U.S. Senate from Ohio in 1974 and served until his retirement in 1999, becoming the longest-serving senator from Ohio during the twentieth century. As a senator, Glenn gained a reputation as a hard worker and effective legislator, and in 1984 ran unsuccessfully for President in the Democratic Party primaries. His connections to Savings and Loan officials may have somewhat diminished his stature when that industry experienced financial scandal in the late 1980s, although he retired from the Senate in 1999 with a strong reputation in that institution and in his home state. In the fall of 1998, he returned to space as the oldest astronaut to date aboard a shuttle as part of NASA's attempt to study the effect of weightlessness on an aging astronaut.

In 1998 the John Glenn Institute for Public Service and Public Policy was established at The Ohio State University to house Glenn's voluminous archives, to curate memorabilia from his military and political careers, and to promote education and training in public service for both students and elected officials as well as to support research on issues concerning the public interest. He and his wife, Annie, are actively associated with the university as they are with Muskingum College, located in New Concord, Ohio, where they met as students and from which they graduated.

Sources and Further Reading: John Glenn, *A Memoir* (1999); Barbara Kramer, *John Glenn: A Space Biography* (1998).

Thomas Hughes
Maxwell Air Force Base, Montgomery, Alabama

Index

Page numbers in bold refer to main encyclopedia entries; page numbers in italics refer to illustrations.

About the Editors

Richard Sisson, a native midwesterner, is Provost and Professor of Political Science Emeritus at The Ohio State University where he held the Board of Trustees Chair in Comparative Politics. A member of the faculty at UCLA for twenty-five years, he also served as Senior Vice Chancellor for Academic Affairs. His more recent books include *War and Secession* (with Leo E. Rose); *The Evolution of Political Knowledge*, 2 vols. (with Edward D. Mansfield); and *Ohio and the World, 1753–2053* (with Geoffrey Parker and William Russell Coil).

Christian Zacher is Professor of English at The Ohio State University and Director of its Institute for Collaborative Research and Public Humanities. A scholar of medieval English literature, he is author or co-editor of various essays and books on medieval literature and culture, including *Critical Studies of Sir Gawain and the Green Knight* (with Donald Howard), *The Idea of Medieval Literature* (with James Dean), and *Curiosity and Pilgrimage*. Like his fellow general editors, he brings to the encyclopedia a longtime resident's knowledge of the Midwest. At the institute he is co-organizer of a living history Chautauqua program and oversees other projects designed to extend the humanities to the general public.

Andrew Cayton is Distinguished Professor of History at Miami University, Oxford, Ohio. He is author or editor of numerous books, including *The Dominion of War: Empire and Liberty in North America, 1500–2000* (with Fred Anderson); *Frontier Indiana; Ohio: The History of a People; The Midwest and the Nation: Rethinking the History of an American Region* (with Peter S. Onuf); and *The American Midwest: Essays on Regional History* (edited with Susan E. Gray).